A London Bibliography of the Social Sciences

BRITISH LIBRARY OF POLITICAL AND ECONOMIC SCIENCE

A London Bibliography of the Social Sciences

Twenty-second Supplement

1987

VOLUME XLV

MANSELL, LONDON AND NEW YORK, 1988

This Bibliography has been published for the British Library of
Political and Economic Science by Mansell Publishing Limited
6 All Saints Street, London N1 9RL, England

Library of Congress Card Number 31-9970

© 1988 The British Library of Political and Economic Science

British Library Cataloguing in Publication Data

British Library of Political and Economic Science
   A London bibliography of the social sciences
   1. Social sciences—Bibliographies
   I. Title
   016.3

   ISSN 0076–051X
   ISBN 0–7201–1958–8

This book has been printed in Great Britain by the University
Press, Cambridge.

Preface

This supplement to *A London Bibliography of the Social Sciences* is the eighth to be produced since the entry of the British Library of Political and Economic Science into the University of London Shared Cataloguing System in January 1980.

The Library acknowledges the assistance of the British Library in the production of computer typesetting tapes and also wishes to acknowledge the British Library (BLAISE) data base as a source of centrally catalogued data.

January 1988   C. J. Hunt
                                                                                                                           Librarian

Notes to users

The final section of this volume is a list of subject headings so that users can more easily determine whether a subject is covered in the bibliography. The presence of a particular subject heading indicates that there is at least one entry under that heading in the volume. However the list of subject headings contains only those cross-references used for the first time in 1987; users are advised to consult the published *Library of Congress Subject Headings*, ninth edition (1980), in order to select the correct form of subject headings under which a search is to be made. Readers are also referred to the notes on pages vi-vii of Volume XXXVIII of the *Bibliography* (1980) for details of those changes in the form of subject headings necessitated by the participation of the British Library of Political and Economic Science in the University of London Shared Cataloguing System from January 1980 onwards. In addition, frequent revision of subject headings is undertaken in order to bring already established headings into line with the Library of Congress's changes in practice. Some headings may therefore appear in variant forms.

Contents of the series

VOLUMES I–IV. *Original compilation.* Holdings up to 1929 of the British Library of Political and Economic Science; Edward Fry Library of International Law; Goldsmiths' Library of Economic Literature, University of London; National Institute of Industrial Psychology; Royal Anthropological Institute; Royal Institute of International Affairs; and Royal Statistical Society. Included additionally are special collections in the libraries of The Reform Club (political and historical pamphlets); University College, London (the Hume, Ricardo and other economic and political collections); and The University of London (works on economics and related subjects).

VOLUME V. *First supplement.* Additions from 1929 to 1931 to the collections included in Volumes I–IV.

VOLUME VI. *Second supplement.* Additions from 1931 to 1936 to the British Library of Political and Economic Science (BLPES), Edward Fry Library of International Law (EFLIL) and Goldsmiths' Library of Economic Literature.

VOLUMES VII–IX. *Third supplement.* Additions from 1936 to 1950, other than works in the Russian language, to BLPES and EFLIL.

VOLUMES X–XI. *Fourth supplement.* Additions from 1950 to 1955 in all languages, and from 1936 to 1950 in Russian, to BLPES and EFLIL.

VOLUMES XII–XIV. *Fifth supplement.* Additions from 1955 to 1962 to BLPES and EFLIL.

VOLUMES XV–XXI. *Sixth supplement.* Additions from 1962 to 1968 to BLPES and EFLIL with indexes.

VOLUMES XXII–XXVIII. *Seventh supplement.* Additions from 1969 to 1972 to BLPES and EFLIL with index.

VOLUMES XXIX–XXXI. *Eighth supplement*. Additions during 1972 and 1973 to BLPES and EFLIL with index.

VOLUME XXXII. *Ninth supplement*. Additions during 1974 to BLPES and EFLIL with index.

VOLUME XXXIII. *Tenth supplement*. Additions during 1975 to BLPES and EFLIL with index.

VOLUME XXXIV. *Eleventh supplement*. Additions during 1976 to BLPES and EFLIL with index.

VOLUME XXXV. *Twelfth supplement*. Additions during 1977 to BLPES and EFLIL with index.

VOLUME XXXVI. *Thirteenth supplement*. Additions during 1978 to BLPES and EFLIL with index.

VOLUME XXXVII. *Fourteenth supplement*. Additions during 1979 to BLPES and EFLIL with index.

VOLUME XXXVIII. *Fifteenth supplement*. Additions during 1980 to BLPES and EFLIL with index.

VOLUME XXXIX. *Sixteenth supplement*. Additions during 1981 to BLPES and EFLIL with index.

VOLUME XL. *Seventeenth supplement*. Additions during 1982 to BLPES and EFLIL with index.

VOLUME XLI. *Eighteenth supplement*. Additions during 1983 to BLPES and EFLIL with index.

VOLUME XLII. *Nineteenth supplement*. Additions during 1984 to BLPES and EFLIL with index.

VOLUME XLIII. *Twentieth supplement*. Additions during 1985 to BLPES and EFLIL with index.

VOLUME XLIV. *Twenty-first supplement*. Additions during 1986 to BLPES and EFLIL with index.

VOLUME XLV. *Twenty-second supplement*. Additions during 1987 to BLPES and EFLIL with index.

PERIODICAL LISTS. An alphabetical list of the periodicals in the British Library of Political and Economic Science in 1929 is given in Volume IV; supplementary lists up to 1936 are given in Volumes V and VI, after which they have been discontinued.

AUTHOR INDEXES. Author indexes are given in Volumes IV (for Volumes I–III), V, and VI, but not in later volumes.

PUBLISHERS OF VOLUMES I–XIV. The British Library of Political and Economic Science, 10 Portugal Street, London WC2A 2HD published the first fourteen volumes.

A London Bibliography of the Social Sciences

A NICARAGUA — Social conditions — 1979-
ROOPER, Alison
Fragile victory : Nicaraguan community at war / Alison Rooper. — London : Weidenfeld and Nicolson, 1987. — xx,229p. — *Bibliography: p [228]-229*

AALBORG (DENMARK) — Civic improvement
DENMARK. Udvalget vedrørende byudviklingsplan for Aalborgegnen
Betaenkning vedrørende byudviklingsplan for Aalborgegnen. — Aalborg : Aksel Schølin, [1953]. — 30p. — *Maps in end-pocket*

ABDUCTION
SACHS, Christina
Child abduction / Christina Sachs. — London : Jordan & Sons, 1987. — xx,126p. — (Guide and practice series)

ABDUL RAHMAN, Tunku, Putra Al-Haj
ABDULLAH AHMAD, Datuk
Tengku Abdul Rahman and Malaysia's foreign policy, 1963-1970 / Dato' Abdullah Ahmad. — Kuala Lumpur : Berita Publishing, 1985. — ix, 182 p.. — *Includes index. — Bibliography: 157-167*

ABERDEEN (GRAMPIAN) — History
New light on medieval Aberdeen / edited by J.S. Smith. — Aberdeen : Aberdeen University Press, 1985. — xi,66p

ABERDEEN (GRAMPIAN) — Social conditions
From lairds to louns : country and burgh life in Aberdeen 1600-1800 / edited by David Stevenson. — Aberdeen : Aberdeen University Press, 1986. — 90p

ABIDJAN (IVORY COAST) — Population — Statistics
ANTOINE, Philippe
Enquête démographique à passages répétés : agglomération d'Abidjan / Philippe Antoine, Claude Herry. — [Abidjan] : Direction de la Statistique, 1982. — 419p

Recensement géneral de la population 1975. — Abidjan : Direction de la Statistique
Vol. 1: Département d'Abidjan, Agglomération du Grand Abidjan : Résultats definitifs. — 1978. — 280p

ABIDJAN (IVORY COAST) — Statistics, vital
ANTOINE, Philippe
Enquête démographique à passages répétés : agglomération d'Abidjan / Philippe Antoine, Claude Herry. — [Abidjan] : Direction de la Statistique, 1982. — 419p

ABNORMALITIES, HUMAN — Denmark — Statistics
Misdannelsesregisteret : foreløbig rapport 1983. — [København] : Sundhedsstyrelsen, 1984. — 46p. — (Vitalstatistik / Sundhedsstyrelsen ; I:9:1984). — *Summary and table headings in English*

ABOLITION OF DOMESTIC RATES ETC. [SCOTLAND] BILL 1986-87
GREAT BRITAIN. Parliament. House of Commons. Library. Research Division
Abolition of Domestic Rates etc. [Scotland] Bill, Bill 9 of 1986-87 / Barry Winetrobe, Rob Clements. — [London] : the Division, 1986. — 20p. — (Reference sheet ; no.86/16)

ABOLITIONISTS
DRESCHER, Seymour
Capitalism and antislavery : British mobilization in comparative perspective / Seymour Drescher ; foreword by Christine Bolt. — London : Macmillan, 1986. — [368]p. — (The second Anstey memorial lecture in the University of Kent at Canterbury ; 1984). — *Includes bibliography and index*

ABOLITIONISTS — History — 19th century — Sources
The Black abolitionist papers / C. Peter Ripley, editor ; Jeffrey S. Rossbach, associate editor ... [et al.]. — Chapel Hill : University of North Carolina Press, c1985-. — p. cm. — *Includes index. — Contents: v. 1. The British Isles, 1830-1865*

ABOLITIONISTS — Great Britain — History
WALVIN, James
England, slaves and freedom, 1776-1838 / James Walvin. — Basingstoke : Macmillan, 1986. — [176]p. — *Includes index*

ABOLITIONISTS — United States — History
NEWMAN, Francis Wilson
Anglo-Saxon abolition of Negro slavery / by F. W. Newman. — New York : Negro Universities Press, 1969. — 135p. — *Originally published in 1889*

ABOLITIONISTS — United States — History — 19th century — Sources
The Black abolitionist papers / C. Peter Ripley, editor ; Jeffrey S. Rossbach, associate editor ... [et al.]. — Chapel Hill : University of North Carolina Press, c1985-. — p. cm. — *Includes index. — Contents: v. 1. The British Isles, 1830-1865*

The black abolitionist papers / C. Peter Ripley, Editor. — Chapel Hill ; London : University of North Carolina Press
Vol.2: Canada, 1830-1865. — 1986. — xxviii,560p

ABORTION
FEMMES EN LUTTE
Nous voulons des enfants désirés. — 2nd ed. — Lausanne : Femmes en Lutte, 1976. — 88p

HURSTHOUSE, Rosalind
Beginning lives / Rosalind Hursthouse. — Oxford : Basil Blackwell in association with the Open University, 1987. — [288]p. — *Includes index*

KENYON, F. E.
The dilemma of abortion / Edwin Kenyon. — London : Faber, 1986. — 282p. — *Includes index*

ABORTION — Law and legislation — Great Britain
GREAT BRITAIN. Parliament. House of Commons. Library. Research Division
Abortion (Amendment) Bill 1979/80 (Bill 7 and Bill 110) / [Julia Lourie]. — [London] : the Division, 1980. — 3leaves. — (Reference sheet ; no.80/7)

GREAT BRITAIN. Parliament. House of Commons. Library. Research Division
Abortion law reform. — [London] : the Division, [1976]. — 10p. — (Background paper ; no.50)

ABORTION — Moral and ethical aspects
IMBER, Jonathan B.
Abortion and the private practice of medicine / Jonathan B. Imber. — New Haven : Yale University Press, c1986. — xviii, 164 p.. — *Includes index. — Bibliography: p. 147-160*

ABORTION — Political aspects
The New politics of abortion / edited by Joni Lovenduski and Joyce Outshoorn. — London : Sage, 1986. — 175p. — (Sage modern politics series ; v.2). — *Includes bibliography and index*

ABORTION — Political aspects — United States
PETCHESKY, Rosalind Pollack
Abortion and woman's choice / Rosalind Pollack Petchesky. — London : Verso, 1986, c1984. — [442]p. — (Questions for feminism). — *Originally published: New York ; London : Longman, 1984. — Includes index*

ABORTION — Social aspects — United States
PETCHESKY, Rosalind Pollack
Abortion and woman's choice / Rosalind Pollack Petchesky. — London : Verso, 1986, c1984. — [442]p. — (Questions for feminism). — *Originally published: New York ; London : Longman, 1984. — Includes index*

ABORTION — Great Britain
Termination of pregnancy, England 1984 : women from the Republic of Ireland / G. Dean [et al.]. — Dublin : Medico-Social Research Board, 1985. — [41p]

ABORTION — United States
DAVIS, Nanette J
From crime to choice : the transformation of abortion in America / Nanette J. Davis. — Westport, Conn. : Greenwood Press, c1985. — p. cm. — (Contributions in women's studies ; no. 60). — *Includes index. — Bibliography: p*

IMBER, Jonathan B.
Abortion and the private practice of medicine / Jonathan B. Imber. — New Haven : Yale University Press, c1986. — xviii, 164 p.. — *Includes index. — Bibliography: p. 147-160*

ABORTION — United States — History — 19th century
PETCHESKY, Rosalind Pollack
Abortion and woman's choice / Rosalind Pollack Petchesky. — London : Verso, 1986, c1984. — [442]p. — (Questions for feminism). — *Originally published: New York ; London : Longman, 1984. — Includes index*

ABORTION (AMENDMENT) BILL 1979-80
GREAT BRITAIN. Parliament. House of Commons. Library. Research Division
Abortion (Amendment) Bill 1979/80 (Bill 7 and Bill 110) / [Julia Lourie]. — [London] : the Division, 1980. — 3leaves. — (Reference sheet ; no.80/7)

ABORTION, INDUCED — United States
IMBER, Jonathan B.
Abortion and the private practice of medicine / Jonathan B. Imber. — New Haven : Yale University Press, c1986. — xviii, 164 p.. — *Includes index. — Bibliography: p. 147-160*

ABSENTEEISM (LABOR) — Great Britain

GREAT BRITAIN. Joint DHSS/NHS Manpower Planning and Personnel Information Sub Group
Absence from work : second report of joint DHSS/NHS Sub-Group. — [London] : Department of Health and Social Security, 1977. — 45p. — (Manpower planning and personnel information ; no.2). — *Bibliography: p43-44*

ABSENTEEISM (LABOR) — Québec (Province)

CÔTÉ-DESBIOLLES, Louise H.
L'absence du travail / par Louise H. Côté-Desbiolles ; avec la collaboration de Réal Morissette. — Québec : Centre de recherche et de statistiques sur le marché du travail, 1985. — 88p. — *Bibliographical references: p87-88*

ABSTRACT DATA TYPES (COMPUTER SCIENCE)

IFIP WG 2.6 WORKING CONFERENCE ON DATA SEMANTICS (DS-1) (1985 : Hasselt)
Database semantics (DS-1) : proceedings of the IFIP WG 2.6 Working Conference on Data Semantics (DS-1) Hasselt, Belgium, 7-11 January, 1985 / edited by T.B. Steel, Jr., R. Meersman. — Amsterdam ; Oxford : North-Holland, 1986. — x,323p. — *Cover title: Database semantics. — Includes bibliographies*

ABSTRACTING AND INDEXING SERVICES — Great Britain — Directories

STEPHENS, J.
Inventory of abstracting and indexing services produced in the U.K. / J. Stephens. — London : British Library, c1986. — vii,238p. — (British Library information guide ; v.2) (British Library information guide ; v.2). — *Updated version of report of same name. London : British Library, R & D Dept., 1983. — Includes index*

ABUSED AGED — Services for — United States — Directories

JOHNSON, Tanya F
Elder neglect and abuse : an annotated bibliography / compiled by Tanya F. Johnson, James G. O'Brien, and Margaret F. Hudson. — Westport, Conn. : Greenwood Press, 1985. — xxvi, 223 p.. — (Bibliographies and indexes in gerontology ; no. 1). — *Includes index*

ABUSED WIVES — Services for — Québec (Province)

BEAUDRY, Micheline
Battered women / Micheline Beaudry ; translated by Lorne Huston and Margaret Heap. — Montréal ; Buffalo, N.Y. : Black Rose Books, 1985. — 118p

ACADEMIC FREEDOM

ROGERS, Carl R
Freedom to learn for the 80's / Carl R. Rogers ; with special contributions by Julie Ann Allender ... [et al.]. — Columbus, Ohio : C.E. Merrill Pub. Co., c1983. — viii, 312 p.. — *Rev. ed. of: Freedom to learn. 1969. — Includes bibliographies and index*

ACADEMIC FREEDOM — South Africa

COOVADIA, H. M.
From ivory tower to a people's university / H. M. Coovadia. — [Cape Town] : University of Cape Town, 1986. — 25 p. — *"The twenty-seventh T. B. Davie Memorial Lecture delivered in the Jameson Hall, University of Cape Town on 25 September 1986"*

ACADEMIC FREEDOM — United States

ARONS, Stephen
Compelling belief : the culture of American schooling / Stephen Arons. — 1st paperback ed. — Amherst : University of Massachusetts Press, 1986, c1983. — xii, 228 p.. — *: Reprint. Originally published: New York : McGraw-Hill, c1983. — Includes index*

ACADEMIC FREEDOM — United States — History — 20th century

SCHRECKER, Ellen
No ivory tower : McCarthyism and the universities / Ellen Schrecker. — New York : Oxford University Press, 1986. — p. cm. — *Includes index. — Bibliography: p*

ACADÉMIE ROYALE DES SCIENCES (Paris)

HAHN, Roger
The anatomy of a scientific institution : the Paris Academy of Sciences, 1666-1803 / by Roger Hahn. — Berkeley ; London (2 Brook St., W1Y 1AA) : University of California Press, 1971. — xiv,433,[4]p. — *Ill. on lining papers. — Bibliographyp.321-418. — Includes index*

ACADIA — History

MACDONALD, M. A.
Fortune and La Tour : the civil war in Acadia / M. A. MacDonald. — Toronto : Methuen, 1986. — xii,228p. — *Bibliography: p219-224*

ACADIA — Lieutenant-governors — Biography

MACDONALD, M. A.
Fortune and La Tour : the civil war in Acadia / M. A. MacDonald. — Toronto : Methuen, 1986. — xii,228p. — *Bibliography: p219-224*

ACCIDENT LAW — England

ATIYAH, P. S.
Atiyah's accidents, compensation and the law / Peter Cane. — 4th ed. — London : Weidenfeld and Nicholson, 1987. — 639p

ACCIDENT LAW — England — Greater Manchester

GENN, Hazel
Meeting legal needs? : an evaluation of a scheme for personal injury victims / Hazel Genn. — Oxford : SSRC Centre for Socio-Legal Studies, 1982. — ix,69p. — *A report commissioned by the Greater Manchester Legal Services Committee*

ACCION ESPANOLA

MORODO, Raúl
Los orígines ideologicos del franquismo : Acción Española / Raúl Morodo. — Madrid : Alianza, 1985. — 227p. — (Alianza universidad ; 429)

ACCIÓN NACIONALISTA VASCA

GRANJA, José Luis de la
Nacionalismo y II República en el País Vasco : estatutos de autonomía, partidos y elecciones : historia de Acción Nacionalista Vasca: 1930-1936 / por José Luis de la Granja Sainz. — Madrid : Centro de Investigaciones Sociologicas : Siglo vientiuno de España, 1986. — xxiv,687p. — *Bibliography: p[641]-659*

ACCIÓN SINDICAL URUGUAYA — History

BOTTARO, José R.
25 años de movimiento Sindical Uruguayo : suplemento especial de Avanzada / José R. Bottaro. — Montevideo : Acción Sindical Uruguaya, [1985]. — 288p

ACCOUNTANTS — Denmark

Revisorerhvervet : struktur, takster og indtjening. — København : Monopoltilsynet, 1985. — 61p

Revisoreshvervet : struktur takster og indtjening. — København : Monopoltilsynet, 1978. — 35p

ACCOUNTANTS — Great Britain

MARGERISON, Tom
The making of a profession / Tom Margerison. — London : Institute of Chartered Accountants in England and Wales, 1980. — 43p

ACCOUNTING

AMERICAN ACCOUNTING ASSOCIATION. Meeting (71st : 1986 : New York)
Accounting and culture : plenary session papers and discussants' comments from the 1986...meeting... / edited by Barry E. Cushing. — [Sarasota, Fla.] : American Accounting Association, 1987. — viii,102p. — *Bibliographies*

BROWN, Lawrence D
The modern theory of financial reporting / Lawrence D. Brown. — Plano, Tex. : Business Publications, 1987. — x, 460 p.. — *Bibliography: p. 441-460*

FASB technical bulletin / Financial Accounting Standards Board. — Stamford, Conn. : Financial Accounting Standards Board, 1986-. — (Financial accounting series). — *Irregular*

GLAUTIER, M. W. E.
Accounting theory and practice / M.W.E. Glautier, B. Underdown. — 3rd ed. — London : Pitman, 1986. — xvii,732p. — *Previous ed.: 1982. — Includes bibliography and index*

HOPWOOD, Tony
Accounting and the domain of the public : some observations on current developments / Anthony G. Hopwood. — Leeds : University of Leeds, 1985. — 19p. — *The Price Waterhouse Public lecture on Accounting, University of Leeds. — Bibliography: p19*

International accounting and transnational decisions / edited by S.J. Gray. — London ; Boston : Butterworth, 1983. — 500p. — *Includes bibliographical references. — Includes index*

International accounting standards. — London : International Accounting Standards Committee, 1975-

LEE, G. A.
Modern financial accounting / G.A. Lee. — 4th ed. — Wokingham : Van Nostrand Reinhold, 1986. — ix.621p. — *Previous ed.: Walton-on-Thames : Nelson, 1981. — Includes index*

LEWIS, Richard, 1941 Sept. 30-
Advanced financial accounting. — 2nd ed. / Richard Lewis, David Pendrill. — London : Pitman, c1985. — xii,729p. — *Previous ed.: 1981. — Includes bibliographies and index*

MEIGS, Walter B
Accounting, the basis for business decisions / Walter B. Meigs, Robert F. Meigs. — 6th ed. — New York : McGraw-Hill, c1984. — xxiii, 1104 p.. — *Includes index*

MOSICH, A. N
Intermediate accounting / A.N. Mosich, E. John Larsen. — 6th ed. — New York : McGraw-Hill, c1986. — p. cm. — *Includes index*

MOSICH, A. N
Modern advanced accounting / A.N. Mosich, E. John Larsen. — 3rd ed. — New York : McGraw-Hill, c1983. — xxi, 872 p.. — *Rev. ed. of: Modern advanced accounting / Walter B. Meigs, A.N. Mosich, E. John Larsen. c1979. — Includes bibliographical references and index*

Statement of financial accounting standards. — Stamford, Conn : Financial Accounting Standards Board. — (Financial accounting series ; no.46)
no.92: Regulated enterprises-accounting for phase-in plans: an amendment of FASB statement no.71. — 1987. — 32p

Statement of financial accounting standards. — Stamford, Conn. : Financial Accounting Standards Board. — (Financial accounting series ; no.47)
no.93: Recognition of depreciation by not-for-profit organizations. — 1987. — 19p

ACCOUNTING
continuation

STILLING, P. J.
Manual of financial reporting and accounting / P.J. Stilling, J.B. Stevenson, A.W. Guida. — London : Butterworths, c1985. — xi, 379p. — *Previous ed: 1982*

WATTS, Ross L.
Positive accounting theory / Ross L. Watts, Jerold L. Zimmerman. — Englewood Cliffs, N.J. : Prentice-Hall, c1986. — p. cm. — *Includes index. — Bibliography: p*

WOLK, Harry I
Accounting theory : a conceptual and institutional approach / Harry I. Wolk, Jere R. Francis, Michael G. Tearney. — Boston, Mass. : Kent Pub. Co., c1984. — xiv, 609 p.. — *Includes bibliographies and index*

ACCOUNTING — Bibliography

TANTRAL, Panadda
Accounting literature in non-accounting journals : an annotated bibliography / Panadda Tantral. — New York : Garland, 1984. — ix, 233 p.. — (Accounting history and the development of a profession). — *: Originally presented as chapter 6 of the author's theses (Ph. D.--New York University, 1983). — Includes index*

ACCOUNTING — Books of Account

KORTE, J. P. de
De jaarlijkse financiele verantwoording in de VOC : Verenigde Oostindische Compagnie / door J. P. de Korte. — Leiden : Martinus Nijhoff, 1984. — xiv,95p,76 leaves. — (Werken uitgegeven door de Vereeniging het Nederlandsch Economisch-Historisch Archief ; 17)

ACCOUNTING — Data processing

BHASKAR, Krish
The impact of microprocessors on the small accounting practice / K.N. Bhaskar and B.C. Williams. — Englewood Cliffs, N.J. ; London : Prentice-Hall in association with the Institute of Chartered Accountants in England & Wales, c1986. — xvi,167p. — (Research studies in accounting). — *Bibliography: p143-162. — Includes index*

HOSKIN, Robert E.
Financial accounting with Lotus 1-2-3 / Robert E. Hoskin, Resa A. Labbe. — Englewood Cliffs, N.J. : Prentice-Hall, c1986. — p. cm. — *Includes index*

WILKINSON, Joseph W
Information systems for accounting and management : concepts, applications, and technology / Joseph W. Wilkinson, Dan C. Kneer. — Englewood Cliffs, N.J. : Prentice-Hall, c1987. — x, 338 p.. — *Includes bibliographies*

ACCOUNTING — Information storage and retrieval systems

KAYE, G. R.
The impact of IT on accountants / G. R. Kaye. — London : Institute of Cost and Management Accountants, 1987. — 36p. — *Bibliography: p33*

ACCOUNTING — Research

GRAY, R. H.
Accounting for R and D : a review of experiences with SSAP13 / R. H. Gray. — [S.l] : Institute of Chartered Accountants in England and Wales, 1985. — 155p. — *Bibliography: p142-155*

INSTITUTE OF CHARTERED ACCOUNTANTS IN ENGLAND AND WALES
Statement of standard accounting practice. — London : Institute of Chartered Accountants in England and Wales
no.13: Accounting for research and development. — 1977. — 6p

ACCOUNTING — Standards

Availability of financial statements. — Paris : OECD, 1987. — 37p. — (Working document / OECD Working Group on Accounting Standards ; no.2). — *Includes bibliographical references*

Statement of financial accounting standards. — Stamford, Conn. : Financial Accounting Standards Board. — (Financial accounting series)
no.90: Regulated enterprises accounting for abandonments and disallowances of plant costs: an amendment of FASB Statement no.71. — 1986. — 33p

Statement of financial accounting standards. — Stanford, Conn. : Financial Accounting Standards Board. — (Financial accounting series)
no.91: Accounting for non refundable fees and costs associated with originating or acquiring loans and initial direct costs of leases: an amendment of FASB Statements No.13, 60, and 65 and a rescission of FASB Statement No.17. — 1986. — 49p

ACCOUNTING — Standards — Great Britain

TAYLOR, Peter, 1929-
The regulation of accounting / Peter Taylor and Stuart Turley. — Oxford : Basil Blackwell, 1986. — x,215p. — (Modern developments in accounting and finance). — *Includes bibliographies and index*

ACCOUNTING — Standards — United States

BELKAOUI, Ahmed
Public policy and the practice and problems of accounting / Ahmed Belkaoui. — Westport, Conn. : Quorum Books, c1985. — p. cm. — *Includes index. — Bibliography: p*

MILLER, Paul B. W.
The FASB : the people, the process, and the politics / Paul B. W. Miller, Rodney J. Redding. — Homewood, Ill. : Irwin, 1986. — xvi,145p

ACCOUNTING — Denmark

Revisorerhvervet : struktur, takster og indtjening. — København : Monopoltilsynet, 1985. — 61p

Revisoreshvervet : struktur takster og indtjening. — København : Monopoltilsynet, 1978. — 35p

ACCOUNTING — Europe

OLDHAM, K. Michael
Accounting systems and practice in Europe / K. Michael Oldham. — 3rd ed. — Aldershot : Gower, c1987. — [290]p. — *Previous ed.: 1981. — Includes bibliography and index*

ACCOUNTING — Japan

Accounting and financial reporting in Japan current issues and future prospects in a world economy / edited by Frederick D.S. Choi and Kazuo Hiramatsu. — Wokingham : Van Nostrand Reinhold, 1987. — xix,276p. — *Includes index*

ACCOUNTING — Spain — Effect of inflation upon

MARTÍNEZ MÉNDEZ, Pedro
Los gastos financieros y los resultados empresariales en condiciones de inflación / Pedro Martínez Méndez. — [Madrid] : Banco de España, 1986. — 134p. — (Estudios económicos / Banco de España, Servicio de Estudios ; no.39). — *Bibliography: p129-131*

ACCOUNTING AND PRICE FLUCTUATIONS

BAXTER, W. T.
Inflation accounting / W.T. Baxter. — Oxford : Philip Allan, 1984. — viii,296p. — *Includes index*

GEORGES, W
Analytical contribution accounting : the interface of cost accounting and pricing policy / Walter Georges and Robert W. McGee. — New York : Quorum Books, 1987. — xii, 254 p.. — *Includes index. — Bibliography: p. [225]-249*

ACCOUNTING FIRMS — South Africa — Statistics

Census of accounting, auditing and bookkeeping services = Sensus van rekening-, oudit-en boekhoudienste / Central Statistical Services, South Africa. — Pretoria : Government Printer, 1975-. — *Irregular. — in English and Afrikaans*

ACCOUNTING LITERATURE

TANTRAL, Panadda
Accounting literature in non-accounting journals : an annotated bibliography / Panadda Tantral. — New York : Garland, 1984. — ix, 233 p.. — (Accounting history and the development of a profession). — *: Originally presented as chapter 6 of the author's theses (Ph. D.--New York University, 1983). — Includes index*

ACCULTURATION — Congresses

INTERNATIONAL CONGRESS OF ANTHROPOLOGICAL AND ETHNOLOGICAL SCIENCES ((10th : 1978 : New Delhi, India)
The tribal world and its transformation / edited by Bhupinder Singh, J.S. Bhandari. — New Delhi : Concept, 1980, c1978. — xx, 276 p.. — (Xth ICAES series ; no. 1). — *Includes bibliographical references and index*

ACCULTURATION — Ethiopia — Case studies

HAMER, John H.
Humane development : participation and change among the Sadáma of Ethiopia / John H. Hamer. — Tuscaloosa, Ala. : University of Alabama Press, c1987. — xi, 281 p.. — *Includes index. — Bibliography: p. 267-276*

ACCULTURATION — United States

CARLSON, Robert A.
The Americanization syndrome : a quest for conformity / Robert A. Carlson. — [Rev. and updated ed.]. — London : Croom Helm, c1987. — 197p. — (Croom Helm series on theory and practice of adult education in North America). — *Previous ed.: published as the quest for conformity. New York : London : Wiley, 1975. — Includes index*

ACEH (INDONESIA) — History — Autonomy and independence movements

SJAMSUDDIN, Nazaruddin
The republican revolt : a study of the Acehnese rebellion / Nazaruddin Sjamsuddin. — Singapore : Institute of Southeast Asian Studies, c1985. — x, 359 p., [1] leaf of plates. — *: Revision of the author's thesis (doctoral)--Monash University. — Bibliography: p. [341]-359*

ACHIEVEMENT MOTIVATION

LEVINE, David O.
The American college and the culture of aspiration, 1915-1940 / David O. Levine. — Ithaca : Cornell University Press, 1986. — 281 p.. — *Includes index. — Bibliography: p. 255-275*

MAEHR, Martin L
The motivation factor : a theory of personal investment / Martin L. Maehr, Larry A. Braskamp. — Lexington, Mass. : Lexington Books, c1986. — p. cm. — *Includes index. — Bibliography: p*

ACID PRECIPITATION

PEARCE, Fred
Acid rain / Fred Pearce. — Harmondsworth : Penguin, 1987. — 162p. — (A Penguin special). — *Bibliography: p.[148]-159*

ACID RAIN
VALROFF, Jean
Pollution atmosphérique et pluies acides : rapport au premier ministre / Jean Valroff, Philippe Le Lourd, Philippe Derexel. — Paris : La Documentation Française, 1985. — 340p. — (Collection des rapports officiels). — *Bibliography: p315-322*

VAN LIER, Irene H.
Acid rain and international law / by Irene H. van Lier. — Toronto : Bunsel Environmental Consultants, [1981?]. — xxii,278p. — *Originally presented as the author's thesis (LL.M.) - Dalhousie University 1980.* — *Bibliography: p.257-266*

ACID RAIN — Bibliography
STOPP, G. Harry
Acid rain : a bibliography of research annotated for easy access / by G. Harry Stopp, Jr. — Metuchen, N.J. : Scarecrow Press, 1985. — p. cm. — *Includes index*

ACID RAIN — Environmental aspects
PEARCE, Fred
Acid rain / Fred Pearce. — Harmondsworth : Penguin, 1987. — 162p. — (A Penguin special) . — *Bibliography: p.[148]-159*

ACID RAIN — Environmental aspects — Government policy — Canada
Acid rain and friendly neighbors : the policy dispute between Canada and the United States / edited by Jurgen Schmandt and Hilliard Roderick. — Durham : Duke University Press, 1985. — xiii, 332 p.. — (Duke Press policy studies). — *Includes index.* — *Bibliography: [292]-322*

ACID RAIN — Environmental aspects — Government policy — United States
Acid rain and friendly neighbors : the policy dispute between Canada and the United States / edited by Jurgen Schmandt and Hilliard Roderick. — Durham : Duke University Press, 1985. — xiii, 332 p.. — (Duke Press policy studies). — *Includes index.* — *Bibliography: [292]-322*

ACID RAIN — Environmental aspects — Canada
Acid rain and friendly neighbors : the policy dispute between Canada and the United States / edited by Jurgen Schmandt and Hilliard Roderick. — Durham : Duke University Press, 1985. — xiii, 332 p.. — (Duke Press policy studies). — *Includes index.* — *Bibliography: [292]-322*

ACID RAIN — Environmental aspects — United States
Acid rain and friendly neighbors : the policy dispute between Canada and the United States / edited by Jurgen Schmandt and Hilliard Roderick. — Durham : Duke University Press, 1985. — xiii, 332 p.. — (Duke Press policy studies). — *Includes index.* — *Bibliography: [292]-322*

ACID RAIN — Law and legislation
Transboundary air pollution : international legal aspects of the co-operation of states / editors, K. Flinterman, B. Kwiatkowska, and J. Lammers. — Dordrecht ; Boston : M. Nijhoff, 1987. — p. cm. — *Includes bibliographies and index*

ACORN (Organization)
DELGADO, Gary
Organizing the movement : the roots and growth of ACORN / Gary Delgado ; with a foreword by Richard A. Cloward and Frances Fox Piven. — Philadelphia : Temple University Press, 1986. — xx, 269 p.. — (Labor and social change). — *Includes index.* — *Bibliography: p. 253-261*

ACQUIRED IMMUNE DEFICIENCY SYNDROME
BLACKIE, Duncan
Aids : the Socialist view / Duncan Blackie and Ian Taylor. — London : Socialist Workers' Party, 1987. — 32p

ACQUIRED IMMUNODEFICIENCY SYNDROME
Mobilizing against AIDS : the unfinished story of a virus / Institute of Medicine, National Academy of Sciences ; Eve K. Nichols, writer. — Cambridge, Mass. : Harvard University Press, 1986. — x, 212 p.. — *Drawn from the 1985 Annual Meeting of the Institute of Medicine.* — *Includes index.* — *Bibliography: p. 189-190*

ACQUIRED IMMUNODEFICIENCY SYNDROME — psychology
BAUMGARTNER, Gail Henderson
AIDS, psychosocial factors in the acquired immune deficiency syndrome / by Gail Henderson Baumgartner. — Springfield, Ill., U.S.A. : Thomas, c1986. — 113p. — *Includes index.* — *Bibliography: p.85-101*

ACQUIRED IMMUNODEFICIENCY SYNDROME — psychology — congresses
What to do about AIDS : physicians and mental health professionals discuss the issues / edited by Leon McKusick. — Berkeley : University of California Press, c1987. — p. cm. — *Papers from a conference convened in San Francisco Sept. 13-14, 1985, by the AIDS Clinical Research Center at the University of California, San Francisco.* — *Includes index*

ACQUISITION OF AUDIO-VISUAL MATERIALS
PINION, Catherine F.
Legal deposit of non-book materials / Catherine F. Pinion. — London : British Library, 1986. — 1v.. — (Library and information research report ; 49). — *Includes bibliography*

ACQUISITIONS (LIBRARIES)
Selection of library materials in the humanities, social sciences, and sciences / Patricia A. McClung, editor ; section editors, William Hepfer ... [et al.]. — Chicago : American Library Association, 1985. — xiv, 405 p.. — *Includes bibliographies and index*

SPILLER, David
Book selection : an introduction to principles and practice / David Spiller ; with an introduction by Brian Baumfield. — 4th ed. — London : Bingley, 1986. — ix,235p. — *Previous ed.: 1980.* — *Bibliography: p206-223.* — *Includes index*

ACTING — Social aspects
MAST, Sharon
Stages of identity : a study of actors / Sharon Mast. — Aldershot : Published for the London School of Economics and Political Science by Gower, c1986. — vfiii,217p. — *Bibliography: p203-213.* — *Includes index*

ACTION DIRECTE
HAMON, Alain
Action directe : du terrorisme français a l'euroterrorisme / Alain Hamon, Jean Charles Marchand. — Paris : Le Seuil, 1986. — 251p

ACTION RESEARCH
ARGYRIS, Chris
Action science / Chris Argyris, Robert Putnam, Diana McLain Smith. — 1st ed. — San Francisco : Jossey-Bass, 1985. — xx, 480 p.. — (The Jossey-Bass social and behavioral science series)(The Jossey-Bass management series). — *Includes index.* — *Bibliography: p. 451-465*

ACTIONS AND DEFENSES — Great Lakes Region
MULDOON, Paul R.
Cross-border litigation : environmental rights in the Great Lakes ecosystem / by Paul R. Muldoon, with David A. Scriven and James B. Olson. — Toronto : Carswell, 1986. — xxxv,410p

ACTRESSES — Soviet Union — Biography
VOLOKHOVA, N. A.
"Fenomen" : stranitsy zhizni i deiatel'nosti M. F. Andreevoi / N. A. Volokhova. — Izd. 2-e, ispr. i dop.. — Leningrad : Lenizdat, 1986. — 317p. — *Bibliography: p315-[318]*

ACUPUNCTURE — Great Britain — Professional ethics
SAKS, Michael Paul
Professions and the public interest : the response of the medical profession to acupuncture in nineteenth and twentieth century Britain / Michael Paul Saks. — 676 leaves. — *PhD(Arts) 1986 LSE*

ADAMS, JOHN BODKIN — Trials, litigation, etc.
DEVLIN, Patrick Devlin, Baron
Easing the passing : the trial of Dr John Bodkin Adams / Patrick Devlin. — London : Bodley Head, 1985. — [256]p

ADAMS, JOHN QUINCY
HARGREAVES, Mary W. M.
The presidency of John Quincy Adams / Mary W.M. Hargreaves. — Lawrence, Kan. : University Press of Kansas, c1985. — xv, 398 p.. — (American presidency series). — *Includes index.* — *Bibliography: p. 325-380*

RICHARDS, Leonard L
The life and times of Congressman John Quincy Adams / Leonard L. Richards. — New York : Oxford University Press, 1986. — viii, 245 p.. — *Includes index.* — *Bibliography: p. 205-238*

ADELAIDE (SOUTH AUSTRALIA) — Planning
SOUTH AUSTRALIA. City of Adelaide Development Committee
City of Adelaide interim development control : second statement of policy, 18th July, 1975. — Adelaide : the Committee, 1975. — 63p

ADENAUER, KONRAD
ADENAUER, Konrad
Memoirs, 1945-53 / translated by Beate Ruhm von Oppen. — London : Weidenfeld and Nicolson, 1966. — 478p

KÖHLER, Henning
Adenauer und die rheinische Republik : der erste Anlauf 1918-1924 / Henning Köhler. — Opladen : Westdeutscher Verlag, 1986. — 287p . — *Bibliography: p281-284*

ADJUSTMENT (PSYCHOLOGY)
BREAKWELL, Glynis M.
Coping with threatened identities / Glynis M. Breakwell. — London : Methuen, 1986. — [232]p. — *Includes index*

ADMINISTRATIVE AGENCIES — Data processing
STEVENS, John M
Information systems and public management / by John M. Stevens. — New York : Praeger, 1985. — p. cm. — *Includes index.* — *Bibliography: p*

ADMINISTRATIVE AGENCIES — Data processing — Congresses
EXPERT SYSTEMS IN GOVERNMENT SYMPOSIUM (1985 : McLean, Va.)
Expert Systems in Government Symposium / Kamal N. Karna, editor ; IEEE Computer Society, The MITRE Corporation, The Institute of Electrical and Electronics Engineers, inc., in association with AIAA National Capital Section. — Washington, D.C. : IEEE Computer Society Press, c1985. — xxiii, 694 p.. — *Includes bibliographies and index*

ADMINISTRATIVE AGENCIES — Handbooks, manuals, etc — Bibliography
KORMAN, Richard I
Checklist of government directories, lists, and rosters / compiled by Richard I. Korman. — Westport, CT : Meckler Pub. ; Cambridge, Eng. : Chadwyck-Healey, c1982. — x, 51 p.. — *"The collections of the Library of Congress are the source of the nearly 300 titles cited"--P. x.* — *Includes index*

ADMINISTRATIVE AGENCIES — Legal status, laws, etc. — Ecuador

ECUADOR
[Laws, etc.]. Ley de la Comisión de Valores - Corporación Financiera Nacional / codificada por José Iturralde Arteaga. — [Quito] : Comision de Valores - Corporación Financiera Nacional, 1975. — 29p

ADMINISTRATIVE AGENCIES — Legal status, laws, etc. — Peru

PERU
[Laws, etc.]. Ley orgánica [del Instituto Nacional de Administración Pública] : Decreto-ley no.20316. — [Lima] : Instituto Nacional de Administración Pública, [ca.1973]. — 25p

PERU
[Laws, etc.]. Junta de Supervigilancia de Películas y su reglamento. — Lima : Oficina Central de Información, 1974. — 25p

PERU
[Laws, etc]. Ley orgánica de la Empresa Editora Perú : Decreto-ley no.21420. — Lima : [Empresa Editora Perú, ca.1976]. — 14p

ADMINISTRATIVE AGENCIES — Australia — Economic aspects

The economics of bureaucracy and statutory authorities : the edited proceedings of a CIS policy forum held in Melbourne on July 8th, 1981 / contributors: Gordon Tullock...[et al.]. — Sydney : Centre for Independent Studies, 1983. — viii,104p. — (CIS Policy Forums ; 1). — *Bibliographies*

ADMINISTRATIVE AGENCIES — Great Britain — Bibliography

GREAT BRITAIN. Civil Service Department. Central Management Library
Fringe bodies (quangos). — London : the Library, 1978. — 3p. — (Policy science documentation. Reading list series ; A90)

ADMINISTRATIVE AGENCIES — Peru

PERU. Servicio del Empleo y Recursos Humanos
Junta Nacional de Mano de Obra. — [Lima : the Servicio, ca.1970]. — [12p]

ADMINISTRATIVE AGENCIES — Puerto Rico — Handbooks, manuals, etc.

PUERTO RICO. Office of the Governor
Manual de servicios de las agencias gubernamentales. — [San Juan] : the Office, [ca.1971]. — vi,346p

ADMINISTRATIVE AGENCIES — Sweden

RESSNER, Ulla
Group organised work in the automated office / Ulla Ressner and Evy Gunnarsson. — Aldershot : Gower, c1986. — 122p. — *Bibliography: p111-122*

ADMINISTRATIVE AGENCIES — United States

CLARKE, Jeanne Nienaber
Staking out the terrain : power differentials among natural resource management agencies / Jeanne Nienaber Clarke, Daniel McCool. — Albany : State University of New York Press, c1985. — p. cm. — (SUNY series in environmental public policy). — *Includes index. — Bibliography: p*

FITZGERALD, Randall
Porkbarrel : the unexpurgated Grace Commission story of congressional profligacy / Randall Fitzgerald and Gerald Lipson. — Washington, D.C. : Cato Institute, c1984. — xxxv, 114 p.. — *"This report was originally prepared under the title The cost of congressional encroachment"--T.p. verso*

ADMINISTRATIVE AGENCIES — United States — History

ROHR, John A
To run a constitution : the legitimacy of the administrative state / John A. Rohr. — Lawrence, Kan. : University Press of Kansas, c1986. — xv, 272 p.. — (Studies in government and public policy). — *Includes index. — Bibliography: p. 215-264*

ADMINISTRATIVE AGENCIES — United States — Management — Decision making

MAGAT, Wesley A
Rules in the making : a statistical analysis of regulatory agency behavior / Wesley A. Magat, Alan J. Krupnick, Winston Harrington. — Washington, D.C. : Resources for the Future, c1986. — xiii, 182 p.. — *Includes bibliographies and index*

ADMINISTRATIVE AND POLITICAL DIVISIONS — Dictionaries

FISHER, Morris
Provinces and provincial capitals of the world / compiled by Morris Fisher. — 2nd ed. — Metuchen, N.J. : Scarecrow, 1985. — ix, 248 p. . — *Includes index*

ADMINISTRATIVE COURTS

AMERASINGHE, C. F.
Index of decisions of international administrative tribunals / C. F. Amerasinghe, D. Bellinger. — 2nd ed. — Washington, D. C. : International Bank for Reconstruction and Development, 1985. — vi,149p. — *Cover title. — Previous ed: 1981*

ADMINISTRATIVE COURTS — Australia

FLICK, Geoffrey A.
Natural justice : principles and practical application / by Geoffrey A. Flick. — 2nd ed. — Sydney : Butterworths, 1984. — xliv,212p

ADMINISTRATIVE DISCRETION — Great Britain

GALLIGAN, D. J.
Discretionary powers : a legal study of official discretion / D.J. Galligan. — Oxford : Clarendon, 1986. — xxi,401p. — *Bibliography: p383-396. — Includes index*

ADMINISTRATIVE LAW — Argentina

DROMI, José Roberto
Administración territorial y economiá : (la provincia, la región y el municipio en Argentina / José Roberto Dromi. — Madrid : Instituto de Estudios de Administración Local, 1983. — 423p. — (Autores Hispanoamericanos de Derecho Público)

ADMINISTRATIVE LAW — Australia

SHARPE, Jennifer M.
The Administrative Appeals Tribunal and policy review / by Jennifer M. Sharpe. — Sydney : The Law Book Company Limited, 1986. — xxvi,232p

WILLIAMS, David John Parry
Investigations by administrative agencies / by David John Parry Williams. — Sydney : Law Book Company, 1987. — cxiii,1099p

ADMINISTRATIVE LAW — Canada

DUSSAULT, René
Administrative law : a treatise / by René Dussault and Louis Borgeat ; translated by Murray Rankin. — 2nd ed. — Toronto : Carswell
Vol.1. — 1985. — xcvii,643p

ADMINISTRATIVE LAW — England

FOULKES, David, 1924-
Administrative law / David Foulkes. — 6th ed. — London : Butterworths, 1986. — xxxv,477p. — *Previous ed.: 1982. — Includes index*

GARNER, J. F.
Garner's administrative law. — 6th ed. / J.F. Garner, B.L. Jones. — London : Butterworths, 1985. — [552]p. — *Previous ed.: published as Administrative law. 1979. — Includes bibliography and index*

HAWKE, Neil
An introduction to administrative law / Neil Hawke. — Oxford : ESC, 1984. — xxix,255p

ADMINISTRATIVE LAW — France

FRANCE
[Code administratif]. Code administratif. — 18e éd. — Paris : Dalloz, 1985. — 1494,23p. — (Petits codes Dalloz). — *Previous ed.: 1983. — Includes index*

ADMINISTRATIVE LAW — Great Britain

CANE, Peter
An introduction to administrative law / Peter Cane. — Oxford : Clarendon, 1986. — xxii,325p. — (Clarendon law series). — *Includes index*

GANZ, Gabriele
Quasi-legislation : recent developments in secondary legislation / by Gabriele Ganz. — 2nd ed. — London : Sweet & Maxwell, 1987. — xiv,114p. — (Modern legal studies). — *New ed. — Previous ed.: published as Administrative procedures. 1974. — Includes index*

ADMINISTRATIVE LAW — India

BASU, Durga Das
Administrative law / Durga Das Basu. — 2nd ed. — New Delhi : Prentice-Hall of India, 1986. — lxxi,622p

ADMINISTRATIVE LAW — Ireland

MORGAN, David Gwynn
Administrative Law / by David Gwynn Morgan and Gerard Hogan. — London : Sweet & Maxwell, 1986. — li,422p. — (Irish law texts). — *Includes index*

ADMINISTRATIVE LAW — Netherlands

WETENSCHAPPELIJKE RAAD VOOR HET REGERINGSBELEID
De organisatie van het openbaar bestuur : enkele aspecten, knelpunten en voorstellen. — 's-Gravenhage : Staatsuitgeverij, 1975. — 195p. — (Rapporten aan de Regering / Wetenschappelijke Raad voor het Regeringsbeleid ; 6)

ADMINISTRATIVE LAW — Peru

PERU
[Laws, etc.]. Ley orgánica [del Instituto Nacional de Administración Pública] : Decreto-ley no.20316. — [Lima] : Instituto Nacional de Administración Pública, [ca.1973]. — 25p

ADMINISTRATIVE LAW — Quebec (Province)

DUSSAULT, René
Administrative law : a treatise / by René Dussault and Louis Borgeat ; translated by Murray Rankin. — 2nd ed. — Toronto : Carswell
Vol.1. — 1985. — xcvii,643p

ADMINISTRATIVE LAW — Spain

GARCÍA DE ENTERRÍA, Eduardo
Curso de derecho administrativo / Eduardo Garcia de Enterria, Tomás-Ramón Fernández. — Madrid : Editoria Civitas
1. — Madrid : Editoria Civitas. — 766p

GARRIDO FALLA, Fernando
Tratado de derecho administrativo / Fernando Garrido Falla. — Reimpresión de la 7a ed. — Madrid : Centro de Estudios Constitucionales
Vol. 2: (Parte general: conclusión). — 1986. — 628p

GONZALEZ PEREZ, Jesus
Régimen jurídico de la Administración local / Jesus Gonzalez Perez. — Madrid : Abella, 1985. — 867p

El sistema juridico de las comunidades autonomas / Eliseo Aja...[et al.]. — Madrid : Tecnos, 1985. — 476p. — *Bibliograhies*

ADMINISTRATIVE LAW — United States — Dictionaries

SHAFRITZ, Jay M
The Facts on File dictionary of public administration / Jay M. Shafritz. — New York, N.Y. : Facts on File, c1985. — 610 p.. — *Includes bibliographies*

ADMINISTRATIVE PROCEDURE — Economic aspects — United States

MAGAT, Wesley A
Rules in the making : a statistical analysis of regulatory agency behavior / Wesley A. Magat, Alan J. Krupnick, Winston Harrington. — Washington, D.C. : Resources for the Future, c1986. — xiii, 182 p.. — *Includes bibliographies and index*

ADMINISTRATIVE PROCEDURE — Australia
FLICK, Geoffrey A.
Natural justice : principles and practical application / by Geoffrey A. Flick. — 2nd ed. — Sydney : Butterworths, 1984. — xliv,212p

ADMINISTRATIVE REMEDIES — Australia
SHARPE, Jennifer M.
The Administrative Appeals Tribunal and policy review / by Jennifer M. Sharpe. — Sydney : The Law Book Company Limited, 1986. — xxvi,232p

ADMINISTRATIVE REMEDIES — India
DUBHASHI, P. R.
Administrative reforms / P. R. Dubhashi. — Delhi : B. R. Publishing Corporation, 1986. — 207p

ADMINISTRATIVE RESPONSIBILITY — Great Britain
DAY, Patricia, 19---
Accountabilities : five public services / Patricia Day, Rudolf Klein. — London : Tavistock, 1987. — 259p. — (Social science paperbacks). — *Includes index*

ADMINSTRATIVE LAW — Spain
GARRIDO FALLA, Fernando
Tratado de derecho adminstrativo / Fernando Garrido Falla. — 9a ed. — Madrid : Centro de Estudios Constitucionales
Vol.1: (Parte general). — 1985. — 748p

ADMIRALS — Great Britain — Biography
HUNT, Barry D.
Sailor-scholar : Admiral Sir Herbert Richmond 1871-1946 / Barry D. Hunt. — Waterloo, Ont. : Wilfred Laurier University Press ; Gerrards Cross : distributed by Smythe, c1982. — xii,259p. — *Bibliography: p238-248. — Includes index*

ZIEGLER, Philip
Mountbatten : the official biography / Philip Ziegler. — London : Collins, 1985. — 786p,[48]p of plates. — *Geneal.table on lining papers. — Bibliography: p751-756. — Includes index*

ADMIRALTY — South Africa
SHAW, D. J.
Admiralty jurisdiction and practice in South Africa / by D. J. Shaw. — Cape Town : Juta, 1987. — xxvii,264p. — *Bibliography: p. xi. - Includes index*

ADOLESCENCE
ADELSON, Joseph
Inventing adolescence : the political psychology of everyday schooling / Joseph Adelson. — New Brunswick, N.J., U.S.A. : Transaction Books, c1986. — ix, 296 p.. — *Includes bibliographical references*

COLEMAN, John C.
The nature of adolescence / John C. Coleman. — London : Methuen, 1980. — ix,214p. — (University paperbacks). — *Bibliography: p191-206. - Includes index*

LEFRANÇOIS, Guy R
Adolescents / Guy R. Lefrancois ; [cartoonist, Tony Hall]. — 2d ed. — Belmont, Calif. : Wadsworth Pub. Co., c1981. — p. cm. — *Includes index. — Bibliography: p*

ADOLESCENCE — Congresses
Development in adolescence : psychological, social, and biological aspects / [edited by] W. Everaerd ... [et al.]. — Boston ; Lancaster : Nijhoff, c1983. — x, 254 p.. — *Based on a postgraduate course for medical practitioners, held in Leiden, Nov. 1981, which was entitled, Adolescence: psychological, social, and biological aspects. — Includes bibliographical references and index*

ADOLESCENCE — Physiological aspects — Addresses, essays, lectures
Development in adolescence : psychological, social, and biological aspects / [edited by] W. Everaerd ... [et al.]. — Boston ; Lancaster : Nijhoff, c1983. — x, 254 p.. — *Based on a postgraduate course for medical practitioners, held in Leiden, Nov. 1981, which was entitled, Adolescence: psychological, social, and biological aspects. — Includes bibliographical references and index*

ADOLESCENCE — Social aspects — Addresses, essays, lectures
Development in adolescence : psychological, social, and biological aspects / [edited by] W. Everaerd ... [et al.]. — Boston ; Lancaster : Nijhoff, c1983. — x, 254 p.. — *Based on a postgraduate course for medical practitioners, held in Leiden, Nov. 1981, which was entitled, Adolescence: psychological, social, and biological aspects. — Includes bibliographical references and index*

ADOLESCENT BEHAVIOR
Suicide in adolescence : suicidal behaviour among adolescents / edited by René F.W. Diekstra and Keith Hawton. — Dordrecht ; Boston : Nijhoff, 1986. — p. cm. — *Includes indexes*

ADOLESCENT PSYCHOLOGY
HAWTON, Keith
Suicide and attempted suicide among children and adolescents / by Keith Hawton. — Beverly Hills ; London : Sage, c1986. — 159 p.. — (Developmental clinical psychology and psychiatry series ; v. 5). — *Includes index. — Bibliography: p. 145-153*

LEFRANÇOIS, Guy R
Adolescents / Guy R. Lefrancois ; [cartoonist, Tony Hall]. — 2d ed. — Belmont, Calif. : Wadsworth Pub. Co., c1981. — p. cm. — *Includes index. — Bibliography: p*

ADOLESCENT PSYCHOLOGY — Addresses, essays, lectures
Development in adolescence : psychological, social, and biological aspects / [edited by] W. Everaerd ... [et al.]. — Boston ; Lancaster : Nijhoff, c1983. — x, 254 p.. — *Based on a postgraduate course for medical practitioners, held in Leiden, Nov. 1981, which was entitled, Adolescence: psychological, social, and biological aspects. — Includes bibliographical references and index*

ADOLESCENT PSYCHOLOGY — Congresses
Development in adolescence : psychological, social, and biological aspects / [edited by] W. Everaerd ... [et al.]. — Boston ; Lancaster : Nijhoff, c1983. — x, 254 p.. — *Based on a postgraduate course for medical practitioners, held in Leiden, Nov. 1981, which was entitled, Adolescence: psychological, social, and biological aspects. — Includes bibliographical references and index*

ADOLESCENT PSYCHOPATHOLOGY — Addresses, essays, lectures
Development in adolescence : psychological, social, and biological aspects / [edited by] W. Everaerd ... [et al.]. — Boston ; Lancaster : Nijhoff, c1983. — x, 254 p.. — *Based on a postgraduate course for medical practitioners, held in Leiden, Nov. 1981, which was entitled, Adolescence: psychological, social, and biological aspects. — Includes bibliographical references and index*

ADOPTION — Law and legislation — Scotland
MCNEILL, Peter G. B.
Adoption of children in Scotland / Peter G. B. McNeill. — 2nd ed.. — Edinburgh : W. Green & Son, 1986. — xxvii,218p

ADOPTION — Psychological aspects
CROOK, Marion
The face in the mirror : teenagers talk about adoption / Marion Crook. — Toronto : NC Press, 1986. — 116p. — *Bibliography: p114-116*

ADOPTION — Great Britain
THOBURN, June
Permanence in child care / June Thoburn, Anne Murdoch, Alison O'Brien. — Oxford : Basil Blackwell, 1986. — xii,202p. — (The practice of social work ; 15). — *Bibliography: p193-198. — Includes index*

ADOPTION — Great Britain — Bibliography
HARRIS, Kevin
Transracial adoption : a bibliography / Kevin Harris. — London : British Agencies for Adoption and Fostering, 1985. — 122p

ADORNO, THEODOR W.
ADORNO-SYMPOSIUM (1984 : Hamburg)
Hamburger Adorno-Symposium / herausgegeben von Michael Löbig und Gerhard Schweppenhäuser. — Lüneberg : Dietrich zu Klampen Verlag, 1984. — 169p. — *Includes bibliographic notes*

ADULT CHILDREN — United States
LITTWIN, Susan
The postponed generation : why America's kids are growing up later / Susan Littwin. — New York : Morrow, c1986. — p. cm

ADULT EDUCATION
Adult education : international perspectives from China / edited by Chris Duke. — London : Croom Helm, c1987. — 254p. — (Croom Helm series in international adult education). — *Conference papers. — Includes bibliographies and index*

LINDEMAN, Eduard
Learning democracy : Eduard Lindeman on adult education and social change / [edited by] Stephen Brookfield. — London : Croom Helm, c1987. — 238p. — (Croom Helm series on theory and practice of adult education in North America). — *Bibliography: p221-231. — Includes index*

Planning adult learning : issues, practices and directions / edited by W.M. Rivera. — London : Croom Helm, c1987. — 189p. — (Croom Helm series on theory and practice of adult education in North America). — *Includes index*

Twentieth century thinkers in adult education / edited by Peter Jarvis. — London : Croom Helm, c1987. — 326p. — (International perspectives on adult and continuing education) . — *Includes bibliographies and index*

ADULT EDUCATION — Government policy — Great Britain
GRIFFIN, Colin
Adult education : as social policy / Colin Griffin. — London : Croom Helm, c1987. — 274p. — *Bibliography: p255-267. — Includes index*

ADULT EDUCATION — Government policy — Great Britain — History — 20th century
EVANS, Brendan
Radical adult education : a political critique / Brendan Evans. — Beckenham : Croom Helm, c1987. — [272]p. — (Radical forum on adult education series). — *Includes index*

ADULT EDUCATION — Africa, West
CALCOTT, David
The education of adults at all levels / by David Calcott. — London : Commonwealth Secretariat, 1970. — 16p. — *At head of title page Commonwealth Conference on Education in Rural Areas. — Bibliography: p15-16. — CRE(70)C/4*

ADULT EDUCATION — Alberta
ROBERTS, Hayden
Culture and adult education : a study of Alberta and Quebec / Hayden Roberts. — Edmonton, Alta., Canada : University of Alberta Press, c1982. — xiv, 274 p.. — *Includes bibliographies and index*

ADULT EDUCATION — Developing countries

CALCOTT, David
The education of adults at all levels / by David Calcott. — London : Commonwealth Secretariat, 1970. — 16p. — *At head of title page Commonwealth Conference on Education in Rural Areas.* — *Bibliography: p15-16.* — CRE(70)C/4

ADULT EDUCATION — England

ADVISORY COUNCIL FOR ADULT AND CONTINUING EDUCATION
Volunteers in adult education : a research report for the Advisory Council / by Dorothea Hall ; assisted by Ieuan Hughes and Colette Laplace under the direction of Barry Elsey. — Leicester : ACACE, c1983. — viii,132p. — *Bibliography: p109-110*

MCDONALD, Joan
Education for unemployed adults : problems and good practice : a paper / by Joan McDonald. — [London] : Department of Education and Science, [1985?]. — 36p

ADULT EDUCATION — England — Liverpool (Merseyside)

EDWARDS, Judith
Working class adult education in Liverpool : a radical approach : an evaluation of Second Chance to Learn / Judith Edwards. — Manchester : University of Manchester Centre for Adult and Higher Education, 1986. — (Manchester monographs ; 25)

ADULT EDUCATION — Finland — Statistics

HAVÉN, Heikki
Participation in adult education [1980] / Heikki Havén, Risto Syvänperä. — Helsinki : Tilastokeskus, 1984. — 98p. — (Tutkimuksia / Finland. Tilastokeskus ; no.92)

ADULT EDUCATION — France

TOYNBEE, W. S.
Adult education and the voluntary associations in France / W. S. Toynbee. — Nottingham : University of Nottingham. Department of Adult Education, 1985. — iv,44p. — (Nottingham working papers in the education of adults ; no.7)

ADULT EDUCATION — Great Britain

Adult education with the unemployed / edited by Bruce Spencer. — Leeds : University of Leeds. Department of Adult and Continuing Education, 1986. — 90p

GREAT BRITAIN. Department of Education and Science. Inspectorate of Schools
NAFE : non-advanced further education in practice : (an HMI survey). — London : H.M.S.O., 1987. — 110p

SENIOR, Barbara
Educational responses to adult unemployment / Barbara Senior and John Naylor. — London : Croom Helm, c1987. — 174p. — (Radical forum on adult education series). — *Includes index*

ADULT EDUCATION — Ireland

MCCARTHY, J. R.
Study while you work : vocational courses in further education for 16-19 year old employees / J. R. McMarthy, R. H. McDowell and C. J. McIlheney. — Belfast : Northern Ireland Council for Educational Research, 1985. — vi,59p. — (Publications of the Northern Ireland Council for Educational Research ; 31). — *Bibliography: p.59*

ADULT EDUCATION — New York (N.Y.) — History

RUTKOFF, Peter M.
New School : a history of the New School for Social Research / Peter M. Rutkoff, William B. Scott. — New York : Free Press ; London : Collier Macmillan, c1986. — xiv, 314p, [16]p of plates. — *Includes bibliographical references and index*

ADULT EDUCATION — Québec (Province)

ROBERTS, Hayden
Culture and adult education : a study of Alberta and Quebec / Hayden Roberts. — Edmonton, Alta., Canada : University of Alberta Press, c1982. — xiv, 274 p.. — *Includes bibliographies and index*

ADULT EDUCATION — United States

LONG, Huey, 1935-
New perspectives on the education of adults in the United States / Huey Long. — London : Croom Helm, c1987. — 263p. — (Croom Helm series in international adult education). — *Bibliography: p225-254.* — *Includes index*

ADULT EDUCATION OF WOMEN — Great Britain

You're learning all the time / edited by Pam Flynn ... [et al.]. — Nottingham : Spokesman, 1986. — 146p. — (Britain's regions in crisis ; 2). — *Bibliography: p143-144.* — *Includes bibliographies*

ADULTERY — United States

RICHARDSON, Laurel Walum
The new other woman : contemporary single women in affairs with married men / Laurel Richardson. — New York : Free Press ; London : Collier Macmillan, c1985. — p. cm. — *Includes index.* — *Bibliography: p*

ADULTHOOD — Michigan — Psychological aspects — Longitudinal studies

MORTIMER, Jeylan T.
Work, family, and personality : transition to adulthood / Jeylan T. Mortimer, Jon Lorence, Donald S. Kumka. — Norwood, N.J. : Ablex Pub. Corp., c1986. — viii, 267 p.. — (Modern sociology). — *Includes index.* — *Bibliography: p. 231-255*

ADVANCED SCHOOL FOR GIRLS (South Australia)

MACKINNON, Alison
One foot on the ladder : origins and outcomes of girls' secondary schooling in South Australia / Alison Mackinnon. — St. Lucia ; New York : University of Queensland Press, 1984. — xii, 209 p.. — (The University of Queensland Press scholars' library). — *Includes index.* — *Bibliography: p. [197]-205*

ADVENTURE AND ADVENTURES — Africa, Central

HARMAN, Nicholas
Bwana Stokesi and his African conquests / Nicholas Harman. — London : Cape, 1986. — xv,272p,[16]p of plates. — *Includes index*

ADVERTISING

JONES, John Philip
What's in a name? : Advertising and the concept of brands / John Philip Jones. — Lexington, Mass. : Lexington Books, c1986. — p. cm. — *Includes index*

ADVERTISING — Charities — Great Britain

Advertising by charities : a practical guide to raising money by press advertising, direct mail, posters, radio and television appeals and telephone selling / edited by Ken Burnett. — London : Directory of Social Changes, 1986. — vii,152p

ADVERTISING — Economic aspects

VAILE, Roland S
Economics of advertising / Roland S. Vaile. — New York : Garland Pub., 1985, [c1927]. — xi, 183 p.. — (The History of advertising). — : Reprint. Originally published: New York : Ronald Press Co., c1927. — *Includes index*

ADVERTISING — Psychological aspects

DYER, Gillian
Advertising as communication / Gillian Dyer. — London : Methuen, 1982. — (Studies in communication)

ADVERTISING — Research

LUCAS, Darrell Blaine
Measuring advertising effectiveness / Darrell Blaine Lucas, Steuart Henderson Britt. — New York : Garland, 1985, c1963. — xi, 399 p.. — (The History of advertising). — : Reprint. Originally published: New York : McGraw-Hill, c1963. — *Includes bibliographical references and index*

ADVERTISING — Social aspects

DYER, Gillian
Advertising as communication / Gillian Dyer. — London : Methuen, 1982. — (Studies in communication)

JHALLY, Sut
The codes of advertising : fetishism and the political economy of meaning in the consumer society / by Sut Jhally. — London : Pinter, 1987. — [200]p. — *Includes bibliography and index*

ADVERTISING — Tobacco trade

CHAPMAN, Simon
Great expectorations : advertising and the tobacco industry / Simon Chapman. — London : Comedia, 1986. — 158p. — *Includes bibliography*

ADVERTISING — Great Britain — Case studies

Advertising works : papers from the IPA Advertising Effectiveness Awards, Institute of Practitioners in Advertising, 1980 / edited and introduced by Simon Broadbent. — London : Holt, Rinehart and Winston, 1981. — xvi,207p. — *Includes index*

Advertising works 2 : papers from the IPA Advertising Effectiveness Awards, Institute of Practitioners in Advertising, 1982 / edited and introduced by Simon Broadbent. — London : Holt, Rinehart and Winston, May 1983. — xv,240p

Advertising works 3 : papers from the IPA Advertising Effectiveness Awards, Institute of Practitioners in Advertising, 1984 / edited and introduced by Charles Channon. — London : Holt, Rinehart and Winston, 1985. — xv,317p. — *Includes index*

ADVERTISING — Québec (Province)

Positionnement de l'industrie de la publicité au Québec / CEGIR. — Québec : Ministère des communications, 1986. — 137p. — *Written by CEGIR for the Confederation générale de la publicité*

ADVERTISING — United States — History

MARCHAND, Roland
Advertising the American dream : making way for modernity, 1920-1940- / Roland Marchand. — Berkeley, Calif ; London : University of California Press, c1985. — xxii, 448p. — *Includes index.* — *Bibliography: p.419-426*

ADVERTISING LAWS — Peru

PERU
[Laws, etc.]. Normas de publicidad : decreto supremo no.003-74-OCI. — Lima : Sistema Nacional de Información, [ca.1974]. — 12p

ADVERTISING LAWS — United States

ROME, Edwin P
Corporate and commercial free speech : first amendment protection of expression in business / Edwin P. Rome and William H. Roberts. — Westport, Conn. : Quorum Books, c1985. — p. cm. — *Includes index.* — *Bibliography: p*

ADVERTISING MEDIA PLANNING

LUCAS, Darrell Blaine
Measuring advertising effectiveness / Darrell Blaine Lucas, Steuart Henderson Britt. — New York : Garland, 1985, c1963. — xi, 399 p.. — (The History of advertising). — : Reprint. Originally published: New York : McGraw-Hill, c1963. — *Includes bibliographical references and index*

ADVERTISING, POLITICAL

New perspectives on political advertising / edited by Lynda Lee Kaid, Dan Nimmo, Keith R. Sanders. — Carbondale, Ill. : Southern Illinois University Press, 1986. — xxvi,370p. — *Bibliography: p347-370*

ADVERTISING, POLITICAL — United States

New perspectives on political advertising / edited by Lynda Lee Kaid, Dan Nimmo, Keith R. Sanders. — Carbondale, Ill. : Southern Illinois University Press, 1986. — xxvi,370p. — *Bibliography: p347-370*

ADVISORY, CONCILIATION AND ARBITRATION SERVICE

GRAHAM, Cosmo
The role of ACAS conciliation in equal pay and sex discrimination cases / Cosmo Graham, Norman Lewis ; [for the] Equal Opportunities in Commission. — Manchester : Equal Opportunities Commission, 1985. — 70p. — *Bibliographical references: p69-70*

AER LINGUS

SHARE, Bernard
The flight of the Iolar : the Aer Lingus experience 1936-1986 / Bernard Share. — Dublin : Gill and Macmillan, 1986. — xii,306p

AERONAUTICS — Law and legislation

Air worthy : liber amicorum, honouring Professor Dr. I.H.Ph. Diederiks-Verschoor / editors J.W.E. Storm van's Gravesande and A. van der Veen Vonk. — Deventer : Kluwer, 1985. — xv,301p. — *Bibliography: p.293-301*

DIEDERIKS-VERSCHOOR, I.H. Ph.
[Inleiding tot het luchtrecht. English]. An introduction to air law / by I.H. Ph. Diederiks-Verschoor. — 2nd rev. ed. — Deventer, Netherlands ; Boston : Kluwer Law and Taxation Publishers, c1985. — xxii, 185p. — *Translation of: Inleiding tot het luchtrecht. — Includes index. — Bibliography: p*

AERONAUTICS — European Economic Community Countries

MCGOWAN, Francis
European aviation : a common market? / Francis McGowan and Chris Trengore. — London : Institute for Fiscal Studies, 1986. — 156p. — (IFS report series ; no.23). — *Bibliography: p152-154*

AERONAUTICS AND STATE — Canada

GILLEN, David W
Canadian airline deregulation and privatization : assessing effects and prospects / by David W. Gillen, Tae H. Oum, Michael W. Tretheway. — Vancouver, Canada : Centre for Transportation Studies, University of British Columbia, c1985. — vi, 300 p.. — *Bibliography: p. 297-300*

AERONAUTICS AND STATE — Canada — History

STEVENSON, Garth
The politics of Canada's airlines : from Diefenbaker to Mulroney / Garth Stevenson. — Toronto : University of Toronto Press, 1987. — xviii,236p. — (The state and economic life ; 9). — *Includes bibliographical references*

AERONAUTICS, COMMERCIAL

SAWERS, David
Competition in the air : what Europe can learn from the USA / David Sawers. — London : Institute of Economic Affairs, 1987. — 83p. — (Research monographs / Institute of Economic Affairs ; 41). — *Bibliography: p.80-81*

SHAW, Stephen
Airline marketing and management / Stephen Shaw. — 2nd ed. — London : Pitman, 1985. — 296p. — *2nd ed. of "Air transport: a marketing perspective" (1982)*

AERONAUTICS, COMMERCIAL — Government policy — Canada — History

STEVENSON, Garth
The politics of Canada's airlines : from Diefenbaker to Mulroney / Garth Stevenson. — Toronto : University of Toronto Press, 1987. — xviii,236p. — (The state and economic life ; 9). — *Includes bibliographical references*

AERONAUTICS, COMMERCIAL — Law and legislation

DIEDERIKS-VERSCHOOR, I.H. Ph.
[Inleiding tot het luchtrecht. English]. An introduction to air law / by I.H. Ph. Diederiks-Verschoor. — 2nd rev. ed. — Deventer, Netherlands ; Boston : Kluwer Law and Taxation Publishers, c1985. — xxii, 185p. — *Translation of: Inleiding tot het luchtrecht. — Includes index. — Bibliography: p*

WASSENBERGH, H. A.
Regulatory reform in international air transport : address by H.A. Wassenbergh on the occasion of the introduction of the International Institute of Air and Space Law of the State University at Leyden 17 March 1986. — Deventer ; London : Kluwer Law and Taxation Publishers, c1986. — 10p

AERONAUTICS, COMMERCIAL — Political aspects — History

JÖNSSON, Christer
International aviation and the politics of regime change / Christer Jönsson. — London : Pinter, 1987. — [200]p. — *Includes index*

AERONAUTICS, COMMERCIAL — Europe, Western

WHEATCROFT, Stephen
Air transport in a competitive European market : problems, prospects and strategies / by Stephen Wheatcroft and Geoffrey Lipman. — London : Economist Intelligence Unit, 1986. — xi,218p. — (Travel and tourism report ; no.3) (Special report ; no.1060). — *Text, ports on inside covers. — Bibliography: p214-218*

AERONAUTICS, COMMERCIAL — Great Britain — Freight — Statistics

Air freight and mail. — London : HMSO, 1968-1972. — (Business monitor. CA ; 3). — *Monthly. — Continued by: CAA monthly statistics; and, CAA annual statistics. — Includes annual summary*

AERONAUTICS, COMMERCIAL — Great Britain — Passenger traffic — Statistics

Air passengers : international and cabotage. — London : HMSO, 1968-1972. — (Business monitor. CA ; 7). — *Quarterly. — Continued by: CAA monthly statistics; and, CAA annual statistics. — Includes annual summary*

Air passengers. — Lodon : HMSO, 1968-1972. — (Business monitor. CA ; 2). — *Monthly. — Continued by: CAA monthly statistics; and, CAA annual statistics. — Includes annual summary*

Domestic passenger traffic. — London : HMSO, 1968-1972. — (Business monitor. CA ; 6). — *Quarterly. — Continued by: CAA monthly statistics; and, CAA annual statistics. — Includes annual summary*

AEROSPACE INDUSTRIES

TODD, Daniel
World aerospace : a statistical handbook / Daniel Todd and Ronald D. Humble. — London : Croom Helm, c1987. — 226p. — *Includes index*

AEROSPACE INDUSTRIES — Australia

The Australian aerospace industry : structure, performance and economic issues. — Canberra : Australian Government Publishing Service, 1986. — xxvi,425p. — (Research report / Bureau of Industry Economics ; 20). — *Bibliography: p405-425*

AEROSPACE INDUSTRIES — Great Britain — Statistics

GREAT BRITAIN. Business Statistics Office
Survey of the United Kingdom aerospace industry, 1975 / ... Business Statistics Office. — London : H.M.S.O., 1975. — vi,45p. — (Business monitor. M ; 9) (M9)

AESTHETICS

LANGERBEIN, Berthold
Roman und Revolte : zur Grundlegung der ästhetischen Theorie Herbert Marcuses und ihrer Stellung in seinem politisch-anthropologischen Denken / Berthold Langerbein. — Pfaffenweiler : Centaurus, 1985. — 115p. — (Reihe Sprach- und Literaturwissenschaft ; Bd.3)

MAQUET, Jacques
The aesthetic experience : an anthropologist looks at the visual arts / Jacques Maquet. — New Haven ; London : Yale University Press, c1986. — xi,272p. — *Bibliography: p256-260. — Includes index*

AFFIRMATIVE ACTION PROGRAMS — England — London

GREATER LONDON COUNCIL. Contract Compliance Equal Opportunities Unit
Information pack. — [London : the Council, 1983-85]. — 7pts.

AFFIRMATIVE ACTION PROGRAMS — United States — Congresses

Affirmative action : theory, analysis, and prospects / edited by Michael W. Combs and John Gruhl. — Jefferson, N.C. : McFarland & Co., c1986. — vi, 185 p.. — *"Consists of selected papers that were presented at the Eighth Annual Hendricks Symposium which was sponsored by the Department of Political Science, University of Nebraska--Lincoln"--Acknowledgements. — Includes bibliographies and index*

AFGHANISTAN — Constitutional law

KAMALI, Mohammad Hashim
Law in Afghanistan : a study of the Constitutions, matrimonial law and judiciary / by Mohammad Hashim Kamali. — Leiden : E. J. Brill, 1985. — viii,265p. — (Social, economic and political studies of the Middle East ; Vol.36). — *Bibliography: p[254]-259*

AFGHANISTAN — Description and travel

NIKOLAEV, Lev Nikolaevich
Afghanistan : between the past and the future / Lev Nikolayev ; translated from the Russian by Vic Schneierson. — Moskva : Progress Publishers, c1986. — 206 p.. — *Title on t.p. verso: Afghanistan--mezhdu proshlym i budushchim*

AFGHANISTAN — Ethnic relations — Congresses

The State, religion, and ethnic politics : Afghanistan, Iran, and Pakistan / edited by Ali Banuazizi and Myron Weiner. — 1st ed. — [Syracuse, N.Y.] : Syracuse University Press, 1986. — xi, 390 p.. — (Contemporary issues in the Middle East). — *"Sponsored by the Joint Committee on the Near and Middle East and the Committee on South Asia of the American Council of Learned Societies and the Social Science Research Council.". — Includes bibliographies and index*

AFGHANISTAN — Foreign relations

BHASIN, V. K.
Soviet intervention in Afghanistan : its background and implications / V. K. Bhasin. — New Delhi : S. Chand, [1984]. — x,304p. — *Bibliography: p[286]-300*

WAKMAN, Mohammad Amin
Afghanistan, non-alignment and the super powers / by Mohammad Amin Wakman. — New Delhi : Radiant Publishers, 1985. — xiv, 169 p.. — *Includes index. — Bibliography: p.[147]-164*

AFGHANISTAN — Foreign relations — Pakistan
KULWANT KAUR
Pak-Afghanistan relations / Kulwant Kaur. — New Delhi : Deep & Deep Publications, c1985. — viii, 252 p.. — *Includes index. Bibliography: p. [224]-250*

AFGHANISTAN — Foreign relations — Soviet Union
RASHIDOV, R. T.
Sovetsko-afganskie otnosheniia i ikh burzhuaznye fal'sifikatory (1978-1983) / R. T. Rashidov. — Tashkent : "Fan" Uzbekskoi SSR, 1986. — 114p

SHAMS-UD-DIN
Soviet Afghan relations / Shams Ud Din. — Calcutta ; New Delhi : K. P. Bagchi, 1985,1984. — vii,168p. — *Bibliography: p [155]-160*

TRASK, Roger
Afghanistan : grasping of the nettle of peace / Roger Trask. — London : Morning Star, 1987. — 24p

VOLODARSKII, M. I.
Sovety i ikh iuzhnye sosedi Iran i Afganistan (1917-1933) / M. I. Volodarskii ; predislovie S. Mogilevskogo. — London : Overseas Publications Interchange, 1985. — 241p. — *Bibliography: p235*

AFGHANISTAN — History — Soviet occupation, 1979-
SHAMS-UD-DIN
Soviet Afghan relations / Shams Ud Din. — Calcutta ; New Delhi : K. P. Bagchi, 1985,1984. — vii,168p. — *Bibliography: p [155]-160*

Afghan resistance : the politics of survival / edited by Grant M. Farr, John G. Merriam. — Boulder, Colo. : Westview Press, 1987. — p. cm. — (Westview special studies in international relations). — *Bibliography: p*

BURES, A. de
Le défi Afghan : l'Urss en échec / A. de Bures, J. M. Chaligny ; préface de Laurent Schwartz. — Paris : Anthropos : Bureau International Afghanistan, 1986. — 309p. — *Bibliography: p301-305*

MUKHERJEE, Sadhan
Afghanistan from tragedy to triumph / Sadhan Mukherjee. — New Delhi : Sterling, c1984. — vii, 258 p.. — *Map on lining papers. — Includes index*

NIKOLAEV, Lev Nikolaevich
Afghanistan : between the past and the future / Lev Nikolayev ; translated from the Russian by Vic Schneierson. — Moskva : Progress Publishers, c1986. — 206 p.. — *Title on t.p. verso: Afghanistan--mezhdu proshlym i budushchim*

AFGHANISTAN — History — Soviet Occupation, 1979-
The Red Army on Pakistan's border : policy implications for the United States / Theodore L. Eliot, Jr. ... [et al.]. — Washington : Pergamon-Brassey's, 1986. — p. cm. — (Special report). — "May 1986.". — "A joint publication of the Institute for Foreign Policy Affairs, Inc. and the Center for Asian Pacific Affairs, the Asia Foundation."

AFGHANISTAN — History — Soviet occupation, 1979-
ROY, Oliver
Islam and resistance in Afghanistan / Olivier Roy. — Cambridge : Cambridge University Press, c1986. — vi,253p. — (Cambridge Middle East library). — *Translation of: L'Afghanistan. — Bibliography: p243-249. — Includes index*

AFGHANISTAN — History — Soviet occupation — 1979-
BHASIN, V. K.
Soviet intervention in Afghanistan : its background and implications / V. K. Bhasin. — New Delhi : S. Chand, [1984]. — x,304p. — *Bibliography: p[286]-300*

AFGHANISTAN — Politics and government
ROY, Oliver
Islam and resistance in Afghanistan / Olivier Roy. — Cambridge : Cambridge University Press, c1986. — vi,253p. — (Cambridge Middle East library). — *Translation of: L'Afghanistan. — Bibliography: p243-249. Includes index*

TRASK, Roger
Afghanistan : grasping of the nettle of peace / Roger Trask. — London : Morning Star, 1987. — 24p

AFGHANISTAN — Politics and government — 1973- — Congresses
The State, religion, and ethnic politics : Afghanistan, Iran, and Pakistan / edited by Ali Banuazizi and Myron Weiner. — 1st ed. — [Syracuse, N.Y.] : Syracuse University Press, 1986. — xi, 390 p.. — (Contemporary issues in the Middle East). — "Sponsored by the Joint Committee on the Near and Middle East and the Committee on South Asia of the American Council of Learned Societies and the Social Science Research Council.". — *Includes bibliographies and index*

AFRICA
GUNTHER, John
Inside Africa / John Gunther. — London : Hamilton, 1955. — 960p

AFRICA — Bibliography
Africa bibliography. — Manchester : Manchester University Press, 1984-. — *Annual*

African studies : papers presented at a colloquium at the British Library 7-9 January 1985 / edited by Ilse Sternberg and Patricia M. Larby. — London : British Library, 1986. — [370]p. — (British Library occasional papers ; 6)

African studies information resources directory / compiled and edited by Jean E. Meeh Gosebrink. — Oxford : Published for the African Studies Association [by] Hans Zell, 1986. — [585]p. — *Bibliography: p505-519. — Includes index*

AFRICA — Civilization
MAZRUI, Ali A.
The Africans : a triple heritage / Ali A. Mazrui. — London : BBC Publications, 1986. — 336p

AFRICA — Civilization — Islamic influences
MAZRUI, Ali A.
The Africans : a triple heritage / Ali A. Mazrui. — London : BBC Publications, 1986. — 336p

AFRICA — Civilization — Occidental influences
MAZRUI, Ali A.
The Africans : a triple heritage / Ali A. Mazrui. — London : BBC Publications, 1986. — 336p

AFRICA — Colonization
AUSTIN, Dennis
Africa repartitioned? / Dennis Austin. — London : Centre for Security and Conflict Studies, 1986. — 33p. — (Conflict studies ; no.193)

German imperialism in Africa : from the beginnings until the Second World War / edited by Helmuth Stoecker ; translated from the German by Bernd Zöllner. — London : Hurst, 1986. — 446p. — *Translation of: Drang nach Afrika. — Includes bibliography and index*

AFRICA — Constitutional history
NWABUEZE, B. O
Presidentialism in commonwealth Africa / by B. O. Nwabueze. — New York : St. Martin's Press, 1974. — xiii, 442 p.. — *Includes bibliographical references and index*

AFRICA — Description and travel — To 1900
ESSNER, Cornelia
Deutsche Afrikareisende im neunzehnten Jahrhundert : zur Sozialgeschichte des Reisens / Cornelia Essner. — Stuttgart : Steiner-Verlag-Wiesbaden, 1985. — 235p. — (Beiträge zur Kolonial- und Überseegeschichte ; Bd.32). — *Bibliography: p210-235*

AFRICA — Economic conditions
Africa index: selected articles on socio-economic development / United Nations. Economic Commission for Africa. — Addis Ababa : United Nations. Economic Commission for Africa, 1971-. — *3 times a year. — Text in English and French*

AUSTEN, Ralph A.
African economic history : internal development and external dependency / Ralph A. Austen. — London : James Currey, 1987. — ix,294p. — *Includes bibliographies and index*

ECA index: bibliography of selected ECA documents / United Nations. Economic Commission for Africa. — Addis Ababa : United Nations. Economic Commission for Africa, 1975-. — *Annual. — Text in English and French*

HARRISON, Paul, 1945-
The greening of Africa : breaking through in the battle for land and food / Paul Harrison. — London : Paladin [for] International Institute for Environment and Development-Earthscan, 1987. — 380p. — *[Commissioned by the International Institute for Environment and Development - Earthscan]. — At foot of title: "International Institute for Environment and Development - Earthscan". — Bibliography: p359-371. — Includes index*

SENDER, John
The development of capitalism in Africa / John Sender and Sheila Smith. — London : Methuen, 1986. — xi,177p. — *Bibliography: p.134-158. — Includes index*

WICKINS, Peter Lionel
Africa 1880-1980 : an economic history / Peter Lionel Wickins. — Cape Town : Oxford University Press, 1986. — ix,321p. — *Bibliography: p312-313*

AFRICA — Economic conditions — Bibliography
Le développement économique industriel et commercial en Afrique: bibliographie / Chambre de Commerce et d'Industrie de la Region du Cap-Vert, Dakar (Senegal). — Dakar : Chambre de Commerce et d'Industrie de la Region du Cap-Vert, 1980-. — *Annual*

AFRICA — Economic conditions — 1945-1960
Economically active population : estimates and projections : 1950-2025 = Evaluations et projections de la population active : 1950-2025 = Estimaciones y proyecciones de la población económicamente activa : 1950-2025. — 3rd ed. — Geneva : International Labour Office V.2: Africa. — 1986. — xxvi,210p. — *Introduction and table headings in English, French and Spanish*

AFRICA — Economic conditions — 1960-
Africa in economic crisis / edited by John Ravenhill. — Basingstoke : Macmillan, 1986. — xiii,359p. — (Macmillan international political economy series). — *Includes index*

African crisis areas and U.S. foreign policy / edited by Gerald J. Bender, James S. Coleman, Richard L. Sklar. — Berkeley : University of California Press, 1986, c1985. — p. cm. — *Includes index. — Bibliography: p*

AFRICA — Economic conditions — 1960-
continuation

Afrika zwischen Subsistenzökonomie und Imperialismus / Georg Elwert, Roland Felt (hg.) ; [mit Beiträgen von C. Meillassoux...[et al.]]. — Frankfurt/Main : Campus, 1982. — 295p. — *Bibliographies*

AKYEAMPONG, Yaw A
African development, a positive direction / Yaw A. Akyeampong. — Tema, Ghana : Ghana Pub. Corp., 1980. — 81 p.. — *Includes bibliographical references*

Economically active population : estimates and projections : 1950-2025 = Evaluations et projections de la population active : 1950-2025 = Estimaciones y proyecciones de la población económicamente activa : 1950-2025. — 3rd ed. — Geneva : International Labour Office V.2: Africa. — 1986. — xxvi,210p. — *Introduction and table headings in English, French and Spanish*

NJOKU, John E. Eberegbulam
Malthusianism, an African dilemma : hunger, drought, and starvation in Africa / by John E. Eberegbulam Njoku. — Metuchen, N.J. : Scarecrow Press, 1986. — xxix, 181 p.. — *Bibliography: p. [163]-181*

OLOKO, Olatunde
Dilemma of African modernisation : an inaugural lecture delivered at the University of Lagos, on Friday, 27th May, 1979 / by Olatunde Oloko. — [Lagos] : University of Lagos Press, 1981. — 54 p.. — (Inaugural lecture series / Lagos University Press)

World recession and the food crisis in Africa / edited by Peter Lawrence. — London : Currey [for the] Review of African Political Economy, 1986. — 314p. — *Bibliography: p300-311. — Includes index*

AFRICA — Economic policy

AKYEAMPONG, Yaw A
African development, a positive direction / Yaw A. Akyeampong. — Tema, Ghana : Ghana Pub. Corp., 1980. — 81 p.. — *Includes bibliographical references*

OLOKO, Olatunde
Dilemma of African modernisation : an inaugural lecture delivered at the University of Lagos, on Friday, 27th May, 1979 / by Olatunde Oloko. — [Lagos] : University of Lagos Press, 1981. — 54 p.. — (Inaugural lecture series / Lagos University Press)

AFRICA — Economic policy — Congresses

Development options for Africa in the 1980s and beyond / edited by P. Ndegwa, L.P. Mureithi, R.H. Green. — Nairobi : Oxford University Press in association with the Society for International Development, Kenya Chapter, 1985. — xii, 260 p.. — *Papers presented at the Symposium on Development Options for Africa in the 1980s and Beyond, organized by the Kenya Chapter of the Society for International Development, held at the Kenyatta Conference Centre, Nairobi, Mar. 7-9, 1983. — Includes bibliographies and index*

INTER-AFRICAN PUBLIC ADMINISTRATION SEMINAR (6th : 1967 : Greenhill (Ghana))
The task of the administrator in developing societies of Africa : report of the...Seminar / [edited by] James Nti. — Tema (Ghana) : Ghana Publishing Corporation, 1978. — 152p. — *First published by Ghana Institute of Public Administration, 1968*

AFRICA — Economic policy — Public opinion

OLOKO, Olatunde
Dilemma of African modernisation : an inaugural lecture delivered at the University of Lagos, on Friday, 27th May, 1979 / by Olatunde Oloko. — [Lagos] : University of Lagos Press, 1981. — 54 p.. — (Inaugural lecture series / Lagos University Press)

AFRICA — Emigration and immigration

KIBREAB, Gaim
African refugees : reflections on the African refugee problem / Gaim Kibreab. — Trenton, N.J. : Africa World Press, 1985. — 125p. — *Previously published as: Reflections on the African refugee problem, (1983)*

AFRICA — Famines

Drought and hunger in Africa : denying famine a future / edited by Michael H. Glantz. — Cambridge : Cambridge University Press, 1987. — xx,457p. — *Conference proceedings. — Includes bibliographies and index*

LESTOR, Joan
Beyond Band Aid : charity is not enough / Joan Lestor [and] David Ward. — London : Fabian Society, 1987. — 22 p. — (Fabian tract ; 520)

AFRICA — Famines — Bibliography

SEELEY, J. A.
Famine in Africa : a guide to bibliographies and resource centres / compiled by J.A. Seeley. — Cambridge : African Studies Centre, University of Cambridge, 1986. — x,86p. — (Cambridge African occasional papers ; no.1). — *Includes index*

AFRICA — Famines — Information services

SEELEY, J. A.
Famine in Africa : a guide to bibliographies and resource centres / compiled by J.A. Seeley. — Cambridge : African Studies Centre, University of Cambridge, 1986. — x,86p. — (Cambridge African occasional papers ; no.1). — *Includes index*

AFRICA — Foreign economic relations

WALLERSTEIN, Immanuel
Africa and the modern world / Immanuel Wallerstein. — Trenton, N.J. : Africa World Press ; Nottingham : Spokesman, 1986. — 209p. — *Bibliographies*

AFRICA — Foreign economic relations — Japan

MOSS, Joanna
Emerging Japanese economic influence in Africa : implications for the United States / Joanna Moss & John Ravenhill. — Berkeley : Institute of International Studies, University of California, c1985. — xi, 150 p.. — (Policy papers in international affairs ; no. 21). — *Includes index. — Bibliography: p. 139-143*

AFRICA — Foreign economic relations — United States

MOSS, Joanna
Emerging Japanese economic influence in Africa : implications for the United States / Joanna Moss & John Ravenhill. — Berkeley : Institute of International Studies, University of California, c1985. — xi, 150 p.. — (Policy papers in international affairs ; no. 21). — *Includes index. — Bibliography: p. 139-143*

AFRICA — Foreign relations

WALLERSTEIN, Immanuel
Africa and the modern world / Immanuel Wallerstein. — Trenton, N.J. : Africa World Press ; Nottingham : Spokesman, 1986. — 209p. — *Bibliographies*

AFRICA — Foreign relations — 1960-

African crisis areas and U.S. foreign policy / edited by Gerald J. Bender, James S. Coleman, Richard L. Sklar. — Berkeley : University of California Press, 1986, c1985. — p. cm. — *Includes index. — Bibliography: p*

MCKAY, Vernon
Africa in world politics / Vernon McKay. — New York : Harper and Row, [1963]. — xii,468p

AFRICA — Foreign relations — Germany

German imperialism in Africa : from the beginnings until the Second World War / edited by Helmuth Stoecker ; translated from the German by Bernd Zöllner. — London : Hurst, 1986. — 446p. — *Translation of: Drang nach Afrika. — Includes bibliography and index*

AFRICA — Foreign relations — Soviet Union

LAÏDI, Zaki
Les contraintes Dûne rivalité : les superpuissances et lÁfríque (1960-1985) / Zaki Laïdi. — Paris : La Découverte, 1986. — 299p. — *Bibliography: p284-292*

AFRICA — Foreign relations — United States

African crisis areas and U.S. foreign policy / edited by Gerald J. Bender, James S. Coleman, Richard L. Sklar. — Berkeley : University of California Press, 1986, c1985. — p. cm. — *Includes index. — Bibliography: p*

LAÏDI, Zaki
Les contraintes Dûne rivalité : les superpuissances et lÁfríque (1960-1985) / Zaki Laïdi. — Paris : La Découverte, 1986. — 299p. — *Bibliography: p284-292*

AFRICA — Historiography — Addresses, essays, lectures

African historiographies : what history for which Africa? / edited by Bogumil Jewsiewicki and David Newbury. — Beverly Hills ; London : Sage Publications, c1985. — 320p. — (Sage series on African modernization and development ; v. 12). — *Bibliography: p 279-316*

AFRICA — History

The Cambridge history of Africa. — Cambridge : Cambridge University Press. — *In 8 vols.*
Vol.8: From c.1940 to c.1975 / edited by Michael Crowder. — 1984. — xvi,1011p. — *Bibliography: p905-961. — Includes index*

AFRICA — History — To 1498

DIOP, Cheikh Anta
[Afrique noire pré-coloniale. English]. Precolonial Black Africa : a comparative study of the political and social systems of Europe and Black Africa, from antiquity to the formation of modern states / Cheikh Anta Diop ; translated by Harold J. Salemson. — Westport, Conn. : L. Hill, 1986. — p. cm. — *Translation of: L´Afrique noire pré-coloniale*

AFRICA — History — 19th century — Sources

GAVIN, R. J., comp
The scramble for Africa : documents on the Berlin West African Conference and related subjects, 1884/1885 / compiled, edited and translated from the French and German, by R. J. Gavin and J. A. Betley. — [Ibadan, Nigeria] : Ibadan University Press, 1973. — xxxiv, 429 p. — *Includes bibliographical references*

AFRICA — History — 1884-1960

Africa and the First World War / edited by Melvin E. Page. — London : Macmillan, 1987. — [270]p. — *Includes bibliography and index*

MEREDITH, Martin
The first dance of freedom : black Africa in the postwar era / Martin Meredith. — London : Hamilton, 1984. — xiv,412p. — *Bibliography: p384-393. — Includes index*

AFRICA — History — 1960-

MEREDITH, Martin
The first dance of freedom : black Africa in the postwar era / Martin Meredith. — London : Hamilton, 1984. — xiv,412p. — *Bibliography: p384-393. — Includes index*

AFRICA — Industries

Bulletin of the Industrial Development Decade for Africa / prepared by the Public Information Section of the United Nations Industrial Development Organization in co-operation with the Co-ordination Unit for the Industrial Development Decade for Africa. — Vienna : Public Information Section, UNIDO, 1985-

AFRICA — Industries — Bibliography
Le développement économique industriel et commercial en Afrique: bibliographie / Chambre de Commerce et d'Industrie de la Region du Cap-Vert, Dakar (Senegal). — Dakar : Chambre de Commerce et d'Industrie de la Region du Cap-Vert, 1980-. — *Annual*

AFRICA — Politics and government
AUSTIN, Dennis
Africa repartitioned? / Dennis Austin. — London : Centre for Security and Conflict Studies, 1986. — 33p. — (Conflict studies ; no.193)

MBOUKOU, Jean-Pierre Makouta
Lettre à la nation africaine : pour que símpose l'humanisme negre / Jean-Pierre Makouta Mboukou. — Paris : Presses de la Fondation du Prix Mondial de la Paix, 1986. — 23p

Revolution africaine. — Hydra : Front de Liberation Nationale, 1985-. — *Weekly*

TORDOFF, William
Government and politics in Africa / William Tordoff. — London : Macmillan, 1984. — xix,352p. — *Bibliography: p321-337. — Includes index*

AFRICA — Politics and government — 1960-
Africa in world politics : changing perspectives / edited by Stephen Wright and Janice N. Brownfoot. — Basingstoke : Macmillan, 1987. — xvi,214p. — *Bibliography: p207-209. — Includes index*

Elections in independent Africa / edited by Fred M. Hayward. — Boulder, Colo. : Westview Press, 1987. — p. cm. — (Westview special studies on Africa)

MARABLE, Manning
African and Caribbean politics from Kwame Nkrumah to the Grenada revolution / Manning Marable. — London : Verso, 1987. — [300]p. — (Haymarket series). — *Includes index*

NWABUEZE, B. O
Presidentialism in commonwealth Africa / by B. O. Nwabueze. — New York : St. Martin's Press, 1974. — xiii, 442 p.. — *Includes bibliographical references and index*

Politics & government in African states, 1960-1985 / edited by Peter Duignan and Robert H. Jackson. — London : Croom Helm, 1986. — 442p. — *Bibliography: p430-434. — Includes index*

AFRICA — Politics and government — 1960- — Congresses
INTER-AFRICAN PUBLIC ADMINISTRATION SEMINAR (6th : 1967 : Greenhill (Ghana))
The task of the administrator in developing societies of Africa : report of the...Seminar / [edited by] James Nti. — Tema (Ghana) : Ghana Publishing Corporation, 1978. — 152p. — *First published by Ghana Institute of Public Administration, 1968*

AFRICA — Population — Statistics
Economically active population : estimates and projections : 1950-2025 = Evaluations et projections de la population active : 1950-2025 = Estimaciones y proyecciones de la población económicamente activa : 1950-2025. — 3rd ed. — Geneva : International Labour Office
V.2: Africa. — 1986. — xxvi,210p. — *Introduction and table headings in English, French and Spanish*

AFRICA — Presidents
NWABUEZE, B. O
Presidentialism in commonwealth Africa / by B. O. Nwabueze. — New York : St. Martin's Press, 1974. — xiii, 442 p.. — *Includes bibliographical references and index*

AFRICA — Relations — United States
East African university student views on international and continental issues. — [Washington, D.C.] : United States Information Agency, 1965. — vii,25p. — *R-39-65*

AFRICA — Religion
Theoretical explorations in African religion / edited by Wim van Binsbergen and Matthew Schoffeleers. — London : KPI, 1985. — x,389p. — (Monographs from the African Studies Centre, Leiden). — *Includes bibliographies and index*

AFRICA — Social conditions
Africa index: selected articles on socio-economic development / United Nations. Economic Commission for Africa. — Addis Ababa : United Nations. Economic Commission for Africa, 1971-. — *3 times a year. — Text in English and French*

ECA index: bibliography of selected ECA documents / United Nations. Economic Commission for Africa. — Addis Ababa : United Nations. Economic Commission for Africa, 1975-. — *Annual. — Text in English and French*

AFRICA — Social policy — Congresses
INTER-AFRICAN PUBLIC ADMINISTRATION SEMINAR (6th : 1967 : Greenhill (Ghana))
The task of the administrator in developing societies of Africa : report of the...Seminar / [edited by] James Nti. — Tema (Ghana) : Ghana Publishing Corporation, 1978. — 152p. — *First published by Ghana Institute of Public Administration, 1968*

AFRICA — Yearbooks
Jahrbuch Asien - Afrika - Lateinamerika : Bilanz und Chronik des Jahres 1985 / L. Rathmann [hrsg.]. — Berlin : VEB Deutscher Verlag der Wissenschaften, 1986. — 329p. — *Table of contents in German, Russian, English, French and Spanish. — "Im Auftrag des Zentralen Rates für Asien-, Afrika-, und Lateinamerikawissenschaften in der DDR". — Bibliography: p[296]-326*

AFRICA — History — Bibliography
SIMS, Michael
American and Canadian doctoral dissertations and master's theses on Africa, 1886-1974 / compiled by Michael Sims and Alfred Kagan. — Waltham, Mass. : African Studies Association, 1976. — 365p

AFRICA, CENTRAL — Courts and courtiers
PALMEIRIM, Maria Manuela Mestre Marques
The sterile mother : aspects of court symbolism among the Lunda of Mwant Yaav (Aruund) / Manuela M. Palmeirim. — 128 leaves. — *MPhil (Econ) 1986 LSE*

AFRICA, CENTRAL — History — To 1884
HARMAN, Nicholas
Bwana Stokesi and his African conquests / Nicholas Harman. — London : Cape, 1986. — xv,272p,[16]p of plates. — *Includes index*

AFRICA, EAST — Bibliography
OFCANSKY, Thomas P.
British East Africa, 1856-1963 : an annotated bibliography / Thomas P. Ofcansky. — New York : Garland Pub., 1985. — xxiii, 474 p.. — (Themes in European expansion ; vol. 7) (Garland reference library of social science ; vol. 158). — *Includes index*

AFRICA, EAST — Description and travel
MACIEL, Mervyn
Bwana Karani / Mervyn Maciel ; with foreword by Sir Richard Turnbull. — Braunton : Merlin, 1985. — 262p

AFRICA, EAST — Foreign relations
YILMA MAKONNEN
The Nyerere doctrine of state succession : Dar es Salaam to Vienna / Yilma Makonnen. — Arusha ; New York : Eastern Africa Publications, 1985. — p. cm. — *Includes bibliographies and index*

AFRICA, EAST — History — To 1886
BENNETT, Norman Robert
Arab versus European : diplomacy and war in nineteenth-century east central Africa / Norman Robert Bennett. — New York ; London : Africana Publishing, 1986. — 325p. — *Includes index. — Bibliography: p*

AFRICA, EAST — Officials and employees — Biography
MACIEL, Mervyn
Bwana Karani / Mervyn Maciel ; with foreword by Sir Richard Turnbull. — Braunton : Merlin, 1985. — 262p

AFRICA, EAST — Politics and government
MAIR, Lucy Philip
Primitive government : a study of traditional political systems in eastern Africa / Lucy Mair. — Rev. ed. — Bloomington : Indiana University Press, c1977. — 244 p.. — *Includes index. — Bibliography: p. 238-239*

AFRICA, EAST — Politics and government — 1884-1960
NYE, Joseph S.
Pan-Africanism and East African integration / Joseph S. Nye. — Cambridge, Mass. : Harvard University Press, 1965. — xvi,307p

AFRICA, EASTERN — Economic integration
KISANGA, Eliawony Joseph
International politics of industrial cooperation in Eastern Africa : 1967-1984 / by Eliawony J. Kisanga. — 480 leaves. — *PhD (Econ) 1986 LSE*

AFRICA, EASTERN — Industries
KISANGA, Eliawony Joseph
International politics of industrial cooperation in Eastern Africa : 1967-1984 / by Eliawony J. Kisanga. — 480 leaves. — *PhD (Econ) 1986 LSE*

AFRICA, NORTH — Emigration and immigration
COLLOQUE "DES ÉTRANGERS QUI FONT AUSSI LA FRANCE"
Les Nord-Africains en France / ouvrage réalisé sous la direction de Magali Morsy. — Paris : CHEAM, 1984. — 200p. — (Publications du CHEAM ; 3). — *Includes bibliographical references*

AFRICA, NORTH — Politics and government
The Government and politics of the Middle East and North Africa / edited by David E. Long and Bernard Reich. — Boulder, Colo. : Westview Press, 1980. — xiv, 480 p.. — *Includes bibliographies and index*

AFRICA, NORTHEAST — Politics and government
MAKINDA, Samuel M.
Superpower diplomacy in the Horn of Africa / Samuel M. Makinda. — London : Croom Helm, c1987. — 241p. — *Bibliography: p225-234. — Includes index*

AFRICA, PORTUGUESE-SPEAKING — Economic conditions — Bibliography
Portuguese-speaking Africa 1900-1979 : a select bibliography. — Braamfontein : South African Institute of International Affairs. — (Bibliographical series / South African Institute of International Affairs ; 11). — *Bound with volume 4*
Vol.3: Portuguese Guinea/Guinea Bissau, Cape Verde, Sao Tomé e Principe, Portuguese-speaking Africa as a whole / Susan Jean Gowan. — 1983. — xvi,350p

Portuguese-speaking Africa 1900-1979 : a select bibliography. — Braamfontein : South African Institute of International Affairs. — (Bibliographical series / South African Institute of International Affairs ; 11). — *Bound with volume 3*
Vol.4: United Nations documentation on Portuguese-speaking Africa / Elna Schoeman. — 1983. — xvi,350p,44p

AFRICA, PORTUGUESE-SPEAKING — Foreign relations — Bibliography

Portuguese-speaking Africa 1900-1979 : a select bibliography. — Braamfontein : South African Institute of International Affairs. — (Bibliographical series / South African Institute of International Affairs ; 11). — *Bound with volume 4*
Vol.3: Portuguese Guinea/Guinea Bissau, Cape Verde, Sao Tomé e Principe, Portuguese-speaking Africa as a whole / Susan Jean Gowan. — 1983. — xvi,350p

Portuguese-speaking Africa 1900-1979 : a select bibliography. — Braamfontein : South African Institute of International Affairs. — (Bibliographical series / South African Institute of International Affairs ; 11). — *Bound with volume 3*
Vol.4: United Nations documentation on Portuguese-speaking Africa / Elna Schoeman. — 1983. — xvi,350,44p

AFRICA, PORTUGUESE-SPEAKING — History — Bibliography

Portuguese-speaking Africa 1900-1979 : a select bibliography. — Braamfontein : South African Institute of International Affairs. — (Bibliographical series / South African Institute of International Affairs ; 11). — *Bound with volume 4*
Vol.3: Portuguese Guinea/Guinea Bissau, Cape Verde, Sao Tomé e Principe, Portuguese-speaking Africa as a whole / Susan Jean Gowan. — 1983. — xvi,350p

Portuguese-speaking Africa 1900-1979 : a select bibliography. — Braamfontein : South African Institute of International Affairs. — (Bibliographical series / South African Institute of International Affairs ; 11). — *Bound with volume 3*
Vol.4: United Nations documentation on Portuguese-speaking Africa / Elna Schoeman. — 1983. — xvi,350,44p

AFRICA, PORTUGUESE-SPEAKING — Politics and government — Bibliography

Portuguese-speaking Africa 1900-1979 : a select bibliography. — Braamfontein : South African Institute of International Affairs. — (Bibliographical series / South African Institute of International Affairs ; 11). — *Bound with volume 4*
Vol.3: Portuguese Guinea/Guinea Bissau, Cape Verde, Sao Tomé e Principe, Portuguese-speaking Africa as a whole / Susan Jean Gowan. — 1983. — xvi,350p

Portuguese-speaking Africa 1900-1979 : a select bibliography. — Braamfontein : South African Institute of International Affairs. — (Bibliographical series / South African Institute of International Affairs ; 11). — *Bound with volume 3*
Vol.4: United Nations documentation on Portuguese-speaking Africa / Elna Schoeman. — 1983. — xvi,350,44p

AFRICA, SOUTHERN — Dependency on South Africa

BUTTS, Kent Hughes
The geopolitics of southern Africa : South Africa as regional superpower / Kent Hughes Butts and Paul R. Thomas. — Boulder : Westview Press, 1986. — xiv, 193 p.. — (Westview special studies on Africa). — *Includes bibliographies and index*

AFRICA, SOUTHERN — Economic integration

KOESTER, Ulrich
Regional cooperation to improve food security in the southern and eastern African countries / Ulrich Koester. — Washington, D.C. : International Food Policy Research Institute, c1986. — 89 p. — (Research report / International Food Policy Research Institute ; 53). — ″July 1986.″. — *Bibliography: p. 85-89*

AFRICA, SOUTHERN — Economic policy

SEMINAR ON EDUCATION, DEVELOPMENT AND SOCIAL TRANSFORMATION (982)
[Proceedings of the] seminar...jointly organized by the National Institute of Research, Gaborone, Botswana [and] the Foundation of Education with Production, Gaborone, Botswana. — Gaborone : National Institute of Research : Foundation for Education with Production, [1982]. — 233p

AFRICA, SOUTHERN — Foreign economic relations — South Africa

BUTTS, Kent Hughes
The geopolitics of southern Africa : South Africa as regional superpower / Kent Hughes Butts and Paul R. Thomas. — Boulder : Westview Press, 1986. — xiv, 193 p.. — (Westview special studies on Africa). — *Includes bibliographies and index*

Confrontation and liberation in southern Africa : regional directions after the Nkomati Accord / edited by Ibrahim S. R. Msabaha and Timothy M. Shaw. — Boulder, Colo : Westview Press, 1987. — xii, 315 p., [1] leaf of plates. — (Westview special studies on Africa). — *Bibliography: p. [307]-315*

AFRICA, SOUTHERN — Foreign relations — 1975-

NEWSUM, H. E.
United States foreign policy towards Southern Africa : Andrew Young and beyond / H.E. Newsum and Olayiwola Abegunrin. — Basingstoke : Macmillan, 1987. — ix,164p. — *Bibliography: p156-157. - Includes index*

AFRICA, SOUTHERN — Foreign relations — South Africa

BUTTS, Kent Hughes
The geopolitics of southern Africa : South Africa as regional superpower / Kent Hughes Butts and Paul R. Thomas. — Boulder : Westview Press, 1986. — xiv, 193 p.. — (Westview special studies on Africa). — *Includes bibliographies and index*

Confrontation and liberation in southern Africa : regional directions after the Nkomati Accord / edited by Ibrahim S. R. Msabaha and Timothy M. Shaw. — Boulder, Colo : Westview Press, 1987. — xii, 315 p., [1] leaf of plates. — (Westview special studies on Africa). — *Bibliography: p. [307]-315*

South African review 3 / edited and compiled by SARS (South African Research Service). — Johannesburg : Ravan Press, 1986. — xiv,397p

AFRICA, SOUTHERN — Foreign relations — United States

NEWSUM, H. E.
United States foreign policy towards Southern Africa : Andrew Young and beyond / H.E. Newsum and Olayiwola Abegunrin. — Basingstoke : Macmillan, 1987. — ix,164p. — *Bibliography: p156-157. - Includes index*

AFRICA, SOUTHERN — History

OMER-COOPER, J. D.
History of Southern Africa / J.D. Omer-Cooper. — London : James Currey, 1987. — [320]p. — *Includes bibliography and index*

AFRICA, SOUTHERN — Military relations — South Africa

Destructive engagement : Southern Africa at war / editors Phyllis Johnson and David Martin ; foreword by Julius K. Nyerere. — Harare : Zimbabwe Publishing House for the Southern African Research and Documentation Centre, 1986. — xxi,378p

AFRICA, SOUTHERN — Politics and government

Destructive engagement : Southern Africa at war / editors Phyllis Johnson and David Martin ; foreword by Julius K. Nyerere. — Harare : Zimbabwe Publishing House for the Southern African Research and Documentation Centre, 1986. — xxi,378p

SHAW, Timothy M.
Southern Africa in crisis : an analysis and bibliography / Timothy M. Shaw. — Halifax, N.S. : Dalhousie University Centre for Foreign Policy Studies, 1986. — vi,48p. — *Bibliography: p19-48*

AFRICA, SOUTHERN — Politics and government — Bibliography

SHAW, Timothy M.
Southern Africa in crisis : an analysis and bibliography / Timothy M. Shaw. — Halifax, N.S. : Dalhousie University Centre for Foreign Policy Studies, 1986. — vi,48p. — *Bibliography: p19-48*

AFRICA, SOUTHERN — Politics and government — 1975-

CARTER, Gwendolen M.
Continuity and change in Southern Africa / Gwendolen M. Carter. — [S.l.] : African Studies Association ; [Gainesville, Fla.] : Center for African Studies, University of Florida, 1985. — x,117p. — (Carter lectures on Africa). — *Includes bibliographies*

AFRICA, SOUTHERN — Social conditions

Children on the front line : the impact of apartheid, destabilization and warfare on children in Southern Africa : a report prepared for UNICEF / by Reginal Herbold Green...[et al.]. — [New York?] : UNICEF, 1987. — v,[29] leaves. — *Bibliographical references: p.[27-28]*

AFRICA, SOUTHERN — Social policy

SEMINAR ON EDUCATION, DEVELOPMENT AND SOCIAL TRANSFORMATION (982)
[Proceedings of the] seminar...jointly organized by the National Institute of Research, Gaborone, Botswana [and] the Foundation of Education with Production, Gaborone, Botswana. — Gaborone : National Institute of Research : Foundation for Education with Production, [1982]. — 233p

AFRICA, SUB-SAHARAN — Armed Forces — Political activity

Military power and politics in black Africa / edited by Simon Baynham. — London : Croom Helm, c1986. — [352]p. — *Includes index*

AFRICA, SUB-SAHARAN — Economic conditions — 1960-

LIEBENOW, J. Gus
African politics : crises and challenges / J. Gus Liebenow ; maps by Cathryn L. Lombardi. — Bloomington : Indiana University Press, c1986. — p. cm. — *Includes index*

Structural distortions and adjustment programmes in the poor countries of Africa : a challenge for development policy / Hartmut Brandt ... [et al.]. — Berlin : German Development Institute, 1985. — xxxi, 377 p.. — (Occasional papers of the German Development Institute (GDI) ; no. 85). — *Includes bibliographies*

AFRICA, SUB-SAHARAN — Economic conditions — 1960- — Bibliography

COOK, Gillian P.
Development in Africa south of the Sahara 1970-1980 : a select annotated bibliography / compiled by Gillian Patricia Cook. — [Cape Town] : University of Cape Town Libraries, 1983. — ix,410p. — (Bibliographical series / University of Cape Town, School of Librarianship)

COOK, Gillian Patricia
Development in Africa, South of the Sahara, 1970-1980 : a select annotated bibliography / compiled by Gillian Patricia Cook. — [Cape Town] : University of Cape Town Libraries, 1984. — ix, 410 p.. — (Bibliographical series / University of Cape Town School of Librarianship). — ″*Presented in partial fulfilment of the requirements for the final diploma in Library and Information Science, 1983*″--T.p. verso. — *Includes indexes*

AFRICA, SUB-SAHARAN — Economic policy

Financing adjustment with growth in Sub-Saharan Africa, 1986-90. — Washington, D.C. : The World Bank, 1986. — x,120p

INTERNATIONAL BANK FOR RECONSTRUCTION AND DEVELOPMENT
Financing adjustment with growth in sub-Saharan Africa, 1986-90. — Washington, D.C. : World Bank, c1986. — p. cm. — *Bibliography: p*

Structural distortions and adjustment programmes in the poor countries of Africa : a challenge for development policy / Hartmut Brandt ... [et al.]. — Berlin : German Development Institute, 1985. — xxxi, 377 p.. — (Occasional papers of the German Development Institute (GDI) ; no. 85). — *Includes bibliographies*

AFRICA, SUB-SAHARAN — Economic policy — Bibliography

COOK, Gillian Patricia
Development in Africa, South of the Sahara, 1970-1980 : a select annotated bibliography / compiled by Gillian Patricia Cook. — [Cape Town] : University of Cape Town Libraries, 1984. — ix, 410 p.. — (Bibliographical series / University of Cape Town School of Librarianship). — *"Presented in partial fulfilment of the requirements for the final diploma in Library and Information Science, 1983"--T.p. verso. — Includes indexes*

AFRICA, SUB-SAHARAN — Famines — Bibliography

SEELEY, J. A.
Famine in sub-Saharan Africa : a select bibliography (excluding the Sahel) from 1978 / compiled by J.A. Seeley. — Cambridge : African Studies Centre, University of Cambridge, 1986. — vi,176p. — (Cambridge African occasional papers ; no.3). — *Includes index*

AFRICA, SUB-SAHARAN — Politics and government

DIOP, Cheikh Anta
[Afrique noire pré-coloniale. English]. Precolonial Black Africa : a comparative study of the political and social systems of Europe and Black Africa, from antiquity to the formation of modern states / Cheikh Anta Diop ; translated by Harold J. Salemson. — Westport, Conn. : L. Hill, 1986. — p. cm. — *Translation of: L'Afrique noire pré-coloniale*

AFRICA, SUB-SAHARAN — Politics and government — Addresses, essays, lectures

The African liberation reader / edited by Aquino de Bragança and Immanuel Wallerstein. — London : Zed Press, June 1982. — (Africa series). — *Translated from Portuguese*
Vol.2: The national liberation movements. — 1982. — vi,196p

AFRICA, SUB-SAHARAN — Politics and government — 1960-

LIEBENOW, J. Gus
African politics : crises and challenges / J. Gus Liebenow ; maps by Cathryn L. Lombardi. — Bloomington : Indiana University Press, c1986. — p. cm. — *Includes index*

Military power and politics in black Africa / edited by Simon Baynham. — London : Croom Helm, c1986. — [352]p. — *Includes index*

AFRICA, SUB-SAHARAN — Population

Population growth and policies in Sub-Saharan Africa. — Washington, D.C. : The World Bank, 1986. — x,102p. — (A World Bank policy study). — *Bibliography: p76-82*

AFRICA, SUB-SAHARAN — Population policy

Population growth and policies in Sub-Saharan Africa. — Washington, D.C. : The World Bank, 1986. — x,102p. — (A World Bank policy study). — *Bibliography: p76-82*

AFRICA, SUB-SAHARAN — Economic policy

Financing adjustment with growth in Sub-Saharan Africa, 1986-90. — Washington, D.C. : The World Bank, 1986. — x,120p

AFRICA, SUB-SARHARAN — Economic conditions — 1960-

MCNAMARA, Robert S.
The challenges for Sub-Saharan Africa / by Robert S. McNamara. — Washington, D.C. : [World Bank], 1985. — 49p

AFRICA, WEST — Discovery and exploration

JOHNSTON, Sir Harry
Pioneers in West Africa / by Sir Harry Johnston. — New York : Negro Universities Press, 1969. — xiv,336p. — *Originally published in 1912*

AFRICA, WEST — Economic integration

The Economic integration of West Africa / edited by E.C. Edozien, E. Osagie. — Ibadan, Nigeria : Ibadan University Press, [1982]. — xvii, 192 p.. — *Includes bibliographical references and index*

AFRICA, WEST — Economic integration — History

ASANTE, S. K. B
The political economy of regionalism in Africa : a decade of the Economic Community of West African States (ECOWAS) / S.K.B. Asante. — New York : Praeger, 1985. — p. cm. — *Includes index. — Bibliography: p*

AFRICA, WEST — Economic policy

Croissance et ajustement : les problèmes de l'Afrique de l'Ouest / préparée par Patrick Guillaumont. — Paris : Economica, 1985. — 248p. — *Includes bibliographies*

AFRICA, WEST — Foreign economic relations

INGHAM, Barbara
Colonialism and the economy of the Gold Coast 1919-1945 / Barbara Ingham. — Salford : University of Salford, 1986. — 51,i-iv leaves. — (Salford papers in economics ; 86-5)

AFRICA, WEST — History — To 1884

History of West Africa / edited by J.F.A. Ajayi and Michael Crowder. — 3rd ed. — Harlow : Longman. — *Previous ed.: 1976. — Includes bibliographies and index*
Vol.I. — 1985. — x,742p

AFRICA, WEST — Kings and rulers — Folklore

African art & leadership / Edited by Douglas Fraser and Herbert M. Cole. — Madison : University of Wisconsin Press, [1972]. — xvii, 332 p. — *Fourteen papers, 6 of which were presented at a symposium entitled The aristocratic traditions in African art, held at Columbia University, May 1965. — Includes bibliographies*

AFRICA, WEST — Politics and government — 1960-

ZOLBERG, Aristide R.
Creating political order : the party-states of West Africa / Aristide R. Zolberg. — Chicago : Rand McNally, [1966]. — vi,168p

AFRICAN STUDENTS — Relations — United States

African student outlook : a comparison of findings at English and French-speaking universities. — [Washington, D.C.] : United States Information Agency, 1965. — vi,29p. — *R-115-65*

AFRICAN STUDENTS — Attitudes

African student outlook : a comparison of findings at English and French-speaking universities. — [Washington, D.C.] : United States Information Agency, 1965. — vi,29p. — *R-115-65*

East African university student views on international and continental issues. — [Washington, D.C.] : United States Information Agency, 1965. — vii,25p. — *R-39-65*

AFRICANS — Sudan — Bibliography

ABD AL-RAHIM NASR, Ahmad
A bibliography of West African settlement and development in the Sudan / Ahmad Abd al-Rahim Nasr and Mark R. Duffield. — Khartoum : University of Khartoum. Faculty of Economic and Social Studies. Development Studies and Research Centre, 1980. — 24p. — (Monograph series / University of Khartoum. Faculty of Economic and Social Studies. Development Studies and Research Centre ; no.13)

AFRIKANERS — South Africa — Gamkaskloof Valley

DU TOIT, Brian M.
People of the valley : life in an isolated Afrikaner community in South Africa / by Brian M. du Toit ; with an introductory statement by Solon T. Kimball. — Cape Town : Balkema (A. A.), 1974. — 134 p., [8] p. of plates. — *Includes index. — Bibliography: p. 126-129*

AFRO-AMERICAN COLLEGE STUDENTS — Political activity — History — 20th century

EXUM, William H.
Paradoxes of protest : black student activism in a White university / William H. Exum. — Philadelphia : Temple University Press, 1985. — p. cm. — *Includes index. — Bibliography: p*

AFRO-AMERICAN COMMUNISTS — History — Sources

American communism and Black Americans : a documentary history, 1919-1929 / edited by Philip S. Foner and James S. Allen. — Philadelphia : Temple University Press, 1987. — xvi, 235 p.. — *Includes bibliographical references and index*

AFRO-AMERICAN ENTERTAINERS — Biography

BOSKIN, Joseph
Sambo : the rise & demise of an American jester / Joseph Boskin. — New York : Oxford University Press, 1986. — ix, 252 p. [8] p. of plates. — *Includes index. — Bibliography: p. 225-243*

AFRO-AMERICAN FAMILIES

EDELMAN, Marian Wright
Families in peril : an agenda for social change / Marian Wright Edelman. — Cambridge, Mass. : Harvard University Press, 1987. — xii, 127 p.. — (The W.E.B. Du Bois lectures ; 1986). — *Includes index. — Bibliography: p. [115]-122*

MARTIN, Elmer P.
The black extended family / Elmer P. Martin, Joanne Mitchell Martin. — Chicago ; London : University of Chicago Press, 1978. — ix,129p. — *Bibliography: p.121-124. — Includes index*

ZOLLAR, Ann Creighton
A member of the family : strategies for Black family continuity / Ann Creighton Zollar. — Chicago : Nelson-Hall, 1984. — p. cm. — *Includes index. — Bibliography: p*

AFRO-AMERICAN FAMILIES — Bibliography

DAVIS, Lenwood G
The Black family in the United States : a revised, updated, selectively annotated bibliography / compiled by Lenwood G. Davis. — New York : Greenwood Press, 1986. — x, 234 p.. — (Bibliographies and indexes in Afro-American and African studies ; no. 14). — *Includes index*

AFRO-AMERICAN FAMILIES — Case studies

STACK, Carol B
All our kin: strategies for survival in a Black community / [by] Carol B. Stack. — [1st ed.]. — New York : Harper & Row, [1974]. — xxi, 175 p. — *Bibliography: p. [160]-167*

AFRO-AMERICAN FAMILIES — History
JONES, Jacqueline
  Labor of love, labor of sorrow : Black women, work, and the family from slavery to the present / Jacqueline Jones. — New York : Basic Books, c1985. — p. cm. — *Includes index. — Bibliography: p*

AFRO-AMERICAN HISTORIANS — History — 20th century — Addresses, essays, lectures
MEIER, August
  Black history and the historical profession, 1915-80 / August Meier and Elliott Rudwick. — Urbana : University of Illinois Press, c1986. — p. cm. — (Blacks in the New World). — *Includes index. — Bibliography: p*

AFRO-AMERICAN IRON AND STEEL WORKERS — Pennsylvania — History
DICKERSON, Dennis C.
  Out of the crucible : Black steelworkers in western Pennsylvania, 1875-1980 / Dennis C. Dickerson. — Albany : State University of New York Press, c1986. — xiv, 323 p.. — (SUNY series in Afro-American studies). — *Includes index. — Bibliography: p. 307-318*

AFRO-AMERICAN SCIENTISTS — United States
PEARSON, Willie
  Black scientists, white society, and colorless science : a study of universalism in American science / Willie Pearson, Jr. — Millwood, N.Y. : Associated Faculty Press, c1985. — xi, 201 p. . — *Includes index. — Bibliography: p. 181-196*

AFRO-AMERICAN SOCIOLOGISTS — United States — Biography
Race, class, and the world system : the sociology of Oliver C. Cox / Herbert M. Hunter and Sameer Y. Abraham, eds. — New York : Monthly Review Press, 1987. — p. cm. — *Bibliography: p*

AFRO-AMERICAN SOLDIERS — Congresses
Values in conflict : Blacks and the American ambivalence toward violence / edited by Charles A. Frye. — Washington, D.C. : University Press of America, c1980. — iii, 169 p.. — *Includes bibliographies and index*

AFRO-AMERICAN SOLDIERS — Correspondence
MCGUIRE, Phillip
  Taps for a Jim Crow army : letters from black soldiers in World War II / Phillip McGuire ; with a foreword by Benjamin Quarles. — Santa Barbara, Calif. : ABC-Clio, c1983. — li, 278 p. . *Includes index. — Bibliography: p. 263*

AFRO-AMERICAN STUDENT MOVEMENTS
EXUM, William H.
  Paradoxes of protest : black student activism in a White university / William H. Exum. — Philadelphia : Temple University Press, 1985. — p. cm. — *Includes index. — Bibliography: p*

AFRO-AMERICAN STUDENT MOVEMENTS — New York (N.Y.) — Case studies
EXUM, William H.
  Paradoxes of protest : black student activism in a White university / William H. Exum. — Philadelphia : Temple University Press, 1985. — p. cm. — *Includes index. — Bibliography: p*

AFRO-AMERICAN WOMEN
Slipping through the cracks : the status of black women / edited by Margaret C. Simms and Julianne Molveaux. — New Brunswick ; Oxford : Transaction Books, 1986. — 302p

AFRO-AMERICAN WOMEN — Employment — History
JONES, Jacqueline
  Labor of love, labor of sorrow : Black women, work, and the family from slavery to the present / Jacqueline Jones. — New York : Basic Books, c1985. — p. cm. — *Includes index. — Bibliography: p*

AFRO-AMERICAN WOMEN — History
JONES, Jacqueline
  Labor of love, labor of sorrow : Black women, work, and the family from slavery to the present / Jacqueline Jones. — New York : Basic Books, c1985. — p. cm. — *Includes index. — Bibliography: p*

AFRO-AMERICAN YOUTH — Employment — Congresses
FREEMAN, Richard B
  The Black youth employment crisis / Richard B. Freeman and Harry J. Holzer. — Chicago : University of Chicago Press, 1986. — p. cm. — (A National Bureau of Economic Research project report). — *Includes bibliographies and indexes*

AFRO-AMERICANS
FARLEY, Reynolds
  Growth of the Black population : a study of demographic trends. — Chicago : Markham Pub. Co, [1970]. — v, 286 p. — (Markham sociology series). — *Includes bibliographical references*

SOUTHERN, David W
  Gunnar Myrdal and Black-white relations : the use and abuse of An American dilemma, 1944-1969 / David W. Southern. — Baton Rouge : Louisiana State University Press, c1987. — xviii, 341 p.. — *Includes index. — Bibliography: p. 311-330*

AFRO-AMERICANS — Addresses, essays, lectures
DU BOIS, W. E. B
  Against racism : unpublished essays, papers, addresses, 1887-1961 / by W.E.B. Du Bois ; edited by Herbert Aptheker. — Amherst : University of Massachusetts Press, 1985. — xx, 325 p.. — *Includes bibliographical references and index*

AFRO-AMERICANS — Biography
The black book : the true political philosophy of Malcolm X (El Hajj Malik el Shabazz / edited and compiled by Y. N. Kly. — Ottawa ; Atlanta : Clarity Press, 1986. — viii,91p. — *Bibliography: p89-91*

FORMAN, James
  The making of Black revolutionaries / James Forman. — 2d ed. — Washington, DC : Open Hand Pub., c1985. — xxiii, 568 p.. — *Includes index*

HORNE, Gerald
  Black and red : W.E.B. Du Bois and the Afro-American response to the Cold War, 1944-1963 / Gerald Horne. — Albany, N.Y. : State University of New York Press, c1985. — xii, 457p. — (SUNY series in Afro-American society). — *Includes index. — Bibliography: p.437-440*

LANDESS, Tom
  Jesse Jackson and the politics of race / Thomas H. Landess, Richard M. Quinn. — Ottawa, Ill. : Jameson Books, c1985. — 269p. — *Includes index*

STEIN, Judith
  The world of Marcus Garvey : race and class in modern society / Judith Stein. — Baton Rouge ; London : Louisiana State University Press, c1986. — xii, 294p. — *Includes index. — Bibliography: p.281-284*

WASHINGTON, Johnny
  Alain Locke and philosophy : a quest for cultural pluralism / Johnny Washington. — Westport, Conn. : Greenwood Press, c1986. — p. cm. — (Contributions in Afro-American and African studies ; no. 94). — *Includes index. — Bibliography: p*

AFRO-AMERICANS — Civil rights
ANDERSON, Alan B.
  Confronting the color line : the broken promise of the civil rights movement in Chicago / Alan B. Anderson, George W. Pickering. — Athens : University of Georgia Press, c1986. — xii, 515 p., [16] p. of plates. — *Includes index. — Bibliography: p. 459-500*

BLOOM, Jack M
  Class, race, and the Civil Rights Movement / Jack M. Bloom. — Bloomington : Indiana University Press, c1987. — x, 267 p.. — (Blacks in the diaspora). — *Includes index. — Bibliography: p. [225]-237*

BOGGS, James
  Racism and the class struggle : further pages from a black worker's notebook. — New York : [Monthly Review Press, 1970]. — 190 p

FORMAN, James
  The making of Black revolutionaries / James Forman. — 2d ed. — Washington, DC : Open Hand Pub., c1985. — xxiii, 568 p.. — *Includes index*

MCDONALD, Laughlin
  Racial equality / Laughlin McDonald. — Skokie, Ill. : National Textbook Co., c1977. — xi, 155 p.. — (To protect these rights). — *Includes bibliographical references and index*

AFRO-AMERICANS — Civil rights — Addresses, essays, lectures
KING, Martin Luther
  A testament of hope : the essential writings of Martin Luther King, Jr. / edited by James Melvin Washington. — 1st ed. — San Francisco : Harper & Row, c1986. — xxvi, 676 p.. — *Includes index. — Bibliography: p. 654-661*

AFRO-AMERICANS — Civil rights — Case studies
MONTI, Daniel J
  A semblance of justice : St. Louis school desegregation and order in urban America / Daniel J. Monti. — Columbia : University of Missouri Press, 1985. — xiv, 221 p.. — *Includes index. — Bibliography: p. 208-215*

AFRO-AMERICANS — Civil rights — History
CURTIS, Michael Kent
  No state shall abridge : the 14th amendment and the Bill of Rights / Michael Kent Curtis. — Durham, N.C. : Duke University Press, 1986. — xii, 275 p.. — *Includes index. — Bibliography: p. [221]-266*

KACZOROWSKI, Robert J
  The politics of judicial interpretation : the federal courts, Department of Justice and civil rights, 1866-1876 / by Robert J. Kaczorowski. — Dobbs Ferry, N.Y. : Oceana Publications, 1985. — xiv, 241 p.. — (New York University School of Law series in legal history). — "New York University School of Law, Linden studies in legal history.". — *Includes bibliographies and index*

AFRO-AMERICANS — Civil rights — Alabama — Tuskegee
NORRELL, Robert J
  Reaping the whirlwind : the civil rights movement in Tuskegee / Robert J. Norrell. — 1st ed. — New York : Knopf : Distributed by Random House, 1985. — x, 254 p., [8] p. of plates. — : *Revision of author's thesis (Ph. D.)--University of Virginia. — Includes index. — Bibliography: p. 237-242*

AFRO-AMERICANS — Civil rights — Illinois — Chicago
ANDERSON, Alan B.
  Confronting the color line : the broken promise of the civil rights movement in Chicago / Alan B. Anderson, George W. Pickering. — Athens : University of Georgia Press, c1986. — xii, 515 p., [16] p. of plates. — *Includes index. — Bibliography: p. 459-500*

AFRO-AMERICANS — Economic conditions
CAYTON, Horace Roscoe
  Black metropolis / by Horace R. Cayton and St. Clair Drake. — London : Cape, 1946. — 809p. — *Bibliography: p793-796*

AFRO-AMERICANS — Economic conditions *continuation*

HILL, Robert Bernard
Economic policies and black progress : myths and realities / Robert B. Hill. — Washington, D.C. (733 15th St., N.W., Suite 1020, Washington 20005) : National Urban League, Research Dept., c1981. — vi, 144 p.. — *Bibliography: p. 90-99*

SMITH, James P.
Closing the gap : forty years of economic progress for Blacks / James P. Smith, Finis R. Welch. — Santa Monica, CA : Rand, [1986]. — xxxvii, 128 p.. — *"Prepared for the U.S. Department of Labor."*. — *"February 1986."*. — *"R-3330-DOL."*. — *Bibliography: p. 127-128*

AFRO-AMERICANS — Economic conditions — Bibliography

OBUDHO, Robert A
Afro-American demograpy and urban issues : a bibliography / compiled by R.A. Obudho and Jeannine B. Scott. — Westport, Conn. : Greenwood Press, 1985. — xxxix, 433 p.. — (Bibliographies and indexes in Afro-American and African studies ; no. 8). — *Includes index*

AFRO-AMERICANS — Education

WASHINGTON, Johnny
Alain Locke and philosophy : a quest for cultural pluralism / Johnny Washington. — Westport, Conn. : Greenwood Press, c1986. — p. cm. — (Contributions in Afro-American and African studies ; no. 94). — *Includes index*. — *Bibliography: p*

AFRO-AMERICANS — Employment — Pennsylvania — History

DICKERSON, Dennis C.
Out of the crucible : Black steelworkers in western Pennsylvania, 1875-1980 / Dennis C. Dickerson. — Albany : State University of New York Press, c1986. — xiv, 323 p.. — (SUNY series in Afro-American studies). — *Includes index*. — *Bibliography: p. 307-318*

AFRO-AMERICANS — Historiography — Addresses, essays, lectures

MEIER, August
Black history and the historical profession, 1915-80 / August Meier and Elliott Rudwick. — Urbana : University of Illinois Press, c1986. — p. cm. — (Blacks in the New World). — *Includes index*. — *Bibliography: p*

AFRO-AMERICANS — History

FRANKLIN, John Hope
From slavery to freedom : a history of Negro Americans / John Hope Franklin. — 5th ed. — New York : Knopf, 1980. — xxvii, 554, xxxix, p.. — *Includes index*. — *Bibliography: p. 507-546*

AFRO-AMERICANS — History — To 1863 — Sources

The Black abolitionist papers / C. Peter Ripley, editor ; Jeffrey S. Rossbach, associate editor ... [et al.]. — Chapel Hill : University of North Carolina Press, c1985-. — p. cm. — *Includes index*. — *Contents: v. 1. The British Isles, 1830-1865*

AFRO-AMERICANS — History — 1877-1964 — Sources

American communism and Black Americans : a documentary history, 1919-1929 / edited by Philip S. Foner and James S. Allen. — Philadelphia : Temple University Press, 1987. — xvi, 235 p.. — *Includes bibliographical references and index*

AFRO-AMERICANS — Legal status, laws, etc.

MCDONALD, Laughlin
Racial equality / Laughlin McDonald. — Skokie, Ill. : National Textbook Co., c1977. — xi, 155 p.. — (To protect these rights). — *Includes bibliographical references and index*

AFRO-AMERICANS — Politics and government

COLLINS, Sheila D
From melting pot to rainbow coalition : the future of race in American politics / Sheila D. Collins. — New York : Monthly Review Press, 1986. — p. cm. — *Includes index*. — *Bibliography: p*

HORNE, Gerald
Black and red : W.E.B. Du Bois and the Afro-American response to the Cold War, 1944-1963 / Gerald Horne. — Albany, N.Y. : State University of New York Press, c1985. — xii, 457p. — (SUNY series in Afro-American society). — *Includes index*. — *Bibliography: p.437-440*

WALTON, Hanes
Invisible politics : Black political behavior / Hanes Walton, Jr. — Albany : State University of New York Press, c1985. — xxii, 366 p.. — (SUNY series in Afro-American society). — *Includes index*. — *Bibliography: p. [323]-358*

WASHINGTON, Johnny
Alain Locke and philosophy : a quest for cultural pluralism / Johnny Washington. — Westport, Conn. : Greenwood Press, c1986. — p. cm. — (Contributions in Afro-American and African studies ; no. 94). — *Includes index*. — *Bibliography: p*

AFRO-AMERICANS — Politics and government — Addresses, essays, lectures

Race, politics, and culture : critical essays on the radicalism of the 1960's / edited by Adolph Reed, Jr. — Westport, Conn. : Greenwood Press, 1986. — xii, 287 p.. — (Contributions in Afro-American and African studies ; no. 95). — *Includes bibliographies and index*

AFRO-AMERICANS — Politics and suffrage

CARMICHAEL, Stokely
Black power : the politics of liberation in America / [by] Stokely Carmichael & Charles V. Hamilton. — New York : Random House, [1967]. — xii, 198 p. — *Bibliography: p. 187-189*

AFRO-AMERICANS — Race identity

STEIN, Judith
The world of Marcus Garvey : race and class in modern society / Judith Stein. — Baton Rouge ; London : Louisiana State University Press, c1986. — xii, 294p. — *Includes index*. — *Bibliography: p.281-284*

AFRO-AMERICANS — Social conditions — Bibliography

OBUDHO, Robert A
Afro-American demograpy and urban issues : a bibliography / compiled by R.A. Obudho and Jeannine B. Scott. — Westport, Conn. : Greenwood Press, 1985. — xxxix, 433 p.. — (Bibliographies and indexes in Afro-American and African studies ; no. 8). — *Includes index*

AFRO-AMERICANS — Social conditions — To 1964

CAYTON, Horace Roscoe
Black metropolis / by Horace R. Cayton and St. Clair Drake. — London : Cape, 1946. — 809p. — *Bibliography: p793-796*

AFRO-AMERICANS — Social conditions — 1964-

RAINWATER, Lee
Behind ghetto walls : Black families in a federal slum. — Chicago : Aldine Pub. Co, [1970]. — xi, 446 p. — *Bibliography: p. 427-440*

AFRO-AMERICANS — Social conditions — 1975-

ZOLLAR, Ann Creighton
A member of the family : strategies for Black family continuity / Ann Creighton Zollar. — Chicago : Nelson-Hall, 1984. — p. cm. — *Includes index*. — *Bibliography: p*

AFRO-AMERICANS — Social life and customs

RAINWATER, Lee
Behind ghetto walls : Black families in a federal slum. — Chicago : Aldine Pub. Co, [1970]. — xi, 446 p. — *Bibliography: p. 427-440*

AFRO-AMERICANS — Statistics, Vital

FARLEY, Reynolds
Growth of the Black population : a study of demographic trends. — Chicago : Markham Pub. Co, [1970]. — v, 286 p. — (Markham sociology series). — *Includes bibliographical references*

AFRO-AMERICANS — Study and teaching (Higher) — United States — History — 20th century — Addresses, essays, lectures

MEIER, August
Black history and the historical profession, 1915-80 / August Meier and Elliott Rudwick. — Urbana : University of Illinois Press, c1986. — p. cm. — (Blacks in the New World). — *Includes index*. — *Bibliography: p*

AFRO-AMERICANS — Suffrage

The Voting Rights Act : consequences and implications / edited by Lorn S. Foster. — New York : Praeger, 1985. — p. cm. — *Includes index*

WALTON, Hanes
Invisible politics : Black political behavior / Hanes Walton, Jr. — Albany : State University of New York Press, c1985. — xxii, 366 p.. — (SUNY series in Afro-American society). — *Includes index*. — *Bibliography: p. [323]-358*

AFRO-AMERICANS — Alabama — Tuskegee — Politics and government

NORRELL, Robert J
Reaping the whirlwind : the civil rights movement in Tuskegee / Robert J. Norrell. — 1st ed — New York : Knopf : Distributed by Random House, 1985. — x, 254 p., [8] p. of plates. — : Revision of author's thesis (Ph. D.)--University of Virginia. — *Includes index*. — *Bibliography: p. 237-242*

AFRO-AMERICANS — Chicago

CAYTON, Horace Roscoe
Black metropolis / by Horace R. Cayton and St. Clair Drake. — London : Cape, 1946. — 809p. — *Bibliography: p793-796*

AFRO-AMERICANS — Georgia — History — 19th century

DUNCAN, Russell
Freedom's shore : Tunis Campbell and the Georgia freedmen / by Russell Duncan. — Athens : University of Georgia Press, c1986. — p. cm. — *Includes index*. — *Bibliography: p*

AFRO-AMERICANS — Georgia — Politics and suffrage

DRAGO, Edmund L.
Black politicians and reconstruction in Georgia : a splendid failure / Edmund L. Drago. — Baton Rouge ; London : Louisiana State University Press, c1982. — xii,201p

AFRO-AMERICANS — Sea Islands — History — 19th century

HAWKS, Esther Hill
A woman doctor's Civil War : Esther Hill Hawks' diary / edited with a foreword and afterword by Gerald Schwartz. — 1st ed. — Columbia, S.C. : University of South Carolina Press, c1984. — p. cm. — *Bibliography: p283-288*. — *Bibliography: p*

AFRO-AMERICANS — St. Louis

RAINWATER, Lee
Behind ghetto walls : Black families in a federal slum. — Chicago : Aldine Pub. Co, [1970]. — xi, 446 p. — *Bibliography: p. 427-440*

AFRO-AMERICANS — Tennessee — History — 19th century
CIMPRICH, John
Slavery's end in Tennessee, 1861-1865 / John Cimprich. — University, Ala. : University of Alabama Press, c1985. — 191 p.. — *Includes index. — Bibliography: p. 181-185*

AFRO-AMERICANS IN THE PERFORMING ARTS
BOSKIN, Joseph
Sambo : the rise & demise of an American jester / Joseph Boskin. — New York : Oxford University Press, 1986. — ix, 252 p. [8] p. of plates. — *Includes index. — Bibliography: p. 225-243*

AFRO-AMERICANS IN THE PERFORMING ARTS — Bibliography
HILL, George H
Blacks on television : a selectively annotated bibliography / by George H. Hill and Sylvia Saverson Hill. — Metuchen, N.J. : Scarecrow Press, 1985. — xiv, 223 p.. — *Includes indexes*

AFRO-AMERICANS IN THE TELEVISION INDUSTRY — Bibliography
HILL, George H
Blacks on television : a selectively annotated bibliography / by George H. Hill and Sylvia Saverson Hill. — Metuchen, N.J. : Scarecrow Press, 1985. — xiv, 223 p.. — *Includes indexes*

AFRO-AMERICANS, RELIGION
X, Malcolm
The autobiography of Malcolm X / with the assistance of Alex Haley. — Harmondsworth : Penguin, by arrangement with Hutchinson of London, 1968. — 512p

AGE
ASSOCIATION OF SOCIAL ANTHROPOLOGISTS OF THE COMMONWEALTH. Conference (1977 : Swansea)
Sex and age as principles of social differentiation / edited by J.S. La Fontaine. — London : Academic Press, 1978. — vii,188p. — (Monographs / Association of Social Anthropologists of the Commonwealth ; 17). — *'The papers presented here represent six out of eight papers delivered at the Conference of the Association of Social Anthropologists at Swansea in April 1977' - Preface. — Includes bibliographies and index*

AGE AND EMPLOYMENT — Great Britain
BOSANQUET, Nicholas
A generation in limbo : government, the economy and the 55-65 age group in Britain / Nick Bosanquet. — London : Public Policy Centre, 1987. — xiii,49p. — *Bibliography: p48-49*

MELLOR, Hugh W.
Work in later life : a plea for flexible retirement / Hugh Mellor. — London : Employment Institute, 1987. — 32p. — *Bibliography: p29-30*

AGE AND EMPLOYMENT — United States
Work, health, and income among the elderly / Gary Burtless, editor. — Washington, D.C. : Brookings Institution, c1987. — xiii, 276 p.. — (Studies in social economics). — *Includes bibliographical references and index*

AGE DISCRIMINATION IN EMPLOYMENT — Australia
FREY, Dianne
Survey of sole parent pensioners' workforce barriers / Dianne Frey. — Woden, ACT : Department of Social Security, 1986. — 40p. — (Background/discussion paper / Social Security Review ; no.12). — *Includes bibliographical references*

AGE DISTRIBUTION (DEMOGRAPHY)
HELLER, Peter S.
Ageing and social expenditure in the major industrial countries, 1980-2025 / by Peter S. Heller, Richard Hemming and Peter W. Kohnert. — Washington, D.C. : The World Bank, 1986. — viii,76p. — (Occasional paper / International Monetary Fund ; no.47). — *Bibliographical references: p74-76*

AGE DISTRIBUTION (DEMOGRAPHY) — Statistics
Age-sex composition of world population by major region and country, based on United Nations' population projections as assessed in 1978. — Tokyo : Institute of Population Problems, 1981. — iv,97p. — (Research series / Institute of Population Problems ; no.225). — *In Japanese with contents and forword also in English*

AGE DISTRIBUTION (DEMOGRAPHY) — Canada
MCDANIEL, Susan A.
Canada's aging population / by Susan A. McDaniel. — Toronto ; Boston : Butterworths, c1986. — xix, 136 p.. — (Butterworths perspectives on individual and population aging). — *Includes index. — Bibliography: p. 121-131*

AGE DISTRIBUTION (DEMOGRAPHY) — United States — Addresses, essays, lectures
Our aging society : paradox and promise / edited by Alan Pifer and Lydia Bronte. — 1st ed. — New York, N.Y. : W.W. Norton, c1986. — viii, 438 p.. — *Includes bibliographies and index*

AGE DISTRIBUTION (DEMOGRAPHY) — United States — Statistics
ROSENWAIKE, Ira
The extreme aged in America : a portrait of an expanding population / Ira Rosenwaike, with the assistance of Barbara Logue. — Westport, Conn. ; London : Greenwood Press, 1985. — xix, 253 p.. — (Contributions to the study of aging ; no. 3). — *Includes index. — Bibliography: p. [229]-241*

AGE FACTORS
MERCER, Ramona Thieme
First-time motherhood : experiences from teens to forties / Ramona T. Mercer. — New York : Springer Pub. Co., c1986. — xv, 384 p.. — *Includes index. — Bibliography: p. 357-374*

AGE GROUPS — Classification
Provisional guidelines on standard international age classifications. — New York : United Nations, 1982. — iv,28p. — ([Document] / United Nations ; ST/ESA/STAT/SER.M/74). — *Includes bibliographical references. — Sales no.: E.82.XVII.5*

AGE GROUPS — Developing countries — Statistics
ZOUGHLAMI, Younès
The demographic characteristics of household populations / Younès Zoughlami, Diana Allsopp. — Voorburg : International Statistical Institute, 1985. — 82p. — (Comparative studies / World Fertility Survey ; no.45). — *Bibliographical references: p31*

AGED — England — Liverpool (Merseyside) — Crimes against
JONKER, Joan
Victims of violence / Joan Jonker. — London : Fontana, 1986. — 223p

AGED
The elderly : victims and deviants / edited by Carl D. Chambers ... [et al.]. — Athens, Ohio : Ohio University Press, 1987. — p. cm. — *Includes bibliographies*

GUBRIUM, Jaber F
Oldtimers and Alzheimer's : the descriptive organization of senility / by Jaber F. Gubrium. — Greenwich, Conn. : JAI Press, c1986. — xii, 222 p.. — (Contemporary ethnographic studies). — *Includes index. — Bibliography: p. 211-219*

VICTOR, Christina R.
Old age in modern society : a textbook of social gerontology / Christina R. Victor. — London : Croom Helm, c1987. — [352]p. — *Includes bibliography and index*

AGED — Care — Great Britain
TESTER, Susan
Ill informed? : a study of information and support for elderly people in the inner city / Susan Tester, Barbara Meredith. — London : Policy Studies Institute, 1987. — 124p. — (PSI report ; 670)

AGED — Care and hygiene
Ageing and social policy : a critical assessment / edited by Chris Phillipson and Alan Walker. — Aldershot : Gower, c1986. — xiv,334p. — (Studies in social policy and welfare ; 28). — *Bibliography: p291-320. — Includes index*

Dependency and interdependency in old age : theoretical perspectives and policy alternatives / edited by Chris Phillipdon, Miriam Bernard and Patricia Strang. — London : Croom Helm in association with the British Society of Gerontology, c1986. — 371p. — *Conference proceedings. — Includes bibliographies*

Welfare provision for the elderly and the role of the state : proceedings of an Anglo-German conference 1985 / introduced by Rosalind Brooke Ross. — [London] : Anglo-German Foundation for the Study of Industrial Society, 1985. — 130p

AGED — Care and hygiene — Great Britain
WRIGHT, Fay D.
Left to care alone / Fay D. Wright. — Aldershot : Gower, c1986. — [214]p. — *Includes bibliography and index*

AGED — Care and hygiene — Wales
NATIONAL UNION OF PUBLIC EMPLOYEES. Joint Working Party on Care of the Elderly
Dignity or despair? : a NUPE report on care of the elderly in Wales. — [Wales] : National Union of Public Employees, [1985?]. — 36p. — *Cover title. — Report of the National Union of Public Employees Joint Working Party on Care of the Elderly. — Bibliography on rear inside cover*

AGED — Employment
SULLEROT, Evelyne
L'âge de travailler / Evelyne Sullerot. — [Paris] : Fayard, 1986. — 224p

AGED — Employment — Australia
FREY, Dianne
Survey of sole parent pensioners' workforce barriers / Dianne Frey. — Woden, ACT : Department of Social Security, 1986. — 40p. — (Background/discussion paper / Social Security Review ; no.12). — *Includes bibliographical references*

AGED — Employment — United States
KAHNE, Hilda
Reconceiving part-time work : new perspectives for older workers and women / Hilda Kahne. — Totowa, N.J. : Rowman & Allanheld, 1985. — xv, 180 p.. — *Includes index. — Bibliography: p. [160]-174*

Work, health, and income among the elderly / Gary Burtless, editor. — Washington, D.C. : Brookings Institution, c1987. — xiii, 276 p.. — (Studies in social economics). — *Includes bibliographical references and index*

AGED — Family relationships
GREENE, Roberta
Social work with the aged and their families / Roberta Greene. — New York : Aldine de Gruyter, c1986. — p. cm. — *Includes index. — Bibliography: p*

AGED — Government policy — Great Britain
GREAT BRITAIN. Department of Health and Social Security
Conference on the Elderly, 26 July 1977 : background paper. — [London] : the Department, [1977]. — 13,[7]p

AGED — Health and hygiene — United States
Work, health, and income among the elderly / Gary Burtless, editor. — Washington, D.C. : Brookings Institution, c1987. — xiii, 276 p.. — (Studies in social economics). — *Includes bibliographical references and index*

AGED — Home care — France
THIRIAT, Marie-Paule
Les services de soins infirmiers à domicile pour personnes agées : caractéristiques, activité, clientèle 1984 / Marie-Paule Thiriat. — [Paris : Ministère des Affaires sociales et de la Solidarité nationale, 1986]. — 87p. — (Solidarité santé. Cahiers statistiques ; 8)

AGED — Home care — Great Britain
CHALLIS, David
Case management in community care : an evaluated experiment in the home care of the elderly / David Challis & Bleddyn Davies. — Aldershot : Gower, c1986. — xvi,289p. — *Bibliography: p268-281. — Includes index*

AGED — Home care — United States
STEPHENS, Susan A.
Informal care of the elderly / Susan A. Stephens, Jon B. Christianson. — Lexington, Mass. : Lexington Books, c1986. — xii, 174 p.. — *Includes index. — Bibliography: p. [165]-169*

AGED — Hospital care — England — London
Policies, practices and projects : hospital discharge and aftercare initiatives in London. — London (54 Knatchbull Road, SE5 9QY) : Age Concern Greater London, 1985. — 34p. — *Cover title. — At head of title: ACGL Health Forum. — Bibliography: p31-32*

AGED — Institutional care — Great Britain
GREAT BRITAIN. Department of Health and Social Security. Social Services Inspectorate. Development Group
Assessment procedures for elderly people referred for local authority residential care : a Development Group project 1984-1985. — [London : the Department], 1985. — 23,vi,17p. — *Bibliography: end pages 1-17*

Residential care for elderly people : research contributions to the development of policy and practice : a collection of papers presented to a DHSS seminar on 'Residential Care for the Elderrly' in October 1983 / edited by Ken judge and Ian Sinclair. — London : H.M.S.O., 1986. — iv,224p. — *At head of t.p. : Department of Health and Social Security*

AGED — Medical care — Great Britain
WHEELER, Rose
Housing and health in old age : a research agenda / Rose Wheeler. — York : University of York. Centre for Health Economics, 1986. — 26p. — (Discussion paper / University of York. Centre for Health Economics ; 21). — *Bibliography: p25-26*

AGED — Medical care — United States — Addresses, essays, lectures
Our aging society : paradox and promise / edited by Alan Pifer and Lydia Bronte. — 1st ed. — New York, N.Y. : W.W. Norton, c1986. — viii, 438 p.. — *Includes bibliographies and index*

AGED — Mental health services — Great Britain
The rising tide : developing services for mental illness in old age / Health Advisiory Service. — Sutton : NHS Health Advisory Service, 1983

AGED — Psychology
COLEMAN, Peter G.
Ageing and reminiscence processes : social and clinical implications / Peter G. Coleman. — Chichester : Wiley, c1986. — x,172p. — *Bibliography: p161-167. — Includes index*

KAUFMAN, Sharon R
The ageless self : sources of meaning in late life / Sharon R. Kaufman. — Madison, Wis. : University of Wisconsin Press, 1986. — xii, 208 p.. — (Life course studies). — *Includes index. — Bibliography: p. 199-204*

AGED — Services for — Great Britain
Developing services for the elderly / [editor, Joyce Lishman with Gordon Horobin]. — 2nd ed. — London : Kogan Page, 1985. — 179p. — (Research highlights in social work ; 3). — *Previous ed.: Aberdeen : University of Aberdeen, Department of Social Work, 1982. — Includes bibliographies*

PERSONAL SOCIAL SERVICES COUNCIL. Policy Group on the Elderly
Comments on "A happier old age". — London : the Council, [ca.1978]. — 25p. — *Bibliographical references: p24-25*

AGED — Services for — United States
BURT, Martha R
Testing the social safety net : the impact of changes in support programs during the Reagan administration / Martha R. Burt, Karen J. Pittman. — Washington, D.C. : Urban Institute Press, c1985. — xix, 183 p.. — (The Changing domestic priorities series). — *Includes bibliographical references*

HUTTMAN, Elizabeth D.
Social services for the elderly / Elizabeth D. Huttman. — New York : Free Press, c1985. — p. cm. — *Includes bibliographical references and index*

AGED — Suicidal behavior — Bibliography
OSGOOD, Nancy J
Suicide and the elderly : an annotated bibliography and review / compiled by Nancy J. Osgood and John L. McIntosh. — New York : Greenwood Press, 1986. — xiii, 193 p.. — (Bibliographies and indexes in gerontology ; no. 3). — *Includes indexes*

AGED — Australia — Economic conditions
CROMPTON, Cathy
Too old for a job, too young for a pension? : income support for older people out of work / Cathy Crompton. — Canberra : Australian Government Publishing Service, 1986. — x,69p. — (Issues paper / Social Security Review ; no.2). — *Bibliogaphy: p67-69*

AGED — Australia — Social conditions
Ageing and families : a support networks perspective / edited by Hal L. Kendig. — London : Allen & Unwin, 1986. — [248]p

AGED — Australia — Brisbane — Case studies
JOB, Eena
Eighty plus : outgrowing the myths of old age / Eena Job. — St Lucia, Queensland : University of Queensland Press ; Lawrence, Mass. : Distributed in the USA and Canada by Technical Impex, 1984. — viii, 235 p.. — *Includes index. — Bibliography: p. [219]-227*

AGED — Australia — Sydney (N.S.W.) — Family relationships
DAY, Alice Taylor
We can manage : expectations about care and varieties of family support among people 75 years and over / Alice T. Day. — Melbourne : Institute of Family Studies, c1985. — xii, 168 p.. — (Institute of Family Studies monograph ; no. 5). — *"February 1985.". — Bibliography: p. 162-168*

AGED — Australia — Sydney (N.S.W.) — Social conditions
DAY, Alice Taylor
We can manage : expectations about care and varieties of family support among people 75 years and over / Alice T. Day. — Melbourne : Institute of Family Studies, c1985. — xii, 168 p.. — (Institute of Family Studies monograph ; no. 5). — *"February 1985.". — Bibliography: p. 162-168*

AGED — California — Los Angeles — Case studies
SMITHERS, Janice A.
Determined survivors : community life among the urban elderly / by Janice A. Smithers. — New Brunswick, N.J. : Rutgers University Press, c1985. — p. cm. — *Includes index. — Bibliography: p*

AGED — Canada
MCDANIEL, Susan A.
Canada's aging population / by Susan A. McDaniel. — Toronto ; Boston : Butterworths, c1986. — xix, 136 p.. — (Butterworths perspectives on individual and population aging). — *Includes index. — Bibliography: p. 121-131*

MARSHALL, Victor W.
Aging in Canada : social perspectives / Victor W. Marshall [editor]. — 2nd ed. — Markham, Ontario : Fitzhenry & Whiteside, 1987. — ii,613p

AGED — Canada — Social conditions
NOVAK, Mark
Successful aging : the myths, realities and future of aging in Canada / Mark Novak. — Ontario : Penguin, 1985. — 368p. — *Bibliography: p[345]-361*

AGED — Denmark — Dwellings
[Oversigt over institutions- og boligforhold for aeldre og handicappede]. Institutions and housing for the elderly and the handicapped in Denmark. — Copenhagen : Housing Committee for Handicapped, 1979. — 23p. — *Translation of:Oversigt over institutions- og boligforhold for aeldre og handicappede*

AGED — Denmark — Odense — Services for
PLATZ, Merete
Laengst muligt i eget hjem... : en undersøgelse blandt aeldre i Odense. — København : Socialforskningsinstituttet, 1987. — 138p. — (Publikation / Socialforskningsinstituttet ; 157). — *Bibliography: p132-134*

AGED — England — Hampshire — Mental health services
Something to look forward to : an evaluation of a travelling day hospital for elderly mentally ill people / Neil Evans...[et al.]. — Portsmouth : Social Services Research and Intelligence Unit, 1986. — x,254p. — (SSRIU Report ; No.15). — *Bibliography: p[251]-254*

AGED — England — Sheffield (South Yorkshire) — Care and hygiene
BENNETT, D.
Review of residents and routines in elderly persons homes in Sheffield / D. Bennett, R. Browne [and] M. Oldfield. — Sheffield : Family and Community Services Department, 1982. — 69p. — (Report / Sheffield. Family and Community Services Department ; no.13). — *At head of title: Research and Information*

AGED — England — Shropshire — Care and hygiene
BERNARD, Miriam
Shropshire's demonstration development district project : a joint Health Authority/Social Services Department initiative for care of the elderly mentally ill / Miriam Bernard. — Shrewsbury : Shropshire Health Authority/Shropshire County Council Social Services Department, 1985. — vii,75p. — *Bibliography: p64-66*

AGED — England — West Sussex — Care and hygiene
WEST SUSSEX. County Council
Accomodation for the elderly : rest homes, nursing homes and private sheltered housing in West Sussex. — Chichester : [the Council], 1986. — 93p

AGED — Europe — Dwellings
HOGLUND, David J.
Housing for the elderly : privacy and independence / J. David Hoglund. — New York : Van Nostrand Reinhold, c1985. — p. cm. — *Includes index. — Bibliography: p*

AGED — France — Economic conditions
BORKOWSKI, Jean-Louis
Les inégalités et leurs cumuls parmi les personnes agées : niveau de vie, santé et isolement / Jean-Louis Borkowski. — Paris : I.N.S.E.E., 1985. — 174p. — (Archives et documents / France. Institut national de la statistique et des études économiques ; no.142)

AGED — France — Social conditions
BORKOWSKI, Jean-Louis
Les inégalités et leurs cumuls parmi les personnes agées : niveau de vie, santé et isolement / Jean-Louis Borkowski. — Paris : I.N.S.E.E., 1985. — 174p. — (Archives et documents / France. Institut national de la statistique et des études économiques ; no.142)

AGED — France — Normandy — Care and hygiene
CAPLAIN, Fernand
Accueil des personnes âgées / rapport présenté par Fernand Caplain, Patrice Leblond. — [Rouen] : Comité économique et social de Haute-Normandie, 1985. — 1v (various pagings). — *Cover title*

AGED — Germany (West) — Political activity
UNRUH, Trude
Aufruf zur Rebellion : Graue Panther machen Geschichte / Trude Unruh. — [Essen] : Klartext Verlag, 1984. — 142p

AGED — Great Britain — Care and Hygiene
Residential care for elderly people : research contributions to the development of policy and practice : a collection of papers presented to a DHSS seminar on 'Residential Care for the Elderrly' in October 1983 / edited by Ken judge and Ian Sinclair. — London : H.M.S.O., 1986. — iv,224p. — *At head of t.p. : Department of Health and Social Security*

AGED — Great Britain — Dwellings
AGE CONCERN ENGLAND
Sheltered housing for older people : the report of a working party...to examine the role of sheltered housing within the spectrum of care and accommodation needed by elderly people / Age Concern. — Mitcham : Age Concern England, 1984. — 94p. — *Chairman of the Working Party: Michael Wakeford*

WHEELER, Rose
Housing and health in old age : a research agenda / Rose Wheeler. — York : University of York. Centre for Health Economics, 1986. — 26p. — (Discussion paper / University of York. Centre for Health Economics ; 21). — *Bibliography: p25-26*

AGED — Great Britain — Dwellings — Quality control
KANE, Eddie
Quality control in public and private homes for the elderly / Eddie Kane. — Norwich : University of East Anglia, 1985. — 40 leaves. — (Social work monographs ; 39). — *Bibliography: p40*

AGED — Great Britain — Economic aspects
FALKINGHAM, Jane
Britain's ageing population : the engine behind increased dependency? / Jane Falkingham. — London : Suntory Toyota International Centre for Economics and Related Disciplines, 1987. — 26p. — (Welfare State Programme ; no.17). — *Bibliography: p25*

AGED — Great Britain — Family relationships
WRIGHT, Fay D.
Left to care alone / Fay D. Wright. — Aldershot : Gower, c1986. — [214]p. — *Includes bibliography and index*

AGED — Great Britain — Services for
TESTER, Susan
Ill informed? : a study of information and support for elderly people in the inner city / Susan Tester, Barbara Meredith. — London : Policy Studies Institute, 1987. — 124p. — (PSI report ; 670)

AGED — Great Britain — Social conditions
MIDWINTER, Eric
Redefining old age : a review of CPA's recent contributions to social policy / Eric Midwinter. — London : Centre for Policy on Ageing, 1987. — v,46p. — (CPA papers ; 1)

NORMAN, A. J.
Aspects of ageism: a discussion paper / Alison Norman. — London : Centre for Policy on Ageing, 1987. — ii,25p. — (CPA papers ; 2). — *Bibliography: p23*

AGED — Great Britain — Statistics
GREAT BRITAIN. Office of Population Censuses and Surveys
Britain's elderly population : 1981 Census / [prepared by the Office of Population Censuses and Surveys and the Central Office of Information]. — London : HMSO, 1984. — 12p. — (Census guide ; 1)

AGED — Great Britain — Transportation
MCTAVISH, A. D.
Survey of concessionary bus fares for the elderly, blind and disabled in England and Wales / A. D. McTavish and P. Mullen. — London : Department of Transport, 1977. — 2,21p. — (Local transport note ; 77/1)

AGED — India — Social conditions
SOUZA, Alfred de
The social organisation of aging among the urban poor / Alfred de Souza. — New Delhi : Indian Social Institute, 1982. — 78p. — *Bibliography: p72-75*

AGED — Ireland — Dublin (Dublin)
HORKAN, Mary
This is our world : perspectives of some elderly people on life in suburban Dublin / Mary Horkan, Audrey Woods. — Dublin : Stationery Office, [1986]. — 80p. — (Report / National Council for the Aged ; no.12). — *Bibliography: p75-77*

AGED — London — Chelsea — Dwellings
SMITH, Karen
'I'm not complaining' : the housing conditions of elderly private tenants / by Karen Smith. — [London] : Kensington and Chelsea Staying Put for the Elderly in association with SHAC, [1986]. — 84p

AGED — London — Kensington — Dwellings
SMITH, Karen
'I'm not complaining' : the housing conditions of elderly private tenants / by Karen Smith. — [London] : Kensington and Chelsea Staying Put for the Elderly in association with SHAC, [1986]. — 84p

AGED — Netherlands — Statistics
De leefsituatie van de nederlandse bevolking van 55 jaar en ouder 1982. — 's-Gravenhage : Staatsuitgeverij. — *Summary in English. — Title on back cover: Well-being of the elderly population in the Netherlands 1982 : a survey on people aged 55 years and over : Part 1B : Key figures*
d. 1B: Kerncijfers : betaald en onbetaald werk, sociale relaties, vrijetijdsbesteding, maatschappelijke participatie. — 1984. — 104p

AGED — Oceania
Aging and its transformations : moving toward death in pacific societies / edited by Dorothy Ayers Counts, David R. Counts. — Lanham, MD : University Press of America, c1985. — 336 p., [2] p. of plates. — (ASAO monograph ; no. 10). — *"Co-published by arrangement with the Association for Social Anthropology in Oceania"--T.p. verso. — Includes index. — Bibliography: p. [275]-313*

AGED — Poland — Statistics
Wybrane uwarunkowania i konsekwencje procesu starzenia się ludności Polski / Ewa Frątczak...[et al.]. — Warszawa : Szkoła Główna Planowania i Statystyki, 1987. — 231p. — (Kształtowanie procesów demograficznych a rozwój społeczno-gospodarczy Polski) (Monografie i opracowania / Szkoła Główna Planowania i Statystyki ; 223/10). — *Contents and summary in English and Russian*

AGED — Scotland
TROUP, Gill
Information and older people in Scotland : needs and strategies : a research report / Gill Troup. — Edinburgh : Scottish Community Education Council, 1985. — 151p

AGED — South Asia — Social conditions
CAIN, Mead
Consequences of reproductive failure : dependence, mobility, and mortality among the elderly in rural South Asia / Mead Cain. — New York : Population Council, 1985. — 30p. — (Working papers / Population Council. Center for Policy Studies ; no.119)

AGED — Spain — Political activity
JUSTEL, Manuel
Los viejos y la política / Manuel Justel. — Madrid : Centro de Investigaciones Sociológicas, 1983. — 268p. — (Colección 'Monografías' ; no. 64). — *Bibliography: p253-264*

AGED — Spain — Social conditions
JUSTEL, Manuel
Los viejos y la política / Manuel Justel. — Madrid : Centro de Investigaciones Sociológicas, 1983. — 268p. — (Colección 'Monografías' ; no. 64). — *Bibliography: p253-264*

AGED — United States
The elderly : victims and deviants / edited by Carl D. Chambers ... [et al.]. — Athens, Ohio : Ohio University Press, 1987. — p. cm. *Includes bibliographies*

AGED — United States — Abuse of
The elderly : victims and deviants / edited by Carl D. Chambers ... [et al.]. — Athens, Ohio : Ohio University Press, 1987. — p. cm. *Includes bibliographies*

AGED — United States — Abuse of — Bibliography
JOHNSON, Tanya F
Elder neglect and abuse : an annotated bibliography / compiled by Tanya F. Johnson, James G. O'Brien, and Margaret F. Hudson. — Westport, Conn. : Greenwood Press, 1985. — xxvi, 223 p.. — (Bibliographies and indexes in gerontology ; no. 1). — *Includes index*

AGED — United States — Congresses
COMMITTEE ON AN AGING SOCIETY (U.S.)
Productive roles in an older society / Committee on an Aging Society, Institute of Medicine and National Research Council. — Washington, D.C. : National Academic Press, 1986. — vii, 154 p.. — (America's aging). — *"This report ... presents the papers commissioned for the May 1983 Symposium on Unpaid Productive Roles in an Aging Society"--Pref. — Includes bibliographies and index*

AGED — United States — Crimes against
The elderly : victims and deviants / edited by Carl D. Chambers ... [et al.]. — Athens, Ohio : Ohio University Press, 1987. — p. cm. *Includes bibliographies*

YIN, Peter
Victimization and the aged / Peter Yin. — Springfield, Ill. : Thomas, c1985. — ix, 211 p.. — *Includes indexes. — Bibliography: p. 175-188*

AGED — United States — Drug use
The elderly : victims and deviants / edited by Carl D. Chambers ... [et al.]. — Athens, Ohio : Ohio University Press, 1987. — p. cm. — *Includes bibliographies*

AGED — United States — Dwellings
NEWMAN, Sandra J
Federal policy and the mobility of older homeowners : the effects of the one-time capital gains exclusion / Sandra Newman, James Reschovsky ; project manager, Robert Marans. — Ann Arbor, Mich. : Survey Research Center, Institute for Social Research, University of Michigan, 1985. — p. cm. — (Research report series / Institute for social research). — ″ISR code no. 9020″--T.p. verso. — *Bibliography: p*

AGED — United States — Dwellings — Addresses, essays, lectures
Housing an aging society : issues, alternatives, and policy / edited by Robert J. Newcomer, M. Powell Lawton, Thomas O. Byerts. — New York : Van Nostrand Reinhold, c1986. — p. cm. — *Includes index*

AGED — United States — Dwellings — Addressses, essays, lectures
Housing the elderly / edited by Judith Ann Hancock. — New Brunswick, N.J. : Center for Urban Policy Research, c1986. — xliv, 324 p. — *Includes index.* — *Bibliography: p. 287-313*

AGED — United States — Economic conditions
SCHULZ, James H
The economics of aging / James H. Schulz. — 3rd ed. — New York : Van Nostrand Reinhold, [1985]. — p. cm. — *Includes index.* — *Bibliography: p*

AGED — United States — Economic conditions — Addresses, essays, lectures
Our aging society : paradox and promise / edited by Alan Pifer and Lydia Bronte. — 1st ed. — New York, N.Y. : W.W. Norton, c1986. — viii, 438 p. — *Includes bibliographies and index*

AGED — United States — Family relationships
MORONEY, Robert
Shared responsibility : families and social policy / Robert M. Moroney. — New York : Aldine Pub. Co., c1986. — xi, 218 p. — *Includes index.* — *Bibliography: p. 177-211*

STEPHENS, Susan A.
Informal care of the elderly / Susan A. Stephens, Jon B. Christianson. — Lexington, Mass. : Lexington Books, c1986. — xii, 174 p. — *Includes index.* — *Bibliography: p. [165]-169*

AGED — United States — Family relationships — Addresses, essays, lectures
Our aging society : paradox and promise / edited by Alan Pifer and Lydia Bronte. — 1st ed. — New York, N.Y. : W.W. Norton, c1986. — viii, 438 p. — *Includes bibliographies and index*

AGED — United States — Family relationships — History
Old age in a bureaucratic society : the elderly, the experts, and the state in American history / edited by David Van Tassel and Peter N. Stearns. — Westport, Conn. : Greenwood Press, c1986. — xx, 259 p. — (Contributions to the study of aging ; no. 4). — *Includes bibliographies and index*

AGED — United States — Interviews
MATTHEWS, Sarah H
Friendships through the life-course : oral biographies in old age / by Sarah H. Matthews. — Beverly Hills : Sage Publications, c1986. — p. cm. — (Sage library of social research ; v. 161). — *Includes index.* — *Bibliography: p*

AGED — United States — Social conditions
Old age in a bureaucratic society : the elderly, the experts, and the state in American history / edited by David Van Tassel and Peter N. Stearns. — Westport, Conn. : Greenwood Press, c1986. — xx, 259 p. — (Contributions to the study of aging ; no. 4). — *Includes bibliographies and index*

AGED — United States — Social conditions — Addresses, essays, lectures
Our aging society : paradox and promise / edited by Alan Pifer and Lydia Bronte. — 1st ed. — New York, N.Y. : W.W. Norton, c1986. — viii, 438 p.. — *Includes bibliographies and index*

AGED — United States — Statistics
ROSENWAIKE, Ira
The extreme aged in America : a portrait of an expanding population / Ira Rosenwaike, with the assistance of Barbara Logue. — Westport, Conn. ; London : Greenwood Press, 1985. — xix, 253 p.. — (Contributions to the study of aging ; no. 3). — *Includes index.* — *Bibliography: p. [229]-241*

AGED — United States — Statistics — Handbooks, manuals, etc
Statistical handbook on aging Americans / edited by Frank L. Schick. — Phoenix, AZ : Oryx Press, 1986. — xviii, 294 p. — *Includes index.* — *Bibliography: p. [269]-287*

AGED — Wales — South Glamorgan
SOUTH GLAMORGAN
1986 social survey : selected characteristics of pensionable age population : county electoral divisions. — [Cardiff] : [the Council], 1987. — ii,35p

AGED — Wales — Torfaen (Gwent) — Dwellings
HUNT, John
Housing and care for elderly people / John Hunt. — Cwmbran : Cwmbran Development Corporation ; Torfaen : Torfaen Borough Council, 1985. — xv,109p

AGED — West Sussex — Dwellings — England
WEST SUSSEX. County Council
Accomodation for the elderly : rest homes, nursing homes and private sheltered housing in West Sussex. — Chichester : [the Council], 1986. — 93p

AGED MEN — United States
RUBINSTEIN, Robert L
Singular paths : old men living alone / Robert L. Rubinstein. — New York : Columbia University Press, 1986. — viii, 265 p.. — (Columbia studies of social gerontology and aging). — *Includes index.* — *Bibliography: p. [257]-261*

AGED OFFENDERS — United States
The elderly : victims and deviants / edited by Carl D. Chambers ... [et al.]. — Athens, Ohio : Ohio University Press, 1987. — p. cm. — *Includes bibliographies*

AGED OFFENDERS — United States — Case studies
SHOVER, Neal
Aging criminals / by Neal Shover. — Beverly Hills [Calif.] : Sage Publications, c1985. — p. cm. — (Sociological observations ; v. 17). — *Includes index.* — *Bibliography: p*

AGED WOMEN
FORD, Janet, 1944-
Sixty years on : women talk about old age / Janet Ford and Ruth Sinclair. — London : Women's, 1987. — 168p

AGENCIA DE PUBLICIDAD DEL ESTADO (Peru) — Legal status, laws, etc.
PERU
[Decreto ley no.21099]. Ley orgánica de la Agencia de Publicidad del Estado : decreto ley no.21099. — [Lima : Presidencia?, 1975]. — 9leaves

AGGRESSION (INTERNATIONAL LAW)
The current legal regulation of the use of force / edited by A. Cassese. — Dordrecht ; Lancaster : Martinus Nijhoff, 1986. — xiv,536p. — (Developments in international law). — *Includes bibliographical references*

The current legal regulation of the use of force / edited by A. Cassese. — Dordrecht ; Lancaster : Martinus Nijhoff, 1986. — xiv,536p. — (Developments in international law). — *Includes bibliographical notes*

KHARE, Subhas Chandra
Use of force under U.N. Charter / Subhas C. Khare ; foreword by Nagendra Singh. — 1st ed. — New Delhi, India : Metropolitan, 1985. — xii, 444 p.. — Spine title: Use of force under United Nations Charter. — : Originally presented as the author's thesis (LL. D.--Lucknow University). — *Includes index. Bibliography: p. [425]-439*

AGGRESSIVENESS IN CHILDREN
BJÖRKQVIST, Kaj
Violent films, anxiety and aggression : experimental studies of the effect of violent films on the level of anxiety and aggressiveness in children / Kaj Björkqvist. — Helsinki : Societas Scientiarum Fennica, 1985. — 75p. — (Commentationes Scientarum Socialium ; 30). — *Bibliography: p71-75*

AGGRESSIVENESS IN CHILDREN — Cross-cultural studies
Television and the aggressive child : a cross-national comparison / edited by L. Rowell Huesmann, Leonard D. Eron. — Hillsdale, N.J. : L. Erlbaum Associates, 1986. — p. cm. — *Includes bibliographies and index*

AGGRESSIVENESS (PSYCHOLOGY)
Altruism and aggression : biological and social orgins / edited by Carolyn Zahn-Waxler, E. Mark Cummings, Ronald Iannotti. — Cambridge : Cambridge University Press, 1986. — xiii,337p. — (Cambridge studies in social and emotional development). — *Includes bibliographies and index*

GOLDSTEIN, Jeffrey H
Aggression and crimes of violence / Jeffrey H. Goldstein. — 2nd ed. — New York : Oxford University Press, 1986. — ix, 230p. — *Includes index.* — *Bibliography: p.[189]-215*

Violent transactions : the limits of personality / edited by Anne Campbell and John J. Gibbs. — Oxford : Basil Blackwell, 1986. — vi,267p. — *Includes bibliographies and index*

AGGRESSIVENESS (PSYCHOLOGY) — Congresses
Development of antisocial and prosocial behavior : research, theories, and issues / edited by Dan Olweus, Jack Block, Marian Radke-Yarrow. — Orlando : Academic Press, 1986. — xiii, 432 p. — (Developmental psychology series). — *Based on a conference on the development of antisocial and prosocial behavior, held at Voss, Norway, 7/4-10/82. — Includes bibliographies and indexes*

AGGRESSIVENESS (PSYCHOLOGY) — Testing
OLDHAM, Helen
Hostility and assaultiveness / Helen Oldham, Barry McGurk and Richard Magaldi. — London : Home Office, Prison Department, Directorate of Psychological Services, 1976. — 13p. — (DPS report. Series 1 ; no.7). — *Bibliography: p[13]*

AGING
NOVAK, Mark
Successful aging : the myths, realities and future of aging in Canada / Mark Novak. — Ontario : Penguin, 1985. — 368p. — *Bibliography: p[345]-361*

AGING continuation
RYBASH, John M
Adult cognition and aging : developmental changes in processing, knowing and thinking / John M. Rybash, William J. Hoyer, Paul A. Roodin. — New York : Pergamon Press, c1986. — x, 194 p.. — (Pergamon general psychology series ; 139) (Pergamon international library of science, technology, engineering, and social studies). — *Includes indexes. — Bibliography: p. 165-185*

AGING — Psychological aspects
BAYLES, Kathryn A.
Communication and cognition in normal aging and dementia / Kathryn A. Bayles and Alfred W. Kaszniak with the assistance of Cheryl K. Tomoeda. — London : Taylor & Francis, c1987. — xvi,400p. — *Includes bibliographies and index*

Later life : the social psychology of aging / edited by Victor W. Marshall. — Beverly Hills, Calif. : Sage, c1986. — 352 p.. — *Includes bibliographies and indexes. — Contents: Dominant and emerging paradigms in the social psychology of aging / Victor W. Marshall -- The subjective construction of self and society / Carol D. Ryff -- Socialization in old age--a Meadian perspective / Neena Chappell and Harold L. Orbach -- Some contributions of symbolic interaction to the study of growing old / Don Spence -- A sociological perspective on aging and dying / Victor Marshall -- The old person as stranger / James J. Dowd -- Social networks and social support / Barry Wellman and Alan Hall -- Friendships in old age / Sarah H. Matthews -- The world we forgot / Martin Kohli -- Comparative perspectives on the microsociology of aging / Vern L. Bengtson*

RYBASH, John M
Adult cognition and aging : developmental changes in processing, knowing and thinking / John M. Rybash, William J. Hoyer, Paul A. Roodin. — New York : Pergamon Press, c1986. — x, 194 p.. — (Pergamon general psychology series ; 139) (Pergamon international library of science, technology, engineering, and social studies). — *Includes indexes. — Bibliography: p. 165-185*

AGING — Social aspects
Later life : the social psychology of aging / edited by Victor W. Marshall. — Beverly Hills, Calif. : Sage, c1986. — 352 p.. — *Includes bibliographies and indexes. — Contents: Dominant and emerging paradigms in the social psychology of aging / Victor W. Marshall -- The subjective construction of self and society / Carol D. Ryff -- Socialization in old age--a Meadian perspective / Neena Chappell and Harold L. Orbach -- Some contributions of symbolic interaction to the study of growing old / Don Spence -- A sociological perspective on aging and dying / Victor Marshall -- The old person as stranger / James J. Dowd -- Social networks and social support / Barry Wellman and Alan Hall -- Friendships in old age / Sarah H. Matthews -- The world we forgot / Martin Kohli -- Comparative perspectives on the microsociology of aging / Vern L. Bengtson*

Social bonds in later life : aging and interdependence / editors Warren A. Peterson and Jill Quadagno. — Beverly Hills ; London : Sage in co-operation with the Midwest Council for Social Research in Aging, c1985. — 447p. — *Bibliography: p419-447*

AGING — Social aspects — Addresses, essays, lectures
Handbook of aging and the social sciences / editors, Robert H. Binstock, Ethel Shanas ; with the assistance of associate editors George L. Maddox, George C. Myers, James H. Schulz. — 2nd ed. — New York ; Wokingham : Van Nostrand Reinhold, c1985. — xiv, 809p. — *Includes indexes*

AGING — Social aspects — Canada
MARSHALL, Victor W.
Aging in Canada : social perspectives / Victor W. Marshall [editor]. — 2nd ed. — Markham, Ontario : Fitzhenry & Whiteside, 1987. — ii,613p

AGRESSIVENESS IN CHILDREN
VOORT, T. H. A. van der
Television violence : a child's-eye view / T.H.A. van der Voort. — Amsterdam ; Oxford : North-Holland, 1986. — xiii, 440p. — (Advances in psychology ; 32). — *Includes indexes. — Bibliography: p 403-423*

AGRICULTURAL ASSISTANCE
SINGER, H. W.
Food aid : the challenge and the opportunity / Hans Singer, John Wood, Tony Jennings. — Oxford : Clarendon, 1987. — [256]p. — *Includes bibliography and index*

AGRICULTURAL ASSISTANCE, AMERICAN
REVEL, Alain
[États-Unis et la stratégie alimentaire mondiale. English]. American green power / by Alain Revel and Christophe Riboud ; translated by Edward W. Tanner. — Baltimore : Johns Hopkins University Press, c1986. — p. cm. — *Translation of: Les États-Unis et la stratégie alimentaire mondiale. — Includes bibliographical references and index*

AGRICULTURAL ASSISTANCE, BRITISH — Africa
ALL PARTY PARLIAMENTARY GROUP ON OVERSEAS DEVELOPMENT
UK aid to African agriculture : report of the Working Party established by the All Party Parliamentary Group on Overseas Development. — London : Overseas Development Institute, 1985. — 63p

AGRICULTURAL ASSISTANCE, CANADIAN — Bibliography
VANDERWAL, Andrew
Canadian development assistance : a selected bibliography 1978-1984 / Andrew Vanderwal ; edited by Rede Widstrand and Vivian Cummins. — Ottawa : Norman Paterson School of International Affairs, [1985]. — 39p. — (Bibliography series / Norman Paterson School of International Affairs ; 7)

AGRICULTURAL COLONIES — Legal status, laws, etc — Ecuador
ECUADOR
[Laws, etc]. Ley de tierras baldias y colonización : decreto supremo no.2172. — Quito : [Presidencia], 1964. — 40p

AGRICULTURAL COLONIES — Legal status, laws, etc. — Ecuador
ECUADOR
[Laws, etc.]. Ley de reforma agraria y colonización : decreto supremo no.1480. — Quito : [Presidencia], 1964. — 107p

AGRICULTURAL COLONIES — Big Sioux River Valley (S.D. and Iowa) — History — 19th century
HARNACK, Curtis
Gentlemen on the prairie / Curtis Harnack. — Ames : Iowa State University Press, c1985. — viii, 254 p.. — *Includes index. — Bibliography: p. 239-248*

AGRICULTURAL CONSERVATION
BLAIKIE, Piers M.
Land degradation and society / Piers Blaikie and Harold Brookfield ; with contributions by Bryant Allen ... [et al.]. — London : Methuen, 1987. — xxiv,296p. — *Bibliography: p251-284. — Includes index*

AGRICULTURAL COOPERATIVE CREDIT ASSOCIATIONS — India
HAQUE, T
Agrarian reforms and institutional changes in India / T. Haque, A.S. Sirohi. — New Delhi : Concept Pub. Co., 1986, c1985. — xvi, 268 p.. — *Includes index. — Bibliography: p. [249]-262*

AGRICULTURAL CREDIT — Addresses, essays, lectures
Rural financial markets in developing countries : their use and abuse / edited by J.D. Von Pischke, Dale W. Adams, Gordon Donald. — Baltimore : Published for the Economic Development Institute of the World Bank [by] the Johns Hopkins University Press, c1983. — xiii,441p. — (EDI series in economic development). — *Includes bibliographies and index*

AGRICULTURAL CREDIT — Colombia
INSTITUTO COLOMBIANO DE LA REFORMA AGRARIA
Crédito supervisado : que es y para que sirve. — [Bogotá : the Instituto, 1966]. — 20p. — (Serie materiales de enseñanza ; 6)

AGRICULTURAL CREDIT — India
HAQUE, T
Agrarian reforms and institutional changes in India / T. Haque, A.S. Sirohi. — New Delhi : Concept Pub. Co., 1986, c1985. — xvi, 268 p.. — *Includes index. — Bibliography: p. [249]-262*

JHA, Nand Kishore
Bank finance & green revolution in India / Nand Kishore Jha. — Delhi : Amar Prakashan, 1985. — xi, 358 p.. — *Bibliography: p. [351]-358*

PANDA, R. K.
Agricultural indebtedness and institutional finance / R.K. Panda. — New Delhi, India : Ashish, 1985. — xv, 180 p.. — *Includes index. — Bibliography: p. 172-175*

AGRICULTURAL CREDIT — Peru
PERU. Sub-Dirección de Asistencia Crediticia
Manual de crédito. — Lima : Comité Nacional de Crédito, Programa de Crédito de Promoción Comunal Agrario, Oficina Nacional de Desarrollo Comunal, Proyecto de Desarrollo e Integración de la Población Campesina, 1971. — 38leaves

AGRICULTURAL CREDIT — Romania
ȘANDRU, D.
Creditul agricol în România (1918-1944) / D. Șandru. — București : Editura Academiei Republicii Socialiste România, 1985. — 179p. — (Biblioteca istorică / Institutul de Istorie și Arheologie "A. D. Xenopol" Iași ; 64). — *Summary in English*

AGRICULTURAL CREDIT — Sierra Leone
JOHNNY, Michael
Informal credit for integrated rural development in Sierra Leone / Michael Johnny. — Hamburg : Weltarchiv, 1985. — xviii,212p. — (Studien zur integrierten ländlichen Entwicklung ; 6). — *Bibliography: p199-212*

(AGRICULTURAL) DEVELOPMENT PROJECTS
TIMBERLAKE, Lloyd
Only one earth : living for the future / Lloyd Timberlake. — London : BBC : Earthscan, 1987. — 168p. — *Bibliography: p160-161*

AGRICULTURAL DEVELOPMENT PROJECTS — Developing countries
BENJAMIN, McDonald P.
Investment projects in agriculture : principles and case studies / McDonald P. Benjamin. — London : Longman, 1981 (1985 [printing]). — 297p. — *Bibliography: p284-285. — Includes index*

AGRICULTURAL DEVELOPMENT PROJECTS — Evaluation — Statistical methods
SCOTT, Chris
Sampling for monitoring and evaluation / Chris Scott. — Washington, D.C. : The World Bank, 1985. — iii,44p. — *"A technical supplement to 'Monitoring and evaluation of agriculture and rural development projects' by Dennis J. Casley and Denis A. Lury". — Includes bibliographical references*

AGRICULTURAL DEVELOPMENT PROJECTS — Management — Statistical methods

SCOTT, Chris
Sampling for monitoring and evaluation / Chris Scott. — Washington, D.C. : The World Bank, 1985. — iii,44p. — "A technical supplement to 'Monitoring and evaluation of agriculture and rural development projects' by Dennis J. Casley and Denis A. Lury". — Includes bibliographical references

AGRICULTURAL DEVELOPMENT PROJECTS — Political aspects — Africa

COLLOQUE DE LA SORBONNE "PARTICIPATION PAYSANNE ET DÉVELOPPEMENT AGRICOLE: L'EXEMPLE DES POLITIQUES DE L'EAU EN AFRIQUE" (1983 : Paris)
Les politiques de l'eau en Afrique : développement agricole et participation paysanne / actes du Colloque de la Sorbonne (organise par le) Centre d'Études Juridiques et Politiques du Monde Africain sous la direction de Gérard Conac, Claudette Savonnet-Guyot [et] Françoise Conac. — Paris : Economica, 1985. — 767p

COLLOQUE DE LA SORBONNE "PARTICIPATION PAYSANNE ET DÉVELOPPEMENT AGRICOLE: L'EXEMPLE DES POLITIQUES DE L'EAU EN AFRIQUE" (1983 : Paris)
Les politiques de l'eau en Afrique : développement agricole et participation paysanne / actes du Colloque de la Sorbonne (organise par le) Centre d'Études Juridiques et Politiques du Monde Africai sous la direction de Gérard Conac, Claudette Savonnet-Guyot [et] Françoise Conac. — Paris : Economica, 1985. — 767p

AGRICULTURAL DEVELOPMENT PROJECTS — Africa

HARRISON, Paul, 1945-
The greening of Africa : breaking through in the battle for land and food / Paul Harrison. — London : Paladin [for] International Institute for Environment and Development-Earthscan, 1987. — 380p. — [Commissioned by the International Institute for Environment and Development - Earthscan]. — At foot of title: "International Institute for Environment and Development - Earthscan". — Bibliography: p359-371. — Includes index

AGRICULTURAL DEVELOPMENT PROJECTS — Developing countries

Démarches de recherche-développement appliquées au secteur de la production rurale des pays en voie de développement / [Alain Lalau-Keraly...et al.]. — [Paris] : Bureau de liaison des agents de la coopération technique...[etc.], c1984. — 91p. — (Collection des ateliers technologique et développement ; no.2). — Ce texte fait suite à un séminaire conçu par Alain Lalau-Keraly et Didier Pillot, avec rédaction finale par Jacques Bodichon. — Bibliography: p81-84

AGRICULTURAL DEVELOPMENT PROJECTS — Developing countries — Cost effectiveness

GITTINGER, J. Price
Economic analysis of agricultural projects / J. Price Gittinger. — 2nd ed. — Baltimore : Johns Hopkins University Press for the Economic Development Institute of the World Bank, 1982. — xxi,505p. — (EDI series in economic development). — Bibliography: p445-455

AGRICULTURAL DEVELOPMENT PROJECTS — Sierra Leone

JOHNNY, Michael
Informal credit for integrated rural development in Sierra Leone / Michael Johnny. — Hamburg : Weltarchiv, 1985. — xviii,212p. — (Studien zur integrierten ländlichen Entwicklung ; 6). — Bibliography: p199-212

AGRICULTURAL DEVELOPMENT PROJECTS — Taiwan

HSIEH, S. C.
An analytical review of agricultural development in Taiwan : an input-output and productivity approach / by S. C. Hsieh and T. H. Lee. — Taipei : Chinese-American Joint Commission on Rural Reconstruction, 1958. — [vi],84p. — (Economic digest series / Joint Commission on Rural Reconstruction ; no.12)

AGRICULTURAL ECOLOGY

WORLD COMMISSION ON ENVIRONMENT AND DEVELOPMENT. Advisory Panel on Food Security, Agriculture, Forestry and Environment
Food 2000 : global policies for sustainable agriculture / report for the World Commission on Environment and Development. — London : Zed, 1987. — [192]p

AGRICULTURAL ECOLOGY — Africa

HARRISON, Paul, 1945-
The greening of Africa : breaking through in the battle for land and food / Paul Harrison. — London : Paladin [for] International Institute for Environment and Development-Earthscan, 1987. — 380p. — [Commissioned by the International Institute for Environment and Development - Earthscan]. — At foot of title: "International Institute for Environment and Development - Earthscan". — Bibliography: p359-371. — Includes index

AGRICULTURAL ECOLOGY — Developing countries

The Green Revolution revisited : critique and alternatives / edited by Bernhard Glaeser. — London : Allen & Unwin, 1987. — xv,206p. — Includes bibliographies and index

AGRICULTURAL ECOLOGY — Great Britain

GREAT BRITAIN. Countryside Commission
Countryside Commission submission to the Ministry of Agriculture, Fisheries and Food's Advisory Council for Agriculture and Horticulture in England and Wales : countryside inquiry. — Cheltenham : the Commission, 1977. — [6] leaves

AGRICULTURAL ECOLOGY — Kenya

YEAGER, Rodger
Wildlife, wild death : land use and survival in eastern Africa / Rodger Yeager, Norman N. Miller. — Albany, NY : State University of New York Press in association with the African-Caribbean Institute, 1986. — p. cm. — Includes index. — Bibliography: p

AGRICULTURAL ECOLOGY — Tanzania

YEAGER, Rodger
Wildlife, wild death : land use and survival in eastern Africa / Rodger Yeager, Norman N. Miller. — Albany, NY : State University of New York Press in association with the African-Caribbean Institute, 1986. — p. cm. — Includes index. — Bibliography: p

AGRICULTURAL EDUCATION — Developing countries

WILSON, Fergus B.
Education and training for agricultural development / by Fergus B. Wilson. — London : Commonwealth Secretariat, 1970. — 11p. — At head of title page: Commonwealth Conference on Education in Rural Areas. — CRE(70)LEAD/3

AGRICULTURAL ESTIMATING AND REPORTING

POATE, C. D.
Estimating crop production in development projects : methods and limitations / C. D. Poate and Dennis J. Casley. — Washington, D.C. : The World Bank, 1985. — iii,34p. — "A technical supplement to 'Monitoring and evaluation of agriculture and rural development projects' by Dennis J. Casley and Dennis A. Lury". — Includes bibliographical references

AGRICULTURAL ESTIMATING AND REPORTING — Taiwan

HSIEH, S. C.
Application of linear programming to crop competition study in Taiwan (with special reference to rice and sugarcane competition in central Taiwan) / by S. C. Hsieh. — Taipei : Chinese-American Joint Commission on Rural Reconstruction, 1957. — [iv],95p. — (Economic digest series / Joint Commission on Rural Reconstruction ; no.10)

AGRICULTURAL EXTENSION WORK

Perspectives on farming systems research and extension / edited by Peter E. Hildebrand. — Boulder, Colo. : L. Rienner, 1986. — p. cm

AGRICULTURAL EXTENSION WORK — Economic aspects

EVENSON, Robert E.
The international agricultural research centers : their impact on spending for national agricultural research and extension / Robert E. Evenson. — Washington, D.C. : The World Bank, 1987. — vii,73p. — (Study paper / Consultative Group on International Agricultural Research ; no.22). — Bibliographical references: p73

AGRICULTURAL EXTENSION WORK — Asia — Congresses

Research-extension-farmer : a two-way continuum for agricultural development / edited by Michael M. Cernea, John K. Coulter, John F. A. Russell. — Washington, D.C. : The World Bank, 1985. — xvi,171p. — Cover: "A World Bank and UNDP Symposium". — Includes bibliographical references

AGRICULTURAL EXTENSION WORK — Developing countries

WILSON, Fergus B.
Education and training for agricultural development / by Fergus B. Wilson. — London : Commonwealth Secretariat, 1970. — 11p. — At head of title page: Commonwealth Conference on Education in Rural Areas. — CRE(70)LEAD/3

AGRICULTURAL EXTENSION WORK — Developing countries — Evaluation

WORLD BANK. Operations Evaluation Department
Agricultural research and extension : an evaluation of the World Bank's experience. — Washington, D.C., U.S.A. : World Bank, 1985. — p. cm

AGRICULTURAL EXTENSION WORK — Puerto Rico

IRIZARRY, Guillermo
The operations and relationships of the agricultural services in Puerto Rico : final report / Guillermo Irizarry. — San Juan : Bureau of the Budget, 1961. — xvi,199p. — With separate map in end pocket

AGRICULTURAL GEOGRAPHY — England — History

THIRSK, Joan
Agricultural regions and agrarian history in England, 1500-1750 / prepared for the Economic History Society by Joan Thirsk. — Basingstoke : Macmillan Education, 1987. — 77p. — (Studies in economic and social history). — Bibliography: p66-74. — Includes index

AGRICULTURAL HOLDINGS BILL 1983-84

GREAT BRITAIN. Parliament. House of Commons. Library. Research Division
Agricultural Holdings Bill (HL) Bill 110 of 1983-84 / Priscilla Baines. — [London] : the Division, 1983. — 12p. — (Reference sheet ; no.84/4). — Bibliographical references: p11-12

AGRICULTURAL IMPLEMENTS — Hungary — Economic aspects

CSIKÓS-NAGY, Béla
Eszközgazdálkodás és árrendszer / Csikós-Nagy Béla. — [Budapest] : Kossuth Könyvkiadó, 1964. — 179p. — Bibliography: p175-[177]

AGRICULTURAL INDUSTRIES — Government policy — Colombia

HELMSING, A. H. J.
Firms, farms, and the state in Colombia : a study of rural, urban, and regional dimensions of change / A.H.J. Helmsing. — Boston : Allen & Unwin, 1986. — xix, 297 p.. — *Includes index. — Bibliography: p. 275-288*

AGRICULTURAL INDUSTRIES — Developing countries — Case studies

Agricultural household models : extensions, applications, and policy / Inderjit Singh. — Baltimore : Johns Hopkins University Press for the World Bank, 1986. — xi,335p. — *Includes bibliographical references*

AGRICULTURAL INDUSTRIES — Soviet Union

KALNYN'SH, A. A.
Razvitie agropromyshennoi integratsii i ekonomicheskogo mekhanizma / sostaviteli: A. Kalnin'sh i V. Tsibul'skii. — Riga : Avots, 1986. — 191p. — (Voprosy agropromyshlennoi integratsii)

LITVIN, Valentin
The Soviet agro-industrial complex : structure and performance / Valentin Litvin. — Boulder, Colo. : Westview Press, 1987. — p. cm. — (Delphic monograph series). — *Includes index. — Bibliography: p*

AGRICULTURAL INDUSTRIES — Soviet Union — Dictionaries

Ekonomicheskii slovar' agropromyshlennogo kompleksa / pod redaktsiei A. A. Storozha. — Kiev : Urozhai, 1986. — 333p

AGRICULTURAL INDUSTRIES — Soviet Union — Management

KULISH, N. E.
Upravlenie agro-promyshlennymi ob"edineniiami v usloviiakh integrirovannoi ekonomiki / N. E. Kulish. — Kiev ; Odessa : Vyshcha Shkola, 1985. — 174p. — (Voprosy agropromyshlennoi integratsii). — *Bibliography: p168-[173]*

AGRICULTURAL INNOVATIONS

Perspectives on farming systems research and extension / edited by Peter E. Hildebrand. — Boulder, Colo. : L. Rienner, 1986. — p. cm

AGRICULTURAL INNOVATIONS — Africa, Sub-Saharan

JAHNKE, Hans E.
The impact of agricultural research in tropical Africa : a study of the collaboration between the international and national research systems / Hans E. Jahnke, Dieter Kirschke and Johannes Lagemann ; in collaboration with K. J. Billing, J. Gromotka, S. N. Lyongo, B. Ndunguru, A. Negewo, G. M. Rillga, D. Sène, H. Shawel, G. Tacher. — Washington, D.C. : The World Bank, 1987. — xvi,175p. — (Study paper / Consultative Group on International Agricultural Research ; no.21). — *Bibliographical references: p159-175*

AGRICULTURAL INNOVATIONS — Asia — Congresses

Research-extension-farmer : a two-way continuum for agricultural development / edited by Michael M. Cernea, John K. Coulter, John F. A. Russell. — Washington, D.C. : The World Bank, 1985. — xvi,171p. — *Cover: "A World Bank and UNDP Symposium". — Includes bibliographical references*

AGRICULTURAL INNOVATIONS — India — Punjab

CHADHA, G. K
The state and rural transformation : the case of Punjab, 1950-85 / G.K. Chadha. — New Delhi ; Beverly Hills : Sage Publications, 1986. — p. cm. — *Includes index. — Bibliography: p*

AGRICULTURAL LABORERS — Government policy — Developing countries — Case studies

Agricultural household models : extensions, applications, and policy / Inderjit Singh. — Baltimore : Johns Hopkins University Press for the World Bank, 1986. — xi,335p. — *Includes bibliographical references*

AGRICULTURAL LABORERS — Argentina — History — 20th century

MASCALI, Humberto
Desocupación y conflictos laborales en el campo argentino (1940-1965) / Humberto Mascali. — Buenos Aires : Centro Editor de América Latina, 1986. — 127p. — (Biblioteca Política Argentina ; 139). — *Bibliography: p121-127*

AGRICULTURAL LABORERS — Byelorussian S.S.R.

KOSTIUK, M. P.
Trudovoi vklad krest'ianstva v pobedu i uprochenie sotsializma : na materialakh BSSR / M. P. Kostiuk ; nauchnyi redaktor I. M. Ignatenko. — Minsk : Nauka i tekhnika, 1986. — 236p

AGRICULTURAL LABORERS — Developing countries

Third World peasantry : a continuing saga of deprivation / editors, R.P. Misra & Nguyen Tri Dung. — New Delhi : Sterling Publishers, c1986. — 2 v.. — *Includes bibliographies and indexes*

AGRICULTURAL LABORERS — Developing countries — Case studies

Agricultural household models : extensions, applications, and policy / Inderjit Singh. — Baltimore : Johns Hopkins University Press for the World Bank, 1986. — xi,335p. — *Includes bibliographical references*

AGRICULTURAL LABORERS — France — Statistics

RÉGNIER, Élisabeth
La pluriactivité en agriculture en 1981 / Élisabeth Régnier. — Paris : I.N.S.E.E., 1986. — 77p. — (Archives et documents / Institut national de la statistique et des études économiques)

AGRICULTURAL LABORERS — India

CHATTOPADHYAY, Manabendu
Conditions of labour in Indian agriculture : apparent and real / Manabendu Chattopadhyay. — Calcutta : K. P. Bagchi & Company, 1985. — 146p. — *Bibliography: p [137]-144*

AGRICULTURAL LABORERS — India — Hyderabad (State) — History

BHASKARA RAO, V.
Agrarian and industrial relations in Hyderabad State / V. Bhaskara Rao. — New Delhi : Associated Pub. House, c1985. — xi, 179 p.. — *Includes index. — Bibliography: p. [169]-173*

AGRICULTURAL LABORERS — Indonesia — Jawa Tengah

HART, Gillian Patricia
Power, labor, and livelihood : processes of change in rural Java / Gillian Hart. — Berkeley : University of California Press, c1986. — xvi, 228 p.. — *Includes index. — Bibliography: p. 213-222*

AGRICULTURAL LABORERS — Mexico

DE ROUFFIGNAC, Ann Elizabeth Lucas
The contemporary peasantry in Mexico : a class analysis / by Ann Elizabeth Lucas de Rouffignac. — New York : Praeger, 1985. — xix, 203p. — *Includes index. — Bibliography: p[186]-196*

AGRICULTURAL LABORERS — Mexico — History — Congresses

Haciendas in central Mexico from late colonial times to the revolution : labour conditions, hacienda management, and its relation to the state / R. Buve, ed. — Amsterdam : Centre for Latin American Research and Documentation, 1984. — 307 p.. — (CEDLA incidentele publicaties ; 28). — *Text in English and Spanish. — Contributions from the International Conference of "The Hacienda in Mexican History," held on 10 May 1982 in Amsterdam, organized by the Interunivrsity Centre for Study and Documentation of Latin America. — Includes bibliographies*

AGRICULTURAL LABORERS — Soviet Union — History

Istoriia sovetskogo krest'ianstva / redkollegiia: V. P. Sherstobitov...[et al.]. — Moskva : Nauka. — (Istoriia krest'ianstva SSSR) 2: Sovetskoe krest'ianstvo v period sotsialisticheskoi rekonstruktsii narodnogo khoziaistva. Konets 1927-1937 / redkollegiia: I. E. Zelenin...[et al.]. — 1986. — 448p

AGRICULTURAL LABORERS — Spain — Andalusia

Land and liberty : the struggle of the agricultural workers of Andalusia. — Basel : Comité Européen pour la Défense des Réfugiés et Immigrés, 1985. — 66p

AGRICULTURAL LABORERS — United States — Congresses

Farm work and fieldwork : American agriculture in anthropological perspective / edited by Michael Chibnik. — Ithaca : Cornell University Press, 1987. — 293 p.. — (Anthropology of contemporary issues). — *Includes bibliographies and index*

AGRICULTURAL LAWS AND LEGISLATION — Ecuador

ECUADOR
[Laws, etc.]. Reforma agraria, ley y reglamento. — Quito : Ministerio de Agricultura y Ganadería, 1974. — 128p

AGRICULTURAL LAWS AND LEGISLATION — European Economic Community countries

Recueil des actes agricoles. — Luxembourg : Office des publications officielles des Communautés européennes, 1985-. — 14v (in 34 parts). — *Contents: Tome 1. Céréales - Riz - t.2. FEOGA - t.3. Politique des structures - t.4. Fruits et légumes - t.5. Généralités - t.6. Harmonisation des législations - t.7. Harmonisation des législations - t.8. Tabac-Houblon - t.9. Matières grasses - t.10. Produits laitiers - t.11. Viande bovine - t.12. Viande de porc - t.13. Sucre - t.14. Vin*

AGRICULTURAL LAWS AND LEGISLATION — Peru

PERU
[Laws, etc]. Texto único de la ley de reforma agraria. — [Lima : Empresa Editora del Diario Oficial "El Peruano", ca.1970]. — 66p

PERU
[Laws, etc]. Estatuto de comunidades campesinas del Perú : Decreto supremo no.37-70-A. — Lima : [Empresa Editora del Diario Oficial "El Peruano"], 1970. — 27p

AGRICULTURAL MACHINERY — Hungary — Economic aspects

CSIKÓS-NAGY, Béla
Eszközgazdálkodás és árrendszer / Csikós-Nagy Béla. — [Budapest] : Kossuth Könyvkiadó, 1964. — 179p. — *Bibliography: p175-[177]*

AGRICULTURAL MARKETING BILL 1982-83

GREAT BRITAIN. Parliament. House of Commons. Library. Research Division
Agricultural Marketing Bill (Bill 7 of 1982-83) / [Priscilla Baines]. — [London] : the Division, [1982]. — 8p. — (Reference sheet ; no.82/12)

AGRICULTURAL POLICY

CAIN, Mead
Population growth and agrarian outcomes / Mead Cain [and] Geoffrey McNicoll. — New York : Population Council, 1986. — 25p. — (Working papers / Population Council. Center for Policy Studies ; no.128). — *Bibliography: p20-21*

AGRICULTURAL POLICY — Mexico

Mexican agriculture : rural crisis and policy response / Louis W. Goodman [et al.]. — Washington, D.C. : Woodrow Wilson International Center for Scholars, 1985. — xii,72,[32p]. — (Working papers / Wilson Centre. Latin American Program ; no.168)

AGRICULTURAL PRICES — Government policy — Bolivia

Bolivia : agricultural pricing and investment policies. — Washington, D.C., U.S.A. : World Bank, c1984. — xlii,130p. — (A World Bank country study). — *Summaries in French and Spanish.* — *Includes bibliographical references*

AGRICULTURAL PRICES — Government policy — Developing countries — Congresses

Agricultural marketing strategy and pricing policy / edited by Dieter Elz. — Washington, D.C. : The World Bank, 1987. — xiii,132p. — (A World Bank symposium). — *Includes bibliographical references.* — *Based on papers from a seminar held in Washington, D.C., May 6-17, 1985*

AGRICULTURAL PRICES — Government policy — Philippines

BAUTISTA, Romeo M.
Production incentives in Philippine agriculture : effects of trade and exchange rate policies / Romeo M. Bautista. — Washington, D.C. : International Food Policy Research Institute, 1987. — p. cm. — (Research report ; 59). — *Bibliography: p*

AGRICULTURAL PRICES — Government policy — United States

TIMMER, C. Peter
Getting prices right : the scope and limits of agricultural price policy / C. Peter Timmer. — Ithaca : Cornell University Press, 1986. — 160 p.. — (Cornell paperbacks). — *Includes index.* — *Bibliography: p. 151-155*

AGRICULTURAL PRICES — France — Statistics

LEBRUN, André
Les indices de prix à la production des industries agricoles et alimentaires / André Lebrun. — [Paris] : INSEE, 1985. — 217p. — (Archives et documents / Institut National de la Statistique et des Études Économiques ; no.129)

AGRICULTURAL PRICES — Great Britain

GODDEN, David Ponsonby
Technological change and demand for output at the farm level in United Kingdom agriculture, 1950-80 / David Ponsonby Godden. — 368 leaves. — PhD (Econ) 1986 LSE. — *Leaves 328-355 are appendices*

AGRICULTURAL PRICES — Poland

MAŁYSZ, Jerzy
Ceny rolne w Polsce / Jerzy MaŁysz. — Warszawa : Książka i Wiedza, 1986. — 254p

AGRICULTURAL PROCESSING INDUSTRIES — France — Energy consumption — Statistics

Les consommations d'énergie dans les industries agricoles et alimentaires / Ministère de l'Agriculture, Service Central des Enquêtes et Études Statistiques. — Paris : Ministère de l'Agriculture. Service Central des Enquêtes et Études Statistiques, 1982-. — *Annual*

AGRICULTURAL PROCESSING INDUSTRIES — France — Statistics

Enquête annvelle d'entreprise: industries agricoles et alimentaires: resultats sectoriels et régionaux / Ministère de l'Agriculture, Service Central des Enquêtes et Etudes Statistiques. — Paris : Ministère de l'Agriculture. Service Central des Enquêtes et Etudes Statistiques, 1982-. — *Annual*

AGRICULTURAL PROCESSING INDUSTRIES — Soviet Union

LITVIN, Valentin
The Soviet agro-industrial complex : structure and performance / Valentin Litvin. — Boulder, Colo. : Westview Press, 1987. — p. cm. — (Delphic monograph series). — *Includes index.* — *Bibliography: p*

AGRICULTURAL PRODUCTIVITY

EVENSON, Robert E.
The international agricultural research centers : their impact on spending for national agricultural research and extension / Robert E. Evenson. — Washington, D.C. : The World Bank, 1987. — vii,73p. — (Study paper / Consultative Group on International Agricultural Research ; no.22). — *Bibliographical references: p73*

AGRICULTURAL PRODUCTIVITY — Africa

LOWE, R. G.
Agricultural revolution in Africa? : impediments to change and implications for farming, for education and for society / R.G. Lowe. — London : Macmillan, 1986. — viii,295p. — *Includes index*

AGRICULTURAL PRODUCTIVITY — Africa, Sub-Saharan

JAHNKE, Hans E.
The impact of agricultural research in tropical Africa : a study of the collaboration between the international and national research systems / Hans E. Jahnke, Dieter Kirschke and Johannes Lagemann ; in collaboration with K. J. Billing, J. Gromotka, S. N. Lyongo, B. Ndunguru, A. Negewo, G. M. Rillga, D. Sène, H. Shawel, G. Tacher. — Washington, D.C. : The World Bank, 1987. — xvi,175p. — (Study paper / Consultative Group on International Agricultural Research ; no.21). — *Bibliographical references: p159-175*

AGRICULTURAL PRODUCTIVITY — Africa, Sub-Saharan — Congresses

Accelerating food production in Sub-Saharan Africa / edited by John W. Mellor, Christopher L. Delgado, Malcolm J. Blackie. — Baltimore : Published for the International Food Policy Research Institute [by] Johns Hopkins University Press, c1987. — xix, 417 p. . — *Papers and commentaries from a conference sponsored by the Dept. of Land Management of the University of Zimbabwe and the International Food Policy Research Institute, held at Victoria Falls, Zimbabwe in Aug. 1983.* — *Includes index.* — *Bibliography: p. 377-396*

AGRICULTURAL PRODUCTIVITY — China — Hunan Province — History

PERDUE, Peter C.
Exhausting the earth : state and peasant in Hunan, 1500-1850 / Peter C. Perdue. — Cambridge, Mass. : Council on East Asian Studies, Harvard University : Distributed by Harvard University Press, 1987. — p. cm. — (Harvard East Asian monographs ; 1987). — *Includes index.* — *Bibliography: p*

AGRICULTURAL PRODUCTIVITY — Communist countries

WONG, Lung-Fai
Agricultural productivity in the Socialist countries / Lung-Fai Wong. — Boulder, Colo. : Westview Press, [1986]. — p. cm. — (Westview special studies in agriculture science and policy). — *Bibliography: p*

AGRICULTURAL PRODUCTIVITY — Communist countries — Case studies

WONG, Lung-Fai
Agricultural productivity in the Socialist countries / Lung-Fai Wong. — Boulder, Colo. : Westview Press, [1986]. — p. cm. — (Westview special studies in agriculture science and policy). — *Bibliography: p*

AGRICULTURAL PRODUCTIVITY — Denmark

Arbejdsforbruget til landbrugets driftsgrene. — København : I kommission hos Landhusholdningsselskabets Forlag, 1977. — 77p. — (Undersøgelse / Det landøkonomiske Driftsbureau ; nr.32). — *Includes summary in English*

JØRGENSEN, Aage
Graense produkter i landbrugets produktion / Aage Jørgensen & Holger Reenberg. — København : I kommission hos Landhusholdningsselskabets Forlag, 1972. — 45p. — (Memorandum / Det landøkonomiske Driftsbureau ; nr.4). — *Includes summary in English.* — *Bibliography: p.35*

AGRICULTURAL PRODUCTIVITY — India — Bihar

RESERVE BANK OF INDIA. Committee on Agricultural Productivity in Eastern India
Agricultural productivity in Eastern India / report of the Committee on Agricultural Productivity in Eastern India. — Bombay : The Committee, 1984. — 2v

AGRICULTURAL PRODUCTIVITY — India — Orissa

RESERVE BANK OF INDIA. Committee on Agricultural Productivity in Eastern India
Agricultural productivity in Eastern India / report of the Committee on Agricultural Productivity in Eastern India. — Bombay : The Committee, 1984. — 2v

AGRICULTURAL PRODUCTIVITY — India — Uttar Pradesh

RESERVE BANK OF INDIA. Committee on Agricultural Productivity in Eastern India
Agricultural productivity in Eastern India / report of the Committee on Agricultural Productivity in Eastern India. — Bombay : The Committee, 1984. — 2v

AGRICULTURAL PRODUCTIVITY — India — West Bengal

RESERVE BANK OF INDIA. Committee on Agricultural Productivity in Eastern India
Agricultural productivity in Eastern India / report of the Committee on Agricultural Productivity in Eastern India. — Bombay : The Committee, 1984. — 2v

AGRICULTURAL PRODUCTIVITY — Nepal

JAIN, S. C.
Nepal : the land question / S. C. Jain. — Indore : Profulla Jain for Development Publishers, 1985. — iv,80p

AGRICULTURAL PRODUCTIVITY — Philippines

BAUTISTA, Romeo M.
Production incentives in Philippine agriculture : effects of trade and exchange rate policies / Romeo M. Bautista. — Washington, D.C. : International Food Policy Research Institute, 1987. — p. cm. — (Research report ; 59). — *Bibliography: p*

AGRICULTURAL RESOURCES

Gene banks and the world's food / Donald L. Plucknett... [et al.]. — Princeton, N.J. : Princeton University Press, c1987. — p. cm. — *Includes index.* — *Bibliography: p*

AGRICULTURAL SOCIETIES — Poland

JAKÓBCZYK, Witold
Wielkopolskie kólka Rolnicze 1866-1939 / Witold Jakóbczyk. — [Poznań] : Krajowa Agencja Wydawnicza, [1982]. — 39p. — (Z dziejów Wielkopolski)

AGRICULTURAL SYSTEMS
Perspectives on farming systems research and extension / edited by Peter E. Hildebrand. — Boulder, Colo. : L. Rienner, 1986. — p. cm

AGRICULTURAL SYSTEMS — Research
Perspectives on farming systems research and extension / edited by Peter E. Hildebrand. — Boulder, Colo. : L. Rienner, 1986. — p. cm

SIMMONDS, Norman W.
Farming systems research : a review / Norman W. Simmonds. — Washington, D.C. : The World Bank, 1985. — xii,97p. — (World Bank technical paper ; no.43). — *Bibliography: p88-97*

Social sciences and farming systems research : methodological perspectives on agricultural development / edited by Jeffrey R. Jones, Ben J. Wallace. — Boulder : Westview Press, 1986. — p. cm

AGRICULTURAL SYSTEMS — Tropics
SIMMONDS, Norman W.
Farming systems research : a review / Norman W. Simmonds. — Washington, D.C. : The World Bank, 1985. — xii,97p. — (World Bank technical paper ; no.43). — *Bibliography: p88-97*

AGRICULTURAL SYSTEMS — Africa, Sub-Saharan
PINGALI, Prabhu L.
Agricultural mechanization and the evolution of farming systems in Sub-Saharan Africa / Prabhu Pingali, Yves Bigot, Hans P. Binswanger. — Baltimore : Johns Hopkins Press for the World Bank, 1987. — viii,216p. — *Bibliographical references: p191-206*

AGRICULTURE — Thailand — Statistics
1983 intercensal survey of agriculture : whole kingdom. — [Bangkok] : National Statistical Office, [1984]. — 54p. — *In English and Thai*

AGRICULTURE — Bibliography
DAVID LUBIN MEMORIAL LIBRARY
FAO documentation : plant production and protection : 1979-1983 = Documentation de la FAO : production et protection des végétaux : 1979-1983 = Documentacion de la FAO : produccion y proteccion de plantas : 1979-1983. — Rome : Food and Agriculture Organization, 1985. — 112,13,34,12p. — *In English with introductions also in French and Spanish*

AGRICULTURE — Economic aspects
BENNETT, Jon
The hunger machine : the politics of food / Jon Bennett ; introduction and conclusion by Susan George. — Cambridge : Polity in association with Channel Four Television and Yorkshire Television, 1987. — 232p. — *Bibliography: p221-222. — Includes index*

CARLES, Roland
La situation financière de l'entreprise agricole / Roland Carles. — Grignon : Institut nationale de la recherche agronomique, [1981]. — 105p. — *Bibliography: p102*

CHAĪANOV, A.
A.V. Chayanov on the theory of peasant economy / edited by Daniel Thorner, Basile Kerblay, R.E.F. Smith ; with a foreword by Teodor Shanin. — Manchester : Manchester University Press, c1986. — v,316p,[1]leaf of plates. — *Translation of: Organizatsiia krest'īaskogo khozīaistva. — Originally published: Hometown : R.D. Irwin for the American Economic Association, 1966. — Bibliography: p279-296. — Includes index*

GITTINGER, J. Price
Economic analysis of agricultural projects / J. Price Gittinger. — 2nd ed. — Baltimore : Johns Hopkins University Press for the Economic Development Institute of the World Bank, 1982. — xxi,505p. — (EDI series in economic development). — *Bibliography: p445-455*

AGRICULTURE — Economic aspects — Northwest, Pacific — History
GIBSON, James R
Farming the frontier : the agricultural opening of the Oregon country, 1786-1846 / James R. Gibson. — Seattle : University of Washington Press, c1985. — 265 p.. — *Maps on lining papers. — Includes index. — Bibliography: p.[215]-226*

AGRICULTURE — Economic aspects — Africa, Southern
DUGGAN, William R
An economic analysis of southern African agriculture / William R. Duggan. — New York : Praeger, 1985. — p. cm. — *Includes index. — Bibliography: p*

AGRICULTURE — Economic aspects — Africa, Sub-Saharan
JAHNKE, Hans E.
The impact of agricultural research in tropical Africa : a study of the collaboration between the international and national research systems / Hans E. Jahnke, Dieter Kirschke and Johannes Lagemann ; in collaboration with K. J. Billing, J. Gromotka, S. N. Lyongo, B. Ndunguru, A. Negewo, G. M. Rillga, D. Sène, H. Shawel, G. Tacher. — Washington, D.C. : The World Bank, 1987. — xvi,175p. — (Study paper / Consultative Group on International Agricultural Research ; no.21). — *Bibliographical references: p159-175*

AGRICULTURE — Economic aspects — Argentina
JACOBS, Eduardo
La industría de semillas en la Argentina / Eduardo Jacobs, Marta Gutierrez. — [Buenos Aires] : CISEA, [1986]. — 242p. — (Documentos del CISEA ; 85). — *Bibliography: p239-242*

AGRICULTURE — Economic aspects — Argentina — History
La Argentina que no fue / Juan José Llach (Selección e introducción. — Buenos Aires : Ediciones del IDES. — (Ediciones del IDES ; 1)
t.i: Las fragilidades de la Argentina agroexportadora (1918-1930). — 1985. — 166p. — *"[una] selección de trabajos aparecidos en la 'Revista de Economía Argentina' (1918-1952)"*

AGRICULTURE — Economic aspects — Australia
Economic development in East and South-east Asia : implications for Australian agriculture in the 1980s / [contributors, Mike Adams ... et al.]. — Canberra : Australian Govt. Pub. Service, 1984. — x, 237 p.. — *At head of title: Bureau of Agricultural Economics, Canberra. — Includes bibliographies*

HIGGS, Peter John
Adaptation and survival in Australian agriculture : a computable general equilibrium analysis of the impact of economic shocks originating outside the domestic agricultural sector / Peter J. Higgs. — Melbourne, Vic. ; Oxford : Oxford University Press, 1986. — 320p. — *Bibliography: p302-310*

AGRICULTURE — Economic aspects — Bangladesh
DE VYLDER, Stefan
Agriculture in chains : Bangladesh : a case study in contradictions and constraints / Stefan de Vylder. — London : Zed Press, 1982. — xii,164p. — *Bibliography: p157-164*

AGRICULTURE — Economic aspects — Bangladesh — History — 20th century
BOYCE, James K.
Agrarian impasse in Bengal : institutional constraints to technological change / James K. Boyce. — Oxford : Oxford University Press, 1987. — xviii,308p. — (The Library of political economy). — *Bibliography: p283-301. — Includes index*

AGRICULTURE — Economic aspects — Bolivia
Bolivia : agricultural pricing and investment policies. — Washington, D.C., U.S.A. : World Bank, c1984. — xlii,130p. — (A World Bank country study). — *Summaries in French and Spanish. — Includes bibliographical references*

AGRICULTURE — Economic aspects — Burkina Faso
LECAILLON, Jacques
Economic policies and agricultural performance : the case of Burkina Faso / by Jacques Lecaillon and Christian Morrisson. — [Paris] : Development Centre of the Organisation for Economic Co-operation and Development, [1986]. — 158p. — (Development Centre papers). — *Bibliography: p.153-156*

AGRICULTURE — Economic aspects — Canada
GIANGRANDE, Carole
Down to earth : the crisis in Canadian farming / Carole Giangrande. — Toronto : Anansi, 1986. — 196p

AGRICULTURE — Economic aspects — Congo (Brazzaville)
NGUYEN, Gregory Tien Hung
Agriculture and rural development in the People's Republic of Congo / Gregory N.T. Hung. — Boulder : Westview Press, 1986. — p. cm. — (Westview special studies on Africa). — *Includes index. — Bibliography: p*

AGRICULTURE — Economic aspects — Denmark
Arbejdsforbruget til landbrugets driftsgrene. — København : I kommission hos Landhusholdningsselskabets Forlag, 1977. — 77p. — (Undersøgelse / Det landøkonomiske Driftsbureau ; nr.32). — *Includes summary in English*

Etablering på 12 landrug : kapital- og finansieringsforhold. — København : I kommission hos Landhusholdningsselskabets Forlag, 1974. — 28p. — (Meddelelse / Det landøkonomiske Driftsbureau ; nr.16)

AGRICULTURE — Economic aspects — Denmark — Mathematical models
JØRGENSEN, Aage
Graense produkter i landbrugets produktion / Aage Jørgensen & Holger Reenberg. — København : I kommission hos Landhusholdningsselskabets Forlag, 1972. — 45p. — (Memorandum / Det landøkonomiske Driftsbureau ; nr.4). — *Includes summary in English. — Bibliography: p.35*

AGRICULTURE — Economic aspects — Developing countries — Congresses
AGRICULTURE SECTOR SYMPOSIUM ((5th : 1985 : World Bank)
Proceedings of the Fifth Agriculture Sector Symposium : population and food / Ted J. Davis, editor. — Washington, D.C., U.S.A. : World Bank, c1985. — viii,230p. — *Includes bibliographies*

AGRICULTURE — Economic aspects — England — History
THIRSK, Joan
Agricultural regions and agrarian history in England, 1500-1750 / prepared for the Economic History Society by Joan Thirsk. — Basingstoke : Macmillan Education, 1987. — 77p. — (Studies in economic and social history). — *Bibliography: p66-74. — Includes index*

AGRICULTURE — Economic aspects — Europe — Societies, etc.
Directory of European agricultural organizations / documentation prepared by the General Secretariat of the Economic and Social Committee of the European Communities. — London : Kogan Page, 1984. — 718p

AGRICULTURE — Economic aspects — European Economic Community Countries

CAPDEVILA BATLLES, José
Agricultura e industria española frente a la CEE : aspectos jurídicos, económicos y políticos / José Capdevila Batlles ; prólogo de Edgard Pisani. — Barcelona : Editorial Aedos, 1985. — 252p. — *Bibliography: p245-252*

AGRICULTURE — Economic aspects — European Economic Commynity countries — Mathematical models

Agricultural data and economic analysis : databases, forecasting and policy analysis in the context of public administration / [edited by] A. Dubgaard, B. Grassmugg, K. J. Munk. — [Maastricht ; Copenhagen] : European Institute of Public Administration : Statens Jordbrugsøkonomiske Institut, 1984. — *Report of a seminar organized by the European Institute of Public Administration, Maastricht, and the Statens Jordbrugsøkonomiske Institut, Copenhagen 3-5 May 1984. — Includes bibliographical references*

AGRICULTURE — Economic aspects — Fiji

BROOKFIELD, Harold Chillingworth
Land, cane and coconuts : papers on the rural economy of Fiji / H. C. Brookfield, F. Ellis, R. G. Ward. — Canberra [A.C.T.] : Australian National University, 1985. — 251p. — (Australian National University Department of Human Geography Publication ; HG/17). — *Includes bibliographies*

AGRICULTURE — Economic aspects — France

Valeur et rentabilité des biens fonciers agricoles / [par Jean-Jacques Malpot [et al.]]. — [Paris] : La Documentation française, 1985. — 162p. — (Documents du Centre dÉtude des Revenus et des Coûts ; no.74)

VERT, Eric
Les revenus fiscaux des agriculteurs en 1979 / Eric Vert. — [Paris] : INSEE, 1985. — 194p. — (Archives et documents / Institut National de la Statistique et des Études Économiques ; no.131)

AGRICULTURE — Economic aspects — Great Britain

HILL, Berkeley
Economics for agriculture : food, farming and the rural economy / Berkeley Hill and Derek Ray. — Basingstoke : Macmillan Education, 1987. — [288]p. — *Includes bibliography and index*

Investing in rural harmony : a critique : proceedings of a seminar organised by the Centre for Agricultural Strategy to consider an Alternative Package of Agricultural Subsidies and Incentives for England and Wales / edited by A. Korbey. — Reading : University of Reading. Centre for Agricultural Strategy, 1984. — 69p. — *Bibliographies*

AGRICULTURE — Economic aspects — India

Indian agricultural development since independence : a collection of essays / [editors], M.L. Dantwala and others. — New Delhi : Oxford & IBH Pub. Co., c1986. — viii, 519 p.. — *Includes bibliographies and index*

AGRICULTURE — Economic aspects — India — Case studies

SRIVASTAVA, G. C
Urbanization, capital formation, and labour productivity in agriculture : a case study of Ranchi / by G.C. Srivastava. — New Delhi : Radiant Publishers, 1986. — xii, 205 p.. — *Bibliography: p. [198]-205*

AGRICULTURE — Economic aspects — India — Punjab

CHADHA, G. K
The state and rural transformation : the case of Punjab, 1950-85 / G.K. Chadha. — New Delhi ; Beverly Hills : Sage Publications, 1986. — p. cm. — *Includes index. — Bibliography: p*

AGRICULTURE — Economic aspects — India — Rānchī — Case studies

SRIVASTAVA, G. C
Urbanization, capital formation, and labour productivity in agriculture : a case study of Ranchi / by G.C. Srivastava. — New Delhi : Radiant Publishers, 1986. — xii, 205 p.. — *Bibliography: p. [198]-205*

AGRICULTURE — Economic aspects — India — West Bengal — History — 20th century

BOYCE, James K.
Agrarian impasse in Bengal : institutional constraints to technological change / James K. Boyce. — Oxford : Oxford University Press, 1987. — xviii,308p. — (The Library of political economy). — *Bibliography: p283-301. Includes index*

AGRICULTURE — Economic aspects — Japan

HAYAMI, Yūjirō
A century of agricultural growth in Japan : its relevance to Asian development / Yujiro Hayami, in association with Masakatsu Akino, Masahiko Shintani, Saburo Yamada. — Minneapolis : University of Minnesota Press, c1975. — xvii, 248 p.. — *Includes bibliographical references and index*

AGRICULTURE — Economic aspects — Japan — History

SMETHURST, Richard J
Agricultural development and tenancy disputes in Japan, 1870-1940 / Richard J. Smethurst. — Princeton, N.J. : Princeton University Press, c1986. — xii, 472 p.. — *Includes index. — Bibliography: p. 437-450*

AGRICULTURE — Economic aspects — Jordan

The Agricultural sector of Jordan : policy & systems studies / [edited by] A.B. Zahlan, Subhi Qasem. — London : Published for the Abdul Hameed Shoman Foundation, Amman by Ithaca, 1985. — xvii,411p. — ([The Abdul Hameed Shoman Foundation series on Arab agriculture]). — *Includes bibliographies*

AGRICULTURE — Economic aspects — Mali

LECAILLON, Jacques
Economic policies and agricultural performance : the case of Mali, 1960-1983 / by Jacques Lecaillon and Christian Morrisson. — Paris : Development Centre of the Organisation for Economic Co-operation and Development, 1986. — 174p. — (Development Centre papers) . — *Bibliography: p155-157*

AGRICULTURE — Economic aspects — Nepal

SVEJNAR, Jan
Economic policies and agricultural performance : the case of Nepal, 1960-1982 / Jan Svejnar and Erik Thorbecke. — Paris : Development Centre of the Organisation for Economic Co-operation and Development, 1986. — 167p. — (Development Centre papers). — *Bibliography: p129-131*

AGRICULTURE — Economic aspects — Nicaragua

COLBURN, Forrest D
Post-revolutionary Nicaragua : state, class, and the dilemmas of agrarian policy / Forrest D. Colburn. — Berkeley : University of California Press, c1986. — xi, 145p. — *Includes index. — Bibliography: p.133-138*

AGRICULTURE — Economic aspects — Nigeria

State, oil, and agriculture in Nigeria / Michael Watts, editor. — Berkeley : Institute of International Studies, University of California, c1987. — xiv, 327 p. — (Research series ; no. 66). — *Includes index. — Bibliography: p. 297-317*

AGRICULTURE — Economic aspects — Pakistan

NABI, Ijaz
The agrarian economy of Pakistan : issues and policies / Ijaz Nabi, Navid Hamid, Shahid Zahid. — Karachi ; Oxford : Oxford University Press, 1986. — 337p. — *Bibliography: p319-324*

AGRICULTURE — Economic aspects — Peru

La cuestión rural en el Perú / Javier Iguíñiz. — 2a ed. — Lima : Pontifica Universidad Católica del Perú Fondo Editorial, 1986. — 332p. — *"Una recopilación de ensayos elaborados por profesores - investigadores de los Departamentos de Economiá y Ciencias Sociales de la Pontifica Universidad Católica del Perú". — Includes bibliographies*

AGRICULTURE — Economic aspects — Portugal

Portuguese agriculture in transition / by Scott R. Pearson ... [et al.]. — Ithaca, N.Y. : Cornell University Press, 1987. — p. cm. — *Includes index*

AGRICULTURE — Economic aspects — Romania

ŞANDRU, D.
Creditul agricol în România (1918-1944) / D. Şandru. — Bucureşti : Editura Academiei Republicii Socialiste România, 1985. — 179p. — (Biblioteca istorică / Institutul de Istorie şi Arheologie "A. D. Xenopol" Iaşi ; 64). — *Summary in English*

AGRICULTURE — Economic aspects — South Africa — History

KEEGAN, Timothy J.
Rural transformations in industrializing South Africa : the Southern Highveld to 1914 / Timothy J. Keegan. — Basingstoke : Macmillan, 1987. — xviii,302p. — *Bibliography: p272-291. — Includes index*

AGRICULTURE — Economic aspects — South Australia

SOUTH AUSTRALIA. Department of Agriculture. Economics Division
Agriculture in the South Australian economy / by the Economics Division. — [Adelaide] : Department of Agriculture, 1983. — iv,92p. — (Technical report / Department of Agriculture ; no.25). — *Bibliographical references: p92*

AGRICULTURE — Economic aspects — South Australia — Research

SOUTH AUSTRALIA. Department of Agriculture. Research Policy Advisory Committee
Research priorities in the Economics Division. — Adelaide : the Department, 1982. — ii,60 leaves. — (Technical report / Department of Agriculture ; no.11). — *Includes bibliographical references*

AGRICULTURE — Economic aspects — Southern States

Agricultural change : consequences for southern farms and rural communities / edited by Joseph J. Molnar. — Boulder : Westview Press, c1986. — xxii, 440 p.. — (Westview special studies in agricultural science and policy). — *Includes bibliographies and indexes*

HEALY, Robert G
Competition for land in the American South : agriculture, human settlement, and the environment / Robert G. Healy. — Washington, D.C. : Conservation Foundation, c1985. — xxxii, 333 p.. — *Includes bibliographies and index*

AGRICULTURE — Economic aspects — Soviet Union

CHAIÀNOV, A.
A.V. Chayanov on the theory of peasant economy / edited by Daniel Thorner, Basile Kerblay, R.E.F. Smith ; with a foreword by Teodor Shanin. — Manchester : Manchester University Press, c1986. — v,316p,[1]leaf of plates. — Translation of: Organizatsiia krest'iàskogo khoziàistva. — Originally published: Hometown : R.D. Irwin for the American Economic Association, 1966. — Bibliography: p279-296. — Includes index

KALNYN'SH, A. A.
Razvitie agropromyshennoi integratsii i ekonomicheskogo mekhanizma / sostaviteli: A. Kalnyn'sh i V. Tsibul'skii. — Riga : Avots, 1986. — 191p. — (Voprosy agropromyshlennoi integratsii)

LITVIN, Valentin
The Soviet agro-industrial complex : structure and performance / Valentin Litvin. — Boulder, Colo. : Westview Press, 1987. — p. cm. — (Delphic monograph series). — Includes index. — Bibliography: p

Spravochnik ekonomista sel'skogo khoziaistva / pod redaktsiei N. P. Kononenko. N. Ia. Kushvida. — Kiev : Urozhai, 1985. — 528p

AGRICULTURE — Economic aspects — Soviet Union — Dictionaries

Ekonomicheskii slovar' agropromyshlennogo kompleksa / pod redaktsiei A. A. Storozha. — Kiev : Urozhai, 1986. — 333p

AGRICULTURE — Economic aspects — Spain

CAPDEVILA BATLLES, José
Agricultura e industria española frente a la CEE : aspectos jurídicos, económicos y políticos / José Capdevila Batlles ; prólogo de Edgard Pisani. — Barcelona : Editorial Aedos, 1985. — 252p. — Bibliography: p245-252

AGRICULTURE — Economic aspects — Spain — Andalucia

LORING MIRÓ, Jaime
Los sectores agrarios de Andalucia ante la integración en la C.E.E. / Jaime Loring Miró, Luis Godoy López, Jose J. Romero Rodríguez. — Madrid : [Mundi-Prensa Libros], 1984. — 303p. — At head of title: Banco de Crédito Agrícola

AGRICULTURE — Economic aspects — Sudan

SØRBØ, Gunnar M.
Tenants and nomads in Eastern Sudan : a study of economic adaptations in the New Halfa Scheme / Gunnar M. Sørbø. — Uppsala : Scandinavian Institute of African Studies, 1985. — 159p

The Agricultural sector of Sudan : policy & systems studies / [edited by] A.B. Zahlan, W.Y. Magar. — London : Published for the Abdul Hameed Shoman Foundation by Ithaca Press, 1986. — xvii,423p. — ([The Abdul Hameed Shoman Foundation series on Arab agriculture]). — Includes bibliographies

AGRICULTURE — Economic aspects — Swaziland

TESTERINK-MAAS, E. M. W. M.
Demographic response on commercialization in agriculture : a case study of Swaziland / E. M. W. M. Testerink-Maas. — Kwaluseni : Kwaluseni Campus, 1985. — iii,76p. — (Research paper / University of Swaziland. Social Science Research Unit ; no.16). — Bibliography: p76

AGRICULTURE — Economic aspects — Taiwan

HSIEH, S. C.
An analytical review of agricultural development in Taiwan : an input-output and productivity approach / by S. C. Hsieh and T. H. Lee. — Taipei : Chinese-American Joint Commission on Rural Reconstruction, 1958. — [vi],84p. — (Economic digest series / Joint Commission on Rural Reconstruction ; no.12)

SHEN, T. H.
Agricultural planning and production / T. H. Shen. — Taipei : Committee D, Economic Stabilization Board, 1958. — [ii],42p

SHEN, T. H.
Economic significance of agricultural development in Taiwan / by T. H. Shen. — Taipei : Committee D, Economic Stabilization Board, 1955. — 41p

TSUI, Y. C.
A summary report on farm income of Taiwan in 1957 in comparison with 1952 / by Y. C. Tsui. — Taipei : Chinese-American Joint Commission on Rural Reconstruction, 1959. — [iii],67p. — (Economic digest series / Joint Commission on Rural Reconstruction ; no.13)

AGRICULTURE — Economic aspects — United States

GOLDSCHMIDT, Yaaqov
The impact of inflation of financial activity in business, with applications to the U.S. farming sector / Yaaqov Goldschmidt, Leon Sashua, Jimmye S. Hillman. — Totowa, N.J. : Rowman & Allanheld, 1986. — p. cm. — Includes index. — Bibliography: p

AGRICULTURE — Economic aspects — United States — History — 19th century

ATACK, Jeremy
To their own soil : agriculture in the Antebellum North / Jeremy Atack, Fred Bateman. — 1st ed. — Ames : Iowa State University Press, 1987. — xi, 322 p.. — (The Henry A. Wallace series on agricultural history and rural studies). — Includes index. — Bibliography: p. 299-312

MCGUIRE, Robert A
An empirical investigation of farmers' behavior under uncertainty : income, price, and yield variability for late-nineteenth century American agriculture / Robert A. McGuire. — New York : Garland Pub., 1985. — 324 p.. — (American economic history). — Thesis (Ph. D.)--University of Washington, 1978. — Bibliography: p. [182]-193

AGRICULTURE — Research — Economic aspects

EVENSON, Robert E.
The international agricultural research centers : their impact on spending for national agricultural research and extension / Robert E. Evenson. — Washington, D.C. : The World Bank, 1987. — vii,73p. — (Study paper / Consultative Group on International Agricultural Research ; no.22). — Bibliographical references: p73

AGRICULTURE — Research — Government policy

EVENSON, Robert E.
The international agricultural research centers : their impact on spending for national agricultural research and extension / Robert E. Evenson. — Washington, D.C. : The World Bank, 1987. — vii,73p. — (Study paper / Consultative Group on International Agricultural Research ; no.22). — Bibliographical references: p73

AGRICULTURE — Research — International cooperation

BAUM, Warren C.
Partners against hunger : the Consultative Group on International Agricultural Research / Warren C. Baum ; with the collaboration of Michael L. Lejeune. — Washington, D.C. : The World Bank for the CGIAR, 1986. — xiii,337p

EL-AKHRASS, Hisham
Syria and the CGIAR centers : a study of the collaboration in agricultural research / Hisham El-Akhrass. — Washington, D.C. : The World Bank, 1986. — x,51p. — (Study paper / Consultative Group on International Agricultural Research ; no.13). — Bibliographical references: p51

EVENSON, Robert E.
The international agricultural research centers : their impact on spending for national agricultural research and extension / Robert E. Evenson. — Washington, D.C. : The World Bank, 1987. — vii,73p. — (Study paper / Consultative Group on International Agricultural Research ; no.22). — Bibliographical references: p73

GOMEZ, Arturo A.
Philippines and the CGIAR centers : a study of their collaboration in agricultural research / Arturo A. Gomez. — Washington, D.C. : The World Bank, 1986. — xii,70p. — (Study paper / Consultative Group on International Agricultural Research ; no.15). — Bibliographical references: p69-70

ISARANGKURA, Rungruang
Thailand and the CGIAR centers : a study of their collaboration in agricultural research / Rungruang Isarangkura. — Washington, D.C. : The World Bank, 1986. — x,94p. — (Study paper / Consultative Group on International Agricultural Research ; no.16)

JAHNKE, Hans E.
The impact of agricultural research in tropical Africa : a study of the collaboration between the international and national research systems / Hans E. Jahnke, Dieter Kirschke and Johannes Lagemann ; in collaboration with K. J. Billing, J. Gromotka, S. N. Lyongo, B. Ndunguru, A. Negewo, G. M. Rillga, D. Sène, H. Shawel, G. Tacher. — Washington, D.C. : The World Bank, 1987. — xvi,175p. — (Study paper / Consultative Group on International Agricultural Research ; no.21). — Bibliographical references: p159-175

KYAW ZIN
Burma and the CGIAR centers : a study of their collaboration in agricultural research / Kyaw Zin. — Washington, D.C. : The World Bank, 1986. — xiv,105p. — (Study paper / Consultative Group on International Agricultural Research ; no.19). — Bibliographical references: p103-105

MAHAPATRA, Ishwar Chandra
India and the international crops research institute for the semi-arid tropics : a study of their collaboration in agricultural research / Ishwar Chandra Mahapatre, Dev Raj Bhumbla, Shriniwas Dattatraya Bokil. — Washington, D.C. : The World Bank, 1986. — x,48p. — (Study paper / Consultative group on International Agricultural Research ; no.18)

OUALI, Ibrahim Firmin
Burkina Faso and the CGIAR Centers : a study of their collaboration in agricultural research / Ibrahim Firmin Ouali. — Washington, D.C. : The World Bank, 1987. — xiv,112p. — (Study paper / Consultative Group on International Agricultural Research ; no.23). — Bibliographical references: p109

PAZ SILVA, Luis J.
Peru and the CGIAR centers : a study of their collaboration in agricultural research / Luis J. Paz Silva. — Washington, D.C. : The World Bank, 1986. — xii,136p. — (Study paper / Consultative Group on International Agricultural Research ; no.12)

POSADA TORRES, Rafael
Ecuador and the CGIAR centers : a study of their collaboration in agricultural research / Rafael Posada Torres. — Washington, D.C. : The Workd Bank, 1986. — x,75p. — (Study paper / Consultative Group on International Agricultural Research ; no.11). — Bibliographical references: p75

SANCHEZ, Pedro A.
Cuba and the CGIAR centers : a study of their collaboration in agricultural research / Pedro A. Sanchez, Grant M. Scobie. — Washington, D.C. : The World Bank, 1986. — xiv,120p. — (Study paper / Consultative Group on International Agricultural Research ; no.14). — Bibliographical references: p117-120

AGRICULTURE — Research — International cooperation
continuation
VENEZIAN, Eduardo
Chile and the CGIAR Centers : a study of their collaboration in agricultural research / Eduardo Venezian. — Washington, D.C. : The World Bank, 1987. — xii,190p. — (Study paper / Consultative Group on International Agricultural Research ; no.20). — *Bibliographical references: p137-141*

AGRICULTURE — Research — On-farm
SIMMONDS, Norman W.
Farming systems research : a review / Norman W. Simmonds. — Washington, D.C. : The World Bank, 1985. — xii,97p. — (World Bank technical paper ; no.43). — *Bibliography: p88-97*

AGRICULTURE — Research — Philippines
GOMEZ, Arturo A.
Philippines and the CGIAR centers : a study of their collaboration in agricultural research / Arturo A. Gomez. — Washington, D.C. : The World Bank, 1986. — xii,70p. — (Study paper / Consultative Group on International Agricultural Research ; no.15). — *Bibliographical references: p69-70*

AGRICULTURE — Research — Syria
EL-AKHRASS, Hisham
Syria and the CGIAR centers : a study of their collaboration in agricultural research / Hisham El-Akhrass. — Washington, D.C. : The World Bank, 1986. — x,51p. — (Study paper / Consultative Group on International Agricultural Research ; no.13). — *Bibliographical references: p51*

AGRICULTURE — Research — Africa, Sub-Saharan
JAHNKE, Hans E.
The impact of agricultural research in tropical Africa : a study of the collaboration between the international and national research systems / Hans E. Jahnke, Dieter Kirschke and Johannes Lagemann ; in collaboration with K. J. Billing, J. Gromotka, B. Ndunguru, A. Negewo, G. M. Rillga, D. Sène, H. Shawel, G. Tacher. — Washington, D.C. : The World Bank, 1987. — xvi,175p. — (Study paper / Consultative Group on International Agricultural Research ; no.21). — *Bibliographical references: p159-175*

AGRICULTURE — Research — Asia — Congresses
Research-extension-farmer : a two-way continuum for agricultural development / edited by Michael M. Cernea, John K. Coulter, John F. A. Russell. — Washington, D.C. : The World Bank, 1985. — xvi,171p. — *Cover: "A World Bank and UNDP Symposium".* — *Includes bibliographical references*

AGRICULTURE — Research — Burkina Faso
OUALI, Ibrahim Firmin
Burkina Faso and the CGIAR Centers : a study of their collaboration in agricultural research / Ibrahim Firmin Ouali. — Washington, D.C. : The World Bank, 1987. — xiv,112p. — (Study paper / Consultative Group on International Agricultural Research ; no.23). — *Bibliographical references: p109*

AGRICULTURE — Research — Burma
KYAW ZIN
Burma and the CGIAR centers : a study of their collaboration in agricultural research / Kyaw Zin. — Washington, D.C. : The World Bank, 1986. — xiv,105p. — (Study paper / Consultative Group on International Agricultural Research ; no.19). — *Bibliographical references: p103-105*

AGRICULTURE — Research — Chile
VENEZIAN, Eduardo
Chile and the CGIAR Centers : a study of their collaboration in agricultural research / Eduardo Venezian. — Washington, D.C. : The World Bank, 1987. — xii,190p. — (Study paper / Consultative Group on International Agricultural Research ; no.20). — *Bibliographical references: p137-141*

AGRICULTURE — Research — Cuba
SANCHEZ, Pedro A.
Cuba and the CGIAR centers : a study of their collaboration in agricultural research / Pedro A. Sanchez, Grant M. Scobie. — Washington, D.C. : The World Bank, 1986. — xiv,120p. — (Study paper / Consultative Group on International Agricultural Research ; no.14). — *Bibliographical references: p117-120*

AGRICULTURE — Research — Developing countries — Evaluation
WORLD BANK. Operations Evaluation Department
Agricultural research and extension : an evaluation of the World Bank's experience. — Washington, D.C., U.S.A. : World Bank, 1985. — p. cm

AGRICULTURE — Research — Ecuador
POSADA TORRES, Rafael
Ecuador and the CGIAR centers : a study of their collaboration in agricultural research / Rafael Posada Torres. — Washington, D.C. : The Workd Bank, 1986. — x,75p. — (Study paper / Consultative Group on International Agricultural Research ; no.11). — *Bibliographical references: p75*

AGRICULTURE — Research — Peru
PAZ SILVA, Luis J.
Peru and the CGIAR centers : a study of their collaboration in agricultural research / Luis J. Paz Silva. — Washington, D.C. : The World Bank, 1986. — xii,136p. — (Study paper / Consultative Group on International Agricultural Research ; no.12)

AGRICULTURE — Research — Thailand
ISARANGKURA, Rungruang
Thailand and the CGIAR centers : a study of their collaboration in agricultural research / Rungruang Isarangkura. — Washington, D.C. : The World Bank, 1986. — x,94p. — (Study paper / Consultative Group on International Agricultural Research ; no.16)

AGRICULTURE — Social aspects — United States — Congresses
Farm work and fieldwork : American agriculture in anthropological perspective / edited by Michael Chibnik. — Ithaca : Cornell University Press, 1987. — 293 p.. — (Anthropology of contemporary issues). — *Includes bibliographies and index*

AGRICULTURE — Statistical methods
Guidelines for the computation of selected statistical indicators. — Rome : FAO, 1986. — vii,71p. — (FAO economic and social development paper ; 60)

AGRICULTURE — Taxation — Belgium
Revenus et fiscalité des agriculteurs en Belgique : politique agricole commune / G. Bublot...[et al.] ; textes rassemblés par Max Frank. — [Bruxelles] : Université de Bruxelles, c1982. — 126p. — *At head of title: Politique agricole commune.* — *Bibliography: p126*

AGRICULTURE — Africa, sub-Saharan — Addresses, essays, lectures
Food in sub-Saharan Africa / edited by Art Hansen and Della E. McMillan. — Boulder,Colo. : Lynne Rienner, 1986. — xvi,410p. — (Food in Africa series)

AGRICULTURE — Albania
SKARSO, Kozma
Agriculture in the People's Socialist Republic of Albania / Kosma Skarso. — Tirana : 8 Nentori Publishing House, 1984. — 97p

AGRICULTURE — Argentina
FIGUEIRAS, Horacio
Bases de discusión para una política rural / Horacio Figueiras, Daniel Adrogue, Raúl Druetta. — Buenos Aires : Editorial Hernandiana : Fundación Alimentaria Argentina, c1985. — 175p. — (Serie política / Fundación Alimentaria Argentina)

AGRICULTURE — Argentina — History — 1943-
LATTUADA, Mario J.
La política agraria peronista (1943-1983) / Mario J. Lattuada. — Buenos Aires : Centro Editor de América Latina. — (Biblioteca Politica Argentina ; 132)
t.1. — 1986. — 142p

AGRICULTURE — Asia
ETIENNE, Gilbert
[Développement rural en Asie. English]. Rural development in Asia : meetings with peasants / Gilbert Etienne ; translated by Arati Sharma. — Rev. ed. — New Delhi ; Beverly Hills, CA : Sage Publications, 1985. — 276 p.. — *Translation of: Développement rural en Asie.* — *Bibliography: p. [272]-276*

AGRICULTURE — Australia
AUSTRALIA. Commonwealth Bureau of Census and Statistics
Agricultural sector: structure of operating units. — Canberra : [the Bureau], 1974/5-1980/81. — *Annual*

AGRICULTURE — Australia — Finance
AUSTRALIA. Commonwealth Bureau of Census and Statistics
Agricultural Sector: financial statistics. — Canberra : [the Bureau], 1974/5-1980/81. — *Annual*

AGRICULTURE — Australia — Tasmania
TASMANIA. Commonwealth Bureau of Census and Statistics. Tasmanian Office
Agricultural industry. — Hobart : [the office], 1973/74-1979/80. — *Annual*

AGRICULTURE — Bangladesh — Economic aspects
MUQTADA, M.
Social and economic formations in Bangladesh agriculture : a historical perspective / M. Muqtada. — Dacca : University of Dacca, 1986. — 68p. — (Research reports / University of Dacca. Bureau of Economic Research ; 3). — *Bibliography: p61-63*

AGRICULTURE — Botswana — Statistics
1982 Botswana agricultural census. — [Gabarone] : Central Statistical Office, 1983. — 102p

AGRICULTURE — Brazil — Statistics
Séries estatísticas retrospectivas. — Rio de Janeiro : IBGE
V.2: O Brasil, suas riquezas naturais, suas industrias
T.2: Indústria agrícolo. — 1986. — 470p. — *Facsimile of 1908 original*

AGRICULTURE — Burkina Faso
LECAILLON, Jacques
Economic policies and agricultural performance : the case of Burkina Faso / by Jacques Lecaillon and Christian Morrisson. — [Paris] : Development Centre of the Organisation for Economic Co-operation and Development, [1986]. — 158p. — (Development Centre papers). — *Bibliography: p.153-156*

AGRICULTURE — Canada
GIANGRANDE, Carole
Down to earth : the crisis in Canadian farming / Carole Giangrande. — Toronto : Anansi, 1986. — 196p

AGRICULTURE — Colombia — Statistics
COLOMBIA. Departamento Administrativo Nacional de Estadística
Encuesta agropecuaria nacional 1965 / Alberto Charry Lara...[et al.]. — Bogotá : the Departamento, 1966. — 26p

COLOMBIA. Departamento Administrativo Nacional de Estadística
Muestra agropecuaria nacional 1964 / Alberto Charry Lara...[et al.]. — Bogotá : the Departamento, 1965. — 32p

AGRICULTURE — Czechoslovakia — History

JELEČEK, Leoš
Zemědělství a půdní fond v Čechách ve 2. polovině 19. století / Leoš Jeleček. — Praha : Academia, 1985. — 283p. — *Summary in English and Russian. — Bibliography: p262-273*

AGRICULTURE — Denmark — History

BRYLD, Carl-Johan
Det agrare Danmark 1680-1980'erne / Carl-Johan Bryld & Harry Haue. — Herning : Systime, 1982. — 332p. — (Historiske kildehæfter). — *Bibliography: p325-327*

AGRICULTURE — Developing countries — Addresses, essays, lectures

Work, income, and inequality : payments systems in the Third World / edited by Frances Stewart. — New York : St. Martin's Press, 1983. — x, 333 p.. — *Includes bibliographical references and index*

AGRICULTURE — Developing countries — Technology transfer — Evaluation

WORLD BANK. Operations Evaluation Department
Agricultural research and extension : an evaluation of the World Bank's experience. — Washington, D.C., U.S.A. : World Bank, 1985. — p. cm

AGRICULTURE — England — Bedfordshire

HOWE, Jonathan
Bedfordshire new agricultural landscape project. — [Bedford] : Bedfordshire County Planning Department, 1987. — 36p

AGRICULTURE — European Economic Community Countries

Agricultural review for Europe. — New York : United Nations, 1983/84-. — *Annual. — Continues: Review of the agricultural situation in Europe and Agricultural trade in Europe. — In 6 vols. Vol.I: General review, Vol.II: Agricultural trade, Vol.III: The Grain Market, Vol.IV: The Livestock and meat market, Vol.V: The milk and dairy products market, Vol.VI: The egg market*

Agricultural trade in Europe : prepared by the FAO/ECE Agriculture and Timber Division of the Secretariat of the Economic Commission for Europe. — New York : United Nations, 1964-1983. — *Annual. — Continued by: Agricultural review for Europe*

AGRICULTURE — European Economic Community countries

FENNELL, Rosemary
The common agricultural policy : a synthesis of opinion / Rosemary Fennell. — Wye : Wye College, School of Rural Economics and Related Studies, [1973]. — vi,106p. — (Reports / Wye College. Centre for European Agricultural Studies ; no.1). — *Bibliography: p.100-106*

Pour un role actif de la Communauté Économique Européen e sur la scene agricole internationale : rapport du groupe de travail sur la prospective des échanges mondiaux agricoles / présidé par B. Auberger. — Paris : La Documentation Français, 1986. — 184p. — *Bibliography: p180-184*

AGRICULTURE — European Economic Community Countries

Review of the agricultural situation in Europe / prepared by the ECE/FAO Agriculture and Timber Division of the Secretariat of The Economic Commission for Europe. — New York : United Nations, 1958-1981. — *Annual. — Continued by: Agricultural review for Europe. — In 2 vols*

AGRICULTURE — European Economic Community countries — Accounting

Agricultural data and economic analysis : databases, forecasting and policy analysis in the context of public administration / [edited by] A. Dubgaard, B. Grassmugg, K. J. Munk. — [Maastricht ; Copenhagen] : European Institute of Public Administration : Statens Jordbrugsøkonomiske Institut, 1984. — *Report of a seminar organized by the European Institute of Public Administration, Maastricht, and the Statens Jordbrugsøkonomiske Institut, Copenhagen 3-5 May 1984. — Includes bibliographical references*

AGRICULTURE — Finland

Suomen taloushistovia. — Helsinki : Kustannusosakeyhtiö Tammi
Vol.1: Agraarinen Suomi / toimittaneet Eino Jutikkala, Yrjö Kaukiainen, Sven-Erik Åström. — 1980. — 494p. — *Bibliography: p488-491*

AGRICULTURE — Finland — Accounting

MÄKELÄ, Pekka
Kansantalouden tilinpito : maa-, metsä- ja kalatalous sekä metsästys kansantalouden tilinpidossa = National accounts : agriculture, forestry, fishing and hunting in national accounts. — Helsinki : Tilastokeskus, 1980. — 126p. — (Tutkimuksia / Finland. Tilastokeskus ; no.61). — *Summary and table headings in English and Swedish*

AGRICULTURE — Finland — Statistics

FINLAND. Tilastokeskus
Maa- ja metsätalous : Maa- ja metsätalouden taloastilasto 1964-1978 = Agriculture and forestry : Economy statistics of agriculture and forestry 1964-1978. — Helsinki : Tilastokeskus, 1979. — 85p. — (Suomen virallinen tilasto = Official statistics of Finland ; 39 ; 5). — *In Finnish, Swedish and English*

AGRICULTURE — France

CHAVAGNE, Yves
Lågriculture industrielle en crise / Yves Chavagne. — [Paris : Syros, c1984]. — 125p. — (Alternatives économiques)

LAFONT, Jean
Paysannerie et capitalisme : analyse des principales tendances du développement récent de l'agriculture française / Jean Lafont. — Paris : Centre D'Études Prospectives D'Économie Mathématique Appliquées à la Planification, 1976. — 116p. — (Centre D'Études Prospectives D'Économie Mathématique Appliquées à la Planification ; 7701)

LANDELL MILLS ASSOCIATES
Exports to France : the market for British farm supplies / Landell Mills Associates. — London : British Overseas Trade Board, Overseas Trade Division 3/Exports to Europe Branch, Department of Trade, 1982. — 2v.(in 1). — *Cover title: Plough into the French market*

AGRICULTURE — France — Statistics

BRESSON, Denis
Les industries agricoles et alimentaires en 1984 : séries statistiques 1977-1984 / Denis Bresson. — [Paris] : INSEE, 1985. — 113p. — (Archives et documents / Institut National de la Statistique et des Études Économiques ; no.130)

AGRICULTURE — Great Britain

BYNG, Julian
Distant views of William Waldegrave's Oxford speech / Julian Byng, Tony Paterson [and] Graham Pye. — London : Centre for Policy Studies, 1986. — 63p

AGRICULTURE — Great Britain — Technological innovations

GODDEN, David Ponsonby
Technological change and demand for output at the farm level in United Kingdom agriculture, 1950-80 / David Ponsonby Godden. — 368 leaves. — *PhD (Econ) 1986 LSE. — Leaves 328-355 are appendices*

AGRICULTURE — Guadeloupe — Statistics

L'évolution des productions agricoles en Guadeloupe : 1952-1977. — [Basse-Terre?] : Direction départmentale de l'agriculture : Atelier départmental d'études économiques et d'aménagement rural, 1979. — 135p. — *Bibliography: p133*

Recensement général de l'agriculture : 1980-1981 : inventaires par commune et par zone agricole : Guadeloupe. — [Basse-Terre?] : Service départemental de statistique agricole de Guadeloupe, [1984]. — 95p

AGRICULTURE — Hungary

A magyar buza minösége, ára és értékesítése : a Magyar Közgazdasági Társaság ankétja / contributions by Éber Antal...[et al.]. — Budapest : Gergely R., 1930. — 202p. — (Közgazdasági Könyvtár ; köt.9). — *Proceedings of a conference "A magyar buza minösége, ára és értékesítése", [Budapest?], 1929-1930 ????????*

AGRICULTURE — India — Statistics

INDIA. Agricultural Census Division
All-India report on agricultural census 1976-77. — New Delhi : Agricultural Census Division, Ministry of Agriculture, 1983. — 119p

INDIA. Ministry of Agriculture and Irrigation. Directorate of Economics and Statistics
Indian livestock census. — [New Delhi] : Ministry of Agriculture and Irrigation, Directorate of Economics and Statistics
vol.2: Detailed tables. — [1976?]. — 3v.

AGRICULTURE — Ireland — History

BELL, Jonathan
Irish farming : implements and techniques, 1750-1900 / Jonathan Bell and Mervyn Watson. — Edinburgh : John Donald, 1986. — viii,256p. — *Bibliography: p240-250*

AGRICULTURE — Italy — Statistics

3 censimento generale dell'agricoltura 24 ottobre 1982. — Roma : I.S.T.A.T.
Tipologia delle aziende agricole : campione al 10% dei questionari di azienda. — 1986. — 114p

ITALY, Istituto Centrale di Statistica
3 censimento generale dell' agricoltura 24 ottobre 1982. — Roma : the Istituto
v.2: Caratteristiche strutturali delle aziende agricole
t.2: fascicoli regionali. — 1986-. — 19V.

AGRICULTURE — Japan

Aspects of the relationship between agriculture and industrialisation in Japan / edited by Janet Hunter. — London : Suntory-Toyota International Centre for Economics and Related Disciplines, 1986. — 51p. — (International Studies ; 1986/4)

AGRICULTURE — Jordan — Statistics

JORDAN. Department of Statistics
General results of the agricultural census 1983. — [Amman] : the Department, 1985. — 1v. (various pagings). — *Text in Arabic with contents list and table headings in English*

The preliminary results of the agricultural census 1983. — [Amman] : Department of Statistics, 1984. — 83p. — *In Arabic with English table headings*

AGRICULTURE — Malawi — Statistics

National sample survey of agriculture 1980-81 : customary land in rural areas only. — Zomba : National Statistical Office
vol. 2: Crops and yield. — 1984. — 28p

National sample survey of agriculture 1980-81 : customary land in rural areas only. — Zomba : National Statistical Office
vol. 3: Income and expenditure, crop storage, livestock, resources and nutrition. — 1984. — 41p

AGRICULTURE — Malawi — Statistics
continuation

National sample survey of agriculture 1980-1981 : Customary land in rural areas only. — Zomba : National Statistical Office vol. 1: Household characteristics, labour availability and garden details. — 1984. — 28p

AGRICULTURE — Mexico

Mexican agriculture : rural crisis and policy response / Louis W. Goodman [et al.]. — Washington, D.C. : Woodrow Wilson International Center for Scholars, 1985. — xii,72,[32p]. — (Working papers / Wilson Centre. Latin American Program ; no.168)

AGRICULTURE — New Caledonia — Statistics

Recensement général de l'agriculture 1983-1984. — Nouméa : Direction territoriale de la statistique et des études économiques t.1: Inventaires communaux. — [1986]. — 141,8p. — (Notes et documents / Direction territoriale de la statistique et des études économiques ; no.36-37)

Recensement général de l'agriculture 1983-1984. — Nouméa : Direction territoriale de la statistique et des études économiques t.1 ter: Inventaires par région. — [1985]. — 29p. — (Notes et documents / Direction territoriale de la statistique et des études économiques ; no.38 Bis)

Recensement général de l'agriculture 1983-1984. — Nouméa : Institut territoriale de la statistique et des études économiques t.2: Résultats
Pt.1: Exploitations agricoles et productions animales. — [1986]. — 91p. — (Notes et documents / Institut territoriale de la statistique et des études économiques ; no.40)

AGRICULTURE — New Zealand — Statistics

Selected agriculture statistics 1949-1983 : prepared for the Minister of Agriculture / prepared by the Statistics Unit ; edited by B. M. Broxc. — Wellington : Economics Division, New Zealand Ministry of Agriculture and Fisheries, 1984. — 18 leaves. — (Research paper / Economics Division, Ministry of Agriculture and Fisheries ; 5/84)

AGRICULTURE — Nigeria — Statistics

National integrated survey of households (Nish): report of rural agricultural sample survey / Agricultural Survey Unit, Nigeria. — Lagos : Agricultural Survey Unit, 1981/82-. — *Annual*

AGRICULTURE — Oregon — History

GIBSON, James R
Farming the frontier : the agricultural opening of the Oregon country, 1786-1846 / James R. Gibson. — Seattle : University of Washington Press, c1985. — 265 p.. — *Maps on lining papers. — Includes index. — Bibliography: p. [215]-226*

AGRICULTURE — Pakistan

PAKISTAN. Agricultural Enquiry Committee
Report of the Agricultural Enquiry Committee. — [Islamabad] : Ministry of Food and Agriculture, 1975. — [iii],62p

AGRICULTURE — Portugal

Portuguese agriculture in transition / by Scott R. Pearson ... [et al.]. — Ithaca, N.Y. : Cornell University Press, 1987. — p. cm. — *Includes index*

AGRICULTURE — Puerto Rico

IRIZARRY, Guillermo
The operations and relationships of the agricultural services in Puerto Rico : final report / Guillermo Irizarry. — San Juan : Bureau of the Budget, 1961. — xvi,199p. — *With separate map in end pocket*

AGRICULTURE — Russian S.F.S.R. — Moscow — Statistics

MOSCOW (R.S.F.S.R.). Sovet deputatov trudiashchikhsia. Statisticheskii otdel
Statisticheskii ezhegodnik g. Moskvy i Moskovskoi gubernii, 1914-1923 = Annuaire statistique de la ville et gouvernement de Moscou, 1914-1923. — Moskva : Izd. Statisticheskogo Otdela Moskovskogo Soveta. — (Rare printed material relating to Moscow, 1887-1923)
Vyp.1: Sel'skokhoziaistvennyi obzor Moskovskoi gubernii za 1916-1923 gg.. — 1925. — xii,288p

AGRICULTURE — Sahel — Congresses

COLLOQUIUM ON THE EFFECTS OF DROUGHT ON THE PRODUCTIVE STRATEGIES OF SUDANO-SAHELIAN HERDSMEN AND FARMERS (1975 : Université de Niamey)
Report / Colloquium on the Effects of Drought on the Productive Strategies of Sudano-Sahelian Herdsmen and Farmers ; edited by Michael M. Horowitz. — Binghamton, N.Y. : Institute for Development Anthropology, [1976]. — xiii, 96 p.. — *Cover title*

AGRICULTURE — San Marino — Statistics

3° censimento generale dell'agricoltura : 31 ottobre 1975. — San Marino : Ufficio Statale di Statistica, 1977. — xii,213 leaves

AGRICULTURE — Scotland

ANDERSON, John
Profitability of farming in south east Scotland 1985/86 / John Anderson. — Edinburgh : East of Scotland College of Agriculture, 1987. — 76p. — (Economics and management series ; no.22)

SINCLAIR, John
A feeling for the land / John Sinclair [and] Berkeley Heppel. — London : BB Communications, 1986. — 119p

AGRICULTURE — Sierra Leone

JOHNNY, Michael
Informal credit for integrated rural development in Sierra Leone / Michael Johnny. — Hamburg : Weltarchiv, 1985. — xviii,212p. — (Studien zur integrierten ländlichen Entwicklung ; 6). — *Bibliography: p199-212*

AGRICULTURE — Soviet Union — Statistics

Spravochnik ekonomista sel'skogo khoziaistva / pod redaktsiei N. P. Kononenko. N. Ia. Kushvida. — Kiev : Urozhai, 1985. — 528p

VASHCHUKOV, L. I.
Razvitie sel'skogo khoziaistva SSR : tsifry i fakty : spravochnoe izdanie / L. I. Vashchukov. — Moskva : Finansy i statistika, 1986. — 93p

AGRICULTURE — Spain

GJELTEN, Tom
To improve Spanish farming without hurting Spanish farmers : a report on agricultural development strategies in Spain / Tom Gjelten. — Langholm : Arkleton Trust, 1984. — 52p

AGRICULTURE — Spain — History

LLUCH, Ernest
Agronomía y fisiocracia en España (1750-1820) / Ernest Lluch y Lluís Argemí d 'Abadal ; prólogo y epílogo por Fabian Estapé. — Valencia : Institución Alfonso el Magnánimo : Institució Valenciana d'estudis i Investigació, [1985]. — lxi,215p. — (Estudios universitarios ; 11)

AGRICULTURE — Spain — History — 19th century

Historia agraria de la España contemporánea. — Barcelona : Crítica. — (Crítica/historia ; 33)
2: Expansión y crisis (1850-1900) / editores Ramón Garrabou y Jesús Sanz Fernández. — c1985. — 542p

AGRICULTURE — Spain — Statistics

[Resultados por comunidades autónomas pluriprovinciales!]. Censo agrario de España 1982. — Madrid : Instituto Nacional de Estadística t.2. — 1985. — 10v

Censo agrario de España 1982. — Madrid : Instituto Nacional de Estadística t.3: Resultados provinciales. — 1984. — 50v

AGRICULTURE — Spain — El Ejido

PONCE MOLINA, Pedro
Agricultura y sociedad de El Ejido en el siglo XVI / Pedro Ponce Molina. — [El Ejido] : Ayuntamiento de El Ejido, 1983. — 199p. — *Bibliography: p[191]-199*

AGRICULTURE — Sri Lanka — Statistics

Sri Lanka census of agriculture 1982 : small holding sector. — [Colombo] : Department of Census and Statistics, [1984-85]. — 15pts

AGRICULTURE — Syria — Statistics

1970-1971 Agriculture census data : first stage : Basic data in Syrian Arab Republic. — [Damascus] : Central Bureau of Statistics, [ca. 1973]. — 182p. — *In English and Arabic*

AGRICULTURE — Taiwan

New spirit for a new China in Agriculture. — Taipei : Joint Commission on Rural Reconstruction, 1957. — 18p

SHEN, T. H.
Agricultural and land programs in free China : increase production and farmer security / by T. H. Shen. — Taipei : Government Information Bureau, 1954. — 85p

AGRICULTURE — Taiwan — Planning

SHEN, T. H.
Agricultural planning and production / T. H. Shen. — Taipei : Committee D, Economic Stabilization Board, 1958. — [ii],42p

AGRICULTURE — Tanzania

The agricultural policy of Tanzania 1983. — Dar es Salaam : Ministry of Agriculture, 1983. — 35p

ÖSTBERG, Wilhelm
The Kondoa transformation : coming to grips with soil erosion in Central Tanzania / Wilhelm Östberg. — Uppsala : Scandinavian Institute of African Studies, 1986. — 99p. — (Research reports / Scandinavian Institute of African Studies ; no.76). — *Bibliography: p97-99*

The Tanzania national agricultural policy. — Dar es Salaam : Ministry of Agriculture, 1982. — 241p

AGRICULTURE — Trinidad and Tobago — Statistics

Agricultural census 1963. — [Port of Spain?] : Central Statistical Office, [1968]
Vol.2
Pt.C: Production and sales of crops : 10 acres and over. — vii,32p

Agricultural report / Central Statistical Office, Trinidad and Tobago. — Port of Spain : Central Statistical Office, 1984-. — *Annual. — Continues: Quarterly agricultural report*

Quarterly agricultural report / Central Statistical Office, Trinidad and Tobago. — Port of Spain : Central Statistical Office, 1974-1983. — *Quarterly. Annual from 1980. — Continued by: Agricultural report*

AGRICULTURE — Wales — Clwyd

CLWYD. County Council
Clwyd county structure plan : public participation seminar : agriculture, woodlands and forestry : report of proceedings. — Mold : [the Council], 1975. — 41p

AGRICULTURE — Zaire

Plan de relance agricole 1982-1984. — [Kinshasa : Département de l'Agriculture et du Développement Rural], 1982. — 199p

AGRICULTURE — Zaire — Economic aspects

TSHIBAKA, Tshikala B.
The effects of trade and exchange rate policies on agriculture in Zaire / Tshikala B. Tshibaka. — Washington, D.C. : International Food Policy Research Institute, 1986. — 65p. — (Research report / International Food Policy Research Institute ; 56). — *Bibliography: p63-65*

AGRICULTURE AND POLITICS — Germany (West)

JOHN, Antonius
Bauernköpfe 1946-1986 / Antonius John. — Bonn : Deutscher Agrar-Verlag, 1986. — 204p

AGRICULTURE AND POLITICS — South Africa — History

KEEGAN, Timothy J.
Rural transformations in industrializing South Africa : the Southern Highveld to 1914 / Timothy J. Keegan. — Basingstoke : Macmillan, 1987. — xviii,302p. — *Bibliography: p272-291. — Includes index*

AGRICULTURE AND STATE

World food policies : toward agricultural interdependence / edited by William P. Browne and Don. F. Hadwiger. — Boulder, Colo. : L. Rienner, 1986. — x, 220p. — *Includes index. — Includes bibliographies*

AGRICULTURE AND STATE — Congresses

INTERNATIONAL CONFERENCE OF AGRICULTURAL ECONOMISTS (19th : 1985 : Málaga)
Agriculture in a turbulent world economy : proceedings of the Nineteenth International Conference of Agricultural Economists held at Málaga, Spain 26 August-4 September 1985 / edited by Allen Maunder and Ulf Renborg [for] International Association of Agricultural Economists, Institute of Agricultural Economics, University of Oxford. — Aldershot : Gower, 1986. — xvi,820p. — *Includes bibliographies and index*

AGRICULTURE AND STATE — Africa

Afrika zwischen Subsistenzökonomie und Imperialismus / Georg Elwert, Roland Felt (hg.) ; [mit Beiträgen von C. Meillassoux...[et al.]]. — Frankfurt/Main : Campus, 1982. — 295p. — *Bibliographies*

AGRICULTURE AND STATE — Africa, Sub-Saharan

HINDERINK, J.
Agricultural commercialization and government policy in Africa / J. Hinderink and J. J. Sterkenburg. — London : KPI, 1987. — xii,328p. — (Monographs from the African Studies Centre, Leiden). — *Bibliography: p281-307*

INTERNATIONAL BANK FOR RECONSTRUCTION AND DEVELOPMENT
Financing adjustment with growth in sub-Saharan Africa, 1986-90. — Washington, D.C. : World Bank, c1986. — p. cm. — *Bibliography: p*

AGRICULTURE AND STATE — Africa, Sub-Saharan — Congresses

Accelerating food production in Sub-Saharan Africa / edited by John W. Mellor, Christopher L. Delgado, Malcolm J. Blackie. — Baltimore : Published for the International Food Policy Research Institute [by] Johns Hopkins University Press, c1987. — xix, 417 p. . — *Papers and commentaries from a conference sponsored by the Dept. of Land Management of the University of Zimbabwe and the International Food Policy Research Institute, held at Victoria Falls, Zimbabwe in Aug. 1983. — Includes index. — Bibliography: p. 377-396*

AGRICULTURE AND STATE — Argentina

FIGUEIRAS, Horacio
Bases de discusión para una política rural / Horacio Figueiras, Daniel Adrogue, Raúl Druetta. — Buenos Aires : Editorial Hernandiana : Fundación Alimentaria Argentina, c1985. — 175p. — (Serie política / Fundación Alimentaria Argentina)

LATTUADA, Mario J.
La política agraria peronista (1943-1983) / Mario J. Lattuada. — Buenos Aires : Centro Editor de América Latina. — (Biblioteca Politica Argentina ; 132)
t.1. — 1986. — 142p

AGRICULTURE AND STATE — Argentina — History

La Argentina que no fue / Juan José Llach (Selección e introducción. — Buenos Aires : Ediciones del IDES. — (Ediciones del IDES ; 1)
t.i: Las fragilidades de la Argentina agroexportadora (1918-1930). — 1985. — 166p. — *"[una] selección de trabajos aparecidos en la 'Revista de Economía Argentina' (1918-1952)"*

MASCALI, Humberto
Desocupación y conflictos laborales en el campo argentino (1940-1965) / Humberto Mascali. — Buenos Aires : Centro Editor de América Latina, 1986. — 127p. — (Biblioteca Política Argentina ; 139). — *Bibliography: p121-127*

AGRICULTURE AND STATE — Asia — Congresses

Research-extension-farmer : a two-way continuum for agricultural development / edited by Michael M. Cernea, John K. Coulter, John F. A. Russell. — Washington, D.C. : The World Bank, 1985. — xvi,171p. — *Cover: "A World Bank and UNDP Symposium". — Includes bibliographical references*

AGRICULTURE AND STATE — Canada

FORBES, James D.
Institutions and influence groups in Canadian farm and food policy / J. D. Forbes. — Toronto : Institute of Public Administration of Canada, 1985. — 131p. — (Monographs on Canadian public administration ; no.10). — *Includes bibliographical references*

GIANGRANDE, Carole
Down to earth : the crisis in Canadian farming / Carole Giangrande. — Toronto : Anansi, 1986. — 196p

SKOGSTAD, Grace
The politics of Agricultural policy-making in Canada / Grace Skogstad. — Toronto : University of Toronto Press, 1987. — ix,229p

AGRICULTURE AND STATE — China — Hunan Province — History

PERDUE, Peter C.
Exhausting the earth : state and peasant in Hunan, 1500-1850 / Peter C. Perdue. — Cambridge, Mass. : Council on East Asian Studies, Harvard University : Distributed by Harvard University Press, 1987. — p. cm. — (Harvard East Asian monographs ; 1987). — *Includes index. — Bibliography: p*

AGRICULTURE AND STATE — Colombia — Addresses, essays, lectures

THOMAS, Vinod
Linking macroeconomic and agricultural policies for adjustment with growth : the Colombian experience / Vinod Thomas with contributions from Sebastian Edwards ... [et al.]. — Baltimore : Published for the World Bank [by] the Johns Hopkins University Press, c1985. — p. cm. — *"A World Bank publication.". — Includes index*

AGRICULTURE AND STATE — Developing countries

Food policy : integrating supply, distribution, and consumption / edited by J. Price Gittinger, Joanne Leslie, Caroline Hoisington. — Baltimore : Johns Hopkins University Press for the World Bank, 1987. — xiv,567p. — (EDI series in economic development). — *Bibliography: p509-555*

Food, the state, and international political economy : developing country dilemmas / F. LaMond Tullis and W. Ladd Hollist, editors. — Lincoln : University of Nebraska Press, c1985. — p. cm. — *Bibliography: p*

AGRICULTURE AND STATE — Egypt

COMMANDER, Simon
The state & agricultural development in Egypt since 1973 / Simon Commander. — London : Published for the Overseas Development Institute by Ithaca, 1987. — xii,319p. — (Middle East science policy studies ; no.11). — *Bibliography: p302-319*

AGRICULTURE AND STATE — Ethiopia

MARIAM, Mesfin Wolde
Rural vulnerability to famine in Ethiopia, 1958-1977 / Mesfin Wolde Mariam. — London : Intermediate Technology Publications, 1986. — xii,191p

AGRICULTURE AND STATE — Europe, Eastern

DEUTSCH, Robert
The food revolution in the Soviet Union and Eastern Europe / Robert Deutsch. — Boulder, Colo. ; London : Westview Press, 1986. — xxi, 256p. — (Westview special studies on the Soviet Union and Eastern Europe). — *Includes index. — Bibliography: p.149-241*

AGRICULTURE AND STATE — European Economic Community countries

Agricultural data and economic analysis : databases, forecasting and policy analysis in the context of public administration / [edited by] A. Dubgaard, B. Grassmugg, K. J. Munk. — [Maastricht ; Copenhagen] : European Institute of Public Administration : Statens Jordbrugsøkonomiske Institut, 1984. — *Report of a seminar organized by the European Institute of Public Administration, Maastricht, and the Statens Jordbrugsøkonomiske Institut, Copenhagen 3-5 May 1984. — Includes bibliographical references*

ECONOMIC AND SOCIAL COMMITTEE OF THE EUROPEAN COMMUNITIES
Agricultural structural policy : opinion / Economic and Social Committee of the European Communities. — Brussels : General Secretariat of the Economic and Social Committee, 1979. — ii,88p

Pour un role actif de la Communauté Économique Européen e sur la scene agricole internationale : rapport du groupe de travail sur la prospective des échanges mondiaux agricoles / présidé par B. Auberger. — Paris : La Documentation Français, 1986. — 184p. — *Bibliography: p180-184*

STOECKEL, Andy
Intersectoral effects of the CAP : growth, trade and unemployment / Andy Stoeckel. — Canberra : Australian Government Publishing Service, 1985. — vi,58p. — (Occasional paper / Bureau of Agricultural Economics ; no.95). — *Bibliographical references: p56-58*

AGRICULTURE AND STATE — European Economic Community countries — Sources — Bibliography

PRICE, Wendy
Common Agricultural Policy : a guide to sources / prepared by Wendy Richard. — [s.l.] : Association of EDC Librarians, [1985?]. — [7p]. — (European Communities information ; no.10)

AGRICULTURE AND STATE — France

CHAVAGNE, Yves
Lågriculture industrielle en crise / Yves Chavagne. — [Paris : Syros, c1984]. — 125p. — (Alternatives économiques)

NAYLOR, Eric L.
Socio-structural policy in French agriculture / Eric L. Naylor. — Aberdeen : Department of Geography, University of Aberdeen, 1985. — ix,179p. — (O'Dell memorial monograph ; no.18). — *Bibliography: p168-174*

AGRICULTURE AND STATE — France
continuation

SMITH, Malcolm
Agriculture and nature conservation in conflict : the less favoured areas of France and the UK / by Malcolm Smith. — Langholm : The Arkleton Trust, 1985. — viii,110p. —
Bibliography: p105-106

AGRICULTURE AND STATE — Germany — History — 20th century

MOELLER, Robert G
German peasants and agrarian politics, 1914-1924 : the Rhineland and Westphalia / Robert G. Moeller. — Chapel Hill ; London : University of North Carolina Press, c1986. — xv, 286p. — *Includes index.* — *Bibliography: p 241-279*

AGRICULTURE AND STATE — Ghana

KONINGS, Piet
The State and rural class formation in Ghana : a comparative analysis / Piet Konings. — London : KPI, 1986. — xvi,391p. —
Bibliography: p356-377

AGRICULTURE AND STATE — Great Britain

Agriculture : people and policies / edited by Graham Cox, Philip Lowe and Michael Winter. — London : Allen & Unwin, 1986. — 238p. — *Conference proceedings.* — *Includes bibliographies and index*

GREAT BRITAIN. Ministry of Agriculture, Fisheries and Food
Farming UK. — London H.M.S.O., 1987. — 39p. — *One of five publications in folder entitled Farming and rural enterprise*

SMITH, Malcolm
Agriculture and nature conservation in conflict : the less favoured areas of France and the UK / by Malcolm Smith. — Langholm : The Arkleton Trust, 1985. — viii,110p. —
Bibliography: p105-106

AGRICULTURE AND STATE — Honduras

Honduras confronts its future : contending perspectives on critical issues / edited by Mark B. Rosenberg and Philip L. Shepherd. — Boulder, Colo. : L. Rienner Publishers, 1986. — xii, 268p. — *Essays first presented at "Honduras: An International Dialogue", in Miami, Fla., December 1984.* — *Includes bibliographical references and index*

AGRICULTURE AND STATE — Hungary

MATOLCSY, Mátyás
Agrárpolitikai feladatok Magyarországon / írta Matolcsy Mátyás ; [elöszóval ellátta Szekfü Gyula]. — [Budapest] : Soli Deo Gloria Szövetség, [c1934]. — 151p

AGRICULTURE AND STATE — India

HAQUE, T
Agrarian reforms and institutional changes in India / T. Haque, A.S. Sirohi. — New Delhi : Concept Pub. Co., 1986, c1985. — xvi, 268 p.. — *Includes index.* — *Bibliography: p. [249]-262*

AGRICULTURE AND STATE — India — Haryana

WESTLEY, John Richard
Agriculture and equitable growth : the case of Punjab-Haryana / John R. Westley. — Boulder : Westview Press, 1986. — p. cm. — (Westview special studies in agriculture science and policy). — *Includes index.* —
Bibliography: p

AGRICULTURE AND STATE — India — Punjab

CHADHA, G. K
The state and rural transformation : the case of Punjab, 1950-85 / G.K. Chadha. — New Delhi ; Beverly Hills : Sage Publications, 1986. — p. cm. — *Includes index.* — *Bibliography: p*

WESTLEY, John Richard
Agriculture and equitable growth : the case of Punjab-Haryana / John R. Westley. — Boulder : Westview Press, 1986. — p. cm. — (Westview special studies in agriculture science and policy). — *Includes index.* —
Bibliography: p

AGRICULTURE AND STATE — Jordan

Agricultural policy in Jordan / edited by Alison Burrell. — London : Published for the Abdul Hameed Shoman Foundation by Ithaca, 1986. — [160]p. — (Middle East science policy studies ; no.7) (Abdul Hameed Shoman Foundation series on Arab agriculture ; no.7)

AGRICULTURE AND STATE — Kazakh S.S.R.

KOVAL'SKII, S. L.
Osvoenie tselinnykh zemel' v Kazakhstane : (istoriko-partiinyi aspekt) / S. L. Koval'skii, Kh. M. Madanov. — Alma-Ata : "Nauka" Kazakhskoi SSR, 1986. — 223p. —
Bibliography: p214-[222]

AGRICULTURE AND STATE — Lithuania

LOIKO, I. I.
Za podėm i intensifikatsiiu sel'skogo khoziaistva : (opyt rukovodstva Kompartii Litvy otrasl'iu v 1952-1970 gg.) / I. Loiko. — Vil'nius : Mintis, 1986. — 214p

AGRICULTURE AND STATE — Mexico

DE ROUFFIGNAC, Ann Elizabeth Lucas
The contemporary peasantry in Mexico : a class analysis / by Ann Elizabeth Lucas de Rouffignac. — New York : Praeger, 1985. — xix, 203p. — *Includes index.* — *Bibliography: p[186]-196*

Food policy in Mexico : the search for self-sufficiency / edited by James E. Austin and Gustavo Esteva. — Ithaca, N.Y. : Cornell University Press, 1987. — p. cm. — *Includes index*

AGRICULTURE AND STATE — Mongolia (Mongolian People's Republic)

ULYMZHIEV, D. B.
Put' mongol'skogo aratstva k sotsializmu / D. B. Ulymzhiev ; otv. redaktory I. I. Kuznetsov, Sh. B. Chimitdorzhiev. — Novosibirsk : Nauka, Sibirskoe otdelenie, 1987. — 283p

AGRICULTURE AND STATE — Near East

Food, states, and peasants : analyses of the agrarian question in the Middle East / edited by Alan Richards. — Boulder : Westview Press, 1986. — p. cm. — (Westview special studies on the Middle East). — *Includes index*

AGRICULTURE AND STATE — Nigeria

OYEJIDE, T. Ademola
The effects of trade and exchange rate policies on agriculture in Nigeria / T. Ademola Oyejide. — Washington, D.C. : International Food Policy Research Institute, 1986. — p. cm. — (Research report ; 55). — *Bibliography: p*

State, oil, and agriculture in Nigeria / Michael Watts, editor. — Berkeley : Institute of International Studies, University of California, c1987. — xiv, 327 p.. — (Research series ; no. 66). — *Includes index.* — *Bibliography: p. 297-317*

AGRICULTURE AND STATE — Organisation for Economic Co-operation and Development countries

National policies and agricultural trade. — Paris : OECD, 1987. — 333p. — *Includes bibliographical references*

AGRICULTURE AND STATE — Pakistan

NABI, Ijaz
The agrarian economy of Pakistan : issues and policies / Ijaz Nabi, Navid Hamid, Shahid Zahid. — Karachi ; Oxford : Oxford University Press, 1986. — 337p. —
Bibliography: p319-324

PAKISTAN. Agricultural Enquiry Committee
Report of the Agricultural Enquiry Committee. — [Islamabad] : Ministry of Food and Agriculture, 1975. — [iii],62p

Pakistan : reforms and development. — [Islamabad : Department of Films and Publications, Ministry of Information and Broadcasting, 1974?]. — 45p

AGRICULTURE AND STATE — Panama

Panama : structural change and growth prospects. — Washington, D.C., U.S.A. : World Bank, 1985. — xxv,307p. — (A World Bank country study). — "Report no. 5236-PAN.". — "February 28, 1985."

AGRICULTURE AND STATE — Portugal

Portuguese agriculture in transition / by Scott R. Pearson ... [et al.]. — Ithaca, N.Y. : Cornell University Press, 1987. — p. cm. — *Includes index*

AGRICULTURE AND STATE — Puerto Rico

IRIZARRY, Guillermo
The operations and relationships of the agricultural services in Puerto Rico : final report / Guillermo Irizarry. — San Juan : Bureau of the Budget, 1961. — xvi,199p. —
With separate map in end pocket

AGRICULTURE AND STATE — Russsian S.F.S.R. — Ural Mountains region

Sovkhozy Urala v period sotsializma (1938-1985 gg.) : sbornik nauchnykh trudov / [otv. redaktor R. P. Tolmacheva]. — Sverdlovsk : AN SSR, Ural'skii nauchnyi tsentr, 1986. — 77p

AGRICULTURE AND STATE — Soviet Union

DEUTSCH, Robert
The food revolution in the Soviet Union and Eastern Europe / Robert Deutsch. — Boulder, Colo. ; London : Westview Press, 1986. — xxi, 256p. — (Westview special studies on the Soviet Union and Eastern Europe). — *Includes index.* — *Bibliography: p.149-241*

LITVIN, Valentin
The Soviet agro-industrial complex : structure and performance / Valentin Litvin. — Boulder, Colo. : Westview Press, 1987. — p. cm. — (Delphic monograph series). — *Includes index.* — *Bibliography: p*

AGRICULTURE AND STATE — Soviet Union — History

SIMONOVA, M. S.
Krizis agrarnoi politiki tsarizma nakanune pervoi rossiiskoi revoliutsii / M. S. Simonova ; otv. redaktor A. M. Anfimov. — Moskva : Nauka, 1987. — 252p

AGRICULTURE AND STATE — Spain

BIGLINO CAMPOS, Paloma
El socialismo español y la cuestion agraria (1890-1936) / Paloma Biglino Campos. — Madrid : Centro de Publicaciones, Ministerio de Trabajo y Seguridad Social, 1986. — 564p. — *Bibliography: p543-564*

España en Europa : aspectos agrícolas de la integración en la CEE / [Danial de Busturia...et al.]. — [Madrid : Audiovisual y Prensa, 1982]. — 116p

AGRICULTURE AND STATE — Spain — Andalucia

Andalucia y la Comunidad Europea : aspectos relevantes / trabajo dirigido por Rafael Illescas Ortiz. — Sevilla : Instituto de Desarrollo Regional, 1981. — xxxix,903p. — ([Publicaciones] / Universidad de Sevilla, Instituto de Desarrollo Regional ; No.21). — *Bibliographies*

LORING MIRÓ, Jaime
Los sectores agrarios de Andalucia ante la integración en la C.E.E. / Jaime Loring Miró, Luis Godoy López, Jose J. Romero Rodríguez. — Madrid : [Mundi-Prensa Libros], 1984. — 303p. — *At head of title: Banco de Crédito Agricola*

AGRICULTURE AND STATE — Tanzania
The agricultural policy of Tanzania 1983. — Dar es Salaam : Ministry of Agriculture, 1983. — 35p

The Tanzania national agricultural policy. — Dar es Salaam : Ministry of Agriculture, 1982. — 241p

AGRICULTURE AND STATE — United States
GALSTON, William A.
A tough row to hoe : the 1985 Farm Bill and beyond / by William A. Galston. — [Lanham, MD] : Hamilton Press ; Washington, D.C. : Roosevelt Center for American Policy Studies, c1985. — p. cm

JOHNSON, D. Gale
Agricultural policy and trade : adjusting domestic programs in an international framework : a task force report to the Trilateral Commission / authors, D. Gale Johnson, Kenzo Hemmi, Pierre Lardinois ; special consultants, T.K. Warley, P.A.J. Wijnmaalen. — New York : New York University Press, 1985. — xi, 132 p.. — (The Triangle papers ; 29). — *Includes bibliographies*

AGRICULTURE AND STATE — United States — History
POPPENDIECK, Janet
Breadlines knee deep in wheat : food assistance in the Great Depression / Janet Poppendieck. — New Brunswick, N.J. : Rutgers University Press, c1986. — xvii, 306p. — *Includes index.* — *Bibliography: p.[257]-259*

AGRICULTURE AND STATE — Uzbek S.S.R.
MINBAEV, B.
Osushchestvlenie agrarnoi politiki KPSS v Uzbekistane / B. Minbaev. — Tashkent : Uzbekistan, 1985. — 140p

AGRICULTURE AND STATE — Zaire
Plan de relance agricole 1982-1984. — [Kinshasa : Département de l'Agriculture et du Développement Rural], 1982. — 199p

AGRICULTURE, COOPERATIVE
Cooperation in world agriculture : experiences, problems and perspectives / edited by Theodor Bergmann and Takekazu B. Ogura. — Tokyo : Food and Agriculture Policy Research Centre, 1985. — vii,367p. — *Bibliography: p346-348*

AGRICULTURE, COOPERATIVE — Byelorussian S.S.R.
KOSTIUK, M. P.
Trudovoi vklad krest'ianstva v pobedu i uprochenic sotsializma : na materialakh BSSR / M. P. Kostiuk ; nauchnyi redaktor I. M. Ignatenko. — Minsk : Nauka i tekhnika, 1986. — 236p

AGRICULTURE, COOPERATIVE — Developing countries — Finance
TURTIAINEN, Turto
Investment and finance in agricultural service cooperatives / Turto Turtiainen and J. D. Von Pischke. — Washington, D. C. : The World Bank, 1986. — x,173p. — (World Bank technical paper ; no.50). — *Bibliography: p120-122*

AGRICULTURE, COOPERATIVE — European Economic Community countries
The cooperative, mutual and non-profit sector and its organizations in the European Community. — Luxembourg : Office for Official Publications of the European Communities, 1986. — xxvii,900p. — *At head of title: Economic and Social Consultative Assembly*

AGRICULTURE, COOPERATIVE — Mongolia (Mongolian People's Republic)
ULYMZHIEV, D. B.
Put' mongol'skogo aratstva k sotsializmu / D. B. Ulymzhiev ; otv. redaktory I. I. Kuznetsov, Sh. B. Chimitdorzhiev. — Novosibirsk : Nauka, Sibirskoe otdelenie, 1987. — 283p

AGRICULTURE, COOPERATIVE — Soviet Union — History
Istoriia sovetskogo krest'ianstva / redkollegiia: V. P. Sherstobitov...[et al.]. — Moskva : Nauka. — (Istoriia krest'ianstva SSSR) 2: Sovetskoe krest'ianstvo v period sotsialisticheskoi rekonstruktsii narodnogo khoziaistva. Konets 1927-1937 / redkollegiia: I. E. Zelenin...[et al.]. — 1986. — 448p

AGRICULTURE, PREHISTORIC — Congresses
Irrigation's impact on society / collaborating authors, Robert McC. Adams ... [et al.] ; editors, Theodore E. Downing and McGuire Gibson. — Tucson : University of Arizona Press, 1974. — xi, 181 p.. — (Anthropological papers of the University of Arizona ; no. 25). — *Papers from a symposium presented at the 1972 meeting of the Southwestern Anthropological Association, Long Beach, Calif.* — *Includes bibliographies and index*

AGRICULTUREAL DEVELOPMENT PROJECTS — Developing countries — Evaluation
WORLD BANK. Operations Evaluation Department
Agricultural research and extension : an evaluation of the World Bank's experience. — Washington, D.C., U.S.A. : World Bank, 1985. — p. cm

AGRICULTUREOFF. PUBNS. — Employment — European Economic Community countries 986
Employment in agriculture : study. — Brussels : Economic and Social Committee, 1978. — ii,135p

AGUARUNA INDIANS — Ethnobotany
BROWN, Michael
Tsewa's gift : magic and meaning in an Amazonian society / Michael F. Brown. — Washington, D.C. : Smithsonian Institution Press, 1985. — p. cm. — (Smithsonian series in ethnographic inquiry). — *Includes index.* — *Bibliography: p*

AGUARUNA INDIANS — Magic
BROWN, Michael
Tsewa's gift : magic and meaning in an Amazonian society / Michael F. Brown. — Washington, D.C. : Smithsonian Institution Press, 1985. — p. cm. — (Smithsonian series in ethnographic inquiry). — *Includes index.* — *Bibliography: p*

AGUARUNA INDIANS — Religion and mythology
BROWN, Michael
Tsewa's gift : magic and meaning in an Amazonian society / Michael F. Brown. — Washington, D.C. : Smithsonian Institution Press, 1985. — p. cm. — (Smithsonian series in ethnographic inquiry). — *Includes index.* — *Bibliography: p*

AIDS (DISEASE) — Congresses
Mobilizing against AIDS : the unfinished story of a virus / Institute of Medicine, National Academy of Sciences ; Eve K. Nichols, writer. — Cambridge, Mass. : Harvard University Press, 1986. — x, 212 p.. — *Drawn from the 1985 Annual Meeting of the Institute of Medicine.* — *Includes index.* — *Bibliography: p. 189-190*

AIDS (DISEASE) — Political aspects — Great Britain
FITZPATRICK, Michael
The truth about the Aids panic / Michael Fitzpatrick, Don Milligan. — London : Junius, 1987. — 66p. — *Bibliography: p65-66*

AIDS (DISEASE) — Political aspects — United States
PATTON, Cindy
Sex & germs : the politics of AIDS / Cindy Patton. — 1st ed. — Boston : South End Press, c1985. — 182 p.. — *Includes index.* — *Bibliography: p. 175-178*

AIDS (DISEASE) — Psychological aspects
BAUMGARTNER, Gail Henderson
AIDS, psychosocial factors in the acquired immune deficiency syndrome / by Gail Henderson Baumgartner. — Springfield, Ill., U.S.A. : Thomas, c1986. — 113p. — *Includes index.* — *Bibliography: p.85-101*

AIDS (DISEASE) — Psychological aspects — Congresses
What to do about AIDS : physicians and mental health professionals discuss the issues / edited by Leon McKusick. — Berkeley : University of California Press, c1987. — p. cm. — *Papers from a conference convened in San Francisco Sept. 13-14, 1985, by the AIDS Clinical Research Center at the University of California, San Francisco.* — *Includes index*

AIDS (DISEASE) — See Acquired immune deficiency syndrome

AIDS (DISEASE) — Social aspects
BAUMGARTNER, Gail Henderson
AIDS, psychosocial factors in the acquired immune deficiency syndrome / by Gail Henderson Baumgartner. — Springfield, Ill., U.S.A. : Thomas, c1986. — 113p. — *Includes index.* — *Bibliography: p.85-101*

AIDS (DISEASE) — Social aspects — United States
PATTON, Cindy
Sex & germs : the politics of AIDS / Cindy Patton. — 1st ed. — Boston : South End Press, c1985. — 182 p.. — *Includes index.* — *Bibliography: p. 175-178*

AIDS (DISEASE) — Transmission
ROBERTSON, Roy
Heroin, AIDS and society / Roy Robertson. — London : Hodder and Stoughton, 1987. — 133p. — *Bibliography: p124-128.* — *Includes index*

AIDS (DISEASE — Developing countries
AIDS and the third world. — Rev. ed. — [London : Panos Institute, 1987]. — 83p. — (Panos dossier ; 1). — *Cover title*

AIDS (DISEASE) — Europe
Guidelines on AIDS in Europe. — 1st rev. ed. — Copenhagen : World Health Organization, 1986. — iii,42p. — *Includes bibliographical references*

AIDS (DISEASE) — Great Britain — Prevention
GREAT BRITAIN. Department of Health and Social Security
AIDS : monitoring response to the public education campaign February 1986-February 1987 : report on four surveys during the first year of advertising. — London : H.M.S.O., 1987. — 141p. — *Research programme designed and executed by British Market Research Bureau Ltd..* — *Four microfiches in end pocket*

AIR — Pollution
Air-borne sulphur pollution : effects and control : report prepared within the framework of the Convention on Long-range Transboundary Air Pollution. — New York : United Nations, 1984. — xiii,265p. — (Air pollution studies ; no.1). — *Sales no: E.84.II.E.8*

Air pollution / issued by the Department of Trade and Industry. — London : Department of Trade and Industry
Part 4: Australia, China, Colombia, Egypt, India, Mexico and Saudi Arabia. — 1984. — 80p. — (Technology and the environment ; no.12, 1982. Reports from overseas posts). — *Includes bibliographical references*

ELSOM, Derek M.
Atmospheric pollution : causes, effects and control policies / Derek Elsom. — Oxford : Basil Blackwell, 1987. — x,319p. — *Bibliography: p284-311.* — *Includes index*

AIR — Pollution
continuation

NATIONAL SOCIETY FOR CLEAN AIR
NSCA reference book / compiled and edited by Jane Dunmore; assistant editor Penny Gilbert. — 2nd rev. ed. — Brighton : National Society for Clean Air, 1987. — viii,303p

AIR — Pollution — Government policy — Europe

BRACKLEY, Peter
Acid deposition and vehicle emissions : European environmental pressures on Britain / Peter Brackley. — Aldershot : Gower, c1987. — xii,124p. — (Energy papers ; no.22). — *Text on inside covers*

AIR — Pollution — Law and legislation

Transboundary air pollution : international legal aspects of the co-operation of states / editors, K. Flinterman, B. Kwiatkowska, and J. Lammers. — Dordrecht ; Boston : M. Nijhoff, 1987. — p. cm. — *Includes bibliographies and index*

VAN LIER, Irene H.
Acid rain and international law / by Irene H. van Lier. — Toronto : Bunsel Environmental Consultants, [1981?]. — xxii,278p. — *Originally presented as the author's thesis (LL.M.) - Dalhousie University 1980.* — *Bibliography: p.257-266*

AIR — Pollution — Law and legislation — Great Britain

NATIONAL SOCIETY FOR CLEAN AIR. Workshop (1984 : Oxford)
Regulating the impact of air pollution / [contributions by M. T. Westaway...et al.]. — Brighton : The Society, 1984. — Various pagings. — *Papers of a workshop held at Lincoln College, Oxford, 28 and 29 March 1984*

AIR — Pollution — Physiological effect

BELLINI, James
High tech holocaust / James Bellini. — Newton Abbot : David & Charles, c1986. — 255p

AIR — Pollution — England — London — History

BRIMBLECOMBE, Peter
The big smoke : a history of air pollution in London since medieval times / Peter Brimblecombe. — London : Methuen, 1987. — xii,185p. — *Bibliography: p179.* — *Includes index*

AIR — Pollution — England — London — Statistics

GREATER LONDON COUNCIL. Air Pollution Group
Air pollution statistics for Greater London : nitrogen dioxide and nitric oxide at 12 sites (1980-1984). — [London] : the Council, 1985. — 752p. — (Statistical series / Greater London Council ; no.42)

AIR — Pollution — France

Air pollution / issued by the Department of Industry. — London : Department of Industry Part 1: France, Germany and Italy. — 1982. — 54p. — (Technology and the environment ; no.12, 1982. Reports from overseas posts). — *Includes bibliographies*

AIR — Pollution — Germany (West)

Air pollution / issued by the Department of Industry. — London : Department of Industry Part 1: France, Germany and Italy. — 1982. — 54p. — (Technology and the environment ; no.12, 1982. Reports from overseas posts). — *Includes bibliographies*

AIR — Pollution — Great Britain

Study of coal / evidence by the HSE to the Commission on Energy and the Environment concerning public health and amenity in the external environment. — London : H.M.S.O., 1980. — iii,43p. — (HSE report). — *At head of title: Health & Safety Commission*

AIR — Pollution — Italy

Air pollution / issued by the Department of Industry. — London : Department of Industry Part 1: France, Germany and Italy. — 1982. — 54p. — (Technology and the environment ; no.12, 1982. Reports from overseas posts). — *Includes bibliographies*

AIR — Pollution — Japan

Air pollution / issued by the Department of Trade and Industry. — London : Department of Trade and Industry Part 3: Japan, USA and USSR. — 1983. — 56p. — (Technology and the environment ; no.12, 1982. Reports from overseas posts). — *Includes bibliographical references*

AIR — Pollution — Organisation for Economic Co-operation and Development countries

LÜBKERT, Barbara
Control of toxic substances in the atmosphere : Benzene / by Barbara Lübkert, Willfried Dulson and Luellen Olsen. — [Paris] : OECD, 1986. — 105p. — (OECD environment monographs ; no.5). — *Bibliography: p96-105*

AIR — Pollution — Scandinavia

Air pollution / issued by the Department of Industry. — London : Department of Industry Part 2: Denmark, Finland, Norway and Sweden. — 1982. — 44p. — (Technology and the environment ; no.12, 1982. Reports from overseas posts). — *Includes bibliographical references*

AIR — Pollution — Soviet Union

Air pollution / issued by the Department of Trade and Industry. — London : Department of Trade and Industry Part 3: Japan, USA and USSR. — 1983. — 56p. — (Technology and the environment ; no.12, 1982. Reports from overseas posts). — *Includes bibliographical references*

AIR — Pollution — United States

Air pollution / issued by the Department of Trade and Industry. — London : Department of Trade and Industry Part 3: Japan, USA and USSR. — 1983. — 56p. — (Technology and the environment ; no.12, 1982. Reports from overseas posts). — *Includes bibliographical references*

AIR — Pollution

VALROFF, Jean
Pollution atmosphérique et pluies acides : rapport au premier ministre / Jean Valroff, Philippe Le Lourd, Philippe Derexel. — Paris : La Documentation Française, 1985. — 340p. — (Collection des rapports officiels). — *Bibliography: p315-322*

AIR LINES — Government policy — Canada

GILLEN, David W
Canadian airline deregulation and privatization : assessing effects and prospects / by David W. Gillen, Tae H. Oum, Michael W. Tretheway. — Vancouver, Canada : Centre for Transportation Studies, University of British Columbia, c1985. — vi, 300 p.. — *Bibliography: p. 297-300*

AIR LINES — Government policy — Canada — History

STEVENSON, Garth
The politics of Canada's airlines : from Diefenbaker to Mulroney / Garth Stevenson. — Toronto : University of Toronto Press, 1987. — xviii,236p. — (The state and economic life ; 9). — *Includes bibliographical references*

AIR LINES — Management

SAWERS, David
Competition in the air : what Europe can learn from the USA / David Sawers. — London : Institute of Economic Affairs, 1987. — 83p. — (Research monographs / Institute of Economic Affairs ; 41). — *Bibliography: p.80-81*

AIR LINES — Canada — History

NEWBY, Jill
The sky's the limit : the story of the Canadian Air Line Flight Attendants' Association / by Jill Newby. — Vancouver : The Association, 1986. — 113p

AIR LINES — Great Britain — Finance — Statistics

Airline financial statistics. — London : HMSO, 1968-1971. — (Business monitor. CA ; 8). — *Annual.* — *Continued by: Financial resources of UK airlines 1968-1974; and, CAA annual statistics*

AIR LINES — Great Britain — Statistics

Airline operations. — London : HMSO, 1968-1972. — (Business monitor. CA ; 4). — *Monthly.* — *Continued by: CAA monthly statistics; and, CAA annual statistics.* — *Includes annual summary*

Airline operations (quarterly). — London : HMSO, 1968-1972. — (Business monitor. CA ; 5). — *1968 title: Airlines (quarterly).* — *Continued by: CAA monthly statistics; and, CAA annual statistics.* — *Includes annual summary*

Airport activity. — London : HMSO, 1968-1972. — (Business monitor. CA ; 1). — *Monthly.* — *Continued by: CAA monthly statistics; and, CAA annual statistics.* — *Includes annual summary*

AIR LINES — Ireland — History

SHARE, Bernard
The flight of the Iolar : the Aer Lingus experience 1936-1986 / Bernard Share. — Dublin : Gill and Macmillan, 1986. — xii,306p

AIR MAIL SERVICE — Great Britain — Statistics

Air freight and mail. — London : HMSO, 1968-1972. — (Business monitor. CA ; 3). — *Monthly.* — *Continued by: CAA monthly statistics; and, CAA annual statistics.* — *Includes annual summary*

AIR POWER

BROWN, Neville
The future of air power / Neville Brown. — London : Croom Helm, c1986. — [304]p

COOPER, Malcolm, 19---
The birth of independent air power : British policy in the First World War / Malcolm Cooper. — London : Allen & Unwin, 1986. — xix,169p,[16]p of plates. — *Bibliography: p158-165.* — *Includes index*

AIR QUALITY — Statistics

Air quality statistics : methods and principles : Finland, Hungary , Sweden. — Helsinki : Tilastokeskus, 1983. — 101p. — (Tutkimuksia / Finland. Tilastokeskus ; no.102). — *Bibliography: p87-89*

AIR QUALITY AND MANAGEMENT — Great Britain

NATIONAL SOCIETY FOR CLEAN AIR. Workshop (1984 : Oxford)
Regulating the impact of air pollution / [contributions by M. T. Westaway...et al.]. — Brighton : The Society, 1984. — Various pagings. — *Papers of a workshop held at Lincoln College, Oxford, 28 and 29 March 1984*

AIR QUALITY MANAGEMENT — International cooperation

Transboundary air pollution : international legal aspects of the co-operation of states / editors, K. Flinterman, B. Kwiatkowska, and J. Lammers. — Dordrecht ; Boston : M. Nijhoff, 1987. — p. cm. — *Includes bibliographies and index*

AIR TRAVEL — Great Britain — Statistics

Air passengers : international and cabotage. — London : HMSO, 1968-1972. — (Business monitor. CA ; 7). — *Quarterly.* — *Continued by: CAA monthly statistics; and, CAA annual statistics.* — *Includes annual summary*

AIR-TURBINES — European Economic Community countries
MUSGROVE, P.
Wind energy evaluation for the European Communities / P. Musgrove. — Luxembourg : Office for the Official Publications of the European Communities, 1984. — vii,136p. — (EUR ; 8996). — *Bibliographical references: p102-107. — Contract no.: XVII/AR/82/255*

AIRCRAFT INDUSTRY — Corrupt practices
PIERCE, Christine
How to solve the Lockheed case / Christine Pierce. — Bowling Green, OH : Social Philosophy and Policy Center ; New Brunswick, USA : Transaction Books, 1986. — 41 p.. — (Original papers / Social Philosophy and Policy Center ; no. 5). — *Bibliography: p. 37-41*

AIRCRAFT INDUSTRY — Technological innovations
The Competitive status of the U.S. civil aviation manufacturing industry : a study of the influences of technology in determining international industrial competitive advantage / prepared by the U.S. Civil Aviation Manufacturing Industry Panel, Committee on Technology and International Economic and Trade Issues of the Office of the Foreign Secretary, National Academy of Engineering and the Commission on Engineering and Technical Systems, National Research Council ; Frederick Seitz, chairman ; Lowell W. Steele, rapporteur. — Washington, DC : National Academy Press, 1985. — xii, 151 p.. — *Includes bibliographies*

AIRCRAFT INDUSTRY — United States
The Competitive status of the U.S. civil aviation manufacturing industry : a study of the influences of technology in determining international industrial competitive advantage / prepared by the U.S. Civil Aviation Manufacturing Industry Panel, Committee on Technology and International Economic and Trade Issues of the Office of the Foreign Secretary, National Academy of Engineering and the Commission on Engineering and Technical Systems, National Research Council ; Frederick Seitz, chairman ; Lowell W. Steele, rapporteur. — Washington, DC : National Academy Press, 1985. — xii, 151 p.. — *Includes bibliographies*

AIRPORTS — Employees — Scotland
BRITISH AIRPORTS AUTHORITY
1976 survey on airport workers: Aberdeen, Edinburgh, Glasgow and Prestwick. — [London] : the Authority, 1976. — 23 leaves

AIRPORTS — Law and legislation — Great Britain
GREAT BRITAIN. Parliament. House of Commons. Library. Research Division
Airports Bill (Bill 60 of 1985/86) / Priscilla Baines. — [London] : the Division, 1986. — 31p. — (Reference sheet ; no.86/4). — *Bibliographical references: p27-31*

AIRPORTS — England — Location
GREAT BRITAIN. Parliament. House of Commons. Library. Research Division
Third London airport / [Christopher Barclay]. — [London] : the Division, 1980. — 10p. — (Reference sheet ; no.80/3). — *Bibliography: p8-10*

AIRPORTS — England — Price policy
NATIONAL ECONOMIC RESEARCH ASSOCIATES
Economic regulation of the British Airports Authority Plc : a report prepared for the Department of Transport / National Economic Research Associates. — [London : Department of Transport], 1986. — 77p. — *Bibliographical references: p77*

AIRPORTS — Great Britain — Statistics
Airport activity. — London : HMSO, 1968-1972. — (Business monitor. CA ; 1). — *Monthly. — Continued by: CAA monthly statistics; and, CAA annual statistics. — Includes annual summary*

AIRPORTS BILL 1985-86
GREAT BRITAIN. Parliament. House of Commons. Library. Research Division
Airports Bill (Bill 60 of 1985/86) / Priscilla Baines. — [London] : the Division, 1986. — 31p. — (Reference sheet ; no.86/4). — *Bibliographical references: p27-31*

AIT ATTA (BERBER TRIBE)
HART, David
The Ait ʿAtta of Southern Morocco : daily life and recent history / by David Hart. — Wisbech : Menas Press, 1984. — xxviii,219p

AKADEMIIA NAUK UKRAINSKOI SSR. Institut ekonomiki
Institut ekonomiki AN USSR : dostizheniia za 50 let 1936-1986 / [otv.redaktor: I. I. Lukinov]. — Kiev : Naukova dumka, 1986. — 237p

AKAN POETRY
NKETIA, J.H.Kwabena
Funeral dirges of the Akan people / J.H.Nketia. — New York : Negro Universities Press, 1969. — v,296p. — *Reprint of 1955 edition. — Bibliography: p295-296*

AL-HIZB AL-SHUYŪʿĪ AL-ʿIRĀQĪ
BATATU, Hanna
The old social classes and the revolutionary movements of Iraq : a study of Iraq's old landed and commercial classes and of its Communists, Baʿthists, and Free Officers / Hanna Batatu. — Princeton, N.J. : Princeton University Press, c1978. — xxiv, 1283 p., [8] leaves of plates. — (Princeton studies on the Near East). — *Includes indexes. Bibliography: p. [1231]-1252*

AL - QADHDHĀFĪ, MUʿAMMAR
BLUNDY, David
Qaddafi and the Libyan revolution / David Blundy and Andrew Lycett. — London : Weidenfeld and Nicolson, 1987

AL-QADHDHAFI, MUʿAMMAR
AYOUB, Mahmoud M.
Islam and the Third Universal Theory : the religious thought of Muʿammar al-Qadhdhafi / Mahmoud M. Ayoub. — London : KPI, 1987. — 155p. — *Bibliography: p148-150*

ALABAMA — Politics and government
MARTIN, David L
Alabama's state and local governments / David L. Martin. — 2nd ed. — University, Ala. : University of Alabama Press, c1985. — xii, 230 p.. — *Includes bibliographies and index*

ALASKA — Economic conditions — Addresses, essays, lectures
Contemporary Alaskan native economies / edited by Steve J. Langdon. — Lanham, MD : University Press of America, c1986. — ix, 183 p.. — *Includes bibliographies. — Contents: Economic growth and development strategies for rural Alaska / Bradford H. Tuck and Lee Huskey -- Subsistence as an economic system in Alaska / Thomas D. Lonner -- Contradictions in Alaskan native economy and society / Steve J. Langdon -- Limited entry policy and impacts on Bristol Bay fishermen / J. Anthony Koslow -- The Cape Romanzoff project / Dean F. Olson -- The Pribilof Island Aleuts / Michael K. Orbach and Beverly Holmes -- The economic efficiency of food production in a western Alaska Eskimo population / Robert J. Wolfe -- Subsistence and the North Slope Inupiat / John A. Kruse -- Subsistence beluga whale hunting in Alaska / Kerry D. Feldman -- Traditional subsistence activities and systems of exchange among the Nelson Island Yupʿik / Ann Fienup-Riordan*

ALASKA — History — To 1867
Russia's American colony / edited by S. Frederick Starr. — Durham : Duke University Press, 1987. — p. cm. — (A Special study of the Kennan Institute for Advanced Russian Studies of the Woodrow Wilson International Center for Scholars). — *Includes index. Bibliography: p*

ALASKA HIGHWAY — History — Congresses
ALASKA HIGHWAY 40TH ANNIVERSARY SYMPOSIUM (1982 : Northern Lights College)
The Alaska Highway : papers of the 40th Anniversary Symposium / edited by Kenneth Coates. — Vancouver : University of British Columbia Press, 1985. — xvi, 208 p., [13] p. of plates. — *Papers presented at the Alaska Highway 40th Anniversary Symposium, held in June 1982 at Northern Lights College, Ft. St. John, B.C. — Includes bibliographies and index*

ALBA, FERNANDO ALVAREZ DE TOLEDO, duque de
MALTBY, William S.
Alba : a biography of Fernando Alvarez de Toledo, third Duke of Alba, 1507-1582 / William S. Maltby. — Berkeley, Calif. ; London : University of California Press, c1983. — xvii, 377p, [8]p of plates. — *Bibliographical notes: p.321-361. — Includes index*

ALBANIA — Economic policy — Congresses
NATIONAL CONFERENCE ON PROBLEMS OF THE DEVELOPMENT OF THE ECONOMY IN THE SEVENTH FIVE-YEAR PLAN (1983 : Tirana)
[Proceedings]. — Tirana : 8 Nentori Publishing House, 1983. — 273p

ALBANIA — Foreign relations
BIBERAJ, Elez
Albania between east and west / Elez Biberaj. — London : Institute for the Study of Conflict, 1986. — 26p. — (Conflict studies ; no.190)

ALBANIA — Foreign relations — 1944-
BIBERAJ, Elez
Albania and China : a study of an unequal alliance / Elez Biberaj. — Boulder : Westview Press, 1986. — xi, 183 p.. — (Westview special studies in international relations). — *Includes index. — Bibliography: p. 167-179*

ALBANIA — Foreign relations — China
BIBERAJ, Elez
Albania and China : a study of an unequal alliance / Elez Biberaj. — Boulder : Westview Press, 1986. — xi, 183 p.. — (Westview special studies in international relations). — *Includes index. — Bibliography: p. 167-179*

ALBANIA — Politics and government
Albania today : political and informative review. — Tirana : [Party of Labour of Albania], 1987-. — *Bimonthly*

ALBANIA — Population
MISJA, Vladimir
Demographic development in the People's Socialist Republic of Albania / Vladimir Misja [and] Ylli Vejsiu. — Tirana : 8 Nentori Publishing House, 1985. — 99p

ALBANIA — Relations — Yugoslavia
VUKOVIʿC, Ilija
Autonomaštvo i separatizam na Kosovu / Ilija Vukoviʿc. — Beograd : Nova Knjiga, 1985. — 238p

ALBANIANS — Yugoslavia
The status of a republic for Kosova is a just demand: article of the newspaper "Zëri i popullit", organ of the CC of the PLA, May 17, 1981. — Tirana : 8 Nentori Publishing House, 1981. — 54p

ALBANY (N.Y.) — Industries — History — 19th century
GREENBERG, Brian
Worker and community : response to industrialization in a nineteenth-century American city, Albany, New York, 1850-1884 / Brian Greenberg. — Albany : State University of New York Press, c1985. — ix, 227 p.. — (SUNY series in American social history). — *Maps on endpapers. — Includes index. — Bibliography: p. 211-220*

ALBERTA — Apropriations and expenditures
Estimates of expenditure / Alberta. Treasury. — Edmonton : Alberta Treasury, 1982/3-. — *Annual*

ALBERTA — Economic conditions — Addresses, essays, lectures
Environment and economy : essays on the human geography of Alberta / edited by B.M. Barr, P.J. Smith. — Edmonton, Alta., Canada : Pica Pica Press, c1984. — xx, 180 p.. — *Includes bibliographies*

ALBERTA — Economic conditions — Statistics
ALBERTA. Bureau of Statistics
Alberta economic accounts. — Edmonton : Alberta. Bureau of Statistics, 1980-. — *Annual*

ALBERTA — Politics and government
WOOD, David G.
The Lougheed legacy / David G. Wood. — Toronto, Ont., Canada : Key Porter Books, c1985. — v, 250 p., [16] p. of plates. — *Includes index*

ALBERTA. Bureau of Statistics
ALBERTA. Bureau of Statistics
Alberta economic accounts. — Edmonton : Alberta. Bureau of Statistics, 1980-. — *Annual*

ALBERTA. Treasury
ALBERTA. Treasury
Government estimates. — Edmonton : [the Treasury], 1983/84-. — *Annual*

ALBERTA AGENCY FOR INTERNATIONAL DEVELOPMENT
ALBERTA AGENCY FOR INTERNATIONAL DEVELOPMENT
Annual review / Alberta Agency for International Development. — Edmonton ; Edmonton : the Agency for International Development, 1985/86-. — *Annual*

ALCHEMY
ELIADE, Mircea
[Forgerons et alchimistes. English]. The forge and the crucible / Mircea Eliade ; translated from the French by Stephen Corrin. — 2d ed. — Chicago : University of Chicago Press, 1978. — 238 p.. — *Subtitle on cover: The origins and structures of alchemy. — Translation of Forgerons et alchimistes. — Includes bibliographical references and index*

ALCOHOL — Physiological effect
DENNEY, Ronald C.
Alcohol and accidents / Ronald C. Denney. — Wilmslow, Cheshire : Sigma Press, 1986. — viii,172p

ALCOHOL DRINKING — dictionaries
SPEARS, Richard A
The slang and jaron of drugs and drink / by Ricard A. Spears. — Metuchen, N.J. : Scarecrow Press, 1986. — xv, 585 p.. — *Bibliography: p. [562]-575*

ALCOHOL FUEL INDUSTRY — Brazil
BARZELAY, Michael
The politicized market economy : alcohol in Brazil's energy strategy / Michael Barzelay. — Berkeley : University of California Press, c1986. — xiv, 289p. — (Studies in international political economy). — *Includes index. — Bibliography: p.267-276*

ALCOHOLICS — Legal status, laws, etc — Australia
CARNEY, Terry
Drug users and the law in Australia : from crime control to welfare / by T. Carney ; with a foreword by Dr. Neal Blewett. — Sydney : Law Book Company, 1987. — lxi,390p. — *Bibliography: pxxxvii-xlvii*

ALCOHOLICS — Rehabilitation — Australia
CARNEY, Terry
Drug users and the law in Australia : from crime control to welfare / by T. Carney ; with a foreword by Dr. Neal Blewett. — Sydney : Law Book Company, 1987. — lxi,390p. — *Bibliography: pxxxvii-xlvii*

ALCOHOLICS — Middle Atlantic States — Case studies
RUDY, David R
Becoming alcoholic : Alcoholics Anonymous and the reality of alcoholism / David R. Rudy. — Carbondale : Southern Illinois University Press, c1986. — xviii, 173 p.. — *Includes indexes. — Bibliography: p. [143]-165*

ALCOHOLICS ANONYMOUS — Case studies
RUDY, David R
Becoming alcoholic : Alcoholics Anonymous and the reality of alcoholism / David R. Rudy. — Carbondale : Southern Illinois University Press, c1986. — xviii, 173 p.. — *Includes indexes. — Bibliography: p. [143]-165*

ALCOHOLISM
The Misuse of alcohol : crucial issues in dependence, treatment & prevention / edited by Nick Heather, Ian Robertson & Phil Davies on behalf of New Directions in the Study of Alcohol Group. — London : Croom Helm, c1985. — 284p. — *Includes bibliographies and index*

ALCOHOLISM — Addresses, essays, lectures
Social thought on alcoholism : a comprehension review / Thomas D. Watts ; with a foreword by Richard L. Rachin. — Original ed. — Malabar, Fla. : R.E. Krieger Pub. Co., 1986. — x, 154 p.. — *Includes bibliographies and index*

ALCOHOLISM — Law and legislation
PORTER, L.
The law and treatment of drug- and alcohol-dependent persons : a comparative study of existing legislation / by L. Porter, A. E. Arif, W. J. Curran. — Geneva : World Health Organization, 1986. — 216p. — *Bibliography: p209-216*

ALCOHOLISM — Study and teaching — England — West Country
Educating about alcohol : professional perspectives and practice in south west England / Robin Means ... [et al.]. — Bristol : University of Bristol, School for Advanced Urban Studies, 1986. — 191p. — (Occasional paper / School for Advanced Urban Studies ; 25)

ALCOHOLISM — Treatment
PORTER, L.
The law and treatment of drug- and alcohol-dependent persons : a comparative study of existing legislation / by L. Porter, A. E. Arif, W. J. Curran. — Geneva : World Health Organization, 1986. — 216p. — *Bibliography: p209-216*

ALCOHOLISM — Denmark
Redegørelse fra situationen vedrørende alkohol- og narkotikamisbruget 1983. — [København] : Alkohol- og Narkotikarådet, 1984. — 27p. — (Alkohol- og Narkotikarådets skriftserie ; 3)

ALCOHOLISM — France — Statistical methods
DAMIANI, Paul
Étude sur l'alcoolisme : données générales et applications de methodes d'analyse statistique / Paul Damiani. — Paris : I.N.S.E.E., 1986. — 129p. — (Archives et documents / Institut national de la statistique et des études économiques ; no.169). — *Includes bibliographical references*

ALCOHOLISM — France — Statistics
DAMIANI, Paul
Étude sur l'alcoolisme : données générales et applications de methodes d'analyse statistique / Paul Damiani. — Paris : I.N.S.E.E., 1986. — 129p. — (Archives et documents / Institut national de la statistique et des études économiques ; no.169). — *Includes bibliographical references*

ALCOHOLISM — Great Britain
CHRISTIAN ECONOMIC AND SOCIAL RESEARCH FOUNDATION
Drink offences : chief constables' reports: England and Wales; and Scotland. — Ilford : Christian Economic and Social Research Foundation, 1985. — [16p]. — *33rd annual report*

ALCOHOLISM — United States — Prevention
Towards the prevention of alcohol problems : government, business and community action : summary of a conference held under the auspices of the Panel on Alternative Policies affecting the Prevention of Alcohol Abuse and Alcoholism [and the] Commission on Behavioral and Social Sciences and Education [of the] National Research Council / Dean R. Gerstein, editor. — Washington : National Academy Press, 1984. — xii,174p. — *Bibliography: p162-169*

ALCOHOLISM AND EMPLOYMENT
SCANLON, Walter F
Alcoholism and drug abuse in the workplace : employee assistance programs / Walter F. Scanlon. — New York : Praeger, 1986. — xiii, 146 p.. — *Includes bibliographies and index*

ALEMÁN, MIGUEL
La clase obrera en la historia de México. — México : Siglo Veintiuno
11: Del avilacamachismo al alemanismo (1940-1952) / Jorge Basurto. — 1984. — 291p

ALGEBRA, ABSTRACT
CROWN, Gary D.
Abstract algebra / Gary D. Crown, Maureen H. Fenrick, Robert J. Valenza. — New York : M. Dekker, c1986. — p. cm. — (Monographs and textbooks in pure and applied mathematics ; 99). — *Includes index. — Bibliography: p*

MCCOY, Neal Henry
Introduction to modern algebra / [by] Neal H. McCoy. — 3d ed. — Boston : Allyn and Bacon, [1975]. — xii, 271 p. — *Bibliography: p. 265-266*

ALGEBRAS, LINEAR
ANTON, Howard
Elementary linear algebra / Howard Anton. — 5th ed. — New York : Wiley, c1987. — xv, 475, 48, 6 p.. — *Includes index*

GROSSMAN, Stanley I
Elementary linear algebra / Stanley I. Grossman. — 2nd ed. — Belmont, Calif. : Wadsworth Pub. Co., c1984. — xv, 426 p.. — *Includes bibliographical references and index*

ALGERIA — Emigration and immigration
ZEHRAOUI, Ahsène
L'Algerie et l'immigration Algerienne en France / Ahsène Zehraoui, Mohamed Mazouz. — [Paris] : Agence de développement des relations interculturelles, 1984. — 48p. — *Includes bibliographical references*

ALGERIA — Foreign relations — France
BEN KHEDDA, Bengoucef
Les accords d'Évian / Bengoucef Ben Khedda. — Alger : Publisud, [1986]. — 119p

LACOUTURE, Jean
Algérie, la guerre est finie / Jean Lacouture avec la collaboration de Catherine Grönblatt. — Bruxelles : Complexe, [1985]. — 207p

ALGERIA — Foreign relations — Soviet Union
SHVEDOV, A. A.
Sovetsko-alzhirskie otnosheniia / A. A. Shvedov, A. B. Podtserob. — Moskva : Progress, 1986. — 260p. — *Bibliography: p247-[261]*

ALGERIA — History — Dictionaries
HEGGOY, Alf Andrew
Historical dictionary of Algeria / Alf Andrew Heggoy with Robert R. Crout. — Metuchen, N.J. : Scarecrow Press, 1981. — x, 237 p.. — (African historical dictionaries ; no. 28). — *Includes index*. — *Bibliography: p. 185-205*

ALGERIA — History — Revolution, 1954-1962
HORNE, Alistair
A savage war of peace : Algeria 1954-1962 / Alistair Horne. — Rev. ed. — London : Papermac, 1987. — 606p,[16]p of plates. — Previous ed.: London : Macmillan, 1977. — *Bibliography: p572-577. — Includes index*

LEVINE, Michel
Les ratonnades d'octobre : un meurtre collectif à Paris en 1961 / Michel Levine. — Paris : Editions Ramsay, 1985. — 309p

ALGERIA — History — 1962-
TLEMCANI, Rachid
State and revolution in Algeria / Rachid Tlemcani. — London : Zed, 1986. — [256]p. — *Includes bibliography and index*

ALGERIA — Population — Statistics
Projections provisoires de la population Algérienne de 1970 à 1985. — Algiers : Secretariat D'Etat Au Plan, Direction Des Statistiques, 1972. — 53p. — (Document de Travail)

ALGERIA — Social conditions
FANON, Frantz
[An v [i.e. cinq] de la Révolution algérienne. English]. Studies in a dying colonialism : with an introd. by Adolfo Gilly / Translated from the French by Haakon Chevalier. — New York : Monthly Review Press, [1965]. — 181 p. — Translation of L'an v [i.e cinq] de la Révolution algérienne

ALGERIA — Statistics
Statistiques industrielle / Office National des Statistiques. — Algers : Office National des Statistiques, 1984-. — *Quarterly*

ALGERIANS — France
ZEHRAOUI, Ahséne
L'Algerie et l'immigration Algerienne en France / Ahsène Zehraoui, Mohamed Mazouz. — [Paris] : Agence de développement des relations interculturelles, 1984. — 48p. — *Includes bibliographical references*

ALGERIANS — France — Congress
GROUPEMENT DE RECHERCHES COORDONNÉES SUR LES MIGRATIONS INTERNATIONALES. Colloque (Grenoble : 1983)
Les algériens en France : genèse et devenir d'une migration / Jacqueline Costa-Lascoux et Emile Temime, coordonnateurs. — Paris : Publisud, [1985]. — 371p

ALGERIANS — France — Paris
LEVINE, Michel
Les ratonnades d'octobre : un meurtre collectif à Paris en 1961 / Michel Levine. — Paris : Editions Ramsay, 1985. — 309p

ALGORITHMS
GONNET, G. H.
Handbook of algorithms and data structures / G.H. Gonnet. — London : Addison-Wesley, c1984. — xi,286p. — (International computer science series). — *Bibliography: p218-253. — Includes index*

MUNDEL, Marvin Everett
Measuring total productivity in manufacturing organizations : algorithms and P-C programs / Marvin E. Mundel. — Tokyo, Japan : Asian Productivity Organization, c1986. — iv[i.e.vi], 155p. — *Includes index*

WETZEL, Gregory F.
The algorithmic process : an introduction to problem solving / Gregory F. Wetzel, William G. Bulgren. — Chicago : Science Research Associates, c1985. — p. cm. — *Includes index*. — *Bibliography: p*

ALICANTE (SPAIN) — Politics and government
GUTIÉRREZ LLORET, Rosa Ana
Republicanos y liberales : la revolución de 1868 y la I.a República en Alicante / Rosa Ana Gutiérrez Lloret. — Alicante : Instituto Juan Gil-Albert, 1985. — 188p. — *Bibliography: p175-185*

ALICANTE (SPAIN: PROVINCE) — Economic conditions
Materiales para la historia economica de Alicante (1850-1900) / introducción y selección de textos Javier Vidal Olivares. — Alicante : Instituto de Estudios Juan Gil-Albert, 1986. — 420p. — (Colección Documental ; 5)

ALIEN LABOR — Government policy — France
EDYE, Dave
Immigrant labour and government policy : the cases of the Federal Republic of Germany and France / Dave Edye. — Aldershot : Gower, c1987. — vi,157p. — *Bibliography: p147-157*

ALIEN LABOR — Government policy — Germany (West)
EDYE, Dave
Immigrant labour and government policy : the cases of the Federal Republic of Germany and France / Dave Edye. — Aldershot : Gower, c1987. — vi,157p. — *Bibliography: p147-157*

ALIEN LABOR — Social aspects — Denmark
DENMARK. Arbejdsgruppe om udenlandske arbejderes sociale og samfundsmaessige tilpasning her i landet
Betaenkning om udenlandske arbejderes sociale og samfundsmaessige tilpasning her i landet / afgivet af en af Socialministeriet nedsat arbejdsgruppe. — [København : Statens Trykningkontor], 1975. — 55p. — (Betaenkning ; nr.761)

ALIEN LABOR — Denmark
Fremmede iblandt os : fremmedarbejderne i Danmark / [Danske Missionsselskab]. — Hellerup : DMS, 1975. — 56p. — (Danske Missionsselskab ; Synspunkt 23). — *Bibliography: p56*

ALIEN LABOR — Europe
"Dritte Welt" in Europa : Probleme der Arbeitsimmigration / Jochen Blaschke/Kurt Greussing (Hg.). — Berlin : Express Edition, 1985. — 126p

ALIEN LABOR — Europe — Congresses
Situation juridique et sociale des travailleurs migrants en Europe : conference internationale / organisée par l'Association Internationale des Juristes Démocrates. — Bruxelles : Association Internationale des Juristes Democrates, 1977. — 224p

ALIEN LABOR — Germany — Government policy
HERBERT, Ulrich
Fremdarbeiter : Politik und Praxis des "Ausländer-Einsatzes" in der Kriegswirtschaft des Dritten Reiches / Ulrich Herbert. — Berlin : J. H. W. Dietz, 1985. — 494p. — *Bibliography: p454-478*

ALIEN LABOR — Germany — History
HERBERT, Ulrich
Fremdarbeiter : Politik und Praxis des "Ausländer-Einsatzes" in der Kriegswirtschaft des Dritten Reiches / Ulrich Herbert. — Berlin : J. H. W. Dietz, 1985. — 494p. — *Bibliography: p454-478*

ALIEN LABOR — Germany — History — 19th century
Population, labour and migration in 19th- and 20th-century Germany / edited by Klaus J. Bade. — Leamington Spa : Berg, 1987. — xii,200p. — (German historical perspectives ; 1). — *Bibliography: p189-196*

ALIEN LABOR — Germany — History — 20th century
Population, labour and migration in 19th- and 20th-century Germany / edited by Klaus J. Bade. — Leamington Spa : Berg, 1987. — xii,200p. — (German historical perspectives ; 1). — *Bibliography: p189-196*

ALIEN LABOR — Germany (West)
Ausländische Arbeitnehmer und Immigranten : sozialwissenschaftliche Beiträge zur Diskussion eines aktuellen Problems / herausgegeben von Marita Rosch ; mit einem Vorwort von Alexander Thomas. — Weinheim : Beltz, 1985. — xiv,279p. — *Bibliography: p277-278*

ALIEN LABOR — Great Britain — History
RAMDIN, Ron
The making of the black working class in Britain / Ron Ramdin. — Aldershot, Gower, c1987. — x,626p. — *Bibliography: p559-605. — Includes index*

ALIEN LABOR CRIMINALS — Netherlands
BRAND-KOOLEN, M. J. M.
Migrants in detention / Maria Brand-Koolen. — The Hague : : Research and Documentation Centre, Ministry of Justice, 1985. — [32]p. — ([Reports, papers, articles] ; 81). — *Bibliography: p27-29*

JUNGER-TAS, J.
Young immigrants in the Netherlands and their contacts with the police / Josine Junger-Tas. — The Hague : Research and Documentation Centre, Ministry of Justice, 1985. — 21p. — ([Reports, papers, articles] ; 85a). — *Bibliography: p21*

ALIEN LABOR, HAITIAN — Dominican Republic
PLANT, Roger
Sugar and modern slavery : a tale of two countries / Roger Plant. — London : Zed, 1987. — [208]p. — *Includes bibliography and index*

ALIEN LABOR, ITALIAN — Bibliography
BRIANI, Vittorio
Italian immigrants abroad : a bibliography on the Italian experience outside Italy in Europe, the Americas, Australia, and Africa = Emigrazione e lavoro italiano all'estero : repertorio bibliografico / by Vittorio Briani ; edited and with a new introd. and supplemental bibliography by Francesco Cordasco. — Detroit : B. Ethridge Books, c1979. — xlix, 229 p.. — Edition of 1967 published under title: Emigrazione e lavoro italiano all'estero. — *Includes indexes*

ALIEN LABOR, MEXICAN — California, Northern
GONZALEZ, Juan L
Mexican and Mexican American farm workers : the California agricultural industry / Juan L. Gonzalez, Jr. — New York : Praeger, c1985. — p. cm. — *Includes index*

ALIEN LABOR, PHILIPPINE
The Labour trade : Filipino migrant workers around the world / Catholic Institute for International Relations. — London : CIIR, 1987. — [200]p

ALIEN LABOR, TURKISH — Germany (West)
WALLRAFF, Günter
Ganz unten / Günter Wallraff. — Köln : Kiepenheuer & Witsch, c1985. — 254 p

ALIEN PROPERTY
SORNARAJAH, M
The pursuit of nationalized property / M. Sornarajah. — Dordrecht ; Boston : M. Nijhoff, 1985. — p. cm. — (Developments in international law). — *Bibliography: p*

ALIENATION (PHILOSOPHY)
DER DERIAN, James
On diplomacy : a genealogy of Western estrangement / James Der Derian. — Oxford : Basil Blackwell, 1987. — 258p. — *Bibliography: p246-253. — Includes index*

ALIENATION (SOCIAL PSYCHOLOGY)
SCHWALBE, Michael L.
The psychosocial consequences of natural and alienated labor / Michael L. Schwalbe. — Albany, N.Y. : State University of New York Press, c1986. — ix, 233 p.. — (SUNY series in the sociology of work). — *Includes index. — Bibliography: p. 215-227*

SILVER, Marc L.
Under construction : work and alienation in the building trades / Marc L. Silver. — Albany : State University of New York Press, c1986. — xi, 251 p.. — (SUNY series in the sociology of work). — *Includes indexes. — Bibliography: p. 229-242*

ALIENATION (SOCIAL PSYCHOLOGY) — France
LAGRÉE, Jean-Charles
La galère : marginalisations juvéniles et collectivités locales / par Jean-Charles Lagrée et Paula Lew-Foi. — Paris : Centre National de la Recherche Scientifique, 1985. — 280p

ALIENS — Legal status, laws, etc.
DAWSON, Frank Griffith
International law, national tribunals, and the rights of aliens / [by] Frank Griffith Dawson and Ivan L. Head. With the collaboration of Peter E. Herzog. — [1st ed.]. — Syracuse, N.Y.] : Syracuse University Press, [1971]. — xvi, 334 p. — (The Procedural aspects of international law series ; 10). — *Includes bibliographical references*

ALIENS — France — Public opinion
SCHOR, Ralph
L'opinion française et les étrangers en France 1919-1939 / par Ralph Schor. — [Paris] : Publications de la Sorbonne, 1985. — xi,761p. — (Publications de la Sorbonne / Série ″France XIXe-XXe siècles″ ; No.22). — *Bibliography: p745-748*

ALIENS — Germany (West)
KOCH-ARZBERGER, Claudia
Die schwierige Integration : die bundesrepublikanische Gesellschaft und ihre 5 Millionen Ausländer / Claudia Koch-Arzberger. — Opladen : Westdeutscher Verlag, 1985. — 211p. — (Beiträge zur sozialwissenschaften Forschung ; Bd.80). — *Bibliography: p197-211*

ALIENS — Great Britain — History
BIRD, J. C
Control of enemy alien civilians in Great Britain, 1914-1918 / J.C. Bird. — New York : Garland Pub., 1986. — 355 p.. — (Outstanding theses from the London School of Economics and Political Science). — *Bibliography: p. 346-355*

ALIENS, ILLEGAL — Nigeria
CHHANGANI, R. C.
Illegal aliens under Nigerian law / R.C. Chhangani. — Jodhpur : Associated Law Publications, 1983. — 91p. — *Includes index*

ALIENS, ILLEGAL — United States
HARWOOD, Edwin
In liberty's shadow : illegal aliens and immigration law enforcement / Edwin Harwood. — Stanford, Calif. : Hoover Institution Press, Stanford University, c1986. — xvi, 224 p.. — (Hoover Press publication ; 331). — *Includes index. — Bibliography: p. [193]-220*

ALIENS, ILLEGAL — United States — Bibliography
CORDASCO, Francesco
The new American immigration : evolving patterns of legal and illegal emigration : a bibliography of selected references / Francesco Cordasco. — New York : Garland, 1987. — xxviii, 418 p.. — (Garland reference library of social science ; vol. 376). — *Includes index*

ALKALI INDUSTRY AND TRADE — Energy conservation
TSEUNG, A. C. C.
Energy conservation in the chlor-alkali industry / A. C. C. Tseung, J. A. Antonian, A. R. Goodson. — Luxembourg : Commission of the European Communities, 1985. — ix,79p. — (EUR ; 10085). — *Series title: Energy. — Bibliographical references: p42-43. — Contract no. EEB/1/111/80/UK (H)*

ALKALI INDUSTRY AND TRADE — Taiwan
Chlorine-Alkali industry in Taiwan, Republic of China. — [Taipei : Ministry of Economic Affairs, 1958]. — [12]p

ALLIANCES
FREY, Eric G
Division and detente : the Germanies and their alliances / Eric G. Frey. — New York : Praeger, 1987. — xvi, 194 p.. — *Includes index. — Bibliography: p. 173-183*

ALLIANCES — Psychological aspects
NELSON, Daniel N.
Alliance behavior in the Warsaw Pact / Daniel N. Nelson. — Boulder : Westview Press, 1986. — xvii, 134 p.. — (Westview special studies on the Soviet Union and Eastern Europe). — *Includes index. — Bibliography: p. [123]-127*

ALLIED HEALTH PERSONNEL — Legal status, laws, etc. — Commonwealth of Nations
PAXMAN, John M.
The use of paramedicals for primary health in the Commonwealth : a survey of medical-legal issues and alternatives / John M. Paxman and Francis M. Shattock and N.R.E. Fendall. — London : Commonwealth Secretariat, 1979. — 129p

ALMIRALL, VALENTÍ
FIGUERES, Josep M.
El primer Congrés Catalanista i Valentí Almirall : materials per a l'estudi dels orígens del catalanisme / Josep M. Figueres. — [Barcelona] : Generalitat de Catalunya, Departament de la Presidència, 1985. — 282p. — *Bibliography: p267-280*

ALSACE (FRANCE) — Population — Statistics
FRANCE. Institut national de la statistique et études économiques. Direction régionale de Strasbourg
De la population active à l'emploi : des résultats pour 108 agglomérations, 1968-1975. — Strasbourg : INSEE, [1984?]. — 45p. — (Documents pour l'Alsace)

ALTERNATIVE MEDICINE *See* Therapeutic systems

ALTRUISM
Altruism and aggression : biological and social orgins / edited by Carolyn Zahn-Waxler, E. Mark Cummings, Ronald Iannotti. — Cambridge : Cambridge University Press, 1986. — xiii,337p. — (Cambridge studies in social and emotional development). — *Includes bibliographies and index*

BADCOCK, C. R.
The problem of altruism : Freudian-Darwinian solutions / C.R. Badcock. — Oxford : Basil Blackwell, 1986. — [270]p. — *Includes bibliography and index*

ALUMINIUM INDUSTRY AND TRADE — European Economic Community countries
NOWAK, S.
Aluminium industry in the European Economic Community / S. Nowak. — Luxembourg : Office for Official Publications of the European Communities, 1984. — 2microfiches. — (EUR ; 8813) (Energy audit ; no.2). — *Contract no.: XVII/AR/81/156*

ALUMINIUM INDUSTRY AND TRADE — Ghana
Essays from the Ghana-Valco renegotiations, 1982-85 / edited by Fui S. Tsikata. — [Accra] : Ghana Publishing Corporation, 1986. — viii,163p. — *Bibliographies*

AMALGAMATED CLOTHING AND TEXTILE WORKERS UNION — Case studies
DOUGLAS, Sara U
Labor's new voice : unions and the mass media / by Sara U. Douglas. — Norwood, N.J. : Ablex, 1986. — p. cm. — (Communication and information science). — *Includes index. — Bibliography: p*

AMALGAMATED ENGINEERING UNION
AEU journal / Amalgamated Engineering Union. — London : Amalgamated Engineering Union, 1986-. — *Monthly. — Continues: AUEW journal*

Amalgamated Engineering Union monthly journal / Amalgamated Engineering Union. — London : Amalgamated Engineering Union, 1920-1970. — *Monthly. — Title varies - later issues entitled AEU journal. — Continues: Amalgamated engineers monthly journal/Amalgamated Society of Engineers . Continued by: AUEW journal*

AMALGAMATED SOCIETY OF ENGINEERS
Amalgamated engineers monthly journal / Amalgamated Society of Engineers. — London : Amalgamated Society of Engineers, 1897-1920 . — *Monthly. — Title varies. — Continued by: Amalgamated Engineering Union monthly journal*

AMALGAMATED UNION OF ENGINEERING WORKERS
AUEW journal / Amalgamated Union of Engineering Workers. — London : Amalgamated Union of Engineering Workers, 1970-1986. — *Monthly. — Continues: Amalgamated Engineering Union monthly journal. Continued by AEU journal*

AMALGAMATED UNION OF ENGINEERING WORKERS. Technical, Administrative and Supervisory Section
TASS news and journal / Amalgamated Union of Engineering Workers. Technical, Administrative and Supervisory Section. — London : TASS, 1986-. — *Irregular*

AMALGAMATED UNION OF OPERATIVE BAKERS, CONFECTIONERS AND ALLIED WORKERS
BAKERS, FOOD AND ALLIED WORKERS' UNION
Annual report / Bakers, Food and Allied Workers' Union. — Welwyn Garden City : The Union, 1928-. — *Issuing body varies. 1928-1963 Issuing body known as The Amalgamated Union of Operative Bakers, Confectioners and Allied Workers. 1965-76 Issuing body known as The Bakers' Union*

AMBASSADORS — Finland — Biography
JAKOBSON, Max
Trettioåttonde våningen : hågkomster och anteckningar 1965-1971 / Max Jakobson ; översättning av Henrik von Bonsdorff. — Helsinki : Holger Schildts, 1983. — 351p. — *Translated into Swedish from Finnish. — Originally published Helsinki Keuruu, 1983*

AMBASSADORS — United States — Biography
FINDLING, John E
Dictionary of American diplomatic history / John E. Findling. — Westport, Conn. : Greenwood Press, 1980. — xviii, 622 p.. — *Includes bibliographies and index*

HEINRICHS, Waldo H
American ambassador : Joseph C. Grew and the development of the United States diplomatic tradition / Waldo H. Heinrichs, Jr. — New York : Oxford University Press, 1986, c1966. — p. cm. — : *Reprint. Originally published: Boston : Little, Brown, 1966. — Includes index. — Bibliography: p*

AMBIGUITY
CONNOLLY, William E
Politics and ambiguity / William E. Connolly. — Madison, Wis. : University of Wisconsin Press, 1987. — xiii, 168 p.. — (Rhetoric of the human sciences). — *Includes bibliographical references and index*

AMERICA — Emigration and immigration — Congresses
The Americas in the new international division of labor / edited by Steven E. Sanderson. — New York, N.Y. : Holmes & Meier, 1985. — p. cm. — *Includes index. — Bibliography: p*

AMERICA — Foreign economic relations — Spain — Valencia — History — 18th century
RIBES, Vicent
Los valencianos y América : el comercio valenciano con Indias en el siglo XVIII / Vicent Ribes. — Valencia : Diputació Provincial de València, [1985]. — 193p. — (Història i societat ; 2)

AMERICAN DILEMMA
SOUTHERN, David W
Gunnar Myrdal and Black-white relations : the use and abuse of An American dilemma, 1944-1969 / David W. Southern. — Baton Rouge : Louisiana State University Press, c1987. — xviii, 341 p.. — *Includes index. — Bibliography: p. 311-330*

AMERICAN FEDERATION OF LABOR
AFL-CIO news: official weekly publication of the American Federation of Labor and Congress of Industrial Organizations. — Washington, DC. : AFL-CIO, 1986-. — *Weekly*

AMERICAN FEDERATION OF LABOR — History
MINK, Gwendolyn
Old labor and new immigrants in American political development : union, party, and state, 1875-1920 / Gwendolyn Mink. — Ithaca, N.Y. : Cornell University Press, 1986. — p. cm. — *Includes index. — Bibliography: p*

AMERICAN JEWISH COMMITTEE
Commentary / American Jewish Committee. — New York : American Jewish Committee, 1987-. — *Monthly*

AMERICAN LITERATURE — 20th century
Cultural change in the United States since World War II / edited by Maurice Gonnand, Sergio Perosa, Christopher W.E. Bigsby ; with contributions from Zoltan Abadi-Nagy...[et al.]. — Amsterdam : Free University Press, 1986. — 102p. — (European contributions to American studies ; 9). — *Includes bibliographies*

AMERICAN LITERATURE — 20th century — History and criticism
HOMBERGER, Eric
American writers and radical politics, 1900-39 : equivocal commitments / Eric Homberger. — Basingstoke : Macmillan, 1986. — xiii,268p. — (Macmillan studies in American literature). — *Bibliography: p242-260. — Includes index*

AMERICAN MISSIONARY ASSOCIATION
RICHARDSON, Joe Martin
Christian reconstruction : the American Missionary Association and Southern Blacks, 1861-1890 / Joe M. Richardson. — Athens : University of Georgia Press, c1986. — ix, 348 p., [16] p. of plates. — *Includes index. — Bibliography: p. 323-335*

AMERICAN NATIONAL RED CROSS — History
WOODRUFF, Nan Elizabeth
As rare as rain : federal relief in the great southern drought of 1930-31 / Nan Elizabeth Woodruff. — Urbana : University of Illinois Press, 1985. — xii, 203 p., [8] p. of plates. — *Includes index. — Bibliography: p. 183-189*

AMERICAN PROSE LITERATURE — Colonial period, ca. 1600-1775 — History and criticism
HOLSTUN, James
A rational millennium : Puritan utopias of seventeenth-century England and America / James Holstun. — New York : Oxford University Press, 1987. — p. cm. — *Includes index. — Bibliography: p*

AMERICAN PROSE LITERATURE — Puritan authors — History and criticism
HOLSTUN, James
A rational millennium : Puritan utopias of seventeenth-century England and America / James Holstun. — New York : Oxford University Press, 1987. — p. cm. — *Includes index. — Bibliography: p*

AMERICAN TELEPHONE AND TELEGRAPH COMPANY
Breaking up Bell : essays on industrial organisation and regulation / [a CERA research study] ; edited by David S. Evans ; with contributions by Robert Bornholz ... [et al.]. — New York ; Oxford : North-Holland, c1983. — xiv,298p. — *Bibliography: p283-291. — Includes index*

AMERICAN TELEPHONE AND TELEGRAPH COMPANY — Reorganization
Telecommunications in the post-divestiture era : essays in honor of Jasper N. Dorsey and Ben T. Wiggins / edited by Albert L. Danielsen, David R. Kamerschen. — [Lexington, Mass.] : Lexington Books, c1986. — xiv, 252 p.. — *Includes bibliographies and index*

AMERICANISMS — Dictionaries
New dictionary of American slang / edited by Robert L. Chapman. — London : Macmillan, 1987, c1986. — xxxvi,485p. — *Based on Dictionary of American slang. Compiled and edited by Harold Wentworth and Stuart Berg Flexner. — 2nd supplemented ed. New York : Crowell, 1975. — Originally published: New York : Harper & Row, 1986*

AMERICANIZATION
CARLSON, Robert A.
The Americanization syndrome : a quest for conformity / Robert A. Carlson. — [Rev. and updated ed.]. — London : Croom Helm, c1987. — 197p. — (Croom Helm series on theory and practice of adult education in North America). — *Previous ed.: published as the quest for conformity. New York : London : Wiley, 1975. — Includes index*

AMERICANS — Employment — Nicaragua
EVERETT, Melissa
Bearing witness, building bridges : interviews with North Americans living and working in Nicaragua / Melissa Everett ; photographs: Michael Kopec. — Philadelphia, Pa. : New Society, 1986. — xviii,169p

AMERICANS — Foreign countries — Australia
AITCHISON, Raymond
The Americans in Australia / Ray Aitchison. — Melbourne (Vic.) : Australasian Educa Press, 1986. — 165p. — (Australian ethnic heritage series). — *Bibliography: p162-163*

AMERICANS — Nicaragua
EVERETT, Melissa
Bearing witness, building bridges : interviews with North Americans living and working in Nicaragua / Melissa Everett ; photographs: Michael Kopec. — Philadelphia, Pa. : New Society, 1986. — xviii,169p

AMISTAD (Schooner)
JONES, Howard
Mutiny on the Amistad : the saga of a slave revolt and its impact on American abolition, law, and diplomacy / Howard Jones. — New York : Oxford University Press, 1987. — ix, 271 p., [12] p. of plates. — *Includes index. — Bibliography: p. 221-259*

AMMONIA INDUSTRY — Great Britain — Employees
HARRIS, Rosemary, 1930-
Power and powerlessness in industry : an analysis of the social relations of production / Rosemary Harris. — London : Tavistock, 1987. — viii,245p. — *Bibliography: p238-239. — Includes index*

AMUESHA INDIANS — Religion and mythology
SANTOS GRANERO, Fernando
The power of love : the moral use of knowledge amongst the Amuesha of Central Peru / Fernando Santos Granero. — 395 leaves. — *PhD (Econ) 1986 LSE. — Leaves 374-384 are appendices*

AMUSEMENTS — Europe — History
STRONG, Roy
Art and power : Renaissance festivals 1450-1650 / Roy Strong. — Woodbridge : Boydell, 1984. — xiii,227p,[ca.100]p of plates. — *Revision of: Splendour at court. London : Weidenfeld and Nicolson, 1973. — Includes index*

ANAA (TUAMOTU ISLANDS) — Population — Statistics
Tableaux normalisés du recensement général de la population : 15 octobre 1983. — [Papeete] : Institut territorial de la statistique Résultats de la commune de Anaa. — [1985?]. — 4p,11 leaves

ANALYSIS OF VARIANCE — Mathematical models
LONG, J. Scott
Covariance structure models : an introduction to LISREL / J. Scott Long. — Beverly Hills : Sage Publications, c1983. — 95 p.. — (Sage university papers series. Quantitative applications in the social sciences ; no. 07-034). — *Bibliography: p. 91-93*

ANALYSIS (PHILOSOPHY)
Language, mind and logic / edited by Jeremy Butterfield. — Cambridge : Cambridge University Press, 1986. — xi,232p. — *Includes bibliographies and index*

ANARCHISM
The anarchist papers / edited by Dimitrios I. Roussopoulos. — Montréal ; Buffalo, N.Y. : Black Rose Books, 1986. — 175p. — *Includes references*

The anarchists / edited with an introduction by Irving Louis Horowitz. — New York : Dell, 1964. — 640p

Critical anarchy. — [Newcastle upon Tyne] : LOS, 1987. — (The Future in the present ; no.1). — *Text, ill on inside covers*
No.1: Critical anarchy. — 64p

ANARCHISM — History
WOODCOCK, George, 1912-
Anarchism : a history of libertanian ideas and movements / George Woodcock. — New ed. — Harmondsworth : Penguin, 1986. — 446p. — (A Pelican book). — *Previous ed.: London? P. Smith, 1962. — Bibliography: p423-432. — Includes index*

ANARCHISM — Spain — History
GÓMEZ CASAS, Juan
[Historia de la FAI. English]. Anarchist organisation : the history of the F.A.I. / Juan Gómez Casas ; translated by Abe Bluestein. — Montréal ; Buffalo : Black Rose Books, c1986. — 261 p.. — *Translation of: Historia de la FAI. — Includes bibliographies*

ANARCHISM AND ANARCHISTS
Anarchist encyclopaedia. — Cambridge : Cambridge Free Press, 1985-. — *Irregular*

FREEMAN, Jo
Untying the knot : feminism, anarchism and organisation / Jo Freeman [and] Cathy Levine. — London : Dark Star/Rebel Press, 1984. — 23p

GROUPE LIBERTAIRE LOUISE MICHEL
Des luttes de liberation nationale : à l'anarchisme. — Paris : Editions La Rue, 1985. — 55p

PUENTE, Issac
Libertarian communism / Issac Puente. — Sydney : Monty Miller Press, 1985. — 32p. — (Rebel worker pamphlet ; 5)

VANEIGEM, R.
[De la grève sauvage à l'autogestione généralisée. English]. Contributions to the revolutionary struggle intended to be discussed, corrected, and principally put into practise without delay / R. Vaneigem ; translated by Paul Sharkey. — London : Bratach Dubh Editions, 1981. — 45p

ANARCHISM AND ANARCHISTS — Bibliography
A short guide to the anarchist publishers. — London : Black Flag/Anarchist Black Cross, [1987]. — [8p]

ANARCHISM AND ANARCHISTS — History — 19th century
BARKER, Jeffrey H.
Individualism and community : the state in Marx and early anarchism / Jeffrey H. Barker. — New York : Greenwood Press, 1986. — xiv, 235 p.. — (Contributions in political science ; no. 143). — *Includes index. — Bibliography: p. [221]-229*

ANARCHISM AND ANARCHISTS — Argentina
BAYER, Osvaldo
Los anarquístas expropriadores y otros ensayos / Osvaldo Bayer. — Buenos Aires : Editorial Legasa, [1986]. — 190p

ANARCHISM AND ANARCHISTS — China
DROWNED RAT COLLECTIVE
Chinese anarchist movement. — [s.l.] : Drowned Rat Collective, 1985. — 20p

ANARCHISM AND ANARCHISTS — England — London
DIG. — London : [S.n.], 1987-. — *Monthly*

ANARCHISM AND ANARCHISTS — France — History
NATAF, André
La vie quotidienne des anarchistes en France 1880-1910 / André Nataf. — Paris : Hachette, 1986. — 350p. — *Bibliography: p337-340*

ANARCHISM AND ANARCHISTS — Great Britain
THAMES VALLEY ANARCHISTS
Vote Labour and still die horribly. — Reading : Thames Valley Anarchists, 1986. — [8p]

ANARCHISM AND ANARCHISTS — Italy
Armed struggle in Italy : a chronology. — London : Bratach Dubh, 1979. — 94p. — (Anarchist pamphlets ; no.4)

MALATESTA, Errico
[Fra Contadini: dialogo sull Ånarchia. English]. Fra Contadini : a dialogue on anarchy / Errico Malatesta ; translated by Jean Weir. — London : Bratach Dubh Editions, 1981. — 43p. — (Bratach Dubh Editions: anarchist pamphlets ; no.6)

ANARCHISM AND ANARCHISTS — Soviet Union
MAXIMOFF, Gregory Petrovich
"My social credo" / G. P. Maximoff. — Sydney : Monty Miller Press, 1983. — 15p. — (Rebel worker pamphlet ; 3). — *Translated into English by H. Frank it appeared in the book Constructive Anarchism by Maximoff, published by the 'Maximoff Memorial Publishing Committee'*

ANARCHISM AND ANARCHISTS — Soviet Union — History
KANEV, S. N.
Revoliutsiia i anarkhism : iz istorii bor'by revoliutsionnykh demokratov i bol'shevikov protiv anarkhizma [1840-1917 gg.] / S. N. Kanev. — Moskva : Mysl', 1987. — 327p

ANARCHISM AND ANARCHISTS — Spain
A day mournful and overcast : an "uncontrollable" from the Iron Column. — [s.l] : [s.n], 1987. — 27p. — *Originally published, by Nosotros, the daily newspaper in Valencia of the Iron Column in 1937*

FERRER, Rai
Durruti, 1896-1936 / Rai Ferrer (Onomatopeya). — Barcelona : Planeta, 1985. — 198p. — *Bibliography: p193-194*

KELSEY, Graham
Civil war and civil peace : libertarian Aragon 1936-37 / Graham Kelsey. — Cambridge : Cambridge Free Press, 1985. — 78p. — (Anarchist encyclopaedia ; monograph 1). — *Bibliography: p73-78*

ANARCHISM AND ANARCHISTS — Spain — Aragon — History
CASANOVA, Julian
Anarquismo y revolución en la sociedad rural aragonesa, 1936-1938 / por Julian Casanova. — Madrid : Siglo Veintiuno, 1985. — 368p. — (Historia de los movimientos sociales)

ANARCHISTS — Germany (West) — Biography
MIERMEISTER, Jürgen
Rudi Dutschke : mit Selbstzeugnissen und Bilddokumenten / Jügen Miermeister. — Reinbek bei Hamburg : Rowohlt, 1986. — 154p. — *Bibliography: p142-151*

ANARCHISTS — Great Britain — Addresses, essays, lectures
GODWIN, William
The anarchist writings of William Godwin / edited with an introduction by Peter Marshall. — London : Freedom Press, 1986. — 182p. — *Bibliography: p180-181*

ANAS, MOHAMMAD
Spectrum of modern geography : essays in memory of Prof. Mohammad Anas / edited by Mohammad Shafi, Mehdi Raza. — New Delhi : Concept Pub. Co., 1986, c1985. — xxvii, 492 p.. — *Summary: Festschrift honoring Mohammad Anas, 1925-1983, professor of geography, Aligarh Muslim University; comprises articles mostly in Indian context. — Includes bibliographies and index*

ANC *See* African National Congress

ANDALUCIA (SPAIN) — Economic ploicy
Andalucia y la Comunidad Europea : aspectos relevantes / trabajo dirigido por Rafael Illescas Ortiz. — Sevilla : Instituto de Desarrollo Regional, 1981. — xxxix,903p. — ([Publicaciones] / Universidad de Sevilla, Instituto de Desarrollo Regional ; No.21). — *Bibliographies*

ANDALUSIA (SPAIN) — Biography
PEINADO PEINADO, Rufino
Recuerdos de un carlista andaluz : un cruzado de la causa / [Rufino Peinado Peinado] ; Rafael Alvarez de Morales y Ruiz. — Córdoba : Instituto de H.a de Andalucía, [1982?]. — 245 p.. — (Publicaciones Instituto de Historia de Andalucía ; no. 13). — *Includes index*

ANDALUSIA (SPAIN) — Civilization
CUENCA TORIBIO, José Manuel
La Andalucía de la transición 1975-1984 : política y cultura / José Manuel Cuenca Toribio. — [Madrid : Mezquita, 1984]. — ix,230p. — (Serie historia ; 31)

ANDALUSIA (SPAIN) — Economic conditions
CUENCA TORIBIO, José Manuel
La Andalucía de la transición 1975-1984 : política y cultura / José Manuel Cuenca Toribio. — [Madrid : Mezquita, 1984]. — ix,230p. — (Serie historia ; 31)

VINCENT, Bernard
Audalucía en la edad moderna : economía y sociedad. — Granada : Diputación Provincial de Granada, [1985]. — 313p

ANDALUSIA (SPAIN) — History
CUENCA TORIBIO, José Manuel
La Andalucía de la transición 1975-1984 : política y cultura / José Manuel Cuenca Toribio. — [Madrid : Mezquita, 1984]. — ix,230p. — (Serie historia ; 31)

VINCENT, Bernard
Audalucía en la edad moderna : economía y sociedad. — Granada : Diputación Provincial de Granada, [1985]. — 313p

ANDALUSIA (SPAIN) — Politics and government
CUENCA TORIBIO, José Manuel
La Andalucía de la transición 1975-1984 : política y cultura / José Manuel Cuenca Toribio. — [Madrid : Mezquita, 1984]. — ix,230p. — (Serie historia ; 31)

ANDALUSIA (SPAIN) — Social conditions
VINCENT, Bernard
Audalucía en la edad moderna : economía y sociedad. — Granada : Diputación Provincial de Granada, [1985]. — 313p

ANDAMAN AND NICOBAR ISLANDS (INDIA) — Population — Statistics
Census of India 1981 / B. K. Singh, Director of Census Operations. — [Delhi : Controller of Publications]
Series 24: Andaman and Nicobar Islands. — [1985-]

ANDES REGION — Rural conditions
La cuestión rural en el Perú / Javier Iguiñiz. — 2a ed. — Lima : Pontifica Universidad Católica del Perú Fondo Editorial, 1986. — 332p. — *"Una recopilación de ensayos elaborados por profesores - investigadores de los Departamentos de Economía y Ciencias Sociales de la Pontifica Universidad Católica del Perú". — Includes bibliographies*

ANDES REGION — Social conditions — Addresses, essays, lectures
Anthropological history of Andean politics / edited by John V. Murra, Nathan Wachtel and Jacques Revel. — Cambridge : Cambridge University Press, 1986. — x,383p. — *Translation of Anthropologie historique des sociétés andines, a special double issue of Annales ; v.33, nos. 5-6 (1978)*

ANDHRA PRADESH (INDIA) — Economic conditions — Maps

Planning atlas of Andhra Pradesh / sponsors, Department of Finance & Planning, Government of Andhra Pradesh [and] Pilot Map Production Plant (C.S.T. & M.P.), Survey of India, Hyderabad [and] Department of Geography, Osmania University, Hyderabad. — Scales differ ; (E 77°–E 85°/N 20°–N 13°). — [S.l. : s.n.]. — *Editor: Afzal Mohammad. "Andhra Pradesh Planning Atlas Project (Supplement) 1978-1980"--Page following verso t.p. — "Reg. no. 1200 PPE '79 (P.M.P. 34 -- 1: = 2,500,000) 520 '79-80"--Verso t.p. — "Based upon Survey of India maps, with the permission of the Surveyor general of India"--Verso t.p. — : "Revised maps ... mostly pertain to socio-economic characteristics"--Foreword. — Contents: Location & administrative divisions -- Land use -- Economic characteristics -- Socio-economic infrastructure Supplement.* — c1980 (Hyderabad, A.P. : Print. Group of the Pilot Map Production Plant, Survey of India). — 1 atlas (xxi p., 40 leaves of plates)

ANDHRA PRADESH (INDIA) — Social conditions — Maps

Planning atlas of Andhra Pradesh / sponsors, Department of Finance & Planning, Government of Andhra Pradesh [and] Pilot Map Production Plant (C.S.T. & M.P.), Survey of India, Hyderabad [and] Department of Geography, Osmania University, Hyderabad. — Scales differ ; (E 77°–E 85°/N 20°–N 13°). — [S.l. : s.n.]. — *Editor: Afzal Mohammad. "Andhra Pradesh Planning Atlas Project (Supplement) 1978-1980"--Page following verso t.p. — "Reg. no. 1200 PPE '79 (P.M.P. 34 -- 1: = 2,500,000) 520 '79-80"--Verso t.p. — "Based upon Survey of India maps, with the permission of the Surveyor general of India"--Verso t.p. — : "Revised maps ... mostly pertain to socio-economic characteristics"--Foreword. — Contents: Location & administrative divisions -- Land use -- Economic characteristics -- Socio-economic infrastructure Supplement.* — c1980 (Hyderabad, A.P. : Print. Group of the Pilot Map Production Plant, Survey of India). — 1 atlas (xxi p., 40 leaves of plates)

ANDORRA — Economic conditions — Statistics

ANDORRA
Recull estadístic 85 / a cura de Albert de Rovira i Mola. — [Andorra la Vella] : M. I. Govern, [1985]. — 275p

ANDORRA — Social conditions — Statistics

ANDORRA
Recull estadístic 85 / a cura de Albert de Rovira i Mola. — [Andorra la Vella] : M. I. Govern, [1985]. — 275p

ANDREEV, A. A.

ANDREEV, A. A.
Vospominaniia, pis'ma / A. A. Andreev ; [sost.: N. A. Andreeva]. — Moskva : Politizdat, 1985. — 333p

ANDREEVA, M. F.

VOLOKHOVA, N. A.
"Fenomen" : stranitsy zhizni i deiatel'nosti M. F. Andreevoi / N. A. Volokhova. — Izd. 2-e, ispr. i dop.. — Leningrad : Lenizdat, 1986. — 317p. — *Bibliography: p315-[318]*

ANGLICAN CHURCH OF CANADA — History

PULKER, Edward
We stand on their shoulders : the growth of social concern in Canadian Anglicanism / Edward Pulker. — Toronto : Anglican Book Centre, 1986. — 188p. — *Includes bibliographic references*

ANGLICAN COMMUNION — England — History — 16th century

TYACKE, Nicholas
Anti-Calvinists : the rise of English Arminianism c.1590-1640 / Nicholas Tyacke. — Oxford : Clarendon, 1987. — [300]p,[4]p of plates. — (Oxford historical monographs). — *Includes bibliography and index*

ANGLICAN COMMUNION — England — History — 17th century

TYACKE, Nicholas
Anti-Calvinists : the rise of English Arminianism c.1590-1640 / Nicholas Tyacke. — Oxford : Clarendon, 1987. — [300]p,[4]p of plates. — (Oxford historical monographs). — *Includes bibliography and index*

ANGLO AMERICAN CORPORATION OF SOUTH AFRICA — History

PALLISTER, David
South Africa Inc : the Oppenheimer empire / David Pallister, Sarah Stewart, Ian Lepper. — London : Simon & Schuster, 1987. — [256]p. — *Includes bibliography and index*

ANGLO-FRENCH WAR, 1755-1763 — Economic aspects — France

RILEY, James C
The Seven Years War and the old regime in France : the economic and financial toll / James C. Riley. — Princeton, N.J. : Princeton University Press, 1986. — xxii, 256p. — *Includes index*

ANGLO-SAXONS

Knowing and telling history : the Anglo-Saxon debate / edited by F. R. Ankersmit. — Middletown, Conn. : Wesleyan University, 1986. — 100p. — (History and theory ; Beiheft 25)

Place-name evidence for the Anglo-Saxon invasion and Scandinavian settlements : eight studies / collected by Kenneth Cameron ; introduction by Margaret Gelling. — [Nottingham] ([c/o School of English Studies, The University, Nottingham NG7 2RD]) : English Place-Name Society, 1975. — [3],v,171p. — *Cover title*

ANGOLA — History — Dictionaries

MARTIN, Phyllis
Historical dictionary of Angola / Phyllis M. Martin. — Metuchen, N.J. : Scarecrow Press, 1980. — xxi, 174 p.. — (African historical dictionaries ; no. 26). — *Includes index. — Bibliography: p. 94-165*

ANGOLA — History — Revolution, 1961-1975

KHAZANOV, A. M.
Agostinho Neto / A. M. Khazanov ; translated from the Russian by Cynthia Carlile. — Moscow : Progress Publishers, 1986. — 302p

ANGOLA — History — Civil War, 1975-

DÖHNING, W
UNITA : União Nacional para a Independência Total de Angola / text by W. Döhning ; photographs by Cloete Breytenbach. — [Angola] : Kwacha Unita Press, 1984. — 93 p.

ANGOLA — Politics and government

HAMILL, James
The challenge to the M.P.L.A. : Angola's war: 1980-1986 / James Hamill. — Coventry : University of Warwick, 1986. — 74p. — (Working paper / University of Warwick. Department of Politics ; no.41)

ANGOLA — Politics and government — 1961-1975

KHAZANOV, A. M.
Agostinho Neto / A. M. Khazanov ; translated from the Russian by Cynthia Carlile. — Moscow : Progress Publishers, 1986. — 302p

ANGRY BRIGADE

The Angry Brigade, 1967-1984 : documents and chronology / introduction by Jean Weir. — London : Elephant Editions, 1985. — 73p. — (Anarchist pocketbooks ; 3). — *First published in 1978 by Bratach Dubh Anarchist Pamphlets*

ANIMAL BEHAVIOR

DAWKINS, Marian Stamp
Unravelling animal behaviour / Marian Stamp Dawkins. — Harlow : Longman, 1986. — x,159p. — *Bibliography: p149-159. — Includes index*

ANIMAL BEHAVIOR — Measurement

MARTIN, Paul, 1958-
Measuring behaviour : an introductory guide / Paul Martin, Patrick Bateson. — Cambridge : Cambridge University Press, 1986. — xii, 200p. — *Includes index. — Bibliography: p.[163]-193*

ANIMAL COMMUNICATION

AKMAJIAN, Adrian
Linguistics, an introduction to language and communication / Adrian Akmajian, Richard A. Demers, Robert M. Harnish. — 2nd ed. — Cambridge, Mass. ; London : MIT Press, c1984. — xvi, 547 p.. — *Includes bibliographies and index*

ANIMAL INDUSTRY — Bibliography

DAVID LUBIN MEMORIAL LIBRARY
FAO documentation : animal production : 1979-1983 = Documentation de la FAO : production animale : 1979-1983 = Documentacion de la FAO : produccion animal : 1979-1983. — Rome : Food and Agriculture Organization, 1985. — 46,6,15,4p. — *In English with French and Spanish introductions*

ANIMAL INDUSTRY — China

China, the livestock sector. — Washington, D.C., U.S.A. : World Bank, 1987. — [xx], 195p. — (A World Bank country study). — *Includes bibliographical references*

ANIMAL INDUSTRY — Developing countries — Forecasting

SARMA, J. S
Cereal feed use in the Third World : past trends and projections to 2000 / J.S Sarma. — Washington, D.C. : International Food Policy Research Institute, c1987. — p. cm. — (Research report ; 57). — *Bibliography: p*

ANIMAL INDUSTRY — Latin America

JARVIS, Lovell S.
Livestock development in Latin America / Lovell S. Jarvis. — Washington, D.C. : The World Bank, 1986. — x,214p. — *Bibliography: p200-207*

ANIMAL INDUSTRY — New Caledonia — Statistics

Recensement général de l'agriculture 1983-1984. — Nouméa : Institut territoriale de la statistique et des études économiques t.2: Résultats
Pt.1: Exploitations agricoles et productions animales. — [1986]. — 91p. — (Notes et documents / Institut territoriale de la statistique et des études économiques ; no.40)

ANIMAL INTELLIGENCE — Addresses, essays, lectures

Minds, machines and evolution : philosophical studies / edited by Christopher Hookway. — Cambridge : Cambridge University Press, 1984. — xi,177p. — *Includes bibliographies and index*

ANIMAL PRODUCTS — Canada

PRESCOTT-ALLEN, Christine
The first resource : wild species in the North American economy / Christine Prescott-Allen and Robert Prescott-Allen. — New Haven : Yale University Press, c1986. — xv, 529 p.. — *"Published with support from the World Wildlife Fund and Philip Morris Incorporated.". — Includes index. — Bibliography: p. 463-507*

ANIMAL PRODUCTS — United States
PRESCOTT-ALLEN, Christine
The first resource : wild species in the North American economy / Christine Prescott-Allen and Robert Prescott-Allen. — New Haven : Yale University Press, c1986. — xv, 529 p.. — "Published with support from the World Wildlife Fund and Philip Morris Incorporated.". — Includes index. — Bibliography: p. 463-507

ANIMAL TRACTION — Africa, Sub-Saharan
PINGALI, Prabhu L.
Agricultural mechanization and the evolution of farming systems in Sub-Saharan Africa / Prabhu Pingali, Yves Bigot, Hans P. Binswanger. — Baltimore : Johns Hopkins Press for the World Bank, 1987. — viii,216p. — Bibliographical references: p191-206

ANIMALS, PROSECUTION AND PUNISHMENT OF — Europe — History
EVANS, E. P.
The criminal prosecution and capital punishment of animals / E.P. Evans. — London : Faber, 1987, c1906. — xxxi,336p. — Facsim of: ed. published London : Heinemann, 1906. — Bibliography: p314-323. — Includes index

ANIMALS, TREATMENT OF
SINGER, Peter, 1946-
The animal liberation movement : its philosophy, its achievements, and its future / Peter Singer. — Nottingham : Old Hammond Press, 1986. — 21p. — Bibliography: p20

ANIMALS, TREATMENT OF — England — History
LANSBURY, Coral
The old brown dog : women, workers, and vivisection in Edwardian England / Coral Lansbury. — Madison, Wis. : University of Wisconsin Press, 1985. — p. cm. — Includes index

ANISEMITISM — United States — History — Addresses, essays, lectures
Anti-Semitism in American history / edited by David A. Gerber. — Urbana : University of Illinois Press, c1986. — p. cm. — Includes index. — Bibliography: p

ANNUITIES
DONALD, David William Alexander
Compound interest and annuities-certain / David William Donald. — Cambridge : Cambridge University Press, 1963. — 300p

ANSCHLUSS MOVEMENT, 1918-1938
LOW, Alfred D.
The Anschluss movement, 1931-1938, and the Great Powers / by Alfred D. Low. — Boulder : East European Monographs ; New York : Distributed by Columbia University Press, c1985. — xv, 507p. — (East European monographs ; no.185). — Bibliography: p.[476]-496

ANSELLS BREWERY STRIKE, GREAT BRITAIN, 1981
WADDINGTON, David P.
Trouble brewing : a social psychological analysis of the Ansells Brewery dispute / David P. Waddington. — Aldershot : Avebury, c1987. — x,164p. — Bibliography: p150-160. — Includes index

ANTARCTIC REGIONS
SABIN, Francene
Arctic and Antarctic regions / by Francene Sabin ; illustrated by Allan Eitzen. — Mahwah, N.J. : Troll Associates, c1985. — p. cm. — Summary: Briefly describes the frozen regions around the North Pole and the South Pole, which are alike in many ways and different in many others

ANTARCTIC REGIONS — Discovery and exploration — Congresses
WORKSHOP ON THE ANTARCTIC TREATY SYSTEM (1985 : Beardmore South Field Camp)
Antarctic treaty system : an assessment : proceedings of a workshop...sponsored by the Polar Research Board [of the] Commission on Physical Sciences, Mathematics and Resources [of the] National Research Council. — Washington : National Academy Press, 1985. — xv,435p. — Bibliographies

ANTARCTIC REGIONS — International status
MYHRE, Jeffrey D
The Antarctic Treaty system : politics, law, and diplomacy / Jeffrey D. Myhre. — Boulder : Westview Press, 1986. — p. cm. — (Westview special studies in international relations). — Includes index. — Bibliography: p

TRIGGS, Gillian D.
International law and Australian sovereignty in Antarctica / by Gillian D. Triggs. — Sydney : Legal Books, 1986. — xxix,403p. — Bibliography: p.379-391. - Includes index

ANTARCTIC REGIONS — International status — Congresses
Antarctic challenge II : conflicting interests, cooperation, environmental protection, economic development : proceedings of an inter-disciplinary symposium, September 27th-21st, 1985 / organized by the Institut für Internationales Recht an der Universität Kiel and the Alfred-Wegener-Institut für Polar- und Meeresforschung, Bremerhaven; edited by Rüdiger Wolfrum, assistant editors: Klaus Bockslaff and Ingrid L. Jahn. — Berlin : Duncker & Humblot, 1986. — 465p. — (Veröffentlichungen des Instituts für Internationales Recht an der Universität Kiel ; 95)

WORKSHOP ON THE ANTARCTIC TREATY SYSTEM (1985 : Beardmore South Field Camp)
Antarctic treaty system : an assessment : proceedings of a workshop...sponsored by the Polar Research Board [of the] Commission on Physical Sciences, Mathematics and Resources [of the] National Research Council. — Washington : National Academy Press, 1985. — xv,435p. — Bibliographies

ANTENUPTIAL CONTRACTS — United States
WEITZMAN, Lenore J
The marriage contract : spouses, lovers and the law / Lenore J. Weitzman. — New York : Free Press, c1981. — p. cm. — Includes index

ANTHROPO-GEOGRAPHY
CARR, Michael
Patterns : process and change in human geography / Michael Carr. — Basingstoke : Macmillan, 1987. — [256]p. — Includes index

Changing Britain, changing world : geographical perspectives. — Milton Keynes : Open University Press. — (Social sciences : a second level course) (D205; Units 1-3). — At head of title: Open University
Section 1: Introduction: issues and themes
Block 1: Introduction: issues and themes / Susan Cunningham...[et al.]. — 1985. — Various pagings

Changing Britain, changing world : geographical perspectives. — Milton Keynes : Open University Press. — (Social services : a second level course) (D205; Units 4-7). — At head of title: Open University
Section 2: Analysis: aspects of the geography of society
Block 2: Industry and resources / Piers Blaikie...[et al.]. — 1985. — Various pagings

Changing Britain, changing world : geographical perspectives. — Milton Keynes : Open University Press. — (Social sciences : a second level course) (D205; Units 21-25). — At head of title : Open University
Section 3: Synthesis: uniqueness and interdependence of place
Block 6: Uneven development and the world order / John Allen...[et al.]. — 1985. — Various pagings

Changing Britain, changing world : geographical perspectives. — Milton Keynes : Open University Press. — (Social sciences : a second level course) (D205; Units 26-29). — At head of title: Open University
Section 4: Geography matters
Block 7: The impact of geography on society / James Anderson...[et al.]. — 1985. — Various pagings

COATES, B. E.
Geography and inequality / B.E. Coates, R.J. Johnston and P.L. Knox. — Oxford : Oxford University Press, 1977. — [8],292p. — Bibliography: p.258-279. — Includes index

CROSBY, Alfred W.
Ecological imperialism : the biological expansion of Europe, 900-1900 / Alfred W. Crosby. — Cambridge : Cambridge University Press, 1986. — xiv,368p,[16]p of plates. — (Studies in environment and history). — Includes index

DODGSHON, Robert A.
The European past : social evolution and spatial order / Robert A. Dodgshon. — Basingstoke : Macmillan Education, 1987. — xi,403p. — (Critical human geography). — Bibliography: p362-393. — Includes index

Geography matters! / edited by Doreen Massey and John Allen with James Anderson ... [et al.]. — Cambridge University Press in association with the Open University, 1984. — vi,204p. — Includes bibliographies and index

GOLD, John R.
An introduction to behavioural geography / John R. Gold. — Oxford : Oxford University Press, 1980. — [9],290p. — Bibliography: p.253-286. — Includes index

GOLLEDGE, Reginald G.
Analytical behavioural geography / Reginald G. Golledge and Robert J. Stimson. — London : Croom Helm, c1987. — 245p. — (Croom Helm series in geography and environment). — Bibliography: p315-337. — Includes index

Humanistic geography / edited by David Ley and Marwyn S. Samuels. — London : Croom Helm, 1978. — x,337p. — Also published: Chicago : Maaroufa Press, 1978

SMITH, David M. (David Marshall)
Where the grass is greener : living in an unequal world / David M. Smith. — Harmondsworth : Penguin, 1979. — 3-386p,[8]p of plates. — (Pelican books. geography and environmental studies). — Bibliography: p.369-380. — Includes index

Social geography : progress and prospect / edited by Michael Pacione. — London : Croom Helm, c1987. — [336]p. — (Croom Helm progress in geography series)

ANTHROPO-GEOGRAPHY — Addresses, essays, lectures
World patterns of modern urban change : essays in honor of Chauncy D. Harris / edited by Michael P. Conzen. — Chicago : University of Chicago, Dept. of Geography, 1985. — p. cm. — (Research paper / the University of Chicago, Department of Geography ; no. 217-218). — Includes index

ANTHROPO-GEOGRAPHY — Dictionaries
GOODALL, Brian
The Penguin dictionary of human geography / Brian Goodall. — Harmondsworth : Penguin, 1987. — 509p. — (Penguin reference books). — Also published under the title: Facts on file dictionary of human geography

ANTHROPO-GEOGRAPHY — Alberta — Addresses, essays, lectures
Environment and economy : essays on the human geography of Alberta / edited by B.M. Barr, P.J. Smith. — Edmonton, Alta., Canada : Pica Pica Press, c1984. — xx, 180 p.. — *Includes bibliographies*

ANTHROPO-GEOGRAPHY — Amazon Valley
MEGGERS, Betty Jane
Amazonia: man and culture in a counterfeit paradise / [by] Betty J. Meggers. — Chicago : Aldine, Atherton, [1971]. — viii, 182 p. — (Worlds of man). — *Bibliography: p. 169-173*

ANTHROPO-GEOGRAPHY — Europe
ILBERY, Brian W.
Western Europe : a systematic human geography / Brian W. Ilbery. — 2nd ed. — Oxford : Oxford University Press, 1986. — [xi,220]p. — *Previous ed.: 1981. — Includes bibliography and index*

ANTHROPO-GEOGRAPHY — France
PINCHEMEL, Philippe
France : a geographical, social and economic survey / Philippe Pinchemel with Chantal Balley ... [et al.] ; translated by Dorothy Elkins with T.H. Elkins. — Cambridge : Cambridge University Press, 1987. — xxvi,660p. — *Translation of: La France. — Bibliography: p605-649. — Includes index*

ANTHROPO-GEOGRAPHY — Great Britain
Changing Britain, changing world : geographical perspectives. — Milton Keynes : Open University Press. — (Social Sciences : a second level course)
Section 2: Analysis: aspects of the geography of society
Block 4: Culture and conflict: views of space, place and nature. — 1985. — 28,27,25,32,24p. — (D205 ; 12/16). — *Contents: Unit 12: Whose land?/Doreen Massey - Unit 13: Place and perception/Phil Sarre - Unit 14: Environment and politics in a capitalist society/Andrew Blowers - Unit 15: Environment and politics in a state socialist society/Allan Cochrane - Unit 16: Geopolitics/John Short*

The Human geography of contemporary Britain / edited by John R. Short and Andrew Kirby. — London : Macmillan, 1984. — 186p. — *Bibliography: p174-178. — Includes index*

ANTHROPO-GEOGRAPHY — Nigeria
BUCHANAN, Keith
Land and people in Nigeria : the human geography of Nigeria and its environmental background / K. M. Buchanan and J. C. Pugh ; with a contribution by A. Brown and a foreword by L. Dudley Stamp. — London : University of London Press, [1955]. — xii,259p

ANTHROPO-GEOGRAPHY — United States
MEINIG, D. W.
The shaping of America : a geographical perspective on 500 years of history / D.W. Meinig. — New Haven ; London : Yale University Press
Vol.1: Atlantic America, 1492-1800. — c1986. — xxii,500p. — *Map on lining papers. — Bibliography: p461-479. — Includes index*

ANTHROPOLOGICAL ETHICS
Advocacy and anthropology : first encounters / edited by Robert Paine. — St. John's Newfoundland : Institute of Social and Economic Research, 1985. — xviii,278p. — *Bibliography: p[260]-278*

ANTHROPOLOGICAL LINGUISTICS
HAARMANN, Harald
Language in ethnicity : a view of basic ecological relations / by Harald Haarmann. — Berlin ; New York : Mouton de Gruyter, c1986. — p. cm. — (Contributions to the sociology of language ; 44). — *Includes indexes. — Bibliography: p*

ANTHROPOLOGY
Advocacy and anthropology : first encounters / edited by Robert Paine. — St. John's Newfoundland : Institute of Social and Economic Research, 1985. — xviii,278p. — *Bibliography: p[260]-278*

Critique of anthropology. — London : University College. Department of Anthropology, 1986-. — *3 per year*

Man, culture and society / edited by Harry L. Shapiro. — Revised ed. — London : Oxford University Press, 1971. — viii,456p. — *Previous ed. 1956. — Bibliographyp.441-443. — Includes index*

ANTHROPOLOGY — Dictionaries
SEYMOUR-SMITH, Charlotte
Macmillan dictionary of anthropology / Charlotte Seymour-Smith. — London : Macmillan Reference, 1986. — vi,305p. — *Bibliography: p293-305*

ANTHROPOLOGY — History — Congresses
Ideas and trends in world anthropology / edited by Charles Frantz. — New Delhi : Concept, 1981. — xxii, 173 p.. — (Xth ICAES series ; no. 4). — *Selection of papers presented at the 10th International Congress of Anthropological and Ethnological Sciences held at New Delhi in 1978. — Includes bibliographies and index*

ANTHROPOLOGY — Philosophy
JARVIE, I. C.
Thinking about society : theory and practice / I. C. Jarvie. — Dordrecht : Reidel, 1986. — xviii,519p. — (Boston studies in the philosophy of science ; v.93)

ANTHROPOLOGY — Philosophy — Congresses
Ideas and trends in world anthropology / edited by Charles Frantz. — New Delhi : Concept, 1981. — xxii, 173 p.. — (Xth ICAES series ; no. 4). — *Selection of papers presented at the 10th International Congress of Anthropological and Ethnological Sciences held at New Delhi in 1978. — Includes bibliographies and index*

ANTHROPOLOGY — Research — Finance — Directories
CANTRELL, Karen
Funding for anthropological research / Karen Cantrell, Denise Wallen. — Phoenix, AZ : Oryx Press, 1986. — p. cm. — *Includes index. — Bibliography: p*

ANTHROPOLOGY — Research grants — United States — Directories
CANTRELL, Karen
Funding for anthropological research / Karen Cantrell, Denise Wallen. — Phoenix, AZ : Oryx Press, 1986. — p. cm. — *Includes index. — Bibliography: p*

ANTHROPOLOGY, CULTURAL — Nepal
JUSTICE, Judith
Policies, plans, and people : culture and health development in Nepal / Judith Justice. — Berkeley : University of California Press, c1986. — p. cm. — (Comparative studies of health systems and medical care). — *Includes index. — Bibliography: p*

ANTHROPOLOGY-GEOGRAPHY — Great Britain
REED, Michael, 1930-
The age of exuberance 1550-1700 / Michael Reed. — London : Routledge & Kegan Paul, 1986. — [320]p. — (The Making of Britain, 1066-1939)

ANTI-APARTHEID MOVEMENTS — Biography
HAIN, Peter
A Putney plot? Peter Hain. — Nottingham : Spokesman, 1987. — 158p. — *Includes index*

ANTI-CATHOLICISM — Scotland — History
BRUCE, Steve
No pope of Rome : anti-catholicism in modern Scotland / Steve Bruce. — Edinburgh : Mainstream, 1985. — 270p. — *Includes bibliographical notes*

ANTI-COMMUNIST MOVEMENTS — France — History
BECKER, Jean Jacuqes
Histoire de l'anti communisme en France / Jean Jacques Becker, Serge Berstein. — Paris : Olivier Orban
T.1: 1917-1940. — 1987. — 407p. — *Bibliography: p389-[395]*

ANTI-COMMUNIST MOVEMENTS — Soviet Union
ANDREYEV, Catherine
Vlasov and the Russian Liberation Movement : Soviet reality and émigré theories / Catherine Andreyev. — Cambridge : Cambridge University Press, 1987. — xiv,251p. — (Soviet and East European studies). — *Bibliography: p224-239. — Includes index*

GRIGOR'EV, V. K.
Razgrom melkoburzhuaznoi kontrrevoliutsii v Kazakhstane (1920-1922 gg.) / V. K. Grigor'ev. — Alma-Ata : Kazakhstan, 1984. — 174p

ANTI-COMMUNIST MOVEMENTS — United States — History
SCHRECKER, Ellen
No ivory tower : McCarthyism and the universities / Ellen Schrecker. — New York : Oxford University Press, 1986. — p. cm. — *Includes index. — Bibliography: p*

ANTI-COMMUNIST MOVEMENTS — United States — History — 20th century
EWALD, William Bragg
McCarthyism and consensus / William Bragg Ewald, Jr. — Lanham [Md.] : University Press of America, c1986. — viii, 68 p.. — (The Credibility of institution, policies and leadership ; v. 13). — *"Co-published by arrangement with the White Burkett Miller Center of Public Affairs, University of Virginia"--T.p. verso. — Contents: Rotunda lecture: "McCarthyism revisited" / William Bragg Ewald, Jr. -- Miller Center discussion: "McCarthyism and consensus."*

ANTI-COMMUNIST MOVEMENTS — Yugoslavia
Savez komunista u borbi protiv antisocijalističkih delovanja i antikomunističkih ideologija / redakcioni odbor David Atlagić...[et al.]. — Beograd : Izdavački centar Komunist, 1986. — viii,555p

ANTI-FASCIST MOVEMENTS — Europe
SSSR v bor'be protiv fashistskoi agressii 1933-1945 / otv. redaktor A. L. Norochnitskii. — 2-e izd., perer. i dop.. — Moskva : Nauka, 1986. — 349p. — *1st ed. 1976*

ANTI-FASCIST MOVEMENTS — Hungary
PINTÉR, István
Hungarian anti-fascism and resistance, 1941-1945 / by István Pintér. — Budapest : Akadémiai Kiadó, 1986. — 234p

ANTI-FASCIST MOVEMENTS — Spain — Catalonia
COLOMER, Josep M.
La ideologia de l'antifranquisme / Josep M. Colomer. — Barcelona : Edicions 62, [1985]. — 158p. — (L'escorpí ; 57)

ANTI-NAZI MOVEMENT
KOMMUNISTISCHE PARTEI DEUTSCHLANDS
Der Sieg des Faschismus in Deutschland und seine Lehren für unseren gegenwärtigen Kampf / herausgegeben vom Zentralkomitee der Kommunistischen Partei Deutschlands. — Berlin : [KPD], [1945?]. — 21p. — (Vortragsdisposition ; Nr.1)

ANTI-NAZI MOVEMENT
continuation

RÖSCH, Augustin
Kampf gegen den Nationalsozialismus / Augustin Rösch ; herausgegeben von Roman Bleistein. — Frankfurt am Main : Josef Knecht, 1985. — 492p. — *Bibliography: p481-484*

Widerstand gegen Krieg und Faschismus! / FIR: Fédération Internationale des Résistants/Der Internationale Vereinigungskongress der Widerstandskämpfer. — Berlin : VVN, [1951]. — 55p. — *Cover half-title: Congrès Inter[national] de la Résistance, Vienne 1951*

ANTI-NAZI MOVEMENT — Germany

Der antifaschistische Widerstandskampf unter Führung der KPD in Mecklenburg 1933 bis 1945 / [Horst Bendig...et al.]. — Berlin : Dietz Verlag, 1985. — 343p

BUCHSTAB, Günter
Verfolgung und Widerstand 1933-1945 : Christliche Demokraten gegen Hitler / Günter Buchstab, Brigitte Kaff, Hans-Otto Kleinmann. — Düsseldorf : Droste Verlag, 1986. — 288p. — *Bibliography: p282-283*

HELMERS, Gerrit
"Wenn die Messer blitzen und die Naziš flitzen..." : der Widerstand von Arbeiterjugendcliquen und -banden in der Weimarer Republik und im 'Dritten Reich' / Gerrit Helmers, Alfons Kenkmann. — Lippstadt : Leimeier, c1984. — iv,267p. — *Bibliography: p256-267*

RÖSCH, Augustin
Kampf gegen den Nationalsozialismus / Augustin Rösch ; herausgegeben von Roman Bleistein. — Frankfurt am Main : Josef Knecht, 1985. — 492p. — *Bibliography: p481-484*

Der Widerstand gegen den Nazionalsozialismus : die deutsche Gesellschaft und der Widerstand gegen Hitler / herausgegeben von Jürgen Schmädeke und Peter Steinbach ; im Auftrage der Historischen Kommission zu Berlin in Zusammenarbeit mit der Gedenkstätte Deutscher Widerstand. — München : Piper, 1985. — xxxviii,1185p. — (Publikationen der Historischen Kommission zu Berlin). — *[Die Internationale Konferenz zum 40. Jahrestag des 20. Juli 1944, "Die deutsche Gesellschaft und der Widerstand gegen Hitler - eine Bilanz nach 40 Jahren" vom 2-6 Juli 1984 in Berlin]*

ANTI-NAZI MOVEMENT — Germany (West) — Munich

DUMBACH, Annette E
Shattering the German night : the story of the White Rose / by Annette E. Dumbach and Jud Newborn. — 1st ed. — Boston : Little, Brown, c1986. — xi, 259 p.. — *Includes index. — Bibliography: p. 243-247*

ANTI-SATELLITE WEAPONS — Soviet Union

STARES, Paul B
Space and national security / Paul B. Stares. — Washington, D.C. : Brookings Institution, c1987. — p. cm. — *Includes bibliographical references and index*

ANTI-SATELLITE WEAPONS — United States

STARES, Paul B
Space and national security / Paul B. Stares. — Washington, D.C. : Brookings Institution, c1987. — p. cm. — *Includes bibliographical references and index*

ANTIGUA AND BARBUDA — Economic conditions

Antigua and Barbuda : economic report. — Washington, D.C., U.S.A. : World Bank, 1985. — [xii],90p. — (A World Bank country study). — *Includes bibliographical references*

ANTIGUA AND BARBUDA — Economic policy

Antigua and Barbuda : economic report. — Washington, D.C., U.S.A. : World Bank, 1985. — [xii],90p. — (A World Bank country study). — *Includes bibliographical references*

ANTIMISSILE MISSILES

DURCH, William J.
The future of the ABM treaty / William J. Durch. — London : International Institute for Strategic Studies, 1987. — 80p. — (Adelphi papers ; 223)

ANTINUCLEAR MOVEMENT

FEHÉR, Ferenc
Doomsday or deterrence / by Ferenc Feher and Agnes Heller. — Armonk, N.Y. : M.E. Sharpe, Inc, c1986. — p. cm

The Nuclear age : power, proliferation, and the arms race. — Washington, D.C. : Congressional Quarterly, c1984. — xii, 253 p.. — *Bibliography: p241-243. — Bibliography: p. 241-243*

ROUSSOPOULOS, Dimitrios I
The coming of World War Three / Dimitrios I. Roussopoulos. — Montréal ; Buffalo : Black Rose Books, c1986-. — v. <1 >. — *Includes bibliographies. — Contents: v. 1. From protest to resistance : the international war system*

ANTINUCLEAR MOVEMENT — Australia

SUTER, Keith D.
The Australian campaign for a Ministry for Peace / Keith D. Suter. — [Sydney] : United Nations Association of Australia, 1984. — iv,153p. — *Notes and references: p145-153*

ANTINUCLEAR MOVEMENT — Germany (West)

HAASKEN, Georg
Protest in der Klemme : soziale Bewegungen in der Bundesrepublik / Georg Haasken, Michael Wigbers. — Frankfurt am Main : Verlag Neue Kritik, 1986. — 212p. — *Bibliography: p203-[212]*

ANTINUCLEAR MOVEMENT — Great Britain

MERCER, Paul
'Peace' of the dead : the truth behind the nuclear disarmaments / Paul Mercer ; foreword by Lord Chalfont. — London : Policy Research Publications, 1986. — 465p. — *Bibliography: p[422]-438*

Preparing for nonviolent direct action / Howard Clark...et al.. — [Nottingham] : Peace News ; [London] : CND, 1984. — 80p

ANTINUCLEAR MOVEMENT — United States

DEMING, Barbara
Prisons that could not hold / Barbara Deming ; introduction by Grace Paley ; photo essay edited by Joan E. Biren. — San Francisco : Spinsters Ink, 1985. — 230p

LOEB, Paul Rogat
Hope in hard times : America's peace movement and the Reagan era / by Paul Rogat Loeb. — Lexington, Mass. : Lexington Books, [1986], c1987. — ix, 322 p.. — *Includes index. — Bibliography: p. [305]-306*

ANTINUCLEAR MOVEMENT — Washington (State)

SUGAI, Wayne H
Nuclear power and ratepayer protest : the Washington Public Power Supply System / Wayne H. Sugai. — Boulder : Westview Press, 1987. — p. cm. — (Westview special studies in public policy and public systems management). — *Bibliography: p*

ANTINUCLEAR MOVEMENT — Washington (State) — Addresses, essays, lectures

We are ordinary women : a chronicle of the Puget Sound Women's Peace Camp / by Peace Camp participants. — 1st ed. — Seattle : Seal Press, 1985. — p. cm

ANTINUCLEAR MOVEMENTS — Great Britain

FRIENDS OF THE EARTH
Critical decision : should Britain buy the pressurised water reactor? : a report on the Sizewell Inquiry by Friends of the Earth / edited by Walt Patterson, Stewart Boyle, Juliette Majot. — London : Friends of the Earth Trust, 1986. — 135p. — *Bibliography: p103-109*

ANTISEMITISM

The bible,racism and anti-semitism / John Austin Baker [et al.] ; edited by Kenneth Leech. — London : Race, Pluralism and Community Group, Board for Social Responsibility, 1985. — iv,54p. — (Theology and racism ; 1)

LEWIS, Bernard, 1916-
Semites and anti-semites : an inquiry into conflict and prejudice / Bernard Lewis. — London : Weidenfeld and Nicolson, c1986. — 283p. — *Includes index*

The Persisting question : sociological perspectives and social contexts of modern antisemitism / edited by Helen Fein. — Berlin ; New York : De Gruyter, 1987. — p. cm. — (Current research on antisemitism ; v. 1)

ANTISEMITISM — History — 20th century

SEIDEL, Gill
The Holocaust denial : antisemitism, racism & the new right / Gill Seidel. — Leeds : Beyond the Pale Collective, 1986. — xxx,202p. — *Includes index*

ANTISEMITISM — Argentina — History — 20th century

SENKMAN, Leonardo
El antisemitismo en la Argentina / Leonardo Senkman. — Buenos Aires : Centro Editor de América Latina. — (Biblioteca Política Argentina ; 146)
t.1. — 1986. — 128p

SENKMAN, Leonardo
El antisemitismo en la Argentina / Leonard Senkman. — Buenos Aires : Centro Editor de América Latina. — (Biblioteca Política Argentina ; 149). — *Bibliography: p233-235*
t.2. — 1986. — 129-250p

ANTISEMITISM — Canada

FRANCQ, Henri G.
Hitler's holocaust : a fact of history / Henri G. Francq. — Vancouver : New Star Books, 1986. — 255p. — *Bibliography: p249-252*

ANTISEMITISM — France

WILSON, Nelly
Bernard-Lazare : l'antisémitisme, l'affaire Dreyfus, et la recherche de l'identité juive / Nelly Wilson ; traduit de l'anglais par Christiane et Douglas Gallagher. — Paris : Albin Michel, [1985]. — 461p. — *Bibliography: p435-450*

ANTISEMITISM — France — Biography

BUSI, Frederick
The pope of antisemitism : the career and legacy of Edouard-Adolphe Drumont / Frederick Busi. — Lanham ; London : University Press of America, 1987. — [242]p. — *Includes bibliography and index*

ANTISEMITISM — Germany — Congresses

The Jewish response to German culture : from the enlightenment to the Second World War / edited by Jehuda Reinharz and Walter Schatzberg. — Hanover, NH : Published for Clark University by University Press of New England, 1985. — xii, 362p. — *"Essays based on papers delivered at the International Conference on German Jews, held at Clark University, Worcester, Massachusetts, October 8-11, 1983.". — Includes index*

ANTISEMITISM — Germany — History — 19th century
ZIMMERMANN, Mosche
[Vilhelm Mar, "ha-paṭri'arkh shel ha-Anṭishemiyut". English]. Wilhelm Marr, the patriarch of Antisemitism / by Moshe Zimmermann. — New York : Oxford University Press, 1986. — p. cm. — Translation of: Vilhelm Mar, "ha-paṭri'arkh shel ha-Anṭishemiyut.". — Includes index

ANTISEMITISM — Soviet Union
KLIER, John
Russia gathers her Jews : the origins of the "Jewish question" in Russia, 1772-1825 / John Doyle Klier. — DeKalb, Ill. : Northern Illinois University Press, 1986. xxiv, 236p. — Map on lining papers. — Includes index. — Bibliography: p. [213]-223

ANTITRUST LAW — Economic aspects — United States
Antitrust policy in transition : the convergence of law and economics / edited by Eleanor M. Fox and James T. Halverson. — United States : American Bar Association, 1984. — xv,488p

ANTITRUST LAW — Canada
NOZICK, Robert S.
The annotated Competition Act / commentary prepared by Robert S. Nozick ; annotations and index prepared by Charlotte Neff. — Toronto : Carswell, 1987. — xviii,290p

Reaction : the new Combines Investigation Act / contributors include: Reuven Brenner....[et al.] ; edited by Walter Block. — [Vancouver] : The Fraser Institute, 1986. — xxix,208p. — Bibliography: p203-208

ANTITRUST LAW — European Economic Community countries
GREEN, Nicholas
Commercial agreements and competition law : practice and procedure in the UK and EEC / Nicholas Green. — London : Graham & Trotman, 1986. — lxxviii,763p. — Bibliography: p.lxix-lxx - Includes index

KORAH, Valentine
An introductory guide to EEC Competition law and practice / Valentine Korah. — 3rd ed. — Oxford : ESC Publishing, 1986. — xxi,177p. — Cover title: EEC competition law and practice. — Includes bibliographies and index

ANTITRUST LAW — Great Britain
GREEN, Nicholas
Commercial agreements and competition law : practice and procedure in the UK and EEC / Nicholas Green. — London : Graham & Trotman, 1986. — lxxviii,763p. — Bibliography: p.lxix-lxx - Includes index

ANTITRUST LAW — United States
ARMENTANO, Dominick T
Antitrust policy : the case for repeal / by D.T. Armentano. — Washington, D.C. : Cato Institute, 1986. — p. cm. — Includes bibliographical references and index

HJELMFELT, David C
Antitrust and regulated industries / David C. Hjelmfelt. — New York : Wiley Law Publications, c1985. — xxi, 465 p.. — (Federal practice library). — Includes bibliographical references and index

LEE, Mark R.
Antitrust law and local government / Mark R. Lee. — Westport, Conn. : Quorum Books, c1985. — p. cm. — Includes index. — Bibliography: p

SCHMALENSEE, Richard
On the use of economic models in anti-trust : the Realemon case / Richard Schmalensee. — [S.l.] : University of Pennsylvania Law Review, 1979. — 994-1049p

WILLIAMSON, Oliver E.
Antitrust economics : mergers, contracting and strategic behavior / Oliver Williamson. — Oxford : Basil Blackwell, 1987. — viii,363p. — Bibliography: p344-351 — Includes index

ANXIETY IN CHILDREN
BJÖRKQVIST, Kaj
Violent films, anxiety and aggression : experimental studies of the effect of violent films on the level of anxiety and aggressiveness in children / Kaj Björkqvist. — Helsinki : Societas Scientiarum Fennica, 1985. — 75p. — (Commentationes Scientarum Socialium ; 30). — Bibliography: p71-75

APARTHEID
BREWER, John D.
After Soweto : an unfinished journey / John D. Brewer. — Oxford : Clarendon, 1986. — [416]p. — Includes bibliography and index

COUNTER INFORMATION SERVICES
Consolidated Gold Fields PLC : partner in apartheid / Counter Information Services. — London : Counter Information Services, 1986. — 48p. — Bibliography: p48

Edinburgh united against apartheid : speeches from a rally against British collaboration with apartheid, Summer1985. — Edinburgh : Rally Against Apartheid Organising Committee, 1985. — 54p

HARRIES, Ann
The child is not dead : youth resistance in South Africa 1976-86 / compiled by Ann Harries, Roger Diski [and] Alasdair Brown. — London : British Defence and Aid Fund for Southern Africa : Inner London Education Authority, 1986. — 64p. — Bibliography: p62

Women and children under apartheid newsletter / ANC Women's Section. — Lusaka : ANC Women's Section, 1986-

APARTHEID — Congresses
South Africa, a chance for liberalism? : papers presented during a seminar of the Friedrich Naumann Foundation in December 1983. — 1. Aufl. — Sankt Augustin [Germany] : Liberal Verlag, 1985. — vi, 407 p.. — (Schriften der Friedrich-Naumann-Stiftung. Liberale Texte). — Includes bibliographies

APARTHEID — Economic aspects — Namibia
Activities of transnational corporations in South Africa and Namibia and the responsibilities of home countries with respect to their operations in this area. — New York : United Nations, 1986. — iii,59p. — ([Document] / United Nations ; ST/CTC/84). — Bibliographical references. — Sales no.: E.85.II.A.16

APARTHEID — Economic aspects — South Africa
Activities of transnational corporations in South Africa and Namibia and the responsibilities of home countries with respect to their operations in this area. — New York : United Nations, 1986. — iii,59p. — ([Document] / United Nations ; ST/CTC/84). — Bibliographical references. — Sales no.: E.85.II.A.16

STADLER, Alf
The political economy of modern South Africa. — London : Croom Helm, 1987. — 197p. — Bibliography: p190-193. — Includes index

APARTHEID — Legal status, laws, etc. — South Africa
Legal aspects of apartheid : a selective bibliography of books and articles and United Nations documentation in English, 1950-1983. — New York : United Nations, 1984. — i,49p. — ([Document] / United Nations ; ST/LIB/SER.B/34)

APARTHEID — Religious aspects
TUTU, Desmond
Crying in the wilderness : the struggle for justice in South Africa / Desmond Tutu ; introduced and edited by John Webster ; foreword by Trevor Huddleston. — Rev. and updated. — London : Mowbray, 1986. — xix,124p,[8]p of plates. — (Mowbrays popular Christian paperbacks). — Previous ed.: published as Bishop Desmond Tutu : the voice of one crying in the wilderness. 1982. — Bibliography: p124

APARTHEID — Religious aspects — Christianity
A Call for an end to unjust rule / edited by Allan Boesak and Charles Villa-Vicencio. — Edinburgh : Saint Andrew Press, 1986. — 189p

APARTHEID — South Africa
HANLON, Joseph
The sanctions handbook : for or against? / Joseph Hanlon and Roger Omond. — Harmondsworth : Penguin Books, 1987. — 399p

LEMON, Anthony
Apartheid in transition / Anthony Lemon. — Aldershot : Gower, 1987. — [410]p. — Includes bibliography and index

MANDELA, Nelson
No easy walk to freedom : articles, speeches and trial addresses of Nelson Mandela / with a foreword by Ruth First. — Harare : Zimbabwe Publishing House, 1983. — 189p. — First published 1965

MATHABANE, Mark
Kaffir boy : growing out of apartheid / Mark Mathabane. — London : Pan, 1987. — xii,354p

MATHEWS, Anthony S.
Freedom, state security and the rule of law : dilemmas of the apartheid society / Anthony S. Mathews. — Cape Town : Juta, 1986. — xxv,312p. — Bibliography: p.xi-xiv. - Includes index

SAMPSON, Anthony
Black & gold : tycoons, revolutionaries and apartheid / Anthony Sampson. — London : Hodder & Stoughton, 1987. — 280p. — Includes index

SAUL, John S.
The crisis in South Africa / by John S. Saul and Stephen Gelb. — Rev. ed. — London : Zed, c1986. — 245p. — Previous ed.: New York : Monthly Review, 1981

South Africa : a plural society in transition / editors, D.J. van Vuuren ... [et al.]. — Durban ; Stoneham, MA : Butterworths, c1985. — 510 p.. — Includes bibliographies and index

South Africa in crisis / edited by Jesmond Blumenfeld. — London : Croom Helm for the Royal Institute of International Affairs, 1987. — x,207p. — Includes index

TUTU, Desmond
Crying in the wilderness : the struggle for justice in South Africa / Desmond Tutu ; introduced and edited by John Webster ; foreword by Trevor Huddleston. — Rev. and updated. — London : Mowbray, 1986. — xix,124p,[8]p of plates. — (Mowbrays popular Christian paperbacks). — Previous ed.: published as Bishop Desmond Tutu : the voice of one crying in the wilderness. 1982. — Bibliography: p124

APARTHEID — South Africa — Bibliography
Apartheid : a selective bibliography on the racial policies of the government of the Republic of South Africa. — New York : United Nations, 1970. — 57p. — ([Document] / United Nations ; ST/LIB/22/Rev.1). — In various languages. — Prepared by the Dag Hammarskjöld Library

APARTHEID — South Africa — History
DENMAN, Earl
 The fiercest fight : a documented account of the struggle against apartheid in South Africa / by Earl Denman ; foreword by Gonville ffrench-Beytagh. — Worthing : Churchman, 1985. — xxii,190p

LAPPING, Brian
 Apartheid : a history / Brian Lapping in association with Granada Television. — London : Grafton, 1986. — xxi,200p,[32]p of plates. — *Bibliography : p185-190 — Includes index*

APARTHEID — South Africa — Religious aspects — Catholic Church
The Church and apartheid. — Sydney : Australian Catholic Relief ; London : Catholic Fund for Overseas Development, c1985. — 12p. — (Church in the world ; 20)

APARTMENT HOUSES — Law and legislation — Great Britain
GREAT BRITAIN. Parliament. House of Commons. Library. Research Division
 Landlord and Tenant (No.2) Bill [Bill 98 of session 1986/87] / Oonagh Gay. — [London] : the Division, 1987. — 26p. — (Reference sheet ; no.87/1). — *Bibliographical references: p24-26*

APARTMENT HOUSES — England — London
GREATER LONDON COUNCIL
 'They who pay the piper...' : evidence submitted by the Greater London Council to the Committee of Inquiry into the Management of Privately Owned Blocks of Flats. — [London] : the Council, 1984. — 27p

APPALACHIAN REGION — Economic conditions
Who owns Appalachia? : landownership and its impact / the Appalachian Land Ownership Task Force ; with an introduction by Charles C. Geisler. — Lexington, Ky. : University Press of Kentucky, c1983. — xxxii, 235 p.. — *Map on lining papers. — Includes bibliographies and index*

APPALACHIAN REGION — Social conditions
Who owns Appalachia? : landownership and its impact / the Appalachian Land Ownership Task Force ; with an introduction by Charles C. Geisler. — Lexington, Ky. : University Press of Kentucky, c1983. — xxxii, 235 p.. — *Map on lining papers. — Includes bibliographies and index*

APPELLATE PROCEDURE — European Economic Community Countries
Article 177 EEC : experiences and problems / edited by Henry G. Schermers...[et al.]. — Amsterdam : North-Holland, 1987. — xxxiv,441p. — (Asser Institute Colloquium on European Law ; 15). — *Proceedings of an international conference "Experiences and Problems in Applying the Preliminary Proceedings of Article 177 EEC", organized by the T.M.C. Asser Institute, the Hague, 5 and 6 September 1985*

APPETITE DISORDERS
Fed up and hungry : women, oppression and food / Marilyn Lawrence (editor) ; with a foreword by Susie Orbach. — London : Women's Press, 1987. — 236p

APPLE — Canada — Marketing
Apple market review = Revue de marché des pommes / Agriculture Canada, Marketing and Economics Branch. — Ottawa : Agriculture Canada, 1984-. — *Annual. — Text in English and French*

APPLIED ANTHROPOLOGY
Anthropological contributions to planned change and development / edited by Harald O. Skar. — Göteborg, Sweden : Acta Universitatis Gothoburgensis, 1985. — iv, 191 p.. — (Gothenburg studies in social anthropology ; 8). — *Includes bibliographies*

Collaborative research and social change : applied anthropology in action / edited by Donald D. Stull, Jean J. Schensul. — Boulder, CO : Westview Press, 1986. — p. cm. — (Westview special studies in applied anthropology). — *Includes index*

APPLIED ANTHROPOLOGY — Addresses, essays, lectures
Indigenous knowledge systems and development / edited by David Brokensha, D. M. Warren, and Oswald Werner. — Washington, D.C. : University Press of America, c1980. — vii, 466 p.. — *Includes indexes. — Bibliography: p. 415-449*

APPLIED ANTHROPOLOGY — Case studies
Practicing development anthropology / edited by Edward C. Green. — Boulder, Colo. : Westview Press, 1986. — xi, 283 p.. — (Westview special studies in applied anthropology). — *Includes bibliographies and index*

APPRENTICES — France — Champagne-Ardenne
Programme régional de formation professionnelle et d'apprentissage 1986-1987. — [Châlons-sur-Marne : Conseil régional], 1986. — 224p. — *Cover title*

APPRENTICES — United States — History
RORABAUGH, W. J
 The craft apprentice : from Franklin to the machine age in America / W.J. Rorabaugh. — New York : Oxford University Press, 1986. — p. cm. — *Includes index*

AQUACULTURE — Waste disposal
EDWARDS, Peter
 Aquaculture : a component of low cost sanitation technology / Peter Edwards. — Washington, D.C. : The World Bank, 1985. — xi,45p. — (World Bank technical paper ; no.36) (UNDP project management report ; no.3) (Integrated resource recovery series ; no.3). — *At head of cover: "Integrated resource recovery". — Bibliographical references: p45*

AQUITAINE BASIN (FRANCE) — Economic policy
Région et aménagement du territoire : mélanges offerts à Joseph Lajugie par ses collègues, ses élèves et ses amis. — Bordeaux : Editions Bière, 1985. — 898p. — *Bibliographies*

AQUITAINE BASIN (FRANCE) — Politics and government
Région et aménagement du territoire : mélanges offerts à Joseph Lajugie par ses collègues, ses élèves et ses amis. — Bordeaux : Editions Bière, 1985. — 898p. — *Bibliographies*

AQUITAINE (FRANCE) — Politics and government
SAVARY, Gilles
 Naissance d'une region, Rue Esprit des Lois : la construction régionale en Aquitaine à travers l'action économique 1982-1985 / Gilles Savary. — [Bordeaux] : Le Mascaret, 1986. — 274p

ARAB AMERICANS — History
NAFF, Alixa
 Becoming American : the early Arab immigrant experience / Alixa Naff. — Carbondale : Southern Illinois University Press, c1985. — p. cm. — (M.E.R.I. special studies). — *Includes index. — Bibliography: p*

ARAB COUNTRIES — Foreign economic relations — United States — Addresses, essays, lectures
U.S.-Arab economic relations : a time of transition / edited by Michael R. Czinkota and Scot Marciel. — New York : Praeger, 1985. — p. cm. — *Includes index*

ARAB COUNTRIES — Foreign relations — Soviet Union — History — 20th century
BEHBEHANI, Hashim S. H.
 The Soviet Union and Arab nationalism, 1917-1966 / Hashim S. H. Behbehani. — London : KPI, 1986. — 252p. — *Bibliography: p237-247*

ARAB COUNTRIES — Intellectual life
KH̄URĪ, Raʾif
 [Al-Fikr al-ʿArabī al-Hadīth-Athār al-Thawra al-Firinsiyya fī Tawjīhihi wa al-Ijitimāʿi. English]. Modern Arab thought : channels of the French revolution to the Arab East / Raʾif Khūrī ; translated by Ihsān ʿAbbās. — Princeton, N.J. : Kingston Press, 1983. — 227p. — (Leaders, politics and social change in the Islamic World ; vol. 4)

ARAB COUNTRIES — Politics and government
KH̄URĪ, Raʾif
 [Al-Fikr al-ʿArabī al-Hadīth-Athār al-Thawra al-Firinsiyya fī Tawjīhihi al Siyāsī wa al-Ijitimāʿi. English]. Modern Arab thought : channels of the French revolution to the Arab East / Raʾif Khūrī ; translated by Ihsān ʿAbbās. — Princeton, N.J. : Kingston Press, 1983. — 227p. — (Leaders, politics and social change in the Islamic World ; vol. 4)

ARAB COUNTRIES — Politics and government — 1945-
DAWISHA, A. I
 The Arab radicals / by Adeed Dawisha. — New York : Council on Foreign Relations, 1986. — p. cm. — *Includes index*

Pan-Arabism and Arab nationalism : the continuing debate / edited by Tawfic E. Farah ; foreword by James A. Bill. — Boulder : Westview Press, 1987. — xvi, 208 p.. — *Includes bibliographies and index*

ARAB COUNTRIES — Population
Population bulletin of ESCWA / United Nations Economic Commission for Western Asia. — Baghdad : United Nations and Social Commission for Western Asia, 1982-. — *Semi-annual*

ARAB COUNTRIES — Relations — Egypt
GERSHONI, I
 Egypt, Islam, and the Arabs : the search for Egyptian nationhood, 1900-1930 / Israel Gershoni and James P. Jankowski. — New York : Oxford University Press, 1986, c1987. — xviii, 346 p.. — (Studies in Middle Eastern history). — *"In cooperation with the Dayan Center and the Shiloah Institute for Middle Eastern and African Studies, Tel Aviv University.". — Includes index. — Bibliography: p. 326-335*

ARAB COUNTRIES — Social conditions
Arab society : social science perspectives / edited by Saad Eddin Ibrahim, Nicholas S. Hopkins. — Cairo : American University in Cairo Press, [1985]. — 507p. — *Rev. ed. of Arab society in transition*

Forbidden agendas : intolerance and defiance in the Middle East / selected and introduced by Jon Rothschild. — London : Al Saqi Books ; London : Zed Press [distributor], 1984. — 400p . — *" The articles in this anthology were first published in the journal 'Khamsin' 1976-83"*

ARABIAN PENINSULA — Commerce — History
CRONE, Patricia
 Meccan trade and the rise of Islam / Patricia Crone. — Princeton, N.J. : Princeton University Press, c1986. — vii, 300p. — *Includes index. — Bibliography: p.271-291*

ARABIAN PENINSULAR — Economic conditions
OSAMA, Abdul Rahman
 The dilemma of development in the Arabian peninsula / Abdul Rahman Osama. — London : Croom Helm, c1987. — 203p. — *Bibliography: p187-195. — Includes index*

ARABIAN PENINSULAR — Economic policy
OSAMA, Abdul Rahman
The dilemma of development in the Arabian peninsula / Abdul Rahman Osama. — London : Croom Helm, c1987. — 203p. — *Bibliography: p187-195. — Includes index*

ARABIAN PENINSULAR — Politics and government
OSAMA, Abdul Rahman
The dilemma of development in the Arabian peninsula / Abdul Rahman Osama. — London : Croom Helm, c1987. — 203p. — *Bibliography: p187-195. — Includes index*

ARABIC LANGUAGE — Addresses, Forms of
PARKINSON, Dilworth B.
Constructing the social context of communication : terms of address in Egyptian Arabic / by Dilworth B. Parkinson. — Berlin ; New York : Mouton de Gruyter, c1985. — 239 p.. — (Contributions to the sociology of language ; 41). — *Includes index. — Bibliography: p. [226]-234*

ARABIC LANGUAGE — Dialects — Egypt
PARKINSON, Dilworth B.
Constructing the social context of communication : terms of address in Egyptian Arabic / by Dilworth B. Parkinson. — Berlin ; New York : Mouton de Gruyter, c1985. — 239 p.. — (Contributions to the sociology of language ; 41). — *Includes index. — Bibliography: p. [226]-234*

ARABIC LANGUAGE — Social aspects — Egypt
PARKINSON, Dilworth B.
Constructing the social context of communication : terms of address in Egyptian Arabic / by Dilworth B. Parkinson. — Berlin ; New York : Mouton de Gruyter, c1985. — 239 p.. — (Contributions to the sociology of language ; 41). — *Includes index. — Bibliography: p. [226]-234*

ARABISM
BERQUE, Jacques
Arab rebirth : pain and ecstasy / Jacques Berque ; translated by Quintin Hoare. — London : Al Saqi, 1983. — 138p. — *Translation of: Les arabes*

ARABS
INGHAM, Bruce
Bedouin of Northern Arabia : traditions of the Al-Dhafir / Bruce Ingham. — London ; New York : KPI, 1986. — xvi,136p

ARABS — History
BERQUE, Jacques
Arab rebirth : pain and ecstasy / Jacques Berque ; translated by Quintin Hoare. — London : Al Saqi, 1983. — 138p. — *Translation of: Les arabes*

LEWIS, Bernard, 1916-
The Arabs in history / Bernard Lewis. — Rev.ed.. — London : Hutchinson, 1958. — 199p. — *Bibliography: p.184-190*

ARABS — Social life and customs
BERQUE, Jacques
Arab rebirth : pain and ecstasy / Jacques Berque ; translated by Quintin Hoare. — London : Al Saqi, 1983. — 138p. — *Translation of: Les arabes*

ARABS — Africa, East — History — 19th century
BENNETT, Norman Robert
Arab versus European : diplomacy and war in nineteenth-century east central Africa / Norman Robert Bennett. — New York ; London : Africana Publishing, 1986. — 325p. — *Includes index. — Bibliography: p*

ARABS — Australia — Public opinion
Migrant attitudes survey : a study of the attitudes of Australians and recently arrived migrants from Asia and the Middle East, in close neighbourhoods in Sydney and Adelaide. — Canberra : Australian Government Publishing Service
V.1: summary findings. — 1986. — vii,71p. — *Bibliography references: p37-38*

Migrant attitudes survey : a study of the attitudes of Australians and recently arrived migrants from Asia and the Middle East, in close neighbourhoods in Sydney and Adelaide. — Canberra : Australian Government Publishing Service
V.2: Overall findings. — 1986. — xxiv,280p

ARABS — Sahara — History
NORRIS, H. T.
The Arab conquest of the Western Sahara : studies of the historical events, religious beliefs and social customs which made the remotest Sahara a part of the Arab world / H.T. Norris. — Harlow : Longman, 1986. — xxvi,309p,[8]p of plates. — (Arab background series). — *Geneal.table on lining papers. — Bibliography: p295-297. — Includes index*

ARABS — Tanzania — Zanzibar — History — 19th century
BENNETT, Norman Robert
Arab versus European : diplomacy and war in nineteenth-century east central Africa / Norman Robert Bennett. — New York ; London : Africana Publishing, 1986. — 325p. — *Includes index. — Bibliography: p*

ARAFAT, YASIR
MISHAL, Shaul
The PLO under 'Arafat : between gun and olive branch / Shaul Mishal. — New Haven ; London : Yale University Press, c1986. — xiv, 190p. — *Includes index*

ARAGON (SPAIN) — Economic conditions
DIPUTACIÓN GENERAL DE ARAGÓN
Libro blanco sobre las repercusiones en Aragón de la integración de España en la CEE / [José María Serrano Sanz...et al.]. — [Zaragoza] : the Diputación, [ca.1985]. — 747p

PEREZ PEREZ, Luis
Approche méthodologique pour une délimitation des zones défavorisées : application au cas de la communauté autonome dÁragon / par Luis Perez Perez. — Montpellier : Institut Ayonomique Méditerranéen de Montpellier, 1985. — 148p. — (Collection "Thèses M. Sc." / Institut Agronomique Mèditerranéen de Montpellier). — *Bibliography:p65-68*

ARAGON (SPAIN) — Economic policy
DIPUTACIÓN GENERAL DE ARAGÓN
Libro blanco sobre las repercusiones en Aragón de la integración de España en la CEE / [José María Serrano Sanz...et al.]. — [Zaragoza] : the Diputación, [ca.1985]. — 747p

ARAGON (SPAIN) — History — Autonomy and Independence movements
CASANOVA, Julian
Anarquismo y revolución en la sociedad rural aragonesa, 1936-1938 / por Julian Casanova. — Madrid : Siglo Veintiuno, 1985. — 368p. — (Historia de los movimientos sociales)

ARAGON (SPAIN) — Politics and government
KELSEY, Graham
Civil war and civil peace : libertarian Aragon 1936-37 / Graham Kelsey. — Cambridge : Cambridge Free Press, 1985. — 78p. — (Anarchist encyclopaedia ; monograph 1). — *Bibliography: p73-78*

ARAPESH TRIBE — Religion
TUZIN, Donald F.
The voice of the Tambaran : truth and illusion in Ilahita Arapesh religion / Donald F. Tuzin. — Berkeley ; London : University of California Press, c1980. — xxi,355p. — *Bibliography: p341-346. — Includes index*

ARBEJDERNES OPLYSNINGSFORBUND
PETERSEN, Jens Peter Østerby
Arbejderne og krisen : forholdet mellem AOF's arbejderuddannelse, reformismen og arbejderbevidstheden i 30 'erne / Jens Peter Østerby Petersen & Jens Skovholm. — København : Litteratur & Samfund, 1978. — 240p. — *Bibliography: p237-239*

ARBITRAGE
HARRINGTON, Diana R.
Modern portfolio theory, the capital asset pricing model, and arbitrage pricing theory : a user's guide / Diana R. Harrington. — 2nd ed. — Englewood Cliffs, N.J. : Prentice-Hall, 1986, c1987. — p. cm. — *: Previous ed. published as: Modern portfolio theory and the capital asset pricing model. 1983. — Includes bibliographies and index*

ARBITRATION AND AWARD — England
BERNSTEIN, Ronald
Handbook of arbitration practice / by Ronald Bernstein, contributors John Tackaberry ... [et al.] ; foreword by Sir John Donaldson ; introduction by Sir Michael Kerr. — London : Sweet & Maxwell in conjunction with the Chartered Institute of Arbitrators, 1987. — xxv,575p. — *Bibliography: p563-564. — Includes index*

LEE, Eric
Encyclopedia of arbitration law / Eric Lee. — London : Lloyd's, c1984. — 1v(looseleaf). — *Includes index*

ARBITRATION AND AWARD, INTERNATIONAL
Contemporary problems in international arbitration / edited by Julian D. M. Lew. — London : Queen Mary College, Centre for Commercial Law Studies. School of International Arbitration, 1986. — xlv, 380p. — *Based on papers presented at a conference organised by the School of International Arbitration, Queen Mary College. — Includes bibliographical references and index*

DORE, Isaak I.
Arbitration and conciliation under the UNCITRAL rules : a textual analysis / Issaak I. Dore. — Dordrecht ; Boston : Nijhoff, 1986. — p. cm

REDFERN, Alan
Law and practice of international commercial arbitration / by Alan Redfern, Martin Hunter ; foreword by Sir Robert Jennings. — London : Sweet & Maxwell, 1986. — xliii,462p. — *Includes index*

ARBITRATION, INDUSTRIAL — Australia
Alternatives to arbitration / edited by Richard Blandy and John Niland ; Industrial Relations Research Centre [and] National Institute of Labour Studies. — Sydney ; London : Allen & Unwin, 1986. — [460]p. — (Australian studies in industrial relations). — *Conference proceedings. — Includes bibliography and index*

HUTSON, Jack
Penal colony to penal powers / by Jack Hutson. — rev. ed. — [Surrey Hills, N.S.W.] : [Amalgamated Metals Foundry and Shipwrights Union], 1983. — 359p

ARBITRATION, INDUSTRIAL — United States
GOULD, William B
Strikes, dispute procedures, and arbitration : essays on labor law / William B. Gould IV. — Westport, Conn. : Greenwood Press, c1985. — p. cm. — (Contributions in American studies ; no. 82). — *Includes index. — Bibliography: p*

ARBITRATION, INDUSTRIAL — United States — Congresses

The Changing law of fair representation / Jean T. McKelvey, editor. — Ithaca, NY : ILR Press, New York State School of Industrial and Labor Relations, Cornell University, 1985. — iv, 298 p.. — *Papers presented at a national conference sponsored by the Extension Division of the New York State School of Industrial and Labor Relations, Cornell University, October 20 and 21, 1983. — Includes bibliographical references and indexes*

ARBITRATION, INTERNATIONAL

LAUTERPACHT, Sir Hersch
Private law sources and analogies on international law / with special reference to international arbitration. — [Hamden, Conn.] : Archon Books, 1970. — xxiv, 326 p. — *Reprint of the 1927 ed. — Bibliography: p. 307-312*

SHORE, William I
Fact-finding in the maintenance of international peace / by William I. Shore. Pref. by A. J. P. Tammes. — Dobbs Ferry, N.Y. : Oceana Publications, 1970. — ii, 183 p. — *Bibliography: p. 154-167*

ARCHAEOLOGISTS — Biography

GREEN, Sally
Prehistorian : a biography of V. Gordon Childe / Sally Green ; with a foreword by Jack Lindsay. — Bradford-on-Avon : Moonraker, 1981. — xxii,200p. — *Bibliography: p176-190. — Includes index*

ARCHITECTS — Germany (West) — Taxation

Kostenstruktur bei Rechtsanwälten und Anwaltsnotaven, bei Wirtschaftsprüfern, Steuerberatern und Steuerbevollmächtigten, bei Architekten und Beratenden Ingenieuren. — Wiesbaden : Statistisches Bundesamt, 1975-. — (Unternehmen und Arbeitsstätten ; Reihe 1.6.2) . — *Every 4 years. — Title varies*

ARCHITECTURE — Environmental aspects — United States

Home environments / edited by Irwin Altman and Carol M. Werner. — New York ; London : Plenum Press, c1985. — xxii, 339p. — (Human behavior and environment ; v. 8). — *Includes index. — Bibliography: p.330-331*

ARCHITECTURE — Human factors

HOGLUND, David J.
Housing for the elderly : privacy and independence / J. David Hoglund. — New York : Van Nostrand Reinhold, c1985. — p. cm. — *Includes index. — Bibliography: p*

ARCHITECTURE — Indian — Lucknow — History

LLEWELLYN-JONES, Rosie
A fatal friendship : the Nawabs, the British and the city of Lucknow / Rosie Llewellyn-Jones. — Delhi ; Oxford : Oxford University Press, c1985. — xii,284p,[12]p of plates. — *Bibliography: p269-276. — Includes index*

ARCHITECTURE — United States — Human factors

Home environments / edited by Irwin Altman and Carol M. Werner. — New York ; London : Plenum Press, c1985. — xxii, 339p. — (Human behavior and environment ; v. 8). — *Includes index. — Bibliography: p.330-331*

ARCHITECTURE AND SOCIETY — United States

CLARK, Clifford Edward
The American family home, 1800-1960 / by Clifford Edward Clark, Jr. — Chapel Hill : University of North Carolina Press, c1986. — p. cm. — *Includes index. — Bibliography: p*

ARCHITECTURE AND THE AGED — Europe

HOGLUND, David J.
Housing for the elderly : privacy and independence / J. David Hoglund. — New York : Van Nostrand Reinhold, c1985. — p. cm. — *Includes index. — Bibliography: p*

ARCHITECTURE, INDUSTRIAL — Great Britain

JONES, Edgar, 1953-
Industrial architecture in Britain 1750-1939 / Edgar Jones. — New York : Facts on File, 1985. — 239p. — *Bibliography: p225-233*

ARCHITECTURE, MODERN — 19th century — Austria — Vienna

OLSEN, Donald J.
The city as a work of art : London, Paris, Vienna / Donald J. Olsen. — New Haven ; London : Yale University Press, c1986. — xiii,341p,[8]p of plates. — *Bibliography: p329-335. — Includes index*

ARCHITECTURE, MODERN — 19th century — England — London

OLSEN, Donald J.
The city as a work of art : London, Paris, Vienna / Donald J. Olsen. — New Haven ; London : Yale University Press, c1986. — xiii,341p,[8]p of plates. — *Bibliography: p329-335. — Includes index*

ARCHITECTURE, MODERN — 19th century — France — Paris

OLSEN, Donald J.
The city as a work of art : London, Paris, Vienna / Donald J. Olsen. — New Haven ; London : Yale University Press, c1986. — xiii,341p,[8]p of plates. — *Bibliography: p329-335. — Includes index*

ARCHITECTURE, MODERN — 20th century — Austria — Vienna

OLSEN, Donald J.
The city as a work of art : London, Paris, Vienna / Donald J. Olsen. — New Haven ; London : Yale University Press, c1986. — xiii,341p,[8]p of plates. — *Bibliography: p329-335. — Includes index*

ARCHITECTURE, MODERN — 20th century — England — London

OLSEN, Donald J.
The city as a work of art : London, Paris, Vienna / Donald J. Olsen. — New Haven ; London : Yale University Press, c1986. — xiii,341p,[8]p of plates. — *Bibliography: p329-335. — Includes index*

ARCHITECTURE, MODERN — 20th century — France — Paris

OLSEN, Donald J.
The city as a work of art : London, Paris, Vienna / Donald J. Olsen. — New Haven ; London : Yale University Press, c1986. — xiii,341p,[8]p of plates. — *Bibliography: p329-335. — Includes index*

ARCHITECTURE, MODERN — 20th century — Great Britain

JONES, Edgar, 1953-
Industrial architecture in Britain 1750-1939 / Edgar Jones. — New York : Facts on File, 1985. — 239p. — *Bibliography: p225-233*

ARCHITECTURE, SCOTTISH — History — 20th century

MCKEAN, Charles
The Scottish Thirties : an architectural introduction / Charles McKean. — Edinburgh : Scottish Academic Press, 1987. — 200p. — *Bibliography: p191*

ARCHITECTURE, VICTORIAN — England

GIROUARD, Mark
The Victorian country house / Mark Girouard. — Revised and enlarged ed. — New Haven ; London : Yale University Press, 1979. — x,467p. — *Facsims on lining papers. — Previous ed.: Oxford : Clarendon Press, 1971. — Includes index*

ARCHIVES — Administration — Addresses, essays, lectures

A Modern archives reader : basic readings on archival theory and practice / edited by Maygene F. Daniels and Timothy Walch. — Washington, D.C. : National Archives and Records Service, U.S. General Services Administration, 1984. — xv, 357p. — *Includes index*

ARCHIVES — Data processing

COOK, Michael, 1931-
Archives and the computer / Michael Cook. — 2nd ed. — London : Butterworths, 1986. — [176]p. — *Previous ed.: 1980. — Includes bibliography and index*

ARCHIVES — Dictionaries — Polyglot

Dictionary of archival terminology = Dictionnaire de terminologie archivistique : English and French with equivalents in Dutch, German, Italian, Russian and Spanish / edited by Peter Walne ; compiled by Frank B. Evans, François-J. Himly and Peter Walne. — München ; London : Saur, 1984. — 226p. — (ICA handbooks series ; v.3). — *At head of title: International Council on Archives*

ARCHIVES — Law and legislation — Great Britain

KNIGHTBRIDGE, A. A. H.
Archive legislation in the United Kingdom / A. A. H. Knightbridge. — Winchester : Society of Archivists, 1985. — [8p]. — (Society of Archivists information leaflet ; 3)

ARCHIVES — Reference services

Reference services in archives / Lucille Whalen, editor. — New York : Haworth Press, c1986. — 210 p.. — *Published also as no. 13, fall 1985/winter 1985-86 of The reference librarian. — Includes bibliographies*

ARCHIVES — United States — Administration — Addresses, essays, lectures

Archival choices : managing the historical record in an age of abundance / edited by Nancy E. Peace. — Lexington, Mass. : Heath, c1984. — 164 p. — (The Lexington books special series in libraries and librarianship)

ARCHTECTURE, MODERN — 19th century — Great Britain

JONES, Edgar, 1953-
Industrial architecture in Britain 1750-1939 / Edgar Jones. — New York : Facts on File, 1985. — 239p. — *Bibliography: p225-233*

ARCTIC REGIONS

SABIN, Francene
Arctic and Antarctic regions / by Francene Sabin ; illustrated by Allan Eitzen. — Mahwah, N.J. : Troll Associates, c1985. — p. cm. — *Summary: Briefly describes the frozen regions around the North Pole and the South Pole, which are alike in many ways and different in many others*

ARENDT, HANNAH

FRIEDMANN, Friedrich Georg
Hannah Arendt : eine deutsche Jüdin im Zeitalter des Totalitarismus / Friedrich Georg Friedmann. — München : Piper, 1985. — 160p

ARGENTINA — Armed Forces — Appropriations and expenditures

LOONEY, Robert E
The political economy of Latin American defense expenditures : case studies of Venezuela and Argentina / Robert E. Looney. — Lexington, Mass. : Lexington Books, c1986. — xxii, 325 p.. — *Includes index. — Bibliography: p. [309]-314*

ARGENTINA — Boundaries

SABATÉ LICHTSCHEIN, Domingo
Problemas argentinos de soberanía territorial / Domingo Sabaté Lichtschein. — 3a edición. — Buenos Aires : Abeledo-Perrot, [ca.1985]. — 453p. — *Publicado originalmente en 1976*

ARGENTINA — Boundaries — Chile
DESTEFANI, Laurio H.
Lo que debe saberse del Beagle : síntesis del conflicto de límites austral entre Argentina y Chile / Laurio H. Destefani. — [Buenos Aires] : Platero, [ca.1984]. — 93p. — *Bibliography: p91-93*

ARGENTINA — Census, 1980
INSTITUTO NACIONAL DE ESTADISTICA Y CENSOS (Argentina)
Censo nacional de poblacion y vivienda 1980 : serie C : vivienda. — Buenos Aires : the Instituto, [1981-]. — 3v

ARGENTINA — Commerce
Comercio exterior / Instituto Nacional de Estadistica y Censos, Argentina. — Buenos Aires : Instituto Nacional de Estadistica y Censos, 1964-1972. — *Quarterly.* — *Continued by: Intercambio comercial*

Intercambio comercial / Instituto Nacional de Estadistica y Censos, Argentina. — Buenos Aires : Instituto Nacional de Estadistica y Censos, 1973-1984. — *Monthly.* — *Continues: Comercio exterior-. Continued by Estadistica mensual*

ARGENTINA — Commerce — Statistics
ALADI / Instituto Nacional de Estadistica y Censos, Argentina. — [Buenos Aires] : Instituto Nacional de Estadistica y Censos, 1982-. — *Annual.* — *Continues: ALALC*

ALALC / Instituto Nacional de Estadistica y Censos, Argentina. — [Buenos Aires] : Instituto Nacional de Estadistica y Censos, 1966-1980. — *Annual.* — *Continues: Intercambio commercial argentino con los paisde la ALALC. Continued by: ALADI*

Intercambio commercial argentino con los paises de la ALALC / Instituto Nacional de Estadistica y Censos. — Buenos Aires : Instituto Nacional de Estadistica y Censos, 1962-1965. — *Quarterly.* — *Continued by: ALALC*

ARGENTINA — Defenses
LOONEY, Robert E
The political economy of Latin American defense expenditures : case studies of Venezuela and Argentina / Robert E. Looney. — Lexington, Mass. : Lexington Books, c1986. — xxii, 325 p.. — *Includes index.* — *Bibliography: p. [309]-314*

ARGENTINA — Economic conditions
La Crisis de 1873 / selección y prólogo, José Panettieri. — Buenos Aires : Centro editor de America latina, 1984. — 91p. — (Historia testimonial argentina ; 17)

ARGENTINA — Economic conditions — Statistics
Estadistica mensual / Instituto Nacional de Estadistica y Censos, Argentina. — Buenos Aires : Instituto Nacional de Estadistica y Censos, 1985-. — *Monthly.* — *Continues: Indice de precios al consumidor, Indice de precios al por mayor, Costo de la construccion, Indices de salarios, Intercambio comercial argentino*

ARGENTINA — Economic conditions — 1918-
JUSTO, Liborio
Argentina y Brasil en la integración continental / Liborio Justo. — [Buenos Aires] : Centro Editor de América Latina, c1983. — 183p. — (Biblioteca política argentina ; 37)

U.S. military intelligence reports : Argentina, 1918-1941. — Frederick, MD : University Publications of America, Inc., 1985. — 4microfilms. — *Contents: Documents from the National Archives and Record Services, Military Intelligence Division*

ARGENTINA — Economic conditions — 1918- — Bibliography
U.S. military intelligence reports : Argentina, 1918-1941 / edited by Dale Reynolds. — Frederick, Md. : University Publications of America, 1985. — 30p. — *Contents: Index to documents from the National Archives and Record Services on microfilm*

ARGENTINA — Economic conditions — 1945-1983
FISCHER, Bernhard
Argentina : the economic crisis in the 1980's / Bernhard Fischer, Ulrich Hiemenz, Peter Trapp. — Tübingen : J. C. B. Mohr, 1985. — x,102p. — (Kieler Studien ; 197). — *Bibliography: p98-102*

JOZAMI, Eduardo
Crisis de la dictadura argentina : política económica y cambio social 1976-1983 / Eduardo Jozami, Pedro Paz, Juan Villarreal. — México : Siglo Veintiuno, c1985. — 283p. — (Sociología y política)

SALEÑO, Nicanor
La Argentina : productividad tecnológica y cambio social; escenario prospectivo para el tercer milenio / Nicanor Saleño. — [Buenos Aires?] : Pleamar, c1984. — 199p. — (Economía y sociedad)

ARGENTINA — Economic conditions — 1945-
CONESA, Eduardo R.
The economic solution for Argentina (taking into account internal-political as well as external constraints) / Eduardo R.Conesa. — Amherst (Mass.) : International Area Studies Programs. University of Massachusetts at Amherst, 1985. — 24p. — (Program in Latin American studies. Occasional papers series ; no.17)

FERRER, Aldo
Living within our means : an examination of the Argentine economic crisis / Aldo Ferrer ; translated by Maria-Ines Alvarez and Nick Caistor. — London : Third World Foundation, 1985. — [112]p. — *Translation from the Spanish*

From military rule to liberal democracy in Argentina / edited by Carlos H. Waisman, Mónica Peralta-Ramos. — Boulder, Colo. : Westview Press, 1986. — xvi, 175p. — (Westview special studies on Latin America and the Caribbean). — *Includes bibliographical references and index*

FUCHS, Jaime
Argentina, estructura económico-social actual / Jaime Fuchs. — 2a edición revisada y actualizada. — Buenos Aires : Cartago, 1985. — 364p. — *Publicado originalmente en 1981*

KÜHL, Livio Guillermo
Una política industrial para la Argentina / director Livio Guillermo Kühl ; supervisión general Horacio R. Rieznik ; investigadores y redactores Rodolfo E. Biasca, Roberto Iglesias. — Buenos Aires : Club de Estudio, c1983. — 2v. — *Vol.2 is a summary of vol.1*

PLA, Alberto J.
La década trágica : ocho ensayos sobre la crisis argentina, 1973-1983 / Alberto J. Pla...[et al.]. — [Buenos Aires] : Tierra del Fuego, 1984. — 252p

SOURROUILLE, Juan V.
Transnacionalización y política económica en la Argentina / Juan V. Sourrouille, Bernardo P. Kosacoff, Jorge Lucangeli. — [Buenos Aires] : Bibliotecas Universitarias, Centro Editor de América Latina : Centro de Economía Transnacional, c1985. — 164p. — (Economía). — *Bibliography: p161-164*

UNITED NATIONS. Economic Commission for Latin America
Internacionalización de empresas y tecnología de origen argentino / Eduardo R. Ablin...[et al.]. — Buenos Aires : CEPAL : EUDEBA, c1985. — 331p

ARGENTINA — Economic policy
FIGUEIRAS, Horacio
Bases de discusión para una política rural / Horacio Figueiras, Daniel Adrogue, Raúl Druetta. — Buenos Aires : Editorial Hernandiana : Fundación Alimentaria Argentina, c1985. — 175p. — (Serie política / Fundación Alimentaria Argentina)

FISCHER, Bernhard
Argentina : the economic crisis in the 1980's / Bernhard Fischer, Ulrich Hiemenz, Peter Trapp. — Tübingen : J. C. B. Mohr, 1985. — x,102p. — (Kieler Studien ; 197). — *Bibliography: p98-102*

JOZAMI, Eduardo
Crisis de la dictadura argentina : política económica y cambio social 1976-1983 / Eduardo Jozami, Pedro Paz, Juan Villarreal. — México : Siglo Veintiuno, c1985. — 283p. — (Sociología y política)

RAPOPORT, Mario
De Pellegrini a Martínez de Hoz : el modelo liberal / Mario Rapoport. — Buenos Aires : Centro Editor de América Latina, c1984. — 199p. — (Biblioteca política argentina ; 61)

WYNIA, Gary W.
La Argentina de posguerra / Gary W. Wynia. — [Buenos Aires] : Editorial de Belgrano, c1986. — 407p. — *Publicado originalmente en inglés con el título: "Argentina in the postwar era: political and economic policy making in a divided society", por University of New Mexico Press, Albuquerque, en 1978.* — *Bibliography: p394-406*

ARGENTINA — Emigration and immigration
GURRIERI, Jorge
Scarce skills and international migration in Argentina / by Jorge Gurrieri, Silvia Lépore, Lelio Mármora. — Geneva : International Labour Office, 1986. — iv,58p. — (Working paper / International Migration for Employment). — *Bibliography: p54-56*

ARGENTINA — Emigration and Immigration
La inmigración Italiana en la Argentina / Fernando Devoto, Gianfausto Rosoli (compiladores). — Buenos Aires : Editorial Biblos, 1985. — 270p

ARGENTINA — Emigration and immigration
PILDAIN SALAZAR, María Pilar
Ir a América : la emigración vasca a América (Guipúzcoa 1840-1870) / María Pilar Pildain Salazar. — San Sebastián : Donostia, 1984. — xii,245p. — (Monografías / Grupo Doctor Camino de Historia de San Sebastián ; 22). — *Bibliography: p82-83*

ARGENTINA — Emigration and immigration — History
Presencia alemana y austríaca en la Argentina = Deutsche und österreichische Präsenz in Argentina / proyecto y dirección Manrique Zago. — Buenos Aires : Manrique Zago, [1985]. — 220p

ARGENTINA — Foreign economic relations — Brazil
JUSTO, Liborio
Argentina y Brasil en la integración continental / Liborio Justo. — [Buenos Aires] : Centro Editor de América Latina, c1983. — 183p. — (Biblioteca política argentina ; 37)

ARGENTINA — Foreign population
Presencia alemana y austríaca en la Argentina = Deutsche und österreichische Präsenz in Argentina / proyecto y dirección Manrique Zago. — Buenos Aires : Manrique Zago, [1985]. — 220p

ARGENTINA — Foreign population — History — 19th century

CARRON, Alexandre
Nos cousins d'Amérique : histoire de l'émigration valaisanne au XIXe siècle / Alexandre Carron [et] Christophe Carron. — Sierre : Monographic SA, 1986. — 300p

ARGENTINA — Foreign relations — Great Britain

CERÓN, Sergio
Malvinas : ¿Gesta heroica o derrota vergonzosa? / Sergio Cerón. — Buenos Aires : Editorial Sudamericana, [ca.1984]. — 344p

FERRER VIEYRA, Enrique
Las islas Malvinas y el derecho internacional : los títulos argentinos y británicos, la convención de Nootka, la prescripción adquisitiva, la libre determinación de los pueblos, las Malvinas y la Antártica Argentina / Enrique Ferrer Vieyra. — Buenos Aires : Depalma, 1984. — xvi, 364p. — *Bibliography: p.333-364*

GREAT BRITAIN. Parliament. House of Commons. Library. International Affairs Section
The Falkland Islands and Dependencies / Richard Ware. — [London] : the Library, 1982. — 21p. — (Background paper / House of Commons. Library. [Research Division] ; no.101). — *Updated and expanded version of paper first issued on 5th April 1982*

ARGENTINA — History — 1810-

TORRES MOLINA, Ramón
Unitarios y Federales en la historia argentina / Ramón Torres Molina. — Buenos Aires : Editorial Contrapunto, 1986. — 134p. — (Colección La historia revisada)

ARGENTINA — History — 1817-1860

TORRES MOLINA, Ramón
Unitarios y Federales en la historia argentina / Ramón Torres Molina. — Buenos Aires : Editorial Contrapunto, 1986. — 134p. — (Colección La historia revisada)

ARGENTINA — History — 1910-1943

ALEN LASCANO, Luis C
Yrigoyen, Sandino y el panamericanismo / Luis C. Alen Lascano. — Buenos Aires : Centro Editor de América Latina, 1986. — 138p. — (Biblioteca Política Argentina ; 131). — *Bibliography: p138*

U.S. military intelligence reports : Argentina, 1918-1941. — Frederick, MD : University Publications of America, Inc., 1985. — 4microfilms. — *Contents: Documents from the National Archives and Record Services, Military Intelligence Division*

ARGENTINA — History — 1910-1943 — Bibliography

U.S. military intelligence reports : Argentina, 1918-1941 / edited by Dale Reynolds. — Frederick, Md. : University Publications of America, 1985. — 30p. — *Contents: Index to documents from the National Archives and Record Services on microfilm*

ARGENTINA — History — 1943-

CRASSWELLER, Robert D.
Perón and the enigmas of Argentina / Robert D. Crassweller. — New York : W. W. Norton, 1987. — xi,432p. — *Bibliography: p406-[420]*

ARGENTINA — History — 1955-1983

AREVALO, Oscar
Malvinas ; Beagle; Atlantico Sur; : Madryn, jaque a la OTAN-OTAS / Oscar Arevalo. — Buenos Aires : Anteo, 1985. — 167p. — (Colección Argentina : temas de actualidad)

ARGENTINA — History — 1955-

GOLDAR, Ernesto
John William Cooke y el peronismo revolucionario / Ernesto Goldar. — Buenos Aires : Centro Editor de América Latina, 1985. — 140p. — (Biblioteca Política Argentina ; 99)

ARGENTINA — History — 1943-

CHÁVEZ, Fermín
Perón y el peronismo en la historia contemporánea / Fermín Chávez. — Buenos Aires : Editorial Oriente. — *Includes bibliographical references*
t.2. — 1984. — 298p

ARGENTINA — History, Naval

PIERROU, Enrique J.
La Armada Argentina en la Antártida / Enrique J. Pierrou. — Buenos Aires : Centro Naval, Instituto de Publicaciones Navales, c1981. — 951p. — (Colección historia / Centro Naval, Instituto de Publicaciones Navales ; 12). — *Bibliography: p947-951*

ARGENTINA — Politics and government

MERLO, Arturo
Argentina totalitaria / Arturo Merlo. — Buenos Aires : Editorial Occidente, 1984. — 253p. — *Bibliography: p251-253*

ARGENTINA — Politics and government — 1860-1910

FALCÓN, Ricardo
Los orígenes del movimiento obrero (1857-1899) / Ricardo Falcón. — Buenos Aires : Centro Editor de América Latina, c1984. — 129p. — (Biblioteca política argentina ; 53). — *Includes bibliographical references*

ARGENTINA — Politics and government — 20th century

RAPOPORT, Mario
De Pellegrini a Martínez de Hoz : el modelo liberal / Mario Rapoport. — Buenos Aires : Centro Editor de América Latina, c1984. — 199p. — (Biblioteca política argentina ; 61)

ARGENTINA — Politics and government — 1910-1943

GARCÍA MOLINA, Fernando
El general Uriburu y el petróleo / Fernando García Molina, Carlos A. Mayo. — Buenos Aires : Centro Editor de América Latina, 1985. — 156p. — (Biblioteca Política Argentina ; 96) . — *Bibliographical notes: p129-156*

MAZO, Gabriel del
La segunda presidencia de Yrigoyen / Gabriel del Mazo. Antecedentes de la crisis de 1930 / Roberto Etchepareborda. — Buenos Aires : Centro Editor de America Latina, 1981. — 159p. — (Biblioteca politica Argentina ; 52. Las presidencias radicales)

ARGENTINA — Politics and government — 1910-

U.S. military intelligence reports : Argentina, 1918-1941. — Frederick, MD : University Publications of America, Inc., 1985. — 4microfilms. — *Contents: Documents from the National Archives and Record Services, Military Intelligence Division*

ARGENTINA — Politics and government — 1910- — Bibliography

U.S. military intelligence reports : Argentina, 1918-1941 / edited by Dale Reynolds. — Frederick, Md. : University Publications of America, 1985. — 30p. — *Contents: Index to documents from the National Archives and Record Services on microfilm*

ARGENTINA — Politics and government — 1943-1955

LUNA, Félix
Perón y su tiempo / Félix Luna. — Buenos Aires : Editorial Sudamericana
Vol.1: La Argentina era una fiesta 1946-1949. — 1984. — 607p. — *Includes 'Cronología - 4 de junio 1946 - 31 de diciembre 1949', p519-592*

LUNA, Félix
Perón y su tiempo / Félix Luna. — Buenos Aires : Editorial Sudamericana
Vol.2: La comunidad organizada, 1950-1952. — 1985. — 424p. — *Includes 'Cronología 1 de enero de 1950 - 31 de diciembre de 1952,' p [353]-393*

MACEYRA, Horacio
La segunda presidencia de Perón / Horacio Maceyra. — Buenos Aires : Centro Editor de América Latina, c1984. — 167 p.. — (Biblioteca Política argentina ; 51) (Biblioteca Política argentina ; 51Las Presidencias peronistas). — *"Volumen especial (E)"--P. [4] of cover. — Includes bibliographies*

ARGENTINA — Politics and government — 1943-

NARVAJA, Aurelio
Cuarenta años de Peronismo / Aurelio Narvaja, Angel Perelman, Jorge Abelardo Ramos. — Buenos Aires : Ediciones del Mar Dulce, 1985. — 158p

PAVÓN PEREYRA, Enrique
Perón tal como fue / Enrique Pavón Pereyra. — Buenos Aires : Centro Editor de América Latina. — (Biblioteca Política Argentina ; 137)
t.1. — 1986. — 139p

WYNIA, Gary W.
La Argentina de posguerra / Gary W. Wynia. — [Buenos Aires] : Editorial de Belgrano, c1986. — 407p. — *Publicado originalmente en inglés con el título: "Argentina in the postwar era: political and economic policy making in a divided society", por University of New Mexico Press, Albuquerque, en 1978. — Bibliography: p394-406*

ARGENTINA — Politics and government — 1955-1983

O'DONNELL, Guillermo A
Modernization and bureaucratic-authoritarianism : studies in South American politics / [by] Guillermo A. O'Donnell. — Berkeley : Institute of International Studies, University of California, [1973]. — xv, 219 p. — (Politics of modernization series ; no. 9). — *Bibliography: p. 201-219*

OLLIER, Maria Matilde
El fenómeno insurreccional y la cultura política (1969-1973) / Maria Matilde Ollier. — Buenos Aires : Centro Editor de América Latina, 1986. — 141p. — (Biblioteca Política Argentina ; 145). — *Bibliography: p139-141*

ARGENTINA — Politics and government — 1955-

From military rule to liberal democracy in Argentina / edited by Carlos H. Waisman, Mónica Peralta-Ramos. — Boulder, Colo. : Westview Press, 1986. — xvi, 175p. — (Westview special studies on Latin America and the Caribbean). — *Includes bibliographical references and index*

PLA, Alberto J.
La década trágica : ocho ensayos sobre la crisis argentina, 1973-1983 / Alberto J. Pla...[et al.]. — [Buenos Aires] : Tierra del Fuego, 1984. — 252p

ARGENTINA — Politics and government — 1983-

BURNS, Jimmy
The land that lost its heroes : the Falklands, the post-war and Alfonsín / Jimmy Burns. — London : Bloomsbury, 1987. — 1v.. — *Includes bibliography and index*

WYNIA, Gary W.
Argentina : illusions and realities / Gary W. Wynia. — New York : Holmes & Meier, 1986. — x, 207 p.

ARGENTINA — Presidents — Wives — Biography

La historia de Eva Perón : un ejemplo de amor entre una mujer y un pueblo. — Buenos Aires : Sánchez Teruelo
Tomo 1. — [1983]. — 320p

La historia de Eva Perón : un ejemplo de amor entre una mujer y un pueblo. — Buenos Aires : Sánchez Teruelo
Tomo 2. — 1985. — 321-560p

ARGENTINA — Relations — Soviet Union
ECHAGÜE, Carlos
El socialimperialismo Ruso en la Argentina / Carlos Echagüe. — Buenos Aires : Agora, 1984. — 367p

VACS, Aldo César
Los socios discretos : el nuevo carácter de las relaciones internacionales entre la Argentina y la Unión Soviética / Aldo César Vacs. — Buenos Aires : Sudoamericana, 1984. — 183p. — *Bibliography: p[187-193]*

ARGENTINA — Relations — Spain
SABSAY, Fernando Leónidas
La sociedad argentina : España y el Rió de la Plata / Fernando L. Sabsay. — Buenos Aires : Ediciones Macchi, [1984]. — 288p. — (Colección Ciencias Economicas). — *Bibliography: p[287]-288*

ARGENTINA — Social conditions — 1945-1983
JOZAMI, Eduardo
Crisis de la dictadura argentina : política económica y cambio social 1976-1983 / Eduardo Jozami, Pedro Paz, Juan Villarreal. — México : Siglo Veintiuno, c1985. — 283p. — (Sociología y política)

ARGENTINA — Social conditions — 1945-
From military rule to liberal democracy in Argentina / edited by Carlos H. Waisman, Mónica Peralta-Ramos. — Boulder, Colo. : Westview Press, 1986. — xvi, 175p. — (Westview special studies on Latin America and the Caribbean). — *Includes bibliographical references and index*

FUCHS, Jaime
Argentina, estructura económico-social actual / Jaime Fuchs. — 2a edición revisada y actualizada. — Buenos Aires : Cartago, 1985. — 364p. — *Publicado originalmente en 1981*

ARGENTINA. Armada — History
PIERROU, Enrique J.
La Armada Argentina en la Antártida / Enrique J. Pierrou. — Buenos Aires : Centro Naval, Instituto de Publicaciones Navales, c1981. — 951p. — (Colección historia / Centro Naval, Instituto de Publicaciones Navales ; 12). — *Bibliography: p947-951*

ARICAN NATIONAL CONGRESS
MANDELA, Nelson
No easy walk to freedom : articles, speeches and trial addresses of Nelson Mandela / with a foreword by Ruth First. — Harare : Zimbabwe Publishing House, 1983. — 189p. — *First published 1965*

ARID REGIONS AGRICULTURE — Congresses
AGRICULTURE SECTOR SYMPOSIUM (6th : 1986 : World Bank)
Development of rainfed agriculture under arid and semiarid conditions : proceedings of the Sixth Agriculture Sector Symposium / Ted J. Davis, editor. — Washington, D.C., U.S.A. : World Bank, 1986. — viii,412p. — *Proceedings held Jan. 6-10, 1986 at the World Bank.* — *Includes bibliographical references*

ARID REGIONS AGRICULTURE — Developing countries — Congresses
AGRICULTURE SECTOR SYMPOSIUM (6th : 1986 : World Bank)
Development of rainfed agriculture under arid and semiarid conditions : proceedings of the Sixth Agriculture Sector Symposium / Ted J. Davis, editor. — Washington, D.C., U.S.A. : World Bank, 1986. — viii,412p. — *Proceedings held Jan. 6-10, 1986 at the World Bank.* — *Includes bibliographical references*

ARISTOTELES
ROSS, William David
Aristotle / by W. D. Ross. — London : Methuen & co., ltd, [1923]. — vii, 300 p. — *Bibliography: p. 291-295*

ARISTOTLE
EVANS, J. D. G.
Aristotle / J.D.G. Evans. — Brighton : Harvester, 1987. — xii,208p. — (Philosophers in context). — *Bibliography: p188-193. Includes index*

ARMADA, 1588 — History — Sources
The great enterprise : the history of the Spanish Armada / as revealed in contemporary documents selected and edited by Stephen Usherwood. — London : Folio Society, 1978. — 192p

ARMAGH PRISON — Security measures
Strip searching : an inquiry into the strip searching of women remand prisoners at Armagh Prison between 1982 and 1985. — London : National Council for Civil Liberties, c1986. — 36p

ARMAMENTS
SIVARD, Ruth Leger
World military and social expenditures 1985 / Ruth Leger Sivard. — Washington D. C. : World Priorities, 1985. — 52p

ARMAMENTS — Economic aspects — Congresses
Economic effects of militarism / edited by Girish Mishoa. — New Delhi : Allied Publishers, 1984. — xii,108p

ARMAMENTS — Economic aspects — Italy — History — 20th century
RASPIN, Angela
The Italian war economy, 1940-1943 : with particular reference to Italian relations with Germany / Angela Raspin. — New York : Garland Pub., 1986. — p. cm. — (Outstanding theses from the London School of Economics and Political Science). — *Thesis (Ph. D.)--London University, 1980.* — *Bibliography: p*

ARMED FORCES
L'année strategique. — [Paris] : Editions Maritimes, 1985-. — *Annual*

FARINGDON, Hugh
Confrontation : the strategic geography of NATO and the Warsaw Pact / Hugh Faringdon. — London : Routledge & Kegan Paul, 1986. — [352]p. — *Includes bibliography and index*

SHEEHAN, Michael
The Economist pocket guide to defence / Michael Sheehan and James H. Wyllie. — Oxford : Basil Blackwell, 1986. — 269p. — *Bibliography: p269*

ARMED FORCES — Appropriations and expenditures
The Economics of military expenditures : military expenditures, economic growth and fluctuations : proceedings of a conference held by the International Economic Association in Paris, France / edited by Christian Schmidt. — Basingstoke : Macmillan, 1987. — xxiii,391p. — *Includes bibliographies and index*

ARMED FORCES — Political activity
KUKREJA, Veena
Military intervention in politics : a case study of Pakistan / Veena Kukreja ; foreword by Mahendra Prasad Singh. — New Delhi : Mrs. A. H. Marwah for NBO Publisher's Distributors, 1985. — 223p. — *Bibliography: p200-219*

ARMED FORCES — Spain — Political activity
BALLBÉ, Manuel
Orden público y militarismo en la España constitucional (1812-1983) / Manuel Ballbé ; prólogo de Eduardo García de Enterría. — 2a ed. — Madrid : Alianza, 1985. — iv,488p

SECO SERRANO, Carlos
Militarismo y civilismo en la España contemporánea / Carlos Seco Serrano. — Madrid : Instituto de Estudios Económicos, 1984. — 458p

ARMENIA — History
PASDERMADJIAN, H.
Histoire de l'Arménie : depuis les origines jusqu'au Traité de Lausanne / H. Pasdermadjian. — 4e éd.. — Paris : Librairie Orientale H. Samuelian, 1986. — 437p

ARMENIA — History — 1801-1900
SONYEL, Salahi Ramsdan
The Ottoman Armenians : victims of great power diplomacy / by Salahi Ramsdan Sonyel. — London : K. Rustem, 1987. — xv,426p. — *Bibliography: p[365]-386*

ARMENIA — History — 1901-
SONYEL, Salahi Ramsdan
The Ottoman Armenians : victims of great power diplomacy / by Salahi Ramsdan Sonyel. — London : K. Rustem, 1987. — xv,426p. — *Bibliography: p[365]-386*

ARMENIA — History — 1901- — Addresses, essays, lectures
The Armenian genocide in perspective / edited by Richard G. Hovannisian ; introduction by Terrence Des Pres ; preface by Israel W. Charny. — New Brunswick, N.J. ; Oxford : Transaction Books, 1986. — vi, 215p

ARMENIA — Relations — Turkey
SONYEL, Salahi Ramsdan
The Ottoman Armenians : victims of great power diplomacy / by Salahi Ramsdan Sonyel. — London : K. Rustem, 1987. — xv,426p. — *Bibliography: p[365]-386*

ARMENIAN MASSACRES, 1915-1923 — Turkey — Addresses, essays, lectures
The Armenian genocide in perspective / edited by Richard G. Hovannisian ; introduction by Terrence Des Pres ; preface by Israel W. Charny. — New Brunswick, N.J. ; Oxford : Transaction Books, 1986. — vi, 215p

ARMENIAN QUESTION
GUNTER, Michael M
"Pursuing the just cause of their people" : a study of contemporary Armenian terrorism / Michael M. Gunter. — New York : Greenwood Press, 1986. — viii, 182 p.. — (Contributions in political science ; no. 152). — *Includes index.* — *Bibliography: p. [159]-169*

SONYEL, Salahi Ramsdan
The Ottoman Armenians : victims of great power diplomacy / by Salahi Ramsdan Sonyel. — London : K. Rustem, 1987. — xv,426p. — *Bibliography: p[365]-386*

ARMENIAN S.S.R — Population
KARAPETIAN, S. A.
Regional'nye osobennosti sotsial'no-demograficheskogo razvitiia Armianskai SSR / S. A. Karapetian, R. L. Ovsepian. — Erevan : Aiastan, 1986. — 215p

ARMINIANISM — England — History — 16th century
TYACKE, Nicholas
Anti-Calvinists : the rise of English Arminianism c.1590-1640 / Nicholas Tyacke. — Oxford : Clarendon, 1987. — [300]p,[4]p of plates. — (Oxford historical monographs). — *Includes bibliography and index*

ARMINIANISM — England — History — 17th century
TYACKE, Nicholas
Anti-Calvinists : the rise of English Arminianism c.1590-1640 / Nicholas Tyacke. — Oxford : Clarendon, 1987. — [300]p,[4]p of plates. — (Oxford historical monographs). — *Includes bibliography and index*

ARMOUR, J. B. — Archives
MCMINN, J. R. B.
Against the tide : a calendar of the papers of Rev. J. B Armour, Irish Presbyterian minister and Home Ruler, 1869-1914. — Belfast : PRONI, 1985. — lxii,225p

ARMS CONTROL

Armed peace : the search for world security / edited by Josephine O'Connor Howe. — London : Macmillan, 1984. — xvii,191p. — *Includes index*

Arms and disarmament : SIPRI findings / edited by Marek Thee. — Oxford : Oxford University Press, 1986. — 491p. — *Includes index*

Arms control and the strategic defense initiative : three perspectives. — Muscatine, Iowa : Stanley Foundation, 1985. — 32p. — (Occasional paper / Stanley Foundation ; 36). — *Contents: Soviet interpretation and response/Jerry F. Hough - A new dilemma for NATO/Stanley R. Sloan - Breaking the deadlock/Paul C. Warnke and David Linebaugh*

Arms control in Asia / edited by Gerald Segal. — Basingstoke : Macmillan, 1987. — [210]p. — *Includes index*

BULL, Hedley
Hedley Bull on arms control / selected and introduced by Robert O'Neill and David N. Schwartz. — Basingstoke : Macmillan in association with the International Institute for Strategic Studies, 1987. — 302p,1leaf of plates. — (Studies in international security ; 25). — *Bibliography: p285-292. — Includes index*

The Chemical industry and the projected chemical weapons convention : proceedings of a SIPRI/Pugwash conference. — Oxford : Published on behalf of Stockholm International Peace Research Institute by Oxford University Press, 1986. — 2v.. — (SIPRI chemical & biological warfare studies ; 4-5). — *Includes bibliography*

Chemical weapon free zones? / edited by Ralf Trapp. — Oxford : Oxford University Press [on behalf of] Stockholm International Peace Research Institute, 1987. — x,211p. — (SIPRI Chemical & biological warfare studies ; no.7)

DEAN, Jonathan
Watershed in Europe : dismantling the East-West military confrontation / Jonathan Dean. — Lexington, Mass. : Lexington Books, 1986, c1987. — p. cm. — *Includes index*

GOETZE, Bernd A
Security in Europe : a crisis of confidence / Bernd A. Goetze. — New York : Praeger, 1984. — p. cm. — *Includes index. — Bibliography: p*

GOODIN, Robert E.
Mood matching and arms control / by Robert E. Goodin. — Colchester : Department of Government University of Essex, 1987. — 27 p. — (Essex papers in politics and government ; no. 41)

GREAT BRITAIN. Parliament. House of Commons. Library. International Affairs Section
Arms control after the Geneva summit / Richard Ware. — [London] : the Library, 1986. — 14p. — (Background paper / House of Commons. Library. [Research Division] ; no.177)

GREAT BRITAIN. Parliament. House of Commons. Library. Research Division
Arms control : the state of the negotiations / Richard Ware. — [London] : the Division, 1987. — 35p. — (Background paper ; no.196)

HALL, Christopher, 1956-
Britain, America and arms control,1921-37 / Christopher Hall. — Basingstoke : Macmillan, 1987. — vii,295p. — *Bibliography: p276-285. — Includes index*

MASTNY, Vojtech
Helsinki, human rights, and European security : analysis and documentation / Vojtech Mastny. — Durham : Duke University Press, 1986. — xvi, 389 p.. — *Includes index*

MÜLLER, Harald
Nuclear proliferation : facing reality / Harald Müller. European security and the role of arms control / Johan Jørgen Holst. — Bruxelles : Centre for European Policy Studies, 1984. — 68p. — (CEPS papers ; no.14/15)

NEW ZEALAND. Ministry of Foreign Affairs
Disarmament and arms control. — Wellington : the Ministry, 1986. — 45p. — (Information bulletin ; no.18)

Power and policy : doctrine, the alliance and arms control. — London : International Institute for Strategic Studies. — (IISS annual conference papers)
Part 1. — 1986. — 72p. — (Adelphi papers ; 205)

Power and policy : doctrine, the alliance and arms control. — London : International Institute for Strategic Studies. — (IISS annual conference papers)
Part 2. — 1986. — 78p. — (Adelphi papers ; 206)

Power and policy : doctrine, the alliance and arms control. — London : International Institute for Strategic Studies. — (IISS annual conference papers)
Part 3. — 1986. — 76p. — (Adelphi papers ; 207)

PROBLEMS DE SEGURIDAD EUROPEA Y DESPLIEGUE DE SISTEMAS DE ALCANCE MEDIO (1984 : Madrid)
Problemas de seguridad europea y despliegue de sistemas de alcance medio : simposio internacional celebrado en el Auditorio del Ministerio de Hacienda, Madrid, mayo de 1984. — [Madrid] : Instituto de Cuestiones Internacionales : Fundación Friedrich Ebert, c1984. — 303p

Strategic defense : folly or future? / [edited by] P. Edward Haley, Jack Merritt. — Boulder : Westview Press, 1986. — p. cm. — *Includes index. — Bibliography: p*

VAN OUDENAREN, John
Soviet policy toward western Europe : objectives, instruments, results / John Van Oudenaren. — Santa Monica, CA : Rand, [1986]. — xi, 118 p.. — "A Project Air Force report, prepared for the United States Air Force.". — "February 1986.". — "R-3310-AF.". — *Bibliography: p. 117-118*

ARMS CONTROL — Congresses

International security and arms control / edited by Ellen Propper Mickiewicz and Roman Kolkowicz. — New York : Praeger, 1986. — xii, 171 p.. — *Includes index*

ARMS CONTROL — Verification

Satellites for arms control and crisis monitoring / edited by Bhupendra Jasani and Toshibomi Sakata. — Oxford : Oxford University Press, 1987. — xv,176p. — *Under the auspices of Sipri. — Includes index*

ARMS CONTROL — Verification — Congresses

Arms control verification : the technologies that make it possible / edited by Kosta Tsipis, David W. Hafemeister, and Penny Janeway. — Washington : Pergamon-Brassey's International Defense Publishers, c1986. — xvi, 419 p.. — *"Published in cooperation with the Program in Science and Technology for International Security, Massachusetts Institute of Technology.". — Papers presented at a conference held at M.I.T., Feb. 1984. — Includes bibliographies and index*

ARMS RACE

Arms control and the arms race : readings from Scientific American / with introductions by Bruce Russett, Fred Chernoff. — New York : W.H. Freeman, c1985. — viii, 229 p.. — *Includes index. — Bibliography: p. [217]-222*

MALCOLMSON, Robert W
Nuclear fallacies : how we have been misguided since Hiroshima / Robert W. Malcolmson. — Kingston : McGill-Queen's University Press, c1985. — xi, 152 p. — *Includes index. — Bibliography: p. [117]-127*

ARMS RACE — History — 20th century

Apocalypse no : an Australian guide to the arms race and the peace movement / edited by Rachel Sharp. — Sydney : Pluto Press in association with Rosa Research Associates, 1984. — 294 p.. — *Includes bibliographies and index*

Arms and disarmament : SIPRI findings / edited by Marek Thee. — Oxford : Oxford University Press, 1986. — 491p. — *Includes index*

The Nuclear age : power, proliferation, and the arms race. — Washington, D.C. : Congressional Quarterly, c1984. — xii, 253 p.. — *Bibliography: p241-243. — Bibliography: p. 241-243*

ARMS RACE — Caribbean Area — History — 20th century

Militarization in the non-Hispanic Caribbean / edited by Alma H. Young and Dion E. Phillips. — Boulder, Colo. : Lynne Rienner Publishers, 1986. — ix, 178p. — *Includes index. — Bibliography: p.160-173*

ARMS RACE — Europe — History — 19th century

HAMILTON, W. Mark
The nation and the navy : methods and organization of British navalist propaganda, 1889-1914 / W. Mark Hamilton. — New York : Garland Pub., 1986. — p. cm. — (Outstanding theses from the London School of Economics and Political Science). — *Thesis (Ph.D.)--University of London, 1977. — Bibliography: p*

ARMS RACE — Europe — History — 20th century

HAMILTON, W. Mark
The nation and the navy : methods and organization of British navalist propaganda, 1889-1914 / W. Mark Hamilton. — New York : Garland Pub., 1986. — p. cm. — (Outstanding theses from the London School of Economics and Political Science). — *Thesis (Ph.D.)--University of London, 1977. — Bibliography: p*

ARMS RACE — Soviet Union

The second superpower : the arms race and the Soviet Union / edited by Gerard Holden. — London : CND Publications, 1985. — 107p. — *Bibliography: p96-100*

ARNIM, HEINRICH ALEXANDER VON — Biography

BUSSCHE, Albrecht von dem
Heinrich Alexander von Arnim : Liberalismus, Polenfrage und deutsche Einheit : das 19. Jahrhundert im Spiegel einer Biographie des preussischen Staatsmannes / von Albrecht von dem Bussche. — Osnabrück : Biblio Verlag, 1986. — x,426p. — *Bibliography: p339-344*

AROMANIANS — History

WINNIFRITH, T. J.
The Vlachs : the history of a Balkan people / T.J. Winnifrith. — London : Duckworth, 1987. — [170]p. — *Includes bibliography and index*

ARON, RAYMOND

COLQUHOUN, Robert, 1938-
Raymond Aron / Robert Colquhoun. — London : Sage, 1986. — 2v.. — *Includes bibliography and index. — Contents: Vol.1. The philosopher in history, 1905—1955 - Vol.2. The sociologist in society, 1955—1983*

ARREST OF SHIPS

Arrest of ships 3 : Malta, Panama, Sweden, United Arab Emirates / by Max Ganado ... [et al.]. — London : Lloyd's of London, 1987. — [xx,110]p

ARROW, KENNETH J.

Arrow and the ascent of modern economic theory / edited by George R. Feiwel. — Basingstoke : Macmillan, 1987. — liv,698p[1] leaf of plates. — *Includes bibliographies and index*

Arrow and the foundations of the theory of economic policy / edited by George R. Feiwel. — Basingstoke : Macmillan, 1987. — lxiii,758p,[1]leaf of plates. — *Includes bibliographies and index*

ART — Addresses, essays, lectures

PANOFSKY, Erwin
Meaning in the visual arts / Erwin Panofsky. — Phoenix ed. — Chicago : University of Chicago Press, 1982, c1955. — xviii, 364 p., [62] p. of plates. — : *Reprint. Originally published: Garden City, N.Y. : Doubleday, 1955. — Includes index. — Bibliography: p. v-viii*

ART — Psychological aspects

WILSON, Robert N
Experiencing creativity : on the social psychology of art / Robert N. Wilson. — New Brunswick, N.J., U.S.A. : Transaction Books, c1986. — vii, 171 p.. — *Includes bibliographies and index*

ART — Psychology

ARNHEIM, Rudolf
Art and visual perception : a psychology of the creative eye / Rudolf Arnheim. — New version, expanded and rev. ed. — Berkeley : University of California Press, [1974]. — x, 508 p., [2] leaves of plates. — *Includes index. — Bibliography: p. [487]-501*

ART — Sociological aspects

BECKER, Howard S.
Art worlds / Howard S. Becker. — Berkeley ; London : University of California Press, 1984, c1982. — xiv,392p. — *Bibliography: p373-384*

ART — Africa, West

African art & leadership / Edited by Douglas Fraser and Herbert M. Cole. — Madison : University of Wisconsin Press, [1972]. — xvii, 332 p. — *Fourteen papers, 6 of which were presented at a symposium entitled The aristocratic traditions in African art, held at Columbia University, May 1965. — Includes bibliographies*

ART — Oceania

Exploring the visual art of Oceania : Australia, Melanesia, Micronesia, and Polynesia / edited by Sidney M. Mead ; assisted by Isabelle Brymer and Susan Martich. — Honolulu : University Press of Hawaii, c1979. — xviii, 455 p.. — *Includes index. — Bibliography: p. [419]-450*

ART AND SCIENCE

INTERDISCIPLINARY CONGRESS ON M.C.ESCHER (1985 : Rome, Italy)
M.C. Escher, art and science : proceedings of the Interdisciplinary Congress on M.C. Escher, Rome, Italy, 26-28 March 1985 / edited by H.S.M. Coxeter ... [et al.]. — Amsterdam ; New York : North-Holland ; New York, N.Y., U.S.A. : Sole distributors for the U.S.A. and Canada, Elsevier Science Pub. Co., 1986. — p. cm

ART AND SOCIETY

HEWISON, Robert
Too much : art and society in the Sixties 1960-75 / Robert Hewison. — London : Methuen, 1986. — [300]p. — *Includes index*

ART AND SOCIETY — Congresses

SCHEMATISATION IN ART (Conference : 1974 : Canberra)
Form in indigenous art : schematisation in the art of Aboriginal Australia and prehistoric Europe / edited by Peter J. Ucko. — Canberra : Australian Institute of Aboriginal Studies ; London : Duckworth [etc.], 1977. — [6],486p. — (Prehistory and material culture series ; no.13). — '... "Schematisation in Art" was the first symposium ... of the Biennial Conference of the Australian Institute of Aboriginal Studies ... [held in 1974 in Canberra]' - Opening remarks. — *Includes bibliographies and index*

ART AND STATE — Great Britain

MULGAN, Geoff
Saturday night or Sunday morning? : from arts to industry : new forms of cultural policy / by Geoff Mulgan and Ken Worpole. — London : Comedia, 1986. — 132p. — *Bibliography: p133*

SHAW, Roy
The arts and the people / Roy Shaw. — London : Cape, 1987. — 147p

ART AUCTIONS

HOGREFE, Jeffrey
"Wholly unacceptable" : the bitter battle for Sotheby's / Jeffrey Hogrefe. — 1st ed. — New York : W. Morrow, c1986. — 238 p.. — *Includes index*

ART, AUSTRALIAN (ABORIGINAL) — Congresses

SCHEMATISATION IN ART (Conference : 1974 : Canberra)
Form in indigenous art : schematisation in the art of Aboriginal Australia and prehistoric Europe / edited by Peter J. Ucko. — Canberra : Australian Institute of Aboriginal Studies ; London : Duckworth [etc.], 1977. — [6],486p. — (Prehistory and material culture series ; no.13). — '... "Schematisation in Art" was the first symposium ... of the Biennial Conference of the Australian Institute of Aboriginal Studies ... [held in 1974 in Canberra]' - Opening remarks. — *Includes bibliographies and index*

ART CENTERS — Great Britain

HUTCHISON, Robert
Arts centres in the United Kingdom / Robert Hutchison, Susan Forrester. — London : Policy Studies Institute, 1987. — 236p. — (PSI research report ; no.668)

ART CRITICISM — History

BARRELL, John
The political theory of painting from Reynolds to Hazlitt : the body of the public / John Barrell. — New Haven ; London : Yale University Press, 1986. — [352]p. — *Includes index*

ART CRITICISM — History — 20th century

GOMBRICH, E. H.
Meditations on a hobby horse and other essays on the theory of art / E.H. Gombrich. — 4th ed. — Oxford : Phaidon, 1985. — [x,182,64]p of plates. — *Previous ed.: 1978. — Includes index*

ART, EUROPEAN — Congresses

SCHEMATISATION IN ART (Conference : 1974 : Canberra)
Form in indigenous art : schematisation in the art of Aboriginal Australia and prehistoric Europe / edited by Peter J. Ucko. — Canberra : Australian Institute of Aboriginal Studies ; London : Duckworth [etc.], 1977. — [6],486p. — (Prehistory and material culture series ; no.13). — '... "Schematisation in Art" was the first symposium ... of the Biennial Conference of the Australian Institute of Aboriginal Studies ... [held in 1974 in Canberra]' - Opening remarks. — *Includes bibliographies and index*

ART HISTORIANS — Great Britain — Biography

PENROSE, Barrie
Conspiracy of silence : the secret life of Anthony Blunt / Barrie Penrose and Simon Freeman. — London : Grafton, 1986. — xix,588p,[20]p of plates. — *Bibliography: p565-567. — Includes index*

ART, MODERN — 17th-18th centuries — Europe

WIND, Edgar
Pagan mysteries in the Renaissance / by Edgar Wind. — [2nd (enlarged) ed.]. — Oxford : Oxford University Press, 1980. — xiii,345p,[64]p of plates. — (Oxford paperbacks). — *This ed. originally published : Harmondsworth : Penguin, 1967. — Bibliography: p.305-315. — Includes index*

ART PATRONAGE — United States — Addresses, essays, lectures

Nonprofit enterprise in the arts : studies in mission and constraint / [edited by] Paul J. DiMaggio. — New York : Oxford University Press, 1986. — xv, 370 p.. — (Yale studies on nonprofit organizations). — *Includes bibliographies and index*

ART, PRIMITIVE

BIEBUYCK, Daniel Prosper
Tradition and creativity in tribal art / edited and with an introduction by Daniel P. Biebuyck. — Berkeley ; London (2 Brook St., W1Y 1AA) : University of California Press, 1969. — xx,236p,64plates. — *bibl p215-224*

ART, PRIMITIVE — Africa, West

African art & leadership / Edited by Douglas Fraser and Herbert M. Cole. — Madison : University of Wisconsin Press, [1972]. — xvii, 332 p. — *Fourteen papers, 6 of which were presented at a symposium entitled The aristocratic traditions in African art, held at Columbia University, May 1965. — Includes bibliographies*

ART, PRIMITIVE — New Guinea

GERBRANDS, Adrian A.
Wow-ipits : eight Asmat woodcarvers of New Guinea / Adrian A. Gerbrands ; [translated from the dutch by Inez Wolf Seeger]. — The Hague : Mouton, c1967. — 191p. — (Art in its context : studies in ethno-aesthetics. field reports ; v.3). — *Bibliography: p[173]-174*

ART, PRIMITIVE — Oceania

Exploring the visual art of Oceania : Australia, Melanesia, Micronesia, and Polynesia / edited by Sidney M. Mead ; assisted by Isabelle Brymer and Susan Martich. — Honolulu : University Press of Hawaii, c1979. — xviii, 455 p.. — *Includes index. — Bibliography: p. [419]-450*

ART, PRIMITIVE — Papua New Guinea

BOWDEN, Ross
Yena : art and ceremony in a Sepik society / Ross Bowden ; with a foreword by Rodney Needham. — Oxford : Pitt Rivers Museum, 1983. — xii,179p, 32 plates. — (Monograph / Pitt Rivers Museum ; 3)

ART, RENAISSANCE

WIND, Edgar
Pagan mysteries in the Renaissance / by Edgar Wind. — [2nd (enlarged) ed.]. — Oxford : Oxford University Press, 1980. — xiii,345p,[64]p of plates. — (Oxford paperbacks). — *This ed. originally published : Harmondsworth : Penguin, 1967. — Bibliography: p.305-315. — Includes index*

ART, SENUFO (AFRICAN PEOPLE)

GLAZE, Anita J.
Art and death in a Senufo village / Anita J. Glaze. — Bloomington : Indiana University Press, c1981. — xvi, 267 p., [2] leaves of plates. — (Traditional arts of Africa). — *Includes index. — Bibliography: p. [246]-254*

ARTIC OCEAN — Congresses
LAW OF THE SEA INSTITUTE. Workshop (1981 : Mackinac Island, Michigan)
Artic Ocean issues in the 1980's : proceedings, Law of the Sea Institute, University of Hawaii, and Dalhousie Ocean Studies Programme, Dalhousie University ... Workshop, June 10-12, 1981, Mackinac Island, Michigan / edited by Douglas M. Johnston. — Honolulu : The Institute, 1982. — iii,60p

ARTIFICAL INTELLIGENCE
GUNDERSON, Keith
Mentality and machines / Keith Gunderson. — 2nd ed. — London : Croom Helm, 1985. — xxii,260p. — Bibliography: p[249]-255

ARTIFICIAL INSEMINATION, HUMAN — Social aspects
COREA, Gena
The mother machine : reproductive technologies from artificial insemination to artificial wombs / Gena Corea. — 1st ed. — New York : Harper & Row, c1985. — p. cm. — Includes index. — Bibliography: p

ARTIFICIAL INTELLIGENCE
ALEKSANDER, Igor
Designing intelligence systems : an introduction / Igor Aleksander. — London : Kogan Page, 1984. — 166p. — ([New technology modular series])

ARBIB, Michael A
In search of the person : philosophical explorations in cognitive science / Michael A. Arbib. — Amherst : University of Massachusetts, 1985. — xii, 156 p.. — Includes index. — Bibliography: p. [137]-149

Artificial intelligence : the case against / edited by Rainer Born. — London : Croom Helm, c1987. — xxxv,220p. — Bibliography: p214-216. — Includes index

Artificial intelligence for society / edited by Karamjit S. Gill. — Chichester : Wiley, c1986. — [300]p. — Includes index

BODEN, Margaret A
Artificial intelligence and natural man / Margaret A. Boden. — 2nd ed., expanded. — New York : Basic Books, c1987. — xii, 576 p.. — Includes index. — Bibliography: p. [501]-528

FORSYTH, Richard
Machine learning : applications in expert systems and information retrieval / R. Forsyth and R. Rada. — Chichester : Ellis Horwood, 1986. — 277p. — (Ellis Horwood series in artificial intelligence). — Text on lining papers. — Bibliography: p264-273. — Includes index

GALAMBOS, James A
Knowledge structures / James A. Galambos, Robert P. Abelson, John B. Black. — Hillsdale, N.J. : Lawrence Erlbaum Associates, 1986. — p. cm. — Includes index. — Bibliography: p

Impacts of artificial intelligence : scientific, technological, military, economic, societal, cultural, and political / edited by R. Trappl ; with contributions by Michael A. Arbib ... [et al.]. — Amsterdam ; New York : North-Holland ; New York, N.Y., U.S.A. : Sole distributors for the U.S.A. and Canada, Elsevier Science Pub. Co., 1986. — p. cm. — Includes indexes. — Bibliography: p

Induction : processes of inference, learning, and discovery / John H. Holland ... [et al.]. — Cambridge, Mass. : MIT Press, c1986. — xvi, 385p. — (Computational models of cognition and perception). — Includes index. — Bibliography: p.357-372

Intelligent machinery : theory and practice / edited by Ian Benson ; illustrated by Benny Kandler. — Cambridge : Cambridge University Press, 1986. — xi,168p. — Conference papers. — Includes bibliographies and index

INTERNATIONAL CONFERENCE ON "LOGIC, INFORMATICS, LAW" (2nd : 1985 : Florence, Italy)
Automated analysis of legal texts : logic, informatics, law : edited versions of selected papers from the Second International Conference on "Logic, Informatics, Law,"Florence, Italy, September 1985 / edited by Antonio A. Martino, Fiorenza Socci Natali ; editorial assistant, Simona Binazzi. — Amsterdam ; New York : North-Holland ; New York, N.Y., U.S.A. : Sole distributors for the U.S.A. and Canada, Elsevier Science Pub. Co., 1986. — xxii, 938 p.. — Includes bibliographies and index

Machine learning : an artificial intelligence approach / contributing authors, John Anderson ... [et al.] ; editors, Ryszard S. Michalski, Jaime G. Carbonell, Tom M. Mitchell. — Los Altos, Calif. : Morgan Kaufmann, 1986, c1983. — p. cm. — : Reprint. Originally published: Palo Alto, Calif. : Tioga Pub. Co., c1983. — Includes index. — Bibliography: p

RAUCH-HINDIN, Wendy B
Artificial intelligence in business, science, and industry / Wendy B. Rauch-Hindin. — Englewood Cliffs, N.J. : Prentice-Hall, <c1985- >. — p. cm. — "Computer vision, chapter 11 in volume II, by Harvey J. Hindin.". — Includes index. — Bibliography: v. 2, p. — Contents: -- v. 2. Applications

Readings in knowledge representation / edited by Ronald J. Brachman and Hector J. Levesque. — [Los Altos, Calif.] : M. Kaufmann Publishers, 1985. — p. cm. — Includes index. — Bibliography: p

SOWA, John F.
Conceptual structures : information processing in mind and machine / John F. Sowa. — Reading, Mass. ; London : Addison-Wesley, 1984. — (The Systems programming series)

ARTIFICIAL INTELLIGENCE — Addresses, essays, lectures
Mind design : philosophy, psychology, artificial intelligence / edited by John Haugeland. — Cambridge, Mass. ; London : MIT Press, 1981. — xii,368p. — A Bradford book

Minds, machines and evolution : philosophical studies / edited by Christopher Hookway. — Cambridge : Cambridge University Press, 1984. — xi,177p. — Includes bibliographies and index

ARTIFICIAL INTELLIGENCE — Data processing
BRATKO, I.
Prolog programming for artificial intelligence / Ivan Bratko. — Wokingham : Addison-Wesley, 1986. — xvii,423p. — (International computer science series). — Includes bibliographies and index

ARTIFICIAL INTELLIGENCE — Scientific applications
CONFERENCE 'ARTIFICIAL INTELLIGENCE IN SIMULATION' (1985 : Ghent)
AI applied to simulation : proceedings of the European Conference at the University of Ghent, February 25-28 1985, Ghent, Belgium / edited by E. J. H. Kerckhoffs, G. C. Vansteenkiste, B. P. Zeigler. — San Diego : Society for Computer Simulation, 1986. — xii,205p. — (Simulation Series ; 18, no.1)

ARTIFICIAL SATELLITES IN TELECOMMUNICATION
POWELL, Jon T
International broadcasting by satellite : issues of regulation, barriers to communication / Jon T. Powell ; foreword by Hale Montgomery. — Westport, Conn. : Quorum Books, 1985. — xviii, 300 p. — Includes index. — Bibliography: p. [287]-290

ARTIFICIAL SATELLITES IN TELECOMMUNICATION — Congresses
IFIP WG 7.3 INTERNATIONAL SEMINAR ON COMPUTER NETWORKING AND PERFORMANCE EVALUATION (1985 : Tokyo, Japan)
Computer networking and performance evaluation : proceedings of the IFIP WG 7.3 International Seminar on Computer Networking and Performance Evaluation, 18-20 September 1985, Tokyo, Japan / edited by T. Hasegawa, H. Takagi, Y. Takahashi. — Amsterdam ; New York : North-Holland ; New York, N.Y., U.S.A. : Sole distributors for the U.S.A. and Canada, Elsevier Science Pub. Co., 1986. — p. cm

Tracing new orbits : cooperation and competition in global satellite development / edited by Donna A. Demac. — New York : Columbia University Press, 1986. — p. cm. — (Columbia studies in business, government, and society). — Includes index. — Bibliography: p

ARTIFICIAL SATELLITES IN TELECOMMUNICATION — Law and legislation
TAISHOFF, Marika Natasha
State responsibility and the direct broadcast satellite / Marika Natasha Taishoff. — London : Pinter, 1987. — xii,203p. — "A publication of the Graduate Institute of International Studies". — Half t.p. verso. — Bibliography: p183-197. — Includes index

ARTIFICIAL SATELLITES IN TELECOMMUNICATION — Australia
Satellite broadcasting : answers to the questions most often asked. — Canberra : Australian Government Publishing Service, 1986. — iv,65p

ARTISANS — Italy — Statistics
ITALY. Istituto Centrale di Statistica
6 censimento generale dell'industria, del commercio, dei servizi e dell'artigianato 26 ottobre 1981. — Roma : the Istituto vol.3: Atti del censimento. — 1985. — 264p

ARTIST COLONIES — Switzerland — Ascona
GREEN, Martin Burgess
Mountain of truth : the counterculture begins, Ascona, 1900-1920 / Martin Green. — Hanover, N.H. : Published for Tufts University by University Press of New England, 1986. — 287 p., [12] p. of plates. — Includes index. — Bibliography: p. [275]-281

ARTISTS — Homes and haunts — United States
LIPSKE, Mike
Artist's housing : creating live/work space that lasts / by Mike Lipske. — Washington, D.C. : Design Arts Programs, National Endowment for the Arts, 1987. — p. cm. — Bibliography: p

ARTISTS — Psychology
KRIS, Ernst
Legend, myth and magic in the image of the artist : a historical experiment / Ernst Kris and Otto Kurz ; [translated from the German by Alastair Laing and revised by Lottie M. Newman] ; preface by E.H. Gombrich. — New Haven ; London : Yale University Press, 1979. — xvi,159p. — Translation and revision of: 'Die Legende vom Künstler'. Vienna : Krystall Verlag, 1934. — Bibliography: p.133-147. — Includes index

ARTISTS' STUDIOS — United States
LIPSKE, Mike
Artist's housing : creating live/work space that lasts / by Mike Lipske. — Washington, D.C. : Design Arts Programs, National Endowment for the Arts, 1987. — p. cm. — Bibliography: p

ARTS — Political aspects — England — History — 17th century
ROWSE, A. L.
Reflections on the Puritan Revolution / A.L. Rowse. — London : Methuen, 1986. — [256]p. — Includes index

ARTS — Political aspects — Great Britain
MILES, Peter
Cinema, literature & society : elite and mass culture in interwar Britain / Peter Miles and Malcolm Smith. — London : Croom Helm, c1987. — 271p. — *Bibliography: p257-266. — Includes index*

ARTS — England — London
Greater London Arts : annual report and accounts. — London : Greater London Arts, 1984/5-. — *Annual*

ARTS — Finland — Statistics
FINLAND. Tilastokeskus
Kulttuaritilasto : Tilastotietoja taiteesta, tiedonvälityksestä, vapaa-ajasta, urheilusta ja nuorisotoiminnasta vuosilta 1930-1977 = Cutlural statistics : Statistical information on arts, communication, leisure, sports and youth activities in 1930-1977. — Helsinki : Tilastokeskus, 1978. — 256p. — (Tilastollisia tiedonantoja = Statistical surveys ; no.60). — *In Finnish, Swedish and English*

FINLAND. Tilastokeskus
Kulttuuritilasto 1981 : Tilastotietoja taiteesta, tiedonvälityksestä, vapaa-ajasta, urheilusta ja nuorisotojmminnasta = Cultural statistics 1981 : Statistical information on arts, communication, leisure, sports and youth activities. — Helsinki : Tilastokeskus, 1984. — 683p. — (Tilastollisia tiedonantoja = Statistical surveys ; no.73). — *In Finnish, Swedish and English*

ARTS — Great Britain — Finance
The arts: the next move forward : a plurality of riches: a plurality of funding / Robert Banks [et al.]. — London : Conservative Political Centre, 1987. — 40p

ARTS — Switzerland — Ascona
GREEN, Martin Burgess
Mountain of truth : the counterculture begins, Ascona, 1900-1920 / Martin Green. — Hanover, N.H. : Published for Tufts University by University Press of New England, 1986. — 287 p., [12] p. of plates. — *Includes index. — Bibliography: p. [275]-281*

ARTS — United States — Finance — Addresses, essays, lectures
Nonprofit enterprise in the arts : studies in mission and constraint / [edited by] Paul J. DiMaggio. — New York : Oxford University Press, 1986. — xv, 370 p.. — (Yale studies on nonprofit organizations). — *Includes bibliographies and index*

ARTS AND CRAFTS MOVEMENT — Exhibitions
Life by design : Delaware Art Museum, November 9, 1984-January 6, 1985 / [photography by Rick Echelmeyer ; editor, Richard J. Mulrooney]. — Wilmington, Del. (2301 Kentmere Pkwy., Wilmington 19806) : The Museum, c1984. — iv, 31 p.. — *At head of title: The Byrdcliffe Arts and Crafts Colony. — Cover title: The Byrdcliffe Arts & Crafts Colony : life by design. — Catalogue of an exhibition held at the Delaware Art Museum, Nov. 9, 1984-Jan. 6, 1985 and at the Edith C. Blum Art Institute, Jan. 15-Mar. 31, 1985. — Includes bibliographies*

ARTS AND CRAFTS MOVEMENT — United States
BORIS, Eileen
Art and labor : Ruskin, Morris, and the craftsman ideal in America / Eileen Boris. — Philadelphia : Temple University Press, 1986. — xviii, 261 p.. — (American civilization). — *Includes index. — Bibliography: p. 195-247*

ARTS AND SOCIETY
BECKER, Howard S.
Art worlds / Howard S. Becker. — Berkeley ; London : University of California Press, 1984, c1982. — xiv,392p. — *Bibliography: p373-384*

WILSON, Robert N
Experiencing creativity : on the social psychology of art / Robert N. Wilson. — New Brunswick, N.J., U.S.A. : Transaction Books, c1986. — vii, 171 p.. — *Includes bibliographies and index*

ARTS AND SOCIETY — Great Britain — History — 20th century
MILES, Peter
Cinema, literature & society : elite and mass culture in interwar Britain / Peter Miles and Malcolm Smith. — London : Croom Helm, c1987. — 271p. — *Bibliography: p257-266. — Includes index*

ARTS AND SOCIETY — United States
LYNES, Russell
The lively audience : a social history of American visual and performing arts, 1890-1950 / Russell Lynes. — 1st ed. — New York ; London : Harper and Row, c1985. — x, 489p. — *Includes index. — Bibliography: p.[463]-472*

ARTS, AUSTRALIAN — History — 18th century
DIXON, Robert
The course of empire : neo-classical culture in New South Wales 1788-1860 / Robert Dixon. — Melbourne : Oxford University Press, 1986. — x,213p. — *Bibliography and picture sources: p201-208*

ARTS, AUSTRALIAN — History — 19th century
DIXON, Robert
The course of empire : neo-classical culture in New South Wales 1788-1860 / Robert Dixon. — Melbourne : Oxford University Press, 1986. — x,213p. — *Bibliography and picture sources: p201-208*

ARTS, ENGLISH
ROWSE, A. L.
Reflections on the Puritan Revolution / A.L. Rowse. — London : Methuen, 1986. — [256]p. — *Includes index*

ARTS FACILITIES — Great Britain
HUTCHISON, Robert
Arts centres in the United Kingdom / Robert Hutchison, Susan Forrester. — London : Policy Studies Institute, 1987. — 236p. — (PSI research report ; no.668)

ARTS, GERMAN — Congresses
Blacks and German culture : essays / edited by Reinhold Grimm and Jost Hermand. — Madison, Wis. : Published for Monatshefte [by] University of Wisconsin Press, 1986. — vii, 184 p.. — (Monatshefte occasional volumes ; no. 4) . — : *Revised and enlarged papers read at the 15th Wisconsin Workshop, held at the University of Wisconsin-Madison Oct. 5-6, 1984. — Includes bibliographies*

ARTS, MODERN — 20th century — Addresses, essays, lectures
The Female body in western culture : contemporary perspectives / Susan Rubin Suleiman, editor. — Cambridge, Mass. : Harvard University Press, 1986. — p. cm. — *Includes bibliographies*

ARTS, MODERN — 20th century — Germany — Congresses
Blacks and German culture : essays / edited by Reinhold Grimm and Jost Hermand. — Madison, Wis. : Published for Monatshefte [by] University of Wisconsin Press, 1986. — vii, 184 p.. — (Monatshefte occasional volumes ; no. 4) . — : *Revised and enlarged papers read at the 15th Wisconsin Workshop, held at the University of Wisconsin-Madison Oct. 5-6, 1984. — Includes bibliographies*

ARUE (TAHITI : REGION) — Population — Statistics
Tableaux normalisés du recensement général de la population : 15 octobre 1983. — [Papeete] : Institut territorial de la statistique Résultats de la commune de Arue. — [1985?]. — 4p,ll leaves

ARUNACHAL PRADESH (INDIA) — Population — Statistics
Census of India 1981. — [Delhi : Controller of Publications]
Series 25: Arunachal Pradesh. — [1985]

ARUTUA (TUAMOTU ISLANDS) — Population — Statistics
Tableaux normalisés du recensement général de la population : 15 octobre 1983. — [Papeete] : Institut territorial de la statistique Résultats de la commune de Arutua. — [1985?]. — 4p,ll leaves

ASBESTOS
Asbestos materials in buildings. — London : HMSO, 1983. — 33p. — *At head of title: Department of the Environment*

DOLL, Sir Richard
Effects of health or exposure to asbestos / Richard Doll, Julian Peto ; [for the] Health and Safety Commission. — London : H.M.S.O., 1985. — 58p. — *Cover title: Asbestos: effects on health of exposure to asbestos. — Bibliographical references: p55-57*

ASBESTOS — Environmental aspects
MCCULLOCH, Jock
Asbestos--its human cost : the anatomy and pathology of an industry / Jock McCulloch. — St Lucia, Qld., Australia ; Manchester, NH, USA : University of Queensland Press, 1986. — p. cm. — *Includes index. — Bibliography: p*

ASBESTOS — Toxicology
MCCULLOCH, Jock
Asbestos--its human cost : the anatomy and pathology of an industry / Jock McCulloch. — St Lucia, Qld., Australia ; Manchester, NH, USA : University of Queensland Press, 1986. — p. cm. — *Includes index. — Bibliography: p*

ASBESTOS INDUSTRY — Australia — Employees — Diseases and hygiene
MCCULLOCH, Jock
Asbestos--its human cost : the anatomy and pathology of an industry / Jock McCulloch. — St Lucia, Qld., Australia ; Manchester, NH, USA : University of Queensland Press, 1986. — p. cm. — *Includes index. — Bibliography: p*

ASCONA (SWITZERLAND) — Intellectual life
GREEN, Martin Burgess
Mountain of truth : the counterculture begins, Ascona, 1900-1920 / Martin Green. — Hanover, N.H. : Published for Tufts University by University Press of New England, 1986. — 287 p., [12] p. of plates. — *Includes index. — Bibliography: p. [275]-281*

ASEAN
ASEAN-South Asia economic relations / edited by Charan D. Wadhva and Mukul G. Asher. — Singapore : Institute of Southeast Asian Studies, c1985. — 384 p

IRACENTIRAN, Ma
ASEAN's foreign relations : the shift to collective action / M. Rajendran. — Kuala Lumpur : Arenabuku, 1985. — xii, 330 p.. — *Based on author's thesis (Ph. D.--Griffith University, 1983). — Includes index. — Bibliography: p. [309]-322*

Multilateral treaties between ASEAN countries / editor-in-chief Visu Sinnadurai. — Singapore : Butterworth, 1986. — 235p. — (ASEAN law series)

SOLIDUM, Estrella D
Bilateral summitry in ASEAN / Estrella D. Solidum. — Manila, Philippines : Foreign Service Institute, 1982. — 44 p.. — *Bibliography: p. 44*

WONG, John
Asian economic handbook / John Wong. — London : Euromonitor, 1986. — [300]p. — *Includes index*

ASEAN — Addresses, essays, lectures
THAMBIPILLAI, Pushpa
ASEAN negotiations : two insights / Pushpa Thambipillai and J. Saravanamuttu. — Singapore : ASEAN Economic Research Unit, Institute of Southeast Asian Studies, 1985. — viii, 56 p.. — (ASEAN political studies). — *Includes bibliographical references*

ASEAN — Congresses

The ASEAN success story : social, economic, and political dimensions : based on the East-West Center's 25th Anniversary Conference on ASEAN and the Pacific Basin, held in Honolulu, Hawaii from 29 October to 1 November 1985 / edited by Linda G. Martin. — Honolulu, Hawaii : The Center : Distributed by the University of Hawaii Press, c1987. — p. cm. — *Includes index.* — *Bibliography: p*

ASEAN — Emigration and immigration

POPE, David
ASEAN-Australian immigration and the demise of 'white Australia' / David Pope [and] Peter Shergold. — Kuala Lumpur ; Canberra : ASEAN-Australia Joint Research Project, 1985. — 60p. — (ASEAN-Australia economic papers ; no.17). — *Bibliography: p59-60*

ASEAN — Foreign relations — New Zealand

NEW ZEALAND. Ministry of Foreign Affairs
ASEAN and New Zealand. — Wellington : the Ministry, 1986. — 31p. — (Information bulletin ; no.17)

ASEAN — History

Understanding ASEAN / edited by Alison Broinowski. — London : Macmillan, 1982

ASHANTIS (AFRICAN PEOPLE)

RATTRAY, R. S.
Ashanti / R. S. Rattray. — Oxford : Clarendon Press, 1923. — 348p

RATTRAY, R. S.
Ashanti law and constitution / R. S. Rattray. — Oxford : Clarendon, 1929. — xx,420p

ASIA — Cities and towns

Basic needs and the urban poor : the provision of communal services / edited by P. J. Richards and A. M. Thomson. — London : Croom Helm, 1984. — 276p. — *Includes bibliographical references.* — *A study prepared for the International Labour Office within the framework of the World Employment Programme*

ASIA — Commerce

AHMAD, Ehtisham
Trade regimes and export strategies with reference to South Asia / E. Ahmad. — London : Suntory-Toyota International Centre for Economics and Related Disciplines, 1987. — 35p. — (Development Research Programme / London School of Economics and Political Science. Suntory-Toyota International Centre for Economics and Related Disciplines ; no.4)

ASIA, — Commerce — Statistics

External trade bulletin of the ESCWA region / United Nations. Economic and Social Commission for Western Asia. — Baghdad : ESCWA, 1985-. — *Annual*

ASIA — Commercial policy

TYERS, Rodney
Economic growth and agricultural protection in east and southeast Asia / Rodney Tyers [and] Kym Anderson. — Kuala Lumpur ; Canberra : ASEAN-Australia Joint Research Project, 1985. — 49p. — (ASEAN-Australia economic papers ; no.21). — *Bibliography: p37-38*

ASIA — Economic conditions — Social aspects

BUSS, Andreas E.
Max Weber and Asia : contributions to the sociology of development / Andreas E. Buss. — München ; London : Weltforum Verlag, 1985. — 115p. — (Materialien zu Entwicklung und Politik ; 27). — *Bibliography: p107-115*

ASIA — Economic conditions — 1945-

Economically active population : estimates and projections : 1950-2025 = Evaluations et projections de la population active : 1950-2025 = Estimaciones y proyecciones de la población económicamente activa : 1950-2025. — 3rd ed. — Geneva : International Labour Office
V.1: Asia. — 1986. — xxvi,176p. — *Introduction and table headings in English, French and Spanish*

Unreal growth : critical studies on Asian development / edited with an introduction by Ngo Manh-Lan. — Delhi : Hindustan Publishing Corporation. — *Vol.1 of two volumes*
Vol.1. — 1984. — xviii,561p

Unreal growth : critical studies in Asian development / edited with an introduction by Ngo Manh-Lan. — Delhi : Hindustan Publishing Corporation. — *Vol.2 of two volumes*
Vol.2. — 1985. — xviii,898p

WONG, John
Asian economic handbook / John Wong. — London : Euromonitor, 1986. — [300]p. — *Includes index*

ASIA — Economic policy

Case studies on poverty programmes in Asia / edited by Swapna Mukhopadhyay. — Kuala Lumpur : Asian and Pacific Development Centre, 1985. — xv,271p. — *Bibliographies*

MEIER, Gerald M
Financing Asian development : performance and prospects / by Gerald M. Meier. — Lanham, MD : University Press of America ; New York, N.Y. : Asia Society, c1986. — xvi, 72 p.. — (Asian agenda report ; 6). — *Bibliography: p. 71*

Unreal growth : critical studies on Asian development / edited with an introduction by Ngo Manh-Lan. — Delhi : Hindustan Publishing Corporation. — *Vol.1 of two volumes*
Vol.1. — 1984. — xviii,561p

Unreal growth : critical studies in Asian development / edited with an introduction by Ngo Manh-Lan. — Delhi : Hindustan Publishing Corporation. — *Vol.2 of two volumes*
Vol.2. — 1985. — xviii,898p

ASIA — Economic policy — Social aspects

BUSS, Andreas E.
Max Weber and Asia : contributions to the sociology of development / Andreas E. Buss. — München ; London : Weltforum Verlag, 1985. — 115p. — (Materialien zu Entwicklung und Politik ; 27). — *Bibliography: p107-115*

ASIA — Foreign relations — Great Britain — History

FREY, Werner
Sir Valentine Chirol : die britische Postition und Politik in Asien 1895-1925. — Zürich : Juris Druck und Verlag, 1976. — viii,255p. — *Dissertation-Universität Zürich, 1975.* — *Bibliography: p230-255*

ASIA — Industries

The Rural non-farm sector in Asia / edited by Swapna Mukhopadhyay, Chee Peng Lim. — Kuala Lumpur, Malaysia : Asian and Pacific Development Centre, 1985. — xiv, 417 p.. — (The Human resource mobilization programme publications). — *Includes bibliographies*

ASIA — Politics and government

BEASLEY, W. G.
Aspects of pan-Asianism / W. G. Beasley, J. Y. Wong [and] Masaki Miyake ; edited by Janet Hunter. — London : Suntory Toyota International Centre for Economics and Related Disciplines, 1987. — 50p. — (International studies ; 1987/11)

PISCATORI, James P
International relations of the Asian Muslim states / by James Piscatori. — Lanham [Md.] : University Press of America ; New York : The Asia Society, c1986. — ix, 41 p.. — *Bibliography: p. 39*

PYE, Lucian W.
Asian power and politics : the cultural dimensions of authority / Lucian W. Pye with Mary W. Pye. — Cambridge, Mass. : Belknap Press, 1985. — p. cm. — *Includes index.* — *Bibliography: p*

Unreal growth : critical studies on Asian development / edited with an introduction by Ngo Manh-Lan. — Delhi : Hindustan Publishing Corporation. — *Vol.1 of two volumes*
Vol.1. — 1984. — xviii,561p

Unreal growth : critical studies in Asian development / edited with an introduction by Ngo Manh-Lan. — Delhi : Hindustan Publishing Corporation. — *Vol.2 of two volumes*
Vol.2. — 1985. — xviii,898p

ASIA — Population

Asia-Pacific population journal / United Nations. Economic and Social Commission for Asia and the Pacific. — Bangkok : ESCAP, 1986-. — *Quarterly*

Fertility in Asia : assessing the impact of development projects / edited by John Stoeckel and Anrudh K. Jain. — London : Pinter, 1986. — xix,177p. — *Includes bibliographies and index*

ASIA — Population — Statistics

Economically active population : estimates and projections : 1950-2025 = Evaluations et projections de la population active : 1950-2025 = Estimaciones y proyecciones de la población económicamente activa : 1950-2025. — 3rd ed. — Geneva : International Labour Office
V.1: Asia. — 1986. — xxvi,176p. — *Introduction and table headings in English, French and Spanish*

ASIA — Religion

Equality and the religious traditions of Asia / edited by R. Siriwardena. — London : Pinter, 1987. — 173p. — *Conference papers.* — *Includes index*

ASIA — Rural conditions

ETIENNE, Gilbert
[Développement rural en Asie. English]. Rural development in Asia : meetings with peasants / Gilbert Etienne ; translated by Arati Sharma. — Rev. ed. — New Delhi ; Beverly Hills, CA : Sage Publications, 1985. — 276 p.. — *Translation of: Développement rural en Asie.* — *Bibliography: p. [272]-276*

The Rural non-farm sector in Asia / edited by Swapna Mukhopadhyay, Chee Peng Lim. — Kuala Lumpur, Malaysia : Asian and Pacific Development Centre, 1985. — xiv, 417 p.. — (The Human resource mobilization programme publications). — *Includes bibliographies*

ASIA — Social conditions

PYE, Lucian W.
Asian power and politics : the cultural dimensions of authority / Lucian W. Pye with Mary W. Pye. — Cambridge, Mass. : Belknap Press, 1985. — p. cm. — *Includes index.* — *Bibliography: p*

ASIA — Strategic aspects

Arms control in Asia / edited by Gerald Segal. — Basingstoke : Macmillan, 1987. — [210]p. — *Includes index*

ASIA — Study and teaching — Germany

Max Weber in Asian studies / edited by Andreas E. Buss. — Leiden : Brill, 1985. — 252p. — (International Studies in Sociology and Social Anthropology ; 42). — *Bibliographies*

ASIA — Yearbooks

Jahrbuch Asien - Afrika - Lateinamerika : Bilanz und Chronik des Jahres 1985 / L. Rathmann [hrsg.]. — Berlin : VEB Deutscher Verlag der Wissenschaften, 1986. — 329p. — *Table of contents in German, Russian, English, French and Spanish. — "Im Auftrag des Zentralen Rates für Asien-, Afrika-, und Lateinamerikawissenschaften in der DDR". — Bibliography: p[296]-326*

ASIA, EASTERN — Foreign relations

East Asia, the west and international security: prospects for peace. — London : International Institute for Strategic Studies. — (Adelphi papers ; 216). — *Papers resented to the 28th IISS Annual Conference held in Kyoto, Japan from 8th to 11th September 1986 Part 1.* — 1987. — 84p

ASIA, SOUTH — Social life and customs

FÜRER-HAIMENDORF, Christoph von
Tribal populations and cultures of the Indian subcontinent / by C. Von Fürer-Haimendorf. — Leiden : E.J. Brill, 1985. — vi, 182 p.. — (Handbuch der Orientalistik. Zweite Abteilung. Indien ; 7. Bd). — *Includes bibliographies and index*

ASIA, SOUTHEASTERN — Civilization

The Chinese in Southeast Asia / edited by L. A. Peter Gosling and Linda Y. C. Lim. — Singapore : Maruzen Asia, 1983. — *Consists mainly of papers from a conference on 'The Chinese in Southeast Asia: Ethnicity and Economic Activity', held by the Center for South and Southeast Asian Studies, University of Michigan, at Aan Arbor on 20th and 21st September 1980. — Includes bibliographical references*
v.2: Identity, culture and politics. — vii,284p

ASIA, SOUTHEASTERN — Commerce

OOI, Guat Tin
Towards a liberal trade regime / Ooi Guat Tin. — Kuala Lumpur : Institute of Strategic and International Studies, 1986. — 18p. — (ISIS ASEAN series). — *Bibliography: p17-18*

Far east-European liner trade. — Tokyo : Japan Maritime Research Institute, 1987. — 49p. — (Jamri report ; no.20)

ASIA, SOUTHEASTERN — Defenses

DJIWANDONO, J. Soedjati
Southeast Asia as a nuclear-weapons-free zone / J Soedjati Djiwandono. — Kuala Lumpur : Institute of Strategic and International Studies, 1986. — 7p. — (ISIS ASEAN series)

MAK, J. N.
Directions for greater defence co-operation / J. N. Mak. — Kuala Lumpur : Institute of Strategic and International Studies, 1986. — 32p. — (ISIS ASEAN series)

ASIA, SOUTHEASTERN — Economic conditions

AIKMAN, David
Pacific Rim : area of change, area of opportunity / by David Aikman. — 1st ed. — Boston : Little, Brown, 1986. — p. cm

CROUCH, Harold
Economic change, social structure and the political system in Southeast Asia : Philippine development compared with the other ASEAN countries / Harold Crouch. — Singapore : Institute of Southeast Asian Studies. Southeast Asian Studies Program, 1985. — 68p. — *Bibliography: p61-68*

Economic development in East and South-east Asia : implications for Australian agriculture in the 1980s / [contributors, Mike Adams ... et al.]. — Canberra : Australian Govt. Pub. Service, 1984. — x, 237 p.. — *At head of title: Bureau of Agricultural Economics, Canberra. — Includes bibliographies*

Survey of major western Pacific economies. — 4th ed. — Canberra : Australian Government Publishing Service, 1986. — v,156p

ASIA, SOUTHEASTERN — Economic conditions — Congresses

The ASEAN success story : social, economic, and political dimensions : based on the East-West Center's 25th Anniversary Conference on ASEAN and the Pacific Basin, held in Honolulu, Hawaii from 29 October to 1 November 1985 / edited by Linda G. Martin. — Honolulu, Hawaii : The Center : Distributed by the University of Hawaii Press, c1987. — p. cm. — *Includes index. — Bibliography: p*

Southeast Asia, an emerging center of world influence? : economic and resource considerations / edited by Wayne Raymond and K. Mulliner. — Athens : Ohio University Center for International Studies, 1977. — vii, 136 p.. — (Papers in international studies : Southeast Asia series ; no. 42). — *Papers presented at a symposium on May 7-8, 1976 at Ohio University, Athens, hosted by the Southeast Asia Studies Program. — Includes bibliographical references*

ASIA, SOUTHEASTERN — Economic integration — Congresses

The ASEAN success story : social, economic, and political dimensions : based on the East-West Center's 25th Anniversary Conference on ASEAN and the Pacific Basin, held in Honolulu, Hawaii from 29 October to 1 November 1985 / edited by Linda G. Martin. — Honolulu, Hawaii : The Center : Distributed by the University of Hawaii Press, c1987. — p. cm. — *Includes index. — Bibliography: p*

ASIA, SOUTHEASTERN — Economic policy

PRESTON, P. W.
Making sense of development : an introduction to classical and contemporary theories of development and their application to Southeast Asia / P. W. Preston. — London : Routledge & Kegan Paul, 1986. — 319 p

ASIA, SOUTHEASTERN — Foreign economic relations — Addresses, essays, lectures

THAMBIPILLAI, Pushpa
ASEAN negotiations : two insights / Pushpa Thambipillai and J. Saravanamuttu. — Singapore : ASEAN Economic Research Unit, Institute of Southeast Asian Studies, 1985. — viii, 56 p.. — (ASEAN political studies). — *Includes bibliographical references*

ASIA, SOUTHEASTERN — Foreign economic relations — South Asia

ASEAN-South Asia economic relations / edited by Charan D. Wadhva and Mukul G. Asher. — Singapore : Institute of Southeast Asian Studies, c1985. — 384 p

ASIA, SOUTHEASTERN — Foreign relations

IRACENTIRAN, Ma
ASEAN's foreign relations : the shift to collective action / M. Rajendran. — Kuala Lumpur : Arenabuku, 1985. — xii, 330 p.. — *Based on author's thesis (Ph. D.--Griffith University, 1983). — Includes index. — Bibliography: p. [309]-322*

TILMAN, Robert O
Southeast Asia and the enemy beyond : ASEAN perceptions of external threats / Robert O. Tilman. — Boulder, Colo. : Westview Press, 1986. — p. cm — (Westview special studies on South and Southeast Asia). — *Includes index*

ASIA, SOUTHEASTERN — Foreign relations — Treaties

Multilateral treaties between ASEAN countries / editor-in-chief Visu Sinnadurai. — Singapore : Butterworth, 1986. — 235p. — (ASEAN law series)

ASIA, SOUTHEASTERN — Foreign relations — Kampuchea

PARIBATRA, Sukhumbhand
Kampuchea without delusion / Sukhumbhand Paribatra. — Kuala Lumpur : Institute of Strategic and International Studies, 1986. — 27p. — (ISIS ASEAN series)

ASIA, SOUTHEASTERN — Foreign relations — Soviet Union

MCLANE, Charles B.
Soviet strategies in southeast Asia : an exploration of eastern policy under Lenin and Stalin / Charles B. McLane. — Princeton : Princeton University Press, 1966. — 563p

ASIA, SOUTHEASTERN — Foreign relations — United States

HESS, Gary R
The United States' emergence as a Southeast Asian power, 1940-1950 / Gary R. Hess. — New York : Columbia University, 1987. — p. cm. — *Includes index. — Bibliography: p*

ASIA, SOUTHEASTERN — Industries

CHONG, Li Choy
Fostering industrial development through market freedom and consumer emancipation / Chong Li Choy. — Kuala Lumpur : Institute of Strategic and International Studies, 1986p. — 18p. — (ISIS ASEAN Series). — *Bibliography: p17-18*

The Pacific challenge in international business / edited by W. Chan Kim and Philip K.Y. Young ; with a foreword by Vern Terpstra. — Ann Arbor, Mich. : UMI Research Press, 1987. — viii, 342 p.. — (Research for business decisions ; no. 72). — *Includes bibliographies and index*

ASIA, SOUTHEASTERN — Library resources — Great Britain

CAREY, Peter
Maritime Southeast Asian studies in the United Kingdom : a survey of their post-war development and current resources / [researched and compiled by] Peter Carey. — Oxford : JASO, 1986. — vii,115p. — (JASO Occasional Papers ; no.6)

ASIA, SOUTHEASTERN — Manufactures

The Pacific challenge in international business / edited by W. Chan Kim and Philip K.Y. Young ; with a foreword by Vern Terpstra. — Ann Arbor, Mich. : UMI Research Press, 1987. — viii, 342 p.. — (Research for business decisions ; no. 72). — *Includes bibliographies and index*

ASIA, SOUTHEASTERN — Politics and government

AIKMAN, David
Pacific Rim : area of change, area of opportunity / by David Aikman. — 1st ed. — Boston : Little, Brown, 1986. — p. cm

CROUCH, Harold
Economic change, social structure and the political system in Southeast Asia : Philippine development compared with the other ASEAN countries / Harold Crouch. — Singapore : Institute of Southeast Asian Studies. Southeast Asian Studies Program, 1985. — 68p. — *Bibliography: p61-68*

JOO-JOCK, Lim
Territorial power domains, southeast Asia, and China : the geo-strategy of an overarching massif / Lim Joo-Jock. — Singapore : Institute of Southeast Asian Studies, 1984. — 230p. — *Bibliography: p215-229*

NEW ZEALAND. Ministry of Foreign Affairs
ASEAN and New Zealand. — Wellington : the Ministry, 1986. — 31p. — (Information bulletin ; no.17)

SOLIDUM, Estrella D
Bilateral summitry in ASEAN / Estrella D. Solidum. — Manila, Philippines : Foreign Service Institute, 1982. — 44 p.. — *Bibliography: p. 44*

ASIA, SOUTHEASTERN — Politics and government — Congresses
The ASEAN success story : social, economic, and political dimensions : based on the East-West Center's 25th Anniversary Conference on ASEAN and the Pacific Basin, held in Honolulu, Hawaii from 29 October to 1 November 1985 / edited by Linda G. Martin. — Honolulu, Hawaii : The Center : Distributed by the University of Hawaii Press, c1987. — p. cm. — Includes index. — Bibliography: p

ASIA, SOUTHEASTERN — Relations — China
SURYADINATA, Leo
China and the ASEAN states : the ethnic Chinese dimension / Leo Suryadinata. — [Singapore] : Singapore University Press, National University of Singapore, [c1985]. — xiii, 230 p., [4] p. of plates. — Includes index. — Bibliography: p. 218-226

ASIA, SOUTHEASTERN — Religion
VON DER MEHDEN, Fred R
Religion and modernization in Southeast Asia / Fred R. von der Mehden. — 1st ed. — Syracuse, N.Y. : Syracuse University Press, c1986. — viii, 240 p.. — Includes index. — Bibliography: p. 225-233

ASIA, SOUTHEASTERN — Rural conditions
Rice societies : Asian problems and prospects / edited by Irene Nørlund, Sven Cederroth, Ingela Gerdin. — London : Curzon, 1986. — x,321p. — (Studies on Asian topics ; 10). — Includes bibliographies

SCOTT, James Cameron
The moral economy of the peasant : rebellion and subsistence in Southeast Asia / James C. Scott. — New Haven ; London : Yale University Press, 1976 [i.e. 1977]. — ix,246p. — Published in the United States: 1976. — Includes index

ASIA, SOUTHEASTERN — Social conditions — Congresses
The ASEAN success story : social, economic, and political dimensions : based on the East-West Center's 25th Anniversary Conference on ASEAN and the Pacific Basin, held in Honolulu, Hawaii from 29 October to 1 November 1985 / edited by Linda G. Martin. — Honolulu, Hawaii : The Center : Distributed by the University of Hawaii Press, c1987. — p. cm. — Includes index. — Bibliography: p

ASIA, SOUTHEASTERN — Study and teaching — Great Britain
CAREY, Peter
Maritime Southeast Asian studies in the United Kingdom : a survey of their post-war development and current resources / [researched and compiled by] Peter Carey. — Oxford : JASO, 1986. — vii,115p. — (JASO Occasional Papers ; no.6)

ASIA, SOUTHEASTERN — Study and teaching — United States — Congresses
Southeast Asian studies : options for the future / edited by Ronald A. Morse. — Lanham : University Press of America ; Washington, D.C. : Asia Program, Wilson Center, c1984. — 192 p.. — Papers presented at a conference held at the Woodrow Wilson International Center for Scholars, March 26, 1984. — Includes bibliographies

ASIAN AMERICANS — History — Addresses, essays, lectures
Dictionary of Asian American history / edited by Hyung-Chan Kim. — New York : Greenwood Press, 1986. — xv, 627 p.. — Includes index. — Bibliography: p. [565]-577

ASIAN AMERICANS — History — Dictionaries
Dictionary of Asian American history / edited by Hyung-Chan Kim. — New York : Greenwood Press, 1986. — xv, 627 p.. — Includes index. — Bibliography: p. [565]-577

ASIAN PRODUCTIVITY ORGANIZATION — Bibliography
APO publications catalogue / Asian Productivity Organization. — Tokyo : Asian Productivity Organization, 1985-. — Annual

ASIANS — Housing — Great Britain
PETTIT, Michael
Housing centres and the Asian community / Michael Pettit. — London : Commission for Racial Equality, 1978. — [2]p. — First published by the Community Relations Commission, 1975

ASIANS — Medical care — Great Britain
Report on the role of an Asian advocate within the health services (a report an a project carried out within the area of the West Lambeth Health Authority). — London : Cicely Northcote Trust, 1987. — 42p

ASIANS — Australia — Public opinion
Migrant attitudes survey : a study of the attitudes of Australians and recently arrived migrants from Asia and the Middle East, in close neighbourhoods in Sydney and Adelaide. — Canberra : Australian Government Publishing Service
V.1: summary findings. — 1986. — vii,71p. — Bibliography references: p37-38

Migrant attitudes survey : a study of the attitudes of Australians and recently arrived migrants from Asia and the Middle East, in close neighbourhoods in Sydney and Adelaide. — Canberra : Australian Government Publishing Service
V.2: Overall findings. — 1986. — xxiv,280p

ASIANS — Canada
JOHNSTON, Hugh
The East Indians in Canada / Hugh Johnston. — Ottawa : Canadian Historical Association, 1984. — 24p. — (Canadian Historical Association booklet ; no.5). — Bibliography: p24

ASIANS — England
WANDSWORTH COUNCIL FOR COMMUNITY RELATIONS
Asians & the health service : a directory of measures implemented by area health authorities to meet the needs of the Asian community. — London : Commission for Racial Equality for Wandsworth Council for Community Relations, 1978. — iv,30p

ASIANS — Great Britain
DAVIES, J. G.
Asian housing in Britain / J. G. Davies. — London : Social Affairs Unit, 1984. — 23p. — (Research reports / Social Affairs Unit ; 6). — Bibliography: p19

GREAT BRITAIN. Community Relations Commission
Background of Asian minority groups / prepared with the assistance of Praful Patel, S. A. Pasha and Harmindar Singh. — London : Commission for Racial Equality, 1978. — 4p. — (Fact paper / Commission for Racial Equality ; 3). — Written at the request of the Trades Union Advisory Group of the former Community Relations Commission. — Bibliography: p[4]

ASIANS — Great Britain — Social conditions
Report on the role of an Asian advocate within the health services (a report an a project carried out within the area of the West Lambeth Health Authority). — London : Cicely Northcote Trust, 1987. — 42p

ASIATIC MODE OF PRODUCTION
THANH-HUNG, Nguyen
Zur Theorie der vorkapitalistischen Produktionsweisen bei K. Marx und F. Engels : dargestellt anhand der Probleme der "asiatischen Produktionsweise" / Nguyen Thanh-Hung. — Gaiganz : Politladen, 1975. — 119p. — (Politladen Typoskript ; 9). — Bibliography: p110-119

ASMAT (Tribe) — New Guinea — Art
GERBRANDS, Adrian A.
Wow-ipits : eight Asmat woodcarvers of New Guinea / Adrian A. Gerbrands ; [translated from the dutch by Inez Wolf Seeger]. — The Hague : Mouton, c1967. — 191p. — (Art in its context : studies in ethno-aesthetics. field reports ; v.3). — Bibliography: p[173]-174

ASQUITH, H. H.
JENKINS, Roy
Asquith / Roy Jenkins. — 3rd ed. — London : Collins, 1986. — [576]p. — Previous ed.: 1978. — Includes index

ASSAM (INDIA) — Politics and government
DEV, Bimal J.
Assam Muslims : politics & cohesion / Bimal J. Dev, Dilip K. Lahiri. — Delhi, India : Mittal Publications : Distributed by Mittal Publishers' Distributors, 1985. — 220 p.. — Includes bibliographies and index

ASSAM (INDIA) — Rural conditions — Case studies
BORAH, K. C
Income, expenditure, and saving in rural India : a micro-level study / K.C. Borah. — Delhi, India : Mittal Publications : Distributed by Mittal Publishers' Distributors, 1985. — xviii, 221 p.. — : Revision of the author's thesis (Ph. D.--Dibrugarh University, 1977). — Summary: Based on survey conducted in Sibsagar District, Assam. — Includes index. — Bibliography: p. [209]-217

ASSASSINATION
Disappeared! : technique of terror : a report / for the Independent Commission on International Humanitarian Issues ; preface by Simone Veil. — London : Zed, 1986. — [112]p

ASSASSINATION — France — Paris
LEVINE, Michel
Les ratonnades d'octobre : un meurtre collectif à Paris en 1961 / Michel Levine. — Paris : Editions Ramsay, 1985. — 309p

ASSEMBLER LANGUAGE (COMPUTER PROGRAM LANGUAGE)
LEMONE, Karen A
Assembly language and systems programming for the IBM personal computer / by Karen A. Lemone. — Boston : Little, Brown, 1985. — p. cm. — (The Little, Brown microcomputer bookshelf). — Includes index

ROLLINS, Dan
IBM-PC 8088 MACRO Assembler programming / Dan Rollins. — New York ; Macmillan ; London : Collier Macmillan, c1985. — xxiii,435p. — Includes index

ASSIMILATION (SOCIOLOGY) — Addresses, essays, lectures
BLAUNER, Robert
Racial oppression in America / Robert Blauner. — New York ; London : Harper and Row, 1972. — x,309p. — Includes index

ASSIMILATION (SOCIOLOGY) — History
MÖRNER, Magnus
Adventurers and proletarians : the story of migrants in Latin America / Magnus Mörner with the collaboration of Harold Sims. — Pittsburgh, PA : University of Pittsburgh Press ; [Paris, France] : Unesco, 1985. — p. cm. — (Pitt Latin American series). — Includes index. — Bibliography: p

ASSISTANCE IN EMERGENCIES — Planning — Congresses
CONFERENCE ON EMERGENCY PLANNING (1985 : San Diego, Calif.)
Emergency planning : proceedings of the Conference on Emergency Planning, 24-26 January 1985, San Diego, California / edited by John M. Carroll. — La Jolla, Calif. (P.O. Box 2228, La Jolla 92038) : Society for Computer Simulation, c1985. — ix, 155 p.. — (Simulation series ; v. 15, no. 1 (January 1985)) . — Includes bibliographies and index

ASSOCIATION OF COUNTY COUNCILS
ASSOCIATION OF COUNTY COUNCILS
The voice of county government : a guide to the work of the ACC. — London : Association of County Councils, 1986. — 18p. — *Bibliography: p17-18*

ASSOCIATION OF PROFESSIONAL, EXECUTIVE, CLERICAL AND COMPUTER STAFF
APEX / Association of Professional, Executive, Clerical and Computer Staff. — London : Association of Professional, Executive, Clerical and Computer Staff, 1986-. — *Bimonthly*

ASSOCIATION OF UNIVERSITY TEACHERS
AUT woman / Association of University Teachers. — London : Association of University Teachers, 1984-. — *Quarterly*

ASSOCIATIONS, INSTITUTIONS, — Great Britain
WEBB, Sidney
The sphere of voluntary agencies in the prevention of destitution / by Sidney and Beatrice Webb. — London : National Committee for the Prevention of Destitution, 1911. — 46p

ASSOCIATIONS, INSTITUTIONS, ETC. — Europe — Finance — Handbooks, manuals, etc.
DAVISON, Ann
Grants from Europe : how to get money and influence policy / written for ERICA by Ann Davison. — 3rd ed.. — London : Bedford Square Press, 1986. — ix, 86p

ASSOCIATIONS, INSTITUTIONS, ETC. — European Economic Community countries — Directories
MORRIS, Brian
The European Community : a practical directory and guide for business, industry and trade / Brian Morris and Klaus Boehm ; editor M ara M. Vilčinskas. — 2nd ed. — [London] : Macmillan, 1986. — xi,348p

ASSOCIATIONS, INSTITUTIONS, ETC. — France
TOYNBEE, W. S.
Adult education and the voluntary associations in France / W. S. Toynbee. — Nottingham : University of Nottingham. Department of Adult Education, 1985. — iv,44p. — (Nottingham working papers in the education of adults ; no.7)

ASSOCIATIONS, INSTITUTIONS, ETC. — Germany — History
Lexikon zur Parteiengeschichte : die bürgerlichen und kleinbürgerlichen Parteien und Verbände in Deutschland (1789-1945) : in vier Bänden / hrsg. von Dieter Fricke (Leiter des Herausgeberkollektivs)...[et al.]. — Köln : Pahl-Rugenstein. — (Geschichte der bürgerlichen und kleinbürgerlichen Parteien und Verbände)
Bd.4: Reichsverband der Deutschen Industrie - Zweckverband der freien Deutschturnsvereine. — 1986. — 743p. — *Includes bibliographies*

ASSOCIATIONS, INSTITUTIONS, ETC. — Great Britain — Bibliography
HARRIS, Margaret
Organising voluntary agencies : a guide through the literature / Margaret Harris and David Billis. — [London] : Bedford Square Press : NCVO, [1986]. — 125p

ASSOCIATIONS, INSTITUTIONS, ETC. — Ireland — Directories
Directory of national voluntary organisations, social service agencies and other useful public bodies. — 5th ed. (1985)-. — Dublin (71 Lower Leeson St., Dublin 2) : NSSB, 1985-. — v.. — *Full name of the body: National Social Service Board. — Continues: Directory of social service organisations*

ASSOCIATIONS, INSTITUTIONS, ETC — United States
LIPNACK, Jessica
The networking book : people connecting with people / Jessica Lipnack and Jeffrey Stamps. — New York : Routledge & Kegan Paul, 1986. — xv, 192 p.. — *Includes index. — Bibliography: p. 179-182*

ASSOCIATIVE STORAGE
STÜTTGEN, Heinrich J.
A hierarchical associative processing system / Heinrich J. Stüttgen. — Berlin ; New York : Springer-Verlag, c1985. — p. cm. — (Lecture notes in computer science ; 195). — *Bibliography: p*

ASTRONAUTICS — Soviet Union — History
MCDOUGALL, Walter A.
The heavens and the earth : a political history of the space age / Walter A. McDougall. — New York : Basic Books, c1985. — xviii, 555p. — *Includes index. — Bibliography: p [466]-536*

ASTRONAUTICS — United States — History
MCDOUGALL, Walter A.
The heavens and the earth : a political history of the space age / Walter A. McDougall. — New York : Basic Books, c1985. — xviii, 555p. — *Includes index. — Bibliography: p [466]-536*

ASTRONAUTICS AND CIVILIZATION
MARSH, Peter, 1952-
The space business : a manual on the commercial uses of space / Peter Marsh. — Harmondsworth : Penguin, 1985. — 232p. — *Further reading: p[211]-217*

ASTRONAUTICS AND STATE — France
CHABBERT, Bernard
Les fils d'Ariane / Bernard Chabbert. — Paris : Plon, 1986. — 248p

ASTRONAUTICS AND STATE — Soviet Union
MCDOUGALL, Walter A.
The heavens and the earth : a political history of the space age / Walter A. McDougall. — New York : Basic Books, c1985. — xviii, 555p. — *Includes index. — Bibliography: p [466]-536*

ASTRONAUTICS AND STATE — United States
MCDOUGALL, Walter A.
The heavens and the earth : a political history of the space age / Walter A. McDougall. — New York : Basic Books, c1985. — xviii, 555p. — *Includes index. — Bibliography: p [466]-536*

ASTRONAUTICS IN METEOROLOGY — Congresses
Space applications for the acquisition and dissemination of disaster-related data : expert meeting, Geneva, 14-17 June 1983. — [Geneva] : Office of the United Nations Disaster Relief Co-ordinator, [1983]. — ii,111p. — *"October 1983"--P. 4 of cover*

ASTRONAUTICS, MILITARY — Soviet Union
JOHNSON, Nicholas L.
Soviet military strategy in space / Nicholas L. Johnson. — London : Jane's, 1987. — 287p

STARES, Paul B
Space and national security / Paul B. Stares. — Washington, D.C. : Brookings Institution, c1987. — p. cm. — *Includes bibliographical references and index*

ASTRONAUTICS, MILITARY — United States
STARES, Paul B
Space and national security / Paul B. Stares. — Washington, D.C. : Brookings Institution, c1987. — p. cm. — *Includes bibliographical references and index*

ASTRONOMY
The Nature of scientific discovery : a symposium commemorating the 500th anniversary of the birth of Nicolaus Copernicus / Edited by Owen Gingerich. — [1st ed.]. — Washington : Smithsonian Institution Press ; [distributed by G. Braziller, New York, 1975]. — 616 p. — (Smithsonian international symposia series ; 5). — *"The fifth international symposium of the Smithsonian Institution organized jointly with the National Academy of Sciences in cooperation with the Copernicus Society of America.". — Bibliography: p. 23-26*

ASTURIAS (SPAIN) — Economic conditions
VAZQUEZ GARCÍA, Juan Antonio
La cuestión hullera en Asturias (1918-1935) / por Juan Antonio Vazquez García ; b prólogo José Luis García Delgado. — Oviedo : Instituto de Estudios Asturianos, 1985. — 222p . — *Bibliography: p219-222*

ASTURIAS (SPAIN) — Emigration and Immigration — Economic aspects — History
OJEDA, Germán
Campesinos, emigrantes, indianos : emigración y economía en Asturias, 1830-1930 / Germán Ojeda, José Luis San Miguel. — Salinas : Ayalga Ediciones, 1985. — 157p. — ("Colección Monografías de Asturias" ; 1). — *Bibliography: p152-157*

ASTURIAS (SPAIN) — History
CARANTOÑA ALVAREZ, Francisco
La guerra de la independencia en Asturias / Francisco Carantoña Alvarez. — Madrid : Silverio Cañada, 1983. — 250p. — (Biblioteca Julio Somoza. Temas de Investigación Asturiana ; 11). — *"Este libro ha sido redacto en base a la Tesis de Licenciatura que...fue presentada ante el Tribunal correspondiente en junio de 1981". — Bibliography: p[181]-190*

DÍAZ FERNÁNDEZ, José
Octubre rojo en Asturias / prólogo de J. Díaz Fernández ; introducción de José Manuel López de Abiada. — Gijon : Silverio Cañada, 1984. — l,205p. — (Colección Reconquista : Libros de Asturias recuperados ; 4). — *Reprint of original edition published by Agencia General de Libreria y Artes Gráficas, with a foreword by J. Díaz Fernández - Madrid, 1935*

Octubre 1934 : cincuenta años para la reflexión / [por] G. Jackson ... [et al.]. — Madrid : Siglo Veintiuno, 1985. — viii,344p. — *'En la edición de la presente obra ha colaborado la Fundación José Barreiro, de Oviedo' — half-title. Bibliography: p.[320]-344*

ASTURIAS (SPAIN) — History — Autonomy and independence movements
CARANTOÑA ALVAREZ, Francisco
La guerra de la independencia en Asturias / Francisco Carantoña Alvarez. — Madrid : Silverio Cañada, 1983. — 250p. — (Biblioteca Julio Somoza. Temas de Investigación Asturiana ; 11). — *"Este libro ha sido redacto en base a la Tesis de Licenciatura que...fue presentada ante el Tribunal correspondiente en junio de 1981". — Bibliography: p[181]-190*

ASTURIAS (SPAIN) — History — Revolution, 1934
BARCO TERUEL, Enrique
El "golpe" socialista del 6 de Octubre de 1934 / Enrique Barco Teruel. — Madrid : Dyrsa, 1984. — 361p

ASTURIAS (SPAIN) — Industries — History
OJEDA, Germán
Asturias en la industrialización española, 1833-1907 / por Germán Ojeda. — Madrid : Siglo veintiuno ; Oviedo : Universidad de Oviedo, Servicio de publicaciones, 1985. — xi,472p. — *Bibliography: p[437]-459*

ASTURIAS (SPAIN) — Social conditions
SHUBERT, Adrian
Hacia la revolución : orígenes sociales del movimiento obrero en Asturias, 1860-1934 / Adrian Shubert ; traducción castellana de Agueda Palacios Honorato. — Barcelona : Crítica, 1984. — 235p. — *Bibliography: p [215]-223*

ASYLUM, RIGHT OF — Biblical teaching — Congresses
Sanctuary : a resource guide for understanding and participating in the Central American refugees' struggle / Gary MacEoin, editor. — 1st ed. — San Francisco : Harper & Row, c1985. — 217 p.. — *Papers derived from the Inter-American Symposium on Sanctuary, held in Tucson, Ariz., Jan. 23-24, 1985, and sponsored by the Tucson Ecumenical Council's Task Force for Central America and others.* — *Bibliography: p. 207-211*

ASYLUM, RIGHT OF — Congresses
Sanctuary : a resource guide for understanding and participating in the Central American refugees' struggle / Gary MacEoin, editor. — 1st ed. — San Francisco : Harper & Row, c1985. — 217 p.. — *Papers derived from the Inter-American Symposium on Sanctuary, held in Tucson, Ariz., Jan. 23-24, 1985, and sponsored by the Tucson Ecumenical Council's Task Force for Central America and others.* — *Bibliography: p. 207-211*

ASYLUM, RIGHT OF — Germany (West)
KLAUSMEIER, Simone
Vom Asylbewerber zum "Scheinasylanten" : Asylrecht und Asylpolitik in der Bundesrepublik Deutschland seit 1973 / Simone Klausmeier. — Berlin : Express Edition, 1984. — 127p. — *Bibliography: p121-127*

ASYLUMS — France
RIPA, Yannick
La ronde des folles : femme, folie et enfermement au XIXe siècle, (1838-1870) / Yannick Ripa. — Paris : Aubier, 1986. — 216p

ATATÜRK, KAMÂL
VOLKAN, Vamik D.
The immortal Atatürk : a psychobiography / Vamik D. Volkan and Norman Itzkowitz. — Chicago ; London : University of Chicago Press, 1984. — xxv,374p. — *Bibliography: p361-368.* — *Includes index*

ATHEISM — Soviet Union
Ateizm v SSSR : stanovlenie i razvitie / [G. V. Vorontsov...et al., otv. redaktor A. F. Okulov]. — Moskva : Mysl', 1986. — 235p

ATHENS (GREECE) — Politics and government
CARTER, L. B.
The quiet Athenian / L.B. Carter. — Oxford : Clarendon, 1986. — [ix,224]p. — *Includes bibliography*

ATLANTIC FISHERIES RESTRUCTURING ACT 1983
Atlantic Ffisheries Rrestructuring Act annual report = sur la restructuration du secteur des pêches de l'Atlantique: rapport annuel / Fisheries and Oceans, Canada. — Ottawa : Department of Fisheries and Oceans, 1983/4-. — *Annual.* — *In English and French*

ATLANTIC OCEAN — Commerce
Technical conservation measures : measures in force in the zones under the fisheries jurisdiction of contracting parties and in the regulatory area of the Commission. — London : North-East Atlantic Fisheries Commission, 1986. — 1v (loose-leaf)

ATLANTIC SALMON — Congresses
INTERNATIONAL ATLANTIC SALMON SYMPOSIUM (2nd : 1978 : Edinburgh)
Atlantic salmon, its future : proceedings of the second International Atlantic Salmon Symposium, Edinburgh 1978, sponsored by the International Atlantic Salmon Foundation and the Atlantic Salmon Research Trust / editor A.E.J. Went. — Farnham : Fishing News, 1980. — xi,253p. — *Includes bibliographies and index*

ATLASES
The Times concise atlas of the world / maps prepared and printed by John Bartholomew and Son Ltd.. — 5th ed. — London : Times Books, 1986. — 44p,148 maps,96p

ATOMIC BOMB
BOYER, Paul S
By the bomb's early light : American thought and culture at the dawn of the atomic age / Paul Boyer. — New York : Pantheon, 1985. — xx, 440p. — *Includes bibliographical references and index*

ATOMIC BOMB — Moral and ethical aspects
BOYER, Paul S
By the bomb's early light : American thought and culture at the dawn of the atomic age / Paul Boyer. — New York : Pantheon, 1985. — xx, 440p. — *Includes bibliographical references and index*

ATOMIC ENERGY
LIBERAL PARTY
For a future thatś safe : the Liberal alternative to nuclear power : the campaign pact. — London : Liberal Party, 1986. — [36p]

The Nuclear age : power, proliferation, and the arms race. — Washington, D.C. : Congressional Quarterly, c1984. — xii, 253 p.. — *Bibliography: p241-243.* — *Bibliography: p. 241-243*

ATOMIC POWER
IBRÜGGER, Lothar
General report on East-West scientific co-operation, the Chernobyl accident, and nuclear waste / Lothar Ibrügger. — Brussels : North Atlantic Assembly, 1986. — ii,33p

ATOMIC POWER — Law and legislation — Mexico
HALVAS, J.
El programa de protección radiológica de la República Mexicana / J. Halvas, R. Díaz Perches, R. González Constandse. — México : Comisión Nacional de Energía Nuclear, 1964. — 8p. — ([Publicación] / Comisión Nacional de Energía Nuclear ; num.160). — *Text in Spanish and English.* — *Presentado al Décimo Congreso Internacional de Radiología en Montreal, el 26 de agosto al 1 de septiembre de 1962*

ATOMIC POWER-PLANTS
Les centrales nucléaires dans le monde = nuclear power plants in the world / Commissariat a l'Energie Atomique. — Paris : Commissariat a L'Energie Atomique, 1986-. — *Annual.* — *Text in English and French*

ATOMIC POWER PLANTS — England — Sizewell (Suffolk)
FRIENDS OF THE EARTH
Critical decision : should Britain buy the pressurised water reactor? : a report on the Sizewell Inquiry by Friends of the Earth / edited by Walt Patterson, Stewart Boyle, Juliette Majot. — London : Friends of the Earth Trust, 1986. — 135p. — *Bibliography: p103-109*

ATOMIC POWER-PLANTS — Great Britain — Accidents — Economic aspects
NECTOUX, Francois
Accidents will happen... : an inquiry into the economic and social consequences of a nuclear accident at Sizewell 'B' / Francois Nectoux, William Cannell. — London : Earth Resources Research : Friends of the Earth Trust, 1984. — 109p

ATOMIC POWER-PLANTS — Great Britain — Accidents — Social aspects
NECTOUX, Francois
Accidents will happen... : an inquiry into the economic and social consequences of a nuclear accident at Sizewell 'B' / Francois Nectoux, William Cannell. — London : Earth Resources Research : Friends of the Earth Trust, 1984. — 109p

ATOMIC WARFARE
FALK, Jim
Taking Australia off the map : facing the threat of nuclear war / Jim Falk. — Melbourne : W. Heinemann Australia, 1983. — xii, 290 p., [16] p. of plates. — *Includes index.* — *Bibliography: p. [252]-254*

ATOMIC WARFARE — Moral and ethical aspects
HOLLENBACH, David
Nuclear ethics : a Christian moral argument / David Hollenbach. — New York : Paulist Press, c1983. — v, 100 p.

ATOMIC WARFARE — Moral and religious aspects
The challenge of nuclear armaments : essays dedicated to Niels Bohr and his appeal for an open world / edited by A. Boserup, L. Christensen and O. Nathan. — Copenhagen : Rhodos International for the University of Copenhagen, 1986. — 346p

ATOMIC WARFARE — Religious aspects — Catholic Church
HOLLENBACH, David
Nuclear ethics : a Christian moral argument / David Hollenbach. — New York : Paulist Press, c1983. — v, 100 p.

ATOMIC WARFARE — Religious aspects — Catholic Church — Addresses, essays, lectures
Catholics and nuclear war : a commentary on The challenge of peace, the U.S. Catholic bishops' pastoral letter on war and peace / edited by Philip J. Murnion ; foreword by Theodore M. Hesburgh. — New York : Crossroad, 1983. — xxii, 346 p. — *"A National Pastoral Life Center publication.".* — *Includes bibliographical references*

ATOMIC WEAPONS
GREEN, William
Soviet nuclear weapons policy : a research guide / William Green. — Boulder, Colo. : Westview Press, 1987, c1983. — p. cm. — (A Westview replica edition). — *Includes bibliographies and indexes*

The Nuclear age : power, proliferation, and the arms race. — Washington, D.C. : Congressional Quarterly, c1984. — xii, 253 p.. — *Bibliography: p241-243.* — *Bibliography: p. 241-243*

SABIN, Philip A. G.
Shadow or substance? : perceptions and symbolism in nuclear force planning / Philip A. G. Sabin. — London : International Institute for Strategic Studies, 1987. — 72p. — (Adelphi papers ; 222)

SIVARD, Ruth Leger
World military and social expenditures 1985 / Ruth Leger Sivard. — Washington D. C. : World Priorities, 1985. — 52p

Study on Israeli nuclear armament. — New York : United Nations, 1982. — vii,22p. — (Disarmament. study series ; 6) [Document] / United Nations ; A/36/431). — *Includes bibliographical references.* — *Sales no.: E.82.IX.2*

ATOMIC WEAPONS — Testing
DANIELSSON, Bengt
Poisoned reign : French nuclear colonialism in the Pacific / Bengt Danielsson and Mariè-Thérèse Danielsson. — 2nd rev. ed. — Ringwood, Victoria : Penguin, 1986. — xiv,323p. — *First published in Paris, 1974, under the title "Moruroa Mon Amour"*

ATOMIC WEAPONS AND DISARMAMENT
CARTWRIGHT, John
Interim report [of the Special Committee on Nuclear Strategy and Arms Control] / John Cartwright. — Brussels : North Atlantic Assembly, 1986. — iii,67p

DJIWANDONO, J. Soedjati
Southeast Asia as a nuclear-weapons-free zone / J Soedjati Djiwandono. — Kuala Lumpur : Institute of Strategic and International Studies, 1986. — 7p. — (ISIS ASEAN series)

GILBERT, Tony
Star wars / Tony Gilbert. — London : Liberation, 1985. — 31p

NATIONAL UNION OF MINEWORKERS
Miners United for peace. — London : National Union of Mineworkers, 1987. — [22p]. — (Campaign briefing ; 3)

The Nuclear age : power, proliferation, and the arms race. — Washington, D.C. : Congressional Quarterly, c1984. — xii, 253 p.. — Bibliography: p241-243. — Bibliography: p. 241-243

The nuclear freeze : a strategic assessment / George C. Betts [et al.]. — Toronto : Canadian Institute of Strategic Studies, 1986. — 38p. — (Issues in strategy)

SMITH, Peter
Real defence : Britain without the bomb / Peter Smith [and] Mike Gapes ; foreword by Joan Ruddock. — Leeds : Independent Labour Publications, 1984. — iii,40p

ATTACHMENT BEHAVIOR IN CHILDREN
Attachment in social networks : contributions to the Bowlby-Ainsworth attachment theory / edited by Louis W.C. Tavecchio and Marinus H. van IJzendoorn. — Amsterdam ; New York : North-Holland ; New York, N.Y., U.S.A. : Sole distributors for the U.S.A. and Canada, Elsevier Science Pub. Co., 1987. — xx, 483 p.. — (Advances in psychology ; 44). — Includes bibliographies and indexes

ATTENTION — Congresses
Attention and performance XI / edited by Michael I. Posner, Oscar S.M. Marin. — Hillsdale, N.J. : Lawrence Erlbaum Associates, 1985. — xxiii, 675p. — "Proceedings of the Eleventh International Symposium on Attention and Performance, Eugene, Oregon, July 1-8, 1984"--P. — Includes bibliographies and indexes

ATTIKÍ (GREECE) — Politics and government
WHITEHEAD, David, 19---
The demes of Attica, 508/7-ca. 250 B.C. : a political and social study / by David Whitehead. — Princeton, N.J. : Princeton University Press, c1985. — xxvii,485p. — Bibliography: p.455-459

ATTIKÍ (GREECE) — Social conditions
WHITEHEAD, David, 19---
The demes of Attica, 508/7-ca. 250 B.C. : a political and social study / by David Whitehead. — Princeton, N.J. : Princeton University Press, c1985. — xxvii,485p. — Bibliography: p.455-459

ATTITUDE CHANGE
Cognitive responses in persuasion / edited by Richard E. Petty, Thomas M. Ostrom, and Timothy C. Brock. — Hillsdale, N.J. : L. Erlbaum Associates, 1981. — xv,476p. — Includes index. — Bibliography: p

PETTY, Richard E
Communication and persuasion : central and peripheral routes to attitude change / Richard E. Petty, John T. Cacioppo. — New York : Springer-Verlag, c1986. — xiv, 262 p.. — (Springer series in social psychology). — Includes indexes. — Bibliography: p. [225]-247

ZIMBARDO, Philip G.
Influencing attitudes and changing behaviour : an introduction to method, theory, and applications of social control & personal power / Philip G. Zimbardo, Ebbe B. Ebbesen [and] Christina Maslach. — 2nd ed. — New York : Random House, 1977. — xv,271p. — (Topics in social psychology). — Originally published 1969. — Bibliography: p243-252

ATTITUDE (PSYCHOLOGY) — Testing
OPPENHEIM, Abraham Naftali
Questionnaire design and attitude measurement / [by] A. N. Oppenheim. — New York : Basic Books, [1966]. — ix, 298 p. — (Basic topics in sociological method). — Includes bibliographies

ATTORNEYS-GENERAL — Ontario — History
ROMNEY, Paul
Mr. Attorney : the Attorney General for Ontario in court, cabinet and legislature 1791-1899 / Paul Romney. — Toronto : Published for The Osgoode Society by University of Toronto Press, 1986. — xiii,396p. — Notes: p[337]-381

ATTRIBUTION (SOCIAL PSYCHOLOGY)
The Development of social cognition / edited by John B. Pryor, Jeanne D. Day. — New York : Springer-Verlag, c1985. — xiv, 239p. — Includes bibliographies and indexes

AUCTIONS
HOGREFE, Jeffrey
"Wholly unacceptable" : the bitter battle for Sotheby's / Jeffrey Hogrefe. — 1st ed. — New York : W. Morrow, c1986. — 238 p.. — Includes index

AUDIT COMMISSION FOR LOCAL AUTHORITIES IN ENGLAND AND WALES
Watchdogs' tales : the District Audit Service - the first 138 years / edited by R.U. Davies. — London : H.M.S.O., 1987. — viii, 250p. — At head of title: The District Auditors' Society

AUDITING
WOOLF, Emile
Auditing today / Emile Woolf. — 3rd ed. — Englewood Cliffs, N.J. ; London : Prentice-Hall, c1986. — xv,524p. — Previous ed.: 1982. — Includes index

AUDITING — Data processing
BEST, Peter J.
Auditing computer-based accounting systems / Peter J. Best, Peter G. Barrett. — Sydney : Prentice-Hall of Australia, c1983. — 247 p.. — Includes index. — Bibliography: p. 241-243

AUDITING — Research
GWILLIAM, David R.
A survey of auditing research / David R. Gwilliam. — Englewood Cliffs ; London : Prentice Hall International in association with the Institute of Chartered Accountants in England and Wales, c1987. — xi,467p. — (Research studies in accounting)

AUDITING — Standards — United States
BELKAOUI, Ahmed
Public policy and the practice and problems of accounting / Ahmed Belkaoui. — Westport, Conn. : Quorum Books, c1985. — p. cm. — Includes index. — Bibliography: p

AUDITORS' REPORTS — Great Britain
HOPKINS, Leon
The audit report / Leon Hopkins ; with a foreword by Brandon Gough. — London : Butterworths, 1984. — x,243p

AUGUSTA REGION (GA.) — Economic conditions
HARRIS, J. William
Plain folk and gentry in a slave society : white liberty and Black slavery in Augusta's hinterlands / J. William Harris. — 1st ed. — Middletown, Conn. : Wesleyan University Press ; Scranton, Pa. : Distributed by Harper & Row, 1985. — xv, 274 p. — : Originally presented as the author's thesis (Ph. D.--Johns Hopkins University, 1982.). — Includes index. — Bibliography: p. 253-261

AUGUSTA REGION (GA.) — Social conditions
HARRIS, J. William
Plain folk and gentry in a slave society : white liberty and Black slavery in Augusta's hinterlands / J. William Harris. — 1st ed. — Middletown, Conn. : Wesleyan University Press ; Scranton, Pa. : Distributed by Harper & Row, 1985. — xv, 274 p. — : Originally presented as the author's thesis (Ph. D.--Johns Hopkins University, 1982.). — Includes index. — Bibliography: p. 253-261

AUSTEN, JANE — Criticism and interpretation
SCHAPERA, Isaac
Kinship terminology in Jane Austen's novels / I. Schapera. — London : Royal Anthropological Institute, 1977. — viii,24p. — (Occasional papers / Royal Anthropological Institute ; no.33)

AUSTIN MOTOR COMPANY — History
LAMBERT, Z. E.
Lord Austin : the man / by Z. E. Lambert and R. J. Wyatt ; with a foreword by Miles Thomas. — London : Sidgwick and Jackson, 1968. — 187p

AUSTIN OF LONGBRIDGE, HERBERT AUSTIN, Baron
LAMBERT, Z. E.
Lord Austin : the man / by Z. E. Lambert and R. J. Wyatt ; with a foreword by Miles Thomas. — London : Sidgwick and Jackson, 1968. — 187p

AUSTRAL ISLANDS — Population — Statistics
Tableaux normalisés du recensement général de la population : 15 octobre 1983. — [Papeete] : Institut territorial de la statistique Résultats de la subdivision administrative des Iles Australes. — [1985?]. — 4p,11 leaves

AUSTRALIA. Broadcasting and Television Act 1942
Freedom of expression and section 116 of the Broadcasting and Television Act 1942. — Canberra : Australian Government Publishing Service, 1985. — vii,22p. — (Report / Human Rights Commission ; no.16)

AUSTRALIA. Migration Act 1958
Human rights and the Migration Act 1985. — Canberra : Australian Government Publishing Service, 1985. — xiv,211p. — (Report / Human Rights Commission ; no.13)

AUSTRALIA — Appropriations and expenditures
Public sector expenditure in Australia. — Canberra : Economic Planning Advisory Council, 1985. — v,19p. — (Council paper / Economic Planning Advisory Council ; no.5)

AUSTRALIA — Bibliography
Australian and New Zealand studies : papers presented at a colloquium at the British Library 7-9 February 1984 / edited by Patricia McLaren-Turner. — London : The Library, 1985. — [232]p. — (British Library occasional papers ; 4)

BLOOMFIELD, Valerie
Resources for Australian and New Zealand studies : a guide to library holdings in the United Kingdom / Valerie Bloomfield. — London : Australian Studies Centre, 1986. — xvi,284p. — Bibliography: p264. — Includes index

AUSTRALIA — Civilization

CLARK, Manning
A history of Australia / C.M.H. Clark. — Carlton, Vic. : Melbourne University Press 3: The beginning of an Australian civilization, 1824-1851. — 1973

AUSTRALIA — Commerce

International trade policy. — Canberra : Economic Planning Advisory Council, 1986. — v,36p. — (Council paper / Economic Planning Advisory Council ; no.18). — *Bibliographical references: p34*

AUSTRALIA — Commerce — Statistics

AUSTRALIA. Commonwealth Bureau of Census and Statistics
Overseas trade. — Melbourne : [the Bureau], 1921/22-1971/72. — *Annual.* — *Continues Australia. Commonwealth Bureau of Census and Statistics. Trade and customs returns*

AUSTRALIA. Commonwealth Bureau of Census and Statistics
Trade and customs amd excise revenue of the Commonwealth of Australia. — Melbourne : [the Bureau], 1903/4-1920/21. — *Annual.* — *Title varies.* — *Continued by Australia. Commonwealth Bureau of Census and Statistics. Overseas trade*

AUSTRALIA — Commerce — New Zealand

NEW ZEALAND. Ministry of Foreign Affairs
CER : the Australia and New Zealand closer economic relations trade agreement. — Wellington : the Ministry, 1986. — 22p. — (Information bulletin ; no.15)

AUSTRALIA — Constitution

AUSTRALIA
[Constitution (1977)]. The constitution as altered to 1 December 1977 together with Statute of Westminster Adoption Act 1942 and index. — [Canberra : Australian Government Publishing Service, 1977]. — 74p

LANE, P. H.
Lane's commentary on the Australian Constitution / P. H. Lane ; with a foreword by Sir Garfield Barwick. — Sydney : Law Book Company, 1986. — xxxviii,766p

AUSTRALIA — Constitutional law

HANKS, P. J.
Australian constitutional law / by P.J. Hanks. — 3rd ed. — Sydney : Butterworths, 1985. — xxix,792p. — *Previous ed.: 1980, published as Fajgenbaum and Hanks' Australian constitutional law.* — *Includes bibliographical references and index*

AUSTRALIA — Defenses

AUSTRALIA. Department of Defence
The defence of Australia 1987 : presented to Parliament by the Minister for Defence the Honourable Kim C. Beazley, M.P. : March 1987. — Canberra : Australian Government Publishing Service, 1987. — x,112p

MARTIN, David
Armed neutrality for Australia / David Martin. — Blackburn, Vic., Australia : Dove Communications, 1984. — xii, 294 p.. — *"A Drummond book.".* — *Includes index.* — *Bibliography: p. 278-279*

AUSTRALIA — Economic condition

So much hard work : women and prostitution in Australian history / edited by Kay Daniels. — Sydney : Fontana : Collins, 1984. — 394 p.. — *Includes bibliographies*

AUSTRALIA — Economic conditions

Uneven development and the geographical transfer of value / D.K. Forbes, P.J. Rimmer (eds.). — Canberra : Research School of Pacific Studies, The Australian National University, 1984. — 297p. — (Publication / Research School of Pacific Studies, Department of Human Geography, Australian National University ; HG/16). — *Original papers given at a Workshop on Geographical Transfer of Value held at ... the Australian National University in 1981*

AUSTRALIA — Economic conditions — 1945-

The medium-term international outlook : an economic, technological and sectoral analysis. — Canberra : Economic Planning Advisory Council, 1986. — v,37p. — (Council paper / Economic Planning Advisory Council ; no.1). — *Bibliography: p36-37*

AUSTRALIA — Economic conditions — Maps

Atlas of Australian resources. Third series. — Canberra : Division of National Mapping, 1986 Vol.4: Climate. — 60p

AUSTRALIA — Economic conditions — Mathematical models

HIGGS, Peter John
Adaptation and survival in Australian agriculture : a computable general equilibrium analysis of the impact of economic shocks originating outside the domestic agricultural sector / Peter J. Higgs. — Melbourne, Vic. ; Oxford : Oxford University Press, 1986. — 320p. — *Bibliography: p302-310*

AUSTRALIA — Economic conditions — 1945-

ECONOMIC PLANNING ADVISORY COUNCIL (Australia)
Medium to longer-term trends affecting Australia's economic growth. — [Canberra] : the Council, 1986. — 59p

GUTMAN, G. O.
Retreat of the dodo : Australian problems and prospects in the 80s / G. O. Gutman. — Canberra : Brian Clouston, 1982. — viii,195p

RICH, David C.
The industrial geography of Australia / David C. Rich. — London : Croom Helm, c1987. — [400]p. — (Croom Helm industrial geography series). — *Bibliography: p350-372.* — *Includes index*

Survey of major western Pacific economies. — 4th ed. — Canberra : Australian Government Publishing Service, 1986. — v,156p

AUSTRALIA — Economic policy

AUSTRALIA
Economic and rural policy : a Government policy statement. — Canberra : Australian Government Publishing Service, 1986. — 89p

AUSTRALIA. Bureau of Industry Economics. Conference on Revitalising Australian Industry (1986 : Sydney)
Revitalising Australian industry : the paths and prospects for long-term growth : conference papers and proceedings Sydney 8-9 April 1986. — Canberra : Australian Government Publishing Service, 1986. — viii,224p. — *Includes bibliographical references*

Directions for imporved long-term growth. — Canberra : Economic Planning Advisory Council, 1986. — v,15p. — (Council paper / Economic Planning Advisory Council ; no.8). — *Bibliographical references: p13-14*

ECONOMIC PLANNING ADVISORY COUNCIL (Australia)
Medium to longer-term trends affecting Australia's economic growth. — [Canberra] : the Council, 1986. — 59p

GUTMAN, G. O.
Retreat of the dodo : Australian problems and prospects in the 80s / G. O. Gutman. — Canberra : Brian Clouston, 1982. — viii,195p

The size of government and economic performance : international comparisons. — Canberra : Economic Planning Advisory Council, 1985. — v,20p. — (Council paper / Economic Planning Advisory Council ; no.4). — *Bibliography: p13*

WHITWELL, Greg
The Treasury line / Greg Whitwell. — London : Allen & Unwin, 1986. — [320]p. — *Includes bibliography and index*

AUSTRALIA — Economic policy — 1976-

Australian overseas aid : future directions / edited by Philip Eldridge, Dean Forbes and Doug Porter. — Sydney ; London : Croom Helm, 1986. — xxix,284p. — *Bibliography: p265-284*

AUSTRALIA — Emigration and immigration

Immigration and ethnicity in the 1980s / edited by I.H. Burnley, S. Encel, and Grant McCall. — Melbourne, Australia : Longman Cheshire, 1985. — vi, 285 p.. — (Australian studies). — *Includes bibliographies and index*

PRENTIS, Malcolm D
The Scots in Australia : a study of New South Wales, Victoria and Queensland, 1788-1900 / Malcolm D. Prentis. — Sydney : Sydney University Press ; Beaverton, Or. : distributed by International Scholarly Book Services, 1983. — xv, 304 p.. — *Includes index.* — *Bibliography: p. 290-294*

RAO, G. Lakshmana
Immigrants in Canada and Australia / edited by: Anthony H. Richmond and Freda Richmond. — Repr. ed. — [Ontario : Institute for Behavioural Research Ethnic Research Programme. — *Bibliography: p113-124* Vol.1: Demographic aspects and education / co-authors: G. Lakshmana Rao, Anthony H. Richmond, Jerzy Zubrzycki. — 1984. — v,125p

RICHMOND, Anthony H.
Immigrants in Canada and Australia / edited by Anthony H. Richmond and Freda Richmond. — [Ontario : Institute for Behaviourol Research, Ethnic Research Programme. — *Bibliography: p135-143* Vol.2: Economic adaptation / co-authors: Anthony H. Richmond and Jerzy Zubrzycki. — 1984. — vi,144p

AUSTRALIA — Emigration and immigration — Education

AUSTRALIA. Committee of Review of the Adult Migrant Education Program
Towards active voice : report / of the Committee of Review of the Adult Migrant Education Program. — Canberra : Australian Government Publishing Service, 1986. — 237p. — *Bibliographical references: p230-237*

AUSTRALIA — Emigration and immigration — Government policy

POPE, David
ASEAN-Australian immigration and the demise of 'white Australia' / David Pope [and] Peter Shergold. — Kuala Lumpur ; Canberra : ASEAN-Australia Joint Research Project, 1985. — 60p. — (ASEAN-Australia economic papers ; no.17). — *Bibliography: p59-60*

WILTON, Janis
Old worlds and new Australia : the post-war migrant experience / Janis Wilton and Richard Bosworth. — Ringwood, Vic. ; Harmondsworth : Penguin, 1985, c1984. — 215p

AUSTRALIA — Emigration and immigration — History

Australia and Ireland 1788-1988 : bicentenary essays / edited by Colm Kiernan. — Dublin : Gill and Macmillan, c1986. — xviii,309p. — *Includes index*

AUSTRALIA — Emigration and immigration — Legal status, laws, etc

AUSTRALIA. Administrative Review Council
Review of migration decisions. — Canberra : Australian Government Publishing Service, 1986. — xii,139p. — (Report to the Attorney-General / Administrative Review Council ; no.25)

AUSTRALIA — Emigration and immigration — Public opinion

Migrant attitudes survey : a study of the attitudes of Australians and recently arrived migrants from Asia and the Middle East, in close neighbourhoods in Sydney and Adelaide. — Canberra : Australian Government Publishing Service
V.1: summary findings. — 1986. — vii,71p. — *Bibliography references: p37-38*

Migrant attitudes survey : a study of the attitudes of Australians and recently arrived migrants from Asia and the Middle East, in close neighbourhoods in Sydney and Adelaide. — Canberra : Australian Government Publishing Service
V.2: Overall findings. — 1986. — xxiv,280p

AUSTRALIA — Emigration and immigration — Social aspects

YOUNG, Christabel
Selection and survival : immigrant mortality in Australia / Dr. Christabel Young. — Canberra : Australian Government Publishing Service, 1986. — xiii,251p. — *Bibliography: p132-150*

AUSTRALIA — Emigration and Immigration — United States

AITCHISON, Raymond
The Americans in Australia / Ray Aitchison. — Melbourne (Vic.) : Australasian Educa Press, 1986. — 165p. — (Australian ethnic heritage series). — *Bibliography: p162-163*

AUSTRALIA — Ethnic relations

Immigration and ethnicity in the 1980s / edited by I.H. Burnley, S. Encel, and Grant McCall. — Melbourne, Australia : Longman Cheshire, 1985. — vi, 285 p.. — (Australian studies). — *Includes bibliographies and index*

AUSTRALIA — Exiles

HUGHES, Robert, 1938-
The fatal shore : a history of the transportation of convicts to Australia, 1787-1868 / Robert Hughes. — London : Collins Harvill, 1987, c1986. — 680,[32]p of plates. — *Originally published: New York : Knopf, 1986.* — *Bibliography: p656-670.* — *Includes index*

AUSTRALIA — Foreign economic relations

CONLON, R. M
Distance and duties : determinants of manufacturing in Australia and Canada / by R.M. Conlon. — Ottawa, Canada : Carleton University Press, c1985. — ix, 217 p.. — (Carleton library series ; 135). — *Bibliography: p. 210-217*

AUSTRALIA — Foreign Economic Relations — European Economic Community countries

BURNETT, Alan
Australia and the European Communities in the 1980s / Alan Burnett. — Canberra : Australian National University, 1983. — xi, 255p. — (Canberra studies in world affairs ; no.12)

AUSTRALIA — Foreign economic relations — Great Britain

MCDOUGALL, F. L
Letters from a 'secret service agent' : F. L. McDougall to S. M. Bruce, 1924-1929 / W. J. Hudson and Wendy Way, editors. — Canberra : Australian Government Publishing Service, 1986. — xix,937p

AUSTRALIA — Foreign opinion, American

Australia through American eyes, 1935-1945 : observations by American diplomats / selected, edited and with an introduction by P.G. Edwards. — St Lucia : University of Queensland Press ; Hemel Hempstead : Distributed by Prentice-Hall, 1979. — xi,104p. — *Bibliography: p.97-101.* — *Includes index*

AUSTRALIA — Foreign population

RAO, G. Lakshmana
Immigrants in Canada and Australia / edited by: Anthony H. Richmond and Freda Richmond. — Repr. ed. — [Ontario : Institute for Behavioural Research Ethnic Research Programme. — *Bibliography: p113-124*
Vol.1: Demographic aspects and education / co-authors: G. Lakshmana Rao, Anthony H. Richmond, Jerzy Zubrzycki. — 1984. — v,125p

RICHMOND, Anthony H.
Immigrants in Canada and Australia / edited by Anthony H. Richmond and Freda Richmond. — [Ontario : Institute for Behaviourol Research, Ethnic Research Programme. — *Bibliography: p135-143*
Vol.2: Economic adaptation / co-authors: Anthony H. Richmond and Jerzy Zubrzycki. — 1984. — vi,144p

WILTON, Janis
Old worlds and new Australia : the post-war migrant experience / Janis Wilton and Richard Bosworth. — Ringwood, Vic. ; Harmondsworth : Penguin, 1985, c1984. — 215p

AUSTRALIA — Foreign relations

DUNN, Michael
Australia and the empire : from 1788 to the present / Michael Dunn. — Sydney : Fontana/Collins, 1984. — vi, 228 p.. — *Includes index.* — *Bibliography: p. 216-218*

AUSTRALIA — Foreign relations — 1945-

HENDERSON, Paul
Parliament and politics in Australia : political institutions and foreign relations / P. Henderson. — 3rd ed. — Richmond : Heinemann Educational Australia, 1985. — vii,440p

REDNER, Harry
Anatomy of the world : the impact of the atom on Australia and the world / Harry Redner, Jill Redner. — [Melbourne?] : Fontana/Collins, 1983. — 368p. — *Includes chronology (1945-1981): p331-345*

AUSTRALIA — Foreign relations — Great Britain

DAY, David
Menzies & Churchill at war : a controversial new account of the 1941 struggle for power / David Day. — North Ryde : Angus & Robertson, 1986. — xii,271p

MCDOUGALL, F. L.
Letters from a 'secret service agent' : F. L. McDougall to S. M. Bruce, 1924-1929 / W. J. Hudson and Wendy Way, editors. — Canberra : Australian Government Publishing Service, 1986. — xix,937p

MARKWELL, D. J.
The Crown and Australia / D. J. Markwell. — London : Australian Studies Centre, 1987. — 26p. — *Trevor Reese Memorial Lecture, 1987.* — *Bibliography: p25-26*

AUSTRALIA — Foreign relations — Indochina

ROSS, Estelle
Australia, the Indochina problem, and the derecognition of the Pol Pot regime / Estelle Ross. — Nathan, Australia : Centre for the Study of Australian-Asian Relations, School of Modern Asian Studies, Griffith University, [1984]. — iii, 65 p.. — (Research paper ; no. 28). — "September 1984.". — *Bibliography: p. 64-65*

AUSTRALIA — Foreign relations — New Zealand — Sources

KAY, Robin
The Australian-New Zealand agreement 1944 / edited by Robin Kay. — Wellington : Historical Publications Branch, 1972. — xxxvi, 297 p. — (Documents on New Zealand external relations ; v. 1). — *Includes the Agreement establishing the South Pacific Commission.* — *Includes bibliographical footnotes*

AUSTRALIA — History

DUNN, Michael
Australia and the empire : from 1788 to the present / Michael Dunn. — Sydney : Fontana/Collins, 1984. — vi, 228 p.. — *Includes index.* — *Bibliography: p. 216-218*

A New history of Western Australia / edited by C.T. Stannage. — Nedlands, W.A. : University of Western Australia Press, 1981. — xxi, 836p. — *Bibliography: p.783-801.* — *Includes index*

AUSTRALIA — History — Sources

CROWLEY, Francis Keble
A documentary history of Australia / Frank Crowley. — West Melbourne [Australia] : Nelson
Vol.1: Colonial Australia 1788-1840. — 1980. — 621p

CROWLEY, Francis Keble
A documentary history of Australia / Frank Crowley. — West Melbourne [Australia] : Nelson
Vol.2: Colonial Australia 1841-1874. — 1980. — 675p

CROWLEY, Francis Keble
A documentary history of Australia / Frank Crowley. — West Melbourne [Australia] : Nelson
Vol.3: Colonial Australia 1875-1900. — 1980. — 645p

AUSTRALIA — History — 1788-1851

CLARK, Manning
A history of Australia / C.M.H. Clark. — Carlton, Vic. : Melbourne University Press
3: The beginning of an Australian civilization, 1824-1851. — 1973

FLETCHER, Brian, 1931-
Ralph Darling : a governor maligned / Brian H. Fletcher. — Melbourne ; Oxford : Oxford University Press, 1984. — xxi,473p. — *Ill on lining papers.* — *Bibliography: p441-467.* — *Includes index*

AUSTRALIA — History — 1788-1900

CLARK, Manning
A history of Australia / C.M.H. Clark. — Carlton, Vic. : Melbourne University Press
4: The earth abideth for ever, 1851-1888. — 1978

CROWLEY, Francis Keble
A documentary history of Australia / Frank Crowley. — West Melbourne [Australia] : Nelson
Vol.1: Colonial Australia 1788-1840. — 1980. — 621p

CROWLEY, Francis Keble
A documentary history of Australia / Frank Crowley. — West Melbourne [Australia] : Nelson
Vol.2: Colonial Australia 1841-1874. — 1980. — 675p

CROWLEY, Francis Keble
A documentary history of Australia / Frank Crowley. — West Melbourne [Australia] : Nelson
Vol.3: Colonial Australia 1875-1900. — 1980. — 645p

AUSTRALIA — History — 20th century

YONG, C. F
The new gold mountain : the Chinese in Australia, 1901-1921 / C. F. Yong. — Richmond, Australia : Raphael Arts, 1977. — xii, 301 p.. — *Includes index.* — *Bibliography: p. 276-290*

AUSTRALIA — Industries

AUSTRALIA. Bureau of Industry Economics. Conference on Revitalising Australian Industry (1986 : Sydney)
Revitalising Australian industry : the paths and prospects for long-term growth : conference papers and proceedings Sydney 8-9 April 1986. — Canberra : Australian Government Publishing Service, 1986. — viii,224p. — *Includes bibliographical references*

AUSTRALIA — Industries *continuation*

TERRY, Chris
Australian microeconomics : policies and industry cases / Chris Terry, Ross Jones, Richard Braddock. — 2nd ed. — Sydney : Prentice-Hall of Australia, c1985. — xi, 362 p.. — *Includes bibliographies*

AUSTRALIA — Industries — Location

RICH, David C.
The industrial geography of Australia / David C. Rich. — London : Croom Helm, c1987. — [400]p. — (Croom Helm industrial geography series). — *Bibliography: p350-372. — Includes index*

AUSTRALIA — Manufactures

CONLON, R. M
Distance and duties : determinants of manufacturing in Australia and Canada / by R.M. Conlon. — Ottawa, Canada : Carleton University Press, c1985. — ix, 217 p., — (Carleton library series ; 135). — *Bibliography: p. 210-217*

AUSTRALIA — Maps

Atlas of Australian resources. Third series. — Canberra : Division of National Mapping, 1986 Vol.4: Climate. — 60p

AUSTRALIA — Military policy

The Anzac connection / edited by Desmond Ball. — Sydney ; London ; Boston : George Allen & Unwin, 1985. — xvi,169p

AUSTRALIA. Department of Defence
The defence of Australia 1987 : presented to Parliament by the Minister for Defence the Honourable Kim C. Beazley, M.P. : March 1987. — Canberra : Australian Government Publishing Service, 1987. — x,112p

MARTIN, David
Armed neutrality for Australia / David Martin. — Blackburn, Vic., Australia : Dove Communications, 1984. — xii, 294 p.. — "A Drummond book.". — *Includes index. — Bibliography: p. 278-279*

AUSTRALIA — Moral conditions

So much hard work : women and prostitution in Australian history / edited by Kay Daniels. — Sydney : Fontana : Collins, 1984. — 394 p.. — *Includes bibliographies*

AUSTRALIA — National security

FALK, Jim
Taking Australia off the map : facing the threat of nuclear war / Jim Falk. — Melbourne : W. Heinemann Australia, 1983. — xii, 290 p., [16] p. of plates. — *Includes index. — Bibliography: p. [252]-254*

AUSTRALIA — Native races

Indigenous peoples and the nation-state : 'fourth world' politics in Canada, Australia, and Norway / edited by Noel Dyck. — St. John's, Nfld., Canada : Institute of Social and Economic Research, Memorial University of Newfoundland, c1985. — 263 p.. — (Social and economic papers ; no. 14). — *Bibliography: 242-259*

AUSTRALIA — Neutrality

MARTIN, David
Armed neutrality for Australia / David Martin. — Blackburn, Vic., Australia : Dove Communications, 1984. — xii, 294 p.. — "A Drummond book.". — *Includes index. — Bibliography: p. 278-279*

AUSTRALIA — Politics and government

BRUGGER, Bill
Australian politics : theory and practice / Bill Brugger and Dean Jaensch. — Sydney ; London : Allen & Unwin, 1985. — [272]p. — *Includes bibliography and index*

Essays in the political economy of Australian capitalism / edited by E. L. Wheelwright and Ken Buckley. — Sydney : Australia & New Zealand Book Company vol.5. — 1983. — 304p

Working papers in Australian studies / Insitute of Commonwealth Studies, Australian Studies Centre. — London : Australian Studies Centre, Insitute of Commonwealth Studies, 1986-

AUSTRALIA — Politics and government — Addresses, essays, lectures

Government, politics, and power in Australia : an introductory reader / edited by Dennis Woodward, Andrew Parkin, John Summers. — 3rd ed. — Melbourne, Australia : Longman Cheshire, 1985. — xiii, 373 p.. — *Includes bibliographies and index*

AUSTRALIA — Politics and government — Bibliography

GOOT, Murray
Henry Mayer's "Immortal works" : scholarly, semi-scholarly and nor very scholarly at all : a descriptive bibliography, with index, 1940-1985 / Murray Goot. — Canberra, A.C.T. : Australian National University for the Australasian Political Studies Association, 1986. — 245p

AUSTRALIA — Politics and government — Congresses

ACADEMY OF THE SOCIAL SCIENCES IN AUSTRALIA (Symposium : 6th : 1982 : Canberra, ACT)
Bigger or smaller government? : papers from the sixth symposium of the Academy of the Social Sciences in Australia, 1982 / edited by Glenn Withers. — Canberra : Academy of the Social Sciences in Australia, 1983. — ix,115p. — *Includes references*

AUSTRALIA — Politics and government — 20th century

RYDON, Joan
A federal legislature : the Australian Commonwealth Parliament 1901-1980 / Joan Rydon. — Melbourne : Oxford University Press, 1986. — 290p. — *Bibliography: p [281]-284*

AUSTRALIA — Politics and government — 1945-

GUTMAN, G. O.
Retreat of the dodo : Australian problems and prospects in the 80s / G. O. Gutman. — Canberra : Brian Clouston, 1982. — viii,195p

HENDERSON, Paul
Parliament and politics in Australia : political institutions and foreign relations / P. Henderson. — 3rd ed. — Richmond : Heinemann Educational Australia, 1985. — vii,440p

WEST, Katharine
The revolution in Australian politics / Katharine West. — Ringwood (Victoria) : Penquin, 1984. — 116p

WHITLAM, E. Gough
The Whitlam government, 1972-1975 / Gough Whitlam. — [Ringwood, Victoria] : Viking, [1985]. — 787p

WHITLAM, Nicholas
Nest of traitors : the Petrov affair / Nicholas Whitlam, John Stubbs. — 2nd ed. — St. Lucia ; New York : University of Queensland Press, 1985. — xii, 259 p., [16] p. of plates. — *Includes index. — Bibliography: p. 251-253*

AUSTRALIA — Population

HUGO, Graeme
Australia's changing population : trends and implications / Graeme Hugo. — Melbourne : Oxford University Press, 1986. — 354p. — *Bibliography: p[329]-347*

AUSTRALIA — Population policy

HUGO, Graeme
Australia's changing population : trends and implications / Graeme Hugo. — Melbourne : Oxford University Press, 1986. — 354p. — *Bibliography: p[329]-347*

AUSTRALIA — Rural conditions — Government policy

AUSTRALIA
Economic and rural policy : a Government policy statement. — Canberra : Australian Government Publishing Service, 1986. — 89p

AUSTRALIA — Social conditions

GUTMAN, G. O.
Retreat of the dodo : Australian problems and prospects in the 80s / G. O. Gutman. — Canberra : Brian Clouston, 1982. — viii,195p

MACINTYRE, Stuart
Winners and losers : the pursuit of social justice in Australian history / Stuart Macintyre. — Sydney ; London : Allen & Unwin, 1985. — xxii,174p. — *Includes index*

AUSTRALIA — Social policy

GOODIN, Robert E.
The middle class infiltration of the welfare state : some evidence from Australia / Robert E. Goodin and Julian Le Grand. — London : Welfare State Programme. Suntory-Toyota International Centre for Economics and Related Disciplines, 1986. — 29p. — (Discussion paper / Welfare State Programme. Suntory-Toyota International Centre for Economics and Related Disciplines ; no.10). — *Bibliography: p27-29*

GUTMAN, G. O.
Retreat of the dodo : Australian problems and prospects in the 80s / G. O. Gutman. — Canberra : Brian Clouston, 1982. — viii,195p

AUSTRALIA — Statistics

AUSTRALIA. Commonwealth Bureau of Census and Statistics
Pocket compendium of Australia statistics. — Canberra : [the Bureau], 1982

AUSTRALIA. Commonwealth Bureau of Census and Statistics
Seasonally adjusted indicators. — Canberra : [the Bureau], 1971-1982. — *Annual*

AUSTRALIA — Statistics, Vital

YOUNG, Christabel
Selection and survival : immigrant mortality in Australia / Dr. Christabel Young. — Canberra : Australian Government Publishing Service, 1986. — xiii,251p. — *Bibliography: p132-150*

AUSTRALIA — Study and teaching — Great Britain — Directories

BLOOMFIELD, Valerie
Resources for Australian and New Zealand studies : a guide to library holdings in the United Kingdom / Valerie Bloomfield. — London : Australian Studies Centre, 1986. — xvi,284p. — *Bibliography: p264. — Includes index*

AUSTRALIA. Administrative Appeals Tribunal

SHARPE, Jennifer M.
The Administrative Appeals Tribunal and policy review / by Jennifer M. Sharpe. — Sydney : The Law Book Company Limited, 1986. — xxvi,232p

AUSTRALIA. Bureau of Agricultural Economics

AUSTRALIA. Bureau of Agricultural Economics
Coarse grains: situation and outlook. — Canberra : [the Bureau], 1954-1984. — *Annual. — Title varies*

AUSTRALIA. Bureau of Agricultural Economics
Eggs: situation and outlook. — Canberra : [the Bureau], 1954/55-1984. — *Annual. — Title varies*

AUSTRALIA. Bureau of Agricultural Economics
Meat: situation and outlook. — Canberra : [the Bureau], 1972-1980. — *Annual. — Continues: Australia. Bureau of Agricultural Economics: Beef situation and Mutton and Lamb situation*

AUSTRALIA. Bureau of Agricultural Economics
Wheat: situation and outlook. — Canberra : [the Bureau], 1951-1980. — *Annual*

AUSTRALIA. Bureau of Industry Economics. Conference on Evaluation of Public Support for Industrial Research and Development (1986 : Canberra)
AUSTRALIA. Bureau of Industry Economics. Conference on Evaluation of Public Support for Industrial Research and Development (1986 : Canberra)
    Evaluation of public support for industrial research and development : conference papers and proceedings Canberra 2 May 1986. — Canberra : Australian Government Publishing Service, 1986. — [vi,]113p. — *Bibliography: p31*

AUSTRALIA. Bureau of Industry Economics. Conference on Revitalising Australian Industry (1986 : Sydney)
AUSTRALIA. Bureau of Industry Economics. Conference on Revitalising Australian Industry (1986 : Sydney)
    Revitalising Australian industry : the paths and prospects for long-term growth : conference papers and proceedings Sydney 8-9 April 1986. — Canberra : Australian Government Publishing Service, 1986. — viii,224p. — *Includes bibliographical references*

AUSTRALIA. Committee of Review of Aboriginal Employment and Training Programs
AUSTRALIA. Committee of Review of Aboriginal Employment and Training Programs
    Aboriginal employment and training programs : report of the Committee of Review. — Canberra : Australian Government Publishing Service, 1985. — ix,453p

AUSTRALIA. Commonwealth Bureau of Census and Statistics
AUSTRALIA. Commonwealth Bureau of Census and Statistics
    Agricultural land use, improvements and labour. — Canberra : [the Bureau], 1979/80-1980/81. — *Annual*

AUSTRALIA. Commonwealth Bureau of Census and Statistics
    Agricultural Sector: financial statistics. — Canberra : [the Bureau], 1974/5-1980/81. — *Annual*

AUSTRALIA. Commonwealth Bureau of Census and Statistics
    Agricultural sector: structure of operating units. — Canberra : [the Bureau], 1974/5-1980/81. — *Annual*

AUSTRALIA. Commonwealth Bureau of Census and Statistics
    Livestock statistics, Australia. — Canberra : [the Bureau], 1974-1980/81. — *Irregular. — Title varies. — Continues: Statistical bulletin: Livestock numbers Australia*

AUSTRALIA. Commonwealth Bureau of Census and Statistics
    Overseas trade. — Melbourne : [the Bureau], 1921/22-1971/72. — *Annual. — Continues Australia. Commonwealth Bureau of Census and Statistics. Trade and customs returns*

AUSTRALIA. Commonwealth Bureau of Census and Statistics
    Pocket compendium of Australia statistics. — Canberra : [the Bureau], 1982

AUSTRALIA. Commonwealth Bureau of Census and Statistics
    Seasonally adjusted indicators. — Canberra : [the Bureau], 1971-1982. — *Annual*

AUSTRALIA. Commonwealth Bureau of Census and Statistics
    Statistical bulletin: livestock numbers, Australia / Commonwealth Bureau of Census and Statistics, Australia. — Canberra : [the Bureau], 1953-1970. — *Irregular. — Continues: A summary of live-stock statistics, Australia continued by Livestock statistics, Australia*

AUSTRALIA. Commonwealth Bureau of Census and Statistics
    University statistics. — Canberra : [the Bureau], 1978-1980. — *Annual*

AUSTRALIA. Federal Court
SMITH, Matthew
    ABC guide to the Federal Court of Australia / by Matthew Smith. — [Sydney] : The Law Book Company Limited, 1986. — xvii,230p

AUSTRALIA. Industries Assistance Commission
Review of the Industries Assistance Commission. — Canberra : Australian Government Publishing Service
Vol.2: Submissions to the review
Pt.1. — 1984. — *1v (various pagings)*

Review of the Industries Assistance Commission. — Canberra : Australian Government Publishing Service
Vol.3: Submissions to the review
Pt.2. — 1984. — *1v (various pagings)*

AUSTRALIA. Joint Select Committee on an Australia Card
AUSTRALIA. Parliament. Joint Select Committee on an Australia Card
    Report of the Joint Select Committee of an Australia Card. — Canberra : Australian Government Publishing Service, 1986. — xxiv,324p. — *Includes bibliographical references*

AUSTRALIA. Parliament. House of Representatives — Rules and practice
AUSTRALIA. Parliament. House of Representatives
    House of Representatives practice / editor, J.A. Pettifer ; assistant editors, A.R. Browning, J.K. Porter. — Canberra : Australian Govt. Pub. Service, 1981. — xxxvii, 966 p.. — *Includes index. — Bibliography: p. 891-942*

AUSTRALIA. Parliament. House of Representavies — Elections, 1984
Election statistics 1984. — Canberra : Australian Government Publishing Service, 1986. — 15v. — *Contents: Voting statistics for the Australian Senate and House of Representatives from the Australian Capital Territory, Northern Territory, Victoria, Western Australia, Queensland, South Australia, New South Wales (3 vols) and Tasmania*

AUSTRALIA. Parliament. Senate — Elections, 1984
Election statistics 1984. — Canberra : Australian Government Publishing Service, 1986. — 15v. — *Contents: Voting statistics for the Australian Senate and House of Representatives from the Australian Capital Territory, Northern Territory, Victoria, Western Australia, Queensland, South Australia, New South Wales (3 vols) and Tasmania*

AUSTRALIA. Royal Commission into British Nuclear Tests in Australia
AUSTRALIA. Royal Commission into British Nuclear Tests in Australia
    The report of the Royal Commission into British Nuclear Tests in Australia. — Canberra : Australian Government Publishing Service, 1985. — 2v. — *President: J. R. McClelland. — Includes bibliography*

AUSTRALIA. Royal Commission into British Nuclear Tests in Australia
    The report of the Royal Commission into British Nuclear Tests in Australia : conclusions and recommendations. — Canberra : Australian Government Publishing Service, 1985. — 32p. — *President: J. R. McClelland*

AUSTRALIA AND NEW ZEALAND BANKING GROUP
MERRETT, D. T.
    ANZ Bank : a history of the Australia and New Zealand Banking Group Limited and its constituents / D.T. Merrett. — Sydney ; London : Allen & Unwin, 1985. — xiv,325p,[4]p of plates. — *Ill on lining papers. — Includes index*

AUSTRALIA CONSTITUTIONAL LAW
LANE, P. H.
    Lane's commentary on the Australian Constitution / P. H. Lane ; with a foreword by Sir Garfield Barwick. — Sydney : Law Book Company, 1986. — xxxviii,766p

AUSTRALIAN ABORIGINES
MASSOLA, Aldo
    The aboriginal people. — Melbourne : Cypress Books, [1969]. — 69 p. — (Historical backgrounds, no. 2). — *Bibliography: p. 65*

AUSTRALIAN ABORIGINES — Congresses
Resource managers : North American and Australian hunter-gatherers / edited by Nancy M. Williams and Eugene S. Hunn. — Canberra : Australian Institute of Aboriginal Studies, 1982. — xii,267p. — (AAAS selected symposia series). — *Based on a symposium of the American Association for the Advancement of Science 1980. — Bibliography at end of each paper*

AUSTRALIAN ABORIGINES — Economic conditions
FISK, E. K.
    The aboriginal economy in town and country / E. K. Fisk. — Sydney : Allen & Unwin, 1985. — xiii,143p. — *Bibliography: p138-139*

AUSTRALIAN ABORIGINES — Education — Case studies
HARKER, Richard K
    Education as cultural artifact : studies in Maori and Aboriginal education / R.K. Harker & K.R. McConnochie. — Palmerston North, N.Z. : Dunmore Press ; Sydney, N.S.W. : Distributed in Australia by Hedley Australia, 1985. — 198 p.. — *Includes index. Bibliography: p. [183]-192*

AUSTRALIAN ABORIGINES — Employment
AUSTRALIA. Committee of Review of Aboriginal Employment and Training Programs
    Aboriginal employment and training programs : report of the Committee of Review. — Canberra : Australian Government Publishing Service, 1985. — ix,453p

AUSTRALIAN ABORIGINES — Employment — South Australia
SOUTH AUSTRALIA. Committee on Aboriginal Employment
    Report of the Committee on Aboriginal Employment. — Adelaide : Equal Opportunities Branch, Public Service Board, [1983]. — 34 leaves. — *Includes bibliographical references*

AUSTRALIAN ABORIGINES — Law and legislation
THAIDAY, Willie
    Under the Act / Willie Thaiday. — Townsville : N.Q. Black Publishing, 1981. — 50p

AUSTRALIAN ABORIGINES — Legal status, laws, etc
HARKINS, Joseph P.
    Inquiry into Aboriginal legal aid. — Canberra : Australian Government Publishing Service
    V.1: General issues / Jodseph P. Harkins. — 1986. — lvii,160p

HARKINS, Joseph P.
    Inquiry into Aboriginal legal aid. — Canberra : Australian Government Publishing Service
    V.2: Legal aid in the states and territories / Joseph P. Harkins. — 1986. — xii,642p

HARKINS, Joseph P.
    Inquiry into Aboriginal legal aid. — Canberra : Australian Government Publishing Service
    V.3: Appendixes / Joseph P. Harkins. — 1986. — iii,486p

AUSTRALIAN ABORIGINES — Legal status, laws, etc. — Australia

The recognition of Aboriginal customary laws. — Canberra : Australian Government Publishing Service. — (Report / Law Reform Commission no.31) (Parliamentary paper ; no.136/1986)
Vol.1. — 1986. — xxxix, 507p

The recognition of Aboriginal customary laws. — Canberra : Australian Government Publishing Service
Vol.2. — 1986. — xvi,415p. — (Report / Law Reform Commission ; no.31) (Parliamentary paper ; no.137/1986). — *Bibliography: p358-397*

AUSTRALIAN ABORIGINES — Religion

DURKHEIM, Emile
The elementary forms of the religious life / Emile Durkheim ; translated [from the French] by Joseph Ward Swain. — 2nd ed. / introduction by Robert Nisbet. — London : Allen and Unwin, 1976. — xix,456p. — *This translation originally published as 1st ed.: 1915. - Translation of: 'Les Formes élémentaires de la vie religieuse, le système totémique en Australiè. Paris : F. Alcan, 1912. — Includes index*

AUSTRALIAN ABORIGINES — Social conditions

FISK, E. K.
The aboriginal economy in town and country / E. K. Fisk. — Sydney : Allen & Unwin, 1985. — xiii,143p. — *Bibliography: p138-139*

AUSTRALIAN ABORIGINES — Social conditions — Congresses

We are bosses ourselves : the status and role of Aboriginal women today / edited by Fay Gale. — Canberra : Australian Institute of Aboriginal Studies ; Atlantic Highlands, NJ : Sold and distributed in North and South America by Humanities Press, 1983. — x, 175 p.. — (AIAS new series ; no. 41). — *Collection from first Australia-wide meeting of Aboriginal women at 1980 ANZAAS Conference in Adelaide*

AUSTRALIAN ABORIGINES — Training of

AUSTRALIA. Committee of Review of Aboriginal Employment and Training Programs
Aboriginal employment and training programs : report of the Committee of Review. — Canberra : Australian Government Publishing Service, 1985. — ix,453p

AUSTRALIAN ABORIGINES — Australia — Western Australia

BATES, Daisy
The native tribes of Western Australia / Daisy Bates ; edited by Isobel White. — Canberra : National Library of Australia, 1985. — xii, 387 p., [12] p. of plates. — *Includes index. — Bibliography: p. 373-378*

AUSTRALIAN ABORIGINES — South Australia — Education

SOUTH AUSTRALIA. Education Department. Statistical Information Unit
Aboriginal enrolments in South Australian schools. — Adelaide : Directorate of Research and Planning, 1983. — 27 leaves. — (Information bulletin / Directorate of Research and Planning ; 15)

AUSTRALIAN HOSPITAL ASSOCIATION

DICKENSON, Mary
Hospitals and politics : the Australian Hospital Association 1946-86 / Mary Dickenson and Catherine Mason. — Deakin, A.C.T. : The Association, 1986. — 144p. — *Notes and references p133-138*

AUSTRALIAN LABOR PARTY

PERCY, Jim
Socialist election strategy today / Jim Percy. — Chippendale, NSW : Pathfinder Press, 1984. — 22p

AUSTRALIAN OVERSEAS AID PROGRAM

Australian overseas aid : future directions / edited by Philip Eldridge, Dean Forbes and Doug Porter. — Sydney ; London : Croom Helm, 1986. — xxix,284p. — *Bibliography: p265-284*

AUSTRALIAN UNIVERSITIES COMMISSION — History

GALLAGHER, A. P.
Coordinating Australian university development : a study of the Australian Universities Commission, 1959-1970 / A.P. Gallagher. — St. Lucia ; New York : University of Queensland Press, c1982. — xii, 244 p.. — (The University of Queensland Press scholars' library). — *Includes index. — Bibliography: p. [230]-238*

AUSTRALIAN VICE-CHANCELLORS' COMMITTEE

AUSTRALIAN VICE-CHANCELLORS' COMMITTEE
AVCC response to the Commonwealth Tertiary Education Commission : review of efficiency and effectiveness in higher education. — Canberra : AVCC, 1986. — 15 leaves

AUSTRALIANS — Fiji — History — 19th century

YOUNG, John
Adventurous spirits : Australian migrant society in pre-cession Fiji / John Young. — St. Lucia, Qld. : University of Queensland Press ; Lawrence, Mass. : Distributed in the USA and Canada by Technical Impex Corp., 1984. — 417 p.. — *Includes index. — Bibliography: p. 395-408*

AUSTRIA — Bibliography

SALT, Denys
Austria / Denys Salt, compiler ; with the assistance of Arthur Farrand Radley. — Oxford : Clio, c1986. — xxxviiip. — (World bibliographical series ; v.66). — *Includes index*

AUSTRIA — Economic conditions

Quarterly economic review: Austria / Economist Intelligence Unit. — London : Economist Intelligence Unit, 1953-1976. — 1977 on microfiche at R (Microfiche) B91. — *Quarterly. — Has supplement Quarterly economic review: Austria: Annual supplement*

Quarterly economic review: Austria: Annual supplement / Economist Intelligence Unit. — London : Economnist Intelligence Unit, 1955-1976. — *Annual. — Is supplement of Quarterly economic review: Austria*

AUSTRIA — Economic conditions — 1945-

BOCK, Fritz
Österreich zuliebe : der Staat, den alle wollten / Fritz Bock, Hertha Firnberg, Willfried Gredler. — Wien : Paul Zsolnay, 1985. — 208p

AUSTRIA — Foreign relations — 18th century

MCKAY, Derek
Allies of convenience : diplomatic relations between Great Britain and Austria, 1714-1719 / Derek McKay. — New York : Garland Pub., 1986. — 378 p.. — (Outstanding theses from the London School of Economics and Political Science). — *Bibliography: p. 350-378*

AUSTRIA — Foreign relations — 19th century

BERTIER DE SAUVIGNY, Guillaume de
Metternich / Guillaume de Bertier de Sauvigny. — Paris : Fayard, 1986. — 535p

AUSTRIA — Foreign relations — 1955-

Österreichbewusstsein - bewusst Österreicher sein? : Materialien zur Entwicklung des Österreichbewusstseins seit 1945 / herausgegeben von Dirk Lyon...[et al.]. — Wien : Österreichischer Bundesverlag, 1985. — 198p. — *Bibliography: p194-[199]*

AUSTRIA — Foreign relations — Great Britain

MCKAY, Derek
Allies of convenience : diplomatic relations between Great Britain and Austria, 1714-1719 / Derek McKay. — New York : Garland Pub., 1986. — 378 p.. — (Outstanding theses from the London School of Economics and Political Science). — *Bibliography: p. 350-378*

AUSTRIA — History — 1867-1918

GALÁNTAI, József
A Habsburg-monarchia alkonya : osztrák-magyar dualizmus 1867-1918 / Galántai József. — [Budapest] : Kossuth Könyvkiadó, 1985. — 386p. — *References: p367-[387]*

AUSTRIA — History — Allied occupation, 1945-1955

INSTITUT FÜR WISSENSCHAFT UND KUNST. Symposium (1985 : Wien)
Verdrängte Schuld, verfehlte Sühne : Entnazifizierung in Österreich 1945-1955 / Symposion... ; herausgegeben von Sebastian Meissl, Klaus-Dieter Mulley und Oliver Rathkolb. — München : Oldenbourg, 1986. — 365p. — *Bibliographical notes*

WHITNAH, Donald Robert
The American occupation of Austria : planning and early years / Donald R. Whitnah and Edgar L. Erickson. — Westport, Conn. ; London : Greenwood Press, c1985. — xiv, 352p, [12]p of plates. — (Contributions in military history ; no. 46). — *Includes index. — Bibliography: p.[329]-333*

AUSTRIA — History — 1918-1938

LOW, Alfred D.
The Anschluss movement, 1931-1938, and the Great Powers / by Alfred D. Low. — Boulder : East European Monographs ; New York : Distributed by Columbia University Press, c1985. — xv, 507p. — (East European monographs ; no.185). — *Bibliography: p.[476]-496*

AUSTRIA — History, Military

DIXON, Joe C
Defeat and disarmament : allied diplomacy and the politics of military affairs in Austria, 1918-1922 / Joe C. Dixon. — Newark : University of Delaware Press, c1986. — 167p. — *Includes index. — Bibliography: p.150-161*

AUSTRIA — Military policy

DIXON, Joe C
Defeat and disarmament : allied diplomacy and the politics of military affairs in Austria, 1918-1922 / Joe C. Dixon. — Newark : University of Delaware Press, c1986. — 167p. — *Includes index. — Bibliography: p.150-161*

AUSTRIA — Politics and government

LOW, Alfred D.
The Anschluss movement, 1931-1938, and the Great Powers / by Alfred D. Low. — Boulder : East European Monographs ; New York : Distributed by Columbia University Press, c1985. — xv, 507p. — (East European monographs ; no.185). — *Bibliography: p.[476]-496*

AUSTRIA — Politics and government — 1918-1938

DIXON, Joe C
Defeat and disarmament : allied diplomacy and the politics of military affairs in Austria, 1918-1922 / Joe C. Dixon. — Newark : University of Delaware Press, c1986. — 167p. — *Includes index. — Bibliography: p.150-161*

AUSTRIA — Politics and government — 1918-

HERZ, Martin Florian
Understanding Austria : the political reports and analyses of Martin F. Herz / edited by Reinhold Wagnleither. — Salzburg : Wolfgang Neugebauer, 1984. — x,653p. — (Quellen zur Geschichte des 19 und 20 Jahrhunderts ; Band4)

AUSTRIA — Politics and government — 1945-

BOCK, Fritz
Österreich zuliebe : der Staat, den alle wollten / Fritz Bock, Hertha Firnberg, Willfried Gredler. — Wien : Paul Zsolnay, 1985. — 208p

HACKL, Dietrich
Im Zentrum der Politik : als Parlamentsstenograph im Hohen Haus / Dietrich Hackl. — Wien : Böhlau, 1984. — 133p

INSTITUT FÜR WISSENSCHAFT UND KUNST. Symposium (1985 : Wien)
Verdrängte Schuld, verfehlte Sühne : Entnazifizierung in Österreich 1945-1955 / Symposion... ; herausgegeben von Sebastian Meissl, Klaus-Dieter Mulley und Oliver Rathkolb. — München : Oldenbourg, 1986. — 365p. — Bibliographical notes

AUSTRIA — Social conditions

BRUCKMÜLLER, Ernst
Sozialgeschichte Österreichs / Ernst Bruckmüller. — Wien : Herold, 1985. — 648p. — Bibliography: p537-598

WEIDENHOLZER, Josef
Der sorgende Staat : zur Entwicklung der Sozialpolitik von Joseph II. bis Ferdinand Hanusch / Josef Weidenholzer. — Wien : Europaverlag, 1985. — 365p. — Bibliography: p349-365

AUSTRIA — Statistics — Bibliography

AUSTRIA. Statistisches Zentralamt
Veröffentlichungen des österreichischen Statistischen Zentralamtes, 1945-1985 : eine Spezialbibliographie. — Wien : Statistisches Zentralamt, 1986. — 432p. — Preface and contents list in English and French

AUSTRIA — 1918-1938

CARSTEN, F. L.
The first Austrian Republic 1918-1938 : a study based on British and Austrian documents / F.L. Carsten. — Aldershot : Gower, c1986. — 309p. — Bibliography: p294-296. — Includes index

AUSTRIAN SCHOOL OF ECONOMISTS

Studies in Austrian capital theory, investment, and time / edited by M. Faber ; with contributions by P. Bernholz ... [et al.]. — Berlin ; New York : Springer-Verlag, c1986. — vi,316p. — (Lecture notes in economics and mathematical systems ; 277). — Supplements and continues: Introduction to modern Austrian capital theory / Malte Faber. — Bibliography: p313-316

AUSTRIANS — Spain — History

Für Spaniens Freiheit : Österreicher an der Seite der Spanischen Republik 1936-1939 : eine Dokumentation / Herausgeber: Dokumentationsarchiv des österreichischen Widerstandes ; Auswahl und Bearbeitung: Mag. Brigitte Galanda...[et al.]. — Wien : Österreichischer Bundesverlag : Jugend und Volk Verlagsges, 1986. — 462p,[32p] of ill. — (Österreicher im Exil 1934-1945)

AUSTRO-HUNGARIAN MONARCHY

GALÁNTAI, József
A Habsburg-monarchia alkonya : osztrák-magyar dualizmus 1867-1918 / Galántai József. — [Budapest] : Kossuth Könyvkiadó, 1985. — 386p. — References: p367-[387]

AUTHORITARIANISM

FALK, Richard A.
A world order perspective on authoritarian tendencies / Richard A. Falk. — New York : Institute for World Order, 1980. — 67p. — (World Order Models Project working paper ; no.10)

O'DONNELL, Guillermo A
Modernization and bureaucratic-authoritarianism : studies in South American politics / [by] Guillermo A. O'Donnell. — Berkeley : Institute of International Studies, University of California, [1973]. — xv, 219 p. — (Politics of modernization series ; no. 9). — Bibliography: p. 201-219

AUTHORITARIANISM — Case studies

Transitions from authoritarian rule : comparative perspectives / edited by Guillermo O'Donnell, Philippe C. Schmitter, and Laurence Whitehead. — Baltimore : Johns Hopkins University Press, c1986. — xii, 190 p.. — Includes index. — Bibliography: p. 165-184. — Contents: Pt. 1, Southern Europe -- Pt. 2, Latin America -- Pt. 3, Comparative perspectives -- Pt. 4, Tentative conclusions and uncertain democracies

AUTHORITARIANISM — Brazil — Addresses, essays, lectures

Authoritarian Brazil: origins, policies, and future / Edited by Alfred Stepan. — New Haven : Yale University Press, 1973. — xi, 265 p. — : Revision of papers originally presented at a workshop on contemporary Brazil held at Yale University in Apr. 1971. — Includes bibliographical references

AUTHORITARIANISM — Europe, Southern — Case studies

Transitions from authoritarian rule / edited by Guillermo O'Donnell, Philippe C. Schmitter, and Laurence Whitehead ; [with a foreword by Abraham F. Lowenthal]. — Baltimore : Johns Hopkins University Press. — Papers originally commissioned for conferences or meetings sponsored by the Latin American Program of the Woodrow Wilson International Center for Scholars between 1979 and 1981. — Includes index. — Bibliography: p. 187-212. — Contents: An introduction to southern European transitions from authoritarian rule : Italy, Greece, Portugal, Spain, and Turkey / Philippe C. Schmitter -- Political economy, legitimation, and the state in southern Europe / Salvador Giner -- The demise of the first Fascist regime and Italy's transition to democracy, 1943-1948 / Gianfranco Pasquino -- Political change in Spain and the prospects for democracy / José María Maravall and Julián Santamaría -- Regime overthrow and the prospects for democratic transition in Portugal / Kenneth Maxwell -- Regime change and the prospects for democracy in Greece, 1974-1983 / P. Nikiforos Diamandouros -- Democracy in Turkey : problems and prospects / Ilkay Sunar and Sabri Sayari
Southern Europe. — c1986. — xii, 218 p.

AUTHORITARIANISM — Latin America — Addresses, essays, lectures

Promise of development : theories of change in Latin America / edited by Peter F. Klarén and Thomas J. Bossert. — Boulder, Colo. : Westview Press, 1986. — xiii, 350p. — Includes index. — Includes bibliographical references

AUTHORITARIANISM — Latin America — Case studies

Transitions from authoritarian rule / edited by Guillermo O'Donnell, Philippe C. Schmitter, Laurence Whitehead. — Baltimore : Johns Hopkins University Press. — Papers originally commissioned for a conference sponsored by the Latin American Program of the Woodrow Wilson International Center for Scholars between 1979 and 1980. — Includes index. — Bibliography: p. — Contents: International aspects of democratization / Laurence Whitehead -- Some problems in the study of the transition to democracy / Adam Przeworski -- Paths toward redemocratization / Alfred Stepan -- Liberalization and democratization in South America ; perspectives from the 1970s / Robert R. Kaufman -- Demilitarization and the institutionalization of military-dominated polities in Latin America / Alain Rouquié -- Entrepreneurs and the transition process : the Brazilian case / Fernando H. Cardoso -- Economic policies and the prospects for successful transition from authoritarian rule in Latin America / John Sheahan
Comparative perspectives. — c1986. — p. cm

Transitions from authoritarian rule / edited by Guillermo O'Donnell, Philippe C. Schmitter, and Laurence Whitehead ; [with a foreword by Abraham F. Lowenthal. — Baltimore : Johns Hopkins University Press. — Papers originally commissioned for a conference sponsored by the Latin American Program of the Woodrow Wilson International Center for Scholars between 1979 and 1981. — Includes index. — Bibliography: p. 221-236. — Contents: Introduction to the Latin American cases / Guillermo O'Donnell -- Political cycles in Argentina since 1955 / Marcelo Cavarozzi -- Bolivia's failed democratization, 1977-1980 / Laurence Whitehead -- The "liberalization" of authoritarian rule in Brazil / Luciano Martins -- The political evolution of the Chilean military regime and problems in the transition to democracy / Manuel Antonio Garretón -- Political liberalization in an authoritarian regime; the case of Mexico / Kevin J. Middlebrook -- Military interventions and "transfer of power to civilians" in Peru / Julio Cotler -- Uruguay's transition from collegial military-technocratic rule / Charles G. Gillespie -- Petroleum and political pacts : the transition to democracy in Venezuela / Terry Lynn Karl
Latin America. — c1986. — xii, 244 p.

AUTHORITY

Authority revisited / edited by J. Roland Pennock and John W. Chapman. — New York : New York University Press, 1987. — xii, 344 p.. — (Nomos ; 29). — Includes bibliographies and index

CONNOLLY, William E
Politics and ambiguity / William E. Connolly. — Madison, Wis. : University of Wisconsin Press, 1987. — xiii, 168 p.. — (Rhetoric of the human sciences). — Includes bibliographical references and index

FENN, Richard K
The spirit of revolt : anarchism and the cult of authority / Richard K. Fenn. — Totowa, NJ : Rowman & Littlefield, 1986. — p. cm. — Includes index. — Bibliography: p

The frailty of authority / edited by Myron J. Aronoff. — New Brunswick, N.J. : Transaction Books, 1986. — 213p. — (Political anthropology ; Vol.5). — Bibliographies

PYE, Lucian W.
Asian power and politics : the cultural dimensions of authority / Lucian W. Pye with Mary W. Pye. — Cambridge, Mass. : Belknap Press, 1985. — p. cm. — Includes index. — Bibliography: p

ROSENBAUM, Alan S
Coercion and autonomy : philosophical foundations, issues, and practices / Alan S. Rosenbaum. — New York : Greenwood Press, 1986. — xii, 196 p.. — (Contributions in philosophy ; no. 31). — Includes index. — Bibliography: p. [187]-188

AUTHORS — Biography — Directories
The International authors and writers who's who / editorial director Ernest Kay. — 10th ed. — Cambridge : International Biographical Centre, 1986. — 879p

AUTHORS — Directories
The writers directory. — Chicago ; London : St. James Press, 1986-88

AUTHORS — Legal status, laws, etc. — Australia
GOLVAN, Colin
Writers and the law / Colin Golvan and Michael McDonald; consultant: Alan Kirsner ; with a foreword by David Williamson. — Sydney : Law Book Company, 1986. — xix,262p. — *Bibliography: pxix*

AUTHORS AND PUBLISHERS
ANESKO, Michael
"Friction with the market" : Henry James and the profession of authorship / Michael Anesko. — New York : Oxford University Press, 1986. — xii, 258 p.. — *Includes index. — Bibliography: p. 245-249*

AUTHORS AND PUBLISHERS — Addresses, essays, lectures
BARZUN, Jacques
On writing, editing, and publishing : essays, explicative and hortatory / Jacques Barzun ; with a foreword by Morris Philipson. — 2nd ed., expanded. — Chicago : University of Chicago Press, 1986. — xi, 148 p.. — (Chicago guides to writing, editing, and publishing)

AUTHORS AND PUBLISHERS — Australia
GOLVAN, Colin
Writers and the law / Colin Golvan and Michael McDonald; consultant: Alan Kirsner ; with a foreword by David Williamson. — Sydney : Law Book Company, 1986. — xix,262p. — *Bibliography: pxix*

AUTHORS AND READERS
ANESKO, Michael
"Friction with the market" : Henry James and the profession of authorship / Michael Anesko. — New York : Oxford University Press, 1986. — xii, 258 p.. — *Includes index. — Bibliography: p. 245-249*

AUTHORS, ENGLISH — Homes and haunts
BLYTHE, Ronald
Divine landscapes / Ronald Blythe ; illustrated with photographs by Edwin Smith. — [Harmondsworth] : Viking, 1986. — 253p. — *Bibliography: p248-250. — Includes index*

AUTHORS, ENGLISH — 19th century Biography
CARROLL, Lewis
Lewis Carroll and the House of Macmillan / edited by Morton N. Cohen and Anita Gandolfo. — Cambridge : Cambridge University Press, 1987. — [392]p. — (Cambridge studies in publishing and printing history). — *Includes index*

AUTHORS, FRENCH — 18th century Biography
MASON, Haydn Trevor
Voltaire : a biography / Haydn Mason. — Baltimore, Md. : Johns Hopkins University Press, 1981. — xiii, 194 p., [8] p. of plates. — *Includes index. — Bibliography: p. 186-187*

AUTHORS, POLISH
Pisarz na obczyźnie / praca zbiorowa pod redakcją Tadeusza Bujnickiego i Wojciecha Wyskiela. — Wrocław : Ossolineum, 1985. — 207p. — (Biblioteka polonijna ; 14). — *Summaries in English*

AUTHORS, RUSSIAN — Biography
TROYAT, Henri
Gorki / Henri Troyat. — Paris : Flammarion, 1986. — 260p. — *Bibliography: p[247]-249*

AUTHORS, SPANISH — Biography
POSADA, Adolfo
Fragmentos de mis memorias / Adolfo Posada. — [Oviedo] : Universidad de Oviedo, Servicio de Publicaciones, Cátedra Aledo, c1983. — 363p. — *Bibliography: p355-363*

AUTHORSHIP — Addresses, essays, lectures
BARZUN, Jacques
On writing, editing, and publishing : essays, explicative and hortatory / Jacques Barzun ; with a foreword by Morris Philipson. — 2nd ed., expanded. — Chicago : University of Chicago Press, 1986. — xi, 148 p.. — (Chicago guides to writing, editing, and publishing)

AUTHORSHIP — Data processing — Handbooks, manuals, etc
Chicago guide to preparing electronic manuscripts for authors and publishers. — Chicago : University of Chicago Press, 1986. — xi, 143p. — (Chicago guides to writing, editing, and publishing). — *Includes index. — Bibliography: p 131*

AUTHORSHIP — Economic aspects
ANESKO, Michael
"Friction with the market" : Henry James and the profession of authorship / Michael Anesko. — New York : Oxford University Press, 1986. — xii, 258 p.. — *Includes index. — Bibliography: p. 245-249*

AUTHORSHIP — Social aspects
ANESKO, Michael
"Friction with the market" : Henry James and the profession of authorship / Michael Anesko. — New York : Oxford University Press, 1986. — xii, 258 p.. — *Includes index. — Bibliography: p. 245-249*

AUTHORSHIP — Style manuals
ALLEN & UNWIN
Author's guide to typescript preparation, house style and proof correction / George Allen & Unwin Ltd. ; [cCompiled by Malcolm Barnes]. — London : George Allen & Unwin, 1973. — 32p

AUTOMATION — Economic aspects
Automation and industrial workers : a fifteen nation study. — Oxford : Pergamon Vol.2 / edited by Frank Adler ... [et al.] for the European Coordination Centre for Research and Documentation in Social Sciences. — 1986. — 2v.(xxiv,866p). — *Vol.2 has sub-title: A cross-national comparison of fifteen countries*

AUTOMATION — Economic aspects — France — Normandy
BOCQUET, Jacques
L'automatisation dans les entreprises régionales et ses conséquences notamment sur l'emploi et la formation / rapport présenté par Jacques Bocquet, Bernard Cuillier. — [Rouen : Comité économique et social, 1985]. — 47p. — *Cover title. — Bibliography: p47*

AUTOMATION — Social aspects
Automation and industrial workers : a fifteen nation study. — Oxford : Pergamon Vol.2 / edited by Frank Adler ... [et al.] for the European Coordination Centre for Research and Documentation in Social Sciences. — 1986. — 2v.(xxiv,866p). — *Vol.2 has sub-title: A cross-national comparison of fifteen countries*

AUTOMATION — Social aspects — France — Normandy
BOCQUET, Jacques
L'automatisation dans les entreprises régionales et ses conséquences notamment sur l'emploi et la formation / rapport présenté par Jacques Bocquet, Bernard Cuillier. — [Rouen : Comité économique et social, 1985]. — 47p. — *Cover title. — Bibliography: p47*

AUTOMOBILE INDUSTRY AND TRADE — Forecasting — Congresses
ROUND TABLE ON TRANSPORT ECONOMICS
The future of the use of the car : 55th, 56th and 57th Round Tables on Transport Economics / Economic Research Centre. — Paris : European Conference of Ministers of Transport, 1982. — 233p. — *Bibliography: p165-168. — Contents: Round Table 55, Forecasts for the ownership and use of a car -- Round Table 56, Cost of using a car (perception and fiscal policy) -- Round Table 57, Interrelationships between car use and changing space-time patterns*

AUTOMOBILE INDUSTRY AND TRADE — Government policy — United States
WINSTON, Clifford
Blind intersection? : policy and the automobile industry / Clifford Winston and associates. — Washington, D.C. : Brookings Institution, c1987. — xii, 108 p. — *Includes bibliographical references and index*

AUTOMOBILE INDUSTRY AND TRADE — History
The Automobile industry and its workers : between Fordism and flexibility / edited by Steven Tolliday and Jonathan Zeitlin. — Cambridge : Polity in association with Blackwell, 1986. — [300]p. — *Includes index*

AUTOMOBILE INDUSTRY AND TRADE — Law and legislation — Peru
PERU
[Laws, etc]. Ley de industria automotriz. — [Lima] : Ministerio de Industria y Comercio, [ca.1970]. — 10p

AUTOMOBILE INDUSTRY AND TRADE — Management
CASSON, Mark
International divestment and restructuring decisions (with special reference to the motor industry) / by Mark Casson. — Geneva : International Labour Office, 1986. — 46p. — (Working paper / Multinational Enterprises Programme ; no.40). — *Bibliography: p[38]-39*

AUTOMOBILE INDUSTRY AND TRADE — Australia
AUTOMOTIVE INDUSTRY AUTHORITY (Australia)
Report on the state of the automotive industry. — Canberra : Australian Government Publishing Service, 1986. — ix,97p. — *Cover title: Report on the State of the automotive industry 1985*

AUTOMOBILE INDUSTRY AND TRADE — Germany — History
POHL, Hans
Die Daimler-Benz AG in den Jahren 1933 bis 1945 : eine Dokumentation / Hans Pohl, Stephanie Habeth, Beate Brüninghaus. — Stuttgart : Franz Steiner Verlag Wiesbaden, 1986. — vii,394p. — (Zeitschrift für Unternehmensgeschichte ; Beiheft 47). — *Bibliography: p[360]-384*

AUTOMOBILE INDUSTRY AND TRADE — Great Britain
Motor industry local authority network. — Birmingham : Economic Planning Group Development Department. — (Economic policy and research papers ; no.1)
no.1: Visit to Austin Rover. — 1987. — 6p

Motor industry local authority network. — Birmingham : Economic Planning Group Development Department. — (Economic policy and research papers ; no.2)
no.2: Visit to General Motors. — 1987. — 5p

WILLIAMS, Karel
The breakdown of Austin Rover : a case-study in the failure of business strategy and industrial policy / Karel Williams, John Williams, Colin Haslam. — Leamington Spa : Berg, 1987. — [160]p

AUTOMOBILE INDUSTRY AND TRADE — Latin America

JENKINS, Rhys, 1948-
Transnational corporations and the Latin American automobile industry / Rhys Jenkins. — London : Macmillan, 1987. — xiv,270p. — (Latin American studies series).
Bibliography: p254-263. — Includes index

AUTOMOBILE INDUSTRY AND TRADE — Michigan — Case studies

JONES, Bryan D
The sustaining hand : community leadership and corporate power / Bryan D. Jones and Lynn W. Bachelor with Carter Wilson. — Lawrence, Kan. : University Press of Kansas, c1986. — xii, 247 p.. — (Studies in government and public policy). — *Includes index.*
Bibliography: p. 223-239

AUTOMOBILE INDUSTRY AND TRADE — Sweden

Volvo Kalmar revisited : ten years of experience / Stefan Agurén [et al.]. — Stockholm : Efficiency and Participation Development Council, 1984. — 107p

AUTOMOBILE INDUSTRY AND TRADE — United States — Automation — History

GARTMAN, David
Auto slavery : the labor process in the American automobile industry, 1897-1950 / David Gartman. — New Brunswick, N.J. : Rutgers University Press, c1986. — xv, 348 p.. — (Class and culture). — *Includes index.*
Bibliography: p. 299-337

AUTOMOBILE INDUSTRY AND TRADE — United States — History

ABODAHER, David
Iacocca / David Abodaher. — London : W.H. Allen, 1986. — 276p,[8]p of plates. — (A Star book). — *Originally published: New York : Macmillan, 1982*

AUTOMOBILE INDUSTRY AND TRADE — United States — Management — History — 20th century

KUHN, Arthur J
GM passes Ford, 1918-1938 : designing the General Motors performance-control system / Arthur J. Kuhn. — University Park : Pennsylvania State University Press, 1986. — p. cm. — *Includes indexes. — Bibliography: p*

AUTOMOBILE INDUSTRY WORKERS — England — Stoke-on-Trent (Staffordshire)

Re-employment experiences of redundant Michelin workers / L. Fishman [et al.]. — Keele : University of Keele, 1986. — 187p. — *Bibliography: p147-148*

AUTOMOBILE INDUSTRY WORKERS — Great Britain — Political activity

THORNETT, Alan
From militancy to marxism : a personal and political account of organising car workers / Alan Thornett. — London : Left View Books, 1987. — 280p

AUTOMOBILE INDUSTRY WORKERS — Sweden

Volvo Kalmar revisited : ten years of experience / Stefan Agurén [et al.]. — Stockholm : Efficiency and Participation Development Council, 1984. — 107p

AUTOMOBILE INDUSTRY WORKERS — United States — History

GARTMAN, David
Auto slavery : the labor process in the American automobile industry, 1897-1950 / David Gartman. — New Brunswick, N.J. : Rutgers University Press, c1986. — xv, 348 p.. — (Class and culture). — *Includes index.*
Bibliography: p. 299-337

AUTOMOBILE OWNERSHIP — Forecasting — Congresses

ROUND TABLE ON TRANSPORT ECONOMICS
The future of the use of the car : 55th, 56th and 57th Round Tables on Transport Economics / Economic Research Centre. — Paris : European Conference of Ministers of Transport, 1982. — 233p. — *Bibliography: p165-168. — Contents: Round Table 55, Forecasts for the ownership and use of a car -- Round Table 56, Cost of using a car (perception and fiscal policy) -- Round Table 57, Interrelationships between car use and changing space-time patterns*

AUTOMOBILE OWNERSHIP — Ireland — Statistics

FEENEY, B. P.
A survey of car ownership and use 1982 / B.P. Feeney, C. Hynes. — Dublin : National Institute for Physical Planning & Construction Research, 1985. — v,36p

AUTOMOBILE PARKING — Law and legislation — Great Britain

GREAT BRITAIN. Department of Transport
Additional powers for local authorities to control off-street parking. — [London : the Department, 1977]. — 10p

AUTOMOBILES — Marketing — Congresses

INTERNATIONAL CONFERENCE ON BUSINESS HISTORY (7th : 1981 : Fuji Education Center)
Development of mass marketing : the automobile and retailing industries : proceedings of the Fuji Conference / edited by Akio Okochi, Koichi Shimokawa. — Tokyo : University of Tokyo Press, 1981. — xiii,308p. — *Includes references*

AUTOMOBILES — Registration and transfer — Great Britain — Statistics

Motor vehicles registrations. — London : HMSO, 1969-. — (Business monitor. MM ; 1) (Business monitor. M ; 1). — *Monthly*

AUTOMOBILES — Great Britain — Statistics

Motor vehicles registrations. — London : HMSO, 1969-. — (Business monitor. MM ; 1) (Business monitor. M ; 1). — *Monthly*

AUTOMOBILES — South Australia — Statistics

Motor vehicle census : 30th September, 1976 / South Australia. — Adelaide : Australian Bureau of Statistics, 1976. — 23p

AUTOMOBILES, COMPANY — Taxation — Great Britain

GREAT BRITAIN. Board of Inland Revenue
The taxation of cars and petrol as benefits in kind : a consultative paper. — [London] : the Board, 1979. — 7p

AUTOMOBILES, COMPANY — England — London

GREATER LONDON COUNCIL. Transportation and Development Department
Company assisted motoring in London. — [London] : the Council, 1985. — 1v. (various pagings). — (Reviews and studies series / Greater London Council ; no.27)

AUTONOMY

CLARK, Gordon L
Judges and the cities : interpreting local autonomy / Gordon L. Clark. — Chicago : University of Chicago Press, c1985. — xv, 247 p.. — *Includes index. — Bibliography: p. 231-242*

Native power : the quest for autonomy and nationhood of indigenous peoples / edited by Jens Brøsted...[et al.]. — Bergen : Universitetsforlaget As, 1985. — 350p. — *Includes bibliography of Helge Kleivan: p.342-348*

ROSENBAUM, Alan S
Coercion and autonomy : philosophical foundations, issues, and practices / Alan S. Rosenbaum. — New York : Greenwood Press, 1986. — xii, 196 p.. — (Contributions in philosophy ; no. 31). — *Includes index. — Bibliography: p. [187]-188*

AUTONOMY (PSYCHOLOGY)

HAWORTH, Lawrence
Autonomy : an essay in philosophical psychology and ethics / Lawrence Haworth. — New Haven ; London : Yale University Press, c1986. — vii, 248p. — *Includes index. — Bibliography: p.233-242*

AVILA CAMACHO, MANUEL

La clase obrera en la historia de México. — México : Siglo Veintiuno
11: Del avilacamachismo al alemanismo (1940-1952) / Jorge Basurto. — 1984. — 291p

AVILA (SPAIN) — Economic conditions

Estructura socioeconomica de la provincia de Avila / [Antonio Jose Delgado Piera...et al.]. — Avila : Institución Gran Duque de Alba, 1985. — 335,[248]

AVILA (SPAIN) — Social conditions

Estructura socioeconomica de la provincia de Avila / [Antonio Jose Delgado Piera...et al.]. — Avila : Institución Gran Duque de Alba, 1985. — 335,[248]

AYER, A. J.. Language, truth and logic

Fact, science and morality : essays on A.J. Ayer's Language, truth and logic / edited by Graham Macdonald and Crispin Wright. — Oxford : Basil Blackwell, 1986. — 314p. — *Includes bibliographies and index*

AZERBAIJAN (IRAN) — Relations — Soviet Union

NISSMAN, David B.
The Soviet Union and Iranian Azerbaijan : the use of nationalism for political penetration / David B. Nissman. — Boulder, Colo. : Westview Press, 1987. — ix,123p. — (Westview special studies on the Soviet Union and Eastern Europe). — *Bibliography: p109-113*

AZTECS — Economic conditions

HASSIG, Ross
Trade, tribute, and transportation : the sixteenth-century political economy of the Valley of Mexico / by Ross Hassig. — Norman : University of Oklahoma Press, c1985. — xvi, 364p. — (Civilization of the American Indian series ; v. 171). — *Includes index. — Bibliography: p 319-350*

BAARD, FRANCIS

BAARD, Frances
My spirit is not banned : as told by Frances Baard to Barbie Schreiner. — Harare : Zimbabwe Publishing House, 1986. — 92p

BABY FOODS — Composition

GREAT BRITAIN. Working Party on the Composition of Foods for Infants and Young Children
Artificial feeds for the young infant / report of the Working Party on the Composition of Foods for Infants and Young Children, Committee on Medical Aspects of Food Policy. — London : H.M.S.O., 1980. — viii,104p. — (Report on health and social subjects ; no.18). — *Cover title. — Bibliography: p84-104*

BADAJOZ (SPAIN) — Economic conditions — 19th century

BOHOYO VELÁZQUEZ, Isidoro Francisco
Situación socio-económica y condiciones de vida en la provincia de Badajoz (1880-1902) / Isidoro Francisco Bohoyo Velázquez. — Badajoz : Universitas Editorial, 1984. — 149p. — (Biblioteca Popular Extremeña). — *Bibliography: p146-149*

BADAJOZ (SPAIN) — Social conditions — 19th century

BOHOYO VELÁZQUEZ, Isidoro Francisco
  Situación socio-económica y condiciones de vida en la provincia de Badajoz (1880-1902) / Isidoro Francisco Bohoyo Velázquez. — Badajoz : Universitas Editorial, 1984. — 149p. — (Biblioteca Popular Extremeña). — *Bibliography: p146-149*

BADEN-POWELL OF GILWELL, ROBERT STEPHENSON SMYTH BADEN-POWELL, Baron

ROSENTHAL, Michael
  The character factory : Baden-Powell and the origins of the Boy Scout movement / Michael Rosenthal. — New York : Pantheon Books, 1986. — p. cm. — *Includes index*

BAGEMDER (ETHIOPIA) — Economic conditions — Case studies

BAKER, Jonathan
  The rural-urban dichotomy in the developing world : a case study from northern Ethiopia / Jonathan Baker. — Oslo : Norwegian University Press : Oxford ; New York : Distributed world-wide excluding Scandinavia by Oxford University Press, c1986. — 372 p.. — *Bibliography: p. [365]-372*

BAGEMDER (ETHIOPIA) — Economic conditions — Regional disparities — Case studies

BAKER, Jonathan
  The rural-urban dichotomy in the developing world : a case study from northern Ethiopia / Jonathan Baker. — Oslo : Norwegian University Press : Oxford ; New York : Distributed world-wide excluding Scandinavia by Oxford University Press, c1986. — 372 p.. — *Bibliography: p. [365]-372*

BAGEMDER (ETHIOPIA) — Social conditions — Case studies

BAKER, Jonathan
  The rural-urban dichotomy in the developing world : a case study from northern Ethiopia / Jonathan Baker. — Oslo : Norwegian University Press : Oxford ; New York : Distributed world-wide excluding Scandinavia by Oxford University Press, c1986. — 372 p.. — *Bibliography: p. [365]-372*

BAGUIO, PHILIPPINES — Markets

DAVIS, William G.
  Social relations in a Philippine market : self-interest and subjectivity / William G. Davis. — Berkeley ; London : University of California Press, 1973. — [1],xiii,315p. — (Publications / University of California. Center for South and South-east Asia Studies). — *Bibliography: p.293-308. — Includes index*

BAGUIO, PHILIPPINES — Social conditions

DAVIS, William G.
  Social relations in a Philippine market : self-interest and subjectivity / William G. Davis. — Berkeley ; London : University of California Press, 1973. — [1],xiii,315p. — (Publications / University of California. Center for South and South-east Asia Studies). — *Bibliography: p.293-308. — Includes index*

BAHAMAS — Census, 1980

Commonwealth of the Bahama Islands : report of the 1980 census of population. — Nassau : Ministry of Finance
V.1: Demographic and social characteristics. — [1986]. — xxx,588p

Commonwealth of the Bahama Islands : report of the 1980 census of population. — Nassau : Ministry of Finance
V.2: Economic activity and income. — [1986]. — xlvi,673p

Commonwealth of the Bahama Islands : report of the 1980 census of population. — Nassau : Ministry of Finance
V.4: Fertility and union status. — [1986]. — xxv,396p

Commonwealth of the Bahama Islands : report of the 1980 census of population. — Nassau : Ministry of Finance
V.3: Migration. — [1986]. — xxxxi,804p

BAHAMAS — Economic conditions

The Bahamas : economic report. — Washington, D.C. : World Bank, 1986. — [xiv],117p. — (A World Bank country study)

BAHAMAS — Economic conditions — Statistics

Commonwealth of the Bahama Islands : report of the 1980 census of population. — Nassau : Ministry of Finance
V.2: Economic activity and income. — [1986]. — xlvi,673p

BAHAMAS — Emigration and immigration — Statistics

Commonwealth of the Bahama Islands : report of the 1980 census of population. — Nassau : Ministry of Finance
V.3: Migration. — [1986]. — xxxxi,804p

BAHAMAS — Population — Statistics

Commonwealth of the Bahama Islands : report of the 1980 census of population. — Nassau : Ministry of Finance
V.1: Demographic and social characteristics. — [1986]. — xxx,588p

Commonwealth of the Bahama Islands : report of the 1980 census of population. — Nassau : Ministry of Finance
V.2: Economic activity and income. — [1986]. — xlvi,673p

BAHAMAS — Social conditions — Statistics

Commonwealth of the Bahama Islands : report of the 1980 census of population. — Nassau : Ministry of Finance
V.1: Demographic and social characteristics. — [1986]. — xxx,588p

BAHIA (BRAZIL: STATE) — Economic conditions — Statistics

Informe conjuntural / Centro de Estatística e Informações, Bahia. — Salvador : Centro de Estatística e Informações, 1983-. — *Irregular*

BAHRAIN — Census, 1971

Statistics of the population census 1971. — [Manama] : Statistical Bureau, 1972. — 67p

BAHRAIN — Population — Statistics

Statistics of the population census 1971. — [Manama] : Statistical Bureau, 1972. — 67p

BAIL — England

CHATTERTON, Clifford E. M.
  Bail : law and practice / Clifford Chatterton. — London : Butterworths, 1986. — xxiii,277p. — *Includes index*

BAIL — South Africa

VAN DER BERG, J.
  Bail : a practitioner's guide / J. Van der Berg. — Cape Town : Juta, 1986. — xix,186p. — *Bibliography: pxi-xii*

BAKERS AND BAKERIES — Great Britain

BAKERS, FOOD AND ALLIED WORKERS' UNION
  Annual report / Bakers, Food and Allied Workers' Union. — Welwyn Garden City : The Union, 1928-. — *Issuing body varies. 1928-1963 Issuing body known as The Amalgamated Union of Operative Bakers, Confectioners and Allied Workers. 1965-76 Issuing body known as The Bakers' Union*

BAKERS', FOOD AND ALLIED WORKERS' UNION

BAKERS, FOOD AND ALLIED WORKERS' UNION
  Annual report / Bakers, Food and Allied Workers' Union. — Welwyn Garden City : The Union, 1928-. — *Issuing body varies. 1928-1963 Issuing body known as The Amalgamated Union of Operative Bakers, Confectioners and Allied Workers. 1965-76 Issuing body known as The Bakers' Union*

BAKERS' UNION

BAKERS, FOOD AND ALLIED WORKERS' UNION
  Annual report / Bakers, Food and Allied Workers' Union. — Welwyn Garden City : The Union, 1928-. — *Issuing body varies. 1928-1963 Issuing body known as The Amalgamated Union of Operative Bakers, Confectioners and Allied Workers. 1965-76 Issuing body known as The Bakers' Union*

BAKONGO (AFRICAN PEOPLE) — Religion

MACGAFFEY, Wyatt
  Religion and society in central Africa : the BaKongo of lower Zaire / Wyatt MacGaffey. — Chicago : University of Chicago Press, 1986. — xi, 295 p. — *Includes index. — Bibliography: p. 273-287*

BAKUNIN, MIKHAIL

LEHNING, Arthur
  Bakounine et les historiens / Arthur Lehning. — Geneve : C.I.R.A. : Editions Noir, [1970]. — 32p

BALANCE OF PAYMENTS

GREAT BRITAIN. Parliament. House of Commons. Library. Research Division
  The international monetary system and the world debt crisis / Christopher Barclay. — [London] : the Division, 1983. — 18p. — (Background paper ; no.126)

INTERNATIONAL MONETARY FUND. Board of Governors. Committee on Reform of the International Monetary System and Related Issues
  International monetary reform : documents of the Committee of Twenty. — Washington, D.C. : the Fund, 1974. — viii,253p. — *Includes the Report to the Board of Governors, Outline of Reform and accompanying Annexes, Reports of Technical groups, and related documents*

KINDLEBERGER, Charles P.
  International capital movements : based on the Marshall Lectures given at the University of Cambridge 1985 / Charles P. Kindleberger. — Cambridge : Cambridge University Press, 1987. — 1v. — *Includes bibliography and index*

LIPSEY, Richard G.
  Global imbalances and U.S. policy responses : a Canadian perspective / Richard G. Lipsey and Murray G. Smith. — Toronto, Ontario : C.D. Howe Institute ; Washington, D.C. : National Planning Association, 1987. — vii,51p

POOL, John Charles
  The ABCs of international finance : understanding the trade and debt crisis / John Charles Pool, Steve Stamos. — Lexington, Mass. : Lexington Books, c1987. — xii, 138 p.. — *Includes index. — Bibliography: p. [131]-132*

BALANCE OF PAYMENTS — Africa, West

Croissance et ajustement : les problèmes de l'Afrique de l'Ouest / préparée par Patrick Guillaumont. — Paris : Economica, 1985. — 248p. — *Includes bibliographies*

BALANCE OF PAYMENTS — Canada

Balance of payments : Canada's international investment position = Balance des paiements : le bilan canadien des investissements internationaux / Statistics Canada. — Ottawa : Statistics Canada, 1982/85-. — *Annual. — Text in English and French*

BALANCE OF PAYMENTS — Developing countries
DE VRIES, Margaret Garritsen
Balance of payments adjustment, 1945 to 1986 : the IMF experience / Margaret Garritsen de Vries. — Washington, D.C. : International Monetary Fund, 1987. — xi,336p. — *Bibliography: p310-322*

BALANCE OF PAYMENTS — Great Britain
BRITTON, Andrew, 1940-
Full employment and the balance of payments / Andrew Britton. — London : Employment Institute, 1987. — 28p. — *At head of title: Employment Institute*

GREAT BRITAIN. Parliament. House of Commons. Library. Research Division
The economic background to the March 1986 budget : oil and the UK economy / Christopher Barclay. — [London] : the Division, 1986. — 13p. — (Background paper ; no.181)

BALANCE OF PAYMENTS — Hong Kong
BALASSA, Bela A
Adusting to success : balance of payments policies in the East Asian NICs / Bela Balassa, John Williamson. — Washington, DC : Institute for International Economics, 1987. — p. cm. — (Policy analyses in international economics ; 17). — *Bibliography: p*

BALANCE OF PAYMENTS — Hungary
FELLNER, Frigyes
A nemzetközi fizetési mérleg és alakulása Magyarországon / a Magyar Tudományos Akadémia megbízásából irta Fellner Frigyes. — Budapest : Politzer-féle Könyvkiadóvállalat, 1908. — 181p. — (Magyar Közgazdasági Könyvtár ; Köt.5)

BALANCE OF PAYMENTS — Japan
YOSHITOMI, Masaru
Japan as capital exporter and the world economy / Masaru Yoshitomi. — New York : Group of Thirty, 1986. — 32p. — (Occasional papers / Group of Thirty ; no.18)

BALANCE OF PAYMENTS — Korea (South)
BALASSA, Bela A
Adusting to success : balance of payments policies in the East Asian NICs / Bela Balassa, John Williamson. — Washington, DC : Institute for International Economics, 1987. — p. cm. — (Policy analyses in international economics ; 17). — *Bibliography: p*

BALANCE OF PAYMENTS — Peru
SCHEETZ, Thomas Edward
Peru and the International Monetary Fund / Thomas Scheetz. — Pittsburgh, PA : University of Pittsburgh Press, c1986. — xi, 257 p.. — (Pitt Latin American series). — *Includes index. — Bibliography: p. 251-254*

BALANCE OF PAYMENTS — Singapore
BALASSA, Bela A
Adusting to success : balance of payments policies in the East Asian NICs / Bela Balassa, John Williamson. — Washington, DC : Institute for International Economics, 1987. — p. cm. — (Policy analyses in international economics ; 17). — *Bibliography: p*

BALANCE OF PAYMENTS — Taiwan
BALASSA, Bela A
Adusting to success : balance of payments policies in the East Asian NICs / Bela Balassa, John Williamson. — Washington, DC : Institute for International Economics, 1987. — p. cm. — (Policy analyses in international economics ; 17). — *Bibliography: p*

BALANCE OF PAYMENTS — United States
LIPSEY, Richard G.
Global imbalances and U.S. policy responses : a Canadian perspective / Richard G. Lipsey and Murray G. Smith. — Toronto, Ontario : C.D. Howe Institute ; Washington, D.C. : National Planning Association, 1987. — vii,51p

BALANCE OF PAYMENTS — United States — Mathematical models
GOLUB, Stephen S
The current-account balance and the dollar, 1977-78 and 1983-84 / Stephen S. Golub. — Princeton, N.J. : Dept. of Economics, Princeton University, 1986. — p. cm. — (Princeton studies in international finance ; no. 57). — *Bibliography: p*

RICHARDSON, Pete
Tracking the U. S. external deficit, 1980-1985 : experience with the OECD interlink model / by Pete Richardson. — Paris : OECD, 1987. — iii,38p. — (Working papers / OECD Department of Economics and Statistics ; no.38). — *Bibliographical references: p36-38*

BALANCE OF POWER
LANG, Daniel George
Foreign policy in the early republic : the law of nations and the balance of power / Daniel George Lang. — Baton Rouge : Louisiana State University Press, c1985. — 175 p.. — (Political traditions in foreign policy series). — *Includes index. — Bibliography: p. 165-170*

LIDER, Julian
Correlation of forces : an analysis of Marxist-Leninist concepts / Julian Lider. — Aldershot : Gower, c1986. — vii,384p. — (Swedish studies in international relations). — *Bibliography: p347-372. — Includes index*

BALANCE OF TRADE
LIPSEY, Richard G.
Global imbalances and U.S. policy responses : a Canadian perspective / Richard G. Lipsey and Murray G. Smith. — Toronto, Ontario : C.D. Howe Institute ; Washington, D.C. : National Planning Association, 1987. — vii,51p

BALANCE OF TRADE — Hungary
FELLNER, Frigyes
A nemzetközi fizetési mérleg és alakulása Magyarországon / a Magyar Tudományos Akadémia megbízásából irta Fellner Frigyes. — Budapest : Politzer-féle Könyvkiadóvállalat, 1908. — 181p. — (Magyar Közgazdasági Könyvtár ; Köt.5)

BALANCE OF TRADE — United States
LIPSEY, Richard G.
Global imbalances and U.S. policy responses : a Canadian perspective / Richard G. Lipsey and Murray G. Smith. — Toronto, Ontario : C.D. Howe Institute ; Washington, D.C. : National Planning Association, 1987. — vii,51p

SOLOMON, Anthony M
The dollar, debt, and the trade deficit / Anthony M. Solomon. — New York : New York University Press, 1986, c1987. — p. cm. — (The Joseph I. Lubin memorial lectures ; no. 3)

BALANCE OF TRADE — United States — Mathematical models
RICHARDSON, Pete
Tracking the U. S. external deficit, 1980-1985 : experience with the OECD interlink model / by Pete Richardson. — Paris : OECD, 1987. — iii,38p. — (Working papers / OECD Department of Economics and Statistics ; no.38). — *Bibliographical references: p36-38*

BALDWIN OF BEWDLEY, STANLEY BALDWIN, Earl
JENKINS, Roy
Baldwin / Roy Jenkins. — London : Collins, 1987. — 204p,[16]p of plates. — *Bibliography: p193-195. — Includes index*

BALI (INDONESIA : PROVINCE) — Population
STREATFIELD, K
Fertility decline in a traditional society : the case of Bali / Kim Streatfield. — [Canberra, ACT] : Dept. of Demography, Australian National University : Distributed by Bibliotech, 1986. — xvii, 177 p.. — (Indonesian population monograph series ; no. 4). — *Bibliography: p. 161-173*

BALKAN PENINSULA — History — Autonomy and independence movements
War and society in East Central Europe. — Boulder, Colo. : Social Science Monographs ; New York : distributed by Columbia University Press. — (East European Monographs ; no.197) (Brooklyn College Studies on Society and Change ; no.36) (Atlantic studies)
Vol.17: Insurrections, wars, and the Eastern crisis in the 1870s / Bela K. Kiraly and Gale Stokes, editors. — 1985. — xxii,421p

BALKAN PENINSULA — History — 19th century
War and society in East Central Europe. — Boulder, Colo. : Social Science Monographs ; New York : distributed by Columbia University Press. — (East European Monographs ; no.197) (Brooklyn College Studies on Society and Change ; no.36) (Atlantic studies)
Vol.17: Insurrections, wars, and the Eastern crisis in the 1870s / Bela K. Kiraly and Gale Stokes, editors. — 1985. — xxii,421p

BALKAN PENINSULA — History, Military
War and society in East Central Europe. — Boulder, Colo. : Social Science Monographs ; New York : distributed by Columbia University Press. — (East European Monographs ; no.197) (Brooklyn College Studies on Society and Change ; no.36) (Atlantic studies)
Vol.17: Insurrections, wars, and the Eastern crisis in the 1870s / Bela K. Kiraly and Gale Stokes, editors. — 1985. — xxii,421p

BALLISTIC MISSILE DEFENSES
Space weapons and international security / edited by Bhupendra Jasani. — Oxford : Oxford University Press, 1986. — xvi,366p. — *Written for the Stockholm International Peace Research Institute. — Bibliography: p353-354 Includes index*

BALLISTIC MISSILE DEFENSES — North America — History
LINDSEY, George
The strategic defence of North America / George R. Lindsey. — [Toronto, Ont., Canada] : Canadian Institute of Strategic Studies, [c1986]. — 40 p.. — (Issues in strategy). — *Bibliography: p. 40*

BALLISTIC MISSILE DEFENSES — Soviet Union
VAN CLEAVE, William R
Fortress U.S.S.R. : the Soviet strategic defense initiative and the U.S. strategic defense reponse / William R. Van Cleave. — Stanford, Calif. : Hoover Institution Press, Stanford University, c1986. — 60 p.. — *Bibliography: p. [57]-60*

BALLISTIC MISSILE DEFENSES — United States
"Zvezdnye voiny" : illiuzii i opasnosti / [redaktor L. I. Dvinina]. — Moskva : Voennoe izd-vo, 1985. — 55p

BALTIC SEA — Defenses
LINDHARDT, Bjarne Fr.
Allied Command Baltic Approaches : a survey / Bjarne Fr. Lindhardt. — Copenhagen : Information and Welfare Service of the Danish Defence, 1987. — 40p. — (People and defence)

BALTIC STATES — Annexation to the Soviet Union
VIZULIS, I. Joseph
Nations under duress : the Baltic States / I. Joseph Vizulis. — Port Washington (New York) ; London : Associated Faculty Press, 1985. — vi,209p

BALTIC STATES — Foreign relations — Germany
HIDEN, John
The Baltic states and Weimar Ostpolitik / John Hiden. — Cambridge : Cambridge University Press, 1987. — xi,296p. — *Bibliography: p243-265 — Includes index*

BALTIC STATES — History
DELLEBRANT, Jan-Åke
The Baltic Republics : years of integration, 1940-1980 / Jan Åke Dellebrant [and] Sten Berglund. — Åbo : Åbo Akademi, 1986. — 29p. — (Meddelanden från Economisk-Statsvetens-kapliga Fakulteten vid Åbo Akademi. ser.A ; 227)

BALTIC STATES — History — German occupation, 1941-1944
VIZULIS, I. Joseph
Nations under duress : the Baltic States / I. Joseph Vizulis. — Port Washington (New York) ; London : Associated Faculty Press, 1985. — vi,209p

BALTIC STATES — Politics and government
Newsletter from behind the Iron Curtain: reports on communist activities in Eastern Europe. — Stockholm : Estonian Information Center and Latvian National Foundation, 1986- . — Monthly

BALTIMORE (MD.) — Economic conditions — Econometric models
DRENNAN, Matthew P.
Modeling metropolitan economies for forecasting and policy analysis / Matthew P. Drennan. — New York : New York University Press, 1985. — p. cm. — Includes index. — Bibliography: p

BANCA CATALANA
BAIGES, Francesc
Banca Catalana : Más que un banco, más que una crisis / Francesc Baiges, Enric Gonzalez, Jaume Reixach. — Barcelona : Plaza & Janes, 1985. — 243p

BARATECH, Feliciano
Banca Catalana(1959-1984) : toda la verdad / Feliciano Baratech. — Barcelona : Planeto, 1985. — 207p

BANDARANAIKE, Family — History
GOONERATNE, Yasmine
Relative merits : a personal memoir of the Bandaranaike family of Sri Lanka / Yasmine Gooneratne. — London : Hurst, 1986. — 269p. — Bibliography: p251-253

BANGKOK (THAILAND) — Social conditions
THORBEK, Susanne
Voices from the city : women of Bangkok / Susanne Thorbek. — London : Zed, 1987. — [224]p. — Includes bibliography and index

BANGLADESH — Commerce — Statistics
Foreign trade statistics of Bangladesh / Bangladesh Bureau of Statistics. — Dhaka : Bangladesh Bureau of Statistics, 1976/77-. — Irregular

BANGLADESH — Economic policy
RAHMAN, M. Akhlaqur
External assistance, saving and resource mobilization in Bangladesh / M. Akhlaqur Rahman, K. Mustahidur Rahman. — [Dacca] : External Resources Division, Ministry of Finance and Planning, [ca.1983]. — 95p. — Bibliography: p94-95

BANGLADESH — History — Revolution, 1971 — Sources
History of Bangladesh war of independence : documents. — Dhaka : Ministry of Information, 1982-1985. — 15v. — Some documents in English, some in Hindi

BANGLADESH — Politics and government
ADDY, Premen
Bangladesh: distortions challenged : Sheikh Mujib's place in history and the truth about his opponents / Dr. Premen Addy, Dr. Gowher Rizvi [and] Abdul Matin. — London : Radical Asia Publications, 1986. — 30p. — (Bangladesh political scene ; no.4)

Ershad's election fraud / edited by Abdul Matin. — London : Radical Asia Publications, 1986. — 31p. — (Bangladesh political scene ; no.3)

HASINA, Sheikh
Address by Sheikh Hasina, President, Bangladesh Awami League at the inaugural session of Awami League's National Council on 1 January 1987. — London : Radical Asia Publications, 1987. — 16p

KHAN, D. G. A
Disintegration of Pakistan / D.G.A. Khan. — Meerut : Meenakshi Prakashan, c1985. — vi, 252 p.. — Includes index. — Bibliography: p. [242]-246

BANGLADESH — Rural conditions
AFSARUDDIN, Mohammad
Rural life in Bangladesh : a study of five selected villages / Mohammad Afsaruddin. — 2nd ed. — Dacca : Nawroze Kitabistan, 1979. — 114 p., [4] p. of plates. — First ed. published in 1964 under title: Rural life in East Pakistan. — Bibliography: p. 105-114

JAHANGIR, B. K.
Rural society, power structure and class practice / B. K. Jahangir. — Dacca : Centre for Social Studies, 1982. — 165p. — Bibliography: p158-165

JANSEN, Eirik G.
Rural Bangladesh : competition for scarce resources / Eirik G. Jansen. — Oslo : Norwegian University Press ; Oxford : Distributed by Oxford University Press, c1986. — xii,351p. — Bibliography: p334-341. — Includes index

RAHMAN, Atiur
Peasants and classes : a study in differentiation in Bangladesh / Atiur Rahman ; preface by Terry Byres. — London : Zed, 1986. — [272]p. — Includes bibliography and index

BANGLADESH — Social life and customs
AFSARUDDIN, Mohammad
Rural life in Bangladesh : a study of five selected villages / Mohammad Afsaruddin. — 2nd ed. — Dacca : Nawroze Kitabistan, 1979. — 114 p., [4] p. of plates. — First ed. published in 1964 under title: Rural life in East Pakistan. — Bibliography: p. 105-114

BANK DEPOSITS — Developing countries
VOGEL, Robert C.
Mobilizing small-scale savings : approaches, costs, and benefits / Robert C. Vogel and Paul Burkett. — Washington, D.C. : The World Bank, 1986. — vii,38p. — (Industry and finance series ; v.15). — Bibliographical references: p30-38

BANK DEPOSITS — United States
Responses to deregulation : retail deposit pricing from 1983 through 1985 / Patrick I. Mahoney...[et al.]. — Washington, D. C. : Board of Governors of the Federal Reserve System, 1987. — 29p. — (Staff study / Board of Governors of the Federal Reserve System ; 151). — Includes bibliographical references

BANK EMPLOYEES — United States — Supply and demand — Forecasting
The Impact of office automation on clerical employment, 1985-2000 : forecasting techniques and plausible futures in banking and insurance / J. David Roessner ... [et al.]. — Westport, Conn. : Quorum Books, c1986. — p. cm. — Includes index. — Bibliography: p

BANK FAILURES — United States
SPRAGUE, Irvine H
Bailout : an insider's account of bank failures and rescues / Irvine H. Sprague. — New York : Basic Books, c1986. — p. cm. — Includes index. — Bibliography: p

BANK INVESTMENTS — Great Britain
TURNER, Dennis
An investment bank for the UK / Dennis Turner [and] Charles Williams. — London : Fabian Society, 1987. — 31 p. — (Fabian tract ; no.518)

BANK LOANS
The international interbank market : a descriptive study. — Basle : Bank for International Settlements, 1983. — 44p. — (BIS economic papers ; no.8)

VENUGOPAL REDDY, Y
World Bank, borrowers' perspectives / Y. Venugopal Reddy. — New Delhi : Sterling Publishers, c1985. — x, 143 p.. — Includes index

BANK LOANS — Mathematical models
CLEMENZ, Gerhard
Credit markets with asymmetric information / Gerhard Clemenz. — Berlin ; New York : Springer-Verlag, c1986. — viii, 212 p.. — (Lecture notes in economics and mathematical systems ; 272). — Bibliography: p. [204]-212

BANK LOANS — European Economic Community countries
The Contribution of credit institutions to the renewal of the economy : proceedings of the conference held in Luxembourg, 28-29 November 1985 / edited by J.M. Gibb. — London : Kogan Page, c1986. — 135p. — English text, French and German summaries. — Organised jointly by The Commission of the European Communities, Directorate General Information Market and Innovation and the Institut Universitaire International Luxembourg

BANK LOANS — United States
BRADY, Thomas F.
The role of the prime rate in the pricing of business loans by commercial banks, 1977-84 / Thomas F. Brady. — Washington, D.C. : Board of Governors of the Federal Reserve System, 1985. — 25p. — (Staff study / Board of Governors of the Federal Reserve System (U.S.) ; 146)

BANK MARKAZI JOMHOURI IRAN
BANK MARKAZI IRAN
Bulletin / Bank Markazi Iran. — Tehran : Bank Markazi Iran, 1962-. — 6 per year. Quarterly from 1973. — From 1983 issuing body entitled Bank Markazi Jomhouri Islami Iran

BANK OF BARODA
TRIPATHI, Dwijendra
Towards a new frontier : history of the Bank of Baroda 1908-1983 / Dwijendra Tripathi, Priti Misra. — New Delhi : Manohar, 1985. — xvi,313p. — Bibliography: p299-309

BANK OF CANADA — Officials and employees — Biography
FULLERTON, Douglas H.
Graham Towers and his times : a biography / by Douglas H. Fullerton. — Toronto : McClelland and Stewart, 1986. — 348p

BANK OF ENGLAND
GEDDES, Philip
Inside the Bank of England / Philip Geddes. — London : Boxtree, 1987. — xi,179p. — Bibliography: p171-172

BANK OF ENGLAND — History
ROTELLI, Claudio
Le origini della controversia monetaria (1797-1844) / Claudio Rotelli. — Bologna : Il Mulino, 1982. — 258p. — (Saggi ; 236)

BANK OF UGANDA
BANK OF UGANDA
Annual report / Bank of Uganda. — Kampala : Bank of Uganda, 1983-. — Annual

BANKERS — Biography
CAROSSO, Vincent P
The Morgans : private international bankers 1854-1913 / Vincent P. Carosso ; with the assistance of Rose C. Carosso. — Cambridge, Mass. ; London : Harvard University Press, 1987. — xvi, 888p, [12]p of plates. — (Harvard studies in business history ; 38). — Includes index. — Bibliography: p.649-653

BANKERS — Canada — Biography
FULLERTON, Douglas H.
Graham Towers and his times : a biography / by Douglas H. Fullerton. — Toronto : McClelland and Stewart, 1986. — 348p

BANKERS — Great Britain — Biography
ATTALI, Jacques
A man of influence : Sir Siegmund Warburg 1902-82 / Jacques Attali ; translated by Barbara Ellis. — London : Weidenfeld and Nicholson, 1986. — vii,346p. — *Translation of: Un homme d'influence*

BANKERS — Switzerland — Biography
SOMARY, Felix
The raven of Zürich : the memoirs of Felix Somary / translated from the German by A.J. Sherman ; with a foreword by Otto Von Habsburg. — London : Hurst, c1986. — xii,310p,[1]p of plates. — *Translation of: Erinnerungen aus meinem Leben. — Includes index*

BANKING — England
VENTRIS, F. M.
Banker's documentary credits : issued in accordance with the Uniform customs and practice (1974 revision) of the International Chamber of Commerce / by F.M. Ventris. — 2nd ed. — London : Lloyd's of London Press, 1983. — xxi,350p. — *Previous ed.: 1980. — With supplement 1985. — Includes index*

BANKING LAW — Ecuador
ECUADOR
[Laws, etc.]. Ley general de bancos. — Quito : Corporación de Estudios y Publicaciones, 1973. — [70]p

BANKING LAW — Germany (West)
The German banking system : an introduction to the German banking system and the law on banking supervision with German text and synoptic English translation of the Banking Act, the Federal Bank Act and other legal provisions = Das Bankwesen in Deutschland : eine Einführung in das deutsche Kreditwesen un Bankenaufsichtsrecht mit deutsch-englischer Textausgabe des KWG, des Bundesbankgesetzes und anderer Rechtscorschriften / [edited by] Hannes Schneider, Hans-Jürgen Hellwig, David J. Kingsman. — 3rd ed. — Frankfurt am Main : Knapp, 1985. — 344p

BANKING LAW — Great Britain
HAMBLIN, C.
Banking law / by Clive Hamblin. — London : Sweet & Maxwell, 1985. — xxvii,377p. — (Concise college texts). — *Includes index*

BANKING LAW — United States
CARL, Notger
Strategic planning of U.S. commercial banks in a changing legal environment / Notger Carl. — Idstein [Germany] : Schulz-Kirchner, 1985. — xiii, 303 p. — (Wissenschaftliche Schriften im Wissenschaftlichen Verlag Dr. Schulz-Kirchner. Reihe 2. Betriebswirtschaftliche Beiträge ; Bd. 101). — *Bibliography: p. 284-303*

BANKING LAW (ISLAMIC LAW)
IQBAL, Zubair
Islamic banking / by Zubair Iqbal and Abbas Mirakhor. — Washington, D. C. : International Monetary Fund, 1987. — v,62p. — (Occasioinal paper / Intetnational Monetary Fund ; no.49). — *Bibliography: p60-62*

BANKRUPTCY — Great Britain
GREAT BRITAIN. Parliament. House of Commons. Library. Research Division
The reform of insolvency law / Tim Edmonds. — [London] : the Division, 1985. — 31p. — (Background paper ; no.164)

BANKRUPTCY — Netherlands
BERGHUIS, A. C.
Abuse of Dutch private companies (BVs) : an empirical study / A. C. Berghuis, G. Paulides. — The Hague : Research and Documentation Centre, Ministry of Justice, 1985. — 35p. — ([Reports, papers, articles] ; 77). — *Includes bibliographical references*

BANKS AND BANKING
AUERBACH, Robert D
Money, banking, and financial markets / Robert D. Auerbach. — 2nd ed. — New York : Macmillan ; London : Collier Macmillan, c1985. — xvii, 650, 17 p.. — *Includes bibliographies and index*

HOWCROFT, J. B.
Retail banking : the new revolution in structure and strategy / J.B. Howcroft and J. Lavis. — Oxford : Basil Blackwell, 1986. — ix,216p. — *Bibliography: p208-211. — Includes index*

The international interbank market : a descriptive study. — Basle : Bank for International Settlements, 1983. — 44p. — (BIS economic papers ; no.8)

SIMON, Claude
Les banques / Claude Simon. — Paris : La Découverte, 1984. — 127p. — *Bibliography: p123-124*

BANKS AND BANKING — Accounting — Mathematical models
ROSE, John T.
Statistical cost accounting models in banking : a reexamination and an application / John T. Rose, John D. Wolken. — Washington, D.C. : Board of Governors of the Federal Reserve System, 1986. — 13p. — (Staff study / Board of Governors of the Federal Reserve System ; 150). — *Bibliography: p12-13*

BANKS AND BANKING — Archival resources — Great Britain
PRESSNELL, L. S.
A guide to the historical records of British banking / L.S. Pressnell and John Orbell with the assistance of Rosemary Ashbee ... [et al.]. — Aldershot : Gower, c1985. — xxv,130p. — (A Grafton book). — *Bibliography: p118-122 — Includes index*

BANKS AND BANKING — Directories
Who owns what in world banking. — London : Financial Times Business Publishing, c1983. — ix,186p. — *Includes index*

BANKS AND BANKING — Government guaranty of deposits
SPRAGUE, Irvine H
Bailout : an insider's account of bank failures and rescues / Irvine H. Sprague. — New York : Basic Books, c1986. — p. cm. — *Includes index. — Bibliography: p*

BANKS AND BANKING — Service charges
CANNER, Glenn B.
Service charges as a source of bank income and their impact on consumers / Glenn B. Canner and Robert D. Kurtz. — Washington, D.C. : Board of Governors of the Federal Reserve System, 1985. — 31p. — (Staff study / Board of Governors of the Federal Reserve System (U.S.) ; 145). — *Includes bibliographical references*

BANKS AND BANKING — Statistics
Bank profitability: Statistical supplement = Rentabilité des banques: supplement statistique / Organisation for Economic Co-operation and Development. — Paris : Organisation for Economic Co-operation and Development, 1981/85-. — *Annual. — Text in English and French*

BANKS AND BANKING — Australia — History
MERRETT, D. T.
ANZ Bank : a history of the Australia and New Zealand Banking Group Limited and its constituents / D.T. Merrett. — Sydney ; London : Allen & Unwin, 1985. — xiv,325p,[4]p of plates. — *Ill on lining papers. — Includes index*

BANKS AND BANKING — Brazil
BANCO CENTRAL DO BRAZIL
Relatorio / Banco Central do Brazil. — Rio de Janeiro : Banco Central do Brazil, 1965-1979. — *Annual. — Continued by: Central Bank of Brazil. Annual report*

CENTRAL BANK OF BRAZIL
Annual report / Central Bank of Brazil. — Brasilia : Central Bank of Brazil, 1980-. — *Annual. — Continues: Banco Central do Brazil. Relatorio*

BANKS AND BANKING — British Virgin Islands — Statistics
Banking statistics / British Virgin Islands. — Tortola : Statistics Division, 1984-. — *Annual*

BANKS AND BANKING — Chile — Statistics
MAMALAKIS, Markos
Historical statistics of Chile / compiled by Markos J. Mamalakis. — Westport, Conn. : Greenwood Press
vol.5: Money, banking, and financial services. — 1985. — xcii,532p

BANKS AND BANKING — Developing countries
VOGEL, Robert C.
Mobilizing small-scale savings : approaches, costs, and benefits / Robert C. Vogel and Paul Burkett. — Washington, D.C. : The World Bank, 1986. — vii,38p. — (Industry and finance series ; v.15). — *Bibliographical references: p30-38*

BANKS AND BANKING — England — History — 20th century
MORRIS, Timothy
Innovations in banking : business strategies and employee relations / Timothy Morris. — London : Croom Helm, c1986. — 137p. — *Bibliography: p128-132. — Includes index*

BANKS AND BANKING — England — Hertfordshire
PARKER, Jack
'Nothing for nothing for nobody' : a history of Hertfordshire banks and banking / Jack Parker. — Stevenage : Hertfordshire Publications, 1986. — 59p

BANKS AND BANKING — England — Sussex — History
JENKINS, Peter R.
Sussex money : a history of banking in Sussex / by Peter R. Jenkins. — Pulborough : Dragonwheel, 1987. — [80]p. — *Includes bibliography*

BANKS AND BANKING — France
LÉVÊQUE, Jean-Maxime
En première ligne / Jean-Maxime Lévêque. — Paris : Albin Michel, [1986]. — 202p

BANKS AND BANKING — France — Statistics
BANQUE DE FRANCE
Statistiques monétaires annuelles. — Paris : Banque de France, 1984-. — *Annual. — Includes Banque de France. Statistiques monétaires: séries retrospectives*

BANKS AND BANKING — Germany — Hamburg
ANDRESEN, Bruno W. F.
Mit Stehpult und Tintenfass : Erinnerungen aus dem Kontor einer Hamburger Merchant-Bank / Bruno W. F. Andresen. — Hamburg : Christians, 1984. — 239p

BANKS AND BANKING — Great Britain
BARCLAYS BANK
Report and accounts. — London : Barclays Bank PLC, 1984. — *Annual. — Continues Barclays Bank International. Report and accounts*

BARCLAYS BANK (DOMINION, COLONIAL AND OVERSEAS)
Report of the Directors. — London : Barclays Bank (Dominion, Colonial and Overseas), 1917. — *Annual, with gaps. — Continued by Barclays Bank International. Report and Accounts*

BANKS AND BANKING — Great Britain
continuation

BARCLAYS BANK INTERNATIONAL
Report and accounts. — London : Barclays Bank International, 1972-. — *Annual.* — *Continues Barclays Bank (Dominion, Colonial and Overseas). Report of the Directors. Continued by Barclays Bank. Report and accounts*

FRAZER, Patrick
Plastic and electronic money : new payment systems and their implications / Patrick Frazer. — Cambridge, Woodhead-Faulkner, 1985. — [272]p. — *Includes bibliography and index*

GEDDES, Philip
Inside the Bank of England / Philip Geddes. — London : Boxtree, 1987. — xi,179p. — *Bibliography: p171-172*

MORAN, Michael, 1946-
The politics of banking : the strange case of competition and credit control / Michael Moran. — 2nd ed. — Basingstoke : Macmillan, 1986. — ix,205p. — (Studies in policy-making). — *Previous ed.: 1984. — Includes index*

MULLINEUX, A. W.
U.K. banking after deregulation / A.W. Mullineux. — London : Croom Helm, c1987. — 180p. — *Bibliography: p166-171. Includes index*

NATIONAL GIRO
Evidence to the Committee to Review the Functioning of Financial Institutions. — [London?] : National Giro, 1977. — 29p

BANKS AND BANKING — Great Britain — Directories

British banking directory 1986-87 / compiled and edited by Anthony B. Capstick. — London : Financial Times Business Information, 1986. — 398p

BANKS AND BANKING — Great Britain — History

GOODHART, C. A. E.
The business of banking, 1891-1914 / C.A.E. Goodhart. — Aldershot : Gower in association with the London School of Economics and Political Science, c1986. — [642]p. — *Originally published: London : Weidenfeld, 1972. — Bibliography: p613-621. — Includes index*

HOLMES, A. R.
Midland : 150 years of banking business / A.R. Holmes & Edwin Green. — London : B.T. Batsford, 1986. — xvi, 352p, 41p of plates

BANKS AND BANKING — Great Britain — Statistics

Abstract of banking statistics / Statistical Unit, Committee of London Clearing Bankers. — London : Committee of London Clearing Bankers. Statistical Unit, 1985-. — *Annual*

BANKS AND BANKING — Great Britain — Technological innovations

TAYLOR, Alan
New technology : banking, insurance and finance / Alan Taylor. — Hammersmith : [the Council], 1983. — 35p. — (Research report / Hammersmith and Fulham ; 59)

BANKS AND BANKING — Hong Kong

GHOSE, T. K.
The banking system of Hong Kong / T. K. Ghose. — Singapore : Butterworths, 1987. — viii,282p

BANKS AND BANKING — Hungary

DOMÁNY, Gyula
Az önálló jegybank felállítása / írta Domány Gyula. — Budapest : Benkö Gyula Könyvkereskedése, 1918. — 45p

SZÁDECZKY-KARDOSS, Tibor
A magyarországi pénzintézetek fejl"odése / írta Szádeczky-Kardoss Tibor. — Budapest : [Pallas részvénytársaság nyomdája], 1928. — vii,212p. — (Közgazdasági Könyvtár ; köt.4)

BANKS AND BANKING — India — History

TRIPATHI, Dwijendra
Towards a new frontier : history of the Bank of Baroda 1908-1983 / Dwijendra Tripathi, Priti Misra. — New Delhi : Manohar, 1985. — xvi,313p. — *Bibliography: p299-309*

BANKS AND BANKING — Iran

Annual report and balance sheet / Bank Markazi Iran. — Tehran : Bank Markazi Iran, 1969-1980. — *Annual. — Continued by: Economic report and balance sheet*

BANK MARKAZI IRAN
Bulletin / Bank Markazi Iran. — Tehran : Bank Markazi Iran, 1962-. — *6 per year. Quarterly from 1973. — From 1983 issuing body entitled Bank Markazi Jomhouri Islami Iran*

Economic report and balance sheet / Bank Markazi Jomhouri, Islami Iran. — Tehran : Bank Markazi Jomhouri Islami Iran, 1981-. — *Annual. — Continues: Annual report and balance sheet*

IQBAL, Zubair
Islamic banking / by Zubair Iqbal and Abbas Mirakhor. — Washington, D. C. : International Monetary Fund, 1987. — v,62p. — (Occasioinal paper / Intetnational Monetary Fund ; no.49). — *Bibliography: p60-62*

BANKS AND BANKING — Islamic countries

EL-ASHKER, Ahmed Abdel-Fattah
The Islamic business enterprise / Ahmed Abdel-Fattah El-Ashker. — London : Croom Helm, c1987. — xi,242p. — *Bibliography: p233-240. — Includes index*

HOMOUD, S. H. (Sami Hassan)
Islamic banking : the adaptation of banking practice to conform with Islamic law / S.H. Homoud. — London : Arabian Information, 1985. — [300]p. — *Translated from the Arabic*

IQBAL, Zubair
Islamic banking / by Zubair Iqbal and Abbas Mirakhor. — Washington, D. C. : International Monetary Fund, 1987. — v,62p. — (Occasioinal paper / Intetnational Monetary Fund ; no.49). — *Bibliography: p60-62*

Islamic banking and finance / Butterworths editorial staff. — London : Butterworths, 1986. — xii,149p. — *Conference papers. — Includes index*

BANKS AND BANKING — Italy

BARINA, Marco
Changes in the degree of concentration of the Italian banking system : an international comparison / by Marco Barina and Silvano Carletti ; editing: Elio Lancieri ; computer programmes by Giovanni Porcelli. — Rome : Banca Nazionale del Lavoro. Economic Research Department, 1986. — [90]p. — (Research papers / Banca Nazionale del Lavoro. Economic Research Department ; no.5). — *Bibliography: p87-[90]*

BANKS AND BANKING — Malaysia

LEE, Sheng-yi
The monetary and banking development of Singapore and Malaysia / Lee Shen-yi. — 2nd ed. — [Singapore] : Singapore University Press, 1986. — 298p

PANG, Johnson Yok
Banking in Malaysia / Johnson Pang Yok, Nathaniel G. Savarimuthu. — Kuala Lumpur : Heinemann (Malaysia), 1986. — xi, 186 p.

BANKS AND BANKING — Netherlands — Statistics

Vierde algemene bedrijfstelling, 1978. — 's-Gravenhage : Staatsuitgeverij. — *Rear cover title: Fourth general economic census, 1978: volume 2, part E: banking, insurance and services*
d. 2: Algemene sectorale gegevens
E: bank- en verzekeringswezen; dienstverlening. — 1985. — 107p

BANKS AND BANKING — New Zealand — History

MERRETT, D. T.
ANZ Bank : a history of the Australia and New Zealand Banking Group Limited and its constituents / D.T. Merrett. — Sydney ; London : Allen & Unwin, 1985. — xiv,325p,[4]p of plates. — *Ill on lining papers. — Includes index*

BANKS AND BANKING — Nigeria — Congresses

Rural banking in Nigeria / edited by Adeniyi Osuntogun and Wole Adewunmi. — London ; New York : Longman, 1982. — p. cm. — *Selected papers from a seminar held at the University of Ife, Mar. 29-Apr. 1, 1979, which was sponsored by the Nigerian Institute of Bankers. — Includes index*

BANKS AND BANKING — Organisation for Economic Co-operation and Development countries — State supervision

PECCHIOLI, R. M.
Prudential supervision in banking / by R. M. Pecchioli. — Paris : Organisation for Economic Co-operation and Development, 1987. — 298p. — (Trends in banking structure and regulation in OECD countries). — *Bibliography: p279-298*

BANKS AND BANKING — Pakistan

IQBAL, Zubair
Islamic banking / by Zubair Iqbal and Abbas Mirakhor. — Washington, D. C. : International Monetary Fund, 1987. — v,62p. — (Occasioinal paper / Intetnational Monetary Fund ; no.49). — *Bibliography: p60-62*

BANKS AND BANKING — Singapore

LEE, Sheng-yi
The monetary and banking development of Singapore and Malaysia / Lee Shen-yi. — 2nd ed. — [Singapore] : Singapore University Press, 1986. — 298p

BANKS AND BANKING — South Africa

BARCLAYS SHADOW BOARD
Barclays Shadow report 1986. — London : End loans to South Africa, 1986. — 18p

BANKS AND BANKING — Spain

FANJUL, Oscar
La eficiencia del sistema bancario español / Oscar Fanjul y Fernando Maravall ; prólogo de Enrique Fuentes Quintana. — Madrid : Alianza Editorial, 1985. — 275p. — *Bibliographies*

GIL, Gonzalo
Sistema financiero español / Gonzalo Gil. — 4a ed. — [Madrid] : Banco de España, 1986. — 206p. — (Estudios económicos / Banco de España, Servicio de Estudios ; no.29)

BANKS AND BANKING — Spain — Catalonia

BAIGES, Francesc
Banca Catalana : Más que un banco, más que una crisis / Francesc Baiges, Enric Gonzalez, Jaume Reixach. — Barcelona : Plaza & Janes, 1985. — 243p

BARATECH, Feliciano
Banca Catalana(1959-1984) : toda la verdad / Feliciano Baratech. — Barcelona : Planeto, 1985. — 207p

BANKS AND BANKING — Sweden

Bankaktiebolagen Fondkommissionärerna Fondbörsen och VPC = Banking and Stock-exchange statistics / Statistika Centralbyrån Sweden. — Stockholm : Kungl Bankinspektionen, 1970-. — *Annual. — Text in Swedish and English. — Title varies. — Continues: Bankerna Fondkommissionärer och Fondbörsen*

BANKS AND BANKING — Sweden
continuation

Bankerna Fond kommissionarer och Fond borsen = Banking and stock-exchange statistics / Statistika Centralbyrån Sweden. — Stockholm : Kungl. Bankinspektionen, 1968-1969. — *Annual.* — *Text in Swedish and English.* — *Continues: Uppgifter om bankerna samt uppgifter om Fondkommissionařer och Fondbörs.* — *Continued by: Bankaktiebolagen Fondkommissionařerna Fondbörsen och VPC*

Uppgifter om bankerna samt uppgifter om Fondkommissionařer och Fondbörs = Yearly banking and stock exchange statistics / Sweden Statistika Centralbyrån. — Stockholm : Kung. Bankinspektionen, 1935-1967. — *Annual.* — *Text in Swedish and English.* — *1935-1952 issuing body entitled Statistika Meddelanden.* — *continued by: Bankerna Fondkommissionärer och Fondbörsen*

BANKS AND BANKING — Switzerland

CHRISTENSEN, Benedicte Vibe
Switzerland's role as an international financial center / by Benedicte Vibe Christensen. — Washington, D. C. : International Monetary Fund, 1986. — v,40p. — (Occasional paper / International Monetary Fund ; no.45). — *Bibliography: p39-40*

BANKS AND BANKING — Turkey — Statistics

Istatistik ve degerlendirme bülteni = Monthly statistical and evaluation bulletin / Turkiye Cumhuriyet Merkez Bankasi. — Ankara : Turkiye Cumhuriyet Merkez Bankasi, 1987-. — *Monthly.* — *Text in English and Turkish*

BANKS AND BANKING — United States

CARL, Notger
Strategic planning of U.S. commercial banks in a changing legal environment / Notger Carl. — Idstein [Germany] : Schulz-Kirchner, 1985. — xiii, 303 p.. — (Wissenschaftliche Schriften im Wissenschaftlichen Verlag Dr. Schulz-Kirchner. Reihe 2. Betriebswirtschaftliche Beiträge ; Bd. 101). — *Bibliography: p. 284-303*

COHEN, Benjamin J
In whose interest? : international banking and American foreign policy / Benjamin J. Cohen. — New Haven ; London : Yale University Press, c1986. — xi, 347p. — *"A Council on Foreign Relations book.".* — *Includes index*

HULBERT, Mark
Interlock : the untold story of American banks, oil interests, the Shah's money, debts and the astounding connections between them / Mark Hulbert. — New York : Richardson and Snyder, 1982. — 272p

ROSE, Peter S
The changing structure of American banking / Peter S. Rose. — New York : Columbia University Press, 1987. — p. cm. — (Columbia studies in business, government, and society). — *Includes bibliographies and index*

BANKS AND BANKING — United States — Accounting — Mathematical models

ROSE, John T.
Statistical cost accounting models in banking : a reexamination and an application / John T. Rose, John D. Wolken. — Washington, D.C. : Board of Governors of the Federal Reserve System, 1986. — 13p. — (Staff study / Board of Governors of the Federal Reserve System ; 150). — *Bibliography: p12-13*

BANKS AND BANKING — United States — Service charges

CANNER, Glenn B.
Service charges as a source of bank income and their impact on consumers / Glenn B. Canner and Robert D. Kurtz. — Washington, D.C. : Board of Governors of the Federal Reserve System, 1985. — 31p. — (Staff study / Board of Governors of the Federal Reserve System (U.S.) ; 145). — *Includes bibliographical references*

BANKS AND BANKING — United States — State supervision

ROBERTSON, Ross M
The Comptroller and bank supervision: a historical appraisal / [by] Ross M. Robertson. — Washington : Office of the Comptroller of the Currency, [1968]. — x,262p. — *Bibliography: p247-253*

BANKS AND BANKING — United States — Statistics

Banking and monetary statistics : 1914-1941. — Washington, D.C. : Board of Governors of the Federal Reserve System, 1976. — 682p

BOARD OF GOVERNORS OF THE FEDERAL RESERVE SYSTEM (U.S.)
Banking and monetary statistics, 1941-1970. — Washington : Board of Governors of the Federal Reserve System, 1976. — vii,1168p

BANKS AND BANKING — Uruguay

ROCCA, José
La captación de excedentes financieros por el sistema bancario comercial. Uruguay, 1974-1982 / José Rocca, Jorge Simon. — Montevideo : Centro Interdisciplinario de Estudios sobre el Desarrollo Uruguay, 1985. — 198p. — (Serie Investigaciones / Centro Interdisciplinario de Estudios sobre el Desarrollo Uruguay ; no.19). — *Bibliography: p198*

BANKS AND BANKING 4Z ASIA SOUTHEASTERN

SKULLY, Michael T
Merchant banking in ASEAN : a regional examination of its development and operations / Michael T. Skully. — rev. ed. — Singapore ; Oxford : Oxford University Press, 1986. — viii,204p

BANKS AND BANKING, AUSTRALIA

SKULLY, Michael T.
The diversification of Australia's trading banks / M. T. Skully. — Lindfield : Kuring-gai College of Advanced Education, Centre for Securities Industry Studies, 1979. — 61p. — (Working papers / Kuring-gai College of Advanced Education, Centre for Securities Industry Studies ; no.2)

BANKS AND BANKING, BRITISH

TURNER, Dennis
An investment bank for the UK / Dennis Turner [and] Charles Williams. — London : Fabian Society, 1987. — 31 p. — (Fabian tract ; no.518)

BANKS AND BANKING, BRITISH — Iran

JONES, Geoffrey, 1952-
Banking and oil : the history of the British Bank of the Middle East, v.2 / Geoffrey Jones ; research by Frances Bostock, Grigori Gerenstein, Judith Nichol. — Cambridge : Cambridge University Press, 1987. — xxi,357,[40]p of plates. — (HongKong Bank Group history series). — *Bibliography: p348-350.* — *Includes index*

BANKS AND BANKING, BRITISH — Near East

JONES, Geoffrey, 1952-
Banking and oil : the history of the British Bank of the Middle East, v.2 / Geoffrey Jones ; research by Frances Bostock, Grigori Gerenstein, Judith Nichol. — Cambridge : Cambridge University Press, 1987. — xxi,357,[40]p of plates. — (HongKong Bank Group history series). — *Bibliography: p348-350.* — *Includes index*

BANKS AND BANKING, CENTRAL

GROUP OF THIRTY
How central banks manage their reserves : a study by the office of the Group of Thirty on behalf of the Multiple Reserve Currency Study Group. — New York : Group of Thirty, 1982. — 35 leaves

Money and the economy : central bankers' views / edited by Pierluigi Ciocca. — Basingstoke : Macmillan, 1987. — x,331p. — *Translation of: La moneta e l'economia.* — *Includes index*

BANKS AND BANKING, CENTRAL — Decision making

Central bankers, bureaucratic incentives, and monetary policy / editors, Eugenia Froedge Toma, Mark Toma. — Dordrecht ; Boston : Martinus Nijhoff, 1987. — p. cm. — (Financial and monetary policy studies ; v. 13)

BANKS AND BANKING, CENTRAL — France

BANQUE DE FRANCE
La Banque de France et la monnaie. — 4th ed. — [Paris] : Banque de France, [1986]. — 208p

BANKS AND BANKING, COOPERATIVE — France

CAISSE CENTRALE DES BANQUES POPULAIRES
Exercice / Caisse Centrale des Banques Populaires. — Paris : Caisse Centrale des Banques Populaires, 1954-. — *Annual.* — *In English from 1985*

BANKS AND BANKING, COOPERATIVE — Germany (West)

ASCHHOFF, Gunther
Das deutshe Genossenschaftswesen : Entwicklung, Struktur, wirtschaftliches Potential / Gunther Aschhoff, Eckart Henningsen. — Frankfurt : Fritz Knapp, 1985. — 167p. — (Veröffentlichungen der Deutsche Genossenschaftsbank ; Bd.15). — *Bibliography: p151-156*

BANKS AND BANKING, COOPERATIVE — India

JHA, Nand Kishore
Bank finance & green revolution in India / Nand Kishore Jha. — Delhi : Amar Prakashan, 1985. — xi, 358 p.. — *Bibliography: p. [351]-358*

BANKS AND BANKING, INTERNATIONAL

BIRD, Graham, 1947-
International financial policy and economic development : a disaggregated approach / Graham Bird. — Basingstoke : Macmillan, 1987. — xvi,348p. — *Bibliography: p338-343.* — *Includes index*

CHO, Kang Rae
Multinational banks : their identities and determinants / by Kang Rae Cho. — Ann Arbor, Mich. : UMI Research Press, c1985. — p. cm. — (Research in business economics and public policy ; no. 8). — : *Revision of thesis--University of Washington, 1983.* — *Includes index.* — *Bibliography: p*

CHRISTENSEN, Benedicte Vibe
Switzerland's role as an international financial center / by Benedicte Vibe Christensen. — Washington, D. C. : International Monetary Fund, 1986. — v,40p. — (Occasional paper / International Monetary Fund ; no.45). — *Bibliography: p39-40*

COHEN, Benjamin J
In whose interest? : international banking and American foreign policy / Benjamin J. Cohen. — New Haven ; London : Yale University Press, c1986. — xi, 347p. — *"A Council on Foreign Relations book.".* — *Includes index*

DALE, Richard
How safe is the banking system? / Richard Dale. — Midlothian : David Hume Institute, 1986. — v,16p. — (Hume occasional paper ; no.4). — *Bibliography: p15-16*

GUTTENTAG, Jack M.
Disaster myopia in international banking / Jack M. Guttentag and Richard J. Herring. — Princeton, N.J. : Princeton University. Department of Economics. International Finance Section, 1986. — 40p. — (Essays in international finance ; no.164). — *Bibliography: p34-*

BANKS AND BANKING, INTERNATIONAL
continuation

International capital markets : development and prospects / by Maxwell Watson...[et al.]. — Washington, D. C. : International Monetary Fund, 1986. — ix,152p. — (World economic and financial surveys). — *Includes Bibliographical references*

KAMBATA, Dara
The practice of multinational banking : macro-policy issues and key international concepts / Dara M. Khambata. — Westport, Conn. : Quorum Books, c1986. — p. cm. — *Includes bibliographies and index*

MULLINEUX, A. W.
International money and banking : the creation of a new order / A.W. Mullineux. — Brighton : Wheatsheaf, 1987. — [224]p. — *Includes bibliography and index*

Recent innovations in international banking / prepared by a Study Group established by the Central Banks of the Group of Ten Countries. — [Basle] : Bank for International Settlements, 1986. — ix.270p

Strategic planning and international banking / edited by Paolo Savona and George Sutija. — Basingstoke : Macmillan in association with the Stalian Banking Association, 1986. — xiv,229p. — *Includes index*

WELLONS, Philip A
Passing the buck : banks, governments, and Third World debt / Philip A. Wellons. — Boston, Mass. : Harvard Business School Press, c1987. — xiv, 342 p.. — *Includes bibliographical references and index*

BANKS AND BANKING, INTERNATIONAL — Accounting
International bank accounting / prepared by Ernst & Whinney. — London : Euromoney Publications, 1986. — xix,358p

BANKS AND BANKING, INTERNATIONAL — History
CAROSSO, Vincent P
The Morgans : private international bankers 1854-1913 / Vincent P. Carosso ; with the assistance of Rose C. Carosso. — Cambridge, Mass. ; London : Harvard University Press, 1987. — xvi, 888p, [12]p of plates. — (Harvard studies in business history ; 38). — *Includes index. — Bibliography: p.649-653*

BANKS AND BANKING, INTERNATIONAL — Law and legislation
RYDER, F. R.
Legal problems of international banking / by F.R. Ryder. — London : Sweet & Maxwell, 1986. — [70]p

BANKS AND BANKING, INTERNATIONAL — Statistics — Sources
LANDELL-MILLS, Joslin
The Fund's international banking statistics / Joslin Landell-Mills. — Washington, D.C. : International Monetary Fund, 1986. — v,54p. — *Bibliographical references: p54*

BANQUE DE FRANCE
BANQUE DE FRANCE
La Banque de France et la monnaie. — 4th ed. — [Paris] : Banque de France, [1986]. — 208p

BANQUE DE FRANCE — Statistics
BANQUE DE FRANCE
Statistiques monétaires annuelles. — Paris : Banque de France, 1984-. — *Annual. — Includes Banque de France. Statistiques monétaires: séries retrospectives*

Communique de la Banque de France. — Paris : Banque de France. Direction Générale des Études. — *Monthly*

BANYORO
BEATTIE, John, 1915-
Understanding an African kingdom : Bunyoro / John Beattie. — New York : Holt, Rinehart and Winston, [1965]. — 61p

BAPTISTS — Georgia
GREENHOUSE, Carol J.
Praying for justice : faith, order, and community in an American town / Carol J. Greenhouse. — Ithaca : Cornell University Press, 1986. — p. cm. — (Anthropology of contemporary issues). — *Includes index. — Bibliography: p*

BARBADOS — Census, 1970
Commonwealth Caribbean population census 1970 : Barbados : preliminary bulletin : housing. — St. Michael : Barbados Statistical Service, 1972. — iii,17p

Commonwealth Caribbean population census 1970 : Barbados : preliminary bulletin : education. — St. Michael : Barbados Statistical Service, 1974. — ii,21p

BARBADOS — Census, 1980
Barbados 1980 population census : preliminary count by parish and sex. — [St. Michael? : Barbados Statistical Service?, 1982]. — 3 leaves

BARBADOS — Economic conditions
HOPE, Kempe R
Economic development in the Caribbean / Kempe Ronald Hope. — New York : Praeger, 1986. — xv, 215p. — *Includes bibliographical references and index*

BARBADOS — Economic policy
Physical development plan for Barbados. — [Bridgetown?] : Town and Country Development Planning Office, 1970. — vii,134p

BARBADOS — population — Statistics
Barbados 1980 population census : preliminary count by parish and sex. — [St. Michael? : Barbados Statistical Service?, 1982]. — 3 leaves

BARBADOS. Legislature. House of Assembly — Elections, 1981
Report on the general election, 1981. — [Bridgetown] : Supervisor of Elections, 1981. — 52p

BARBIE, KLAUS
LINKLATER, Magnus
The Fourth Reich : Klaus Barbie and the neo-Fascist connection / Magnus Linklater, Isabel Hilton and Neal Ascherson with Mark Hosenball in Washington, Jon Swain in Paris and Tana de Zulueta in Rome. — London : Hodder and Stoughton, 1984 (1985 [printing]). — [iv,448]p. — (Coronet books)

BARBOSA, RUY, 1849-1923
LACOMBE, Américo Jacobina
À sombra de Rui Barbosa / Américo Jacobina Lacombe. — [São Paulo] : Companhia Editora Nacional ; [Brasília : Instituto Nacional do Livro, MEC, 1978]. — x,226p. — (Brasiliana ; volume 365)

BARCELONA (SPAIN) — Economic conditions
MASSANA, Carme
Indústria, ciutat i propietat : política econòmica i propietat urbana a l'àrea de Barcelona (1901-1939) / Carme Massana. — Barcelona : Curial, 1985. — 431p. — (Biblioteca de cultura catalana ; 57)

BARCELONA (SPAIN) — Social conditions
MCDONOGH, Gary W
Good families of Barcelona : a social history of power in the industrial era / Gary Wray McDonogh. — Princeton, N.J. : Princeton University Press, c1986. — xiv, 262 p. — *Includes index. — Bibliography: p. [227]-251*

BARCLAYS BANK
BARCLAYS SHADOW BOARD
Barclays Shadow report 1986. — London : End loans to South Africa, 1986. — 18p

BARCLAYS BANK INTERNATIONAL
BARCLAYS BANK
Report and accounts. — London : Barclays Bank PLC, 1984. — *Annual. — Continues Barclays Bank International. Report and accounts*

BARCLAYS BANK (DOMINION, COLONIAL AND OVERSEAS)
Report of the Directors. — London : Barclays Bank (Dominion, Colonial and Overseas), 1917. — *Annual, with gaps. — Continued by Barclays Bank International. Report and Accounts*

BARCLAYS BANK INTERNATIONAL
Report and accounts. — London : Barclays Bank International, 1972-. — *Annual. — Continues Barclays Bank (Dominion, Colonial and Overseas). Report of the Directors. Continued by Barclays Bank. Report and accounts*

BARNSLEY WOMEN AGAINST PIT CLOSURES
BARNSLEY WOMEN AGAINST PIT CLOSURES
Barnsley Women Against Pit Closures. — Barnsley (Barnsley Women Against Pit Closures). — (Women Against Pit Closures ; vol.2) (People's History of Yorkshire ; no.12) vol.2. — 1985. — 109p

BAROTSE (AFRICAN PEOPLE) — See
Lozi (Afican people)

BARRE, RAYMOND
LEBACQZ, Albert
Journal politique de 1985 : le retour de Raymond Barre / Albert Lebacqz. — Paris : Editions France-Empire, 1986. — 279p

BARRY (SOUTH GLAMORGAN) — History
Barry : the centenary book / edited by Donald Moore. — 2nd ed, rev.. — Barry (22 Redbrink Crescent, Barry Island, South Glamorgan) : Barry Centenary Book Committee, c1985. — xxi, 496p. — *Col. map on lining papers*

BARTER — Addresses, essays, lectures
Barter in the world economy / edited by Bart S. Fisher, Kathleen M. Harte. — New York : Praeger, 1985. — p. cm. — *Includes indexes. — Bibliography: p*

BARUYA (PAPUAN PEOPLE) — Social life and customs
GODELIER, Maurice
The making of great men : male domination and power among the New Guinea Baruya / Maurice Godelier ; translated by Rupert Suryer. — Cambridge : Cambridge University Press, 1986. — xv,251p. — (Cambridge studies in social anthropology ; 56)

BASEL (SWITZERLAND) — Industries
FINK, Paul
Vom Passementerhandwerk zur Bandindustrie : ein Beitrag zur Geschichte des alten Basel / Paul Fink ; herausgegeben von der Gesellschaft für das Gute und Gemeinnützige. — Basel : in Kommission bei Helbing & Lichtenhahn, 1979. — 101p. — *Bibliography: p100-101*

BASIC (COMPUTER PROGRAM LANGUAGE)
MUNDEL, Marvin Everett
BASIC, a personal computer language for improving productivity / Marvin E. Mundel and David Danner. — Tokyo, Japan : Asian Productivity Organization, c1986. — v,322p. — *Includes index*

BASIC NEEDS
Basic needs and the urban poor : the provision of communal services / edited by P. J. Richards and A. M. Thomson. — London : Croom Helm, 1984. — 276p. — *Includes bibliographical references. — A study prepared for the International Labour Office within the framework of the World Employment Programme*

BASIC NEEDS — Africa
The Challenge of employment : and basic needs in Africa : essays in honour of Shyam B. L. Nigam and to mark the tenth anniversary of JASPA. — Nairobi : Oxford University Press, 1986. — xii,379p. — *Includes bibliographical references*

BASIC NEEDS — Brazil
KNIGHT, Peter T.
Brazil / Peter T. Knight and Ricardo Moran. — [Washington, D.C. : World Bank], 1981. — 101p. — (Poverty and basic needs series). — *Includes bibliographical references*

BASIC NEEDS — Kenya
GHAI, Dharam Pal
Planning for basic needs in Kenya : performance, policies and prospects / Dharam Ghai, Martin Godfrey [and] Franklyn Lisk. — Geneva : International Labour Office, 1979. — x, 166p

BASILDON (ESSEX) — History
LUCAS, Peter
Basildon : birth of a city : background to the development of Basildon New Town (Essex) / Peter Lucas. — Basildon : Peter Lucas, 1986. — 222p

BASQUE PROVINCES — History
COLLINS, Roger
The Basques / Roger Collins. — Oxford : Basil Blackwell, 1986. — 1v.. — (The Peoples of Europe). — *Includes index*

BASQUE PROVINCES (SPAIN) — Boundaries — France
FERNANDEZ DE CASADEVANTE ROMANI, Carlos
La frontera hispano-francesca y las relaciones de vecindad : (especial refrencia al sector fronterizo del País Vasco / Carlos Fernandez de Casadevante Romani. — [Bilbao] : Universidad del País Vasco, 1985. — xx,547p. — *Bibliography: p[507]-539*

BASQUE PROVINCES (SPAIN) — Economic conditions — Congresses
COLOQUIO VASCO-CATALÁN DE HISTORIA (1 : 1982 : Sitges, Spain)
Industrialización y nacionalismo : análisis comparativos / edición a cargo de Manuel González Portilla, Jordi Maluquer de Motes, Borja de Riquer Permanyer. — Bellaterra : Servicio de Publicacions de la Universidad Autónoma de Barcelona, 1985. — 610p. — *In Spanish, with some papers in Catalan*

BASQUE PROVINCES (SPAIN) — History — Autonomy and independence movements
GRANJA, José Luis de la
Nacionalismo y II República en el País Vasco : estatutos de autonomía, partidos y elecciones : historia de Acción Nacionalista Vasca: 1930-1936 / por José Luis de la Granja Sainz. — Madrid : Centro de Investigaciones Sociologicas : Siglo vientiuno de España, 1986. — xxiv,687p. — *Bibliography: p[641]-659*

BASQUE PROVINCES (SPAIN) — History — 20th century
FUSI, Juan Pablo
El País Vasco : pluralismo y nacionalidad / Juan Pablo Fusi. — Madrid : Alianza Editorial, 1984. — 255p

BASQUE PROVINCES (SPAIN) — History — Autonomy and independence movements
Conflicto en Euskadi / Juan J. Linz con la colaboración de Manuel Gómez-Reino, Francisco Andrés Orizo y Darío Vila. — Madrid : Espasa Calpe, 1986. — 699p

GURRUCHAGA, Ander
El código nacionalista vasco durante el franquismo / Ander Gurruchaga ; prólogo de Alfonso Pérez-Agote. — Barcelona : Anthropos, 1985. — 456p. — *Bibliography: p439-456*

BASQUE PROVINCES (SPAIN) — Politics and government
Conflicto en Euskadi / Juan J. Linz con la colaboración de Manuel Gómez-Reino, Francisco Andrés Orizo y Darío Vila. — Madrid : Espasa Calpe, 1986. — 699p

GARCÍA DAMBORENEA, Ricardo
La encrucijada vasca / Ricardo Damborenea García. — Barcelona : Argos Vergara, 1984. — 250p

LLERA RAMO, Francisco José
"Postfranquismo y fuerzas politicas en Euskadi" : sociología electoral del País Vasco / Francisco José Llera Ramo. — Bilbao : Universidad del País Vasco, 1985. — 596p. — *Bibliography: p363-366*

REAL CUESTA, Javier
El carlismo vasco 1876-1900 / por Javier Real Cuesta. — Madrid : Siglo ventinuo, 1985. — xiii,338p. — *"El carlismo vasco, 1876-1900 es el resumen de una tesis doctoral que con el mismo título fue presentada en la Universidad de Zaragoza en 1983". — Bibliography: p [311]-321*

REINARES, Fernando
Violencia y politica en Euskadi / Fernando Reinares. — Bilbao : Désclee de Brouwer, 1984. — 254p. — *Bibliography: p251-252*

BASQUES
ATABIZKAR
Les Basques : un peuple, une nation : Euskadi dans l'Europe / Atabizkar. — [s.l.] : Editions Elkar, [1970]. — 63p

BASQUES — Argentina — History
PILDAIN SALAZAR, María Pilar
Ir a América : la emigración vasca a América (Guipúzcoa 1840-1870) / María Pilar Pildain Salazar. — San Sebastián : Donostia, 1984. — xii,245p. — (Monografías / Grupo Doctor Camino de Historia de San Sebastián ; 22). — *Bibliography: p82-83*

BASQUES — Latin America — History
PILDAIN SALAZAR, María Pilar
Ir a América : la emigración vasca a América (Guipúzcoa 1840-1870) / María Pilar Pildain Salazar. — San Sebastián : Donostia, 1984. — xii,245p. — (Monografías / Grupo Doctor Camino de Historia de San Sebastián ; 22). — *Bibliography: p82-83*

BASTÜRK, ABDULLAH
Defence of Abdullah Bastürk : trade unionism on trial in Turkey. — [s.l.] : Public Services International, 1981. — 199p

BATH (AVON) — City planning
NATHANIEL LICHFIELD AND PARTNERS
Bath minimum physical change study, final report / [Nathaniel Lichfield and Partners]. — London (2 Old Brewery Mews, Hampstead High St., NW3 1PZ) : Nathaniel Lichfield and Partners, 1976. — [5],iii,51p

NATHANIEL LICHFIELD AND PARTNERS
Bath minimum physical change study, technical appendices / [Nathaniel Lichfield and Partners]. — London (2 Old Brewery Mews, Hampstead High St., NW3 1PZ) : Nathaniel Lichfield and Partners, 1976. — [3],98p

BATH PARTY *See* Hizb al-Báth al-Árabī al-Ishtirāki (Syria)

BAUER, OTTO — History and criticism
SCHÖLER, Uli
"Otto Bauer - nein danke"? : Austromarxismusdiskussion und historische Bezüge für eine Standortbestimmung marxistischer Sozialdemokraten / Uli Schöler. — Berlin : Demokratische Verlagskooperative, 1984. — 89p. — *Bibliography: p87-89*

BAVARIA (GERMANY) — Politics and government — 1918-1945
HARRISON, E. D. R.
Gauleiter Bürckel and the Bavarian Palatinate 1933-40 / E. D. R. Harrison. — Leeds : Leeds Philosophical and Literary Society, 1986. — p273-291. — (Proceedings of the Leeds Philosophical and Literary Society, Literary and Historical Section ; vol.10, part 3). — *Bibliography: p290-291*

BAYESIAN STATISTICAL DECISION THEORY
Bayesian inference and decision techniques : essays in honor of Bruno de Finetti / edited by Prem K. Croel [and] Arnold Zellner. — Amsterdam : North Holland, 1986. — 496p. — (Studies in Bayesian econometrics and statistics ; 6)

BAYESIAN STATISTICAL DECISION THEORY — Congresses
UNIVERSITY OF CALIFORNIA, IRVINE, CONFERENCE ON POLITICAL ECONOMY ((2nd : 1983)
Information pooling and group decision making : proceedings of the Second University of California, Irvine, Conference on Political Economy / edited by Bernard Grofman, Guillermo Owen. — Greenwich, Conn. : JAI Press, c1986. — xii, 279 p.. — (Decision research ; v. 2). — *Includes index. — Bibliography: p. 231-264*

BAZAINE, ACHILLE FRANÇOIS, 1811-1888
BAUMONT, Maurice
Bazaine : les secrets d'un maréchal 1811/1888. — Paris : Imprimere nationale, 1978. — 425p. — (Collection "Personnages"). — *Includes index. — Bibliography: p401-406*

BEAGLE CHANNEL — International status
DESTEFANI, Laurio H.
Lo que debe saberse del Beagle : síntesis del conflicto de límites austral entre Argentina y Chile / Laurio H. Destefani. — [Buenos Aires] : Platero, [ca.1984]. — 93p. — *Bibliography: p91-93*

BEBEL, AUGUST
JUNG, Werner
August Bebel : deutscher Patriot und internationaler Sozialist : seine Stellung zu Patriotismus und Internationalismus / Werner Jung. — Pfaffenweiler : Centaurus-Verlagsgesellschaft, 1986. — 539p. — (Reihe Geschichtswissenschaft ; Bd.6). — *Bibliography: p521-538*

BED AND BREAKFAST ACCOMODATIONS — England — London
It's the limit : an exposé of pricing in London's B and B land. — London : CHAR, 1986. — 40p

BEDFORDSHIRE — Population
STOTT, David
Bedfordshire 1981 census : commuting / David Stott. — Bedford : Bedfordshire County Planning Department, 1986. — 18p

BEDFORDSHIRE (ENGLAND) — Population
BEDFORDSHIRE. County Council
Population change 1985 : update supplement 1987. — [Bedford] : [the Council], 1985. — 12p

BEDLINGTON (NORTHUMBERLAND) — Social life and customs
WADE, Mary
To the miner born / by Mary Wade. — Stocksfield : Oriel, 1984. — 130p,[16]p of plates

BEDOUINS
INGHAM, Bruce
Bedouin of Northern Arabia : traditions of the Āl-Dhafir / Bruce Ingham. — London ; New York : KPI, 1986. — xvi,136p

BEEF INDUSTRY — Botswana
HUBBARD, Michael
Agricultural exports and economic growth : a study of the Botswana beef industry / Michael Hubbard. — London : KPI, 1986. — xx,284p

BEEF INDUSTRY — Central America
WILLIAMS, Robert G
Export agriculture and the crisis in Central America / by Robert G. Williams. — Chapel Hill : University of North Carolina Press, c1986. — xvi, 257p. — *Includes index. — Bibliography: p.[239]-248*

BEHAVIOR

Handbook of environmental psychology / edited by Daniel Stokols, Irwin Altman. — New York : Wiley, c1987. — 2 vols. — "A Wiley-Interscience publication.". — Includes bibliographies and indexes

LEARY, Mark R
Social psychology and dysfunctional behavior : origins, diagnosis, and treatment / Mark R. Leary and Rowland S. Miller. — New York : Springer-Verlag, c1986. — xiii, 262 p. — (Springer series in social psychology). — Includes indexes. — Bibliography: p. [203]-244

MEISTER, David
Behavioral analysis and measurement methods / David Meister. — New York : Wiley, c1985. — xiii, 509 p.. — "A Wiley-Interscience publication.". — Includes bibliographies and index

BEHAVIOR MODIFICATION

JEHU, Derek
Learning theory and social work / Derek Jehu. — London : Routledge and Kegan Paul, 1967. — viii,139p. — Bibliography: p122-136. — Includes index

STUMPHAUZER, Jerome S
Helping delinquents change : a treatment manual of social learning approaches / Jerome S. Stumphauzer. — New York : Haworth Press, c1986. — p. cm. — "Published also as v. 8, no. 1/2 of the Child & youth services.". — Includes index. — Bibliography: p

BEHAVIOR THERAPY

HERBERT, Martin
Behavioural treatment of children with problems : a practice manual / Martin Herbert. — 2nd ed. — London : Academic Press, 1987. — [250]p. — Previous ed.: published as Behavioural treatment of problem children. 1981. — Includes bibliography and index

BEHAVIORAL ASSESSMENT

LAKE, Dale G
Measuring human behavior : tools for the assessment of social functioning / [by] Dale G. Lake, Matthew B. Miles [and] Ralph B. Earle, Jr. — New York : Teachers College Press, [1973]. — xviii, 422 p. — Includes bibliographies

BEHAVIORAL ASSESSMENT OF CHILDREN

Children's social behavior : development, assessment, and modification / edited by Phillip S. Strain, Michael J. Guralnick, Hill M. Walker. — Orlando [Fla.] : Academic Press, 1986. — xiii, 460 p.. — Includes bibliographies and index

BEHAVIORISM (PSYCHOLOGY) — Congresses

Constraints on learning : limitations and predispositions, based on a conference sponsored by St John's College, Cambridge, England / edited by R.A. Hinde and J. Stevenson-Hinde. — London : Academic Press, 1973. — xv,488p. — 'The conference was held in ... [St John's] College between April 4th and 7th, 1972' - Preface. — Includes bibliographies and index

BEHAVIORISM (PSYCHOLOGY) — History

O'DONNELL, John M.
The origins of behaviorism : American psychology, 1870-1920 / John M. O'Donnell. — New York ; London : New York University Press, 1985. — xii, 299p. — (The American social experience series ; 3). — Includes bibliographical references and index

BEHRSTOCK, JULIAN

BEHRSTOCK, Julian
The eighth case : troubled times at the United Nations / Julian Behrstock. — Lanham : University Press of America, c1987. — p. cm. — Includes bibliographical references and index

BEIRUT — Politics and government

JOHNSON, Michael
Class & client in Beirut : the Sunni Muslim community and the Lebanese state, 1840-1985 / Michael Johnson. — London : Ithaca, c1986. — xvii,243p. — Includes index

BELFAST (NORTHERN IRELAND) — City planning

DAWSON, Gerry
Planning in the shadow of urban civil conflict : a case study from Belfast / by Gerry Dawson. — Liverpool : University of Liverpool, Dept. of Civic Design, 1984. — 48 leaves. — (Working paper / Dept. of Civic Design, University of Liverpool ; WP24)

BELFAST (NORTHERN IRELAND) — City planning — History

HENDRY, John, 1934-
Belfast - who cares? : an inaugural lecture delivered before the Queen's University of Belfast on 15 January 1985 / John Hendry. — [Belfast] : Queen's University of Belfast, c1985. — 18p. — (New lecture series ; no.139)

BELFAST (NORTHERN IRELAND) — Social life and customs

ADAMS, Gerry
Falls memories / Gerry Adams. — Rev. ed. — Dingle, Co. Kerry : Brandon, 1983. — 144p. — Originally published: 1982. — Bibliography: p143-144

MUNCK, Ronnie
Belfast in the thirties : an oral history / Ronnie Munck & Bill Rolston with Gerry Moore. — Belfast : Blackstaff, 1987. — 209p. — Bibliography: p206-209

BELGIANS — South Africa — History

GORIS, J. M.
België en de Boerenrepublieken : Belgisch-Zuidafrikaanse betrekkingen (ca.1835-1895) / J. M. Goris. — Retie : Kempische Boekhandel, 1983. — 620p. — (Belgie Zuid-Afrika ; Deel 1)

BELGIUM — Census, 1981

BELGIUM. Institut national de statistique
Recensement de la population [au] 1 [er] mars 1981. — Bruxelles : Institut national de statistique
t.5: Population selon l'état civil et par âge. — [1985]. — 2v

Recensement de la population et des logements au 1er mars 81. — Bruxelles : Institut national de statistique
Résultats généraux
Population scolaire et niveau d'instruction. — [1986]. — 307p

Recensement de la population et des logements au 1er mars 81. — Bruxelles : Institut national de statistique
Résultats généraux
Population scolaire et niveau d'instruction. — 1986. — 307p

Recensement de la population et des logements au 1er mars 1981. — Bruxelles : Institut national de statistique. — Cover title
t.2: Royaume, régions, provinces et arrondissements. — [1986]. — 378p

Recensement de la population et des logements au 1er mars 81. — Bruxelles : Institut national de statistique
Résultats généraux
Population active. — 1986. — 305p

BELGIUM — Commerce — Statistics

BELGIUM. Institut national de statistique
Recensement de l'industrie et du commerce : 31 décembre 1970. — Bruxelles : Institut national de statistique, 1975-

BELGIUM — Economic conditions — 1945- — Congresses

CONGRÈS DES ÉCONOMISTES BELGES DE LANGUE FRANÇAISE (4 : 1980 : Mons)
Les conditions de l'initiative économique. — Charleroi : Centre interuniversitaire de formation permanente
Actes. — [1980]. — 239p

CONGRÈS DES ÉCONOMISTES BELGES DE LANGUE FRANÇAISE (4 : 1980 : Mons)
Les conditions de l'initiative économique. — Charleroi : Centre interuniversitaire de formation permanente
Allocation optimale des ressources, rentabilité et initiative économique; rapport préparatoire / Commission 4. — [1980]. — 125p

CONGRÈS DES ÉCONOMISTES BELGES DE LANGUE FRANÇAISE (4 : 1980 : Mons)
Les conditions de l'initiative économique. — Charleroi : Centre interuniversitaire de formation permanente
Contexte réglementaire et institutionnel de l'initiative économique; rapport préparatoire / Commission 5. — [1980]. — 143p

CONGRÈS DES ÉCONOMISTES BELGES DE LANGUE FRANÇAISE (4 : 1980 : Mons)
Les conditions de l'initiative économique. — Charleroi : Centre interuniversitaire de formation permanente
Les motivations à l'initiative économique; rapport préparatoire / Commission 1. — 1980. — 70p

CONGRÈS DES ÉCONOMISTES BELGES DE LANGUE FRANÇAISE (4 : 1980 : Mons)
Les conditions de l'initiative économique. — Charleroi : Centre interuniversitaire de formation permanente
L'innovation et l'initiative économique; rapport préparatoire / Commission 2. — [1980]. — 56p

CONGRÈS DES ÉCONOMISTES BELGES DE LANGUE FRANÇAISE (4 : 1980 : Mons)
Les conditions de l'initiative économique. — Charleroi : Centre interuniversitaire de formation permanente
Orientations et moyens d'action d'une stratégie régionale de redéploiement économique: l'exemple de la Wallonie; rapport préparatoire / Commission de Base. — [1980]. — 178p

CONGRÈS DES ÉCONOMISTES BELGES DE LANGUE FRANÇAISE (4 : 1980 : Mons)
Les conditions de l'initiative économique. — Charleroi : Centre interuniversitaire de formation permanente
Présentation générale. — [1980]. — 21p

CONGRÈS DES ÉCONOMISTES BELGES DE LANGUE FRANÇAISE (4 : 1980 : Mons)
Les conditions de l'initiative économique. — Charleroi : Centre interuniversitaire de formation permanente
Réduction progressive des heures et partage du travail; rapport préparatoire / Commission 3. — [1980]. — 87p

BELGIUM — Economic conditions — 1945- — Mathematical models

D'ALCANTARA, G.
Serena : a microeconomic sectoral, regional and national accounting econometric model for the Belgian economy / G. d'Alcantara. — Leuven : Acco, 1983. — 588p

BELGIUM — Economic policy — Congresses

CONGRÈS DES ÉCONOMISTES BELGES DE LANGUE FRANÇAISE (4 : 1980 : Mons)
Les conditions de l'initiative économique. — Charleroi : Centre interuniversitaire de formation permanente
Actes. — [1980]. — 239p

CONGRÈS DES ÉCONOMISTES BELGES DE LANGUE FRANÇAISE (4 : 1980 : Mons)
Les conditions de l'initiative économique. — Charleroi : Centre interuniversitaire de formation permanente
Allocation optimale des ressources, rentabilité et initiative économique; rapport préparatoire / Commission 4. — [1980]. — 125p

**BELGIUM — Economic policy —
Congresses** *continuation*
CONGRÈS DES ÉCONOMISTES BELGES DE
LANGUE FRANÇAISE (4 : 1980 : Mons)
 Les conditions de l'initiative économique. —
 Charleroi : Centre interuniversitaire de
 formation permanente
 Contexte réglementaire et institutionnel de
 l'initiative économique; rapport préparatoire /
 Commission 5. — [1980]. — 143p

CONGRÈS DES ÉCONOMISTES BELGES DE
LANGUE FRANÇAISE (4 : 1980 : Mons)
 Les conditions de l'initiative économique. —
 Charleroi : Centre interuniversitaire de
 formation permanente
 Les motivations à l'initiative économique;
 rapport préparatoire / Commission 1. — 1980.
 — 70p

CONGRÈS DES ÉCONOMISTES BELGES DE
LANGUE FRANÇAISE (4 : 1980 : Mons)
 Les conditions de l'initiative économique. —
 Charleroi : Centre interuniversitaire de
 formation permanente
 L'innovation et l'initiative économique; rapport
 préparatoire / Commission 2. — [1980]. — 56p

CONGRÈS DES ÉCONOMISTES BELGES DE
LANGUE FRANÇAISE (4 : 1980 : Mons)
 Les conditions de l'initiative économique. —
 Charleroi : Centre interuniversitaire de
 formation permanente
 Orientations et moyens d'action d'une stratégie
 régionale de redéploiement économique:
 l'exemple de la Wallonie; rapport préparatoire
 / Commission de Base. — [1980]. — 178p

CONGRÈS DES ÉCONOMISTES BELGES DE
LANGUE FRANÇAISE (4 : 1980 : Mons)
 Les conditions de l'initiative économique. —
 Charleroi : Centre interuniversitaire de
 formation permanente
 Présentation générale. — [1980]. — 21p

CONGRÈS DES ÉCONOMISTES BELGES DE
LANGUE FRANÇAISE (4 : 1980 : Mons)
 Les conditions de l'initiative économique. —
 Charleroi : Centre interuniversitaire de
 formation permanente
 Réduction progressive des heures et partage du
 travail; rapport préparatoire / Commission 3.
 — [1980]. — 87p

BELGIUM — Foreign economic relations
FÉDÉRATION DES ENTREPRISES DE
BELGIQUE
 La Belgique dans le monde. — Bruxelles :
 Fédération des Entreprises de Belgique, 1973.
 — 60p

BELGIUM — History — To 1555
NICHOLAS, David
 The domestic life of a medieval city : women,
 children, and the family in fourteenth-century
 Ghent / David Nicholas. — Lincoln :
 University of Nebraska Press, c1985. — p. cm.
 — *Includes index.* — *Bibliography: p*

**BELGIUM — History — Revolution,
1789-1790**
POLASKY, Janet L
 Revolution in Brussels, 1787-1793 / by Janet
 L. Polasky. — Brussels : Académie royale de
 Belgique ; Hanover : Published for the
 University of New Hampshire by University
 Press of New England, 1987. — 315 p., [2]
 leaves of plates (1 folded). — (Mémoires de la
 Classe des lettres. Collection in-8o ; 2e sér., t.
 66, fasc. 4-1985). — *Includes index.* —
 Bibliography: p. [277]-299

BELGIUM — History — Invasion of 1792
POLASKY, Janet L
 Revolution in Brussels, 1787-1793 / by Janet
 L. Polasky. — Brussels : Académie royale de
 Belgique ; Hanover : Published for the
 University of New Hampshire by University
 Press of New England, 1987. — 315 p., [2]
 leaves of plates (1 folded). — (Mémoires de la
 Classe des lettres. Collection in-8o ; 2e sér., t.
 66, fasc. 4-1985). — *Includes index.* —
 Bibliography: p. [277]-299

VERSTEGEN, Vedastus
 Lokeren onder de Franse overheersing /
 Vedastus Verstegen. — Hasselt : Provinciale
 Bibliothek, 1971. — (Mededelingen van het
 Centrum voor Studie van de Boerenkrijg ; 79)
 11: De finantiële toestand. — 72p

BELGIUM — History — 19th century
VERSCHAEREN, J.
 Julius Vuylsteke (1836-1903) : Klavwaard &
 Geus / J. Verschaeren. — Kortrijk : Van
 Ghemmert, 1984. — 486p. — *Bibliography:
 p12-21*

BELGIUM — Industries
FÉDÉRATION DES ENTREPRISES DE
BELGIQUE
 La Belgique dans le monde. — Bruxelles :
 Fédération des Entreprises de Belgique, 1973.
 — 60p

BELGIUM — Industries — Statistics
BELGIUM. Institut national de statistique
 Recensement de l'industrie et du commerce :
 31 décembre 1970. — Bruxelles : Institut
 national de statistique, 1975-

**BELGIUM — Languages — Political
aspects**
MCRAE, Kenneth D.
 Conflict and compromise in multilingual
 societies : Belgium / Kenneth D.McRae. —
 Waterloo, Ont. : Wilfrid Laurier University
 Press, 1986. — xiv, 387p

BELGIUM — Politics and government
MCRAE, Kenneth D.
 Conflict and compromise in multilingual
 societies : Belgium / Kenneth D.McRae. —
 Waterloo, Ont. : Wilfrid Laurier University
 Press, 1986. — xiv, 387p

BELGIUM — Population — Statistics
BELGIUM. Direction de l'étude des problèmes
du travail
 Estimation de la population active belge au 30
 juin des années 1970-1984 : nouvelle série
 N.A.C.E. = Raming van de Belgische
 beroepsbevolking op 30 juni der jaren
 1970-1984 : nieuwe reeks N.A.C.E.. —
 [Bruxelles] : Direction de l'étude des problèmes
 de travail, 1986. — [47] leaves. — *In French
 and Flemish*

BELGIUM. Institut national de statistique
 Recensement de la population [au] 1 [er] mars
 1981. — Bruxelles : Institut national de
 statistique
 t.5: Population selon l'état civil et par âge. —
 [1985]. — 2v

Recensement de la population et des logements
 au 1er mars 81. — Bruxelles : Institut national
 de statistique
 Résultats généraux
 Population scolaire et niveau d'instruction. —
 [1986]. — 307p

Recensement de la population et des logements
 au 1er mars 1981. — Bruxelles : Institut
 national de statistique. — *Cover title*
 t.2: Royaume, régions, provinces et
 arrondissements. — [1986]. — 378p

BELGIUM — Social conditions — 1945-
MCRAE, Kenneth D.
 Conflict and compromise in multilingual
 societies : Belgium / Kenneth D.McRae. —
 Waterloo, Ont. : Wilfrid Laurier University
 Press, 1986. — xiv, 387p

BELGIUM — Social policy
MORAUX, B.
 Si mupa, modèle dâide a la décision dans un
 secteur social / B.Moraux [et] B. Meunier. —
 Namur : Facultés Universitaires Notre-Dame
 de la Paix, 1985. — 21p. — (Cahiers de la
 Faculté des Sciences Economiques et Sociales
 de Namur. Série recherche ; no.67). —
 Bibliography: p19-21

BELIZE — Description and travel
British Honduras : general description with
 map and illustrations. — London : The West
 Indian and Atlantic Group Committee for the
 Government of British Honduras, [1923]. —
 15p. — *Reprint of a lecture by Algernon
 Aspinall*

BELIZE — Economic conditions
Belize, economic report. — Washington, D.C.,
 U.S.A. : World Bank, c1984. — xxxiv,111p. —
 (A World Bank country study). — *Summary in
 English, French, and Spanish*

DEVELOPMENT FINANCE CORPORATION
(Belize). Investment Promotion Unit
 Communication, transport and public utilities
 in Belize. — Belize City : the Corporation,
 1980. — 11 leaves

BELIZE — Economic policy
Belize, economic report. — Washington, D.C.,
 U.S.A. : World Bank, c1984. — xxxiv,111p. —
 (A World Bank country study). — *Summary in
 English, French, and Spanish*

BELIZE — Foreign economic relations
Belize, economic report. — Washington, D.C.,
 U.S.A. : World Bank, c1984. — xxxiv,111p. —
 (A World Bank country study). — *Summary in
 English, French, and Spanish*

BELIZE — Population — Statistics
1980-1981 population census of the
 Commonwealth Caribbean. — [Jamaica?] :
 Caricom
 Belize. — 1980

BELIZE — Social conditions
DEVELOPMENT FINANCE CORPORATION
(Belize). Investment Promotion Unit
 Living in Belize. — Belize City : the
 Corporation, 1980. — 9 leaves

BELIZE — Statistics, Vital
1980-1981 population census of the
 Commonwealth Caribbean. — [Jamaica?] :
 Caricom
 Belize. — 1980

BELLO, Sir AHMADU
PADEN, John N.
 Ahmadu Bello, Sardauna of Sokoto : values
 and leadership in Nigeria / John N. Paden. —
 London : Hodder and Stoughton, 1986. —
 xi,799p,[24]p of plates. — *Includes
 bibliographies and index*

BEN-GURION, DAVID
TEVETH, Shabtai
 Ben-Gurion and the Palestinian Arabs : from
 peace to war / Shabtai Teveth. — Oxford :
 Oxford University Press, 1985. — x,234p

**BENDE (NIGERIA) — Politics and
government**
JONES, G. I. (Gwilym Iwan)
 Annual reports of the Bende Division, South
 Eastern Nigeria, 1905-1912 : with a
 commentary by G.I. Jones. — Cambridge :
 African Studies Centre, University of
 Cambridge, 1986. — iv,99p. — (Cambridge
 African occasional papers ; no.2). — *Two maps
 on folded leaves in pocket*

BENEŠ, EDVARD
PECHÁČEK, Jaroslav
 Masaryk - Beneš -Hrad : Masarykovy dopisi
 Benešovi / Jaroslav Pecháček. — München :
 České Slovo, 1984. — 182p

BENEVOLENCE
VANDEVEER, Donald
 Paternalistic intervention : the moral bounds of
 benevolence / Donald VanDeVeer. —
 Princeton, N.J. : Princeton University Press,
 c1986. — xii, 452 p.. — (Studies in moral,
 political, and legal philosophy). — *Includes
 bibliographical references and index*

BENEVOLENCE — Moral and ethical aspects

Beneficence, philanthropy and the public good / edited by Ellen Frankel Paul...[et at]. — Oxford : Basil Blackwell for the Social Philosphy and Policy Center, Bowling Green State University, 1987. — 141p

BENGAL (INDIA) — Rural conditions

BOSE, Sugata
Agrarian Bengal : economy, social structure and politics, 1919-1947 / Sugata Bose. — Cambridge : Cambridge University Press, 1986. — xii,306p. — (Cambridge South Asian studies ; [no.36]). — *Bibliography: p285-292. — Includes index*

BENGAL (INDIA) — Social conditions

BOSE, Sugata
Agrarian Bengal : economy, social structure and politics, 1919-1947 / Sugata Bose. — Cambridge : Cambridge University Press, 1986. — xii,306p. — (Cambridge South Asian studies ; [no.36]). — *Bibliography: p285-292. — Includes index*

BENIN CITY, NIGERIA — Kings and rulers

BRITISH MUSEUM
Divine kingship in Africa / William Fagg. — London : British Museum, 1970. — 60p. — ´...[catalogue of an exhibition of] the British Museum´s entire Benin collection...´ - Preface and dedication. — bibl p60

BENNETT, RICHARD BEDFORD BENNETT, 1st viscount

WILBUR, J. Richard H
The Bennett administration 1930-1935 / by Richard Wilbur. — Ottawa : Canadian Historical Association, 1969. — 23 p. — (Canadian Historical Association booklets, no. 24). — *Includes bibliographical references*

BENNETT, WILLIAM R

GARR, Allen
Tough guy : Bill Bennett and the taking of British Columbia / by Allen Garr. — Toronto, Ont., Canada : Key Porter Books, c1985. — ix, 197 p., [16] p. of plates. — *Includes index. — Bibliography: p. 191-192*

BENTHAM, JEREMY

POSTEMA, Gerald J.
Bentham and the common law tradition / Gerald J. Postema. — Oxford : Clarendon, 1986. — xvi,490p. — (Clarendon law series). — *Bibliography: p465-476. — Includes indexes*

STEPHEN, Sir Leslie
The English utilitarians / by Sir Leslie Stephen. — New York : Kelley
Vol.1: Jeremy Bentham. — 1968. — 326p

BENZENE — Environmental aspects — Organisation for Economic Co-operation and Development countries

LÜBKERT, Barbara
Control of toxic substances in the atmosphere : Benzene / by Barbara Lübkert, Willfried Dulson and Luellen Olsen. — [Paris] : OECD, 1986. — 105p. — (OECD environment monographs ; no.5). — *Bibliography: p96-105*

BERBERS

Regards sur le Maroc : actualité de Robert Montagne. — Paris : CHEAM, 1986. — 239p. — (Publications du CHEAM ; 9). — *Bibliography: p233-239. — Contents: La vie sociale et politique des Berberes/Robert Montagne - The Berbers: their social and political organisation /Ernest Gellner, David Seddon - Robert Montagne et les structures politiques du Maroc pre-colonial/Mohamed Berdouzi*

BEREAVEMENT

MARRIS, Peter
Loss and change / Peter Marris. — rev. ed. — London : Routledge and Kegan Paul, 1986. — xiv,178p. — (Reports / Institute of Community Studies). — *Bibliography: p172-174*

BEREAVEMENT — Psychological aspects

KNAPP, Ronald J
Beyond endurance : when a child dies / Ronald J. Knapp. — New York : Schocken Books, 1986. — xv, 271 p.. — *Includes index. — Bibliography: p. 263-265*

BERGEN-BELSEN (GERMANY: CONCENTRATION CAMP)

KOLB, Eberhard
Bergen-Belsen : vom "Aufenthaltslager" zum Konzentrationslager 1943-1945 / Eberhard Kolb. — Göttingen : Vandenhoek und Rupredit, 1985. — 105 (12)p

BERKELEY, GEORGE

FLAGE, Daniel E.
Berkeley´s doctrine of notions : a reconstruction based on his theory of meaning / Daniel E. Flage. — London : Croom Helm, c1987. — 226p. — *Bibliography: p221-224. — Includes index*

BERKSHIRE COUNTY (MASS.) — History

MCGAW, Judith A.
Most wonderful machine : mechanization and social change in Berkshire paper making, 1801-1885 / Judith A. McGaw. — Princeton, N.J. : Princeton University Press, c1987. — xv, 439 p.. — *Includes index. — Bibliography: p. [413]-425*

BERLIN. Conference (1884-1885)

GAVIN, R. J., comp
The scramble for Africa : documents on the Berlin West African Conference and related subjects, 1884/1885 / compiled, edited and translated from the French and German, by R. J. Gavin and J. A. Betley. — [Ibadan, Nigeria] : Ibadan University Press, 1973. — xxxiv, 429 p. — *Includes bibliographical references*

BERLIN (GERMANY) — Archives

Berlin in Geschichte und Gegenwart: Jahrbuch des Landesarchivs, Berlin. — Berlin : Wolf Jobst Siedler, 1982-. — *Annual*

BERLIN (GERMANY) — History

Berlin : pivot of German destiny / translated and edited by Charles B. Robson ; introduction by Willy Brandt. — Chapel Hill, N.C. : University of North Carolina Press, 1960. — 233p

Berlin in Geschichte und Gegenwart: Jahrbuch des Landesarchivs, Berlin. — Berlin : Wolf Jobst Siedler, 1982-. — *Annual*

BERLIN (GERMANY) — History — Allied occupation, 1945-

KEITHLY, David M
Breakthrough in the Ostpolitik : the 1971 Quadripartite Agreement / David M. Keithly. — Boulder : Westview Press, 1986. — p. cm. — (Westview special studies in international relations). — *Includes index. — Bibliography: p*

BERLIN (GERMANY) — Politics and government

Berlin between two worlds / edited by Ronald A. Francisco and Richard L. Merritt. — Boulder, Colo. ; London : Westview Press, 1986. — xiii,184p

BERLIN (GERMANY) — Politics and government — 1945-

GELB, Norman
The Berlin Wall / Norman Gelb. — London : Joseph, 1986. — [320]p. — *Includes bibliography and index*

BERLIN QUESTION (1945-)

Berlin : pivot of German destiny / translated and edited by Charles B. Robson ; introduction by Willy Brandt. — Chapel Hill, N.C. : University of North Carolina Press, 1960. — 233p

BERLIN QUESTION (1945-)

KEITHLY, David M
Breakthrough in the Ostpolitik : the 1971 Quadripartite Agreement / David M. Keithly. — Boulder : Westview Press, 1986. — p. cm. — (Westview special studies in international relations). — *Includes index. — Bibliography: p*

WETZLAUGK, Udo
Berlin und die deutsche Frage / Udo Wetzlaugk. — Köln : Verlag Wissenschaft und Politik, 1985. — 272p. — *Bibliography: p257-272*

BESANT, ANNIE

DINNAGE, Rosemary
Annie Besant / Rosemary Dinnage. — Harmondsworth : Penguin, 1986. — 127p,[8]p of plates. — (Lives of modern women). — *Bibliography: p124. — Includes index*

BESEDOVSKIĬ, GRIGORIĬ ZINOV´EVICH

BESEDOVSKIĬ, Grigoriĭ Zinov´evich
[Na putīakh k termidoru. English]. Revelations of a Soviet diplomat / by Grigory Bessedovsky ; translated by Matthew Norgate. — Westport, Conn. : Hyperion Press, 1977. — 276 p.. — Abridged translation of Na putīakh k termidoru. — Reprint of the 1931 ed. published by Williams & Norgate, London. — *Includes index*

BEVAN, ANEURIN

CAMPBELL, John, 1947-
Nye Bevan and the mirage of British socialism / John Campbell. — London : Weidenfeld and Nicolson, c1987. — 430 p.. — *Bibliography: p.411-417*

BEVERAGE INDUSTRY — European Economic Community countries

MARFELS, Christian
Concentration, competition and competitiveness in the beverages industries of the European Community / by Professor Christian Marfels. — Luxembourg : Office for Official Publications of the European Communities, 1984. — xii,122p. — *At head of title page: Commission of the European Communities*

BEVERAGE INDUSTRY

Primary commodities : market developments and outlook / by the Commodities Division of the Research Department. — Washington, D.C. : International Monetary Fund, 1986. — vii,74p. — (World economic and financial surveys)

BEVERAGE INDUSTRY — Political aspects — Great Britain

CANNON, Geoffrey
The politics of food : the secret world of Whitehall and the food giants which threaten your health / Geoffrey Cannon. — London : Century, 1987. — [408]p. — *Includes index*

BHARAT HEAVY ELECTRICALS LIMITED

KUNDU, Amitabh
Location of public enterprises and regional development / Amitabh Kundu, Girish K. Misra, Rajkishor Meher. — New Delhi : Concept Pub. Co., 1986. — xv, 178 p.. — *Summary: Economic study of the impact of Bharat Heavy Electricals Limited on Bhopal City. — Includes index. — Bibliography: p. [170]-174*

BHARIAS

KURUP, Ayyappan Madhava
Continuity and change in a little community : a study of the Bharias of Patalkot in Madhya Pradesh / A. M. Kurup. — New Delhi : Concept Publishing, 1985. — 140p. — *Includes references*

BHILAI STEEL PLANT

SURESH KUMAR
Social mobility in industrializing society / Suresh Kumar. — Jaipur : Rawat Publications, 1986. — x, 188 p.. — *Includes bibliographies and index*

BHOPAL UNION CARBIDE PLANT DISASTER, BHOPAL, INDIA, 1984

SUFRIN, Sidney C.
Bhopal, its setting, responsibility, and challenge / Sidney C. Surfin. — Delhi : Ajanta Publications : Distributors, Ajanta Books International, 1985. — 98 p.. — *60-9*

MOREHOUSE, Ward
The Bhopal tragedy : what really happened and what it means for American workers and communities at risk / by Ward Morehouse and M. Arun Subramaniam. — [New York] : [Council on International and Public Affairs], [1986]. — xiii,190p. — *A report for the Citizens Commission on Bhopal. — Bibliography: p139-144*

WEIR, David
The Bhopal syndrome : pesticide manufacturing and the Third World / by David Weir ; with an afterword by Claude Alvares. — Penang : International Organization of Consumers Union Regional Office for Asia and the Pacific, 1986. — vii,117p

BHUTTO, ZULFIKAR ALI

KAUSHIK, Surendra Nath
Pakistan under Bhutto's leadership / by Serundra Nath Kaushik. — New Dehli : Uppal, 1985. — xii,363p. — *Bibliography: p [335]-356*

KAUSHIK, Surendra Nath
Politics in Pakistan, with special reference to rise and fall of Bhutto / Surendra Nath Kaushik. — Jaipur : Aalekh, 1985. — iv, 152 p.. — (South Asian studies series). — *Summary: On the political scene of Pakistan under the leadership of Zulfikar Ali Bhutto. — Includes index. — Bibliography: p. [144]-146*

BIBLE — Versions

[Bible. English. Authorized. 1984]. The Holy Bible : containing the Old and New Testaments [and Apocrypha] translated out of the original tongues and with the former translations diligently compared and revised by His Majesty's Special command; appointed to be read in churches. — Oxford : Oxford University Press, [1984]. — 1158,348,272,[3],9p . — *Includes set of 9 maps*

BIBLIOGRAPHICAL SERVICES — Directories

Encyclopedia of information systems and services / edited by John Schmittroth, Jr. ; Amy F. Lucas and Annette Novallo, associate editors ; Kathleen Young Marcaccio, contributing editor. — 6th ed. — Detroit, Mich. : Gale Research Co., c1985-. — v. <1 >. — *At head of title: 1985-86. — Includes indexes. — Contents: v. 1. International volume*

BIBLIOGRAPHY — Bibliography — Afro-Americans

OBUDHO, Robert A
Afro-American demograpy and urban issues : a bibliography / compiled by R.A. Obudho and Jeannine B. Scott. — Westport, Conn. : Greenwood Press, 1985. — xxxix, 433 p.. — (Bibliographies and indexes in Afro-American and African studies ; no. 8). — *Includes index*

BIBLIOGRAPHY — Bibliography — Catalogs

COMMISSION OF THE EUROPEAN COMMUNITIES. Library
List of additions to the Library : supplement. — [Luxembourg : Office for Official Publications of the European Communities] 1981/2: Selection of bibliographies available in the Library. — 1981. — vp,72 columns. — *In Community languages*

BIBLIOGRAPHY — Bibliography — History

HENIGE, David P
Serial bibliographies and abstracts in history : an annotated guide / compiled by David Henige. — Westport, Conn. ; London : Greenwood Press, c1986. — xiv, 220p. — (Bibliographies and indexes in world history ; no. 2). — *Includes index*

BIBLIOGRAPHY — Bibliography — Sociology, Rural

BERNDT, Judy
Rural sociology : a bibliography of bibliographies / by Judy Berndt. — Metuchen, N.J. : Scarecrow, 1986. — viii, 177 p.. — *Includes indexes*

BIBLIOGRAPHY — Rare books

DROZ, E.
Complément à la bibliographie de Pierre Haultin / E. Droz. — Genève : E. Droz, 1961. — p.375-394. — (Bibliothèque d'humanisme et renaissance. travaux et documents ; Tome 23). — *Offprint*

BIBLIOGRAPHY — Soviet Union

Kniga i sotsial'nyi progress / otv. redaktor N. M. Sikorskii. — Moskva : Nauka, 1986. — 227p. — *Kniga podgotovlennaia po materialam Piatoi Vsesoiuznoi nauchnoi konferentsii po knigovedeniiu (Moskva, 1984)*

BIBLIOGRAPHY, NATIONAL — Catalogs

BELL, Barbara L.
An annotated guide to current national bibliographies / Barbara L. Bell. — Cambridge : Chadwyck-Healey, 1986. — [450]p. — (Government documents bibliographies)

BIBLIOGRAPHY, NATIONAL — Directories

Inventaire général des bibliographies nationales rétrospectives = retrospective national bibliographies : an international directory / edité par = edited by Marcelle Beaudiquez. — Munich ; London : K.G. Saur, 1986. — 189p. — (IFLA publications ; 35)

BICULTURALISM — Québec (Province)

SANCTON, Andrew
Governing the Island of Montreal : language differences and metropolitan politics / Andrew Sancton. — Berkeley : University of California Press, c1985. — xxxviii, 213 p.. — (Lane studies in regional government) (A Publication of the Franklin K. Lane Memorial Fund, Institute of Governmental Studies, University of California, Berkeley). — *"Published for the Institute of Governmental Studies and the Institute of International Studies, University of California, Berkeley.". — Includes bibliographical references and index*

BIG BUSINESS — History — 20th century

DUNNING, John H.
The world's largest industrial enterprises 1962-1983 / John H. Dunning, Robert D. Pearce. — 2nd ed. — Aldershot : Gower, c1985. — v,186p. — *Previous ed.: 1981*

BIG BUSINESS — United States

ADAMS, Walter
The bigness complex : industry, labor, and government in the American economy / Walter Adams and James W. Brock. — 1st ed. — New York : Pantheon Books, 1986. — xiii, 426 p.. — *Includes indexes. — Bibliography: p. 381-413*

NADER, Ralph
The big boys : portraits of corporate power / Ralph Nader and William Taylor. — New York : Pantheon Books, 1986. — xix, 571p. — *Includes index. — Bibliography: p.523-553*

BIG SIOUX RIVER VALLEY (S.D. AND IOWA) — History

HARNACK, Curtis
Gentlemen on the prairie / Curtis Harnack. — Ames : Iowa State University Press, c1985. — viii, 254 p.. — *Includes index. — Bibliography: p. 239-248*

BIHAR (INDIA) — Economic conditions

ROY, Ramashray
Dialogues on development : individuals, society, and the political order / Ramashray Roy and R.K. Srivastava. — New Delhi ; Beverly Hills : Sage Publications, 1985. — p. cm

BIHAR (INDIA) — Population density

SINGH, Ram Dayal
Population structure of Indian cities : a case study of the cities of Bihar / Ram Dayal Singh. — New Delhi : Inter-India Publications, 1985. — x,173p. — *Bibliography: p[158]-167*

BILBO, THEODORE GILMORE

MORGAN, Chester M
Redneck liberal : Theodore G. Bilbo and the New Deal / Chester M. Morgan. — Baton Rouge : Louisiana State University Press, c1985. — p. cm. — *Includes index. — Bibliography: p*

BILINGUALISM

APPEL, René
Language contact and bilingualism / René Appel and Pieter Muysken. — London : Edward Arnold, 1987. — [224]p. — *Includes bibliography and index*

LAPONCE, J. A.
Languages and their territories / J. A. Laponce ; translated from the French by Anthony Martin-Sperry. — Toronto : University of Toronto Press, 1987. — x,265p. — *Bibliography: p[211]-249*

BILINGUALISM — Political aspects — Manitoba — History

DOERN, Russell
The battle over bilingualism : the Manitoba language question 1983-1985 / Russell Deorn. — Winnipeg : Cambridge Publishers, 1985. — 227p

BILINGUALISM — Belgium — Brussels

The Interdisciplinary study of urban bilingualism in Brussels / edited by Els Witte and Hugo Baetens Beardsmore. — Clevedon : Multilingual Matters, c1987. — 241p. — (Multilingual matters ; 28). — *Includes bibliographies and index*

BILINGUALISM — Mexico — Statistics

MARTÍNEZ RUIZ, Jesús
Densidad territorial de los monolingües y bilingües de México, en 1960-1970 : estadísticas del Proyecto Sociolingüístico elaboradas por Jesús Martínez Ruiz. — México : Instituto de Investigaciones Sociales, U.N.A.M., 1977. — 228p

BILL DRAFTING

THORNTON, G. C.
Legislative drafting / G.C. Thornton. — 3rd ed. — London : Butterworth, 1987. — [396]p. — *Previous ed.: 1979. — Includes index*

BILLS, LEGISLATIVE — Canada

PARLIAMENT. House of Commons
Status of Bills = État des projets de loi. — Ottawa : Canadian Government Publishing, 1987-. — *Irregular. — Text in English and French*

BILLS OF LADING

TODD, Paul, 1954-
Modern bills of lading / Paul Todd. — London : Collins, 1986. — [256]p. — *Includes index*

BILLS, PRIVATE — Great Britain

MARSH, Dave
The government and Private Members' Bills : wolves in sheep's clothing / by Dave Marsh and Melvyn Read (with Bernard Myers). — Colchester : Department of Government University of Essex, 1987. — 24 p. — (Essex papers in politics and government ; no.43)

BINANDELI (PAPUAN PEOPLE)

ITEANU, André
La ronde des échanges : de la circulation aux valeurs chez les Orokaiva / André Iteanu. — Cambridge : Publié avec le concours du Centre national de la recherche scientifique [by] Cambridge University Press, c1983. — 335p. — (Atelier d'anthropologie sociale). — *Bibliography: p311-318. — Includes index*

BINGHAM, THOMAS HENRY. Report on the supply of petroleum and petroleum products to Rhodesia — Bibliography
GREAT BRITAIN. Parliament. House of Commons. Library. International Affairs Section
The Bingham Report : a background bibliography / [Carole B. Mann]. — [London] : the Library, 1978. — 6leaves. — (Reference sheet / House of Commons. Library. Research Division ; no.78/9)

GREAT BRITAIN. Parliament. House of Commons. Library. International Affairs Section
The Bingham Report : a background bibliography; addenda: November 1978-January 1979 / [Carole B. Mann]. — [London] : the Library, 1979. — 2leaves. — ([Reference sheet] / House of Commons. Library. [Research Division] ; no.78/9: Addenda)

BIOETHICS
ENGELHARDT, H. Tristram
The foundations of bioethics / by H. Tristram Engelhardt, Jr. — New York : Oxford University Press, 1986. — p. cm. — *Includes bibliographies and index*

FRANCE
Éthique et recherche biomédicale : rapport 1985. — [Paris] : Documentation française, [1986]. — 170p

BIOGAS — Developing countries
GUNNERSON, Charles G.
Anaerobic digestion : principles and practices for biogas systems / Charles G. Gunnerson and David C. Stuckey. — Washington, D.C. : The World Bank, 1986. — xv,154p. — (World Bank technical paper ; no.49) (UNDP project management report ; no.5) (Integrated resource recovery series ; no.5). — *At head of cover: "Integrated resource recovery". — Bibliographical references: p137-154*

BIOLOGICAL WARFARE
SIMS, Nicholas A.
Biological and toxin weapons : issues in the 1986 review / Nicholas A. Sims. — London : Council for Arms Control, 1986. — ii, 26p. — (Faraday discussion paper ; no.7). — *Bibliography: p23-26*

BIOLOGY — Philosophy — History
GREENE, John C.
Science, ideology, and world view : esssays in the history of evolutionary ideas / John C. Greene. — Berkeley ; London : University of California Press, c1981. — x,202p. — *Includes index*

BIOLOGY — Social aspects
Journal of social and biological structures: studies in human social biology. — London : Academic Press, 1986-. — *Quarterly*

KAYE, Howard L.
The social meaning of modern biology : from social Darwinism to sociobiology / Howard L. Kaye. — New Haven ; London : Yale University Press, c1986. — ix,184p.. — *Bibliography: p167-180. — Includes index*

BIOLOGY, ECONOMIC — Canada
PRESCOTT-ALLEN, Christine
The first resource : wild species in the North American economy / Christine Prescott-Allen and Robert Prescott-Allen. — New Haven : Yale University Press, c1986. — xv, 529 p.. — *"Published with support from the World Wildlife Fund and Philip Morris Incorporated.". — Includes index. — Bibliography: p. 463-507*

BIOLOGY, ECONOMIC — United States
PRESCOTT-ALLEN, Christine
The first resource : wild species in the North American economy / Christine Prescott-Allen and Robert Prescott-Allen. — New Haven : Yale University Press, c1986. — xv, 529 p.. — *"Published with support from the World Wildlife Fund and Philip Morris Incorporated.". — Includes index. — Bibliography: p. 463-507*

BIOMASS ENERGY — Congresses
SOUTHERN BIOMASS ENERGY RESEARCH CONFERENCE ((3rd : 1985 : Gainesville, Fla.)
Biomass energy development / edited by Wayne H. Smith. — New York : Plenum Press, c1986. — p. cm. — *"Proceedings of the Third Southern Biomass Energy Research Conference, held March 12-14, 1985, in Gainesville, Florida"--T.p. verso. — Includes index. — Bibliography: p*

BIOMASS ENERGY — European Economic Community countries
Biomass : recent economic studies [a seminar in the CEC research programme on energy in agriculture, held in Brussels, Belgium, 10-11 October 1985] / [sponsored by the Commission of the European Communities, Directorate-General for Agriculture, Coordination of Agricultural Research] ; edited by J.-C. Sourie and L. Killen. — London : Elsevier Applied Science, c1986. — x,187p. — *Includes bibliographies*

BIOPOLITICS
Biology and bureaucracy : public administration and public policy from the perspective of evolutionary, genetic and neurobiological theory / edited by Elliott White and Joseph Losco. — Lanham ; London : University Press of America, 1987. — [652]p. — *Includes bibliography and index*

Politics and the life sciences: the journal of the Association for Politics and the Life Sciences. — Dekalb (Ill.) : Association for Politics and the Life Sciences, 1986-. — *Semi-annual*

BIOTECHNOLOGY
KENNEY, Martin
Biotechnology : the university-industrial complex / Martin Kenney. — New Haven ; London : Yale University Press, c1986. — xv,306p. — *Bibliography: p261-293. — Includes index*

BIOTECHNOLOGY — Developing countries
The Biotechnological challenge / [edited by] S. Jacobsson, A. Jamison, H. Rothman. — Cambridge : Cambridge University Press, 1986. — 181p. — *Includes bibliographies and index*

BIOTECHNOLOGY — Europe — Government policy
SHARP, Margaret, 1938-
The new biotechnology : European governments in search of a strategy / Margaret Sharp. — [Brighton] : Science Policy Research Unit, University of Sussex, c1985. — 149p. — (Sussex European paper ; no.15) (Industrial adjustment and policy ; 6). — *Bibliography: p135-140*

BIOTECHNOLOGY INDUSTRIES
KENNEY, Martin
Biotechnology : the university-industrial complex / Martin Kenney. — New Haven ; London : Yale University Press, c1986. — xv,306p. — *Bibliography: p261-293. — Includes index*

BIOTECHNOLOGY INDUSTRIES — Europe
SHARP, Margaret, 1938-
The new biotechnology : European governments in search of a strategy / Margaret Sharp. — [Brighton] : Science Policy Research Unit, University of Sussex, c1985. — 149p. — (Sussex European paper ; no.15) (Industrial adjustment and policy ; 6). — *Bibliography: p135-140*

BIRLA, G. D.
ROSS, Alan
The emissary : G.D. Birla, Gandhi and independence / Alan Ross. — London : Collins Harvill, 1986. — [288]p. — *Includes bibliography and index*

BIRTH CONTROL
DRAPER, Elizabeth
Birth control in the modern world : the role of the individual in population control / Elizabeth Draper. — Harmondsworth : Penguin, 1965. — 332p

HARRIS, Marvin
Death, sex, and fertility : population regulation in preindustrial and developing societies / Marvin Harris and Eric B. Ross. — New York : Columbia University Press, 1987. — p. cm. — *Incldues index. — Bibliography: p*

Population reports: Series J: family planning programs. — Washington, D.C. : George Washington University Medical Center - Population Information Program, 1986. — *5 times per year*

WHICKER, Marcia Lynn
Sex role changes : technology, politics, and policy / Marcia Lynn Whicker, Jennie Jacobs Kronenfeld. — New York : Praeger, 1985. — p. cm. — *Includes indexes. — Bibliography: p*

WORLD HEALTH ORGANIZATION. Regional Office for Europe
Training in family planning for health personnel : report on a W.H.O. meeting, Paris, 6-11 July 1981 / World Health Organization, Regional Office for Europe. — Copenhagen : World Health Organization, 1985. — 99p. — (Public health in Europe ; 20)

BIRTH CONTROL — Cross-cultural studies
KASARDA, John D
Status enhancement and fertility : reproductive responses to social mobility and educational opportunity / John D. Kasarda, John O.G. Billy, Kirsten West. — Orlando, Fla. : Academic Press, 1986. — xii, 266 p.. — (Studies in population). — *Includes indexes. — Bibliography: p.216-250*

Women's medicine : a cross-cultural study of indigenous fertility regulation / Lucile F. Newman, editor, with the assistance of James M. Nyce. — New Brunswick, N.J. : Rutgers University Press, c1985. — x, 203 p.. — (The Douglass series on women's lives and the meaning of gender). — *Includes bibliographies*

BIRTH CONTROL — Evaluation — Methodology
Evaluation of the impact of family planning programmes on fertility : sources of variance. — New York : United Nations, 1982. — xxi,290p. — (Population studies / Department of International Economic and Social Affairs ; no. 76). — *"A project of the Population Division of the Department of International Economic and Social Affairs of the United Nations Secretariat, in collaboration with the Committee for the Analysis of Family Planning Programmes of the International Union for the Scientific Study of Population.". — "Related to the work of the Second Expert Group Meeting on Methods of Measuring the Impact of Family Planning Programmes on Fertility, which was convened at Geneva, Switzerland, from 19 to 26 March 1979"--P. iii. — "ST/ESA/SER.A/76.". — "United Nations publication sales no. E.81.XIII.9"--Verso t.p. — Includes bibliographical references*

BIRTH CONTROL — Government policy — Louisiana
WARD, Martha Coonfield
Poor women, powerful men : America's great experiment in family planning / Martha C. Ward. — Boulder : Westview Press, 1986. — p. cm. — *Includes index. — Bibliography: p*

BIRTH CONTROL — Africa, Sub-Saharan
Population growth and policies in Sub-Saharan Africa. — Washington, D.C. : The World Bank, 1986. — x,102p. — (A World Bank policy study). — *Bibliography: p76-82*

BIRTH CONTROL — Africa, Subsaharan
FRANK, Odile
The demand for fertility control in Sub-Saharan Africa / Odile Frank. — New York : Population Council, 1985. — 50p. — (Working papers / Population Council. Center for Policy Studies ; no.117). — *Bibliography: p46-50*

BIRTH CONTROL — India
KANGAS, Georgia Lee
Population dilemma : India's struggle for survival / Georgia Lee Kangas. — New Delhi : Arnold-Heinemann, 1985. — 152 p.. — *Bibliography: p. [146]-150*

BIRTH CONTROL — India — Bibliography
Population and family planning in India : a select bibliography / compiled and edited by G. C. Kendadamath. — Gurgaon : Indian Documentation Service, 1985. — xxii,162p

BIRTH CONTROL — India — Congresses
PLANNING SEMINAR ON FAMILY WELFARE IN INDIA (1980 : Dhārwār, India)
Seminar on Family Welfare (Planning) in India / edited by A.P. Katti. — Dharwad : Population Research Centre, Institute of Economic Research, [1980]. — xviii, 222 p.. — *Includes statistical tables. — Includes bibliographical references*

BIRTH CONTROL — Indonesia — Bali (Province)
STREATFIELD, K
Fertility decline in a traditional society : the case of Bali / Kim Streatfield. — [Canberra, ACT] : Dept. of Demography, Australian National University : Distributed by Bibliotech, 1986. — xvii, 177 p.. — (Indonesian population monograph series ; no. 4). — *Bibliography: p. 161-173*

BIRTH CONTROL — Louisiana
WARD, Martha Coonfield
Poor women, powerful men : America's great experiment in family planning / Martha C. Ward. — Boulder : Westview Press, 1986. — p. cm. — *Includes index. — Bibliography: p*

BIRTH CONTROL — Pakistan
SOOMRO, Ghulam Yasin
Prevalence of knowledge and use of contraception in Pakistan / Ghulam Yasin Soomro [and] Syed Mubashir Ali. — Islamabad : Pakistan Institute of Development Economics, 1986. — 43,[1]p. — (Studies in population, labour force and migration project report ; no.3). — *Bibliography: p[44]*

BIRTH CONTROL — United States — History — Bibliography
MOORE, Gloria
Margaret Sanger and the birth control movement : a bibliography, 1911-1984 / by Gloria Moore and Ronald Moore. — Metuchen, N.J. : Scarecrow Press, 1986. — xvii, 211 p.. — *Includes indexes. — Bibliography: xi-xii*

BIRTH INTERVALS — Great Britain
NEWELL, Marie-Louise
The next job after the first baby : occupational transition among women born in 1946 / Marie-Louise and Heather Joshi. — London : London School of Hygiene and Tropical Medicine, 1986. — 68p. — (CPS research paper ; 86-3). — *Bibliography: p37-38*

BIRTH INTERVALS — Jordan
ABDEL-AZIZ, Abdallah
A study of birth intervals in Jordan / Abdallah Abdel-Aziz. — Voorburg : International Statistical Institute, 1983. — 33p. — (Scientific reports / World Fertility Survey ; no.46)

BISERICA ORTODOXA ROMANA — History
PĂCURARIU, Mircea
Politica statului ungar față de Biserica românească din Transilvania în perioada dualismului (1867-1918) / Mircea Păcurariu. — Sibiu : Editura Institutului Biblic și de Misiune al Bisericii Ortodoxe Române, 1986. — 301p

BISMARCK, OTTO, Fürst von
EYCK, Erich
Bismarck and the German empire / Erich Eyck. — 3rd ed. — London : Allen and Unwin, 1968. — x,327p

GALL, Lothar
Bismarck : the white revolutionary / Lothar Gall ; translated from the German by J.A. Underwood. — London : Allen & Unwin. — *Translation of: Bismarck. — Originally published under the title, Bismarck der weiss Revolutionaär, Frankfurt am Main : Ullstein, 1980*
Vol.1: 1815-1871. — 1986. — [640]p. — *Includes bibliography and index*

GALL, Lothar
Bismarck : the white revolutionary / Lothar Gall ; translated from the German by J.A. Underwood. — London : Allen & Unwin
Vol.2: 1871-1898. — 1987. — [384]p. — *Translation of: Bismarck. — Includes bibliography and index*

STERN, Fritz Richard
Gold and iron : Bismarck, Bleichroder and the building of the German empire / Fritz R. Stern. — London : Allen and Unwin, 1977. — 620p

BISMARK, OTTO, Fürst von
ENGELBERG, Ernst
Bismarck : Urpreusse und Reichsgründer / Ernst Engelberg. — Berlin : Siedler, 1985. — xvi,839p

BITBURG (GERMANY) — Addresses, essays, lectures
Bitburg in moral and political perspective / edited by Geoffrey H. Hartman. — Bloomington : Indiana University Press, c1986. — xvi, 284 p.. — *Bibliography: p. [281]-282*

BLACK ENGLISH — United States
Black English : educational equity and the law / edited by John W. Chambers, Jr. ; with a foreword by Julian Bond. — Ann Arbor, Mich. : Karoma, 1983. — xiv,170p

BLACK FAMILIES — United States
WILLIE, Charles Vert
Black and white families : a study in complementarity / Charles Vert Willie. — New York : General Hall, 1985. — v,308p — *Bibliographies*

BLACK MARKET
MATTERA, Philip
Off the books : the rise of the underground economy / Philip Mattera. — London : Pluto, 1985. — [v,160]p. — *Includes bibliography and index*

BLACK MARKET — Great Britain
GREAT BRITAIN. Parliament. House of Commons. Library. Research Division
The black economy / Jennifer Tanfield. — [London] : the Division, 1984. — 10p. — (Background paper ; no.151). — *Bibliographical references: p9-10*

BLACK MILITANT ORGANIZATIONS — France
DEWITTE, Philippe
Les mouvements nègres en France 1919-1939 / Philippe Dewitte. — Paris : Editions L'Harmattan, [1985]. — 416p. — *Bibliography: p396-405*

BLACK MUSLIMS
MROZEK, Anna
Social functions of black Islam / Anna Mrozek. — Warsaw : Polish Academy of Sciences. Center for Studies on Non-European Countries, 1984. — 41p. — *Bibliography: p39-41*

BLACK MUSLIMS — Biography
The black book : the true political philosophy of Malcolm X (El Hajj Malik el Shabazz / edited and compiled by Y. N. Kly. — Ottawa ; Atlanta : Clarity Press, 1986. — viii,91p. — *Bibliography: p89-91*

BLACK MUSLIMS — United States
X, Malcolm
The autobiography of Malcolm X / with the assistance of Alex Haley. — Harmondsworth : Penguin, by arrangement with Hutchinson of London, 1968. — 512p

BLACK NATIONALISM
The black book : the true political philosophy of Malcolm X (El Hajj Malik el Shabazz / edited and compiled by Y. N. Kly. — Ottawa ; Atlanta : Clarity Press, 1986. — viii,91p. — *Bibliography: p89-91*

BLACK NATIONALISM — United States
X, Malcolm
The autobiography of Malcolm X / with the assistance of Alex Haley. — Harmondsworth : Penguin, by arrangement with Hutchinson of London, 1968. — 512p

BLACK NATIONALISM — United States — History
STEIN, Judith
The world of Marcus Garvey : race and class in modern society / Judith Stein. — Baton Rouge ; London : Louisiana State University Press, c1986. — xii, 294p. — *Includes index. — Bibliography: p.281-284*

BLACK POWER
BOGGS, James
Racism and the class struggle : further pages from a black worker's notebook. — New York : [Monthly Review Press, 1970]. — 190 p

CARMICHAEL, Stokely
Black power : the politics of liberation in America / [by] Stokely Carmichael & Charles V. Hamilton. — New York : Random House, [1967]. — xii, 198 p. — *Bibliography: p. 187-189*

BLACK THEOLOGY
KRETZSCHMAR, Louise
The voice of black theology in South Africa / Louise Kretzschmar. — Johannesburg : Ravan Press, 1986. — xiii,136p. — *Bibliography: p [116]-134*

BLACKBURN (LANCASHIRE) — Social life and customs
LEWIS, Brian, 1965-
Life in a cotton town : Blackburn, 1818-48 / Brian Lewis. — [Preston] ([24 Ribblesdale Place, Preston PR1 3NA]) : Carnegie, c1985. — 64p

BLACKS
MYRDAL, Gunnar
Value in social theory : a selection of essays on methodology / by Gunnar Myrdal ; edited by Paul Streeten. — London : Routledge and Kegan Paul, 1958. — (International library of sociology and social reconstruction)

BLACKS — Civil rights — South Africa
Urban black law : being a series of articles by a team of authors, first published in Acta Juridica 1984 / editorial board: T. W. Bennett...[et al.]. — Cape Town : Juta, 1985. — x,269p

BLACKS — Education — Great Britain
Towards the decolonization of the British education system / Amon Saba Saakana, Adetokunbo Pearse, editors. — London : Frontline Journal : Karnak House, 1986. — 128p. — *Includes bibliographies*

BLACKS — Education — South Africa
Black advancement in the South African economy / edited by Roy Smollan. — Basingstoke : Macmillam, 1986. — 256p. — *Bibliography: p243-250*

BLACKS — Employment — Law and legislation — South Africa
Urban black law : being a series of articles by a team of authors, first published in Acta Juridica 1984 / editorial board: T. W. Bennett...[et al.]. — Cape Town : Juta, 1985. — x,269p

BLACKS — Employment — South Africa
Black advancement in the South African economy / edited by Roy Smollan. — Basingstoke : Macmillam, 1986. — 256p. — *Bibliography: p243-250*

BLONDEL, Alain
The parrot's egg / Alain Blondel and Shena Lamb ; photographs by Ali Hashemian. — Johannesburg : Ravan Press, 1985. — 159p. — *Bibliography: p158-159*

SCHNEIER, Steffen
Occupational mobility among Blacks in South Africa / Steffen Schneier. — Cape Town : Southern Africa Labour and Development Research Unit, [1983]. — vi, 219 p.. — (Saldru working paper ; no. 58). — *"November 1983."*. — *Bibliography: p. 214-219*

BLACKS — Services for — Great Britain — Case studies
PANEL TO PROMOTE THE CONTINUING DEVELOPMENT OF TRAINING FOR PART-TIME AND VOLUNTARY YOUTH AND COMMUNITY WORKERS
Working with black youth : complementary or competing perspectives? / the report of the Panel to Promote the Continuing Development of Training for Part-time and Voluntary Youth and Community Workers ; written by Gus John and Nigel Parkes. — Leicester : National Youth Bureau, 1984. — 11p. — (Extension report ; no.2). — *Bibliography: p11*

BLACKS — Africa — Religion
Theoretical explorations in African religion / edited by Wim van Binsbergen and Matthew Schoffeleers. — London : KPI, 1985. — x,389p. — (Monographs from the African Studies Centre, Leiden). — *Includes bibliographies and index*

BLACKS — Africa, Sub-Saharan — Psychology
KRIEL, Abraham
Roots of African thought / Abraham Kriel. — Cape Town : A.A. Balkema, 1984-. — v. <1 >. — *Bibliography: v. 1, p. 165-168*. — *Contents: 1. Manipulating actions*

BLACKS — England
KING, Michael, 1942-
Black magistrates : a study of selection and appointment / by Michael King and Colin May. — London : Cobden Trust, 1985. — 198p. — *Includes bibliography*

BLACKS — England — London
HOWES, Eileen
Black and ethic minority population estimates / Eileen Howes. — Hackney : London Borough of Hackney. Research and Intelligence Section. Chief Executive's Office, 1986. — 27p. — (Research note / Hackney. Chief Executive's Office. Research and Intelligence Section ; 10). — *At head of cover title: Research in Hacknry*

The London Labour plan : black workers. — London : London Strategic Policy Unit, 1986. — 51p. — *Bibliography: p49*

TIPLER, Jonathan
Is justice colour blind? : a study of the impact of race in the juvenile justice system in Hackney / Jonathan Tipler. — Hackney : London Borough of Hackney. Directorate of Social Services. Research, Development and Programming, 1985. — 25p. — (Social services research note / Hackney. Directorate of Social Services. Research, Development and Programming ; 6). — *At head of cover title: Research in Hackney*

BLACKS — England — London — Political activity
ACKERS, Helen Louise
Racism and political marginalisation in the metropolis : the relationship between black people and the Labour Party in London / Louise Ackers. — 280 leaves. — *Labour Party leaflet and 'Anti-racism action sheets' are in end pocket.* — *PhD (Econ) 1986 LSE.* — *Leaves 240-261 are appendices*

BLACKS — England — London — Social conditions
ACKERS, Helen Louise
Racism and political marginalisation in the metropolis : the relationship between black people and the Labour Party in London / Louise Ackers. — 280 leaves. — *Labour Party leaflet and 'Anti-racism action sheets' are in end pocket.* — *PhD (Econ) 1986 LSE.* — *Leaves 240-261 are appendices*

BLACKS — France — History — 20th century
DEWITTE, Philippe
Les mouvements nègres en France 1919-1939 / Philippe Dewitte. — Paris : Editions L'Harmattan, [1985]. — 416p. — *Bibliography: p396-405*

BLACKS — Great Britain
Black and in care: conference report (report of a conference organized by the Black and In Care Steering Group held in October 1984). — London : Black and In Care Steering Group, 1985. — 45p

BLACK WORKERS' PLANNING GROUP
Black workers in the north west : a report of a conference held on 3rd November 1984. — Manchester : Black Workers' Planning Group, 1984. — 19p

BLACKS — Great Britain — Education
RUNNYMEDE TRUST
Education for some : a summary of the Eggleston Report on the educational and vocational experiences of young black people. — London : Runnymede Trust, 1986. — iv,57p

BLACKS — Great Britain — Language
The Language of the black experience : cultural expression through word and sound in the Caribbean and black Britain / edited by David Sutcliffe and Ansel Wong. — Oxford : Blackwell, 1986. — x,214p. — *Bibliography: p.192-207.* — *Includes index*

BLACKS — Great Britain — Political activity
FITZGERALD, Marian
Black people and party politics in Britain / Marian Fitzgerald. — London : Runnymede Trust, 1987. — 51p. — (Runnymede research report)

BLACKS — Great Britain — Politics and government
HOWE, Darcus
Black sections in the Labour Party / Darcus Howe. — London : Race Today Publications, 1985. — 16p

BLACKS — Haiti
GARRETT, Mitchell Bennett
The French colonial question 1789-1791 : dealings of the constituent assembly with problems arising from the revolution in the West Indies / by Mitchell Bennett Garrett. — New York : Negro Universities Press, 1970. — iv,167p. — *Reprint of 1916 edition.* — *Bibliography: p[135]-160*

BLACKS — Panama — History — 20th century
CONNIFF, Michael L
Black labor on a white canal : Panama, 1904-1981 / Michael L. Conniff. — Pittsburgh : University of Pittsburgh Press, 1985. — p. cm . — *Includes index.* — *Bibliography: p*

BLACKS — South Africa
BADSHA, Omar
Imijondolo : a photographic essay on forced removals in South Africa / Omar Badsha ; text by Heather Hughes ; foreword by Bishop Desmond Tutu. — Johannesburg : Afrapix, 1985. — 78p

BLACKS — South Africa — Biography
TOM, Petrus
My life struggle : the story of Petrus Tom. — Braamfontein, South Africa : Ravan Press, 1985. — 68 p., [1] leaf of plates. — (Ravan worker series)

BLACKS — South Africa — Civil rights
South Africa : a plural society in transition / editors, D.J. van Vuuren ... [et al.]. — Durban ; Stoneham, MA : Butterworths, c1985. — 510 p. — *Includes bibliographies and index*

BLACKS — South Africa — Economic conditions
ORKIN, Mark
Disinvestment, the struggle, and the future : what black South Africans really think / Mark Orkin. — Johannesburg : Ravan Press, 1986. — xii, 78 p.. — *A CASE/IBR study.* — *Includes bibliographies and index*

BLACKS — South Africa — History
CORNEVIN, Marianne
Apartheid : power and historical falsification / Marianne Cornevin. — Paris : Unesco, 1980. — 144 p.. — (Insights). — *Bibliography: p. [139]-144*

BLACKS — South Africa — Politics and government
FATTON, Robert
Black consciousness in South Africa : the dialectics of ideological resistance to white supremacy / Robert Fatton, Jr. — Albany : State University of New York Press, c1986. — ix, 189 p.. — (SUNY series in African politics and society). — : *Revision of the author's thesis (Ph.D.)--University of Notre Dame.* — *Includes index.* — *Bibliography: p. 171-185*

TATZ, Colin Martin
Shadow and substance in South Africa : a study in land and franchise policies affecting Africans, 1910-1960 / Colin Tatz. — Pietermaritzburg : University of Natal Press, 1962. — vi,238p

BLACKS — South Africa — Race identity
FATTON, Robert
Black consciousness in South Africa : the dialectics of ideological resistance to white supremacy / Robert Fatton, Jr. — Albany : State University of New York Press, c1986. — ix, 189 p.. — (SUNY series in African politics and society). — : *Revision of the author's thesis (Ph.D.)--University of Notre Dame.* — *Includes index.* — *Bibliography: p. 171-185*

BLACKS — South Africa — Religion
KRETZSCHMAR, Louise
The voice of black theology in South Africa / Louise Kretzschmar. — Johannesburg : Ravan Press, 1986. — xiii,136p. — *Bibliography: p [116]-134*

BLACKS — South Africa — Relocation
PLATZKY, Laurine
The surplus people : forced removals in South Africa / Laurine Platzky and Cherryl Walker for the Surplus People Project. — Johannesburg : Ravan Press, 1985. — xxxiii, 446 p., [12] p. of plates. — *Includes index.* — *Bibliography: p. [404]-408*

BLACKS — South Africa — Relocation — History — 20th century
UNTERHALTER, Elaine
Forced removal : the division, segregation and control of the people of South Africa / Elaine Unterhalter. — London : International Defence and Aid Fund for Southern Africa, 1987. — viii,177p,[8]p of plates. — *Bibliography: p156-167.* — *Includes index*

BLACKS — South Africa — Segregation
Apartheid in crises / edited by Mark A. Uhlig. — Harmondsworth : Penguin Books, 1986. — viii,334p

DANAHER, Kevin
In whose interest? : a guide to U.S.-South Africa relations / Kevin Danaher. — 1st ed. — Washington, D.C. : Institute for Policy Studies, c1985. — p. cm. — *Includes index.* — *Bibliography: p*

LOUW, Leon
South Africa, the solution / Leon Louw and Frances Kendall. — Bisho, Ciskei : Amagi, [1986]. — xvi,237p. — *Bibliography: p235-237*

SMITH, David M. (David Marshall)
Update : apartheid in South Africa / David M. Smith. — London : Dept. of Geography and Earth Science, Queen Mary College, 1983. — 76p. — (Special publication / Queen Mary College, Department of Geography and Earth Science ; 6). — *Bibliography: p. 74-76*

BLACKS — South Africa — Social conditions
Black advancement in the South African economy / edited by Roy Smollan. — Basingstoke : Macmillam, 1986. — 256p. — *Bibliography: p243-250*

FATTON, Robert
Black consciousness in South Africa : the dialectics of ideological resistance to white supremacy / Robert Fatton, Jr. — Albany : State University of New York Press, c1986. — ix, 189 p.. — (SUNY series in African politics and society). — : *Revision of the author's thesis (Ph.D.)--University of Notre Dame.* — *Includes index.* — *Bibliography: p. 171-185*

BLACKS — South Africa — Natal
ROBBINS, David
Inside the last outpost / David Robbins, Wyndham Hartley. — 1st ed. — Pietermaritzburg [South Africa] : Shuter & Shooter, 1985. — 198 p.. — *Bibliography: p. 196-198*

BLACKS IN ART — Congresses
Blacks and German culture : essays / edited by Reinhold Grimm and Jost Hermand. — Madison, Wis. : Published for Monatshefte [by] University of Wisconsin Press, 1986. — vii, 184 p.. — (Monatshefte occasional volumes ; no. 4) . — : *Revised and enlarged papers read at the 15th Wisconsin Workshop, held at the University of Wisconsin-Madison Oct. 5-6, 1984.* — *Includes bibliographies*

BLACKS IN LITERATURE — Congresses
Blacks and German culture : essays / edited by Reinhold Grimm and Jost Hermand. — Madison, Wis. : Published for Monatshefte [by] University of Wisconsin Press, 1986. — vii, 184 p.. — (Monatshefte occasional volumes ; no. 4) . — : *Revised and enlarged papers read at the 15th Wisconsin Workshop, held at the University of Wisconsin-Madison Oct. 5-6, 1984.* — *Includes bibliographies*

BLEICHRODER, GERSON VON
STERN, Fritz Richard
Gold and iron : Bismarck, Bleichroder and the building of the German empire / Fritz R. Stern. — London : Allen and Unwin, 1977. — 620p

BLOCK GRANTS — England
Understanding block grant : guide and glossary / Association of County Councils. — 1985-86-. — London (66a Eaton Sq., SW1H 9BH) : The Association, 1985-. — v.. — *Annual*

BLUMENFELD, HANS — Congresses
The Metropolis : proceedings of a conference in honour of Hans Blumenfeld, University of Toronto, November 4-5, 1983 / edited by John R. Hitchcock, Anne McMaster, with the assistance of Judith Kjellberg. — [Toronto] : Dept. of Geography and Centre for Urban and Community Studies, University of Toronto, c1985. — 249 p.. — *"The writings of Hans Blumenfeld": p. 241-249.* — *Includes bibliographies*

BLUNT, ANTHONY
PENROSE, Barrie
Conspiracy of silence : the secret life of Anthony Blunt / Barrie Penrose and Simon Freeman. — London : Grafton, 1986. — xix,588p,[20]p of plates. — *Bibliography: p565-567.* — *Includes index*

BMDP (COMPUTER SYSTEM)
HILL, MaryAnn
BMDP user's digest : a condensed guide to the BMDP computer programs / MaryAnn Hill. — 3rd ed. — Los Angeles : BMDP Statistical Software, 1984. — 177p

BOARD OF GOVERNORS OF THE FEDERAL RESERVE SYSTEM (U.S.)
Central bankers, bureaucratic incentives, and monetary policy / editors, Eugenia Froedge Toma, Mark Toma. — Dordrecht ; Boston : Martinus Nijhoff, 1987. — p. cm. — (Financial and monetary policy studies ; v. 13)

KETTL, Donald F
Leadership at the Fed / Donald F. Kettl. — New Haven ; London : Yale University Press, c1986. — xiii, 218p. — *Includes index*

BOARD OF GOVERNORS OF THE FEDERAL RESERVE SYSTEM (U.S.)
BOARD OF GOVERNORS OF THE FEDERAL RESERVE SYSTEM (U.S.)
Annual report / Board of Governors of the Federal Reserve System (U.S.). — Washington, D.C. : [the Board], 1985-. — *Annual*

BODICHON, BARBARA LEIGH SMITH
HERSTEIN, Sheila R
A mid-Victorian feminist, Barbara Leigh Smith Bodichon / Sheila R. Herstein. — New Haven : Yale University Press, c1985. — p. cm. — : *Revision of thesis (doctoral)--City University of New York.* — *Includes index.* — *Bibliography: p*

BODIN, JEAN
COLLOQUE INTERDISCIPLINAIRE 'JEAN BODIN' &K1984 (Angers)
Jean Bodin : actes .... — [S.l.] : Presses de LÙniversite DAngers, 1985. — 2v

BODY, HUMAN — Social aspects — United States
SCHWARTZ, Hillel
Never satisified : a cultural history of diets, fantasies, and fat / Hillel Schwartz. — New York : Free Press ; London : Collier Macmillan, c1986. — p. cm. — *Bibliography: p*

BODY IMAGE
SCHWARTZ, Hillel
Never satisified : a cultural history of diets, fantasies, and fat / Hillel Schwartz. — New York : Free Press ; London : Collier Macmillan, c1986. — p. cm. — *Bibliography: p*

BOER WAR, 1899-1902 *See* South African War, 1899-1902

BOGOTÁ (COLOMBIA) — Economic conditions
MOHAN, Rakesh
Work, wages, and welfare in a developing, metropolis : some consequences of growth in Bogotá, Colombia / by Rakesh Mohan. — Washington, D.C. : World Bank, 1986. — xi,403p. — *Bibliographical references: p382-395*

BOGOTÁ (COLOMBIA) — History
BRAUN, Herbert
The assassination of Gaitán : public life and urban violence in Colombia / Herbert Braun. — Madison, Wis. : University of Wisconsin Press, 1985. — xiii, 282p. — *Includes index.* — *Bibliography: p.257-271*

BOHEMIAN FLATS (MINNEAPOLIS, MINN.) — Social life and customs
The Bohemian Flats / compiled by the workers of the Writers' Program of the Work Projects Administration in the State of Minnesota ; with an introduction by Thaddeus Radzilowsky. — St. Paul : Minnesota Historical Society Press, 1986. — p. cm. — (Borealis books). — : *Reprint. Originally published: Minneapolis : University of Minnesota Press, 1941. With new introd. and index.* — *Bibliography: p[189]-203*

BOHEMIANISM — France — Paris — History — 19th century
SEIGEL, Jerrold E.
Bohemian Paris : culture, politics, and the boundaries of bourgeois life, 1830-1930 / Jerrold Seigel. — New York, N.Y., U.S.A. : Viking, 1986. — ix, 453 p.. — "Elisabeth Sifton books.". — *Includes index.* — *Bibliography: p. 405-440*

BOHR, NIELS
Niels Bohr : a centenary volume / edited by A.P.French and P.J.Kennedy. — Cambridge, Mass. ; London : Harvard University Press, 1985

BOLIVIA — Politics and government — 1879-1938
KNUDSON, Jerry W
Rolivia, press and revolution, 1932-1964 / by Jerry W. Knudson. — Lanham, MD : University Press of America, c1986. — x, 488p. — *Includes bibliographical footnotes and index*

BOLIVIA — Politics and government — 1938-1952
KNUDSON, Jerry W
Bolivia, press and revolution, 1932-1964 / by Jerry W. Knudson. — Lanham, MD : University Press of America, c1986. — x, 488p. — *Includes bibliographical footnotes and index*

BOLIVIA — Politics and government — 1952-1982
KNUDSON, Jerry W
Bolivia, press and revolution, 1932-1964 / by Jerry W. Knudson. — Lanham, MD : University Press of America, c1986. — x, 488p. — *Includes bibliographical footnotes and index*

BOLIVIA — Rural conditions
HAVET, José
The diffusion of power : rural elites in a Bolivian province / José Havet. — Ottawa : University of Ottawa Press, 1985. — xvi,156p. — (International Development ; 3). — *Bibliography: p145-150*

BOLIVIAN NEWSPAPERS — History — 20th century
KNUDSON, Jerry W
Bolivia, press and revolution, 1932-1964 / by Jerry W. Knudson. — Lanham, MD : University Press of America, c1986. — x, 488p. — *Includes bibliographical footnotes and index*

BOLLISHE MISSILE DEFENSES — United States
PAYNE, Keith B
Strategic defense : "star wars" in perspective / [by Keith B. Payne ; foreword by Zbigniew Brzezinski]. — Lanham, MD : Hamilton Press, c1986. — xviii, 250 p. — *Includes bibliographies and index*

BOLOGNA (ITALY) — Politics and government
ANDERLINI, Fausto
Territorio e comportamento e lettorale : una analisi delle regionali '85 e delle politiche '83 nei communi dell'Emilia-Romagna e nella città di Bologna / Fausto Anderlini. — Bologna : Servizio Studi e Programmazione, Assessorato Programmazione, 1986. — 157p. — *Includes 10 folded maps*

BOMBAY (INDIA) — Social conditions
JHA, S. S.
Structure of urban poverty : the case of Bombay slums / S. S. Jha. — London : Sangam Books, 1986. — xvii,184p

BOMBING INVESTIGATION — England — Guildford (Surrey)
KEE, Robert
Trial and error : the Maguires, the Guildford pub bombings and British justice / Robert Kee. — London : Hamish Hamilton, 1986. — 284p. — *Includes index*

BOMBINGS — England — Birmingham (West Midlands) — History — 20th century
MULLIN, Chris
Error of judgment : the Birmingham bombings / by Chris Mullin. — London : Chatto & Windus, 1986. — [224]p

BOND, JAMES (FICTITIOUS CHARACTER)
BENNETT, Tony
Bond and beyond : the political career of a popular hero / Tony Bennett and Janet Woollacott. — Basingstoke : Macmillan Education, 1987. — xi,315p. — (Communications and culture). — *Includes index*

BONUZZI, PIERRE
Pierre Bonuzzi 1908-1970. — Zurich : Les Archives Sociales Suisses, 1973. — 67p

BOOK DESIGN
NATIONAL BOOK DEVELOPMENT COUNCIL OF SINGAPORE
Report : training seminar on book design and illustration 1980 / National Book Development Council of Singapore. — Singapore : the Council, c1980. — 51p

BOOK INDUSTRIES AND TRADE
Book trade year book / Publishers Association. — London : Publishhers Association, 1985-. — *Annual*

BOOK INDUSTRIES AND TRADE — Management
BAILEY, Herbert Smith
The art and science of book publishing / Herbert S. Bailey. — New York : Harper and Row, [1970]. — xii,216p. — *Bibliography: p203-208*

BOOK INDUSTRIES AND TRADE — Commonwealth of Nations
COMMOMWEALTH SECRETARIAT
Training for book development : incorporating a directory of Commonwealth opportunities for the training of book personnel. — London : the Secretariat, c1973. — vii,52p

BOOK INDUSTRIES AND TRADE — Soviet Union
Kniga i sotsial′nyi progress / otv. redaktor N. M. Sikorskii. — Moskva : Nauka, 1986. — 227p. — *Kniga podgotovlennaia po materialam Piatoi Vsesoiuznoi nauchnoi konferentsii po knigovedeniiu (Moskva, 1984)*

BOOK REVIEWING
Reviews and reviewing : a guide / edited by A.J. Walford. — London : Mansell, 1986. — [208]p. — *Includes index*

BOOK SELECTION
Selection of library materials in the humanities, social sciences, and sciences / Patricia A. McClung, editor ; section editors, William Hepfer ... [et al.]. — Chicago : American Library Association, 1985. — xiv, 405 p.. — *Includes bibliographies and index*

SPILLER, David
Book selection : an introduction to principles and practice / David Spiller ; with an introduction by Brian Baumfield. — 4th ed. — London : Bingley, 1986. — ix,235p. — *Previous ed.: 1980. — Bibliography: p206-223. — Includes index*

BOOKS — History — Dictionaries
FEATHER, John
A dictionary of book history / John Feather. — London : Croom Helm, c1986. — [288]p

BOOKS — Purchasing — Statistics
NEW ZEALAND BOOK TRADE ORGANISATION
Survey of book buying in New Zealand / New Zealand Book Trade Organisation. — Wellington, N.Z. : the Organisation, 1976. — 34p

BOOKS — France — Prices
L'évolution des librairies et le prix unique du livre / Edith Archambault [and others]. — [Paris] : La Documentation française, [1987]. — 171p. — *Bibliography: p129-130*

BOOKS — Great Britain — Conservation and restoration
ANDERSON, Hazel
Planning manual for disaster control in Scottish libraries & record offices / Hazel Anderson, John E. McIntyre. — Edinburgh : National Library of Scotland, 1985. — 75p. — *Bibliography: p71-72. — Includes index*

BOOKS — Great Britain — Mutilation, defacement, etc.
ANDERSON, Hazel
Planning manual for disaster control in Scottish libraries & record offices / Hazel Anderson, John E. McIntyre. — Edinburgh : National Library of Scotland, 1985. — 75p. — *Bibliography: p71-72. — Includes index*

BOOKS — Great Britain — Prices
Average prices of British academic books / Centre for Library and Information Management, Loughborough University of Technology. — Loughborough : Publications Department. Centre for Library Information Management, Loughborough University of Technology, 1986-. — *Semi-annual*

BOOKS — New Zealand — Statistics
NEW ZEALAND BOOK TRADE ORGANISATION
Survey of book buying in New Zealand / New Zealand Book Trade Organisation. — Wellington, N.Z. : the Organisation, 1976. — 34p

BOOKS — Soviet Union
Kniga i sotsial′nyi progress / otv. redaktor N. M. Sikorskii. — Moskva : Nauka, 1986. — 227p. — *Kniga podgotovlennaia po materialam Piatoi Vsesoiuznoi nauchnoi konferentsii po knigovedeniiu (Moskva, 1984)*

BOOKS — Sweden — History
LINDBERG, Sten G.
Svenska böcker 1483-1983 : bokhistoria i f°agelperspektiv / Sten G. Lindberg. — Stockholm : Bokbranschens marknadsinst, [1983]. — 61p

BOOKS AND READING — Addresses, essays, lectures
SALISBURY, Harrison Evans
The book enchained / Harrison E. Salisbury. — Washington : Library of Congress, 1984. — 9p. — (The Center for the Book viewpoint series ; 10). — *"A lecture sponsored by The Center for the Book in the Library of Congress and the Authors League of America; presented at the Library of Congress September 28, 1983."*

BOOKS AND READING — Soviet Union — History
BROOKS, Jeffrey
When Russia learned to read : literacy and popular literature, 1861-1917 / Jeffrey Brooks. — Princeton, N.J. : Princeton University Press, c1985. — xxii, 450 p.. — *Includes index. — Bibliography: p. 415-435*

BOOKSELLERS AND BOOKSELLING — France
L'évolution des librairies et le prix unique du livre / Edith Archambault [and others]. — [Paris] : La Documentation française, [1987]. — 171p. — *Bibliography: p129-130*

LINDON, Jérome
La FNAC et les livres / Jérome Lindon. — Paris : Editions de Minuit, 1978. — 16p

BOOKSELLERS AND BOOKSELLING — Great Britain — Directories
GERALD COE
Small booksellers directory 1966. — Wilbarston : Gerald Coe, 1966. — 60p

BOOKSELLERS AND BOOKSELLING — Latin America
BLOCK, David
Directory of vendors of Latin American library materials / David Block [and] Howard L. Karno. — 2nd ed.. — Madison : University of Wisconsin-Madison, 1986. — 46p. — (Seminar on the acquisition of Latin American library materials bibliography and reference series ; 16)

BOOKSELLERS AND BOOKSELLING — London (England) — Directories
GERALD COE
Coe′s guide to London bookshops. — Wilbarston : Gerald Coe, 1967. — (xii),44,(xvi)p

BOOKSELLERS AND BOOKSELLING — Sweden — History
MENNANDER, Carl Fridric
Tal om bok-handeln i Sverige, hållit för Kongl. Vetenskaps Academien vid Praesidii afl°aggande, den 8 Maji, 1756 / af Carl Fridric Mennander ; efterskrift, Hans Küntzel. — [s.l. : Almqvist & Wiksell, 1968]. — 29(2)p. — *Facsimile reprint of original published in 1756 by the Kongl. Vetenskaps Academien*

BOPHUTHATSWANA (AFRICAN PEOPLE) — Social life and customs
SCHAPERA, Isaac
The Tswana : by I. Schapera / with a supplementary chapter by John L. Comaroff ; and a supplementary bibliography by Adam Kuper. — London : KPI in association with the International African Institute, 1984. — 93p

BORA-BORA (SOCIETY ISLANDS) — Population — Statistics
Tableaux normalisés du recensement général de la population : 15 octobre 1983. — [Papeete] : Institut territorial de la statistique

BORIS III, King of Bulgaria
DIMITROFF, Pashanko
Boris III of Bulgaria : toiler, citizen, king, 1894-1943 / Pashanko Dimitroff. — Lewes : Book Guild, 1986. — 202p

BOROUGH (LONDON, ENGLAND) — Social conditions
BOULTON, J. P.
Neighbourhood and society : a London suburb in the seventeenth century / J.P. Boulton. — Cambridge : Cambridge University Press, 1987. — [352]p. — (Cambridge studies in population, economy and society in past time ; 5). — *Includes bibliography and index*

BOSTON (MASS.) — Commerce — History — 18th century
TYLER, John W.
Smugglers & patriots : Boston merchants and the advent of the American Revolution / John W. Tyler. — Boston : Northeastern University Press, c1986. — xiv, 349p. — *Includes index. — Bibliography: p 319-335*

BOSTON (MASS.) — History — Revolution, 1775-1783 — Economic aspects
TYLER, John W.
Smugglers & patriots : Boston merchants and the advent of the American Revolution / John W. Tyler. — Boston : Northeastern University Press, c1986. — xiv, 349p. — *Includes index. — Bibliography: p 319-335*

BOSTON (MASS.) — Race relations
LUKAS, J. Anthony
Common ground : a turbulent decade in the lives of three American Families / J. Anthony Lukas. — New York : Vintage Books, 1986. — xiv,674p. — *Originally published: New York : Random House, 1985*

BOTHA, PIETER WILLEM
DE VILLIERS, Dirk
PW / Dirk en Johanna de Villiers. — Kaapstad : Tafelberg, 1984. — 376p

BOTSWANA — Census, 1981
1981 population and housing census : guide to the villages and towns of Botswana. — Gaborone : Central Statistics Office, [1983]. — 1 vol.(various pagings)

1981 population and housing census : census administrative/technical report and national statistical tables. — Gaborone : Central Statistics Office, [1983]. — 1 vol. (various pagings)

BOTSWANA — Commerce
HUBBARD, Michael
Agricultural exports and economic growth : a study of the Botswana beef industry / Michael Hubbard. — London : KPI, 1986. — xx,284p

BOTSWANA — Economic conditions
Country profile : Botswana 1985. — Gaborone : Central Statistics Office, 1986. — 114p

RODEN, Hanne
The World Bank : introduction to its involvement in urbanisation in the 3rd World : the care of Botswana / Hanne Roden. — Copenhagen : [s.n.], 1984. — 186p

BOTSWANA — Economic conditions — 1966-
HUBBARD, Michael
Agricultural exports and economic growth : a study of the Botswana beef industry / Michael Hubbard. — London : KPI, 1986. — xx,284p

BOTSWANA — Foreign relations — South Africa
NYELELE, Libero
The raid on Gaborone : June 14, 1985, a memorial / Libero Nyelele and Ellen Drake. — Gaborone : Nyelele and Drake, 1985. — 39p

BOTSWANA — Social conditions
Country profile : Botswana 1985. — Gaborone : Central Statistics Office, 1986. — 114p

BOUNDARIES
PRESCOTT, J. R. V.
Political frontiers and boundaries / J.R.V. Prescott. — London : Allen & Unwin, 1987. — [320]p. — *Some material based on: Boundaries and frontiers. London : Croom Helm, 1978. — Includes bibliography and index*

BOUNDARIES — Legal status, laws, etc.
SCHOFIELD, Richard N.
Evolution of the Shatt al-'Arab boundary dispute / by Richard N. Schofield. — Wisbech : Middle East and North African Studies Press, 1986. — viii,111p. — *Bibliography: p87-94*

BOUNDARIES — Political aspects
Maritime boundaries and ocean resources / edited by Gerald Blake ; International Geographical Union Study Group on the World Political Map. — London : Croom Helm, c1987. — 284p. — *Bibliography: p257-271. — Includes index*

BOY SCOUTS — Biography
ROSENTHAL, Michael
The character factory : Baden-Powell and the origins of the Boy Scout movement / Michael Rosenthal. — New York : Pantheon Books, 1986. — p. cm. — *Includes index*

BOY SCOUTS — History
ROSENTHAL, Michael
The character factory : Baden-Powell and the origins of the Boy Scout movement / Michael Rosenthal. — New York : Pantheon Books, 1986. — p. cm. — *Includes index*

BOYES, GEORGE THOMAS WILLIAM BLAMEY
The diaries and letters of G. T. W. B. Boyes. — Melbourne ; Auckland : Oxford University Press. — *Bibliography: p647-657*
vol.1: 1820-1832 / edited by Peter Chapman. — 1985. — xxvi,692p

BOYS — Psychology — Longitudinal studies
GREEN, Richard
The "sissy boy syndrome" and the development of homosexuality / Richard Green. — New Haven : Yale University Press, c1987. — x, 416 p.. — *Includes index. — Bibliography: p. 399-409*

BRADFORD (WEST YORKSHIRE) — Economic conditions
GRAHAM MOSS ASSOCIATES
Bradford integrated operations study : the final report of a study commissioned by Bradford City Council with support from the European Commission. — Bristol : Graham Moss Associates, 1986. — xv,335p

BRADFORD (WEST YORKSHIRE) — Politics and government
WRIGHT, D. G.
The Chartist risings in Bradford / D.G. Wright. — Bradford : Bradford Libraries and Information Service, 1987. — 72p. — *Bibliography: p66-67. — Includes index*

BRAIN
RESTAK, Richard M.
The infant mind / Richard M. Restak. — 1st ed. — Garden City, N.Y. : Doubleday, 1986. — xi, 274 p.. — *Includes index. — Bibliography: p. [255]-264*

THOMPSON
The brain : an introduction to neuroscience / Richard F. Thompson. — New York : W.H. Freeman, c1985. — p. cm. — *Includes bibliographies and index*

BRAIN — popular works
RESTAK, Richard M.
The infant mind / Richard M. Restak. — 1st ed. — Garden City, N.Y. : Doubleday, 1986. — xi, 274 p.. — *Includes index. — Bibliography: p. [255]-264*

BRAIN DRAIN — Argentina
GURRIERI, Jorge
Scarce skills and international migration in Argentina / by Jorge Gurrieri, Silvia Lépore, Lelio Mármora. — Geneva : International Labour Office, 1986. — iv,58p. — (Working paper / International Migration for Employment). — *Bibliography: p54-56*

BRAND NAME PRODUCTS
JONES, John Philip
What's in a name? : Advertising and the concept of brands / John Philip Jones. — Lexington, Mass. : Lexington Books, c1986. — p. cm. — *Includes index*

BRAZIL — Church history
COOK, Guillermo
The expectation of the poor : base ecclesial communities in Protestant perspective / Guillermo Cook. — Maryknoll, NY : Orbis Books, c1985. — p. cm. — *Includes index. — Bibliography: p*

MAINWARING, Scott
The Catholic Church and politics in Brazil, 1916-1985 / Scott Mainwaring. — Stanford, Calif. : Stanford University Press, 1986. — xv, 328p. — *Includes index. — Bibliography: p.[297]-319*

BRAZIL — Civilization
FREYRE, Gilberto
[Sobrados e mucambos. English]. The mansions and the shanties : the making of modern Brazil / by Gilberto Freyre ; translated from the Portuguese and edited by Harriet de Onís ; with an introduction by Frank Tannenbaum, new introduction by E. Bradford Burns. — Berkeley : University of California Press, c1986. — p. cm. — *Translation of: Sobrados e mucambos. — : Originally published: New York : Knopf, 1963. — Includes index. — Bibliography: p*

BRAZIL — Civilization — 19th century
FREYRE, Gilberto
[Ordem e progresso. English]. Order and progress : Brazil from Monarchy to Republic / edited and translated from the Portuguese by Rod W. Horton ; new introduction by Ludwig Lauerhass, Jr. — Berkeley : University of California Press, c1986. — p. cm. — *Translation of: Ordem e progresso*

BRAZIL — Civilization — 20th century
FREYRE, Gilberto
[Ordem e progresso. English]. Order and progress : Brazil from Monarchy to Republic / edited and translated from the Portuguese by Rod W. Horton ; new introduction by Ludwig Lauerhass, Jr. — Berkeley : University of California Press, c1986. — p. cm. — *Translation of: Ordem e progresso*

BRAZIL — Economc policy
MARTONE, Celso L.
Macroeconomic policies, debt accumulation, and adjustment in Brazil, 1965-84 / Celso L. Martone. — Washington, D.C. : The World Bank, 1987. — 43p. — (World Bank discussion papers ; no.8). — *Includes bibliographical references*

BRAZIL — Economic conditions
FREYRE, Gilberto
[Ordem e progresso. English]. Order and progress : Brazil from Monarchy to Republic / edited and translated from the Portuguese by Rod W. Horton ; new introduction by Ludwig Lauerhass, Jr. — Berkeley : University of California Press, c1986. — p. cm. — *Translation of: Ordem e progresso*

GOMES, Gustavo Maia
The roots of state intervention in the Brazilian economy / Gustavo Maia Gomes. — New York : Praeger, 1986. — xvii, 376 p.. — *Includes indexes. — Bibliography: p. 353-367*

BRAZIL — Economic conditions — 19th century
COSTA, Emília Viotti da
[Da monarquia à república. English]. The Brazilian Empire : myths and histories / Emilia Viotti da Costa. — Chicago ; London : University of Chicago Press, 1985. — xxv, 287p. — *: Revised translation of: Da monarquia à república. — Includes index. — Bibliographical notes: p.249-278*

BRAZIL — Economic conditions — 1918-
JUSTO, Liborio
Argentina y Brasil en la integración continental / Liborio Justo. — [Buenos Aires] : Centro Editor de América Latina, c1983. — 183p. — (Biblioteca política argentina ; 37)

BRAZIL — Economic conditions — 1964-1985
Brazil, financial systems review. — Washington, D.C., U.S.A. : World Bank, c1984. — xcix,150p. — (A World Bank Country study). — *Summaries in French, Portuguese, and Spanish. — Bibliography: p144-149*

BRAZIL — Economic conditions — 1964-
KNIGHT, Peter T.
Brazil / Peter T. Knight and Ricardo Moran. — [Washington, D.C. : World Bank], 1981. — 101p. — (Poverty and basic needs series). — *Includes bibliographical references*

BRAZIL — Economic policy

BARZELAY, Michael
The politicized market economy : alcohol in Brazil's energy strategy / Michael Barzelay. — Berkeley : University of California Press, c1986. — xiv, 289p. — (Studies in international political economy). — Includes index. — Bibliography: p.267-276

GOMES, Gustavo Maia
The roots of state intervention in the Brazilian economy / Gustavo Maia Gomes. — New York : Praeger, 1986. — xvii, 376 p.. — Includes indexes. — Bibliography: p. 353-367

TOPIK, Steven
The political economy of the Brazilian State, 1889-1930 / by Steven Topik. — 1st ed. — Austin : University of Texas Press, 1987. — p. cm. — (Latin American monographs / Institute of Latin American Studies, the University of Texas at Austin ; no. 71). — Includes index. — Bibliography: p

BRAZIL — Economic policy — Addresses, essays, lectures

Authoritarian Brazil: origins, policies, and future / Edited by Alfred Stepan. — New Haven : Yale University Press, 1973. — xi, 265 p. — : Revision of papers originally presented at a workshop on contemporary Brazil held at Yale University in Apr. 1971. — Includes bibliographical references

BRAZIL — Foreign economic relations

FRITSCH, Winston
Brazil and the Great War, 1914-1918 / Winston Fritsch. — Rio de Janeiro, RJ : Departamento de Economia, Pontifícia Universidade Católica do Rio de Janeiro, [1984]. — 54 leaves. — (Texto para discussão / Departamento de Economia, PUC/RJ ; no. 62) . — "January 1984.". — Includes bibliographical references

BRAZIL — Foreign economic relations — Argentina

JUSTO, Liborio
Argentina y Brasil en la integración continental / Liborio Justo. — [Buenos Aires] : Centro Editor de América Latina, c1983. — 183p. — (Biblioteca política argentina ; 37)

BRAZIL — Foreign relations — Netherlands

STRAATEN, Harald S. van der
Brazil - a destiny : Dutch contacts through the ages. — The Hague : Government Publishing Office, 1984. — 164p. — (Ethnological serie "Verre naasten naderbij"). — Bibliography: p163-164

BRAZIL — History — 1763-1821

MACAULAY, Neill
Dom Pedro : the struggle for liberty in Brazil and Portugal, 1798-1834 / Neill Macaulay. — Durham, [N.C.] : Duke University Press, 1986. — xiv, 361 p.. — Includes index. — Bibliography: p. [339]-344

BRAZIL — History — 1822-1889

MACAULAY, Neill
Dom Pedro : the struggle for liberty in Brazil and Portugal, 1798-1834 / Neill Macaulay. — Durham, [N.C.] : Duke University Press, 1986. — xiv, 361 p.. — Includes index. — Bibliography: p. [339]-344

BRAZIL — History — 1889-1930

TOPIK, Steven
The political economy of the Brazilian State, 1889-1930 / by Steven Topik. — 1st ed. — Austin : University of Texas Press, 1987. — p. cm. — (Latin American monographs / Institute of Latin American Studies, the University of Texas at Austin ; no. 71). — Includes index. — Bibliography: p

BRAZIL — Industries — Statistics

Séries estatísticas retrospectivas. — Rio de Janeiro : IBGE
V.2: O Brasil, suas riquezas naturais, suas indústrias
T.3: Indústria de transportes, indústria fabril. — 1986. — 273,148p. — Facsimile of 1909 edition

Séries estatísticas retrospectivas. — Rio de Janeiro : IBGE
V.2: O Brasil, suas riquezas naturais, suas indústrias
Introdução - indústria extrativa. — 1986. — vi,216,353,552p. — Facsimile of 1907 original

BRAZIL — Kings and rulers — Biography

MACAULAY, Neill
Dom Pedro : the struggle for liberty in Brazil and Portugal, 1798-1834 / Neill Macaulay. — Durham, [N.C.] : Duke University Press, 1986. — xiv, 361 p.. — Includes index. — Bibliography: p. [339]-344

BRAZIL — Politics and government

LAMOUNIER, Bolivar
Political parties and democratic consolidation : the Brazilian case / Bolivar Lamounier [and] Rachel Meneguello. — Washington, D.C. : Latin American Program of the Woodrow Wilson International Center for Scholars, Smithsonian Institution and the World Peace Foundation, 1985. — 37p. — (Working papers / Woodrow Wilson International Center for Scholars. Latin American Program ; no.165). — Bibliography: p32-37

BRAZIL — Politics and government — 1822-1889

BRAZIL. Imperador
Falas do trono desde o ano de 1823 até o ano do 1889 : acompanhadas dos respectivos votos de graça da Câmara Temporária / prefácio de Pedro Calmon. — [Brasília] : Instituto Nacional do Livro, Ministério da Educação e Cultura, [1977]. — 544p. — Com "diferentes informações e esclarecimentos sobre todas as sessões extraordinárias, adiamentos, dissoluções, sessões secretas e fusões com un quadro das épocas e motivos que deram lugar à reunião das duas câmaras e competente histórico, coligades na Secretaria da Câmara dos Deputados"

COSTA, Emília Viotti da
[Da monarquia à república. English]. The Brazilian Empire : myths and histories / Emilia Viotti da Costa. — Chicago ; London : University of Chicago Press, 1985. — xxv, 287p. — : Revised translation of: Da monarquia à república. — Includes index. — Bibliographical notes: p.249-278

BRAZIL — Politics and government — 1889-1930

COSTA, Emília Viotti da
[Da monarquia à república. English]. The Brazilian Empire : myths and histories / Emilia Viotti da Costa. — Chicago ; London : University of Chicago Press, 1985. — xxv, 287p. — : Revised translation of: Da monarquia à república. — Includes index. — Bibliographical notes: p.249-278

BRAZIL — Politics and government — 20th century

MAINWARING, Scott
The Catholic Church and politics in Brazil, 1916-1985 / Scott Mainwaring. — Stanford, Calif. : Stanford University Press, 1986. — xv, 328p. — Includes index. — Bibliography: p.[297]-319

BRAZIL — Politics and government — 1930-1954

SKIDMORE, Thomas E
Politics in Brazil, 1930-1964 : an experiment in democracy / [by] Thomas E. Skidmore. — New York : Oxford University Press, 1967. — xviii, 446p. — Includes bibliographical references

BRAZIL — Politics and government — 1954-1964

SKIDMORE, Thomas E
Politics in Brazil, 1930-1964 : an experiment in democracy / [by] Thomas E. Skidmore. — New York : Oxford University Press, 1967. — xviii, 446p. — Includes bibliographical references

BRAZIL — Politics and government — 1964-1985 — Addresses, essays, lectures

Authoritarian Brazil: origins, policies, and future / Edited by Alfred Stepan. — New Haven : Yale University Press, 1973. — xi, 265 p. — : Revision of papers originally presented at a workshop on contemporary Brazil held at Yale University in Apr. 1971. — Includes bibliographical references

BRAZIL — Race relations

FREYRE, Gilberto
[Sobrados e mucambos. English]. The mansions and the shanties : the making of modern Brazil / by Gilberto Freyre ; translated from the Portuguese and edited by Harriet de Onís ; with an introduction by Frank Tannenbaum, new introduction by E. Bradford Burns. — Berkeley : University of California Press, c1986. — p. cm. — Translation of: Sobrados e mucambos. — : Originally published: New York : Knopf, 1963. — Includes index. — Bibliography: p

BRAZIL — Social conditions

FREYRE, Gilberto
[Ordem e progresso. English]. Order and progress : Brazil from Monarchy to Republic / edited and translated from the Portuguese by Rod W. Horton ; new introduction by Ludwig Lauerhass, Jr. — Berkeley : University of California Press, c1986. — p. cm. — Translation of: Ordem e progresso

FREYRE, Gilberto
[Sobrados e mucambos. English]. The mansions and the shanties : the making of modern Brazil / by Gilberto Freyre ; translated from the Portuguese and edited by Harriet de Onís ; with an introduction by Frank Tannenbaum, new introduction by E. Bradford Burns. — Berkeley : University of California Press, c1986. — p. cm. — Translation of: Sobrados e mucambos. — : Originally published: New York : Knopf, 1963. — Includes index. — Bibliography: p

BRAZIL — Social conditions — 19th century

COSTA, Emília Viotti da
[Da monarquia à república. English]. The Brazilian Empire : myths and histories / Emilia Viotti da Costa. — Chicago ; London : University of Chicago Press, 1985. — xxv, 287p. — : Revised translation of: Da monarquia à república. — Includes index. — Bibliographical notes: p.249-278

BRAZIL — Social conditions — 1964-

KNIGHT, Peter T.
Brazil / Peter T. Knight and Ricardo Moran. — [Washington, D.C. : World Bank], 1981. — 101p. — (Poverty and basic needs series). — Includes bibliographical references

BRAZIL — Social policy

PASSARINHO, Jarbas G.
Discurso de posse... na Pasta do Trabalho e Previdência Social / Jarbas Passarinho. — [Brasília] : Ministério do Trabalho e Previdência Social, Serviço de Documentação, Seção de Publicação, 1967. — [4]p

PASSARINHO, Jarbas G.
Discurso... na 51a. sessão da Conferência Internacional do Trabalho (Genebra - 1967) / Jarbas Passarinho. — [Brasília] : Ministério do Trabalho e Previdência Social, Serviço de Documentação, Seção de Publicação, 1967. — 6p

BRAZIL — Statistics

Séries estatíticas retrospectivos. — Rio de Janeiro : IBGE. — Facsimile edition of 1941 original
V.1: Repertório estatístico do Brasil : quadros retrospectivos. — Rio de Janeiro : IBGE. — xvi,138p. — Facsimile edition of 1941 original

BRAZIL, NORTH — Population — Statistics

Contribuiç̃oes para o estudo da demografia do Norte. — [Rio de Janeiro : IGBE, 1956]. — 58p

BREACH OF CONTRACT — Canada
GEVA, Benjamin
Financing consumer sales and product defences in Canada and the United States / by Benjamin Geva. — [Agincourt, Ont.] : Carswell Legal Publications, 1984. — xlii, 340 p.. — "Text on part V of the Bills of Exchange Act, FTC Trade Regulation Rule, provincial, federal, and uniform state legislation, legal doctrines and statutes pertaining to financing assignee, holder for value, holder in due course, direct lender, or credit card issuer, and related topics.". — Includes bibliographical references and index

BREACH OF CONTRACT — England
GREAT BRITAIN. Law Commission
Transfer of land : the rule in Bain v. Fothergill / The Law Commission. — London : H.M.S.O., 1986. — iv,49p. — (Working paper / Law Commission ; no. 98). — Includes bibliographical references

BREACH OF THE PEACE — Great Britain
CARD, Richard
Public order — the new law / Richard Card. — London : Butterworths, 1987. — [170]p. — Includes index

STAUNTON, Marie
Free to walk together? : a guide to the Government's public order proposals for voluntary organisations, campaigners and church groups / Marie Staunton. — London : National Council for Civil Liberties, c1985. — 41p

THORNTON, Peter, 1946-
We protest : the public order debate / Peter Thornton. — London : National Council for Civil Liberties, 1985. — [96]p

BREAD
Nutritional aspects of bread and flour / report of the Panel on Bread, Flour and other Cereal Products, Committee on Medical Aspects of Food Policy. — London : H.M.S.O., 1981. — x,64p. — (Report on health and social subjects ; 23). — At head of title: Department of Health and Social Security. — Bibliography: p55-64

BREAST — Cancer
Breast cancer screening : report to the Health Ministers of England, Wales, Scotland & Northern Ireland / by a working group chaired by Sir Patrick Forrest. — London : H.M.S.O., 1986. — 102p. — At head of title page: Department of Health and Social Security. — Bibliography: p95-98

BREAST — Radiography
Breast cancer screening : report to the Health Ministers of England, Wales, Scotland & Northern Ireland / by a working group chaired by Sir Patrick Forrest. — London : H.M.S.O., 1986. — 102p. — At head of title page: Department of Health and Social Security. — Bibliography: p95-98

BREAST FEEDING
Breastfeeding, child health & child spacing : cross-cultural perspectives / edited by Valerie Hull & Mayling Simpson. — London : Croom Helm, c1985. — 216p. — Includes bibliographies and index

BREAST FEEDING — Pakistan
KHAN, Zabeda
Breast-feeding in Pakistan / Zabeda Khan. — Islamadad : Pakistan Institute of Development Economics, 1986. — 25,[41] leaves. — (Studies in population, labour force and migration project report ; no.10). — Bibliography: p [26-27]

BREATH TESTS — Great Britain
COBB, P. G. W.
Report on the performance of the Lion Intoximeter 3000 and the Camic Breath Analyser evidential breath alcohol measuring instruments during the period 16 April 1984 to 15 October 1984 / P. G . W. Cobb, M . D .G. Dabbs, with a foreword by Sir William Paton ; [for the] Home Office. — London : H.M.S.O., 1985. — 70p. — Cover title: Report on breath alcohol measuring instruments

BRENT (LONDON, ENGLAND) — Social policy
BRENT. Education Department
Brent religious education now and tomorrow. — Brent : [the Department], 1986. — 26p

BRENT. Social Services Department
Comparative provision levels. — Brent : [the Department]
Report no. 1/86 to Social Services Committee from the Director of Social Services. — 1986. — 5-17p

BREWERY WORKERS — Effect of technological innovations on
GHOBADIAN, Abby
The effects of new technological change on shift work in the brewing industry / Abby Ghobadian. — Aldershot : Gower, c1986. — xiv,192p. — Includes bibliography

BREWING INDUSTRY — Great Britain — Corrupt practices
KOCHAN, Nick
The Guinness affair : anatomy of a scandal / Nick Kochan & Hugh Pym. — Bromley : Helm, c1987. — [224]p. — Includes index

BREWING INDUSTRY — Great Britain — History
PUDNEY, John
A draught of contentment : the story of the Courage Group / John Pudney. — London : New English Library, 1971. — 152p

BRICKMAKING — European Economic Community countries — Energy consumption
BRITISH CERAMIC RESEARCH ASSOCIATION LTD.
Clay-brick industry in the European Economic Community / British Ceramic Research Association Ltd.. — Luxembourg : Commission of the European Communities, 1985. — iii,69p. — (EUR ; 9469) (Energy audit ; no.5). — Series title: Energy. — Bibliographical references: p47-48. — Contract no. XVII/AR/82/599

BRIDGES — England — London — Drawings
PENTON, Howard
County of London sketches of bridges over the Thames / sketches by Howard Penton ; letterpress by Charles Palmer. — [London : Walter Emden, 1903]. — [24] leaves of plates. — Spine title: Sketches of bridges over the Thames. — Printed protectives include notes on each bridge

BRIGGS, RAYMOND. When the wind blows
KILBORN, Richard W.
The multi-media melting pot : marketing When the wind blows / by Richard Kilborn. — London : Comedia, 1986. — 117p. — Bibliography: p114-117

BRIGGS, RAYMOND — Adaptations
KILBORN, Richard W.
The multi-media melting pot : marketing When the wind blows / by Richard Kilborn. — London : Comedia, 1986. — 117p. — Bibliography: p114-117

BRIGHOUSE (YORKSHIRE) — Civic improvement
GREAT BRITAIN. Department of the Environment. Yorkshire and Humberside Regional Office
A study of the environment in Brighouse. — [Leeds] : the Office, [1973]. — 99p

BRIGHT, JOHN
READ, Donald
Cobden and Bright : a Victorian political partnership / Donald Read. — London : Edward Arnold, 1967. — 275p

BRISBANE (QLD.) — History
COLE, John R.
Shaping a city : Greater Brisbane 1925-1985 / by John R. Cole. — Eagle Farm (Qld.) : William Brooks Queensland, 1984. — 416p. — Bibliography: p411-416

BRISBANE STOCK EXCHANGE — History
LOUGHEED, A. L
The Brisbane Stock Exchange, 1884-1984 / A.L. Lougheed. — Brisbane, Qld. : Boolarong Publications, 1984. — xiii, 182 p.. — Includes bibliographical references

BRISTOL (AVON) — Economic conditions
BODDY, Martin
Sunbelt city? : a study of economic change in Britain's M4 growth corridor / Martin Boddy, John Lovering and Keith Bassett. — Oxford : Clarendon Press, 1986. — vii,235p. — (Inner Cities Research Programme series ; 3). — Bibliography: p22l-226. — Includes index

BRISTOL (AVON) — Economic policy
BODDY, Martin
Sunbelt city? : a study of economic change in Britain's M4 growth corridor / Martin Boddy, John Lovering and Keith Bassett. — Oxford : Clarendon Press, 1986. — vii,235p. — (Inner Cities Research Programme series ; 3). — Bibliography: p22l-226. — Includes index

BRITISH — Argentina
MÍGUEZ, Eduardo José
Las tierras de los ingleses en la Argentina (1870-1914) / Eduardo José Míguez. — [Buenos Aires] : Editorial de Belgrano, 1985. — 348p. — "El presente libro es una traducción y adaptación de mi tesis doctoral, titulada 'British interests in Argentine Land Development, 1870-1914. A study of British investment in Argentina', defendida en la Universidad de Oxford en abril de 1981.". — Bibliography: p[331]-342

BRITISH — Australia — Social conditions
HUGHES, Robert, 1938-
The fatal shore : a history of the transportation of convicts to Australia, 1787-1868 / Robert Hughes. — London : Collins Harvill, 1987, c1986. — 680,[32]p of plates. — Originally published: New York : Knopf, 1986. — Bibliography: p656-670. — Includes index

BRITISH — Big Sioux River Valley (S.D. and Iowa) — History — 19th century
HARNACK, Curtis
Gentlemen on the prairie / Curtis Harnack. — Ames : Iowa State University Press, c1985. — viii, 254 p.. — Includes index. — Bibliography: p. 239-248

BRITISH — Canada
COWAN, Helen I.
British immigration before Confederation / Helen I. Cowan. — Ottawa : Canadian Historical Association, 1978. — 22p. — (Canadian Historical Association booklets ; no.22)

BRITISH — China
ATWELL, Pamela
British mandarins and Chinese reformers : the British administration of Weihaiwei (1898-1930) and the territory's return to Chinese rule / Pamela Atwell ; with a foreword by N. J. Miners. — Hong Kong : Oxford University Press, 1985. — xviii,302p. — (East Asian historical monographs). — Bibliography: p[284]-294

BRITISH — Spain — History — 20th century

FYRTH, Jim
The signal was Spain : the Spanish aid Movement in Britain, 1936-39 / Jim Fyrth. — London : Lawrence and Wishart ; New York : St. Martin's Press, 1986. — 344p. — *Cover and spine title: The signal was Spain: the Aid Spain movement in Britain, 1936-39*

BRITISH — United States

VAN VUGT, William
British emigration during the early 1850's : with special reference to emigration to the USA / by William E. Van Vugt. — 351 leaves. — *PhD (Econ) 1986 LSE. — Leaves 287-322 are appendices*

BRITISH AIRPORTS AUTHORITY — Price policy

NATIONAL ECONOMIC RESEARCH ASSOCIATES
Economic regulation of the British Airports Authority Plc : a report prepared for the Department of Transport / National Economic Research Associates. — [London : Department of Transport], 1986. — 77p. — *Bibliographical references: p77*

BRITISH BANK OF THE MIDDLE EAST — history

JONES, Geoffrey, 1952-
Banking and oil : the history of the British Bank of the Middle East, v.2 / Geoffrey Jones ; research by Frances Bostock, Grigori Gerenstein, Judith Nichol. — Cambridge : Cambridge University Press, 1987. — xxi,357,[40]p of plates. — (HongKong Bank Group history series). — *Bibliography: p348-350. — Includes index*

BRITISH BROADCASTING CORPORATION

WOLFE, Kenneth M.
The churches and the British Broadcasting Corporation, 1922-1956 : the politics of broadcast religion / Kenneth M. Wolfe. — London : SCM Press, 1984. — xxiv, 627p

BRITISH BROADCASTING CORPORATION — History

LEAPMAN, Michael
The last days of the Beeb / Michael Leapman. — London : Allen & Unwin, 1986. — [316]p

RENIER, Olive
Assigned to listen : the Evesham experience 1939-43 / by Olive Renier, Vladimir Rubinstein. — [S.l.] : B.B.C. External Services, 1986. — 154p

BRITISH COLUMBIA — Appropriations and expenditures — Statistics

British Columbia economic accounts 1971-1984. — [Victoria] : Central Statistics Bureau, [1986]. — 119p

BRITISH COLUMBIA — Commerce

External trade report / Ministry of Industry and Small Business Development, British Columbia. — Victoria (B.C.) : Ministry of Industry and Small Business Development, 1969-. — Annual. — Title varies. — *Continues: Preliminary annual statement of external trade through British Columbia customs ports/Department of Economic Development, British Columbia*

Preliminary annual statement of external trade through British Columbia customs ports / Department of Economic Development, British Columbia. — Victoria : Department Of Economic Development, 1947/48-1968. — Annual. — *Continued by: External trade report/Ministry of Industry and Small Business Development. British Columbia*

BRITISH COLUMBIA — Economic conditions

After Bennett : a new politics for British Columbia / edited by Warren Magnusson ... [et al.]. — Vancouver, B.C. : New Star Books, 1986. — 429 p.. — *Bibliography: p. 392-423*

The New reality : the politics of restraint in British Columbia / edited by Warren Magnusson ... [et al.]. — Vancouver : New Star Books, c1984. — 311 p.. — *Includes bibliographical references*

BRITISH COLUMBIA — Economic conditions — Statistics

British Columbia economic accounts 1971-1984. — [Victoria] : Central Statistics Bureau, [1986]. — 119p

BRITISH COLUMBIA — Economic policy

After Bennett : a new politics for British Columbia / edited by Warren Magnusson ... [et al.]. — Vancouver, B.C. : New Star Books, 1986. — 429 p.. — *Bibliography: p. 392-423*

The New reality : the politics of restraint in British Columbia / edited by Warren Magnusson ... [et al.]. — Vancouver : New Star Books, c1984. — 311 p.. — *Includes bibliographical references*

BRITISH COLUMBIA — Politics and government

After Bennett : a new politics for British Columbia / edited by Warren Magnusson ... [et al.]. — Vancouver, B.C. : New Star Books, 1986. — 429 p.. — *Bibliography: p. 392-423*

BLAKE, Donald E.
Two political worlds : parties and voting in British Columbia / Donald E. Blake, with the collaboration of David J. Elkins and Richard Johnston. — Vancouver : University of British Columbia Press, 1985. — x, 205 p.. — *On spine: 2 political worlds. — Includes bibliographical references and index*

GARR, Allen
Tough guy : Bill Bennett and the taking of British Columbia / by Allen Garr. — Toronto, Ont., Canada : Key Porter Books, c1985. — ix, 197 p., [16] p. of plates. — *Includes index. Bibliography: p. 191-192*

BRITISH COLUMBIA — Politics and government — 1975-

The New reality : the politics of restraint in British Columbia / edited by Warren Magnusson ... [et al.]. — Vancouver : New Star Books, c1984. — 311 p.. — *Includes bibliographical references*

BRITISH GAS CORPORATION

GREAT BRITAIN. Department of Energy
Authorisation granted and directions given by the Secretary of State for Energy to the British Gas Corporation under the Gas Act 1986. — London : H.M.S.O., 1986. — 44p

BRITISH GAS CORPORATION — Legal status, laws, etc.

GREAT BRITAIN. Parliament. House of Commons. Library. Research Division
The Gas Bill (Bill 13 of 1985/6) / Christopher Barclay, Caroline Gilmour. — [London] : the Division, 1985. — 30p. — (Reference sheet ; no.85/10). — *Bibliography: p28-30*

BRITISH GENERAL TARIFF (1932)

DOWNS, André
General import restrictions and the behaviour of domestic prices and wages : the case of the British General Tariff of 1932 / by André Downs. — 245 leaves. — *PhD (Econ) 1986 LSE. — Leaves 210-245 are appendices*

BRITISH HOSPITALS CONTRIBUTORY SCHEMES ASSOCIATION

PALLISER, Gordon
The charitable work of hospital contributory schemes / Gordon Palliser [et al.]. — Bristol : British Hospitals Contributory Schemes Association, 1984. — 129p

BRITISH LEYLAND MOTOR CORPORATION — History

WILLIAMS, Karel
The breakdown of Austin Rover : a case-study in the failure of business strategy and industrial policy / Karel Williams, John Williams, Colin Haslam. — Leamington Spa : Berg, 1987. — [160]p

BRITISH NATIONAL OIL CORPORATION

BRITISH NATIONAL OIL CORPORATION
The British National Oil Corporation. — [Glasgow] : the Corporation, 1978. — 12p

BRITISH NATIONAL OIL CORPORATION
Report and accounts / British National Oil Corporation. — London : the Corporation, 1976-1984. — Annual. — *Continued by Britoil annual report*

BRITISH NEWSPAPERS — History — Bibliography

The Newspaper press in Britain : an annotated bibliography / edited by David Linton and Ray Boston. — London : Mansell, 1987. — [350]p. — *Includes index*

BRITISH NORTH AMERICA ACT, 1867

GREAT BRITAIN. Parliament. House of Commons. Library. International Affairs Section
Patriation of the Canadian constitution / Simon Young. — [London] : the Library, 1980. — 9p. — (Background paper / House of Commons. Library. [Research Division] ; no.84). — *Bibliography: p9*

GREAT BRITAIN. Parliament. House of Commons. Library. International Affairs Section
Patriation of the Canadian constitution / Simon Young. — [London] : the Library, 1981. — 23p. — (Background paper / House of Commons. Library. [Research Division] ; no.96). — *Replaces Background Paper no.84. — Bibliography: p21-23*

BRITISH NUCLEAR FUELS LIMITED

Folio 1 / British Nuclear Fuels Limited. — Warrington : British Nuclear Fuels, 1986-. — *Semi-annual*

BRITISH RAIL

LONDON REGIONAL PASSENGERS' COMMITTEE
The clandestine railway : a report / by the London Regional Passengers' Committee. — London : London Regional Passengers' Committee, [1986]. — 24p. — *Cover title*

WEISBERG, Jacob
Labour turnover : a case study of early quits in British Rail / by Jacob Weisberg. — 333 leaves . — *PhD (Econ) 1986 LSE. — Leaves 272-300 are appendices*

BRITISH RAIL — History

GOURVISH, T. R.
British railways, 1948-73 : a business history / T.R. Gourvish ; research by N. Blake ... [et al.]. — Cambridge : Cambridge University Press, 1986. — xxvii,781p,[17]p of plates (1folded). — *Bibliography: p756-763. — Includes index*

BRITISH RAIL. Scottish Region — Management

STEWART, Valerie
Changing trains : messages for management from the ScotRail challenge / Valerie Stewart and Vivian Chadwick. — Newton Abbot : David & Charles, c1987. — 190p

BRITISH SHIPBUILDERS

GREAT BRITAIN. Parliament. House of Commons. Library. Research Division
Shipbuilding in crisis : Christopher Barclay. — [London] : the Division, 1983. — 12p. — (Background paper ; no.133)

GREAT BRITAIN. Parliament. House of Commons. Library. Research Division
The shipbuilding industry / Christopher Barclay, Samantha Bennett. — [London] : the Division, 1985. — 14p. — (Background paper ; no.173)

BRITISH SOCIOLOGICAL ASSOCIATION

Network: newsletter of the British Sociological Association. — London : British Sociological Association, 1975-. — *3 per year*

BRITISH STEEL CORPORATION
BANK, John
Worker directors speak / by the British Steel Corporation employee directors with John Bank and Ken Jones. — Farnborough, Hants. : Gower Press, 1977. — *Based on group discussions and interviews*

GREAT BRITAIN. Parliament. House of Commons. Library. Research Division
The British Steel Corporation and the steel industry / [Christopher Barclay]. — [London] : the Division, 1980. — 18p. — *Bibliography: p16-18*

MAUNDERS, A. R.
A process of struggle : the campaign for Corby steelmaking in 1979 / Allen Maunders. — Gower : Aldershot, c1987. — [295]p. — *Includes bibliography*

BRITISH STEEL CORPORATION — Legal status, laws, etc.
GREAT BRITAIN. Parliament. House of Commons. Library. Research Division
The Iron and Steel Bill / Christopher Barclay. — [London] : the Division, 1981. — 9p. — (Reference sheet ; no.81/11). — *Bibliography: p7-9*

BRITISH TELECOM
HEUVERMANN, Arnulf
Die Liberalisierung des britischen Telekommunikationsmarktes / Arnulf Heuermann, Karl-Heinz Neumann. — Berlin : Springer-Verlag, 1985. — xii,401p. — (Schriftenreihe des Wissenschaftlichen Instituts für Kommunikationsdienste der Deutschen Bundespost ; Bd.3). — *Bibliography: p [395]-401*

BRITISH TELECOM — Legal status, laws, etc.
GREAT BRITAIN. Parliament. House of Commons. Library. Research Division
Telecommunications Bill 1983/84 (Bill 5) / Christopher Barclay. — [London] : the Division, 1983. — 15p. — (Reference sheet ; no.83/11). — *Bibliography: p11-13*

GREAT BRITAIN. Parliament. House of Commons. Library. Research Division
Telecommunications Bill (Bill 15) / Christopher Barclay. — [London] : the Division, 1982. — 12p. — (Reference sheet ; no.82/15). — *Bibliography: p11-12*

BRITISH TRANSPORT COMMISSION — History
BONAVIA, Michael R.
The nationalisation of British transport : the early history of the British Transport Commission, 1948-53 / Michael R. Bonavia. — London : Macmillan in association with the London School of Economics and Political Science, 1987. — xii,192p. — *Includes index*

BRITISH VIRGIN ISLANDS — Economic policy
Management and utilization of the marine resources of the British Virgin Islands : a study conducted by the Dalhousie Ocean Studies Programme on behalf of the Government of the British Virgin Islands with funding from the Special Programs Division of the Canadian International Development Agency (CIDA). — Halifax, N.S. [Nova Scotia] : Dalhousie Ocean Studies Programme, Dalhousie University, 1985. — xi,125p

BRITISH WATERWAYS BOARD
BRITISH WATERWAYS BOARD
Government observations on the fourth report of the Select Committee on Nationalised Industries : a memorandum. — [London] : the Board, 1978. — 6p

GREAT BRITAIN. Countryside Commission
Memorandum to Secretaries of State for Environment and for Wales on the future organisation of water and sewage services. — [Cheltenham] : the Commission, 1972. — 9p

BRITOIL PLC
Britoil annual report. — Glasgow : Britoil, 1985-. — *Annual.* — *Continues: Report and accounts/British National Oil Corporation*

BRITTANY (FRANCE)
FLATRÈS, Pierre
La Bretagne / par Pierre Flatrès. — Paris : Presses Universitaires de France, 1986. — 183p. — (La question régionale)

BRITTANY (FRANCE) — Economic conditions — Statistics
L´espace Breton. — Rennes : INSEE, 1985. — 135p. — (Les dossiers d´Octant ; no.10)

BRIXTON (LONDON, ENGLAND) — Riot, 1981
SCARMAN, Leslie George Scarman, Baron
The Brixton disorders 10-12 April 1981 : report of an enquiry / by Lord Scarman. — London : H.M.S.O., 1981. — viii,168p. — (Cmnd. ; 8427). — *At head of title: Home Office Police Act 1964.* — *Map on folded sheet attached to inside cover.* — *Bibliography: p164-168*

BROADCASTING
WEDELL, George
Media in competition : the future of print and electronic media in 22 countries / George Wedell and Georg-Michael Luyken ; with contributions by Alberto Cavallari...[et al.]. — Manchester : European Institute for the Media, 1986. — 173p. — (Euromedia Indicator ; No.1). — *Includes summaries in French and German*

BROADCASTING — History
LEWIS, Peter M.
Media & power : from Marconi to Murdoch : a graphic guide / Peter M. Lewis and Corinne Pearlman. — London : Camden Press, 1986. — 187p. — (Graphic guides)

BROADCASTING — Law and legislation — Canada
KAUFMAN, Donna Soble
Broadcasting law in Canada : fairness in the administrative process / Donna Soble Kaufman. — Toronto : Carswell, 1987. — xv,82p. — *Bibliography: p[75]-78*

BROADCASTING — Law and legislation — Ecuador
ECUADOR
[Laws, etc.] Ley de radiodifusión y televisión : registro oficial no.785, viernes 18 de abril de 1975. — Quito : [Secretaría Nacional de Información Pública], 1976. — 37p

BROADCASTING — Law and legislation — United States — Digests
BENSMAN, Marvin R.
Broadcast regulation : selected cases and decisions / Marvin R. Bensman. — 2nd ed. — Lanham, MD : University Press of America, c1985. — v, 192 p.. — *Includes index*

BROADCASTING — Management
SHERMAN, Barry L.
Telecommunications management : the broadcast & cable industries / Barry L. Sherman. — New York ; London : McGraw—Hill, 1987. — (McGraw-Hill series in mass communication)

BROADCASTING — Political aspects — Germany — History
KUTSCH, Arnulf
Rundfunkwissenschaft im Dritten Reich : Geschichte des Instituts für Rundfunkwissenschaft der Universität Freiburg / Arnulf Kutsch. — München : Saur, 1985. — x,600p. — (Rundfunkstudien ; 2). — *Bibliography: p548-569*

BROADCASTING — Social aspects
LEWIS, Peter M.
Media & power : from Marconi to Murdoch : a graphic guide / Peter M. Lewis and Corinne Pearlman. — London : Camden Press, 1986. — 187p. — (Graphic guides)

BROADCASTING — Africa, Sub-Saharan
Making broadcasting useful : the African experience : the development of radio and television in Africa in the 1980s / George Wedell, editor ; James Kangwana and Lawrence Lawler, assistant editors. — Manchester : Manchester University Press [for] European Institute for the Media, c1986. — xii,306p. — *Bibliography: p301-302.* — *Includes index*

BROADCASTING — Australia
Satellite broadcasting : answers to the questions most often asked. — Canberra : Australian Government Publishing Service, 1986. — iv,65p

BROADCASTING — Developing countries
KATZ, Elihu
Broadcasting in the Third World : promise and performance / Elihu Katz and George Wedell, with Michael Pilsworth and Dov Shinar. — Cambridge : Harvard University Press, 1977. — xvi, 305 p.. — *Includes bibliographical references and index*

BROADCASTING — Great Britain — Public opinion
MORRISON, David, 1944-
Invisible citizens : British public opinion and the future of broadcasting / David Morrison. — London : Libbey, 1986. — 89p. — (Broadcasting Research Unit monograph)

BROADCASTING AND TELEVISION ACT 1942
Freedom of expression and section 116 of the Broadcasting and Television Act 1942. — Canberra : Australian Government Publishing Service, 1985. — vii,22p. — (Report / Human Rights Commission ; no.16)

BROADCASTING BILL 1979-80
GREAT BRITAIN. Parliament. House of Commons. Library. Research Division
Broadcasting 1980 / [Fiona Poole]. — [London] : the Division, 1980. — 15p. — (Reference sheet ; no.80/8). — *Includes bibliographical references*

BROADCASTING POLICY — Germany — History
KUTSCH, Arnulf
Rundfunkwissenschaft im Dritten Reich : Geschichte des Instituts für Rundfunkwissenschaft der Universität Freiburg / Arnulf Kutsch. — München : Saur, 1985. — x,600p. — (Rundfunkstudien ; 2). — *Bibliography: p548-569*

BROCK, WILLIAM REES
BROCK, Peter Jeffry
William Rees Brock, 1836-1917 : paradise regained : an odyssey in Canadian business / by Peter Jeffry Brock. — Toronto : National Press, 1984. — 382p

BROCKDORFF-RANTZAU, ULRICH, Graf von — Biography
HAUPTS, Leo
Graf Brockdorff-Rantzou : Diplomat und Minister in Kaiser-reich und Republik / Leo Haupts. — Göttingen : Muster-Schmidt, c1984. — 106p. — (Persönlichkeit und Geschichte ; Bd.116/117). — *Bibliography: p103-106*

BROCKWAY, FENNER
BROCKWAY, Fenner
98 not out / Fenner Brockway. — London : Quartet, 1986. — [140]p. — *Includes index*

BROILERS (POULTRY) — Trinidad and Tobago — Statistics
The broiler industry in Trinidad and Tobago : 1969-1971. — [Port of Spain] : Central Statistical Office, 1974. — iii,38p

BROKEN HILL (N.S.W.) — History
KENNEDY, Brian Ernest
A tale of two mining cities : Johannesburg and Broken Hill 1885-1925 / Brian Kennedy. — Johannesburg : Ad. Donker, 1984. — xiii,146p. — *Bibliography: p136-142*

BROKEN HILL (N.S.W.) — Race relations — History
KENNEDY, Brian Ernest
A tale of two mining cities : Johannesburg and Broken Hill 1885-1925 / Brian Kennedy. — Johannesburg : Ad. Donker, 1984. — xiii,146p. — *Bibliography: p136-142*

BROKEN HOMES — Denmark
KOCH-NIELSEN, Inger
Familiemønstre efter skilsmisse / Inger Koch-Nielsen, Henning Transgaard. — København : Socialforskningsinstituttet, 1987. — 120p. — (Publikation / Socialforskningsinstituttet ; 155). — *Bibliography: p112-115*

BROKERS — United States
AULETTA, Ken
Greed and glory on Wall Street : the fall of the house of Lehman / Ken Auletta. — Harmondsworth : Penguin Books, 1986. — xi,253p

BROWN, ED — Trials, litigation, etc
CORTNER, Richard C
A "Scottsboro" case in Mississippi : the Supreme Court and Brown v. Mississippi / by Richard C. Cortner. — Jackson : University of Mississippi, c1986. — xiii, 174 p.. — *Includes index. — Bibliography: p. 170*

BRUCE, S. M.
MCDOUGALL, F. L.
Letters from a 'secret service agent' : F. L. McDougall to S. M. Bruce, 1924-1929 / W. J. Hudson and Wendy Way, editors. — Canberra : Australian Government Publishing Service, 1986. — xix,937p

BRUGMANS, HENDRIK
Liber amicorum Henri Brugmans : au service de l'Europe : études et témoignages édités à l'occasion de son soixante-quinzième anniversaire = Liber amicorum Henri Brugmans : striving for Europe : studies and tributes published on the occasion of his seventy-fifth birthday. — Amsterdam : European Cultural Foundation, 1981. — 590p

BRUNEI — Constitution
BRUNEI. State Secretariat
[Constitution (1959-60)]. Brunei constitutional documents. — Kuala Lumpur : [State Secretariat?, 1960]. — iii,277p. — *Contains all constitutional documents which came into force on September 29, 1959 and before July 1, 1960*

BRUNEI — Economic conditions
ARIEF, Sritua
The Brunei economy / Sritua Arief. — East Balmain : Rosecons, for the Southeast Asia Research and Development Institute, 1986. — xiii,233p. — *Bibliography: p231*

BRUNEI — Economic policy
ARIEF, Sritua
The Brunei economy / Sritua Arief. — East Balmain : Rosecons, for the Southeast Asia Research and Development Institute, 1986. — xiii,233p. — *Bibliography: p231*

BRUNEI
Development report, January, 1956. — Kuching : Government Printer, 1956. — iii,60p

BRUNEI
Five year development plan : summary of proposals. — [Kuching : Government Printing Dept., 1953]. — 6p

BRUSSELS (BELGIUM) — History
POLASKY, Janet L
Revolution in Brussels, 1787-1793 / by Janet L. Polasky. — Brussels : Académie royale de Belgique ; Hanover : Published for the University of New Hampshire by University Press of New England, 1987. — 315 p., [2] leaves of plates (1 folded). — (Mémoires de la Classe des lettres. Collection in-8o ; 2e sér., t. 66, fasc. 4-1985). — *Includes index. — Bibliography: p. [277]-299*

BRYANT, JOHN EMORY
CURRIE-MCDANIEL, Ruth
Carpetbagger of conscience : a biography of John Emory Bryant / Ruth Currie-McDaniel. — Athens : University of Georgia Press, c1987. — 238 p.. — *Includes index. — Bibliography: p. [221]-231*

BRYANT & MAY — History
BRYANT & MAY
The match makers / Patrick Beaver. — London : Published for Bryant & May by Melland, c1985. — 128p. *Includes index*

BUBBITT, IRVING, 1865-1933
RYN, Claes G.
Will, imagination, and reason : Irving Babbitt and the problem of reality / by Claes G. Ryn. — Chicago, IL : Regnery Gateway, [1986]. — p. cm. — *Bibliography: p*

BUCHANAN, JAMES M.
ATKINSON, A. B.
James Buchanan's contribution to economics / A. B. Atkinson. — [London : London School of Economics and Political Science], 1986. — 13p. — (Taxation, incentives and the distribution of income ; no.100). — *Economic and Social Research Council programme. — Bibliographical references: p11-13*

BUDGET
BAXTER, W. T.
Discount and budgets : with constant prices and inflation / W.T.Baxter. — London : Published for the Chartered Association of Certified Accountants by Certified Accountant Publications, 1986. — 49p

BEAN, Charles R.
Budget deficits, interest rates and the incentive effects of income tax cuts / C. R. Bean and S. V. Wijnbergen. — London : Centre for Labour Economics, London School of Economics, 1987. — 37p. — (Discussion paper / London School of Economics and Political Science. Centre for Labour Economics ; no.270)

WILDAVSKY, Aaron B
Budgeting : a comparative theory of budgetary processes / Aaron Wildavsky. — 2nd, rev. ed. — New Brunswick (U.S.A.) : Transaction Books, c1986. — xii, 403 p.. — *Includes bibliographies and index*

BUDGET — Law and legislation — United States
CEBULA, Richard J
The deficit problem in perspective / Richard J. Cebula. — Lexington, Mass. : Lexington Books, c1987. — p. cm. — *Includes index*

BUDGET — Political aspects
WILDAVSKY, Aaron B
Budgeting : a comparative theory of budgetary processes / Aaron Wildavsky. — 2nd, rev. ed. — New Brunswick (U.S.A.) : Transaction Books, c1986. — xii, 403 p.. — *Includes bibliographies and index*

BUDGET — Australia
Issues in medium-term budgetary policy. — Canberra : Economic Planning Advisory Council, 1986. — v,26p. — (Council paper / Economic Planning Advisory Council ; no.16). — *Bibliographical references: p24*

BUDGET — Canada
SWANKEY, Ben
The Tory budget and the corporate plan to restructure Canada : and how the system really works / by Ben Swankey. — Vancouver : Centre for Socialist Education, 1985. — xi,246p

BUDGET — China — Congresses
CHINA. Ch'üan kuo jen min tai piao ta hui [Chung-hua jen min kung ho kuo ti 6 chieh ch'üan kuo jen min tai piao ta hui ti 2 tz'u hui i chu yao wen chien. English]. The second session of the Sixth National People's Congress (main documents). — 1st ed. — Beijing : Foreign Languages Press : Distributed by China International Book Trading Corp., 1984. — 102 p.. — (Chinese documents). — *Colophon title in Chinese: Chung-hua jen min kung ho kuo ti 6 chieh ch'üan kuo jen min tai piao ta hui ti 2 tz'u hui i chu yao wen chien. — Translation of: Chung-hua jen min kung ho kuo ti 6 chieh ch'üan kuo jen min tai piao ta hui ti 2 tz'u hui i chu yao wen chien*

BUDGET — Ecuador
SEMINARIO NACIONAL "PLANIFICACIÓN Y PRESUPUESTO DEL SECTOR PÚBLICO" (1973 : Quito)
Seminario Nacional "Planificación y Presupuesto del Sector Público" : Hotel Colon Internacional, enero 25,26 y 27, 1973, Quito, Ecuador. — Quito : Programa "Administración para el Desarrollo", CICAP, Proyecto 214, O.E.A. : Oficina de Presupuesto, Ministerio de Finanzas, 1973. — 257p

BUDGET — France
GRANDJEAT, Pierre
Les chambres régionales des comptes : analyse d'une pratique / Pierre Grandjeat, Yves Détraigne. — [Paris : La Documentation Française]. — 126p. — (Notes et études documentaires ; no.4826). — *Bibliography: p125*

LINOTTE, Didier
La rationalisation des choix budgétaires de la police nationale / Didier Linotte. — Paris : Presses Universitaires de France, 1975. — 82p. — (Travaux et Recherches de l'Université de Droit, d'Economie et de Sciences Sociales de Paris / Série sciences administrative ; 8). — *Bibliography: p79-80*

BUDGET — Great Britain
CHILD POVERTY ACTION GROUP
A budget to unite a divided Britain : memorandum to the Chancellor of the Exchequer from the Child Poverty Action Group. — London : Child Poverty Action Group, 1985. — 9p

CHILD POVERTY ACTION GROUP
Building one nation : memorandum to the Chancellor of the Exchequer. — London : Child Poverty Action Group, 1987. — 16p

CONFEDERATION OF BRITISH INDUSTRY
Technical budget representations 1987. — London : Confederation of British Industry, 1986. — 31p

GREAT BRITAIN. Parliament. House of Commons. Library. Research Division
The April 1979 Budget - forcasts made for the Budget debate using the Treasury model / [Liz Spilsbury, Christopher Barclay]. — [London] : the Division, [1979]. — 21p. — (Background paper ; 69)

GREAT BRITAIN. Parliament. House of Commons. Library. Research Division
Economic background to the March 1982 budget / Christopher Barclay. — [London] : the Division, 1982. — 26p. — (Background paper ; no.99)

GREAT BRITAIN. Parliament. House of Commons. Library. Research Division
The economic background to the March 1984 Budget / Christopher Barclay. — [London] : the Division, 1984. — 16p. — (Background paper ; no.136)

GREAT BRITAIN. Parliament. House of Commons. Library. Research Division
The economic background to the March 1985 Budget / Christopher Barclay. — [London] : the Division, 1985. — 18p. — (Background paper ; no.165)

BUDGET — Great Britain
continuation

GREAT BRITAIN. Parliament. House of Commons. Library. Research Division
Economic forecasts and the March 1980 budget / Christopher Barclay. — [London] : the Division, 1980. — 22p. — (Background paper ; no.78)

GREAT BRITAIN. Parliament. House of Commons. Library. Research Division
Economic forecasts and the March 1981 budget / Christopher Barclay, Paul Hutt. — [London] : the Division, 1981. — 41p. — (Background paper ; no.89)

GREAT BRITAIN. Parliament. House of Commons. Library. Research Division
Economic forecasts and the March 1983 budget / Christopher Barclay. — [London] : the Division, 1983. — 18p. — (Background paper ; no.113)

GREAT BRITAIN. Parliament. House of Commons. Library. Research Division
The impact of the 1982 budget on individual incomes and real income movements since 1979 / Jennifer Tanfield. — [London] : the Division, 1982. — 22p. — (Background paper ; no.100)

GREAT BRITAIN. Parliament. House of Commons. Library. Research Division
The impact of the 1983 Budget on individual incomes and real income movements since 1979 / Jennifer Tanfield. — [London] : the Division, 1983. — 22p. — (Background paper ; no.115)

BUDGET — Hungary
State budget / Ministry of Finance, Hungary. — Budapest : Ministry of Finance, 1983-. — (Public finance in Hungary). — *Annual*

BUDGET — Mauritius
Budget speech / Mauritius. — Port Luis : Government Printer, 1979-. — *Annual*

BUDGET — Mexico
VÁZQUEZ ARROYO, Francisco
Presupuestos por programas para el sector público de México / Francisco Vázquez Arroyo. — México : Universidad Nacional Autónoma de México, 1979. — 325p. — *Publicado originalmente en 1971.* — *Bibliography: p315-318*

BUDGET — Mexico — Mexico (State)
MEXICO (Mexico: State). Dirección General de Hacienda
Informática municipal. — Toluca : the Dirección, [ca.1975]. — 93p

BUDGET — Nigeria
NIGERIA
Budget. — Lagos : [s.n.], 1986-. — *Annual*

BUDGET — Puerto Rico
PUERTO RICO. Office of Budget and Management
Reseña histórica y evolución del proceso presupuestario de Puerto Rico = Historical background and evolution of the budgeting process in Puerto Rico. — [San Juan] : the Office, [198-]. — [23]p. — *Paralled Spanish and English texts*

BUDGET — Sudan
AZHAR, B. A.
Development budgeting in the Sudan / Dr. B. A. Azhar. — Khartoum : University of Khartoum. Faculty of Economic and Social Studies. Development Studies and Research Centre, 1977. — iv,45p. — (Monograph series / University of Khartoum. Faculty of Economic and Social Studies. Development Studies and Research Centre ; no.4)

BUDGET — United States
COHEN, Joshua
Inequity and intervention : the federal budget and Central America / Joshua Cohen and Joel Rogers. — 1st ed. — Boston, MA : South End Press, c1986. — xi, 66 p.. — (PACCA series on the domestic roots of United States foreign policy). — *Bibliographical notes: p.57-62*

BUDGET DEFICITS — Canada
CARMICHAEL, Edward A
Tackling the federal deficit / Edward A. Carmichael. — Toronto : C.D. Howe Institute, [1984]. — 88 p.. — (Observation ; no. 26). — *Includes bibliographical references*

BUDGET DEFICITS — Europe
DORNBUSCH, Rudiger
Dollars, debts, and deficits / Rudiger Dornbusch. — 1st MIT Press ed. — Leuven, Belgium : Leuven University Press ; Cambridge, Mass. : MIT Press, 1986. — 240 p. . — *The Professor Dr. Gaston Eyskens lectures delivered at the Katholieke Universiteit Leuven, Belgium in the fall of 1984.* — *Includes bibliographies and index*

BUDGET DEFICITS — United States
CEBULA, Richard J
The deficit problem in perspective / Richard J. Cebula. — Lexington, Mass. : Lexington Books, c1987. — p. cm. — *Includes index*

GREAT BRITAIN. Parliament. House of Commons. Library. Research Division
The U.S. budget deficit and its consequences for the world / Christopher Barclay. — [London] : the Division, 1984. — 17p. — (Background paper ; no.145)

MAKIN, John H
U.S. fiscal policy : its effects at home and abroad / John H. Makin. — Washington, D.C. : American Enterprise Institute for Public Policy Research, [1986]. — p. cm. — (AEI studies ; 447)

BUDGETS, PERSONAL — Netherlands — Methodology
NETHERLANDS. Centraal Bureau voor de Statistiek
Werknemersbudgetonderzoek 1974-75. — s-Gravenhage : Staatsuitgeverij. — *Contents list in English.* — *Title on back cover: Workers' budget survey 1974-75. Part 5. Methodology. Appendix 1. Instruments and instructions for data collection*
deel 5: Methodologie
bijlage 1: Enquêtedocumenten. — 1980. — 187p

NETHERLANDS. Centraal Bureau voor de Statistiek
Werknemersbudgetonderzoek, 1974-75. — s-Gravenhage : Staatsuitgeverij, 1980. — *Contents list in English.* — *Title on back cover: Workers' budget survey 1974-75. Part 5. Methodology.* — *Bibliography: p86*
deel 5: Methodologie. — 86p

BUDGETS, PERSONAL — Netherlands — Statistics
NETHERLANDS
Budgetonderzoek 1980. — s-Gravenhage : Staatsuitgeverij, 1985. — 172p. — *Title on back cover: Budgetsurvey 1980*

BUFFER STATES
Buffer states in world politics / edited by John Chay, Thomas E. Ross. — Boulder : Westview Press, 1986. — p. cm. — (Westview special studies in international relations). — *Includes index*

BUILDING — Estimates — Finland
Rakennuskustannusindeksit 1980=100 = Building cost indices 1980=100. — Helsinki : Tilastokeskus, 1981. — 59p. — (Tutkimuksia / Finland. Tilastokeskus ; no.70). — *Contents list, summary and table headings in English*

BUILDING — Great Britain — Safety measures
Asbestos materials in buildings. — London : HMSO, 1983. — 33p. — *At head of title: Department of the Environment*

BUILDING — Nigeria — Statistics
Report of building and Construction Survey 1980. — Lagos : Federal Office of Statistics, General Economic Statistics Division, 1985. — 22p

BUILDING AND LOAN ASSOCIATIONS — Law and legislation — Great Britain
BUILDING SOCIETIES ASSOCIATION
The Building Societies Bill : BSA commentary. — London : the Association, 1985. — viii,206p

BUILDING AND LOAN ASSOCIATIONS — France — History
LESCURE, Michel
Les sociétés immobilières en France au XIXe siècle : contribution à l'histoire de la mise en valeur du sol urbain en économie capitaliste / Michel Lescure. — Paris : Université de Paris I, Panthéon Sorbonne, 1980. — 84p. — (Publications de la Sorbonne. Série étude ; no.15)

BUILDING AND LOAN ASSOCIATIONS — Great Britain
BOLÉAT, Mark
The building society industry / Mark Boléat. — 2nd ed. — London : Allen & Unwin, 1986. — [220]p. — *Previous ed.:1982.* — *Includes bibliography and index*

COLES, Adrian
Building Societies and the savings market / b Adrian Coles. — London : Building Societies Association, 1986. — 32p

GREAT BRITAIN. Parliament. House of Commons. Library. Research Division
Building societies / Timothy Edmonds. — [London] : the Division, 1984. — 13p. — (Background paper ; no.149)

HAWES, Derek
Building societies- the way forward / Derek Hawes. — Bristol : University of Bristol, School for Advanced Urban Studies, c1986. — ii,84p. — (Occasional paper ; 26). — *Bibliography: p81-84*

BUILDING AND LOAN ASSOCIATIONS — Great Britain — Statistics
BUILDING SOCIETIES ASSOCIATION
A compendium of Building Society statistics / the Building Societies Association. — 6th ed. — London : Building Societies Association, 1985. — ii,195p

BUILDING LAWS — Great Britain
GREAT BRITAIN. Parliament. House of Commons. Library. Research Division
The Housing and Building Control Bill (Bill 3, session 1983/84) / [Christine Gillie, Barry Winetrobe]. — [London] : the Division, 1983. — 21p. — (Reference sheet ; no.83/10). — *Includes bibliographical references*

BUILDING LAWS — Illinois — Chicago
JONES, Bryan D
Governing buildings and building government : a new perspective on the old party / Bryan D. Jones. — University, Ala. : University of Alabama Press, c1985. — p. cm. — *Includes index.* — *Bibliography: p*

BUILDING MATERIALS — Prices — Peru
PERU. Dirección de Planificación Estadística
Indices de precios de materiales de construcción e indices de costo de mano de obra, noviembre 1975. — Lima : the Dirección, [1976]. — 9p. — (Serie de indices de precios al por mayor). — *Cover title: Materiales de construcción y costo de mano de obra*

BUILDING RESEARCH ESTABLISHMENT
Information directory / Building Research Establishment. — Watford : Building Research Establishment, 1973-1982. — *Annual*

BUILDING TRADES — Social aspects — United States
SILVER, Marc L.
Under construction : work and alienation in the building trades / Marc L. Silver. — Albany : State University of New York Press, c1986. — xi, 251 p.. — (SUNY series in the sociology of work). — *Includes indexes.* — *Bibliography: p. 229-242*

BUILDINGS — England — Maintenance
RESEARCH INSTITUTE FOR CONSUMER AFFAIRS
The consumers' view of building maintenance : a report / Harvey Sheldon, May Clark. — London : Department of the Environment, Directorate of Research and Information, 1971. — xi,189p. — *Report produced for the Ministry of Public Building and Works*

BUILDINGS — Great Britain — Repair and reconstruction
GREEN, Howard
Redundant space : a productive asset : converting property for small business use / Howard Green and Paul Foley. — London : Harper & Rowe on behalf of the Small Business Research Trust, 1986. — 140p. — *Bibliography: p136. — Includes index*

BULGARIA — Civilization
ZHIVKOVA, Liudmila
S aprilsko vdŭkhnovenie v borbata za mir i sotsializŭm, za edinstvo, tvorchestvo i krasota : dokladi, rechi, statii i izkazvaniia / Liudmila Zhivkova. — Sofiia : Partizdat, 1982-1983. — 3vols

BULGARIA — Foreign relations — 1878-1944
FREIDRICH, Wolfgang-Uwe
Bulgarien und die Mächte 1913-1915 : ein Beitrag zur Weltkriegs- und Imperialismusgescgichte / Wolfgang-Uwe Freidrich. — Stuggart : Steiner Verlag Wiesbaden, 1985. — xxii,453p. — (Quellen und Studien zur Geschichte des östlichen Europa ; Bd.21). — *Bibliography: p435-453*

BULGARIA — History — 1878-1944
CRAMPTON, R. J.
A short history of modern Bulgaria / R.J. Crampton. — Cambridge : Cambridge University Press, 1987. — xiii,221p. — *Bibliography: p210-213. — Includes index*

BULGARIA — History — 1944-
CRAMPTON, R. J.
A short history of modern Bulgaria / R.J. Crampton. — Cambridge : Cambridge University Press, 1987. — xiii,221p. — *Bibliography: p210-213. — Includes index*

BULGARIA — Politics and government — 1878-1944
FREIDRICH, Wolfgang-Uwe
Bulgarien und die Mächte 1913-1915 : ein Beitrag zur Weltkriegs- und Imperialismusgescgichte / Wolfgang-Uwe Freidrich. — Stuggart : Steiner Verlag Wiesbaden, 1985. — xxii,453p. — (Quellen und Studien zur Geschichte des östlichen Europa ; Bd.21). — *Bibliography: p435-453*

BULGARIA — Politics and government — 1944-
ZHIVKOV, Todor, 1911-
Marxist concepts and practices : a series of lectures on theoretical problems and practical approaches to the construction of a developed socialist society in the People's Republic of Bulgaria / by Todor Zhivkov. — Oxford : Pergamon, 1984. — xi,201p. — *Translated from the Bulgarian. — Includes index*

BULGARIA — Population
Kharakteristika na bŭlgarskoto naselenie : trudovi vŭzmozhnosti i realizatsiia : pod obshchata redaktsiia Minko Minkov. — Sofiia : Dŭrzhavno izd-vo nauka i izkustvo, 1984. — 483p. — *Summary in Russian and French*

BULGARIA — Relations — Soviet Union
Internatsional'noe sotrudnichestvo KPSS i BKP : istoriia i sovremennost' / pod obshchei redaktsiei A. G. Egorova (SSSR) i D. Elazara (NRB). — Moskva : Politizdat, 1985. — 415p

BŬLGARSKA KOMUNISTICHESKA PARTIIA
Internatsional'noe sotrudnichestvo KPSS i BKP : istoriia i sovremennost' / pod obshchei redaktsiei A. G. Egorova (SSSR) i D. Elazara (NRB). — Moskva : Politizdat, 1985. — 415p

BŬLGARSKA KOMUNISTICHESKA PARTIIA — History
Istoriia na Bŭlgarskata komunisticheska partiia / redaktsionna komisiia: Ruben Abramov...[et al.]. — 4-o dop. izd.. — Sofiia : Partizdat, 1984. — 791p

ROTHSCHILD, Joseph
The Communist Party of Bulgaria : origins and development, 1883-1936 / Joseph Rothschild. — [New York : AMS Press, 1972]. — viii, 354 p. — *Reprint of the ed. originally published: New York: Columbia University Press, 1959. — Bibliography: p. [313]-333*

BULK CARRIER CARGO SHIPS
Bulk shipping and terminal logistics / Ernst G. Frankel...[et al.]. — Washington, D.C. : The World Bank, 1985. — xvi,288p. — (World Bank technical paper ; no.38)

BULK SOLIDS — Transportation
Bulk shipping and terminal logistics / Ernst G. Frankel...[et al.]. — Washington, D.C. : The World Bank, 1985. — xvi,288p. — (World Bank technical paper ; no.38)

BUNGE & BORN
GREEN, Raúl
Bunge & Born : puissance et secret dans l'agro-alimentaire / Raúl Green, Catherine Laurent. — Paris : Publisud, [1985]. — 180p. — *Bibliography: p169-180*

BURDEN OF PROOF — Great Britain
Burden of proof / general editor Albert Kiralfry. — Abingdon : Professional, 1987. — [200]p. — *Includes index*

BUREAUCRACY
BEETHAM, David
Bureacracy / David Beetham. — Milton Keynes : Open University Press, 1987. — [112] p. — (Concepts in the social sciences). — *Includes bibliography and index*

O'DONNELL, Guillermo A
Modernization and bureaucratic-authoritarianism : studies in South American politics / [by] Guillermo A. O'Donnell. — Berkeley : Institute of International Studies, University of California, [1973]. — xv, 219 p. — (Politics of modernization series ; no. 9). — *Bibliography: p. 201-219*

BUREAUCRACY — Congresses
Public expenditure : the key issues / edited by John Bristow and Declan McDonagh. — Dublin, Ireland : Institute of Public Administration, 1986. — 138 p.. — *Proceedings of National Conference on Public Expenditure: the Key Issues, held Nov. 1985 in Dublin, organized by the Institute. — Includes bibliographies. — Contents: Public expenditure and public debt / Vito Tanzi -- The political economy of public expenditure / Alan Peacock -- Public employment and public expenditure / Richard Rose -- Public expenditure and the bureaucracy / Peter Jackson -- An Irish overview / Alan Dukes*

BUREAUCRACY — Arabian Peninsula
OSAMA, Abdul Rahman
The dilemma of development in the Arabian peninsula / Abdul Rahman Osama. — London : Croom Helm, c1987. — 203p. — *Bibliography: p187-195. — Includes index*

BUREAUCRACY — China — History
MANN, Susan
Local merchants and the Chinese bureaucracy, 1750-1950 / Susan Mann. — Stanford, Calif. : Stanford University Press, 1987. — viii, 278 p.. — *Includes index. — Bibliography: p. [255]-267*

BUREAUCRACY — Hongkong
PALMIER, Leslie H
The control of bureaucratic corruption : case studies in Asia / Leslie Palmier. — New Delhi : Allied Publishers, 1985. — xi, 292 p.. — *Includes bibliographies and index*

BUREAUCRACY — India
MISRA, B. B.
Government and bureaucracy in India, 1947-1976 / B. B. Misra. — Delhi ; Oxford : Oxford University Press, 1986. — 416 p

PALMIER, Leslie H
The control of bureaucratic corruption : case studies in Asia / Leslie Palmier. — New Delhi : Allied Publishers, 1985. — xi, 292 p.. — *Includes bibliographies and index*

BUREAUCRACY — Indonesia
PALMIER, Leslie H
The control of bureaucratic corruption : case studies in Asia / Leslie Palmier. — New Delhi : Allied Publishers, 1985. — xi, 292 p.. — *Includes bibliographies and index*

BUREAUCRACY — Italy — Florence — History
LITCHFIELD, R. Burr
Emergence of a bureaucracy : the Florentine patricians, 1530-1790 / R. Burr Litchfield. — Princeton, N.J. : Princeton University Press, 1986. — xiii, 407 p., [8] p. of plates. — *Includes index. — Bibliography: p. 383-396*

BUREAUCRACY — Mexico — History
LEIBY, John S.
Colonial bureaucrats and the Mexican economy : growth of a patrimonial state, 1763-1821 / John S. Leiby. — New York : P. Lang, c1986. — xvii, 252 p.. — (American university studies. Series IX. History ; vol. 13). — *Bibliography: p. [239]-252*

BUREAUCRACY — United States
CLARKE, Jeanne Nienaber
Staking out the terrain : power differentials among natural resource management agencies / Jeanne Nienaber Clarke, Daniel McCool. — Albany : State University of New York Press, c1985. — p. cm. — (SUNY series in environmental public policy). — *Includes index. — Bibliography: p*

BURGLARY — Great Britain
WALSH, Dermot
Heavy business : commercial burglary and robbery / Dermot Walsh. — London : Routledge & Kegan Paul, 1986. — xii,188p. — *Bibliography: p178-184. — Includes index*

BURIAT A.S.S.R. (R.S.F.S.R.) — Social conditions
MITUPOV, K. B-M.
Stanovlenie sotsialisticheskoi sotsial'noi struktury Buriatii 1938-1960 gg. / K. B-M. Mitupov ; otv.redaktor V. B. Tel'pukhovskii. — Novosibirsk : Nauka, Sibirskoe otdelenie, 1986. — 133p

BURKINA FASO — Census, 1975
Recensement général de la population, décembre 1975 : résultats définitifs. — [Ouagadougou] : Institut National de la Statistique et de la Démographie, 1978. — 2v. — *Contents: v.1. Les données nationales - v.2. Les données départementales*

BURKINA FASO — Census, 1985
Recensement général de la population du 10 au 20 décembre 1985 : résultats provisoires. — Ouagadougou : Institut National de la Statistique et de la Démographie, 1986. —

BURKINA FASO — Economic conditions
Elements caractéristiques des entreprises du Burkina Faso. — Ouagadougou : Institut National de Statistique et de la Démographie, [1986]. — 31p

BURKINA FASO — Economic conditions — Statistics
Annuaire statistique du Burkina Faso / Institut National de la Statistique et de la Demographie. — Ouagadougou : Institut National de la Statistique et de la Demographie, 1984-. — *Annual*

BURKINA FASO — Economic conditions — Statistics *continuation*
Bulletin d'information statistique et économique / Institut National de la Statistique et de la Démographie. — Ouagadougou : Institut National de la Statistique et de la Demographie, 1985-. — *3 per year*

BURKINA FASO — Economic policy
LECAILLON, Jacques
Economic policies and agricultural performance : the case of Burkina Faso / by Jacques Lecaillon and Christian Morrisson. — [Paris] : Development Centre of the Organisation for Economic Co-operation and Development, [1986]. — 158p. — (Development Centre papers). — *Bibliography: p.153-156*

Premier plan quinquennal de développement populaire 1986-1990. — [Ouagadougou : Ministère de la Planification et du Développement Populaire], [1986?]
Vol. 1: Rapport général de synthèse. — 279p

Premier plan quinquennal de développement populaire 1986-1990. — [Ouagadougou : Ministère de la Planification et du Développement Populaire]
vol. 2: Politiques sectorielles. — [1986?]. — 422p

Programme populaire de développement Octobre 1984-Decembre 1985 : Bilan final. — [Ouagadougou] : Ministère de la Planification et du Développement Populaire, 1986. — 2v

Programme populaire de développement Octobre1984-Decembre 1985. — [Ouagadougou] : Ministère de la Planification et du Développement Populaire, [1984?]. —

BURKINA FASO — Population — Statistics
Recensement général de la population, décembre 1975 : résultats définitifs. — [Ouagadougou] : Institut National de la Statistique et de la Démographie, 1978. — 2v. — *Contents: v.1. Les données nationales - v.2. Les données départementales*

Recensement général de la population du 10 au 20 décembre 1985 : résultats provisoires. — Ouagadougou : Institut National de la Statistique et de la Démographie, 1986. —

BURKINA FASO — Social conditions — Statistics
Annuaire statistique du Burkina Faso / Institut National de la Statistique et de la Demographie. — Ougadougou : Institut National de la Statistique et de la Demographie, 1984-. — *Annual*

BURKINA FASO — Social policy
Premier plan quinquennal de développement populaire 1986-1990. — [Ouagadougou : Ministère de la Planification et du Développement Populaire], [1986?]
Vol. 1: Rapport général de synthèse. — 279p

Premier plan quinquennal de développement populaire 1986-1990. — [Ouagadougou : Ministère de la Planification et du Développement Populaire]
vol. 2: Politiques sectorielles. — [1986?]. — 422p

Programme populaire de développement Octobre 1984-Decembre 1985 : Bilan final. — [Ouagadougou] : Ministère de la Planification et du Développement Populaire, 1986. — 2v

Programme populaire de développement Octobre1984-Decembre 1985. — [Ouagadougou] : Ministère de la Planification et du Développement Populaire, [1984?]. —

BURKINA FASO — Statistics
Annuaire statistique du Burkina Faso / Institut National de la Statistique et de la Demographie. — Ougadougou : Institut National de la Statistique et de la Demographie, 1984-. — *Annual*

BURMA — History — 1948-
TINKER, Hugh
The Union of Burma : a study of the first years of independence / Hugh Tinker. — 3rd ed. — London : Oxford University Press, 1957. — 424p

BURMA — Rural conditions
SCOTT, James Cameron
The moral economy of the peasant : rebellion and subsistence in Southeast Asia / James C. Scott. — New Haven ; London : Yale University Press, 1976 [i.e. 1977]. — ix,246p. — *Published in the United States: 1976. — Includes index*

BURTON, JOHN W — Addresses, essays, lectures
Conflict in world society : a new perspective on international relations / edited by Michael Banks ; foreword by Herbert Kelman. — New York : St. Martin's Press, 1984. — xx, 234 p.. — *Essays written in honor of John Burton. — Includes indexes. — Bibliography: p. [209]-225*

BURTON, ORMOND
CRANE, Ernest
I can do no other : a biography of the Reverend Ormond Burton / Ernest Crane. — Auckland ; London : Hodder and Stoughton, 1986. — xii,338p. — *Bibliography: p328-9*

BURUNDI — Economic Policy
4me plan quinquennal de dévelopment économique et social 1983-1987. — [Bujumbura], [ca. 1983]. — 321p

BURUNDI — Social Policy
4me plan quinquennal de dévelopment économique et social 1983-1987. — [Bujumbura], [ca. 1983]. — 321p

BUS DRIVERS — Great Britain
GREAT BRITAIN. Working Group on Violence to Road Passenger Transport Staff
Assaults on bus staff and measures to prevent such assaults : report on the Working Group...under the chairmanship of the Department of Transport. — London : H.M.S.O., 1986. — iii,77,21p

GREAT BRITAIN. Working Group on Violence to Road Passenger Transport Staff
Assaults on bus staff and measures to prevent such assaults : a summary of the findings and recommendations of the 1986 report of the Working Group under the chairmanship of the Department of Transport. — London : H.M.S.O., 1986. — 19p

BUS LINES — Law and legislation — Great Britain
DOUGLAS, Neil J.
A welfare assessment of transport deregulation : the case of the express coach market in 1980 / Neil J. Douglas. — Aldershot : Gower, c1987. — xxiv,349p. — (Institute for Transport Studies ; 2). — *Bibliography: p335-349*

GREAT BRITAIN. Parliament. House of Commons. Library. Research Division
Transport Bill, Bill 68 of 1984-85 / Priscilla Baines. — [London] : the Division, 1985. — 34p. — (Reference sheet ; no.85/4). — *Includes bibliographical references*

SAVAGE, Ian
The deregulation of bus services / Ian Savage. — Aldershot : Gower, c1985. — 267p. — (Institute for Transport Studies ; 1)

BUS LINES — Licenses — Great Britain
GREAT BRITAIN. Department of Transport
Proposals for relaxing the bus licensing system : (policy document). — [London] : the Department, 1979. — 4leaves

BUS LINES — Australia
AUSTRALIA. Bureau of Transport Economics. Seminar on Australian Long Distance Surface Passenger Transport (1985 : Canberra)
Papers and proceedings. — Canberra : Australian Government Publishing Service, 1985. — viii,90p. — *Includes bibliographical references*

BUS LINES — Great Britain
DOUGLAS, Neil J.
A welfare assessment of transport deregulation : the case of the express coach market in 1980 / Neil J. Douglas. — Aldershot : Gower, c1987. — xxiv,349p. — (Institute for Transport Studies ; 2). — *Bibliography: p335-349*

SAVAGE, Ian
The deregulation of bus services / Ian Savage. — Aldershot : Gower, c1985. — 267p. — (Institute for Transport Studies ; 1)

BUS LINES — Great Britain — Fares — Special rates
MCTAVISH, A. D.
Survey of concessionary bus fares for the elderly, blind and disabled in England and Wales / A. D. McTavish and P. Mullen. — London : Department of Transport, 1977. — 2,21p. — (Local transport note ; 77/1)

BUS LINES — Scotland — History
HUNTER, D. L. G.
From S.M.T. to Eastern Scottish : an 80th anniversary story / D. L. G. Hunter. — Edinburgh : John Donald, 1987. — viii,198p

BUS LINES — Wales, South — History
HOLDING, David
South Wales / David Holding & Tony Moyes. — London : Ian Allan, 1986. — 128p. — (History of British bus services). — *Includes index*

BUSAN CITY (KOREA (SOUTH)) — Statistics
1970 population and housing census report (complete). — [Seoul] : Economic Planning Board. — *In Korean and English*
Vol.12-3: Busan City. — 1972. — 126p

BUSES — England — London
COLIN BUCHANAN AND PARTNERS
Bus priorities in London : final report / Colin Buchanan and Partners ; [for] London Regional Transport. — [London : London Regional Transport], 1986. — 1v (various pagings). — *Bibliographical references: Appendix C*

BUSES — Great Britain
GREAT BRITAIN. Working Group on Bus Demonstration Projects. Technical Sub-Committee
Bus detection : bus priorities at traffic control signals. — London : Department of the Environment, [1973]. — 10p. — (Bus Demonstration Project summary report ; No.1)

BUSINESS
KAMPFRAATH, A. A.
Bronnen van welvaart en welzijn / A. A. Kampfraath. — Alphen aan den Rijn : Sansom, 1970. — 24p. — *Rede uitgesproken bij de aanvaarding van het ambt van gewoon hoogleraar in de industriële bedrijfskunde en organisatieleer aan de Landbouwhogeschool te Wageningen op donderdag 23 april 1970. — Bibliography: p23-24*

KIDRON, Michael
The book of business, money and power / Michael Kidron and Ronald Segal. — London : Pluto Projects, 1987. — 187p

Views from the top : establishing the foundation for the future of business / edited by Jerome M. Rosow. — London : Sphere, 1987. — xv,[208]p. — *Originally published: Facts on File, 1985*

BUSINESS — Archives
Newsletter / Business Archives Council. — London : Business Archives Council, 1986-. — *Quarterly*

BUSINESS — Data processing
BUGG, Phillip W
Microcomputers in the corporate environment / Phillip W. Bugg. — Englewood Cliffs, N.J. : Prentice-Hall, c1986. — xv, 192 p.. — *Includes index*

BUSINESS — Data processing
continuation

WELDON, Jay-Louise
Data base administration / Jay-Louise Weldon. — New York ; London : Plenum, c1981. — xii,250p. — (Applications of modern technology in business). — *Includes index*

BUSINESS — Dictionaries

Harrap's business French-English dictionary = dictionnaire anglais-français / edited by Françoise Laurendeau-Collin, Jane Pratt [and] Peter Collin. — London ; Paris : Harrap, 1986. — xiv,224p

MITSUBISHI SHŌJI KABUSHIKI KAISHA
Japanese business language : an essential dictionary / compiled by the Mitsubishi Corporation ; introduction by Kaori O'Connor. — London : KPI ; London : Routledge and Kegan Paul, 1987. — xiii,221p

Shorter Cambridge-Eichborn German dictionary : business and business law, economics, administration. — Cambridge : Cambridge University Press, 1984. — 2v.

BUSINESS — Dictionaries — German

Shorter Cambridge-Eichborn German dictionary : business and business law, economics, administration. — Cambridge : Cambridge University Press, 1984. — 2v.

BUSINESS — Information services

FOSTER, Allan
Online business sourcebook / by Allan Foster and Gerry Smith. — Hartlepool : Headland, 1985. — 1v.(looseleaf). — *Includes index*

Legal industrial espionage : a sourcebook and guide to finding company information / edited by Tony Reid. — Northill, Beds. : Eurofi (UK), 1985. — 158p

BUSINESS — Information services — Directories

The International directory of business information sources and services. — London : Europa, 1986. — ix,377p. — *Includes index*

BUSINESS — Information services — Great Britain — Directories

TUDOR, James
Macmillan directory of business information sources / James Tudor. — London : Macmillan, 1987. — [300]p

BUSINESS — Law and legislation

International business lawyer: journal of the section on business law of the International Bar Association. — London : International Bar Association, 1986-. — *Monthly*

Revue de droit des affaires internationales. International business law journal. — Paris : Librairie Generale de Droit et de Jurisprudence, 1986-. — *Quarterly. — Text in French and English*

BUSINESS — Periodicals — Indexes

Canadian business index. — Toronto, Ont. : Micromedia, 1984-. — *Monthly*

BUSINESS AND POLITICS — Europe

The Politicisation of business in western Europe / edited by M.C.P.M. van Schendelen and R.J. Jackson. — London : Croom Helm, c1987. — 185p. — *Includes bibliographies and index*

BUSINESS AND POLITICS — France — Reims — History — 19th century

GORDON, David M.
Merchants and capitalists : industrialization and provincial politics in mid-nineteenth century France / by David M. Gordon. — University, Ala. : University of Alabama Press, c1985. — ix, 249p. — *Includes index. — Bibliography: p.232-239*

BUSINESS AND POLITICS — France — Saint Étienne (Loire) — History — 19th century

GORDON, David M.
Merchants and capitalists : industrialization and provincial politics in mid-nineteenth century France / by David M. Gordon. — University, Ala. : University of Alabama Press, c1985. — ix, 249p. — *Includes index. — Bibliography: p.232-239*

BUSINESS AND POLITICS — Great Britain

CONFEDERATION OF BRITISH INDUSTRY
Working with politicians / CBI. — London : Confederation of British Industry, 1985. — 135p. — *Includes supplement of updating information, May 1986*

GRANT, Wyn
Business and politics in Britain / Wyn Grant with Jane Sargent. — Basingstoke : Macmillan, 1987. — [288]p. — *Includes bibliography and index*

BUSINESS AND POLITICS — Michigan — Case studies

JONES, Bryan D
The sustaining hand : community leadership and corporate power / Bryan D. Jones and Lynn W. Bachelor with Carter Wilson. — Lawrence, Kan. : University Press of Kansas, c1986. — xii, 247 p.. — (Studies in government and public policy). — *Includes index. — Bibliography: p. 223-239*

BUSINESS AND POLITICS — United States

LEE, Dwight R
Regulating government : a preface to constitutional economics / Dwight R. Lee, Richard B. McKenzie. — Lexington, Mass. : Lexington Books, c1987. — xiv, 192 p.. — *Includes bibliographical references and index*

LEONE, Robert A
Who profits : winners, losers, and government regulation / Robert A. Leone. — New York : Basic Books, 1986. — xiii, 248 p.. — *Includes index. — Bibliography: p. 231-237*

BUSINESS ARCHIVES COUNCIL

Newsletter / Business Archives Council. — London : Business Archives Council, 1986-. — *Quarterly*

BUSINESS CYCLES

ALOGOSKOUFIS, George S.
Competitiveness, oil prices and government expenditure in the United Kingdom business cycle / George Alogoskoufis. — London : Centre for Economic Policy Research, 1987. — 28p. — (Discussion paper series / Centre for Economic Policy Research ; no.184). — *Bibliography: p22-23*

BOWER, Joseph L
When markets quake : the management challenge of restructuring industry / Joseph L. Bower. — Boston, Mass. : Harvard Business School Press, c1986. — xi, 240 p.. — *Includes bibliographies and index*

CIRET. Conference (17th : 1985 : Vienna)
CIRET. Conference (17th : 1985 : Vienna)

Business cycle surveys in the assessment of economic activity : papers presented at the 17th CIRET Conference proceedings, Vienna, 1985 / edited by Karl Heinrich Oppenländer and Günter Poser. — Aldershot : Gower, c1986. — xi,664p

GOUREVITCH, Peter Alexis
Politics in hard times : comparative responses to international economic crises / Peter Gourevitch. — Ithaca : Cornell University Press, 1986. — p. cm. — (Cornell studies in political economy). — *Includes index*

Real business cycles, real exchange rates and actual policies / editors, Karl Brunner [and] Allan H. Meltzer. — Amsterdam : North-Holland, 1986. — 304p. — (Carnegie-Rochester Conference Series on Public Policy ; vol.25)

BUSINESS CYCLES — Congresses

INTERNATIONAL ASSOCIATION OF ENERGY ECONOMISTS. North American Meeting (1985 : Philadelphia, Pa.)
World energy markets : stability or cyclical change? : proceedings, Seventh Annual North American Meeting, International Association of Energy Economists, Philadelphia, Pennsylvania, December 1985 / edited by William F. Thompson and David J. DeAngelo. — Boulder : Westview Press, 1985. — xiii, 690 p.. — (Westview special studies in natural resources and energy management). — *Includes bibliographies*

BUSINESS CYCLES — History

RAPOŠ, Pavel
Die kranke Wirtschaft : Kapitalismus und krise / Pavel Rapoš ; Übersetzung aus dem Slowakischen: Intertext. — Köln : Pahl-Rugenstein, 1984. — 321p. — *Originally published: Bratislava: Pravda, 1981*

BUSINESS CYCLES — Mathematical models

LUCAS, Robert E.
Models of business cycles / Robert E. Lucas Jr. — Oxford : Basil Blackwell, 1987. — 115p. — (Yrjö Jahnsson lectures). — *Includes index*

BUSINESS CYCLES — Mathematical models — Congresses

Competition, instability, and nonlinear cycles : proceedings of an international conference, New School for Social Research, New York, USA, March 1985 / edited by Willi Semmler. — Berlin ; New York : Springer-Verlag, c1986. — p. cm. — (Lecture notes in economics and mathematical systems ; 275)

BUSINESS CYCLES — Europe

HIBBS, Douglas A.
The political economy of industrial democracies / Douglas A. Hibbs, Jr. — Cambridge, Mass. ; London : Harvard University Press, 1987. — viii, 327 p.. — *Includes bibliographical references and index*

BUSINESS CYCLES — Europe — Congresses

ROUND TABLE ON TRANSPORT ECONOMICS (41st : 1978 : Paris)
The role of transport in counter-cyclical policy : report of the forty-first Round Table on Transport Economics, held in Paris on 2nd-3rd March, 1978 ... — Paris : Organisation for Economic Co-operation and Development. — 61p. — *At head of title: Economic Research Centre. — Bibliography: p47-48*

BUSINESS CYCLES — United States

HIBBS, Douglas A.
The political economy of industrial democracies / Douglas A. Hibbs, Jr. — Cambridge, Mass. ; London : Harvard University Press, 1987. — viii, 327 p.. — *Includes bibliographical references and index*

BUSINESS CYCLES — United States — Addresses, essays, lectures

The American business cycle : continuity and change / edited by Robert J. Gordon. — Chicago : University of Chicago Press, 1986. — p. cm. — *Includes bibliographies and index*

BUSINESS EDUCATION — United States

The official guide to MBA programs, admissions, and careers / Graduate Management Admission Council. — Princeton, N.J. : Graduate Management Admission Council

BUSINESS EDUCATION GRADUATES — United States

The official guide to MBA programs, admissions, and careers / Graduate Management Admission Council. — Princeton, N.J. : Graduate Management Admission Council

BUSINESS ENTERPRISES

Research in international business and international relations. — Greenwich, Conn. : Jai Press, 1986. — *Annual*

BUSINESS ENTERPRISES
continuation

UNION DES INDUSTRIES DE LA COMMUNAUTÉ EUROPEENNE
Rôle et avenir des petites et moyennes entreprises industrielles. — Bruxelles : U.N.I.C.E., [1970]. — 32p

BUSINESS ENTERPRISES — Accounting

Statement of financial accounting standards. — Stamford, Conn. : Financial Accounting Standards Board. — (Financial accounting series)
no.90: Regulated enterprises accounting for abandonments and disallowances of plant costs: an amendment of FASB Statement no.71. — 1986. — 33p

BUSINESS ENTERPRISES — Employment — Organization for Economic Co-operation and Development countries

The role of large firms in local job creation. — [Paris] : Organisation for Economic Co-operation and Development, 1986. — 31p. — (Local initiatives for employment creation)

BUSINESS ENTERPRISES — Finance

The Economics of the firm / edited by Roger Clarke and Tony McGuinness. — Oxford : Basil Blackwell, 1987. — 190p. — *Bibliography : p174-185. — Includes index*

HIGSON, C. J.
Business finance / C.J. Higson. — London : Butterworths, 1986. — [iii,450]p. — *Includes bibliographies and index*

Modern finance and industrial economics : papers in honor of J. Fred Weston / edited by Thomas E. Copeland. — Oxford : Basil Blackwell, 1987. — xii,253p. — *Includes bibliographies and index*

BUSINESS ENTERPRISES — Finance — Data processing

MCLAUGHLIN, Hugh S
Financial management with Lotus 1-2-3 / Hugh S. McLaughlin, J. Russell Boulding. — Englewood Cliffs, N.J. : Prentice-Hall, c1986. — p. cm. — *On t.p. the circled symbol "R" is superscript following "Lotus" and "1-2-3" in the title. — Includes bibliographies and index*

THOMAS, Tom E.
Financial decision making with VisiCalc and SuperCalc / Tom E. Thomas. — Englewood Cliffs, N.J. : Prentice-Hall, 1985. — p. cm. — *Includes index*

BUSINESS ENTERPRISES — Finance — Research

Symposium on business finance research : discussion papers. — [Glasgow] : Department of Accountancy, University of Glasgow, 1984. — 65p. — (Accounting, auditing and business finance research symposium ; no.2). — *Includes bibliographies*

BUSINESS ENTERPRISES — Foreign Government ownership — Bibliography

Nationalization or take-over of foreign enterprises : a select bibliography = Nationalisation ou reprise des entreprises étrangères : bibliographie sélective. — New York : United Nations, 1974. — 17p. — ([Document] / United Nations ; ST/LIB/35). — *In various languages*

BUSINESS ENTERPRISES — Political aspects — France

WEISS, Dimitri
Centralité de l'entreprise et partis politiques / Dimitri Weiss. — [S.l.] : Revue française de Gestion, 1977. — 122p

BUSINESS ENTERPRISES — Research

Research approaches on business enterprises : proceedings of the Second Summer Seminar of the Group on the Theory of the Firm, 6-7 June 1985, Espoo Finland / Kari Lilja, Keijo Räsänen, Risto Tainio (eds.). — Helsinki : Helsinki School of Economics, 1985. — 101p. — (Publications of the Research Group on the Theory of the Firm ; no.4)

BUSINESS ENTERPRISES — Belgium

FÉDÉRATION DES ENTREPRISES DE BELGIQUE
La Belgique dans le monde. — Bruxelles : Fédération des Entreprises de Belgique, 1973. — 60p

BUSINESS ENTERPRISES — Belgium — History — 19th century

KURGAN-VAN HENTENRYK, G
Rail, finance et politique : les entreprises Philippart, 1865-1890 / G. Kurgan-van Hentenryk. — Bruxelles, Belgique : Editions de l'Université de Bruxelles, 1982. — 392 p.. — (Université libre de Bruxelles, Faculté de philosophie et lettres ; 84). — *Includes index. — Bibliography: p. 366-370*

BUSINESS ENTERPRISES — Belize — Rules and practice

DEVELOPMENT FINANCE CORPORATION (Belize). Investment Promotion Unit
Formation and conduct of commercial entities in Belize. — Belize City : the Corporation, 1980. — 4 leaves

BUSINESS ENTERPRISES — Burkina Faso

Elements caractéristiques des entreprises du Burkina Faso. — Ouagadougou : Institut National de Statistique et de la Démographie, [1986]. — 31p

BUSINESS ENTERPRISES — England — London

WILSON, Peter E. B.
Black business in Brent : a study of Inner London black minority enterprise / Peter Wilson and John Stanworth. — London : Small Business Research Trust, 1985. — 57p. — *Bibliography: p37-38*

BUSINESS ENTERPRISES — France

MORVILLE, Pierre
Les nouvelles politiques sociales du patronat / Pierre Morville. — Paris : La Découverte, 1985. — 127p. — *Bibliography: p124-125*

BUSINESS ENTERPRISES — France — Statistics

MONFORT, Jean Alain
La concentration des activités économiques : les établissements, les entreprises et les groupes / Jean Alain Monfort, Laurent Vassille. — Paris : Institut national de la statistique et des études économiques, 1985. — 171p. — (Les collections de l'INSEE. Série E ; no.98)

BUSINESS ENTERPRISES — Germany

German yearbook on business history / edited by the German Society for Business History, Cologne in cooperation with the Institute for Bank-Historical Research, Frankfurt/Main. — Berlin : Springer-Verlag, 1985-. — *Annual*

BUSINESS ENTERPRISES — Great Britain

COOKE, R. M.
Establishing a business in the United Kingdom / R. M. Cooke and D. C. Borer. — 3rd ed. — London : Institute of Chartered Accountants, 1986. — viii,226p

DONNELLY, Graham
The firm in society / Graham Donnelly. — 2nd ed. — London : Pitman, 1987. — [384]p. — *Previous ed.: London : Longman, 1981. — Includes index*

HART, P. E.
Job generation and size of firm / P. E. Hart. — London : National Institute of Economic and Social Research, 1987. — 24p. — (Discussion paper / National Institute of Economic and Social Research ; no.125). — *Bibliography: p22*

BUSINESS ENTERPRISES — Great Britain — History — Bibliography

Debrett's bibliography of business history / edited by Stephanie Zarach ; foreword by Theo Barker. — Basingstoke : Macmillan in association with Debrett's History Research, 1987. — xv,278p. — *Includes index*

GOODALL, Francis
A bibliography of British business histories / Francis Goodall ; with an introduction by Geoffrey Jones ... [et al.]. — Aldershot : Gower, c1987. — v,638p. — ([Business history series]). — *Includes index*

BUSINESS ENTERPRISES — Great Britain — History — 19th century

CHECKLAND, S. G.
The city and the businessman viewed historically : an aspect of the performance of capitalism / by Sydney Checkland. — Leicester : Victorian Studies Centre, University of Leicester, 1985. — 24p. — (The H.J. Dyos memorial lecture ; 1985)

BUSINESS ENTERPRISES — Hungary

Koncepció és kritika : vita Liska Tibor "szocialista vállalkozási szektor" javaslatáról / szerkesztette síklaky István. — Budapest : Magvetö kiadó, [1985]. — 387p. — (Gyorsuló idö)

BUSINESS ENTERPRISES — India — Statistics

INDIA. Central Statistical Organisation
Economic census 1980 : all-India report. — [New Delhi] : Central Statistical Organisation, [1985]. — 101p

INDIA. Central Statistical Organisation
Economic census 1980 : districtwise aggregates of principal characteristics of enterprises. — [New Delhi] : Central Statistical Organisation, 1986. — 302p

BUSINESS ENTERPRISES — Manitoba

MANITOBA. Business Development and Tourism Department
Annual report / Business Development and Tourism Department, Manitoba. — Winnipeg : [the Department], 1983/84-. — *Annual*

BUSINESS ENTERPRISES — Netherlands

Voorjaarsnota / Raad voor het Midden-en Kleinbedrijf. — 's-Gravenhage : Raad voor het Midden-en Keinbedrijf, 1984-. — *Annual*

BUSINESS ENTERPRISES — Netherlands — Corrupt practices

BERGHUIS, A. C.
Abuse of Dutch private companies (BVs) : an empirical study / A. C. Berghuis, G. Paulides. — The Hague : Research and Documentation Centre, Ministry of Justice, 1985. — 35p. — ([Reports, papers, articles] ; 77). — *Includes bibliographical references*

BUSINESS ENTERPRISES — Norway

HALVORSEN, Ragnar
Lønnsomhetskrav : Strategi for lønnsom vekst sett fra Dyno Industrier A.S' side / Ragnar Halvorsen. — Bergen : Norges handelshøyskole, 1985. — 34p. — (Kristofer Lehmkuhl Forelesning ; 1985)

BUSINESS ENTERPRISES — Spain

La empresa española ante la CEE / selección de textos y coordinación Eduardo Bueno Campos. — Madrid : Instituto de Estudios Económicos, 1984. — xxvii,184p. — *Revista del Instituto de Estudios Económicos, 1984, No.2*

La empresa española en las Comunidades Europeas : temas clave de gestión / por Lluís Riera i Figueras...[et al.] ; prólogo por Manuel Marín. — Barcelona : Editorial Hispano Europea, 1986. — 423p. — (Colección ESADE " Estudios de la Empresa). — *Bibliographies*

LAMPREAVE PEREZ, Jose Luis
La empresa española ante el impuesto sobre el valor añadido : medidas de adaptación y ajuste / Jose Luis Lampreave Perez, Juan Antonio Gimeno Ullastres y Alberto Terol Esteban ; prologo: César Albiñana García-Quintana. — Madrid : Instituto de Estudios Fiscales, 1985. — 493p

BUSINESS ENTERPRISES — Spain — Finance
GUTIÉRREZ, Fernando
La empresa española y su financiación (1963-1982) : (análisis elaborado a partir de una muestra de 21 empresas cotizadas en Bolsa) / Fernando Gutiérrez, Eduardo Fernández. — [Madrid] : Banco de España, 1985. — 128p. — (Estudios económicos / Banco de España, servicio de Estudios ; no.38). — *Bibliography: p128*

BUSINESS ENTERPRISES — Switzerland
WALSER, Rudolf
Les réglementations publiques : un fardeau pour les PME : données du problème et solutions possibles / Rudolf Walser [and] Urs Hunkeler. — Zurich : Union Suisse du Commerce et de l'Industrie, 1986. — 28p

BUSINESS ENTERPRISES, FOREIGN — Yugoslavia
YUGOSLAVIA
[Laws etc]. The law on exports and imports of goods and services ; The decree on requirements for the opening and work of representative offices of foreign persons in Yugoslavia. — Belgrade : Jugoslovenski pregled, 1986. — 103p

BUSINESS ENTREPRISES — Ile-de-France (France)
Les mouvements des entreprises en Ile-de-France. — Paris : Institut d'aménagement et d'urbanisme de la région d'Ile-de-France, 1984. — 95 leaves

BUSINESS ETHICS
BRAYBROOKE, David
Ethics in the world of business / David Braybrooke. — Totowa, N.J. : Rowman and Littlefield, 1982. — xvii, 488p. — (Philosophy and society). — *Includes bibliographic references and index*

BUSINESS ETHICS — Addresses, essays, lectures
Corporations and the common good / edited by Robert B. Dickie and Leroy S. Rouner. — Notre Dame, Ind. : University of Notre Dame Press, c1986. — xii, 147 p.. — "Published with the School of Management, Boston University.". — *Includes bibliographies. — Contents: Introduction -- The moral crisis of capitalism / Peter Berger -- Realities and appearances in capitalism / Robert Heil-broner -- Perfecting capitalism / James E. Post -- The large corporation and the new American ideology / George C. Lodge -- The multinational corporation / Kenneth Mason -- Ethics and corporate strategy / Edwin A. Murray, Jr. -- Sanctions, incentives, and corporate behavior / Peter T. Jones -- Epilogue : can managers be taught to be ethical? / Henry Morgan*

BUSINESS ETHICS — Congresses
NATIONAL CONFERENCE ON BUSINESS ETHICS (1985 : Waltham, Mass.)
Ethics and the multinational enterprise : proceedings of the Sixth National Conference on Business Ethics, October 10 and 11, 1985 / sponsored by Center for Business Ethics, Bentley College, Waltham, Massachusetts ; edited by W. Michael Hoffman, Ann E. Lange, David A. Fedo. — Lanham, MD : University Press of America, c1986. — xlix, 530 p.. — *Includes bibliographies*

BUSINESS FORECASTING
SAUNDERS, John A.
Practical business forecasting / John A. Saunders, John A. Sharp and Stephen F. Witt. — Aldershot : Gower, c1987. — xii, 340p. — *Includes bibliographies and index*

BUSINESS INTELLIGENCE
FREEMANTLE, Brian
The steal : counterfeiting and industrial espionage / Brian Freemantle. — London : Joseph, 1986. — [256]p. — *Includes bibliography and index*

Legal industrial espionage : a sourcebook and guide to finding company information / edited by Tony Reid. — Northill, Beds. : Eurofi (UK), 1985. — 158p

BUSINESS MATHEMATICS
MCCUTCHEON, J. J.
An introduction to the mathematics of finances / J. J. McCutcheon and W.F. Scott. — London : Published for the Institute of Actuaries and the Faculty of Actuaries [by] Heinemann, 1986. — x, 46ep. — *Bibliography: p310-312. — Includes index*

BUSINESS MATHEMATICS — Data processing
MUNDEL, Marvin Everett
BASIC, a personal computer language for improving productivity / Marvin E. Mundel and David Danner. — Tokyo, Japan : Asian Productivity Organization, c1986. — v, 322p. — *Includes index*

BUSINESS RECORDS
ARMSTRONG, John, 1944-
Business documents : their origins, sources and uses in historical research / John Armstrong and Stephanie Jones. — London : Mansell, 1987. — xvi, 251p. — *Bibliography: p231-235. — Includes index*

BUSINESS TAX — Germany (West)
Local business taxes in Britain and Germany : report on an Anglo-German conference 8-9 April 1986, [London] / [edited by R. J. Bennett and H. Zimmermann]. — London : Anglo-German Foundation for the Study of Industrial Society, 1986. — 186p

BUSINESS TAX — Great Britain
Local business taxes in Britain and Germany : report on an Anglo-German conference 8-9 April 1986, [London] / [edited by R. J. Bennett and H. Zimmermann]. — London : Anglo-German Foundation for the Study of Industrial Society, 1986. — 186p

BUSINESSMEN — Canada — Biography
BROCK, Peter Jeffry
William Rees Brock, 1836-1917 : paradise regained : an odyssey in Canadian business / by Peter Jeffry Brock. — Toronto : National Press, 1984. — 382p

BUSINESSMEN — Great Britain — Biography
BRADLEY, Ian, 1950-
Enlightened entrepreneurs / Ian Campbell Bradley. — London : Weidenfeld and Nicolson, 1987. — xii, 207p, 12p of plates. — *Bibliography: p202*

FORTE, Charles
Forte : the autobiography of Charles Forte. — London : Sidgwick and Jackson, 1986. — x, 235p

Geoffrey Heyworth : Baron Heyworth of Oxton : a memoir. — [London] ([PO Box 68, Unilever Hse., Blackfriars, EC4P 4BQ]) : [Unilever], c1985. — 71p

GOLDSMITH, Walter
The new elite : Britain's top chief executives / Walter Goldsmith and Berry Ritchie. — London : Weidenfeld and Nicolson, 1987. — ix, 179p

BUSINESSMEN — great Britain — Biography
KAY, William
Tycoons : where they came from and how they made it / William Kay. — London : Pan, 1986. — 208p

BUSINESSMEN — Great Britain — Biography
REDHEAD, Brian
The Summers of Shotton / Brian Redhead & Sheila Gooddie. — London : Hodder and Stoughton, 1987. — 160p. — *Map on lining papers. — Bibliography: p156. — Includes index*

BUSINESSMEN — Great Britain — Political activity
CONFEDERATION OF BRITISH INDUSTRY
Working with politicians / CBI. — London : Confederation of British Industry, 1985. — 135p. — *Includes supplement of updating information, May 1986*

BUSINESSMEN — India — Case studies
NAFZIGER, E. Wayne
Entrepreneurship, equity, and economic development / by E. Wayne Nafziger. — Greenwich, Conn. : JAI Press, c1986. — p. cm. — (Contemporary studies in economic and financial analysis ; v. 53). — *Includes index. — Bibliography: p*

BUSINESSMEN — Japan — Biography
MORITA, Akio
Made in Japan : Akio Morita and Sony / Akio Morita with Edwin M. Reingold and Mitsuko Shimomura. — London : Collins, 1987. — viii, 309p, [8]p of plates. — *Includes index*

BUSINESSMEN — Mexico — History
WALKER, David W
Kinship, business, and politics : the Martínez del Río family in Mexico, 1824-1867 / by David W. Walker. — 1st ed. — Austin : University of Texas Press, 1986. — x, 278 p.. — (Latin American monographs / Institute of Latin American Studies, University of Texas at Austin ; no.70). — *Includes index. — Bibliography: p. [259]-267*

BUSINESSMEN — Nigeria — Case studies
NAFZIGER, E. Wayne
Entrepreneurship, equity, and economic development / by E. Wayne Nafziger. — Greenwich, Conn. : JAI Press, c1986. — p. cm. — (Contemporary studies in economic and financial analysis ; v. 53). — *Includes index. — Bibliography: p*

BUSINESSMEN — Pennsylvania — Philadelphia — History — 18th century
DOERFLINGER, Thomas M
A vigorous spirit of enterprise : merchants and economic development in Revolutionary Philadelphia / Thomas M. Doerflinger. — Chapel Hill : Published for the Institute of Early American History and Culture, Williamsburg, Va. by the University of North Carolina Press, c1986. — xvi, 413 p.. — *Includes index. — Bibliography: p. [383]-398*

BUSINESSMEN — United States
BAUER, Raymond A.
American business and public policy : the politics of foreign trade / Raymond A. Bauer, Ithiel de Sola Pool, Lewis Anthony Dexter. — New York : Atherton Press, 1963. — xxvii, 499p

NADER, Ralph
The big boys : portraits of corporate power / Ralph Nader and William Taylor. — New York : Pantheon Books, 1986. — xix, 571p. — *Includes index. — Bibliography: p.523-553*

BUSINESSMEN — United States — Biography
ABODAHER, David
Iacocca / David Abodaher. — London : W.H. Allen, 1986. — 276p, [8]p of plates. — (A Star book). — *Originally published: New York : Macmillan, 1982*

HAMMER, Armand
Witness to history / by Armand Hammer with Neil Lyndon. — New York ; London : Simon & Schuster, 1987. — [512]p. — *Includes index*

MERCER, Lloyd J
E.H. Harriman, master railroader / Lloyd J. Mercer. — Boston, Mass. : Twayne Publishers, c1985. — p. cm. — (The Evolution of American business). — *Includes index. — Bibliography: p*

BUSING FOR SCHOOL INTEGRATION — Law and legislation — United States
DIMOND, Paul R
Beyond busing : inside the challenge to urban segregation / Paul R. Dimond. — Ann Arbor : University of Michigan Press, c1985. — p. cm. — *Bibliography: p*

BUSING FOR SCHOOL INTEGRATION — Massachusetts — Boston
LUKAS, J. Anthony
Common ground : a turbulent decade in the lives of three American Families / J. Anthony Lukas. — New York : Vintage Books, 1986. — xiv,674p. — *Originally published: New York : Random House, 1985*

BUSING FOR SCHOOL INTEGRATION — Tennessee — Nashville — History
PRIDE, Richard A
The burden of busing : the politics of desegregation in Nashville, Tennessee / Richard A. Pride, J. David Woodard. — Knoxville : University of Tennessee Press, [1985]. — xii, 302p. — *Includes index.* — *Bibliography: p 287-296*

BUSOGA (UGANDA) — Social life and customs
Towards a reconstructed past : historical texts from Busoga, Uganda / [compiled by] David William Cohen. — Oxford : Published for the British Academy by Oxford University Press, c1986. — 363p. — (Union Academique Internationale fontes historiae Africanae. Series varia ; 3). — *Parallel, Luganda text and English translation.* — *Includes index*

BUTLER, RICHARD AUSTEN BUTLER, Baron
HOWARD, Anthony
Rab : the life of R.A. Butler / Anthony Howard. — London : Cape, 1987. — xv,422p,[24]p of plates. — *Bibliography: p407-410.* — *Includes index*

BYELORUSSIAN S.S.R. — History — February Revolution, 1917
IGNATENKO, I. M.
Fevral'skaia burzhuazno-demokraticheskaia revoliutsiia v Belorussii / I. M. Ignatenko. — Minsk : Nauka i tekhnika, 1986. — 341p

BYELORUSSIAN S.S.R. — Politics and government
Kommunisticheskaia partiia Belorussii v rezoliutsiiakh i resheniiakh s"ezdov i plenumov TsK / [pod obshchei redaktsiei G. G. Bartoshevicha...et al.]. — Minsk : Belarus' T.4: 1945-1955. — 1986. — 615p

MARTIUKHOVA, M. A.
Na perelome revoliutsii : obshchestvenno-politicheskoe dvizhenie v Belorussii v sviazi s uchrezhdeniem Gosudarstvennoi dumy v Rossii (avgust 1905-iiul' 1906 g.) / M. A. Martiukhova ; pod redaktsiei T. E. Solodkova. — Minsk : Nauka i Tekhnika, 1986. — 140p

BYELORUSSIAN S.S.R. — Religion
Katolitsizm v Belorussii : traditsionalizm i prisposoblenie / pod redaktsiei A. S. Maikhrovicha, E. S. Prokoshinoi. — Minsk : Nauka i tekhnika, 1987. — 238p

BYRDCLIFFE (Art colony) — Exhibitions
Life by design : Delaware Art Museum, November 9, 1984-January 6, 1985 / [photography by Rick Echelmeyer ; editor, Richard J. Mulrooney]. — Wilmington, Del. (2301 Kentmere Pkwy., Wilmington 19806) : The Museum, c1984. — iv, 31 p.. — *At head of title: The Byrdcliffe Arts and Crafts Colony.* — *Cover title: The Byrdcliffe Arts & Crafts Colony : life by design.* — *Catalogue of an exhibition held at the Delaware Art Museum, Nov. 9, 1984-Jan. 6, 1985 and at the Edith C. Blum Art Institute, Jan. 15-Mar. 31, 1985.* — *Includes bibliographies*

BYZANTINE EMPIRE — History
OSTROGORSKY, Georg
History of the Byzantine state / Georg Ostrogorsky ; translated by Joan Hussey. — Oxford : Blackwell, 1956. — xxvii,548p

C O B O L (COMPUTER PROGRAM LANGUAGE)
MCCRACKEN, Daniel D.
A simplified guide to structured COBOL programming / Daniel D. McCracken. — New York ; London : Wiley, 1976. — [9],390p. — *With answers to starred exercises.* — *Includes index*

C.1673-1717
LIDDELL, Henry
The Letters of Henry Liddell to William Cotesworth / edited by J. M. Ellis. — [Durham?] : Surtees Society, 1987. — xvi,293p. — (Publications of the Surtees Society ; v.197)

CABINET MINISTERS — Canada — Biography
CONRAD, Margaret
George Nowlan : Maritime Conservative in national politics / Margaret Conrad. — Toronto : University of Toronto Press, 1986. — xviii,357p. — *Notes: p[309]-343*

MACLAREN, Roy
Honourable mentions : the uncommon diary of an M.P. / Roy MacLaren. — Toronto : Deneau, 1986. — 226p

WHELAN, Eugene
Whelan : the man in the green stetson / by Eugene Whelan ; with Rick Archbold. — Toronto : Irwin Publishing, 1986. — 322p

CABINET OFFICERS — Handbooks, manuals, etc
TRUHART, Peter
Regents of nations : systematic chronology of states and their political representives in past and present : a biographical reference book = Regenten der Nationen : systematische Chronologie die Sraaten und ihrer politischen Repräsentanten in Vergangenheit und Gegenwart : ein biographisches Nachgeschlagewerk / Peter Truhart. — München : K.G. Saur. — *Headings in English and German*
Pt.3
1: Mittel-, Ost-, Nord-, Süd-, Südosteuropa. — 1986. — xii,2280-3357

CABINET OFFICERS — Canada — Biography
CAHILL, Jack
John Turner : the long run / by Jack Cahill. — Toronto, Ont. : McClelland and Stewart, c1984. — 234 p., [24] p. of plates. — *Includes index*

CHRÉTIEN, Jean
Straight from the heart / Jean Chrétien. — Toronto, Ont., Canada : Key Porter Books, c1985. — 231 p. — *Includes index*

FLEMING, Donald M
So very near : the political memoirs of the Honourable Donald M. Fleming. — Toronto, Ont. : McCelland and Stewart, c1985. — 2 v.. — *Includes index.* — *Contents: v. 1. The rising years--v. 2. The summit years*

CABINET OFFICERS — Great Britain
ROSE, Richard, 1933-
Ministers and ministries : a functional analysis / Richard Rose. — Oxford : Clarendon, 1987. — [256]p. — *Includes bibliography and index*

CABINET OFFICERS — Great Britain — History — 19th century
British foreign secretaries and foreign policy : from Crimean War to First World War / edited by Keith M. Wilson. — London : Croom Helm, c1987. — v,218p. — *Includes index*

CABINET OFFICERS — Great Britain — History — 20th century
British foreign secretaries and foreign policy : from Crimean War to First World War / edited by Keith M. Wilson. — London : Croom Helm, c1987. — v,218p. — *Includes index*

CABINET OFFICERS — Ontario — Biography
OLIVER, Peter
Unlikely Tory : the life and politics of Allan Grossman / Peter Oliver. — 1st ed. — Toronto, Ont. : L. & O. Dennys, c1985. — xi, 322 p., [8] p. of plates. — *Includes bibliographical references and index*

CABINET OFFICERS — Poland
KONARSKI, Marek
Stanowisko ministra w PRL : zagadnienia prawno-konstytucyjne / Marek Konarski. — Warszawa : Państwowe Wydawnictwo Naukowe, 1986. — 287p. — *Bibliography: p283-286*

CABINET OFFICERS — United States — Biography
GREENYA, John
The real David Stockman / by John Greenya and Anne Urban ; introduction by Ralph Nader. — New York : St. Martin's Press, 1986. — p. cm. — *On t.p. "real" is italicized*

CABINET SYSTEM — Great Britain
BUTLER, David, 1924-
Governing without a majority : dilemmas for hung parliaments in Britain / David Butler. — 2nd ed. — Basingstoke : Macmillan, 1986. — [156]p. — *Previous ed.: London : Collins, 1983.* — *Includes index*

ROSE, Richard, 1933-
Ministers and ministries : a functional analysis / Richard Rose. — Oxford : Clarendon, 1987. — [256]p. — *Includes bibliography and index*

CABLE TELEVISION — Management
SHERMAN, Barry L.
Telecommunications management : the broadcast & cable industries / Barry L. Sherman. — New York ; London : McGraw—Hill, 1987. — (McGraw-Hill series in mass communication)

CABLE TELEVISION — Canada — Statistics
Cable television = Télédistribution / Statistics Canada. — Ottawa : Minister of Supply and Services Canada, 1984-. — *Annual.* — *Text in English and French*

CABLE TELEVISION — Great Britain
GREAT BRITAIN. Parliament. House of Commons. Library. Research Division
Television and cable / J. M. Fiddick. — [London] : the Division, 1982. — 32p. — (Background paper ; no.106)

HARPER, J. M.
Telecommunications and computing : the uncompleted revolution : a survey in plain English of the state of the common ground of telecommunications, computing, office machinery and cable television in the UK / J. M. Harper. — London : Communications Educational Services, 1986. — xix,200p

CACAO
Cocoa production : present constraints and priorities for research / R. A. Lass and G. A. R. Wood, editors. — Washington, D.C. : The World Bank, 1985. — xi,95p. — (World Bank technical paper ; no.39)

CACAO — Research
Cocoa production : present constraints and priorities for research / R. A. Lass and G. A. R. Wood, editors. — Washington, D.C. : The World Bank, 1985. — xi,95p. — (World Bank technical paper ; no.39)

CADASTERS — Soviet Union — History — 17th century

MILOV, L. V.
Tendentsii agrarnogo razvitiia Rossii pervoi poloviny XVII stoletiia : istoriografiia, komp'iuter i metody issledovaniia / L. V. Milov, M. B. Bulgakov, I. M. Garskova. — Moskva : Izd-vo Moskovskogo universiteta, 1986. — 299p

CÁDIZ (SPAIN) — Politics and government — History — 19th century

LA PARRA LÓPEZ, Emilio
La libertad de prensa en las Cortes de Cádiz / Emilio La Parra López. — Valencia : NAU llibres, 1984. — 130p. — *Includes references*

CAJUNS — Louisiana — Henderson — Social conditions

ESMAN, Marjorie R
Henderson, Louisiana : cultural adaptation in a Cajun community / by Marjorie R. Esman. — New York : Holt, Rinehart, and Winston, c1985. — xv, 137 p.. — (Case studies in cultural anthropology). — *Includes index. — Bibliography: p. 133-134*

CALCULUS

ALLEN, R. G. D.
Mathematical analysis for economists / R.G.D. Allen. — London : Macmillan ; New York : St. Martin's Press, 1962. — 548p.,ill.,23cm. — (Studies in statistics and scientific method ; no.3) (Papermacs ; no.34). — *Originally published 1938*

COURANT, Richard
Differential and integral calculus / Richard Courant ; translated by E. J. McShane. — 2nd ed. — London : Blackie. — *First published in 1936*
Vol.1. — 1960. — xiii,616p

MENTZENIOTIS, Dionisios
Three views concerning continuity and infinitesimals : non-standard analysis, topos theory and intuitionism / by Dionisios Mentzeniotis. — 251 leaves. — *PhD (Econ) 1987 LSE. — Leaves 218-234 are appendices*

CALCULUS, DIFFERENTIAL

COURANT, Richard
Differential and integral calculus / Richard Courant ; translated by E. J. McShane. — 2nd ed. — London : Blackie. — *First published in 1936*
Vol.1. — 1960. — xiii,616p

CALCULUS, INTEGRAL

COURANT, Richard
Differential and integral calculus / Richard Courant ; translated by E. J. McShane. — 2nd ed. — London : Blackie. — *First published in 1936*
Vol.1. — 1960. — xiii,616p

CALCULUS OF VARIATIONS

TIKHOMIROV, V. M.
Fundamental principles of the theory of extremal problems / by Vladimir M. Tikhomirov ; translated by Bernd Luderer. — Chichester : Wiley, 1986. — 136p. — *Translation of: Grundprinzien der Theorie der Extremalaufgaben. — Bibliography: p127-132. — Includes index*

CALI (COLOMBIA) — Economic conditions

MOHAN, Rakesh
Work, wages, and welfare in a developing, metropolis : some consequences of growth in Bogotá, Colombia / by Rakesh Mohan. — Washington, D.C. : World Bank, 1986. — xi,403p. — *Bibliographical references: p382-395*

CALIFORNIA, SOUTHERN — History

STARR, Kevin
Inventing the dream : California through the Progressive Era / Kevin Starr. — New York : Oxford University Press, 1985. — p. cm. — *Includes index. — Bibliography: p*

CALIFORNIA, SOUTHERN — Social life and customs

STARR, Kevin
Inventing the dream : California through the Progressive Era / Kevin Starr. — New York : Oxford University Press, 1985. — p. cm. — *Includes index. — Bibliography: p*

CALIFORNIA STATE UNIVERSITIES AND COLLEGES — Faculty — Statistics

BEAUMONT, Marion S
Salary systems in public higher education : a microeconomic analysis / Marion S. Beaumont. — New York : Praeger, 1985. — p. cm. — *Includes index. — Bibliography: p*

CALLAGHAN, JAMES

CALLAGHAN, James
Time and chance / James Callaghan. — London : Collins, 1987. — [420]p. — *Includes index*

CALVINISTS — England — South East — History — 16th century

PETTEGREE, Andrew
Foreign Protestant communities in sixteenth-century London / Andrew Pettegree. — Oxford : Clarendon, 1986. — ix,329p. — *Bibliography: p310-318. — Includes index*

CALVINISTS — England — South East — Social conditions

PETTEGREE, Andrew
Foreign Protestant communities in sixteenth-century London / Andrew Pettegree. — Oxford : Clarendon, 1986. — ix,329p. — *Bibliography: p310-318. — Includes index*

CALVINSIM — France — History

HELLER, Henry
The conquest of poverty : the Calvinist revolt in sixteenth century France / by Henry Heller. — Leiden : Brill, 1986. — xiii, 281p. — (Studies in medieval and reformation thought ; v.35). — *Bibliography: p.[259]-274*

CAMBODIA — Biography

MAY, Someth
Cambodian witness : the autobiography of Someth May / edited and with an introduction by James Fenton. — London : Faber, 1986. — [300]p

CAMBODIA — History — 20th century

BECKER, Elizabeth
When the war was over : the voices of Cambodia's revolution and its people / by Elizabeth Becker. — New York : Simon and Schuster, c1986. — 502 p., [8] p. of plates. — *Includes index. — Bibliography: p. 449-478*

CAMBODIA — History — Civil War, 1970-1975

SHAWCROSS, William
Sideshow : Kissinger, Nixon and the destruction of Cambodia / William Shawcross. — New ed. — London : Hogarth, 1986. — 524p,[16]p of plates. — *Previous ed.: London : Deutsch, 1979. — Bibliography: p493-495. — Includes index*

CAMBODIA — History — 1975-

CHANG, Pao-min
Kampuchea between China and Vietnam / Chang Pao-min. — Singapore : Singapore University Press, National University of Singapore, c1985. — xi, 204 p.. — *Includes bibliographical references and index*

SZYMUSIAK, Molyda
The stones cry out : a Cambodian childhood 1975-1980 / Molyda Szymusiak ; translated by Linda Coverdale. — London : Cape, 1987, c1986. — [272]p. — *Translation of: Les pierres crieront*

CAMBODIA — Politics and government

SHAWCROSS, William
Sideshow : Kissinger, Nixon and the destruction of Cambodia / William Shawcross. — New ed. — London : Hogarth, 1986. — 524p,[16]p of plates. — *Previous ed.: London : Deutsch, 1979. — Bibliography: p493-495. — Includes index*

CAMBODIA — Social life and customs

SZYMUSIAK, Molyda
The stones cry out : a Cambodian childhood 1975-1980 / Molyda Szymusiak ; translated by Linda Coverdale. — London : Cape, 1987, c1986. — [272]p. — *Translation of: Les pierres crieront*

CAMBODIAN-VIETNAMESE CONFLICT, 1977-

THAILAND. Ministry of Foreign Affairs. Department of Political Affairs
Documents on the Kampuchean problem 1979-1985. — Bangkok : the Ministry, [1985]. — ix,189p

CAMBRIDGE (CAMBRIDGESHIRE) — Intellectual life

SINCLAIR, Andrew
The red and the blue : intelligence, treason and the universities / Andrew Sinclair. — London : Weidenfeld and Nicolson, 1986. — 179p. — *Bibliography: p162-168. — Includes index*

CAMBRIDGE SCIENTIFIC INSTRUMENT COMPANY — History

CATTERMOLE, M. J. G.
Horace Darwin's shop : a history of the Cambridge Scientific Instrument Company 1878 to 1968 / M.J.G. Cattermole, A.F. Wolfe. — Bristol : Hilger, c1987. — xvi,285p. — *Bibliography: p258-276. — Includes index*

CAMBRIDGE UNIVERSITY — History — 20th century

SINCLAIR, Andrew
The red and the blue : intelligence, treason and the universities / Andrew Sinclair. — London : Weidenfeld and Nicolson, 1986. — 179p. — *Bibliography: p162-168. — Includes index*

CAMDEN. Borough Council

CAMDEN. Borough Council
Annual report and budget consultation / Camden Council. — London : London Borough of Camden, 1984/85-

CAMDEN. Housing Department

CAMDEN. Housing Department. Policy and Information Unit
London Borough of Camden : organisation of the housing department. — Camden : [the Unit], 1987. — 36p. — (Policy and information paper / Camden. Housing Department. Policy and Information Unit)

CAMDEN (LONDON, ENGLAND) — Economic conditions — Statistics

WALKER, David
Borough plan inquiry 1985/86, statistical annex : population, employment and the economy (Document E) / David Walker. — Camden : Department of Planning and Communications, 1986. — 18p. — (Planning and Communication notes)

CAMDEN (LONDON, ENGLAND) — Population

WALKER, David
Population estimates and projections 1986 / David Walker. — Camden : Department of Planning and Communications, 1987. — 25p. — (Planning and Communication notes)

CAMDEN (LONDON, ENGLAND) — Population — Statistics

Analysis of 1981 census data. — Camden : Department of Planning and Communications. — (Planning and Communication notes)
Part 2: Ward profiles / Elizabeth Pope [et al.]. — 1983. — 85 leaves

LAND, Peter
Analysis of 1981 census data for Camden. — Camden : Department of Planning and Communications. — (Planning and Communication notes)
Part 3: 10% sample borough and ward profiles / Peter Land and Richard Elliott. — 1983. — iv,83p

CAMDEN (LONDON, ENGLAND) — Population — Statistics
continuation

LAND, Peter
Analysis of 1981 census data for Camden. — Camden : Planning and Communications Department. — (Planning and Communication notes)
Part 4: Census atlas. — 1985. — 58p

LAND, Peter
Analysis of the 1981 census data for Camden. — Camden : Department of Planning and Communications. — (Planning and Communication notes)
Part 5: Ward comparisons. — 1985. — 33p

POPE, Elizabeth
Analysis of 1981 census data for Camden. — Camden : Department of Planning and Communications. — (Planning and Communication notes)
Part 1: 100% small area statistics / Elizabeth Pope, Jane Hamilton [and] David Walker. — 1982. — 59p

WALKER, David
Analysis of 1981 census data for Camden. — Camden : Department of Planning and Communications. — (Planning and Communication notes)
Part 6: Council tenants. — 1987. — 18p

WALKER, David
Borough plan inquiry 1985/86, statistical annex : population, employment and the economy (Document E) / David Walker. — Camden : Department of Planning and Communications, 1986. — 18p. — (Planning and Communication notes)

CAMEROON — Bibliography
LE VINE, Victor T
Historical dictionary of Cameroon / by Victor T. Le Vine and Roger P. Nye. — Metuchen, N.J. : Scarecrow Press, 1974. — xii, 198 p. — (African historical dictionaries ; no. 1). — *Bibliography: p. 151-198*

CAMEROON — Constitution
CAMEROON
[Constitution (1972)]. Constitution of the Republic of Cameroon. — Yaounde : General Secretariat, [1972]. — 30,30p. — *Text in English and French*

CAMEROON — Economic conditions — Statistics
Bulletin trimestriel de conjoncture / Direction de la Statistique et de la Comptabilité Nationale, Cameroon. — Yaoundé : Direction de la Statistique et de la Comptabilité Nationale, 1983-. — *Quarterly*

CAMEROON — Economic Conditions 1960- — Statistics
Le Cameroun en chiffres 1985. — Yaoundé : Direction de la Statistique et de la Comptabilité Nationale, 1985. — 26p

CAMEROON — History — Chronology
LE VINE, Victor T
Historical dictionary of Cameroon / by Victor T. Le Vine and Roger P. Nye. — Metuchen, N.J. : Scarecrow Press, 1974. — xii, 198 p. — (African historical dictionaries ; no. 1). — *Bibliography: p. 151-198*

CAMEROON — History — Dictionaries
LE VINE, Victor T
Historical dictionary of Cameroon / by Victor T. Le Vine and Roger P. Nye. — Metuchen, N.J. : Scarecrow Press, 1974. — xii, 198 p. — (African historical dictionaries ; no. 1). — *Bibliography: p. 151-198*

CAMEROON — Politics and government
Republique du Cameroun : annuaire national = Republic of Cameroon : national year-book / Department of Press and Information, Cameroon. — Yaoundé : Societé de Presse et d'Édition du Cameroun, 1986-. — *Annual*

CAMEROON — Population — Bibliography
GUBRY, Patrick
Bibliographie générale des études de population au Cameroun : arretée au 31 mars 1984 = General bibliography of population studies in Cameroon : as at 31st March 1984 / par Patrick Gubry. — Yaoundé : Ministère de l'enseignement superieur et de la recherche scientifique, 1984. — 382p. — (Travaux et documents de l'Institut des science humaines) (Collection études bibliographiques et recherches en bibliothéconomie ; no.8). — *In French, English and German with introduction in French*

CAMEROON — Population — Statistics
The Cameroon Fertility Survey, 1978 : a summary of findings. — Voorburg : International Statistical Institute, 1983. — 14p. — (World Fertility Survey ; no.41)

CAMEROON — Population — Statistics — Evaluation
SANTOW, Gigi
An evaluation of the Cameroon Fertility Survey / Gigi Santow, A. Bioumla. — Voorburg : International Statistical Institute, 1984. — 46p. — (Scientific reports / World Fertility Survey ; no.64)

CAMEROON — Statistics
Le Cameroun en chiffres 1985. — Yaoundé : Direction de la Statistique et de la Comptabilité Nationale, 1985. — 26p

CAMPAIGN FOR A SCOTTISH ASSEMBLY
CAMPAIGN FOR A SCOTTISH ASSEMBLY [Discussion papers on the Scottish constitutional convention]. — Edinburgh : Campaign for a Scottish Assembly, 1985. — 8 leaflets

CAMPAIGN FOR NUCLEAR DISARMAMENT
REEVE, Gillian
Offence of the realm : how peace campaigners get bugged / Gillian Reeve [and] Joan Smith. — London : CND Publications, 1986. — 44p

CAMPAIGN FOR NUCLEAR DISARMAMENT — History
MERCER, Paul
'Peace' of the dead : the truth behind the nuclear disarmaments / Paul Mercer ; foreword by Lord Chalfont. — London : Policy Research Publications, 1986. — 465p. — *Bibliography: p[422]-438*

CAMPAIGN FUNDS — United States
BENNETT, James T
Destroying democracy : how government funds partisan politics / James T. Bennett, Thomas J. DiLorenzo. — Washington, D.C. : Cato Institute, c1985. — xiii, 561 p.. — *Includes index.* — *Bibliography: p. 505-543*

CAMPALANS, ALBERT
BALCELLS, Albert
Rafael Campalans, socialisme català : biografia i textos / Albert Balcells. — [Barcelona?] : L'Abadia de Montserrat, 1985. — 444p

CAMPBELL, JOHN LOGAN
STONE, R. C. J.
Young Logan Campbell / R.C.J. Stone. — [Auckland] : Auckland University Press ; [Oxford] : Oxford University Press, 1982. — 287p,[24]p of plates. — *Bibliography: p273-280.* — *Includes index*

CAMPBELL, TUNIS
DUNCAN, Russell
Freedom's shore : Tunis Campbell and the Georgia freedmen / by Russell Duncan. — Athens : University of Georgia Press, c1986. — p. cm. — *Includes index.* — *Bibliography: p*

CAMRAN (YEMEN) — Social conditions
STEVENSON, Thomas B.
Social change in a Yemeni highlands town / Thomas B. Stevenson. — Salt Lake City : University of Utah Press, c1985. — xxiii, 190 p.. — *Includes index.* — *Bibliography: p. [181]-184*

CAMRAN (YEMEN) — Social life and customs
STEVENSON, Thomas B.
Social change in a Yemeni highlands town / Thomas B. Stevenson. — Salt Lake City : University of Utah Press, c1985. — xxiii, 190 p.. — *Includes index.* — *Bibliography: p. [181]-184*

CANADA. Atlantic Fisheries Restructuring Act 1983
Atlantic Ffisheries Rrestructuring Act annual report = sur la restructuration du secteur des pêches de l'Atlantique: rapport annuel / Fisheries and Oceans, Canada. — Ottawa : Department of Fisheries and Oceans, 1983/4-. — *Annual.* — *In English and French*

CANADA. Canada Health Act 1984
Canada Health Act: annual report = Loi canadienne sur la santé: rapport annual / Health and Welfare Canada. — Ottawa : Health and Welfare Canada, 1984/5-. — *Annual.* — *In English and French*

CANADA. Canadian Charter of Rights and Freedoms
Charterwatch : reflections on equality / edited by Christine L. M. Boyle...[et al.]. — Toronto : Carswell, 1986. — ix,356p

GIBSON, Dale
The law of the Charter : general principles / Dale Gibson. — Toronto : Carswell, 1986. — xxxiii,302p

CANADA. Constitution Act, 1982
CHEFFINS, Ronald I.
The revised Canadian constitution : politics as law / Ronald I. Cheffins, Patricia A. Johnson. — Toronto : McGraw-Hill Ryerson, 1986. — 244p

CANADA. Constitutional Act 1982
MEEKISON, J. Peter
Origins and meanings of Section 92A : the 1982 Constitutional Amendment on Resources / J. Peter Meekison, Roy J. Romanow [and] William D. Moull. — Montreal : Institute for Research on Public Policy/L'Institut de Recherches Politiques, 1985. — xxii,77p

CANADA. Public Service Superannuation Act (Canada)
CANADA. Treasury Board
Report on the administration of the Public Service Superannuation Act. — Ottawa : Canada. Treasury Board, 1984-. — *Annual.* — *Text in English and French*

CANADA — Air defenses, Military
BYERS, R. B
Aerospace defence : Canada's future role? / R.B. Byers, John Hamre, G.R. Lindsey. — Toronto, Canada : Canadian Institute of International Affairs, 1985. — 56 p.. — (Wellesley papers ; 9/1985). — *Includes bibliographies.* — *Contents: Defending North America / G.R. Lindsey -- Continental air defence, United States security policy, and Canada-United States defence relations / John Hamre -- NORAD, Star Wars, and strategic doctrine / R.B. Byers*

CANADA — Bibliography
Canadian studies : papers presented at a colloquium at the British Library, 17-19 August 1983 / edited by Patricia McLaren-Turner. — London : British Library, 1984. — vii,210p,[8]p of plates. — (British Library occasional papers ; 1). — *Includes bibliographies*

Canadian who's who in microfiche, incorporating Canadian men and women of the time. — Toronto : University of Toronto Press, 1898-1975

CANADA — Canadian Charter of Rights and Freedoms
The media, the courts and the Charter / edited by Philip Anisman and Allen M. Linden. — Toronto : Carswell, 1986. — xiv,521p

CANADA — Civilization — 1945- — Congresses

Se connaître : politics and culture in Canada / edited by John Lennox. — North York, Ontario : Robarts Centre for Canadian Studies, 1985. — 119p. — *Papers presented at a conference held at York University [Ontario], May 15-16, 1985. — Includes some text in French*

CANADA — Combines Investigation Act

Reaction : the new Combines Investigation Act / contributors include: Reuven Brenner....[et al.] ; edited by Walter Block. — [Vancouver] : The Fraser Institute, 1986. — xxix,208p. — *Bibliography: p203-208*

CANADA — Commerce

DALY, D. J.
Canadian manufactured exports : constraints and opportunities / D. J. Daly [and] D. C. Maccharles. — Montreal : The Institute for Research on Public Policy/L'Institut de recherches politiques. — xxviii,180p. — *Bibliography: p155-168*

CANADA — Commerce — History

BLISS, Michael
Northern enterprise : five centuries of Canadian business / Michael Bliss. — Toronto : McClelland and Stewart, 1987. — 640p. — *Bibliography: p585-618*

CANADA — Commerce — Communist countries

Canada's trade with the Soviet Union bloc : the report of a Working Group of the CIIA; Aldo Nicolai, chairman. — Toronto : Canadian Institute of International Affairs, 1985. — vi,50p. — (CIIA working group reports ; 3)

CANADA — Commerce — European Economic Community

PAPADOPOULOS, N. G.
Canada and the European Community : an uncomfortable partnership? / N. G. Papadopoulos. — Montreal : Institute for Research on Public Policy / L'Institut de recherches politiques, 1986. — xxix,136p. — (Essays in international economics / Institute for Research on Public Policy / L'Institut de recherches politiques). — *Bibliography: p111-136*

CANADA — Commerce — France — History — 18th century

BOSHER, J. F.
The Canada merchants 1713-1763 / J.F. Bosher. — Oxford : Clarendon, 1987. — viii,234p. — *Includes index*

CANADA — Commerce — Great Britain

NADEAU, Bertrand
Britain's entry into the European Economic Community and its effect on Canada's agricultural exports / Bertrand Nadeau. — Montreal : The Institute for Research on Public Policy/LInstitut de recherches politiques, 1985. — xx,111p. — (Essays in international economics). — *Foreword and summary in English and French. — Bibliography: p95-100*

CANADA — Commerce — Japan

WRIGHT, Richard W.
Japanese business in Canada : the elusive alliance / Richard W. Wright. — Montreal : The Institute for Research on Public Policy/L'Institut de recherches politiques, 1984. — xxxi,110p. — *Summary in French and English. — Bibliography: p99-100*

CANADA — Commerce — United States

Building a Canadian-American free trade area : papers / by Donald S. MacDonald...[et al.] ; edited by Edward R. Fried, Frank Stone, Philip H. Trezise. — Washington, D.C. : Brookings Institution, 1987. — xii,217p. — (Brookings dialogues on public policy)

LIPSEY, Richard G.
Taking the initative : Canada's trade options in a turbulent world / Richard G. Lipsey and Murray G. Smith. — Toronto : C.D. Howe Institute, 1985. — xi.183p. — (Observation / C.D. Howe Institute ; no.27). — *Includes references*

WINHAM, Gilbert R.
Canada - U.S. sectoral trade study : the impact of free trade : a background paper prepared for Royal Commission on the Economic Union and Development Prospects for Canada, Ottawa, Ontario - April 1985 / Gilbert R. Winham ; with the assistance of David Black...[et al.]. — Halifax, N.S. : Dalhousie University, Centre for Foreign Policy Studies, 1986. — viii,323p

WONNACOTT, Ronald J
Aggressive U.S. reciprocity evaluated with a new analytical approach to trade conflicts / R.J. Wonnacott. — Montreal, Quebec : Institute for Research on Public Policy, c1984. — xxi, 68 p.. — (Essays in international economics). — *Bibliography: p. 57-58*

CANADA — Commercial policy

GORECKI, Paul K.
The objectives of canadian competition policy 1888-1983 / Paul K. Gorecki and W. T. Stanbury. — Montreal : The Institute for Research on Public Policy, [1984]. — xxviii,236p. — *Bibliography: p189-206*

HART, Michael
Some thoughts on Canada-United States sectoral free trade / Michael Hart. — Montreal, Quebec : Institute for Research on Public Policy, c1985. — xiii, 54 p.. — (Essays in international economics). — *Bibliography: p. 43-44*

LIPSEY, Richard G.
Taking the initative : Canada's trade options in a turbulent world / Richard G. Lipsey and Murray G. Smith. — Toronto : C.D. Howe Institute, 1985. — xi.183p. — (Observation / C.D. Howe Institute ; no.27). — *Includes references*

STONE, Frank
Canada, the GATT and the international trade system / Frank Stone. — Montreal, Quebec : Institute for Research on Public Policy, [1985] c1984. — xix, 236 p.. — (Essays in international economics). — *Bibliography: p. 217-224*

WONNACOTT, Paul
The United States and Canada : the quest for freer trade : an examination of selected issues / Paul Wonnacott ; with an appendix by John Williamson. — Washington, DC : Institute for International Economics, 1987. — p. cm. — (Policy analyses in international economics ; 16). — *Bibliography: p*

CANADA — Commercial policy — History — 19th century

FORSTER, Jakob Johann Benjamin
A conjunction of interests : business, politics, and tariffs, 1825-1879 / Ben Forster. — Toronto ; Buffalo : University of Toronto Press, c1986. — vi, 288 p.. — (The State and economic life ; 8). — *Includes index. — Bibliography: p. [259]-276*

CANADA — Constitution

GREAT BRITAIN. Parliament. House of Commons. Library. International Affairs Section
Patriation of the Canadian constitution / Simon Young. — [London] : the Library, 1980. — 9p. — (Background paper / House of Commons. Library. [Research Division] ; no.84). — *Bibliography: p9*

GREAT BRITAIN. Parliament. House of Commons. Library. International Affairs Section
Patriation of the Canadian constitution / Simon Young. — [London] : the Library, 1981. — 23p. — (Background paper / House of Commons. Library. [Research Division] ; no.96). — *Replaces Background Paper no.84. — Bibliography: p21-23*

CANADA — Constitutional law

CHEFFINS, Ronald I.
The revised Canadian constitution : politics as law / Ronald I. Cheffins, Patricia A. Johnson. — Toronto : McGraw-Hill Ryerson, 1986. — 244p

HOGG, Peter W
Constitutional law of Canada / by Peter W. Hogg. — 2nd ed. — Toronto, Canada : Carswell, 1985. — lxxv, 988 p.. — *Includes indexes. — Bibliography: p. 915-925*

CANADA — Constitutional law — Amendments

Charterwatch : reflections on equality / edited by Christine L. M. Boyle...[et al.]. — Toronto : Carswell, 1986. — ix,356p

CHEFFINS, Ronald I.
The revised Canadian constitution : politics as law / Ronald I. Cheffins, Patricia A. Johnson. — Toronto : McGraw-Hill Ryerson, 1986. — 244p

GIBSON, Dale
The law of the Charter : general principles / Dale Gibson. — Toronto : Carswell, 1986. — xxxiii,302p

MEEKISON, J. Peter
Origins and meanings of Section 92A : the 1982 Constitutional Amendment on Resources / J. Peter Meekison, Roy J. Romanow [and] William D. Moull. — Montreal : Institute for Research on Public Policy/L'Institut de Recherches Politiques, 1985. — xxii,77p

CANADA — Cultural policy — Congresses

Se connaître : politics and culture in Canada / edited by John Lennox. — North York, Ontario : Robarts Centre for Canadian Studies, 1985. — 119p. — *Papers presented at a conference held at York University [Ontario], May 15-16, 1985. — Includes some text in French*

CANADA — Defenses

BYERS, R. B.
Canadian security and defence : the legacy and the challenges / R. B. Byers. — London : International Institute for Strategic Studies, 1986. — 88p. — (Adelphi papers ; 214)

CANADA. Dept. of National Defence
Defence = Défense / Dept. of National Defence, Canada. — Ottawa : [the Department], 1986-. — *Annual. — Text in English and French*

COX, David
Trends in continental defence : a Canadian perspective / David Cox. — Ottawa : Canadian Institute for International Peace and Security, 1986. — 50p. — (Occasional paper / Canadian Institute for International Peace and Security ; no.2)

CANADA — Department of Industry, Trade and Commerce

Annual reports / Department of Industry, Trade and Commerce, Department of Regional Economic Expansion and Department of Regional Industrial Expansion. — Ottawa : Minister of Supply and Services Canada, 1983/84-. — *Annual. — Text in English and French. — Continues: Annual report/Department of Regional Economic Expansion and Annual review/Department of Industry, Trade and Commerce*

CANADA — Department of Regional Economic Expansion

Annual reports / Department of Industry, Trade and Commerce, Department of Regional Economic Expansion and Department of Regional Industrial Expansion. — Ottawa : Minister of Supply and Services Canada, 1983/84-. — *Annual. — Text in English and French. — Continues: Annual report/Department of Regional Economic Expansion and Annual review/Department of Industry, Trade and Commerce*

CANADA — Department of Regional Industrial Expansion
Annual reports / Department of Industry, Trade and Commerce, Department of Regional Economic Expansion and Department of Regional Industrial Expansion. — Ottawa : Minister of Supply and Services Canada, 1983/84-. — Annual. — Text in English and French. — Continues: Annual report/Department of Regional Economic Expansion and Annual review/Department of Industry, Trade and Commerce

CANADA — Diplomatic and consular service — History
DELONG, Linwood
A guide to Canadian diplomatic relations 1925-1983 / Linwood DeLong. — Ottawa : Canadian Library Association, 1985. — 58p

CANADA — Economic conditions
LYONS, Brian
Canadian microeconomics : problems and policies / Brian Lyons. — 3rd ed. — Scarborough, Ontario : Prentice-Hall Canada, 1987. — xvi,388p

CANADA — Economic conditions — Addresses, essays, lectures
Explorations in Canadian economic history : essays in honour of Irene M. Spry / edited by Duncan Cameron. — Ottawa, Canada : University of Ottawa Press, 1985. — 330 p.. — *Bibliography: p. 327-330*

CANADA — Economic conditions — Bibliography
The New practical guide to Canadian political economy / edited by Daniel Drache & Wallace Clement. — Toronto : J. Lorimer, 1985. — xxiv, 243 p.. — *Rev. ed. of: A practical guide to Canadian political economy / Wallace Clement & Daniel Drache. — Includes bibliographies and index*

CANADA — Economic conditions — Statistics
The national balance sheet accounts = les comptes du bilan national / Statistics Canada. — Ottawa : Minister of Supply and Services Canada, 1961-. — Annual. — *Text in English and French*

CANADA — Economic conditions — 1918-1945
BROWN, Lorne
When freedom was lost : the unemployed, the agitator, and the state / Lorne Brown. — Montréal : Black Rose Books, 1987. — 208p. — *Includes bibliographic references*

CANADA — Economic conditions — 1918-
HORN, Michiel
The Great Depression of the 1930s in Canada / Michiel Horn. — Ottawa : Canadian Historical Association, 1984. — 24 p.. — (Historical booklet / Canadian Historical Association ; no. 39). — *Bibliography: p. 21-22*

PIERSON, Ruth Roach
They're still women after all : the Second World War and Canadian womanhood / Ruth Roach Pierson. — Toronto, Ont. : McClelland and Stewart, c1986. — 301 p.. — (The Canadian social history series). — *Includes index. — Bibliography: p. 221-236*

CANADA — Economic conditions — 1945-
BRYAN, Ingrid A
Economic policies in Canada / Ingrid A. Bryan. — 2nd ed. — Toronto : Butterworths, c1986. — xi, 309 p.. — *Includes bibliographies and indexes*

The Canadian economy : a regional perspective / edited by Donald J. Savoie. — Toronto ; London : Methuen, 1986. — 291p

COHEN, Maxwell
The Dominion-Provincial Conference : some basic issues / by Maxwell Cohen. — Toronto : Ryerson Press, 1945. — 39p

Economically active population : estimates and projections : 1950-2025 = Evaluations et projections de la population active : 1950-2025 = Estimaciones y proyecciones de la población económicamente activa : 1950-2025. — 3rd ed. — Geneva : International Labour Office V.4: Northern America, Europe, Oceania and USSR. — 1986. — xxvi,177p. — *Introduction and table headings in English, French and Spanish*

The Other MacDonald report : the consensus on Canada's future that the Macdonald Commission left out / edited by Daniel Drache and Duncan Cameron. — Toronto : J. Lorimer, 1985. — xxxix, 225 p.. — *Bibliography: p. [214]-225*

SAVOIE, Donald J.
Regional economic development : Canada's search for solutions / Donald J. Savoie. — Toronto ; London : University of Toronto Press, 1986. — 212p

CANADA — Economic conditions — 1945- — Regional disparities
Regionalism in Canada / edited by Robert J. Brym. — Toronto, Canada : Irwin Pub., c1986. — viii, 213 p.. — *Bibliography: p. 208-211*

CANADA — Economic conditions — 1971-
The Canadian economy : problems and policies / [edited by] G. C. Ruggeri. — 3rd ed. — Toronto : Gage Educational Publishing Company, 1987. — xiii,474p. — *Bibliography: p468-474*

CARMICHAEL, Edward A.
Confronting global challenges : policy review and outlook, 1987 / Edward A. Carmichael. — Toronto : C.D. Howe Institute, 1987. — iv,74p. — (Policy review and outlook ; 1987)

GONICK, Cy
The great economic debate : failed economics and a future for Canada / Cy Gonick. — Toronto : James Lorimer & Company, 1987. — xii,425p. — *Notes: p[389]-409*

CANADA — Economic policy
BARRADOS, John P.
A key to the Canadian economy / John P. Barrados. — Lanham, MD : University Press of America, c1966. — p. cm. — *Includes index*

BRYAN, Ingrid A
Economic policies in Canada / Ingrid A. Bryan. — 2nd ed. — Toronto : Butterworths, c1986. — xi, 309 p.. — *Includes bibliographies and indexes*

BRYCE, Robert B.
Maturing in hard times : Canada's Department of Finance through the Great Depression / Robert B. Bryce. — Kingston ; Montreal : McGill-Queen's University Press : Institute of Public Administration of Canada, 1986. — xii,278p. — (Canadian public administration series)

The Canadian economy : a regional perspective / edited by Donald J. Savoie. — Toronto ; London : Methuen, 1986. — 291p

CULLINGWORTH, J. B
Urban and regional planning in Canada / J. Barry Cullingworth. — New Brunswick, U.S.A. : Transaction Books, c1987. — p. cm. — *Includes index. — Bibliography: p*

GILLIES, James
Facing reality : consultation, consensus and making economic policy for the 21st century / James M. Gillies. — Montreal : The Institute for Research on Public Policy/L'Institut de recherches politiques, 1986. — xxxviii,221p. — *Bibliography: p199-221*

LESLIE, Peter M.
Federal state, national economy / Peter M. Leslie. — Toronto : University of Toronto Press, [1987]. — xvi,213p. — *Notes: p[191]-205*

MANZER, Ronald A
Public policies and political development in Canada / Ronald Manzer. — Toronto ; Buffalo : University of Toronto Press, c1985. — x, 240 p.. — *Includes index. — Bibliography: p. [191]-228*

MILNE, David
Tug of war : Ottawa and the provinces under Trudeau and Mulroney / David Milne. — Toronto : J. Lorimer, 1986. — viii, 275 p.. — *Includes index. — Bibliography: p. [239]-269*

Mining communities : hard lessons for the future : proceedings of the twelfth CRS policy discussion seminar, Kingston, Ontario, September 27-29, 1983. — [Kingston, Ont.] : [Centre for Resource Studies, Queen's University], 1984. — v,205p. — (Proceedings / Centre for Resource Studies, Queen's University ; no.14)

The Other MacDonald report : the consensus on Canada's future that the Macdonald Commission left out / edited by Daniel Drache and Duncan Cameron. — Toronto : J. Lorimer, 1985. — xxxix, 225 p.. — *Bibliography: p. [214]-225*

OWRAM, Doug
The government generation : Canadian intellectuals and the state 1900-1945 / Doug Owram. — Toronto ; London : University of Toronto Press, 1986. — 402p

ROBERTS, John
Agenda for Canada : towards a new liberalism / John Roberts. — 1st ed. — Toronto, Ont., Canada : Lester & Orpen Dennys, c1985. — 239 p.. — *Bibliography: p. 237-239*

SAVOIE, Donald J.
Regional economic development : Canada's search for solutions / Donald J. Savoie. — Toronto ; London : University of Toronto Press, 1986. — 212p

CANADA — Economic policy — Congresses
The Integration question : political economy and public policy in Canada and North America / edited by Jon H. Pammett and Brian W. Tomlin. — Don Mills, Ont. ; Reading, Mass. : Addison-Wesley Publishers, c1984. — 262 p.. — : *Revised papers of the Conference on Integration and Fragmentation in Canada and North America held March, 1982 at Carleton University, and sponsored by the Carleton Dept. of Political Science in cooperation with Norman Paterson School of International Affairs. — Includes bibliographies and index*

Se connaître : politics and culture in Canada / edited by John Lennox. — North York, Ontario : Robarts Centre for Canadian Studies, 1985. — 119p. — *Papers presented at a conference held at York University [Ontario], May 15-16, 1985. — Includes some text in French*

CANADA — Economic policy — 1971-
The Canadian economy : problems and policies / [edited by] G. C. Ruggeri. — 3rd ed. — Toronto : Gage Educational Publishing Company, 1987. — xiii,474p. — *Bibliography: p468-474*

CARMICHAEL, Edward A.
Confronting global challenges : policy review and outlook, 1987 / Edward A. Carmichael. — Toronto : C.D. Howe Institute, 1987. — iv,74p. — (Policy review and outlook ; 1987)

SWANKEY, Ben
The Tory budget and the corporate plan to restructure Canada : and how the system really works / by Ben Swankey. — Vancouver : Centre for Socialist Education, 1985. — xi,246p

CANADA — Economics condition — 1945-
A social frame work for economics : development from the ground up : submission of the Vanier Institute of the Family to the Royal Commission on the Economic Union and Development Prospects for Canada. — Ottawa, Ont. : Vanier Institute of the Family, 1983. — 76p

CANADA — Emigration and immigration

BUMSTED, J. M.
The Scots in Canada / J.M. Bumsted. — Ottawa : Canadian Historical Association, 1982. — 19p. — (Canada's ethnic groups. booklet ; no. 1)

COWAN, Helen I.
British immigration before Confederation / Helen I. Cowan. — Ottawa : Canadian Historical Association, 1978. — 22p. — (Canadian Historical Association booklets ; no.22)

DANYS, Matilda
D. P. [Displaced Persons] : Lithuanian immigration to Canada after the second world war / Matilda Danys. — Toronto : Multicultural History Society of Ontario, 1986. — 365p. — (Studies in ethnic and immigration history). — *Bibliography: p[352]-353*

CANADA — emigration and immigration

HIGGS, David
The Portuguese in Canada / David Higgs. — Ottawa : Canadian Historical Association, 1982. — 18p. — (Canada's ethnic groups. booklet ; n. 2)

CANADA — Emigration and immigration

RAO, G. Lakshmana
Immigrants in Canada and Australia / edited by: Anthony H. Richmond and Freda Richmond. — Repr. ed. — [Ontario : Institute for Behavioural Research Ethnic Research Programme. — *Bibliography: p113-124*
Vol.1: Demographic aspects and education / co-authors: G. Lakshmana Rao, Anthony H. Richmond, Jerzy Zubrzycki. — 1984. — v,125p

RICHMOND, Anthony H.
Immigrants in Canada and Australia / edited by Anthony H. Richmond and Freda Richmond. — [Ontario : Institute for Behaviourol Research, Ethnic Research Programme. — *Bibliography: p135-143*
Vol.2: Economic adaptation / co-authors: Anthony H. Richmond and Jerzy Zubrzycki. — 1984. — vi,144p

WARD, W. Peter
The Japanese in Canada / W. Peter Ward. — Ottawa : Canadian Historical Association, 1982. — 21p. — (Canada's ethnic groups. booklet ; no. 3)

CANADA — Emigration and immigration — History

PETRYSHYN, Jaroslav
Peasants in the promised land : Canada and the Ukrainians, 1891-1914 / Jaroslav Petryshyn with L. Dzubak. — Toronto : James Lorimer, 1985. — xi,265p. — *Bibliography: p[240]-255*

CANADA — Foreign economic relations

CONLON, R. M
Distance and duties : determinants of manufacturing in Australia and Canada / by R.M. Conlon. — Ottawa, Canada : Carleton University Press, c1985. — ix, 217 p.. — (Carleton library series ; 135). — *Bibliography: p. 210-217*

CANADA — Foreign economic relations — United States

CLARKSON, Stephen
Canada and the Reagan challenge : crisis and adjustment, 1981-85 / Stephen Clarkson. — New updated ed. — Toronto : J. Lorimer, 1985. — xv, 431 p.. — *Includes index. — Bibliography: p. 378-409*

GWYN, Richard J.
The 49th paradox : Canada in North America / Richard Gwyn. — Toronto, Ont. : McClelland and Stewart, c1985. — 362 p.. — *Includes index. Bibliography: p. 341-348*

The legal framework for Canada-United States trade / edited by Maureen Irish and Emily F. Carasco. — Toronto : Carswell, 1987. — xxxviii,275p

WONNACOTT, Paul
The United States and Canada : the quest for freer trade : an examination of selected issues / Paul Wonnacott ; with an appendix by John Williamson. — Washington, DC : Institute for International Economics, 1987. — p. cm. — (Policy analyses in international economics ; 16). — *Bibliography: p*

CANADA — Foreign economic relations — United States — Congresses

The Integration question : political economy and public policy in Canada and North America / edited by Jon H. Pammett and Brian W. Tomlin. — Don Mills, Ont. ; Reading, Mass. : Addison-Wesley Publishers, c1984. — 262 p.. — : *Revised papers of the Conference on Integration and Fragmentation in Canada and North America held March, 1982 at Carleton University, and sponsored by the Carleton Dept. of Political Science in cooperation with Norman Paterson School of International Affairs. — Includes bibliographies and index*

CANADA — Foreign population

AVERY, D. H.
The Poles in Canada / D.H.Avery and J.K.Fedorowicz. — Ottawa : Canadian Historical Association, 1982. — 22p. — (Canada's ethnic groups. booklet ; no.4)

BUMSTED, J. M.
The Scots in Canada / J.M. Bumsted. — Ottawa : Canadian Historical Association, 1982. — 19p. — (Canada's ethnic groups. booklet ; no. 1)

HIGGS, David
The Portuguese in Canada / David Higgs. — Ottawa : Canadian Historical Association, 1982. — 18p. — (Canada's ethnic groups. booklet ; n. 2)

RAO, G. Lakshmana
Immigrants in Canada and Australia / edited by: Anthony H. Richmond and Freda Richmond. — Repr. ed. — [Ontario : Institute for Behavioural Research Ethnic Research Programme. — *Bibliography: p113-124*
Vol.1: Demographic aspects and education / co-authors: G. Lakshmana Rao, Anthony H. Richmond, Jerzy Zubrzycki. — 1984. — v,125p

RICHMOND, Anthony H.
Immigrants in Canada and Australia / edited by Anthony H. Richmond and Freda Richmond. — [Ontario : Institute for Behaviourol Research, Ethnic Research Programme. — *Bibliography: p135-143*
Vol.2: Economic adaptation / co-authors: Anthony H. Richmond and Jerzy Zubrzycki. — 1984. — vi,144p

WARD, W. Peter
The Japanese in Canada / W. Peter Ward. — Ottawa : Canadian Historical Association, 1982. — 21p. — (Canada's ethnic groups. booklet ; no. 3)

CANADA — Foreign relations

FOX, William T. R
A continent apart : the United States and Canada in world politics / William T.R. Fox. — Toronto ; Buffalo : University of Toronto Press, c1985. — xv, 188 p.. — (The Bissell lectures ; 1982-3). — *Includes bibliographical references and index*

Roots of peace : the movement against militarism in Canada / edited by Eric Shragge, Ronald Babin, and Jean-Guy Vaillancourt. — Toronto : Between The Lines, 1986. — 203p. — *Bibliography: p181-194*

SOWARD, F. H.
The Department of External Affairs and Canadian autonomy, 1899-1939 / F. H. Soward. — Ottawa : Canadian Historical Association, 1979. — 24p. — (Canadian Historical Association booklets ; no.7)

CANADA — Foreign relations — Congresses

Groups and governments in Canadian foreign policy : proceedings of a conference, Ottawa, Canada, 9-11 June 1982 / edited by Don Munton. — Toronto, Ont. : Canadian Institute of International Affairs, c1985. — x, 115 p.. — *Includes bibliographical references*

CANADA — Foreign relations — History

DELONG, Linwood
A guide to Canadian diplomatic relations 1925-1983 / Linwood DeLong. — Ottawa : Canadian Library Association, 1985. — 58p

CANADA — Foreign relations — 1945-

BARROS, James
No sense of evil : espionage, the case of Herbert Norman / James Barros. — Toronto : Deneau, 1986. — xi,259p

HALSTEAD, John G. H.
Canada's international relations : the report of a Working Group of the National Capital Branch / John G. H. Halstead [and] Michael Jarvis. — Toronto : Canadian Institute of International Affairs, 1986. — 30p

Parliament and Canadian foreign policy / edited by David Taras. — Toronto, Canada : Canadian Institute of International Affairs, c1985. — ix, 121 p.. — *"Domestic sources of Canadian foreign policy, 2"--CIP data. — Includes bibliographies*

CANADA — Foreign relations — 1945- — Citizen participation

RIDDELL-DIXON, Elizabeth
The domestic mosaic : domestic groups and Canadian foreign policy / Elizabeth Riddell-Dixon. — Toronto, Canada : Canadian Institute of International Affairs, c1985. — xii, 120 p.. — *"Domestic sources of Canadian foreign policy ; 1"--Can. CIP. — Includes index. — Bibliography: p. 76-78*

CANADA — Foreign relations — Great Britain

GREAT BRITAIN. Parliament. House of Commons. Library. International Affairs Section
Patriation of the Canadian constitution / Simon Young. — [London] : the Library, 1980. — 9p. — (Background paper / House of Commons. Library. [Research Division] ; no.84). — *Bibliography: p9*

GREAT BRITAIN. Parliament. House of Commons. Library. International Affairs Section
Patriation of the Canadian constitution / Simon Young. — [London] : the Library, 1981. — 23p. — (Background paper / House of Commons. Library. [Research Division] ; no.96). — *Replaces Background Paper no.84. — Bibliography: p21-23*

CANADA — Foreign relations — South Africa

BABB, Glenn
South Africa: where we stand / Glenn Babb. Clark's South Africa policy: a Canadian disgrace / Kenneth H. W. Hilborn. — Toronto : Citizens for Foreign Aid Reform, 1987. — [20p]. — (C. FAR Canadian Issues Series ; 15)

Canada and South Africa : challenge and response / editor: Douglas G. Anglin. — Ottawa : The Norman Paterson School of International Affairs, Carleton University, 1986. — vii,64p. — (Carleton International Proceedings). — *Proceedings of a Forum held in Ottawa, Ontario, March 1986*

CANADA — Foreign relations — United States

CLARKSON, Stephen
Canada and the Reagan challenge : crisis and adjustment, 1981-85 / Stephen Clarkson. — New updated ed. — Toronto : J. Lorimer, 1985. — xv, 431 p.. — *Includes index. — Bibliography: p. 378-409*

CANADA — Foreign relations — United States *continuation*

DORAN, Charles F
Canada and Congress : lobbying in Washington / by Charles F. Doran, Joel J. Sokolsky. — Halifax, N.S., Canada : Centre for Foreign Policy Studies, Dalhousie University, 1985. — vi, 257 p.. — *Includes bibliographies*

FOX, William T R
A continent apart : the United States and Canada in world politics / William T.R. Fox. — Toronto ; Buffalo : University of Toronto Press, c1985. — xv, 188 p.. — (The Bissell lectures ; 1982-3). — *Includes bibliographical references and index*

MARTIN, Lawrence
The presidents and the prime ministers : Washington and Ottawa face to face : the myth of bilateral bliss 1867-1982 / Lawrence Martin. — PaperJacks ed. — Toronto : PaperJacks, 1983,c1982. — 300p. — *Originally published: Toronto: Doubleday Canada, 1982*

CANADA — Foreign relations — Vietnam

LEVANT, Victor
Quiet complicity : Canadian involvement in the Vietnamese War / Victor Levant. — Toronto : Between The Lines, 1986. — 322p. — *Bibliography: p297-313*

CANADA — Foreign relations administration

NOSSAL, Kim Richard
The politics of Canadian foreign policy / Kim Richard Nossal. — Scarborough, Ont. : Prentice-Hall, 1985. — xvi,232p. — *Includes bibliographical notes*

CANADA — Government publications

Microlog index : Canadian government publications and reports = Microlog index : rapports et publications gouvernementales canadiennes. — Toronto, Ont. : Micromedia Ltd, 1986-. — *Monthly*

CANADA — Historiography

BERGER, Carl
The writing of Canadian history : aspects of English-Canadian historical writing since 1900 / Carl Berger. — 2nd ed. — Toronto : University of Toronto Press, 1986. — x,364p. — *Bibliographical note and references: p [320]-352*

CANADA — History

Interpreting Canada's past / edited by J. M. Bumsted. — Toronto : Oxford University Press . — *Includes references*
vol.1: Before Confederation. — 1986. — x,420p

Interpreting Canada's past. — Toronto : Oxford University Press. — *Includes references*
Vol.2: After confederation / edited by J.M. Bumsted. — 1986. — x,471p

LEHMANN, Heinz
The German Canadians, 1750-1937 : immigration, settlement & culture / Heinz Lehmann ; translated, edited & introduced by Gerhard P. Bassler. — St. John's, Nfld. : Jesperson Press, 1986. — lxii, 541 p., [24] p. of plates. — *Col. map on lining paper. — One folded col. map in pocket. — Includes index. — Bibliography: p. 459-496*

CANADA — History — To 1763

BOSHER, J. F.
The Canada merchants 1713-1763 / J.F. Bosher. — Oxford : Clarendon, 1987. — viii,234p. — *Includes index*

CANADA — History — To 1763 (New France)

TRIGGER, Bruce G.
Natives and newcomers : Canada's "Heroic age" reconsidered / Bruce G. Trigger. — Manchester : Manchester University Press, 1986. — xiii, 430p

CANADA — History — 1867-1914

BOTHWELL, Ian
Canada, 1900-1945 / Robert Bothwell, Ian Drummond, John English. — Toronto : University of Toronto Press, 1987. — x,427p. — *Bibliography: p[401]-410*

RIEL, Louis
[[Works]]. The collected writings of Louis Riel = Les ecrits complets de Louis Riel / Louis Riel ; general editor George F. G. Stanley. — Edmonton : University of Alberta Press. — *Text in English and French*
Vol.1: 29 December 1861 - 7 December 1875 / editor Raymond Huel. — 1985. — 546p. — *Bibliography and index in Vol.5*

RIEL, Louis
[[Works]]. The collected writings of Louis Riel = Les ecrits complets de Louis Riel / Louis Riel ; general editor George F. G. Stanley. — Edmonton : University of Alberta Press. — *Text in English and French*
Vol.2: 8 December 1875 - 4 June 1884 / editor Gilles Martel. — 1985. — 482p. — *Bibliography and index in Vol.5*

RIEL, Louis
[[Works]]. The collected writings of Louis Riel = Les ecrits complets de Louis Riel / Louis Riel ; general editor George F. G. Stanley. — Edmonton : University of Alberta Press. — *Text in English and French*
Vol.3: 5 June 1884 - 16November 1885 / editor Thomas Flanagan. — Edmonton : University of Alberta Press. — 637p. — *Text in English and French*

RIEL, Louis
[[Works]]. The collected writings of Louis Riel = Les ecrits complets de Louis Riel / Louis Riel ; general editor George F. G. Stanley. — Edmonton : University of Alberta Press. — *Text in English and French*
Vol.4: Poetry / editor Glen Campbell. — 1985. — 544p. — *Bibliography and index in Vol.5*

RIEL, Louis
[[Works]]. The collected writings of Louis Riel = Les ecrits complets de Louis Riel / Louis Riel ; general editor George F. G. Stanley. — Edmonton : University of Alberta Press. — *Text in English and French*
Vol.5: Reference / editors George F. G. Stanley, Thomas Flanagan, Claude Rocan. — 1985. — 360p. — *Contains bibliography, p131-205 and biographical index, p207-360*

CANADA — History — 1914-1945

BOTHWELL, Ian
Canada, 1900-1945 / Robert Bothwell, Ian Drummond, John English. — Toronto : University of Toronto Press, 1987. — x,427p. — *Bibliography: p[401]-410*

CANADA — Indexes

CANADA
Personal information index / Canada. — Ottawa : Canadian Government Publishing Centre, 1986-. — *Annual*

CANADA — Indian Act — 1984

HAWLEY, Donna Lea
The Indian Act annotated / by Donna Lea Hawley. — 2nd ed. — Toronto : Carswell, 1986. — xvii,103p

CANADA — Industries — Statistics

System of national accounts: gross domestic product by industry = Système de comptabilité nationale: produit intérieur brut par industrie / Statistics Canada. — Ottawa : Statistics Canada, 1984-. — *Annual. — Text in English and French*

CANADA — Intellectual life — History

SHORE, Marlene
The science of social redemption : McGill, Chicago School, and the origins of social research in Canada. — Toronto : University of Toronto Press, 1987. — xviii,340p. — *Bibliographical notes: p[275]-324*

CANADA — Library resources — Europe

BLOOMFIELD, Valerie
Guide to resources for Canadian studies in Britain : with some reference to relevant collections in Europe / by Valerie Bloomfield. — 2nd ed. — London : British Association for Canadian Studies, c1983. — xxi,252p. — *Previous ed.: Ottawa : Dept. of External Affairs, 1979. — Bibliography: p238. — Includes index*

CANADA — Manufactures

CONLON, R. M
Distance and duties : determinants of manufacturing in Australia and Canada / by R.M. Conlon. — Ottawa, Canada : Carleton University Press, c1985. — ix, 217 p.. — (Carleton library series ; 135). — *Bibliography: p. 210-217*

CANADA — Manufactures — Statistics

Census of manufactures = Recensement des manufactures / Statistics Canada. — Ottawa : Statistics Canada, 1985-. — *Annual. — Text in English and French*

CANADA — Maps

Surveys and mapping = Levés et cartographie / Energy, Mines and Resources Canada. — Ottawa : Surveys and Mapping Branch, Energy Mines and Resources, 1984-. — *Annual. — Text in English and French*

CANADA — Military policy

BYERS, R. B
Aerospace defence : Canada's future role? / R.B. Byers, John Hamre, G.R. Lindsey. — Toronto, Canada : Canadian Institute of International Affairs, 1985. — 56 p. — (Wellesley papers ; 9/1985). — *Includes bibliographies. — Contents: Defending North America / G.R. Lindsey -- Continental air defence, United States security policy, and Canada-United States defence relations / John Hamre -- NORAD, Star Wars, and strategic doctrine / R.B. Byers*

JOCKEL, Joseph T
Canada and collective security : odd man out / Joseph T. Jockel, Joel J. Sokolsky ; foreword by John G.H. Halstead. — New York : Praeger, 1986. — xv, 118 p.. — (The Washington papers ; 121). — *"Published with the Center for Strategic and International Studies, Georgetown University, Washington, D.C.". — Bibliography: p. 117-118*

CANADA — Military policy — Economic aspects

CANADIAN CENTRE FOR ARMS CONTROL AND DISARMAMENT
The economics of the strategic defence initiative : critical questions for Canada. — Ottawa, Ont. : Canadian Centre for Arms Control and Disarmament, 1985. — vi,16p. — (Issue brief / Canadian Centre for Arms Control and Disarmament ; no.4)

CANADA — Military relations — United States

BYERS, R. B
Aerospace defence : Canada's future role? / R.B. Byers, John Hamre, G.R. Lindsey. — Toronto, Canada : Canadian Institute of International Affairs, 1985. — 56 p.. — (Wellesley papers ; 9/1985). — *Includes bibliographies. — Contents: Defending North America / G.R. Lindsey -- Continental air defence, United States security policy, and Canada-United States defence relations / John Hamre -- NORAD, Star Wars, and strategic doctrine / R.B. Byers*

LITTLETON, James
Target nation : Canada and the western intelligence network / James Littleton. — 1st ed. — Toronto, Canada : L. & O. Dennys : CBC Enterprises, c1986. — viii, 228 p.. — *Includes index. — Bibliography: p. 209-220*

CANADA — National security — Congresses

Canada's strategies for the Pacific Rim / edited by Brian MacDonald. — Toronto, Ont., Canada : Canadian Institute of Strategic Studies, c1985. — 145 p.. — *Papers presented at a conference held in Victoria, B.C., Oct. 1984. — On cover: Proceedings, Fall 1984. — Includes bibliographies*

CANADA — Native races — Bibliography

PETERS, Evelyn J.
Aboriginal self-government in Canada : a bibliography 1986 / Evelyn J. Peters. — Kingston, Ont. : Queens University Institute of Intergovernmental Relations, 1986. — ix,112p. — (Aboriginal peoples and constitutional reform). — *English text with French summary*

CANADA — Occupations

CHEN, Mervin Yaotsu
Work in the changing Canadian society / Mervin Y.T. Chen, Thomas G. Regan. — Toronto : Butterworths, c1985. — xiv, 289 p.. — *Includes index. — Bibliography: p. [245]-286*

CANADA — Officials and employees

MORGAN, Nicole
Implosion : an analysis of the growth of the federal public service in Canada (1945-1985) / Nicole Morgan. — Montreal : The Institute for Research on Public Policy/L'Institut de recherches politiques. — xxv,160p. — *Prefatory material in English and French. — Issued also in French under title: 'Implosion: analyse de la croissance de la Fonction publique fédérale canadienne, 1945-1985'*

CANADA — Politics and government

ADIE, Robert F.
Canadian public administration : problematical perspectives / Robert F. Adie, Paul G. Thomas. — 2nd ed. — Scarborough, Ontario : Prentice-Hall Canada, 1987. — x,629p. — *Bibliography: p597-603*

DONALDSON, Gordon
Eighteen men : the prime ministers of Canada / by Gordon Donaldson. — Toronto, Ont. : Doubleday Canada ; Garden City, N.Y. : Doubleday, 1985. — p. cm. — *Rev. ed. of: Sixteen men. — Includes index. — Bibliography: p*

JACKSON, Robert J.
Politics in Canada : culture, institutions, behaviour and public policy / Robert J. Jackson, Doreen Jackson, Nicolas Baxter-Moore. — Scarborough, Ontario : Prentice-Hall Canada Inc., 1986. — xv,778p. — *Bibliography: p675-681*

MANZER, Ronald A
Public policies and political development in Canada / Ronald Manzer. — Toronto ; Buffalo : University of Toronto Press, c1985. — x, 240 p.. — *Includes index. — Bibliography: p. [191]-228*

MORGAN, Nicole
Implosion : an analysis of the growth of the federal public service in Canada (1945-1985) / Nicole Morgan. — Montreal : The Institute for Research on Public Policy/L'Institut de recherches politiques. — xxv,160p. — *Prefatory material in English and French. — Issued also in French under title: 'Implosion: analyse de la croissance de la Fonction publique fédérale canadienne, 1945-1985'*

MORRISON, William R
Showing the flag : the Mounted Police and Canadian sovereignty in the north, 1894-1925 / William R. Morrison. — Vancouver : University of British Columbia Press, 1985. — xix, 220 p., [16] p. of plates. — *Includes index. — Bibliography: p. [209]-216*

National politics and community in Canada / edited by R. Kenneth Carty and W. Peter Ward. — Vancouver : University of British Columbia Press, 1986. — 200 p.. — *Includes bibliographical references. — Contents: Canada as political community / R. Kenneth Carty & W. Peter Ward -- The Origins of Canadian politics and John A. Macdonald / Gordon Stewart -- Networks and associations and the nationalizing of sentiment in English Canada / Margaret Prang -- The Making of a Canadian political citizenship / R. Kenneth Carty & W. Peter Ward -- National political parties and the growth of the national political community / David E. Smith -- Leadership conventions and the development of the national political community in Canada / John C. Courtney -- Ceremonial politics / Christopher Armstrong -- Becoming Canadians / P.B. Waite -- Managing the periphery / Donald E. Blake -- The "French lieutenant" in Ottawa / John English*

PROSS, A. Paul
Group politics and public policy / A. Paul Pross. — Toronto : Oxford University Press, 1986. — xi,343p. — *Bibliography: p321-333*

CANADA — Politics and government — 1867-1896

FRIEDLAND, Martin L.
The case of Valentine Shortis : a true story of crime and politics in Canada / Martin L. Friedland. — Toronto : University of Toronto Press, 1986. — xi,324p

CANADA — Politics and government — 20th century

BOTHWELL, Ian
Canada, 1900-1945 / Robert Bothwell, Ian Drummond, John English. — Toronto : University of Toronto Press, 1987. — x,427p. — *Bibliography: p[401]-410*

The Canadian House of Commons : essays in honour of Norman Ward / edited by John C. Courtney. — Calgary, Alberta : University of Calgary Press, 1985. — xv,217p. — *Papers from a conference held at the University of Saskatchewan, Nov. 16-17, 1984. — Bibliography: p201-214*

LÉVESQUE, René
Memoirs / René Levesque ; translated by Philip Stratford. — Toronto : McClelland and Stewart, 1986. — 368p. — *Issued also in French under title: Mémoires*

NOSSAL, Kim Richard
The politics of Canadian foreign policy / Kim Richard Nossal. — Scarborough, Ont. : Prentice-Hall, 1985. — xvi,232p. — *Includes bibliographical notes*

OWRAM, Doug
The government generation : Canadian intellectuals and the state 1900-1945 / Doug Owram. — Toronto ; London : University of Toronto Press, 1986. — 402p

SCOTT, Frank R.
A new endeavour : selected political essays, letters, and addresses / edited and introduced by Michiel Horn. — Toronto : University of Toronto Press, 1986. — xlix,144p

CANADA — Politics and government — 1914-1945

WILBUR, J. Richard H
The Bennett administration 1930-1935 / by Richard Wilbur. — Ottawa : Canadian Historical Association, 1969. — 23 p. — (Canadian Historical Association booklets, no. 24). — *Includes bibliographical references*

CANADA — Politics and government — 1945-1980

BLAKE, Donald E.
Two political worlds : parties and voting in British Columbia / Donald E. Blake, with the collaboration of David J. Elkins and Richard Johnston. — Vancouver : University of British Columbia Press, 1985. — x, 205 p.. — *On spine: 2 political worlds. — Includes bibliographical references and index*

CAHILL, Jack
John Turner : the long run / by Jack Cahill. — Toronto, Ont. : McClelland and Stewart, c1984. — 234 p., [24] p. of plates. — *Includes index*

CHRÉTIEN, Jean
Straight from the heart / Jean Chrétien. — Toronto, Ont., Canada : Key Porter Books, c1985. — 231 p.. — *Includes index*

FLEMING, Donald M
So very near : the political memoirs of the Honourable Donald M. Fleming. — Toronto, Ont. : McCelland and Stewart, c1985. — 2 v.. — *Includes index. — Contents: v. 1. The rising years--v. 2. The summit years*

GOSSAGE, Patrick
Close to the charisma : my years between the press and Pierre Elliott Trudeau / Patrick Gossage. — Toronto : McClelland and Stewart, c1986. — 271 p., [16] p. of plates

PICKERSGILL, J. W.
The road back : by a Liberal in opposition / J. W. Pickersgill. — Toronto : University of Toronto Press, 1986. — 320p

CANADA — Politics and government — 1945-

COHEN, Maxwell
The Dominion-Provincial Conference : some basic issues / by Maxwell Cohen. — Toronto : Ryerson Press, 1945. — 39p

JEROME, James
Mr. Speaker / James Jerome. — Toronto, Ont. : McClelland and Stewart, c1985. — 175 p., [8] p. of plates. — *Includes index*

CANADA — Politics and government — 1957-1963

CONRAD, Margaret
George Nowlan : Maritime Conservative in national politics / Margaret Conrad. — Toronto : University of Toronto Press, 1986. — xviii,357p. — *Notes: p[309]-343*

CANADA — Politics and government — 1963-1968

LOOMIS, D. G.
Not much glory : quelling the F.L.Q. / Dan G. Loomis. — Toronto : Deneau, 1984. — 199p

CANADA — Politics and government — 1963-

Authority and influence : institutions, issues and concepts in Canadian politics / edited by Carla Cassidy, Phyllis Clarke and Wayne Petrozzi. — Oakville, Ont. : Mosaic Press, 1986. — 569p

JOHNSTON, Donald J
Up the hill / Donald Johnston. — Montréal : Optimum, c1986. — vii, 304 p.. — *Includes index. — Bibliography: p. 289-295*

SMILEY, Donald V.
The federal condition in Canada / Donald V. Smiley. — Toronto : Mcgraw-Hill Ryerson, 1987. — xii,202p. — (McGraw-Hill Ryerson series in Canadian politics). — *Includes bibliographical references*

CANADA — Politics and government — 1968-1969

LOOMIS, D. G.
Not much glory : quelling the F.L.Q. / Dan G. Loomis. — Toronto : Deneau, 1984. — 199p

CANADA — Politics and government — 1980-1984

BRIMELOW, Peter
The patriot game : national dreams & political realities / Peter Brimelow. — Toronto : Key Porter Books, 1986. — 310p. — *Bibliography: p[293]-299*

CANADA — Politics and government — 1980-

GAGNON, Lysiane
Chroniques politiques / Lysiane Gagnon. — Montréal : Boréal Express, 1985. — 461p

CANADA — Politics and government — 1980- *continuation*

GOSSAGE, Patrick
Close to the charisma : my years between the press and Pierre Elliott Trudeau / Patrick Gossage. — Toronto : McClelland and Stewart, c1986. — 271 p., [16] p. of plates

GRAHAM, Ron
One-eyed kings : promise & illusion in Canadian politics / Ron Graham. — Toronto : Collins, 1986. — 441 p.. — *Includes index*

GRANATSTEIN, J. L
Sacred trust? : Brian Mulroney and the Conservative Party in power / by J.L. Granatstein, David Bercuson, William Young. — 1st ed. — Toronto, Canada : Doubleday Canada ; Garden City, N.Y. : Doubleday, 1986. — p. cm. — *Includes index*

MILNE, David
Tug of war : Ottawa and the provinces under Trudeau and Mulroney / David Milne. — Toronto : J. Lorimer, 1986. — viii, 275 p.. — *Includes index. — Bibliography: p. [239]-269*

ROBERTS, John
Agenda for Canada : towards a new liberalism / John Roberts. — 1st ed. — Toronto, Ont., Canada : Lester & Orpen Dennys, c1985. — 239 p.. — *Bibliography: p. 237-239*

SNIDER, Norman
The changing of the guard : how the Liberals fell from grace and the Tories rose to power / Norman Snider. — Toronto : Lester & Orpen Denys, 1985. — 206p

CANADA — Politics and government — 1981-

CHRÉTIEN, Jean
Straight from the heart / Jean Chrétien. — Toronto, Ont., Canada : Key Porter Books, c1985. — 231 p.. — *Includes index*

CANADA — Politics and government — 1984-

BRIMELOW, Peter
The patriot game : national dreams & political realities / Peter Brimelow. — Toronto : Key Porter Books, 1986. — 310p. — *Bibliography: p[293]-299*

FRIZZELL, Alan
The Canadian general election of 1984 : politicians, parties, press and polls / Alan Frizzell, Anthony Westell ; with contributions by Nick Hills, Jeffrey Simpson, and Val Sears. — Ottawa : Carleton University Press, 1985. — vii,139p

CANADA — Population

FRIESEN, John W.
When cultures clash : case studies in multiculturalism / John W. Friesen. — Calgary, Alberta : Detselig Enterprises, 1985. — 171p

HILLER, Harry H.
Canadian society : a macro analysis / Harry H. Hiller. — Scarborough, Ont. : Prentice-Hall Canada, c1986. — x, 245 p.. — *Includes index. — Bibliography: p. 234-241*

CANADA — Population — Bibliography

WAI, Lokky
Annotated bibliography of Canadian demography 1966-1982 / Lokky Wai, Suzanne Shiel, T. R. Balakrishnan. — London, Ont. : University of Western Ontario, Centre for Canadian Population Studies, 1984. — v,314p

CANADA — Race relations

BOLARIA, B. Singh
Racial oppression in Canada / B. Singh Bolaria, Peter S. Li. — Toronto, Canada : Garamond Press, c1985. — 232 p.. — *Bibliography: p. 199-221. Includes index*

CANADA — Relations — East Asia

DOWNTON, Eric
Pacific challenge : Canada's future in the new Asia / Eric Downton. — Toronto : Stoddart, 1986. — 258p. — *Bibliography: p[247]-251*

CANADA — Relations — Foreign countries

LOOMIS, D. G.
Not much glory : quelling the F.L.Q. / Dan G. Loomis. — Toronto : Deneau, 1984. — 199p

CANADA — Relations — Newfoundland

MACKENZIE, David Clark
Inside the Atlantic Triangle : Canada and the entrance of Newfoundland into confederation, 1939-1949 / David MacKenzie. — Toronto ; Buffalo : University of Toronto Press, c1986. — xi, 285 p. — *Includes index. — Bibliography: p. [263]-273*

CANADA — Relations — Pacific Ocean Region — Congresses

Canada's strategies for the Pacific Rim / edited by Brian MacDonald. — Toronto, Ont., Canada : Canadian Institute of Strategic Studies, c1985. — 145 p.. — *Papers presented at a conference held in Victoria, B.C., Oct. 1984. — On cover: Proceedings, Fall 1984. — Includes bibliographies*

CANADA — Relations — United States

GWYN, Richard J.
The 49th paradox : Canada in North America / Richard Gwyn. — Toronto, Ont. : McClelland and Stewart, c1985. — 362 p.. — *Includes index. — Bibliography: p. 341-348*

LEYTON-BROWN, David
Weathering the storm : Canadian-U.S. relations, 1980-83 / by David Leyton-Brown. — Toronto, Ont. : Canadian-American Committee, [1985]. — xi, 86 p.. — *Includes bibliographical references*

Southern exposure : Canadian perspectives on the United States / edited with an introduction by David H. Flaherty, William R. McKercher. — Toronto : McGraw-Hill Ryerson, 1986. — x,246p. — *Bibliography: p233-237*

CANADA — Religion

MOL, Hans
Faith and fragility : religion and identity in Canada / Hans Mol. — Burlington, Ont., Canada : Trinity Press, c1985. — viii, 354 p.. — *Includes index. — Bibliography: p. 301-338*

CANADA — Social conditions

Interpreting Canada's past / edited by J. M. Bumsted. — Toronto : Oxford University Press . — *Includes references*
vol.1: Before Confederation. — 1986. — x,420p

Interpreting Canada's past. — Toronto : Oxford University Press. — *Includes references*
Vol.2: After confederation / edited by J.M. Bumsted. — 1986. — x,471p

CANADA — Social conditions — 20th century

SCOTT, Frank R.
A new endeavour : selected political essays, letters, and addresses / edited and introduced by Michiel Horn. — Toronto : University of Toronto Press, 1986. — xlix,144p

CANADA — Social conditions — 1945-

CHEN, Mervin Yaotsu
Work in the changing Canadian society / Mervin Y.T. Chen, Thomas G. Regan. — Toronto : Butterworths, c1985. — xiv, 289 p.. — *Includes index. — Bibliography: p. [245]-286*

METTRICK, Alan
Last in line : on the road and out of work-- a desperate journey with Canada's unemployed / by Alan Mettrick. — Toronto, Ont., Canada : Key Porter Books, c1985. — x, 201 p.

CANADA — Social policy

The Canadian state : evolution and transition / edited by Jacqueline S. Ismael. — Edmonton, Alberta : University of Alberta Press, 1987. — xxv,390p

MANZER, Ronald A
Public policies and political development in Canada / Ronald Manzer. — Toronto ; Buffalo : University of Toronto Press, c1985. — x, 240 p.. — *Includes index. — Bibliography: p. [191]-228*

MILNE, David
Tug of war : Ottawa and the provinces under Trudeau and Mulroney / David Milne. — Toronto : J. Lorimer, 1986. — viii, 275 p.. — *Includes index. — Bibliography: p. [239]-269*

CANADA — Social policy — Congresses

Canadian social welfare policy : federal and provincial dimensions / edited by Jacqueline S. Ismael. — Kingston : McGill-Queen's University Press, 1985. — xviii, 187 p.. — (Canadian public administration series = Collection Administration publique canadienne). — *"The Institute of Public Administration of Canada.". — Proceedings of the First Conference on Provincial Social Welfare Policy, held at the University of Calgary, May 1982. — Includes bibliographies and index*

CANADA — Study and teaching — Europe

BLOOMFIELD, Valerie
Guide to resources for Canadian studies in Britain : with some reference to relevant collections in Europe / by Valerie Bloomfield. — 2nd ed. — London : British Association for Canadian Studies, c1983. — xxi,252p. — *Previous ed.: Ottawa : Dept. of External Affairs, 1979. — Bibliography: p238. — Includes index*

CANADA. Agriculture Canada. Research Branch

CANADA. Agriculture Canada. Research Branch
[Report] / Research Branch, Agriculture Canada. — Ottawa : Agriculture Canada. Research Branch, 1985-. — *Annual. — Text in English and French*

CANADA. Canadian armed forces — History

LOOMIS, D. G.
Not much glory : quelling the F.L.Q. / Dan G. Loomis. — Toronto : Deneau, 1984. — 199p

CANADA. Chief Electoral Officer

CANADA. Chief Electoral Officer
Statutory report of the Chief Electoral Officer of Canada = Rapport statutaire du Directeur Général des Élections du Canada. — Ottawa : Chief Electoral Officer of Canada, 1986-. — *Annual*

CANADA. Commission of Inquiry on War Criminals

TOLSTOY, Nikolai
Trial and error : Canada's Commission of Inquiry on War Criminals and the Soviets / Nikolai Tolstoy. — Toronto : Justinian Press, 1986. — 28p

CANADA. Department of External Affairs

SOWARD, F. H.
The Department of External Affairs and Canadian autonomy, 1899-1939 / F. H. Soward. — Ottawa : Canadian Historical Association, 1979. — 24p. — (Canadian Historical Association booklets ; no.7)

CANADA. Department of Finance — History

BRYCE, Robert B.
Maturing in hard times : Canada's Department of Finance through the Great Depression / Robert B. Bryce. — Kingston ; Montreal : McGill-Queen's University Press : Institute of Public Administration of Canada, 1986. — xii,278p. — (Canadian public administration series)

CANADA. Department of Industry, Trade and Commerce

CANADA. Department of Industry, Trade and Commerce
Annual report / Department of Industry, Trade and Commerce, Canada. — Ottawa : Department of Industry, Trade and Commerce, 1970-1974. — Annual. — Text in English and French. — Continued by: Annual review/Department of Industry, Trade and Commerce, Canada

CANADA. Department of Industry, Trade and Commerce
Annual review / Department of Industry, Trade and Commerce, Canada. — Ottawa : Department of Industry, Trade and Commerce, 1974-1981/82. — Annual. — Text in English and French. — Continues: Annual report/Department of Industry, Trade and Commerce, Canada. Continued by: Annual reports/Department of Industry, Trade and Commerce, Department of Regional Economic Expansion and Department of Regional Industrial Expansion

CANADA. Department of Regional Economic Expansion

CANADA. Department of Regional Economic Expansion
Annual report / Department of Regional Economic Expansion, Canada. — Ottawa : Department of Regional Economic Expansion, 1968/69-1981/82. — Annual. — Text in English and French. — Continued by: Annual reports/Department of Industry, Trade and Commerce, Department of Regional Economic Expansion and Department of Regional Industrial Expansion

CANADA. Department of Regional Industrial Expansion

CANADA. Department of Regional Industrial Expansion
Annual report / Department of Regional Industrial Expansion, Canada. — Ottawa : [the Department], 1984/85-. — Annual. — Text in English and French

CANADA. Emergency Planning Canada

CANADA. Emergency Planning Canada
Annual review = Revue annuelle / Emergency Planning Canada. — Ottawa : Emergency Planning Canada, 1985-. — Annual. — Text in English and French

CANADA. Indian Affairs Branch — History

TITLEY, E. Brian
A narrow vision : Duncan Campbell Scott and the Administration of Indian affairs in Canada / E. Brian Titley. — Vancouver : University of British Columbia Press, 1986. — viii,245p

CANADA. Investment Canada

CANADA. Investment Canada
Annual report / Investment Canada. — Ottawa : Investment Canada, 1985-. — Annual. — Text in English and French

CANADA. Northern Pipeline Agency

CANADA. Northern Pipeline Agency
Annual report. — Ottawa : Northern Pipeline Agency, 1984-. — Annual. — Text in English and French

CANADA. Parlament. House of Commons. Standing Committee on External Affairs and National Defence

Parliament and Canadian foreign policy / edited by David Taras. — Toronto, Canada : Canadian Institute of International Affairs, c1985. — ix, 121 p.. — "Domestic sources of Canadian foreign policy, 2"--CIP data. — Includes bibliographies

CANADA. Parliament — Elections, 1984

COMBER, Mary Anne
The newsmongers : how the media distort the political news / Mary Anne Comber and Robert S. Mayne. — Toronto : McClelland and Stewart, 1986. — 178p. — Bibliography: p177-178

JOHNSTON, Donald J
Up the hill / Donald Johnston. — Montréal : Optimum, c1986. — vii, 304 p.. — Includes index. — Bibliography: p. 289-295

FRIZZELL, Alan
The Canadian general election of 1984 : politicians, parties, press and polls / Alan Frizzell, Anthony Westell ; with contributions by Nick Hills, Jeffrey Simpson, and Val Sears. — Ottawa : Carleton University Press, 1985. — vii,139p

SNIDER, Norman
The changing of the guard : how the Liberals fell from grace and the Tories rose to power / Norman Snider. — Toronto : Lester & Orpen Denys, 1985. — 206p

CANADA. Parliament. House of Commons

The Canadian House of Commons : essays in honour of Norman Ward / edited by John C. Courtney. — Calgary, Alberta : University of Calgary Press, 1985. — xv,217p. — Papers from a conference held at the University of Saskatchewan, Nov. 16-17, 1984. — Bibliography: p201-214

CANADA. Parliament. House of Commons — Biography

PICKERSGILL, J. W.
The road back : by a Liberal in opposition / J. W. Pickersgill. — Toronto : University of Toronto Press, 1986. — 320p

CANADA. Parliament. House of Commons — Speaker — Biography

JEROME, James
Mr. Speaker / James Jerome. — Toronto, Ont. : McClelland and Stewart, c1985. — 175 p., [8] p. of plates. — Includes index

CANADA. Parliament. House of Commons. Standing Committee on Finance and Economic Affairs

CANADA. Parliament. House of Commons. Standing Committee on Elections, Privileges and Procedure
Minutes of proceedings and evidence = Procès-verbaux et témoignages / Standing Committee on Elections, Privileges and Procedure. — Ottawa : Queen's Printer for Canada, 1986-. — Irregular. — Text in English and French. — Continues: Canada. Parliament. House of Commons. Standing Committee on Privileges and Elections. Minutes of proceedings and evidence

CANADA. Parliament. House of Commons. Standing Committee on Finance and Economic Affairs
Minutes of proceedings and evidence = Procès-verbaux et témoignages / Standing Committee on Finance and Economic Affairs, Canada. — Ottawa : Queen's Printer for Canada, 1986-. — Irregular. — Text in English and French. — Continues: Canada. Parliament. House of Commons. Standing Committee on Finance, Trade and Economic Affairs. Minutes of proceedings and evidence

CANADA. Parliament. House of Commons. Standing Committee on Finance, Trade and Economic Affairs
Minutes of proceedings and evidence = Procès-verbaux et témoignages / Standing Committee on Finance, Trade and Economic Affairs, Canada. — Ottawa : Queen's Printer for Canada, 1984-1986. — Continued by: Canada. Parliament. House of Commons. Standing Committee on Finance and Economic Affairs. Minutes of proceedings and evidence

CANADA. Parliament. House of Commons. Standing Committee on Justice and Legal Affairs

CANADA. Parliament. House of Commons. Standing Committee on Justice and Legal Affairs
Minutes of proceedings and evidence = Procès-verbaux et témoignages / Standing Committee on Justice and Legal Affairs, Canada. — Ottawa : Queen's Printer for Canada, 1984-1986. — Continued by: Canada. Parliament. House of Commons. Standing Committee on Justice and Solicitor General. Minutes of proceedings and evidence

CANADA. Parliament. House of Commons. Standing Committee on Justice and Solicitor General

CANADA. Parliament. House of Commons. Standing Committee on Justice and Solicitor General
Minutes of proceedings and evidence = Procès-verbaux et témoignages / Standing Committee on Justice and Solicitor General, Canada. — Ottawa : Queen's Printer for Canada, 1986-. — Irregular. — Text in English and French. — Continues: Canada Parliament. House of Commons. Standing Committee on Justice and Legal Affairs. Minutes of proceedings and evidence

CANADA. Parliament. House of Commons. Standing Committee on Labour, Employment and Immigration

CANADA. Parliament. House of Commons. Standing Committee on Labour, Employment and Immigration
[Minutes of proceedings and evidence] / Standing Committee on Labour, Employment and Immigration. — Ottawa : [the Committee], 1985-. — Irregular. — Continues: Canada. Parliament. House of Commons. Standing Committee on Labour, Manpower and Immigration. [Minutes of proceedings and evidence]

CANADA. Parliament. House of Commons. Standing Committee on Labour, Manpower and Immigration

CANADA. Parliament. House of Commons. Standing Committee on Labour, Manpower and Immigration
[Minutes of proceedings and evidence] / Standing Committee on Labour, Manpower and Immigration, Canada. — Ottawa : [the Committee], 1968-1985. — Irregular. — Continued by: Canada. Parliament. House of Commons. Standing Committee on Labour, Employment and Immigration. [Minutes of proceedings and evidence]

CANADA. Parliament. House of Commons. Standing Committee on Priviledges and Elections

CANADA. Parliament. House of Commons. Standing Committee on Priviledges and Elections
Minutes of proceedings and evidence = Procès-verbaux et témoignages / Standing Committee on Priviledges and Elections, Canada. — Ottawa : Queen's Printer for Canada, 1984-1986. — Continued by: Canada. Parliament. House of Commons. Standing Committee on Elections, Priviledges and Procedure

CANADA. Parliament. House of Commons. Standing Committee on Secretary of State

CANADA. Parliament. House of Commons. Standing Committee on Secretary of State
Minutes of proceedings and evidence. Procès-verbaux et témoignages. — Ottawa : Canadian Government Publishing Centre, 1986-. — Irregular. — Text in English and French

CANADA. Parliament. Senate — Biography

DAVEY, Keith
The rainmaker : a passion for politics / Keith Davey. — Toronto : Stoddart, 1986. — xii,383p

CANADA. Parliament. Senate. Standing Committee on Foreign Affairs

Parliament and Canadian foreign policy / edited by David Taras. — Toronto, Canada : Canadian Institute of International Affairs, c1985. — ix, 121 p.. — "Domestic sources of Canadian foreign policy, 2"--CIP data. — Includes bibliographies

CANADA. Petroleum Incentives Administration

CANADA. Petroleum Incentives Administration
Annual report / Petroleum Incentives Administration. — Ottawa : Energy, Mines and Resources Canada, 1984-. — Annual

CANADA. Royal Commission on Equality in Employment
BLOCK, Walter
On employment equity : a critique of the Abella Royal Commission Report / by Walter Block and Michael A. Walker. — [Vancouver] : The Fraser Institute, 1985. — 111p. — (Focus / Fraser Institute (Vancouver, B.C.) ; no.17). — References: p[91]-111

CANADA. Security Intelligence Review Committee
Annual report / Security Intelligence Review Committee, Canada. — Hawa : Security Intelligence Review Committee, 1985/86-. — *Annual*

CANADA. Supreme Court — History
SNELL, James G.
The Supreme Court of Canada : history of the institution / James G. Snell and Frederick Vaughan. — Toronto ; London : Published for the Osgoode Society by University of Toronto Press, c1985. — xv,319p,[8]p of plates. — *Includes index*

CANADA, EASTERN — Commerce — New England
Trade and investment across the northeast boundary : Quebec, the Atlantic provinces, and New England / edited by William D. Shipman. — Montreal : The Institute for Research on Public Policy/L'Institute de Recherches Politique 260.01/1, 1986. — xxi,315p

CANADA EMPLOYMENT AND IMMIGRATION ADVISORY COUNCIL
CANADA EMPLOYMENT AND IMMIGRATION ADVISORY COUNCIL
Annual review = Revue annuelle / Canada Employment and Immigration Advisory Council. — Hull (Quebec) : [the Council], 1984-. — *Annual. — Text in English and French*

CANADA HEALTH ACT 1984
Canada Health Act: annual report = Loi canadienne sur la santé: rapport annuel / Health and Welfare Canada. — Ottawa : Health and Welfare Canada, 1984/5-. — *Annual. — In English and French*

CANADA LABOUR RELATIONS BOARD
FOISY, Claude H.
Canada Labour Relations Board policies and procedures / Claude H. Foisy, Daniel E. Lavery and Luc Martineau. — Toronto ; Vancouver : Butterworths, 1986. — li,553p

CANADA, NORTHERN — History
MORRISON, William R
Showing the flag : the Mounted Police and Canadian sovereignty in the north, 1894-1925 / William R. Morrison. — Vancouver : University of British Columbia Press, 1985. — xix, 220 p., [16] p. of plates. — *Includes index. — Bibliography: p. [209]-216*

CANADA OIL AND GAS LANDS ADMINISTRATION
CANADA OIL AND GAS LANDS ADMINISTRATION
Annual Report / Canada Oil and Gas Lands Administration. — Ottawa : Canada Oil and Gas Lands Administration, 1985-. — *Annual*

CANADA-ONTARIO-INDUSTRY ROCKBURST PROJECT
Annual report of the Canada-Ontario-industry Rockburst project / Energy, Mines and Resources Canada [and] Centre for Mineral and Energy Technology, Canada. — Ottawa : Energy, Mines and Resources Canada, 1985-. — *Annual*

CANADA, WESTERN — Bibliography
ARTIBISE, Alan F. J
Western Canada since 1870 : a select bibliography and guide / Alan F. J. Artibise. — Vancouver : University of British Columbia Press, c1978. — xii, 294 p.. — *Includes indexes*

CANADA, WESTERN — History — Bibliography
ARTIBISE, Alan F. J
Western Canada since 1870 : a select bibliography and guide / Alan F. J. Artibise. — Vancouver : University of British Columbia Press, c1978. — xii, 294 p.. — *Includes indexes*

CANADIAN AIR LINE FLIGHT ATTENDANTS' ASSOCIATION — History
NEWBY, Jill
The sky's the limit : the story of the Canadian Air Line Flight Attendants' Association / by Jill Newby. — Vancouver : The Association, 1986. — 113p

CANADIAN AVIATION SAFETY BOARD
CANADIAN AVIATION SAFETY BOARD
Annual report. — Ottawa : Minister of Supply and Services, Canada, 1984-. — *Annual. — Text in English and French*

CANADIAN BAR ASSOCIATION
CANADIAN BAR ASSOCIATION
Report of the special committee on bilingualism in the courts = Rapport du comite special sur le bilinguisme dans les cours de justice. — [S.l.] : [Canadian Bar Association], 1974. — [28p]

CANADIAN HUMAN RIGHTS COMMISSION
CANADIAN HUMAN RIGHTS COMMISSION
Annual report / Canadian Human Rights Commission. — Ottawa : the Commission, 1984-. — *Annual. — Text in English and French*

CANADIAN SEAMEN'S UNION
KAPLAN, William
Everything that floats : Pat Sullivan, Hal Banks, and the Seamen's Unions of Canada / William Kaplan. — Toronto : University of Toronto Press, 1987. — xii,241p. — *Bibliography: p[227]-231*

CANADIAN SEAMEN'S UNION — History
GREEN, Jim
Against the tide : the story of the Canadian Seamen's Union / Jim Green. — Toronto : Progress Books, 1986. — 324p. — *Bibliography: p297-316*

CANADIAN SECURITY INTELLIGENCE SERVICE
LITTLETON, James
Target nation : Canada and the western intelligence network / James Littleton. — 1st ed. — Toronto, Canada : L. & O. Dennys : CBC Enterprises, c1986. — viii, 228 p.. — *Includes index. — Bibliography: p. 209-220*

CANADIAN WHO'S WHO — Indexes
MCMANN, Evelyn de R.
Canadian who's who index 1898-1984 : incorporating Canadian men and women of the time / Evelyn de R. McMann. — Toronto ; London : University of Toronto Press, c1986. — 528p

CANALS — Law and legislation — Egypt
The Egyptian Canal Act. — Cairo : Ministry of Public Works, 1915. — xv,22p

CANALS — Great Britain — Recreational use
INLAND WATERWAYS AMENITY ADVISORY COUNCIL
Policy framework for structure plans. — London : the Council, [1979]. — 2p

CANARY ISLANDS — Appropriations and expenditures
Contabilidad regional de Canarias / Consejería de Economía ye Comercio, Gobierno de Canarias. — Las Palmas : Gobierno de Canarias. Consejería de Economía y Comercio,, 1985-. — *Annual*

Ley de presupuestos generales de la comunidad autonoma de Canarias. — Las Palmas : Consejeria de Hacienda, 1983-. — *Annual*

CANARY ISLANDS — Commerce
GUIMERÁ RAVINA, Agustín
Burgesía extranjera y comercio atlántico : la empresa comercial irlandesa en Canarias : 1703-1771 / Agustín Guimerá Ravina. — Tenerifè : Consejería de Cultura y Deportes, 1985. — 478p

CANARY ISLANDS — Politics and government
Ley de presupuestos generales de la comunidad autonoma de Canarias. — Las Palmas : Consejeria de Hacienda, 1983-. — *Annual*

CANBERRA (A.C.T.) — History
PEGRUM, Roger
The bush capital : how Australia chose Canberra as its federal city / Roger Pegrum. — Sydney, NSW : Hale & Iremonger, c1983. — 192 p... — *Includes bibliographical references and index*

CANCER — Government policy — United States — History
RUSHEFSKY, Mark R.
Making cancer policy / Mark R. Rushefsky. — Albany : State University of New York Press, c1986. — xiii, 257 p.. — (SUNY series in public administration in the 1980s). — *Includes index. — Bibliography: p. 225-245*

CANCER — Mortality — Netherlands — Statistics
Atlas van de kankersterfte in Nederland 1969-1978 = Atlas of cancer mortality in the Netherlands 1969-1978. — 's-Gravenhage : Staatsvitgeverij, 1980. — xxxii,171p. — *Table of contents, summary, description of methods and layout, table headings, all in English. — Bibliography: pxxxi*

CANCER — Reporting — Great Britain
GREAT BRITAIN. Advisory Committee on Cancer Registration
Report of the Advisory Committee on Cancer Registration : cancer registration in the 1980s. — London : H.M.S.O., 1981. — v,39p. — (Series MB1 / Office of Population Censuses and Surveys ; no.6). — *Bibliography: p26*

CANCER — England — Cumbria
GREAT BRITAIN. Committee on Medical Aspects of Radiation in the Environment
First report : the implications of the new data on the releases from Sellafield in the 1950s for the conclusions of the report on the investigation of the possible increased incidence of cancer in West Cumbria / chairman: M. Bobrow. — London : H.M.S.O., 1986. — 42p. — *Bibliographical references: p25-26*

CANCER — England — West Cumbria
Investigation of the possible increased incidence of cancer in West Cumbria : report of the independent advisory group / chairman Sir Douglas Black. — London : H.M.S.O., 1984. — 103p

CANCER — Great Britain — Statistics
Cancer incidence and mortality in the vicinity of nuclear installations England and Wales 1959-80 / P. J. Cook-Mozaffari...[et al.] ; [for the] Office of Population Censuses and Surveys. — London : H.M.S.O., 1987. — xiii,280p. — 27microfiches in end pocket. — (Studies on medical and population subjects ; no.51). — *Bibliographical references: p266-274*

Childhood cancer in Britain : incidence, survival and mortality / G. J. Draper...[et al.] ; [for the] Office of Population Censuses and Surveys. — London : H.M.S.O., 1982. — vii,87p. — (Studies on medical and population subjects ; no.37). — *Bibliographical references: p87*

CANCER — Great Britain — Statistics
continuation
GREAT BRITAIN. Office of Population Censuses and Surveys
Cancer statistics : incidence, survival and mortality in England and Wales / Office of Population Censuses and Surveys, Cancer Research Campaign. — London : H.M.S.O., 1981. — xxviii,114p. — (Studies on medical and population subjects ; no.43)

CANCER — United States — Statistics
GOULD, Jay M
Quality of life in American neighborhoods : levels of affluence, toxic waste, and cancer mortality in residential Zip code areas / Jay M. Gould ; edited by Alice Tepper Marlin. — Boulder : Westview Press, 1986. — ix, 402 p.. — *"Published in cooperation with the Council on Economic Priorities."*

CANNABIS
DU TOIT, Brian M.
Drug use and South African students / by Brian M. Du Toit. — [Athens] : Ohio University Center for International Studies, Africa Program, 1978. — 127 p.. — (Papers in international studies : Africa series ; no. 35). — *Bibliography: p. 126-127*

CANNABIS — Physiological effect
EDWARDS, Griffith
Cannabis and the criteria for legalisation of a currently prohibited recreational drug : groundwork for a debate / Griffith Edwards. — Copenhagen : Munksgaard, 1974. — 62 p.. — (Supplementum - Acta psychiatrica Scandinavica ; 251). — *Bibliography: p. 56-62*

CANNIBALISM
ARENS, W.
The man-eating myth : anthropology & anthropophagy / W. Arens. — New York : Oxford University Press, 1979. — vii, 206 p.. — *Includes index.* — *Bibliography: p. [187]-201*

CANNIBALISM — Congresses
The Ethnography of cannibalism / edited by Paula Brown and Donald Tuzin. — Washington, D.C. : Society for Psychological Anthropology, c1983. — 108 p.. — *Essays from a symposium held Dec. 1980 in Washington, D.C., sponsored by the Society for Psychological Anthropology.* — *Includes bibliographies*

CANNING AND PRESERVING — Industry and trade — Hawaii — History
HAWKINS, Richard Adrian
Economic diversification in the American Pacific Territory of Hawai'i, 1893-1941 / Richard Adrian Hawkins. — 576 leaves. — *PhD (Econ) 1986 LSE.* — *Leaves 547-576 are appendices*

CANTABRIA (SPAIN) — History
ORTIZ REAL, Javier
Cantabria en el siglo XV : aproximación al estudio de los conflictos sociales / Javier Ortiz Real. — Santander : Tantín, 1985. — 212p. — *Bibliography: p207-212*

CANTABRIA (SPAIN) — History — 20th century
ARGOS VILLAR, José Carlos
El movimiento obrero en Cantabria (1955-1977) / José Carlos Argos Villar, José Emilio Gómez Díaz ; prólogo de J. R. Saiz Viadero. — Santander : Puntal Libros, [1982]. — 227p

CANTABRIA (SPAIN) — Social conditions
ORTIZ REAL, Javier
Cantabria en el siglo XV : aproximación al estudio de los conflictos sociales / Javier Ortiz Real. — Santander : Tantín, 1985. — 212p. — *Bibliography: p207-212*

CANTERBURY CATHEDRAL — History
SMITH, R. A. L.
Canterbury Cathedral priory : a study in monastic administration / Reginald Anthony Lenden Smith. — Cambridge : Cambridge University Press, 1943. — 237p

CANTILLON, RICHARD
MURPHY, Antoin E.
Richard Cantillon : entrepreneur and economist / Antoin E. Murphy. — Oxford : Clarendon, 1986. — [ix,470]p. — *Includes index*

CANVASSING
ASSOCIATION OF LIBERAL COUNCILLORS
Knocking on doors : why do we do it?. — Hebden Bridge : Association of Liberal Councillors, [1983]. — 11p. — (ALC activists' guide ; no.3)

CAPE OF GOOD HOPE (SOUTH AFRICA) — Frontier troubles
MACLENNAN, Ben
A proper degree of terror : John Graham and the Capeś Eastern frontier / Ben Maclennan. — Braamfontein : Ravan Press, 1986. — 252p

CAPE OF GOOD HOPE (SOUTH AFRICA) — History — 1795-1872
MACLENNAN, Ben
A proper degree of terror : John Graham and the Capeś Eastern frontier / Ben Maclennan. — Braamfontein : Ravan Press, 1986. — 252p

CAPE VERDE — Bibliography
LOBBAN, Richard
Historical dictionary of the Republics of Guinea-Bissau and Cape Verde / Richard Lobban. — Metuchen, N.J. : Scarecrow Press, 1979. — xv, 193 p.. — (African historical dictionaries ; no. 22). — *Bibliography: p. 121-184*

CAPE VERDE — Census, 1970
1° recenseamento geral da população e Haabitaçáo-1980. — Praia : Direcçáo de Recenseamento e Inqueritos
Vol.5: Recenseamento geral da populaçáo-1970. — 1983. — 292p

CAPE VERDE — Census, 1980
1° recenseamento geral da popula,áo e habitaçáo. — Praia : Direcçáo de Recenseamentos e Inqueritos
Vol.3: População activa. — 1983. — 401p

1° recenseamento geral da população-1980 e habitaçao. — Praia : Direcçào de Recenseamento e Inqueritos
Vol.2: Estruturas da popula,áo. — 1983. — 277p

1° recenseamento geral da populaçao e habitaçáo-1980. — Praia : Direcçào de Recenseamentos e Inqueritos. — 1983
Vol.1: Populaçao global. — 82p

1° recenseamento geral da populacáo e habitaçáo-1980. — Praia : Direcçáo de Recenseamento e Inqueritos
Vol.4: Habitaçáo. — 1983. — 177p

1° recenseamentogeral da populaçáo e habitaço-1980. — Praia : Direcçào de Recenseamontos e Inqueritos
b Vol.6: Anaálise dos resultados a popula,áo de Cabo Verde. — 1983. — 332p

CAPE VERDE — Commerce — Statistics
Boletim trimestral do comércia externo / Direcçáo-Geral de Estatística, Cape Verde. — [Praia] : Direcçáo-Geral de Estatística, 1984-. — *Quarterly*

CAPE VERDE — History — Dictionaries
LOBBAN, Richard
Historical dictionary of the Republics of Guinea-Bissau and Cape Verde / Richard Lobban. — Metuchen, N.J. : Scarecrow Press, 1979. — xv, 193 p.. — (African historical dictionaries ; no. 22). — *Bibliography: p. 121-184*

CAPE VERDE — Politics and government
CABO VERDE
Sessoes legislativas. — Praia : Imprensa Nacional, 1981-1983. — *Annual*

CAPE VERDE — Population — Statistics
1° recenseamento geral da população-1980 e habitaçao. — Praia : Direcçào de Recenseamento e Inqueritos
Vol.2: Estruturas da popula,áo. — 1983. — 277p

1° recenseamento geral da população e Haabitaçáo-1980. — Praia : Direcçáo de Recenseamento e Inqueritos
Vol.5: Recenseamento geral da populaçáo-1970. — 1983. — 292p

1° recenseamento geral da populaçao e habitaçáo-1980. — Praia : Direcçáo de Recenseamentos e Inqueritos. — 1983
Vol.1: Populaçao global. — 82p

1° recenseamentogeral da populaçáo e habitaço-1980. — Praia : Direcçáo de Recenseamentos e Inqueritos
b Vol.6: Anaálise dos resultados a popula,áo de Cabo Verde. — 1983. — 332p

CAPITAL
FOLEY, Duncan K
Understanding capital : Marx's economic theory / Duncan K. Foley. — Cambridge, Mass. ; London : Harvard University Press, 1986. — viii, 183p. — *Includes index.* — *Bibliography: p.[177]-180*

MARX, Karl, 1818-1883
Capital : a critique of political economy. — London : Lawrence and Wishart. — *Based on the 1893 German edition*
Vol.2: The process of circulation of capital / edited by Friedrich Engels. — 1956. — xii,551p

PLOEG, Frederick van der
Capital accumulation, inflation and long-run conflict in international objectives / F. van der Ploeg. — London : Centre for Labour Economics, London School of Economics, 1986. — 29p. — (Discussion paper / London School of Economics and Political Science. Centre for Labour Economics ; no.250). — *Bibliography: p28-29*

RUTTERFORD, Janette Marie
An empirical investigation into the effects of corporate and personal taxes on company capital structure / by Janette Rutterford. — 563 leaves. — *PhD (Econ) 1986 LSE*

Studies in Austrian capital theory, investment, and time / edited by M. Faber ; with contributions by P. Bernholz ... [et al.]. — Berlin ; New York : Springer-Verlag, c1986. — vi,316p. — (Lecture notes in economics and mathematical systems ; 277). — *Supplements and continues: Introduction to modern Austrian capital theory / Malte Faber.* — *Bibliography: p313-316*

CAPITAL — Mathematical models
Measurement issues and behavior of productivity variables / edited by Ali Dogramaci. — Boston : Kluwer Nijhoff ; Hingham, MA, USA : Distributors for the United States and Canada, Kluwer Academic Publishers, c1986. — ix, 262 p.. — (Studies in productivity analysis). — *Includes bibliographies and indexes*

CAPITAL — Canada
CARROLL, William K.
Corporate power and Canadian capitalism / William K. Carroll. — Vancouver : University of British Columbia Press, 1986. — xvii,284p. — *Bibliography: p[257]-276*

CAPITAL — Great Britain
WADHWANI, Sushil B.
The U.K. capital stock : new estimates of premature scrapping / S. Wadhwani and M. Wall. — London : Centre for Labour Economics, London School of Economics, 1986. — 31p. — (Discussion paper / London School of Economics and Political Science. Centre for Labour Economics ; no.245). — *Bibliography: p31-*

CAPITAL — India
BIRLA INSTITUTE OF SCIENTIFIC RESEARCH. Economic Research Division
Capital and technological progress in the Indian economy, 1950/51 - 1980/81. — New Delhi : Radiant Publishers, 1985. — xvi,198p. — *Bibliography: p192-198*

CAPITAL — Soviet Union
LAFONT, Jean
L'accumulation du capital et les crises dans l'URSS contemporaine : une première approche / Jean Lafont et Danièle Leborgne. — Paris : Centre D'Études Prospectives d'Économie Mathématique Appliquées à la Planification, 1979. — 98p. — (Centre d'Études Prospectives d'Économie Mathématique Appliquées à la Planification ; 7910). — *Bibliography: p93-98*

CAPITAL — United States
Measurement issues and behavior of productivity variables / edited by Ali Dogramaci. — Boston : Kluwer Nijhoff ; Hingham, MA, USA : Distributors for the United States and Canada, Kluwer Academic Publishers, c1986. — ix, 262 p.. — (Studies in productivity analysis). — *Includes bibliographies and indexes*

CAPITAL — United States — Congresses
Financing corporate capital formation / edited by Benjamin M. Friedman. — Chicago : University of Chicago Press, 1986. — 127 p.. — (A National Bureau of Economic Research project report). — *Papers presented at a conference held at Williamsburg, Va., Sept. 20-21, 1984, sponsored by the National Bureau of Economic Research. — Includes bibliographies and index*

CAPITAL ASSETS PRICING MODEL
HARRINGTON, Diana R.
Modern portfolio theory, the capital asset pricing model, and arbitrage pricing theory : a user's guide / Diana R. Harrington. — 2nd ed. — Englewood Cliffs, N.J. : Prentice-Hall, 1986, c1987. — p. cm. — : *Previous ed. published as: Modern portfolio theory and the capital asset pricing model. 1983. — Includes bibliographies and index*

CAPITAL BUDGET
AULD, D. A. L.
Budget reform : should there be a capital budget for the public sector? / D. A. L. Auld. — Toronto : C.D. Howe Institute, 1985. — vi,36p

BOWER, Joseph L
Managing the resource allocation process : a study of corporate planning and investment / Joseph L. Bower. — Boston, Mass. : Harvard Business School Press, c1986. — p. cm. — (Harvard Business School classics ; 3). — *Bibliography: p[349]-353. — Bibliography: p*

CAPITAL GAINS TAX — Law and legislation — United States
NEWMAN, Sandra J
Federal policy and the mobility of older homeowners : the effects of the one-time capital gains exclusion / Sandra Newman, James Reschovsky ; project manager, Robert Marans. — Ann Arbor, Mich. : Survey Research Center, Institute for Social Research, University of Michigan, 1985. — p. cm. — (Research report series / Institute for social research). — *"ISR code no. 9020"--T.p. verso. — Bibliography: p*

CAPITAL GAINS TAX — Great Britain
GREAT BRITAIN. Board of Inland Revenue
Capital gains tax : partnerships. — London : the Board, 1975. — 8leaves

CAPITAL INVESTMENTS
BOWER, Joseph L
Managing the resource allocation process : a study of corporate planning and investment / Joseph L. Bower. — Boston, Mass. : Harvard Business School Press, c1986. — p. cm. — (Harvard Business School classics ; 3). — *Bibliography: p[349]-353. — Bibliography: p*

PITELIS, Christos
Corporate capital : control, ownership, saving and crisis / Christos Pitelis. — Cambridge : Cambridge University Press, 1987. — [220]p. — *Includes bibliography and index*

CAPITAL INVESTMENTS — Evaluation
ENGLISH, J. Morley
Project evaluation : a unified approach for the analysis of capital investments / J. Morley English. — New York : Macmillan, c1984. — p. cm. — *Bibliography: p*

CAPITAL INVESTMENTS — Colombia
Colombia, the investment banking system and related issues in the financial sector. — Washington, D.C., U.S.A. : World Bank, c1985. — xl,82p. — (A World Bank country study). — *Preface and summary in English and Spanish. — Includes bibliographical references*

CAPITAL INVESTMENTS — Finland
KOSKENKYLÄ, Heikki
Investment behaviour and market imperfections with an application to the Finnish corporate sector / Heikki Koskenkylä. — Helsinki : Bank of Finland, 1985. — 65p. — *Bibliography: p52-65*

CAPITAL INVESTMENTS — Great Britain
CHICK, Martin John
Economic planning, managerial decision-making and the role of fixed capital in the investment in the economic recovery of the United Kingdom, 1945-1955 / Martin John Chick. — 313 leaves. — *PhD (Econ) 1986 LSE*

CAPITAL LEVY
AGNELL, Jonas
Tax reforms and asset markets / Jonas Agnell. — Stockholm : Industrial Institute for Economic and Social Research : Distributed by Almqvist & Wiksell, 1985. — 181p. — *Bibliography: p170-181*

RUTTERFORD, Janette Marie
An empirical investigation into the effects of corporate and personal taxes on company capital structure / by Janette Rutterford. — 563 leaves. — *PhD (Econ) 1986 LSE*

CAPITAL LEVY — Mathematical models
LEAPE, Jonathan
Taxes and transaction costs in asset market equilibrium / Jonathan Leape. — Rev. ed. — [London : London School of Economics and Political Science], 1986. — 34p. — (Taxation, incentives and the distribution of income ; no.97). — *Economic and Social Research Council programme. — Bibliographical references: p33-34*

CAPITAL LEVY — Turkey
OKTE, Faik
The tragedy of the Turkish capital tax / Faik Ökte ; translated by Geoffrey Cox. — Beckenham : Croom Helm, c1987. — xx,95p. — *Translation from the Turkish*

CAPITAL LEVY — United States
NATIONAL BUREAU OF ECONOMIC RESEARCH
Taxes and capital formation : NBER summary report. — Cambridge (Mass.) : National Bureau of Economic Research, 1986. — 40p. — *This report summarizes the papers discussed at the NBER's conference on the effects of taxation on capital formation held on February 13-16 1986, in Palm Beach, Florida*

CAPITAL MARKET
CRAWFORD, Vincent P.
International lending, long-term credit relationships, and dynamic contract theory / Vincent P. Crawford. — Princeton, N.J. : International Finance Section, Dept. of Economics, Princeton University, 1987. — p. cm. — (Princeton studies in international finance ; no. 59 (March 1987)). — *Bibliography: p*

FUKAO, Mitsuhiro
Internationalisation of financial markets : some implications for macroeconomic policy and for the allocation of capital / by Mitsuhiro Fukao and Masaharu Hanazaki. — [Paris] : OECD, 1986. — 97p. — (Working papers / OECD Department of Economics and Statistics ; no.37). — *Bibliographical references: p36-40*

International trade in services : securities. — Paris : Organisation for Economic Co-operation and Development, 1987. — 125p

KOBOLD, Klaus
Interest rate futures markets and capital market theory : theoretical concepts and empirical evidence / Klaus Kobold. — Berlin ; New York : W. de Gruyte, 1986. — p. cm. — (Series D--Economcis =Economique ; 1)

KROUSE, Clement G
Capital markets and prices : valuing uncertain income streams / Clement G. Krouse. — Amsterdam ; New York : North-Holland ; New York, N.Y. : Sole distributors for U.S.A. and Canada, Elsevier Science Pub. Co., 1986. — p. cm. — (Advanced textbooks in economics ; v. 25). — *Includes index*

STRONG, Norman
Information and capital markets / Norman Strong and Martin Walker. — Oxford : Basil Blackwell, 1987. — [240]p. — *Includes bibliography and index*

CAPITAL MARKET — Australia
Business investment and the capital stock. — Canberra : Economic Planning Advisory Council, 1986. — v,27p. — (Council paper / Economic Planning Advisory Council ; no.10). — *Bibliographical references: p25*

CAPITAL MOVEMENTS
CUDDINGTON, John T
Capital flight : estimates, issues, and explanations / John T. Cuddington. — Princeton, N.J. : International Finance Section, Dept. of Economics, Princeton University, c1986. — 44 p.. — (Princeton studies in international finance ; no. 58 (Dec. 1986). — *Bibliography: p. 39-40*

International capital markets : development and prospects / by Maxwell Watson...[et al.]. — Washington, D. C. : International Monetary Fund, 1986. — ix,152p. — (World economic and financial surveys). — *Includes Bibliographical references*

KINDLEBERGER, Charles P.
International capital movements : based on the Marshall Lectures given at the University of Cambridge 1985 / Charles P. Kindleberger. — Cambridge : Cambridge University Press, 1987. — 1v. — *Includes bibliography and index*

CAPITAL MOVEMENTS — Law and legislation — Organisation for Economic Co-operation and Development countries
Code of liberalisation of capital movements. — Paris : Organisation for Economic Co-operation and Development, 1986. — 122p. — *Incorporates all changes in obligations and positions of Member countries to 31st August 1986*

Introduction to the OECD codes of liberalisation. — Paris : Organisation for Economic Co-operation and Development, 1987. — 42p. — *Bibliographical references: p30-32*

CAPITAL MOVEMENTS — Japan
YOSHITOMI, Masaru
Japan as capital exporter and the world economy / Masaru Yoshitomi. — New York : Group of Thirty, 1986. — 32p. — (Occasional papers / Group of Thirty ; no.18)

CAPITAL MOVEMENTS — Organisation for Economic Co-operation and Development countries — Statistics
Flows and stocks of fixed capital : 1960-1985 = Flux et stocks de capital fixe : 1960-1985. — Paris : Organisation for Economic Co-operation and Development, 1987. — 39p

CAPITAL MOVEMENTS — Pacific Area

GOLDBERG, Michael A
The Chinese connection : getting plugged in to Pacific Rim real estate, trade, and capital markets / Michael A. Goldberg. — Vancouver : University of British Columbia Press, 1985. — xi, 158 p.. — *Includes indexes. — Bibliography: p. [121]-158*

CAPITAL PRODUCTIVITY — Norway

HALVORSEN, Ragnar
Lønnsomhetskrav : Strategi for lønnsom vekst sett fra Dyno Industrier A.S' side / Ragnar Halvorsen. — Bergen : Norges handelshøyskole, 1985. — 34p. — (Kristofer Lehmkuhl Forelesning ; 1985)

CAPITAL PUNISHMENT — Great Britain

GREAT BRITAIN. Parliament. House of Commons. Library. Research Division
Capital punishment / Patrick Nealon. — [London] : the Division, 1983. — 30p. — (Background paper ; no.122). — *Updating of Background Paper no.104 of May 1982*

CAPITAL PUNISHMENT — Great Britain — History — 20th century

BABINGTON, Anthony
For the sake of example : capital courts martial, 1914-1920 / Anthony Babington ; with a postscript by...Frank Richardson. — London : Paladin Grafton Books, 1985. — x,309p. — *Bibliography: p301-304*

CAPITAL STOCK — Great Britain

SMITH, A. D.
A current cost accounting measure of the stock of equipment in British manufacturing industry / A. D. Smith. — London : National Institute of Economic and Social Research, 1986. — 25p. — (Discussion paper / National Institute of Economic and Social Research ; no.115)

SMITH, A. D.
The feasibility of fire insurance measures of capital stock / A. D. Smith. — London : National Institute of Economic and Social Research, 1986. — 25p. — (Discussion paper / National Institute of Economic and Social Research ; no.116)

CAPITAL STOCK — Organisation for Economic Co-operation and Development countries — Statistics

Flows and stocks of fixed capital : 1960-1985 = Flux et stocks de capital fixe : 1960-1985. — Paris : Organisation for Economic Co-operation and Development, 1987. — 39p

CAPITALISM

ANDERSEN, Alfred F.
Liberating the early American dream : a way to transcend the capitalist/communist dilemma nonviolently / by Alfred F. Andersen. — Ukiah, Calif. : Tom Paine Institute, c1985. — p. cm. — *Rev. ed. of: Updating the early American dream. c1984. — Includes index. — Bibliography: p*

BERBEROGLU, Berch
The international of capital : imperialism and capitalist development on a world scale / Berch Berberoglu. — New York : Praeger, 1987. — p. cm. — *Bibliography: p*

BERGER, Peter L.
The capitalist revolution : fifty propositions about prosperity, equality and liberty / Peter L. Berger. — Aldershot : Gower, c1987. — [350]p. — *Includes bibliography and index*

BERGER, Peter L.
The capitalist revolution : fifty propositions about prosperity, equality, and liberty / Peter L. Berger. — Aldershot : Wildwood House, [1987]. — 262p

BOTTOMORE, Tom
Theories of modern capitalism / Tom Bottomore. — London : Allen & Unwin, 1985. — [96]p. — (Controversies in sociology ; 17). — *Includes bibliography and index*

BOWLES, Samuel
Democracy and capitalism : property, community, and the contradictions of modern social thought / Samuel Bowles, Herbert Gintis. — London : Routledge & Kegan Paul, 1986. — x,244p. — *Includes index*

BOWLES, Samuel
Understanding capitalism : competition, command, and change in the U.S. economy / by Samuel Bowles and Richard Edwards. — New York, NY : Harper & Row, c1985. — p. cm. — *Includes index*

BOYER, Robert
La crise actuelle : une mise en perspective historique : quelques reflexions à partir d'une analyse du capitalisme français en longue période / Robert Boyer. — Paris : Centre d'Études Prospectives D'Économie Mathématique Appliquées à la Planification, 1979. — 126p. — (Centre d'Études Prospectives d'Économie Mathematique Appliquées à la Planification ; no.7909). — *Bibliography: p115-128*

CHARLTON, William
The Christian response to industrial capitalism / William Charlton, Tatiana Mallinson, Robert Oakeshott. — London : Sheed & Ward, 1986. — 263p

DICKHUT, Willi
Krisen und Klassenkampf / Willi Dickhut. — Stuttgart : Verlag Neuer Weg, 1985. — 292p

FOLEY, Duncan K
Money, accumulation, and crisis / Duncan K. Foley. — Chur, Switzerland ; New York : Harwood Academic Publishers, c1986. — 60 p.. — (Fundamentals of pure and applied economics ; vol. 2 Marxian economics section). — *Includes index. — Bibliography: p. 55-58*

FOSTER, John Bellamy
The theory of monopoly capitalism : an elaboration of Marxian political economy / John Bellamy Foster. — New York : Monthly Review Press, c1986. — 280 p.. — *Includes index. — Bibliography: p. 225-263*

GREEN, Francis
The profit system : [the economics of capitalism] / Francis Green and Bob Sutcliffe. — Harmondsworth : Penguin, 1987. — [xiii],389p. — *Bibliography: p[381]-382*

GREENBERG, Edward S.
Capitalism and the American political ideal / by Edward S. Greenberg. — Armonk, N.Y. : M.E. Sharpe, 1985. — p. cm

International capitalism and industrial restructuring : a critical analysis / edited by Richard Peet. — Boston ; London : Allen & Unwin, 1987. — [224]p. — *Includes bibliography and index*

KOSTOPOULOS, Tryphon
Beyond capitalism : toward nomocracy / Tryphon Kostopoulos. — New York : Praeger, c1986. — p. cm. — *Includes index. — Bibliography: p*

LASH, Scott
The end of organized capitalism / Scott Lash and John Urry. — Cambridge : Polity, 1987. — [330]p. — *Includes index*

Lenin and imperialism : an appraisal of theories and contemporary reality / edited by Prabhat Patnaik. — London : Sangam Books, 1986. — 414p

MILES, Robert
Capitalism and unfree labour : anomaly or necessity? / Robert Miles. — London : Tavistock, 1987. — [viii,272]p. — *Includes bibliography and index*

MOORE, Barrington
Authority and inequality under capitalism and socialism / Barrington Moore Jr. — Oxford : Clarendon, 1987. — x,142p. — *Includes index*

O'CONNOR, James
The meaning of crisis : a theoretical introduction / James O'Connor. — Oxford : Basil Blackwell, 1987. — [192]p v,197p. — *Includes index*

Science, technology and the labour process : Marxist studies / edited by Les Levidow and Bob Young. — London : Free Association Books
Vol.2. — 1985. — v,232p. — *Includes bibliographies*

SCOTT, John, 1949-
Corporations, classes and capitalism / John Scott. — 2nd, completely rev., ed. — London : Hutchinson, 1985. — 319p. — (Hutchinson university library). — *Previous ed.: 1979. — Bibliography: p270-312. — Includes index*

THANH-HUNG, Nguyen
Zur Theorie der vorkapitalistischen Produktionsweisen bei K. Marx und F. Engels : dargestellt anhand der Probleme der "asiatischen Produktionsweise" / Nguyen Thanh-Hung. — Gaiganz : Politladen, 1975. — 119p. — (Politladen Typoskript ; 9). — *Bibliography: p110-119*

CAPITALISM — Addresses, essays, lectures

Corporations and the common good / edited by Robert B. Dickie and Leroy S. Rouner. — Notre Dame, Ind. : University of Notre Dame Press, c1986. — xii, 147 p.. — *"Published with the School of Management, Boston University.". — Includes bibliographies. — Contents: Introduction -- The moral crisis of capitalism / Peter Berger -- Realities and appearances in capitalism / Robert Heilbroner -- Perfecting capitalism / James E. Post -- The large corporation and the new American ideology / George C. Lodge -- The multinational corporation / Kenneth Mason -- Ethics and corporate strategy / Edwin A. Murray, Jr. -- Sanctions, incentives, and corporate behavior / Peter T. Jones -- Epilogue : can managers be taught to be ethical? / Henry Morgan*

CAPITALISM — Congresses

The Dynamics of market economies / edited by Richard H. Day and Gunnar Eliasson. — New York : North Holland Pub. Co. ; New York, N.Y. : Sole distributors for the U.S.A. and Canada, Elsevier Science Pub. Co., 1985. — p. cm. — *"Papers and discussion of a conference on the dynamics of decentralized, market economies held at the Grand Hotel, Saltsjöbaden near Stockholm, August 29-31, 1983 ... sponsored by the Marcus Wallenberg Foundation for International Cooperation in Science"--P*

CAPITALISM — History

LITTLER, Craig R.
The development of the labour process in capitalist societies : a comparative study of the transformation of work organization in Britain, Japan and the USA / Craig R. Littler. — Aldershot : Gower, 1986, c1982. — [240]p. — *Originally published: London : Heinemann Educational, 1982*

RAPOŠ, Pavel
Die kranke Wirtschaft : Kapitalismus und krise / Pavel Rapoš ; Übersetzung aus dem Slowakischen: Intertext. — Köln : Pahl-Rugenstein, 1984. — 321p. — *Originally published: Bratislava: Pravda, 1981*

CAPITALISM — Moral and ethical aspects

MCKENZIE, Richard B
The fairness of markets : a search for justice in a free society / Richard B. McKenzie. — Lexington, Mass. : Lexington Books, c1987. — xiv, 235 p.. — *Includes bibliographies and index*

CAPITALISM — Religious aspects
WEBER, Max
The Protestant ethic and the spirit of capitalism / Max Weber ; translated by Talcott Parsons ; introduction by Anthony Giddens. — London : Unwin Paperbacks, 1985. — [320]p. — (Counterpoint). — *Translation of: Die protestantische Ethik und der 'Geist' des Kapitalismus. — Originally published: London : Allen & Unwin, 1930. — Includes index*

CAPITALISM — Australia
Essays in the political economy of Australian capitalism / edited by E. L. Wheelwright and Ken Buckley. — Sydney : Australia & New Zealand Book Company vol.5. — 1983. — 304p

CAPITALISM — China — History — 19th century
HAO, Yen-p'ing
The commercial revolution in nineteenth-century China : the rise of Sino-Western mercantile capitalism / Yen-p'ing Hao. — Berkeley : University of California Press, c1986. — xv, 394 p.. — *Includes index. — Bibliography: p. 364-380*

CAPITALISM — Developing countries
Capitalism and equality in the Third World / edited by Peter L. Berger. — Lanham, MD : Hamilton Press ; [Washington, D.C.] : Institute for Educational Affairs, <1987- >. — p. cm. — *Bibliography: p. — Contents: -- v. 2. Modern capitalism*

CAPITALISM — Hungary
Koncepció és kritika : vita Liska Tibor "szocialista vállalkozási szektor" javaslatáról / szerkesztette síklaky István. — Budapest : Magvetö kiadó, [1985]. — 387p. — (Gyorsuló idö)

CAPITALISM — Ivory coast — History
The African bourgeoisie : capitalist development in Nigeria, Kenya, and the Ivory Coast / edited by Paul M. Lubeck. — Boulder, Colo. : L. Rienner Publishers, 1986. — p. cm. — *Includes bibliographies and index*

CAPITALISM — Kenya — History
The African bourgeoisie : capitalist development in Nigeria, Kenya, and the Ivory Coast / edited by Paul M. Lubeck. — Boulder, Colo. : L. Rienner Publishers, 1986. — p. cm. — *Includes bibliographies and index*

CAPITALISM — Latin America
CHILCOTE, Ronald H
Latin America : capitalist and socialist perspectives of development and underdevelopment / Ronald H. Chilcote and Joel C. Edelstein. — Boulder ; London : Westview Press, 1986. — xv, 175p. — (Latin American perspectives series ; no. 3). — *"This is a complete revision and expansion of our introduction to Latin America : the struggle with dependency and beyond, published in 1974"--Pref. — Includes index. — Bibliography: p.153-164*

CAPITALISM — Latin America — History
KINSBRUNER, Jay
Petty capitalism in Spanish America : the Pulperos of Puebla, Mexico City, Caracas, and Buenos Aires / Jay Kinsbruner. — Boulder, Colo. ; London : Westview Press, 1987. — xxii,159p. — (Dellplain Latin American studies ; no.21). — *Bibliography: p[143]-152*

CAPITALISM — Nigeria — History
The African bourgeoisie : capitalist development in Nigeria, Kenya, and the Ivory Coast / edited by Paul M. Lubeck. — Boulder, Colo. : L. Rienner Publishers, 1986. — p. cm. — *Includes bibliographies and index*

CAPITALISM — North Carolina — History
WOOD, Phillip J.
Southern capitalism : the political economy of North Carolina, 1880-1980 / Phillip J. Wood. — Durham, N.C. : Duke University Press, 1986. — xi, 272 p.. — *Includes index. — Bibliography: p. [250]-267*

CAPITALISM — Puerto Rico — History
DIETZ, James L.
Economic history of Puerto Rico : institutional change and capitalist development / James L. Dietz. — Princeton, N.J. : Princeton University Press, c1986. — xxiii, 337p, [11]p of plates. — *Includes index. — Bibliography: p.[311]-326*

CAPITALISM — South Africa
Contending ideologies in South Africa / edited by James Leatt, Theo Kneifel, and Klaus Nürnberger. — Grand Rapids : W.B. Eerdmans, 1986. — x, 318 p.. — *Includes index. — Bibliography: p. [303]-309*

CAPITALISM — Soviet Union — History
DRUZHININ, N. M.
Izbrannye trudy / N. M. Druzhinin. — Moskva : Nauka
[2]: Sotsial'no-ekonomicheskaia istoriia Rossii / otv. redaktor S. S. Dmitriev. — 1987. — 421p

CAPITALISTS AND FINANCIERS — Ivory Coast — History
The African bourgeoisie : capitalist development in Nigeria, Kenya, and the Ivory Coast / edited by Paul M. Lubeck. — Boulder, Colo. : L. Rienner Publishers, 1986. — p. cm. — *Includes bibliographies and index*

CAPITALISTS AND FINANCIERS — Kenya — History
The African bourgeoisie : capitalist development in Nigeria, Kenya, and the Ivory Coast / edited by Paul M. Lubeck. — Boulder, Colo. : L. Rienner Publishers, 1986. — p. cm. — *Includes bibliographies and index*

CAPITALISTS AND FINANCIERS — Nigeria — History
The African bourgeoisie : capitalist development in Nigeria, Kenya, and the Ivory Coast / edited by Paul M. Lubeck. — Boulder, Colo. : L. Rienner Publishers, 1986. — p. cm. — *Includes bibliographies and index*

CAPITALISTS AND FINANCIERS — Southern States — History — 19th century
SHORE, Laurence
Southern capitalists : the ideological leadership of an elite, 1832-1885 / by Laurence Shore. — Chapel Hill : University of North Carolina Press, c1986. — p. cm. — (The Fred W. Morrison series in southern studies). — *Includes index. — Bibliography: p*

CAPITALISTS AND FINANCIERS — United States — Biography
HAMMER, Armand
Witness to history / by Armand Hammer with Neil Lyndon. — New York ; London : Simon & Schuster, 1987. — [512]p. — *Includes index*

MERCER, Lloyd J
E.H. Harriman, master railroader / Lloyd J. Mercer. — Boston, Mass. : Twayne Publishers, c1985. — p. cm. — (The Evolution of American business). — *Includes index. — Bibliography: p*

CAPITALS (CITIES) — Dictionaries
FISHER, Morris
Provinces and provincial capitals of the world / compiled by Morris Fisher. — 2nd ed. — Metuchen, N.J. : Scarecrow, 1985. — ix, 248 p. . — *Includes index*

CARACAS (VENEZUELA) — History
MCKINLEY, P. Michael
Pre-revolutionary Caracas : politics, economy and society 1777-1811 / P. Michael McKinley. — Cambridge : Cambridge University Press, 1985. — xiv,245p. — (Cambridge Latin American studies ; 56). — *Bibliography: p212-217. — Includes index*

CARDANHA (PORTUGAL) — Population, Rural — History
AMORIM, Norberta
Método de exploração dos livros de registos paroquiais, e Cardanha e a sua população de 1573 a 1800 / por Norberta Amorim. — Lisboa : Instituto Nacional de Estatística, 1980. — 135p. — (Publicações do Centro de Estudos Demográficos). — *Bibliogrpahy: p127*

CARDANHA (PORTUGAL) — Statistics, Vital — History
AMORIM, Norberta
Método de exploração dos livros de registos paroquiais, e Cardanha e a sua população de 1573 a 1800 / por Norberta Amorim. — Lisboa : Instituto Nacional de Estatística, 1980. — 135p. — (Publicações do Centro de Estudos Demográficos). — *Bibliogrpahy: p127*

CARDIAC PACEMAKER INDUSTRY — France
Les stimulateurs cardiaques. — [Paris] : La Documentation française, 1985. — 232p

CARDIGANSHIRE — Industries — Statistics
BURT, Roger, 1942-
The mines of Cardiganshire : metalliferous and associated minerals 1845-1913 / Roger Burt, Peter Waite, Ray Burnley. — Exeter : Department of Economic History, University of Exeter, in association with the Northern Mine Research Society, [1985]. — xxviii, 92p

CARDINALS — Poland — Biography
KĄKOL, Kazimierz
Kardynał Stefan Wyszyński jakim go znałem / Kazimierz Kąkol. — Warszawa : Instytut Wydawniczy Związków Zawodowych, 1985. — 145,[30]p

CARDIOVASCULAR SYSTEM — Diseases — Nutritional aspects
PANEL ON DIET IN RELATION TO CARDIOVASCULAR DISEASE
Diet and cardiovascular disease : report of the Panel on Diet in Relation to Cardiovascular Disease. — London : HMSO, 1984. — viii,32. — (Report on Health and social subjects / Great Britain. Department of Health and Social Security ; 28)

CAREER DEVELOPMENT — United States
Women's career development / editors, Barbara A. Gutek and Laurie Larwood. — Newbury Park, Calif. : Sage Publications, c1987. — 191 p.. — *Includes bibliographies and index*

CAREER EDUCATION — European Economic Community countries
MCMULLEN, I. R.
Guidance and orientation in secondary schools / I. R. McMullen. — Luxembourg : Office for Official Publications of the European Communities, 1977. — 60p. — (Education series / Commission of the European Communities ; no.2)

CAREER EDUCATION — Great Britain
WEBB, Sylvia P.
Personal development in information work / Sylvia P. Webb. — London : Aslib, 1986. — [128]p. — *Includes index*

CAREER EDUCATION — Great Britain — Management
RANSON, Stewart
The management of change in the careers service / by Stewart Ranson and Peter Ribbins ; with Lesley Chesterfield and Tony Smith. — Birmingham : INLOGOV, 1986. — 200p

CARIB INDIANS — Saint Vincent — Folklore
GULLICK, C. J. M. R.
Myths of a minority : the changing traditions of the Vincentian Caribs / C. J. M. R. Gullick. — Assen : Van Gorcum, 1985. — 211p. — (Studies of developing countries ; 30). — *Bibliography: p196-211*

CARIBBEAN AREA — Archival resources

Research guide to Central America and the Caribbean / Kenneth Grieb, editor-in-chief ; associate editors, Ralph Lee Woodward, Jr., Graeme S. Mount, Thomas Mathews. — Madison, Wis. : University of Wisconsin Press, 1985. — xv, 431p. — *Includes bibliographical references and index*

CARIBBEAN AREA — Armed Forces

Militarization in the non-Hispanic Caribbean / edited by Alma H. Young and Dion E. Phillips. — Boulder, Colo. : Lynne Rienner Publishers, 1986. — ix, 178p. — *Includes index*. — *Bibliography: p.160-173*

CARIBBEAN AREA — Census — Handbooks, manuals, etc

GOYER, Doreen S.
The handbook of national population censuses : Latin America and the Caribbean, North America, and Oceania / Doreen S. Goyer and Eliane Domschke. — Westport, Conn. : Greenwood Press, 1983. — xii, 711 p.. — *Includes index*. — *Bibliography: p. 28-30*

CARIBBEAN AREA — Congresses

CANADIAN ASSOCIATION FOR LATIN AMERICAN AND CARIBBEAN STUDIES. Conference (1983 : Ottawa)
Latin America and the Caribbean : geopolitics, development and culture : conference proceedings / edited by Arch R. M. Ritter. — Ottawa : CALACS, 1984. — viii,355p. — *Includes chapters in French and Spanish.* — *Conference cosponsored by the Ontario Cooperative Program for Latin American and Caribbean Studies*

CARIBBEAN AREA — Economic conditions — 1945- — Congresses

Crises in the Caribbean basin : past and present / edited by Richard Tardanico. — Beverly Hills [Calif.] : Sage Publications, c1986. — p. cm. — (Political economy of the world-system annuals ; v. 9). — *"Based on papers presented at the ninth annual Conference on the Political Economy of the World-System, Tulane University, March 18-20, 1985"--Pref*

CARIBBEAN AREA — Foreign relations

BAUMAN, Everett A.
The strengths and weaknesses of Contadora as regional diplomacy in the Caribbean basis / Everett A. Bauman. — Washington, D.C. : Latin American Program, the Wilson Centre, 1985. — 62p. — (Working papers / Wilson Centre. Latin American Program ; 167)

CARIBBEAN AREA — Foreign relations — Soviet Union

MANFARLANE, S. Neil
Superpower rivalry and Soviet policy in the Caribbean Basin / S. N. MacFarlane. — Ottawa : Canadian Institue for International Peace and Security, 1986. — 70p. — (Occasional papers / Canadian Institute for International Peace and Security ; no.1)

CARIBBEAN AREA — Foreign relations — United States

POLICY ALTERNATIVES FOR THE CARIBBEAN AND CENTRAL AMERICA
Changing course : blueprint for peace in Central America and the Caribbean / PACCA. — Washington D.C. : Institute for Policy Studies, 1984. — 116p

CARIBBEAN AREA — Politics and government — 1945-

MARABLE, Manning
African and Caribbean politics from Kwame Nkrumah to the Grenada revolution / Manning Marable. — London : Verso, 1987. — [300]p. — (Haymarket series). — *Includes index*

CARIBBEAN AREA — Politics and government — 1945- — Congresses

Crises in the Caribbean basin : past and present / edited by Richard Tardanico. — Beverly Hills [Calif.] : Sage Publications, c1986. — p. cm. — (Political economy of the world-system annuals ; v. 9). — *"Based on papers presented at the ninth annual Conference on the Political Economy of the World-System, Tulane University, March 18-20, 1985"--Pref*

CARIBBEAN AREA — Relations — Europe

HULME, Peter
Colonial encounters : Europe and the native Caribbean, 1492-1797 / Peter Hulme. — London : Methuen, 1986. — xv,348p. — *Includes index*. — *Bibliography: p329-348*

CARIBBEAN AREA — Research

Research guide to Central America and the Caribbean / Kenneth Grieb, editor-in-chief ; associate editors, Ralph Lee Woodward, Jr., Graeme S. Mount, Thomas Mathews. — Madison, Wis. : University of Wisconsin Press, 1985. — xv, 431p. — *Includes bibliographical references and index*

CARIBBEAN AREA — Social conditions — 1945-

Dual legacies in the contemporary Caribbean : continuing aspects of British and French dominion / edited by Paul Sutton. — London : Cass, 1986. — [280]p. — (Legacies of West Indian slavery). — *Conference papers*

CARINTHIA (AUSTRIA) — Ethnic relations

ZWITTER, Fran
To destroy Nazism or to reward it? : an aspect of the question of Slovene Carinthia / Fran Zwitter. — Beograd : Yugoslav Institute for International Affairs, 1947. — 30p

CARINTHIA (AUSTRIA) — Politics and government

Carinthischer Herbst = Koroška jesen. — Klagenfurt : Karel Smolle, [1978?]. — 31p. — *Text in German and Slovene*

ZWITTER, Fran
To destroy Nazism or to reward it? : an aspect of the question of Slovene Carinthia / Fran Zwitter. — Beograd : Yugoslav Institute for International Affairs, 1947. — 30p

CARINTHIA (AUSTRIA) — Social conditions

Carinthischer Herbst = Koroška jesen. — Klagenfurt : Karel Smolle, [1978?]. — 31p. — *Text in German and Slovene*

CARLISTS

REAL CUESTA, Javier
El carlismo vasco 1876-1900 / por Javier Real Cuesta. — Madrid : Siglo ventiuno, 1985. — xiii,338p. — *"El carlismo vasco, 1876-1900 es el resumen de una tesis doctoral que con el mismo título fue presentada en la Universidad de Zaragoza en 1983"*. — *Bibliography: p [311]-321*

CARLISTS — Biography

PEINADO PEINADO, Rufino
Recuerdos de un carlista andaluz : un cruzado de la causa / [Rufino Peinado Peinado] ; Rafael Alvarez de Morales y Ruiz. — Córdoba : Instituto de H.a de Andalucía, [1982?]. — 245 p.. — (Publicaciones Instituto de Historia de Andalucía ; no. 13). — *Includes index*

CARLOS, Prince of Bourbon

PEINADO PEINADO, Rufino
Recuerdos de un carlista andaluz : un cruzado de la causa / [Rufino Peinado Peinado] ; Rafael Alvarez de Morales y Ruiz. — Córdoba : Instituto de H.a de Andalucía, [1982?]. — 245 p.. — (Publicaciones Instituto de Historia de Andalucía ; no. 13). — *Includes index*

CARRERO BLANCO, LUIS

EL PAÍS. Equipo de Investigación
Golpe mortal : asesinato de Carrero y agonía del franquismo / El País, Equipo de Investigación ; Ismael Fuente, Javier García y Joaquín Prieto. — [Madrid : Promotora de Informaciones], 1983. — 374p

CARROLL, LEWIS — Biography

CARROLL, Lewis
Lewis Carroll and the House of Macmillan / edited by Morton N. Cohen and Anita Gandolfo. — Cambridge : Cambridge University Press, 1987. — [392]p. — (Cambridge studies in publishing and printing history). — *Includes index*

CARTER, JIMMY — Views on civil rights

MURAVCHIK, Joshua
The uncertain crusade : Jimmy Carter and the dilemmas of human rights policy / Joshua Muravchik ; foreword by Jeane Kirkpatrick. — Lanham, Md. ; London : Hamilton Press, c1986. — xxii, 247p. — *Includes bibliographies and index*

CARTOGRAPHY

Elements of cartography / Arthur H. Robinson ... [et al.]. — 5th ed. — New York ; Chichester : Wiley, 1984. — 544 p.. — : *Revision of: Robinson, A.H. Elements of cartography. 4th ed. c1978*. — *Includes bibliographies and index*

CARTOGRAPHY — Data processing

AUTO CARTO LONDON (1986)
Proceedings / edited by Michael Blakemore. — London : Auto Carto London. — *Subtitle: International conference on the acquisition, management and presentation of spatial data, 14-19 September, 1986*
Vol.1: Hardware, data capture and management techniques. — 1986. — 597p

AUTO CARTO LONDON (1986)
Proceedings / edited by Michael Blakemore. — London : Auto Carto London, 1986. — *Subtitle: International conference on the acquisition, management and presentation of spatial data, 14-19 September, 1986*
Vol.2: Digital mapping and spatial information systems. — 565p

CARTULARIES

Reading Abbey cartularies : British Library manuscripts - Egerton 3031, Harley 1708 and Cotton Vespasian Exxv / edited by B.R. Kemp. — London : Royal Historical Society 2: Berkshire documents, Scottish charters and miscellaneous documents. — 1987. — [440]p. — (Camden fourth series ; v.33). — *Includes bibliography and index*

CASELY HAYFORD, ADELAIDE SMITH

CROMWELL, Adelaide M.
An African Victorian feminist : the life and times of Adelaide Smith Casely Hayford 1868-1960 / Adelaide M. Cromwell. — London : Cass, 1986. — xvi,235p,[13]p of plates. — *Includes index*

CASEY, RICHARD GARDINER CASEY, Baron

HUDSON, W. J.
Casey / W. J. Hudson. — Melbourne : Oxford University Press, 1986. — xii,361p

CASH FLOW

KING, Mervyn A.
The cash flow corporate income tax / Mervyn A. King. — [London : London School of Economics and Political Science], 1986. — 35p. — (Taxation, incentives and the distribution of income ; no.95). — *Economic and Social Research Council programme*. — *Paper prepared for the NBER Conference on the Effects of Taxation on Capital Formation, Palm Beach*. — *Bibliographical references: p29-30*

CASH FLOW — Accounting

LEE, T. A.
Cash flow accounting / Tom Lee. — Wokingham : Van Nostrand Reinhold, 1984. — xii,154p. — (The VNR series in accounting and finance). — *Bibliography: p139-142*. — *Includes index*

CASH FLOW — Great Britain — Management
AUDIT COMMISSION FOR LOCAL AUTHORITIES IN ENGLAND AND WALES
Improving cash flow management in local government : a report. — London : H.M.S.O., 1986. — 80p

CASSAVA INDUSTRY — India — Kerala
NINAN, K. N.
Cereal substitutes in a developing economy : a study of tapioca, Kerala State / K.N. Ninan. — New Delhi : Concept Pub. Co., 1986. — xviii, 252 p.. — : Revision of the author's thesis (Ph. D.--Mysore University. 1984). — Includes index. — Bibliography: p. [241]-248

CAST
HEATHFIELD, David F.
An introduction to cost and production functions / David F. Heathfield and Sören Wibe. — Basingstoke : Macmillan, 1987. — 193p. — Bibliography: p183-189. — Includes index

CAST-IRON — Economic aspects
BHAT, B. A.
Choice of technique in iron founding / B.A. Bhat and C.C. Prendergast. — Edinburgh : Scottish Academic Press, 1984. — xiv,110p. — (David Livingstone Institute series on choice of technique in developing countries ; v.8). — Bibliography: p104-105. — Includes index

CASTE — India
GUPTA, S. K.
The scheduled castes in modern Indian politics : their emergence as a political power / S. K. Gupta. — New Delhi : Munshiram Manoharlal, 1985. — xi,355p. — Bibliography: p[333]-342

PRAKASH, Om
Caste Hindu and scheduled caste children in rural India / Om Prakash and Arun K. Sen. — New Delhi : Ess Ess Publications, 1985. — xiv, 184 p.. — Spine title: Hindu caste and scheduled caste children in rural India. — Includes index. — Bibliography: p. [155]-182

SARKAR, J.
Caste, occupation and change / J. Sarkar. — Delhi : B. R. Publishing Corporation, 1984. — 112p. — Bibliography: p[107]-110

CASTE — India — Bengal
DASGUPTA, Satadal
Caste, kinship and community : social system of a Bengal caste / Satadal Dasgupta. — London : Sangam Books Ltd., 1986. — xii,291p. — Bibliography: p[283]-286

CASTE — India — Nagpur
SHAMKUNWAR, M. R.
Scheduled castes : socio-economic survey / by M. R. Shamkunwar. — Allahabad [India] : Kitab Mahal, 1985. — vii,151p. — Bibliography: p[141]-143

CASTELLÓN DE LA PLANA (SPAIN) — Politics and government
MARTÍ, Manuel
Cossieros i anticossieros : burgesia i política local, Castelló de la Plana, 1875-1891 / Manuel Martí. — [Castelló] : Diputació Provincial de Castelló, 1985. — 333 p.. — (Col·lecció universitària). — : Originally presented as the author's thesis (llicenciatura--Universitat de València, 1984) under the title: Burgesia i política local, Castelló de la Plana, 1875-1891. — Bibliography: p. 323-333

CASTILE (SPAIN) — Economic conditions
MARCOS MARTÍN, Alberto
Economía, sociedad, pobreza en Castilla : Palencia, 1500-1814 / Alberto Marcos Martín. — Palencia : Diputación Provincial
1. — 1985. — 358p

MARCOS MARTÍN, Alberto
Economía, sociedad, pobreza en Castilla : Palencia, 1500-1814 / Alberto Marcos Martín. — Palencia : Diputación Provincial.
Bibliography: p[691]-715
2. — 1985. — p369-742

CASTILLA-LA MANCHA (SPAIN) — Politics and government
IZQUIERDO COLLADO, Juan de Dios
Las elecciones de la transición en Castilla-La Mancha / Juan de Dios Izquierdo Collado. — Albacete : Instituto de Estudios Albacetenses : Confederación Española de Centros de Estudios Locales
Vol.1: Albacete. — (Serie 1 : Ensayos históricos y científicos / Instituto de Estudios Albacetenses ; núm.19)
Tomo 1: 1976-79. — 1984. — 348p

IZQUIERDO COLLADO, Juan de Dios
Las elecciones de la transición en Castilla-La Mancha / Juan de Dios Izquierdo Collado. — Albacete : Instituto de Estudios Albacetenses : Confederación Española de Centros de Estudios Locales
Vol.1: Albacete. — (Serie 1 : Ensayos históricos y científicos / Instituto de Estudios Albacetenses ; núm.19)
Tomo 2: 1979-83. — 1984. — 407p. — Bibliography: p405-407

CASTILLO RIVAS, ANA MARÍA — Biography
ALEGRÍA, Claribel
They won't take me alive : Salvadorean women in struggle for national liberation / Claribel Alegria ; translated by Amanda Hopkinson. — London : Women's Press, c1987. — 145p. — Translation of: No me agarran viva

CASTRO, FIDEL
BOURNE, Peter G.
[Fidel : una biografia de Fidel Castro. English]. Castro : a biography of Fidel Castro / Peter Bourne. — London : Macmillan, 1987, c1986. — xii,332,[17]p of plates. — Originally published: New York : Dodd, Mead, 1986. — Bibliography: p319-322. — Includes index

CASTRO, Fidel
Fidel Castro : nothing can stop the course of history / interview by Jeffrey M. Elliot and Mervyn M. Dymally. — New York ; London : Pathfinder Press, 1986. — 258p

HARNECKER, Marta
Fidel Castro's political strategy : from Moncada to victory / by Marta Harnecker. — New York ; London : Pathfinder Press, 1987. — 157p. — Includes "History will absolve me" by Fidel Castro

CASTRO, FIDEL — Psychology
GONZALEZ, Edward
Castro, Cuba, and the world / Edward Gonzalez, David Ronfeldt. — Santa Monica, CA. : Rand, 1986. — xx, 133 p.. — "June 1986.". — "R-3420.". — Includes bibliographical references

CASTRO, FIDEL — Public opinion — Congresses
The Selling of Fidel Castro : the media and the Cuban Revolution / edited by William E. Ratliff. — New Brunswick, N.J., U.S.A. : Transaction Books, c1986. — p. cm. — Presented as part of a conference held on November 16-17, 1984, in Washington, D.C. — "Prepared in cooperation with the Cuban American National Foundation ... Washington, D.C."--Verso t.p

CATALAN LANGUAGE — Political aspects — Spain
FERRER I GIRONÈS, Francesc
La persecució política de la llengua catalana : història de les mesures preses contra el seu ús des de la Nova Planta fins avui / Francesc Ferrer i Gironès. — Barcelona : Edicions 62, 1985. — 309p. — Bibliography: p[295]-300

CATALANS — Ethnic identity
FERRER I GIRONÈS, Francesc
La persecució política de la llengua catalana : història de les mesures preses contra el seu ús des de la Nova Planta fins avui / Francesc Ferrer i Gironès. — Barcelona : Edicions 62, 1985. — 309p. — Bibliography: p[295]-300

CATALOGS, ON-LINE
MITEV, Nathalie Nadia
Designing an online public access catalogue : Okapi, a catalogue on a local area network / Nathalie Nadia Mitev, Gillian M. Venner, Stephen Walker. — London : British Library, 1985. — xiii,254p. — (Library and information research report ; 39). — Bibliography: p211-231. — Includes index

Online public access to library files : conference proceedings / edited by Janet Kinsella. — Oxford : Elsevier International Bulletins, 1985. — [200]p. — Includes bibliographies and index

Online public access to library files : second national conference : [proceedings] / Janet Kinsella, editor. — Oxford : Elsevier International Bulletins, 1986. — 141p. — Includes bibliographies

CATALOGS, UNION — United States
WILLIAMS, Lee H
The Allende years : a union list of Chilean imprints, 1970-1973, in selected North American libraries, with a supplemental holdings list of books published elsewhere for the same period by Chileans or about Chile or Chileans / compiled by Lee H. Williams, Jr. — Boston : G. K. Hall, c1977. — vii, 339 p.. — Includes index

CATALONIA (SPAIN) — Economic conditions
GIBERNAU, J. A
L'any 2000, un repte per a Catalunya / J.A. Gibernau ; pròleg Ramon Vila-Abadal. — 1a ed. — Barcelona : El Llamp, c1982. — 157 p.. — (Col·lecció "La Rella")

GRANELL, Francesc
Cataluña, sus relaciones económicas transnacionales y la C.E.E. / Francesc Granell ; prólogo: Jordi Pujol. — Barcelona : Vicens-Vives, 1986. — 151p

CATALONIA (SPAIN) — Economic conditions — Congresses
COLOQUIO VASCO-CATALÁN DE HISTORIA (1 : 1982 : Sitges, Spain)
Industrialización y nacionalismo : análisis comparativos / edición a cargo de Manuel González Portilla, Jordi Maluquer de Motes, Borja de Riquer Permanyer. — Bellaterra : Servicio de Publicaciones de la Universidad Autónoma de Barcelona, 1985. — 610p. — In Spanish, with some papers in Catalan

CATALONIA (SPAIN) — Emigration and immigration
CANDEL, Francesc
Els altres catalans vint anys després / Francesc Candel ; pròleg d'Oriol Badia. — Barcelona : edicions 62, [1985]. — 281p. — (Llibres a l'abast ; 210)

CATALONIA (SPAIN) — Foreign economic relations
GRANELL, Francesc
Cataluña, sus relaciones económicas transnacionales y la C.E.E. / Francesc Granell ; prólogo: Jordi Pujol. — Barcelona : Vicens-Vives, 1986. — 151p

CATALONIA (SPAIN) — History
MUNIESA, Bernat
La burguesía catalana ante la II República española / Bernat Muniesa ; prólogo de Antoni Jutglar. — Barcelona : Anthropos. — (Historia, ideas y textos ; 10)
1: "Il trovatore" frente a Wotan. — 1985. — 321p

MUNIESA, Bernat
La burguesía catalana ante la II República española (1931-1936) / Bernat Muniesa. — Barcelona : Anthropos. — (Historia, ideas y textos ; 12)
2: El triunfo de Wagner sobre Verdi. — 1986. — 262p

CATALONIA (SPAIN) — History
continuation

SERRA Y MORET, Manuel
Introducción al "Manifiesto del Partido Comunista" y otros escritos / Manuel Serra y Moret ; estudio preliminar y notas aríticas a crgo de Antoni Jutglar. — [Barcelona] : Anthropos, Editorial del Hombre, 1984. — 279p. — (Historia, ideas y textos ; 9)

TARÍN-IGLESIAS, Manuel
Los años rojos / Manuel Tarín-Iglesias. — Barcelona : Planeta, 1985. — 251p

CATALONIA (SPAIN) — History — Autonomy and independence movements

AMETLLA, Claudi
Catalunya paradís perdut : (la guerra civil i revolució anarco-comunista) / Claudi Ametlla ; pròleg del Molt Honorable President de la Generalitat Jordi Pujol. — Barcelona : Editorial Selecta, 1984. — 228p

CATALONIA (SPAIN) — History — 20th century

COLOMER, Josep M.
La ideologia de l'antifranquisme / Josep M. Colomer. — Barcelona : Edicions 62, [1985]. — 158p. — (L'escorpí ; 57)

CATALONIA (SPAIN) — History — Autonomy and independence movements

FIGUERES, Josep M.
El primer Congrés Catalanista i Valentí Almirall : materials per a l'estudi dels orígens del catalanisme / Josep M. Figueres. — [Barcelona] : Generalitat de Catalunya, Departament de la Presidència, 1985. — 282p. — *Bibliography: p267-280*

LORÉS, Jaume
La transició a Catalunya (1977-1984) : el pujolisme i els altres / Jaume Lorés. — Barcelona : Editorial Empúries, 1985. — 228p

CATALONIA (SPAIN) — Politics and government

AMETLLA, Claudi
Catalunya paradís perdut : (la guerra civil i revolució anarco-comunista) / Claudi Ametlla ; pròleg del Molt Honorable President de la Generalitat Jordi Pujol. — Barcelona : Editorial Selecta, 1984. — 228p

BALCELLS, Albert
Rafael Campalans, socialisme català : biografia i textos / Albert Balcells. — [Barcelona?] : L'Abadia de Montserrat, 1985. — 444p

BARCELÓ I SERRAMALERA, Mercè
El pensament polític de Serra i Moret : nació, democràcia i socialisme / Mercè Barceló i Serramalera ; pròleg d'Isidre Molas. — Barcelona : Edicions 62, 1986. — 205p. — *Bibliography: p191-205*

CAMINAL I BADIA, Miquel
Joan Comorera / Miquel Caminal i Badia. — Barcelona : Empúries. — (Biblioteca universal Empúries)
Volum 2: Guerra i revolució (1936-1939). — [1984]. — 294p

CAMINAL I BADIA, Miquel
Joan Comorera / Miquel Caminal i Badia. — Barcelona : Empúries. — (Biblioteca universal Empúries)
Volum 3: Comunisme i nacionalisme (1939-1958). — [1985]. — 393p

CULLA I CLARÀ, Joan B.
El republicanisme lerrouxista a Catalunya (1901-1923) / per Joan B. Culla i Clarà. — Barcelona : Curial, 1986. — 493p. — (Documents de cultura ; 19). — *Bibliography: p[465]-478*

Les eleccions al Parlament de Catalunya : una experiència interdisciplinar a BUP / Joana Amengual...[et al.]. — Barcelona : Rosa Sensat : Edicions 62, 1985. — 169p

GIBERNAU, J. A
L'any 2000, un repte per a Catalunya / J.A. Gibernau ; pròleg Ramon Vila-Abadal. — 1a ed. — Barcelona : El Llamp, c1982. — 157 p.. — (Col·lecció "La Rella")

LORÉS, Jaume
El 1984 de Catalunya : una crònica apassionada / Jaume Lorés. — Barcelona : Edicions 62, [1985]. — 203p. — (Llibres a l'abast ; 206)

LORÉS, Jaume
La transició a Catalunya (1977-1984) : el pujolisme i els altres / Jaume Lorés. — Barcelona : Editorial Empúries, 1985. — 228p

Nuestra utopía : PSVC: cincuenta años de historia de Cataluña / colaboran: Andreu Mayayo...[et al.]. — Barcelona : Planeta, 1986. — 279p. — *At head of title: Nous Horitzons*

SERRA Y MORET, Manuel
Introducción al "Manifiesto del Partido Comunista" y otros escritos / Manuel Serra y Moret ; estudio preliminar y notas aríticas a crgo de Antoni Jutglar. — [Barcelona] : Anthropos, Editorial del Hombre, 1984. — 279p. — (Historia, ideas y textos ; 9)

CATALONIA (SPAIN) — Politics and government — 20th century

COLOMER, Josep M.
La ideologia de l'antifranquisme / Josep M. Colomer. — Barcelona : Edicions 62, [1985]. — 158p. — (L'escorpí ; 57)

CATALONIA (SPAIN) — Public works — History

GENERALITAT DE CATALUNYA (Spain). Departament de Política Territorial i Obres Públiques
Pla general d'obres públiques any 1935. — [Barcelona] : the Department, 1982. — 124p

CATALONIA (SPAIN) — Relations — Europe

POU I SERRADELL, Victor
Catalunya i Europa / Victor Pou i Serradell. — Barcelona : Sirocco, 1985. — 58p. — (Els europeus ; no.1)

CATALONIA (SPAIN) — Social conditions

CANDEL, Francesc
Els altres catalans vint anys després / Francesc Candel ; pròleg d'Oriol Badia. — Barcelona : edicions 62, [1985]. — 281p. — (Llibres a l'abast ; 210)

Conflict in Catalonia : images of an urban society / edited by Gary W. McDonogh. — Gainesville : University Presses of Florida, University of Florida Press, c1986. — 102 p.. — (University of Florida monographs. Social sciences ; no. 71). — *Includes bibliographies and index*

JUTGLAR, Antoni
[Els burgesos catalans. Spanish]. Historia crítica de la burguesía en Cataluña / Antoni Jutglar. — Edición ampliada. — [Barcelona] : Anthropos, [1984]. — 554p. — (Historia, ideas y textos ; 8). — *Publicado originalmente en catalán por Editorial Norfeu, Barcelona, 1966. — Con un "Prólogo para no catalanes" y "Unas últimas reflexiones: en turno a unas posibles claves para la comprensión de la burguesía catalana actual"*

CATERERS AND CATERING — Great Britain

Waiting for change? : working in hotel and catering / edited by Dominic Byrne. — London : Low Pay Unit, 1986. — v,66p. — (Low pay pamphlet ; no.42). — *Bibliography: p65-86*

CATERERS AND CATERING — Great Britain — Statistics

Catering trades. — London : HMSO, 1971-. — (Business monitor. SD ; 5) (Business monitor. SDQ ; 5). — *Monthly (1971-76); quarterly (1977-79)*

HOTEL AND CATERING INDUSTRY TRAINING BOARD

Manpower in the hotel and catering industry. — [Wembley] : the Board, [ca.1977]. — 47p

CATHOLIC CHURCH — Doctrines

HOLLENBACH, David
Nuclear ethics : a Christian moral argument / David Hollenbach. — New York : Paulist Press, c1983. — v, 100 p.

MCLEAN, Edward B
Roman Catholicism and the right to work / Edward B. McLean. — Lanham : University Press of America, c1985. — ix, 175 p.. — *Bibliography: p. 167-175*

CATHOLIC CHURCH — Doctrines — Addresses, essays, lectures

Catholics and nuclear war : a commentary on The challenge of peace, the U.S. Catholic bishops' pastoral letter on war and peace / edited by Philip J. Murnion ; foreword by Theodore M. Hesburgh. — New York : Crossroad, 1983. — xxii, 346 p. — "A National Pastoral Life Center publication.". — *Includes bibliographical references*

CATHOLIC CHURCH — History — 20th century

KURTZ, Lester R
The politics of heresy : the modernist crisis in Roman Catholicism / Lester R. Kurtz. — Berkeley : University of California Press, c1986. — xii, 267 p.. — *Includes index. — Bibliography: p. [229]-254*

ZABŁOCKI, Janusz
Kościoł i świat współczesny : wprowadzenie do soborowej konstytucji pastoralnej "Gaudium et spes" / Janusz Zabłocki. — 2nd ed. — Warszawa : Ośrodek Dokumentacji i Studiów Społecznych, 1986. — 457p

CATHOLIC CHURCH — Argentina — History

RECALDE, Héctor
La iglesia y la cuestión social (1874-1910) / Héctor Recalde. — Buenos Aires : Centro Editor de América Latina, 1985. — 157p. — (Biblioteca Política Argentina ; 110)

CATHOLIC CHURCH — Brazil — History

COOK, Guillermo
The expectation of the poor : base ecclesial communities in Protestant perspective / Guillermo Cook. — Maryknoll, NY : Orbis Books, c1985. — p. cm. — *Includes index. — Bibliography: p*

CATHOLIC CHURCH — Brazil — History — 20th century

MAINWARING, Scott
The Catholic Church and politics in Brazil, 1916-1985 / Scott Mainwaring. — Stanford, Calif. : Stanford University Press, 1986. — xv, 328p. — *Includes index. — Bibliography: p.[297]-319*

CATHOLIC CHURCH — Byelorussian S.S.R.

Katolitsizm v Belorussii : traditsionalizm i prisposoblenie / pod redaktsiei A. S. Maikhrovicha, E. S. Prokoshinoi. — Minsk : Nauka i tekhnika, 1987. — 238p

CATHOLIC CHURCH — Guatemala — History

VAN OSS, Adriaan C.
Catholic colonialism : a parish history of Guatemala, 1524-1821 / Adriaan C. van Oss. — Cambridge : Cambridge University Press, 1986. — xx,248p. — (Cambridge Latin American studies ; 57). — *Bibliography: p227-236. — Includes index*

CATHOLIC CHURCH — Ireland — History

INGLIS, Tom
Moral monopoly : the Catholic Church in modern Irish society / Tom Inglis. — Dublin : Gill and Macmillan, c1987. — 251p. — *Includes index*

CATHOLIC CHURCH — Latin America — History — 20th century — Addresses, essays, lectures

Religion and political conflict in Latin America / edited by Daniel H. Levine. — Chapel Hill : University of North Carolina Press, 1986. — xiii, 266p. — *Includes index.* — *Bibliography: p.257-260*

CATHOLIC CHURCH — Nicaragua

BRADSTOCK, Andrew
Saints and Sandinistas : the Catholic Church in Nicaragua and its response to the revolution / Andrew Bradstock. — London : Epworth, 1987. — [96]p. — *Includes bibliography*

CATHOLIC CHURCH — Nicaragua — History — 20th century

O'SHAUGHNESSY, Laura Nuzzi
The church and revolution in Nicaragua / Laura Nuzzi O'Shaughnessy & Luis H. Serra. — Athens, Ohio : Ohio University, Center for International Studies, Latin America Studies Program, 1986, c1985. — p. cm. — (Monographs in international studies. Latin America series ; no. 11). — *Bibliography: p*

CATHOLIC CHURCH — Poland

KĄKOL, Kazimierz
Kardynał Stefan Wyszyński jakim go znałem / Kazimierz Kąkol. — Warszawa : Instytut Wydawniczy Związków Zawodowych, 1985. — 145,[30]p

CATHOLIC CHURCH — Poland — Clergy

POPIEŁUSZKO, Jerzy
Zapiski 1980-1984 / Jersey Popiełuszko. — Paris : Editions Spotkania, 1985. — Various pagings

CATHOLIC CHURCH — Poland — Clergy — Biography

SIKORSKA, Grażyna
Prawda warta życie : Ks. Jerzy Popiełuszko / Grażyna Sikorska. — Londyn : Polska Fundacja Kulturalna, 1985. — xvi,148p

CATHOLIC CHURCH — Spain

ARBELOA, Víctor Manuel
Separación de Iglesia-Estado en España / Víctor Manuel Arbeloa. — Madrid : Mañana, 1977. — 76p. — (Colección Aperos del cristianismo ; 13). — *On cover: Separación de la Iglesia y el Estado en España.* — *Appendices (p. 46-[77]) contain legislation.* — *Includes bibliographical references*

CATHOLIC CHURCH — Spain — Congresses

SEMANA DE HISTORIA ECLESIÁSTICA DE ESPAÑA CONTEMPORÁNEA (6 : 1981 : Madrid)
Iglesia, sociedad y política en la España contemporánea / M. Espadas Burgos...[et al.]. — [Madrid] : Ediciones Escurialenses, Real Monasterio de El Escorial, 1983. — 407p. — (Biblioteca "La ciudad de Dios". Pax veritatis) (Varios ; 34)

CATHOLIC CHURCH — Spain — History

LANNON, Frances
Privilege, persecution and prophecy : the Catholic Church in Spain, 1875-1975 / Frances Lannon. — Oxford : Clarendon, 1987. — [350]p. — *Includes bibliography and index*

CATHOLIC CHURCH — Spain — History — Congresses

SEMANA DE HISTORIA ECLESIÁSTICA DE ESPAÑA CONTEMPORÁNEA (6 : 1981 : Madrid)
Iglesia, sociedad y política en la España contemporánea / M. Espadas Burgos...[et al.]. — [Madrid] : Ediciones Escurialenses, Real Monasterio de El Escorial, 1983. — 407p. — (Biblioteca "La ciudad de Dios". Pax veritatis) (Varios ; 34)

SIMPOSIO INTERNACIONAL "LA INQUISICIÓN ESPAÑOLA Y LA MENTALIDAD INQUISITORIAL" (1983 : New York)
Inquisición española y mentalidad inquisitorial : ponencias del Simposio Internacional sobre Inquisición, Nueva York, abril de 1983 / Angel Alcalá y otros. — Barcelona : Ariel, [1984]. — 618p. — (Ariel - historia)

CATHOLIC CHURCH — Spain — History — 20th century

RUÍZ GIMÉNEZ, Joaquín
Iglesia, Estado y sociedad en España. 1930-1982 / Joaquín Ruíz Giménez. — Barcelona : Editorial Argos Vergara, 1984. — 402p

CATHOLIC CHURCH — United States

MOSQUEDA, Lawrence J.
Chicanos, Catholicism and political ideology / Lawrence J. Mosqueda. — Lanham ; London : University Press of America, c1986. — vii,219p . — *Bibliography: p199-213.* — *Includes index*

CATHOLIC CHURCH. National Conference of Catholic Bishops. Challenge of peace — Addresses, essays, lectures

Catholics and nuclear war : a commentary on The challenge of peace, the U.S. Catholic bishops' pastoral letter on war and peace / edited by Philip J. Murnion ; foreword by Theodore M. Hesburgh. — New York : Crossroad, 1983. — xxii, 346 p.. — *"A National Pastoral Life Center publication."*. — *Includes bibliographical references*

CATHOLIC CHURCH. National Conference of Catholic Bishops

BLOCK, Walter
The U.S. bishops and their critics : an economic and ethical perspective / Walter Block. — Vancouver : Fraser Institute, 1986. — 127p

CATHOLIC CHURCH (Poland)

MONTICONE, Ronald C.
The Catholic Church in communist Poland, 1945-1985 : forty years of church-state [relations] / Ronald C. Monticone. — Boulder : East European Monographs, 1986. — viii,227p. — (East European Monographs ; No.205). — *Bibliography: p219-224*

CATHOLIC CHURCH — Social aspects

ESCRIVA DE BALAGUER, Josemaría
Conversations with Mgr Escriva de Balaguer : [recent interviews] / [by Pedro Rodriguez...[et al.]. — Dublin : Scepter Books, 1968. — 146p

CATHOLIC CHURCH — Argentina — Social aspects

RECALDE, Héctor
La iglesia y la cuestión social (1874-1910) / Héctor Recalde. — Buenos Aires : Centro Editor de América Latina, 1985. — 157p. — (Biblioteca Política Argentina ; 110)

CATHOLIC CHURCH AND WORLD POLITICS — History — 20th century

HANSON, Eric O
The Catholic Church in world politics / Eric O. Hanson. — Princeton, N.J. : Princeton University Press, c1987. — p. cm. — *Includes index.* — *Bibliography: p*

CATHOLICS — England — History — 20th century

HORNSBY-SMITH, Michael P.
Roman Catholics in England : studies in social structure since the Second World War / Michael P. Hornsby-Smith. — Cambridge : Cambridge University Press, 1987. — [264]p. — *Includes bibliography and index*

CATHOLICS — Ireland — History

CORISH, Patrick J.
The Irish Catholic experience : a historical survey / Patrick J. Corish. — Dublin : Gill and Macmillan, c1985. — ix,283p. — *Includes index*

CATHOLICS — Northern Ireland — History

BIGGS-DAVISON, John
The cross of St Patrick : the Catholic Unionist tradition in Ireland / John Biggs-Davison and George Chowdharay-Best. — Bourne End : Kensal, c1984. — 487p,[8]p of plates. — *Bibliography: p453-471.* — *Includes index*

CATHOLICS — United States — Attitudes

MCAULEY, E. Nancy
Faith without form : beliefs of Catholic youth / E. Nancy McAuley and Moira Mathiesen ; introduction, George Gallup. — Kansas City : Sheed and Ward, 1986. — vi,166p. — *Bibliography: p165-6*

CATT, CARRIE CHAPMAN

FOWLER, Robert Booth
Carrie Catt : feminist politician / Robert Booth Fowler. — Boston : Northeastern University Press, c1986. — xx, 226 p.. — *Includes index.* — *Bibliography: p. 201-218*

CATTLE — Prices — Peru

PERU. Dirección de Planificación Estadística
Indices de precios de productos pecuarios, julio-agosto-setiembre 1975. — Lima : the Dirección, [1976]. — 14p. — (Serie de indices de precios al por mayor). — *Cover title: Productos pecuarios*

CATTLE — Denmark

Investering i kvaeghold. — København : I kommission hos Landhusholdningsselskabets Forlag, 1977. — 20p. — (Meddelelse / Det Landøkonomiske Driftsbureau ; nr.25)

CATTLE TRADE — Central America

WILLIAMS, Robert G
Export agriculture and the crisis in Central America / by Robert G. Williams. — Chapel Hill : University of North Carolina Press, c1986. — xvi, 257p. — *Includes index.* — *Bibliography: p.[239]-248*

CAUCASIAN RACE

KATZ, Judy H.
White awareness : handbook for anti-racism training / by Judy H. Katz. — 1st ed. — Norman : University of Oklahoma Press, c1978. — x, 211 p.. — *Includes index.* — *Bibliography: p. 201-205*

CAUSATION

FLEW, Antony
Agency and necessity / Antony Flew and Godfrey Vesey. — Oxford : Basil Blackwell, 1987. — [224]p. — (Great debates in philosophy). — *Includes bibliography and index*

MACKIE, J. L.
The cement of the universe : a Study of Causation / J.L. Mackie. — [1st ed. reprinted] / with new preface, additional notes and additional bibliography. — Oxford : Clarendon Press, 1980. — xvii,329p. — (Clarendon library of logic and philosophy). — *Originally published: 1974.* — *Bibliography: p.323-326.* — *Includes index*

Mind, causation & action / edited by Leslie Stevenson, Roger Squires, John Haldane. — Oxford : Blackwell, 1986. — viii,190p. — *Includes index*

CAYMAN ISLANDS — Census, 1960

Cayman Islands, April, 1960. — [George Town? : Government Information Service, 1960?]. — i, 8 leaves

CAYMAN ISLANDS — Census, 1979

CAYMAN ISLANDS
Population census, 1979. — [George Town? : s.n., 1980]. — 354p

CAYMAN ISLANDS — Population — Statistics

CAYMAN ISLANDS
Population census, 1979. — [George Town? : s.n., 1980]. — 354p

CAYMAN ISLANDS — Population — Statistics *continuation*
Cayman Islands, April, 1960. — [George Town? : Government Information Service, 1960?]. — i, 8 leaves

CAYMAN ISLANDS. Legislative Assembly — Elections, 1976
Results of general election, Cayman Islands : 10th November, 1976. — [George Town] : Supervisor of Elections, 1976. — 1 sheet

CELTIC LANGUAGES
ELLIS, Peter Berresford
The Celtic revolution : a study in anti-imperialism / Peter Berresford Ellis. — Talybont : Y Lolfa, 1985. — 218p. — *Bibliography: p215-217*

CELTS — Political activity
ELLIS, Peter Berresford
The Celtic revolution : a study in anti-imperialism / Peter Berresford Ellis. — Talybont : Y Lolfa, 1985. — 218p. — *Bibliography: p215-217*

CELTS — Great Britain
ELLIS, Peter Berresford
The Celtic revolution : a study in anti-imperialism / Peter Berresford Ellis. — Talybont : Y Lolfa, 1985. — 218p. — *Bibliography: p215-217*

CEMENT INDUSTRIES
YOSHIDA, Shigeru
Status of cement exports/imports in the world and Japan as well as the shipping industry / Shigeru Yoshida. — Tokyo : Japan Maritime Research Institute, 1987. — 48p. — (Jamri report ; no.22)

CEMENT INDUSTRIES — Japan
YOSHIDA, Shigeru
Status of cement exports/imports in the world and Japan as well as the shipping industry / Shigeru Yoshida. — Tokyo : Japan Maritime Research Institute, 1987. — 48p. — (Jamri report ; no.22)

CENSORSHIP
Pressefreiheit / herausgegeben von Jürgen Wilke. — Darmstadt : Wissenschaftliche Buchgesellschaft, 1984. — vii,525p. — (Wege der Forschung ; Bd.625). — *Bibliography: p493-521*

Women against censorship / edited by Varda Burstyn ; essays by Varda Burstyn ... [et al.]. — Vancouver : Douglas & McIntyre, c1985. — 210 p.. — *Bibliography: p. 201-205*

CENSORSHIP — Addresses, essays, lectures
SALISBURY, Harrison Evans
The book enchained / Harrison E. Salisbury. — Washington : Library of Congress, 1984. — 9p. — (The Center for the Book viewpoint series ; 10). — "A lecture sponsored by The Center for the Book in the Library of Congress and the Authors League of America; presented at the Library of Congress September 28, 1983."

CENSORSHIP — Great Britain — History
SUTHERLAND, J. A. (John Andrew)
Offensive literature : decensorship in Britain, 1960-1982 / John Sutherland. — London : Junction Books, 1982. — 207p

CENSORSHIP — United States
ARONS, Stephen
Compelling belief : the culture of American schooling / Stephen Arons. — 1st paperback ed. — Amherst : University of Massachusetts Press, 1986, c1983. — xii, 228 p.. — : Reprint. Originally published: New York : McGraw-Hill, c1983. — *Includes index*

SPITZER, Matthew Laurence
Seven dirty words and six other stories : controlling the content of print and broadcast / Matthew Laurence Spitzer. — New Haven : Yale University Press, 1986. — p. cm. — *Includes index*

CENSUS — Handbooks, manuals, etc
GOYER, Doreen S.
The handbook of national population censuses : Latin America and the Caribbean, North America, and Oceania / Doreen S. Goyer and Eliane Domschke. — Westport, Conn. : Greenwood Press, 1983. — xii, 711 p.. — *Includes index. — Bibliography: p. 28-30*

CENSUS — Methodology
Principles and recommendations for population and housing censuses. — New York : United Nations, 1980. — xiv,330p. — (Statistical papers / United Nations, Statistical Office. Series M ; no.67) ([Document] (United Nations) ; ST/ESA/STAT/SER.M/67). — *Sales no.: E.80.XVII.8*

CENTRAL AFRICAN REPUBLIC — History — Dictionaries
KALCK, Pierre
Historical dictionary of the Central African Republic / by Pierre Kalck ; translated by Thomas E. O'Toole. — Metuchen, N.J. : Scarecrow Press, 1980. — p. cm. — (African Historical dictionaries ; no. 27). — *Bibliography: p*

CENTRAL AMERICA — Archival resources
Research guide to Central America and the Caribbean / Kenneth Grieb, editor-in-chief ; associate editors, Ralph Lee Woodward, Jr., Graeme S. Mount, Thomas Mathews. — Madison, Wis. : University of Wisconsin Press, 1985. — xv, 431p. — *Includes bibliographical references and index*

CENTRAL AMERICA — Economic conditions
FEINBERG, Richard E
Development postponed : the political economy of Central America in the 1980s / Richard E. Feinberg and Bruce M. Bagley. — Boulder : Westview Press, 1986. — xiii, 65 p.. — (SAIS papers in Latin American studies). — *Bibliography: p. 51-60*

WEEKS, John
The economies of Central America / John Weeks. — New York : Holmes & Meier, 1985. — 209p. — *Includes bibliographies and index*

CENTRAL AMERICA — Economic conditions — 1979- — Congresses
Crises in the Caribbean basin : past and present / edited by Richard Tardanico. — Beverly Hills [Calif.] : Sage Publications, c1986. — p. cm. — (Political economy of the world-system annuals ; v. 9). — "Based on papers presented at the ninth annual Conference on the Political Economy of the World-System, Tulane University, March 18-20, 1985"--Pref

CENTRAL AMERICA — Economic integration
UNITED STATES. Agency for International Development. Regional Office for Central America and Panama Affairs
A collection of some of the most important economic integration treaties of Central America : Unofficial translations. — [Rev.]. — Guatemala, 1966. — 186p. — *Cover title: Economic integration treaties of Central America*

CENTRAL AMERICA — Foreign relations — 1979-
BERRYMAN, Phillip
Inside Central America : the essential facts past and present on El Salvador, Nicaragua, Honduras, Guatemala and Costa Rica / Phillip Berryman. — London : Pluto, 1985. — [176]p. — *Includes bibliography and index*

BEST, Edward
US policy and regional security in Central America / Edward Best. — [London] : IISS, c1987. — 182p. — *Includes index*

Conflict in Central America : approaches to peace and security / edited by Jack Child. — London : published for the International Peace Academy by Hurst, c1986. — xiv,208p. — *Includes index*

CENTRAL AMERICA — Foreign relations — United States
BERRYMAN, Phillip
Inside Central America : the essential facts past and present on El Salvador, Nicaragua, Honduras, Guatemala and Costa Rica / Phillip Berryman. — London : Pluto, 1985. — [176]p. — *Includes bibliography and index*

BEST, Edward
US policy and regional security in Central America / Edward Best. — [London] : IISS, c1987. — 182p. — *Includes index*

COHEN, Joshua
Inequity and intervention : the federal budget and Central America / Joshua Cohen and Joel Rogers. — 1st ed. — Boston, MA : South End Press, c1986. — xi, 66 p.. — (PACCA series on the domestic roots of United States foreign policy). — *Bibliographical notes: p.57-62*

Confronting revolution : security through diplomacy in Central America / Morris Blachman, William LeoGrande, and Kenneth Sharpe, editors. — New York : Pantheon Books, [1986]. — ix, 438p. — *Includes bibliographies and index*

FAGEN, Richard R.
Forging peace : the challenge of Central America / Richard R. Fagen ; foreword by George McGovern. — Oxford : Basil Blackwell, 1987. — [160]p. — (A PACCA book). — *Includes index*

POLICY ALTERNATIVES FOR THE CARIBBEAN AND CENTRAL AMERICA
Changing course : blueprint for peace in Central America and the Caribbean / PACCA. — Washington D.C. : Institute for Policy Studies, 1984. — 116p

SAUVAGE, Léo
Les États-Unis face à l'Amerique centrale / Léo Sauvage. — Paris : Balland, [1985]. — 285p

WILLIAMS, Robert G
Export agriculture and the crisis in Central America / by Robert G. Williams. — Chapel Hill : University of North Carolina Press, c1986. — xvi, 257p. — *Includes index. — Bibliography: p.[239]-248*

CENTRAL AMERICA — History — 1951-
SCHOOLEY, Helen
Conflict in Central America / by Helen Schooley. — Harlow : Longman, 1987. — xxiii,326p. — (Keesing's international studies). — *Bibliography: p315-317. — Includes index*

CENTRAL AMERICA — Politics and government
FEINBERG, Richard E
Development postponed : the political economy of Central America in the 1980s / Richard E. Feinberg and Bruce M. Bagley. — Boulder : Westview Press, 1986. — xiii, 65 p.. — (SAIS papers in Latin American studies). — *Bibliography: p. 51-60*

CENTRAL AMERICA — Politics and government — 1979-
FERRIS, Elizabeth G
The Central American refugees / Elizabeth G. Ferris. — New York : Praeger, 1986. — p. cm

NUCCIO, Richard
What's wrong, who's right in Central America? : a citizen's guide / by Richard A. Nuccio. — New York, N.Y. : Facts on File, 1986. — xvi, 136p. — *Includes index*

WILLIAMS, Robert G
Export agriculture and the crisis in Central America / by Robert G. Williams. — Chapel Hill : University of North Carolina Press, c1986. — xvi, 257p. — *Includes index. — Bibliography: p.[239]-248*

CENTRAL AMERICA — Politics and government — 1979- — Congresses
Crises in the Caribbean basin : past and present / edited by Richard Tardanico. — Beverly Hills [Calif.] : Sage Publications, c1986. — p. cm. — (Political economy of the world-system annuals ; v. 9). — *"Based on papers presented at the ninth annual Conference on the Political Economy of the World-System, Tulane University, March 18-20, 1985"--Pref*

CENTRAL AMERICA — Relations (Military) — United States
¡ Basta! : no mandate for war : a pledge of resistance handbook / by the Emergency Response Network ; edited by Ken Butigan, Terry Messman-Rucker, and Marie Pastrick. — Philadelphia : New Society, 1986. — 83,ivp. — *Bibliography: pi-iv*

CENTRAL AMERICA — Research
Research guide to Central America and the Caribbean / Kenneth Grieb, editor-in-chief ; associate editors, Ralph Lee Woodward, Jr., Graeme S. Mount, Thomas Mathews. — Madison, Wis. : University of Wisconsin Press, 1985. — xv, 431p. — *Includes bibliographical references and index*

CENTRAL COMPUTER AND TELECOMMUNICATIONS AGENCY
CENTRAL COMPUTER AND TELECOMMUNICATIONS AGENCY
Central Computer and Telecommunications Agency : progress report. — London : H.M.S.O., 1985. — vi,41p. — (Information technology in the civil service. IT series ; no.11)

CENTRAL COUNCIL FOR EDUCATION AND TRAINING IN SOCIAL WORK
CCETSW reporting / Central Council for Education and Training in Social Work. — London : CCETSW, 1985-. — *Irregular*

CENTRAL COUNCIL FOR EDUCATION AND TRAINING IN SOCIAL WORK
Council policy on training for community work within the personal social services. — [London] : the Council, 1979. — 14p

CENTRAL EUROPEAN CANADIANS — Congresses
Central and East European ethnicity in Canada : adaptation and preservation / T. Yedlin, editor. — Edmonton : Central and East European Studies Society of Alberta, 1985. — viii,178p. — *Papers presented at the conference on Central and East European Ethnicity in Canada, sponsored by the Central and East European Studies Society of Alberta, the Central and East European Studies Association of Canada and the Department of Slavic and East European Studies, University of Alberta at February 1983, held in Edmonton, Alberta*

CENTRAL INTELLIGENCE AGENCY
RANELAGH, John
The agency : the rise and decline of the CIA / John Ranelagh. — London : Weidenfeld and Nicolson, 1986. — 847p. — *Bibliography: p795-807*

CENTRAL PLANNING — Communist countries
PRYBYLA, Jan S
Market and plan under socialism : the bird in the cage / Jan S. Prybyla. — Stanford, Calif. : Hoover Institution Press, Stanford University, c1987. — xv, 348 p. — (Hoover Press publication ; 335). — *Includes index. — Bibliography: p. [317]-335*

CENTRAL PLANNING — Great Britain
CHICK, Martin John
Economic planning, managerial decision-making and the role of fixed capital in the investment in the economic recovery of the United Kingdom, 1945-1955 / Martin John Chick. — 313 leaves. — *PhD (Econ) 1986 LSE*

CENTRAL PLANNING — Poland
KARPIŃSKI, Andrzej
40 lat planowania w Polsce : problemy, ludzie, refleksje / Andrzej Karpiński. — Warszawa : Państwowe Wydawnictwo Ekonomiczne, 1986. — 421p. — *Bibliography: p413-[416]*

CENTRAL PLANNING — Soviet Union
BECKER, Abraham Samuel
Soviet central decisionmaking and economic growth : a summing up / Abraham S. Becker. — Santa Monica, CA : Rand, [1986]. — xi, 53 p.. — *"A Project Air Force report prepared for the United States Air Force.". — "January 1986.". — "R-3349-AF.". — Includes bibliographical references*

DZIUBIK, S. D.
Rynok sredstv proizvodstva v sisteme planomerno organizovannoi ekonomiki / S. D. Dziubik. — L'vov : Vyshcha shkola, 1984. — 157p

Planovoe upravlenie ekonomikoi razvitogo sotsializma / redaktsionnaia kollegiia: A. S. Emel'ianov...[et al.]. — Kiev : Naukova dumka . — *V piati tomakh*
T.1: Narodno-khoziaistvennye proportsii, ikh planirovanie i prognozirovanie / otv. redaktor A. S. Emel'ianov. — 1985. — 316p. — *Bibliography: p311-[314]*

Planovoe upravlenie ekonomikoi razvitogo sotsializma / redaktsionnaia kollegiia: A. S. Emel'ianov...[et al.]. — Kiev : Naukova dumka . — *V piati tomakh. — Bibliography: p303-[307]*
T.2: Resursy narodnogo khoziaistva: planirovanie i effektivnost' ispol'zovaniia / redaktsionnaia kollegiia: I. K. Bondar'...[et al.]. — 1985. — 308p

Planovoe upravlenie ekonomikoi razvitogo sotsializma / redaktsionnaia kollegiia: A. S. Emel'ianov...[et al.]. — Kiev : Naukova dumka . — *V piati tomath*
T.3: Nauchno-tekhnicheskii progress i planovoe investirovanie v narodnoe khoziaistvo / otv. redaktor S. M. Iampol'skii. — 1986. — 307p. — *Bibliography: p305-[308]*

Planovoe upravlenie ekonomikoi razvitogo sotsializma / redaktsionnaia kollegiia: A. S. Emel'ianov...[et al.]. — Kiev : Naukova dumka . — *V piati tomakh*
T.4: Nauchno-metodicheskie osnovy planirovaniia i prognozirovaniia razvitiia ekonomiki / otv. redaktor V. F. Besedin. — 1986. — 322p. — *Bibliography: p318-[323]*

Planovoe upravlenie ekonomikoi razvitogo sotsializma / redaktsionnaia kollegiia: A. S. Emel'ianov...[et al.]. — Kiev : Naukova dumka . — *V piati tomakh*
T.5: Otraslevye problemy planovogo razvitiia ekonomiki respubliki / otv. redaktor A. S. Emel'ianov. — 1986. — 403p. — *Bibliography: p299-[302]*

CENTRAL PLANNING — Soviet Union — Data processing
URINSON, Ia. M.
Sovershenstvovanie tekhnologii narodnokhoziaistvennogo planirovaniia / Ia. M. Urinson. — Moskva : Ekonomika, 1986. — 197p

CENTRAL PLANNING — Ukraine
Planovoe upravlenie ekonomikoi razvitogo sotsializma / redaktsionnaia kollegiia: A. S. Emel'ianov...[et al.]. — Kiev : Naukova dumka . — *V piati tomakh*
T.1: Narodno-khoziaistvennye proportsii, ikh planirovanie i prognozirovanie / otv. redaktor A. S. Emel'ianov. — 1985. — 316p. — *Bibliography: p311-[314]*

Planovoe upravlenie ekonomikoi razvitogo sotsializma / redaktsionnaia kollegiia: A. S. Emel'ianov...[et al.]. — Kiev : Naukova dumka . — *V piati tomath*
T.3: Nauchno-tekhnicheskii progress i planovoe investirovanie v narodnoe khoziaistvo / otv. redaktor S. M. Iampol'skii. — 1986. — 307p. — *Bibliography: p305-[308]*

Planovoe upravlenie ekonomikoi razvitogo sotsializma / redaktsionnaia kollegiia: A. S. Emel'ianov...[et al.]. — Kiev : Naukova dumka . — *V piati tomakh*
T.4: Nauchno-metodicheskie osnovy planirovaniia i prognozirovaniia razvitiia ekonomiki / otv. redaktor V. F. Besedin. — 1986. — 322p. — *Bibliography: p318-[323]*

Planovoe upravlenie ekonomikoi razvitogo sotsializma / redaktsionnaia kollegiia: A. S. Emel'ianov...[et al.]. — Kiev : Naukova dumka . — *V piati tomakh*
T.5: Otraslevye problemy planovogo razvitiia ekonomiki respubliki / otv. redaktor A. S. Emel'ianov. — 1986. — 403p. — *Bibliography: p299-[302]*

CENTRAL PROVINCE (PAPUA NEW GUINEA) — Population — Statistics
1980 national population census : final figures : provincial summary : Central Province. — Port Moresby : National Statistical Office, 1985. — iii,103p

CENTRE FOR POLICY RESEARCH (New Delhi, India)
MARATHE, Shared S.
Regulation and development : India's experience of controls over industry / Shared S. Marathe ; under the auspices of the Centre for Policy Research. — New Delhi ; Beverly Hills : Sage Publications, 1986. — p. cm. — *Includes index. — Bibliography: p*

CENTRE ON INTEGRATED RURAL DEVELOPMENT FOR ASIA AND THE PACIFIC
CIRDAP newsletter / Centre on Integrated Rural Development for Asia and the Pacific. — Dhaka : Centre on Integrated Rural Development for Asia and the Pacific, 1986-. — *Quarterly*

CEREAL PRODUCTS — European Economic Community countries
The production and use of cereal and potato starch in the EEC / prepared by Centre for European Agricultural Studies. — Luxembourg : Office for Official Publications of the European Communities, 1986. — 123p. — *At head of title: Commission of the European Communities*

CEREMONIAL EXCHANGE — Papua New Guinea
FEIL, D. K.
Ways of exchange : the Enga tee of Papua New Guinea / D.K. Feil. — St. Lucia, Qld. : University of Queensland Press ; Lawrence, Mass. : Distributed in the USA and Canada by Technical Impex Corp., 1984. — xvi, 269 p.. — *Bibliography: p[253]-261. — Bibliography: p. [253]-261*

CHAADAEV, P. IA.
LAZAREV, V. V.
Chaadaev. — Moskva : Iuridicheskaia literatura, 1986. — 110p. — (Iz istorii politicheskoi i pravovoi mysli). — *Bibliography: p107-[110]*

CHACO WAR, 1932-1935 — Campaigns
MACHUCA, Vicente
La Guerra del Chaco : desde la terminación del armisticio hasta el fin de la contienda / Vicente Machuca. — Asunción : NAPA, [1983]. — 562 p., [28] p. of plates. — (Colección Prisma). — *Includes bibliographical references*

CHAD — Bibliography
DECALO, Samuel
Historical dictionary of Chad / by Samuel Decalo. — Metuchen, N.J. : Scarecrow Press, 1977. — xxiv, 413 p.. — (African historical dictionaries ; no. 13). — *Bibliography: p. 301-413*

CHAD — History — Dictionaries
DECALO, Samuel
Historical dictionary of Chad / by Samuel Decalo. — Metuchen, N.J. : Scarecrow Press, 1977. — xxiv, 413 p.. — (African historical dictionaries ; no. 13). — *Bibliography: p. 301-413*

CHAD — Social conditions
HASSAN KHAYAR, Issa
Tchad : regards sur les élites ouaddaïennes / par Issa Hassan Khayar. — Paris : Centre National de la Recherche Scientifique, 1984. — 231p. — (Contributions à la connaissance des élites africaines ; 3). — *Bibliography: p215-231*

CHAFEE, ZECHARIAH
SMITH, Donald L.
Zechariah Chafee, Jr., defender of liberty and law / Donald L. Smith. — Cambridge, Mass. : Harvard University Press, 1986. — x, 355 p.. — *Includes index. — Bibliography: p. [283]-343*

CHAGA (AFRICAN PEOPLE) — Social life and customs
MOORE, Sally Falk
Social facts and fabrications : "customary" law on Kilimanjaro, 1880-1980 / Sally Falk Moore. — Cambridge : Cambridge University Press, 1986. — xvi,397p. — (The Lewis Henry Morgan Lectures ; 1981). — *Bibliography: p376-384. — Includes index*

CHAIANOV, A. V.
CHAĪANOV, A.
A.V. Chayanov on the theory of peasant economy / edited by Daniel Thorner, Basile Kerblay, R.E.F. Smith ; with a foreword by Teodor Shanin. — Manchester : Manchester University Press, c1986. — v,316p,[1]leaf of plates. — *Translation of: Organizatsiia krestīaskogo khoziāistva. — Originally published: Hometown : R.D. Irwin for the American Economic Association, 1966. — Bibliography: p279-296. — Includes index*

CHALLENGE OF PEACE
Catholics and nuclear war : a commentary on The challenge of peace, the U.S. Catholic bishops' pastoral letter on war and peace / edited by Philip J. Murnion ; foreword by Theodore M. Hesburgh. — New York : Crossroad, 1983. — xxii, 346 p.. — *"A National Pastoral Life Center publication.". — Includes bibliographical references*

CHAMBRI (PAPUA NEW GUINEA PEOPLE)
GEWERTZ, Deborah B.
Sepik river societies : a historical ethnography of the Chambri and their neighbours / Deborah B. Gewertz. — New Haven : Yale University Press, 1983

CHANGE (PSYCHOLOGY)
MARRIS, Peter
Loss and change / Peter Marris. — rev. ed. — London : Routledge and Kegan Paul, 1986. — xiv,178p. — (Reports / Institute of Community Studies). — *Bibliography: p172-174*

CHANNEL ISLANDS — Economic conditions
A people of the sea : the maritime history of the Channel Islands / edited by A.G. Jamieson. — London : Methuen, 1986. — xxxvi, 528p, [41]p of plates (some col.). — *Includes index. — Bibliography: p.[482]-502*

CHANNEL ISLANDS — History
A people of the sea : the maritime history of the Channel Islands / edited by A.G. Jamieson. — London : Methuen, 1986. — xxxvi, 528p, [41]p of plates (some col.). — *Includes index. — Bibliography: p.[482]-502*

CHANNEL TUNNEL
KENT. County Council
The Channel Tunnel and the future for Kent. — Maidstone : [the Council], 1987. — [8]p

LONDON STRATEGIC POLICY UNIT. Transport Group
The Channel Tunnel and London : an examination of British Rail's plans for London terminal facilities. — London : [the Group], 1987. — iv,84p. — *Bibliography: p77*

CHARITABLE USES, TRUSTS, AND FOUNDATIONS — United States — History
NIELSEN, Waldemar A
The golden donors : a new anatomy of the great foundations / by Waldemar A. Nielsen. — 1st ed. — New York : E.P. Dutton, c1985. — xi, 468p. — *"A Truman Talley book.". — Includes bibliographical references and index*

CHARITABLE USES, TRUSTS, AND FOUNDATIONS (ISLAMIC LAW) — India
KOZLOWSKI, Gregory C.
Muslim endowments and society in British India / Gregory C. Kozlowski. — Cambridge : Cambridge University Press, 1985. — x,211p. — (Cambridge South Asian studies ; 35). — *Bibliography: p197-208. — Includes index*

CHARITIES — History
MOLLAT, Michel
[Pauvres au Moyen Age. English]. The poor in the Middle Ages : an essay in social history / Michel Mollat ; translated by Arthur Goldhammer. — New Haven : Yale University Press, c1986. — p. cm. — *Translation of: Les Pauvres au Moyen Age. — Includes index. — Bibliography: p*

CHARITIES — Denmark
JEPPESEN, Kirsten Just
Private hjaelpeorganisationer : på det sociale område / Kirsten Just Jeppesen, Dorte Høeg. — København : Socialforskningsinstituttet, 1987. — 182p. — (Publikation / Socialforskningsinstituttet ; 160). — *Bibliography: p179-180*

CHARITIES — England
BURGESS, Andrew C.
Tolley's charities manual / Andrew C. Burgess, Martin J. Crane, Richard J. Fox. — Croydon : Tolley Publishing, 1986. — xx,306p

CHARITIES — England — Cambridge (Cambridgeshire) — History
RUBIN, Miri
Charity and community in medieval Cambridge / Miri Rubin. — Cambridge : Cambridge University Press, 1987. — xiv,365p. — (Cambridge studies in medieval life and thought. Fourth series). — *Bibliography: p304-353. — Includes index*

CHARITIES — France — Grenoble — History — 17th century
NORBERG, Kathryn
Rich and poor in Grenoble, 1600-1814 / Kathryn Norberg. — Berkeley ; London : University of California Press, c1985. — xii, 366p. — *Includes index. — Bibliography: p.345-352*

CHARITIES — France — Grenoble — History — 18th century
NORBERG, Kathryn
Rich and poor in Grenoble, 1600-1814 / Kathryn Norberg. — Berkeley ; London : University of California Press, c1985. — xii, 366p. — *Includes index. — Bibliography: p.345-352*

CHARITIES — Great Britain
Efficiency scrutiny of the supervision of charities : report to the Home Secretary and the Economic Secretary to the Treasury / Sir Philip Woodfield...[et al.]. — London : H.M.S.O., 1987. — v,96p

WEBB, Sidney
The sphere of voluntary agencies in the prevention of destitution / by Sidney and Beatrice Webb. — London : National Committee for the Prevention of Destitution, 1911. — 46p

CHARITIES — Great Britain — Finance
Raising money from government / edited by Michael Norton. — 2nd ed. — London : Directory of Social Change, 1985. — [144]p. — *Previous ed.: 1981*

CHARITIES — Spain — Valladolid — History
MAZA ZORRILLA, Elena
Valladolid : sus pobres y la respuesta institucional (1750-1900) / Elena Maza Zorrilla. — Valladolid : Universidad de Valladolid : Junta de Castille y León, 1985. — 405p. — *Bibliography: p381-392*

CHARITIES — United States
SOSIN, Michael
Private benefits : material assistance in the private sector / Michael Sosin. — Orlando : Academic Press, 1986. — xvii, 195 p.. — (Institute for Research on Poverty monograph series). — *Includes index. — Bibliography: p. 179-184*

CHARITIES, MEDICAL — Great Britain
PALLISER, Gordon
The charitable work of hospital contributory schemes / Gordon Palliser [et al.]. — Bristol : British Hospitals Contributory Schemes Association, 1984. — 129p

CHARITY LAWS AND LEGISLATION — Great Britain
Efficiency scrutiny of the supervision of charities : report to the Home Secretary and the Economic Secretary to the Treasury / Sir Philip Woodfield...[et al.]. — London : H.M.S.O., 1987. — v,96p

CHARTER-PARTIES — Great Britain
VENTRIS, F. M.
Tanker voyage charter parties / by F. M. Ventris. — [S.l.] : Kluwer Law Publishers ; [chichester] : Barry Rose, 1986. — xvi,411p

CHARTERED ASSOCIATION OF CERTIFIED ACCOUNTANTS
CHARTERED ASSOCIATION OF CERTIFIED ACCOUNTANTS
List of members in practice / Chartered Association of Certified Accountants. — London : Chartered Association of Certified Accountants. — *Annual*

CHARTISM
ROYLE, Edward
Chartism / Edward Royle. — 2nd ed. — London : Longman, 1986. — v,153p. — (Seminar studies in history). — *Previous ed.: 1980. — Bibliography: p140-149. — Includes index*

WRIGHT, D. G.
The Chartist risings in Bradford / D.G. Wright. — Bradford : Bradford Libraries and Information Service, 1987. — 72p. — *Bibliography: p66-67. — Includes index*

CHARWOMEN AND CLEANERS — India — Delhi — Economic conditions
KARLEKAR, Malavika
Poverty and women's work : a study of sweeper women in Delhi / Malavika Karlekar. — New Delhi : Vikas Pub. House, c1982. — vi, 158 p.. — *Includes index. — Bibliography: p. [149]-152*

CHASE MANHATTAN BANK, N.A — History — 20th century
WILSON, John Donald
The Chase : the Chase Manhattan Bank, N.A., 1945-1985 / John Donald Wilson. — Boston, Mass. : Harvard Business School Press, c1986. — x, 432 p., [23] p. of plates. — *Includes index. — Bibliography: p. 373-407*

CHEBYSHEV APPROXIMATION
ALPERN, S.
A mixed strategy minimax theorem / Steve Alpern and Shmuel Gal. — London : Suntory Toyota Internation Centre for Economics and Related Disciplines, 1987. — 10p. — (Theoretical economics ; 87/157)

CHECKS — Legal status, laws, etc. — Ecuador
ECUADOR
[Laws, etc.]. Ley de cheques codificada. — [Quito] : Superintendencia de Bancos, 1975. — 8p

CHEMICAL INDUSTRY — Government policy — Germany — History
STRATMANN, Freidrich
Chemische Industrie unter Zwang? : Staatliche Einflussnahme am Beispiel der chemischen Industrie Deutschlands 1933-1949 / Friedrich Stratmann. — Stuttgart : Franz Steiner Verlag Wiesbaden, 1985. — [xv],531p. — (Zeitschrift für Unternehmensgeschichte ; Beiheft 43). — *Bibliography: p495-519*

CHEMICAL INDUSTRY — Government policy — Ukraine
SOKOLOV, V. N.
Kursom na sotsialisticheskuiu industrializatsiiu / V. N. Sokolov. — Kiev : Vyshcha shkola, 1985. — 158p. — *Bibliography: p154-[159]*

CHEMICAL INDUSTRY — Germany — History
Geschichte der Farbwerke Hoechst und der chemischen Industrie in Deutschland : ein Lesebuch aus der Arbeiterbildung. — Offenbach : Verlag 2000, c1984. — 176p. — *Bibliography: p174-176*

STRATMANN, Freidrich
Chemische Industrie unter Zwang? : Staatliche Einflussnahme am Beispiel der chemischen Industrie Deutschlands 1933-1949 / Friedrich Stratmann. — Stuttgart : Franz Steiner Verlag Wiesbaden, 1985. — [xv],531p. — (Zeitschrift für Unternehmensgeschichte ; Beiheft 43). — *Bibliography: p495-519*

CHEMICAL INDUSTRY — Germany (West) — History
Geschichte der Farbwerke Hoechst und der chemischen Industrie in Deutschland : ein Lesebuch aus der Arbeiterbildung. — Offenbach : Verlag 2000, c1984. — 176p. — *Bibliography: p174-176*

CHEMICAL INDUSTRY — Switzerland — History
RIEDL-EHRENBERG, Renate
Alfred Kern (1850-1893) : Edouard Sandoz (1853-1928) : Gründer der Sandoz AG, Basel / Renate Riedl-Ehrenberg. — Zürich : Verein für wirtschaftshistorische Studien, 1986. — 90p. — (Schweizer Pioniere der Wirtschaft und Technik ; 44). — *Bibliography: p84*

CHEMICAL INDUSTRY — Ukraine
SOKOLOV, V. N.
Kursom na sotsialisticheskuiu industrializatsiiu / V. N. Sokolov. — Kiev : Vyshcha shkola, 1985. — 158p. — *Bibliography: p154-[159]*

CHEMICAL WARFARE
The Chemical industry and the projected chemical weapons convention : proceedings of a SIPRI/Pugwash conference. — Oxford : Published on behalf of Stockholm International Peace Research Institute by Oxford University Press, 1986. — 2v.. — (SIPRI chemical & biological warfare studies ; 4-5). — *Includes bibliography*

Chemical weapon free zones? / edited by Ralf Trapp. — Oxford : Oxford University Press [on behalf of] Stockholm International Peace Research Institute, 1987. — x,211p. — (SIPRI Chemical & biological warfare studies ; no.7)

CHEMICAL WARFARE — History
ANGERER, Jo
Chemische Waffen in Deutschland : Missrauch einer Wissenschaft / Jo Angerer. — Darmstadt : Hermann Luchterhand, 1985. — 299p

CHEMICAL WARFARE — Germany (West)
ANGERER, Jo
Chemische Waffen in Deutschland : Missrauch einer Wissenschaft / Jo Angerer. — Darmstadt : Hermann Luchterhand, 1985. — 299p

CHEMICAL-WEAPON-FREE ZONES
Chemical weapon free zones? / edited by Ralf Trapp. — Oxford : Oxford University Press [on behalf of] Stockholm International Peace Research Institute, 1987. — x,211p. — (SIPRI Chemical & biological warfare studies ; no.7)

CHEMICALS — Hygienic aspects
The language of risk : conflicting perspectives on occupational health / edited by Dorothy Nelkin. — Beverly Hills : Sage Publications, c1985. — p. cm. — (Sage Focus edition ; v. 71). — *Includes bibliographies and index*

CHEMISTRY, FORENSIC
Without a trace : a forensics manual for you and me. — [S.l.] : Hooligan Press, 1986. — 32p

CHEMISTRY, FORENSIC — England
RAMSAY, Malcolm
The effectiveness of the Forensic Science Service / by Malcolm Ramsay. — London : H.M.S.O., 1987. — v,93p. — (Home Office research study ; 92). — *A Home Office Research and Planning Unit report*

CHENG, NIEN
CHENG, Nien
Life and death in Shanghai / Nien Cheng. — London : Grafton, 1986. — 496p. — *Includes index*

CHESHIRE — History
A History of the county of Chester / edited by B.E. Harris assisted by A.T. Thacker. — Oxford : Published for the Institute of Historical Research by Oxford University Press. — (The Victoria history of the counties of England)
Vol.1: Physique, prehistory, Roman, Anglo-Saxon and Domesday. — 1987. — xvi,391p,[12]p of plates. — *Includes index*

CHESHIRE (ENGLAND) — Population
CHESHIRE. Planning Department
Cheshire population report 1986 : the present and future population. — Chester : [the Department], 1986. — iii,48p

CHIANG, KAI-SHEK
SIÉ, Chéou-kang
President Chiang Kai-shek : his childhood and youth / by Chéou-kang Sié. — Taipei : China Cultural Service, [1954?]. — x,131p

CHICAGO (Ill.). Department of Buildings
JONES, Bryan D
Governing buildings and building government : a new perspective on the old party / Bryan D. Jones. — University, Ala. : University of Alabama Press, c1985. — p. cm. — *Includes index. — Bibliography: p*

CHICAGO (ILL.) — Ethnic relations
PADILLA, Felix M
Latino ethnic consciousness : the case of Mexican Americans and Puerto Ricans in Chicago / Felix M. Padilla. — Notre Dame, Ind. : University of Notre Dame Press, c1985. — ix, 187 p.. — *Includes index. — Bibliography: p. 173-183*

CHICAGO (ILL.) — Race relations
ANDERSON, Alan B.
Confronting the color line : the broken promise of the civil rights movement in Chicago / Alan B. Anderson, George W. Pickering. — Athens : University of Georgia Press, c1986. — xii, 515 p., [16] p. of plates. — *Includes index. — Bibliography: p. 459-500*

The ethnic frontier : essays in the history of group survival in Chicago and the Midwest / edited by Melvin G. Holli and Peter d'A. Jones. — Grand Rapids : Eerdmans, c1977. — 422p. — *Includes bibliographical references and index*

CHICAGO SCHOOL OF ECONOMICS
GREAT BRITAIN. Parliament. House of Commons. Library. Research Division
Monetary policy and monetarism / [Christopher Barclay]. — [London] : the Division, [1979]. — 20p. — (Background paper ; no.72). — *Bibliography: p19-20*

RAYACK, Elton
Not so free to choose : the political economy of Milton Friedman and Ronald Reagan / Elton Rayack.. — New York : Praeger, 1987. — x, 215 p.. — *Includes index. — Bibliography: p. 203-208*

ROBINSON, Derek, 1932 Feb. 9-
Monetarism and the labour market / Derek Robinson. — Oxford : Clarendon, 1986. — 1v.. — (The Library of political economy)

CHICAGO SCHOOL OF ECONOMISTS
SMITH, David
The rise and fall of monetarism / David Smith. — Harmondsworth : Penguin, 1987. — 186p. — *Bibliography: p177-179*

CHICAGO SCHOOL OF SOCIOLOGY — History
SHORE, Marlene
The science of social redemption : McGill, the Chicago School, and the origins of social research in Canada. — Toronto : University of Toronto Press, 1987. — xviii,340p. — *Bibliographical notes: p[275]-324*

CHILD ABUSE
FINKELHOR, David
A sourcebook on child sexual abuse / David Finkelhor and associates. — Beverly Hills : Sage Publications, c1986. — p. cm. — *Includes index. — Bibliography: p*

Sexual abuse of children in the 1980's : ten essays and an annotated bibliography / edited by Benjamin Schlesinger. — Toronto : University of Toronto Press, 1986. — 201p. — *Annotated bibliography: p[95]-189*

Understanding child abuse / David N. Jones [editor] ... [et al.]. — 2nd ed. — Basingstoke : Macmillan Education, 1987. — xi,357p. — *Previous ed.: Sevenoaks : Teach Yourself, 1982. — Bibliography: p328-347. — Includes index*

CHILD ABUSE — Bibliography
COOPER, A. B.
Selected references on child abuse 1968-1975 / compiled by A. B. Cooper and S. M. Rugg. — [London] : Department of Health and Social Security Library, 1975. — 9,3p. — (Bibliography series ; no.B2). — *Includes supplement compiled by Nerida J. S. Clarke, 1975*

SHRIGLEY, Sheila
Selected British references on child abuse 1966-1976 / compiled by Sheila M. Shrigley. — [London] : Department of Health and Social Security Library, 1976. — 17 leaves. — (Bibliography series ; no.B37). — *Includes index*

SHRIGLEY, Sheila
Selected references on non-accidental injury to children / compiled by Sheila M. Shrigley and Susan M. Rugg. — London : Department of Health and Social Security Library, 1978. — 16p. — (Bibliography series / Department of Health and Social Security Library ; no.B81)

CHILD ABUSE — Congresses
CIOMS ROUND TABLE CONFERENCE (19th : 1985 : Berne, Switzerland)
Battered children and child abuse : proceedings of the XIXth CIOMS Round Table Conference, Berne, Switzerland, 4-6 December 1985 / edited by Z. Bankowski and M. Carballo ; organized jointly by the Council for International Organizations of Medical Sciences and the World Health Organization. — Geneva, Switzerland : CIOMS, c1986. — xiii, 174 p.. — *Includes bibliographies*

CHILD ABUSE — Psychological aspects
Psychological maltreatment of children and youth / [compiled by] Marla R. Brassard, Robert Germain, Stuart N. Hart. — New York ; Oxford : Pergamon, 1987. — xii, 296p. — (Pergamon general psychology series ; 143). — *Includes index*

CHILD ABUSE — Services
MCGLOIN, Paul
Parent participation in child abuse review conferences : a research report / Paul McGloin and Annmarie Turnbull. — London : Directorate of Social Services, 1986. — 70p. — (Planning and research). — *Bibliography: p [71-73]*

CHILD ABUSE — Services — Scotland
WORKING GROUP ON SOCIAL WORK ISSUES IN CHILD ABUSE
Child abuse : report. — [Edinburgh] : Social Work Services Group, [1985]. — [56]p

CHILD ABUSE — Canada
No safe place : violence against women and children / edited by Connie Guberman & Margie Wolfe. — Toronto, Ont. : Women's Press, c1985. — 165 p.. — *Includes bibliographical references*

Sexual abuse of children in the 1980's : ten essays and an annotated bibliography / edited by Benjamin Schlesinger. — Toronto : University of Toronto Press, 1986. — 201p. — *Annotated bibliography: p[95]-189*

CHILD ABUSE — Great Britain
GREAT BRITAIN. Welsh Office. Health and Social Work Department
Violence to children - a response to the First Report from the Select Committee on Violence in the Family. — Cardiff : the Office, 1978. — 2,[5]leaves. — (Circular / Welsh Office ; no.78/56) ([Health circular] ; WHC (78)14)

CHILD ABUSE — Great Britain — Bibliography
SHRIGLEY, Sheila
Selected British references on child abuse 1966-1976 / compiled by Sheila M. Shrigley. — [London] : Department of Health and Social Security Library, 1976. — 17 leaves. — (Bibliography series ; no.B37). — *Includes index*

CHILD ABUSE — South Africa
LAWYERS COMMITTEE FOR HUMAN RIGHTS
The war against children : South Africa's youngest victims / Lawyers Committee for Human Rights ; with a foreword by Bishop Desmond Tutu. — New York : Lawyers Committee for Human Rights, [1986]. — vi,151p

CHILD ABUSE — United States
BILLER, Henry B
Child maltreatment and paternal deprivation / Henry Biller, Richard Solomon. — Lexington, Mass. : Lexington Books, c1986. — p. cm. — *Includes indexes. — Bibliography: p*

No safe place : violence against women and children / edited by Connie Guberman & Margie Wolfe. — Toronto, Ont. : Women's Press, c1985. — 165 p.. — *Includes bibliographical references*

CHILD ABUSE — United States — Addresses, essays, lectures
Unhappy families : clinical and research perspectives on family violence / [edited by] Eli H. Newberger, Richard Bourne. — Littleton, Mass. : PSG, c1985. — p. cm. — *Includes index*

CHILD CARE
SCARR, Sandra
Mother care/ other care : [the child-care dilemma for women and children] / Sandra Scarr and Judy Dunn. — 2nd ed. — Harmondsworth : Penguin, 1987. — 239p. — *Originally published: New York: Basic Books, 1984. — Bibliography: [p221]-229*

CHILD CARE — Law and legislation — Great Britain
HOGGETT, Brenda M.
Parents and children : the law of parental responsibility / Brenda M. Hoggett. — 3rd ed. — London : Sweet and Maxwell, 1987. — xxvi,213p. — *Previous ed.: 1981. — Bibliography: p193-204*

CHILD CARE — Great Britain
KASTELL, Jean
Casework in child care / by Jean Kastell ; foreword by M. Brooke Willis. — London : Routledge and Kegan Paul, 1962. — [xii].306p

CHILD CARE — Great Britain — Case studies
HILL, Malcolm
Sharing child care in early parenthood / Malcolm Hill. — London : Routledge & Kegan Paul, 1987. — [360]p. — *Includes bibliography and index*

CHILD CARE SERVICES — Government policy
Childcare and equal opportunities : some policy perspectives : papers delivered at a workshop organised by the Equal Opportunities Commission / edited by Bronwen Cohen and Karen Clarke. — London : H.M.S.O., 1986. — 87p. — *Includes bibliographical references*

CHILD CARE SERVICES — Government policy — Great Britain
Childcare and equal opportunities : some policy perspectives : papers delivered at a workshop organised by the Equal Opportunities Commission / edited by Bronwen Cohen and Karen Clarke. — London : H.M.S.O., 1986. — 87p. — *Includes bibliographical references*

CHILD CARE SERVICES — England — London
GREATER LONDON COUNCIL. Economic Policy Group
Child care : meeting needs and making jobs. — [London] : the Council, 1983. — 23p. — (Strategy document ; no.14)

CHILD CARE SERVICES — Great Britain
KASTELL, Jean
Casework in child care / by Jean Kastell ; foreword by M. Brooke Willis. — London : Routledge and Kegan Paul, 1962. — [xii].306p

CHILD DEVELOPMENT
CONNOLLY, Kevin J.
The lost children : poverty and human development / Kevin Connolly. — [Exeter] : University of Exeter, 1985. — 20p. — (The Hugh Greenwood lecture ; 1985). — *Bibliography: p19-20*

HODGE, Robert
Children and television : a semiotic approach / Robert Hodge and David Tripp. — Cambridge : Polity, 1986. — vi,233p. — *Bibliography: p219-225. — Includes index*

MERCER, Ramona Thieme
First-time motherhood : experiences from teens to forties / Ramona T. Mercer. — New York : Springer Pub. Co., c1986. — xv, 384 p.. — *Includes index. — Bibliography: p. 357-374*

NATO CONFERENCE ON THE ACQUISITION OF SYMBOLIC SKILLS (1982 : University of Keele)
The acquisition of symbolic skills / [proceedings of a NATO Conference on the Acquisition of Symbolic Skills, held July 5-10, 1982, at the University of Keele, Keele, England] ; edited by Don Rogers and John A. Sloboda. — New York ; London : Published in cooperation with NATO Scientific Affairs Division [by] Plenum, c1983. — xii,623p. — (NATO conference series. III, Human factors ; v.22). — *Includes bibliographies and index*

PALMER, Patricia
The lively audience : a study of children around the TV set / Patricia Palmer. — London : Allen & Unwin, 1986. — x,166p. — *Bibliography: p154-164. — Includes index*

SANTROCK, John W.
Child development : an introduction / John W. Santrock and Steven R. Yussen. — 3rd ed. — Dubuque, Iowa : W.C. Brown, c1987. — xxxii,652p. — *Originally published 1978. — Bibliography: p595-628*

STERN, Daniel N
The interpersonal world of the infant : a view from psychoanalysis annd developmental psychology / Daniel N. Stern. — New York : Basic Books, c1985. — x, 304p. — *Includes index. — Bibliography: p.278-294*

CHILD DEVELOPMENT — Congresses
Questions on social explanation : Piagetian themes reconsidered / edited by Luigia Camaioni and Cláudia de Lemos. — Amsterdam ; Philadelphia : J. Benjamins Pub. Co., 1985. — 141 p.. — (Pragmatics & beyond ; VI:4). — *Selection of the papers presented at the international conference in honour of Jean Piaget, held in Rome, 9-10 Oct. 1981, and sponsored by Rome University. — Bibliography: p. [131]-141*

CHILD DEVELOPMENT — popular works
RESTAK, Richard M.
The infant mind / Richard M. Restak. — 1st ed. — Garden City, N.Y. : Doubleday, 1986. — xi, 274 p.. — *Includes index. — Bibliography: p. [255]-264*

CHILD DEVELOPMENT — Testing
Risk in intellectual and psychosocial development / edited by Dale C. Farran, James D. McKinney. — Orlando [FL] : Academic Press, 1986. — xii, 331 p.. — (Developmental psychology series). — *Includes bibliographies and indexes*

CHILD DEVELOPMENT — Great Britain — Case studies
HILL, Malcolm
Sharing child care in early parenthood / Malcolm Hill. — London : Routledge & Kegan Paul, 1987. — [360]p. — *Includes bibliography and index*

CHILD DEVELOPMENT — Japan
HENDRY, Joy
Becoming Japanese : the world of the pre-school child / Joy Hendry. — Manchester : Manchester University Press, c1986. — 194p,[8]p of plates. — (Nihon kenkyū = Japanese studies). — *Bibliography: p182-188. — Includes index*

CHILD DEVELOPMENT DEVIATIONS — Diagnosis
Risk in intellectual and psychosocial development / edited by Dale C. Farran, James D. McKinney. — Orlando [FL] : Academic Press, 1986. — xii, 331 p.. — (Developmental psychology series). — *Includes bibliographies and indexes*

CHILD HEALTH SERVICES — Africa, Sub-Saharan
Within human reach : a future for Africa's children. — New York : United Nations Children's Fund, 1985. — xiii,93p. — *"... prepared by Manzoor Ahmed with the collaboration of many people ... " - t.p. verso*

CHILD HEALTH SERVICES — United States
VALDEZ, Robert Otto Burciaga
The effects of cost sharing on the health of children / Robert Otto Burciaga Valdez. — Santa Monica, CA : Rand, 1986. — xiv, 117 p.. — (Health insurance experiment series). — *"March 1986.". — "R-3270-HHS.". — Bibliography: p. 109-117*

CHILD HEALTH SERVICES — United States — Cost control
VALDEZ, Robert Otto Burciaga
The effects of cost sharing on the health of children / Robert Otto Burciaga Valdez. — Santa Monica, CA : Rand, 1986. — xiv, 117 p.. — (Health insurance experiment series). — *"March 1986.". — "R-3270-HHS.". — Bibliography: p. 109-117*

CHILD HEALTH SERVICES — Wales
GREAT BRITAIN. Welsh Office. Health and Social Work Department
Health service development : the Court Report on child health services. — Cardiff : the Office, 1978. — 5,iileaves. — (Welsh Office circular ; 78/19) ([Health circular] ; WHC (78)4)

CHILD LABOR
Children at work / edited by Elías Mendelievich. — Geneva : International Labour Office, c1979. — ix, 176 p., [6] leaves of plates. — *Bibliography: p. 175-176*

CHILD LABOR — Case studies
Children at work / edited by Elías Mendelievich. — Geneva : International Labour Office, c1979. — ix, 176 p., [6] leaves of plates. — *Bibliography: p. 175-176*

CHILD LABOR — Statistics
Children at work / edited by Elías Mendelievich. — Geneva : International Labour Office, c1979. — ix, 176 p., [6] leaves of plates. — *Bibliography: p. 175-176*

CHILD MOLESTERS
FINKELHOR, David
A sourcebook on child sexual abuse / David Finkelhor and associates. — Beverly Hills : Sage Publications, c1986. — p. cm. — *Includes index. — Bibliography: p*

CHILD MOLESTING
ENNEW, Judith
The sexual exploitation of children / Judith Ennew. — Cambridge : Polity, 1986. — [200]p. — *Includes index*

FINKELHOR, David
Child sexual abuse : new theory and research / David Finkelhor. — New York : Free Press, c1984. — xii, 260 p.. — *Includes index. — Bibliography: p. 240-255*

FINKELHOR, David
A sourcebook on child sexual abuse / David Finkelhor and associates. — Beverly Hills : Sage Publications, c1986. — p. cm. — *Includes index. — Bibliography: p*

Sexual abuse of children in the 1980's : ten essays and an annotated bibliography / edited by Benjamin Schlesinger. — Toronto : University of Toronto Press, 1986. — 201p. — *Annotated bibliography: p[95]-189*

CHILD MOLESTING — Investigation
GOLDSTEIN, Seth L
The sexual exploitation of children : a practical guide to assessment, investigation, and intervention / Seth L. Goldstein. — New York : Elsevier, c1987. — xix, 433 p.. — (Elsevier series in practical aspects of criminal and forensic investigations). — *Includes bibliographies and index*

CHILD MOLESTING — South Australia
SOUTH AUSTRALIA. Task Force on Child Sexual Abuse
Community disscussion paper. — Adelaide : South Australian Health Commission, 1985. — 89p. — *Includes bibliography references*

SOUTH AUSTRALIA. Task Force on Child Sexual Abuse
Final report of the Task Force on Child Sexual Abuse. — Adelaide : South Australian Health Commission, 1986. — viii,358p. — *Bibliography: p347-358*

CHILD MOLESTING — United States
GOLDSTEIN, Seth L
The sexual exploitation of children : a practical guide to assessment, investigation, and intervention / Seth L. Goldstein. — New York : Elsevier, c1987. — xix, 433 p.. — (Elsevier series in practical aspects of criminal and forensic investigations). — *Includes bibliographies and index*

CHILD MOLESTING — United States — Addresses, essays, lectures
Unhappy families : clinical and research perspectives on family violence / [edited by] Eli H. Newberger, Richard Bourne. — Littleton, Mass. : PSG, c1985. — p. cm. — *Includes index*

CHILD POVERTY ACTION GROUP
Annual report / Child Poverty Action Group. — London : Child Poverty Action Group, 1984/5-. — *Annual*

CHILD POVERTY ACTION GROUP
A budget to unite a divided Britain : memorandum to the Chancellor of the Exchequer from the Child Poverty Action Group. — London : Child Poverty Action Group, 1985. — 9p

CHILD PSYCHOLOGY
AUSUBEL, David Paul
Theory and problems of child development. — 3rd ed. / [by] David P. Ausubel, Edmund V. Sullivan, S. William Ives. — New York ; London : Grune and Stratton, 1980. — ix,652p . — *Previous ed.: / by David P. Ausubel and Edmund V. Sullivan. New York : Grune and Stratton, 1970. — Bibliography: p.484-596. — Includes index*

The Future of Piagetian theory : the neo-Piagetians / edited by Valerie L. Shulman, Lillian C.R. Restaino-Baumann and Loretta Butler. — New York ; London : Plenum, c1985. — xxv,222p. — *Includes bibliographies and index*

SANTROCK, John W.
Child development : an introduction / John W. Santrock and Steven R. Yussen. — 3rd ed. — Dubuque, Iowa : W.C. Brown, c1987. — xxxii,652p. — *Originally published 1978. — Bibliography: p595-628*

STERN, Daniel N
The interpersonal world of the infant : a view from psychoanalysis annd developmental psychology / Daniel N. Stern. — New York : Basic Books, c1985. — x, 304p. — *Includes index. — Bibliography: p.278-294*

TIZARD, Barbara
Young children learning : talking and thinking at home and at school / Barbara Tizard and Martin Hughes. — London : Fontana, 1984. — 286p

CHILD PSYCHOLOGY — Addresses, essays, lectures
The Child's construction of social inequality / edited by Robert L. Leahy. — New York ; London : Academic Press, 1983. — xv, 349p. — (Developmental psychology series). — *Includes bibliographies and indexes*

CHILD PSYCHOLOGY — popular works
RESTAK, Richard M.
The infant mind / Richard M. Restak. — 1st ed. — Garden City, N.Y. : Doubleday, 1986. — xi, 274 p.. — *Includes index. — Bibliography: p. [255]-264*

CHILD PSYCHOTHERAPY
HODGES, William F
Interventions for children of divorce : custody, access, and psychotherapy / William F. Hodges. — New York, N.Y. : Wiley, c1986. — p. cm. — (Wiley series on personality processes). — *"A Wiley-Interscience publication.". — Includes indexes. — Bibliography: p*

CHILD PSYCHOTHERAPY — Residential treatment
Psychotherapy with severely deprived children / edited by Mary Boston and Rolene Szur. — London ; Boston : Routledge & K. Paul, 1983. — p. cm. — *Includes index. — Bibliography: p*

CHILD PSYCHOTHERAPY — Residential treatment — England — London Metropolitan Area
Psychotherapy with severely deprived children / edited by Mary Boston and Rolene Szur. — London ; Boston : Routledge & K. Paul, 1983. — p. cm. — *Includes index. — Bibliography: p*

CHILD REARING — Economic aspects — Great Britain
ROLL, Jo
Babies & money : birth trends and costs / Jo Roll. — London : Family Policy Studies Centre, 1986. — 60p. — (Occasional paper ; no.4). — *Bibliography: p53-60*

CHILD REARING — Great Britain — Case studies
HILL, Malcolm
Sharing child care in early parenthood / Malcolm Hill. — London : Routledge & Kegan Paul, 1987. — [360]p. — *Includes bibliography and index*

CHILD REARING — United States
FALLOWS, Deborah
A mother's work / Deborah Fallows. — Boston : Houghton-Mifflin, 1985. — p. cm. — *"A Richard Todd book"--*

CHILD SUPPORT — Great Britain
ROLL, Jo
Babies & money : birth trends and costs / Jo Roll. — London : Family Policy Studies Centre, 1986. — 60p. — (Occasional paper ; no.4). — *Bibliography: p53-60*

CHILD WELFARE — Bibliography
UNICEF
Geographical index to UNICEF documents 1946 to 1972. — New York : UNICEF, 1974. — 324p. — (Documents / United Nations ; E/ICEF/INDEX/2) ([Document] - United Nations ; E/ICEF/Index/2). — *Cover title*

CHILD WELFARE — Government policy — Australia — History — 20th century
BRENNAN, Deborah
Caring for Australia's children : political and industrial issues in child care / Deborah Brennan and Carol O'Donnell. — Sydney ; London : Allen & Unwin, 1986. — [200]p

CHILD WELFARE — Law and legislation — England
DINGWALL, Robert
Care proceedings : a practical guide for social workers, health visitors and others / Robert Dingwall and John Eekelaar. — Oxford : Basil Blackwell, 1982. — viii,140p. — *Bibliography: p135-136. — Includes index*

HOLDEN, Alan S.
Children in care : the Association of Directors of Social Services guide to personal social services legislation / Alan S. Holden. — 2nd ed. — [Leamington Spa] : Comyn, 1985. — 257p. — *Previous ed.: 1980. — Includes index*

CHILD WELFARE — Canada
The Challenge of child welfare / edited by Kenneth L. Levitt and Brian Wharf. — Vancouver : University of British Columbia Press, 1985. — xiii, 310 p.. — *Includes index. — Bibliography: p. [302]-305*

CHILD WELFARE — Developing countries — History
BLACK, Maggie
The children and the nations : the story of UNICEF / by Maggie Black. — New York : UNICEF, 1986. — x,502p. — *Includes bibliographical references*

CHILD WELFARE — England
Lost in care : the problems of maintaining links between children in care and their families / Spencer Millham ... [et al.]. — Aldershot : Gower, c1986. — ix,258p. — *Includes index*

CHILD WELFARE — England — History — 20th century
DWORK, Deborah
War is good for babies and other young children : a history of the infant and child welfare movement in England 1898-1918 / Deborah Dwork. — London : Tavistock, 1987. — 307p. — *Bibliography: p268-295. — Includes index*

CHILD WELFARE — France — Nomenclature
FRANCE. Comité des Nomenclatures
Etat des nomenclatures applicables aux établissements sanitaires et sociaux : période de validité: exercice 1986 : nomenclatures concernées, catégories d'établissements, statuts juridiques. — [Paris : Ministère des Affaires sociales et de la Solidarité nationale, 1986]. — 105p

CHILD WELFARE — Great Britain
FISHER, Mike
In and out of care : the experiences of children, parents and social workers / Mike Fisher, Peter Marsh and David Phillips with Eric Sainsbury. — London : Batsford in association with British Agencies for Adoption and Fostering, 1986. — 154p. — (Child care policy and practice). — *Bibliography: p146-150.* — *Includes index*

HENWOOD, Melanie
Benefit or burden? : the objectives and impact of child support / Melanie Henwood and Malcolm Wicks. — London : Family Policy Studies Centre, 1986. — 62p. — (Occasional paper / Family Policy Studies Centre ; no.3). — *Bibliography: p57-63*

RYAN, Mary
A guide to care and related proceedings / Mary Ryan. — 3rd ed. — London : Family Rights Group, 1985. — 83p

VERNON, Jeni
In care : a study of social work decision making / Jeni Vernon & David Fruin. — London : National Children's Bureau, 1986. — 157p

CHILD WELFARE — United States
BURT, Martha R
Testing the social safety net : the impact of changes in support programs during the Reagan administration / Martha R. Burt, Karen J. Pittman. — Washington, D.C. : Urban Institute Press, c1985. — xix, 183 p.. — (The Changing domestic priorities series). — *Includes bibliographical references*

KIMMICH, Madeleine H
America's children, who cares? : growing needs and declining assistance in the Reagan era / Madeleine H. Kimmich. — Washington, D.C. : Urban Institute Press, c1985. — xvii 112 p.. — (The Changing domestic priorities series). — *Includes bibliographical references*

CHILD WELFARE — United States — Addresses, essays, lectures
The Media, social science, and social policy for children / Eli A. Rubinstein and Jane D. Brown, editors. — Norwood, N.J. : Ablex Pub. Corp., 1985. — xv, 240 p.. — (Child and family policy ; v. 5). — *Includes bibliographies and indexes*

CHILDBIRTH — Psychology
LUPTON, Carol
Women's experience of antenatal care : a report of research conducted in collaboration with Portsmouth and South-East Hampshire Community Health Council / Carol Lupton, Graham Moon and Ian Mountifield. — Portsmouth : Social Services Research and Intelligence Unit, 1985. — vi,76p. — (SSRIU occasional paper ; no.12)

CHILDBIRTH — Great Britain — History
LEWIS, Judith Schneid
In the family way : childbearing in the British aristocracy, 1760-1860 / Judith Schneid Lewis. — New Brunswick, N.J. : Rutgers University Press, c1986. — xi, 313 p.. — *Includes index*. — *Bibliography: p. 291-303*

CHILDBIRTH — Great Britain — Statistics
GREAT BRITAIN. Office of Population Censuses and Surveys
Birth statistics : historical series of statistics from registrations of births in England and Wales, 1837-1983. — London : H.M.S.O., 1987. — x,206p. — (Series FM1 / Office of Population Censuses and Surveys ; no.13)

GREAT BRITAIN. Office of Population Censuses and Surveys
Period and cohort birth order statistics : period analyses for years from 1938-85 and cohort analyses for women born in each year from 1920 (England and Wales). — London : H.M.S.O., 1987. — iii,30p. — (Series FM1 ; no.14). — *7 microfiches in end pocket.* — *Bibliographical references: p13*

CHILDE, V. GORDON
GREEN, Sally
Prehistorian : a biography of V. Gordon Childe / Sally Green ; with a foreword by Jack Lindsay. — Bradford-on-Avon : Moonraker, 1981. — xxii,200p. — *Bibliography: p176-190.* — *Includes index*

CHILDHOOD FRIENDSHIP
Conversations of friends : speculations on affective development / edited by John M. Gottman and Jeffrey G. Parker. — Cambridge : Cambridge University Press, 1987. — [416]p. — (Studies in emotion and social interaction). — *Includes index*

CHILDREN
Children first! / UNICEF (U.K.). — London : UNICEF (U.K.), 1986-. — *Quarterly*

CHILDREN — Attitudes — Addresses, essays, lectures
The Child's construction of social inequality / edited by Robert L. Leahy. — New York ; London : Academic Press, 1983. — xv, 349p. — (Developmental psychology series). — *Includes bibliographies and indexes*

CHILDREN — Care and hygiene
MAYALL, Berry
Keeping children healthy : the role of mothers and professionals / Berry Mayall. — London ; Boston : Allen & Unwin, 1986. — xiv,258p. — *Bibliography: p[251]-258*

NATIONAL COUNCIL FOR ONE PARENT FAMILIES
Time-off for child care : evidence to the House of Lords on the European Commission's proposed directive on parental leave and leave for family reasons. — London : National Council for One Parent Families, 1984. — 24p

The state of the world's children / United Nations Children's Fund. — London : Published for UNICEF by the Oxford University Press 1981-. — *Annual*

CHILDREN — Care and hygiene — Denmark
The Children and Young Persons Act, 1964. — [Copenhagen : Ministry of Social Affairs?], 1964. — 33 leaves

CHILDREN — Care and hygiene — Developing countries
Child health & survival : the UNICEF GOBI-FFF program / edited by Richard Cash, Gerald T. Keusch and Joel Lamstein. — London : Croom Helm, c1987. — x,253p. — *Conference proceedings*

CHILDREN — Care and hygiene — France — Costs
EUVRARD, Françoise
Mères de famille : coûts et revenus de lâctivité professionnelle / [étude...réalisée par Françoise Euvrard...Marie-Gabrielle David et Kristof Starzek. — [Paris] : Centre dÉtude des Revenus et des Coûts, 1985. — 163p. — (Documents du Centre dÉtude des Revenus et des Coûts ; no.75)

CHILDREN — Death — Psychological aspects
KNAPP, Ronald J
Beyond endurance : when a child dies / Ronald J. Knapp. — New York : Schocken Books, 1986. — xv, 271 p.. — *Includes index.* — *Bibliography: p. 263-265*

CHILDREN — Economic aspects — Sri Lanka
DEATON, Angus
Three essays on a Sri Lanka household survey / Angus Deaton. — Washington, D.C., U.S.A. : World Bank, 1985 printing, c1981. — [iv],87p. — (LSMS working papers ; no.11). — *Bibliographical references: p85-87*

CHILDREN — Employment
Child labour : a briefing manual. — Geneva : International Labour Office, 1986. — [83]. — *Includes bibliographical references*

CHILDREN — Employment — Bibliography
Annotated bibliography on child labour. — Geneva : International Labour Office, 1986. — 69p

CHILDREN — Employment — Bangladesh
KABEER, Naila
The functions of children in the household economy and levels of fertility : a case study of a village in Bangladesh / Naila Kabeer. — 311 leaves. — *PhD (Econ) 1986 LSE.* — *Leaves 260-301 are appendices*

CHILDREN — Government policy — Great Britain
ROLL, Jo
Babies & money : birth trends and costs / Jo Roll. — London : Family Policy Studies Centre, 1986. — 60p. — (Occasional paper ; no.4). — *Bibliography: p53-60*

CHILDREN — Institutional care — Law and legislation — England
GREAT BRITAIN. Department of Health and Social Security
Review of child care law : publication of interim discussion papers by the inter-Departmental working party / Department of Health and Social Security. — [London] : The Department, 1986. — 1v.(various pagings)

CHILDREN — Institutional care — Australia
AUSTRALIA. Parliament. Senate. Standing Committee on Social Welfare
Children in institutional and other forms of care : a national perspective : report of the Senate Standing Committee on Social Welfare. — Canberra : Australian Government Publishing Service, 1985. — xii,121p. — *Includes bibliographical references*

CHILDREN — Institutional care — Denmark
ANDERSEN, Bjarne Hjorth
Dagpasning for de 6-10-årige. — København : Socialforskninginstituttet, 1987. — 105p. — (Publikation / Socialforskningsinstituttet ; 159). — *Bibliography: p102*

CHILDREN — Institutional care — England
LOVEDAY, Susan
Reflections on care / Susan Loveday. — London : Children's Society, 1985. — [232]p. — *Includes bibliography and index*

CHILDREN — Institutional care — England — Congresses
QUALITY OF CARE PROJECT
Seminar at the Dalmeny Hotel, St Anne's-on-Sea, 6th-8th November, 1979. — [S.l.] : Department of Health and Social Security
Part 1: The collected papers. — [ca.1979]. — 42p

QUALITY OF CARE PROJECT
Seminar at the Dalmeny Hotel, St. Anne's-on-Sea, 6th-8th November, 1979. — [S.l.] : Department of Health and Social Security
Part 2: Being in care: a consumer view: digest of discussions on key issues. — [ca.1979]. — 20p

CHILDREN — Institutional care — England — Formby (Lancashire)
St. Vincent's Community Home, Formby, Lancashire / report of the working party. — [London : Department of Health and Social Security], 1975. — 12p

CHILDREN — Institutional care — Great Britain
Black and in care: conference report (report of a conference organized by the Black and In Care Steering Group held in October 1984). — London : Black and In Care Steering Group, 1985. — 45p

CHILDREN — Institutional care — Great Britain *continuation*

CAWSON, Pat
Young offenders in care / Pat Cawson. — [London] : Department of Health and Social Security, Social Research Branch, 1978. — iii,38p. — *Bibliography: p23*

GREAT BRITAIN. Department of Health and Social Security. Social Work Service
Inspection of secure accommodation for children and young persons : guidance for Social Work Service. — [London : the Department], 1979. — 77p. — *The report of a Working Group set up to provide information for Social Work Service. — Bibliography: p75-77*

GREAT BRITAIN. Law Commission
Family law : review of child law : Care, supervision and interim orders in custody proceedings / The Law Commission. — London : H.M.S.O., 1987. — v,80p. — (Working paper / Law Commission ; no.100)

KASTELL, Jean
Casework in child care / by Jean Kastell ; foreword by M. Brooke Willis. — London : Routledge and Kegan Paul, 1962. — [xii].306p

VERNON, Jeni
In care : a study of social work decision making / Jeni Vernon & David Fruin. — London : National Children's Bureau, 1986. — 157p

CHILDREN — Institutional care — Scotland

PETRIE, Cairine
The nowhere girls / Cairine Petrie. — Aldershot : Gower, c1986. — [364]p. — *Bibliography: p325-343. — Includes index*

CHILDREN — Interviews

GREEN, Richard
The "sissy boy syndrome" and the development of homosexuality / Richard Green. — New Haven : Yale University Press, c1987. — x, 416 p.. — *Includes index. — Bibliography: p. 399-409*

CHILDREN — Language

Language acquisition : studies in first language development / edited by Paul Fletcher and Michael Garman. — 2nd ed. — Cambridge : Cambridge University Press, 1986. — [625]p. — *Previous ed.: 1979. — Includes bibliography and index*

CHILDREN — Language — Congresses

INTERNATIONAL CONGRESS FOR THE STUDY OF CHILD LANGUAGE (2nd : 1981 : Vancouver)
Proceedings of the Second International Congress for the Study of Child Language. — Lanham ; London : University Press of America
Vol.2 / edited by Carol Larson Thew, Carolyn Echols Johnson. — c1984. — viii,520p. — *Includes bibliographies*

CHILDREN — Legal status, laws, etc

Law and the status of the child / [edited by] Anna Mamalakis Pappas. — New York, N.Y. (801 United Nations Plaza, New York 10017) : United Nations Institute for Training and Research (UNITAR), c1983. — 2 v. (lv, 743 p.). — *Published also as v. 13, no. 1-2 of the Columbia human rights law review. — United Nations sales no. E.83.XV.RR/29. — Includes bibliographical references*

CHILDREN — Legal status, laws, etc — Canada

SAMMON, William J.
Advocacy in child welfare cases : a practitioner's guide / William J. Sammon. — Toronto, Canada : Carswell Co., 1985. — xvii, 191 p.. — *Includes bibliographical references and indexes*

CHILDREN — Legal status, laws, etc. — Great Britain

CRONIN, Kathryn
Children, nationality and immigration : a handbook on nationality, immigration and international family law affecting children and young people / written by Kathryn Cronin for the Children's Legal Centre. — London : Children's Legal Centre, 1985. — 146p. — *Bibliography: p127-132*

RAE, Maggie
First rights : a guide to legal rights for young people / Maggie Rae, Patricia Hewitt and Barry Hugill ; illustrated by Corinne Pearlman. — 3rd ed. — London : National Council for Civil Liberties, 1985. — [128]p. — *Previous ed.: 1981. — Includes bibliography and index*

CHILDREN — Mortality — Social aspects — Bangladesh

AL–KABIR, Ahmed
Effects of community factors on infant and child mortality in rural Bangladesh / Ahmed Al–Kabir. — Voorburg : International Statistical Institute, 1984. — 33p. — (Scientific reports / World Fertility Survey ; no.56)

CHILDREN — Mortality — Statistical methods

COCHRANE, Susan Hill
Procedures for collecting and analyzing mortality data in LSMS / Susan H. Cochrane, William D. Kalsbeek, Jeremiah M. Sullivan. — Washington, D.C. : World Bank, Development Research Dept., 1982, c1981. — 148p. — (LSMS working papers ; no.16). — *Bibliography: p64-69*

CHILDREN — Nutrition

MAYALL, Berry
Keeping children healthy : the role of mothers and professionals / Berry Mayall. — London ; Boston : Allen & Unwin, 1986. — xiv,258p. — *Bibliography: p[251]-258*

CHILDREN — Suicidal behavior

HAWTON, Keith
Suicide and attempted suicide among children and adolescents / by Keith Hawton. — Beverly Hills ; London : Sage, c1986. — 159 p.. — (Developmental clinical psychology and psychiatry series ; v. 5). — *Includes index. — Bibliography: p. 145-153*

CHILDREN — Africa — Mortality — Bibliography

HILL, Allan G.
A review of materials and methods for the study of infant and child mortality in Africa / Allan G. Hill and Georgia L. Kaufmann. — London : London School of Hygiene and Tropical Medicine, Centre for Population Studies, 1987. — 38p. — (CPS research paper ; 87-1)

CHILDREN — Africa, Southern

Children on the front line : the impact of apartheid, destabilization and warfare on children in Southern Africa : a report prepared for UNICEF / by Reginal Herbold Green...[et al.]. — [New York?] : UNICEF, 1987. — v,[29] leaves. — *Bibliographical references: p.[27-28]*

CHILDREN — Africa, Sub-saharan — Care and hygiene

FRANK, Odile
A child health questionnaire for sub-saharan Africa / Odile Frank. — New York : Population Council, 1987. — 119p. — (Working papers / Population Council. Center for Policy Studies ; no.132). — *Bibliography: p105-116*

CHILDREN — Africa, Subsaharan — Mortality

FRANK, Odile
Child survival in sub-saharan Africa : structural means and individual capacity : [a case study in Burkina Faso] / Odile Frank [and] Mathias Dakuyo. — New York : Population Council, 1985. — 76p. — (Working papers / Population Council. Center for Policy Studies ; no.122). — *Bibliography: p69-76*

CHILDREN — Belgium — Ghent — History

NICHOLAS, David
The domestic life of a medieval city : women, children, and the family in fourteenth-century Ghent / David Nicholas. — Lincoln : University of Nebraska Press, c1985. — p. cm. — *Includes index. — Bibliography: p*

CHILDREN — Ecuador — Mortality

BORJA M., Eduardo
Factores determinantes de una mortalidad prematura en Ecuador / Eduardo Borja M.. — Voorburg : International Statistical Institute, 1985. — 31p. — (Scientific reports / World Fertility Survey ; no.74)

CHILDREN — England — Buckinghamshire — Longitudinal studies

MITCHELL, Sheila, 1926-
Nine-year-olds grow up : a follow-up study of schoolchildren / Sheila Mitchell. — London : Tavistock, 1987. — viii,181p. — *Includes index*

CHILDREN — Great Britain — History

A Lasting relationship : parents and children over three centuries / [compiled by] Linda Pollock. — London : Fourth Estate, 1986. — [320]p. — *Includes bibliography and index*

CHILDREN — Great Britain — Nutrition

GREAT BRITAIN. Committee on Medical Aspects of Food Policy. Sub-Committee on Nutritional Surveillance
Second report. — London : H.M.S.O., 1981. — 143p. — (Report on health and social subjects ; 21). — *Includes bibliographical references*

CHILDREN — Great Britain — Social conditions

LISTER, Ruth
Opportunity lost : a response to the Green Paper on the Reform of Personal Taxation from the Child Poverty Action Group / Ruth Lister and Fran Bennett. — London : Child Poverty Action Group, 1986. — 34p

NATIONAL CHILDREN'S HOME. Child and Family Policy Unit
Children in danger : an NCH factfile about children today / compiled by the NCH Child and Family Policy Unit ; edited by Patrick Lyons. — London : National Children's Home, 1987. — 32p

PIACHAUD, David
Poor children : a tale of two decades / David Piachaud. — London : Child Poverty Action Group, 1986. — 16p. — *Bibliography: p15-16*

CHILDREN — Guyana — Mortality

EBANKS, G. Edward
Infant and child mortality and fertility : Trinidad and Tobago, Guyana and Jamaica / G. Edward Ebanks. — Voorburg : International Statistical Institute, 1985. — 68p. — (Scientific reports / World Fertility Survey ; no.75)

CHILDREN — Haiti — Mortality — Statistics

ROUSSEAU, J. A.
La mortalité infantile et juvénile en Haïti / J. A. Rousseau. — Voorburg : International Statistical Institute, 1985. — 23p. — (Scientific reports / World Fertility Survey ; no.82)

CHILDREN — India

PRAKASH, Om
Caste Hindu and scheduled caste children in rural India / Om Prakash and Arun K. Sen. — New Delhi : Ess Ess Publications, 1985. — xiv, 184 p.. — *Spine title: Hindu caste and scheduled caste children in rural India. — Includes index. — Bibliography: p. [155]-182*

CHILDREN — Jamaica — Mortality

EBANKS, G. Edward
Infant and child mortality and fertility : Trinidad and Tobago, Guyana and Jamaica / G. Edward Ebanks. — Voorburg : International Statistical Institute, 1985. — 68p. — (Scientific reports / World Fertility Survey ; no.75)

CHILDREN — Northern Ireland

CAIRNS, Ed
Caught in crossfire : children and the Northern Ireland conflict / Ed Cairns. — Belfast : Appletree, 1987. — [176]p. — *Includes bibliography and index*

CHILDREN — Peru — Mortality — Statistics

MOSER, Kath
Levels and trends in child and adult mortality in Peru / Kath Moser. — Voorburg : International Statistical Institute, 1985. — 42p. — (Scientific reports / World Fertility Survey ; no.77)

CHILDREN — Scotland

Inequalities and childhood : the proceedings of a conference held on 26 April 1985 at the Queen's Hall, Edinburgh / edited by Eric Wilkinson and Rachel Jenkins. — Edinburgh : Scottish Child and Family Alliance, 1986. — 57p

CHILDREN — Scotland — Care and hygiene

SCOTTISH CHILD AND FAMILY ALLIANCE. Study Conference (2nd : 1985 : Glasgow)
Care by the Community: residential resources. — Edinburgh : Scottish Child and Family Alliance, 1985. — 42p. — (Conference paper ; 2). — *Bibliography: p42.* — *Contents: Residential communities: a radical choice/Keith White - Residential communities; fossil or phoenix/Spencer Millham*

CHILDREN — Spain

Infancia y sociedad en España / [J. L.] Aranguren...[et al.]. — Jaen : Hesperia, c1983. — 311p. — (Colección "Ciencias sociales")

CHILDREN — Syria — Mortality — Statistics

VAIDYANATHAN, K. E.
Estimation of infant and child mortality in Syria from the 1970 Census data / K. E. Vaidyanathan. — Damascus : Central Bureau of Statistics, 1976. — 17p. — (Syrian Population Studies Series ; No.2)

CHILDREN — Trinidad and Tobago — Mortality

EBANKS, G. Edward
Infant and child mortality and fertility : Trinidad and Tobago, Guyana and Jamaica / G. Edward Ebanks. — Voorburg : International Statistical Institute, 1985. — 68p. — (Scientific reports / World Fertility Survey ; no.75)

CHILDREN — Uganda — Social conditions

War, violence, and children in Uganda / edited by Cole P. Dodge and Magne Raundalen. — Oslo : Norwegian University Press ; Oxford : Oxford University Press [distributor], c1987. — xvi,159p. — *Includes bibliographies*

CHILDREN — United States — History

A Lasting relationship : parents and children over three centuries / [compiled by] Linda Pollock. — London : Fourth Estate, 1986. — [320]p. — *Includes bibliography and index*

CHILDREN, ADOPTED — Canada — Interviews

CROOK, Marion
The face in the mirror : teenagers talk about adoption / Marion Crook. — Toronto : NC Press, 1986. — 116p. — *Bibliography: p114-116*

CHILDREN AND DEATH

WILCOX, Sandra Galdieri
Understanding death and dying : an interdisciplinary approach / Sandra Galdieri Wilcox and Marilyn Sutton. — 3rd ed. — Palo Alto ; London : Mayfield, c1985. — xxii,428p

CHILDREN AND WAR — Bibliography

SHRIGLEY, Sheila
Selected references on children in war time and other social disturbances / compiled by Sheila M. Shrigley. — [London] : Department of Health and Social Security Library, 1975. — 3p. — (Bibliography series ; no.B25)

CHILDREN AND YOUNG PERSONS ACT, 1964

The Children and Young Persons Act, 1964. — [Copenhagen : Ministry of Social Affairs?], 1964. — 33 leaves

CHILDREN, BLACK — South Africa

LAWYERS COMMITTEE FOR HUMAN RIGHTS
The war against children : South Africa's youngest victims / Lawyers Committee for Human Rights ; with a foreword by Bishop Desmond Tutu. — New York : Lawyers Committee for Human Rights, [1986]. — vi,151p

CHILDREN, DEAF — Language

Teaching and talking with deaf children / by David Wood ... [et al.] with contributions by Margaret Tait and Sue Lewis. — Chichester : Wiley, c1986. — xiii,199p. — (Wiley series in developmental psychology and its applications). — *Bibliography: p187-193.* — *Includes index*

CHILDREN, FIRST-BORN

MERCER, Ramona Thieme
First-time motherhood : experiences from teens to forties / Ramona T. Mercer. — New York : Springer Pub. Co., c1986. — xv, 384 p.. — *Includes index.* — *Bibliography: p. 357-374*

CHILDREN OF DIVORCED PARENTS — Finance

GRIFFITHS, Bob
Overseas countries' maintenance provisions / Bob Griffiths, Shelley Cooper and Neil McVicar. — Woden, ACT : Department of Social Security, 1986. — [45]p. — (Background/discussion paper / Social Security Review ; no.13). — *Bibliography: p[40-41]*

CHILDREN OF DIVORCED PARENTS — Mental health

HODGES, William F
Interventions for children of divorce : custody, access, and psychotherapy / William F. Hodges. — New York, N.Y. : Wiley, c1986. — p. cm. — (Wiley series on personality processes). — *"A Wiley-Interscience publication."*. — *Includes indexes.* — *Bibliography: p*

CHILDREN OF DIVORCED PARENTS — Denmark

Parent-child relationship, post-divorce : a seminar report. — [Copenhagen : Socialforskningsinstituttet, 1984]. — 301p

CHILDREN OF DIVORCED PARENTS — United States

GROSSMAN, Tracy Barr
Mothers and children facing divorce / by Tracy Barr Grossman. — Ann Arbor, Mich. : UMI Research Press, c1986. — 208 p.. — (Research in clinical psychology ; no. 15). — : Revision of thesis (Ph.D.)--University of Michigan, 1984. — *Includes index.* — *Bibliography: p. [203]-205*

CHILDREN OF HOLOCAUST SURVIVORS — Austria — Biography

SICHROVSKY, Peter
[Wir wissen nicht was morgen wird, wir wissen wohl was gestern war. English]. Strangers in their own land : young Jews in Germany and Austria today / Peter Sichrovsky ; translated by Jean Steinberg. — New York : Basic Books, c1986. — ix, 165 p.. — *Translation of: Wir wissen nicht was morgen wird, wir wissen wohl was gestern war*

CHILDREN OF HOLOCAUST SURVIVORS — Germany (West) — Biography

SICHROVSKY, Peter
[Wir wissen nicht was morgen wird, wir wissen wohl was gestern war. English]. Strangers in their own land : young Jews in Germany and Austria today / Peter Sichrovsky ; translated by Jean Steinberg. — New York : Basic Books, c1986. — ix, 165 p.. — *Translation of: Wir wissen nicht was morgen wird, wir wissen wohl was gestern war*

CHILDREN OF IMMIGRANTS — Education — Organisation for Economic Co-operation and Development countries

Immigrants' children at school. — Paris : OECD, 1987. — 322p. — *At head of title: Centre for Educational Research and Innovation (CERI).* — *Includes bibliographical references*

CHILDREN OF IMMIGRANTS — France

MINCES, Juliette
La génération suivante (les enfants de l'immigration) / Juliette Minces. — Paris : Flammarion, 1986. — 209p

CHILDREN OF INTERRACIAL MARRIAGE — Great Britain

WILSON, Anne, 19---
'Mixed race' children : a study of identity / Anne Wilson. — London : Allen & Unwin, 1987. — [172]p. — *Includes bibliography and index*

CHILDREN OF MIGRANT LABORERS — Education — Germany (West) — Munich

GEIPEL, Robert
Schools, space and social policy : educational provision for the children of migrant workers in Munich / R. Geipel ; translated by N.M. Beattie. — [Liverpool] : Liverpool University Press, 1986. — viii,40p. — (International monographs in community and educational policy studies). — *Translation of: Bildungsgeographische Probleme bei der Schulversorgung von Kinder ausländischer Arbeitnehmer*

CHILDREN OF MIGRANT LABORERS — European Economic Community countries

The children of migrant workers. — Luxembourg : Office for Official Publications of the European Communities, 1977. — 53p. — (Education series / Commission of the European Communities ; no.1)

CHILDREN OF MINORITIES — Government policy — Great Britain

DALE, David
Denying homes to black children : Britain's new race adoption policies / David Dale. — London : Social Affairs Unit, [1987]. — 45p. — (Research report ; 8)

CHILDREN OF MINORITIES — Great Britain

GREAT BRITAIN. Commission for Racial Equality
Child benefit - but not for all? : comments on the Child Benefit Scheme. — London : the Commission, 1978. — 10p. — (Occasional paper / Commission for Racial Equality ; no.4)

CHILDREN OF MINORITIES — Great Britain — Books and reading

GREAT BRITAIN. Commission for Racial Equality
Books for under fives in multi-racial Britain. — London : the commission, 1978. — 6p. — *First published by the Community Relations Commission*

CHILDREN OF PRISONERS — Great Britain

SHAW, Roger
Children of imprisoned fathers / Roger Shaw. — London : Hodder and Stoughton, 1987. — vi,89p. — *Bibliography: p[83]-87*

CHILDREN OF WORKING MOTHERS — United States
BERG, Barbara J
The crisis of the working mother : resolving the conflict between family and work / by Barbara Berg. — New York : Summit Books, c1986. — p. cm. — *Includes bibliographical references*

CHILDREN OF WORKING PARENTS — United States
GROLLMAN, Earl A
The working parent dilemma : how to balance the responsibilities of children and careers / Earl A. Grollman and Gerri L. Sweder. — 1st ed. — Boston : Beacon Press, 1986. — xv, 190 p.. — *Includes index.* — *Bibliography: p. 181-185*

CHILDREN'S ACCIDENTS — Prevention
MAYALL, Berry
Keeping children healthy : the role of mothers and professionals / Berry Mayall. — London ; Boston : Allen & Unwin, 1986. — xiv,258p. — *Bibliography: p[251]-258*

CHILDREN'S CLUBS
Woodcraft focus: a journal for youth leaders and parents. — London : Woodcraft Folk, 1987-. — *Quarterly*

CHILDREN'S LITERATURE
MICHEL, Andrée
Down with stereotypes! : eliminating sexism from children's literature and school textbooks / Andrée Michel. — Paris : Unesco, 1986. — 105p. — *Bibliography: p103-105*

CHILDREN'S LITERATURE — Great Britain
NAIDOO, Beverley
Censoring reality : an examination of books on South Africa / by Beverley Naidoo. — [London] (Mawbey School, Coopers Rd. SE1) : [ILEA Centre for Anti-Racist Education and the British Defence and Aid Fund for Southern Africa], c1984. — 44p. — *Text on inside covers.* — *Bibliography: p44*

CHILE — Bibliography — Union lists
WILLIAMS, Lee H
The Allende years : a union list of Chilean imprints, 1970-1973, in selected North American libraries, with a supplemental holdings list of books published elsewhere for the same period by Chileans or about Chile or Chileans / compiled by Lee H. Williams, Jr. — Boston : G. K. Hall, c1977. — vii, 339 p.. — *Includes index*

CHILE — Biography — 20th century
Diccionario biográfico de Chile. — 18a ed. — Santiago, Chile : Empresa Periodística Chile, [1985]. — xvi, 1276p

CHILE — Boundaries — Argentina
DESTEFANI, Laurio H.
Lo que debe saberse del Beagle : síntesis del conflicto de límites austral entre Argentina y Chile / Laurio H. Destefani. — [Buenos Aires] : Platero, [ca.1984]. — 93p. — *Bibliography: p91-93*

CHILE — Commerce
Chile: principales exportaciones y paises de destino = Chile: list of selected Chilean export commodities and countries of destination / Banco Central de Chile. — Santiago : Banco Central de Chile, 1980-1982. — *Annual.* — *Text in English and Spanish*

CHILE — Commerce — Great Britain — History — 19th century
MAYO, John
British merchants and Chilean development, 1851-1886 / John Mayo. — Boulder, Colo : Westview Press, 1986. — p. cm. — (Dellplain Latin American studies ; 22). — *Bibliography: p*

CHILE — Constitutional history
INTERNATIONAL COMMISSION OF JURISTS
Chile : the new constitution and human rights. — London : Chile Solidarity Campaign, 1981. — [4p]

CHILE — Ecnmic policy
EDWARDS, Sebastián
Monetarism and liberalization : the Chilean experiment / Sebastian Edwards and Alejandra Cox Edwards. — Cambridge, MA : Ballinger Pub. Co., c1987. — xxi, 233 p.. — *Includes index.* — *Bibliography: p. 211-226*

CHILE — Economic conditions — 1970-
BITAR, Sergio
Chile : experiment in democracy / Sergio Bitar ; translated by Sam Sherman. — Philadelphia : Institute for the Study of Human Issues, 1985. — xvi, 243p. — (Inter-American politics series ; v. 6). — *Includes bibliographical references and index*

EDWARDS, Sebastián
Monetarism and liberalization : the Chilean experiment / Sebastian Edwards and Alejandra Cox Edwards. — Cambridge, MA : Ballinger Pub. Co., c1987. — xxi, 233 p.. — *Includes index.* — *Bibliography: p. 211-226*

CHILE — Economic conditions — 1970- — Addresses, essays, lectures
Chile after 1973 : elements for the analysis of military rule / edited by David E. Hojman. — Liverpool : Centre for Latin-American Studies, University of Liverpool, 1985. — 151p. — (Monograph series / Centre for Latin-American Studies, University of Liverpool ; no.12)

CHILE — History — 1824-1920
SATER, William F.
Chile and the War of the Pacific / William F. Sater. — Lincoln ; London : University of Nebraska Press, 1986. — 343p. — *Includes index.* — *Bibliography: p.[323]-335*

CHILE — History — 1920-
WINN, Peter
Weavers of revolution : the Yarur workers and Chile's road to socialism / Peter Winn. — New York : Oxford University Press, 1986. — xiv, 328 p.. — *Includes index.* — *Bibliography: p. 300-315*

CHILE — History — Coup d'état, 1973
CHAVKIN, Samuel
Storm over Chile : the Junta under siege / Samuel Chavkin ; with foreword by Hortensia de Allende. — Westport, Conn. : L. Hill, 1985. — 303p. — *Rev. ed. of 'The murder of Chile'.* New York: Everest House, c1982. — *Includes index*

CHILE — Imprints — Union lists
WILLIAMS, Lee H
The Allende years : a union list of Chilean imprints, 1970-1973, in selected North American libraries, with a supplemental holdings list of books published elsewhere for the same period by Chileans or about Chile or Chileans / compiled by Lee H. Williams, Jr. — Boston : G. K. Hall, c1977. — vii, 339 p.. — *Includes index*

CHILE — Politics and government
CHILE SOLIDARITY CAMPAIGN
Chile : trade unions and the coup. — London : Chile Solidarity Campaign, 1974. — 12p

CHILE SOLIDARITY CAMPAIGN
Chile's demand : 1986, the manifesto of the National Civil Assembly, 1986. — London : Chile Solidarity Campaign, 1986. — 6p

MITCHELL, Adrian
Tourist snapshots of Chile / Adrian Mitchell. — [London] : Chile Solidarity Campaign, 1987. — [8p]

VALENZUELA, Arturo
Origins and characteristics of the Chilean party system : a proposal for a parliamentary form of government / Arturo Valenzuela. — Washington, D.C. : Latin American Program of the Woodrow Wilson International Center for Scholars, Smithsonian Institution and the World Peace Foundation, 1985. — 43p. — (Working papers / Woodrow Wilson International Center for Scholars. Latin American Program ; no.164)

CHILE — Politics and government — 1970-1973
BITAR, Sergio
Chile : experiment in democracy / Sergio Bitar ; translated by Sam Sherman. — Philadelphia : Institute for the Study of Human Issues, 1985. — xvi, 243p. — (Inter-American politics series ; v. 6). — *Includes bibliographical references and index*

CHILE — Politics and government — 1970-
CHAVKIN, Samuel
Storm over Chile : the Junta under siege / Samuel Chavkin ; with foreword by Hortensia de Allende. — Westport, Conn. : L. Hill, 1985. — 303p. — *Rev. ed. of 'The murder of Chile'.* New York: Everest House, c1982. — *Includes index*

Chile now : initial report of the labour movement delegation, September 1984. — London : Chile Solidarity Campaign, 1984. — 40p

FARRELL, Joseph P
The National Unified School in Allende's Chile : the role of education in the destruction of a revolution / Joseph P. Farrell. — Vancouver : University of British Columbia Press in association with the Centre for Research on Latin America and the Caribbean, York University, 1986. — viii, 268 p.. — (Latin American and Caribbean studies ; 1). — *Includes index.* — *Bibliography: p. [259]-263*

CHILE — Politics and government — 1973- — Addresses, essays, lectures
Chile after 1973 : elements for the analysis of military rule / edited by David E. Hojman. — Liverpool : Centre for Latin-American Studies, University of Liverpool, 1985. — 151p. — (Monograph series / Centre for Latin-American Studies, University of Liverpool ; no.12)

CHILE — Social conditions
Chile now : initial report of the labour movement delegation, September 1984. — London : Chile Solidarity Campaign, 1984. — 40p

CHILE — Statistics
MAMALAKIS, Markos
Historical statistics of Chile / compiled by Markos J. Mamalakis. — Westport, Conn. : Greenwood Press
vol.5: Money, banking, and financial services. — 1985. — xcii,532p

CHILEANS — Scotland
KAY, Diana
Chileans in exile : private struggles, public lives / Diana Kay. — Basingstoke : Macmillan, 1987. — ix,225p. — (Edinburgh studies in sociology). — *Bibliography: p220-223.* — *Includes index*

CHIMBU PROVINCE (PAPUA NEW GUINEA) — Population — Statistics
1980 national population census : final figures : provincial summary : Chimbu Province. — Port Moresby : National Statistical Office, 1985. — iii,132p

CHINA
China in the 1980s - and beyond / edited by Birthe Arendrup, Carsten Boyer Thøgersen, Anne Wedell-Wedellsborg. — London : Curzon, 1986. — vii,175p. — (Studies on Asian topics ; no.9). — *Conference proceedings.* — *Includes bibliographies*

CHINA *continuation*
PAN, Lynn
The new Chinese revolution / by Lynn Pan. — London : Hamilton, 1987. — 246p. — *Map on lining papers.* — *Includes index*

CHINA — Armed Forces
China's military reforms : international and domestic implications / edited by Charles D. Lovejoy, Jr., Bruce W. Watson. — Boulder, Colo. : Westview Press, 1986. — p. cm. — (Westview special studies in military affairs). — *Includes index*

CHINA — Biography
BARTKE, Wolfgang
Who's who in the People's Republic of China : by Wolfgang Bartke. — 2nd ed. — München ; London : K. G. Saur, 1987. — ix,786p

CHINA — Boundaries — India
BANERJEE, D. K.
Sino-Indian border dispute / D. K. Banerjee. — New Delhi : Intellectual Publishing House, 1985. — xii,116p. — *Bibliography: p[110]-112*

LU, Chih H
The Sino-Indian border dispute : a legal study / Chih H. Lu. — New York : Greenwood Press, 1986. — x, 143 p.. — (Contributions in political science ; no. 139). — *Includes index.* — *Bibliography: p. [125]-134*

CHINA — Civilization — Congresses
Chinese culture and mental health / edited by Wen-Shing Tseng, David Y.H. Wu. — Orlando : Academic Press, 1985. — xxiii, 412 p.. — *Derived from a conference held in Hawaii, Mar. 1-6, 1982, and sponsored by the Culture Learning Institute of the East-West Center, the Dept. of Psychiatry, University of Hawaii School of Medicine, and the Queen's Medical Center in Honolulu.* — *Includes bibliographies and index*

CHINA — Commerce — History — 19th century
HAO, Yen-p'ing
The commercial revolution in nineteenth-century China : the rise of Sino-Western mercantile capitalism / Yen-p'ing Hao. — Berkeley : University of California Press, c1986. — xv, 394 p.. — *Includes index.* — *Bibliography: p. 364-380*

CHINA — Commerce — Great Britain — History — 19th century
CHINA AND THE RED BARBARIANS: AMERICAN AND BRITISH RELATIONS WITH CHINA IN THE 19TH CENTURY (Symposium : 1972 : London)
China and the red barbarians : [papers read at the Symposium]. — London : National Maritime Museum, 1973. — 26p. — (Maritime monographs and reports ; no.8)

CHINA — Commerce — United States — History — 19th century
CHINA AND THE RED BARBARIANS: AMERICAN AND BRITISH RELATIONS WITH CHINA IN THE 19TH CENTURY (Symposium : 1972 : London)
China and the red barbarians : [papers read at the Symposium]. — London : National Maritime Museum, 1973. — 26p. — (Maritime monographs and reports ; no.8)

CHINA — Commercial policy
MANN, Susan
Local merchants and the Chinese bureaucracy, 1750-1950 / Susan Mann. — Stanford, Calif. : Stanford University Press, 1987. — viii, 278 p.. — *Includes index.* — *Bibliography: p. [255]-267*

CHINA — Description and travel — To 1900
MORRISON, G. E.
An Australian in China / G. E. Morrison ; with an introduction by David Bonavia. — Hong Kong : Oxford University Press, 1985. — 299p. — (Oxford in Asia paperbacks). — *A reprint of the ed. published, London: Horace Cox, 1895*

CHINA — Descriptions and travel — 1949-
LEYS, Simon
Chinese shadows / Simon Leys ; [translated from the French]. — Harmondsworth : Penguin, 1978. — *This translation originally published: New York : Viking Press, 1977.* - *Translation of: 'Ombres chinoises'. Paris : Union générale d'éditions, 1974*

CHINA — Econmic conditions — 1976-
PERKINS, Dwight Heald
China, Asia's next economic giant? / Dwight H. Perkins. — Seattle : University of Washington Press, c1986. — x, 98 p.. — (The Henry M. Jackson lectures in modern Chinese studies). — *Includes index.* — *Bibliography: p. 91-93*

CHINA — Economic conditions
CHEUNG, Steven N. S.
Will China go 'capitalist' ? : an economic analysis of property rights and institutional change / Steven N.S.Cheung. — 2nd ed.. — London : Institute of Economic Affairs, 1986. — 80p. — (Hobart paper ; 94). — *Previous ed.: 1982*

LIPPIT, Victor D
The economic development of China / by Victor D. Lippit. — Armonk, N.Y. : M.E. Sharpe, c1987. — p. cm. — *Includes bibliographies and index*

SENESE, Donald J.
Sweet and sour capitalism : an analysis of 'socialism with Chinese characteristics' / Donald J. Senese. — Washington, D.C. : Council for Social and Economic Studies, 1985. — vii,159p

CHINA — Economic conditions — 1912-1949
HONIG, Emily
Sisters and strangers : women in the Shanghai cotton mills, 1919-1949 = [Shang-hai sha ch'ang nü kung] / Emily Honig. — Stanford, Calif. : Stanford University Press, 1986. — ix, 299 p.. — *Parallel title in Chinese characters.* — *Includes index.* — *Bibliography: p. [279]-289*

CHINA — Economic conditions — 1949-1976
China's socialist economy : an outline history (1949-1984) / editors Liu Suinian, Wu Qungan. — Beijing : Beijing Review, 1986. — vi,700p

CHINA — Economic conditions — 1949-
GRUMMITT, Karsten
China economic handbook / [Karsten Grummitt]. — London : Euromonitor, 1986. — 246p. — *Includes index*

Review of the economic situation of the Chinese mainland provinces during the year 1954. — [Taipei] : Economic Stabilization Board, 1955. — 92p

RISKIN, Carl
China's political economy : the quest for development since 1949 / Carl Riskin. — Oxford : Oxford University Press, 1987. — xvi,418p. — (Economies of the world). — *Bibliography: p380-401.* — *Includes index*

CHINA — Economic conditions — 1976-
China's socialist economy : an outline history (1949-1984) / editors Liu Suinian, Wu Qungan. — Beijing : Beijing Review, 1986. — vi,700p

GOODMAN, David S. G.
The China challenge : adjustment and reform / David S. G. Goodman, Martin Lockett and Gerald Segal. — London : Routledge & Kegan Paul, [for the] Royal Institute of International Affairs, 1986. — 86p. — (Chatham House papers ; 32)

Learning from China? : development and environment in Third World countries / edited by Bernhard Glaeser. — London : Allen & Unwin, 1987. — xvii,282p,[8]p of plates. — *Conference papers.* — *Includes bibliographies and index*

Survey of recent developments in China (Mainland and Taiwan), 1985-1986 / edited by Hungdah Chiu ; with the assistance of Jaw-ling Joanne Chang. — Baltimore : University of Maryland School of Law in cooperation with the American Association for Chinese Studies, 1987. — 223p. — (Occasional papers/reprints series in contemporary Asian studies ; 1987, no.2(79))

CHINA — Economic policy
CHEUNG, Steven N. S.
Will China go 'capitalist' ? : an economic analysis of property rights and institutional change / Steven N.S.Cheung. — 2nd ed.. — London : Institute of Economic Affairs, 1986. — 80p. — (Hobart paper ; 94). — *Previous ed.: 1982*

LIPPIT, Victor D
The economic development of China / by Victor D. Lippit. — Armonk, N.Y. : M.E. Sharpe, c1987. — p. cm. — *Includes bibliographies and index*

CHINA — Economic policy — 1976-
BATTAT, Joseph Y
Management in post-Mao China : an insider's view / by Joseph Y. Battat. — Ann Arbor, Mich. : UMI Research Press, c1986. — xiii, 182 p.. — (Research for business decisions ; no. 76). — *Includes index.* — *Bibliography: p. [173]-176*

China's socialist modernization / edited by Yu Guangyuan. — Beijing : Foreign Languages Press, 1984. — 775p

Economic relations in the Asian-Pacific region : report of a conference cosponsored by the Chinese Academy of Social Sciences and the Brookings Institution, June 1985 / edited by Bruce Dickson and Harry Harding. — Washington,D.C. : Brookings Institution, 1987. — ix,91p. — (Brookings dialogues on public policy)

MA, Hung
[Chung-kuo ching chi fa chan ti hsin chan lüeh. English]. New strategy for China's economy / by Ma Hong ; translated by Yang Lin. — 1st ed. — Beijing, China : New World Press : Distributed by China Publications Centre, 1983. — 166 p.. — (China studies series). — *Translation of: Chung-kuo ching chi fa chan ti hsin chan lüeh.* — *Includes bibliographical references and index*

Modernization in China : the case of the Shenzhen special economic zone / editors Kwan-yiu Wong, David K.Y. Chu. — Oxford : Oxford University Press, 1986. — xi,229p. — *Bibliography: p[218]-224*

PERKINS, Dwight Heald
China, Asia's next economic giant? / Dwight H. Perkins. — Seattle : University of Washington Press, c1986. — x, 98 p.. — (The Henry M. Jackson lectures in modern Chinese studies). — *Includes index.* — *Bibliography: p. 91-93*

SEMINAR ON CHINA : MODERNIZATION AND DIPLOMACY (1979 : Hong Kong)
Modernization and diplomacy of China : selections from proceedings of the seminar / edited by Kuang-Sheng Liao. — Hong Kong : Public Affairs Research Centre, Chinese University of Hong Kong, 1981. — 161p

CHINA — Economic policy — 1976- — Congresses
CHINA. Ch'üan kuo jen min tai piao ta hui [Chung-hua jen min kung ho kuo ti 6 chieh ch'üan kuo jen min tai piao ta hui ti 2 tz'u hui i chu yao wen chien. English]. The second session of the Sixth National People's Congress (main documents). — 1st ed. — Beijing : Foreign Languages Press : Distributed by China International Book Trading Corp., 1984. — 102 p.. — (Chinese documents). — *Colophon title in Chinese: Chung-hua jen min kung ho kuo ti 6 chieh ch'üan kuo jen min tai piao ta hui ti 2 tz'u hui i chu yao wen chien.* — *Translation of: Chung-hua jen min kung ho kuo ti 6 chieh ch'üan kuo jen min tai piao ta hui ti 2 tz'u hui i chu yao wen chien*

CHINA — Emigration and immigration — History

YEN, Ch'ing-huang
Coolies and mandarins : China's protection of overseas Chinese during the late Ch'ing period (1851-1911) / Yen Ching-Hwang. — Singapore : Singapore University Press, National University of Singapore, c1985. — xvi, 413 p.. — Includes index. — Bibliography: p. 360-398

CHINA — Foreign economic relations

ENG, Robert Y.
Economic imperialism in China : silk production and exports, 1861-1932 / Robert Y. Eng. — Berkeley, (Calif.) : University of California. Institute of East Asian Studies, 1986. — (China research monograph ; 31). — Bibliography: p205-243

HAO, Yen-p'ing
The commercial revolution in nineteenth-century China : the rise of Sino-Western mercantile capitalism / Yen-p'ing Hao. — Berkeley : University of California Press, c1986. — xv, 394 p.. — Includes index. — Bibliography: p. 364-380

CHINA — Foreign economic relations — United States

Economic relations in the Asian-Pacific region : report of a conference cosponsored by the Chinese Academy of Social Sciences and the Brookings Institution, June 1985 / edited by Bruce Dickson and Harry Harding. — Washington,D.C. : Brookings Institution, 1987. — ix,91p. — (Brookings dialogues on public policy)

CHINA — Foreign relations — 1644-1912

EDWARDS, E. W.
British diplomacy and finance in China, 1895-1914 / E.W. Edwards. — Oxford : Clarendon, 1987. — 212p. — Bibliography: p202-208. — Includes index

JOSEPH, Philip
Foreign diplomacy in China, 1894-1900 : a study in political and economic relations with China / Philip Joseph. — London : Allen and Unwin, 1928. — 458p

CHINA — Foreign relations — 1949-1976

FITZGERALD, C. P.
The Chinese view of their place in the world / C. P. Fitzgerald. — London : Oxford University Press, 1965. — 72p

CHINA — Foreign relations — 1949-

HART, Thomas G.
Sino-Soviet relations : re-examining the prospects for normalization / Thomas G. Hart. — Aldershot : Gower, 1987. — [170]p. — (Swedish studies in international relations). — Bibliography: p121-126. — Includes index

YAHUDA, Michael B.
China's role in world affairs / Michael B. Yahuda. — London : Croom Helm, 1978. — 298,[2]p. — Bibliography: p.286-288. — Includes index

CHINA — Foreign relations — 1976-

China's military reforms : international and domestic implications / edited by Charles D. Lovejoy, Jr., Bruce W. Watson. — Boulder, Colo. : Westview Press, 1986. — p. cm. — (Westview special studies in military affairs). — Includes index

DALLY, Peter
The Sino-Soviet split : a trap for the West / by Peter Dally. — Cheltenham (31 Seneca Way, Cheltenham, Glos. GL50 45F) : British Anti-Communist Council, c1984. — 67p

HSIUNG, James Chieh
Beyond China's independent foreign policy : challenge for the U.S. and its Asian allies / James C. Hsiung. — New York : Praeger, 1985. — p. cm. — "Published under the auspices of the Contemporary U.S.-Asia Research Institute, Inc., New York, NY.". — Includes index. — Bibliography: p

MACKAY, Louis
China : a power for peace = Wei hu shi jie he ping / Louis Mackay. — London : Merlin, 1986. — 83p

SEMINAR ON CHINA : MODERNIZATION AND DIPLOMACY (1979 : Hong Kong)
Modernization and diplomacy of China : selections from proceedings of the seminar / edited by Kuang-Sheng Liao. — Hong Kong : Public Affairs Research Centre, Chinese University of Hong Kong, 1981. — 161p

Survey of recent developments in China (Mainland and Taiwan), 1985-1986 / edited by Hungdah Chiu ; with the assistance of Jaw-ling Joanne Chang. — Baltimore : University of Maryland School of Law in cooperation with the American Association for Chinese Studies, 1987. — 223p. — (Occasional papers/reprints series in contemporary Asian studies ; 1987, no.2(79))

CHINA — Foreign relations — 1976- — Addresses, essays, lectures

The End of an isolation : China after Mao / edited by Harish Kapur. — Dordrecht ; Boston : M. Nijhoff Publishers, 1985. — xiv, 371 p.. — (International relations of socialist countries ; v. 1). — Includes bibliographies and index

CHINA — Foreign relations — Albania

BIBERAJ, Elez
Albania and China : a study of an unequal alliance / Elez Biberaj. — Boulder : Westview Press, 1986. — xi, 183 p.. — (Westview special studies in international relations). — Includes index. — Bibliography: p. 167-179

CHINA — Foreign relations — Great Britain

EDWARDS, E. W.
British diplomacy and finance in China, 1895-1914 / E.W. Edwards. — Oxford : Clarendon, 1987. — 212p. — Bibliography: p202-208. — Includes index

JONES, A. Phillip
Britain's search for Chinese cooperation in the First World War / A. Phillip Jones. — New York : Garland, 1986. — p. cm. — (Outstanding theses from the London School of Economics and Political Science). — Thesis (Ph.D.)--University of London, 1976. — Bibliography: p

CHINA — Foreign relations — Indochina

CHANG, Pao-min
Kampuchea between China and Vietnam / Chang Pao-min. — Singapore : Singapore University Press, National University of Singapore, c1985. — xi, 204 p.. — Includes bibliographical references and index

CHINA — Foreign relations — Nepal

HUSAIN, Asad
Conflict in Asia : a case study of Nepal / Asad Husain, Asifa Anwar ; foreword by Q. Ahmad. — New Delhi : Classical Publications, 1979. — x, 88 p.. — Includes bibliographical references and index

CHINA — Foreign relations — Soviet Union

DALLY, Peter
The Sino-Soviet split : a trap for the West / by Peter Dally. — Cheltenham (31 Seneca Way, Cheltenham, Glos. GL50 45F) : British Anti-Communist Council, c1984. — 67p

HART, Thomas G.
Sino-Soviet relations : re-examining the prospects for normalization / Thomas G. Hart. — Aldershot : Gower, 1987. — [170]p. — (Swedish studies in international relations). — Bibliography: p121-126. — Includes index

LEDOVSKII, A. M.
Kitaiskaia politika SShA i sovetskaia diplomatiia 1942-1954 / A. M. Ledovskii. — Moskva : Nauka (IVL), 1985. — 286p. — English summary

CHINA — Foreign relations — Sri Lanka

KUMAR, Vijay
India and Sri Lanka-China Relations (1948-84) / Vijay Kumar. — New Delhi : Uppal Publishing House, 1986. — 196p. — Bibliography: p181-187

CHINA — Foreign relations — Tibet (China)

WALT VAN PRAAG, M. C. van
The status of Tibet : history, rights, and prospects in international law / by Michael C. Van Walt, van Praag ; with a foreword by Franz Michael and an introduction by Rikhi Jaipal. — Boulder, Colo. : Westview Press, 1987. — xxiv, 381 p., [1] p. of plates. — Includes index. — Bibliography: p. 343-359

CHINA — Foreign relations — United States

ANSCHEL, Eugene
Homer Lea, Sun Yat-sen, and the Chinese revolution / by Eugene Anschel. — New York : Praeger, 1984. — xvi, 269 p.. — Includes index. — Bibliography: p. 253-262

CHANG, Jaw-ling Joanne
United States-China normalization : an evaluation of foreign policy decision making / Jaw-ling Joanne Chang. — [Baltimore] : School of Law, University of Maryland, 1986. — 246p. — (Occasional papers?reprints series in contemporary Asian studies ; 1986; no.4(75)). — Bibliography: p205-225

The China Hands' legacy : ethics and diplomacy / edited by Paul Gordon Lauren. — Boulder : Westview Press, 1987. — xi, 196 p.. — Includes bibliographies and index

GREGOR, A. James
The China connection : U.S. policy and the People's Republic of China / A. James Gregory. — Stanford, Calif. : Hoover Institution Press, Stanford University, 1986. — x, 263 p.. — Map on lining papers. — Includes index. — Bibliography: p. [241]-254

HALLENBERG, Jan
Foreign policy change : United States foreign policy toward the Soviet Union and the People's Republic of China, 1961-1980 / Jan Hallenberg. — [Stockholm] : Dept. of Political Science, University of Stockholm, 1984. — 347 p.. — (Stockholm studies in politics ; 25). — Errata slip inserted. — : Originally presented as the author's thesis (doctoral--University of Stockholm, 1984). — Bibliography: p. 333-347

KUSANO, Atsushi
Two Nixon shocks and Japan-U.S. relations / Atsushi Kusano. — Princeton, N.J. : Princeton University. Woodrow Wilson School of Public and International Affairs, 1987. — 46p. — (Research monograph / Princeton University. Woodrow Wilson School of Public and International Affairs ; no.50)

LEDOVSKII, A. M.
Kitaiskaia politika SShA i sovetskaia diplomatiia 1942-1954 / A. M. Ledovskii. — Moskva : Nauka (IVL), 1985. — 286p. — English summary

CHINA — Foreign relations — United States — Case studies

STOESSINGER, John George
Nations in darkness--China, Russia, and America / John G. Stoessinger. — 4th ed. — New York : Random House, 1986. — x, 301 p. . — Includes index. — Bibliography: p. 281-286

CHINA — History — 1861-1912

ANSCHEL, Eugene
Homer Lea, Sun Yat-sen, and the Chinese revolution / by Eugene Anschel. — New York : Praeger, 1984. — xvi, 269 p.. — Includes index. — Bibliography: p. 253-262

CHINA — History — Hsüan-t'ung, 1908-1912

POWER, Brian
The puppet Emperor : the life of Pu Yi, last Emperor of China / Brian Power. — London : Peter Owen, 1986. — 230p

CHINA — History — Revolution, 1911-1912

ANSCHEL, Eugene
Homer Lea, Sun Yat-sen, and the Chinese revolution / by Eugene Anschel. — New York : Praeger, 1984. — xvi, 269 p.. — *Includes index. — Bibliography: p. 253-262*

CHINA — History — Revolution, 1911-1912 — Addresses, essays, lectures

HU, Sheng
[Hsin hai ko ming. English]. The 1911 Revolution : a retrospective after 70 years / by Hu Sheng, Liu Danian and others. — 1st ed. — Beijing, China : New World Press, 1983. — 222 p.. — (China studies series). — *Translation of: Hsin hai ko ming*

CHINA — History — Republic, 1912-1949 — Addresses, essays, lectures

China, seventy years after the 1911 Hsin-Hai Revolution / edited by Hungdah Chiu with Shao-Chuan Leng. — Charlottesville : University Press of Virginia, 1984. — x, 601 p.. — *Papers from the Tenth Annual Meeting of the Mid-Atlantic Regional Conference of the Association for Asian Studies, held at the University of Maryland, Oct. 17-18, 1981 and the Twenty-third Annual Meeting of the American Association for Chinese Studies, held at Ohio State University, Nov. 7-8, 1981. — Includes bibliographical references and index*

CHINA — History — May Fourth Movement, 1919

SCHWARCZ, Vera
The Chinese enlightenment : intellectuals and the legacy of the May Fourth movement of 1919 / Vera Schwarcz. — Berkeley : University of California Press, c1986. — xvi, 393 p.. — *Includes index. — Bibliography: p. 358-375*

CHINA — History — 1937-1945

GILLIN, Donald G.
Falsifying China's history : the case of Sterling Seagrave's the Soong Dynasty / Donald G. Gillin. — Stanford, Calif. : Stanford University. Hoover Institution, 1986. — 24p

CHINA — History — Civil war, 1945-1949

LEVINE, Steven I
Anvil of victory : the Communist revolution in Manchuria, 1945-1948 / Steven I. Levine. — New York : Columbia University Press, 1987. — p. cm. — (Studies of the East Asian Institute, Columbia University). — *Based on the author's thesis (Ph.D.)--Harvard University. — Includes index. — Bibliography: p*

CHINA — History — 1949- — Addresses, essays, lectures

China, seventy years after the 1911 Hsin-Hai Revolution / edited by Hungdah Chiu with Shao-Chuan Leng. — Charlottesville : University Press of Virginia, 1984. — x, 601 p.. — *Papers from the Tenth Annual Meeting of the Mid-Atlantic Regional Conference of the Association for Asian Studies, held at the University of Maryland, Oct. 17-18, 1981 and the Twenty-third Annual Meeting of the American Association for Chinese Studies, held at Ohio State University, Nov. 7-8, 1981. — Includes bibliographical references and index*

CHINA — History — 1949- — Chronology

CHENG, Peter
Chronology of the People's Republic of China, 1970-1979 / by Peter P. Cheng. — Metuchen, N.J. : Scarecrow Press, 1986. — viii, 621 p.. — *Continues: A chronology of the People's Republic of China from October 1, 1949. — Includes indexes. — Bibliography: p. 569-572*

CHINA — Industries — Research

POLLACK, Jonathan D.
The R and D process and technological innovation in the Chinese industrial system / Jonathan D. Pollack. — Santa Monica (Calif.) : Rand, 1985. — iii,12p

CHINA — Intellectual life — 20th century

SCHWARCZ, Vera
The Chinese enlightenment : intellectuals and the legacy of the May Fourth movement of 1919 / Vera Schwarcz. — Berkeley : University of California Press, c1986. — xvi, 393 p.. — *Includes index. — Bibliography: p. 358-375*

CHINA — Kings and rulers — Biography

POWER, Brian
The puppet Emperor : the life of Pu Yi, last Emperor of China / Brian Power. — London : Peter Owen, 1986. — 230p

CHINA — Library resources — Europe

MA, John T.
Chinese collections in western Europe : survey of their technical and readers' service / John T. Ma. — Zug : Inter Documentation Company, 1985. — 90p. — (Bibliotheca Asiatica ; 18)

CHINA — Politics and government

CHANG, Shuhua
Communications and China's national integration : an analysis of the People's Daily and the Central Daily News on the China reunification issue / Shuhua Chang. — Dever, Colo. : University of Denver Monograph Series in World Affairs ; Baltimore : University of Maryland School of Law Occasional Papers/Reprint[s] Series in Contempory Asian Studies, 1986. — 205p. — (Occasional papers/reprints series in contemporary Asian studies ; 1986,no.5(76))

China Daily. — Beijing : Pergamon Journals, 1986

CHINA — Politics and government — 1368-1644

SOUZA, George Bryan
The survival of empire : Portuguese trade and society in China and the South China Sea, 1630-1754 / George Bryan Souza. — Cambridge : Cambridge University Press, 1986. — xx,282p. — *Bibliography: p262-275. — Includes index*

CHINA — Politics and government — 1644-1912

Ideal and reality : social and political change in modern China, 1860-1949 / edited by David Pong and Edmund S.K. Fung. — Lanham, MD : University Press of America, c1985. — xiii, 386 p.. — *Includes index. — Bibliography: p. 365-371*

SOUZA, George Bryan
The survival of empire : Portuguese trade and society in China and the South China Sea, 1630-1754 / George Bryan Souza. — Cambridge : Cambridge University Press, 1986. — xx,282p. — *Bibliography: p262-275. — Includes index*

CHINA — Politics and government — 1912-1949

FORBES, Andrew D. W.
Warlords and Muslims in Chinese Central Asia : a political history of republican Sinkiang, 1911-1949 / Andrew D.W. Forbes. — Cambridge : Cambridge University Press, 1986. — xvi,376p. — *Bibliography: p345-364. — Includes index*

Ideal and reality : social and political change in modern China, 1860-1949 / edited by David Pong and Edmund S.K. Fung. — Lanham, MD : University Press of America, c1985. — xiii, 386 p.. — *Includes index. — Bibliography: p. 365-371*

CHINA — Politics and government — 1949-1976

GARDNER, John, 1939-
China under Deng / John Gardner. — London : Centre for Security and Conflict Studies, 1986. — 26p. — (Conflict studies ; 197)

MAO, Zedong
The writings of Mao Zedong, 1949-1976 / edited by Michael Y.M. Kau, John K. Leung. — Armonk, N.Y. ; London : M.E. Sharpe. — *Translated from the Chinese*
Vol.1: September 1949-December 1955. — c1986. — xli,771p. — *Bibliography: p755-771*

CHINA — Politics and government — 1949-

China's provincial leaders 1949-1985 / editor David S.G. Goodman. — Cardiff : University College Cardiff Press. — (Studies on East Asia)
Vol.1: Directory. — 1986. — [xii,298]p. — *Includes index*

DITTMER, Lowell
China's continuous revolution : the post-liberation epoch, 1949-1981 / Lowell Dittmer. — Berkeley : University of California Press, c1987. — p. cm. — *Includes index. — Bibliography: p*

LAMPTON, David M
Paths to power : elite mobility in contemporary China / by David M. Lampton with the assistance of Yeung Sai-cheung. — Ann Arbor : Center for Chinese Studies, Unversity of Michigan, 1985. — p. cm. — (Michigan monographs in Chinese studies ; no. 55). — *Includes index. — Bibliography: p*

SENESE, Donald J.
Democracy in mainland China : the myth and the reality / by Donald J. Senese. — Washington : Council for Social and Economic Studies, 1986. — 96p

YAHUDA, Michael B.
China's role in world affairs / Michael B. Yahuda. — London : Croom Helm, 1978. — 298,[2]p. — *Bibliography: p.286-288. — Includes index*

CHINA — Politics and government — 1976-

CHIANG, Ching-kuo
China's reunification and World peace / Chiang Ching-kuo. — Taipei : [Kuomintang], 1986. — 14p

China's military reforms : international and domestic implications / edited by Charles D. Lovejoy, Jr., Bruce W. Watson. — Boulder, Colo. : Westview Press, 1986. — p. cm. — (Westview special studies in military affairs). — *Includes index*

CHOU, Wen-ch'ing
Where are the Chinese communists headed / by Chou Wen-ching. — [Taipei, Taiwan] : World Anti-Communist League, China Chapter : Asian Peoples' Anti-Communist League, Republic of China, [1981]. — 90 p.. — *Cover title. — "September 1981."*

GATES, Millicent Anne
The dragon & the snake : an American account of the turmoil in China, 1976-1977 / by Millicent Anne Gates and E. Bruce Geelhoed ; with a foreword by Gerald R. Ford. — Philadelphia : University of Pennsylvania Press, 1986. — p. cm. — *Includes index. — Bibliography: p*

GOODMAN, David S. G.
The China challenge : adjustment and reform / David S. G. Goodman, Martin Lockett and Gerald Segal. — London : Routledge & Kegan Paul, [for the] Royal Institute of International Affairs, 1986. — 86p. — (Chatham House papers ; 32)

Groups and politics in the People's Republic of China / edited by David S.G. Goodman. — Cardiff : University College Cardiff Press, 1984. — v,217p

Survey of recent developments in China (Mainland and Taiwan), 1985-1986 / edited by Hungdah Chiu ; with the assistance of Jaw-ling Joanne Chang. — Baltimore : University of Maryland School of Law in cooperation with the American Association for Chinese Studies, 1987. — 223p. — (Occasional papers/reprints series in contemporary Asian studies ; 1987, no.2(79))

CHINA — Politics and government — 1976- — Congresses

CHINA. Ch'üan kuo jen min tai piao ta hui [Chung-hua jen min kung ho kuo ti 6 chieh ch'üan kuo jen min tai piao ta hui ti 2 tz'u hui i chu yao wen chien. English]. The second session of the Sixth National People's Congress (main documents). — 1st ed. — Beijing : Foreign Languages Press : Distributed by China International Book Trading Corp., 1984. — 102 p.. — (Chinese documents). — *Colophon title in Chinese: Chung-hua jen min kung ho kuo ti 6 chieh ch'üan kuo jen min tai piao ta hui ti 2 tz'u hui i chu yao wen chien. — Translation of: Chung-hua jen min kung ho kuo ti 6 chieh ch'üan kuo jen min tai piao ta hui ti 2 tz'u hui i chu yao wen chien*

CHINA — Politics and government — 1949-

SEYMOUR, James D
China's satellite parties / James D. Seymour. — Armonk, N.Y. : M.E. Sharpe, c1987. — xi, 149 p.. — (Studies of the East Asian Institute). — *"An East-gate book."*. — *Includes index. — Bibliography: p. 135-144*

CHINA — Population density — History

CHAO, Kang
Man and land in Chinese history : an economic analysis / Kang Chao. — Stanford, Calif. : Stanford University Press, 1986. — xii, 268 p.. — *Includes index. — Bibliography: p. 255-263*

CHINA — Presidents — Biography

WONG, J. Y
The origins of an heroic image : Sun Yatsen in London, 1896-1897 / J.Y. Wong. — Hong Kong ; Oxford : Oxford University Press, 1986. — xviii, 330p, [8]p of plates. — (East Asian historical monographs). — *Includes index. — Bibliography: p.299-319*

CHINA — Relations — Asia, Southeastern

SURYADINATA, Leo
China and the ASEAN states : the ethnic Chinese dimension / Leo Suryadinata. — [Singapore] : Singapore University Press, National University of Singapore, [c1985]. — xiii, 230 p., [4] p. of plates. — *Includes index. — Bibliography: p. 218-226*

CHINA — Relations — India

BINDRA, S. S
India and her neighbours : a study of political, economic, and cultural relations, and interactions / S.S. Bindra. — New Delhi : Deep & Deep, c1984. — 404 p.. — *Includes index. — Bibliography: p. [364]-398*

CHINA — Relations — United States

Confidential U.S. State Department Central Files : United States-China relations, 1940-1949 / edited by Paul Kesaris. — Frederick, MD : University Publications of America, 1985. — 7microfilms. — *Contents: Documents from the records of the Department of State, Central Files: China*

CHINA — Relations — United States — Bibliography

Confidential U.S. State Department Central Files : United States - China relations, 1940-1949 / edited by Robert Lester. — Frederick, Md. : University Publications of America, 1985. — 7p. — *Contents: Index to documents from Department of State Central Files*

CHINA — Religion

WELLER, Robert P.
Unities and diversities in Chinese religion / Robert P. Weller. — Basingstoke : Macmillan, 1987. — viii,215p,[8]p of plates. — *Bibliography: p199-207. — Includes index*

CHINA — Religious life and customs

WELLER, Robert P.
Unities and diversities in Chinese religion / Robert P. Weller. — Basingstoke : Macmillan, 1987. — viii,215p,[8]p of plates. — *Bibliography: p199-207. — Includes index*

CHINA — Social conditions

TSAI, Wen-hui
From tradition to modernity : a socio-historical interpretation on China's struggle toward modernization since the mid-19th century / Wen-hui Tsai. — Baltimore : University of Maryland School of Law, 1986. — 76p. — (Occasional papers/reprint series in contemporary Asian studies. 1986 ; no.1 (72))

CHINA — Social conditions — 1644-1912

Ideal and reality : social and political change in modern China, 1860-1949 / edited by David Pong and Edmund S.K. Fung. — Lanham, MD : University Press of America, c1985. — xiii, 386 p.. — *Includes index. — Bibliography: p. 365-371*

CHINA — Social conditions — 1912-1949

Ideal and reality : social and political change in modern China, 1860-1949 / edited by David Pong and Edmund S.K. Fung. — Lanham, MD : University Press of America, c1985. — xiii, 386 p.. — *Includes index. — Bibliography: p. 365-371*

CHINA — Social conditions — 1976-

The Re-emergence of the Chinese peasantry : aspects of rural decollectivisation / edited by Ashwani Saith. — London : Croom Helm, c1987. — ix,277p. — *Includes bibliographies and index*

Survey of recent developments in China (Mainland and Taiwan), 1985-1986 / edited by Hungdah Chiu ; with the assistance of Jaw-ling Joanne Chang. — Baltimore : University of Maryland School of Law in cooperation with the American Association for Chinese Studies, 1987. — 223p. — (Occasional papers/reprints series in contemporary Asian studies ; 1987, no.2(79))

CHINA — Social life and customs — Addresses, essays, lectures

Kinship organization in late imperial China, 1000-1940 / edited by Patricia Buckley Ebrey and James L. Watson. — Berkeley : University of California Press, c1986. — p. cm. — (Studies on China ; 5). — *Includes index. — Bibliography: p*

CHINA — Study and teaching — Taiwan

KUO, Tai-Chün
Understanding Communist China : Communist China studies in the United States and the Republic of China, 1949-1978 / Tai-Chün Kuo and Ramon H. Myers. — Stanford, Calif. : Hoover Institution Press, Stanford University, c1986. — xi, 172 p.. — (Hoover Press publication ; 334). — *Includes index. — Bibliography: p. [135]-165*

CHINA — Study and teaching — United States

KUO, Tai-Chün
Understanding Communist China : Communist China studies in the United States and the Republic of China, 1949-1978 / Tai-Chün Kuo and Ramon H. Myers. — Stanford, Calif. : Hoover Institution Press, Stanford University, c1986. — xi, 172 p.. — (Hoover Press publication ; 334). — *Includes index. — Bibliography: p. [135]-165*

CHINA. Chung-kuo jen min chieh fang chün — Biography

P'ENG, Te-huai
[P'eng Te-huai tzu shu. English]. Memoirs of a Chinese marshal : the autobiographical notes of Peng Dehuai (1898-1974) / translated by Zheng Longpu ; English text edited by Sara Grimes. — 1st ed. — Beijing : Foreign Languages Press, 1984. — vi, 523 p., [15] p. of plates. — *Translation of: P'eng Te-huai tzu shu*

CHINA. National People's Congress

CHINA. National Peoples Congress
National Peoples Congress : documents. — Peking : Foreign Languages Press, 1955-. — *Irregular*

CHINA — History — 1912-1937

JOHNSTON, Reginald F.
Twilight in the forbidden city / Reginald F. Johnston ; with an introduction by Pamela Atwell. — Hong Kong : Oxford University Press, 1985. — xi,486p. — *Reprint of original published by Victor Gollancz in 1934*

CHINA, SOUTHWEST — Politics and government

GOODMAN, David S. G.
Centre and province in the People's Republic of China : Sichuan and Guizhou, 1955-1965 / David S. G. Goodman. — Cambridge : Cambridge University Press, 1986. — [301]p. — (Contemporary China Institute publications). — *Bibliography: p290-301*

CHINESE — Asia, Southeastern

The Chinese in Southeast Asia / edited by L. A. Peter Gosling and Linda Y. C. Lim. — Singapore : Maruzen Asia, 1983. — *Consists mainly of papers from a conference on 'The Chinese in Southeast Asia: Ethnicity and Economic Activity', held by the Center for South and Southeast Asian Studies, University of Michigan, at Aan Arbor on 20th and 21st September 1980. — Includes bibliographical references*
v.2: Identity, culture and politics. — vii,284p

GOLDBERG, Michael A
The Chinese connection : getting plugged in to Pacific Rim real estate, trade, and capital markets / Michael A. Goldberg. — Vancouver : University of British Columbia Press, 1985. — xi, 158 p.. — *Includes indexes. — Bibliography: p. [121]-158*

CHINESE — East Asia

GOLDBERG, Michael A
The Chinese connection : getting plugged in to Pacific Rim real estate, trade, and capital markets / Michael A. Goldberg. — Vancouver : University of British Columbia Press, 1985. — xi, 158 p.. — *Includes indexes. — Bibliography: p. [121]-158*

CHINESE — Foreign countries — History

YEN, Ch'ing-huang
Coolies and mandarins : China's protection of overseas Chinese during the late Ch'ing period (1851-1911) / Yen Ching-Hwang. — Singapore : Singapore University Press, National University of Singapore, c1985. — xvi, 413 p.. — *Includes index. — Bibliography: p. 360-398*

CHINESE — Great Britain

Chinese children. — London : Commission for Racial Equality, 1980. — [2]p. — *Summary of work by Brian Jackson and Anne Garvey. — Reprint from Education & community relations, November, 1974*

"Chinese community in Britain" : conference report. — London : Chinese Information and Advice, 1985. — 35p

The Chinese community in Britain : the Home Affairs Committee report in context. — London : Runnymede Trust, 1986. — 21p. — (Runnymede Research Report). — *Bibliography: p21*

CHINESE — Singapore — Economic conditions

CHENG, Lim Keak
Social change and the Chinese in Singapore : a socio-economic geography with special reference to bāng structure / Cheng Lim-Keak. — Singapore : Singapore University Press : National University of Singapore, c1985. — xix, 235 p., [8] p. of plates. — : *Revision of the author's thesis (Ph. D.--University of London, 1979). — Includes index. — Bibliography: p. 206-228*

CHINESE — Singapore — History

SONG, Ong Siang
One hundred years' history of the Chinese in Singapore / Song Ong Siang ; introduction by Edwin Lee. — Singapore ; Oxford : Oxford University Press, 1984. — xxii,602p,[113]leaves of plates. — *Facsim of: 1st ed. London : John Murray, 1923. — Includes index*

CHINESE — Singapore — Social conditions
CHENG, Lim Keak
Social change and the Chinese in Singapore : a socio-economic geography with special reference to bāng structure / Cheng Lim-Keak. — Singapore : Singapore University Press : National University of Singapore, c1985. — xix, 235 p., [8] p. of plates. — : Revision of the author's thesis (Ph. D.--University of London, 1979). — Includes index. — Bibliography: p. 206-228

CHINESE — Singapore — Societies, etc
CHENG, Lim Keak
Social change and the Chinese in Singapore : a socio-economic geography with special reference to bāng structure / Cheng Lim-Keak. — Singapore : Singapore University Press : National University of Singapore, c1985. — xix, 235 p., [8] p. of plates. — : Revision of the author's thesis (Ph. D.--University of London, 1979). — Includes index. — Bibliography: p. 206-228

CHINESE — South Africa
HUMAN, L. N
The Chinese people of South Africa : freewheeling on the fringes / Linda Human. — Pretoria : University of South Africa, 1984. — 129 p.. — (Miscellanea / UNISA ; 42). — Bibliography: p. 124-129

CHINESE — United States — History — 19th century
CHINA AND THE RED BARBARIANS: AMERICAN AND BRITISH RELATIONS WITH CHINA IN THE 19TH CENTURY (Symposium : 1972 : London)
China and the red barbarians : [papers read at the Symposium]. — London : National Maritime Museum, 1973. — 26p. — (Maritime monographs and reports ; no.8)

CHINESE AMERICANS — Ethnic identity
LYMAN, Stanford M
Chinatown and Little Tokyo : power, conflict, and community among Chinese and Japanese immigrants to America / Stanford Morris Lyman. — Millwood, N.Y. : Associated Faculty Press, c1986. — xiv, 282 p.. — (Minority structures and race and ethnic relations series). — Bibliography: p. 255-272

CHINESE AMERICANS — History
TSAI, Shih-shan Henry
The Chinese experience in America / Shih-shan Henry Tsai. — Bloomington : Indiana University Press, c1986. — xv, 223 p.. — (Minorities in modern America). — Includes index. — Bibliography: p. 214-219

CHINESE AMERICANS — Social conditions
LYMAN, Stanford M
Chinatown and Little Tokyo : power, conflict, and community among Chinese and Japanese immigrants to America / Stanford Morris Lyman. — Millwood, N.Y. : Associated Faculty Press, c1986. — xiv, 282 p.. — (Minority structures and race and ethnic relations series). — Bibliography: p. 255-272

CHINESE IN AUSTRALIA — History
YONG, C F
The new gold mountain : the Chinese in Australia, 1901-1921 / C. F. Yong. — Richmond, Australia : Raphael Arts, 1977. — xii, 301 p.. — Includes index. — Bibliography: p. 276-290

CHINESE REUNIFICATION QUESTION, 1949-
CHANG, Shuhua
Communications and China's national integration : an analysis of the People's Daily and the Central Daily News on the China reunification issue / Shuhua Chang. — Dever, Colo. : University of Denver Monograph Series in World Affairs ; Baltimore : University of Maryland School of Law Occasional Papers/Reprint[s] Series in Contempory Asian Studies, 1986. — 205p. — (Occasional papers/reprints series in contemporary Asian studies ; 1986,no.5(76))

CHIROL, VALENTINE
FREY, Werner
Sir Valentine Chirol : die britische Postition und Politik in Asien 1895-1925. — Zürich : Juris Druck und Verlag, 1976. — viii,255p. — Dissertation-Universität Zürich, 1975. — Bibliography: p230-255

CHLORIDES
TSEUNG, A. C. C.
Energy conservation in the chlor-alkali industry / A. C. C. Tseung, J. A. Antonian, A. R. Goodson. — Luxembourg : Commission of the European Communities, 1985. — ix,79p. — (EUR ; 10085). — Series title: Energy. — Bibliographical references: p42-43. — Contract no. EEB/1/111/80/UK (H)

CHLORINE INDUSTRY — Taiwan
Chlorine-Alkali industry in Taiwan, Republic of China. — [Taipei : Ministry of Economic Affairs, 1958]. — [12]p

CHOICE OF TRANSPORTATION
ROUND TABLE ON TRANSPORT ECONOMICS (68th : 1984 : Paris)
Changes in transport users' motivations for modal choice : passenger transport. — Paris : European Conference of Ministers of Transport, 1985. — 102p. — Includes bibliographies

CHOICE (PSYCHOLOGY) — Congresses
The reasoning criminal : rational choice perspectives on offending / edited by Derek B. Cornish, Ronald V. Clarke. — New York : Springer-Verlag, c1986. — p. cm. — (Research in criminology). — Includes index. — Bibliography: p

CHOLERA, ASIATIC — France — Paris — History — 19th century
DELAPORTE, François
Disease and civilization : the cholera in Paris, 1832 / François Delaporte ; translated by Arthur Goldhammer ; foreword by Paul Rabinow. — Cambridge, Mass. : MIT Press, c1986. — xiii, 250 p.. — Includes index. — Bibliography: p. [201]-234

CHOU, EN-LAI
FANG, Percy Jucheng
Zhou Enlai : a profile / Percy Jucheng Fang, Lucy Guinong J. Fang. — 1st ed. — Beijing : Foreign Languages Press : Distributed by China International Book Trading Corporation, c1986. — iii, 238 p., [1] leaf of plates. — Colophon title: Chou En-lai chuan lüeh. — Bibliography: p. 199-212

CHRÉTIEN, JEAN
CHRÉTIEN, Jean
Straight from the heart / Jean Chrétien. — Toronto, Ont., Canada : Key Porter Books, c1985. — 231 p.. — Includes index

CHRISTIAN COMMUNITIES — Catholic Church
COOK, Guillermo
The expectation of the poor : base ecclesial communities in Protestant perspective / Guillermo Cook. — Maryknoll, NY : Orbis Books, c1985. — p. cm. — Includes index. — Bibliography: p

CHRISTIAN COMMUNITIES — Brazil
COOK, Guillermo
The expectation of the poor : base ecclesial communities in Protestant perspective / Guillermo Cook. — Maryknoll, NY : Orbis Books, c1985. — p. cm. — Includes index. — Bibliography: p

CHRISTIAN COMMUNITIES — Philippines
BATANGAN, Enrique P.
Faith and social change : basic Christian communities in the Philippines / Enrique P. Batangan. — London : Catholic Institute for International Relations, 1985. — 14p. — (CIIR justice papers ; no.7)

CHRISTIAN LIFE
LEWIS, C. S.
A grief observed / Clive Staples Lewis. — London : Faber, 1961. — 60p

CHRISTIAN SAINTS — Biography
FARMER, David Hugh
The Oxford dictionary of saints / David Hugh Farmer. — 2nd ed. — Oxford : Oxford University Press, 1987. — [512]p. — Previous ed.: Oxford : Clarendon, 1978. — Includes bibliography

CHRISTIAN SAINTS — Dictionaries
FARMER, David Hugh
The Oxford dictionary of saints / David Hugh Farmer. — 2nd ed. — Oxford : Oxford University Press, 1987. — [512]p. — Previous ed.: Oxford : Clarendon, 1978. — Includes bibliography

CHRISTIAN SOCIALIST MOVEMENT — History
NORMAN, E. R.
The Victorian Christian Socialists / Edward Norman. — Cambridge : Cambridge University Press, 1987. — [v,315]p. — Includes index

CHRISTIAN ZIONISM — History of doctrines — 20th century
HALSELL, Grace
Prophecy and politics : militant evangelists on the road to nuclear war / Grace Halsell. — Westport, Conn. : Lawrence Hill & Co., c1986. — 210 p.. — Includes index

CHRISTIANITY
LEWIS, C. S.
A grief observed / Clive Staples Lewis. — London : Faber, 1961. — 60p

CHRISTIANITY — Psychology
COHEN, Charles Lloyd
God's caress : the psychology of Puritan religious experience / Charles Lloyd Cohen. — New York : Oxford University Press, 1986. — p. cm. — Includes index. — Bibliography: p

CHRISTIANITY — Canada — 19th century
COOK, Ramsay
The regenerators : social criticism in late Victorian English Canada / Ramsay Cook. — Toronto : University of Toronto Press, 1985. — x,291p. — Includes bibliographical references

CHRISTIANITY — Great Britain — Attitudes
Views from the pews : Lent' 86 and local ecumenism. — London : British Council of Churches ; London : Catholic Truth Society, 1986. — viii,88p. — Bibliography: p88

CHRISTIANITY — Philippines
DE LA TORRE, Edicio
Touching ground, taking root : theological and political reflections on the Philippine struggle / Edicio de la Torre. — London : Catholic Institute for International Relations in association with British Council of Churches, 1986. — ix,214p

CHRISTIANITY — Sweden
Aktiva i Svenska kyrkan : en livsstilstudie / [Hans L. Zetterberg...et al.]. — [s.l.] : Verbum, 1983. — 236p

CHRISTIANITY AND ECONOMICS
Finance and ethics / Ronald Preston [et al.]. — Edinburgh : University of Edinburgh. Centre for Theology and Public Issues, 1987. — 56p. — (Occasional paper / University of Edinburgh. Centre for Theology and Public Issues ; no.11)

CHRISTIANITY AND JUSTICE — Georgia
GREENHOUSE, Carol J.
Praying for justice : faith, order, and community in an American town / Carol J. Greenhouse. — Ithaca : Cornell University Press, 1986. — p. cm. — (Anthropology of contemporary issues). — Includes index. — Bibliography: p

CHRISTIANITY AND POLITICS
BIGGS-DAVISON, John
The cross of St Patrick : the Catholic Unionist tradition in Ireland / John Biggs-Davison and George Chowdharay-Best. — Bourne End : Kensal, c1984. — 487p,[8]p of plates. — Bibliography: p453-471. — Includes index

CLIFFORD, Paul Rowntree
Politics and the Christian vision / Paul Rowntree Clifford. — London : SCM, 1984. — x,175p. — Includes index

KUITERT, H. M.
Everything is politics but politics is not everything : a theological perspective on faith and politics / H.M. Kuitert. — London : SCM Press, 1986. — 183p. — Translation of: Alles is politiek maar politiek is niet alles. — Includes bibliographies

LEFEVER, Ernest W.
Ethics and United States foreign policy / Ernest W. Lefever. — Lanham : University Press of America ; London : Distributed by Eurospan, c1986. — [236]p. — Includes bibliography and index

MÍGUEZ BONINO, José
Toward a Christian political ethics / José Míguez Bonino. — London : SCM Press, 1983. — 126p.

The new right and Christian values [a one day seminar, Wednesday, 13 February 1985, Martin Hall, New College, The Mound, Edinburgh]. — Edinburgh : University of Edinburgh. Department of Christian Ethics and Practical Theology, 1985. — [48]p. — (Occasional paper / Edinburgh University. Centre for Theology and Public Issues ; no.5)

SPRING, William
The long fields : Zimbabwe since independence / William Spring. — Basingstoke : Pickering, 1986. — 191p

CHRISTIANS — Soviet Union
Aufstehen! das Gericht kommt! : Gerichtsprozesse gegen Christen in der UdSSR / zusammengestellt und bearbeitet von H. Hartfeld. — Gummersbach : Friedenstimme, 1981. — 154p

CHRISTLICH DEMOKRATISCHE VOLKSPARTEI DER SCHWEIZ
PDC : programme dåction 1975. — [s.l.] : PDC, 1975. — 95p

CHRONIC DISEASES — Epidemiology
Western diseases, their emergence and prevention / edited by H. C. Trowell, D. P. Burkitt ; foreword by John R. K. Robson. — Cambridge, Mass. : Harvard University Press, 1981. — xix, 456 p.. — Includes bibliographies and index

CHRONICALLY SICK AND DISABLED PERSONS (AMENDMENT) BILL 1983-84
GREAT BRITAIN. Parliament. House of Commons. Library. Research Division
The Chronically Sick and Disabled Persons (Amendment) Bill (Bill 15, Session 1983/84) / Christine Gillie. — [London] : the Division, 1983. — 13p. — (Reference sheet ; no.83/20). — Bibliographical references: p12-13

CHRONOLOGY, HISTORICAL
STEINBERG, S. H.
Historical tables : 58 B.C.-A.D. 1985 / by S.H. Steinberg. — 11th ed / updated by John Paxton ; foreword by G.P. Gooch. — London : Macmillan Reference, 1986. — ix,277p. — Previous ed.: 1979. — Includes index

CHRONOLOGY, HISTORICAL — Charts, diagrams, etc
Handbook of dates for students of English history / edited by C. R. Cheney. — London : Royal Historical Society, 1978. — xviii,164p. — (Royal Historical Society Guides and Handbooks ; no.4)

CHRYSLER CORPORATION — History
JEFFERYS, Steve
Management and managed : fifty years of crisis at Chrysler / Steve Jefferys. — Cambridge : Cambridge University Press, 1986. — xiv,290p. — Bibliography: p275-282. — Includes index

CH'UNG, HSUAN-T'UNG, Emperor of China, 1906-1967
JOHNSTON, Reginald F.
Twilight in the forbidden city / Reginald F. Johnston ; with an introduction by Pamela Atwell. — Hong Kong : Oxford University Press, 1985. — xi,486p. — Reprint of original published by Victor Gollancz in 1934

CHUNGCHEONG BUG DO (KOREA (SOUTH)) — Statistics
1970 population and housing census report (complete). — [Seou] : Economic Planning Board. — In Korean and English
Vol.12-6: Chungcheong Bug Do. — 1972. — 202p

CHUNGCHEONG NAM DO (KOREA (SOUTH)) — Statistics
1970 population and housing census report (complete). — [Seoul] : Economic Planning Board. — In Korean and English
Vol.12-7: Chungcheong Nam Do. — 1972. — 126p

CHURCH AND LABOR
MCLEAN, Edward B
Roman Catholicism and the right to work / Edward B. McLean. — Lanham : University Press of America, c1985. — ix, 175 p.. — Bibliography: p. 167-175

CHURCH AND LABOR — Spain
DOMINGUEZ, Javier
Organizaciones obreras cristianas en la oposición al franquismo (1951-1975) : (con 65 documentos clandestinos e inéditos) / Javier Dominquez. — Bilbao : Mensajero, 1985. — 479p

CHURCH AND MINORITIES — Great Britain
HOLDEN, Tony
People, churches and multi-racial projects : an account of English Methodism's response to plural Britain / Tony Holden. — London : Division of Social Responsibility, Methodist Church, [1985]. — 151p. — Bibliography: p142-151

CHURCH AND RACE PROBLEMS — Great Britain
LEECH, Kenneth
The fields of charity and sin / Kenneth Leech. — London : Race, Pluralism and Community Group Board for Social responsibility, 1986. — 14p. — (Theology and racism ; 3). — Bibliography: p13

CHURCH AND SOCIAL PROBLEMS
CHARLTON, William
The Christian response to industrial capitalism / William Charlton, Tatiana Mallinson, Robert Oakeshott. — London : Sheed & Ward, 1986. — 263p

CHURCH AND SOCIAL PROBLEMS — Anglican Church of Canada — History
PULKER, Edward
We stand on their shoulders : the growth of social concern in Canadian Anglicanism / Edward Pulker. — Toronto : Anglican Book Centre, 1986. — 188p. — Includes bibliographic references

CHURCH AND SOCIAL PROBLEMS — Catholic Church
BLOCK, Walter
The U.S. bishops and their critics : an economic and ethical perspective / Walter Block. — Vancouver : Fraser Institute, 1986. — 127p

CHURCH AND SOCIAL PROBLEMS — Great Britain
CHURCH OF ENGLAND. Industrial and Economic Affairs Committee
Growth, justice and work : the report of the...committee. — London : CIO Publishing, 1985. — 50p

Options for youth / John Fethney (ed.) ; with a foreword by Philip Morgan. — [Chichester] : Angel, [c1985]. — 144p. — Cover title

CHURCH AND SOCIAL PROBLEMS — Scotland
Faith in the Scottish city : the Scottish relevance of the report of the Archbishop's Commission on Urban Priority Areas / Richard O'Brien [et al.]. — Edinburgh : University of Edinburgh. Department of Christian Ethics and Practical Theology, 1986. — 30p. — (Occasional papers / University of Edinburgh. Department of Christian Ethics and Practical Theology ; no.8)

CHURCH AND SOCIAL PROBLEMS — South Africa
LEE, Peter, 1944-
Guard her children : hope for South Africa today / Peter Lee. — Eastbourne : Kingsway, 1986. — 256p. — Bibliography: p254-256

CHURCH AND SOCIAL PROBLEMS — United States
BLOCK, Walter
The U.S. bishops and their critics : an economic and ethical perspective / Walter Block. — Vancouver : Fraser Institute, 1986. — 127p

CHURCH AND STATE
Church-state relations : tensions and transitions / edited by Thomas Robbins and Roland Robertson. — New Brunswick : Transaction Books, c1986. — p. cm. — Includes index

CHURCH AND STATE — Bibliography
Religion and church and state : a bibliography selected from the ATLA religion database / edited by Albert E. Hurd. — rev. ed. — Chicago : American Theological Library Association, 1986. — 602p

CHURCH AND STATE — Brazil — History — 20th century
MAINWARING, Scott
The Catholic Church and politics in Brazil, 1916-1985 / Scott Mainwaring. — Stanford, Calif. : Stanford University Press, 1986. — xv, 328p. — Includes index. — Bibliography: p.[297]-319

CHURCH AND STATE — Germany — History — 1933-1945
[BELL, George Kennedy Allen]
A letter to my friends in the Evangelical Church in Germany / from the Bishop of Chichester. — London : S.C.M. Press, [1946]. — 12p

NOORMANN, Harry
Protestantismus und politisches Mandat 1945-1949 / Harry Noormaan. — Gütersloh : Gütersloher Verlagshaus. — Bibliography: p295-317
Bd.1: Grundriss. — 1985. — 317p

NOORMANN, Harry
Protestantismus und politisches Mandat 1945-1949 / Harry Noormann. — Gütersloh : Gütersloher Verlagshaus Mohn
Bd.2: Dokumente und Kommentare. — 1985. — 287p

CHURCH AND STATE — Great Britain — History
PARRY, J. P. (Jonathan Philip)
Democracy and religion : Gladstone and the Liberal Party, 1867-1875 / J.P. Parry. — Cambridge : Cambridge University Press, 1986. — xiii,504p. — (Cambridge studies in the history and theory of politics). — Bibliography: p453-492. — Includes index

CHURCH AND STATE — Great Britain — History — 16th century — Sources

KNOX, John
The political writings of John Knox : The first blast of the trumpet against the monstrous regiment of women and other selected works / edited and with an introduction by Marvin A. Breslow. — Washington : Folger Shakespeare Library ; London : Associated University Presses, c1985. — 160 p.. — "Folger books.". — Includes bibliographies. — Contents: The first blast of the trumpet against the monstrous regiment of women (1558) -- Letter to the Regent of Scotland (1558) -- Appellation to the nobility (1558) -- Letter to the commonalty of Scotland (1558) -- The second blast (1558)

CHURCH AND STATE — Great Britain — History — 19th century

MACHIN, G. I. T.
Politics and the churches in Great Britain 1869 to 1921 / G.I.T. Machin. — Oxford : Clarendon, 1987. — x,376p. — Bibliography: p332-362. — Includes index

CHURCH AND STATE — Great Britain — History — 20th century

MACHIN, G. I. T.
Politics and the churches in Great Britain 1869 to 1921 / G.I.T. Machin. — Oxford : Clarendon, 1987. — x,376p. — Bibliography: p332-362. — Includes index

CHURCH AND STATE — Nicaragua

BRADSTOCK, Andrew
Saints and Sandinistas : the Catholic Church in Nicaragua and its response to the revolution / Andrew Bradstock. — London : Epworth, 1987. — [96]p. — Includes bibliography

CHURCH AND STATE — Nicaragua — History — 20th century

O'SHAUGHNESSY, Laura Nuzzi
The church and revolution in Nicaragua / Laura Nuzzi O'Shaughnessy & Luis H. Serra. — Athens, Ohio : Ohio University, Center for International Studies, Latin America Studies Program, 1986, c1985. — p. cm. — (Monographs in international studies. Latin America series ; no. 11). — Bibliography: p

CHURCH AND STATE — Poland — History

MONTICONE, Ronald C.
The Catholic Church in communist Poland, 1945-1985 : forty years of church-state [relations] / Ronald C. Monticone. — Boulder : East European Monographs, 1986. — viii,227p. — (East European Monographs ; No.205). — Bibliography: p219-224

CHURCH AND STATE — Scotland

The Scottish churches and the political process today / edited by Alison Elliot and Duncan B. Forrester. — Edinburgh : University of Edinburgh. Centre for Theology and Public Issues and Unit for the Study of Government in Scotland, 1986. — 94p

CHURCH AND STATE — Soviet Union — History — 20th century

BUSS, Gerald
The bear's hug : religious belief and the Soviet state / Gerald Buss. — London : Hodder and Stoughton, 1987. — 223p,[4]p of plates. — Bibliography: p215-218. — Includes index

CHURCH AND STATE — Spain

MANTELLI, Roberto
The political, religious, and historiographical ideas of Juan Francisco Masdeu, S.J., 1744-1817 / Roberto Mantelli. — New York : Garland, 1987. — p. cm. — (Political theory and political philosophy). — Thesis (Ph. D.)--University of London, 1978. — Bibliography: p

RUÍZ GIMÉNEZ, Joaquín
Iglesia, Estado y sociedad en España. 1930-1982 / Joaquín Ruíz Giménez. — Barcelona : Editorial Argos Vergara, 1984. — 402p

CHURCH AND STATE — Spain — Congresses

SEMANA DE HISTORIA ECLESIÁSTICA DE ESPAÑA CONTEMPORÁNEA (6 : 1981 : Madrid)
Iglesia, sociedad y política en la España contemporánea / M. Espadas Burgos...[et al.]. — [Madrid] : Ediciones Escurialenses, Real Monasterio de El Escorial, 1983. — 407p. — (Biblioteca "La ciudad de Dios". Pax veritatis) (Varios ; 34)

CHURCH AND STATE IN GREAT BRITAIN

EDGAR, David
The new right and the church / David Edgar, Kenneth Leech and Paul Weller. — London : Jubilee Group, 1985-. — 58p — Bibliographies

CHURCH AND THE POOR

ELLIOTT, Charles, 1939-
Comfortable compassion? / Charles Elliott. — London : Hodder & Stoughton, 1987. — 194p

NEAL, Marie Augusta
The just demands of the poor : essays in socio-theology / Marie Augusta Neal. — New York : Paulist Press, c1987. — v, 142 p.. — Bibliography: p. 113-132

SADOWSKY, James
The Christian response to poverty : working with God's economic laws / James Sadowsky. — London : Social Affairs Unit, [1985]. — 16p. — (Taking thought for the poor). — Cover title

CHURCH AND THE POOR — Scotland

Faith in the Scottish city : the Scottish relevance of the report of the Archbishop's Commission on Urban Priority Areas / Richard O'Brien [et al.]. — Edinburgh : University of Edinburgh. Department of Christian Ethics and Practical Theology, 1986. — 30p. — (Occasional papers / University of Edinburgh. Department of Christian Ethics and Practical Theology ; no.8)

CHURCH AND THE WORLD

LANNON, Frances
Privilege, persecution and prophecy : the Catholic Church in Spain, 1875-1975 / Frances Lannon. — Oxford : Clarendon, 1987. — [350]p. — Includes bibliography and index

CHURCH CHARITIES — United States

MCKINLEY, Edward H
Somebody's brother : a history of the Salvation Army Men's Social Service Department, 1891-1985 / E.H. McKinley. — Lewiston [N.Y.] : Edwin Mellen Press, c1986. — xiii, 273 p., [40] p. of plates. — (Studies in American religion ; v. 21). — Includes index. — Bibliography: p. 217-260

CHURCH HISTORY

ECCLESIASTICAL HISTORY SOCIETY. Summer Meeting (1985 : Lady Margaret Hall, Oxford)
Voluntary religion : papers read at the 1985 Summer Meeting and the 1986 Winter Meeting of the Ecclesiastical History Society / edited by W.J. Sheils and Diana Wood. — Oxford : Published for the Ecclesiastical History Society by Basil Blackwell, 1986. — xvi,521p. — (Studies in church history ; v.23). — Includes index

CHURCH HISTORY — Middle Ages, 600-1500

HAMILTON, Bernard
Religion in the medieval West / Bernard Hamilton. — London : Edward Arnold, 1986. — vii,216p. — Bibliography: p202-212. — Includes index

CHURCH LANDS — England — Reading (Berkshire)

Reading Abbey cartularies : British Library manuscripts - Egerton 3031, Harley 1708 and Cotton Vespasian Exxv / edited by B.R. Kemp. — London : Royal Historical Society 2: Berkshire documents, Scottish charters and miscellaneous documents. — 1987. — [440]p. — (Camden fourth series ; v.33). — Includes bibliography and index

CHURCH OF ENGLAND

MOORE, Charles, 19---
The Church in crisis / Charles Moore, A.N. Wilson, Gavin Stamp. — London : Hodder and Stoughton, 1986. — 223p

CHURCH OF ENGLAND — History — 16th century

TYACKE, Nicholas
Anti-Calvinists : the rise of English Arminianism c.1590-1640 / Nicholas Tyacke. — Oxford : Clarendon, 1987. — [300]p,[4]p of plates. — (Oxford historical monographs). — Includes bibliography and index

CHURCH OF ENGLAND — History — 17th century

TYACKE, Nicholas
Anti-Calvinists : the rise of English Arminianism c.1590-1640 / Nicholas Tyacke. — Oxford : Clarendon, 1987. — [300]p,[4]p of plates. — (Oxford historical monographs). — Includes bibliography and index

CHURCH OF SCOTLAND — Doctrines — Addresses, essays, lectures

KNOX, John
The political writings of John Knox : The first blast of the trumpet against the monstrous regiment of women and other selected works / edited and with an introduction by Marvin A. Breslow. — Washington : Folger Shakespeare Library ; London : Associated University Presses, c1985. — 160 p.. — "Folger books.". — Includes bibliographies. — Contents: The first blast of the trumpet against the monstrous regiment of women (1558) -- Letter to the Regent of Scotland (1558) -- Appellation to the nobility (1558) -- Letter to the commonalty of Scotland (1558) -- The second blast (1558)

CHURCH RECORDS AND REGISTERS — Portugal

AMORIM, Norberta
Método de exploração dos livros de registos paroquiais, e Cardanha e a sua população de 1573 a 1800 / por Norberta Amorim. — Lisboa : Instituto Nacional de Estatística, 1980. — 135p. — (Publicações do Centro de Estudos Demográficos). — Bibliogrpahy: p127

CHURCH RENEWAL — Catholic church

ZABŁOCKI, Janusz
Kościoł i świat współczesny : wprowadzenie do soborowej konstytucji pastoralnej "Gaudium et spes" / Janusz Zabłocki. — 2nd ed. — Warszawa : Ośrodek Dokumentacji i Studiów Społecznych, 1986. — 457p

CHURCH SCHOOLS — United States

PRASZAŁOWICZ, Dorota
Ameryka'nska etniczna szkoła parafialna : studium porównawcze frzech wybranych odmian instytucji / Dorota Praszałowicz. — Wrocław : Ossolineum, 1986. — 226p. — (Biblioteka polonijna ; 15). — Summaries in English

CHURCH SOCIETIES — Directories

UK Christian handbook. — 1987/88 ed. / Peter Brierley, editor ; David Longley, assistant editor. — 1987/88 ed. — London : MARC Europe, 1986. — 649p. — Includes index

CHURCH WORK WITH ALCOHOLICS — United States

MCKINLEY, Edward H
Somebody's brother : a history of the Salvation Army Men's Social Service Department, 1891-1985 / E.H. McKinley. — Lewiston [N.Y.] : Edwin Mellen Press, c1986. — xiii, 273 p., [40] p. of plates. — (Studies in American religion ; v. 21). — Includes index. — Bibliography: p. 217-260

CHURCH WORK WITH YOUTH — United States — Catholic Church

MCAULEY, E. Nancy
Faith without form : beliefs of Catholic youth / E. Nancy McAuley and Moira Mathiesen ; introduction, George Gallup. — Kansas City : Sheed and Ward, 1986. — vi,166p. — Bibliography: p165-6

CHURCHES, ANGLICAN — London — History — 18th century — Sources
COMMISSION FOR BUILDING FIFTY NEW CHURCHES
The Commissions for Building Fifty New Churches : the minute books, 1711-27 : a calendar / edited by M.H.Port. — London : London Record Society, 1986. — xl, 193p. — (London Record Society publications ; v.23)

CHURCHILL, Sir WINSTON
HARBUTT, Fraser J
The iron curtain : Churchill, America, and the origins of the Cold War / Fraser J. Harbutt. — New York ; Oxford : Oxford University Press, 1986. — xiv, 370p. — *Includes index. — Bibliography: p.341-353*

CHURCHILL, WINSTON S.
GILBERT, Martin
Winston S. Churchill / by Martin Gilbert. — London : Heinemann
Vol. 7: Road to victory, 1941-1945. — 1986. — 1417 p.

CHURCHILL, WINSTON S. (Winston Spencer), 1874-1965
DAY, David
Menzies & Churchill at war : a controversial new account of the 1941 struggle for power / David Day. — North Ryde : Angus & Robertson, 1986. — xii, 271p

CICERO, MARCUS TULLIUS
COWELL, F. R.
Cicero and the Roman Republic. — London : Pitman, 1948. — xiv, 306p

COWELL, F. R.
Cicero and the Roman Republic. — 3rd ed. — Harmondsworth : Penguin, 1964. — xvii, 398p.

CIGAR INDUSTRY — Germany — History
BUSCHAK, Willy
Von Menschen, die wie Menschen leben wollten : die Geschichte der Gewerkschaft Nahrung-Genuss-Gaststätten und ihrer Vorläufer / Willy Buschak ; Vorwork: Günter Döding. — Köln : Bund, 1985. — 645p. — *Bibliography: p634-639*

CIGAR MAKERS — Germany — Social conditions
BUSCHAK, Willy
Von Menschen, die wie Menschen leben wollten : die Geschichte der Gewerkschaft Nahrung-Genuss-Gaststätten und ihrer Vorläufer / Willy Buschak ; Vorwork: Günter Döding. — Köln : Bund, 1985. — 645p. — *Bibliography: p634-639*

CIGARETTE HABIT
JACOBSON, Bobbie
Beating the ladykillers : women and smoking / Bobbie Jacobson. — London : Pluto, 1986. — [192]p. — *Includes index*

CILICIA (TURKEY) — History
SAAKIAN, R. G.
Franko-turetskie otnosheniia i Kilikiia v 1918-1923 gg. / R. G. Saakian. — Erevan : Izd-vo AN Armianskoi SSR, 1986. — 281p. — *Summary in French. — Bibliography: p245-272*

CINCINNATI (OHIO) — Politics and government
THOMAS, John Clayton
Between citizen and city : neighborhood organizations and urban politics in Cincinnati / John Clayton Thomas. — Lawrence : University Press of Kansas, c1986. — xii, 196 p.. — (Studies in government and public policy). — *Includes index. — Bibliography: p. 179-188*

CIRCULAR VELOCITY OF MONEY — Great Britain
CAPIE, Forrest
The long run behaviour of velocity in the U.K. / Forrest H. Capie and Geoffrey E. Wood. — London : Centre for Banking and International Finance, City University, 1986. — 16p. — (Monetary history discussion paper series ; no.23). — *Bibliography: p15-16*

CIRCUMCISION
BLOCH, Maurice
From blessing to violence : history and ideology in the circumcision ritual of the Merina of Madagascar / Maurice Bloch. — Cambridge : Cambridge University Press, 1986. — x,214p. — (Cambridge studies in social anthropology ; 61). — *Bibliography: p200-205*

CITIES AND TOWNS
BOOKCHIN, Murray
The limits of the city : with a new introduction / Murray Bookchin. — 2nd rev, ed. — Montreal ; Buffalo N.Y. : Black Rose Books, 1986. — xi,194p. — *First published: New York: Harper & Row, 1974. — Includes bibliography*

Geography and the urban environment : progress in research and applications. — Chichester : Wiley. — *Includes bibliographies and index*
Vol. 3 / edited by D.T. Herbert and R.J. Johnston. — c1980. — xiii,428p

Geography and the urban environment : progress in research and applications. — Chichester : Wiley. — c1981
Vol.4 / edited by D.T. Herbert and R.J. Johnston. — xiii,354p. — *Includes bibliographies and index*

LEY, David
A social geography of the city / David Ley. — New York : Harper & Row, c1983. — xii,449p. — (Harper & Row series in geography). — *Bibliography: p.401-441*

MUMFORD, Lewis
The culture of cities / Lewis Mumford. — New York : Harcourt, Brace, 1938. — xii,586p

MUMFORD, Lewis
The culture of cities / Lewis Mumford. — London : Secker, 1940. — xii,530p

Perspectives in urban geography. — New Delhi : Concept Publishing
Vol.1: New directions in urban geography / edited by C. S. Yadav. — 1986. — 347p. — *Includes bibliographies and index*

Perspectives in urban geography. — New Delhi : Concept Publishing
Vol.3: Comparative urbanization : city growth and change / edited by C. S. Yadav. — 1986. — 420p. — *Includes bibliographies and index*

Perspectives in urban geography. — New Delhi : Concept Publishing
Vol. 5: Urban research methods : central place, hierarchical and city size models / edited by C. S. Yadav. — 1986. — 320p. — *Includes bibliographies and index*

Social process and the city / edited by Peter Williams. — London : Allen & Unwin, 1983. — 233p. — (Urban studies yearbook ; 1)

CITIES AND TOWNS — Addresses, essays, lectures
World patterns of modern urban change : essays in honor of Chauncy D. Harris / edited by Michael P. Conzen. — Chicago : University of Chicago, Dept. of Geography, 1985. — p. cm. — (Research paper / the University of Chicago, Department of Geography ; no. 217-218). — *Includes index*

CITIES AND TOWNS — Congresses
Pouvoir local et urbanisme : Colloque de Lyon - 16-17 Octobre 1980 / Christian Barbier...[et al.]. — Lyon : Université Lyon II, U.E.R. Sciences juridiques, Centre de recherches sur les institutions publiques : Presses universitaires de Lyon, 1981. — 170p

CITIES AND TOWNS — Growth
BOOKCHIN, Murray
The limits of the city : with a new introduction / Murray Bookchin. — 2nd rev, ed. — Montreal ; Buffalo N.Y. : Black Rose Books, 1986. — xi,194p. — *First published: New York: Harper & Row, 1974. — Includes bibliography*

CITIES AND TOWNS — Growth — Congresses
INTERNATIONAL SYMPOSIUM ON THE CRISIS OF THE CENTRAL CITY AND THE TAKE-OFF OF SUBURBIA (1984 : Munich & Vienna)
The take-off of suburbia and the crisis of the central city : proceedings of the International Symposium in Munich and Vienna 1984 / edited by Günter Heinritz and Elisabeth Lichtenberger. — Stuttgart : Steiner, 1986. — [viii],301p. — (Erdkundliches Wissen ; Heft 76)

CITIES AND TOWNS — Growth — History
KONVITZ, Josef W
The urban millennium : the city-building process from the early Middle Ages to the present / Josef W. Konvitz. — Carbondale : Southern Illinois University Press, c1985. — p. cm. — *Includes index. — Bibliography: p*

CITIES AND TOWNS — Handbooks, manuals, etc
MARLIN, John Tepper
Book of world city rankings / John Tepper Marlin, Immanuel Ness, and Stephen T. Collins. — New York : Free Press ; London : Collier Macmillan, c1986. — xiii, 604 p.. — *Includes bibliographies*

CITIES AND TOWNS — History
KONVITZ, Josef W
The urban millennium : the city-building process from the early Middle Ages to the present / Josef W. Konvitz. — Carbondale : Southern Illinois University Press, c1985. — p. cm. — *Includes index. — Bibliography: p*

CITIES AND TOWNS — Mathematical models
FOOT, David, 1939-
Operational urban models : an introduction / David Foot. — London : Methuen, 1981. — xviii,231p. — *Bibliography: p214-220. — Includes index*

Urban systems : contemporary approaches to modelling / edited by C.S. Bertuglia ... [et al.]. — London : Croom Helm, c1987. — 677p. — *Bibliography: p597-650. — Includes index*

CITIES AND TOWNS — Quotations, maxims, etc — Dictionaries
CLAPP, James A
The city, a dictionary of quotable thought on cities and urban life / James A. Clapp. — New Brunswick, N.J. : Center for Urban Policy Research, c1984. — xxv, 288 p... — *Includes indexes*

CITIES AND TOWNS — Research
Perspectives in urban geography. — New Delhi : Concept Publishing
Vol.2: Comparative urban research / edited by C. S. Yadav. — 1986. — 219p. — *Includes bibliographies and index*

CITIES AND TOWNS — Research — Great Britain
GREAT BRITAIN. Department of the Environment
Brief for external research on inner city areas. — [London : the Department, 1977]. — 8 leaves

GREAT BRITAIN. Department of the Environment
Invitation to submit proposals for research on inner city areas. — London : the Department, 1977. — 4 leaves

CITIES AND TOWNS — Social conditions
Perspectives in urban geography. — New Delhi : Concept Publishing
Vol.7: Slums, urban decline and revitalization / edited by C. S. Yadav. — 1987. — 288p. — *Includes bibliographies and index*

CITIES AND TOWNS — Statistics

MARLIN, John Tepper
Book of world city rankings / John Tepper Marlin, Immanuel Ness, and Stephen T. Collins. — New York : Free Press ; London : Collier Macmillan, c1986. — xiii, 604 p.. — *Includes bibliographies*

CITIES AND TOWNS — Africa

Feeding African cities : studies in regional social history / edited by Jane I. Guyer. — Manchester : Manchester University Press for the International African Institute, London, c1987. — x,249p. — (International African library ; 2). — *Includes bibliographies and index*

CITIES AND TOWNS — Africa — Bibliography

AJAEGBU, Hyacinth I.
African urbanization : a bibliography / compiled by Hyacinth I. Ajaegbu. — London : International African Institute, 1972. — vi,78p

CITIES AND TOWNS — Ahmedabad

DOSHI, Harish
Traditional neighbourhood in a modern city / Harish Doshi. — New Delhi : Abhinav Publications, 1974. — x,154p. — *Bibliographic references: p[147]-150*

CITIES AND TOWNS — Arab countries

Middle Eastern cities in comparative perspective = Points de vue sur les villes du Maghreb et du Machrek : Franco-British Symposium London, 10-14 May 1984 / edited by Kenneth Brown ... [et al.]. — London : Ithaca, 1986. — 341p. — (Middle Eastern cultures series ; 11). — *Text in English and French. — Includes bibliographies and index*

CITIES AND TOWNS — Australia

SANDERCOCK, Leonie
Urban political economy : the Australian case / Leonie Sandercock, Michael Berry. — Sydney ; Boston : G. Allen & Unwin, 1983. — xi, 193 p.. — *Includes index. — Bibliography: p. 179-187*

CITIES AND TOWNS — Australia — Growth

Urban Australia : planning issues and policies / [edited by] Stephen Hamnett and Raymond Bunker. — London : Mansell, 1987, c1986. — [208]p. — *Includes index*

CITIES AND TOWNS — Australia — Brisbane (Qld.) — Growth

COLE, John R.
Shaping a city : Greater Brisbane 1925-1985 / by John R. Cole. — Eagle Farm (Qld.) : William Brooks Queensland, 1984. — 416p. — *Bibliography: p411-416*

CITIES AND TOWNS — Botswana — Statistics

1981 population and housing census : guide to the villages and towns of Botswana. — Gaborone : Central Statistics Office, [1983]. — 1 vol.(various pagings)

CITIES AND TOWNS — Brazil — History

SALGADO, Plínio
Como nasceram as cidades do Brasil / Plínio Salgado. — 5a. edição. — São Paulo : Voz do Oeste ; [Brasília] : Instituto Nacional do Livro, MEC, 1978. — xxi,195p. — *Publicado originalmente em Lisboa por Ática, 1946. — Bibliography: pxvii-xxi*

CITIES AND TOWNS — Canada

GOLDBERG, Michael A.
The myth of the North American city : continentalism challenged / Michael A. Goldberg and John Mercer. — Vancouver : University of British Columbia Press, 1986. — xx,308p

CITIES AND TOWNS — Canada — Growth

CARELESS, J. M. S.
The rise of cities in Canada before 1914 / J. M. S. Careless. — Ottawa : Canadian Historical Association, 1978. — 26, [2] p.. — (Historical booklet / Canadian Historical Association ; no.32). — *Bibliography: p.[27]*

CITIES AND TOWNS — Canada — Growth — Addresses, essays, lectures

Power and place : Canadian urban development in the North American context / edited by Gilbert A. Stelter and Alan F. J. Artibise. — Vancouver : University of British Columbia Press, 1986. — 398p. — *Based on papers presented at the Canadian-American Urban Development Conference held at the University of Guelph in August 1982*

CITIES AND TOWNS — Canada — History

CARELESS, J. M. S.
The rise of cities in Canada before 1914 / J. M. S. Careless. — Ottawa : Canadian Historical Association, 1978. — 26, [2] p.. — (Historical booklet / Canadian Historical Association ; no.32). — *Bibliography: p.[27]*

CITIES AND TOWNS — Canada — History — Addresses, essays, lectures

Power and place : Canadian urban development in the North American context / edited by Gilbert A. Stelter and Alan F. J. Artibise. — Vancouver : University of British Columbia Press, 1986. — 398p. — *Based on papers presented at the Canadian-American Urban Development Conference held at the University of Guelph in August 1982*

CITIES AND TOWNS — Caribbean Area — Growth

HOPE, Kempe R
Urbanization in the Commonwealth Caribbean / Kempe Ronald Hope. — Boulder, Colo. : Westview Press, 1986. — p. cm. — (Westview special studies on Latin America and the Caribbean). — *Includes index. — Bibliography: p*

CITIES AND TOWNS — China — Growth

Chinese cities : the growth of the metropolis since 1949 / editor, Victor F. S. Sit ; contributors, Dong Liming ... [et al.]. — Oxford : Oxford University Press, 1985. — xvi,239p

CITIES AND TOWNS — Developing countries

LOWDER, Stella
Inside Third World cities / Stella Lowder. — London : Croom Helm, c1986. — [288]p. — *Includes bibliography and index*

Small and intermediate urban centres : their role in regional and national development in the Third World / edited by Jorge E. Hardoy and David Satterthwaite. — London : Hodder and Stoughton in association with the United Nations University, 1986. — [416]p. — *Includes bibliography and index*

CITIES AND TOWNS — Ethiopia — Bagēmder — Case studies

BAKER, Jonathan
The rural-urban dichotomy in the developing world : a case study from northern Ethiopia / Jonathan Baker. — Oslo : Norwegian University Press : Oxford ; New York : Distributed world-wide excluding Scandinavia by Oxford University Press, c1986. — 372 p.. — *Bibliography: p. [365]-372*

CITIES AND TOWNS — Europe — Growth — History

WRIGLEY, E. A.
People, cities and wealth : the transformation of traditional society / E.A. Wrigley. — Oxford : Basil Blackwell, 1987. — [400]p. — *Includes bibliography and index*

CITIES AND TOWNS — Finland

Ways of Life in Finland and Poland : comparative studies on urban populations / edited by J.P. Roos and Andrzej Sicinski. — Aldershot : Avebury, c1987. — viii,203p. — *Includes bibliographies*

CITIES AND TOWNS — France

OSTROWETSKY, Sylvia
L'imaginaire bâtisseur : les villes nouvelles françaises / préface de Louis Marin. — Paris : Librairie des Méridiens, 1983. — viii,345p. — *Bibliography: p331-342*

CITIES AND TOWNS — Great Britain

Critical issues in urban economic development / edited by Victor A. Hausner. — Oxford : Clarendon. — (Publications in the inner cities research programme series ; 8)
Vol.1. — 1986. — [240]p. — *Includes index*

TOWN AND COUNTRY PLANNING ASSOCIATION
Whose responsibility? : reclaiming the inner cities. — London : TCPA, 1986. — 40p

CITIES AND TOWNS — Great Britain — Conservation and restoration

GREAT BRITAIN. Department of the Environment. Yorkshire and Humberside Regional Office
Positive urban conservation. — [Leeds] : the Office, [1974]. — v,90p. — *Produced for European Architectural Heritage Year 1975*

CITIES AND TOWNS — Great Britain — History

LAWLESS, Paul
Urban growth and change in Britain : an introduction / Paul Lawless and Frank Brown. — London : Harper & Row, 1986. — 247p. — *Includes bibliographies*

CITIES AND TOWNS — India

Indian cities : ecological perspectives / edited by Vinod K. Tewari, Jay A. Weinstein, V. L. S. Prakasa Rao. — New Delhi : Concept Publishing Company, 1986. — 289p. — *Bibliography: p273-284*

CITIES AND TOWNS — India — Growth

MILLS, Edwin S
Studies in Indian urban development / Edwin S. Mills, Charles M. Becker ; with a contribution by Satyendra Verma. — Washington, D.C. : Published for the World Bank [by] Oxford University Press, 1986. — viii, 214 p.. — (A World Bank research publication). — *Includes bibliographies and index*

MILLS, Edwin S.
Studies in Indian urban development / Edwin S. Mills, Charles M. Becker. — New York : OUP for the World Bank, 1986. — viii,214p. — *Includes bibliographical references*

CITIES AND TOWNS — India — History

NAQVI, Hameeda Khatoon
Urbanisation and urban centres under the Great Mughals 1556-1707 : an essay in interpretation / Hameeda Khatoon Naqvi. — Simla : Indian Institute of Advanced Study
Vol.1. — 1971. — 210p. — *Bibliography: p [187]-192*

CITIES AND TOWNS — India — Bihar — Growth

SINGH, Ram Dayal
Population structure of Indian cities : a case study of the cities of Bihar / Ram Dayal Singh. — New Delhi : Inter-India Publications, 1985. — x,173p. — *Bibliography: p[158]-167*

CITIES AND TOWNS — India — Growth

Urban growth and urban planning : political context and people's priorities / edited by Alfred de Souza. — New Delhi : Indian Social Institute, c1983. — xi, 163 p.. — *Includes index. — Bibliography: p. [155]-160. — Contents: The challenge of urbanisation and the response / C.S. Chandrasekhara -- Patterns of urban growth, 1971-81 / Ashish Bose -- An approach to urban land policy / Louis Menezes -- Planning for the urban poor: basic needs and priorities / E.F.N. Ribeiro -- Ahmedabad slums: redefining strategies for action / Kirtee Shah -- Rural-urban migration of women: some implications for urban planning / Andrea Menefee Singh -- Urban growth and urban planning / Alfred de Souza*

CITIES AND TOWNS — Mexico

RAMOS G., Sergio
Urbanización y servicios públicos en México / Sergio Ramos G.. — México D.F. : Universidad Nacional Autónoma de México, Instituto de Investigaciones Sociales, 1972. — 192p

CITIES AND TOWNS — Middle West — Case studies

ELAZAR, Daniel Judah
Cities of the prairie revisited : the closing of the metropolitan frontier / Daniel J. Elazar with Rozann Rothman ... [et al.]. — Lincoln : University of Nebraska Press, c1986. — 288 p.. — *Sequel to: Cities of the prairie. Includes index. — Bibliography: p. [269]-276*

CITIES AND TOWNS — Middle West — Economic conditions

The Metropolitan Midwest : policy problems and prospects for change / edited by Barry Checkoway and Carl V. Patton. — Urbana : University of Illinois Press, c1985. — 309 p.. — *Includes bibliographies*

CITIES AND TOWNS — Middle West — Social conditions

The Metropolitan Midwest : policy problems and prospects for change / edited by Barry Checkoway and Carl V. Patton. — Urbana : University of Illinois Press, c1985. — 309 p.. — *Includes bibliographies*

CITIES AND TOWNS — Poland

DĘBSKI, Jerzy
Integracja wielkich miast Polski w zakresie powiązań towarowych / Jerzy Dębski. — Wrocław : Ossolineum, 1980. — 125p. — (Prace geograficzne / Polska Akademia Nauk. Instytut Geografii i Przestrzennego Zagospodarowania ; Nr.135). — *Summary in Russian and English. — Bibliography: p115-119*

Ways of Life in Finland and Poland : comparative studies on urban populations / edited by J.P. Roos and Andrzej Sicinski. — Aldershot : Avebury, c1987. — viii,203p. — *Includes bibliographies*

CITIES AND TOWNS — Poland — Growth

KOTER, Marek
Geneza układu przestrzennego Łodzi przemysłowej / Marek Koter. — Warszawa : Państwowe Wydawnictwo Naukowe, 1969. — 134p. — (Prace geograficzne / Polska Akademia Nauk. Instytut Geografii ; Nr.79). — *Summary in Russian and English. — Bibliography: p118-[121]*

Studia nad migracjami i przemianami systemu osadniczego w Polsce : opracowanie zbiorowe / pod redakcją Kazimierza Dziewoʹnskiego i Piotra Korcellego. — Wrocław : Ossolineum, 1981. — 267p. — (Prace geograficzne / Polska Akademia Nauk. Instytut Geografii i Przestrzennego Zagospodarowania ; Nr.140). — *Summaries in Russian and English. — Bibliographies*

CITIES AND TOWNS — Russian S.F.S.R. — Moscow

SAUSHKIN, Iu. G.
Moskva sredi gorodov mira : ekonomiko-geograficheskoe issledovanie / Iu. G. Saushkin, V. G. Glushkova. — Moskva : Mysl', 1983. — 282p

CITIES AND TOWNS — Russian S.F.S.R. — Siberia

Urbanizatsiia sovetskoi Sibiri / otv. redaktor V. V. Alekseev. — Novosibirsk : Nauka, Sibirskoe otdelenie, 1987. — 222p

CITIES AND TOWNS — Scotland — History — 16th century

The Early modern town in Scotland / edited by Michael Lynch. — London : Croom Helm, c1987. — 262p. — *Bibliography: p245-249. Includes index*

CITIES AND TOWNS — Scotland — History — 17th century

The Early modern town in Scotland / edited by Michael Lynch. — London : Croom Helm, c1987. — 262p. — *Bibliography: p245-249. Includes index*

CITIES AND TOWNS — Soviet Union

ROMANENKOVA, G. M.
Trudovye resursy krupnogo goroda / G. M. Romanenkova ; pod redaktsiei V. R. Polozova. — Leningrad : Nauka, Leningradskoe otdelenie, 1986. — 159p

CITIES AND TOWNS — Soviet Union — History — Addresses, essays, lectures

The City in late imperial Russia / edited by Michael F. Hamm. — Bloomington : Indiana University Press, c1986. — viii, 372p. — (Indiana-Michigan series in Russian and East European studies). — *Papers from a meeting of the American Association for the Advancement of Slavic Studies, held in Kansas City, Mo., Oct. 1983. Includes index. — Bibliography: p.[355]-359*

CITIES AND TOWNS — Sunbelt States — Growth

ABBOTT, Carl
The new urban America : growth and politics in Sunbelt cities / Carl Abbott. — Rev. ed. — Chapel Hill : University of North Carolina Press, c1987. — p. cm. — *Includes index. — Bibliography: p*

CITIES AND TOWNS — United States

The Egalitarian city : issues of rights, distribution, access, and power / edited by Janet K. Boles. — New York : Praeger, 1986. — xiv, 223 p.. — *Includes bibliographies*

GOLDBERG, Michael A.
The myth of the North American city : continentalism challenged / Michael A. Goldberg and John Mercer. — Vancouver : University of British Columbia Press, 1986. — xx,308p

STERNLIEB, George
Patterns of development / by George Sternlieb. — New Brunswick, N.J. : Center for Urban Policy Research, c1986. — p. cm. — *Includes index. — Bibliography: p*

Urban ethnicity in the United States : new immigrants and old minorities / edited by Lionel Maldonado and Joan Moore. — Beverly Hills ; London : Sage Publications, c1985. — 304p. — (Urban affairs annual reviews ; v. 29). — *"Published in cooperation with the Urban Research Center, University of Wisconsin--Milwaukee.". — Bibliography: p 277-301*

CITIES AND TOWNS — United States — Addresses, essays, lectures

Internal structure of the city : readings on urban form, growth, and policy / edited by Larry S. Bourne. — 2nd ed. — New York : Oxford University Press, 1982. — xi, 629 p.. — *Bibliography: p. 619-629*

The Urban predicament / edited by William Gorham, Nathan Glazer. — Washington : Urban Institute, c1976. — xix, 363 p.. — *Includes bibliographical references and index*

CITIES AND TOWNS — United States — Growth

LOGAN, John R.
Urban fortunes : the political economy of place / John R. Logan, Harvey L. Molotch. — Berkeley, CA : University of California Press, 1987. — p. cm. — *Includes index. — Bibliography: p*

CITIES AND TOWNS — United States — Growth — Case studies

AMOS, Harriet E.
Cotton City : urban development in antebellum Mobile / Harriet E. Amos. — University, Ala. : University of Alabama Press, c1985. — xvi, 311 p.. — *Includes index. — Bibliography: p. 287-297*

CITIES AND TOWNS — United States — History — 19th century

SCHUYLER, David
The new urban landscape : the redefinition of city form in nineteenth-century America / David Schuyler. — Baltimore ; London : Johns Hopkins University Press, c1986. — xiv, 237p. — (New studies in American intellectual and cultural history). — *Includes index. — Bibliography: p.227-232*

CITIES AND TOWNS — United States — History — 20th century

KIRSCHNER, D. S.
The paradox of professionalism : reform and public service in urban America, 1900-1940 / by D.S. Kirschner. — Westport, Conn. ; London : Greenwood, 1987. — [224]p. — (Contributions in American history ; no.119). — *Includes bibliography and index*

TEAFORD, Jon C
The twentieth-century American city : problem, promise, and reality / Jon C. Teaford. — Baltimore ; London : Johns Hopkins University Press, c1986. — x, 177p. — (The American moment). — *Includes index. — Bibliography: p.[157]-169*

CITIES AND TOWNS — Uzbek S.S.R. — History

MUKMINOVA, R. G.
Sotsial'naia differentsiatsiia naseleniia gorodov Uzbekistana, konets XV-XVI v. / R. G. Mukminova. — Tashkent : "Fan" Uzbekskoi SSR, 1985. — 135p

CITIES AND TOWNS — Wales — Clwyd

CLWYD. County Council
Clwyd county structure plan : public participation seminar : urban communities : report of proceedings. — Mold : [the Council], 1975. — 23p

CITIES AND TOWNS, ISLAMIC — Middle East — History — Congresses

The Middle East city : ancient traditions confront a modern world / edited by Abdulaziz Y. Saqqaf. — New York : Paragon House, c1987. — xx, 393 p.. — *Proceedings of a conference sponsored by the Middle East Chapter of the Professors World Peace Academy. — "A PWPA book.". — Includes bibliographies and index*

CITIES AND TOWNS, MEDIEVAL — England — Winchester (Hampshire)

KEENE, Derek
Survey of medieval Winchester / Derek Keene with a contribution by Alexander R. Rumble. — Oxford : Clarendon, 1985. — 2v.(xxxviii,1490p,[10]p of plates). — (Winchester studies ; 2). — *Maps (6 folded sheets) and table (1 folded sheet) in pocket in first volume. — Includes index*

CITIESA AND TOWNS — Vanuatu — Statistics

Report of the Vanuatu urban census 1986. — [Port Vila?] : National Planning and Statistics Office, 1986. — 157p

CITIZENS' ASSOCIATIONS — England — London
CHILDS, Di
Citizens' advice : a study of who uses London's Citizens Advice Bureaux and the service they receive / Di Childs, Angela Hickey [and] Jane Winter ; edited by Barbara Fletcher. — London : Greater London Citizens' Advice Bureau, 1985. — 46p

CITIZENS' ASSOCIATIONS — Missouri — Kansas City
SHARP, Elaine B
Citizen demand-making in the urban context / Elaine B. Sharp. — University, AL : University of Alabama Press, c1986. — p. cm. — *Includes index. — Bibliography: p*

CITIZENS' ASSOCIATIONS — Ohio — Cincinnati
THOMAS, John Clayton
Between citizen and city : neighborhood organizations and urban politics in Cincinnati / John Clayton Thomas. — Lawrence : University Press of Kansas, c1986. — xii, 196 p.. — (Studies in government and public policy). — *Includes index. — Bibliography: p. 179-188*

CITIZENS' ASSOCIATIONS — United States
WILLIAMS, Michael R.
Neighborhood organizations : seeds of a new urban life / Michael R. Williams. — Westport, Conn. : Greenwood Press, 1985. — xiii, 278 p.. — (Contributions in political science ; no. 131). — *Includes index. — Bibliography: p. [261]-269*

CITIZENSHIP — France
FRANCE. Ministere de la Justice
La nationalité française : textes et documents. — Paris : La Documentation Française, 1985. — 327p

CITIZENSHIP — France — Philosophy
VERNON, Richard
Citizenship and order : studies in French political thought / Richard Vernon. — Toronto ; Buffalo : University of Toronto Press, c1986. — 264 p.. — *Includes index. — Bibliography: p. [253]-260*

CITIZENSHIP — Great Britain
CRONIN, Kathryn
Children, nationality and immigration : a handbook on nationality, immigration and international family law affecting children and young people / written by Kathryn Cronin for the Children's Legal Centre. — London : Children's Legal Centre, 1985. — 146p. — *Bibliography: p127-132*

GRAY, Kevin J.
Property, divorce and retirement pension rights / by K.J. Gray. British nationality and the right of abode 1948-1983 / by C.C. Turpin. — Deventer ; London : Kluwer, 1986. — vii,269p. — (Cambridge-Tilburg law lectures ; 5th ser., 1982). — *Includes bibliographical references*

GREAT BRITAIN. Parliament. House of Commons. Library. Research Division
Nationality / [Fiona Poole]. — [London] : the Division, 1980. — 19p. — (Reference sheet ; no.80/15). — *Bibliographical references: p18-19*

CITIZENSHIP — Puerto Rico
FUSTER, Jaime B.
Deberes y obligaciones del ciudadano responsable / Jaime B. Fuster. — Segunda edición revisada. — San Juan : Comision de Derechos Civiles, 1974. — ix,49p. — *Publicado originalmente en 1973*

CITIZENSHIP — United States
COLLINS, Donald E
Native American aliens : renunciation of citizenship by Japanese Americans during World War II / Donald E. Collins. — Westport, Conn. : Greenwood Press, c1985. — p. cm. — (Contributions in legal studies ; no. 32). — *Includes index. — Bibliography: p*

CITY AND TOWN LIFE
The Quality of urban life : social, psychological, and physical conditions / edited by Dieter Frick in cooperation with Hans-Wolfgang Hoefert ... [et al.]. — Berlin ; New York : De Gruyter, 1986. — x, 262 p.. — *Includes bibliographies and index*

CITY AND TOWN LIFE — Canada
MCGAHAN, Peter
Urban sociology in Canada / Peter McGahan. — 2nd ed. — Toronto : Butterworths, 1986. — vi,334p. — *Bibliography: p[271]-323*

CITY AND TOWN LIFE — European Economic Community countries
Living conditions in urban areas : an overview of factors influencing urban life in the European Community. — Luxembourg : Office for Official Publications of the European Communities, 1986. — v, 163, 47p

CITY AND TOWN LIFE — Spain — Catalonia
Conflict in Catalonia : images of an urban society / edited by Gary W. McDonogh. — Gainesville : University Presses of Florida, University of Florida Press, c1986. — 102 p.. — (University of Florida monographs. Social sciences ; no. 71). — *Includes bibliographies and index*

CITY OF LONDON — Periodicals
The City Press : the City of London newspaper. — London : The City Press, 1945-1975. — *Weekly*

CITY PLANNING
BRACKEN, Ian
Urban planning methods : research and policy analysis / Ian Bracken. — London : Methuen, 1981. — xii,400p. — *Bibliography: p357-388. — Includes index*

ELSON, Martin J.
Green belts : conflict mediation in the urban fringe / Martin J. Elson. — London : Heinemann, 1986. — xxxi,304p. — *Includes index*

FALUDI, Andreas
A decision-centred view of environmental planning / by Andreas Faludi. — Oxford : Pergamon, 1987. — xiii,240p. — (Urban and regional planning series ; v.38). — *Includes bibliographies and index*

OWENS, Susan E.
Energy, planning and urban form / Susan Owens. — London : Pion, c1986. — 118p. — *Bibliography: p107-116. — Includes index*

RAMSAY, Anthony
Planning new towns : a review of ideas, policies, plans and programmes relating to new towns together with a guide to relevant documents and organisations / compiled by Anthony Ramsay. — Edinburgh : Capital Planning Information Limited, 1985. — 33p. — (CPI topicguides ; no.6). — *Bibliography: p.19-31*

CITY PLANNING — Addresses, essays, lectures
Strengthening urban management : international perspectives and issues / edited by Thomas L. Blair. — New York : Plenum Press, c1985. — p. cm. — (Urban innovation abroad). — "Published in cooperation with the International Union of Local Authorities, The Hague, Netherlands.". — *Includes indexes. — Bibliography: p*

CITY PLANNING — Congresses
INTERNATIONAL SYMPOSIUM ON THE CRISIS OF THE CENTRAL CITY AND THE TAKE-OFF OF SUBURBIA (1984 : Munich & Vienna)
The take-off of suburbia and the crisis of the central city : proceedings of the International Symposium in Munich and Vienna 1984 / edited by Günter Heinritz and Elisabeth Lichtenberger. — Stuttgart : Steiner, 1986. — [viii],301p. — (Erdkundliches Wissen ; Heft 76)

CITY PLANNING — Dictionaries — Polyglot
LOGIE, Gordon
Glossary of land resources : English-French-Italian-Dutch-German-Swedish / Gordon Logie. — Amsterdam ; New York : Elsevier, 1984. — xxvii, 303 p.. — (International planning glossaries ; 4). — *Includes indexes. — Bibliography: p. 299-300*

CITY PLANNING — Dictionaries, Polyglot
LOGIE, Gordon
Glossary of planning and development : English-French-Italian-Dutch-German-Swedish / Gordon Logie. — Amsterdam ; Oxford : Elsevier, 1986. — xxv,254p. — (International planning glossaries ; 5). — *Text in English and various other European languages. — Bibliography: p251-252*

CITY PLANNING — Economic aspects — Zambia — Lusaka
PASTEUR, D.
Management for the absorption of newcomers in Lusaka / D. Pasteur. — Norwich : Geo Books ; Birmingham : Development Administration Group, Institute of Local Government Studies, University of Birmingham, [ca.1976]. — 98p. — (Papers in the administration of development ; no.2)

CITY PLANNING — Environmental aspects — United States — History — 19th century
SCHUYLER, David
The new urban landscape : the redefinition of city form in nineteenth-century America / David Schuyler. — Baltimore ; London : Johns Hopkins University Press, c1986. — xiv, 237p. — (New studies in American intellectual and cultural history). — *Includes index. — Bibliography: p.227-232*

CITY PLANNING — Evaluation — Handbooks, manuals, etc.
BAMBERGER, Michael
A manager's guide to monitoring and evaluating urban development programs : a handbook for program managers and researchers / Michael Bamberger and Eleanor Hewitt. — Washington, D.C. : The World Bank, 1987. — v,22p. — (World Bank technical paper ; no.54). — *Includes bibliographical references*

CITY PLANNING — Evaluation — Handbooks, manuals, etc
BAMBERGER, Michael
Monitoring and evaluating urban development programs : a handbook for program managers and researchers / Michael Bamberger and Eleanor Hewitt. — Washington, D.C. : The World Bank, 1986. — xxvii,263p. — (World Bank technical paper ; no.53). — *Bibliographical references: p257-263*

CITY PLANNING — History
KONVITZ, Josef W
The urban millennium : the city-building process from the early Middle Ages to the present / Josef W. Konvitz. — Carbondale : Southern Illinois University Press, c1985. — p. cm. — *Includes index. — Bibliography: p*

RELPH, Edward
The modern urban landscape / Edward Relph. — London : Croom Helm, c1987. — 279p. — *Bibliography: p268-273. — Includes index*

CITY PLANNING — Mathematical models
LEE, Colin
Models in planning : an introduction to the use of quantitative models in planning / C. Lee. — Oxford : Pergamon, 1973. — x,142p. — (Urban and regional planning series ; v.4). — *Includes index*

CITY PLANNING — Mathematical models — Congresses

Advances in urban systems modelling / editors, Bruce Hutchinson and Michael Batty. — Amsterdam ; New York : North-Holland ; New York, N.Y., U.S.A. : Sole distributors for the U.S.A. and Canada, Elsevier Science Pub. Co., 1986. — xi, 432 p.. — (Studies in regional science and urban economics ; v. 15). — *Based on the papers originally presented at the International Symposium on New Directions in Urban Systems Modelling held at the University of Waterloo in July, 1983. — Includes bibliographies*

CITY PLANNING — Moral and ethical aspects

Ethics in planning / edited by Martin Wachs. — New Brunswick, N.J. : Center for Urban Policy Research, c1985. — xxi, 372 p. — *Includes index. — Bibliography: p. 356-365*

CITY PLANNING — Asia — Congresses

Cities in conflict : studies in the planning and management of Asian cities / edited by John P. Lea and John M. Courtney. — Washington, D.C., U.S.A. : World Bank, 1985. — p. cm. — (A World Bank symposium). — *Outgrowth of a symposium held in Sydney, Australia, June 13-17, 1983, sponsored by the World Bank in association with the Commonwealth Association of Architects and the Royal Australian Institute of Architects. — Bibliography: p*

CITY PLANNING — Australia

Urban Australia : planning issues and policies / [edited by] Stephen Hamnett and Raymond Bunker. — London : Mansell, 1987, c1986. — [208]p. — *Includes index*

With conscious purpose : a history of town planning in South Australia / edited by Alan Hutchings and Raymond Bunker. — Netley : Wakefield Press in association with Royal Australian Planning Institute (South Australian Division), 1986, 1986. — xiv,122p. — *Bibliography: p117-118*

CITY PLANNING — Canada

CULLINGWORTH, J. B
Urban and regional planning in Canada / J. Barry Cullingworth. — New Brunswick, U.S.A. : Transaction Books, c1987. — p. cm. — *Includes index. — Bibliography: p*

CITY PLANNING — Canada — Addresses, essays, lectures

Power and place : Canadian urban development in the North American context / edited by Gilbert A. Stelter and Alan F. J. Artibise. — Vancouver : University of British Columbia Press, 1986. — 398p. — *Based on papers presented at the Canadian-American Urban Development Conference held at the University of Guelph in August 1982*

CITY PLANNING — Canada — History — 19th century

ARTIBISE, Alan F. J
Prairie urban development, 1870-1930 / Alan F.J. Artibise. — Ottawa : Canadian Historical Association, 1981. — 42 p.. — (Historical booklet / Canadian Historical Association ; no.34). — *Bibliography: p. 24-25*

CITY PLANNING — Canada — History — 20th century

ARTIBISE, Alan F. J
Prairie urban development, 1870-1930 / Alan F.J. Artibise. — Ottawa : Canadian Historical Association, 1981. — 42 p.. — (Historical booklet / Canadian Historical Association ; no.34). — *Bibliography: p. 24-25*

CITY PLANNING — China

Chinese cities : the growth of the metropolis since 1949 / editor, Victor F. S. Sit ; contributors, Dong Liming ... [et al.]. — Oxford : Oxford University Press, 1985. — xvi,239p

CITY PLANNING — Denmark — Abstracts

Urban and regional research in Denmark 1981-1983 : an annotated list / prepared by the Danish Building Research Institute, Urban and Regional Planning Division, for the Group of Experts on Urban and Regional Research, United Nations Economic Commission for Europe. — Hørsholm : Danish Building Research Institute, 1984. — 11,66 leaves

CITY PLANNING — Developing countries — Evaluation — Handbooks, manuals, etc.

BAMBERGER, Michael
A manager's guide to monitoring and evaluating urban development programs : a handbook for program managers and researchers / Michael Bamberger and Eleanor Hewitt. — Washington, D.C. : The World Bank, 1987. — v,22p. — (World Bank technical paper ; no.54). — *Includes bibliographical references*

CITY PLANNING — Developing countries — Evaluation — Handbooks, manuals, etc,

BAMBERGER, Michael
Monitoring and evaluating urban development programs : a handbook for program managers and researchers / Michael Bamberger and Eleanor Hewitt. — Washington, D.C. : The World Bank, 1986. — xxvii,263p. — (World Bank technical paper ; no.53). — *Bibliographical references: p257-263*

CITY PLANNING — England

BRUTON, M. J.
Local planning in practice / Michael Bruton and David Nicholson. — London : Hutchinson, 1987. — 452p. — (The Built environment series). — *Bibliography: p421-440. — Includes index*

CITY OF LONDON. Department of Architecture and Planning
City of London local plan : written statement and proposals map. — London : [the Department], 1986. — 226p. — *Includes modifications to the revised plan*

GREENWICH. Planning Department
The people's plan : a community-based local plan for the London Borough of Greenwich. — Greenwich : [the Department], 1986. — 314p. — *Includes two maps*

LAMBETH
Lambeth local plan : Lambeth council's response to the inspector's report on the public local inquiry. — Lambeth : [the Council], 1986. — 133p

LAMBETH
Lambeth local plan July 1984 : inspector's report on the public local inquiry, October 1985. — Lambeth : [the Council], 1986. — 56p

NATHANIEL LICHFIELD AND PARTNERS
Bath minimum physical change study, final report / [Nathaniel Lichfield and Partners]. — London (2 Old Brewery Mews, Hampstead High St., NW3 1PZ) : Nathaniel Lichfield and Partners, 1976. — [5],iii,51p

NATHANIEL LICHFIELD AND PARTNERS
Bath minimum physical change study, technical appendices / [Nathaniel Lichfield and Partners]. — London (2 Old Brewery Mews, Hampstead High St., NW3 1PZ) : Nathaniel Lichfield and Partners, 1976. — [3],98p

CITY PLANNING — England — Central Lancashire New Town (Lancashire) — Citizen participation

WOODCOCK, Geoffrey L.
Planning, politics and communications : a study of the Central Lancashire New Town / Geoffrey L. Woodcock. — Aldershot : Gower, c1986. — ix,235p. — *Bibliography: p222-235*

CITY PLANNING — England — Hertfordshire

MCNAMARA, Paul
Restraint policy and development interests : housing in Dacorum and North Hertfordshire / by Paul McNamara. — [Oxford : Oxford Polytechnic, Dept. of Town Planning], 1982. — iii,75p. — (Working paper / Oxford Polytechnic, Dept. of Town Planning ; no.76). — *Cover title: Housing in Dacorum & North Hertfordshire : restraint policy & development interests. — "... the eighth working paper forming part of an SSRC sponsored study entitled "Land release and development in areas of restraint" - p.i*

Welwyn Garden City : town centre study : a report for public discussion / David Overton with the assistance of the County Surveyor. — Hertford : Hertfordshire County Council, 1973. — 22p. — *Includes folded map*

CITY PLANNING — England — Leicestershire

LEICESTER POLYTECHNIC. School of Land and Building Studies. Research Unit
Development planning in Leicestershire : policies and problems / SLABS Research Unit. — Leicester : School of Land and Building Studies, Leicester Polytechnic, 1984. — iii,51 leaves. — (Housing land in urban areas ; Working paper no.2)

CITY PLANNING — England — London

HACKNEY. Planning Division
The draft Hackney borough plan. — Hackney : [the Division], 1986. — 114p. — *Cover title: London Borough of Hackney: local plan: consultation draft. — Includes folded map in back pocket*

TOWER HAMLETS. Planning Department
Tower Hamlets borough plan, adopted 12th March, 1986. — Tower Hamlets : [the Department], 1986. — v,190,A35p. — *Cover title: Adopted borough plan*

CITY PLANNING — England — Redditch

ANSTIS, Gordon
Redditch : success in the heart of England : the history of Redditch New Town, 1964-1985 / Gordon Anstis ; preface by Sir Edward Thompson ; foreword by Sir Michael Edwardes. — Stevenage, Herts. : Publications for Companies, 1985. — xvi,264p

CITY PLANNING — France — History — Congresses

FRANCO-IRISH SEMINAR OF SOCIAL AND ECONOMIC HISTORIANS (4th : 1984 : Trinity College Dublin)
Cities and merchants : French and Irish perspectives on urban development, 1500-1900 : proceedings of the fourth Franco-Irish Seminar of Social and Economic Historians / edited by P. Butel and L. M. Cullen. — Dublin : Department of Modern History, Trinity College Dublin, 1986. — 259p. — *English and French text. — Maps on lining papers*

CITY PLANNING — Great Britain

Contemporary issues in town planning / edited by K.G. Willis. — Aldershot : Gower, c1986. — [220]p. — *Includes bibliographies*

FRIEND, John Kimball
Local government and strategic choice : an operational research approach to the processes of public planning / J. K. Friend and W. N. Jessop. — 2d ed. — Oxford ; New York : Pergamon Press, 1977. — xxvi, 304 p., [1] leaf of plates (fold.). — (Urban and regional planning series ; v. 14) (Pergamon international library of science, technology, engineering and social studies). — *Includes index. — Bibliography: p. 297-298*

GREAT BRITAIN. Department of the Environment
Demonstration sites in the United Kingdom. — [London] : the Department, 1976. — 19p. — (Planning in the United Kingdom). — *Paper presented at the United Nations Conference on Human Settlements, 1976, Vancouver*

CITY PLANNING — Great Britain
continuation

GREAT BRITAIN. Department of the Environment
United Kingdom memorandum on current trends and policies in the fields of housing, building and planning during the year 1975. — [London] : the Department, [1976]. — ii,28p. — *Prepared for the thirty-seventh session of the Committee on Housing, Building and Planning, United Nations Economic Commission for Europe*

GREAT BRITAIN. Parliament. House of Commons. Library. Research Division
Town and country planning : the Dobry reports and the Community Land Bill. — [London] : the Division, 1975. — 11 leaves. — (Background paper ; no.42)

GREAT BRITAIN. Parliament. House of Commons. Library. Research Division
Town and country planning : conservation and European Architectural Heritage Year 1975. — [London] : the Division, [1975]. — 18 leaves. — (Background paper ; no.46). — *Bibliographical references: leaf 18*

PETRELLI, Robert
Structure planning and the coordination of policies within British local authorities. — 316 leaves. — *PhD (Econ) 1986 LSE*

Planning control : philosophies, prospects and practice / edited by M.L. Harrison and R. Mordey. — London : Croom Helm, c1987. — 234p. — (Croom Helm series in geography and environment). — *Bibliography: p227-232. — Includes index*

READE, Eric
British town and country planning / Eric Reade. — Milton Keynes : Open University Press, 1987. — xiii,270p. — *Bibliography: p243-266. — Includes index*

CITY PLANNING — Great Britain — Citizen participation

GREAT BRITAIN. Department of the Environment
Public participation in the statutory planning process : United Kingdom research programme. — [London] : the Department, 1976. — [11]p. — (Planning in the United Kingdom). — *Paper presented at the United Nations Conference on Human Settlements, 1976, Vancouver*

HUTTON, N. R.
Lay participation in a public local inquiry : a sociological case study / Neil Hutton. — Aldershot : Gower, c1986. — x,203p. — *Bibliography: p199-203*

ROYAL TOWN PLANNING INSTITUTE. Public Participation Working Party
The public and planning : means to better participation : final report of the Public Participation Working Party, Royal Town Planning Institute. — London : The Institute, 1982. — 96p

CITY PLANNING — Great Britain — History

HALL, Peter, 1932-
Urban and regional planning / Peter Hall. — 2nd ed. — London : Allen & Unwin, 1985, c1982. — [xv,336]p. — *Originally published: Harmondsworth : Penguin, 1982. — Includes index*

CITY PLANNING — India

MILLS, Edwin S
Studies in Indian urban development / Edwin S. Mills, Charles M. Becker ; with a contribution by Satyendra Verma. — Washington, D.C. : Published for the World Bank [by] Oxford University Press, 1986. — viii, 214 p.. — (A World Bank research publication). — *Includes bibliographies and index*

MILLS, Edwin S.
Studies in Indian urban development / Edwin S. Mills, Charles M. Becker. — New York : OUP for the World Bank, 1986. — viii,214p. — *Includes bibliographical references*

Urban growth and urban planning : political context and people's priorities / edited by Alfred de Souza. — New Delhi : Indian Social Institute, c1983. — xi, 163 p.. — *Includes index. — Bibliography: p. [155]-160. — Contents: The challenge of urbanisation and the response / C.S. Chandrasekhara -- Patterns of urban growth, 1971-81 / Ashish Bose -- An approach to urban land policy / Louis Menezes -- Planning for the urban poor: basic needs and priorities / E.F.N. Ribeiro -- Ahmedabad slums: redefining strategies for action / Kirtee Shah -- Rural-urban migration of women: some implications for urban planning / Andrea Menefee Singh -- Urban growth and urban planning / Alfred de Souza*

CITY PLANNING — Ireland — History — Congresses

FRANCO-IRISH SEMINAR OF SOCIAL AND ECONOMIC HISTORIANS (4th : 1984 : Trinity College Dublin)
Cities and merchants : French and Irish perspectives on urban development, 1500-1900 : proceedings of the fourth Franco-Irish Seminar of Social and Economic Historians / edited by P. Butel and L. M. Cullen. — Dublin : Department of Modern History, Trinity College Dublin, 1986. — 259p. — *English and French text. — Maps on lining papers*

CITY PLANNING — London metropolitan area — Westminster

PIMLICO NEIGHBOURHOOD AID CENTRE HOUSING GROUP
Planning, policy and eviction in Pimlico : a report / by the Pimlico Neighbourhood Aid Centre Housing Group. — London : Pimlico Neighbourhood Aid Centre, 1974. — 13p

CITY PLANNING — Middle West

The Metropolitan Midwest : policy problems and prospects for change / edited by Barry Checkoway and Carl V. Patton. — Urbana : University of Illinois Press, c1985. — 309 p.. — *Includes bibliographies*

CITY PLANNING — Northern Ireland — History — 20th century

HENDRY, John, 1934-
Belfast - who cares? : an inaugural lecture delivered before the Queen's University of Belfast on 15 January 1985 / John Hendry. — [Belfast] : Queen's University of Belfast, c1985. — 18p. — (New lecture series ; no.139)

CITY PLANNING — Northern Ireland — Belfast

DAWSON, Gerry
Planning in the shadow of urban civil conflict : a case study from Belfast / by Gerry Dawson. — Liverpool : University of Liverpool, Dept. of Civic Design, 1984. — 48 leaves. — (Working paper / Dept. of Civic Design, University of Liverpool ; WP24)

CITY PLANNING — Quebec (Province)

DIVAY, Gérard
Les promoteurs d'habitation dans la région de Montréal : présentation partielle et préliminaire / Gérard Divay et Luc Hurtubise. — Quebec : Université du Quebec. Institut National de la Recherche Scientifique, 1972. — 41 leaves. — (Notes de recherche / INRS Urbanisation ; no.1)

CITY PLANNING — South Australia — Adelaide

SOUTH AUSTRALIA. City of Adelaide Development Committee
City of Adelaide interim development control : second statement of policy, 18th July, 1975. — Adelaide : the Committee, 1975. — 63p

CITY PLANNING — Sweden

General plan för Malmö / verkställd på stadsingenjörskontoret av Martin Weibull. — Malmö : Stadsingenjörskontoret
Del 2: Inventering av näringsliv och allmänna institutioner. — 1952. — 353,41p

CITY PLANNING — Turkey — Ankara

DANIELSON, Michael N
The politics of rapid urbanization : government and growth in modern Turkey / Michael N. Danielson, Ruşen Keleş. — New York : Holmes & Meier, 1984. — p. cm. — *Includes index. — Bibliography: p*

CITY PLANNING — Turkey — Istanbul

DANIELSON, Michael N
The politics of rapid urbanization : government and growth in modern Turkey / Michael N. Danielson, Ruşen Keleş. — New York : Holmes & Meier, 1984. — p. cm. — *Includes index. — Bibliography: p*

CITY PLANNING — United States

CHRISTENSEN, Carol A
The American garden city and the new towns movement / by Carol A. Christensen. — Ann Arbor, Mich. : UMI Research Press, c1986. — x, 203p. — (Architecture and urban design ; no. 13). — : *Revision of author's thesis (Ph.D.)--University of Minnesota, 1977. — Includes index. — Bibliography: p. [179]-190*

CITY PLANNING — United States — History

FOGLESONG, Richard E.
Planning the capitalist city : the colonial era to thhe 1920s / by Richard E. Foglesong. — Princeton, N.J. : Princeton University Press, c1986. — x, 286 p.. — *Includes index. — Bibliography: p. 258-279*

CITY PLANNING — Wales — Glamorgan

MID GLAMORGAN. County Council
Position and prospects 1975 : an analysis of the special problems of Mid Glamorgan and their solution / Mid Glamorgan County Council. — Cardiff : Mid Glamorgan County Council
Vol.1. — 1975. — [xi],20p

MID GLAMORGAN. County Council
Position and prospects 1975 : an analysis of the special problems of Mid Glamorgan and their solution / Mid Glamorgan County Council. — Cardiff : Mid Glamorgan County Council
Vol.2. — 1975. — [viii],138,vp

CITY PLANNING AND REDEVELOPMENT LAW — Canada

MAKUCH, Stanley M
Canadian municipal and planning law / Stanley M. Makuch. — Toronto, Canada : Carswell Co., 1983. — xxxiii, 325 p.. — *Includes bibliographical references and index*

CITY PLANNING AND REDEVELOPMENT LAW — England

GRANT, Malcolm
Urban planning law : first supplement, up to date to July 30, 1986 / by Malcolm Grant. — London : Sweet & Maxwell, 1986. — [114]p

GREAT BRITAIN. Department of the Environment
Speeding planning appeals : the handling of inquiries planning appeals : action plan [and review] / Department of the Environment. — London : H.M.S.O., 1986. — iv,182p

HEAP, Sir Desmond
An outline of planning law / Sir Desmond Heap. — 9th ed. — London : Sweet & Maxwell, 1987. — [350]p. — *Previous ed.: 1982. — Includes index*

CITY PLANNING AND REDEVELOPMENT LAW — Europe

Planning law in Western Europe / edited by J.F. Garner and N.P. Gravells. — 2nd. rev. ed. — Amsterdam ; New York : North-Holland ; New York, N.Y., U.S.A. : Sole distributors for the U.S.A. and Canada, Elsevier Science Pub. Co., 1986. — p. cm. — *Bibliography: p*

CITY PLANNING AND REDEVELOPMENT LAW — France
FRANCE
[Code de l'urbanisme]. Code de l'urbanisme / documentation commentée par Franck Moderne et Hubert Charles. — 4e éd. — Paris : Dalloz, 1985. — vi,901,9p. — (Petits codes Dalloz). — *Previous ed.: 1982. — Includes index*

CITY PLANNING AND REDEVELOPMENT LAW — Great Britain
Challenging decision : papers from a conference held at Oxford, September 1985 / organised by the Bar Council, the Law Society and the Royal Institution of Chartered Surveyors. — London : Sweet & Maxwell, 1986. — vi,101p. — (Journal of planning and environmental law occasional papers ; no.12). — *Conference paper*

GREAT BRITAIN. Parliament. House of Commons. Library. Research Division
Housing and Planning Bill (Bill 63 of 1985/86) / Oonagh Gay, Barry Winetrobe, Betty Miller. — [London] : the Division, 1986. — 38p. — (Reference sheet ; no.86/5). — *Bibliographical references: p30-38*

CITY PLANNING AND REDEVELOPMENT LAW — Nigeria
OLA, C. S
Town and country planning and environmental laws in Nigeria / C.S. Ola. — 2nd ed. — Jericho, Ibadan, Nigeria : University Press, 1984. — xx, 275 p.. — *Rev. ed. of: Town and country planning law in Nigeria. 1977. — Based on a small part of author's thesis--University College, London. — Includes index. — Bibliography: p. 265-269*

CITY-STATES — Greece
GLOTZ, Gustave
The Greek city and its institutions / Gustave Glotz ; foreword by Henri Berr; translated by N. Mallinson. — London : Kegan Paul, Trench and Trubner, 1929. — xx,416p

CITY TRAFFIC — Mathematical models
VAUGHAN, Rodney
Urban spatial traffic patterns / Rodney Vaughan. — London : Pion, 1987. — 334p. — *Bibliography: p[315]-330*

CIUDAD JUAREZ (MEXICO) — Economic conditions
The social ecology and economic development of Ciudad Juarez / edited by Gay Young. — Boulder ; London : Westview, 1986. — xiv,171p. — *Bibliographies*

CIUDAD JUAREZ (MEXICO) — Social conditions
The social ecology and economic development of Ciudad Juarez / edited by Gay Young. — Boulder ; London : Westview, 1986. — xiv,171p. — *Bibliographies*

CIVICS — Study and teaching (Secondary) — United States
BATTISTONI, Richard M
Public schooling and the education of democratic citizens / Richard M. Battistoni. — Jackson : University Press of Mississippi, c1985. — viii, 200 p.. — *Includes bibliographies and index*

CIVIL DEFENSE — History — 20th century
VALE, Lawrence J.
The limits of civil defence in the USA, Switzerland, Britain and the Soviet Union : the evolution of policies since 1945 / Lawrence J. Vale. — Basingstoke : Macmillan, 1987. — xii,268p. — *Bibliography: p233-257. — Includes index*

CIVIL ENGINEERING — Cold weather conditions
HARRIS, Stuart A.
The permafrost environment / Stuart A. Harris. — London : Croom Helm, c1986. — 276p. — (The Croom Helm natural environment. Problems and management series) . — *Bibliography: p235-270. — Includes index*

CIVIL LAW
CAŁUS, Andrzej
Prawo cywilne i handlowe państw obcych / Andrzej Całus. — [2nd ed.] — Warszawa : Państwowe Wydawnictwo Ekonomiczne, 1985. — 483p. — *Table of contents in English and Russian*

CIVIL LAW — Congresses
Drafting and enforcing contracts in civil and common law jurisdictions / edited by Kojo Yelpaala, Mauro Rubino-Sammartano, Dennis Campbell. — Deventer, Netherlands ; Boston : Kluwer Law and Taxation Publishers, c1986. — 275 p.. — *Papers presented at the Third Annual Waidring Conference, McGeorge School of Law, 1986*

CIVIL LAW — Economic aspects
BISHOP, William Dutton
Aspects of the economics of private law / William Dutton Bishop. — 356 leaves. — *PhD (Econ) 1986 LSE*

CIVIL LAW — California — History
BAKKEN, Gordon Morris
The development of law in frontier California : civil law and society, 1850-1890 / Gordon Morris Bakken. — Westport, Conn. : Greenwood Press, 1985. — 162 p.. — (Contributions in legal studies ; no. 33). — *Includes index. — Bibliography: p. [113]-154*

CIVIL LAW — England — History — Sources
Sources of English legal history : private law to 1750 / (compiled by) J.H. Baker, S.F.C. Milsom. — London : Butterworths, 1986. — xl,698p. — *Includes index*

CIVIL LAW — France
FRANCE
[Code civil]. Code civil. — 85e éd. — Paris : Dalloz, 1985. — viii,1556p. — (Petits codes Dalloz). — *Previous ed.: 1983. — Includes index*

FRANCE
[Code civil]. Code civil. — 86e éd.. — Paris : Dalloz, 1986. — viii,1589,2p. — (Codes Dalloz). — *Includes index*

CIVIL LAW — Hungary
HUNGARY
[Polgári törvénykönyv. English]. Civil code of the Hungarian People's Republic. — [Budapest] : Ministry of Justice of the Hungarian People's Republic, c1982. — 298 p. — (The Statutes of the Hungarian People's Republic)

CIVIL LAW — Spain
DÍEZ-PICAZO, Luis
Sistema de derecho civil / Luis Díez-Picazo y Antonio Gullón. — 5a ed. — Madrid : Tecnos Vol.1. — 1985. — 575p

DÍEZ-PICAZO, Luis
Sistema de derecho civil / Luis Díez-Picazo y Antonio Gullón. — 4a.ed. — Madrid : Tecnos Vol.2. — 1983. — 665p

CIVIL-MILITARY RELATIONS — Latin America
BLACK, Jan Knippers
Sentinels of empire : United States and Latin American militarism / Jan Knippers Black. — Westport, Conn. : Greenwood Press, 1986. — xix, 240p. — (Contributions in political science ; no. 144). — *Includes index. — Bibliography: p.[221]-236*

CIVIL-MILITARY RELATIONS — Latin America — History — 20th century
Armies and politics in Latin America / edited by Abraham F. Lowenthal and J. Samuel Fitch. — Rev. ed. — New York : Holmes & Meier Publishers, 1986. — p. cm. — *Includes index. — Bibliography: p*

CIVIL-MILITARY RELATIONS — Spain
BALLBÉ, Manuel
Orden público y militarismo en la España constitucional (1812-1983) / Manuel Ballbé ; prólogo de Eduardo García de Enterría. — 2a ed. — Madrid : Alianza, 1985. — iv,488p

LLEIXÀ, Joaquim
Cien años de militarismo en España : funciones estatales confiadas al Ejército en la Restauración y el franquismo / Joaquim Lleixà. — Barcelona : Editorial Anagrama, 1986. — 217p

CIVIL MILITARY RELATIONS — Spain
SECO SERRANO, Carlos
Militarismo y civilismo en la España contemporánea / Carlos Seco Serrano. — Madrid : Instituto de Estudios Económicos, 1984. — 458p

CIVIL-MILITARY RELATIONS — United States — History — 20th century — Addresses, essays, lectures
The national strategy : its theory and practice in the United States, 1945-1960 / edited by Norman A. Graebner. — New York : Oxford University Press, 1986. — p. cm. — *Includes index*

CIVIL PROCEDURE — England
JACOB, Sir Jack I. H.
The fabric of English civil justice / by Sir Jack I.H. Jacob. — London : Stevens, 1987. — [100]p. — (The Hamlyn lectures ; 38). — *Includes index*

O'HARE, John, 1949-
Civil litigation / John O'Hare, Robert N. Hill. — 4th ed. — London : Longman, 1986. — xxvi,507p. — *Previous ed.: Oyez Longman, 1985. — Includes index*

CIVIL RIGHTS — New Zealand
ELKIND, Jerome B
A standard for justice : a critical commentary on the proposed Bill of Rights for New Zealand / Jerome B. Elkind and Antony Shaw ; with a foreword by P.T. Mahon. — Auckland ; New York : Oxford University Press, 1986. — xvi, 238 p.. — *Includes bibliographies and indexes*

CIVIL RIGHTS
The Diplomacy of human rights / edited by David D. Newsom. — Lanham, MD. : University Press of America ; [Washington, D.C.] : Institute for the Study of Diplomacy, c1986. — p. cm. — *Includes bibliographies*

Food as a human right / edited by Asbjorn Eide ... [et al.]. — Tokyo : United Nations University, c1984. — xi,289p

Law, rights and the welfare state / edited by C.J.G. Sampford and D.J. Galligan. — London : Croom Helm, c1986. — xv,215p. — *Bibliography: p200-207. — Includes index*

MACFARLANE, L. J.
The theory and practice of human rights / Leslie J. Macfarlane. — London : Temple Smith, 1985. — 193p. — *Includes index*

MILNE, A. J. M.
Human rights and human diversity : an essay in the philosophy of human rights / A.J.M. Milne. — London : Macmillan, 1986. — [240]p . — *Includes index*

SINGH, Nagendra
Enforcement of human rights in peace and war and the future of humanity / Nagendra Singh. — Dordrecht ; Boston : Nijhoff ; Calcutta : Eastern Law House Private Ltd., 1986. — p. cm

South African journal on human rights. — Braamfontein : Ravan Press, 1985-. — *Annual*

URIBE VARGAS, Diego
La troisième génération des droits de l'homme et la paix / Diego Uribe Vargas. — Paris : C.I.E.M., [1985]. — 83p

VEATCH, Henry B.
Human rights : fact or fancy? / Henry B. Veatch. — Baton Rouge : Louisiana State University Press, c1985. — xi, 258p. — *Includes index. — Bibliography: p.251-253*

CIVIL RIGHTS
continuation

VINCENT, R. J.
Human rights and international relations / R.J. Vincent. — Cambridge : Published in association with the Royal Institute of International Affairs by Cambridge University Press, 1986. — 1v.. — *Includes index*

CIVIL RIGHTS — Addresses, essays, lectures

The Child's construction of social inequality / edited by Robert L. Leahy. — New York ; London : Academic Press, 1983. — xv, 349p. — (Developmental psychology series). — *Includes bibliographies and indexes*

Government violence and repression : an agenda for research / edited by Michael Stohl and George A. Lopez. — New York : Greenwood Press, 1986. — viii, 278 p.. — (Contributions in political science ; no. 148). — *Includes index. — Bibliography: p. [269]-270*

CIVIL RIGHTS — Bibliography

Human rights : an international and comparative law bibliography / compiled and edited by Julian R. Friedman and Marc I. Sherman. — Westport, Conn. ; London : Greenwood, 1985. — xxvii,868p. — (Bibliographies and indexes in law and political science ; no.4). — *English translations provided for foreign language entries*

TAY, Alice Erh-Soon
Human rights for Australia : a survey of literature and developments, and a select and annotated bibliography of recent literature in Australia and abroad / Alice Erh-Soon Tay. — Canberra : Australian Government Publishing Service, 1986. — xvi, 360p. — (Monograph series / Human Rights Commission ; no.1). — *Bibliography: p131-343*

VERSTAPPEN, Berth
Human rights reports : an annotated bibliography of fact-finding missions / by Berth Verstappen. — London : Zell, 1987. — [400]p. — *Includes index*

CIVIL RIGHTS — Evaluation

THOOLEN, Hans
Human rights missions : a study of the fact-finding practice of non-governmental organizations / Hans Thoolen and Berth Verstappen. — Dordrecht ; Boston : M. Nijhoff, 1986. — p. cm. — (International studies in human rights)

CIVIL RIGHTS — Legal status, laws, etc. — Indonesia

INTERNATIONAL COMMISSION OF JURISTS
Indonesia and the rule of law : twenty years of 'New Order' government : a study / prepared by the International Commission of Jurists and the Netherlands Institute of Human Rights ; edited by Hans Thoolen. — London : Pinter, 1987. — xii,208p. — *Includes index*

CIVIL RIGHTS — Moral and ethical aspects

The Moral foundations of civil rights / edited by Robert K. Fullinwider and Claudia Mills. — Totowa, NJ : Rowman & Littlefield, 1986. — p. cm. — (Maryland studies in public philosophy). — *Includes index*

CIVIL RIGHTS — Africa

HOWARD, Rhoda E.
Human rights in Commonwealth Africa / Rhoda E. Howard. — Totowa, N.J. : Rowman & Littlefield, 1986. — xiii, 250 p.. — *Includes index. — Bibliography: p. [231]-239*

CIVIL RIGHTS — America

Handbook of existing rules pertaining to human rights in the inter-American system / Inter-American Commission on Human Rights. — Washington, D.C. : Organization of American States, 1977-. — *Biennial. — Title varies*

INTER-AMERICAN COURT OF HUMAN RIGHTS
Serie A: Fallos y opiniones = Series A: Judgments and opinions / Inter-American Court of Human Rights. — ; San José, Costa Rica : Secretariat of the Court, 1982-. — *Annual. — Text in Spanish and English*

INTER-AMERICAN COURT OF HUMAN RIGHTS
Serie B: Memorias, argumentos orales y documentos = Series B: Pleadings, oral arguments and documents / Inter-American Court of Human Rights. — San José, Costa Rica : Secretariat of the Court, 1983-. — *Annual. — Text in Spanish and English*

CIVIL RIGHTS — Argentina

INTER-AMERICAN COMMISSION ON HUMAN RIGHTS
Informe sobre la situacion de los derechos humanos en Argentina. — Washington, D.C. : Secretaría General, Organización de los Estados Americanos, 1980. — iii,294p. — *Includes bibliographical references. — OEA/Ser.L/V/II.49 doc.19*

INTER-AMERICAN COMMISSION ON HUMAN RIGHTS
Report on the situation of human rights in Argentina. — Washington, D.C. : General Secretoriat, Organization of American States, 1980. — iii,266p. — *English translation of: Informe sobre la situacion de los derechos humanos en Argentina. — Includes bibliographical references. — OEA/Ser.L/V/II.49 doc.19 corr.1*

CIVIL RIGHTS — Asia

ASIAN COALITION OF HUMAN RIGHTS ORGANIZATIONS
Human rights activism in Asia : some perspectives, problems and approaches. — New York : Council on International and Public Affairs, 1984. — 79p

CIVIL RIGHTS — Australia

Human rights and the Migration Act 1985. — Canberra : Australian Government Publishing Service, 1985. — xiv,211p. — (Report / Human Rights Commission ; no.13)

TAY, Alice Erh-Soon
Human rights for Australia : a survey of literature and developments, and a select and annotated bibliography of recent literature in Australia and abroad / Alice Erh-Soon Tay. — Canberra : Australian Government Publishing Service, 1986. — xvi, 360p. — (Monograph series / Human Rights Commission ; no.1). — *Bibliography: p131-343*

CIVIL RIGHTS — Australia — Bibliography

TAY, Alice Erh-Soon
Human rights for Australia : a survey of literature and developments, and a select and annotated bibliography of recent literature in Australia and abroad / Alice Erh-Soon Tay. — Canberra : Australian Government Publishing Service, 1986. — xvi, 360p. — (Monograph series / Human Rights Commission ; no.1). — *Bibliography: p131-343*

CIVIL RIGHTS — Canada

CANADIAN HUMAN RIGHTS COMMISSION
Annual report / Canadian Human Rights Commission. — Ottawa : the Commission, 1984-. — *Annual. — Text in English and French*

Charterwatch : reflections on equality / edited by Christine L. M. Boyle...[et al.]. — Toronto : Carswell, 1986. — ix,356p

Equality rights and the Canadian Charter of Rights and Freedoms / edited by Anne F. Bayefsky and Mary Eberts. — Toronto : Carswell, 1985. — xliv, 661 p.. — *Includes bibliographical references and indexes*

GIBSON, Dale
The law of the Charter : general principles / Dale Gibson. — Toronto : Carswell, 1986. — xxxiii,302p

MORGAN, Nicole
Implosion : an analysis of the growth of the federal public service in Canada (1945-1985) / Nicole Morgan. — Montreal : The Institute for Research on Public Policy/L'Institut de recherches politiques. — xxv,160p. — *Prefatory material in English and French. — Issued also in French under title: 'Implosion: analyse de la croissance de la Fonction publique fédérale canadienne, 1945-1985'*

CIVIL RIGHTS — Canada — History

SALHANY, Roger E
The origin of rights / by Roger E. Salhany. — Toronto : Carswell, 1986. — viii, 175 p.. — *Includes index. — Bibliography: p. [163]-171*

CIVIL RIGHTS — Chile

CHAVKIN, Samuel
Storm over Chile : the Junta under siege / Samuel Chavkin ; with foreword by Hortensia de Allende. — Westport, Conn. : L. Hill, 1985. — 303p. — *Rev. ed. of 'The murder of Chile'. New York: Everest House, c1982. — Includes index*

INTER-AMERICAN COMMISSION ON HUMAN RIGHTS
Informe sobre la situacion de los derechos humanos en Chile. — Washington, D.C. : Secretaría General, Organización de los Estados Americanos, 1985. — ix,371p. — *Bibliographical references: p336-371. — OEA/Ser.L/V/II.66 doc.17*

INTER-AMERICAN COMMISSION ON HUMAN RIGHTS
Report on the situation of human rights in Chile. — Washington, D.C. : General Secretariat, Organization of American States, 1985. — xiii,336p. — *English translation of: Informe sobre la situacion de los derechos humanos en Chile. — Bibliographical references: p306-336. — OAS/Ser.L/V/II.66 Doc.17*

INTERNATIONAL COMMISSION OF JURISTS
Chile : the new constitution and human rights. — London : Chile Solidarity Campaign, 1981. — [4p]

CIVIL RIGHTS — Communist countries

Sotsialisticheskaia kontseptsiia prav cheloveka / otv. redaktory V. M. Chkhikvadze, E. A. Lukasheva. — Moskva : Nauka, 1986. — 220p

CIVIL RIGHTS — Cuba

INTER-AMERICAN COMMISSION ON HUMAN RIGHTS
La situacion de los derechos humanos en Cuba : septimo informe. — Washington, D.C. : Secretaría General, Organización de los Estados Americanos, 1983. — vii,241p. — *Includes bibliographical references. — OEA/Ser.L/V/II.61 Doc.29 rev.1*

INTER-AMERICAN COMMISSION ON HUMAN RIGHTS
The situation of human rights in Cuba : seventh report. — Washington, D.C. : General Secretariat, Organization of American States, 1983. — ix,183p. — *English translation of: La situacion de los derechos humanos en Cuba: septimo informe. — Includes bibliographical references. — OEA/Ser.L/V/II.61 Doc.29 rev.1*

CIVIL RIGHTS — Developing countries

FRANCK, Thomas M
Human rights in Third World perspective / Thomas M. Franck. — Dobbs Ferry, NY : Oceana Publications, 1982. — 3vols.

Human rights in developing countries : a yearbook on countries receiving Norwegian aid. — Oslo : Norwegian University Press, 1986-. — *Annual*

CIVIL RIGHTS — Developing countries — Addresses, essays, lectures

Human rights and Third World development / edited by George W. Shepherd, Jr. and Ved P. Nanda. — Westport, Conn. : Greenwood Press, c1985. — viii, 330 p.. — (Studies in human rights ; no. 5). — Includes index. — Bibliography: p. [309]-321

CIVIL RIGHTS — England — London

NATIONAL COUNCIL FOR CIVIL LIBERTIES
No way in Wapping : the effect of the policing of the News International dispute on Wapping residents. — London : National Council for Civil Liberties, 1986. — 40p

CIVIL RIGHTS — Europe

GREAT BRITAIN. Parliament. House of Commons. Library. International Affairs Section
The European Convention on Human Rights / Chris Bowlby. — [London] : the Library, 1986. — 16p. — (Background paper / House of Commons. Library. [Research Division] ; no.179). — Bibliography: p16

CIVIL RIGHTS — Europe, Eastern

MASTNY, Vojtech
Helsinki, human rights, and European security : analysis and documentation / Vojtech Mastny. — Durham : Duke University Press, 1986. — xvi, 389 p.. — Includes index

CIVIL RIGHTS — Finland

TÖRNUDD, Klaus
Finland and the international norms of human rights / K. Törnudd. — Dordrecht ; Boston : M. Nijhoff, 1986. — p. cm. — (International studies in human rights). — Bibliography: p

CIVIL RIGHTS — Great Britain

Freedom of information — freedom of the individual?. — London : Papermac, 1987. — 110p. — (Days of decision)

GREAT BRITAIN. Paliament. House of Commons. Library. Research Division
A bill of rights. — [London] : the Division, 1976. — 10p. — (Background paper ; no.49). — Bibliography: p9-10

GREAT BRITAIN. Parliament. House of Commons. Library. International Affairs Section
The European Convention on Human Rights / Chris Bowlby. — [London] : the Library, 1986. — 16p. — (Background paper / House of Commons. Library. [Research Division] ; no.179). — Bibliography: p16

NATIONAL COUNCIL FOR CIVIL LIBERTIES
Stonehenge : a report into the civil liberties implications of the events relating to the convoys of summer 1985 and 1986. — London : National Council for Civil Liberties, 1986. — 43p

SCAFFARDI, Sylvia
Fire under the carpet : working for civil liberties in the thirties / Sylvia Scaffardi. — London : Lawrence and Wishart, 1986. — 208p

SDP-LIBERAL ALLIANCE
Government, law and justice : the case for a Ministry of Justice. — Hebden Bridge : Hebden Royd Publications, 1985. — 14p. — (Alliance paper ; no.1)

THORNTON, Peter, 1946-
The civil liberties of the Zircon affair : Peter Thornton. — London : National Council for Civil Liberties, 1987. — 23p

CIVIL RIGHTS — Great Britain — History

SALHANY, Roger E
The origin of rights / by Roger E. Salhany. — Toronto : Carswell, 1986. — viii, 175 p.. — Includes index. — Bibliography: p. [163]-171

CIVIL RIGHTS — Guatemala

INTER-AMERICAN COMMISSION ON HUMAN RIGHTS
Informe sobre la situacion de los derechos humanos en Guatemala. — Washington, D.C. : Secretaría General, Organización de los Estados Americanos, 1983. — ii,144p. — Includes bibliographical references. — OEA/Ser.L/V/II.61 Doc.47

INTER-AMERICAN COMMISSION ON HUMAN RIGHTS
Report on the situation of human rights in the Republic of Guatemala. — Washington, D.C. : General Secretariat, Organization of American States, 1983. — ii,134p. — English translation of: Informe sobre la situacion de los derechos humanos en Guatemala. — Includes bibliographical references. — OEA/Ser.L/V/II.61 Doc.47 rev.1

CIVIL RIGHTS — Haiti

INTER-AMERICAN COMMISSION ON HUMAN RIGHTS
Informe sobre la situación de los derechos humanos en Haití. — Washington, D.C. : Secretaría General, Organización de los Estados Americanos, 1979. — ii,77p. — Spanish translation of: Rapport sur la situation de droits des l'homme en Haiti. — Includes bibliographical references. — OEA/Ser.L/V/II.46 doc.66 rev.1

INTER-AMERICAN COMMISSION ON HUMAN RIGHTS
Report on the situation of human rights in Haiti. — Washington, D.C. : General Secretariat, Organization of American States, 1979. — ii,81p. — English translation of: Rapport sur la situation des droits de l'homme en Haiti. — Includes bibliographical references. — OEA/Ser.L/V/II.46 doc.66 rev.1

CIVIL RIGHTS — Honduras

Honduras confronts its future : contending perspectives on critical issues / edited by Mark B. Rosenberg and Philip L. Shepherd. — Boulder, Colo. : L. Rienner Publishers, 1986. — xii, 268p. — Essays first presented at "Honduras: An International Dialogue", in Miami, Fla., December 1984. — Includes bibliographical references and index

CIVIL RIGHTS — India

HINGORANI, R. C.
Human rights in India / R.C. Hingorani. — New Delhi : Oxford & IBH, c1985. — vii, 181 p.. — Includes bibliographical references and index

Violation of democratic rights in India / editor,A. R. Desai. — London : Sangam volume 1. — 1986. — 624p

CIVIL RIGHTS — Japan — History

UPHAM, Frank K
Law and social change in postwar Japan / Frank K. Upham. — Cambridge, Mass. : Harvard University Press, 1987. — p. cm. — Includes index

CIVIL RIGHTS — Korea (South) — History

PAE, Sung M
Testing democratic theories in Korea / Sung M. Pae. — Lanham, MD : University Press of America, c1986. — xvii, 300 p.. — Includes index. — Bibliography: p. [281]-289

CIVIL RIGHTS — Mexico

Mexico : human rights in rural areas : exchange of documents with the Mexico government on human rights violations in Oaxaca and Chiapas. — London : Amnesty International Publications, 1986. — 136p

CIVIL RIGHTS — Namibia

INTERNATIONAL SOCIETY FOR HUMAN RIGHTS
Namibia : human rights in conflict: documentation. — Frankfurt : International Society for Human Rights, 1985. — 27p

CIVIL RIGHTS — New Zealand

ELKIND, Jerome B
A standard for justice : a critical commentary on the proposed Bill of Rights for New Zealand / Jerome B. Elkind and Antony Shaw ; with a foreword by P.T. Mahon. — Auckland ; New York : Oxford University Press, 1986. — xvi, 238 p.. — Includes bibliographies and indexes

CIVIL RIGHTS — Nicaragua

Human rights in Nicaragua : 1986. — New York, NY : Americas Watch Committee, c1987. — iii, 174 p.. — (An Americas Watch report). — "February 1987.". — Bibliography: p. 171-174

Human rights in Nicaragua 1985-1986. — Washington, D.C. : America's Watch Committee, 1986. — iii,149p

INTER-AMERICAN COMMISSION ON HUMAN RIGHTS
Informe sobre la situacion de los derechos humanos de un sector de la poblacion Nicaragüense de origen Miskito y resolucion sobre el procedimiento de solucion amistosa sobre la situacion de los derechos humanos de un sector de la poblacion Nicaragüense de origen Miskito. — Washington, D.C. : Secretaría General, Organización de los Estados Americanos, 1984. — ii,150p. — Includes bibliographical references. — OEA/Ser.L/V/II.62 doc.10 rev.3 and doc.26

INTER-AMERICAN COMMISSION ON HUMAN RIGHTS
Report on the situation of human rights of a segment of the Nicaraguan population of Miskito origin and resolution on the friendly settlement procedure regarding the human rights situation of a segment of the Nicaraguan population of Miskito origin. — Washington, D.C. : General Secretariat, Organization of American States, 1984. — 142p. — English translation of: Informe sobre la situacion de los derechos humanos de un sector de la poblacion Nicaragüense de origen Miskito.... — Includes bibliographical references. — OEA/Ser.L/V/II.62 doc.10 rev. 3 and doc.26

CIVIL RIGHTS — Philippines

LAWYERS COMMITTEE FOR INTERNATIONAL HUMAN RIGHTS
The Philippines : a country in crisis / a report by the Lawyers Committee for International Human Rights. — New York : the Committee, 1983. — iii,142p

CIVIL RIGHTS — Puerto Rico

FUSTER, Jaime B.
Deberes y obligaciones del ciudadano responsable / Jaime B. Fuster. — Segunda edición revisada. — San Juan : Comision de Derechos Civiles, 1974. — ix,49p. — Publicado originalmente en 1973

FUSTER, Jaime B.
Los derechos civiles reconocidos en el sistema de vida puertorriqueño / Jaime B. Fuster. — Quinta edición revisada. — San Juan : Comisión de Derechos Civiles, 1974. — xi,231p . — Bibliography: p219-221

CIVIL RIGHTS — Scandinavia

Mänskliga rättigheter i Norden : andra nordiska seminariet rörande forskning, undervisning och information om de mänskliga rättigheterna, Åbo 7-9 juni 1982 / red. Heli Pelkonen & Allan Rosas. — Åbo : Åbo Akademi, 1983. — (Meddelanden från Stiftelsens för Åbo Akademi Forskningsinstitut ; nr.82)

CIVIL RIGHTS — South Africa

LOVE, Janice
The U.S. anti-apartheid movement : local activism in global politics / Janice Love. — New York : Praeger, 1985. — p. cm. — Includes index. — Bibliography: p

MATHEWS, Anthony S.
Freedom, state security and the rule of law : dilemmas of the apartheid society / Anthony S. Mathews. — Cape Town : Juta, 1986. — xxv,312p. — Bibliography: p.xi-xiv. - Includes index

CIVIL RIGHTS — South Africa
continuation

South Africa. — London : Amnesty International, 1986. — 17p. — (Amnesty International briefing). — *Text on inside covers*

South African journal on human rights. — Braamfontein : Ravan Press, 1985-. — *Annual*

SUTTNER, Raymond
30 years of the Freedom Charter / Raymond Suttner, Jeremy Cronin. — Johannesburg : Ravan Press, 1985. — xi,266p

CIVIL RIGHTS — Soviet Union

Forced labor in the Soviet Union. — [Washington, D.C.] : United States Information Service, [1952?]. — vi,63p

INTERNATIONAL SAKHAROV HEARING (5th : 1985 : London)
Proceedings : April, 1985 / Fifth International Sakharov Hearing ; edited by Allan Wynn ; associate editors, Martin Dewhirst, Harold Stone. — London : Deutsch, 1986. — 214p

MASTNY, Vojtech
Helsinki, human rights, and European security : analysis and documentation / Vojtech Mastny. — Durham : Duke University Press, 1986. — xvi, 389 p.. — *Includes index*

PARCHOMENKO, Walter
Soviet images of dissidents and nonconformists / Walter Parchomenko. — New York ; London : Praeger, 1986. — xv, 251 p.. — *"Praeger special studies. Praeger scientific.". — Includes index. — Bibliography: p. 213-243*

CIVIL RIGHTS — Spain — Congresses

Libertades publicas y fuerzas armadas : actas de las jornadas de estudio celebradas en el Instituto de Derechos Humanos de la Universidad Complutense, Madrid, 4-24 Febrero, 1984 / presentación y edición a cargo de Luis Prieto y Carlos Bruquetas. — Madrid : Centro de Publicaciones del Ministerio de Educación y Ciencia, 1985. — 926p. — *Bibliography: p915-917*

CIVIL RIGHTS — Surinam

INTER-AMERICAN COMMISSION ON HUMAN RIGHTS
Segundo informe sobre la situacion de los derechos humanos en Suriname. — Washington, D.C. : Secretaría General, Organización de los Estados Americanos, 1985. — iii,73p. — *Translation of: Second report on the human rights situation in Suriname. — Includes bibliographical references. — OEA/Ser.L/V/II.66 doc.21, rev.1*

INTER-AMERICAN COMMISSION ON HUMAN RIGHTS
Informe sobre la situacion de los derechos humanos en Suriname. — Washington, D.C. : Organización de los Estados Americanos, 1983. — 48p. — *Spanish translation of: Report on the situation of human rights in Suriname. — OEA/Ser/L/II/61 doc.6 rev.1*

INTER-AMERICAN COMMISSION ON HUMAN RIGHTS
Second report on the human rights situation in Suriname. — Washington, D.C. : General Secretariat, Organization of American States, 1985. — ii,69p. — *OAS/Ser.L/V/II.66 doc.21 rev.1*

CIVIL RIGHTS — Switzerland

PARTI LIBÉRAL SUISSE
Droits populaires et gouvernement : résumé des rapports présentés au Congrès du Parti libéral suisse à Cressier/NE le 26 mars 1977. — Berne : Parti Libéral Suisse, 1977. — 28p

CIVIL RIGHTS — United States

MORGAN, Richard E.
Disabling America : the "rights industry" in our time / Richard E. Morgan. — New York : Basic Books, c1984. — ix, 245 p.. — *Includes indexes. — Bibliography: p. 215-234*

SCHEINGOLD, Stuart A
The politics of rights : lawyers, public policy, and political change / Stuart A. Scheingold. — New Haven : Yale University Press, 1974. — xiv, 224 p.. — *Includes bibliographical references and index*

SMITH, Donald L.
Zechariah Chafee, Jr., defender of liberty and law / Donald L. Smith. — Cambridge, Mass. : Harvard University Press, 1986. — x, 355 p.. — *Includes index. — Bibliography: p. [283]-343*

WARBY, Stephen L.
Civil liberties : policy and policy making / Stephen L. Warby. — Lanham : University Press of America ; London : Distributed by Eurospan, c1986. — [272]p. — *Includes index*

CIVIL RIGHTS — United States — History

BIGEL, Alan I.
The Supreme Court on emergency powers, foreign affairs, and protection of civil liberties, 1935-1975 / Alan I. Bigel. — Lanham, MD : University Press of America, c1986. — xv, 211 p.. — *: Originally presented as the author's thesis (doctoral--New School for Social Research). — Includes indexes. — Bibliography: p. 194-203*

SALHANY, Roger E
The origin of rights / by Roger E. Salhany. — Toronto : Carswell, 1986. — viii, 175 p.. — *Includes index. — Bibliography: p. [163]-171*

CIVIL RIGHTS — Zambia

Civil liberties cases in Zambia / [compiled] by Muna Ndulo and Kaye Turner. — Oxford : African Law Reports, 1984. — xxii,579p. — *Includes index*

CIVIL RIGHTS AND SOCIALISM

Sotsialisticheskaia kontseptsiia prav cheloveka / otv. redaktory V. M. Chkhikvadze, E. A. Lukasheva. — Moskva : Nauka, 1986. — 220p

CIVIL RIGHTS DEMONSTRATIONS — United States

DEMING, Barbara
Prisons that could not hold / Barbara Deming ; introduction by Grace Paley ; photo essay edited by Joan E. Biren. — San Francisco : Spinsters Ink, 1985. — 230p

CIVIL RIGHTS (INTERNATIONAL LAW)

DILLOWAY, James
Is world order evolving? : an adventure into human potential / by James Dilloway. — Oxford : Pergamon, 1986. — [220]p. — (Systems science and world order library). — *Includes index*

FAWCETT, J. E. S.
The application of the European Convention on Human Rights / by J.E.S. Fawcett. — 2nd ed. — Oxford : Clarendon, 1987. — xiii,444p. — *Previous ed.: 1969. — Includes index*

Mänskliga rättigheter i Norden : andra nordiska seminariet rörande forskning, undervisning och information om de mänskliga rättigheterna, Åbo 7-9 juni 1982 / red. Heli Pelkonen & Allan Rosas. — Åbo : Åbo Akademi, 1983. — (Meddelanden från Stiftelsens för Åbo Akademi Forskningsinstitut ; nr.82)

MERON, Theodor
Human rights law-making in the United Nations : a critique of instruments and process / Theodor Meron. — Oxford : Clarendon, 1986. — [350]p. — *Includes index*

MOWER, A. Glenn
International cooperation for social justice : global and regional protection of economic/social rights / A. Glenn Mower, Jr. — Westport, Conn. : Greenwood Press, c1985. — p. cm. — (Studies in human rights ; no. 6). — *Includes index. — Bibliography: p*

MURAVCHIK, Joshua
The uncertain crusade : Jimmy Carter and the dilemmas of human rights policy / Joshua Muravchik ; foreword by Jeane Kirkpatrick. — Lanham, Md. ; London : Hamilton Press, c1986. — xxii, 247p. — *Includes bibliographies and index*

RODLEY, Nigel S.
The treatment of prisoners under international law / Nigel S. Rodley. — Paris : Unesco ; Oxford : Clarendon, 1987. — xxii,374. — *Includes index*

TÖRNUDD, Klaus
Finland and the international norms of human rights / K. Törnudd. — Dordrecht ; Boston : M. Nijhoff, 1986. — p. cm. — (International studies in human rights). — *Bibliography: p*

CIVIL RIGHTS (INTERNATIONAL LAW) — Bibliography

Human rights : an international and comparative law bibliography / compiled and edited by Julian R. Friedman and Marc I. Sherman. — Westport, Conn. ; London : Greenwood, 1985. — xxvii,868p. — (Bibliographies and indexes in law and political science ; no.4). — *English translations provided for foreign language entries*

CIVIL RIGHTS (INTERNATIONAL LAW) — Cases

HUMAN RIGHTS COMMITTEE (International Covenant on Civil and Political Rights (1966))
Selected decisions under the optional protocol : second to sixteenth sessions / Human Rights Committee. — New York : United Nations, 1985. — v, 167 p.. — *"International Covenant on Civil and Political Rights and Optional Protocol":-p. 147-154. — At head of title: International Covenant on Civil and Political Rights. — "CCPR/C/OP/1; United Nations publication sales no. E.84.XIV.2; O165OP"--T.p. verso. — Includes indexes*

CIVIL RIGHTS (INTERNATIONAL LAW) — Developing Countries

CHOURAQUI, Gilles
Report of the Working Group of Governmental Experts on the Right to Development / Rapporteur: Mr. Gilles Chouraqui (France). — Geneva : United Nations, 1982. — 17p. — *United Nations. Economic and Social Council. Commission on Human Rights. Thirty-ninth session, 31 January-11 March 1983. Item 8 of the provisional agenda. — U.N. document E/CN.4/1983/11 dated 9 December 1982*

CIVIL RIGHTS MOVEMENTS — Southern States

BARKAN, Steven E.
Protesters on trial : criminal justice in the Southern civil rights and Vietnam antiwar movements / Steven E. Barkan. — New Brunswick, N.J. : Rutgers University Press, c1985. — p. cm. — (Crime, law, and deviance series). — *Includes index. — Bibliography: p*

CIVIL RIGHTS MOVEMENTS — United States — History — 20th century

HAMMERBACK, John C
A war of words : Chicano protest in the 1960s and 1970s / John C. Hammerback, Richard J. Jensen, and Jose Angel Gutierrez. — Westport, Conn. ; London : Greenwood Press, 1985. — x, 187p. — (Contributions in ethnic studies ; no. 12). — *Includes index. — Bibliography: p.[173]-178*

CIVIL RIGHTS WORKERS — United States — Biography

LANDESS, Tom
Jesse Jackson and the politics of race / Thomas H. Landess, Richard M. Quinn. — Ottawa, Ill. : Jameson Books, c1985. — 269p. — *Includes index*

CIVIL SERVICE
Public/private interplay in social protection : a comparative study / edited by Martin Rein and Lee Rainwater ; with Ellen Immergut, Michael O'Higgins, and Harald Russig. — Armonk, N.Y. : M.E. Sharpe, c1986. — viii, 215 p.. — (Comparative public policy analysis). — *Includes bibliographies*

CIVIL SERVICE — Congresses
Public expenditure : the key issues / edited by John Bristow and Declan McDonagh. — Dublin, Ireland : Institute of Public Administration, 1986. — 138 p.. — *Proceedings of National Conference on Public Expenditure: the Key Issues, held Nov. 1985 in Dublin, organized by the Institute. — Includes bibliographies. — Contents: Public expenditure and public debt / Vito Tanzi -- The political economy of public expenditure / Alan Peacock -- Public employment and public expenditure / Richard Rose -- Public expenditure and the bureaucracy / Peter Jackson -- An Irish overview / Alan Dukes*

CIVIL SERVICE — Training of — Denmark
DENMARK. Udvalget vedrørende centraladministrationens personalepolitik
Efteruddannelse af statens og kommunernes administrative personale : I. betaenkning afgivet af Udvalget vedrørende centraladministrationens personalepolitik. — [København : Statens Trykningskontor], 1962. — 39p. — (Betaenkning ; nr.311)

CIVIL SERVICE — Denmark — Study and teaching
Efteruddannelse af akademiske tjenestemaend i centraladministrationen : betaenkning til forvaltningsnaevnet fra den af naevnet 1 januar 1957 nedsatte arbejdsgruppe. — [København : Statens Trykningskontor], 1960. — 49p. — (Betaenkning ; nr.256)

CIVIL SERVICE — Europe — Effect of technological innovations on
New technology in the public service : consolidated report. — Luxembourg : Office for Official Publications of the European Communities, 1986. — 75p

CIVIL SERVICE — Great Britain
ROSE, Richard, 1933-
Giving direction to civil servants : signals from the law, expertise, the market, and the electorate / Professor Richard Rose. — Glasgow : Centre for the Study of Public Policy, University of Strathclyde, 1986. — 24p. — (Studies in public policy ; 156)

CIVIL SERVICE — Great Britain — Bibliography
GREAT BRITAIN. Civil Service Department. Central Management Library
Policy making in the Civil Service. — London : the Library, 1977. — 4p. — (Policy science documentation. Bibliography series ; B10)

CIVIL SERVICE — Great Britain — Communication systems
CENTRAL COMPUTER AND TELECOMMUNICATIONS AGENCY
Central Computer and Telecommunications Agency : progress report. — London : H.M.S.O., 1985. — vi,41p. — (Information technology in the civil service. IT series ; no.11)

CIVIL SERVICE — Great Britain — Effect of technological innovations on
New technology in the public service : United Kingdom. — Shankill, Co.Dublin : European Foundation for the Improvement of Living and Working Conditions, 1986. — 103p

CIVIL SERVICE — Great Britain — Management
GREAT BRITAIN. Civil Service Department. Staff Inspection and Evaluation Branch
Staff inspection in the civil service : an instrument of manpower control and an aid to management efficiency. — London : the Department, 1975. — 10p

CIVIL SERVICE — Great Britain — Management — Evaluation
HUMPHREY, P. B.
The development of a methodology for the evaluation of management by objectives in the British civil service / P. B. Humphrey, M. C. Davey, N. M. Hardinge. — [London?] : Civil Service Department, Behavioural Sciences Research Division, 1974. — 66p. — (BSRD report ; no. 17). — *Bibliography: p65-66*

CIVIL SERVICE — India — History
SIKKA, Ram Parkash
The civil service in India : Europeanisation and Indianisation under the East India Company, 1765-1857 / Ram Parkash Sikka. — New Delhi : Uppal Pub. House, c1984. — xii, 2494, p.. — *Includes index. — Bibliography: p. [221]-241*

CIVIL SERVICE — India — History — 20th century
POTTER, David, 1931 Nov. 3-
India's political administrators 1919-1983 / David C. Potter. — Oxford : Clarendon, 1986. — xv,289p. — *Bibliography: p253-277. — Includes index*

CIVIL SERVICE — New Zealand
State servants and the public in the 1980s / edited by R. M. Alley. — Wellington : New Zealand Institute of Public Administration, 1980. — 127p. — (Studies in public administration ; no.25). — *Includes bibliographical references*

CIVIL SERVICE — Peru
PERU. Dirección nacional de Personal. Programa Participación de los TAP
Nueva política de incentivos para los trabajadores de la administración pública. — [Lima] : the Dirección, [197-?]. — 35p. — *Documento de trabajo. — Bibliography: p[35]*

CIVIL SERVICE — South Australia — Minority employment
SOUTH AUSTRALIA. Public Service Board
The ethnic composition of the South Australian public service. — [Adelaide] : the Board, 1982. — iii,102,4p

CIVIL SERVICE — Spain — History — 20th century
ALVÁREZ ALVÁREZ, Julian
Burocracia y poder político en el regimen franquista : el papel de los Cuerpos de funcionarios en 1938 y 1975 / Julian Alvárez Alvárez. — [Madrid : Instituto Nacional de Administración Pública, c1984. — 130p. — (Publicaciones del Instituto Nacional de Administración Pública) (Biblioteca básica de administración pública. Serie general). — *Bibliography: p127-128*

CIVIL SERVICE — Trinidad and Tobago — Statistics
The growth of the public service 1973-1978 and projected growth 1979-1983. — [Port of Spain?] : Personnel Department, [1980]. — 27p

CIVIL SERVICE — United States — History — 19th century
ARON, Cindy Sondik
Ladies and gentlemen of the civil service : middle-class workers in Victorian America / Cindy Sondik Aron. — New York : Oxford University Press, 1987. — viii, 234 p.. — *Includes index. — Bibliography: p. 195-227*

CIVIL SERVICE PENSIONS — Canada
CANADA. Treasury Board
Report on the administration of the Public Service Superannuation Act. — Ottawa : Canada. Treasury Board, 1984-. — *Annual. — Text in English and French*

CIVIL SERVICE POSITIONS — Great Britain — Bibliography
GREAT BRITAIN. Civil Service Department. Central Management Library
Professionals, specialists and generalists in the Civil Service. — London : the Library, 1979. — ii,24p. — (Policy science documentation. Bibliography series ; B30-B40/2)

CIVIL SERVICE RECRUITING — Great Britain
GREAT BRITAIN. Civil Service Commission. Working Party on the Selection of Specialists
Report of the Working Party on the Selection of Specialists. — [London] : the Commission, 1977. — 19p

CIVIL SERVICE REFORM — United States
Fraud, waste, and abuse in government : causes, consequences, and cures / edited by Jerome B. McKinney and Michael Johnston. — Philadelphia : Institute for the Study of Human Issues, 1986. — p. cm. — *Includes index*

CIVIL SUPREMACY OVER THE MILITARY — Great Britain — History — 19th century
Sword and mace : twentieth century civil-military relations in Britain / edited by John Sweetman. — London : Brassey's Defence, 1986. — [228]p

CIVIL SUPREMACY OVER THE MILITARY — Great Britain — History — 20th century
Sword and mace : twentieth century civil-military relations in Britain / edited by John Sweetman. — London : Brassey's Defence, 1986. — [228]p

CIVIL SUPREMACY OVER THE MILITARY — Nigeria
NWANKWO, Arthur A.
Civilianized soldiers : army-civilian government for Nigeria / Arthur A. Nwankwo. — Enugu : Fourth Dimension Publications, 1984. — iv,70p

CIVIL WAR
ASSEFA, Hizkias
Mediation of civil wars / Hizkias Assefa. — Boulder, Colo. : Westview Press, 1986. — p. cm. — (Westview special studies in peace, conflict, and conflict resolution). — *Includes index. — Bibliography: p*

DUNÉR, Bertil, 1942-
Military intervention in civil wars : the 1970s / Bertil Dunér. — Aldershot : Gower, c1985. — xiii,197p. — (Swedish studies in international relations ; 14). — *Bibliography: p173-191. — Includes index*

CIVILIZATION
Patterns of modernity / edited by S.N. Eisenstadt. — London : Pinter
Vol.2: Beyond the West. — 1987. — vii,223p. — *Includes index*

SPENGLER, Oswald
[Der Untergang des Abendlandes. English]. The decline of the west : Oswald Spengler / authorized translation with notes by C. F. Atkinson. — London : George Allen and Unwin
vol.1: Form and actuality. — 1926. — xviii,442p

SPENGLER, Oswald
[Der Untergang des Abendlandes. English]. The decline of the west / Oswald Spengler ; authorized translation with notes by C. F. Atkinson. — London : George Allen and Unwin
vol.2: Perspectives of world history. — 1928. — xi,507,xxxiip

CIVILIZATION — Congresses
The Burden of being civilized : an anthropological perspective on the discontents of civilization / Miles Richardson and Malcolm C. Webb, editors. — Athens : University of Georgia Press, c1986. — x, 156 p.. — (Southern Anthropological Society proceedings ; no. 18). — *Includes papers presented at a symposium, held in Baton Rouge, Feb. 12-14, 1983, as part of the annual meeting of the Southern Anthropological Society. — Includes index. — Bibliography: p. [127]-145*

CIVILIZATION — History — Congresses

Irrigation civilizations : a comparative study : a symposium on method and result in cross-cultural regularities / [by] Julian H. Steward ... [et al.]. — Westport, Conn. : Greenwood Press, [1981]. — v, 78 p.. — : Reprint. Originally published: Washington, D.C. : Social Science Section, Dept. of Cultural Affairs, Pan American Union, 1955. (Social science monographs ; 1). — Includes bibliographies. — Contents: Introduction / by Julian H. Steward -- Developmental stages in ancient Mesopotamia / by Robert M. Adams -- Development of civilization on the coast of Peru / by Donald Collier -- The agricultural bases of urban civilization in Mesoamerica / by Angel Palerm -- Developmental aspects of hydraulic societies / by Karl A. Wittfogel -- Discussion: symposium on irrigation civilizations / by Ralph L. Beals -- Some implications of the symposium / by Julian H. Steward

CIVILIZATION — Philosophy

DUERR, Hans Peter
Dreamtime : concerning the boundary between wilderness and civilization / Hans Peter Duerr ; translated by Felicitas Goodman. — Oxford : Blackwell, 1985. — xi,462p. — Translation of: Traumzeit. — Bibliography: p371-457. — Includes index

CIVILIZATION — Philosophy — Congresses

Irrigation civilizations : a comparative study : a symposium on method and result in cross-cultural regularities / [by] Julian H. Steward ... [et al.]. — Westport, Conn. : Greenwood Press, [1981]. — v, 78 p.. — : Reprint. Originally published: Washington, D.C. : Social Science Section, Dept. of Cultural Affairs, Pan American Union, 1955. (Social science monographs ; 1). — Includes bibliographies. — Contents: Introduction / by Julian H. Steward -- Developmental stages in ancient Mesopotamia / by Robert M. Adams -- Development of civilization on the coast of Peru / by Donald Collier -- The agricultural bases of urban civilization in Mesoamerica / by Angel Palerm -- Developmental aspects of hydraulic societies / by Karl A. Wittfogel -- Discussion: symposium on irrigation civilizations / by Ralph L. Beals -- Some implications of the symposium / by Julian H. Steward

CIVILIZATION, ANCIENT

CHILDE, V. Gordon
Man makes himself / Vere Gordon Childe. — London : Watts, 1936. — xii,275p

MAZZARINO, Santo
The end of the ancient world / Santo Mazzarino ; translated by George Holmes. — London : Faber, 1966. — 198p

CIVILIZATION, ANGLO-SAXON

CAMPBELL, James
Essays in Anglo-Saxon history / James Campbell. — London : Hambledon Press, 1986. — xi,240p. — (History series ; 26)

CIVILIZATION, CELTIC

ELLIS, Peter Berresford
The Celtic revolution : a study in anti-imperialism / Peter Berresford Ellis. — Talybont : Y Lolfa, 1985. — 218p. — Bibliography: p215-217

CIVILIZATION, CLASSICAL

SAXONHOUSE, Arlene W
Women in the history of political thought : ancient Greece to Machiavelli / Arlene W. Saxonhouse. — New York ; Eastbourne : Praeger, 1985. — xii, 210p. — (Women and politics series). — Includes index. — Bibliography: p.199-204

CIVILIZATION, ISLAMIC

ROY, Manabendra Nath
The historical role of Islam / M. N. Roy. — Delhi : Ajanta Books, 1939. — 91p

SARDAR, Ziauddin
The future of Muslim civilisation / Ziauddin Sardar. — 2nd ed. — London : Mansell, 1987. — [250]p. — (Islamic futures and policy studies). — Previous ed.: London : Croom Helm, 1979. — Includes bibliography and index

CIVILIZATION, ISLAMIC — History

HODGSON, Marshall Goodwin Simms
The venture of Islam : conscience and history in a world civilisation / Marshall G.S. Hodgson. — Chicago ; London : University of Chicago Press, 1974. — 3v.(xii,532p;vii,609p;vi,469p). — Maps on lining papers. — Includes bibliographies and index

CIVILIZATION, ISLAMIC — Occidental influences

Revolt against modernity : Muslim zealots and the West / Michael Youssef. — Leiden : Brill, 1985. — 189p. — (Social, economic and political studies of the Middle East ; v. 39). — Bibliography: p182-184

YOUSSEF, Michael
Revolt against modernity : Muslim zealots and the West / Michael Youssef. — Leiden : Brill, 1985. — 189p. — (Social, economic and political studies of the Middle East ; v.39). — Bibliography: p182-184

CIVILIZATION, MEDIEVAL

Aspects of late medieval government and society : essays presented to J.R. Lander / edited by J. G. Rowe. — Toronto ; London : published in association with the University of Western Ontario by University of Toronto Press, 1986. — xx,276p

CIVILIZATION, MODERN — 19th century

LOVE, Nancy Sue
Marx, Nietzsche, and modernity / Nancy S. Love. — New York : Columbia University Press, 1986. — xii, 264 p. — Includes index. — Bibliography: p. [243]-255

CIVILIZATION, MODERN — 20th century

KOHN, Hans
The twentieth century / Hans Kohn. — London : Gollancz, 1950. — xi,242p

PYM, Denis
The employment question, & other essays / Denis Pym. — London : Freedom Press, 1986. — 68p

Shaping the future : thoughts on the world to come / by the...Bishop of Birmingham...[et al.]. — Wellington, N.Z. : Progressive Publishing Society, 1943. — 55p

CIVILIZATION, MODERN — 1950-

CAREY, George W. (George Westcott)
Order, freedom and the polity : critical essays on the open society / George W. Carey. — Lanham : University Press of America ; London : Distributed by Eurospan, c1986. — [196]p

The revolution of everyday life : a new translation...of Traité de savoir-vivre à l'usage des jeunes générations / Raoul Vaneigem ; [translated by] Donald Nicholson-Smith. — [London?] : Left Bank Books : Rebel Press, 1983. — 216p

CIVILIZATION, OCCIDENTAL

CAREY, George W. (George Westcott)
Order, freedom and the polity : critical essays on the open society / George W. Carey. — Lanham : University Press of America ; London : Distributed by Eurospan, c1986. — [196]p

TRASK, Haunani-Kay
Eros and power : the promise of feminist theory / Haunani-Kay Trask. — Philadelphia : University of Pennsylvania Press, c1986. — xiv, 186 p.. — Includes bibliographies and index

CIVILIZATION, OCCIDENTAL — Addresses, essays, lectures

The Female body in western culture : contemporary perspectives / Susan Rubin Suleiman, editor. — Cambridge, Mass. : Harvard University Press, 1986. — p. cm. — Includes bibliographies

CIVILIZATION, ORIENTAL

Patterns of modernity / edited by S.N. Eisenstadt. — London : Pinter
Vol.2: Beyond the West. — 1987. — vii,223p. — Includes index

CK COACHES

PUNNETT, L. M.
Bus service competition in action — the rise and fall of CK Coaches Ltd. : a report of a study conducted on behalf of the Rees Jeffreys Road Fund : by L.M. Punnett. — [Cardiff : Transport & Traffic Studies Unit, Department of Town Planning, UWIST, [1983]. — v,63p,[4] leaves of plates

CLAIMS

LILLICH, Richard B
International claims : their settlement by lump sum agreements / Richard B. Lillich and Burns H. Weston. — 1st ed. — Charlottesville : University Press of Virginia, 1975. — 2 v. — (The Procedural aspects of international law series ; 12). — Includes index. — Bibliography: v. 1, p. [335]-350. — Contents: pt. 1. The commentary.--pt. 2. The agreements

CLANS — Indonesia — Mamboru

NEEDHAM, Rodney
Mamboru : history and structure in a domain of Northwestern Sumba / Rodney Needham. — Oxford : Clarendon, 1987. — xxv,202p,[6]p of plates. — Bibliography: p194-200. — Includes index

CLANS AND CLAN SYSTEMS — Scotland — History

BROWN, Keith M.
Bloodfeud in Scotland, 1573-1625 : violence, justice and politics in an early modern society / Keith M. Brown. — Edinburgh : John Donald, c1986. — x, 299p. — Bibliography: p 285-293

CLARK, WILLIAM, 1916-1985

CLARK, William, 1916-1985
From three worlds : memoirs / William Clark. — London : Sidgwick & Jackson, [1986]. — xi,292p

CLASS ACTIONS (CIVIL PROCEDURE) — United States

SCHUCK, Peter H
Agent Orange on trial : mass toxic disasters in the courts / Peter H. Schuck. — Cambridge, Mass. : Belknap Press of Harvard University Press, 1986. — ix, 347 p. — Includes index. — Bibliography: p. [301]-335

CLASS CONSCIOUSNESS — Norway

Styrk fagbevegelsens kampkraft : faglig studiebok fra AKP (m-l). — Oslo : Forlaget Oktober, 1975. — 205p

CLASSICAL SCHOOL OF ECONOMICS

HSIEH, Ching-Yao
A search for synthesis in economic theory / by Ching-Yao Hsieh and Stephen L. Mangum. — Armonk, N.Y. : M.E. Sharpe, c1986. — p. cm. — Bibliography: p

CLASSICAL SCHOOL OF ECONOMICS — History

O'DONELL, Margaret G.
The educational thought of the classical political economists / by Margaret G. O'Donnell. — Lanham [MD] : University Press of America, c1985. — p. cm. — Includes index

CLASSIFICATION
DURKHEIM, Émile
Primitive classification / by Émile Durkheim and Marcel Mauss ; translated from the French and edited with an introduction by Rodney Needham. — 2nd ed. — London : Cohen and West, 1970. — xlviii,96p. — *Second ed. originally published 1969. Previous ed. of this translation 1963. Originally published as 'De quelques formes primitives de classification' in 'Année Sociologique', 1903. — bibl p89-93*

CLASSIFICATION, PRIMITIVE — Addresses, essays, lectures
Indigenous knowledge systems and development / edited by David Brokensha, D. M. Warren, and Oswald Werner. — Washington, D.C. : University Press of America, c1980. — vii, 466 p.. — *Includes indexes. — Bibliography: p. 415-449*

CLAUSEWITZ, CARL VON
Clausewitz and modern strategy / edited by Michael I. Handel. — London : Cass, 1986. — [320]p. — (Journal of strategic studies ; 9, no.1 & 2). — *Includes index*

CLAY — Biography
CLAY, Cassius Marcellus
The life of Cassius Marcellus Clay : memoirs, writings, and speeches showing his conduct in the overthrow of American slavery, the salvation of the Union, and the restoration of the autonomy of the states / [by Cassius Marcellus Clay]. — New York : Negro Universities Press. — *Reprint of 1886 edition* [Vol.1]. — 1969. — xiii,600p

CLAY INDUSTRIES — European Economic Community countries — Energy consumption
BRITISH CERAMIC RESEARCH ASSOCIATION LTD.
Clay-brick industry in the European Economic Community / British Ceramic Research Association Ltd.. — Luxembourg : Commission of the European Communities, 1985. — iii,69p. — (EUR ; 9469) (Energy audit ; no.5). — *Series title: Energy. — Bibliographical references: p47-48. — Contract no. XVII/AR/82/599*

CLERGY — England
HEATH, Peter
The English parish clergy on the eve of the reformation / Peter Heath. — London : Routledge and Kegan Paul, 1969. — xiii,249p

CLERGY — Great Britain — Directories
Crockford's clerical directory : a directory of the serving and retired clergy of the Church of England, the Church in Wales, and the Scottish Episcopal Church. — London : Oxford University Press, 1927-. — *Irregular. — Sub-title varies. — From 1985 published by Church House Publishing for the Church Commissioners for England and the Central Board of Finance of the Church of England*

CLERGY — Great Britain — Minor orders — History
DENTON, Jeffrey H.
Representatives of the lower clergy in Parliament, 1295-1340 / J.H. Denton and J.P. Dooley. — Woodbridge : Boydell, 1987. — [viii,256]p. — (Royal Historical Society studies in history series ; no.50). — *At foot of t.p.: Royal Historical Society. — Includes bibliography and index*

CLERGY — Northern Ireland — Biography
BRUCE, Steve
God save Ulster : the religion and politics of Paisleyism / Steve Bruce. — Oxford : Clarendon, 1986. — xv,308p. — *Includes index*

CLERKS — Salaries, pensions, etc — Great Britain
RAHMAN, Nasreen
Council non-manual workers and low pay / Nasreen Rahman. — London : Low Pay Unit, 1986. — 32p. — (Low pay pamphlet ; no.41)

CLERKS — France
STEEDMAN, Hilary
Vocational training in France and Britain : office work / Hilary Steedman. — London : National Institute of Economic and Social Research, 1986. — 23p. — (Discussion paper / National Institute of Economic and Social Research ; no.114)

CLERKS — Germany — History
SPEIER, Hans
[Angestellten vor dem Nationalsozialismus. English]. German white-collar workers and the rise of Hitler / Hans Speier. — New Haven : Yale University Press, c1986. — xxv, 208 p.. — *Translation of: Die Angestellten vor dem Nationalsozialismus. — Includes index. — Bibliography: p. 191-203*

CLERKS — Great Britain
BAIN, George Sayers
The growth of white-collar unionism / by George Sayers Bain. — Oxford : Clarendon P, 1970. — xvi,233p,fold plate. — *bibl p219-220*

STEEDMAN, Hilary
Vocational training in France and Britain : office work / Hilary Steedman. — London : National Institute of Economic and Social Research, 1986. — 23p. — (Discussion paper / National Institute of Economic and Social Research ; no.114)

CLEVELAND — Economic conditions
CLEVELAND. County Council. Research and Intelligence Unit
Cleveland 1987-1991 : an economic, demographic and social review. — Middlesbrough : [the Unit], 1987. — 17p. — *Bibliography: p17*

CLEVELAND. Planning Department
Employment trends and forecasts. — Middlesbrough : [the] Department, 1983. — 20,[12]p. — (Monitoring note report / Cleveland Planning Department ; no.234)

CLEVELAND. Planning Department
Employment trends and forecasts. — Middlesbrough : [the Department], 1987. — [6]p. — (Monitoring note / Cleveland. Planning Department ; 87/2)

CLEVELAND — Population
CLEVELAND. County Council. Research and Intelligence Unit
Cleveland 1987-1991 : an economic, demographic and social review. — Middlesbrough : [the Unit], 1987. — 17p. — *Bibliography: p17*

CLEVELAND. County Council. Research and Intelligence Unit
Population projections for Cleveland and its boroughs, 1986-2001: detailed report. — Middlesbrough : [the Unit], 1987. — 23,[40]p

CLEVELAND. County Council. Research and Intelligence Unit
Population projections for electoral divisions, wards and other small areas in Cleveland, 1987-2001. — [Middlesbrough] : [the Unit], 1987. — 4,[22]p. — *Includes folded map*

CLEVELAND — Social conditions
CLEVELAND. County Council. Research and Intelligence Unit
Cleveland 1987-1991 : an economic, demographic and social review. — Middlesbrough : [the Unit], 1987. — 17p. — *Bibliography: p17*

CLIMATIC CHANGES — Economic aspects
Social and economic responses to climatic variability in the UK / by K.T. Parker...[et al.]. — London : Technical Change Centre, 1986. — iii, 160p. — *Bibliography: p.144-154*

CLIMATIC CHANGES — Social aspects
Social and economic responses to climatic variability in the UK / by K.T. Parker...[et al.]. — London : Technical Change Centre, 1986. — iii, 160p. — *Bibliography: p.144-154*

CLIMATIC CHANGES — Great Britain
Social and economic responses to climatic variability in the UK / by K.T. Parker...[et al.]. — London : Technical Change Centre, 1986. — iii, 160p. — *Bibliography: p.144-154*

CLIMATOLOGY — Economic aspects
MAUNDER, W. J., 1932-
The uncertainty business : risks and opportunities in weather and climate / W.J. Maunder ; with a foreword by John R. Mather. — London : Methuen, 1986. — xxviii,420p. — *Bibliography: p361-403. — Includes indexes*

CLOSE COLONY (IOWA) — History
HARNACK, Curtis
Gentlemen on the prairie / Curtis Harnack. — Ames : Iowa State University Press, c1985. — viii, 254 p.. — *Includes index. — Bibliography: p. 239-248*

CLOTHING, PROTECTIVE
LABOUR RESEARCH DEPARTMENT
A guide to protective clothing. — London : LRD Publications, 1986. — 38p

CLOTHING TRADE — Great Britain — Statistics
Clothing and footwear shops. — London : HMSO, 1970-79. — (Business monitor. SD ; 2) (Business monitor. SDM ; 2). — *Monthly. — Continued by: Retail sales*

CLOTHING TRADE — New York (N.Y.)
WALDINGER, Roger David
Through the eye of the needle : immigrants and enterprise in New York's garment trades / Roger D. Waldinger. — New York : New York University Press, 1986. — p. cm. — *Includes index. — Bibliography: p*

CLOTHING WORKERS
Social and labour practices of multinational enterprises in the textiles, clothing, and footwear industries. — Geneva : International Labour Office, 1984. — xii,184p. — *Includes bibliographies*

CLOTHING WORKERS — New York (N.Y.)
WALDINGER, Roger David
Through the eye of the needle : immigrants and enterprise in New York's garment trades / Roger D. Waldinger. — New York : New York University Press, 1986. — p. cm. — *Includes index. — Bibliography: p*

CLUSTER ANALYSIS
ALDENDERFER, Mark S.
Cluster analysis / by Mark S. Aldenderfer and Roger K. Blashfield. — Beverly Hills : Sage, 1984. — (Quantitative applications in the social sciences ; 44)

EVERITT, Brian
Cluster analysis / Brian Everitt. — 2nd ed. — Aldershot : Published on behalf of the Social Science Research Council by Gower, 1986, c1980. — 136p. — (Reviews of current research ; 11). — *Previous ed.: London : Heinemann Educational for the Social Science Research Council, 1974. — Bibliography: p119-132. — Includes index*

CLWYD (WALES) — Economic conditions
CLWYD. County Council
Clwyd county structure plan : public participation seminar : employment : report of proceedings. — Mold : [the Council], 1975. — 24p

CLWYD (WALES) — Population
CLWYD. County Council
Clwyd county structure plan : report of survey. — Mold [the Council]. — 1978. — *Includes folded maps*
Technical appendix: population, housing and settlements. — 64p

CLWYD (WALES) — Rural conditions
CLWYD. County Council
Clwyd county structure plan : public participation seminar : rural communities : report of proceedings. — Mold : [the Council], 1975. — 25p

CLYDESIDE (STRATHCLYDE) — Economic conditions

The city in transition : policies and agencies for the economic regeneration of Clydeside / edited by William Lever and Chris Moore. — Oxford : Clarendon Press, 1986. — xvi,173p. — (Inner Cities Research Programme series ; 4). — Bibliography: p163-167. — Includes index

CLYDESIDE (STRATHCLYDE) — Economic policy

The city in transition : policies and agencies for the economic regeneration of Clydeside / edited by William Lever and Chris Moore. — Oxford : Clarendon Press, 1986. — xvi,173p. — (Inner Cities Research Programme series ; 4). — Bibliography: p163-167. — Includes index

CO-OPERATIVE COMMONWEALTH FEDERATION — History — Congresses

"Building the Co-operative Commonwealth" : essays on the Democratic Socialist tradition in Canada / edited by J. William Brennan. — Regina : University of Regina, Canadian Plains Research Center, 1985. — xiii,255p. — (Canadian Plains proceedings ; 13). — "Based on papers delivered at the Regina Conference, June 23-25, 1983, commemorating the 50th anniversary of the Regina Manifesto". — Includes references

CO-OPERATIVE PARTY

The Co-operative Party : what's it all about?. — London : Co-operative Party, 1987. — 27p

CO-OPERATIVE PRODUCTION — Great Britain

CLARKE, Peter, 1949-
Co-operative enterprise and the social economy / Peter Clarke and Will Watkins. — London : Co-operative Party, 1984. — 12p. — (Co-operative briefing)

CO-OPERATIVE SOCIETIES — Canada

MACPHERSON, Ian
The co-operative movement of the Prairies, 1900-1955 / Ian Macpherson. — Ottawa : Canadian Historical Association, 1979. — 21p. — (Canadian Historical Association booklets ; no.33). — Bibliography: p21

CO-OPERATIVE SOCIETIES — Great Britain — Finance

MACFARLANE, Richard
Councils support co-ops : Local authority support for worker co-ops : the past and the future / Richard Macfarlane. — Manchester : CLES, 1986. — 64p. — (CLES report ; no2)

COACHING — Great Britain — History

AUSTEN, Brian
British mail-coach services, 1784-1850 / Brian Austen. — New York : Garland Pub., 1986. — p. cm. — (Outstanding theses from the London School of Economics and Political Science). — : Originally presented as the author's thesis (Ph. D.)--University of London, 1979. — Bibliography: p

COAL — Economic aspects — Great Britain

NATIONAL SOCIETY FOR CLEAN AIR. Workshop (1983 : Sheffield)
Coal and the Community / [contributions by G. R. Millington...et al.]. — Brighton : The Society, [c1983]. — various pagings. — Papers of a workshop held in Sheffield, 23 and 24 March 1983

COAL — Environmental aspects — Great Britain

NATIONAL SOCIETY FOR CLEAN AIR. Workshop (1983 : Sheffield)
Coal and the Community / [contributions by G. R. Millington...et al.]. — Brighton : The Society, [c1983]. — various pagings. — Papers of a workshop held in Sheffield, 23 and 24 March 1983

Study of coal / evidence by the HSE to the Commission on Energy and the Environment concerning public health and amenity in the external environment. — London : H.M.S.O., 1980. — iii,43p. — (HSE report). — At head of title: Health & Safety Commission

COAL — Environmental aspects — International Energy Agency countries

Clean coal technology : programmes and issues. — Paris : International Energy Agency, 1987. — 174p

COAL — Environmental aspects — Organisation for Economic Co-operation and Development countries

IEA COAL INDUSTRY ADVISORY BOARD
Coal use and the environment. — Paris : International Energy Agency. — Bibliography: pC1
Vol.1. — 1983. — 66p

COAL MINERS — England — Thurcroft (South Yorkshire) — Interviews

Thurcroft : a village and the miners' strike : an oral history / the people of Thurcroft. — Nottingham : Spokesman, 1986. — 276p. — (Britain's regions in crisis ; 1). — Includes index

COAL MINERS — France — Decazeville — History

REID, Donald, 1952-
The miners of Decazeville : a genealogy of deindustrialization / Donald Reid. — Cambridge, Mass. ; London : Harvard University Press, 1985. — vi,333p. — Includes index

COAL-MINERS — Great Britain

BEAN, Charles R.
Employment in the British coal industry : a test of the labour demand model / C. R. Bean and P. J. Turnbull. — London : London School of Economics, Centre for Labour Economics, 1987. — 36p. — (Discussion paper / London School of Economics and Political Science. Centre for Labour Economics ; no.274). — Bibliography: p34-36

COAL MINERS — Spain — Asturias — History — 20th century

SHUBERT, Adrian
Hacia la revolución : orígenes sociales del movimiento obrero en Asturias, 1860-1934 / Adrian Shubert ; traducción castellana de Agueda Palacios Honorato. — Barcelona : Crítica, 1984. — 235p. — Bibliography: p [215]-223

COAL MINERS' STRIKE, GREAT BRITAIN, 1984-1985

JACKSON, Bernard
The battle for Orgreave / Bernard Jackson with Tony Wardle. — Brighton : Vanson Wardle Productions, [1986?]. — x,129p

COAL MINERS' WIVES — England — Nottinghamshire

WITHAM, Joan
Hearts and minds : the story of the women of Nottinghamshire in the miners' strike, 1984-1985 / Joan Witham. — London : Canary, 1986. — 217p. — Includes index

COAL MINERS' WIVES — Great Britain

MILLER, Jill
You can't kill the spirit : women in a Welsh mining village / Jill Miller. — London : Women's Press, c1986. — 142p

STEAD, Jean
Never the same again : women and the miner's strike 1984-85 / Jean Stead. — London : Women's Press, 1987. — 177p,[8]p of plates. — Includes index

COAL MINES AND MINING — Economic aspects — Great Britain

GLYN, Andrew
The economic case against pit closures / prepared for the National Union of Mineworkers by Andrew Glyn. — [Sheffield : N.U.M., 1984]. — 25p

COAL MINES AND MINING — Environmental aspects — Bibliography

GREAT BRITAIN. Department of Energy. Library
Direct effects of coal production on land use / [compiled by A. E. Cunningham]. — London : the Library, [1979]. — 7 leaves

COAL MINES AND MINING — Environmental aspects — England — Woolley

GREAT BRITAIN. Department of the Environment. Yorkshire and Humberside Regional Office
Woolley Colliery : study report. — [Leeds : the Office, 1973]. — 12p

COAL MINES AND MINING — Environmental aspects — Great Britain

NATIONAL SOCIETY FOR CLEAN AIR. Workshop (1983 : Sheffield)
Coal and the Community / [contributions by G. R. Millington...et al.]. — Brighton : The Society, [c1983]. — various pagings. — Papers of a workshop held in Sheffield, 23 and 24 March 1983

COAL MINES AND MINING — Environmental aspects — Organisation for Economic Co-operation and Development countries

Coal : environmental policies and institutions. — Paris : OECD, 1987. — 108p. — Includes bibliographical references

COAL MINES AND MINING — Government ownership — Great Britain

NATIONAL COAL BOARD
Coal consumers' councils : statement by the National Coal Board at the inaugural meetings. — [London : the Board, 1947]. — 19p

COAL MINES AND MINING — England — Newcastle-upon-Tyne (Tyne and Wear) — History

LIDDELL, Henry
The Letters of Henry Liddell to William Cotesworth / edited by J. M. Ellis. — [Durham?] : Surtees Society, 1987. — xvi,293p. — (Publications of the Surtees Society ; v.197)

COAL MINES AND MINING — England — Vale of Belvoir (Leicestershire: District) — Designs and plans

Belvoir prospect / National Coal Board, South Nottinghamshire and South Midlands areas. — [London? : National Coal Board?]
Vol.2: Surface works report / Leonard and Partners in association with Owen Luder Partnership
Appendices
Plans. — 1977. — 1v. of plans

Belvoir prospect / National Coal Board, South Nottinghamshire and South Midlands areas. — [London? : National Coal Board?]
Vol.2: Surface works report / Leonard and Partners in association with Owen Luder Partnership
Plans. — 1977. — 50plans

COAL MINES AND MINING — England — Vale of Belvoir (Leicestershire: District) — Planning

Belvoir prospect / National Coal Board, South Nottinghamshire and South Midlands areas. — [London? : National Coal Board?]
Vol.1: Surface and underground works, joint conclusion / Leonard and Partners with Owen Luder Partnership, Thyssen (G.B.) Ltd.. — 1977. — [2] leaves, 1 map

Belvoir prospect / National Coal Board, South Nottinghamshire and South Midlands areas. — [London? : National Coal Board?]
Vol.2: Surface works report / Leonard and Partners in association with Owen Luder Partnership. — 1977. — 96p

COAL MINES AND MINING — England — Vale of Belvoir (Leicestershire: District) — Planning *continuation*

Belvoir prospect / National Coal Board, South Nottinghamshire and South Midlands areas. — [London? : National Coal Board?] Surface works report / Leonard and Parners in association with Owen Luder Partnership Appendices. — 1977. — *352p*

COAL MINES AND MINING — France — Decazeville — history

REID, Donald, 1952-
The miners of Decazeville : a genealogy of deindustrialization / Donald Reid. — Cambridge, Mass. ; London : Harvard University Press, 1985. — vi,333p. — *Includes index*

COAL MINES AND MINING — Great Britain

GLYN, Andrew
Colliery results and closures after the 1984-85 coal dispute / Andrew Glyn. — Oxford : Institute of Economics and Statistics, 1987. — 22p. — (Applied economics discussion paper ; no.24)

COAL MINES AND MINING — Great Britain — History

The History of the British coal industry. — Oxford : Clarendon
Vol.5: 1946-1982: the nationalized industry / by William Ashworth with the assistance of Mark Pegg. — 1986. — xix,710p,[12]p of plates. — *Bibliography: p689-695. — Includes index*

COAL MINES AND MINING — Spain — Asturias

VAZQUEZ GARCÍA, Juan Antonio
La cuestión hullera en Asturias (1918-1935) / por Juan Antonio Vazquez García ; b prólogo José Luis García Delgado. — Oviedo : Instituto de Estudios Asturianos, 1985. — 222p. — *Bibliography: p219-222*

COAL STRIKE, GREAT BRITAIN, 1984-5

The enemy within : pit villages and the miners' strike of 1984-5 / edited by Raphael Samuel, Barbara Bloomfield, Guy Boanas. — London : Routledge & Kegan Paul, 1986. — xxiii, 260p. — (History Workshop series)

COAL STRIKE, GREAT BRITAIN, 1984-1985

ADENEY, Martin, 19---
The miners' strike : 1984-5 : loss without limit / Martin Adeney and John Lloyd. — London : Routledge & Kegan Paul, 1986. — vii,319p. — *Includes index*

BARNSLEY WOMEN AGAINST PIT CLOSURES
Barnsley Women Against Pit Closures. — Barnsley (Barnsley Women Against Pit Closures). — (Women Against Pit Closures ; vol.2) (People's History of Yorkshire ; no.12) vol.2. — 1985. — 109p

GOODMAN, Geoffrey
The miners' strike / Geoffrey Goodman. — London : Pluto, 1985. — [224]p. — *Includes index*

LEVY, Catriona
A very hard year : the 1984-85 miners' strike in Mauchline / compiled by Catriona Levy and Mauchline miners' wives. — Glasgow : Workers' Educational Association, [1985]. — 34p

MACGREGOR, Ian
The enemies within : the story of the miners' strike, 1984-5 / Ian MacGregor with Rodney Tyler. — London : Collins, 1986. — 384p,[8]p of plates

MILLER, Jill
You can't kill the spirit : women in a Welsh mining village / Jill Miller. — London : Women's Press, c1986. — 142p

STEAD, Jean
Never the same again : women and the miner's strike 1984-85 / Jean Stead. — London : Women's Press, 1987. — 177p,[8]p of plates. — *Includes index*

Thurcroft : a village and the miners' strike : an oral history / the people of Thurcroft. — Nottingham : Spokesman, 1986. — 276p. — (Britain's regions in crisis ; 1). — *Includes index*

A year of our lives : a colliery community in the great coal strike of 1984/85 / compiled and narrated by David John Douglass. — [S.l.] : Hooligan Press, [1986]. — [100]p

COAL STRIKE, GREAT BRITAIN, 1984-1985 — Social aspects

PARKER, Tony
Red Hill : a mining community / Tony Parker. — London : Heinemann, 1986. — [xi],196p. — *Bibliography: p[191]-192*

COAL STRIKE, GREAT BRITAIN, 1984-1985 — England — Nottinghamshire

WITHAM, Joan
Hearts and minds : the story of the women of Nottinghamshire in the miners' strike, 1984-1985 / Joan Witham. — London : Canary, 1986. — 217p. — *Includes index*

COAL TRADE

GORDON, Richard L.
World coal : economics, politics and prospects / Richard L. Gordon. — Cambridge : Cambridge University Press, 1987. — [225]p. — (Cambridge energy studies). — *Includes bibliography and index*

COAL TRADE — Great Britain — Economic aspects

BEAN, Charles R.
Employment in the British coal industry : a test of the labour demand model / C. R. Bean and P. J. Turnbull. — London : London School of Economics, Centre for Labour Economics, 1987. — 36p. — (Discussion paper / London School of Economics and Political Science. Centre for Labour Economics ; no.274). — *Bibliography: p34-36*

COAL TRADE — Scotland — Hamilton (Strathclyde) — History

WALLACE, William, 1916-
Some notes on the coal industry in Hamilton / by William Wallace. — Hamilton : Bell College, 1985. — 23p. — (Occasional papers / Bell College Library). — *Bibliography: p22*

COALITION GOVERNMENTS — Europe

Coalitional behaviour in theory and practice : an inductive model for Western Europe / edited by Geoffrey Pridham. — Cambridge : Cambridge University Press, 1986. — [500]p. — Conference proceedings. — *Includes bibliography and index*

LUEBBERT, Gregory M
Comparative democracy : policy making and governing coalitions in Europe and Israel / Gregory M. Luebbert. — New York : Columbia University Press, 1986. — xiv, 341 p. . — *Includes index. — Bibliography: p. [313]-325*

COALITION GOVERNMENTS — Great Britain

BUTLER, David, 1924-
Governing without a majority : dilemmas for hung parliaments in Britain / David Butler. — 2nd ed. — Basingstoke : Macmillan, 1986. — [156]p. — Previous ed.: London : Collins, 1983. — *Includes index*

COALITION GOVERNMENTS — Israel

LUEBBERT, Gregory M
Comparative democracy : policy making and governing coalitions in Europe and Israel / Gregory M. Luebbert. — New York : Columbia University Press, 1986. — xiv, 341 p. . — *Includes index. — Bibliography: p. [313]-325*

COALITION (POLITICAL SCIENCE)

WINEMAN, Steven
The politics of human services : radical alternatives to the welfare state / by Steven Wineman. — 1st ed. — Boston, MA : South End Press, c1984. — iv, 272 p.. — *Bibliography: p. 249-272*

COASTAL ZONE MANAGEMENT — Greece

APOSTOLOPOULOS, Yannis N.
Maritime industrial area : a new investment concept for shipping and industry / Yannis N. Apostolopoulos. — Athens : Industrial Development Division, Hellenic Industrial Development Bank, 1984. — 135p. — *Bibliography: p133-135*

COASTAL ZONE MANAGEMENT — United States — Congresses

Cities on the beach : management issues of developed coastal barriers / edited by Rutherford H. Platt, Sheila G. Pelczarski, Barbara K.R. Burbank. — Chicago, Ill. : Department of Geography, University of Chicago, 1987. — p. cm. — (Research paper / University of Chicago. Dept. of Geography ; no. 224). — *Bibliography: p*

COBBETT, WILLIAM

GREEN, Daniel
Great Cobbett : the noblest agitator / Daniel Green. — Oxford : Oxford University Press, 1985. — ix,496p. — *Bibliography: p483-486*

COBDEN, RICHARD

EDSALL, Nicholas C
Richard Cobden, independent radical / Nicholas C. Edsall. — Cambridge, Mass. ; London : Harvard University Press, 1986. — xiv, 465p. — *Includes index. — Bibliography: p.[429]-433*

HINDE, Wendy
Richard Cobden : a Victorian outsider : a biography / by Wendy Hinde. — New Haven : Yale University Press, 1987. — p. cm. — *Includes index. — Bibliography: p*

READ, Donald
Cobden and Bright : a Victorian political partnership / Donald Read. — London : Edward Arnold, 1967. — 275p

COBOL (COMPUTER PROGRAM LANGUAGE)

PARKIN, Andrew, 1941-
COBOL for students / Andrew Parkin. — 2nd ed., including structured program design. — London : Edward Arnold, 1982. — vi,212p. — Previous ed.: 1975. — *Includes index*

COCA-COLA

GATEHOUSE, Mike
Soft drink, hard labour : Guatemalan workers take on Coca-Cola / [by Mike Gatehouse and Miguel Angel Reyes] ; [editing and additional material by James Painter]. — London : Latin America Bureau, 1987. — 38p

COCA-COLA — Marketing

OLIVER, Thomas, 1950-
The real Coke : the real story / Thomas Oliver. — London : Elm Tree, 1986. — 195p

COCA-COLA COMPANY — History

OLIVER, Thomas, 1950-
The real Coke : the real story / Thomas Oliver. — London : Elm Tree, 1986. — 195p

COCAINE

The Steel drug : cocaine in perspective / Patricia G. Erickson ... [et al.]. — Lexington, Mass. : Lexington Books, c1987. — xviii, 169 p.. — *Includes index. — Bibliography: p. [151]-159*

COCAINE HABIT

The Steel drug : cocaine in perspective / Patricia G. Erickson ... [et al.]. — Lexington, Mass. : Lexington Books, c1987. — xviii, 169 p.. — *Includes index. — Bibliography: p. [151]-159*

COCAINE HABIT — Canada
The Steel drug : cocaine in perspective / Patricia G. Erickson ... [et al.]. — Lexington, Mass. : Lexington Books, c1987. — xviii, 169 p.. — *Includes index. — Bibliography: p. [151]-159*

COCAINE HABIT — United States
The Steel drug : cocaine in perspective / Patricia G. Erickson ... [et al.]. — Lexington, Mass. : Lexington Books, c1987. — xviii, 169 p.. — *Includes index. — Bibliography: p. [151]-159*

WISOTSKY, Steven
Breaking the impasse in the war on drugs / Steven Wisotsky ; foreword by Thomas Szasz. — New York : Greenwood Press, 1986. — xxiv, 279 p.. — (Contributions in political science ; no. 159). — *Includes index. — Bibliography: p. [263]-271*

COCKBURN, CLAUDE
Cockburn in Spain : despatches from the Spanish Civil War / edited by James Pettifer. — London : Lawrence and Wishart, 1986. — 208p

COCOA
Cocoa production : present constraints and priorities for research / R. A. Lass and G. A. R. Wood, editors. — Washington, D.C. : The World Bank, 1985. — xi,95p. — (World Bank technical paper ; no.39)

COCOA — Research
Cocoa production : present constraints and priorities for research / R. A. Lass and G. A. R. Wood, editors. — Washington, D.C. : The World Bank, 1985. — xi,95p. — (World Bank technical paper ; no.39)

COCOA TRADE — Ghana
KONINGS, Piet
The State and rural class formation in Ghana : a comparative analysis / Piet Konings. — London : KPI, 1986. — xvi,391p. — *Bibliography: p356-377*

COCONUT — Fiji
BROOKFIELD, Harold Chillingworth
Land, cane and coconuts : papers on the rural economy of Fiji / H. C. Brookfield, F. Ellis, R. G. Ward. — Canberra [A.C.T.] : Australian National University, 1985. — 251p. — (Australian National University Department of Human Geography Publication ; HG/17). — *Includes bibliographies*

COD-FISHERIES — Economic aspects — Newfoundland
RYAN, Shannon
Fish out of water : the Newfoundland saltfish trade 1814-1914 / Shannon Ryan. — St. John's (Nfld.) : Breakwater, 1986. — 320p,[24]p of plates. — (Newfoundland history series ; 2). — *Bibliography: p301-310*

COFFEE — Guatemala — History — 19th century
CAMBRANES, J. C
[Café y campesinos en Guatemala, 1853-1897. English]. Coffee and peasants : the origins of the modern plantation economy in Guatemala, 1853-1897 / J.C. Cambranes ; [English version revised by Carla Clason-Höök]. — Stockholm, Sweden : Institute of Latin American Studies, c1985. — 334 p.. — (Monografías / Institute of Latin American Studies ; no.10). — *Translation of: Café y campesinos en Guatemala, 1853-1897. — Bibliography: p. 327-332*

COFFEE TRADE — Brazil — History
CONRAD, Robert Edgar
World of sorrow : the African slave trade to Brazil / Robert Edgar Conrad. — Baton Rouge : Louisiana State University Press, c1986. — 215 p.. — *Includes index. — Bibliography: p. 197-212*

COFFEE TRADE — Colombia — Addresses, essays, lectures
THOMAS, Vinod
Linking macroeconomic and agricultural policies for adjustment with growth : the Colombian experience / Vinod Thomas with contributions from Sebastian Edwards ... [et al.]. — Baltimore : Published for the World Bank [by] the Johns Hopkins University Press, c1985. — p. cm. — *"A World Bank publication.". — Includes index*

COFFEE TRADE — Guatemala — History — 19th century
CAMBRANES, J. C
[Café y campesinos en Guatemala, 1853-1897. English]. Coffee and peasants : the origins of the modern plantation economy in Guatemala, 1853-1897 / J.C. Cambranes ; [English version revised by Carla Clason-Höök]. — Stockholm, Sweden : Institute of Latin American Studies, c1985. — 334 p.. — (Monografías / Institute of Latin American Studies ; no.10). — *Translation of: Café y campesinos en Guatemala, 1853-1897. — Bibliography: p. 327-332*

COGENERATION OF ELECTRIC POWER AND HEAT — Great Britain
SCHAFFER, I. R.
Combined heat and power and electricity generation in British industry, 1983-1988 : a statistical and economic survey / I. R. Schaffer ; technical consultant, R.W. Clayton. — London : H.M.S.O. [for the Energy Efficiency Office, Dept. of Energy], 1986. — [ca.190]p in various pagings. — (Energy efficiency series ; 5)

COGNITION
ARBIB, Michael A
In search of the person : philosophical explorations in cognitive science / Michael A. Arbib. — Amherst : University of Massachusetts, 1985. — xii, 156 p.. — *Includes index. — Bibliography: p. [137]-149*

BEST, John B
Cognitive psychology / John B. Best. — St. Paul : West Pub. Co., c1986. — xv, 547p. — *Includes index. — Bibliography: p.502-525*

Cognitive aspects of skilled typewriting / edited by William E. Cooper. — New York : Springer-Verlag, c1983. — xii, 417 p.. — *Includes bibliographies and indexes*

Cognitive psychology : new directions / edited by Guy Claxton. — London : Routledge & Kegan Paul, 1980. — [334]p. — (International library of psychology)

Cognitive responses in persuasion / edited by Richard E. Petty, Thomas M. Ostrom, and Timothy C. Brock. — Hillsdale, N.J. : L. Erlbaum Associates, 1981. — xv,476p. — *Includes index. — Bibliography: p*

The Development of social cognition / edited by John B. Pryor, Jeanne D. Day. — New York : Springer-Verlag, c1985. — xiv, 239p. — *Includes bibliographies and indexes*

GALAMBOS, James A
Knowledge structures / James A. Galambos, Robert P. Abelson, John B. Black. — Hillsdale, N.J. : Lawrence Erlbaum Associates, 1986. — p. cm. — *Includes index. — Bibliography: p*

GREENE, Judith
Language understanding : a cognitive approach / Judith Greene. — Milton Keynes : Open University, 1986. — 158p. — (Open guides to psychology). — *Includes index. — Bibliography: p.153-155*

Handbook of social cognition / edited by Robert S. Wyer, Jr., Thomas K. Srull. — Hillsdale, N.J. ; London : L. Erlbaum Associates, 1984. — 3v. — *Includes bibliographies and indexes*

MCCLELLAND, James L.
Parallel distributed processing : explorations in the microstructure of cognition. — Cambridge, Mass. : MIT Press. — (Computational models of cognition and perception) Vol.2: Psychological and biological models / James L. McClelland, David E. Rumelhart and the PDP Research Group. — 1986. — xii,611p . — *Bibliography: p[553]-579*

New directions in cognitive science / edited by Theodore M. Shlechter and Michael P. Toglia. — Norwood, N.J. : Ablex Pub. Corp., 1985. — viii, 309p. — *Includes bibliographical references and index*

PAIVIO, Allan
Mental representations : a dual coding approach / Allan Paivio. — New York : Oxford University Press ; Oxford : Clarendon Press, 1986. — x, 322p. — (Oxford psychology series ; no. 9). — *Includes index. — Bibliography: p.277-305*

RUMELHART, David E.
Parallel distributed processing : explorations in the microstructure of cognition. — Cambridge, Mass. ; London : MIT Press. — (Computational models of cognition and perception) (A Bradford book) Vol.1: Foundations / David E. Rumelhart, James L. McClelland and the PDP Research Group ; Chisato Asanuma ..: [et al.]. — c1986. — xx,547p. — *Bibliography: p507-516. — Includes index*

SOWA, John F.
Conceptual structures : information processing in mind and machine / John F. Sowa. — Reading, Mass. ; London : Addison-Wesley, 1984. — (The Systems programming series)

COGNITION — Age factors
RYBASH, John M
Adult cognition and aging : developmental changes in processing, knowing and thinking / John M. Rybash, William J. Hoyer, Paul A. Roodin. — New York : Pergamon Press, c1986. — x, 194 p.. — (Pergamon general psychology series ; 139) (Pergamon international library of science, technology, engineering, and social studies). — *Includes indexes. — Bibliography: p. 165-185*

COGNITION — Congresses
Questions on social explanation : Piagetian themes reconsidered / edited by Luigia Camaioni and Cláudia de Lemos. — Amsterdam ; Philadelphia : J. Benjamins Pub. Co., 1985. — 141 p.. — (Pragmatics & beyond ; VI:4). — *Selection of the papers presented at the international conference in honour of Jean Piaget, held in Rome, 9-10 Oct. 1981, and sponsored by Rome University. — Bibliography: p. [131]-141*

COGNITION — Handbooks
Handbook of social cognition / edited by Robert S. Wyer, Jr., Thomas K. Srull. — Hillsdale, N.J. ; London : L. Erlbaum Associates, 1984. — 3v. — *Includes bibliographies and indexes*

COGNITION — in adulthood
RYBASH, John M
Adult cognition and aging : developmental changes in processing, knowing and thinking / John M. Rybash, William J. Hoyer, Paul A. Roodin. — New York : Pergamon Press, c1986. — x, 194 p.. — (Pergamon general psychology series ; 139) (Pergamon international library of science, technology, engineering, and social studies). — *Includes indexes. — Bibliography: p. 165-185*

COGNITION — physiology
RYBASH, John M
Adult cognition and aging : developmental changes in processing, knowing and thinking / John M. Rybash, William J. Hoyer, Paul A. Roodin. — New York : Pergamon Press, c1986. — x, 194 p.. — (Pergamon general psychology series ; 139) (Pergamon international library of science, technology, engineering, and social studies). — *Includes indexes. — Bibliography: p. 165-185*

COGNITION — Research
New directions in cognitive science / edited by Theodore M. Shlechter and Michael P. Toglia. — Norwood, N.J. : Ablex Pub. Corp., 1985. — viii, 309p. — *Includes bibliographical references and index*

COGNITION — Social aspects
BANDURA, Albert
Social foundations of thought and action : a social cognitive theory / Albert Bandura. — Englewood Cliffs, N.J. : Prentice-Hall, c1986. — p. cm. — (Prentice-Hall series in social learning theory). — *Includes index. — Bibliography: p*

WERTSCH, James V
Vygotsky and the social formation of mind / James V. Wertsch. — Cambridge, Mass. : Harvard University Press, 1985. — p. cm. — *Includes index. — Bibliography: p*

COGNITION IN CHILDREN
Blueprints for thinking : the role of planning in cognitive development / edited by Sarah L. Friedman, Ellin Kofsky Scholnick, Rodney R. Cocking. — Cambridge : Cambridge University Press, 1987. — xv,559p. — *Includes bibliographies and index*

CASE, Robbie
Intellectual development : birth to adulthood / Robbie Case. — Orlando : Academic Press, 1985. — xix, 460 p.. — (Developmental psychology series). — *Includes indexes. — Bibliography: p. 433-450*

Culture, communication and cognition : Vygotskian perspectives / edited by James V. Wertsch. — Cambridge : Cambridge University Press, 1985. — x,379p. — *Bibliographies*

GINSBURG, Herbert
Piaget´s theory of intellectual development / Herbert Ginsburg, Sylvia Opper. — 2nd ed. — Englewood Cliffs ; London : Prentice-Hall, 1979. — xvi,253p. — *Previous ed.: 1969. — Bibliography: p.239-244. — Includes index*

NATO CONFERENCE ON THE ACQUISITION OF SYMBOLIC SKILLS (1982 : University of Keele)
The acquisition of symbolic skills / [proceedings of a NATO Conference on the Acquisition of Symbolic Skills, held July 5-10, 1982, at the University of Keele, Keele, England] ; edited by Don Rogers and John A. Sloboda. — New York ; London : Published in cooperation with NATO Scientific Affairs Division [by] Plenum, c1983. — xii,623p. — (NATO conference series. III, Human factors ; v.22). — *Includes bibliographies and index*

Thinking and learning skills / edited by Judith W. Segal, Susan F. Chipman, Robert Glaser. — Hillsdale, N.J. ; London : Erlbaum
Volume 1: Relating instruction to research. — 1985. — xii,554p

Thinking and learning skills / edited by Susan F. Chipman, Judith W. Segal, Robert Glaser. — Hillsdale, N.J. ; London : Erlbaum
Volume 2: Research and open questions. — 1985. — xii,639p

COLLECTION DEVELOPMENT (LIBRARIES)
Selection of library materials in the humanities, social sciences, and sciences / Patricia A. McClung, editor ; section editors, William Hepfer ... [et al.]. — Chicago : American Library Association, 1985. — xiv, 405 p.. — *Includes bibliographies and index*

COLLECTIVE BARGAINING
CABLE, John
Control, technology and the social efficiency of traditional production : a bargaining model of the capital-labour relationship / John Cable. — Coventry : University of Warwick, 1987. — 35p. — (Warwick economic research papers ; no.279)

Collective bargaining : a workers´ education manual. — 2nd (revised) ed.. — Geneva : International Labour Office, 1986. — ix,112p. — *Bibliography: p111-112*

Collective bargaining in industrialised market economies : a reappraisal. — Geneva : International Labour Office, 1987. — xii,333p. — *Bibliography: p325-333. — Contents: Part 1 : A comparative study/John P. Windmuller - Part 2: Country studies/W. Albeda...[et al.]*

FOX, Alan
Man mismanagement / Alan Fox. — London : Hutchinson, 1974. — 178p. — (Industry in action)

INTERNATIONAL LABOUR OFFICE
Collective bargaining : a response to the recession in industrialised market economy countries. — Geneva : I.L.O., 1984

INTERNATIONAL LABOUR OFFICE
Collective bargaining in industrialised market economies. — Geneva : International Labour Office, 1973. — vi, 415 p.. — (Studies and reports / International Labour Office. new series ; no. 80). — *Bibliography: p. 409-415*

ROOTS, Paul
Collective bargaining : opportunities for a new approach / Paul Roots. — Coventry : University of Warwick. School of Industrial and Business Studies. Industrial Relations Research Unit, 1985. — 8 leaves. — (Warwick papers in industrial relations ; no.5)

COLLECTIVE BARGAINING — Government employees — Great Britain
GREAT BRITAIN. Department of Health and Social Security
McCarthy report "Making Whitley work" : position paper. — [London : the Department], 1978. — 10p

COLLECTIVE BARGAINING — International business enterprises — Asia — Congresses
ASIAN REGIONAL CONFERENCE ON INDUSTRIAL RELATIONS (6th : 1975 : Tokyo)
Foreign investment and labor in Asian countries : proceedings of the 1975 Asian Regional Conference on Industrial Relations, Tokyo, Japan, 1975. — [Tokyo] : Japan Institute of Labour, [1976]. — iii, 240 p.. — *Held March 17-20, 1975; co-sponsored by the Japan Institute of Labour and the Japan Industrial Relations Research Association. — Includes bibliographical References*

COLLECTIVE BARGAINING — Mathematical models
The Economics of bargaining / edited by Ken Binmore and Partha Dasgupta. — Oxford : Basil Blackwell, 1987. — 260p. — *Includes bibliographies and index*

COLLECTIVE BARGAINING — Transportation — New Zealand
Industrial relations in transport : proceedings of a seminar / edited by Kevin Hince. — Wellington : Victoria University of Wellington. Industrial Relations Centre : Chartered Institute of Transport in New Zealand, 1985. — 55p

COLLECTIVE BARGAINING — Canada
CARROTHERS, A. W. R.
Collective bargaining law in Canada / A. W. R. Carrothers, E. E. Palmer, W. B. Rayner. — 2nd ed. — Toronto : Butterworths, 1986. — cliii,785p

COLLECTIVE BARGAINING — Great Britain
ADVISORY, CONCILIATION AND ARBITRATION SERVICE
Collective bargaining in Britain : its extent and level. — [London : the Service], 1983. — 28p. — (Discussion paper ; no.2). — *Bibliographical references: p23-25*

FERRY, Alex
Bargaining : 1984 and beyond / Alex Ferry. — Nottingham : Trent Polytechnic, 1984. — 39p. — *Trent Business School. Open lectures on industrial relations: the changing contours of collective bargaining*

LEE, Kevin
An empirical investigation of the frequency of industrial wage change in the U.K. / Kevin Lee. — London : Centre for Labour Economics, London School of Economics, 1987. — 46p. — (Discussion paper / London School of Economics and Political Science ; no.271). — *Bibliography: p44-46*

SCHULLER, Tom
Pensions, bargaining and corporate policy / Tom Schuller. — Coventry : University of Warwick. School of Industrial and Business Studies. Industrial Relations Research Unit, 1986. — 17 leaves. — (Warwick papers in industrial relations ; no.12). — *Bibliography: p16*

COLLECTIVE BARGAINING — United States
Collective bargaining in the U.S. : structures, practices and accomplishments / by Otis Brubaker...[et al.]. — London : Labour Information Office, U.S. Information Service, 1957. — 23p. — *A reprint of three articles originally published in "Labour news from the U.S.", Oct. and Nov., 1957*

COLLECTIVE BARGAINING UNIT — United States
WILLIAMS, Robert E.
NLRB regulation of election conduct / by Robert E. Williams ; with acknowledgement to Peter A. Janus and Kenneth C. Huhn. — Rev ed. — Philadelphia, Pa. : Industrial Research Unit, Wharton School, University of Pennsylvania, c1985. — xv, 539 p.. — (Labor relations and public policy series ; no. 8). — *Includes bibliographical references and index*

COLLECTIVE FARMS — Soviet Union — Officials and employees
VIOLA, Lynne
The best sons of the fatherland : workers in the vanguard of soviet collectivization / Lynne Viola. — New York : Oxford University Press, 1987. — p. cm. — *Includes index. — Bibliography: p*

COLLECTIVE LABOR AGREEMENTS — European Economic Community countries
PERONE, Gian Carlo
The law of collective agreements in the countries of the European Community / report submitted by Gian Carlo Perone ; with the assistance of Antonio Vallebona. — Luxembourg : Office for Official Publications of the European Communities, 1984. — 42p. — *At head of title page: Commission of the European Communities*

COLLECTIVE LABOR AGREEMENTS — Great Britain
BURROWS, Giles
No-strike agreements and pendulum arbitration / Giles Burrows. — London : Institute of Personnel Management, 1986. — [88]p. — *Includes bibliography*

COLLECTIVE SETTLEMENTS
MELNYK, George
The search for community : from utopia to a co-operative society / George Melnyk. — Montréal ; Buffalo : Black Rose Books, c1985. — xv, 170 p.. — *Includes bibliographical references and index*

SHENKER, Barry
Intentional communities : ideology and alienation in communal societies / Barry Shenker. — London : Routledge & Kegan Paul, 1986. — [320]p. — (The International library of group psychotherapy and group process. Therapeutic communities). — *Includes index*

COLLECTIVE SETTLEMENTS — United States — History
Utopias : the American experience / edited by Gairdner B. Moment & Otto F. Kraushaar. — Metuchen ; London : Scarecrow Press ; [Folkestone] : [Distributed by Bailey and Swinfen], 1980. — [1],vii,251p. — *Includes bibliographies and index*

COLLECTIVIZATION OF AGRICULTURE — Soviet Union — History
VIOLA, Lynne
The best sons of the fatherland : workers in the vanguard of soviet collectivization / Lynne Viola. — New York : Oxford University Press, 1987. — p. cm. — *Includes index. — Bibliography: p*

COLLEGE CREDITS — Europe
COX, Edwin H.
Academic recognition of diplomas in the European Community : present state and prospects / by Edwin Cox. — Brussels : Commission of the European Communities, 1977c1979. — 75p. — (Education series / Commission of the European Communities ; no. 10)

COLLEGE GRADUATES — Employment — Great Britain
CONNOR, Helen
The graduate milkround : its changing role and pattern of use / Helen Connor and Geoffrey Prior-Wandesforde. — Brighton : Institue of Manpower Studies. University of Sussex, 1986. — vi,41p. — (IMS report ; no.124). — *Bibliography: p41*

CONNOR, Helen
The labour market for IT postgraduates / by Helen Connor and Richard Pearson. — Brighton : Institute of Manpower Studies, 1986. — vi,108p. — (IMS report ; No.118)

MABEY, Christopher, 1951-
Graduates into industry : a survey of changing graduate attitudes / Christopher Mabey. — Aldershot : Gower, c1986. — ix,182p. — *Bibliography: p174-182*

PEARSON, Richard, 1948-
Monitoring graduate recruitment / Richard Pearson and Geoffrey Prior-Wandesforde. — Brighton : Institute of Manpower Studies, University of Sussex, 1986. — iv,35p. — (IMS report ; no.123). — *Bibliography: p31-32*

COLLEGE GRADUATES — United States
LITTWIN, Susan
The postponed generation : why America's kids are growing up later / Susan Littwin. — New York : Morrow, c1986. — p. cm

COLLEGE INTEGRATION — New York (N.Y.) — Case studies
EXUM, William H.
Paradoxes of protest : black student activism in a White university / William H. Exum. — Philadelphia : Temple University Press, 1985. — p. cm. — *Includes index. — Bibliography: p*

COLLEGE LIBRARIANS — Great Britain
British journal of academic librarianship. — London : Taylor Graham, 1986-. — *3 per year*

COLLEGE STUDENTS — Finland — Statistics
KOLARI, Risto
Korkeakouluopiskelu : korkeakoulututkinnot ja opintojen keskeyttäminen 1966-1979 = University studies : university degrees and interruption of studies 1966-1979. — Helsinki : Tilastokeskus, 1982. — 98p. — (Tutkimuksia / Finland. Tilastokeskus ; no.84). — *In Finnish and English*

COLLEGE STUDENTS — Germany — Political activity — History — 20th century
WEBER, R. G. S.
The German student corps in the Third Reich / R.G.S. Weber. — Basingstoke : Macmillan, 1986. — ix,209p. — *Bibliography: p196-202. — Includes index*

COLLEGE STUDENTS — South Africa
DU TOIT, Brian M.
Drug use and South African students / by Brian M. Du Toit. — [Athens] : Ohio University Center for International Studies, Africa Program, 1978. — 127 p.. — (Papers in international studies : Africa series ; no. 35). — *Bibliography: p. 126-127*

COLLEGE STUDENTS, BLACK — South Africa — Intellectual life — History
NKOMO, Mokubung O
Student culture and activism in black South African universities : the roots of resistance / Mokubung O. Nkomo ; foreword by Johnnetta B. Cole. — Westport, Conn. : Greenwood Press, 1984. — xxiii, 209 p.. — (Contributions in Afro-American and African studies ; no. 78) . — *Includes index. — Bibliography: p. [179]-200*

COLLEGE STUDENTS, JEWISH — Connecticut — New Haven — History
OREN, Dan A.
Joining the club : a history of Jews and Yale / Dan A. Oren. — New Haven : Yale University Press, c1985. — xiv, 440 p.. — (The Yale scene. University series ; 4). — *Published in cooperation with the American Jewish Archives. — Includes index. — Bibliography: p. 397-423*

COLLEGE STUDENTS' SOCIO-ECONOMIC STATUS — Australia — Statistics
ANDERSON, Don
Access to privilege : patterns of participation in Australian post-secondary education / D.S. Anderson and A.E. Vervoorn. — Canberra, Australia ; Miami, Fla., USA : Australian National University Press, 1983. — xii, 197 p.. — *Includes index. — Bibliography: p. [177]-185*

COLLEGE TEACHERS — Political activity
AUERNHEIMER, Gustav
Genosse Herr Doktor : zur Rolle von Akademikern in der deutschen Sozialdemokratie 1890 bid 1933 / Gustav Auernheimer. — Giessen : Focus-verlag, 1985. — 240p. — *Bibliography: p223-240*

COLLEGE TEACHERS — Salaries, pensions, etc — California — Statistics
BEAUMONT, Marion S
Salary systems in public higher education : a microeconomic analysis / Marion S. Beaumont. — New York : Praeger, 1985. — p. cm. — *Includes index. — Bibliography: p*

COLLEGE TEACHERS — Tenure — Great Britain
Academic tenure : luxury or necessity? / a report by the Council for Science and Society. — London : The Council, c1985. — 26p. — (CSS report)

COLLEGE TEACHERS — Australia
HIREMATH, S. G
Sociology of academics in India and abroad / S.G. Hiremath. — Delhi : Sundeep Prakashan, 1983. — 10, 294 p.. — *Includes index. — Bibliography: p. [282]-290*

COLLEGE TEACHERS — Germany — History
AUERNHEIMER, Gustav
Genosse Herr Doktor : zur Rolle von Akademikern in der deutschen Sozialdemokratie 1890 bid 1933 / Gustav Auernheimer. — Giessen : Focus-verlag, 1985. — 240p. — *Bibliography: p223-240*

COLLEGE TEACHERS — Germany — Political activity — History — 20th century
GALLIN, Alice
Midwives to Nazism : university professors in Weimar Germany, 1925-1933 / Alice Gallin. — Macon, Ga. : Mercer, c1986. — viii, 134 p.. — *Includes index. — Bibliography: p. [115]-128*

COLLEGE TEACHERS — India
HIREMATH, S. G
Sociology of academics in India and abroad / S.G. Hiremath. — Delhi : Sundeep Prakashan, 1983. — 10, 294 p.. — *Includes index. — Bibliography: p. [282]-290*

COLLEGE TEACHERS — Spain — Biography
POSADA, Adolfo
Fragmentos de mis memorias / Adolfo Posada. — [Oviedo] : Universidad de Oviedo, Servicio de Publicaciones, Cátedra Aledo, c1983. — 363p. — *Bibliography: p355-363*

COLLEGE TEACHERS — Spain — Catalonia — Biography
BALCELLS, Albert
Rafael Campalans, socialisme català : biografia i textos / Albert Balcells. — [Barcelona?] : L'Abadia de Montserrat, 1985. — 444p

COLLEGE TEACHERS — United States — Political activity — History — 20th century
SCHRECKER, Ellen
No ivory tower : McCarthyism and the universities / Ellen Schrecker. — New York : Oxford University Press, 1986. — p. cm. — *Includes index. — Bibliography: p*

COLLEGE TEACHING — Vocational guidance — Australia
HIREMATH, S. G
Sociology of academics in India and abroad / S.G. Hiremath. — Delhi : Sundeep Prakashan, 1983. — 10, 294 p.. — *Includes index. — Bibliography: p. [282]-290*

COLLEGE TEACHING — Vocational guidance — India
HIREMATH, S. G
Sociology of academics in India and abroad / S.G. Hiremath. — Delhi : Sundeep Prakashan, 1983. — 10, 294 p.. — *Includes index. — Bibliography: p. [282]-290*

COLLISIONS AT SEA — Cases
HOLDERT, H. M. C.
Collision cases : judgments and diagrams / by H.M.C. Holdert and F.J. Buzek. — London : Lloyd's, 1984. — xvii,190p

COLLISIONS AT SEA — Prevention
STURT, R. H. B.
The collision regulations : the application and enforcement of the Merchant Shipping (Distress Signals and Prevention of Collisions) Regulations 1983 / by R.H.B. Sturt ; illustrations by Ann L. Sturt. — 2nd ed.. — London : Lloyd's of London Press, 1984. — xlvi,177p, 5p of plates. — *Previous ed.: 1977. — Includes index*

COLLOQUE NATIONAL SUR LA FÉCONDITÉ EN TUNISIE
COLLOQUE NATIONAL SUR LA FÉCONDITÉ EN TUNISIE (1985 : Tunis)
La fécondité en Tunisie : situation actuelle et perspectives : actes du Colloque National. — Tunis : Office National de la Famille et de la Population, 1985. — 351p. — *In French with summary in Arabic*

COLOMBIA — Administrative and political divisions
COLOMBIA. Registraduría Nacional del Estado Civil
Circunscripciones electorales y división político administrativa de Colombia 1968. — [Bogotá] : the Registraduría, 1968. — 269p

COLOMBIA — Comnmercial policy — Addresses, essays, lectures
THOMAS, Vinod
Linking macroeconomic and agricultural policies for adjustment with growth : the Colombian experience / Vinod Thomas with contributions from Sebastian Edwards ... [et al.]. — Baltimore : Published for the World Bank [by] the Johns Hopkins University Press, c1985. — p. cm. — *"A World Bank publication.". — Includes index*

COLOMBIA — Constitution

COLOMBIA
[Laws, etc]. Constitución política de Colombia acordada con la reforma plebiscitaria, los actos legislativos 1 y 2 de 1959, y el número 1 de 1968. — Bogotá : Cámara de Rrepresentantes, 1970. — 170p

COLOMBIA — Constitutional history

RESTREPO PIEDRAHITA, Carlos
Constituciones de la primera república liberal 1853-1856 / Carlos Restrepo Piedrahita. — [Bogotá] : Universidad Externado de Colombia
t.1: Constituciones provinciales : Antioquia-Choco. — [1979]. — xli,608p. — *Bibliography: p[239]-248*

RESTREPO PIEDRAHITA, Carlos
Constituciones de la primera república liberal 1853-1856 / Carlos Restrepo Piedrahita. — [Bogotá] : Universidad Externado de Colombia
t.2: Constituciones provinciales : García Rovira-Zipaquirá. — [1979]. — 618-1189p

RESTREPO PIEDRAHITA, Carlos
Constituciones de la primera república liberal 1855-1885 / Carlos Restrepo Piedrahita. — [Bogotá] : Universidad Externado de Colombia
t.3: Constituciones federales : Antioquia-Bolívar. — [1985]. — 762p. — *Bibliography: p[261]-267*

RESTREPO PIEDRAHITA, Carlos
Constituciones de la primera república liberal 1855-1885 / Carlos Restrepo Piedrahita. — [Bogotá] : Universidad Externado de Colombia
t.4(1): Constituciones Federales : Boyaca-Magdalena. — [1985]. — 774-1272p

RESTREPO PIEDRAHITA, Carlos
Constituciones de la primera república liberal 1855-1885 / Carlos Restrepo Piedrahita. — Bogotá : Universidad Externado de Colombia
t.4(2): Constituciones federales Panama-Tolima. — 1985. — [1277]-1853p

URIBE VARGAS, Diego
Las constituciones de Colombia / Diego Uribe Vargas. — 2a ed. ampliada y actualizada. — Madrid : Ediciones Cultura Hispanica, Instituto de Cooperación Iberamericana
Vol.1: Perspectiva historica y sociologica. — 1985. — 321p. — *Bibliography: p303-309*

URIBE VARGAS, Diego
Las constituciones de Colombia / Diego Uribe Vargas. — 2a ed. ampliada y actualizada. — Madrid : Ediciones Cultura Hispanica, Instituto de Cooperación Iberoamericana
Vol. 3: Textos, 1886-1985. — 1985. — p1091-1471

URIBE VARGAS, Diego
Las constituciones de Colombia / Diego Uribe Vargas. — 2a ed. ampliada y actualizada. — Madrid : Ediciones Cultura Hispanica, Instituto de Cooperación Iberoamericana
Textos, 1810-1876. — 1985. — p333-1079

COLOMBIA — Constitutional law

COLOMBIA
[Laws, etc]. Constitución política de Colombia acordada con la reforma plebiscitaria, los actos legislativos 1 y 2 de 1959, y el número 1 de 1968. — Bogotá : Cámara de Rrepresentantes, 1970. — 170p

COLOMBIA — Economic conditions

OCAMPO, José Antonio
Colombia y la economía mundial, 1830-1910 / por José Antonio Ocampo. — Bogotá : Siglo Veintiuno, 1984. — 456p. — (Economía y demografía)

COLOMBIA — Economic conditions — Regional disparities

HELMSING, A. H. J.
Firms, farms, and the state in Colombia : a study of rural, urban, and regional dimensions of change / A.H.J. Helmsing. — Boston : Allen & Unwin, 1986. — xix, 297 p.. — *Includes index. — Bibliography: p. 275-288*

COLOMBIA — Economic conditions — Statistics

Boletin de estadistica / Departmento Administrativo Nacional de Estadistica, Colombia. — Bogota : Departmento Administrativo Nacional de Estadistica, 1985. — *Quarterly. — Continues: Boletin mensual de estadistica*

Boletin mensual de estadistica / Departamento Administrativo Nacional de Estadistica, Colombia. — Bogota : Departamento Administrativo Nacional de Estadistica, 1952-1984. — *Monthly. — Continued by: Boletin de estadistica*

COLOMBIA — Economic conditions — 1970-

Colombia : economic development and policy under changing conditions. — Washington, D.C. : World Bank, c1984. — lxxxv,282p. — (A World Bank country study). — *"Report is based on the findings of an economic mission which visited Colombia during June/July 1982"--P. [iv]. — Includes bibliographical references*

COLOMBIA — Economic policy

Colombia : economic development and policy under changing conditions. — Washington, D.C. : World Bank, c1984. — lxxxv,282p. — (A World Bank country study). — *"Report is based on the findings of an economic mission which visited Colombia during June/July 1982"--P. [iv]. — Includes bibliographical references*

COLOMBIA — Economic policy — Addresses, essays, lectures

THOMAS, Vinod
Linking macroeconomic and agricultural policies for adjustment with growth : the Colombian experience / Vinod Thomas with contributions from Sebastian Edwards ... [et al.]. — Baltimore : Published for the World Bank [by] the Johns Hopkins University Press, c1985. — p. cm. — *"A World Bank publication.". — Includes index*

COLOMBIA — Manufactures

WALLACE, Brian F
Ownership and development : a comparison of domestic and foreign firms in Colombian manufacturing / by Brian F. Wallace. — Athens, Ohio : Ohio University Center for International Studies, 1987. — p. cm. — (Monographs in international studies. Latin America series ; no. 12). — *Bibliography: p*

COLOMBIA — Politics and government — 1930-1946

BRAUN, Herbert
The assassination of Gaitán : public life and urban violence in Colombia / Herbert Braun. — Madison, Wis. : University of Wisconsin Press, 1985. — xiii, 282p. — *Includes index. — Bibliography: p.257-271*

COLOMBIA — Politics and government — 1946-1974

BRAUN, Herbert
The assassination of Gaitán : public life and urban violence in Colombia / Herbert Braun. — Madison, Wis. : University of Wisconsin Press, 1985. — xiii, 282p. — *Includes index. — Bibliography: p.257-271*

COLOMBIA
[Laws, etc]. Constitución política de Colombia acordada con la reforma plebiscitaria, los actos legislativos 1 y 2 de 1959, y el número 1 de 1968. — Bogotá : Cámara de Rrepresentantes, 1970. — 170p

COLOMBIA. Registraduría Nacional del Estado Civil
Circunscripciones electorales y división político administrativa de Colombia 1968. — [Bogotá] : the Registraduría, 1968. — 269p

COLOMBIA — Politics and government — 1946-

COLOMBIA. División de Asistencia Técnica Departamental y Municipal
Regiones para la descentralización adminstrativa. — Bogotá : the División. — (Documento / Departamento Nacional de Planeación, Unidad de Desarrollo Regional y Urbano, División de Asistencia Técnica Departamental y Municipal ; 76/3)
Parte 2: Anexo - aspectos metodológicos. — 1976. — 23,16leaves

COLOMBIA. División de Asistencia Técnica Departamental y Municipal
Regiones para la descentralización adminstrativa. — Bogotá : the División. — (Documento / Departamento Nacional de Planeación, Unidad de Desarrollo Regional y Urbano, División de Asistencia Técnica Departamental y Municipal ; 76/3)
Parte 1. — 1976. — 24leaves

COLOMBIA — Politics and government — 1974-

DIX, Robert H
The politics of Colombia / Robert H. Dix. — New York : Praeger, 1987. — xv, 247 p.. — (Politics in Latin America). — *"Copublished with Hoover Institution Press, Stanford University, Stanford, California.". — Includes index. — Bibliography: p. 227-238*

COLOMBIA — Rural conditions

LEGRAND, Catherine
Frontier expansion and peasant protest in Colombia, 1850-1936 / Catherine LeGrand. — 1st ed. — Albuquerque : University of New Mexico Press, c1986. — xviii, 302p. — *Includes index. — Bibliography: p.267-289*

COLOMBIA — Social conditions

COLOMBIA. Unidad de Desarrollo Regional y Urbano
Estudio sobre algunos indicadores socioeconómicos para centros urbanos con población superior a 20.000 habitantes. — Bogotá : the Unidad, 1973. — 54leaves. — (Documento / Departamento Nacional de Planeación, Unidad de Desarrollo Regional y Urbano, División de Estudios Regionales ; 73/3)

COLOMBIA — Social conditions — Statistics

Boletin de estadistica / Departmento Administrativo Nacional de Estadistica, Colombia. — Bogota : Departmento Administrativo Nacional de Estadistica, 1985. — *Quarterly. — Continues: Boletin mensual de estadistica*

Boletin mensual de estadistica / Departamento Administrativo Nacional de Estadistica, Colombia. — Bogota : Departamento Administrativo Nacional de Estadistica, 1952-1984. — *Monthly. — Continued by: Boletin de estadistica*

COLOMBIA — Statistics

Boletin de estadistica / Departmento Administrativo Nacional de Estadistica, Colombia. — Bogota : Departmento Administrativo Nacional de Estadistica, 1985. — *Quarterly. — Continues: Boletin mensual de estadistica*

Boletin mensual de estadistica / Departamento Administrativo Nacional de Estadistica, Colombia. — Bogota : Departamento Administrativo Nacional de Estadistica, 1952-1984. — *Monthly. — Continued by: Boletin de estadistica*

COLOMBIA. Departamento Administrativo Nacional de Estadística
El país en cifras. — Segunda edición. — Bogotá : the Departamento, 1964. — 27leaves. — *Publicado originalmente en 1963*

Colombia estadistica. — Bogota : Departamento Administrativo Nacional de Estadística, 1985-. — *Annual*

COLOMBIA — Statistics, vital
COLOMBIA. Departamento Administrativo Nacional de Estadística
El país en cifras. — Segunda edición. — Bogotá : the Departamento, 1964. — 27leaves. — *Publicado originalmente en 1963*

COLONIAL ADMINISTRATORS — Africa — Biography
YOUÉ, Christopher P.
Robert Thorne Coryndon : proconsular imperialism in Southern and Eastern Africa 1897-1925 / Christopher P. Youé. — Gerrards Cross : Smythe, 1986. — [xiv,236]p. — *Bibliography: p215-229. — Includes index*

COLONIAL ADMINISTRATORS — Great Britain — Biography
ROBERTS, Shirley
Charles Hotham : a biography / Shirley Roberts. — Carlton : Melbourne University Press ; Ashford : HB Sales [distributor], 1985. — xi,201p. — *Bibliography: p193-195. — Includes index*

YOUÉ, Christopher P.
Robert Thorne Coryndon : proconsular imperialism in Southern and Eastern Africa 1897-1925 / Christopher P. Youé. — Gerrards Cross : Smythe, 1986. — [xiv,236]p. — *Bibliography: p215-229. — Includes index*

COLONIES
FANON, Frantz
The wretched of the earth / Frantz Fanon ; translated from the French by Constance Farrington. — London : MacGibbon and Kee, 1965. — 255p

KIERNAN, V. G
The lords of human kind : black man, yellow man, and white man in an age of empire / V.G. Kiernan. — Columbia University Press morningside ed. — New York : Columbia University Press, 1987, c1969. — 336p, [16]p of plates. — *: Reprint. Originally published: Boston : Little, Brown, 1969. — Includes bibliographical references*

COLONIES — History
FABIAN, Johannes
Language and colonial power : the appropriation of Swahili in the former Belgian Congo 1880-1938 / Johannes Fabian. — Cambridge : Cambridge University Press, 1986. — viii,206p. — (African studies series ; 48). — *Bibliography: p188-199. — Includes index*

COLONIES — Africa
UMOZURIKE, U. O.
International law and colonialism in Africa / U. O. Umozurike. — Enugu : Nwamife, 1979. — x,173p. — *Bibliography: p[162]-167*

COLONIES (INTERNATIONAL LAW)
UMOZURIKE, U. O.
International law and colonialism in Africa / U. O. Umozurike. — Enugu : Nwamife, 1979. — x,173p. — *Bibliography: p[162]-167*

COLONIES (INTERNATIONAL LAW) — Bibliography
Granting of independence to colonial countries and peoples : selective bibliography 1960-1980 = L'octroi de l'independance aux pays et aux peuples coloniaux : bibliographie sélective 1960-1980 / Dag Hammarskjöld Library. — New York : United Nations, 1981. — xiii,92p. — (Bibliographical series / Dag Hammarskjöld Library ; no. 31) ([Document] / United Nations ; ST/LIB/SER.B/31)

COLORED PEOPLE (SOUTH AFRICA) — Addresses, essays, lectures
VAN DER ROSS, R. E
Coloured viewpoint : a series of articles in the Cape times, 1958-1965 / by R.E. van der Ross ; compiled by J.L. Hattingh, H.C. Bredekamp. — Bellville : Western Cape Institute for Historical Research (IHR), University of the Western Cape, 1984. — xii, 279 p.. — (Publication series / Western Cape Institute for Historical Research (IHR) ; B2)

COLORED PEOPLE (SOUTH AFRICA) — Relocation
PLATZKY, Laurine
The surplus people : forced removals in South Africa / Laurine Platzky and Cherryl Walker for the Surplus People Project. — Johannesburg : Ravan Press, 1985. — xxxiii, 446 p., [12] p. of plates. — *Includes index. — Bibliography: p. [404]-408*

COLUMBIA — Politics and government — 1863-1885
PARK, James William
Rafael Núñez and the politics of Colombian regionalism, 1863-1886 / James William Park. — ; Baton Rouge ; London : Louisiana State University Press, c1985. — xii, 304p. — *Includes index. — Bibliography: p.[279]-296*

COMBINATORIAL ANALYSIS
KRISHNAMURTHY, V.
Combinatorics : theory and applications / V. Krishnamurthy. — Chichester : Ellis Horwood, 1986. — xxxii,483p. — (Ellis Horwood series in mathematics and its applications. Statistics and its operational research). — *Bibliography: p459-476. — Includes index*

COMBINATORIAL OPTIMIZATION
CHUANG, Min Hwei
A sparse matrix implementation of the simplex method : its application to a class of combinatorial optimization problems / by Chuang Min Hwei. — 210 leaves. — *PhD (Econ) 1986 LSE*

COMMERCE
CANTILLON, Richard
Essai sur la nature du commerce au général / edited with an English translation and other material by Henry Higgs. — New York : Kelley, 1964. — viii,394p. — (Reprints of economic classics). — *Reprint of edition published: London : Macmillan, 1931*

CLAUSEN, A. W.
International trade and global economic growth : the critical relationship : address before the Economic Club of Detroit / by A. W. Clausen. — Washington, D.C. : World Bank, 1984. — 20p

CONNOLLY, Michael B
International trade and lending / Michael B. Connolly. — New York, NY, USA : Praeger, 1985. — xi, 131 p.. — *Includes bibliographies and index*

DIECKMANN, Norbert
Das Britische Exportfinanzierungs-system : eine landeskundliche Untersuchung / Norbert Dieckmann. — Hamburg : Hamburger Buchagentur, 1985. — 250p. — (Anglo-Amerikanische Wirtschaftsstudien ; Bd.2). — *Bibliography: p230-250*

GANDOLFO, Giancarlo
International economics / Giancarlo Gandolfo. — Berlin ; New York : Springer-Verlag, c1986. — p. cm

HAZARI, Bharat R.
International trade : theoretical issues / Bharat R. Hazari. — London : Croom Helm, c1986. — 372p. — *Includes bibliographies and index*

Inflation, trade and taxes : essays in honor of Alice Bourneuf / edited by David A. Belsley...[et al.]. — Columbus : Ohio State University Press, 1976. — 252p

LOVETT, William Anthony
World trade rivalry : trade equity and competing industrial policies / William A. Lovett. — Lexington, Mass. : Lexington Books, c1987. — p. cm. — *Includes index. — Bibliography: p*

COMMERCE — Classification
Standard International Trade Classification. — Rev.3. — New York : United Nations, 1986. — xvii,106,31,25p. — (Document ; ST/ESA/STAT/SER.M/34/REV.3) (Statistical papers. series M / Statistical Office ; no.34/Rev.3). — *Sales no.: E.86.XVII.12*

COMMERCE — Congresses
Foreign languages and international trade : a global perspective / edited by Samia I. Spencer. — Athens : University of Georgia Press, c1987. — xxiv, 255 p.. — *Collection of papers derived from an international symposium held in the spring of 1983, sponsored by the Committee for the Humanities in Alabama and Auburn University. — Includes bibliographies*

Trade in transit : world trade and world economy--past, present, and future / edited by Hans Visser, Evert Schoorl. — Dordrecht ; Boston : Kluwer Academic Publishers, 1987. — xvii, 338 p.. — *Based on papers presented at the World Trade Conference 1985, organized by the World Trade Center Amsterdam, the University of Amsterdam, and the Free University at Amsterdam, held in Amsterdam, Sept. 4-6, 1985. — Includes bibliographies*

COMMERCE — Dictionaries
DIETL, Clara-Erika
Wörterbuch für Rechts, Wirtschaft und Politik : mit erläuternden und rechtsvergleichenden Kommentaren. — 4., völlig n. bearbeitete und erw. Aufl.. — München : Beck ; New York : Bender
T.1: Englisch-Deutsch: einschliesslich der Besonderheiten des amerikanischen Sprachgebrauchs / von Clara-Erika Dietl, Anneliese A. Moss, Egon Lorenz ; unter Mitarbeit von Wiebke Buxbaum. — 1987. — lxxi,911p. — *English and German text. — Title on added title page : Dictionary of legal, commercial and political terms*

COMMERCE — Dictionaries — Russian
VOSKRESENSKAIA, I. V.
Russian-English foreign trade dictionary = Russko-angliiskii vneshnetorgovyi slovar' / I. V. Voskresenskaia, V. I. Mitrokhina, L. G. Pamukhina. — Moscow : Russky Yazyk, 1986. — 494p

COMMERCE — Directories
World diplomatic guide : directory of the diplomatic and trade missions of all nations / Emmanuel Okoro; editor. — London : Irving and Skinner, 1985. — xiv,826p

COMMERCE — Directories — Bibliography
SCIENCE REFERENCE AND INFORMATION SERVICE
Trade directory information in journals / Business Information Service. — 6th ed. — London : Science Reference and Information Service, 1986. — 50p. — *Previous ed.: 1985*

COMMERCE — Econometric models
ITALIANER, Alexander
Theory and practice of international trade linkage models / by Alexander Italianer. — Dordrecht ; Boston : M. Nijhoff, 1986. — xi,393p. — (Advanced studies in theoretical and applied economics ; 9). — *Bibliography: p [365]-382*

COMMERCE 650/2INVESTMENTS,
HOLLAND, Stuart
The global economy : from meso to macroeconomics / Stuart Holland. — London : Weidenfeld and Nicolson, c1987. — x, 443p. — *Bibliography: p.[424]-434*

COMMERCE, PRIMITIVE — Nepal — Dolpā
FISHER, James F
Trans-Himalayan traders : economy, society, and culture in northwest Nepal / James F. Fisher. — Berkeley : University of California Press, c1986. — xiv, 232 p., [8] p. of plates. — *Includes index. — Bibliography: p. 219-223*

COMMERCE, PRIMITIVE — New Guinea
RUBEL, Paula G
Your own pigs you may not eat : a comparative study of New Guinea societies / Paula G. Rubel, Abraham Rosman. — Chicago : University of Chicago Press, 1978. — xiv, 368 p. — *Includes index. — Bibliography: p. 347-359*

COMMERCIAL ASSOCIATIONS — Switzerland

Wirtschaftsverbände in der Schweiz : Organisation und Aktivitäten von Wirtschaftsverbänden in vier Sektoren der Industrie / Peter Farago, Hanspeter Kriesi (Hrsg.) ; mit Beiträgen von: Marcos Buser...[et al.]. — Grüsch : Rüegger, 1986. — xv,294p. — *Bibliography: p283-292*

COMMERCIAL CRIMES — Soviet Union

EVEL'SON, Evgeniia
Sudebnye protsessy po ekonomicheskim delam v SSSR (shestidesiatye gody) / Evgeniia Evel'son. — London : Overseas Publications Interchange, 1986. — 370p. — *Published in conjunction with the Soviet and East European Research Centre of the Hebrew University, Jerusalem. — Bibliography: p365-370*

COMMERCIAL CRIMES — United States

COLEMAN, James William
The criminal elite : the sociology of white collar crime / James W. Coleman. — New York : St. Martin's Press, c1985. — xi, 260 p.. — *Includes bibliographies and index*

COMMERCIAL FINANCE COMPANIES — Great Britain — Statistics

Assets and liabilities of finance houses and other consumer credit companies. — London : HMSO, 1974-. — (Business monitor. SD ; 7) (Business monitor. SDQ ; 7). — *Quarterly. — Title from 1974-75 is: Assets and liabilities of finance houses*

Credit business of finance houses and the specialist consumer credit grantors. — London : HMSO, 1979-. — (Business monitor. SDM ; 6). — *Monthly. — Continues: Instalment credit business of finance houses*

Instalment credit business of finance houses. — London : HMSO, 1974-78. — (Business monitor. SD ; 6) (Business monitor. SDM ; 6). — *Monthly. — Continued by: Credit business of finance houses and other specialist consumer credit grantors*

COMMERCIAL LAW

CAŁUS, Andrzej
Prawo cywilne i handlowe państw obcych / Andrzej Całus. — [2nd ed]. — Warszawa : Państwowe Wydawnictwo Ekonomiczne, 1985. — 483p. — *Table of contents in English and Russian*

FRANCE
[Code de commerce]. Code de commerce. — 81e éd. — Paris : Dalloz, 1985. — viii,1552p. — (Petits codes Dalloz). — *Previous ed.: 1984. — Includes index*

LOWENFELD, Andreas F.
International economic law. — New York : Matthew Bender
Vol.1: International private trade / Andreas F. Lowenfeld. — 2nd ed. — 1981. — xi,183,177,7,8p. — *Includes Documents Supplement*

LOWENFELD, Andreas F.
International economic law. — New York : Matthew Bender
Vol.2: International private investment / Andreas F. Lowenfeld. — 2nd ed. — 1982. — xi,207,355,2,12p. — *Includes Documents Supplement*

LOWENFELD, Andreas F.
International economic law. — New York : Matthew Bender
Vol.3: Trade controls for political ends / Andreas F. Lowenfeld. — 2nd ed. — 1983. — x,621,910,5,21p. — *Includes Documents Supplement*

LOWENFELD, Andreas F.
International economic law. — New York : Matthew Bender
Vol.4: The international monetary system / Andreas F. Lowenfeld. — 2nd ed. — 1984. — xvi,404,473,4,17p. — *Includes Documents Supplement*

LOWENFELD, Andreas F.
International economic law. — New York : Matthew Bender
Vol.6: Public controls on international trade / Andreas F. Lowenfeld. — 2nd ed. — 1983. — xvii,457,775,4,22p. — *Includes Documents Supplement*

TILLINGHAST, David R.
International economic law. — New York : Matthew Bender
Vol.5: Tax aspects of international transactions / David R. Tillinghast. — 2nd ed. — 1984. — xv,473,177,12,10p. — *Bibliography*

COMMERCIAL LAW — Bibliography

KUDEJ, Blanka
International trade law : international law bibliography / prepared by Blanka Kudej. — New York : Oceana Publications, 1984. — p. cm. — (A Collection of bibliographic and research resources)

COMMERCIAL LAW — Congresses

CONGRESS ON PRIVATE LAW (2d : 1976 : Rome)
New directions in international trade law : acts and proceedings of the 2nd Congress on Private Law held by the International Institute for the Unification of Private Law, UNIDROIT, Rome, 9-15 September, 1976. — Dobbs Ferry, N.Y. : Oceana Publications, 1977. — 2 v. (xliii, 793 p.). — *English or French. — Contents: v. 1. Reports.--v. 2. Written communications and oral interventions*

COMMERCIAL LAW — Australia

Equity and commercial relationships / edited by P. D. Finn. — Sydney : Law Book Company, 1987. — xxvii,320p

COMMERCIAL LAW — Belgium

RAUCQ, Albert
Sociétés anonymes / par Albert Raucq. — Bruxelles : Larcier, 1982. — 382p. — (Répertoire notarial ; T.12. Droit commercial ; Livre 3). — *Ouvrage mis à jour au 15 juin 1981 par Gilberte Raucq. — In French and Flemish. — First published 1972*

COMMERCIAL LAW — England

SMITH, Kenneth, 1910-1966
Smith and Keenan's mercantile law. — 6th ed. / Dennis Keenan. — London : Pitman, 1985 (1986 [printing]). — xxxii,628p. — *Previous ed. published as: Mercantile law. 1982. — Includes index*

COMMERCIAL LAW — European Economic Community countries

VANDAMME, J
La politique de la concurrence dans la C.E.E. / J.A. Van Damme. — Kortrijk, Belgique : UGA, [1980]. — 658 p., [1] leaf of plates. — (Cours / Centre international d'études et de recherches européennes ; 1977). — *At head of title: Institut universitaire international, Luxembourg. — Bibliography: p. 589-658*

COMMERCIAL LAW — France

FRANCE
[Code de commerce]. Code de commerce. — 82e éd.. — Paris : Dalloz, 1986. — ix,1630p. — (Codes Dalloz). — *Includes index*

COMMERCIAL LAW — Great Britain

COOKE, R. M.
Establishing a business in the United Kingdom / R. M. Cooke and D. C. Borer. — 3rd ed. — London : Institute of Chartered Accountants, 1986. — viii,226p

COMMERCIAL LAW — Iran

AMIN, Sayed Hassan
Commercial law of Iran : by Sayed Hassan Amin. — Tehran : Vahid Publications, 1986. — vii,144p. — *Bibliography: p137-140*

COMMERCIAL LAW — Korea (South)

Business laws in Korea : investment, taxation, and industrial property / Chan-jin Kim, editor. — Seoul, Korea : Panmun Book Co., 1982. — xii, 799 p.. — *Includes bibliographical references*

COMMERCIAL LAW — Nigeria

ACHIKE, Okay
Commercial law in Nigeria / by Okay Achike. — Enugu : Fourth Dimension, 1985. — xxii,496p. — *Includes bibliographical references*

COMMERCIAL LAW — Singapore

WOON, Walter C. M.
Commercial law of Singapore : an introduction / Walter C.M. Woon. — Cambridge : Woodhead-Faulkner, 1986. — [256]p. — *Includes bibliography and index*

COMMERCIAL LAW — Spain

GARRIGUES, Joaquin
Curso de derecho mercantil. — Madrid : Imprenta Aguirre
Tomo II. — 8a ed. / revisada con la colaboración de Fernando Sanchez Calero. — 1983. — xxxi,861p. — *Includes bibliographies and index*

COMMERCIAL LAW — Yugoslavia

YUGOSLAVIA
[Laws etc]. The law on exports and imports of goods and services ; The decree on requirements for the opening and work of representative offices of foreign persons in Yugoslavia. — Belgrade : Jugoslovenski pregled, 1986. — 103p

COMMERCIAL LAW — Zimbabwe

CHRISTIE, R. H.
Business law in Zimbabwe / R. H. Christie. — Cape Town : Juta, 1985. — lvii,575p

COMMERCIAL POLICY

ATSÉ, David
Commodity futures trading and international market stabilization / David Atsé. — Uppsala : Uppsala Universitet, 1986. — 151p. — (Acta Universitatis Upsaliensis. Studia oeconomica Upsaliensia ; 10). — *Bibliography: p144-151*

International trade policy. — Canberra : Economic Planning Advisory Council, 1986. — v,36p. — (Council paper / Economic Planning Advisory Council ; no.18). — *Bibliographical references: p34*

MUKHERJEE, Santosh
Restructuring of industrial economies and trade with developing countries / Santosh Mukherjee, assisted by Charlotte Feller. — Geneva : International Labour Office, 1978. — x,110p. — *Bibliography: p83-84*

Protection and competition in international trade : essays in honour of W.M. Corden / edited by Henryk Kierzkowski. — Oxford : Basil Blackwell, 1987. — [256]p. — *Includes index*

STONE, Frank
Canada, the GATT and the international trade system / Frank Stone. — Montreal, Quebec : Institute for Research on Public Policy, [1985] c1984. — xix, 236 p.. — (Essays in international economics). — *Bibliography: p. 217-224*

WALDMANN, Raymond J
Managed trade : the new competition between nations / Raymond J. Waldmann. — Cambridge, Mass. : Ballinger Pub. Co., [1986]. — p. cm. — *Includes index. — Bibliography: p*

WINHAM, Gilbert R
International trade and the Tokyo Round negotiation / Gilbert R. Winham. — Princeton, N.J. : Princeton University Press, c1986. — xiv, 449 p.. — *Includes index. — Bibliography: p. 425-437*

COMMERCIAL POLICY — Addresses, essays, lectures

Strategic trade policy and the new international economics / edited by Paul R. Krugman. — Cambridge, Mass ; London : MIT Press, c1986. — 313p. — *Includes bibliographies and index*

COMMERCIAL PRODUCTS

Primary commodities : market developments and outlook / by the Commodities Division of the Research Department. — Washington, D.C. : International Monetary Fund, 1987. — vii,91p. — (World economic and financial surveys). — *Includes bibliographical references*

COMMERCIAL PRODUCTS — Classification

Classification by broad economic categories : defined in terms of SITC, Rev.3. — New York : United Nations, 1986. — x,68p. — (Statistical papers / United Nations, Statistical Office. Series M ; no.53, Rev.2) ([Document] / United Nations ; ST/ESA/STAT/SER.M/53/Rev.2). — *Sales no.: E.86.XVII.24*

Commodity indexes for the Standard International Trade Classification : revision 2. — New York : United Nations. — (Statistical papers / Statistical Office of the United Nations. Series M ; no.38/Rev.; Vol.1) ([Document] / United Nations ; ST/ESA/STAT/SER.M/38/Rev.; Vol.1) V.1. — 1981. — xiii,587p. — *Sales no.: E.81.XVII.3*

Commodity indexes for the Standard International Trade Classification : revision 2. — New York : United Nations. — (Statistical papers / Statistical Office of the United Nations. Series M ; no.38/Rev.; Vol.2) ([Document] / United Nations ; ST/ESA/STAT/SER.M/38/Rev., Vol.2) V.2. — 1981. — lxxvii,525p. — *Sales no.: E.81.XVII.4*

COMMERCIAL PRODUCTS — Prices — Mathematical models

HOLTHAM, Gerald
OECD economic activity and non-oil commodity prices : reduced-form equations for INTERLINK / by Gerald Holtham, Martine Durand. — Paris : OECD, 1987. — 24p. — (Working papers / OECD Department 0f Economics and Statistics ; no.42). — *Bibliographical references: p24*

COMMERCIAL PRODUCTS — Netherlands — Nomenclature

NETHERLANDS. Centraal Bureau voor de Statistiek
Werknemersbudgetonderzoek 1974-75. — s-Gravenhage : Staatsuitgeverij. — *Title on back cover: Workers' budget survey 1974-75. Part 5. Methodology. Appendix 2. Draft for a nomenclature of consumer goods deel 5: Methodologie bijlage 2: Proeve van een verbruiksgoederennomenclatuur.* — 1980. — 217p

COMMERCIAL PRODUCTS — Soviet Union

MEDVEDEV, G. I.
Proizvodstvo tovarov narodnogo potrebleniia : rezervy predpriiatii / G. I. Medvedev. — Leningrad : Lenizdat, 1978. — 175p. — *Bibliography: p173-[174]*

COMMERCIAL STATISTICS

International trade statistics : concepts and definitions. — Rev.1. — New York : United Nations, 1982. — ii,71p. — (Statistical papers / United Nations Statistical Office. Series M ; no.52,REv.1) ([Document] United Nations) ; ST/ESA/STAT/SER.M/52/Rev.1 538Sales.: E.82.XVII.14). — *Includes bibliographical references*

Price and quantity measurement in external trade : two studies of national practice. — New York : United Nations, 1983. — v,108p. — (Statistical papers / United Nations, Statistical Office. Series M ; no.76) ([Document] / United Nations ; ST/ESA/STAT/SER.M/78). — *Bibliography: p39.* — *Sales no.: E.83.XVII.7*

COMMERCIAL STATISTICS — Bibliography

Bibliography of industrial and distributive-trade statistics. — New York : United Nations, 1981. — iv,149p. — (Statistical papers / United Nations, Statistical Office. Series M ; no.36, Rev. 5) ([Document] (United Nations) ; ST/ESA/STAT/SER.M/36,Rev.5). — *Sales no.: E.81.XVII.5*

COMMERCIAL STATISTICS — Methodology

Strategies for price and quantity measurement in external trade : a technical report. — New York : United Nations, 1981. — vi,67p. — (Statistical papers / United Nations Statistical Office. Series M ; no.69) ([Document] (United Nations) ; ST/ESA/STAT/SER.M/69). — *Sales no.: E.82.XVII.3*

COMMERCIAL TREATIES

GENERAL AGREEMENT ON TARIFFS AND TRADE (Organization)
Text of the General Agreement. — Geneva : the Organization, 1986. — vi,96p

The texts of the Tokyo Round Agreements. — Geneva : General Agreement on Tariffs and Trade, 1986. — vii,208p

COMMERCIAL TREATIES — Congresses

The legal framework for Canada-United States trade / edited by Maureen Irish and Emily F. Carasco. — Toronto : Carswell, 1987. — xxxviii,275p

COMMISSION FOR BUILDING FIFTY NEW CHURCHES

COMMISSION FOR BUILDING FIFTY NEW CHURCHES
The Commissions for Building Fifty New Churches : the minute books, 1711-27 : a calendar / edited by M.H.Port. — London : London Record Society, 1986. — xl, 193p. — (London Record Society publications ; v.23)

COMMISSION OF THE EUROPEAN COMMUNITIES

COMMISSION OF THE EUROPEAN COMMUNITIES
Bulletin of energy prices = Bulletin des prix de l'energie / Commission of the European Communities. — Luxembourg : Office for Official Publications of the European Communities, 1985-. — *Irregular*

COMMISSION OF THE EUROPEAN COMMUNITIES
SCAD bibliographies / Commission of the European Communities. — Luxembourg : Office for Official Publications of the European Communities, 1985-. — *Irregular.* — *Text in Community languages.* — *Continues: The Commission's Documentation bulletin: Series B*

COMMISSION OF THE EUROPEAN COMMUNITIES
SCAD dossier bibliographique. — Luxembourg : Office for Official publications of the European Communities, 1985-. — *Irregular.* — *Text in Community languages.* — *Continues: The Commission's Documentation bulletin: Series C*

COMMISSION OF THE EUROPEAN COMMUNITIES — Documentation — Bibliography

HOPKINS, Michael, 1945-
Commission documents : a guide to sources / prepared by Dr. Mike Hopkins. — [s.l.] : Association of EDC Librarians, [1984?]. — 6p. — (European Communities information ; no.6)

COMMISSION OF THE EUROPEAN COMMUNITIES. Library — Catalogs

COMMISSION OF THE EUROPEAN COMMUNITIES. Library
List of additions to the Library : supplement. — [Luxembourg : Office for Official Publications of the European Communities] 1981/2: Selection of bibliographies available in the Library. — 1981. — vp,72 columns. — *In Community languages*

COMMISSION OF THE EUROPEAN COMMUNITIES. London Information Office

PAU, Giancarlo
London Information Office of the European Commission / prepared by Giancarlo Pau. — [s.l.] : Association of EDC Librarians, [1984]. — 4p. — (European Communities information ; no.5)

COMMITTEE FOR COORDINATION OF INVESTIGATIONS OF THE LOWER MEKONG BASIN

COMMITTEE FOR COORDINATION OF INVESTIGATIONS OF THE LOWER MEKONG BASIN
Annual report / Committee for Coordination of Investigations of the Lower Mekong Basin. — New York : ESCAP, 1983-. — *Annual*

COMMODITY CONTROL

ATSÉ, David
Commodity futures trading and international market stabilization / David Atsé. — Uppsala : Uppsala Universitet, 1986. — 151p. — (Acta Universitatis Upsaliensis. Studia oeconomica Upsaliensia ; 10). — *Bibliography: p144-151*

COMMODITY CONTROL — Bibliography

Commodities : a select bibliography, 1965-1975 = Produits de base : bibliographie sélective, 1965-1975. — New York : United Nations, 1975. — 69p. — ([Document] / United Nations ; ST/LIB/SER.B/19). — *In various languages.* — *Prepared by the Dag Hammarskjöld Library*

COMMODITY EXCHANGES

BROWN, Stewart L
Trading energy futures : a manual for energy industry professionals / Stewart L. Brown and Steven Errera. — New York : Quorum Books, c1986. — p. cm. — *Includes index.* — *Bibliography: p*

CLUBLEY, Sally
Trading in oil futures / Sally Clubley. — Cambridge : Woodhead-Faulkner, 1986. — [112]p. — *Includes index*

KROUSE, Clement G
Capital markets and prices : valuing uncertain income streams / Clement G. Krouse. — Amsterdam ; New York : North-Holland ; New York, N.Y. : Sole distributors for U.S.A. and Canada, Elsevier Science Pub. Co., 1986. — p. cm. — (Advanced textbooks in economics ; v. 25). — *Includes index*

LANGHOLM, Odd
The Aristotelian analysis of usury / Odd Langholm. — Bergen : Universitetsforlaget ; London : [Distributed by] Global Book Resources, c1984. — 153p. — *Bibliography: p.[152]-153*

STEIN, Jerome L.
The economics of futures markets / Jerome L. Stein. — Oxford : Basil Blackwell, 1986. — [250]p. — *Includes bibliography and index*

COMMODITY EXCHANGES — Law and legislation — United States — History

MARKHAM, Jerry W
The history of commodity futures trading and its regulation / Jerry W. Markham. — New York : Praeger, 1987. — xiv, 305 p.. — *Includes index.* — *Bibliography: p. 277-285*

COMMODITY EXCHANGES — Mathematical models

GHOSH, S.
Stabilizing speculative commodity markets / S. Ghosh, C.L. Gilbert and A.J. Hughes Hallett. — Oxford : Clarendon, 1987. — [448]p. — *Includes bibliography and index*

COMMODITY EXCHANGES — United States — History

MARKHAM, Jerry W
The history of commodity futures trading and its regulation / Jerry W. Markham. — New York : Praeger, 1987. — xiv, 305 p.. — *Includes index.* — *Bibliography: p. 277-285*

COMMON AGRICULTURAL POLICY See
Agriculture and state - European Economic Community countries

COMMON LAW — Congresses
Drafting and enforcing contracts in civil and common law jurisdictions / edited by Kojo Yelpaala, Mauro Rubino-Sammartano, Dennis Campbell. — Deventer, Netherlands ; Boston : Kluwer Law and Taxation Publishers, c1986. — 275 p.. — *Papers presented at the Third Annual Waidring Conference, McGeorge School of Law, 1986*

COMMON LAW — England — History and criticism
MILSOM, S. F. C.
Studies in the history of the common law / S.F.C. Milsom. — London : Hambledon, c1985. — xii,335p. — ([History series]). — *Includes index*

COMMON LAW — Great Britain
COSGROVE, Richard A.
Our lady the common law : an Anglo-American legal community, 1870-1930 / Richard A. Cosgrove. — New York : New York University Press, c1987. — x, 330 p.. — *Includes index. — Bibliography: p. 295-326*

COMMON LAW — United States
COSGROVE, Richard A.
Our lady the common law : an Anglo-American legal community, 1870-1930 / Richard A. Cosgrove. — New York : New York University Press, c1987. — x, 330 p.. — *Includes index. — Bibliography: p. 295-326*

COMMON MARKET See European Economic Community

COMMONWEALTH DEVELOPMENT CORPORATION
Partners in development: finance plus management / Commonwealth Development Corporation. — London : Commonwealth Development Corporation, 1973-1981. — *Annual*

COMMONWEALTH FOUNDATION
COMMONWEALTH FOUNDATION
The first five years, 1966-1971. — London : Commonwealth Foundation, 1971. — 89p

COMMONWEALTH OF NATIONS
MOORE, R. J. (Robin James)
Making the new Commonwealth / R.J. Moore. — Oxford : Clarendon, 1987. — [224]p. — *Includes bibliography and index*

Regional co-operation: recent developments / Commonwealth Secretariat. — London : Commonwealth Secretariat, 1984-. — *Irregular*

COMMONWEALTH OF NATIONS — Constitutional History
SWINFEN, David B.
Imperial appeal : the debate on the appeal to the Privy Council, 1833-1986 / David B. Swinfen. — Manchester : Manchester University Press, c1987. — viii,268p. — *Bibliography: p255-260. — Includes index*

COMMONWEALTH OF NATIONS — Foreign relations
MILLER, John Donald Bruce
The Commonwealth in the world / John Donald Bruce. — London : Duckworth, 1958. — 308p

COMMONWEALTH OF NATIONS — History
LAPPING, Brian
End of Empire / Brian Lapping. — London : Granada in association with Channel Four Television Company and Granada Television, 1985. — xvi,560p. — *Based on the television series. — Maps on the lining papers. — Bibliography: p539-550. — Includes index*

COMMONWEALTH OF NATIONS — Research — Bibliography
Theses in progress in Commonwealth studies / Institute of Commonwealth Studies Library, University of London. — London : University of London. Institute of Commonwealth Studies Library, [196-?]-. — *Annual*

COMMONWEALTH OF NATIONS
COMMONWEALTH SECRETARIAT
The Commonwealth today. — [Rev. ed.]. — London : the Secretariat, 1983. — 40p

COMMONWEALTH PARLIAMENTARY ASSOCIATION — History
GREY, Ian
The parliamentarians : the history of the Commonwealth Parliamentary Association, 1911-1985 / Ian Grey. — Aldershot : Gower, c1986. — xiii,319p,[8]p of plates. — *Includes index*

COMMONWEALTH SCIENTIFIC AND INDUSTRIAL RESEARCH ORGANIZATION (Australia)
AUSTRALIAN SCIENCE AND TECHNOLOGY COUNCIL
Future directions for CSIRO : a report to the Prime Minister / by the Australian Science and Technology Council (ASTEC). — Canberra : Australian Government Publishing Service, 1985. — viii,94p. — *Bibliographical references: p62-64*

COMMONWEALTH YOUTH PROGRAMME
COMMONWEALTH SECRETARIAT. Youth Division
Commonwealth youth programme. — [London] : the Secretariat, [1978]. — [12]p

COMMUNICABLE DISEASES — Mortality — History
MCKEOWN, Thomas
The modern rise of population / Thomas McKeown. — London : Edward Arnold, 1976. — [5],168p. — *Includes index*

COMMUNICATION
Communication research. — Newbury Park (Calif.) : Sage Publications, 1987-. — *6 per year*

Communication studies : an introductory reader / edited by John Corner and Jeremy Hawthorn. — 2nd ed. — London : Edward Arnold, 1985. — vi,218p. — *Previous ed.: 1980. — Includes bibliographies and index*

LINDSAY, Peter H.
Human information processing : An introduction to psychology / Peter H. Lindsay and Donald A. Norman. — 2d ed. — New York : Academic Press, c1977. — xxiii, 777 p. — *Includes indexes. — Bibliography: p. [734]-762*

The Myth of the information revolution : social and ethical implications of communication technology / edited by Michael Traber. — London : Sage, 1986. — viii,146p. — (Sage communications in society series). — *Includes index*

TAN, Alexis S
Mass communication theories and research / Alexis S. Tan. — 2nd ed. — New York : Wiley, c1985. — p. cm. — *Includes index*

WILDEN, Anthony
The rules are no game : the strategy of communication / by Anthony Wilden. — London : Routledge & Kegan Paul, 1987. — xv,432p. — *"Introduced by The naming of parts and the 20th century war by Anthony Wilden". — Bibliography: p323-398. — Includes index. — Includes: Women in production : the chorus line, 1932-1980 / by Rhonda Hammer and Anthony Wilden ; The naming of parts and the 20th century war / by Anthony Wilden*

COMMUNICATION — Dictionaries
DEVITO, Joseph A.
The communication handbook : a dictionary / Joseph A. DeVito. — New York : Harper & Row, c1986. — p. cm. — *Includes bibliographical references and index*

COMMUNICATION — International cooperation
MCPHAIL, Thomas L
Electronic colonialism : the future of international broadcasting and communication / Thomas L. McPhail. — Rev. 2nd ed. — Newbury Park, Calif. : Sage Publications, c1987. — 311 p.. — (Sage library of social research ; v. 126). — *Includes bibliographies and index*

MEHRA, Achal
Free flow of information : a new paradigm / Achal Mehra. — New York : Greenwood Press, 1986. — xiii, 225 p.. — (Contributions to the study of mass media and communications ; no. 7). — *Includes index. — Bibliography: p. [209]-214*

COMMUNICATION — International cooperation — Addresses, essays, lectures
Communication and domination : essays to honor Herbert I. Schiller / edited by Jörg Becker, Göran Hedebro, Leena Paldán. — Norwood, N.J. : Ablex, 1986. — p. cm. — *Includes index. — Bibliography: p*

COMMUNICATION — International cooperation — Bibliography
The New World Information and Communication Order : a selective bibliography = Le nouvel ordre mondial de l'information et de la communication : une bibliographie sélective. — New York : United Nations, 1984. — viii,152p. — (Bibliographical series / Dag Hammarskjöld Library ; no.35 = Série bibliographique / Bibliothèque Dag Hammarskjöld ; no.35) ([Document] / United Nations ; ST/LIB/SER.B/35). — *Sales no: E/F.84.I.15*

COMMUNICATION — International cooperation — Congresses
Communications for national development : lessons from experience / [edited by] Robert D. Graff. — Cambridge, Mass. : Oelgeschlager, Gunn & Hain, c1983. — ix, 395 p.. — *Based on papers and discussions of three successive Salzburg Seminars, held Sept. 1979, Sept. 1980, and Mar. 1981 in Salzburg, Austria. — Bibliography: p. 373-380*

COMMUNICATION — Philosophy
INGRAM, David
Habermas and the dialectic of reason / David Ingram. — New Haven, CT : Yale University Press, c1987. — xvii, 263p. — *Includes index. — Bibliography: p.243-254*

COMMUNICATION — Political aspects — Addresses, essays, lectures
Communication and domination : essays to honor Herbert I. Schiller / edited by Jörg Becker, Göran Hedebro, Leena Paldán. — Norwood, N.J. : Ablex, 1986. — p. cm. — *Includes index. — Bibliography: p*

COMMUNICATION — Political aspects — United States
DENTON, Robert E., Jr
Political communication in America / Robert E. Denton, Gary C. Woodward. — New York : Praeger, 1985. — p. cm. — *Includes index*

COMMUNICATION — Psychological aspects
PETTY, Richard E
Communication and persuasion : central and peripheral routes to attitude change / Richard E. Petty, John T. Cacioppo. — New York : Springer-Verlag, c1986. — xiv, 262 p.. — (Springer series in social psychology). — *Includes indexes. — Bibliography: p. [225]-247*

COMMUNICATION — Research — Latin America

Communication and Latin American society : trends in critical research, 1960-1985 / edited by Rita Atwood and Emile McAnany. — Madison, Wis. : University of Wisconsin Press, 1986. — p. cm. — (Studies in communication and society). — *Includes bibliographies and index.* — *Contents: Assessing critical mass communication scholarship in the Americas / Rita Atwood -- Seminal ideas in Latin American critical communication research in its historical context / Cristina Schwarz and Oscar Jaramillo -- Transnational communication and culture / Rafael Roncagliolo -- Transnational communication and Brazilian culture / Carlos Eduardo Lins Da Silva -- Means of communication and construction of hegemony / Javier Esteinou Madrid -- Transnational advertising / Noreene Janus -- Commercial television as an educational and political institution / Alberto Montoya Martín Del Campo and Maria Antonieta Rebeil Corella -- Trends in alternative communication research in Latin America / Maximo Simpson Grinberg -- Alternative communication, solidarity, and development in the face of transnational expansion / Fernando Reyes Matta*

COMMUNICATION — Sex differences

Communication, gender, and sex roles in diverse interaction contexts / edited by Lea P. Stewart and Stella Ting-Toomey. — Norwood, N.J. : Ablex Pub. Corp., c1987. — xii, 264 p.. — (Communication and information science). — *Includes bibliographies and indexes*

COMMUNICATION — Social aspects

QVORTRUP, Lars
The social significance of telematics : an essay on the information society / Lars Qvortrup ; translated by Philip Edmonds. — Amsterdam ; Philadelphia : J. Benjamins Pub. Co., 1984. — xviii, 228 p.. — (Pragmatics & beyond ; V:7). — *Bibliography: p. [221]-228*

COMMUNICATION — Social aspects — Congresses

The Communication of ideas / edited by J.S. Yadava, Vinayshil Gautam. — New Delhi : Concept, 1980, c1978. — xx, 276 p.. — (Xth ICAES series ; no. 3). — *Selection of papers presented at the 10th International Congress of Anthropological and Ethnological Sciences held at New Delhi, 1978.* — *Includes bibliographies and index*

COMMUNICATION — Social aspects — United States

BENIGER, James R
The control revolution : technological and economic origins of the information society / James R. Beniger. — Cambridge, Mass. : Harvard University Press, 1986. — x, 493 p.. — *Includes index.* — *Bibliography: p. [439]-476*

COMMUNICATION — Technological innovations

QVORTRUP, Lars
The social significance of telematics : an essay on the information society / Lars Qvortrup ; translated by Philip Edmonds. — Amsterdam ; Philadelphia : J. Benjamins Pub. Co., 1984. — xviii, 228 p.. — (Pragmatics & beyond ; V:7). — *Bibliography: p. [221]-228*

COMMUNICATION — Technological innovations — Addresses, essays, lectures

Communication and domination : essays to honor Herbert I. Schiller / edited by Jörg Becker, Göran Hedebro, Leena Paldán. — Norwood, N.J. : Ablex, 1986. — p. cm. — *Includes index.* — *Bibliography: p*

COMMUNICATION — Finland — Accounting

HAMUNEN, Eeva
Kansantalouden tilinpito : liikenne kansantalouden tilinpidossa = National accounts : transport and communication in national accounts / Eeva Hamunen. — Helsinki : Tilastokeskus, 1982. — 77p. — (Tutkimuksia / Finland. Tilastokeskus ; no.85). — *In Finnish and English*

COMMUNICATION — Finland — Statistics

FINLAND. Tilastokeskus
Kulttuuritilasto : Tilastotietoja taiteesta, tiedonvälityksestä, vapaa-ajasta, urheilusta ja nuorisotoiminnasta vuosilta 1930-1977 = Cutlural statistics : Statistical information on arts, communication, leisure, sports and youth activities in 1930-1977. — Helsinki : Tilastokeskus, 1978. — 256p. — (Tilastollisia tiedonantoja = Statistical surveys ; no.60). — *In Finnish, Swedish and English*

FINLAND. Tilastokeskus
Kulttuuritilasto 1981 : Tilastotietoja taiteesta, tiedonvälityksestä, vapaa-ajasta, urheilusta ja nuorisotojminnasta = Cultural statistics 1981 : Statistical information on arts, communication, leisure, sports and youth activities. — Helsinki : Tilastokeskus, 1984. — 683p. — (Tilastollisia tiedonantoja = Statistical surveys ; no.73). — *In Finnish, Swedish and English*

COMMUNICATION — Iran

BEEMAN, William O
Language, status, and power in Iran / William O. Beeman. — Bloomington : Indiana University Press, c1986. — xx, 255 p.. — (Advances in semiotics). — *Includes indexes.* — *Bibliography: p. 213-235*

COMMUNICATION — United States — Statistics

RUBIN, Michael Rogers
The knowledge industry in the United States, 1960-1980 / Michael Rogers Rubin and Mary Taylor Huber with Elizabeth Lloyd Taylor. — Princeton, N.J. : Princeton University Press, c1986. — p. cm. — *Includes index*

COMMUNICATION — West Bank

SHINAR, Dov
Palestinian voices : communication and nation building in the West Bank / Dov Shinar. — Boulder, Colo. : L. Rienner, 1987. — xi, 211 p.. — *Includes index.* — *Bibliography: p. 201-202*

COMMUNICATION AND TRAFFIC

MCLUHAN, Marshall
Understanding media : the extensions of man / Marshall McLuhan ; Marshall McLuhan. — London : ARK, 1987. — 359 p

COMMUNICATION AND TRAFFIC — India

SUKHWAL, B. L.
India : economic resource base and contemporary political patterns / B.L. Sukhwal. — 1st ed. — New York : Envoy Press, 1987. — viii, 200 p.. — *Includes index.* — *Bibliography: p. [189]-192*

COMMUNICATION AND TRAFFIC — Taiwan

Communications in the Republic of China. — [Taipei] : Ministry of Communications, 1958. — 49p

COMMUNICATION DISORDERS — Age factors

BAYLES, Kathryn A.
Communication and cognition in normal aging and dementia / Kathryn A. Bayles and Alfred W. Kaszniak with the assistance of Cheryl K. Tomoeda. — London : Taylor & Francis, c1987. — xvi,400p. — *Includes bibliographies and index*

COMMUNICATION IN ECONOMIC DEVELOPMENT — Malaysia

KAUR, Amarjit
Bridge and barrier : transport and communications in colonial Malaya 1870-1957 / Amarjit Kaur. — Oxford : Oxford University Press, 1985. — 235p

COMMUNICATION IN MANAGEMENT

ANDREWS, David
Th hidden manager : communication technology and information networks in business organisations / David Andrews and John Kent. — London : Taylor Graham, 1986. — 90p

COMMUNICATION IN MANAGEMENT — Congresses

Communication and group decision-making / edited by Randy Y. Hirokawa and Marshall Scott Poole ; foreword by James H. Davis. — Beverly Hills : Sage Publications, c1986. — 315 p.. — (Sage focus editions ; 77). — *Developed from discussions at the Conference on Research in Small Group Communication, held at the Pennsylvania State University, Apr. 29-30, 1982.* — *Bibliography: p. 293-312*

COMMUNICATION IN MANAGEMENT — Great Britain

Employee communications in the public sector / edited by Geoff Perkins. — London : Institute of Personnel Management, 1986. — 89p. — *Bibliography: p62-67*

COMMUNICATION IN MARRIAGE

Intimate relationships : development, dynamics, and deterioration / edited by Daniel Perlman, Steve Duck. — Beverly Hills : Sage Publications, c1987. — 320 p.. — (Sage focus editions ; v. 80). — *Includes bibliographies and index*

COMMUNICATION IN MEDICINE

Doctor-patient communication / edited by David Pendleton and John Hasler. — London : Academic Press, c1983. — x,293p. — *Includes bibliographies and index*

COMMUNICATION IN ORGANIZATIONS

BINSTED, Don
Developments in interpersonal skills training / Don Binsted. — Aldershot : Gower, c1986. — vi,208p. — *Bibliography: p206-208*

COMMUNICATION IN ORGANIZATIONS — Addresses, essays, lectures

Organization--communication : emerging perspectives / Lee Thayer, editor. — Norwood, N.J. : Ablex Pub. Corp., c1986-. — v. <1, >. — (People, communication, organization). — *Includes bibliographies and indexes*

COMMUNICATION IN POLITICS

Political communication research : approaches, studies, assessments / edited by David L. Paletz. — Norwood, N.J. : Ablex Pub. Corp., c1987. — xii, 276 p.. — (Communication and information science). — *Includes bibliographies and indexes*

COMMUNICATION IN POLITICS — Addresses, essays, lectures

Mass media and political thought : an information-processing approach / edited by Sidney Kraus, Richard M. Perloff. — Beverly Hills : Sage Publications, c1985. — 350 p.. — *Includes bibliographies and index*

COMMUNICATION IN POLITICS — France

CAYROL, Roland
La nouvelle communication politique / Roland Cayrol. — Paris : Larousse, [1986]. — 214p

COMMUNICATION IN POLITICS — Great Britain

BLUMLER, Jay G.
Political communication and the young voter : a panel study, 1970-1971, examining the role of election communication in the political socialisation of first time voters / Jay G. Blumler, Denis McQuail and T. J. Nossiter ; report to the Social Science Research Council, October 1975. — [London : Social Science Research Council, 1975]. — 1v. (various pagings). — *Bibliographical references: end of vol.*

COMMUNICATION IN POLITICS — Great Britain *continuation*
BLUMLER, Jay G.
Political communication and the young voter in the general election of February 1974 : a panal study, 1970-1974, examining influences on the political socialisation of young voters between their first and second election campaigns / Jay G. Blumler, Denis McQuail and T. J. Nossiter ; report to the Social Science Research Council, July 1976. — [London : Social Science Research Council, 1976]. — 99 leaves. — *Bibliographical references: p98-99*

COMMUNICATION IN POLITICS — United States
DENTON, Robert E., Jr
Presidential communication : description and analysis / Robert E. Denton, Jr. and Dan F. Hahn. — New York : Praeger, 1986. — xxiii, 332 p.. — *Includes bibliographies and index*

COMMUNICATION IN RURAL DEVELOPMENT — Developing countries
BOWERS, John
Communication and rural development / by John Bowers. — London : Commonwealth Secretariat, 1970. — 17p. — *At head of title page: Commonwealth Conference on Education in Rural Areas.* — CRE(70)B/3 and C/5

COMMUNICATION IN SCIENCE
AILES, Catherine P.
Cooperation in science and technology : an evaluation of the U.S.-Soviet agreement / Catherine P. Ailes and Arthur E. Pardee. — Boulder : Westview, 1986. — xxiii,334p

COMMUNICATION IN THE HUMANITIES — Great Britain
KATZEN, May
Recent initiatives in communication in the humanities / M. Katzen and S.M. Howley. — London : British Library Research & Development Department, 1984. — xii,125p. — (Library and information research report ; 11)

KATZEN, May
Technology and communication in the humanities : training and services in universities and polytechnics in the UK / M. Katzen. — London : British Library, c1985. — x,121p. — (Library and information research report ; 32)

COMMUNICATION IN THE HUMANITIES — United States
KATZEN, May
Recent initiatives in communication in the humanities / M. Katzen and S.M. Howley. — London : British Library Research & Development Department, 1984. — xii,125p. — (Library and information research report ; 11)

COMMUNICATION IN THE SOCIAL SCIENCES
HOROWITZ, Irving Louis
Communicating ideas : the crisis of publishing in a post-industrial society / Irving Louis Horowitz. — New York : Oxford University Press, 1986. — x, 240 p.. — *Includes index.* — *Bibliography: p. 217-230*

COMMUNICATION IN THE SOCIAL SCIENCES — Case studies
LENGYEL, Peter
International social science, the UNESCO experience / Peter Lengyel. — New Brunswick, U.S.A. : Transaction Books, c1986. — xii, 133 p.. — *Includes index.* — *Bibliography: p. 123-129*

COMMUNICATION, INTERNATIONAL
MCPHAIL, Thomas L
Electronic colonialism : the future of international broadcasting and communication / Thomas L. McPhail. — Rev. 2nd ed. — Newbury Park, Calif. : Sage Publications, c1987. — 311 p.. — (Sage library of social research ; v. 126). — *Includes bibliographies and index*

MOWLANA, Hamid
Global information and world communication : new frontiers in international relations / Hamid Mowlana. — New York ; London : Longman, c1985. — viii, 248p. — (Annenberg/Longman communication books). — *Includes index.* — *Bibliography: p.[223]-237*

POWELL, Jon T
International broadcasting by satellite : issues of regulation, barriers to communication / Jon T. Powell ; foreword by Hale Montgomery. — Westport, Conn. : Quorum Books, 1985. — xviii, 300 p.. — *Includes index.* — *Bibliography: p. [287]-290*

COMMUNICATION, INTERNATIONAL — Congresses
Communication and interaction in global politics / edited by Claudio Cioffi-Revilla, Richard L. Merritt, Dina A. Zinnes. — Beverly Hills : Sage Publications, c1985. — p. cm. — (Advances in political science ; v. 5). — *Includes index*

COMMUNICATION MANAGERS' ASSOCIATION
Annual report [and supplement] / Communication Managers' Association. — Reading : Communication Managers' Association, 1986-. — *Annual.* — *Part of New Management the Journal of the Communication Managers' Association*

COMMUNICATION OF TECHNICAL INFORMATION
AILES, Catherine P.
Cooperation in science and technology : an evaluation of the U.S.-Soviet agreement / Catherine P. Ailes and Arthur E. Pardee. — Boulder : Westview, 1986. — xxiii,334p

COMMUNICATION POLICY — Congresses
Communications for national development : lessons from experience / [edited by] Robert D. Graff. — Cambridge, Mass. : Oelgeschlager, Gunn & Hain, c1983. — ix, 395 p.. — *Based on papers and discussions of three successive Salzburg Seminars, held Sept. 1979, Sept. 1980, and Mar. 1981 in Salzburg, Austria.* — *Bibliography: p. 373-380*

COMMUNICATION, PRIMITIVE — Congresses
The Communication of ideas / edited by J.S. Yadava, Vinayshil Gautam. — New Delhi : Concept, 1980, c1978. — xx, 276 p.. — (Xth ICAES series ; no. 3). — *Selection of papers presented at the 10th International Congress of Anthropological and Ethnological Sciences held at New Delhi, 1978.* — *Includes bibliographies and index*

COMMUNICATIONS WORKERS OF AMERICA — History
SCHACHT, John N.
The making of telephone unionism, 1920-1947 / John N. Schacht. — New Brunswick, N.J. : Rutgers University Press, c1985. — p. cm. — *Includes index.* — *Bibliography: p*

COMMUNISM
Analytical Marxism / edited by John Roemer. — Cambridge : Cambridge University Press, 1986. — [324]p. — (Studies in Marxism and social theory). — *Includes bibliography*

BERG, Hermann von
Marxismus-Leninismus : das Elend der halb deutschen, halb russischen Ideologie. — 2., überarbeitete Aufl.. — Köln : Bund-Verlag, 1987. — 320p

CASTORIADIS, Cornelius
The imaginary institution of society / Cornelius Castoriadis ; translated by Kathleen Blamey. — Cambridge : Polity, 1987. — vii,418p. — *Translation of: L'institution imaginaire de la société.* — *Includes index*

CONWAY, David
A farewell to Marx : an outline and appraisal of his theories / David Conway. — Harmondsworth : Penguin, 1987. — 230p. — (Pelican books). — *Bibliography: p.221-224*

GERAS, Norman
Literature of revolution : essays on Marxism / Norman Geras. — London : Verso, 1986. — [288]p. — *Includes index*

GRLIČKOV, Aleksandar
Raskršća socijalizma / Aleksandar Grličkov. — Beograd : Izdavački centar Komunist, 1984. — 358p

Irish political review. — Dublin : Irish Political Review, 1986-. — *Monthly.* — *Continues the Communist and the Irish communist*

JACOBY, Russell
Stalin, marxism-Leninism and the left : Russell Jacoby. — Somerville, Mass. : New England Free Press, 1976. — 63p

Journal of communist studies. — London : Frank Cass, 1985-. — *Quarterly*

Karl Marx, the Materialist Messiah / edited by Kevin B. Nowlan. — Dublin : Published in collaboration with Radio Telefís Éireann, 1984. — 99p. — (The Thomas Davis lecture series). — *Bibliography: p98-99*

KOMMUNISTISCHE ORGANISATIE ROTTERDAM EN OMSTREKEN (MARXISTISCH-LENINISTISCH)
Politieke stellingname beginselverklaring doel en taken / von de Kommunistische Organisatie Rotterdam en Omstreken (marxistisch-leninistisch). — Rotterdam : Koro (ml), 1974. — 16p

KRIEGEL, Annie
Le système communiste mondial / Annie Kriegel. — Paris : Presses Universitaires de France, 1984. — 271p. — (Perspectives internationales)

LICHTHEIM, George
[Selections. 1986]. Thoughts among the ruins : collected essays on Europe and beyond / George Lichtheim ; new introduction by Walter Laqueur. — New Brunswick (U.S.A.) : Transaction Books, [1986], c1973. — xxix, 492 p.. — *"First paperback edition"--T.p. verso.* — *"Introduction ... first appeared in Commentary magazine, August 1973"--T.p. verso.* — : Reprint. Originally published: Collected essays. New York : Viking Press, 1973

LIDER, Julian
Correlation of forces : an analysis of Marxist-Leninist concepts / Julian Lider. — Aldershot : Gower, c1986. — vii,384p. — (Swedish studies in international relations). — *Bibliography: p347-372.* — *Includes index*

MARX, Karl, 1818-1883
[Manifest der Kommunistischen Partei. English]. Manifesto of the Communist Party / Karl Marx. with an appendix, Principles of Communism / Friedrich Engels. — 2nd ed. — Moscow : Progress, 1977. — 106p. — *This edition is a reproduction of the translation made by Samuel Moore in 1888 from the original German text of 1848 and edited by Friedrich Engels.* — *Originally published 1971*

Marx refuted : the verdict of history / edited by Ronald Duncan and Colin Wilson. — Bath : Ashgrove Press, 1987. — 284p

Marxism and liberalism / edited by Ellen Frankel Paul ... [et al.]. — Oxford : Basil Blackwell for the Social Philosophy and Policy Center, Bowling Green State University, 1986. — xii,223p

Marxist policies today : in socialist and capitalist countries / edited by Edwin Dowdy. — St. Lucia ; London : University of Queensland Press, 1986. — viii,234p. — *Includes bibliographies and index*

COMMUNISM
continuation

Marx...ou pas? : réflexions sur un centenaire / Denis Woronoff...[et al.]. — Paris : Etudes et documentation internationales, 1986. — 340p

NIN, Andrés
Les dictadures dels nostres dies / Andreu Nin. — 2a edició. — Sant Boi de Llobregat : Lluita, 1984. — 211p. — (Collecció espurna ; 3)

POPOV, M.V.
Planomernoe razreshenie protivorechii razvitiia sotsializma kak pervoi fazy kommunizma / M.V. Popov. — Leningrad : Izd-vo Leningradskogo universiteta, 1986. — 156p

POTIER, Jean-Pierre
Lectures italiennes de Marx : les conflits d'interpretation chez les économistes et les philosophes, 1883-1983 / Jean-Pierre Potier. — Lyon : Presses Universitaires de Lyon, 1986. — 500p. — *Bibliography: p471-492*

Problèmes du mouvement communiste international / édité par le Comité Central de Parti Communiste Français. — [Paris] : Parti Communiste Français, 1963. — 95p

PUENTE, Issac
Libertarian communism / Issac Puente. — Sydney : Monty Miller Press, 1985. — 32p. — (Rebel worker pamphlet ; 5)

SASSOON, Anne Showstack
Gramsci's politics / Anne Showstack Sassoon. — 2nd ed. — London : Hutchinson Education, 1987. — [261]p. — (Contemporary politics). — *Previous ed.: London : Croom Helm, 1980. — Includes bibliography and index*

COMMUNISM — Dictionaries
Dictionnaire critique du marxisme / Georges Labica et Gérard Bensussan; directeurs de la production. — 2nd ed. — Paris : Presses Universitaires de France, 1985. — xi,1240p

[Nauchnyi kommunizm]. A Dictionary of scientific communism / [translated from the Russian]. — Moscow : Progress Publishers, c1984. — 288 p.. — *Translation of: Nauchnyĭ kommunizm*

COMMUNISM — History
Pervyi kongress Kominterna : Velikii Oktiabr' i rozhdenie mezhdunarodnogo kommunisticheskogo dvizheniia / [otv. redaktor K. K. Shirinia]. — Moskva : Politizdat, 1986. — (Osnovnye etapy istorii mezhdunarodnogo kommunisticheskogo dvizheniia)

COMMUNISM — History — 20th century
BEILHARZ, Peter
Trotsky, Trotskyism and the transition to socialism / Peter Beilharz. — London : Croom Helm, c1987. — 197p. — *Includes index*

COMMUNISM — History — 20th century — Sources
A Documentary history of communism / edited, with an introduction, notes and original translations, by Robert V. Daniels. — London : Tauris, 1986, c1985. — 2v.. — *Translated from various languages. — Originally published: Hanover : University Press of New England for the University of Vermont, 1984. — Includes index*

COMMUNISM — 1945-
OELEK, Sambal
Die Linke in den Wechseljahren : Gedankensplitter im Theorievakuum / Sambal Oelek. — Zürich : Rotpunktverlag, 1985. — 174p. — *Bibliography: p170-171, 174*

COMMUNISM — 1945- — Bibliography
Communism in the world since 1945 : an annotated bibliography / Susan K. Kinnell, editor ; foreword by Herbert J. Ellison. — Santa Barbara, Calif. : ABC-CLIO, c1987. — xiii, 415 p.. — (Clio bibliography series). — *Includes indexes*

COMMUNISM — Argentina — History — 20th century
COGGIOLA, Osvaldo
El trotskismo en la Argentina (1960-1985) / Osvaldo Coggiola. — Buenos Aires : Centro Editor de América Latina. — (Biblioteca Política Argentina ; 133). — *Bibliography: p101-104*
t.1. — 1986. — 104p

COGGIOLA, Osvaldo
Historia del trotskismo argentino (1929-1960) / Osvaldo Coggiola. — Buenos Aires : Centro Editor de América Latina, 1985. — 159p. — (Biblioteca Política Argentina ; 91). — *Bibliographical notes: p154-158*

COMMUNISM — Austria
SCHÖLER, Uli
"Otto Bauer - nein danke"? : Austromarxismusdiskussion und historische Bezüge für eine Standortbestimmung marxistischer Sozialdemokraten / Uli Schöler. — Berlin : Demokratische Verlagskooperative, 1984. — 89p. — *Bibliography: p87-89*

COMMUNISM — Bulgaria
SLAVOV, Slavi Dimitrov
Georgi Dimitrov : opit za teoreticheski portret / Slavi Slavov. — Sofiia : Izd-vo na Bŭlgarskata Akademiia na Naukite, 1983. — 207p. — *Summary in Russian and German. — Bibliography: p195-201*

ZHIVKOV, Todor, 1911-
Marxist concepts and practices : a series of lectures on theoretical problems and practical approaches to the construction of a developed socialist society in the People's Republic of Bulgaria / by Todor Zhivkov. — Oxford : Pergamon, 1984. — xi,201p. — *Translated from the Bulgarian. — Includes index*

COMMUNISM — Bulgaria — History
Istoriia na Bŭlgarskata komunisticheska partiia / redaktsionna komisiia: Ruben Abramov...[et al.]. — 4-o dop. izd.. — Sofiia : Partizdat, 1984. — 791p

COMMUNISM — China
CHIANG, Kai-shek, 1887-1975
President Chiang Kai-shek's selected speeches and messages in 1962. — [Taipei] : Government Information Office, 1963. — 59p

China's socialist economy : an outline history (1949-1984) / editors Liu Suinian, Wu Qungan. — Beijing : Beijing Review, 1986. — vi,700p

SENESE, Donald J.
Democracy in mainland China : the myth and the reality / by Donald J. Senese. — Washington : Council for Social and Economic Studies, 1986. — 96p

COMMUNISM — Cuba
Cuban Communism / edited by Irving Louis Horowitz. — 6th ed. — New Brunswick, U.S.A. : Transaction Books, c1987. — xvi, 743 p.. — *Includes bibliographies*

COMMUNISM — Cuba — History
LISTER, John
Cuba : radical face of Stalinism / John Lister. — London : Left View Books, 1985. — 168p. — *Bibliography: p165-168. — Includes chronology (1868-1985): p149-164*

COMMUNISM — Developing countries
Marxian theory and the third world / edited by Diptendra Banerjee. — New Delhi ; Beverly Hills : Sage Publications, 1985. — 325 p.. — *Includes bibliographical references*

COMMUNISM — Egypt
GOLDBERG, Ellis
Tinker, tailor, and textile worker : class and politics in Egypt, 1930-1952 / Ellis Goldberg. — Berkeley : University of California Press, 1986. — p. cm. — *Includes index. — Bibliography: p*

COMMUNISM — Europe
DOUGHERTY, James E.
Eurocommunism and the Atlantic Alliance / James E. Dougherty and Diane K. Pfaltzgraff. — Cambridge, Mass : Institute for Foreign Policy Analysis, 1977. — xiv, 66 p. — (Special Report - Institute for Foreign Policy Analysis). — *Includes bibliographical references*

FEHÉR, Ferenc
Eastern left : western left : a contribution to the morphology of a problematic relationship / Ferenc Fehér [and] Agnes Heller. — Munchen : Projekt 'Crises in Soviet-type systems', 1986. — 40p. — (Research project Crises in Soviet-type systems ; Study no.10)

COMMUNISM — Europe — History — 20th century
SPRIANO, Paolo
Stalin and the European communists / Paolo Spriano ; translated by Jon Rothschild. — London : Verso, 1985. — 315p. — *Translation of: I comunisti europei e Stalin. — Includes index*

COMMUNISM — Europe — History — 20th century — Bibliography
NARKIEWICZ, Olga A.
Eurocommunism 1968-1986 : a select bibliography / Olga A. Narkiewicz. — London : Mansell, 1987. — [230]p. — *Includes index*

COMMUNISM — Europe, Eastern
PIREC, Dušan
Kriza realnog socijalizma? : društveno-ekonomske karakteristike i protivurečnosti istočnoevropskih socijalističkih zemalja / Dušan Pirec. — Beograd : Ekonomika, 1985. — 412p. — *Bibliography: p369-392*

SETON-WATSON, Hugh
The East European revolution / Hugh Seton-Watson. — Boulder : Westview Press, 1985. — xix, 451 p.. — "Westview encore reprint.". — : *Reprint. Originally published: New York : Praeger, 1951. — Includes index. — Bibliography: p. 416-423*

COMMUNISM — France
AVENAS, Denise
"Lutte ouvrière" et la révolution mondiale / Denise Avenas. — Paris : François Maspero, 1971. — 45p. — (Série "Marx ou crève" ; 3) (Cahiers rouges)

La nation socialiste : cahiers du communisme démocratique et national : revue mensuelle. — Paris : National Socialiste, 1956. — 96p

ORGANISATION COMMUNISTE INTERNATIONALISTE
Programme d'action de la classe ouvrière pour le socialisme, pour le gouvernement ouvrier. — Paris : Selio, 1968. — 22p. — (Documents de l'OCI ; no.1)

COMMUNISM — France — History
BECKER, Jean Jacuqes
Histoire de l'anti communisme en France / Jean Jacques Becker, Serge Berstein. — Paris : Olivier Orban
T.1: 1917-1940. — 1987. — 407p. — *Bibliography: p389-[395]*

COMMUNISM — France — History — 20th century
READER, Keith
Intellectuals and the Left in France since 1968 / Keith A. Reader. — Basingstoke : Macmillan, 1987. — xii,154p. — *Bibliography: p148-150. — Includes index*

COMMUNISM — Germany — History
AGURSKY, Mikhail
The third Rome : national Bolshevism in the USSR / Mikhail Agursky ; foreword by Leonard Shapiro. — Boulder : Westview Press, 1987. — p. cm. — *Includes index. — Bibliography: p*

COMMUNISM — Germany (East)
GLAESSNER, Gert-Joachim
Bürokratische Herrschaft : Konflikt-bewältigung in der DDR / Gert-Joachim Glaessner. — München : Spendenkonto Projekt, 1986. — 64p. — (Krisen in den Systemen Sowjetischen typs ; Studie nr.13). — *Bibliography: p63-64*

COMMUNISM — Germany (West) — History and criticism
DOZEKAL, Egbert
Von der 'Rekonstruktion' der Marxschen Theorie zur 'Krise des Marxismus' : Darstellung und Kritik eines Diskussionsprozesses in der Bundesrepublik von 1967 bis 1984 / Egbert Dozekal. — Köln : Pahl-Rugenstein, 1985. — 301p. — (Pahl-Rugenstein Hochschulschriften Gesellschafts- und Naturwissenschaften ; 204). — *Bibliography: p294-301*

COMMUNISM — Great Britain — History
WOODHOUSE, Michael
Essays on the history of communism in Britain / by Michael Woodhouse and Brian Pearce. — London : New Park Publications, 1975. — xv,248p. — *Spine title: Communism in Britain. — Includes index*

COMMUNISM — Great Britain — History — 20th century
CALLAGHAN, John
The far left in British politics / John Callaghan. — Oxford : Basil Blackwell, 1987. — xi,249p. — *Includes index*

MACINTYRE, Stuart
A proletarian science : Marxism in Britain 1917-1933 / Stuart Macintyre. — Paperback ed, with corrections. — London : Lawrence and Wishart, 1986. — [xiii],286p. — *Originally published: Cambridge: Cambridge University Press, 1980. — Bibliography: p[271]-280*

COMMUNISM — India
JOSHI, P. C.
Marxism and social revolution in India and other essays / P. C. Joshi. — New Delhi : Patriot Publishers, 1986. — xiv,227p

COMMUNISM — Ireland — History
CLIFFORD, Brendan
James Connolly : an adventurous socialist : May Day address, Cork 1984 / Brendan Clifford. — [Cork] (26, Church Ave., Roman St., Cork) : Labour Comment, [1984?]. — 15p

COMMUNISM — Italy — History — 20th century
DE GRAND, Alexander J.
In Stalin's shadow : Angelo Tasca and the crisis of the left in Italy and France, 1910-1945 / Alexander J. De Grand. — Dekalb, Ill. : Northern Illinois University Press, 1986. — viii, 231p. — *Includes index. — Contains bibliographical references*

COMMUNISM — Japan — History
MIYAMOTO, Kenji
Selected works / Kenji Miyamoto. — Tokyo : Japan Press Service, 1985. — v,560p

COMMUNISM — Japan — History — 20th century
HOSTON, Germaine A.
Marxism and the crisis of development in prewar Japan / Germaine A. Hoston. — Princeton, N.J. : Princeton University Press, c1986. — xviii, 401 p.. — *Includes index. — Bibliography: p. 357-386*

COMMUNISM — Mexico
SCHMITT, Karl M.
Communism in Mexico : a study in political frustration / Karl M. Schmitt. — Austin : University of Texas Press, 1965. — xii,290p. — *Bibliography: p251-262*

COMMUNISM — Netherlands
KOMMUNISTISCHE ORGANISATIE ROTTERDAM EN OMSTREKEN (MARXISTISCH-LENINISTISCH)
Politieke stellingname beginselverklaring doel en taken / von de Kommunistische Organisatie Rotterdam en Omstreken (marxistisch-leninistisch). — Rotterdam : Koro (ml), 1974. — 16p

COMMUNISM — New York (N.Y.) — History — 20th century
COONEY, Terry A
The rise of the New York Intellectuals : Partisan review and its circle / Terry A. Cooney. — Madison, Wis. : University of Wisconsin Press, 1986. — xi, 350p. — (History of American thought and culture). — *Includes index. — Bibliography: p.331-333*

COMMUNISM — Norway — History
LORENZ, Einhart
Det er ingen sak å få partiet lite : NKP 1923-1931 / Einhart Lorenz. — Olso : Pax, 1983. — 301p. — *Bibliography: p280-287*

COMMUNISM — Paraguay
PRIETO YEGROS, Leandro
La infiltración comunista en los partidos politicos paraguayos : caso del "Bloque Liberación" del Partido Revolucionario Febrerista : (version documental / Leandro Prieto Yegros. — [Asunción] : Cuadernos Republicanos, [1985]. — 521p

COMMUNISM — Poland
KARPIŃSKI, Jakub
Ustrój komunistyczny w Polsce / Jakub Karpiński. — Londyn : Aneks, 1985. — 228p

COMMUNISM — Poland — History
Komunistyczna Partia Polski (1918-1938) : zarys historii / Antoni Czubiński. — Warszawa : Wydawnictwa Szkolne i Pedagogiczne, 1985. — 283p. — *Bibliography: p275-[281]*

COMMUNISM — Portugal
Comment les communistes ont essayé de s'emparer du pouvoir au Portugal : supplément de Est et Ouest / edité par le Centre dArchives et de Documentation Politiques et Sociales. — Paris : Centre dArchives et de Documentation Politiques et Sociales, 1975. — 32p

COMMUNISM — Russia
WEBB, Sidney
Soviet communism : a new civilisation / by Sidney and Beatrice Webb. postscript added to the second edition. — [London] : Privately printed by the authors, 1937. — 72,33p

COMMUNISM — South Africa
Contending ideologies in South Africa / edited by James Leatt, Theo Kneifel, and Klaus Nürnberger. — Grand Rapids : W.B. Eerdmans, 1986. — x, 318 p.. — *Includes index. — Bibliography: p. [303]-309*

COMMUNISM — Soviet Union
Ekonomicheskie problemy razvitogo sotsializma / red. kollegiia I. I. Lukinov...[et al.]. — Kiev : Naukova dumka
T.4: Ekonomicheskaia struktura obshchestva i razitie sotsialisticheskogo obraza zhizni / red. kollegiia V. E. Kozak...[et al.]. — 1985. — 270p

Kalendar'-ezhegodnik kommunista na 1931 god. — Moskva : Moskovskii rabochii, 1931

LUDWIKOWSKI, Rett R
The crisis of communism : its meaning, origins, and phases / Rett R. Ludwikowski. — Washington : Pergamon-Brassey's International Defense Publishers, 1986. — xii, 84 p.. — (Foreign policy report). — *"A Publication of the Institute for Foreign Policy Analysis, Inc.". — Includes bibliographical references*

POPOV, M.V.
Planomernoe razreshenie protivorechii razvitiia sotsializma kak pervoi fazy kommunizma / M.V. Popov. — Leningrad : Izd-vo Leningradskogo universiteta, 1986. — 156p

RAȚIU, Ion
Moscow challenges the world / Ion Rațiu ; with an introduction by Brian Crozier. — London : Sherwood Press, 1986. — [vi],410p. — *Bibliography: p381-388*

Razvitoi sotsializm : voprosy teorii i istorii / otv. redaktor S. S. Khromov. — Moskva : Nauka, 1986. — 245p

SHISHKINA, I. M.
Partiia i rabochii klass v sotsialisticheskom obshchestve : izmyshleniia sovetologov i deistvitel'nost' / I. M. Shishkina. — Leningrad : Lenizdat, 1986. — 260p

SOUVARINE, Boris
[Staline. English]. Stalin : a critical survey of Bolshevism. — New York : Arno Press, 1972 [c1939]. — xiv, 690 p. — (World affairs: national and international viewpoints)

Voprosyteorii i praktiki ideologicheskoi raboty / Akademiia obshchestvennykh nauk pri TSK KPSS. — Moskva : Akademiia obshchestvennykh nauk pri TSK KPSS, 1972-. — *Annual. — Vyp.1-13 entitled Voprosyteorii i metodov idealogicheskoi raboty*

COMMUNISM — Soviet Union — History
AGURSKY, Mikhail
The third Rome : national Bolshevism in the USSR / Mikhail Agursky ; foreword by Leonard Shapiro. — Boulder : Westview Press, 1987. — p. cm. — *Includes index. — Bibliography: p*

BUBIS, Mordecai Donald
The Soviet Union and Stalinism in the ideological debates of American Trotskyism (1937-51) / by Mordecai Donald Bubis. — 330 leaves. — *PhD (Econ) 1986 LSE*

WILLIAMS, Robert Chadwell
The other Bolsheviks : Lenin and his critics, 1904-1914 / Robert C. Williams. — Bloomington : Indiana University Press, c1986. — 233 p.. — *Includes index. — Bibliography: p. 222-228*

COMMUNISM — Spain — Congresses
PARTIDO COMUNISTA DE ESPAÑA
Asamblea para la Unidad de los Comunistas, 19-20 de Octubre de 1985 : texto íntegro. — Madrid : Ahora, 1985. — 177p

COMMUNISM — Spain — History
ANDRADE, Juan
Notas sobre la guerra civil : (actuación del POUM) / Juan Andrade. — Madrid : Ediciones Libertarias, 1986. — 158p

MONREAL, Antoni
El pensamiento político de Joaquín Maurín / Antoni Monreal. — [Barcelona] : Península, [1984]. — 204p. — (Historia, ciencia, sociedad ; 190)

MORÁN, Gregorio
Miseria y grandeza del Partido Comunista de España, 1939-1985 / Gregorio Morán. — Barcelona : Planeta, 1986. — 648p. — (Espejo de España ; 122)

VILAR, Sergio
Porque se ha destruido el PCE / Sergio Vilar. — Barcelona : Plaza & Janes Editores, 1986. — 281p

COMMUNISM — Sweden — History
HERMANSSON, Jörgen
Kommunism på svenska? : SKP/VPK:s idéutveckling efter Komintern / Jörgen Hermansson. — Uppsala : Uppsala universitet ; Stockholm : Distributed by Almqvist & Wiksell, 1984. — 388p. — (Acta Universitatis Upsaliensis). — *With English summary. — Doktorsavhandling framlagd vid Uppsala universitet 1984*

Marx i Sverige : 100 år med Marx i svensk historia, vetenskap och politik / redigerad ar Lars Vikström. — Stockholm : Arbetarkultur, 1983. — 258p. — (Teori & praxis ; 6)

COMMUNISM — Switzerland
La critique des communistes aux initiatives 40 heures : l'aventurisme parlementaire et l'opportunisme contre l'organisation autonome de la classe ouvriere. — [S.l.] : Coopérative d'Impressions Nouvelles, 1970. — 22p

OELEK, Sambal
Die Linke in den Wechseljahren : Gedankensplitter im Theorievakuum / Sambal Oelek. — Zürich : Rotpunktverlag, 1985. — 174p. — *Bibliography: p170-171, 174*

COMMUNISM — Turkey — History
HARRIS, George S
The origins of communism in Turkey / [by] George S. Harris. — Stanford, Calif. : Hoover Institution on War, Revolution and Peace, 1967. — 215 p. — (Hoover Institution publications). — *Bibliography: p. 186-201*

COMMUNISM — United States — History
BUBIS, Mordecai Donald
The Soviet Union and Stalinism in the ideological debates of American Trotskyism (1937-51) / by Mordecai Donald Bubis. — 330 leaves. — *PhD (Econ) 1986 LSE*

BUHLE, Paul
Marxism in the United States : remapping the history of the American left / Paul Buhle. — London : Verso, 1987. — [290]p. — (Haymarket series)

COMMUNISM — United States — History — Sources
American communism and Black Americans : a documentary history, 1919-1929 / edited by Philip S. Foner and James S. Allen. — Philadelphia : Temple University Press, 1987. — xvi, 235 p.. — *Includes bibliographical references and index*

COMMUNISM — United States — History — 20th century
SCALES, Junius Irving
Cause at heart : a former Communist remembers / Junius Irving Scales and Richard Nickson ; foreword by Telford Taylor. — Athens : University of Georgia Press, c1987. — xxxv, 427 p.. — *Includes index*

COMMUNISM — United States — 1917-
SCHRECKER, Ellen
No ivory tower : McCarthyism and the universities / Ellen Schrecker. — New York : Oxford University Press, 1986. — p. cm. — *Includes index.* — *Bibliography: p*

COMMUNISM — Yugoslavia
Savez komunista u borbi protiv antisocijalističkih delovanja i antikomunističkih ideologija / redakcioni odbor David Atlagić...[et al.]. — Beograd : Izdavački centar Komunist, 1986. — viii,555p

Socijalistički savez radnog naroda u razvoju socijalističkog samoupravnog društva / redakcioni odbor: Ilija Globačnik...[et al.]. — Beograd : Izdavački centar Komunist ; Ljubljana : Jugoslovenski centar za teoriju i praksu samoupravljanja "Edvard Kardelj", [1986]. — 902p. — *U zborniku objavljuju se saopštenja i diskusije sa naučnog skupa, 26. i 27. januara 1984 godine u okviru Teorijskih rasprava "Misao i revolucionarno delo Edvarda Kardelja". — Summaries in Serbian, Croat, Macedonian, Hungarian, Albanian and English*

COMMUNISM — Yugoslavia — History
Istorija Saveza komunista Jugoslavije / autori: Janko Pleterski...[et al.] ; redaktsioni odbor: Takhir Abdulji...[et al.]. — Beograd : Izdavački centar komunist : Narodna knjiga : Rad, 1985. — xv,485p

COMMUNISM AND CHRISTIANITY
LYON, David, 1948-
Marx and the microchip / David Lyon. — Leicester : UCCF Associates on behalf of the Historians' Study Group, [1985?]. — 11p

COMMUNISM AND CHRISTIANITY — Catholic Church — Poland
MONTICONE, Ronald C.
The Catholic Church in communist Poland, 1945-1985 : forty years of church-state [relations] / Ronald C. Monticone. — Boulder : East European Monographs, 1986. — viii,227p. — (East European Monographs ; No.205). — *Bibliography: p219-224*

COMMUNISM AND CHRISTIANITY — History
MCLELLAN, David
Marxism and religion : a description and assessment of the Marxist critique of Christianity / David McLellan. — Basingstoke : Macmillan, 1987. — [192]p. — *Includes bibliography and index*

COMMUNISM AND CULTURE — Hungary
HERNÁDI, Miklós
Olyan amilyen? : körkép új kultúránkról / Hernádi Miklós. — Budapest : Kozmosz Könyvek, 1984. — 285p. — (Az én világom)

COMMUNISM AND INTELLECTUALS — China — Addresses, essays, lectures
China's establishment intellectuals / edited by Carol Lee Hamrin and Timothy Cheek. — Armonk, N.Y. : M.E. Sharpe, c1986. — xix, 266 p.. — *"An East gate book"--facing t.p. — "East gate books"--T.p. verso. — Includes bibliographical references and index*

COMMUNISM AND INTELLECTUALS — Soviet Union
BURBANK, Jane
Intelligentsia and revolution : Russian views of Bolshevism, 1917-1922 / Jane Burbank. — New York : Oxford University Press, 1986. — viii, 340 p.. — *Includes index.* — *Bibliography: p. 315-326*

COMMUNISM AND NUCLEAR WARFARE
INTERNATIONAL SYMPOSIUM ON STRUGGLE FOR PREVENTING NUCLEAR WAR AND ELIMINATING NUCLEAR WEAPONS (1985 : Tokyo)
Struggle for preventing nuclear war and eliminating nuclear weapons : [papers presented at the Symposium]. — Tokyo : Japan Press Service, 1985. — vii,555p

COMMUNISM AND PHILOSOPHY
SUCHTING, W. A.
Marx and philosophy : three studies / W.A. Suchting. — London : Macmillan, 1986. — [160]p. — *Includes index*

COMMUNISM AND RELIGION
Ateizm v SSSR : stanovlenie i razvitie / [G. V. Vorontsov...et al., otv. redaktor A. F. Okulov]. — Moskva : Mysl', 1986. — 235p

COMMUNISM AND SCIENCE — Soviet Union
HOFFMANN, Erik P.
Technocratic socialism : the Soviet Union in the advanced industrial era / Erik P. Hoffmann and Robbin F. Laird. — Durham : Duke University Press, 1985. — 228 p. — (Duke Press policy studies). — *Includes index.* — *Bibliography: p.[201]-225*

COMMUNIST COUNTRIES
Newsletter from behind the Iron Curtain: reports on communist activities in Eastern Europe. — Stockholm : Estonian Information Center and Latvian National Foundation, 1986- . — *Monthly*

COMMUNIST COUNTRIES — Commerce
Effektivnost' sotsialisticheskoi vnutrennei torgovli / R. A. Maksimento...[et al.] ; pod redaktsiei V. I. Ivanitskogo i L. Rendosha. — Kiev : Vyshcha shkola, 1985. — 174p

COMMUNIST COUNTRIES — Commerce — Canada
Canada's trade with the Soviet Union bloc : the report of a Working Group of the CIIA; Aldo Nicolai, chairman. — Toronto : Canadian Institute of International Affairs, 1985. — vi,50p. — (CIIA working group reports ; 3)

COMMUNIST COUNTRIES — Economic conditions
BROMLEI, N. Ia.
Obraz zhizni v usloviiakh sovershenstvovaniia sotsializma : opyt istoriko-sravnitel'nogo issledovaniia / N. Ia. Bromlei ; otv. redaktor E. I. Kapustin. — Moskva : Nauka, 1986. — 222p

Power, purpose, and collective choice : economic strategy in socialist states / Ellen Comisso and Laura D'Andrea Tyson, editors. — Ithaca : Cornell University Press, 1986. — p. cm. — (Cornell studies in political economy) . — *Published also as v. 40, no. 2 of the journal International organization*

THALHEIM, Karl C.
Stagnation or change in communist economies? / Karl C. Thalheim ; a note by Gregory Grossman. — London : Centre for Research into Communist Economies, 1986. — 54p. — (The State of communist economies ; 1). — *Translation of: Wirtschaftsreformen in Ostblockländern. — Text on inside covers*

WINIECKI, Jan
Economic prospects - East and West : a view from the East / Jan Winiecki ; comment: Roger Clarke. — London : Centre for Research into Communist Economies, 1987. — 136p. — (Understanding economic systems ; 3) . — *Bibliography: 123-127*

COMMUNIST COUNTRIES — Economic policy
Economie politique de la planification en système socialiste / coordonnées par Marie Lavigne. — Paris : Economica, 1978. — 327p. — (Recherches Panthéon-Sorbonne. Série sciences économiques)

Intensifikatsiia i effektivnost' sotsialisticheskogo vosproizvodstva / [redkol.: A. Braun...et al.]. — Moskva : Politizdat, 1986. — 350p

Power, purpose, and collective choice : economic strategy in socialist states / Ellen Comisso and Laura D'Andrea Tyson, editors. — Ithaca : Cornell University Press, 1986. — p. cm. — (Cornell studies in political economy) . — *Published also as v. 40, no. 2 of the journal International organization*

PRYBYLA, Jan S
Market and plan under socialism : the bird in the cage / Jan S. Prybyla. — Stanford, Calif. : Hoover Institution Press, Stanford University, c1987. — xv, 348 p.. — (Hoover Press publication ; 335). — *Includes index.* — *Bibliography: p. [317]-335*

RADNÓTI, Éva
Árpolitikai koncepciók és gazdaságunk fejlődése / Radnóti Éva. — Budapest : Közgazdasági és Jogi Könyvkiadó, 1984. — 233p. — (Időszerű közgazdasági kérdések). — *Bibliography: p229-[234]*

Soglasovanie ekonomicheskoi politiki stran SEV / otv. redaktor O. T. Bogomolov. — Moskva : Nauka, 1986. — 287p

COMMUNIST COUNTRIES — Foreign economic relations
BUCHAN, David
Incidences stratégiques du commerce est-ouest / David Buchan ; traduction de R. Manicacci. — Paris : Bosquet, [1985]. — 169p

East-West economic relations in the changing global environmental : proceedings of a conference held by the International Economic Association in Budapest, Hungary, and Vienna, Austria / edited by Béla Csikós-Nagy and David G. Young. — Basingstoke : Macmillan, 1986. — xxiv,429p. -- *Includes index*

COMMUNIST COUNTRIES — Foreign economic relations — Cuba

Kuba v mezhdunarodnom sotsialisticheskom razdelenii truda / otv. redaktor M. A. Manasov. — Moskva : Nauka, 1986. — 146p

COMMUNIST COUNTRIES — Foreign economic relations — Nicaragua

BERRIOS, Ruben
Economic relations between Nicaragua and the socialist countries / Ruben Berrios. — Washington, D.C. : Latin American Program of the Woodrow Wilson International Center for Scholars, 1985. — 23p. — (Working papers / Woodrow Wilson International Center for Scholars. Latin American Program ; 166)

COMMUNIST COUNTRIES — Foreign relations

HALLIDAY, Fred
The making of the second cold war / Fred Halliday. — 2nd ed. — London : Verso, 1986. — [256]p. — *Previous ed.: 1983. — Includes bibliography and index*

COMMUNIST COUNTRIES — Politics and government

Communist politics : a reader / edited by Stephen White and Daniel Nelson. — London : Macmillan, 1986. — xii,416p. — *Bibliography: p380-410. — Includes index*

NELSON, Daniel N.
Alliance behavior in the Warsaw Pact / Daniel N. Nelson. — Boulder : Westview Press, 1986. — xvii, 134 p.. — (Westview special studies on the Soviet Union and Eastern Europe). — *Includes index. Bibliography: p. [123]-127*

COMMUNIST COUNTRIES — Social conditions

BROMLEI, N. Ia.
Obraz zhizni v usloviiakh sovershenstvovaniia sotsializma : opyt istoriko-sravnitel'nogo issledovaniia / N. Ia. Bromlei ; otv. redaktor E. I. Kapustin. — Moskva : Nauka, 1986. — 222p

COMMUNIST COUNTRIES — Social policy

Obraz zhizni i planirovanie sotsial'nykh protsessov / pod redaktsiei G. Assmana, I. Ia. Pisarenko. — Minsk : Izd-vo "Universitetskoe", 1986. — 366p

COMMUNIST EDUCATION — Soviet Union

Voprosyteorii i praktiki ideologicheskoi raboty / Akademiia obshchestvennykh nauk pri TSK KPSS. — Moskva : Akademiia obschestvennykh nauk pri TSK KPSS, 1972-. — Annual. — Vyp.1-13 entitled Voprosyteorii i metodov idealogicheskoi raboty

COMMUNIST INTERNATIONAL See also Third International

COMMUNIST INTERNATIONAL

Pervyi kongress Kominterna : Velikii Oktiabr' i rozhdenie mezhdunarodnogo kommunisticheskogo dvizheniia / [otv. redaktor K. K. Shirinia]. — Moskva : Politizdat, 1986. — (Osnovnye etapy istorii mezhdunarodnogo kommunisticheskogo dvizheniia)

COMMUNIST INTERNATIONAL — Biography — Dictionaries

LAZIĆ, Branko M
Biographical dictionary of the Comintern / by Branko Lazitch in collaboration with Milorad M. Drachkovitch. — New, rev. and expanded ed. — Stanford, Calif. : Hoover Institution Press, 1986. — lv, 532 p.. — *Bibliography: p. xxii-xxiii*

COMMUNIST INTERNATIONAL — History — Sources

The German revolution and the debate on Soviet power : documents, 1918-1919 : preparing the founding conference / edited by John Riddell. — New York : Anchor : Distributed by Pathfinder Press, 1986. — xx,540p. — (The Communist International in Lenin's time). — *Bibliography: p528*

COMMUNIST INTERNATIONAL. Congress (7th : 1935)

Istoricheskoe znachenie VII kongressa Kominterna : materialy nauchnoi konferentsii, posviashchennoi 50-letiiu VII kongressa Kommunisticheskogo Internatsionala. Moskva, 16-17 iiulia 1985 g. / [otv. redaktor P. A. Rodionov]. — Moskva : Politizdat, 1986. — 357p

COMMUNIST LEADERSHIP — Russian S.F.S.R. — Biography — Directories

HELF, Gavin
A biographical directory of Soviet regional party leaders / compiled by Gavin Helf. — Munich : Radio Liberty Research, RFE/RL Part 1: RSFSR oblasts, krais, and ASSRs. — 1987. — 90p

COMMUNIST ORGANISATION IN THE BRITISH ISLES

COMMUNIST ORGANISATION IN THE BRITISH ISLES
Platform of the Communist Organisation in the British Isles. — Edinburgh (c/o J. Maisels, 3 May Court, Edinburgh EH4 4SD) : C.O.B.I., 1976. — [1],24p

COMMUNIST PARTIES

DOUGHERTY, James E.
Eurocommunism and the Atlantic Alliance / James E. Dougherty and Diane K. Pfaltzgraff. — Cambridge, Mass : Institute for Foreign Policy Analysis, 1977. — xiv, 66 p. — (Special Report - Institute for Foreign Policy Analysis). — *Includes bibliographical references*

KULINCHENKO, V. A.
Demokraticheskii tsentralizm i razvitie vnutripartiinykh otnoshenii / V. A. Kulinchenko. — Moskva : Mysl', 1985. — 277p

COMMUNIST PARTIES — Directories

HOBDAY, Charles
Communist and Marxist parties of the world / compiled and written by Charles Hobday. — Harlow : Longman, 1986. — 529p. — (A Keesing's reference publication). — *Bibliography: p508-513. — Includes index*

COMMUNIST PARTIES — Communist countries

Ruling Communist parties and their status under law / edited by D.A. Loeber (editor in chief) ... [et al.]. — The Hague ; Boston : M. Nijhoff ; Hingham, MA : Distributors for the U.S. and Canada, Kluwer Academic Publishers, 1986, c1984. — p. cm. — (Law in Eastern Europe ; no. 31). — *Includes bibliographies and index*

COMMUNIST PARTIES — Soviet Union

Ruling Communist parties and their status under law / edited by D.A. Loeber (editor in chief) ... [et al.]. — The Hague ; Boston : M. Nijhoff ; Hingham, MA : Distributors for the U.S. and Canada, Kluwer Academic Publishers, 1986, c1984. — p. cm. — (Law in Eastern Europe ; no. 31). — *Includes bibliographies and index*

COMMUNIST PARTY OF GREAT BRITAIN

COMMUNIST PARTY OF GREAT BRITAIN
How to beat the Tories and go one better! : Communist election manifesto. — London : Communist Party of Great Britain, 1987. — [4p]

News and views: Communist Party monthly. — London : Communist Party of Great Britain, 1987-. — *Monthly*

COMMUNIST PARTY OF GREAT BRITAIN — History

BRULEY, Sue
Leninism, Stalinism, and the women's movement in Britain, 1920-1939 / Susan Bruley. — New York : Garland Pub., 1986. — p. cm. — (Outstanding theses from the London School of Economics and Political Science). — Thesis (Ph.D.)--University of London, 1980. — *Bibliography: p*

COMMUNIST PARTY OF GREAT BRITAIN — History — Addresses, essays, lectures

WOODHOUSE, Michael
Essays on the history of communism in Britain / by Michael Woodhouse and Brian Pearce. — London : New Park Publications, 1975. — xv,248p. — *Spine title: Communism in Britain. — Includes index*

COMMUNIST STATE

IONESCU, Ghita
The politics of the European Communist states / by Ghiţa Ionescu. — London : Weidenfeld & Nicolson, 1969. — viii,304p. — (Weidenfeld goldbacks). — *Originally published (B67-14569) 1967. — bibl p291-297*

LENIN, V. I.
The state and revolution : the Marxist theory of the State and the tasks of the proletariat in the revolution / V. I. Lenin. — Moscow : Progress Publishers, 1949. — 139p

COMMUNIST STATE — History — 19th century

BARKER, Jeffrey H.
Individualism and community : the state in Marx and early anarchism / Jeffrey H. Barker. — New York : Greenwood Press, 1986. — xiv, 235 p.. — (Contributions in political science ; no. 143). — *Includes index. — Bibliography: p. [221]-229*

COMMUNIST STATES — Politics and government

FURTAK, Robert K.
The political systems of the socialist states : an introduction to Marxist-Leninist regimes / Robert K. Furtak. — Brighton : Wheatsheaf Books, 1986. — xi, 308p. — *Contains bibliographies*

COMMUNIST STRATEGY

KHRUSHCHEV, N.
For victory in peaceful competition with capitalism : with a special preface written for the English edition / Nikita S. Khrushchev. — London : Hutchinson, 1960. — 784p

RAŢIU, Ion
Moscow challenges the world / Ion Raţiu ; with an introduction by Brian Crozier. — London : Sherwood Press, 1986. — [vi],410p. — *Bibliography: p381-388*

COMMUNIST STRATEGY — Congresses

The Red orchestra : instruments of Soviet policy in Latin America and the Caribbean / Dennis L. Bark, editor. — Stanford, Calif. : Hoover Institution Press, Stanford University, c1986. — ix, 139p. — *Includes bibliographies and index*

COMMUNISTS — Biography

Biographical dictionary of Marxism / edited by Robert A. Gorman. — Westport, Conn. : Greenwood ; London : Mansell, 1986. — 1v.. — *Includes bibliographies and index*

DRAPER, Hal
The Marx-Engels chronicle : a day-by-day chronology of Marx and Engels' life and activity / by Hal Draper ; with the assistance of the Center for Socialist History. — New York : Schocken Books, 1985. — xxii, 297 p. — (The Marx-Engels cyclopedia ; v. 1)

COMMUNISTS — Biography — Dictionaries
LAZIĆ, Branko M
Biographical dictionary of the Comintern / by Branko Lazitch in collaboration with Milorad M. Drachkovitch. — New, rev., and expanded ed. — Stanford, Calif. : Hoover Institution Press, 1986. — lv, 532 p.. — *Bibliography: p. xxii-xxiii*

COMMUNISTS — Argentina
COGGIOLA, Osvaldo
Historia del trotskismo argentino (1929-1960) / Osvaldo Coggiola. — Buenos Aires : Centro Editor de América Latina, 1985. — 159p. — (Biblioteca Política Argentina ; 91). — *Bibliographical notes: p154-158*

COGGIOLA, Osvaldo
El trotskismo en la Argentina (1960-1985) / Osvaldo Coggiola. — Buenos Aires : Centro Editor de América Latina. — (Biblioteca Política Argentina ; 133). — *Bibliography: p101-104*
t.1. — 1986. — 104p

COMMUNISTS — Bulgaria — Addresses, essays, lectures
ZHIVKOV, Todor
Velik sin na Bŭlgariia : dokladi, statii, rechi, razmisli za Georgi Dimitrov / Todor Zhivkov. — Sofiia : Partizdat, 1982. — 454p

COMMUNISTS — Bulgaria — Biography
Georgi Dimitrov : biografiia / [Dobrin Michev...et al.]. — []2. dop. izd.]. — Sofiia : Partizdat, 1982. — 663p

SLAVOV, Slavi Dimitrov
Georgi Dimitrov : opit za teoreticheski portret / Slavi Slavov. — Sofiia : Izd-vo na Bŭlgarskata Akademiia na Naukite, 1983. — 207p. — *Summary in Russian and German.* — *Bibliography: p195-201*

COMMUNISTS — Czechoslovakia — Biography
Klement Gottwald : revolucionař a politik : sborník statí / [redakční rada: Ivan Krempa, Antonín Faltys, Květoslava Volková]. — Praha : Nakladatelství Svoboda, 1986. — 353p

KODEŠ, Jiří
Gustav Kliment / Jiří Kodeš. — Praha : Práce, 1986. — 187p

COMMUNISTS — France
GANIER-RAYMOND, Philippe
L'affiche rouge / Philippe Ganier Raymond. — Verviers, Belgium : Marabout, [1985]. — 251p

ROBRIEUX, Phillippe
Låffaire Manouchian : vie et mort dűn héros communiste / Philippe Robrieux. — Paris : Fazard, [1986]. — 434p

COMMUNISTS — Great Britain — Directories
COMMON CAUSE PUBLICATIONS
The far left guide : directory of organisations and supporters. — Fleet, Hants : Common Cause Publications, 1985. — vi,33p

COMMUNISTS — Ireland — History
O'RIORDAN, Manus
Larkinism in perspective : from communism to evolutionary socialism / Manus O'Riordan. — Dublin : Labour History Workshop, 1983. — 20 leaves

COMMUNISTS — Italy — Biography
DE GRAND, Alexander J.
In Stalin's shadow : Angelo Tasca and the crisis of the left in Italy and France, 1910-1945 / Alexander J. De Grand. — Dekalb, Ill. : Northern Illinois University Press, 1986. — viii, 231p. — *Includes index.* — *Contains bibliographical references*

COMMUNISTS — Poland — Interviews
TORAŃSKA, Teresa
Oni / Teresa Torańska. — Londyn : Aneks, 1985. — 365p

COMMUNISTS — Russian S.F.S.R. — Moscow — Biography
Nezabyvaemye 30-e : vospominaniia veteranov partii-moskvichei / [sostavitel': N. B. Ivushkin]. — Moskva : Moskovskii rabochii, 1986. — 303p

COMMUNISTS — Russian S.F.S.R. — Tatar A.S.S.R.
SHARAPOV, Ia. Sh.
Iz iskry-plamia : (V. I. Lenin i kazanskie bol'sheviki / Ia. Sh. Sharapov. — Kazan' : Tatarskoe knizhnoe izd-vo, 1985. — 255p. — (Leniniana Sovetskoi Tatarii ; T.2)

COMMUNISTS — Soviet Union — Biography
VOLOKHOVA, N. A.
"Fenomen" : stranitsy zhizni i deiatel'nosti M. F. Andreevoi / N. A. Volokhova. — Izd. 2-e, ispr. i dop. — Leningrad : Lenizdat, 1986. — 317p. — *Bibliography: p315-[318]*

COMMUNISTS — Soviet Union — History
BADAYEV, A. Y.
Bolsheviks in the Tsarist Duma / A. Y. Badayev ; [with an introduction by Tony Cliff]. — London : Bookmarks, 1987. — 248p. — *Includes bibliographical notes*

COMMUNISTS — Spain — Biography
IBÁRRURI, Dolores
Memorias de Dolores Ibárruri : Pasionaria: La Lucha y la vida / Dolores Ibárruri. — Barcelona : Planeta, 1985. — 763p. — *Contents: Elúnico camino, Me faltaba España*

MONREAL, Antoni
El pensamiento político de Joaquín Maurín / Antoni Monreal. — [Barcelona] : Península, [1984]. — 204p. — (Historia, ciencia, sociedad ; 190)

COMMUNISTS — United States — Biography
SCALES, Junius Irving
Cause at heart : a former Communist remembers / Junius Irving Scales and Richard Nickson ; foreword by Telford Taylor. — Athens : University of Georgia Press, c1987. — xxxv, 427 p.. — *Includes index*

COMMUNISTS — United States — Biography — Dictionaries
Biographical dictionary of the American Left / edited by Bernard K. Johnpoll and Harvey Klehr. — Westport, Conn. : Greenwood Press, 1986. — xiii, 493 p.. — *Includes index*

COMMUNITY
Ideology and national competitiveness : an analysis of nine countries / edited by George C. Lodge and Ezra F. Vogel. — Boston, Mass. : Harvard Business School Press, c1987. — x, 350 p.. — *Includes index.* — *Bibliography: p. 327-342*

NANCY, Jean-Luc
La communauté désoeuvrée / Jean-Luc Nancy. — Paris : Bourgois, 1986. — 197p

Symbolising boundaries : identity and diversity in British cultures / edited by Anthony P. Cohen. — Manchester : Manchester University Press, c1986. — x,189p. — (Anthropological studies of Britain ; no.2). — *Includes index*

COMMUNITY AND SCHOOL — Great Britain
Education and community / Ruth Jonathan [et al.]. — Edinburgh : University of Edinburgh. Department of Christian Ethics and Practical Theology, 1986. — 31p. — (Occasional papers / University of Edinburgh. Department of Christian Ethics and Practical Theology ; no.9)

COMMUNITY AND SCHOOL — Virginia — History — 19th century
LINK, William A
A hard country and a lonely place : schooling, society, and reform in rural Virginia, 1870-1920 / William A. Link. — Chapel Hill : University of North Carolina Press, c1986. — p. cm. — (The Fred W. Morrison series in Southern studies). — *Includes index.* — *Bibliography: p*

COMMUNITY AND SCHOOL — Virginia — History — 20th century
LINK, William A
A hard country and a lonely place : schooling, society, and reform in rural Virginia, 1870-1920 / William A. Link. — Chapel Hill : University of North Carolina Press, c1986. — p. cm. — (The Fred W. Morrison series in Southern studies). — *Includes index.* — *Bibliography: p*

COMMUNITY ART PROJECTS — England — Lancashire
HIGNEY, Clare
' — Not a bed of roses' : an arts development officer in the trade union movement / by Clare Higney. — London : Calouste Gulbenkian Foundation, 1985. — 51p

COMMUNITY-BASED CORRECTIONS — Europe
BOL, Menke W.
C.S.O.'s in the Netherlands / Menke W. Bol. — The Hague : Research and Documentation Centre, Ministry of Justice, 1985. — 38p. — ([Reports, papers, articles] ; 76). — *Bibliographical references: p35-37*

COMMUNITY-BASED CORRECTIONS — Massachusetts
MILLER, Alden D
Delinquency and community : creating opportunities and controls / Alden D. Miller, Lloyd E. Ohlin. — Beverly Hills : Sage Publications, c1985. — 208 p.. — *Includes bibliographies*

COMMUNITY-BASED CORRECTIONS — Netherlands
BOL, Menke W.
C.S.O.'s in the Netherlands / Menke W. Bol. — The Hague : Research and Documentation Centre, Ministry of Justice, 1985. — 38p. — ([Reports, papers, articles] ; 76). — *Bibliographical references: p35-37*

COMMUNITY DEVELOPMENT
CHEKKI, Dan A.
Participatory democracy in action : international profiles of community development / Dan A. Chekki. — Sahibabad : Vikas Publishing House PVT, [1979]. — xvi,306p. — *Bibliography: p293-300*

Community and cooperatives in participatory development / edited by Yair Levi and Howard Litwin. — Aldershot : Gower, c1986. — xii,261p. — *Conference proceedings.* — *Includes bibliographies and index*

SCHAEFER, Christopher
Vision in action : the art of taking and shaping initiatives / Christopher Schaefer [and] Tijno Voors. — Stroud : Hawthorn Press, 1986. — 206p

COMMUNITY DEVELOPMENT — Research — Case studies
LENGYEL, Peter
International social science, the UNESCO experience / Peter Lengyel. — New Brunswick, U.S.A. : Transaction Books, c1986. — xii, 133 p.. — *Includes index.* — *Bibliography: p. 123-129*

COMMUNITY DEVELOPMENT — Brazil — São Paulo (State) — History
KUZNESOF, Elizabeth Anne
Household economy and urban development : São Paulo, 1765 to 1836 / Elizabeth Anne Kuznesof. — Boulder ; London : Westview Press, 1986. — xvii, 216p. — (Dellplain Latin American studies ; 18). — *Includes index.* — *Bibliography: p199-211*

COMMUNITY DEVELOPMENT — Developing countries
MIDGLEY, James
Community participation, social developments and the state / James Midgley with Anthony Hall, Margaret Hardiman and Dhanpaul Narine. — London : Methuen, 1986. — [200]p. — *Includes bibliography and index*

COMMUNITY DEVELOPMENT — Developing countries — Evaluation

FEUERSTEIN, Marie-Thérèse
Partners in evaluation : evaluating development and community programmes with participants / Marie-Thérèse Feuerstein. — London : Macmillan, 1986. — xii,196p. — *Bibliography: p187-190. — Includes index*

COMMUNITY DEVELOPMENT — England — London

GREENWICH. Planning Department
The people's plan : a community-based local plan for the London Borough of Greenwich. — Greenwich : [the Department], 1986. — 314p. — *Includes two maps*

Introducing community and voluntary services. — Croydon : Community and Voluntary Services, Croydon Social Services Dept., 1986. — 18p

COMMUNITY DEVELOPMENT — Great Britain

ASSOCIATION OF COUNTY COUNCILS
Strategies for community care. — London : Association of County Councils, 1985. — 8p

A Community social worker's handbook / Roger Hadley ... [et al.]. — London : Tavistock, 1987. — [224]p. — *Includes bibliography and index*

MARRIS, Peter
Meaning and action : community planning and conceptions of change / Peter Marris. — 2nd rev. ed. — London : Routledge & Kegan Paul, 1987. — ix,181p. — *Previous ed.: published as Community planning and conceptions of change. 1982. — Bibliography: p172-176. — Includes index*

UNELL, Judith
Opportunity costs : government funding and volunteering by unemployed young people / Judith Unell. — Leicester : National Youth Bureau, 1984. — 24p. — *Bibliography: p24*

COMMUNITY DEVELOPMENT — Ireland

EIPPER, Chris
The ruling trinity : a community study of church, state and business in Ireland / Chris Eipper. — Aldershot : Gower, c1986. — viii,230p. — *Bibliography: p225-230*

SCOTT, Ian, 19---
The periphery is the centre : a study of community development practice in the west of Ireland, 1983/84 / by Ian Scott. — Langholm (Langholm, Dumfriesshire, DG13 0HL) : Arkleton Trust, c1985. — x,93p,[4]p of plates. — *Bibliography: p86-89*

COMMUNITY DEVELOPMENT — Nicaragua

MELROSE, Dianna
Nicaragua : the threat of a good example? / by Dianna Melrose. — Oxford : Oxfam, 1985. — 68p

COMMUNITY DEVELOPMENT — Norway

TORSTENSON, Joel S.
Urbanization and community building in modern Norway / by Joel S. Torstenson, Michael F. Metcalf, Tor Fr. Rasmussen. — Oslo : Urbana, 1985. — xviii,313p. — *Bibliographies*

COMMUNITY DEVELOPMENT — South Australia

SOUTH AUSTRALIA. Department for Community Welfare
Regional community welfare services : a plan of development. — [Adelaide] : the Department, 1983. — [40]p. — *Cover title. — Submission to the National Commission on Social Welfare*

COMMUNITY DEVELOPMENT — Wales — Cardiff

WILLIAMSON, Howard
Strategies for intervention : an approach to youth and community work in an area of social deprivation / Howard Williamson [and] Kaye Weatherspoon. — Cardiff : University College, Social Research Unit, 1985. — 99p. — *Bibliography: p99*

COMMUNITY DEVELOPMENT — Wales — West Glamorgan

WEST GLAMORGAN. County Council
Community facilities : what are the issues?. — Swansea : [the Council], 1976. — 31p

COMMUNITY DEVELOPMENT, URBAN — Case studies

UNIVERSITY COLLEGE LONDON. Development Planning Unit
Evaluating community participation in urban development projects : proceedings of a workshop held at the DPU 14th January 1983 / edited by Caroline O. N. Moser. — London : Development Planning Unit, Bartlett School of Architecture and Planning, University College London, 1983. — 67p. — (Working paper / University College London, Development Planning Unit ; No.14)

COMMUNITY DEVELOPMENT, URBAN — Study and teaching — Great Britain

CENTRAL COUNCIL FOR EDUCATION AND TRAINING IN SOCIAL WORK
Council policy on training for community work within the personal social services. — [London] : the Council, 1979. — 14p

COMMUNITY DEVELOPMENT, URBAN — Asia

SIVARAMAKRISHNAN, K. C.
Metropolitan management : the Asian experience / K. C. Sivaramakrishnan and Leslie Green. — New York : Oxford University Press for the Economic Development Institute of the World Bank, 1986. — xiv,290p. — (EDI series in economic development). — *Includes bibliographical references*

COMMUNITY DEVELOPMENT, URBAN — India

Indian cities : ecological perspectives / edited by Vinod K. Tewari, Jay A. Weinstein, V. L. S. Prakasa Rao. — New Delhi : Concept Publishing Company, 1986. — 289p. — *Bibliography: p273-284*

COMMUNITY DEVELOPMENT, URBAN — Pakistan — Lahore

SHAH, Nasra M
Basic needs, woman, and development : a survey of squatters in Lahore, Pakistan / by Nasra M. Shah and Muhammad Anwar. — Honolulu : East-West Population Institute, East-West Center ; Ottawa : International Development Research Centre, c1986. — xii, 163 p.. — *Bibliography: p. [159]-163*

COMMUNITY DEVELOPMENT, URBAN — United States

DELGADO, Gary
Organizing the movement : the roots and growth of ACORN / Gary Delgado ; with a foreword by Richard A. Cloward and Frances Fox Piven. — Philadelphia : Temple University Press, 1986. — xx, 269 p.. — (Labor and social change). — *Includes index. — Bibliography: p. 253-261*

VARADY, David P
Neighborhood upgrading : a realistic assessment / David P. Varady. — Albany : State University of New York Press, c1986. — p. cm. — (SUNY series on urban public policy). — *Includes index. — Bibliography: p*

WILLIAMS, Michael R.
Neighborhood organizations : seeds of a new urban life / Michael R. Williams. — Westport, Conn. : Greenwood Press, 1985. — xiii, 278 p.. — (Contributions in political science ; no. 131). — *Includes index. — Bibliography: p. [261]-269*

COMMUNITY HEALTH AIDES — Tanzania

Community health workers : the Tanzanian experience / Kris Heggenhougen ... [et al.] ; with special assistance from M.P. Mandara ; foreword by A.D. Chiduo. — Oxford : Oxford University Press, 1987. — xii,205p. — (Oxford medical publications). — *Bibliography: p197-202. — Includes index*

COMMUNITY HEALTH SERVICES

Collaboration in community care : a discussion document / [prepared by Central Health Services Council and Personal Social Services Council]. — London : H.M.S.O., 1978. — 64p. — *At head of title page: Department of Health & Social Security. — Bibliography*

COMMUNITY HEALTH SERVICES — Case studies

Practising health for all / edited by David Morley, Jon E. Rohde, Glynn Williams. — Oxford ; New York : Oxford University Press, 1983. — p. cm. — (Oxford medical publications). — *Includes bibliographies and index*

COMMUNITY HEALTH SERVICES — Developing countries — Case studies

Practising health for all / edited by David Morley, Jon E. Rohde, Glynn Williams. — Oxford ; New York : Oxford University Press, 1983. — p. cm. — (Oxford medical publications). — *Includes bibliographies and index*

COMMUNITY HEALTH SERVICES — Developing countries — Finance — Evaluation

MACH, E. P
Planning the finances of the health sector : a manual for developing countries / by E.P. Mach, B. Abel-Smith. — Geneva : World Health Organization, 1983. — 124p. — *Bibliography: p105-106*

COMMUNITY HEALTH SERVICES — England

KENNER, Charmian
Whose needs count? : community action for health / written for Community Health Initiatives Resource Unit by Charmian Kenner. — London : Bedford Square Press, 1986. — vii,110p

Wallingford Community Hospital research project : report of an ad-hoc Working Party formed to consider detailed proposals for the pattern of medical working appropriate to this new concept. — [Oxford] : Oxford Regional Hospital Board, 1973. — 30, [11]leaves. — *Chairman: A. E. Bennett*

COMMUNITY HEALTH SERVICES — Europe

WORLD HEALTH ORGANIZATION. Meeting on Primary Health Care in Undergraduate Medical Education (1983 : Exeter)
Primary health care in undergraduate medical education : report on a WHO meeting : Exeter, 18-22 July 1983. — Copenhagen : World Health Organization, 1984. — 64p. — *Includes summaries in French, German and Russian. — Bibliography: p40*

COMMUNITY HEALTH SERVICES — Great Britain

Collaboration in community care : a discussion document. — London : H.M.S.O., 1978. — [6],64p. — *'The Working Party on Collaboration between the health and social services in Community Care was the joint creation of the Standing Medical and the Standing Nursing and Midwifery Advisory Committees of the Central Health Services Council, and the Personal Social Services Council' - Introduction. — Chairman of the working party: Dame Albertine Winner. — Bibliography: p55-59*

COMMUNITY HEALTH SERVICES — Great Britain — Bibliography
Studies on community health and personal social services / Department of Health and Social Security Library, Great Britain. — London : DHSS, 1972. — *Annual*

COMMUNITY HEALTH SERVICES — Great Britain — Citizen participation — Bibliography
PRICE, C. J.
Selected references on consumer and community participation in health care / compiled by C. J. Price. — London : Department of Health and Social Security Library, 1979. — 5p. — (Bibliography series ; no.B120)

COMMUNITY HEALTH SERVICES — United States
GINZBERG, Eli
Local health policy in action : the Municipal Health Services Program / Eli Ginzberg, Edith Davis, Miriam Ostow. — Totowa, N.J. : Rowman & Allanheld, c1985. — xiv, 136 p.. — (LandMark studies). — *Includes bibliographies and index*

COMMUNITY HEALTH SERVICES FOR CHILDREN — Africa, Sub-Saharan
Within human reach : a future for Africa's children. — New York : United Nations Children's Fund, 1985. — xiii,93p. — *"... prepared by Manzoor Ahmed with the collaboration of many people ... " - t.p. verso*

COMMUNITY HEALTH SERVICES FOR THE AGED — Great Britain
PERSONAL SOCIAL SERVICES COUNCIL. Policy Group on the Elderly
Comments on "A happier old age". — London : the Council, [ca.1978]. — 25p. — *Bibliographical references: p24-25*

COMMUNITY MENTAL HEALTH SERVICES — organization & administration — United States
The Organization of mental health services : societal and community systems / edited by W. Richard Scott and Bruce L. Black. — Beverly Hills, Calif. : Sage Publications, c1986. — 311 p.. — (Sage focus editions ; v. 78). — *Includes bibliographies*

COMMUNITY MENTAL HEALTH SERVICES — China — Congresses
Chinese culture and mental health / edited by Wen-Shing Tseng, David Y.H. Wu. — Orlando : Academic Press, 1985. — xxiii, 412 p.. — *Derived from a conference held in Hawaii, Mar. 1-6, 1982, and sponsored by the Culture Learning Institute of the East-West Center, the Dept. of Psychiatry, University of Hawaii School of Medicine, and the Queen's Medical Center in Honolulu. — Includes bibliographies and index*

COMMUNITY MENTAL HEALTH SERVICES — Great Britain
PETER BEDFORD TRUST
Community care : which community?, what care? / a report to the House of Commons. Social Services Committee. — London : [the Trust], 1984. — 24p

COMMUNITY MENTAL HEALTH SERVICES — United States — Management — Addresses, essays, lectures
The Organization of mental health services : societal and community systems / edited by W. Richard Scott and Bruce L. Black. — Beverly Hills, Calif. : Sage Publications, c1986. — 311 p.. — (Sage focus editions ; v. 78). — *Includes bibliographies*

COMMUNITY ORGANIZATION — Great Britain
HENDERSON, Paul, 1942-
Skills in neighbourhood work / Paul Henderson, David N. Thomas. — 2nd ed. — London : Allen & Unwin, 1987. — xviii,358p. — *Previous ed.: 1980. — Bibliography : p334-346. — Includes index*

What a way to run a railroad : an analysis of radical failure / by Charles Landry ... [et al.]. — London : Comedia, 1985. — vi,101p

COMMUNITY ORGANIZATION — North Carolina
BEAVER, Patricia D
Rural community in the Appalachian South / Patricia Duane Beaver. — Lexington, KY : University Press of Kentucky, c1996. — p. cm. — *Includes index. — Bibliography: p*

COMMUNITY ORGANIZATION — United States
WILLIAMS, Michael R.
Neighborhood organizations : seeds of a new urban life / Michael R. Williams. — Westport, Conn. : Greenwood Press, 1985. — xiii, 278 p.. — (Contributions in political science ; no. 131). — *Includes index. — Bibliography: p. [261]-269*

COMMUNITY ORGANIZATION — United States — Case studies
DELGADO, Gary
Organizing the movement : the roots and growth of ACORN / Gary Delgado ; with a foreword by Richard A. Cloward and Frances Fox Piven. — Philadelphia : Temple University Press, 1986. — xx, 269 p.. — (Labor and social change). — *Includes index. — Bibliography: p. 253-261*

COMMUNITY POWER
Community power : directions for future research / edited by Robert J. Waste. — Beverly Hills : Sage Publications, 1986. — p. cm. — (Sage focus editions ; v. 79). — *Includes bibliographies*

COMMUNITY SCHOOLS
WIDLAKE, Paul
Reducing educational disadvantage / Paul Widlake. — Milton Keynes : Open University Press, 1986. — vi,146p. — (Innovations in education). — *Includes index*

COMMUNITY SCHOOLS — England — Coventry (West Midlands)
School and community in Coventry. — London : Commission for Racial Equality, [1980?]. — [2]p. — *Reprint from Education & community relations, December 1974*

COMMUNITY SCHOOLS — Great Britain
COWBURN, Will
Class ideology and community education / Will Cowburn. — London : Croom Helm, c1986. — 235p. — (Radical forum on adult education series). — *Includes index*

COMMUTING — England
RESEARCH PROJECTS LIMITED
The outer suburban commuter : the study at Berkhamsted and Harpenden / research undertaken by David Hollings...[et al.]. — London : Research Projects Limited, 1970. — 1v(various pagings). — *Prepared for the Passenger Departments, British Railways Board and London Midland Region, B. R.*

COMMUTING — England — Bedfordshire
STOTT, David
Bedfordshire 1981 census : commuting / David Stott. — Bedford : Bedfordshire County Planning Department, 1986. — 18p

COMMUTING — England — Surrey
SURREY. County Planning Department
Employment and commuting in Surrey 1971-1981. — [Kingston upon Thames] : The [Department], 1985. — [93 leaves]. — (Technical report / Surrey. County Planning Department ; no.1/85). — *Bound with Structure plan monitoring: Employment and commercial data*

COMMUTING — Spain — Statistics
DIEZ NICOLAS, Juan
Movimientos de población en áreas urbanas españolas / Juan Díez Nicolás, Francisco Alvira Martín. — Madrid : Centro de Estudios de Ordenación del Territorio y Medio Ambiente, 1985. — 666p. — (Monografías / Centro de Estudios de Ordenación del Territorio y Media Ambiente ; 18)

COMORERA, JOAN, 1895-1958
CAMINAL I BADIA, Miquel
Joan Comorera / Miquel Caminal i Badia. — Barcelona : Empúries. — (Biblioteca universal Empúries)
Volum 2: Guerra i revolució (1936-1939). — [1984]. — 294p

CAMINAL I BADIA, Miquel
Joan Comorera / Miquel Caminal i Badia. — Barcelona : Empúries. — (Biblioteca universal Empúries)
Volum 3: Comunisme i nacionalisme (1939-1958). — [1985]. — 393p

COMOROS
Recensement général de la population et de l'habitat 15 Septembre 1980. — Moroni : Direction de la Statistique. — *On front cover: Bureau Central de Recensement*
vol.1: Caracteristiques demographiques et movements de la population. — 1984. — 149p

COMOROS — Census, 1980
Recensement général de la population et de l'habitat 15 septembre 1980. — Moroni : Direction de la statistique. — *On front cover: Bureau Central de Recensement*
vol.2: Tableaux statistiques du recensement de la population. — 1984. — 296p

Recensement général de la population et de l'habitat 15 septembre 1980. — Moroni : Direction de la Statistique. — *On front cover: Bureau Central de Recensement*
vol.3: Analyse des resultats du recensement d l'habitat et tableaux. — 1984. — 26p

COMOROS — Economic conditions
Plan intérimaire de développement économique et social 1983-1986. — Moroni : Direction Générale du Plan, 1983. — 4v

COMOROS — Economic policy
Plan intérimaire de développement économique et social 1983-1986. — Moroni : Direction Générale du Plan, 1983. — 4v

COMOROS — Population — Statistics
Recensement général de la population et de l'habitat 15 Septembre 1980. — Moroni : Direction de la Statistique. — *On front cover: Bureau Central de Recensement*
vol.1: Caracteristiques demographiques et movements de la population. — 1984. — 149p

Recensement général de la population et de l'habitat 15 septembre 1980. — Moroni : Direction de la Statistique. — *On front cover: Bureau Central de Recensement*
vol.3: Analyse des resultats du recensement d l'habitat et tableaux. — 1984. — 26p

COMOROS — Population — Statistiques
Recensement général de la population et de l'habitat 15 septembre 1980. — Moroni : Direction de la statistique. — *On front cover: Bureau Central de Recensement*
vol.2: Tableaux statistiques du recensement de la population. — 1984. — 296p

COMOROS — Social conditions
Plan intérimaire de développement économique et social 1983-1986. — Moroni : Direction Générale du Plan, 1983. — 4v

COMOROS — Social policy
Plan intérimaire de développement économique et social 1983-1986. — Moroni : Direction Générale du Plan, 1983. — 4v

COMPANIES ACT 1985
RENSHALL, Michael
The Companies Act 1985 : a guide to the accounting and reporting requirements / Michael Renshall, John Aldis. — London : Peat, Marwick, Mitchell, 1985. — xxx,274p. — *Includes index*

COMPARATIVE ACCOUNTING
BELKAOUI, Ahmed
International accounting : issues and solutions / Ahmed Belkaoui. — Westport, Conn. : Quorum Books, 1985. — xiv, 364 p.. — *Includes bibliographies and index*

COMPARATIVE ADVANTAGE (COMMERCE) — Case studies
States versus markets in the world-system / edited by Peter Evans, Dietrich Rueschemeyer, Evelyne Huber Stephens. — Beverly Hills, Calif. : Sage Publications, c1985. — 295 p.. — (Political economy of the world-system annuals ; v. 8). — *Includes bibliographies*

COMPARATIVE ECONOMICS
GREGORY, Paul R
Comparative economic systems / Paul R. Gregory, Robert C. Stuart. — 2nd ed. — Boston : Houghton Mifflin, c1985. — xii, 575 p.. — *Includes bibliographies and index*

Khoziaistvennyi mekhanizm obshchestvennykh formatsii / pod obshchei redaktsiei L. I. Abalkina. — Moskva : Mysl', 1986. — 268p

KRAVIS, Irving B.
World product and income : international comparisons of real gross product / Irving B. Kravis, Alan Heston, Robert Summers. — Baltimore : John Hopkins University Press for the World Bank, 1982. — x,388p. — *At head of title: United Nations International Comparison Project, phase III. — Produced by the Statistical Office of the United Nations and the World Bank*

Socialist economy and economic policy / edited by G. Fink. — Wien : Springer-Verlag, 1985. — 279p. — (Studien über Wirtschafts- und Systemvergleiche ; Bd.13). — *"Essays in honour of Friedrich Levcik". — Includes bibliographies*

Tratat de economie contemporană / colegiul de coordonare: I. V. Totu...[et al.]. — București : Editura politică. — *Contents in English, French, German, Russian and Spanish. — Bibliography: p[771]-792*
Vol.1: Sistemul științelor economice și sistemele economice contemporane / colegiul de redacție: N. N. Constantinescu....[et al.]. — 1986. — 858p

COMPARATIVE EDUCATION — Congresses
The School and the university : an international perspective / edited by Burton R. Clark. — Berkeley : University of California Press, c1985. — xii, 337 p.. — *Based on a seminar held at the University of California, July 1983. — Includes bibliographies and index*

COMPARATIVE GOVERNMENT
BERTSCH, Gary K
Comparing political systems : power and policy in three worlds / Gary K. Bertsch, Robert P. Clark, David M. Wood. — 3rd ed. — New York : Wiley, c1986. — xxviii, 555 p.. — *Includes bibliographies and index*

Communist politics : a reader / edited by Stephen White and Daniel Nelson. — London : Macmillan, 1986. — xii,416p. — *Bibliography: p380-410. — Includes index*

EISENSTADT, S. N.
Centre formation, protest movements, and class structure in Europe and the United States / S.N. Eisenstadt, L. Roniger and A. Seligman. — London : Pinter, 1987. — 187p. — *Includes index*

LANE, Jan-Erik
Politics and society in Western Europe / by Jan-Erik Lane & Svante O. Ersson. — London : Sage, 1986. — [352]p. — *Includes index*

LUEBBERT, Gregory M
Comparative democracy : policy making and governing coalitions in Europe and Israel / Gregory M. Luebbert. — New York : Columbia University Press, 1986. — xiv, 341 p. . — *Includes index. — Bibliography: p. [313]-325*

MACRIDIS, Roy C
Modern political regimes : patterns and institutions / Roy C. Macridis. — Boston : Little, Brown, c1986. — x, 292 p.. — *Includes bibliographies and index*

Political parties : electoral change and structural response / edited by Alan Ware. — Oxford : Basil Blackwell, 1987. — [240]p. — *Includes index*

Public access to government-held information : a comparative symposium / general editor, Norman S. Marsh. — London : Published under the auspices of the British Institute of International & Comparative Law [by] Stevens, 1987. — xxi,342p. — *Includes index*

ROBERTS, Geoffrey K. (Geoffrey Keith), 1936-
An introduction to comparative politics / Geoffrey K. Roberts. — London : Edward Arnold, 1986. — [v,192]p. — *Includes bibliography and index*

WOOD, David M.
Power and policy in Western European democracies / David M. Wood. — New York ; Chichester : Wiley, 1978. — ix,177p. — *Includes bibliographies and index*

COMPARATIVE GOVERNMENT — Addresses, essays, lectures
Handbook of legislative research / edited by Gerhard Loewenberg, Samuel C. Patterson, Malcolm E. Jewell. — Cambridge, Mass. : Harvard University Press, 1985. — x, 810 p.. — *Includes bibliographies and index*

COMPARATIVE LAW
The Law of tort : policies and trends in liability for damage to property and economic loss / edited by Michael Furmston. — London : Duckworth, 1986. — vi,231p. — (Colston papers ; no.36). — *Conference proceedings. — Includes index*

Legal traditions and systems : an international handbook / edited by Alan N. Katz. — New York : Greenwood Press, 1986. — viii, 450 p.. — *Includes bibliographies and index*

STEIN, Peter, 1926-
Legal institutions : the development of dispute settlement / Peter Stein. — London : Butterworths, 1984. — ix,236p. — *Includes index*

COMPARATIVE MANAGEMENT — Addresses, essays, lectures
BJØRN-ANDERSEN, Niels
Managing computer impact : an international study of management and organizations / by Niels Bjørn-Andersen, Ken Eason, Daniel Robey. — Norwood, N.J. : Ablex, 1986. — viii, 248p. — *Includes index. — Bibliography: p.233-239*

COMPASS
FANNING, A. E.
Steady as she goes : a history of the Compass Department of the Admiralty / by A.E. Fanning. — London : H.M.S.O., c1986. — xlv, 462p. — *"The National Maritime Museum...sponsored the writing and publication" - foreword. — Bibliography: p.[445]-446*

COMPENSATION (LAW)
LILLICH, Richard B
International claims : their settlement by lump sum agreements / Richard B. Lillich and Burns H. Weston. — 1st ed. — Charlottesville : University Press of Virginia, 1975. — 2 v.. — (The Procedural aspects of international law series ; 12). — *Includes index. — Bibliography: v. 1, p. [335]-350. — Contents: pt. 1. The commentary.--pt. 2. The agreements*

COMPENSATION (LAW) — England
ATIYAH, P. S.
Atiyah's accidents, compensation and the law / Peter Cane. — 4th ed. — London : Weidenfeld and Nicholson, 1987. — 639p

COMPENSATION (LAW) — England — Greater Manchester
GENN, Hazel
Meeting legal needs? : an evaluation of a scheme for personal injury victims / Hazel Genn. — Oxford : SSRC Centre for Socio-Legal Studies, 1982. — ix,69p. — *A report commissioned by the Greater Manchester Legal Services Committee*

COMPENSATION (LAW) — Great Britain
BAILEY, Suzanne
Remedies for victims of crime / Suzanne Bailey, David Tucker. — London : Legal Action Group, 1984. — xxxi,133p. — (Law and Practice guide ; No.7)

COMPETITION
Competitive ethnic relations / edited by Susan Olzak, Joane Nagel. — Orlando : Academic Press, 1986. — ix, 252 p. — *Includes bibliographies and index*

CONFEDERATION OF BRITISH INDUSTRY
Issues in UK competition policy : a discussion document. — London : Confederation of British Industry, 1986. — 44p. — *Bibliography: p33-35*

FOSTER, Richard N.
Innovation : the attacker's advantage / Richard N. Foster. — London : Macmillan, 1986. — [320]p. — *Includes bibliography and index*

Industrie mondiale : la compétitivité à tout prix / sous la direction de Michel Fouquin. — [Paris : Economica, 1986]. — xxiv,332p

IRELAND, Norman J.
Product differentiation and non-price competition / Norman Ireland. — Oxford : Basil Blackwell, 1987. — 1v.. — *Includes bibliography and index*

SHAKED, Avner
Multiproduct firms and market structure / Avner Shaked and John Sutton. — London : Suntory Toyota International Centre for Economics and Related Disciplines, 1987. — 20p. — (Theoretical economics)

WITTMANN, Walter
How social is the market economy? / Walter Wittmann. — London : Centre for Research into Communist Economics, 1985. — 50p. — (Understanding economic systems ; 2). — *Bibliography: p49*

COMPETITION — Congresses
Innovation and entrepreneurship in organizations : strategies for competitiveness, deregulation, and privatization / edited by Richard M. Burton and Børge Obel. — Amsterdam ; New York : Elsevier ; New York, NY, U.S.A. : Distributors for the U.S. and Canada, Elsevier Science Pub. Co., 1986. — vii, 207 p.. — *Chiefly papers presented at a seminar held at the European Institute for Advanced Studies in Management, Brussels, in May 1985. — "Has been published in a special issue of Technovation, vol 5 (1986), issues 1-3.". — Includes bibliographies and index*

COMPETITION — Law and legislation — European Economic Community Countries
CASTELL BORRAS, Brigitte
La defensa de la competencia en la C.E.E. : Artículo 85 del Tratado de Roma / Brigitte Castell Borras. — Barcelona : Editorial Praxis, 1986. — xx,522p. — *Bibliography: p497-519*

COMPETITION — Mathematical models
BOWRING, Joseph
Competition in a dual economy / Joseph Bowring. — Princeton, N.J. : Princeton University Press, c1986. — p. cm. — *Includes index. — Bibliography: p*

COMPETITION — Mathematical models — Congresses

Competition, instability, and nonlinear cycles : proceedings of an international conference, New School for Social Research, New York, USA, March 1985 / edited by Willi Semmler. — Berlin ; New York : Springer-Verlag, c1986. — p. cm. — (Lecture notes in economics and mathematical systems ; 275)

COMPETITION — Europe

CEPS CONFERENCE [ON] U.S. COMPETITIVENESS AND ITS IMPLICATIONS FOR EUROPE (1984 : Frankfurt)
US competitiveness and its implications for Europe : [papers presented at conference] / Robert Z. Lawrence...[et al.] ; with an introduction by Alexis Jacquemin. — Bruxelles ; Louvain : Centre for European Policy Studies, [1985]. — 80p. — (CEPS Papers ; Nos.11-13)

COMPETITION — European Economic Community countries

Community competition policy : opinion. — Brussels : Economic and Social Committee, 1981. — ii,86p

SCHINA, Despina
State aids under the EEC treaty articles 92 to 94 / Despina Schina. — Oxford : ESC Publishing, 1987. — xviii, 221p. — (European competition law monographs). — *Bibliography: p.179-185. - Includes index*

VANDAMME, J
La politique de la concurrence dans la C.E.E. / J.A. Van Damme. — Kortrijk, Belgique : UGA, [1980]. — 658 p., [1] leaf of plates. — (Cours / Centre international d'études et de recherches européennes ; 1977). — *At head of title: Institut universitaire international, Luxembourg. — Bibliography: p. 589-658*

COMPETITION — Organisation for Economic Co-operation and Development countries

ORGANISATION FOR ECONOMIC CO-OPERATION AND DEVELOPMENT. Committee of Experts on Restrictive Business Practices
Competition policy and deregulation : developments since the adoption of the 1979 Council recommendation on competition policy and exempted or regulated sectors. — Paris : OECD, 1986. — 35p

COMPETITION — United States

ADAMS, Walter
The bigness complex : industry, labor, and government in the American economy / Walter Adams and James W. Brock. — 1st ed. — New York : Pantheon Books, 1986. — xiii, 426 p.. — *Includes indexes. — Bibliography: p. 381-413*

CEPS CONFERENCE [ON] U.S. COMPETITIVENESS AND ITS IMPLICATIONS FOR EUROPE (1984 : Frankfurt)
US competitiveness and its implications for Europe : [papers presented at conference] / Robert Z. Lawrence...[et al.] ; with an introduction by Alexis Jacquemin. — Bruxelles ; Louvain : Centre for European Policy Studies, [1985]. — 80p. — (CEPS Papers ; Nos.11-13)

LEE, Dwight R
Regulating government : a preface to constitutional economics / Dwight R. Lee, Richard B. McKenzie. — Lexington, Mass. : Lexington Books, c1987. — xiv, 192 p.. — *Includes bibliographical references and index*

COMPETITION — United States — Case studies

RAMSEY, Douglas K.
The corporate warriors / Douglas K. Ramsey. — London : Grafton, 1987. — xxi,261p. — *Bibliography: p261*

COMPETITION, IMPERFECT

GREENHUT, M. L.
The economics of imperfect competition : a spatial approach / Melvin L. Greenhut, George Norman and Chao-shun Hung. — Cambridge : Cambridge University Press, 1987. — xix,408p. — *Bibliography: p389-399. — Includes index*

COMPETITION, IMPERFECT — Mathematical models

CRIPPS, Martin William
Imperfect competition and strategic information transmission / Martin William Cripps. — 201 leaves. — *PhD (Econ) 1986 LSE*

COMPETITION, INTERNATIONAL

CEPS CONFERENCE [ON] U.S. COMPETITIVENESS AND ITS IMPLICATIONS FOR EUROPE (1984 : Frankfurt)
US competitiveness and its implications for Europe : [papers presented at conference] / Robert Z. Lawrence...[et al.] ; with an introduction by Alexis Jacquemin. — Bruxelles ; Louvain : Centre for European Policy Studies, [1985]. — 80p. — (CEPS Papers ; Nos.11-13)

CLAUSEN, A. W.
International trade and global economic growth : the critical relationship : address before the Economic Club of Detroit / by A. W. Clausen. — Washington, D.C. : World Bank, 1984. — 20p

Competition in global industries / edited by Michael E. Porter. — Boston, Mass. : Harvard Business School Press, c1986. — x, 581 p.. — (Research colloquium / Harvard Business School). — *Includes bibliographies and index*

The Competitive status of the U.S. civil aviation manufacturing industry : a study of the influences of technology in determining international industrial competitive advantage / prepared by the U.S. Civil Aviation Manufacturing Industry Panel, Committee on Technology and International Economic and Trade Issues of the Office of the Foreign Secretary, National Academy of Engineering and the Commission on Engineering and Technical Systems, National Research Council ; Frederick Seitz, chairman ; Lowell W. Steele, rapporteur. — Washington, DC : National Academy Press, 1985. — xii, 151 p.. — *Includes bibliographies*

FLAMM, Kenneth
Targeting the computer : government support and international competition / Kenneth Flamm. — Washington, D.C. : Brookings Institution, c1987. — xiii, 266 p.. — *Includes index*

Ideology and national competitiveness : an analysis of nine countries / edited by George C. Lodge and Ezra F. Vogel. — Boston, Mass. : Harvard Business School Press, c1987. — x, 350 p.. — *Includes index. — Bibliography: p. 327-342*

LOVETT, William Anthony
World trade rivalry : trade equity and competing industrial policies / William A. Lovett. — Lexington, Mass. : Lexington Books, c1987. — p. cm. — *Includes index. — Bibliography: p*

Protection and competition in international trade : essays in honour of W.M. Corden / edited by Henryk Kierzkowski. — Oxford : Basil Blackwell, 1987. — [256]p. — *Includes index*

STIGUM, Marcia L
The impact of the European Economic Community on the French cotton and electrical engineering industries / Marcia Lee Stigum. — New York : Arno Press, 1981. — xi, 258 p.. — (Dissertations in European economic history). — *: Originally presented as the author's thesis, Massachusetts Institute of Technology, 1961. — Bibliography: p. 250-258*

VANDAMME, J
La politique de la concurrence dans la C.E.E. / J.A. Van Damme. — Kortrijk, Belgique : UGA, [1980]. — 658 p., [1] leaf of plates. — (Cours / Centre international d'études et de recherches européennes ; 1977). — *At head of title: Institut universitaire international, Luxembourg. — Bibliography: p. 589-658*

WALDMANN, Raymond J
Managed trade : the new competition between nations / Raymond J. Waldmann. — Cambridge, Mass. : Ballinger Pub. Co., [1986]. — p. cm. — *Includes index. — Bibliography: p*

COMPETITION, UNFAIR — Canada

GORECKI, Paul K.
The objectives of canadian competition policy 1888-1983 / Paul K. Gorecki and W. T. Stanbury. — Montreal : The Institute for Research on Public Policy, [1984]. — xxviii,236p. — *Bibliography: p189-206*

NOZICK, Robert S.
The annotated Competition Act / commentary prepared by Robert S. Nozick ; annotations and index prepared by Charlotte Neff. — Toronto : Carswell, 1987. — xviii,290p

Reaction : the new Combines Investigation Act / contributors include: Reuven Brenner....[et al.] ; edited by Walter Block. — [Vancouver] : The Fraser Institute, 1986. — xxix,208p. — *Bibliography: p203-208*

COMPETITION, UNFAIR — European Economic Community countries

KORAH, Valentine
An introductory guide to EEC Competition law and practice / Valentine Korah. — 3rd ed. — Oxford : ESC Publishing, 1986. — xxi,177p. — *Cover title: EEC competition law and practice. — Includes bibliographies and index*

COMPOST

OBENG, Letitia A.
The co-composting of domestic solid and human wastes / Letitia A. Obeng and Frederick W. Wright. — Washington, D.C. : The World Bank, 1987. — xii,101p. — (World Bank technical paper ; no.57) (UNDP project management report ; no.7) (Intergrated resource recovery series ; no.7). — *At head of cover: "Integrated resource recovery"*

COMPREHENSION

VOSS, Bernd
Slips of the ear : investigations into the speech perception behaviour of German speakers of English / Bernd Voss. — Tübingen : G. Narr, c1984. — 184 p.. — (Tübinger Beiträge zur Linguistik ; 254). — *Bibliography: p. 126-134*

COMPREHENSIVE HIGH SCHOOLS — England

SHAW, Beverley
Comprehensive schooling : the impossible dream? / Beverley Shaw. — Oxford : Blackwell, 1983. — v,176p. — *Bibliography: p167-171. — Includes index*

COMPROMISE (LAW) — England

FOSKETT, David
The law and practice of compromise / by David Foskett. — 2nd ed. — London : Sweet & Maxwell, 1985. — xlvii,388p. — *Previous ed.: 1980. — Includes index*

COMPUTABLE FUNCTIONS — Data processing

MALLOZZI, John S.
Computability with Pascal / John S. Mallozzi, Nicholas J. De Lillo. — Englewood Cliffs : Prentice-Hall, 1984. — xii, 193p. — *Includes index. — Bibliography: p186-187*

COMPUTER-AIDED DESIGN

Information pack including bibliography on advanced manufacturing technology / compiled by Lucy Hamilton and John Devine ; foreword by Peter Willows. — London : Institution of Mechanical Engineers, 1986. — vi,98p. — (Information Pack ; 1). — *Annotated bibliography: p47-98*

COMPUTER ARCHITECTURE

BRITISH COMPUTER SOCIETY. Human Computer Interaction Specialist Group. Conference (2nd : 1986 : University of York)
People and computers : designing for usability : proceedings of the Second Conference of the British Computer Society, Human Computer Interaction Specialist Group, University of York, 23-26 September 1986 / edited by M.D. Harrison, A.F. Monk. — Cambridge : Cambridge University Press on behalf of the British Computer Society, 1986. — xiii,650p. — (The British Computer Society Workshop series). — *Bibliography: p615-644. — Includes index*

Computer architecture / [by] D. D. Gajski...[et al.]. — Washington : IEEE Computer Press for IEEE Computer Society, [1986]. — ix,593p. — (Tutorial). — *Variant title: Tutorial: computer architecture. — Bibliographies*

GORSLINE, George W.
Computer organization : hardware/software / G.W. Gorsline. — 2nd ed. — Englewood Cliffs, N.J. : Prentice-Hall, c1986. — xvi, 623p. — *Includes index. — Bibliography: p.607-616*

STÜTTGEN, Heinrich J.
A hierarchical associative processing system / Heinrich J. Stüttgen. — Berlin ; New York : Springer-Verlag, c1985. — p. cm. — (Lecture notes in computer science ; 195). — *Bibliography: p*

COMPUTER ASSISTED INSTRUCTION

Applications of cognitive psychology : problem solving, education, and computing / edited by Dale E. Berger, Kathy Pezdek, William P. Banks. — Hillsdale, N.J. : L. Erlbaum Associates, 1987. — xii, 235 p.. — *Includes bibliographies and indexes*

COMPUTER-ASSISTED INSTRUCTION

GARSON, G. David
Academic microcomputing : a resource guide / G. David Garson. — Beverly Hills : Sage Publications, c1987. — 175 p.. — *Includes bibliographies*

PAPERT, Saymour
Mindstorms : children, computers, and powerful ideas / Seymour Papert. — New York : Basic Books ; Brighton, Sussex : Harvester Press, c1980. — p. cm. — (Harvester studies in cognitive science ; 14). — *Includes bibliographical references and index*

WOODHOUSE, David
Computers : promise and challenge in education / David Woodhouse [and] Anne McDougall. — Melbourne : Blackwell Scientific Publications, 1986. — ix,308p. — *Bibliography: p[294]-301*

COMPUTER-ASSISTED INSTRUCTION — Addresses, essays, lectures

BORK, Alfred M
Learning with personal computers / by Alfred Bork. — New York : Harper & Row, c1987. — p. cm

COMPUTER-ASSISTED INSTRUCTION — European Economic Community countries

HANSEN, Jørgen
Teaching and training the handicapped through the new information technology : computeraided special education / Jørgen Hansen. — Luxembourg : Office for Official Publications of the European Communities, 1984. — 119p. — *At head of title page: Commission of the European Communities*

COMPUTER-ASSISTED INSTRUCTION — Great Britain

INFORMATION TECHNOLOGY ADVISORY PANEL
Learning to live with IT : an overview of the potential of information technology for education and training. — London : H.M.S.O., 1986. — 44p

COMPUTER CRIMES

BEQUAI, August
Technocrimes / by August Bequai. — Lexington, Mass. : Lexington Books, c1987. — p. cm. — *Includes index. — Bibliography: p*

Countering computer fraud. — London : Institute of Chartered Accountants in England and Wales, 1987. — 80p. — *Bibliography: p77-80*

SIEBER, Ulrich
The international handbook on computer crime : computer related economic crime and the infringements of privacy / Ulrich Sieber. — Chichester : Wiley, c1986. — xiv,276p. — *Bibliography: p184-196. — Includes index*

COMPUTER CRIMES — Legal status, laws, etc. — Organisation for Economic Co-operation and Development countries

Information, computer, communications policy. — Paris : Organisation for Economic Co-operation and Development 10: Computer-related crime : analysis of legal policy. — 1986. — 71p

COMPUTER CRIMES — United States

BEQUAI, August
Technocrimes / by August Bequai. — Lexington, Mass. : Lexington Books, c1987. — p. cm. — *Includes index. — Bibliography: p*

COMPUTER ENGINEERING

CHI '85 CONFERENCE (San Francisco)
Human factors in computing systems II : proceedings of the CHI '85 conference held San Francisco, C.A., U.S.A., 14-18 April 1985, sponsored by the association for Computing Machinery's Special Interest Group on Computer and Human Interaction (ACH/SIGCHI) in cooperation with the Human Factors Society edited by Lorraine Borman and Bill Curtis. — Amsterdam ; Oxford : North-Holland, 1985. — vii,231p. — *Includes index*

COMPUTER GRAPHICS

LEWELL, John
Computer graphics : a survey of current techniques and applications / John Lewell. — London : Orbis, 1985. — 160p. — *Bibliography: p157*

SMITH, Brian Reffin
Soft computing : art and design / Brian Reffin Smith. — Wokingham : Addison-Wesley, c1984. — 196p,[4]p of plates. — (Small computer series). — *Bibliography: p190-194. — Includes index*

COMPUTER INDUSTRY — Government policy — United States

FLAMM, Kenneth
Targeting the computer : government support and international competition / Kenneth Flamm. — Washington, D.C. : Brookings Institution, c1987. — xiii, 266 p.. — *Includes index*

COMPUTER INDUSTRY — Canada

LESSER, Barry
Computer communications and the mass market in Canada / Barry Lesser, Louis Vagianos. — Montreal, Quebec : Institute for Research on Public Policy, c1985. — xxiii, 163 p.. — *Includes bibliographies*

COMPUTER INDUSTRY — Great Britain

KELLY, Tim, 19---
The British computer industry : crisis and development / Tim Kelly. — London : Croom Helm, c1987. — 267p. — *Bibliography: p234-257. — Includes index*

COMPUTER INDUSTRY — United States — History

WANG, An
Lessons, an autobiography / An Wang ; with Eugene Linden. — Reading, Mass. : Addison-Wesley, 1986. — p. cm. — *Includes index*

COMPUTER INDUSTRY — United States — Technological innovations

FLAMM, Kenneth
Targeting the computer : government support and international competition / Kenneth Flamm. — Washington, D.C. : Brookings Institution, c1987. — xiii, 266 p.. — *Includes index*

COMPUTER INTEGRATED MANUFACTURING SYSTEMS

Modelling and design of flexible manufacturing systems / edited by Andrew Kusiak. — Amsterdam : Elsevier, 1986. — ix,431p. — (Manufacturing research and technology ; 3)

COMPUTER NETWORK PROTOCOLS — Bibliography

THOMAS SLATNER AND CO.
Citations from the NTIS database : computer network protocols (1973-1984). — Springfield, VA : National Technical Information Service, [1984]. — v,16,166,39p. — *A bibliography containing "citations concerning the design, network analysis, and formulation of computer network protocols"*

COMPUTER NETWORKS

Computer networks : international computer state of the art report. — Maidenhead : Infotech Information Limited, 1971. — v,623. — (Infotech State of the Art Report ; 6). — *Bibliography: p577-605*

DA SILVA, Ed
Introduction to data communications and LAN technology / Ed da Silva. — London : Collins Professional and Technical, 1986. — [160]p. — *Includes bibliography and index*

HILTZ, Starr Roxanne
The network nation : human communication via computer / Starr Roxanne Hiltz, Murray Turoff ; with forewords by Suzanne Keller and Herbert R.J. Grosch. — Reading, Mass. ; London : Addison-Wesley, 1978. — xxxv,528 [i.e.536]p. — *Text on lining paper. — Bibliography(21p.). — Includes index*

MARSDEN, Brian W.
Communication network protocols / Brian W. Marsden. — [2nd ed.]. — Bromley, Kent : Chartwell—Bratt, 1986. — 343p

COMPUTER NETWORKS — Congresses

IFIP WG 7.3 INTERNATIONAL SEMINAR ON COMPUTER NETWORKING AND PERFORMANCE EVALUATION (1985 : Tokyo, Japan)
Computer networking and performance evaluation : proceedings of the IFIP WG 7.3 International Seminar on Computer Networking and Performance Evaluation, 18-20 September 1985, Tokyo, Japan / edited by T. Hasegawa, H. Takagi, Y. Takahashi. — Amsterdam ; New York : North-Holland ; New York, N.Y., U.S.A. : Sole distributors for the U.S.A. and Canada, Elsevier Science Pub. Co., 1986. — p. cm

COMPUTER NETWORKS — Great Britain

HOLLIGAN, Patrick J.
Access to academic networks / Patrick J. Holligan. — London : Taylor Graham on behalf of the Primary Communications Research Centre, c1986. — 91p. — *Bibliography: p87-91*

COMPUTER PROGRAMMING MANAGEMENT

JONES, Capers
Programming productivity / Capers Jones. — New York : McGraw-Hill, c1986. — p. cm. — (McGraw-Hill series in software engineering and technology). — *Includes bibliographies and index*

COMPUTER PROGRAMS

DE JONG, Lucy
Statistical package for social sciences : a summary or facilities available and a guide to their use / Lucy de Jong. — [London?] : Civil Service Department, Behavioural Sciences Research Division, 1974. — 15p. — (BSRD statistical and computer paper ; no.13)

COMPUTER PROGRAMS *continuation*
SOMMERVILLE, Ian
Software engineering / I Sommerville. — 2nd ed. — Wokingham : Addison-Wesley, c1985. — xi,334p. — (International computer science series). — *Previous ed.: c1982.* — *Bibliography: p319-327.* — *Includes index*

COMPUTER PROGRAMS — Simulation methods
CHEW, Sew Tee
Program generators for discrete event digital simulation modelling / See Tee Chew. — 352 leaves. — PhD(Econ) 1986 LSE. — *Leaves 159-342 are appendices*

COMPUTER PROGRAMS — Specifications
Software specification techniques / [edited by] Narain Gehani, Andrew McGettrick. — Wokingham : Addison-Wesley, c1986. — xii,477p. — (International computer science series). — *Bibliography: p455-477*

COMPUTER PROGRAMS — Testing
ABBOTT, Joe
Software testing techniques / Joe Abbott. — Manchester : NCC, 1986. — [140]p. — *Includes bibliography and index*

COMPUTER SCIENCE LITERATURE — Indexes
CMCI compumath citation index. — Philadelphia : Institute for Scientific Information, 1985. — *Annual*

COMPUTER SERVICE INDUSTRY — Great Britain — Statistics
Computer services. — London : HMSO, 1973-. — (Business monitor. SD ; 9) (Business monitor. SDQ ; 9). — *Quarterly*

COMPUTER SIMULATION
CONFERENCE 'ARTIFICIAL INTELLIGENCE IN SIMULATION' (1985 : Ghent)
AI applied to simulation : proceedings of the European Conference at the University of Ghent, February 25-28 1985, Ghent, Belgium / edited by E. J. H. Kerckhoffs, G. C. Vansteenkiste, B. P. Zeigler. — San Diego : Society for Computer Simulation, 1986. — xii,205p. — (Simulation Series ; 18, no.1)

COMPUTER SOFTWARE
GORSLINE, George W.
Computer organization : hardware/software / G.W. Gorsline. — 2nd ed. — Englewood Cliffs, N.J. : Prentice-Hall, c1986. — xvi, 623p. — *Includes index.* — *Bibliography: p.607-616*

COMPUTER SOFTWARE — Design
MACRO, Allen
The craft of software engineering / Allen Macro, John Buxton. — Wokingham : Addison-Wesley, c1987. — [376]p. — (International computer science series). — *Includes index*

COMPUTER SOFTWARE — Development
AGRESTI, William W.
New paradigms for software development / William W. Agresti. — Washington : IEEE Computer Society Press for IEEE Computer Society, [1986]. — viii,295p. — (Tutorial). — *Bibliographies*

CAMERON, John R.
JSP & JSD : the Jackson approach to software development / John R. Cameron. — New York : IEEE Computer Society Press, 1983. — (A monograph in the Computer Society Press series)

COMPUTER SOFTWARE — Development — Mathematical models
JONES, Cliff B.
Systematic software development using VDM / Cliff B. Jones. — Englewood Cliffs ; London : Prentice-Hall, c1986. — xvi,300p. — (Prentice-Hall international series in computer science). — *Bibliography: p294-296.* — *Includes index*

COMPUTER SOFTWARE INDUSTRY — Great Britain
Software : a vital key to UK competitiveness. — London : H.M.S.O., 1986. — viii,87p. — (An ACARD report). — *At head of title: Cabinet Office, Advisory Council for Applied Research and Development*

COMPUTERS *See also* Electronic digital computers

COMPUTERS
AUSTING, Richard H
Computers in focus / Richard Austing, Lillian Cassel. — Monterey, Calif. : Brooks/Cole Pub. Co., 1986. — p. cm. — *Includes index*

GRAHAM, Neill
The mind tool : computers and their impact on society / Neill Graham. — 4th ed. — St. Paul : West Pub. Co., c1986. — p. cm. — *Includes bibliographical references and index*

International journal of man-machine studies. — London : Academic Press, 1986-. — *Monthly*

NICKERSON, Raymond S
Using computers : human factors in information systems / Raymond S. Nickerson. — Cambridge, Mass. ; London : MIT Press, c1986. — xiv, 434p. — *"A Bradford book."*

ROSENBERG, Richard S
Computers and the information society / Richard S. Rosenberg. — New York ; Chichester : Wiley, c1986. — xxv, 397p. — *Includes bibliographies and index*

SANDERS, Donald H
Computers today / Donald H. Sanders. — 2nd ed. — New York : McGraw-Hill, c1985. — p. cm. — *Includes index*

SAVAGE, John E.
The mystical machine : issues and ideas in computing / John E. Savage, Susan Magidson, Alex M. Stein. — 1st ed. — Reading, Mass. : Addison-Wesley, c1986. — xvi, 407 p. — *Ill. on lining papers.* — *Includes bibliographies and index*

WOODHOUSE, David
Computer science / David Woodhouse, Greg Johnstone, Anne McDougall. — 2nd ed. — Milton, Qld. : Jacaranda Press, 1984. — xv,588p

COMPUTERS — Access control
CAMPBELL, Duncan, 1952-
On the record : surveillance, computers and privacy : the inside story / Duncan Campbell and Steve Connor. — London : Joseph, 1986. — 347p,[8]p of plates. — *Includes index*

COMPUTERS — Bibliography
BRAMER, M. A.
The fifth generation : an annotated bibliography / Max & Dawn Bramer. — Wokingham : Addison-Wesley, c1984. — 119p. — *Includes indexes*

COMPUTERS — Congresses
Computer culture : the scientific, intellectual, and social impact of the computer / edited by Heinz R. Pagels. — New York, N.Y. : New York Academy of Sciences, 1984. — p. cm. — (Annals of the New York Academy of Sciences ; v. 426). — *Papers presented at a symposium sponsored by the New York Academy of Sciences, held Apr. 5-8, 1983.* — *Includes indexes.* — *Bibliography: p*

Philosophy and technology II : information technology and computers in theory and practice / edited by Carl Mitcham and Alois Huning. — Dordrecht ; Boston : Reidel ; Hingham, MA, U.S.A. : sold and distributed in the U.S.A. and Canada by Kluwer Academic Publisher, c1986. — xxii, 352 p.. — (Boston studies in the philosophy of science ; v. 90). — *Selected proceedings of an international conference held in New York, September 3-7, 1983, and organized by the Philosophy & Technology Studies Center of the Polytechnic Institute of New York in conjunction with the Society for Philosophy and Technology. — "A German-language version has appeared under the title: Technikphilosophie im Zeitalter der Informationstechnik (Braunschweig: Vieweg, 1985)"--Pref.* — *Includes indexes.* — *Bibliography: p. 307-339*

COMPUTERS — Economic aspects — Organisation for Economic Co-operation and Development countries
KIMBEL, Dieter
Information technology and economic prospects / [Dieter Kimbel, Paul Stoneman]. — Paris : OECD, 1987. — 221p. — (Information, computer, communications policy ; 12). — *Bibliography: p219-220*

COMPUTERS — History
WILLIAMS, M. R. (Michael Roy)
A history of computing technology / Michael R. Williams. — Englewood Cliffs ; London : Prentice-Hall, c1985. — xi,432p. — (Prentice-Hall series in computational mathematics). — *Includes bibliographies and index*

COMPUTERS — Law and legislation
Information technology & the law / [edited by] Chris Edwards and Nigel Savage. — Basingstoke : Macmillan, 1986. — viii,283p. — *Includes index*

COMPUTERS — Management
BANERJEE, Utpal K.
Computer management and planning / Utpal K. Banerjee. — New Delhi : Tata McGraw-Hill, 1985. — xi,330p

COMPUTERS — Research — Government policy — United States
FLAMM, Kenneth
Targeting the computer : government support and international competition / Kenneth Flamm. — Washington, D.C. : Brookings Institution, c1987. — xiii, 266 p.. — *Includes index*

COMPUTERS — Social aspects
LYON, David, 1948-
The silicon society / David Lyon. — Tring : Lion, 1986. — 127p. — (London lectures in contemporary Christianity ; 1985). — *Includes index*

COMPUTERS — Social aspects — Congresses
The Computer culture : a symposium to explore the computer's impact on society / edited by Denis P. Donnelly. — Rutherford : Fairleigh Dickinson University Press, c1985. — p. cm. — *Edited proceedings of the Computer Culture Symposium.* — *Bibliography: p*

IFIP TC9 CONFERENCE ON HUMAN CHOICE AND COMPUTERS ((3rd : 1985 : Stockholm, Sweden)
Comparative worldwide national computer policies : proceedings of the Third IFIP TC9 Conference on Human Choice and Computers, Stockholm, Sweden, 2-5 September 1985 / edited by Harold Sackman. — Amsterdam ; New York : North-Holland ; New York, N.Y., U.S.A. : Sole distributors for the U.S.A. and Canada, Elsevier Science Pub. Co., 1986. — xi, 486 p.. — *Conference sponsored by the International Federation for Information Processing and UNESCO.* — *Includes bibliographies*

COMPUTERS — Study and teaching
SKOK, Walter
Education and training for users of computer systems : development and evaluation of a systems training tool / Walter Skok. — 247 leaves. — *PhD (Econ) 1986 LSE. — Leaves 138-247 are appendices, leaves 178-247 being computer listing*

COMPUTERS — Study and teaching — Great Britain
Core skills in YTS. — [Sheffield : Manpower Services Commission] 260.01/1, [1985] Part 2: Computer and information technology. — 11p. — (Youth Training Scheme manual)

COMPUTERS — Vocational guidance
DEAKIN, Rose
Women and computing : the golden opportunity / Rose Deakin. — London : Macmillan, 1984. — 149p. — (Papermac computer library). — *Includes index*

COMPUTERS — Great Britain
HARPER, J. M.
Telecommunications and computing : the uncompleted revolution : a survey in plain English of the state of the common ground of telecommunications, computing, office machinery and cable television in the UK / J. M. Harper. — London : Communications Educational Services, 1986. — xix,200p

COMPUTERS — Scotland
PILLEY, Christopher
Computers, communication and the community / Christopher Pilley [and] Margaret Sutherland. — Edinburgh : Scottish Community Education Council, 1985. — 50p

COMPUTERS — United States — Access control
LAUDON, Kenneth C.
Dossier society : value choices in the design of national information systems / Kenneth C. Laudon. — New York : Columbia University Press, 1986. — xi, 421 p.. — (CORPS (computing, organizations, policy, and society) series). — *Includes index. — Bibliography: p. [403]-414*

COMPUTERS AND CHILDREN
Children and computers / Elisa L. Klein; editor. — San Francisco : Jossey-Bass, 1985. — 129p. — (New directions for child development ; no.28). — *Bibliographies*

COMPUTERS AND CIVILIZATION
BENIGER, James R
The control revolution : technological and economic origins of the information society / James R. Beniger. — Cambridge, Mass. : Harvard University Press, 1986. — x, 493 p.. — *Includes index. — Bibliography: p. [439]-476*

BESSANT, J. R.
Microprocessors in production processes / John Bessant. — London : Policy Studies Institute, 1982. — 134p. — (P.S.I. ; no.609)

Compulsive technology : computers as culture / edited by Tony Solomonides and Les Levidow. — London : Free Association, 1985. — 160p. — (Radical science series ; no.18). — *Bibliography: p139-143*

DREYFUS, Hubert L.
Mind over machine : the power of human intuition and expertise in the era of the computer / Hubert L. Dreyfus, Stuart E. Dreyfus with Tom Athanasiou. — Oxford : Basil Blackwell, 1986. — xviii,231p. — *Includes index*

ENNALS, J. R.
Star Wars : a question of initiative / Richard Ennals. — Chichester : Wiley, c1986. — xiv,236p. — *Includes index*

GRAHAM, Neill
The mind tool : computers and their impact on society / Neill Graham. — 4th ed. — St. Paul : West Pub. Co., c1986. — p. cm. — *Includes bibliographical references and index*

LYON, David, 1948-
The silicon society / David Lyon. — Tring : Lion, 1986. — 127p. — (London lectures in contemporary Christianity ; 1985). — *Includes index*

NATIONAL ECONOMIC DEVELOPMENT COUNCIL. Economic Development Committee for the Information Technology Industry. Long-Term Perspectives Group
IT futures : what current forecasting literature says about the social impact of information technology : a report / prepared by John Bessant ... [et al.] for the Long-Term Perspectives Group [of the Information Technology Economic Development Committee]. — London : National Economic Development Office, 1985. — vi,118p. — *Chairman: Alan Benjamin*

ROSENBERG, Richard S
Computers and the information society / Richard S. Rosenberg. — New York ; Chichester : Wiley, c1986. — xxv, 397p. — *Includes bibliographies and index*

SIEGEL, Lenny
The high cost of high tech : the dark side of the chip / by Lenny Siegel and John Markoff. — 1st ed. — New York : Harper & Row, c1985. — p. cm. — *"A Cornelia and Michael Bessie book.". — Includes index*

CONACHER, J. B
The Gladstonian turn of mind : essays presented to J.B. Conacher / edited by Bruce L. Kinzer. — Toronto ; London : University of Toronto Press, c1985. — xv, 294 p.. — *"James Blennerhasset Conacher publications, 1947-84 / compiled by N. Merrill Distad" --p. [265]-271. — Includes bibliographies and index*

CONCEICAO, MANUEL DA
COMITÉ DE SOLIDARITÉ AVEC LE PEUPLE BRÉSILIEUN
[Manuel da Conceiçao]. — Geneve : Comité de Solidarité avec le Peuple Brésilieun, 1973. — 10p

CONCEICAO, Manuel da
Il était une fois dans le nord-est... / Manual da Conceiçao. — [S.l.] : Comité de Solidarité avec le Peuple brésilieu, 1976. — 18p

CONCENTRATION CAMPS — France
MONTSENY, Federica
El exodo : pasión y muerte de españoles en el exilio / Federica Montseny. — 1. ed. — Barcelona : Galba, 1977. — 305p. — (Memorias) (Galba ; 20)

CONCENTRATION CAMPS — Germany — History — 20th century
PLANT, Richard
The pink triangle : the Nazi war against homosexuals / Richard Plant. — 1st ed. — New York : H. Holt, c1986. — x, 257 p.. — *"A New Republic book.". — Includes index. — Bibliography: p. 236-248*

CONCENTRATION CAMPS — Great Britain — History
BIRD, J. C
Control of enemy alien civilians in Great Britain, 1914-1918 / J.C. Bird. — New York : Garland Pub., 1986. — 355 p.. — (Outstanding theses from the London School of Economics and Political Science). — *Bibliography: p. 346-355*

CONCEPTS
NELSON, Katherine
Making sense : the acquisition of shared meaning / Katherine Nelson. — Orlando [Fla.] : Academic Press, 1985. — p. cm. — *Includes index*

CONCERT OF EUROPE
KISSINGER, Henry A.
A world restored : Metternich, Castlereagh and the problems of peace, 1812-22 / Henry Alfred Kissinger. — New York : Grosset and Dunlap, 1964. — 354p

CONDEGA (NICARAGUA) — Social conditions
ROOPER, Alison
Fragile victory : Nicaraguan community at war / Alison Rooper. — London : Weidenfeld and Nicolson, 1987. — xx,229p. — *Bibliography: p [228]-229*

CONDUCT OF COURT PROCEEDINGS — Australia
SMITH, Matthew
ABC guide to the Federal Court of Australia / by Matthew Smith. — [Sydney] : The Law Book Company Limited, 1986. — xvii,230p

CONDUCT OF LIFE
EKKEN, Kaibara Atsunobu
The way of contentment ; and Women and wisdom of Japan [Greater learning for women] / Kaibara Ekken ; translated from the Japanese by Ken Hoshino. — Washington, D.C. : University Publications of America, 1979. — 124,64p. — (Studies in Japanese history and civilization). — *At head of title: Wisdom of the East. — Reprint the way of contentment (London: John Murray, 1913) and Women and wisdom of Japan [Greater learning for women] (London: John Murray, 1905)*

CONFEDERACION NACIONAL DE TRABAJO (SPAIN)
Que es la C.N.T.?. — Barcelona : Federacion Local de Barcelona, 1977. — 9p

CONFEDERATE STATES OF AMERICA — Historiography — Addresses, essays, lectures
Why the South lost the Civil War / Richard E. Beringer ... [et al.]. — Athens : University of Georgia Press, c1986. — xi, 582 p., [24] p. of plates. — *Includes index. — Bibliography: p. [537]-555*

CONFÉDÉRATION FRANÇAISE DEMOCRATIQUE DU TRAVAIL
SMITH, W. Rand
Crisis in the French labour movement : a grassroots' perspective / W. Rand Smith. — Basingstoke : Macmillan, 1987. — xiii,272p. — *Bibliography: p258-269. — Includes index*

CONFÉDÉRATION GÉNÉRALE DU TRAVAIL
SMITH, W. Rand
Crisis in the French labour movement : a grassroots' perspective / W. Rand Smith. — Basingstoke : Macmillan, 1987. — xiii,272p. — *Bibliography: p258-269. — Includes index*

CONFEDERATION OF BRITISH INDUSTRY
CONFEDERATION OF BRITISH INDUSTRY
Building a better Britain. — London : Confederation of British Industry, 1986. — 44p. — (Fabric of the nation ; 3)

CONFEDERATION OF BRITISH INDUSTRY
Business manifesto. — London : Confederation of British Industry, 1986. — [18p]

CONFEDERATION OF BRITISH INDUSTRY
Change to succeed : action now. — London : Confederation of British Industry, 1986. — 23p

CONFEDERATION OF BRITISH INDUSTRY
Issues in UK competition policy : a discussion document. — London : Confederation of British Industry, 1986. — 44p. — *Bibliography: p33-35*

CONFEDERATION OF BRITISH INDUSTRY
Late payment of trade debts : questionnaire results. — London : Confederation of British Industry, 1986. — 22p

CONFEDERATION OF BRITISH INDUSTRY
Planning and working together : report of the Joint Working Party on Planning of the National Development Control Forum and the CBI. — London : Confederation of British Industry, 1986. — 24p

CONFEDERATION OF BRITISH INDUSTRY *continuation*

CONFEDERATION OF BRITISH INDUSTRY
Technical budget representations 1987. — London : Confederation of British Industry, 1986. — 31p

CONFEDERATION OF BRITISH INDUSTRY
Vision 2010 : a preliminary report by the CBI under-35s group. — London : Confederation of British Industry, 1986. — 30p

CONFEDERATION OF BRITISH INDUSTRY
Working with politicians / CBI. — London : Confederation of British Industry, 1985. — 135p. — *Includes supplement of updating information, May 1986*

CONFEDERATION OF THE SOCIALIST PARTIES OF THE EUROPEAN COMMUNITY

CONFEDERATION OF THE SOCIALIST PARTIES OF THE EUROPEAN COMMUNITY
Manifesto : adopted by the XIIIth Congress of the Confederation of the Socialist Parties of the European Community. — Bruxelles : Confederation of the Socialist Parties of the European Community, 1984. — 32p

CONFERENCE ON INTERNATIONAL COMPARISONS OF THE DISTRIBUTION OF HOUSEHOLD WEALTH (1983 : New York, N.Y.)

International comparisons of the distribution of household wealth / edited by Edward N. Wolff. — Oxford : Clarendon, 1987. — xii,283p. — *Includes bibliographies and index*

CONFERENCE ON SECURITY AND CO-OPERATION IN EUROPE

CONFERENCE ON SECURITY AND CO-OPERATION IN EUROPE
Final Act. — Helsinki : 1975. — 397p [viii]. — *Text also available in English in British Parliamentary Papers, Command Paper Cmnd 6198. — Text of the Final Act is given in German, English, Spanish, French, Italian and Russian, the English text being between pages 73 and 135*

CONFERENCE ON SECURITY AND CO-OPERATION IN EUROPE. Stage I (1973 : Helsinki)
Documents. — [Helsinki], 1973. — *Restricted distribution documents CSCE/I/1-CSCE/I/30*

CONFERENCE ON SECURITY AND CO-OPERATION IN EUROPE. Stage I (1973 : Helsinki)
Verbatim records : July 3-7, 1973 : Open sessions. — [Helsinki], 1973. — various paginations. — *Restricted distribution documents CSCE/I/PV.1-CSCE/I/PV.8*

CONFERENCE ON SECURITY AND CO-OPERATION IN EUROPE. Stage I (1973 : Helsinki)
Verbatim records : July 3-7, 1973 : Private sessions. — [Helsinki], 1973. — Various paginations. — *Restricted distribution documents CSCE/I/CM/PV.1-CSCE/I/CM/PV.7*

CONFERENCE ON SECURITY AND CO-OPERATION IN EUROPE. Stage III (1975 : Helsinki)
Verbatim records and documents. — [Helsinki], 1975. — Various paginations. — *Restricted distribution documents CSCE/III/PV.1-CSCE/III/PV.7 and CSCE/III/1 and CSCE/III/2*

CONFERENCE SUR LA SECURITÉ ET LA COOPERATION EN EUROPE. Phase I (1973 : Helsinki)
Liste des participants. — Helsinki, 1973. — 39p

CONFERENCE SUR LA SECURITÉ ET LA COOPERATION EN EUROPE. Phase III (1975 : Helsinki)
Liste des participants. — Helsinki, 1975. — 74p

HELSINKI CONSULTATIONS

Final recommendations of the Helsinki consultations. — Helsinki, 1973. — 6 language versions separately paginated. — *Text of the Helsinki Consultations' recommendations on the holding of the Conference on Security and Co-operation in Europe given in each language version in the order: German, English, Spanish, French, Italian and Russian*

CONFERENCE ON SECURITY AND COOPERATION IN EUROPE

GOETZE, Bernd A
Security in Europe : a crisis of confidence / Bernd A. Goetze. — New York : Praeger, 1984. — p. cm. — *Includes index. — Bibliography: p*

CONFERENCE ON SECURITY AND COOPERATION IN EUROPE — Addresses, essays, lectures

Ten years after Helsinki : the making of the European security regime / edited by Kari Möttölä. — Boulder, Colo. : Westview Press, 1986. — x, 184 p.. — (Westview special studies in international security). — *"Published in cooperation with the Finnish Institute of International Affairs"--P. [iv]. — Includes bibliographies and index*

CONFERENCE ON SECURITY AND COOPERATION IN EUROPE (1975 : Helsinki, Finland)

MASTNY, Vojtech
Helsinki, human rights, and European security : analysis and documentation / Vojtech Mastny. — Durham : Duke University Press, 1986. — xvi, 389 p.. — *Includes index*

CONFESSION (LAW) — England

MIRFIELD, Peter
Confessions / by Peter Mirfield. — London : Sweet & Maxwell, 1985. — [165]p. — (Modern legal studies). — *Includes index*

CONFESSION (LAW) — United States

CORTNER, Richard C
A "Scottsboro" case in Mississippi : the Supreme Court and Brown v. Mississippi / by Richard C. Cortner. — Jackson : University of Mississippi, c1986. — xiii, 174 p.. — *Includes index. — Bibliography: p. 170*

CONFLICT MANAGEMENT

Escalation and intervention : multilateral security and its alternatives / edited by Arthur R. Day and Michael W. Doyle. — Boulder, Colo. : Westview ; London : Mansell, 1986. — x,181p. — (Westview special studies in international security). — *Published in cooperation with the United Nations Association of the United States of America. — Includes index*

MOORE, Christopher W.
The mediation process : practical strategies for resolving conflict / Christopher W. Moore. — 1st ed. — San Francisco : Jossey-Bass, 1986. — p. cm. — (The Jossey-Bass social and behavioral science series). — *Includes index. — Bibliography: p*

ZIEGENHAGEN, Eduard A.
The regulation of political conflict / Eduard A. Ziegenhagen. — New York : Praeger, 1986. — xix, 224 p.. — *Includes bibliographies and index*

CONFLICT MANAGEMENT — Mathematical models

Analysing conflict and its resolution : some mathematical contributions : based on the proceedings of a conference organized by the Institute of Mathematics and its Applications on the Mathematics of Conflict and its resolution, held at Churchill College, Cambridge in December, 1984 / edited by P.G. Bennett. — Oxford : Clarendon, 1987. — xvi,349p. — (The Institute of Mathematics and its Applications conference series. New series). — *Includes bibliographies*

Axiomatics and pragmatics of conflict analysis / edited by J.H.P. Paelinck and P.H. Vossen. — Aldershot : Gower, c1987. — ix,316p. — (Issues in interdisciplinary studies ; 3). — *Includes bibliographies*

CONFLICT MANAGEMENT — Europe — History

The Settlement of disputes in early medieval Europe / edited by Wendy Davies and Paul Fouracre. — Cambridge : Cambridge University Press, 1986. — [549]p. — *Includes index*

CONFLICT MANAGEMENT — Georgia

GREENHOUSE, Carol J.
Praying for justice : faith, order, and community in an American town / Carol J. Greenhouse. — Ithaca : Cornell University Press, 1986. — p. cm. — (Anthropology of contemporary issues). — *Includes index. — Bibliography: p*

CONFLICT OF LAWS

LOWENFELD, Andreas F.
International economic law. — New York : Matthew Bender
Vol.1: International private trade / Andreas F. Lowenfeld. — 2nd ed. — 1981. — xi,183,177,7,8p. — *Includes Documents Supplement*

LOWENFELD, Andreas F.
International economic law. — New York : Matthew Bender
Vol.2: International private investment / Andreas F. Lowenfeld. — 2nd ed. — 1982. — xi,207,355,2,12p. — *Includes Documents Supplement*

LOWENFELD, Andreas F.
International economic law. — New York : Matthew Bender
Vol.3: Trade controls for political ends / Andreas F. Lowenfeld. — 2nd ed. — 1983. — x,621,910,5,21p. — *Includes Documents Supplement*

LOWENFELD, Andreas F.
International economic law. — New York : Matthew Bender
Vol.4: The international monetary system / Andreas F. Lowenfeld. — 2nd ed. — 1984. — xvi,404,473,4,17p. — *Includes Documents Supplement*

LOWENFELD, Andreas F.
International economic law. — New York : Matthew Bender
Vol.6: Public controls on international trade / Andreas F. Lowenfeld. — 2nd ed. — 1983. — xvii,457,775,4,22p. — *Includes Documents Supplement*

TILLINGHAST, David R.
International economic law. — New York : Matthew Bender
Vol.5: Tax aspects of international transactions / David R. Tillinghast. — 2nd ed. — 1984. — xv,473,177,12,10p. — *Bibliography*

CONFLICT OF LAWS — Competition, Unfair

EDINBURGH INSTITUTE ON INTERNATIONAL BUSINESS TRANSACTIONS (1984)
Legal aspects of international business transactions, II : the Edinburgh Institute on International Business Transactions, 1984 / edited by D. Campbell and C. Rohwer. — Amsterdam ; New York : North Holland ; New York : Elsevier Science Pub. Co., distributor, 1985. — p. cm. — *"A project of University of the Pacific, McGeorge School of Law, International Programs."*

CONFLICT OF LAWS — Persons — Africa, Southern

BENNETT, T. W.
The application of customary law in southern Africa : the conflict of personal laws / T.W. Bennett. — Cape Town : Juta, 1985. — xxxvii,250p. — *Bibliography: p.xv-xxi. - Includes index*

CONFLICT OF LAWS — Products liability
EDINBURGH INSTITUTE ON INTERNATIONAL BUSINESS TRANSACTIONS (1984)
Legal aspects of international business transactions, II : the Edinburgh Institute on International Business Transactions, 1984 / edited by D. Campbell and C. Rohwer. — Amsterdam ; New York : North Holland ; New York : Elsevier Science Pub. Co., distributor, 1985. — p. cm. — "A project of University of the Pacific, McGeorge School of Law, International Programs."

CONFLICT OF LAWS — Canada — Cases
CASTEL, Jean Gabriel
Conflict of laws : cases, notes and materials / by J.-G. Castel. — 5th ed. — Toronto : Butterworths, 1984. — xxiv,various pagings

CONFLICT OF LAWS — England
CHESHIRE, G. C. (Geoffrey Chevalier), 1886-1978
Cheshire and North private international law. — 11th ed. / P.M. North and J.J. Fawcett. — London : Butterworths, 1987. — xcviii,940p. — Previous ed.: 1979. — Bibliography: pxv-xvi. — Includes index

CONFLICT OF LAWS — European Economic Community countries
L'influence des Communautés européennes sur le droit international privé des Etats membres = The influence of the European Communities upon private international law of the member states / [papers by] P. Bourel [et al.]. — Bruxelles : F. Larcier, 1981. — 266p

LASOK, D.
Conflict of laws in the European Community / D. Lasok and P. A. Stone. — Abingdon : Professional Books, 1987. — xx,460p. — Bibliography: p xviii-xx

CONFLICT OF LAWS — Great Britain — Cases
CASTEL, Jean Gabriel
Conflict of laws : cases, notes and materials / by J.-G. Castel. — 5th ed. — Toronto : Butterworths, 1984. — xxiv,various pagings

CONFUCIANISM — Korea — Rituals
PALMER, Spencer J.
Confucian rituals in Korea / Spencer J. Palmer. — Berkeley, Calif. : Asian Humanities Press ; Seoul : Po Chin Chai, [1984?]. — 270p. — (Religions of Asia series ; no.3). — Bibliography: p[234]-252

CONGLOMERATE CORPORATIONS
SHAKED, Avner
Multiproduct firms and market structure / Avner Shaked and John Sutton. — London : Suntory Toyota International Centre for Economics and Related Disciplines, 1987. — 20p. — (Theoretical economics)

CONGO (BRAZZAVILLE) — Economic policy
NGUYEN, Gregory Tien Hung
Agriculture and rural development in the People's Republic of Congo / Gregory N.T. Hung. — Boulder : Westview Press, 1986. — p. cm. — (Westview special studies on Africa). — Includes index. — Bibliography: p

CONGRÉS CATALANISTA (1st : 1880 : Barcelona)
FIGUERES, Josep M.
El primer Congrés Catalanista i Valentí Almirall : materials per a l'estudi dels orígens del catalanisme / Josep M. Figueres. — [Barcelona] : Generalitat de Catalunya, Departament de la Presidència, 1985. — 282p. — Bibliography: p267-280

CONGRÈS INTERNATIONAL DE LA RÉSISTANCE (1951 : Vienne)
Widerstand gegen Krieg und Faschismus! / FIR: Fédération Internationale des Résistants/Der Internationale Vereinigungskongress der Widerstandskämpfer. — Berlin : VVN, [1951]. — 55p. — Cover half-title: Congrès Inter[national] de la Résistance, Vienne 1951

CONGRESS OF INDUSTRIAL ORGANIZATIONS
AFL-CIO news: official weekly publication of the American Federation of Labor and Congress of Industrial Organizations. — Washington, DC. : AFL-CIO, 1986-. — Weekly

CONGRESS OF VIENNA (1814-1815)
NICOLSON, Harold
The congress of Vienna : a study in allied unity, 1812-1822 / Harold Nicolson. — London : Constable, 1946. — 312p

NICOLSON, Harold
The Congress of Vienna : a study in allied unity, 1812-1822 / Harold Nicolson. — London : Methuen, 1961. — 312p

CONJUGAL VIOLENCE — Bibliography
ENGELDINGER, Eugene A
Spouse abuse : an annotated bibliography of violence between mates / by Eugene A. Engeldinger. — Metuchen, N.J. : Scarecrow Press, 1986. — xiv, 317 p.. — Includes indexes

CONJUGAL VIOLENCE — United States
SHUPE, Anson D
Violent men, violent couples : the dynamics of domestic violence / Anson Shupe, William A. Stacey, Lonnie R. Hazlewood. — Lexington, Mass. : Lexington Books, c1987. — x, 152 p.. — Includes index. — Bibliography: p. [143]-150

CONNOLLY, JAMES
CLIFFORD, Brendan
James Connolly : an adventurous socialist : May Day address, Cork 1984 / Brendan Clifford. — [Cork] (26, Church Ave., Roman St., Cork) : Labour Comment, [1984?]. — 15p

ZAGLADINA, Kh. T
Dzheims Konnoli / Kh. T. Zagladina. — Moskva : Mysl', 1985. — 165p

CONQUISTA DEL ESTADO, LA (PERIODICAL)
LEDESMA RAMOS, Ramiro
Escritos politicos : La Conquista del Estado, 1931 / Ramiro Ledesma Ramos. — Madrid : Trinidad Ledesma Ramos, 1986. — 329p

CONRAD HINRICH DONNER (MERCHANT BANK)
ANDRESEN, Bruno W. F.
Mit Stehpult und Tintenfass : Erinnerungen aus dem Kontor einer Hamburger Merchant-Bank / Bruno W. F. Andresen. — Hamburg : Christians, 1984. — 239p

CONSCIENTIOUS OBJECTORS — Legal status, laws, etc — United States — History
KOHN, Stephen M
Jailed for peace : the history of American draft law violators, 1658-1985 / Stephen M. Kohn. — Westport, Conn. : Greenwood Press, 1986. — xii, 169 p.. — (Contributions in military studies ; no. 49). — Includes index. — Bibliography: p. [145]-158

CONSCIENTIOUS OBJECTORS — United States — History
KOHN, Stephen M
Jailed for peace : the history of American draft law violators, 1658-1985 / Stephen M. Kohn. — Westport, Conn. : Greenwood Press, 1986. — xii, 169 p.. — (Contributions in military studies ; no. 49). — Includes index. — Bibliography: p. [145]-158

CONSCIOUSNESS
Altered states of consciousness : a book of readings / Charles T. Tart, editor. — New York : Wiley, 1969. — 575p

NEUMANN, Erich
The origins and history of consciousness / [by] Erich Neumann ; with a foreword by C. G. Jung ; translated from the German by R. F. C. Hull. — Princeton, N.J. : Princeton University Press, 1970. — xxiv,493p. — (Bollingen Series ; 42). — Originally published in German as 'Ursprungsgeschichte des Bewussteins': Zurich: Rascher Verlag: 1949

CONSCIOUSNESS — Addresses, essays, lectures
TART, Charles T., comp
Altered states of consciousness / Edited by Charles T. Tart. — Garden City, N.Y. : Doubleday, 1972. — ix, 589 p. — Bibliography: p. 531-570

CONSEIL NATIONAL DE LA RÉSISTANCE (France) — Congresses
Jean Moulin et le Conseil national de la Résistance : études et témoignages / sous la direction de François Bédarida et Jean-Pierre Azéma ; textes de Daniel Cordier ; interventions de C. Andrieu ... [et al.]. — Paris : Institut d'histoire du temps présent, Editions du Centre national de la recherche scientifique, 1983. — 192 p.. — "Journée d'études sur le Conseil national de la Résistance, Sorbonne, 9 juin 1983"--P. [5]. — Bibliography: p. 133-180

CONSEIL NATIONAL DES CHARGEURS DU CAMEROUN
Les cahiers statistiques du C.N.C.C. / Conseil National des Chargeurs du Cameroun. — [Douala] : Conseil National des Chargeurs du Cameroun, 1982-. — Irregular

CONSEJO NACIONAL PARA LA SEGURIDAD SOCIAL (Peru)
CONSEJO NACIONAL PARA LA SEGURIDAD SOCIAL (Peru)
Consejo Nacional para la Seguridad Social. — [Lima] : the Consejo, [197-?]. — 9p

CONSENT (LAW)
MONAHAN, Arthur P.
Consent, coercion, and limit : the medieval origins of parliamentary democracy / Arthur P. Monahan. — Kingston ; Montreal : McGill-Queen's University Press, 1987. — xx,345p. — (McGill-Queen's studies in the history of ideas ; 10). — Bibliography: p [265]-325

YOUNG, Peter W.
The law of consent / by Peter W. Young. — Sydney : Law Book Company, 1986. — xxxvi,228p

CONSERVATION OF HUMAN RESOURCES PROJECT (Columbia University)
GINZBERG, Eli
From health dollars to health services : New York City, 1965-1985 / Eli Ginzberg and the Conservation of Human Resources staff. — Totowa, N.J. : Rowman & Allanheld, c1986. — xii, 163 p.. — ([Conservation of human resources series ; 25]) (Land Mark studies). — First series from jacket. — Includes index. — Bibliography: p. [155]

CONSERVATION OF NATURAL RESOURCES
World conservation strategy : living resource conservation for sustainable development / prepared by the International Union for Conservation of Nature and Natural Resources (IUCN) ... [et al.]. — Gland : International Union for Conservation of Nature and Natural Resources, 1980. — vii, [59]p

CONSERVATION OF NATURAL RESOURCES — Citizen participation
TIMBERLAKE, Lloyd
Only one earth : living for the future / Lloyd Timberlake. — London : BBC : Earthscan, 1987. — 168p. — Bibliography: p160-161

CONSERVATION OF NATURAL RESOURCES — Law and legislation — France
PLANEL-MARCHAND, Aloméee
La protection des sites / Alomée Planel-Marchand. — [Paris : Presses universitaires de France, 1981]. — 127p. — (Que sais-je? ; 1921). — *Bibliography: p125*

CONSERVATION OF NATURAL RESOURCES — Europe
European environmental yearbook 1987 : nature conservation, protection of the environment, town and country planning in Belgium, Demark, the Federal Republic of Germany, France, Greece, Ireland, Italy, Luxembourg, The Netherlands, Portugal, Spain and the United Kingdom, with a special survey of USA policy / Docter ; Yearbook director Achille Cutrera. — London : Docter International U.K., 1987. — xx,815p. — *Prepared with the co-operation of and financial assistance from the Commission of the European Communities*

CONSERVATION OF NATURAL RESOURCES — France
PLANEL-MARCHAND, Alomée
La protection des sites / Alomée Planel-Marchand. — [Paris : Presses universitaires de France, 1981]. — 127p. — (Que sais-je? ; 1921). — *Bibliography: p125*

CONSERVATION OF NATURAL RESOURCES — Great Britain
MACEWEN, Ann
Greenprints for the countryside? : the story of Britain's national parks / Ann and Malcolm MacEwen. — London : Allen & Unwin, 1987. — [224]p. — *Includes bibliography and index*

CONSERVATION OF NATURAL RESOURCES — Southern States
HEALY, Robert G
Competition for land in the American South : agriculture, human settlement, and the environment / Robert G. Healy. — Washington, D.C. : Conservation Foundation, c1985. — xxxii, 333 p.. — *Includes bibliographies and index*

CONSERVATION OF NATURAL RESOURCES — Switzerland
Energie, Umweltschäden und Umweltschutz in der Schweiz / René L. Frey...[et al.]. — Grüsch : Rüegger, 1985. — 128p. — (Basler Sozialökonomische Studien ; Bd.27). — *Bibliography: p[119]-128*

CONSERVATION OF NATURAL RESOURCES — United States
LUTEN, Daniel B
Progress against growth : Daniel B. Luten on the American landscape / edited by Thomas R. Vale ; introduction by Garrett Hardin ; drawings by Faye Field ; figures by Adrienne Morgan. — New York : Gilford Press, c1986. — p. cm. — *Includes index. — Bibliography: p*

CONSERVATISM
GREEN, David G.
The new right : the counter-revolution in political, economic and social thought / David G. Green. — Brighton : Wheatsheaf, 1987. — xi,238p. — *Bibliography: p221-232. — Includes index*

NISBET, Robert, 1913-
Conservatism : dream and reality / Robert Nisbet. — Milton Keynes : Open University Press, 1986. — x,118p. — (Concepts in the social sciences). — *Bibliography: p110-112. — Includes index*

CONSERVATISM — Analysis
The new right : image and reality / Gerald Cohen...[et al.] ; with an introduction by Nicholas Deakin. — London : Runnymede Trust, 1986. — 55p

CONSERVATISM — Germany
Leitbilder des deutschen Konservatismus : Schopenhauer, Nietzsche, Spengler, Heidegger, Schelsky, Rohrmoser, Kaltenbrunner u.a. / Ludwig Elm (Hrsg.). — Cologne : Pahl-Rugenstein, 1984. — 285p. — *Includes bibliographic notes*

CONSERVATISM — Germany (West)
PECHMANN, Alexander von
Konservatismus in der Bundesrepublik : Geschichte und Ideologie / Alexander von Pechmann. — Frankfurt am Main : Verlag Marxistische Blätter, 1985. — 188p. — (Marxismus aktuell ; 181). — *Includes bibliographic notes*

CONSERVATISM — Great Britain
WALKER, Peter, 1932-
Trust the people : the selected essays and speeches of Peter Walker / edited by Neale Stevenson ; with an introduction by Robert Rhodes James. — London : Collins, 1987. — 206p

CONSERVATISM — Great Britain — History — Sources
British conservatism : conservative thought from Burke to Thatcher / [compiled and with an introduction by] Frank O'Gorman. — London : Longman, 1986. — xvi,237p. — (Documents in political ideas). — *Bibliography: p231-237*

CONSERVATISM — Great Britain — History — 19th century
FABER, Richard
Young England / Richard Faber. — London : Faber, 1987. — [260]p. — *Includes index*

CONSERVATISM — Great Britain — History — 20th century
WEBBER, G. C.
The ideology of the British Right, 1918-1939 / G.C. Webber. — London : Croom Helm, c1986. — 185p. — *Bibliography: p166-177. — Includes index*

CONSERVATISM — Israel
MERGUI, Raphael
Israel's ayatollahs : Meir Kahane and the far right in Israel / Raphael Mergui & Philippe Simonnot. — London : Saqi, 1987. — [176]p. — *Translation of: Meir Kahane: le Rabbin qui fait peur aux Juifs. — Includes index*

CONSERVATISM — Poland
KOZUB-CIEMBRONIEWICZ, Wiesław
Austria a Polska w konserwatyzmie Antoniego Z. Helcla, 1846-1865 / Wiesław Kozub-Ciembroniewicz. — Kraków : Krajowa Agencja Wydawnicza, 1986. — 215p. — *Summary in German. — Bibliography: p191-[200]*

CONSERVATISM — Poland — History
JASZCZUK, Andrzej
Spór pozytywistów z konserwatystami o przysałość Polski 1870-1903 / Andrzej Jaszczuk. — Warszawa : Państwowe Wydawnictwo Naukowe, 1986. — 292p. — (Polska XIX i XX wieku : dzieje społeczne)

CONSERVATISM — United States
MACEDO, Stephen
The New Right v. the Constitution / Stephen Macedo. — Washington, D.C. : Cato Institute, c1986. — xiv, 60 p.. — *Includes bibliographical references*

CONSERVATISM — United States — History — 20th century
EAST, John P
The American Conservative movement : the philosophical founders / John P. East. — Chicago : Regnery Books, c1986. — 279 p.. — *Bibliography: p. 237-273*

FURGURSON, Ernest B.
Hard right : the rise of Jesse Helms / by Ernest B. Furgurson. — 1st ed. — New York : Norton, c1986. — p. cm

GOTTFRIED, Paul
The search for historical meaning : Hegel and the postwar American right / Paul Edward Gottfried. — DeKalb, Ill. : Northern Illinois University Press, 1986. — xv, 178 p.. — *Includes index. — Bibliography: p. [163]-170*

IDE, Arthur Frederick
Tomorrow's tyrants : the radical right & the politics of hate / by Arthur Frederick Ide. — Dallas : Monument Press, 1985. — p. cm. — *Includes bibliographical references and index*

CONSERVATISM — United States — Periodicals — Bibliography
SKIDMORE, Gail
From radical left to extreme right : a bibliography of current periodicals of protest, controversy, advocacy, or dissent, with dispassionate content-summaries to guide librarians and other educators. — 3rd ed., completely rev. / by Gail Skidmore and Theodore Jurgen Spahn. — Metuchen, N.J. : Scarecrow Press, 1987. — p. cm. — *Rev. ed. of: From radical left to extreme right. 2nd ed. / by Robert H. Muller, Theodore Jurgen Spahn, and Janet M. Spahn. 1970-1976. — Includes indexes*

CONSERVATIVE PARTY
BIFFEN, John
Forward from conviction : the second Disraeli lecture / John Biffen. — London : Conservative Political Centre, 1986. — 12p

CAMPBELL, Beatrix
The iron ladies : why do women vote Tory? / Beatrix Campbell. — London : Virago, 1987. — 314p.

CONSERVATIVE PARTY
The next moves forward : the Conservative manifesto 1987. — London : Conservative Central Office, 1987. — 77p

CONSERVATIVE PARTY
Our first eight years. — London : Conservative Central Office, 1987. — 26p

CONSERVATIVE STUDY GROUP ON CRIME
Prison. — London : Conservative Study Group on Crime, 1986. — 16p

CREWE, Ivor
Thatcherism : its origins, electoral impact and implications for Down's theory of party strategy / Ivor Crewe and Donald D. Searing. — Colchester : University of Essex. Department of Government, 1986. — [48p]. — (Essex papers in politics and government ; no.37)

EDGAR, David
The new right and the church / David Edgar, Kenneth Leech and Paul Weller. — London : Jubilee Group, 1985-. — 58p. — *Bibliographies*

MOUNT, Ferdinand
The practice of liberty / Ferdinand Mount. — London : Conservative Political Centre, 1986. — 15p

The road to reform : thoughts for a third term / edited by Christopher Frazer. — London : Conservative Political Centre, 1987. — 52p

Save our schools / by the 'no turning back' group of Conservative MPs. — London : Conservative Political Centre, 1986. — 32p

TYLER, Rodney
Campaign! : the selling of the Prime Minister / by Rodney Tyler. — London : Grafton, 1987. — 251p

CONSERVATIVE PARTY (Great Britain)
SELF, Robert C.
Tories and tariffs : the Conservative Party and the politics of tariff reform, 1922-1932 / Robert C. Self. — New York : Garland Pub., 1986. — xxv, 817 p.. — (Outstanding theses from the London School of Economics and political Science). — *Bibliography: p. [784]-817*

CONSOLIDATED GOLD FIELDS
COUNTER INFORMATION SERVICES
Consolidated Gold Fields PLC : partner in apartheid / Counter Information Services. — London : Counter Information Services, 1986. — 48p. — *Bibliography: p48*

CONSOLIDATED GOLD FIELDS LIMITED — History
JOHNSON, Paul, 1928-
Consolidated Gold Fields : a centenary portrait / Paul Johnson. — London : Weidenfeld and Nicolson, c1987. — 256p

CONSOLIDATION AND MERGER OF CORPORATIONS — Denmark
Fusioner og virksomhedsovertagelser i Dansk erhvervsliv 1984. — København : Monopoltilsynet, 1985. — 63p. — (Redegørelse fra monopoltilsynet)

CONSOLIDATION AND MERGER OF CORPORATIONS — Great Britain
CHIPLIN, Brian
The logic of mergers : the competitive market in corporate control in theory and practice / Brian Chiplin and Mike Wright. — London : Institute of Economic Affairs, 1987. — 91p. — (Hobart paper ; 107). — *Bibliography: p89-90*

MORGAN, Edward Victor
Economic issues in merger policy / E. Victor Morgan. — Edinburgh : David Hume Institute, 1987. — 12p. — (Hume occasional paper ; no.5)

CONSOLIDATION AND MERGER OF CORPORATIONS — Great Britain — Statistics
Acquisitions and mergers of industrial and commercial companies. — London : HMSO, 1974-. — (Business monitor. MQ ; 7) (Business monitor. M ; 7). — *Quarterly*

CONSOLIDATION AND MERGER OF CORPORATIONS — United States — Bibliography
WARSHAWSKY, Mark J.
Determinants of corporate merger activity : A review of the literature / Mark J. Warshawsky. — Washington, D. C. : Board of Governors of the Federal Reserve System, 1987. — 18p. — (Staff study / Board of Governors of the Federal Reserve System ; 152). — *Bibliography: p14-18*

CONSPIRACIES — United States — History — Miscellanea
ROGIN, Michael Paul
"Ronald Reagan," the movie : and other episodes in political demonology / Michael Rogin. — Berkeley : University of California Press, 1987. — p. cm. — *Includes index*

CONSTABLES — England — History — 16th century
KENT, Joan R.
The English village constable 1580-1642 : a social and administrative study / Joan R. Kent. — Oxford : Clarendon, 1986. — [xi,320]p. — *Includes index*

CONSTABLES — England — History — 17th century
KENT, Joan R.
The English village constable 1580-1642 : a social and administrative study / Joan R. Kent. — Oxford : Clarendon, 1986. — [xi,320]p. — *Includes index*

CONSTITUTION
Beyond confederation : origins of the constitution and American national identity / edited by Richard Beeman, Stephen Botein, and Edward C. Carter II. — Chapel Hill : University of North Carolina Press, c1987. — p. cm. — *"Published for the Institute of Early American History and Culture, Williamsburg, Virginia.". — Includes index*

CONSTITUTIONAL LAW
BRENNAN, Geoffrey
The reason of rules : constitutional political economy / Geoffrey Brennan [and] James M. Buchanan. — Cambridge : Cambridge University Press, 1985. — xiv,153p

MONAHAN, Arthur P.
Consent, coercion, and limit : the medieval origins of parliamentary democracy / Arthur P. Monahan. — Kingston ; Montreal : McGill-Queen's University Press, 1987. — xx,345p. — (McGill-Queen's studies in the history of ideas ; 10). — *Bibliography: p [265]-325*

CONSTITUTIONAL LAW — Interpretation and construction
ANTIEAU, Chester James
Adjudicating constitutional issues / Chester James Antieau. — London : Oceana Publications, 1985. — xxviii,441p

CONSTITUTIONS
PEASLEE, Amos Jenkins
Constitutions of nations / by Amos J. Peaslee. — Rev. 4th ed. / prepared by Dorothy Peaslee Xydis. — Dordecht ; Lancaster : M. Nijhoff Vol. 2: Asia, Australia and Oceania. — 1985. — 2v

CONSTITUTIONS, STATE — Colombia
RESTREPO PIEDRAHITA, Carlos
Constituciones de la primera república liberal 1853-1856 / Carlos Restrepo Piedrahita. — [Bogotá] : Universidad Externado de Colombia t.1: Constituciones provinciales : Antioquia-Choco. — [1979]. — xli,608p. — *Bibliography: p[239]-248*

RESTREPO PIEDRAHITA, Carlos
Constituciones de la primera república liberal 1853-1856 : Carlos Restrepo Piedrahita. — [Bogotá] : Universidad Externado de Colombia t.2: Constituciones provinciales : García Rovira-Zipaquirá. — [1979]. — 618-1189p

RESTREPO PIEDRAHITA, Carlos
Constituciones de la primera república liberal 1855-1885 / Carlos Restrepo Piedrahita. — [Bogotá] : Universidad Externado de Colombia t.3: Constituciones federales : Antioquia-Bolívar. — [1985]. — 762p. — *Bibliography: p[261]-267*

RESTREPO PIEDRAHITA, Carlos
Constituciones de la primera república liberal 1855-1885 / Carlos Restrepo Piedrahita. — [Bogotá] : Universidad Externado de Colombia t.4(1): Constituciones Federales : Boyaca-Magdalena. — [1985]. — 774-1272p

RESTREPO PIEDRAHITA, Carlos
Constituciones de la primera república liberal 1855-1885 / Carlos Restrepo Piedrahita. — Bogotá : Universidad Externado de Colombia t.4(2): Constituciones federales Panama-Tolima. — 1985. — [1277]-1853p

CONSTRUCTION INDUSTRY
HILLEBRANDT, Patricia M.
Economic theory and the construction industry / Patricia M. Hillebrandt. — 2nd ed. — London : Macmillan, 1985. — [192]p. — *Previous ed.: 1974. — Includes index*

CONSTRUCTION INDUSTRY — Economic aspects — Northeastern States — Mathematical models
CROW, Robert Thomas
A model of output, income and employment in contract construction in the Northeast Corridor region / by Robert Thomas Crow and Margaret Ann Burns. — [Washington, D.C.] : U.S. Department of Commerce, 1966. — 24,3p. — (Northeast Corridor Transportation Project technical paper ; no.3). — *Bibliography: p1-3*

CONSTRUCTION INDUSTRY — Social aspects — United States
SILVER, Marc L.
Under construction : work and alienation in the building trades / Marc L. Silver. — Albany : State University of New York Press, c1986. — xi, 251 p.. — (SUNY series in the sociology of work). — *Includes indexes. — Bibliography: p. 229-242*

CONSTRUCTION INDUSTRY — Argentina — Costs
Costa de la construcción / Instituto Nacional de Estadistica y Censos, Argentina. — Buenos Aires : Instituto Nacional de Estadistica y Censos, 1969-1984. — *Monthly. — Continued by: Estadistica mensual*

CONSTRUCTION INDUSTRY — Australia — New South Wales
NEW SOUTH WALES. Commonwealth Bureau of Census and Statistics. New South Wales Office
Building. — Sydney : [the Bureau], 1958-1979/80. — *Annual. — Supercedes in part 'Social condition' in the bound volume Statistical register*

CONSTRUCTION INDUSTRY — Australia — Tasmania
TASMANIA. Commonwealth Bureau of Census and Statistics. Tasmanian Office
Building industry. — Hobart : [the Office], 1972/3-1980/81. — *Annual*

CONSTRUCTION INDUSTRY — Australia — Western Australia
WESTERN AUSTRALIA. Commonwealth Bureau of Census and Statistics. Western Australian Office
Building and housing. — Perth : [Office], 1968/9-. — *Annual. — Supercedes in part its Statistical register of Western Australia: part 12. Retail prices, wages, employment and miscellaneous*

CONSTRUCTION INDUSTRY — Employment — European Economic Community countries
Employment and housing renovation in Europe / by Euro—Construct. — Luxembourg : Office for Official Publications of the European Communities, 1986. — 89p. — *At head of title: Commission of the European Communities*

CONSTRUCTION INDUSTRY — Finland — Accounting
LEPPÄNEN, Veli-Jukka
Kansantalouden tilinpito : rakennustoiminta kansantalouden tilinpidossa = National accounts : construction in national accounts / Veli-Jukka Leppänen, Henry Takala. — Helsinki : Tilastokeskus, 1982. — 109p. — (Tutkimuksia / Finland. Tilastokeskus ; no.73). — *In Finnish with English summary and table headings*

CONSTRUCTION INDUSTRY — Great Britain
GREAT BRITAIN. Department of the Environment
Local authority direct labourconsultation paper. — [London : the Department, 1979?]. — 7 leaves

GREAT BRITAIN. Department of the Environment
United Kingdom memorandum on current trends and policies in the fields of housing, building and planning during the year 1975. — [London] : the Department, [1976]. — ii,28p. — *Prepared for the thirty-seventh session of the Committee on Housing, Building and Planning, United Nations Economic Commission for Europe*

GREAT BRITAIN. Working Party on Direct Labour Organisations
Final report. — [London] : Department of the Environment, 1978. — 98p

CONSTRUCTION INDUSTRY — Hungary — Budapest

25 [ie. huszonöt] éve az állami építöiparban a 100 éves Budapestért 1948-1973 / Kisvári János, and 43 sz. állami építöipari vállalat. — Budapest : Révai Nyomda, [1973?]. — 119p

CONSTRUCTION INDUSTRY — Netherlands — Statistics

Vierde algemene bedrijfstelling, 1978. — 's-Gravenhage : Staatsuitgeverij. — *Rear cover title: Fourth general economic census, 1978: volume 2, part A: mining and quarrying, manufacturing, public utilities, construction and installation on construction projects*
d.2: Algemene sectorale gegevens A: Delfstoffenwinning, industrie, openbare nutsbedrijven, bouwnijverheid en bouwinstallatie. — 1985. — 87p

CONSTRUCTION INDUSTRY — Nigeria — Statistics

Report of building and Construction Survey 1980. — Lagos : Federal Office of Statistics, General Economic Statistics Division, 1985. — 22p

CONSTRUCTION WORKERS — Diseases and hygiene — West Virginia — Gauley Bridge

CHERNIACK, Martin
The Hawk's Nest incident : America's worst industrial disaster / Martin Cherniack ; foreword by Phillip Landrigan and Anthony Robbins. — New Haven : Yale University Press, c1986. — x, 194p, [16]p of plates. — *Includes index. — Bibliography: p.184-188*

CONSTRUCTION WORKERS — United States

SILVER, Marc L.
Under construction : work and alienation in the building trades / Marc L. Silver. — Albany : State University of New York Press, c1986. — xi, 251 p.. — (SUNY series in the sociology of work). — *Includes indexes. — Bibliography: p. 229-242*

CONSULTATIVE GROUP ON INTERNATIONAL AGRICULTURAL RESEARCH

BAUM, Warren C.
Partners against hunger : the Consultative Group on International Agricultural Research / Warren C. Baum ; with the collaboration of Michael L. Lejeune. — Washington, D.C. : The World Bank for the CGIAR, 1986. — xiii,337p

EL-AKHRASS, Hisham
Syria and the CGIAR centers : a study of the collaboration in agricultural research / Hisham El-Akhrass. — Washington, D.C. : The World Bank, 1986. — x,51p. — (Study paper / Consultative Group on International Agricultural Research ; no.13). — *Bibliographical references: p51*

EVENSON, Robert E.
The international agricultural research centers : their impact on spending for national agricultural research and extension / Robert E. Evenson. — Washington, D.C. : The World Bank, 1987. — vii,73p. — (Study paper / Consultative Group on International Agricultural Research ; no.22). — *Bibliographical references: p73*

GOMEZ, Arturo A.
Philippines and the CGIAR centers : a study of their collaboration in agricultural research / Arturo A. Gomez. — Washington, D.C. : The World Bank, 1986. — xii,70p. — (Study paper / Consultative Group on International Agricultural Research ; no.15). — *Bibliographical references: p69-70*

ISARANGKURA, Rungruang
Thailand and the CGIAR centers : a study of their collaboration in agricultural research / Rungruang Isarangkura. — Washington, D.C. : The World Bank, 1986. — x,94p. — (Study paper / Consultative Group on International Agricultural Research ; no.16)

JAHNKE, Hans E.
The impact of agricultural research in tropical Africa : a study of the collaboration between the international and national research systems / Hans E. Jahnke, Dieter Kirschke and Johannes Lagemann ; in collaboration with K. J. Billing, J. Gromotka, S. N. Lyongo, B. Ndunguru, A. Negewo, G. M. Rillga, D. Sène, H. Shawel, G. Tacher. — Washington, D.C. : The World Bank, 1987. — xvi,175p. — (Study paper / Consultative Group on International Agricultural Research ; no.21).
Bibliographical references: p159-175

KYAW ZIN
Burma and the CGIAR centers : a study of their collaboration in agricultural research / Kyaw Zin. — Washington, D.C. : The World Bank, 1986. — xiv,105p. — (Study paper / Consultative Group on International Agricultural Research ; no.19). — *Bibliographical references: p103-105*

MAHAPATRA, Ishwar Chandra
India and the international crops research institute for the semi-arid tropics : a study of their collaboration in agricultural research / Ishwar Chandra Mahapatre, Dev Raj Bhumbla, Shriniwas Dattatraya Bokil. — Washington, D.C. : The World Bank, 1986. — x,48p. — (Study paper / Consultative group on International Agricultural Research ; no.18)

OUALI, Ibrahim Firmin
Burkina Faso and the CGIAR Centers : a study of their collaboration in agricultural research / Ibrahim Firmin Ouali. — Washington, D.C. : The World Bank, 1987. — xiv,112p. — (Study paper / Consultative Group on International Agricultural Research ; no.23). — *Bibliographical references: p109*

PAZ SILVA, Luis J.
Peru and the CGIAR centers : a study of their collaboration in agricultural research / Luis J. Paz Silva. — Washington, D.C. : The World Bank, 1986. — xii,136p. — (Study paper / Consultative Group on International Agricultural Research ; no.12)

POSADA TORRES, Rafael
Ecuador and the CGIAR centers : a study of their collaboration in agricultural research / Rafael Posada Torres. — Washington, D.C. : The Workd Bank, 1986. — x,75p. — (Study paper / Consultative Group on International Agricultural Research ; no.11). — *Bibliographical references: p75*

SANCHEZ, Pedro A.
Cuba and the CGIAR centers : a study of their collaboration in agricultural research / Pedro A. Sanchez, Grant M. Scobie. — Washington, D.C. : The World Bank, 1986. — xiv,120p. — (Study paper / Consultative Group on International Agricultural Research ; no.14). — *Bibliographical references: p117-120*

VENEZIAN, Eduardo
Chile and the CGIAR Centers : a study of their collaboration in agricultural research / Eduardo Venezian. — Washington, D.C. : The World Bank, 1987. — xii,190p. — (Study paper / Consultative Group on International Agricultural Research ; no.20). — *Bibliographical references: p137-141*

CONSUMER CREDIT — Law and legislation — Canada

GEVA, Benjamin
Financing consumer sales and product defences in Canada and the United States / by Benjamin Geva. — [Agincourt, Ont.] : Carswell Legal Publications, 1984. — xlii, 340 p.. — *"Text on part V of the Bills of Exchange Act, FTC Trade Regulation Rule, provincial, federal, and uniform state legislation, legal doctrines and statutes pertaining to financing assignee, holder for value, holder in due course, direct lender, or credit card issuer, and related topics.". — Includes bibliographical references and index*

CONSUMER CREDIT — Law and legislation — Great Britain

GREAT BRITAIN. Department of Prices and Consumer Protection
Consumer Credit Act 1974 : guide on appeals from licensing determinations of the Director General of Fair Trading. — London : the Department, [1976]. — 6p

CONSUMER CREDIT — Licenses — Great Britain

GREAT BRITAIN. Department of Prices and Consumer Protection
Consumer Credit Act 1974 : guide on appeals from licensing determinations of the Director General of Fair Trading. — London : the Department, [1976]. — 6p

CONSUMER CREDIT — Great Britain — Statistics

Assets and liabilities of finance houses and other consumer credit companies. — London : HMSO, 1974-. — (Business monitor. SD ; 7) (Business monitor. SDQ ; 7). — *Quarterly. Title from 1974-75 is: Assets and liabilities of finance houses*

Consumer credit business of retailers. — London : HMSO, 1979-. — (Business monitor. SDM ; 8). — *Monthly. — Continues: Instalment credit business of retailers*

Credit business of finance houses and the specialist consumer credit grantors. — London : HMSO, 1979-. — (Business monitor. SDM ; 6). — *Monthly. — Continues: Instalment credit business of finance houses*

Instalment credit business of finance houses. — London : HMSO, 1974-78. — (Business monitor. SD ; 6) (Business monitor. SDM ; 6). — *Monthly. — Continued by: Credit business of finance houses and other specialist consumer credit grantors*

CONSUMER CREDIT ACT 1974

GREAT BRITAIN. Department of Prices and Consumer Protection
Consumer Credit Act 1974 : guide on appeals from licensing determinations of the Director General of Fair Trading. — London : the Department, [1976]. — 6p

CONSUMER EDUCATION

GREAT BRITAIN. Ministry of Agriculture, Fisheries and Food
Survey of consumer attitudes to food additives. — London : HMSO
Vol.1: Reports prepared for the Ministry of Agriculture, Fisheries and Food, Food Science Division / by Research Surveys of Great Britain Limited. — c1987. — 51p

GREAT BRITAIN. Ministry of Agriculture, Fisheries and Food
Survey of consumer attitudes to food additives. — London : HMSO
Vol.2: Reports prepared for the Ministry of Agriculture, Fisheries and Food, Food Science Division : computer tabulations of fieldwork questionnaires conducted by Research Surveys of Great Britain, 10 to 13 July 1986. — c1987. — various paging

CONSUMER PANELS

SUDMAN, Seymour
Consumer panels / Seymour Sudman, Robert Ferber. — Chicago : American Marketing Association, c1979. — ix, 123 p.. — *Bibliography: p. 119-123*

CONSUMER PRICE INDEXES — Peru — Arequipa (City)

PERU. Dirección General de Indicadores Económicos y Sociales
Indices de precios al consumidor de la ciudad de Arequipa, enero 1976. — Lima : the Dirección, [1976]. — 23p. — *Base 1966 = 100.00*

CONSUMER PRICE INDEXES — Peru — Chiclayo
PERU. Dirección de Planificación Estadística. Division de Precios e Indices
Indices de precios al consumidor de la ciudad de Chiclayo, diciembre 1975. — Lima : the División, [1976]. — 15p. — *Base 1966 = 100.00*

CONSUMER PRICE INDEXES — Peru — Cuzco (City)
PERU. Dirección General de Indicadores Económicos y Sociales. Area de Indices de Precios al Consumidor
Indices de precios al consumidor de la ciudad del Cuzco, enero 1976. — Lima : the Area, [1976]. — 17p. — *Base 1966 = 100.00*

CONSUMER PRICE INDEXES — Peru — Huancayo
PERU. Dirección de Planificación Estadística. División de Precios e Indices
Indices de precios al consumidor de la ciudad de Huancayo, diciembre 1975. — Lima : the División, [1976]. — 14p. — *Base 1966 = 100.00*

CONSUMER PRICE INDEXES — Peru — Iquitos
PERU. Dirección General de Indicadores Económicos y Sociales. Area de Indices de Precios al Consumidor
Indices de precios al consumidor de la ciudad de Iquitos. — Lima : the Area, [1976]. — 16p. — *Base 1966 = 100.00*

CONSUMER PRICE INDEXES — Peru — Piura (City)
PERU. Dirección General de Indicadores Económicos y Sociales. Area de Indices de Precios al Consumidor
Indices de precios al consumidor de la ciudad de Piura, enero 1976. — Lima : the Area, [1976]. — 19p. — *Base 1969 = 100.00*

CONSUMER PRICE INDEXES — Peru — Trujillo
PERU. Dirección de Planificación Estadística. División de Precios e Indices
Indices de precios al consumidor de la ciudad de Trujillo, diciembre 1975. — Lima : the División, [1976]. — 15p. — *Base 1968 = 100.00*

CONSUMER PROTECTION — Law and legislation — European Economic Community Countries
KRÄMER, L.
EEC consumer law / L. Krämer. — Bruxelles : Story-Scientia ; Louvain : Centre de droit de la consommation, 1986. — xviii,432p. — (Droit et consommation ; 10)

CONSUMER PROTECTION — Law and legislation — Great Britain
STANESBY, Anne
Consumer rights / Anne Stanesby. — London : Pluto, 1986. — [256]p. — (Pluto Press workers' handbooks). — *Includes bibliography and index*

CONSUMER PROTECTION — Law and legislation — United States
HASIN, Bernice Rothman
Consumers, commissions, and Congress : law, theory, and the Federal Trade Commission, 1968-1985 / Bernice Rothman Hasin. — New Brunswick (U.S.A.) : Transaction Books, c1987. — ix, 236 p.. — *Based on the author's doctoral dissertation, University of California.* — *Includes bibliographies and index*

CONSUMER PROTECTION — European Economic Community countries
Producer–consumer dialogue : opinion. — Brussels : Economic and Social Committee. Press, Information and Publications Division, 1984. — 55p. — *At head of title page: Economic and Social Committee of the European Communities*

Ten years of Community consumer policy : a contribution to a People's Europe. — Luxembourg : Office for Official Publications of the European Communities, 1985. — 1v.(various pagings). — *At head of title page: Commission of the European Communities*

CONSUMER PROTECTION — United States
HASIN, Bernice Rothman
Consumers, commissions, and Congress : law, theory, and the Federal Trade Commission, 1968-1985 / Bernice Rothman Hasin. — New Brunswick (U.S.A.) : Transaction Books, c1987. — ix, 236 p.. — *Based on the author's doctoral dissertation, University of California.* — *Includes bibliographies and index*

CONSUMERS
BAYE, Michael R.
Consumer behavior, cost of living measures, and the income tax / Michael R. Baye, Dan A. Black. — Berlin ; New York : Springer-Verlag, c1986. — 119 p.. — (Lecture notes in economics and mathematical systems ; 276). — *Bibliography: p. [112]-119*

MAHATOO, Winston H
The dynamics of consumer behavior / Winston H. Mahatoo. — Toronto ; New York : J. Wiley, c1985. — xix, 428 p.. — *Includes bibliographies and index*

CONSUMERS — Addresses, essays, lectures
The Collection and analysis of economic and consumer behavior data : in memory of Robert Ferber / edited by Seymour Sudman and Mary A. Spaeth. — Champaign, Ill. : Bureau of Economic and Business Research & Survey Research Laboratory, University of Illinois, c1984. — x, 406 p.. — *Includes bibliographies*

CONSUMERS — Attitudes
GREAT BRITAIN. Ministry of Agriculture, Fisheries and Food
Survey of consumer attitudes to food additives. — London : HMSO
Vol.1: Reports prepared for the Ministry of Agriculture, Fisheries and Food, Food Science Division / by Research Surveys of Great Britain Limited. — c1987. — 51p

GREAT BRITAIN. Ministry of Agriculture, Fisheries and Food
Survey of consumer attitudes to food additives. — London : HMSO
Vol.2: Reports prepared for the Ministry of Agriculture, Fisheries and Food, Food Science Division : computer tabulations of fieldwork questionnaires conducted by Research Surveys of Great Britain, 10 to 13 July 1986. — c1987. — various paging

CONSUMERS — Research — Addresses, essays, lectures
Perspectives on methodology in consumer research / [edited] by David Brinberg, Richard J. Lutz. — New York : Springer-Verlag, c1986. — p. cm. — *Includes bibliographies and indexes*

CONSUMERS — Argentina — Statistics
Indice de precios al consumidor, capital federal / Instituto Nacional de Estadistica y Censos, Argentina. — Buenos Aires : Instituto Nacional de Estadistica y Censos, 1973-1984. — *Monthly.* — *Continues: Costa di vida-*. *Continued by Estadistica mensual*

CONSUMERS — England — Attitudes
RESEARCH INSTITUTE FOR CONSUMER AFFAIRS
The consumers' view of building maintenance : a report / Harvey Sheldon, May Clark. — London : Department of the Environment, Directorate of Research and Information, 1971. — xi,189p. — *Report produced for the Ministry of Public Building and Works*

CONSUMERS — Great Britain
DROBNY, A.
An investigation of the long-run properties of aggregate non-durable consumers' expenditure in the U.K. / A. Drobny and S. G. Hall. — London : National Institute of Economic and Social Research, 1987. — 44p. — (Discussion paper / National Institute of Economic and Social Research ; no.128). — *Bibliography: p42-44*

LABOUR PARTY (Great Britain)
Labour's charter for consumers. — London : Labour Party, 1986. — 27p. — (Labour's Jobs and Industry campaign)

CONSUMERS — India
GHATAK, Anita
Consumer behaviour in India / by Anita Ghatak. — New Delhi : D. K. Agencies P. Ltd., 1985. — 231p. — *Bibliography: p [218]-225*

CONSUMERS — India — Statistical methods
GHATAK, Anita
Consumer behaviour in India / by Anita Ghatak. — New Delhi : D. K. Agencies P. Ltd., 1985. — 231p. — *Bibliography: p [218]-225*

CONSUMERS — Pakistan
AHMAD, E.
Demand response in Pakistan : a modification of the linear expenditure system for 1976 / E. Ahmad, H. M. Leung and N. H. Stern. — London : Suntory Toyota International Centre for Economics and Related Disciplines, 1987. — 18p. — (Development research programme / London School of Economics and Political Science. Suntory Toyota International Centre for Economics and Related Disciplines ; no.6). — *Bibliography: p17*

CONSUMERS' PREFERENCES
GREAT BRITAIN. Ministry of Agriculture, Fisheries and Food
Survey of consumer attitudes to food additives. — London : HMSO
Vol.1: Reports prepared for the Ministry of Agriculture, Fisheries and Food, Food Science Division / by Research Surveys of Great Britain Limited. — c1987. — 51p

GREAT BRITAIN. Ministry of Agriculture, Fisheries and Food
Survey of consumer attitudes to food additives. — London : HMSO
Vol.2: Reports prepared for the Ministry of Agriculture, Fisheries and Food, Food Science Division : computer tabulations of fieldwork questionnaires conducted by Research Surveys of Great Britain, 10 to 13 July 1986. — c1987. — various paging

CONSUMPTION (ECONOMICS)
CAMPBELL, Donald E.
Resource allocation mechanisms / Donald E. Campbell. — Cambridge : Cambridge University Press, 1987. — xiii,183p. — *Bibliography: p171-177*. — *Includes index*

HOLTHAM, G. H.
Wealth and inflation effects in the aggregate consumption function / by G. H. Holtham, H. Kato. — [Paris] : OECD, 1986. — 37p. — (Working papers / OECD Department of Economics and Statistics ; no.35). — *Bibliographical references: p19*

ROTH, Timothy P
The present state of consumer theory / Timothy P. Roth. — Lanham, MD : University Press of America, c1987. — vi, 168 p.. — *Bibliography: p. 155-168*

SMITH, Martin, 1951-
The consumer case for socialism / Martin Smith. — London : Fabian Society, 1986. — 32p. — (Fabian tract ; 513)

UUSITALO, Liisa
Environmental impacts of consumption patterns / Liisa Uusitalo. — Aldershot : Gower, c1986. — 184p. — *Bibliography: p172-184*

CONSUMPTION (ECONOMICS) — Mathematical models
Analysis of a market-split model / by A. J. Goldman...[et al.]. — [Washington, D.C.] : U.S. Department of Transportation, 1967. — 38p. — (Northeast Corridor Transportation Project technical paper ; no.8)

DEATON, Angus
Life-cycle models of consumption : is the evidence consistent with the theory? / Angus Deaton. — Cambridge, MA : NBER, 1986. — 47p. — (NBER working paper series ; no.1910) . — *Bibliography: p40-43*

HADJIMATHEOU, G.
Consumer economics after Keynes : theory and evidence of the consumption function / George Hadjimatheou. — Brighton : Wheatsheaf, 1987. — [272]p. — *Includes bibliography and index*

CONSUMPTION (ECONOMICS) — Surveys
GROOTAERT, Christiaan
The conceptual basis of measures of household welfare and their implied survey data requirements / Christiaan Grootaert. — Washington, D.C. : Development Research Dept., World Bank, c1982. — 42p. — (LSMS working papers ; no.19). — *Bibliographical references: p41-42*

CONSUMPTION (ECONOMICS) — France
Revenus et consommation des Français : le grand tournant / sous la direction de Michel Gaspard. — Paris : La Documentation française, 1985. — 187p. — (Notes et études documentaires ; no.4800)

CONSUMPTION (ECONOMICS) — France — Statistics
La consommation des ménages: séries de la comptabilité nationale / Institut National de la Statistique et des Etudes Economiques. — Paris : INSEE, 1985-. — (Les collections de l'Insée. série C). — *Annual*

CONSUMPTION (ECONOMICS) — Great Britain
GREAT BRITAIN. Office of Population Censuses and Surveys
Contract law and minors : expenditure of 16 and 17 year olds in the FES; report to the Law Commission / W.F.F. Kemsley. — [London : the Office, 1978]. — 9leaves

CONSUMPTION (ECONOMICS) — Hungary — Statistics
A fogyasztói árak valtozása a lakosság föbb rétegeinél. — Budapest : Központi Statisztikai Hivatal, 1980-. — *Annual*

CONSUMPTION (ECONOMICS) — India
GHATAK, Anita
Consumer behaviour in India / by Anita Ghatak. — New Delhi : D. K. Agencies P. Ltd., 1985. — 231p. — *Bibliography: p [218]-225*

CONSUMPTION (ECONOMICS) — Japan — Statistics
JAPAN. Statistics Bureau
1984 national survey of family income and expenditure. — [Tokyo] : Statistics Bureau, [1985-1987]. — *Text in Japanese and English*

CONSUMPTION (ECONOMICS) — Jordan — Statistics
JORDAN. Department of Statistics
Family expenditure survey 1980. — [Amman] : the Department, ca.1982. — 1v (various pagings). — *Text in Arabic with table headings in English*

CONSUMPTION (ECONOMICS) — Latin America
MUSGROVE, Philip
The ECIEL study of household income and consumption in urban Latin America : an analytical history / Philip Musgrove. — Washington, D.C. : World Bank, Development Research Center, 1982, c1981. — 72p. — (LSMS working papers ; no.12). — *Bibliography: p67-72*

CONSUMPTION (ECONOMICS) — Nepal
Employment, income distribution, and consumption patterns in Nepal : results of a survey conducted by the National Planning Commission, Nepal, March-July 1977. — Kathmandu, Nepal : His Majesty's Govt., National Planning Commission Secretariat, 1983. — xiv,122p. — *Cover title: A survey of employment, income distribution, and consumption patterns in Nepal*

CONSUMPTION (ECONOMICS) — Netherlands — Statistics
NETHERLANDS. Centraal Bureau voor de Statistiek
Werknemersbudgetonderzoek, 1974-75. — s-Gravenhage : Staatsuitgeverij. — *Contents list and summary in English.* — Title on back cover: Workers' budget survey 1974-75. Part 3. Family consumption by place of purchase deel 3: Gezinsverbruik naar aankoopplaats. — 1979. — 55p

CONSUMPTION (ECONOMICS) — Soviet Union
MEDVEDEV, G. I.
Proizvodstvo tovarov narodnogo potrebleniia : rezervy predpriiatii / G. I. Medvedev. — Leningrad : Lenizdat, 1978. — 175p. — *Bibliography: p173-[174]*

CONTADINI, FRA
MALATESTA, Errico
[Fra Contadini: dialogo sull Ánarchia. English]. Fra Contadini : a dialogue on anarchy / Errico Malatesta ; translated by Jean Weir. — London : Bratach Dubh Editions, 1981. — 43p. — (Bratach Dubh Editions: anarchist pamphlets ; no.6)

CONTAINERIZATION
MAHONEY, John H.
Intermodel freight transportation / John H. Mahoney. — Westport, Conn. : Eno Foundation for Transportation, 1985. — xix, 214p

CONTEMPT OF COURT — Legal status, laws, etc. — Great Britain
GREAT BRITAIN. Parliament. House of Commons. Library. Research Division
Contempt of Court Bill (Bill 74) / [Patrick Nealon]. — [London] : the Division, 1981. — 22p. — (Reference sheet ; no.81/10). — *Bibliography: p17-22*

CONTEMPT OF COURT — Australia
Contempt and family law. — Sydney : Law Reform Commission, 1985. — 76p. — (Discussion paper / Law Reform Commission ; no.24)

CONTEMPT OF COURT BILL 1980-1981
GREAT BRITAIN. Parliament. House of Commons. Library. Research Division
Contempt of Court Bill (Bill 74) / [Patrick Nealon]. — [London] : the Division, 1981. — 22p. — (Reference sheet ; no.81/10). — *Bibliography: p17-22*

CONTENTMENT
EKKEN, Kaibara Atsunobu
The way of contentment ; and Women and wisdom of Japan [Greater learning for women] / Kaibara Ekken ; translated from the Japanese by Ken Hoshino. — Washington, D.C. : University Publications of America, 1979. — 124,64p. — (Studies in Japanese history and civilization). — *At head of title: Wisdom of the East.* — Reprint the way of contentment (London: John Murray, 1913) and Women and wisdom of Japan [Greater learning for women] (London: John Murray, 1905)

CONTINENTAL SHELF — United States
Offshore lands : oil and gas leasing and conservation on the outer continental shelf / Walter J. Mead ... [et al.] ; foreword by Stephen L. McDonald. — San Francisco, Calif. : Pacific Institute for Public Policy Research, c1985. — xxviii, 169 p.. — (Pacific studies in public policy). — *Includes index.* — *Bibliography: p. 157-162*

CONTINGENCY TABLES
FACHEL, Jandyra Maria Guimarães
The C-type distribution as an underlying model for categorical data and its use in factor analysis / by Jandyra Maria Guimarães Fachel. — 255 leaves. — *PhD (Econ) 1986 LSE.* — *Microfiches are in end pocket*

CONTINUING EDUCATION — Philosophy
WAIN, Kenneth
Philosophy of lifelong education / Kenneth Wain. — London : Croom Helm, c1987. — [272]p. — (Croom Helm series in international adult education). — *Bibliography: p242-249.* — *Includes index*

CONTRACEPTION — Guyana
ABDULAH, Norma
Contraceptive use and fertility in the Commonwealth Caribbean / Norma Abdulah, Jack Harewood. — Voorburg : International Statistical Institute, 1984. — 55p. — (Scientific reports / World Fertility Survey ; no.60)

CONTRACEPTION — Jamaica
ABDULAH, Norma
Contraceptive use and fertility in the Commonwealth Caribbean / Norma Abdulah, Jack Harewood. — Voorburg : International Statistical Institute, 1984. — 55p. — (Scientific reports / World Fertility Survey ; no.60)

CONTRACEPTION — Trinidad and Tobago
ABDULAH, Norma
Contraceptive use and fertility in the Commonwealth Caribbean / Norma Abdulah, Jack Harewood. — Voorburg : International Statistical Institute, 1984. — 55p. — (Scientific reports / World Fertility Survey ; no.60)

CONTRACT LABOR — History
YEN, Ch'ing-huang
Coolies and mandarins : China's protection of overseas Chinese during the late Ch'ing period (1851-1911) / Yen Ching-Hwang. — Singapore : Singapore University Press, National University of Singapore, c1985. — xvi, 413 p.. — *Includes index.* — *Bibliography: p. 360-398*

CONTRACT LABOR — Canada
DANYS, Matilda
D. P. [Displaced Persons] : Lithuanian immigration to Canada after the second world war / Matilda Danys. — Toronto : Multicultural History Society of Ontario, 1986. — 365p. — (Studies in ethnic and immigration history). — *Bibliography: p[352]-353*

CONTRACT SYSTEM (LABOR) — Great Britain
GREAT BRITAIN. Department of the Environment
Local authority direct labourconsultation paper. — [London : the Department, 1979?]. — 7 leaves

GREAT BRITAIN. Working Party on Direct Labour Organisations
Final report. — [London] : Department of the Environment, 1978. — 98p

CONTRACTING OUT — Great Britain
ASCHER, Kate Julie
Contracting out in local authorities and the NHS : developments under the Conservative governments 1979-1985 / Kate J. Ascher. — 378 leaves. — *PhD.(Econ) 1986 LSE.* — *Leaves 333-350 are appendices*

Using private enterprise in government : report of a multi-departmental review of competitive tendering and contracting for services in government departments. — London : H.M.S.O., 1986. — 41p. — *At head of title page: HM Treasury*

CONTRACTING OUT — Great Britain — Auditing
AUDIT COMMISSION FOR LOCAL AUTHORITIES IN ENGLAND AND WALES
Competitiveness and contracting out of local authorities' services. — [London : H.M.S.O.], 1987. — 7p. — (Occasional papers ; no.3)

CONTRACTING PARTIES TO THE GENERAL AGREEMENT ON TARIFFS AND TRADE

The European Community and GATT / edited by Meinhard Hilf, Francis G. Jacobs, and Ernst-Ulrich Petersmann. — Deventer, the Netherlands ; Boston : Kluwer, c1986. — xvii, 398 p.. — (Studies in transnational economic law ; v. 4). — *Includes bibliographical references and index*

CONTRACTS

BOLTON, Patrick
The role of contracts in industrial organisation theory / by Patrick Bolton. — 182 leaves. — PhD (Econ) 1986 LSE

CRAWFORD, Vincent P.
International lending, long-term credit relationships, and dynamic contract theory / Vincent P. Crawford. — Princeton, N.J. : International Finance Section, Dept. of Economics, Princeton University, 1987. — p. cm. — (Princeton studies in international finance ; no. 59 (March 1987)). — *Bibliography: p*

CONTRACTS — Congresses

Drafting and enforcing contracts in civil and common law jurisdictions / edited by Kojo Yelpaala, Mauro Rubino-Sammartano, Dennis Campbell. — Deventer, Netherlands ; Boston : Kluwer Law and Taxation Publishers, c1986. — 275 p.. — *Papers presented at the Third Annual Waidring Conference, McGeorge School of Law, 1986*

CONTRACTS — Economic aspects

Contract and organization : legal analysis in the light of economic and social theory / edited by Terence Daintith and Gunther Teubner. — Berlin ; New York : W. de Gruyter, 1986. — p. cm. — (Series A--Law =Droit ; 5). — *Includes index. — Bibliography: p*

CONTRACTS — Australia

GOLVAN, Colin
Writers and the law / Colin Golvan and Michael McDonald; consultant: Alan Kirsner ; with a foreword by David Williamson. — Sydney : Law Book Company, 1986. — xix,262p. — *Bibliography: pxix*

CONTRACTS — Canada

CLARK, Robert W.
Inequality of bargaining power : judicial intervention in improvident and unconscionable bargains / Robert W. Clark. — Toronto : Carswell, 1987. — xxxvii,255p

CONTRACTS — Canada — Cases

Contracts : cases and commentaries / edited by Christine Boyle and David R. Percy. — 2nd ed. — Toronto : Burroughs, 1981. — lviii, 843 p.

CONTRACTS — England

ADAMS, John N.
Understanding contract law / John N. Adams and Roger Brownsword. — London : Fontana, 1987. — 229p. — (Understanding law). — *Bibliography: p213-216*

BURROWS, A. S.
Remedies for torts and breach of contract / A.S. Burrows. — London : Butterworths, 1987. — lviii,435p. — *Includes index*

CHESHIRE, G. C.
Cheshire, Fifoot and Furmston's Law of contract. — 11th ed. / M.P. Furmston ; historical introduction, A.W.B. Simpson. — London : Butterworth, 1986. — [620]p. — *Previous ed.: published as Cheshire and Fifoot's law of contract. 1981. — Includes index*

GOODE, R. M.
Proprietary rights and insolvency in sales transactions / by R.M. Goode. — London : Sweet & Maxwell, 1985. — xv,137p. — *Includes index*

TREITEL, G. H.
The law of contract / by G.H. Treitel. — 7th ed. — London : Stevens, 1987. — [850]p. — *Previous ed.: 1983. — Includes index*

YATES, David, 1946-
Standard business contracts : exclusions and related devices / by David Yates and A.J. Hawkins. — London : Sweet & Maxwell, 1986. — [450]p. — *Includes index*

CONTRACTS — England — Cases

SMITH, J. C. (John Cyril)
Smith and Thomas : a casebook on contract. — 8th ed. / by J.C. Smith. — London : Sweet & Maxwell, 1987. — [600]p. — *Previous ed.: published as A casebook on contract. 1982. — Includes index*

CONTRACTS — Great Britain

ATIYAH, P. S.
Essays on contract / P.S. Atiyah. — Oxford : Clarendon, 1986. — vi,363p. — *Includes index*

CLARK, Robert W.
Inequality of bargaining power : judicial intervention in improvident and unconscionable bargains / Robert W. Clark. — Toronto : Carswell, 1987. — xxxvii,255p

CONTRACTS — Ireland

CLARK, Robert, 19---
Contract / by Robert Clark. — 2nd ed. — London : Sweet & Maxwell, 1986. — 1v.. — (Irish law texts). — *Previous ed.: 1982. — Includes index*

CONTRACTS — Switzerland

SWISS-AMERICAN CHAMBER OF COMMERCE
Swiss contract law : Swiss code of obligations : English translation of official texts. — 2nd ed enlarged. — Zurich : Swiss-American Chamber of Commerce, 1984. — 143p

CONTRACTS, LETTING OF

Procurement of goods. — [Washington, D.C.? : World Bank?], 1983. — iii,44p. — (Sample bidding documents)

CONTRACTS, MARITIME — Great Britain

VENTRIS, F. M.
Tanker voyage charter parties / by F. M. Ventris. — [S.l.] : Kluwer Law Publishers ; [chichester] : Barry Rose, 1986. — xvi,411p

CONTRIBUTIONS IN POLITICAL SCIENCE

KAVKA, Gregory S.
Hobbesian moral and political theory / Gregory S. Kavka. — Princeton, N.J. : Princeton University Press, c1986. — xviii, 460p. — (Studies in moral, political, and legal philosophy). — *Includes index. — Includes bibliographical references*

CONTROL THEORY

MANOHAR RAO, M. J
Filtering and control of macroeconomic systems : a control system incorporating the Kalman filter for the Indian economy / M.J. Manohar Rao. — Amsterdam ; New York : North-Holland ; New York, N.Y., U.S.A. : Sole distributors for the U.S.A. and Canada, Elsevier Science Pub. Co., 1987. — p. cm. — (Contributions to economic analysis ; 160). — *Includes indexes. — Bibliography: p*

CONTROL THEORY — Econometric models — Congresses

Developments of control theory for economic analysis / Carlo Carraro and Domenico Sartore, editors. — Dordrecht ; Boston : M. Nijhoff, 1987. — p. cm. — (Advanced studies in theoretical and applied econometrics ; v. 7). — *"Proceedings of the Conference on "Economic Policy and Control Theory" which was held at the University of Venice (Italy) on 27 January-1 February 1985"--Pref*

CONVENTION ON A CODE OF CONDUCT FOR LINER CONFERENCES

STURMEY, S. G.
Workbook on the application of the Unctad Code / by S.G. Sturmey. — 2nd ed. — London : Seatrade Academy, 1985. — ix,159p, [40]p. — *Includes index*

JUDA, Lawrence
The UNCTAD Liner Code : United States maritime policy at the crossroads / Lawrence Juda. — Boulder, Colo. : Westview Press, 1983. — xiv, 234 p.. — (A Westview replica edition). — *"Appendix 1: The Convention on a Code of Conduct for Liner Conferences, and the Resolutions adopted by the United Nations Conference of Plenipotentiaries": p. 169-207. — Includes index. — Bibliography: p. 215-229*

CONVERSATION

Talk and social organisation / edited by Graham Button and John R.E. Lee. — Clevedon : Multilingual Matters, c1987. — 335p. — (Intercommunication ; 1). — *Bibliography: p323-327. — Includes index*

TAYLOR, Talbot J.
Analysing conversation : rules and units in the structure of talk / by Talbot J. Taylor and Deborah Cameron. — Oxford : Pergamon, 1987. — viii,169p. — (Language & communication library ; v9). — *Bibliography: p163-165. — Includes index*

CONVERSION

COHEN, Charles Lloyd
God's caress : the psychology of Puritan religious experience / Charles Lloyd Cohen. — New York : Oxford University Press, 1986. — p. cm. — *Includes index. — Bibliography: p*

WHITEHEAD, Harriet
Renunciation and reformulation : a study of conversion in an American sect / Harriet Whitehead. — Ithaca : Cornell University Press, 1987. — 299 p.. — (Anthropology of contemporary issues). — *Includes index. — Bibliography: p. 287-291*

CONVEYANCING — England

GREAT BRITAIN. Law Commission
Transfer of land : the rule in Bain v. Fothergill / The Law Commission. — London : H.M.S.O., 1986. — iv,49p. — (Working paper / Law Commission ; no. 98). — *Includes bibliographical references*

CONVICT LABOR — New York (State) — Albany — History — 19th century

GREENBERG, Brian
Worker and community : response to industrialization in a nineteenth-century American city, Albany, New York, 1850-1884 / Brian Greenberg. — Albany : State University of New York Press, c1985. — ix, 227 p.. — (SUNY series in American social history). — *Maps on endpapers. — Includes index. — Bibliography: p. 211-220*

CONWAY, MONCURE

BROCKWAY, Fenner
Moncure Conway : his life and message for today / Fenner Brockway ; introduction by Michael Foot. — London : South Place Ethical Society, 1986. — 11p

COOK ISLANDS — Census, 1981

COOK ISLANDS. Statistics Office
Cook Islands census of population and dwellings : demographic characteristics of the population of the Cook Islands. — Rarotonga : the Office, 1982. — 16p. — CPD-82

COOK ISLANDS. Statistics Office
Cook Islands census of population and dwellings 1981 : comparison of the Cook Islands population at successive censuses 1961-1981. — Rarotonga : the Office, 1984. — 21p. — CPD11-84

COOK ISLANDS — Population — Statistics

COOK ISLANDS. Statistics Office
Cook Islands census of population and dwellings : demographic characteristics of the population of the Cook Islands. — Rarotonga : the Office, 1982. — 16p. — *CPD-82*

COOK ISLANDS. Statistics Office
Cook Islands census of population and dwellings 1981 : comparison of the Cook Islands population at successive censuses 1961-1981. — Rarotonga : the Office, 1984. — 21p. — *CPD11-84*

COOKE, JOHN WILLIAM

GOLDAR, Ernesto
John William Cooke y el peronismo revolucionario / Ernesto Goldar. — Buenos Aires : Centro Editor de América Latina, 1985. — 140p. — (Biblioteca Política Argentina ; 99)

COOKERY — England — Yorkshire

BREARS, Peter
Traditional food in Yorkshire / Peter Brears. — Edinburgh : John Donald, c1987. — vii,232p

COOPERATION — Great Britain — History

WEBB, Beatrice
The Co-operative Movement in Great Britain / Beatrice Potter. — Aldershot : Gower, c1987. — xxxvii,260p. — *Facsim of ed. published: London : Sonnenschein, 1891. — Bibliography: p243-245. — Includes index*

COOPERATION

Community and cooperatives in participatory development / edited by Yair Levi and Howard Litwin. — Aldershot : Gower, c1986. — xii,261p. — *Conference proceedings. — Includes bibliographies and index*

MELNYK, George
The search for community : from utopia to a co-operative society / George Melnyk. — Montréal ; Buffalo : Black Rose Books, c1985. — xv, 170 p.. — *Includes bibliographical references and index*

COOPERATION — European Economic Community countries

The cooperative, mutual and non-profit sector and its organizations in the European Community. — Luxembourg : Office for Official Publications of the European Communities, 1986. — xxvii,900p. — *At head of title: Economic and Social Consultative Assembly*

COOPERATION — Finland

A quarter of a century of co-operation in Finland : published for the twenty-fifth anniversary of the Pellervo Society, 2.10.1924. — Helsinki : [Government Printing Office], 1924. — 45p

COOPERATION — Germany — Biography

ARNOLD, Walter
Friedrich Wilhelm Raiffeisen : einer für alle - alle für einen / Walter Arnold, Fritz H. Lamparter. — Neuhausen-Stuttgart : Hänssler, 1985. — 209p. — *Bibliography: p192-193*

COOPERATION — Germany (West)

ASCHHOFF, Gunther
Das deutshe Genossenschaftswesen : Entwicklung, Struktur, wirtschaftliches Potential / Gunther Aschhoff, Eckart Henningsen. — Frankfurt : Fritz Knapp, 1985. — 167p. — (Veröffentlichungen der Deutsche Genossenschaftsbank ; Bd.15). — *Bibliography: p151-156*

COOPERATION — Nigeria — Addresses, essays, lectures

New trends in African cooperatives : the Nigerian experience / [edited by M.O. Ijere]. — Enugu, Nigeria : Fourth Dimension (Publishers), [1975?]. — 142 p.. — *Imprint from label on verso t.p. — Includes bibliographical references*

COOPERATION — Poland

GRYNBERG, Michał
Żydowska spóŁdzielczość prazy w Polsce w latach 1945-1949 / Michał Grynberg. — Warszawa : Państwowe Wydawnictwo Naukowe, 1986. — 183p. — *Bibliography: p174-176*

KOWALSKI, Witold
Wkład PPR i PPS w rozwój spółdzielczości w Polsce w latach 1944-1948 / Witold Kowalski. — Warszawa : Książka i Wiedza, 1986. — 425p. — *Bibliography: p394-[413]*

COOPERATIVE SOCIETIES

MCKENNA, Dermot
Create employment : start worker co-operatives / Fr. Dermot McKenna. — Dublin : Irish Messenger Publications, 1985. — 30p

MELNYK, George
The search for community : from utopia to a co-operative society / George Melnyk. — Montréal ; Buffalo : Black Rose Books, c1985. — xv, 170 p.. — *Includes bibliographical references and index*

PFEIFFER, Lucien
Libre entreprise et socialismes. — Paris : Nouvelle Société des Éditions Encre, 1986. — 192p

WATKINS, W. P.
Co-operative principles : today and tomorrow / by W.P. Watkins ; with an introduction by T.F. Carbery. — Manchester : Holyoake, 1986. — [140]p. — *Includes index*

COOPERATIVE SOCIETIES — Government policies — Hungary

PRUGBERGER, Tamás
A szövetkezetek gazdaságirányítása és állami felügyelete / Prugberger Tamás. — Budapest : Közgazdasági és Jogi Kňyvkiadó, 1985. — 329p

COOPERATIVE SOCIETIES — Law and legislation — Hungary

PRUGBERGER, Tamás
A szövetkezetek gazdaságirányítása és állami felügyelete / Prugberger Tamás. — Budapest : Közgazdasági és Jogi Kňyvkiadó, 1985. — 329p

COOPERATIVE SOCIETIES — Canada — Auditing — Social aspects

Social auditing : a manual for co-operative organizations / prepared under the direction of the Social Audit Task Force of the Co-operative Union of Canada. — Ottawa : Co-operative Union of Canada, 1985. — vi,86p. — *Bibliography: p85-86*

COOPERATIVE SOCIETIES — Canada — History

MACPHERSON, Ian
Building and protecting the co-operative movement : a brief history of the Co-operative Union of Canada, 1909-1984 / by Ian MacPherson. — Ottawa, Ont. : Co-operative Union of Canada, [1984]. — xii, 254 p.. — *Includes bibliographical references*

COOPERATIVE SOCIETIES — European Economic Community countries

The cooperative, mutual and non-profit sector and its organizations in the European Community. — Luxembourg : Office for Official Publications of the European Communities, 1986. — xxvii,900p. — *At head of title: Economic and Social Consultative Assembly*

Prospects for workers' co-operatives. — Luxembourg : Office for Official Publications of the European Communities. — *At head of title page: Commission of the European Communities*
Vol. 1: Overview / by Mutual Aid Center, London. — 1984. — 1v.(various pagings)

Prospects for workers' co-operatives. — Luxembourg : Office for Official Publications of the European Communities. — *At head of title page: Commission of the European Communities*
Vol. 2: Country reports - first series : Denmark; Greece; Republic of Ireland; Netherlands; Spain: United Kingdom / by Mutual Aid Center, London. — 1984. — 1v.(various pagings)

Prospects for workers' co-operatives. — Luxembourg : Office for Official Publications of the European Communities. — *At head of title page: Commission of the European Communities*
Vol. 3: Country reports - second series : Belgium; France; Federal Republic of Germany; Italy / by Ten Cooperative de Conseils, Paris. — 1984. — 1v.(various pagings)

COOPERATIVE SOCIETIES — France

Forms of organisation, type of employment, working conditions and industrial relations in co-operatives, any collectiveness or other self-managing structures of the EEC. — Luxembourg : Office for Official Publications of the European Communities, 1986. — i,119,C.102p. — (Programme of research and actions on the development of the labour market). — *At head of title: Commission of the European Communities*

COOPERATIVE SOCIETIES — Germany (West)

ASCHHOFF, Gunther
Das deutshe Genossenschaftswesen : Entwicklung, Struktur, wirtschaftliches Potential / Gunther Aschhoff, Eckart Henningsen. — Frankfurt : Fritz Knapp, 1985. — 167p. — (Veröffentlichungen der Deutsche Genossenschaftsbank ; Bd.15). — *Bibliography: p151-156*

COOPERATIVE SOCIETIES — Great Britain

Forms of organisation, type of employment, working conditions and industrial relations in co-operatives, any collectiveness or other self-managing structures of the EEC. — Luxembourg : Office for Official Publications of the European Communities, 1986. — i,119,C.102p. — (Programme of research and actions on the development of the labour market). — *At head of title: Commission of the European Communities*

TRADES UNION CONGRESS
Trade Unions and co-operatives : TUC statement and guidelines on worker co-operatives. — [London] : Trades Union Congress, 1985. — [10p]

COOPERATIVE SOCIETIES — Italy

Forms of organisation, type of employment, working conditions and industrial relations in co-operatives, any collectiveness or other self-managing structures of the EEC. — Luxembourg : Office for Official Publications of the European Communities, 1986. — i,119,C.102p. — (Programme of research and actions on the development of the labour market). — *At head of title: Commission of the European Communities*

COOPERATIVE UNION OF CANADA — History

MACPHERSON, Ian
Building and protecting the co-operative movement : a brief history of the Co-operative Union of Canada, 1909-1984 / by Ian MacPherson. — Ottawa, Ont. : Co-operative Union of Canada, [1984]. — xii, 254 p.. — *Includes bibliographical references*

COOPERATIVES — Africa — Addresses, essays, lectures

New trends in African cooperatives : the Nigerian experience / [edited by M.O. Ijere]. — Enugu, Nigeria : Fourth Dimension (Publishers), [1975?]. — 142 p.. — *Imprint from label on verso t.p. — Includes bibliographical references*

COPENHAGEN (DENMARK) — Economic conditions — Statistics
Københavnernes indkomster 1980-1983. — [København : Københavns Statistiske Kontor, 1985]. — 98p. — (Undersøgelser fra Københavns Statistiske Kontor ; nr.23)

COPERNICUS (Nicolaus)
The Nature of scientific discovery : a symposium commemorating the 500th anniversary of the birth of Nicolaus Copernicus / Edited by Owen Gingerich. — [1st ed.]. — Washington : Smithsonian Institution Press ; [distributed by G. Braziller, New York, 1975]. — 616 p. — (Smithsonian international symposia series ; 5). — "The fifth international symposium of the Smithsonian Institution organized jointly with the National Academy of Sciences in cooperation with the Copernicus Society of America.". — Bibliography: p. 23-26

COPPER INDUSTRY AND TRADE — Mathematical models
GHOSH, S.
Stabilizing speculative commodity markets / S. Ghosh, C.L. Gilbert and A.J. Hughes Hallett. — Oxford : Clarendon, 1987. — [448]p. — Includes bibliography and index

COPPER INDUSTRY AND TRADE — Poland
BARTOSIK, Zygmunt
Przemysł miedziowy / Zygmunt Bartosik. — Wrocław : Ossolineum, 1981. — 259p

COPPS, SHEILA, 1952-
COPPS, Sheila
Nobody's baby : a survival guide to politics / Sheila Copps. — Toronto : Deneau, 1986. — 192p

COPYRIGHT — Computer programs
BORKING, John J.
Third party protection of software and firmware : direct protection of zeros and ones / John J. Borking. — Amsterdam ; Oxford : North-Holland, 1985. — xx,521p. — Bibliography: p491-510. — Includes index

COPYRIGHT — Music — Canada
SANDERSON, Paul
Musicians and the law in Canada / by Paul Sanderson. — [Toronto] : Carswell, 1985. — xxxi,258p

COPYRIGHT — Australia
GOLVAN, Colin
Writers and the law / Colin Golvan and Michael McDonald; consultant: Alan Kirsner ; with a foreword by David Williamson. — Sydney : Law Book Company, 1986. — xix,262p. — Bibliography: pxix

COPYRIGHT — Great Britain
STERLING, J. A. L.
Copyright law in the United Kingdom and the rights of performers, authors and composers in Europe / by J.A.L. Sterling and M.C.L. Carpenter. — London : Legal Books, 1986. — cxi,749p

CORBY (NORTHAMPTONSHIRE) — Industries
MAUNDERS, A. R.
A process of struggle : the campaign for Corby steelmaking in 1979 / Allen Maunders. — Gower : Aldershot, c1987. — [295]p. — Includes bibliography

CORDAGE INDUSTRY — Mexico — Yucatán — History
BRANNON, Jeffery
Agrarian reform & public enterprise in Mexico : the political economy of Yucatán's henequen industry / Jeffery Brannon, Eric N. Baklanoff ; a foreword by Edward H. Moseley. — Tuscaloosa, Ala. : University of Alabama Press, c1987. — xv, 237 p.. — Includes index. — Bibliography: p. 220-230

CORN — Indonesia
The Corn economy of Indonesia / edited by C. Peter Timmer. — Ithaca : Cornell University Press, 1987. — 302 p.. — Includes index. — Bibliography: p. [287]-293

CORN — Indonesia — Utilization
The Corn economy of Indonesia / edited by C. Peter Timmer. — Ithaca : Cornell University Press, 1987. — 302 p.. — Includes index. — Bibliography: p. [287]-293

CORN INDUSTRY — Indonesia
The Corn economy of Indonesia / edited by C. Peter Timmer. — Ithaca : Cornell University Press, 1987. — 302 p.. — Includes index. — Bibliography: p. [287]-293

CORONERS
JUSTICE
Coroners courts in England and Wales : a report / by JUSTICE ; Chairman of Committee Evan Stone. — London : JUSTICE, 1986. — 28p

CORPORAL PUNISHMENT — Legal status, laws, etc. — Great Britain
GREAT BRITAIN. Parliament. House of Commons. Library. Research Division
Education (Corporal Punishment) Bill [Bill 57 of 1984/85] / Kay Andrews. — [London] : the Division, 1985. — 25p. — (Reference sheet ; no.85/2). — Bibliography: p21-25

CORPORATE CULTURE
DYER, W. Gibb
Cultural change in family firms : anticipating and managing business and family transitions / W. Gibb Dyer, Jr. — 1st ed. — San Francisco : Jossey-Bass, 1986. — xxi, 179 p.. — (The Jossey-Bass management series) (The Jossey-Bass social and behavioral science series) . — Includes index. — Bibliography: p. 167-171

SCHEIN, Edgar H
Organizational culture and leadership : a dynamic view / Edgar H. Schein. — 1st ed. — San Franciso : Jossey-Bass Publishers, c1985. — p. cm. — (A Joint publication in the Jossey-Bass management series and the Jossey-Bass social and behavioral science series) . — Includes index. — Bibliography: p

CORPORATE CULTURE — United States
HOWARD, Robert
Brave new workplace / Robert Howard. — New York : Penguin Books, 1986, c1985. — p. cm. — "Elisabeth Sifton books.". — Includes index

CORPORATE DIVESTITURE
CASSON, Mark
International divestment and restructuring decisions (with special reference to the motor industry) / by Mark Casson. — Geneva : International Labour Office, 1986. — 46p. — (Working paper / Multinational Enterprises Programme ; no.40). — Bibliography: p[38]-39

CORPORATE IMAGE — United States — History
NYE, David E.
Image worlds : corporate identities at General Electric, 1890-1930 / David E. Nye. — Cambridge, Mass. ; London : MIT Press, c1985. — xiv, 188p, [38]p of plates. — Includes index. — Bibliography: p.[161]-182

CORPORATE PLANNING
AMEY, Lloyd R
Corporate planning : a systems view / Lloyd R. Amey. — New York : Praeger, 1986. — xiv, 272 p.. — Includes bibliographies and indexes

GLUECK, William F
Strategic management and business policy / William F. Glueck, Lawrence R. Jauch. — 2nd ed. — New York : McGraw-Hill, c1984. — xiii, 447 p.. — (McGraw-Hill series in management). — Includes bibliographical references and index

KAMPFRAATH, A. A.
Bronnen van welvaart en welzijn / A. A. Kampfraath. — Alphen aan den Rijn : Sansom, 1970. — 24p. — Rede uitgesproken bij de aanvaarding van het ambt van gewoon hoogleraar in de industriële bedrijfskunde en organisatieleer aan de Landbouwhogeschool te Wageningen op donderdag 23 april 1970. — Bibliography: p23-24

NAYLOR, Thomas H.
The corporate strategy matrix / Thomas H. Naylor. — New York : Basic Books, c1986. — xii, 290 p.. — Includes index. — Bibliography: p. 276-280

WHITE, Jonathan Peter
Roles of boundary-spanning individuals in decision-making involving organization-environment communication / by Jonathan Peter White. — 318 leaves. — PhD (Econ) 1986 LSE. — Leaves 289-318 are appendices

CORPORATE PLANNING — Addresses, essays, lectures
Readings on strategic management / edited by Arnoldo C. Hax. — Cambridge, Mass. : Ballinger Pub. Co., 1984. — x, 224 p.. — Includes bibliographies and index

CORPORATE PLANNING — Case studies
GRAYSON, Leslie E
Who and how in planning for large companies / by Leslie E. Grayson. — New York : St. Martin's Press, 1986. — p. cm. — Includes index

CORPORATE PROFITS
RAPPAPORT, Alfred
Creating shareholder value : the new standard for business performance / Alfred Rappaport. — New York : Free Press ; London : Collier Macmillan, c1986. — xv, 270 p.. — Includes index. — Bibliography: p. 241-257

CORPORATE RE-ORGANIZATIONS
GHERTMAN, Michel
Decision-making regarding restructuring in multinational enterprises / by Michel Ghertman. — Geneva : International Labour Office, 1986. — 69p. — (Working paper / Multinational Enterprises Programme ; no.39). — Includes bibliographical references

CORPORATE STATE
NEWELL, A.
Corporatism, the laissez-faire and the rise in unemployment / A. Newell and J. S. V. Symons. — London : Centre for Labour Economics, London School of Economics, 1986. — 62p. — (Discussion paper / London School of Economics and Political Science. Centre for Labour Economics ; no.260). — Bibliography: p60-62

CORPORATE STATE — Congresses
Economic and social partnership and incomes policy = : Pacto social e política de rendimentos / edited by Aníbal A. Cavaco Silva. — Lisboa : Faculdade de Ciências Humanas da Universidade Católica Portuguesa, c1984. — 304 p.. — English, French, and Portuguese. — Papers and comemntary presented at the Conference on "Economic and Social Partnership and Incomes Policy" organized by the Austrian Embassy in Portugal and the Faculty of Social Sciences of the Portuguese Catholic University, held Mar. 15-16, 1983, in Lisbon. — Includes bibliographical references

CORPORATE STATE — Europe
Political stability and neo-corporatism : corporatist integration and societal cleavages in Western Europe / edited by Ilja Scholten. — London : Sage, 1987. — x,276p. — (Sage series in neo-corporatism). — Includes bibliographies and index

CORPORATE STATE — Latin America — Addresses, essays, lectures

Promise of development : theories of change in Latin America / edited by Peter F. Klarén and Thomas J. Bossert. — Boulder, Colo. : Westview Press, 1986. — xiii, 350p. — Includes index. — Includes bibliographical references

CORPORATION — Great Britain — Accounting — Study and teaching

RUTHERFORD, B. A.
Cases in company financial reporting / B.A. Rutherford, R.T. Wearing. — London : Harper & Row, 1987. — xxi, 186p. — (Harper & Row series in accounting and finance). — Includes bibliographies

CORPORATION LAW — Austria

The Austrian law on companies with limited liability, as of January 1, 1984, with excerpted provisions of other relevant laws and annotations / editor Julie Goldberg. — Deventer ; Antwerp : Kluwer Law and Taxation Publishers, c1985. — 122p. — (Series on international corporate law ; 1). — Bibliography: p122

CORPORATION LAW — Belgium

RAUCQ, Albert
Sociétés anonymes / par Albert Raucq. — Bruxelles : Larcier, 1982. — 382p. — (Répertoire notarial ; T.12. Droit commercial ; Livre 3). — Ouvrage mis à jour au 15 juin 1981 par Gilberte Raucq. — In French and Flemish. — First published 1972

CORPORATION LAW — Canada — Cases

Cases and materials on partnerships and Canadian business corporations / by Stanley M. Beck ... [et al.]. — Toronto, Canada : Carswell, 1983. — xxix, 938 p.. — "Table of cases": p. xxiii-xxix

CORPORATION LAW — France

FRANCE
[Code des sociétés]. Code des sociétés. — 6e éd. — Paris : Dalloz, 1985. — viii, 1421, 17p. — (Petits codes Dalloz). — Includes index

CORPORATION LAW — Great Britain

Butterworths company law handbook / 5th ed. / consultant editor, Keith Walmsley. — London : Butterworths, 1986. — viii, 1141, 16p

Company law in change / edited by B.G. Pettet. — London : Stevens, 1987. — [144]p. — (Current legal problems). — Includes index

JOHNSON, Barry
Accounting provisions of the Companies Act 1985 / Barry Johnson, Matthew Patient ; legal consultant editor: Mary Arden. — [London : Farringdon], c1985. — xix, 908p

MAYSON, Stephen W.
A practical approach to company law / Stephen W. Mayson and Derek French. — 3rd ed. — London : Financial Training, 1986. — lxii, 617p

MAYSON, Stephen W.
A practical approach to company law / Stephen W. Mayson, Derek French and Christopher L. Ryan. — 4th ed. — London : Financial Training, 1987. — lxvii, 618p

NORTHEY, J. F.
Northey & Leigh's introduction to company law. — 4th ed / L.H. Leigh, V.H. Joffe, D. Goldberg. — London : Butterworths, 1987. — [546]p. — Previous ed.: 1983. — Includes index

RANKING, D. F. de l'Hoste
Ranking and Spicer's Company law. — 13th ed. / J.M. Gullick. — London : Butterworths, 1987. — xxix, 331p. — Previous ed: London : HFL in association with Chart Foulks Lynch, 1981. — Includes index

RENSHALL, Michael
The Companies Act 1985 : a guide to the accounting and reporting requirements / Michael Renshall, John Aldis. — London : Peat, Marwick, Mitchell, 1985. — xxx, 274p. — Includes index

THOMAS, Colin
Company law for accountants / C.D. Thomas. — London : Butterworths, 1985. — xxxv, 501p. — Includes index

CORPORATION LAW — Great Britain — Accounting

JOHNSON, Barry
Accounting provisions of the Companies Act 1985 / Barry Johnson, Matthew Patient ; legal consultant editor: Mary Arden. — [London : Farringdon], c1985. — xix, 908p

CORPORATION LAW — Great Britain — Cases

HAHLO, H. R.
Hahlo's case and materials on company law. — 3rd ed. / by the late H.R. Hahlo and John H. Farrar. — London : Sweet & Maxwell, 1987. — xxxvi, 674p. — Previous ed: published as Hahlo's casebook on company law, 1977. — Includes index

CORPORATION LAW — Great Britain — Handbooks, manuals, ect.

Butterworths company law handbook / consultant editor Keith Walmsley. — 6th ed. — London : Butterworths, 1987. — 1358, 37p

CORPORATION LAW — Great Britain — Handbooks, manuals, etc

PENNINGTON, Robert R.
The Companies Acts 1980 and 1981 : a practitioners' manual / by Robert R. Pennington. — London : Lloyds of London Press, 1983. — lxii, 313p. — Includes index

CORPORATION LAW — Hong Kong

WALLACE, Pauline
Company law in Hong Kong / Pauline Wallace. — Singapore : Butterworths, 1986. — xxvii, 366p

CORPORATION LAW — United States

ROME, Edwin P
Corporate and commercial free speech : first amendment protection of expression in business / Edwin P. Rome and William H. Roberts. — Westport, Conn. : Quorum Books, c1985. — p. cm. — Includes index. — Bibliography: p

CORPORATION REPORTS — France

ORDRE DES EXPERTS COMPTABLES ET DES COMPTABLES AGRÉÉS
Les rapports annuels des sociétés françaises : année 1984 : analyse de l'information comptable et financière contenue dans les rapports annuels de 150 sociétés françaises / Ordre des Experts Comptables et des Comptables Agréés. — [France] : Éditions Comptables Malesherbes
T.L: [Les comptes annuels]. — 1986. — xi, 160p

ORDRE DES EXPERTS COMPTABLES ET DES COMPTABLES AGRÉÉS
Les rapports annuels des sociétés françaises : année 1984 : analyse de l'information comptable et financière contenue dans les rapports annuels de 150 sociétés françaises / Ordre des Experts Comptables et des Comptables Agréés. — [France] : Éditions Comptables Malesherbes
T.2: [Les comptes consolidés]. — 1986. — xi, 188p

CORPORATIONS

MARGINSON, Paul
Labour and the modern corporation : mutual interest or control? / Paul Marginson. — Coventry : University of Warwick. School of Industrial and Business Studies. Industrial Relations Research Unit, 1985. — 15 leaves. — (Warwick papers in industrial relations ; no.9). — Bibliography: p15

MUELLER, Dennis C
The modern corporation / D.C. Mueller. — Lincoln : University of Nebraska Press, 1966. — p. cm. — Bibliography: p

RICKETTS, Martin J. H.
The economics of business enterprise : new approaches to the firm / Martin Ricketts. — Brighton : Wheatsheaf, 1987. — xii, 306p. — Bibliography: p282-299p. — Includes index

CORPORATIONS — Accounting

BUDWORTH, D. W.
Rewinding the mainspring : a discussion paper on innovation expenditure in company accounts / D. W. Budworth. — London : Technical Change Centre, 1987. — vii, 53p

Financial reporting 1985-86 : a survey of UK published accounts / edited by L. C. L. Skerratt and D. J. Tonkin. — London : Institute of Chartered Accountants in England and Wales, 1986. — xvii, 165p

CORPORATIONS — Accounting — Law and legislation — Ireland

POWER, B. J.
Accounting law and practice for Limited companies : format and disclosure requirements under the Irish Companies Acts 1963 to 1986, and accounting standards / B.J. Power. — Dublin : Gill and Macmillan, c1987. — xvii, 219p. — Includes index

CORPORATIONS — Addresses, essays, lectures

Corporations and the common good / edited by Robert B. Dickie and Leroy S. Rouner. — Notre Dame, Ind. : University of Notre Dame Press, c1986. — xii, 147 p.. — "Published with the School of Management, Boston University.". — Includes bibliographies. — Contents: Introduction -- The moral crisis of capitalism / Peter Berger -- Realities and appearances in capitalism / Robert Heil-broner -- Perfecting capitalism / James E. Post -- The large corporation and the new American ideology / George C. Lodge -- The multinational corporation / Kenneth Mason -- Ethics and corporate strategy / Edwin A. Murray, Jr. -- Sanctions, incentives, and corporate behavior / Peter T. Jones -- Epilogue : can managers be taught to be ethical? / Henry Morgan

CORPORATIONS — Charitable contributions — Great Britain

COWTON, Christopher J.
A study of the disclosure of charitable donations by companies in the United Kingdom / Christopher J. Cowton. — London : Institute of Chartered Accountants, 1986. — 52p. — Bibliography: p46-52

CORPORATIONS — Corrupt practices — Bibliography

WALKER, Christine
Corruption in police forces, business & government. — [London] : Home Office Library, 1978. — 6leaves. — (Reading list / Home Office, Library)

CORPORATIONS — Finance

British readings in financial management / edited by Stewart Ivison, Caroline Moss and Mary Simpson. — London : Harper & Row, 1986. — ix, 385. — Includes index

Midland corporate finance journal / Midland Bank PLC. — New York : Stern Stewart Management Services, 1985-. — Quarterly

PITELIS, Christos
Corporate capital : control, ownership, saving and crisis / Christos Pitelis. — Cambridge : Cambridge University Press, 1987. — [220]p. — Includes bibliography and index

The Revolution in corporate finance / edited by Joel M. Stern and Donald H. Chew Jr. — Oxford : Basil Blackwell, 1986. — [400] pxiii, 455p. — Bibliography: p453. — Includes index

CORPORATIONS — Finance — Data processing
MCLAUGHLIN, Hugh S
Financial management with Lotus 1-2-3 / Hugh S. McLaughlin, J. Russell Boulding. — Englewood Cliffs, N.J. : Prentice-Hall, c1986. — p. cm. — On t.p. the circled symbol "R" is superscript following "Lotus" and "1-2-3" in the title. — Includes bibliographies and index

CORPORATIONS — History — 20th century
DUNNING, John H.
The world's largest industrial enterprises 1962-1983 / John H. Dunning, Robert D. Pearce. — 2nd ed. — Aldershot : Gower, c1985. — v,186p. — Previous ed.: 1981

CORPORATIONS — Social aspects
Corporate social responsibility : contemporary viewpoints / Suzanne Robitaille Ontiveros, editor ; foreword by Joan L. Bavaria. — Santa Barbara, Calif. : ABC-CLIO, c1986. — xv, 229 p.. — (The Dynamic organization series). — Includes indexes

CORPORATIONS — Social aspects — Spain
SÁNCHEZ CREUS, Fernando
Estudio socio-laboral de la empresa española : segundo análisis / estudio dirigido por Fernando Sánchez Creus y Emilio Arevalo Eizaguirre. — [Madrid] : Asociación para el Progreso de la Dirección, 1983. — 259p

CORPORATIONS — Statistics
DUNNING, John H.
The world's largest industrial enterprises 1962-1983 / John H. Dunning, Robert D. Pearce. — 2nd ed. — Aldershot : Gower, c1985. — v,186p. — Previous ed.: 1981

CORPORATIONS — Taxation
KING, Mervyn A.
The cash flow corporate income tax / Mervyn A. King. — [London : London School of Economics and Political Science], 1986. — 35p. — (Taxation, incentives and the distribution of income ; no.95). — Economic and Social Research Council programme. — Paper prepared for the NBER Conference on the Effects of Taxation on Capital Formation, Palm Beach. — Bibliographical references: p29-30

MAJD, Saman
Tax asymmetrics and corporate income tax reform / Saman Majd, Stewart C. Myers. — Cambridge, Mass. : NBER, 1986. — 38p. — (NBER working paper series ; no.1924). — Bibliography: p37-38

CORPORATIONS — Taxation — Germany (West)
Local business taxes in Britain and Germany : report on an Anglo-German conference 8-9 April 1986, [London] / [edited by R. J. Bennett and H. Zimmermann]. — London : Anglo-German Foundation for the Study of Industrial Society, 1986. — 186p

CORPORATIONS — Taxation — Great Britain
GAMMIE, Malcolm
Tax strategy for companies. — 4th ed / by Malcolm Gammie. — London : Longman Professional, 1986. — xxviii,511p. — Previous ed.: 1983. — Includes index

Local business taxes in Britain and Germany : report on an Anglo-German conference 8-9 April 1986, [London] / [edited by R. J. Bennett and H. Zimmermann]. — London : Anglo-German Foundation for the Study of Industrial Society, 1986. — 186p

MORGAN, Eleanor J.
Corporate taxation and investment : the implications of the 1984 tax reform / Eleanor J. Morgan. — Aldershot : Gower, c1986. — x,220p. — Bibliography: p214-216

CORPORATIONS — Valuation
RAPPAPORT, Alfred
Creating shareholder value : the new standard for business performance / Alfred Rappaport. — New York : Free Press ; London : Collier Macmillan, c1986. — xv, 270 p.. — Includes index. — Bibliography: p. 241-257

CORPORATIONS — Australia — Finance
Trends in the composition of corporate finance in Australia. — Canberra : Economic Planning Advisory Council, 1985. — v,14p. — (Council paper / Economic Planning Advisory Council ; no.3). — Bibliography: p10

CORPORATIONS — Canada
CARROLL, William K.
Corporate power and Canadian capitalism / William K. Carroll. — Vancouver : University of British Columbia Press, 1986. — xvii,284p. — Bibliography: p[257]-276

CORPORATIONS — Canada — Charitable contributions
MARTIN, Samuel A
An essential grace : funding Canada's health care, education, welfare, religion, and culture / by Samuel A. Martin. — Toronto : McClelland and Stewart, c1985. — xvii, 322 p.. — Includes index

CORPORATIONS — European Economic Community countries — Finance
The Contribution of credit institutions to the renewal of the economy : proceedings of the conference held in Luxembourg, 28-29 November 1985 / edited by J.M. Gibb. — London : Kogan Page, c1986. — 135p. — English text, French and German summaries. — Organised jointly by The Commission of the European Communities, Directorate General Information Market and Innovation and the Institut Universitaire International Luxembourg

CORPORATIONS — France
BOUVIER-AJAM, Maurice
Recherches sur la genese et la date d'apparition des corporations medievales en France / Maurice Bouvier-Ajam. — Paris : Librairie Generale de Droit et de Jurisprudence, 1978. — 33p

CORPORATIONS — Great Britain
SCOTT, John
Corporate control in Britain : an analysis of 250 large companies / John Scott. — Leicester : University of Leicester. Department of Sociology, 1985. — 19p. — (Working paper for the company analysis report)

CORPORATIONS — Great Britain — Accounting
FLINT, David
A true and fair view in company accounts / by David Flint. — London : Published for the Institute of Chartered Accountants of Scotland by Gee, 1982. — vi,47p. — Bibliography: p46-47

WALTON, Peter, 19---
Corporate reports : their interpretation and use in business / Peter Walton and Michael Bond. — London : Hutchinson, 1986. — vii,386p. — (Hutchinson management studies). — Includes index

CORPORATIONS — Great Britain — Charitable contributions
A Guide to company giving / edited by Michael Norton ; research by Helene Bellofattee ... [et al.] ; additional contributions from Keith Bantick ... [et al.]. — 1986-87 ed. — London : Directory of Social Change, 1986. — 187p. — Previous ed.: 1984

CORPORATIONS — Great Britain — Finance
CHOWDHURY, G.
An empirical model of companies' debt and dividend decisions : evidence from company accounts data / G. Chowdhury and D. K. Miles. — London : Bank of England, 1987. — 34p. — (Bank of England discussion papers ; no. 28)

CHOWDHURY, G.
An empirical model of company short-term financial decisions : evidence from company accounts data / G. Chowdhury, C. J. Green and D. K. Miles. — London : Bank of England, 1986. — 65p. — (Bank of England discussion papers ; no.26) (Discussion paper / Bank of England ; no.26). — Bibliography: p63-65

Company finance. — London : HMSO, 1969-. — (Business monitor. MA ; 3) (Business monitor. M ; 3). — Annual

Model financial statements for public and private companies / Stoy Hayward. — London : Butterworth, 1986. — [120]p

PARKER, Lee D.
Communicating financial information through the Annual Report / Prof. Lee D. Parker. — London : Institute of Chartered Accountants, 1986. — iii,86p

CORPORATIONS — Great Britain — Finance — Mathematical models
KELLY, Christopher
Factor prices in the Treasury model / Christopher Kelly, David Owen. — London : HM Treasury, 1985. — 81p. — (Government Economic Service working paper ; no.83) (Treasury working paper ; no.37). — Bibliographical references: p73-74

CORPORATIONS — India
HANDA, Jagdish
The economic behaviour of industrial corporations : an econometric study of four Indian industries / Jagdish Handa, Chandra Prakash Khetan, Ramesh R. Waghmare. — Delhi : Macmillan India, 1985. — xii, 123 p.. — 74-9. — Bibliography: p. [119]-123

CORPORATIONS — Japan — Finance
BANK OF JAPAN. Research and Statistics Department
Further relaxation of financial conditions and structural changes in corporate finance. — Tokyo : Bank of Japan. Research and Statistics Department, 1986. — 38p. — (Special paper / Bank of Japan. Research and Statistics Department ; no.145)

CORPORATIONS — Netherlands — Corrupt practices
BERGHUIS, A. C.
Abuse of Dutch private companies (BVs) : an empirical study / A. C. Berghuis, G. Paulides. — The Hague : Research and Documentation Centre, Ministry of Justice, 1985. — 35p. — ([Reports, papers, articles] ; 77). — Includes bibliographical references

CORPORATIONS — United States
Patterns of power : an introductory study of corporate control for the members of the Securities and Exchange Commission. — [Hampton, Va.] (532 Settlers Landing Rd., P.O. Box 302, Hampton 23669) : Foundation for the Study of Philanthropy, c1982. — 3, ii-v, 151 leaves. — Includes index. — Bibliography: leaves 135-140

Views from the top : establishing the foundation for the future of business / edited by Jerome M. Rosow. — London : Sphere, 1987. — xv,[208]p. — Originally published: Facts on File, 1985

CORPORATIONS — United States — Case studies
PAUL, Ronald N
The 101 best performing companies in America / Ronald N. Paul, James W. Taylor. — Chicago, Ill. : Probus Pub. Co., c1986. — vii, 382 p. — Includes bibliographical references and index

RAMSEY, Douglas K.
The corporate warriors / Douglas K. Ramsey. — London : Grafton, 1987. — xxi,261p. — Bibliography: p261

CORPORATIONS — United States — Finance

DYCKMAN, Thomas R.
Efficient capital markets and accounting : a critical analysis. — 2nd ed. / Thomas R. Dyckman, Dale Morse. — Englewood Cliffs ; London : Prentice-Hall, c1986. — xiv,129p. — (Prentice-Hall contemporary topics in accounting series). — *Previous ed.: 1975.* — *Bibliography: p92-105.* — *Includes index*

CORPORATIONS — United States — Finance — Congresses

Financing corporate capital formation / edited by Benjamin M. Friedman. — Chicago : University of Chicago Press, 1986. — 127 p.. — (A National Bureau of Economic Research project report). — *Papers presented at a conference held at Williamsburg, Va., Sept. 20-21, 1984, sponsored by the National Bureau of Economic Research.* — *Includes bibliographies and index*

Issues in pension economics / edited by Zvi Bodie, John B. Shoven, and David A. Wise. — Chicago : University of Chicago Press, 1987. — ix, 376 p.. — (A National Bureau of Economic Research project report). — *Includes bibliographies and indexes*

CORPORATIONS — United States — Investor relations

Patterns of power : an introductory study of corporate control for the members of the Securities and Exchange Commission. — [Hampton, Va.] (532 Settlers Landing Rd., P.O. Box 302, Hampton 23669) : Foundation for the Study of Philanthropy, c1982. — 3, ii-v, 151 leaves. — *Includes index.* — *Bibliography: leaves 135-140*

CORPORATIONS — United States — Political activity

RYAN, Mike H.
Corporate strategy, public policy and the Fortune 500 : how America´s major corporations influence government / Mike H. Ryan, Carl L. Swanson and Rogene A. Buchholz. — Oxford : Basil Blackwell, 1987. — 1v.. — *Includes index*

CORPORATIONS, BRITISH

British multinationals : origins, management and performance / edited by Geoffrey Jones. — Aldershot : Gower, c1986. — [200]p. — (Business history series). — *Includes index*

CORPORATIONS, DEVELOPING COUNTRIES´

Multinationals of the south : new actors in the international economy / edited by Khushi M. Khan. — London : Pinter, 1986. — xi,250p. — *Includes index*

CORPORATIONS, EUROPEAN — Management

European approaches to international management / Klaus Macharzina and Wolfgang H.Staehle. — Berlin : Walter de Gruyter, 1986

CORPORATIONS, FOREIGN — Taxation

ARNOLD, Brian J
The taxation of controlled foreign corporations : an international comparison / Brian J. Arnold. — Toronto, Ont. : Canadian Tax Foundation, c1986. — xxiii, 816. — (Canadian tax paper ; no. 78). — *Includes index.* — *Bibliography: p. 797-811*

CORPORATIONS, FOREIGN — Taxation — Canada

ARNOLD, Brian J
The taxation of controlled foreign corporations : an international comparison / Brian J. Arnold. — Toronto, Ont. : Canadian Tax Foundation, c1986. — xxiii, 816. — (Canadian tax paper ; no. 78). — *Includes index.* — *Bibliography: p. 797-811*

CORPORATIONS, FOREIGN — Asia — Personnel management — Congresses

ASIAN REGIONAL CONFERENCE ON INDUSTRIAL RELATIONS (6th : 1975 : Tokyo)
Foreign investment and labor in Asian countries : proceedings of the 1975 Asian Regional Conference on Industrial Relations, Tokyo, Japan, 1975. — [Tokyo] : Japan Institute of Labour, [1976]. — iii, 240 p.. — *Held March 17-20, 1975; co-sponsored by the Japan Institute of Labour and the Japan Industrial Relations Research Association.* — *Includes bibliographical References*

CORPORATIONS, FOREIGN — South Africa

SAMPSON, Anthony
Black & gold : tycoons, revolutionaries and apartheid / Anthony Sampson. — London : Hodder & Stoughton, 1987. — 280p. — *Includes index*

CORPORATIONS, GOVERNMENT — Great Britain

Employee communications in the public sector / edited by Geoff Perkins. — London : Institute of Personnel Management, 1986. — 89p. — *Bibliography: p62-67*

CORPORATIONS, GOVERNMENT — Great Britain — Accounting — Effect of inflation on

Accounting for economic costs and changing prices : a report to HM Treasury by an Advisory Group. — London : H.M.S.O., 1986. — 2v.(in 1). — *Chairman: I. C. R. Byatt.* — *Bibliography: v.2, p137*

CORPORATIONS, GOVERNMENT — Great Britain — Finance

GREAT BRITAIN. Parliament. House of Commons. Library. Research Division
The financing of nationalised industries / Christopher Barclay. — [London] : the Division, 1979. — 21p. — (Reference sheet ; no79/9)

GREAT BRITAIN. Parliament. House of Commons. Library. Research Division
The financing of nationalised industries / C. R. Barclay. — [London] : the Division, 1980. — 26p. — (Background paper ; no.88). — *Includes bibliographical references*

GREAT BRITAIN. Parliament. House of Commons. Library. Research Division
The financing of nationalised industries / C. R. Barclay. — [New ed.]. — [London] : the Division, 1982. — 21p. — (Background paper ; no.103)

CORPORATIONS, GOVERNMENT — Great Britain — Management — Employee participation

GREAT BRITAIN. Parliament. House of Commons. Library. Research Division
Worker participation in the public sector. — [London] : the Division, 1977. — 17p. — (Reference sheet ; no.77/13). — *Bibliography:p13-17*

CORPORATIONS, JAPANESE — European Economic Community countries

The Internationalization of Japanese business : European and Japanese perspectives / edited by Malcolm Trevor. — Boulder : Westview Press, 1986. — p. cm

CORPORATIONS, JAPANESE — United States

YOSHIDA, Mamoru
Japanese direct manufacturing investment in the United States / Mamoru Yoshida. — New York : Praeger, 1987. — xiv, 220 p.. — : *Originally presented as the author's thesis (doctoral--University of Miami).* — *Includes index.* — *Bibliography: p. 209-216*

CORPORATIONS, NONPROFIT — Finland — Accounting

RITVANEN, Kari
Kansantalouden tilinpito : voittoa tavoittelemattomat yhteisöt kansantalouden tilinpidossa = National accounts : non-profit institutions in national accounts / Kari Ritvanen. — Helsinki : Tilastokeskus, 1982. — 67p. — (Tutkimuksia / Finland. Tilastokeskus ; no.77)

CORPORATIONS, NONPROFIT

VERRUCOLI, Piero
Non-profit organizations : a comparative approach / Piero Verrucoli. — Milano : A. Giuffrè, 1985. — 132 p.. — (Studies in comparative law ; 28). — *Summary in French.* — *Includes bibliographical references*

CORPORATIONS, NONPROFIT — Legal status, laws, etc. — France

GALIMARD, Michel
Les sociétés civiles / Michel et Bertrand Galimard. — [Paris : Presses universitaires de France, 1981]. — 127p. — (Que sais-je? ; 1979) . — *Bibliography: p127*

CORPORATIONS, NONPROFIT — Management

MCLAUGHLIN, Curtis P
The management of nonprofit organizations / Curtis P. McLaughlin. — 1st ed. — New York : Wiley, c1986. — p. cm. — (Wiley series in managment). — *Includes indexes*

CORPORATIONS, NONPROFIT — Management — Case studies

MCLAUGHLIN, Curtis P
The management of nonprofit organizations / Curtis P. McLaughlin. — 1st ed. — New York : Wiley, c1986. — p. cm. — (Wiley series in managment). — *Includes indexes*

CORPORATIONS, NONPROFIT — United States — Finance — Addresses, essays, lectures

Nonprofit enterprise in the arts : studies in mission and constraint / [edited by] Paul J. DiMaggio. — New York : Oxford University Press, 1986. — xv, 370 p.. — (Yale studies on nonprofit organizations). — *Includes bibliographies and index*

CORPORATIONS — Taxation — United States

Tax reform and U.S. economy / papers by Henry J. Aaron...[et al.] ; edited by Joseph A. Pechman. — Washington, D.C. : Brookings Institution, 1987. — 107p. — (Brookings dialogues on public policy). — *Papers presented at a conference at the Brookings institution, December 2, 1986*

CORRECTIONAL PERSONNEL — Addresses, essays, lectures

LYLE, William H., comp
Behavioral science and modern penology : a book of readings / edited by William H. Lyle, Jr., and Thetus W. Horner. — Springfield, Ill. : Thomas, [1973]. — xvi, 355 p. — *Includes bibliographical references*

CORRECTIONS — Addresses, essays, lectures

LYLE, William H., comp
Behavioral science and modern penology : a book of readings / edited by William H. Lyle, Jr., and Thetus W. Horner. — Springfield, Ill. : Thomas, [1973]. — xvi, 355 p. — *Includes bibliographical references*

CORRECTIONS — Canada

GAMBERG, Herbert
The illusion of prison reform : corrections in Canada / Herbert Gamberg and Anthony Thomson. — New York : P. Lang, c1984. — 161 p.. — (American university studies. Series XI. Anthropology/sociology ; vol. 5). — *Bibliography: p. [145]-161*

CORRECTIONS — Canada
continuation

PLECAS, Darryl Blair
Federal corrections in Canada : a comprehensive introduction / Darryl B. Plecas ; edited by Joanne Broatch. — Vancouver : Good 80's Enterprises, 1986. — vii,148p. — *Includes references*

CORRECTIONS — Great Britain — History — 19th century

FORSYTHE, W. J. (William James)
The reform of prisoners 1830-1900 / William James Forsythe. — London : Croom Helm, c1987. — 234p. — *Includes index*

CORRECTIONS — New York (State)

MCELENEY, Barbara Lavin
Correctional reform in New York : the Rockefeller years and beyond / Barbara Lavin McEleney. — Lanham : University Press of America, c1985. — ix, 173 p.. — *Includes index. — Bibliography: p. 155-167*

CORRECTIONS — United States

THOMAS, Charles Wellington
Corrections in America : problems of the past and the present / Charles W. Thomas. — Newbury Park, Ca. : Sage Publications, 1987. — 159p. — (Law and criminal justice series ; v.7). — *Bibliography: p148-154*

CORRESPONDENCE SCHOOLS AND CLASSES — Addresses, essays, lectures

Alternative routes to formal education : distance teaching for school equivalency / edited by Hilary Perraton. — Baltimore : Johns Hopkins University Press for the World Bank, 1982. — xiii,329p. — *Includes bibliographical references*

CORRUPTION (IN POLITICS) — Bibliography

WALKER, Christine
Corruption in police forces, business & government. — [London] : Home Office Library, 1978. — 6leaves. — (Reading list / Home Office, Library)

CORRUPTION (IN POLITICS) — Africa, Sub. Saharan

WILLIAMS, Robert, 1946-
Political corruption in Africa / Robert Williams. — Aldershot : Gower, c1987. — [251]p. — *Includes bibliography and index*

CORRUPTION (IN POLITICS) — Canada

MALVERN, Paul
Persuaders : influence peddling, lobbying and political corruption in Canada / Paul Malvern. — Toronto ; London : Methuen, 1985. — 350p . — *Includes bibliographical notes*

CORRUPTION (IN POLITICS) — Great Britain

KNIGHTLEY, Phillip
An affair of state : the Profumo case and the framing of Stephen Ward / by Phillip Knightley and Caroline Kennedy. — London : Cape, 1987. — [304]p. — *Includes bibliography and index*

CORRUPTION (IN POLITICS) — Hong Kong — History

LETHBRIDGE, H. J.
Hard graft in Hong Kong : scandal; corruption; the ICAC / H. J. Lethbridge. — Hong Kong ; Oxford : Oxford University Press, 1985. — viii,247p. — *Bibliography: p232-243*

CORRUPTION (IN POLITICS) — Hongkong

PALMIER, Leslie H
The control of bureaucratic corruption : case studies in Asia / Leslie Palmier. — New Delhi : Allied Publishers, 1985. — xi, 292 p.. — *Includes bibliographies and index*

CORRUPTION (IN POLITICS) — Illinois — Chicago

JONES, Bryan D
Governing buildings and building government : a new perspective on the old party / Bryan D. Jones. — University, Ala. : University of Alabama Press, c1985. — p. cm. — *Includes index. — Bibliography: p*

CORRUPTION (IN POLITICS) — India

PALMIER, Leslie H
The control of bureaucratic corruption : case studies in Asia / Leslie Palmier. — New Delhi : Allied Publishers, 1985. — xi, 292 p.. — *Includes bibliographies and index*

CORRUPTION (IN POLITICS) — Indonesia

PALMIER, Leslie H
The control of bureaucratic corruption : case studies in Asia / Leslie Palmier. — New Delhi : Allied Publishers, 1985. — xi, 292 p.. — *Includes bibliographies and index*

CORRUPTION (IN POLITICS) — United States

Fraud, waste, and abuse in government : causes, consequences, and cures / edited by Jerome B. McKinney and Michael Johnston. — Philadelphia : Institute for the Study of Human Issues, 1986. — p. cm. — *Includes index*

CORRUPTION (IN POLITICS) — United States — 20th century

DUNAR, Andrew J.
The Truman scandals and the politics of morality / Andrew J. Dunar. — Columbia : University of Missouri Press, 1984. — viii, 213p. — *Bibliography: p.199-205*

CORRUPTION INVESTIGATION — Hong Kong — History

LETHBRIDGE, H. J.
Hard graft in Hong Kong : scandal; corruption; the ICAC / H. J. Lethbridge. — Hong Kong ; Oxford : Oxford University Press, 1985. — viii,247p. — *Bibliography: p232-243*

CORSICA — History — French Revolution, 1789-1793

GREGORY, Desmond
The ungovernable rock : a history of the Anglo-Corsican Kingdom and its role in Britain's Mediterranean strategy during the Revolutionary War, 1793-1797 / Desmond Gregory. — Rutherford : Fairleigh Dickinson University Press ; London ; Cranbury, NJ : Associated University Presses, c1985. — 211p. — *Bibliography: p202-206*

CORSICA — History — British occupation, 1794-1796

GREGORY, Desmond
The ungovernable rock : a history of the Anglo-Corsican Kingdom and its role in Britain's Mediterranean strategy during the Revolutionary War, 1793-1797 / Desmond Gregory. — Rutherford : Fairleigh Dickinson University Press ; London ; Cranbury, NJ : Associated University Presses, c1985. — 211p. — *Bibliography: p202-206*

CORYNDON, ROBERT THORNE

YOUÉ, Christopher P.
Robert Thorne Coryndon : proconsular imperialism in Southern and Eastern Africa 1897-1925 / Christopher P. Youé. — Gerrards Cross : Smythe, 1986. — [xiv,236]p. — *Bibliography: p215-229. — Includes index*

COSSACKS — History

MCNEAL, Robert H.
Tsar and Cossack, 1855-1914 / Robert H. McNeal. — London : Macmillan in association with St Antony's College, Oxford, 1987. — 262p. — (St Antony's/Macmillan series) (St Antony's / Macmillan series). — *Bibliography: p223-226. — Includes index*

COST ACCOUNTING

COST ACCOUNTING FOR THE '90S: THE CHALLENGE OF TECHNOLOGICAL CHANGE (Conference : 1986 : Boston)
Cost accounting for the '90s.... — Montvale, N.J. : National Association of Accountants, 1986. — v,164p

GEORGES, W
Analytical contribution accounting : the interface of cost accounting and pricing policy / Walter Georges and Robert W. McGee. — New York : Quorum Books, 1987. — xii, 254 p.. — *Includes index. — Bibliography: p. [225]-249*

MALLINSON, Derek
Understanding current cost accounting : a guide for those preparing and using financial statements / by Derek Mallinson. — London : Butterworth, 1980. — xviii,428p. — *Includes: Current cost accounting / Institute of Chartered Accountants in England and Wales - Guidance notes on SSAP 16, current cost accounting / Accounting Standards Committee*

OLIVER, E. Eugene
Cost accounting : a practical approach / E. Eugene Oliver. — Englewood Cliffs, N.J. : Prentice-Hall, c1987. — p. cm. — *Includes index*

COST ACCOUNTING — Technological innovations

COST ACCOUNTING FOR THE '90S: THE CHALLENGE OF TECHNOLOGICAL CHANGE (Conference : 1986 : Boston)
Cost accounting for the '90s.... — Montvale, N.J. : National Association of Accountants, 1986. — v,164p

COST AND STANDARD OF LIVING

BAYE, Michael R.
Consumer behavior, cost of living measures, and the income tax / Michael R. Baye, Dan A. Black. — Berlin ; New York : Springer-Verlag, c1986. — 119 p.. — (Lecture notes in economics and mathematical systems ; 276). — *Bibliography: p. [112]-119*

BIRDSALL, Nancy
Child schooling and the measurement of living standards / Nancy Birdsall. — Washington, D.C., U.S.A. : World Bank, c1982 ((1985 printing)). — 84p. — (LSMS working papers ; no.14) (LSMS working papers ; no. 14). — *Bibliographical references: p80-84*

DEATON, Angus
The measurement of welfare : theory and practical guidelines / Angus Deaton. — Washington, D.C., U.S.A. : World Bank, 1985 printing, c1980. — 82p. — (LSMS working papers ; no.7) (LSMS working papers ; no. 7). — *Bibliographical references: p79-82*

HO, Teresa J.
Measuring health as a component of living standards / Teresa J. Ho. — Washington, D.C., U.S.A. : World Bank, c1982 ((1985 printing)). — 58p. — (LSMS working papers ; no.15) (LSMS working papers ; no. 15). — *Bibliography: p56-58*

COST AND STANDARD OF LIVING — Statistical methods

CHANDER, R
Living standards surveys in developing countries / Ramesh Chander, statistical adviser, Christiaan Grootaert, economist, Graham Pyatt, senior adviser. — Washington, D.C. : World Bank, 1980. — 27p. — (LSMS working papers ; no.1). — *Based on a paper originally presented at an Aug. 1980 meeting of the American Statistical Association*

GROOTAERT, Christiaan
Household expenditure surveys : some methodological issues / Christiaan N. Grootaert, K.F. Cheung. — Washington, D.C., U.S.A. : World Bank, c1985. — ix,72p. — (LSMS working paper ; no.22) — *Includes bibliographical references*

COST AND STANDARD OF LIVING — Statistical methods
continuation

GROOTAERT, Christiaan
The role of employment and earnings in analyzing levels of living / Christiaan Grootaert. — Washington D.C. : The World Bank, 1986. — xiv,278p. — (LSMS working papers ; no.27). — *Bibliographical references: p269-278*

MEHRAN, Farhad
Employment data for the measurement of living standards / Farhad Mehran. — Washington, D.C., U.S.A. : World Bank, 1985 printing, c1980. — 14p. — (LSMS working papers ; no.8) (LSMS working papers ; no. 8). — *Includes bibliographical references*

Towards more effective measurement of levels of living; and, Review of work of the United Nations Statistical Office (UNSO) related to statistics of levels of living / United Nations Statistical Office. — Washington, D.C., U.S.A. : World Bank, Development Research Dept., [1985], c1980. — 61p. — (LSMS working papers ; no.4) (LSMS working paper ; no. 4 (Oct. 1980)). — *Includes bibliographical references*

WOOD, G. Donald
The collection of price data for the measurement of living standards / G. Donald Wood, Jr., Jane A. Knight. — Washington, D.C., U.S.A. : The World Bank, c1985. — viii,61p. — (LSMS working papers ; no.21) (LSMS working papers ; no. 21). — *Summary in French and Spanish. — Bibliographical references: p61*

COST AND STANDARD OF LIVING — Africa

BOOKER, William
Household survey experience in Africa / William Booker, Parmeet Singh, Landing Savane. — Washington, D.C., U.S.A. : World Bank, 1985 printing, c1980. — 54p. — (LSMS working papers ; no.6) (LSMS working papers ; no. 6). — *Includes bibliographical references*

COST AND STANDARD OF LIVING — Armenian S.S.R.

KARAPETIAN, S. A.
Regional'nye osobennosti sotsial'no-demograficheskogo razvitiia Armianskai SSR / S. A. Karapetian, R. L. Ovsepian. — Erevan : Aiastan, 1986. — 215p

COST AND STANDARD OF LIVING — Asia

VISARIA, Pravin M
Poverty and living standards in Asia : an overview of the main results and lessons of selected household surveys / Pravin Visaria assisted by Shyamalendu Pal. — Washington, D.C., U.S.A. : World Bank, 1986 printing, c1980. — xii,224p. — (LSMS working papers ; no.2). — *Includes bibliographical references*

COST AND STANDARD OF LIVING — Bulgaria — Statistics

BULGARIA, 10, Komitet za sotsialna informatsiia pri Ministerskiia Svet
Biudzheti na domakinstvata v NR Bulgaria (1965-1984g.). — Sofiia : Komitet za sotsialna informatsii, 1985. — 233p

COST AND STANDARD OF LIVING — Developing countries

ACHARYA, Meena
Time use data and the living standards measurement study / Meena Acharya. — Washington, D.C., U.S.A. : World Bank, c1982 ((1985 printing)). — 72p. — (LSMS working papers ; no.18) (LSMS working papers ; no. 18). — *Bibliographical references: p69-72*

MARTORELL, Reynaldo
Nutrition and health status indicators : suggestions for surveys of the standard of living in developing countries / Reynaldo Martorell. — Washington, D.C., U.S.A. : World Bank, Development Research Center, c1981. — 97p. — (LSMS working papers ; no.13). — *"February 1982.". — Bibliography: p91-97*

COST AND STANDARD OF LIVING — Developing countries — Case studies

SCOTT, Christopher
Conducting surveys in developing countries : practical problems and experience in Brazil, Malaysia, and the Philippines / Christopher Scott, Paulo T.A. de Andre, Ramesh Chander. — Washington, D.C., U.S.A. : World Bank, 1986 printing, c1980. — 113p. — (LSMS working papers ; no.5). — *Includes bibliographical references*

COST AND STANDARD OF LIVING — Developing countries — Congresses

SAUNDERS, Christopher Thomas
Reflections on the LSMS group meeting / Christopher Saunders, Christiaan Grootaert. — Washington, D.C., U.S.A. : World Bank, 1985 printing, c1980. — 76p. — (LSMS working papers ; no.10) (LSMS working papers ; no. 10). — *Includes bibliographical references*

COST AND STANDARD OF LIVING — Developing countries — Methodology

ABDUL WAHAB, Mohammed
Income and expenditure surveys in developing countries : sample design and execution / Mohammed Abdul Wahab. — Washington, D.C., U.S.A. : World Bank, 1985 printing, c1980. — 126p. — (LSMS working papers ; no.9) (LSMS working papers ; no. 9). — *Bibliography: p. 124-216*

COST AND STANDARD OF LIVING — France

Revenus et consommation des Français : le grand tournant / sous la direction de Michel Gaspard. — Paris : La Documentation française, 1985. — 187p. — (Notes et études documentaires ; no.4800)

COST AND STANDARD OF LIVING — Germany (West) — Statistics

GERMANY (Federal Republic). Statistisches Bundesamt
Einkommens- und Verbrauchsstichprobe 1983. — Wiesbaden : the Bundesamt. — (Wirtschaftsrechnungen)
Heft 2: Vermögenbestände und Schulden privater Haushalte. — 1986. — 540p

COST AND STANDARD OF LIVING — Hong Kong — Statistics

Report of the household expenditure survey, 1984-85. — Hong Kong : Census and Statistics Department, 1986. — viii,153p. — *Cover title: Report on the household expenditure survey, 1984-85*

COST AND STANDARD OF LIVING — Hungary — Statistical methods — Congresses

SCIENTIFIC CONFERENCE ON STATISTICAL PROBLEMS. Branch B (1961 : Budapest)
The standard of living : some problems of analysis and of international comparison / edited by M. Mód...[et al.]. — Budapest : Akadémiai Kiadó, 1962. — 294p

COST AND STANDARD OF LIVING — India — Assam — Case studies

BORAH, K. C
Income, expenditure, and saving in rural India : a micro-level study / K.C. Borah. — Delhi, India : Mittal Publications : Distributed by Mittal Publishers' Distributors, 1985. — xviii, 221 p.. — : *Revision of the author's thesis (Ph. D.--Dibrugarh University, 1977). — Summary: Based on survey conducted in Sibsagar District, Assam. — Includes index. — Bibliography: p. [209]-217*

COST AND STANDARD OF LIVING — India — Sibsägar District — Case studies

BORAH, K. C
Income, expenditure, and saving in rural India : a micro-level study / K.C. Borah. — Delhi, India : Mittal Publications : Distributed by Mittal Publishers' Distributors, 1985. — xviii, 221 p.. — : *Revision of the author's thesis (Ph. D.--Dibrugarh University, 1977). — Summary: Based on survey conducted in Sibsagar District, Assam. — Includes index. — Bibliography: p. [209]-217*

COST AND STANDARD OF LIVING — Italy

LECALDANO SASSO LA TERZA, E.
Households' saving and the real rate of interest : the Italian experience, 1970-1983 / E. Lecaldano Sasso la Terza, G. Marotta, R. S. Masera. — [Roma] : Banca d'Italia, 1985. — 33p , addenda. — (Temi di discussione ; 47) (Servizio studi della Banca d'Italia). — *Bibliography: p32-33*

COST AND STANDARD OF LIVING — Ivory Coast

GROOTAERT, Christian
Measuring and analyzing levels of living in developing countries : an annotated questionnaire / Christian Grootaert. — Washington, D.C. : The World Bank, 1986. — x,139p. — (LSMS working papers ; no.24)

COST AND STANDARD OF LIVING — Ivory Coast — Statistical methods

AINSWORTH, Martha
The Côte d'Ivoire living standards survey / Martha Ainsworth and Juan Munõz. — Washington, D.C. : The World Bank, 1986. — vii,43p. — (LSMS working papers ; no.26)

COST AND STANDARD OF LIVING — Japan — Statistics

JAPAN. Statistics Bureau
1984 national survey of family income and expenditure. — [Tokyo] : Statistics Bureau, [1985-1987]. — *Text in Japanese and English*

COST AND STANDARD OF LIVING — Jordan — Statistics

JORDAN. Department of Statistics
Family expenditure survey 1980. — [Amman] : the Department, ca.1982. — 1v (various pagings). — *Text in Arabic with table headings in English*

COST AND STANDARD OF LIVING — Latin America

ALTIMIR, Oscar
Measuring levels of living in Latin America : an overview of main problems / Oscar Altimir, Juan Sourrouille. — Washington, D.C., U.S.A. : World Bank, 1986 printing, c1980. — 75p. — (LSMS working papers ; no.3). — *Includes bibliographical references*

COST AND STANDARD OF LIVING — Malaysia

GROOTAERT, Christiaan
The role of employment and earnings in analyzing levels of living / Christiaan Grootaert. — Washington D.C. : The World Bank, 1986. — xiv,278p. — (LSMS working papers ; no.27). — *Bibliographical references: p269-278*

COST AND STANDARD OF LIVING — Netherlands — Methodology

NETHERLANDS. Centraal Bureau voor de Statistiek
Werknemersbudgetonderzoek 1974-75. — s-Gravenhage : Staatsuitgeverij. — *Contents list in English. — Title on back cover: Workers' budget survey 1974-75. Part 5. Methodology. Appendix 1. Instruments and instructions for data collection*
deel 5: Methodologie
bijlage 1: Enquêtedocumenten. — 1980. — 187p

NETHERLANDS. Centraal Bureau voor de Statistiek
Werknemersbudgetonderzoek, 1974-75. — s-Gravenhage : Staatsuitgeverij, 1980. — *Contents list in English. — Title on back cover: Workers' budget survey 1974-75. Part 5. Methodology. — Bibliography: p86*
deel 5: Methodologie. — 86p

COST AND STANDARD OF LIVING — Netherlands — Statistics

De leefsituatie van de nederlandse bevolking van 55 jaar en ouder 1982. — 's-Gravenhage : Staatsuitgeverij. — *Summary in English. — Title on back cover: Well-being of the elderly population in the Netherlands 1982 : a survey on people aged 55 years and over : Part 1B : Key figures*
d. 1B: Kerncijfers : betaald en onbetaald werk, sociale relaties, vrijetijdsbesteding, maatschappelijke participatie. — 1984. — 104p

NETHERLANDS
Budgetonderzoek 1980. — s-Gravenhage : Staatsuitgeverij, 1985. — 172p. — *Title on back cover: Budgetsurvey 1980*

NETHERLANDS. Centraal Bureau voor de Statistiek
Werknemersbudgetonderzoek, 1974-75. — s-Gravenhage : Staatsuitgeverij. — *Contents list and summary in English. — Title on back cover: Workers' budget survey 1974-75. Part 3. Family consumption by place of purchase*
deel 3: Gezinsverbruik naar aankooppplaats. — 1979. — 55p

NETHERLANDS. Centraal Bureau voor de Statistiek
Werknemersbudgetonderzoek, 1974-75. — s-Gravenhage : Staatsuitgeverij. — *Contents list and summary in English. — Title on back cover: Workers' budget survey 1974-75. Part 4. Food bought; quantities and prices*
deel 4: Gekochte voedingsmiddelen; hoeveelheid en prijs. — 1979. — 43p

COST AND STANDARD OF LIVING — Norway — Statistics

Levekårsundersøkelsen 1983 = Survey of level of living 1983. — Oslo : Statistisk Sentralbyrå, 1985. — 223p. — (Norges offisielle statistikk ; B511). — *In Norwegian and English*

COST AND STANDARD OF LIVING — Sri Lanka

DEATON, Angus
Three essays on a Sri Lanka household survey / Angus Deaton. — Washington, D.C., U.S.A. : World Bank, 1985 printing, c1981. — [iv],87p. — (LSMS working papers ; no.11). — *Bibliographical references: p85-87*

COST AND STANDARD OF LIVING — Thailand

GROOTAERT, Christiaan
The role of employment and earnings in analyzing levels of living / Christiaan Grootaert. — Washington D.C. : The World Bank, 1986. — xiv,278p. — (LSMS working papers ; no.27). — *Bibliographical references: p269-278*

COST CONTROL

ROBERTS, Stephen A.
Cost management for library and information services / Stephen A. Roberts. — London : Butterworths, 1985. — 181 p

COST CONTROL — trends — United States

GINZBERG, Eli
American medicine : the power shift / Eli Ginzberg. — Totowa, N.J. : Rowman & Allanheld, 1985. — xv, 207 p.. — *Includes index. — Bibliography: p. [194]-199*

COST EFFECTIVENESS

CAMPEN, James T
Benefit, cost, and beyond : the political economy of benefit-cost analysis / James T. Campen. — Cambridge, Mass. : Ballinger Pub. Co., 1986. — p. cm. — *Includes index. — Bibliography: p*

DUVIGNEAU, J. Christian
Guidelines for calculating financial amd economic rates of return for DFC projects / J. Christian Duvigneau and Ranga N. Prasad. — Washington, D.C. : The World Bank, 1984. — xii,149p. — (World Bank technical paper ; no.33) (Industry and finance series ; v.9). — *Bibliography: p148-149*

MERKHOFER, Miley W.
Decision science and social risk management : a comparative evaluation of cost-benefit analysis, decision analysis, and other formal decision-aiding approaches / Miley W. Merkhofer. — Dordrecht ; Boston : D. Reidel ; Norwell, MA : Sold and distributed in the U.S.A. and Canada by Kluwer Academic Publishers, 1986. — p. cm. — (Technology, risk, and society). — *Includes index. — Bibliography: p*

COSTA RICA — Census, 1984

Censo de poblacion 1984. — San José : Ministerio de Gobernacion y Policia, 1986. — 2v

COSTA RICA — Population

ROSERO, Luis
The determinants of fertility decline in Costa Rica, 1964—76 / Luis Rosero, Miguel Gómez, Virginia Rodríguez. — Voorburg : International Statistical Institute, [1984?]. — 14p. — *Translated from Determinantes de la fecundidad en Costa Rica: analisis longitudinal de tres encuestas*

COSTA RICA — Population — Psychological aspects

STYCOS, J. Mayone
Putting back the K and A in KAP : a study of the implications of knowledge and attitudes for fertility in Costa Rica / J. Mayone Stycos. — Voorburg : International Statistical Institute, 1984. — 45p. — (Scientific reports / World Fertility Survey ; no.48)

COSTA RICA — Population — Statistics

Censo de poblacion 1984. — San José : Ministerio de Gobernacion y Policia, 1986. — 2v

COSTA RICA. Dirección General de Estadística y Censos
Encuesta de hogares por muestreo : zonas urbanas de Costa Rica, julio de 1967 a junio de 1968. — [San José] : the Dirección, 1970. — 75p

COSTS, INDUSTRIAL — Great Britain — Mathematical models

KELLY, Christopher
Factor prices in the Treasury model / Christopher Kelly, David Owen. — London : HM Treasury, 1985. — 81p. — (Government Economic Service working paper ; no.83) (Treasury working paper ; no.37). — *Bibliographical references: p73-74*

COSTS, INDUSTRIAL — United States

LEONE, Robert A
Who profits : winners, losers, and government regulation / Robert A. Leone. — New York : Basic Books, 1986. — xiii, 248 p.. — *Includes index. — Bibliography: p. 231-237*

COSTUME — Social aspects

JOSEPH, Nathan
Uniforms and nonuniforms : communication through clothing / Nathan Joseph. — New York : Greenwood Press, 1986. — vi, 248 p.. — (Contributions in sociology ; no. 61). — *Includes index. — Bibliography: p. [221]-238*

COTTAGE INDUSTRIES — Cyprus — Statistics

CYPRUS. Department of Statistics and Research
Census of cottage industry 1982. — [Nicosia] : Department of Statistics and Research, [1983]. — 76p. — (Industrial statistics / Department of Statistics and Research. Series 8 (Cottage) ; Report no.3)

COTTAGE INDUSTRIES — Italy, Northern — History — 19th century

DEWERPE, Alain
L'industrie aux champs : essai sur la proto-industrialisation en Italie du Nord (1800-1880) / Alain Dewerpe. — [Rome] : Ecole Française de Rome, 1985. — xxxv,543p. — (Collection de l'École Française de Rome ; 85). — *Bibliographie: p483-530*

COTTON TRADE — Alabama — Mobile — History — 19th century

AMOS, Harriet E.
Cotton City : urban development in antebellum Mobile / Harriet E. Amos. — University, Ala. : University of Alabama Press, c1985. — xvi, 311 p.. — *Includes index. — Bibliography: p. 287-297*

COTTON TRADE — Central America

WILLIAMS, Robert G
Export agriculture and the crisis in Central America / by Robert G. Williams. — Chapel Hill : University of North Carolina Press, c1986. — xvi, 257p. — *Includes index. — Bibliography: p.[239]-248*

COTTON TRADE — European Economic Community countries

STIGUM, Marcia L
The impact of the European Economic Community on the French cotton and electrical engineering industries / Marcia Lee Stigum. — New York : Arno Press, 1981. — xi, 258 p.. — (Dissertations in European economic history). — *— : Originally presented as the author's thesis, Massachusetts Institute of Technology, 1961. — Bibliography: p. 250-258*

COTTON TRADE — France

STIGUM, Marcia L
The impact of the European Economic Community on the French cotton and electrical engineering industries / Marcia Lee Stigum. — New York : Arno Press, 1981. — xi, 258 p.. — (Dissertations in European economic history). — *— : Originally presented as the author's thesis, Massachusetts Institute of Technology, 1961. — Bibliography: p. 250-258*

COUNCIL FOR MUTUAL ECONOMIC ASSISTANCE

CRANE, Keith
The Soviet economic dilemma of eastern Europe / Keith Crane. — Santa Monica, CA : Rand, [1986]. — xiii, 70 p.. — *"A Project Air Force report prepared for the United States Air Force.". — "R-3368-AF.". — "May 1986.". — Bibliography: p. 65-70*

DEUTSCH, Robert
The food revolution in the Soviet Union and Eastern Europe / Robert Deutsch. — Boulder, Colo. ; London : Westview Press, 1986. — xxi, 256p. — (Westview special studies on the Soviet Union and Eastern Europe). — *Includes index. — Bibliography: p.149-241*

COUNCIL FOR NATIONAL ACADEMIC AWARDS

BOURNER, Tom
Entry qualifications and degree performance : the technical report of a research project on the relationship between entry qualifications and degree performance on CNAA first degree courses / Tom Bourner and Mahmoud Hamed. — London : CNAA, 1987. — 77p. — (CNAA development sevices publications ; 10). — *Bibliography: p68-69*

COUNCIL FOR NATIONAL PARKS

COUNCIL FOR NATIONAL PARKS
50 years for national parks. — London : Council for National Parks, 1986. — 32p

COUNCIL OF EUROPE. Parliamentary Assembly — Comparative studies

KREMAIER, Franz
Das Europäische Parlament der EG und die Parlamentarische Versammlung des Europarates : eine vergleichende Strukturanalyse zur Begrifflichkeit... / Franz Kremaier. — München : Florentz, 1985. — (Europarecht - Völkerrecht ; Bd.9). — *Bibliographical notes*

COUNCIL OF EUROPE. Symposium on Legal Data Processing in Europe (8th : 1985 : Luxembourg)

SYMPOSIUM ON LEGAL DATA PROCESSING IN EUROPE (8th : 1985 : Luxembourg)
Access to legal data bases in Europe : reports presented at the Symposium. — Strasbourg : Council of Europe, 1986. — 226p

COUNCIL OF MINISTERS OF THE EUROPEAN COMMUNITIES — Sources — Bibliography
WILLS, Grahame
Council of Ministers : a guide to sources / prepared by Grahame Wills. — [s.l.] : Association of EDC Librarians, [1984]. — 5p. — (European Communities information ; no.4)

COUNCIL OF THE EUROPEAN COMMUNITIES — History
BULMER, Simon
The European Council : decision-making in European politics / Simon Bulmer and Wolfgang Wessels. — Basingstoke : Macmillan, 1987. — xii,174p. — *Includes index*

COUNSELING
LEARY, Mark R
Social psychology and dysfunctional behavior : origins, diagnosis, and treatment / Mark R. Leary and Rowland S. Miller. — New York : Springer-Verlag, c1986. — xiii, 262 p.. — (Springer series in social psychology). — *Includes indexes. — Bibliography: p. [203]-244*

MAPLE, Frank F
Dynamic interviewing : an introduction to counseling / by Frank F. Maple. — Beverly Hills ; London : Sage Publications, c1985. — 174p. — (Sage Human services guides ; 41). — *Bibliography: p 173-174*

MURGATROYD, Stephen
Counselling and helping / Stephen Murgatroyd. — Leicester : British Psychological Society, 1985. — 165p. — (Psychology in action). — *Includes bibliographies and index*

COUNTERFACTUALS (LOGIC) — History — 18th century
WILSON, Fred
Laws and other worlds : a Humean account of laws and counterfactuals / Fred Wilson. — Dordrecht ; Lancaster : Reidel, c1986. — xv, 328 p.. — (The University of Western Ontario series in philosophy of science ; v. 31). — *Includes index. — Bibliography: p. 315-321*

COUNTERINSURGENCY
CABLE, Larry E.
Conflict of myths : the development of American counterinsurgency doctrine and the Vietnam War / Larry E. Cable. — New York : New York University Press, 1986. — p. cm. — *Includes index. — Bibliography: p*

COUNTERINSURGENCY — United States — History — 20th century — Bibliography
BEEDE, Benjamin R
Intervention and counterinsurgency : an annotated bibliography of the small wars of the United States, 1898-1984 / Benjamin R. Beede. — New York : Garland Pub., 1985. — xxxviii, 321 p.. — (Wars of the United States ; vol. 5) (Garland reference library of social science ; vol. 251). — *Includes indexes*

COUNTERREVOLUTIONS — Nicaragua
[Contra. English]. The Contras : interviews with anti-Sandinistas / [edited] Dieter Eich and Carlos Rincón. — San Francisco : Synthesis Publications, c1985. — iv, 193 p.. — *Translation of: La contra*

GROSSMAN, Karl
Nicaragua, America's new Vietnam? / text and photos by Karl Grossman. — Sag Harbor, N.Y. : Permanent Press, c1984. — 228 p.. — *Bibliography: p. 227-228*

COUNTERTRADE
ELDERKIN, Kenton W
Creative countertrade : a guide to doing business worldwide / Kenton E. Elderkin, Warren E. Norquist. — Cambridge, Mass. : Ballinger Pub. Co., c1987. — xv, 221 p.. — *Includes bibliographies and index*

COUNTERTRADE — Congresses
International countertrade / edited by Christopher M. Korth. — New York : Quorum Books, c1987. — p. cm. — *Results of a conference held at the College of Business, University of South Carolina, Spring, 1985 ; co-sponsored by the U.S. Dept. of Education. — Includes bibliographies and index*

COUNTRY HOMES — England — History — 19th century
GIROUARD, Mark
The Victorian country house / Mark Girouard. — Revised and enlarged ed. — New Haven ; London : Yale University Press, 1979. — x,467p. — *Facsims on lining papers. — Previous ed.: Oxford : Clarendon Press, 1971. — Includes index*

COUNTRY LIFE — England — History
NEWBY, Howard, 1947-
Country life : a social history of rural England / Howard Newby. — London : Weidenfeld and Nicolson, 1987. — 250p. — *Bibliography: p238-241*

COUNTY COURTS — Great Britain
The county court practice. — London : Butterworths, 1982-. — *Annual*

DEIGHAN, Maurice
County Court practice and procedure / by Maurice Deighan. — London : Fourmat, 1980. — xv, 125p. — (Lawyers' practice and procedure)

COUPS DE'ÉTAT — Spain
SANCHIS DE LOS SANTOS, Ramón de
Los golpes de Estado en España : de Espoz y Mina a Miláns del Bosch, pasando por Espartero, Prim y otros / Ramón de Sanchis de los Santos ; prologo de: Ramón Serrano Suñer. — Madrid : Vassallo de Mumbert, 1985. — 431p

COUPS D'ÉTAT
O'KANE, Rosemary H. T.
The likelihood of coups / Rosemary H.T. O'Kane. — Aldershot : Gower, 1987. — [169]p. — *Includes bibliography and index*

COUPS D'ÉTAT — History — 20th century
FERGUSON, Gregor
Coup d'etat : a practical manual / by Gregor Ferguson. — London : Arms and Armour, 1987. — [224]p. — *Includes bibliography and index*

COUPS D'ÉTAT — Developing countries
DAVID, Steven R
Third World coups d'état and international security / Steven R. David. — Baltimore : Johns Hopkins University Press, c1987. — p. cm. — *Includes index. — Bibliography: p*

COUPS D'ÉTAT — Latin America — History — 20th century
Armies and politics in Latin America / edited by Abraham F. Lowenthal and J. Samuel Fitch. — Rev. ed. — New York : Holmes & Meier Publishers, 1986. — p. cm. — *Includes index. — Bibliography: p*

COURT ADMINISTRATION — England
JUSTICE
The administration of the courts : JUSTICE / a report by John Macdonald, Chairman of committee. — London : JUSTICE, 1986. — 46p

COURT OF JUSTICE OF THE EUROPEAN COMMUNITIES
Article 177 EEC : experiences and problems / edited by Henry G. Schermers...[et al.]. — Amsterdam : North-Holland, 1987. — xxxiv,441p. — (Asser Institute Colloquium on European Law ; 15). — *Proceedings of an international conference "Experiences and Problems in Applying the Preliminary Proceedings of Article 177 EEC", organized by the T.M.C. Asser Institute, the Hague, 5 and 6 September 1985*

BUFFET-TCHAKALOFF, Marie France
La France devant la Cour de Justice des Communautes européennes / Marie France Buffet-Tchakaloff ; préface de Louis Dubois. — Paris : Economica ; Aix-en-Provence : Presses universitaires d'Aix-Marseille, 1985. — 404p. — (Collection droit public positif). — *Bibliography: p[379]-394*

COURT OF JUSTICE OF THE EUROPEAN COMMUNITIES
Digest of case-law relating to the European Communities: A series: judgements of the Courts of Justice of the European Communities excluding cases connected with the European civil service and cases on the Convention of 27 September 1968 on Jurisdiction and the Enforcement of Judgements in Civil and Commercial Matters. — Luxembourg : Office for Official Publications of the European Communities, 1983-

Information on the Court of Justice of the European Communities. — Luxembourg : Information Office, Court of Justice of the European Communities, 1977-1982. — *Quarterly*

RASMUSSEN, Hjalte
On law and policy in the European Court of Justice : a comparative study in judicial policymaking / by Hjalte Rasmussen. — Dordrecht ; Boston : M. Nijhoff ; Hingham, MA, USA : Distributors, for the U.S. and Canada, Kluwer Academic Publishers, 1986. — xxv, 555 p.. — *Summary in Danish. — Thesis (doctoral)--University of Copenhagen, 1985. — Includes bibliographies and indexes*

Synopsis of case-law: the EEC convention of 27 September 1968 on jurisdiction and the enforcement of judgements in civil and commercial matters. — Luxembourg : Documentation Branch, Court of Justice, 1977. — *Annual. — Continued by: Digest of case-law relating to the European Communities: Series D*

VOLCANSEK, Mary L.
Judicial politics in Europe : an impact analysis / Mary L. Volcansek. — New York : P. Lang, c1986. — xi, 325 p.. — (American university studies. Series X, Political science ; vol. 7). — *Includes index. — Bibliography: p. [295]-313*

COURT OF JUSTICE OF THE EUROPEAN COMMUNITIES — Sources — Bibliography
SAINSBURY, Ian
The Court of Justice : a guide to sources / prepared by Ian Sainsbury. — [s.l.] : Association of EDC Librarians, [1985]. — 5p. — (European Communities information ; no.3)

COURT RECORDS — England — History
GUY, J. A.
The Court of Star Chamber and its records to the reign of Elizabeth I / by J. A. Guy. — London : H.M.S.O., 1985. — 112 p. — (Public Record Office handbooks ; no. 21)

COURT RULES — Australia
SMITH, Matthew
ABC guide to the Federal Court of Australia / by Matthew Smith. — [Sydney] : The Law Book Company Limited, 1986. — xvii,230p

COURTS
ANTIEAU, Chester James
Adjudicating constitutional issues / Chester James Antieau. — London : Oceana Publications, 1985. — xxviii,441p

DAMAŠKA, Mirjan R.
The faces of justice and state authority : a comparative approach to the legal process / Mirjan R. Damaška. — New Haven : Yale University Press, c1986. — xi, 247 p.. — *Includes bibliographical references and index*

COURTS — England
JUSTICE
The administration of the courts : JUSTICE / a report by John Macdonald, Chairman of committee. — London : JUSTICE, 1986. — 46p

COURTS — European Economic Community Countries

Article 177 EEC : experiences and problems / edited by Henry G. Schermers...[et al.]. — Amsterdam : North-Holland, 1987. — xxxiv,441p. — (Asser Institute Colloquium on European Law ; 15). — *Proceedings of an international conference "Experiences and Problems in Applying the Preliminary Proceedings of Article 177 EEC", organized by the T.M.C. Asser Institute, the Hague, 5 and 6 September 1985*

COURTS — European Economic Community countries

VOLCANSEK, Mary L.
Judicial politics in Europe : an impact analysis / Mary L. Volcansek. — New York : P. Lang, c1986. — xi, 325 p.. — (American university studies. Series X, Political science ; vol. 7). — *Includes index. — Bibliography: p. [295]-313*

COURTS — France

ABRAHAM, Henry Julian
The judicial process : an introductory analysis of the courts of the United States, England, and France / Henry J. Abraham. — 5th ed. — New York : Oxford University Press, 1985. — p. cm. — *Includes indexes. — Bibliography: p*

COURTS — Great Britain

ABRAHAM, Henry Julian
The judicial process : an introductory analysis of the courts of the United States, England, and France / Henry J. Abraham. — 5th ed. — New York : Oxford University Press, 1985. — p. cm. — *Includes indexes. — Bibliography: p*

COURTS — Great Britain — Directories

Hazell's guide to the judiciary and the courts. With, The Holborn Law Society's list of barristers by chambers. — 1986. — Henley-on-Thames : Hazell & Co., 1986. — 314p

COURTS — Northern Ireland — History

GREER, S. C.
Abolishing the Diplock courts : the case for restoring jury trial to scheduled offences in Northern Ireland / S.C. Greer, A. White. — London : Cobden Trust, c1986. — x,133p. — *Includes index*

COURTS — United States

ABRAHAM, Henry Julian
The judicial process : an introductory analysis of the courts of the United States, England, and France / Henry J. Abraham. — 5th ed. — New York : Oxford University Press, 1985. — p. cm. — *Includes indexes. — Bibliography: p*

CARP, Robert A.
The federal courts / Robert A. Carp, Ronald Stidham. — Washington, D.C. : CQ Press, c1985. — xi, 258 p.. — *Includes index. — Bibliography: p. 239-246*

DELORIA, Vine
American Indians, American justice / by Vine Deloria, Jr. and Clifford M. Lytle. — 1st ed. — Austin : University of Texas Press, 1983. — xiii, 262 p.. — *Includes indexes. — Bibliography: p. [247]-249*

HARRINGTON, Christine B
Shadow justice : the ideology and institutionalization of alternatives to court / Christine B. Harrington. — Westport, Conn. : Greenwood Press, c1985. — p. cm. — (Contributions in political science ; no. 133). — *Includes index. — Bibliography: p*

COURTS — United States — History

HENDERSON, Dwight F.
Congress, courts, and criminals : the development of federal criminal law, 1801-1829 / Dwight F. Henderson. — Westport, Conn. : Greenwood Press, c1985. — x, 257 p.. — (Contributions in American history ; no. 113). — *Includes index. — Bibliography: p. [221]-233*

COURTS — Zambia

Law in Zambia / Muna Ndulo, ed. — Nairobi, Kenya : East African Pub. House, 1984. — 308 p.. — *Includes bibliographies*

COURTS AND COURIERS

The Courts of Europe : politics, patronage, and royalty, 1400-1800 / [edited by A.G. Dickens ; with texts by A.G. Dickens ... et al.]. — New York : Greenwich House : Distributed by Crown Publishers, 1984. — p. cm. — *Includes index. — Bibliography: p*

COURTS AND COURTIERS — History

STRONG, Roy
Art and power : Renaissance festivals 1450-1650 / Roy Strong. — Woodbridge : Boydell, 1984. — xiii,227p,[ca.100]p of plates. — *Revision of: Splendour at court. London : Weidenfeld and Nicolson, 1973. — Includes index*

COURTS, ISLAMIC — Afghanistan

KAMALI, Mohammad Hashim
Law in Afghanistan : a study of the Constitutions, matrimonial law and judiciary / by Mohammad Hashim Kamali. — Leiden : E. J. Brill, 1985. — viii,265p. — (Social, economic and political studies of the Middle East ; Vol.36). — *Bibliography: p[254]-259*

COURTS, JEWISH

QUINT, Emanuel B.
Jewish jurisprudence : its sources and modern applications / Emanuel B. Quint and Neil S. Hecht. — Chur : Harwood Academic Publishers
Vol.2. — 1986. — xvii,237p

COURTS-MARTIAL AND COURTS OF INQUIRY — Great Britain — History — 20th century

BABINGTON, Anthony
For the sake of example : capital courts martial, 1914-1920 / Anthony Babington ; with a postscript by...Frank Richardson. — London : Paladin Grafton Books, 1985. — x,309p. — *Bibliography: p301-304*

COURTSHIP

PERPER, Timothy
Sex signals : the biology of love / Timothy Perper. — Philadelphia : ISI Press, c1985. — xvi, 323 p.. — *Includes index. — Bibliography: p. 296-314*

COURTSHIP — Great Britain — History

GILLIS, John R.
For better, for worse : British marriages, 1600 to the present / John R. Gillis. — New York ; Oxford : Oxford University Press, 1985. — 417 p.

COVENTRY (WEST MIDLANDS, ENGLAND) — History

The Early records of medieval Coventry / edited and introduced by Peter R. Coss. — London : Published for the British Academy by Oxford University Press, c1986. — xlii,450p,[4]p of plates. — (Records of social and economic history. New series ; 11). — *Includes Latin text. — Includes index. — Partial contents: The Hundred Rolls of 1280 / edited and introduced by Trevor John*

Life and labour in a twentieth century city : the experience of Coventry / edited by Bill Lancaster and Tony Mason. — Coventry : Cryfield Press, Centre for the Study of Social History, University of Warwick, [1986?]. — 372p

COVENTRY (WEST MIDLANDS, ENGLAND) — Population — Statistics

MCCHESNEY, N. P.
A statistical digest of ethnic minority population / N. P. McChesney, M. Z. Hassan [and] F. Prevc. — Coventry : Department of Economic Development and Planning. Forward Planning Division, 1986. — 50p. — (Coventry-trends)

COWAN, JAMES

HARNACK, Curtis
Gentlemen on the prairie / Curtis Harnack. — Ames : Iowa State University Press, c1985. — viii, 254 p.. — *Includes index. — Bibliography: p. 239-248*

COWAN, WALTER

HARNACK, Curtis
Gentlemen on the prairie / Curtis Harnack. — Ames : Iowa State University Press, c1985. — viii, 254 p.. — *Includes index. — Bibliography: p. 239-248*

COWLES COMMISSION FOR RESEARCH IN ECONOMICS

HILDRETH, Clifford
The Cowles Commission in Chicago, 1939-1955 / Clifford Hildreth. — Berlin ; New York : Springer-Verlag, c1986. — 176 p.. — (Lecture notes in economics and mathematical systems ; 271). — *Includes index. — Bibliography: p. [138]-163*

COX, JAMES M

CEBULA, James E.
James M. Cox : journalist and politician / James E. Cebula. — New York : Garland, 1985. — 181 p.. — (Modern American history) . — *Includes index. — Bibliography: p. 171-173*

COX, OLIVER C

Race, class, and the world system : the sociology of Oliver C. Cox / Herbert M. Hunter and Sameer Y. Abraham, eds. — New York : Monthly Review Press, 1987. — p. cm. — *Bibliography: p*

COX, REAVIS

Marketing management technology as a social process / edited by George Fisk. — New York : Praeger, 1986. — xvi, 301 p.. — *"Significant issues ... analyzed by purpose of publications of Reavis Cox compared to papers in this book"--P. xii. — Includes bibliographies and index*

CREATIVE ABILITY

SCHLESINGER, Arthur M. (Arthur Meier), 1917-
Creativity in statecraft / by Arthur Schlesinger, Jr. — Washington : Library of Congress, 1983. — iii,34p. — (Occasional papers of the Council of Scholars ; no. 1). — *Includes bibliographical references*

CREATIVE ABILITY IN SCIENCE

GRUBER, Howard E
Darwin on man : a psychological study of scientific creativity / Howard E. Gruber ; foreword to the 1st ed. by Jean Piaget. — 2d ed. — Chicago : University of Chicago Press, 1981. — xxvii, 310 p.. — *First ed., published in 1974, entered under title: Darwin on man. — Includes bibliographical references and index*

The Nature of scientific discovery : a symposium commemorating the 500th anniversary of the birth of Nicolaus Copernicus / Edited by Owen Gingerich. — [1st ed.]. — Washington : Smithsonian Institution Press ; [distributed by G. Braziller, New York, 1975]. — 616 p. — (Smithsonian international symposia series ; 5). — *"The fifth international symposium of the Smithsonian Institution organized jointly with the National Academy of Sciences in cooperation with the Copernicus Society of America.". — Bibliography: p. 23-26*

CREDIT

CRAWFORD, Vincent P.
International lending, long-term credit relationships, and dynamic contract theory / Vincent P. Crawford. — Princeton, N.J. : International Finance Section, Dept. of Economics, Princeton University, 1987. — p. cm. — (Princeton studies in international finance ; no. 59 (March 1987)). — *Bibliography: p*

CREDIT — Dictionaries — Russian

Finansovo-kreditnyi slovar' : v 3-kh t. / glavnyi redaktor V. F. Garbuzov. — Moskva : Finansy i statistika
T.2: K-P. — 1986. — 511p

CREDIT — Management
BATHORY, Alexander
The analysis of credit : foundations and development of corporate credit assessment / Alexander Bathory. — London : McGraw-Hill, c1987. — xiii,385p. — Bibliography: p357-358. — Includes index

CREDIT — Brazil
Brazil, financial systems review. — Washington, D.C., U.S.A. : World Bank, c1984. — xcix,150p. — (A World Bank Country study). — Summaries in French, Portuguese, and Spanish. — Bibliography: p144-149

CREDIT — Communist countries
MOLCHANOVA, O. A.
Kreditnyi mekhanizm sotsialisticheskogo obshchestva : (politekonomicheskii aspekt) / O. A. Molchanova. — Leningrad : Izd-vo Leningradskogo universiteta, 1986. — 134p

CREDIT — Great Britain — Statistics
Credit business of finance houses and the specialist consumer credit grantors. — London : HMSO, 1979-. — (Business monitor. SDM ; 6). — Monthly. — Continues: Instalment credit business of finance houses

Instalment credit business of finance houses. — London : HMSO, 1974-78. — (Business monitor. SD ; 6) (Business monitor. SDM ; 6). — Monthly. — Continued by: Credit business of finance houses and other specialist consumer credit grantors

CREDIT — Peru
PERU. Sub-Dirección de Asistencia Crediticia
Manual de crédito. — Lima : Comité Nacional de Crédito, Programa de Crédito de Promoción Comunal Agrario, Oficina Nacional de Desarrollo Comunal, Proyecto de Desarrollo e Integración de la Población Campesina, 1971. — 38leaves

CREDIT — Soviet Union — Bibliography
DREMINA, Z. E.
Finansy, den'gi i kredit SSSR : bibliograficheskii ukazatel' 1976-1985 gg. / [sostaviteli: Z. E. Dremina, A. V. Golousenko, G. M. Klimova; otv. redaktor V. S. Kulikov]. — Moskva : Finansy i statistika, 1986. — 287p

CREDIT — Uruguay
GONZÁLEZ GARCÍA, José I.
La segmentación del mercado del credito y sus impactos sobre la distribución del ingreso / José I. González. — Montevideo : Centro Interdisciplinario de Estudios sobre el Desarollo Uruguay, 1984. — 123p. — (Serie Investigaciones / Centro Interdisciplinario de Estudios sobre el Desarollo Uruguay ; no.18). — Bibliography: p89-92

CREDIT CONTROL — Mathematical models
CLEMENZ, Gerhard
Credit markets with asymmetric information / Gerhard Clemenz. — Berlin ; New York : Springer-Verlag, c1986. — viii, 212 p.. — (Lecture notes in economics and mathematical systems ; 272). — Bibliography: p. [204]-212

CREDIT CONTROL — Developing countries
GYLFASON, Thorvaldur
Credit policy and economic activity in developing countries with IMF stabilization programs / Thorvaldur Gylfason. — Princeton, N.J. : International Finance Section, Dept. of Economics, Princeton University, 1987. — p. cm. — (Princeton studies in international finance ; no. 60 (August 1987)). — Bibliography: p

CREDIT CONTROL — United States
BOSWORTH, Barry
The economics of federal credit programs / Barry P. Bosworth, Andrew S. Carron, Elisabeth H. Rhyne. — Washington, D.C. : Brookings Institution, c1987. — xii, 214 p. — Includes bibliographical references and index

CREOLE DIALECTS
MÜHLHÄUSLER, Peter
Pidgin & creole linguistics / Peter Mühlhäusler. — Oxford : Blackwell, 1986. — 320p. — (Language in society ; 11). — Bibliography: p297-317. — Includes index

CRICHEL DOWN (WIMBORNE, DORSET) — History
NICOLSON, I. F.
The mystery of Crichel Down / I.F. Nicolson. — Oxford : Clarendon, 1986. — [344]p. — Includes bibliography and index

CRIME
Ecologic-biochemical approaches to treatment of delinquents and criminals / edited by Leonard J. Hippchen. — New York : Van Nostrand Reinhold Co., c1978. — xx,396p. — Bibliography: p389-392. — Bibliography: p. 389-392

CRIME AND AGE — Case studies
SHOVER, Neal
Aging criminals / by Neal Shover. — Beverly Hills [Calif.] : Sage Publications, c1985. — p. cm. — (Sociological observations ; v. 17). — Includes index. — Bibliography: p

CRIME AND CRIMINALS
KAISER, Günther
Kriminologie : eine Einführung in die Grundlagen / Günther Kaiser. — 7. Auflage. — Heidelberg : C. F. Müller Juristischer Verlag, c1985. — xviii,393p. — First published 1971

MANNHEIM, Hermann
Comparative criminology : a text book / Hermann Mannheim. — London : Routledge and Kegan Paul, 1965. — 2v

MORRIS, Allison
Women, crime and criminal justice / Allison Morris. — Oxford : Basil Blackwell, 1987. — [256]p. — Includes bibliography and index

TRASLER, Gordon
The explanation of criminality. — Routledge & K.Paul, 1962. — 134p.,23cm. — (International library of sociology and social reconstruction)

VETTER, Harold J.
Criminology and crime : an introduction / Harold J. Vetter, Ira J. Silverman. — New York, NY : Harper & Row, c1986. — p. cm. — Includes bibliographies and index

WILSON, James Q
Crime and human nature / James Q. Wilson and Richard J. Herrnstein. — New York : Simon and Schuster, c1985. — p. cm. — Includes index. — Bibliography: p

CRIME AND CRIMINALS — Addresses, essays, lectures
Ecologic-biochemical approaches to treatment of delinquents and criminals / edited by Leonard J. Hippchen. — New York : Van Nostrand Reinhold Co., c1978. — xx,396p. — Bibliography: p389-392. — Bibliography: p. 389-392

CRIME AND CRIMINALS — Congresses
Critique and explanation : essays in honor of Gwynne Nettler / edited by Timothy F. Hartnagel and Robert A. Silverman. — New Brunswick, U.S.A. : Transaction Books, c1986. — vii, 215 p.. — Bibliography: p. 187-214

INTERNATIONAL CONFERENCE ON PRISON ABOLITION (2nd : 1985 : Amsterdam)
Abolitionism : towards a non-repressive approach to crime : proceedings of the Second International Conference on Prison Abolition, Amsterdam, 1985 / edited by Herman Bianchi, René van Swaaningen. — Amsterdam : Free University Press, 1986. — 247p

The reasoning criminal : rational choice perspectives on offending / edited by Derek B. Cornish, Ronald V. Clarke. — New York : Springer-Verlag, c1986. — p. cm. — (Research in criminology). — Includes index. — Bibliography: p

CRIME AND CRIMINALS — Developing countries
HUGGINS, Martha Knisely
From slavery to vagrancy in Brazil : crime and social control in the Third World / Martha Knisely Huggins. — New Brunswick, N.J. : Rutgers University Press, c1984. — xix, 183p. — (Crime, law, and deviance series). — Includes index. — Bibliography: p 159-167

CRIME AND CRIMINALS — Public opinion
CRIMINOLOGICAL RESEARCH CONFERENCE (13th : 1978)
Public opinion on crime and criminal justice : reports presented to the Thirteenth Criminological Research Conference (1978). — Strasbourg : Council of Europe, 1979. — 200p. — (Collected studies in criminological research ; v.17). — Includes bibliographies

Obshchestvennoe mnenie i prestuplenie / G. Kh. Efremova...[et al.]. — Tbilisi : Metsniereba, 1984. — 298p

CRIME AND CRIMINALS — Research
Crime and justice: an annual review of research. — Chicago : University of Chicago, 1979-. — Annual

CRIME AND CRIMINALS — Social aspects
BOX, Steven
Recession, crime and punishment / Steven Box. — London : Macmillan Education, 1987. — [240]p. — Includes index

Crime and justice : a review of research / edited by Michael Tonry and Norval Morris with the support of the National Institute of Justice. — Chicago ; London : The University of Chicago Press
Vol.8: Communities and crime / edited by Albert J. Reiss and Michael Tonry. — 1986. — viii,421p

CRIME AND CRIMINALS — Social aspects — Great Britain
SMITH, Susan J.
Crime, space and society / Susan J. Smith. — Cambridge : Cambridge University Press, 1986. — xii,228p. — (Cambridge human geography). — Bibliography: p197-221. — Includes index

CRIME AND CRIMINALS — Sociological aspects
ANDENÆS, Johs.
Kriminalitet og samfunn : artikler og foredrag / Johs. Andenæs, Anders Bratholm og Nils Christie. — 5. oppl.. — Oslo : Pax, 1978. — 187p. — First published 1966

CRIME AND CRIMINALS — Africa, Southern
Crime and power in South Africa : Critical studies in criminology / edited by Dennis Davis and Mana Slabbert. — Cape Town : David Philip ; London : Distributed by Global Book Resources, 1985. — 138p.. — Includes index

CRIME AND CRIMINALS — Australia
HALL, Richard
Disorganized crime / Richard Hall. — St. Lucia ; New York : University of Queensland Press, 1986. — 280 p., [7] p. of plates. — Includes index. — Bibliography: p. [273]-276

CRIME AND CRIMINALS — Brazil — Pernambuco — History — 19th century
HUGGINS, Martha Knisely
From slavery to vagrancy in Brazil : crime and social control in the Third World / Martha Knisely Huggins. — New Brunswick, N.J. : Rutgers University Press, c1984. — xix, 183p. — (Crime, law, and deviance series). — Includes index. — Bibliography: p 159-167

CRIME AND CRIMINALS — Canada
Criminology : a Canadian perspective / Rick Linden [general editor]. — Toronto : Holt, Rinehart and Winston of Canada, 1987. — 368p. — Bibliography: p[337]-357

CRIME AND CRIMINALS — Canada
continuation

MCKECHNIE, Gail
Native North Americans : crime, conflict and criminal justice : a research bibliography / prepared by Gail McKechnie. — 3rd ed. — [Burnaby] : Northern Conference Resource Centre, 1986. — 156p (loose-leaf)

SILVERMAN, Robert A.
Crime in Canadian society / Robert A. Silverman [and] James J. Teevan. — 3rd ed. — xii,340p. — *Bibliography: p303-340*

CRIME AND CRIMINALS — Canada — History

FRIEDLAND, Martin L.
The case of Valentine Shortis : a true story of crime and politics in Canada / Martin L. Friedland. — Toronto : University of Toronto Press, 1986. — xi,324p

CRIME AND CRIMINALS — Council of Europe countries — Congresses

COUNCIL OF EUROPE. Criminological Colloquium (5th : 1981)
Trends in crime : comparative studies and technical problems : reports presented to the fifth Criminological Colloquium. — Strasbourg : Council of Europe, 1983. — 119p. — (Collected studies in criminological research ; v.20) (Legal affairs). — *On cover: European Committee on Crime Problems*

CRIME AND CRIMINALS — Council of Europe countries — History — Congresses

COUNCIL OF EUROPE. Criminological Colloquium (6th : 1983)
Historical research on crime and criminal justice : reports presented to the sixth Criminological Colloquium (1983). — Strasbourg : Council of Europe, 1985. — 167p. — (Collected studies in criminological research ; v.22). — *At head of cover: Council of Europe, Legal Affairs. — Also on cover: European Committee on Crime Problems*

CRIME AND CRIMINALS — Council of Europe countries — Public opinion

CRIMINOLOGICAL RESEARCH CONFERENCE (13th : 1978)
Public opinion on crime and criminal justice : reports presented to the Thirteenth Criminological Research Conference (1978). — Strasbourg : Council of Europe, 1979. — 200p. — (Collected studies in criminological research ; v.17). — *Includes bibliographies*

CRIME AND CRIMINALS — Cyrprus — Statistics

Criminal statistics / Department of Statistics and Research, Cyprus. — Nicosia : Department of Statistics and Research, 1984-. — *Annual*

CRIME AND CRIMINALS — England — London

DEUTSCH, Francis
Street crime in London 1981 / Francis Deutsch. — London : Commission for Racial Equality, 1982. — 12p

GREAT BRITAIN. Department of Transport
Crime on the London Underground / report of a study by the Department of Transport in conjunction with London Underground ... [et al.]. — London : H.M.S.O., 1986. — 118p

CRIME AND CRIMINALS — England — London — History

MCMULLAN, John L.
The canting crew : London's criminal underworld, 1550-1700 / John L. McMullan. — New Brunswick, N.J. : Rutgers University Press, c1984. — ix, 226 p.. — (Crime, law, and deviance series). — *Includes index. — Bibliography: p. 197-213*

CRIME AND CRIMINALS — France

DESDEVISES, Marie-Clet
La delinquance etrangere (analyse statistique) / Marie-Clet Desdevises. — Grenoble : Université des Sciences Sociales de Grenoble. Service de Reproduction des Theses, 1968. — 51p

CRIME AND CRIMINALS — France — Statistics

Aspects de la criminalité en France / Direction Generale de la Police Nationale [et] Direction Centrale de la Police Judiciaire. — Paris : Documentation Française, 1982-. — *Annual*

CRIME AND CRIMINALS — Great Britain

BOTTOMLEY, A. Keith
Crime and punishment : interpreting the data / A. Keith Bottomley, Ken Pease. — Milton Keynes : Open University Press, 1986. — xviii,185p. — *Bibliography: p171-180. — Includes index*

CRIME AND CRIMINALS — India — Assam

Crime perspective in north-east India / edited by B. Datta Ray, D. N. Majumdar, D. Doley. — New Delhi : Omsons Publications, 1986. — vi,111p. — *Bibliography: p[105]-108*

CRIME AND CRIMINALS — India — Meghalaya

Crime perspective in north-east India / edited by B. Datta Ray, D. N. Majumdar, D. Doley. — New Delhi : Omsons Publications, 1986. — vi,111p. — *Bibliography: p[105]-108*

CRIME AND CRIMINALS — Nepal

VAIDYA, Tulasi Ram
Crime and punishment in Nepal : a historical perspective / Tulasi Ram Vaidya, Tri Ratna Manandhar. — Kathmandu : Bin Vaidya and Purna Devi Manandhar, 1985. — 302p. — *Bibliography: p295-300*

CRIME AND CRIMINALS — Netherlands

Democratie en geweld : probleemanalyse naar aanleiding van de gebeurtenissen in Amsterdam op 30 april 1980. — 's-Gravenhage : Staatsuitgeverij, 1980. — 32 p. — (Rapporten aan de regering ; 20). — *Prepared by the Wetenschappelijke Raad voor het Regeringsbeleid. — Includes bibliographical references*

CRIME AND CRIMINALS — Netherlands — Citizen participation

STEINMETZ, C. H. D.
Bystanders of crime : some results from a national survey / Carl H. D. Steinmetz. — The Hague : Research and Documentation Centre, Ministry of Justice, 1986. — p.441-460. — ([Reports, papers, articles] ; 92). — *Reprinted from: Victimology: an international journal, vol.10,1985. — Bibliographical references: p459-460*

CRIME AND CRIMINALS — Netherlands — Public opinion

DIJK, J. J. M. van
What we say - what we do / Jan J. M. van Dijk, Nicolette Neijenhuis. — The Hague : Research and Documentaton Centre, Ministry of Justice, 1985. — [19]p. — ([Reports, papers, articles] ; 86). — *Bibliography: p[19]. — "A study of the correspondence between verbal attitudes and actual behaviour in anxiety feelings as regards criminality"*.

CRIME AND CRIMINALS — Norway

ANDENÆS, Johs.
Kriminalitet og samfunn : artikler og foredrag / Johs. Andenæs, Anders Bratholm og Nils Christie. — 5. oppl.. — Oslo : Pax, 1978. — 187p. — *First published 1966*

CRIME AND CRIMINALS — Prussia — History

BLASIUS, Dirk
Bürgerliche Gesellschaft und Kriminalität : zur Sozialgeschichte Preussens im Vormärz / Dirk Blasius. — Göttingen : Vandenhoeck und Ruprecht, 1976. — 203 p. — (Kritische Studien zur Geschichtswissenschaft ; Bd. 22). — *Includes index. Habilitationsschrift--Düsseldorf. — Bibliography: p. 186-198*

CRIME AND CRIMINALS — Soviet Union — Case studies

ROSNER, Lydia S
The Soviet way of crime : beating the system in the Soviet Union and the U.S.A. / Lydia S. Rosner. — South Hadley, Mass. : Bergin & Garvey Publishers, 1986. — xvii, 140 p.. — *Includes bibliographies and index*

CRIME AND CRIMINALS — Soviet Union — Public opinion

Obshchestvennoe mnenie i prestuplenie / G. Kh. Efremova...[et al.]. — Tbilisi : Metsniereba, 1984. — 298p

CRIME AND CRIMINALS — United States

CURRIE, Elliott
Confronting crime : an American challenge / Elliott Currie. — 1st ed. — New York : Pantheon Books, c1985. — viii, 326 p.. — *Includes index. — Bibliography: p. 279-316*

FARRINGTON, David P
Understanding and controlling crime : toward a new research strategy / David P. Farrington, Lloyd E. Ohlin, James Q. Wilson. — New York : Springer-Verlag, c1986. — p. cm. — (Research in criminology). — *Includes index. — Bibliography: p*

GOLDSTEIN, Jeffrey H
Aggression and crimes of violence / Jeffrey H. Goldstein. — 2nd ed. — New York : Oxford University Press, 1986. — ix, 230p. — *Includes index. — Bibliography: p.[189]-215*

MCKECHNIE, Gail
Native North Americans : crime, conflict and criminal justice : a research bibliography / prepared by Gail McKechnie. — 3rd ed. — [Burnaby] : Northern Conference Resource Centre, 1986. — 156p (loose-leaf)

The Social ecology of crime / edited by James M. Byrne and Robert J. Sampson. — New York : Springer-Verlag, c1986. — p. cm. — (Research in criminology). — *Includes index. — Bibliography: p*

THOMAS, Charles Wellington
Corrections in America : problems of the past and the present / Charles W. Thomas. — Newbury Park, Ca. : Sage Publications, 1987. — 159p. — (Law and criminal justice series ; v.7). — *Bibliography: p148-154*

VETTER, Harold J.
Criminology and crime : an introduction / Harold J. Vetter, Ira J. Silverman. — New York, NY : Harper & Row, c1986. — p. cm. — *Includes bibliographies and index*

WRIGHT, James D
Armed and considered dangerous : a survey of felons and their firearms / James D. Wright, Peter H. Rossi. — New York : Aldine de Gruyter, c1986. — xvi, 247 p.. — (Social institutions and social change). — *Includes index. — Bibliography: p. 239-242*

WRIGHT, Kevin N
The great American crime myth / Kevin N. Wright. — Westport, Conn. ; London : Greenwood Press, 1985. — x, 227p. — (Contributions in criminology and penology ; no. 9). — *Includes index. — Bibliography: p [217]-220*

CRIME AND CRIMINALS — United States — Bibliography

Crime and punishment in America : a historical bibliography / [this bibliography was conceived and compiled from the periodicals database of the American Bibliographical Center by editors at ABC-Clio Information Services] ; [Lance Klass and Susan Kinnell, project coordinators ...]. — Santa Barbara, Calif. ; Oxford : The Information Service, c1984. — xii,346p. — (ABC-Clio research guides). — *Includes index*

CRIME AND CRIMINALS — United States — Case studies
MERRY, Sally Engle
Urban danger : life in a neighborhood of strangers / Sally Engle Merry. — Philadelphia : Temple University Press, 1981. — x, 278 p.. — Includes index. — Bibliography: p. [259]-272

CRIME AND CRIMINALS — United States — Congresses
Values in conflict : Blacks and the American ambivalence toward violence / edited by Charles A. Frye. — Washington, D.C. : University Press of America, c1980. — iii, 169 p.. — Includes bibliographies and index

CRIME AND CRIMINALS — United States — History — 19th century
HARTSFIELD, Larry K
The American response to professional crime, 1870-1917 / Larry K. Hartsfield. — Westport, Conn. ; London : Greenwood Press, c1985. — x, 226p. — (Contributions in criminology and penology ; no. 8). — Includes index. — Bibliography: p.[209]-215p

CRIME AND CRIMINALS — United States — History — 20th century
HARTSFIELD, Larry K
The American response to professional crime, 1870-1917 / Larry K. Hartsfield. — Westport, Conn. ; London : Greenwood Press, c1985. — x, 226p. — (Contributions in criminology and penology ; no. 8). — Includes index. — Bibliography: p.[209]-215p

CRIME AND CRIMINALS — United States — Public opinion
LEWIS, Dan A
Fear of crime : incivility and the production of a social problem / Dan A. Lewis and Greta Salem. — New Brunswick, U.S.A. : Transaction Books, c1986. — p. cm. — Includes index. — Bibliography: p

CRIME AND CRIMINALS — United States — Public opinion — History
HARTSFIELD, Larry K
The American response to professional crime, 1870-1917 / Larry K. Hartsfield. — Westport, Conn. ; London : Greenwood Press, c1985. — x, 226p. — (Contributions in criminology and penology ; no. 8). — Includes index. — Bibliography: p.[209]-215p

CRIME AND CRIMINALS — United States — Research
FARRINGTON, David P
Understanding and controlling crime : toward a new research strategy / David P. Farrington, Lloyd E. Ohlin, James Q. Wilson. — New York : Springer-Verlag, c1986. — p. cm. — (Research in criminology). — Includes index. — Bibliography: p

CRIME AND THE PRESS — United States
LOFTON, John
Justice and the press. — Boston : Beacon Press, [1966]. — xiv, 462 p. — Bibliography: p. [433]-447

CRIME IN TELEVISION
CARLSON, James M
Prime time law enforcement : crime show viewing and attitudes toward the criminal justice system / by James M. Carlson. — New York : Praeger, 1985. — p. cm. — Includes index. — Bibliography: p

CRIME LABORATORIES — England
RAMSAY, Malcolm
The effectiveness of the Forensic Science Service / by Malcolm Ramsay. — London : H.M.S.O., 1987. — v,93p. — (Home Office research study ; 92). — A Home Office Research and Planning Unit report

CRIME PREVENTION — Congresses
Situational crime prevention : from theory into practice / edited by Kevin Heal and Gloria Laycock. — London : H.M.S.O., 1986. — vii,159p. — At head of t.p.: Home Office Research and Planning Unit. — Bibliography: p.135-146. - Includes indexes

CRIME PREVENTION — Netherlands — Evaluation
SKOGAN, Wesley G.
Evaluating neighborhood crime prevention programs / Prof. Wesley G. Skogan. — The Hague : Research and Documentation Centre, Ministry of Justice, 1985. — 53p. — ([Reports, papers, articles] ; 88). — Bibliography: p50-53

CRIME PREVENTION — United States
Community crime prevention / edited by Dennis P. Rosenbaum. — Beverly Hills : Sage Publications, c1986. — p. cm. — (Sage criminal justice system annuals ; v. 22)

FARRINGTON, David P
Understanding and controlling crime : toward a new research strategy / David P. Farrington, Lloyd E. Ohlin, James Q. Wilson. — New York : Springer-Verlag, c1986. — p. cm. — (Research in criminology). — Includes index. — Bibliography: p

CRIME PREVENTION — United States — Citizen participation
Community crime prevention / edited by Dennis P. Rosenbaum. — Beverly Hills : Sage Publications, c1986. — p. cm. — (Sage criminal justice system annuals ; v. 22)

CRIMEAN WAR, 1853-1856 — Diplomatic history
WETZEL, David
The Crimean War : a diplomatic history / David Wetzel. — Boulder : East European Monographs ; New York : Distributed by Columbia University Press, 1985. — viii, 255 p.. — (East European monographs ; no. 193). — Includes index. — Bibliography: p. 217-241

CRIMES ABOARD BUSES — Great Britain
GREAT BRITAIN. Working Group on Violence to Road Passenger Transport Staff
Assaults on bus staff and measures to prevent such assaults : report on the Working Group...under the chairmanship of the Department of Transport. — London : H.M.S.O., 1986. — iii,77,21p

GREAT BRITAIN. Working Group on Violence to Road Passenger Transport Staff
Assaults on bus staff and measures to prevent such assaults : a summary of the findings and recommendations of the 1986 report of the Working Group under the chairmanship of the Department of Transport. — London : H.M.S.O., 1986. — 19p

CRIMINAL ANTHROPOLOGY
WILSON, James Q
Crime and human nature / James Q. Wilson and Richard J. Herrnstein. — New York : Simon and Schuster, c1985. — p. cm. — Includes index. — Bibliography: p

CRIMINAL BEHAVIOR
BAYLEY, David H
Social control and political change / by David H. Bayley. — [Princeton, N.J.] : Center of International Studies, Woodrow Wilson School of Public and International Affairs, Princeton University, c1985. — 135 p.. — (Research monograph / Center for International Studies, Woodrow Wilson School of Public and International Affairs ; no. 49). — "December 1985.". — Includes bibliographical references

CRIMINAL BEHAVIOR — Congresses
Development of antisocial and prosocial behavior : research, theories, and issues / edited by Dan Olweus, Jack Block, Marian Radke-Yarrow. — Orlando : Academic Press, 1986. — xiii, 432 p.. — (Developmental psychology series). — Based on a conference on the development of antisocial and prosocial behavior, held at Voss, Norway, 7/4-10/82. — Includes bibliographies and indexes

CRIMINAL BEHAVIOR, PREDICTION OF
WILSON, James Q
Crime and human nature / James Q. Wilson and Richard J. Herrnstein. — New York : Simon and Schuster, c1985. — p. cm. — Includes index. — Bibliography: p

CRIMINAL BEHAVIOR, PREDICTION OF — Statistical methods
GABOR, Thomas
The prediction of criminal behaviour : statistical approaches / Thomas Gabor. — Toronto : University of Toronto Press, 1986. — viii,119p. — Bibliography: p[91]-105

CRIMINAL COURTS — England
MIRFIELD, Peter
Confessions / by Peter Mirfield. — London : Sweet & Maxwell, 1985. — [165]p. — (Modern legal studies). — Includes index

CRIMINAL IINVESTIGATION — Canada
STOBER, Michael I.
Entrapment in Canadian criminal law / by Michael I. Stober. — Toronto : Carswell Legal Publications, 1985. — xxx, 228 p.. — (Carswell's criminal law series). — Includes bibliographical references and indexes

CRIMINAL INVESTIGATION
PHILLIPS, J. H.
Forensic science and the expert witness / by J.H. Phillips, J.K. Bowen ; with a foreword by Sir Daryl Dawson. — North Ryde, N.S.W. : Law Book Company ; London : Sweet & Maxwell, 1985. — ix,114p. — Includes index

STOBER, Michael I.
Entrapment in Canadian criminal law / by Michael I. Stober. — Toronto : Carswell Legal Publications, 1985. — xxx, 228 p.. — (Carswell's criminal law series). — Includes bibliographical references and indexes

CRIMINAL INVESTIGATION — England
BANTON, Michael
Investigating robbery / Michael Banton. — Aldershot : Gower, c1985. — [vii,126]p. — Bibliography: p109-110. — Includes index

CRIMINAL INVESTIGATION — England — Birmingham (West Midlands) — History — 20th century
MULLIN, Chris
Error of judgment : the Birmingham bombings / by Chris Mullin. — London : Chatto & Windus, 1986. — [224]p

CRIMINAL INVESTIGATION — Great Britain
The Police : powers, procedures and proprieties / edited by John Benyon and Colin Bourn ; with a foreword by Lord Scarman. — Oxford : Pergamon, 1986. — xxiv,334p. — Bibliography: p299-312. — Includes index

CRIMINAL JURISDICTION — Canada
WHITLEY, Stuart James
Jurisdiction in criminal law / by Stuart James Whitley. — Calgary, Alta. : Carswell Legal Publications, 1985. — xxxviii, 240 p.. — (Carswell's criminal law series). — Includes indexes. — Bibliography: p. [229]-235

CRIMINAL JUSTICE, ADMINISTRATION OF
Crime, justice & codification : essais à la mémoire de Jaques Fortin = essays in commemoration of Jaques Fortin / edited by /reponsable de Patrick Fitzgerald. — Toronto : Carswell, 1986. — vii,196p. — Text in English and French

MORRIS, Allison
Women, crime and criminal justice / Allison Morris. — Oxford : Basil Blackwell, 1987. — [256]p. — Includes bibliography and index

CRIMINAL JUSTICE, ADMINISTRATION OF — Bibliography

LUTZKER, Marilyn
Criminal justice research in libraries : strategies and resources / Marilyn Lutzker and Eleanor Ferrall ; foreword by Edward Sagarin. — Westport, Conn. : Greenwood Press, c1986. — p. cm. — *Includes indexes*

CRIMINAL JUSTICE, ADMINISTRATION OF — Religious aspects — Christianity

SPELLER, Adrian
Breaking out : a Christian critique of criminal justice / Adrian Speller. — London : Hodder and Stoughton, 1986. — [192]p. — *Includes index*

CRIMINAL JUSTICE, ADMINISTRATION OF — Social aspects — United States

CARLSON, James M
Prime time law enforcement : crime show viewing and attitudes toward the criminal justice system / by James M. Carlson. — New York : Praeger, 1985. — p. cm. — *Includes index. — Bibliography: p*

CRIMINAL JUSTICE, ADMINISTRATION OF — Canada

PLECAS, Darryl Blair
Federal corrections in Canada : a comprehensive introduction / Darryl B. Plecas ; edited by Joanne Broatch. — Vancouver : Good 80's Enterprises, 1986. — vii,148p. — *Includes references*

CRIMINAL JUSTICE, ADMINISTRATION OF — England

GREAT BRITAIN. Home Office
Criminal justice : a working paper. — [London] : Home Office, [1984]. — 36p. — *"Prepared for the Home Office by the Central Office of Information"*

GREAT BRITAIN. Home Office
Criminal justice : a working paper. — Rev. ed.. — [London] : H.M.S.O., 1986. — 51p. — *"Designed and produced for the Home Office by the Central Office of Information"*

Panel services for offenders : comparative studies of England and Poland 1984/85 / edited by Thelma Wilson. — Aldershot : Avebury, c1987. — ix,103p. — *Bibliography: p96-103*

CRIMINAL JUSTICE, ADMINISTRATION OF — England — London

TIPLER, Jonathan
Is justice colour blind? : a study of the impact of race in the juvenile justice system in Hackney / Jonathan Tipler. — Hackney : London Borough of Hackney. Directorate of Social Services. Research, Development and Programming, 1985. — 25p. — (Social services research note / Hackney. Directorate of Social Services. Research, Development and Programming ; 6). — *At head of cover title: Research in Hackney*

TIPLER, Jonathan
Juvenile justice in Hackney / Jonathan Tipler. — Hackney : Directorate of Social Services. Research, Development and Programming, 1985. — 31p. — *At head of cover title: Research in Hackney*

CRIMINAL JUSTICE, ADMINISTRATION OF — Great Britain

GREAT BRITAIN. Parliament. House of Commons. Library. Research Division
The Criminal Justice Bill 1986/87 [Bill 2] / Mary Baber. — [London] : the Division, 1986. — 23p. — (Reference sheet ; no.86/14). — *Bibliographical references: p21-23*

PRISON REFORM TRUST
Commentary on the White Paper 'Criminal justice: plans for legislation' (Cmnd.9658). — [London] : Prison Reform Trust, 1986. — 18 leaves

CRIMINAL JUSTICE, ADMINISTRATION OF — India

SHARMA, P. D.
Police and criminal justice administration in India / P. D. Sharma. — New Delhi : Upper Publishing House, 1985. — xv,247p. — *Bibliography: p227-236*

CRIMINAL JUSTICE, ADMINISTRATION OF — Poland

Panel services for offenders : comparative studies of England and Poland 1984/85 / edited by Thelma Wilson. — Aldershot : Avebury, c1987. — ix,103p. — *Bibliography: p96-103*

CRIMINAL JUSTICE, ADMINISTRATION OF — Prussia — History

BLASIUS, Dirk
Bürgerliche Gesellschaft und Kriminalität : zur Sozialgeschichte Preussens im Vormärz / Dirk Blasius. — Göttingen : Vandenhoeck und Ruprecht, 1976. — 203 p. — (Kritische Studien zur Geschichtswissenschaft ; Bd. 22). — *Includes index. — Habilitationsschrift--Düsseldorf. — Bibliography: p. 186-198*

CRIMINAL JUSTICE, ADMINISTRATION OF — United States

BARKAN, Steven E.
Protesters on trial : criminal justice in the Southern civil rights and Vietnam antiwar movements / Steven E. Barkan. — New Brunswick, N.J. : Rutgers University Press, c1985. — p. cm. — (Crime, law, and deviance series). — *Includes index. — Bibliography: p*

CULLEN, Francis T
Reaffirming rehabilitation / Francis T. Cullen, Karen E. Gilbert ; foreword by Donald R. Cressey. — Cincinnati, Ohio : Anderson Pub. Co., c1982. — xxx, 315 p.. — (Criminal justice studies). — *Includes bibliographical references and indexes*

CURRIE, Elliott
Confronting crime : an American challenge / Elliott Currie. — 1st ed. — New York : Pantheon Books, c1985. — viii, 326 p.. — *Includes index. — Bibliography: p. 279-316*

ROSS, Robert R.
Female offender : correctional afterthoughts / by Robert R. Ross, Elizabeth A. Fabiano. — Jefferson, N.C. : McFarlane, 1986. — p. cm. — *Includes index. — Bibliography: p*

THOMAS, Charles Wellington
Corrections in America : problems of the past and the present / Charles W. Thomas. — Newbury Park, Ca. : Sage Publications, 1987. — 159p. — (Law and criminal justice series ; v.7). — *Bibliography: p148-154*

WRIGHT, Kevin N
The great American crime myth / Kevin N. Wright. — Westport, Conn. ; London : Greenwood Press, 1985. — x, 227p. — (Contributions in criminology and penology ; no. 9). — *Includes index. — Bibliography: p [217]-220*

CRIMINAL JUSTICE, ADMINISTRATION OF — United States — Addresses, essays, lectures

Probation and justice : reconsideration of mission / edited by Patrick D. McAnany, Doug Thomson, David Fogel. — Cambridge, Mass. : Oelgeschlager, Gunn & Hain, c1984. — xi, 411 p.. — *Includes bibliographies and index*

CRIMINAL JUSTICE, ADMINISTRATION OF — United States — Bibliography

Crime and punishment in America : a historical bibliography / [this bibliography was conceived and compiled from the periodicals database of the American Bibliographical Center by editors at ABC-Clio Information Services] ; [Lance Klass and Susan Kinnell, project coordinators ...]. — Santa Barbara, Calif. ; Oxford : The Information Service, c1984. — xii,346p. — (ABC-Clio research guides). — *Includes index*

CRIMINAL JUSTICE, ADMINISTRATION OF — United States — Data processing

LAUDON, Kenneth C.
Dossier society : value choices in the design of national information systems / Kenneth C. Laudon. — New York : Columbia University Press, 1986. — xi, 421 p.. — (CORPS (computing, organizations, policy, and society) series). — *Includes index. — Bibliography: p. [403]-414*

CRIMINAL JUSTICE, ADMINISTRATION OF — United States — Mathematical models

NAGEL, Stuart S.
Law, policy, and optimizing analysis / Stuart S. Nagel. — New York : Quorum Books, 1986. — xix, 328 p.. — *Includes indexes. — Bibliography: p. [313]-320*

CRIMINAL JUSTICE BILL 1981-82

GREAT BRITAIN. Parliament. House of Commons. Library. Research Division
Criminal Justice Bill 1981-82 [Bill 32] / [Patrick Nealon]. — [London] : the Division, 1982. — 25p. — (Reference sheet ; no.82/3). — *Bibliography: p18-25*

CRIMINAL JUSTICE BILL 1986-87

GREAT BRITAIN. Parliament. House of Commons. Library. Research Division
The Criminal Justice Bill 1986/87 [Bill 2] / Mary Baber. — [London] : the Division, 1986. — 23p. — (Reference sheet ; no.86/14). — *Bibliographical references: p21-23*

CRIMINAL LAW

Crime, justice & codification : essais à la mémoire de Jaques Fortin = essays in commemoration of Jaques Fortin / edited by /reponsable de Patrick Fitzgerald. — Toronto : Carswell, 1986. — vii,196p. — *Text in English and French*

CRIMINAL LAW — Congresses, conferences, etc.

INTERNATIONAL CONGRESS OF CRIMINAL LAW
Actes / International Congress of Criminal Law. — Paris : Association Internationale de Droit Pénal, 1926-1947. — Irregular. — *Continued by: Couptes rendues/International Congress of Criminal Law*

INTERNATIONAL CONGRESS OF CRIMINAL LAW
Comptes rendues / International Congress of Criminal Law. — Paris : Association International de Droit Pénal, 1953-. — *Irregular. — Continues: Actes/International Congress of Criminal Law*

CRIMINAL LAW — Moral and religious aspects

FEINBERG, Joel
The moral limits of the criminal law / Joel Feinberg. — New York ; Oxford : Oxford University Press
Vol.1: Harm to others. — 1984. — xiii,269p. — *Includes index*

FEINBERG, Joel
The moral limits of the criminal law / Joel Finberg. — New York ; Oxford : Oxford University Press
Vol.3: Harm to self. — 1986. — xxiii,420p

CRIMINAL LAW — Philosophy
FEINBERG, Joel
The moral limits of the criminal law / Joel Finberg. — New York ; Oxford : Oxford University Press
Vol.3: Harm to self. — 1986. — xxiii,420p

CRIMINAL LAW — Public opinion
CRIMINOLOGICAL RESEARCH CONFERENCE (13th : 1978)
Public opinion on crime and criminal justice : reports presented to the Thirteenth Criminological Research Conference (1978). — Strasbourg : Council of Europe, 1979. — 200p. — (Collected studies in criminological research ; v.17). — Includes bibliographies

CRIMINAL LAW — Canada
COLVIN, Eric
Principles of criminal law / Eric Colvin. — Toronto : Carswell, 1986. — xxix,340p

CRIMINAL LAW — China
The criminal law and the criminal procedure law of the People's Republic of China. — Beijing : Foreign Languages Press, 1984. — ii,298p

CRIMINAL LAW — England
CLARKSON, C. M. V.
Understanding criminal law / C. M. V. Clarkson. — London : Fontana, 1987. — 224p. — (Understanding law) (Understanding law). — Bibliography: p201-205

CRIMINAL LAW — England — Cases
SMITH, J. C. (John Cyril)
Criminal law : cases and materials / J.C. Smith, Brian Hogan. — 3rd ed. — London : Butterworths, 1986. — [700]p. — Previous ed.: 1980. — Includes index

CRIMINAL LAW — England — Digests
COCKBURN, J. S.
Calendar of assize records : home circuit indictments : Elizabeth I and James I... / by J.S. Cockburn. — London : H.M.S.O. Introduction. — 1985. — x, 334p

CRIMINAL LAW — Europe
Criminal law in action : an overview of current issues in Western societies / edited by Jan van Dijk ... [et al.]. — Arnhem : Gouda Quint ; Deventer : Kluwer, 1986. — 440p. — Includes bibliographical references

CRIMINAL LAW — France
FRANCE
[Code pénal]. Code pénal. — 83e éd. — Paris : Dalloz, 1985. — viii,1248,3p. — (Petits codes Dalloz). — Previous ed.: 1984. — Includes index

FRANCE
[Code pénal]. Code pénal. — 84e éd.. — Paris : Dalloz, 1986. — viii,1294,4p. — (Codes Dalloz). — Includes index

CRIMINAL LAW — Great Britain — Congresses
Justice and comparative law : Anglo-Soviet perspectives on criminal law, evidence, procedure, and sentencing policy / edited by W.E. Butler. — Dordrecht ; Boston : M. Nijhoff, 1986. — p. cm. — Includes index

CRIMINAL LAW — Indonesia
INTERNATIONAL COMMISSION OF JURISTS
Indonesia and the rule of law : twenty years of 'New Order' government : a study / prepared by the International Commission of Jurists and the Netherlands Institute of Human Rights ; edited by Hans Thoolen. — London : Pinter, 1987. — xii,208p. — Includes index

CRIMINAL LAW — Soviet Union — Cases
UNION OF SOVIET SOCIALIST REPUBLICS. Verkhovnyi sud
Sbornik postanovlenii Plenuma i opredelenii Kollegii Verkhovnogo suda SSSR po ugolovnym delam, 1971-1979 / [sostaviteli: E. A. Smolentsev (otv. redaktor)...et al.]. — Moskva : Izd-vo "Izvestiia Sovetov narodnykh deputatov SSSR, 1981. — 992p

CRIMINAL LAW — Soviet Union — Congresses
Justice and comparative law : Anglo-Soviet perspectives on criminal law, evidence, procedure, and sentencing policy / edited by W.E. Butler. — Dordrecht ; Boston : M. Nijhoff, 1986. — p. cm. — Includes index

CRIMINAL LAW — United States
THOMAS, Charles Wellington
Criminal law : understanding basic principles / Charles W. Thomas, Donna A. Bishop. — Newbury Park, Calif. : Sage Publications, c1987. — 159 p.. — (Law and criminal justice series ; v. 8). — Includes index. — Bibliography: p. 147-150

CRIMINAL LAW — United States — History
HENDERSON, Dwight F.
Congress, courts, and criminals : the development of federal criminal law, 1801-1829 / Dwight F. Henderson. — Westport, Conn. : Greenwood Press, c1985. — x, 257 p.. — (Contributions in American history ; no. 113). — Includes index. — Bibliography: p. [221]-233

CRIMINAL LIABILITY — Council of Europe countries
COUNCIL OF EUROPE. Criminological Colloquium (7th : 1985)
Studies on criminal responsibility and psychiatric treatment of mentally ill offenders : reports presented to the seventh Criminological Colloquium (1985). — Strasbourg : Council of Europe, 1986. — 103p. — (Collected studies in criminological research ; v.24) (Legal affairs). — On cover: European Committee on Crime Problems

CRIMINAL PROCEDURE — Canada
WHITLEY, Stuart James
Jurisdiction in criminal law / by Stuart James Whitley. — Calgary, Alta. : Carswell Legal Publications, 1985. — xxxviii, 240 p.. — (Carswell's criminal law series). — Includes indexes. — Bibliography: p. [229]-235

CRIMINAL PROCEDURE — Canada — History
STENNING, Philip C
Appearing for the Crown : a legal and historical review of criminal prosecutorial authority in Canada : a study conducted for the Law Reform Commission of Canada by Philip C. Stenning. — Cowansville, Qué. : Brown Legal Publications, c1986. — 426 p.. — Includes indexes. — Bibliography: p. 385-396

CRIMINAL PROCEDURE — China
The criminal law and the criminal procedure law of the People's Republic of China. — Beijing : Foreign Languages Press, 1984. — ii,298p

CRIMINAL PROCEDURE — England
EMMINS, Christopher J.
A practical approach to criminal procedure / Christopher J. Emmins. — 3rd ed. — London : Financial Training, 1985. — xxxiii,473p. — Includes index

CRIMINAL PROCEDURE — Europe — Congresses
EUROPEAN SEMINAR ON NON-PROSECUTION IN EUROPE (1986 : Helsinki)
Non-prosecution in Europe : report of the European seminar. — Helsinki : Helsinki Institute for Crime Prevention and Control, 1986. — 338p. — (Publication series / Helsinki Institute for Crime Prevention and Control ; no.9)

CRIMINAL PROCEDURE — Great Britain
GREAT BRITAIN. Parliament. House of Commons. Library. Research Division
Police and Criminal Evidence Bill (Bill 16, session 1982-83) / [Patrick Nealon]. — [London] : the Division, [1982]. — 25p. — (Reference sheet ; no.82/17). — Includes bibliographical references

The Police : powers, procedures and proprieties / edited by John Benyon and Colin Bourn ; with a foreword by Lord Scarman. — Oxford : Pergamon, 1986. — xxiv,334p. — Bibliography: p299-312. — Includes index

CRIMINAL PROCEDURE — Great Britain — Congresses
Justice and comparative law : Anglo-Soviet perspectives on criminal law, evidence, procedure, and sentencing policy / edited by W.E. Butler. — Dordrecht ; Boston : M. Nijhoff, 1986. — p. cm. — Includes index

CRIMINAL PROCEDURE — Soviet Union — Cases
UNION OF SOVIET SOCIALIST REPUBLICS. Verkhovnyi sud
Sbornik postanovlenii Plenuma i opredelenii Kollegii Verkhovnogo suda SSSR po ugolovnym delam, 1971-1979 / [sostaviteli: E. A. Smolentsev (otv. redaktor)...et al.]. — Moskva : Izd-vo "Izvestiia Sovetov narodnykh deputatov SSSR, 1981. — 992p

CRIMINAL PROCEDURE — Soviet Union — Congresses
Justice and comparative law : Anglo-Soviet perspectives on criminal law, evidence, procedure, and sentencing policy / edited by W.E. Butler. — Dordrecht ; Boston : M. Nijhoff, 1986. — p. cm. — Includes index

CRIMINAL PROCEDURE — Spain
SORIANO, Ramón
El nuevo jurado español / Ramón Soriano. — Barcelona : Ariel, 1985. — 157p

CRIMINAL PROCEDURE (INTERNATIONAL LAW)
International criminal law / edited by M. Cherif Bassiouni. — Dobbs Ferry, N.Y. : Transnational Publishers
Vol.2: Procedure. — 1986. — xvii,552p

CRIMINAL PSYCHOLOGY
BRAND-KOOLEN, M. J. M.
"At the government's pleasure" : trends and developments in the compulsory treatment of mentally disturbed offender in the Netherlands / Dr. Maria J. M. Brand-Koolen. — The Hague : Research and Documentation Centre, Ministry of Justice, 1986. — 18p. — ([Report, papers, articles] ; 91). — Bibliography: p16-18

EMMERICK, J. L. van
Recidivism among psychiatric offenders / Jos L. van Emmerik. — The Hague : Research and Documentation Centre, Ministry of Justice, 1985. — 20p. — ([Reports, papers, articles] ; 87). — Bibliographical references: p14. — "A summary of a survey of persons who were discharged between 1974 and 1979"

HALLECK, Seymour L
Psychiatry and the dilemmas of crime : a study of causes, punishment, and treatment / [by] Seymour L. Halleck. — [1st paperback ed.]. — Berkeley : University of California Press, 1971 [c1967]. — xiv, 382 p. — Bibliography: p. 351-370

CRIMINAL PSYCHOLOGY — Addresses, essays, lectures
Ecologic-biochemical approaches to treatment of delinquents and criminals / edited by Leonard J. Hippchen. — New York : Van Nostrand Reinhold Co., c1978. — xx,396p. — Bibliography: p389-392. — Bibliography: p. 389-392

CRIMINAL PSYCHOLOGY — Congresses
The reasoning criminal : rational choice perspectives on offending / edited by Derek B. Cornish, Ronald V. Clarke. — New York : Springer-Verlag, c1986. — p. cm. — (Research in criminology). — Includes index. — Bibliography: p

CRIMINAL PSYCHOLOGY — Congresses
continuation
Reconstructing the past : the role of psychologists in criminal trials / edited by Arne Trankell. — Deventer, The Netherlands : Kluwer, [1982]. — 398p. — *"This book contains papers and panels from the first international conference on Witness Psychology...Stockholm...September 1981"*

CRIMINAL PSYCHOLOGY — Testing
OLDHAM, Helen
Hostility and assaultiveness / Helen Oldham, Barry McGurk and Richard Magaldi. — London : Home Office, Prison Department, Directorate of Psychological Services, 1976. — 13p. — (DPS report. Series 1 ; no.7). — *Bibliography: p[13]*

CRIMINAL REGISTERS — Australia
Criminal records. — Sydney : Law Reform Commission, 1985. — 117p. — (Discussion paper / Law Reform Commission ; no.25)

CRIMINAL STATISTICS — Netherlands
[Honderd jaar strafrecht in statistieken, 1886-1986. English]. One hundred years of penal code in the Netherlands : a statistical view of 1886-1986. — The Hague : Staatsuitgeverij : cbs-publications, 1986. — 46p. — *Translation of: Honderd jaar strafrecht in statistieken, 1886-1986*

CRIMINAL STATISTICS — Northern Ireland
GREAT BRITAIN. Northern Ireland Office. Statistics Branch
A commentary on Northern Ireland crime statistics 1983-1984 / prepared by Northern Ireland Office Statistics Branch. — Belfast : Her Majesty's Stationary Office, 1985. — ix,78p

CRIMINAL STATISTICS — United States
O'BRIEN, Robert M
Crime and victimization data / Robert M. O'Brien. — Beverly Hills, Calif. : SAGE Publications, c1985. — 127 p.. — (Law and criminal justice series ; v. 4). — *Includes index. — Bibliography: p. 115-121*

CRIMINOLOGISTS — England — Biography
ROLPH, C. H.
Further particulars / C.H. Rolph. — Oxford : Oxford University Press, 1987. — [288]p. — *Includes index*

CRISES
BOYER, Robert
La crise actuelle : une mise en perspective historique : quelques reflexions à partir d'une analyse du capitalisme français en longue période / Robert Boyer. — Paris : Centre d'Études Prospectives D'Économie Mathématique Appliquées à la Planification, 1979. — 126p. — (Centre d'Études Prospectives d'Économie Mathematique Appliquées à la Planification ; no.7909). — *Bibliography: p115-128*

LAFONT, Jean
L'accumulation du capital et les crises dans l'URSS contemporaine : une première approche / Jean Lafont et Danièle Leborgne. — Paris : Centre D'Études Prospectives d'Économie Mathématique Appliquées à la Planification, 1979. — 98p. — (Centre d'Études Prospectives d'Économie Mathématique Appliquées à la Planification ; 7910). — *Bibliography: p93-98*

MBIYE, Tshiunza
La douce negligence et les crises actuelles / Tshiunza Mbiye. — Kinshasa : "Zaire-Afrique", 1975. — 40p

CRITICAL CARE MEDICINE — Moral and ethical aspects — Congresses
Ethics and critical care medicine / edited by John C. Moskop and Loretta Kopelman. — Dordrecht ; Lancaster : D. Reidel, c1985. — xx, 236p. — (Philosophy and medicine ; v. 19). — *Based on papers presented at a symposium held at East Carolina University School of Medicine in Greenville, N.C. on Mar. 17-19, 1983; sponsored by the East Carolina University School of Medicine and others. — Includes bibliographies and index*

CRITICAL CARE MEDICINE — Social aspects — Congresses
Ethics and critical care medicine / edited by John C. Moskop and Loretta Kopelman. — Dordrecht ; Lancaster : D. Reidel, c1985. — xx, 236p. — (Philosophy and medicine ; v. 19). — *Based on papers presented at a symposium held at East Carolina University School of Medicine in Greenville, N.C. on Mar. 17-19, 1983; sponsored by the East Carolina University School of Medicine and others. — Includes bibliographies and index*

CRITICISM
BERGER, Arthur Asa
Media analysis techniques / Arthur Asa Berger. — Beverly Hills : Sage Publications, c1982. — 160 p.. — (The Sage commtext series ; v. 10). — *Bibliography: p. 158-159*

CRITICISM — Social aspects
SWINGEWOOD, Alan
Sociological poetics and aesthetic theory / Alan Swingewood. — Basingstoke : Macmillan, 1986. — [144]p. — *Includes bibliography and index*

CRITICISM (PHILOSOPHY)
ALVESSON, Mats
[Organisationsteori och teknokratiskt medvetande. English]. Organization theory and technocratic consciousness : rationality, ideology, and quality of work / Mats Alvesson. — Berlin ; New York : W. De Gruyter, 1987. — p. cm. — (De Gruyter studies in organization ; 8). — *Translation of: Organisationsteori och teknokratiskt medvetande. — Includes index. — Bibliography: p*

FAY, Brian
Critical social science : liberation and its limits / Brian Fay. — Ithaca, N.Y. : Cornell University Press, [1987]. — p. cm. — *Includes index. — Bibliography: p*

CRITIQUE DE LA RAISON DIALECTIQUE. 1, THÉORIE DES ENSEMBLES PRATIQUES
CATALANO, Joseph S
A commentary on Jean-Paul Sartre's Critique of dialectical reason, volume 1, Theory of practical ensembles / Joseph S. Catalano. — Chicago : University of Chicago Press, 1986. — x, 282 p.. — *Includes index. — Bibliography: p. [269]-273*

CROP YIELDS
Crop production levels and fertilizer use. — Rome : Food and Agriculture Organization of the United Nations, 1981. — ix, 69 p.. — (FAO fertilizer and plant nutrition bulletin ; 2). — *"Fertilizer and Plant Nutrition Service. Land and Water Development Division.". — Bibliography: p. 53-54*

CROP YIELDS — Malawi — Statistics
National sample survey of agriculture 1980-81 : customary land in rural areas only. — Zomba : National Statistical Office
vol. 2: Crops and yield. — 1984. — 28p

CROP YIELDS — Soviet Union
DESAI, Padma
Weather and grain yields in the Soviet Union / Padma Desai. — Washington, D.C. : International Food Policy Research Institute, 1986. — p. cm. — (Research report ; 54). — *Bibliography: p*

CROP YIELDS — Zimbabwe — Statistics
1985 census of resettlement schemes : crops, fertilizer, equipment and persons on normal intensive and accelerated schemes and model B-Co-operatives (by scheme / Co-operative. — Harare : Central Statistical Office, [1986?]. — 316p

CROPS — Nutrition
Fertilizer and plant nutrition guide / Fertilizer and Plant Nutrition Service, Land and Water Development Division. — Rome : Food and Agriculture Organization of the United Nations, 1984. — xiv, 176 p.. — (FAO fertilizer and plant nutrition bulletin ; 9). — *Bibliography: p. 173-176*

CROPS — Nutrition — Congresses
EXPERT CONSULTATION ON BETTER EXPLOITATION OF PLANT NUTRIENTS (1977 : Rome City)
Improved use of plant nutrients : report of the expert consultation on better exploitation of plant nutrients held in Rome 18-22 April 1977. — Rome : Food and Agriculture Organization of the United Nations, 1978. — vii, 152 p.. — (FAO soils bulletin ; 37). — *On t.p.: Soil Resources, Management and Conservation Service, Land and Water Development Division. — Includes bibliographies*

CROPS — Research — India
MAHAPATRA, Ishwar Chandra
India and the international crops research institute for the semi-arid tropics : a study of their collaboration in agricultural research / Ishwar Chandra Mahapatre, Dev Raj Bhumbla, Shriniwas Dattatraya Bokil. — Washington, D.C. : The World Bank, 1986. — x,48p. — (Study paper / Consultative group on International Agricultural Research ; no.18)

CROPS — Fiji
BROOKFIELD, Harold Chillingworth
Land, cane and coconuts : papers on the rural economy of Fiji / H. C. Brookfield, F. Ellis, R. G. Ward. — Canberra [A.C.T.] : Australian National University, 1985. — 251p. — (Australian National University Department of Human Geography Publication ; HG/17). — *Includes bibliographies*

CROPS AND SOILS
Fertilizer and plant nutrition guide / Fertilizer and Plant Nutrition Service, Land and Water Development Division. — Rome : Food and Agriculture Organization of the United Nations, 1984. — xiv, 176 p.. — (FAO fertilizer and plant nutrition bulletin ; 9). — *Bibliography: p. 173-176*

CROWN AGENTS FOR OVERSEA GOVERNMENTS AND ADMINISTRATIONS
Annual report and accounts / Crown Agents for Oversea Governments and Administrations. — Sutton : Crown Agents for Oversea Governments and Administrations, 1984-. — *Annual*

CROWN LANDS — Hong Kong
Hong Kong in transition / editor Joseph Y.S. Cheng ; contributors Albert H.Y. Chen ... [et al.]. — Hong Kong ; Oxford : Oxford University Press, 1986. — xvi,457p. — *Includes bibliographies and index*

CROYDON (LONDON, ENGLAND) — Social policy
Introducing community and voluntary services. — Croydon : Community and Voluntary Services, Croydon Social Services Dept., 1986. — 18p

CRUELTY TO CHILDREN — England — London
HILLINGDON
Report of the review panel of the London Borough of Hillingdon Area Review Committee on Child Abuse into the death of Heidi Koseda. — Hillingdon : [the Council], 1986. — 66p

CRUSADES
RUNCIMAN, Steven
A history of the Crusades. — Cambridge : Cambridge University Press
Vol.2: The Kingdom of Jerusalem and the Frankish East,1100-1187. — 1952. — 523p.,ill.,22cm

CRUSADES — First, 1096-1099
RILEY-SMITH, Jonathan
The first crusade and the idea of crusading / Jonathan Riley-Smith. — London : Athlone, 1986. — 227p. — *Bibliography: p204-213. — Includes index*

CRUTCHFIELD, JAMES ARTHUR
Natural resources economics and policy applications : essays in honor of James A. Crutchfield / edited by Edward Miles, Robert Pealy, and Robert Stokes ; foreword by Brewster C. Denny. — Seattle : Institute for Marine Studies of the University of Washington : Distributed by the University of Washington Press, c1986. — p. cm. — (Public policy issues in resource management). — *Includes index. — Bibliography: p*

CRYPTOGRAPHY — History
Codebreaking and signals intelligence / edited by Christopher Andrew. — London : Cass, 1985. — [128]p. — (Intelligence and national security ; 1)

CUBA — Armed forces
Cuban Communism / edited by Irving Louis Horowitz. — 6th ed. — New Brunswick, U.S.A. : Transaction Books, c1987. — xvi, 743 p.. — *Includes bibliographies*

CUBA — Economic conditions — 1959-
Cuban Communism / edited by Irving Louis Horowitz. — 6th ed. — New Brunswick, U.S.A. : Transaction Books, c1987. — xvi, 743 p.. — *Includes bibliographies*

CUBA — Economic conditions — 1959- — Statistics
Cuba quarterly economic report / Comite Estatal de Estadísticas and Banco Nacional de Cuba. — Havana : Comite Estatal de Estadisticas, 1984-. — *Semi-annual*

CUBA — Foreign economic relations — Communist Countries
Kuba v mezhdunarodnom sotsialisticheskom razdelenii truda / otv. redaktor M. A. Manasov. — Moskva : Nauka, 1986. — 146p

CUBA — Foreign relations
CASTRO, Fidel
Fidel Castro : nothing can stop the course of history / interview by Jeffrey M. Elliot and Mervyn M. Dymally. — New York ; London : Pathfinder Press, 1986. — 258p

CUBA — Foreign relations — 1959-
GONZALEZ, Edward
Castro, Cuba, and the world / Edward Gonzalez, David Ronfeldt. — Santa Monica, CA. : Rand, 1986. — xx, 133 p.. — *"June 1986.". — "R-3420.". — Includes bibliographical references*

CUBA — Foreign relations — Puerto Rica
Castro's Puerto Rican obsession. — Washington, D.C. : Cuban-American National Foundation, 1987. — 53p

CUBA — Foreign relations — United States
PÉREZ, Louis A.
Cuba under the Platt Amendment, 1902-1934 / Louis A. Pérez, Jr. — Pittsburg, Pa. : University of Pittsburgh Press, c1986. — xiii, 410p. — (Pitt Latin American series). — *Includes index. — Bibliography: p.[387]-402*

CUBA — History — Revolution, 1959
LISTER, John
Cuba : radical face of Stalinism / John Lister. — London : Left View Books, 1985. — 168p. — *Bibliography: p165-168. — Includes chronology (1868-1985): p149-164*

CUBA — History — 1878-1895
PÉREZ, Louis A.
Cuba between empires, 1878-1902 / Louis A. Pérez, Jr. — Pittsburgh, Pa. : University of Pittsburgh Press, c1983. — xx, 490 p.. — (Pitt Latin American series). — *Includes index. — Bibliography: p. 449-480*

CUBA — History — Revolution, 1895-1898
PÉREZ, Louis A.
Cuba between empires, 1878-1902 / Louis A. Pérez, Jr. — Pittsburgh, Pa. : University of Pittsburgh Press, c1983. — xx, 490 p.. — (Pitt Latin American series). — *Includes index. — Bibliography: p. 449-480*

CUBA — History — 1899-1906
PÉREZ, Louis A.
Cuba between empires, 1878-1902 / Louis A. Pérez, Jr. — Pittsburgh, Pa. : University of Pittsburgh Press, c1983. — xx, 490 p.. — (Pitt Latin American series). — *Includes index. — Bibliography: p. 449-480*

CUBA — History — Revolution, 1959 — Journalists — Congresses
The Selling of Fidel Castro : the media and the Cuban Revolution / edited by William E. Ratliff. — New Brunswick, N.J., U.S.A. : Transaction Books, c1986. — p. cm. — *Presented as part of a conference held on November 16-17, 1984, in Washington, D.C. — "Prepared in cooperation with the Cuban American National Foundation ... Washington, D.C."--Verso t.p*

CUBA — Politics and government — 1933-1959
HARNECKER, Marta
Fidel Castro's political strategy : from Moncada to victory / by Marta Harnecker. — New York ; London : Pathfinder Press, 1987. — 157p. — *Includes "History will absolve me" by Fidel Castro*

CUBA — Politics and government — Revolution, 1959
HARNECKER, Marta
Fidel Castro's political strategy : from Moncada to victory / by Marta Harnecker. — New York ; London : Pathfinder Press, 1987. — 157p. — *Includes "History will absolve me" by Fidel Castro*

CUBA — Politics and government — 1959-
Cuban Communism / edited by Irving Louis Horowitz. — 6th ed. — New Brunswick, U.S.A. : Transaction Books, c1987. — xvi, 743 p.. — *Includes bibliographies*

GONZALEZ, Edward
Castro, Cuba, and the world / Edward Gonzalez, David Ronfeldt. — Santa Monica, CA. : Rand, 1986. — xx, 133 p.. — *"June 1986.". — "R-3420.". — Includes bibliographical references*

CUBA — Relations — Soviet Union
DUNCAN, W. Raymond
The Soviet Union and Cuba : interests and influence / by W. Raymond Duncan. — New York : Praeger, 1985. — xv, 220p. — (Studies of influence in international relations). — *Includes index. — Bibliography: p.205-209*

Letopis' vazhneishikh sobytii sovetskokubinskoi druzhby i sotrudnichestva 1959-1985 / [sostavitel': M. V. Grishchenko; otv. redaktor I. N. Mel'nikova]. — Kiev : Naukova dumka, 1987. — 136p

CUBA — Relations — United States
FREDERICK, Howard H
Cuban-American radio wars : ideology in international telecommunications / Howard H. Frederick. — Norwood, N.J. : Ablex Pub. Corporation, c1986. — viii, 200 p.. — (Communication and information science). — *Includes indexes. — Bibliography: p. 177-193*

CUBA — Social conditions — 1959-
Cuban Communism / edited by Irving Louis Horowitz. — 6th ed. — New Brunswick, U.S.A. : Transaction Books, c1987. — xvi, 743 p.. — *Includes bibliographies*

MARSHALL, Peter H.
Cuba libre : breaking the chains? / by Peter Marshall. — London : Gollancz, 1987. — viii,310p,[16]p of plates. — *Bibliography: p291-298. — Includes index*

CUBA — History
Cuban Communism / edited by Irving Louis Horowitz. — 6th ed. — New Brunswick, U.S.A. : Transaction Books, c1987. — xvi, 743 p.. — *Includes bibliographies*

CUBA — Politics and government — 1909-1933
PÉREZ, Louis A.
Cuba under the Platt Amendment, 1902-1934 / Louis A. Pérez, Jr. — Pittsburg, Pa. : University of Pittsburgh Press, c1986. — xiii, 410p. — (Pitt Latin American series). — *Includes index. — Bibliography: p.[387]-402*

CUBA. Treaties, etc. United States (1903 May 22)
PÉREZ, Louis A.
Cuba under the Platt Amendment, 1902-1934 / Louis A. Pérez, Jr. — Pittsburg, Pa. : University of Pittsburgh Press, c1986. — xiii, 410p. — (Pitt Latin American series). — *Includes index. — Bibliography: p.[387]-402*

CUBAN MISSILE CRISIS, OCT. 1962
GRIFFITHS, John, 1942 Apr. 5-
The Cuban missile crisis / John Griffiths. — Hove : Wayland, 1986. — [80]p. — (Flashpoints). — *Includes bibliography and index*

CUBAN MISSILE CRISIS, OCT. 1962 — Bibliography
The "Cuban crisis" of 1962 : selected documents, chronology, and bibliography / David L. Larson. — 2nd ed. — Lanham, MD : University Press of America, c1986. — xix, 461 p.. — *Bibliography: p. 451-461*

CUBAN MISSILE CRISIS, OCT. 1962 — Sources
The "Cuban crisis" of 1962 : selected documents, chronology, and bibliography / David L. Larson. — 2nd ed. — Lanham, MD : University Press of America, c1986. — xix, 461 p.. — *Bibliography: p. 451-461*

CUBEO INDIANS
GOLDMAN, Irving
The Cubeo Indians of the Northwest Amazon / Irving Goldman. — 2d ed. — Urbana : University of Illinois Press, 1979. — 315 p.. — (Illini books edition). — *Includes index. — Bibliography: p. 295-297*

CULTS
Cults, sects, and new religious movements : a bibliography of religions from the ATLA Religion Database / edited by Erica Treesh. — Chicago : American Theological Library Association, 1985. — 223p

SHUPE, Anson D.
A documentary history of the anti-cult movement / Anson D. Shupe and David G. Bromley. — Arlington : University of Texas. Center for Social Research, 1985. — [400p]

CULTS — Congresses
Religious movements : genesis, exodus, and numbers / edited by Rodney Stark. — New York : Paragon House Publishers, c1985. — v, 354 p.. — *"A New ERA book.". — "Essays ... were originally prepared for an international conference held in May 1982 on Orcas Island, Washington"--Editor's introd. — Includes bibliographies and index*

CULTS — Controversial literature — History and criticism
MELTON, J. Gordon
The encyclopedic handbook of cults in America / J. Gordon Melton. — New York : Garland Pub., 1986. — x, 272 p.. — (Garland reference library of social science ; v. 213). — *Includes bibliographies and index*

CULTS — United States

MELTON, J. Gordon
The encyclopedic handbook of cults in America / J. Gordon Melton. — New York : Garland Pub., 1986. — x, 272 p.. — (Garland reference library of social science ; v. 213). — *Includes bibliographies and index*

CULTURAL PROPERTY EXPORT AND IMPORT ACT (CANADA)

CANADA. Department of Communications
Cultural Property Export and Import Act : annual report. — Ottawa : Department of Communications, 1983-. — *Annual. — Text in English and French*

CULTURAL RELATIONS

MITCHELL, J. M.
International cultural relations / J.M. Mitchell. — London : Allen & Unwin, 1986. — [256]p. — (Key concepts in international relations ; 3). — *Includes bibliography and index*

ZHIVKOVA, Liudmila
S aprilsko vdŭkhnovenie v borbata za mir i sotsializŭm, za edinstvo, tvorchestvo i krasota : dokladi, rechi, statii i izkazvaniia / Liudmila Zhivkova. — Sofiia : Partizdat, 1982-1983. — 3vols

CULTURAL RELATIONS — Addresses essays, lectures

BOORSTIN, Daniel J.
The invisible world : libraries and the myth of cultural exchange / Daniel J. Boorstin. — Washington, D. C. : Library of Congress, 1985. — 14p. — (The Center for the Book viewpoint series ; no.15). — *"Remarks at the IFLA General Conference, August 19, 1985"*

CULTURE

COHEN, Bernice
The cultural science of man / Bernice Cohen. — London : Codek
Vol.1: The seamless web : discovering cultural man. — c1987. — xvii,384p. — *Bibliography: p359-372. — Includes index*

Doing cross-national research. — Birmingham : Aston Modern Languages Club. — (Cross-national research papers). — *Bibliographies*
3: Language and culture in cross-national research / edited by Linda Hantrais [and] Steen Mangen. — 1987. — x,62p

GRAMSCI, Antonio
Selections from cultural writings / Antonio Gramsci ; edited by David Forgacs and Geoffrey Nowell-Smith ; translated by William Boelhower. — London : Lawrence and Wishart, 1985. — xvi,448p

SCHEIN, Edgar H
Organizational culture and leadership : a dynamic view / Edgar H. Schein. — 1st ed. — San Franciso : Jossey-Bass Publishers, c1985. — p. cm. — (A Joint publication in the Jossey-Bass management series and the Jossey-Bass social and behavioral science series). — *Includes index. — Bibliography: p*

WAGNER, Roy
Symbols that stand for themselves / Roy Wagner. — Chicago : University of Chicago Press, 1986. — p. cm. — *Sequel to: The invention of culture. — Includes index. — Bibliography: p*

CURIEL, HENRI

GAUCHER, Roland
Le réseau Curiel = ou, La subversion humanitaire / Roland Gaucher. — Paris : Editions Jean Picollec, 1981. — 433p

CURRAGH (KILDARE : COUNTY) MUTINY, 1914

The Army and the Curragh incident / edited by Ian F.W. Beckett. — London : Bodley Head for the Army Records Society, 1986. — [448]p. — *Includes bibliography and index*

CURRENCY QUESTION

DOMÁNY, Gyula
Nemzetközi pénzügyi kapcsolatok / írta Domány Gyula. — Budapest : Grill-féle udvari könyvkereskedés kiadása, 1936. — 36p. — *Bibliography: p[35]-36*

INTERNATIONAL MONETARY FUND. Board of Governors. Committee on Reform of the International Monetary System and Related Issues
International monetary reform : documents of the Committee of Twenty. — Washington, D.C. : the Fund, 1974. — viii,253p. — *Includes the Report to the Board of Governors, Outline of Reform and accompanying Annexes, Reports of Technical groups, and related documents*

CURRENCY QUESTION — History

DOMÁNY, Gyula
A háborus valuta / írta Domány Gyula. — Budapest : Benkö Gyula cs. és kir. udvari könyvkereskedése, 1917. — 141p

CURRENCY QUESTION — Germany

BALOGH, Tamás
A német pénzromlás oknyomozó története / írta Balogh Tamás ; Navratil Ákos előszavával. — Budapest : Gergely R. Könyvkereskedése, 1928. — 104p. — (Közgazdasági Könyvtár ; Köt.5). — *Bibliography: p103-104*

CURRENCY QUESTION — Great Britain — History

ROTELLI, Claudio
Le origini della controversia monetaria (1797-1844) / Claudio Rotelli. — Bologna : Il Mulino, 1982. — 258p. — (Saggi ; 236)

CURRENCY QUESTION — Hungary

FELLNER, Frigyes
A valuta rendezése Magyarországon : különös tekintettel a készpénzfizetések megkezdésére / a Magyar Tudományos Akadémia megbízásából írta Fellner Frigyes. — Budapest : Grill Károley Könyvkiadó-vállalet, 1911. — 287p. — (Magyar Közgazdasági Könyvtár ; köt.6)

IVÁN, Miklós
A Koronától az aranypengöig : a pénzválság bonctana / írta Iván Miklós. — Budapest : Gergely R., 1934. — 104p

CURRENCY QUESTION — Hungary — Congress

MAGYARORSZÁG KÖZÉPEURÓPAI IUTÉZETE. Conference (Budapest : 1936)
A dunai államok valutarendezése / Magyarország Középeurópa Intézete ; [contributions by] Hantos Elemér...[et al.]. — Budapest : Szeged Városi Nyomda, 1936. — 72p

CURRENCY QUESTION — Poland

SUŁKOWSKA, Wanda
Koncepcje społeczno-ekonomiczne i działalność Feliksa Młynarskiego / Wanda Sułkowska. — Wrocław Ossolineum, 1985. — 104p. — (Prace Komisji Nauk Ekonomicznch / Polska Akademia Nauk. Oddział w Krakowie ; Nr13). — *Summary in French and English. — Bibliography: p[96]-99*

CURRENCY QUESTION — Soviet Union — History

GALIMDSÁN, Tagán
Oroszország valutája a háború alatt és a háború után / írta Tagán Galimdsán, Heller Farkas. — Budapest : Légrády Testvérek nyomdai müintézete, 1929. — 112p. — (Közgazdasági Könyvtár ; köt.8). — *Contains summary in German, p[99]-112*

CURRENT COST ACCOUNTING

MALLINSON, Derek
Understanding current cost accounting : a guide for those preparing and using financial statements / by Derek Mallinson. — London : Butterworth, 1980. — xviii,428p. — *Includes: Current cost accounting / Institute of Chartered Accountants in England and Wales - Guidance notes on SSAP 16, current cost accounting / Accounting Standards Committee*

CURRENT VALUE ACCOUNTING — Great Britain

Accounting for economic costs and changing prices : a report to HM Treasury by an Advisory Group. — London : H.M.S.O., 1986. — 2v.(in 1). — *Chairman: I. C. R. Byatt. — Bibliography: v.2, p137*

CURRICULUM PLANNING

Changing the curriculum / edited by John F. Kerr. — London : University of London Press, c1968. — 112p. — *Bibliographies*

GREAT BRITAIN. Department of Education and Science
The school curriculum / Department of Education and Science, Welsh Office. — London : H.M.S.O., 1981

CURRICULUM PLANNING — England — Suffolk

VOICE, John
The whole curriculum : review and analysis / John Voice. — [Ipswich] : Education Department, [1987]. — 53,[20]p. — (Research paper / Suffolk. Education Department ; no.2). — *Bibliography: p73*

CURRICULUM PLANNING — United States

FRANKLIN, Barry M.
Building the American community : the school curriculum and the search for social control / Barry M. Franklin. — London : Falmer, 1986. — 176p. — (Studies in curriculum history ; 4). — *Includes index*

CURRYS GROUP PLC — History

LERNER, Harry
Currys : the first 100 years / Harry Lerner. — Cambridge : Woodhead-Faulkner, 1984. — 112p

CURTIN, PHILIP D

Africans in bondage : studies in slavery and the slave trade : essays in honor of Philip D. Curtin on the occasion of the twenty-fifth anniversary of African Studies at the University of Wisconsin / edited by Paul E. Lovejoy. — Madison : African Studies Program, University of Wisconsin-Madison : Distributed by the University of Wisconsin Press, c1986. — 378p. — *Includes index. — Includes bibliographies*

CURZON, GEORGE NATHANIEL CURZON, Marquess

NICOLSON, Harold
Curzon : the last phase, 1919-1925 : a study in post-war diplomacy / Harold Nicolson. — 2nd ed. — London, 1937. — 416p

CUSTODY OF CHILDREN

HODGES, William F
Interventions for children of divorce : custody, access, and psychotherapy / William F. Hodges. — New York, N.Y. : Wiley, c1986. — p. cm. — (Wiley series on personality processes). — *"A Wiley-Interscience publication.". — Includes indexes. — Bibliography: p*

CUSTODY OF CHILDREN — Psychological aspects

HODGES, William F
Interventions for children of divorce : custody, access, and psychotherapy / William F. Hodges. — New York, N.Y. : Wiley, c1986. — p. cm. — (Wiley series on personality processes). — *"A Wiley-Interscience publication.". — Includes indexes. — Bibliography: p*

CUSTODY OF CHILDREN — England

GREAT BRITAIN. Law Commission
Family law : review of child law : Care, supervision and interim orders in custody proceedings / The Law Commission. — London : H.M.S.O., 1987. — v,80p. — (Working paper / Law Commission ; no.100)

CUSTODY OF CHILDREN — England
continuation

GREAT BRITAIN. Law Commission
Family law : review of child law : custody / The Law Commission. — London : H.M.S.O., 1986. — viii,233p. — (Working paper / Law Commission ; no. 96). — *Includes bibliographical references*

Lesbian mothers's legal handbook / Rights of Women Lesbian Custody Group. — London : Women's, 1986. — [214]p. — *Includes bibliography and index*

CUSTODY OF CHILDREN — Great Britain

FREEMAN, M. D. A.
The law and practice of custodianship / by Michael D.A. Freeman. — London : Sweet & Maxwell, 1986. — xviii,156p. — *Includes index*

PRIEST, J. A.
Custody law in practice in the divorce and domestic courts / by J.A. Priest and J.C. Whybrow. — London : H.M.S.O., 1986. — vii,113p. — *Supplement to: Working paper no. 96, entitled Family law: review of child law: custody*

RYAN, Mary
A guide to care and related proceedings / Mary Ryan. — 3rd ed. — London : Family Rights Group, 1985. — 83p

CUSTODY OF CHILDREN — United States

CHESLER, Phyllis
Mothers on trial : the battle for children and custody / Phyllis Chesler. — New York : McGraw-Hill Book Co., c1986. — xviii, 651 p.. — *Bibliography: p. 457-621. — Includes index*

WEITZMAN, Lenore J
The divorce revolution : the unexpected social and economic consequences for women and children in America / Lenore J. Weitzman. — New York : Free Press ; London : Collier Macmillan, c1985. — p. cm

CUSTOMARY LAW — Africa, Southern

BENNETT, T. W.
The application of customary law in southern Africa : the conflict of personal laws / T.W. Bennett. — Cape Town : Juta, 1985. — xxxvii,250p. — *Bibliography: p.xv-xxi. - Includes index*

CUSTOMARY LAW — Australia

The recognition of Aboriginal customary laws. — Canberra : Australian Government Publishing Service. — (Report / Law Reform Commission no.31) (Parliamentary paper ; no.136/1986)
Vol.1. — 1986. — xxxix, 507p

The recognition of Aboriginal customary laws. — Canberra : Australian Government Publishing Service
Vol.2. — 1986. — xvi,415p. — (Report / Law Reform Commission ; no.31) (Parliamentary paper ; no.137/1986). — *Bibliography: p358-397*

CUSTOMARY LAW — Tanzania — Kilimanjaro

MOORE, Sally Falk
Social facts and fabrications : "customary" law on Kilimanjaro, 1880-1980 / Sally Falk Moore. — Cambridge : Cambridge University Press, 1986. — xvi,397p. — (The Lewis Henry Morgan Lectures ; 1981). — *Bibliography: p376-384. — Includes index*

CUSTOMER SERVICE — Great Britain — Management

Are they being served? : quality consciousness in service industries / edited by Brian Moores. — Oxford : Philip Allan, 1986. — 305p. — *Bibliography: p296-299. — Includes index*

CUSTOMS ADMINISTRATION — China — History

HALL, B. Foster
The Chinese Maritime Customs : an international service, 1854-1950 / B. Foster Hall. — [London] : National Maritime Museum, 1977. — iv,46p. — (Maritime monographs and reports ; no.26)

CUSTOMS UNIONS

Building a Canadian-American free trade area : papers / by Donald S. MacDonald...[et al.] ; edited by Edward R. Fried, Frank Stone, Philip H. Trezise. — Washington, D.C. : Brookings Institution, 1987. — xii,217p. — (Brookings dialogues on public policy)

OVERTURF, Stephen Frank
The economic principles of European integration / Stephen Frank Overturf. — New York : Praeger, 1986. — xiii, 173 p.. — *Includes index. — Bibliography: p. 167*

CYBERNETICS

KUHN, Arthur J
Organizational cybernetics and business policy : System design for performance control / Arthur J. Kuhn. — University Park : Pennsylvania State University Press, 1986. — p. cm. — *Includes index. — Bibliography: p*

CYPRIOTES — England — London — Ethnic identity

BRIDGWOOD, Ann
Marriage, honour and property : Turkish Cypriots in North London / Ann Bridgwood. — 486 leaves. — *Only 1 set of photographs deposited. — PhD (Econ) 1986 LSE. — Photographs are shelved with thesis. — Leaves 452-477 are appendices*

CYPRIOTES — England — London — Social life and customs

BRIDGWOOD, Ann
Marriage, honour and property : Turkish Cypriots in North London / Ann Bridgwood. — 486 leaves. — *Only 1 set of photographs deposited. — PhD (Econ) 1986 LSE. — Photographs are shelved with thesis. — Leaves 452-477 are appendices*

CYPRUS — Economic conditions

Cyprus : a long-term development perspective. — Washington, D.C. : The World Bank, 1987. — xvii,79p. — (A World Bank country study)

CYPRUS — Economic policy

Cyprus : a long-term development perspective. — Washington, D.C. : The World Bank, 1987. — xvii,79p. — (A World Bank country study)

CYPRUS — Ethnic relations

JOSEPH, Joseph S.
Cyprus : ethnic conflict and international concern / Joseph S. Joseph. — New York : P. Lang, c1985. — xiv, 300 p.. — (American university studies. Series X, Political science ; vol. 6). — *Includes index. — Bibliography: p. [285]-291*

CYPRUS — Foreign relations

JOSEPH, Joseph S.
Cyprus : ethnic conflict and international concern / Joseph S. Joseph. — New York : P. Lang, c1985. — xiv, 300 p.. — (American university studies. Series X, Political science ; vol. 6). — *Includes index. — Bibliography: p. [285]-291*

CYPRUS — History

JOSEPH, Joseph S.
Cyprus : ethnic conflict and international concern / Joseph S. Joseph. — New York : P. Lang, c1985. — xiv, 300 p.. — (American university studies. Series X, Political science ; vol. 6). — *Includes index. — Bibliography: p. [285]-291*

VANEZIS, Procopios Nichola
Cyprus : the unfinished agony / P.N. Vanezis. — London : Abelard-Schuman, 1977. — x,141p,[4]p of plates. — *Bibliography: p.112-115*

CYPRUS — History — Cyprus crisis, 1974-

HALLEY, Laurence
Ancient affections : ethnic groups and foreign policy / Laurence Halley. — New York : Praeger, 1985. — viii, 180 p.. — *Includes index. — Bibliography: p. 172-174*

CYPRUS — Politics and government

JOSEPH, Joseph S.
Cyprus : ethnic conflict and international concern / Joseph S. Joseph. — New York : P. Lang, c1985. — xiv, 300 p.. — (American university studies. Series X, Political science ; vol. 6). — *Includes index. — Bibliography: p. [285]-291*

KOUMOULIDES, John T. A.
Cyprus in transition, 1960-1985 / editor John T.A. Koumoulides ; contributors Lord Carver ... [et al.]. — London : Trigraph, 1986. — xv,173p. — *Bibliography: p157-158. — Includes index*

REDDAWAY, John
Burdened with Cyprus : the British connection / John Reddaway. — London : Weidenfeld & Nicolson, c1986. — 37p. — *Includes index*

VANEZIS, Procopios Nichola
Cyprus : the unfinished agony / P.N. Vanezis. — London : Abelard-Schuman, 1977. — x,141p,[4]p of plates. — *Bibliography: p.112-115*

CYPRUS — Population — Statistics

CYPRUS. Department of Statistics and Research
Demographic survey, 1980/1981. — [Nicosia] : the Department, [1984]. — 349p. — (Population statistics / Cyprus. Department of Statistics and Research. Series 3 ; Report no.4)

CYPRUS — Statistics, Vital

AGATHANGELOU, Alecos
Mortality in Cyprus / by Alecos Agathangelou. — [Nicosia] : Department of Statistics and Research, [1985]. — 56p. — (Population statistics / Department of Statistics and Research. Series 3 ; Report no.5). — *Bibliography: p55-56*

CZECH AMERICANS — Minnesota — Minneapolis — Social life and customs

The Bohemian Flats / compiled by the workers of the Writers' Program of the Work Projects Administration in the State of Minnesota ; with an introduction by Thaddeus Radzilowsky. — St. Paul : Minnesota Historical Society Press, 1986. — p. cm. — (Borealis books). — : Reprint. Originally published: Minneapolis : University of Minnesota Press, 1941. With new introd. and index. — *Bibliography: p[189]-203*

CZECH SOCIALIST REPUBLIC (CZECHOSLOVAKIA) — Census — 1980

CZECH SOCIALIST REPUBLIC. Czechoslovakia. Český Statistický Úřad
[Census]. Sčítání lidu, domů a bytů 1980. — Praha : Český Statistický Úřad, 1982. — 303p

CZECH SOCIALIST REPUBLIC (CZECHOSLOVAKIA) — Statistics

CZECH SOCIALIST REPUBLIC. Czechoslovakia. Český Statistický Úřad
[Census]. Sčítání lidu, domů a bytů 1980. — Praha : Český Statistický Úřad, 1982. — 303p

CZECHOSLAVAKIA — Presidents — Correspondence

PECHÁČEK, Jaroslav
Masaryk - Beneš -Hrad : Masarykovy dopisi Benešovi / Jaroslav Pecháček. — München : České Slovo, 1984. — 182p

CZECHOSLOVAKIA

HUSÁK, Gustáv
Gustáv Husák, President of Czechoslovakia, speeches and writings. — Oxford : Pergamon, 1986. — xxiii,267p,[32]p of plates. — (Leaders of the world). — *Translated from the Czech. — Includes index*

CZECHOSLOVAKIA — Bibliography

SHORT, David, 19---
Czechoslovakia / David Short, compiler. — Oxford : Clio, c1986. — xxv,409p. — (World bibliographical series ; v.68). — *Includes index*

CZECHOSLOVAKIA — Census — 1980

CZECHOSLOVAKIA. Federální Statistický Úřad
[Census]. Sčítání lidu, domů a bytů 1.11.1980 : rychlé výsledky. — Praha : Federální Statistický Úřad, 1981. — 200p

CZECHOSLOVAKIA. Federální Statistický Úřad
[Census]. Sčítání lidu, domů a bytů, 1.11.1980. — Praha : Federální Statistický Úřad, 1982. — 15microfiches

CZECHOSLOVAKIA. Federální Statistický Úřad
[Census]. Vývoj společnosti ČSSR : (podle výsledků sčítání lidu, domů a bytů 1980) : tabulková část. — [Praha] : Federální Statistický Úřad, 1985. — 141p

CZECHOSLOVAKIA. Federální Statistický Úřad
[Census]. Vývoj společnosti ČSSR : (podle výsledků sčítání lidu, domů a bytů 1980) : textová část. — [Praha] : Federální Statistický Úřad, 1985. — 238p

CZECHOSLOVAKIA — Census — 1980-

CZECHOSLOVAKIA. Federální Statistický Úřad
[Census]. Sčítání lidu, domů a bytů 1.11.1980 : střediskovost, sídelní typy a velikostní skupiny obcí. — Praha : Federální Statistický Úřad, 1982. — 164 leaves. — (Československá statistika)

CZECHOSLOVAKIA — Commerce

Czechoslovak foreign trade. — Praha : Rapid Czechoslovak Advertising Agency, 1987-. — *Monthly*

Effektivnost' sotsialisticheskoi vnutrennei torgovli / R. A. Maksimento...[et al.] ; pod redaktsiei V. I. Ivanitskogo i L. Rendosha. — Kiev : Vyshcha shkola, 1985. — 174p

CZECHOSLOVAKIA — Foreign relations — Germany

KŘEN, Jan
Integration oder Ausgrenzung : Deutsche und Tschechen 1890-1945 / J. Křen, V. Kural [und] D. Brandes ; mit einen Vorwort von Dieter Beyran. — Bremen : Donat und Temmen, 1986. — 156p. — *Bibliographical notes*

CZECHOSLOVAKIA — Foreign relations — Soviet Union

FLORIA, B. N.
Rossiia i cheshskoe vosstanie protiv Gabsburgov / B. N. Floria ; otv. redaktor A. S. Myl'nikov. — Moskva : Nauka, 1986. — 206p

CZECHOSLOVAKIA — History

MICHEL, Bernard
La mémoire de Prague : conscience nationale et intelligentsia dans l'histoire tchèque et slovaque / Bernard Michel. — Paris : Librairie Académique Perrin, 1986. — 220p

CZECHOSLOVAKIA — History — 1918-1938

KALVODA, Josef
The genesis of Czechoslovakia / Josef Kalvoda. — Boulder, Colo. : East European Monographs ; New York : distributed by Columbia University Press, 1986. — viii,673p. — (East European Monographs ; no.209). — *Bibliography: p611-648*

CZECHOSLOVAKIA — History — 1938-1945

KŘEN, Jan
Integration oder Ausgrenzung : Deutsche und Tschechen 1890-1945 / J. Křen, V. Kural [und] D. Brandes ; mit einen Vorwort von Dieter Beyran. — Bremen : Donat und Temmen, 1986. — 156p. — *Bibliographical notes*

NESVADBA, František
Proč nezahřměla děla / František Nesvadba. — [Praha] : Naše vojsko, 1986. — 397p. — (Živá minulost ; sv.85). — *Bibliography: p389-394*

CZECHOSLOVAKIA — History — 1938-1945 — Sources

Kampf - Widerstand - Verfolgung der sudetendeutschen Sozialdemokraten : Dokumentation der deutschen Sozialdemokraten aus der Tschechoslowakei im Kampf gegen Henlein und Hitler / erarbeitet von Adolf Hasenöhrl. — Stuttgart : Seliger-Gemeinde, 1983. — 649p

CZECHOSLOVAKIA — History — Intervention, 1968

ZEMAN, Zbynek Anthony Bohuslav
Prague spring : a report on Czechoslovakia, 1968 / Z. A. B. Zeman. — Harmondsworth : Penguin Books, 1969. — 169p

CZECHOSLOVAKIA — Intellectual life

MICHEL, Bernard
La mémoire de Prague : conscience nationale et intelligentsia dans l'histoire tchèque et slovaque / Bernard Michel. — Paris : Librairie Académique Perrin, 1986. — 220p

CZECHOSLOVAKIA — Intellectual life — 1945-

Václav Havel, or, Living in truth : twenty-two essays published on the occasion of the award of the Erasmus Prize to Václav Havel / edited by Jan Vladislav. — London : Faber, 1987. — xix,315p. — *Translation from various European languages*

CZECHOSLOVAKIA — Politics and government

KAPLAN, Karel
The overcoming of the regime crisis after Stalin's death in Czechoslovakia, Poland and Hungary / Karel Kaplan. — Munchen : Projekt 'Crises in Soviet-type systems', 1986. — 119p. — (Research project Crises in Soviet-type systems ; Study no.11)

CZECHOSLOVAKIA — Politics and government — 1938-1945

FEIERABEND, Ladislav
Soumrak československé demokracie / Ladislav Feierabend. — Londyn : Rozmluvy. — *Vyšlo v červenci 1986 jako 30. svazek edice časopisu Rozmluvy*
[1]. — 1986. — 321p

CZECHOSLOVAKIA — Politics and government — 1945-

KAPLAN, Karel
The short march : the communist take-over in Czechoslovakia : 1945-1948 / Karel Kaplan. — London : Hurst, c1987. — xiv,207p. — *Translation of: Der Kurze Marsch.* — *Bibliography: p195-200. — Includes index*

CZECHOSLOVAKIA — Presidents — Biography

Klement Gottwald : revolucionař a politik : sborník statí / [redakční rada: Ivan Krempa, Antonín Faltys, Květoslava Volková]. — Praha : Nakladatelství Svoboda, 1986. — 353p

CZECHOSLOVAKIA — Presidents — Correspondence

PECHÁČEK, Jaroslav
Masaryk - Beneš -Hrad : Masarykovy dopisi Benešovi / Jaroslav Pecháček. — München : České Slovo, 1984. — 182p

CZECHOSLOVAKIA — Social conditions

CZECHOSLOVAKIA. Federální Statistický Úřad
[Census]. Vývoj společnosti ČSSR : (podle výsledků sčítání lidu, domů a bytů 1980) : tabulková část. — [Praha] : Federální Statistický Úřad, 1985. — 141p

DEYL, Zdeněk
Sociální vývoj Československa 1918-1938 / Zdeněk Deyl. — Praha : Academia, 1985. — 221p. — *Summary in German.* — *Bibliography: p212-216*

CZECHOSLOVAKIA — Social policy

DEYL, Zdeněk
Sociální vývoj Československa 1918-1938 / Zdeněk Deyl. — Praha : Academia, 1985. — 221p. — *Summary in German.* — *Bibliography: p212-216*

CZECHOSLOVAKIA — Statistics

CZECHOSLOVAKIA. Federální Statistický Úřad
[Census]. Sčítání lidu, domů a bytů 1.11.1980 : rychlé výsledky. — Praha : Federální Statistický Úřad, 1981. — 200p

CZECHOSLOVAKIA. Federální Statistický Úřad
[Census]. Sčítání lidu, domů a bytů 1.11.1980 : střediskovost, sídelní typy a velikostní skupiny obcí. — Praha : Federální Statistický Úřad, 1982. — 164 leaves. — (Československá statistika)

CZECHOSLOVAKIA. Federální Statistický Úřad
[Census]. Vývoj společnosti ČSSR : (podle výsledků sčítání lidu, domů a bytů 1980) : tabulková část. — [Praha] : Federální Statistický Úřad, 1985. — 141p

CZECHOSLOVAKIA. Federální Statistický Úřad
[Census]. Vývoj společnosti ČSSR : (podle výsledků sčítání lidu, domů a bytů 1980) : textová část. — [Praha] : Federální Statistický Úřad, 1985. — 238p

DACCA (BANGLADESH) — Social conditions

AHMED, Sharif Uddin
Dacca : a study in urban history and development / Sharif Uddin Ahmed. — London : Curzon, 1986. — xii,266p,[8]p of plates. — (London studies on South Asia ; no.4). — *Bibliography: p248-262. — Includes index*

DADRA AND NAGAR HAVELI (INDIA) — Population — Statistics

Census of India 1981 / S. K. Gandhe, Director of Census Operations, Dadra and Nagar Haveli. — [Delhi : Controller of Publications] Series 27: Dadra & Nagar Haveli. — [1985-]

DAIMLER-BENZ AKTIENGESELLSCHAFT — History

POHL, Hans
Die Daimler-Benz AG in den Jahren 1933 bis 1945 : eine Dokumentation / Hans Pohl, Stephanie Habeth, Beate Brüninghaus. — Stuttgart : Franz Steiner Verlag Wiesbaden, 1986. — vii,394p. — (Zeitschrift für Unternehmensgeschichte ; Beiheft 47). — *Bibliography: p[360]-384*

DAIRY CATTLE — Denmark

Malkekvaeghold i en billig løsdriftstald : den tekniske og økonomiske udvikling på en ejendom 1964-74. — København : I kommission hos Landhusholdningsselskabets Forlag, 1975. — 27p. — (Meddelelse / Det landøkonomiske Driftsbureau ; nr.19)

DAIRY FARMING — England — West Country — Finance

NIXON, B. R.
Dairy farm incomes : a study of 46 farms in South West England 1979-80 to 1983-84 / B.R. Nixon and K.I. Robbins. — Exeter (Lafrowda House, St. German's Rd, Exeter EX4 6TL) : University of Exeter, Agricultural Economics Unit, 1985. — i,57p

DAIRY PRODUCTS — Statistics
Milk and milk products balances in OECD countries. Bilans de lait et des produits laitiers dans les pays de l'OCDE / Organisation for Economic Co-operation and Development. — Paris : OECD, 1985-. — Annual. — Text in French and English

DAIRYING — Economic aspects — European Economic Community Countries
MEYNELL, Peter John
Milk producer organisations in the E.E.C. : current trends in organisational structure and member relations / Peter John Meynell. — Oxford : Plunkett Foundation for Co-operative Studies, 1986. — 32,[11]p. — Bibliography: p [33-35]

DAIRYING — Denmark
Investering i kvaeghold. — København : I kommission hos Landhusholdningsselskabets Forlag, 1977. — 20p. — (Meddelelse / Det Landøkonomiske Driftsbureau ; nr.25)

Malkekvaeghold i en billig løsdriftstald : den tekniske og økonomiske udvikling på en ejendom 1964-74. — København : I kommission hos Landhusholdningsselskabets Forlag, 1975. — 27p. — (Meddelelse / Det landøkonomiske Driftsbureau ; nr.19)

DALHOUSIE OCEAN STUDIES PROGRAMME
Management and utilization of the marine resources of the British Virgin Islands : a study conducted by the Dalhousie Ocean Studies Programme on behalf of the Government of the British Virgin Islands with funding from the Special Programs Division of the Canadian International Development Agency (CIDA). — Halifax, N.S. [Nova Scotia] : Dalhousie Ocean Studies Programme, Dalhousie University, 1985. — xi,125p

DALTON, HUGH
DALTON, Hugh
The political diary of Hugh Dalton, 1918-40, 1945-60 / edited by Ben Pimlott. — London : Cape in association with the London School of Economics and Political Science, 1986. — 737p,[16]p of plates. — Includes index

DANSKE BOGHANDLERMEDHJÆLPERFORENING
JØRGENSEN, Niels Chr.
BMFs historie 1883-1983 / Niels Chr. Jørgensen & Niels Erik Knudsen. — København : den Danske Boghandlermedhjælperforening, 1983. — 144p. — Bibliography: p143

DANVILLE (VA.) — Economic conditions
SIEGEL, Frederick F
The roots of southern distinctiveness : tobacco and society in Danville, Virginia, 1780-1865 / by Frederick F. Siegel. — Chapel Hill, N.C. : University of North Carolina Press, c1987. — p. cm. — Includes index. — Bibliography: p

DANVILLE (VA.) — Social conditions
SIEGEL, Frederick F
The roots of southern distinctiveness : tobacco and society in Danville, Virginia, 1780-1865 / by Frederick F. Siegel. — Chapel Hill, N.C. : University of North Carolina Press, c1987. — p. cm. — Includes index. — Bibliography: p

DARIBI
WAGNER, Roy
Symbols that stand for themselves / Roy Wagner. — Chicago : University of Chicago Press, 1986. — p. cm. — Sequel to: The invention of culture. — Includes index. — Bibliography: p

DARLING, Sir RALPH
FLETCHER, Brian, 1931-
Ralph Darling : a governor maligned / Brian H. Fletcher. — Melbourne ; Oxford : Oxford University Press, 1984. — xxi,473p. — Ill on lining papers. — Bibliography: p441-467. — Includes index

DARRÉ, WALTHUR
BRAMWELL, Anna
Blood and soil : Richard Walther Darré and Hitler's 'Green Party' / [Anna Bramwell]. — Bourne End : Kensal, c1985. — viii,288p,[8]p of plates. — Bibliography: p265-282. — Includes index

DARWIN, CHARLES
BETZIG, L. L
Despotism and differential reproduction : a Darwinian view of history / L.L. Betzig. — New York : Aldine Pub., 1986. — p. cm. — Bibliography: p

GRUBER, Howard E
Darwin on man : a psychological study of scientific creativity / Howard E. Gruber ; foreword to the 1st ed. by Jean Piaget. — 2d ed. — Chicago : University of Chicago Press, 1981. — xxvii, 310 p.. — First ed., published in 1974, entered under title: Darwin on man. — Includes bibliographical references and index

DARWIN, CHARLES — Influence
HOLBROOK, David
Evolution and the humanities / David Holbrook. — Aldershot : Gower, c1987. — [230]p. — (Avebury series in philosophy). — Includes bibliography and index

YOUNG, Robert M. (Robert Maxwell)
Darwin's metaphor : nature's place in Victorian culture / Robert M. Young. — Cambridge : Cambridge University Press, 1985. — xvii,341p . — Bibliography: p287-332. — Includes index

DAS KAPITAL
SHAW, George Bernard
Bernard Shaw & Karl Marx : a symposium, 1884-1889. — Folcroft, Pa. : Folcroft Library Editions, 1977. — ix, 200 p., [1] fold. leaf of plates. — Reprint of the 1930 ed. printed for Random House by R. W. Ellis, The Georgian Press, New York

DATA BASE MANAGEMENT
BRITISH NATIONAL CONFERENCE ON DATABASES (5th : 1986 : University of Kent at Canterbury)
Proceedings of the Fifth British National Conference on Databases (BNCOD 5) : University of Kent at Canterbury, 14-16 July 1986 / edited by E.A. Oxborrow. — Cambridge : Cambridge University Press on behalf of the British Computer Society, 1986. — [210]p. — (The British Computer Society Workshop series)

Data base directory. — White Plains, N.Y. : Published by Knowledge Industry Publications in cooperation with the American Society for Information Science, 1985-. — Semi-annual. — Includes monthly update, Data Base Alert

DATE, C. J.
An introduction to database systems / C.J. Date. — 4th ed. — Reading, Mass. ; Wokingham : Addison-Wesley. — (Addison-Wesley Systems programming series) Vol.1. — c1986. — xx, 639p. — Contains bibliographical references

DEEN, S. M.
Principles and practice of database systems / S.M. Deen. — Basingstoke : Macmillan Education, 1985. — [350]p. — (Macmillan computer science series)

GILLENSON, Mark L.
Database : step-by-step / Mark L. Gillenson. — New York ; Chichester : Wiley, c1985. — xviii,386p. — Includes bibliographies and index

HAWRYSZKIEWYCZ, I. T
Database analysis and design / I.T. Hawryszkiewycz. — Chicago : Science Research Associates, c1984. — xx, 578 p.. — Includes index. — Bibliography: p. 561-571

JONES, J. A. (John Anthony)
Databases in theory and practice / J.A. Jones. — London : Kogan Page, 1986. — 324p. — ([New technology modular series]). — Bibliography: p317-320. — Includes index

KORTH, Henry F
Database system concepts / Henry F. Korth, Abraham Silberschatz. — New York : McGraw-Hill, c1986. — p. cm. — (McGraw-Hill computer science series). — Includes index. — Bibliography: p

MARTIN, James, 1933-
Computer data-base organization / James Martin. — 2nd ed. — Englewood Cliffs ; London : Prentice-Hall, 1977. — xviii,713p. — (Prentice-Hall series in automatic computation) . — Col. ill. on lining papers. — Previous ed.: 1975. — Includes index

New applications of data bases / edited by G. Gardarin, E. Gelenbe. — London : Academic, 1984. — xii,273p. — Conference papers

PERKINSON, Richard C
Data analysis : the key to data base design / Richard C. Perkinson. — Wellesley, Mass. : QED Information Sciences, c1984. — xvii, 285 p.. — Bibliography: p. 283-285

SIMPSON, Alan
Understanding dBase III / Alan Simpson. — Berkeley ; London : Sybex, c1985. — xvi,300p

SIMPSON, Alan
Understanding dBASE III PLUS / Alan Simpson. — Berkeley : SYBEX, c1986. — xxiv, 415 p.. — (SYBEX computer books). — Includes index

TOWNSEND, Carl
Mastering dBase III : a structured approach / Carl Townsend. — Berkeley ; London : Sybex, c1985. — xvi,338p

WELDON, Jay-Louise
Data base administration / Jay-Louise Weldon. — New York ; London : Plenum, c1981. — xii,250p. — (Applications of modern technology in business). — Includes index

DATA BASES — Models
KORTH, Henry F
Database system concepts / Henry F. Korth, Abraham Silberschatz. — New York : McGraw-Hill, c1986. — p. cm. — (McGraw-Hill computer science series). — Includes index. — Bibliography: p

DATA LIBRARIES — Congresses
INTERNATIONAL CONFERENCE ON DATABASES IN THE HUMANITIES AND SOCIAL SCIENCES (4th : 1983 : New Brunswick, N.J.)
The International Conference on Databases in the Humanities and Social Sciences 1983 / edited by Robert F. Allen. — Osprey, Fla. : Paradigm Press, 1985. — 434p. — Cover title: Databases in the humanities and social sciences. — Bibliographical references

DATA PROTECTION — Great Britain
CORNWELL, Roger
Data protection : putting the record straight : the NCCL guide to the Data Protection Act / Roger Cornwell and Marie Staunton. — London : National Council for Civil Liberties, c1985. — 122p. — Bibliography: p106. — Includes index

GREAT BRITAIN. Parliament. House of Commons. Library. Research Division
Data protection and privacy / Barry K. Winetrobe. — [London] : the Division, 1982. — 23p. — (Background paper ; no.107)

GREAT BRITAIN. Parliament. House of Commons. Library. Research Division
Data Protection Bill, Bill 51, 1983-84 / Barry K. Winetrobe. — [London] : the Division, 1984. — 10p. — (Reference sheet ; no.84/1). — Bibliographical references: p7-10

GREAT BRITAIN. Parliament. House of Commons. Library. Research Division
Data Protection Bill (HL), Bill 117 of 1982-83 / Barry K. Winetrobe. — [London] : the Division, 1983. — 11p. — (Reference sheet ; no.83/8). — Bibliographical references: p2-5

DATA PROTECTION — Great Britain
continuation
GREATER LONDON COUNCIL. Central Computer Service
The Data Protection Act : implications, security, registration, training. — [London : the Council, 1985]. — 50 leaves

GULLEFORD, Kenneth
Data protection in practice / Kenneth Gulleford. — London : Butterworths, 1986. — xi,306p. — *Includes index*

DATA PROTECTION ACT
GREATER LONDON COUNCIL. Central Computer Service
The Data Protection Act : implications, security, registration, training. — [London : the Council, 1985]. — 50 leaves

DATA PROTECTION ACT 1984
CORNWELL, Roger
Data protection : putting the record straight : the NCCL guide to the Data Protection Act / Roger Cornwell and Marie Staunton. — London : National Council for Civil Liberties, c1985. — 122p. — *Bibliography: p106. — Includes index*

GULLEFORD, Kenneth
Data protection in practice / Kenneth Gulleford. — London : Butterworths, 1986. — xi,306p. — *Includes index*

DATA PROTECTION BILL 1982-83
GREAT BRITAIN. Parliament. House of Commons. Library. Research Division
Data Protection Bill (HL), Bill 117 of 1982-83 / Barry K. Winetrobe. — [London] : the Division, 1983. — 11p. — (Reference sheet ; no.83/8). — *Bibliographical references: p2-5*

DATA PROTECTION BILL 1983-84
GREAT BRITAIN. Parliament. House of Commons. Library. Research Division
Data Protection Bill, Bill 51, 1983-84 / Barry K. Winetrobe. — [London] : the Division, 1984. — 10p. — (Reference sheet ; no.84/1). — *Bibliographical references: p7-10*

DATA REDUCTION
EHRENBERG, A. S. C
A primer in data reduction : an introductory statistics textbook / A.S.C. Ehrenberg. — Chichester [West Sussex] ; New York : Wiley, c1982. — p. cm. — *Includes index*

DATA STRUCTURES (COMPUTER SCIENCE)
IFIP WG 2.6 WORKING CONFERENCE ON DATA SEMANTICS (DS-1) (1985 : Hasselt)
Database semantics (DS-1) : proceedings of the IFIP WG 2.6 Working Conference on Data Semantics (DS-1) Hasselt, Belgium, 7-11 January, 1985 / edited by T.B. Steel, Jr., R. Meersman. — Amsterdam ; Oxford : North-Holland, 1986. — x,323p. — *Cover title: Database semantics. — Includes bibliographies*

REINGOLD, Edward M.
Data structures in Pascal / Edward M. Reingold, Wilfred J. Hansen. — Boston : Little, Brown, c1986. — xvi, 505 p.. — (Little, Brown computer systems series). — *Includes bibliographies and index*

TREMBLAY, Jean-Paul
An introduction to data structures with applications / Jean-Paul Tremblay, Paul G. Sorenson. — 2nd ed. — New York ; London : McGraw Hill, 1984. — xviii,861p. — (McGraw-Hill computer science series). — *Previous ed.: 1976. Bibliography: p840-842. — Includes index*

DATA TRANSMISSION EQUIPMENT INDUSTRY — Canada
LESSER, Barry
Computer communications and the mass market in Canada / Barry Lesser, Louis Vagianos. — Montreal, Quebec : Institute for Research on Public Policy, c1985. — xxiii, 163 p.. — *Includes bibliographies*

DATABASE MANAGEMENT
Database: the magazine of database reference and review. — Western (CT) : Online, Inc, 1986. — *6 times per year*

Online: the magazine of online information systems. — Weston : On-Line, Inc., 1986-. — *6 times a year*

DATING (SOCIAL CUSTOMS)
MURSTEIN, Bernard I
Paths to marriage / by Bernard I. Murstein. — Beverly Hills, Calif. : Sage Publications, c1986. — p. cm. — (Family studies text series ; v. 5). — *Includes index*

DAUPHINÉ (FRANCE) — Economic conditions
HICKEY, Daniel
The coming of French absolutism : the struggle for tax reform in the Province of Dauphiné, 1540-1650 / Daniel Hickey. — Toronto ; London : University of Toronto Press, c1986. — 273 p.

DAUPHINÉ (FRANCE) — History
HICKEY, Daniel
The coming of French absolutism : the struggle for tax reform in the Province of Dauphiné, 1540-1650 / Daniel Hickey. — Toronto ; London : University of Toronto Press, c1986. — 273 p.

DAVEY, KEITH
DAVEY, Keith
The rainmaker : a passion for politics / Keith Davey. — Toronto : Stoddart, 1986. — xii,383p

DAVIS, WILLIAM G
HOY, Claire
Bill Davis : a biography / by Claire Hoy. — Toronto : New York : Methuen, c1985. — 413 p., [16] p. of plates. — *Includes index*

DAY CARE CENTERS — Denmark
ANDERSEN, Bjarne Hjorth
Dagpasning for de 6-10-årige. — København : Socialforskninginstituttet, 1987. — 105p. — (Publikation / Socialforskningsinstituttet ; 159). — *Bibliography: p102*

DAY CARE CENTERS — England
BONE, Margaret
Pre-school children and the need for day-care : a survey carried out on behalf of the Department of Health and Social Security / Margaret Bone. — London : H.M.S.O., 1977. — vi,95p. — *At head of title: Office of Population Censuses and Surveys, Social Survey Division*

DAY CARE CENTERS — European Economic Community countries
PICHAULT, Camille
Day-care facilities and services for children under the age of three in the European Community / by Camille Pichault. — Luxembourg : Office for Official Publications of the European Communities, 1984. — ii,143p . — *At head of title page: Commission of the European Communities*

DAY CARE CENTERS — United States
FALLOWS, Deborah
A mother's work / Deborah Fallows. — Boston : Houghton-Mifflin, 1985. — p. cm. — *"A Richard Todd book"--*

DBASE III (COMPUTER PROGRAM)
COWART, Robert
The ABC's of dBASE III PLUS / Robert Cowart. — Berkeley : Sybex, [1986]. — 264p

DBASE III (COMPUTER PROGRAM)
SIMPSON, Alan
Understanding dBase III / Alan Simpson. — Berkeley ; London : Sybex, c1985. — xvi,300p

DBASE III (COMPUTER PROGRAM)
TOWNSEND, Carl
Mastering dBase III : a structured approach / Carl Townsend. — Berkeley ; London : Sybex, c1985. — xvi,338p

TOWNSEND, Carl
Mastering dBASE III PLUS : a structural approach / Carl Townsend. — Berkeley : Sybex, [1986]. — 342p

DBASE III PLUS (COMPUTER PROGRAM)
SIMPSON, Alan
Understanding dBASE III PLUS / Alan Simpson. — Berkeley : SYBEX, c1986. — xxiv, 415 p.. — (SYBEX computer books). — *Includes index*

SIMPSON, Alan, 1953-
Advanced techniques in dBASE III PLUS / Alan Simpson. — Berkeley ; London : SYBEX, c1986. — xxiii,454p. — *Includes index*

DE FINETTI, BRUNO
Bayesian inference and decision techniques : essays in honor of Bruno de Finetti / edited by Prem K. Croel [and] Arnold Zellner. — Amsterdam : North Holland, 1986. — 496p. — (Studies in Bayesian econometrics and statistics ; 6)

DE GASPERI, ALEIDE
DE GASPERI, Maria Romana
Mio caro padre : con otto testimonianze / Maria Romana de Gasperi. — 3 ed. — Brescia : Morcelliana, 1981. — 223p. — *First published 1979*

DE SECONDAT, CHARLES, baron de Montesquieu *See* Montesquieu, Charles de Secondat, baron de

DE TOCQUEVILLE, ALEXIS *See* Tocqueville, Alexis de

DEAF — Means of communication
Teaching and talking with deaf children / by David Wood ... [et al.] with contributions by Margaret Tait and Sue Lewis. — Chichester : Wiley, c1986. — xiii,199p. — (Wiley series in developmental psychology and its applications). — *Bibliography: p187-193. — Includes index*

DEAF — Great Britain — Public opinion
BUNTING, Claire
Public attitudes to deafness : a survey carried out on behalf of the Department of Health and Social Security / Claire Bunting. — London : H.M.S.O., 1981. — vi,43p. — *At head of title: Office of Population Censuses and Surveys Social Survey Division*

DEAF — United States — Biography
LANE, Harlan L
When the mind hears : a history of the deaf / Harlan Lane. — 1st ed. — New York : Random House, c1984. — xvii, 537 p.. — *Includes index. — Bibliography: p. [457]-518*

DEAF — United States — History
LANE, Harlan L
When the mind hears : a history of the deaf / Harlan Lane. — 1st ed. — New York : Random House, c1984. — xvii, 537 p.. — *Includes index. — Bibliography: p. [457]-518*

DEATH — Political aspects — France — History — 18th century
KELLY, George Armstrong
Mortal politics in eighteenth-century France / George Kelly Armstrong. — Waterloo, Ontario : University of Waterloo Press, 1986. — xxiii,334p. — *Bibliographical note: p[318]*

DEATH — Proof and certification — United States
CANTOR, Norman L
Legal frontiers of death and dying / by Norman L. Cantor. — Bloomington : Indiana University Press, c1987. — p. cm. — (Medical ethics series). — *Includes index*

DEATH — Psychological aspects
WILCOX, Sandra Galdieri
Understanding death and dying : an interdisciplinary approach / Sandra Galdieri Wilcox and Marilyn Sutton. — 3rd ed. — Palo Alto ; London : Mayfield, c1985. — xxii,428p

DEATH — Social aspects
WILCOX, Sandra Galdieri
Understanding death and dying : an interdisciplinary approach / Sandra Galdieri Wilcox and Marilyn Sutton. — 3rd ed. — Palo Alto ; London : Mayfield, c1985. — xxii,428p

DEATH — Social aspects — Oceania
Aging and its transformations : moving toward death in pacific societies / edited by Dorothy Ayers Counts, David R. Counts. — Lanham, MD : University Press of America, c1985. — 336 p., [2] p. of plates. — (ASAO monograph ; no. 10). — "Co-published by arrangement with the Association for Social Anthropology in Oceania"--T.p. verso. — Includes index. — Bibliography: p. [275]-313

DEBREU, GERARD
Contributions to mathematical economics in honor of Gérard Debreu / edited by Werner Hildenbrand, Andreau Mas-Colell. — Amsterdam ; New York : North Holland ; New York, N.Y., U.S.A. : Sole distributors for the U.S.A. and Canada, Elsevier Science Pub. Co., 1986. — p. cm

DEBT — Brazil
MARTONE, Celso L.
Macroeconomic policies, debt accumulation, and adjustment in Brazil, 1965-84 / Celso L. Martone. — Washington, D.C. : The World Bank, 1987. — 43p. — (World Bank discussion papers ; no.8). — Includes bibliographical references

DEBT — Germany (West) — Statistics
GERMANY (Federal Republic). Statistisches Bundesamt
Einkommens- und Verbrauchsstichprobe 1983. — Wiesbaden : the Bundesamt. — (Wirtschaftsrechnungen)
Heft 2: Vermögenbestände und Schulden privater Haushalte. — 1986. — 540p

DEBT — Great Britain
CONFEDERATION OF BRITISH INDUSTRY
Late payment of trade debts : questionnaire results. — London : Confederation of British Industry, 1986. — 22p

DEBT RELIEF
MENDELSOHN, Stefan
Commercial banks and the restructuring of cross-border debt / by M.S. Mendelsohn. — New York : Group of Thirty, 1983. — 36 p.. — "This study is based partly on interviews with commercial banks and supervisors in the United States and Europe by Mario Deaglio, Karl Grun, Jenny Ireland, Roshanak Khalili, and Ann Tutwiler."

DEBT RELIEF — Brazil
BATISTA JUNIOR, Paulo Nogueira
International financial flows to Brazil since the late 1960s : an analysis of debt expansion and payments problems / Paulo Nogueira Batista. — Washington, D.C. : The World Bank, 1987. — vi,66p. — (World Bank discussion papers ; 7). — Bibliographical references: p59-66

DEBT RELIEF — Developing countries
CARVOUNIS, Chris C
The foreign debt/national development conflict : external adjustment and internal disorder in the developing nations / Chris C. Carvounis. — New York : Quorum Books, 1986. — xxiii, 243 p.. — Includes index. — Bibliography: p. [223]-235

DEBTOR AND CREDITOR — England
OUGH, Richard N.
The Mareva injunction and Anton Piller order : practice and precedents / by Richard N. Ough. — London : Butterworths, 1987. — xxii,175p. — Includes index

DEBTOR AND CREDITOR — Scotland
GREGORY, Janet
Survey of defenders in debt actions in Scotland / Janet Gregory and Janet Monk. — London : H.M.S.O., 1981. — ix,109p. — (Research report for the Scottish Law Commission / Great Britain. Office of Population Censuses and Surveys. Social Survey Division ; no. 6). — Includes index

DEBTS, EXTERNA
MENDELSOHN, Stefan
Commercial banks and the restructuring of cross-border debt / by M.S. Mendelsohn. — New York : Group of Thirty, 1983. — 36 p.. — "This study is based partly on interviews with commercial banks and supervisors in the United States and Europe by Mario Deaglio, Karl Grun, Jenny Ireland, Roshanak Khalili, and Ann Tutwiler."

DEBTS, EXTERNAL
GREAT BRITAIN. Parliament. House of Commons. Library. Research Division
The international monetary system and the world debt crisis / Christopher Barclay. — [London] : the Division, 1983. — 18p. — (Background paper ; no.126)

HEFFERNAN, Shelagh A.
Sovereign risk analysis / Shelagh A. Heffernan. — London : Allen & Unwin, 1986. — [200]p. — Includes index

International borrowing : negotiating and structuring international debt transactions / Daniel D. Bradlow, editor. — 2nd ed. — Washington, D.C. : International Law Institute, c1986. — 499p. — (International negotiation and development : sourcebooks on policy and practice ; 1)

KRAYENBUEHL, Thomas E.
Country risk : assessment and monitoring / Thomas E. Krayenbuehl. — Cambridge : Woodhead-Faulkner, 1985. — x,180p. — Bibliography: p169. — Includes index

DEBTS, EXTERNAL — Dictionaries — Polyglot
Borrowing and lending terminology : English-French-Spanish = Terminologie des emprunts et des prêts : Français-anglais-espagnol = Terminología de empréstitos y prśetamos : Español-inglés-francés. — Washington, D.C. : The World Bank, 1984. — vii,56p. — (A World Bank glossary). — In English, French and Spanish

DEBTS, EXTERNAL — Reporting — Handbooks, manuals, etc.
World Bank Debt reporting system manual. — Washington, D.C. : World Bank, 1980. — 30p

DEBTS, EXTERNAL — Brazil
BATISTA JUNIOR, Paulo Nogueira
International financial flows to Brazil since the late 1960s : an analysis of debt expansion and payments problems / Paulo Nogueira Batista. — Washington, D.C. : The World Bank, 1987. — vi,66p. — (World Bank discussion papers ; 7). — Bibliographical references: p59-66

FRAGA, Arminio
German reparations and Brazilian debt : a comparative study / Arminio Fraga. — Princeton, N.J. : Princeton University. Department of Economics. International Finance Section, 1986. — 34p. — (Essays in international finance ; no.163). — Bibliography: p28-29

DEBTS, EXTERNAL. — Brazil
MARTONE, Celso L.
Macroeconomic policies, debt accumulation, and adjustment in Brazil, 1965-84 / Celso L. Martone. — Washington, D.C. : The World Bank, 1987. — 43p. — (World Bank discussion papers ; no.8). — Includes bibliographical references

DEBTS, EXTERNAL — Caribbean Area
CASTRO, Fidel
Speech at closing session [of the] meeting on the foreign debt of Latin America and the Caribbean / Fidel Castro. — La Habana : Editora Politica, 1985. — 53p

DEBTS, EXTERNAL — Developing countres
CUDDINGTON, John T
Capital flight : estimates, issues, and explanations / John T. Cuddington. — Princeton, N.J. : International Finance Section, Dept. of Economics, Princeton University, c1986. — 44 p.. — (Princeton studies in international finance ; no. 58 (Dec. 1986). — Bibliography: p. 39-40

DEBTS, EXTERNAL — Developing countries
CARVOUNIS, Chris C
The foreign debt/national development conflict : external adjustment and internal disorder in the developing nations / Chris C. Carvounis. — New York : Quorum Books, 1986. — xxiii, 243 p.. — Includes index. — Bibliography: p. [223]-235

CLAUSEN, A. W.
Third World debt and global recovery : the 1983 Jodidi Lecture at the Center for International Affairs, Harvard University / by A. W. Clausen. — Washington, D.C. : World Bank, 1983. — 22p

DORNBUSCH, Rudiger
Dollars, debts, and deficits / Rudiger Dornbusch. — 1st MIT Press ed. — Leuven, Belgium : Leuven University Press ; Cambridge, Mass. : MIT Press, 1986. — 240 p. . — The Professor Dr. Gaston Eyskens lectures delivered at the Katholieke Universiteit Leuven, Belgium in the fall of 1984. — Includes bibliographies and index

Economic report of the people / Center for Popular Economics. — 1st ed. — Boston : South End Press, c1986. — xvii, 260 p.. — The crossed out word "President" appears in the title before the word "people.". — Includes bibliographies and index

GHARTEY, J. B.
Crisis accountability and development in the Third World : the case of Africa / J.B. Ghartey. — Aldershot : Gower, c1987. — [259]p. — Includes bibliography and index

LOXLEY, John
Debt and disorder : external financing for development / John Loxley. — Boulder : Westview Press, 1986. — p. cm. — (Westview special studies in social, political, and economic development). — Includes index. — Bibliography: p

MILLER, Morris
Coping is not enough! : the international debt crisis and the roles of the World Bank and International Monetary Fund / Morris Miller. — Homewood, Ill. : Dow Jones-Irwin, c1986. — xiii, 268 p.. — Includes bibliographical references and index

POOL, John Charles
The ABCs of international finance : understanding the trade and debt crisis / John Charles Pool, Steve Stamos. — Lexington, Mass. : Lexington Books, c1987. — xii, 138 p.. — Includes index. — Bibliography: p. [131]-132

SCHATAN, Jacobo
World debt : who is to pay? / Jacobo Schatan with the collaboration of Gilda Schatan. — London : Zed, 1987. — [144]p. — Translation of: America Latina, deuda extema y desarrollo. — Includes bibliography and index

WATKINS, Alfred J.
Till debt do us part : who wins, who loses, and who pays for the international debt crisis / Alfred J. Watkins. — London : University Press of America, 1987. — [108]p

WELLONS, Philip A
Passing the buck : banks, governments, and Third World debt / Philip A. Wellons. — Boston, Mass. : Harvard Business School Press, c1987. — xiv, 342 p.. — Includes bibliographical references and index

DEBTS, EXTERNAL — Developing countries — Congresses

SEMINÁRIO "AJUSTAMENTO E CRESCIMENTO NA ACTUAL CONJUNTURA ECONÓMICA MUNDIAL" (1985 : Estoril)
Ajustamento e crescimento na actual conjuntura económica mundial / editado por José de Silva Lopes. — Washington, D.C. : International Monetary Fund, 1985. — xi,200p. — *Includes bibliographical references*

DEBTS, EXTERNAL — Developing countries — Management

ALL PARTY PARLIAMENTARY GROUP ON OVERSEAS DEVELOPMENT. Second Working Party
Managing Third World debt : report of the Second Working Party established by the All Party Parliamentary Group on Overseas Development. — London : Overseas Development Institute, 1987. — 76p

DEBTS, EXTERNAL — Developing countries — Statistics

Developoment and debt service : dilemma of the 1980s. — Washington, D.C. : The World Bank, 1986. — xlv,26p. — *"An abridged version of 'World debt tables' 1985-86 edition"*

DEBTS, EXTERNAL — Germany

FRAGA, Arminio
German reparations and Brazilian debt : a comparative study / Arminio Fraga. — Princeton, N.J. : Princeton University. Department of Economics. International Finance Section, 1986. — 34p. — (Essays in international finance ; no.163). — *Bibliography: p28-29*

DEBTS, EXTERNAL — Latin America

CASTRO, Fidel
Speech at closing session [of the] meeting on the foreign debt of Latin America and the Caribbean / Fidel Castro. — La Habana : Editora Politica, 1985. — 53p

CONFERENCE "BEYOND THE DEBT CRISIS - LATIN AMERICA: THE NEXT TEN YEARS" (1986 : London)
Beyond the debt crisis - Latin America : the next ten years. — London : Inter-American Development Bank : Internationl Herald Tribune, 1986. — 146p

External debt in Latin America : adjustment policies and renegotiation / Economic Commission for Latin America and the Caribbean. — Boulder, Colo. : L. Rienner Publishers, 1985. — viii, 125p. — *Includes index.* — *Bibliography: p.117-122*

Latin American debt and the adjustment crisis / edited by Rosemary Thorp and Laurence Whitehead. — Basingstoke : Macmillan in association with St Antony's College, Oxford, 1987. — xv,359p. — (St Antony's/Macmillan series). — *Includes bibliographies and index*

WIARDA, Howard J.
Latin America at the crossroads : debt, development, and the future / Howard J. Wiarda. — Boulder, Colo. : Westview Press ; Washington, D.C. : American Enterprise Institute for Public Policy Research, 1987. — xiii, 114 p.. — *Includes index.* — *Bibliography: p. 99-105*

DEBTS, EXTERNAL — United States

SOLOMON, Anthony M
The dollar, debt, and the trade deficit / Anthony M. Solomon. — New York : New York University Press, 1986, c1987. — p. cm. — (The Joseph I. Lubin memorial lectures ; no. 3)

DEBTS, PUBLIC

HEFFERNAN, Shelagh A.
Sovereign risk analysis / Shelagh A. Heffernan. — London : Allen & Unwin, 1986. — [200]p. — *Includes index*

KRAYENBUEHL, Thomas E.
Country risk : assessment and monitoring / Thomas E. Krayenbuehl. — Cambridge : Woodhead-Faulkner, 1985. — x,180p. — *Bibliography: p169.* — *Includes index*

DEBTS, PUBLIC — Congresses

INTERNATIONAL INSTITUTE OF PUBLIC FINANCE. Congress (1984 : Innsbruck, Austria)
Public finance and public debt = : Finances publiques et endettement public : proceedings of the 40th Congress of the International Institute of Public Finance, Innsbruck, 1984 / edited by Bernard P. Herber. — Detroit, Mich. : Wayne State University Press, c1985. — p. cm. — *English and French*

Public expenditure : the key issues / edited by John Bristow and Declan McDonagh. — Dublin, Ireland : Institute of Public Administration, 1986. — 138 p.. — *Proceedings of National Conference on Public Expenditure: the Key Issues, held Nov. 1985 in Dublin, organized by the Institute.* — *Includes bibliographies.* — *Contents: Public expenditure and public debt / Vito Tanzi -- The political economy of public expenditure / Alan Peacock -- Public employment and public expenditure / Richard Rose -- Public expenditure and the bureaucracy / Peter Jackson -- An Irish overview / Alan Dukes*

DEBTS, PUBLIC — Australia

Australia's foreign and public sector debt. — Canberra : Economic Planning Advisory Council, 1985. — v,29p. — (Council paper / Economic Plannning Advisory Council ; no.6). — *Bibliographical references: p18-19*

DEBTS, PUBLIC — Germany

ERHARD, Ludwig
Kriegsfinanzierung und Schuldenkonsolidierung / Ludwig Erhard ; mit Vorbemerkungen von Ludwig Erhard, Theodor Eschenburg, Günter Schmölders. — Faks.-Dr. d. Denkschr. von 1943-44. — Frankfurt/M ; Berlin ; Wien : Propyläen, 1977. — xxxiv, 268 p. — *On spine: Denkschrift 1943/44.* — *"Eine Veröffentlichung der Ludwig-Erhard-Stiftung e.V. Bonn. Materialien zur Zeitgeschichte."*

DEBTS, PUBLIC — India

MISHRA, D. K.
Public debt and economic development in India / D.K. Mishra. — Lucknow : Print House (India), c1985. — xii, 552 p.. — *Includes bibliographical references and index*

DEBTS, PUBLIC — United States

MALKIN, Lawrence
The national debt / Lawrence Malkin. — 1st ed. — New York : Holt, c1987. — ix, 309 p.. — *Includes index.* — *Bibliography: p. 277-298*

DEBTS,PUBLIC — Organisation for Economic Co-operation and Development countries

CHOURAQUI, Jean-Claude
Public debt in a medium-term context and its implications for fiscal policy / by Jean-Claude Chouraqui, Brian Jones and Robert Bruce Montador. — [Paris] : OECD, 1986. — 67P. — (Working papers / OECD. Department of Economics and Statistics ; no.30). — *Bibliographical references: p.32-37*

DEBUGGING IN COMPUTER SCIENCE

PERRY, William E
Cleaning up a computer mess : a guide to diagnosing and correcting computer problems / William E. Perry. — New York : Van Nostrand Reinhold, c1986. — xii, 255 p.. — *Includes index*

WRAY, William C
What every engineer should know about microcomputer systems design and debugging / Bill Wray and Bill Crawford. — New York, N.Y. : M. Dekker, c1984. — ix, 183 p.. — (What every engineer should know ; v. 12). — *Includes index*

DECAZEVILLE (FRANCE) — Industries — History

REID, Donald, 1952-
The miners of Decazeville : a genealogy of deindustrialization / Donald Reid. — Cambridge, Mass. ; London : Harvard University Press, 1985. — vi,333p. — *Includes index*

DECEDENTS' FAMILY MAINTENANCE — England

ROSS MARTYN, John G.
Family provision : law and practice / by John G. Ross Martyn. — 2nd ed. — London : Sweet & Maxwell, 1985. — xviii,187p. — *Previous ed.: published as The modern law of family provision. 1978.* — *Includes index*

DECEMBRISTS

DRUZHININ, N. M.
Izbrannye trudy / N. M. Druzhinin. — Moskva : Nauka
[1]: Revoliutsionnoe dvizhenie v Rossii v XIX v. / otv. redaktor S. S. Dmitriev. — 1985. — 484p

NEVELEV, G. A.
"Istina sil'nee Tsaria..." : A. S. Pushkin v rabote nad istoriei dekabristov / G. A. Nevelev. — Moskva : Mysl', 1985. — 203p

Obshchestvennaia mysl' v Rossii XIX v. / [redaktsionnaia kollegiia: A. N. Tsamutali...[et al.]. — Leningrad : Nauka, Leningradskoe otdelenie, 1986. — 244p. — (Trudy / Institut istorii SSSR, Leningradskoe otdelenie ; Vyp.16) . — *Contains chart: "Skhema razvitiia dekabristskikh i sviazannykh s nimi organizatsii."*

DECENTRALISATION IN GOVERNMENT — Europe

Decentralisation of local government at neighbourhood level / ... prepared by the Secretariat of the Steering Committee for Regional and Municipal Matters with the assistance of Sven-Runo Bergqvist. — Strasbourg : Council of Europe, 1981. — 30p. — (Study series local and regional authorities in Europe ; study no. 27)

Functional decentralisation at local and regional level / report prepared by the Steering Committee for Regional and Municipal Matters. — Strasbourg : Council of Europe, 1981. — i,29p. — (Study series local and regional authorities in Europe ; study no. 26)

Methods of consulting citizens on municipal affairs. — Strasbourg : Council of Europe, 1979. — iii,43p. — (Study series local and regional authorities in Europe ; study no. 18). — *"Prepared by the Secretariat of the Steering Committee for Regional and Municipal Matters with the assistance of two consultants, Mr. Bart (France) and Mr. Couchepin (Switzerland)"*

DECENTRALISATION IN GOVERNMENT — France — Bordeaux

GARRISH, Stephen
Centralisation and decentralisation in England and France / Stephen Garrish. — Bristol : University of Bristol, School for Advanced Urban Studies, 1986. — xvi,160p. — (Occasional paper / University of Bristol, School for Advanced Urban Studies ; 27)

DECENTRALIZATION IN GOVERNMENT — England — Bristol

GARRISH, Stephen
Centralisation and decentralisation in England and France / Stephen Garrish. — Bristol : University of Bristol, School for Advanced Urban Studies, 1986. — xvi,160p. — (Occasional paper / University of Bristol, School for Advanced Urban Studies ; 27)

DECENTRALIZATION IN GOVERNMENT — England — London

GREGORY, Sarah
Decentralisation in London / Sarah Gregory. — [London] : Greater London Council, 1985. — 52p. — (Reviews and studies series / Greater London Council ; no.26)

DECENTRALIZATION IN GOVERNMENT — Europe
Regionalism in Europe / European Centre for Political Studies ; edited by Roger Morgan. — London : Policy Studies Institute, 1986. — [208]p. — *Includes bibliography*

DECENTRALIZATION IN GOVERNMENT — France
Centralismo y descentralización : modelos y procesos históricos en Francia y en España : Coloquio Franco-Español (Madrid, 10-14 octubre 1984). — Madrid : Ministerio de Administración Territorial, Instituto de Estudios de Administración Local, 1985. — 427p. — *At head of title: Comité français des sciences historiques [and] Comité español de Ciencias históricas. — In French or Spanish*

KEATING, Michael, 1950-
Decentralisation and change in contemporary France / Michael Keating and Paul Hainsworth. — Aldershot : Gower, c1986. — [143]p. — *Bibliography: p136-140. — Includes index*

SAVARY, Gilles
Naissance d'une region, Rue Esprit des Lois : la construction régionale en Aquitaine à travers l'action économique 1982-1985 / Gilles Savary. — [Bordeaux] : Le Mascaret, 1986. — 274p

DECENTRALIZATION IN GOVERNMENT — Great Britain
Decentralisation and democracy : localising public services / edited by Paul Hoggett, Robin Hambleton. — Bristol : University of Bristol, School for Advanced Urban Studies, c1987. — 269p. — (Occasional paper ; no.28). — *Bibliography: p267-269*

GREAT BRITAIN, Parliament, House of Commons, Library, Research Division
The devolution question - regional statistics. — [London] : the Division, [1979]. — 28p. — (Background paper ; no.67)

GREAT BRITAIN. Parliament. House of Commons. Library. Research Division
Devolution proposals 1973-1976. — [London] : the Division, [1976]. — 18p. — (Background paper ; no.54)

DECENTRALIZATION IN GOVERNMENT — Iran — Case studies
GOODELL, Grace E
The elementary structures of political life : rural development in Pahlavi Iran / Grace E. Goodell. — New York : Oxford University Press, 1986. — vii, 362 p.. — *Includes index. — Bibliography: p. 345-350*

DECENTRALIZATION IN GOVERNMENT — Spain
Centralismo y descentralización : modelos y procesos históricos en Francia y en España : Coloquio Franco-Español (Madrid, 10-14 octubre 1984). — Madrid : Ministerio de Administración Territorial, Instituto de Estudios de Administración Local, 1985. — 427p. — *At head of title: Comité français des sciences historiques [and] Comité español de Ciencias históricas. — In French or Spanish*

DECISION-MAKING
Behavioral decision making / edited by George Wright. — New York ; London : Plenum Press, c1985. — xix, 407p. — *Includes bibliographies and index. — Bibliography: p*

CHICK, Martin John
Economic planning, managerial decision-making and the role of fixed capital in the investment in the economic recovery of the United Kingdom, 1945-1955 / Martin John Chick. — 313 leaves. — *PhD (Econ) 1986 LSE*

DECISION MAKING
DAVIS, Morton D.
The art of decision-making / Morton Davis. — New York : Springer-Verlag, c1985. — p. cm. — *Includes index. — Bibliography: p*

DECISION-MAKING
Empirical research on organizational decision-making / edited by E. Witte, H.-J. Zimmermann. — Amsterdam ; New York : North-Holland ; New York : Sole distributors for the U.S.A. and Canada, Elsevier Science Pub. Co., 1986. — x, 408 p.. — *Includes bibliographies*

DECISION MAKING
FISHER, Sue
In the patient's best interest : women and the politics of medical decisions / Sue Fisher. — New Brunswick, N.J. : Rutgers University Press, c1986. — ix, 214 p.. — *Includes index. — Bibliography: p. 195-207*

DECISION-MAKING
JUDGE, George G
Improved methods of inference in econometrics / George G. Judge and Thomas A. Yancey. — Amsterdam ; New York : North-Holland ; New York, N.Y., U.S.A. : Elsevier Science Pub. Co. [distributor], 1986. — xvi, 291 p.. — (Studies in mathematical and managerial economics ; v. 34). — *Includes bibliographies and indexes*

Judgment and decision making : an interdisciplinary reader / edited by Hal R. Arkes, Kenneth R. Hammond. — Cambridge : Cambridge University Press, 1986. — xiv,818p. — *Bibliography: p739-799. — Includes index*

DECISION MAKING
MARCH, James G.
Ambiguity and choice in organizations / by James G. March and Johan P. Olsen; with contributions by Søren Christensen...[et al.]. — 2nd ed. — Bergen : Universitetsforlaget, 1979. — 408p. — *Bibliography: p397-402*

DECISION-MAKING
MARSHALL, G. P.
Economics of managerial decision-making / G.P. Marshall and B.J. McCormick. — Oxford : Blackwell, 1986. — [v,470]p. — *Includes index*

MERKHOFER, Miley W.
Decision science and social risk management : a comparative evaluation of cost-benefit analysis, decision analysis, and other formal decision-aiding approaches / Miley W. Merkhofer. — Dordrecht ; Boston : D. Reidel ; Norwell, MA : Sold and distributed in the U.S.A. and Canada by Kluwer Academic Publishers, 1986. — p. cm. — (Technology, risk, and society). — *Includes index. — Bibliography: p*

New directions in research on decision making / edited by Berndt Brehmer ... [et al.]. — Amsterdam ; New York : North-Holland ; New York, N.Y. : Sole distributors for the U.S.A. and Canada, c1986. — p. cm. — *Includes indexes. — Bibliography: p*

Project appraisal: wage, means and experiences. — Guildford : Beech Tree Publishing, 1986-. — *Quarterly*

RAIFFA, Howard
Decision analysis : introductory lectures on choices under uncertainty / Howard Raiffa. — New York : Random House, 1968. — xxiii,309p. — (Behavioral science: quantitative methods). — *Bibliography: p298-300*

SENGUPTA, Jatikumar
Stochastic optimization and economic models / Jati K. Sengupta. — Dordrecht ; Boston : D. Reidel ; Norwell, MA, U.S.A. : Sold and distributed in the U.S.A. and Canada by Kluwer Academic, c1986. — x, 373 p.. — (Theory and decision library. Series B. Mathematical and statistical methods). — *Includes bibliographies and indexes*

DECISION MAKING
SHRADER-FRECHETTE, K. S.
Risk analysis and scientific method : methodological and ethical problems with evaluating societal hazards / K.S. Shrader-Frechette. — Dordrecht ; Boston : D. Reidel ; Hingham, MA, U.S.A. : Sold and distributed in the U.S.A. and Canada by Kluwer Academic Publishers, c1985. — x, 232 p.. — *Includes indexes. — Bibliography: p. 217-226*

DECISION-MAKING
SLOAN, Tod Stratton
Deciding : self-deception in life choices / Tod Stratton Sloan. — New York ; London : Methuen, 1987, c1986. — xii,170p. — *Bibliography: p160-168. — Includes index*

VON WINTERFELDT, Detlof
Decision analysis and behavioral research / Detlof von Winterfeldt, Ward Edwards. — Cambridge : Cambridge University Press, 1986. — xv,604p. — *Bibliography: p575-594. — Includes index*

DECISION MAKING
WHITE, Jonathan Peter
Roles of boundary-spanning individuals in decision-making involving organization-environment communication / by Jonathan Peter White. — 318 leaves. — *PhD (Econ) 1986 LSE. — Leaves 289-318 are appendices*

DECISION MAKING — Case studies
NEUSTADT, Richard E
Thinking in time : the uses of history for decision-makers / Richard E. Neustade, Ernest R. May. — New York : Free Press ; London : Collier Macmillan, c1986. — p. cm. — *Includes index. — Bibliography: p*

DECISION-MAKING — Congresses
INTERNATIONAL INSTITUTE FOR APPLIED SYSTEMS ANALYSIS IIASA SUMMER STUDY ON PLURAL RATIONALITY AND INTERACTIVE DECISION PROCESSES (1984 : Sopron, Hungary)
Plural rationality and interactive decision processes : proceedings of an IIASA (International Institute for Applied Systems Analysis) Summer Study on Plural Rationality and Interactive Decision Processes, held at Sopron, Hungary, August 12-16, 1984 / edited by M. Grauer, M. Thompson, and A.P. Wierzbicki. — Berlin ; New York : Springer-Verlag, c1985. — vi, 353 p.. — (Lecture notes in economics and mathematical systems ; 248). — *Includes bibliographies and index*

Multiple criteria decision methods and applications : selected readings of the First International Summer School, Acireale, Sicily, September, 1983 / edited by Günter Fandel and Jaap Spronk in collaboration with Benedetto Matarazzo. — Berlin ; New York : Springer-Verlag, c1985. — p. cm. — *Sponsored by CREST (EEC) ... and others. — Based on a selection of papers from the First International Summer School on Multiple Criteria Decision Making Methods, Applications and Software. — Includes bibliographies and index*

The reasoning criminal : rational choice perspectives on offending / edited by Derek B. Cornish, Ronald V. Clarke. — New York : Springer-Verlag, c1986. — p. cm. — (Research in criminology). — *Includes index. — Bibliography: p*

DECISION-MAKING — Mathematical models
ARROW, Kenneth Joseph
Social choice and multicriterion decision-making / Kenneth J. Arrow and Hervé Raynaud. — Cambridge, Mass. : MIT Press, c1986. — p. cm. — *Includes index. — Bibliography: p*

BHATTACHARYA, Keron
The new frontiers for business analysis / Keron Bhattacharya. — Basingstoke : Macmillan, c1987. — x,166p. — *Includes index*

DECISION-MAKING — Mathematical models *continuation*

Decision and organization : a volume in honor of Jacob Marschak / edited by C.B. McGuire and Roy Radner ; contributors, Kenneth J. Arrow ... [et al.]. — 2nd ed. — Minneapolis : University of Minnesota Press, c1986. — p. cm . — Includes indexes. — ″Publications of Jacob Marschak″: p. — Bibliography: p

DECISION MAKING — mathematical models

ROUBENS, Marc
Preference Modelling / Marc Roubens [and] PHilippe Vincke. — Berlin : Springer-Verlag, 1985. — vi,94p. — (Lecture notes in economics and mathematical systems ; 250)

DECISION-MAKING — Mathematical models — Congresses

INTERNATIONAL CONFERENCE ON MULTIPLE CRITERIA DECISION MAKING ((6th : 1984 : Case Western Reserve University)
Decision making with multiple objectives : proceedings of the Sixth International Conference on Multiple-Criteria Decision Making, held at the Case Western University, Cleveland, Ohio, USA, June 4-8, 1984 / edited by Yacov Y. Haimes and Vira Chankong. — Berlin ; New York : Springer-Verlag, c1985. — xi, 571 p.. — (Lecture notes in economics and mathematical systems ; 242). — Includes bibliographies

UNIVERSITY OF CALIFORNIA, IRVINE, CONFERENCE ON POLITICAL ECONOMY ((2nd : 1983)
Information pooling and group decision making : proceedings of the Second University of California, Irvine, Conference on Political Economy / edited by Bernard Grofman, Guillermo Owen. — Greenwich, Conn. : JAI Press, c1986. — xii, 279 p.. — (Decision research ; v. 2). — Includes index. — Bibliography: p. 231-264

DECISION-MAKING (ETHICS)

HÖFFE, Otfried
Strategien der Humanität : zur Ethik öffentlicher Entscheidungsprozesse / Otfried Höffe. — Frankfurt am Main : Suhrkamp, 1985. — 372p. — Published Freiburg: Karl Alber, 1975. — Bibliography: p341-362

DECISION-MAKING, GROUP — Congresses

Communication and group decision-making / edited by Randy Y. Hirokawa and Marshall Scott Poole ; foreword by James H. Davis. — Beverly Hills : Sage Publications, c1986. — 315 p.. — (Sage focus editions ; 77). — Developed from discussions at the Conference on Research in Small Group Communication, held at the Pennsylvania State University, Apr. 29-30, 1982. — Bibliography: p. 293-312

Experimental social dilemmas / Henk A.M. Wilke, Dave M. Messick, Christel G. Rutte, eds. — Frankfurt am Main ; New York : P. Lang, c1986. — vi, 234 p.. — (Psychologie des Entscheidungsverhaltens und des Konfliktes =Psychology of decisions and conflict ; Bd. 3). — Papers were presented at a conference held at the University of Groningen in the spring of 1984. — Includes bibliographies

INTERNATIONAL INSTITUTE FOR APPLIED SYSTEMS ANALYSIS IIASA SUMMER STUDY ON PLURAL RATIONALITY AND INTERACTIVE DECISION PROCESSES (1984 : Sopron, Hungary)
Plural rationality and interactive decision processes : proceedings of an IIASA (International Institute for Applied Systems Analysis) Summer Study on Plural Rationality and Interactive Decision Processes, held at Sopron, Hungary, August 12-16, 1984 / edited by M. Grauer, M. Thompson, and A.P. Wierzbicki. — Berlin ; New York : Springer-Verlag, c1985. — vi, 353 p.. — (Lecture notes in economics and mathematical systems ; 248). — Includes bibliographies and index

DECISION SUPPORT SYSTEMS

MITTRA, Sitansu S
Decision support systems : tools and techniques / Sitansu S. Mittra. — New York : Wiley, 1986. — xviii, 433 p.. — ″A Wiley-Interscience publication.″. — Includes bibliographies and index

DECLARATION ON THE RIGHT TO DEVELOPMENT [DRAFT]

CHOURAQUI, Gilles
Report of the Working Group of Governmental Experts on the Right to Development / Rapporteur: Mr. Gilles Chouraqui (France). — Geneva : United Nations, 1982. — 17p. — United Nations. Economic and Social Council. Commission on Human Rights. Thirty-ninth session, 31 January-11 March 1983. Item 8 of the provisional agenda. — U.N. document E/CN.4/1983/11 dated 9 December 1982

DECOLONIZATION — History

British imperial policy and decolonization, 1938-64 / [edited by] A.N. Porter and A.J. Stockwell. — Basingstoke : Macmillan. — (Cambridge commonwealth series) Vol.1: 1938-51. — 1987. — xvii,403p. — Bibliography: p390-393. — Includes index

DECORATION AND ORNAMENT — Psychological aspects

GOMBRICH, E. H.
The sense of order : a study in the psychology of decorative art / E. H. Gombrich. — 2nd ed. — Oxford : Phaidon, 1984. — xii,411p. — ″... the ninth volume of the Wrightsman lectures ...″ - t.p. verso

DECORATIONS OF HONOR — Great Britain

WALKER, John
The Queen has been pleased : the British honours system at work / John Walker. — London : Secker & Warburg, 1986. — viii,216p

DECORATIVE ARTS — England

Huguenots in Britain and their French background, 1550-1800 / edited by Irene Scouloudi. — Totowa, N.J. : Barnes & Noble, 1987. — p. cm. — Includes index

DECORATIVE ARTS — New York (State) — Woodstock — History — 20th century — Exhibitions

Life by design : Delaware Art Museum, November 9, 1984-January 6, 1985 / [photography by Rick Echelmeyer ; editor, Richard J. Mulrooney]. — Wilmington, Del. (2301 Kentmere Pkwy., Wilmington 19806) : The Museum, c1984. — iv, 31 p.. — At head of title: The Byrdcliffe Arts and Crafts Colony. — Cover title: The Byrdcliffe Arts & Crafts Colony : life by design. — Catalogue of an exhibition held at the Delaware Art Museum, Nov. 9, 1984-Jan. 6, 1985 and at the Edith C. Blum Art Institute, Jan. 15-Mar. 31, 1985. — Includes bibliographies

DECORATIVE ARTS, HUGUENOT — England

Huguenots in Britain and their French background, 1550-1800 / edited by Irene Scouloudi. — Totowa, N.J. : Barnes & Noble, 1987. — p. cm. — Includes index

DEFAULT (FINANCE) — New York (N.Y.)

SHEFTER, Martin
Political crisis, fiscal crisis : the collapse and revival of New York City / Martin Shefter. — New York : Basic Books, c1985. — p. cm. — Includes index. — Bibliography: p

DEFECTORS — Poland

BŁAŻYŃSKI, Zbigniew
Mówi Józef Światło : za kulisami bezpieki i partii 1940-1955 / Zbigniew Błażyński ; słowo wstępne: Jan Nowak-Jezioranski. — Wyd. 3 (z erratami i uzupełnieniem). — Londyn : Polska Fundacja Kulturalna, 1986. — xv,319p. — Part of the material contained in this book was published by Radio Free Europe as a pamphlet in 1955 and dropped over Poland from balloons, under the title ″Za kulisami bezpieki i partii″. Reprinted under title ″Kulisy bezpieki i partii″ in Warsaw 1979 by the clandestine Publishing House NOWA

DEFECTORS — Poland — Biography

SPASOWSKI, Romuald
The liberation of one / Romuald Spasowski. — 1st ed. — San Diego : Harcourt Brace Jovanovich, c1986. — 687 p., [16] p. of plates. — Includes index

DEFECTORS — United States — Biography

SPASOWSKI, Romuald
The liberation of one / Romuald Spasowski. — 1st ed. — San Diego : Harcourt Brace Jovanovich, c1986. — 687 p., [16] p. of plates. — Includes index

DEFENSES — Technological innovations

IBRÜGGER, Lothar
General report on strategic defence : technology issues / Lothar Ibrügger. — Brussels : North Atlantic Assembly, 1986. — ii,30p

DEFICIT FINANCING — Canada

CARMICHAEL, Edward A
Tackling the federal deficit / Edward A. Carmichael. — Toronto : C.D. Howe Institute, [1984]. — 88 p.. — (Observation ; no. 26). — Includes bibliographical references

DEFICIT FINANCING — India

SEN, Pradip K
Deficit financing and development planning / Pradip K. Sen. — New Delhi : Criterion Publications : Distributed by Deep & Deep Publications, 1985. — xvi, 341 p. — Includes index. — Bibliography: p. [319]-338

DEFICIT FINANCING — United States

Deficits / edited by James M. Buchanan, Charles K. Rowley and Robert D. Tollison. — Oxford : Basil Blackwell, 1987, c1986. — x,417p. — Includes bibliographies and index

DEFORESTATION

The Vanishing forest : the human consequences of deforestation : a report for the Independent Commission on International Humanitarian Issues / preface by Sadruddin Aga Khan. — London : Zed Books, 1986. — [96]p. — Translation of: La Déforestation. — Includes bibliography

DEFORESTATION — Social aspects

The Vanishing forest : the human consequences of deforestation : a report for the Independent Commission on International Humanitarian Issues / preface by Sadruddin Aga Khan. — London : Zed Books, 1986. — [96]p. — Translation of: La Déforestation. — Includes bibliography

DEGREES, ACADEMIC — Europe

COX, Edwin H.
Academic recognition of diplomas in the European Community : present state and prospects / by Edwin Cox. — Brussels : Commission of the European Communities, 1977c1979. — 75p. — (Education series / Commission of the European Communities ; no. 10)

DELAUNAY, VADIM

DELAUNAY, Vadim
Portrety v koliuchei rame = Portraits in a barbed wire frame / Vadim Delone ; predislovie Vladimira Bukovskogo. — London : Overseas Publications Interchange, 1984. — 217p

DELEGATED LEGISLATION — Great Britain
GANZ, Gabriele
Quasi-legislation : recent developments in secondary legislation / by Gabriele Ganz. — 2nd ed. — London : Sweet & Maxwell, 1987. — xiv,114p. — (Modern legal studies). — *New ed.* — *Previous ed.: published as Administrative procedures. 1974.* — *Includes index*

DELHI (INDIA) — History
Delhi through the ages : essays in urban history, culture, and society / edited by R.E. Frykenberg. — Delhi ; New York : Oxford University Press, 1986. — xli, 524 p., [8] p. of plates. — *Maps on lining papers.* — *Includes bibliographies and index*

DELIERY OF HEALTH CARE — trends — United States
CALIFANO, Joseph A.
America's health care revolution : who lives? who dies? who pays? / Joseph A. Califano, Jr. — 1st ed. — New York : Random House, c1986. — x, 241 p.. — *Includes index.* — *Bibliography: p. [227]-230*

DELINQUENT GIRLS — Scotland
PETRIE, Cairine
The nowhere girls / Cairine Petrie. — Aldershot : Gower, c1986. — [364]p. — *Bibliography: p325-343.* — *Includes index*

DELIVERY OF HEALTH CARE
ENGELHARDT, H. Tristram
The foundations of bioethics / by H. Tristram Engelhardt, Jr. — New York : Oxford University Press, 1986. — p. cm. — *Includes bibliographies and index*

DELIVERY OF HEALTH CARE — economics — United States
GINZBERG, Eli
American medicine : the power shift / Eli Ginzberg. — Totowa, N.J. : Rowman & Allanheld, 1985. — xv, 207 p.. — *Includes index.* — *Bibliography: p. [194]-199*

SORKIN, Alan L
Health care and the changing economic environment / Alan L. Sorkin. — Lexington, Mass. : Lexington Books, c1986. — xiv, 161 p.. — *Includes bibliographies and index*

DELIVERY OF HEALTH CARE — history — Great Britain
HOLLINGSWORTH, J. Rogers
A political economy of medicine : Great Britain and the United States / J. Rogers Hollingsworth. — Baltimore : Johns Hopkins University Press, c1986. — xix, 312 p.. — *Includes index.* — *Bibliography: p. 275-303*

DELIVERY OF HEALTH CARE — history — United States
HOLLINGSWORTH, J. Rogers
A political economy of medicine : Great Britain and the United States / J. Rogers Hollingsworth. — Baltimore : Johns Hopkins University Press, c1986. — xix, 312 p.. — *Includes index.* — *Bibliography: p. 275-303*

DELIVERY OF HEALTH CARE — trends — United States — congresses
CORNELL UNIVERSITY MEDICAL COLLEGE CONFERENCE ON HEALTH POLICY (1985 : New York, N.Y.)
The U.S. health care system : a look to the 1990s / Cornell University Medical College Conference on Health Policy, March 7-8, 1985, New York City ; Eli Ginzberg, editor. — Totowa, N.J. : Rowman & Allanheld, 1985. — x, 133 p.. — (Conservation of human resources series ; 26) (Land Mark studies). — *Includes index.* — *Bibliography: p. 115-123*

DEMENTIA
HENDERSON, A. S.
The problem of dementia in Australia / by A. S. Henderson and A. F. Jorm. — Canberra : Australian Government Publishing Service, 1986. — v,56p. — *Bibliographical references: p53-56*

DEMING, BARBARA
DEMING, Barbara
Prisons that could not hold / Barbara Deming ; introduction by Grace Paley ; photo essay edited by Joan E. Biren. — San Francisco : Spinsters Ink, 1985. — 230p

DEMOCRACY
ANTCZAK, Frederick J.
Thought and character : the rhetoric of democratic education / Frederick J. Antczak. — 1st ed. — Ames : Iowa State University Press, 1985. — viii, 242 p. — *Includes index.* — *Bibliography: p. 229-235*

BOBBIO, Norberto
The future of democracy : a defence of the rules of the game / Norberto Bobbio ; translated by Roger Griffin ; edited and introduced by Richard Bellamy. — Cambridge : Polity, 1987. — 184p. — *Translation of: Il futuro della democrazia.* — *Includes index*

BOWLES, Samuel
Democracy and capitalism : property, community, and the contradictions of modern social thought / Samuel Bowles, Herbert Gintis. — London : Routledge & Kegan Paul, 1986. — x,244p. — *Includes index*

DAHL, Robert A.
Democracy, liberty and equality / Robert A. Dahl. — Oslo : Norwegian University Press ; Oxford : Distributed by Oxford University Press, c1986. — 286p. — (Scandinavian library). — *Includes index*

Democracy in contemporary Japan / edited by Gavan McCormack & Yoshio Sugimoto. — Armonk, N.Y. ; London : M.E. Sharpe, 1987. — 1v.

Development, democracy, and the art of trespassing : essays in honor of Albert O. Hirschman / edited by Alejandro Foxley, Michael S. McPherson, and Guillermo O'Donnell. — Notre Dame, Ind. : Published for the Helen Kellogg Institute for International Studies by University of Notre Dame Press, c1986. — vii, 379 p.. — *Bibliography: p. 375-379*

EVANS, Sara M
Free spaces : the sources of democratic change in America / Sara M. Evans and Harry C. Boyte. — 1st ed. — New York : Harper & Row, c1986. — xi, 228 p. — *Includes index.* — *Bibliography: p. [203]-219*

Extremismus und streitbare Demokratie mit Beiträgen von Uwe Backes und Eckhard Jesse / herausgegeben von Wolfgang Michalka. — Stuttgart : Franz Steiner, 1987. — 128p. — (Neue politische Literatur. Beihefte Forschungsberichte zur internationalen Literatur ; 4)

GABRIEL, Ralph Henry
The course of American democratic thought / Ralph Henry Gabriel. — 3rd ed. / with Robert H. Walker. — New York : Greenwood Press, 1986. — xix, 568 p.. — (Contributions in American studies ; no. 87). — *Includes index.* — *Bibliography: p. 541-547*

HATTERSLEY, Roy
Choose freedom : the future for democratic socialism / Roy Hattersley. — London : Joseph, 1987. — [352]p. — *Includes index*

HELD, David
Models of democracy / David Held. — Cambridge : Polity in association with Blackwell, 1987. — xii,321p. — *Bibliography: p301-312.* — *Includes index*

HIRST, Paul Q.
Law, socialism and democracy / Paul Q. Hirst. — London : Allen & Unwin, 1986. — [200]p. — *Includes bibliography and index*

HOLCOMBE, Randall G
An economic analysis of democracy / Randall G. Holcombe. — Carbondale : Southern Illinois University Press, c1985. — xiii, 269 p.. — (Political and social economy). — *Includes index.* — *Bibliography: p. 257-266*

MONAHAN, Arthur P.
Consent, coercion, and limit : the medieval origins of parliamentary democracy / Arthur P. Monahan. — Kingston ; Montreal : McGill-Queen's University Press, 1987. — xx,345p. — (McGill-Queen's studies in the history of ideas ; 10). — *Bibliography: p [265]-325*

New forms of democracy / edited by David Held and Christopher Pollitt. — London : Sage in association with the Open University, 1987. — [256]p. — *Includes bibliography and index*

Opposition in Western Europe / edited by Eva Kolinsky. — London : Croom Helm, c1987. — [416]p. — *Includes bibliography and index*

ORLOW, Dietrich
Weimar Prussia, 1918-1925 : the unlikely rock of democracy / Dietrich Orlow. — Pittsburgh, Pa. : University of Pittsburgh Press, 1985. — xii, 363p. — *Includes index.* — *Bibliography: p.333-355*

OSTROGORSKI, M.
Democracy and the organization of political parties / with a preface by...James Bryce ; edited...by Seymour Martin Lipset. — Chicago : Quadrangle
volume 1: England. — 1964. — lxxxii,350p. — *First published in English in 1902*

OSTROGORSKI, M.
Democracy and the organization of political parties / with a preface by...James Bryce ; edited...by Seymour Martin Lipset. — Chicago : Quadrangle
volume 2: United States. — 1964. — lxxvii,418p. — *First published in English in 1902*

PACHER-THEINBURG, Regina
The concept of consent and its role in liberal democratic theory / by Regina Pacher-Theinburg. — 201 leaves. — *PhD (Econ) 1986 LSE*

PICARD, Robert G
The press and the decline of democracy : the democratic socialist response in public policy / Robert G. Picard. — Westport, Conn. ; London : Greenwood Press, 1985. — 173p. — (Contributions to the study of mass media and communications ; no. 4). — *Includes index.* — *Bibliography: p [153]-168*

QUALTER, Terence H.
Conflicting political ideas in liberal democracies / Terence H. Qualter. — Toronto : Methuen, 1986. — ix,294p

SARTORI, Giovanni
The theory of democracy revisited / Giovanni Sartori. — Chatham, N.J. : Chatham House Publishers, c1987. — 3v(xiv,253,viiip, p257-542)

Die Unternehmung in der demokratischen Gesellschaft = : The business corporation in the democratic society / herausgegeben von Wolfgang Dorow. — Berlin ; New York : W. de Gruyter, 1987. — xiii, 390 p.. — *"Günter Dlugos zum 65. Geburtstagegewidmet."*. — *English and German.* — *Includes bibliographies*

WOLFE, Joel D
Workers, participation, and democracy : internal politics in the British union movement / Joel D. Wolfe. — Westport, Conn. ; London : Greenwood Press, c1985. — xii, 258p. — (Contributions in political science ; no. 136). — *Includes index.* — *Bibliography: p.[219]-243*

DEMOCRACY — Addresses, essays, lectures
Essays on democratic theory / edited by Dag Anckar, Erkki Berndtson. — [Helsinki, Finland] : Finnish Political Science Association, [1984]. — 166 p.. — *Includes bibliographies*

DEMOCRACY — Case studies

Transitions from authoritarian rule : comparative perspectives / edited by Guillermo O'Donnell, Philippe C. Schmitter, and Laurence Whitehead. — Baltimore : Johns Hopkins University Press, c1986. — xii, 190 p.. — Includes index. — Bibliography: p. 165-184. — Contents: Pt. 1, Southern Europe -- Pt. 2, Latin America -- Pt. 3, Comparative perspectives -- Pt. 4, Tentative conclusions and uncertain democracies

Transitions from authoritarian rule / edited by Guillermo O'Donnell, Philippe C. Schmitter, Laurence Whitehead. — Baltimore : Johns Hopkins University Press. — Papers originally commissioned for a conference sponsored by the Latin American Program of the Woodrow Wilson International Center for Scholars between 1979 and 1980. — Includes index. — Bibliography: p. — Contents: International aspects of democratization / Laurence Whitehead -- Some problems in the study of the transition to democracy / Adam Przeworski -- Paths toward redemocratization / Alfred Stepan -- Liberalization and democratization in South America ; perspectives from the 1970s / Robert R. Kaufman -- Demilitarization and the institutionalization of military-dominated polities in Latin America / Alain Rouquié -- Entrepreneurs and the transition process : the Brazilian case / Fernando H. Cardoso -- Economic policies and the prospects for successful transition from authoritarian rule in Latin America / John Sheahan
Comparative perspectives. — c1986. — p. cm

Transitions from authoritarian rule / edited by Guillermo O'Donnell, Philippe C. Schmitter, and Laurence Whitehead ; [with a foreword by Abraham F. Lowenthal]. — Baltimore : Johns Hopkins University Press. — Papers originally commissioned for a conference sponsored by the Latin American Program of the Woodrow Wilson International Center for Scholars between 1979 and 1981. — Includes index. — Bibliography: p. 221-236. — Contents: Introduction to the Latin American cases / Guillermo O'Donnell -- Political cycles in Argentina since 1955 / Marcelo Cavarozzi -- Bolivia's failed democratization, 1977-1980 / Laurence Whitehead -- The "liberalization" of authoritarian rule in Brazil / Luciano Martins -- The political evolution of the Chilean military regime and problems in the transition to democracy / Manuel Antonio Garretón -- Political liberalization in an authoritarian regime; the case of Mexico / Kevin J. Middlebrook -- Military interventions and "transfer of power to civilians" in Peru / Julio Cotler -- Uruguay's transition from collegial military-technocratic rule / Charles G. Gillespie -- Petroleum and political pacts : the transition to democracy in Venezuela / Terry Lynn Karl
Latin America. — c1986. — xii, 244 p.

Transitions from authoritarian rule / edited by Guillermo O'Donnell, Philippe C. Schmitter, and Laurence Whitehead ; [with a foreword by Abraham F. Lowenthal]. — Baltimore : Johns Hopkins University Press. — Papers originally commissioned for conferences or meetings sponsored by the Latin American Program of the Woodrow Wilson International Center for Scholars between 1979 and 1981. — Includes index. — Bibliography: p. 187-212. — Contents: An introduction to southern European transitions from authoritarian rule : Italy, Greece, Portugal, Spain, and Turkey / Philippe C. Schmitter -- Political economy, legitimation, and the state in southern Europe / Salvador Giner -- The demise of the first Fascist regime and Italy's transition to democracy, 1943-1948 / Gianfranco Pasquino -- Political change in Spain and the prospects for democracy / José María Maravall and Julián Santamaría -- Regime overthrow and the prospects for democratic transition in Portugal / Kenneth Maxwell -- Regime change and the prospects for democracy in Greece, 1974-1983 / P. Nikiforos Diamandouros -- Democracy in Turkey : problems and prospects / Ilkay Sunar and Sabri Sayari
Southern Europe. — c1986. — xii, 218 p.

DEMOCRACY — Congresses

Parlamento y democracia : problemas y perspectivas en los años 80 : textos del coloquio organizado por la Fundación Pablo Iglesias durante los días 23, 24 y 25 de septiembre de 1981 / Pierre Birnbaum ... [et al.] ; edición preparada por Mónica Threlfall. — Madrid : Editorial P. Iglesias, [1982?]. — 170 p.

DEMOCRACY — Economic aspects

DOWNS, Anthony
An economic theory of democracy. — New York : Praeger, 1957. — ix,310p

DEMOCRACY — History

KLOPPENBERG, James T
Uncertain victory : social democracy and progressivism in European and American thought, 1870-1920 / James T. Kloppenberg. — New York : Oxford University Press, 1986. — x, 546 p.. — Includes index. — Bibliography: p. [511]-528

PAE, Sung M
Testing democratic theories in Korea / Sung M. Pae. — Lanham, MD : University Press of America, c1986. — xvii, 300 p.. — Includes index. — Bibliography: p. [281]-289

DEMOCRACY — Public opinion

CARTER, L. B.
The quiet Athenian / L.B. Carter. — Oxford : Clarendon, 1986. — [ix,224]p. — Includes bibliography

DEMOCRATIC CENTRALISM

KULINCHENKO, V. A.
Demokraticheskii tsentralizm i razvitie vnutripartiinykh otnoshenii / V. A. Kulinchenko. — Moskva : Mysl', 1985. — 277p

DEMOCRATIC PARTY (Ill.)

JONES, Bryan D
Governing buildings and building government : a new perspective on the old party / Bryan D. Jones. — University, Ala. : University of Alabama Press, c1985. — p. cm. — Includes index. — Bibliography: p

DEMOCRATIC PARTY (N.Y.) — History — 20th century

WESSER, Robert F
A response to progressivism : the Democratic Party and New York politics, 1902-1918 / Robert F. Wesser. — New York : New York University Press, c1986. — p. cm. — Includes index. — Bibliography: p

DEMOCRATIC PARTY (U.S.) — History

MINK, Gwendolyn
Old labor and new immigrants in American political development : union, party, and state, 1875-1920 / Gwendolyn Mink. — Ithaca, N.Y. : Cornell University Press, 1986. — p. cm. — Includes index. — Bibliography: p

DEMOGRAPHERS — Biography

PETERSEN, William
Dictionary of demography / William Petersen and Renee Petersen ; with the collaboration of an international panel of demographers. — Westport, Conn. : Greenwood Press. — Includes index. — Bibliography: p. — Contents: v. 1. A-L -- v. 2. M-Z
Biographies. — c1985. — p. cm

DEMOGRAPHERS — Soviet Union — Directories

VORONITSYN, Sergei
A directory of prominent Soviet economists, sociologists, and demographers by institutional affiliation / compiled by Sergei Voronitsyn ; edited by: Robert Farrell. — Munich : Radio Liberty, 1987. — 118p

DEMOGRAPHIC ANTHROPOLOGY

Culture and reproduction : an anthropological critique of demographic transition theory / edited by W. Penn Handwerker. — Boulder, Colo. : Westview Press, 1986. — xix, 389 p.. — Based on papers presented at a conference held Dec. 2, 1981 at the University of California, Los Angeles. — Includes index. — Bibliography: p. 350-382

HARRIS, Marvin
Death, sex, and fertility : population regulation in preindustrial and developing societies / Marvin Harris and Eric B. Ross. — New York : Columbia University Press, 1987. — p. cm. — Incldues index. — Bibliography: p

DEMOGRAPHIC SURVEYS

BILSBORROW, Richard E.
Migration surveys in low income countries : guidelines for survey and questionnaire design : a study prepared for the International Labour Organisation within the framework of the World Employment Programme with the financial support of the United Nations Fund for Population Activities / Richard E. Bilsborrow, A.S. Oberai and Guy Standing. — London : Croom Helm, c1984. — 552p. — Bibliography: p499-535. — Includes index

Principles and recommendations for population and housing censuses. — New York : United Nations, 1980. — xiv,330p. — (Statistical papers / United Nations, Statistical Office. Series M ; no.67) ([Document] (United Nations) ; ST/ESA/STAT/SER.M/67). — Sales no.: E.80.XVII.8

WORLD FERTILITY SURVEY. Seminar on Collection and Analyis of Data on Community and Institutional Factors (1983 : London)
The Collection and analysis of community data / edited by John B. Casterline. — Voorburg : International Statistical Institute : World Fertility Survey, 1985. — xvi, 286p. — Includes bibliographical references

DEMOGRAPHIC SURVEYS — Data processing

Software user's manual. — Voorburg : International Statistical Institute, 1984. — 269p. — (Basic documentation / World Fertility Survey ; no.12)

DEMOGRAPHIC SURVEYS — Cyprus

CYPRUS. Department of Statistics and Research
Demographic survey, 1980/1981. — [Nicosia] : the Department, [1984]. — 349p. — (Population statistics / Cyprus. Department of Statistics and Research. Series 3 ; Report no.4)

DEMOGRAPHIC SURVEYS — Yugoslavia — Vojvodina

YUGOSLAVIA. Savezni zavod za statistiku
Uticaj popisivača na rezultate probnog istraživanja u SAP Vojvodini 1976. godine = Enumerators influence on pilot inquiry results in SAP Vojvodini 1976 / Živojin Jevtić, Zlatinka Leković. — Beograd : Savezni zavod za statistiku, 191980. — 161p. — (Studije, analize i prikazi / Savezni zavod za statistiku ; 103). — Summary in English

DEMOGRAPHIC TRANSITION

Culture and reproduction : an anthropological critique of demographic transition theory / edited by W. Penn Handwerker. — Boulder, Colo. : Westview Press, 1986. — xix, 389 p.. — Based on papers presented at a conference held Dec. 2, 1981 at the University of California, Los Angeles. — Includes index. — Bibliography: p. 350-382

DEMOGRAPHIC TRANSITION — Congresses

Pre-industrial population change : the mortality decline and short-term population movements / edited by Tommy Bengtsson, Gunnar Fridlizius and Rolf Ohlsson. — Stockholm : Almqvist and Wiksell, 1984. — 419p. — Conference papers

DEMOGRAPHIC TRANSITION — England
LEVINE, David, 1946-
Reproducing families : the political economy of English population history / David Levine. — Cambridge : Cambridge University Press, 1987. — [272]p. — (Themes in the social sciences). — Includes index

DEMOGRAPHIC TRANSITION — India
SHARMA, A. K.
Social inequality and demographic processes / A.K. Sharma. — Delhi, India : Mittal Publications : Distributed by Mittal Publishers' Distributors, 1985. — x, 170 p.. — Includes bibliographies and index

DEMOGRAPHY
DEMENY, Paul George
The world demographic situation / Paul Demeny. — New York : Population Council, 1985. — 52p. — (Working papers / Population Council. Center for Policy Studies ; no.121)

MAITRA, Priyatosh
Population, technology and development : a critical analysis / Priyatosh Maitra. — Aldershot : Gower, c1986. — [216]p. — Includes bibliography and index

TREBICI, Vladimir
Demografie şi etnografie / Vladimir Trebici, Ion Ghinoiu. — Bucureşti : Editura Ştiinţifică şi Enciclopedică, 1986. — 325p. — Bibliography: p321-[325]

DEMOGRAPHY — Cross-cultural studies
Migration and settlement : a multiregional comparative study / edited by Andrei Rogers and Frans J. Willekens. — Dordrecht ; Lancaster : Reidel, 1986. — xiii, 496p. — (The Geojournal library). — Bibliography: p.475-489

DEMOGRAPHY — Data processing
BONGAARTS, John
The Population Council target-setting model : a user's manual / John Bongaarts [and] John Stover. — New York : Population Council, 1986. — 100p. — (Working papers / Population Council. Center for Policy Studies ; no.130). — Bibliography: p96-97

DEMOGRAPHY — Dictionaries — Polyglot
PETERSEN, William
Dictionary of demography / William Petersen and Renee Petersen with the collaboration of an international panel of demographers. — Westport, Conn ; London : Greenwood Press, 1985
Multilingual glossary. — 1985. — 259p

DEMOGRAPHY — History
SHELESTOV, D. K.
Demography in the mirror of history / Dmitry Shelestov. — Moscow : Progress, 1987. — 214p

DEMOGRAPHY — Mathematical models
ROGERS, Andrei
Regional population models / Andrei Rogers. — Beverley Hills ; London : Sage, c1985. — 96p. — (Scientific geography series ; v.4). — Bibliography: p95-96

DEMOGRAPHY — Statistical methods
BRASS, William
Advances in methods for estimating fertility and mortality from limted and defective data / William Brass. — London : London School of Hygiene and Tropical Medicine, Centre for Population Studies, 1985. — 103p. — (Occasional publication / Centre for Population Studies, London School of Hygiene and Tropical Medicine)

DEMOGRAPHY — Canada — Bibliography
WAI, Lokky
Annotated bibliography of Canadian demography 1966-1982 / Lokky Wai, Suzanne Shiel, T. R. Balakrishnan. — London, Ont. : University of Western Ontario, Centre for Canadian Population Studies, 1984. — v,314p

DEMOGRAPHY — Europe — Bibliography
POLSKA AKADEMIA NAUK. Komitet Nauk Demograficznych. Sekcja Demografii Historycznej
Przeszło's'c demograficzna Polski : materiały i studia / [komitet redakcyjny: Irena Gieysztorowa, Egon Vielrose (red. naczelny)...et al.]. — Warszawa : Pa'nstwowe Wydawnictwo Naukowe
12. — 1980. — 236p. — Table of contents in English. — Contains "Bibliography of European historical demography 1971-1977", pt.1

POLSKA AKADEMIA NAUK. Komitet Nauk Demograficznych. Sekcja Demografii Historycznej
Przeszło's'e demograficzna Polski : materiały i studia / [komitet redakcyjny: Stanisław Gierszewski, Egon Vielrose (red. naczelny)...et al.]. — Warszawa : Pa'nstwowe Wydawnictwo Naukowe
13. — 1981. — 185p. — Table of contents in English. — Contains "Bibliography of European historical demography 1971-1977", pt.2

DEMOGRAPHY — Finland — Bibliography
INTERNATIONAL UNION FOR THE SCIENTIFIC STUDY OF POPULATION
National population bibliography of Finland 1945-1978 / [editorial group: Altti Majava...et.al.]. — Helsinki : Finnish Demographic Society for the International Union for the Scientific Study of Population, 1984. — 296p

DEMOGRAPHY — Great Britain — History
NISSEL, Muriel
People count : a history of the General Register Office / Muriel Nissel : [for the] Office of Population Censuses and Surveys. — London : H.M.S.O., 1987. — 157p. — Includes index

DEMOGRAPHY — North America
THORNTON, Russell
We shall live again : the 1870 and 1890 ghost dance movements as demographic revitalization / Russell Thornton. — Cambridge : Cambridge University Press, 1986. — xiii,95p. — (The Arnold and Caroline Rose monograph series of the American Sociology Association). — Bibliography: p.85-92. — Includes index

DEMOGRAPHY — Poland
LINK, Krzysztof
Społeczno-ekonomiczne czynniki tworzenia gospodarstw domowych / Krzysztof Link. — Warszawa : Szkoła Główna Planowania i Statystyki, 1986. — 155p. — (Kształtowanie procesów demograficznych a rozwój społeczno-gospodarczy Polski) (Monografie i opracowania / Szkoła Główna Planowania i Statystyki). — Contents and summary in English and Russian

OCHOCKI, Andrzej
Wpływ migracji na rozmieszczenie zasobów pracy w latach 1970-1983 / Andrzej Ochocki. — Warszawa : Szkoła Główna Planowania i Statystyki, 1986. — 155p. — (Kształtowanie procesów demograficznych a rozwój społeczno-gospodarczy Polski) (Monografie i opracowania / Szkoła Główna Planowania i Statystyki ; 221/8). — Summary and contents in English and Russian

POLSKA AKADEMIA NAUK. Komitet Nauk Demograficznych. Sekcja Demografii Historycznej
Przeszło's'c demograficzna Polski : materiały i studia / [komitet redakcyjny: Irena Gieysztorowa, Egon Vielrose (red. naczelny)...et al.]. — Warszawa : Pa'nstwowe Wydawnictwo Naukowe
12. — 1980. — 236p. — Table of contents in English. — Contains "Bibliography of European historical demography 1971-1977", pt.1

POLSKA AKADEMIA NAUK. Komitet Nauk Demograficznych. Sekcja Demografii Historycznej
Przeszło's'e demograficzna Polski : materiały i studia / [komitet redakcyjny: Stanisław Gierszewski, Egon Vielrose (red. naczelny)...et al.]. — Warszawa : Pa'nstwowe Wydawnictwo Naukowe
13. — 1981. — 185p. — Table of contents in English. — Contains "Bibliography of European historical demography 1971-1977", pt.2

Wybrane uwarunkowania i konsekwencje procesu starzenia się ludności Polski / Ewa Frątczak...[et al.]. — Warszawa : Szkoła Główna Planowania i Statystyki, 1987. — 231p. — (Kształtowanie procesów demograficznych a rozwój społeczno-gospodarczy Polski) (Monografie i opracowania / Szkoła Główna Planowania i Statystyki ; 223/10). — Contents and summary in English and Russian

DEMOGRAPHY — Russian S.F.S.R. — Ural Mountains region
Osobennosti vosproizvodstva i migratsii naseleniia na Urale : sbornik nauchnykh trudov / [otv. redaktor I. P. Mokerov]. — Sverdlovsk : AN SSSR, Ural'skii nauchnyi tsentr, 1986. — 101p

DEMOGRAPHY — Soviet Union
Dinamika naseleniia SSSR 1960-1980gg. / [E. K. Vasil'eva...et al.]. — Moskva : Finansy i statistika, 1985. — 174p. — Bibliography: p [172-173]

DROBIZHEV, V. Z.
U istokov sovetskoi demografii. — Moskva : Mysl', 1987. — 221p. — Bibliography: p192-[199]

DEMOGRAPHY — Soviet Union — History
SHELESTOV, D. K.
Demography in the mirror of history / Dmitry Shelestov. — Moscow : Progress, 1987. — 214p

DEMOGRAPHY — Soviet Union — Study and teaching
ZHURAVLEVA, N. I.
Antisovetizm burzhuaznoi demografii / N. I. Zhuravleva. — Moskva : Mysl', 1987. — 189p. — (Kritika burzhuaznoi ideologii i revizionizma). — Bibliography: p177-[190]

DEMONSTRATIONS — Germany (West)
HAASKEN, Georg
Protest in der Klemme : soziale Bewegungen in der Bundesrepublik / Georg Haasken, Michael Wigbers. — Frankfurt am Main : Verlag Neue Kritik, 1986. — 212p. — Bibliography: p203-[212]

DENAZIFICATION
BILLSTEIN, Reinhold
Neubeginn ohne Neuordnung : Dokumente und Materialien zur politischen Weichenstellung in den Westzonen nach 1945 / Reinhold Billstein. — Köln : Pahl-Rugenstein, 1984. — 351p. — Bibliography: p340-349

INSTITUT FÜR WISSENSCHAFT UND KUNST. Symposium (1985 : Wien)
Verdrängte Schuld, verfehlte Sühne : Entnazifizierung in Österreich 1945-1955 / Symposion... ; herausgegeben von Sebastian Meissl, Klaus-Dieter Mulley und Oliver Rathkolb. — München : Oldenbourg, 1986. — 365p. — Bibliographical notes

DENG, XIAOPING
GARDNER, John, 1939-
China under Deng / John Gardner. — London : Centre for Security and Conflict Studies, 1986. — 26p. — (Conflict studies ; 197)

DENMARK — Administrative and political divisions — Population — Statistics
Folke- og boligtaellingen 1 januar 1981. — København : Danmarks Statistik. — Table headings and summary in English
L3: Danmarks administrative inddeling / Danmarks Statistik. — 1986. — 323p

DENMARK — Census, 1981
Folke- og boligtaellingen 1 januar 1981. — København : Danmarks Statistik. — Table headings and summary in English L3: Danmarks administrative inddeling / Danmarks Statistik. — 1986. — 323p

DENMARK — Commerce — Statistics
Import-, beskaeftigelses- og energimultiplikatover. Import-, employment- and energy multipliers / Danmarks Statistik, Nationalregnskabssektionen. — København : Danmarks Statistik. Nationalregnskabssektionen, 1984-. — Annual

DENMARK — Defenses
DENMARK. Forsvarskommissionen Beretning fra Forsvarskommissionen. — København : the Kommissionen, 1972. — 494p

Dyvig-rapporten : Danmarks sikkerhedspolitiske situation i 1980érne med Kommentarer og debat. — [København] : Det Sikkerheds- og Nedrustningspolitiske Udvalg, 1985. — [284]p

ESPERSEN, Mogens
Crossroads / Mogens Espersen. — Copenhagen : Information and Welfare Service of the Danish Defence, 1987. — [33p]. — (People and defence)

LINDHARDT, Bjarne Fr.
Allied Command Baltic Approaches : a survey / Bjarne Fr. Lindhardt. — Copenhagen : Information and Welfare Service of the Danish Defence, 1987. — 40p. — (People and defence)

DENMARK — Defenses — Bibliography
NEVALD, Anna-Lise
Dansk sikkerhedspolitisk bibliografi 1945-1983 / Anna-Lise Nevald ; Redaktion: Bertel Heurlin...[et al.]. — København : Schultz, 1984. — 133p

DENMARK — Diplomatic and consular service
KJØLSEN, Klaus
Dänemarks Auswärtiger Dienst 1770-1970 / von Klaus Kjølsen. — [Kopenhagen] : Presse-und Informationsabteilung, Aussenministerium, 1971]. — 40p

DENMARK — Economic conditions
JOHANSEN, Hans Christian
The Danish economy in the twentieth century / Hans Christian Johansen. — London : Croom Helm, c1987. — 221p. — (Croom Helm series on the contemporary economic history of Europe). — Bibliography: p210-215. — Includes index

DENMARK — Economic conditions — Statistics
Import-, beskaeftigelses- og energimultiplikatover. Import-, employment- and energy multipliers / Danmarks Statistik, Nationalregnskabssektionen. — København : Danmarks Statistik. Nationalregnskabssektionen, 1984-. — Annual

DENMARK — Economic conditions — 1945-
Servicesektorens rolle i dansk økonomi. — København : Industriministeriet, 1984. — 96p

DENMARK — Economic conditions — 1945- — Mathematical models
ADAM oktober 1984 : en oversigt : Danmark Statistiks økonomiske model / redigeret af Niels Fink. — [København] : Danmarks Statistik, 1985. — 159p. — (Arbejdsnotat / Danmarks Statistik ; nr.18)

DENMARK — Economic policy
Firkløver-regeringens program for genopretning af dansk økonomi. — København : Statsministeriet og finansministeriet, 1982. — 44p

DENMARK — Emigration and immigration
HENRIKSEN, Ingrid
Mødet mellem indvandrerfamilier og social- og sundhedssystemet. — København : Socialforskningsinstituttet, 1987. — 208p. — (Publikation / Socialforskningsinstituttet ; 158). — Bibliography: p203-206

DENMARK — Foreign relations
Danmarks strategiske betydning : udarbejdet af Forsvarskommandoen. — [København] : Det Sikkerheds- og Nedrustningspolitiske Udvalg, 1986. — . — (Det Sikkerheds- og Nedrustningspolitiske Udvalgs skriftserie)

DENMARK — History — German occupation, 1940-1945
LUND, Erik
A girdle of truth : the underground news service "Information" 1943-1945 / Erik Lund. — [Copenhagen : Ministry of Foreign Affairs, 1970]. — 25p. — A condensed version of the book "Fire millioner frie ord" by Erik Lund

DENMARK — Military policy
Danmarks strategiske betydning : udarbejdet af Forsvarskommandoen. — [København] : Det Sikkerheds- og Nedrustningspolitiske Udvalg, 1986. — . — (Det Sikkerheds- og Nedrustningspolitiske Udvalgs skriftserie)

Dyvig-rapporten : Danmarks sikkerhedspolitiske situation i 1980érne med Kommentarer og debat. — [København] : Det Sikkerheds- og Nedrustningspolitiske Udvalg, 1985. — [284]p

DENMARK — Military policy — Bibliography
NEVALD, Anna-Lise
Dansk sikkerhedspolitisk bibliografi 1945-1983 / Anna-Lise Nevald ; Redaktion: Bertel Heurlin...[et al.]. — København : Schultz, 1984. — 133p

DENMARK — National security
Danmarks strategiske betydning : udarbejdet af Forsvarskommandoen. — [København] : Det Sikkerheds- og Nedrustningspolitiske Udvalg, 1986. — . — (Det Sikkerheds- og Nedrustningspolitiske Udvalgs skriftserie)

DENMARK. Forsvarskommissionen
Beretning fra Forsvarskommissionen. — København : the Kommissionen, 1972. — 494p

Dyvig-rapporten : Danmarks sikkerhedspolitiske situation i 1980érne med Kommentarer og debat. — [København] : Det Sikkerheds- og Nedrustningspolitiske Udvalg, 1985. — [284]p

DENMARK — Officials and employees
DENMARK. Udvalget vedrørende de for statens tjenestemaend gaeldende regler om arbejdstid, fridage og overarbejde m.v.
Betaenkning afgivet af det af finansministeren den 19. september 1958 nedsatte udvalg til overvejelse af spørgsmålet om eventuelle aendringer i de for statens tjenestemaend gaeldende regler om arbejdstid, fridage og overarbejde m.v.. — [København : Statens Trykningskontor], 1961. — 35p. — (Betaenkning, nr.276)

DENMARK — Politics and government
FRIISBERG, Gregers
Politik : magt eg indflydelse i det politiske system / Gregers Friisberg. — København : Samfundsfagsnyt, 1983. — 232p

DENMARK — Politics and government — 1900-
HOLCH, Mogens
K.Ø. Holch : landets sidste kgl. borgmester / Mogens Holch. — København : Dansk Historisk Håndbogsforlag, c1986. — 200p. — Bibliography: p193

DENMARK — Politics and government — 1940-1945
MEYER, Poul
Dansk politik 1944-1984 : politiske begreber / Poul Meyer. — København : G.E.C. Gad, 1984. — 159p

DENMARK — Politics and government — 1947-
MEYER, Poul
Dansk politik 1944-1984 : politiske begreber / Poul Meyer. — København : G.E.C. Gad, 1984. — 159p

DENMARK — Politics and government — 1972-
GARODKIN, I. J.
Handbog i dansk politik, 1978-79 / I. J. Garodkin. — [Tappernøje] : Mjølner, 1978. — 349p

KONSERVATIVE FOLKEPARTI (Denmark)
En fremtid i frihed : det konservative folkepartis program : ditto partiprogram er vedtaget på Det konservative folkepartis landsråd i Herning i September 1981 / Det konservative folkeparti. — København : Det konservative folkeparti, 1981. — 64p

Urban political theory and the management of fiscal stress / edited by Michael Goldsmith, Søren Villadsen. — Aldershot : Gower, c1986. — xviii,269p

DENMARK — Population
IMPAGLIAZZO, John
Deterministic aspects in mathematical demography / J. Impagliazzo ; with 53 illustrations. — Berlin ; New York : Springer-Verlag, 1985. — p. cm. — (Biomathematics ; v. 13). — Includes index. — Bibliography: p. 179-182

DENMARK — Population — Statistics
Folke- og boligtaellingen 1 januar 1981. — København : Danmarks Statistik. — Table headings and summary in English L3: Danmarks administrative inddeling / Danmarks Statistik. — 1986. — 323p

DENMARK — Social conditions
MØLLER, Iver Hornemann
Klassekamp og sociallovgivning 1850-1970 / Iver Hornemann Møller. — København : Socialistiske Økonomers Forlag, 1981. — 296p

Sociale netvaerk og socialpolitik : en undersøgelse i to lokalområder / Mogens Kjaer Jensen...[et al.]. — København : Socialforskningsinstituttet, 1987. — 202p. — (Publikation / Socialforskningsinstituttet ; 163). — Bibliography: p199-200

DENMARK — Social conditions — 1945-
JØRGENSEN, Jørgen
Betonbørn / Jørgen Jørgensen. — Aarhus : Modtryk, 1978. — 94p

DENMARK — Social policy
Redegørelse '84 om social- og sundhedsplanlaegning 1984-88. — [København] : Socialstyrelsen, 1984. — 177p

DENMARK — Statistics, Vital
JUEL, Knud
Døgelighedsindeks for kommuner og amter 1971-80 = Age-standardized mortality index for Danish municipalities and countries 1971-80. — [København : Dansk Institut for Klinisk Epidemiologi, 1984]. — 156p. — (Vitalstatistik ; 1984:7:1). — Includes summary and table headings in English. — Bibliography: p.116-118

Regionale dødelighedsforskelle i Danmark 1971-79. — København : Danmarks Statistik, 1983. — 136p. — (Statistiske Undersøgelser ; nr.39)

DENMARK. Folketinget. Children and Young Persons Act, 1964
The Children and Young Persons Act, 1964. — [Copenhagen : Ministry of Social Affairs?], 1964. — 33 leaves

DENMARK. Folketinget. Employment Service and Unemployment Insurance Act, 1970
The Employment Service and Unemployment Insurance Act, 1970, as amended. — [Copenhagen : Ministry of Labour?], 1970. — 35p

DENMARK. Folketinget. Holidays with Pay Act, 1971
   The Holidays with Pay Act, 1971. — [Copenhagen : Ministry of Labour?], 1971. — 8 leaves

DENMARK. Folketinget. National Health Security Act, 1975
   National Health Security Act, 1975. — Copenhagen : Ministry of Social Affairs, [1975]. — 14 leaves

DENMARK. Folketinget. Occupational Safety, Health and Welfare (General) Act, 1968
   The Occupational Safety, Health and Welfare (General) Act, 1968. — [Copenhagen : Ministry of Labour], 1968. — 49 leaves. — *Promulgated by the Ministry of Labour on 4th July 1968*

DENMARK. Folketinget. Old Age Pension Act, 1969
   The Old Age Pension Act, 1969. — [Copenhagen : Ministry of Social Affairs], 1970. — 17 leaves. — *Promulgated by the Ministry of Social Affairs on 15th April 1970*

DENMARK. Folketinget. Old Age Pension (Amendment) Act, 1972
   The Old Age Pension (Amendment) Act, 1972. — [Copenhagen : Ministry of Social Affairs?], 1972. — 15 leaves

DENMARK. Folketinget. Public Health Security Act, 1971
   The Public Health Security Act, 1971. — [Copenhagen : Sundhedsstyrelsen?], 1971. — 15 leaves

DENMARK. Folketinget. Rehabilitation Act, 1970
   The Rehabilitation Act, 1970. — [Copenhagen : Ministry of Social Affairs?], 1970. — 11 leaves

DENMARK. Folketinget
   Folketinget håndbog. — København : A/S. J. H. Schultz Bogtrykkeri, 1971-. — *Irregular*

DENMARK. Miljøministeriet
   DENMARK. Miljøministeriet
   The Ministry of the Environment, Denmark. — [Copenhagen : Ministry of the Environment, 1984]. — 40p

DENTAL LAWS AND LEGISLATION — Great Britain
   GREAT BRITAIN. Parliament. House of Commons. Library. Research Division
   Dentists Bill (HL) 1982-83 (Bill 90) / Keith Cuninghame. — [London] : the Division, 1983. — 5p. — (Reference sheet ; no.83/6). — *Bibliographical references: p5*

DENTISTRY AS A PROFESSION
   SPERO, Marlene Elizabeth
   The professionalisation of English dentistry in the 19th century : with comparative reference to France and the United States / Marlene Elizabeth Spero. — 361 leaves. — *Only 1 copy deposited.* — PhD (Econ) 1985 LSE

DENTISTS — England — History — 19th century
   SPERO, Marlene Elizabeth
   The professionalisation of English dentistry in the 19th century : with comparative reference to France and the United States / Marlene Elizabeth Spero. — 361 leaves. — *Only 1 copy deposited.* — PhD (Econ) 1985 LSE

DENTISTS — South Africa — Statistics
   Sensus van ge nee shere en tan dartse = census of medical practitioners and dentists / Central Statistical Services, South Africa. — Pretoria : Government Printer, 1979-. — *Annual. — Text in Afrikaans and English*

DENTISTS BILL 1982-83
   GREAT BRITAIN. Parliament. House of Commons. Library. Research Division
   Dentists Bill (HL) 1982-83 (Bill 90) / Keith Cuninghame. — [London] : the Division, 1983. — 5p. — (Reference sheet ; no.83/6). — *Bibliographical references: p5*

DEPARTMENT STORES — Canada — Statistics
   Retail chain and department stores = Magasins de détail à succursales et les grands magasins / Statistics Canada. — Ottawa : Statistics Canada, 1983-. — *Annual. — Text in English and French*

DEPENDENCY — Addresses, essays, lectures
   Dependency theory and the return of high politics / edited by Mary Ann Tétreault and Charles Frederick Abel. — New York : Greenwood Press, 1986. — xii, 270 p.. — (Contributions in political science ; no. 140). — *Includes index. — Bibliography: p. [255]-260*

DEPORTATION — Sri Lanka
   FRIES, Yvonne
   The undesirables : the expatriation of the Tamil people "of recent Indian origin" from the plantations in Sri Lanka to India / Yvonne Fries, Thomas Bibin. — Calcutta : K P Bagchi, 1984. — 253 p.. — *Bibliography: p [248]-253*

DEPRESSION — psychology
   KLEINMAN, Arthur
   Social origins of distress and disease : depression, neurasthenia, and pain in modern China / Arthur Kleinman. — New Haven : Yale University Press, c1986. — xii, 264 p.. — *Includes index. — Bibliography: p. 241-254*

DEPRESSION, MENTAL — Social aspects
   Social support, life events, and depression / edited by Nan Lin, Alfred Dean, and Walter M. Ensel. — New York : Academic Press, 1986. — p. cm. — *Includes index*

DEPRESSION, MENTAL — Social aspects — Research
   Social support, life events, and depression / edited by Nan Lin, Alfred Dean, and Walter M. Ensel. — New York : Academic Press, 1986. — p. cm. — *Includes index*

DEPRESSION, MENTAL — Somatization — China
   KLEINMAN, Arthur
   Social origins of distress and disease : depression, neurasthenia, and pain in modern China / Arthur Kleinman. — New Haven : Yale University Press, c1986. — xii, 264 p.. — *Includes index. — Bibliography: p. 241-254*

DEPRESSIONS
   The Changing experience of employment : restructuring and recession / edited by Kate Purcell ... [et al.]. — Basingstoke : Macmillan in association with British Sociological Association, 1986. — [256]p. — (Explorations in sociology ; 22). — *Includes bibliography and index*

   DICKHUT, Willi
   Krisen und Klassenkampf / Willi Dickhut. — Stuttgart : Verlag Neuer Weg, 1985. — 292p

   MONTBRIAL, Thierry de
   La revanche de l'histoire / Thierry de Montbrial. — Paris : Julliard, c1985. — 197p. — (Commentaire Julliard)

   O'CONNOR, James
   The meaning of crisis : a theoretical introduction / James O'Connor. — Oxford : Basil Blackwell, 1987. — [192]p v,197p. — *Includes index*

   PRATTEN, C. F.
   Destocking in the recession / Cliff Pratten. — Aldershot : Gower, c1985. — x,147p

   Threats to international financial stability / edited by Richard Portes and Alexander K. Swoboda. — Cambridge : Cambridge University Press, 1987. — xviii,307p. — *Conference proceedings. — Includes bibliographies and index*

DEPRESSIONS — Social aspects — United States
   Nothing else to fear : new perspectives on America in the thirties / edited with an introduction by Stephen W. Baskerville and Ralph Willett. — Manchester : Manchester University Press, c1985. — viii,294p. — *Bibliography: p285-287. — Includes index*

DEPRESSIONS — 1929 — Canada
   BROWN, Lorne
   When freedom was lost : the unemployed, the agitator, and the state / Lorne Brown. — Montréal : Black Rose Books, 1987. — 208p. — *Includes bibliographic references*

   HORN, Michiel
   The Great Depression of the 1930s in Canada / Michiel Horn. — Ottawa : Canadian Historical Association, 1984. — 24 p.. — (Historical booklet / Canadian Historical Association ; no. 39). — *Bibliography: p. 21-22*

DEPRESSIONS — 1929 — Spain
   HERNÁNDEZ ANDREU, Juan
   España y la crisis de 1929 / Juan Hernández Andreu. — Madrid : Espasa-Calpe, 1986. — 260p. — *Bibliography: p[167]-172*

DEPRESSIONS — 1929 — United States
   Nothing else to fear : new perspectives on America in the thirties / edited with an introduction by Stephen W. Baskerville and Ralph Willett. — Manchester : Manchester University Press, c1985. — viii,294p. — *Bibliography: p285-287. — Includes index*

   POPPENDIECK, Janet
   Breadlines knee deep in wheat : food assistance in the Great Depression / Janet Poppendieck. — New Brunswick, N.J. : Rutgers University Press, c1986. — xvii, 306p. — *Includes index. — Bibliography: p.[257]-259*

   WOODRUFF, Nan Elizabeth
   As rare as rain : federal relief in the great southern drought of 1930-31 / Nan Elizabeth Woodruff. — Urbana : University of Illinois Press, 1985. — xii, 203 p., [8] p. of plates. — *Includes index. — Bibliography: p. 183-189*

DEPRESSIONS — 1929 — United States — Bibliography
   The Great Depression : a historical bibliography. — Santa Barbara, Calif. ; Oxford : ABC-Clio Information Services, c1984. — xii, 260p. — (ABC-Clio research guides ; 4). — *Includes index*

DEPRESSIONS — 1929-
   KINDLEBERGER, Charles P.
   The world in depression 1929-1939 / Charles P. Kindleberger. — Harmondsworth : Penguin, 1987. — 355p. — *Bibliography: p307-332*

DEPTS, EXTERNAL — Developing countries
   WOOD, Robert Everett
   From Marshall Plan to debt crisis : foreign aid and development choices in the world economy / Robert E. Wood. — Berkeley : University of California Press, c1986. — p. cm. — (Studies in international political economy). — *Includes index. — Bibliography: p*

DERBYSHIRE — Population
   DERBYSHIRE. County Council
   Social policy indicators : an analysis of the 1981 census for Derbyshire / A. W. Johnson; editor. — [Matlock] : [the Council], 1986. — [vii,160p]. — *Annual*

DERBYSHIRE — Social policy
   DERBYSHIRE. County Council
   Social policy indicators : an analysis of the 1981 census for Derbyshire / A. W. Johnson; editor. — [Matlock] : [the Council], 1986. — [vii,160p]. — *Annual*

DEREGULATION — Germany (West)
ARBEITSGEMEINSCHAFT DEUTSCHER WIRTSCHAFTSWISSENSCHAFTLICHER FORSCHUNGSINSTITUTE (1985 : Bonn)
Deregulierung als ordnungs- und prozesspolitische Aufgabe : Bericht über den wissenschaftlichen Teil der 48. Mitgliederversammlung der Arbeitsgemeinschaft deutscher wirtschaftswissenschaftlicher Forschungsinstitute e.V. in Bonn am 9. und 10. Mai 1985. — Berlin : Duncker and Humblot, [1986]. — 190p. — (Beihefte der Konjunkturpolitik ; Heft 32)

DERRIDA, JACQUES
MELVILLE, Stephen W.
Philosophy beside itself : on deconstruction and modernism / Stephen W. Melville ; foreword by Donald Marshall. — Manchester : Manchester University Press, c1986. — xxix,188p. — (Theory and history of literature ; v.27). — *Bibliography: p173-179. — Includes index*

DESCARTES, RENÉ
COTTINGHAM, John
Descartes / John Cottingham. — Oxford : Basil Blackwell, 1986. — [220]p. — *Includes bibliography and index*

DESERTIFICATION — Control
AHMAD, Yusuf J.
Desertification : financial support for the biosphere / Yusuf J. Ahmad, Mohammed Kassas ; sponsored by the United Nations Environment Programme. — London : Hodder and Stoughton, 1987. — xviii,187p. — *Includes index*

INTERNATIONAL LABOUR ORGANIZATION. Identification and Programming Mission to the Republic of the Sudan (1985)
After the famine : a programme of action to strengthen the survival strategies of affected populations / report of the ILO Identification and Programming Mission to the Republic of the Sudan, September 1985. — Geneva : ILO, c1986. — xi,309p

DESERTIFICATION — China — Control
Combating desertification in China : a report on a seminar sponsored by the Academy of Sciences of the People's Republic of China and the United Nations Environment Programme / edited by James Walls. — Nairobi : United Nations Environment Programme, 1982. — viii, 70p. — (UNEP reports and proceedings series ; 3)

DESERTIFICATION — Sudan
IBRAHIM, Fouad N.
The problem of desertification in the Republic of the Sudan with special reference to Northern Darfar Province / Dr. Fouad N. Ibrahim. — Khartoum : University of Khartoum. Faculty of Economic and Social Studies. Development Studies and Research Centre, 1978. — 54p. — (Monograph series / University of Khartoum. Faculty of Economic and Social Studies. Development Studies and Research Centre ; no.8)

INTERNATIONAL LABOUR ORGANIZATION. Identification and Programming Mission to the Republic of the Sudan (1985)
After the famine : a programme of action to strengthen the survival strategies of affected populations / report of the ILO Identification and Programming Mission to the Republic of the Sudan, September 1985. — Geneva : ILO, c1986. — xi,309p

DESHMUKH, DURGABAI
Social development : essays in honour of SMT Durgabai Deshmukh / edited by B. N. Ganguli. — New Delhi : Sterling Publishers : Council for Social Development, 1977. — viii,303p. — *Bibliography: p287-290*

DESIGN, INDUSTRIAL — Management
Design and innovation : policy and management / edited by Richard Langdon and Roy Rothwell. — London : Pinter, 1985. — [220]p. — *Includes bibliography*

DESIGN, INDUSTRIAL — Great Britain — History
STEWART, Richard
Design and British industry / Richard Stewart. — London : Murray, 1987. — 256p. — *Bibliography: p251-253. — Includes index*

DESIGN, INDUSTRIAL — United States — History
PULOS, Arthur J
American design ethic : a history of industrial design to 1940 / Arthur J. Pulos. — Cambridge, Mass. : MIT Press, c1983. — 441 p.. — *Includes index. — Bibliography: p. 426-433*

DESPOTISM — Cross-cultural studies
BETZIG, L. L
Despotism and differential reproduction : a Darwinian view of history / L.L. Betzig. — New York : Aldine Pub., 1986. — p. cm. — *Bibliography: p*

DESRAMAULT, LUC
VLAEMYNCK, Carlos H.
Naar Engeland gedeporteerd : Vlaamse geïnterneerden van het eiland Man 1940-1945 / Carlos H. Vlaemynck. — Antwerpen : De Nederlandsche Boekhandel, 1984. — 80p. — *Bibliography: p75-76*

DET NORSKE TOTALARHOLDSSELSKAPS BARNEFORBUND
KAASALIA, T. H.
Med skjold og fakkel : det Norske Totalavholdsselskaps barnearbeid i 100 år : 1874/1974 / T. H. Kaasalia. — [s.l.] : Magne, 1974. — 48p

DETECTIVES
KLOCKARS, Carl B
The idea of police / by Carl Klockars. — Beverly Hills, Calif. : Sage Publications, c1985. — p. cm. — (Law and criminal justice series ; v. 2). — *Includes index*

DETENTE
FREY, Eric G
Division and detente : the Germanies and their alliances / Eric G. Frey. — New York : Praeger, 1987. — xvi, 194 p.. — *Includes index. — Bibliography: p. 173-183*

JOHNSON, A. Ross
The impact of eastern Europe on Soviet policy toward western Europe / A. Ross Johnson. — Santa Monica, CA. : Rand, [1986]. — xv, 79 p. . — *"A project Air Force report prepared for the United States Air Force.". — "March 1986.". — "R-3332-AF.". — Includes bibliographical references*

Prospectus for a habitable planet / edited by Dan Smith and E. P. Thompson. — Harmondsworth : Penguin, 1987. — 240p

The second superpower : the arms race and the Soviet Union / edited by Gerard Holden. — London : CND Publications, 1985. — 107p. — *Bibliography: p96-100*

DETENTION OF PERSONS — Great Britain
GRAHAM, Finlay
Young persons remanded in custody : can the numbers safely be reduced? / F. Graham. — London : Home Office, Prison Department, Directorate of Psychological Services, 1979. — 17p. — (DPS report. Series 1 ; no.14). — *Bibliography: p17*

DETENTION OF PERSONS — Scotland
CURRAN, J. H.
Detention or voluntary attendance? : police use of detention under section 2, Criminal Justice (Scotland) Act 1980 / Joseph H. Curran, James K. Carnie. — Edinburgh : H.M.S.O., 1986. — xiv,94p. — (A Scottish Office social research study). — *Prepared under the auspices of the Scottish Office, Central Research Unit. — Bibliography: p93-94*

DETERMINISM (PHILOSOPHY)
EARMAN, John
A primer on determinism / John Earman. — Dordrecht ; Lancaster : Reidel, c1986. — xiv, 273p. — (University of Western Ontario series in philosophy of science ; v. 32). — *Includes index. — Bibliography: p 257-269*

DETERRENCE (STATEGY)
DEMILLE, Dianne
Challenges to deterrence : doctrines, technologies and public concerns : a conference report / Dianne DeMille. — Ottawa : Canadian Institute for International Peace and Security, 1985. — iv,69p. — (Report / Canadian Institute for International Peace and Security ; no.2)

DETERRENCE (STRATEGY)
CHARLTON, Michael
From deterrence to defence : the inside story of strategic policy / Michael Charlton. — Cambridge, Mass. : Harvard University Press, 1987, c1986. — p. cm. — *Based on the author's BBC radio series, The Star wars history. — Includes index*

The Strategic Defense Initiative : new perspectives on deterrence / edited by Dorinda G. Dallmeyer ; in association with Daniel S. Papp. — Boulder : Westview Press, 1986. — xi, 112 p.. — (A Dean Rusk Center monograph). — *Includes index*

YANIV, A
Deterrence without the bomb : the politics of Israeli strategy / Avner Yaniv. — Lexington, Mass. : Lexington Books, 1986, c1987. — x, 324p. — *Includes index. — Bibliography: p.[304]-313*

ZAGARE, Frank C
The dynamics of deterrence / Frank C. Zagare. — Chicago : University of Chicago Press, 1987. — p. cm. — *Includes index. — Bibliography: p*

DETERRENCE (STRATEGY) — Congresses
Nuclear deterrence--new risks, new opportunities / edited by Catherine Kelleher, Frank J. Kerr, and George Quester. — Washington : Pergamon-Brassey's International Defense Publishers, 1986. — p. cm. — *Revision of papers, presented at a conference which was convened by the University of Maryland's International Security Project in Sept. 1984 at College Park, Md*

DETERRENCE (STRATEGY) — Moral and ethical aspects
FINNIS, J. M.
Nuclear deterrence, morality and realism / John Finnis, Joseph M. Boyle, Jr., Germain Grisez. — Oxford : Clarendon, 1987. — xv,429p. — *Bibliography: p391-411. — Includes index*

DEUTSCHE DEMOKRATISCHE PARTEI — History
FRYE, Bruce B.
Liberal Democrats in the Weimar Republic : the history of the German Democratic Party and the German State Party / Bruce B. Frye. — Carbondale : Southern Illinois University Press, c1985. — p. cm. — *Includes index. — Bibliography: p*

DEUTSCHE STAATSPARTEI — History

FRYE, Bruce B.
Liberal Democrats in the Weimar Republic : the history of the German Democratic Party and the German State Party / Bruce B. Frye. — Carbondale : Southern Illinois University Press, c1985. — p. cm. — Includes index. — Bibliography: p

DEVALUATION OF CURRENCY

KOVÁCS, Lipót
A pénz lényege és értékcsökkenésének okai / írta Kovács Lipót. — Budapest : Lampel R. Könyvkereskedése, 1911. — 162p

DEVALUATION OF CURRENCY — Australia

AUSTRALIA. Bureau of Industry Economics
The depreciation of the Australian dollar : its impact on importers and manufacturers. — Canberra : Australian Government Publishing Service, 1986. — xviii,167p. — Bibliographical references: p165-167

DEVALUATION OF CURRENCY — Germany

BALOGH, Tamás
A német pénzromlás oknyomozó története / írta Balogh Tamás ; Navratil Akos előszavával. — Budapest : Gergely R. Könyvkereskedése, 1928. — 104p. — (Közgazdasági Könyvtár ; Köt.5). — Bibliography: p103-104

DEVELOPING COUNTRIES

FEUER, Guy
Droit international du développement / Guy Feuer [et] Hervé Cassan. — Paris : Dalloz, 1985. — xxx,644p.

The Guardian Third World review : voices from the South / editors Victoria Brittain and Michael Simmons. — London : Hodder and Stoughton, 1987. — xii,269p

GUHA, Amalendu
Development alternative / Amalendu Guha, Franklin Vivekananda. — Stockholm : Bethany Books for Institute for Alternative Development Research, 1985. — 328p

HOLLY, Daniel
L'Unesco : le tiers-monde et l'économie mondiale / Daniel A. Holly. — Montréal : Presses de l'Université de Montréal ; Genève : Institute Universitaire de Hautes Études Internationales, 1981. — 176p. — Bibliography: p161-172

KOOPMAN, J.
Nouvelle forme de coopération en vue du développement / J. Koopman [et] A. Schmidt. — Budapest : Centre pour la Recherche de l'Afro-Asie de l'Académie des Sciences de Hongrie, 1972. — 86p. — (Etudes sur les pays en voie de developpement ; no.56)

LACOSTE, Yves
Contre les anti-tiers mondistes et contre certains tiers-mondistes / Yves Lacoste. — Paris : La Découverte, 1986. — 142p

SZENTES, Tamás
Une interpretation restreinte du dualisme dans les theories du sous-développement / Tamás Szentes. — Budapest : Centre pour la Recherche de l'Afro-Asie de l'Académie des Sciences de Hongrie, 1971. — 17p. — (Etudes sur les pays en voie de developpement ; no.45)

TIMMERMANN, Vincenz
A socio-economic path model with latent variables for the study of growth and development in underdeveloped countries / Vincenz Timmermann and Eberhard Scholing. — Hamburg : Sozialökonomisches Seminar der Universität Hamburg, 1986. — 96p. — Bibliography: p86-96

DEVELOPING COUNTRIES — Abstracts

International development abstracts. — Norwich : Geo Abstracts, 1985-. — 6 per year. — Includes index

DEVELOPING COUNTRIES — Armed Forces — Appropriations and expenditures

Defence, security and development / edited by Saadet Deger and Robert West. — London : Pinter, 1987. — xiii,219p. — Bibliography: p207-214. — Includes index

DEVELOPING COUNTRIES — Armed forces — Appropriations and expenditures — Economic aspects

DEGER, Saadet
Military expenditure in Third World countries : the economic effects / Saadet Deger. — London : Routledge and Kegan Paul, 1986. — xv,288p. — Bibliography: p273-281

DEVELOPING COUNTRIES — Colonial influence

BRUCKNER, Pascal
Le sanglot de l'homme blanc : Tiers-monde, culpabilité, haine de soi / Pascal Bruckner. — Paris : Editions du Seuil, c1983. — 309 p.. — (L'Histoire immédiate). — Includes bibliographical references

BRUCKNER, Pascal
[Sanglot de l'homme blanc. English]. The tears of the white man : compassion as contempt / Pascal Bruckner ; translated with an introduction by William R. Beer. — New York : Free Press, c1986. — xx, 244 p.. — Translation of: Le sanglot de l'homme blanc. — Includes bibliographical references and index

DEVELOPING COUNTRIES — Commerce

BRZOSKA, Michael
Arms transfers to the Third World, 1971-85 / Michael Brzoska and Thomas Ohlson. — Oxford : Oxford University Press, 1987. — [440]p. — Written for the Stockholm International Peace Research Institute. — Includes bibliography and index

ELDERKIN, Kenton W
Creative countertrade : a guide to doing business worldwide / Kenton W. Elderkin, Warren E. Norquist. — Cambridge, Mass. : Ballinger Pub. Co., c1987. — xv, 221 p.. — Includes bibliographies and index

HAQUANI, Zalmaï
Industrialisation et commerce du Tiers monde / Zalmaï Haquani. — Paris : La Documentation française, 1986. — 144p. — (Notes et études documentaires ; no.4808). — Bibliography: p136-139

MANLEY, Michael
Up the down escalator : development and the international economy : a Jamaican case study / Michael Manley. — London : Andre Deutsch, 1987. — xv,332p

Surveys in development economics / edited by Norman Gemmell. — Oxford : Basil Blackwell, 1987. — [500]p

TUSSIE, Diana
The less developed countries and the world trading system : a challenge to the GATT / Diana Tussie. — London : Pinter, 1987. — 162p.. — (Studies in international political economy). — Bibliography: p147-153. — Includes index

DEVELOPING COUNTRIES — Commerce — Statistics

Foreign trade: third countries statistical yearbook = Commerce extérieur: pays tiers annuaire statistique / Statistical Office of the European Communities. — Luxembourg : Office for Official Publications of the European Communities, 1977/83-. — Annual. — Text in English and French. — Continues: Yearbook of foreign trade statistics: third countries. — Contents: Volume A-ACP countries - Volume B-Mediterranean countries

DEVELOPING COUNTRIES — Commerce — European Economic Community countries

The Significance of the EEC's generalised system of preferences : trade effects and links with other community aid policies / Axel Borrmann ... [et al.]. — Hamburg : Verlag Weltarchivi, 1985. — 420 p.. — (Publication of HWWA-Institut für Wirtschaftsforschung-Hamburg). — Bibliography: p. 405-420

DEVELOPING COUNTRIES — Commercial policy

Economic liberalization in developing countries / edited by Armeane M. Choksi and Demetris Papageorgiou. — Oxford : Blackwell, 1986. — 278p. — Conference papers. — Includes index

MUKHERJEE, Santosh
Restructuring of industrial economies and trade with developing countries / Santosh Mukherhee, assisted by Charlotte Feller. — Geneva : International Labour Office, 1978. — x,110p. — Bibliography: p83-84

DEVELOPING COUNTRIES — Defenses

World peace and the developing countries : annals of Pugwash 1985 / edited by Joseph Rotblat and Ubiratan D'Ambrosio. — Basingstoke : Macmillan, 1986. — xix,272p. — Conference proceedings. — Includes index

DEVELOPING COUNTRIES — Defenses — Economic aspects

Economic effects of militarism / edited by Girish Mishoa. — New Delhi : Allied Publishers, 1984. — xii,108p

DEVELOPING COUNTRIES — Economic conditions

Australian overseas aid : future directions / edited by Philip Eldridge, Dean Forbes and Doug Porter. — Sydney ; London : Croom Helm, 1986. — xxix,284p. — Bibliography: p265-284

The Biotechnological challenge / [edited by] S. Jacobsson, A. Jamison, H. Rothman. — Cambridge : Cambridge University Press, 1986. — 181p. — Includes bibliographies and index

Capitalism and equality in the Third World / edited by Peter L. Berger. — Lanham, MD : Hamilton Press ; [Washington, D.C.] : Institute for Educational Affairs, <1987- >. — p. cm. — Bibliography: p. — Contents: -- v. 2. Modern capitalism

Changing Britain, changing world : geographical perspectives. — Milton Keynes : Open University Press. — (Social sciences : a second level course) (D205; Units 21-25). — At head of title : Open University
Section 3: Synthesis: uniqueness and interdependence of place
Block 6: Uneven development and the world order / John Allen...[et al.]. — 1985. — Various pagings

COLMAN, David, 1940-
Economics of change in less developed countries / David Colman and Frederick Nixson. — 2nd ed. — Oxford : Philip Allan, 1986. — ix,445p. — Previous ed.: 1978. — Includes bibliographies and index

DASGUPTA, Ajit Kumar
Economic theory and the developing countries / Ajit K. Dasgupta. — London : Macmillan, 1974. — ix,132p. — Bibliography: p.120-128. — Includes index

Development policies and the crisis of the 1980s / edited by Louis Emmerij. — Paris : OECD, 1987. — 178p. — (Development Centre seminars). — Includes bibliographies. — Contents: papers delivered at a seminar on "Alternative Development Strategies in the Light of Recent Experience", January,1987

DEVELOPING COUNTRIES — Economic conditions *continuation*

GAYLE, Dennis John
The small developing state : comparing political economies in Costa Rica, Singapore and Jamaica / Dennis John Gayle. — Aldershot : Gower, c1986. — [xiii,218]p. — *Includes index*

GRIFFIN, Keith
World hunger and the world economy : and other essays in development economics / Keith Griffin. — London : Macmillan, 1987. — [300]p. — *Includes index*

KAPUR, Basant K.
Studies in inflationary dynamics : financial repression and financial liberalization in less developed countries / Basant K. Kapur. — Singapore : Singapore University Press, 1986. — xviii,146p. — *Bibliography: p142-146*

KEYNES SEMINAR (7th : 1985 : University of Kent at Canterbury)
Keynes and economic development : the Seventh Keynes Seminar Hold at the University of Kent at Canterbury, 1985 / edited by A.P. Thirlwall. — Basingstoke : Macmillan, 1987. — x,186p. — *Includes bibliographies and index*

KRUIJER, Gerald J., d. 1986
Development through liberation : Third World problems and solutions / Gerald J. Kruijer ; translated by Arnold Pomerans. — Basingstoke : Macmillan Education, 1987. — x,257p. — *Translated from the Dutch. — Bibliography: p242-252. — Includes index*

Learning from China? : development and environment in Third World countries / edited by Bernhard Glaeser. — London : Allen & Unwin, 1987. — xvii,282p,[8]p of plates. — *Conference papers. — Includes bibliographies and index*

LIPTON, Michael
Why poor people stay poor : urban bias in world development / Michael Lipton. — Cambridge : Harvard University Press, 1977, c1976. — 467 p.. — *Includes index. — Bibliography: p. 355-357*

LLOYD, Peter C.
Classes, crises and coups : themes in the sociology of developing countries / Peter C. Lloyd. — London : Paladin, 1973, c1971. — 223p. — *Originally published: MacGibbon and Kee, 1971. — Further reading: p205-212*

MASON, Edward Sagendorph
The Harvard Institute for International Development and its antecedents / Edward S. Mason. — [Cambridge, Mass.] : Harvard Institute for International Development, Harvard University ; Lanham, MD : University Press of America, c1986. — x, 97 p.. — *Bibliography: p. 74-78*

PATEL, I. G
On the economics of development : towards a consensus ... by I.G.Patel. — London : University of London, [1985]. — 26p. — *Stamp Memorial Lecture, delivered before the University of London on Thursday 21 November 1985*

POPOV, Iu. N.
Essays in political economy / Yuri Popov ; [translated from the Russion by Yuri Sdobnikov]. — Moscow : Progress Publishers. — (Progress guides to the social sciences)
[1]: Imperialism and developing countries. — 1984. — 292p

Prospects for developing countries, 1978-85 / Helen Hughes...[et al.]. — [Washington, D.C.?] : World Bank, 1977. — 158p

REDCLIFT, Michael
Sustainable development : exploring the contradictions / Michael Redclift. — London : Methuen, 1987. — [viii,200]p. — *Includes index*

REGAN, Colm
75:25, Ireland in an unequal world / by Colm Regan, with Pauline Eccles ... [et al.]. — Dublin, Ireland : Development Education Commission of CONGOOD, c1984. — 208 p.

RIDDELL, Roger
Foreign aid reconsidered / Roger C. Riddell. — Baltimore : The Johns Hopkins University Press ; London : Currey, 1987. — x,309p. — *Bibliography: p279-301. — Includes index*

The Socialist Third World : urban development and territorial planning / edited by Dean Forbes and Nigel Thrift. — Oxford : Basil Blackwell, 1987. — [288]p. — *Includes bibliography and index*

SOTTAS, Eric
The least developed countries : introduction to the LDCs and to the substantial new programme of action for them. — New York : United Nations, 1985. — ix,157p. — (Document ; TAD/INF/PUB/84.2). — *At head of title: United Nations Conference on Trade and Development, Geneva. — Bibliography: p157*

Staff studies for the World Economic Outlook / by the Research Department of the International Monetary Fund. — Washington, D. C. : International Monetary Fund, 1986. — xi,195p. — (World economic and financial surveys). — *Includes bibliographical references. — Contents: Differences in employment behaviour among industrial countries/Charles Adams, Paul R. Fenton and Flemming Larsen - Labor markets, external developments, and unemployment in developing countries/Omotunde E.G. Johnson - Velocity of money and the practice of monetary targeting/Peter Isard and Liliana Rojas-Suarez - Effects of exchange rate changes in industrial countries/James M. Boughton, et al. - Transmission of economic influences from industrial to developing countries/David Goldsbrough and Iqbal Zaidi*

Stagflation, savings, and the state : perspective on the global economy / edited by Deepak Lal and Martin Wolf. — New York ; Oxford : Published for the World Bank [by] Oxford University Press, 1986. — xii,402p. — (A World Bank research publication). — *Includes bibliographies and index*

Surveys in development economics / edited by Norman Gemmell. — Oxford : Basil Blackwell, 1987. — [500]p

THAKUR, Shrinivas Y.
Industrialization and economic development : an appropriate strategy for the underdeveloped countries / Shrinivas Y. Thakur. — London : Sangam Books, 1985. — vii,284p. — *Bibliography: p277-281*

The Third World and the world economic system / V.R. Panchamukhi ... [et al.]. — New Delhi : Radiant Publishers ; Atlantic Highlands, N.J. : Distributed in the U.S.A. by Humanities Press, 1986. — viii, 309 p.. — *Includes bibliographies*

Uneven development and the geographical transfer of value / D.K. Forbes, P.J. Rimmer (eds.). — Canberra : Research School of Pacific Studies, The Australian National University, 1984. — 297p. — (Publication / Research School of Pacific Studies, Department of Human Geography, Australian National University ; HG/16). — *Original papers given at a Workshop on Geographical Transfer of Value held at ... the Australian National University in 1981*

Wage policy issues in economic development : the proceedings of a symposium held by the International Institute for Labour Studies at Egelund, Denmark, 23-27 October 1967 / edited by Anthony D. Smith, with a preface by R. W. Cox. — London : Macmillan, 1969. — xv,408p

DEVELOPING COUNTRIES — Economic conditions — Congresses

IFAC/IFORS CONFERENCE ON SYSTEMS APPROACHES TO DEVELOPING COUNTRIES (1973 : Algiers)
Systems approaches to developing countries : proceedings / Edited by M. A. Cuenod [and] S. Kahne. — Pittsburgh : Distributed by Instrument Society of America, [1973]. — ix, 515 p. — *"A publication of the International Federation of Automatic Control.". — English or French. — Includes bibliographical references*

DEVELOPING COUNTRIES — Economic conditions — Mathematical models — Congresses

Social accounting matrices : a basis for planning / edited by Graham Pyatt and Jeffery I. Round. — Washington, D.C., U.S.A. : World Bank, 1985. — p. cm. — *Bibliography: p*

DEVELOPING COUNTRIES — Economic conditions — Regional disparities

Ethnic preference and public policy in developing states / edited by Neil Nevitte and Charles H. Kennedy. — Boulder, Colo. : Lynne Rienner Publishers, c1986. — p. cm. — *Includes index. — Bibliography: p*

DEVELOPING COUNTRIES — Economic integration

CARL, Beverly May
Economic integration among developing nations : law and policy / Beverly May Carl. — New York : Praeger, 1986. — xx, 285 p.. — *"Praeger special studies. Praeger scientific.". — Includes bibliographies and index*

Cooperation south: the magazine of technical co-operation among developing countries / United Nations. Development Programme. — New York : UNDP, 1985-. — *Quarterly. — Continues:*

Technical cooperation among developing countries news : TCDC news / United Nations. Development Programme. — New York : UNDP, 1979-1984. — *Quarterly. — Continued by: Cooperation south: the magazine of technical co-operation among developing countries*

DEVELOPING COUNTRIES — Economic policy

BULAJIĆ, Milan
Principles of international development law : progressive development of the principles of international law relating to the new international economic order / Milan Bulajić. — Dordrecht, Netherlands ; Boston : Martinus Nijhoff Publishers, 1986. — 403p. — *Bibliography: p.359-366*

CARVOUNIS, Chris C
The foreign debt/national development conflict : external adjustment and internal disorder in the developing nations / Chris C. Carvounis. — New York : Quorum Books, 1986. — xxiii, 243 p.. — *Includes index. — Bibliography: p. [223]-235*

Fund-supported programs, fiscal policy, and income distribution : a study / by the Fiscal Affairs Department of the International Monetary Fund. — Washington, D.C. : International Monetary Fund, 1986. — v,58p. — (Occasional paper / International Monetary Fund ; no.46). — *Bibliographical references: p54-58*

GYLFASON, Thorvaldur
Credit policy and economic activity in developing countries with IMF stabilization programs / Thorvaldur Gylfason. — Princeton, N.J. : International Finance Section, Dept. of Economics, Princeton University, 1987. — p. cm. — (Princeton studies in international finance ; no. 60 (August 1987)). — *Bibliography: p*

DEVELOPING COUNTRIES — Economic policy *continuation*

LOXLEY, John
Debt and disorder : external financing for development / John Loxley. — Boulder : Westview Press, 1986. — p. cm. — (Westview special studies in social, political, and economic development). — Includes index. — *Bibliography: p*

MACESICH, George
Economic nationalism and stability / by George Macesich. — New York : Praeger, 1985. — p. cm. — *Includes bibliographies and index*

Macro policies for appropriate technology in developing countries / edited by Francis Stewart. — Boulder : Westview Press, 1986. — p. cm. — (Westview special studies in social, political, and economic development)

Marxian theory and the third world / edited by Diptendra Banerjee. — New Delhi ; Beverly Hills : Sage Publications, 1985. — 325 p.. — *Includes bibliographical references*

Population and socioeconomic development / [translated from the Russian by Sergeĭ Sosinsky ; authors D. Horlacher ... et al.]. — Moscow : Progress Publishers, 1986. — 186 p.. — *Title on verso of t.p.: Narodonaselenie i sot͡sial'no-ėkonomicheskoe razvitie*

Population growth and economic development : issues and evidence / edited by D. Gale Johnson and Ronald D. Lee. — Madison, Wis. : University of Wisconsin Press, 1987. — xiii, 702 p.. — (Social demography). — *"Working Group on Population Growth and Economic Development; Committee on Population, Commission on Behavioral and Social Sciences and Education, National Research Council.". — Includes bibliographies and index*

Prospects for developing countries, 1978-85 / Helen Hughes...[et al.]. — [Washington, D.C.?] : World Bank, 1977. — 158p

SILVERMAN, Jerry M.
Action-planning workshops for development management : guidelines / Jerry M. Silverman, Merlyn Kettering and Terry D. Schmidt. — Washington, D.C. : The World Bank, 1986. — ix,74p. — (World Bank technical paper ; no.56). — *Bibliography: p49-54*

The State and development in the Third World / edited by Atul Kohli. — Princeton, N.J. : Princeton University Press, 1986. — 288 p.. — (A World politics reader). — *"Essays collected...were published in World politics between 1976 and 1984"--Introd. — Includes bibliographical references*

State trading and development : a perspective view of state trading organizations in developing countries as instruments of national development and channels of international cooperation / edited by Praxy Fernandes. — Ljubljana, Yugoslavia : International Center for Public Enterprises in Developing Countries, 1982. — 277p. — *Includes bibliographical references*

A változó harmadik világ : (valogatás a magyar fejlődés-kutatások műhelyeiből) / szerkesztők: Dobozi István és Láng László. — Budapest : Világgazdasági Kutato Intézet, 1985. — 479p. — (Studies on developing countries ; 118)

DEVELOPING COUNTRIES — Economic policy — Congresses

SEMINÁRIO "AJUSTAMENTO E CRESCIMENTO NA ACTUAL CONJUNTURA ECONÓMICA MUNDIAL" (1985 : Estoril)
Ajustamento e crescimento na actual conjuntura económica mundial / editado por José de Silva Lopes. — Washington, D.C. : International Monetary Fund, 1985. — xi,200p. — *Includes bibliographical references*

DEVELOPING COUNTRIES — Emigration and immigration

TODARO, Michael P.
International migration, domestic unemployment, and urbanization : a three-sector model / Michael P. Todaro. — New York : Population Council, 1986. — 29p. — (Working papers / Population Council, New York. Center for Policy Studies ; no.124). — *Bibliography: p24-25*

TODARO, Michael P.
A theory of illegal international migration from developing countries / Michael P. Todaro. — New York : Population Council, 1986. — 45p. — (Working papers / Population Council, New York. Center for Policy Studies ; no.126). — *Bibliography: p41-42*

DEVELOPING COUNTRIES — Emigration and immigration — History — 20th century

REIMERS, David M
Still the golden door : the third world comes to America / David M. Reimers. — New York : Columbia University Press, c1985. — xviii, 319p. — *Includes index. — Bibliography: p.[219]-312*

DEVELOPING COUNTRIES — Ethnic relations

Ethnic preference and public policy in developing states / edited by Neil Nevitte and Charles H. Kennedy. — Boulder, Colo. : Lynne Rienner Publishers, c1986. — p. cm. — *Includes index. — Bibliography: p*

DEVELOPING COUNTRIES — Foreign economic relations

BERBEROGLU, Berch
The international of capital : imperialism and capitalist development on a world scale / Berch Berberoglu. — New York : Praeger, 1987. — p. cm. — *Bibliography: p*

BOLLECKER-STERN, Brigitte
Droit économique / Brigitte Bollecker-Stern, Maurice Dahan, Lazare Kopelmanas. — Paris : Pedone, 1978. — 166p. — (Cours et travaux / Institut des hautes études internationales de Paris)

IBRAHIM, Tigani E.
Developing countries and the Tokya round / Dr. Tigani E. Ibrahim. — Khartoum : University of Khartoum. Faculty of Economic and Social Studies. Development Studies and Research Centre, [1978]. — iii,52p. — (Occasional papers / University of Khartoum. Faculty of Economic and Social Studies. Development Studies and Research Centre ; no.1)

Positive sum : improving North-South relations / edited by I. William Zartman. — New Brunswick, N.J. : Transaction Books, c1986. — p. cm. — *Includes bibliographies*

RAMPHAL, Shridath S.
For the South, a time to think / Shridath S. Ramphal. — London : Third World Foundation, 1986. — 18p. — (Third World Foundation monograph ; 16)

DEVELOPING COUNTRIES — Foreign economic relations — Bibliography

The Third world and international law : selected bibliography, 1955-1982 / United Nations Library, Geneva = Le Tiers monde et le droit international : bibliographie sélective, 1955-1982 / Nations Unies, Bibliothèque, Genève. — Geneva : United Nations Library, 1983. — 100p. — (Publications / United Nations Library, Geneva. Series C, Special bibliographies, repertoires, and indexes = Publications / Nations Unies, Bibliothèque, Genève. Série C, Bibliographies spéciales, répertoires, et index ; no. 5). — *Includes indexes*

DEVELOPING COUNTRIES — Foreign economic relations — Congresses

SEMINÁRIO "AJUSTAMENTO E CRESCIMENTO NA ACTUAL CONJUNTURA ECONÓMICA MUNDIAL" (1985 : Estoril)
Ajustamento e crescimento na actual conjuntura económica mundial / editado por José de Silva Lopes. — Washington, D.C. : International Monetary Fund, 1985. — xi,200p. — *Includes bibliographical references*

DEVELOPING COUNTRIES — Foreign relations

THOMAS, Caroline, 1959-
In search of security : the Third World in international relations / Caroline Thomas. — Brighton : Wheatsheaf, 1987. — xv,228p. — *Bibliography: p202-220. — Includes index*

DEVELOPING COUNTRIES — Foreign relations — Congresses

East-West tensions in the Third World / Marshall D. Shulman, editor. — 1st ed. — New York : W.W. Norton, c1986. — 243 p.. — *Background papers prepared for the 70th American Assembly at Arden House, Harriman, N.Y., Nov. 21, 1985. — At head of title: American Assembly. — Includes index*

DEVELOPING COUNTRIES — Foreign relations — Soviet Union

FUKUYAMA, Francis
Moscow's post-Brezhnev reassessment of the Third World / Francis Fukuyama. — Santa Monica (Calif.) : Rand, 1986. — xi,91p. — *Bibliography: p87-91*

The Soviet Union and the Third World : the last three decades / edited by Andrzej Korbonski and Francis Fukuyama. — Ithaca, N.Y. : Cornell University Press, c1987. — p. cm. — *"A book from the Rand/UCLA Center for the Study of Soviet International Behavior.". — Includes index*

DEVELOPING COUNTRIES — Foreign relations — Soviet Union — Congresses

East-West tensions in the Third World / Marshall D. Shulman, editor. — 1st ed. — New York : W.W. Norton, c1986. — 243 p.. — *Background papers prepared for the 70th American Assembly at Arden House, Harriman, N.Y., Nov. 21, 1985. — At head of title: American Assembly. — Includes index*

DEVELOPING COUNTRIES — Foreign relations — United States

HALLIDAY, Fred
Beyond Irangate : the Reagan doctrine and the Third World / Fred Halliday. — Amsterdam : Transnational Institute, 1987. — 38p. — (Transnational issues ; 1)

THORNTON, Thomas Perry
The challenge to U.S. policy in the Third World : global responsibilities and regional devolution / Thomas Perry Thornton. — Boulder : Westview Press with the Foreign Policy Institute, School of Advanced International Studies, Johns Hopkins University, 1986. — p. cm. — (SAIS papers in international affairs ; no. 9). — *Includes index*

DEVELOPING COUNTRIES — Foreign relations — United States — Congresses

East-West tensions in the Third World / Marshall D. Shulman, editor. — 1st ed. — New York : W.W. Norton, c1986. — 243 p.. — *Background papers prepared for the 70th American Assembly at Arden House, Harriman, N.Y., Nov. 21, 1985. — At head of title: American Assembly. — Includes index*

DEVELOPING COUNTRIES — Full employment policies — Congresses

Public enterprises and employment in developing countries / edited by W.D. Lakshman. — Ljubljana, Yugoslavia : International Center for Public Enterprises in Developing Countries, c1984. — 182p. — *Papers presented at a meeting held in Amman, Jordan in April 1983. — Includes bibliographies. — Contents: The role of public enterprises in employment generation in underdeveloped countries / W.D. Lakshman -- The role of public enterprises in employment in Latin America / Horacio Boneo -- Conflicts between employment and output growth objectives of public enterprises in developing countries / Frances Stewart -- Public enterprise, technology, and employment in less developed countries / Jeffrey James -- Measurement of indirect employment effects of public enterprises in developing countries through social accounting matrices / Aleš Vahčič -- Thoughts about the probable employment conditions of women in public enterprises / Souad N. Barnouti -- Manpower development through public enterprises / Tayseer Abdel Jaber -- Public enterprises as sources of employment for less developed regions in developing countries / Hassan A. El Tayeb*

DEVELOPING COUNTRIES — History, Military

NEUMAN, Stephanie G
Military assistance in recent wars : the dominance of the superpowers / Stephanie Neuman ; foreword by Ernest Graves. — New York : Praeger, 1986. — p. cm. — (The Washington papers ; 122). — *"Published with the Center for Strategic and International Studies, Georgetown University, Washington, D.C.". — "Praeger special studies. Praeger scientific."*

DEVELOPING COUNTRIES — Industries

HAQUANI, Zalmaï
Industrialisation et commerce du Tiers monde / Zalmaï Haquani. — Paris : La Documentation française, 1986. — 144p. — (Notes et études documentaires ; no.4808). — *Bibliography: p136-139*

HARRIS, Nigel
The end of the Third World : newly industrializing countries and the decline of an ideology / by Nigel Harris. — London : Tauris, 1986. — [220]p. — *Includes bibliography and index*

Industry and development : global report 1986. — Vienna : United Nations Industrial Development Organization, 1986. — xxiii,330p. — (Document ; ID/343). — *Bibliography: p143-145. — Document no.ID/343; Sales no. E.86.II.B.5*

LIPIETZ
Mirages et miracles : problèmes de l'industrialisation dans le tiers monde / Alain Lipietz. — Paris : La Découverte, 1985. — 188p. — *Bibliography: p179-186*

Surveys in development economics / edited by Norman Gemmell. — Oxford : Basil Blackwell, 1987. — [500]p

THAKUR, Shrinivas Y.
Industrialization and economic development : an appropriate strategy for the underdeveloped countries / Shrinivas Y. Thakur. — London : Sangam Books, 1985. — vii,284p. — *Bibliography: p277-281*

DEVELOPING COUNTRIES — Industries — Energy conservation

GAMBA, Julio R.
Industrial energy rationalization in developing countries / Julio R. Gamba, David A. Caplin, John J. Mulckhuyse. — Baltimore : Johns Hopkins University Press for the World Bank, 1986. — x,114p. — *Bibliography: p99-105*

DEVELOPING COUNTRIES — Literatures — History and criticism

HARLOW, Barbara
Resistance literature / Barbara Harlow. — New York ; London : Methuen, 1987. — xx,234p. — *Bibliography: p217-226. — Includes index*

DEVELOPING COUNTRIES — Military relations — Soviet Union

LEONARD, Ellis P
[Orthopedic surgery of the dog and cat]. Leonard's Orthopedic surgery of the dog and cat. — 3rd ed. / J.W. Alexander. — Philadelphia : Saunders, 1985. — ix, 242 p.. — *Includes bibliographies and index*

DEVELOPING COUNTRIES — Military relations — United States

LEONARD, Ellis P
[Orthopedic surgery of the dog and cat]. Leonard's Orthopedic surgery of the dog and cat. — 3rd ed. / J.W. Alexander. — Philadelphia : Saunders, 1985. — ix, 242 p.. — *Includes bibliographies and index*

DEVELOPING COUNTRIES — Politics and government

BRUCKNER, Pascal
Le sanglot de l'homme blanc : Tiers-monde, culpabilité, haine de soi / Pascal Bruckner. — Paris : Editions du Seuil, c1983. — 309 p.. — (L'Histoire immédiate). — *Includes bibliographical references*

BRUCKNER, Pascal
[Sanglot de l'homme blanc. English]. The tears of the white man : compassion as contempt / Pascal Bruckner ; translated with an introduction by William R. Beer. — New York : Free Press, c1986. — xx, 244 p.. — *Translation of: Le sanglot de l'homme blanc. — Includes bibliographical references and index*

Ethnic preference and public policy in developing states / edited by Neil Nevitte and Charles H. Kennedy. — Boulder, Colo. : Lynne Rienner Publishers, c1986. — p. cm. — *Includes index. — Bibliography: p*

Ethnicity, politics, and development / edited by Dennis L. Thompson and Dev Ronen. — Boulder, Colo. : L. Rienner, c1985. — p. cm. — *Includes index. — Bibliography: p*

GAYLE, Dennis John
The small developing state : comparing political economies in Costa Rica, Singapore and Jamaica / Dennis John Gayle. — Aldershot : Gower, c1986. — [xiii,218]p. — *Includes index*

LLOYD, Peter C.
Classes, crises and coups : themes in the sociology of developing countries / Peter C. Lloyd. — London : Paladin, 1973, c1971. — 223p. — *Originally published: MacGibbon and Kee, 1971. — Further reading: p205-212*

SENGUPTA, Jyoti
Non-alignment : search for a destination / Jyoti Sengupta. — Calcutta : Naya Prokash, 1979. — xxii,208p

SOMJEE, A. H.
Parallels and actuals of political development / A.H. Somjee. — London : Macmillan, 1986. — x,141p. — *Includes index*

The State and development in the Third World / edited by Atul Kohli. — Princeton, N.J. : Princeton University Press, 1986. — 288 p.. — (A World politics reader). — *"Essays collected...were published in World politics between 1976 and 1984"--Introd. — Includes bibliographical references*

Understanding political development : an analytic study / general editors, Myron Weiner, Samuel P. Huntington ; contributors, Gabriel A. Almond ... [et al.]. — Boston : Little, Brown, c1987. — xxviii, 514 p.. — (The Little, Brown series in comparative politics). — *Includes bibliographies and indexes*

DEVELOPING COUNTRIES — Population

Fertility in developing countries : an economic perspective on research and policy issues / edited and introduced by Ghazi M. Farooq and George B. Simmons ; foreword by Rafael M. Salas. — London : Macmillan, 1985. — xxiv,533p. — (The Macmillan series of ILO studies). — *"A study prepared for the International Labour Office within the framework of the World Employment Programme ...". — Bibliography: p490-520. — Includes index*

Population growth and economic development : issues and evidence / edited by D. Gale Johnson and Ronald D. Lee. — Madison, Wis. : University of Wisconsin Press, 1987. — xiii, 702 p.. — (Social demography). — *"Working Group on Population Growth and Economic Development; Committee on Population, Commission on Behavioral and Social Sciences and Education, National Research Council.". — Includes bibliographies and index*

DEVELOPING COUNTRIES — Population — Congresses

AGRICULTURE SECTOR SYMPOSIUM ((5th : 1985 : World Bank)
Proceedings of the Fifth Agriculture Sector Symposium : population and food / Ted J. Davis, editor. — Washington, D.C., U.S.A. : World Bank, c1985. — viii,230p. — *Includes bibliographies*

DEVELOPING COUNTRIES — Population — Statistics — Estimates — Handbooks, Manuals, etc

CLAIRIN, Rémy
Handbook for estimating demographic statistics from incomplete data in developing countries / by Rémy Clairin and Julien Condé. — Paris : Development Centre of the Organisation for Economic Co-operation and Development, 1986. — 266p. — (Development Centre papers) . — *Bibliography: p264-266*

DEVELOPING COUNTRIES — Population policy

Population and socioeconomic development / [translated from the Russian by Sergeĭ Sosinsky ; authors D. Horlacher ... et al.]. — Moscow : Progress Publishers, 1986. — 186 p.. — *Title on verso of t.p.: Narodonaselenie i sot͡sial'no-ėkonomicheskoe razvitie*

DEVELOPING COUNTRIES — Rural conditions

Third World peasantry : a continuing saga of deprivation / editors, R.P. Misra & Nguyen Tri Dung. — New Delhi : Sterling Publishers, c1986. — 2 v.. — *Includes bibliographies and indexes*

DEVELOPING COUNTRIES — Rural conditions — Case studies

Agricultural household models : extensions, applications, and policy / Inderjit Singh. — Baltimore : Johns Hopkins University Press for the World Bank, 1986. — xi,335p. — *Includes bibliographical references*

DEVELOPING COUNTRIES — Social conditions

BRUCKNER, Pascal
Le sanglot de l'homme blanc : Tiers-monde, culpabilité, haine de soi / Pascal Bruckner. — Paris : Editions du Seuil, c1983. — 309 p.. — (L'Histoire immédiate). — *Includes bibliographical references*

BRUCKNER, Pascal
[Sanglot de l'homme blanc. English]. The tears of the white man : compassion as contempt / Pascal Bruckner ; translated with an introduction by William R. Beer. — New York : Free Press, c1986. — xx, 244 p.. — *Translation of: Le sanglot de l'homme blanc. — Includes bibliographical references and index*

LLOYD, Peter C.
Classes, crises and coups : themes in the sociology of developing countries / Peter C. Lloyd. — London : Paladin, 1973, c1971. — 223p. — *Originally published: MacGibbon and Kee, 1971. — Further reading: p205-212*

DEVELOPING COUNTRIES — Social conditions *continuation*

MARTON, Imre
Contribution to a critique of an interpretation of specific Third World traits / Imre Marton. — Budapest : Institute for World Economics of the Hungarian Academy of Sciences : sold by Kultúra, 1978. — 120 p.. — (Studies on developing countries ; no. 97). — *Includes bibliographical references*

SOMJEE, A. H.
Parallels and actuals of political development / A.H. Somjee. — London : Macmillan, 1986. — x,141p. — *Includes index*

SZENTES, Tamás
Intérpretations sociologiques du sous-développement / Tamás Szentes. — Budapest : Centre pour la Recherche de l'Afro-Asie de l'Académie des Sciences de Hongrie, 1972. — 37p. — (Études sur les pays en voie de developpement ; no.49)

DEVELOPING COUNTRIES — Social policy

MACPHERSON, Stewart
Comparative social policy and the Third World / Stewart MacPherson and James Midgley. — Brighton : Wheatsheaf, 1987. — x,228p. — (Studies in international social policy and welfare). — *Bibliography: p205-221. — Includes index*

A változó harmadik világ : (valogatás a magyar fejlődés-kutatások műhelyeiből) / szerkesztők: Dobozi István és Láng László. — Budapest : Világgazdasági Kutato Intézet, 1985. — 479p. — (Studies on developing countries ; 118)

DEVELOPING COUNTRIES — Statistics, Vital

INSTITUT NATIONAL D'ETUDES DÉMOGRAPHIQUES
Health policy, social policy and mortality prospects : proceedings of a seminar at Paris, France, February 28-March 4, 1983 / edited by Jacques Vallin and Alan D. Lopez. — [Liège] : Ordina, 1985. — 557p. — *Bibliographies*

ZOUGHLAMI, Younès
The demographic characteristics of household populations / Younès Zoughlami, Diana Allsopp. — Voorburg : International Statistical Institute, 1985. — 82p. — (Comparative studies / World Fertility Survey ; no.45). — *Bibliographical references: p31*

DEVELOPING COUNTRIES — Economic policy

TODARO, Michael P
Economic development in the Third World / Michael P. Todaro. — 3rd ed. — New York : Longman, c1985. — xxxvi, 648 p. — *Includes index. — Bibliography: p. 613-640*

DEVELOPING COUNTRIES — Foreign economic relations

Linking the south : the route to economic cooperation / edited by Bernard Chidzero and Altaf Gauhar. — London : Third World Foundation, 1986. — xviii,344p

DEVELOPING COUNTRIES — Industries — Addresses, essays, lectures

Industrialization and development : a Third World perspective / Pradip K. Ghosh, editor ; foreword by Subbiah Kannappan. — Westport, Conn. : Greenwood Press, c1984. — xxviii, 566 p.. — (International development resource books ; no. 1). — *"Prepared under the auspices of the Center for Advanced Study of International Development, Michigan State University.". — Includes indexes. — Bibliography: p. [381]-516*

DEVELOPING COUNTRIES — Politics and government

SOMJEE, A. H.
Parallels and actuals of political development / A.H. Somjee. — London : Macmillan, 1986. — x,141p. — *Includes index*

DEVELOPMENT BANKS

WELLONS, Phillip
Banks and specialised financial intermediaries in development / by Phillip Wellons, Dimitri Germidis and Bianca Glavanis. — Paris : Organisation for Economic Co—operation and Development, 1986. — 150p. — (Development Centre studies). — *Bibliography: p131-133*

DEVELOPMENT BANKS — Law and legislation

The international law of development : basic documents / compiled and edited by A. Peter Mutharika. — Dobbs Ferry, N.Y. : Oceana Vol.1. — 1978. — x,646p

DEVELOPMENT BANKS — India

SINGH, Vimal Shankar
Development banking in India / Vimal Shankar Singh. — New Delhi : Deep & Deep Publications, c1985. — 376 p.. — *Includes index. — Bibliography: p. [371]-374*

DEVELOPMENT BANKS — Mexico

RAMÍREZ, Miguel D
Development banking in Mexico : the case of the Nacional Financiera, S.A. / Miguel D. Ramírez. — New York : Praeger, 1985. — xix, 228p. — *Includes index. — Bibliography: p.215-221*

DEVELOPMENT BANKS — Puerto Rico

WENDIN, Constance M.
Development banks and corporations / Constance M. Wendin. — [San Juan] : Government Development Bank for Puerto Rico, 1965. — 70p. — (GOVBANK technical papers ; no.4). — *Bibliography: p63-70*

DEVELOPMENT CREDIT CORPORATIONS

DUVIGNEAU, J. Christian
Guidelines for calculating financial amd economic rates of return for DFC projects / J. Christian Duvigneau and Ranga N. Prasad. — Washington, D.C. : The World Bank, 1984. — xii,149p. — (World Bank technical paper ; no.33) (Industry and finance series ; v.9). — *Bibliography: p148-149*

DEVELOPMENT CREDIT CORPORATIONS — Organisation for Economic Co-operation and Development countries

MITSOTAKI, Alexandra Gourdain
Public development finance corporations : their role in the new forms of investment in developing countries / by Alexandra Gourdain Mitsotaki. — [Paris] : Development Centre of the Organisation for Economic Co-operation and Development, [1986]. — 40p. — (Development Centre papers). — *Bibliographical references: p.39-40*

DEVELOPMENTAL PSYCHOLOGY

STERN, Daniel N
The interpersonal world of the infant : a view from psychoanalysis annd developmental psychology / Daniel N. Stern. — New York : Basic Books, c1985. — x, 304p. — *Includes index. — Bibliography: p.278-294*

DEVELOPMENTAL PSYCHOLOGY — Congresses

Life-span developmental psychology : intergenerational relations / edited by Nancy Datan, Anita L. Greene, Hayne W. Reese. — Hillsdale, N.J. ; London : Lawrence Erlbaum Associates, 1986. — xiii, 280p. — *Proceedings of the Ninth West Virginia University Conference on Life-Span Developmental Psychology held in Morgantown on May 10-12, 1984. — Includes bibliographies and index*

DEVELOPMENTAL PSYCHOLOGY — Dictionaries

The Dictionary of developmental and educational psychology / edited by Rom Harré and Roger Lamb ; advisory editors, Peter Bryant, R. Maliphant. — Oxford : Blackwell Reference, 1986. — x,271p. — *Includes bibliographies and index*

DEVIANT BEHAVIOR

PFOHL, Stephen J
Images of deviance and social control : a sociological history / Stephen J. Pfohl. — New York : McGraw-Hill, c1985. — xiii, 402 p.. — *Cover title: Images of deviance & social control. — Includes bibliographies and index*

DEVIANT BEHAVIOR — Congresses

Development of antisocial and prosocial behavior : research, theories, and issues / edited by Dan Olweus, Jack Block, Marian Radke-Yarrow. — Orlando : Academic Press, 1986. — xiii, 432 p.. — (Developmental psychology series). — *Based on a conference on the development of antisocial and prosocial behavior, held at Voss, Norway, 7/4-10/82. — Includes bibliographies and indexes*

DEVIANT BEHAVIOR — History

PFOHL, Stephen J
Images of deviance and social control : a sociological history / Stephen J. Pfohl. — New York : McGraw-Hill, c1985. — xiii, 402 p.. — *Cover title: Images of deviance & social control. — Includes bibliographies and index*

DEVIANT BEHAVIOR IN MASS MEDIA — United States

GILBERT, James Burkhart
A cycle of outrage : juvenile delinquency and mass media in the 1950s / James Gilbert. — New York ; Oxford : Oxford University Press, 1986. — vi, 258p, [6]p of plates. — *Includes bibliographical references and index. — Bibliography: p*

DEVIL — History of doctrines

RUSSELL, Jeffrey Burton
Mephistopheles : the Devil in the modern world / Jeffrey Burton Russell. — Ithaca : Cornell University Press, 1986. — 333 p.. — *Includes index. — Bibliography: p. [303]-323*

DEVON — Statistics

Comparative statistics: Devon v the Shire Counties : based on 1983/84 estimates. — [Exeter] : Central Information Service, Devon County Council, [1983?]. — 33leaves. — *Cover title*

DEVON. County Council

Leisure policies and programmes : a summary report on future possibilities. — Exeter : Devon County Council, 1985. — 28p. — *"This summary report shows the opportunities for future leisure provision by Devon's local authorities. The full report contains the survey material and analysis on which these possibilities are based."*

DHIMAL (NEPALESE PEOPLE) — Social life and customs

REGMI, Rishikeshab Raj
Cultural patterns and economic change : (anthropological study of Dhimals of Nepal) / Rishikeshab Raj Regmi. — Delhi : Motilal Banarasi Dass, 1985. — iii,218p. — *Includes glossary of local terms used: p[212]-218. — Bibliography: p[204]-212*

DHOFAR (OMAN) — Social conditions

JANZEN, Jörg
[Normaden Dhofars/Sultanat Oman. English]. Nomads in the Sultanate of Oman : tradition and development in Dhofar / Jörg Janzen. — Boulder : Westview Press, 1986. — xxiii, 315 p.. — (Westview special studies on the Middle East). — *Translation of: Die Nomaden Dhofars/Sultanat Oman. — Bibliography: p. 299-315*

DIALECTIC

CATALANO, Joseph S
A commentary on Jean-Paul Sartre's Critique of dialectical reason, volume 1, Theory of practical ensembles / Joseph S. Catalano. — Chicago : University of Chicago Press, 1986. — x, 282 p.. — *Includes index. — Bibliography: p. [269]-273*

LORENZEN, Max-Otto
Der Geist der Dialektik oder die Erschöpfung der Kritik / Max-Otto Lorenzen. — Hannover : die Freie Gesellschaft, 1979. — 124p

DIALECTICAL MATERIALISM
CARCHEDI, Guglielmo
Class analysis and social research / Guglielmo Carchedi. — Oxford : Basil Blackwell, 1987. — [224]p. — *Includes bibliography and index*

KAIN, Philip J.
Marx' method, epistemology, and humanism : a study in the development of his thought / Philip J. Kain. — Dordrecht ; Boston : D. Reidel ; Hingham, MA, U.S.A. : Sold and distributed in the U.S.A. and Canada by Kluwer Academic Publishers, c1986. — x, 197 p.. — (Sovietica ; v. 48). — *Includes index.* — *Bibliography: p. 176-184*

KOSTOPOULOS, Tryphon
Beyond capitalism : toward nomocracy / Tryphon Kostopoulos. — New York : Praeger, c1986. — p. cm. — *Includes index.* — *Bibliography: p*

DICKEY, CHRISTOPHER
DICKEY, Christopher
With the Contras : a reporter in the wilds of Nicaragua / Christopher Dickey. — New York : Simon and Schuster, c1985. — 327 p., [9] p. of plates. — *Includes index.* — *Bibliography: p. 273-315*

DICTATORS
NIN, Andrés
Les dictadures dels nostres dies / Andreu Nin. — 2a edició. — Sant Boi de Llobregat : Lluita, 1984. — 211p. — (Collecció espurna ; 3)

DICTATORS — Europe — History — 20th century
LEE, Stephen J.
The European dictatorships 1918-1945 / Stephen J. Lee. — London : Methuen, 1987. — xv,343p. — *Bibliography: p331-334.* — *Includes index*

DICTATORSHIP OF THE PROLETARIAT
LENIN, V. I.
The state and revolution : the Marxist theory of the State and the tasks of the proletariat in the revolution / V. I. Lenin. — Moscow : Progress Publishers, 1949. — 139p

SHISHKINA, I. M.
Partiia i rabochii klass v sotsialisticheskom obshchestve : izmyshleniia sovetologov i deistvitel'nost' / I. M. Shishkina. — Leningrad : Lenizdat, 1986. — 260p

DICTIONARIES — Polyglot
Borrowing and lending terminology : English-French-Spanish = Terminologie des emprunts et des prêts : Français-anglais-espagnol = Terminología de empréstitos y préstamos : Español-inglés-francés. — Washington, D.C. : The World Bank, 1984. — vii,56p. — (A World Bank glossary). — *In English, French and Spanish*

DICTIONARIES, POLYGLOT
Dictionary of archival terminology = Dictionnaire de terminologie archivistique : English and French with equivalents in Dutch, German, Italian, Russian and Spanish / edited by Peter Walne ; compiled by Frank B. Evans, François-J. Himly and Peter Walne. — München ; London : Saur, 1984. — 226p. — (ICA handbooks series ; v.3). — *At head of title: International Council on Archives*

LOGIE, Gordon
Glossary of transport : English, French, Italian, Dutch, German, Swedish / Gordon Logie. — Amsterdam ; New York : Elsevier Scientific Pub. Co. ; New York : distributors for the U.S. and Canada, Elsevier/North-Holland, 1980. — xxvii, 296 p.. — (International planning glossaries ; 2)

PETERSEN, William
Dictionary of demography / William Petersen and Renee Petersen with the collaboration of an international panel of demographers. — Westport, Conn ; London : Greenwood Press, 1985
Multilingual glossary. — 1985. — 259p

DIESEL, RUDOLF
THOMAS, Donald E.
Diesel : technology and society in industrial Germany / Donald E. Thomas, Jr. — Tuscaloosa, Ala. : University of Alabama Press, c1987. — xii, 279 p.. — *Includes index.* — *Bibliography: p. 262-267*

DIESEL MOTOR — History
THOMAS, Donald E.
Diesel : technology and society in industrial Germany / Donald E. Thomas, Jr. — Tuscaloosa, Ala. : University of Alabama Press, c1987. — xii, 279 p.. — *Includes index.* — *Bibliography: p. 262-267*

DIET
PANEL ON DIET IN RELATION TO CARDIOVASCULAR DISEASE
Diet and cardiovascular disease : report of the Panel on Diet in Relation to Cardiovascular Disease. — London : HMSO, 1984. — viii,32. — (Report on Health and social subjects / Great Britain. Department of Health and Social Security ; 28)

WHEELOCK, Verner
The food revolution / J. Verner Wheelock. — Marlow, Bucks : Chalcombe Publications, c1986. — viii,119p

DIET — History
MCKEOWN, Thomas
The modern rise of population / Thomas McKeown. — London : Edward Arnold, 1976. — [5],168p. — *Includes index*

DIET — China
PIAZZA, Alan Lee
Food consumption and nutritional status in the P.R.C. / Alan Piazza. — Boulder : Westview Press, 1986. — p. cm. — (Westview special studies on China). — *Bibliography: p*

DIET — Developing countries
MARTORELL, Reynaldo
Nutrition and health status indicators : suggestions for surveys of the standard of living in developing countries / Reynaldo Martorell. — Washington, D.C., U.S.A. : World Bank, Development Research Center, c1981. — 97p. — (LSMS working papers ; no.13). — "February 1982.". — *Bibliography: p91-97*

DIET — United States
SILVERSTEIN, Brett
Fed up : the food forces that make you fat, sick, and poor / by Brett Silverstein. — Boston, MA : South End Press, c1984. — 160 p.. — *Bibliography: p. 149-160*

DIFFUSION OF INNOVATIONS
ROGERS, Everett M.
Diffusion of innovations / Everett M. Rogers. — 3rd ed.. — New York : Free Press ; London : Collier Macmillan, 1983. — xix, 453p. — Rev. ed. of: Communication of innovations. 2nd ed. 1971. — *Bibliography: p 414-439*

DIGITAL MAPPING
AUTO CARTO LONDON (1986)
Proceedings / edited by Michael Blakemore. — London : Auto Carto London, 1986. — Subtitle: International conference on the acquisition, management and presentation of spatial data, 14-19 September, 1986
Vol.2: Digital mapping and spatial information systems. — 565p

CARTER, James R.
Computer mapping : progress in the '80s / James R. Carter. — Washington, D.C. : Association of American Geographers, c1984. — viii, 86 p.. — (Resource publications in geography). — *Bibliography: p. [79]-82*

DILL, Sir JOHN
DANCHEV, Alex
Very special relationship : Field-Marshall Sir John Dill and the Anglo-American alliance 1941-44 / Alex Danchev. — London : Brassey's Defence, 1986. — xv,201p. — *Bibliography: p183-197.* — *Includes index*

DILTHEY, WILHELM
HODGES, Herbert Arthur
Wilhelm Dilthey : an introduction / by H. A. Hodges. — New York : Howard Fertig, 1969. — x, 174p. — *Bibliography: p. 161-167*

DIMITROV, GEORGI
Georgi Dimitrov : biografiia / [Dobrin Michev...et al.]. — []2. dop. izd.]. — Sofiia : Partizdat, 1982. — 663p

SLAVOV, Slavi Dimitrov
Georgi Dimitrov : opit za teoreticheski portret / Slavi Slavov. — Sofiia : Izd-vo na Bŭlgarskata Akademiia na Naukite, 1983. — 207p. — *Summary in Russian and German.* — *Bibliography: p195-201*

ZHIVKOV, Todor
Velik sin na Bŭlgariia : dokladi, statii, rechi, razmisli za Georgi Dimitrov / Todor Zhivkov. — Sofiia : Partizdat, 1982. — 454p

DINKA (AFRICAN PEOPLE) — Biography
DENG, Francis Mading
The man called Deng Majok : a biography of power, polygyny, and change / Francis Mading Deng. — New Haven : Yale University Press, c1986. — p. cm. — *Includes index*

DIPLOMACY
COHEN, Raymond
Theatre of power : the art of diplomatic signalling / Raymond Cohen. — London : Longman, 1987. — [208]p. — *Includes index*

DER DERIAN, James
On diplomacy : a genealogy of Western estrangement / James Der Derian. — Oxford : Basil Blackwell, 1987. — 258p. — *Bibliography: p246-253.* — *Includes index*

Diplomacy at the UN / edited and introduced by G.R. Berridge and A. Jennings. — London : Macmillan, 1985. — xvii,227p. — *Includes index*

HERZ, Martin Florian
Making the world a less dangerous place : lessons learned from a career in diplomacy / Martin F. Herz. — Washington, D.C. : Georgetown University. Iinstitute for Study of Diplomacy, 1981. — iv,27p. — *Fifth Oscar Iden lecture*

PANIKKAR, Kavalam Madhava
The principles and practice of diplomacy / Kavalam Madhava Panikkar. — Bombay : Asia Publishing House, 1956. — 99p

PLISCHKE, Elmer
Diplomat in chief : the President at the summit / Elmer Plischke. — New York ; Eastbourne : Praeger, 1986. — x,518p. — *Bibliography: p490-494*

Positive sum : improving North-South relations / edited by I. William Zartman. — New Brunswick, N.J. : Transaction Books, c1986. — p. cm. — *Includes bibliographies*

DIPLOMACY — Dictionaries — Russian
Diplomaticheskii slovar' / glavnaia redaktsiia A. A. Gromyko...[et al.]. — 4-e perer. i dop. izd.. — Moskva : Nauka
T.3: S-Ia. — 1986. — 749p

DIPLOMACY — Directories
World diplomatic guide : directory of the diplomatic and trade missions of all nations / Emmanuel Okoro; editor. — London : Irving and Skinner, 1985. — xiv,826p

DIPLOMACY — Moral and ethical aspects
The China Hands' legacy : ethics and diplomacy / edited by Paul Gordon Lauren. — Boulder : Westview Press, 1987. — xi, 196 p.. — *Includes bibliographies and index*

DIPLOMATIC AND CONSULAR SERVICE IN GREAT BRITAIN

LEWIS, Charles J.
State and diplomatic immunity / by Charles J. Lewis. — 2nd ed. — London : Lloyd's of London, 1985. — [xxvi,250]p. — *Previous ed.: 1980. — Includes index*

DIPLOMATIC NEGOTIATIONS IN INTERNATIONAL DISPUTES

Negotiating world order : the artisanship and architecture of global diplomacy / edited by Alan K. Henrikson ; with essays by Gamani Corea ... [et al.]. — Wilmington, Del. : Scholarly Resources, 1986. — xxx, 265 p.. — *Includes bibliographies and index*

DIPLOMATS — United States — Biography

CLAY, Cassius Marcellus
The life of Cassius Marcellus Clay : memoirs, writings, and speeches showing his conduct in the overthrow of American slavery, the salvation of the Union, and the restoration of the autonomy of the states / [by Cassius Marcellus Clay]. — New York : Negro Universities Press. — *Reprint of 1886 edition* [Vol.1]. — 1969. — xiii,600p

DIPLOMATS — Canada — Biography

RITCHIE, Charles
Diplomatic passport : more undiplomatic diaries, 1946-1962 / Charles Rtichie. — Toronto : Macmillan of Canada, 1986. — 200p. — (Macmillan paperbacks ; 12)

DIPLOMATS — Germany — Biography

HAUPTS, Leo
Graf Brockdorff-Rantzou : Diplomat und Minister in Kaiser-reich und Republik / Leo Haupts. — Göttingen : Muster-Schmidt, c1984. — 106p. — (Persönlichkeit und Geschichte ; Bd.116/117). — *Bibliography: p103-106*

DIPLOMATS — Great Britain — Biography

MASTERSON, William H
Tories and Democrats : British diplomats in the pre-Jacksonian America / by William H. Masterson ; foreword by Frank E. Vandiver. — 1st ed. — College Station : Texas A&M University Press, c1985. — xvi, 280p, [8]p of plates. — *Includes index. — Bibliography: p.[259]- 274*

DIPLOMATS — Philippines — Biography

ROMULO, Carlos Peña
Forty years : a Third World soldier at the UN / Carlos P. Romulo with Beth Day Romulo. — Westport, Conn. : Greenwood Press, c1986. — p. cm. — (Studies in freedom ; no. 3). — *Includes index. — Bibliography :*

DIPLOMATS — Russia — Biography

BESEDOVSKIĬ, Grigoriĭ Zinov'evich
[Na putīākh k termidoru. English]. Revelations of a Soviet diplomat / by Grigory Bessedovsky ; translated by Matthew Norgate. — Westport, Conn. : Hyperion Press, 1977. — 276 p.. — *Abridged translation of Na putīākh k termidoru. — Reprint of the 1931 ed. published by Williams & Norgate, London. — Includes index*

DIPLOMATS — United States — Biography

ANSCHEL, Eugene
Homer Lea, Sun Yat-sen, and the Chinese revolution / by Eugene Anschel. — New York : Praeger, 1984. — xvi, 269 p.. — *Includes index. — Bibliography: p. 253-262*

Australia through American eyes, 1935-1945 : observations by American diplomats / selected, edited and with an introduction by P.G. Edwards. — St Lucia : University of Queensland Press ; Hemel Hempstead : Distributed by Prentice-Hall, 1979. — xi,104p. — *Bibliography: p.97-101. — Includes index*

FINDLING, John E
Dictionary of American diplomatic history / John E. Findling. — Westport, Conn. : Greenwood Press, 1980. — xviii, 622 p.. — *Includes bibliographies and index*

DIPLOMATS — United States — History — 18th century

MASTERSON, William H
Tories and Democrats : British diplomats in the pre-Jacksonian America / by William H. Masterson ; foreword by Frank E. Vandiver. — 1st ed. — College Station : Texas A&M University Press, c1985. — xvi, 280p, [8]p of plates. — *Includes index. — Bibliography: p.[259]- 274*

DIPLOMATS — United States — History — 19th century

MASTERSON, William H
Tories and Democrats : British diplomats in the pre-Jacksonian America / by William H. Masterson ; foreword by Frank E. Vandiver. — 1st ed. — College Station : Texas A&M University Press, c1985. — xvi, 280p, [8]p of plates. — *Includes index. — Bibliography: p.[259]- 274*

DIRECT BROADCAST SATELLITE TELEVISION — Australia

Satellite broadcasting : answers to the questions most often asked. — Canberra : Australian Government Publishing Service, 1986. — iv,65p

DIRECTORS OF CORPORATIONS — Legal status, laws etc. — Great Britain

PENNINGTON, Robert R.
Directors' personal liability / Robert R. Pennington. — London : Collins Professional and Technical, 1987. — [256]p. — *Includes index*

WRIGHT, Desmond
Rights and duties of directors / Desmond Wright. — London : Butterworths, 1987. — [140]p. — *Includes index*

DIRECTORS OF CORPORATIONS — Great Britain

TOWERS, Brian
Worker-directors in private manufacturing industry in Great Britain. — [London] : Department of Employment, 1987. — 34p. — (Research paper / Department of Employment ; no.29). — *Bibliography: p33-34*

DIRGES

NKETIA, J.H.Kwabena
Funeral dirges of the Akan people / J.H.Nketia. — New York : Negro Universities Press, 1969. — v,296p. — *Reprint of 1955 edition. — Bibliography: p295-296*

DISABLED PERSONS (SERVICES, CONSULTATION AND REPRESENTATION) BILL 1985-86

GREAT BRITAIN. Parliament. House of Commons. Library. Research Division
Disabled Persons (Services, Consultation and Representation) Bill, session 1985-86 / Christine Gillie. — [London] : the Division, 1986. — 26,xp. — (Reference sheet ; no.86/9). — *Bibliographical references: p22-26*

DISARMAMENT

Across the divide : Liberal values for defence and disarmament / Simon Hughes [et al.]. — Hebden Bridge : Hebden Royd Publications, 1986. — 60p. — (Liberal challenge ; no.8)

BAJUSZ, William
Deterrence, technology and strategic arms control / William Bajusz. — London : International Institute for Strategic Studies, 1987. — 56p. — (Adelphi papers ; 215)

Beyond survival : new directions for the disarmament movement / edited by Michael Albert and David Dellinger. — Boston : South End Press, 1983. — 365p

GREAT BRITAIN. Parliament. House of Commons. Library. International Affairs Section
Arms control after the Geneva summit / Richard Ware. — [London] : the Library, 1986. — 14p. — (Background paper / House of Commons. Library. [Research Division] ; no.177)

GREAT BRITAIN. Parliament. House of Commons. Library. Research Division
Arms control : the state of the negotiations / Richard Ware. — [London] : the Division, 1987. — 35p. — (Background paper ; no.196)

KENT, Bruce
Disarmament : nuclear swords or unilateral ploughshares?. — London : Papermac, 1987. — vii,108p. — (Days of decision) (Papermac). — *Contents: Choices for defence / Lord Carver — Defence and disarmament / Lord Chalfont — A personal viewpoint on a dangerous world / Bruce Kent*

Konzepte zum Frieden : Vorschläge für eine neue Abrüstungs- und Entspannungspolitik der SPD / herausgegeben von Katrin Fuchs, Hajo Hoffmann und Horst Klaus. — Berlin : spw-Verlag, 1985. — 179p

NEW ZEALAND. Ministry of Foreign Affairs
Disarmament and arms control. — Wellington : the Ministry, 1986. — 45p. — (Information bulletin ; no.18)

Roots of peace : the movement against militarism in Canada / edited by Eric Shragge, Ronald Babin, and Jean-Guy Vaillancourt. — Toronto : Between The Lines, 1986. — 203p. — *Bibliography: p181-194*

Status of multilateral arms regulation and disarmament agreements. — New York : United Nations, 1978. — iv,144p. — *At head of title: Department of Political and Security Council Affairs, United Nations Centre for Disarmament. — "Special supplement to The United Nations disarmament yearbook volume II, 1977.". — "United Nations publication: sales no. E.78.IX.2."*

Status of multilateral arms regulation and disarmament agreements. — 2nd ed., 1982. — New York : United Nations, 1983. — iv,176p. — *At head of t.p.: United Nations. Department for Disarmament Affairs. — Sales no.*

SUTER, Keith D.
Peace working : the United Nations and disarmament / Keith D. Suter. — Sydney : United Nations Association of Australia, 1985. — 189p

DISARMAMENT — Congresses

Economic effects of militarism / edited by Girish Mishoa. — New Delhi : Allied Publishers, 1984. — xii,108p

DISARMAMENT — Economic aspects — Sweden

THORSSON, Inga
In pursuit of disarmament : conversion from military to civil production in Sweden / by Inga Thorsson. — Stockholm : [Liber] Vol 1A: Background, facts and analyses. — 1984. — 347p. — *Bibliography: p345-347*

THORSSON, Inga
In pursuit of disarmament : conversion from military to civil production in Sweden / by Inga Thorsson. — Stockholm : [Liber] Vol 1B: Summary, appraisals and recommendations. — 1984. — 66p

DISARMAMENT — History

DINGMAN, Roger
Power in the Pacific : the origins of naval arms limitation, 1914-1922 / Roger Dingman. — Chicago : University of Chicago Press, 1976. — xiii, 318 p.. — *Includes index. — Bibliography: p. 287-310*

The United Nations and disarmament, 1945-1985 / United Nations Department for Disarmament Affairs. — New York : United Nations, 1985. — x, 166 p.. — *"United Nations publication sales no. E.85.IX.6"--T.p. verso*

DISARMAMENT — Public opinion
Perception and reality : an opinion poll on defence and disarmament / with commentaries by Clive Rose and Peter Blaker. — London : Institute for European Defence and Strategic Studies, 1986. — 35p. — (Occasional paper / Institute for European Defence and Strategic Studies ; no.17)

DISASTER HOSPITALS
INTERNATIONAL MEETING ON MOBILE DISASTER UNITS (1984 : Geneva)
Final report. — Geneva : United Nations, 1984. — 68p

INTERNATIONAL MEETING ON MOBILE SISASTER UNITS (1982 : Geneva)
Final report. — Geneva : United Nations, 1982. — ii,18,8,5p

DISASTER RELIEF
Disaster prevention and mitigation : a compendium of current knowledge. — Geneva : New York
V.1: Volcanological aspects. — 1976. — iv,38p. — *Bibliographical references: p33-38. — "UNDRO/28/75"*

Disaster prevention and mitigation : a compendium of current knowledge. — New York : United Nations
V.2: Hydrological aspects. — 1976. — viii,100p. — *Bibliography: p98-100. — "UNDRO/22/76"*

Disaster prevention and mitigation : a compendium of current knowledge. — New York : United Nations
V.3: Seismological aspects. — 1978. — viii,127p. — *Bibliography: p122-127. — "UNDRO/22/76 VOL.III"*

Disaster prevention and mitigation : a compendium of current knowledge. — New York : United Nations
V.4: Meteorological aspects. — 1978. — viii,96p. — *Bibliography: p95-96. — "UNDRO/22/76 VOL.IV"*

Disaster prevention and mitigation : a compendium of current knowledge. — New York : United Nations
V.5: Land use aspects. — 1977. — vii,68p. — *Bibliography: p67-68. — "UNDRO/22/76 VOL.V"*

DRABEK, Thomas E.
Human system responses to disaster : an inventory of sociological findings / Thomas E. Drabek. — New York : Springer-Verlag, c1986. — xvii, 509 p.. — (Springer series on environmental management). — *Includes indexes. — Bibliography: p. [423]-479*

DISASTER RELIEF — Congresses
Space applications for the acquisition and dissemination of disaster-related data : expert meeting, Geneva, 14-17 June 1983. — [Geneva] : Office of the United Nations Disaster Relief Co-ordinator, [1983]. — ii,111p. — *"October 1983"--P. 4 of cover*

DISASTER RELIEF — Economic aspects
Disaster prevention and mitigation : a compendium of current knowledge. — New York : United Nations
V.7: Economic aspects. — 1979. — vii,73p. — *Bibliography: p69-73. — "UNDRO/22/76 Vol.VII"*

DISASTER RELIEF — Equipment and supplies
INTERNATIONAL MEETING ON MOBILE DISASTER UNITS (1984 : Geneva)
Final report. — Geneva : United Nations, 1984. — 68p

INTERNATIONAL MEETING ON MOBILE SISASTER UNITS (1982 : Geneva)
Final report. — Geneva : United Nations, 1982. — ii,18,8,5p

DISASTER RELIEF — Legal status, laws, etc.
Disaster prevention and mitigation : a compendium of current knowledge. — New York : United Nations
V.9: Legal aspects. — 1980. — viii,67p. — *Bibliography: p65-67. — "UNDRO/22/76 VOL.IX"*

DISASTER RELIEF — Management — Congresses
Space applications for the acquisition and dissemination of disaster-related data : expert meeting, Geneva, 14-17 June 1983. — [Geneva] : Office of the United Nations Disaster Relief Co-ordinator, [1983]. — ii,111p. — *"October 1983"--P. 4 of cover*

DISASTER RELIEF — Planning — Congresses
CONFERENCE ON EMERGENCY PLANNING (1985 : San Diego, Calif.)
Emergency planning : proceedings of the Conference on Emergency Planning, 24-26 January 1985, San Diego, California / edited by John M. Carroll. — La Jolla, Calif. (P.O. Box 2228, La Jolla 92038) : Society for Computer Simulation, c1985. — ix, 155 p.. — (Simulation series ; v. 15, no. 1 (January 1985)) . — *Includes bibliographies and index*

DISASTER RELIEF — Public relations
Disaster prevention and mitigation : a compendium of current knowledge. — New York : United Nations
V.10: Public information aspects. — 1979. — ix,142p. — *Bibliography: p137-142. — "UNDRO/22/76 Vol.X"*

DISASTER RELIEF — Social aspects
Disaster prevention and mitigation : a compendium of current knowledge. — New York : United Nations. — *"UNDRO/22/76 (vo.XII)"*
V.12: Social and sociological aspects. — 1986. — viii,48p. — *Includes bibliographical references*

DISASTER RELIEF — Angola
Displaced and drought affected persons in the People's Republic of Angola : assessment of relief operations in the Southern Provinces first emergency phase : 1st October 1981-28th February 1983. — Geneva : UNDRO, 1983. — 72p

DISASTER RELIEF — California — Planning
TURNER, Ralph H
Waiting for disaster : earthquake watching in southern California / Ralph H. Turner, Joanne M. Nigg, Denise Heller Paz. — Berkeley : University of California Press, c1986. — p. cm. — *Includes index*

DISASTER RELIEF — Ethiopia
ETHIOPIA. Relief and Rehabilitation Commission
Pre-disaster planning program / The Relief and Rehabilitation Commission, Government of Ethiopia. — Addis Ababa : [The Commission], 1975. — 20 leaves

DISASTER VICTIMS
Disasters and the disabled. — New York : United Nations, 1982. — 63p. — *Includes bibliographical references*

DISASTERS
DRABEK, Thomas E.
Human system responses to disaster : an inventory of sociological findings / Thomas E. Drabek. — New York : Springer-Verlag, c1986. — xvii, 509 p.. — (Springer series on environmental management). — *Includes indexes. — Bibliography: p. [423]-479*

DISASTERS — Economic aspects
Disaster prevention and mitigation : a compendium of current knowledge. — New York : United Nations
V.7: Economic aspects. — 1979. — vii,73p. — *Bibliography: p69-73. — "UNDRO/22/76 Vol.VII"*

DISASTERS — Law and legislation
HUFFMAN, James
Government liability and disaster mitigation : a comparative study / James Huffman. — London : University Press of America, 1987. — [660]p

DISASTERS — Legal status, laws, etc.
Disaster prevention and mitigation : a compendium of current knowledge. — New York : United Nations
V.9: Legal aspects. — 1980. — viii,67p. — *Bibliography: p65-67. — "UNDRO/22/76 VOL.IX"*

DISASTERS — Planning
DRABEK, Thomas E.
Human system responses to disaster : an inventory of sociological findings / Thomas E. Drabek. — New York : Springer-Verlag, c1986. — xvii, 509 p.. — (Springer series on environmental management). — *Includes indexes. — Bibliography: p. [423]-479*

DISASTERS — Prevention
Disaster prevention and mitigation : a compendium of current knowledge. — New York : United Nations
V.11: Preparedness aspects. — 1984. — vi,218p . — *Includes bibliograpical references. — UNDRO/22/76 Vol.XI*

DISASTERS — Psychological aspects
RAPHAEL, Beverley
When disaster strikes : a handbook for the caring professions / Beverley Raphael. — London : Hutchinson, 1986. — x,342p. — *Bibliography: p317-330. — Includes index*

DISASTERS — Research
DRABEK, Thomas E.
Human system responses to disaster : an inventory of sociological findings / Thomas E. Drabek. — New York : Springer-Verlag, c1986. — xvii, 509 p.. — (Springer series on environmental management). — *Includes indexes. — Bibliography: p. [423]-479*

TURNER, Ralph H
Waiting for disaster : earthquake watching in southern California / Ralph H. Turner, Joanne M. Nigg, Denise Heller Paz. — Berkeley : University of California Press, c1986. — p. cm. — *Includes index*

DISASTERS — United States — Psychological aspects — Case studies
PERRY, Ronald W.
Minority citizens in disasters / Ronald W. Perry, Alvin H. Mushkatel. — London : University of Georgia Press, 1987. — [224]p

DISCOUNT
BAXTER, W. T.
Discount and budgets : with constant prices and inflation / W.T.Baxter. — London : Published for the Chartered Association of Certified Accountants by Certified Accountant Publications, 1986. — 49p

DISCOURSE ANALYSIS
BILMES, Jack
Discourse and behavior / Jack Bilmes. — New York : Plenum Press, c1986. — p. cm. — *Includes index. — Bibliography: p*

Handbook of discourse analysis / edited by Teun A. van Dijk. — London : Academic Press. — *Bibliographies*
Vol.2: Dimensions of discourse. — 1985. — xvii,279p

MISHLER, Elliot George
Research interviewing : context and narrative / Elliot G. Mishler. — Cambridge, Mass. : Harvard University Press, 1986. — xi, 189 p.. — *Includes index. — Bibliography: p. [171]-185*

VENTOLA, Eija
The structure of social interaction : a systemic approach to the semiotics of service encounters / Eija Ventola. — London : Pinter, 1987. — [270]p. — (Open linguistics series). — *Includes bibliography and index*

DISCRIMINATION IN EMPLOYMENT — Great Britain

GREAT BRITAIN. Commission for Racial Equality
Employment. — Rev. ed. — London : the Commission, 1981, 1981. — 4p. — (Fact sheet / Commission for Racial Equality ; 3). — *First published 1976*

DISCRIMINATION

The Sociobiology of ethnocentrism : evolutionary dimensions of xenophobia, discrimination, racism and nationalism / edited by Vernon Reynolds, Vincent Falger and Ian Vine. — London : Croom Helm, c1987. — xx,327p. — *Bibliography: p274-314. — Includes index*

DISCRIMINATION — Great Britain

EDWARDS, John, 1943-
Positive discrimination, social justice and social policy : moral scrutiny of a policy practice / John Edwards ; foreword by Lord Scarman. — London : Tavistock, 1987. — x,243p. — *Bibliography: p222-235. — Includes index*

DISCRIMINATION IN EDUCATION — Law and legislation — United States

DIMOND, Paul R
Beyond busing : inside the challenge to urban segregation / Paul R. Dimond. — Ann Arbor : University of Michigan Press, c1985. — p. cm. — *Bibliography: p*

SALOMONE, Rosemary C
Equal education under law : legal rights and federal policy in the post-Brown era / Rosemary C. Salomone. — New York : St. Martin's Press, c1986. — xiii, 272 p.. — *Includes index. — Bibliography: p. 253-266*

DISCRIMINATION IN EDUCATION — Connecticut — New Haven

OREN, Dan A.
Joining the club : a history of Jews and Yale / Dan A. Oren. — New Haven : Yale University Press, c1985. — xiv, 440 p.. — (The Yale scene. University series ; 4). — *Published in cooperation with the American Jewish Archives. — Includes index. — Bibliography: p. 397-423*

DISCRIMINATION IN EDUCATION — Great Britain

Towards the decolonization of the British education system / Amon Saba Saakana, Adetokunbo Pearse, editors. — London : Frontline Journal : Karnak House, 1986. — 128p. — *Includes bibliographies*

DISCRIMINATION IN EMPLOYMENT

COATES, Mary Lou
Employment equity : issues, approaches and public policy framework / Mary Lou Coates. — Kingston, Ont. : Queen's University at Kingston. Industrial Relations Centre, 1986. — 109p. — (Research and current issues series / Queen's University at Kingston. Industrial Relations Centre ; no.44). — *Bibliographies*

The Manufacture of disadvantage : stigma and social closure / edited by Gloria Lee and Ray Loveridge. — Milton Keynes : Open University Press, 1987. — [320]p. — *Includes bibliography and index*

DISCRIMINATION IN EMPLOYMENT — Canada

BLOCK, Walter
On employment equity : a critique of the Abella Royal Commission Report / by Walter Block and Michael A. Walker. — [Vancouver] : The Fraser Institute, 1985. — 111p. — (Focus / Fraser Institute (Vancouver, B.C.) ; no.17). — *References: p[91]-111*

BOLARIA, B. Singh
Racial oppression in Canada / B. Singh Bolaria, Peter S. Li. — Toronto, Canada : Garamond Press, c1985. — 232 p.. — *Bibliography: p. 199-221. — Includes index*

DISCRIMINATION IN EMPLOYMENT — Cyprus — Statistics

HOUSE, William J.
Discrimination and segregation of women workers in Cyprus / by William J. House. — [Nicosia] : Department of Statistics and Research, [1983?]. — 82p. — *Bibliography: p80-82*

DISCRIMINATION IN EMPLOYMENT — England — London

GREASLEY, Phil
Gay men at work : a report on discrimination against gay men in employment in London / by Phil Greasley ; contributions from: Matt Williams...[et al.]. — [London?] : Lesbian and Gay Employment Rights, 1986. — vi,104p. — *Bibliography: p103-104*

DISCRIMINATION IN EMPLOYMENT — Great Britain

Black youth futures : ethnic minorities and the Youth Training Scheme / edited by Malcolm Cross and Douglas I. Smith. — [S.l.] : National Youth Bureau, 1987. — 113 p

CARR, John
New roads to equality : contract compliance for the UK? / John Carr. — London : Fabian Society, 1987. — 26 p. — (Fabian tract ; 517)

Equal opportunities for men and women in the Civil Service. — London (St Andrews House, 40 Broadway, SW1H OBT) : Council of Civil Service Unions, [1985]. — 38p

NEWNHAM, Anne
Employment, unemployment and black people / Anne Newnham. — London : Runnymede Trust, 1986. — 30p. — (Runnymede research report). — *Bibliography:p.30*

PEARSON, Maggie
Equal opportunities in the NHS : a handbook / by Maggie Pearson. — Leeds : Training in Health and Race, 1985. — 39p

DISCRIMINATION IN EMPLOYMENT — Pennsylvania — History

DICKERSON, Dennis C.
Out of the crucible : Black steelworkers in western Pennsylvania, 1875-1980 / Dennis C. Dickerson. — Albany : State University of New York Press, c1986. — xiv, 323 p.. — (SUNY series in Afro-American studies). — *Includes index. — Bibliography: p. 307-318*

DISCRIMINATION IN HOUSING — Law and legislation — United States

DIMOND, Paul R
Beyond busing : inside the challenge to urban segregation / Paul R. Dimond. — Ann Arbor : University of Michigan Press, c1985. — p. cm. — *Bibliography: p*

Housing desegregation and federal policy / edited by John M. Goering. — Chapel Hill : University of North Carolina Press, c1986. — x, 343 p.. — (Urban and regional policy and development studies). — *Includes bibliographies and index*

DISCRIMINATION IN HOUSING — England

HENDERSON, Jeff
Race, class and state housing : inequality and the allocation of public housing in Britain / Jeff Henderson and Valerie Karn. — Aldershot : Gower, c1987. — xxiii,331p. — (Studies in urban and regional policy ; 4). — *Bibliography: p313-320. — Includes index*

DISCRIMINATION IN HOUSING — Great Britain

New perspectives on race and housing in Britain / edited by Susan J. Smith and John Mercer. — [Glasgow] : Centre for Housing Research, 1987. — 247p. — (Studies in housing ; no.2). — *Bibliographies*

Racial minorities & public housing. — London : Commission for Racial Equality, 1978. — [2] p. — (Research summary / Commission for Racial Equality ; 4). — *Summary of work by David J. Smith and Anne Whalley, published by P.E.P., 1975*

DISCRIMINATION IN HOUSING — London metropolitan area — Tower Hamlets

PHILLIPS, Deborah
What price equality? : a report on the allocation of GLC housing in Tower Hamlets / by Deborah Phillips. — London : Greater London Council, 1986. — 83p. — (GLC housing research and policy report ; no.9). — *Title from cover*

DISCRIMINATION IN HOUSING — United States

Housing desegregation and federal policy / edited by John M. Goering. — Chapel Hill : University of North Carolina Press, c1986. — x, 343 p.. — (Urban and regional policy and development studies). — *Includes bibliographies and index*

Race, ethnicity, and minority housing in the United States / edited by Jamshid A. Momeni ; foreword by Joe T. Darden. — New York : Greenwood Press, 1986. — xxv, 224 p.. — (Contributions in ethnic studies ; no. 16). — *Includes index. — Bibliography: p. [217]-220*

DISEASE — History

Western diseases, their emergence and prevention / edited by H. C. Trowell, D. P. Burkitt ; foreword by John R. K. Robson. — Cambridge, Mass. : Harvard University Press, 1981. — xix, 456 p.. — *Includes bibliographies and index*

DISEASE — Tanzania — Causes and theories of causation — History

TURSHEN, Meredeth
The political ecology of disease in Tanzania / Meredeth Turshen. — New Brunswick, N.J. : Rutgers University Press, c1984. — xiv, 259 p., [2] leaves of plates. — *Includes index. — Bibliography: p. 211-239*

DISEASES — Great Britain

Morbidity and its relationship to resource allocation / edited by Sir John Brotherston. — [Cardiff] ([Crown Building, Cathays Park, Cardiff CF1 3NQ]) : Welsh Office, [1978]. — [1],vii,97p. — *'Papers and proceedings of a workshop held at the Hill Residential College, Abergavenny, Gwent on Tuesday 24 and Wednesday 25 January 1978' - p.i*

DISEASES — Great Britain — Statistics

Morbidity statistics from general practice. — London : HMSO, 1958-62. — 3v. — (Studies on medical and population subjects ; no.14). — *Contents: Vol.1: General/W. P. D. Logan and A. A. Cushion - v.2: Occupation/W. P. D. Logan - v.3: Disease in general practice/Research Committee of the Council of the College of General Practitioners*

Morbidity statistics from general practice 1981-1982 : third national study. — London : HMSO, 1986. — ix,245p. — *Includes 8 microfiches of morbidity tabulations in pocket on rear cover*

DISINFORMATION

DEACON, Richard, 1911-
The truth twisters / Richard Deacon. — London : Macdonald, 1987, c1986. — 240p,[8]p of plates. — *Includes index*

DISINVESTMENTS — South Africa

ORKIN, Mark
Disinvestment, the struggle, and the future : what black South Africans really think / Mark Orkin. — Johannesburg : Ravan Press, 1986. — xii, 78 p.. — *A CASE/IBR study. — Includes bibliographies and index*

DISINVESTMENTS — South Africa — Public opinion
ORKIN, Mark
Disinvestment, the struggle, and the future : what black South Africans really think / Mark Orkin. — Johannesburg : Ravan Press, 1986. — xii, 78 p.. — *A CASE/IBR study.* — *Includes bibliographies and index*

DISPOSITION (PHILOSOPHY)
PRIOR, Elizabeth
Dispositions / Elizabeth Prior. — Aberdeen : Aberdeen University Press, 1985. — [176]p. — (Scots philosophical monographs ; no.7). — *Includes bibliography*

DISPUTE RESOLUTION (LAW) — United States
HARRINGTON, Christine B
Shadow justice : the ideology and institutionalization of alternatives to court / Christine B. Harrington. — Westport, Conn. : Greenwood Press, c1985. — p. cm. — (Contributions in political science ; no. 133). — *Includes index. — Bibliography: p*

DISRAELI, BENJAMIN
BEHRENS, Robert
Benjamin Disraeli and the triumph of imagination / Robert Behrens. — Coventry : University of Warwick, 1987. — 61p. — (Politics working papers / University of Warwick ; no.43). — *Bibliography: p54-62*

DISSENTERS — Argentina
GOLDAR, Ernesto
John William Cooke y el peronismo revolucionario / Ernesto Goldar. — Buenos Aires : Centro Editor de América Latina, 1985. — 140p. — (Biblioteca Política Argentina ; 99)

DISSENTERS — Czechoslovakia
Václav Havel, or, Living in truth : twenty-two essays published on the occasion of the award of the Erasmus Prize to Václav Havel / edited by Jan Vladislav. — London : Faber, 1987. — xix,315p. — *Translation from various European languages*

DISSENTERS — Soviet Union
PARCHOMENKO, Walter
Soviet images of dissidents and nonconformists / Walter Parchomenko. — New York ; London : Praeger, 1986. — xv, 251 p.. — "Praeger special studies. Praeger scientific.". — *Includes index. — Bibliography: p. 213-243*

DISSENTERS — Soviet Union — Biography
NIKOLAEV, E. B.
Predavshie Gippokrata = The betrayal of Hippocrates / Evgenii Nikolaev. — London : Overseas Publications Interchange, 1984. — 324p

DISSENTERS — Spain — La Rioja — History
HERNÁNDEZ GARCÍA, Antonio
La represión en La Rioja durante la Guerra Civil / Antonio Hernández García. — Logroño : A. Hernández García, 1984. — 3v

DISSENTERS — United States — Biography
The Dissenters : voices from contemporary America / [compiled by] John Langston Gwaltney. — 1st ed. — New York : Random House, c1986. — xxviii, 321 p., [8] p. of plates

DISSENTERS — United States — History — 19th century
SHIELDS, Johanna Nicol
The line of duty : maverick congressmen and the development of American political culture, 1836-1860 / Johanna Nicol Shields. — Westport, Conn. : Greenwood Press, c1985. — p. cm. — (Contributions in American studies ; no. 80). — *Includes index. — Bibliography: p*

DISSENTERS, RELIGIOUS
Cults, sects, and new religious movements : a bibliography of religions from the ATLA Religion Database / edited by Erica Treesh. — Chicago : American Theological Library Association, 1985. — 223p

ECCLESIASTICAL HISTORY SOCIETY.
Summer Meeting (1985 : Lady Margaret Hall, Oxford)
Voluntary religion : papers read at the 1985 Summer Meeting and the 1986 Winter Meeting of the Ecclesiastical History Society / edited by W.J. Sheils and Diana Wood. — Oxford : Published for the Ecclesiastical History Society by Basil Blackwell, 1986. — xvi,521p. — (Studies in church history ; v.23). — *Includes index*

DISSERTATIONS, ACADEMIC
A Catalogue of doctoral dissertations / University Microfilms International. — Godstone : University Microfilms International. — *Irregular*

DISSERTATIONS, ACADEMIC — England — London — Bibliography
Theses and dissertations accepted for higher degrees / University of London. — London : University of London, 1959-1977. — *Continues: Theses and dissertations and published work accepted for higher degrees/University of London.- Continued by: Theses and dissertations accepted for the degrees of M. Phil. and Ph.D in the University of London/University of London*

Theses and dissertations accepted for the degrees of M.Phil and Ph.D in the University of London / University of London. — London : University of London Library, 1977-. — *Continues: Theses and dissertations accepted for higher degrees/University of London*

DISSERTATIONS, ACADEMIC — Great Britain
The social science PhD : the ESRC inquiry on submission rates / chairman: Graham Winfield. — London : Economic and Social Research Council
Background papers. — 1987. — 232p

The social science PhD : the ESRC inquiry on submission rates / chairman: Graham Winfield. — London : Economic and Social Research Council
The report. — 1987. — 133p

DISTANCE EDUCATION — Addresses, essays, lectures
Alternative routes to formal education : distance teaching for school equivalency / edited by Hilary Perraton. — Baltimore : Johns Hopkins University Press for the World Bank, 1982. — xiii,329p. — *Includes bibliographical references*

DISTRESS (LAW) — England
GREAT BRITAIN. Law Commission
Distress for rent / the Law Commission. — London : H.M.S.O., 1986. — vi,146p. — (Working paper / Law Commission ; no. 97). — *Includes bibliographical references*

DISTRIBUTION (PROBABILITY THEORY)
FACHEL, Jandyra Maria Guimarães
The C-type distribution as an underlying model for categorical data and its use in factor analysis / by Jandyra Maria Guimarães Fachel. — 255 leaves. — *PhD (Econ) 1986 LSE. — Microfiches are in end pocket*

JOHNSON, Norman L.
Distributions in statistics / Norman L. Johnson, Samuel Kotz. — New York : John Wiley. — (Wiley series in probability and mathematical statistics)
Vol.2: Continuous univariate distributions. — c1970. — xiii,306p

MATÉRN, Bertil
Spatial variation / Bertil Matérn. — 2nd ed. — Berlin ; New York : Springer-Verlag, c1986. — 151 p.. — (Lecture notes in statistics ; v. 36). — *Includes indexes. — Bibliography: p. [140]-144*

DISTRIBUTIVE JUSTICE
Justice : views from the social sciences / edited by Ronald L. Cohen. — New York : Plenum Press, c1986. — p. cm. — (Critical issues in social justice). — *Includes bibliographies and index*

DISTRIBUTIVE JUSTICE — Congresses
Justice in social relations / edited by Hans Werner Bierhoff, Ronald L. Cohen, and Jerald Greenberg. — New York : Plenum Press, c1986. — xvi, 364 p.. — (Critical issues in social justice). — *Includes bibliographies and indexes*

DIVER (Family)
LUKAS, J. Anthony
Common ground : a turbulent decade in the lives of three American Families / J. Anthony Lukas. — New York : Vintage Books, 1986. — xiv,674p. — *Originally published: New York : Random House, 1985*

DIVERSIFICATION IN INDUSTRY — Great Britain
CHISHOLM, Michael
The changing pattern of employment : regional specialisation and industrial localisation in Britain / Michael Chisholm and Jim Oeppen. — London : Croom Helm, 1973. — 127p. — *Bibliography: p.121-124. — Includes index*

DIVERSIFICATION IN INDUSTRY — United States — Case studies
GHOSH, Arabinda
Competition and diversification in the United States petroleum industry / Arabinda Ghosh. — Westport, Conn. : Quorum Books, c1985. — p. cm. — *Includes index. — Bibliography: p*

DIVIDENDS — Australia — Reinvestment
SKULLY, Michael T.
Dividend reinvestment plans : improving shareholder relations while raising new equity / by Michael T. Skully. — Caterham : Australiana, 1981. — 41leaves

DIVIDENDS — Great Britain
WREN-LEWIS, Simon
An approach to dynamic specification when expectations are based on the State Space Form, with an application to U.K. dividend behaviour / Simon Wren-Lewis. — London : National Institute of Economic and Social Research, 1986. — 24p. — (Discussion paper / National Institute of Economic and Social Research ; no.118). — *Bibliography: [p24-25]*

DIVIDENDS — United States — Reinvestment
SKULLY, Michael T.
Dividend reinvestment plans : improving shareholder relations while raising new equity / by Michael T. Skully. — Caterham : Australiana, 1981. — 41leaves

DIVISION OF LABOR — Canada
Work in the Canadian context : continuity despite change / [edited by] Katherina L. P. Lundy and Barbara Warme. — 2nd ed.. — Toronto ; Vancouver : Butterworths, 1986. — xvii,369p. — *Includes bibliographical references*

DIVORCE — Law and legislation — Great Britain
GRAY, Kevin J.
Property, divorce and retirement pension rights / by K.J. Gray. British nationality and the right of abode 1948-1983 / by C.C. Turpin. — Deventer ; London : Kluwer, 1986. — vii,269p. — (Cambridge-Tilburg law lectures ; 5th ser., 1982). — *Includes bibliographical references*

DIVORCE — Law and legislation — Netherlands
BIJLEVELD, W. H.
Erkenning van buitenlandse echtsheidingen : een bedenkelijke ontwikkeling in de nederlandse jurisprudentie / W. H. Bijleveld. — Zwolle : Tjeenk Willink, 1970. — 31p

DIVORCE — Law and legislation — United States
WEITZMAN, Lenore J
The divorce revolution : the unexpected social and economic consequences for women and children in America / Lenore J. Weitzman. — New York : Free Press ; London : Collier Macmillan, c1985. — p. cm

DIVORCE — Australia
WESTERN AUSTRALIA. Commonwealth Bureau of Census and Statistics. Western Australian Office
Divorce / Western Australian Office, Commonwealth Bureau of Census and Statistics. — Perth : [the Office], 1947-1980. — Annual

DIVORCE — Denmark
KOCH-NIELSEN, Inger
Familiemønstre efter skilsmisse / Inger Koch-Nielsen, Henning Transgaard. — København : Socialforskningsinstituttet, 1987. — 120p. — (Publikation / Socialforskningsinstituttet ; 155). — *Bibliography: p112-115*

DIVORCE — England
HOWARD, John, 19---
Conciliation, children and divorce : a family systems approach / John Howard and Graham Shepherd. — London : Batsford, 1987. — [160] p. — (Child care policy and practice). — *Includes bibliography and index*

DIVORCE — Great Britain
BURGOYNE, Jacqueline
Divorce matters / Jacqueline Burgoyne, Roger Ormrod and Martin Richards. — Harmondsworth : Penguin, 1987. — 216p0. — (A Pelican book)

DIVORCE — Netherlands
BIJLEVELD, W. H.
Erkenning van buitenlandse echtsheidingen : een bedenkelijke ontwikkeling in de nederlandse jurisprudentie / W. H. Bijleveld. — Zwolle : Tjeenk Willink, 1970. — 31p

DIVORCE — Trinidad and Tobago — Statistics
Marriages and divorces report, 1979-1983. — [Port of Spain] : Central Statistical Office, 1985. — v,19p

DIVORCE — United States
GROSSMAN, Tracy Barr
Mothers and children facing divorce / by Tracy Barr Grossman. — Ann Arbor, Mich. : UMI Research Press, c1986. — 208 p.. — (Research in clinical psychology ; no. 15). — : Revision of thesis (Ph.D.)--University of Michigan, 1984. — Includes index. — *Bibliography: p. [203]-205*

DIVORCE MEDIATION — Canada
TRANS-ATLANTIC DIVORCE MEDIATION CONFERENCE (Burlington, Vt. : 1986)
The role of mediation in divorce proceedings : a comparative perspective (United States, Canada and Great Britain). — South Royalton, Vt. : Vermont Law School Dispute Resolution Project, 1987. — iv,295p. — *Spine title: Divorce mediation - a comparative perspective*

DIVORCE MEDIATION — Great Britain
TRANS-ATLANTIC DIVORCE MEDIATION CONFERENCE (Burlington, Vt. : 1986)
The role of mediation in divorce proceedings : a comparative perspective (United States, Canada and Great Britain). — South Royalton, Vt. : Vermont Law School Dispute Resolution Project, 1987. — iv,295p. — *Spine title: Divorce mediation - a comparative perspective*

DIVORCE MEDIATION — United States
TRANS-ATLANTIC DIVORCE MEDIATION CONFERENCE (Burlington, Vt. : 1986)
The role of mediation in divorce proceedings : a comparative perspective (United States, Canada and Great Britain). — South Royalton, Vt. : Vermont Law School Dispute Resolution Project, 1987. — iv,295p. — *Spine title: Divorce mediation - a comparative perspective*

DIVORCE SUITS — Great Britain
GREAT BRITAIN. Parliament. House of Commons. Library. Research Division
Matrimonial and Family Proceedings Bill (H.L.) 1983-4 [Bill 96] / [Patrick Nealon]. — [London] : the Division, 1984. — 11p. — (Research note ; no.141)

DIVORCE THERAPY
HODGES, William F
Interventions for children of divorce : custody, access, and psychotherapy / William F. Hodges. — New York, N.Y. : Wiley, c1986. — p. cm. — (Wiley series on personality processes). — *"A Wiley-Interscience publication."*. — Includes indexes. — *Bibliography: p*

DIVORCED MOTHERS — Legal status, laws, etc. — United States
ARENDELL, Terry
Mothers and divorce : legal, economic and social dilemmas / Terry Arendell ; foreword by Arlie Russell Hochschild. — Berkeley, Calif. ; London : University of California Press, 1986. — xiv,221p

DIVORCED MOTHERS — United States
GROSSMAN, Tracy Barr
Mothers and children facing divorce / by Tracy Barr Grossman. — Ann Arbor, Mich. : UMI Research Press, c1986. — 208 p.. — (Research in clinical psychology ; no. 15). — : Revision of thesis (Ph.D.)--University of Michigan, 1984. — Includes index. — *Bibliography: p. [203]-205*

DIVORCED MOTHERS — United States — Economic conditions
ARENDELL, Terry
Mothers and divorce : legal, economic and social dilemmas / Terry Arendell ; foreword by Arlie Russell Hochschild. — Berkeley, Calif. ; London : University of California Press, 1986. — xiv,221p

DIVORCED MOTHERS — United States — Social conditions
ARENDELL, Terry
Mothers and divorce : legal, economic and social dilemmas / Terry Arendell ; foreword by Arlie Russell Hochschild. — Berkeley, Calif. ; London : University of California Press, 1986. — xiv,221p

DIVORCED PARENTS — Denmark
KOCH-NIELSEN, Inger
Familiemønstre efter skilsmisse / Inger Koch-Nielsen, Henning Transgaard. — København : Socialforskningsinstituttet, 1987. — 120p. — (Publikation / Socialforskningsinstituttet ; 155). — *Bibliography: p112-115*

DIVORCED WOMEN — United States — Economic conditions
WEITZMAN, Lenore J
The divorce revolution : the unexpected social and economic consequences for women and children in America / Lenore J. Weitzman. — New York : Free Press ; London : Collier Macmillan, c1985. — p. cm

DIVORCED WOMEN — United States — Social conditions
WEITZMAN, Lenore J
The divorce revolution : the unexpected social and economic consequences for women and children in America / Lenore J. Weitzman. — New York : Free Press ; London : Collier Macmillan, c1985. — p. cm

DLUGOS, GÜNTER
Die Unternehmung in der demokratischen Gesellschaft = : The business corporation in the democratic society / herausgegeben von Wolfgang Dorow. — Berlin ; New York : W. de Gruyter, 1987. — xiii, 390 p.. — *"Günter Dlugos zum 65. Geburtstagegewidmet."*. — English and German. — *Includes bibliographies*

DOCTOR OF PHILOSOPHY DEGREE — Great Britain
The social science PhD : the ESRC inquiry on submission rates / chairman: Graham Winfield. — London : Economic and Social Research Council
Background papers. — 1987. — 232p

DOCUMENTARY CREDIT
VENTRIS, F. M.
Banker's documentary credits : issued in accordance with the Uniform customs and practice (1974 revision) of the International Chamber of Commerce / by F.M. Ventris. — 2nd ed.. — London : Lloyd's of London Press, 1983. — xxi,350p. — *Previous ed.: 1980.* — With supplement 1985. — *Includes index*

DOGON LANGUAGE — Social aspects
CALAME-GRIAULE, Geneviève
[Ethnologie et langage. English]. Words and the Dogon world / Geneviève Calame-Griaule ; translated from the French by Deirdre LaPin. — Philadelphia : Institute for the Study of Human Issues, 1985. — p. cm. — (Translations in folklore studies). — *Translation of: Ethnologie et language.* — *Bibliography: p*

DOGONS (AFRICAN PEOPLE) — Social life and customs
CALAME-GRIAULE, Geneviève
[Ethnologie et langage. English]. Words and the Dogon world / Geneviève Calame-Griaule ; translated from the French by Deirdre LaPin. — Philadelphia : Institute for the Study of Human Issues, 1985. — p. cm. — (Translations in folklore studies). — *Translation of: Ethnologie et language.* — *Bibliography: p*

DOLLAR, AMERICAN
BANK OF JAPAN. Research and Statistics Department
On effective U.S. dollar exchange rate indices. — Tokyo : Bank of Japan. Research and Statistics Department, 1986. — 19p

DORNBUSCH, Rudiger
Dollars, debts, and deficits / Rudiger Dornbusch. — 1st MIT Press ed. — Leuven, Belgium : Leuven University Press ; Cambridge, Mass. : MIT Press, 1986. — 240 p. . — *The Professor Dr. Gaston Eyskens lectures delivered at the Katholieke Universiteit Leuven, Belgium in the fall of 1984.* — *Includes bibliographies and index*

WACHTEL, Howard M
The money mandarins : the making of a new supranational economic order / Howard M. Wachtel. — 1st ed. — New York : Pantheon Books, c1986. — xvi, 254 p.. — *Includes index.* — *Bibliography: p. [227]-245*

DOLPĀ (NEPAL) — Economic conditions
FISHER, James F
Trans-Himalayan traders : economy, society, and culture in northwest Nepal / James F. Fisher. — Berkeley : University of California Press, c1986. — xiv, 232 p., [8] p. of plates. — *Includes index.* — *Bibliography: p. 219-223*

DOLPĀ (NEPAL) — Ethnic relations
FISHER, James F
Trans-Himalayan traders : economy, society, and culture in northwest Nepal / James F. Fisher. — Berkeley : University of California Press, c1986. — xiv, 232 p., [8] p. of plates. — *Includes index.* — *Bibliography: p. 219-223*

DOMESDAY BOOK — Bibliography
BATES, David
A bibliography of Domesday book / David Bates. — Woodbridge : Boydell, 1986, c1985. — xi,166p

DOMESTIC ANIMALS, EFFECT OF RADIATION ON
GREAT BRITAIN. Ministry of Agriculture, Fisheries and Food
Radionuclide levels in food, animals and agricultural products : post Chernobyl monitoring in England and Wales / Ministry of Agriculture, Fisheries and Food, Welsh Office. — London : HMSO, c1987. — ii,203p

DOMESTIC EDUCATION — United States
ARONS, Stephen
Compelling belief : the culture of American schooling / Stephen Arons. — 1st paperback ed. — Amherst : University of Massachusetts Press, 1986, c1983. — xii, 228 p. — : *Reprint. Originally published: New York : McGraw-Hill, c1983. — Includes index*

DOMESTIC RELATIONS
Family law reports. — Bristol : Family Law, 1980-

International journal of law and the family. — Oxford : Oxford University Press, 1987-. — *Biannual*

DOMESTIC RELATIONS — Australia
Contempt and family law. — Sydney : Law Reform Commission, 1985. — 76p. — (Discussion paper / Law Reform Commission ; no.24)

DICKEY, Anthony
Family law / by Anthony Dickey. — North Ryde, N.S.W. : Law Book Company, 1985. — lxxxvii,685p. — *Bibliography: p643-659*

Matrimonial property law. — Sydney : Law Reform Commission, 1985. — 105p. — (Discussion paper / Law Reform Commission ; no.22). — *Includes bibliographical references*

DOMESTIC RELATIONS — Belgium — Ghent — History
NICHOLAS, David
The domestic life of a medieval city : women, children, and the family in fourteenth-century Ghent / David Nicholas. — Lincoln : University of Nebraska Press, c1985. — p. cm. — *Includes index. — Bibliography: p*

DOMESTIC RELATIONS — England
BROMLEY, P. M. (Peter Mann)
Family law / P.M. Bromley, N.V. Lowe. — 7th ed. — London : Butterworths, 1987. — lvi,793p. — *Cover title: Bromley's family law. — Previous ed. 1981. Includes index*

HOGGETT, Brenda M.
The family, law and society : cases and materials / Brenda M. Hoggett, David S. Pearl. — 2nd ed. — London : Butterworths, 1987. — [670]p. — *Previous ed.: 1983. Includes bibliography and index*

DOMESTIC RELATIONS — Hong Kong
PEGG, Leonard
Family law in Hong Kong / Leanard Pegg. — 2nd ed. — Singapore : Buterworths, 1986. — vii,256p. — *Earlier edition held: 1981. Includes index*

DOMESTIC RELATIONS — Ontario — History
KIERAN, Sheila
The family matters : two centuries of family law in Canada / Sheila Kieran. — Toronto : Keyporter Books, 1986. — xiv,178p. — *Bibliography: p[166]-172*

DOMESTIC RELATIONS — Scotland
THOMSON, J. M.
Family law in Scotland / J.M. Thomson. — London : Butterworths, 1987. — xxiv,232p. — *Includes index*

DOMESTIC RELATIONS — United States
RUBIN, Eva R
The Supreme Court and the American Family : ideology and issues / Eva R. Rubin. — New York : Greenwood Press, 1986. — 251 p.. — (Contributions in American studies ; [no. 85]). — *Series no. from jacket. — Includes indexes. — Bibliography: p. [225]-236*

DOMESTIC RELATIONS (ISLAMIC LAW)
PEARL, David
A textbook on Muslim personal law / David Pearl. — 2nd ed. — London : Croom Helm, c1987. — 284p. — *Previous ed.: published as a Textbook on Muslim Law. 1979. Bibliography: p260-265. — Includes index*

DOMESTIC RELATIONS (KURIA LAW) — Tanzania
RWEZAURA, B. A.
Traditional family law and change in Tanzania : a study of the Kuria social system / Barthazar Aloys Rwezaura. — Baden-Baden : Nomos Verlagsgesellschaft, 1985. — xiv,197p. — (Veröffentlichungen aus dem Institut für Internationale Angelegenheiten der Universität Hamburg ; 17). — *Bibliography: p189-197*

DOMICILE IN PUBLIC WELFARE — New York (State) — History — 20th century
CROUSE, Joan M.
The homeless transient in the Great Depression : New York State, 1929-1941 / Joan M. Crouse. — Albany, N.Y. : State University of New York Press, c1986. — xii, 319 p., [8] p. of plates. — : *Revision of thesis (doctoral)--State University of New York at Buffalo. — Includes index. — Bibliography: p. 296-306*

DOMICILE IN PUBLIC WELFARE — United States
REDBURN, F. Stevens
Responding to America's homeless : public policy alternatives / F. Stevens Redburn and Terry F. Buss. — New York : Praeger, 1986. — xvi, 154 p.. — *Includes index. — Bibliography: p. 142-148*

DOMINICA — Economic conditions
Dominica, priorities and prospects for development. — Washington, D.C., U.S.A. : World Bank, c1985. — [xiv],105p. — (World Bank country study)

DOMINICA — Economic policy
Dominica, priorities and prospects for development. — Washington, D.C., U.S.A. : World Bank, c1985. — [xiv],105p. — (World Bank country study)

DOMINICAN REPUBLIC — Census, 1970 — Methodology
DOMINICAN REPUBLIC. Oficina Nacional de Estadística
Censo nacional de población y habitación 9 y 10 enero 1970 : boletín censal. — [Santo Domingo} : the Oficina, 1969-

DOMINICAN REPUBLIC — Commercial policy
Dominican Republic : economic prospects and policies to renew growth. — Washington, D.C., U.S.A. : World Bank, 1985. — xviii,174p. — (A World Bank country study). — *Includes bibliographical references*

DOMINICAN REPUBLIC — Economic policy
Dominican Republic : economic prospects and policies to renew growth. — Washington, D.C., U.S.A. : World Bank, 1985. — xviii,174p. — (A World Bank country study). — *Includes bibliographical references*

VEDOVATO, Claudio
Politics, foreign trade and economic development : a study of the Dominican Republic / Claudio Vedovato. — London : Croom Helm, c1986. — [224]p. — *Includes bibliography*

DOMINICAN REPUBLIC — History
BLACK, Jan Knippers
The Dominican Republic : politics and development in an unsovereign state / Jan Knippers Black. — Boston, [Mass.] ; London : Allen & Unwin, 1986. — xi,164p. — *Bibliography: p151-157. — Includes index*

DOMINICAN REPUBLIC — Population — Statistics — Evaluation
RODRÍGUEZ SEPÚLVEDA, Bienvenida
Evaluación de la Encuesta Nacional de Fecundidad de la República Dominicana de 1980 / Bienvenida Rodríguez Sepúlveda. — Voorburg : International Statistical Institute, 1984. — 72p. — (Scientific reports / World Fertility Survey ; no.63)

DOMINICAN REPUBLIC — Population — Statistics — Methodology
DOMINICAN REPUBLIC. Oficina Nacional de Estadística
Censo nacional de población y habitación 9 y 10 enero 1970 : boletín censal. — [Santo Domingo} : the Oficina, 1969-

DONALD, DAVID HERBERT — Addresses, essays, lectures
A Master's due : essays in honor of David Herbert Donald / edited by William J. Cooper, Jr., Michael F. Holt, and John McCardell. — Baton Rouge : Louisiana State University Press, c1985. — p. cm. — *"The principal writings of David Herbert Donald": p. — Includes index. — Contents: Introduction: David Herbert Donald / Ari Hoogenboom -- The election of 1840, voter mobilization, and the emergence of the second American party system / Michael F. Holt -- "The only door" / William J. Cooper, Jr. -- [etc.] The ceremonies of politics / Jean H. Baker -- American historians and Antebellum southern slavery, 1959-1984 / Peter Kolchin -- Ethnic roots of southern violence / Grady McWhiney -- Family, kinship, and neighborhood in an Antebellum southern community / Robert C. Kenzer -- Trent's Simms / John McCardell -- "Gotta mind to move, a mind to settle down" / Sydney Nathans -- Jazz, segregation, and desegregation / Stanley P. Hirshson -- The "Long march through the institutions" / Irwin Unger*

DONALD — Bibliography
A Master's due : essays in honor of David Herbert Donald / edited by William J. Cooper, Jr., Michael F. Holt, and John McCardell. — Baton Rouge : Louisiana State University Press, c1985. — p. cm. — *"The principal writings of David Herbert Donald": p. — Includes index. — Contents: Introduction: David Herbert Donald / Ari Hoogenboom -- The election of 1840, voter mobilization, and the emergence of the second American party system / Michael F. Holt -- "The only door" / William J. Cooper, Jr. -- [etc.] The ceremonies of politics / Jean H. Baker -- American historians and Antebellum southern slavery, 1959-1984 / Peter Kolchin -- Ethnic roots of southern violence / Grady McWhiney -- Family, kinship, and neighborhood in an Antebellum southern community / Robert C. Kenzer -- Trent's Simms / John McCardell -- "Gotta mind to move, a mind to settle down" / Sydney Nathans -- Jazz, segregation, and desegregation / Stanley P. Hirshson -- The "Long march through the institutions" / Irwin Unger*

DONATION OF ORGANS, TISSUES, ETC. — Great Britain — Attitudes
MARPLAN LTD.
Public attitudes to kidney donation : report of a survey / prepared by Marplan Ltd. ; for the Central Office of Information ; on behalf of the Department of Health and Social Security. — [London? : Department of Health and Social Security?], 1979. — xii,154p

DORSEY, JASPER N
Telecommunications in the post-divestiture era : essays in honor of Jasper N. Dorsey and Ben T. Wiggins / edited by Albert L. Danielsen, David R. Kamerschen. — [Lexington, Mass.] : Lexington Books, c1986. — xiv, 252 p.. — *Includes bibliographies and index*

DOVER, STRAIT OF — International status
CUYVERS, Luc
The strait of Dover / by Luc Cuyvers. — Dordrecht ; Lancaster : Martinus Nijhoff, 1986. — xvi, 150p. — (International straits of the world ; #8)

DOW CHEMICAL COMPANY — Trials, litigation, etc
SCHUCK, Peter H
Agent Orange on trial : mass toxic disasters in the courts / Peter H. Schuck. — Cambridge, Mass. : Belknap Press of Harvard University Press, 1986. — ix, 347 p.. — *Includes index. — Bibliography: p. [301]-335*

DOWNES, JOHN
The slaying of John Downes / issued by Sinn Fein Publicity Department. — Dublin : Republican Publications, 1984. — 30p

DRAINAGE — Government policy — Great Britain
PENNING-ROWSELL, Edmund C.
Floods and drainage : British policies for hazard reduction, agricultural improvement and wetland conservation / E.C. Penning-Rowsell, D.J. Parker, D.M. Harding. — London : Allen & Unwin, 1986. — xx,199p. — (The Risks & hazards series ; v.2). — *Bibliography: p178-192. — Includes index*

DRAMATISTS, IRISH — 19th century — Diaries
SHAW, Bernard
Bernard Shaw : the diaries, 1885-1897 with early autobiographical notebooks and diaries, and an abortive 1917 diary / edited & annotated by Stanley Weintraub ; transliterated by Stanley Rypins, with additional transliterations & transcriptions by Blanche Patch ... [et al.]. — University Park, Pa. : Pennsylvania State University Press, 1986. — p. cm. — *Includes index*

DRENTHE (NETHERLANDS) — Economic policy
NETHERLANDS. Stuurgroep Integraal Structuurplan Noorden des Lands
Het Noorden : een versterkte bevolkingsgroei? Of juist niet! : een bewerking van het rapport Bevolkingsaspecten Noorden des Lands / Samensteller R. Idenburg. — 's-Gravenhage : Staatsuitgeverij, 1974. — 21p

NETHERLANDS. Werkgroep Beleidsdoelstellingen Analyse Noorden
ISP : integraal structuurplan Noorden des lands : rapport van de Werkgroep Beleidsdoelstellingen Analyse Noorden. — [s-Gravenhage] : the Werkgroep 2. — 1974. — 27p

DREYFUS, ALFRED
WILSON, Nelly
Bernard-Lazare : l'antisémitisme, l'affaire Dreyfus, et la recherche de l'identité juive / Nelly Wilson ; traduit de l'anglais par Christiane et Douglas Gallagher. — Paris : Albin Michel, [1985]. — 461p. — *Bibliography: p435-450*

DRINKING AND TRAFFIC ACCIDENTS
DENNEY, Ronald C.
Alcohol and accidents / Ronald C. Denney. — Wilmslow, Cheshire : Sigma Press, 1986. — viii,172p

DRINKING OF ALCOHOLIC BEVERAGES — England — West Country
Educating about alcohol : professional perspectives and practice in south west England / Robin Means ... [et al.]. — Bristol : University of Bristol, School for Advanced Urban Studies, 1986. — 191p. — (Occasional paper / School for Advanced Urban Studies ; 25)

FRANKLIN, Adrian
Pub drinking and the licensed trade : a study of drinking cultures and local community in two areas of south west England / Adrian Franklin. — Bristol : University of Bristol, School for Advanced Urban Studies, 1985. — 64p. — (Occasional paper / School for Advanced Urban Studies ; 21)

DRINKING OF ALCOHOLIC BEVERAGES — Switzerland — Statistics
SCHMID, E.
100 ans de statistique de la consommation de l'alcool : la consommation des boissons alcooliques en Suisse de 1976 à 1980 et durant les périodes antérieures / par E. Schmid et N. Blanchard. — Berne : Regie fédéral des alcools, 1981. — 33p. — *Bibliographical references: p32-33*

DROPOUTS — Tanzania — Bukumbi
KAAYK, Jan
Education, estrangement and adjustment : a study among pupils and school leavers in Bukumbi, a rural community in Tanzania / Jan Kaayk ; [translation, V. A. February]. — The Hague : Mouton, [1976]. — xv, 267 p.. — (Change and continuity in Africa). — *Includes index. — Bibliography: p. 265-267*

DROUGHT RELIEF — Southern States — History
WOODRUFF, Nan Elizabeth
As rare as rain : federal relief in the great southern drought of 1930-31 / Nan Elizabeth Woodruff. — Urbana : University of Illinois Press, 1985. — xii, 203 p., [8] p. of plates. — *Includes index. — Bibliography: p. 183-189*

DROUGHT RELIEF — Sudan
INTERNATIONAL LABOUR ORGANIZATION. Identification and Programming Mission to the Republic of the Sudan (1985)
After the famine : a programme of action to strengthen the survival strategies of affected populations / report of the ILO Identification and Programming Mission to the Republic of the Sudan, September 1985. — Geneva : ILO, c1986. — xi,309p

DROUGHTS
GARCIA, Rolando V.
Drought and man : the 1972 case history. — Oxford : Pergamon
Vol.1: Nature pleads not guilty / by Rolando V. Garcia ; with a section on climatic variability by J. Smagorinsky and special contributions from M. Ellman ... [et al.]. — 1981. — xiv,300p. — *Includes bibliographies and index*

GARCIA, Rolando V.
Drought and man : the 1972 case history. — Oxford : Pergamon. — *Published for the International Federation of Institutes for Advanced Study*
Vol.3: The roots of catastrophe / by Rolando V. Garcia and Pierre Spitz ; with special contributions from P. Bonte ... [et al.] ; edited by J. Ann Zammit. — 1986. — xviii,193p. — *Includes index*

DROUGHTS — Economic aspects
GARCIA, Rolando V.
Drought and man : the 1972 case history / by Rolando V. Garcia and José C. Escudero ; and special contributions by S. Ayalew...[et al.]. — Oxford : Pergamon, Sept.1981
Vol.2: The constant catastrophe / by Rolando V. Garcia and J. E. Escudera. — x, 204p. — *Includes bibliographies*

DROUGHTS — Social aspects
GARCIA, Rolando V.
Drought and man : the 1972 case history / by Rolando V. Garcia and José C. Escudero ; and special contributions by S. Ayalew...[et al.]. — Oxford : Pergamon, Sept.1981
Vol.2: The constant catastrophe / by Rolando V. Garcia and J. E. Escudera. — x, 204p. — *Includes bibliographies*

DROUGHTS — Sahel — Congresses
COLLOQUIUM ON THE EFFECTS OF DROUGHT ON THE PRODUCTIVE STRATEGIES OF SUDANO-SAHELIAN HERDSMEN AND FARMERS (1975 : Université de Niamey)
Report / Colloquium on the Effects of Drought on the Productive Strategies of Sudano-Sahelian Herdsmen and Farmers ; edited by Michael M. Horowitz. — Binghamton, N.Y. : Institute for Development Anthropology, [1976]. — xiii, 96 p.. — *Cover title*

DROUGHTS — Southern States — History
WOODRUFF, Nan Elizabeth
As rare as rain : federal relief in the great southern drought of 1930-31 / Nan Elizabeth Woodruff. — Urbana : University of Illinois Press, 1985. — xii, 203 p., [8] p. of plates. — *Includes index. — Bibliography: p. 183-189*

DROUGHTS — Sudan
INTERNATIONAL LABOUR ORGANIZATION. Identification and Programming Mission to the Republic of the Sudan (1985)
After the famine : a programme of action to strengthen the survival strategies of affected populations / report of the ILO Identification and Programming Mission to the Republic of the Sudan, September 1985. — Geneva : ILO, c1986. — xi,309p

DRUG ABUSE
National drug intelligence estimate = rapport annuel national sur les drogues / Royal Canadian Mounted Police. — Ottawa : Royal Canadian Mounted Police, 1984/85-. — Annual. — *Text in French and English*

PLANT, Martin A.
Drugs in perspective / Martin A. Plant. — London : Hodder and Stoughton, 1987. — xii,176p. — *Originally published: Sevenoaks : Teach Yourself Books, 1981. — Bibliography: p157-169. — Includes index*

WHITAKER, Ben
The global connection : the crisis of drug addiction / Ben Whitaker. — London : Cape, 1987. — 432p. — *Includes index*

DRUG ABUSE — Treatment — Denmark
At møde mennesket hvor det er... : om behandlingen af stofmisbrugere. — [København] : Alkohol- og Narkotikarºadet, 1984. — 204p. — *Bibliography: p.200-204*

DRUG ABUSE — Treatment — Great Britain
ADVISORY COUNCIL ON THE MISUSE OF DRUGS. Treatment and Rehabilitation Working Group
First interim report. — [London] : Department of Health and Social Security, 1977. — 18p

DRUG ABUSE — Canada
National drug intelligence estimate = rapport annuel national sur les drogues / Royal Canadian Mounted Police. — Ottawa : Royal Canadian Mounted Police, 1984/85-. — Annual. — *Text in French and English*

DRUG ABUSE — Denmark
Redegørelse fra situationen vedrørende alkohol- og narkotikamisbruget 1983. — [København] : Alkohol- og Narkotikarådet, 1984. — 27p. — (Alkohol- og Narkotikarådets skriftserie ; 3)

DRUG ABUSE — Germany (West)
BEHR, Hans-Georg
Drogenpolitik in der Bundesrepublik / Hans-Georg Behr, Andreas Juhnke...[et al.]. — Reinbek bei Hamburg : Rowohlt Taschenbuch Verlag, 1985. — 277p

DRUG ABUSE — Scandinavia
Drugs and drug control / edited by Per Stangeland. — Oslo : Norwegian University Press ; Oxford : Oxford University Press [distributor], c1987. — 132p. — (Scandinavian studies in criminology ; v.8). — *Includes bibliographies*

DRUG ABUSE — United States
Chemical dependencies : patterns, costs, and consequences / edited by Carl D. Chambers ... [et al.]. — Athens, Ohio : Ohio University Press, 1987. — p. cm. — *Includes bibliographies*

LEE, Martin A
Acid dreams : the CIA, LSD, and the sixties rebellion / by Martin A. Lee and Bruce Shlain. — 1st Grove Press ed. — New York : Grove Press, 1986. — xxi, 343p, [12] p of plates. — *Includes index. — Bibliography: p.320-329*

STEPHENS, Richard C
Mind-altering drugs : use, abuse, and treatment / Richard C. Stephens. — Newbury Park, Calif. : SAGE Publications, c1987. — 133 p.. — (Law and critical justice series ; v. 9). — *Includes index. — Bibliography: p. 125-128*

DRUG ABUSE — United States
continuation

WISOTSKY, Steven
Breaking the impasse in the war on drugs / Steven Wisotsky ; foreword by Thomas Szasz. — New York : Greenwood Press, 1986. — xxiv, 279 p.. — (Contributions in political science ; no. 159). — *Includes index. — Bibliography: p. [263]-271*

DRUG ABUSE — United States — Prevention

STEPHENS, Richard C
Mind-altering drugs : use, abuse, and treatment / Richard C. Stephens. — Newbury Park, Calif. : SAGE Publications, c1987. — 133 p.. — (Law and critical justice series ; v. 9). — *Includes index. — Bibliography: p. 125-128*

DRUG ABUSE AND CRIME

BRUNO, Francesco
Combatting drug abuse and related crime : comparative research on the effectiveness of socio-legal preventive and control measures in different countries on the interaction between criminal behaviour and drug abuse / by Francesco Bruno. — Rome : Fratelli Palombi, 1984. — 251p. — (Publication / United Nations Social Defence Research Institute ; no. 21). — *'Funded by the United Nations Fund for Drug Abuse'. — Bibliography: p.212-244*

DRUG ABUSE AND CRIME — United States

Chemical dependencies : patterns, costs, and consequences / edited by Carl D. Chambers ... [et al.]. — Athens, Ohio : Ohio University Press, 1987. — p. cm. — *Includes bibliographies*

DRUG ABUSE AND EMPLOYMENT

CONFEDERATION OF BRITISH INDUSTRY
Danger - drugs at work : an employer's guide to drugs misuse. — London : Confederation of British Industry, 1986. — 31p

DRUG ABUSE SURVEYS — Canada

The Steel drug : cocaine in perspective / Patricia G. Erickson ... [et al.]. — Lexington, Mass. : Lexington Books, c1987. — xviii, 169 p.. — *Includes index. — Bibliography: p. [151]-159*

DRUG ABUSE SURVEYS — United States

The Steel drug : cocaine in perspective / Patricia G. Erickson ... [et al.]. — Lexington, Mass. : Lexington Books, c1987. — xviii, 169 p.. — *Includes index. — Bibliography: p. [151]-159*

DRUG TRADE

Adverse effects : women and the pharmaceutical industry / edited by Kathleen McDonnell. — Penang : International Organization of Consumers Unions Regional Office for Asia and the Pacific, 1986. — 217p

RIGONI, Raymond
Les multinationales de la pharmacie : polémiques, perceptions et paradoxes / Raymond Rigoni, Adrian Griffiths, William Laing. — Genève : Institut de Recherche et d'Information sur les Multinationales, [1985]. — 123p. — (Dossiers de l'Institut de Recherche et d'Information sur les Multinationales ; No.5). — *Bibliography: p121-123*

DRUG TRADE — Bangladesh

ROLT, Francis
Pills, policies and profits : reactions to the Bangladesh drug policy / by Francis Rolt. — London : War on Want, 1985. — 114p

DRUG TRADE — Germany (West)

BEHR, Hans-Georg
Drogenpolitik in der Bundesrepublik / Hans-Georg Behr, Andreas Juhnke...[et al.]. — Reinbek bei Hamburg : Rowohlt Taschenbuch Verlag, 1985. — 277p

DRUG TRADE — Great Britain

NATIONAL ECONOMIC DEVELOPMENT COUNCIL. Economic Development Committee for Pharmaceuticals
A new focus on pharmaceuticals. — London : H.M.S.O., 1986. — 36p

DRUG TRADE — Great Britain — History

One hundred years : Wellcome 1880-1980 : in pursuit of excellence / [written by Gilbert Macdonald]. — London : Wellcome Foundation, 1980. — 120p

DRUGS — dictionaries

SPEARS, Richard A
The slang and jaron of drugs and drink / by Ricard A. Spears. — Metuchen, N.J. : Scarecrow Press, 1986. — xv, 585 p.. — *Bibliography: p. [562]-575*

DRUGS — Law and legislation — Great Britain

GREAT BRITAIN. Department of Health and Social Security
The control of medicines in the United Kingdom of Great Britain and Northern Ireland / prepared by the Department of Health and Social Security ; on behalf of the Health Departments of the United Kingdom. — [London : Medicines Division, Department of Health and Social Security], 1977. — 28p

DRUGS — Law and legislation — Northern Ireland

GREAT BRITAIN. Department of Health and Social Security
The control of medicines in the United Kingdom of Great Britain and Northern Ireland / prepared by the Department of Health and Social Security ; on behalf of the Health Departments of the United Kingdom. — [London : Medicines Division, Department of Health and Social Security], 1977. — 28p

DRUGS — Physiological effect

Chemical dependencies : patterns, costs, and consequences / edited by Carl D. Chambers ... [et al.]. — Athens, Ohio : Ohio University Press, 1987. — p. cm. — *Includes bibliographies*

PLANT, Martin A
Drugs in perspective / Martin A. Plant. — London : Hodder and Stoughton, 1987. — xii,176p. — *Originally published: Sevenoaks : Teach Yourself Books, 1981. — Bibliography: p157-169. — Includes index*

DRUGS — Physiological effect — Addresses, essays, lectures

Teen drug use / edited by George Beschner, Alfred S. Friedman. — Lexington, Mass. : Lexington Books, c1986. — x, 243 p.. — *Includes bibliographies and index*

DRUGS — Denmark

Engrosdistributionen af fabriksfremstillede laegemidler. — København : Monopoltilsynet, 1983. — 125p

DRUGS — Germany (West)

BEHR, Hans-Georg
Drogenpolitik in der Bundesrepublik / Hans-Georg Behr, Andreas Juhnke...[et al.]. — Reinbek bei Hamburg : Rowohlt Taschenbuch Verlag, 1985. — 277p

DRUGS AND EMPLOYMENT

SCANLON, Walter F
Alcoholism and drug abuse in the workplace : employee assistance programs / Walter F. Scanlon. — New York : Praeger, 1986. — xiii, 146 p.. — *Includes bibliographies and index*

DRUGS AND PRISONERS — Great Britain

ADVISORY COUNCIL ON THE MISUSE OF DRUGS. Working Group on Treatment and Rehabilitation
Report on drug dependants within the prison system in England and Wales. — London : the Council, 1979. — 20p

DRUGS AND YOUTH — South Africa

DU TOIT, Brian M.
Drug use and South African students / by Brian M. Du Toit. — [Athens] : Ohio University Center for International Studies, Africa Program, 1978. — 127 p.. — (Papers in international studies : Africa series ; no. 35). — *Bibliography: p. 126-127*

DRUMONT, EDOUARD-ADOLPHE

BUSI, Frederick
The pope of antisemitism : the career and legacy of Edouard-Adolphe Drumont / Frederick Busi. — Lanham ; London : University Press of America, 1987. — [242]p. — *Includes bibliography and index*

DRUNK DRIVING — Great Britain

WALLS, H. J.
Drink, drugs and driving / by H.J. Walls and Alistair R. Brownlie. — 2nd ed. — London : Sweet & Maxwell, 1985. — xxix,281p. — *Previous ed.: 1970. — Bibliography: p247-268. — Includes index*

DRUZHININ, N. M.

Sotsial'no-ekonomicheskoe razvitie Rossii : sbornik statei k 100-letiiu so dnia rozhdeniia Nikolaia Mikhailovicha Druzhinina / otv. redaktor S. L. Tikhvinskii. — Moskva : Nauka, 1986. — 267p

DRY FARMING — Research — India

MAHAPATRA, Ishwar Chandra
India and the international crops research institute for the semi-arid tropics : a study of their collaboration in agricultural research / Ishwar Chandra Mahapatre, Dev Raj Bhumbla, Shriniwas Dattatraya Bokil. — Washington, D.C. : The World Bank, 1986. — x,48p. — (Study paper / Consultative group on International Agricultural Research ; no.18)

DU BOIS, W. E. B — Views on world politics

HORNE, Gerald
Black and red : W.E.B. Du Bois and the Afro-American response to the Cold War, 1944-1963 / Gerald Horne. — Albany, N.Y. : State University of New York Press, c1985. — xii, 457p. — (SUNY series in Afro-American society). — *Includes index. — Bibliography: p.437-440*

DUAL-CAREER FAMILIES — United States

PLECK, Joseph H
Working wives, working husbands / Joseph H. Pleck. — Beverly Hills, Calif. : Published in cooperation with the National Council on Family Relations [by] Sage Publications, c1985. — 167 p.. — (New perspectives on family). — *Bibliography: p. 160-167*

DUALITY THEORY (MATHEMATICS)

KLEIN HANEVELD, Willem K.
Duality in stochastic linear and dynamic programming / Willem K. Klein Haneveld. — Berlin ; New York : Springer-Verlag, c1986. — p. cm. — (Lecture notes in economics and mathematical systems ; 274). — *Includes bibliographies and index*

DUARTE, JOSÉ NAPOLEÓN

DUARTE, José Napoleón
Duarte : my story / Jose Napoleon Duarte. — New York : Putnam, 1986. — p. cm

DUHEM, PIERRE MAURICE MARIE, b.1861

Can theories be refuted? : essays on the Duhem-Quine-thesis / [compiled by] S.G. Harding. — Dordrecht-Holland ; Boston : D. Reidel Pub. Co, [1975]. — (Synthese library ; 81). — *Includes bibliographies and index*

DULLES, JOHN FOSTER

TOULOUSE, Mark G.
The transformation of John Foster Dulles : from prophet of realism to priest of nationalism / Mark G. Toulouse. — [Macon, GA] : Mercer University Press, c1985. — xlii, 277 p.. — *Includes index. — Bibliography: p. [255]-269*

DUMFRIES AND GALLOWAY — Economic conditions

DUMFRIES AND GALLOWAY. Regional Council
  Structure plan : report of survey : population, employment and housing (revised). — Dumfries : [the Regional Council], 1979. — 105p

DUMFRIES AND GALLOWAY — Population

DUMFRIES AND GALLOWAY. Regional Council
  Structure plan : report of survey : population, employment and housing (revised). — Dumfries : [the Regional Council], 1979. — 105p

DUMONT

WEINSTEIN, Michael A.
  Culture critique : Fernand Dumont and New Quebec sociology / Michael A. Weinstein. — Montréal : New World Perspectives, 1985. — 123p. — *Bibliography p[124]*

DUNÁNTÚL (HUNGARY) — Industries

MÉREY, Klára T.
  Dél-Dunántúl iparának története a kapitalizmus idején / T. Mérey Klára. — Budapest : Akadémiai Kiadó, 1985. — 289p

DURABLE GOODS, CONSUMER — France — Statistics

BUZULIER, Nadine
  Images economiques des entreprises. — Paris : I.N.S.E.E.. — (Archives et documents / Institut national de la statistique et des études économiques ; no.150)
  Dossier sectoriel no.5: Biens de consommation courante au 1-1-1983 / Nadine Buzulier. — 1986. — 71p

DURABLE GOODS, CONSUMER — Great Britain — Statistics

Durable goods shops. — London : HMSO, 1970-79. — (Business monitor. SD ; 3) (Business monitor. SDM ; 3). — *Monthly. — Continued by: Retail sales*

DURABLE GOODS, CONSUMER — Netherlands — Statistics

Vierde algemene bedrijfstelling, 1978. — 's-Gravenhage : Staatsuitgeverij. — *Rear cover title: Fourth general economic census, 1978: volume 2, part B: trade and repair of consumer goods*
  d.2: Algemene sectorale gegevens. — 1985
  B: groothandel, tussenpersonen in de handel, detailhandel en reparatie van gebruiksgoederen. — 141p

DURBAN METROPOLITAN CHAMBER OF COMMERCE

DURBAN METROPOLITAN CHAMBER OF COMMERCE
  Annual report / Durban Metropolitan Chamber of Commerce. — Durban : Durban Metropolitan Chamber of Commerce, 1986-. — *Annual*

DURESS (LAW)

MONAHAN, Arthur P.
  Consent, coercion, and limit : the medieval origins of parliamentary democracy / Arthur P. Monahan. — Kingston ; Montreal : McGill-Queen's University Press, 1987. — xx,345p. — (McGill-Queen's studies in the history of ideas ; 10). — *Bibliography p [265]-325*

DURHAM (ENGLAND: COUNTY) — Bibliography — Union lists

Durham and Northumberland / county editor F.W.D. Manders. — London : British Library, c1982. — xvi,65p. — (Bibliography of British newspapers). — *"The bibliography of British newspapers is edited by the Reference Special and Information Section of the Library Association". — Includes index*

DURKHEIM, ÉMILE. Suicide

POPE, Whitney
  Durkheim's Suicide : a classic analyzed / Whitney Pope. — Chicago ; London : University of Chicago Press, 1982. — 229 p. — (Midway reprint). — *Originally published: University of Chicago Press, 1976*

DURKHEIM, EMILE

BAUDELOT, Christian
  Durkheim et le suicide / Christian Baudelot et Roger Establet. — [Paris] : Presses universitaires de France, [1984]. — 125p. — (Philosophies ; 3)

DURKHEIM, ÉMILE

GIDDENS ANTHONY
  Durkheim / Anthony Giddens. — London : Fontana, 1978. — 126p. — (Fontana modern masters)

DURKHEIM, EMILE

JONES, Robert Alun
  Emile Durkheim : an introduction to four major works / by Robert Alun Jones. — Beverly Hills : Sage Publications, c1985. — p. cm. — (Masters of social theory ; v. 2). — *Bibliography: p*

DURKHEIMIAN SCHOOL OF SOCIOLOGY

JONES, Robert Alun
  Emile Durkheim : an introduction to four major works / by Robert Alun Jones. — Beverly Hills : Sage Publications, c1985. — p. cm. — (Masters of social theory ; v. 2). — *Bibliography: p*

DURRUTI, BUENAVENTURA

FERRER, Rai
  Durruti, 1896-1936 / Rai Ferrer (Onomatopeya). — Barcelona : Planeta, 1985. — 198p. — *Bibliography: p193-194*

DURY, E. C. (Ernest Charles)

JOHNSTON, Charles M.
  E. C. Drury : agrarian idealist / Charles M. Johnston. — Toronto : University of Toronto Press, 1986. — xii,299p. — (Ontario Historical Studies Series). — *Includes references*

DUTCH — New York (State) — History — 17th century

RINK, Oliver A.
  Holland on the Hudson : an economic and social history of Dutch New York / Oliver A. Rink. — Ithaca, N.Y. : Cornell University Press ; Cooperstown, N.Y. : New York State Historical Association, 1986. — p. cm. — *Includes index. — Bibliography: p*

DUTCH LANGUAGE

VANDEPUTTE, O.
  Dutch : the language of twenty million Dutch and Flemish people / O. Vandeputte, P. Vincent, T. Hermans. — Rekkem, Flanders : Flemish-Netherlands Foundation/Stichting Ons Erfdeel vzw, 1986. — 64p

DUTCH LANGUAGE — Dictionaries

Cassell's English-Dutch/Dutch-English dictionary = Engels-Nederlands/Nederlands-Engels woordenboek / completely revised by J. A. Jockin-la Bastide [and] G. van Kooten. — London : Cassell, 1981. — xiv,602,vii,729p

DUTSCHKE, RUDI

MIERMEISTER, Jürgen
  Rudi Dutschke : mit Selbstzeugnissen und Bilddokumenten / Jügen Miermeister. — Reinbek bei Hamburg : Rowohlt, 1986. — 154p. — *Bibliography: p142-151*

DUTTON, HARRY

Innovation and labour during British industrialisation : a celebration of the life and work of Harry Dutton, 1947-1984. — Cambridge : Huntington, [1985]. — 92p. — *Bibliography: p90*

DUTY

ROBINS, Michael H.
  Promising, intending, and moral autonomy / Michael H. Robins. — Cambridge : Cambridge University Press, 1984. — xii,180p. — (Cambridge studies in philosophy). — *Bibliography: p171-177. — Includes index*

DUTY-FREE IMPORTATION — European Economic Community countries

Reliefs from taxes granted to imports made by private persons : situation 1.7.1984. — Luxembourg : Office for Official Publications of the European Communities, 1984. — 82p. — *At head of title page: Commission of the European Communities*

DWELLINGS — Energy conservation — Econometric models

KHAZZOOM, J. Daniel
  An econometric model integrating conservation measures in the residential demand for electricity / by J. Daniel Khazzoom. — Greenwich, Conn. : JAI Press, c1986. — xx, 305 p.. — (Contemporary studies in energy analysis and policy ; v. 8). — *Includes index. — Bibliography: p. 165-170*

DWELLINGS — Great Britain — Handbooks, manuals, etc.

Ideal home / Jon Preston...[et al.]. — Survival edition. — [London? : Suspect : Hooligan, 1986]. — [127p]

DWELLINGS — Great Britain — Maintenance and repair — Finance

GREAT BRITAIN. Parliament. House of Commons. Library. Research Division
  Improvement policies for private housing / Oonagh Gay. — [London] : the Division, 1985. — 47p. — (Background paper ; no.169)

DWELLINGS — Japan — Statistics

JAPAN. Statistics Bureau
  1983 housing survey of Japan. — [Tokyo] : the Bureau
  Vol.1: Results for whole Japan
  Part 1: Characteristics of dwellings. — [1985]. — xxxv,769,56p. — Text in Japanese and English

DWELLINGS — South Africa — Johannesburg

BARRY, Margaret
  Magnates and mansions : Johannesburg, 1886-1914 / Margaret Barry and Nimmo Law. — Johannesburg : Lowry : Thorold's Africana Books [distributor], 1985. — 162 p.. — *Includes index. — Bibliography: p. 151-152*

DWELLINGS — United States — History — 19th century

CLARK, Clifford Edward
  The American family home, 1800-1960 / by Clifford Edward Clark, Jr. — Chapel Hill : University of North Carolina Press, c1986. — p. cm. — *Includes index. — Bibliography: p*

DWELLINGS — United States — History — 20th century

CLARK, Clifford Edward
  The American family home, 1800-1960 / by Clifford Edward Clark, Jr. — Chapel Hill : University of North Carolina Press, c1986. — p. cm. — *Includes index. — Bibliography: p*

DYNAMIC PROGRAMMING

KLEIN HANEVELD, Willem K.
  Duality in stochastic linear and dynamic programming / Willem K. Klein Haneveld. — Berlin ; New York : Springer-Verlag, c1986. — p. cm. — (Lecture notes in economics and mathematical systems ; 274). — *Includes bibliographies and index*

DYNO INDUSTRIER A.S.

HALVORSEN, Ragnar
  Lønnsomhetskrav : Strategi for lønnsom vekst sett fra Dyno Industrier A.S' side / Ragnar Halvorsen. — Bergen : Norges handelshøyskole, 1985. — 34p. — (Kristofer Lehmkuhl Forelesning ; 1985)

DZERZHINSKII, F. E.
Feliks Edmundovich Dzerzhinskii : biografiia / [redkollegiia: A. S. Velidov...et al.]. — Izd. 3-e, dop.. — Moskva : Politizdat, 1986. — 509p

EARTHQUAKE PREDICTION
Disaster prevention and mitigation : a compendium of current knowledge. — New York : United Nations
V.3: Seismological aspects. — 1978. — viii,127p. — Bibliography: p122-127. — "UNDRO/22/76 VOL.III"

EARTHQUAKE PREDICTION — Social aspects — California
TURNER, Ralph H
Waiting for disaster : earthquake watching in southern California / Ralph H. Turner, Joanne M. Nigg, Denise Heller Paz. — Berkeley : University of California Press, c1986. — p. cm. — Includes index

EARTHQUAKES — Social aspects — California
TURNER, Ralph H
Waiting for disaster : earthquake watching in southern California / Ralph H. Turner, Joanne M. Nigg, Denise Heller Paz. — Berkeley : University of California Press, c1986. — p. cm. — Includes index

EAST ASIA
MICHAEL, Franz
The far east in the modern world / by Franz H. Michael and George E. Taylor. — Rev. ed. — London : Metheun, [1964]. — xiii,850p

EAST ASIA — Commercial policy — Congresses
The 21st Century, the Asian century? / Takeshi Ishida ... [et al.] ; Sung-Jo Park (Hg.). — Berlin : EXpress Edition, c1985. — 140 p.. — Includes bibliographical references

EAST ASIA — Economic conditions
AIKMAN, David
Pacific Rim : area of change, area of opportunity / by David Aikman. — 1st ed. — Boston : Little, Brown, 1986. — p. cm

Economic development in East and South-east Asia : implications for Australian agriculture in the 1980s / [contributors, Mike Adams ... et al.]. — Canberra : Australian Govt. Pub. Service, 1984. — x, 237 p.. — At head of title: Bureau of Agricultural Economics, Canberra. — Includes bibliographies

PERKINS, Dwight Heald
China, Asia's next economic giant? / Dwight H. Perkins. — Seattle : University of Washington Press, c1986. — x, 98 p.. — (The Henry M. Jackson lectures in modern Chinese studies). — Includes index. — Bibliography: p. 91-93

WORONOFF, Jon
Asia's "miracle" economies / by Jon Woronoff. — Armonk, N.Y. ; London : M. E. Sharpe, 1987. — 1v.

EAST ASIA — Economic policy
The Political economy of the new Asian industrialism / edited by Frederic C. Deyo. — Ithaca, N.Y. : Cornell University Press, 1987. — 252 p.. — (Cornell studies in political economy). — Includes bibliographies and index. — Contents: Export-oriented industrializing states in the capitalist world system / Richard E. Barrett and Soomi Chin -- The origins and development of the Northeast Asian political economy / Bruce Cumings -- State and foreign capital in the East Asian NICs / Stephan Haggard and Tun-jen Cheng -- Political institutions and economic performance / Chalmers Johnson -- The interplay of state, social class, and world system in East Asian development / Hagen Koo -- State and labor / Frederic C. Deyo -- Class, state, and dependence in East Asia / Peter Evans -- Coalitions, institutions, and linkage sequencing toward a strategic capacity model of East Asian development / Frederic C. Deyo

The Sun also sets : lessons in 'looking East' / editor, Jomo. — 2nd ed., rev. & expanded. — Kuala Lumpur : INSAN, 1985. — xvi, 415 p.. — Includes bibliographies

EAST ASIA — Economic policy — Congresses
The 21st Century, the Asian century? / Takeshi Ishida ... [et al.] ; Sung-Jo Park (Hg.). — Berlin : EXpress Edition, c1985. — 140 p.. — Includes bibliographical references

EAST ASIA — Foreign economic relations
Economic relations in the Asian-Pacific region : report of a conference cosponsored by the Chinese Academy of Social Sciences and the Brookings Institution, June 1985 / edited by Bruce Dickson and Harry Harding. — Washington,D.C. : Brookings Institution, 1987. — ix,91p. (Brookings dialogues on public policy)

EAST ASIA — Foreign relations
MICHAEL, Franz Henry
The far east in the modern world / Franz H. Michael and George E. Taylor. — New York : Holt, 1956. — xi,724

EAST ASIA — Foreign relations — United States
BISSON, Thomas Arthur
America's far eastern policy / T. A. Bisson. — New York : Institute of Pacific Relations, 1945. — xiii,235p

GRISWOLD, Alfred Whitney
The far eastern policy of the United States / Alfred W. Griswold. — New Haven : Yale University Press, 1962. — 530p

EAST ASIA — History
LATOURETTE, Kenneth Scott
A short history of the far east / Kenneth S. Latourette. — 3rd ed. — New York : Macmillan, 1957. — 745p

VINACKE, Harold Monk
A history of the far east in modern times / Harold M. Vinacke. — New York : Knopf, 1928. — xiv,503p

EAST ASIA — Industries
The Pacific challenge in international business / edited by W. Chan Kim and Philip K.Y. Young ; with a foreword by Vern Terpstra. — Ann Arbor, Mich. : UMI Research Press, 1987. — viii, 342 p.. — (Research for business decisions ; no. 72). — Includes bibliographies and index

EAST ASIA — Manufactures
The Pacific challenge in international business / edited by W. Chan Kim and Philip K.Y. Young ; with a foreword by Vern Terpstra. — Ann Arbor, Mich. : UMI Research Press, 1987. — viii, 342 p.. — (Research for business decisions ; no. 72). — Includes bibliographies and index

EAST ASIA — Politics and government
AIKMAN, David
Pacific Rim : area of change, area of opportunity / by David Aikman. — 1st ed. — Boston : Little, Brown, 1986. — p. cm

IRIYE, Akira
After imperialism : the search for a new order in the far east, 1921-1931 / Akira Iriye. — Cambridge, Mass. : Harvard University Press, 1965. — ix,375p

MOON, Changjoo
The balance of power in Asia and U.S.-Korea relations = : [Asia üi seryŏk kyunhyŏng kwa Han-Mi kwan'gye] / Changjoo Moon. — Seoul, Korea : Gimm-Young Press ; Maple Shade, N.J. : Distributive Office for the U.S.A., Gimm-Young Co., c1983. — 386 p.. — English and Korean. — Includes bibliographical references

EAST ASIA — Politics and government — Congresses
Peace and stability in northeast Asia : achieving international order without violence / edited by Chong-Ki Choi. — Seoul, Korea : Korean Institute of International Studies, 1985. — vii, 400 p.. — Proceedings of the Institute's 14th international conference, held in Seoul, Korea, Oct. 4-6, 1984. — Includes bibliographical references and index

EAST ASIA — Relations — Canada
DOWNTON, Eric
Pacific challenge : Canada's future in the new Asia / Eric Downton. — Toronto : Stoddart, 1986. — 258p. — Bibliography: p[247]-251

EAST BURRA (SCOTLAND) — Social conditions
BYRON, Reginald
Sea change : a Shetland society, 1970-79 / Reginald Byron. — St John's : Institute of Social and Economic Research Memorial University of Newfoundland, 1986. — vii,164p

EAST-CENTRAL STATE (NIGERIA) — Politics and government — Congresses
SEMINAR ON DIVISIONAL ADMINISTRATION, INSTITUTE OF ADMINISTRATION (1971)
A new system of local government : government by the community in the East Central State of Nigeria : a report of the Seminar on Divisional Administration held at the Institute of Administration Enugu, 24th-26th February, 1971 / edited by G. A. Odenigwe, assisted by C. E. Emezi, H. N. Nwosu. — Enugu, Nigeria : Nwamife, 1977. — xxi, 298, [112] p.. — Includes bibliographical references

EAST EUROPEAN CANADIANS — Congresses
Central and East European ethnicity in Canada : adaptation and preservation / T. Yedlin, editor. — Edmonton : Central and East European Studies Society of Alberta, 1985. — viii,178p. — Papers presented at the conference on Central and East European Ethnicity in Canada, sponsored by the Central and East European Studies Society of Alberta, the Central and East European Studies Association of Canada and the Department of Slavic and East European Studies, University of Alberta at February 1983, held in Edmonton, Alberta

EAST INDIA COMPANY — Employees — History
SIKKA, Ram Parkash
The civil service of India : Europeanisation and Indianisation under the East India Company, 1765-1857 / Ram Parkash Sikka. — New Delhi : Uppal Pub. House, c1984. — xii, 2494, p.. — Includes index. Bibliography: p. [221]-241

EAST INDIAN AMERICANS
SARAN, Parmatma
The Asian Indian experience in the United States / Parmatma Saran. — New Delhi : Vikas, 1985. — x,131p. — Bibliography: p [123]-126

EAST INDIANS — Great Britain — Social conditions
VISRAM, Rozina
Ayahs, lascars and princes : Indians in Britain 1700-1947 / Rozina Visram. — London : Pluto, 1986. — x,304p,[16]p of plates. — Includes index

EAST INDIANS — South Africa — Relocation
PLATZKY, Laurine
The surplus people : forced removals in South Africa / Laurine Platzky and Cherryl Walker for the Surplus People Project. — Johannesburg : Ravan Press, 1985. — xxxiii, 446 p., [12] p. of plates. — Includes index. — Bibliography: p. [404]-408

EAST SEPIK (PAPUA NEW GUINEA) — Population — Statistics
1980 national population census : final figures : provincial summary : East Sepik Province. — Port Moresby : National Statistical Office, 1985. — iii,117p

EAST-WEST TRADE (1945-)
East-West economic relations in the changing global environmental : proceedings of a conference held by the International Economic Association in Budapest, Hungary, and Vienna, Austria / edited by Béla Csikós-Nagy and David G. Young. — Basingstoke : Macmillan, 1986. — xxiv,429p. — *Includes index*

EAST-WEST TRADE (1945-)
KÖVES, András
The CMEA countries in the world economy : turning inwards or turning outwards / by András Köves. — Budapest : Akadémiai Kiadó, 1985. — 247p. — *Revised version of Hungarian original (Budapest,1980)*

OGNEV, A. P.
Ekonomicheskie otnosheniia Vostok-Zapad v 80-e gody : novye iavleniia, problemy, perspektivy / A. P. Ognev ; otv. redaktor V. N. Shenaev. — Moskva : Nauka, 1986. — 220p

EAST-WEST TRADE (1945-)
PASZYNSKI, Marian
International organizations, economic security and normalization of east-west economic relations / Marian Paszynski. — Warsaw : Foreign Trade Research Institute, 1986. — 29p

SOKOLOFF, Georges
The economy of détente : the Soviet Union and western capital / Georges Sokoloff ; translated from the French by Jean Kirby. — Leamington Spa : Berg, c1987. — [236]p. — *Translation of: L'économie de la détente. — Includes bibliography and index*

EAST-WEST TRADE (1945-)
STERN, Jonathan P.
Soviet oil and gas exports to the west : commercial transaction or security threat? / Jonathan P. Stern. — Aldershot : Gower, 1987. — xi,123p. — (Energy papers ; no.21). — *Bibliographical notes*

EASTER ISLAND — History
BARTHEL, Thomas S.
[Achte Land. English]. The eighth land : the Polynesian discovery and settlement of Easter Island / Thomas S. Barthel ; translated for the German by Anneliese Martin. — Honolulu : University Press of Hawaii, c1978. — xi, 372 p.. — *Translation of Das achte Land. — Includes index. — Bibliography: p. [357]-362*

EASTERN CAPE (SOUTH AFRICA) — Politics and government
BEINART, William
Hidden struggles in rural South Africa : politics & popular movements in the Transkei & Eastern Cape 1890-1930 / William Beinart, Colin Bundy. — London : Currey, 1987. — xxvi,326p. — *Includes index*

EASTERN HIGHLANDS PROVINCE (PAPUA NEW GUINEA) — Population — Statistics
1980 national population census : final figures : provincial summary : Eastern Highlands Province. — Port Moresby : National Statistical Office, 1985. — 146p

EASTERN QUESTION (BALKAN)
War and society in East Central Europe. — Boulder, Colo. : Social Science Monographs ; New York : distributed by Columbia University Press. — (East European Monographs ; no.197) (Brooklyn College Studies on Society and Change ; no.36) (Atlantic studies)
Vol.17: Insurrections, wars, and the Eastern crisis in the 1870s / Bela K. Kiraly and Gale Stokes, editors. — 1985. — xxii,421p

EASTERN SCOTTISH — History
HUNTER, D. L. G.
From S.M.T. to Eastern Scottish : an 80th anniversary story / D. L. G. Hunter. — Edinburgh : John Donald, 1987. — viii,198p

EASTLEIGH. Council — History
NORRIS, Norman
Eastleigh : an illustrated history of the Council, 1895-1986 / Norman Norris. — Horndean : Milestone, c1986. — 80p. — (Down memory lane). — *Text and port on inside covers*

EAVESDROPPING — Government policy — Great Britain
GREAT BRITAIN. Parliament. House of Commons. Library. Research Division
Telephone tapping and electronic surveillance devices / [Margaret M. Camsell]. — [London] : the Division, 1980. — 14p. — (Reference sheet ; no.80/12)

EAVESDROPPING — Ireland
MUNNELLY, Brendan
Who's bugging you? : inside Ireland's secret world of electronic surveillance / Brendan Munnelly. — Cork : Mercier Press, 1987. — 90p

ECCLESIASTICAL LAW — Spain
ARBELOA, Víctor Manuel
Separación de Iglesia-Estado en España / Víctor Manuel Arbeloa. — Madrid : Mañana, 1977. — 76p. — (Colección Aperos del cristianismo ; 13). — *On cover: Separación de la Iglesia y el Estado en España. — Appendices (p. 46-[77]) contain legislation. — Includes bibliographical references*

ECOLE NATIONALE D'ADMINISTRATION (France)
KESLER, Jean-François
L'E.N.A., La société, l'Etat / Jean-François Kesler. — [Paris] : Berger-Levrault, c1985. — 584p. — (L'administration nouvelle). — *Bibliography: p577-[584]*

ECOLOGY
Écologie et liberté : résumé des rapports présentés au Congrès du Parti Liberal Suisse à Crissier/VD le 4 février 1978. — [S.l.] : Parti liberal suisse, 1978. — 24p

ECOLOGY — Bibliography
An Environmental bibliography : publications issued by UNEP or under its auspices, 1973-1980. — Nairobi : United Nations Environment Programme, 1981. — vi,67p. — (UNEP reference series ; 2). — *Includes indexes*

ECOLOGY — Philosophy
SALE, Kirkpatrick
Dwellers in the land : the bioregional vision / Kirkpatrick Sale. — San Francisco : Sierra Club Books, c1985. — x, 217 p.. — *Includes index. — Bibliography: p. 193-207*

ECOLOGY — Statistics
Syrvey of environment statistics : frameworks, approaches and statistical publications. — New York : United Nations, 1982. — v,115p. — (Statistical papers / United Nations, Statistical Office. Series M ; no.73) ([Document] / United Nations ; ST/ESA/STAT/SER.M/73). — *Includes bibliographical references. — Sales: E.82.XVII.4*

ECOLOGY — Statistics — Bibliography
Directory of environment statistics. — New York : United Nations, 1983. — v,305p. — (Statistical papers / United Nations, Statistical Office. Series M ; no.75) ([Document] (United Nations) ; ST/ESA/STAT/SER.M/75). — *Sales no.: E.83.XVII.12*

ECOLOGY — Germany (West) — Political aspects
Eingriffe im Diesseits : Beiträge zu einer radikalen grünen Realpolitik / herausgegeben von Gabriel Falkenberg und Heiner Kersting. — Essen : Klartext, 1985. — 203p

ECOLOGY — Malaysia
AIKEN, S. Robert
Development and environment in peninsular Malaysia / S. Robert Aiken...[et al.]. — Singapore ; New York : McGraw-Hill International, 1982. — xx,310p. — (McGraw-Hill Southeast Asia series). — *Bibliography: p283-301*

ECONOMETRIC MODELS
ARELLANO GONZALEZ, Manuel
Estimation and testing of dynamic econometric models from panel data / by Manuel Arellano Gonzalez. — 193 leaves. — PhD (Econ) 1986 LSE

BINMORE, K. G.
Remodeled rational players / K. G. Binmore. — London : Suntory Toyota International Centre for Economics and Related Disciplines, 1987. — 54p. — (Theoretical economics). — *Bibliography: p[55-56]*

BÜTTLER, Hans-Jürgen
Estimation of disequilibrium models / Hans-Jürg Büttler, Gertrude Frei, Bernd Schips. — Berlin ; New York : Springer-Verlag, c1986. — p. cm. — (Lecture notes in economics and mathematical systems ; 279). — *Includes bibliographies*

Econometric modeling in economic education research / edited by William E. Becker and William B. Walstad. — Boston, Mass. : Kluwer-Nijhoff Pub., 1986. — p. cm. — (International series in economic modeling). — *Includes index*

HOQUE, Asraul
The exact multiperiod mean-square forecast error for the first-order auto regressive model / Asraul Hoque, Jan R. Magnus and Bahram Pesaran. — London : Suntory-Toyota International Centre for Economics and Related Disciplines, 1986. — 35p. — (Econometrics). — *Bibliography: p26-29*

MARWAHA, S. S.
Some single endogenous variable rational expectation models : asymptotic theory and finite sample simulations compared / S. S. Marwaha and J. D. Sargan. — London : Economic and Social Research Council : London School of Economics, 1986. — [44p]. — (ESRC/LSE econometrics project discussion paper ; A.60)

MARWAHA, Satwent Singh
Practical considerations when solving nonlinear rational expectations models / Satwent Singh Marwaha. — London : Economic and Social Research Council : London School of Economics, 1986. — [44p]. — (ESRC/LSE econometrics project discussion paper ; A.63). — *Bibliography: p13*

RICHARDSON, Pete
Recent developments in OECD's international macroeconomic model / by Pete Richardson. — [Paris] : OECD, 1987. — iv,31p. — (Working papers / OECD Department of Economics and Statistics ; no.46). — *Bibliographical references:p30-31*

RICHARDSON, Pete
A review of the simulation properties of OECD's INTERLINK model / by Pete Richardson. — [Paris] : OECD, 1987. — iv,67p. — (Working papers / OECD Department of Economics and Statistics ; no.47). — *Bibliographical references: p55*

SENGUPTA, Jatikumar
Stochastic optimization and economic models / Jati K. Sengupta. — Dordrecht ; Boston : D. Reidel ; Norwell, MA, U.S.A. : Sold and distributed in the U.S.A. and Canada by Kluwer Academic, c1986. — x, 373 p.. — (Theory and decision library. Series B. Mathematical and statistical methods). — *Includes bibliographies and indexes*

ECONOMETRIC MODELS
continuation

VILARES, Manuel José
Structural change in macroeconomic models : theory and estimation / by Manuel José Vilares. — Dordrecht ; Boston : Martinus Nijhoff, 1986. — p. cm. — (Advanced studies in theoretical and applied econometrics ; v. 6). — : *Originally presented as author's thesis, University of Dijon.* — Bibliography: p

ECONOMETRIC MODELS — Addresses, essays, lectures

Specification analysis in the linear model : (in honour of Donald Cochrane) / edited by Maxwell L. King and David E.A. Giles. — London : Routledge & Kegan Paul, 1987. — ix,358p. — (International library of economics)

ECONOMETRIC MODELS — Congresses

Time series and econometric modelling / Ian B. MacNeill & Gary J. Umphrey, editors ; associate editors, Richard A.L. Carter, A. Ian McLeod, Aman Ullah. — Dordrecht ; Boston : D. Reidel ; Norwell, MA, U.S.A. : Sold and distributed in the U.S.A. and Canada by Kluwer Academic Publishers, c1987. — p. cm. — (Advances in the statistical sciences ; v. 3) (The University of Western Ontario series in philosophy of science ; v. 36)

ECONOMETRICS

Advances in economic theory : fifth world congress / edited by Truman F. Bewley. — Cambridge : Cambridge University Press, 1987. — vii,428p. — (Econometric Society monographs ; no.12). — *Conference papers.* — Includes bibliographies

ALPERN, S.
A mixed strategy minimax theorem / Steve Alpern and Shmuel Gal. — London : Suntory Toyota Internation Centre for Economics and Related Disciplines, 1987. — 10p. — (Theoretical economics ; 87/157)

Annales de l'INSEE / Institut National de la Statistique et des Études Économiques. — Paris : Institut National de la Statistique et des Etudes Économiques, 1969-1985. — *3 per year.* — *Continued by Annales d'Economie et de Statistique/Institut National de la Statistique et des Etudes Economiques*

Annales d'économie et de statistique / Institut National de la Statistique et des Etudes Economiques. — Paris : Institut National de la Statistique et des Études Économiques, 1986-. — *Quarterly.* — *Continues Annales de l'INSEE and Cahiers du Séminaire d'Econométrie*

Cahiers du séminaire d'économétrie / Centre National de la Recherche Scientifique. — Paris : Centre National de la Recherche Scientifique, 1951-1985. — *Annual.* — *Continued by Annales d'économie et de statistique/Institut National de la Statistique et des Études Économiques*

CHOW, Gregory C.
Econometrics / Gregory C. Chow. — New York : McGraw-Hill Book Co., c1983. — xiii, 432p. — (Economics handbook series). — Includes bibliographical references and index

CHRIST, Carl F.
Econometric models and methods. — Wiley, 1966. — 705p.,ill.,24cm

DESAI, Meghnad
An econometric approach to the measurement of poverty / Meghnad Desai and Anup Shah. — London : Welfare State Programme Suntory-Toyota International Centre for Economics and Related Displines, 1985. — 20p. — (Discussion paper / Welfare State Programme. Suntory-Toyota International Centre For Economics and Related Disciplines ; no.2)

Econometric contributions to public policy : proceedings of a conference held by the International Economic Association at Urbino, Italy / edited by Richard Stone and William Peterson. — London : Macmillan, 1978. — [416]p

Econometric Research Program research memorandum / Princeton University. — Princeton, N.J. : Princeton University, 1985-

Econometric Theory. — Cambridge : Cambridge University Press, 1985-. — *3 per year*

Handbook of econometrics. — Amsterdam ; Oxford : North-Holland Vol.3 / edited by Zvi Griliches and Michael D. Intriligator. — 1986. — xxv,p1465-2107. — (Handbooks on economics ; Bk.2). — Includes bibliographies and indexes

Journal of applied econometrics. — Chichester : John Wiley, 1986-. — *Quarterly*

JUDGE, George G
Improved methods of inference in econometrics / George G. Judge and Thomas A. Yancey. — Amsterdam ; New York : North-Holland ; New York, N.Y., U.S.A. : Elsevier Science Pub. Co. [distributor], 1986. — xvi, 291 p.. — (Studies in mathematical and managerial economics ; v. 34). — Includes bibliographies and indexes

KMENTA, Jan
Elements of econometrics / Jan Kmenta. — 2nd ed. — New York : Macmillan ; London : Collier Macmillan, c1986. — xii, 786p. — Includes index

MAGNUS, Jan R.
The bias of forecasts from a first-order autoregression / Jan R. Magnus and Bahram Pesaran. — London : Suntory Toyota International Centre for Economics and Related Disciplines, 1987. — 46p. — (Econometrics ; 87/153)

PUDNEY, S. E.
Frequency of purchase and Engel curve estimation / S. E. Pudney. — London : London School of Economics : Economic and Social Research Council, 1986. — [41]p. — (ESRC/LSE econometrics project discussion paper ; A.56). — Bibliography: p37

SPANOS, Aris
Statistical foundations of econometric modelling / Aris Spanos. — Cambridge : Cambridge University Press, 1986. — xxiii,695p. — Bibliography: p673-688. — Includes index

ECONOMETRICS — Addresses, essays, lectures

Specification analysis in the linear model : (in honour of Donald Cochrane) / edited by Maxwell L. King and David E.A. Giles. — London : Routledge & Kegan Paul, 1987. — ix,358p. — (International library of economics)

ECONOMETRICS — Computer programs

Econometric software register / ESRC Centre in Economic Computing. — London : ESRC Centre in Economic Computing, 1985-. — *Irregular*

ECONOMIC — Computer programs

ESRC Centre in Economic Computing bulletin. — London : ESRC Centre in Economic Computing, 1984-. — *Semi-annual*

ECONOMIC AND SOCIAL COMMITTEE OF THE EUROPEAN COMMUNITIES 986OFF. PUBNS.. (270/2)

ECONOMIC AND SOCIAL COMMITTEE OF THE EUROPEAN COMMUNITIES
Organization and management of community research and development : study / Economic and Social Committee of the European Communities. — Brussels : General Secretariat of the Economic and Social Committee, 1980. — vi,159p

ECONOMIC ANTHROPOLOGY

Beyond the new economic anthropology / edited by John Clammer. — Basingstoke : Macmillan, 1987. — [200]p. — Includes index

GODELIER, Maurice
The mental and the material / by Maurice Godelier ; translated by Martin Thom. — London : Verso, 1986. — [280]p. — *Translation of: L'idéel et le matériel.* — Includes index

ECONOMIC ANTHROPOLOGY — Australia

TESTART, Alain
Le communisme primitif / Alain Testart. — Paris : Editions de la Maison des sciences de l'homme
1: Economie et idéologie. — 1985. — 548p. — Bibliography: p523-[536]

ECONOMIC ANTHROPOLOGY — Indonesia — Saroako

ROBINSON, Kathryn May
Stepchildren of progress : the political economy of development in an Indonesian mining town / Kathryn May Robinson. — Albany, N.Y. : State University of New York Press, c1986. — xvi, 315 p.. — (SUNY series in the anthropology of work). — : *Originally presented as the author's thesis (Ph.D.)--Australian National University, 1983.* — Includes index. — Bibliography: p. 295-307

ECONOMIC ANTHROPOLOGY — Papua New Guinea

SILLITOE, Paul
Give and take : exchange in Wola society / Paul Sillitoe. — New York : St. Martin's Press, 1979. — xiv, 316 p., [4] leaves of plates. — Includes index. — Bibliography: p. [303]-308

ECONOMIC ANTHROPOLOGY — Papua New Guinea — Goroka District

SEXTON, Lorraine
Mothers of money, daughters of coffee : the Wok Meri movement / by Lorraine Sexton. — Ann Arbor, Mich. : UMI Research Press, c1986. — p. cm. — (Studies in cultural anthropology ; no. 10). — : *Revision of thesis (Ph. D.)--Temple University, 1980.* — Includes index. — Bibliography: p

ECONOMIC ASSISTANCE

BIRD, Graham, 1947-
International financial policy and economic development : a disaggregated approach / Graham Bird. — Basingstoke : Macmillan, 1987. — xvi,348p. — Bibliography: p338-343. — Includes index

Die Entwicklungspolitik wichtiger OECD-Staaten : eine Untersuchungung der Systeme und ihrer aussenwirtschaftlichen Implikationen / hrsg. von Manfred Holthus und Dietrich Kebschull. — Hamburg : Verlag Weltarchiv. — (Veröffentlichungen des HWWA. Institut für Wirtschaftsforschung-Hamburg). — Includes bibliographies
Bd.1: Mit Länderbeiträgen über USA, Grossbritannien, Japan, Bundesrepublik Deutschland, Italien / Susanne Erbe...[et al.]. — 1985. — 749p

GORDENKER, Leon
Refugees in international politics / Leon Gordenker. — London : Croom Helm, c1987. — 227p. — (The Croom Helm United Nations and its agencies series). — Bibliography: p215-220. — Includes index

GREAT BRITAIN. Overseas Development Administration. Economic Planning Staff
Project handbook : small-scale enterprises. — [London] : the Adminstration, [1979]. — 10leaves. — Bibliography: leaf[10]

HÖLL, Otmar
Österreichische Entwicklungshilfe 1970-1983 : kritische Analyse und internationale Vergleich / Otmar Höll. — Wien : Braumuller, 1986. — 187p. — (Informationen zur Weltpolitik ; 7). — Bibliography: p183-187

ECONOMIC ASSISTANCE
continuation

The international law of development : basic documents / compiled and edited by A. Peter Mutharika. — Dobbs Ferry, N.Y. : Oceana
Vol.1. — 1978. — x,646p

The international law of development : basic documents / compiled and edited by A. Peter Mutharika. — Dobbs Ferry, N.Y. : Oceana
Vol.4. — 1979. — vii.1999-2620p

The international law of development : basic documents / compiled and edited by A. Peter Mutharika. — Dobbs Ferry, N.Y. : Oceana
Vol.5. — 1985. — xiii,708p

OPEC aid and the challenge of development / edited by Abdelkader Benamara and Sam Ifeagwu. — London : Croom Helm, c1987. — x,130p

PLATTEAU, J. P.
La fonction euphémisante et mystificatrice de làide / Jean-Philippe Platteau. — Namur : Facultés Notre-Dame de la Paix, 1986. — 60p. — (Cahiers de la Faculté des Sciences Economiques et Sociales de Namur. Serie recherche ; no.70). — *Bibliography: p58-60*

WOOD, Robert Everett
From Marshall Plan to debt crisis : foreign aid and development choices in the world economy / Robert E. Wood. — Berkeley : University of California Press, c1986. — p. cm. — (Studies in international political economy). — *Includes index.* — *Bibliography: p*

ECONOMIC ASSISTANCE — Dictionaries

The World Bank glossary = Glossaire de la Banque mondiale. — Washington, D.C. : The World Bank
V.1: English-French, French-English. — 1986. — 429p. — *In English and French*

The World Bank glossary = Glosario del Banco Mundial. — Washington, D.C. : The World Bank
V.2: English-Spanish, Spanish-English. — 1986. — v,360p. — *In English and Spanish*

ECONOMIC ASSISTANCE — Statistics

GREAT BRITAIN. overseas Development Administration. Statistics Division
OECD and multilateral aid : geographical distribution 1977-1982. — [London] : the Administration, 1984. — 135p. — *Produced from an OECD computer tape*

ECONOMIC ASSISTANCE — Developing countries

MOSLEY, Paul
Overseas aid : its defence and reform / Paul Mosley. — Brighton : Wheatsheaf, 1987. — [256]p. — (Studies in political economy ; 1). — *Includes bibliography and index*

ECONOMIC ASSISTANCE — Africa, Sub-Saharan

Financing adjustment with growth in Sub-Saharan Africa, 1986-90. — Washington, D.C. : The World Bank, 1986. — x,120p

INTERNATIONAL BANK FOR RECONSTRUCTION AND DEVELOPMENT
Financing adjustment with growth in sub-Saharan Africa, 1986-90. — Washington, D.C. : World Bank, c1986. — p. cm. — *Bibliography: p*

ECONOMIC ASSISTANCE — Bangladesh

RAHMAN, M. Akhlaqur
External assistance, saving and resource mobilization in Bangladesh / M. Akhlaqur Rahman, K. Mustahidur Rahman. — [Dacca] : External Resources Division, Ministry of Finance and Planning, [ca.1983]. — 95p. — *Bibliography: p94-95*

ECONOMIC ASSISTANCE — Developing countries

ADAMS, Patricia
In the name of progress : the underside of foreign aid / Patricia Adams and Lawrence Solomon. — Toronto, Canada : Energy Probe Research Foundation, 1985. — 229 p.. — ″An energy probe project.″. — *Includes index.* — *Bibliography: p. 168-214*

CASSEN, Robert
Does aid work? : report to an intergovernmental task force / Robert Cassen & associates. — Oxford : Clarendon, 1986. — [350]p. — (The Library of political economy)

Die Entwicklungspolitik wichtiger OECD-Staaten : eine Untersuchungung der Systeme und ihrer aussenwirtschaftlichen Implikationen / hrsg. von Manfred Holthus und Dietrich Kebschull. — Hamburg : Verlag Weltarchiv. — (Veröffentlichungen des HWWA. Institut für Wirtschaftsforschung-Hamburg). — *Includes bibliographies*
Bd.1: Mit Länderbeiträgen über USA, Grossbritannien, Japan, Bundesrepublik Deutschland, Italien / Susanne Erbe...[et al.]. — 1985. — 749p

MORSS, Elliott R
The future of Western development assistance / Elliott R. Morss, Victoria A. Morss. — Boulder : Westview Press, 1986. — xiii, 115 p.. — (Westview special studies in social, political, and economic development). — *Includes bibliographies and index*

RIDDELL, Roger
Foreign aid reconsidered / Roger C. Riddell. — Baltimore : The Johns Hopkins University Press ; London : Currey, 1987. — x,309p. — *Bibliography: p279-301.* — *Includes index*

Shared horizon : interviews with leaders of thought / [edited by] Altaf Gauhar. — London : Third World Foundation for Social and Economic Studies, c1985. — xxv,257p. — *Includes index*

SINGER, H. W.
Food aid : the challenge and the opportunity / Hans Singer, John Wood, Tony Jennings. — Oxford : Clarendon, 1987. — [256]p. — *Includes bibliography and index*

SOTTAS, Eric
The least developed countries : introduction to the LDCs and to the substantial new programme of action for them. — New York : United Nations, 1985. — ix,157p. — (Document ; TAD/INF/PUB/84.2). — *At head of title: United Nations Conference on Trade and Development, Geneva.* — *Bibliography: p157*

WOOD, Robert Everett
From Marshall Plan to debt crisis : foreign aid and development choices in the world economy / Robert E. Wood. — Berkeley : University of California Press, c1986. — p. cm. — (Studies in international political economy). — *Includes index.* — *Bibliography: p*

ECONOMIC ASSISTANCE — European Economic Community countries

SCHINA, Despina
State aids under the EEC treaty articles 92 to 94 / Despina Schina. — Oxford : ESC Publishing, 1987. — xviii, 221p. — (European competition law monographs). — *Bibliography: p.179-185. - Includes index*

ECONOMIC ASSISTANCE — Nepal

POUDYAL, Sriram
Impact of foreign aid on Nepal´s development / Sriram Poudyal. — Kathmandu : Tribhuvan University. Centre for Economic Development and Administration, 1983. — 58p. — *Bibliography: p[59]*

ECONOMIC ASSISTANCE — Rwanda

TABLE RONDE DES AIDES EXTÉRIEURES AU RWANDA (3ème : 1982 : Kigali)
[Report]. — Kigali : Ministère du Plan, [1983?]. — 326p

ECONOMIC ASSISTANCE, AMERICAN

JONES, Joseph Marion
The fifteen weeks : (February 21-June 5, 1947) / Joseph Marion Jones. — San Diego ; London : Harcourt Brace Jovanovich, c1955. — viii,296p

ECONOMIC ASSISTANCE, AMERICAN — Addresses, essays, lectures

The Origins of the cold war and contemporary Europe / edited with an introd. by Charles S. Maier. — New York : New Viewpoints, 1978. — xvi, 255 p.. — (Modern scholarship on European history). — *Includes index.* — *Bibliography: p. 245-248*

ECONOMIC ASSISTANCE, AMERICAN — Developing countries

GUESS, George M.
The politics of United States foreign aid / George M. Guess. — London : Croom Helm, c1987. — 297p. — *Bibliography: p273-289.* — *Includes index*

ECONOMIC ASSISTANCE, AMERICAN — Egypt

WEINBAUM, Marvin G.
Egypt and the politics of U.S. economic aid / Marvin G. Weinbaum. — Boulder ; London : Westview, 1986. — xii,192p. — *Bibliography: p183-187*

ECONOMIC ASSISTANCE, AMERICAN — Europe

WOOD, Robert Everett
From Marshall Plan to debt crisis : foreign aid and development choices in the world economy / Robert E. Wood. — Berkeley : University of California Press, c1986. — p. cm. — (Studies in international political economy). — *Includes index.* — *Bibliography: p*

ECONOMIC ASSISTANCE, AMERICAN — Europe — History

KINDLEBERGER, Charles P.
Marshall Plan days / Charles P. Kindleberger. — Boston ; London : Allen & Unwin, 1987. — [250]p. — *Includes bibliography and index*

ECONOMIC ASSISTANCE, AMERICAN — India

AGARWAL, Sushila
Super powers and the Third World / Sushila Agarwal. — Jaipur, India : Aalekh, 1985. — ii,151p

ECONOMIC ASSISTANCE, AMERICAN — Nepal

20 years of Nepalese-American cooperation : a summary of American aid to Nepal, 1951-1971. — [Kathmandu? : s.n., 1971?]. — 42p. — *Cover title*

ECONOMIC ASSISTANCE, AMERICAN — Vietnam

DACY, Douglas C.
Foreign aid, war, and economic development : South Vietnam, 1955-1975 / Dougxlas C. Dacy. — Cambridge : Cambridge University Press, 1986. — xix,300p. — *Bibliography: p283-293.* — *Includes index*

ECONOMIC ASSISTANCE, AUSTRALIAN — Developing countries

Australian overseas aid : future directions / edited by Philip Eldridge, Dean Forbes and Doug Porter. — Sydney ; London : Croom Helm, 1986. — xxix,284p. — *Bibliography: p265-284*

ECONOMIC ASSISTANCE, BRITISH

GREAT BRITAIN. Overseas Development Administration
United Kingdom memorandum to the Development Assistance Committee of the Organisation for Economic Cooperation and Development. — [London] : the Administration, 1979. — 13p

LESTOR, Joan
Beyond Band Aid : charity is not enough / Joan Lestor [and] David Ward. — London : Fabian Society, 1987. — 22 p. — (Fabian tract ; 520)

ECONOMIC ASSISTANCE, BRITISH — Administration
GREAT BRITAIN. Overseas Development Administration
Minister's seminar on aid procedures : Deputy Secretaries' working group. — [London : the Administration, ca.1979]. — 14p

ECONOMIC ASSISTANCE, BRITISH — Bibliography
GREAT BRITAIN. Ministry of Overseas Development. Library
British aid : a select bibliography. — 5th revised ed. — [London] ([Eland House, Stag Place, SW1E 5DH]) : [The Library], 1978. — [3],27p. — *Previous ed.: / issued by the Overseas Development Administration. 1974*

ECONOMIC ASSISTANCE, BRITISH — Evaluation
GREAT BRITAIN. Overseas Development Administration. Evaluation Unit
Guidelines for the preparation of evaluation studies. — London : the Unit, 1979. — 9,2p

ECONOMIC ASSISTANCE, BRITISH — Africa
ALL PARTY PARLIAMENTARY GROUP ON OVERSEAS DEVELOPMENT
UK aid to African agriculture : report of the Working Party established by the All Party Parliamentary Group on Overseas Development. — London : Overseas Development Institute, 1985. — 63p

ECONOMIC ASSISTANCE, CANADIAN
ALBERTA AGENCY FOR INTERNATIONAL DEVELOPMENT
Annual review / Alberta Agency for International Development. — Edmonton ; Edmonton : the Agency for International Development, 1985/86-. — *Annual*

ECONOMIC ASSISTANCE, CANADIAN — Bibliography
VANDERWAL, Andrew
Canadian development assistance : a selected bibliography 1978-1984 / Andrew Vanderwal ; edited by Rede Widstrand and Vivian Cummins. — Ottawa : Norman Paterson School of International Affairs, [1985]. — 39p. — (Bibliography series / Norman Paterson School of International Affairs ; 7)

ECONOMIC ASSISTANCE, CHINESE
The aid programme of China. — Paris : Organisation for Economic Co-operation and Development, 1987. — 28p. — *Bibliographical references: p28*

ECONOMIC ASSISTANCE, COMMUNIST — Grenada — History
PRYOR, Frederic L
Revolutionary Grenada : a study in political economy / Frederic L. Pryor. — New York : Praeger, 1986. — xx, 395 p.. — *Includes index. — Bibliography: p. 375-382*

ECONOMIC ASSISTANCE, DOMESTIC
LIPTON, Michael
Why poor people stay poor : urban bias in world development / Michael Lipton. — Cambridge : Harvard University Press, 1977, c1976. — 467 p.. — *Includes index. — Bibliography: p. 355-357*

MCCLAM, Warren D.
Adjustment performance of open economies : some international comparisons / by W. D. McClam and P. S. Andersen. — Basle : Bank for International Settlements, 1983. — 100p. — (BIS economic papers ; no.10)

ECONOMIC ASSISTANCE, DOMESTIC — India
HIRWAY, Indira
Abolition of poverty in India : with special reference to target group approach in Gujarat / Indira Hirway. — New Delhi : Vikas Pub. House, c1986. — vi, 284 p. [i.e. 184]. — *Includes bibliographies and index*

ECONOMIC ASSISTANCE, DOMESTIC — India — Congresses
Seventh Plan and development of weaker sections : questions, challenges, and alternatives / edited by Jose Kananaikil. — New Delhi : Indian Social Institute, c1985. — xv, 188 p.. — *Includes index. — Bibliography: p. [171]-186*

ECONOMIC ASSISTANCE, DOMESTIC — India — Chakrabhavi
HADIMANI, R. N
The politics of poverty / R.N. Hadimani. — New Delhi : Ashish, 1984. — xxi, 194 p.. — *Summary: Study of the factors responsible for restricting the efficient implementation of the anti-poverty programs; based on empirical data from a village in Bangalore District, Karnataka. — Includes index. — Bibliography: p. 185-189*

ECONOMIC ASSISTANCE, DOMESTIC — India — Gujarat
HIRWAY, Indira
Abolition of poverty in India : with special reference to target group approach in Gujarat / Indira Hirway. — New Delhi : Vikas Pub. House, c1986. — vi, 284 p. [i.e. 184]. — *Includes bibliographies and index*

ECONOMIC ASSISTANCE, DOMESTIC — United States
ZAREFSKY, David
President Johnson's war on poverty : rhetoric and history / David Zarefsky. — University, Ala. : University of Alabama Press, c1986. — xxiii, 275p. — *Includes index. — Bibliography: p 256-266*

ECONOMIC ASSISTANCE, NORWEGIAN
Human rights in developing countries : a yearbook on countries receiving Norwegian aid. — Oslo : Norwegian University Press, 1986-. — *Annual*

ECONOMIC ASSISTANCE, RUSSIAN — India
AGARWAL, Sushila
Super powers and the Third World / Sushila Agarwal. — Jaipur, India : Aalekh, 1985. — ii,151p

ECONOMIC COMMUNITY OF WEST AFRICAN STATES — History
ASANTE, S. K. B
The political economy of regionalism in Africa : a decade of the Economic Community of West African States (ECOWAS) / S.K.B. Asante. — New York : Praeger, 1985. — p. cm. — *Includes index. — Bibliography: p*

ECONOMIC CONDITIONS — Burkina Faso — Statistics
Statistiques Sociales. — Ouagadougou : Institut National de la Statistique et de la Démographie, 1984. — 108p

ECONOMIC COOPERATION
The international law of development : basic documents / compiled and edited by A. Peter Mutharika. — Dobbs Ferry, N.Y. : Oceana Vol.3. — 1979. — vii,1305-1997p

ECONOMIC DEVELOPMENT
AHN, Chung-si
Social development and political violence : a cross-national causal analysis / by Chung-si Ahn. — [Seoul?] : Seoul National University Press, c1981. — xviii, 191 p. — (International studies series ; no. 3). — *Includes indexes. — Bibliography: p. [175]-182*

Anthropological contributions to planned change and development / edited by Harald O. Skar. — Göteborg, Sweden : Acta Universitatis Gothoburgensis, 1985. — iv, 191 p.. — (Gothenburg studies in social anthropology ; 8) . — *Includes bibliographies*

BOOTH, Douglas E
Regional long waves, uneven growth, and the cooperative alternative / Douglas E. Booth. — New York : Praeger, 1987. — 121 p.. — *Includes index. — Bibliography: p. 109-115*

BRUNO, Michael
Economics of worldwide stagflation / Michael Bruno and Jeffrey D. Sachs. — Cambridge, Mass. : Harvard University Press, 1985. — 315p. — *Includes index. — Bibliography: p.[297]-310*

BRYDEN, John
Tourism and development : a case study of the Commonwealth Caribbean / John M. Bryden. — London : Cambridge University Press, 1973. — xii,236p. — *Bibliographyp.222-227. — Includes index*

CHENERY, Hollis Burnley
Industrialization and growth : a comparative study / Hollis Chenery, Sherman Robinson, Moshe Syrquin. — New York : Published for the World Bank [by] Oxford University Press, c1986. — x,387p. — *Bibliographical references: p361-377. — Bibliography: p*

CLAUSEN, A. W.
Population growth and economic and social development : addresses / by A. W. Clausen. — Washington, D.C. : World Bank, 1984. — 36p. — *Contents: Address to the National Leader's Seminar on Population and Development, Nairobi, Kenya, July 11, 1984 - Address to the International Population Conference, Mexico City, August 7, 1984*

Development, democracy, and the art of trespassing : essays in honor of Albert O. Hirschman / edited by Alejandro Foxley, Michael S. McPherson, and Guillermo O'Donnell. — Notre Dame, Ind. : Published for the Helen Kellogg Institute for International Studies by University of Notre Dame Press, c1986. — vii, 379 p.. — *Bibliography: p. 375-379*

Development is for people / edited by Jan K. Coetzee. — Braamfontein : Macmillan, 1986. — 253p. — *Bibliography: p241-250*

Development policies and the crisis of the 1980s / edited by Louis Emmerij. — Paris : OECD, 1987. — 178p. — (Development Centre seminars). — *Includes bibliographies. — Contents: papers delivered at a seminar on "Alternative Development Strategies in the Light of Recent Experience", January,1987*

Economic progress : proceedings of a conference held by the International Economic Association at Santa Margherita Ligure, Italy. — 2nd ed. / edited by Austin Robinson. — London : Macmillan, 1986. — [580]p. — *Previous ed.: Louvain : Institut de recherches économiques et sociales, 1955. — Includes index*

Ethnicity, politics, and development / edited by Dennis L. Thompson and Dev Ronen. — Boulder, Colo. : L. Rienner, c1985. — p. cm. — *Includes index. — Bibliography: p*

GHARAJEDAGHI, Jamshid
A prologue to national development planning / Jamshid Gharajedaghi, in collaboration with Russell L. Ackoff. — New York : Greenwood Press, 1986. — xiii, 210 p.. — (Contributions in economics and economic history ; no. 70). — *Includes index. — Bibliography: p. [201]-204*

GOULET, Denis
Three rationalities in development decisions / Denis Goulet. — Budapest : Institute for World Economics of the Hungarian Academy of Sciences, 1986. — 25p. — (Studies on developing countries ; no.122)

Growth and distribution : intergenerational problems / edited by Villy Bergström, Seppo Honkapohja and Jan Södersten. — Oxford : Basil Blackwell in cooperation with Scandinavian Journal of Economics, 1986. — 340p. — (Topics in contemporary economic analysis). — *Includes bibliographies and index*

GUHA, Amalendu
Development alternative / Amalendu Guha, Franklin Vivekananda. — Stockholm : Bethany Books for Institute for Alternative Development Research, 1985. — 328p

ECONOMIC DEVELOPMENT
continuation

HERSHLAG, Z. Y.
The philosophy of development revisited / by Z.Y. Hershlag. — Leiden : Brill, 1984. — x, 130p. — *Bibliography: p.112-121*

HOSELITZ, Berthold Frank
Sociological aspects of economic growth / Berthold Frank Hoselitz. — Glencoe, Ill. : Free Press, [1960]. — vii,250p

The insurance industry in economic development / Bernard Wasow and Raymond D. Hill, editors. — New York : New York University Press, c1986. — p. cm. — *Includes bibliographies and index*

International development policies : review of the activities of international organisations / Commonwealth Secretariat. — London : Commonwealth Secretariat, 1983. — *Quarterly*

The international law of development : basic documents / compiled and edited by A. Peter Mutharika. — Dobbs Ferry, N.Y. : Oceana
Vol.1. — 1978. — x,646p

The international law of development : basic documents / compiled and edited by A. Peter Mutharika. — Dobbs Ferry, N.Y. : Oceana
Vol.2. — 1978. — vii,647-1303p

The international law of development : basic documents / compiled and edited by A. Peter Mutharika. — Dobbs Ferry, N.Y. : Oceana
Vol.3. — 1979. — vii,1305-1997p

The international law of development : basic documents / compiled and edited by A. Peter Mutharika. — Dobbs Ferry, N.Y. : Oceana
Vol.4. — 1979. — vii.1999-2620p

The international law of development : basic documents / compiled and edited by A. Peter Mutharika. — Dobbs Ferry, N.Y. : Oceana
Vol.5. — 1985. — xiii,708p

KOHR, Leopold
The breakdown of nations / Leopold Kohr ; foreword by Ivan Illich. — London : Routledge & Kegan Paul, 1986. — xxvi,244p. — *First published 1957. — Bibliography: p235-237*

LAROUCHE, Lyndon H.
There are no limits to growth / Lyndon H. LaRouche. — New York : New Benjamin Franklin House, 1983. — xix,225p

LAVOIE, Don
National economic planning : what is left? / Don Lavoie. — Cambridge, Mass. : Ballinger Pub. Co., c1985. — xii, 291 p. — *Includes index. — Bibliography: p. 267-279*

The living economy : a new economics in the making / edited by Paul Ekins. — London : Routledge and Kegan Paul, 1986. — xviii,398p. — *Bibliography: p379-390*

Machinery and economic development / edited by Martin Fransman. — Basingstoke : Macmillan, 1986. — xvii,274p. — *Includes bibliographies and index*

MANLEY, Michael
Up the down escalator : development and the international economy : a Jamaican case study / Michael Manley. — London : Andre Deutsch, 1987. — xv,332p

MAUNDER, W. J., 1932-
The uncertainty business : risks and opportunities in weather and climate / W.J. Maunder ; with a foreword by John R. Mather. — London : Methuen, 1986. — xxviii,420p. — *Bibliography: p361-403. — Includes indexes*

MICHAÏLOF, Serge
Les apprentis sorciers du développement / Serge Michaïlof. — Paris : ACCT, 1984. — 266p. — *Bibliography: p255-262*

MORSS, Elliott R
The future of Western development assistance / Elliott R. Morss, Victoria A. Morss. — Boulder : Westview Press, 1986. — xiii, 115 p.. — (Westview special studies in social, political, and economic development). — *Includes bibliographies and index*

MUÑOZ MARÍN, Luis
The will to develop : address...before the Sixth World Conference of the Society for International Development / Luis Muñoz Marín. — [San Juan : Government Development Bank for Puerto Rico, ca.1964]. — 10p. — *Address delivered by Sr. Muñoz Marín's representative, Dr. Rafael Pico*

NAFZIGER, E. Wayne
Entrepreneurship, equity, and economic development / by E. Wayne Nafziger. — Greenwich, Conn. : JAI Press, c1986. — p. cm. — (Contemporary studies in economic and financial analysis ; v. 53). — *Includes index. — Bibliography: p*

NERLOVE, Marc
Household and economy : welfare economics of endogenous fertility / Marc Nerlove, Assaf Razin, Efraim Sadka. — Boston : Academic Press, 1987. — xiii, 155 p.. — (Economic theory, econometrics, and mathematical economics). — *Includes bibliographies and indexes*

NJOKU, John E. Eberegbulam
Malthusianism, an African dilemma : hunger, drought, and starvation in Africa / by John E. Eberegbulam Njoku. — Metuchen, N.J. : Scarecrow Press, 1986. — xxix, 181 p.. — *Bibliography: p. [163]-181*

OCRAN, Tawia Modibo
Law in aid of development : issues in legal theory, institution building, and economic development in Africa / Tawia Modibo Ocran. — Tema, Ghana : Ghana Pub. Corp., 1978. — xii, 247 p.. — *Includes bibliographical references*

PRESTON, P. W.
Making sense of development : an introduction to classical and contemporary theories of development and their application to Southeast Asia / P. W. Preston. — London : Routledge & Kegan Paul, 1986. — 319 p

RIDDLE, Dorothy I
Service-led growth : the role of the service sector in world development / Dorothy I. Riddle. — New York : Praeger, 1985. — p. cm. — *Includes index. — Bibliography: p*

SILVERMAN, Jerry M.
Action-planning workshops for development management : guidelines / Jerry M. Silverman, Merlyn Kettering and Terry D. Schmidt. — Washington, D.C. : The World Bank, 1986. — ix,74p. — (World Bank technical paper ; no.56). — *Bibliography: p49-54*

STEIDLMEIER, Paul
The paradox of poverty : a reappraisal of economic development policy / Paul Steidlmeier. — Cambridge, Mass. : Ballinger, 1987. — p. cm. — *Includes bibliographies and index*

Surveys in development economics / edited by Norman Gemmell. — Oxford : Basil Blackwell, 1987. — [500]p

SZENTES, Tamás
Une interpretation restreinte du dualisme dans les theories du sous-développement / Tamás Szentes. — Budapest : Centre pour la Recherche de l'Afro-Asie de l'Académie des Sciences de Hongrie, 1971. — 17p. — (Etudes sur les pays en voie de developpement ; no.45)

TODARO, Michael P
Economic development in the Third World / Michael P. Todaro. — 3rd ed. — New York : Longman, c1985. — xxxvi, 648 p.. — *Includes index. — Bibliography: p. 613-640*

TOYE, John
Dilemmas of development : reflections on the counter-revolution in development theory and policy / John Toye. — Oxford : Basil Blackwell, 1987. — [224]p. — *Includes bibliography and index*

WEITZ, Ranaan
New roads to development / Raanan Weitz ; foreword by M.J. Rossant. — Westport, Conn. : Greenwood Press, c1986. — p. cm. — (Contributions in economics and economic history ; no. 64). — *"A Twentieth Century Fund essay.". — Includes index. — Bibliography: p*

WOOD, Robert Everett
From Marshall Plan to debt crisis : foreign aid and development choices in the world economy / Robert E. Wood. — Berkeley : University of California Press, c1986. — p. cm. — (Studies in international political economy). — *Includes index. — Bibliography: p*

ECONOMIC DEVELOPMENT — Addresses, essays, lectures

Industrialization and development : a Third World perspective / Pradip K. Ghosh, editor ; foreword by Subbiah Kannappan. — Westport, Conn. : Greenwood Press, c1984. — xxviii, 566 p.. — (International development resource books ; no. 1). — *"Prepared under the auspices of the Center for Advanced Study of International Development, Michigan State University.". — Includes indexes. — Bibliography: p. [381]-516*

Pioneers in development / edited by Gerald M. Meier and Dudley Seers. — New York : OUP for the World Bank, 1985. — x,372p. — *Included bibliographical references*

The Political economy of international technology transfer / edited by John R. McIntyre and Daniel S. Papp. — Westport, Conn. : Quorum Books, c1986. — p. cm. — *Includes index. — Bibliography: p*

ECONOMIC DEVELOPMENT — Case studies

GOODELL, Grace E
The elementary structures of political life : rural development in Pahlavi Iran / Grace E. Goodell. — New York : Oxford University Press, 1986. — vii, 362 p.. — *Includes index. — Bibliography: p. 345-350*

ROY, Ramashray
Dialogues on development : individuals, society, and the political order / Ramashray Roy and R.K. Srivastava. — New Delhi ; Beverly Hills : Sage Publications, 1985. — p. cm

ECONOMIC DEVELOPMENT — Congresses

IFAC/IFORS CONFERENCE ON SYSTEMS APPROACHES TO DEVELOPING COUNTRIES (1973 : Algiers)
Systems approaches to developing countries : proceedings / Edited by M. A. Cuenod [and] S. Kahne. — Pittsburgh : Distributed by Instrument Society of America, [1973]. — ix, 515 p. — *"A publication of the International Federation of Automatic Control.". — English or French. — Includes bibliographical references*

ECONOMIC DEVELOPMENT — Dictionaries

The World Bank glossary = Glossaire de la Banque mondiale. — Washington, D.C. : The World Bank
V.1: English-French, French-English. — 1986. — 429p. — *In English and French*

The World Bank glossary = Glosario del Banco Mundial. — Washington, D.C. : The World Bank
V.2: English-Spanish, Spanish-English. — 1986. — v,360p. — *In English and Spanish*

ECONOMIC DEVELOPMENT — Effect of education on
PSACHAROPOULOS, George
Education for development : an analysis of investment choices / George Psacharopoulos, Maureen Woodhall. — New York : OUP for the World Bank, 1985. — ix,337p. — *Includes bibliographical references*

ECONOMIC DEVELOPMENT — Effect of education on — Congresses
The Quality of education and economic development / edited by Stephen P. Heyneman, Daphne Siev White. — Washington, D.C., U.S.A. : World Bank, 1986. — xi,59p. — (A World Bank symposium). — *"The papers were originally prepared for a conference on school quality sponsored by the World Bank's Research Committee and held in Harper's Ferry, West Virginia, in May 1983"--Foreword.* — *Bibliography: p57-59*

ECONOMIC DEVELOPMENT — Environmental aspects
LUTEN, Daniel B
Progress against growth : Daniel B. Luten on the American landscape / edited by Thomas R. Vale ; introduction by Garrett Hardin ; drawings by Faye Field ; figures by Adrienne Morgan. — New York : Gilford Press, c1986. — p. cm. — *Includes index.* — *Bibliography: p*

WORLD COMMISSION ON ENVIRONMENT AND DEVELOPMENT
Our common future / World Commission on Environment and Development. — Oxford : Oxford University Press, 1987. — [320]p

ECONOMIC DEVELOPMENT — Mathematical models
The Globus model : computer simulation of worldwide political and economic developments / edited by Stuart A. Bremer. — Boulder : Westview Press, 1986. — p. cm. — *Includes index.* — *Bibliography: p*

NERLOVE, Marc
Population policy and individual choice : a theoretical investigation / Marc Nerlove, Assaf Razin, and Efraim Sadka. — Washington, D.C. : International Food Policy Research Institute, 1987. — p. cm. — (Research report / International Food Policy Research Institute ; 60). *"June 1987."*. — *Bibliography: p*

ECONOMIC DEVELOPMENT — Religious aspects
VON DER MEHDEN, Fred R
Religion and modernization in Southeast Asia / Fred R. von der Mehden. — 1st ed. — Syracuse, N.Y. : Syracuse University Press, c1986. — viii, 240 p. — *Includes index.* — *Bibliography: p. 225-233*

ECONOMIC DEVELOPMENT — Research
ORGANISATION FOR ECONOMIC CO-OPERATION AND DEVELOPMENT. Development Centre
Programme of research, 1987-1989. — Paris : OECD Development Centre, 1987. — 77p

ECONOMIC DEVELOPMENT — Social aspects
Global restructuring and territorial development / edited by Jeffrey Henderson and Manuel Castells. — London : Sage, 1987. — 272p. — *Includes index*

ROSS, David P
From the roots up : economic development as if community mattered / David P. Ross and Peter J. Usher ; with a foreword by George McRobie. — Croton-on-Hudson, N.Y. : Bootstrap Press, c1986. — xviii, 173 p.. — *Bibliography: p. 167-172*

ECONOMIC DEVELOPMENT — Social aspects — Addresses, essays, lectures
Essays on economic development and cultural change in honor of Bert F. Hoselitz / Manning Nash, editor. — [Chicago : University of Chicago Press], 1977. — vi,460p. — (Economic development and cultural change ; v.25. Supplement)

ECONOMIC DEVELOPMENT — Social aspects — Developing countries — Case studies — Congresses
Social accounting matrices : a basis for planning / edited by Graham Pyatt and Jeffery I. Round. — Washington, D.C., U.S.A. : World Bank, 1985. — p. cm. — *Bibliography: p*

ECONOMIC DEVELOPMENT — Statistics
Industry and development: global report / United Nations Industrial Development Organization. — Vienna : United Nations Industrial Development Organisation, 1985-. — *Annual*

ECONOMIC DEVELOPMENT — Caribbean Area
HOPE, Kempe R
Urbanization in the Commonwealth Caribbean / Kempe Ronald Hope. — Boulder, Colo. : Westview Press, 1986. — p. cm. — (Westview special studies on Latin America and the Caribbean). — *Includes index.* — *Bibliography: p*

ECONOMIC DEVELOPMENT — India
MILLS, Edwin S.
Studies in Indian urban development / Edwin S. Mills, Charles M. Becker. — New York : OUP for the World Bank, 1986. — viii,214p. — *Includes bibliographical references*

ECONOMIC DEVELOPMENT PROJECTS
CLAUSEN, A. W
The development challenge of the eighties : A.W. Clausen at the World Bank : major policy addresses, 1981-1986. — Washington, D.C., U.S.A. : The Bank, 1986. — p. cm

CLAUSEN, A. W.
The development challenge of the eighties : A. W. Clausen at the World Bank : major policy addresses, 1981-1986 / A. W. Clausen. — Washington, D.C. : The World Bank, 1986. — xxvii,496p. — *Contents: Addresses to various bodies by A. W. Clausen, ex-President of the World Bank*

ECONOMIC DEVELOPMENT PROJECTS — Environmental aspects
Environmental assessment and development assistance. — [Paris] : Environment Directorate, Organisation for Economic Co-operation and Development, 1986. — 103p. — (OECD environment monographs ; no.4). — *Bibliographical references: p52-53*

ECONOMIC DEVELOPMENT PROJECTS — Evaluation
Annual review of project performance audit results. — Washington, DC : World Bank, 1982-1983

DUVIGNEAU, J. Christian
Guidelines for calculating financial amd economic rates of return for DFC projects / J. Christian Duvigneau and Ranga N. Prasad. — Washington, D.C. : The World Bank, 1984. — xii,149p. — (World Bank technical paper ; no.33) (Industry and finance series ; v.9). — *Bibliography: p148-149*

ENGLISH, J. Morley
Project evaluation : a unified approach for the analysis of capital investments / J. Morley English. — New York : Macmillan, c1984. — p. cm. — *Bibliography: p*

ECONOMIC DEVELOPMENT PROJECTS — Evaluation — Bibliography
LEISTRITZ, Larry
Social impact assessment and management : an annotated bibliography / Larry Leistritz and Brenda L. Ekstrom ; with Robert A. Chase, Ronald Bisset, and John M. Halstead. — New York : Garland Pub., 1986. — xxiii, 343 p.. — (Garland reference library of social science ; vol. 205Applied social science bibliographies ; vol. 3). — *Includes indexes*

ECONOMIC DEVELOPMENT PROJECTS — Finance
Disbursement handbook. — Washington D. C. : The World Bank, 1986. — iv,58p

ECONOMIC DEVELOPMENT PROJECTS — Finance — Kenya
Guidelines for the preparation, appraisal and approval of new public sector investment projects. — Nairobi : Ministry of Economic Planning and Development, 1983. — 49p

ECONOMIC DEVELOPMENT PROJECTS — Social aspects — Bibliography
LEISTRITZ, Larry
Social impact assessment and management : an annotated bibliography / Larry Leistritz and Brenda L. Ekstrom ; with Robert A. Chase, Ronald Bisset, and John M. Halstead. — New York : Garland Pub., 1986. — xxiii, 343 p.. — (Garland reference library of social science ; vol. 205Applied social science bibliographies ; vol. 3). — *Includes indexes*

ECONOMIC DEVELOPMENT PROJECTS — Asia
Fertility in Asia : assessing the impact of development projects / edited by John Stoeckel and Anrudh K. Jain. — London : Pinter, 1986. — xix,177p. — *Includes bibliographies and index*

ECONOMIC DEVELOPMENT PROJECTS — Bolivia — La Paz — Evaluation
SALMEN, Lawrence F.
Listen to the people : participant-observer evaluation of development projects / Lawrence F. Salmen. — New York : Oxford University Press for the World Bank, 1987. — x,149p. — *Bibliography: p140-144*

ECONOMIC DEVELOPMENT PROJECTS — Caribbean area
Integrating women into development programs : a guide for implementation for Latin America and the Caribbean / by Karen White...[et al.] ; tables prepared by Roxana Moayedi. — Washington, D.C. : International Centre for Research on Women, 1986. — iv,87p. — *Prepared for the Bureau for Latin America and the Caribbean, U.S. Agency for International Development*

ECONOMIC DEVELOPMENT PROJECTS — Developing countries
Fund-supported programs, fiscal policy, and income distribution : a study / by the Fiscal Affairs Department of the International Monetary Fund. — Washington, D.C. : International Monetary Fund, 1986. — v,58p. — (Occasional paper / International Monetary Fund ; no.46). — *Bibliographical references: p54-58*

HEAVER, Richard
Country commitment to development projects / Richard Heaver, Arturo Israel. — Washington, D.C. : The World Bank, 1986. — 32p. — (World Bank discussion papers ; no.4). — *Includes bibliographical references*

MASON, Edward Sagendorph
The Harvard Institute for International Development and its antecedents / Edward S. Mason. — [Cambridge, Mass.] : Harvard Institute for International Development, Harvard University ; Lanham, MD : University Press of America, c1986. — x, 97 p.. — *Bibliography: p. 74-78*

ECONOMIC DEVELOPMENT PROJECTS — Developing countries — Citizen participation
PAUL, Samuel
Community participation in development projects : the World Bank experience / Samuel Paul. — Washington, D.C. : The World Bank, 1987. — 37p. — (World Bank discussion papers ; no.6). — *Includes bibliographical references*

ECONOMIC DEVELOPMENT PROJECTS — Developing countries — Evaluation

SALMEN, Lawrence F.
Listen to the people : participant-observer evaluation of development projects / Lawrence F. Salmen. — New York : Oxford University Press for the World Bank, 1987. — x,149p. — *Bibliography: p140-144*

ECONOMIC DEVELOPMENT PROJECTS — Ecuador — Guayaquil — Evaluation

SALMEN, Lawrence F.
Listen to the people : participant-observer evaluation of development projects / Lawrence F. Salmen. — New York : Oxford University Press for the World Bank, 1987. — x,149p. — *Bibliography: p140-144*

ECONOMIC DEVELOPMENT PROJECTS — Egypt

NIEUWENHUIJZE, C. A. O. van
The poor man's model of development : development potential at low levels of living in Egypt / by C. A. O. van Nieuwenhuijze, M. Fathalla al-Khatib, Adel Azer. — Leiden : E. J. Brill, 1985. — viii,206p. — (Social, economic and political studies of the Middle East ; 40)

ECONOMIC DEVELOPMENT PROJECTS — European Economic Community countries

Aims and priorities of a common research and development policy : study. — Brussels : Economic and Social Committee, 1982. — 2,59p. — *At head of title: 'Economic and Social Committee of the European Communities'*

ECONOMIC DEVELOPMENT PROJECTS — Latin America

Integrating women into development programs : a guide for implementation for Latin America and the Caribbean / by Karen White...[et al.] ; tables prepared by Roxana Moayedi. — Washington, D.C. : International Centre for Research on Women, 1986. — iv,87p. — *Prepared for the Bureau for Latin America and the Caribbean, U.S. Agency for International Development*

ECONOMIC DEVELOPMENT PROJECTS — Saint Kitts-Nevis

St. Christopher and Nevis : economic report. — Washington, D.C., U.S.A. : World Bank, 1985. — xii,82p. — (World Bank country study)

ECONOMIC DEVELOPMENTECONOMIC DEVELOPMENT — Social aspects

Development is for people / edited by Jan K. Coetzee. — Braamfontein : Macmillan, 1986. — 253p. — *Bibliography: p241-250*

ECONOMIC FORECASTING

Judgmental forecasting / edited by George Wright and Peter Ayton. — Chichester : Wiley, c1987. — ix,293p. — *Includes bibliographies and index*

ROYAL SOCIETY. Symposium (1986 : [London?])
Predictability in science and society : a joint symposium of the Royal Society and the British Academy held on 20 and 21 March 1986 / organized and edited by John Mason, P. Mathias, and J. H. Westcott. — London : Royal Society : British Academy, 1986. — viii,145p. — *Includes bibliographies*

ECONOMIC FORECASTING — Computer programs

RICHARDSON, Pete
Recent developments in OECD's international macroeconomic model / by Pete Richardson. — [Paris] : OECD, 1987. — iv,31p. — (Working papers / OECD Department of Economics and Statistics ; no.46). — *Bibliographical references:p30-31*

RICHARDSON, Pete
A review of the simulation properties of OECD's INTERLINK model / by Pete Richardson. — [Paris] : OECD, 1987. — iv,67p. — (Working papers / OECD Department of Economics and Statistics ; no.47). — *Bibliographical references: p55*

ECONOMIC FORECASTING — Mathematical models

Catastrophe or new society? : a Latin American world model / Amílcar O. Herrera ... [et al.]. — Ottawa : International Development Research Centre, c1976. — 108 p.. — *"IDRC-064e."*. — *Includes bibliographical references*

ECONOMIC FORECASTING — Bahamas

The Bahamas : economic report. — Washington, D.C. : World Bank, 1986. — [xiv],117p. — (A World Bank country study)

ECONOMIC FORECASTING — Great Britain

GREAT BRITAIN. Parliament. House of Commons. Library. Research Division
The April 1979 Budget - forcasts made for the Budget debate using the Treasury model / [Liz Spilsbury, Christopher Barclay]. — [London] : the Division, [1979]. — 21p. — (Background paper ; 69)

GREAT BRITAIN. Parliament. House of Commons. Library. Research Division
Economic forecasts and the March 1980 budget / Christopher Barclay. — [London] : the Division, 1980. — 22p. — (Background paper ; no.78)

GREAT BRITAIN. Parliament. House of Commons. Library. Research Division
Economic forecasts and the March 1981 budget / Christopher Barclay, Paul Hutt. — [London] : the Division, 1981. — 41p. — (Background paper ; no.89)

GREAT BRITAIN. Parliament. House of Commons. Library. Research Division
Economic forecasts and the March 1983 budget / Christopher Barclay. — [London] : the Division, 1983. — 18p. — (Background paper ; no.113)

ECONOMIC FORECASTING — Great Britain — Simulation methods

GREAT BRITAIN. Parliament. House of Commons. Library. Research Division
Ready reckoners on the Treasury Model / Christopher Barclay. — [London] : the Division, 1981. — 26 leaves. — (Background paper ; no.95)

GREAT BRITAIN. Parliament. House of Commons. Library. Research Division
Ready reckoners on the Treasury Model / Christopher Barclay. — [London] : the Division, 1982. — 39p. — (Background paper ; no.108). — *Updates Background Paper no.95*

GREAT BRITAIN. Parliament. House of Commons. Library. Research Division
Ready reckoners on the Treasury Model / Christopher Barclay. — [London] : the Division, 1984. — 21p. — (Background paper ; no.157)

ECONOMIC FORECASTING — Hong Kong

Long-term economic and agricultural commodity projections for Hong Kong, 1970, 1975, and 1980. — Jerusalem : Publications Services Division of the Israel Program for Scientific Translations for the U.S. Department of Agriculture, 1969. — iv,248p. — *Contents: A contract study...for the United States Department of Agriculture under the principal research directorship of Anthony M. Tang*

ECONOMIC FORECASTING — Netherlands

WETENSCHAPPELIJKE RAAD VOOR HET REGERINGSBELEID
A policy-oriented survey of the future : towards a better perspective : summary of the twenty-fifth report to the government. — The Hague : Netherlands Scientific Council for Government Policy, [1983?]. — 80p. — *English translation of: Beleidsgerichte toekomstverkenning: een verruiming van perspectief.* — *Bibliography: p76-80*

ECONOMIC FORECASTING — New Zealand

SEMINAR ON ECONOMIC MODELLING IN NEW ZEALAND (1984 : Wellington)
Economic modelling in New Zealand : proceedings of a seminar sponsored by the New Zealand Planning Council, Wellington, December 1984 / edited by Brian Silverstone and Graeme Wells. — Wellington : New Zealand Planning Council, 1986. — viii,131p. — *Includes bibliographical references*

Towards 1995 : patterns of national and sectoral development. — Wellington : New Zealand Planning Council, 1986. — ii,86p. — (Planning paper / New Zealand Planning Council ; no.26). — *Includes bibliographical references*

ECONOMIC FORECASTING — Soviet Union

Planovoe upravlenie ekonomikoi razvitogo sotsializma / redaktsionnaia kollegiia: A. S. Emel'ianov...[et al.]. — Kiev : Naukova dumka . — *V piati tomakh*
T.4: Nauchno-metodicheskie osnovy planirovaniia i prognozirovaniia razvitiia ekonomiki / otv. redaktor V. F. Besedin. — 1986. — 322p. — *Bibliography: p318-[323]*

ECONOMIC FORECASTING — Spain — Catalonia

GIBERNAU, J. A
L'any 2000, un repte per a Catalunya / J.A. Gibernau ; pròleg Ramon Vila-Abadal. — 1a ed. — Barcelona : El Llamp, c1982. — 157 p.. — (Col·lecció "La Rella")

ECONOMIC FORECASTING — Thailand

INTERNATIONAL BANK FOR RECONSTRUCTION AND DEVELOPMENT
Thailand : managing public resources for structural adjustment. — Washington, D.C., U.S.A. : World Bank, c1984. — Lxviii,275p. — (A World Bank country study). — *Summaries in English, French, and Spanish*. — *Includes bibliographical references*

ECONOMIC HISTORY

ASHWORTH, William, 1920-
A short history of the international economy since 1850 / William Ashworth. — 4th ed. — London : Longman, 1987. — [304]p. — *Previous ed.: 1975*. — *Includes index*

MONTBRIAL, Thierry de
La revanche de l'histoire / Thierry de Montbrial. — Paris : Julliard, c1985. — 197p. — (Commentaire Julliard)

ECONOMIC HISTORY — Congresses

INTERNATIONAL ECONOMIC HISTORY CONGRESS (9th : 1986 : Bern)
Ninth International Economic History Congress, Bern 1986 : debates and controversies / [Autoren: I. T. Berend...[et al.]]. — Zürich : Verlag der Fachvereine, 1986. — vii,179p. — *Includes one chapter in French*

Trade in transit : world trade and world economy--past, present, and future / edited by Hans Visser, Evert Schoorl. — Dordrecht ; Boston : Kluwer Academic Publishers, 1987. — xvii, 338 p.. — *Based on papers presented at the World Trade Conference 1985, organized by the World Trade Center Amsterdam, the University of Amsterdam, and the Free University at Amsterdam, held in Amsterdam, Sept. 4-6, 1985*. — *Includes bibliographies*

ECONOMIC HISTORY — 1600-1750
EKELUND, Robert B
Mercantilism as a rent-seeking society : economic regulation in historical perspective / by Robert B. Ekelund and Robert D. Tollison. — 1st ed. — College Station, Tex. : Texas A&M University Press, 1981. — xiii, 169 p.. — (Texas A & M University economics series ; no. 5). — Includes index. — Bibliography: p. [157]-164

ECONOMIC HISTORY — 1750-1918
NEUBAUER, Gyula
A világgazdaság válaszúton : a budapesti szabadegyetemen tartott tíz elöadás / Neubauer Gyula. — Budapest : Toldi Lajos bizománya, 1943. — 371p. — A series of ten lectures held at the Open University of Budapest in the autumn of 1942

POLANYI, Karl
The great transformation / Karl Polanyi ; foreword by Robert M. MacIver. — Boston : Beacon Press, 1957. — xii,315p

ECONOMIC HISTORY — 19th century
NEUBAUER, Gyula
A világgazdaság válaszúton : a budapesti szabadegyetemen tartott tíz elöadás / Neubauer Gyula. — Budapest : Toldi Lajos bizománya, 1943. — 371p. — A series of ten lectures held at the Open University of Budapest in the autumn of 1942

ECONOMIC HISTORY — 20th century
Economic statistics 1900-1983 : United Kingdom, United States of America, France, Germany, Italy, Japan / compiled and written by Thelma Liesner. — London : Economist Publications, c1985. — ix,142p. — Includes index

NEUBAUER, Gyula
A világgazdaság válaszúton : a budapesti szabadegyetemen tartott tíz elöadás / Neubauer Gyula. — Budapest : Toldi Lajos bizománya, 1943. — 371p. — A series of ten lectures held at the Open University of Budapest in the autumn of 1942

ECONOMIC HISTORY — 20th century — Environmental aspects
DUMONT, René
Les raisons de la colère, ou L'utopie et les Verts / René Dumont ; avec Charlotte Paquet. — Paris : Éditions Entente, 1986. — 137p. — Bibliography: p135-137

ECONOMIC HISTORY — 1918-1945
KINDLEBERGER, Charles P.
The world in depression 1929-1939 / Charles P. Kindleberger. — Harmondsworth : Penguin, 1987. — 355p. — Bibliography: p307-332

MATTHEWS, K. G. P.
The inter-war economy : an equilibrium analysis / K.G.P. Matthews. — Aldershot : Gower, c1986. — xiv,244p. — Bibliography: p235-244

NEWELL, A.
Wages and employment between the wars / A. Newell and J. S. V. Symons. — London : Centre for Labour Economics, London School of Economics, 1986. — 36p. — (Discussion paper / London School of Economics and Political Science. Centre for Labour Economics ; no.257)

ECONOMIC HISTORY — 1945-1971
The Third World and the world economic system / V.R. Panchamukhi ... [et al.]. — New Delhi : Radiant Publishers ; Atlantic Highlands, N.J. : Distributed in the U.S.A. by Humanities Press, 1986. — viii, 309 p.. — Includes bibliographies

ECONOMIC HISTORY — 1945-
Contributi alla ricerca economica: servizio studi della Banca d'Italia. — Roma : Banca d'Italia, 1972-1976. — Annual

The Economic bulletin / Business School, Robert Gordon's Institute of Technology, Aberdeen. — Aberdeen : Business School, 1984-. — Annual

WACHTEL, Howard M
The money mandarins : the making of a new supranational economic order / Howard M. Wachtel. — 1st ed. — New York : Pantheon Books, c1986. — xvi, 254 p.. — Includes index. — Bibliography: p. [227]-245

ECONOMIC HISTORY — 1945- — Congresses
Futures for the welfare state / edited by Norman Furniss. — Bloomington : Indiana University Press, c1986. — vi, 444 p.. — Bibliography: p. 404-431

ECONOMIC HISTORY — 1971-
LIPIETZ, Alain
Mirages and miracles : the crises of global Fordism / Alain Lipietz ; translated by David Macey. — London : Verso, 1987. — 226p. — Translation of: Mirages et miracles. — Includes index

ECONOMIC HISTORY — 1971- — Congresses
The Global economy : divergent perspectives on economic change / edited by Edward W. Gondolf, Irwin M. Marcus, and James P. Dougherty. — Boulder : Westview Press, 1986. — xvii, 212 p.. — (Westview special studies in international economics and business). — 'Essays ... drawn from a conference on 'Industry and society' at Indiana University of Pennsylvania"--Acknowledgments

ECONOMIC HISTORY — 1971- — Mathematical models
The Globus model : computer simulation of worldwide political and economic developments / edited by Stuart A. Bremer. — Boulder : Westview Press, 1986. — p. cm. — Includes index. — Bibliography: p

ECONOMIC HISTORY — Great Britain — History
COLEMAN, D. C.
History and the economic past : an account of the rise and decline of economic history in Britain / D.C. Coleman. — Oxford : Clarendon, 1987. — 150p. — Includes index

ECONOMIC INDICATORS — Paraguay
HERKEN-KRAUER, Juan Carlos
Economic indicators for the Paraguayan economy, 1869-1932 : isolation and the world economy / by Juan Carlos Herken-Krauer. — 280 leaves. — PhD (Econ) 1986 LSE

ECONOMIC PLANNING
Discussion paper series / Centre for Economic Policy Research. — London : Centre for Economic Policy Research, 1986-

ECONOMIC POLICY
ATKINSON, Rodney
Government against the people : the economics of exploitation / Rodney Atkinson. — Swalwell Industrial Estate, Tyne and Wear : Compuprint e, 1986. — 160p

BELTRÁN, Lucas
La nueva economía liberal : un horizonte para la economía española / Lucas Bettrán. — [Madrid] : Instituto de Economía de Mercado : Fundación Canovas del Castillo, c1982. — 188p. — (Biblioteca del pensamiento conservador. Moderna). — Bibliography: p183-185

CAIRNCROSS, Sir Alec
Economics and economic policy / Alec Cairncross. — Oxford : Basil Blackwell, 1986. — [300]p. — Includes index

COTTA, Alain
Les 5 erreurs / Alain Cotta. — Paris : Orban, [1985]. — 245p

Current controversies in economics / edited by Howard Vane and Terry Caslin. — Oxford : Basil Blackwell, 1987. — xii,319p. — Includes bibliographies and index

Economic policy in theory and practice / edited by Assaf Razin and Efraim Sadka. — Basingstoke : Macmillan, 1987. — xli,552p. — Includes bibliographies and index

FUKAO, Mitsuhiro
Internationalisation of financial markets : some implications for macroeconomic policy and for the allocation of capital / by Mitsuhiro Fukao and Masaharu Hanazaki. — [Paris] : OECD, 1986. — 97p. — (Working papers / OECD Department of Economics and Statistics ; no.37). — Bibliographical references: p36-40

GHARAJEDAGHI, Jamshid
A prologue to national development planning / Jamshid Gharajedaghi, in collaboration with Russell L. Ackoff. — New York : Greenwood Press, 1986. — xiii, 210 p.. — (Contributions in economics and economic history ; no. 70). — Includes index. — Bibliography: p. [201]-204

GOUREVITCH, Peter Alexis
Politics in hard times : comparative responses to international economic crises / Peter Gourevitch. — Ithaca : Cornell University Press, 1986. — p. cm. — (Cornell studies in political economy). — Includes index

Grüne Wirtschaftspolitik, machbare Utopien / Frank Beckenbach...[et al.] ; mit einem Vorwort von Otto Schily. — [Originalausg.]. — Köln : Kiepenheuer und Witsch, 1985. — 363p . — Bibliographies

HENNING, C. Randall
Macroeconomic diplomacy in the 1980s : domestic politics and international conflict among the United States, Japan, and Europe / C. Randall Henning. — London : Croom Helm for the Atlantic Institute for International Affairs, c1987. — [96]p. — (Atlantic paper ; no.65)

JACKMAN, Richard
Innovative supply-side policies to reduce unemployment / R. Jackman and R. Layard. — London : Centre for Labour Economics, London School of Economics, 1987. — 34p. — (Discussion paper / London School of Economics and Political Science. Centre for Labour Economics ; no.281). — Bibliography: p33-34

KALECKI, Michał
Selected essays on economic planning / Michal Kalecki ; edited, translated and introduced by Jan Toporowski. — Cambridge : Cambridge University Press, 1986. — [vi],[196]p. — Translation of the Polish. — Includes index

LAVOIE, Don
National economic planning : what is left? / Don Lavoie. — Cambridge, Mass. : Ballinger Pub. Co., c1985. — xii, 291 p.. — Includes index. — Bibliography: p. 267-279

LEVAČIĆ, Rosalind
Economic policy-making / Rosalind Levačić. — Brighton : Wheatsheaf, 1987. — xii,372p. — Bibliography: p363-365. — Includes index

MACESICH, George
Economic nationalism and stability / by George Macesich. — New York : Praeger, 1985. — p. cm. — Includes bibliographies and index

MCKENZIE, Richard B
The fairness of markets : a search for justice in a free society / Richard B. McKenzie. — Lexington, Mass. : Lexington Books, c1987. — xiv, 235 p.. — Includes bibliographies and index

ECONOMIC POLICY
continuation

The Management of interlinkages / edited by Ricardo Acosta Suárez. — Ljubljana, Yugoslavia : International Center for Public Enterprises in Developing Countries, c1985. — 272p. — *Includes bibliographies.* — *Contents: Towards management of interlinkages / Ricardo Acosta Suárez -- Interlinkages / Horacio Boneo -- The management of interlinkages / Praxy J. Fernandes -- Patterns of strategic behaviour and models for strategic planning in state enterprises in some developing countries / M.S.S. El-Namaki -- Some theoretical and operational aspects of interlinkage planning / Aleš Vahčič -- Empirical evaluation of macroeconomic linkages between public and private sectors / Boris Pleskovič and Gustavo Treviño -- Public enterprise interlinkages / Georg Sørensen*

The medium-term international outlook : an economic, technological and sectoral analysis. — Canberra : Economic Planning Advisory Council, 1986. — v,37p. — (Council paper / Economic Planning Advisory Council ; no.1). — *Bibliography: p36-37*

MILLS, Edwin S
The burden of government / Edwin S. Mills. — Stanford, Calif. : Hoover Institution Press, c1986. — p. cm. — *Includes index.* — *Bibliography: p*

MORISHIMA, Michio
Ideology and economic activity / Michio Morishima. — London : Suntory-Toyota International Centre for Economics and Related Disciplines, 1986. — 38p. — (Japanese studies). — *Bibliography: p37-38*

NEUBAUER, Gyula
A világgazdaság válaszúton : a budapesti szabadegyetemen tartott tíz elöadás / Neubauer Gyula. — Budapest : Toldi Lajos bizománya, 1943. — 371p. — *A series of ten lectures held at the Open University of Budapest in the autumn of 1942*

PETERSEN, Uwe
Arbeitslosigkeit unser Schicksal? : Wirtschaftspolitik in der Stagflation / Uwe Petersen. — Frankfurt am Main : Peter Lang, 1985. — 133p. — (Europöische Hochschulschriften. Reihe 5, Volks- und Betriebswirtschaft ; Bd.661). — *Bibliography: p130-133*

Planning perspectives: an international journal of history, planning and the environment. — London : E. & F. N. Spoon, 1986-. — *3 per year*

Staat und Politische Ökonomie heute : Horst Claus Recktenwald zum 65. Geburtstag = Public sector and political economy today: essays in honour of Horst Claus Recktenwald / herausgegeben von Horst Hanusch, Karl W. Roskamp, Jack Wiseman. — Stuttgart : Gustav Fischer, 1985. — xii,393p. — *Includes bibliographies*

STEIDLMEIER, Paul
The paradox of poverty : a reappraisal of economic development policy / Paul Steidlmeier. — Cambridge, Mass. : Ballinger, 1987. — p. cm. — *Includes bibliographies and index*

STIGLER, George J.
The regularities of regulation / George J. Stigler. — Glencorse : David Hume Institute, 1986. — vi,12p. — (Hume occasional paper ; no.3). — *Bibliography: p11*

STIGLITZ, Joseph E.
Economics of the public sector / Joseph E. Stiglitz. — New York ; London : Norton, 1986. — xxiii,509p. — *Bibliography: p577-586*

THOMPSON, Grahame
Economic calculation and policy formation / Grahame Thompson. — London : Routledge & Kegan Paul, 1986. — 191p. — (Economy and society paperbacks). — *With a chapter by Angelo Reati. — Includes bibliographies*

TICKNER, J. Ann
Self-reliance versus power politics : the American and Indian experience in building nation states / J. Ann Tickner. — New York : Columbia University Press, 1987. — xi, 282 p.. — (The Political economy of international change). — *Includes index.* — *Bibliography: p. [231]-267*

VEGA MORENO, Néstor
Ensayos sobre desarrollo económico / Néstor Vega Moreno. — Quito : Junta Nacional de Planificación y Coordinación Económica, [ca.1967]. — 338p

WEITZ, Ranaan
New roads to development / Raanan Weitz ; foreword by M.J. Rossant. — Westport, Conn. : Greenwood Press, c1986. — p. cm. — (Contributions in economics and economic history ; no. 64). — *"A Twentieth Century Fund essay.".* — *Includes index.* — *Bibliography: p*

WHITELEY, Paul
Political control of the macroeconomy : the political economy of public policy making / by Paul Whiteley. — London : Sage, 1986. — 212p. — *Bibliogrpahy: p191-201.* — *Includes index*

WITTMANN, Walter
How social is the market economy? / Walter Wittmann. — London : Centre for Research into Communist Economics, 1985. — 50p. — (Understanding economic systems ; 2). — *Bibliography: p49*

The World Bank economic review / World Bank. — Washington, D.C. : International Bank for Reconstruction and Development, 1986-. — *Quarterly*

ECONOMIC POLICY — Addresses, essays, lectures

Natural resource economics : policy problems and contemporary analysis / edited by Daniel W. Bromley. — Hingham, MA, USA : Kluwer-Nijhoff : Distributors for the U.S. and Canada, Kluwer Academic Publishers, c1986. — xiv, 234 p.. — (Recent economic thought series). — *Includes index.* — *Bibliography: p. 226-229*

ECONOMIC POLICY — Case studies

ROY, Ramashray
Dialogues on development : individuals, society, and the political order / Ramashray Roy and R.K. Srivastava. — New Delhi ; Beverly Hills : Sage Publications, 1985. — p. cm

ECONOMIC POLICY — Congresses

CONGRÈS DES ÉCONOMISTES BELGES DE LANGUE FRANÇAISE (4 : 1980 : Mons)
Les conditions de l'initiative économique. — Charleroi : Centre interuniversitaire de formation permanente
Actes. — [1980]. — 239p

CONGRÈS DES ÉCONOMISTES BELGES DE LANGUE FRANÇAISE (4 : 1980 : Mons)
Les conditions de l'initiative économique. — Charleroi : Centre interuniversitaire de formation permanente
Allocation optimale des ressources, rentabilité et initiative économique; rapport préparatoire / Commission 4. — [1980]. — 125p

CONGRÈS DES ÉCONOMISTES BELGES DE LANGUE FRANÇAISE (4 : 1980 : Mons)
Les conditions de l'initiative économique. — Charleroi : Centre interuniversitaire de formation permanente
Contexte réglementaire et institutionnel de l'initiative économique; rapport préparatoire / Commission 5. — [1980]. — 143p

CONGRÈS DES ÉCONOMISTES BELGES DE LANGUE FRANÇAISE (4 : 1980 : Mons)
Les conditions de l'initiative économique. — Charleroi : Centre interuniversitaire de formation permanente
Les motivations à l'initiative économique; rapport préparatoire / Commission 1. — 1980. — 70p

CONGRÈS DES ÉCONOMISTES BELGES DE LANGUE FRANÇAISE (4 : 1980 : Mons)
Les conditions de l'initiative économique. — Charleroi : Centre interuniversitaire de formation permanente
L'innovation et l'initiative économique; rapport préparatoire / Commission 2. — [1980]. — 56p

CONGRÈS DES ÉCONOMISTES BELGES DE LANGUE FRANÇAISE (4 : 1980 : Mons)
Les conditions de l'initiative économique. — Charleroi : Centre interuniversitaire de formation permanente
Orientations et moyens d'action d'une stratégie régionale de redéploiement économique: l'exemple de la Wallonie; rapport préparatoire / Commission de Base. — [1980]. — 178p

CONGRÈS DES ÉCONOMISTES BELGES DE LANGUE FRANÇAISE (4 : 1980 : Mons)
Les conditions de l'initiative économique. — Charleroi : Centre interuniversitaire de formation permanente
Présentation générale. — [1980]. — 21p

CONGRÈS DES ÉCONOMISTES BELGES DE LANGUE FRANÇAISE (4 : 1980 : Mons)
Les conditions de l'initiative économique. — Charleroi : Centre interuniversitaire de formation permanente
Réduction progressive des heures et partage du travail; rapport préparatoire / Commission 3. — [1980]. — 87p

The Dynamics of market economies / edited by Richard H. Day and Gunnar Eliasson. — New York : North Holland Pub. Co. ; New York, N.Y. : Sole distributors for the U.S.A. and Canada, Elsevier Science Pub. Co., 1985. — p. cm. — *"Papers and discussion of a conference on the dynamics of decentralized, market economies held at the Grand Hotel, Saltsjöbaden near Stockholm, August 29-31, 1983 ... sponsored by the Marcus Wallenberg Foundation for International Cooperation in Science"--P*

The Global economy : divergent perspectives on economic change / edited by Edward W. Gondolf, Irwin M. Marcus, and James P. Dougherty. — Boulder : Westview Press, 1986. — xvii, 212 p.. — (Westview special studies in international economics and business). — *"Essays ... drawn from a conference on 'Industry and society' at Indiana University of Pennsylvania"--Acknowledgments*

ECONOMIC POLICY — Decision making — Congresses

International macroeconomic modelling for policy decisions / edited by P. Artus and O. Guvenen in collaboration with F. Gagey. — Dordrecht ; Boston : M. Nijhoff, 1986. — viii, 269 p.. — (Advanced studies in theoretical and applied econometrics ; v. 5). — *"Based on an international conference organised by the Applied Econometric Association (AEA) ... which was held in Brussels at the Commission of the European Communities in December 1983"--Pref.* — *Includes bibliographies and index*

ECONOMIC POLICY — Econometric models

Econometric contributions to public policy : proceedings of a conference held by the International Economic Association at Urbino, Italy / edited by Richard Stone and William Peterson. — London : Macmillan, 1978. — [416]p

ECONOMIC POLICY — Econometric models — Congresses

Developments of control theory for economic analysis / Carlo Carraro and Domenico Sartore, editors. — Dordrecht ; Boston : M. Nijhoff, 1987. — p. cm. — (Advanced studies in theoretical and applied econometrics ; v. 7). — *"Proceedings of the Conference on "Economic Policy and Control Theory" which was held at the University of Venice (Italy) on 27 January-1 February 1985"--Pref*

ECONOMIC POLICY — Mathematical models

Macroeconomics [i.e. Macroeconimic] impacts of energy shocks / edited by Bert G. Hickman, Hillard G. Huntington, and James L. Sweeney. — Amsterdam ; New York : North-Holland ; New York, N.Y., U.S.A. : Sole distributors for the U.S.A. and Canada, Elsevier Science Pub. Co., 1987. — xvi, 331 p.. — (Contributions to economic analysis ; 163). — *Includes bibliographical references*

ECONOMIC RECOVERY TAX ACT

BRAYTON, Flint
The macroeconomic and sectoral effects of the Economic Recovery Tax Act : some simulation results / Flint Brayton, Peter B. Clark. — Washington, D.C. : Board of Governors of the Federal Reserve System, 1985. — 17p. — (Staff study / Board of Governors of the Federal Reserve System (U.S.) ; 148)

ECONOMIC RESEARCH

Cowles Foundation discussion paper / Cowles Foundation for Research in Economics at Yale University. — New Haven, Conn. : Cowles Foundation for Research in Economics at Yale University, 1986-

LONDON SCHOOL OF ECONOMICS AND POLITICAL SCIENCE. Centre for Labour Economics
Review of the year's work, 1985-86. — London : Centre for Labour Economics, London School of Economics, 1986. — 30p. — (Discussion paper / London School of Economics and Political Science. Centre for Labour Economics ; no.263)

ECONOMIC SANCTIONS — South Africa

GREAT BRITAIN. Parliament. House of Commons. Library. International Affairs Section
The South African crisis / Chris Bowlby. — [London] : the Library, 1987. — 49p. — (Background paper / House of Commons. Library. [Research Division] ; no.192). — *Bibliography: p49*

HAYES, J. P.
Economic effects of sanctions on Southern Africa / by J.P. Hayes. — Aldershot : Gower, for the Trade Policy Research Centres, 1987. — xii,100p. — (Thames essay ; no.53). — *Bibliography: p94-95*

ECONOMIC SANCTIONS — South Africa — Bibliography

Sanctions against South Africa : a selective bibliography = Les sanctions contre l'Afrique du Sud : bibliographie selective. — New York : United Nations, 1981. — vii,28p. — (Bibliographical series / Dag Hammarskjöld Library ; no.32 = Série bibliographique / Bibliothèque Dag Hammarskjöld ; no.32) ([Document] / United Nations ; ST/LIB/SER.B/32). — *In English, French, German, Italian and Russian. — Sales no: E/F/81.I.13*

ECONOMIC SANCTIONS — Zimbabwe — Bibliography

GREAT BRITAIN. Parliament. House of Commons. Library. International Affairs Section
The Bingham Report : a background bibliography / [Carole B. Mann]. — [London] : the Library, 1978. — 6leaves. — (Reference sheet / House of Commons. Library. Research Division ; no.78/9)

GREAT BRITAIN. Parliament. House of Commons. Library. International Affairs Section
The Bingham Report : a background bibliography; addenda: November 1978-January 1979 / [Carole B. Mann]. — [London] : the Library, 1979. — 2leaves. — ([Reference sheet] / House of Commons. Library. [Research Division] ; no.78/9: Addenda)

ECONOMIC STABILIZATION

DORNBUSCH, Rudiger
Inflation, exchange rates, and stabilization / Rudiger Dornbusch. — Princeton, N.J. : International Finance Section, Dept. of Economics, Princeton University, 1986. — p. cm. — (Essays in international finance ; no. 165 (Oct. 1986)). — *Bibliography: p*

ECONOMIC STABILIZATION — Mathematical models

GHOSH, S.
Stabilizing speculative commodity markets / S. Ghosh, C.L. Gilbert and A.J. Hughes Hallett. — Oxford : Clarendon, 1987. — [448]p. — *Includes bibliography and index*

ECONOMIC STABILIZATION — Africa, West

Croissance et ajustement : les problèmes de l'Afrique de l'Ouest / préparée par Patrick Guillaumont. — Paris : Economica, 1985. — 248p. — *Includes bibliographies*

ECONOMIC STABILIZATION — Central America

FEINBERG, Richard E
Development postponed : the political economy of Central America in the 1980s / Richard E. Feinberg and Bruce M. Bagley. — Boulder : Westview Press, 1986. — xiii, 65 p.. — (SAIS papers in Latin American studies). — *Bibliography: p. 51-60*

ECONOMIC STABILIZATION — Chile

EDWARDS, Sebastián
Monetarism and liberalization : the Chilean experiment / Sebastian Edwards and Alejandra Cox Edwards. — Cambridge, MA : Ballinger Pub. Co., c1987. — xxi, 233 p.. — *Includes index. — Bibliography: p. 211-226*

ECONOMIC STABILIZATION — Developing countries

DORNBUSCH, Rudiger
Dollars, debts, and deficits / Rudiger Dornbusch. — 1st MIT Press ed. — Leuven, Belgium : Leuven University Press ; Cambridge, Mass. : MIT Press, 1986. — 240 p. . — *The Professor Dr. Gaston Eyskens lectures delivered at the Katholieke Universiteit Leuven, Belgium in the fall of 1984. — Includes bibliographies and index*

GYLFASON, Thorvaldur
Credit policy and economic activity in developing countries with IMF stabilization programs / Thorvaldur Gylfason. — Princeton, N.J. : International Finance Section, Dept. of Economics, Princeton University, 1987. — p. cm. — (Princeton studies in international finance ; no. 60 (August 1987)). — *Bibliography: p*

The IMF and stabilisation : developing country experiences / directed and edited by Tony Killick ; contributors : Graham Bird ... [et al.]. — London : Gower in association with the Overseas Development Institute, 1985, c1984. — viii,216p. — *Originally published: London : Heinemann Educational in association with the Overseas Development Institute, 1984. — Includes bibliographies*

MACESICH, George
Economic nationalism and stability / by George Macesich. — New York : Praeger, 1985. — p. cm. — *Includes bibliographies and index*

The Quest for economic stabilisation : the IMF and the Third World / directed and edited by Tony Killick ; contributors Graham Bird ... [et al.]. — Aldershot : Gower in association with the Overseas Development Institute, 1985, c1984. — [xii,352]p. — *Originally published: London : Heinemann, 1984. — Bibliography: p321-331. — Includes index*

ECONOMIC STABILIZATION — Developing countries — Congresses

Economic adjustment and exchange rates in developing countries / edited by Sebastian Edwards and Liaquat Ahamed. — Chicago : University of Chicago Press, c1986. — p. cm. — (A National Bureau of Economic Research conference report). — *"Papers ... presented at a joint National Bureau of Economic Research-World Bank conference held in Washington, D.C., 29 November through 1 December, 1984."--. — Includes index. — Bibliography: p*

ECONOMIC STABILIZATION — Latin America

Economic reform and stabilization in Latin America / edited by Michael Connolly, Claudio González-Vega. — New York : Praeger, [1987]. — xxiii, 348 p.. — *"Second Dominican Republic Conference on Trade and Financial Liberalization in Latin America held in Santo Domingo, March 22-24, 1985"--P. iii. — Includes bibliographies*

ECONOMIC STABILIZATION — Peru

SCHEETZ, Thomas Edward
Peru and the International Monetary Fund / Thomas Scheetz. — Pittsburgh, PA : University of Pittsburgh Press, c1986. — xi, 257 p.. — (Pitt Latin American series). — *Includes index. — Bibliography: p. 251-254*

ECONOMIC STABILIZATION — Southern Cone of South America

RAMOS, Joseph R
Neoconservative economics in the southern cone of Latin America, 1973-1983 / Joseph Ramos. — Baltimore : Johns Hopkins University Press, c1986. — xviii, 200p. — (The Johns Hopkins studies in development). — *Includes index. — Bibliography: p.185-191*

ECONOMIC STABILIZATION — Switzerland

GENBERG, Hans
External influences on the Swiss economy under fixed and flexible exchange rates / Hans Genberg and Alexander K. Swoboda. — Grüsch : Rüegger, c1985. — ii, 182 p.. — (Schweizerisches Institut für Aussenwirtschafts-, Struktur- und Regionalforschung an der Hochschule St. Gallen ; Bd. 10). — *Bibliography: p. 178-182*

ECONOMIC SURVEYS

CHANDER, R
Living standards surveys in developing countries / Ramesh Chander, statistical adviser, Christiaan Grootaert, economist, Graham Pyatt, senior adviser. — Washington, D.C. : World Bank, 1980. — 27p. — (LSMS working papers ; no.1). — *Based on a paper originally presented at an Aug. 1980 meeting of the American Statistical Association*

GROOTAERT, Christiaan
Household expenditure surveys : some methodological issues / Christiaan N. Grootaert, K.F. Cheung. — Washington, D.C., U.S.A. : World Bank, c1985. — ix,72p. — (LSMS working paper ; no.22). — *Includes bibliographical references*

ECONOMIC ZONES (MARITIME LAW)

AKAHA, Tsuneo
Japan in global ocean politics / Tsuneo Akaha. — Honolulu : University of Hawaii Press and Law of the Sea Institute, University of Hawaii, c1985. — xii, 224 p.. — *Includes index. Bibliography: p. [203]-213*

ATTARD, David Joseph
The exclusive economic zone in international law / David Joseph Attard. — Oxford : Clarendon, 1987. — [256]p. — (Oxford monographs in international law). — *Includes index*

The law of the sea : national legislation on the exclusive economic zone, the economic zone and the exclusive fishery zone. — New York : United Nations, 1986. — xv,337p

ECONOMIC ZONES (MARITIME LAW)
continuation

LAW OF THE SEA INSTITUTE. Conference (1984 : San Francisco, Calif.)LAW OF THE SEA INSTITUTE. Conference (18th : 1984 : San Francisco, Calif.)
The developing order of the oceans : proceedings / Law of the Sea Institute Eighteenth Annual Conference ; co-sponsored by the University of San Francisco, October 24-27, 1984, San Francisco ; edited by Robert B. Krueger, Stefan A. Riesenfeld. — Honolulu : Law of the Sea Institute, William S. Richardson School of Law, University of Hawaii, 1986. — p. cm. — (Sea grant cooperative report ; UNIHI-SEAGRANT-CR-85-03). — *Includes bibliographies*

SMITH, Robert W
Exclusive economic zone claims : an analysis and primary documents / Robert W. Smith. — Dordrecht ; Boston : M. Nijhoff ; Hingham, MA, USA : Distributors for the U.S. and Canada, Kluwer Academic, 1986. — xiv, 501 p., [1] folded leaf of plates. — *Includes bibliographies and indexes*

ECONOMIC ZONES (MARITIME LAW) — Japan

AKAHA, Tsuneo
Japan in global ocean politics / Tsuneo Akaha. — Honolulu : University of Hawaii Press and Law of the Sea Institute, University of Hawaii, c1985. — xii, 224 p.. — *Includes index.* — *Bibliography: p. [203]-213*

ECONOMIC ZONING — Congresses

SEMANA ECONÓMICA INTERNACIONAL (1st : 1970 : Barcelona)
La región y el desarrollo : (en España y a nivel internacional) / Selección y supervisión general de Ramón Roca-Sastre Moncunill. — [1. ed. — Barcelona] : DOPESA, [1972]. — 288p. — (Documento económico, 2). — *At head of title: Organizada por el semanario Mundo*

ECONOMIC ZONING — China

Modernization in China : the case of the Shenzhen special economic zone / editors Kwan-yiu Wong, David K.Y. Chu. — Oxford : Oxford University Press, 1986. — xi,229p. — *Bibliography: p[218]-224*

ECONOMIC ZONING — Spain — Congresses

SEMANA ECONÓMICA INTERNACIONAL (1st : 1970 : Barcelona)
La región y el desarrollo : (en España y a nivel internacional) / Selección y supervisión general de Ramón Roca-Sastre Moncunill. — [1. ed. — Barcelona] : DOPESA, [1972]. — 288p. — (Documento económico, 2). — *At head of title: Organizada por el semanario Mundo*

ECONOMICS

Advances in economic theory : fifth world congress / edited by Truman F. Bewley. — Cambridge : Cambridge University Press, 1987. — vii,428p. — (Econometric Society monographs ; no.12). — *Conference papers.* — *Includes bibliographies*

ARNE RYDE SYMPOSIUM (8th : 1985 : Frostavallen)
Incentives and economic systems : proceedings of the Eighth Arne Ryde Symposium, Frostavallen, 26-27 August 1985 / edited by Stefan Hedlund. — London : Croom Helm, c1987. — 372p. — *Includes index*

Arrow and the ascent of modern economic theory / edited by George R. Feiwel. — Basingstoke : Macmillan, 1987. — liv,698p[1] leaf of plates. — *Includes bibliographies and index*

Arrow and the foundations of the theory of economic policy / edited by George R. Feiwel. — Basingstoke : Macmillan, 1987. — lxiii,758p,[1]leaf of plates. — *Includes bibliographies and index*

BEGG, David K. H.
Economics. — 2nd ed. [i.e. 2nd British ed.] / David Begg and Stanley Fischer, Rudiger Dornbusch. — London : McGraw-Hill, c1987. — xx,770p. — *Previous ed.: / Stanley Fischer, Rudiger Dornbusch. 1983.* — *Includes index*

BOWLES, Samuel
Understanding capitalism : competition, command, and change in the U.S. economy / by Samuel Bowles and Richard Edwards. — New York, NY : Harper & Row, c1985. — p. cm. — *Includes index*

CANTILLON, Richard
Essai sur la nature du commerce au général / edited with an English translation and other material by Henry Higgs. — New York : Kelley, 1964. — viii,394p. — (Reprints of economic classics). — *Reprint of edition published: London : Macmillan, 1931*

CHARLES, Susan
The economic approach to social policy / S.T. Charles, A.L. Webb. — Brighton : Wheatsheaf, 1986. — xii,247p. — *Includes index*

DAY, A. C. L.
Economic strategies : Keynes, Friedman and their disciples / Alan Day. — [London] : Banking World, 1986. — 48p. — *At head of title: Alan Day report*

Discussion paper series / Centre for Economic Policy Research. — London : Centre for Economic Policy Research, 1986-

Discussion paper series / Harvard Institute of Economic Research, Harvard University. — Cambridge, Mass. : Harvard Insitute of Economic Research, 1986-

Discussion papers in economics / Princeton University. Woodrow Wilson School of Public and International Affairs. — Princeton, N.J. : Woodrow Wilson School of Public and International Affairs, 1986-

Economics and philosophy. — Cambridge ; New York : Cambridge University Press, 1985- . — *Semi-annual*

FRIEDMAN, Milton
The essence of Friedman / edited by Kurt R. Leube ; foreword by W. Glenn Campbell. — Stanford, Calif. : Hoover Institution Press, 1987. — p. cm. — (Hoover Press publication ; 366). — *Includes index.* — *Bibliography: p*

GENETSKI, Robert J.
Taking the voodoo out of economics / by Robert J. Genetski. — Chicago : Regnery Books, 1986. — 189p. — *Bibliographical notes: p187-189*

HSIEH, Ching-Yao
A search for synthesis in economic theory / by Ching-Yao Hsieh and Stephen L. Mangum. — Armonk, N.Y. : M.E. Sharpe, c1986. — p. cm. — *Bibliography: p*

The journal of economic perspectives : a journal of the American Economic Association. — Nashville : American Economic Association, 1987-. — *Quarterly*

Journal of interdisciplinary economics. — Berkhamsted : AB Academic Publishers, 1985-. — *Irregular*

KEYNES, John Maynard
The collected writings of John Maynard Keynes. — [New standard ed.]. — London : Macmillan for the Royal Economic Society Vol.28: Social, political and literary writings / edited by Donald Moggridge. — c1982. — xiii,470p,[1]leaf of plates. — *Includes index*

KRIESLER, Peter
Kalecki's microanalysis : the development of Kalecki's analysis of pricing and distribution / Peter Kriesler. — Cambridge : Cambridge University Press, 1987. — [140]p. — *Includes bibliography and index*

LINDERT, Peter H.
International economics / Peter H. Lindert. — 8th ed. — Homewood, Ill. : Irwin, 1986. — xxii,576p. — (Irwin publications in Economics) . — *Bibliography: pR1-R11*

LIPSEY, Richard G.
Economics / Richard G. Lipsey, Peter O. Steiner, Douglas D. Purvis. — 8th ed. — New York : Harper & Row, c1987. — xxvii, 942 p.. — *Includes index*

The living economy : a new economics in the making / edited by Paul Ekins. — London : Routledge and Kegan Paul, 1986. — xviii,398p. — *Bibliography: p379-390*

MARX, Karl, 1818-1883
Capital : a critique of political economy. — London : Lawrence and Wishart. — *Based on the 1893 German edition*
Vol.2: The process of circulation of capital / edited by Friedrich Engels. — 1956. — xii,551p

MEERHAEGHE, Marcel Alfons Gilbert van
Economic theory : a critic's companion / M.A.G. van Meerhaeghe. — 2nd rev. ed. — Dordrecht ; Boston : Martinus Nijhoff, 1986. — p. cm. — *Includes bibliographies and indexes*

MORISHIMA, Michio
Ideology and economic activity / Michio Morishima. — London : Suntory-Toyota International Centre for Economics and Related Disciplines, 1986. — 38p. — (Japanese studies). — *Bibliography: p37-38*

NBER working paper series / National Bureau of Economic Research. — Cambridge (Mass.) : National Bureau of Economic Research, 1985-

PÄTZOLD, Jürgen
Stabilisierungspolitik : Grundlagen der nachfrage- und angebotsorientierten Wirtschaftspolitik / Jürgen Pätzold. — Bern : Haupt, 1985. — 340p. — *Bibliography: p326-334*

PHELPS, Edmund S
Political economy : an introductory text / Edmund S. Phelps. — 1st ed. — New York : Norton, c1985. — p. cm

PYM, Denis
The employment question, & other essays / Denis Pym. — London : Freedom Press, 1986. — 68p

REISMAN, David
The economics of Alfred Marshall / David Reisman ; foreword by G.L.S. Shackle. — London : Macmillan, 1986. — [384]p. — *Includes index*

ROBBINS, Lionel Charles Robbins, Baron
An essay on the nature and significance of economic science / Lord Robbins ; Lord Robbins. — 3rd ed. / foreword by William J. Baumol. — New York : New York University Press, 1984. — xliii, 160p. — *Includes bibliographical references and index*

RUBINSTEIN, Ariel
The complexity of strategies and the resolution of conflict : an introduction / Ariel Rubinstein. — London : Suntory Toyota International Centre for Economics and Related Disciplines, 1987. — 26p. — (Theoretical economics ; 87/150). — *Bibliography: p25-26*

SCITOVSKY, Tibor
Human desire and economic satisfaction : essays on the frontiers of economics / Tibor Scitovsky. — Brighton : Wheatsheaf, 1986. — [208]p. — *Includes index*

Seminar papers / Institute for International Economic Studies, University of Stockholm. — Stockholm : University of Stockholm. Institute for International Studies, 1986-

SIJBEN, J.J
Money and finance : a blurring of disciplines / Jac J. Sijben. — Tilburg : Tilburg University Press, 1986. — 43p

ECONOMICS *continuation*

SMITH, Adam, 1723-1790
The essential Adam Smith / edited and with introductory readings by Robert L. Heilbroner with the assistance of Laurence J. Malone. — Oxford : Oxford University Press, 1986. — vii, 341p.. — *Includes index*

Staat und Politische Ökonomie heute : Horst Claus Recktenwald zum 65. Geburtstag = Public sector and political economy today: essays in honour of Horst Claus Recktenwald / herausgegeben von Horst Hanusch, Karl W. Roskamp, Jack Wiseman. — Stuttgart : Gustav Fischer, 1985. — xii,393p. — *Includes bibliographies*

Technical working papers / National Bureau of Economic Research. — Cambridge (Mass.) : National Bureau of Economic Research, 1985-

TOBIN, James
Policies for prosperity : essays in a Keynesian mode / James Tobin ; edited by P.M. Jackson. — Brighton : Wheatsheaf, 1987. — xiv,508p. — *Includes index*

TURGOT, Anne Robert Jacques, baron de l'Aulne
[Reflexions sur la formation et la distribution des richesses. English]. Reflections on the formation and the distribution of riches [1770] / Translated by William J. Ashley. — New York : A. M. Kelley, 1971. — xxii, 112 p. — (Reprints of economic classics). — *Reprint of the 1898 ed.* — *Translation of Reflexions sur la formation et la distribution des richesses*

WILLIAMSON, John, 1937-
Political economy and international money : selected essays of John Williamson / edited by Chris Milner. — Brighton : Wheatsheaf, 1987. — [320]p. — *Includes bibliography and index*

WINTERBERGER, Gerhard
L'économie, l'état et la politique / Gerhard Winterberger. — Zurich : Union Suisse du Commerce et de l'Industrie, 1986. — 20p. — (Publication du Vorort ; no.44)

WONNACOTT, Paul
Economics / Paul Wonnacott, Ronald Wonnacott. — 3rd ed. — New York ; London : McGraw-Hill, c1986. — xxxii, 830p. — *Includes bibliographical references and index*

Working paper / Department of Economics, Massachusetts Institute of Technology. — Cambridge, Mass. : Massachusetts Institute of Technology, 1985-

Working papers in economics / Domestic Studies Program, Hoover Institution Stanford, University. — Stanford, Calif. : Stanford University. Hoover Institution, 1986-

ECONOMICS — Addresses, essays, lectures

The philosophy of economics : an anthology / edited by Daniel M. Hausman. — Cambridge : Cambridge University Press, 1984. — viii, 415p . — *Bibliography: p.389-405*

ECONOMICS — Collected works

SAMUELSON, Paul A.
The collected scientific papers / edited by Kate Crowley. — Cambridge, Massachusetts ; London : MIT Press
Vol.5. — 1986. — xii,1052p

ECONOMICS — Congresses

Economy and society in the transformation of the world / edited by Mike Gonzalez, Salustiano del Campo Urbano, Roberto Mesa. — London : United Nations University in association with Macmillan, 1984. — viii,206p. — ('The Transformation of the world' series ; v.2). — *Conference proceedings.* — *Includes index*

Law and economics and the economics of legal regulation / edited by J.-Matthias Graf v.d. Schulenburg, Göran Skogh. — Dordrecht ; Boston : M. Nijhoff, 1986. — p. cm. — (International studies in economics and econometrics ; 13). — *"Selected papers of a conference of the International Institute of Management Wissenschaftszentrum Berlin."*. — *Includes index.* — *Contents: Law and economics and the economics of legal regulation / Göran Skogh -- Efficiency, equity, and inalienability / Susan Rose-Ackerman -- Negotiated settlement / Gordon Tullock -- Economic efficiency and the common law / Peter H. Aranson -- Default risk and the optimal pricing of court enforcement services / Hugh Gravelle -- Transaction cost and communincation / Michael Hutter -- Regulatory measures to enforce quality production of self-employed professinals / J.-Matthias Graf v.d. Schulenburg -- Controlling insider trading in Europe and America / David D. Haddock, Jonathan R. Macey -- The regulatin of shop opening hours in the United Kingdom / Susan M. Jaffer, John A. Kay Belgian public policy towards the retailing trade / Roger Van den Bergh -- Assessing the effectiveness of economic efficiency of an E.E.C. pollution control directive / John Ashworth, Ivy Papps, David J. Storey*

Marx, Schumpeter, and Keynes : a centenary celebration of dissent / Suzanne W. Helburn and David F. Bramhall, editors. — Armonk, N.Y. : M.E. Sharpe, c1986. — xii, 343 p.. — *Papers presented at a symposium held Apr. 20-22, 1983 at the University of Colorado at Denver.* — *Includes bibliographies*

ECONOMICS — Decision making

DRÈZE, Jacques H.
Essays on economic decisions under uncertainty / Jacques H. Drèze. — Cambridge : Cambridge University Press, c1987. — xxvii,424p. — *Includes bibliographies and index*

Surveys in the economics of uncertainty / edited by John D. Hey and Peter J. Lambert. — Oxford : Basil Blackwell, 1987. — 232p. — *Includes bibliographies and index*

ECONOMICS — Dictionaries — Swedish

EDSTRÖM, N. F.
Ekonomi ordbok : svensk-engelsk fackordbok för ekonomifunktionen med begreppsförklaringar / N.F. Edström, L.A. Samuelson, O.K. Böök. — 2. uppl. — Stockholm : Norstedt & Söners, 1984. — 145p

ECONOMICS — Dictionaries, indexes, etc.

MALTHUS, T. R.
[Works]. The works of Thomas Robert Malthus / edited by E. A. Wrigley and David Souden. — London : Pickering
Vol.8: Definitions in political economy with index to the Works of Malthus. — 1986. — iii,165p. — *Bibliography: p123*

ECONOMICS — History

BREMS, Hans
Pioneering economic theory, 1630-1980 : a mathematical restatement / Hans Brems. — Baltimore : Johns Hopkins University Press, c1986. — xv, 411 p.. — *Includes bibliographies and indexes*

POLANYI, Karl
The great transformation / Karl Polanyi ; foreword by Robert M. MacIver. — Boston : Beacon Press, 1957. — xii,315p

ECONOMICS — History — To 1800

BHARADWAJ, Krishna
Classical political economy and rise to dominance of supply and demand theories / Krishna Bharadwaj. — 2nd rev. ed. — London : Sangain Books, 1986. — viii,88p

ECONOMICS — History — 19th century

BHARADWAJ, Krishna
Classical political economy and rise to dominance of supply and demand theories / Krishna Bharadwaj. — 2nd rev. ed. — London : Sangain Books, 1986. — viii,88p

MALTHUS, T. R.
[Works]. The works of Thomas Robert Malthus / edited by E. A. Wrigley and David Souden. — London : Pickering
Vol.8: Definitions in political economy with index to the Works of Malthus. — 1986. — iii,165p. — *Bibliography: p123*

ECONOMICS — History — 20th century

AFANAS'EV, V. S.
Burzhuaznaia ekonomicheskaia mysl' 30-80-kh godov XX veka : ocherk teorii / V. S. Afanas'ev. — Izd. 2-e, dop. i perer. — Moskva : Ekonomika, 1986. — 350p

BELKA, Marek
Doktryna ekonomiczno-społeczna Miltona Friedmana / Marek Belka. — Warszawa : Państwowe Wydawnictwo Naukowe, 1986. — 387p. — (Ekonomia XX wieku). — *Bibliography: p364-[373]*

Tratat de economie contemporană / colegiul de coordonare: I. V. Totu...[et al.]. — București : Editura politică. — *Contents in English, French, German, Russian and Spanish.* — *Bibliography: p[771]-792*
Vol.1: Sistemul științelor economice și sistemele economice contemporane / colegiul de redacție: N. N. Constantinescu....[et al.]. — 1986. — 858p

ECONOMICS — Law and legislation

Journal of law, economics, and organization. — New Haven : Yale University Press, 1986-. — *Semi-annual*

ECONOMICS — Mathematical models

BREMS, Hans
Pioneering economic theory, 1630-1980 : a mathematical restatement / Hans Brems. — Baltimore : Johns Hopkins University Press, c1986. — xv, 411 p.. — *Includes bibliographies and indexes*

RUBINOV, A. M.
Matematicheskie modeli rasshirennogo vosproizvodstva : A. M. Rubinov. — Leningrad : Nauka, Leningradskoe otdelenie, 1983. — 186p. — *Bibliography: p183-[185]*

ECONOMICS — Mathematical models — Congresses

Models of economic dynamics : proceedings of a workshop held at the IMA, University of Minnesota, Minn., October 24-28, 1983 / edited by Hugo F. Sonnenschein. — Berlin : Springer, 1986. — [v],212p. — (Lecture notes in economics and mathematical systems ; 264)

ECONOMICS — Methodology

Appraisal and criticism in economics : a book of readings / edited by Bruce J. Caldwell. — Boston, [Mass.] ; London : Allen & Unwin, 1984. — xiv,490p. — *Bibliography: p473-490*

Economic imperialism : the economic approach applied outside the field of economics / edited by Gerard Radnitzky and Peter Bernholz. — New York : Paragon House Publishers, c1986. — ix, 421 p.. — *"A Professors World Peace Academy book."*. — *Includes bibliographies and index*

JOHNSON, Glenn L.
Research methodology for economists : philosophy and practice / Glenn L. Johnson. — New York : Macmillan ; London : Collier Macmillan, c1986. — xx, 252p. — *Includes bibliographies and index*

KOLM, Serge - Christophe
Philosophie de l'économie / Serge - Christophe Kolm. — Paris : Seuil, [1986]. — 322p

ECONOMICS — Methodology — Addresses, essays, lectures

The philosophy of economics : an anthology / edited by Daniel M. Hausman. — Cambridge : Cambridge University Press, 1984. — viii, 415p . — *Bibliography: p.389-405*

ECONOMICS — Moral and ethical aspects

MCKENZIE, Richard B
The fairness of markets : a search for justice in a free society / Richard B. McKenzie. — Lexington, Mass. : Lexington Books, c1987. — xiv, 235 p.. — *Includes bibliographies and index*

SEN, Amartya
On ethics and economics / Amartya Sen. — Oxford : Basil Blackwell, 1987. — 131p. — (The Royer lectures). — *Bibliography: p90-122. — Includes index*

ECONOMICS — Periodicals — Bibliography

SICHEL, Beatrice
Economics journals and serials : an analytical guide / compiled by Beatrice Sichel and Werner Sichel. — Westport, Conn. : Greenwood Press, c1986. — xxiii, 285p. — (Annotated bibliographies of serials ; no. 5). — *Includes indexes*

ECONOMICS — Periodicals — Indexes

SICHEL, Beatrice
Economics journals and serials : an analytical guide / compiled by Beatrice Sichel and Werner Sichel. — Westport, Conn. : Greenwood Press, c1986. — xxiii, 285p. — (Annotated bibliographies of serials ; no. 5). — *Includes indexes*

ECONOMICS — Philosophy

JOHNSON, Glenn L.
Research methodology for economists : philosophy and practice / Glenn L. Johnson. — New York : Macmillan ; London : Collier Macmillan, c1986. — xx, 252p. — *Includes bibliographies and index*

O'SULLIVAN, Patrick J.
Economic methodology and freedom to choose / Patrick J. O'Sullivan. — London : Allen & Unwin, 1987. — [320]p. — *Includes bibliography and index*

ECONOMICS — Philosophy — Addresses, essays, lectures

The philosophy of economics : an anthology / edited by Daniel M. Hausman. — Cambridge : Cambridge University Press, 1984. — viii, 415p . — *Bibliography: p.389-405*

ECONOMICS — Political aspects

BRENNAN, Geoffrey
The reason of rules : constitutional political economy / Geoffrey Brennan [and] James M. Buchanan. — Cambridge : Cambridge University Press, 1985. — xiv,153p

ECONOMICS — Psychological aspects

Economic psychology : intersections in theory and application / edited by Alan J. and Heather W. MacFadyen. — Amsterdam ; New York : North-Holland ; New York, N.Y., U.S.A. : Sole distributors for the U.S.A. and Canada, Elsevier Science Pub. Co., 1986. — viii, 697 p.. — *Includes bibliographies and indexes*

LEA, S. E. G.
The individual in the economy a textbook of economic psychology / Stephen E.G. Lea, Roger M. Tarpy, Paul Webley. — Cambridge : Cambridge University Press, 1987. — xxiii,627p. — *Bibliography: p545-609. — Includes index*

ECONOMICS — Religious aspects — Islam

EL-ASHKER, Ahmed Abdel-Fattah
The Islamic business enterprise / Ahmed Abdel-Fattah El-Ashker. — London : Croom Helm, c1987. — xi,242p. — *Bibliography: p233-240. — Includes index*

MANNAN, Muhammad Abdul
Islamic economics : theory and practice / Muhammad Abdul Mannan. — Sevenoaks : Hodder and Stoughton, 1986. — [426]p. — *Includes bibliography and index*

ECONOMICS — Research

JOHNSON, Glenn L.
Research methodology for economists : philosophy and practice / Glenn L. Johnson. — New York : Macmillan ; London : Collier Macmillan, c1986. — xx, 252p. — *Includes bibliographies and index*

ECONOMICS — Statistical methods — Addresses, essays, lectures

The Collection and analysis of economic and consumer behavior data : in memory of Robert Ferber / edited by Seymour Sudman and Mary A. Spaeth. — Champaign, Ill. : Bureau of Economic and Business Research & Survey Research Laboratory, University of Illinois, c1984. — x, 406 p.. — *Includes bibliographies*

ECONOMICS — Study and teaching

Econometric modeling in economic education research / edited by William E. Becker and William B. Walstad. — Boston, Mass. : Kluwer-Nijhoff Pub., 1986. — p. cm. — (International series in economic modeling). — *Includes index*

Economics education : research and development issues : papers presented at the international research seminar held at the University of London Institute of Education, 30 July-1 August 1985 / edited for the Economics Association by Steve Hodkinson and David J. Whitehead. — London : Longman, 1986. — ix,308p. — *Includes bibliographies and index*

ECONOMICS — Study and teaching — Ukraine

Institut ekonomiki AN USSR : dostizheniia za 50 let 1936-1986 / [otv.redaktor: I. I. Lukinov]. — Kiev : Naukova dumka, 1986. — 237p

ECONOMICS — Study and teaching (Higher) — Thailand

NITSMER, Samart
Economics curricula and their relevance to policy-making in Thailand / Samart Nitsmer. — Singapore : Regional Institute of Higher Education and Development, 1984. — 197p. — (RIHED Research Series). — *Bibliography: p [147]-152*

ECONOMICS — Denmark — Bibliography

SVENNEVIG, Palle
Dansk økonomisk bibliograf: 1975-1977 / Palle Svennevig. — København : Akademisk Forlag, 1978. — 431p

SVENNEVIG, Palle
Danske økonomisk bibliografi 1978-1979. — København : Akademisk Forlag, 1980. — 342p

ECONOMICS — France — History — 20th century

RUEFF, Jacques
Oeuvres complètes de Jacques Rueff. — Paris : Plon. — *Bibliography: p436-438*
Tome 1: De l'aube au crépuscule : autobiographie de l'auteur. — [1977]. — 443p

ECONOMICS — Great Britain — History

BRITISH ASSOCIATION FOR THE ADVANCEMENT OF SCIENCE. Section F (Economics). Meeting (1985 : Strathclyde)
Ideas in economics : proceedings of Section F (Economics) of the British Association for the Advancement of Science, Strathclyde, 1985 / edited by R.D. Collison Black. — Basingstoke : Macmillan, c1986. — x,246p. — *Includes bibliographies and index*

DAVIS, Lance E.
Mammon and the pursuit of empire : the political economy of British imperialism, 1860-1912 / Lance E. Davis and Robert A. Huttenback with the assistance of Susan Gray Davis. — Cambridge : Cambridge University Press, 1986. — x,394p. — (Interdisciplinary perspectives on modern history). — *Bibliography: p365-388. — Includes index*

ECONOMICS — Great Britain — History — 19th century

David Ricardo : critical assessments / edited by John Cunningham Wood. — London : Croom Helm, c1985. — 4v. — (Croom Helm critical assessments of leading economists). — *In slipcase*

John Stuart Mill critical assessments / edited by John Cunningham Wood. — London : Croom Helm, 1986, c1987. — 4v. — (The Croom Helm critical assessments of leading economists)

Thomas Robert Malthus : critical assessments / edited by John Cunningham Wood. — London : Croom Helm, c1986. — 4v.([2000]p). — (The Croom Helm critical assessments of leading economists)

WINCH, Donald
Malthus / Donald Winch. — Oxford : Oxford University Press, 1987. — [144]p. — (Past masters). — *Includes bibliography and index*

ECONOMICS — Great Britain — History — 19th century — Sources

Critics of capitalism : Victorian reactions to 'political economy' / edited by Elisabeth Jay and Richard Jay. — Cambridge : Cambridge University Press, 1986. — vii,268p. — (Cambridge English prose texts). — *Bibliography: p262-268*

ECONOMICS — Great Britain — History — 20th century

STEWART, Michael, 1933-
Keynes and after / Michael Stewart. — 3rd ed. — Harmondsworth : Penguin, 1986. — 230p. — (Pelican books). — *Previous ed.: 1972*

ECONOMICS — Soviet Union

ABALKIN, L. I.
Novyi tip ekonomicheskogo myshleniia / L. I. Abalkin. — Moskva : Ekonomika, 1987. — 189p

ECONOMICS, MATHEMATICAL

Advances in economic theory : fifth world congress / edited by Truman F. Bewley. — Cambridge : Cambridge University Press, 1987. — vii,428p. — (Econometric Society monographs ; no.12). — *Conference papers. — Includes bibliographies*

AGNELL, Jonas
Tax reforms and asset markets / Jonas Agnell. — Stockholm : Industrial Institute for Economic and Social Research : Distributed by Almqvist & Wiksell, 1985. — 181p. — *Bibliography: p170-181*

ALLEN, R. G. D.
Mathematical analysis for economists / R.G.D. Allen. — London : Macmillan ; New York : St. Martin's Press, 1962. — 548p.,ill.,23cm. — (Studies in statistics and scientific method ; no.3) (Papermacs ; no.34). — *Originally published 1938*

BAUMOL, William J.
Economic theory and operations analysis / William J. Baumol. — 4th ed. — Englewood Cliffs, N.J : Prentice-Hall, c1977. — xxi, 695 p. — (Prentice-Hall international series in management). — *Includes bibliographies and index*

BIRCHENHALL, Chris
Mathematics for modern economics / Chris Birchenhall and Paul Grout. — Deddington : Philip Allan, 1984. — xii,412p. — *Bibliography: p406-408. — Includes index*

Economic organizations as games / edited by Ken Binmore and Partha Dasgupta. — Oxford : Basil Blackwell, 1986. — 219p.. — *Includes bibliography and index*

Matekon: translations of Russian and East European mathematical economics. — New York : International Arts and Sciences Press, 1969-. — *Quarterly. — Continues: Mathematical studies in economics and statistics in the USSR and Eastern Europe*

ECONOMICS, MATHEMATICAL
continuation
Mathematical studies in economics and statistics in the USSR and Eastern Europe. — New York : International Arts and Sciences Press, 1964-1968. — *Quarterly. — Continued by: Matekon: translations of Russian and East European mathematical economics*

RASHID, Salim
Economies with many agents : an approach using nonstandard analysis / Salim Rashid. — Baltimore : Johns Hopkins University Press, c1987. — xii, 160 p.. — *Includes indexes. — Bibliography: p. [149]-156*

Technical report series / Institute for Mathematical Studies in the Social Sciences. — Stanford, Calf. : Institute for Mathematical Studies in the Social Sciences, 1986-. — (Economics series / Institute for Mathematical Studies in the Social Sciences)

ECONOMICS, MATHEMATICAL — Addresses, essays, lectures
Contributions to mathematical economics in honor of Gérard Debreu / edited by Werner Hildenbrand, Andreau Mas-Colell. — Amsterdam ; New York : North Holland ; New York, N.Y., U.S.A. : Sole distributors for the U.S.A. and Canada, Elsevier Science Pub. Co., 1986. — p. cm

ECONOMICS, MATHEMATICAL — Congresses
Dynamic games and applications in economics / edited by T.Basar. — Berlin : Springer-Verlag, 1986. — vii,288p. — (Lecture notes in economics and mathematical systems ; 265)

ECONOMICS, MATHEMATICAL — Research
HILDRETH, Clifford
The Cowles Commission in Chicago, 1939-1955 / Clifford Hildreth. — Berlin ; New York : Springer-Verlag, c1986. — 176 p.. — (Lecture notes in economics and mathematical systems ; 271). — *Includes index. — Bibliography: p. [138]-163*

ECONOMICS, MEDICAL — history — Great Britain
HOLLINGSWORTH, J. Rogers
A political economy of medicine : Great Britain and the United States / J. Rogers Hollingsworth. — Baltimore : Johns Hopkins University Press, c1986. — xix, 312 p.. — *Includes index. — Bibliography: p. 275-303*

ECONOMICS, MEDICAL — history — United States
HOLLINGSWORTH, J. Rogers
A political economy of medicine : Great Britain and the United States / J. Rogers Hollingsworth. — Baltimore : Johns Hopkins University Press, c1986. — xix, 312 p.. — *Includes index. — Bibliography: p. 275-303*

ECONOMICS, MEDICAL — trends — United Staes
SORKIN, Alan L
Health care and the changing economic environment / Alan L. Sorkin. — Lexington, Mass. : Lexington Books, c1986. — xiv, 161 p.. — *Includes bibliographies and index*

ECONOMICS, MEDICAL — trends — United States
CALIFANO, Joseph A.
America's health care revolution : who lives? who dies? who pays? / Joseph A. Califano, Jr. — 1st ed. — New York : Random House, c1986. — x, 241 p.. — *Includes index. — Bibliography: p. [227]-230*

FEIN, Rashi
Medical care, medical costs : the search for a health insurance policy / Rashi Fein. — Cambridge, Mass. : Harvard University Press, 1986. — viii, 240 p.. — *Includes index*

GINZBERG, Eli
American medicine : the power shift / Eli Ginzberg. — Totowa, N.J. : Rowman & Allanheld, 1985. — xv, 207 p.. — *Includes index. — Bibliography: p. [194]-199*

ECONOMICS, MEDICAL — United States — congresses
The Price of health / edited by George J. Agich and Charles E. Begley. — Dordrecht ; Boston : D. Reidel Pub. Co. ; Hingham, MA, U.S.A. : Sold and distributed in the U.S.A. and Canada by Kluwer Academic Publishers, c1987. — p. cm. — (Philosophy and medicine ; v. 21). — *Based on a conference entitled "The price of health: economics and ethics in medicine," held at the School of Public Health, University of Texas Health Science Center, Houston, Tex., June 24-26, 1985. — Includes bibliographies and index*

ECONOMIS ASSISTANCE
The international law of development : basic documents / compiled and edited by A. Peter Mutharika. — Dobbs Ferry, N.Y. : Oceana
Vol.3. — 1979. — vii,1305-1997p

ECONOMISTS — Biography
BLAUG, Mark
Great economists before Keynes : an introduction to the lives & works of one hundred great economists of the past / Mark Blaug. — Brighton : Wheatsheaf, 1986. — xi,286p. — *Includes index*

Lives of the laureates / edited by William Breit and Roger W. Spencer. — Cambridge, Mass. : MIT Press, c1986. — p. cm. — *Bibliography: p*

ECONOMISTS — Austria — Biography
SOMARY, Felix
The raven of Zürich : the memoirs of Felix Somary / translated from the German by A.J. Sherman ; with a foreword by Otto Von Habsburg. — London : Hurst, c1986. — xii,310p,[1]p of plates. — *Translation of: Erinnerungen aus meinem Leben. — Includes index*

ECONOMISTS — Germany — Biography
HENDERSON, W. O.
Friedrich List : economist and visionary 1789-1846 / W.O. Henderson. — London : Cass, 1983. — xi,288p,[5]p of plates. — *Bibliography: p262-273. — Includes index*

ECONOMISTS — Great Britain — Biography
HUBBACK, David
No ordinary press baron : a life of Walter Layton / David Hubback. — London : Weidenfeld and Nicolson, c1985. — [240]p. — *Includes index*

MACDOUGALL, Donald
Don and mandarin : memoirs of an economist / Donald MacDougall. — London : Murray, 1987. — [312]p. — *Includes index*

VAIZEY, John
Scenes from institutional life and other writings / John Vaizey. — London : Weidenfeld and Nicolson, 1986. — vi,164p. — *Bibliography: p163-164*

ECONOMISTS — Great Britain — History
BRITISH ASSOCIATION FOR THE ADVANCEMENT OF SCIENCE. Section F (Economics). Meeting (1985 : Strathclyde)
Ideas in economics : proceedings of Section F (Economics) of the British Association for the Advancement of Science, Strathclyde, 1985 / edited by R.D. Collison Black. — Basingstoke : Macmillan, c1986. — x,246p. — *Includes bibliographies and index*

ECONOMISTS — Poland
SUŁKOWSKA, Wanda
Koncepcje społeczno-ekonomiczne i działalność Feliksa Młynarskiego / Wanda Sułkowska. — Wrocław Ossolineum, 1985. — 104p. — (Prace Komisji Nauk Ekonomicznch / Polska Akademia Nauk. Oddział w Krakowie ; Nr13) . — *Summary in French and English. — Bibliography: p[96]-99*

ECONOMISTS — Poland — Biography
ZARĘBA, Janusz
Reforma w testamencie : rzecz o Oskarze Langem / Janusz Zaręba. — Warszawá : Młodziezowa Agencja Wydawnicza, 1985. — 230p

ECONOMISTS — Scotland — Correspondence
SMITH, Adam, 1723-1790
The correspondence of Adam Smith / edited by Ernest Campbell Mossner and Ian Simpson Ross. — [2nd ed.]. — Oxford : Clarendon, 1987. — xxxi,464p. — (The Glasgow edition of the works and correspondence of Adam Smith ; 6). — *Previous ed.: 1977. — Includes index*

ECONOMISTS — Soviet Union — Directories
VORONITSYN, Sergei
A directory of prominent Soviet economists, sociologists, and demographers by institutional affiliation / compiled by Sergei Voronitsyn ; edited by: Robert Farrell. — Munich : Radio Liberty, 1987. — 118p

ECONOMISTS — Spain — Biography
BARRENECHEA, José Manuel
Valentín de Foronda, reformador y economista ilustrado / José Manuel Barrenechea. — [S.l.] : Diputación Foral de Alava, Departamento de Publicaciones, [ca.1984]. — xxiv,519p. — *Bibliography: P477-503*

ECONOMISTS — United States — Biography
GALBRAITH, John Kenneth
A view from the stands : of people, politics, military power, and the arts / John Kenneth Galbraith ; with notes by the author ; arranged and edited by Andrea D. Williams. — Boston : Houghton Mifflin, 1986. — p. cm. — *Includes index*

ECONOMISTS — United States — Collected works
SAMUELSON, Paul A.
The collected scientific papers / edited by Kate Crowley. — Cambridge, Massachusetts ; London : MIT Press
Vol.5. — 1986. — xii,1052p

ECUADOR — Economic conditions — 1918-1972
VEGA MORENO, Néstor
Ensayos sobre desarrollo económico / Néstor Vega Moreno. — Quito : Junta Nacional de Planificación y Coordinación Económica, [ca.1967]. — 338p

ECUADOR — Economic policy
SEMINARIO NACIONAL "PLANIFICACIÓN Y PRESUPUESTO DEL SECTOR PÚBLICO" (1973 : Quito)
Seminario Nacional "Planificación y Presupuesto del Sector Público" : Hotel Colon Internacional, enero 25,26 y 27, 1973, Quito, Ecuador. — Quito : Programa "Administración para el Desarrollo", CICAP, Proyecto 214, O.E.A. : Oficina de Presupuesto, Ministerio de Finanzas, 1973. — 257p

VEGA MORENO, Néstor
Ensayos sobre desarrollo económico / Néstor Vega Moreno. — Quito : Junta Nacional de Planificación y Coordinación Económica, [ca.1967]. — 338p

ECUADOR — Politics and government — 1944-
MARTZ, John D
Politics and petroleum in Ecuador / John D. Martz. — New Brunswick, N.J. : Transaction, c1986. — p. cm. — *Includes index. — Bibliography: p*

ECUADOR — Social policy
SEMINARIO NACIONAL "PLANIFICACIÓN Y PRESUPUESTO DEL SECTOR PÚBLICO" (1973 : Quito)
Seminario Nacional "Planificación y Presupuesto del Sector Público" : Hotel Colon Internacional, enero 25,26 y 27, 1973, Quito, Ecuador. — Quito : Programa "Administración para el Desarrollo", CICAP, Proyecto 214, O.E.A. : Oficina de Presupuesto, Ministerio de Finanzas, 1973. — 257p

ECUADOR — Statistics, Vital
BORJA M., Eduardo
Factores determinantes de una mortalidad prematura en Ecuador / Eduardo Borja M.. — Voorburg : International Statistical Institute, 1985. — 31p. — (Scientific reports / World Fertility Survey ; no.74)

ECUADOR. Comisión de Valores - Corporación Financiera Nacional — Legal status, laws, etc.
ECUADOR
[Laws, etc.]. Ley de la Comisión de Valores - Corporación Financiera Nacional / codificada por José Iturralde Arteaga. — [Quito] : Comisión de Valores - Corporación Financiera Nacional, 1975. — 29p

EDEL, ABRAHAM
Ethics, science, and democracy : the philosophy of Abraham Edel / edited by Irving Louis Horowitz and H. Standish Thayer. — New Brunswick, N.J., U.S.A. : Transaction Books, c1986. — viii, 318p. — "Festschrift honoring Abraham Edel"--Pref. — "Abraham Edel: philosophical bibliography, 1930-1985": p

EDEN, ANTHONY
JAMES, Robert Rhodes
Anthony Eden / Robert Rhodes James. — London : Weidenfeld and Nicolson, c1986. — xiv,665,[16]p of plates. — Includes index

SHUCKBURGH, Sir Evelyn
Descent to Suez : diaries, 1951-56 / Evelyn Shuckburgh ; selected for publication by John Charmley. — London : Weidenfeld and Nicolson, 1986. — x,380p,[12]p of plates

EDEN, ANTHONY — Career in international relations
PETERS, A. R.
Anthony Eden at the Foreign Office, 1931-1938 / A.R. Peters. — Aldershot : Gower, 1986. — viii,402p. — Bibliography: p383-392. — Includes index

EDITING
SHILLINGSBURG, Peter L
Scholarly editing in the computer age : theory and practice / Peter L. Shillingsburg. — Athens : University of Georgia Press, c1986. — x, 178 p.. — "Lectures delivered at the University of New South Wales, Royal Military College, Duntroon, Australian Capital Territory, June through October 1984"--Pref. — Includes bibliographical references and index

EDITORS — Addresses, essays, lectures
BARZUN, Jacques
On writing, editing, and publishing : essays, explicative and hortatory / Jacques Barzun ; with a foreword by Morris Philipson. — 2nd ed., expanded. — Chicago : University of Chicago Press, 1986. — xi, 148 p.. — (Chicago guides to writing, editing, and publishing)

EDMONDS, LLOYD — Correspondence
EDMONDS, Lloyd
Letters from Spain / Lloyd Edmonds ; edited by Amirah Inglis. — Sydney ; London : Allen & Unwin, 1985. — xiv,200p

EDUCATION
FURTER, Pierre
Les espaces de la formation : essais de microcomparaison et de microplanification / Pierre Furter ; préface de Gaston Pineau. — Lausanne : Presses Polytechniques Romandes, 1983. — 286p

SEMINAR ON EDUCATION, DEVELOPMENT AND SOCIAL TRANSFORMATION (1982)
[Proceedings of the] seminar...jointly organized by the National Institute of Research, Gaborone, Botswana [and] the Foundation of Education with Production, Gaborone, Botswana. — Gaborone : National Institute of Research : Foundation for Education with Production, [1982]. — 233p

EDUCATION — Aims and objectives
Essays on quality in education / edited by B. S. Crittenden and J. V. D'Cruz. — Richmond, Vic. : Primary Education (Publishing), 1976. — viii, 121 p.. — Simultaneously published as summer 1975 issue of Twentieth century. — Includes bibliographies

EDUCATION — Aims and objectives — Congresses
The Quality of education and economic development / edited by Stephen P. Heyneman, Daphne Siev White. — Washington, D.C., U.S.A. : World Bank, 1986. — xi,59p. — (A World Bank symposium). — "The papers were originally prepared for a conference on school quality sponsored by the World Bank's Research Committee and held in Harper's Ferry, West Virginia, in May 1983"--Foreword. — Bibliography: p57-59

EDUCATION — Data processing
Applications of cognitive psychology : problem solving, education, and computing / edited by Dale E. Berger, Kathy Pezdek, William P. Banks. — Hillsdale, N.J. : L. Erlbaum Associates, 1987. — xii, 235 p.. — Includes bibliographies and indexes

WOODHOUSE, David
Computers : promise and challenge in education / David Woodhouse [and] Anne McDougall. — Melbourne : Blackwell Scientific Publications, 1986. — ix,308p. — Bibliography: p[294]-301

EDUCATION — Data processing — Addresses, essays, lectures
BORK, Alfred M
Learning with personal computers / by Alfred Bork. — New York : Harper & Row, c1987. — p. cm

EDUCATION — Economic aspects
Education: a framework for choice : papers on historical, economic and administrative aspects of choice in education and its finance / by A. C. F. Beales [and others]. — 2nd ed. / with an appraisal by Rhodes Boyson. — London : Institute of Economic Affairs, 1970. — xvi,100p. — (Readings in political economy ; 1). — Previous ed. 1967. — bibl p100

Education, recession and the world village : a comparative political economy of education / edited and introduced by Frederick M. Wirt, Grant Harmann. — London : Falmer Press, 1986. — vii,191p. — (Contemporary analysis in education series)

EDUCATION — Economic aspects — Bibliography
PAULSTON, Rolland G.
Educación y desarrollo socio-económico de la selva peruana : buna bibliografía anotada / Rolland G. Paulston. — Lima : Ministerio de Educación Pública, Dirección General de Educación, Centro de Investigaciones Pedagógicas, 1967. — 14leaves. — ([Informe] / Centro de Investigaciones Pedagógicas ; no.1)

EDUCATION — Economic aspects — Congresses
The Quality of education and economic development / edited by Stephen P. Heyneman, Daphne Siev White. — Washington, D.C., U.S.A. : World Bank, 1986. — xi,59p. — (A World Bank symposium). — "The papers were originally prepared for a conference on school quality sponsored by the World Bank's Research Committee and held in Harper's Ferry, West Virginia, in May 1983"--Foreword. — Bibliography: p57-59

EDUCATION — Economic aspects — Developing countries
JIMENEZ, Emmanuel
Pricing policy in the social sectors : cost recovery for education and health in developing countries / Emmanuel Jimenez. — Baltimore : Johns Hopkins University Press for the World Bank, 1987. — v,170p. — Bibliographical references: p155-163

EDUCATION — Economic aspects — Europe — History
O'DONELL, Margaret G.
The educational thought of the classical political economists / by Margaret G. O'Donnell. — Lanham [MD] : University Press of America, c1985. — p. cm. — Includes index

EDUCATION — Economic aspects — India
ANSARI, M. M.
Education and economic development : perspectives for policy planning / M. M. Ansari. — New Delhi : Association of Indian Universities, 1987. — 57p

EDUCATION — Economic aspects — Sudan
BESHIR, Mohamed Omer
Educational policy and the employment problem in the Sudan / M. O. Beshir. — Khartoum : University of Khartoum. Faculty of Economic and Social Studies. Development Studies and Research Centre, 1977. — 68p. — (Monograph series / University of Khartoum. Faculty of Economic and Social Studies. Development Studies and Research Centre ; no.3). — Bibliography: p[69]

EDUCATION — Experimental methods
ROGERS, Carl R
Freedom to learn for the 80's / Carl R. Rogers ; with special contributions by Julie Ann Allender ... [et al.]. — Columbus, Ohio : C.E. Merrill Pub. Co., c1983. — viii, 312 p.. — Rev. ed. of: Freedom to learn. 1969. — Includes bibliographies and index

EDUCATION — Finance — Law and legislation — Great Britain
GREAT BRITAIN. Parliament. House of Commons. Library. Research Division
The Education (Grants and Awards) Bill [Bill 40 of 1983-84] / Kay Andrews. — [London] : the Division, 1983. — 27p. — (Reference sheet ; no.83/19). — Bibliographical references: p23-27

EDUCATION — Philosophy — History
O'DONELL, Margaret G.
The educational thought of the classical political economists / by Margaret G. O'Donnell. — Lanham [MD] : University Press of America, c1985. — p. cm. — Includes index

STABLER, Ernest
Founders : innovators in education, 1830-1980 / Ernest Stabler. — Edmonton : University of Alberta Press, 1987. — xiii,306p. — Bibliography: p297-306

EDUCATION — Philosophy — 1965-
Philosophers on education / edited by Roger Straughan and John Wilson. — Basingstoke : Macmillan, 1987. — x,180p. — Includes index

SCHEFFLER, Israel
Of human potential : an essay in the philosophy of education / Israel Scheffler. — Boston, Mass. ; London : Routledge & Kegan Paul, 1985. — xiii,141p. — Includes index

EDUCATION — Research
Interviewing in educational research / Janet Powney ... [et al.]. — London : Routledge & Kegan Paul, 1987. — [210]p. — (Routledge education books). — Includes bibliography and index

Thinking and learning skills / edited by Judith W. Segal, Susan F. Chipman, Robert Glaser. — Hillsdale, N.J. ; London : Erlbaum Volume 1: Relating instruction to research. — 1985. — xii,554p

EDUCATION — Research
continuation
Thinking and learning skills / edited by Susan F. Chipman, Judith W. Segal, Robert Glaser. — Hillsdale, N.J. ; London : Erlbaum
Volume 2: Research and open questions. — 1985. — xii,639p

EDUCATION — Research — France
FRANCE. Ministère de la recherche et de l'enseignement supérieur. Programme mobilisateur technologie, emploi, travail
L'introuvable relation formation/emploi : un état des recherches en France / sous la direction de Lucie Tanguy. — [Paris] : Documentation française, [1986]. — 302p. — *Bibliography: p271-300*

EDUCATION — Social aspects
LYNCH, James
Prejudice reduction and the schools / James Lynch. — New York : Nichols Pub., 1987. — p. cm. — *Includes indexes. — Bibliography: p*

EDUCATION — Social aspects — Canada
Social change and education in Canada / [edited by] Ratna Ghosh and Douglas Ray. — Don Mills, Ont. : Harcourt Brace Jovanovich, 1987. — viii,288p. — *Includes references*

EDUCATION — Social aspects — Europe — History — 19th century
MAYNES, Mary Jo
Schooling in Western Europe : a social history / Mary Jo Maynes. — Albany : State University of New York, 1985. — p. cm. — *Includes index. — Bibliography: p*

EDUCATION — Social aspects — Peru — Bibliography
PAULSTON, Rolland G.
Educación y desarrollo socio-económico de la selva peruana : buna bibliografía anotada / Rolland G. Paulston. — Lima : Ministerio de Educación Pública, Dirección General de Educación, Centro de Investigaciones Pedagógicas, 1967. — 14leaves. — ([Informe] / Centro de Investigaciones Pedagógicas ; no.1)

PAULSTON, Rolland G.
Investigaciones sobre la escuela y la comunidad peruana rural / Rolland G.Paulston. — [Lima] : Ministerio de Educación Pública, Dirección General de Educación, Centro de Investigaciones Pedagógicas, [1967]. — 46p. — (Informe / Centro de Investigaciones Pedagógicas ; no.2)

EDUCATION — Social aspects — United States
APPLE, Michael W.
Teachers and texts : a political economy of class and gender relations in education / Michael W. Apple. — New York ; London : Routledge & Kegan Paul, 1986. — viii,259p. — *Bibliography: p241-254. — Includes index*

Schooling in social context : qualitative studies / edited by George W. Noblit, William T. Pink. — Norwood, N.J. : Ablex Pub. Corp., c1987. — xviii, 332 p.. — *Includes bibliographies and indexes*

EDUCATION — Social aspects — United States — History
PETERSON, Paul E
The politics of school reform, 1870-1940 / Paul E. Peterson. — Chicago : University of Chicago Press, 1985. — x, 241 p.. — *Includes index. — Bibliography: p. [227]-234*

EDUCATION — Africa, Southern
SEMINAR ON EDUCATION, DEVELOPMENT AND SOCIAL TRANSFORMATION (982)
[Proceedings of the] seminar...jointly organized by the National Institute of Research, Gaborone, Botswana [and] the Foundation of Education with Production, Gaborone, Botswana. — Gaborone : National Institute of Research : Foundation for Education with Production, [1982]. — 233p

EDUCATION — Australia
Essays on quality in education / edited by B. S. Crittenden and J. V. D'Cruz. — Richmond, Vic. : Primary Education (Publishing), 1976. — viii, 121 p.. — *Simultaneously published as summer 1975 issue of Twentieth century. — Includes bibliographies*

EDUCATION — Australia — New South Wales
NEW SOUTH WALES. Australian Bureau of Statistics. New South Wales Office
Schools. — Sydney : [the Office], 1981-. — Annual. — *Continues in part New South Wales. Commonwelath Bureau of Census and Statistics. New South Wales. Education*

NEW SOUTH WALES. Commonwealth Bureau of Census and Statistics. New South Wales Office
Education / New South Wales Office, Commonwealth Bureau of Census and Statistics. — Sydney : [the Office], 1976-1980. — Annual. — *Continued by New South Wales. Australian Bureau of Statistics. New South Wales Office. Schools*

EDUCATION — Bahamas — Statistics
Commonwealth of the Bahama Islands : report of the 1980 census of population. — Nassau : Ministry of Finance
V.5: Education. — [1987]. — xvi,231p

EDUCATION — Barbados — Statistics
Commonwealth Caribbean population census 1970 : Barbados : preliminary bulletin : education. — St. Michael : Barbados Statistical Service, 1974. — ii,21p

EDUCATION — Canada
The political economy of Canadian schooling / edited by Terry Wotherspoon. — Toronto : Methuen, 1987. — 327p. — *Includes bibliographical references*

EDUCATION — Cuba — History — 20th century
MACDONALD, Theodore H
Making a new people : education in revolutionary Cuba / Theodore MacDonald. — Vancouver : New Star Books, c1985. — 248 p.. — *Includes index. — Bibliography: p. 242-245*

EDUCATION — Developing countries — Aims and objectives
FULLER, Bruce
Raising school quality in developing countries : what investments boost learning? / Bruce Fuller. — Washington, D.C. : The World Bank, 1986. — 81p. — (World Bank disscussion papers ; no.2). — *Includes bibliographical references*

EDUCATION — Developing countries — Congresses
The Quality of education and economic development / edited by Stephen P. Heyneman, Daphne Siev White. — Washington, D.C., U.S.A. : World Bank, 1986. — xi,59p. — (A World Bank symposium). — *"The papers were originally prepared for a conference on school quality sponsored by the World Bank's Research Committee and held in Harper's Ferry, West Virginia, in May 1983"--Foreword. — Bibliography: p57-59*

EDUCATION — Developing countries — Finance
Financing education in developing countries : an exploration of policy options. — Washington, D.C. : The World Bank, 1986. — iv,67p. — *Bibliography: p64-67*

FULLER, Bruce
Raising school quality in developing countries : what investments boost learning? / Bruce Fuller. — Washington, D.C. : The World Bank, 1986. — 81p. — (World Bank disscussion papers ; no.2). — *Includes bibliographical references*

PSACHAROPOULOS, George
Education for development : an analysis of investment choices / George Psacharopoulos, Maureen Woodhall. — New York : OUP for the World Bank, 1985. — ix,337p. — *Includes bibliographical references*

EDUCATION — Developing countries — Political aspects
MANDI, Peter
Quantité et qualité dans la politique de l'education poursuivre pour les pays en voie de développement / Peter Mandi. — Budapest : Centre pour la Recherche de l'Afro-Asie de l'Académie des Sciences de Hongrie, 1969. — 16p. — (Etudes sur les pays en voie de developpement ; no.29)

EDUCATION — England
HALL, Rachel
Education in Japan and England : a personal view / Rachel Hall. — London : Suntory Toyota International Centre for Economics and Related Disciplines, 1987. — 31p. — (Japanese studies). — *Bibliography: p27-31*

EDUCATION — England — London
BRENT. Education Department
Brent religious education now and tomorrow. — Brent : [the Department], 1986. — 26p

The London Labour plan : education and training. — London : London Strategic Policy Unit, 1986. — 77p. — *Bibliography: p75*

EDUCATION — Europe — History — 19th century
The Rise of the modern educational system : structural change and social reproduction 1870-1920 / [edited by] Detlef K. Müller, Fritz Ringer, Brian Simon. — Cambridge : Cambridge University Press, 1987. — xiv,264p. — *Includes index*

EDUCATION — Europe — History — 20th century
The Rise of the modern educational system : structural change and social reproduction 1870-1920 / [edited by] Detlef K. Müller, Fritz Ringer, Brian Simon. — Cambridge : Cambridge University Press, 1987. — xiv,264p. — *Includes index*

EDUCATION — Gambia — Statistics
Education statistics / Central Statistics Department, Ministry of Economic Planning and Industrial Development, Gambia. — Banjul : Ministry of Economic Planning and Industrial Development. Central Statistics Department, 1983-. — *Annual*

EDUCATION — Germany (West) — Curricula
GREAT BRITAIN. Department of Education and Science. Inspectorate of Schools
Education in the Federal Republic of Germany : aspects of curriculum and assessment : a paper by HMI. — London : H.M.S.O., 1986. — 49p

EDUCATION — Great Britain
COWBURN, Will
Class ideology and community education / Will Cowburn. — London : Croom Helm, c1986. — 235p. — (Radical forum on adult education series). — *Includes index*

Education, the Labour Party and the election campaign : the principles of the Labour Party's 1988 Education Act. — London : Socialist Educational Association, 1987. — 12p

SCRUTON, Roger
Education and indoctrination : an attempt at definition and a review of social and political implications / Roger Scruton, Angela Ellis-Jones and Dennis O'Keeffe. — Harrow : Education Research Centre, 1985. — 64p

SDP/LIBERAL ALLIANCE
The essential investment : Liberal/SDP Alliance Policies for Education. — Hebden Bridge : Hebden Royd Publications, [1987]. — [12 leaves]

EDUCATION — Great Britain — Aims and objectives
Education for capability / edited for the RSA (the Royal Society for the Encouragement of Arts, Manufactures and Commerce) by Tyrrell Burgess. — Windsor : NFER-Nelson, 1985. — ix,201p

EDUCATION — Great Britain — Curricula
GREAT BRITAIN. Department of Education and Science
The school curriculum / Department of Education and Science, Welsh Office. — London : H.M.S.O., 1981

EDUCATION — Great Britain — History — 19th century
MARSDEN, W. E.
Unequal educational provision in England and Wales : the nineteenth-century roots / W.E. Marsden. — London : Woburn, 1987. — [xvi,272]p. — Includes index

EDUCATION — Great Britain — Models
MOSER, C. A.
A computable model of the educational system in England and Wales / C. A. Moser and P. Redfern. — Beograd : International Statistical Institute, 1965. — 20p

EDUCATION — India — History — Sources
Development of education in India : a historical survey of educational documents before and after independence / [compiled by] A. Biswas, S.P. Agrawal. — New Delhi : Concept Pub. Co., 1986, c1985. — xv, 936 p.. — 87-9 . — Includes bibliographical references and index

EDUCATION — Japan
HALL, Rachel
Education in Japan and England : a personal view / Rachel Hall. — London : Suntory Toyota International Centre for Economics and Related Disciplines, 1987. — 31p. — (Japanese studies). — Bibliography: p27-31

EDUCATION — Japan — History
PASSIN, Herbert
Society and education in Japan / Herbert Passin. — 1st pbk. ed. — Tokyo ; New York : Kodansha International ; New York, N.Y. : distributed in the U.S. by Kodansha International/U.S.A. through Harper & Row, 1982. — 347 p.. — Includes index. — Bibliography: p. 327-337

EDUCATION — Mauritius — Statistics
1983 housing and population census of Mauritius : analysis report. — Rose Hill : Central Statistical Office
vol.2: Education: characteristics, prospects and some implications : (Island of Mauritius). — 1986. — 57p

EDUCATION — Morocco — Statistics
Caractéristiques socio-économiques de la population d'après le recensement général de la population et de l'habitat de 1982 : niveau national : sondage au 1/20e. — Rabat : Direction de la Statistique, 1984. — 185p

EDUCATION — New Brunswick — History
NEW BRUNSWICK. Department of Education
Two centuries of educational progress in New Brunswick : 1784-1984 = Deux siècles de progrès en éducation au Nouveau-Brunswick : 1784-1984. — [Moncton?]. : the Department, [1985?]. — 30,30p. — In English and French. — Bibliography: p30

EDUCATION — Nicaragua
ARNOVE, Robert F
Education and revolution in Nicaragua / Robert F. Arnove. — New York : Praeger, 1986. — xii, 160 p.. — (Praeger special studies series in comparative education). — "Praeger special studies. Praeger scientific.". — Includes index. — Bibliography: p. 145-153

EDUCATION — Organisation for Economic Co-operation and Development countries
Multicultural education. — Paris : Organisation for Economic Co-operation and Development, 1987. — 349p. — Includes bibliographies

EDUCATION — Peru — Bibliography
PAULSTON, Rolland G.
Educación y desarrollo socio-económico de la selva peruana : buna bibliografía anotada / Rolland G. Paulston. — Lima : Ministerio de Educación Pública, Dirección General de Educación, Centro de Investigaciones Pedagógicas, 1967. — 14leaves. — ([Informe] / Centro de Investigaciones Pedagógicas ; no.1)

PAULSTON, Rolland G.
Investigaciones sobre la escuela y la comunidad peruana rural / Rolland G.Paulston. — [Lima] : Ministerio de Educación Pública, Dirección General de Educación, Centro de Investigaciones Pedagógicas, [1967]. — 46p. — (Informe / Centro de Investigaciones Pedagógicas ; no.2)

EDUCATION — Quebec (Province)
MILNER, Henry
The long road to reform : restructuring public education in Quebec / Henry Milner. — Kingston ; Montreal : McGill-Queen's University Press, 1986. — xi,170p. — Bibliographical notes: p[141]-165

EDUCATION — Scotland
HUMES, Walter M.
The leadership class in Scottish education / Walter M. Humes. — Edinburgh : Donald, c1986. — x,228p. — Bibliography: p213-216. — Includes index

EDUCATION — South Africa — History
CHRISTIE, Pam
The right to learn : the struggle for education in South Africa / prepared for Sached by Pam Christie. — Braamfontein, South Africa : Ravan Press ; Johannesburg, South Africa : Sached Trust, [1985]. — 272 p.. — (A People's college book). — Includes bibliographies

EDUCATION — Southern States — History — Congresses
The Web of southern social relations : women, family, & education / edited by Walter J. Fraser, Jr., R. Frank Saunders, Jr., and Jon L. Wakelyn. — Athens : University of Georgia Press, c1985. — xvii, 257 p.. — Includes bibliographies and index

EDUCATION — Soviet Union — Aims and objectives — Addresses, essays, lectures
SORRENTINO, Frank M.
Soviet politics and education / Frank M. Sorrentino and Frances R. Curcio. — Lanham, MD : University Press of America, c1985. — p. cm. — Bibliography: p

EDUCATION — Soviet Union — Curricula — Addresses, essays, lectures
SORRENTINO, Frank M.
Soviet politics and education / Frank M. Sorrentino and Frances R. Curcio. — Lanham, MD : University Press of America, c1985. — p. cm. — Bibliography: p

EDUCATION — Spain — History — 20th century
CÁMARA VILLAR, Gregorio
Nacional - Catolicismo y escuela : 1a socialización política del franquismo : 1936-1951 / Gregorio Camara Villar. — [Jaén] : Hesperia, c1984. — 421p. — (Colección "Ciencias sociales"). — Bibliography:p411-421

FERNÁNDEZ SORIA, Juan Manuel
Educación y cultura en la Guerra Civil : (España 1936-39) / Juan Manuel Fernández Soria. — Valencia : NAU Llibres, 1984. — 311p

EDUCATION — Spain — Castile
HERNÁNDEZ, J. M.
La educación en Castilla y León / J. M. Hernández, M. Grande, A. Infestas. — Valladolid : Ambito ed, [1984]. — 192p. — (Colección AMBITO Castilla y León ; 22)

EDUCATION — Spain — Catalonia — History
BALCELLS, Albert
Rafael Campalans, socialisme català : biografia i textos / Albert Balcells. — [Barcelona?] : L'Abadia de Montserrat, 1985. — 444p

EDUCATION — Spain — León
HERNÁNDEZ, J. M.
La educación en Castilla y León / J. M. Hernández, M. Grande, A. Infestas. — Valladolid : Ambito ed, [1984]. — 192p. — (Colección AMBITO Castilla y León ; 22)

EDUCATION — Sweden — Addresses, essays, lectures
HARTMANN, Jürgen
Youth in the welfare society : a reader on theoretical concepts and empirical studies in youth research / Jürgen Hartmann. — Uppsala, Sweden : Distribution, Dept. of Sociology, Uppsala University, [1984]. — 103 p.. — Includes bibliographies

EDUCATION — Taiwan
Elementary and compulsory education : Republic of China : 1959. — Taipei : Ministry of Education, 1959. — 24,12 leaves. — Contents: Answers to a Unesco "questionnaire for a Survey of primary and compulsory education in South and Southeast Asia"

EDUCATION — Tanzania — Bukumbi
KAAYK, Jan
Education, estrangement and adjustment : a study among pupils and school leavers in Bukumbi, a rural community in Tanzania / Jan Kaayk ; [translation, V. A. February]. — The Hague : Mouton, [1976]. — xv, 267 p.. — (Change and continuity in Africa). — Includes index. — Bibliography: p. 265-267

EDUCATION — Thailand — Statistics
1974 statistics on general stream of education by province. — [Bangkok] : National Statistical Office, [1974?]. — 18 leaves, 170p. — In English and Thai

EDUCATION — Togo — Statistics
Recensement général de la population et de l'habitat 9-22 novembre 1981. — [Lomé] : Bureau Central du Recensement
vol.2: Caractéristiques socio-culturelles : résultats définitifs. — 1985. — 327p

EDUCATION — Trinidad and Tobago — Statistics
Report on education statistics / Central Statistical Office, Republic of Trinidad and Tobago. — Port of Spain : Central Statistical Office, 1979/80-. — Annual. — Continues: Report on enrolment in educational institutions/Central Statistical Office, Republic of Trinidad and Tobago

Report on enrolment in educational institutions / Central Statistical Office, Republic of Trinidad and Tobago. — Port of Spain : Central Statistical Office, 1973/74-1978/79. — Annual. — Data previously included in Trinidad and Tobago. Central Statistical Office. Digest of Statistics and education Continued by Report on education statistics/Central Statistical Office, Republic of Trinidad and Tobago

EDUCATION — United States — Aims and objectives
Excellence in education : perspectives on policy and practice / edited by Philip G. Altbach, Gail P. Kelly, Lois Weis. — Buffalo, N.Y. : Prometheus Books, 1985. — 290 p.. — (Frontiers in education). — "The excellence debates: a select bibliography, Kowsar P. Chowdhury and Philip G. Altbach" p. [274]-287

EDUCATION — United States — Aims and objectives *continuation*

Schooling in social context : qualitative studies / edited by George W. Noblit, William T. Pink. — Norwood, N.J. : Ablex Pub. Corp., c1987. — xviii, 332 p.. — *Includes bibliographies and indexes*

EDUCATION — United States — Curricula

The Hidden curriculum and moral education : deception or discovery? / edited by Henry Giroux and David Purpel. — Berkeley, Calif. : McCutchan Pub. Corp., c1983. — x, 425 p.. — *Includes bibliographical references*

EDUCATION — United States — Evaluation — Methodology

WORTHEN, Blaine R
Evaluating educational and social programs : guidelines for proposal review, onsite evaluation, evaluation contracts, and technical assistance / Blaine R. Worthen, Karl R. White. — Boston : Kluwer-Nijhoff ; Norwell, MA : Distributors for North America, Kluwer Academic, c1987. — xi, 347 p.. — (Evaluation in education and human services). — *Includes index. — Bibliography: p. [342]-344*

EDUCATION — United States — Finance

Political science and school politics : the princes and pundits / edited by Samuel K. Gove, Frederick M. Wirt. — Lexington, Mass. : Lexington Books, c1976. — x, 143 p.. — (Policy Studies Organization series ; 12). — *Includes bibliographical references and index*

EDUCATION — United States — History

ANTCZAK, Frederick J.
Thought and character : the rhetoric of democratic education / Frederick J. Antczak. — 1st ed. — Ames : Iowa State University Press, 1985. — viii, 242 p.. — *Includes index. — Bibliography: p. 229-235*

PETERSON, Paul E
The politics of school reform, 1870-1940 / Paul E. Peterson. — Chicago : University of Chicago Press, 1985. — x, 241 p.. — *Includes index. — Bibliography: p. [227]-234*

EDUCATION — United States — Statistics

RUBIN, Michael Rogers
The knowledge industry in the United States, 1960-1980 / Michael Rogers Rubin and Mary Taylor Huber with Elizabeth Lloyd Taylor. — Princeton, N.J. : Princeton University Press, c1986. — p. cm. — *Includes index*

EDUCATION (AMENDMENT) BILL 1985-86

GREAT BRITAIN. Parliament. House of Commons. Library. Research Division
Education (Amendment) Bill, [Bill 12 of 1985/86] / Kay Andrews. — [London] : the Division, 1985. — 18p. — (Reference sheet ; no.85/8). — *Bibliographical references: p17-18*

EDUCATION AND STATE

Education: a framework for choice : papers on historical, economic and administrative aspects of choice in education and its finance / by A. C. F. Beales [and others]. — 2nd ed. / with an appraisal by Rhodes Boyson. — London : Institute of Economic Affairs, 1970. — xvi,100p. — (Readings in political economy ; 1). — *Previous ed. 1967. — bibl p100*

Education, recession and the world village : a comparative political economy of education / edited and introduced by Frederick M. Wirt, Grant Harmann. — London : Falmer Press, 1986. — vii,191p. — (Contemporary analysis in education series)

SEXTON, Stuart
Our schools : a radical policy / Stuart Sexton. — Warlingham : Institute of Economic Affairs. Education Unit, 1987. — 50p

EDUCATION AND STATE — California — San Francisco

FINE, Doris R
When leadership fails : desegregation and demoralization in the San Francisco schools / Doris R. Fine. — New Brunswick, U.S.A. : Transaction Books, c1986. — ix, 222 p.. — (Observations in education). — *Includes bibliographical references and index*

EDUCATION AND STATE — Chile — History — 20th century

FARRELL, Joseph P
The National Unified School in Allende's Chile : the role of education in the destruction of a revolution / Joseph P. Farrell. — Vancouver : University of British Columbia Press in association with the Centre for Research on Latin America and the Caribbean, York University, 1986. — viii, 268 p.. — (Latin American and Caribbean studies ; 1). — *Includes index. — Bibliography: p. [259]-263*

EDUCATION AND STATE — Cuba — History — 20th century

MACDONALD, Theodore H
Making a new people : education in revolutionary Cuba / Theodore MacDonald. — Vancouver : New Star Books, c1985. — 248 p.. — *Includes index. — Bibliography: p. 242-245*

EDUCATION AND STATE — Europe — History

O'DONELL, Margaret G.
The educational thought of the classical political economists / by Margaret G. O'Donnell. — Lanham [MD] : University Press of America, c1985. — p. cm. — *Includes index*

EDUCATION AND STATE — Great Britain

BARLOW, John Robert
Central-local government relations : the role of finance in influencing local policy making in education and housing in England : with special reference to the period 1974-1982 / John Robert Barlow. — 459 leaves. — *PhD (Econ) 1986 LSE*

GREAT BRITAIN. Parliament. House of Commons. Library. Research Division
The Education (Grants and Awards) Bill [Bill 40 of 1983-84] / Kay Andrews. — [London] : the Division, 1983. — 27p. — (Reference sheet ; no.83/19). — *Bibliographical references: p23-27*

RADICE, Giles
Equality and quality : socialist plan for education / Giles Radice. — London : Fabian Society, 1986. — 19 p. — (Fabian tract ; no.514)

Save our schools / by the 'no turning back' group of Conservative MPs. — London : Conservative Political Centre, 1986. — 32p

EDUCATION AND STATE — Nicaragua

ARNOVE, Robert F
Education and revolution in Nicaragua / Robert F. Arnove. — New York : Praeger, 1986. — xii, 160 p.. — (Praeger special studies series in comparative education). — "Praeger special studies. Praeger scientific.". — *Includes index. — Bibliography: p. 145-153*

VILAS, Carlos M.
The Sandinista revolution : national liberation and social transformation in Central America / Carlos M. Vilas ; translated by Judy Butler. — New York : Monthly Review Press ; Berkeley, Calif. : Centre for the Study of the Americans, 1986. — 317p. — *Originally published as 'Perfiles de la revolución Sandinista: Liberación nacional y transformaciones sociales en Centroamérica' by Editorial Legasa, Madrid. — Bibliography: p293-307*

EDUCATION AND STATE — Pakistan

PAKISTAN. Ministry of Education
Action plan for educational development : 1983-88. — Islamabad : the Ministry 260.01/1, 1984. — 117p

EDUCATION AND STATE — Papua New Guinea

BACCHUS, M. K.
Educational policy and development strategy in the Third World / M. Kazil Bacchus. — Aldershot : Avebury, c1987. — xi,233p

EDUCATION AND STATE — South Africa — History

CHRISTIE, Pam
The right to learn : the struggle for education in South Africa / prepared for Sached by Pam Christie. — Braamfontein, South Africa : Ravan Press ; Johannesburg, South Africa : Sached Trust, [1985]. — 272 p.. — (A People's college book). — *Includes bibliographies*

EDUCATION AND STATE — Soviet Union — Addresses, essays, lectures

SORRENTINO, Frank M.
Soviet politics and education / Frank M. Sorrentino and Frances R. Curcio. — Lanham, MD : University Press of America, c1985. — p. cm. — *Bibliography: p*

EDUCATION AND STATE — Spain

Spain. — Paris : Organisation for Economic Co-operation and Development, 1986. — 107p. — (Reviews of national policies for education). — *Includes bibliographical references*

EDUCATION AND STATE — Spain — History

CÁMARA VILLAR, Gregorio
Nacional - Catolicismo y escuela : la socialización política del franquismo : 1936-1951 / Gregorio Camara Villar. — [Jaén] : Hesperia, c1984. — 421p. — (Colección "Ciencias sociales"). — *Bibliography:p411-421*

EDUCATION AND STATE — United States

ARONS, Stephen
Compelling belief : the culture of American schooling / Stephen Arons. — 1st paperback ed. — Amherst : University of Massachusetts Press, 1986, c1983. — xii, 228 p. — : Reprint. *Originally published: New York : McGraw-Hill, c1983. — Includes index*

CARNEGIE COUNCIL ON POLICY STUDIES IN HIGHER EDUCATION
The federal role in postsecondary education : unfinished business, 1975-1980 / a report by the Carnegie Council on Policy Studies in Higher Education. — San Francisco ; Washington : Jossey-Bass, 1975. — xi,97p. — (Carnegie Council series). — *Bibliography: p [89]-92*

Excellence in education : perspectives on policy and practice / edited by Philip G. Altbach, Gail P. Kelly, Lois Weis. — Buffalo, N.Y. : Prometheus Books, 1985. — 290 p.. — (Frontiers in education). — "The excellence debates: a select bibliography, Kowsar P. Chowdhury and Philip G. Altbach" p. [274]-287

Political science and school politics : the princes and pundits / edited by Samuel K. Gove, Frederick M. Wirt. — Lexington, Mass. : Lexington Books, c1976. — x, 143 p.. — (Policy Studies Organization series ; 12). — *Includes bibliographical references and index*

School days, rule days : the legislation and regulation of education / edited by David L. Kirp. — London : Falmer Press, 1985

Schooling in social context : qualitative studies / edited by George W. Noblit, William T. Pink. — Norwood, N.J. : Ablex Pub. Corp., c1987. — xviii, 332 p.. — *Includes bibliographies and indexes*

STEIN, Colman B
Sink or swim : the politics of bilingual education / Colman Brez Stein, Jr. — New York : Praeger, 1986. — xii, 237 p.. — "Praeger special studies. Praeger scientific.". — *Includes index. — Bibliography: p. 203-206*

EDUCATION AND STATE — United States — History
SHARPES, Donald K.
Education and the US government / Donald K. Sharpes. — London : Croom Helm, c1987. — 190p. — (Croom Helm educational management series). — *Bibliography: p183-184.* — *Includes index*

EDUCATION, BILINGUAL — Political aspects — United States
STEIN, Colman B
Sink or swim : the politics of bilingual education / Colman Brez Stein, Jr. — New York : Praeger, 1986. — xii, 237 p.. — "Praeger special studies. Praeger scientific.". — *Includes index.* — *Bibliography: p. 203-206*

EDUCATION, BILINGUAL — United States
STEIN, Colman B
Sink or swim : the politics of bilingual education / Colman Brez Stein, Jr. — New York : Praeger, 1986. — xii, 237 p.. — "Praeger special studies. Praeger scientific.". — *Includes index.* — *Bibliography: p. 203-206*

EDUCATION, BILINGUAL — Wales
BAKER, Colin, 1949-
Aspects of bilingualism in Wales / Colin Baker. — Clevedon : Multilingual Matters, c1985. — xii,209p. — (Multilingual matters ; 19). — *Bibliography: p197-204.* — *Includes index*

EDUCATION BILL 1980-81
GREAT BRITAIN. Parliament. House of Commons. Library. Research Division
Education Bill (Bill 48 of 1980/81) / [Kay Andrews]. — [London] : the Division, 1981. — 20p. — (Reference sheet ; no.81/5). — *Bibliography: p16-20*

EDUCATION BILL 1985-86
GREAT BRITAIN. Parliament. House of Commons. Library. Research Division
Education Bill (HL) [Bill 87 of 1985-86] / Kay Andrews. — [London] : the Division, 1986. — 37p. — (Reference sheet ; no.86/8). — *Bibliographical references: p31-37*

EDUCATION (CORPORAL PUNISHMENT) BILL 1984-85
GREAT BRITAIN. Parliament. House of Commons. Library. Research Division
Education (Corporal Punishment) Bill [Bill 57 of 1984/85] / Kay Andrews. — [London] : the Division, 1985. — 25p. — (Reference sheet ; no.85/2). — *Bibliography: p21-25*

EDUCATION (FEES AND AWARDS) BILL 1982-83
GREAT BRITAIN. Parliament. House of Commons. Library. Research Division
Education (Fees and Awards) Bill (Bill 135 of 1982/83) / Kay Andrews. — [London] : the Division, 1983. — 16p. — (Reference sheet ; no.83/9). — *Bibliographical references: p14-16*

EDUCATION (GRANTS AND AWARDS) BILL 1983-84
GREAT BRITAIN. Parliament. House of Commons. Library. Research Division
The Education (Grants and Awards) Bill [Bill 40 of 1983-84] / Kay Andrews. — [London] : the Division, 1983. — 27p. — (Reference sheet ; no.83/19). — *Bibliographical references: p23-27*

EDUCATION, HIGHER — Congresses
The School and the university : an international perspective / edited by Burton R. Clark. — Berkeley : University of California Press, c1985. — xii, 337 p.. — Based on a seminar held at the University of California, July 1983. — *Includes bibliographies and index*

EDUCATION, HIGHER — Data processing
GARSON, G. David
Academic microcomputing : a resource guide / G. David Garson. — Beverly Hills : Sage Publications, c1987. — 175 p. — *Includes bibliographies*

EDUCATION, HIGHER — Political aspects — Argentina — History — 20th century
MANGONE, Carlos
Universidad y peronismo (1946-1955) / Carlos Mongone y Jorge A. Warley. — Buenos Aires : Centro Editor de América Latina, 1986. — 161p. — (Biblioteca Política Argentina ; 83)

EDUCATION, HIGHER — Social aspects — United States — History
WALLENFELDT, E. C
Roots of special interests in American higher education : a social psychological historical perspective / E.C. Wallenfeldt. — Lanham, MD : University Press of America, c1986. — p. cm. — *Includes index.* — *Bibliography: p*

EDUCATION, HIGHER — Africa
Higher education in Africa : manual for refugees = Enseignement supérieur en Afrique : Manuel pour les réfugiés. — [Geneva?] : World University Service International, 1986. — xiii,784p

EDUCATION, HIGHER — Africa, Sub-Saharan
HINCHLIFFE, Keith
Higher education in sub-Saharan Africa / Keith Hinchliffe. — London : Croom Helm, c1987. — 189p. — *Bibliography: p173-180.* — *Includes index*

EDUCATION, HIGHER — Australia
AUSTRALIAN VICE-CHANCELLORS' COMMITTEE
AVCC response to the Commonwealth Tertiary Education Commission : review of efficiency and effectiveness in higher education. — Canberra : AVCC, 1986. — 15 leaves

EDUCATION, HIGHER — China
China : management and finance of higher education. — Washington, D.C. : The World Bank, 1986. — [xxiii],126p. — (A World Bank country study). — *Bibliographical references: p124-126*

EDUCATION, HIGHER — Denmark
Higher education in Denmark : a short survey of the organization and activities of the universities and other institutions of higher education in Denmark. — Copenhagen : Danish Ministry of Education, 1954. — 55p

EDUCATION, HIGHER — Denmark — Planning
Skitse for udbygningen af de højere uddannelser i tiden indtil 1980. — [København] : Planlaegningsrådet for de højere uddannelser, 1967. — [269]p. — *Includes summary in English*

EDUCATION, HIGHER — England
GREAT BRITAIN. Department of Education and Science
Higher education in England outside the Universities : policy, funding and management : a consultative document issued by the Secretary of State for Education and Science. — [London] : the Department, 1981. — 14p

EDUCATION, HIGHER — Europe 1965-
CERYCH, Ladislav
Great expectations and mixed performance : the implementation of higher education reforms in Europe / Ladislav Cerych and Paul Sabatier. — Stoke-on-Trent : Trentham Books, 1986. — xx,276p

EDUCATION, HIGHER — European Economic Community countries
NEAVE, Guy
Nouveaux modèles d'enseignement supérieur et égalité des chances : prospectives internationales / par Guy Neave. — Luxembourg : Office des Publications Officielles des Communautés Européennes, 1978. — 134p. — (Série éducation / Commission of the European Communities ; no.6)

EDUCATION, HIGHER — France — History
BROCKLISS, L. W. B.
French higher education in the seventeenth and eighteenth centuries : a cultural history / L.W.B. Brockliss. — Oxford : Clarendon, 1987. — xiii,544p. — *Bibliography: p486-523.* — *Includes index*

EDUCATION, HIGHER — Great Britain
BOURNER, Tom
Entry qualifications and degree performance : the technical report of a research project on the relationship between entry qualifications and degree performance on CNAA first degree courses / Tom Bourner and Mahmoud Hamed. — London : CNAA, 1987. — 77p. — (CNAA development sevices publications ; 10). — *Bibliography: p68-69*

MARRIS, Robin L.
The higher education crisis : a Sermon for Conservatives and socialists / Robin L. Marris. — London : Suntory-Toyota International Centre for Economics and Related Disciplines. London School of Economics and Political Science, 1986. — 41p

REDPATH, R. U.
Young people's intentions to enter higher education : the report of a survey carried out by the Social Survey Division of OPCS on behalf of the Department of Education and Science / Bob Redpath, Barbara Harvey. — London : H.M.S.O., 1987. — xii,111p. — *Social Survey no.: SS1231*

EDUCATION, HIGHER — Great Britain — Supply and demand — Forecasting
GREAT BRITAIN. Department of Education and Science
Projections of demand for higher education in Great Britain 1986-2000. — [London] : the Department, 1986. — 26p

EDUCATION, HIGHER — Kenya
HUGHES, Rees
Higher education and employment in Kenya : a liberal interpretation of the literature / Rees Hughes [and] James Gituro Wahome. — Nairobi : University of Nairobi. Institute for Development Studies, 1985. — 34p. — (Working paper / University of Nairobi. Institute for Development Studies ; no.426). — *Bibliography: p[35-36]*

EDUCATION, HIGHER — Soviet Union
ZIUZIN, D. I.
Kachestvo podgotovki spetsialistov kak sotsial'naia problema / D. I. Ziuzin. — Moskva : Nauka, 1978. — 164p

EDUCATION, HIGHER — United States — History
WALLENFELDT, E. C
Roots of special interests in American higher education : a social psychological historical perspective / E.C. Wallenfeldt. — Lanham, MD : University Press of America, c1986. — p. cm. — *Includes index.* — *Bibliography: p*

EDUCATION, HIGHER — United States — Philosophy
BLOOM, Allan David
The closing of the American mind / Allan Bloom. — New York : Simon and Schuster, c1987. — 392p. — *Includes index*

EDUCATION, HIGHER — Wales — Management
GREAT BRITAIN. Welsh Office. Education Department
The management of higher education in the maintained sector in Wales : consultative document. — [Cardiff : the Office, 1978]. — 4,3leaves

EDUCATION, HIGHER — West Bank
ANABTAWI, Samir N.
Palestinian higher education in the West Bank and Gaza : a critical assessment / Samir N. Anabtawi. — London : KPI, 1986. — 94p

EDUCATION OF CHILDREN

BIRDSALL, Nancy
Child schooling and the measurement of living standards / Nancy Birdsall. — Washington, D.C., U.S.A. : World Bank, c1982 ((1985 printing)). — 84p. — (LSMS working papers ; no.14) (LSMS working papers ; no. 14). — *Bibliographical references: p80-84*

EDUCATION, PRIMARY — Brazil — Finance

Brazil : finance of primary education. — Washington, D.C. : The World Bank, 1986. — 78p. — (A World Bank country study). — *Bibliographical references: p55-56*

EDUCATION, PRIMARY — England — London

INNER LONDON EDUCATION AUTHORITY. Research and Statistics Branch
The junior school project. — [London : the Authority]. — *Bibliographical references: p139-143*
Part C: Understanding school effectiveness. — [1986]. — 143,122p

INNER LONDON EDUCATION AUTHORITY. Research and Statistics Branch
The junior school project. — [London : the Authority]. — *Bibliographical references: p77-81*
Part A: Pupils' progress and development. — [1986]. — 81p

INNER LONDON EDUCATION AUTHORITY. Research and Statistics Branch
The junior school project. — [London : the Authority]. — *Bibliographical references: p225-228*
Part B: Differences between junior schools. — [1986]. — 228p

INNER LONDON EDUCATION AUTHORITY. Research and Statistics Branch
The junior school project. — [London : the Authority]
Technical appendices. — [1986]. — 247p

EDUCATION, PRIMARY — England — Suffolk

LILEY, D.
A study in contraction in the primary school : its effect on groupings in the classroom / D. Liley. — [Ipswich] : Education Department, [1987]. — 34p. — (Research paper / Suffolk. Education Department ; no.5)

REDMONDS, Jo
A study of co-operative teaching in primary schools / Jo Redmonds. — [Ipswich] : Education Department, 1987. — 53,iip. — (Research paper / Suffolk. Education Department ; no.6). — *Bibliography: pi-ii*

EDUCATION, PRIMARY — Great Britain

COMMITTEE ON PRIMARY EDUCATION
Improving primary schools : report of the Committee on Primary Education / chaired by Norman Thomas. — [London] : Inner London Education Authority, 1985

LUNN, Joan C. Barker
Streaming in the primary school : a longitudinal study of children in streamed and non-streamed junior schools / Joan C. Barker Lunn. — Slough : National Foundation for Educational Research in England and Wales, 1970. — xxiii,508p

EDUCATION, RURAL — Africa, West

CALCOTT, David
The education of adults at all levels / by David Calcott. — London : Commonwealth Secretariat, 1970. — 16p. — *At head of title page Commonwealth Conference on Education in Rural Areas.* — *Bibliography: p15-16.* — CRE(70)C/4

EDUCATION, RURAL — Developing countries

CALCOTT, David
The education of adults at all levels / by David Calcott. — London : Commonwealth Secretariat, 1970. — 16p. — *At head of title page Commonwealth Conference on Education in Rural Areas.* — *Bibliography: p15-16.* — CRE(70)C/4

LEWIS, Leonard John
The school and the rural environment / by L. J. Lewis. — London : Commonwealth Secretariat, 1970. — 10p. — *At head of title page: Commonwealth Conference on Education in Rural Areas.* — CRE(70)LEAD/1

EDUCATION, RURAL — Developing countries — Communication systems

BOWERS, John
Communication and rural development / by John Bowers. — London : Commonwealth Secretariat, 1970. — 17p. — *At head of title page: Commonwealth Conference on Education in Rural Areas.* — CRE(70)B/3 and C/5

EDUCATION, RURAL — India

RAO, Sudha V.
Education and rural development / Sudha V. Rao ; foreword by T. Scarlett Epstein. — New Delhi ; London : Sage, 1985. — 334p. — *Bibliography: p321-328. — Includes index*

EDUCATION, RURAL — Virginia — History — 19th century

LINK, William A
A hard country and a lonely place : schooling, society, and reform in rural Virginia, 1870-1920 / William A. Link. — Chapel Hill : University of North Carolina Press, c1986. — p. cm. — (The Fred W. Morrison series in Southern studies). — *Includes index. — Bibliography: p*

EDUCATION, RURAL — Virginia — History — 20th century

LINK, William A
A hard country and a lonely place : schooling, society, and reform in rural Virginia, 1870-1920 / William A. Link. — Chapel Hill : University of North Carolina Press, c1986. — p. cm. — (The Fred W. Morrison series in Southern studies). — *Includes index. — Bibliography: p*

EDUCATION, RURAL — Wales

GREAT BRITAIN. Welsh Education Office. Inspectors of Schools
Primary education in rural Wales = Addysg gynradd yn y Gymru wledig / [H.M. Inspectors of Schools]. — Cardiff (Government Buildings, Tŷ Glas Rd, Llanishen, Cardiff CF4 5PF) : Welsh Office, Education Department, 1978. — 122p. — (Surveys / Great Britain. Welsh Education Office ; no.6). — *Parallel English and Welsh text. - Col. map (fold. sheet) in pocket*

EDUCATION (SCOTLAND) BILL 1980-81

GREAT BRITAIN. Parliament. House of Commons. Library. Research Division
Education (Scotland) Bill, Bill 14 of 1980-81 / [Keith Cuninghame]. — [London] : the Division, 1981. — 13p. — (Reference sheet ; no.81/2). — *Includes bibliographical references*

EDUCATION, SECONDARY — Australia — South Australia — History — Case studies

MACKINNON, Alison
One foot on the ladder : origins and outcomes of girls' secondary schooling in South Australia / Alison Mackinnon. — St. Lucia ; New York : University of Queensland Press, 1984. — xii, 209 p. — (The University of Queensland Press scholars' library). — *Includes index. — Bibliography: p. [197]-205*

EDUCATION, SECONDARY — Colombia — Curricula — Case studies

PSACHAROPOULOS, George
Diversified secondary education and development : evidence from Colombia and Tanzania / George Psacharopoulos and William Loxley. — Baltimore : Johns Hopkins University Press for the World Bank, 1985. — x,243p. — *Bibliographical references: p229-238*

EDUCATION, SECONDARY — Denmark — Copenhagen — Statistics

Unges uddannelses- og beskaeftigelsesforhold i København, 1981. — [København : Københavns Statistiske Kontor, 1984. — 26p. — (Undersøgelser fra Københavns Statistiske Kontor ; nr.22). — *Includes English summary*

EDUCATION, SECONDARY — England

SHAW, Beverley
Comprehensive schooling : the impossible dream? / Beverley Shaw. — Oxford : Blackwell, 1983. — v,176p. — *Bibliography: p167-171. — Includes index*

EDUCATION, SECONDARY — England — History — 19th century

ROACH, John, 1920-
A history of secondary education in England, 1800-1870 / John Roach. — London : Longman, 1986. — xv,342p. — *Bibliography: p308-334. — Includes index*

EDUCATION, SECONDARY — England — London — History

BRYANT, Margaret E.
The London experience of secondary education / Margaret E. Bryant. — London : Athlone, 1986. — xiii,553p,[12]p of plates. — *Bibliography: p505-528. — Includes index*

EDUCATION, SECONDARY — England — Suffolk

MACDONALD, Ian L.
Educational provision for the 16 + age group : a research study on behalf of Suffolk County Council / Ian L. Macdonald. — [Ipswich] : [Education Department], 1987. — 52,[80p]. — (Research paper / Suffolk. Education Department ; no.4)

VOICE, John
The whole curriculum : review and analysis / John Voice. — [Ipswich] : Education Department, [1987]. — 53,[20]p. — (Research paper / Suffolk. Education Department ; no.2). — *Bibliography: p73*

EDUCATION, SECONDARY — Great Britain

Education and youth / edited and introduced by David Marsland. — London ; Philadelphia : Falmer Press, 1987. — (Contemporary analysis in education series ; 14)

GREAT BRITAIN. Parliament. House of Commons. Library. Research Division
Education and assessment : proposals for reform / Kay Andrews. — [London] : the Division, 1984. — 22p. — (Background paper ; no.146)

GREAT BRITAIN. Parliament. House of Commons. Library. Research Division
Education, training and income support for young people / Kay Andrews, Richard Cracknell, Christine Gillie. — [London] : the Division, 1985. — 52p. — (Background paper ; no.167). — *Bibliographical references: p50-52*

VAN DYKE, Ruth Marie
Secondary school careers advice, examination choices and adult aspirations : the maintenance of gender stratification / Ruth Marie Van Dyke. — 472 leaves. — *PhD (Econ) 1986 LSE. — Leaves 373-447 are appendices*

EDUCATION, SECONDARY — Great Britain — Curricula

The Wayward curriculum : a cause for parents' concern? / edited by Dennis O'Keeffe. — [London] : [Social Affairs Unit], c1986. — 227p

EDUCATION, SECONDARY — Great Britain — 1945- — Social aspects

REID, Ivan
The sociology of school and education / Ivan Reid. — London : Fontana Press, 1986. — 320p. — *Bibliography: p294-314*

EDUCATION, SECONDARY — Papua New Guinea
BACCHUS, M. K.
Educational policy and development strategy in the Third World / M. Kazil Bacchus. — Aldershot : Avebury, c1987. — xi,233p

EDUCATION, SECONDARY — Tanzania — Curricula — Case studies
PSACHAROPOULOS, George
Diversified secondary education and development : evidence from Colombia and Tanzania / George Psacharopoulos and William Loxley. — Baltimore : Johns Hopkins University Press for the World Bank, 1985. — x,243p. — *Bibliographical references: p229-238*

EDUCATION, SECONDARY — Wales — Cardiff (South Glamorgan) — Administration — History — 20th century
GEEN, A. G.
Decision making and secondary education : a case study / by A.G. Geen. — Cardiff : University of Wales Press, 1986. — 160p

EDUCATION SOCIOLOGY — Canada
The political economy of Canadian schooling / edited by Terry Wotherspoon. — Toronto : Methuen, 1987. — 327p. — *Includes bibliographical references*

EDUCATION, URBAN — United States — History
PETERSON, Paul E
The politics of school reform, 1870-1940 / Paul E. Peterson. — Chicago : University of Chicago Press, 1985. — x, 241 p.. — *Includes index. — Bibliography: p. [227]-234*

EDUCATIONAL ACCOUNTABILITY
KOGAN, Maurice
Education accountability : an analytic overview / Maurice Kogan. — London : Hutchinson, 1986. — 178p. — *Bibliography: p155-171. — Includes index*

EDUCATIONAL ACCOUNTABILITY — United States
WORTHEN, Blaine R
Evaluating educational and social programs : guidelines for proposal review, onsite evaluation, evaluation contracts, and technical assistance / Blaine R. Worthen, Karl R. White. — Boston : Kluwer-Nijhoff ; Norwell, MA : Distributors for North America, Kluwer Academic, c1987. — xi, 347 p.. — (Evaluation in education and human services). — *Includes index. — Bibliography: p. [342]-344*

EDUCATIONAL ANTHROPOLOGY
The cultural transition : human experience and social transformation in the Third World and Japan / edited by Merry I. White and Susan Pollack. — London : Routledge and Kegan Paul, 1986. — xiii,302p

EDUCATIONAL EQUALIZATION
Equality and freedom in education : a comparative study / edited by Brian Holmes. — London : Allen & Unwin, 1985. — ix,259p. — *Includes bibliographies and index*

GAMBETTA, Diego
Were they pushed or did they jump? : individual decision mechanisms in education / Diego Gambetta. — Cambridge : Cambridge University Press, 1987. — ix,234p. — (Studies in rationality and social change). — *Bibliography: p218-231. — Includes index*

EDUCATIONAL EQUALIZATION — Social aspects — England
SANDERSON, Michael, 1939 Jan. 23-
Educational opportunity and social change in England / Michael Sanderson. — London : Faber, 1987. — xv,164p. — (Historical handbooks). — *Bibliography: p152-157 — Includes index*

EDUCATIONAL EQUALIZATION — England — History — 20th century
SANDERSON, Michael, 1939 Jan. 23-
Educational opportunity and social change in England / Michael Sanderson. — London : Faber, 1987. — xv,164p. — (Historical handbooks). — *Bibliography: p152-157 — Includes index*

EDUCATIONAL EQUALIZATION — European Economic Community countries
NEAVE, Guy
Nouveaux modèles d'enseignement supérieur et égalité des chances : prospectives internationales / par Guy Neave. — Luxembourg : Office des Publications Officielles des Communautés Européennes, 1978. — 134p. — (Série éducation / Commission of the European Communities ; no.6)

EDUCATIONAL EQUALIZATION — Great Britain
RADICE, Giles
Equality and quality : socialist plan for education / Giles Radice. — London : Fabian Society, 1986. — 19 p. — (Fabian tract ; no.514)

EDUCATIONAL EQUALIZATION — Texas — History — 20th century
SAN MIGUEL, Guadalupe
"Let all of them take heed" : Mexican Americans and the campaign for educational equality in Texas, 1910-1981 / by Guadalupe San Miguel, Jr. — 1st ed. — Austin : University of Texas Press, 1987. — p. cm. — (Mexican American monograph ; 11). — *Includes index. — Bibliography:*

EDUCATIONAL EQUALIZATION — United States
Black English : educational equity and the law / edited by John W. Chambers, Jr. ; with a foreword by Julian Bond. — Ann Arbor, Mich. : Karoma, 1983. — xiv,170p

Excellence in education : perspectives on policy and practice / edited by Philip G. Altbach, Gail P. Kelly, Lois Weis. — Buffalo, N.Y. : Prometheus Books, 1985. — 290 p.. — (Frontiers in education). — *"The excellence debates: a select bibliography, Kowsar P. Chowdhury and Philip G. Altbach" p. [274]-287*

Policy controversies in higher education / edited by Samuel K. Gove and Thomas M. Stauffer ; prepared under the auspices of the Policy Studies Organization. — New York : Greenwood Press, 1986. — xi, 274 p.. — (Contributions to the study of education ; no. 19). — *Includes index. — Bibliography: p. [261]-264*

EDUCATIONAL EQUALIZATION — United States — Case studies
MONTI, Daniel J
A semblance of justice : St. Louis school desegregation and order in urban America / Daniel J. Monti. — Columbia : University of Missouri Press, 1985. — xiv, 221 p.. — *Includes index. — Bibliography: p. 208-215*

EDUCATIONAL EXCHANGES — Bibliography
ALTBACH, Philip G
Bibliography of foreign students and international study / by Philip G. Altbach, David H. Kelly, and Y. G-M. Lulat. — New York : Praeger, 1985. — p. cm. — (The Praeger special studies series in comparative education). — *"Published in cooperation with the Comparative Education Center, State University of New York, Buffalo."*

EDUCATIONAL EXCHANGES — European Economic Community countries — Congresses
Pupil exchange in the European Community : Venice Colloquium, 24—28 October 1977. — Luxembourg : Office for Official Publications of the European Communities, 1978. — 68p. — (Education series / Commission of the European Communities ; no.5)

EDUCATIONAL INNOVATIONS
ROGERS, Carl R
Freedom to learn for the 80's / Carl R. Rogers ; with special contributions by Julie Ann Allender ... [et al.]. — Columbus, Ohio : C.E. Merrill Pub. Co., c1983. — viii, 312 p.. — *Rev. ed. of: Freedom to learn. 1969. — Includes bibliographies and index*

EDUCATIONAL INNOVATIONS — Great Britain
Alternative educational futures / edited by Clive Harber, Roland Meighan, Brian Roberts. — London : Holt, Rinehart and Winston, c1984. — xii,180p. — (Holt education). — *Includes bibliographies and index*

EDUCATIONAL LAW AND LEGISLATION — Great Britain
GREAT BRITAIN. Parliament. House of Commons. Library. Research Division
Education Bill (Bill 48 of 1980/81) / [Kay Andrews]. — [London] : the Division, 1981. — 20p. — (Reference sheet ; no.81/5). — *Bibliography: p16-20*

GREAT BRITAIN. Parliament. House of Commons. Library. Research Division
Education Bill (HL) [Bill 87 of 1985-86] / Kay Andrews. — [London] : the Division, 1986. — 37p. — (Reference sheet ; no.86/8). — *Bibliographical references: p31-37*

EDUCATIONAL LAW AND LEGISLATION — Scotland
GREAT BRITAIN. Parliament. House of Commons. Library. Research Division
Education (Scotland) Bill, Bill 14 of 1980-81 / [Keith Cuninghame]. — [London] : the Division, 1981. — 13p. — (Reference sheet ; no.81/2). — *Includes bibliographical references*

EDUCATIONAL LAW AND LEGISLATION — United States
School days, rule days : the legislation and regulation of education / edited by David L. Kirp. — London : Falmer Press, 1985

EDUCATIONAL PLANNING
FURTER, Pierre
Les espaces de la formation : essais de microcomparaison et de microplanification / Pierre Furter ; préface de Gaston Pineau. — Lausanne : Presses Polytechniques Romandes, 1983. — 286p

EDUCATIONAL PLANNING — Statistical methods
Methods and statistical needs for educational planning. — Paris : Organisation for Economic Co-operation and Development, 1967. — 363p

EDUCATIONAL PLANNING — Papua New Guinea
BACCHUS, M. K.
Educational policy and development strategy in the Third World / M. Kazil Bacchus. — Aldershot : Avebury, c1987. — xi,233p

EDUCATIONAL PLANNING — Peru — Congresses
CURSO NACIONAL DE PLANIFICACIÓN EDUCATIVA (1 : 1965 : Lima)
Informe final presentado...en la Ceremonia de Clausura, realizada en la Casa de la Cultura / Carlos Pestana Zevallos. — Lima : Instituto Nacional de Planificación, 1965. — 89p

EDUCATIONAL PSYCHOLOGY
EDWARDS, Derek
Common knowledge : the development of understanding in the classroom / Derek Edwards and Neil Mercer. — London : Methuen, 1987. — x,193p. — (Open University set book). — *Bibliography: p182-187. — Includes index*

EDUCATIONAL SOCIOLOGY
Critical pedagogy and cultural power / David W. Livingstone & contributors ; introduction by Paulo Freire and Henry Giroux. — Basingstoke : Macmillan, 1987. — xvi,342p. — *Bibliography: p293-335. — Includes index*

EDUCATIONAL SOCIOLOGY *continuation*

GAMBETTA, Diego
Were they pushed or did they jump? : individual decision mechanisms in education / Diego Gambetta. — Cambridge : Cambridge University Press, 1987. — ix,234p. — (Studies in rationality and social change). — *Bibliography: p218-231.* — *Includes index*

Handbook of theory and research for the sociology of education / edited by John G. Richardson. — New York : Greenwood Press, 1986. — xxiv, 377 p.. — *Includes bibliographies and indexes*

The Social psychology of education : current research and theory / edited by Robert S. Feldman. — Cambridge : Cambridge University Press, 1986. — 381p. — *Includes bibliographies and index*

Structures of knowing / edited by Richard C. Monk. — Lanham ; London : University Press of America, 1987. — [522]p. — *Includes index*

EDUCATIONAL SOCIOLOGY — Australia

KING, R. J. R.
A systematic sociology of Australian education / R.J.R. King and R.E. Young. — London : Allen & Unwin, 1986. — [204]p

EDUCATIONAL SOCIOLOGY — Great Britain

Education and community / Ruth Jonathan [et al.]. — Edinburgh : University of Edinburgh. Department of Christian Ethics and Practical Theology, 1986. — 31p. — (Occasional papers / University of Edinburgh. Department of Christian Ethics and Practical Theology ; no.9)

Handbook of theory and research for the sociology of education / edited by John G. Richardson. — New York : Greenwood Press, 1986. — xxiv, 377 p.. — *Includes bibliographies and indexes*

EDUCATIONAL SOCIOLOGY — Japan — History

PASSIN, Herbert
Society and education in Japan / Herbert Passin. — 1st pbk. ed. — Tokyo ; New York : Kodansha International ; New York, N.Y. : distributed in the U.S. by Kodansha International/U.S.A. through Harper & Row, 1982. — 347 p.. — *Includes index.* — *Bibliography: p. 327-337*

EDUCATIONAL SOCIOLOGY — United States

Handbook of theory and research for the sociology of education / edited by John G. Richardson. — New York : Greenwood Press, 1986. — xxiv, 377 p.. — *Includes bibliographies and indexes*

EDUCATIONAL STATISTICS

Drawing inferences from self-selected samples / edited by Howard Wainer. — New York : Springer-Verlag, c1986. — xii, 163 p.. — *Papers from a conference sponsored by Educational Testing Service.* — *Includes indexes.* — *Bibliography: p. [153]-157*

EDUCATIONAL SURVEYS

BIRDSALL, Nancy
Child schooling and the measurement of living standards / Nancy Birdsall. — Washington, D.C., U.S.A. : World Bank, c1982 ((1985 printing)). — 84p. — (LSMS working papers ; no.14) (LSMS working papers ; no. 14). — *Bibliographical references: p80-84*

EDUCATIONAL SURVEYS — United States

WORTHEN, Blaine R
Evaluating educational and social programs : guidelines for proposal review, onsite evaluation, evaluation contracts, and technical assistance / Blaine R. Worthen, Karl R. White. — Boston : Kluwer-Nijhoff ; Norwell, MA : Distributors for North America, Kluwer Academic, c1987. — xi, 347 p.. — (Evaluation in education and human services). — *Includes index.* — *Bibliography: p. [342]-344*

EDUCATIONAL TECHNOLOGY

Aspects of educational technology. — London : Kogan Page
Vol.19: Educational training and information technologies : economics and other realities / edited for the Association of Educational and Training Technology by Nick Rushby and Anne Howe. — 1986. — [180]p. — *Includes index*

EDUCATIONAL VOUCHERS

HOLLAND, Peter F.
Education vouchers : the radical approach to educational reform? / by Peter F. Holland. — [Sheffield] : PAVIC Publications, [c1985]. — 56p. — (POPSA ; 4). — *Cover title.* — *Bibliography: p53-56*

EDUCATORS — Biography

STABLER, Ernest
Founders : innovators in education, 1830-1980 / Ernest Stabler. — Edmonton : University of Alberta Press, 1987. — xiii,306p. — *Bibliography: p297-306*

EDUCATORS — History

STABLER, Ernest
Founders : innovators in education, 1830-1980 / Ernest Stabler. — Edmonton : University of Alberta Press, 1987. — xiii,306p. — *Bibliography: p297-306*

EDUCATORS — Denmark — Biography

Grundtvig's ideas in North America : influences and parallels / edited by Det Danske Selskab/The Danish Institute. — Copenhagen : Det Danske Selskab, 1983. — 173p. — *Bibliography: p167*

EDUCATORS — Sierra Leone — Biography

CROMWELL, Adelaide M.
An African Victorian feminist : the life and times of Adelaide Smith Casely Hayford 1868-1960 / Adelaide M. Cromwell. — London : Cass, 1986. — xvi,235p,[13]p of plates. — *Includes index*

EEC *See* European Economic Community

EFFICIENCY, INDUSTRIAL

Die Unternehmung in der demokratischen Gesellschaft = : The business corporation in the democratic society / herausgegeben von Wolfgang Dorow. — Berlin ; New York : W. de Gruyter, 1987. — xiii, 390 p.. — "Günter Dlugos zum 65. Geburtstagegewidmet.". — *English and German.* — *Includes bibliographies*

EFFICIENCY, INDUSTRIAL — Soviet Union

Ekonomicheskie problemy razvitogo sotsializma / red. kollegiia I. I. Lukinov...[et al.]. — Kiev : Naukova dumka
T.3: Povyshenie effektivnosti sotsialisticheskogo vosproizvodstva / red. kollegiia V. I. Kononenko...[et al.]. — 1985. — 270p

MAKOVETSKAIA, M. I.
Effektivnost' sotsialisticheskogo vosproizvodstva : (sushchnost', kriterii, izmerenie) / M. I. Makovetskaia ; otv. redaktor I. P. Suslov. — Novosibirsk : Nauka, Sibirskoe otdelenie, 1982. — 112p. — *Bibliography: p109-112*

Rezervy povysheniia effektivnosti proizvodstva / [A. N. Zolotarev...et al.]. — Kiev : Naukova dumka, 1983. — 200p. — *Bibliography: p196-[201]*

EFFICIENCY, INDUSTRIAL — United States

ADAMS, Walter
The bigness complex : industry, labor, and government in the American economy / Walter Adams and James W. Brock. — 1st ed. — New York : Pantheon Books, 1986. — xiii, 426 p.. — *Includes indexes.* — *Bibliography: p. 381-413*

EFFICIENCY, INDUSTRIAL — United States — Case studies

PAUL, Ronald N
The 101 best performing companies in America / Ronald N. Paul, James W. Taylor. — Chicago, Ill. : Probus Pub. Co., c1986. — vii, 382 p.. — *Includes bibliographical references and index*

EGG TRADE — Australia

AUSTRALIA. Bureau of Agricultural Economics
Eggs: situation and outlook. — Canberra : [the Bureau], 1954/55-1984. — *Annual.* — *Title varies*

EGG TRADE — European Economic Community Countries

Agricultural review for Europe. — New York : United Nations, 1983/84-. — *Annual.* — *Continues: Review of the agricultural situation in Europe and Agricultural trade in Europe.* — *In 6 vols. Vol.I: General review, Vol.II: Agricultural trade, Vol.III: The Grain Market, Vol.IV: The Livestock and meat market, Vol.V: The milk and dairy products market, Vol.VI: The egg market*

EGGLESTON, JOHN

RUNNYMEDE TRUST
Education for some : a summary of the Eggleston Report on the educational and vocational experiences of young black people. — London : Runnymede Trust, 1986. — iv,57p

EGGLESTON REPORT

RUNNYMEDE TRUST
Education for some : a summary of the Eggleston Report on the educational and vocational experiences of young black people. — London : Runnymede Trust, 1986. — iv,57p

EGGPLANT INDUSTRY — Mexico

MEXICO. Dirección General de Economía Agrícola
Programa siembra-exportación de berenjena, temporada 1983-84. — [México] : the Dirección, [ca.1985]. — 25p. — *Cover title: Berenjena, programa siembra exportación 1983-1984*

EGNA PROVINCE (PAPUA NEW GUINEA) — Population — Statistics

1980 national population census : final figures : provincial summary : Enga Province. — Port Moresby : National Statistical Office, 1985. — iii,123p

EGYPT — Boundaries

La frontière occidentale de l'Egypte : accord Italo-Egyptien du 6 Décembre 1925. — Le Caire : Ministère des Affaires Étrangères, 1927. — 22p. — (Documents réservés ; no.1)

EGYPT — Census, 1976

1976 population and housing census : total republic. — Cairo : Central Agency for Public Mobilisation and Statistics
Vol. 1. — 1980. — 478p

1976 Population and housing census : total Republic. — Cairo : Central Agency for Public Mobilisation and Statistics
Vol. 2: Fertility and internal migration and movement of workers and students. — 1980. — 440p

EGYPT — Economic policy

COOPER, Mark N
The transformation of Egypt / Mark N. Cooper. — Baltimore, Md. : Johns Hopkins University Press, 1982. — 278 p.. — *Includes bibliographical references and index*

EGYPT — Economic policy *continuation*

WEINBAUM, Marvin G.
Egypt and the politics of U.S. economic aid / Marvin G. Weinbaum. — Boulder ; London : Westview, 1986. — xii,192p. — *Bibliography: p183-187*

EGYPT — Foreign relations — Italy

La frontière occidentale de l'Egypte : accord Italo-Egyptien du 6 Décembre 1925. — Le Caire : Ministère des Affaires Étrangères, 1927. — 22p. — (Documents réservés ; no.1)

EGYPT — Foreign relations — Saudi Arabia

BADEEB, Saeed M
The Saudi-Egyptian conflict over North Yemen, 1962-1970 / Saeed M. Badeeb ; foreword by J.E. Peterson. — Boulder, Colo. : Westview Press ; Washington, D.C. : American-Arab Affairs Council, 1986. — xv, 148 p., [1] p. of plates. — *Includes index.* — *Bibliography: p. 137-142*

EGYPT — Foreign relations — United States

WEINBAUM, Marvin G.
Egypt and the politics of U.S. economic aid / Marvin G. Weinbaum. — Boulder ; London : Westview, 1986. — xii,192p. — *Bibliography: p183-187*

EGYPT — History — British occupation, 1882-1936

EGYPT. Delegation to the Paris Peace Conference (1919-1920)
Discours prononcés au déjeuner offert par la délégation Égyptienne le 2 aout 1919. — [Paris : the Delegation, 1919]. — 24p

EGYPT. Delegation to the Paris Peace Conference (1919-1920)
The Egyptian national claims : a memorandum presented to the Peace Conference by the Egyptian Delegation charged with the defence of Egyptian Independence. — [Paris : the Delegation, 1919]. — 31p

EGYPT — History — British Occupation 1882-1936

EGYPT. Delegation to the Paris Peace Conference (1919-1920)
Note présentée le 9 juin 1919 à l'"Internationale Socialiste". — [Paris : the Delegation, 1919]. — 18p

EGYPT — History — Insurrection, 1919

EGYPT. Delegation to the Paris Peace Conference (1919-1920)
Rapport presenté a la Conférence de la Paix sur la répression par les troupes Britanniques du mouvement national Egyptien du mois de mars 1919. — Paris : Délégation Egyptienne, 1919. — 102p

EGYPT. Delegation to the Paris Peace Conference (1919-1920)
Report presented on March the 30th 1919 by the Egyptian delegation to His Excellency the General Sir Edmund-Henry-Hymman Allenby, British High Commissioner. — [Paris : the Delegation, 1919]. — 8p

EGYPT — History — 19th century

HUNTER, F. Robert
Egypt under the khedives, 1805-1879 : from household government to modern bureaucracy / F. Robert Hunter. — Pittsburgh, PA : University of Pittsburgh Press, c1984. — xv, 283 p.. — *Includes index.* — *Bibliography: p. 267-277*

EGYPT — History — Intervention, 1956

FAWZI, Mahmoud
Suez 1956 : an Egyptian perspective / by Mahmoud Fawzi. — London : Shorouk International, [1986]. — 149p

HEIKAL, Mohamed
Cutting the lion's tail : Suez through Egyptian eyes / Mohamed H. Heikal. — London : Deutsch, 1986. — xiv,238p,12p of plates. — *Includes index*

REID, Escott
Hungary and Suez 1956 : a view from New Delhi / Escott Reid. — Oakville [Ontario] : Mosaic Press, 1986. — 163p

SHUCKBURGH, Sir Evelyn
Descent to Suez : diaries, 1951-56 / Evelyn Shuckburgh ; selected for publication by John Charmley. — London : Weidenfeld and Nicolson, 1986. — x,380p,[12]p of plates

EGYPT — Industries

Emploi de l'energie électrique dans les établissements industriels : conditions générales concernant les établissements industriels (usines et ateliers) régis par la loi du 28 Août 1904, sur les établissements incommodes, insalubres et dangereux, et par l'arrêté ministériel du 29 Août 1904. — Le Caire : Ministère de l'Intérieur, 1923. — 10p

EGYPT — Politics and government — 640-1882

HUNTER, F. Robert
Egypt under the khedives, 1805-1879 : from household government to modern bureaucracy / F. Robert Hunter. — Pittsburgh, PA : University of Pittsburgh Press, c1984. — xv, 283 p.. — *Includes index.* — *Bibliography: p. 267-277*

EGYPT — Politics and government — 1882-1936

GERSHONI, I
Egypt, Islam, and the Arabs : the search for Egyptian nationhood, 1900-1930 / Israel Gershoni and James P. Jankowski. — New York : Oxford University Press, 1986, c1987. — xviii, 346 p.. — (Studies in Middle Eastern history). — "In cooperation with the Dayan Center and the Shiloah Institute for Middle Eastern and African Studies, Tel Aviv University.". — *Includes index.* — *Bibliography: p. 326-335*

EGYPT — Politics and government — 1952-

ANSARI, Hamied
Egypt, the stalled society / Hamied Ansari. — Albany : State University of New York Press, c1986. — xiv, 308 p.. — (SUNY series in Near Eastern studies). — *Includes indexes.* — *Bibliography: p. 291-295*

COOPER, Mark N
The transformation of Egypt / Mark N. Cooper. — Baltimore, Md. : Johns Hopkins University Press, 1982. — 278 p.. — *Includes bibliographical references and index*

EGYPT — Population

Population studies: quarterly review / Population and Family Planning Board. — Cairo : Population and Family Planning Board. Research Office, 1983-. — *Quarterly*

EGYPT — Population — Statistics

1976 population and housing census : total republic. — Cairo : Central Agency for Public Mobilisation and Statistics
Vol. 1. — 1980. — 478p

1976 Population and housing census : total Republic. — Cairo : Central Agency for Public Mobilisation and Statistics
Vol. 2: Fertility and internal migration and movement of workers and students. — 1980. — 440p

The Egyptian Fertility Survey, 1980 : a summary of findings. — Voorburg : International Statistical Institute, 1983. — 33p. — (World Fertility Survey ; no.42)

NASSEF, Abdel-Fattah
Demographic developments in Egypt, 1960-76 / Abdel-Fattah Nassef. — Geneva : International Labour Office, 1983. — viii,40p. — (Employment opportunities and equity in Egypt ; no.2). — *Bibliographical references: p39-40.* — *A technical paper of the ILO/UNDP comprehensive employment strategy mission to Egypt, 1980*

EGYPT — Relations — Arab countries

GERSHONI, I
Egypt, Islam, and the Arabs : the search for Egyptian nationhood, 1900-1930 / Israel Gershoni and James P. Jankowski. — New York : Oxford University Press, 1986, c1987. — xviii, 346 p.. — (Studies in Middle Eastern history). — "In cooperation with the Dayan Center and the Shiloah Institute for Middle Eastern and African Studies, Tel Aviv University.". — *Includes index.* — *Bibliography: p. 326-335*

EGYPT — Rural conditions

ANSARI, Hamied
Egypt, the stalled society / Hamied Ansari. — Albany : State University of New York Press, c1986. — xiv, 308 p.. — (SUNY series in Near Eastern studies). — *Includes indexes.* — *Bibliography: p. 291-295*

EGYPT — Statistics, Vital

NASSEF, Abdel-Fattah
Demographic developments in Egypt, 1960-76 / Abdel-Fattah Nassef. — Geneva : International Labour Office, 1983. — viii,40p. — (Employment opportunities and equity in Egypt ; no.2). — *Bibliographical references: p39-40.* — *A technical paper of the ILO/UNDP comprehensive employment strategy mission to Egypt, 1980*

EGYPT. Legislative Council. Egyptian Canal Act

The Egyptian Canal Act. — Cairo : Ministry of Public Works, 1915. — xv,22p

EGYPTIAN CANAL ACT

The Egyptian Canal Act. — Cairo : Ministry of Public Works, 1915. — xv,22p

EHRLICH, EUGEN

REHBINDER, Manfred
Die Begründung der Rechtssoziologie durch Eugen Ehrlich / von Manfred Rehbinder. — 2nd ed. — Berlin : Duncker and Humblot, [1986]. — 147p. — (Schriftenreihe zur Rechtssoziologie und Rechtstatschenforschung ; Bd.6). — *Bibliography: p143-147*

EIGHT-HOUR MOVEMENT

STEINISCH, Irmgard
Arbeitszeitverkürzung und sozialer Wandel : der Kampf um die Achtstundenschicht in der deutschen und amerikanischen Eisen- und Stahlindustrie 1880-1929 / Irmgard Steinisch. — Berlin : de Gruyter, 1986. — xiv,640p. — (Veröffentlichungen der Historischen Kommission zu Berlin ; Bd.65) (Beiträge zu Inflation und Wiederaufbau in Deutschland und Europa 1914-1924 ; Bd.6). — *Bibliography: p577-620*

EINSTEIN, ALBERT — Views on realism

FINE, Arthur
The shaky game : Einstein, realism, and the quantum theory / Arthur Fine. — Chicago : University of Chicago Press, c1986. — xi, 186 p.. — (Science and its conceptual foundations). — *Includes index.* — *Bibliography: p. 173-179*

EISENHOWER, DWIGHT D

BRENDON, Piers
Ike, his life and times / Piers Brendon. — 1st ed. — New York : Harper & Row, c1986. — xvi, 478 p., [16] p. of plates. — *Includes index.* — *Bibliography: p. [461]-462*

BURK, Robert Fredrick
Dwight D. Eisenhower, hero & politician / Robert F. Burk. — Boston : Twayne Publishers, c1986. — xii, 207 p., [14] p. of plates. — (Twayne's twentieth-century American biography series ; no. 2). — *Includes index.* — *Bibliography: p. 178-199*

EISENHOWER, DWIGHT D.

EISENHOWER, David
Eisenhower : at war 1943-1945 / David Eisenhower. — London : Collins, 1986. — xxvii,977p,[32]p of plates. — *Bibliography: p847-857.* — *Includes index*

EL EJIDO (SPAIN) — Social conditions
PONCE MOLINA, Pedro
Agricultura y sociedad de El Ejido en el siglo XVI / Pedro Ponce Molina. — [El Ejido] : Ayuntamiento de El Ejido, 1983. — 199p. — *Bibliography: p[191]-199*

EL SALVADOR — Description and travel
COXSEDGE, Joan
Thank God for the revolution : a journey through Central America / Joan Coxsedge ; foreword by Noam Chomsky. — Sydney ; London : Pluto Press, 1986. — xiv,175p

EL SALVADOR — Dictionaries and encyclopedias
FLEMION, Philip F
Historical dictionary of El Salvador / by Philip F. Flemion. — Metuchen, N.J. : Scarecrow Press, 1972. — 157 p. — (Latin American historical dictionaries, no. 5). — *Bibliography: p. 149-157*

EL SALVADOR — Foreign relations — United States
REED, Roger
El Salvador and the crisis in Central America / Roger Reed. — Washington, D.C. : Council for Inter-American Security, c1984. — 59 p.. — *Includes bibliographical references*

EL SALVADOR — History — 1944-1979
ALEGRÍA, Claribel
They won't take me alive : Salvadorean women in struggle for national liberation / Claribel Alegria ; translated by Amanda Hopkinson. — London : Women's Press, c1987. — 145p. — *Translation of: No me agarran viva*

EL SALVADOR — History — 1979-
ALEGRÍA, Claribel
They won't take me alive : Salvadorean women in struggle for national liberation / Claribel Alegria ; translated by Amanda Hopkinson. — London : Women's Press, c1987. — 145p. — *Translation of: No me agarran viva*

EL SALVADOR — Politics and government — 1979-
CLEMENTS, Charles
Witness to war : an American doctor in El Salvador / Charles Clements. — London : Fontana, 1985, c1984. — xiv,306p,[8]p of plates. — *Originally published: Toronto : Bantam, 1984*

COXSEDGE, Joan
Thank God for the revolution : a journey through Central America / Joan Coxsedge ; foreword by Noam Chomsky. — Sydney ; London : Pluto Press, 1986. — xiv,175p

DUARTE, José Napoleón
Duarte : my story / Jose Napoleon Duarte. — New York : Putnam, 1986. — p. cm

GREAT BRITAIN. Parliament. House of Commons. Library. International Affairs Section
The crisis in El Salvador / Richard Ware. — [London] : the Library, 1981. — 12p. — (Background paper / House of Commons. Library. [Research Division] ; no.90). — *Bibliographical references: p12*

REED, Roger
El Salvador and the crisis in Central America / Roger Reed. — Washington, D.C. : Council for Inter-American Security, c1984. — 59 p.. — *Includes bibliographical references*

EL SALVADOR — Presidents — Biography
DUARTE, José Napoleón
Duarte : my story / Jose Napoleon Duarte. — New York : Putnam, 1986. — p. cm

ELECTIC UTILITIES — Great Britain — Bibliography
ELECTRICITY COUNCIL. Intelligence Section
Select list of references to publications bearing on the economic appraisal and planning of the Generating Board's system. — London : the Section, [1969]. — 10p. — (Bibliographies / Electricity Council, Intelligence Section ; B30)

ELECTION DISTRICTS — Great Britain
WALLER, Robert
The almanac of British politics / Robert Waller. — 3rd ed. — London : Croom Helm, c1987. — [640]p. — *Previous ed.: 1983*

ELECTION DISTRICTS — Wales
GREAT BRITAIN. Welsh Office
Areas of parliamentary constituencies in Wales : (areas in terms of new local authorities; areas in terms of former local authorities). — [Cardiff : the Office, 1974]. — [7]leaves

ELECTION LAW
FRANCE
[Code électoral]. Code électoral. — 3e éd. — Paris : Dalloz, 1986. — viii,375p. — (Codes Dalloz). — *Previous ed.: 1984. Includes index*

ELECTION LAW — France
FRANCE
Code électoral : mise à jour au 1er janvier 1986. — Nouvelle éd. complétée par des textes annexes. — Paris : Berger-Levrault, 1986. — xiv,256p

ELECTION LAW — Germany (West)
JESSE, Eckhard
Wahlrecht zwischen Kontinuität und Reform : eine Analyse der Wahlsystemdiskussion und der Wahlrechtsänderungen in der Bundesrepublik Deutschland 1949-1983 / Eckhard Jesse ; [herausgegeben von der Kommission für Geschichte des Parlamentarismus und der politischen Parteien]. — Düsseldorf : Droste, 1985. — 440p. — (Beiträge zur Geschichte des Parlamentarismus und der politischen Parteien ; Bd.78)

ELECTION LAW — Great Britain
GREAT BRITAIN. Parliament. House of Commons. Library. Research Division
Representation of the People Bill [Bill 153 of 1980-81] / [Rosamund Coates]. — [London] : the Division, 1981. — 18p. — (Reference sheet ; no.81/16)

ELECTIONEERING — History — 20th century
Ideology, strategy and party change : spatial analyses of post-war election programmes in 19 democracies / edited by Ian Budge, David Robertson, Derek Hearl. — Cambridge : Cambridge University Press, 1987. — xvii,494p . — *Bibliography: p472-483. — Includes index*

ELECTIONEERING — United States
MAISEL, Louis Sandy
Parties and elections in America : the electoral process / Louis Sandy Maisel. — New York : Random House, 1986. — p. cm. — *Includes index. — Bibliography: p*

ELECTIONS
Do elections matter? / Benjamin Ginsberg and Alan Stone, editors. — Armonk, N.Y. : M.E. Sharpe, c1986. — 240 p.. — *Includes bibliographies*

GINSBERG, Benjamin
The captive public : how mass opinion promotes state power / Benjamin Ginsberg. — New York : Basic Books, c1986. — xi, 272 p.. — *Includes index. — Bibliography: p. [233]-249*

Political parties : electoral change and structural response / edited by Alan Ware. — Oxford : Basil Blackwell, 1987. — [240]p. — *Includes index*

ELECTIONS — History
PRZEWORSKI, Adam
Paper stones : a history of electoral socialism / Adam Przeworski and John Sprague. — Chicago : University of Chicago Press, 1986. — vi, 224 p.. — *Includes indexes. — Bibliography: p. [203]-216*

ELECTIONS — Maps
LEONARD, Dick
World atlas of elections : voting patterns in 39 democracies / Dick Leonard and Richard Natkiel. — London : Economist Publications, c1986. — 159p. — *Bibliography: p5-8*

ELECTIONS — Social aspects — Spain — Basque Provinces
LLERA RAMO, Francisco José
"Postfranquismo y fuerzas politicas en Euskadi" : sociología electoral del País Vasco / Francisco José Llera Ramo. — Bilbao : Universidad del País Vasco, 1985. — 596p. — *Bibliography: p363-366*

ELECTIONS — Social aspects — Wales — Brecknock (Powys)
BRADBURY, Farel
The Brecon mandate : portrait of an electorate / Farel Bradbury. — Ross-on-Wye : Hydatum, 1986. — ix,99p. — *Subtitle: An analysis of 159,137 replies to the Voice of the People (VP) policy survey by the Electorate at the Parliamentary by-election for the constituency of Brecon and Radnor, 4th July, 1985. — "Voice of the People...Policy Survey" sample form in rear pocket*

ELECTIONS — Social aspects — Wales — Radnor (Powys)
BRADBURY, Farel
The Brecon mandate : portrait of an electorate / Farel Bradbury. — Ross-on-Wye : Hydatum, 1986. — ix,99p. — *Subtitle: An analysis of 159,137 replies to the Voice of the People (VP) policy survey by the Electorate at the Parliamentary by-election for the constituency of Brecon and Radnor, 4th July, 1985. — "Voice of the People...Policy Survey" sample form in rear pocket*

ELECTIONS — Africa — History — 20th century
Elections in independent Africa / edited by Fred M. Hayward. — Boulder, Colo. : Westview Press, 1987. — p. cm. — (Westview special studies on Africa)

ELECTIONS — Arab countries
Elections in the Middle East : implications of recent trends / edited by Linda L. Layne. — Boulder, Colo. ; London : Westview Press, 1987. — xi,226p. — (Westview special studies on the Middle East). — *Bibliography: p215-223*

ELECTIONS — Australia — Statistics
Election statistics 1984. — Canberra : Australian Government Publishing Service, 1986. — 15v. — *Contents: Voting statistics for the Australian Senate and House of Representatives from the Australian Capital Territory, Northern Territory, Victoria, Western Australia, Queensland, South Australia, New South Wales (3 vols) and Tasmania*

ELECTIONS — Australia — New South Wales
The Wran model : electoral politics in New South Wales 1981 and 1984 / edited by Ernie Chaples, Helen Nelson [and] Ken Turner. — Melbourne : Oxford University Press, 1985. — vi,289p

ELECTIONS — Canada
JOHNSTON, Donald J
Up the hill / Donald Johnston. — Montréal : Optimum, c1986. — vii, 304 p.. — *Includes index. — Bibliography: p. 289-295*

ELECTIONS — England — History — Bibliography
SEATON, Janet
English constituency histories, 1265-1832 : a guide to printed sources / by Janet Seaton. — London : H.M.S.O., 1986. — xvii, 143p. — (House of Commons Library document ; no.15)

ELECTIONS — England — History — 17th century

KISHLANSKY, Mark A.
Parliamentary selection : social and political choice in early modern England / Mark A. Kishlansky. — Cambridge : Cambridge University Press, 1986. — 1v.. — *Includes bibliography and index*

ELECTIONS — France

SINCLAIR, Philippe
Les idées de mars 1986 : que choisir? / Philippe Sinclair. — Paris : Flammarion, [1985]. — 213p

ELECTIONS — France — Statistics

BAGUENARD, Jacques
La France electorale / Jacques Baguenard. — Paris : Presses Universitaires de France, 1986. — viii,725p

ELECTIONS — France — Meaux

LOGRE, Bernard
Jozon-Menier : récit d'une campagne électorale : les élections législatives de 1876 dans l'arrondissement de Meaux / Bernard Logre. — Dammarie-les-Lys : Editions Amatteis, 1986. — 111p

ELECTIONS — Germany (West)

JESSE, Eckhard
Wahlrecht zwischen Kontinuität und Reform : eine Analyse der Wahlsystemdiskussion und der Wahlrechtsänderungen in der Bundesrepublik Deutschland 1949-1983 / Eckhard Jesse ; [herausgegeben von der Kommission für Geschichte des Parlamentarismus und der politischen Parteien]. — Düsseldorf : Droste, 1985. — 440p. — (Beiträge zur Geschichte des Parlamentarismus und der politischen Parteien ; Bd.78)

ELECTIONS — Great Britain

BBC newsnight constituency survey : Greenwich survey 21 February 1987. — London : BBC, 1987. — 11p

BRADBURY CONTROLS LTD
Manifesto of manifestos U.K. general election 11th June, 1987 : a concise listing of the election policies extracted from the official party manifestos. — 4th ed.. — Ross-on-Wye : Hydatum, 1987. — iv,32p

GREAVES, Tony
[Leaflet delivery] / Tony Greaves. — Hebden Bridge : Association of Liberal Councillors, 1985. — [8p]. — (Activists' guide ; no.4)

GREAVES, Tony
Polling day: a guide to organisation / Tony Greaves. — Hebden Bridge : Association of Liberal Councillors, 1982. — 15p. — (ALC activists'guide ; no.2)

LABOUR PARTY (Great Britain)
Britain will win : Labour manifesto, June 1987. — London : The Party, 1987. — 17 p

LABOUR PARTY (Great Britain)
How to fight local elections. — London : Labour Party, 1985. — 72p

SCARBROUGH, Elinor
The British electorate twenty years on : reviewing electoral change and election surveys / by Elinor Scarbrough. — Colchester : Department of Government University of Essex, 1986. — 34 p. — (Essex papers in politics and government ; no.35)

SDP-LIBERAL ALLIANCE
Britain united : the time has come : the SDP/Liberal Alliance programme for government. — London : The Alliance, [1987]. — [24] p.

WORKERS POWER
The class struggle and the elections : a workers' manifesto. — London : Workers Power, 1987. — 58p

ELECTIONS — Great Britain — History — 19th century

Chronology of British parliamentary by-elections 1833-1987 / compiled and edited by F.W.S. Craig. — Chichester : Parliamentary Research Services, c1987. — xvi,383p. — *Includes index*

ELECTIONS — Great Britain — History — 20th century

Chronology of British parliamentary by-elections 1833-1987 / compiled and edited by F.W.S. Craig. — Chichester : Parliamentary Research Services, c1987. — xvi,383p. — *Includes index*

ELECTIONS — Great Britain — Law and legislation

RAYMOND, Brian
Election law : a campaigner's guideBrian Raymond. — London : CND Publications, 1987. — 28p

ELECTIONS — India

BUTLER, David
A compendium of Indian elections / David Butler, Ashok Lahiri, Prannoy Roy. — New Delhi : Arnold-Heinemann, 1984. — 281 p.. — *Includes statistical tables. — Bibliography: p. [267]-281*

GUPTA, R. L.
Electoral politics in India / R. L. Gupta. — Delhi : Discovery, 1985. — xv,175p. — *Bibliography: p[161]-170*

ELECTIONS — Israel — Addresses, essays, lectures

Israel at the polls, 1981 : a study of the Knesset elections / edited by Howard R. Penniman and Daniel J. Elazar. — Washington : American Enterprise Institute for Public Policy Research ; Bloomington : Indiana University Press, c1986. — xiii, 280 p.. — (Jewish political and social studies). — *Includes bibliographies and index*

ELECTIONS — Italy

Italy at the polls, 1979 : a study of the parliamentary elections / [edited by Howard R. Penniman]. — Washington, D.C. : American Enterprise Institute for Public Policy Research, c1981. — xiv, 335 p.. — (At the polls) (AEI studies ; 321) (Studies in political and social processes). — *Includes bibliographical references and index*

ELECTIONS — Italy — Emilia Romagna

ANDERLINI, Fausto
Territorio e comportamento e lettorale : una analisi delle regionali '85 e delle politiche '83 nei communi dell'Emilia-Romagna e nella città di Bologna / Fausto Anderlini. — Bologna : Servizio Studi e Programmazione, Assessorato Programmazione, 1986. — 157p. — *Includes 10 folded maps*

ELECTIONS — Kenya

ALILA, Patrick O.
Kenya's parliamentary elections : ethnic politics in two rural constituencies in Nyanza / Patrick O. Alila. — Nairobi : University of Nairobi. Institute for Development Studies, 1986. — 37p. — (Discussion paper / University of Nairobi. Institute for Development Studies ; no.282)

WANJOHI, N. Gatheru
The politics of ideology and personality rivalry in Muranga district, Kenya: a study of electoral competition / N. Gatheru Wanjohi. — Nairobi : University of Nairobi. Institute for Development Studies, 1984. — 37p. — (Working paper / University of Nairobi. Institute for Development Studies ; no.411)

ELECTIONS — Near East

Elections in the Middle East : implications of recent trends / edited by Linda L. Layne. — Boulder, Colo. ; London : Westview Press, 1987. — xi,226p. — (Westview special studies on the Middle East). — *Bibliography: p215-223*

ELECTIONS — New Zealand — Administration

1984 early general election : review. — Lower Hutt : Chief Electoral Office, 1985. — 27 leaves

ELECTIONS — Nigeria

ADAMU, Haroun
Nigeria : the meaning of the presidential system : 1979 General Elections / Haroun Adamu, Alaba Ogunsanwo. — Kano, Nigeria : Triumph Pub. Co., [1982?]. — x, 267 p.

ELECTIONS — North Carolina — History — 20th century

SNIDER, William D
Hunt and Helms : North Carolina chooses a Senator / by William D. Snider. — Chapel Hill : University of North Carolina Press, c1985. — p. cm. — *Includes index*

ELECTIONS — Norway — Statistics

Stortingsvalget 1985 = Storting elections 1985. — Oslo : Statistisk Sentralbyr˚a. — (Norges offisielle statistikk ; B594). — *Contents list, details of survey design and main results, table headings in English*
Hefte 1. — 1986. — 145p

ELECTIONS — Puerto Rico — Statistics

PUERTO RICO. Commonwealth Board of Elections
Estadísticas de las elecciones generales celebradas en Puerto Rico el 8 de noviembre de 1960. — [San Juan] : the Board, [ca.1961]. — viii,37p

ELECTIONS — Spain

CACIAGLI, Mario
Elecciones y partidos en la transición española / por Mario Caciagli. — Madrid : Centro de Investigaciones Sociologicas : Siglo Vientiuno, 1986. — x,292p

ELECTIONS — Spain — History — 20th century

TUSELL GÓMEZ, Javier
Las constituyentes de 1931 : unas elecciones de transición / Javier Tusell ; [con la colaboración de Octavio Ruiz Manjón y Genoveva García Queipo de Llano]. — Madrid : Centro de Investigaciones Sociológicas, 1982. — 206p. — (Colección monografías / Centro de Investigaciones sociológicas ; núm.59). — *Publicado originalmente en Madrid por Universidad Nacional de Educación a Distancia, 1981-1982*

ELECTIONS — Spain — Basque Provinces

LLERA RAMO, Francisco José
"Postfranquismo y fuerzas politicas en Euskadi" : sociología electoral del País Vasco / Francisco José Llera Ramo. — Bilbao : Universidad del País Vasco, 1985. — 596p. — *Bibliography: p363-366*

ELECTIONS — Spain — Castilla-La Mancha

IZQUIERDO COLLADO, Juan de Dios
Las elecciones de la transición en Castilla-La Mancha / Juan de Dios Izquierdo Collado. — Albacete : Instituto de Estudios Albacetenses : Confederación Española de Centros de Estudios Locales
Vol.1: Albacete. — (Serie 1 : Ensayos históricos y científicos / Instituto de Estudios Albacetenses ; núm.19)
Tomo 1: 1976-79. — 1984. — *348p*

IZQUIERDO COLLADO, Juan de Dios
Las elecciones de la transición en Castilla-La Mancha / Juan de Dios Izquierdo Collado. — Albacete : Instituto de Estudios Albacetenses : Confederación Española de Centros de Estudios Locales
Vol.1: Albacete. — (Serie 1 : Ensayos históricos y científicos / Instituto de Estudios Albacetenses ; núm.19)
Tomo 2: 1979-83. — 1984. — *407p. — Bibliography: p405-407*

ELECTIONS — Spain — Catalonia

Les eleccions al Parlament de Catalunya : una experiència interdisciplinar a BUP / Joana Amengual...[et al.]. — Barcelona : Rosa Sensat : Edicions 62, 1985. — 169p

ELECTIONS — Spain — Galicia — Statistics

BRABO CASTELLS, Pilar
Atlas electoral de España / Pilar Brabo Castells, Carmen Ortiz Corulla. — Madrid : Fundación IESA
t.2: Comunidad autónoma de Galicia. — 1985. — 344p

ELECTIONS — Spain — Lerida

MIR, Conxita
Lleida (1890-1936) : caciquisme polític i lluita electoral / Conxita Mir. — Barcelona : Publicaciones de l'Abadia de Montserrat, 1985. — 778p. — Maps in end pocket. — Bibliography: p[753]-760

ELECTIONS — Spain — Madrid (Province) — Statistics

BRABO CASTELLS, Pilar
Atlas electoral de España / Pilar Brabo Castells, Carmen Ortiz Corulla. — Madrid : Fundación IESA
t.1: Comunidad autónoma de Madrid. — 1985. — 74p, 75 leaves of statistical tables and maps

ELECTIONS — Switzerland

PARTI RADICAL-DÉMOCRATIQUE SUISSE
Objectifs 1975 : securité et liberté. — Lausanne : Parti Radical-Démocratique Suisse, 1975. — 68p

ELECTIONS — Uganda

BWENGYE
The agony of Uganda : from Idi Amin to Obote : repressive rule and bloodshed : causes, effects and the cure / Francis Aloysius Wazarwalu Bwengye ; foreword by Grove Stuart Ibingira. — London : Regency Press, 1985. — xx,379p. — Bibliography: p374-379

ELECTIONS — United States

ABRAMSON, Paul R
Change and continuity in the 1984 elections / Paul R. Abramson, John H. Aldrich, David W. Rohde. — Rev. ed. — Washington, D.C. : CQ Press, c1987. — xvi, 378 p.. — Includes index. — Bibliography: p. 359-367

MAISEL, Louis Sandy
Parties and elections in America : the electoral process / Louis Sandy Maisel. — New York : Random House, 1986. — p. cm. — Includes index. — Bibliography: p

NEUMAN, W. Russell
The paradox of mass politics : knowledge and opinion in the American electorate / W. Russell Neuman. — Cambridge, Mass. : Harvard University Press, 1986. — 241 p.. — Includes index. — Bibliography: p. [222]-236

ELECTIONS — United States — Addresses, essays, lectures

The Election of 1984 : reports and interpretations / Gerald M. Pomper ... [et al.]. — Chatham, N.J. : Chatham House Publishers, c1985. — p. cm. — Includes bibliographies and index

ELECTIONS — United States — History — Bibliography

The American electorate : a historical bibliography. — Santa Barbara, Calif. : ABC-Clio Information Services, 1983. — xii, 388 p.. — (ABC-Clio research guides ; 8). — Includes indexes. — "This bibliography was conceived and compiled from the periodicals database of the American Bibliographical Center by editors at ABC-Clio Information Services."

ELECTRIC INDUSTRIES — European Economic Community countries

STIGUM, Marcia L
The impact of the European Economic Community on the French cotton and electrical engineering industries / Marcia Lee Stigum. — New York : Arno Press, 1981. — xi, 258 p.. — (Dissertations in European economic history). — : Originally presented as the author's thesis, Massachusetts Institute of Technology, 1961. — Bibliography: p. 250-258

ELECTRIC INDUSTRIES — France

STIGUM, Marcia L
The impact of the European Economic Community on the French cotton and electrical engineering industries / Marcia Lee Stigum. — New York : Arno Press, 1981. — xi, 258 p.. — (Dissertations in European economic history). — : Originally presented as the author's thesis, Massachusetts Institute of Technology, 1961. — Bibliography: p. 250-258

ELECTRIC INDUSTRIES — Portugal

Estatística das instal a ções eléctricas em Portugal (Continente e A çores). — Lisboa : Direcção-Geral de Energia, 1983-. — Annual. — Title varies slightly. — 1935-1982 Issuing body entitled: Direcção-Geral dos Serviçõs Eléctricos

ELECTRIC LIGHTING — England — Godalming (Surrey) — History

HAVERON, Francis
'The brilliant ray' or 'How the electric light was brought to Godalming in 1881' / by Francis Haveron. — [Godalming] ([c/o Francis Haveron, 5 Hill Court, Ballfield Rd, Godalming, Surrey]) : Godalming Electricity Centenary Celebrations Committee, c1981. — 36p. — Text on inside covers. — Bibliography: on inside cover

ELECTRIC NETWORKS

Network user (incorporating Network). — London : British Telecommunications, 1986-. — Quarterly

ELECTRIC POWER — Congresses

The Future of electrical energy : a regional perspective of an industry in transition / edited by Sidney Saltzman and Richard E. Schuler. — New York : Praeger, 1986. — xviii, 372 p.. — "Praeger special studies. Praeger scientific.". — Includes bibliographies and index

ELECTRIC POWER — Conservation

Electric utility conservation programs / edited by Clark W. Gellings and Dilip R. Limaye. — New York : Praeger, 1986. — xi, 255 p.. — Includes bibliographies and index

ELECTRIC POWER — Environmental aspects — Great Britain

HAWKINS, Arthur
Electricity supply and the environment / by Arthur Hawkins ; researched and edited by A. J. Clarke. — [London : Central Electricity Generating Board, 1974]. — 64p. — Based on a paper given at the Institute of Fuel Conference "Fuel and the environment", Eastbourne, November 1973

ELECTRIC POWER — Egypt

Emploi de l'energie électrique dans les établissements industriels : conditions générales concernant les établissements industriels (usines et ateliers) régis par la loi du 28 Août 1904, sur les établissements incommodes, insalubres et dangereux, et par l'arrêté ministériel du 29 Août 1904. — Le Caire : Ministère de l'Intérieur, 1923. — 10p

ELECTRIC POWER CONSUMPTION — Bibliography

ELECTRICITY COUNCIL. Intelligence Section
Price elasticity and electricity demand : select list of references, 1957-January 1974. — London : the Section, [1974]. — [4]p. — (Bibliographies / Electricity Council, Intelligence Section ; B88)

ELECTRIC POWER CONSUMPTION — Econometric models

KHAZZOOM, J. Daniel
An econometric model integrating conservation measures in the residential demand for electricity / by J. Daniel Khazzoom. — Greenwich, Conn. : JAI Press, c1986. — xx, 305 p.. — (Contemporary studies in energy analysis and policy ; v. 8). — Includes index. — Bibliography: p. 165-170

ELECTRIC POWER CONSUMPTION — Forecasting — Economic aspects — United States

ENERGY ENGINEERING BOARD (U.S.). Committee on Electricity in Economic Growth
Electricity in Economic Growth : a report. — Washington, D.C. : National Academic Press, 1986. — xx,165p

ELECTRIC POWER-PLANTS — Load — Mathematical models

MITCHELL, Bridger M
Projecting the demand for electricity : a survey and forecast / Bridger M. Mitchell, Rolla Edward Park, Francis Labrune. — Santa Monica, CA : Rand, [1986]. — xiii, 67 p.. — "Prepared for the Private Sector Sponsors Program.". — "February 1986.". — "R-3312-PSSP.". — Bibliography: p. 63-67

ELECTRIC POWER PRODUCTION — Economic aspects — United States

ENERGY ENGINEERING BOARD (U.S.). Committee on Electricity in Economic Growth
Electricity in Economic Growth : a report. — Washington, D.C. : National Academic Press, 1986. — xx,165p

ELECTRIC POWER PRODUCTION — Great Britain

SCHAFFER, I. R.
Combined heat and power and electricity generation in British industry, 1983-1988 : a statistical and economic survey / I. R. Schaffer ; technical consultant, R.W. Clayton. — London : H.M.S.O. [for the Energy Efficiency Office, Dept. of Energy], 1986. — [ca.190]p in various pagings. — (Energy efficiency series ; 5)

ELECTRIC UTILITIES — Environmental aspects — Great Britain

HAWKINS, Arthur
Electricity supply and the environment / by Arthur Hawkins ; researched and edited by A. J. Clarke. — [London : Central Electricity Generating Board, 1974]. — 64p. — Based on a paper given at the Institute of Fuel Conference "Fuel and the environment", Eastbourne, November 1973

ELECTRIC UTILITIES — Government ownership — United States — History

SCHAP, David
Municipal ownership in the electric utility industry : a centennial view / David Schap. — New York : Praeger, 1986. — xiii, 128 p.. — "Praeger special studies. Praeger scientific.". — Includes index. — Bibliography: p. 117-126

ELECTRIC UTILITIES — Rates

TURVEY, Ralph
Electricity economics : essays and case studies / Ralph Turvey and Dennis Anderson. — Baltimore ; London : John Hopkins University Press for the World Bank, 1977. — xvii,364p. — (Research publications / World Bank). — Bibliography: p.290-296. — Includes index

ELECTRIC UTILITIES — Rates — Bibliography

ELECTRICITY COUNCIL. Intelligence Section
Price elasticity and electricity demand : select list of references, 1957-January 1974. — London : the Section, [1974]. — [4]p. — (Bibliographies / Electricity Council, Intelligence Section ; B88)

ELECTRIC UTILITIES — Asia — Costs
REGIONAL POWER UTILITY TARIFF SYMPOSIUM (1982 : Manila)
Costing and pricing electricity in developing countries : proceedings of the Asian Development Bank Regional Power Utility Tariff Symposium, August 1982 / edited by Mohan Munasinghe, Shyam Rungta. — Manila : Asian Development Bank, 1984. — xvii,648p. — Includes bibliographical references

ELECTRIC UTILITIES — Asia — Rates
REGIONAL POWER UTILITY TARIFF SYMPOSIUM (1982 : Manila)
Costing and pricing electricity in developing countries : proceedings of the Asian Development Bank Regional Power Utility Tariff Symposium, August 1982 / edited by Mohan Munasinghe, Shyam Rungta. — Manila : Asian Development Bank, 1984. — xvii,648p. — Includes bibliographical references

ELECTRIC UTILITIES — Australia
DAWSON, Ken
The electricity supply industry in Australia, 1955-2000 / Ken Dawson. — [Canberra? : National Energy Advisory Committee?], 1981. — 88,4,6 leaves

ELECTRIC UTILITIES — Developing countries — Costs
REGIONAL POWER UTILITY TARIFF SYMPOSIUM (1982 : Manila)
Costing and pricing electricity in developing countries : proceedings of the Asian Development Bank Regional Power Utility Tariff Symposium, August 1982 / edited by Mohan Munasinghe, Shyam Rungta. — Manila : Asian Development Bank, 1984. — xvii,648p. — Includes bibliographical references

ELECTRIC UTILITIES — Developing countries — Rates
REGIONAL POWER UTILITY TARIFF SYMPOSIUM (1982 : Manila)
Costing and pricing electricity in developing countries : proceedings of the Asian Development Bank Regional Power Utility Tariff Symposium, August 1982 / edited by Mohan Munasinghe, Shyam Rungta. — Manila : Asian Development Bank, 1984. — xvii,648p. — Includes bibliographical references

ELECTRIC UTILITIES — Europe — Bibliography
ELECTRICITY COUNCIL. Intelligence Section
The prospects in Europe for the electricity supply industry : select list of references. — London : the Section, [1974]. — 11p. — (Bibliographies / Electicity Council, Intelligence Section ; B87)

ELECTRIC UTILITIES — Great Britain
DALE, Paul
Technical change and electricity generation and supply in Great Britain since 1960-1980 : with special reference to the evaluation of schemes for the combined production of electricity and heat / by Paul Dale. — 461 leaves. — PhD (Econ) 1986 LSE

EDEN, Richard
Electricity supply in the UK / Richard Eden and Nigel Evans. — Aldershot : Gower, c1986. — [103]p. — (Energy papers ; 20)

ELECTRIC UTILITIES — Great Britain — Bibliography
ELECTRICITY COUNCIL. Intelligence Section
Select list of references on the electricity supply industry in Great Britain. — London : the Section, [1974]. — 14p. — (Bibliographies / Electricity Council, Intelligence Section ; B100)

ELECTRIC UTILITIES — Great Britain — History
BYERS, Anthony
Centenary of service : a history of electricity in the home / by Anthony Byers. — London : The Electricity Council, 1981. — 96p

GORDON, Bob, 1911-
One hundred years of electricity supply 1881-1981 : a brief account of some aspects of growth and development over the past century / by Bob Gordon. — Hove : South Eastern Electricity Board, 1981. — 83p. — (A Milne Museum booklet). — Bibliography: p83

ELECTRIC UTILITIES — Great Britain — History — Bibliography
ELECTRICITY COUNCIL. Intelligence Section
Select list of references on historical development of electric power generation and supply in Great Britain. — London : the Section, [1969]. — 24p. — (Bibliographies / Electricity Council, Intelligence Section ; B25)

ELECTRIC UTILITIES — Great Britain — Technological innovations — Bibliography
ELECTRICITY COUNCIL. Intelligence Section
Electricity supply industry : technological development since 1948; list of references 1948-74. — London : the Section, [1974]. — 80p. — (Bibliographies / Electricity Council, Intelligence Section ; B113)

ELECTRIC UTILITIES — Mexico — Energy consumption
Energy efficiency and conservation in Mexico : perspectives on efficiency and conservation policies / edited by Oscar Guzmán, Antonio Yúnez-Naude, Miguel S. Wionczek. — Boulder, Colo. : Westview Press, 1986. — p. cm. — (Westview special studies on Latin America and the Caribbean). — Bibliography: p

ELECTRIC UTILITIES — Organisation for Economic Co-operation and Development countries — Costs
Projected costs of generating electricity from nuclear and coal-fired power stations for commissioning in 1995 : a report / by an Expert Group. — Paris : Nuclear Energy Agency, 1986. — 72p. — Bibliographical references: p70

ELECTRIC UTILITIES — Sweden
VATTENFALL
Annual report / Vattenfall, Sweden. — Vällingby : Vattenfall, 1984-. — Annual

ELECTRIC UTILITIES — Washington (State) — Rates — Public opinion
SUGAI, Wayne H
Nuclear power and ratepayer protest : the Washington Public Power Supply System / Wayne H. Sugai. — Boulder : Westview Press, 1987. — p. cm. — (Westview special studies in public policy and public systems management). — Bibliography: p

ELECTRICITY — Prices — European Economic Community Countries
Electricity prices / Statistical Office of the European Communities. — Luxembourg : Statistical Office of the European Communities, 1984-. — Annual. — Table headings in European Community languages

ELECTRIFICATION — Finland
CHRISTIERNIN, Georg
Finland's water-power and electrification / Georg Christiernin. — Helsingfors : Government Printing Office, 1924. — 11p

ELECTRONIC DATA PROCESSING
ADDIS, T. R.
Designing knowledge-based systems / T.R. Addis. — London : Kogan Page, 1985. — 322p. — Bibliography: p303-310. — Includes index

ARNOLD, Erik
Parallel convergence : national strategies in information technology / Erik Arnold and Ken Guy. — London : Pinter, 1986. — [230]p. — Includes bibliography and index

BEHAN, Kate
Understanding information technology : text, readings, and cases / Kate Behan, Diana Holmes. — Englewood Cliffs, N.J. : Prentice-Hall, c1986. — xiv, 493 p.. — Includes bibliographies and indexes

BOHL, Marilyn
Information processing / Marilyn Bohl. — 4th ed. — Chicago : Science Research Associates, c1984. — xvii, 558 p.. — Includes index

CHI '85 CONFERENCE (San Francisco)
Human factors in computing systems II : proceedings of the CHI '85 conference held San Francisco, C.A., U.S.A., 14-18 April 1985, sponsored by the association for Computing Machinery's Special Interest Group on Computer and Human Interaction (ACH/SIGCHI) in cooperation with the Human Factors Society edited by Lorraine Borman and Bill Curtis. — Amsterdam ; Oxford : North-Holland, 1985. — vii,231p. — Includes index

Data processing. — Guildford : Butterworths, 1981-1986. — 10 per year. — Continued by: Information and software technology

Decision support systems : the international journal. — Amsterdam : North-Holland, 1985-. — Quarterly

ELDER, John, 1949-
Construction of data processing software / John Elder. — Englewood Cliffs ; London : Prentice-Hall, 1984. — xiv,432p. — (Prentice-Hall international series in computer science). — Bibliography: p418-419. — Includes index

Handbook of information technology and office systems / edited by A.E. Cawkell. — Amsterdam ; New York : North-Holland ; New York, N.Y., U.S.A. : Sole distributors for the U.S.A. and Canada, Elsevier Science Pub. Co., 1986. — x, 996 p.. — Includes bibliographies and index

Information and software technology. — Guildford : Butterworth Scientific, 1987-. — 10 per year. — Continues: Data processing

MANDELL, Steven L
Computers and data processing : concepts and applications / Steven L. Mandell. — 3rd ed. — St. Paul, Minn. : West Pub. Co., c1985. — xvi, 512, [20] p.. — Includes index

MEGARRY, Jacquetta
Inside information : computers, communications and people / Jacquetta Megarry. — London : British Broadcasting Corporation, 1985. — 224p. — Includes index

NICKERSON, Raymond S
Using computers : human factors in information systems / Raymond S. Nickerson. — Cambridge, Mass. ; London : MIT Press, c1986. — xiv, 434p. — "A Bradford book."

SANDERS, Donald H
Computers today / Donald H. Sanders. — 2nd ed. — New York : McGraw-Hill, c1985. — p. cm. — Includes index

SAVAGE, John E.
The mystical machine : issues and ideas in computing / John E. Savage, Susan Magidson, Alex M. Stein. — 1st ed. — Reading, Mass. : Addison-Wesley, c1986. — xvi, 407 p.. — Ill. on lining papers. — Includes bibliographies and index

WEBSTER, Frank
Information technology : a luddite analysis / Frank Webster Kevin Robins. — Norwood, N.J. : Ablex Pub. Corp., 1986. — x,387p.. — (Communication and information science). — Bibliography: p.349-375. — Bibliography: p

WERNER, Oswald
Systematic fieldwork / Oswald Werner, G. Mark Schoepfle. — Newbury Park [Calif.] ; London : Sage
Vol.2: Ethnographic analysis and data management. — 1987. — 355p. — Bibliography: p339-345

WOODHOUSE, David
Computer science / David Woodhouse, Greg Johnstone, Anne McDougall. — 2nd ed. — Milton, Qld. : Jacaranda Press, 1984. — xv,588p

ELECTRONIC DATA PROCESSING — Addresses, essays, lectures

Trends in information systems : an anthology of papers from conferences of the IFIP Technical Committee 8 "Information Systems" to commemorate their tenth anniversary / edited by B. Langefors, A.A. Verrijn-Stuart, G. Bracchi. — Amsterdam ; New York : North-Holland ; New York : Sole distributors for the U.S.A. and Canada Elsevier Science Pub. Co., 1986. — xv, 469 p.. — *Includes bibliographies*

ELECTRONIC DATA PROCESSING — Congresses

Philosophy and technology II : information technology and computers in theory and practice / edited by Carl Mitcham and Alois Huning. — Dordrecht ; Boston : Reidel ; Hingham, MA, U.S.A. : sold and distributed in the U.S.A. and Canada by Kluwer Academic Publisher, c1986. — xxii, 352 p.. — (Boston studies in the philosophy of science ; v. 90). — *Selected proceedings of an international conference held in New York, September 3-7, 1983, and organized by the Philosophy & Technology Studies Center of the Polytechnic Institute of New York in conjunction with the Society for Philosophy and Technology. — "A German-language version has appeared under the title: Technikphilosophie im Zeitalter der Informationstechnik (Braunschweig: Vieweg, 1985)"--Pref. — Includes indexes. — Bibliography: p. 307-339*

ELECTRONIC DATA PROCESSING — Directories

Encyclopedia of information systems and services / edited by John Schmittroth, Jr. ; Amy F. Lucas and Annette Novallo, associate editors ; Kathleen Young Marcaccio, contributing editor. — 6th ed. — Detroit, Mich. : Gale Research Co., c1985-. — v. <1 >. — *At head of title: 1985-86. — Includes indexes. — Contents: v. 1. International volume*

ELECTRONIC DATA PROCESSING — Distributed processing

CHAMPINE, George A.
Distributed computer systems : impact on management, design, and analysis / George A. Champine with Ronald D. Coop, Russell C. Heinselman. — Amsterdam ; Oxford : North-Holland, 1980. — xvi,380p. — *Bibliography: p341-369. — Includes index*

ELECTRONIC DATA PROCESSING — Economic research

INFOTECH INFORMATION LIMITED
Computing economics : international computer state of the art report / Infotech Information Limited. — Maidenhead (Nicholson House, Maidenhead, Berks. SL6 1LD) : Infotech Information Limited, 1973. — vi,600p. — ([Infotech state of the art report]). — *Bibliography: p.563-584. — Includes index*

ELECTRONIC DATA PROCESSING — Government policy — Congresses

IFIP TC9 CONFERENCE ON HUMAN CHOICE AND COMPUTERS ((3rd : 1985 : Stockholm, Sweden)
Comparative worldwide national computer policies : proceedings of the Third IFIP TC9 Conference on Human Choice and Computers, Stockholm, Sweden, 2-5 September 1985 / edited by Harold Sackman. — Amsterdam ; New York : North-Holland ; New York, N.Y., U.S.A. : Sole distributors for the U.S.A. and Canada, Elsevier Science Pub. Co., 1986. — xi, 486 p.. — *Conference sponsored by the International Federation for Information Processing and UNESCO. — Includes bibliographies*

ELECTRONIC DATA PROCESSING — Handbooks, manuals, etc

SAS INSTITUTE
SAS introductory guide for personal computers. — Version 6 ed. — Cary, N.C. : SAS Institute, 1985. — 111p

SAS INSTITUTE
SAS language guide for personal computers. — Version 6 ed. — Cary, N.C. : SAS Institute, 1985. — 429p

SAS INSTITUTE
SAS procedures guide for personal computers. — Version 6 ed. — Cary, N.C. : SAS Institute, 1985. — 373p

ELECTRONIC DATA PROCESSING — Research

Critical issues in information systems research / edited by R.J. Boland, Jr., R.A. Hirschheim. — Chichester : Wiley, c1987. — xv,394p. — (John Wiley information systems series). — *Includes bibliographies index*

ELECTRONIC DATA PROCESSING — Social aspects

Information technology & people : designing for the future / edited by Frank Blackler and David Oborne. — Leicester : British Psychological Society, 1987. — 262 p

ELECTRONIC DATA PROCESSING — Social sciences

HAYES, Brian
A design sketch of a parallel "MSDOS" computer for use by social scientists / Brian Hayes. — London : Suntory-Toyota International Centre for Economics and Related Disciplines, 1987. — 31p. — (Information technology). — *Bibliography: p29-31*

ELECTRONIC DATA PROCESSING — Structured techniques

WARD, Paul T.
Structured development for real-time systems / by Paul T. Ward and Stephen J. Mellor. — New York : Yourden Press
Vol.1: Introduction and tools. — 1985. — 156p

ELECTRONIC DATA PROCESSING — Vocational guidance

Computing manpower : international computer state of the art report. — Maidenhead : Infotech Information, 1973. — 526p. — (Infotech state of the art report ; 16). — *Bibliography: p475-507*

ELECTRONIC DATA PROCESSING DEPARTMENTS — Auditing

BEST, Peter J.
Auditing computer-based accounting systems / Peter J. Best, Peter G. Barrett. — Sydney : Prentice-Hall of Australia, c1983. — 247 p.. — *Includes index. — Bibliography: p. 241-243*

ELECTRONIC DATA PROCESSING DEPARTMENTS — Management

PERRY, William E
Cleaning up a computer mess : a guide to diagnosing and correcting computer problems / William E. Perry. — New York : Van Nostrand Reinhold, c1986. — xii, 255 p. — *Includes index*

ELECTRONIC DATA PROCESSING IN RESEARCH

MADRON, Thomas W.
Using microcomputers in research / Thomas Wm Madron, C. Neal Tate [and] Robert G. Brookshire. — Beverly Hills ; London : Sage, 1985. — 87 p. — (Quantitative applications in the social sciences ; 52)

ELECTRONIC DATA PROCESSING PERSONNEL

Computing manpower : international computer state of the art report. — Maidenhead : Infotech Information, 1973. — 526p. — (Infotech state of the art report ; 16). — *Bibliography: p475-507*

ELECTRONIC DIGITAL COMPUTERS
See also Computers

ELECTRONIC DIGITAL COMPUTERS

BOHL, Marilyn
Information processing / Marilyn Bohl. — 4th ed. — Chicago : Science Research Associates, c1984. — xvii, 558 p.. — *Includes index*

Computer users' data book / B.C. Walsh ... [et al.]. — Oxford : Blackwell Scientific, 1986. — vii,177p. — *Bibliography: p169. — Includes index*

Designing for human-computer communication / edited by M.E. Sime and M.J. Coombs. — London : Academic Press, 1983. — x,338p. — (Computers and people). — *Includes bibliographies and index*

INFOTECH INFORMATION LIMITED
Computing economics : international computer state of the art report / Infotech Information Limited. — Maidenhead (Nicholson House, Maidenhead, Berks. SL6 1LD) : Infotech Information Limited, 1973. — vi,600p. — ([Infotech state of the art report]). — *Bibliography: p.563-584. — Includes index*

MANDELL, Steven L
Computers and data processing : concepts and applications / Steven L. Mandell. — 3rd ed. — St. Paul, Minn. : West Pub. Co., c1985. — xvi, 512, [20] p.. — *Includes index*

STEVENS, Richard, 1946-
Understanding computers / Richard Stevens. — Oxford : Oxford University Press, 1986. — 218p. — *Includes bibliography and index*

ELECTRONIC DIGITAL COMPUTERS — Programming

BORNAT, Richard
Programming from first principles / Richard Bornat. — Englewood Cliffs, N.J. ; London : Prentice-Hall International, c1987. — xviii,538p. — (Prentice-Hall International series in computer science). — *Includes index*

GILBERT, Philip
Software design and development / Philip Gilbert. — Chicago : Science Research Associates, c1983. — xvi, 681 p.. — (SRA computer science series). — *Includes bibliographies and index*

JONES, Capers
Programming productivity / Capers Jones. — New York : McGraw-Hill, c1986. — p. cm. — (McGraw-Hill series in software engineering and technology). — *Includes bibliographies and index*

MACRO, Allen
The craft of software engineering / Allen Marco, John Buxton. — Wokingham : Addison-Wesley, c1987. — [376]p. — (International computer science series). — *Includes index*

TREMBLAY, Jean-Paul
An introduction to data structures with applications / Jean-Paul Tremblay, Paul G. Sorenson. — 2nd ed. — New York ; London : McGraw Hill, 1984. — xviii,861p. — (McGraw-Hill computer science series). — *Previous ed.: 1976. — Bibliography: p840-842. — Includes index*

WETZEL, Gregory F.
The algorithmic process : an introduction to problem solving / Gregory F. Wetzel, William G. Bulgren. — Chicago : Science Research Associates, c1985. — p. cm. — *Includes index. — Bibliography: p*

ELECTRONIC DIGITAL COMPUTERS — Developing countries

Computers and computer applications in developing countries / edited by Ukandi G. Damachi, H. Ray Souder and Nicholas A. Damachi. — London : Macmillan, 1987. — [256]p. — *Includes index*

ELECTRONIC FUNDS TRANSFERS — Australia

AUSTRALIA. Working Group Examining the Rights and Obligations of the Users and Providers of Electronic Funds Transfer Systems
Report. — Canberra : Australian Government Publishing Service, 1986. — 88p

ELECTRONIC FUNDS TRANSFERS — Australia *continuation*

AUSTRALIAN SCIENCE AND TECHNOLOGY COUNCIL. Technological Change Committee
Towards a cashless society? : a report to the Prime Minister / by the Australian Science and Technology Council (ASTEC) prepared by the Technological Change Committee. — Canberra : Australian Government Publishing Service, 1986. — xi,175p. — *Includes bibliographies*

ELECTRONIC FUNDS TRANSFERS — Great Britain

KIRKMAN, P. R. A.
Electronic funds transfer systems : the revolution in cashless banking and payment methods / Patrick Kirkman. — Oxford : Basil Blackwell, 1987. — 1v.

ELECTRONIC INDUSTRIES — Great Britain

GREAT BRITAIN. Parliament. House of Commons. Library. Research Division
The UK information technology industry / C. R. Barclay. — [London] : the Division, 1987. — 33p. — (Background paper ; no.194). — *Bibliography: p33*

ELECTRONIC INDUSTRIES — Japan — Technological innovations

GREGORY, Gene
Japanese electronics technology : enterprise and innovation / by Gene Gregory. — 2nd ed. — Chichester : Wiley, 1986. — xiv,458p. — *Previous ed.: Tokyo : Japan Times, 1985.* — *Includes index*

ELECTRONIC INTELLIGENCE

MUNNELLY, Brendan
Who's bugging you? : inside Ireland's secret world of electronic surveillance / Brendan Munnelly. — Cork : Mercier Press, 1987. — 90p

ELECTRONIC OFFICE MACHINES — Great Britain

HARPER, J. M.
Telecommunications and computing : the uncompleted revolution : a survey in plain English of the state of the common ground of telecommunications, computing, office machinery and cable television in the UK / J. M. Harper. — London : Communications Educational Services, 1986. — xix,200p

ELECTRONIC PUBLISHING

BLEND-5 : the computer human factors journal / journal editors: B. Shackel, J. Florentin, P. Wright ... ; this report was collated and edited by David J. Pullinger and produced with the help of Wendy Buckland. — London : British Library, c1986. — xi,221p. — (Library and information research report ; 47). — *Includes bibliographies*

PULLINGER, D. J.
BLEND-4 : user-system interaction / D.J. Pullinger with B. Shackel ... [et al.]. — [London] : British Library, c1985. — xi,76p. — (Library and information research report ; 45). — *Bibliography: p67-69*

ELECTRONIC PUBLISHING — Costs

PULLINGER, D. J.
BLEND-8 : cost appraisal / D.J. Pullinger. — London : British Library Research and Development Dept., c1987. — ix,41p. — (Library and information research report ; 53)

ELECTRONIC PUBLISHING — Directories

Encyclopedia of information systems and services / edited by John Schmittroth, Jr. ; Amy F. Lucas and Annette Novallo, associate editors ; Kathleen Young Marcaccio, contributing editor. — 6th ed. — Detroit, Mich. : Gale Research Co., c1985-. — v. <1 >. — *At head of title: 1985-86.* — *Includes indexes.* — *Contents: v. 1. International volume*

ELECTRONIC PUBLISHING — Handbooks, manuals, etc

Chicago guide to preparing electronic manuscripts for authors and publishers. — Chicago : University of Chicago Press, 1986. — xi, 143p. — (Chicago guides to writing, editing, and publishing). — *Includes index.* — *Bibliography: p 131*

ELECTRONIC PUBLISHING — Great Britain

Electronic publishing & the UK : prospects, economics & constraints : proceedings of a conference held in London in December 1984 / organised by the British Library in conjunction with the International Electronic Publishing Research Centre ... [et al.]. — London : British Library, c1986. — v,113p

ELECTRONIC TRAFFIC CONTROLS

GREAT BRITAIN. Working Group on Bus Demonstration Projects. Technical Sub-Committee
Bus detection : bus priorities at traffic control signals. — London : Department of the Environment, [1973]. — 10p. — (Bus Demonstration Project summary report ; No.1)

ELECTRONICS — Study and teaching — Addresses, essays, lectures

ROBERTS, D. H.
Electronics - the interdependence of industry and academia / by D. H. Roberts. — [Southampton] : University of Southampton, 1986. — 19 p.. — *"The thirty-first Fawley Foundation lecture".* — *At head of title: The Fawley Foundation*

ELEMENTARY SCHOOLS — Wales

GREAT BRITAIN. Welsh Education Office. Inspectors of Schools
Primary education in rural Wales = Addysg gynradd yn y Gymru wledig / [H.M. Inspectors of Schools]. — Cardiff (Government Buildings, Tŷ Glas Rd, Llanishen, Cardiff CF4 5PF) : Welsh Office, Education Department, 1978. — 122p. — (Surveys / Great Britain. Welsh Education Office ; no.6). — *Parallel English and Welsh text.* - *Col. map (fold. sheet) in pocket*

ELGIN (NAME)

Elgin international / compiled by Morag Pirie. — Aberdeen : Aberdeen University Press, 1985. — [70]p

ELITE (SOCIAL SCIENCES)

ALBERTONI, Ettore A.
Mosca and the theory of elitism / Ettore A. Albertoni ; translated by Paul Goodrick. — Oxford : Basil Blackwell, 1987. — xvii,194p. — *Translation of: Dottrina della classe politica e teoria delle elites.* — *Bibliography: p186-191.* — *Includes index*

Community power : directions for future research / edited by Robert J. Waste. — Beverly Hills : Sage Publications, 1986. — p. cm. — (Sage focus editions ; v. 79). — *Includes bibliographies*

ELITE (SOCIAL SCIENCES) — Research

Research methods for elite studies / edited by George Moyser and Margaret Wagstaffe. — London : Allen & Unwin, 1987. — [240]p. — (Contemporary social research series ; 14). — *Includes bibliography*

ELITE (SOCIAL SCIENCES) — Bolivia

HAVET, José
The diffusion of power : rural elites in a Bolivian province / José Havet. — Ottawa : University of Ottawa Press, 1985. — xvi,156p. — (International Development ; 3). — *Bibliography: p145-150*

ELITE (SOCIAL SCIENCES) — Brazil — History — 19th century

COSTA, Emília Viotti da
[Da monarquia à república. English]. The Brazilian Empire : myths and histories / Emilia Viotti da Costa. — Chicago ; London : University of Chicago Press, 1985. — xxv, 287p. — : *Revised translation of: Da monarquia à república.* — *Includes index.* — *Bibliographical notes: p.249-278*

ELITE (SOCIAL SCIENCES) — Canada

CARROLL, William K.
Corporate power and Canadian capitalism / William K. Carroll. — Vancouver : University of British Columbia Press, 1986. — xvii,284p. — *Bibliography: p[257]-276*

ELITE (SOCIAL SCIENCES) — China — Case studies

LAMPTON, David M
Paths to power : elite mobility in contemporary China / by David M. Lampton with the assistance of Yeung Sai-cheung. — Ann Arbor : Center for Chinese Studies, Unversity of Michigan, 1985. — p. cm. — (Michigan monographs in Chinese studies ; no. 55). — *Includes index.* — *Bibliography: p*

ELITE (SOCIAL SCIENCES) — China — History

LIPPIT, Victor D
The economic development of China / by Victor D. Lippit. — Armonk, N.Y. : M.E. Sharpe, c1987. — p. cm. — *Includes bibliographies and index*

ELITE (SOCIAL SCIENCES) — Developing countries

KLITGAARD, Robert E
Elitism and meritocracy in developing countries : selection policies for higher education / Robert Klitgaard. — Baltimore : Johns Hopkins University Press, c1986. — xi, 191 p.. — (The Johns Hopkins studies in development). — *Includes index.* — *Bibliography: p. 161-183*

ELITE (SOCIAL SCIENCES) — Germany — History

MOSSE, W. E.
Jews in the German economy : the German-Jewish economic élite, 1820-1935 / W.E. Mosse. — Oxford : Clarendon, 1987. — 420p. — *Bibliography: p406-409.* — *Includes index*

ELITE (SOCIAL SCIENCES) — India — Punjab

PURI, Nina
Political elite and society in the Punjab / Nina Puri. — New Delhi : Vikas, 1985. — vi,218p. — *Bibliography: p[194]-211*

ELITE (SOCIAL SCIENCES) — Italy — Florence — History

LITCHFIELD, R. Burr
Emergence of a bureaucracy : the Florentine patricians, 1530-1790 / R. Burr Litchfield. — Princeton, N.J. : Princeton University Press, 1986. — xiii, 407 p., [8] p. of plates. — *Includes index.* — *Bibliography: p. 383-396*

ELITE (SOCIAL SCIENCES) — Mexico

CAMP, Roderic Ai
Intellectuals and the state in twentieth-century Mexico / by Roderic A. Camp. — Austin : University of Texas Press, 1985. — ix, 279p. — (Latin American monographs ; no. 65). — *Includes index.* — *Bibliography: p.[233]-265*

ELITE (SOCIAL SCIENCES) — Mexico — History

TUTINO, John
From insurrection to revolution in Mexico : social bases of agrarian violence, 1750-1940 / John Tutino. — Princeton, N.J. : Princeton University Press, c1986. — xx, 425 p.. — *Includes index.* — *Bibliography: p. [399]-417*

ELITE (SOCIAL SCIENCES) — Ouaddai (Chad)

HASSAN KHAYAR, Issa
Tchad : regards sur les élites ouaddaïennes / par Issa Hassan Khayar. — Paris : Centre National de la Recherche Scientifique, 1984. — 231p. — (Contributions à la connaissance des élites africaines ; 3). — *Bibliography: p215-231*

ELITE (SOCIAL SCIENCES) — Soviet Union

KOLLMANN, Nancy Shields
Kinship and politics : the making of the Muscovite political system, 1345-1547 / Nancy Shields Kollmann. — Stanford, Calif. : Stanford University Press, 1987. — x, 324 p.. — *Includes index. — Bibliography: p. [289]-308*

ELITE (SOCIAL SCIENCES) — Spain

MOYA, Carlos
Señas de Leviatán : estado nacional y sociedad industrial : España 1936-1980 / Carlos Moya. — Madrid : Alianza, 1984. — 356p. — *Bibliographies*

ELITE (SOCIAL SCIENCES) — Spain — Barcelona — History

AMELANG, James S.
Honored citizens of Barcelona : patrician culture and class relations, 1490-1714 / James S. Amelang. — Princeton, N.J. : Princeton University Press, c1986. — xxvi, 259p. — *Includes index. — Bibliography: p.223-252*

MCDONOGH, Gary W
Good families of Barcelona : a social history of power in the industrial era / Gary Wray McDonogh. — Princeton, N.J. : Princeton University Press, c1986. — xiv, 262 p.. — *Includes index. — Bibliography: p. [227]-251*

ELITE (SOCIAL SCIENCES) — Syria

DAM, Nikolaos van
The struggle for power in Syria : sectarianism, regionalism and tribalism in politics, 1961—1980 / Nikolaos van Dam. — 2nd ed. — London : Croom Helm, c1981. — 169 p

ELITE (SOCIAL SCIENCES) — Turkey — History

DAVIS, Fanny
The Ottoman lady : a social history from 1718 to 1918 / Fanny Davis. — Westport, Conn. : Greenwood Press, c1986. — xv, 321 p.. — (Contributions in women's studies ; no. 70). — *Includes bibliographies and index*

ELITE (SOCIAL SCIENCES) — United States

GROSS, Bertram
Friendly fascism : the new face of power in America / Bertram Gross. — Montréal : Black Rose Books, 1985. — xxvii,409p

NEUMAN, W. Russell
The paradox of mass politics : knowledge and opinion in the American electorate / W. Russell Neuman. — Cambridge, Mass. : Harvard University Press, 1986. — 241 p.. — *Includes index. — Bibliography: p. [222]-236*

ELITE (SOCIAL SCIENCES) — United States — Addresses, essays, lectures

Power elites and organizations / edited by G. William Domhoff and Thomas R. Dye. — Beverly Hills : Sage Publications, c1986. — p. cm. — (Sage focus editions ; 82). — *Includes index*

EMBARGO

LUNDBORG, Per
The economics of export embargo : the case of the US-Soviet grain suspension / Per Lundborg. — London : Croom Helm, c1987. — xi,127p. — *Bibliography: p119-122. — Includes index*

EMIGRANT REMITTANCES — Portugal — History

CHANEY, Rick
Regional emigration and remittances in underdeveloped countries : the Portugese experience / by Rick Chaney. — New York : Praeger, 1986. — p. cm. — *Includes index. — Bibliography: p*

EMIGRATION AND IMMIGRATION

The future of migration. — Paris : OECD, 1987. — 319p

EMIGRATION AND IMMIGRATION — Government policy

DOWTY, Alan
The new serfdom : contemporary control of emigration and expulsion / Alan Dowty. — New Haven : Yale University Press, c1987. — p. cm. — (A Twentieth Century Fund report). — *Includes index*

EMIGRATION AND IMMIGRATION — History — Congresses

Migration across time and nations : population mobility in historical contexts / edited by Ira Glazier and Luigi De Rosa. — New York ; London : Holmes & Meier, c1986. — viii, 384p . — *Papers presented at a session of the Eighth International Congress on Economic History held in Budapest in 1982. — Contains bibliographies*

EMIGRATION AND IMMIGRATION — Religious aspects — Christianity

JENKINS, Keith
The closed door : a Christian critique of Britain's immigration policies / by Keith Jenkins. — London : British Council of Churches, 1984. — iii,45,[2]p. — *Bibliography: p[2]*

EMIGRATION AND IMMIGRATION — Denmark — Public opinion

KÖRMENDI, Eszter
Os og de andre : Danskernes holdinger til indvandrere og flygtninge = Danish attitudes towards immigrants and refugees / Eszter Körmendi. — København : Socialforskningsinstituttet, 1986. — 180p. — (Publikation / Socialforskningsinstituttet ; 153). — *In Danish, with English summary. — Bibliography: p176-177*

EMIGRATION AND IMMIGRATION LAW — Australia

Human rights and the Migration Act 1985. — Canberra : Australian Government Publishing Service, 1985. — xiv,211p. — (Report / Human Rights Commission ; no.13)

EMIGRATION AND IMMIGRATION LAW — Great Britain

CRONIN, Kathryn
Children, nationality and immigration : a handbook on nationality, immigration and international family law affecting children and young people / written by Kathryn Cronin for the Children's Legal Centre. — London : Children's Legal Centre, 1985. — 146p. — *Bibliography: p127-132*

GRANT, Lawrence
Immigration law and practice / Lawrence Grant, Ian Martin. — London : Cobden Trust 1st supplement. — 1985. — xxxiii,174p. — *Includes index*

GREAT BRITAIN. Parliament. House of Commons. Library. Research Division
Immigration control / [Fiona Poole]. — [London] : the Division, 1979. — 26p. — (Reference sheet ; no.79/10). — *Bibliography: p18-25*

LEGOMSKY, Stephen H.
Immigration and the judiciary : law and politics in Britain and America / Stephen H. Legomsky. — Oxford : Clarendon, 1987. — xxxix,345p. — *Bibliography: p327-345*

MACDONALD, Ian A. (Ian Alexander), 1939-
Immigration law and practice in the United Kingdom / Ian A. Macdonald. — 2nd ed. — London : Butterworths, 1987. — [560]p. — *Previous ed.: 1983. — Includes index*

Worlds apart : women under immigration and nationality law / edited by Jacqueline Bhabha, Francesca Klug and Sue Shutter. — London : Pluto, 1985. — [vi,176]p. — *At head of title: The Women, Immigration and Nationality Group. — Includes bibliography*

EMIGRATION AND IMMIGRATION LAW — Great Britain — Handbooks, manuals, etc

Immigration law handbook. — Rewritten 3rd ed. — [Birmingham] : Handsworth Law Centre, [1985]. — 144p. — *First ed. published in 1979*

EMIGRATION AND IMMIGRATION LAW — New Zealand

NEW ZEALAND. Immigration Division
Immigration and New Zealand : a statement of current immigration policy. — Wellington : the Division, 1986. — ii,23,2p

EMIGRATION AND IMMIGRATION LAW — Organisation for Economic Co-operation and Development countries

CONDÉ, Julien
Les migrations internationales Sud-Nord : evolution jusqu'en 1981 des lois et règlements concernant l'immigration dans les pays Membres de l'OCDE : examen par pays / par Julien Condé et Carlos Taveres-Gravato. — Paris : Centre de Developpement de l'OCDE, 1986. — 23v in 1. — (Textes de travail non revisés). — *Includes bibliographies and references. — Contents: Australie, Autriche, Belgique, Canada, Danemark, Espagne,États-Unis d'Amérique, Finlande, France, Gréce, Italie, Japon, Luxembourg, Norvège, Nouvelle-Zélande, Pays-Bas, Portugal, République Féderale d'Allemagne, Royaume-Uni, Suède, Turquie, Suisse, Yougoslavie*

CONDÉ, Julien
South-North international migrations : the development of immigration laws and regulations in OECD Member countries / by Julien Condé. — Paris : Development Centre of the Organisation for Economic Co-operation and Development, 1986. — 43p. — (Development Centre papers). — *Includes bibliographical references*

EMIGRATION AND IMMIGRATION LAW — United States

HARWOOD, Edwin
In liberty's shadow : illegal aliens and immigration law enforcement / Edwin Harwood. — Stanford, Calif. : Hoover Institution Press, Stanford University, c1986. — xvi, 224 p.. — (Hoover Press publication ; 331). — *Includes index. — Bibliography: p. [193]-220*

LEGOMSKY, Stephen H.
Immigration and the judiciary : law and politics in Britain and America / Stephen H. Legomsky. — Oxford : Clarendon, 1987. — xxxix,345p. — *Bibliography: p327-345*

EMILIA ROMAGNA (ITALY) — Politics and government

ANDERLINI, Fausto
Territorio e comportamento e lettorale : una analisi delle regionali '85 e delle politiche '83 nei communi dell'Emilia-Romagna e nella città di Bologna / Fausto Anderlini. — Bologna : Servizio Studi e Programmazione, Assessorato Programmazione, 1986. — 157p. — *Includes 10 folded maps*

EMINANT DOMAIN — Sudan
EL RAHMAN, Fath
Compensation paid to foreign nationalised banks and companies in the Sudan / Fath El Rahman [and] Abdalla El Sheikh. — Khartoum : University of Khartoum. Faculty of Economic and Social Studies. Development Studies and Research Centre, 1983. — 52p. — (Monograph series / University of Khartoum. Faculty of Economic and Social Studies. Development Studies and Research Centre ; no.14)

EMINENT DOMAIN — Great Britain
Compensation for compulsory purchase : papers from a conference organized by the Law Society, the Bar Council and the Royal Institution of Chartered Surveyors. — London : Sweet and Maxwell, 1975. — 53p. — (Journal of planning and environment law occasional papers)

EMINENT DOMAIN — Malaysia
KHUBLALL, N.
Law of compulsory purchase and compensation - Singapore and Malaysia / N. Khublall. — Singapore : Butterworths, 1984. — xxviii,310p. — *Bibliography p.293-294. - Includes index*

EMINENT DOMAIN — Singapore
KHUBLALL, N.
Law of compulsory purchase and compensation - Singapore and Malaysia / N. Khublall. — Singapore : Butterworths, 1984. — xxviii,310p. — *Bibliography p.293-294. - Includes index*

EMINENT DOMAIN — United States
PAUL, Ellen Frankel
Property rights and eminent domain / Ellen Frankel Paul. — New Brunswick, U.S.A. : Transaction Books, 1987. — 276 p. — ([Social & moral thought series]). — *Series statement from jacket. — Includes bibliographies and indexes*

EMINENT DOMAIN (INTERNATIONAL LAW)
FRIEDMAN, Samy
[L'expropriation en droit international public. English]. Expropriation in international law / by S. Friedman. — Westport, Conn. : Greenwood Press, 1981. — xv,236p. — *Translation of L'Expropriation en droit international public. — Reprint of the 1953 ed. published by Stevens, London, as no.20 of the Library of world affairs. — Bibliography: p.223-229*

SORNARAJAH, M
The pursuit of nationalized property / M. Sornarajah. — Dordrecht ; Boston : M. Nijhoff, 1985. — p. cm. — (Developments in international law). — *Bibliography: p*

EMOTIONS
Experiencing emotion : a cross cultural study / edited by Klaus R. Scherer, Harald G. Wallbott and Angela B. Summerfield. — Cambridge : Cambridge University Press, 1986. — xiii,302p. — (European monographs in social psychology). — *Bibliography: p282-292. — Includes index*

The Social construction of emotions / edited by Rom Harré. — Oxford : Basil Blackwell, 1986. — viii,316p. — *Includes bibliographies and index*

EMPIRICISM
MOSER, Paul K.
Empirical justification / Paul K. Moser. — Dordrecht ; Boston : D. Reidel Pub. Co. ; Hingham MA, U.S.A. : Sold and distributed in the U.S.A. and Canada by Kluwer Boston, c1985. — x, 263p. — (Philosophical studies series in philosophy ; v. 34). — *Includes indexes*

EMPLOYEE ASSISTANCE PROGRAMS
SCANLON, Walter F
Alcoholism and drug abuse in the workplace : employee assistance programs / Walter F. Scanlon. — New York : Praeger, 1986. — xiii, 146 p.. — *Includes bibliographies and index*

EMPLOYEE FRINGE BENEFITS
Public/private interplay in social protection : a comparative study / edited by Martin Rein and Lee Rainwater ; with Ellen Immergut, Michael O'Higgins, and Harald Russig. — Armonk, N.Y. : M.E. Sharpe, c1986. — viii, 215 p.. — (Comparative public policy analysis). — *Includes bibliographies*

ZOETEWEIJ, H
Indirect remuneration : an international overview / H. Zoeteweij. — Geneva : International Labour Office, 1986. — viii,82p. — *Includes bibliographies*

EMPLOYEE FRINGE BENEFITS — Taxation — Great Britain
GREAT BRITAIN. Board of Inland Revenue
The taxation of cars and petrol as benefits in kind : a consultative paper. — [London] : the Board, 1979. — 7p

EMPLOYEE FRINGE BENEFITS — Great Britain
Fringe benefits, labour costs and social security / edited by Graham L Reid and Donald J. Robertson. — London : Allen and Unwin, 1965. — 336p

EMPLOYEE FRINGE BENEFITS — Japan
FUJITA, Yoshitaka
Employee benefits and industrial relations / Yoshitaka Fujita. — Tokyo : Japan Institute of Labour, 1984. — 47p. — (Japanese industrial relations series ; 12)

EMPLOYEE MOTIVATION
MAEHR, Martin L
The motivation factor : a theory of personal investment / Martin L. Maehr, Larry A. Braskamp. — Lexington, Mass. : Lexington Books, c1986. — p. cm. — *Includes index. — Bibliography: p*

Motivation and work behavior / [compiled by] Richard M. Steers, Lyman W. Porter. — 4th ed. — New York : McGraw-Hill, c1987. — xii, 595 p.. — (McGraw-Hill series in management) . — *Includes bibliographies and indexes*

EMPLOYEE MOTIVATION — Germany (West)
SCHMIDTCHEN, Gerhard
Neue Technik neue Arbeitsmoral : eine sozialpsychologische Untersuchung über Motivation in der Metallindustrie / Gerhard Schmidtchen. — Köln : Deutscher Instituts-Verlag, 1984. — 382p

EMPLOYEE OWNERSHIP
BLANCHFLOWER, D. G.
Shares for employees : a test of their effects / D. G. Blanchflower and A. J. Oswald. — London : Centre for Labour Economics, London School of Economics, 1987. — 36p. — (Discussion paper / London School of Economics and Political Science. Centre for Labour Economics ; no.273). — *Bibliography: p34-36*

PFEIFFER, Lucien
Libre entreprise et socialismes. — Paris : Nouvelle Société des Éditions Encre, 1986. — 192p

REGIONAL TRADE UNION SEMINAR (1967 : Florence)
Workers' negotiated savings plans for capital formation: regional trade union seminar, Florence, 23rd-24th May 1967: final report. — Paris : Organisation for Economic Co-operation & Development ; London : H.M.S.O, 1970. — 174p. — (International seminars / Organisation for Economic Co-operation and Development ; 1967-2)

EMPLOYEE OWNERSHIP — Chile — Santiago
WINN, Peter
Weavers of revolution : the Yarur workers and Chile's road to socialism / Peter Winn. — New York : Oxford University Press, 1986. — xiv, 328 p.. — *Includes index. — Bibliography: p. 300-315*

EMPLOYEE OWNERSHIP — Great Britain
BRADLEY, Keith
The success story of the John Lewis Partnership : a study of comparative performance : a research report / prepared by Keith Bradley and Saul Estrin for Partnership Research Ltd.. — London : [Partnership Research Ltd.], 1986. — 29 leaves

COPEMAN, George
Shared ownership : how to use capital incentives to sustain business growth / George Copeman, Peter Moore, Carol Arrowsmith. — Aldershot : Gower, c1984. — vii,251p. — *Bibliography: p237-240. — Includes index*

HELLER, Robert
Shares for employees / by Robert Heller. — London : Poland Street Publications, 1984. — 131p

Shares for employees / prepared by Deloitte Haskins & Sells. — 3rd ed. — London : Deloitte Haskins & Sells, 1984. — 65p. — *Previous ed.: 1983*

EMPLOYEE OWNERSHIP — United States
ROSEN, Corey
Employee ownership in America : the equity solution / Corey Rosen, Katherine J. Klein, Karen M. Young. — Lexington, Mass. : Lexington Books, 1985. — p. cm. — (Issues in organization and management series). — *Includes bibliographies and index*

EMPLOYEE SELECTION
SMITH, Mike, 1945-
The theory and practice of systematic staff selection / Mike Smith and Ivan T. Robertson. — Basingstoke : Macmillan, 1986. — xii,321p. — *Bibliography: p291-313. — Includes index*

EMPLOYEE SELECTION — Great Britain
GREAT BRITAIN. Equal Opportunities Commission
Fair and efficient selection : guidance on equal opportunities policies in recruitment and selection procedures. — London : H.M.S.O., 1986. — 50p

EMPLOYEE STOCK OPTIONS — Legal status, Laws, etc. — Great Britain
KOPPEL, Michael
Tolley's share options and incentives for directors and employees / by Michael Koppel, Peter Wolstenholme. — Croydon : Tolley, 1986. — xi,108p

EMPLOYEES, DISMISSAL OF
Redundancy, layoffs and plant closures : their character, causes and consequences / edited by Raymond M. Lee. — London : Croom Helm, c1987. — 339p. — *Includes bibliographies and index*

EMPLOYEES, DISMISSAL OF — Law and legislation — Great Britain
RUBENSTEIN, Michael
Unfair dismissal : a guide to relevant case law / by Michael Rubenstein and Yvonne Frost. — 5th ed. — London : Industrial Relations Services, [1987?]. — 91p

UPEX, Robert
Termination of employment / Robert Upex. — 2nd ed. / section on taxation of damages, Denise M. Catterall. — London : Sweet & Maxwell, 1986. — xlii,148p. — *Previous ed.: 1983. — Includes index*

EMPLOYEES, DISMISSAL OF — Great Britain — Law and legislation
KOMIYA, Fumito
Comparative analysis of the law on dismissal in Great Britain, Japan and the U.S.A. / Fumito Komiya. — London : Suntory Toyota International Centre for Economics and Related Disciplines, 1986. — 58p. — (Comparative industrial relations). — *Bibliography: p50-58*

EMPLOYEES, DISMISSAL OF — Japan — Law and legisatlion

KOMIYA, Fumito
Comparative analysis of the law on dismissal in Great Britain, Japan and the U.S.A. / Fumito Komiya. — London : Suntory Toyota International Centre for Economics and Related Disciplines, 1986. — 58p. — (Comparative industrial relations). — *Bibliography: p50-58*

EMPLOYEES, DISMISSAL OF — United States — Law and legislation

KOMIYA, Fumito
Comparative analysis of the law on dismissal in Great Britain, Japan and the U.S.A. / Fumito Komiya. — London : Suntory Toyota International Centre for Economics and Related Disciplines, 1986. — 58p. — (Comparative industrial relations). — *Bibliography: p50-58*

EMPLOYEES, DISMISSAL OF — Wales, South

HARRIS, C. C.
Redundancy and recession in South Wales / C.C. Harris and the Redundancy and Unemployment Research Group, School of Social Studies, University College of Swansea. — Oxford : Basil Blackwell, 1987. — [256]p. — *Includes bibliography and index*

EMPLOYEES' REPRESENTATION IN MANAGEMENT

FOX, Alan
Man mismanagement / Alan Fox. — London : Hutchinson, 1974. — 178p. — (Industry in action)

EMPLOYEES' REPRESENTATION IN MANAGEMENT — England — Liverpool (Merseyside)

MCTIERNAN, M. P.
Workers' alternative plans : a case study at United Biscuits Liverpool plant / M. P. McTiernan. — Coventry : University of Warwick. School of Industrial and Business Studies. Industrial Relations Research Unit, 1986. — 13p. — (Warwick papers in industrial relations ; no.7). — *Bibliography: p13*

EMPLOYEES' REPRESENTATION IN MANAGEMENT — Great Britain

BANK, John
Worker directors speak / by the British Steel Corporation employee directors with John Bank and Ken Jones. — Farnborough, Hants. : Gower Press, 1977. — *Based on group discussions and interviews*

BATE, Paul
Exploring participation / Paul Bate and Lain Mangham. — Chichester : Wiley, c1981. — xii,290p. — *Bibliography: p275-283.* — *Includes index*

WADHWANI, Sushil B.
Profit-sharing and Meade's discriminating labour-capital partnerships : a review article / S. Wadhwani. — London : Centre for Labour Economics, London School of Economics, 1987. — 42p. — (Discussion paper / London School of Economics and Political Science. Centre for Labour Economics ; no.276). — *Bibliography: p38-42*

EMPLOYEES' REPRESENTATION IN MANAGEMENT — Poland

LEWANDOWSKI, Janusz
Samorząd w dobie "Solidarności" : współpraca samorządów pracowniczych Pomorza Gdańskiego na tle sytuacji w kraju w latach 1980/81 / opracował Janusz Lewandowski przy współpracy Jana Szomburga. — Londyn : Odnowa, 1985. — 109p

EMPLOYEE'S REPRESENTATION IN MANAGEMENT — Quebec (Province)

FÉDÉRATION DES TRAVAILLEURS DU QUÉBEC. Conference (13th : 1973 : Montréal)
Notre place dans l'entreprise : les droits des travailleurs dans l'entreprise. — Montreal : Fédération des Travailleurs du Québec, 1973. — 41p

EMPLOYEES' REPRESENTATION IN MANAGEMENT — Sweden — Case studies

TÖRNER, Pär
[Matforsrapporten. English]. The Matfors report : experimental activities with changed organization at SCA-Matfors : final report from the reference group / Pär Törner. — Stockholm : Swedish Employers' Confederation, Technical department, 1976. — 107 p.

EMPLOYEES, TRAINING OF

BINSTED, Don
Developments in interpersonal skills training / Don Binsted. — Aldershot : Gower, c1986. — vi,208p. — *Bibliography: p206-208*

EMPLOYEES, TRAINING OF — Commonwealth of Nations

COMMOMWEALTH SECRETARIAT
Training for book development : incorporating a directory of Commonwealth opportunities for the training of book personnel. — London : the Secretariat, c1973. — vii,52p

EMPLOYEES, TRAINING OF — England — Bolton (Greater Manchester)

THURNHAM, Peter
Operation long-stop : a time limit to unemployment : a redirection of the Community Programme based on the Bolton Pilot Scheme / Peter Thurnham. — London : Conservative Political Centre, 1987. — 55p. — *Bibliography: p52-53*

EMPLOYEES, TRAINING OF — England — Humberside

KENDRA, Neil
Training across the region : evaluation of the Yorkshire and Humberside training scheme : the report of the Panel to Promote the Continuing Development of Training for Part-time and Voluntary Youth and Community Workers / Neil Kendra. — Leicester : National Youth Bureau, 1985. — 15p. — (Extension report / National Youth Bureau ; no.6)

EMPLOYEES, TRAINING OF — England — London

ISLINGTON. Council
Making the most of your abilities : a training plan for Islington. — Islington : [the Council], 1987. — 69p

The London Labour plan : education and training. — London : London Strategic Policy Unit, 1986. — 77p. — *Bibliography: p75*

EMPLOYEES, TRAINING OF — England — Yorkshire

KENDRA, Neil
Training across the region : evaluation of the Yorkshire and Humberside training scheme : the report of the Panel to Promote the Continuing Development of Training for Part-time and Voluntary Youth and Community Workers / Neil Kendra. — Leicester : National Youth Bureau, 1985. — 15p. — (Extension report / National Youth Bureau ; no.6)

EMPLOYEES, TRAINING OF — France

Formation emploi / Centre d'Études et de Recherches sur les Qualifications. — Paris : La Documentation Française, 1986-. — *Quarterly*

EMPLOYEES, TRAINING OF — Great Britain

COOPERS & LYBRAND (Firm)
A challenge to complacency : changing attitudes to training : a report to the Manpower Services Commission and the National Economic Development Office / Coopers & Lybrand Associates. — [Sheffield : Manpower Services Commission, 1985]. — 31p

EMPLOYEES, TRAINING OF — Great Britain — Evaluation

GREAT BRITAIN. Civil Service Department
Evaluation of training in the civil service : a survey. — [London] : the Department, 1977. — 126p. — *Bibliography: p126*

EMPLOYEES, TRAINING OF — Great Britain — History — 20th century

PERRY, P. J. C.
Sand in the sandwich : and other editorials from the BACIE journal 1970-1984 / by P.C.J. Perry ; with a foreword by H.R.H. The Prince Philip Duke of Edinburgh ; and a postscript by Sir Adrian Cadbury. — London : British Association for Commercial and Industrial Education, 1984. — xvi,131p. — *Includes index*

SHELDRAKE, John
The history of industrial training in Britain / John Sheldrake and Sarah Vickerstaff. — Aldershot : Avebury, c1987. — v,75p. — *Bibliography: p66-71.* — *Includes index*

EMPLOYEES, TRAINING OF — London

DAVIES, Tom
Shutting out the inner city worker : recruitment and training practices of large employers in central London / Tom Davies, Charlie Mason. — Bristol : University of Bristol, School for Advanced Urban Studies, 1986. — 50p. — (Occasional paper / University of Bristol, School for Advanced Urban Studies ; 23)

EMPLOYEES, TRANSFER OF

PICKAVANCE, Rachel
Employee utilisation and deployment / Rachel Pickavance. — Brighton : Institute of Manpower Studies, University of Sussex, 1985. — iv,32p. — (IMS report ; no.115)

EMPLOYERS' ASSOCIATIONS — Germany (West)

GRANT, Wyn
Why employer organisation matters : a comparative analysis of business association activity in Britain and West Germany / Wyn Grant. — Coventry : University of Warwick, 1986. — 29p. — (Working paper / University of Warwick ; no.42). — *Bibliography: p28-29*

EMPLOYERS' ASSOCIATIONS — Great Britain

GRANT, Wyn
Why employer organisation matters : a comparative analysis of business association activity in Britain and West Germany / Wyn Grant. — Coventry : University of Warwick, 1986. — 29p. — (Working paper / University of Warwick ; no.42). — *Bibliography: p28-29*

EMPLOYERS' ASSOCIATIONS — Great Britain — Directories

Directory of employers' associations, trade unions, joint organisations, &c / Department of Employment. — London : H.M.S.O., 1986-. — 1v.(loose-leaf). — *Includes index*

EMPLOYMENT — Research — France

FRANCE. Ministère de la recherche et de l'enseignement supérieur. Programme mobilisateur technologie, emploi, travail
L'introuvable relation formation/emploi : un état des recherches en France / sous la direction de Lucie Tanguy. — [Paris] : Documentation française, [1986]. — 302p. — *Bibliography: p271-300*

EMPLOYMENT — Manitoba

MANITOBA LABOUR
Annual report / Manitoba Labour. — Winnipeg : Manitoba Labour, 1984-. — *Continues: Manitoba. Department of Labour and Employment Services. Annual report*

EMPLOYMENT — Norway — Statistics

SKREDE, Kari
Sosialøkonomisk klassifisering av yrker i Norge, 1960 / Kari Skrede. — [s.l.] : Institutt for anvendt sosialvitenskapelig forskning, 1971. — (ii),66p. — (INAS report ; no.71-1)

EMPLOYMENT AGENCIES

MCKEE, William L
Where the jobs are : identification and analysis of local employment opportunities / William L. McKee, Richard C. Froeschle. — Kalamazoo, MI : W.E. Upjohn Institute for Employment Research, c1985. — xii, 175 p.

EMPLOYMENT AGENCIES — Denmark
The Employment Service and Unemployment Insurance Act, 1970, as amended. — [Copenhagen : Ministry of Labour?], 1970. — 35p

EMPLOYMENT AGENCIES — France — History — 19th century
SCHÖTTLER, Peter
Naissance des Bourses du travail : un appareil idéologique d'État à la fin du XIXe siècle / Peter Schöttler ; traduction française de Jean-Pierre Lefebvre et de l'auteur. — Paris : Presses Universitaires de France, 1982. — 294p

EMPLOYMENT AGENCIES — Great Britain
GREAT BRITAIN. Employment Division
Development of the employment service : paper by the Chief Executive, Employment Division. — [Sheffield : the Division, 1984]. — fo.[20]. — Includes summary. — MSC: 84/22

GREAT BRITAIN. Employment Division
Development of the employment service : paper by the Chief Executive, Employment Division. — [Sheffield : the Division, 1984]. — 9p, fo.[6]. — MSC: 84/60

GREAT BRITAIN. Manpower Services Commission
Development of the employment service : consultation. — [Sheffield : the Commission, 1984]. — 1v. (various pagings)

EMPLOYMENT BILL 1979-80
GREAT BRITAIN. Parliament. House of Commons. Library. Research Division
Employment Bill (Bill 97, 1979-80) / Celia Nield. — Rev. ed. — [London] : the Division, 1980. — 53p. — (Reference sheet ; no.79/17). — First Published in 1979. — Includes bibliographical references

EMPLOYMENT BILL 1981-82
GREAT BRITAIN. Parliament. House of Commons. Library. Research Division
Employment Bill (Bill 56 1981-82) / Celia Nield. — [London] : the Division, 1982. — 30p. — (Reference sheet ; no.82/5). — Bibliography: p28-30

EMPLOYMENT (ECONOMIC THEORY)
ARMSTRONG, Harvey
Regional policy : the way forward / Harvey Armstrong and Jim Taylor. — London : Employment Institute, [1987]. — 55 p. — At head of title: Employment Institute

CARTTER, Allan Murray
Theory of wages nd employment / by Allan M. Cartter. — Homewood, Ill. : Irwin, 1959. — xii,193p

GAUSDEN, Robert
Real wages and employment : a survey of studies based on the Granger-Causality testing approach / Robert Gausden. — London : National Institute of Economic and Social Research, 1986. — 40p. — (Discussion paper / National Institute of Economic and Social Research ; no.123). — Bibliography: p39-40

HELD, Daniel
Marché de l'emploi : entreprises et régions / Daniel Held et Denis Maillat. — [Lausanne] : Presses Polytechniques Romandes, 1984. — 205p. — (Collection "villes, régions et sociétés")

LEADBEATER, Charles
In search of work / Charles Leadbeater and John Lloyd. — Harmondsworth : Penguin, 1987. — 232p. — 'Based on a special report "Work - the way ahead", published by the Financial Times in 1986'. — Bibliography: p [214]-218

PYM, Denis
The employment question, & other essays / Denis Pym. — London : Freedom Press, 1986. — 68p

UNIVERSITY OF OXFORD. Institute of Economics and Statistics
The economics of full employment : six studies in applied economics. — Oxford : Blackwell, 1944. — 213p

Work, employment and society / British Sociological Association. — London : British Sociological Association, 1987-. — Quarterly

EMPLOYMENT (ECONOMIC THEORY) — Graphic methods
OSWALD, A. J.
Efficient contracts are on the labour demand curve : theory and facts / Andrew J. Oswald. — Princeton : Industrial Relations Section, Princeton University, 1984. — 43p. — (Working Paper / Princeton University. Industrial Relations Section ; 178). — Bibliography: leaves 33-36

EMPLOYMENT FORECASTING
MCKEE, William L
Where the jobs are : identification and analysis of local employment opportunities / William L. McKee, Richard C. Froeschle. — Kalamazoo, MI : W.E. Upjohn Institute for Employment Research, c1985. — xii, 175 p.

EMPLOYMENT FORECASTING — France
HELD, Daniel
Marché de l'emploi : entreprises et régions / Daniel Held et Denis Maillat. — [Lausanne] : Presses Polytechniques Romandes, 1984. — 205p. — (Collection "villes, régions et sociétés")

EMPLOYMENT FORECASTING — Ireland
HENRY, E. W.
Multisector modelling of the Irish economy : with special reference to employment projections / E. W. Henry. — Dublin : Economic and Social Research Institute, 1986. — 169p. — (Paper / Economic and Social Research Institute ; 128)

EMPLOYMENT FORECASTING — United States — Econometric models
DRENNAN, Matthew P.
Modeling metropolitan economies for forecasting and policy analysis / Matthew P. Drennan. — New York : New York University Press, 1985. — p. cm. — Includes index. — Bibliography: p

EMPLOYMENT SERVICE AND UNEMPLOYMENT INSURANCE ACT, 1970
The Employment Service and Unemployment Insurance Act, 1970, as amended. — [Copenhagen : Ministry of Labour?], 1970. — 35p

EMPLOYMENT STABILIZATION — Australia
Community Employment Program : the first year. — Canberra : Australian Government Publishing Service, 1984. — ix,101p

EMPRESA DE RADIODIFUSIÓN (Peru) — Legal status, laws, etc.
PERU
[Decreto supremo no.007-74-OCI]. Decreto supremo no.007-74-OCI. — [Lima : Presidencia?, 1974]. — 10leaves

EMPRESA EDITORA PERÚ — Legal status, laws, etc.
PERU
[Laws, etc]. Ley orgánica de la Empresa Editora Perú : Decreto-ley no.21420. — Lima : [Empresa Editora Perú, ca.1976]. — 14p

ENCOMIENDAS (LATIN AMERICA)
COLE, Jeffrey A
The Potosí mita, 1573-1700 : compulsory Indian labor in the Andes / Jeffrey A. Cole. — Stanford, Calif. : Stanford University Press, 1985. — xi, 206p. — Includes index. — Bibliography: p.187-196

END OF THE WORLD
HALSELL, Grace
Prophecy and politics : militant evangelists on the road to nuclear war / Grace Halsell. — Westport, Conn. : Lawrence Hill & Co., c1986. — 210 p.. — Includes index

ENDOWMENTS — Directories
The international foundation directory. — 4th ed. / consultant editor H. V. Hodson. — London : Europa, 1986. — 434 p

ENDOWMENTS — Canada
MARTIN, Samuel A
An essential grace : funding Canada's health care, education, welfare, religion, and culture / by Samuel A. Martin. — Toronto : McClelland and Stewart, c1985. — xvii, 322 p.. — Includes index

ENDOWMENTS — United States — History
NIELSEN, Waldemar A
The golden donors : a new anatomy of the great foundations / by Waldemar A. Nielsen. — 1st ed. — New York : E.P. Dutton, c1985. — xi, 468p. — "A Truman Talley book.". — Includes bibliographical references and index

ENERGY CONSERVATION
Energy 2000 : a global strategy for sustainable development : a report for the World Commission on Environment and Development. — London : Zed, 1987. — [96]p

HAYES, Denis, 1944-
Rays of hope : the transition to a post-petroleum world / Denis Hayes. — 1st ed. — New York : Norton, c1977. — 240 p. — "A Worldwatch Institute book.". — Includes bibliographical references and index

OWENS, Susan E.
Energy, planning and urban form / Susan Owens. — London : Pion, c1986. — 118p. — Bibliography: p107-116. — Includes index

ENERGY CONSERVATION — Great Britain
DAVIS, John, 1923-
As though people mattered : a prospect for Britain / John Davis and Alan Bollard. — London : Intermediate Technology Publications, 1986. — xv, 184p

ENERGY CONSERVATION — Great Britain — Bibliography
GREAT BRITAIN. Department of Energy. Library
Energy conservation in the United Kingdom : bibliography 1974-75. — [London : the Library, 1976]. — 14leaves

ENERGY CONSERVATION — International Energy Agency countries
Energy conservation in IEA countries. — Paris : International Energy Agency, 1987. — 259p. — Bibliography: p243-259

ENERGY CONSERVATION — Mexico
Energy efficiency and conservation in Mexico : perspectives on efficiency and conservation policies / edited by Oscar Guzmán, Antonio Yúnez-Naude, Miguel S. Wionczek. — Boulder, Colo. : Westview Press, 1986. — p. cm. — (Westview special studies on Latin America and the Caribbean). — Bibliography: p

ENERGY CONSUMPTION
HEDLEY, Don
World energy : the facts reassessed / Don Hedley. — 2nd ed. — London : Euromonitor, 1985. — [350]p. — Previous ed.: 1981. — Includes bibliography

ENERGY CONSUMPTION — Environmental aspects — Switzerland
GYSIN, Christoph H.
Externe Kosten der Energie in der Schweiz : methodische Grundlagen und Versuch einer Schätzung / Christoph H. Gysin. — Grüsch : Verlag Rüegger, 1985. — xi,220p. — Bibliography: p205-220

ENERGY CONSUMPTION — Brazil
BRAZIL. Secretaria de Tecnologia
Balanço de energia útil. — [Brasília] : the Secretaria, 1984. — 46p

ENERGY CONSUMPTION — France — Statistics
FRANCE. Observatoire de l'Energie
Bilans de l'énergie, 1970 à 1984. — Paris : Observatoire de l'Energie, 1985. — 45p. — (Collection chiffres et documents)

ENERGY CONSUMPTION — Mexico
Energy efficiency and conservation in Mexico : perspectives on efficiency and conservation policies / edited by Oscar Guzmán, Antonio Yúnez-Naude, Miguel S. Wionczek. — Boulder, Colo. : Westview Press, 1986. — p. cm. — (Westview special studies on Latin America and the Caribbean). — *Bibliography: p*

ENERGY CONSUMPTION — Netherlands — Statistics
De Nederlandse energiehuishouding 1982-1983 : nieuwe opzet en tijdreeksen. — 's-Gravenhage : Staatsuitgevrij, 1985. — 199p. — *Contents list in English. — Title on back cover: Energy supply in the Netherlands 1982-1983: new version and time series*

ENERGY CONSUMPTION — Scotland
HAMPSON, S. F.
Recent trends in the Scottish energy market / S.F. Hampson, L.H. Thomson. — [Edinburgh] : [Economics and Statistics Unit, Scottish Economic Planning Department], [1977?]. — 54p. — (ESU discussion paper ; no.1)

ENERGY CONSUMPTION — Switzerland
Energie, Umweltschäden und Umweltschutz in der Schweiz / René L. Frey...[et al.]. — Grüsch : Rüegger, 1985. — 128p. — (Basler Sozialökonomische Studien ; Bd.27). — *Bibliography: p[119]-128*

ENERGY CONSUMPTION — Zambia — Statistics
NATIONAL ENERGY COUNCIL (Zambia)
Energy production and consumption in Zambia 1978-1983. — [Lusaka] : National Energy Council, [1984?]. — 39p

ENERGY DEVELOPMENT — Asia — Statistics
Asian energy problems : an Asian Development Bank survey. — New York : Praeger, 1982. — xxxviii,363p. — *Includes bibliographical references*

ENERGY DEVELOPMENT — Soviet Union
KELLY, William J
Energy research and development in the USSR : preparations for the twenty-first century / William J. Kelly, Hugh L. Shaffer, and J. Kenneth Thompson. — Durham, N.C. : Duke University Press, 1986. — p. cm. — (Duke Press policy studies). — *Includes bibliographies and index*

ENERGY DEVELOPMENT — United States — Addresses, essays, lectures
The Politics of energy research and development / edited by John Byrne and Daniel Rich. — New Brunswick, U.S.A. : Transaction Books, c1986. — 181 p.. — (Energy policy studies ; v. 3). — *Includes bibliographies*

ENERGY INDUSTRIES
BROWN, Stewart L
Trading energy futures : a manual for energy industry professionals / Stewart L. Brown and Steven Errera. — New York : Quorum Books, c1986. — p. cm. — *Includes index. — Bibliography: p*

HEDLEY, Don
World energy : the facts reassessed / Don Hedley. — 2nd ed. — London : Euromonitor, 1985. — [350]p. — *Previous ed.: 1981. — Includes bibliography*

ENERGY INDUSTRIES — Congresses
INTERNATIONAL ASSOCIATION OF ENERGY ECONOMISTS. North American Meeting (1985 : Philadelphia, Pa.)
World energy markets : stability or cyclical change? : proceedings, Seventh Annual North American Meeting, International Association of Energy Economists, Philadelphia, Pennsylvania, December 1985 / edited by William F. Thompson and David J. DeAngelo. — Boulder : Westview Press, 1985. — xiii, 690 p.. — (Westview special studies in natural resources and energy management). — *Includes bibliographies*

ENERGY INDUSTRIES — Economic aspects — Spain — Congresses
ESTRATEGIA PARA EL SECTOR ENERGÉTICO ESPAÑOL (1983 : Madrid)
Estrategia para el sector energético español : Madrid, 20 y 21 de junio de 1983 / organizado por: Price Waterhouse [y] Instituto de Empresa. — [Madrid : Instituto de Empresa, 1984]. — 334p. — *In Spanish, with some contributions in English*

ENERGY INDUSTRIES — Forecasting — Case studies
The Politics of energy forecasting : a comparative study of energy forecasting in Western Europe and North America / edited by Thomas Baumgartner and Atle Midttun. — Oxford : Clarendon, 1987. — xiii,314p. — *Includes bibliographies and index*

ENERGY INDUSTRIES — Government policy
Energy, markets and regulation : essays in honor of M.A. Adelman / edited by Richard L. Gordon, Henry D. Jacoby, and Martin B. Zimmerman. — Cambridge, Mass. : MIT Press, c1987. — p. cm. — *Includes index. — Bibliography: p*

ENERGY INDUSTRIES — Government policy — United States
Energy, markets and regulation : essays in honor of M.A. Adelman / edited by Richard L. Gordon, Henry D. Jacoby, and Martin B. Zimmerman. — Cambridge, Mass. : MIT Press, c1987. — p. cm. — *Includes index. — Bibliography: p*

ENERGY INDUSTRIES — Political aspects — Europe
JENTLESON, Bruce W.
Pipeline politics : the complex political economy of East-West energy trade / Bruce W. Jentleson. — Ithaca, N.Y. : Cornell University Press, 1986. — 263 p.. — (Cornell studies in political economy). — *Includes index. — Bibliography: p. 247-256*

ENERGY INDUSTRIES — Political aspects — Soviet Union
JENTLESON, Bruce W.
Pipeline politics : the complex political economy of East-West energy trade / Bruce W. Jentleson. — Ithaca, N.Y. : Cornell University Press, 1986. — 263 p.. — (Cornell studies in political economy). — *Includes index. — Bibliography: p. 247-256*

ENERGY INDUSTRIES — Brazil
BRAZIL. Secretaria de Tecnologia
Balanço de energia útil. — [Brasília] : the Secretaria, 1984. — 46p

ENERGY INDUSTRIES — Developing countries
Major stages and steps in energy manpower analysis : a practical framework. — Geneva : International Labour Office, 1986. — viii,80p. — *Bibliographical references: p[74]-80*

ENERGY INDUSTRIES — Germany (West)
SCHIFFER, Hans-Wilhelm
Struktur und Wandel der Energiewirtschaft in der Bundesrepublik Deutschland / Hans-Wilhelm Schiffer. — Köln : Verlag TÜV Rheinland, 1985. — xi,185p

ENERGY INDUSTRIES — Great Britain
Energy technologies for the United Kingdom : 1986 appraisal of research, development and demonstration. — London : H.M.S.O., 1987. — vii,25p. — (Energy paper / Department of Energy ; 54). — *Prepared at the request of the Secretary of State for Energy's Advisory Council on Research and Development by the Chief Scientist's Group of the Energy Technology Support Unit*

ENERGY INDUSTRIES — Scotland
HAMPSON, S. F.
Recent trends in the Scottish energy market / S.F. Hampson, L.H. Thomson. — [Edinburgh] : [Economics and Statistics Unit, Scottish Economic Planning Department], [1977?]. — 54p. — (ESU discussion paper ; no.1)

ENERGY INDUSTRIES — Siberia, Western (R.S.F.S.R.) — Government policy
CHUNG, Han-Ku
Interest representation in Soviet policy-making : a case study of a Siberian energy coalition, 1969-1981 / Han-Ku Chung. — 176 leaves. — *PhD (Econ) 1986 LSE*

ENERGY INDUSTRIES — Spain — Congresses
ESTRATEGIA PARA EL SECTOR ENERGÉTICO ESPAÑOL (1983 : Madrid)
Estrategia para el sector energético español : Madrid, 20 y 21 de junio de 1983 / organizado por: Price Waterhouse [y] Instituto de Empresa. — [Madrid : Instituto de Empresa, 1984]. — 334p. — *In Spanish, with some contributions in English*

ENERGY INDUSTRIES — United States
PEIRCE, William Spangar
Economics of the energy industries / William Spangar Peirce. — Belmont, Calif. : Wadsworth Pub. Co., c1986. — p. cm. — *Includes index*

ENERGY POLICY
CROWN AGENTS FOR OVERSEAS GOVERNMENTS AND ADMINISTRATIONS
Energy crisis in the eighties. — London : the Agents, 1980. — 48p. — *Crown Agents special review, July 1980*

INTERNATIONAL ASSOCIATION OF ENERGY ECONOMISTS. International Conferences (6th : Churchill College, Cambridge : 1982)
International energy policy : the potential for change / selected papers from the Sixth Annual International Conference of the International Association of Energy Economists hosted by its UK affiliate, the British Institute of Energy Economics, held in Churchill College, Cambridge, on 9-11 April 1984. — Bedford : Cranfield Press, 1985

ENERGY POLICY — Case studies
The Politics of energy forecasting : a comparative study of energy forecasting in Western Europe and North America / edited by Thomas Baumgartner and Atle Midttun. — Oxford : Clarendon, 1987. — xiii,314p. — *Includes bibliographies and index*

ENERGY POLICY — Congresses
IAEE CONFERENCE ((7th : 1985 : Bonn, Germany)
Energy and economy, global interdependences : papers of the plenary sessions of the 1985 International Conference of the International Association of Energy Economists (IAEE) and its German Chapter, the Gesellschaft für Energiewissenschaft und Energiepolitik (GEE) / Mark Baier (Hrsg.). — Köln : Verlag TÜV Rheinland, c1986. — 183 p.. — *Includes bibliographies*

ENERGY POLICY — Economic aspects
The Economics of choice between energy sources : proceedings of a conference held by the International Economic Association in Tokyo, Japan / edited by Pierre Maillet, Douglas Hague and Chris Rowland. — Basingstoke : Macmillan, 1987. — xvi,493p. — *Includes index*

ENERGY POLICY — Environmental aspects — Australia
JAMES, D.
Energy development and environment quality management / D. James. — Canberra : Australian Government Publishing Service, 1985. — xvi,78p. — (Environment papers / Department of Arts, Heritage and Environment). — *Bibliographical references: p71-72*

ENERGY POLICY — Statistics
ORGANIZATION OF THE PETROLEUM EXPORTING COUNTRIES
Facts and figures: a graphical analysis of world energy up to 1985 / Organization of Petroleum Exporting Countries. — Vienna : OPEC, 1981-. — *Annual. — Sub-title varies*

ENERGY POLICY — Asia — Congresses
PACIFIC TRADE AND DEVELOPMENT CONFERENCE (13th : 1983 : Manila, Philippines)
Energy and structural change in the Asia Pacific region : papers and proceedings of the Thirteenth Pacific Trade and Development Conference held in Manila, Philippines, January 24-28, 1983 / edited by Romeo M. Bautista and Seiji Naya. — [Manila, Philippines] : Philippine Institute for Development Studies : Asian Development Bank, 1984. — xxii,532p. — *Bibliography: p423-532*

ENERGY POLICY — Brazil
BARZELAY, Michael
The politicized market economy : alcohol in Brazil's energy strategy / Michael Barzelay. — Berkeley : University of California Press, c1986. — xiv, 289p. — (Studies in international political economy). — *Includes index. — Bibliography: p.267-276*

ENERGY POLICY — Canada
Canada's energy policy, 1985 and beyond / Edward A. Carmichael, Corina M. Herrera (Editors). — Toronto : C. D. Howe Institute, 1984. — 95p

ENERGY POLICY — Denmark
Energy in Denmark : a report on energy planning, 1983. — [Copenhagen] : Ministry of Energy, 1983. — 90p

ENERGY POLICY — Denmark — Statistics
Import-, beskaeftigelses- og energimultiplikatover. Import-, employment- and energy multipliers / Danmarks Statistik, Nationalregnskabssektionen. — København : Danmarks Statistik. Nationalregnskabssektionen, 1984-. — *Annual*

ENERGY POLICY — Europe — Bibliography
ELECTRICITY COUNCIL. Intelligence Section
The prospects in Europe for the electricity supply industry : select list of references. — London : the Section, [1974]. — 11p. — (Bibliographies / Electicity Council, Intelligence Section ; B87)

ENERGY POLICY — European Economic Community
COMMISSION OF THE EUROPEAN COMMUNITIES
Bulletin of energy prices = Bulletin des prix de l'energie / Commission of the European Communities. — Luxembourg : Office for Official Publications of the European Communities, 1985-. — *Irregular*

ENERGY POLICY — European Economic Community Countries
COMMISSION OF THE EUROPEAN COMMUNITIES. Directorate-General for Energy
Energy in Europe : energy policies and trends in the European Community. — Luxembourg : Office for Official Publications of the European Communities, 1985-. — *3 per year*

ENERGY POLICY — European Economic Community countries
DAINTITH, Terence
Energy strategy in Europe : the legal framework / by Terence Daintith and Leigh Hancher. — Berlin : W. de Gruyter, 1986. — ix,190p. — (Series A, Law / European University Institute ; 4). — *Includes bibliographical references and index*

ENERGY POLICY — European Economic Community countries — Congresses
SECTOR ENERGETICO ESPAÑOL ANTE LA ENTRADA EN LA CEE (Conferencia : 1985 : Madrid)
El sector energetico español ante la entrada en la CEE : conferencia, Madrid 20 y 21 de febrero de 1985 / organizada por: Instituto de Empresa. — Madrid : Instituto de Empresa, 1985. — 135p

ENERGY POLICY — France
Les consommations d'énergie dans l'industrie. — Paris : Documentation Française, 1982-. — (Traits fondamentaux du système industriel français) (Collection chiffres et documents: Serie industrie). — *Annual*

FABERON, Jean-Yves
La maîtrise de l'énergie : cadre juridique et bilan / Jean-Yves Faberon. — [Paris : La Documentation française, 1986]. — 111p. — (Notes et études documentaires ; no.4823). — *Bibliography: p108-109*

Les perspectives énergétiques de la France à l'horizon 2000. — Paris : the Ministère, 1987. — 5,92,74p

ENERGY POLICY — Great Britain
LYNK, Edward L.
The demand for energy by U.K. manufacturing industry / Edward L. Lynk. — Oxford : Oxford Institute for Energy Studies, 1985. — 27p. — *Bibliography: p26-27*

PORTER, Andy
The energy fix : towards a socialist energy strategy / Andy Porter, Martin Spence, Roy Thompson. — London : Pluto, 1986. — [224]p. — *Includes index*

ENERGY POLICY — Pacific Area — Congresses
PACIFIC TRADE AND DEVELOPMENT CONFERENCE (13th : 1983 : Manila, Philippines)
Energy and structural change in the Asia Pacific region : papers and proceedings of the Thirteenth Pacific Trade and Development Conference held in Manila, Philippines, January 24-28, 1983 / edited by Romeo M. Bautista and Seiji Naya. — [Manila, Philippines] : Philippine Institute for Development Studies : Asian Development Bank, 1984. — xxii,532p. — *Bibliography: p423-532*

ENERGY POLICY — Scotland — Strathclyde
STRATHCLYDE. Regional Council
Babcock Energy PLC : economic and social importance of Babcock Energy's power division to Strathclyde, Scotland and the United Kingdom : submission to the Secretary of State for Scotland by Strathclyde Regional Council. — Glasgow : [the Council], 1987. — 15p. — *Cover title: Babcock Power : the case for government action*

ENERGY POLICY — Soviet Union
CHUNG, Han-Ku
Interest representation in Soviet policy-making : a case study of a Siberian energy coalition, 1969-1981 / Han-Ku Chung. — 176 leaves. — *PhD (Econ) 1986 LSE*

ENERGY POLICY — Spain — Congresses
SECTOR ENERGETICO ESPAÑOL ANTE LA ENTRADA EN LA CEE (Conferencia : 1985 : Madrid)
El sector energetico español ante la entrada en la CEE : conferencia, Madrid 20 y 21 de febrero de 1985 / organizada por: Instituto de Empresa. — Madrid : Instituto de Empresa, 1985. — 135p

ENERGY POLICY — Sweden
Energy ahead: Vattenfall annual R and D report. — Vallingby : Vattenfall, 1984-. — *Annual*

LÖNNROTH, Mans
Energy in transition : a report on energy policy and future options / Mans Lönnroth, Peter Steen and Thomas Johansson. — Berkeley ; London : University of California Press, 1980. — 171p. — *Bibliography: p.165-167. — Includes index*

ENERGY POLICY — Switzerland
GYSIN, Christoph H.
Externe Kosten der Energie in der Schweiz : methodische Grundlagen und Versuch einer Schätzung / Christoph H. Gysin. — Grüsch : Verlag Rüegger, 1985. — xi,220p. — *Bibliography: p205-220*

PARTI LIBÉRAL SUISSE
Pour une politique libérale de l'énergie : rapport d'une commission d'étude du Parti libéral suisse, 6 octobre 1978. — Berne : Parti Libéral Suisse, 1978. — 31p

ENERGY POLICY — United States — Addresses, essays, lectures
The Politics of energy research and development / edited by John Byrne and Daniel Rich. — New Brunswick, U.S.A. : Transaction Books, c1986. — 181 p.. — (Energy policy studies ; v. 3). — *Includes bibliographies*

ENFIELD (MASS.) — Social life and customs
UNDERWOOD, Francis Henry
Quabbin : the story of a small town with outlooks upon Puritan life / by Francis H. Underwood ; with a foreword by Robert A. Gross. — Northeastern University Press ed. — Boston : Northeastern University Press, 1986. — xxxv, 375 p., [4] p. of plates. — : Reprint. Originally published: London : Bliss, Sands & Foster, 1893. — *Bibliography: p. xxxiii-xxxv*

ENGA (NEW GUINEA PEOPLE) — Commerce
FEIL, D. K.
Ways of exchange : the Enga tee of Papua New Guinea / D.K. Feil. — St. Lucia, Qld. : University of Queensland Press ; Lawrence, Mass. : Distributed in the USA and Canada by Technical Impex Corp., 1984. — xvi, 269 p.. — *Bibliography: p[253]-261. — Bibliography: p. [253]-261*

ENGA (NEW GUINEA PEOPLE) — Rites and ceremonies
FEIL, D. K.
Ways of exchange : the Enga tee of Papua New Guinea / D.K. Feil. — St. Lucia, Qld. : University of Queensland Press ; Lawrence, Mass. : Distributed in the USA and Canada by Technical Impex Corp., 1984. — xvi, 269 p.. — *Bibliography: p[253]-261. — Bibliography: p. [253]-261*

ENGELS, FRIEDERICH — Bibliography
DRAPER, Hal
The Marx-Engels register : a complete bibliography of Marx and Engels' individual writings / by Hal Draper with the assistance of the Center for Socialist History. — New York : Schocken Books, 1985. — xxx, 271 p.. — (Marx-Engels cyclopedia ; v. 2). — *Includes index*

ENGELS, FRIEDRICH
Engels revisited : new feminist essays / edited by Janet Sayers, Mary Evans, and Nanneke Redclift. — London : Tavistock, 1987. — 172p. — *Includes bibliographies and index*

MARX, Karl, 1818-1883
[Collected works]. Werke, Artikel, Entwurfe : Juli 1851 bis Dezember 1852 / Karl Marx, Friedrich Engels ; [Bearbeitung des Bandes: Martin Hundt...et al.]. — Berlin : Dietz, 1985. — 2v. — (Karl Marx Friedrich Engels Gesamtausgabe (MEGA). 1 Abt. ; Bd.11)

ENGELS, FRIEDRICH — Chronology
DRAPER, Hal
The Marx-Engels chronicle : a day-by-day chronology of Marx and Engels' life and activity / by Hal Draper ; with the assistance of the Center for Socialist History. — New York : Schocken Books, 1985. — xxii, 297 p.. — (The Marx-Engels cyclopedia ; v. 1)

ENGELS, FRIEDRICH — Language — Glossaries, etc
DRAPER, Hal
The Marx-Engels glossary : glossary to the chronicle and register, annd index to the glossary / by Hal Draper ; with the assistance of the Center for Socialist History. — New York : Schocken Books, 1986. — xx, 249 p.. — (The Marx-Engels encyclopedia ; v. 3). — Includes index

ENGINEERING — Great Britain — Employees
FREEMAN, Christopher
Engineering and vehicles / Christopher Freeman, Daniel R. Jones ; edited by Christopher Freeman. — Aldershot : Gower, c1985. — xvii,199p. — (Technological trends and employment ; 4)

ENGINEERING DESIGN — Data processing
Information pack including bibliography on advanced manufacturing technology / compiled by Lucy Hamilton and John Devine ; foreword by Peter Willows. — London : Institution of Mechanical Engineers, 1986. — vi,98p. — (Information Pack ; 1). — Annotated bibliography: p47-98

ENGINEERING FIRMS — Great Britain — Employees
GLOVER, Ian A.
Engineers in Britain : a sociological study of the engineering dimension / Ian A. Glover, Michael P. Kelly. — London : Allen & Unwin, 1987. — [288]p. — Includes bibliography and indexes

ENGINEERS — England — Supply and demand
INSTITUTE OF MANPOWER STUDIES
Craftsmen and draughtsmen : the end of shortages?. — [Sheffield : Manpower Services Commission, 1983]. — 21p

ENGINEERS — Germany (West) — Taxation
Kostenstruktur bei Rechtsanwälten und Anwaltsnotaven, bei Wirtschaftsprüfern, Steuerberatern und Steuerbevollmäch tigten, bei Architekten und Beratenden Ingenieuren. — Wiesbaden : Statistisches Bundesamt, 1975-. — (Unternehmen und Arbeitsstätten ; Reihe 1.6.2) . — Every 4 years. — Title varies

ENGINEERS — Russian S.F.S.R. — Siberia
MOZYREVA, T. A.
Tekuchest' i stabilizatsiia inzhenernotekhnicheskikh rabotnikov na predpriiatiiakh Sibiri / T. A. Mozyreva ; otv. redaktor E. G. Antosenkov. — Novosibirsk : Nauka, Sibirskoe otdelenie, 1986. — 156p

ENGLAND — Census, 1676
The Compton census of 1676 : a critical edition / edited by Anne Whiteman with the assistance of Mary Clapinson. — London : Published for the British Academy by Oxford University Press, 1986. — cxxiv,801p,[8]p of plates. — (Records of social and economic history. New series ; 10). — Bibliography: p647-655. Includes index

ENGLAND — Church history — Modern period, 1485-
RUPP, Gordon
Religion in England 1688-1791 / Gordon Rupp. — Oxford : Clarendon, 1986. — [xiv,520]p. — (Oxford history of the Christian Church). — Includes bibliography and index

ENGLAND — Church history — 16th century
TYACKE, Nicholas
Anti-Calvinists : the rise of English Arminianism c.1590-1640 / Nicholas Tyacke. — Oxford : Clarendon, 1987. — [300]p,[4]p of plates. — (Oxford historical monographs). — Includes bibliography and index

ENGLAND — Church history — 17th century
TYACKE, Nicholas
Anti-Calvinists : the rise of English Arminianism c.1590-1640 / Nicholas Tyacke. — Oxford : Clarendon, 1987. — [300]p,[4]p of plates. — (Oxford historical monographs). — Includes bibliography and index

ENGLAND — Church history — 20th century
HASTINGS, Adrian
A history of English Christianity 1920-1985 / Adrian Hastings. — London : Collins, 1986. — 720p. — Includes index

ENGLAND — Civilization
NEWMAN, Gerald
The rise of English nationalism : a cultural history, 1720-1830 / Gerald Newman. — New York : St. Martin's Press, 1987. — xxiii, 294 p. . — Includes index. — Bibliography: p. [269]-280

ENGLAND — Civilization — 19th century
WIENER, Martin J.
English culture and the decline of the industrial spirit, 1850-1980 / Martin J. Wiener. — Harmondsworth : Penguin, 1985. — xi,217p. — (Pelican book)

ENGLAND — Civilization — 20th century
WIENER, Martin J.
English culture and the decline of the industrial spirit, 1850-1980 / Martin J. Wiener. — Harmondsworth : Penguin, 1985. — xi,217p. — (Pelican book)

ENGLAND — Constitutional law — Historiography
POCOCK, J. G. A.
The ancient constitution and the feudal law : a study of English historical thought in the seventeenth century / J.G.A. Pocock. — Reissue with a retrospect [i.e. 2nd ed.]. — Cambridge : Cambridge University Press, 1987. — xv,402p. — Previous ed.: 1957. — Includes index

ENGLAND — Economic conditions — Medieval period, 1066-1485
MCINTOSH, Marjorie Keniston
Autonomy and community : the Royal Manor of Havering, 1200-1500 / Marjorie Keniston McIntosh. — Cambridge : Cambridge University Press, 1986. — [460]p. — (Cambridge studies in medieval life and thought. Fourth series). — Includes bibliography and index

ENGLAND — Emigration and immigration — History
Huguenots in Britain and their French background, 1550-1800 / edited by Irene Scouloudi. — Totowa, N.J. : Barnes & Noble, 1987. — p. cm. — Includes index

ENGLAND — Emigration and immigration — History — 19th century
MARGRAVE, Richard Dobson
The emigration of silk workers from England to the United States in the nineteenth century : with special reference to Coventry, Macclesfield, Paterson, New Jersey, and South Manchester, Connecticut / Richard Dobson Margrave. — New York : Garland, 1986. — 421 p.. — (Outstanding theses from the London School of Economics and Political Science). — Thesis (Ph. D.)--London School of Economics and Political Science, 1981. — Bibliography: p. [384]-421

ENGLAND — History — Medieval period, 1066-1485
GIVEN-WILSON, Chris
The English nobility in the late Middle Ages : the fourteenth-century political community / Chris Given-Wilson. — London : Routledge and Kegan Paul, 1987. — xxii,222p

ENGLAND — Nobility — History
BECKETT, J. V.
The aristocracy in England 1660-1914 / J.V. Beckett. — Oxford : Basil Blackwell, 1986. — 1v.. — Includes index

GIVEN-WILSON, Chris
The English nobility in the late Middle Ages : the fourteenth-century political community / Chris Given-Wilson. — London : Routledge and Kegan Paul, 1987. — xxii,222p

ENGLAND — Population
SERPLAN
Department of the Environment 1983-based household projections : implications for the south east region. — London : SERPLAN, 1986. — [8p]

ENGLAND — Population — History
LEVINE, David, 1946-
Reproducing families : the political economy of English population history / David Levine. — Cambridge : Cambridge University Press, 1987. — [272]p. — (Themes in the social sciences). — Includes index

ENGLAND — Population — History — Addresses, Essays, Lectures
Population and history : from the traditional to the modern world : edited by Robert I. Rotberg and Theodore K. Rabb / guest editors: Roger S. Schofield and E. Anthony Wrigley ; contributors: Michael Anderson ... [et al.]. — Cambridge : Cambridge University Press, 1986. — [iv],219p. — (Studies in interdisciplinary history)

ENGLAND — Population, rural
PARSONS, D. J.
Rural gentrification : the influence of rural settlement planning policies / D. J. Parsons. — [Brighton : University of Sussex, 1980]. — 36p. — (University of Sussex Research Papers in Geography)

ENGLAND — Race relations
ROSE, E. J. B.
Colour and citizenship : a report on British race relations / E.J.B. Rose ... [et al.]. — London : Oxford University Press for the Institute of Race Relations, 1969. — xxiii,815p. — Bibliography: p.797-805

ENGLAND — Royal household — History
GIVEN-WILSON, Chris
The royal household and the King's affinity : service, politics and finance in England 1360-1413 / Chris Given-Wilson. — New Haven ; London : Yale University Press, 1986. — viii,327p. — Bibliography: p316-320. Includes index

ENGLAND — Rural conditions
HORN, Pamela
Life and labour in rural England 1760-1850 / Pamela Horn. — Basingstoke : Macmillan, 1987. — x,184p. — (Context and commentary). — Bibliography: p175-180. — Includes index

NEWBY, Howard, 1947-
Country life : a social history of rural England / Howard Newby. — London : Weidenfeld and Nicolson, 1987. — 250p. — Bibliography: p238-241

PARSONS, D. J.
Rural gentrification : the influence of rural settlement planning policies / D. J. Parsons. — [Brighton : University of Sussex, 1980]. — 36p. — (University of Sussex Research Papers in Geography)

ENGLAND — Social conditions

MACFARLANE, Alan
The culture of capitalism / Alan Macfarlane. — Oxford : Basil Blackwell, 1987. — [256]p. — *Includes bibliography and index*

ENGLAND — Social conditions — Medieval period, 1066-1485

CHIBNALL, Marjorie
Anglo-Norman England 1066-1166 / Marjorie Chibnall. — Oxford : Blackwell, 1986. — 240p. — *Bibliography: p224-231. — Includes index*

GIVEN-WILSON, Chris
The English nobility in the late Middle Ages : the fourteenth-century political community / Chris Given-Wilson. — London : Routledge and Kegan Paul, 1987. — xxii,222p

MCINTOSH, Marjorie Keniston
Autonomy and community : the Royal Manor of Havering, 1200-1500 / Marjorie Keniston McIntosh. — Cambridge : Cambridge University Press, 1986. — [460]p. — (Cambridge studies in medieval life and thought. Fourth series). — *Includes bibliography and index*

ENGLAND — Social conditions — 19th century

DINWIDDY, J. R.
From Luddism to the First Reform Bill : reform in England 1810-1832 / J.R. Dinwiddy. — Oxford : Basil Blackwell, 1986. — [96]p. — (Historical Association studies). — *Includes bibliography and index*

ROSENTHAL, Michael
The character factory : Baden-Powell and the origins of the Boy Scout movement / Michael Rosenthal. — New York : Pantheon Books, 1986. — p. cm. — *Includes index*

ENGLAND — Social life and customs

CORRIGAN, Philip
The great arch : English state formation as cultural revolution / Philip Corrigan and Derek Sayer ; with a foreword by G.E. Aylmer. — Oxford : Blackwell, 1985. — x,268p. — *Bibliography: p233-264. — Includes index*

NEWBY, Howard, 1947-
Country life : a social history of rural England / Howard Newby. — London : Weidenfeld and Nicolson, 1987. — 250p. — *Bibliography: p238-241*

ENGLAND — Social life and customs — 16th century

SHARPE, J. A.
Early modern England : a social history 1550-1760 / J.A. Sharpe. — London : Edward Arnold, 1987. — [400]p. — *Includes bibliography and index*

ENGLAND — Social life and customs — 17th century

SHARPE, J. A.
Early modern England : a social history 1550-1760 / J.A. Sharpe. — London : Edward Arnold, 1987. — [400]p. — *Includes bibliography and index*

ENGLAND — Social life and customs — 18th century

SHARPE, J. A.
Early modern England : a social history 1550-1760 / J.A. Sharpe. — London : Edward Arnold, 1987. — [400]p. — *Includes bibliography and index*

ENGLAND. Court of Star Chamber — History

GUY, J. A.
The Court of Star Chamber and its records to the reign of Elizabeth I / by J. A. Guy. — London : H.M.S.O., 1985. — 112 p. — (Public Record Office handbooks ; no. 21)

ENGLAND. Parliament. House of Commons — History — Bibliography

SEATON, Janet
English constituency histories, 1265-1832 : a guide to printed sources / by Janet Seaton. — London : H.M.S.O., 1986. — xvii, 143p. — (House of Commons Library document ; no.15)

ENGLAND — Church history — 16th century

HEATH, Peter
The English parish clergy on the eve of the reformation / Peter Heath. — London : Routledge and Kegan Paul, 1969. — xiii,249p

ENGLAND AND WALES. Army. New Model Army — History

WOOLRYCH, Austin
Soldiers and statesmen : the General Council of the Army and its debates 1647-1648 / Austin Woolrych. — Oxford : Clarendon, 1987. — [250]p. — *Includes bibliography and index*

ENGLAND AND WALES. Court of Star Chamber — History

GUY, J. A.
The Court of Star Chamber and its records to the reign of Elizabeth I / by J. A. Guy. — London : H.M.S.O., 1985. — 112 p. — (Public Record Office handbooks ; no. 21)

ENGLAND AND WALES. Parliamant. House of Commons — History — Bibliography

SEATON, Janet
English constituency histories, 1265-1832 : a guide to printed sources / by Janet Seaton. — London : H.M.S.O., 1986. — xvii, 143p. — (House of Commons Library document ; no.15)

ENGLAND AND WALES. Parliament — History

ELTON, G. R.
The Parliament of England, 1559-1581 / G.R. Elton. — Cambridge : Cambridge University Press, 1986. — [411]p. — *Includes index*

GRAVES, Michael A. R.
Elizabethan parliaments, 1559-1601 / Michael A. R. Graves. — London : Longman, 1987. — v,123p. — (Seminar studies in history). — *Text on inside cover. — Bibliography: p114-118. Includes index*

THOMPSON, Christopher, 19---
Parliamentary history in the 1620s : in or out of perspective? / by Christopher Thompson. — Wivenhoe : Orchard, c1986. — 26leaves

ENGLISH — Spain — Valverde — History

RAMÍREZ COPEIRO DEL VILLAR, Jesús
Ingleses en Valverde : aspecto humano de la minería inglesa en la provincia de Huelva / por Jesús Ramírez Copeiro del Villar. — Huelva : Jesús Ramírez Copeiro del Villar, Granada no.13, Valverde de Camino (Huelva), 1985. — 281p. — *Bibliography: p279-281*

ENGLISH CHANNEL (ENGLAND AND FRANCE) — History

A people of the sea : the maritime history of the Channel Islands / edited by A.G. Jamieson. — London : Methuen, 1986. — xxxvi, 528p, [41]p of plates (some col.). — *Includes index. — Bibliography: p.[482]-502*

ENGLISH DRAMA — 20th century

Plays by women. — London : Methuen. — (A Methuen theatrefile)
Vol.1 / edited and introduced by Michelene Wandor. — 1982. — 136p. — *Contents: Vinegar Tom / by Caryl Churchill. — Dusa, fish, stas and VI / by Pam Gems. — Tissue / by Louise Page. — Aurora Leigh / by Michelene Wandor*

ENGLISH IMPRINTS

HORAK, Stephan M.
Russia, the USSR, and Eastern Europe : a bibliographic guide to English language publications, 1975-1980 / Stephan M. Horak. — Littleton, Colo. : Libraries Unlimited, 1982. — 279 p.. — *Supplements: Russia, the USSR, and Eastern Europe : a bibliographic guide to English language publications, 1964-1974 / Stephan M. Horak. 1978. — Includes index*

ENGLISH LANGUAGE — Data processing

GRISHMAN, Ralph
Computational linguistics : an introduction / Ralph Grishman. — Cambridge : Cambridge University Press, 1986. — [vii,409]p. — (Studies in natural language processing). — *Includes bibliography and index*

ENGLISH LANGUAGE — Dialects

EDWARDS, Viv
Language in a black community / Viv Edwards. — Clevedon : Multilingual Matters, c1986. — 169p. — (Multilingual matters ; 24). — *Bibliography: p153-164. — Includes index*

ENGLISH LANGUAGE — Dictionaries

Cassell's English-Dutch/Dutch-English dictionary = Engels-Nederlands/Nederlands-Engels woordenboek / completely revised by J. A. Jockin-la Bastide [and] G. van Kooten. — London : Cassell, 1981. — xiv,602,vii,729p

Longman dictionary of contemporary English. — New ed. — Harlow : Longman, 1987. — [1360]p. — *Previous ed.: 1978*

ENGLISH LANGUAGE — Dictionaries — French

GORSE, Jean Eugène
A World Bank glossary : forestry terms : English-French = Glossaire de la Banque mondiale : terminologie forestière : français-anglais. — Washington, D.C. : World Bank, 1984. — v,42p. — *In English and French*

KETTRIDGE, J. O.
French dictionary : French-English, English-French / compiled by J.O. Kettridge. — Rev. ed / completely revised by Alec Strahan, Wyn Johnson and Sarah Edwards. — London : Routledge & Kegan Paul, 1986. — x,566p. — *Previous ed.: i.e. New rev. ed. published as Kettridge's French-English, English-French dictionary. New York : New American Library, 1984*

Population terminology = Terminologie de la population = Terminología de población. — Washington, D.C. : The World Bank, 1986. — iii,27p. — (A World Bank glossary)

ENGLISH LANGUAGE — Dictionaries — German

BESELER, Dora von
Law dictionary : technical dictionary of the Anglo-Americal legal terminology including commercial and political terms : English-German / von Beseler/Jacobs-Wüstefeld. — 4th rev. and enl. ed. / by Barbara Wüstefeld (nee Jacobs). — Berlin ; New York : W. de Gruyter, 1986. — p. cm

Shorter Cambridge-Eichborn German dictionary : business and business law, economics, administration. — Cambridge : Cambridge University Press, 1984. — 2v.

ENGLISH LANGUAGE — Dictionaries — Greek language, Modern

PRING, J. T.
The Oxford dictionary of modern Greek : English-Greek / compiled by J.T. Pring. — Oxford : Clarendon, 1982. — x,370p

ENGLISH LANGUAGE — Dictionaries — Spanish

Population terminology = Terminologie de la population = Terminología de población. — Washington, D.C. : The World Bank, 1986. — iii,27p. — (A World Bank glossary)

ENGLISH LANGUAGE — Gender
BARON, Dennis E
Grammar and gender / Dennis Baron. — New Haven : Yale University Press, c1986. — p. cm . — *Includes index. — Bibliography: p*

ENGLISH LANGUAGE — Jargon
SPEARS, Richard A
The slang and jaron of drugs and drink / by Ricard A. Spears. — Metuchen, N.J. : Scarecrow Press, 1986. — xv, 585 p.. — *Bibliography: p. [562]-575*

ENGLISH LANGUAGE — Jargon — Dictionaries
GREEN, Jonathon
Newspeak : a dictionary of jargon / Jonathon Green. — London : Routledge & Kegan Paul, 1984. — xii,263p. — *Bibliography: p261-263*

ENGLISH LANGUAGE — Modality
PREISLER, Bent
Linguistic sex roles in conversation : social variation in the expression of tentativeness in English / Bent Preisler. — Berlin ; New York : Mouton de Gruyter, c1986. — p. cm. — (Contributions to the sociology of language ; 45). — *Includes indexes. — Bibliography: p*

ENGLISH LANGUAGE — Reform
BARON, Dennis E
Grammar and gender / Dennis Baron. — New Haven : Yale University Press, c1986. — p. cm . — *Includes index. — Bibliography: p*

ENGLISH LANGUAGE — Rhetoric
BORN, Roscoe C
The suspended sentence : a guide for writers / Roscoe C. Born. — New York : Scribner, c1986. — x, 214 p.. — *Includes index*

ENGLISH LANGUAGE — Sex differences
BARON, Dennis E
Grammar and gender / Dennis Baron. — New Haven : Yale University Press, c1986. — p. cm . — *Includes index. — Bibliography: p*

PREISLER, Bent
Linguistic sex roles in conversation : social variation in the expression of tentativeness in English / Bent Preisler. — Berlin ; New York : Mouton de Gruyter, c1986. — p. cm. — (Contributions to the sociology of language ; 45). — *Includes indexes. — Bibliography: p*

ENGLISH LANGUAGE — Slang — Dictionaries
SPEARS, Richard A
The slang and jaron of drugs and drink / by Ricard A. Spears. — Metuchen, N.J. : Scarecrow Press, 1986. — xv, 585 p.. — *Bibliography: p. [562]-575*

ENGLISH LANGUAGE — Social aspects
Discourse among cultures : strategies in world Englishes / edited by Larry E. Smith. — Hemel Hempstead : Prentice-Hall International, 1987. — 1v.. — (English in the international context series). — *Includes bibliography and index*

PREISLER, Bent
Linguistic sex roles in conversation : social variation in the expression of tentativeness in English / Bent Preisler. — Berlin ; New York : Mouton de Gruyter, c1986. — p. cm. — (Contributions to the sociology of language ; 45). — *Includes indexes. — Bibliography: p*

ENGLISH LANGUAGE — Social aspects — Great Britain
The Language of the black experience : cultural expression through word and sound in the Caribbean and black Britain / edited by David Sutcliffe and Ansel Wong. — Oxford : Blackwell, 1986. — x,214p. — *Bibliography: p.192-207. — Includes index*

ENGLISH LANGUAGE — Spoken English
PREISLER, Bent
Linguistic sex roles in conversation : social variation in the expression of tentativeness in English / Bent Preisler. — Berlin ; New York : Mouton de Gruyter, c1986. — p. cm. — (Contributions to the sociology of language ; 45). — *Includes indexes. — Bibliography: p*

VOSS, Bernd
Slips of the ear : investigations into the speech perception behaviour of German speakers of English / Bernd Voss. — Tübingen : G. Narr, c1984. — 184 p.. — (Tübinger Beiträge zur Linguistik ; 254). — *Bibliography: p. 126-134*

ENGLISH LANGUAGE — Spoken English — Australia — Social aspects
HORVATH, Barbara M.
Variation in Australian English : the sociolects of Sydney / Barbara M. Horvath. — Cambridge : Cambridge University Press, 1985. — xi,200p. — (Cambridge studies in linguistics ; 45). — *Bibliography: p190-196. — Includes index*

ENGLISH LANGUAGE — Study and teaching — German speakers
VOSS, Bernd
Slips of the ear : investigations into the speech perception behaviour of German speakers of English / Bernd Voss. — Tübingen : G. Narr, c1984. — 184 p.. — (Tübinger Beiträge zur Linguistik ; 254). — *Bibliography: p. 126-134*

ENGLISH LANGUAGE — Style
The Economist pocket style book. — London : Economist Publications, 1986 (1987 [printing]). — xi,96p. — *Bibliography: p92. — Includes index*

ENGLISH LANGUAGE — Synonyms and antonyms
Chambers 20th century thesaurus : a comprehensive word-finding dictionary / edited by M.A. Seaton ... [et al.]. — Edinburgh : Chambers, c1986. — [750]p

ENGLISH LANGUAGE — Tense
NEEDHAM, Paul
Temporal perspective : a logical analysis of temporal reference in English / Paul Needham. — Uppsala : [Philosophical Society : Dept. of Philosophy, University of Uppsala], 1975. — 112 p.. — (Philosophical studies ; no. 25). — Thesis--Uppsala. — *Includes index. — Bibliography: p. 108-109*

ENGLISH LANGUAGE — Word formation
SELKIRK, Elisabeth O.
The syntax of words / Elisabeth O. Selkirk. — Cambridge, Mass. : MIT Press, c1982. — x, 136 p. — (Linguistic inquiry monographs ; 7). — *Bibliography: p. [132]-136*

ENGLISH LANGUAGE — United States — Dictionaries
HORNBY, A. S.
[Oxford student's dictionary of American English]. The Oxford paperback American dictionary / A.S. Hornby with the assistance of Christina A. Ruse. — Oxford : Oxford University Press, 1983 (1986 [printing]). — xxi,714p. — (Oxford paperback reference). — *Text on inside covers*

ENGLISH LANGUAGE — United States — Slang — Dictionaries
New dictionary of American slang / edited by Robert L. Chapman. — London : Macmillan, 1987, c1986. — xxxvi,485p. — Based on Dictionary of American slang. Compiled and edited by Harold Wentworth and Stuart Berg Flexner. — 2nd supplemented ed. New York : Crowell, 1975. — Originally published: New York : Harper & Row, 1986

ENGLISH LITERATURE — Dictionaries
The Oxford companion to English literature. — 5th ed. / edited by Margaret Drabble. — Oxford : Oxford University Press, 1985. — xii,1155p. — *Previous ed.: 1967*

ENGLISH LITERATURE — 19th century — History and criticism
SWINDELLS, Julia
Victorian writing and working women : the other side of silence / Julia Swindells. — Cambridge : Polity, 1985. — [240]p. — *Includes index*

ENGLISH LITERATURE — 20th century
FYVEL, T. R.
And there my trouble began : uncollected writings, 1945-1985 / T. R. Fyvel. — London : Weidenfeld and Nicolson, 1986. — xii,240p

ENGLISH NEWSPAPERS — History — 17th century
SUTHERLAND, James
The Restoration newspaper and its development / James Sutherland. — Cambridge : Cambridge University Press, 1986. — ix,262p. — *Bibliography: p233-234. — Includes index*

ENGLISH NEWSPAPERS — History — 18th century
SUTHERLAND, James
The Restoration newspaper and its development / James Sutherland. — Cambridge : Cambridge University Press, 1986. — ix,262p. — *Bibliography: p233-234. — Includes index*

ENGLISH NEWSPAPERS — England — Derbyshire — Bibliography
Derbyshire / county editors, Anne Mellors, Jean Radford. — London : British Library, c1987. — xx,74p. — (Bibliography of British newspapers). — *Bibliography: pxv. — Includes index*

ENGLISH NEWSPAPERS — England — Kent — Bibliography
Kent / county editors: Winifred F. Bergess, Barbara R.M. Riddell, John Whyman. — London : British Library, c1982. — xviii,139p. — (Bibliography of British newspapers). — *Includes index*

ENGLISH NEWSPAPERS — England — Nottinghamshire — Bibliography
Nottinghamshire / county editor, Michael Brook. — London : British Library, c1987. — xvii,62p. — (Bibliography of British newspapers). — *Bibliography: pxiii. — Includes index*

ENGLISH NEWSPAPERS — England — Wiltshire — Bibliography — Union lists
Wiltshire / county editor: R.K. Bluhm. — London : Library Association Special, Reference and Information Section, 1975. — 28p. — (Bibliography of British newspapers)

ENGLISH NEWSPAPERS — England, Northern — Bibliography
Durham and Northumberland / county editor F.W.D. Manders. — London : British Library, c1982. — xvi,65p. — (Bibliography of British newspapers). — *"The bibliography of British newspapers is edited by the Reference Special and Information Section of the Library Association". — Includes index*

ENGLISH NEWSPAPERS — Japan
FÄLT, Olavi K
Fascism, militarism, or Japanism? : the interpretation of the crisis years of 1930-1941 in the Japanese English-language press / Olavi K. Fält ; [translated by Malcolm Hicks]. — Rovaniemi : Pohjois-Suomen Historiallinen Yhdistys : Societas Historica Finlandiae Septentrionalis, 1985. — 150 p.. — (Studia historica septentrionalia ; 8). — *Includes index. — Bibliography: p. 146-148*

ENGLISH PERIODICALS — History — 17th century
NELSON, C. (Carolyn)
Periodical publications, 1641-1700 : a survey with illustrations / by C. Nelson & M. Seccombe. — London : Bibliographical Society, 1986. — [xii,113]p. — (Occasional papers of the Bibliographical Society ; no.2)

ENGLISH PROSE LITERATURE — Puritan authors — History and criticism
HOLSTUN, James
A rational millennium : Puritan utopias of seventeenth-century England and America / James Holstun. — New York : Oxford University Press, 1987. — p. cm. — *Includes index. — Bibliography: p*

ENGLISH PROSE LITERATURE — 17th century — History and criticism
HOLSTUN, James
A rational millennium : Puritan utopias of seventeenth-century England and America / James Holstun. — New York : Oxford University Press, 1987. — p. cm. — *Includes index. — Bibliography: p*

ENGLISH WIT AND HUMOR
The Oxford book of political anecdotes / edited by Paul Johnson. — Oxford : Oxford University Press, 1986. — [352]p. — *Includes index*

ENTEBBE AIRPORT RAID, 1976
STEVENSON, William
90 minutes at Entebbe / by William Stevenson ; with material by Uri Dan. — New York : Bantam Books, 1976. — 216p

ENTERPRISE ZONES — Great Britain
GREAT BRITAIN. Department of the Environment
Enterprise zone information 1984-1985. — London : H.M.S.O., 1986. — viii,111p

Local employment initiatives : local enterprise agencies in Great Britain : a study of their impact, operational lessons and policy implications / by Community Initiatives Research Trust (CIRT) Liverpool. — Luxembourg : Office for Official Publications of the European Communities, 1985. — iv, 61p. — (Programme of research and action on the development of the labour market). — *At head of title: Commission of the European Communities*

MORISON, Hugh
The regeneration of local economies / Hugh Morison. — Oxford : Clarendon, 1987. — viii,212p. — *Bibliography: p199-205. — Includes index*

ENTERPRISE ZONES — Greece
APOSTOLOPOULOS, Yannis N.
Maritime industrial area : a new investment concept for shipping and industry / Yannis N. Apostolopoulos. — Athens : Development Division, Hellenic Industrial Development Bank, 1984. — 135p. — *Bibliography: p133-135*

ENTRAPMENT (CRIMINAL LAW)
STOBER, Michael I.
Entrapment in Canadian criminal law / by Michael I. Stober. — Toronto : Carswell Legal Publications, 1985. — xxx, 228 p.. — (Carswell's criminal law series). — *Includes bibliographical references and indexes*

ENTRAPMENT (CRIMINAL LAW) — Canada
STOBER, Michael I.
Entrapment in Canadian criminal law / by Michael I. Stober. — Toronto : Carswell Legal Publications, 1985. — xxx, 228 p.. — (Carswell's criminal law series). — *Includes bibliographical references and indexes*

ENTREPRENEUR
Entrepreneurship & technology : world experiences and policies / editors, Wayne S. Brown & Roy Rothwell. — Harlow : Longman, 1986. — 222p. — *Includes bibliographies*

Entrepreneurship and social change / edited by Sidney M. Greenfield, Arnold Strickon. — London : University Press of America/Eurospan, 1986. — [278]p. — (Monographs in economic anthropology ; no.2). — *Conference proceedings*

NAFZIGER, E. Wayne
Entrepreneurship, equity, and economic development / by E. Wayne Nafziger. — Greenwich, Conn. : JAI Press, c1986. — p. cm. — (Contemporary studies in economic and financial analysis ; v. 53). — *Includes index. — Bibliography: p*

SMILES, Samuel
Self-help : with illustrations of conduct and perseverence / by Samuel Smiles ; abridged by George Bull ; with an introduction by Sir Keith Joseph. — Harmondsworth : Penguin, 1986. — 251p. — (Penguin business library. Management classics). — *Full ed. originally published: London : s.n., 1859. — Includes index*

SMILOR, Raymond W
The new business incubator : linking talent, technology, capital, and know-how / Raymond W. Smilor, Michael Doud Gill, Jr. — Lexington, Mass. : Lexington Books, c1986. — xiii, 199 p.. — *Includes index. — Bibliography: p. [183]-187*

ENTREPRENEUR — Addresses, essays, lectures
Entrepreneurship, intrapreneurship, and venture capital : the foundation of economic renaissance / edited by Robert D. Hisrich. — Lexington, Mass. : Lexington Books, c1986. — xiv, 144 p.. — *Includes bibliographies. — Contents: Importance of entrepreneurship in economic development / Howard H. Stevenson and William A. Sahlman -- Role of entrepreneurship in economic development / Donald L. Sexton -- Building indigenous companies / Raymond W. Smilor -- Entrepreneurship and intrapreneurship / Robert D. Hisrich -- The role of venture capital in the economic renaissance of an area / Barry M. Davis -- Entrepreneurs, angels, and economic renaissance / William E. Wetzel, Jr*

ENTREPRENEUR — Biography
HUGHES, Jonathan R. T
The vital few : the entrepreneur and American economic progress / Jonathan Hughes. — Expanded ed. — New York : Oxford University Press, 1986. — p. cm. — *Includes index. — Bibliography: p*

ENTREPRENEUR — Social aspects
Entrepreneurship and social change / edited by Sidney M. Greenfield, Arnold Strickon. — London : University Press of America/Eurospan, 1986. — [278]p. — (Monographs in economic anthropology ; no.2). — *Conference proceedings*

ENTREPRENEURSHIP — Europe
Entrepreneurship in Europe : the social processes / edited by Robert Goffee and Richard Scase. — London : Croom Helm, c1987. — 197p. — (Social analysis). — *Includes bibliographies and index*

ENVIRONMENT
Handbook of environmental psychology / edited by Daniel Stokols, Irwin Altman. — New York : Wiley, c1987. — 2 vols. — "A Wiley-Interscience publication.". — *Includes bibliographies and indexes*

ENVIRONMENTAL ARCHAEOLOGY
Landscape and culture : geographical and archaeological perspectives / edited by J.M. Wagstaff. — Oxford : Basil Blackwell, 1987. — [v,256]p. — *Includes bibliography and index*

ENVIRONMENTAL EDUCATION
GRAY, David B
Ecological beliefs and behaviors : assessment and change / David B. Gray, in collaboration with Richard J. Borden and Russell H. Weigel ; foreword by Riley E. Dunlap. — Westport, Conn. : Greenwood Press, c1985. — p. cm. — (Contributions in psychology ; no. 4). — *Includes index. — Bibliography: p*

ENVIRONMENTAL HEALTH
BASSETT, W. H.
Environmental health procedures / W.H. Bassett. — 2nd ed. — London : H.K. Lewis, 1987. — xxi, 405p

ENVIRONMENTAL HEALTH — Moral and ethical aspects
The Environment of the workplace and human values / editor, Sheldon W. Samuels. — New York : Liss, c1986. — vii, 118 p.. — *Published also as the American journal of industrial medicine, v. 9, no. 1, 1986. — Conference cosponsored by the Labor Policy Institute and the Marshall-Wythe School of Law at the College of William and Mary, May 20-22, 1982. — Includes bibliographical references and index*

ENVIRONMENTAL HEALTH — Statistics — Bibliography
Directory of environment statistics. — New York : United Nations, 1983. — v,305p. — (Statistical papers / United Nations, Statistical Office. Series M ; no.75) ([Document] (United Nations) ; ST/ESA/STAT/SER.M/75). — *Sales no.: E.83.XVII.12*

ENVIRONMENTAL IMPACT ANALYSIS
Differential social impacts of rural resource development / editor Pamela D. Elkind-Savatsky ; associate editor Judith D. Kaufman. — Boulder, Colo. ; London : Westview Press, 1986. — xvii,293p. — (Social Impact Assessment Series ; no.13)

ENVIRONMENTAL IMPACT ANALYSIS — Australia
Compendium of case studies on using cost-benefit analysis in the environment impact assessment process. — Canberra : Australian Government Publishing Service, 1985. — v,29p. — *Includes bibliographical references*

ENVIRONMENTAL IMPACT ANALYSIS — Canada
New directions in environmental impact assessment in Canada / edited by Virginia W. Maclaren [and] Joseph B. Whitney. — Toronto : Methuen, 1985. — xiv,245p. — *Includes references*

ENVIRONMENTAL IMPACT ANALYSIS — Great Britain
GREAT BRITAIN. Department of the Environment
UK national report : environmental assessment procedures and methods for development projects. — [London : the Department, 1976]. — 15 leaves. — *Prepared for the tenth meeting of the Group on the Urban Environment, Paris, 10th, 11th, and 12th May, 1976*

ENVIRONMENTAL IMPACT ANALYSIS — United States
PROJECT APPRAISAL FOR DEVELOPMENT CONTROL RESEARCH TEAM
Environmental impact assessment in the USA : a critical review; report prepared for the Scottish Development Department, the Department of the Environment and the Welsh Office / B. D. Clark...[et al.]. — London : Department of the Environment, c1978. — xii,74p. — (Research report / Departments of the Environment and Transport ; 26). — *Bibliography: p61-[74]*

ENVIRONMENTAL IMPACT STATEMENTS — United States
CULHANE, Paul J.
Forecasts and environmental decisionmaking : the contents and predictive accuracy of environmental impact statements / Paul J. Culhane, H. Paul Friesema and Janice A. Beecher. — Boulder, Col. : Westview, 1987. — x,306p. — *Bibliography: p287-300*

ENVIRONMENTAL LAW
BASSETT, W. H.
Environmental health procedures / W.H. Bassett. — 2nd ed. — London : H.K. Lewis, 1987. — xxi, 405p

ENVIRONMENTAL LAW — Great Lakes Region

MULDOON, Paul R.
Cross-border litigation : environmental rights in the Great Lakes ecosystem / by Paul R. Muldoon, with David A. Scriven and James B. Olson. — Toronto : Carswell, 1986. — xxxv,410p

ENVIRONMENTAL LAW — New Zealand

A guide to environmental law in New Zealand / editor, N. E. Wells for Legal Information Service (Inc). — 2nd ed. — Wellington : Brooker and Friend Ltd for Commission for the Environment, 1984. — xiii,172p

ENVIRONMENTAL LAW — Nigeria

OLA, C. S
Town and country planning and environmental laws in Nigeria / C.S. Ola. — 2nd ed. — Jericho, Ibadan, Nigeria : University Press, 1984. — xx, 275 p.. — *Rev. ed. of: Town and country planning law in Nigeria. 1977. — Based on a small part of author's thesis--University College, London. — Includes index. — Bibliography: p. 265-269*

ENVIRONMENTAL LAW — United States — Cases

FINDLEY, Roger W
Environmental law : cases and materials / by Roger W. Findley, Daniel A. Farber. — 2nd ed. — St. Paul, Minn. : West Pub. Co., 1985. — p. cm. — (American casebook series). — *Includes index*

ENVIRONMENTAL LAW, INTERNATIONAL

Selected multilateral treaties in the field of the environment / editor, Alexandre Charles Kiss. — Nairobi : United Nations Environment Programme, 1983, c1982. — ix,525p. — (UNEP reference series ; 4). — *On cover: UNEP reference series 3. — Issued also in French*

VAN LIER, Irene H.
Acid rain and international law / by Irene H. van Lier. — Toronto : Bunsel Environmental Consultants, [1981?]. — xxii,278p. — *Originally presented as the author's thesis (LL.M.) - Dalhousie University 1980. — Bibliography: p.257-266*

ENVIRONMENTAL POLICY

The avoidance and adjustment of environmental disputes : summary of discussions of a conference, July 1974, Villa Serbélloni, Bellagio (Italy). — Washington, D.C. : American Society of International Law, 1975. — 23p

HARTWICK, John M
The economics of natural resource use / John Hartwick, Nancy Olewiler. — New York, NY : Harper & Row, c1986. — p. cm. — *Includes bibliographies*

LEE, James A.
The environment, public health, and human ecology : considerations for economic development / James A. Lee. — Baltimore : Johns Hopkins University Press for the World Bank, 1985. — x,288p. — *Bibliography: p233-288*

Natural resources economics and policy applications : essays in honor of James A. Crutchfield / edited by Edward Miles, Robert Pealy, and Robert Stokes ; foreword by Brewster C. Denny. — Seattle : Institute for Marine Studies of the University of Washington : Distributed by the University of Washington Press, c1986. — p. cm. — (Public policy issues in resource management). — *Includes index. — Bibliography: p*

Red and green : a new politics of the environment / edited by Joe Weston. — London : Pluto, 1986. — [192]p. — *Includes bibliography and index*

RÖMPCZYK, Elmar
International environmental policy as a challenge to the politics of development / Elmar Römpczyk. — Bonn : Research Institute of the Friedrich-Ebert-Stiftung, Department of Development Research, 1987. — 39p. — (International politics)

Social responses to technological change / edited by Augustine Brannigan and Sheldon Goldenberg. — Westport, Conn. : Greenwood Press, c1985. — p. cm. — (Contributions in sociology ; no. 56). — *Includes index. — Bibliography: p*

ENVIRONMENTAL POLICY — Economic aspects — Australia

Fiscal measures and the environment impacts and potential. — Canberra : Australian Government Publishing Service, 1985. — x,25p. — (Environment papers / Department of Arts, Heritage and Environment). — *Bibliographical references: p23*

ENVIRONMENTAL POLICY — Information services — Developing countries

VIEIRA, Anna da Soledade
Environmental information in developing nations : politics and policies / Anna da Soledade Vieira. — Westport, Conn. : Greenwood Press, c1985. — p. cm. — (Contributions in librarianship and information science ; no. 51). — *Includes index. — Bibliography: p*

ENVIRONMENTAL POLICY — Statistics — Standards

A framework for the development of environment statistics. — New York : United Nations, 1984. — vi,28p. — (Statistical papers / United Nations, Statistical Office. Series M ; no.78) ([Document] ; ST/ESA/STAT/SER.M/78). — *Bibliography: p27-28. — Sales no.: E.84.XVII.12*

ENVIRONMENTAL POLICY — Antarctic regions — Congresses

WORKSHOP ON THE ANTARCTIC TREATY SYSTEM (1985 : Beardmore South Field Camp)
Antarctic treaty system : an assessment : proceedings of a workshop...sponsored by the Polar Research Board [of the] Commission on Physical Sciences, Mathematics and Resources [of the] National Research Council. — Washington : National Academy Press, 1985. — xv,435p. — *Bibliographies*

ENVIRONMENTAL POLICY — Denmark

DENMARK. Miljøministeriet
The Ministry of the Environment, Denmark. — [Copenhagen : Ministry of the Environment, 1984]. — 40p

ENVIRONMENTAL POLICY — Developing countries

Multinational corporations, environment, and the Third World : business matters / edited by Charles S. Pearson. — Durham, NC : Duke University Press, 1987. — xvi, 295 p.. — (Duke Press policy studies). — *"A World Resources Institute book.". — Based on an international meeting held in 1984 and sponsored by the World Resources Institute. — Includes index. — Bibliography: p. 261-284*

TEXLER, Jiri
Environmental hazards in Third World development / Jiri Texler. — Budapest : Institute for World Economy of the Hungarian Academy of Sciences, 1986. — 48p. — (Studies on developing countries ; no.120)

ENVIRONMENTAL POLICY — Europe

European environmental yearbook 1987 : nature conservation, protection of the environment, town and country planning in Belgium, Demark, the Federal Republic of Germany, France, Greece, Ireland, Italy, Luxembourg, The Netherlands, Portugal, Spain and the United Kingdom, with a special survey of USA policy / Docter ; Yearbook director Achille Cutrera. — London : Docter International U.K., 1987. — xx,815p. — *Prepared with the co-operation of and financial assistance from the Commission of the European Communities*

HAWKE, Neil
Environmental impact assessment : North American and European developments / Neil Hawke. — Leicester : Leicester Polytechnic. School of Law, 1987. — 17p

ENVIRONMENTAL POLICY — European Economic Community countries

Britain, Europe and the environment : contributions to a conference held at Imperial College of Science and Technology / edited by Richard Macrory. — London : Imperial College Centre for Environmental Technology, 1983. — 130p

COMMISSION OF THE EUROPEAN COMMUNITIES. Consumer Protection and Nuclear Safety
The state of the environment in the European Community, 1986 / Commission of the European Communities, Directorate-General Environment, Consumer Protection and Nuclear Safety. — Luxembourg : Commission of the European Communities, 1987. — xvi,370p

Producer—consumer dialogue : opinion. — Brussels : Economic and Social Committee. Press, Information and Publications Division, 1984. — 55p. — *At head of title page: Economic and Social Committee of the European Communities*

ENVIRONMENTAL POLICY — Germany (West)

Eingriffe im Diesseits : Beiträge zu einer radikalen grünen Realpolitik / herausgegeben von Gabriel Falkenberg und Heiner Kersting. — Essen : Klartext, 1985. — 203p

ENVIRONMENTAL POLICY — Great Britain

CONFEDERATION OF BRITISH INDUSTRY
Clean up : its good business. — London : Confederation of British Industry, 1986. — 43p

GREAT BRITAIN. Environmental Board
Report of the Environmental Board's meeting at the Civil Service College, Sunningdale, 27 and 28 January 1978. — [London : Department of the Environment], 1978. — 5leaves

LIBERAL PARTY ENVIRONMENTAL CO-ORDINATING GROUP
Survival : the liberal way to an environment for the future. — Hebden Bridge : Hebden Royd Publications, 1986. — 35p

ENVIRONMENTAL POLICY — Great Britain — Finance

GREAT BRITAIN. Urban Affairs Division I
Grant aid for voluntary bodies in the environmental field. — [London] : the Division, 1975. — 16p

ENVIRONMENTAL POLICY — Great Britain — History

Green Britain or industrial wasteland? / edited by Edward Goldsmith and Nicholas Hildyard. — Cambridge : Polity, 1986. — xv,374p. — *Includes index*

ENVIRONMENTAL POLICY — Japan — Tokyo

TOKYO. Somukyoku. Shōgai Kankōbu. Gaijika
Tokyo fights pollution / [English text by Mitsuo Shono ; edited by the Liaison and Protocol Section, Bureau of General Affairs, Tokyo Metropolitan Government]. — Rev. ed. — [Tokyo : Tokyo Metropolitan Government], 1977. — ix, 222 p.. — (TMG municipal library ; no. 13). — *Revised translation of Tōkyō-to Kōgai Kenkyūjo Kōgai to Tōkyō-to*

ENVIRONMENTAL POLICY — North America

HAWKE, Neil
Environmental impact assessment : North American and European developments / Neil Hawke. — Leicester : Leicester Polytechnic. School of Law, 1987. — 17p

ENVIRONMENTAL POLICY — Organisation for Economic Co-operation and Development countries

Improving the enforcement of environmental policies. — Paris : Organisation for Economic Co-operation and Development, 1987. — 60p. — (OECD environment monographs ; no.8). — *Bibliographical references: p60*

OECD and the environment. — Paris : Organisation for Economic Co-operation and Development, 1986. — 220p. — *Bibliography: p193-220*

ENVIRONMENTAL POLICY — Organisation for Economic Co-operation and Development countries — Statistics

OECD environmental data : compendium 1987 = Données OCDE sur l'environnement : compendium 1987. — Paris : Organisation for Economic Co-operation and Development, 1987. — 365p. — *In English and French.* — *Bibliographical references: p320*

ENVIRONMENTAL POLICY — Pakistan — Statistics

Environment statistics of Pakistan / Federal Bureau of Statistics, Pakistan. — Karachi : Federal Bureau of Statistics, 1984-

ENVIRONMENTAL POLICY — Soviet Union

Ekonomicheskie i demograficheskie voprosy sovershenstvovaniia prirodopol'zovaniia / pod redaktsiei R. V. Tatevosova. — Moskva : Izd-vo Moskovskogo universiteta, 1977. — 99p

ZIEGLER, Charles E.
Environmental policy in the USSR / Charles E. Ziegler. — London : Pinter, 1987. — 195p. — *Includes index*

ENVIRONMENTAL POLICY — Sudan

INTERNATIONAL LABOUR ORGANIZATION. Identification and Programming Mission to the Republic of the Sudan (1985)
After the famine : a programme of action to strengthen the survival strategies of affected populations / report of the ILO Identification and Programming Mission to the Republic of the Sudan, September 1985. — Geneva : ILO, c1986. — xi,309p

ENVIRONMENTAL POLICY — United States

CLARKE, Jeanne Nienaber
Staking out the terrain : power differentials among natural resource management agencies / Jeanne Nienaber Clarke, Daniel McCool. — Albany : State University of New York Press, c1985. — p. cm. — (SUNY series in environmental public policy). — *Includes index.* — *Bibliography: p*

LUTEN, Daniel B
Progress against growth : Daniel B. Luten on the American landscape / edited by Thomas R. Vale ; introduction by Garrett Hardin ; drawings by Faye Field ; figures by Adrienne Morgan. — New York : Gilford Press, c1986. — p. cm. — *Includes index.* — *Bibliography: p*

Resources / Resources for the Future. — Washington, D.C. : Resruces for the Future, 1986-. — *Quarterly*

ENVIRONMENTAL POLICY — United States — Addresses, essays, lectures

Controversies in environmental policy / edited by Sheldon Kamieniecki, Robert O'Brien, and Michael Clarke. — Albany : State University of New York Press, c1986. — vi, 322 p. — (SUNY series in environmental public policy). — *Includes bibliographies and index*

ENVIRONMENTAL POLICY — United States — History

RUSHEFSKY, Mark R.
Making cancer policy / Mark R. Rushefsky. — Albany : State University of New York Press, c1986. — xiii, 257 p.. — (SUNY series in public administration in the 1980s). — *Includes index.* — *Bibliography: p. 225-245*

ENVIRONMENTAL POLICY — United States — History — 20th century

HAYS, Samuel P.
Beauty, health and permanence : environmental politics in the United States, 1955-1985 / Samuel P. Hays in collaboration with Barbara D. Hays. — Cambridge : Cambridge University Press, 1987. — [648]p. — (Studies in environment and history). — *Includes index*

ENVIRONMENTAL POLICY — Wales — Statistics

Environmental digest for Wales = Crynhoad o ystadegau'r amgylchedd / Welsh Office. — Cardiff : Economic and Statistical Services Division, Welsh Office, 1984-. — *Annual*

ENVIRONMENTAL POLICY — Yugoslavia

Environmental policies in Yugoslavia : a review / by the OECD and its Environment Committee. — Paris : Organisation for Economic Co-operation and Development, 1986. — 160p

ENVIRONMENTAL PROTECTION

LEE, James A.
The environment, public health, and human ecology : considerations for economic development / James A. Lee. — Baltimore : Johns Hopkins University Press for the World Bank, 1985. — x,288p. — *Bibliography: p233-288*

MORONE, Joseph G
Averting catastrophe : strategies for regulating risky technologies / Joseph G. Morone and Edward J. Woodhouse. — Berkeley : University of California Press, 1985, c1986. — p. cm. — *Includes index.* — *Bibliography: p*

SMIL, Vaclav
Energy, food, environment : realities, myths, options / Vaclav Smil. — Oxford : Clarendon, 1987. — [390]p. — *Includes bibliography and index*

TIMBERLAKE, Lloyd
Only one earth : living for the future / Lloyd Timberlake. — London : BBC : Earthscan, 1987. — 168p. — *Bibliography: p160-161*

ENVIRONMENTAL PROTECTION — Bibliography

An Environmental bibliography : publications issued by UNEP or under its auspices, 1973-1980. — Nairobi : United Nations Environment Programme, 1981. — vi,67p. — (UNEP reference series ; 2). — *Includes indexes*

ENVIRONMENTAL PROTECTION — Information services — Developing countries

VIEIRA, Anna da Soledade
Environmental information in developing nations : politics and policies / Anna da Soledade Vieira. — Westport, Conn. : Greenwood Press, c1985. — p. cm. — (Contributions in librarianship and information science ; no. 51). — *Includes index.* — *Bibliography: p*

ENVIRONMENTAL PROTECTION — Moral and ethical aspects

TAYLOR, Paul W
Respect for nature : a theory of environmental ethics / Paul W. Taylor. — Princeton, N.J. : Princeton University Press, c1986. — p. cm. — (Studies in moral, political, and legal philosophy). — *Includes index.* — *Bibliography: p*

ENVIRONMENTAL PROTECTION — Africa

HARRISON, Paul, 1945-
The greening of Africa : breaking through in the battle for land and food / Paul Harrison. — London : Paladin [for] International Institute for Environment and Development-Earthscan, 1987. — 380p. — *[Commissioned by the International Institute for Environment and Development - Earthscan].* — *At foot of title: "International Institute for Environment and Development - Earthscan".* — *Bibliography: p359-371.* — *Includes index*

ENVIRONMENTAL PROTECTION — Africa, Sub-Saharan — Bibliography

SEELEY, J. A.
Conservation in sub-Saharan Africa : an introductory bibliography for the social sciences / compiled by J.A. Seeley. — Cambridge : African Studies Centre, University of Cambridge, 1985. — xii,207p. — (Cambridge African monographs ; 5). — *Includes index*

ENVIRONMENTAL PROTECTION — Europe

European environmental yearbook 1987 : nature conservation, protection of the environment, town and country planning in Belgium, Demark, the Federal Republic of Germany, France, Greece, Ireland, Italy, Luxembourg, The Netherlands, Portugal, Spain and the United Kingdom, with a special survey of USA policy / Docter ; Yearbook director Achille Cutrera. — London : Docter International U.K., 1987. — xx,815p. — *Prepared with the co-operation of and financial assistance from the Commission of the European Communities*

ENVIRONMENTAL PROTECTION — France — Statistics

FRANCE. Institut national de la statistique et des études économiques
Les comptes satellites de l'environment : méthodes et résultats. — [Paris] : I.N.S.E.E., 1986. — 146p. — (Les collections de l'INSEE. Série C. Comptes et planification ; no.130). — *At head of title: Les comptes satellites du SECN*

ENVIRONMENTAL PROTECTION — Great Britain

Environmental economy / editors, Richard Brooker and Matthew Corder. — London : Spon, 1986. — [200]p. — *Includes bibliography and index*

ENVIRONMENTAL PROTECTION — Switzerland

Office fédéral de la protection de l'environnement 1971-1981 : textes rédigés à l'occasion de son dixième anniversaire. — Berne : the Office, 1981. — 160p

ENVIRONMENTAL PROTECTION — Ukraine

UK-USSR Environmental Protection Agreement: area III (land reclamation) : report of a visit to the USSR (by a UK delegation) in 1976. — London : Planning, Regional and Minerals Directorate, Department of the Environment, [1977]. — 24p

ENVIRONMENTAL PSYCHOLOGY

Environmental stress / edited by Gary W. Evans. — Cambridge [Cambridgeshire] ; New York : Cambridge University Press, 1982. — xiv, 386 p.. — *Includes bibliographies and indexes*

ENVIRONMENTAL PSYCHOLOGY
continuation

FISHER, Jeffrey D.
Environmental psychology. — 2nd ed. / Jeffrey D. Fisher, Paul A. Bell, Andrew Baum. — New York ; London : Holt, Rinehart and Winston, c1984. — xvii,472p. — *Previous ed.: / by Paul A. Bell, Jeffrey D. Fisher, Ross J. Loomis. Philadelphia ; London : Saunders, 1978. — Bibliography: p407-447. — Includes index*

GOLD, John R.
An introduction to behavioural geography / John R. Gold. — Oxford : Oxford University Press, 1980. — [9],290p. — *Bibliography: p.253-286. — Includes index*

GRAY, David B
Ecological beliefs and behaviors : assessment and change / David B. Gray, in collaboration with Richard J. Borden and Russell H. Weigel ; foreword by Riley E. Dunlap. — Westport, Conn. : Greenwood Press, c1985. — p. cm. — (Contributions in psychology ; no. 4). — *Includes index. — Bibliography: p*

Handbook of environmental psychology / edited by Daniel Stokols, Irwin Altman. — New York : Wiley, c1987. — 2 vols. — "A Wiley-Interscience publication.". — *Includes bibliographies and indexes*

ROSE, Nikolas Simon
The psychological complex : psychology, politics and society in England, 1869-1939 / Nikolas Rose. — London : Routledge and Kegan Paul, 1985. — 293p. — *Bibliography: p255-285*

SEAMON, David
A geography of the lifeworld : movement, rest, and encounter / David Seamon. — New York : St. Martin's Press, 1979. — 227 p.. — *Includes index. — Bibliography: p. 211-222*

ENVIRONMENTAL PSYCHOLOGY — Congresses

Environmental psychology : directions and perspectives / edited by Nickolaus R. Feimer and E. Scott Geller. — New York, NY, U.S.A. : Praeger, 1983. — 356 p.. — *Includes papers originally presented at the Third Annual Symposium on Applied Behavioral Science, held in 1980 at the Virginia Polytechnic Institute and State University, and sponsored by the Psychology Dept. of that institution. — Includes bibliographies and indexes*

EPIDEMICS — History — 18th century

RILEY, James C., 1943-
The eighteenth-century campaign to avoid disease / James C. Riley. — Basingstoke : Macmillan, 1987. — xvii,213p. — *Bibliography: p177-200. — Includes index*

EPIDEMICS — Mathematical models

CLIFF, A. D.
Spatial aspects of influenza epidemics / A. D. Cliff, P. Haggett, J. K. Ord. — London : Pion, 1986. — [xii],280p. — *Bibliography: p[269]-275*

EPIDEMICS — Japan — History

JANNETTA, Ann Bowman
Epidemics and mortality in early modern Japan / Ann Bowman Jannetta. — Princeton, N.J. : Princeton University Press, c1986. — p. cm. — *Includes index. — Bibliography: p*

EPIDEMIOLOGY

ALDERSON, Michael
An introduction to epidemiology / Michael Alderson. — 2nd. ed. — London : Macmillan, 1983. — xiv,335p. — *Previous ed.: 1976*

CLIFF, A. D.
Spatial aspects of influenza epidemics / A. D. Cliff, P. Haggett, J. K. Ord. — London : Pion, 1986. — [xii],280p. — *Bibliography: p[269]-275*

EPIDEMIOLOGY — Government policy

Epidemiology and health policy / edited by Sol Levine and Abraham M. Lilienfeld. — New York ; London : Tavistock, 1987. — xvi,301p. — (Contemporary issues in health, medicine, and social policy). — *Includes bibliographies and index*

EPIDEMIOLOGY — England — West Cumbria

Investigation of the possible increased incidence of cancer in West Cumbria : report of the independent advisory group / chairman Sir Douglas Black. — London : H.M.S.O., 1984. — 103p

EPILEPSY — Great Britain

GREAT BRITAIN. Working Group on Services for People with Epilepsy
Report of the working group on services for people with epilepsy : a report to the Department of Health and Social Security, the Department of Education and Science and the Welsh Office. — London : H.M.S.O., 1986. — 77p. — *Chairman: P. M. C. Winterton*

EPILEPTICS — Services for — Great Britain

MORGAN, John
Special services for people with epilepsy in the 1970s / John Morgan, Zarrina Kurtz ; [for the] Department of Health and Social Security. — London : H.M.S.O., 1987. — xi,186p. — *Bibliographical references: p180-186*

EPISTEMICS

MOSER, Paul K.
Empirical justification / Paul K. Moser. — Dordrecht ; Boston : D. Reidel Pub. Co. ; Hingham MA, U.S.A. : Sold and distributed in the U.S.A. and Canada by Kluwer Boston, c1985. — x, 263p. — (Philosophical studies series in philosophy ; v. 34). — *Includes indexes*

EQUAL PAY FOR EQUAL WORK

ALDRICH, Mark
The economics of comparable worth / Mark Aldrich, Robert Buchele. — Cambridge, Mass. : Ballinger Pub. Co., 1986. — p. cm. — *Includes bibliographies and index*

Equal pay for women : progress and problems in seven countries / edited by Barrie O. Pettman with the assistance of John Fyfe. — Bradford (200 Keighley Rd, Bradford, W. Yorkshire BD9 4JZ) : MCB Books [for] the International Institute of Social Economics, 1975. — ix,173p

SHAMIE, Stephen
Narrowing the gender wage gap : is equal value legislation the answer? / Stephen Shamie. — Kingston, Ont. : Queen's University at Kingston. Industrial Relations Centre, 1986. — 41p. — (Research and current issues series / Queen's University at Kingston. Industrial Relations Centre ; no.46). — *Bibliography: p39-41*

EQUAL PAY FOR EQUAL WORK — Law and legislation

SHAMIE, Stephen
Narrowing the gender wage gap : is equal value legislation the answer? / Stephen Shamie. — Kingston, Ont. : Queen's University at Kingston. Industrial Relations Centre, 1986. — 41p. — (Research and current issues series / Queen's University at Kingston. Industrial Relations Centre ; no.46). — *Bibliography: p39-41*

EQUAL PAY FOR EQUAL WORK — Canada

GANNAGÉ, Charlene
Double day, double bind : women garment workers / by Charlene Gannagé. — Toronto, Ont. : Women's Press, 1986. — 235 p., [1] leaf of plates. — (Women's press issues). — *Bibliography: p. 227-235*

EQUAL PAY FOR EQUAL WORK — Great Britain

GHOBADIAN, Abby
Job evaluation and equal pay / Abby Ghobadian, Michael White, Policy Studies Institute. — [London] : Department of Employment, [1986]. — 177p. — (Research paper / Department of Employment ; no.58)

GILL, Deirdre
Equal pay : the challenge of equal value / Deirdre Gill, Bernard Ungerson. — London : Institute of Personnel Management, 1984. — 58p. — *Bibliography: p58*

GRAHAM, Cosmo
The role of ACAS conciliation in equal pay and sex discrimination cases / Cosmo Graham, Norman Lewis ; [for the] Equal Opportunities in Commission. — Manchester : Equal Opportunities Commission, 1985. — 70p. — *Bibliographical references: p69-70*

TZANNATOS, Z.
A general equilibrium model of discrimination and its effect on incomes / Z. Tzannatos. — London : Centre for Labour Economics, London School of Economics, 1986. — 28p. — (Discussion paper / London School of Economics and Political Science. Centre for Labour Economics ; no.244). — *Bibliography: p26-28*

EQUAL PAY FOR EQUAL WORK — Pennsylvania

PERRIN, Suzanne M.
Comparable worth and public policy : the case of Pennsylvania / by Suzanne M. Perrin. — Philadelphia, Pa : Industrial Research Unit, University of Pennsylvania, 1985. — viii,123p. — (Labor Relations and Public Policy Series ; No.29)

EQUAL PAY FOR EQUAL WORK — United States

CAMERAN, Lougy M.
The comparable worth controversy / Henry J. Aaron and Cameran Lougy. — Washington, D.C. : Brookings Institution, c1986. — p. cm. — *Includes index*

Women's work, men's work : sex segregation on the job / Barbara F. Reskin and Heidi I. Hartmann, editors ; Committee on Women's Employment and Related Social Issues, Commission on Behavioral and Social Sciences and Education, National Research Council. — Washington, D.C. : National Academy Press, 1986. — xii, 173 p.. — *Includes index. — Bibliography: p. 141-161*

EQUAL RIGHTS AMENDMENTS — United States

MANSBRIDGE, Jane J
Why we lost the ERA / Jane J. Mansbridge. — Chicago : University of Chicago Press, 1986. — p. cm. — *Includes index. — Bibliography: p*

EQUAL RIGHTS AMENDMENTS — United States — Bibliography

BEINBERG, Renee
The Equal Rights Amendment : an annotated bibliography of the issues, 1976-1985 / compiled by Renee Feinberg. — New York : Greenwood Press, 1986. — xiii, 151 p.. — (Bibliographies and indexes in women's studies ; no. 3). — *Includes indexes*

EQUALITY

COATES, B. E.
Geography and inequality / B.E. Coates, R.J. Johnston and P.L. Knox. — Oxford : Oxford University Press, 1977. — [8],292p. — *Bibliography: p.258-279. — Includes index*

The Egalitarian city : issues of rights, distribution, access, and power / edited by Janet K. Boles. — New York : Praeger, 1986. — xiv, 223 p.. — *Includes bibliographies*

Equality and the religious traditions of Asia / edited by R. Siriwardena. — London : Pinter, 1987. — 173p. — *Conference papers. — Includes index*

EQUALITY *continuation*

HAMILTON, Malcolm
Class and inequality : in pre-industrial, capitalist and communist societies / Malcolm Hamilton, Maria Hirszowicz. — Brighton : Wheatsheaf, 1987. — xv,300p. — *Bibliography: p279-292. — Includes index*

LANE, David
The end of inequality? : stratification under state socialism / David Lane. — Harmondsworth : Penguin, 1971. — 156p. — (Penguin modern sociology monographs) (Penguin education). — *Bibliographyp.141-147. — Includes index*

LIAZOS, Alexander
Sociology : a liberating perspective / Alezander Liazos. — London : Allyn and Bacon, 1985. — xviii,461p. — *Bibliography: p[415]-444*

NORMAN, Richard
Free and equal : a philosophical examination of political values / Richard Norman. — Oxford : Clarendon, 1987. — [192]p. — *Includes index*

SMITH, David M. (David Marshall)
Where the grass is greener : living in an unequal world / David M. Smith. — Harmondsworth : Penguin, 1979. — 3-386p,[8]p of plates. — (Pelican books. geography and environmental studies). — *Bibliography: p.369-380. — Includes index*

EQUALITY — Addresses, essays, lectures

The Child's construction of social inequality / edited by Robert L. Leahy. — New York ; London : Academic Press, 1983. — xv, 349p. — (Developmental psychology series). — *Includes bibliographies and indexes*

EQUALITY — Cross-cultural studies — Congresses

Inequality and contemporary revolutions / Manus I. Midlarsky, editor. — Denver, Colo. : Graduate School of International Studies, University of Denver, c1986. — p. cm. — (Monograph series in world affairs ; v. 22, bk. 2). — *Includes bibliographies*

EQUALITY — Public opinion

KLUEGEL, James R
Beliefs about inequality : Americans' views of what is and what ought to be / James R. Kluegel and Eliot R. Smith. — New York : A. de Gruyter, 1986. — p. cm. — *Includes index. — Bibliography: p*

EQUALITY — Developing countries

Capitalism and equality in the Third World / edited by Peter L. Berger. — Lanham, MD : Hamilton Press ; [Washington, D.C.] : Institute for Educational Affairs, <1987- >. — p. cm. — *Bibliography: p. — Contents: -- v. 2. Modern capitalism*

EQUALITY — India

KAMBLE, J. R.
Pursuit of equality in Indian history / J. R. Kamble. — New Delhi : National Publishing House, 1985. — xi,414p. — *Bibliography: p386-394*

SHARMA, A. K.
Social inequality and demographic processes / A.K. Sharma. — Delhi, India : Mittal Publications : Distributed by Mittal Publishers' Distributors, 1985. — x, 170 p.. — *Includes bibliographies and index*

EQUALITY — Scandinavia

Norden : the passion for equality / edited by Stephen R. Graubard. — Oslo : Norwegian University Press ; Oxford : Distributed by Oxford University Press, c1986. — 323p. — (Scandinavian library)

EQUALITY — United States — Public opinion

KLUEGEL, James R
Beliefs about inequality : Americans' views of what is and what ought to be / James R. Kluegel and Eliot R. Smith. — New York : A. de Gruyter, 1986. — p. cm. — *Includes index. — Bibliography: p*

EQUALITY BEFORE THE LAW — Australia

FLICK, Geoffrey A.
Natural justice : principles and practical application / by Geoffrey A. Flick. — 2nd ed. — Sydney : Butterworths, 1984. — xliv,212p

EQUALITY BEFORE THE LAW — Canada

Charterwatch : reflections on equality / edited by Christine L. M. Boyle...[et al.]. — Toronto : Carswell, 1986. — ix,356p

Equality rights and the Canadian Charter of Rights and Freedoms / edited by Anne F. Bayefsky and Mary Eberts. — Toronto : Carswell, 1985. — xliv, 661 p.. — *Includes bibliographical references and indexes*

EQUALITY BEFORE THE LAW — South Australia

SOUTH AUSTRALIA. Equal Opportunities Branch
Australian equal opportunity legislation. — [Adelaide] : the Branch, 1986. — 3 leaves. — (Equal employment opportunity management planning information sheet)

EQUALITY OF STATES

TUCKER, Robert W
The inequality of nations / Robert W. Tucker. — New York : Basic Books, c1977. — x, 214 p.. — *Includes bibliographical references and index*

EQUATORIAL GUINEA — Bibliography

LINIGER-GOUMAZ, Max
Historical dictionary of Equatorial Guinea / by Max Liniger-Goumaz. — Metuchen, N.J. : Scarecrow Press, 1979. — xxiv, 222 p.. — (African historical dictionaries ; no. 21). — *Bibliography: p. 177-222*

EQUATORIAL GUINEA — Census, 1983

Censos nacionales : I de población y I de vivienda - 4 al 17 de Julio de 1983 : resultados provisionales. — Malabo : Dirección General de Estadística, 1983. — 8p

EQUATORIAL GUINEA — Constitution

EQUATORIAL GUINEA
Ley fundamental de Guinea Ecuatorial. — Malabo : El Departamento de Información de la Presidencia de la República, 1982. — 45p

EQUATORIAL GUINEA — History — Dictionaries

LINIGER-GOUMAZ, Max
Historical dictionary of Equatorial Guinea / by Max Liniger-Goumaz. — Metuchen, N.J. : Scarecrow Press, 1979. — xxiv, 222 p.. — (African historical dictionaries ; no. 21). — *Bibliography: p. 177-222*

EQUATORIAL GUINEA — Population — Statistics

Censos nacionales : I de población y I de vivienda - 4 al 17 de Julio de 1983 : resultados provisionales. — Malabo : Dirección General de Estadística, 1983. — 8p

EQUILIBRIUM (ECONOMICS)

ABREU, Dilip
The Structure of Nash equilibrium in repeated games with finite automata / Dilip Abreu and Ariel Rubinstein. — London : Suntory-Toyota International Centre for Economics and Related Disciplines, 1986. — 36p. — (Theoretical economics). — *Bibliography: p36*

BÖRGERS, Tilman
Perfect equilibrium histories of finite and infinite horizon games / Tilman Börgers. — London : Sontory Toyota International Centre for Economics and Related Disciplines, 1987. — 32p. — (Theoretical economics ; 87/148). — *Bibliography: p32*

BREMS, Hans
Pioneering economic theory, 1630-1980 : a mathematical restatement / Hans Brems. — Baltimore : Johns Hopkins University Press, c1986. — xv, 411 p.. — *Includes bibliographies and indexes*

BÜTTLER, Hans-Jürgen
Estimation of disequilibrium models / Hans-Jürg Büttler, Gertrude Frei, Bernd Schips. — Berlin ; New York : Springer-Verlag, c1986. — p. cm. — (Lecture notes in economics and mathematical systems ; 279). — *Includes bibliographies*

CAMPBELL, Donald E.
Resource allocation mechanisms / Donald E. Campbell. — Cambridge : Cambridge University Press, 1987. — xiii,183p. — *Bibliography: p171-177. — Includes index*

CHING-TO, Ma
Unique implementation of incentive contracts with many agents / Ching-to Ma. — London : Suntory Toyota International Centre for Economics and Related Disciplines, 1986. — 40p. — (Theoretical economics ; 87/146). — *Bibliography: p39-40*

Economic organizations as games / edited by Ken Binmore and Partha Dasgupta. — Oxford : Basil Blackwell, 1986. — 219p.. — *Includes bibliography and index*

HARRIS, Milton
Dynamic economic analysis / Milton Harris. — New York : Oxford University Press, 1987. — p. cm. — *Includes index. — Bibliography: p*

PÄTZOLD, Jürgen
Stabilisierungspolitik : Grundlagen der nachfrage- und angebotsorientierten Wirtschaftspolitik / Jürgen Pätzold. — Bern : Haupt, 1985. — 340p. — *Bibliography: p326-334*

RUBINSTEIN, Ariel
Competitive equilibrium in a market with decentralized trade and strategic behaviour : an introduction / Ariel Rubinstein. — London : Suntory Toyota International Centre for Economics and Related Disciplines, 1986. — 29p. — (Theoretical economics ; 87/147). — *Bibliograhy: p28-29*

EQUILIBRIUM (ECONOMICS) — Mathematical models

BREMS, Hans
Pioneering economic theory, 1630-1980 : a mathematical restatement / Hans Brems. — Baltimore : Johns Hopkins University Press, c1986. — xv, 411 p.. — *Includes bibliographies and indexes*

CRIPPS, Martin William
Imperfect competition and strategic information transmission / Martin William Cripps. — 201 leaves. — *PhD (Econ) 1986 LSE*

GOLUB, Stephen S
The current-account balance and the dollar, 1977-78 and 1983-84 / Stephen S. Golub. — Princeton, N.J. : Dept. of Economics, Princeton University, 1986. — p. cm. — (Princeton studies in international finance ; no. 57). — *Bibliography: p*

SARGENT, Thomas J
Dynamic macroeconomic theory / Thomas J. Sargent. — Cambridge, Mass. : Harvard University Press, 1987. — xii, 369 p.. — *Includes bibliographies and index*

EQUITABLE REMEDIES — Canada

CLARK, Robert W.
Inequality of bargaining power : judicial intervention in improvident and unconscionable bargains / Robert W. Clark. — Toronto : Carswell, 1987. — xxxvii,255p

EQUITABLE REMEDIES — Great Britain

CLARK, Robert W.
Inequality of bargaining power : judicial intervention in improvident and unconscionable bargains / Robert W. Clark. — Toronto : Carswell, 1987. — xxxvii,255p

EQUITY — Australia

Equity and commercial relationships / edited by P. D. Finn. — Sydney : Law Book Company, 1987. — xxvii,320p

EQUITY — Australia — Addresses, Essays, Lectures
Essays in equity / edited by P.D. Finn. — Sydney : Law Book Company, 1985. — xxv,256p

EQUITY — England
HACKNEY, Jeffrey
Understanding equity and trusts / Jeffrey Hackney. — London : Fontana, 1987. — 182p. — (Understanding law) (Understanding law). — *Bibliography: p169-175*

KEETON, George W.
Equity / by George W. Keeton and L.A. Sheridan. — 3rd ed. — [Chichester] : Barry Rose, 1987. — cxxvi,576p. — *Previous ed.: 1976. — Includes index*

ERITREA (ETHIOPIA) — Social conditions
FIREBRACE, James
Never kneel down : drought, development and liberation in Eritrea / James Firebrace with Stuart Holland ; preface by Neil Kinnock. — Nottingham : Spokesman for War on Want, 1984. — 192p. — *Bibliography: p186-189*

EROS AND CIVILIZATION
ROTH, Roland
Rebellische Subjektivität : Herbert Marcuse und die neuen Protestbewegungen / Roland Roth. — Frankfurt : Campus, 1985. — 338p. — *Bibliography: p325-338*

EROTICA — Addresses, essays, lectures
The Female body in western culture : contemporary perspectives / Susan Rubin Suleiman, editor. — Cambridge, Mass. : Harvard University Press, 1986. — p. cm. — *Includes bibliographies*

ERROR ANALYSIS (MATHEMATICS)
Statistical experimentation for household surveys : two case studies of Hong Kong / Christiaan Grootaert ... [et al.]. — Washington, D.C. : World Bank, 1982. — 66p. — (LSMS working papers ; no.20). — *Cover title. — Bibliography: p65-66*

ERSHAD, HOSSAIN MOHAMMAD
Ershad's election fraud / edited by Abdul Matin. — London : Radical Asia Publications, 1986. — 31p. — (Bangladesh political scene ; no.3)

ESCALATION (MILITARY SCIENCE)
Escalation and intervention : multilateral security and its alternatives / edited by Arthur R. Day and Michael W. Doyle. — Boulder, Colo. : Westview ; London : Mansell, 1986. — x,181p. — (Westview special studies in international security). — *Published in cooperation with the United Nations Association of the United States of America. — Includes index*

ESCHER, M. C. — Criticism and interpretation
INTERDISCIPLINARY CONGRESS ON M.C.ESCHER (1985 : Rome, Italy)
M.C. Escher, art and science : proceedings of the Interdisciplinary Congress on M.C. Escher, Rome, Italy, 26-28 March 1985 / edited by H.S.M. Coxeter ... [et al.]. — Amsterdam ; New York : North-Holland ; New York, N.Y., U.S.A. : Sole distributors for the U.S.A. and Canada, Elsevier Science Pub. Co., 1986. — p. cm

ESCRIVA DE BALAGUER, JOSEMARÍA — Interviews
ESCRIVA DE BALAGUER, Josemaría
Conversations with Mgr Escriva de Balaguer : [recent interviews] / [by Pedro Rodriguez...[et al.]. — Dublin : Scepter Books, 1968. — 146p

ESKIMOS — Alaska — Claims
BERGER, Thomas R
Village journey : the report of the Alaska Native Review Commission / by Thomas R. Berger. — New York : Hill and Wang, c1985. — p. cm

ESKIMOS — Alaska — Economic conditions — Addresses, essays, lectures
Contemporary Alaskan native economies / edited by Steve J. Langdon. — Lanham, MD : University Press of America, c1986. — ix, 183 p.. — *Includes bibliographies. — Contents: Economic growth and development strategies for rural Alaska / Bradford H. Tuck and Lee Huskey -- Subsistence as an economic system in Alaska / Thomas D. Lonner -- Contradictions in Alaskan native economy and society / Steve J. Langdon -- Limited entry policy and impacts on Bristol Bay fishermen / J. Anthony Koslow -- The Cape Romanzoff project / Dean F. Olson -- The Pribilof Island Aleuts / Michael K. Orbach and Beverly Holmes -- The economic efficiency of food production in a western Alaska Eskimo population / Robert J. Wolfe -- Subsistence and the North Slope Inupiat / John A. Kruse -- Subsistence beluga whale hunting in Alaska / Kerry D. Feldman -- Traditional subsistence activities and systems of exchange among the Nelson Island Yup'ik / Ann Fienup-Riordan*

ESKIMOS — Alaska — Government relations
BERGER, Thomas R
Village journey : the report of the Alaska Native Review Commission / by Thomas R. Berger. — New York : Hill and Wang, c1985. — p. cm

ESKIMOS — Alaska — Land tenure
BERGER, Thomas R
Village journey : the report of the Alaska Native Review Commission / by Thomas R. Berger. — New York : Hill and Wang, c1985. — p. cm

ESPARTERO, BALDOMERO
INIGO GÍAS, María Pilar
Zaragoza esparterista (1840-1843) / Maria Pilar Inigo Gias. — Zaragoza : Ayuntamiento de Zaragoza, 1983. — 111p. — *Bibliography: p77-81*

ESPIONAGE — Bibliography
IMPERIAL WAR MUSEUM. Library
Bibliography of espionage and treason. — [London] : the Library, [1955]. — 21p. — (Booklist / Imperial War Museum Library ; no.1244)

IMPERIAL WAR MUSEUM. Library
Espionage and treason : a list of selected references. — [London] : the Library, [1963]. — 8p. — (Booklist / Imperial War Museum Llibrary ; no.1244). — *Supplement to booklist published in 1955*

ESPIONAGE — Canada
BARROS, James
No sense of evil : espionage, the case of Herbert Norman / James Barros. — Toronto : Deneau, 1986. — xi,259p

ESPIONAGE — France
FALIGOT, Roger
Service B / Roger Faligot, Rémi Kauffer. — Paris : Fazard, [1985]. — 342p

ESPIONAGE — Germany (West)
KAHL, Werner
Spionage in Deutschland heute / Werner Kahl. — München : Edition Meyster, 1986. — 280p. — *Bibliography: p279-280*

ESPIONAGE — Great Britain — History — 20th century
SINCLAIR, Andrew
The red and the blue : intelligence, treason and the universities / Andrew Sinclair. — London : Weidenfeld and Nicolson, 1986. — 179p. — *Bibliography: p162-168. — Includes index*

ESPIONAGE — Ireland
MUNNELLY, Brendan
Who's bugging you? : inside Ireland's secret world of electronic surveillance / Brendan Munnelly. — Cork : Mercier Press, 1987. — 90p

ESPIONAGE, AMERICAN — Soviet Union — History
BESCHLOSS, Michael R.
Mayday : Eisenhower, Khrushchev and the U-2 affair / Michael R. Beschloss. — London : Faber, 1986. — xvi,494p,[24]p of plates. — *Bibliography: p416-422. — Includes index*

ESPIONAGE, BRITISH
WEST, Nigel
Molehunt : the full story of the Soviet spy in MI5 / Nigel West. — London : Weidenfeld and Nicholson, 1987. — 208p. — *Bibliography: p.197-199*

ESPIONAGE, RUSSIAN
STAAR, Richard Felix
USSR foreign policies after detente / Richard F. Staar. — Rev. ed. — Stanford, Calif. : Hoover Institution Press, Stanford University, c1987. — xxvii, 308 p.. — (Hoover Press publication ; 359). — *Includes index. — Bibliography: p. [275]-295*

ESPIONAGE, RUSSIAN — History — 20th century
PINCHER, Chapman
The secret offensive : active measures : a saga of deception, disinformation, subversion, terrorism, sabotage and assassination / Chapman Pincher. — London : Sidgwick & Jackson, 1985. — 314p,[8]p of plates. — *Bibliography: p306. — Includes index*

ESPIONAGE, RUSSIAN — Australia
WHITLAM, Nicholas
Nest of traitors : the Petrov affair / Nicholas Whitlam, John Stubbs. — 2nd ed. — St. Lucia ; New York : University of Queensland Press, 1985. — xii, 259 p., [16] p. of plates. — *Includes index. — Bibliography: p. 251-253*

ESPIONAGE, RUSSIAN — Great Britain — History — 20th century
GLEES, Anthony
The secrets of the service : British intelligence and Communist subversion 1939-51 / Anthony Glees. — London : Cape, 1987. — 1v.. — *Includes bibliography and index*

PINCHER, Chapman
Their trade is treachery / Chapman Pincher. — [New ed.]. — London : Sidgwick & Jackson, 1982. — xi,317p. — *Previous ed.: 1981. — Includes index*

ESPIONAGECANADA
STAFFORD, David
Camp X / David Stafford. — New York : Dodd, Mead, 1987. — p. cm. — *Includes index. — Bibliography: p*

ESTIMATION THEORY
SILVERMAN, B. W.
Density estimation for statistics and data analysis / B.W. Silverman. — London : Chapman and Hall, 1986. — [200]p. — (Monographs on statistics and applied probability). — *Includes bibliography and index*

ETA
EL PAÍS. Equipo de Investigación
Golpe mortal : asesinato de Carrero y agonía del franquismo / El País, Equipo de Investigación ; Ismael Fuente, Javier García y Joaquín Prieto. — [Madrid] : Promotora de Informaciones], 1983. — 374p

ETHICAL RELATIVISM
KANE, R
Free will and values / R. Kane. — Albany : State University of New York Press, c1985. — vii, 229 p.. — (SUNY series in philosophy). — *Includes indexes. — Bibliography: p. 206-218*

ETHICS
ALMOND, Brenda
Moral concerns / Brenda Almond. — Atlantic Highlands, NJ : Humanities Press International, 1987. — xiii, 152p

ETHICS *continuation*

ARKES, Hadley
First things : an inquiry into the first principles of morals and justice / Hadley Arkes. — Princeton, N.J. : Princeton University Press, c1986. — xii, 432p. — *Includes index*

ATTFIELD, Robin
A theory of value and obligation / Robin Attfield. — London : Croom Helm, c1987. — [iv,256]p. — *Includes bibliography and index*

DOOB, Leonard William
Slightly beyond skepticism : social science and the search for morality / Leonard W. Doob. — New Haven : Yale University Press, c1987. — ix, 319 p.. — *Includes index. — Bibliography: p. 281-306*

HUDSON, Stephen D.
Human character and morality : reflections from the history of ideas / Stephen D. Hudson. — Boston ; London : Routledge & Kegan Paul, 1986. — xvii,164p. — *Bibliography: p153-158. — Includes index*

LARMORE, Charles E.
Patterns of moral complexity / Charles E. Larmore. — Cambridge : Cambridge University Press, 1987. — [208]p

MACINTYRE, Alasdair
After virtue : a study in moral theory / Alasdair MacIntyre. — 2nd ed. — London : Duckworth, 1985. — xi,286p. — *Previous ed.: 1981. — Bibliography: p[279]-281*

ROBINS, Michael H.
Promising, intending, and moral autonomy / Michael H. Robins. — Cambridge : Cambridge University Press, 1984. — xii,180p. — (Cambridge studies in philosophy). — *Bibliography: p171-177. — Includes index*

TRUSTED, Jennifer
Moral principles and social values / Jennifer Trusted. — London : Routledge & Kegan Paul, 1987. — [160]p. — *Includes bibliography and index*

WALZER, Michael
Interpretation and social criticism / Michael Walzer. — Cambridge, Mass. : Harvard University Press, 1987. — viii, 96 p.. — (The Tanner lectures on human values). — *Includes bibliographical references and index*

ETHICS — Addresses, essays, lectures

[Moralisches Urteilen und soziale Umwelt. English]. Moral development and the social environment : studies in the philosophy and psychology of moral judgment and education / edited by Georg Lind, Hans A. Hartmann, and Roland Wakenhut ; general editor and translator, Thomas E. Wren. — Chicago, Ill. : Precedent Pub., c1985. — xvii, 327 p.. — (Precedent studies in ethics and the moral sciences). — *Rev. translation of: Moralisches Urteilen und soziale Umwelt. — Includes indexes. — Bibliography: p. [299]-318*

Morality, reason, and truth : new essays on the foundations of ethics / edited by David Copp and David Zimmerman. — Totowa, NJ : Rowman & Allanheld, 1984. — viii, 331p. — *Includes index. — Bibliography: p 320-328*

ETHICS, MEDICAL

ENGELHARDT, H. Tristram
The foundations of bioethics / by H. Tristram Engelhardt, Jr. — New York : Oxford University Press, 1986. — p. cm. — *Includes bibliographies and index*

ETHICS, MEDICAL — congresses

The Price of health / edited by George J. Agich and Charles E. Begley. — Dordrecht ; Boston : D. Reidel Pub. Co. ; Hingham, MA, U.S.A. : Sold and distributed in the U.S.A. and Canada by Kluwer Academic Publishers, c1987. — p. cm. — (Philosophy and medicine ; v. 21). — *Based on a conference entitled "The price of health: economics and ethics in medicine," held at the School of Public Health, University of Texas Health Science Center, Houston, Tex., June 24-26, 1985. — Includes bibliographies and index*

ETHICS, MEDICAL — United States

IMBER, Jonathan B.
Abortion and the private practice of medicine / Jonathan B. Imber. — New Haven : Yale University Press, c1986. — xviii, 164 p.. — *Includes index. — Bibliography: p. 147-160*

ETHICS, MODERN — 20th century — Addresses, essays, lectures

New directions in ethics : the challenge of applied ethics / edited by Joseph P. MeMarco, Richard M. Fox. — New York ; London : Routledge & Kegan Paul, 1986. ; xi, 335p. — *Includes bibliographical references*

ETHIOPIA — Description and travel — To 1900

GOBAT, Samuel
Journal of three years' residence in Abyssinia : preceded by an introduction geographical and historical, on Abyssinia / by Samuel Gobat ; translated from the French by Sereno D. Clark ; accompanied with a biographical sketch of Bishop Gobat by Robert Baird. — New York : Negro Universities Press, 1969. — xviii,480p. — *Reprint of 1851 edition*

ETHIOPIA — Description and travel — to 1900

PORTAL, Gerald H.
My mission to Abyssinia : with map and illustrations / by Gerald H. Portal. — New York : Negroes University Press, 1969. — vi,261p. — *Originally published in 1892 by Edward Arnold, London*

ETHIOPIA — Famines

CLAY, Jason W.
Politics and the Ethiopian famine 1984-1985 / Jason W. Clay and Bonnie K. Holcomb. — rev. ed. — Cambridge, Mass. : Cultural Survival, 1986. — xvii,237p. — (Cultural survival report ; 20)

ETHIOPIA — Foreign relations — Somalia

SPENCER, John Hathaway
Ethiopia, the Horn of Africa, and U.S. policy / John H. Spencer. — Cambridge, Mass : Institute for Foreign Policy Analysis, 1977. — 69 p. — (Foreign policy report). — *Includes bibliographical references*

ETHIOPIA — Foreign relations — United States

SPENCER, John Hathaway
Ethiopia, the Horn of Africa, and U.S. policy / John H. Spencer. — Cambridge, Mass : Institute for Foreign Policy Analysis, 1977. — 69 p. — (Foreign policy report). — *Includes bibliographical references*

ETHIOPIA — History — Autonomy and independence movements

HENZE, Paul B.
Rebels and separatists in Ethiopia : regional resistance to a Marxist regime / Paul Henze. — Santa Monica, CA : Rand, [1986]. — xv, 98 p.. — *"Prepared for the Office of the Under Secretary of Defense for Policy.". — "R-3347-USDP.". — "December 1985.". — Bibliography: p. 95-98*

ETHIOPIA — History — Dictionaries

ROSENFELD, Chris Prouty
Historical dictionary of Ethiopia / by Chris Prouty and Eugene Rosenfeld. — Metuchen, N.J. : Scarecrow Press, 1981, c1982. — xv, 436 p.. — (African historical dictionaries ; no. 32). — *Includes index. — Bibliography: p. [192]-407*

ETHIOPIA — History — 1889-1974

MARCUS, Harold G
Haile Sellassie I : the formative years, 1892-1936 / Harold G. Marcus. — Berkeley : University of California Press, c1986. — p. cm. — *Includes index. — Bibliography: p*

ETHIOPIA — Kings and rulers — Biography

MARCUS, Harold G
Haile Sellassie I : the formative years, 1892-1936 / Harold G. Marcus. — Berkeley : University of California Press, c1986. — p. cm. — *Includes index. — Bibliography: p*

ETHIOPIA — Politics and government

KAPUŚCIŃSKI, Ryszard
The Emperor : downfall of an autocrat / Ryszard Kapuściński ; translated from the Polish by William R. Brand and Katarzyna Mroczkowska Brand. — London : Quartet, 1983. — 164p. — *Translation of: Cesarz*

The Southern marches of Imperial Ethiopia : essays in history and social anthropology / edited by Donald Donham and Wendy James. — Cambridge : Cambridge University Press, 1986. — xvi,308p. — (African studies series ; 51). — *Bibliography: p295-298. — Includes index*

SPENCER, John Hathaway
Ethiopia, the Horn of Africa, and U.S. policy / John H. Spencer. — Cambridge, Mass : Institute for Foreign Policy Analysis, 1977. — 69 p. — (Foreign policy report). — *Includes bibliographical references*

ETHIOPIA — Politics and government — 1974-

HENZE, Paul B.
Rebels and separatists in Ethiopia : regional resistance to a Marxist regime / Paul Henze. — Santa Monica, CA : Rand, [1986]. — xv, 98 p.. — *"Prepared for the Office of the Under Secretary of Defense for Policy.". — "R-3347-USDP.". — "December 1985.". — Bibliography: p. 95-98*

KAPUŚCIŃSKI, Ryszard
The Emperor : downfall of an autocrat / Ryszard Kapuściński ; translated from the Polish by William R. Brand and Katarzyna Mroczkowska Brand. — London : Quartet, 1983. — 164p. — *Translation of: Cesarz*

ETHNIC GROUPS — Civil rights

DENCH, Geoff
Minorities in the open society : prisoners of ambivalence / Geoff Dench. — London : Routledge & Kegan Paul, 1986. — vii, 275p. — *Bibliography: p.262-268*

ETHNIC GROUPS — Dictionaries and encyclopedias

CARATINI, Roger
La force des faibles : encyclopédie mondiale des minorités / Roger Caratini. — Paris : Larousse, [1986]. — 399p. — *Bibliography: p370-382*

ETHNIC GROUPS — Government policy — Developing countries

Ethnic preference and public policy in developing states / edited by Neil Nevitte and Charles H. Kennedy. — Boulder, Colo. : Lynne Rienner Publishers, c1986. — p. cm. — *Includes index. — Bibliography: p*

ETHNIC GROUPS — Political activity

Ethnicity, politics, and development / edited by Dennis L. Thompson and Dev Ronen. — Boulder, Colo. : L. Rienner, c1985. — p. cm. — *Includes index. — Bibliography: p*

WALZER, Michael
The politics of ethnicity / Michael Walzer...[et al.]. — Cambridge, Mass. ; London : Belknap Press of Harvard University Press, 1982. — vi,142p. — (Dimensions of ethnicity : Selections from the Harvard Encyclopedia of American ethnic groups). — *Bibliography: p [139]-142*

ETHNIC PRESS — Great Britain

Ethnic minority broadcasting and local radio. — Berkhamsted : Volunteer Centre Media Project, 1984. — 17p. — (Social action and the media ; no.18)

ETHNIC PRESS — Great Britain — Directories

GREAT BRITAIN. Commission for Racial Equality
Ethnic minority press. — London : the Commission, 1982. — [2]p

ETHNIC RELATIONS
DENCH, Geoff
Minorities in the open society : prisoners of ambivalence / Geoff Dench. — London : Routledge & Kegan Paul, 1986. — vii, 275p. — *Bibliography: p.262-268*

Ethnic conflict : international perspectives / edited by Jerry Boucher, Dan Landis, Karen Arnold Clark. — Newbury Park, Calif. : Sage Publications, c1987. — 331 p.. — (Sage focus editions ; 84). — *Includes bibliographies and index*

Theories of race and ethnic relations / edited by John Rex and David Mason. — Cambridge : Cambridge University Press, 1986. — [x,526p] p. — (Comparative ethnic and race relations). — *Bibliography: p482-526*

ETHNIC RELATIONS — Political aspects — Case studies
Competitive ethnic relations / edited by Susan Olzak, Joane Nagel. — Orlando : Academic Press, 1986. — ix, 252 p.. — *Includes bibliographies and index*

ETHNICITY
DENCH, Geoff
Minorities in the open society : prisoners of ambivalence / Geoff Dench. — London : Routledge & Kegan Paul, 1986. — vii, 275p. — *Bibliography: p.262-268*

Ethnic Canada : identities and inequalities / [edited by] Leo Driedger. — Toronto : Copp Clark Pitman, 1987. — v,442p. — *Bibliography: p408-433*

HAARMANN, Harald
Language in ethnicity : a view of basic ecological relations / by Harald Haarmann. — Berlin ; New York : Mouton de Gruyter, c1986. — p. cm. — (Contributions to the sociology of language ; 44). — *Includes indexes. — Bibliography: p*

ETHNICITY — Case studies
Competitive ethnic relations / edited by Susan Olzak, Joane Nagel. — Orlando : Academic Press, 1986. — ix, 252 p.. — *Includes bibliographies and index*

ETHNICITY — Economic aspects — Cross-cultural studies
SOWELL, Thomas
Race, politique et économie : une approche internationale / Thomas Sowell ; ouvrage traduit de l'Américain par Raoul Audouin ; avec la collaboration de François Guillaumot. — Paris : Presses Universitaires de France, 1986. — 313p. *Includes bibliographical notes*

ETHNICITY — Political aspects — Cross-cultural studies
SOWELL, Thomas
Race, politique et économie : une approche internationale / Thomas Sowell ; ouvrage traduit de l'Américain par Raoul Audouin ; avec la collaboration de François Guillaumot. — Paris : Presses Universitaires de France, 1986. — 313p. *Includes bibliographical notes*

ETHNICITY — Canada
HILLER, Harry H.
Canadian society : a macro analysis / Harry H. Hiller. — Scarborough, Ont. : Prentice-Hall Canada, c1986. — x, 245 p.. — *Includes index. — Bibliography: p. 234-241*

ETHNICITY — Canada — Congresses
Central and East European ethnicity in Canada : adaptation and preservation / T. Yedlin, editor. — Edmonton : Central and East European Studies Society of Alberta, 1985. — viii,178p. — *Papers presented at the conference on Central and East European Ethnicity in Canada, sponsored by the Central and East European Studies Society of Alberta, the Central and East European Studies Association of Canada and the Department of Slavic and East European Studies, University of Alberta at February 1983, held in Edmonton, Alberta*

ETHNICITY — New Zealand — Statistics
BROWN, P. G.
An investigation of official ethnic statistics / P. G. Brown. — Wellington : Department of Statistics, 1983. — . — (Occasional paper / Department of Statistics ; no.5). *Bibliographical references: p70-71*

ETHNICITY — Singapore
CHEW, Sock Foon
Ethnicity and nationality in Singapore / by Chew Sock Foon. — Athens, Ohio : Ohio University Center for International Studies, Center for Southeast Asian Studies, 1987. — xv, 229 p.. — (Monographs in international studies. Southeast Asia series ; no. 78). — *Bibliography: p. 213-229*

KUO, Eddie C. Y
Ethnicity and fertility in Singapore / by Eddie C.Y. Kuo and Chiew Seen-Kong. — Singapore : Institute of Southeast Asian Studies, 1984. — xv, 180 p.. — (Research notes and discussions paper ; no. 48). — *Bibliography: p. 178-180*

ETHNICITY — Thailand
PRASITHRATHSINT, Suchart
Ethnicity and fertility in Thailand / Suchart Prasithrathsint. — Singapore : Institute of Southeast Asian Studies, 1985. — xviii,270p. — (Research notes and discussions paper ; no.51) (Ethnicity and fertility in Southeast Asia series) . — *Bibliography: p265-270*

ETHNICITY — United States
LAVENDER, Abraham D
Ethnic women and feminist values : toward a "new" value system / Abraham D. Lavender. — Lanham, MD : University Press of America, c1986. — xix, 291 p.. — *Includes index. — Bibliography: p. 247-285*

ETHNOBOTANY — Addresses, essays, lectures
Indigenous knowledge systems and development / edited by David Brokensha, D. M. Warren, and Oswald Werner. — Washington, D.C. : University Press of America, c1980. — vii, 466 p.. — *Includes indexes. — Bibliography: p. 415-449*

ETHNOCENTRISM
The Sociobiology of ethnocentrism : evolutionary dimensions of xenophobia, discrimination, racism and nationalism / edited by Vernon Reynolds, Vincent Falger and Ian Vine. — London : Croom Helm, c1987. — xx,327p. — *Bibliography: p274-314. — Includes index*

ETHNOGRAPHY
TREBICI, Vladimir
Demografie şi etnografie / Vladimir Trebici, Ion Ghinoiu. — Bucureşti : Editura Ştiinţifică şi Enciclopedică, 1986. — 325p. — *Bibliography: p321-[325]*

ETHNOLOGICAL JURISPRUDENCE — Addresses, essays, lectures
Sociology of law and legal anthropology in the Dutch speaking countries / J. van Houtte, editor. — Dordrecht ; Boston : M. Nijhoff Publishers, 1985. — p. cm. — (Nijhoff law specials). — *Bibliography of 'The sociology of law in Dutch-speaking countries': p67-102. — Bibliography of 'Current legal anthropology in the Netherlands': p149-162*

ETHNOLOGISTS — Biography
MOERAN, Brian
Ōkubo diary : portrait of a Japanese valley / Brian Moeran. — Stanford, Calif. : Stanford University, 1985. — p. cm. — *Bibliography: p*

ETHNOLOGY
IZIKOWITZ, Karl Gustav
Compass for fields afar : essays in social anthropology / Karl Gustav Izikowitz ; edited by Göran Aijmer. — Göteborg, Sweden : Acta Universitatis Gothoburgensis, 1985. — vi, 313 p., [1] leaf of plates. — (Gothenburg studies in social anthropology ; 7). — *English and French. — Bibliography: p. 309-313*

LEACH, Sir Edmund Ronald
Social anthropology : a natural science of society? / Sir Edmund Ronald Leach. — London : The British Academy, 1976. — 26p. — *Bibliography*

LÉVI-STRAUSS, Claude
Anthropology and myth : lectures 1951-1982 / Claude Lévi-Strauss ; translated by Roy Willis. — Oxford : Basil Blackwell, 1987. — vi,232p. — *Translation of: Paroles données. — Includes index*

SMITH, Anthony D. (Anthony David)
The ethnic origins of nations / Anthony D. Smith. — Oxford : Basil Blackwell, 1986. — 1v.. — *Includes bibliography and index*

ETHNOLOGY — Biographical methods
WATSON, Lawrence Craig
Interpreting life histories : an anthropological inquiry / Lawrence C. Watson, Maria-Barbara Watson-Franke. — New Brunswick, N.J. : Rutgers University Press, c1985. — x, 228 p.. — *Includes index. — Bibliography: p. [207]-222*

ETHNOLOGY — Field work
EL GUINDI, Fadwa
The myth of ritual : a native's ethnography of Zapotec life-crisis rituals / Fadwa El Guindi, with the collaboration of Abel Hernández Jiménez. — Tucson : University of Arizona Press, c1986. — xvii, 147p. — *Includes index. — Bibliography: p.125-139*

MOERAN, Brian
Ōkubo diary : portrait of a Japanese valley / Brian Moeran. — Stanford, Calif. : Stanford University, 1985. — p. cm. — *Bibliography: p*

ETHNOLOGY — Field work — Case studies
Practicing development anthropology / edited by Edward C. Green. — Boulder, Colo. : Westview Press, 1986. — xi, 283 p.. — (Westview special studies in applied anthropology). — *Includes bibliographies and index*

ETHNOLOGY — Fieldwork
DWYER, Kevin
Moroccan dialogues : anthropology in question / Kevin Dwyer. — Baltimore : Johns Hopkins University Press, c1982. — xxvii, 297 p.. — *Includes dialogues between Kevin Dwyer and Faqir Muhammad. — Includes index. Bibliography: p. 289-292*

WERNER, Oswald
Systematic fieldwork / Oswald Werner, G. Mark Schoepfle. — Newbury Park [Calif.] ; London : Sage
Vol.1: Foundations of ethnography and interviewing. — 1987. — 416p. — *Bibliography: p395-406*

WERNER, Oswald
Systematic fieldwork / Oswald Werner, G. Mark Schoepfle. — Newbury Park [Calif.] ; London : Sage
Vol.2: Ethnographic analysis and data management. — 1987. — 355p. — *Bibliography: p339-345*

ETHNOLOGY — Methodology
Current anthropology in the Netherlands / edited by Peter Kloos and Henri J. M. Claessen. — Rotterdam : Anthropological Branch of the Netherlands Sociological and Anthropological Society. — 184p. — *Includes references*

WERNER, Oswald
Systematic fieldwork / Oswald Werner, G. Mark Schoepfle. — Newbury Park [Calif.] ; London : Sage
Vol.1: Foundations of ethnography and interviewing. — 1987. — 416p. — *Bibliography: p395-406*

ETHNOLOGY — Methodology
continuation

WERNER, Oswald
Systematic fieldwork / Oswald Werner, G. Mark Schoepfle. — Newbury Park [Calif.] ; London : Sage
Vol.2: Ethnographic analysis and data management. — 1987. — 355p. —
Bibliography: p339-345

ETHNOLOGY — Philosophy

FERNANDEZ, James W
Persuasions and performances : the play of tropes in culture / James W. Fernandez. — Bloomington : Indiana University Press, c1986. — xv, 304 p.. — *Includes bibliographies and index*

ETHNOLOGY — Research

WERNER, Oswald
Systematic fieldwork / Oswald Werner, G. Mark Schoepfle. — Newbury Park [Calif.] ; London : Sage
Vol.1: Foundations of ethnography and interviewing. — 1987. — 416p. —
Bibliography: p395-406

ETHNOLOGY — Africa

African worlds : studies in the cosmological ideas and social values of African peoples / edited with an introduction by Daryll Forde. — London : International African Institute, 1954. — 243p

ETHNOLOGY — Africa, Central

COLSON, Elizabeth
Seven tribes of British Central Africa / edited by Elizabeth Colson and Max Gluckman. — London : Oxford University Press, 1951. — xx,409p

ETHNOLOGY — Asia, South

FÜRER-HAIMENDORF, Christoph von
Tribal populations and cultures of the Indian subcontinent / by C. Von Fürer-Haimendorf. — Leiden : E.J. Brill, 1985. — vi, 182 p.. — (Handbuch der Orientalistik. Zweite Abteilung. Indien ; 7. Bd). — *Includes bibliographies and index*

ETHNOLOGY — Asia, Southeastern

Shared wealth and symbol : food, culture, and society in Oceania and Southeast Asia / edited by Lenore Manderson. — Cambridge : Cambridge University Press, 1987. — xii,314p. — *Bibliography: p283-308. — Includes index*

WONG, Aline K
Ethnicity and fertility in Southeast Asia : a comparative analysis / by Aline K. Wong and Ng Shui Meng. — Singapore : Institute of Southeast Asian Studies, 1985. — xii, 393 p.. — (Research notes and discussions paper ; no. 50) (Ethnicity and fertility in Southeast Asia series). — *Bibliography: p. 372-377*

ETHNOLOGY — Australia

Immigration and ethnicity in the 1980s / edited by I.H. Burnley, S. Encel, and Grant McCall. — Melbourne, Australia : Longman Cheshire, 1985. — vi, 285 p.. — (Australian studies). — *Includes bibliographies and index*

ETHNOLOGY — Canada

COSPER, Ronald L.
Ethnicity and occupation in Atlantic Canada : the social and economic implications of cultural diversity / Ronald L. Cosper. — Halifax : International Education Centre, 1984. — 47p. — (Ethnic heritage series ; vol.10). —
Bibliography: p46-47

ETHNOLOGY — Ethiopia — Gamo

BUREAU, Jacques
Les Gamo d´Éthiopie : étude du système politique / Jacques Bureau. — Paris : Société d´ethnographie, 1981. — 303p. — (Histoire et civilisations de l´Afrique Orientale ; 3). —
Bibliography: p277-299

ETHNOLOGY — Europe

Anthropology at home / edited by Anthony Jackson. — London : Tavistick, 1987. — x,221p. — (ASA monographs ; 25). —
Conference papers. — Includes bibliographies and index

ETHNOLOGY — India

FÜRER-HAIMENDORF, Christoph von
Tribal populations and cultures of the Indian subcontinent / by C. Von Fürer-Haimendorf. — Leiden : E.J. Brill, 1985. — vi, 182 p.. — (Handbuch der Orientalistik. Zweite Abteilung. Indien ; 7. Bd). — *Includes bibliographies and index*

THOMAS, Antony
Mahatma Gandhi and the communal problem / Antony Thomas. — New Delhi : Indian Social Institute, 1983. — 29p. — (Monograph series / Indian Social Institute ; 13). —
Bibliography: p28-29

VIDYARTHI, Lalita Prasad
The tribal culture of India / L. P. Vidyarthi, B. K. Rai. — 2nd ed. — New Delhi : Concept Publishing, 1985. — 488p. — *Previous ed: 1976. — Includes bibliographical references*

ETHNOLOGY — India — Research — India

Survey of research in sociology and social anthropology, 1969-1979. — 1st ed. — New Delhi : Satvahan, 1985-1986. — 3 v.. — "A project sponsored by the Indian Council of Social Science Research.". — *Includes bibliographies and indexes*

ETHNOLOGY — India — Madhya Pradesh

KURUP, Ayyappan Madhava
Continuity and change in a little community : a study of the Bharias of Patalkot in Madhya Pradesh / A. M. Kurup. — New Delhi : Concept Publishing, 1985. — 140p. — *Includes references*

ETHNOLOGY — India — West Bengal

BOSE, P. K.
Classes and class relations among tribals of Bengal / Pradip Kumar Bose. — 1st ed. — Delhi : Ajanta Publications : Distributors, Ajanta Books International, 1985. — viii, 132 p.. — *Includes index. — Bibliography: p. [126]-128*

ETHNOLOGY — Indonesia

TAN, Mely G
Ethnicity and fertility in Indonesia / by Mely G. Tan and Budi Soeradji. — Singapore : Institute of Southeast Asian Studies, 1986. — xiv, 143 p.. — (Research notes and discussions paper ; no. 53) (Ethnicity and fertility in Southeast Asia series). — *Bibliography: p. 143*

ETHNOLOGY — Indonesia — Mamboru

NEEDHAM, Rodney
Mamboru : history and structure in a domain of Northwestern Sumba / Rodney Needham. — Oxford : Clarendon, 1987. — xxv,202p,[6]p of plates. — *Bibliography: p194-200. — Includes index*

ETHNOLOGY — Israel

EISENSTADT, S. N.
The development of the ethnic problem in Israeli society : observations and suggestions for research / S. N. Eisenstadt. — Jerusalem : Jerusalem Institute for Israel Studies, 1986. — 45p. — (Jerusalem Institute for Israel Studies ; no.17)

ETHNOLOGY — Japan

MOERAN, Brian
Okubo diary : portrait of a Japanese valley / Brian Moeran. — Stanford, Calif. : Stanford University, 1985. — p. cm. — *Bibliography: p*

ETHNOLOGY — Japan — Ryukyu Islands

OUWEHAND, Cornelius
Hateruma : socio-religious aspects of a South Ryukyuan island culture / C. Ouwehand. — Leiden : Brill, 1985. — 324,(73)p

ETHNOLOGY — Latvia

ZAVARINA, A. A.
Russkoe naselenie vostochnoi Latvii vo vtoroi polovine XIX - nachale XX veka : istoriko-etnograficheskii ocherk / A. A. Zavarina. — Riga : Zinatne, 1986. — 246p

ETHNOLOGY — Mediterranean region

DAVIS, John, 1938-
People of the Mediterranean : an essay in comparative social anthropology / J. Davis. — London : Routledge and Kegan Paul, 1977. — xi,288p. — (Library of man). — *Bibliography: p.261-279. — Includes index*

ETHNOLOGY — Melanesia

ERRINGTON, Frederick Karl
Karavar: masks and power in a Melanesian ritual. — Ithaca [N.Y.] : Cornell University Press, [1974]. — 259 p. — (Symbol, myth, and ritual series). — *Bibliography: p. 255-256*

ETHNOLOGY — Morocco

DWYER, Kevin
Moroccan dialogues : anthropology in question / Kevin Dwyer. — Baltimore : Johns Hopkins University Press, c1982. — xxvii, 297 p.. — *Includes dialogues between Kevin Dwyer and Faqir Muhammad. — Includes index. — Bibliography: p. 289-292*

ETHNOLOGY — Nepal

REGMI, Rishikeshab Raj
Cultural patterns and economic change : (anthropological study of Dhimals of Nepal) / Rishikeshab Raj Regmi. — Delhi : Motilal Banarasi Dass, 1985. — iii,218p. — *Includes glossary of local terms used: p[212]-218. — Bibliography: p[204]-212*

ETHNOLOGY — Netherlands

Current anthropology in the Netherlands / edited by Peter Kloos and Henri J. M. Claessen. — Rotterdam : Anthropological Branch of the Netherlands Sociological and Anthropological Society. — 184p. — *Includes references*

ETHNOLOGY — New Guinea

RUBEL, Paula G
Your own pigs you may not eat : a comparative study of New Guinea societies / Paula G. Rubel, Abraham Rosman. — Chicago : University of Chicago Press, 1978. — xiv, 368 p.. — *Includes index. — Bibliography: p. 347-359*

ETHNOLOGY — New Guinea — Art

GERBRANDS, Adrian A.
Wow-ipits : eight Asmat woodcarvers of New Guinea / Adrian A. Gerbrands ; [translated from the dutch by Inez Wolf Seeger]. — The Hague : Mouton, c1967. — 191p. — (Art in its context : studies in ethno-aesthetics. field reports ; v.3). — *Bibliography: p[173]-174*

ETHNOLOGY — New Zealand — Statistics

BROWN, P. G.
An investigation of official ethnic statistics / P. G. Brown. — Wellington : Department of Statistics, 1983. — . — (Occasional paper / Department of Statistics ; no.5). —
Bibliographical references: p70-71

ETHNOLOGY — Oceania

Cultures of the Pacific : selected readings / edited and with introductions by Thomas G. Harding and Ben J. Wallace. — New York : The Free Press ; London : Collier-Macmillan, [1970]. — xv,496p. — *Includes bibliographical references*

Shared wealth and symbol : food, culture, and society in Oceania and Southeast Asia / edited by Lenore Manderson. — Cambridge : Cambridge University Press, 1987. — xii,314p. — *Bibliography: p283-308. — Includes index*

ETHNOLOGY — Papua New Guinea

ERRINGTON, Frederick Karl
Karavar: masks and power in a Melanesian ritual. — Ithaca [N.Y.] : Cornell University Press, [1974]. — 259 p. — (Symbol, myth, and ritual series). — *Bibliography: p. 255-256*

ETHNOLOGY — Papua New Guinea
continuation

GELBER, Marilyn G
Gender and society in the New Guinea Highlands : an anthropological perspective on antagonism toward women / Marilyn G. Gelber. — Boulder : Westview Press, 1986. — xi, 180 p.. — (Women in cross-cultural perspective). — *Includes index.* — *Bibliography: p. [159]-175*

KAHN, Miriam
Always hungry, never greedy : food and the expression of gender in a Melanesian society / Miriam Kahn. — Cambridge : Cambridge University Press, 1986. — xx,187p. — *Bibliography: p174-181.* — *Includes index*

LEDERMAN, Rena
What gifts engender : social relations and politics in Mendi, Highland Papua New Guinea / Rena Lederman. — Cambridge : Cambridge University Press, 1986. — [297]p. — *Includes bibliography and index*

MUSKO, Mark S.
Quadripartite structures : categories, relations and homologies in Bush Mekeo culture / Mark S. Musko. — Cambridge : Cambridge University Press, 1985. — xiii,298p. — *Bibliography: p278-288.* — *Includes index*

ETHNOLOGY — Papua New Guinea — Field work

READ, Kenneth E
Return to the high valley : coming full circle / Kenneth E. Read. — Berkeley : University of California Press, c1986. — xxi, 269 p., [8] p. of plates. — (Studies in Melanesian anthropology) . — *Includes bibliographical references and index*

ETHNOLOGY — Papua New Guinea — Gawa

MUNN, Nancy D.
The fame of Gawa : a symbolic study of value tranformation in a Massim (Papua New Guinea) society / Nancy D. Munn. — Cambridge : Cambridge University Press, 1987. — xviii,331p. — (The Lewis Henry Morgan lectures ; 1976). — *Bibliography: p317-325.* — *Includes index*

ETHNOLOGY — Scotland

FENTON, Alexander
The shape of the past 1 : essays in Scottish ethnology / Alexander Fenton. — Edinburgh : John Donald, 1985. — viii,186p. — *Bibliography: p176-186*

ETHNOLOGY — Somalia

LEWIS, I. M.
A pastoral democracy : a study of pastoralism and politics among the Northern Somali of the Horn of Africa / I. M. Lewis. — London : Oxford University Press, 1961. — xiii,320p

ETHNOLOGY — South Africa

KUPER, Adam
South Africa and the anthropologist / Adam Kuper. — London : Routledge & Kegan Paul, 1987. — [xii,220]p. — *Includes bibliography and index*

The Politics of race, class and nationalism in twentieth century South Africa / edited by Shula Marks and Stanley Trapido. — Harlow : Longman, 1987. — 1v.. — *Includes index*

ETHNOLOGY — Soviet Union

Sotsial'no kul'turnyi oblik sovetskikh natsii : po rezul'tatam etnosotsiologicheskogo issledovaniia / otv. redaktory: Iu. V. Arutiunian, Iu. V. Bromlei. — Moskva : Nauka, 1986. — 453p. — *Table of contents in English*

Sovremennye etnosotsial'nye protsessy na sele / otv. redaktor Iu. V. Arutiunian. — Moskva : Nauka, 1986. — 247p. — *Table of contents in English*

ETHNOLOGY — Soviet Union, Northern

KUOLJOK, Kerstin Eidlitz
The revolution in the north : Soviet ethnography and nationality policy / Kerstin Eidlitz Kuoljok ; translated by T. J. M. Gray and N. Tomkinson. — Uppsala : [Universitet] ; Stockholm : Almquist and Wiksell, 1985. — x,185p. — (Acta Universitatis Upsaliensis / Studia Multiethnica Upsaliensia ; no.I) (Uppsala Research Reports in Cultural Anthropology ; 1). — *Bibliography: p173-182*

ETHNOLOGY — Spain

FERNANDEZ, James W
Persuasions and performances : the play of tropes in culture / James W. Fernandez. — Bloomington : Indiana University Press, c1986. — xv, 304 p.. — *Includes bibliographies and index*

ETHNOLOGY — Spain — Ronda

CORBIN, J. R.
Urbane thought : culture and class in an Andalusian city / J.R. Corbin and M.P. Corbin. — Aldershot : Gower, c1987. — v,213p. — (Studies in Spanish anthropology ; 2). — *Bibliography: p193-199.* — *Includes index*

ETHNOLOGY — United States — Addresses, essays, lectures

A melting pot or a nation of minorities / [by] Robert L. Payton...[et al.] ; edited by W. Lawson Taitte ; with an introduction by Andrew R. Cecil. — Dallas : University of Texas, 1986. — 205p. — (Andrew R. Cecil Lectures on Moral Values in a Free Society ; vol.7)

ETHNOLOGY — United States — Congresses

Farm work and fieldwork : American agriculture in anthropological perspective / edited by Michael Chibnik. — Ithaca : Cornell University Press, 1987. — 293 p.. — (Anthropology of contemporary issues). — *Includes bibliographies and index*

ETHNOMETHODOLOGICAL

Ethnomethodological studies of work / edited by Harold Garfinkel. — London ; New York : Routledge and Kegan Paul, 1986. — viii,196p

ETHNOMETHODOLOGY

SHARROCK, W. W.
The ethnomethodologists / Wes Sharrock and Bob Anderson. — Chichester : Ellis Horwood, 1986. — xii,121p. — (Key sociologists). — *Includes index*

ETHNOPHILOSOPHY — Africa, Sub-Saharan

KRIEL, Abraham
Roots of African thought / Abraham Kriel. — Cape Town : A.A. Balkema, 1984-. — v. <1 >. — *Bibliography: v. 1, p. 165-168.* — *Contents: 1. Manipulating actions*

ETHNOPSYCHOLOGY

The cultural transition : human experience and social transformation in the Third World and Japan / edited by Merry I. White and Susan Pollack. — London : Routledge and Kegan Paul, 1986. — xiii,302p

WALLACE, Edwin R
Freud and anthropology : a history and reappraisal / Edwin R. Wallace, IV. — New York : International Universities Press, c1983. — xi, 306p. — (Psychological issues ; monograph 55). — *Bibliography: p.281-294.* — *Includes index*

ETHNOPSYCHOLOGY — Case studies

MERRY, Sally Engle
Urban danger : life in a neighborhood of strangers / Sally Engle Merry. — Philadelphia : Temple University Press, 1981. — x, 278 p.. — *Includes index.* — *Bibliography: p. [259]-272*

ETHNOZOOLOGY — Addresses, essays, lectures

Indigenous knowledge systems and development / edited by David Brokensha, D. M. Warren, and Oswald Werner. — Washington, D.C. : University Press of America, c1980. — vii, 466 p.. — *Includes indexes.* — *Bibliography: p. 415-449*

EUGENICS

KEVLES, Daniel J.
In the name of eugenics : genetics and the uses of human heredity / Daniel Jo Kevles. — Harmondsworth : Penguin, 1986. — x,426p. — (Pelican books). — *Previously published: New York : Knopf, 1986*

WARREN, Mary Anne
Gendercide : the implications of sex selection / Mary Anne Warren. — Totowa, N.J. : Rowman & Allanheld, 1985. — viii, 209 p.. — (New feminist perspectives). — *Includes bibliographies and index*

EUORPEAN ECONOMIC COMMUNITY — Spain

MUÑOZ MACHADO, Santiago
El Estado, el derecho interno y la Comunidad Europea / Santiago Muñoz Machado. — Madrid : Editorial Civitas, 1986. — 300p. — *Bibliography: p[291]-300*

EURATOM SUPPLY AGENCY

EURATOM SUPPLY AGENCY
Annual report / Euratom Supply Agency. — Luxembourg : Office for Official Publications of the European Communities, 1983-. — *Annual*

EURO-DOLLAR MARKET

CHITALE, V. P
India and Euro-currency markets / V.P. Chitale. — New Delhi : Economic and Scientific Research Foundation, [1984]. — viii, 150 p.. — *Includes bibliographical references*

JOHNSTON, R. B.
Theories of the growth of the Euro—currency market : a review of the Euro—currency deposit multiplier / by R. B. Johnston. — Basle : Bank for International Settlements, 1981. — 52p. — (BIS economic papers ; no.4)

MCCLAM, Warren D.
US monetary aggregates, income velocity and the euro-dollar market / by Warren D. McClam. — Basle : Bank for International Settlements, 1980. — 43p. — (BIS economic papers ; no.2)

EUROPE — Armed Forces

The Defence of Western Europe / edited by L.H. Gann. — London : Croom Helm, c1987. — 317p. — *Includes index*

EUROPE — Biography

RIEBEN, Henri
Une lettre / Henri Rieben. — Lausanne : Fondation Jean Monnet pour l'Europe. Centre de Recherches Européennes, 1986. — 33p

EUROPE — Church history

HAMILTON, Bernard
Religion in the medieval West / Bernard Hamilton. — London : Edward Arnold, 1986. — vii,216p. — *Bibliography: p202-212.* — *Includes index*

EUROPE — Civilization

Liber amicorum Henri Brugmans : au service de l'Europe : études et témoignages édités a` l'occasion de son soixante-quinzième anniversaire = Liber amicorum Henri Brugmans : striving for Europe : studies and tributes published on the occasion of his seventy-fifth birthday. — Amsterdam : European Cultural Foundation, 1981. — 590p

EUROPE — Civilization
continuation

LICHTHEIM, George
[Selections. 1986]. Thoughts among the ruins : collected essays on Europe and beyond / George Lichtheim ; new introduction by Walter Laqueur. — New Brunswick (U.S.A.) : Transaction Books, [1986], c1973. — xxix, 492 p.. — *"First paperback edition"--T.p. verso. — "Introduction ... first appeared in Commentary magazine, August 1973"--T.p. verso. — : Reprint. Originally published: Collected essays. New York : Viking Press, 1973*

Politics and culture in early modern Europe : essays in honor of H.G. Koenigsberger / edited by Phyllis Mack and Margaret C. Jacob. — Cambridge : Cambridge University Press, 1987. — [538]p. — *Includes bibliography and index*

EUROPE — Civilization — 18th century — Sources

The age of Enlightenment / edited by Simon Eliot and Beverley Stern. — London : Ward Lock [for] the Open University Press, 1979. — (Set books / Open University)
Vol.1. — vi,345p. — *Includes index*

The age of Enlightenment / edited by Simon Eliot and Beverley Stern. — London : Ward Lock [for] the Open University Press, 1979. — (Set books / Open University)
Vol.2. — xv,264p,[16]p of plates. — *Includes index*

EUROPE — Commerce — Japan

MOORHOUSE, James, 1924-
Righting the balance : a new agenda for Euro-Japanese trade / James Moorhouse and Anthony Teasdale. — London : Conservative Political Centre, 1987. — 87p

EUROPE — Defences

FREEDMAN, Lawrence
Arms control : management or reform? / Lawrence Freedman. — London : Routledge & Kegan Paul, 1986. — 102p. — (Chatham House papers ; 31)

EUROPE — Defenses

Arms control and the arms race : readings from Scientific American / with introductions by Bruce Russett, Fred Chernoff. — New York : W.H. Freeman, c1985. — viii, 229 p.. — *Includes index. — Bibliography: p. [217]-222*

BONIFACE, Pascal
La puce, les hommes et la bombe : lÉurope face aux nouveau défis technologiques et militaires / Pascal Boniface, François Heisbourg ; Préface dÁndré Fontaine. — Paris : Hachette, [1986]. — 321p. — *Bibliography: p310-314*

BRECCIA, Alfredo
L'Italia e la difesa dell'Europa : alle origini del "Piano Pleven" / Alfredo Breccia. — Roma : Istituto di Studi Europei A. de Gasperi, 1984. — 274p. — *Bibliography: p257-261*

Evolving European defense policies / edited by Catherine M. Kelleher and Gale A. Mattox. — Lexington, Mass. : Lexington Books, c1987. — p. cm. — *Includes index*

LANGER, Peter H.
Transatlantic discord and NATO's crisis of cohesion / Peter H. Langer. — Washington, D.C. : Pergamon-Brassey's, 1986. — p. cm. — (Foreign policy report). — *"A publication of the Institute for Foreign Policy Analysis, Inc.". — Bibliography: p*

MASTNY, Vojtech
Helsinki, human rights, and European security : analysis and documentation / Vojtech Mastny. — Durham : Duke University Press, 1986. — xvi, 389 p.. — *Includes index*

PROBLEMS DE SEGURIDAD EUROPEA Y DESPLIEGUE DE SISTEMAS DE ALCANCE MEDIO (1984 : Madrid)
Problemas de seguridad europea y despliegue de sistemas de alcance medio : simposio internacional celebrado en el Auditorio del Ministerio de Hacienda, Madrid, mayo de 1984. — [Madrid] : Instituto de Cuestiones Internacionales : Fundación Friedrich Ebert, c1984. — 303p

EUROPE — Defenses — Addresses, essays, lectures

Ten years after Helsinki : the making of the European security regime / edited by Kari Möttölä. — Boulder, Colo. : Westview Press, 1986. — x, 184 p.. — (Westview special studies in international security). — *"Published in cooperation with the Finnish Institute of International Affairs"--P. [iv]. — Includes bibliographies and index*

EUROPE — Defenses — Congresses

ATLANTISCHE COMMISSIE. International Round Table Conference (1985 : Hague, Netherlands)
The future of European defence : proceedings of the Second International Round Table Conference of the Netherlands Atlantic Commission on May 24 and 25, 1985 / Frans Bletz and Rio Praaning [editors]. — Dordrecht ; Boston : M. Nijhoff, 1986. — p. cm

EUROPE — Dependency on foreign countries

Self-reliant development in Europe : theory, problems, actions / edited by Michel Bassand ... [et al.]. — Aldershot : Gower, c1986. — vi,234p. — *Conference proceedings. — Bibliography: p217-234*

EUROPE — Economic and conditions — 1945-

Growth to limits : the western European welfare states since World War II / edited by Peter Flora. — Berlin ; New York : W. de Gruyter, 1986-. — v. <1-2, >. — (Series C--Political and social sciences =Sciences politiques et sociales ; 6). — *Includes bibliographies. — Contents: v. 1. Sweden, Norway, Finland, Denmark -- v. 2. Germany, United Kingdom, Ireland, Italy*

EUROPE — Economic co-operation

BOGNÁR, J.
Politique internationale, securité européenne et coopération económique (faits, rapports de forces et possibilités en été 1972) / J. Bognár. — Budapest : Conseil Scientifique Hongrois D'Économie Mondiale, 1972. — 18p. — (Tendances dans l'économie mondiale ; no.9)

EUROPE — Economic conditions

Annali / Istituto di Studi Europei A. De Gasperi. — Roma : Istituto di Studi Europei A. De Gasperi, 1979-. — *Annual*

Handbuch der Europäischen Wirtschafts- und Sozialgeschichte / herausgegeben von Wolfram Fischer...[et al.]. — Stuttgart : Klett-Cotta
Bd.3: Europäische Wirtschafts- und Sozialgeschichte vom ausgehenden Mittelalter bis zur Mitte des 17. Jahrhunderts / unter Mitarbeit von Norbert Angermann...[et al.] ; herausgegeben von Hermann Kellenbenz. — 1986. — xxvi,1326p

EUROPE — Economic conditions — Statistics

State, economy and society in Western Europe 1815-1975 : a data handbook in two volumes / Peter Flora, Franz Kraus and Winfried Pfenning [compilers]. — Frankfurt : Campus ; London : Macmillan
Vol.2: The growth of industrial societies and capitalist economies. — 1987. — 758p

EUROPE — Economic conditions — To 1492

DAY, John, 1924-
The medieval market economy / John Day. — Oxford : Basil Blackwell, 1987. — [288]p. — *Includes bibliography and index*

EUROPE — Economic conditions — 1945-

Economically active population : estimates and projections : 1950-2025 = Evaluations et projections de la population active : 1950-2025 = Estimaciones y proyecciones de la población económicamente activa : 1950-2025. — 3rd ed. — Geneva : International Labour Office
V.4: Northern America, Europe, Oceania and USSR. — 1986. — xxvi,177p. — *Introduction and table headings in English, French and Spanish*

Europe at the crossroads : agendas of the crisis / edited by Stefan A. Musto, Carl F. Pinkele. — New York : Praeger, 1985. — p. cm

HOGAN, Michael J., 1943-
The Marshall Plan : America, Britain, and the reconstruction of Western Europe, 1947-1952 / Michael J. Hogan. — Cambridge : Cambridge University Press, 1987. — xiv,482p. — *Bibliography: p446-463. — Includes index*

KINDLEBERGER, Charles P.
Marshall Plan days / Charles P. Kindleberger. — Boston ; London : Allen & Unwin, 1987. — [250]p. — *Includes bibliography and index*

Liber amicorum Henri Brugmans : au service de l'Europe : études et témoignages édités a` l'occasion de son soixante-quinzième anniversaire = Liber amicorum Henri Brugmans : striving for Europe : studies and tributes published on the occasion of his seventy-fifth birthday. — Amsterdam : European Cultural Foundation, 1981. — 590p

SCHULTZE, Charles L
Other times, other places : macroeconomic lessons from U.S. and European history / Charles L. Schultze. — Washington, D.C. : Brookings Institution, c1986. — p. cm. — *Includes index*

Self-reliant development in Europe : theory, problems, actions / edited by Michel Bassand ... [et al.]. — Aldershot : Gower, c1986. — vi,234p. — *Conference proceedings. — Bibliography: p217-234*

WINIECKI, Jan
Economic prospects - East and West : a view from the East / Jan Winiecki ; comment: Roger Clarke. — London : Centre for Research into Communist Economies, 1987. — 136p. — (Understanding economic systems ; 3) . — *Bibliography: 123-127*

EUROPE — Economic integration

BARRE, Raymond
Un plan pour l'Europe : la Communauté européenne, problèmes et perspectives / Raymond Barre. — [Nancy] : Presses universitaires de Nancy, c1984. — 59p. — (Travaux du Centre européen universitaire)

BEUGEL, Ernst Hans van der
From Marshall Aid to Atlantic partnership : European integration as a concern of American foreign policy / Ernst Hans van der Beugel. — Amsterdam : Elsevier, 1966. — 480p

KOZMA, F.
Facteurs déterminant caractère des processus d intégration économique en Europe orientale et occidentale / F. Kozma. — Budapest : Conseil Scientifique Hongrois d'Économie Mondiale, 1974. — 63p. — (Tendances dans l'économie mondiale ; no.13)

MENDES, A. J. Marques
Economic integration and growth in Europe / A.J. Marques Mendes. — London : Croom Helm, c1987. — 141p. — *Bibliography: p129-135. — Includes index*

OVERTURF, Stephen Frank
The economic principles of European integration / Stephen Frank Overturf. — New York : Praeger, 1986. — xiii, 173 p.. — *Includes index. — Bibliography: p. 167*

EUROPE — Economic integration — Congresses
Integration and unequal development : the experience of the EEC / edited by Dudley Seers and Constantine Vaitsos, with the assistance of Marja-Liisa Kiljunen. — New York : St. Martin's Press, 1980. — xxi, 359 p.. — (Studies in the integration of Western Europe). — Based on the papers commissioned for discussion at the Institute of Development Studies (IDS) at the University of Sussex in May-June 1979.". — Includes bibliographical references and index

EUROPE — Economic policy
Europe at the crossroads : agendas of the crisis / edited by Stefan A. Musto, Carl F. Pinkele. — New York : Praeger, 1985. — p. cm

EUROPE — Economic policy — Congresses
ROUND TABLE ON TRANSPORT ECONOMICS (41st : 1978 : Paris)
The role of transport in counter-cyclical policy : report of the forty-first Round Table on Transport Economics, held in Paris on 2nd-3rd March, 1978 ... — Paris : Organisation for Economic Co-operation and Development. — 61p. — At head of title: Economic Research Centre. — Bibliography: p47-48

EUROPE — Emigration and immigration
CONSULTATIVE GROUP ON ETHNIC MINORITIES (1983 : The Hague)
Migration and health : towards an understanding of the health care needs of ethnic minorities : proceedings of a Consultative Group on Ethnic Minorities, The Hague, Netherlands 28-30 November 1983 / edited by M. Colledge, H. A. van Geuns and P. -G. Svensson. — Copenhagen : World Health Organization, Regional Office for Europe, 1986. — vii,203p. — Includes bibliographical references

Labour supply and migration in Europe : demographic dimensions 1950-1975 and prospects / prepared by the Secretariat of the Economic Commission for Europe. — New York : United Nations, 1979. — xi,332p. — "Economic survey of Europe in 1977: part II". — Sales no.: E.78.II.E.20

EUROPE — Foreign economic relations
TINBERGEN, Jan
L'Europe et le nouvel ordre economique international / Jan Tinbergen. — Bruxelles : Fondation Paul-Henri Spaak, 1977. — 23p

EUROPE — Foreign economic relations — Eastern Europe
VOGEL, Heinrich
Western economic policy toward Eastern Europe / Heinrich Vogel. — Paris : Atlantic Institute for International Affairs, 1986. — 39p. — (Atlantic papers ; no.61). — Bibliography: p35-37

EUROPE — Foreign economic relations — Latin America — Bibliography
Trade relations between Latin America and Europe = Les relations commerciales entre l'Amérique Latine et l'Europe. — Geneva : United Nations Library, 1978. — 57p

EUROPE — Foreign economic relations — Persian Gulf States
YORKE, Valerie
European interests and Gulf oil / Valerie York and Louis Turner. — Aldershot : Gower, c1986. — x,125p. — (Energy papers ; no.17). — Includes index

EUROPE — Foreign economic relations — United States — Addresses, essays, lectures
New directions in economic and security policy : U.S.-West European relations in a period of crisis and indecision / edited by Werner J. Feld. — Boulder : Westview Press, 1985. — xiii, 93 p.. — "Sixth biannual symposium published in cooperation with the Institute for the Comparative Study of Public Policy, the University of New Orleans/the University of Innsbruck.". — Includes bibliographies

EUROPE — Foreign relations
RUSSELL, Joycelyne G.
Peacemaking in the Renaissance / Joycelyne G. Russell. — London : Duckworth, 1986. — x,278p,[8]p of plates. — Bibliography: p257-267. — Includes index

EUROPE — Foreign relations — 1871-1918
DOCKRILL, M. L
The formulation of a continental foreign policy by Great Britain, 1908-1912 / Michael Lawrence Dockrill. — New York : Garland, 1986. — 407 p.. — (Outstanding theses from the London School of Economics and Political Science). — Bibliography: p. 399-407

EUROPE — Foreign relations — 20th century
Evropa XX veka : problemy mira i bezopasnosti / [red. kollegiia: A. O. Chubarian...et al.]. — Moskva : mezhdunarodnye otnosheniia, 1985. — 268p

EUROPE — Foreign relations — 1945-
CARMOY, Guy de
Western Europe in world affairs : continuity, change, and challenge / Guy de Carmoy and Jonathan Story. — New York ; London : Praeger, 1986. — xx, 220p. — Includes indexes. — Bibliography: p.209-212

Ethics & European security / edited by Barrie Paskins. — London : Croom Helm, c1986. — 199p. — Includes index

Europe and Japan : changing relationships since 1945 / edited by Gordon Daniels and Reinhard Drifte. — Ashford : Norbury, 1985. — 1v.. — Includes index

Overcoming threats to Europe : a new deal for confidence and security / edited by Sverre Lodgaard and Karl Birnbaum. — Oxford : Oxford University Press, 1987. — ix,235p. — Under the auspices of Stockholm International Peace Research Institute. — Includes index

Partners and rivals in Western Europe : Britain, France and Germany / edited by Roger Morgan and Caroline Bray. — Aldershot : Gower, c1986. — [xviii,200]p. — At head of title: Policy Studies Institute (The European Centre for Political Studies). — Includes bibliography and index

EUROPE — Foreign relations — 1945- — Addresses, essays, lectures
Ten years after Helsinki : the making of the European security regime / edited by Kari Möttölä. — Boulder, Colo. : Westview Press, 1986. — x, 184 p.. — (Westview special studies in international security). — "Published in cooperation with the Finnish Institute of International Affairs"--P. [iv]. — Includes bibliographies and index

EUROPE — Foreign relations — Germany — Addresses, essays, lectures
German nationalism and the European response, 1890-1945 / edited by Carole Fink, Isabel V. Hull, and MacGregor Knox. — 1st ed. — Norman : University of Oklahoma Press, c1985. — xv, 299 p.. — Includes bibliographical references and index

EUROPE — Foreign relations — Germany (East)
FREY, Eric G
Division and detente : the Germanies and their alliances / Eric G. Frey. — New York : Praeger, 1987. — xvi, 194 p.. — Includes index. — Bibliography: p. 173-183

EUROPE — Foreign relations — Germany (West)
FREY, Eric G
Division and detente : the Germanies and their alliances / Eric G. Frey. — New York : Praeger, 1987. — xvi, 194 p.. — Includes index. — Bibliography: p. 173-183

EUROPE — Foreign relations — Great Britain
DOCKRILL, M. L
The formulation of a continental foreign policy by Great Britain, 1908-1912 / Michael Lawrence Dockrill. — New York : Garland, 1986. — 407 p.. — (Outstanding theses from the London School of Economics and Political Science). — Bibliography: p. 399-407

EUROPE — Foreign relations — Japan
Europe and Japan : changing relationships since 1945 / edited by Gordon Daniels and Reinhard Drifte. — Ashford : Norbury, 1985. — 1v.. — Includes index

EUROPE — Foreign relations — Near East
GREAT BRITAIN. Parliament. House of Commons. Library. International Affairs Section
Western Europe and the Palestinian question / Richard War. — [London] : the Library, 1981. — 29p. — (Background paper / House of Commons. Library. [Research Division] ; no.94). — Bibliography: p24

EUROPE — Foreign relations — Soviet Union
JENTLESON, Bruce W.
Pipeline politics : the complex political economy of East-West energy trade / Bruce W. Jentleson. — Ithaca, N.Y. : Cornell University Press, 1986. — 263 p.. — (Cornell studies in political economy). — Includes index. — Bibliography: p. 247-256

MINC, Alain
Le syndrone finlandais / Alain Minc. — Paris : Seuil, [1986]. — 232p

PLATT, Alan
Soviet-West European relations : recent trends and near-term prospects / Alan Platt. — Santa Monica (Calif.) : Rand, 1986. — xiii,50p

EUROPE — Foreign relations — United States
BEUGEL, Ernst Hans van der
From Marshall Aid to Atlantic partnership : European integration as a concern of American foreign policy / Ernst Hans van der Beugel. — Amsterdam : Elsevier, 1966. — 480p

JENTLESON, Bruce W.
Pipeline politics : the complex political economy of East-West energy trade / Bruce W. Jentleson. — Ithaca, N.Y. : Cornell University Press, 1986. — 263 p.. — (Cornell studies in political economy). — Includes index. — Bibliography: p. 247-256

LANGER, Peter H.
Transatlantic discord and NATO's crisis of cohesion / Peter H. Langer. — Washington, D.C. : Pergamon-Brassey's, 1986. — p. cm. — (Foreign policy report). — "A publication of the Institute for Foreign Policy Analysis, Inc.". — Bibliography: p

LEFFLER, Melvyn P.
The elusive quest : the America's pursuit of European stability and French security, 1919-1933 / by Melvyn P. Leffler. — Chapel Hill : University of North Carolina Press, c1979. — xvi, 409 p.. — Includes index. — Bibliography: p. 369-393

OLDAG, Andreas
Allianzpolitische Konflikte in der NATO : die sicherheitspolitischen Interessen der USA und Westeuropas zu Beginn der 80er Jahre / Andreas Oldag. — Baden-Baden : Nomos Verlagsgesellschaft, 1985. — vi,185p. — (Darstellungen zur internationalen Politik und Entwicklungspolitik ; 15). — Bibliography: p169-185

WALWORTH, Arthur
Wilson and his peacemakers : American diplomacy at the Paris Peace Conference, 1919 / Arthur Walworth. — New York ; London : W.W. Norton, 1986. — xiii, 618p. — Includes index. — Bibliography: p.572-585

EUROPE — Foreign relations — United States — Congresses

Reagan's leadership and the Atlantic Alliance : views from Europe and America / [edited by] Walter Goldstein. — Washington : Pergamon-Brassey, 1986. — p. cm. — *"Developed with the support of the Standing Conference of Atlantic Organizations.". — Papers presented at the 13th Annual Meeting of the Standing Conference of Atlantic Organizations, Wingspread House, Racine, Wisc., July 1985, sponsored by the Johnson Foundation and the Information Directorate of NATO*

EUROPE — Frontier troubles

Frontier regions in Western Europe / edited by Malcolm Anderson. — London : Cass, 1983. — 136p. — *First appeared in a special issue on 'Frontier regions in Western Europe' of West European politics, Vol.5, no.4*

EUROPE — Gentry — History

The Gentry and lesser nobility in late medieval Europe / edited by Michael Jones and R.L. Storey. — Gloucester : Sutton, 1986. — [192]p

EUROPE — History — 392-814

STAFFORD, Pauline
Queens, concubines, and dowagers : the king's wife in the early Middle Ages / Pauline Stafford. — Athens, Ga. : University of Georgia Press, c1983. — xiii, 248 p.. — *Includes index. — Bibliography: p. 211-226*

EUROPE — History — 15th century

The Gentry and lesser nobility in late medieval Europe / edited by Michael Jones and R.L. Storey. — Gloucester : Sutton, 1986. — [192]p

EUROPE — History — To 1492

DIOP, Cheikh Anta
[Afrique noire pré-coloniale. English]. Precolonial Black Africa : a comparative study of the political and social systems of Europe and Black Africa, from antiquity to the formation of modern states / Cheikh Anta Diop ; translated by Harold J. Salemson. — Westport, Conn. : L. Hill, 1986. — p. cm. — *Translation of: L'Afrique noire pré-coloniale*

EUROPE — History — 1492-1648

Politics and society in Reformation Europe : essays for Sir Geoffrey Elton on his sixty-fifth birthday / edited by Tom Scott and E.I. Kouri. — London : Macmillan, 1986. — [480]p. — *Includes index*

RUSSELL, Joycelyne G.
Peacemaking in the Renaissance / Joycelyne G. Russell. — London : Duckworth, 1986. — x,278p,[8]p of plates. — *Bibliography: p257-267. — Includes index*

ZAGORIN, Perez
Revueltas y revoluciones en la Edad Moderna / Perez Zagorin. — Madrid : Catedra 1: Movimientos campesinos y urbanos. — 1985. — 325p

EUROPE — History — 1648-1789

SHENNAN, J. H.
Liberty and order in early modern Europe : the subject and the State, 1650-1800 / J.H. Shennan. — London : Longman, 1986. — xii, 144p. — (Studies in modern history). — *Bibliography: p.129-136*

TREASURE, G. R. R.
The making of modern Europe : 1648-1780 / Geoffrey Treasure. — London : Methuen, 1985. — xvii,647p. — *Includes index*

EUROPE — History — 18th century

ANDERSON, M. S. (Matthew Smith)
Europe in the eighteenth century, 1713-1783 / M. S. Anderson. — 3rd ed. — London : Longman, 1987. — xii,539p. — (A general history of Europe)

COOK, Chris
The Longman handbook of modern European history 1763-1985 / Chris Cook and John Stevenson. — London : Longman, 1987. — [672]p. — *Includes bibliography and index*

EUROPE — History — 1789-1815

KISSINGER, Henry A.
A world restored : Metternich, Castlereagh and the problems of peace, 1812-22 / Henry Alfred Kissinger. — New York : Grosset and Dunlap, 1964. — 354p

EUROPE — History — 1789-1815 — Dictionaries

Historical dictionary of Napoleonic France, 1799-1815 / edited by Owen Connelly ; Harold T. Parker, Peter W. Becker, and June K. Burton, associate editors ; Janice Seaman Berbin, editorial assistant. — Westport, Conn. : Greenwood Press, 1985. — xiii, 586 p.. — *Includes index. — Bibliography: p. [587]-541*

EUROPE — History — 1789-1900

CRAIG, Gordon A.
Europe since 1815. — alternate ed.. — New York : Holt, Rinehart and Winston, 1974. — xv,620p. — *Bibliography: p575-596*

EUROPE — History — 19th century

COOK, Chris
The Longman handbook of modern European history 1763-1985 / Chris Cook and John Stevenson. — London : Longman, 1987. — [672]p. — *Includes bibliography and index*

EUROPE — History — 1815-1848

KISSINGER, Henry A.
A world restored : Metternich, Castlereagh and the problems of peace, 1812-22 / Henry Alfred Kissinger. — New York : Grosset and Dunlap, 1964. — 354p

EUROPE — History — 1815-1871

GILDEA, Robert
Barricades and borders : Europe, 1800-1914 / Robert Gildea. — Oxford : Oxford University Press, 1987. — [450]p. — (The Short Oxford history of the modern world). — *Includes bibliography and index*

EUROPE — History — 1848-1871

ROBERTSON, Priscilla
Revolutions of 1848 : a social history / Priscilla Robertson. — Princeton : Princeton University Press, 1952. — xi,464p

EUROPE — History — 1871-1918

GILDEA, Robert
Barricades and borders : Europe, 1800-1914 / Robert Gildea. — Oxford : Oxford University Press, 1987. — [450]p. — (The Short Oxford history of the modern world). — *Includes bibliography and index*

EUROPE — History — 20th century

BENNS, Frank Lee
Europe since 1914 in its world setting / Frank Lee Benns. — 8th ed. — New York : Appleton, 1957. — xx,833p

BLACK, C. E.
Twentieth century Europe : a history / C. E. Black and E. C. Helmreich. — 2nd ed. — New York : Alfred A. Knopf, 1964. — xx,865,xxiip

COOK, Chris
The Longman handbook of modern European history 1763-1985 / Chris Cook and John Stevenson. — London : Longman, 1987. — [672]p. — *Includes bibliography and index*

CRAIG, Gordon A.
Europe since 1815. — alternate ed.. — New York : Holt, Rinehart and Winston, 1974. — xv,620p. — *Bibliography: p575-596*

SONTAG, Raymond James
European diplomatic history 1871-1932 / Raymond James Sontag. — London : Century, 1933. — xi,425p

WESTERN, J. R.
The end of European primacy (1871-1945) / John Randle Western. — London : Blandford Press, 1965. — x,573p

WILLIS, F. Roy
France, Germany and the New Europe, 1945—1967 / F. Roy Willis. — Rev. and expanded ed. — Stanford, Calif. : Stanford University Press ; London : Oxford University Press, 1968. — 431 p

EUROPE — History — 1945-

BEYER, Henry
Robert Schuman : l'Europe par la reconciliation franco-allemande / Henry Beyer. — Lausanne : Centre de Recherches Européennes, 1986. — [174]p

NEUBERT, Harald
Europa 1945 - Europa 1985 : Realitäten, Wandlungen, Perspektiven / Harald Neubert. — Berlin : Dietz Verlag, 1985. — 227p

EUROPE — History, Military

HALE, J. R.
Renaissance war studies / J.R. Hale. — London : Hambledon, c1983. — x,524p,[90]p of plates. — (History series ; v.11). — *Includes text in Italian. — Includes index*

EUROPE — History, Military — 17th century

The origins of war in early modern Europe / edited by Jeremy Black. — Edinburgh : John Donald Publishers, 1987. — xiii,271p. — *Bibliography: p261-271*

EUROPE — History, Military — 18th century

The origins of war in early modern Europe / edited by Jeremy Black. — Edinburgh : John Donald Publishers, 1987. — xiii,271p. — *Bibliography: p261-271*

EUROPE — Industries — History

WRIGLEY, E. A.
People, cities and wealth : the transformation of traditional society / E.A. Wrigley. — Oxford : Basil Blackwell, 1987. — [400]p. — *Includes bibliography and index*

EUROPE — Kings and rulers

The Courts of Europe : politics, patronage, and royalty, 1400-1800 / [edited by A.G. Dickens ; with texts by A.G. Dickens ... et al.]. — New York : Greenwich House ; Distributed by Crown Publishers, 1984. — p. cm. — *Includes index. — Bibliography: p*

STRONG, Roy
Art and power : Renaissance festivals 1450-1650 / Roy Strong. — Woodbridge : Boydell, 1984. — xiii,227p,[ca.100]p of plates. — *Revision of: Splendour at court. London : Weidenfeld and Nicolson, 1973. — Includes index*

EUROPE — Literature — History — 19th century

DERRÉ, Jean René
Litterature et politique dans l'Europe du XIXe siècle / Jean René Derré. — Lyon : Presses Universities de Lyon, 1986. — 392p

EUROPE — Literature — Political aspects

DERRÉ, Jean René
Litterature et politique dans l'Europe du XIXe siècle / Jean René Derré. — Lyon : Presses Universities de Lyon, 1986. — 392p

EUROPE — Military policy

España, Europa, occidente : una política integrada de seguridad / textos de: José María de Areilza...[et al.] ; editado por: Bernhard Hagemeyer...[et al.]. — Madrid : Distribución y Comunicación, 1984. — 177p. — *Papers presented at an international colloquium organized by the Konrad Adenauer Stiftung in Madrid, 26-28 October, 1983*

Sicherheit für Westeuropa : alternative Sicherheits- und Militärpolitik / "Generale für Frieden und Abrüstung". — Hamburg : Rasch und Röhring, 1985. — 223p

EUROPE — National security

BOGNÁR, J.
Politique internationale, sécurité européenne et coopération ecónomique (faits, rapports de forces et possibilités en été 1972) / J. Bognár. — Budapest : Conseil Scientifique Hongrois D'Économie Mondiale, 1972. — 18p. — (Tendances dans l'économie mondiale ; no.9)

DEAN, Jonathan
Watershed in Europe : dismantling the East-West military confrontation / Jonathan Dean. — Lexington, Mass. : Lexington Books, 1986, c1987. — p. cm. — *Includes index*

GOETZE, Bernd A
Security in Europe : a crisis of confidence / Bernd A. Goetze. — New York : Praeger, 1984. — p. cm. — *Includes index. — Bibliography: p*

HUNTER, Robert Edwards
Security in Europe / Robert Edwards Hunter. — London : Elek, 1969. — 188p

The Neutral democracies and the new Cold War / edited by Bengt Sundelius. — Boulder, Colo. : Westview Press, 1987. — xi, 245 p.. — (Westview special studies in international relations). — *"Published in cooperation with the Swedish Institute of International Affairs, Stockholm.". — Includes index. — Bibliography: p. 218-220*

Overcoming threats to Europe : a new deal for confidence and security / edited by Sverre Lodgaard and Karl Birnbaum. — Oxford : Oxford University Press, 1987. — ix,235p. — *Under the auspices of Stockholm International Peace Research Institute. — Includes index*

EUROPE — National security — Addresses, essays, lectures

New directions in economic and security policy : U.S.-West European relations in a period of crisis and indecision / edited by Werner J. Feld. — Boulder : Westview Press, 1985. — xiii, 93 p.. — *"Sixth biannual symposium published in cooperation with the Institute for the Comparative Study of Public Policy, the University of New Orleans/the University of Innsbruck.". — Includes bibliographies*

EUROPE — Neutrality

The Neutral democracies and the new Cold War / edited by Bengt Sundelius. — Boulder, Colo. : Westview Press, 1987. — xi, 245 p.. — (Westview special studies in international relations). — *"Published in cooperation with the Swedish Institute of International Affairs, Stockholm.". — Includes index. — Bibliography: p. 218-220*

EUROPE — Occupations — History — Addresses, essays, lectures

Women and work in preindustrial Europe / edited by Barbara A. Hanawalt. — Bloomington : Indiana University Press, c1986. — xviii, 233 p.. — *Includes bibliographies and index*

EUROPE — Politics — 1945-

MORGAN, Roger
West European politics since 1945 : the shaping of the European Community / Roger Morgan. — London : Batsford, 1972. — x,243p. — *Bibliographyp.232-233. — Includes index*

EUROPE — Politics and government

Annali / Istituto di Studi Europei A. De Gasperi. — Roma : Istituto di Studi Europei A. De Gasperi, 1979-. — *Annual*

CARSTENS, Karl
Un souffle de renouveau en Europe / Karl Carstens. — Lausanne : Fondation Jean Monnet pour l'Europe. Centre de Recherches Européennes. — 29p

The Courts of Europe : politics, patronage, and royalty, 1400-1800 / [edited by A.G. Dickens ; with texts by A.G. Dickens ... et al.]. — New York : Greenwich House ; Distributed by Crown Publishers, 1984. — p. cm. — *Includes index. — Bibliography: p*

DIOP, Cheikh Anta
[Afrique noire pré-coloniale. English]. Precolonial Black Africa : a comparative study of the political and social systems of Europe and Black Africa, from antiquity to the formation of modern states / Cheikh Anta Diop ; translated by Harold J. Salemson. — Westport, Conn. : L. Hill, 1986. — p. cm. — *Translation of: L'Afrique noire pré-coloniale*

Les états-unis socialistes d'Europe / brochure diffusée par la Ligue Révolutionnaire des Travailleurs (Belgique), la Ligue Communiste (France) et la Ligue Marxiste Révolutionnaire (Suisse). — Paris : François Maspero, 1972. — 48p. — (Classique rouge ; no.10)

Frontier regions in Western Europe / edited by Malcolm Anderson. — London : Cass, 1983. — 136p. — *First appeared in a special issue on 'Frontier regions in Western Europe' of West European politics, Vol.5, no.4*

HALLSTEIN, Walter
United Europe : challenge and opportunity / Walter Hallstein. — London : Oxford University Press, 1962. — xiii,109p

The Languages of political theory in early-modern Europe / edited by Anthony Pagden. — Cambridge : Cambridge University Press, 1987. — [viii,280]p. — (Ideas in context). — *Includes index*

Les pays d'Europe occidentale / Documentation Française. — Paris : Documentation Française, 1986. — (Notes et études documentaires ; no.4813). — *Annual*

Politics and culture in early modern Europe : essays in honor of H.G. Koenigsberger / edited by Phyllis Mack and Margaret C. Jacob. — Cambridge : Cambridge University Press, 1987. — [538]p. — *Includes bibliography and index*

EUROPE — Politics and government — 1789-1815

NICOLSON, Harold
The congress of Vienna : a study in allied unity, 1812-1822 / Harold Nicolson. — London : Constable, 1946. — 312p

NICOLSON, Harold
The Congress of Vienna : a study in allied unity, 1812-1822 / Harold Nicolson. — London : Methuen, 1961. — 312p

EUROPE — Politics and government — 20th century

Evropa XX veka : problemy mira i bezopasnosti / [red. kollegiia: A. O. Chubarian...et al.]. — Moskva : mezhdunarodnye otnosheniia, 1985. — 268p

EUROPE — Politics and government — 1918-1945

KARSKI, Jan
The Great Powers & Poland, 1919-1945 : from Versailles to Yalta / Jan Karski. — Lanham, MD : University Press of America, c1985. — xvi, 697 p.. — *Includes index. — Bibliography: p. 627-671*

LEE, Stephen J.
The European dictatorships 1918-1945 / Stephen J. Lee. — London : Methuen, 1987. — xv,343p. — *Bibliography: p331-334. — Includes index*

LEFFLER, Melvyn P.
The elusive quest : the America's pursuit of European stability and French security, 1919-1933 / by Melvyn P. Leffler. — Chapel Hill : University of North Carolina Press, c1979. — xvi, 409 p.. — *Includes index. — Bibliography: p. 369-393*

EUROPE — Politics and government — 1945-

BARRE, Raymond
Un plan pour l'Europe : la Communauté européenne, problèmes et perspectives / Raymond Barre. — [Nancy] : Presses universitaires de Nancy, c1984. — 59p. — (Travaux du Centre européen universitaire)

GORDON, Lincoln
Eroding empire : Western relations with Eastern Europe / Lincoln Gordon, with J.F. Brown ... [et al.]. — Washington, D.C. : Brookings Institution, c1987. — xv, 359 p.. — *Includes bibliographical references and index*

Growth to limits : the western European welfare states since World War II / edited by Peter Flora. — Berlin ; New York : W. de Gruyter, 1986-. — v. <1-2, >. — (Series C--Political and social sciences =Sciences politiques et sociales ; 6). — *Includes bibliographies. — Contents: v. 1. Sweden, Norway, Finland, Denmark -- v. 2. Germany, United Kingdom, Ireland, Italy*

LANE, Jan-Erik
Politics and society in Western Europe / by Jan-Erik Lane & Svante O. Ersson. — London : Sage, 1986. — [352]p. — *Includes index*

Liber amicorum Henri Brugmans : au service de l'Europe : études et témoignages édités a` l'occasion de son soixante-quinzième anniversaire = Liber amicorum Henri Brugmans : striving for Europe : studies and tributes published on the occasion of his seventy-fifth birthday. — Amsterdam : European Cultural Foundation, 1981. — 590p

MILJAN, Toivo
The reluctant Europeans : the attitudes of the Nordic countries towards European integration / Toivo Miljan. — London : C. Hurst, 1977. — viii,325p. — *Bibliography: p.301-318. — Includes index*

MINC, Alain
Le syndrone finlandais / Alain Minc. — Paris : Seuil, [1986]. — 232p

NEUBERT, Harald
Europa 1945 - Europa 1985 : Realitäten, Wandlungen, Perspektiven / Harald Neubert. — Berlin : Dietz Verlag, 1985. — 227p

Opposition in Western Europe / edited by Eva Kolinsky. — London : Croom Helm, c1987. — [416]p. — *Includes bibliography and index*

Political stability and neo-corporatism : corporatist integration and societal cleavages in Western Europe / edited by Ilja Scholten. — London : Sage, 1987. — x,276p. — (Sage series in neo-corporatism). — *Includes bibliographies and index*

SAVINOV, K. I.
Varshavskii dogovor - faktor mira, shchit sotsializma / K. I. Savinov. — Moskva : Mezhdunarodnye otnosheniia, 1986. — 267p

SHIPLEY, Peter
Patterns of protest in Western Europe / Peter Shipley. — London : Institute for the Study of Conflict, 1986. — 23p. — (Conflict studies ; no.189)

The Social basis of European fascist movements / edited by Detlef Mühlberger. — London : Croom Helm, c1987. — [384]p. — *Includes index*

WOOD, David M.
Power and policy in Western European democracies / David M. Wood. — New York ; Chichester : Wiley, 1978. — ix,177p. — *Includes bibliographies and index*

EUROPE — Politics and government — 1945- — Addresses, essays, lectures

The Future of party government. — Berlin ; New York : W. de Gruyter, 1986-. — p. cm. — (Series C--Political and social sciences =Sciences politiques et sociales ; 5). — *"A series under the general editorship of Rudolf Wildenmann.". — Includes index (v. 1). — Contents: v. 1. Visions and realities of party government / edited by Francis G. Castles and Rudolf Wildenmann*

EUROPE — Politics and government — 1945- — Addresses, essays, lectures
continuation

The Origins of the cold war and contemporary Europe / edited with an introd. by Charles S. Maier. — New York : New Viewpoints, 1978. — xvi, 255 p.. — (Modern scholarship on European history). — Includes index. — Bibliography: p. 245-248

EUROPE — Politics and government — 1945- — Dictionaries

ROSSI, Ernest E
The European political dictionary / Ernest E. Rossi, Barbara P. McCrea. — Santa Barbara, Calif. : ABC-Clio Information Services, c1985. — p. cm. — (Clio dictionaries in political science ; #7). — Includes index

EUROPE — Popular culture — History

Inquisition and society in early modern Europe / edited and translated by Stephen Haliczer. — London : Croom Helm, c1987. — 196p. — Includes index

MULLETT, Michael A.
Popular culture and popular protest in late medieval and early modern Europe / Michael Mullett. — London : Croom Helm, c1987. — [9],176p. — Bibliography: p170-171. Includes index

EUROPE — Population — Congresses

EUROPEAN POPULATION CONFERENCE (1982 : Strasbourg)
Proceedings of the European Population Conference 1982 : Strasbourg, 21-24 September 1982. — Strasbourg : Council of Europe, 1983. — 473p. — Includes bibliographical references

EUROPE — Public opinion

The standing of the U.S. in West European opinion-1965 : (World Survey III series). — [Washington, D.C.] : United States Information Agency, 1965. — xii,59p. — R-145-65

EUROPE — Race relations

CRANFIELD-WOLFSON COLLOQUIUM ON MULTI-ETHNIC AREAS IN EUROPE (1983 : Cambridge)
Policing and social policy : [papers presented at the]...colloquium / edited by John Brown. — London : Police Review Publishing, [1984]. — 158p

EUROPE — Relations — Caribbean Area

HULME, Peter
Colonial encounters : Europe and the native Caribbean, 1492-1797 / Peter Hulme. — London : Methuen, 1986. — xv,348p. — Includes index. — Bibliography: p329-348

EUROPE — Relations — Soviet Union

JOHNSON, A. Ross
The impact of eastern Europe on Soviet policy toward western Europe / A. Ross Johnson. — Santa Monica, CA. : Rand, [1986]. — xv, 79 p. . — "A project Air Force report prepared for the United States Air Force.". — "March 1986.". — "R-3332-AF.". — Includes bibliographical references

VAN OUDENAREN, John
Soviet policy toward western Europe : objectives, instruments, results / John Van Oudenaren. — Santa Monica, CA : Rand, [1986]. — xi, 118 p.. — "A Project Air Force report, prepared for the United States Air Force.". — "February 1986.". — "R-3310-AF.". — Bibliography: p. 117-118

EUROPE — Relations — Spain

HERRERO DE MIÑON, Miguel
España y la Comunidad Económica Europea : Un sí para... / Miguel Herrero de Miñon. — Barcelona : Planeta, 1986. — 225p

EUROPE — Relations — United States

SERVAN-SCHREIBER, J. J.
The American challenge / J. J. Servan-Schreiber ; translated from the French by Ronald Steel ; with a foreword by Arthur Schlesinger, Jr.. — New York : Atheneum, 1979. — 254p. — Originally published as Le défi américain, by Denöel, 1967

EUROPE — Social conditions

Handbuch der Europäischen Wirtschafts- und Sozialgeschichte / herausgegeben von Wolfram Fischer...[et al.]. — Stuttgart : Klett-Cotta
Bd.3: Europäische Wirtschafts- und Sozialgeschichte vom ausgehenden Mittelalter bis zur Mitte des 17. Jahrhunderts / unter Mitarbeit von Norbert Angermann...[et al.] ; herausgegeben von Hermann Kellenbenz. — 1986. — xxvi,1326p

EUROPE — Social conditions — Statistics

State, economy and society in Western Europe 1815-1975 : a data handbook in two volumes / Peter Flora, Franz Kraus and Winfried Pfenning [compilers]. — Frankfurt : Campus ; London : Macmillan
Vol.2: The growth of industrial societies and capitalist economies. — 1987. — 758p

EUROPE — Social conditions — To 1492

MOORE, R. I.
The formation of a persecuting society : power and deviance in Western Europe, 950-1250 / R.I. Moore. — Oxford : Basil Blackwell, 1987. — [192]p. — Includes bibliography and index

The Settlement of disputes in early medieval Europe / edited by Wendy Davies and Paul Fouracre. — Cambridge : Cambridge University Press, 1986. — [549]p. — Includes index

EUROPE — Social conditions — 20th century

EISENSTADT, S. N.
European civilization in a comparative perspective : a study in the relations between culture and social structure / S.N. Eisenstadt. — Oslo : Norwegian University Press ; Oxford : Oxford University Press [distributors], c1987. — 162p. — (Scandinavian library). — Bibliography: p153-159. — Includes index

Growth to limits : the western European welfare states since World War II / edited by Peter Flora. — Berlin ; New York : W. de Gruyter, 1986-. — v. <1-2, >. — (Series C--Political and social sciences =Sciences politiques et sociales ; 6). — Includes bibliographies. — Contents: v. 1. Sweden, Norway, Finland, Denmark -- v. 2. Germany, United Kingdom, Ireland, Italy

Western Europe. — Rev. and updated / edited by Richard Mayne. — New York ; Oxford : Facts on File, 1987, c1986. — xvii,699p. — (Handbooks to the modern world). — Previous ed.: London : Blond, 1967. — Includes bibliographies and index

EUROPE — Social conditions — 1945-

Liber amicorum Henri Brugmans : au service de l'Europe : études et témoignages édités à l'occasion de son soixante-quinzième anniversaire = Liber amicorum Henri Brugmans : striving for Europe : studies and tributes published on the occasion of his seventy-fifth birthday. — Amsterdam : European Cultural Foundation, 1981. — 590p

EUROPE — Statistics, Vital

LYNGE, Elsebeth
Socio-economic differences in mortality in Europe : newly emerging trends in mortality / Elsebeth Lynge. — Strasbourg : Council of Europe, 1984. — 89p. — (Population studies / Council of Europe ; no.9)

State, economy and society in Western Europe 1815-1975 : a data handbook in two volumes / Peter Flora, Franz Kraus and Winfried Pfenning [compilers]. — Frankfurt : Campus ; London : Macmillan
Vol.2: The growth of industrial societies and capitalist economies. — 1987. — 758p

EUROPE — Strategic aspects

Overcoming threats to Europe : a new deal for confidence and security / edited by Sverre Lodgaard and Karl Birnbaum. — Oxford : Oxford University Press, 1987. — ix,235p. — Under the auspices of Stockholm International Peace Research Institute. — Includes index

EUROPE — Politics and government — 1815-1848

KISSINGER, Henry A.
A world restored / Henry A. Kissinger. — Gloucester, Man. : Peter Smith, 1973. — xi,354p. — Originally published, Houghton Mifflin, 1957. — Bibliography: p333-346

EUROPE, EASTERN

IONESCU, Ghita
The politics of the European Communist states / by Ghiţa Ionescu. — London : Weidenfeld & Nicolson, 1969. — viii,304p. — (Weidenfeld goldbacks). — Originally published (B67-14569) 1967. — bibl p291-297

EUROPE, EASTERN — Bibliography

HORAK, Stephan M.
Russia, the USSR, and Eastern Europe : a bibliographic guide to English language publications, 1975-1980 / Stephan M. Horak. — Littleton, Colo. : Libraries Unlimited, 1982. — 279 p.. — Supplements: Russia, the USSR, and Eastern Europe : a bibliographic guide to English language publications, 1964-1974 / Stephan M. Horak. 1978. — Includes index

EUROPE, EASTERN — Commercial policy

KÖVES, András
The CMEA countries in the world economy : turning inwards or turning outwards / by András Köves. — Budapest : Akadémiai Kiadó, 1985. — 247p. — Revised version of Hungarian original (Budapest,1980)

EUROPE, EASTERN — Description and travel

RUGG, Dean S.
Eastern Europe / Dean S. Rugg ; with a foreword by J.M. Houston. — London : Longman, 1985. — xxii,401p. — (The World's landscapes). — Bibliography: p368-382. — Includes index

EUROPE, EASTERN — Economic conditions

The economic history of Eastern Europe, 1919—1975. — Oxford : Clarendon Press
Vol.2: Interwar policy; The war and reconstruction / edited by M. C. Kaser and E. A. Radice. — 1986. — ix, 666p

KASER, M. C.
The economic history of eastern Europe 1919-1975. — Oxford : Oxford University Press
Vol.3: Institutional change within a planned economy. — July 1984. — [288]p

PIREC, Dušan
Kriza realnog socijalizma? : društveno-ekonomske karakteristike i protivurečnosti istočnoevropskih socijalističkih zemalja / Dušan Pirec. — Beograd : Ekonomika, 1985. — 412p. — Bibliography: p369-392

EUROPE, EASTERN — Economic conditions — 1945-

East European economic handbook. — London : Euromonitor, 1985. — [304]p

The economies of Eastern Europe and their foreign economic relations : colloquium, 9—11 April 1986, Brussels / Philip Joseph, editor = L'économie des pays d'Europe de l'Est et leurs relations economiques extérieures. — Brussels : NATO, 1986. — 363p

Power, purpose, and collective choice : economic strategy in socialist states / Ellen Comisso and Laura D'Andrea Tyson, editors. — Ithaca : Cornell University Press, 1986. — p. cm. — (Cornell studies in political economy) . — Published also as v. 40, no. 2 of the journal International organization

EUROPE, EASTERN — Economic conditions — 1945-
continuation

RESEARCH PROJECT ON NATIONAL INCOME IN EAST CENTRAL EUROPE
Occasional papers Nos.90-94 of the Research Project on National Income in East Central Europe / [by] Thad P. Alton...[et al.]. — New York : L. W. International Financial Research, Inc., 1986. — 1v(various pagings). — *Bibliography: [11p]. — Contents: Economic growth in Eastern Europe, 1970, and 1975-1985: Agricultural output, expenses and depreciation, gross product, and net product in Eastern Europe, 1965, 1970 and 1975-1985: Eastern Europe: Domestic Final Uses of Gross Product, 1970 and 1975-1985: Money Income of the Population and Standard of Living in Eastern Europe, 1970-1985: Measuring Industrial Growth of Yugoslavia, 1970-1985*

EUROPE, EASTERN — Economic integration

SELUCKY, Radoslav
The present dilemma of Soviet-East European integration / Radoslav Selucky. — Munchen : Projekt ´Crises in Soviet-type systems´, 1985. — 24p. — (Research project Crises in Soviet-type systems ; Study no.7)

EUROPE, EASTERN — Economic policy

Planning in Eastern Europe / [edited by] Andrew H. Dawson. — London : Croom Helm, c1987. — 348p. — (Croom Helm series in geography and environment)

Socialist economy and economic policy / edited by G. Fink. — Wien : Springer-Verlag, 1985. — 279p. — (Studien über Wirtschafts- und Systemvergleiche ; Bd.13). — *"Essays in honour of Friedrich Levcik". — Includes bibliographies*

EUROPE, EASTERN — Foreign economic relations

Socialist economy and economic policy / edited by G. Fink. — Wien : Springer-Verlag, 1985. — 279p. — (Studien über Wirtschafts- und Systemvergleiche ; Bd.13). — *"Essays in honour of Friedrich Levcik". — Includes bibliographies*

EUROPE, EASTERN — Foreign economic relations — Europe

VOGEL, Heinrich
Western economic policy toward Eastern Europe / Heinrich Vogel. — Paris : Atlantic Institute for International Affairs, 1986. — 39p. — (Atlantic papers ; no.61). — *Bibliography: p35-37*

EUROPE, EASTERN — Foreign economic relations — Soviet Union

CRANE, Keith
The Soviet economic dilemma of eastern Europe / Keith Crane. — Santa Monica, CA : Rand, [1986]. — xiii, 70 p.. — *"A Project Air Force report prepared for the United States Air Force.". — "R-3368-AF.". — "May 1986.". — Bibliography: p. 65-70*

SELUCKY, Radoslav
The present dilemma of Soviet-East European integration / Radoslav Selucky. — Munchen : Projekt ´Crises in Soviet-type systems´, 1985. — 24p. — (Research project Crises in Soviet-type systems ; Study no.7)

EUROPE, EASTERN — Foreign relations — 1945-

GARRETT, Stephen A.
From Potsdam to Poland : American policy toward Eastern Europe / Stepehn A. Garrett. — New York : Praeger, 1986. — ix, 237 p.. — *Includes index. — Bibliography: p. 221-232*

GORDON, Lincoln
Eroding empire : Western relations with Eastern Europe / Lincoln Gordon, with J.F. Brown ... [et al.]. — Washington, D.C. : Brookings Institution, c1987. — xv, 359 p.. — *Includes bibliographical references and index*

Vneshniaia politika stran Varshavskogo Dogovora : (pervaia polovina 80-kh godov) / otv. redaktor I. I. Orlik. — Moskva : Nauka, 1986. — 319p

EUROPE, EASTERN — Foreign relations — Soviet Union

Dominant powers and subordinate states : the United States in Latin America and the Soviet Union in Eastern Europe / edited by Jan F. Triska. — Durham, [N.C.] : Duke University Press, 1986. — xi, 504 p.. — (Duke Press policy studies). — *Includes index. — Bibliography: p. [471]-498*

FEHÉR, Ferenc
Eastern Europe under the shadow of a new Rapallo / Ferenc Fehér [and] Agnes Heller. — Munchen : Projekt ´Crises in Soviet-type systems´, 1984. — 38p. — (Research project Crises in Soviet-type systems ; Study no.6)

GATI, Charles
Hungary and the Soviet bloc / by Charles Gati. — Durham [N.C.] : Duke University Press, 1986. — 244 p.. — *Includes index. — Bibliography: p. [233]-237*

SSSR v bor'be protiv fashistskoi agressii 1933-1945 / otv. redaktor A. L. Norochnitskii. — 2-e izd., perer. i dop.. — Moskva : Nauka, 1986. — 349p. — *1st ed. 1976*

EUROPE, EASTERN — Foreign relations — United States

GARRETT, Stephen A.
From Potsdam to Poland : American policy toward Eastern Europe / Stepehn A. Garrett. — New York : Praeger, 1986. — ix, 237 p.. — *Includes index. — Bibliography: p. 221-232*

GORDON, Lincoln
Eroding empire : Western relations with Eastern Europe / Lincoln Gordon, with J.F. Brown ... [et al.]. — Washington, D.C. : Brookings Institution, c1987. — xv, 359 p.. — *Includes bibliographical references and index*

EUROPE, EASTERN — History

SETON-WATSON, Hugh
Eastern Europe between the wars, 1918-1941 / by Hugh Seton-Watson. — Boulder : Westview Press, 1986, c1982. — xvii, 425 p.. — *Includes index*

SUBTELNY, Orest
Domination of Eastern Europe : native nobilities and foreign absolutism, 1500-1715 / Orest Subtelny. — Kingston : McGill-Queen´s University Press ; Gloucester : Alan Sutton, 1986. — xii,270p

EUROPE, EASTERN — History — 1945-

SETON-WATSON, Hugh
The East European revolution / Hugh Seton-Watson. — Boulder : Westview Press, 1985. — xix, 451 p.. — *"Westview encore reprint.". — : Reprint. Originally published: New York : Praeger, 1951. — Includes index. — Bibliography: p. 416-423*

EUROPE, EASTERN — Library resources

AMERICAN COUNCIL OF LEARNED SOCIETIES. Joint Committee on Soviet Studies. Subcommittee on Bibliography, Information Retrieval and Documentation
International directory of librarians and library specialists in the Slavic and East European field / prepared under the auspices of the Subcommittee on Bibliography,Information Retrieval and Documentation of the Joint Committee on Soviet Studies of the American Council of Learned Societies and the Social Science Research Council. — New York : American Council of Learned Societies, 1985. — 58p

EUROPE, EASTERN — Military policy

Vneshniaia politika stran Varshavskogo Dogovora : (pervaia polovina 80-kh godov) / otv. redaktor I. I. Orlik. — Moskva : Nauka, 1986. — 319p

EUROPE, EASTERN — Nobility

SUBTELNY, Orest
Domination of Eastern Europe : native nobilities and foreign absolutism, 1500-1715 / Orest Subtelny. — Kingston : McGill-Queen´s University Press ; Gloucester : Alan Sutton, 1986. — xii,270p

EUROPE, EASTERN — Politics and government

FEHÉR, Ferenc
Eastern left, Western left : totalitarianism, freedom and democracy / Ferenc Fehér and Agnes Heller. — Cambridge : Polity, 1987, c1986. — 287p. — *Includes index*

Newsletter from behind the Iron Curtain: reports on communist activities in Eastern Europe. — Stockholm : Estonian Information Center and Latvian National Foundation, 1986-. — *Monthly*

PEASE, Neal
Poland, the United States, and the stabilization of Europe, 1919-1933 / by Neal Pease. — New York ; Oxford : Oxford University Press, 1986. — vii, 238p. — *Includes index. — Bibliography: p.[222]-231*

Sotsial'naia struktura i politicheskie dvizheniia v stranakh Tsentral'noi i Iugo-Vostochnoi Evropy : mezhvoennyi period / otv. redaktor A. Kh. Klevanskii. — Moskva : Nauka, 1986. — 244p

War and society in East Central Europe. — Boulder, Colo. : Social Science Monographs, 1985. — (East European monographs ; no.196) vol.19: East Central European society in World War 1 / Béla K. Király Nándor F. Dreisziger, and Albert A. Nofi; editors. — xi,623p

EUROPE, EASTERN — Politics and government — 1945-

JOHNSON, A. Ross
The impact of eastern Europe on Soviet policy toward western Europe / A. Ross Johnson. — Santa Monica, CA. : Rand, [1986]. — xv, 79 p. . — *"A project Air Force report prepared for the United States Air Force.". — "March 1986.". — "R-3332-AF.". — Includes bibliographical references*

EUROPE, EASTERN — Population policy

HEITLINGER, Alena
Reproduction, medicine and the socialist state / Alena Heitlinger. — Basingstoke : Macmillan, 1987. — xv,318p. — *Bibliography: p280-303. — Includes index*

EUROPE, EASTERN — Relations — Soviet Union

JOHNSON, A. Ross
The impact of eastern Europe on Soviet policy toward western Europe / A. Ross Johnson. — Santa Monica, CA. : Rand, [1986]. — xv, 79 p. . — *"A project Air Force report prepared for the United States Air Force.". — "March 1986.". — "R-3332-AF.". — Includes bibliographical references*

EUROPE, EASTERN — Social conditions

Sotsial'naia struktura i politicheskie dvizheniia v stranakh Tsentral'noi i Iugo-Vostochnoi Evropy : mezhvoennyi period / otv. redaktor A. Kh. Klevanskii. — Moskva : Nauka, 1986. — 244p

The Soviet Union and Eastern Europe / edited by George Schöpflin. — Rev. and updated. — New York ; Oxford : Facts on File, 1986. — xvii,637p. — (Handbooks to the modern world) . — *Previous ed.: London : Blond, 1970. — Includes bibliographies and index*

EUROPE, GERMAN-SPEAKING — Bibliography

KREWSON, Margrit B.
The German-speaking countries of Europe : a selective bibliography / Margrit B. Krewson. — Washington, D.C. : Library of Congress, 1985. — v,121p

EUROPE, NORTHERN — National security

Northern Europe : security issues for the 1990s / edited by Paul M. Cole, Douglas M. Hart. — Boulder : Westview Press, 1986. — p. cm. — (Westview special studies in international relations). — *Includes index*

EUROPE, NORTHERN — National security — Congresses

Security in the North : Nordic and superpower perceptions : papers / presented to a seminar on "The North and the superpowers : mutual security policy perceptions" on March 16, 1983 ; edited by Bo Huldt and Atis Lejins. — Stockholm : Swedish Institute of International Affairs, [1984]. — vii, 78 p.. — (Conference papers / the Swedish Institute of International Affairs ; 5, 1984). — *Includes bibliographies.* — *Contents: Perceptions in international politics and national security / Christer Jönsson -- Nordic perceptions of the great powers and Nordic security / Kari Möttölä -- The USA and security in the Nordic countries / Svein Melby -- Soviet perceptions of Nordic security problems / Bjarne Nörretranders -- The big powers and Nordic security / Sverre Lodgaard*

EUROPE, NORTHERN — Strategic aspects

The Military buildup in the high North : American and Nordic perspectives / edited by Sverre Jervell and Kare Nyblom. — Lanham ; London : Center for International Affairs, Harvard University and University Press of America, c1986. — xiii,159p

EUROPE, SOUTHERN — Economic conditions — Congresses

Semiperipheral development : the politics of southern Europe in the twentieth century / Giovanni Arrighi, editor. — Beverly Hills, Calif. : Sage Publications, c1985. — p. cm. — (Explorations in the world-economy ; v. 5). — *"Different versions of these papers were presented at two colloquia ... held at the Fernand Braudel Center, SUNY-Binghamton, Binghamton, NY, in March 1982 and at the Maison des Sciences de l'Homme, Paris, in June 1983"--Acknowledgements*

EUROPE, SOUTHERN — Economic conditions — Regional disparities

HADJIMICHALIS, Costis
Uneven development and regionalism : state, territory and class in southern Europe / Costis Hadjimichalis. — London : Croom Helm, c1987. — 343p. — (Croom Helm series in geography and environment). — *Bibliography: p310-332.* — *Includes index*

EUROPE, SOUTHERN — Politics and government — Congresses

Semiperipheral development : the politics of southern Europe in the twentieth century / Giovanni Arrighi, editor. — Beverly Hills, Calif. : Sage Publications, c1985. — p. cm. — (Explorations in the world-economy ; v. 5). — *"Different versions of these papers were presented at two colloquia ... held at the Fernand Braudel Center, SUNY-Binghamton, Binghamton, NY, in March 1982 and at the Maison des Sciences de l'Homme, Paris, in June 1983"--Acknowledgements*

EUROPE, WESTERN — Economic conditions

Les pays d'Europe occidentale en 1984-85 : évolution politique, économique et social... / sous la direction d'Alfred Grosser. — [Paris : Documentation française, 1985]. — 333p

EUROPE, WESTERN — Politics and government

Les pays d'Europe occidentale en 1984-85 : évolution politique, économique et social... / sous la direction d'Alfred Grosser. — [Paris : Documentation française, 1985]. — 333p

EUROPE, WESTERN — Social conditions

Les pays d'Europe occidentale en 1984-85 : évolution politique, économique et social... / sous la direction d'Alfred Grosser. — [Paris : Documentation française, 1985]. — 333p

EUROPEAN COMMUNITIES

Europe: magazine of the European Community / Commission of the European Communities. — Washington, D.C. : Commission of the European Communities, 1979-. — *Bimonthly.* — *Continues: European Community*

EUROPEAN COMMUNITIES

Cost projects / European Communities. — Luxembourg : Office for Official Publications of the European Communities, 1983/84-. — *Annual*

European Community / Commission of the European Communities. — Washington, D.C. : Commission of the European Communities, 1971-1978. — *Bimonthly.* — *Continued by: Europe: magazine of the European Community*

Register of current Community legal instruments. — Luxembourg : Office for Official Publications of the European Communities, 1980-1983. — *Continued by: Official journal of the European Communities: Directory of Community legislation in force*

Scad news / Commission of the European Communities. — Luxembourg : Service Central de Documentation, 1986-. — *Monthly.* — *Text in English and French*

EUROPEAN COMMUNITIES — Bibliography

EUROPEAN COMMUNITIES
Documents. — Luxembourg : Office for Official Publications of the European Communities, 1987-. — *Monthly*

The European Community as a publisher. — Luxembourg : Office for Official Publications of the European Communities, 1985/86-. — *Annual*

EUROPEAN COMMUNITIES — Economic and Social Committee

EUROPEAN COMMUNITIES. Economic and Social Committee
The economic and social situation of the Community / Economic and Social Committee, European Communities. — Luxembourg : Office for Official Publications of the European Communities, 1985-. — *Annual*

EUROPEAN COMMUNITIES — Statistics

Structure and activity of industry: data by size of enterprises / Statistical Office of the European Communities. — Luxembourg : Statistical Office of the European Communities, 1979-. — *Annual*

Yearbook of industrial statistics / Statistical Office of the European Communities. — Luxembourg : Statistical Office of the European Communities, 1984-. — *Annual*

EUROPEAN COMMUNITIES. Economic and Social Committee

EUROPEAN COMMUNITIES. Economic and Social Committee
Opinions: Annual catalogue. — Luxembourg : office for Official Publications of the European Communities, 1984-. — *Annual*

EUROPEAN COMMUNITIES

Basic Community laws / edited by Bernard Rudden and Derrick Wyatt. — 2nd ed. — Oxford : Clarendon, 1986. — xvi,407p.. — *Previous ed.: 1980*

BURROWS, F.
Free movement in European Community law / F. Burrows. — Oxford : Clarendon, 1987. — xxxvii,346p. — *Bibliography: xxxvii* — *Includes index*

The European Union treaty : commentary on the draft adopted by the European Parliament on 14 February 1984 / by Francesco Capotorti ... [et al.]. — Oxford : Clarendon, 1986. — xii,327p. — *Translation of: Le Traité d'union européenne.* — *Bibliography: p325-327*

Fact sheets on the European Parliament and the activities of the European Community. — [Luxembourg?] : European Parliament, [1979]. —

Fact sheets on the European Parliament and the activities of the European Community. — 3rd ed. — Luxembourg : Office for Official Publications of the European Communities, 1987. — 1v (various pagings)

GREAT BRITAIN. Parliament. House of Lords. Select Committee on the European Communities
Progress of scrutiny / Select Committee on the European Communities. — London : HMSO, 1982-

EUROPEAN COMMUNITIES — Appropriations and expenditures

GREAT BRITAIN. Parliament. House of Commons. Library. International Affairs Section
The European Community budget 1981 and Britain / Simon Young. — [London] : the Library, 1980. — 13p. — (Background paper / House of Commons. Library. [Research Division] ; no.86). — *Bibliographical references: p12-13*

GREAT BRITAIN. Parliament. House of Commons. Library. Research Division
The Budget of the European Communities / [Robert Clements]. — [London] : the Division, [1979]. — 16p. — (Background paper ; no.73)

EUROPEAN COMMUNITIES — Constitution

Treaties establishing the European Communities : Amending treaties : Other basic instruments. — Abridged ed.. — Luxembourg : Office for Official Publications of the European Communities, 1983. — 542p

EUROPEAN COMMUNITIES — Dictionaries

PAXTON, John
A dictionary of the European Communities / John Paxton. — 2nd ed. — London : Macmillan, 1984. — 282p. — *Previous ed.: published as A dictionary of the European Economic Community. 1977.* — *Bibliography: p279-282*

EUROPEAN COMMUNITIES — Directories

Who's Who : European Communities and other European organizations = Who's Who : communautés européennes et autres organisations européennes = Who's Who : europäische gemeinschaften und andere europäische organisationen. — 3rd ed. — Bruxelles : Editions Delta, 1986. — 216p

EUROPEAN COMMUNITIES — Economic aspects — Bibliography — Catalogs

COMMISSION OF THE EUROPEAN COMMUNITIES. Library
Recent publications on the European Communities received by the Library : supplement. — [Luxembourg : Office for Official Publications of the European Communities]
1985/1: Bibliography on monetary and financial matters. — 1985. — 750,54 columns. — *In Community languages*

EUROPEAN COMMUNITIES — Finance — Bibliography — Catalogs

COMMISSION OF THE EUROPEAN COMMUNITIES. Library
Recent publications on the European Communities received by the Library : supplement. — [Luxembourg : Office for Official Publications of the European Communities]
1985/1: Bibliography on monetary and financial matters. — 1985. — 750,54 columns. — *In Community languages*

EUROPEAN COMMUNITIES — Foreign relations — Bibliography — Catalogs
COMMISSION OF THE EUROPEAN COMMUNITIES. Library
Recent publications on the European Communities received by the Library : supplement. — [Luxembourg : Office for Official Publications of the European Communities]
1985/3: Bibliography on the external relations of the European Communities. — 1985. — 55p,448,31 columns. — *In Community languages*

EUROPEAN COMMUNITIES — Legal status, laws, etc.
GREAT BRITAIN. Parliament. House of Commons. Library c 245.10European Communities (Amendment) Bill (Bill 126 of 1985-86) (Simon Young)
. — [London] : the Library, 1986. — 16p. — (Reference sheet / House of Commons. Library. [Research Division] ; no.86/11). — *Bibliographical references: p15-16*

EUROPEAN COMMUNITIES — Periodicals — Handbooks, manuals, etc.
PAU, Giancarlo
The Official Journal : a guide / prepared by Giancarlo Pau. — [s.l.] : Association of EDC Librarians, [1984?]. — 6p. — (European Communities information ; no.7)

EUROPEAN COMMUNITIES — Sources
PAU, Giancarlo
London Information Office of the European Commission / prepared by Giancarlo Pau. — [s.l.] : Association of EDC Librarians, [1984]. — 4p. — (European Communities information ; no.5)

EUROPEAN COMMUNITIES — Sources — Bibliography
RICHARD, Stephen
Basic sources for libraries and information units / prepared by Stephen Richard. — [s.l.] : Association of EDC Librarians, [1987]. — [ii],26p. — (European Communities information ; no.11)

RICHARD, Stephen
Getting started : prepared by Stephen Richard. — [s.l.] : Association of EDC Librarians, [1984?]. — 10p. — (European Communities information ; no.1)

EUROPEAN COMMUNITIES — Statistics — Bibliography
RAMSAY, Anne
European Communities statistics : a guide to sources / prepared by Anne Ramsay. — [s.l.] : Association of EDC Librarians, [1984]. — 5p. — (European Communities information ; no.8)

EUROPEAN COMMUNITIES — Statistics — Catalogs
STATISTICAL OFFICE OF THE EUROPEAN COMMUNITIES
Catalogue of Eurostat publications. — Luxembourg : Office for Official Publications of the European Communities, 1986. — 48p

EUROPEAN COMMUNITIES — Statistics — Indexes
RAMSAY, Anne
Eurostat index : a detailed keyword subject index to the statistical series published by the Statistical Office of the European Communities with notes on the series / compiled by Anne Ramsay. — 3rd completely rev. and enl. ed. — Stamford : Capital Planning Information, 1986. — 248p. — *Previous ed.: 1983. — Includes bibliography and index*

EUROPEAN COMMUNITIES (AMENDMENT) BILL 1985-86
GREAT BRITAIN. Parliament. House of Commons. Library c 245.10European Communities (Amendment) Bill (Bill 126 of 1985-86) (Simon Young)
. — [London] : the Library, 1986. — 16p. — (Reference sheet / House of Commons. Library. [Research Division] ; no.86/11).
Bibliographical references: p15-16

EUROPEAN COMMUNITIESOFF. PUBNS. — Foreign relations 986
The EEC's external relations - stocktaking and consistency of action : study / rapporteur: Aldo Romoli. — Brussels : Economic and Social Committee, 1982. — ii,139p

EUROPEAN CONVENTION ON HUMAN RIGHTS
FAWCETT, J. E. S.
The application of the European Convention on Human Rights / by J.E.S. Fawcett. — 2nd ed. — Oxford : Clarendon, 1987. — xiii,444p. — *Previous ed.: 1969. — Includes index*

GREAT BRITAIN. Parliament. House of Commons. Library. International Affairs Section
The European Convention on Human Rights / Chris Bowlby. — [London] : the Library, 1986. — 16p. — (Background paper / House of Commons. Library. [Research Division] ; no.179). — *Bibliography: p16*

EUROPEAN COOPERATION
EUROPEAN COMMUNITIES
Cost projects / European Communities. — Luxembourg : Office for Official Publications of the European Communities, 1983/84-. — *Annual*

LANGER, Peter H.
Transatlantic discord and NATO's crisis of cohesion / Peter H. Langer. — Washington, D.C. : Pergamon-Brassey's, 1986. — p. cm. — (Foreign policy report). — *"A publication of the Institute for Foreign Policy Analysis, Inc.". — Bibliography: p*

EUROPEAN COOPERATION — Addresses, essays, lectures
Ten years after Helsinki : the making of the European security regime / edited by Kari Möttölä. — Boulder, Colo. : Westview Press, 1986. — x, 184 p.. — (Westview special studies in international security). — *"Published in cooperation with the Finnish Institute of International Affairs"--P. [iv]. — Includes bibliographies and index*

EUROPEAN COUNCIL *See* Council of the European Communities

EUROPEAN CURRENCY UNIT
The role of the SDR in the international monetary system : studies by the Research and Treasurer's Departments of the International Monetary Fund. — Washington, D. C. : International Monetary Fund, 1987. — vii,62p. — (Occasional paper / International Monetary Fund ; no.51). — *Bibliography: p60-62*

EUROPEAN ECONOMIC COMMUNITY. Laws, statutes, etc
European Communities secondary legislation, English text. — London : H.M.S.O.. — *In 42 parts*
Part 2: Commercial policy / [European Economic Community and European Coal and Steel Community]. — 1972. — 2v.([8],517p)

European Communities secondary legislation, English text. — London : H.M.S.O.. — *In 42 parts*
Part 4: Competition / [European Economic Community and European Coal and Steel Community]. — 1972. — [9],239p

EUROPEAN ECONOMIC COMMUNITY
BARRE, Raymond
Un plan pour l'Europe : la Communauté européenne, problèmes et perspectives / Raymond Barre. — [Nancy] : Presses universitaires de Nancy, c1984. — 59p. — (Travaux du Centre européen universitaire)

BETHELL, Nicholas
Why do we sell butter to Russia? and other common questions from the Common Market / Nicholas Bethell. — London : European Democratic Group, 1986. — [8p]

Britain, Europe and the environment : contributions to a conference held at Imperial College of Science and Technology / edited by Richard Macrory. — London : Imperial College Centre for Environmental Technology, 1983. — 130p

BUTLER, Sir Michael, 1927-
Europe : more than a continent / Michael Butler. — London : Heinemann, 1986. — 184p

CARSTENS, Karl
Un souffle de renouveau en Europe / Karl Carstens. — Lausanne : Fondation Jean Monnet pour l'Europe. Centre de Recherches Européennes. — 29p

FORUTAN SABZAVARI, Faezeh
The EEC steel industry and the mid 1970s crisis : some aspects of trade policy / by Faezeh Forutan Sabzavari. — 348 leaves. — *PhD (Econ) 1986 LSE*

GREAT BRITAIN. Parliament. House of Lords. Select Committee on the European Communities
Progress of scrutiny / Select Committee on the European Communities. — London : HMSO, 1982-

LABOUZ, Marie Françoise
Le système communautaire européen / Marie Françoise Labouz ; préface de Jean Paul Jacqué. — Paris : Berger-Levrault, 1986. — 350p. — (Mondes en devenir ; 18). — *Bibliographies*

NICHOLSON, Frances
From the six to the twelve : the enlargement of the European Communities / by Frances Nicholson and Roger East. — Harlow : Longman, 1987. — xvii,298p. — (Keesing's international studies). — *Includes index*

OVERTURF, Stephen Frank
The economic principles of European integration / Stephen Frank Overturf. — New York : Praeger, 1986. — xiii, 173 p.. — *Includes index. — Bibliography: p. 167*

Single European Act. and, Final Act. — Luxembourg : Office for Official Publications of the European Communities, 1986. — v, 76p. — *Title on cover: Single European Act*

EUROPEAN ECONOMIC COMMUNITY — Bibliography
SIEMERS, J. P
European integration : select international bibliography of theses and dissertations = Europäische Integration : Internationales Auswahlverzeichnis von Dissertationen und Diplomarbeiten = Intégration européenne : bibliographie internationale sélective de thèses et mémoires, 1957-1980 / J.P. Siemers, E.H. Siemers-Hidma ; preface, Ralf Dahrendorf. — 2nd rev. and enl. ed. — The Hague ; Boston : Martinus Nijhoff ; Hingham, MA : Distributors for the United States and Canada, Kluwer Boston, 1981. — xx, 412 p.. — *English, French, German, and Italian. — Includes indexes*

EUROPEAN ECONOMIC COMMUNITY — Commerce — Canada
PAPADOPOULOS, N. G.
Canada and the European Community : an uncomfortable partnership? / N. G. Papadopoulos. — Montreal : Institute for Research on Public Policy / L'Institut de recherches politiques, 1986. — xxix,136p. — (Essays in international economics / Institute for Research on Public Policy / L'Institut de recherches politiques). — *Bibliography: p111-136*

EUROPEAN ECONOMIC COMMUNITY — Congresses

Integration and unequal development : the experience of the EEC / edited by Dudley Seers and Constantine Vaitsos, with the assistance of Marja-Liisa Kiljunen. — New York : St. Martin's Press, 1980. — xxi, 359 p.. — (Studies in the integration of Western Europe). — *Based on the papers commissioned for discussion at the Institute of Development Studies (IDS) at the University of Sussex in May-June 1979.". — Includes bibliographical references and index*

EUROPEAN ECONOMIC COMMUNITY — Economic assistance

A guide to European Community grants and loans 1986/87 : for commerce, industry, local authorities, academic and research institutions / compiled by Gay Scott. — 7th ed. — Newbury : Eurofi (UK), 1986. — 1v.(loose-leaf)

EUROPEAN ECONOMIC COMMUNITY — Economic conditions

EUROPEAN COMMUNITIES. Economic and Social Committee
The economic and social situation of the Community / Economic and Social Committee, European Communities. — Luxembourg : Office for Official Publications of the European Communities, 1985-. — *Annual*

EUROPEAN ECONOMIC COMMUNITY — Economic conditions — Regional disparities

The contribution of infrastructure to regional development. — Luxembourg : Office for Official Publications of the European Communities. — *At head of title: Commission of the European Communities*
Final report / by Dieter Biehl. — 1986. — 73p

EUROPEAN ECONOMIC COMMUNITY — Economic conditions — Regional disparities — Statistics

The contribution of infrastructure to regional development. — Luxembourg : Office for Official Publications of the European Communities. — *At head of title: Commission of the European Communities*
Annex: Companion volume to the Final report / by Infrastructure Study Group. — 1986. — 190p

EUROPEAN ECONOMIC COMMUNITY — Foreign relations

The EEC's external relations - stocktaking and consistency of action : study / rapporteur: Aldo Romoli. — Brussels : Economic and Social Committee, 1982. — ii,139p

EUROPEAN ECONOMIC COMMUNITY — History

KÜSTERS, Hanns Jürgen
Die Gründung der Europöischen Wirtschaftsgemeinschaft / Hanns Jürgen Küsters. — Baden-Baden : Nomos Verlagsgesellschaft, 1982. — 569p. — *Bibliography: p521-563*

MOWAT, Robert Case
Creating the European Community / R.C. Mowat. — London : Blandford Press, 1973. — [10],235p. — *Bibliographyp.223-226. — Includes index*

EUROPEAN ECONOMIC COMMUNITY — Industries

The Community fertiliser industry / joint report by the CMC—Engrais/Commission Services Working Group on Fertilisers. — Luxembourg : Office for Official Publications of the European Communities, 1985. — 50p. — *At head of title: Commission of the European Communities*

MARFELS, Christian
Concentration, competition and competitiveness in the beverages industries of the European Community / by Professor Christian Marfels. — Luxembourg : Office for Official Publications of the European Communities, 1984. — xii,122p. — *At head of title page: Commission of the European Communities*

The production and use of cereal and potato starch in the EEC / prepared by Centre for European Agricultural Studies. — Luxembourg : Office for Official Publications of the European Communities, 1986. — 123p. — *At head of title: Commission of the European Communities*

EUROPEAN ECONOMIC COMMUNITY — Industries — Statistics

Structure and activity of industry: data by size of enterprises / Statistical Office of the European Communities. — Luxembourg : Statistical Office of the European Communities, 1979-. — *Annual*

Yearbook of industrial statistics / Statistical Office of the European Communities. — Luxembourg : Statistical Office of the European Communities, 1984-. — *Annual*

EUROPEAN ECONOMIC COMMUNITY — Information services — Directories

HOGAN, Jim
EEC contacts 1985/86 : sources of information on European Community aspects of policy and legislation affecting business / by Jim Hogan. — Northill, Beds. : Eurofi (UK), 1986. — 204p

EUROPEAN ECONOMIC COMMUNITY — Transportation

Carriage of goods by inland waterways. — Luxembourg : Office for Official Publications of the European Communities, 1985. — *Text in Community languages*
1983. — xxx,170p

EUROPEAN ECONOMIC COMMUNITY — Transportation — Statistics

Carriage of goods by rail. — Luxembourg : Office des Publications Officielles des Communautés Européennes. — *On cover: Eurostat. — Text in Community languages*
1983. — 1985. — xxx, 145p

EUROPEAN ECONOMIC COMMUNITY — Australia

BURNETT, Alan
Australia and the European Communities in the 1980s / Alan Burnett. — Canberra : Australian National University, 1983. — xi, 255p. — (Canberra studies in world affairs ; no.12)

EUROPEAN ECONOMIC COMMUNITY — Europe, Southern — Congresses

Horticultural trade of the expanded European Community : implications for Mediterranean countries / edited by Malcolm D. Bale. — Washington, D.C., U.S.A. : World Bank, 1986. — x,274p. — (A World Bank symposium). — *Based on symposiums held Oct. 1984 at the World Bank of Wahington, D.C. and at the Food and Agriculture Organization in Rome, Italy*

EUROPEAN ECONOMIC COMMUNITY — Germany (West)

BULMER, Simon
The domestic structure of European community policy-making in West Germany / Simon Bulmer. — New York : Garland, 1986. — 403 p.. — (Outstanding theses from the London School of Economics and Political Science). — *Thesis (Ph. D.)--University of London, 1982. — Bibliography: p. 388-400*

BULMER, Simon
The Federal Republic of Germany and the European Community / Simon Bulmer, William Paterson. — London : Allen & Unwin, 1987. — [224]p. — *Includes bibliography and index*

JEUTTER, Peter
EWG - Kein Weg nach Europa : [die Haltung der Freien Demokratischen Partei zu den Römischen Verträgen 1957] / Peter Jeutter. — Bonn : Europa Union Verlag, 1985. — 330p. — (Europäische Studien des Instituts für Europäische Politik ; Bd.14). — *Bibliography: p299-327*

EUROPEAN ECONOMIC COMMUNITY — Great Britain

MAY, Simon
The European Community and the task for the British presidency in 1986 / Simon May. — London : Centre for Policy Studies, 1986. — 8p. — (C.P.S. policy challenge)

NADEAU, Bertrand
Britain's entry into the European Economic Community and its effect on Canada's agricultural exports / Bertrand Nadeau. — Montreal : The Institute for Research on Public Policy/LInstitut de recherches politiques, 1985. — xx,111p. — (Essays in international economics). — *Foreword and summary in English and French. — Bibliography: p95-100*

WEST MIDLANDS. County Council
Visit to EEC and EIB, September 1975, European Economic Community : Economic trends in the West Midlands. — Birmingham : [the Council], 1975. — 36p

EUROPEAN ECONOMIC COMMUNITY — Greece

ECONOMIC AND SOCIAL COMMITTEE OF THE EUROPEAN COMMUNITIES
Enlargement of the European Community: Greece - Spain - Portugal : opinion / Economic and Social Committee of the European Communities. — Brussels : General Secretariat of the Economic and Social Committee, 1979. — 75p

Greece and the EEC : integration and convergence / edited by George N. Yannopoulos. — Basingstoke : Macmillan in association with the Graduate School of European and International Studies, University of Reading, 1986. — xii,178p. — (University of Reading European and international studies). — *Includes bibliographies and index*

EUROPEAN ECONOMIC COMMUNITY — Mexico

The European Economic Community and Mexico / editors, Peter Coffey and Miguel S. Wionczek. — Dordrecht ; Boston : M. Nijhoff, 1987. — p. cm. — (Euro-Latin American relations - the Omagua series). — *Includes index*

EUROPEAN ECONOMIC COMMUNITY — Spain

ALONSO, Antonio
España en el Mercado Común : del Acuerdo del 70 a la Comunidad de Doce / Antonio Alonso ; prólogo de José María de Areilza. — Madrid : Espasa-Calpe, 1985. — 331p. — (Nueva Europa ; 1)

ALONSO, Jose A.
Efectos de la adhesión de España a la CEE sobre las exportaciones de Iberoamerica / Jose A. Alonso, Vicente Donoso. — Madrid : Ediciones Cultura Hispanica, 1983. — 316p. — *Bibliography: p305-310*

Andalucia y la Comunidad Europea : aspectos relevantes / trabajo dirigido por Rafael Illescas Ortiz. — Sevilla : Instituto de Desarrollo Regional, 1981. — xxxix,903p. — ([Publicaciones] / Universidad de Sevilla, Instituto de Desarrollo Regional ; No.21). — *Bibliographies*

CAPDEVILA BATLLES, José
Agricultura e industria española frente a la CEE : aspectos jurídicos, económicos y políticos / José Capdevila Batlles ; prólogo de Edgard Pisani. — Barcelona : Editorial Aedos, 1985. — 252p. — *Bibliography: p245-252*

Derecho de patentes : España y la Comunidad Económica Europea / Alberto Bercovitz...[et al.]. — Barcelona : Ariel, 1985. — 109p

DIPUTACIÓN GENERAL DE ARAGÓN
Libro blanco sobre las repercusiones en Aragón de la integración de España en la CEE / [José María Serrano Sanz...et al.]. — [Zaragoza] : the Diputación, [ca.1985]. — 747p

EUROPEAN ECONOMIC COMMUNITY
— Spain   *continuation*
ECONOMIC AND SOCIAL COMMITTEE OF THE EUROPEAN COMMUNITIES
Enlargement of the European Community: Greece - Spain - Portugal : opinion / Economic and Social Committee of the European Communities. — Brussels : General Secretariat of the Economic and Social Committee, 1979. — 75p

La empresa española ante la CEE / selección de textos y coordinación Eduardo Bueno Campos. — Madrid : Instituto de Estudios Económicos, 1984. — xxvii,184p. — *Revista del Instituto de Estudios Económicos, 1984, No.2*

La empresa española en las Comunidades Europeas : temas clave de gestión / por Lluís Riera i Figueras...[et al.] ; prólogo por Manuel Marín. — Barcelona : Editorial Hispano Europea, 1986. — 423p. — (Colección ESADE " Estudios de la Empresa). — *Bibliographies*

ESCUELA SUPERIOR DE GESTIÓN COMERCIAL Y MARKETING (ESIC). Gabinete de Estudios
Consecuencias para la economia española de la integracion de España en la C.E.E.. — Madrid : Ediciones ESIC, 1986. — 227p. — (Estudios ESIC ; 11)

España en Europa : aspectos agrícolas de la integración en la CEE / [Danial de Busturia...et al.]. — [Madrid : Audiovisual y Prensa, 1982]. — 116p

GIL, Gonzalo
Aspectos financieros y monetarios de la integración española en la Comunidad Economica Europea / Gonzalo Gil. — [Madrid] : Banco de España, 1985. — 187p. — (Estudios económicos / Banco de España, Servicio de Estudios ; no.37)

HERRERO DE MIÑON, Miguel
España y la Comunidad Económica Europea : Un sí para... / Miguel Herrero de Miñon. — Barcelona : Planeta, 1986. — 225p

PARTIDO SOCIALISTA OBRERO ESPAÑOL
España ante el reto de Europa / Partido Socialista Obrero Español. — [Madrid] : PSOE, 1985. — 87p

Tratado de adhesión de España a las Comunidades Europeas. — Madrid : Tecnos, 1986. — xv,583p. — (Practica juridica)

EUROPEAN ECONOMIC COMMUNITY
— Spain — Andalucia
LORING MIRÓ, Jaime
Los sectores agrarios de Andalucia ante la integración en la C.E.E. / Jaime Loring Miró, Luis Godoy López, Jose J. Romero Rodríguez. — Madrid : [Mundi-Prensa Libros], 1984. — 303p. — *At head of title: Banco de Crédito Agrícola*

EUROPEAN ECONOMIC COMMUNITY
— Spain — Catalonia
GRANELL, Francesc
Cataluña, sus relaciones económicas transnacionales y la C.E.E. / Francesc Granell ; prólogo: Jordi Pujol. — Barcelona : Vicens-Vives, 1986. — 151p

POU I SERRADELL, Victor
Catalunya i Europa / Victor Pou i Serradell. — Barcelona : Sirocco, 1985. — 58p. — (Els europeus ; no.1)

EUROPEAN ECONOMIC COMMUNITY
— Switzerland
SCHWAMM, Henri
La pénétration industrielle suisse dans le marché commun / Henri Schwamm. — Lausanne : Feuille dÀvis de Lausanne, 1971. — 19p

EUROPEAN ECONOMIC COMMUNITY
ECONOMIC AND SOCIAL COMMITTEE OF THE EUROPEAN COMMUNITIES
Enlargement of the European Community: Greece - Spain - Portugal : opinion / Economic and Social Committee of the European Communities. — Brussels : General Secretariat of the Economic and Social Committee, 1979. — 75p

MOREAU DEFARGES, Philippe
Quel avenir pour quelle Communauté? / Philippe Moreau Defarges. — Paris : Institut Français des Relations Internationales, 1986. — 230p. — (Travaux et Recherches de l'IFRI). — *Bibliography: p [229]-230*

EUROPEAN ECONOMIC COMMUNITY
— Economic policy
STATISTICAL OFFICE OF THE EUROPEAN COMMUNITIES
Regional accounts ESA : detailed tables by branches : 1981. — Luxembourg : Office for Official Publications of the E.C., 1985. — 125p . — *Includes map of the regions of the European Community*

EUROPEAN ECONOMIC COMMUNITY
— Politics and government
BULMER, Simon
The European Council : decision-making in European politics / Simon Bulmer and Wolfgang Wessels. — Basingstoke : Macmillan, 1987. — xii,174p. — *Includes index*

EUROPEAN ECONOMIC COMMUNITY
— Denmark
DENMARK. Udvalget vedrørende Danmarks forhold til de Europaeiske faellesskaber
Danmark og de Europaeiske faellesskaber : 4. supplerende redegørelse : udviklingen i 1971. — [København] : the Udvalget, 1972. — 432p

EUROPEAN ECONOMIC COMMUNITY
— Portugal
L´Espagne et le Portugal dans la CEE : interrogations et enjeux / Danielle Charles-Le Bihan [et al.]. — Paris : La Documentation française, 1986. — 144p. — (Notes et études documentaires ; no.4819)

EUROPEAN ECONOMIC COMMUNITY
— Spain
L´Espagne et le Portugal dans la CEE : interrogations et enjeux / Danielle Charles-Le Bihan [et al.]. — Paris : La Documentation française, 1986. — 144p. — (Notes et études documentaires ; no.4819)

EUROPEAN ECONOMIC COMMUNITY COUNTRIES
BUTLER, Sir Michael, 1927-
Europe : more than a continent / Michael Butler. — London : Heinemann, 1986. — 184p

L'influence des Communautés européennes sur le droit international privé des Etats membres = The influence of the European Communities upon private international law of the member states / [papers by] P. Bourel [et al.]. — Bruxelles : F. Larcier, 1981. — 266p

EUROPEAN ECONOMIC COMMUNITY COUNTRIES — Commerce — Statistics
External trade: statistical yearbook / Statistical Office of the European Communities. — Luxembourg : Statistical Office of the European Communities, 1985-. — *Annual.* — *Text in Community languages.* — *Continues: Monthly external trade bulletin Special Issue*

Foreign trade : monthly statistics / Statistical Office of the European Communities. — Luxembourg : Statistical Office of the Euopean Communities, 1961-1975. — *Monthly.* — *Continued by: Monthly external trade bulletin*

Monthly external trade bulletin / Statistical Office of the European Communities. — Luxembourg : Statistical Office of the European Communites, 1961-1985. — *Monthly.* — *Text in Community languages.* — *Continues: Foreign trade: monthly statistics.* — *Continued by: Monthly external trade statistics*

Monthly external trade statistics / Statistical Office of the European Communities. — Luxembourg : Statistical Office of the European Communities, 1986-. — *Monthly.* — *Text in Community languages.* — *Continues: Monthly external trade bulletin*

EUROPEAN ECONOMIC COMMUNITY COUNTRIES — Commerce — Developing countries
The Significance of the EEC's generalised system of preferences : trade effects and links with other community aid policies / Axel Borrmann ... [et al.]. — Hamburg : Verlag Weltarchiv, 1985. — 420 p.. — (Publication of HWWA-Institut für Wirtschaftsforschung-Hamburg). — *Bibliography: p. 405-420*

EUROPEAN ECONOMIC COMMUNITY COUNTRIES — Commerce — Great Britain
PERRY, K.
Business in Europe : opportunites for British companies in the EEC / Keith Perry. — London : Heinemann, 1987. — xii,206p. — *Bibliography: p199-200.* — *Includes index*

EUROPEAN ECONOMIC COMMUNITY COUNTRIES — Commerce — Spain
ALONSO, Jose Antonio
La empresa exportadora español frente a Iberoamerica y la CEE / Jose Antonio Alonso, Vicente Donoso. — Madrid : Ediciones Cultura Hispanica del Instituto de Cooperación Iberoamericana, 1985. — xiii,263p. — *Bibliography: p193-199*

EUROPEAN ECONOMIC COMMUNITY COUNTRIES — Commercial policy
VANDAMME, J
La politique de la concurrence dans la C.E.E. / J.A. Van Damme. — Kortrijk, Belgique : UGA, [1980]. — 658 p., [1] leaf of plates. — (Cours / Centre international d'études et de recherches européennes ; 1977). — *At head of title: Institut universitaire international, Luxembourg.* — *Bibliography: p. 589-658*

EUROPEAN ECONOMIC COMMUNITY COUNTRIES — Economic conditions — Regional disparities
CLOUT, Hugh
Regional variations in the European Community / Hugh Clout. — Cambridge : Cambridge University Press, 1986. — 128p. — (Cambridge topics in geography) (Cambridge topics in geography. Second series). — *Bibliography: p124-126.* — *Includes index*

DURU, Gérard
Structures productives européennes : analyse prétopologique des phénomènes de dépendance interindustrielle / Gérard Duru, Michel Mougeot, Jean-Paul Auray. — Paris : Editions du Centre national de la recherche scientifique, 1982. — 327 p.. — *On cover: Centre national de la recherche scientifique, Centre régional de publication Lyon.* — *Bibliography: p. 320-325*

SWEENEY, G. P.
Innovation, entrepreneurs and regional development / G.P. Sweeney. — London : Pinter, 1987. — xvi,271p. — *Includes bibliographies and index*

EUROPEAN ECONOMIC COMMUNITY COUNTRIES — Economic integration
The Dynamics of European union / edited by Roy Pryce. — London : Croom Helm, c1987. — 300p. — *Includes bibliographies and index*

EUROPEAN ECONOMIC COMMUNITY COUNTRIES — Economic policy
BULMER, Simon
The domestic structure of European community policy-making in West Germany / Simon Bulmer. — New York : Garland, 1986. — 403 p.. — (Outstanding theses from the London School of Economics and Political Science). — *Thesis (Ph. D.)--University of London, 1982.* — *Bibliography: p. 388-400*

EUROPEAN ECONOMIC COMMUNITY COUNTRIES — Economic policy
continuation

A Competitive future for Europe? : towards a new European industrial policy / edited by P.R. Beije ... [et al.]. — London : Croom Helm, c1987. — 324p

DELIÈGE-ROTT, Denise
Situation et politique sociales Européennes / Denise Deliège-Rott. — 2è ed. — [Louvain] : Ecole de Santé Publique, Université Catholique de Louvain, 1980. — v,312p

MENDES, A. J. Marques
Economic integration and growth in Europe / A.J. Marques Mendes. — London : Croom Helm, c1987. — 141p. — *Bibliography: p129-135. — Includes index*

Prospects for the '80s : opinion. — Brussels : Economic and Social Committee, 1981. — 58p

VANHOVE, N.
Regional policy : a European approach / N. Vanhove, L.H. Klaassen. — 2nd ed. — Aldershot : Gower, c1987. — [xiv,450]p. — (Studies in spatial analysis). — *Previous ed.: Farnborough, Hampshire : Saxon House, 1980. — Bibliography: p433-448. — Includes index*

EUROPEAN ECONOMIC COMMUNITY COUNTRIES — Foreign economic relations — Australia
BURNETT, Alan
Australia and the European Communities in the 1980s / Alan Burnett. — Canberra : Australian National University, 1983. — xi, 255p. — (Canberra studies in world affairs ; no.12)

EUROPEAN ECONOMIC COMMUNITY COUNTRIES — Foreign economic relations — Hungary
HEDRI, Gabriella
A Közös Piac és a magyar export / Hedri Gabriella. — Budapest : Közgazdasági és Jogi könyvkiadó, 1970. — 178p. — *Bibliography: p173-174*

EUROPEAN ECONOMIC COMMUNITY COUNTRIES — Foreign economic relations — Mexico
The European Economic Community and Mexico / editors, Peter Coffey and Miguel S. Wionczek. — Dordrecht ; Boston : M. Nijhoff, 1987. — p. cm. — (Euro-Latin American relations - the Omagua series). — *Includes index*

EUROPEAN ECONOMIC COMMUNITY COUNTRIES — Foreign economic relations — Scandinavia
MILJAN, Toivo
The reluctant Europeans : the attitudes of the Nordic countries towards European integration / Toivo Miljan. — London : C. Hurst, 1977. — viii,325p. — *Bibliography: p.301-318. — Includes index*

EUROPEAN ECONOMIC COMMUNITY COUNTRIES — Foreign economic relations — United States
LEVINE, Michael K
Inside international trade policy formulation : a history of the 1982 US-EC steel arrangements / by Michael K. Levine. — New York : Praeger, 1985. — p. cm. — *Includes index*

EUROPEAN ECONOMIC COMMUNITY COUNTRIES — Foreign relations — Bibliography — Catalogs
COMMISSION OF THE EUROPEAN COMMUNITIES. Library
Recent publications on the European Communities received by the Library : supplement. — [Luxembourg : Office for Official Publications of the European Communities]
1985/3: Bibliography on the external relations of the European Communities. — 1985. — 55p,448,31 columns. — *In Community languages*

EUROPEAN ECONOMIC COMMUNITY COUNTRIES — Foreign relations — Treaties
AUDRETSCH, H. A. H.
Supervision in European Community law : observance by the member states of their treaty obligations : a treatise on international and supra-national supervision / H.A.H. Audretsch. — 2nd rev. ed. — Amsterdam ; Oxford : North-Holland, 1986. — xix,782p. — *Previous ed.: 1978. — Bibliography: p.591-613. - Includes index*

EUROPEAN ECONOMIC COMMUNITY COUNTRIES — Industries
CAPDEVILA BATLLES, José
Agricultura e industria española frente a la CEE : aspectos jurídicos, económicos y políticos / José Capdevila Batlles ; prólogo de Edgard Pisani. — Barcelona : Editorial Aedos, 1985. — 252p. — *Bibliography: p245-252*

A Competitive future for Europe? : towards a new European industrial policy / edited by P.R. Beije ... [et al.]. — London : Croom Helm, c1987. — 324p

DURU, Gérard
Structures productives européennes : analyse prétopologique des phénomènes de dépendance interindustrielle / Gérard Duru, Michel Mougeot, Jean-Paul Auray. — Paris : Editions du Centre national de la recherche scientifique, 1982. — 327 p.. — *On cover: Centre national de la recherche scientifique, Centre régional de publication Lyon. — Bibliography: p. 320-325*

GREAT BRITAIN. Parliament. House of Commons. Library. Research Division
Why the USA creates new jobs and why Europe does not / Christopher Barclay. — [London] : the Division, 1985. — 25p. — (Background paper ; no.170)

EUROPEAN ECONOMIC COMMUNITY COUNTRIES — Languages
Terminlogie et traduction / Commission des Communautés Européennes. — Luxembourg : Office des publications officielles des Communautés européennes, 1985. — *Annual*

EUROPEAN ECONOMIC COMMUNITY COUNTRIES — Politics and government
HEWSTONE, Miles
Understanding attitudes to the European Community : a social-psychological study in four member states / Miles Hewstone. — Cambridge : Cambridge University Press, 1986. — 1v. — (European monographs in social psychology). — *Includes index*

EUROPEAN ECONOMIC COMMUNITY COUNTRIES — Social conditions
DELIÈGE-ROTT, Denise
Situation et politique sociales Européennes / Denise Deliège-Rott. — 2è ed. — [Louvain] : Ecole de Santé Publique, Université Catholique de Louvain, 1980. — v,312p

Living conditions in urban areas : an overview of factors influencing urban life in the European Community. — Luxembourg : Office for Official Publications of the European Communities, 1986. — v, 163, 47p

EUROPEAN ECONOMIC COMMUNITY COUNTRIES — Social policy
DELIÈGE-ROTT, Denise
Situation et politique sociales Européennes / Denise Deliège-Rott. — 2è ed. — [Louvain] : Ecole de Santé Publique, Université Catholique de Louvain, 1980. — v,312p

EUROPEAN ECONOMIC COMMUNITY COUNTRIES — Statistics
Eurostat news / Statistical Office of the European Communities. — Luxembourg : Statistical Office of the European Communities, 1976-. — *Quarterly*

STATISTICAL OFFICE OF THE EUROPEAN COMMUNITIES
Regional accounts ESA : detailed tables by branches : 1981. — Luxembourg : Office for Official Publications of the E.C., 1985. — 125p . — *Includes map of the regions of the European Community*

EUROPEAN ECONOMIC COMMUNITY COUNTRIES — Statistics — Indexes
RAMSAY, Anne
Eurostat index : a detailed keyword subject index to the statistical series published by the Statistical Office of the European Communities with notes on the series / compiled by Anne Ramsay. — 3rd completely rev. and enl. ed. — Stamford : Capital Planning Information, 1986. — 248p. — *Previous ed.: 1983. — Includes bibliography and index*

EUROPEAN ECONOMIC COMMUNITY COUNTRIES — Terminology
Terminlogie et traduction / Commission des Communautés Européennes. — Luxembourg : Office des publications officielles des Communautés européennes, 1985. — *Annual*

EUROPEAN ECONOMIC COMMUNITY COUNTRIES — Economic conditions
COMMISSION OF THE EUROPEAN COMMUNITIES
The regional development programmes : Brussels / Commission of the European Communities. — [Washington, D.C. : sold by European Community Information Service], 1979. — (Regional policy series ; 17)

EUROPEAN ECONOMIC COMMUNITY COUNTRIES — Social conditions
COMMISSION OF THE EUROPEAN COMMUNITIES
The regional development programmes : Brussels / Commission of the European Communities. — [Washington, D.C. : sold by European Community Information Service], 1979. — (Regional policy series ; 17)

EUROPEAN ECONOMIC COMMUNITY COUNTRIESOFF. PUBNS. — Economic conditions — Regional disparities 986
ECONOMIC AND SOCIAL COMMITTEE OF THE EUROPEAN COMMUNITIES
Agricultural structural policy : opinion / Economic and Social Committee of the European Communities. — Brussels : General Secretariat of the Economic and Social Committee, 1979. — ii,88p

EUROPEAN ECONOMIC COMMUNITY COUNTRIESOFF. PUBNS. — Economic policy 986
Economic pointers for 1982 : opinion. — Brussels : Economic and Social Committee, 1981. — 23p

EUROPEAN ECONOMIC COMMUNITY COUNTRIESOFF. PUBNS. — Social policy 986
Prospects for the '80s : opinion. — Brussels : Economic and Social Committee, 1981. — 58p

EUROPEAN ECONOMIC COMMUNITYOFF. PUBNS. — Portugal 986. (271/6)
ECONOMIC AND SOCIAL COMMITTEE OF THE EUROPEAN COMMUNITIES
Enlargement of the European Community: Greece - Spain - Portugal : opinion / Economic and Social Committee of the European Communities. — Brussels : General Secretariat of the Economic and Social Committee, 1979. — 75p

EUROPEAN FEDERATION
Single European Act. and, Final Act. — Luxembourg : Office for Official Publications of the European Communities, 1986. — v, 76p. — *Title on cover: Single European Act*

BEUGEL, Ernst Hans van der
From Marshall Aid to Atlantic partnership : European integration as a concern of American foreign policy / Ernst Hans van der Beugel. — Amsterdam : Elsevier, 1966. — 480p

EUROPEAN FEDERATION *continuation*

CAMPS, Miriam
European unification in the sixties : from the veto to the crisis / Miriam Camps. — London : Oxford University Press, 1967. — xiii,273p

The Dynamics of European union / edited by Roy Pryce. — London : Croom Helm, c1987. — 300p. — *Includes bibliographies and index*

HALLSTEIN, Walter
United Europe : challenge and opportunity / Walter Hallstein. — London : Oxford University Press, 1962. — xiii,109p

Integration through law : Europe and the American federal experience / under the general editorship of Mauro Cappelletti, Monica Seccombe [and] Joseph Weiler. — Berlin : Walter de Gruyter
Vol. 1: Methods, tools and institutions / edited by Mauro Cappelletti, Monica Seccombe [and] Joseph Weiler
Bk.1: A political, legal and economic overview. — 1986, c1985. — xc,616p. — (Series A. Law ; 2.1.1). — *Bibliographical notes*

JANSEN, Max
The ordeal of unity : the politics of European integration, 1945-1985 / Max Jansen and Johan K. de Vree. — Bilthoven : Prime Press, 1985. — vii,406p

Liber amicorum Henri Brugmans : au service de l'Europe : études et témoignages édités a` l'occasion de son soixante-quinzième anniversaire = Liber amicorum Henri Brugmans : striving for Europe : studies and tributes published on the occasion of his seventy-fifth birthday. — Amsterdam : European Cultural Foundation, 1981. — 590p

MOWAT, Robert Case
Creating the European Community / R.C. Mowat. — London : Blandford Press, 1973. — [10],235p. — *Bibliographyp.223-226. Includes index*

Le traité d'union europeenne : commentaire du projet adopté par le Parlement Européan, le 14 février 1984 / F. Capotorti [et al.]. — Bruxelles : Éditions de l'Université de Bruxelles, 1985. — xiii,307p. — *Bibliography: p299-301*

WILLIS, F. Roy
France, Germany and the new Europe, 1945—1963 / F. Roy Willis. — Stanford : Stanford University Press ; London : Oxford University Press, 1965. — xiv,397p. — *Bibliography: p373-387*

EUROPEAN FEDERATION — Bibliography

SIEMERS, J. P
European integration : select international bibliography of theses and dissertations = Europäische Integration : Internationales Auswahlverzeichnis von Dissertationen und Diplomarbeiten = Intégration européenne : bibliographie internationale sélective de thèses et mémoires, 1957-1980 / J.P. Siemers, E.H. Siemers-Hidma ; preface, Ralf Dahrendorf. — 2nd rev. and enl. ed. — The Hague ; Boston : Martinus Nijhoff ; Hingham, MA : Distributors for the United States and Canada, Kluwer Boston, 1981. — xx, 412 p.. — *English, French, German, and Italian. — Includes indexes*

EUROPEAN FEDERATION — Congresses

WIGNY, Pierre
On the way to an [sic] European political community : report to the Congress of the European Movement / presented by Pierre Wigny. — Brussels : European Movement, [1962]. — 40p

EUROPEAN FEDERATION — History — Documentation

Documents on the history of European integration / edited by Walter Lipgens. — Berlin : Walter de Gruyter
Vol.1: Continental plans for European union 1939-1945. — 1985, c1984. — xxiii,823p. — (Series B. History / European University Institute ; 1.1). — *Bibliographies. — Includes 250 documents in their original language on 6 microfiches in back pocket*

EUROPEAN FOUNDATION FOR THE IMPROVEMENT OF LIVING AND WORKING CONDITIONS

EF news / European Foundation for the Improvement of Living and Working Conditions. — Shankill : European Foundation for the Improvement of Living and Working Conditions, 1986-. — *Bimonthly*

EUROPEAN FOUNDATION FOR THE IMPROVEMENT OF LIVING AND WORKING CONDITIONS

Annual report. — Shankill : European Foundation for the Improvement of Living and Working Conditions, 1984-. — *Annual*

EUROPEAN FREE TRADE ASSOCIATION

DENMARK. Udvalget vedrørende Danmarks forhold til de Europaeiske faellesskaber
Danmark og de Europaeiske faellesskaber : 4. supplerende redegørelse : udviklingen i 1971. — [København] : the Udvalget, 1972. — 432p

EUROPEAN GROUP OF PUBLIC ADMINISTRATION

Bulletin des recherches. Research bulletin / European Group of Public Administration. — Roma : Formez Centro di Formazione e Studi per il Mezzogiorno, 1985-. — *Semi-annual. — Text in French and English*

EUROPEAN INTEGRATION

SIMONIS, Heide
Final report of the Sub-Committee on Economic Co-operation / Heide Simonis. — Brussels : North Atlantic Assembly, 1986. — vi,31p

EUROPEAN PARLIAMENT

COLLOQUE DE L'I[NSTITUT] [D']É[TUDES] J[URIDIQUES] E[UROPÉENNES] SUR LES COMMUNAUTÉS EUROPÉENNES (8° : 1976 : Liège)
Le Parlement Européen : pouvoirs, election, rôle futur : actes du...colloque. — Liège : Université de Liège, Institut d'Études Juridiques Européennes, 1976. — 343p. — (Collection Scientifique de la Faculté de Droit, d'Économie et de Sciences Sociales de l'Université de Liège ; 42)

Fact sheets on the European Parliament and the activities of the European Community. — [Luxembourg?] : European Parliament, [1979]. —

Fact sheets on the European Parliament and the activities of the European Community. — 3rd ed. — Luxembourg : Office for Official Publications of the European Communities, 1987. — 1v (various pagings)

The public image of the European Parliament / edited by Ann Robinson. — London : Policy Studies Institute, 1986. — iv,77p. — (Studies in European politics ; 10). — *Bibliography: p77*

SPITZHÜTTL, Rolf
Das Europäische Parlament : zwischen Chaos und Courage / von Rolf Spitzhüttl und Ulrich Lüke. — Bonn : Europa Union, 1983. — 160p

Le traité d'union europeenne : commentaire du projet adopté par le Parlement Européan, le 14 février 1984 / F. Capotorti [et al.]. — Bruxelles : Éditions de l'Université de Bruxelles, 1985. — xiii,307p. — *Bibliography: p299-301*

EUROPEAN PARLIAMENT — Comparative studies

KREMAIER, Franz
Das Europäische Parlament der EG und die Parlamentarische Versammlung des Europarates : eine vergleichende Strukturanalyse zur Begrifflichkeit... / Franz Kremaier. — München : Florentz, 1985. — (Europarecht - Völkerrecht ; Bd.9). — *Bibliographical notes*

EUROPEAN PARLIAMENT — Sources

BOLTON, Rohan
London Information Office of the European Parliament / prepared by Rohan Bolton. — [s.l.] : Association of EDC Librarians, [1985]. — [4p]. — (European Communities information ; no.9)

EUROPEAN PARLIAMENT — Sources — Bibliography

NEILSON, June
European Parliament : a guide to sources / prepared by June Neilson. — [s.l.] : Association of EDC Librarians, [1984]. — 5p. — (European Communities information ; no.2)

EUROPEAN PARLIAMENT. Information Office

BOLTON, Rohan
London Information Office of the European Parliament / prepared by Rohan Bolton. — [s.l.] : Association of EDC Librarians, [1985]. — [4p]. — (European Communities information ; no.9)

EUROPEAN POPULATION CONFERENCE (1982 : Strasbourg)

EUROPEAN POPULATION CONFERENCE (1982 : Strasbourg)
Proceedings of the European Population Conference 1982 : Strasbourg, 21-24 September 1982. — Strasbourg : Council of Europe, 1983. — 473p. — *Includes bibliographical references*

EUROPEANS — Relations — United States

The standing of the U.S. in West European opinion-1965 : (World Survey III series). — [Washington, D.C.] : United States Information Agency, 1965. — xii,59p. — R-145-65

EUROPEANS — Migrations

CROSBY, Alfred W.
Ecological imperialism : the biological expansion of Europe, 900-1900 / Alfred W. Crosby. — Cambridge : Cambridge University Press, 1986. — xiv,368p,[16]p of plates. — (Studies in environment and history). — *Includes index*

EUROPEN COMMUNITIES

Official journal of the European Communities : Directory of Community legislation in force. — Luxembourg : Office for Official Publications of the European Communities, 1984-. — *Published in annual volumes with supplements. — Continues: Register of current community legal instruments*

EUTHANASIA

Voluntary euthanasia : experts debate the right to die / edited by A.B. Downing and Barbara Smoker. — Rev., enl. ed. — London : Peter Owen, c1986. — 303p. — *Originally published as: Euthanasia and the right to death:the case for voluntary euthanasia, 1969. — Bibliography:p302-303*

EUTHANASIA — Moral and ethical aspects — Congresses

Euthanasia and the newborn : conflicts regarding saving lives / edited by Richard M. McMillan, H. Tristram Engelhardt, Jr., and Stuart F. Spicker. — Dordrecht ; Boston : D. Reidel Pub. Co. ; Norwell, MA, U.S.A. : Sold and distributed in the U.S.A. and Canada by Kluwer Academic Publishers, c1987. — p. cm. — (Philosophy and medicine ; v. 24). — *Based on a symposium entitled "Conflicts with Newborns: Saving Lives, Scarce Resources, and Euthanasis," held May 10-12, 1984, at the Mercer University School of Medicine, Macon, Ga. — Includes bibliographies and index*

EUTROPHICATION — Control
ORGANISATION FOR ECONOMIC CO-OPERATION AND DEVELOPMENT. Water Management Sector Group
Report of the Water Management Sector Group on eutrophication control. — Paris : the Organisation, 1974. — 19p. — *Includes bibliographical references*

EVALUATION RESEARCH (SOCIAL ACTION PROGRAMS)
AHONEN, Pertti
Public policy evaluation as discourse / Perti Ahonen. — Helsinki : Finnish Political Science Association, 1983. — 191 p.. — *Bibliography: p. 187-191*

ROSSI, Peter H.
Evaluation : a systematic approach / Peter H. Rossi, Howard E. Freeman. — 3rd ed. — Beverly Hills : Sage, c1985. — 422p. — *Includes index.* — *Bibliography: p.401-414*

EVALUATION RESEARCH (SOCIAL ACTION PROGRAMS) — Bibliography
LEISTRITZ, Larry
Social impact assessment and management : an annotated bibliography / Larry Leistritz and Brenda L. Ekstrom ; with Robert A. Chase, Ronald Bisset, and John M. Halstead. — New York : Garland Pub., 1986. — xxiii, 343 p.. — (Garland reference library of social science ; vol. 205Applied social science bibliographies ; vol. 3). — *Includes indexes*

EVALUATION RESEARCH (SOCIAL ACTION PROGRAMS) — United States
WORTHEN, Blaine R
Evaluating educational and social programs : guidelines for proposal review, onsite evaluation, evaluation contracts, and technical assistance / Blaine R. Worthen, Karl R. White. — Boston : Kluwer-Nijhoff ; Norwell, MA : Distributors for North America, Kluwer Academic, c1987. — xi, 347 p.. — (Evaluation in education and human services). — *Includes index.* — *Bibliography: p. [342]-344*

EVANGELISCHE KIRCHE IN DEUTSCHLAND — History
[BELL, George Kennedy Allen]
A letter to my friends in the Evangelical Church in Germany / from the Bishop of Chichester. — London : S.C.M. Press, [1946]. — 12p

EVICTION — London — Westminster
PIMLICO NEIGHBOURHOOD AID CENTRE HOUSING GROUP
Planning, policy and eviction in Pimlico : a report / by the Pimlico Neighbourhood Aid Centre Housing Group. — London : Pimlico Neighbourhood Aid Centre, 1974. — 13p

EVICTION — Northern Ireland
DOWLING, J.A.
Ejectment for non-payment of rent / by J. A. Dowling ; with a supplement for the Republic of Ireland by G. McCormack. — Belfast : Faculty of Law, the Queen's University of Belfast, 1986. — xvii,84p

EVIDENCE, CRIMINAL — United States
MOENSSENS, Andre A
Scientific evidence in criminal cases / by Andre A. Moenssens, Fred E. Inbau, James E. Starrs. — 3rd ed. — Mineola, N.Y. : Foundation Press, 1986. — p. cm. — *Includes index*

EVIDENCE, EXPERT — Congresses
Reconstructing the past : the role of psychologists in criminal trials / edited by Arne Trankell. — Deventer, The Netherlands : Kluwer, [1982]. — 398p. — *"This book contains papers and panels from the first international conference on Witness Psychology...Stockholm...September 1981"*

EVIDENCE, EXPERT — United States
MOENSSENS, Andre A
Scientific evidence in criminal cases / by Andre A. Moenssens, Fred E. Inbau, James E. Starrs. — 3rd ed. — Mineola, N.Y. : Foundation Press, 1986. — p. cm. — *Includes index*

Scientific and expert evidence : formerly Scientific and expert evidence in criminal advocacy / edited by Edward J. Imwinkelried. — 2nd ed. — New York City : Practising Law Institute, 1981. — xx, 1353 p.. — *"C3-1168."*. — *Includes bibliographical references and index*

EVIDENCE (LAW) — England
COWSILL, Eric
Evidence : law and practice / Eric Cowsill, John Clegg. — London : Longman Professional, 1985. — xxii,230p. — (Oyez Longam practitioner series. Practice and procedure). — *Includes index*

CROSS, Sir Rupert
Outline of the law of evidence / Cross and Wilkins. — 6th ed / Colin Tapper. — London : Butterworths, 1986. — xxix,307p. — *Previous ed.: 1980.* — *Includes index*

EVIDENCE (LAW) — Scotland
WILKINSON, A. B.
The Scottish law of evidence / A.B. Wilkinson. — London : Butterworths, 1986. — [200]p. — *Includes index*

EVIDENCE (LAW) — United States
Statistics and the law / edited by Morris H. DeGroot, Stephen E. Fienberg, Joseph B. Kadane. — New York : Wiley, c1986. — xviii, 484 p.. — (Wiley series in probability and mathematical statistics. Applied probability and statistics). — *Includes bibliographies and indexes*

EVIDENCE (LAW) — United States — Statistical methods
Statistics and the law / edited by Morris H. DeGroot, Stephen E. Fienberg, Joseph B. Kadane. — New York : Wiley, c1986. — xviii, 484 p.. — (Wiley series in probability and mathematical statistics. Applied probability and statistics). — *Includes bibliographies and indexes*

EVOLUTION
DALY, Martin
Sex, evolution, and behavior / Martin Daly and Margo Wilson. — 2nd ed. — Boston : Willard Grant Press, c1983. — xiv, 402 p.. — *Includes index.* — *Bibliography: p. 345-389*

DARWIN, Charles
The works of Charles Darwin / edited by Paul Barrett. — London : Pickering & Chatto, 1986. — 10v.

GRUBER, Howard E
Darwin on man : a psychological study of scientific creativity / Howard E. Gruber ; foreword to the 1st ed. by Jean Piaget. — 2d ed. — Chicago : University of Chicago Press, 1981. — xxvii, 310 p.. — *First ed., published in 1974, entered under title: Darwin on man.* — *Includes bibliographical references and index*

EVOLUTION — History
GREENE, John C.
Science, ideology, and world view : esssays in the history of evolutionary ideas / John C. Greene. — Berkeley ; London : University of California Press, c1981. — x,202p. — *Includes index*

HOLBROOK, David
Evolution and the humanities / David Holbrook. — Aldershot : Gower, c1987. — [230]p. — (Avebury series in philosophy). — *Includes bibliography and index*

EVOLUTION — Philosophy
RITCHEY, Thomas P.
Towards a theory of non-linear social evolution / Thomas P. Ritchey. — Malmö : Liber, 1983. — 164p. — *Bibliography: p156-164*

EVOLUTION — Philosophy — Addresses, essays, lectures
Minds, machines and evolution : philosophical studies / edited by Christopher Hookway. — Cambridge : Cambridge University Press, 1984. — xi,177p. — *Includes bibliographies and index*

EWE (AFRICAN PEOPLE) — Social conditions
HILL, Polly
Talking with Ewe seine fishermen and shallot farmers / recording and edited by Polly Hill. — Cambridge : African Studies Centre, University of Cambridge, [1986]. — 66p,[11] leaves of plates. — (Cambridge African monographs ; 6). — *Bibliography: p57-58.* — *Includes index*

EX-NUNS — United States
HOLLINGSWORTH, Gerelyn
Ex-nuns : women who have left the convent / by Gerelyn Hollingsworth. — Jefferson, N.C. : McFarland & Co., c1985. — ix, 126 p.. — *Includes index.* — *Bibliography: p. 117-124*

EXAMINATIONS — Great Britain
BOURNER, Tom
Entry qualifications and degree performance : the technical report of a research project on the relationship between entry qualifications and degree performance on CNAA first degree courses / Tom Bourner and Mahmoud Hamed. — London : CNAA, 1987. — 77p. — (CNAA development sevices publications ; 10). — *Bibliography: p68-69*

GREAT BRITAIN. Parliament. House of Commons. Library. Research Division
Education and assessment : proposals for reform / Kay Andrews. — [London] : the Division, 1984. — 22p. — (Background paper ; no.146)

EXAMINERS (ADMINISTRATIVE PROCEDURE) — United States
COFER, M. Donna Price
Judges, bureaucrats, and the question of independence : a study of the Social Security Administration hearing process / Donna Price Cofer. — Westport, Conn. : Greenwood Press, 1985. — xvii, 245 p.. — (Contributions in political science ; no. 130). — *Includes index.* — *Bibliography: p. [231]-235*

EXCHANGE
Production, circulation et monnaie / [par] R. Arena...[et al.] ; introduction: R. Arena, A. Graziani [et] post-face: J. Kregel. — Paris : Presses Universitaires de France, 1985. — 435p. — (Travaux et Recherches du Laboratoire Associé No.301. C.N.R.S.-Université de Nice). — *"Le présent ouvrage est né d'une rencontre...organisée par le L.A.T.A.P.S.E.S. (UA CNRS N°301), les 1 er et 2 février 1984 à l'Université de Nice"*. — *Bibliograhie: p428-430*

EXCHANGE — Social aspects — Papua New Guinea
SILLITOE, Paul
Give and take : exchange in Wola society / Paul Sillitoe. — New York : St. Martin's Press, 1979. — xiv, 316 p., [4] leaves of plates. — *Includes index.* — *Bibliography: p. [303]-308*

EXCHANGES, LITERARY AND SCIENTIFIC — Addresses, essays, lectures
BOORSTIN, Daniel J.
The invisible world : libraries and the myth of cultural exchange / Daniel J. Boorstin. — Washington, D. C. : Library of Congress, 1985. — 14p. — (The Center for the Book viewpoint series ; no.15). — *"Remarks at the IFLA General Conference, August 19, 1985"*

EXECUTIVE ABILITY
CLEVELAND, Harlan
The knowledge executive : leadership in an information society / by Harlan Cleveland. — 1st ed. — New York : Dutton, c1985. — p. cm . — *"A Truman Talley Book."*. — *Includes index.* — *Bibliography: p*

EXECUTIVE ADVISORY BODIES — Netherlands — Directories
WETENSCHAPPELIJKE RAAD VOOR HET REGERINGSBELEID
Overzicht externe adviesorganen van de centrale overheid. — 's-Gravenhage : Staatsuitgeverij, 1976. — 1v. (various pagings). — (Rapporten aan de Regering / Wetenschappelijke Raad voor het Regeringsbeleid ; 11). — *Includes indexes*

EXECUTIVE ADVISORY BODIES — United States
FLITNER, David
The politics of presidential commissions / by David Flitner. — Dobbs Ferry, N.Y. : Transnational Pub., c1986. — xvii, 236 p.. — *Includes index. — Bibliography: p. 221-227*

EXECUTIVE POWER — New Zealand
The accountability of the executive / edited by T. M. Berthold. — Wellington : New Zealand Institute of Public Administration, 1981. — 110p. — *Includes bibliographical references*

EXECUTIVE POWER — France — History
DERFLER, Leslie
President & Parliament : a short history of the French Presidency / Leslie Derfler. — Boca Raton : University Presses of Florida, c1983. — ix, 286 p.. — *"A Florida Atlantic University book.". — Includes index. Bibliography: p. 273-279*

EXECUTIVE POWER — India
CHOUDHARY, Valmiki
President and the Indian Constitution / Valmiki Choudhary. — New Delhi : Allied Publishers, 1985. — x, 379 p.. — 60-9. — *Includes index*

EXECUTIVE POWER — United States
FISHER, Louis
The politics of shared power : Congress and the executive / Louis Fisher. — 2nd ed. — Washington, D.C. : CQ Press, c1987. — xi, 241 p. — *Includes indexes. — Includes bibliographies*

LOFGREN, Charles A
"Government from reflection and choice" : constitutional essays on war, foreign relations, and federalism / Charles A. Lofgren. — New York : Oxford University Press, c1986. — xviii, 235p. — *Includes index*

MERRY, Henry J
The constitutional system : the group character of the elected institutions / Henry J. Merry. — New York : Praeger, 1986. — x, 215 p.. — *Includes bibliographies and index*

MOSHER, Frederick C
Presidential transitions and foreign affairs / Frederick C. Mosher, W. David Clinton, Daniel G. Lang. — Baton Rouge : Louisiana State University Press, c1987. — xvii, 281 p.. — (Miller Center series on the American presidency). — *The recommendations of the Miller Center Commission on Presidential Transitions and Foreign Policy are included in the appendix. — Includes index. — Bibliography: p. [265]-273*

The President, the Congress, and foreign policy / [foreword by] Edmund S. Muskie, Kenneth Rush ; Kenneth W. Thompson [rapporteur]. — Lanham : University Press of America, c1986. — xv, 311 p.. — *"A joint policy project of the Association of Former Members of Congress and the Atlantic Council of the United States. — Includes bibliographies*

EXECUTIVE PRIVILEGE (GOVERNMENT INFORMATION) — United States
DEMAC, Donna A
Keeping America uninformed : government secrecy in the 1980's / Donna A. Demac ; preface by Ben H. Bagdikian. — New York : Pilgrim Press, c1984. — xii, 180 p.. — *Includes index. — Bibliography: p. 169-174*

EXECUTIVES
MUELLER, Dennis C
The modern corporation / D.C. Mueller. — Lincoln : University of Nebraska Press, 1966. — p. cm. — *Bibliography: p*

EXECUTIVES — Addresses, essays, lectures
SRIVASTVA, Suresh
Executive power / Suresh Srivastva and associates. — San Francisco : Jossey-Bass Publishers, 1986. — xxii, 360 p.. — *Includes index. — Bibliography: p. 331-351*

EXECUTIVES — Training of — Developing countries
Management training and development in public enterprises in developing countries : report and papers of a regional workshop held in Karachi, Pakistan, 5-15 January 1981, convened by ICPE in collaboration with the United Nations Industrial Development Organization and the Pakistan Institute of Management / edited by Irshad H. Khan, Shahiruddin Al[v]i and Stane Možina. — Ljubljana, Yugoslavia : International Center for Public Enterprises in Developing Countries, 1982. — 199p. — *Includes bibliographical references*

EXECUTIVES — Europe, Eastern — Training of
Organizatsiia obucheniia khoziaistvennykh rukovoditelei : opyt sotsialisticheskikh stran / pod redaktsiei F. M. Rusinova, T. V. Burgeevoi. — Moskva : Ekonomika, 1986. — 255p

EXECUTIVES — France
MORVILLE, Pierre
Les nouvelles politiques sociales du patronat / Pierre Morville. — Paris : La Découverte, 1985. — 127p. — *Bibliography: p124-125*

EXECUTIVES — Great Britain
CRUM, R. E.
Non—productive activities in U.K. manufacturing industry : a report by the School of Social Studies of the University of East Anglia (Norwich) to the U.K. Department of Industry and the European Economic Community / R. E. Crum [and] G. Gudgin. — Luxembourg : Office for Official Publications of the European Communities, 1977. — ix, 176p. — (Regional policy series ; no.3)

EXECUTIVES — Soviet Union — Training of
Organizatsiia obucheniia khoziaistvennykh rukovoditelei : opyt sotsialisticheskikh stran / pod redaktsiei F. M. Rusinova, T. V. Burgeevoi. — Moskva : Ekonomika, 1986. — 255p

EXECUTIVES — United States
FOUNDATION FOR THE STUDY OF PHILANTHROPY
Are we corrupting our executives?. — Hampton (Va.) : Foundation for the Study of Philanthropy, 1983. — 41 leaves

EXISTENTIALISM
BLACKHAM, H. J.
Six existentialist thinkers / H. J. Blackham. — London : Routledge & Kegan Paul, 1961. — vii,179p. — *First published 1952. — Bibliography: p169-173*

CATALANO, Joseph S
A commentary on Jean-Paul Sartre's Critique of dialectical reason, volume 1, Theory of practical ensembles / Joseph S. Catalano. — Chicago : University of Chicago Press, 1986. — x, 282 p.. — *Includes index. — Bibliography: p. [269]-273*

HEINEMANN, Frederick Henry
Existentialism and the modern predicament / F. H. Heinemann. — Westport, Conn. : Greenwood Press, 1979, c1958. — xix, 229 p.. — *Reprint of the ed. published by Harper, New York, which was issued as no. TB28 of Harper torchbooks. — Includes index. — Bibliography: p. 219-225*

MACQUARRIE, John
Existentialism / John Macquarrie. — Harmondsworth : Penguin, 1973. — xi,252 p. — (Pelican books). — *Originally published: New York : World Publishing Co. ; London : Hutchinson, 1972. — Bibliography: p.239-246. — Includes index*

EXISTENTIALISM — Study and teaching (Higher) — Israel
GORDON, Hayim
Dance, dialogue, and despair : existentialist philosophy and education for peace in Isreal / Haim Gordon. — University, Ala. : University of Alabama Press, c1986. — xvii, 250 p.. — (Judaic studies series). — *Includes index. — Bibliographical essay: p. 240-244*

EXORCISM
DAVIS, Winston Bradley
Dojo : magic and exorcism in modern Japan / Winston Davis. — Stanford, Calif. : Stanford University Press, 1980. — xvi, 332 p.. — *Includes bibliographical references and index*

EXPATRIATION — Israel — History
PALUMBO, Michael
The Palestinian catastrophe : the 1948 expulsion of a people from their homeland / Michael Palumbo. — London : Faber, 1987. — xix,233p. — *Includes index*

EXPENDITURES, PUBLIC
AULD, D. A. L.
Budget reform : should there be a capital budget for the public sector? / D. A. L. Auld. — Toronto : C.D. Howe Institute, 1985. — vi,36p

HELLER, Peter S.
Ageing and social expenditure in the major industrial countries, 1980-2025 / by Peter S. Heller, Richard Hemming and Peter W. Kohnert. — Washington, D.C. : The World Bank, 1986. — viii,76p. — (Occasional paper / International Monetary Fund ; no.47). — *Bibliographical references: p74-76*

EXPENDITURES, PUBLIC — Classification
Classification of the functions of government. — New York : United Nations, 1980. — iii,52p. — (Statistical papers / United Nations, Statistical Office. Series M ; no.70) ([Document] (United Nations) ; ST/ESA/STAT/SER.M/70). — *Sales no.: E.80.XVII.17*

EXPENDITURES, PUBLIC — Congresses
Public expenditure : the key issues / edited by John Bristow and Declan McDonagh. — Dublin, Ireland : Institute of Public Administration, 1986. — 138 p.. — *Proceedings of National Conference on Public Expenditure: the Key Issues, held Nov. 1985 in Dublin, organized by the Institute. — Includes bibliographies. — Contents: Public expenditure and public debt / Vito Tanzi -- The political economy of public expenditure / Alan Peacock -- Public employment and public expenditure / Richard Rose -- Public expenditure and the bureaucracy / Peter Jackson -- An Irish overview / Alan Dukes*

EXPENDITURES, PUBLIC — Forecasting
HELLER, Peter S.
Ageing and social expenditure in the major industrial countries, 1980-2025 / by Peter S. Heller, Richard Hemming and Peter W. Kohnert. — Washington, D.C. : The World Bank, 1986. — viii,76p. — (Occasional paper / International Monetary Fund ; no.47). — *Bibliographical references: p74-76*

EXPERIMENTAL DESIGN
KISH, Leslie
Statistical design for research / Leslie Kish. — New York : Wiley, 1987. — p. cm. — (Wiley series in probability and mathematical statistics. Applied probability and statistics section). — *Includes index. — Bibliography: p*

EXPERIMENTAL THEATER — Great Britain — History
DAVIES, Andrew
Other theatres : the development of alternative and experimental theatre in Britain / Andrew Davies. — London : Macmillan Education, 1987. — xx,249p. — (Communication and culture). — *Includes index*

EXPERT SYSTEMS
KERAVNOU, E. T.
Competent expert systems : a case study in fault diagnosis / E.T. Keravnou & L. Johnson. — London : Kogan Page, 1986. — 320p. — ([New technology modular series]). — Bibliography: p303-311. — Includes index

EXPERT SYSTEMS (COMPUTER SCIENCE)
HART, Anna
Knowledge acquisition for expert systems / Anna Hart. — London : Kogan Page, 1986. — 180p. — ([New technology modular series]). — Bibliography: p165-168. — Includes index

JACKSON, Peter, 1948 Dec. 29-
Introduction to expert systems / Peter Jackson. — Wokingham : Addison-Wesley, c1986. — [250]p. — (International computer science series). — Includes bibliography and index

JOHNSON, L.
Expert systems technology : a guide / L. Johnson, E.T. Keravnou. — Tunbridge Wells : Abacus, 1985 (1986 [printing]). — 184p

EXPERT SYSTEMS (COMPUTER SCIENCE) — Congresses
EXPERT SYSTEMS IN GOVERNMENT SYMPOSIUM (1985 : McLean, Va.)
Expert Systems in Government Symposium / Kamal N. Karna, editor ; IEEE Computer Society, The MITRE Corporation, The Institute of Electrical and Electronics Engineers, inc., in association with AIAA National Capital Section. — Washington, D.C. : IEEE Computer Society Press, c1985. — xxiii, 694 p.. — Includes bibliographies and index

EXPLORERS — Africa
ESSNER, Cornelia
Deutsche Afrikareisende im neunzehnten Jahrhundert : zur Sozialgeschichte des Reisens / Cornelia Essner. — Stuttgart : Steiner-Verlag-Wiesbaden, 1985. — 235p. — (Beiträge zur Kolonial- und Überseegeschichte ; Bd.32). — Bibliography: p210-235

EXPORT CONTROLS
Guidelines for the acquisition of foreign technology in developing countries : with special reference to technology licence agreements. — New York : United Nations, 1973. — xi,55p. — ([Documents] / United Nations ; ID/98). — "Prepared by Rana K.D.N. Singh...in co-operation with the secretariat of UNIDO". — Sales no.: E.73.II.B.1

EXPORT CONTROLS — United States
PANEL ON THE IMPACT OF NATIONAL SECURITY CONTROLS ON INTERNATIONAL TECHNOLOGY TRANSFER
Balancing the national interest : U.S. national security export controls and global economic competition. — Washington : National Academy Press, 1987. — xiii,321p. — Bibliography: p297-309

EXPORT CREDIT
Export credits : developments and prospects / by Eduard Brau...[et al.]. — Washington, D.C. : International Monetary Fund, 1986. — v,34p. — (World economic and financial surveys)

EXPORT CREDIT — Great Britain
DIECKMANN, Norbert
Das Britische Exportfinanzierungs-system : eine landeskundliche Untersuchung / Norbert Dieckmann. — Hamburg : Hamburger Buchagentur, 1985. — 250p. — (Anglo-Amerikanische Wirtschaftsstudien ; Bd.2). — Bibliography: p230-250

EXPORT CREDIT — United States
The Export-Import Bank at fifty : the international environment and the institution's role / edited by Rita M. Rodriguez. — Lexington, Mass. : Lexington Books, c1987. — xii, 206 p.. — Includes bibliographies and index

EXPORT-IMPORT BANK OF THE UNITED STATES
The Export-Import Bank at fifty : the international environment and the institution's role / edited by Rita M. Rodriguez. — Lexington, Mass. : Lexington Books, c1987. — xii, 206 p.. — Includes bibliographies and index

EXPORT MARKETING
Case studies in international marketing / edited by Peter Doyle and Norman A. Hart. — London : Heinemann published on behalf of the CAM Foundation and the Institute of Marketing, 1982. — vii,391p

CATEORA, Philip R
International marketing / Philip R. Cateora. — 6th ed. — Homewood, Ill. : Irwin, 1987. — xvii, 839 p.. — Includes index. — Bibliography: p. 801-805

GILLIGAN, Colin
International marketing : strategy and management / Colin Gilligan and Martin Hird. — London : Croom Helm, c1986. — [336]p. — Includes index

MAJARO, Simon
International marketing : a strategic approach to world markets / Simon Majaro. — Rev. ed. — London : Allen & Unwin, 1982. — 307p. — Previous ed.: 1977. — Bibliography: p299-301. — Includes index

Research in international marketing / edited by Peter W. Turnbull & Stanley J. Paliwoda. — London : Croom Helm, c1986. — 376p. — Includes bibliographies

TERPSTRA, Vern
International marketing / Vern Terpstra. — 3rd ed. — Chicago ; London : Dryden, c1983. — xiii,702p. — (The Dryden Press series in marketing). — Previous ed.: 1978. — Includes index

EXPORT MARKETING — Management
KEEGAN, Warren J
Multinational marketing management / Warren J. Keegan. — 3rd ed. — Englewood Cliffs, N.J. : Prentice-Hall, c1984. — xxii, 698 p.. — (The Prentice-Hall series in management) (Prentice-Hall international series in management). — Includes bibliographies and indexes

EXPORT MARKETING — Canada
DALY, D. J.
Canadian manufactured exports : constraints and opportunities / D. J. Daly [and] D. C. Maccharles. — Montreal : The Institute for Research on Public Policy/L'Institut de recherches politiques. — xxviii,180p. — Bibliography: p155-168

EXPORT MARKETING — European Economic Community countries
PERRY, K.
Business in Europe : opportunites for British companies in the EEC / Keith Perry. — London : Heinemann, 1987. — xii,206p. — Bibliography: p199-200. — Includes index

EXPORT MARKETING — Great Britain
PERRY, K.
Business in Europe : opportunites for British companies in the EEC / Keith Perry. — London : Heinemann, 1987. — xii,206p. — Bibliography: p199-200. — Includes index

EXPORT MARKETING — Sri Lanka
ATHUKORALA, Premachandra
Export instability and growth : problems and prospects for the developing economies / Premachandra Athukorala and Frank Cong Hiep Huynh. — London : Croom Helm, c1987. — 244p. — Bibliography: p221-237. — Includes index

EXPORT MARKETING — United States — Decision making
SOMKID JATUSRIPITAK
The exporting behavior of manufacturing firms / by Somkid Jatusripitak. — Ann Arbor, Mich. : UMI Research Press, c1986. — xii, 115 p.. — (Research for business decisions ; no. 87) . — : A revision of author's thesis (Ph. D.)--Northwestern University, 1984. — Includes index. — Bibliography: p. [107]-112

EXPORT-PROCESSING ZONES — Asia, Southeastern
Transnational corporations in South East Asia and the Pacific. — Sydney : Transnational Corporations Research Project, University of Sydney
vol.7: Transnational corporations and export-oriented industrialization / Ernst Utrecht, editor. — 1985. — 273p

EXPORT PROCESSING ZONES — Caribbean Area
LONG, Frank
Employment effects of multinational enterprises in export processing zones in the Caribbean : a joint ILO/UNCTC research project / by Frank Long. — Geneva : International Labour Office, 1986. — 82p. — Includes bibliographical references

EXPORT-PROCESSING ZONES — Pacific area
Transnational corporations in South East Asia and the Pacific. — Sydney : Transnational Corporations Research Project, University of Sydney
vol.7: Transnational corporations and export-oriented industrialization / Ernst Utrecht, editor. — 1985. — 273p

EXPORT SALES
EDINBURGH INSTITUTE ON INTERNATIONAL BUSINESS TRANSACTIONS (1984)
Legal aspects of international business transactions, II : the Edinburgh Institute on International Business Transactions, 1984 / edited by D. Campbell and C. Rohwer. — Amsterdam ; New York : North Holland ; New York : Elsevier Science Pub. Co., distributor, 1985. — p. cm. — "A project of University of the Pacific, McGeorge School of Law, International Programs."

EXPORT SALES — Legal aspects, laws, etc.
Survey of the international sale of goods / edited by Louis Lafili, Franklin Gevurtz, Dennis Campbell. — Deventer [Netherlands] ; Boston : Kluwer Law and Taxation Publishers, 1985. — p. cm. — Includes bibliographies

EXPORT SALES — Europe
Survey of the international sale of goods / edited by Louis Lafili, Franklin Gevurtz, Dennis Campbell. — Deventer [Netherlands] ; Boston : Kluwer Law and Taxation Publishers, 1985. — p. cm. — Includes bibliographies

EXPORT SALES — Great Britain — Finance
DIECKMANN, Norbert
Das Britische Exportfinanzierungs-system : eine landeskundliche Untersuchung / Norbert Dieckmann. — Hamburg : Hamburger Buchagentur, 1985. — 250p. — (Anglo-Amerikanische Wirtschaftsstudien ; Bd.2). — Bibliography: p230-250

EXPORT SALES — Middle East
Middle Eastern exports : problems and prospects / edited by Rodney Wilson. — [Durham] : University of Durham Centre for Middle Eastern and Islamic Studies, c1986. — 119p. — (Occasional papers series ; no.29)

EXPORT SALES — United States
SOLOMON, Anthony M
The dollar, debt, and the trade deficit / Anthony M. Solomon. — New York : New York University Press, 1986, c1987. — p. cm. — (The Joseph I. Lubin memorial lectures ; no. 3)

EXPORT TRADING COMPANIES
ELDERKIN, Kenton W
Creative countertrade : a guide to doing business worldwide / Kenton W. Elderkin, Warren E. Norquist. — Cambridge, Mass. : Ballinger Pub. Co., c1987. — xv, 221 p.. — *Includes bibliographies and index*

EXPRESS HIGHWAYS — Developing countries
BANISTER, David
Toll road pricing on inter urban highways in developing countries / David Banister. — London : Bartlett School of Architecture and Planning, 1986. — [31]p. — (Town planning discussion paper ; no.46)

EXPRESS HIGHWAYS — France
MAGNAN, René
L'autoroute dans la ville / René Magnan. — Paris : Centre de Recherche d'Urbanisme, 1971. — 53p

EXTERNAL PROBLEMS (MATHEMATICS)
TIKHOMIROV, V. M.
Fundamental principles of the theory of extremal problems / by Vladimir M. Tikhomirov ; translated by Bernd Luderer. — Chichester : Wiley, 1986. — 136p. — *Translation of: Grundprinzien der Theorie der Extremalaufgaben.* — *Bibliography: p127-132.* — *Includes index*

EXTERNALITIES (ECONOMICS) — Addresses, essays, lectures
Natural resource economics : policy problems and contemporary analysis / edited by Daniel W. Bromley. — Hingham, MA, USA : Kluwer-Nijhoff : Distributors for the U.S. and Canada, Kluwer Academic Publishers, c1986. — xiv, 234 p.. — (Recent economic thought series). — *Includes index.* — *Bibliography: p. 226-229*

FAAA (TAHITI : REGION) — Population — Statistics
Tableaux normalisés du recensement général de la population : 15 octobre 1983. — [Papeete] : Institut territorial de la statistique Résultats de la commune de Faaa. — [1985?]. — 12 leaves

FABIAN SOCIETY
Fabian society briefing. — London : Fabian Society, 1986-

FACTORIES — Location — Bibliography
DOMSCHKE, Wolfgang
Location and layout planning : an international bibliography / Wolfgang Domschke, Andreas Drexl. — Berlin ; New York : Springer-Verlag, 1985. — p. cm. — (Lecture notes in economics and mathematical systems ; 238)

FACTORY AND TRADE WASTE
Recycling from municipal refuse : a state-of-the-art review and annotated bibliography / Sanda Johnson Cointreau. — Washington, D.C. : The World Bank, 1984. — xiv,214p. — (World Bank technical paper ; no.30) (UNDP project management report ; no.1) (Integrated resource recovery series ; no.1). — *Bibliography: p25-189*

FACTORY AND TRADE WASTE — Bibliography
Recycling from municipal refuse : a state-of-the-art review and annotated bibliography / Sanda Johnson Cointreau. — Washington, D.C. : The World Bank, 1984. — xiv,214p. — (World Bank technical paper ; no.30) (UNDP project management report ; no.1) (Integrated resource recovery series ; no.1). — *Bibliography: p25-189*

FACTORY AND TRADE WASTE — Economic aspects
WILCOX, Joan
Urban waste : economic aspects of technological alternatives / Joan Wilcox. — London : Department of the Environment, 1976. — 17,[9]leaves. — *Bibliography: second sequence, leaf [9]*

FACTORY AND TRADE WASTE — England
BRITTAN, Yvonne
The impact of water pollution control on industry : a case study of fifty dischargers / Yvonne Brittan. — Oxford : Centre for Socio-Legal Studies, 1984. — vii,115p. — *Bibliography: p107*

FACTORY MANAGEMENT — Germany (West)
SORGE, Arndt
Comparative factory organisation : an Anglo-German comparison of manufacturing, management and manpower / Arndt Sorge and Malcolm Warner. — Aldershot : Gower, c1986. — viii,229p. — *Bibliography: p209-219.* — *Includes index*

FACTORY MANAGEMENT — Great Britain
SORGE, Arndt
Comparative factory organisation : an Anglo-German comparison of manufacturing, management and manpower / Arndt Sorge and Malcolm Warner. — Aldershot : Gower, c1986. — viii,229p. — *Bibliography: p209-219.* — *Includes index*

FACTORY MANAGEMENT — Hungary — History
RÁCZ, János
Az üzemi bizottságok a magyar demokratikus átalakulásban (1944-1948) / Rácz János. — Budapest : Akadémiai Kiadó, 1971. — 159p

F.A.I. (Organization : Spain)
GÓMEZ CASAS, Juan
[Historia de la FAI. English]. Anarchist organisation : the history of the F.A.I. / Juan Gómez Casas ; translated by Abe Bluestein. — Montréal ; Buffalo : Black Rose Books, c1986. — 261 p.. — *Translation of: Historia de la FAI.* — *Includes bibliographies*

FAILURE (PSYCHOLOGY)
BARRETT, Jeffrey W
Impulse to revolution in Latin America / by Jeffrey W. Barrett. — New York : Praeger, 1985. — ix, 357p. — (Praeger special studies)

FAIRBAIRN, JOHN
BOTHA, H. C.
John Fairbairn in South Africa / by H.C. Botha. — Cape Town : Historical Publication Society, c1984. — xviii, 336p. — *Translation of thesis (D.Litt.et Phil.) - University of South Africa, 1980.* — *Bibliography: p.311-329*

FAKARAVA (TUAMOTU ISLANDS) — Population — Statistics
Tableaux normalisés du recensement général de la population : 15 octobre 1983. — [Papeete] : Institut territorial de la statistique Résultats de la commune de Fakarava. — [1985?]. — 4p,ll leaves

FALKLAND ISLAND — International status
FERRER VIEYRA, Enrique
Las islas Malvinas y el derecho internacional : los títulos argentinos y británicos, la convención de Nootka, la prescripción adquisitiva, la libre determinación de los pueblos, las Malvinas y la Antártica Argentina / Enrique Ferrer Vieyra. — Buenos Aires : Depalma, 1984. — xvi, 364p. — *Bibliography: p.333-364*

FALKLAND ISLANDS
ARGENTINA. Secretaría de Información Pública
Islas Malvinas Argentinas. — [Buenos Aires : the Secretaría, 1982]. — [12]p. — *In Spanish and English.* — *"Text based on previous publications of the Public Information Secretariat of the Presidency of the Nation, with the advice of Rear-Admiral Laurio Destefani and Professor Dr. Calixto Armas Barea"*

FALKLAND ISLANDS — Bibliography
GREAT BRITAIN. Parliament. House of Commons. Library. International Affairs Section
The Falkland Islands conflict : political and economic aspects / R. J. Ware. — 2nd issue. — [London] : the Library, 1983. — 11p. — (Reference sheet / House of Commons. Library. [Research Division] ; no.82/19)

GREAT BRITAIN. Parliament. House of Commons. Library. International Affairs Section
The Falkland Islands conflict : political and economic aspects / R.J.Ware. — 3rd issue. — [London] : the Library, 1983. — 14p. — (Reference sheet / House of Commons Library, [Research Division] ; no.83/12)

FALKLAND ISLANDS — Census, 1986
FALKLAND ISLANDS. Census Supervisor
Report of census 1986. — [Stanley : Government Printer], 1986. — 22 leaves

FALKLAND ISLANDS — Economic policy
Report and accounts / Falkland Islands Development Corporation. — Stanley : Falkland Islands Development Corporation, 1984-

FALKLAND ISLANDS — History
AREVALO, Oscar
Malvinas; Beagle; Atlantico Sur; : Madryn, jaque a la OTAN-OTAS / Oscar Arevalo. — Buenos Aires : Anteo, 1985. — 167p. — (Colección Argentina : temas de actualidad)

CERÓN, Sergio
Malvinas : ¿Gesta heroica o derrota vergonzosa? / Sergio Cerón. — Buenos Aires : Editorial Sudamericana, [ca.1984]. — 344p

FALKLAND ISLANDS — International status
DOLZER, Rudolf
Der völkerrechtliche Status der Falkland-Inseln (Malvinas) in Wandel der Zeit / von Rudolf Dolzer. — Heidelberg : R. V. Decker und C. F. Müller, 1986. — xi,239p. — (Heidelberger Forum ; 39). — *Bibliography: p229-235*

FALKLAND ISLANDS — Population — Statistics
FALKLAND ISLANDS. Census Supervisor
Report of census 1986. — [Stanley : Government Printer], 1986. — 22 leaves

FALKLAND ISLANDS DEVELOPMENT CORPORATION
Report and accounts / Falkland Islands Development Corporation. — Stanley : Falkland Islands Development Corporation, 1984-

FALKLAND ISLANDS WAR, 1982
ARGENTINA. Secretaría de Información Pública
Islas Malvinas Argentinas. — [Buenos Aires : the Secretaría, 1982]. — [12]p. — *In Spanish and English.* — *"Text based on previous publications of the Public Information Secretariat of the Presidency of the Nation, with the advice of Rear-Admiral Laurio Destefani and Professor Dr. Calixto Armas Barea"*

CERÓN, Sergio
Malvinas : ¿Gesta heroica o derrota vergonzosa? / Sergio Cerón. — Buenos Aires : Editorial Sudamericana, [ca.1984]. — 344p

FERRER VIEYRA, Enrique
Las islas Malvinas y el derecho internacional : los títulos argentinos y británicos, la convención de Nootka, la prescripción adquisitiva, la libre determinación de los pueblos, las Malvinas y la Antártica Argentina / Enrique Ferrer Vieyra. — Buenos Aires : Depalma, 1984. — xvi, 364p. — *Bibliography: p.333-364*

GAMBA, Virginia
The Falklands / Malvinas War : a model for north-south crisis prevention / Virginia Gamba. — Boston, Mass. ; London : Allen & Unwin, 1987. — xii,212p. — *Bibliography: p195-203.* — *Includes index*

FALKLAND ISLANDS WAR, 1982
continuation

Government popularity and the Falklands War : a reassessment / by David Sanders ... [et al.]. — Colchester : Department of Government University of Essex, 1986. — 33 p. — (Essex papers in politics and government ; no.40)

GREAT BRITAIN. Parliament. House of Commons. Library. International Affairs Section
The Falkland Islands and Dependencies / Richard Ware. — [London] : the Library, 1982. — 21p. — (Background paper / House of Commons. Library. [Research Division] ; no.101). — *Updated and expanded version of paper first issued on 5th April 1982*

MITIAEVA, E. V.
Anglo-argentiiskii konflikt iz-za Folklendskikh (Mal'vinskikh) ostrovov / E. V. Mitiaeva. — Moskva : Mezhdunarodnye otnosheniia, 1985. — 90p. — (Mezhdunarodnaia biblioteka)

FALKLAND ISLANDS WAR, 1982 — Bibliography

GREAT BRITAIN. Parliament. House of Commons. Library. International Affairs Section
The Falkland Islands conflict : political and economic aspects / R. J. Ware. — 2nd issue. — [London] : the Library, 1983. — 11p. — (Reference sheet / House of Commons. Library. [Research Division] ; no.82/19)

FALKLAND ISLANDS WAR, 1982 — Influence

BURNS, Jimmy
The land that lost its heroes : the Falklands, the post-war and Alfonsín / Jimmy Burns. — London : Bloomsbury, 1987. — 1v.. — *Includes bibliography and index*

FALKLAND ISLANDS WAR, 1982 — Journalists

ADAMS, Valerie, 1950-
The media and the Falklands campaign / Valerie Adams. — Basingstoke : Macmillan, 1986. — x,224p. — *Bibliography: p214-217.* — *Includes index*

HOLMES, Deborah
Governing the press : media freedom in the U.S. and Great Britain / Deborah Holmes. — Boulder : Westview Press, 1986. — xi, 107 p.. — (A Westview special study). — *Includes index.* — *Bibliography: p. 93-102*

FALKLAND ISLANDS WAR, 1982 — Political aspects

AREVALO, Oscar
Malvinas; Beagle; Atlantico Sur; : Madryn, jaque a la OTAN-OTAS / Oscar Arevalo. — Buenos Aires : Anteo, 1985. — 167p. — (Colección Argentina : temas de actualidad)

FALKLANDS ISLANDS WAR, 1982 — Bibliography

GREAT BRITAIN. Parliament. House of Commons. Library. International Affairs Section
The Falkland Islands conflict : political and economic aspects / R.J.Ware. — 3rd issue. — [London] : the Library, 1983. — 14p. — (Reference sheet / House of Commons Library, [Research Division] ; no.83/12)

FALKLANDS ISLANDS WAR, 1982 — Economic aspects

MILIA, Juan Guillermo
El valor estrategico y económico del Atlantico sur y la guerra de las Malvinas / Juan Guillermo Milia. — [Buenos Aires] : OIKOS, [1985]. — 34p. — *Bibliography: p[35-36]*

FALLS ROAD (BELFAST, NORTHERN IRELAND)

ADAMS, Gerry
Falls memories / Gerry Adams. — Rev. ed. — Dingle, Co. Kerry : Brandon, 1983. — 144p. — *Originally published: 1982.* — *Bibliography: p143-144*

FALWELL, JERRY

HALSELL, Grace
Prophecy and politics : militant evangelists on the road to nuclear war / Grace Halsell. — Westport, Conn. : Lawrence Hill & Co., c1986. — 210 p.. — *Includes index*

FAME

BRAUDY, Leo
The frenzy of renown : fame & its history / Leo Braudy. — New York : Oxford University Press, 1986. — xiii, 649 p., [32] p. of plates. — *Includes index.* — *Bibliography: p. 599-623*

FAMILY

DE'ATH, Erica
Families and self-help : a resource pack / Erica De'Ath and Gill Webster. — London : National Children's Bureau, 1986. — 1 pamphlet, 10 information sheets, 16 work-cards

Family portraits / edited by Digby Anderson and Graham Dawson. — London : Social Affairs Unit, c1986. — 127p

Family, self, and society : emerging issues, alternatives, and interventions / edited by Douglas B. Gutknecht, Edgar W. Butler. — 2nd ed. — Lanham ; New York ; London : University Press of America, 1985. — xii,373p. — *Includes bibliographies*

Management of work and personal life : problems and opportunities / edited by Mary Dean Lee and Rabindra N. Kanungo. — New York, N.Y. : Praeger, 1984. — p. cm. — *Includes index.* — *Bibliography: p*

Social change and the life course / edited by Gaynor Cohen. — London : Tavistock, 1987. — viii,248p. — *Includes bibliographies and index*

TODD, Emmanuel
The causes of progress : culture, authority and change / Emmanuel Todd ; translated by Richard Boulind. — Oxford : Basil Blackwell, 1987. — [iv,224]p. — (Family, sexuality and social relations in past times). — *Translation of: L'enfance du monde.* — *Includes bibliography and index*

Unhappy families : clinical and research perspectives on family violence / [edited by] Eli H. Newberger, Richard Bourne. — Littleton, Mass. : PSG, c1985. — p. cm. — *Includes index*

FAMILY — Addresses, essays, lectures

Men in families / edited by Robert A. Lewis and Robert E. Salt. — Beverly Hills : Sage Publications, c1985. — p. cm. — (Sage focus editions ; v. 76). — *Includes bibliographical references*

FAMILY — Economic aspects

RAINWATER, Lee
Income packaging in the welfare state : a comparative study of family income / Lee Rainwater, Martin Rein, and Joseph Schwartz. — New York : Oxford University Press, 1986. — p. cm. — *Includes index.* — *Bibliography: p*

FAMILY — Economic aspects — Canada

HARPELL, Cindy
An analysis of dual-earner families in Canada / Cindy Harpell. — Kingston, Ont., Canada : Industrial Relations Centre, Queen's University at Kingston, 1985. — 48 p.. — (School of Industrial Relations research essay series ; no. 2). — *Bibliography: p. 47-48*

FAMILY — Economic aspects — Great Britain — Congresses

BRANNEN, Julia
Give and take in families : studies in resource distribution / Julia Brannen and Gail Wilson. — London : Allen & Unwin, 1987. — [192]p. — *Includes bibliography and index*

FAMILY — Handbooks, manuals, etc

Handbook of marriage and the family / edited by Marvin B. Sussman and Suzanne K. Steinmetz. — New York : Plenum Press, c1986. — p. cm. — *Includes bibliographical references and index*

FAMILY — History

SEGALEN, Martine
Historical anthropology of the family / Martine Segalen ; translated by J.C. Whitehouse and Sarah Matthews. — Cambridge : Cambridge University Press, 1986. — x,328p. — (Themes in the social sciences). — *Translation of: Sociologie de la famille.* — *Includes bibliographies and index*

FAMILY — Research

Family demography : methods and their application / editors John Bongaarts, Thomas K. Burch and Kenneth W. Wachter. — Oxford : Clarendon, 1987. — viii,365p. — (International studies in demography ; 2). — *Conference papers.* — *Includes bibliographies and index*

MILLER, Brent C
Family research methods : a primer / by Brent C. Miller. — Beverly Hills : Sage Publications, c1986. — p. cm. — (Family studies text series ; v. 4). — *Includes index*

VETERE, Arlene
Ecological studies of family life / Arlene Vetere and Anthony Gale with Sue Lewis, Claire Jolly and Shirley Reynolds. — Chichester : Wiley, c1987. — xii,206p. — *Includes bibliographies and index*

FAMILY — Research — Methodology

MILLER, Brent C
Family research methods : a primer / by Brent C. Miller. — Beverly Hills : Sage Publications, c1986. — p. cm. — (Family studies text series ; v. 4). — *Includes index*

FAMILY — Australia — Finance

MOORE, Jim
Trends in the disposable incomes of Australian families : 1964-65 to 1985-86 / Jim Moore and Peter Whiteford. — Woden, ACT : Department of Social Security, 1986. — vii,102p. — (Background/discussion paper / Social Security Review ; no.11) (Research paper / Development Division, Department of Social Security ; no.31). — *Bibliographical references: p35-37*

FAMILY — Australia — Statistics

ROBINSON, Judi
Australian families : current situation and trends; 1969-1985 / Judi Robinson and Bob Griffiths. — Woden, ACT : Department of Social Security, 1986. — 27leaves. — (Background paper / Social Security Review ; no.10) (Research paper / Development Division, Department of Social Security ; no.30). — *Includes bibliographical references*

FAMILY — Belgium — Ghent — History

NICHOLAS, David
The domestic life of a medieval city : women, children, and the family in fourteenth-century Ghent / David Nicholas. — Lincoln : University of Nebraska Press, c1985. — p. cm. — *Includes index.* — *Bibliography: p*

FAMILY — Brazil — Paraíba (State) — Case studies

LEWIN, Linda
Politic and Parentela in Paraíba : a case study of family-based oligarchy in Brazil / Linda Lewin. — Princeton, N.J. : Princeton University Press, c1987. — p. cm. — *Includes index.* — *Bibliography: p*

FAMILY — Caribbean Area

ABBAS, Ibrahim
The proximate determinants of fertility in North Sudan / Ibrahim Abbas, I. Kalule—Sabiti. — Voorburg : International Statistical Institute, 1985. — 35p. — (Scientific reports / World Fertility Survey ; no.73)

FAMILY — Egypt
TADROS, Helmi R
Social security and the family in Egypt / by Helmi R. Tadros. — New York, NY (866 United Nations Plaza, New York 10017) : American University in Cairo, c1984. — ix, 87 p.. — (The Cairo papers in social science ; v. 7, monograph 1). — Summary in Arabic. — Title on added t.p.: al-Ta'minat al-ijtima'iyah fi Misr. — "March 1984.". — Bibliography: p. 49-50

FAMILY — England — History
DAVIDOFF, Leonore
Family fortunes : men and women of the English middle class 1780-1850 / Leonore Davidoff and Catherine Hall. — London : Hutchinson, 1987. — 576p. — Bibliography: p542-559. — Includes index

FAMILY — Europe — History
HERLIHY, David
Medieval households / David Herlihy. — Cambridge, Mass. ; London : Harvard University Press, 1985. — vii, 227p. — (Studies in cultural history). — Includes index. — Bibliography: p.[161]-177

FAMILY — Great Britain
Family expenditure survey / Department of Employment, Great Britain. — London : Department of Employment, 1953-. — Annual. — Continues: Report of an enquiry into household expenditure

GOLDTHORPE, J. E.
Family life in western societies : a historical sociology of family relationships in Britain and North America / J.E. Goldthorpe. — Cambridge : Cambridge University Press, 1987. — [304]p

FAMILY — Great Britain — Case studies
RAPOPORT, Rhona
Dual-career families re-examined : new integrations of work & family / Rhona & Robert N. Rapoport. — New York : Harper & Row, 1977, c1976. — 382 p. — (Harper colophon books ; CN 521). — Sequel to the author's Dual-career families. — Bibliography: p. [373]-382

FAMILY — Great Britain — Congresses
BRANNEN, Julia
Give and take in families : studies in resource distribution / Julia Brannen and Gail Wilson. — London : Allen & Unwin, 1987. — [192]p. — Includes bibliography and index

FAMILY — Great Britain — Finance — Statistics
GREAT BRITAIN. Department of Health and Social Security
Low income families - 1983 : estimated numbers of families and persons with incomes at various levels relative to supplementary benefit level analysed by family type and economic status. — [London] : the Department, 1986. — [12]p

FAMILY — Great Britain — History
LEWIS, Judith Schneid
In the family way : childbearing in the British aristocracy, 1760-1860 / Judith Schneid Lewis. — New Brunswick, N.J. : Rutgers University Press, c1986. — xi, 313 p.. — Includes index. — Bibliography: p. 291-303

FAMILY — Iran
Women and the family in Iran / edited by Asghar Fathi. — Leiden : E. J. Brill, 1985. — 239p. — (Social, economic and political studies of the Middle East ; v.38)

FAMILY — Latin America — Statistics — Methodology
TORRADO, Susana
La familia como unidad de análisis en censos y encuestas de hogares : metodología actual y prospectiva en América Latina / Susana Torrado. — Buenos Aires : Ediciones CEUR, 1983. — xv,277p. — Bibliography: p271-273

FAMILY — London
YOUNG, Michael, 1915-
Family and kinship in East London / Michael Young & Peter Willmott. — London : Routledge & Kegan Paul, 1986. — xxxi,234p. — (Reports of the Institute of Community Studies). — Originally published in 1957, reprinted with a new introduction 1986

FAMILY — Scotland — History
KELSALL, Helen M.
Scottish lifestyle 300 years ago : new light on Edinburgh and Border families / Helen and Keith Kelsall. — Edinburgh : John Donald, 1986. — vii,224p. — Bibliography: p201-202

FAMILY — Southern States — History — Congresses
The Web of southern social relations : women, family, & education / edited by Walter J. Fraser, Jr., R. Frank Saunders, Jr., and Jon L. Wakelyn. — Athens : University of Georgia Press, c1985. — xvii, 257 p.. — Includes bibliographies and index

FAMILY — Sudan
GRUENBAUM, Ellen
Patterns of family living : a case study of two villages on the Rahad River / Ellen Gruenbaum. — Khartoum : University of Khartoum. Faculty of Economic and Social Studies. Development Studies and Research Centre, 1979. — 55p. — (Monograph series / University of Khartoum. Faculty of Economic and Social Studies. Development Studies and Research Centre ; no.12). — Bibliography: p54-55

FAMILY — Switzerland — Law and legislation
GROSSEN, Jacques-Michel
L'egalité du mari et de la femme au regard du droit de la famille / Jacques-Michel Grossen. — Neuchatel : Secrétariat de l'Université, 1957. — 29p

FAMILY — Turkey — History
DAVIS, Fanny
The Ottoman lady : a social history from 1718 to 1918 / Fanny Davis. — Westport, Conn. : Greenwood Press, c1986. — xv, 321 p.. — (Contributions in women's studies ; no. 70). — Includes bibliographies and index

FAMILY — United States
Family, self, and society : emerging issues, alternatives, and interventions / edited by Douglas B. Gutknecht, Edgar W. Butler. — 2nd ed. — Lanham ; New York ; London : University Press of America, 1985. — xii,373p. — Includes bibliographies

GOLDTHORPE, J. E.
Family life in western societies : a historical sociology of family relationships in Britain and North America / J.E. Goldthorpe. — Cambridge : Cambridge University Press, 1987. — [304]p

LAROSSA, Ralph
Becoming a parent / by Ralph LaRossa. — Beverly Hills : Sage Publications, c1986. — p. cm. — (Family studies text series ; v. 3). — Includes index. — Bibliography: p

WILLIE, Charles Vert
Black and white families : a study in complementarity / Charles Vert Willie. — New York : General Hall, 1985. — v,308p. — Bibliographies

FAMILY — United States — Addresses, essays, lectures
MOYNIHAN, Daniel P
Family and nation : the Godkin lectures, Harvard University / Daniel Patrick Moynihan. — 1st ed. — San Diego : Harcourt Brace Jovanovich, c1986. — xii, 207 p.. — Includes index. — Bibliography: p. 195-197

FAMILY — United States — Congresses
In support of families / edited by Michael W. Yogman and T. Berry Brazelton. — Cambridge, Mass. : Harvard University Press, 1986. — 293 p.. — Includes index. — Bibliography: p. [257]-283

FAMILY — United States — History
OGDEN, Annegret S
The great American housewife : from helpmate to wage earner, 1776-1986 / Annegret S. Ogden. — Westport, Conn. : Greenwood Press, 1986. — xxiii, 256 p.. — (Contributions in women's studies ; no. 61). — Includes index. — Bibliography: p. [241]-247

FAMILY — United States — Psychological aspects — Congresses
In support of families / edited by Michael W. Yogman and T. Berry Brazelton. — Cambridge, Mass. : Harvard University Press, 1986. — 293 p.. — Includes index. — Bibliography: p. [257]-283

FAMILY — United States — Religious life — History — 19th century
MCDANNELL, Colleen
The Christian home in Victorian America, 1840-1900 / Colleen McDannell. — Bloomington : Indiana University Press, c1986. — xvii, 193p. — (Religion in North America). — Includes index. — Bibliography: p. 178-186

FAMILY — West Bank
ATA, Ibrahim Wade
The West Bank Palestinian family / Ibrahim Wade Ata. — London : KPI, 1986. — xiii,166p. — Bibliography: p152-160

FAMILY ALLOWANCES — Australia
CASS
Income support for families with children / Bettina Cass. — Canberra : Australian Government Publishing Service, 1986. — xiii,126p. — (Issues paper / Social Security Review ; no.1). — Bibliography: p115-120

RAYMOND, Judy
Bringing up children alone : policies for sole parents / Judy Raymond. — Canberra : Australian Government Publishing Service, 1987. — xi,145p. — (Issues paper / Social Security Review ; no.3). — Bibliography: p139-145

ROBINSON, Judi
Australian families : current situation and trends; 1969-1985 / Judi Robinson and Bob Griffiths. — Woden, ACT : Department of Social Security, 1986. — 27leaves. — (Background paper / Social Security Review ; no.10) (Research paper / Development Division, Department of Social Security ; no.30). — Includes bibliographical references

FAMILY ALLOWANCES — Denmark
Børnetilskud og andre familieydelser i årene 1970-1981. — [København] : Sikringsstyrelsen, 1983. — 64p. — (Sikringsstyrelsens undersøgelser ; nr.8)

FAMILY ALLOWANCES — Great Britain
GREAT BRITAIN. Commission for Racial Equality
Child benefit - but not for all? : comments on the Child Benefit Scheme. — London : the Commission, 1978. — 10p. — (Occasional paper / Commission for Racial Equality ; no.4)

GREAT BRITAIN. Equal Opportunities Commission
Response to the DHSS consultative document 'A fresh look at maternity benefits'. — Manchester : the Commission, 1980. — 15p

GREAT BRITAIN. Parliament. House of Commons. Library. Research Division
Child benefit. — [London] : the Division, [1977]. — 13p. — (Background paper ; no.59)

FAMILY CORPORATIONS — Management
DYER, W. Gibb
Cultural change in family firms : anticipating and managing business and family transitions / W. Gibb Dyer, Jr. — 1st ed. — San Francisco : Jossey-Bass, 1986. — xxi, 179 p.. — (The Jossey-Bass management series) (The Jossey-Bass social and behavioral science series) . — Includes index. — Bibliography: p. 167-171

FAMILY CORPORATIONS — East Asia — History — Congresses

INTERNATIONAL CONFERENCE ON BUSINESS HISTORY ((10th : 1983 : Fuji Education Center)
Family business in the era of industrial growth : its ownership and management : proceedings of the Fuji Conference / the International Conference on Business History, 10 ; edited by Akio Okochi, Shigeaki Yasuoka. — [Tokyo] : University of Tokyo Press, c1984. — xiii, 318 p.. — *Includes bibliographical references and index*

FAMILY CORPORATIONS — Europe — History — Congresses

INTERNATIONAL CONFERENCE ON BUSINESS HISTORY ((10th : 1983 : Fuji Education Center)
Family business in the era of industrial growth : its ownership and management : proceedings of the Fuji Conference / the International Conference on Business History, 10 ; edited by Akio Okochi, Shigeaki Yasuoka. — [Tokyo] : University of Tokyo Press, c1984. — xiii, 318 p.. — *Includes bibliographical references and index*

FAMILY CORPORATIONS — United States — History — Congresses

INTERNATIONAL CONFERENCE ON BUSINESS HISTORY ((10th : 1983 : Fuji Education Center)
Family business in the era of industrial growth : its ownership and management : proceedings of the Fuji Conference / the International Conference on Business History, 10 ; edited by Akio Okochi, Shigeaki Yasuoka. — [Tokyo] : University of Tokyo Press, c1984. — xiii, 318 p.. — *Includes bibliographical references and index*

FAMILY CORPORATIONS — United States — Management

The Family in business / Paul C. Rosenblatt ... [et al.]. — 1st ed. — San Francisco : Jossey-Bass Publishers, 1985. — xxii, 321 p.. — (A Joint publication in the Jossey-Bass management series and the Jossey-Bass social and behavioral science series). — *Includes indexes.* — *Bibliography: p. 303-309*

FAMILY CORPORATIONS — United States — Psychological aspects

The Family in business / Paul C. Rosenblatt ... [et al.]. — 1st ed. — San Francisco : Jossey-Bass Publishers, 1985. — xxii, 321 p.. — (A Joint publication in the Jossey-Bass management series and the Jossey-Bass social and behavioral science series). — *Includes indexes.* — *Bibliography: p. 303-309*

FAMILY DEMOGRAPHY — Methodology

Family demography : methods and their application / editors John Bongaarts, Thomas K. Burch and Kenneth W. Wachter. — Oxford : Clarendon, 1987. — viii,365p. — (International studies in demography ; 2). — *Conference papers.* — *Includes bibliographies and index*

FAMILY FARMS

Perspectives on farming systems research and extension / edited by Peter E. Hildebrand. — Boulder, Colo. : L. Rienner, 1986. — p. cm

FAMILY FARMS — Africa, Sub-Saharan

Understanding Africa's rural households and farming systems / [edited by] Joyce Lewinger Moock. — Boulder : Westview Press, 1986. — p. cm. — (Westview special studies on Africa). — *Bibliography: p*

FAMILY HEALTH FOUNDATION (La.)

WARD, Martha Coonfield
Poor women, powerful men : America's great experiment in family planning / Martha C. Ward. — Boulder : Westview Press, 1986. — p. cm. — *Includes index.* — *Bibliography: p*

FAMILY LIFE EDUCATION — Great Britain

ALLEN, Isobel
Education in sex and personal relationships / Isobel Allen. — London : Policy Studies Institute, 1987. — 238p

FAMILY LIFE EDUCATION — United States — Addresses, essays, lectures

Current controversies in marriage and family studies / edited by Harold Feldman & Margaret Feldman. — Beverly Hill : Sage Publications, c1985. — p. cm

FAMILY LIFE SURVEYS — India — Maps

DHURANDHER, K. P.
An atlas of assets and liabilities of Indian rural households / K. P. Dhurandher. — New Delhi : Vikas, 1985. — 180p. — *Contains 107 black and white maps*

FAMILY LIFE SURVEYS — Pakistan — Lahore

SHAH, Nasra M
Basic needs, woman, and development : a survey of squatters in Lahore, Pakistan / by Nasra M. Shah and Muhammad Anwar. — Honolulu : East-West Population Institute, East-West Center ; Ottawa : International Development Research Centre, c1986. — xii, 163 p.. — *Bibliography: p. [159]-163*

FAMILY LIFE SURVEYS — United States

PLECK, Joseph H
Working wives, working husbands / Joseph H. Pleck. — Beverly Hills, Calif. : Published in cooperation with the National Council on Family Relations [by] Sage Publications, c1985. — 167 p.. — (New perspectives on family). — *Bibliography: p. 160-167*

FAMILY MEDICINE

RUSHTON, Andrée
Social work and health care / Andrée Rushton and Penny Davies. — London : Heinemann Educational, 1984. — 103 p. — (Community care practice handbooks ; 16)

FAMILY MEDICINE — Data processing

Micros in practice : report of an appraisal of GP microcomputer systems / sponsored jointly by the Department of Health and Social Security and the Joint Computer Policy Group. — London : H.M.S.O., 1986. — ii,130, [34]p. — *'User survey ... carried out by a team from the Department of General Practice at Exeter University'* — preface

FAMILY MEDICINE — Great Britain — Data processing

A prescription for change : a report on the longer term use and development of computers in general practice / M. J. Fitter...[et al.] ; [for the] Department of Health and Social Security. — London : H.M.S.O., 1986. — vii,56,50p

FAMILY MEDICINE — Great Britain — Evaluation

What sort of doctor? : assessing quality of care in general practice / Royal College of General Practitioners. — London : The College, 1985. — vi,27p. — (Report from general practice ; 23)

FAMILY MEDICINE — Wales

WELSH CONSUMER COUNCIL
Patient participation in general practice : a study of the Patients' Committee at Aberdare Health Centre, Mid Glamorgan. — Cardiff : the Council, 1978. — 71p. — *Bibliography: p69*

FAMILY PLANNING — history — United States — abstracts

MOORE, Gloria
Margaret Sanger and the birth control movement : a bibliography, 1911-1984 / by Gloria Moore and Ronald Moore. — Metuchen, N.J. : Scarecrow Press, 1986. — xvii, 211 p.. — *Includes indexes.* — *Bibliography: xi-xii*

FAMILY PLANNING — United States

IMBER, Jonathan B.
Abortion and the private practice of medicine / Jonathan B. Imber. — New Haven : Yale University Press, c1986. — xviii, 164 p.. — *Includes index.* — *Bibliography: p. 147-160*

FAMILY POLICY

KAMERMAN, Sheila B.
Child care, family benefits, and working parents : a study in comparative policy / Sheila B. Kamerman, Alfred J. Kahn. — New York ; Guildford : Columbia University Press, 1981. — xii,327p. — *Includes index*

FAMILY POLICY — Australia

HARDING, Ann
Assistance for families with children and the Social Security Review / Ann Harding. — Woden, ACT : Department of Social Security, 1986. — [18] leaves. — (Background/discussion paper / Social Security Review ; no.4). — *Bibliographical references: p [18-19]*

WHITEFORD, Peter
Issues in assistance for families - horizontal and vertical equity considerations / Peter Whiteford. — Woden, ACT : Department of Social Security, 1986. — iii,56p. — (Background/discussion paper / Social Security Review ; no.5) (Research paper / Department of Social Security ; no.29). — *Bibliography: p52-56*

FAMILY POLICY — China — Congresses

Chinese culture and mental health / edited by Wen-Shing Tseng, David Y.H. Wu. — Orlando : Academic Press, 1985. — xxiii, 412 p.. — *Derived from a conference held in Hawaii, Mar. 1-6, 1982, and sponsored by the Culture Learning Institute of the East-West Center, the Dept. of Psychiatry, University of Hawaii School of Medicine, and the Queen's Medical Center in Honolulu.* — *Includes bibliographies and index*

FAMILY POLICY — Germany (East)

HILLE, Barbara
Familie und Sozialisation in der DDR / Barbara Hille. — Opladen : Leske & Budrich, 1985. — 216p. — *Bibliography: p196-216*

KOCH, Petra
Familienpolitik der DDR im Spannungsfeld zwischen Familie und Berufstätigkeit von Frauen / Petra Koch [und] Hans Günther Knöbel. — Pfaffenweiler : Centaurus-Verlagsgesellschaft, 1986. — vii,171p . — *Bibliography: p124-143*

OBERTREIS, Gesine
Familienpolitik in der DDR 1945-1980 / Gesine Obertreis. — Opladen : Leske & Budrich, 1986. — v,378p. — (Forschungstexte Wirtschafts- und Sozialwissenschaften ; Bd.17)

FAMILY POLICY — Great Britain

ASSOCIATION OF COUNTY COUNCILS
Family policy. — London : Association of County Councils, 1986. — 32p

Family impact: 1986 Social Security Bill. — London : Family Policy Studies Centre, 1986. — 16p. — (Family policy briefing papers). — *Bibliography: p16*

FAMILY POLICY STUDIES CENTRE
The Shops Bill: the family dimension. — London : Family Policy Studies Centre, 1986. — 16p

FAMILY POLICY STUDIES CENTRE
The social fund: a briefing. — London : Family Policy Studies Centre, 1986. — 8p. — *Bibliography: p8*

MARSHALL, Kate
Moral panics and Victorian values / Kate Marshall. — 2nd ed. — London : Junius Publications, 1986. — 62p

FAMILY POLICY — United States

EDELMAN, Marian Wright
Families in peril : an agenda for social change / Marian Wright Edelman. — Cambridge, Mass. : Harvard University Press, 1987. — xii, 127 p.. — (The W.E.B. Du Bois lectures ; 1986). — Includes index. — Bibliography: p. [115]-122

KIMMICH, Madeleine H
America's children, who cares? : growing needs and declining assistance in the Reagan era / Madeleine H. Kimmich. — Washington, D.C. : Urban Institute Press, c1985. — xvii 112 p.. — (The Changing domestic priorities series). — Includes bibliographical references

MINDICK, Burton
Social engineering in family matters / Burton Mindick. — New York : Praeger, 1985. — p. cm. — Includes index. — Bibliography: p

MORONEY, Robert
Shared responsibility : families and social policy / Robert M. Moroney. — New York : Aldine Pub. Co., c1986. — xi, 218 p. — Includes index. — Bibliography: p. 177-211

FAMILY POLICY — United States — Addresses, essays, lectures

The Media, social science, and social policy for children / Eli A. Rubinstein and Jane D. Brown, editors. — Norwood, N.J. : Ablex Pub. Corp., 1985. — xv, 240 p.. — (Child and family policy ; v. 5). — Includes bibliographies and indexes

MOYNIHAN, Daniel P
Family and nation : the Godkin lectures, Harvard University / Daniel Patrick Moynihan. — 1st ed. — San Diego : Harcourt Brace Jovanovich, c1986. — xii, 207 p.. — Includes index. — Bibliography: p. 195-197

FAMILY PSYCHOTHERAPY

BURNHAM, John B.
Family therapy : first steps towards a systemic approach / John B. Burnham. — London : Tavistock, 1986. — xii,244p. — (Tavistock library of social work practice). — Bibliography: p225-234. — Includes index

The father's role : applied perspectives / edited by Michael E. Lamb. — New York : J. Wiley, c1986. — xiv, 461 p.. — (Wiley series on personality processes). — "A Wiley-Interscience publication.". — Includes bibliographies and indexes

Psychotherapy with families : an analytic approach / Sally Box ... [et al.]. — London : Routledge & Kegan Paul, 1981. — xii,179p. — Bibliography: p173-176. — Includes index

FAMILY SIZE — Cross-cultural studies

KASARDA, John D
Status enhancement and fertility : reproductive responses to social mobility and educational opportunity / John D. Kasarda, John O.G. Billy, Kirsten West. — Orlando, Fla. : Academic Press, 1986. — xii, 266 p.. — (Studies in population). — Includes indexes. — Bibliography: p.216-250

FAMILY SIZE — Australia — Addresses, essays, lectures

Towards an understanding of contemporary demographic change : a report on semi structured interviews / [by] John Caldwell ... [et al.]. — Canberra : Dept. of Demography, Research School of Social Sciences, Australian National University, 1976. — vii, 143 p. — (Australian family formation project monograph ; no. 4). — Aus. — Bibliography: p. 142-143

FAMILY SIZE — Egypt

TADROS, Helmi R
Social security and the family in Egypt / by Helmi R. Tadros. — New York, NY (866 United Nations Plaza, New York 10017) : American University in Cairo, c1984. — ix, 87 p.. — (The Cairo papers in social science ; v. 7, monograph 1). — Summary in Arabic. — Title on added t.p.: al-Ta'mīnāt al-ijtimā'īyah fī Miṣr. — "March 1984.". — Bibliography: p. 49-50

FAMILY SIZE — Poland

LINK, Krzysztof
Społeczno-ekonomiczne czynniki tworzenia gospodarstw domowych / Krzysztof Link. — Warszawa : Szkoła Główna Planowania i Statystyki, 1986. — 155p. — (Kształtowanie procesów demograficznych a rozwój społeczno-gospodarczy Polski) (Monografie i opracowania / Szkoła Główna Planowania i Statystyki). — Contents and summary in English and Russian

FAMILY SOCIAL WORK

BURNHAM, John B.
Family therapy : first steps towards a systemic approach / John B. Burnham. — London : Tavistock, 1986. — xii,244p. — (Tavistock library of social work practice). — Bibliography: p225-234. — Includes index

Caring : experiences of looking after disabled relatives / edited by Anna Briggs and Judith Oliver. — London : Routledge & Kegan Paul, 1985

Family, self, and society : emerging issues, alternatives, and interventions / edited by Douglas B. Gutknecht, Edgar W. Butler. — 2nd ed. — Lanham ; New York ; London : University Press of America, 1985. — xii,373p. — Includes bibliographies

GREENE, Roberta
Social work with the aged and their families / Roberta Greene. — New York : Aldine de Gruyter, c1986. — p. cm. — Includes index. — Bibliography: p

FAMILY SOCIAL WORK — England

HOWARD, John, 19---
Conciliation, children and divorce : a family systems approach / John Howard and Graham Shepherd. — London : Batsford, 1987. — [160] p. — (Child care policy and practice). — Includes bibliography and index

FAMILY SOCIAL WORK — Great Britain

BARNES, Gill Gorell
Working with families / Gill Gorell Barnes. — Basingstoke : Macmillan, 1984. — ix,133p. — (Practical social work). — Bibliography: p125-131. — Includes index

FAMILY RIGHTS GROUP
The link between prevention and care : papers from a seminar organised by FRG in 1984 for social work managers and practitioners. — London : Family Rights Group, 1985. — 44p

FAMILY SOCIAL WORK — New York (State) — Syracuse — Case studies

MINDICK, Burton
Social engineering in family matters / Burton Mindick. — New York : Praeger, 1985. — p. cm. — Includes index. — Bibliography: p

FAMILY SOCIAL WORK — United States

Family, self, and society : emerging issues, alternatives, and interventions / edited by Douglas B. Gutknecht, Edgar W. Butler. — 2nd ed. — Lanham ; New York ; London : University Press of America, 1985. — xii,373p. — Includes bibliographies

FAMILY VIOLENCE — Law and legislation — South Australia

NAFFIN, Ngaire
Domestic violence and the law : a study of S.99 of the Justices Act (S. A.) / by Naffin. — [Adelaide] : Women's Adviser's Office, Department of the Premier and Cabinet, 1985. — iv,iii,170p. — Includes bibliographical references

FAMILY VIOLENCE — Law and legislation — Council of Europe countries

COUNCIL OF EUROPE. Committee of Ministers
Violence in the family : Recommendation no.R (85) 4 adopted by the Committee of Ministers of the Council of Europe on 26 March 1985 and Explanatory memorandum. — Strasbourg : Council of Europe, 1986. — 15p. — (Legal affairs). — " ... prepared by a select committee of experts under the authority of the European Committee on Crime Problems" - p.[3]

FAMILY VIOLENCE — United States

GELLES, Richard J
Intimate violence in families / Richard J. Gelles and Claire Pedrick Cornell. — Beverly Hills, Calif. : Sage Publications, c1985. — 160 p.. — (Family studies text series ; v. 2). — Includes indexes. — Bibliography: p. 148-154

SHUPE, Anson D
Violent men, violent couples : the dynamics of domestic violence / Anson Shupe, William A. Stacey, Lonnie R. Hazlewood. — Lexington, Mass. : Lexington Books, c1987. — x, 152 p.. — Includes index. — Bibliography: p. [143]-150

Violence in the home : interdisciplinary perspectives / edited by Mary Lystad. — New York : Brunner/Mazel, c1986. — xxxv, 322 p.. — Includes bibliographies and indexes

FAMILY VIOLENCE — United States — Addresses, essays, lectures

Unhappy families : clinical and research perspectives on family violence / [edited by] Eli H. Newberger, Richard Bourne. — Littleton, Mass. : PSG, c1985. — p. cm. — Includes index

FAMILY VIOLENCE — United States — Prevention

Violence in the home : interdisciplinary perspectives / edited by Mary Lystad. — New York : Brunner/Mazel, c1986. — xxxv, 322 p.. — Includes bibliographies and indexes

FAMINES

GARCIA, Rolando V.
Drought and man : the 1972 case history / by Rolando V. Garcia and José C. Escudero ; and special contributions by S. Ayalew...[et al.]. — Oxford : Pergamon, Sept.1981
Vol.2: The constant catastrophe / by Rolando V. Garcia and J. E. Escudera. — x, 204p. — Includes bibliographies

GARCIA, Rolando V.
Drought and man : the 1972 case history. — Oxford : Pergamon. — Published for the International Federation of Institutes for Advanced Study
Vol.3: The roots of catastrophe / by Rolando V. Garcia and Pierre Spitz ; with special contributions from P. Bonte ... [et al.] ; edited by J. Ann Zammit. — 1986. — xviii,193p. — Includes index

FAMINES — Economic aspects

RAVALLION, Martin
Markets and famines / Martin Ravallion. — Oxford : Clarendon, 1987. — [260]p. — Includes bibliography and index

FAMINES — Handbooks, manuals, etc.

LEFTWICH, Adrian
The political economy of famine : a preliminary report on the literature, bibliographic resources, research activities and needs in the UK / by Adrian Leftwich and Dominique Harvie. — York : University of York, 1986. — 66p. — (Discussion paper / University of York. Dept. of Politics ; 116). — References: p63-66

FAMINES — Research
LEFTWICH, Adrian
The political economy of famine : a preliminary report on the literature, bibliographic resources, research activities and needs in the UK / by Adrian Leftwich and Dominique Harvie. — York : University of York, 1986. — 66p. — (Discussion paper / University of York. Dept. of Politics ; 116). — *References: p63-66*

FAMINES — Africa
Drought and hunger in Africa : denying famine a future / edited by Michael H. Glantz. — Cambridge : Cambridge University Press, 1987. — xx,457p. — *Conference proceedings. — Includes bibliographies and index*

FAMINES — Ethiopia
ETHIOPIA. Relief and Rehabilitation Commission
Pre-disaster planning program / The Relief and Rehabilitation Commission, Government of Ethiopia. — Addis Ababa : [The Commission], 1975. — 20 leaves

JANSSON, Kurt
The Ethiopian famine : the story of the emergency relief operation / Kurt Jansson, Michael Harris, Angela Penrose. — London : Zed, 1987. — [256]p

MARIAM, Mesfin Wolde
Rural vulnerability to famine in Ethiopia, 1958-1977 / Mesfin Wolde Mariam. — London : Intermediate Technology Publications, 1986. — xii,191p

FAMINES — Malawi — History
VAUGHAN, Megan
The story of an African famine : gender and famine in twentieth-century Malawi / Megan Vaughan. — Cambridge : Cambridge University Press, 1987. — [192]p. — *Includes bibliography and index*

FAMINES — Sahel — Congresses
COLLOQUIUM ON THE EFFECTS OF DROUGHT ON THE PRODUCTIVE STRATEGIES OF SUDANO-SAHELIAN HERDSMEN AND FARMERS (1975 : Université de Niamey)
Report / Colloquium on the Effects of Drought on the Productive Strategies of Sudano-Sahelian Herdsmen and Farmers ; edited by Michael M. Horowitz. — Binghamton, N.Y. : Institute for Development Anthropology, [1976]. — xiii, 96 p.. — *Cover title*

FAMINES — Ukraine — Congresses
Famine in Ukraine, 1932-1933 / edited by Roman Serbyn and Bohdan Krawchenko. — Edmonton : Canadian Institute of Ukrainian Studies, 1986. — 192p. — (Canadian library in Ukrainian Studies). — *Selected papers from a conference held in 1983 at the Université du Québec à Montréal*

FANGATAU (TUAMOTU ISLANDS) — Population — Statistics
Tableaux normalisés du recensement général de la population : 15 octobre 1983. — [Papeete] : Institut territorial de la statistique Résultats de la commune de Fangatau. — [1985?]. — 4p,ll leaves

FANON, FRANTZ
BULHAN, Hussein Abdilahi
Frantz Fanon and the psychology of oppression / Hussein Abdilahi Bulhan. — New York ; London : Plenum Press, c1985. — xiii, 299p. — (PATH in psychology). — *Includes index. — Includes bibliographical references*

FARM INCOME — Australia — Forecasting
HIGGS, Peter John
Adaptation and survival in Australian agriculture : a computable general equilibrium analysis of the impact of economic shocks originating outside the domestic agricultural sector / Peter J. Higgs. — Melbourne, Vic. ; Oxford : Oxford University Press, 1986. — 320p. — *Bibliography: p302-310*

FARM INCOME — France
Les agriculteurs et leurs revenus. — Paris : La Documentation française. — (Documents du Centre d'Étude des Revenus et des Coûts ; no.78)
1: Familles et exploitations agricoles / ...réalisée par Yves Chassard [et al.]. — 1985. — 108p

Les agriculteurs et leurs revenus. — Paris : La Documentation française. — (Documents du Centre d'Étude des Revenus et des Coûts ; no.79)
2: Composition et emploi des revenus / ...réalisée par Yves Chassard [et al.]. — 1986. — 130p

FARM INCOME — France — Statistics
VERT, Eric
Les revenus fiscaux des agriculteurs en 1979 / Eric Vert. — [Paris] : INSEE, 1985. — 194p. — (Archives et documents / Institut National de la Statistique et des Études Économiques ; no.131)

FARM INCOME — Southern States
Agricultural change : consequences for southern farms and rural communities / edited by Joseph J. Molnar. — Boulder : Westview Press, c1986. — xxii, 440 p.. — (Westview special studies in agricultural science and policy). — *Includes bibliographies and indexes*

FARM INCOME — Taiwan
TSUI, Y. C.
A summary report on farm income of Taiwan in 1957 in comparison with 1952 / by Y. C. Tsui. — Taipei : Chinese-American Joint Commission on Rural Reconstruction, 1959. — [iii],67p. — (Economic digest series / Joint Commission on Rural Reconstruction ; no.13)

FARM MANAGEMENT
Farm management survey / Department of Agricultural Economics, Faculty of Economic and Social Studies, University of Manchester. — Manchester : University of Manchester, 1983/84-. — *Annual*

Successful agribusiness management / edited by John Freivalds. — Aldershot : Gower, c1985. — xiii,245p

FARM MANAGEMENT — Great Britain — Bibliography
The farm as a family business : an annotated bibliography / edited by Andrew Errington ; contributions : Graham Crow ... [et al.]. — [Reading] : [Reading University], 1986. — 33p. — *Published as the result of a workshop organized by the Agricultural Manpower Society at Reading University, February 1985*

FARM MANAGEMENT — Hungary — Economic aspects
CSIKÓS-NAGY, Béla
Eszközgazdálkodás és árrendszer / Csikós-Nagy Béla. — [Budapest] : Kossuth Könyvkiadó, 1964. — 179p. — *Bibliography: p175-[177]*

FARM MANAGEMENT — Soviet Union
SHMELEV, G.
Personal subsidiary farming under socialism / G. Shmelev ; translated from the Russian. — Moscow : Progress Publishers, 1986. — 110p

FARM MECHANIZATION — Economic aspects — Developing countries
BURCH, David, 1942 Jan. 16-
Overseas aid and the transfer of technology : the political economy of agricultural mechanisation in the Third World / David Burch. — Aldershot : Avebury, c1987. — xiv,370p. — *Bibliography: p354-370*

FARM MECHANIZATION — Government policy — Africa
PINGALI, Prabhu L.
Agricultural mechanization and the evolution of farming systems in Sub-Saharan Africa / Prabhu Pingali, Yves Bigot, Hans P. Binswanger. — Baltimore : Johns Hopkins Press for the World Bank, 1987. — viii,216p. — *Bibliographical references: p191-206*

FARM MECHANIZATION — Social aspects — Developing countries
BURCH, David, 1942 Jan. 16-
Overseas aid and the transfer of technology : the political economy of agricultural mechanisation in the Third World / David Burch. — Aldershot : Avebury, c1987. — xiv,370p. — *Bibliography: p354-370*

FARM MECHANIZATION — Africa, Sub-Saharan
PINGALI, Prabhu L.
Agricultural mechanization and the evolution of farming systems in Sub-Saharan Africa / Prabhu Pingali, Yves Bigot, Hans P. Binswanger. — Baltimore : Johns Hopkins Press for the World Bank, 1987. — viii,216p. — *Bibliographical references: p191-206*

FARM MECHANIZATION — Denmark
Arbejdsforbruget til landbrugets driftsgrene. — København : I kommission hos Landhusholdningsselskabets Forlag, 1977. — 77p. — (Undersøgelse / Det landøkonomiske Driftsbureau ; nr.32). — *Includes summary in English*

FARM PRODUCE — Marketing — Government policy — Developing countries — Congresses
Agricultural marketing strategy and pricing policy / edited by Dieter Elz. — Washington, D.C. : The World Bank, 1987. — xiii,132p. — (A World Bank symposium). — *Includes bibliographical references. — Based on papers from a seminar held in Washington, D.C., May 6-17, 1985*

FARM PRODUCE — Prices — Peru
PERU. Dirección de Planificación Estadística
Indice de precios de productos agrícolas, julio-agosto [1975]. — Lima : the Dirección, [ca.1976]. — 15p. — (Serie de indices de precios al por mayor). — *Cover title: Productos agrícolas*

FARM PRODUCE — Central America — Supply and demand — Forecasting
Projections of supply and demand for selected agricultural products in Central America through 1980. — Jerusalem : Publications Services Division of the Israel Program for Scientific Translations for the U.S. Department of Agriculture, 1969. — xxi,261p. — *Includes bibliographical references*

FARM PRODUCE — Chile
Chile : demand and supply projections for agricultural products, 1965-1980. — Jerusalem : Publication Services Division of the Israel Program for Scientific Translations for the U.S. Department of Agriculture, 1969. — xxiii,130p. — *Includes bibliographical references*

FARM PRODUCE — England — London — Marketing
BARTY-KING, Hugh
Making provision : a centenary history of the provision trade / Hugh Barty-King. — London : Quiller Press, 1986. — xiv,171p. — *Bibliography: p163-164*

FARM PRODUCE — Mexico — Marketing
YUNEZ-NAUDE, Antonio
Peasantry and agricultural exchange relations : an enquiry based on data for the Mexican economy / by Antonio Yunez-Naude. — 324 leaves. — *PhD (Econ) 1986 LSE. — Leaves 273-316 are appendices*

FARM RENTS — Legal status, laws, etc — Great Britain
GREAT BRITAIN. Parliament. House of Commons. Library. Research Division
Agricultural Holdings Bill (HL) Bill 110 of 1983-84 / Priscilla Baines. — [London] : the Division, 1983. — 12p. — (Reference sheet ; no.84/4). — *Bibliographical references: p11-12*

FARM SUPPLIES — France — Marketing

LANDELL MILLS ASSOCIATES
Exports to France : the market for British farm supplies / Landell Mills Associates. — London : British Overseas Trade Board, Overseas Trade Division 3/Exports to Europe Branch, Department of Trade, 1982. — 2v.(in 1). — *Cover title: Plough into the French market*

FARM SUPPLIES — Great Britain — Marketing

LANDELL MILLS ASSOCIATES
Exports to France : the market for British farm supplies / Landell Mills Associates. — London : British Overseas Trade Board, Overseas Trade Division 3/Exports to Europe Branch, Department of Trade, 1982. — 2v.(in 1). — *Cover title: Plough into the French market*

FARM TENANCY — Georgia — History — 19th century

BODE, Frederick A.
Farm tenancy and the census in antebellum Georgia / Frederick A. Bode, Donald E. Ginter. — Athens : University of Georgia Press, c1987. — p. cm. — *Includes index. — Bibliography: p*

FARM TENANCY — Great Britain

GREAT BRITAIN. Parliament. House of Commons. Library. Research Division
Agricultural Holdings Bill (HL) Bill 110 of 1983-84 / Priscilla Baines. — [London] : the Division, 1983. — 12p. — (Reference sheet ; no.84/4). — *Bibliographical references: p11-12*

FARMERS — Asia — Congresses

Research-extension-farmer : a two-way continuum for agricultural development / edited by Michael M. Cernea, John K. Coulter, John F. A. Russell. — Washington, D.C. : The World Bank, 1985. — xvi,171p. — *Cover: "A World Bank and UNDP Symposium". — Includes bibliographical references*

FARMERS — Denmark — Socioeconomic status

Landbrugeres supplerende indtjening. — København : I kommission hos Landhusholdningsselskabets Forlag, 1977. — 20p. — (Meddelelse / Det landøkonomiske Driftsbureau ; nr.23)

FARMERS — Ghana — Social conditions

HILL, Polly
Talking with Ewe seine fishermen and shallot farmers / recording and edited by Polly Hill. — Cambridge : African Studies Centre, University of Cambridge, [1986]. — 66p,[11] leaves of plates. — (Cambridge African monographs ; 6). — *Bibliography: p57-58. — Includes index*

FARMERS — India — Political activity

The Peasant movement today / Sunil Sahasrabudhey. — New Delhi : Ashish Pub. House, 1986. — xix, 224 p. — *English and Hindi. — "Under the auspices of Gandhian Institute of Studies, Rajghat, Varanasi"--T.p. verso. — Includes bibliographies and index*

FARMERS — Ireland

HIGGINS, J
A study of part-time farmers in the Republic of Ireland / J. Higgins. — Dublin : An Foras Taluntais, Economics and Rural Welfare Research Centre, [1983]. — 118 p.. — (Socio-economic research series ; no. 3). — *Includes bibliographical references*

FARMERS — United States — Congresses

Farm work and fieldwork : American agriculture in anthropological perspective / edited by Michael Chibnik. — Ithaca : Cornell University Press, 1987. — 293 p.. — (Anthropology of contemporary issues). — *Includes bibliographies and index*

FARMERS INSTITUTES — Africa

BARWELL, C. W.
Education and training for agricultural development : the place of institutional farmer training / by C. W. Barwell. — London : Commonwealth Secretariat, 1970. — 11p. — *At head of title page: Commonwealth Conference on Education in Rural Areas. — CRE(70)D/6*

FARMS — India — Statistics

INDIA. Central Statistical Organisation
Economic census 1980 : districtwise aggregates of principal characteristics of enterprises. — [New Delhi] : Central Statistical Organisation, 1986. — 302p

FARMS — United States — Congresses

Farm work and fieldwork : American agriculture in anthropological perspective / edited by Michael Chibnik. — Ithaca : Cornell University Press, 1987. — 293 p.. — (Anthropology of contemporary issues). — *Includes bibliographies and index*

FARMS, SMALL

Perspectives on farming systems research and extension / edited by Peter E. Hildebrand. — Boulder, Colo. : L. Rienner, 1986. — p. cm

FARMS, SMALL — Soviet Union

SHMELEV, G.
Personal subsidiary farming under socialism / G. Shmelev ; translated from the Russian. — Moscow : Progress Publishers, 1986. — 110p

FAROE ISLANDS — Economic conditions

Færøerne : samfunds- og erhvervsstruktur : import- og eksportforhold. — [København] : Udenrigsministeriets erhvervstjeneste, [1974]. — 36p

Den økonomiske udvikling pa Færøerne / Det Rådgivende Udvalg Vedrørende Færøerne. — København : Statsministeriet, 1983-. — *Annual*

FAROE ISLANDS — Foreign relations

KROGSTRUP, Hanne
Færøernes erhvervspolitik / Hanne Krogstrup og Yvonne Barnholdt Lund. — Aalborg : Aalborg Universitetsforlag, 1983. — 171p. — (Serie om nordatlantiske forhold ; nr.8). — *Bibliography: p168-171*

FAROE ISLANDS — History — 20th Century

KROGSTRUP, Hanne
Færøernes erhvervspolitik / Hanne Krogstrup og Yvonne Barnholdt Lund. — Aalborg : Aalborg Universitetsforlag, 1983. — 171p. — (Serie om nordatlantiske forhold ; nr.8). — *Bibliography: p168-171*

FAROE ISLANDS — Politics and government

KROGSTRUP, Hanne
Færøernes erhvervspolitik / Hanne Krogstrup og Yvonne Barnholdt Lund. — Aalborg : Aalborg Universitetsforlag, 1983. — 171p. — (Serie om nordatlantiske forhold ; nr.8). — *Bibliography: p168-171*

FAROE ISLANDS — Social conditions

Færøerne : samfunds- og erhvervsstruktur : import- og eksportforhold. — [København] : Udenrigsministeriets erhvervstjeneste, [1974]. — 36p

FAROE ISLANDS — Yearbooks

Årbog for Færøerne. — Kobenhavn : Stougaard Jensen, 1983-. — *Annual*

FARRIS (FIRM) — History

KROHN-HOLM, Jan W.
Farriskildene i Larvik gjennem 150 °ar / Jan W. Krohn-Holm. — Larvik : Utgitt av Farris, 1971. — 165p

FASCISM

NIN, Andrés
Les dictadures dels nostres dies / Andreu Nin. — 2a edició. — Sant Boi de Llobregat : Lluita, 1984. — 211p. — (Collecció espurna ; 3)

NS bulletin: official newsletter of the New Order. — Arlington, VA : New Order, 1986-. — *Quarterly. — Continues in part: The National Socialist*

FASCISM — Argentina

NARVAJA, Aurelio
Cuarenta años de Peronismo / Aurelio Narvaja, Angel Perelman, Jorge Abelardo Ramos. — Buenos Aires : Ediciones del Mar Dulce, 1985. — 158p

FASCISM — Europe

ANNE FRANK FOUNDATION
International seminar on the extreme right in Europe and the United States, 16,17 and 18 November, 1984 / Editor: Vera Ebels-Dolanová. — Amsterdam : Anne Frank Stichting, 1985. — vi,132p. — *Cover title: The extreme right in Europe and the United States*

BELL, Andrew
Against racism and fascism in Europe / Andrew Bell. — Strasbourg : Socialist Group. European Parliament, 1986. — 47p

The Social basis of European fascist movements / edited by Detlef Mühlberger. — London : Croom Helm, c1987. — [384]p. — *Includes index*

FASCISM — France

PETITFILS, Jean Christian
L'extrême droite en France / Jean Christian Petitfils. — Paris : [Presses Universitaires de France], 1983. — 127p. — (Que sais-je? ; 2118) . — *Bibliography: p126*

FASCISM — France — History

STERNHELL, Zeev
[Ni droite, ni gauche. English]. Neither right nor left : fascist ideology in France / Zeev Sternhell ; translated by David Maisel. — Berkeley : University of California Press, c1986. — p. cm. — *Translation of: Ni droite, ni gauche. — Includes index. — Bibliography: p*

FASCISM — Germany — History

KERSHAW, Ian
The 'Hitler myth' : image and reality in the Third Reich / Ian Kershaw. — Oxford : Clarendon, 1987. — xii,297p. — *Rev. ed. of: Der Hitler-Mythos. 1980. — Bibliography: p277-287. — Includes index*

FASCISM — Great Britain

EREIRA, Mark
The National Front in Islington : an anti fascist pamphlet / Mark Ereira. — London : Community Education Trust, 1985. — 29p

FASCISM — Great Britain — History

THURLOW, Richard
Fascism in Britain : a history, 1918-1985 / Richard Thurlow. — Oxford : Basil Blackwell, 1987. — xvii,317p,[16]p of plates. — *Bibliography: p305-308. — Includes index*

FASCISM — Italy

Rethinking Italian Fascism : capitalism, populism and culture / edited by David Forgacs. — London : Lawrence and Wishart, [1986]. — xxi,209p

ROMANO, Sergio
Giovanni Gentile : la filosofia al potere / Sergio Romano. — Milano : Bompiani, 1984. — 352p, [32]p of plates

FASCISM — Italy — Turin — History — 20th century

PASSERINI, Luisa
Fascism in popular memory : the cultural experience of the Turin working class / Luisa Passerini ; translated by Bob Lumley and Jude Bloomfield. — Cambridge : Cambridge University Press, 1987. — x,244p. — (Studies in modern capitalism = Etudes sur le capitalisme moderne). — *Translation of: Torino operaia e Fascismo. — Includes index*

FASCISM — New Zealand

SPOONLEY, P.
The politics of nostalgia : racism and the Extreme Right in New Zealand / Paul Spoonley. — Palmerston North : Dunmore Press, 1987. — 318p. — *Bibliography: p267-279*

FASCISM — Spain

LEDESMA RAMOS, Ramiro
Escritos politicos : JONS, 1933-1934 / Ramiro Ledesma Ramos. — Madrid : Trinidad Ledesma Ramos, 1985. — 239,[35]p

LEDESMA RAMOS, Ramiro
Escritos politicos : La Conquista del Estado, 1931 / Ramiro Ledesma Ramos. — Madrid : Trinidad Ledesma Ramos, 1986. — 329p

SAZ CAMPOS, Ismael
Mussolini contra la II República : hostilidad, conspiraciones, intervención (1931-1936) / Ismael Saz. — Valencia : Edicions Alfons el Magnànim, Institució Valenciana d'Estudis i Investigació, 1986. — 265p. — *Bibliography: p [255]-265*

FASCISM — United States

ANNE FRANK FOUNDATION
International seminar on the extreme right in Europe and the United States, 16,17 and 18 November, 1984 / Editor: Vera Ebels-Dolanová. — Amsterdam : Anne Frank Stichting, 1985. — vi,132p. — *Cover title: The extreme right in Europe and the United States*

FASCISM AND WOMEN — Germany

THEWELEIT, Klaus
Male fantasies 1 : women, floods, bodies, history / Klaus Theweleit ; translated by Stephen Conway in collaboration with Erica Carter and Chris Turner ; foreword by Barbara Ehrenreich. — Cambridge : Polity, 1987. — xxii,517p. — *Translation of: Männerphantasien. — Includes index*

FASCIST ETHICS

MOSSE, George L
Nationalism and sexuality : respectability and abnormal sexuality in modern Europe / George L. Mosse. — 1st ed. — New York : H. Fertig, 1985. — viii, 232 p., [10] p. of plates. — *Includes index. — Bibliography: p. 195-223*

FASCISTS — Germany — Attitudes

THEWELEIT, Klaus
Male fantasies 1 : women, floods, bodies, history / Klaus Theweleit ; translated by Stephen Conway in collaboration with Erica Carter and Chris Turner ; foreword by Barbara Ehrenreich. — Cambridge : Polity, 1987. — xxii,517p. — *Translation of: Männerphantasien. — Includes index*

FASCISTS — Great Britain

The murderers are amongst us : the criminal records of Britain's racists. — London : Searchlight Publishing, 1985. — 22p

FATHER AND CHILD

The father's role : applied perspectives / edited by Michael E. Lamb. — New York : J. Wiley, c1986. — xiv, 461 p.. — (Wiley series on personality processes). — *"A Wiley-Interscience publication.". — Includes bibliographies and indexes*

FATHER AND CHILD — Addresses, essays, lectures

Men in families / edited by Robert A. Lewis and Robert E. Salt. — Beverly Hills : Sage Publications, c1985. — p. cm. — (Sage focus editions ; v. 76). — *Includes bibliographical references*

FATHER AND CHILD — United States

LEWIS, Charlie
Becoming a father / Charlie Lewis. — Milton Keynes : Open University Press, 1986. — ix,222p. — *Includes index*

FATHERS

MACKEY, Wade C.
Fathering behaviors : the dynamics of the man-child bond / Wade C. Mackey. — New York ; London : Plenum, c1985. — xviii,203p. — (Perspectives in developmental psychology). — *Bibliography: p185-196. — Includes index*

Reassessing fatherhood : new observations on fathers and the modern family / edited by Charlie Lewis and Margaret O'Brien. — London : Sage, 1987. — 270p. — *Includes bibliographies and index*

FATHERS — Psychology

The father's role : applied perspectives / edited by Michael E. Lamb. — New York : J. Wiley, c1986. — xiv, 461 p.. — (Wiley series on personality processes). — *"A Wiley-Interscience publication.". — Includes bibliographies and indexes*

FATHERS — United States — Psychology

LEWIS, Charlie
Becoming a father / Charlie Lewis. — Milton Keynes : Open University Press, 1986. — ix,222p. — *Includes index*

FATHERS AND DAUGHTERS

NELSON, Sarah
Incest : fact and myth / Sarah Nelson. — 2nd rev. ed. — Edinburgh : Stramullion, 1987. — 128p. — *Previous ed.: 1982. — Bibliography: p122-128*

FATU HIVA (MARQUESAS ISLANDS) — Population — Statistics

Tableaux normalisés du recensement général de la population : 15 ocobre 1983. — [Papeete] : Institut territorial de la statistique Résultats de la commune de Fatu Hiva. — [1985?]. — 4p,11 leaves

FEAR

LEWIS, Dan A
Fear of crime : incivility and the production of a social problem / Dan A. Lewis and Greta Salem. — New Brunswick, U.S.A. : Transaction Books, c1986. — p. cm. — *Includes index. — Bibliography: p*

FEDERACIÓN OBRERA REGIONAL ARGENTINA — History

BILSKY, Edgardo J.
La F.O.R.A. y el movimiento obrero (1900-1910) / Edgardo J. Bilsky. — Buenos Aires : Centro Editor de América Latina. — (Biblioteca Política Argentina ; 97). — *Bibliographic notes: p97-108*
t.1. — 1985. — 108p

BILSKY, Edgardo J.
La F.O.R.A. y el movimiento obrero (1900-1910) / Edgardo J. Bilsky. — Buenos Aires : Centro Editor de América Latina. — (Biblioteca Política Argentina ; 98)
t.2. — 1985. — 109-243p

FEDERAL AID TO CHILD WELFARE — United States

KIMMICH, Madeleine H
America's children, who cares? : growing needs and declining assistance in the Reagan era / Madeleine H. Kimmich. — Washington, D.C. : Urban Institute Press, c1985. — xvii 112 p.. — (The Changing domestic priorities series). — *Includes bibliographical references*

FEDERAL AID TO HIGHER EDUCATION — Australia — History

GALLAGHER, A. P.
Coordinating Australian university development : a study of the Australian Universities Commission, 1959-1970 / A.P. Gallagher. — St. Lucia ; New York : University of Queensland Press, c1982. — xii, 244 p.. — (The University of Queensland Press scholars' library). — *Includes index. — Bibliography: p. [230]-238*

FEDERAL AID TO HIGHER EDUCATION — United States

CARNEGIE COUNCIL ON POLICY STUDIES IN HIGHER EDUCATION
The federal role in postsecondary education : unfinished business, 1975-1980 / a report by the Carnegie Council on Policy Studies in Higher Education. — San Francisco ; Washington : Jossey-Bass, 1975. — xi,97p. — (Carnegie Council series). — *Bibliography: p [89]-92*

FEDERAL AID TO PUBLIC WELFARE — Political aspects — Puerto Rico

GAUTIER, Carmen Eulalia
One aspect of the political dependence of Puerto Rico : the politics of the United States' financed poor relief in Puerto Rico / by Carmen E. Gautier. — 438 leaves. — *PhD (Econ) 1986 Ext*

FEDERAL AID TO RESEARCH — United States — Directories

CANTRELL, Karen
Funding for anthropological research / Karen Cantrell, Denise Wallen. — Phoenix, AZ : Oryx Press, 1986. — p. cm. — *Includes index. — Bibliography: p*

FEDERAL AID TO TRANSPORTATION — Europe

ROUND TABLE ON TRANSPORT ECONOMICS (67th : 1984 : Paris)
Aims and effects of public financial support for passenger transport. — Paris : European Conference of Ministers of Transport, 1984. — 77p. — *Bibliography: p58-61*

FEDERAL-CITY RELATIONS — United States

Intergovernmental relations and public policy / edited by J. Edwin Benton and David R. Morgan ; prepared under the auspices of the Policy Studies Organization. — New York : Greenwood Press, 1986. — viii, 224 p.. — (Contributions in political science ; no. 156). — *Includes index. — Bibliography: p. [213]-216*

FEDERAL-CITY RELATIONS — United States — Addresses, essays, lectures

Urban policy problems : federal policy and institutional change / Mark S. Rosentraub, ed. — New York : Praeger, 1986. — p. cm. — *Published in cooperation with the Policy Studies Organization. — Includes index. — Bibliography: p*

FEDERAL DEPOSIT INSURANCE CORPORATION

SPRAGUE, Irvine H
Bailout : an insider's account of bank failures and rescues / Irvine H. Sprague. — New York : Basic Books, c1986. — p. cm. — *Includes index. — Bibliography: p*

FEDERAL GOVERNMENT

CONFERENCE ON PLURALISM IN FEDERAL STATES (1983 : Kingston, Canada)
[Pluralism in Federal States]. — Kingston, Canada : International Political Science Association, 1983. — 13michrofiches

ELAZAR, Daniel Judah
Exploring federalism / Daniel J. Elazar. — University, Ala. : University of Alabama Press, c1987. — xvi, 335 p.. — *Includes index. — Bibliography: p. 304-326*

FEDERAL GOVERNMENT
continuation

Integration through law : Europe and the American federal experience / series under the general editorship of Mauro Cappelletti, Monica Seccombe, Joseph Weiler. — Berlin ; New York : W. de Gruyter, 1985-<1987 >. — <v. 1-3; in 5 >. — (Series A, Law / European University Institute =Series A, Droit / Institut Universitaire Européen ; 2.1-<2.3 >). — *Includes bibliographical references and indexes.* — *Contents: v. 1. Methods, tools, and institutions. bk. 1. A political, legal, and economic overview. bk. 2. Political organs, integration techniques, and judicial process. bk. 3. Forces and potential for a European identity -- v. 2. Environmental protection policy / by Eckard Rehbinder and Richard Stewart -- v. 3. Consumer law, common markets, and Federalism in Europe and the United States / by Thierry Bourgoignie and David Trubek (with Louise Trubek and Denis Stingl)*

FEDERAL GOVERNMENT — Legal aspects

BASU, Durga Das
Comparative federalism / Durga Das Basu. — New Delhi : Prentice-Hall of India, 1987. — xxv,642p

FEDERAL GOVERNMENT — Canada

DYCK, Rand
Provincial politics in Canada / Rand Dyck. — Scarborough : Prentice-Hall, 1986. — 626p. — *Bibliography: p587-616*

GROUPE SOCIALISTE DES TRAVAILLEURS DU QUÉBEC
La question nationale et la révolution prolétarienne au Canada : définition des mots dòrdre du G.S.T.Q. au Québec dans la lutte pour la destruction de l'État fédéral. — Montreal : Presses Socialistes Internationales, 1978. — 61p. — (Documents du Groupe socialiste des travailleurs du Québec ; 3)

Index to federal programs and services [Canada]. — Ottawa : Supply and Services Canada, 1985-. — *Annual*

LESLIE, Peter M.
Federal state, national economy / Peter M. Leslie. — Toronto : University of Toronto Press, [1987]. — xvi,213p. — *Notes: p[191]-205*

MILNE, David
Tug of war : Ottawa and the provinces under Trudeau and Mulroney / David Milne. — Toronto : J. Lorimer, 1986. — viii, 275 p.. — *Includes index.* — *Bibliography: p. [239]-269*

National politics and community in Canada / edited by R. Kenneth Carty and W. Peter Ward. — Vancouver : University of British Columbia Press, 1986. — 200 p.. — *Includes bibliographical references.* — *Contents: Canada as political community / R. Kenneth Carty & W. Peter Ward -- The Origins of Canadian politics and John A. Macdonald / Gordon Stewart -- Networks and associations and the nationalizing of sentiment in English Canada / Margaret Prang -- The Making of a Canadian political citizenship / R. Kenneth Carty & W. Peter Ward -- National political parties and the growth of the national political community / David E. Smith -- Leadership conventions and the development of the national political community in Canada / John C. Courtney -- Ceremonial politics / Christopher Armstrong -- Becoming Canadians / P.B. Waite -- Managing the periphery / Donald E. Blake -- The "French lieutenant" in Ottawa / John English*

SMILEY, Donald V.
The federal condition in Canada / Donald V. Smiley. — Toronto : Mcgraw-Hill Ryerson, 1987. — xii,202p. — (McGraw-Hill Ryerson series in Canadian politics). — *Includes bibliographical references*

FEDERAL GOVERNMENT — Canada — Congresses

COHEN, Maxwell
The Dominion-Provincial Conference : some basic issues / by Maxwell Cohen. — Toronto : Ryerson Press, 1945. — 39p

FEDERAL GOVERNMENT — European Economic Community countries

Integration through law : Europe and the American federal experience / under the general editorship of Mauro Cappelletti, Monica Seccombe [and] Joseph Weiler. — Berlin : Walter de Gruyter
Vol. 1: Methods, tools and institutions / edited by Mauro Cappelletti, Monica Seccombe [and] Joseph Weiler
Bk.1: A political, legal and economic overview. — 1986, c1985. — xc,616p. — (Series A. Law ; 2.1.1). — *Bibliographical notes*

Integration through law : Europe and the American federal experience / under the general editorship of Mauro Cappelletti, Monica Seccombe [and] Joseph Weiler. — Berlin : Walter de Gruyter
Vol.3: Consumer law, common markets and federalism in Europe and the United States / by Thierry Bourgoignie and David Trubek ; (with Louise Trubek and Denis Stingl). — 1987, c1986. — xxiii,271p. — (Series A. Law / European University Institute ; 2.3). — *Bibliographical references*

FEDERAL GOVERNMENT — Germany (West) — Bibliography

DÖRNER, Dieter
Das föderative System der Bundesrepublik Deutschland : Auswahlbibliographie / Dieter Dörner, Ronald Huth ; mit einem Vorwort von Otto Wilke. — Berlin : EXpress Edition, 1985. — 215p. — (Schriftenreihe zur politischen Bildung)

FEDERAL GOVERNMENT — India

SARKAR, Ranadhir Sarma
Union-state relations in India / R.C.S. Sarkar. — New Delhi, India : National, 1986. — ixv [i.e. xiv], 172 p.. — *Summary: Transcript of the third Dr. Rajendra Prasad memorial lecture delivered under the auspices of the Institute of Constitutional and Parliamentary Studies.* — *Includes bibliographical references and index*

FEDERAL GOVERNMENT — India — Case studies

SATHYAMURTHY, T. V
India since independence : studies in the development of the power of the state / T.V. Sathyamurthy. — 1st ed. — Delhi : Ajanta Publications : Distributors, Ajanta Books International, 1985-. — v. <1- >. — *Includes index.* — *Bibliography: v. 1, p. [457]-474.* — *Contents: v. 1. Centre-state relations: the case of Kerala*

FEDERAL GOVERNMENT — India — Legal aspects

BASU, Durga Das
Comparative federalism / Durga Das Basu. — New Delhi : Prentice-Hall of India, 1987. — xxv,642p

FEDERAL GOVERNMENT — Malaysia

ISIS CONFERENCE ON NATIONAL INTEGRATION (1st : 1985 : Kuala Lumpur)
The bonding of a nation : federalism and territorial integration in Malaysia : proceedings of the first ISIS Conference.... — Kuala Lumpur : Institute of Strategic and International Studies, 1986. — v,131p

FEDERAL GOVERNMENT — Netherlands

WETENSCHAPPELIJKE RAAD VOOR HET REGERINGSBELEID
De organisatie van het openbaar bestuur : enkele aspecten, knelpunten en voorstellen. — 's-Gravenhage : Staatsuitgeverij, 1975. — 195p. — (Rapporten aan de Regering / Wetenschappelijke Raad voor het Regeringsbeleid ; 6)

FEDERAL GOVERNMENT — Nigeria

OYOUBAIRE, Sam Egite
Federalism in Nigeria : a study in the development of the Nigerian state / Sam Egite Oyoubaire. — London : Macmillan, 1985. — xx,306p. — (Contemporary African issues series). — *Bibliography: p285-294.* — *Includes index*

FEDERAL GOVERNMENT — Switzerland

NÜSSLI, Kurt
Föderalismus in der Schweiz : Konzepte, Indikatoren, Daten / Kurt Nüssli. — Zürich : Rüegger, 1985. — 383p. — (Zürcher Beiträge zur politischen Wissenschaft ; Bd.12). — *Bibliography: p367-381*

Relations cantons-confédération : résumé des rapports présentés au Congrès de l'Union libérale-democratique suisse à Neuchâtel le 5 avril 1975. — [S.l.] : Union libérale-démocratique suisse, 1975. — 27p

FEDERAL GOVERNMENT — United States

Integration through law : Europe and the American federal experience / under the general editorship of Mauro Cappelletti, Monica Seccombe [and] Joseph Weiler. — Berlin : Walter de Gruyter
Vol.3: Consumer law, common markets and federalism in Europe and the United States / by Thierry Bourgoignie and David Trubek ; (with Louise Trubek and Denis Stingl). — 1987, c1986. — xxiii,271p. — (Series A. Law / European University Institute ; 2.3). — *Bibliographical references*

Intergovernmental relations and public policy / edited by J. Edwin Benton and David R. Morgan ; prepared under the auspices of the Policy Studies Organization. — New York : Greenwood Press, 1986. — viii, 224 p.. — (Contributions in political science ; no. 156). — *Includes index.* — *Bibliography: p. [213]-216*

PETERSON, Paul E
When federalism works / Paul E. Peterson, Barry G. Rabe, Kenneth K. Wong. — Washington, D.C. : Brookings Institution, c1986. — xvi, 245 p.. — *Includes bibliographical references and index*

State politics and the new federalism : readings and commentary / edited by Marilyn Gittell. — New York : Longman, c1986. — xv, 544 p.. — *Includes index.* — *Bibliography: p. 533-535*

FEDERAL REFORMATORY FOR WOMEN (Alderson (West Virginia))

GIALLOMBARDO, Rose
Society of women : a study of a women's prison / Rose Giallombardo. — New York ; London : Wiley, [1966]. — viii,248p

FEDERAL RESERVE BANKS

The Federal Reserve System : purposes and functions. — Washington, D.C. : Board of Governors of the Federal Reserve System, 1984. — x,120p

FEDERALISM — Argentina — History

TORRES MOLINA, Ramón
Unitarios y Federales en la historia argentina / Ramón Torres Molina. — Buenos Aires : Editorial Contrapunto, 1986. — 134p. — (Colección La historia revisada)

FEDERALISM — European Economic Community countries — History

Documents on the history of European integration / edited by Walter Lipgens. — Berlin : Walter de Gruyter
Vol.1: Continental plans for European union 1939-1945. — 1985, c1984. — xxiii,823p. — (Series B. History / European University Institute ; 1.1). — *Bibliographies.* — *Includes 250 documents in their original language on 6 microfiches in back pocket*

FEDERALIST

WHITE, Morton Gabriel
Philosophy, The Federalist, and the Constitution / Morton White. — New York ; Oxford : Oxford University Press, 1987. — xi, 273p. — *Includes bibliographical references and index*

FEDERALLY ADMINISTERED TRIBAL AREAS (PAKISTAN) — Population — Statistics
1981 census report of Federally Administered Tribal Areas (FATA). — Islamabad : Population Census Organisation, 1984. — 116p. — (Census report ; no.62)

FÉDÉRATION DES ENTREPRISES DE BELGIQUE
FÉDÉRATION DES ENTREPRISES DE BELGIQUE
La FEB et l inflation. — Bruxelles : Fédération des Entreprises, 1974. — 7p

FÉDÉRATION DES ÉTUDIANTS D'AFRIQUE NOIRE EN FRANCE
TRAORE, Sekou
La Fédération des Étudiants d'Afrique Noire en France (F.E.A.N.F.) / Sekou Traore. — Paris : L'Harmattan, 1985. — 102p. — *Bibliography: p97-100*

FÉDÉRATION DES TRAVAILLEURS DU QUÉBEC
FÉDÉRATION DES TRAVAILLEURS DU QUÉBEC. Conference (13th : 1973 : Montréal)
Notre place dans l'entreprise : les droits des travailleurs dans l'entreprise. — Montreal : Fédération des Travailleurs du Québec, 1973. — 41p

FEED ADDITIVE RESIDUES
ERLICHMAN, James
Gluttons for punishment / James Erlichman. — Harmondsworth : Penguin Books, 1986. — 156p

FEIERABEND, LADISLAV
FEIERABEND, Ladislav
Soumrak československé demokracie / Ladislav Feierabend. — Londýn : Rozmluvy. — *Vyšlo v červenci 1986 jako 30. svazek edice časopisu Rozmluvy*
[1]. — 1986. — 321p

FEMALE OFFENDERS
MORRIS, Allison
Women, crime and criminal justice / Allison Morris. — Oxford : Basil Blackwell, 1987. — [256]p. — *Includes bibliography and index*

FEMALE OFFENDERS — Poland
KOLARCZYK, Tadeusz
Przestępczość kobiet : aspekty kryminologiczne i penitencjarne / Tadeusz Kolarczyk, Jacek Roman Kubiak, Piotr Wierzbicki. — Warszawa : Wydawnictwo Prawnicze, 1984. — 312p. — *Summary in English*

FEMALE OFFENDERS — United States
ROSS, Robert R.
Female offender : correctional afterthoughts / by Robert R. Ross, Elizabeth A. Fabiano. — Jefferson, N.C. : McFarlane, 1986. — p. cm. — *Includes index.* — *Bibliography: p*

FEMININITY
WESTCOTT, Marcia
The feminist legacy of Karen Horney / Marcia Westkott. — New Haven : Yale University Press, c1986. — p. cm. — *Includes index.* — *Bibliography: p*

FEMININITY (PSYCHOLOGY)
ELSHTAIN, Jean Bethke
Meditations on modern political thought : masculine/feminine themes from Luther to Arendt / Jean Bethke Elshtain. — New York : Praeger, 1986. — p. cm. — *Includes index.* — *Bibliography: p*

FEMINISM
BASSNETT, Susan
Feminist experiences : the women's movement in four cultures / Susan Bassnett. — London : Allen & Unwin, 1986. — [168]p. — *Includes index*

BERNARD, Jessie Shirley
The female world from a global perspective / by Jessie Bernard. — Bloomington : Indiana University Press, c1987. — p. cm. — *Includes index.* — *Bibliography: p*

Feminism and political economy : women's work, women's struggles / edited by Heather Jon Maroney and Meg Luxton. — Toronto ; New York ; London : Methuen, 1987. — xii,333p. — *Bibliography: p285-318*

For alma mater : theory and practice in feminist scholarship / edited by Paula A. Treichler, Cheris Kramarae, Beth Stafford. — Urbana : University of Illinois Press, c1985. — xv, 450 p., [10] p. of plates. — *Includes bibliographies and index*

FRASER, Arvonne S
The U.N Decade for Women : documents and dialogue / Arvonne S. Fraser. — Boulder : Westview Press, 1987. — p. cm. — (Westview special studies on women in contemporary society)

FREEMAN, Jo
Untying the knot : feminism, anarchism and organisation / Jo Freeman [and] Cathy Levine. — London : Dark Star/Rebel Press, 1984. — 23p

HARDING, Sandra G
The science question in feminism / Sandra Harding. — Ithaca : Cornell University Press, 1986. — p. cm. — *Includes index.* — *Bibliography: p*

HERON, Liz
Changes of heart : reflections on women's independence / Liz Heron. — London : Pandora, 1986. — [224]p

NORRIS, Pippa
Politics and sexual equality : the comparative position of women in Western democracies / Pippa Norris. — Brighton : Wheatsheaf, 1987. — [160]p. — *Includes bibliography and index*

SYDIE, R. A
Natural women, cultured men : a feminist perspective on sociological theory / R.A. Sydie. — Milton Keynes : Open University Press, 1987. — x,268p. — *Bibliography: p247-258.* — *Includes index*

TRASK, Haunani-Kay
Eros and power : the promise of feminist theory / Haunani-Kay Trask. — Philadelphia : University of Pennsylvania Press, c1986. — xiv, 186 p.. — *Includes bibliographies and index*

WARREN, Mary Anne
Gendercide : the implications of sex selection / Mary Anne Warren. — Totowa, N.J. : Rowman & Allanheld, 1985. — viii, 209 p.. — (New feminist perspectives). — *Includes bibliographies and index*

WEEDON, Chris
Feminist practice and poststructuralist theory / Chris Weedon. — Oxford : Basil Blackwell, 1987. — 1v. — *Includes bibliography and index*

Women against censorship / edited by Varda Burstyn ; essays by Varda Burstyn ... [et al.]. — Vancouver : Douglas & McIntyre, c1985. — 210 p.. — *Bibliography: p. 201-205*

Women, social science and public policy / edited by Jacqueline Goodnow & Carole Pateman for the Academy of Social Sciences in Australia. — Sydney ; London : Allen & Unwin, 1985. — xvi,162p

FEMINISM — Congresses
Women's worlds : from the new scholarship / edited by Marilyn Safir ... [et al] ; in cooperation with the Society for the Psychological Study of Social Issues. — New York : Praeger, 1985. — p. cm. — *Papers presented at the First International Interdisciplinary Congress on Women held at the University of Haifa, Haifa, Israel, Dec. 28, 1981-Jan. 1, 1982.* — *Includes index*

FEMINISM — Cross-cultural studies
Women in the world, 1975-1985 : the women's decade / Lynne B. Iglitzin and Ruth Ross, editors. — 2nd rev. ed. — Santa Barbara, Calif. : ABC-Clio Information Services, c1985. — p. cm. — (Studies in international and comparative politics ; 16). — *Includes bibliographies and index*

Women living change / edited by Susan C. Bourque and Donna Robinson Divine. — Philadelphia : Temple University Press, 1985. — p. cm. — (Women in the political economy) . — *Includes index*

FEMINISM — History
GUTIÉRREZ ALVAREZ, José
Mujeres socialistas / José Gutiérrez Alvarez. — Barcelona : Editorial Hacer, [1986]. — 157p

FEMINISM — History — Addresses, essays, lectures
SCHNEIR, Miriam, comp
Feminism : the essential historical writings / Edited, and with an introd. and commentaries, by Miriam Schneir. — [1st ed.]. — New York : Random House, [1972]. — xxi, 360 p. — *Bibliography: p. 356-360*

FEMINISM — History — 20th century
The New women's movement : feminism and political power in Europe and the USA / edited by Drude Dahlerup. — London : Sage, 1986. — 254p. — (Sage modern politics series ; v.12). — *Includes bibliographies and index*

FEMINISM — Periodicals — Bibliography
DOUGHAN, David
Feminist periodicals, 1855-1984 : an annotated critical bibliography of British, Irish, Commonwealth and international titles / David Doughan, Denise Sanchez. — Brighton : Harvester, 1987. — [336]p. — *Includes index*

FEMINISM — Philosophy
DONOVAN, Josephine
Feminist theory : the intellectual traditions of American feminism / Josephine Donovan. — New York : F. Ungar Pub. Co., c1985. — xiii, 237 p.. — *Includes index.* — *Bibliography: p. 217-224*

FEMINISM — Philosphy
KRISTEVA, Julia
The Kristeva reader / Julia Kristeva ; edited by Toril Moi. — Oxford : Basil Blackwell, 1986. — vii,327p. — *Translation of the French.* — *Includes index*

FEMINISM — Australia
Australian women : new feminist perspectives / edited by Norma Grieve and Ailsa Burns. — Melbourne ; New York : Oxford University Press, 1986. — xii, 412 p.. — *Bibliography: p. [358]-395*

Women, social science and public policy / edited by Jacqueline Goodnow & Carole Pateman for the Academy of Social Sciences in Australia. — Sydney ; London : Allen & Unwin, 1985. — xvi,162p

FEMINISM — Europe — History
EVANS, Richard J.
Comrades and sisters : feminism, socialism and pacifism in Europe 1870-1945 / Richard J. Evans. — Brighton : Wheatsheaf, 1987. — [240]p. — *Includes index*

FEMINISM — France
French connections : voices from the women's movement in France / edited and translated by Claire Duchen. — London : Hutchinson, 1987. — 143p. — (Explorations in feminism). — *Translated from the French*

French feminist thought : a reader / edited by Toril Moi. — Oxford : Basil Blackwell, 1987. — [256]p. — *Translated from the French.* — *Includes index*

FEMINISM — France — History

CIXOUS, Hélène
The newly born woman / Hélène Cixous and Catherine Clément ; translation by Betsy Wing ; introduction by Sandra M. Gilbert. — Manchester : Manchester University Press, c1986. — xviii,168p. — (Theory and history of literature (Manchester University Press) ; v.24). — *Translation of: La jeune née.* — *Bibliography: p58-59*

FEMINISM — Germany — History — 19th century

BUSSEMER, Herrad-Ulrike
Frauenemanzipation und Bildungsbürgertum : Sozialgeschichte der Frauenbewegung in der Reichsgründungszeit / Herrad-Ulrike Bussemer. — Weinheim : Beltz Verlag, 1985. — 360p. — (Ergebnisse der Frauenforschung ; Bd.7). — *Bibliography: p[350]-360*

FEMINISM — Great Britain

COOTE, Anna
Sweet freedom : the struggle for women's liberation / Anna Coote and Beatrix Campbell. — 2nd ed. — Oxford : Basil Blackwell, 1987. — [224]p. — *Previous ed.: 1982.* — *Includes index*

PASCALL, Gillian
Social policy : a feminist analysis / Gillian Pascall. — London : Tavistock, 1986. — [v,220]p. — *Includes bibliography and index*

SEGAL, Lynne
Is the future female? : troubled thoughts on contemporary feminism / Lynne Segal. — London : Virago, 1987. — xvi, 272p. — *Includes index*

FEMINISM — Great Britain — History

BANKS, Olive
Becoming a feminist : the social origins of 'first wave' feminism / Olive Banks. — Brighton : Wheatsheaf, 1986. — [176]p. — *Includes bibliography*

BRULEY, Sue
Leninism, Stalinism, and the women's movement in Britain, 1920-1939 / Susan Bruley. — New York : Garland Pub., 1986. — p. cm. — (Outstanding theses from the London School of Economics and Political Science). — *Thesis (Ph.D.)--University of London, 1980.* — *Bibliography: p*

HERSTEIN, Sheila R
A mid-Victorian feminist, Barbara Leigh Smith Bodichon / Sheila R. Herstein. — New Haven : Yale University Press, c1985. — p. cm. — : *Revision of thesis (doctoral)--City University of New York.* — *Includes index.* — *Bibliography: p*

FEMINISM — Great Britain — History — 19th century

Equal or different : women's politics 1800-1914 / edited by Jane Rendall. — Oxford : Basil Blackwell, 1987. — [288]p. — *Includes index*

FEMINISM — Great Britain — History — 19th century — Sources

Barbara Leigh Smith Bodichon and the Langham Place Group / edited by Candida Ann Lacey. — New York ; London : Routledge & Kegan Paul, 1987. — vii,485p.. — (Women's source library). — *Includes index*

FEMINISM — Israel — Congresses

Women's worlds : from the new scholarship / edited by Marilyn Safir ... [et al] ; in cooperation with the Society for the Psychological Study of Social Issues. — New York : Praeger, 1985. — p. cm. *Papers presented at the First International Interdisciplinary Congress on Women held at the University of Haifa, Haifa, Israel, Dec. 28, 1981-Jan. 1, 1982.* — *Includes index*

FEMINISM — Nevada — History — 20th century

HOWARD, Anne Bail
The long campaign : a biography of Anne Martin / Anne Bail Howard. — Reno, Nevada : University of Nevada Press, c1985. — p. cm. — (Nevada studies in history and political science ; no. 20). — *Includes index.* — *Bibliography: p*

FEMINISM — Pakistan — History — 20th century

MUMTAZ, Khawar
Two steps forward, one step back? : women of Pakistan / Khawar Mumtaz and Farida Shaheed. — London : Zed, 1986. — [256]p

FEMINISM — Puerto Rico

The Puerto Rican woman : perspectives on culture, history, and society / edited by Edna Acosta-Belén. — 2nd ed. — New York : Praeger, 1986. — xii, 212 p. — *Includes index.* — *Bibliography: p. 189-208*

FEMINISM — Spain — History

DI FEBO, Giuliana
Resistencia y movimiento de mujeres en España 1936-1976 / Giuliana Di Febo. — [Barcelona] : Icaria, 1979. — 239p

FEMINISM — United States

DONOVAN, Josephine
Feminist theory : the intellectual traditions of American feminism / Josephine Donovan. — New York : F. Ungar Pub. Co., c1985. — xiii, 237 p. — *Includes index.* — *Bibliography: p. 217-224*

FERREE, Myra Marx
Controversy and coalition : the new feminist movement / Myra Marx Ferree, Beth B. Hess. — Boston : Twayne Publishers, c1985. — xi, 215 p. — (Social movements past & present). — *Includes index.* — *Bibliography: p. 185-199*

GELB, Joyce
Women and public policies / Joyce Gelb and Marian Lief Palley. — rev. ed. — Princeton : Princeton University Press, 1987. — xvi,241p

HEWLETT, Sylvia Ann
A lesser life : the myth of women's liberation in America / Sylvia A. Hewlett. — New York, N.Y. : W. Morrow, 1986. — p. cm

LAVENDER, Abraham D
Ethnic women and feminist values : toward a "new" value system / Abraham D. Lavender. — Lanham, MD : University Press of America, c1986. — xix, 291 p.. — *Includes index.* — *Bibliography: p. 247-285*

MACKINNON, Catharine A
Feminism unmodified : discourses on life and law / Catharine A. MacKinnon. — Cambridge, Mass. : Harvard University Press, 1987. — p. cm. — *Includes index.* — *Bibliography: p*

MANSBRIDGE, Jane J
Why we lost the ERA / Jane J. Mansbridge. — Chicago : University of Chicago Press, 1986. — p. cm. — *Includes index.* — *Bibliography: p*

Women and symbolic interaction / edited by Mary Jo Deegan, Michael R. Hill. — Boston, Mass. ; London : Allen & Unwin, 1987. — xii,458p. — *Includes index*

FEMINISM — United States — History — Addresses, essays, lectures

Freedom, feminism, and the state : an overview of individualist feminism / edited by Wendy McElroy ; foreword by Lewis Perry. — Washington, D.C. : Cato Institute, c1982. — xi, 357 p.. — *Includes index.* — *Bibliography: p. 349-352*

FEMINIST LITERARY CRITICISM

For alma mater : theory and practice in feminist scholarship / edited by Paula A. Treichler, Cheris Kramarae, Beth Stafford. — Urbana : University of Illinois Press, c1985. — xv, 450 p., [10] p. of plates. — *Includes bibliographies and index*

FEMINISTS — Biography

GUTIÉRREZ ALVAREZ, José
Mujeres socialistas / José Gutiérrez Alvarez. — Barcelona : Editorial Hacer, [1986]. — 157p

FEMINISTS — England — Biography

SIMON, Joan
Shena Simon : feminist and educationalist / Joan Simon. — [Manchester] : [J. Simon], 1986. — [250 leaves]. — *Bibliography: p[4]*

FEMINISTS — Great Britain — Biography

CURTIN, Patricia R
E. Sylvia Pankhurst : portrait of a radical / by Patricia Romero Curtin. — New Haven : Yale University Press, c1986. — p. cm. — *Includes index.* — *Bibliography: p*

HERSTEIN, Sheila R
A mid-Victorian feminist, Barbara Leigh Smith Bodichon / Sheila R. Herstein. — New Haven : Yale University Press, c1985. — p. cm. — : *Revision of thesis (doctoral)--City University of New York.* — *Includes index.* — *Bibliography: p*

FEMINISTS — Ireland — Biography

FALLON, Charlotte H.
Soul of fire : a biography of Mary MacSwiney / Charlotte H. Fallon. — Cork : Mercier, c1986. — 207p. — *Bibliography: p204-207*

FEMINISTS — Nevada — Biography

HOWARD, Anne Bail
The long campaign : a biography of Anne Martin / Anne Bail Howard. — Reno, Nevada : University of Nevada Press, c1985. — p. cm. — (Nevada studies in history and political science ; no. 20). — *Includes index.* — *Bibliography: p*

FEMINISTS — New Jersey — History — 20th century

GORDON, Felice D.
After winning : the legacy of the New Jersey suffragists, 1920-1947 / Felice D. Gordon. — New Brunswick, N.J. : Rutgers University Press, c1986. — x, 262 p.. — *Includes index.* — *Bibliography: p. [245]-251*

FEMINISTS — Sierra Leone — Biography

CROMWELL, Adelaide M.
An African Victorian feminist : the life and times of Adelaide Smith Casely Hayford 1868-1960 / Adelaide M. Cromwell. — London : Cass, 1986. — xvi,235p,[13]p of plates. — *Includes index*

FENCES — Law and legislation — Australia — New South Wales

COLLINS, C. M
The law of fences and pastures protection, New South Wales / Collins. — 2nd ed. / by H.K. Insall. — Sydney : Law Book Co., 1984. — xxi, 208 p.

FERBER, ROBERT

The Collection and analysis of economic and consumer behavior data : in memory of Robert Ferber / edited by Seymour Sudman and Mary A. Spaeth. — Champaign, Ill. : Bureau of Economic and Business Research & Survey Research Laboratory, University of Illinois, c1984. — x, 406 p.. — *Includes bibliographies*

FERRARO, GERALDINE

FERRARO, Geraldine
Ferraro, my story / Geraldine A. Ferraro, with Linda Bird Francke. — Toronto ; New York : Bantam Books, 1985. — 340 p., [24] p. of plates. — *Includes index*

FERROL DEL CAUDILLO (SPAIN) — Social conditions

PALOMARES IBÁÑEZ, Jesús María
La Comisión de Reformas Sociales y la cuestión social en Ferrol (1884-1903) / Jesús Ma. Palomares Ibáñes, Ma. del Carmen Fernández Casanova. — [Santiago de Compostela] : Universidad de Santiago de Compostela, 1984. — 202p. — (Monografías de la Universidad de Santiago de Compostela ; no.93)

FERTILITY, HUMAN

Culture and reproduction : an anthropological critique of demographic transition theory / edited by W. Penn Handwerker. — Boulder, Colo. : Westview Press, 1986. — xix, 389 p.. — Based on papers presented at a conference held Dec. 2, 1981 at the University of California, Los Angeles. — Includes index. — Bibliography: p. 350-382

Evaluation of the impact of family planning programmes on fertility : sources of variance. — New York : United Nations, 1982. — xxi,290p. — (Population studies / Department of International Economic and Social Affairs ; no. 76). — "A project of the Population Division of the Department of International Economic and Social Affairs of the United Nations Secretariat, in collaboration with the Committee for the Analysis of Family Planning Programmes of the International Union for the Scientific Study of Population.". — "Related to the work of the Second Expert Group Meeting on Methods of Measuring the Impact of Family Planning Programmes on Fertility, which was convened at Geneva, Switzerland, from 19 to 26 March 1979"--P. iii. — "ST/ESA/SER.A/76.". — "United Nations publication sales no. E.81.XIII.9"--Verso t.p. — Includes bibliographical references

HANSEN, Joseph
Too many babies? : the myth of the population explosion / Joseph Hansen. — New York : Pathfinder Press, 1987. — 43p

HARRIS, Marvin
Death, sex, and fertility : population regulation in preindustrial and developing societies / Marvin Harris and Eric B. Ross. — New York : Columbia University Press, 1987. — p. cm. — Incldues index. — Bibliography: p

NERLOVE, Marc
Household and economy : welfare economics of endogenous fertility / Marc Nerlove, Assaf Razin, Efraim Sadka. — Boston : Academic Press, 1987. — xiii, 155 p.. — (Economic theory, econometrics, and mathematical economics). — Includes bibliographies and indexes

FERTILITY, HUMAN — Addresses, essays, lectures

Fertility and mortality : theory, methodology, and emperical issues / edited by K. Mahadevan with P.J. Reddy & D.A. Naidu. — New Delhi ; Beverly Hills ; London : Sage Publications, 1986. — 351p. — Includes bibliographies

FERTILITY, HUMAN — Cross-cultural studies

KASARDA, John D
Status enhancement and fertility : reproductive responses to social mobility and educational opportunity / John D. Kasarda, John O.G. Billy, Kirsten West. — Orlando, Fla. : Academic Press, 1986. — xii, 266 p.. — (Studies in population). — Includes indexes. — Bibliography: p.216-250

FERTILITY, HUMAN — Econometric models

ERMISCH, John
Econometric analysis of birth rate dynamics / John Ermisch. — London : National Institute of Economic and Social Research, 1987. — 38p. — (Discussion paper / National Institute of Economic and Social Research ; no.127). — Bibliography: p36-38

FERTILITY, HUMAN — Economic aspects

MCNICOLL, Geoffrey
Economic growth under non-replacement fertility / Geoffrey McNicoll. — New York : Population Council, 1985. — 39p. — (Working papers / Population Council. Center for Policy Studies ; no.120). — Bibliography: p35-39

FERTILITY, HUMAN — Economic aspects — Mexico — Baviacora

SIMONELLI, Jeanne M.
Two boys, a girl and enough! : reproductive and economic decisionmaking on the Mexican periphery / Jeanne M. Simonelli. — Boulder, Colo. ; London : Westview, 1986. — xxii,231p. — Bibliography: p203-222

FERTILITY, HUMAN — Mathematical models

NERLOVE, Marc
Population policy and individual choice : a theoretical investigation / Marc Nerlove, Assaf Razin, and Efraim Sadka. — Washington, D.C. : International Food Policy Research Institute, 1987. — p. cm. — (Research report / International Food Policy Research Institute ; 60). — "June 1987.". — Bibliography: p

FERTILITY, HUMAN — Political aspects

PETCHESKY, Rosalind Pollack
Abortion and woman's choice / Rosalind Pollack Petchesky. — London : Verso, 1986, c1984. — [442]p. — (Questions for feminism). — Originally published: New York ; London : Longman, 1984. — Includes index

FERTILITY, HUMAN — Research

WOOLF, Myra
The reliability of fertility data obtained from pregnancy histories / Myra Woolf ; [for the] Office of Population Censuses and Surveys. — London : H.M.S.O., 1979. — [4],16p. — (Studies on medical and population subjects ; no.40). — Bibliography: p.16

FERTILITY, HUMAN — Statistical methods

BECKER, Stan
A validation study of backward and foreward pregnancy histories in Matlab, Bangladesh / Stan Becker, Simeen Mahmud. — Voorburg : International Statistical Institute, 1984. — 37p. — (Scientific reports / World Fertility Survey ; no.52)

BRASS, William
Advances in methods for estimating fertility and mortality from limted and defective data / William Brass. — London : London School of Hygiene and Tropical Medicine, Centre for Population Studies, 1985. — 103p. — (Occasional publication / Centre for Population Studies, London School of Hygiene and Tropical Medicine)

Indirect techniques for demographic estimation. — New York : United Nations, 1983. — xxv,304p. — (Population studies / Department of International Economic and Social Affairs ; no. 81). — At head of title: Manual X. — "A collaboration of the Population Division of the Department of International Economic and Social Affairs of the United Nations Secretariat with the Committee on Population and Demography of the National Research Council, United States National Academy of Sciences.". — "ST/ESA/SER.A/81.". — "United Nations publication, sales no. E.83.XIII.2"--T.p. verso. — Includes bibliographical references

FERTILITY, HUMAN — England — History

LEVINE, David, 1946-
Reproducing families : the political economy of English population history / David Levine. — Cambridge : Cambridge University Press, 1987. — [272]p. — (Themes in the social sciences). — Includes index

FERTILITY, HUMAN — Africa, Subsaharan

FRANK, Odile
The demand for fertility control in Sub-Saharan Africa / Odile Frank. — New York : Population Council, 1985. — 50p. — (Working papers / Population Council. Center for Policy Studies ; no.117). — Bibliography: p46-50

FERTILITY, HUMAN — Asia

Fertility in Asia : assessing the impact of development projects / edited by John Stoeckel and Anrudh K. Jain. — London : Pinter, 1986. — xix,177p. — Includes bibliographies and index

FERTILITY, HUMAN — Asia, Southeastern

WONG, Aline K
Ethnicity and fertility in Southeast Asia : a comparative analysis / by Aline K. Wong and Ng Shui Meng. — Singapore : Institute of Southeast Asian Studies, 1985. — xii, 393 p.. — (Research notes and discussions paper ; no. 50) (Ethnicity and fertility in Southeast Asia series). — Bibliography: p. 372-377

FERTILITY, HUMAN — Australia — Addresses, essays, lectures

Towards an understanding of contemporary demographic change : a report on semi structured interviews / [by] John Caldwell ... [et al.]. — Canberra : Dept. of Demography, Research School of Social Sciences, Australian National University, 1976. — vii, 143 p.. — (Australian family formation project monograph ; no. 4). — Aus. — Bibliography: p. 142-143

FERTILITY, HUMAN — Bahamas — Statistics

Commonwealth of the Bahama Islands : report of the 1980 census of population. — Nassau : Ministry of Finance
V.4: Fertility and union status. — [1986]. — xxv,396p

FERTILITY, HUMAN — Bangladesh

KABEER, Naila
The functions of children in the household economy and levels of fertility : a case study of a village in Bangladesh / Naila Kabeer. — 311 leaves. — PhD (Econ) 1986 LSE. — Leaves 260-301 are appendices

FERTILITY, HUMAN — Cameroon

SANTOW, Gigi
An evaluation of the Cameroon Fertility Survey / Gigi Santow, A. Bioumla. — Voorburg : International Statistical Institute, 1984. — 46p. — (Scientific reports / World Fertility Survey ; no.64)

FERTILITY, HUMAN — Cameroon — Statistics

The Cameroon Fertility Survey, 1978 : a summary of findings. — Voorburg : International Statistical Institute, 1983. — 14p. — (World Fertility Survey ; no.41)

FERTILITY, HUMAN — China

GREENHALGH, Susan
Fertility policy in China : future options / Susan Greenhalgh [and] John Bongaarts. — New York : Population Council. Center for Policy Studies, 1986. — 31p. — (Working papers / Population Council, New York. Center for Policy Studies ; no.127). — Bibliography: p26-28

FERTILITY, HUMAN — Costa Rica

ROSERO, Luis
The determinants of fertility decline in Costa Rica, 1964—76 / Luis Rosero, Miguel Gómez, Virginia Rodríguez. — Voorburg : International Statistical Institute, [1984?]. — 14p. — Translated from Determinantes de la fecundidad en Costa Rica: analisis longitudinal de tres encuestas

FERTILITY, HUMAN — Costa Rica — Attitudes

STYCOS, J. Mayone
Putting back the K and A in KAP : a study of the implications of knowledge and attitudes for fertility in Costa Rica / J. Mayone Stycos. — Voorburg : International Statistical Institute, 1984. — 45p. — (Scientific reports / World Fertility Survey ; no.48)

FERTILITY, HUMAN — Developing countries

BONGAARTS, John
The transition in reproductive behavior in the Third World / John Bongaarts. — New York : Population Council, 1986. — 29p. — (Working papers / Population Council, New York. Center for Policy Studies ; no.125)

SAFILIOS-ROTHSCHILD, Constantina
The status of women and fertility in the Third World in the 1970-80 decade / Constantina Safilios-Rothschild. — New York : Population Council, 1985. — 49p. — (Working papers / Population Council. Center for Policy Studies ; no.118). — *Bibliography: p25-28*

FERTILITY, HUMAN — Developing countries — Case studies

ANKER, Richard
Fertility determinants in developing countries : a case study of Kenya / by Richard Anker and James C. Knowles. — Liège (Belgium) : Ordina Editions, c1982. — x, 222 p.. — *Bibliography: p. 203-213*

FERTILITY, HUMAN — Developing countries — Statistical methods

GOLDMAN, Noreen
Assessment of the quality of data in 41 WFS surveys : a comparative approach / Noreen Goldman, Shea Oscar Rutstein, Suseela Singh. — Voorburg : International Statistical Institute, 1985. — 83p. — (Comparative studies / World Fertility Survey ; no.44). — *Bibliography: p81-83*

FERTILITY, HUMAN — Dominican Republic

RODRÍGUEZ SEPÚLVEDA, Bienvenida
Evaluación de la Encuesta Nacional de Fecundidad de la República Dominicana de 1980 / Bienvenida Rodríguez Sepúlveda. — Voorburg : International Statistical Institute, 1984. — 72p. — (Scientific reports / World Fertility Survey ; no.63)

FERTILITY, HUMAN — Ecuador

HERRERA DE RIVADENEIRA, M. Ines
Evaluación de la Encuesta Nacional de Fecundidad de 1979 de Ecuador / M. Ines Herrera de Rivadeneira. — Voorburg : International Statistical Institute, 1984. — 59p. — (Scientific reports / World Fertility Service ; no.51)

FERTILITY, HUMAN — Egypt — Statistics

1976 Population and housing census : total Republic. — Cairo : Central Agency for Public Mobilisation and Statistics
Vol. 2: Fertility and internal migration and movement of workers and students. — 1980. — 440p

The Egyptian Fertility Survey, 1980 : a summary of findings. — Voorburg : International Statistical Institute, 1983. — 33p. — (World Fertility Survey ; no.42)

FERTILITY, HUMAN — England — History

WRIGLEY, E. A.
The local and the general in population history : the sixteenth Harte lecture, delivered in the University of Exeter on 13 May 1983 / by E.A. Wrigley. — [Exeter] : University of Exeter, 1985. — 19p

FERTILITY, HUMAN — England — Cleveland

CLEVELAND. County Council. Research and Intelligence Unit
The birth rate in Cleveland. — [Middlesbrough] : [the Unit], 1986. — 11 leaves. — (Information note / Cleveland. County Council. Research and Intelligence Unit ; 298)

FERTILITY, HUMAN — England — London — Statistics

HILLS, Carole
London borough fertility rates, 1981 / Carole Hills. — [London] : London Research Centre, 1986. — iii,12,[66]p. — (Statistical series ; no.54). — *Bibliographical references: p12*

FERTILITY, HUMAN — Europe — History

WRIGLEY, E. A.
People, cities and wealth : the transformation of traditional society / E.A. Wrigley. — Oxford : Basil Blackwell, 1987. — [400]p. — *Includes bibliography and index*

FERTILITY, HUMAN — France — Statistics

DESPLANQUES, Guy
Recensement général de la population de 1982. — [Paris] : INSEE. — *Bibliography: p55.* — *RP 82/7*
Principaux résultats de l'enquête sur les familles : nuptialité et fécondité : France métropolitaine / par Guy Desplanques. — 1985. — 136p

FERTILITY, HUMAN — Ghana

GAISIE, S. K.
The proximate determinants of fertility in Ghana / S.K. Gaisie. — Voorburg : International Statistical Institute, 1984. — 63p. — (Scientific reports / World Fertility Survey ; no.53)

OWUSU, John Y.
Evaluation of the Ghana Fertility Survey 1979-80 / John Y. Owusu. — Voorburg : International Statistical Institute, 1984. — 44p. — (Scientific reports / World Fertility Survey ; no.69)

FERTILITY, HUMAN — Ghana — Statistics

The Ghana Fertility Survey, 1979—80 : a summary of findings. — Voorburg : International Statistical Institute, 1983. — 16p. — (World Fertility Survey ; no.39)

FERTILITY, HUMAN — Great Britain

BROWNLEE, John
The history of the birth and death rates in England and Wales taken as a whole from 1750 to the present time / John Brownlee. — London : Society of Medical Officers of Health, 1916. — 24p

FERTILITY, HUMAN — Great Britain — Statistics

GREAT BRITAIN. Office of Population Censuses and Surveys
Birth statistics : historical series of statistics from registrations of births in England and Wales, 1837-1983. — London : H.M.S.O., 1987. — x,206p. — (Series FM1 / Office of Population Censuses and Surveys ; no.13)

GREAT BRITAIN. Office of Population Censuses and Surveys
Period and cohort birth order statistics : period analyses for years from 1938-85 and cohort analyses for women born in each year from 1920 (England and Wales). — London : H.M.S.O., 1987. — iii,30p. — (Series FM1 ; no.14). — *7 microfiches in end pocket.* — *Bibliographical references: p13*

FERTILITY, HUMAN — Guyana

ABDULAH, Norma
Contraceptive use and fertility in the Commonwealth Caribbean / Norma Abdulah, Jack Harewood. — Voorburg : International Statistical Institute, 1984. — 55p. — (Scientific reports / World Fertility Survey ; no.60)

HAREWOOD, Jack
Mating and fertility : results from three WFS surveys in Guyana, Jamaica and Trinidad and Tobago / Jack Harewood. — Voorburg : International Statistical Institute, 1984. — 65p. — (Scientific reports / World Fertility Survey ; no.67)

LIGHTBOURNE, Robert E.
Fertility preferences in Guyana, Jamaica and Trinidad and Tobago, from World Fertility Survey, 1975-77 : a multiple indicator approach / R.E. Lightbourne. — Voorburg : International Statistical Institute, 1984. — 128p. — (Scientific reports / World Fertility Survey ; no.68)

SINGH, Susheela
Guyana, Jamaica and Trinidad and Tobago : socio—economic differentials in cumulative fertility / Susheela Singh. — Voorburg : International Statistical Institute, 1984. — 89p. — (Scientific reports / World Fertility Survey ; no.57)

FERTILITY, HUMAN — Haiti

FORTUNAT, F.
Les déterminants proches de la fécondité en Haïti / F. Fortunat. — Voorburg : International Statistical Institute, 1984. — 77p. — (Scientific reports / World Fertility Survey ; no.61)

TARDIEU, Camille
Evaluation des données de l'Enquête Haïtienne sur la Fécondité / Camille Tardieu. — Voorburg : International Statistical Institute, 1984. — 59p. — (Scientific reports / World Fertility Survey ; no.50)

FERTILITY, HUMAN — Haiti — Forecasting

COURBAGE, Youssef
Méthodes d'estimation du niveau futur de la fécondité à partir du nombre d'enfants désirés et des facteurs socio-économiques en Haïti / Youssef Courbage. — Voorburg : International Statistical Institute, 1984. — 29p. — (Scientific reports / World Fertility Survey ; no.66)

FERTILITY, HUMAN — Hungary — Statistics

Summary of the 1986 fertility surveys. — Budapest : Central Statistical Office, 1987. — 21p

FERTILITY, HUMAN — India — Case studies — Addresses, essays, lectures

Fertility and mortality : theory, methodology, and emperical issues / edited by K. Mahadevan with P.J. Reddy & D.A. Naidu. — New Delhi ; Beverly Hills ; London : Sage Publications, 1986. — 351p. — *Includes bibliographies*

FERTILITY, HUMAN — India — Arunachal Pradesh — Statistics

Census of India 1981. — [Delhi : Controller of Publications]
Series 25: Arunachal Pradesh. — [1985]

FERTILITY, HUMAN — India — Gujarat — Statistics

Census of India 1981. — [Delhi : Controller of Publications]
Series 5: Gujarat. — [1985]

FERTILITY, HUMAN — Indonesia

TAN, Mely G
Ethnicity and fertility in Indonesia / by Mely G. Tan and Budi Soeradji. — Singapore : Institute of Southeast Asian Studies, 1986. — xiv, 143 p.. — (Research notes and discussions paper ; no. 53) (Ethnicity and fertility in Southeast Asia series). — *Bibliography: p. 143*

FERTILITY, HUMAN — Indonesia — Bali (Province)

STREATFIELD, K
Fertility decline in a traditional society : the case of Bali / Kim Streatfield. — [Canberra, ACT] : Dept. of Demography, Australian National University : Distributed by Bibliotech, 1986. — xvii, 177 p.. — (Indonesian population monograph series ; no. 4). — *Bibliography: p. 161-173*

FERTILITY, HUMAN — Italy — Statistics

Fertility Survey in Italy, 1979 : a summary of findings. — Voorburg : International Statistical Institute, 1982. — 20p. — (World Fertility Survey ; no.37)

FERTILITY, HUMAN — Italy — Statistics
continuation

Indagine sulla fecondità della donna. — Roma : Instituto Centrale di Statistica, 1974. — (Note e relazioni ; n.50). — *Summary in English*

FERTILITY, HUMAN — Ivory Coast

SOMBO, N'cho
Enquête Ivoirienne sur la fecondité, 1980-81 : rapport d'évaluation / N'cho Sombo. — Voorburg : International Statistical Institute, 1985. — 63p. — (Scientific reports / World Fertility Survey ; no.79)

FERTILITY, HUMAN — Jamaica

ABDULAH, Norma
Contraceptive use and fertility in the Commonwealth Caribbean / Norma Abdulah, Jack Harewood. — Voorburg : International Statistical Institute, 1984. — 55p. — (Scientific reports / World Fertility Survey ; no.60)

HAREWOOD, Jack
Mating and fertility : results from three WFS surveys in Guyana, Jamaica and Trinidad and Tobago / Jack Harewood. — Voorburg : International Statistical Institute, 1984. — 65p. — (Scientific reports / World Fertility Survey ; no.67)

LIGHTBOURNE, Robert E.
Fertility preferences in Guyana, Jamaica and Trinidad and Tobago, from World Fertility Survey, 1975-77 : a multiple indicator approach / R.E. Lightbourne. — Voorburg : International Statistical Institute, 1984. — 128p. — (Scientific reports / World Fertility Survey ; no.68)

SINGH, Susheela
Guyana, Jamaica and Trinidad and Tobago : socio—economic differentials in cumulative fertility / Susheela Singh. — Voorburg : International Statistical Institute, 1984. — 89p. — (Scientific reports / World Fertility Survey ; no.57)

FERTILITY, HUMAN — Jordan

ABDEL-AZIZ, Abdallah
Evaluation of the Jordan Fertility Survey 1976 / Abdallah Abdel-Aziz. — Voorburg : International Statistical Institute, 1983. — 31p. — (Scientific reports / World Fertility Survey ; no. 42)

ABDEL-AZIZ, Abdallah
A study of birth intervals in Jordan / Abdallah Abdel-Aziz. — Voorburg : International Statistical Institute, 1983. — 33p. — (Scientific reports / World Fertility Survey ; no.46)

FERTILITY, HUMAN — Kenya

ANKER, Richard
Fertility determinants in developing countries : a case study of Kenya / by Richard Anker and James C. Knowles. — Liège (Belgium) : Ordina Editions, c1982. — x, 222 p.. — *Bibliography: p. 203-213*

FERRY, Benoit
The proximate determinants of fertility and their effect on fertility patterns : an illustrative analysis applied to Kenya / Benoit Ferry, H.J. Page. — Voorburg : International Statistical Institute, 1984. — 54p. — (Scientific reports / World Fertility Survey ; no.71)

FRANK, Odile
An interpretation of fertility and population policy in Kenya / Odile Frank [and] Geoffrey McNicoll. — New York : Population Council, 1987. — 49p. — (Working papers / Population Council. Center for Policy Studies ; no.131). — *Bibliography: p42-46*

FERTILITY, HUMAN — Korea (South — Satatistics

1970 population and housing census report. — [Seoul] Bureau of Statistics, Economic Planninfg Board. — *In Korean and English*
Vol.2: 10% sample survey. — [Seoul] Bureau of Statistics, Economic Planninfg Board. — *In Korean and English*
Vol.4-2: Fertility. — 1973. — 258p

FERTILITY, HUMAN — Lesotho

MPITI, A. M.
The proximate determinants of fertility in Lesotho / A. M. Mpiti, I. Kalule—Sabiti. — Voorburg : International Statistical Institute, 1985. — 44p. — (Scientific reports / World Fertility Survey ; no.78)

O'MUIRCHEARTAIGH, C. A.
The magnitude and pattern of response variance in the Lesotho Fertility Survey / C.A. O'Muircheartaigh. — Voorburg : International Statistical Institute, 1984. — 43p. — (Scientific reports / World Fertility Survey ; no.70)

TIMAEUS, Ian
Evaluation of the Lesotho Fertility Survey 1977 / Ian Timaeus, K. Balasubramanian. — Voorburg : International Statistical Institute, 1984. — 39p. — (Scientific reports / World Fertility Survey ; no.58)

FERTILITY, HUMAN — Netherlands — Statistics

Onderzoek gezinsvorming 1982 : verantwoording en vitkomsten. — 's-Gravenhage : Staatsuitgeverij, 1984. — 117p. — *Table of contents, summary and table headings in English. — Title on back cover: Netherlands fertility survey 1982*

FERTILITY, HUMAN — Nigeria

MORAH, Benson C.
Evaluation of the Nigeria Fertility Survey 1981-2 / Benson C. Morah. — Voorburg : International Statistical Institute, 1985. — 57p. — (Scientific reports / World Fertility Survey ; no.80)

FERTILITY, HUMAN — Pakistan

ALAM, Iqbal
Fertility levels : trends and differentials in Pakistan / evidence from the population, labour force and migration survey 1979-80 ; Iqbal Alam, Mohammad Irfan [and] Naseem Iqbal Farooqui. — Islamabad : Pakistan Institute of Development Economics, 1986. — 74 leaves. — (Studies in population, labour force and migration project report ; no.1). — *Bibliography: p65-66*

IRFAN, Mohammad
An investigation of household reproductive behaviour in Pakistan / Mohammad Irfan [and] G. M. Farooq. — Islamabad : Pakistan Institute of Development Economics, 1986. — 31,[16] leaves. — (Studies in population, labour force and migration project report ; no.4)

FERTILITY, HUMAN — Paraguay

SCHOEMAKER, Juan F.
Evaluación de la Encuesta Nacional de Fecundidad del Paraguay de 1979 / Juan F. Schoemaker. — Voorburg : International Statistical Institute, 1984. — 56p. — (Scientific reports / World Fertility Survey ; no.62)

FERTILITY, HUMAN — Paraguay — Statistics

The Paraguay Fertility Survey, 1979 : a summary of findings. — Voorburg : International Statistical Institute, 1983. — 16p. — (World Fertility Survey ; no.38)

FERTILITY, HUMAN — Peru — Statistical methods

O'MUIRCHEARTAIGH, C. A.
The magnitude and pattern of response variance in the Peru Fertility survey / C.A. O'Muircheartaigh. — Voorburg : International Statistical Institute, 1984. — 39p. — (Scientific reports / World Fertility Survey ; no.45)

FERTILITY, HUMAN — Portugal — Statistics

The Portugal Fertility Survey, 1979-80 : a summary of findings. — Voorburg : International Statistical Institute, 1983. — 23p. — (World Fertility Survey ; no.40)

FERTILITY, HUMAN — Portugal — Lanhezes — History

BRETTELL, Caroline
Men who migrate, women who wait : population and history in a Portuguese parish / Caroline B. Brettell. — Princeton, N.J. : Princeton University Press, c1986. — xv, 329 p., [8] p. of plates. — *Includes index. — Bibliography: p. [299]-319*

FERTILITY, HUMAN — Senegal

GUEYE, Lamine
Enquête Sénégalaise sur la fécondité : rapport d'évaluation / Lamine Gueye. — Voorburg : International Statistical Institute, 1984. — 57p. — (Scientific reports / World Fertility Service ; no.49)

FERTILITY, HUMAN — Seychelles

PEDERSEN, Jon
The social construction of fertility : population processes on a plantation in the Seychelles / Jon Pedersen. — Oslo : Department of Social Anthropology, Oslo University, 1985. — 230p. — (Oslo occasional papers in social anthropology ; no.10). — *Thesis submitted for the "Magistergrad" at the Institute of Social Anthropology, University of Oslo, April 1982. — Bibliography: p218-230*

FERTILITY, HUMAN — Singapore

KUO, Eddie C. Y
Ethnicity and fertility in Singapore / by Eddie C.Y. Kuo and Chiew Seen-Kong. — Singapore : Institute of Southeast Asian Studies, 1984. — xv, 180 p.. — (Research notes and discussions paper ; no. 48). — *Bibliography: p. 178-180*

FERTILITY, HUMAN — South Asia

CAIN, Mead
Consequences of reproductive failure : dependence, mobility, and mortality among the elderly in rural South Asia / Mead Cain. — New York : Population Council, 1985. — 30p. — (Working papers / Population Council. Center for Policy Studies ; no.119)

FERTILITY, HUMAN — Southern Africa

TIMAEUS, Ian
Labour circulation, marriage and fertility in Southern Africa / Ian Timaeus and Wendy Graham. — London : London School of Hygiene and Tropical Medicine. Centre for Population Studies, 1986. — 30p. — (CPS research paper ; no.86-2). — *Bibliography: p24-30*

FERTILITY, HUMAN — Soviet Union — History — 19th century

JONES, Ellen
Modernization, value change and fertility in the Soviet Union / Ellen Jones, Fred W. Grupp. — Cambridge : Cambridge University Press, 1987. — xiv,420p. — (Soviet and East European studies). — *Includes index*

FERTILITY, HUMAN — Soviet Union — History — 20th century

JONES, Ellen
Modernization, value change and fertility in the Soviet Union / Ellen Jones, Fred W. Grupp. — Cambridge : Cambridge University Press, 1987. — xiv,420p. — (Soviet and East European studies). — *Includes index*

FERTILITY, HUMAN — Statistical methods

MARCKWARDT, Albert M.
Response rates, callbacks and coverage : the WFS experience / Albert M. Marckwardt. — Voorburg : International Statistical Institute, 1984. — 32p. — (Scientific reports / World Fertility Survey ; no.55)

FERTILITY, HUMAN — Sweden — Statistics

Fertility survey in Sweden, 1981 : a summary of findings. — Voorburg : International Statistical Institute, 1984. — 18p. — (World Fertility Survey ; no.43)

FERTILITY, HUMAN — Syria — Statistics

Pregnancy follow-up study in Syria : 1976-1979. — [Damascus] : Central Bureau of Statistics, 1984. — 90p

VAIDYANATHAN, K. E.
Estimation of fertility in Syria from the 1970 Census data on past live births. — Damascus : Central Bureau of Statistics, 1976. — 22p. — (Syrian Population Studies Series ; no. 1)

FERTILITY, HUMAN — Thailand

GOLDSTEIN, Sidney
Migration and fertility-related attitudes and behavior in urban Thailand / Sidney Goldstein, Alice Goldstein [and] Bhassorn Limanonda. — Bangkok : Chulalongkorn University. Institute of Population Studies, 1981. — 71p. — (Paper / Chulalongkorn University. Institute of Population Studies ; no.38)

KNODEL, John
Thailand's continuing fertility decline / John Knodel, Nibhon Rebavalya [and] Peerarsit Kamnuansilpa. — Bangkok : Chulalongkorn University. Institute of Population Studies, 1981. — 41p. — (Paper / Chulalongkorn University. Institute of Population Studies ; no.40). — *Bibliography: p38-41*

PRASITHRATHSINT, Suchart
Ethnicity and fertility in Thailand / Suchart Prasithrathsint. — Singapore : Institute of Southeast Asian Studies, 1985. — xviii,270p. — (Research notes and discussions paper ; no.51) (Ethnicity and fertility in Southeast Asia series). — *Bibliography: p265-270*

FERTILITY, HUMAN — Thailand — Statistics

The survey of population change, 1974-76 : special report on fertility, nuptiality and infant mortality measures. — Bangkok : National Statistical Office, [1979]. — 81p. — *Contents: Estimating fertility in Thailand from information on children ever born/Kenneth Hill - Some indirect estimates of fertility and infant mortality.../Arjun L. Adlakha and Chintana Pejaranonda - Marriage pattern/Chinatana Pejaranonda*

FERTILITY, HUMAN — Trinidad and Tobago

ABDULAH, Norma
Contraceptive use and fertility in the Commonwealth Caribbean / Norma Abdulah, Jack Harewood. — Voorburg : International Statistical Institute, 1984. — 55p. — (Scientific reports / World Fertility Survey ; no.60)

HAREWOOD, Jack
Mating and fertility : results from three WFS surveys in Guyana, Jamaica and Trinidad and Tobago / Jack Harewood. — Voorburg : International Statistical Institute, 1984. — 65p. — (Scientific reports / World Fertility Survey ; no.67)

LIGHTBOURNE, Robert E.
Fertility preferences in Guyana, Jamaica and Trinidad and Tobago, from World Fertility Survey, 1975-77 : a multiple indicator approach / R.E. Lightbourne. — Voorburg : International Statistical Institute, 1984. — 128p. — (Scientific reports / World Fertility Survey ; no.68)

SINGH, Susheela
Guyana, Jamaica and Trinidad and Tobago : socio-economic differentials in cumulative fertility / Susheela Singh. — Voorburg : International Statistical Institute, 1984. — 89p. — (Scientific reports / World Fertility Survey ; no.57)

FERTILITY, HUMAN — Trinidad and Tobago — Statistics

HUNTE, Desmond
Evaluation of the Trinidad and Tobago Fertility Survey 1977 / Desmond Hunte. — Voorburg : International Statistical Institute, 1983. — 55p. — (Scientific reports / World Fertility Survey ; no.44)

FERTILITY, HUMAN — Tunisia — Statistics

COLLOQUE NATIONAL SUR LA FÉCONDITÉ EN TUNISIE (1985 : Tunis)
La fécondité en Tunisie : situation actuelle et perspectives : actes du Colloque National. — Tunis : Office National de la Famille et de la Population, 1985. — 351p. — *In French with summary in Arabic*

FERTILITY, HUMAN — Turkey

ÜNER, Sunday
Evaluation of the Turkish Fertility Survey 1978 / Sunday Üner. — Voorburg : International Statistical Institute, 1983. — 37p. — (Scientific reports / World Fertility Survey ; no. 43)

FERTILITY, HUMAN — Yemen

AL—TOHAMY, Abdel—Malik
Evaluation of the Yemen Arab Republic Fertility Survey 1979 / Abdel—Malik Al—Tohamy, Ishmael Kalule—Sabiti. — Voorburg : International Statistical Institute, 1985. — 47p. — (Scientific reports / World Fertility Survey ; no.76)

FERTILIZATION IN VITRO, HUMAN — Law and legislation

COWEN, Zelman
Reflections on medicine, biotechnology, and the law / Sir Zelman Cowen. — [Lincoln, NE] : University of Nebraska College of Law : Distributed by the University of Nebraska Press, 1986, c1985. — p. cm. — *"Eleventh in the series of Roscoe Pound lectures at the University of Nebraska College of Law"--Foreword*

FERTILIZER INDUSTRY — European Economic Community countries

The Community fertiliser industry / joint report by the CMC—Engrais/Commission Services Working Group on Fertilisers. — Luxembourg : Office for Official Publications of the European Communities, 1985. — 50p. — At head of title: Commission of the European Communities

FERTILIZER INDUSTRY

SHELDRICK, William F.
World nitrogen survey / William F. Sheldrick. — Washington, D.C. : The World Bank, 1987. — xxv,227p. — (Industry and finance series ; v20) (World Bank technical paper ; no.59). — *Includes bibliographical references*

FERTILIZER INDUSTRY — Energy conservation

HEATH, Roger
Potential for energy efficiency in the fertilizer industry / Roger Heath, John Mulckhuyse, and Subrahmanyan Venkataraman. — Washington, D.C. : The World Bank, 1985. — xii,97p. — (World Bank technical paper ; no.35). — *Bibliographical references: p90-97*

FERTILIZER INDUSTRY — Environmental aspects

RPA
Étude concernant les technologies propres dans l'industrie des fertilisants / RPA. — Luxembourg : Commission des Communautés Européennes, 1985. — v,105p. — (EUR ; 9626). — *Series title: Environment et qualité de la vie. — Bibliographical references: p105. — Contrat no.: U/83/229*

FERTILIZER INDUSTRY — Great Britain

Fertiliser report and statistics / Fertiliser Manufacturers' Association. — London : Fertiliser Manufacturers' Association, 1959. — Annual. — *Continued by Fertiliser statistics*

Fertiliser review / Fertiliser Manufacturers' Association. — London : Fertiliser Manufacturers' Association, 1984-. — Annual. — *Continues Fertiliser statistics*

Fertiliser statistics / Fertiliser Manufacturers' Association. — London : Fertiliser Manufacturers' Association, 1960-1982. — Annual. — *Continued by Fertiliser review*

FERTILIZER INDUSTRY — Latin America — Evaluation — Mathematical models

MENNES, L. B. M.
Multicoutry investment analysis / Loet B. M. Mennes, Ardy J. Stoutjesdijk. — Baltimore : Johns Hopkins University Press for the World Bank, 1985. — xii,228p. — (The planning of investment programs ; v.4) (A World Bank research publication). — *Includes bibliographical references*

FERTILIZER INDUSTRY — Taiwan

Taiwan Fertilizer Co., Ltd.. — Taipei : [Government Information Office], 1957. — [20]p

FERTILIZERS

Crop production levels and fertilizer use. — Rome : Food and Agriculture Organization of the United Nations, 1981. — ix, 69 p.. — (FAO fertilizer and plant nutrition bulletin ; 2). — *"Fertilizer and Plant Nutrition Service. Land and Water Development Division.". — Bibliography: p. 53-54*

Fertilizer and plant nutrition guide / Fertilizer and Plant Nutrition Service, Land and Water Development Division. — Rome : Food and Agriculture Organization of the United Nations, 1984. — xiv, 176 p.. — (FAO fertilizer and plant nutrition bulletin ; 9). — *Bibliography: p. 173-176*

FOOD AND AGRICULTURE ORGANIZATION. Fertilizer and Plant Nutrition Service
Maximizing fertilizer use efficiency. — Rome : F.A.O., 1983 [i.e.1984]. — (FAO Fertilizer and Plant Nutrition Bulletin ; no.6)

FERTILIZERS — Congresses

EXPERT CONSULTATION ON BETTER EXPLOITATION OF PLANT NUTRIENTS (1977 : Rome City)
Improved use of plant nutrients : report of the expert consultation on better exploitation of plant nutrients held in Rome 18-22 April 1977. — Rome : Food and Agriculture Organization of the United Nations, 1978. — vii, 152 p.. — (FAO soils bulletin ; 37). — *On t.p.: Soil Resources, Management and Conservation Service, Land and Water Development Division. — Includes bibliographies*

FERTILIZERS — Developing countries

Crop production levels and fertilizer use. — Rome : Food and Agriculture Organization of the United Nations, 1981. — ix, 69 p.. — (FAO fertilizer and plant nutrition bulletin ; 2). — *"Fertilizer and Plant Nutrition Service. Land and Water Development Division.". — Bibliography: p. 53-54*

FERTILIZERS — Economic aspects

Crop production levels and fertilizer use. — Rome : Food and Agriculture Organization of the United Nations, 1981. — ix, 69 p.. — (FAO fertilizer and plant nutrition bulletin ; 2). — *"Fertilizer and Plant Nutrition Service. Land and Water Development Division.". — Bibliography: p. 53-54*

FERTILIZERS — Environmental aspects — Organisation for Economic Co-operation and Development countries

Water pollution by fertilizers and pesticides. — Paris : Organisation for Economic Co-operation and Development, 1986. — 144p. — *Includes bibliographical references*

FERTILIZERS — Developing countries — Price policy — Case studies — Congresses

INTERNATIONAL SEMINAR ON FERTILIZER PRICING POLICIES (1984 : Washington, D.C.)
Fertilizer producer pricing in developing countries : issues and approaches / Edilberto L. Segura, Y. T. Shetty, and Mieko Nishimizu, editors. — Washington, D.C. : The World Bank, 1986. — xiii,250p. — (Industry and finance series ; v.11). — *Includes bibliographical references. — Proceedings of the International Seminar on Fertilizer Pricing Policies, sponsored by the Industry Department of the World Bank in March 1984*

FERTILIZERS — Developing countries — Price policy — Congresses

INTERNATIONAL SEMINAR ON FERTILIZER PRICING POLICIES (1984 : Washington, D.C.)
Fertilizer producer pricing in developing countries : issues and approaches / Edilberto L. Segura, Y. T. Shetty, and Mieko Nishimizu, editors. — Washington, D.C. : The World Bank, 1986. — xiii,250p. — (Industry and finance series ; v.11). — *Includes bibliographical references. — Proceedings of the International Seminar on Fertilizer Pricing Policies, sponsored by the Industry Department of the World Bank in March 1984*

FERTILIZERS — United States

WINES, Richard A
Fertilizer in America : from waste recycling to resource exploitation / Richard A. Wines. — Philadelphia : Temple University Press, 1985. — p. cm. — *Includes index. — Bibliography: p*

FERTILIZERS AND MANURES — Great Britain

Fertiliser report and statistics / Fertiliser Manufacturers' Association. — London : Fertiliser Manufacturers' Association, 1959. — *Annual. — Continued by Fertiliser statistics*

Fertiliser review / Fertiliser Manufacturers' Association. — London : Fertiliser Manufacturers' Association, 1984-. — *Annual. — Continues Fertiliser statistics*

Fertiliser statistics / Fertiliser Manufacturers' Association. — London : Fertiliser Manufacturers' Association, 1960-1982. — *Annual. — Continued by Fertiliser review*

FESTIVALS — Sri Lanka

TANAKA, Masakazu
Sacrifice and divine power : Hindu temple rituals and village festivals in a fishing village, Sri Lanka / by Masakazu Tanaka. — 562 leaves. — *PhD (Econ) 1986 LSE. — Leaves 477-536 are appendices*

FEUDALISM — Soviet Union — History

VOROB'EV, V. M.
Russkoe feodal'noe zemlevladenie ot "smutnogo vremeni" do kanuna petrovskikh reform / V. M. Vorob'ev, A. Ia. Degtiarev ; otv. redaktor A. L. Shapiro. — Leningrad : Izd-vo Leningradskogo universiteta, 1986. — 197p

FICTION — History and criticism

KUMAR, Krishan, 1942-
Utopia and anti-Utopia in modern times / Krishan Kumar. — Oxford : Basil Blackwell, 1986. — [352]p. — *Includes bibliography and index*

FICTION IN ENGLISH

WALKER, John, 19---
The Queen has been pleased : the British honours system at work / John Walker. — London : Secker & Warburg, 1986. — viii,216p . — *Includes index*

FIFE (SCOTLAND) — Antiquities

WALKER, Bruce
Exploring Scotland's heritage : Fife and Tayside / Bruce Walker and Graham Ritchie. — Edinburgh : H.M.S.O., 1987. — 202p. — (Exploring Scotland's heritage). — *At foot of t.p.: The Royal Commission on the Ancient and Historical Monuments of Scotland. — Bibliography: p.196-197*

FIJI — Economic conditions

BRITTON, Stephen G
Tourism and underdevelopment in Fiji / Stephen G. Britton. — Canberra, Australia ; New York, N.Y., U.S.A. : Australian National University ; Canberra : Distributed by ANU Press, 1983. — xiv, 232 p. — (Monograph / Development Studies Centre ; no. 31). *Bibliography: p. 219-226*

FIJI — History

LASAQA, I. Q
The Fijian people before and after independence / Isireli Lasaqa. — Canberra ; New York : Australian National University Press, 1984, c1983. — xvi, 231 p. — *Includes index. — Bibliography: p. [223]-225*

YOUNG, John
Adventurous spirits : Australian migrant society in pre-cession Fiji / John Young. — St. Lucia, Qld. : University of Queensland Press ; Lawrence, Mass. : Distributed in the USA and Canada by Technical Impex Corp., 1984. — 417 p. — *Includes index. — Bibliography: p. 395-408*

FIJI — Industries — Statistics

Census of industrial production / Bureau of Statistics, Fiji. — Suva : Bureau of Statistics, 1979-. — *Annual*

FIJI — Politics and government

Politics in Fiji / edited by Brij V. Lal. — Sydney ; London : Allen & Unwin, 1986. — [156]p. — *Includes index*

FIJI — Social conditions

TOREN, Christina Camden
Symbolic space and the construction of hierarchy : an anthropological and cognitive development study in a Fijian village / by Christina Toren. — 523 leaves. — *PhD (Arts) 1986 LSE. — Leaves 432-512 are appendices*

FIJIAN LANGUAGE — History

SIEGEL, Jeff
Language contact in a plantation environment : a sociolinguistic history of Fiji / Jeff Siegel. — Cambridge : Cambridge University Press, 1987. — [324]p. — (Studies in the social and cultural foundations of language ; 5). — *Includes bibliography and index*

FILE ORGANIZATION (COMPUTER SCIENCE)

BRITISH NATIONAL CONFERENCE ON DATABASES (5th : 1986 : University of Kent at Canterbury)
Proceedings of the Fifth British National Conference on Databases (BNCOD 5) : University of Kent at Canterbury, 14-16 July 1986 / edited by E.A. Oxborrow. — Cambridge : Cambridge University Press on behalf of the British Computer Society, 1986. — [210]p. — (The British Computer Society Workshop series)

DEEN, S. M.
Principles and practice of database systems / S.M. Deen. — Basingstoke : Macmillan Education, 1985. — [350]p. — (Macmillan computer science series)

GILLENSON, Mark L.
Database : step-by-step / Mark L. Gillenson. — New York ; Chichester : Wiley, c1985. — xviii,386p. — *Includes bibliographies and index*

HAWRYSZKIEWYCZ, I. T
Database analysis and design / I.T. Hawryszkiewycz. — Chicago : Science Research Associates, c1984. — xx, 578 p. — *Includes index. — Bibliography: p. 561-571*

New applications of data bases / edited by G. Gardarin, E. Gelenbe. — London : Academic, 1984. — xii,273p. — *Conference papers*

FILMS See Moving-pictures

FILTERS (MATHEMATICS)

MANOHAR RAO, M. J
Filtering and control of macroeconomic systems : a control system incorporating the Kalman filter for the Indian economy / M.J. Manohar Rao. — Amsterdam ; New York : North-Holland ; New York, N.Y., U.S.A. : Sole distributors for the U.S.A. and Canada, Elsevier Science Pub. Co., 1987. — p. cm. — (Contributions to economic analysis ; 160). — *Includes indexes. — Bibliography: p*

FINANCE

AUERBACH, Robert D
Money, banking, and financial markets / Robert D. Auerbach. — 2nd ed. — New York : Macmillan ; London : Collier Macmillan, c1985. — xvii, 650, 17 p. — *Includes bibliographies and index*

Changing money : financial innovation in developed countries / edited by Marcello de Cecco. — Oxford : Basil Blackwell in co-operation with the European University Institute, Florence, 1987. — vii,329p. — *Includes bibliographies and index*

EDMISTER, Robert O
Financial institutions : markets and management / Robert O. Edmister. — 2nd ed. — New York : McGraw-Hill, c1986. — xxi, 521 p.. — (McGraw-Hill series in finance). — *Includes bibliographies and index*

KAUFMAN, George G
The U.S. financial system : money, markets, and institutions / George G. Kaufman. — 3rd ed. — Englewood Cliffs, N.J. : Prentice-Hall, c1986. — xxvii, 668p. — *Includes bibliographical references and index*

KAUFMAN, Henry
Interest rates, the markets, and the new financial world / Henry Kaufman. — London : Tauris, 1986. — [224]p. — *Includes bibliography and index*

The Operation and regulation of financial markets / edited by Charles Goodhart, David Currie and David T. Llewellyn. — Basingstoke : Macmillan in association with the Money Study Group, 1987. — xvii,270p. — (Studies in monetary economics). — *Includes bibliographies*

SIJBEN, J.J
Money and finance : a blurring of disciplines / Jac J. Sijben. — Tilburg : Tilburg University Press, 1986. — 43p

FINANCE — Dictionaries — Russian

Finansovo-kreditnyi slovar' : v 3-kh t. / glavnyi redaktor V. F. Garbuzov. — Moskva : Finansy i statistika
T.2: K-P. — 1986. — 511p

FINANCE — Periodicals

The City Press : the City of London newspaper. — London : The City Press, 1945-1975. — *Weekly*

FINANCE — Africa

SEIDMAN, Ann
Money, banking and public finance in Africa / Ann Seidman. — London : Zed, 1986. — [368]p. — *Includes bibliography and index*

FINANCE — Asia

MEIER, Gerald M
Financing Asian development : performance and prospects / by Gerald M. Meier. — Lanham, MD : University Press of America ; New York, N.Y. : Asia Society, c1986. — xvi, 72 p. — (Asian agenda report ; 6). — *Bibliography: p. 71*

FINANCE — Asia, South-Eastern

NG, Beoy Kui
Some aspects of the informal financial sector in the SEACEN countries / Ng Beoy Kui. — [s.l.] : South-East Asian Central Bank (SEACEN) Research and Training Centre, 1985. — 46p. — (Staff papers / SEACEN ; no.10)

FINANCE — Australia

AUSTRALIAN PAYMENTS SYSTEM COUNCIL
The Australian payments system. — [S.l.] : Australian Payments System Council, 1987. — vi,61p

FINANCE — Bangladesh
RANA, Pradumna B.
Improving domestic resource mobilization through financial development : Bangladesh / Pradumna B. Rana. — Manila : Asian Development Bank, 1986. — [v],52p. — *Includes bibliographical references*

FINANCE — Brazil
Brazil, financial systems review. — Washington, D.C., U.S.A. : World Bank, c1984. — xcix,150p. — (A World Bank Country study). — *Summaries in French, Portuguese, and Spanish. — Bibliography: p144-149*

FINANCE — Canada
NEAVE, Edwin H.
Canada's financial system : a managerial approach / Edwin H. Neave, Jacques Préfontaine. — Toronto : Methuen, 1987. — ix,414p. — *Includes references*

FINANCE — Canada — Statistics
Financial flow accounts = Comptes des flux financiers / Statistics Canada. — Ottawa : Minister of Supply and Services Canada, 1986-. — *Quarterly. — Text in English and French*

FINANCE — Chile — Statistics
MAMALAKIS, Markos
Historical statistics of Chile / compiled by Markos J. Mamalakis. — Westport, Conn. : Greenwood Press
vol.5: Money, banking, and financial services. — 1985. — xcii,532p

FINANCE — Colombia
Colombia, the investment banking system and related issues in the financial sector. — Washington, D.C., U.S.A. : World Bank, c1985. — xl,82p. — (A World Bank country study). — *Preface and summary in English and Spainsh. — Includes bibliographical references*

FINANCE — Communist countries
MOLCHANOVA, O. A.
Kreditnyi mekhanizm sotsialisticheskogo obshchestva : (politekonomicheskii aspekt) / O. A. Molchanova. — Leningrad : Izd-vo Leningradskogo universiteta, 1986. — 134p

VOZNESENSKII, E. A.
Finansy kak stoimostnaia kategoriia / E. A. Voznesenskii. — Moskva : Finansy i statistika, 1985. — 157p

FINANCE — Developing countries
INTERNATIONAL DEVELOPMENT ASSOCIATION
By-laws : as amended through March 2, 1981. — Washington, D.C. : the Association, 1981. — 2p

INTERNATIONAL DEVELOPMENT ASSOCIATION
General conditions applicable to development credit agreements. — [[Washington, D.C.?] : the Association, 1980. — iii,12p

INTERNATIONAL FINANCE CORPORATION
Articles of agreement of the International Finance Corporation : as amended by resolutions effective September 21, 1961 and September 1, 1965. — Washington, D.C. : the Corporation, 1979. — 13p

INTERNATIONAL FINANCE CORPORATION
By-laws of the International Finance Corporation : as amended through February 18, 1980. — Washington, D.C. : the Corporation, 1980. — 4p

WORLD BANK
Articles of agreement of the International Bank for Reconstruction and Development : as amended effective December 17, 1965. — Washington, D.C. : the Bank, 1980. — 24p

WORLD BANK
By-laws of the International Bank for Reconstruction and Development : as amended through September 26, 1980. — Washington, D.C. : the Bank, 1980. — 6p

WORLD BANK
General conditions applicable to loan and guarantee agreements. — [Washington, D.C.] : the Bank, 1974. — iii,18p. — *At head of title page: International Bank for Reconstruction and Development*

WORLD BANK
Loan regulations no.3 : applicable to loans made by the Bank to member governments : dated February 15, 1961 as amended February 9, 1967. — [Washington, D.C.?] : the Bank, 1967. — iv,35p

WORLD BANK
Loan regulations no.4 : applicable to loans made by the Bank to borrowers other than member governments : dated Februrary 15, 1961 as amended February 9, 1967. — [Washington, D.C.?] : the Bank, 1967. — iv,40p

FINANCE — England — London
COGGAN, Philip
The money machine : how the city works / Philip Coggan. — Harmondsworth : Penguin Books, 1986. — 231p. — *Bibliography: p222-[223]*

FINANCE — European Economic Community countries
CARCELÉN CONESA, José Miguel
Las entidades financieras de desarrollo regionl en la Europa comunitaria / José Miguel Carcelén Conesa. — Madrid : Instituto de Estudios de Administración Local, 1982. — 421p. — (Colección estudios / Instituto de Estudios de Administración Local). — *Bibliography: p407-417*

GIL, Gonzalo
Aspectos financieros y monetarios de la integración española en la Comunidad Economica Europea / Gonzalo Gil. — [Madrid] : Banco de España, 1985. — 187p. — (Estudios económicos / Banco de España, Servicio de Estudios ; no.37)

FINANCE — France
MÉTAIS, Joël
Les mutations du système financier français : innovation et déréglementation / Joel Métais, Philippe Szymczak. — Paris : La Documentation franąise, 1986. — 144p. — (Notes et études documentaires ; no.4820). — *Bibliography: p143-144*

ROSA, Jean-Jacques
La répression financière / Jean-Jacques Rosa [and] Michel Dietsch. — Paris : Bonnel Éditions, 1981. — 151p. — *Bibliography: p149-151*

FINANCE — Great Britain
Financial deregulation : the proceedings of a conference held by the David Hume Institute in May 1986 / edited by Richard Dale. — Cambridge : Woodhead Faulkner, 1986. — [96]p

FINANCE — Great Britain — History — 20th century
HOLLOWAY, Edward
Money matters : a modern pilgrim's economic progress / Edward Holloway. — London : Sherwood Press, 1986. — [vii],198p

FINANCE — Great Britain — Statistical services
A Guide to Financial times statistics / editor Alan Greenhorn ; assistant editor S. Cockerill. — London : Financial Times Business Information, 1985. — 64p. — *Includes index*

FINANCE — Indonesia — Statistics
Statistik keuangan. Financial Statistics / Biro Pusat Statistik, Indonesia. — Jakarta : Biro Pusat Statistik, 1977/78-. — *Annual. — Text in Indonesian and English*

Statistik keuangan desa. village government financial statistics / Biro Pusat Statistik, Indonesia. — Jakarta : Biro Pusat Statistik, Indonesia, 1980-. — *Annual. — Text in Indonesian and English*

FINANCE — Japan
HORNE, James
Japan's financial markets : conflict and consensus in policy making / James Horne. — Sidney : George Allen & Unwin in association with the Australia-Japan Research Centre, 1985. — 271p. — *Bibliography: p[234]-266*

FINANCE — Latin America
BALASSA, Bela A
Toward renewed economic growth in Latin America / Bela Balassa ... [et al.]. — Washington, DC : Institute for International Economics, 1986. — p. cm. — *Bibliography: p*

FINANCE — Nepal
MAHAT, R. S
Capital market, financial flows, and industrial finance in Nepal / R.S. Mahat. — 1st ed. — Lalitpur : Sajha Prakashan, 1981. — xvi, 350 p.. — *Bibliography: p. 335-346*

FINANCE — Persian Gulf region
SEZNEC, Jean-François
The financial markets of the Arabian Gulf / Jean-François Seznec. — London : Croom Helm, c1987. — xiii,143p. — *Bibliography: p137-138. — Includes index*

FINANCE — Soviet Union
Soviet financial system / by group of authors at the Moscow Financial Institute directed by D. A. Allakhverdyan. — Moscow : Progress Publishers, 1966. — 353p

FINANCE — Soviet Union — Bibliography
DREMINA, Z. E.
Finansy, denği i kredit SSSR : bibliograficheskii ukazatel' 1976-1985 gg. / [sostaviteli: Z. E. Dremina, A. V. Golousenko, G. M. Klimova; otv. redaktor V. S. Kulikov]. — Moskva : Finansy i statistika, 1986. — 287p

FINANCE — Spain
España : un presente para el futuro. — [Madrid] : Instituto de Estudios Económicos. — (Colección tablero)
2: Las instituciones / E. García de Enterría...[et al.]. — c1984. — 445p

GIL, Gonzalo
Aspectos financieros y monetarios de la integración española en la Comunidad Economica Europea / Gonzalo Gil. — [Madrid] : Banco de España, 1985. — 187p. — (Estudios económicos / Banco de España, Servicio de Estudios ; no.37)

GIL, Gonzalo
Sistema financiero español / Gonzalo Gil. — 4a ed. — [Madrid] : Banco de España, 1986. — 206p. — (Estudios económicos / Banco de España, Servicio de Estudios ; no.29)

FINANCE — United States
KAUFMAN, George G
The U.S. financial system : money, markets, and institutions / George G. Kaufman. — 3rd ed. — Englewood Cliffs, N.J. : Prentice-Hall, c1986. — xxvii, 668p. — *Includes bibliographical references and index*

FINANCE — United States — Statistics
Banking and monetary statistics : 1914-1941. — Washington, D.C. : Board of Governors of the Federal Reserve System, 1976. — 682p

BOARD OF GOVERNORS OF THE FEDERAL RESERVE SYSTEM (U.S.)
Banking and monetary statistics, 1941-1970. — Washington : Board of Governors of the Federal Reserve System, 1976. — vii,1168p

FINANCE COMPANIES — European Economic Community countries
CARCELÉN CONESA, José Miguel
Las entidades financieras de desarrollo regionl en la Europa comunitaria / José Miguel Carcelén Conesa. — Madrid : Instituto de Estudios de Administración Local, 1982. — 421p. — (Colección estudios / Instituto de Estudios de Administración Local). — *Bibliography: p407-417*

FINANCE DEPARTMENTS — Poland
System instytucji prawno-finansowych PRL / redaktor Marian Weralski. — Wrocław : Ossolineum
T.3: Instytucje budżetowe
Cz.2: Dochody i wydatki budżetu. — 1985. — 751p. — Bibliography: p712-748

FINANCE, PERSONAL
DAVIS, E. P.
Portfolio behaviour of the non-financial private sectors in the major economies / by E. P. Davies. — Basle : Bank for International Settlements, 1986. — 140p. — (BIS economic papers ; no.17). — Bibliographical references: p136-139

Personal financial markets : an examination of the evolving markets for personal savings and financing in the United Kingdom and the United States / edited by R.L. Carter and B. Chiplin and M.K. Lewis. — Oxford : Philip Allan, 1986. — viii,279p. — Includes bibliographies and index

Private saving and public debt / edited by Michael J. Boskin, John S. Flemming and Stefano Gorini. — Oxford : Basil Blackwell, 1987. — x,424p. — Includes bibliographies and index

FINANCE, PERSONAL — Great Britain
RAYER, John
Personal financial planning manual 1986-1987. — 3rd ed. / John Rayer, Nicholas Andrew. — London : Butterworths, 1986. — xxiv,279p. — Previous ed.: 1985. — Includes index

FINANCE, PUBLIC
BENARD, Jean
Economie publique / Jean Benard. — Paris : Economica, c1985. — 430p. — (Collection "Economie"). — Bibliography: p[401]-414

Staat und Politische Ökonomie heute : Horst Claus Recktenwald zum 65. Geburtstag = Public sector and political economy today: essays in honour of Horst Claus Recktenwald / herausgegeben von Horst Hanusch, Karl W. Roskamp, Jack Wiseman. — Stuttgart : Gustav Fischer, 1985. — xii,393p. — Includes bibliographies

FINANCE, PUBLIC — Accounting
RUTHERFORD, B. A.
Financial reporting in the public sector / B.A. Rutherford. — London : Butterworths, c1983. — xvi,257p. — Includes bibliographies and index

UNITED NATIONS
National accounts statistics : government accounts and tables / United Nations. — New York : United Nations, 1982-. — Annual

FINANCE, PUBLIC — Accounting — France
CASTILLE, Didier
Les comptes du secteur public concurrentiel séries 1981-1983 / Didier Castille, Denis Cavaud et Pierre Muller. — Paris : I.N.S.E.E., 1985. — 213p. — (Les collections de l'INSEE ; 96)

FINANCE, PUBLIC — Addresses, essays, lectures
MUSGRAVE, Richard A.
Public finance in a democratic society : collected papers / Richard A. Musgrave. — Brighton : Harvester
Vol. 2: Fiscal doctrine, growth and institutions. — 1986. — 400 p

FINANCE, PUBLIC — Congresses
INTERNATIONAL INSTITUTE OF PUBLIC FINANCE. Congress (1984 : Innsbruck, Austria)
Public finance and public debt = : Finances publiques et endettement public : proceedings of the 40th Congress of the International Institute of Public Finance, Innsbruck, 1984 / edited by Bernard P. Herber. — Detroit, Mich. : Wayne State University Press, c1985. — p. cm. — English and French

FINANCE, PUBLIC — Decision making
HOLCOMBE, Randall G
An economic analysis of democracy / Randall G. Holcombe. — Carbondale : Southern Illinois University Press, c1985. — xiii, 269 p.. — (Political and social economy). — Includes index. — Bibliography: p. 257-266

FINANCE, PUBLIC — European Economic Community countries
Les ressources financières de la Communauté Européenne / sous la direction de Guy Isaac ; préface de Jacques Delors. — Paris : Economica, 1986. — vii,464p. — (Travaux de la Commission pour l'Etude des Communautés Européennes)

FINANCE, PUBLIC — Law and legislation — Ecuador
ECUADOR
[Laws, etc.]. Ley orgánica de hacienda codificada. — [Quito] : Superintendencia de Bancos, 1975. — 42p

FINANCE, PUBLIC — Law and legislation — Poland
System instytucji prawno-finansowych PRL / redaktor Marian Weralski. — Wrocław : Ossolineum
T.3: Instytucje budżetowe
Cz.2: Dochody i wydatki budżetu. — 1985. — 751p. — Bibliography: p712-748

FINANCE, PUBLIC — Management
GLYNN, John J.
Public sector financial control and accounting / John Glynn. — Oxford : Basil Blackwell, 1987. — [240]p. — Includes index

FINANCE, PUBLIC — Political aspects — Central Europe — History
Wealth and taxation in Central Europe : the history and sociology of public finance / edited by Peter-Christian Witt. — Leamington Spa : Berg, 1987. — [208]p. — (German historical perspectives ; 2)

FINANCE, PUBLIC — Social aspects — Central Europe — History
Wealth and taxation in Central Europe : the history and sociology of public finance / edited by Peter-Christian Witt. — Leamington Spa : Berg, 1987. — [208]p. — (German historical perspectives ; 2)

FINANCE, PUBLIC — California — San Francisco — History
MCDONALD, Terrence J
The parameters of urban fiscal policy : socio-economic change, political culture, and fiscal policy in San Francisco, 1860-1906. — Berkeley : University of California Press, c1986. — p. cm. — Includes index. — Bibliography: p

FINANCE, PUBLIC — Canada
BARRADOS, John P.
A key to the Canadian economy / John P. Barrados. — Lanham, MD : University Press of America, c1966. — p. cm. — Includes index

FINANCE, PUBLIC — Canada — History
BRYCE, Robert B.
Maturing in hard times : Canada's Department of Finance through the Great Depression / Robert B. Bryce. — Kingston ; Montreal : McGill-Queen's University Press : Institute of Public Administration of Canada, 1986. — xii,278p. — (Canadian public administration series)

FINANCE, PUBLIC — England — London
AUDIT COMMISSION FOR LOCAL AUTHORITIES IN ENGLAND AND WALES
The management of London's authorities : preventing the breakdown of services. — [London : H.M.SO.], 1987. — 16p. — (Occasional papers ; no.2)

FINANCE, PUBLIC — England — London — Statistics
GREATER LONDON COUNCIL
Comparative economic and financial statistics on London and the rest of England. — [Rev. ed]. — [London] : the Council, 1986. — 1v.(unpaged). — (Statistical series ; no.49)

FINANCE, PUBLIC — European Economic Community countries — Bibliography — Catalogs
COMMISSION OF THE EUROPEAN COMMUNITIES. Library
Recent publications on the European Communities received by the Library : supplement. — [Luxembourg : Office for Official Publications of the European Communities]
1985/1: Bibliography on monetary and financial matters. — 1985. — 750,54 columns. — In Community languages

FINANCE, PUBLIC — France — History — 18th century
RILEY, James C
The Seven Years War and the old regime in France : the economic and financial toll / James C. Riley. — Princeton, N.J. : Princeton University Press, 1986. — xxii, 256p. — Includes index

FINANCE, PUBLIC — France — Statistics
Ventilation fonctionnelle des dépenses des administrations publiques : année 1970 et séries 1975-1983. — Paris : I.N.S.E.E., 1986. — 128p. — (Archives et documents / Institut national de la statistique et des études économiques ; no.161)

FINANCE, PUBLIC — Georgia — History — 19th century
WALLENSTEIN, Peter
From slave South to New South : public policy in nineteenth-century Georgia / Peter Wallenstein. — Chapel Hill : University of North Caroline Press, c1987. — xii, 284 p.. — (The Fred W. Morrison series in Southern studies). — Includes index. — Bibliography: p. [257]-272

FINANCE, PUBLIC — Germany
BOELCKE, Willi A.
Die Kosten von Hitlers Krieg : Kriegsfinanzierung und finanzielles Kriegserbe in Deutschland 1933-1948 / Willi A. Boelcke. — Paderborn : Schöningh, 1985. — 220p. — Includes bibliograhical references

ERHARD, Ludwig
Kriegsfinanzierung und Schuldenkonsolidierung / Ludwig Erhard ; mit Vorbemerkungen von Ludwig Erhard, Theodor Eschenburg, Günter Schmölders. — Faks.-Dr. d. Denkschr. von 1943-44. — Frankfurt/M ; Berlin ; Wien : Propyläen, 1977. — xxxiv, 268 p. — On spine: Denkschrift 1943/44. — "Eine Veröffentlichung der Ludwig-Erhard-Stiftung e.V. Bonn. Materialien zur Zeitgeschichte."

FINANCE, PUBLIC — Great Britain
GREAT BRITAIN. Parliament. House of Commons. Library. Research Division
Public expenditure and the economy / [Priscilla Baines, Christopher Barclay, Robert Clements]. — [London] : the Division, 1980. — 19p. — (Background paper ; no.75). — Bibliography: p18-19

New priorities in public spending / edited by M.S. Levitt. — Aldershot : Gower, c1987. — [220]p. — (Joint studies in public policy ; 13). — Conference proceedings. — At head of title: National Institute of Economic and Social Research, Policy Studies Institute, Royal Institute of International Affairs. — Includes bibliography and index

PEACOCK, Alan, 1922-
The growth of public expenditure in the United Kingdom / by Alan T. Peacock and Jack Wiseman assisted by Jindrich Veverka. — 2nd rev. ed.. — Allen & Unwin, 1967. — 213p. — (University of York studies in economics ; 1) (University books). — Previous ed (B62-2055): Oxford U.P. 1962

FINANCE, PUBLIC — Great Britain
continuation

WALSHE, Grahame
Planning public spending in the UK / Grahame Walshe. — Basingstoke : Macmillan Education, 1987. — xi,123p. — *Bibliography: p97-101.* — *Includes index*

FINANCE, PUBLIC — Great Britain — To 1688

CUST, Richard
The forced loan and English politics : 1626-1628 / Richard Cust. — Oxford : Clarendon, 1987. — [380]p. — *Includes bibliography and index*

FINANCE, PUBLIC — Great Britain — To 1688 — Sources

ENGLAND. Exchequer
The Great Roll of the Pipe for the fourth year of the reign of King Henry III, Michaelmas 1220 : (Pipe Roll 64) : now first printed from the original in the Public Record Office / with an introduction by B.E. Harris. — London : Pipe Roll Society, 1987. — xviii,307p. — (Publications of the Pipe Roll Society ; v.85. New series ; v.47). — *Latin text, English introduction and notes*

FINANCE, PUBLIC — Ireland

Comprehensive public expenditure programmes. — Dublin : Stationery Office, 1985-. — *Annual*

Managing public money / edited by Sean Cromien and Aidan Pender. — Dublin : Institute of Public Administration, 1987. — 110p

FINANCE, PUBLIC — Japan

FELDMAN, Robert Alan
Japanese financial markets : deficits, dilemmas, and deregulation / Robert Alan Feldman. — Cambridge, Mass. : MIT Press, c1986. — p. cm. — *Includes index.* — *Bibliography: p*

Public finance in Japan / edited by Tokue Shibata. — Tokyo : University of Tokyo Press, 1986. — xiv,195p. — *Bibliography: p175-179.* — *Includes glossary*

FINANCE, PUBLIC — Mexico

VÁZQUEZ ARROYO, Francisco
Presupuestos por programas para el sector público de México / Francisco Vázquez Arroyo. — México : Universidad Nacional Autónoma de México, 1979. — 325p. — *Publicado originalmente en 1971.* — *Bibliography: p315-318*

FINANCE, PUBLIC — Nepal

JHA, Hari Bansh
Resource mobilisation and economic development in Nepal during the plan period / by Hari Bansh Jha. — Allahabad : Kitab Mahal, 1984. — xiv,199p. — *Revision of author's thesis (PhD: University of Bihar).* — *Bibliography: p[184]-199*

FINANCE, PUBLIC — New York (N.Y.)

SHEFTER, Martin
Political crisis, fiscal crisis : the collapse and revival of New York City / Martin Shefter. — New York : Basic Books, c1985. — p. cm. — *Includes index.* — *Bibliography: p*

FINANCE, PUBLIC — Newfoundland

Mid-year financial report / Government of Newfoundland and Labrador. — [St. John's : Department of Finance], 1983/84-. — *Annual*

FINANCE, PUBLIC — Nigeria

ASHWE, Chiichii
Fiscal federalism in Nigeria / Chiichii Ashwe. — Canberra : The Australian National University of Canberra, Centre for Research on Federal Financial Relations, 1986. — xi,140p. — (Research monograph / Australian National University. Centre for Research on Federal Financial Relations ; no.46). — *Bibliography: p112-125*

FINANCE, PUBLIC — Pakistan — Accounting

The Federal Public Accounts Committee in Pakistan. — [Islamabad] : National Assembly Secretariat ; [1985]. — x,232p

FINANCE, PUBLIC — Panama

Panama : structural change and growth prospects. — Washington, D.C., U.S.A. : World Bank, 1985. — xxv,307p. — (A World Bank country study). — *"Report no. 5236-PAN.".* — *"February 28, 1985."*

FINANCE, PUBLIC — Peru

10Peru. Programa de Adecuación del Sistema Financiero al Desarrollo Regional
Participación en el desarrollo regional. — Lima : the Programa, [ca.1974]. — 37leaves

PERU. Dirección de Política y Programación Financiera
Metodología para el estudio del sistema financiero a nivel regional. — [Lima] : the dirección, 1972. — 47leaves

FINANCE, PUBLIC — Peru — History — 17th century

ANDRIEN, Kenneth J.
Crisis and decline : the Viceroyalty of Peru in the seventeenth century / Kenneth J. Andrien. — 1st ed. — Albuquerque : University of New Mexico Press, c1985. — x, 287 p.. — *Includes index.* — *Bibliography: p. 263-275*

FINANCE, PUBLIC — Peru — Mathematical models

PERU. Dirección de Política y Programación Financiera
Metodología para el estudio del sistema financiero a nivel regional. — [Lima] : the dirección, 1972. — 47leaves

FINANCE, PUBLIC — Poland

System instytucji prawno-finansowych PRL / redaktor Marian Weralski. — Wrocław : Ossolineum
T.3: Instytucje budżetowe
Cz.2: Dochody i wydatki budżetu. — 1985. — 751p. — *Bibliography: p712-748*

FINANCE, PUBLIC — Saint Kitts-Nevis

St. Christopher and Nevis : economic report. — Washington, D.C., U.S.A. : World Bank, 1985. — xii,82p. — (World Bank country study)

FINANCE, PUBLIC — Saint Lucia

St. Lucia : economic performance and prospects. — Washington, D.C., U.S.A. : World Bank, 1985. — [xi],99p. — (World Bank country study). — *"Based on the findings of a World Bank mission to St. Lucia in February 1985"--Pref*

FINANCE, PUBLIC — Soviet Union

Rol' finansov v sotsial'no-ekonomicheskom razvitii strany / pod redaktsiei G. V. Bazarovoi. — Moskva : Finansy i statistika, 1986. — 230p

FINANCE, PUBLIC — Soviet Union — History

POSOSHKÓV, Iván
The book of poverty and wealth / Iván Pososhkóv ; edited and translated by A.P. Vlasto and L.R. Lewitter ; introduction and commentaries by L.R. Lewitter. — London : Athlone, 1987. — 440p. — *Translation of: Kniga o skúdosti i bogátstve.* — *Bibliography: p401-430.* — *Includes index*

FINANCE, PUBLIC — Spain

ALVAREZ BLANCO, Rafael
El sector publico en España : clasificación, fuentes y cuentas / Rafael Alvarez Blanco. — [Madrid] : Banco de España, 1982. — 128p. — (Estudios económicos / Banco de España, Servicio de Estudios ; no.24)

FINANCE, PUBLIC — Spain — Colonies — History — 17th century

ANDRIEN, Kenneth J.
Crisis and decline : the Viceroyalty of Peru in the seventeenth century / Kenneth J. Andrien. — 1st ed. — Albuquerque : University of New Mexico Press, c1985. — x, 287 p.. — *Includes index.* — *Bibliography: p. 263-275*

FINANCE, PUBLIC — United States — Accounting

Fraud, waste, and abuse in government : causes, consequences, and cures / edited by Jerome B. McKinney and Michael Johnston. — Philadelphia : Institute for the Study of Human Issues, 1986. — p. cm. — *Includes index*

FINANCE, PUBLIC — United States — States

Studies in state and local public finance / edited by Harvey S. Rosen. — Chicago : University of Chicago Press, c1986. — ix, 236 p.. — (A National Bureau of Economic Research project report). — *Includes bibliographies and indexes*

FINANCE, PUBLIC — United States — States — Congresses

States under stress : a report on the finances of Massachusetts, Michigan, Texas, and California : California Policy Seminar conference report / Peggy B. Musgrave, editor. — Berkeley : Institute of Governmental Studies, University of California, [c1985]. — vii, 60 leaves. — *"February 1985."*

FINANCIAL ACCOUNTING STANDARDS BOARD

MILLER, Paul B. W.
The FASB : the people, the process, and the politics / Paul B. W. Miller, Rodney J. Redding. — Homewood, Ill. : Irwin, 1986. — xvi,145p

FINANCIAL FUTURES — United States

Financial futures and options in the U.S. economy : a study / by the staff of the Federal Reserve System ; edited by Myron L. Kwast. — [Washington : Board of Governors of the Federal Reserve System], 1986. — [ix],264p. — *Bibliography: p249-264*

FINANCIAL INSTITUTIONS

EDMISTER, Robert O
Financial institutions : markets and management / Robert O. Edmister. — 2nd ed. — New York : McGraw-Hill, c1986. — xxi, 521 p.. — (McGraw-Hill series in finance). — *Includes bibliographies and index*

The GT guide to world equity markets / edited by Charles G. Hildeburn ; editorial advisor David Galloway ; assistant editors Bryan de Caires, Quek Peck Lim, Andrew Luglis-Taylor. — London : Euromoney Publications, 1986. — xi,290p

MAYCOCK, James
Financial conglomerates : the new phenomenon / James Maycock. — Aldershot : Gower, c1986. — [150]p. — (Gower studies in finance and investment ; 2). — *Includes index*

Personal financial markets : an examination of the evolving markets for personal savings and financing in the United Kingdom and the United States / edited by R.L. Carter and B. Chiplin and M.K. Lewis. — Oxford : Philip Allan, 1986. — viii,279p. — *Includes bibliographies and index*

FINANCIAL INSTITUTIONS — Government policy — Japan

HORNE, James
Japan's financial markets : conflict and consensus in policy making / James Horne. — Sidney : George Allen & Unwin in association with the Australia-Japan Research Centre, 1985. — 271p. — *Bibliography: p[234]-266*

FINANCIAL INSTITUTIONS — Law and legislation — Great Britain
GREAT BRITAIN
[Financial Services Act 1986]. The Financial Services Act 1986 : a guide to the new law / Andrew Whittaker, Geoffrey Morse. — London : Butterworths, 1987. — vii,475p. — *Includes index*

A guide to the Financial Services Act 1986 / A.J. Wedgwood ... [et al.]. — London : Financial Training, 1986. — xi,371p. — *Includes index. — Includes the text of the Act*

MULLINEUX, A. W.
U.K. banking after deregulation / A.W. Mullineux. — London : Croom Helm, c1987. — 180p. — *Bibliography: p166-171.* — *Includes index*

FINANCIAL INSTITUTIONS — Law and legislation — Organisation for Economic Co-operation and Development countries
Introduction to the OECD codes of liberalisation. — Paris : Organisation for Economic Co-operation and Development, 1987. — 42p. — *Bibliographical references: p30-32*

FINANCIAL INSTITUTIONS — Asia, South-Eastern
NG, Beoy Kui
Some aspects of the informal financial sector in the SEACEN countries / Ng Beoy Kui. — [s.l.] : South-East Asian Central Bank (SEACEN) Research and Training Centre, 1985. — 46p. — (Staff papers / SEACEN ; no.10)

FINANCIAL INSTITUTIONS — Asia, Southeastern
SKULLY, Michael T
Merchant banking in ASEAN : a regional examination of its development and operations / Michael T. Skully. — rev. ed. — Singapore ; Oxford : Oxford University Press, 1986. — viii,204p

FINANCIAL INSTITUTIONS — Canada
NEAVE, Edwin H.
Canada's financial system : a managerial approach / Edwin H. Neave, Jacques Préfontaine. — Toronto : Methuen, 1987. — ix,414p. — *Includes references*

FINANCIAL INSTITUTIONS — Developing countries
WELLONS, Phillip
Banks and specialised financial intermediaries in development / by Phillip Wellons, Dimitri Germidis and Bianca Glavanis. — Paris : Organisation for Economic Co—operation and Development, 1986. — 150p. — (Development Centre studies). — *Bibliography: p131-133*

FINANCIAL INSTITUTIONS — England — London
COGGAN, Philip
The money machine : how the city works / Philip Coggan. — Harmondsworth : Penguin Books, 1986. — 231p. — *Bibliography: p222-[223]*

WIDLAKE, Brian
In the city / Brian Widlake. — London : Faber, 1986. — 327p. — *Includes index*

FINANCIAL INSTITUTIONS — France
MÉTAIS, Joël
Les mutations du système financier français : innovation et déréglementation / Joel Métais, Philippe Szymczak. — Paris : La Documentation française, 1986. — 144p. — (Notes et études documentaires ; no.4820). — *Bibliography: p143-144*

FINANCIAL INSTITUTIONS — Great Britain
LOMAX, David F.
London markets after the Financial Services Act / David F. Lomax. — London : Butterworths, 1987. — [225]p. — *Includes bibliography and index*

WATKINS, Trevor
Marketing financial services / by Trevor Watkins and Mike Wright. — London : Butterworths, 1986. — ix,170p. — *Bibliography: p159-163. — Includes index*

FINANCIAL INSTITUTIONS — Great Britain — Technological innovations
TAYLOR, Alan
New technology : banking, insurance and finance / Alan Taylor. — Hammersmith : [the Council], 1983. — 35p. — (Research report / Hammersmith and Fulham ; 59)

FINANCIAL INSTITUTIONS — Hong Kong
Hong Kong's financial institutions and markets / editors; Robert Haney Scott, K.A. Wong [and] Yan Ki Ho. — Hong Kong : Oxford University Press, 1986. — xiii,185p. — *Bibliographies*

FINANCIAL INSTITUTIONS — Italy — Statistics
Le principali società italiane. — Milano : Banca di Credito Finanziario, 1985-. — *Annual*

FINANCIAL INSTITUTIONS — Organisation for Economic Co-operation and Development countries — Investments
MITSOTAKI, Alexandra Gourdain
Public development finance corporations : their role in the new forms of investment in developing countries / by Alexandra Gourdain Mitsotaki. — [Paris] : Development Centre of the Organisation for Economic Co-operation and Development, [1986]. — 40p. — (Development Centre papers). — *Bibliographical references: p.39-40*

FINANCIAL INSTITUTIONS — Switzerland
CHRISTENSEN, Benedicte Vibe
Switzerland's role as an international financial center / by Benedicte Vibe Christensen. — Washington, D. C. : International Monetary Fund, 1986. — v,40p. — (Occasional paper / International Monetary Fund ; no.45). — *Bibliography: p39-40*

FINANCIAL STATEMENTS
Availability of financial statements. — Paris : OECD, 1987. — 37p. — (Working document / OECD Working Group on Accounting Standards ; no.2). — *Includes bibliographical references*

BROWN, Lawrence D
The modern theory of financial reporting / Lawrence D. Brown. — Plano, Tex. : Business Publications, 1987. — x, 460 p.. — *Bibliography: p. 441-460*

GREENER, Michael
Between the lines of the balance sheet : the plain man's guide to published accounts / by Michael Greener. — 2nd ed. — Oxford : Pergamon, 1980. — xxiii,221p. — (Pergamon international library). — *Previous ed.: 1968. — Includes index*

MALLINSON, Derek
Understanding current cost accounting : a guide for those preparing and using financial statements / by Derek Mallinson. — London : Butterworth, 1980. — xviii,428p. — *Includes: Current cost accounting / Institute of Chartered Accountants in England and Wales - Guidance notes on SSAP 16, current cost accounting / Accounting Standards Committee*

FINANCIAL STATEMENTS — France
ORDRE DES EXPERTS COMPTABLES ET DES COMPTABLES AGRÉÉS
Les rapports annuels des sociétés françaises : année 1984 : analyse de l'information comptable et financière contenue dans les rapports annuels de 150 sociétés françaises / Ordre des Experts Comptables et des Comptables Agréés. — [France] : Éditions Comptables Malesherbes
T.L: [Les comptes annuels]. — 1986. — xi,160p

FINANCIAL STATEMENTS — Great Britain
FLINT, David
A true and fair view in company accounts / by David Flint. — London : Published for the Institute of Chartered Accountants of Scotland by Gee, 1982. — vi,47p. — *Bibliography: p46-47*

Model financial statements for public and private companies / Stoy Hayward. — London : Butterworth, 1986. — [120]p

FINANCIAL STATEMENTS — Great Britain — Case studies
RUTHERFORD, B. A.
Cases in company financial reporting / B.A. Rutherford, R.T. Wearing. — London : Harper & Row, 1987. — xxi,186p. — (Harper & Row series in accounting and finance). — *Includes bibliographies*

FINANCIAL STATEMENTS — United States
FINANCIAL ACCOUNTING STANDARDS BOARD
Statement of financial accounting standards. — Stamford, Conn. : Financial Accounting Standards Board
No.89: Financial reporting and changing prices. — 1986. — 81p

FINANCIAL STATEMENTS, CONSOLIDATED
TAYLOR, P. A. (Paul A)
Consolidated financial statements : concepts, issues and techniques / P.A. Taylor. — London : Harper & Row, 1987. — xvii,329p. — (Harper & Row series in accounting and finance). — *Bibliography: p315-321.* — *Includes index*

FINANCIAL STATEMENTS, CONSOLIDATED — France
ORDRE DES EXPERTS COMPTABLES ET DES COMPTABLES AGRÉÉS
Les rapports annuels des sociétés françaises : année 1984 : analyse de l'information comptable et financière contenue dans les rapports annuels de 150 sociétés françaises / Ordre des Experts Comptables et des Comptables Agréés. — [France] : Éditions Comptables Malesherbes
T.2: [Les comptes consolidés]. — 1986. — xi,188p

'FINANCIAL TIMES'
A Guide to Financial times statistics / editor Alan Greenhorn ; assistant editor S. Cockerill. — London : Financial Times Business Information, 1985. — 64p. — *Includes index*

FINE GAEL — History
O'BYRNES, Stephen
Hiding behind a face : Fine Gael under Fitzgerald / Stephen O'Byrnes. — Dublin : Gill and Macmillan, 1986. — 330p

FINLAND — Appropriations and expenditures
PIETILÄ, Juha
Statens inkomster och utgifter länsvis 1978 / Juha Pietilä, Aku Alanen. — Helsinki : Tilastokeskus, 1981. — 83p. — (Tutkimuksia / Finland. Tilastokeskus ; no.69)

FINLAND — Census, 1980
PUTKONEN, Carita
Confidence study : population and housing census 1980 : measurement and processing errors / Carita Putkonen. — Helsinki : Tilastokeskus, 1984. — 90p. — (Tutkimuksia / Finland. Tilastokeskus ; no.99)

PUTKONEN, Carita
Luotettavuustutkimus : vaestö- ja och bostadsräkningen 1980 / Carita Putkonen. — Helsinki : Tilastokeskus. — (Tutkimuksia / Finland. Tilastokeskus ; no.99). — *Summary in Swedish*
Osa 1: Selvitys mittaus- ja käsittelyvirheistä = Del 1: Utredning av mätfel och bearbetningsfel. — 1983. — 212p

FINLAND — Census, 1980
continuation

PUTKONEN, Carita
Luotettavuustutkimus : vaesto- ja asuntolaskenta 1980 / Carita Putkonen. — Helsinki : Tilastokeskus. — (Tutkimuksia / Finland. Tilastokeskus ; no.100)
Osa 2: Peittävyysselvitys. — 1984. — 69p

FINLAND — Commerce

ERIKSSON, Gösta A.
Finnish and Swedish iron export to England in the 18th and 19th centuries with an excursus / Gösta A. Eriksson. — °Abo : °Abo Akademis, 1987. — 43p. — (Meddelanden fr°an Ekonomisk-Statsveten skapliga Fakulteten vid °Abo Akademi ; Ser.A.:239). — *Bibliography: p42-43*

FINLAND — Economic conditions

HEIKKINEN, Sakari
Suomen teollisuus ja teollinen käsityö 1860-1913 / Sakari Heikkinen ja Riitta Hjerppe. — Helsinki : Suomen Pankki, 1986. — 140p. — *With summary in English*

Suomen taloushistoria. — Helsinki : Kustannusosakeyhtiö Tammi
Vol.2: Teollistuva Suomi / toimittaneet Jorma Ahvenainen, Erkki Pihkala, Viljo Rasila. — 1982. — 555p. — *Bibliography: p532-537*

Suomen taloushistoria. — Helsinki : Kustannusosakeyhtiö Tammi. — *Text in English and Finnish*
vol.3: Historiallinen tilasto / toimittanut Kaarina Vattula ; English translation by Sinikka Lampivuo. — 1983. — 470p

Suomen taloushistovia. — Helsinki : Kustannusosakeyhtiö Tammi
Vol.1: Agraarinen Suomi / toimittaneet Eino Jutikkala, Yrjö Kaukiainen, Sven-Erik Åström. — 1980. — 494p. — *Bibliography: p488-491*

FINLAND — Economic policy

Finland 1995 : economic prospects. — Helsinki : Economic Planning Centre, 1981. — 85p

FINLAND — Foreign relations — Soviet Union

LUNTINEN, Pertti
F.A. Seyn : a political biography of a Tsarist imperialist as administrator of Finland / Pertti Luntinen. — Helsinki : SHS, 1985. — 343p. — (Studia historica ; 19)

FINLAND — History — 1809-1917

LUNTINEN, Pertti
F.A. Seyn : a political biography of a Tsarist imperialist as administrator of Finland / Pertti Luntinen. — Helsinki : SHS, 1985. — 343p. — (Studia historica ; 19)

FINLAND — History — 20th century

JÄGERSKIÖLD, Stig
Gustaf Mannerheim 1867-1951 / Stig Jägerskiöld. — Helsingfors : Schildtz, 1983. — 235p. — *Bibliography: p235*

FINLAND — Industries — History

HEIKKINEN, Sakari
Suomen teollisuus ja teollinen käsityö 1860-1913 / Sakari Heikkinen ja Riitta Hjerppe. — Helsinki : Suomen Pankki, 1986. — 140p. — *With summary in English*

FINLAND — Industries — History — Statistics

HEIKKINEN, Sakari
Suomen teollisuus ja teollinen käsityö 1860-1913 / Sakari Heikkinen ja Riitta Hjerppe. — Helsinki : Suomen Pankki, 1986. — 140p. — *With summary in English*

FINLAND — Industries — Statistics

HEIKKINEN, Sakari
Suomen teollisuus ja teollinen käsityö 1860-1913 / Sakari Heikkinen ja Riitta Hjerppe. — Helsinki : Suomen Pankki, 1986. — 140p. — *With summary in English*

FINLAND — Military relations — Soviet Union

BERNER, Örjan
[Sovjet & Norden. English]. Soviet policies toward the Nordic countries / Örjan Berner. — Lanham, MD : University Press of America ; [Cambridge, Mass.] : Center for International Affairs, Harvard University, c1986. — xii, 192 p., [1] leaf of plates. — *Shorter version published under title: Sovjet & Norden. c1985.* — *Bibliography: p. 187-192*

FINLAND — Politics and government

JÄGERSKIÖLD, Stig
Gustaf Mannerheim 1918 / Stig Jägerskiöld. — [Stockholm?] : Bonniers, 1967. — 411p. — *Bibliography: p399-402*

MANNERHEIM, Carl
The memoirs of Marshal Mannerheim [/ Carl Mannerheim] ; translated by Count Eric Lewenhaupt. — London : Cassell, 1953. — xi,540p

FINLAND — Politics and government — 1945-

BLÅFIELD, Antti
Maktskiftet / Antti Blåfield, Pekka Vuoristo. — Helsinki : Schildts, 1982. — 243p. — *Translated from Finnish into Swedish*

GRÖNHOLM, Christoffer
Kommunal självstyrelse och demokrati i Finland (inklusive en presentation av femkommunsundersökningen 1982) / Christoffer Grönholm. — Helsinki : Schildt, 1983. — 243p. — *Bibliography: p238-243*

HYVÄRINEN, Matti
The Finnish Communist Party : the failure of attempts to modernize a C.P. / Matti Hyvärinen, Jukka Paastela. — Tampere : Tampereen yliopisto, Politiikan tutkimuksen laitos, 1985. — 42 leaves. — (Tutkielmia / Tampereen yliopisto, Politiikan tutkimuksen laitosOccasional papers / University of Tampere, Department of Political Science ; 39). — *Bibliography: leaves 35-42*

FINLAND — Population — Bibliography

INTERNATIONAL UNION FOR THE SCIENTIFIC STUDY OF POPULATION
National population bibliography of Finland 1945-1978 / [editorial group: Altti Majava...et.al.]. — Helsinki : Finnish Demographic Society for the International Union for the Scientific Study of Population, 1984. — 296p

FINLAND — Population — Statistics

MARJOMAA, Pertti
Väestökehitys ja kotitalouks n kulutusmenot = Demografic [sic] development and household consumption expenditure. — Helsinki : Tilastokeskus, 1982. — 57p. — (Tutkimuksia / Finland. Tilastokeskus ; no.79). — *Bibliography: p56-57*

PUTKONEN, Carita
Confidence study : population and housing census 1980 : measurement and processing errors / Carita Putkonen. — Helsinki : Tilastokeskus, 1984. — 90p. — (Tutkimuksia / Finland. Tilastokeskus ; no.99)

PUTKONEN, Carita
Luotettavuustutkimus : vaestö- ja och bostadsräkningen 1980 / Carita Putkonen. — Helsinki : Tilastokeskus. — (Tutkimuksia / Finland. Tilastokeskus ; no.99). — *Summary in Swedish*
Osa 1: Selvitys mittaus- ja käsittelyvirheistä = Del 1: Utredning av mätfel och bearbetningsfel. — 1983. — 212p

PUTKONEN, Carita
Luotettavuustutkimus : vaesto- ja asuntolaskenta 1980 / Carita Putkonen. — Helsinki : Tilastokeskus. — (Tutkimuksia / Finland. Tilastokeskus ; no.100)
Osa 2: Peittävyysselvitys. — 1984. — 69p

FINLAND — Presidents — Election

BLÅFIELD, Antti
Maktskiftet / Antti Blåfield, Pekka Vuoristo. — Helsinki : Schildts, 1982. — 243p. — *Translated from Finnish into Swedish*

FINLAND — Social policy

Finland 1995 : economic prospects. — Helsinki : Economic Planning Centre, 1981. — 85p

FINLAND. Tilastokeskus

NIITAMO, O. E.
Long-term planning in the Central Statistical Office of Finland / Niitamo, O. E., Laihonen, A., Tiihonen, P.. — Helsinki : Tilastokeskus, 1981. — 53p,[13]p. — (Tutkimuksia / Finland. Tilastokeskus ; no.71)

NIITAMO, Olavi E.
Tilastollinen tietohuolto 1980-luvulla = Statistical information service in the 1980's / Olavi E. Niitamo. — Helsinki : Tilastokeskus, 1981. — 37p. — (Tutkimuksia / Finland. Tilastokeskus ; no.68). — *In Finnish and English*

FIRE-DEPARTMENTS — Great Britain

CENTRAL FIRE BRIGADES ADVISORY COUNCIL FOR ENGLAND AND WALES
Report of the working party to review the experience of the fire service - summer 1976 / Central Fire Brigades Advisory Council for England and Wales, Scottish Central Fire Brigades Advisory Council. — [London] : Home Office, Fire Department, 1978. — [118]p . — *Cover title: Report of the Joint Working Party to review the experience of the Fire Service — summer 1976*

FIRE-DEPARTMENTS — Great Britain — Auditing

AUDIT COMMISSION FOR LOCAL AUTHORITIES IN ENGLAND AND WALES
Value for money in the fire service : some strategic issues to be resolved. — [London : H.M.S.O.], 1986. — [6]p. — (Occasional papers ; no.1)

FIRE PREVENTION — Great Britain

CENTRAL FIRE BRIGADES ADVISORY COUNCIL FOR ENGLAND AND WALES
Report of the working party to review the experience of the fire service - summer 1976 / Central Fire Brigades Advisory Council for England and Wales, Scottish Central Fire Brigades Advisory Council. — [London] : Home Office, Fire Department, 1978. — [118]p . — *Cover title: Report of the Joint Working Party to review the experience of the Fire Service — summer 1976*

FIREARM OWNERSHIP — United States

WRIGHT, James D
Armed and considered dangerous : a survey of felons and their firearms / James D. Wright, Peter H. Rossi. — New York : Aldine de Gruyter, c1986. — xvi, 247 p.. — (Social institutions and social change). — *Includes index.* — *Bibliography: p. 239-242*

FIREARMS — Law and legislation — United States

KRUSCHKE, Earl R
The right to keep and bear arms : a continuing American dilemma / by Earl R. Kruschke. — Springfield, Ill., USA : Thomas, c1985. — p. cm. — *Bibliography: p*

FIRES — Great Britain — Casualties

MELINEK, S. J.
Loss of life expectancy due to fire / by S. J. Melinek. — Borehamwood : Fire Research Station, 1973. — 12p. — (Fire research note ; no.978). — *Bibliographical references: p6*

FIRMS — Great Britain — Archival resources

BUSINESS ARCHIVES COUNCIL
The first five hundred : chronicles and house histories of companies and organisations in the Business Archives Library. — London : Business Archives Council, 1959. — 22p

FIRMS — Great Britain — History — Sources

BUSINESS ARCHIVES COUNCIL
The first five hundred : chronicles and house histories of companies and organisations in the Business Archives Library. — London : Business Archives Council, 1959. — 22p

FISCAL POLICY

BLÖNDAL, Gísli
Fiscal policy in the smaller industrial countries, 1972-82 / by Gísli Blöndal. — Washington, D.C. : International Monetary Fund, 1986. — ix,232p. — *Bibliographical references: p231-232*

HELLER, Peter S.
A review of the fiscal impulse measure / by Peter S. Heller, Richard D. Haas, and Ahsan S. Mansur. — Washington, D.C. : Internation Monetary Fund, 1986. — vii,43p. — (Occasional paper / International Monetary Fund ; no.44). — *Bibliography: p.41-43*

MARINI, Giancarlo
Monetary and fiscal policy in an optimizing model with capital accumulation and finite lives / G. Marini [and] F. van der Ploeg. — London : Centre for Labour Economics, London School of Economics, 1987. — 28p. — (Discussion paper / London School of Economics and Political Science. Centre for Labour Economics ; no.277). — *Bibliography: p27-28*

Private saving and public debt / edited by Michael J. Boskin, John S. Flemming and Stefano Gorini. — Oxford : Basil Blackwell, 1987. — x,424p. — *Includes bibliographies and index*

FISCAL POLICY — Congresses

The Monetary versus fiscal policy debate : lessons from two decades / edited by R.W. Hafer. — Totowa, N.J. : Rowman & Allanheld, 1986. — 171 p.. — *Papers presented at the ninth annual economic policy conference held Oct. 12-13, 1984, sponsored by the Federal Reserve Bank of St. Louis. — Includes bibliographies and index*

FISCAL POLICY — Religious aspects — Islam

AL-SA'ADI, Abdullah Juma'an Saeed
Fiscal policy in the Islamic state : its origins and contemporary relevance / Abdullah Juma'an Saeed al-Sa'adi ; translated by Ahmad al-Anani. — Newcastle under Lyme : Lyme, 1986. — 272p. — *Translation of: Siyasat al-mal fil Islam. — Bibliography: p258-265. — Includes index*

FISCAL POLICY — Australia

Issues in meduim-term budgetary policy. — Canberra : Economic Planning Advisory Council, 1986. — v,26p. — (Council paper / Economic Planning Advisory Council ; no.16). — *Bibliographical references: p24*

FISCAL POLICY — California — San Francisco — History

MCDONALD, Terrence J
The parameters of urban fiscal policy : socio-economic change, political culture, and fiscal policy in San Francisco, 1860-1906. — Berkeley : University of California Press, c1986. — p. cm. — *Includes index. — Bibliography: p*

FISCAL POLICY — Canada

Fiscal and monetary policy / John Sargent, research coordinator. — Toronto : University of Toronto Press, 1986. — xviii,339p

FISCAL POLICY — Communist countries

WERALSKI, Marian
Tendences du développement des systèmes fiscaux dans les pays socialistes / Marian Weralski. — Warszawa : Pántswowe Wydawhictwo Nankowe, 1974. — 15p. — (Conférences fascicule / Académie Polonaise des Sciences. Centre Scientifique à Paris ; 108)

FISCAL POLICY — Developing countries

Fund-supported programs, fiscal policy, and income distribution : a study / by the Fiscal Affairs Department of the International Monetary Fund. — Washington, D.C. : International Monetary Fund, 1986. — v,58p. — (Occasional paper / International Monetary Fund ; no.46). — *Bibliographical references: p54-58*

FISCAL POLICY — Dominican Republic

Dominican Republic : economic prospects and policies to renew growth. — Washington, D.C., U.S.A. : World Bank, 1985. — xviii,174p. — (A World Bank country study). — *Includes bibliographical references*

FISCAL POLICY — Georgia — History — 19th century

WALLENSTEIN, Peter
From slave South to New South : public policy in nineteenth-century Georgia / Peter Wallenstein. — Chapel Hill : University of North Caroline Press, c1987. — xii, 284 p.. — (The Fred W. Morrison series in Southern studies). — *Includes index. — Bibliography: p. [257]-272*

FISCAL POLICY — Islamic countries

AL-SA'ADI, Abdullah Juma'an Saeed
Fiscal policy in the Islamic state : its origins and contemporary relevance / Abdullah Juma'an Saeed al-Sa'adi ; translated by Ahmad al-Anani. — Newcastle under Lyme : Lyme, 1986. — 272p. — *Translation of: Siyasat al-mal fil Islam. — Bibliography: p258-265. — Includes index*

FISCAL POLICY — Nepal

AMATYA, Daman B
Nepal's fiscal issues : new challenges / D.B. Amatya. — New Delhi : Sterling Publishers, c1986. — xiv, 205 p.. — *Includes index. — Bibliography: p. [192]-202*

FISCAL POLICY — Organisation for Economic Co-operation and Development countries

CHOURAQUI, Jean-Claude
Public debt in a medium-term context and its implications for fiscal policy / by Jean-Claude Chouraqui, Brian Jones and Robert Bruce Montador. — [Paris] : OECD, 1986. — 67P. — (Working papers / OECD. Department of Economics and Statistics ; no.30). — *Bibliographical references: p.32-37*

FISCAL POLICY — Thailand

INTERNATIONAL BANK FOR RECONSTRUCTION AND DEVELOPMENT
Thailand : managing public resources for structural adjustment. — Washington, D.C., U.S.A. : World Bank, c1984. — Lxviii,275p. — (A World Bank country study). — *Summaries in English, French, and Spanish. — Includes bibliographical references*

FISCAL POLICY — Turkey

KOPITS, George
Structural reform, stabilization, and growth in Turkey / by George Kopits. — Washington, D.C. : International Monetary Fund : External Relations Dept., Publication Services, IMF [distributor], c1987. — v,46p. — (Occasional paper ; no. 52). — *"May 1987.". — Bibliographical references: p46*

FISCAL POLICY — Unied States

MAKIN, John H
U.S. fiscal policy : its effects at home and abroad / John H. Makin. — Washington, D.C. : American Enterprise Institute for Public Policy Research, [1986]. — p. cm. — (AEI studies ; 447)

FISCAL POLICY — United States

BRAYTON, Flint
The macroeconomic and sectoral effects of the Economic Recovery Tax Act : some simulation results / Flint Brayton, Peter B. Clark. — Washington, D.C. : Board of Governors of the Federal Reserve System, 1985. — 17p. — (Staff study / Board of Governors of the Federal Reserve System (U.S.) ; 148)

CEBULA, Richard J
The deficit problem in perspective / Richard J. Cebula. — Lexington, Mass. : Lexington Books, c1987. — p. cm. — *Includes index*

Tax reform and U.S. economy / papers by Henry J. Aaron...[et al.] ; edited by Joseph A. Pechman. — Washington, D.C. : Brookings Institution, 1987. — 107p. — (Brookings dialogues on public policy). — *Papers presented at a conference at the Brookings institution, December 2, 1986*

FISCAL POLICY — United States — States — Congresses

States under stress : a report on the finances of Massachusetts, Michigan, Texas, and California : California Policy Seminar conference report / Peggy B. Musgrave, editor. — Berkeley : Institute of Governmental Studies, University of California, [c1985]. — vii, 60 leaves. — *"February 1985."*

FISH, MARY

BUEL, Joy Day
The way of duty : a woman and her family in revolutionary America / Joy Day Buel and Richard Buel, Jr. — New York ; London : Norton, c1984. — xviii,309p. — *Bibliography: p299-301. — Includes index*

FISH-CULTURE — Government policy — Great Britain

NATIONAL WATER COUNCIL
Fish farming : observations on the paper "The need for a revision of government policies for the industry" published by the National Farmers' Unions in September 1978. — [London] : the Council, [1979]. — 9leaves

FISH, SALTED — Economic aspects — Newfoundland

RYAN, Shannon
Fish out of water : the Newfoundland saltfish trade 1814-1914 / Shannon Ryan. — St. John's (Nfld.) : Breakwater, 1986. — 320p,[24]p of plates. — (Newfoundland history series ; 2). — *Bibliography: p301-310*

FISH TRADE — Newfoundland — History — 19th century

RYAN, Shannon
Fish out of water : the Newfoundland saltfish trade 1814-1914 / Shannon Ryan. — St. John's (Nfld.) : Breakwater, 1986. — 320p,[24]p of plates. — (Newfoundland history series ; 2). — *Bibliography: p301-310*

FISHERIES — Bibliography

DAVID LUBIN MEMORIAL LIBRARY
FAO documentation : fisheries : 1979-1983 = Documentation de la FAO : pêches : 1979-1983 = Documentacion de la FAO : pesca : 1979-1983. — Rome : Food and Agriculture Organization, 1984. — 156p. — *In English with introductions also in French and Spanish*

FAO documentation : fisheries : 1983-1985 = Documentation de la FAO : fisheries : 1983-1985 = Documentacion de la FAO : pesca : 1983-1985. — Rome : Food and Agriculture Organization, 1986. — 117p. — *In English with introductions also in French and Spanish*

FISHERIES — Economic aspects — Newfoundland

SINCLAIR, Peter R.
From traps to draggers : domestic commodity production in Northwest Newfoundland, 1850-1982 / Peter R. Sinclair. — Newfoundland : Memorial University of Newfoundland, Institute of Social and Economic Research, 1985. — ix,171p. — (Social and Economic Studies / Memorial University of Newfoundland. Institute of Social and Economic Research ; no.31). — *Bibliography: p[157]-167*

FISHERIES — Argentina

ESPOZ ESPOZ, Milciades
Introducción a la pesca argentina : su rol en la economía nacional y mundial / Milciades Espoz Espoz. — [Buenos Aires] : Fundación Atlántica, c1985. — xii,336p. — *Bibliography: p336*

FISHERIES — California — History

MCEVOY, Arthur F.
The fisherman's problem : ecology and law in the California fisheries, 1850-1980 / Arthur F. McEvoy. — Cambridge : Cambridge University Press, 1986. — 1v.. — (Studies in environment and history). — *Includes bibliography and index*

FISHERIES — Canada — History

CLEMENT, Wallace
The struggle to organize : resistance in Canada's fishery / by Wallace Clement. — Toronto, Ont. : McClelland and Stewart, c1986. — 219 p.. — *Includes index. — Bibliography: p. 197-209*

FISHERIES — Finland — Accounting

MÄKELÄ, Pekka
Kansantalouden tilinpito : maa-, metsä- ja kalatalous sekä metsästys kansantalouden tilinpidossa = National accounts : agriculture, forestry, fishing and hunting in national accounts. — Helsinki : Tilastokeskus, 1980. — 126p. — (Tutkimuksia / Finland. Tilastokeskus ; no.61). — *Summary and table headings in English and Swedish*

FISHERIES — Georges Bank

MACLEISH, William H.
Oil and water : the struggle for Georges Bank / by William H. MacLeish. — 1st ed. — Boston : Atlantic Monthly Press, c1985. — 304 p.. — *Includes index*

FISHERIES — Newfoundland — History

SINCLAIR, Peter R.
From traps to draggers : domestic commodity production in Northwest Newfoundland, 1850-1982 / Peter R. Sinclair. — Newfoundland : Memorial University of Newfoundland, Institute of Social and Economic Research, 1985. — ix,171p. — (Social and Economic Studies / Memorial University of Newfoundland. Institute of Social and Economic Research ; no.31). — *Bibliography: p[157]-167*

FISHERIES — North Atlantic Ocean

NORTH-EAST ATLANTIC FISHERIES COMMISSION
Report of the annual meeting. — London : Office of the Commission, 1982-. — *Annual*

FISHERIES — Taiwan

Fisheries of Taiwan, Republic of China. — [Taipei : Ministry of Economic Affairs, 1958]. — [16]p

Taiwan fisheries. — Taipei : Industrial Development Commission, 1955. — 16p

FISHERIES, CO-OPERATIVE — Zimbabwe — Kariba

BOURDILLON, M. F. C.
Inshore fishing co-operatives in the Kariba district / M. F. C. Bourdillon. — Gweru : Mambo Press, 1986. — 33p. — (Mambo occasional papers. socio-economic series ; no.21)

FISHERIES, COOPERATIVE — Canada — History

CLEMENT, Wallace
The struggle to organize : resistance in Canada's fishery / by Wallace Clement. — Toronto, Ont. : McClelland and Stewart, c1986. — 219 p.. — *Includes index. — Bibliography: p. 197-209*

FISHERMEN — Spain — Galicia

VARELA LAFUENTE, Manuel María
Procesos de producción en el sector pesquero en Galicia / Manuel María Varela Lafuente. — Santiago : Universidad de Santiago de Compostela, Diputaciones de La Coruña, Lugo y Pontevedra, 1985. — 315p. — (Monografía de la Universidad de Santiago de Compostela ; no.106). — *Bibliography: p305-315*

FISHERS — Canada — History

CLEMENT, Wallace
The struggle to organize : resistance in Canada's fishery / by Wallace Clement. — Toronto, Ont. : McClelland and Stewart, c1986. — 219 p.. — *Includes index. — Bibliography: p. 197-209*

FISHERS — Ghana — Social conditions

HILL, Polly
Talking with Ewe seine fishermen and shallot farmers / recording and edited by Polly Hill. — Cambridge : African Studies Centre, University of Cambridge, [1986]. — 66p,[11] leaves of plates. — (Cambridge African monographs ; 6). — *Bibliography: p57-58. — Includes index*

FISHERS — Hong Kong

WARD, Barbara E.
Through other eyes : essays in understanding 'conscious models' : mostly in Hong Kong / Barbara E. Ward. — Hong Kong : Chinese University Press ; Boulder : Westview, 1985. — xvi,280p

FISHERY CONSERVATION — Atlantic Ocean — Congresses

INTERNATIONAL ATLANTIC SALMON SYMPOSIUM (2nd : 1978 : Edinburgh)
Atlantic salmon, its future : proceedings of the second International Atlantic Salmon Symposium, Edinburgh 1978, sponsored by the International Atlantic Salmon Foundation and the Atlantic Salmon Research Trust / editor A.E.J. Went. — Farnham : Fishing News, 1980. — xi,253p. — *Includes bibliographies and index*

FISHERY CONSERVATION — North Atlantic Ocean

Technical conservation measures : measures in force in the zones under the fisheries jurisdiction of contracting parties and in the regulatory area of the Commission. — London : North-East Atlantic Fisheries Commission, 1986. — 1v (loose-leaf)

FISHERY LAW AND LEGISLATION — North Atlantic Ocean

Technical conservation measures : measures in force in the zones under the fisheries jurisdiction of contracting parties and in the regulatory area of the Commission. — London : North-East Atlantic Fisheries Commission, 1986. — 1v (loose-leaf)

FISHERY LAW AND LEGISLATION

The law of the sea : national legislation on the exclusive economic zone, the economic zone and the exclusive fishery zone. — New York : United Nations, 1986. — xv,337p

FISHERY LAW AND LEGISLATION — Congresses

LAW OF THE SEA INSTITUTE. Conference (16th : 1982 : Halifax, N.S.)
The law of the sea and ocean industry : new opportunities and restraints : proceedings, Sixteenth Annual Conference / co-sponsored by the Dalhousie Ocean Studies Programme, June 21-24, 1982, Halifax, Nova Scotia ; edited by Douglas M. Johnston and Norman G. Letalik. — Honolulu : Law of the Sea Institute, University of Hawaii, c1983. — p. cm. — (Sea grant cooperative report ; UNIHI-SEAGRANT-CR-83-02). — *Bibliography: p*

FISHERY LAW AND LEGISLATION — California — History

MCEVOY, Arthur F.
The fisherman's problem : ecology and law in the California fisheries, 1850-1980 / Arthur F. McEvoy. — Cambridge : Cambridge University Press, 1986. — 1v.. — (Studies in environment and history). — *Includes bibliography and index*

FISHERY LAW AND LEGISLATION — Caribbean Area

EDESON, W. R
The legal regime of fisheries in the Caribbean region / W.R. Edeson, J.-F. Pulvenis. — Berlin ; New York : Springer-Verlag, 1983. — x, 204 p.. — (Lectures notes in coastal and estuarine studies ; 7). — *Bibliography: p. [197]-204*

FISHERY MANAGEMENT

CHASTON, Ian
Business management in fisheries and aquaculture / Ian Chaston. — Farnham : Fishing News, c1984. — 128p

Natural resources economics and policy applications : essays in honor of James A. Crutchfield / edited by Edward Miles, Robert Pealy, and Robert Stokes ; foreword by Brewster C. Denny. — Seattle : Institute for Marine Studies of the University of Washington : Distributed by the University of Washington Press, c1986. — p. cm. — (Public policy issues in resource management). — *Includes index. — Bibliography: p*

FISHERY MANAGEMENT — California — History

MCEVOY, Arthur F.
The fisherman's problem : ecology and law in the California fisheries, 1850-1980 / Arthur F. McEvoy. — Cambridge : Cambridge University Press, 1986. — 1v.. — (Studies in environment and history). — *Includes bibliography and index*

FISHERY POLICY — Social aspects — Canada

SINCLAIR, Peter R.
State intervention and the Newfoundland fisheries : essays on fisheries policy and social structure / Peter R. Sinclair. — Aldershot : Avebury, c1987. — vi,155p. — *Bibliography: p146-155*

FISHERY POLICY — Social aspects — Newfoundland

SINCLAIR, Peter R.
State intervention and the Newfoundland fisheries : essays on fisheries policy and social structure / Peter R. Sinclair. — Aldershot : Avebury, c1987. — vi,155p. — *Bibliography: p146-155*

FISHERY POLICY — Canada

Atlantic Ffisheries Rrestructuring Act annual report = sur la restructuration du secteur des pêches de l'Atlantique: rapport annuel / Fisheries and Oceans, Canada. — Ottawa : Department of Fisheries and Oceans, 1983/4-. — *Annual. — In English and French*

FISHERY POLICY — France

SHACKLETON, Michael
The politics of fishing in Britain and France / by Michael Shackleton. — Aldershot : Gower, c1986. — [410]p. — *Includes bibliography*

FISHERY POLICY — Great Britain

SHACKLETON, Michael
The politics of fishing in Britain and France / by Michael Shackleton. — Aldershot : Gower, c1986. — [410]p. — *Includes bibliography*

FISHERY POLICY — Spain — Galicia

VARELA LAFUENTE, Manuel María
Procesos de producción en el sector pesquero en Galicia / Manuel María Varela Lafuente. — Santiago : Universidad de Santiago de Compostela, Diputaciones de La Coruña, Lugo y Pontevedra, 1985. — 315p. — (Monografía de la Universidad de Santiago de Compostela ; no.106). — *Bibliography: p305-315*

FISHING VILLAGES — Scotland — Burra (Shetland Islands)
BYRON, Reginald
Sea change : a Shetland society, 1970-79 / Reginald Byron. — St John's : Institute of Social and Economic Research Memorial University of Newfoundland, 1986. — vii,164p

FITZGERALD, GARRET
Ireland in the contemporary world : essays in honour of Garret FitzGerald / edited by James Dooge. — Dublin : Gill and Macmillan, 1986. — [viii],160p

FITZGERALD, GARRET MICHAEL DESMOND
O'BYRNES, Stephen
Hiding behind a face : Fine Gael under Fitzgerald / Stephen O'Byrnes. — Dublin : Gill and Macmillan, 1986. — 330p

FLAGS OF CONVENIENCE
METAXAS, B. N.
Flags of convenience : a study of internationalization / B.N. Metaxas. — Aldershot : Gower, c1985. — x,107p. — *Includes index*

FLAT-RATE INCOME TAX — United States
A Citizen's guide to the new tax reforms : fair tax, simple tax, flat tax / Joseph A. Pechman, editor. — Totowa, N.J. : Rowman & Allanheld, 1985. — p. cm. — *Includes index*

FLEMING, DONALD M
FLEMING, Donald M
So very near : the political memoirs of the Honourable Donald M. Fleming. — Toronto, Ont. : McCelland and Stewart, c1985. — 2 v.. — *Includes index*. — *Contents: v. 1. The rising years--v. 2. The summit years*

FLEMING, IAN, 1908-1964 — Characters — James Bond
BENNETT, Tony
Bond and beyond : the political career of a popular hero / Tony Bennett and Janet Woollacott. — Basingstoke : Macmillan Education, 1987. — xi,315p. — (Communications and culture). — *Includes index*

FLEMINGS — Biography
VERSCHAEREN, J.
Julius Vuylsteke (1836-1903) : Klavwaard & Geus / J. Verschaeren. — Kortrijk : Van Ghemmert, 1984. — 486p. — *Bibliography: p12-21*

FLEMISH MOVEMENT
VERSCHAEREN, J.
Julius Vuylsteke (1836-1903) : Klavwaard & Geus / J. Verschaeren. — Kortrijk : Van Ghemmert, 1984. — 486p. — *Bibliography: p12-21*

FLETCHER, ERIC GEORGE MOLYNEUX, Baron
FLETCHER, Eric George Molyneux, Baron
Random reminiscences / of Lord Fletcher of Islington. — London : Bishopsgate Press, 1986. — xii,269p

FLEXIBLE MANUFACTURING SYSTEMS
Flexible manufacturing : integrating technological and social innovation / by P.T. Bolwijn ... [et al.]. — Amsterdam ; New York : Elsevier, 1986. — p. cm. — (Manufacturing research and technology ; 4). — *Includes bibliographies*

Flexible manufacturing systems : methods and studies / edited by Andrew Kusiak. — Amsterdam ; New York : North-Holland ; New York, N.Y., U.S.A. : Sole distributors for the U.S.A. and Canada, Elsevier Science Pub. Co., 1986. — ix, 408 p.. — (Studies in management science and systems ; v. 12). — *Includes bibliographies*

Information pack including bibliography on advanced manufacturing technology / compiled by Lucy Hamilton and John Devine ; foreword by Peter Willows. — London : Institution of Mechanical Engineers, 1986. — vi,98p. — (Information Pack ; 1). — *Annotated bibliography: p47-98*

Modelling and design of flexible manufacturing systems / edited by Andrew Kusiak. — Amsterdam : Elsevier, 1986. — ix,431p. — (Manufacturing research and technology ; 3)

FLOOD CONTROL
Disaster prevention and mitigation : a compendium of current knowledge. — New York : United Nations
V.2: Hydrological aspects. — 1976. — viii,100p. — *Bibliography: p98-100*. — "UNDRO/22/76"

FLOOD CONTROL — Government policy — Great Britain
PENNING-ROWSELL, Edmund C.
Floods and drainage : British policies for hazard reduction, agricultural improvement and wetland conservation / E.C. Penning-Rowsell, D.J. Parker, D.M. Harding. — London : Allen & Unwin, 1986. — xx,199p. — (The Risks & hazards series ; v.2). — *Bibliography: p178-192*. — *Includes index*

FLORENCE (ITALY) — Politics and government — 1421-1737
LITCHFIELD, R. Burr
Emergence of a bureaucracy : the Florentine patricians, 1530-1790 / R. Burr Litchfield. — Princeton, N.J. : Princeton University Press, 1986. — xiii, 407 p., [8] p. of plates. — *Includes index*. — *Bibliography: p. 383-396*

FLORENCE (ITALY) — Politics and government — 1737-1860
LITCHFIELD, R. Burr
Emergence of a bureaucracy : the Florentine patricians, 1530-1790 / R. Burr Litchfield. — Princeton, N.J. : Princeton University Press, 1986. — xiii, 407 p., [8] p. of plates. — *Includes index*. — *Bibliography: p. 383-396*

FLORENCE (ITALY) — Social conditions
CARMICHAEL, Ann G.
Plague and the poor in Renaissance Florence / Ann G. Carmichael. — Cambridge : Cambridge University Press, 1986. — xv,180p. — (Cambridge history of medicine). — *Bibliography: p166-175*. — *Includes index*

FLOUR
Nutritional aspects of bread and flour / report of the Panel on Bread, Flour and other Cereal Products, Committee on Medical Aspects of Food Policy. — London : H.M.S.O., 1981. — x,64p. — (Report on health and social subjects ; 23). — *At head of title: Department of Health and Social Security*. — *Bibliography: p55-64*

FLOUR AND FEED TRADE — Developing countries — Forecasting
SARMA, J. S
Cereal feed use in the Third World : past trends and projections to 2000 / J.S Sarma. — Washington, D.C. : International Food Policy Research Institute, c1987. — p. cm. — (Research report ; 57). — *Bibliography: p*

FLOW OF FUNDS — Australia
MARZOUK, G. A.
National income and flow of funds accounts : 1959-60 to 1983-84 / G. A. Marzouk. — Sydney : Australian Professional Publications, 1987. — vii,[66p]

FLOW OF FUNDS — Great Britain
HOLMANS, A. E.
Flows of funds associated with house purchase for owner-occupation in the United Kingdom 1977-1984 and equity withdrawal from house purchase finance / A. E. Holmans. — London : Departments of the Environment and Transport, 1986. — 128p. — (Government Economic Service working paper ; no.92)

FLOW OF FUNDS — Great Britain — Econometric models
ALFORD, R. F. G.
Flow of funds : a conceptual framework and some applications / R.F.G. Alford. — Aldershot : Published in association with the London School of Economics and Political Science by Gower, c1986. — viii,188p

FLOW OF FUNDS — Japan
Flow of funds in Japan in 1985. — Tokyo : Bank of Japan. Research and Statistics Department, 1987. — 30p. — (Special paper / Bank of Japan. Research and Statistics Department ; no.142)

FLOW OF FUNDS — Taiwan
Flow of funds in Taiwan district, the Republic of China / Economic Research Department, Central Bank of China. — Taiping : Economic Research Department, Central Bank of China, 1984-. — *Annual*

FM BROADCASTING — Government policy — Australia
AUSTRALIA. Department of Communications. Forward Development Unit
Future directions for commercial radio : interim report : AM/FM conversion. — Canberra : Australian Government Publishing Service, 1986. — xxix,274p

FODIO, USMAN DAN
SULAIMAN, Ibraheem
A revolution in history : the jihad of Usman Dan Fodio / Ibraheem Sulaiman ; with a foreword by Shehu Usman M. Bugaje. — London : Mansell, 1986. — [208]p. — (East-West University Islamic studies)

FOLK ART
BIEBUYCK, Daniel Prosper
Tradition and creativity in tribal art / edited and with an introduction by Daniel P. Biebuyck. — Berkeley ; London (2 Brook St., W1Y 1AA) : University of California Press, 1969. — xx,236p,64plates. — *bibl p215-224*

FOLK MEDICINE — Cross-cultural studies
Women's medicine : a cross-cultural study of indigenous fertility regulation / Lucile F. Newman, editor, with the assistance of James M. Nyce. — New Brunswick, N.J. : Rutgers University Press, c1985. — x, 203 p.. — (The Douglass series on women's lives and the meaning of gender). — *Includes bibliographies*

FOLK MEDICINE — Thailand
GOLOMB, Louis
An anthropology of curing in multiethnic Thailand / Louis Golomb. — Urbana : University of Illinois Press, c1985. — p. cm. — (Illinois studies in anthropology ; no. 15). — *Includes index*. — *Bibliography: p*

FOOD
SILVERSTEIN, Brett
Fed up : the food forces that make you fat, sick, and poor / by Brett Silverstein. — Boston, MA : South End Press, c1984. — 160 p.. — *Bibliography: p. 149-160*

FOOD — Drying
Solar drying : practical methods of food preservation. — Geneva : International Labour Office, 1986. — xii,127p. — *Bibliography: p123-127*

FOOD — Religious aspects
MEIGS, Anna S.
Food, sex, and pollution : a New Guinea religion / Anna S. Meigs. — New Brunswick, N.J. : Rutgers University Press, c1984. — xix, 196 p.. — : *Revision of thesis (Ph. D.)--University of Pennsylvania*. — *Includes index*. — *Bibliography: p. 181-187*

FOOD ADDITIVES
GREAT BRITAIN. Ministry of Agriculture, Fisheries and Food
Survey of consumer attitudes to food additives. — London : HMSO
Vol.1: Reports prepared for the Ministry of Agriculture, Fisheries and Food, Food Science Division / by Research Surveys of Great Britain Limited. — c1987. — 51p

GREAT BRITAIN. Ministry of Agriculture, Fisheries and Food
Survey of consumer attitudes to food additives. — London : HMSO
Vol.2: Reports prepared for the Ministry of Agriculture, Fisheries and Food, Food Science Division : computer tabulations of fieldwork questionnaires conducted by Research Surveys of Great Britain, 10 to 13 July 1986. — c1987. — various paging

FOOD ADULTERATION AND INSPECTION — Law and legislation — New York (State) — History — 19th century
OKUN, Mitchell
Fair play in the marketplace : the first battle for pure food and drugs / Mitchell Okun. — Dekalb, Ill. : Northern Illinois University Press, 1986. — xii, 345 p.. — *Includes index. — Bibliography: p. [307]-323*

FOOD ADULTERATION AND INSPECTION — Law and legislation — United States — History — 19th century
OKUN, Mitchell
Fair play in the marketplace : the first battle for pure food and drugs / Mitchell Okun. — Dekalb, Ill. : Northern Illinois University Press, 1986. — xii, 345 p.. — *Includes index. — Bibliography: p. [307]-323*

FOOD ADULTERATION AND INSPECTION — New York (State) — History — 19th century
OKUN, Mitchell
Fair play in the marketplace : the first battle for pure food and drugs / Mitchell Okun. — Dekalb, Ill. : Northern Illinois University Press, 1986. — xii, 345 p.. — *Includes index. — Bibliography: p. [307]-323*

FOOD ADULTERATION AND INSPECTION — United States — History — 19th century
OKUN, Mitchell
Fair play in the marketplace : the first battle for pure food and drugs / Mitchell Okun. — Dekalb, Ill. : Northern Illinois University Press, 1986. — xii, 345 p.. — *Includes index. — Bibliography: p. [307]-323*

FOOD AND AGRICULTURE ORGANIZATION
Food aid in figures / Food and Agriculture Organization of the United Nations. — Rome : Food and Agriculture Organization of the United Nations, 1983-. — *Annual*

Ideas and action / Food and Agriculture Organization of the United Nations. — Rome : Food and Agriculture Organization of the United Nations, 1985-. — *6 per year*

FOOD AND AGRICULTURE ORGANIZATION — Bibliography
FOOD AND AGRICULTURE ORGANIZATION
List of documents / Food and Agriculture Organization. — Food and Agriculture Organization

FOOD AND AGRICULTURE ORGANIZATION — Catalogs
DAVID LUBIN MEMORIAL LIBRARY
FAO documentation : animal production : 1979-1983 = Documentation de la FAO : production animale : 1979-1983 = Documentacion de la FAO : produccion animal : 1979-1983. — Rome : Food and Agriculture Organization, 1985. — 46,6,15,4p. — *In English with French and Spanish introductions*

DAVID LUBIN MEMORIAL LIBRARY
FAO documentation : plant production and protection : 1979-1983 = Documentation de la FAO : production et protection des végétaux : 1979-1983 = Documentacion de la FAO : produccion y proteccion de plantas : 1979-1983. — Rome : Food and Agriculture Organization, 1985. — 112,13,34,12p. — *In English with introductions also in French and Spanish*

FOOD AND AGRICULTURE ORGANIZATION. Fisheries Department — Catalogs
DAVID LUBIN MEMORIAL LIBRARY
FAO documentation : fisheries : 1979-1983 = Documentation de la FAO : pêches : 1979-1983 = Documentacion de la FAO : pesca : 1979-1983. — Rome : Food and Agriculture Organization, 1984. — 156p. — *In English with introductions also in French and Spanish*

FAO documentation : fisheries : 1983-1985 = Documentation de la FAO : fisheries : 1983-1985 = Documentacion de la FAO : pesca : 1983-1985. — Rome : Food and Agriculture Organization, 1986. — 117p. — *In English with introductions also in French and Spanish*

FOOD AND AGRICULTURE ORGANIZATION. Forestry Department — Catalogs
DAVID LUBIN MEMORIAL LIBRARY
FAO documentation : forestry : 1983-1985 = Documentation de la FAO : forêts : 1983-1985 = Documentacion de la FAO : montes : 1983-1985. — Rome : Food and Agriculture Organization, 1986. — 133p. — *In English with introductions also in French and Spanish*

FOOD AND AGRICULTURE ORGANIZATION. Human Resources, Institutions and Agrarian Reform Division — Catalogs
DAVID LUBIN MEMORIAL LIBRARY
FAO documentation : rural development : 1980-1984 = Documentation de la FAO : developpement rural : 1980-1984 = Documentacion de la FAO : desarrollo rural : 1980-1984. — Rome : Food and Agriculture Organization, 1985. — [47]p. — *In English with introductions in French and Spanish*

FOOD AND AGRICULTURE ORGANIZATION OF THE UNITED NATIONS. Forestry Department
Forest products prices = Prix des produits forestiers = Precios de productos forestales / Food and Agriculture Organization of the United Nations. Forestry Department. — Rome : Food and Agriculture Organization of the United Nations, 1960-. — (FAO forestry paper). — *Annual. — Text in English, French and Spanish*

FOOD CONSUMPTION
The Food consumer / edited by Christopher Ritson, Leslie Gofton and John McKenzie. — Chichester : Wiley, c1986. — xi,262p. — *Includes index*

FOOD CONSUMPTION — History
Food in change : eating habits from the Middle Ages to the present day / edited by Alexander Fenton and Eszter Kisbán. — Edinburgh : John Donald in association with the National Museums of Scotland, 1986. — viii,166p

FOOD CONSUMPTION — Statistical methods
Guidelines for the computation of selected statistical indicators. — Rome : FAO, 1986. — vii,71p. — (FAO economic and social development paper ; 60)

FOOD CONSUMPTION — Statistics
FOOD AND AGRICULTURE ORGANIZATION
Review of food consumption surveys = Recueil d'enquêtes sur la consommation alimentaire = Recopilacion de encuestas de consumo de alimentos. — Rome : F.A.O., [1958]

FOOD AND AGRICULTURE ORGANIZATION
Review of food consumption surveys 1985 : household food consumption by economic groups. — Rome : F.A.O., 1986. — xxiv,212p. — (FAO Food and Nutrition Paper ; no.35)

FOOD CONSUMPTION — Chile
Chile : demand and supply projections for agricultural products, 1965-1980. — Jerusalem : Publication Services Division of the Israel Program for Scientific Translations for the U.S. Department of Agriculture, 1969. — xxiii,130p. — *Includes bibliographical references*

FOOD CONSUMPTION — China
PIAZZA, Alan Lee
Food consumption and nutritional status in the P.R.C. / Alan Piazza. — Boulder : Westview Press, 1986. — p. cm. — (Westview special studies on China). — *Bibliography: p*

FOOD CONSUMPTION — France — Statistics
Consommation et lieux d'achat des produits alimentaires / Institut National de la Statistique et des Etudes Economiques. — Paris : INSEE, 1982-. — (Les collections de l'Insée. Série M). — *Annual*

FOOD CONSUMPTION — Kenya
GREER, Joel
Food poverty and consumption patterns in Kenya / Joel Greer and Erik Thorbecke. — Geneva : International Labour Office, 1986. — xii,170p

FOOD CONSUMPTION — Netherlands — Statistics
NETHERLANDS. Centraal Bureau voor de Statistiek
Werknemersbudgetonderzoek, 1974-75. — s-Gravenhage : Staatsuitgeverij. — *Contents list and summary in English. — Title on back cover: Workers' budget survey 1974-75. Part 4. Food bought; quantities and prices deel 4: Gekochte voedingsmiddelen; hoeveelheid en prijs. — 1979. — 43p*

FOOD CONSUMPTION — Sri Lanka
DEATON, Angus
Three essays on a Sri Lanka household survey / Angus Deaton. — Washington, D.C., U.S.A. : World Bank, 1985 printing, c1981. — [iv],87p. — (LSMS working papers ; no.11). — *Bibliographical references: p85-87*

FOOD CONSUMPTION — Taiwan
YEH, Sing-min
Per capita consumption level of basic food in Taiwan / by Sing-min Yeh. — Taipei : Chinese-American Joint Commission on Rural Reconstruction, 1957. — [vii],47p. — (Economic digest series / Joint Commission on Rural Reconstruction ; no.11)

FOOD CONTAMINATION
ERLICHMAN, James
Gluttons for punishment / James Erlichman. — Harmondsworth : Penguin Books, 1986. — 156p

FOOD CROPS
POATE, C. D.
Estimating crop production in development projects : methods and limitations / C. D. Poate and Dennis J. Casley. — Washington, D.C. : The World Bank, 1985. — iii,34p. — *"A technical supplement to 'Monitoring and evaluation of agriculture and rural development projects' by Dennis J. Casley and Dennis A. Lury". — Includes bibliographical references*

FOOD FROM BRITAIN
FOOD FROM BRITAIN
Annual report / Food from Britain. — London : Food from Britain, 1985/86-. — *Annual*

FOOD HABITS
CHERNIN, Kim
The hungry self : women, eating, and identity / Kim Chernin. — London : Virago, 1986, c1985. — xv,213p. — *Originally published: New York : Times Books, 1985*

FOOD HABITS *continuation*
WHEELOCK, Verner
The food revolution / J. Verner Wheelock. — Marlow, Bucks : Chalcombe Publications, c1986. — viii,119p

FOOD HABITS — England — Yorkshire
BREARS, Peter
Traditional food in Yorkshire / Peter Brears. — Edinburgh : John Donald, c1987. — vii,232p

FOOD HABITS — France — Statistics
MERCIER, Marie-Annick
Repas à l'extérieur et au domicile en 1980 et 1981 / par Marie-Annick Mercier. — Paris : I.N.S.E.E., 1985. — 193p. — (Les collections de l'INSEE. Série M. Ménages ; no.115). — *Bibliography: p193*

FOOD HABITS — Great Britain
COLE-HAMILTON, Isobel
Tightening belts : a report on the impact of poverty on food / Isobel Cole-Hamilton and Tim Long. — 2nd ed. — London : London Food Commission, 1986. — viii,132p. — *Bibliography: p98-110*

FOOD HABITS — Papua New Guinea
KAHN, Miriam
Always hungry, never greedy : food and the expression of gender in a Melanesian society / Miriam Kahn. — Cambridge : Cambridge University Press, 1986. — xx,187p. — *Bibliography: p174-181. — Includes index*

FOOD HABITS — Scotland — History
STEVEN, Maisie
The good Scots diet : what happened to it? / Maisie Steven. — Aberdeen : Aberdeen University Press, 1985. — [176]p. — *Bibliography: p173-176*

FOOD HANDLING
Health service catering / Hotel and Dietetic Services. — London : HMSO Hygiene. — c1986. — 45p

FOOD HISTORY — 19th century — England — Yorkshire
BREARS, Peter
Traditional food in Yorkshire / Peter Brears. — Edinburgh : John Donald, c1987. — vii,232p

FOOD INDUSTRY AND TRADE — European Economic Community countries
The production and use of cereal and potato starch in the EEC / prepared by Centre for European Agricultural Studies. — Luxembourg : Office for Official Publications of the European Communities, 1986. — 123p. — *At head of title: Commission of the European Communities*

FOOD INDUSTRY AND TRADE
BENNETT, Jon
The hunger machine : the politics of food / Jon Bennett ; introduction and conclusion by Susan George. — Cambridge : Polity in association with Channel Four Television and Yorkshire Television, 1987. — 232p. — *Bibliography: p221-222. — Includes index*

GREEN, Raúl
Bunge & Born : puissance et secret dans l'agro-alimentaire / Raúl Green, Catherine Laurent. — Paris : Publisud, [1985]. — 180p. — *Bibliography: p169-180*

Primary commodities : market developments and outlook / by the Commodities Division of the Research Department. — Washington, D.C. : International Monetary Fund, 1986. — vii,74p. — (World economic and financial surveys)

World food marketing systems / edited by Erdener Kaynak. — London : Butterworth, 1986. — [320]p. — *Includes bibliography and index*

YATES, Geoffrey, 19---
Food : need, greed, & myopia : exploitation and starvation in a world of plenty / Geoffrey Yates. — 2nd ed., fully rev. — Ryton : Earthright, 1986. — [104]p. — *Previous ed.: 1980. — Bibliography: p84-90. — Includes index*

FOOD INDUSTRY AND TRADE — Political aspects — Developing countries
Food, the state, and international political economy : developing country dilemmas / F. LaMond Tullis and W. Ladd Hollist, editors. — Lincoln : University of Nebraska Press, c1985. — p. cm. — *Bibliography: p*

FOOD INDUSTRY AND TRADE — Political aspects — Great Britain
CANNON, Geoffrey
The politics of food : the secret world of Whitehall and the food giants which threaten your health / Geoffrey Cannon. — London : Century, 1987. — [408]p. — *Includes index*

FOOD INDUSTRY AND TRADE — Asia
TYERS, Rodney
Economic growth and agricultural protection in east and southeast Asia / Rodney Tyers [and] Kym Anderson. — Kuala Lumpur ; Canberra : ASEAN-Australia Joint Research Project, 1985. — 49p. — (ASEAN-Australia economic papers ; no.21). — *Bibliography: p37-38*

FOOD INDUSTRY AND TRADE — England — London
BARTY-KING, Hugh
Making provision : a centenary history of the provision trade / Hugh Barty-King. — London : Quiller Press, 1986. — xiv,171p. — *Bibliography: p163-164*

FOOD INDUSTRY AND TRADE — France — Energy consumption — Statistics
Les consommations d'énergie dans les industries agricoles et alimentaires / Ministère de l'Agriculture, Service Central des Enquêtes et Études Statistiques. — Paris : Ministère de l'Agriculture. Service Central des Enquêtes et Études Statistiques, 1982-. — *Annual*

FOOD INDUSTRY AND TRADE — France — Statistics
BRESSON, Denis
Les industries agricoles et alimentaires en 1984 : séries statistiques 1977-1984 / Denis Bresson. — [Paris] : INSEE, 1985. — 113p. — (Archives et documents / Institut National de la Statistique et des Études Économiques ; no.130)

Enquête annvelle d'entreprise: industries agricoles et alimentaires: resultats sectoriels et régionaux / Ministère de l'Agriculture, Service Central des Enquêtes et Etudes Statistiques. — Paris : Ministère de l'Agriculture. Service Central des Enquêtes et Etudes Statistiques, 1982-. — *Annual*

FOOD INDUSTRY AND TRADE — Great Britain — Statistics
Food shops. — London : HMSO, 1970-79. — (Business monitor. SD ; 1) (Business monitor. SDM ; 1). — *Monthly. — Continued by: Retail sales*

FOOD INDUSTRY AND TRADE — Soviet Union
LITVIN, Valentin
The Soviet agro-industrial complex : structure and performance / Valentin Litvin. — Boulder, Colo. : Westview Press, 1987. — p. cm. — (Delphic monograph series). — *Includes index. — Bibliography: p*

FOOD INDUSTRY AND TRADE — United States
SILVERSTEIN, Brett
Fed up : the food forces that make you fat, sick, and poor / by Brett Silverstein. — Boston, MA : South End Press, c1984. — 160 p.. — *Bibliography: p. 149-160*

FOOD LAW AND LEGISLATION
LONDON FOOD COMMISSION
Consumer protection and food legislation : a London Food Commission submission to the Ministry of Agriculture, Fisheries and Food. — 2nd ed.. — London : London Food Commission, 1986

FOOD PRICES — Government policy — Dominican Republic
Dominican Republic : economic prospects and policies to renew growth. — Washington, D.C., U.S.A. : World Bank, 1985. — xviii,174p. — (A World Bank country study). — *Includes bibliographical references*

FOOD PRICES — Government policy — United States
TIMMER, C. Peter
Getting prices right : the scope and limits of agricultural price policy / C. Peter Timmer. — Ithaca : Cornell University Press, 1986. — 160 p.. — (Cornell paperbacks). — *Includes index. — Bibliography: p. 151-155*

FOOD PRICES — France — Statistics
JOUVENCEL, Tanneguy de
Prix de détail observation courante et validation sur moyenne période : l'exemple des produits alimentaires / Tanneguy de Jouvencel. — Paris : I.N.S.E.E., 1986. — ii,107p. — (Archives et documents / Institut national de la statistique et des études économiques ; no.157). — *Bibliography: p107*

LEBRUN, André
Les indices de prix à la production des industries agricoles et alimentaires / André Lebrun. — [Paris] : INSEE, 1985. — 217p. — (Archives et documents / Institut National de la Statistique et des Études Économiques ; no.129)

FOOD PRICES — Kenya
GREER, Joel
Food poverty and consumption patterns in Kenya / Joel Greer and Erik Thorbecke. — Geneva : International Labour Office, 1986. — xii,170p

FOOD RELIEF
Ending hunger : an idea whose time has come / the Hunger Project. — New York ; Eastbourne : Praeger, 1985. — 430p. — (Praeger special studies). — *Bibliography: p413-417. — Includes index*

GORDENKER, Leon
Refugees in international politics / Leon Gordenker. — London : Croom Helm, c1987. — 227p. — (The Croom Helm United Nations and its agencies series). — *Bibliography: p215-220. — Includes index*

SINGER, H. W.
Food aid : the challenge and the opportunity / Hans Singer, John Wood, Tony Jennings. — Oxford : Clarendon, 1987. — [256]p. — *Includes bibliography and index*

FOOD RELIEF — Government policy — Sri Lanka
EDIRISINGHE, Neville
The food stamp scheme in Sri Lanka : costs, benefits, and options for modification / Neville Edirisinghe. — Washington, D.C. : International Food Policy Research Institute, 1987. — 85p. — (Research report / International Food Policy Research Institute ; 58). — *Bibliography: p82-85*

FOOD RELIEF — Sri Lanka
EDIRISINGHE, Neville
The food stamp scheme in Sri Lanka : costs, benefits, and options for modification / Neville Edirisinghe. — Washington, D.C. : International Food Policy Research Institute, 1987. — 85p. — (Research report / International Food Policy Research Institute ; 58). — *Bibliography: p82-85*

FOOD RELIEF — United States — History
POPPENDIECK, Janet
Breadlines knee deep in wheat : food assistance in the Great Depression / Janet Poppendieck. — New Brunswick, N.J. : Rutgers University Press, c1986. — xvii, 306p. — *Includes index.* — *Bibliography: p.[257]-259*

FOOD RELIEF, AMERICAN
REVEL, Alain
[États-Unis et la stratégie alimentaire mondiale. English]. American green power / by Alain Revel and Christophe Riboud ; translated by Edward W. Tanner. — Baltimore : Johns Hopkins University Press, c1986. — p. cm. — *Translation of: Les États-Unis et la stratégie alimentaire mondiale.* — *Includes bibliographical references and index*

FOOD STAMP PROGRAM — Sri Lanka
EDIRISINGHE, Neville
The food stamp scheme in Sri Lanka : costs, benefits, and options for modification / Neville Edirisinghe. — Washington, D.C. : International Food Policy Research Institute, 1987. — 85p. — (Research report / International Food Policy Research Institute ; 58). — *Bibliography: p82-85*

FOOD SUPPLY — European Economic Community countries
The production and use of cereal and potato starch in the EEC / prepared by Centre for European Agricultural Studies. — Luxembourg : Office for Official Publications of the European Communities, 1986. — 123p. — *At head of title: Commission of the European Communities*

FOOD SUPPLY
BENNETT, Jon
The hunger machine : the politics of food / Jon Bennett ; introduction and conclusion by Susan George. — Cambridge : Polity in association with Channel Four Television and Yorkshire Television, 1987. — 232p. — *Bibliography: p221-222.* — *Includes index*

Food as a human right / edited by Asbjorn Eide ... [et al.]. — Tokyo : United Nations University, c1984. — xi,289p

KANBUR, S. M. Ravi
Global food balances and individual hunger : three themes in an entitlements based approach / S. M. Ravi Kanbur. — Coventry : University of Warwick. Department of Economics, 1987. -- 43p. — (Warwick economic research papers ; no.277). — *Bibliography: p36-38*

LAPPÉ, Frances Moore
World hunger : twelve myths / by Frances Moore Lappé and Joseph Collins. — New York : Grove Press, 1986. — [x],208p

LOWRY, J. H.
World population and food supply / J.H. Lowry. — 3rd ed. — London : Edward Arnold, 1986. — [128]p. — *Previous ed.: 1976*

REVEL, Alain
[États-Unis et la stratégie alimentaire mondiale. English]. American green power / by Alain Revel and Christophe Riboud ; translated by Edward W. Tanner. — Baltimore : Johns Hopkins University Press, c1986. — p. cm. — *Translation of: Les États-Unis et la stratégie alimentaire mondiale.* — *Includes bibliographical references and index*

TWOSE, Nigel
Cultivating hunger : an Oxfam study of food, power and poverty / Nigel Twose. — Oxford : Oxfam, 1984. — 48p. — *Bibliography: p46-47*

World food policies : toward agricultural interdependence / edited by William P. Browne and Don. F. Hadwiger. — Boulder, Colo. : L. Rienner, 1986. — x, 220p. — *Includes index.* — *Includes bibliographies*

FOOD SUPPLY — Congresses
INTERNATIONAL CONFERENCE OF AGRICULTURAL ECONOMISTS (19th : 1985 : Málaga)
Agriculture in a turbulent world economy : proceedings of the Nineteenth International Conference of Agricultural Economists held at Málaga, Spain 26 August-4 September 1985 / edited by Allen Maunder and Ulf Renborg [for] International Association of Agricultural Economists, Institute of Agricultural Economics, University of Oxford. — Aldershot : Gower, 1986. — xvi,820p. — *Includes bibliographies and index*

FOOD SUPPLY — Government policy — Mexico
Food policy in Mexico : the search for self-sufficiency / edited by James E. Austin and Gustavo Esteva. — Ithaca, N.Y. : Cornell University Press, 1987. — p. cm. — *Includes index*

FOOD SUPPLY — Political aspects
WARNOCK, John W.
The politics of hunger : the global food system / by John W. Warnock. — London : Methuen, 1987. — [328]p. — *Includes index*

FOOD SUPPLY — Statistics
Food aid in figures / Food and Agriculture Organization of the United Nations. — Rome : Food and Agriculture Organization of the United Nations, 1983-. — *Annual*

FOOD SUPPLY — Africa
Feeding African cities : studies in regional social history / edited by Jane I. Guyer. — Manchester : Manchester University Press for the International African Institute, London, c1987. — x,249p. — (International African library ; 2). — *Includes bibliographies and index*

FOOD SUPPLY — Africa, Southern
KOESTER, Ulrich
Regional cooperation to improve food security in the southern and eastern African countries / Ulrich Koester. — Washington, D.C. : International Food Policy Research Institute, c1986. — 89 p.. — (Research report / International Food Policy Research Institute ; 53). — *"July 1986.".* — *Bibliography: p. 85-89*

FOOD SUPPLY — Africa, Sub-Saharan
JAHNKE, Hans E.
The impact of agricultural research in tropical Africa : a study of the collaboration between the international and national research systems / Hans E. Jahnke, Dieter Kirschke and Johannes Lagemann ; in collaboration with K. J. Billing, J. Gromotka, S. N. Lyongo, B. Ndunguru, A. Negewo, G. M. Rillga, D. Sène, H. Shawel, G. Tacher. — Washington, D.C. : The World Bank, 1987. — xvi,175p. — (Study paper / Consultative Group on International Agricultural Research ; no.21). — *Bibliographical references: p159-175*

FOOD SUPPLY — Africa, sub-Saharan — addresses, essays, lectures
Food in sub-Saharan Africa / edited by Art Hansen and Della E. McMillan. — Boulder,Colo. : Lynne Rienner, 1986. — xvi,410p. — (Food in Africa series)

FOOD SUPPLY — Africa, Sub-Saharan — Congresses
Accelerating food production in Sub-Saharan Africa / edited by John W. Mellor, Christopher L. Delgado, Malcolm J. Blackie. — Baltimore : Published for the International Food Policy Research Institute [by] Johns Hopkins University Press, c1987. — xix, 417 p. . — *Papers and commentaries from a conference sponsored by the Dept. of Land Management of the University of Zimbabwe and the International Food Policy Research Institute, held at Victoria Falls, Zimbabwe in Aug. 1983.* *Includes index. Bibliography: p. 377-396*

FOOD SUPPLY — Africa,sub-Saharan
Nourrir les villes en Afrique sub-saharienne / [édité par] N. Bricas...[et al.]; contributions de ce. Arditi...[et al.]. — Paris : Editions L'Harmattan, 1985. — 421p

FOOD SUPPLY — Developing countries
Food policy : integrating supply, distribution, and consumption / edited by J. Price Gittinger, Joanne Leslie, Caroline Hoisington. — Baltimore : Johns Hopkins University Press for the World Bank, 1987. — xiv,567p. — (EDI series in economic development). — *Bibliography: p509-555*

Food, the state, and international political economy : developing country dilemmas / F. LaMond Tullis and W. Ladd Hollist, editors. — Lincoln : University of Nebraska Press, c1985. — p. cm. — *Bibliography: p*

Ideas and action / Food and Agriculture Organization of the United Nations. — Rome : Food and Agriculture Organization of the United Nations, 1985-. — *6 per year*

KENT, George
The political economy of hunger : the silent holocaust / George Kent. — New York ; Eastbourne : Praeger, 1984. — x,163p. — (Praeger special studies). — *Bibliography: p151-161*

PAULINO, Leonardo A.
Food in the Third World : past trends and projections to 2000 / Leonardo A. Paulino. — Washington, D.C. : International Food Policy Research Institute, 1986. — 76p. — (Research report / International Food Policy Research Institute ; 52). — *Bibliography: p76*

Population growth and economic development : issues and evidence / edited by D. Gale Johnson and Ronald D. Lee. — Madison, Wis. : University of Wisconsin Press, 1987. — xiii, 702 p.. — (Social demography). — *"Working Group on Population Growth and Economic Development; Committee on Population, Commission on Behavioral and Social Sciences and Education, National Research Council.".* — *Includes bibliographies and index*

Poverty and hunger : issues and options for food security in developing countries. — Washington, D.C., U.S.A. : World Bank, 1986. — p. cm. — (A World Bank policy study). — *Bibliography: p*

FOOD SUPPLY — Developing countries — Congresses
AGRICULTURE SECTOR SYMPOSIUM ((5th : 1985 : World Bank)
Proceedings of the Fifth Agriculture Sector Symposium : population and food / Ted J. Davis, editor. — Washington, D.C., U.S.A. : World Bank, c1985. — viii,230p. — *Includes bibliographies*

FOOD SUPPLY — England — London
BARTY-KING, Hugh
Making provision : a centenary history of the provision trade / Hugh Barty-King. — London : Quiller Press, 1986. — xiv,171p. — *Bibliography: p163-164*

FOOD SUPPLY — Europe, Eastern
DEUTSCH, Robert
The food revolution in the Soviet Union and Eastern Europe / Robert Deutsch. — Boulder, Colo. ; London : Westview Press, 1986. — xxi, 256p. — (Westview special studies on the Soviet Union and Eastern Europe). — *Includes index.* — *Bibliography: p.149-241*

FOOD SUPPLY — Germany
STÜBER, Gabriele
Der Kampf gegen den Hunger 1945-1950 : der Ernährungslage in der britischken Zone Deutschlands, insbesondere in Schleswig-Holstein und Hamburg / Gabriele Stüber. — Neumunster : Wachholtz, 1984. — 935p. — (Studien zur Wirtschafts- und Sozialgeschichte Schleswig-Holsteins ; Bd.6). — *Bibliography: p824-913*

FOOD SUPPLY — Germany — Schleswig-Holstein

STÜBER, Gabriele
Der Kampf gegen den Hunger 1945-1950 : der Ernährungslage in der britishchen Zone Deutschlands, insbesondere in Schleswig-Holstein und Hamburg / Gabriele Stüber. — Neumunster : Wachholtz, 1984. — 935p. — (Studien zur Wirtschafts- und Sozialgeschichte Schleswig-Holsteins ; Bd.6). — *Bibliography: p824-913*

FOOD SUPPLY — Great Britain

FOOD FROM BRITAIN
Annual report / Food from Britain. — London : Food from Britain, 1985/86-. — *Annual*

FOOD SUPPLY — Soviet Union

DEUTSCH, Robert
The food revolution in the Soviet Union and Eastern Europe / Robert Deutsch. — Boulder, Colo. ; London : Westview Press, 1986. — xxi, 256p. — (Westview special studies on the Soviet Union and Eastern Europe). — *Includes index. — Bibliography: p.149-241*

FOOD SUPPLY — Tanzania

KOESTER, Ulrich
Regional cooperation to improve food security in the southern and eastern African countries / Ulrich Koester. — Washington, D.C. : International Food Policy Research Institute, c1986. — 89 p.. — (Research report / International Food Policy Research Institute ; 53). — *"July 1986.". — Bibliography: p. 85-89*

FOOD, WILD — Canada

PRESCOTT-ALLEN, Christine
The first resource : wild species in the North American economy / Christine Prescott-Allen and Robert Prescott-Allen. — New Haven : Yale University Press, c1986. — xv, 529 p.. — *"Published with support from the World Wildlife Fund and Philip Morris Incorporated.". — Includes index. — Bibliography: p. 463-507*

FOOD, WILD — United States

PRESCOTT-ALLEN, Christine
The first resource : wild species in the North American economy / Christine Prescott-Allen and Robert Prescott-Allen. — New Haven : Yale University Press, c1986. — xv, 529 p.. — *"Published with support from the World Wildlife Fund and Philip Morris Incorporated.". — Includes index. — Bibliography: p. 463-507*

FOOLS AND JESTERS — United States

BOSKIN, Joseph
Sambo : the rise & demise of an American jester / Joseph Boskin. — New York : Oxford University Press, 1986. — ix, 252 p. [8] p. of plates. — *Includes index. — Bibliography: p. 225-243*

FOOTWARE INDUSTRY — Employees

Social and labour practices of multinational enterprises in the textiles, clothing, and footwear industries. — Geneva : International Labour Office, 1984. — xii,184p. — *Includes bibliographies*

FOOTWEAR INDUSTRY — Great Britain — Statistics

Clothing and footwear shops. — London : HMSO, 1970-79. — (Business monitor. SD ; 2) (Business monitor. SDM ; 2). — *Monthly. Continued by: Retail sales*

FORCED LABOR — Bolivia — Potosí (Dept.) — History

COLE, Jeffrey A
The Potosí mita, 1573-1700 : compulsory Indian labor in the Andes / Jeffrey A. Cole. — Stanford, Calif. : Stanford University Press, 1985. — xi, 206p. — *Includes index. — Bibliography: p.187-196*

FORCED LABOR — Brazil — Pernambuco — History — 19th century

HUGGINS, Martha Knisely
From slavery to vagrancy in Brazil : crime and social control in the Third World / Martha Knisely Huggins. — New Brunswick, N.J. : Rutgers University Press, c1984. — xix, 183p. — (Crime, law, and deviance series). — *Includes index. — Bibliography: p 159-167*

FORCED LABOR — Soviet Union

Forced labor in the Soviet Union. — [Washington, D.C.] : United States Information Service, [1952?]. — vi,63p

FORCES LABOR — Dominican Republic

PLANT, Roger
Sugar and modern slavery : a tale of two countries / Roger Plant. — London : Zed, 1987. — [208]p. — *Includes bibliography and index*

FORD (Family) — History

LACEY, Robert
Ford : the men and the machine / Robert Lacey. — London : Heinemann, 1986

FORD MOTOR COMPANY — History

LACEY, Robert
Ford : the men and the machine / Robert Lacey. — London : Heinemann, 1986

FORD MOTOR COMPANY — Management

KUHN, Arthur J
Organizational cybernetics and business policy : System design for performance control / Arthur J. Kuhn. — University Park : Pennsylvania State University Press, 1986. — p. cm. — *Includes index. — Bibliography: p*

FORD MOTOR COMPANY — Management — History — 20th century

KUHN, Arthur J
GM passes Ford, 1918-1938 : designing the General Motors performance-control system / Arthur J. Kuhn. — University Park : Pennsylvania State University Press, 1986. — p. cm. — *Includes indexes. — Bibliography: p*

FORECASTING

ROYAL SOCIETY. Symposium (1986 : [London?])
Predictability in science and society : a joint symposium of the Royal Society and the British Academy held on 20 and 21 March 1986 / organized and edited by John Mason, P. Mathias, and J. H. Westcott. — London : Royal Society : British Academy, 1986. — viii,145p. — *Includes bibliographies*

FOREGIN TRADE REGULATION

LOWENFELD, Andreas F.
International economic law. — New York : Matthew Bender
Vol.1: International private trade / Andreas F. Lowenfeld. — 2nd ed. — 1981. — xi,183,177,7,8p. — *Includes Documents Supplement*

FOREIGN EXCHANGE

ATTANASIO, O.
Non-constant variances and foreign exchange risk : an empirical study / O. Attanasio and M. Edey. — London : Centre for Labour Economics, London School of Economics, 1987. — 23p. — (Discussion paper / London School of Economics and Political Science. Centre for Labour Economics ; no.285). — *Bibliography: p22-23*

BANK OF JAPAN. Research and Statistics Department
On effective U.S. dollar exchange rate indices. — Tokyo : Bank of Japan. Research and Statistics Department, 1986. — 19p

BROOKS, Simon
The exchange rate environment / Simon Brooks, Keith Cuthbertson and David G. Mayes. — London : Crown Helm, c1986. — [320]p. — *Includes bibliography and index*

CURRIE, David A.
A stock/flow model of the determination of the UK effective exchange rate / David Currie and Stephen Hall. — London : National Institute of Economic and Social Research, 1986. — 15p. — (Discussion paper / National Institute of Economic and Social Research ; no.124)

DOMÁNY, Gyula
Nemzetközi pénzügyi kapcsolatok / irta Domámy Gyula. — Budapest : Grill-féle udvari könyvkereskedés kiadása, 1936. — 36p. — *Bibliography: p[35]-36*

DORNBUSCH, Rudiger
Inflation, exchange rates, and stabilization / Rudiger Dornbusch. — Princeton, N.J. : International Finance Section, Dept. of Economics, Princeton University, 1986. — p. cm. — (Essays in international finance ; no. 165 (Oct. 1986)). — *Bibliography: p*

FELDMAN, Robert Alan
Japanese financial markets : deficits, dilemmas, and deregulation / Robert Alan Feldman. — Cambridge, Mass. : MIT Press, c1986. — p. cm. — *Includes index. — Bibliography: p*

GENBERG, Hans
External influences on the Swiss economy under fixed and flexible exchange rates / Hans Genberg and Alexander K. Swoboda. — Grüsch : Rüegger, c1985. — ii, 182 p.. — (Schweizerisches Institut für Aussenwirtschafts-, Struktur- und Regionalforschung an der Hochschule St. Gallen ; Bd. 10). — *Bibliography: p. 178-182*

GREAT BRITAIN. Parliament. House of Commons. Library. Research Division
The exchange rate / Christopher Barclay. — [London] : the Division, 1981. — 25p. — (Background paper ; no.93). — *Bibliography: p24-25*

HEYWOOD, John, 1940-
Foreign exchange and the corporate treasurer / John Heywood. — 4th ed. — London : Black, 1984. — viii,193p. — *Previous ed.: 1978. — Bibliography: p189. — Includes index*

INTERNATIONAL MONETARY FUND. Board of Governors. Committee on Reform of the International Monetary System and Related Issues
International monetary reform : documents of the Committee of Twenty. — Washington, D.C. : the Fund, 1974. — viii,253p. — *Includes the Report to the Board of Governors, Outline of Reform and accompanying Annexes, Reports of Technical groups, and related documents*

International trade and exchange rates in the late eighties / edited by Theo Peeters, Peter Praet and Paul Reding. — Amsterdam : North-Holland ; Bruxelles : Université de Bruxelles, 1985. — xii,418p

KINDLEBERGER, Charles P.
International capital movements : based on the Marshall Lectures given at the University of Cambridge 1985 / Charles P. Kindleberger. — Cambridge : Cambridge University Press, 1987. — 1v. *Includes bibliography and index*

MAYER, Helmut
Official intervention in the exchange markets : stabilising or destabilising / by Helmut Mayer and Hiroo Taguchi. — Basle : Bank for International Settlements, 1983. — 40p. — (BIS economic papers ; no.6)

MAYER, Helmut
The theory and practice of floating exchange rates and the rôle of official exchange—market intervention / by Helmut Mayer. — Basle : Bank for International Settlements, 1982. — 47p. — (BIS economic papers ; no. 5)

Real business cycles, real exchange rates and actual policies / editors, Karl Brunner [and] Allan H. Meltzer. — Amsterdam : North-Holland, 1986. — 304p. — (Carnegie-Rochester Conference Series on Public Policy ; vol.25)

FOREIGN EXCHANGE *continuation*

SACHS, Jeffrey
Wage indexation, flexible exchange rates, and macro-economic policy / by Jeffrey Sachs. — [Washington, D.C. : Board of Governors of the Federal Reserve System], 1979. — 36p. — (International finance discussion papers ; no.137). — *Bibliographical references: p34-36*

Staff studies for the World Economic Outlook / by the Research Department of the International Monetary Fund. — Washington, D. C. : International Monetary Fund, 1986. — xi,195p. — (World economic and financial surveys). — *Includes bibliographical references.* — Contents: Differences in employment behaviour among industrial countries/Charles Adams, Paul R. Fenton and Flemming Larsen - Labor markets, external developments, and unemployment in developing countries/Omotunde E.G. Johnson - Velocity of money and the practice of monetary targeting/Peter Isard and Liliana Rojas-Suarez - Effects of exchange rate changes in industrial countries/James M. Boughton, et al. - Transmission of economic influences from industrial to developing countries/David Goldsbrough and Iqbal Zaidi

FOREIGN EXCHANGE — Accounting

GRAZIANO, Loretta
Currency fluctuations and the perception of corporate performance : a communications approach to financial accounting and reporting / Loretta Graziano. — New York : Quorum Books, c1986. — viii, 183 p.. — *Includes index.* — *Bibliography: p. [175]-179*

FOREIGN EXCHANGE — Law and legislation — Taiwan

YIN, K. Y.
A review of existing foreign exchange and trade control policy and technique / K. Y. Yin. — [Taipei : Foreign Exchange and Trade Control, 1959. — 34p

FOREIGN EXCHANGE — Mathematical models

GOLUB, Stephen S
The current-account balance and the dollar, 1977-78 and 1983-84 / Stephen S. Golub. — Princeton, N.J. : Dept. of Economics, Princeton University, 1986. — p. cm. — (Princeton studies in international finance ; no. 57). — *Bibliography: p*

FOREIGN EXCHANGE — Great Britain

BEAN, Charles R.
Sterling misalignment and British trade performance / C. Bean. — London : Centre for Labour Economics, London School of Economics, 1987. — 49p. — (Discussion paper / London School of Economics and Political Science. Centre for Labour Economics ; no.288). — *Bibliography: p46-49*

TAYLOR, M. P.
Expectations, risk and uncertainty in the foreign exchange market : some results based on survey data / M. P. Taylor. — London : Bank of England, 1987. — 19p. — (Bank of England discussion papers ; no.29). — *Bibliography: p18-19*

FOREIGN EXCHANGE — Great Britain — Government policy

Exchange rate policy for sterling : the Croham Report. — London : Public Policy Centre, 1986. — xv, 81p

FOREIGN EXCHANGE ADMINISTRATION — Addresses, essays, lectures

Alternative monetary regimes / edited by Colin D. Campbell and William R. Dougan. — Baltimore : Johns Hopkins University Press, c1986. — xi, 251 p.. — *Includes bibliographies and index*

FOREIGN EXCHANGE ADMINISTRATION — Developing countries — Congresses

Economic adjustment and exchange rates in developing countries / edited by Sebastian Edwards and Liaquat Ahamed. — Chicago : University of Chicago Press, c1986. — p. cm. — (A National Bureau of Economic Research conference report). — *"Papers ... presented at a joint National Bureau of Economic Research-World Bank conference held in Washington, D.C., 29 November through 1 December, 1984."--.* — *Includes index.* — *Bibliography: p*

FOREIGN EXCHANGE ADMINISTRATION — Latin America

Economic reform and stabilization in Latin America / edited by Michael Connolly, Claudio González-Vega. — New York : Praeger, [1987]. — xxiii, 348 p.. — *"Second Dominican Republic Conference on Trade and Financial Liberalization in Latin America held in Santo Domingo, March 22-24, 1985"--P. iii.* — *Includes bibliographies*

FOREIGN EXCHANGE ADMINISTRATION — Nigeria

OYEJIDE, T. Ademola
The effects of trade and exchange rate policies on agriculture in Nigeria / T. Ademola Oyejide. — Washington, D.C. : International Food Policy Research Institute, 1986. — p. cm. — (Research report ; 55). — *Bibliography: p*

FOREIGN EXCHANGE PROBLEM

CROCKETT, Andrew
Strengthening the international monetary system : exchange rates, surveillance, and objective indicators / by Andrew Crockett and Morris Goldstein. — Washington, D. C. : International Monetary Fund, 1987. — vii,84p. — (Occasional paper / International Monetary Fund ; no.50). — *Bibliographical references: p83-84*

MAYER, Helmut
The theory and practice of floating exchange rates and the rôle of official exchange—market intervention / by Helmut Mayer. — Basle : Bank for International Settlements, 1982. — 47p. — (BIS economic papers ; no. 5)

Monetary and exchange rate policy / edited by Donald R. Hodgman and Geoffrey E. Wood. — London : Macmillan in association with Centre for Banking and International Finance, the City University Business School, 1987. — xv,223p. — (Studies in banking and international finance). — *Includes bibliographies and index*

SIEGEL, Michael H
Foreign exchange risk and direct foreign investment / by Michael H. Siegel. — Ann Arbor, Mich. : UMI Research Press, c1983. — vi, 97 p. — (Research for business decisions ; no. 60). — *Includes index.* — *Bibliography: p. [89]-92*

FOREIGN EXCHANGE PROBLEM — Addresses, essays, lectures

International financial management : theory and application / edited by Donald R. Lessard. — 2nd ed. — New York : Wiley, c1985. — xi, 594 p.. — *Includes bibliographies and indexes*

FOREIGN EXCHANGE PROBLEM — Australia

AUSTRALIA. Bureau of Industry Economics
The depreciation of the Australian dollar : its impact on importers and manufacturers. — Canberra : Australian Government Publishing Service, 1986. — xviii,167p. — *Bibliographical references: p165-167*

FOREIGN EXCHANGE PROBLEM — Developing countries

Floating exchange rates in developing countries : experience with auction and interbank markets / by Peter J. Quirk ... [et al.]. — Washington, D.C. : International Monetary Fund, 1987. — v,43p. — (Occasional paper ; no. 53). — *"May 1987.".* — *Includes bibliographical references*

FOREIGN EXCHANGE PROBLEM — Japan — Congresses

Japan and the United States today : exchange rates, macroeconomic policies, and financial market innovations / Hugh T. Patrick, Ryuichiro Tachi, editors. — New York : Center on Japanese Economy and Business, Columbia University, 1986, c1987. — vii, 234 p.. — *Papers presented at a conference held in New York, June 4-5, 1986, sponsored by the Center on Japanese Economy and Business at the Graduate School of Business, Columbia University, and the Institute of Fiscal and Monetary Policy of the Japanese Ministry of Finance, together with the Foundation for Advanced Information and Research, Japan.* — *Includes bibliographies*

FOREIGN EXCHANGE PROBLEM — Norway

BREKK, Odd Per
Norwegian foreign exchange policy / Odd Per Brekk. — Oslo : Norges Bank, 1987. — 48p. — (Norges Banks skriftserie ; no.16)

FOREIGN EXCHANGE PROBLEM — Sweden

FRANZÉN, Thomas
[Översyn av valutaregleringen. English]. The foreword exchange market / Thomas Franzén ; translated from the Swedish by Martin Naylor. — Stockholm : Sveriges Riksbank, 1987. — 53p. — (Occasional paper / Sveriges Riksbank ; 4). — *This Occasional paper is a direct translation of chapter 17 of the report of the Swedish Foreign Exchange Regulation Committee, Översyn av valutaregleringen*

FOREIGN EXCHANGE PROBLEM — United States

DORNBUSCH, Rudiger
Dollars, debts, and deficits / Rudiger Dornbusch. — 1st MIT Press ed. — Leuven, Belgium : Leuven University Press ; Cambridge, Mass. : MIT Press, 1986. — 240 p. . — *The Professor Dr. Gaston Eyskens lectures delivered at the Katholieke Universiteit Leuven, Belgium in the fall of 1984.* — *Includes bibliographies and index*

MAKIN, John H
U.S. fiscal policy : its effects at home and abroad / John H. Makin. — Washington, D.C. : American Enterprise Institute for Public Policy Research, [1986]. — p. cm. — (AEI studies ; 447)

SOLOMON, Anthony M
The dollar, debt, and the trade deficit / Anthony M. Solomon. — New York : New York University Press, 1986, c1987. — p. cm. — (The Joseph I. Lubin memorial lectures ; no. 3)

WACHTEL, Howard M
The money mandarins : the making of a new supranational economic order / Howard M. Wachtel. — 1st ed. — New York : Pantheon Books, c1986. — xvi, 254 p.. — *Includes index.* — *Bibliography: p. [227]-245*

FOREIGN EXCHANGE PROBLEM — United States — Congresses

Japan and the United States today : exchange rates, macroeconomic policies, and financial market innovations / Hugh T. Patrick, Ryuichiro Tachi, editors. — New York : Center on Japanese Economy and Business, Columbia University, 1986, c1987. — vii, 234 p.. — *Papers presented at a conference held in New York, June 4-5, 1986, sponsored by the Center on Japanese Economy and Business at the Graduate School of Business, Columbia University, and the Institute of Fiscal and Monetary Policy of the Japanese Ministry of Finance, together with the Foundation for Advanced Information and Research, Japan.* — *Includes bibliographies*

FOREIGN EXCHANGE PROBLEMS — Switzerland

GENBERG, Hans
External influences on the Swiss economy under fixed and flexible exchange rates / Hans Genberg and Alexander K. Swoboda. — Grüsch : Rüegger, c1985. — ii, 182 p.. — (Schweizerisches Institut für Aussenwirtschafts-, Struktur- und Regionalforschung an der Hochschule St. Gallen ; Bd. 10). — *Bibliography: p. 178-182*

FOREIGN LICENSING AGREEMENTS

Guidelines for the acquisition of foreign technology in developing countries : with special reference to technology licence agreements. — New York : United Nations, 1973. — xi,55p. — ([Documents] / United Nations ; ID/98). — *"Prepared by Rana K.D.N. Singh...in co-operation with the secretariat of UNIDO". — Sales no.: E.73.II.B.1*

FOREIGN NEWS — Congresses

The Selling of Fidel Castro : the media and the Cuban Revolution / edited by William E. Ratliff. — New Brunswick, N.J., U.S.A. : Transaction Books, c1986. — p. cm. — *Presented as part of a conference held on November 16-17, 1984, in Washington, D.C. — "Prepared in cooperation with the Cuban American National Foundation ... Washington, D.C."--Verso t.p*

FOREIGN NEWS — United States

Outstanding international press reporting : Pulitzer Prize winning articles in foreign correspondence / editor Heinz-Dietrich Fischer. — Berlin ; New York : Walter de Gruyter
Vol.1: 1928-1945, from the consequences of World War I to the end of World War II. — 1984. — liii,368p

Outstanding international press reporting : Pulitzer Prize winning articles in foreign correspondence / editor Heinz-Dietrich Fischer. — Berlin ; New York : Walter de Gruyter
Vol.2: 1946-1962, from the end of World War II to the various stations of the Cold War. — 1985. — lxvii,304p

Outstanding international press reporting : Pulitzer Prize winning articles in foreign correspondence / editor Heinz-Dietrich Fischer. — Berlin ; New York : Walter de Gruyter
Vol.3: 1963-1977, from the escalation of the Vietnam war to the East Asian refugee problems. — 1986. — lxxii,309p

FOREIGN STUDY — Bibliography

ALTBACH, Philip G
Bibliography of foreign students and international study / by Philip G. Altbach, David H. Kelly, and Y. G-M. Lulat. — New York : Praeger, 1985. — p. cm. — (The Praeger special studies series in comparative education). — *"Published in cooperation with the Comparative Education Center, State University of New York, Buffalo."*

FOREIGN TRADE AND EMPLOYMENT

MUKHERJEE, Santosh
Restructuring of industrial economies and trade with developing countries / Santosh Mukherhee, assisted by Charlotte Feller. — Geneva : International Labour Office, 1978. — x,110p. — *Bibliography: p83-84*

FOREIGN TRADE AND EMPLOYMENT — Japan

DORE, R. P.
Structural adjustment in Japan, 1970-82 / R. P. Dore ; with contributions by K. Taira. — Geneva : International Labour Office, 1986. — xii,189p. — (Employment, adjustment and industrialisation ; 1). — *Bibliography: p [183]-189*

FOREIGN TRADE AND EMPLOYMENT — United States

GRAY, H. Peter
International trade, employment and structural adjustment : the United States / H. Peter Gray, Thomas Pugel and Ingo Walter. — Geneva : International Labour Office, 1986. — x,108p. — (Employment, adjustment and industrialisation ; 3). — *Includes bibliographical references*

FOREIGN TRADE PROMOTION — Morocco

Morocco : industrial incentives and export promotion. — Washington, D.C., U.S.A. : World Bank, c1984. — Lxxvii,219p. — (A World Bank country study). — *Report prepared by an economic mission that visited Morocco in Sept. 1982 composed of Bela Balassa and others. — Summaries in French and Spanish. — Includes bibliographical references*

FOREIGN TRADE REGULATION

BOLLECKER-STERN, Brigitte
Droit économique / Brigitte Bollecker-Stern, Maurice Dahan, Lazare Kopelmanas. — Paris : Pedone, 1978. — 166p. — (Cours et travaux / Institut des hautes études internationales de Paris)

EDINBURGH INSTITUTE ON INTERNATIONAL BUSINESS TRANSACTIONS (1984)
Legal aspects of international business transactions, II : the Edinburgh Institute on International Business Transactions, 1984 / edited by D. Campbell and C. Rohwer. — Amsterdam ; New York : North Holland ; New York : Elsevier Science Pub. Co., distributor, 1985. — p. cm. — *"A project of University of the Pacific, McGeorge School of Law, International Programs."*

LOWENFELD, Andreas F.
International economic law. — New York : Matthew Bender
Vol.6: Public controls on international trade / Andreas F. Lowenfeld. — 2nd ed. — 1983. — xvii,457,775,4,22p. — *Includes Documents Supplement*

FOREIGN TRADE REGULATION — Bibliography

KUDEJ, Blanka
International trade law : international law bibliography / prepared by Blanka Kudej. — New York : Oceana Publications, 1984. — p. cm. — (A Collection of bibliographic and research resources)

FOREIGN TRADE REGULATION — Congresses

CONGRESS ON PRIVATE LAW (2d : 1976 : Rome)
New directions in international trade law : acts and proceedings of the 2nd Congress on Private Law held by the International Institute for the Unification of Private Law, UNIDROIT, Rome, 9-15 September, 1976. — Dobbs Ferry, N.Y. : Oceana Publications, 1977. — 2 v. (xliii, 793 p.). — *English or French. — Contents: v. 1. Reports.--v. 2. Written communications and oral interventions*

FOREIGN TRADE REGULATION — Political aspects

LOWENFELD, Andreas F.
International economic law. — New York : Matthew Bender
Vol.3: Trade controls for political ends / Andreas F. Lowenfeld. — 2nd ed. — 1983. — x,621,910,5,21p. — *Includes Documents Supplement*

FOREIGN TRADE REGULATION — Taxation

TILLINGHAST, David R.
International economic law. — New York : Matthew Bender
Vol.5: Tax aspects of international transactions / David R. Tillinghast. — 2nd ed. — 1984. — xv,473,177,12,10p. — *Bibliography*

FOREIGN TRADE REGULATION — European Economic Community countries

BESELER, H. F.
Anti-dumping and anti-subsidy law : the European Communities / by J. [i.e. H.] F. Beseler and A.N. Williams. — London : Sweet & Maxwell, 1986. — xx,438p. — *Includes index*

VANDAMME, J
La politique de la concurrence dans la C.E.E. / J.A. Van Damme. — Kortrijk, Belgique : UGA, [1980]. — 658 p., [1] leaf of plates. — (Cours / Centre international d'études et de recherches européennes ; 1977). — *At head of title: Institut universitaire international, Luxembourg. — Bibliography: p. 589-658*

FOREIGN TRADE REGULATION — Great Britain

GREENAWAY, David
Boosting employment by import controls? / D. Greenaway [and] G. K. Shaw. — Buckingham : University of Buckingham. Employment Research Centre, 1986. — 30p. — (Occasional papers in employment studies / University of Buckingham. Employment Research Centre ; no.5). — *Bibliography: p27-29*

FOREIGN TRADE REGULATION — Great Britain — History

DOWNS, André
General import restrictions and the behaviour of domestic prices and wages : the case of the British General Tariff of 1932 / by André Downs. — 245 leaves. — *PhD (Econ) 1986 LSE. — Leaves 210-245 are appendices*

FOREIGN TRADE REGULATION — Japan — Congresses

Law and trade issues of the Japanese economy : American and Japanese perspectives / edited by Gary R. Saxonhouse and Kozo Yamamura. — Seattle : University of Washington Press ; [Tokyo] : University of Tokyo Press, c1986. — xx, 290 p.. — *Based on a workshop held in Sept. 1983, sponsored by the Committee on Japanese Economic Studies. — Includes bibliographies and index*

FOREIGN TRADE REGULATION — United States — Congresses

Law and trade issues of the Japanese economy : American and Japanese perspectives / edited by Gary R. Saxonhouse and Kozo Yamamura. — Seattle : University of Washington Press ; [Tokyo] : University of Tokyo Press, c1986. — xx, 290 p.. — *Based on a workshop held in Sept. 1983, sponsored by the Committee on Japanese Economic Studies. — Includes bibliographies and index*

FOREIGN TRADE REGULATIONS — European Economic Community countries

The European Community and GATT / edited by Meinhard Hilf, Francis G. Jacobs, and Ernst-Ulrich Petersmann. — Deventer, the Netherlands ; Boston : Kluwer, c1986. — xvii, 398 p.. — (Studies in transnational economic law ; v. 4). — *Includes bibliographical references and index*

FORENSIC PSYCHIATRY — North America

Dangerousness : probability and prediction, psychiatry and public policy / edited by Christopher D. Webster, Mark H. Ben-Aron, Stephen J. Hucker. — Cambridge : Cambridge University Press, 1985. — xiii,236p. — *Includes bibliographies and index*

FOREST AND FORESTRY — Scotland

SHERWWOD, Marika
The British Honduran forestry unit in Scotland 1941-43 / Marika Sherwwod. — London : One Caribbean, 1982. — 51p. — *Bibliography: p.51*

FOREST CONSERVATION — Canada
GILLIS, R. Peter
Lost initiatives : Canada's forest industries, forest policy, and forest conservation / R. Peter Gillis and Thomas R. Roach. — New York : Greenwood Press, 1986. — 326 p., [1] p. of plates. — (Contributions in economics and economic history ; no. 69). — *Includes index.* — *Bibliography: p. [301]-314*

FOREST MANAGEMENT — United States
Forestlands : public and private / edited by Robert T. Deacon, M. Bruce Johnson ; foreword by B. Delworth Gardner. — San Francisco, Calif. : Pacific Institute for Public Policy Research ; Cambridge, Mass. : Ballinger Pub. Co., c1985. — xxvii, 332 p.. — (Pacific studies in public policy). — *Includes index.* — *Bibliography: p. 303-312*

FOREST POLICY — Canada
GILLIS, R. Peter
Lost initiatives : Canada's forest industries, forest policy, and forest conservation / R. Peter Gillis and Thomas R. Roach. — New York : Greenwood Press, 1986. — 326 p., [1] p. of plates. — (Contributions in economics and economic history ; no. 69). — *Includes index.* — *Bibliography: p. [301]-314*

FOREST POLICY — United States
Forestlands : public and private / edited by Robert T. Deacon, M. Bruce Johnson ; foreword by B. Delworth Gardner. — San Francisco, Calif. : Pacific Institute for Public Policy Research ; Cambridge, Mass. : Ballinger Pub. Co., c1985. — xxvii, 332 p.. — (Pacific studies in public policy). — *Includes index.* — *Bibliography: p. 303-312*

FOREST POLICY — United States — History
ROBBINS, William G.
American forestry : a history of national, state, and private cooperation / by William G. Robbins. — Lincoln : University of Nebraska Press, c1985. — xv, 344 p.. — *Includes index.* — *Bibliography: p. 271-326*

FOREST PRODUCTS — Prices
Forest products prices = Prix des produits forestiers = Precios de productos forestales / Food and Agriculture Organization of the United Nations. Forestry Department. — Rome : Food and Agriculture Organization of the United Nations, 1960-. — (FAO forestry paper). — *Annual.* — *Text in English, French and Spanish*

FOREST PRODUCTS INDUSTRY — Canada
GILLIS, R. Peter
Lost initiatives : Canada's forest industries, forest policy, and forest conservation / R. Peter Gillis and Thomas R. Roach. — New York : Greenwood Press, 1986. — 326 p., [1] p. of plates. — (Contributions in economics and economic history ; no. 69). — *Includes index.* — *Bibliography: p. [301]-314*

FOREST PRODUCTS INDUSTRY — New Brunswick — Statistics
A profile of forestry in New Brunswick. — [Fredericton] : New Brunswick Statistics Agency, 1985. — 44 leaves

FORESTS AND FORESTRY — Bibliography
DAVID LUBIN MEMORIAL LIBRARY
FAO documentation : forestry : 1983-1985 = Documentation de la FAO : forêts : 1983-1985 = Documentacion de la FAO : montes : 1983-1985. — Rome : Food and Agriculture Organization, 1986. — 133p. — *In English with introductions also in French and Spanish*

FORESTS AND FORESTRY — Dictionaries
GORSE, Jean Eugène
A World Bank glossary : forestry terms : English-French = Glossaire de la Banque mondiale : terminologie forestière : français-anglais. — Washington, D.C. : World Bank, 1984. — v,42p. — *In English and French*

FORESTS AND FORESTRY — Dictionaries — French
GORSE, Jean Eugène
A World Bank glossary : forestry terms : English-French = Glossaire de la Banque mondiale : terminologie forestière : français-anglais. — Washington, D.C. : World Bank, 1984. — v,42p. — *In English and French*

FORESTS AND FORESTRY — Economic aspects — Southern States
HEALY, Robert G
Competition for land in the American South : agriculture, human settlement, and the environment / Robert G. Healy. — Washington, D.C. : Conservation Foundation, c1985. — xxxii, 333 p.. — *Includes bibliographies and index*

FORESTS AND FORESTRY — Economic aspects — United States
Forestlands : public and private / edited by Robert T. Deacon, M. Bruce Johnson ; foreword by B. Delworth Gardner. — San Francisco, Calif. : Pacific Institute for Public Policy Research ; Cambridge, Mass. : Ballinger Pub. Co., c1985. — xxvii, 332 p.. — (Pacific studies in public policy). — *Includes index.* — *Bibliography: p. 303-312*

FORESTS AND FORESTRY — Asia, Southeastern
WHITMORE, T. C.
Tropical rain forests of the Far East / T.C. Whitmore ; with a chapter on soils by C.P. Burnham. — 2nd ed. — Oxford : Clarendon, 1984. — xvi,352p. — *Previous ed.: 1975.* — *Maps on lining papers.* — *Bibliography: p297-328.* — *Includes index*

FORESTS AND FORESTRY — Finland — c Accounting
MÄKELÄ, Pekka
Kansantalouden tilinpito : maa-, metsä- ja kalatalous sekä metsästys kansantalouden tilinpidossa = National accounts : agriculture, forestry, fishing and hunting in national accounts. — Helsinki : Tilastokeskus, 1980. — 126p. — (Tutkimuksia / Finland. Tilastokeskus ; no.61). — *Summary and table headings in English and Swedish*

FORESTS AND FORESTRY — Finland — Statistics
FINLAND. Tilastokeskus
Maa- ja metsätalous : Maa- ja metsätalouden taloastilasto 1964-1978 = Agriculture and forestry : Economy statistics of agriculture and forestry 1964-1978. — Helsinki : Tilastokeskus, 1979. — 85p. — (Suomen virallinen tilasto = Official statistics of Finland ; 39 ; 5). — *In Finnish, Swedish and English*

FORESTS AND FORESTRY — Great Britain — Statistics
LOCKE, G. M. L.
Census of woodlands and trees 1979-82 / G. M. L. Locke. — London : H.M.S.O., 1987. — v,123p. — (Forestry Commission bulletin ; 63)

FORESTS AND FORESTRY — Taiwan
Forestry Taiwan. — [Taipei : Industrial Development Commission, 1955]. — [13]p

Taiwan's forests. — [Taipei : Ministry of Economic Affairs, 1958]. — 25p

FORESTS AND FORESTRY — United States — History
This well-wooded land : Americans and their forests from colonial times to the present / Thomas R. Cox ... [et al.]. — Lincoln : University of Nebraska Press, c1985. — xvii, 325 p., [22] p. of plates. — *Includes index.* — *Bibliography: p. [303]-312*

FORESTS AND FORESTRY — Wales — Clwyd
CLWYD. County Council
Clwyd county structure plan : public participation seminar : agriculture, woodlands and forestry : report of proceedings. — Mold : [the Council], 1975. — 41p

FORMAN, JAMES
FORMAN, James
The making of Black revolutionaries / James Forman. — 2d ed. — Washington, DC : Open Hand Pub., c1985. — xxiii, 568 p.. — *Includes index*

FORONDA, VALENTÍN DE
BARRENECHEA, José Manuel
Valentín de Foronda, reformador y economista ilustrado / José Manuel Barrenechea. — [S.l.] : Diputación Foral de Alava, Departamento de Publicaciones, [ca.1984]. — xxiv,519p. — *Bibliography: P477-503*

FORTE, CHARLES
FORTE, Charles
Forte : the autobiography of Charles Forte. — London : Sidgwick and Jackson, 1986. — x,235p

FORTRAN (COMPUTER PROGRAM LANGUAGE) — Handbooks, manuals, etc.
PROSPERO SOFTWARE
Pro Fortran-77 user manual : version iid 1.2 for 8086/8088/80186/80286 processor and optional 8087/80287 co-processor with MS-DOS/PC-DOS 2.1 or later / Prospero Software. — London : Prospero Software, 1987, c1986. — 1v.(loose-leaf)

FOSTER HOME CARE — Law and legislation
RYAN, Mary
A guide to care and related proceedings / Mary Ryan. — 3rd ed. — London : Family Rights Group, 1985. — 83p

FOSTER HOME CARE — Great Britain
Black and in care: conference report (report of a conference organized by the Black and In Care Steering Group held in October 1984). — London : Black and In Care Steering Group, 1985. — 45p

THOBURN, June
Permanence in child care / June Thoburn, Anne Murdoch, Alison O'Brien. — Oxford : Basil Blackwell, 1986. — xii,202p. — (The practice of social work ; 15). — *Bibliography: p193-198.* — *Includes index*

FOSTER HOME CARE — Wales
SOME ASPECTS OF FAMILY PLACEMENT (Conference : 1978 : Abergavenny)
Some aspects of family placement : report of the seminar held at The Hill Residential College, Abergavenny, 13-15 February 1978. — [Cardiff] ([Pearl Assurance House, Greyfriars Rd, Cardiff CF1 3JL]) : Welsh Office, Social Work Service, [1978]. — [1],i,61p. — *'... report of a ... seminar on "Some Aspects of Family Placement" organised by the Social Work Service of the Welsh Office ...' - Introduction*

FOUCAULT, MICHEL
Foucault : a critical reader / David Couzens Hoy, editor. — Oxford : Basil Blackwell, 1986. — [280]p. — *Includes index*

Towards a critique of Foucault / edited by Mike Gane. — London ; New York : Routledge & Kegan Paul, 1986. — (Economy and society series)

FOUNDRYMEN — South Africa — History
WEBSTER, Eddie
Cast in a racial mould : labour process and trade unionism in the foundries / Eddie Webster. — Johannesburg : Ravan Press, 1985. — xv, 299 p., [6] p. of plates. — *Includes index.* — *Bibliography: p. [281]-293*

FOURIER, CHARLES
BEECHER, Jonathan
Charles Fourier : the visionary and his world / Jonathan Beecher. — Berkeley : University of California Press, 1987. — p. cm. — *Includes index.* — *Bibliography: p*

FRAGA IRIBARNE, MANUEL
BERNÁLDEZ, José María
El patrón de la derecha : biografía de Fraga / José María Bernáldez. — [Barcelona] : Plaza & Janes, [1985]. — 281p. — (Biografías y memorias)

FRANCE
Journal officiel de la Republique Francaise: documents parlementaires: Assemblée Nationale. — Paris : Government Printer, 1946-. — Irregular. — Continues: Journal officiel de la Republique Francaise: documents de l'Assemblée Nationale Constituante

The Mitterand experiment : continuity and change in modern France / edited by George Ross, Stanley Hoffmann and Sylvia Malzacher. — Oxford : Polity, 1987. — xiii,363p. — (Europe and the international order). — Includes index

RUDÉ, George
Paris and London in the eighteenth century : studies in popular protest / by George Rudé. — London : Collins, 1970. — 350p. — (Fontana history)

FRANCE — Appropriations and expenditures
LÉONARD, Jean G.
Le financement des dépenses publiques en France / Jean G. Léonard. — Lyon : Presses Universitaires de Lyon, [1986]. — 259p

FRANCE — Appropriations and expenditures — Statistics
Ventilation fonctionnelle des dépenses des administrations publiques : année 1970 et séries 1975-1983. — Paris : I.N.S.E.E., 1986. — 128p. — (Archives et documents / Institut national de la statistique et des études économiques ; no.161)

FRANCE — Armed Forces — History — World War, 1939-1945
GAUNSON, A. B.
The Anglo-French clash in Lebanon and Syria, 1940-45 / A.B. Gaunson. — London : Macmillan, 1986. — xi,233p,[8]p of plates. — Bibliography: p219-225. — Includes index

FRANCE — Boundaries — Spain
FERNANDEZ DE CASADEVANTE ROMANI, Carlos
La frontera hispano-francesca y las relaciones de vecindad : (especial referncia al sector fronterizo del País Vasco) / Carlos Fernandez de Casadevante Romani. — [Bilbao] : Universidad del País Vasco, 1985. — xx,547p. — Bibliography: p[507]-539

FRANCE — Cencus, 1982 — Classification
FRANCE. Institut national de la statistique et des études économiques
Recensement général de la population de 1982 : guide d'utilisation. — Paris : I.N.S.E.E. Tome 6: Publications et microfiches : description des tableaux. — [1986]. — 200p

FRANCE — Census, 1982
DESPLANQUES, Guy
Recensement général de la population de 1982. — [Paris] : INSEE. — Bibliography: p55. — RP 82/7
Principaux résultats de l'enquête sur les familles : nuptialité et fécondité : France métropolitaine / par Guy Desplanques. — 1985. — 136p

FRANCE. Institut national de la statistique et des études économiques
Recensement général de la population de 1982 : guide d'utilisation. — [Paris] : I.N.S.E.E.
Tome 4: Description du fichier codifié (exploitation exhaustive). — [1985]. — 169p

GUILLOT, Françoise
Recensement général de la population de 1982. — [Paris] : INSEE. — Sondage au 1/4. — RP 82/8
Les populations des dom-tom en France métropolitaine / par Françoise Guillot, Solange Hémery et Claude-Valentin Marie. — 1985. — 157p

FRANCE — Census, 1982 — Classification
Recensement général de la population de 1982: guide d'utilisation. — Paris : INSEE, [1986]. — Cover title
Tome 5: Chiffrement, saisie, contrôles, redressements, calculs de codes (exploitation-exhaustive). — 162p

FRANCE — Church history — 16th century
HELLER, Henry
The conquest of poverty : the Calvinist revolt in sixteenth century France / by Henry Heller. — Leiden : Brill, 1986. — xiii, 281p. — (Studies in medieval and reformation thought ; v.35). — Bibliography: p.[259]-274

FRANCE — Civilization — Addresses, essays, lectures
POTTS, Denys Campion
French thought since 1600 / D. C. Potts and D. G. Charlton. — Rev. and reprinted from France : a companion to French studies / edited by D. G. Charlton. — London : Methuen ; [New York] : distributed by Harper & Row, 1974. — viii, 96 p. — (University paperbacks ; UP546). — Includes bibliographies and index

FRANCE — Civilization — 1830-1900
WEBER, Eugen
France, fin de siècle / Eugen Weber. — Cambridge, Mass. : Harvard University Press, 1986. — x, 294p. — Includes bibliographical references and index

FRANCE — Colonies
BOUVIER, Jean
L'impérialisme à la française / Jean Bouvier, René Girault, Jacques Thobie. — Paris : Éditions La Découverte
[2]: 1914-1960. — 1986. — 294p

GARRETT, Mitchell Bennett
The French colonial question 1789-1791 : dealings of the constituent assembly with problems arising from the revolution in the West Indies / by Mitchell Bennett Garrett. — New York : Negro Universities Press, 1970. — iv,167p. — Reprint of 1916 edition. — Bibliography: p[135]-160

FRANCE — Commerce
NGUYÊN DUY-TÂN, Joële
Le commerce extérieur de la France : environnement international et instruments juridiques / Joële Nguyên Duy-Tân avec la collaboration de Caroline Pignol et Anita Tiraspolsky. — Paris : La Documentation française, c1986. — 143p. — (Notes et études documentaires ; .no4798). — Bibliography:p.142-143

FRANCE — Commerce — History — Congresses
FRANCO-IRISH SEMINAR OF SOCIAL AND ECONOMIC HISTORIANS (4th : 1984 : Trinity College Dublin)
Cities and merchants : French and Irish perspectives on urban development, 1500-1900 : proceedings of the fourth Franco-Irish Seminar of Social and Economic Historians / edited by P. Butel and L. M. Cullen. — Dublin : Department of Modern History, Trinity College Dublin, 1986. — 259p. — English and French text. — Maps on lining papers

FRANCE — Commerce — Statistics
DEMAILLY, Dominique
Rétropolation 1959-1969 de comptes détaillés des biens et des services / Dominique Demailly, Alain Tranap. — Paris : I.N.S.E.E., 1986. — 71p. — (Archives et documents / Institut national de la statistique et des études économiques ; no.164)

DEPOUTOT, Raoul
Indices de chiffres d'affaires dans le commerce et les services : 1976-1984 / Raoul Depoutot, Marie-Line Honnibal. — Paris : I.N.S.E.E., 1986. — 113p. — (Archives et documents / Institut national de la statistique et des études économiques ; no.163)

ROBIN, Jacqueline
Images économiques des entreprises. — Paris : I.N.S.E.E.. — (Archives et documents / Institut national de la statistique et des études économiques ; no.151)
Dossier sectoriel no.6: Commerce au 1-1-1983 / Jacqueline Robin. — 1986. — 61p

FRANCE — Commerce — Canada — History — 18th century
BOSHER, J. F.
The Canada merchants 1713-1763 / J.F. Bosher. — Oxford : Clarendon, 1987. — viii,234p. — Includes index

FRANCE — Commercial policy
NGUYÊN DUY-TÂN, Joële
Le commerce extérieur de la France : environnement international et instruments juridiques / Joële Nguyên Duy-Tân avec la collaboration de Caroline Pignol et Anita Tiraspolsky. — Paris : La Documentation française, c1986. — 143p. — (Notes et études documentaires ; .no4798). — Bibliography:p.142-143

FRANCE — Constitution
Constitution française du 4 octobre 1958. — [Paris : La Documentation française, 1987]. — 32p. — (Documents d'études. Droit constitutionnel et institutions politiques ; No.1.04). — Cover title

FRANCE — Constitution — Dictionaries
Dictionnaire de la Constitution : les institutions de la Ve République / Raymond Barrillon...[et al.]. — 4e éd, revue et angmentée. — Paris : Editions Cujas, 1986. — xxxviii,606p. — Bibliography: p[605]-606

FRANCE — Description and travel — 1600-1799
LOUGH, John
France observed in the seventeenth century : by British travellers / John Lough. — Stocksfield : Oriel, 1984, c1985. — xvii,372p. — Bibliography: p346. — Includes index

FRANCE — Economic conditions
Avis et rapports du Conseil Economique. — Paris : Government Printer, 1948-1959. — Irregular. — Continued by: Avis et rapports de Conseil Economique et Social

BOYER, Robert
La crise actuelle : une mise en perspective historique : quelques reflexions à partir d'une analyse du capitalisme français en longue période / Robert Boyer. — Paris : Centre d'Études Prospectives D'Économie Mathématique Appliquées à la Planification, 1979. — 126p. — (Centre d'Études Prospectives d'Économie Mathematique Appliquées à la Planification ; no.7909). — Bibliography: p115-128

FRANCE.. Ministère de l'Économie, des Finances et de la Privatisation
Les notes bleues / Ministère de l'Économie, des Finances et de la Privatisation. — Paris : France. Ministère de l'Économie, des Finances et de la Privatisation, 1986. — Fortnightly

Journal Officiel de la Republique Francaise: avis et rapports du Conseil Economique. — Paris : Government Printer, 1948-1959. — Irregular. — Continued by: Journal Officiel de la Republique: avis et rapports du Conseil Economique et Sociale

Journal Officiel [de la Republique Francaise]: avis et rapports du Conseil Economique et Sociale. — Paris : Government Printer, 1959-. — From Jan 1986 on microfiche. — Continues: Journal Officiel de la Republique Francaise: avis et rapports du Conseil Economique

PINCHEMEL, Philippe
France : a geographical, social and economic survey / Philippe Pinchemel with Chantal Balley ... [et al.] ; translated by Dorothy Elkins with T.H. Elkins. — Cambridge : Cambridge University Press, 1987. — xxvi,660p. — Translation of: La France. — Bibliography: p605-649. — Includes index

FRANCE — Economic conditions
continuation

RILEY, James C
The Seven Years War and the old regime in France : the economic and financial toll / James C. Riley. — Princeton, N.J. : Princeton University Press, 1986. — xxii, 256p. — *Includes index*

FRANCE — Economic conditions — Regional disparities

HELD, Daniel
Marché de l'emploi : entreprises et régions / Daniel Held et Denis Maillat. — [Lausanne] : Presses Polytechniques Romandes, 1984. — 205p. — (Collection "villes, régions et sociétés")

FRANCE — Economic conditions — 1918-

NERE, J.
Le problème du mur d'argent : les crises du franc (1924-1926) / J. Nere. — Paris : La Pensée Universelle, 1985. — 159p

FRANCE — Economic conditions — 1945-

FONTENEAU, Alain
La gauche face à la crise / Alain Fonteneau, Pierre Alain Muet. — [Paris] : Presses de la Fondation nationale des sciences politiques, 1985. — 389p. — *Bibliography: p[377]-381*

Géopolitiques des régions françaises / sous la direction de Yves Lacoste ; Yves Lacoste ... [et al.]. — Paris : Fayard, 1986. — 3v. — *Contents: t.1. France septentrionale - t.2. La façade occidentale - t.3. La France du sud-est*

GREAT BRITAIN. Parliament. House of Commons. Library. Research Division
The economic record of the French socialist government since 1981 / Christopher Barclay. — [London] : the Division, 1985. — 18p. — (Background paper ; no.175). — *Bibliography: p18*

Regards sur l'actualité / Direction de la Documentation Française. — Paris : La Documentation Française, 1986-. — *10 per year*

SAVY, Michel
Atlas des français / Michel Savy, Pierre Beckouche. — [Paris] : Hachette, c1985. — 331p. — (Collection Pluriel). — *Bibliography: p[311-312]*

FRANCE — Economic conditions — 1945- — Statistics

Annales d'économie et de statistique / Institut National de la Statistique et des Études Economiques. — Paris : Institut National de la Statistique et des Études Économiques, 1986-. — *Quarterly. — Continues Annales de l'INSEE and Cahiers du Séminaire d'Econométrie*

DEVILLIERS, Michel
Les enquêtes de conjoncture / Michel Devilliers. — [Paris] : INSEE, 1984. — ii,59p. — (Archives et documents / Institut National de la Statistique et des Études Économiques ; no.101)

FRANCE — Economic conditions — 1945- — Statistics Economiques

Annales de l'INSEE / Institut National de la Statistique et des Études Économiques. — Paris : Institut National de la Statistique et des Etudes Économiques, 1969-1985. — *3 per year. — Continued by Annales d'Economie et de Statistique/Institut National de la Statistique et des Etudes Economiques*

FRANCE — Economic policy

ELWITT, Sanford
The Third Republic defended : bourgeois reform in France, 1880-1914 / Sanford Elwitt. — Baton Rouge : Louisiana State University Press, c1986. — xvi, 304 p.. — *Includes bibliographical references and index*

HALL, Peter A.
Governing the economy : the politics of state intervention in Britain and France / Peter A. Hall. — Cambridge : Polity, 1986. — 341p. — (Europe and the international order). — *Bibliography: p292-321. — Includes index*

Innovation policy : France. — Paris : OECD, 1986. — 296p. — *Bibliographical references: p237-242, 296*

ROSA, Jean-Jacques
La répression financière / Jean-Jacques Rosa [and] Michel Dietsch. — Paris : Bonnel Editions, 1981. — 151p. — *Bibliography: p149-151*

FRANCE — Economic policy — 20th century

BLOCH-LAINÉ, François
La France restaurée, 1944-1954 : dialogue sur les choix d'une modernisation / François Bloch-Lainé, Jean Bouvier ; prologue de Jean-Pierre Rioux. — Paris : Fayard, 1986. — 338p

QUINET, Emile
Le plan français : mythe ou nécessité / Émile Quinet [et] Lucien Touzery. — Paris : Economica, 1986. — 300p. — *Bibliography: p289-296*

FRANCE — Economic policy — 1945-

COTTA, Alain
Les 5 erreurs / Alain Cotta. — Paris : Orban, [1985]. — 245p

DATAR: rapport d'activité / Délégation à l'Aménagement du Territoire et à l'Action Régionale. — Paris : DATAR, 1984/85-. — *Annual*

De Monnet à Massé : enjeux politiques et objectifs économiques dans le cadre des quatre premiers Plans (1946-1965) : actes de la table ronde tenue à l'IHTP les 24 et 25 juin 1983 / sous la direction de Henry Rousso. — Paris : Editions du Centre National de la Recherche Scientifique, 1986. — 245p

FABIUS, Laurent
Le coeur du futur / Laurent Fabius. — [Paris] : Calmann-Lévy, 1985. — 263p

FONTENEAU, Alain
La gauche face à la crise / Alain Fonteneau, Pierre Alain Muet. — [Paris] : Presses de la Fondation nationale des sciences politiques, 1985. — 389p. — *Bibliography: p[377]-381*

GREAT BRITAIN. Parliament. House of Commons. Library. Research Division
The economic record of the French socialist government since 1981 / Christopher Barclay. — [London] : the Division, 1985. — 18p. — (Background paper ; no.175). — *Bibliography: p18*

FRANCE — Economic policy — 1965-

BALLADUR, Edouard
Vers la liberté : la réforme économique 1986 / Edouard Balladur. — [Paris : La Documentation française, 1987]. — 103p

FRANCE — Emigration and immigration

COLLOQUE "DES ÉTRANGERS QUI FONT AUSSI LA FRANCE"
Les Nord-Africains en France / ouvrage réalisé sous la direction de Magali Morsy. — Paris : CHEAM, 1984. — 200p. — (Publications du CHEAM ; 3). — *Includes bibliographical references*

HOO KHOA, Le
Les réfugié set immigrés originaires de la péninsule Indochinoise / Le Huu Khoa. — [Paris] : Agence de développement des relations interculturelles, 1984. — 54 leaves. — *Bibliography: p40-51*

JAZOULI, Adil
Dynamiques collectives et initiatives d'intégration sociale chez les jeunes d'origine immigrée / Adil Jazouli. — [Paris] : Agence de développement des relations interculturelles, 1984. — 76 leaves. — *Includes bibliographical references*

MARIE, Claude Valentin
L'immigration étrangère en France / Claude Valentin Marie. — [Paris] : ADRI, 1984. — 177p. — *Bibliography: p173-177*

MARTINS, Vasco Manuel
Le Portugal et l'immigration Portugaise en France / Vasco Manuel Martins. — [Paris] : Agence de développement des relations interculturelles, 1984. — 51 leaves. — *Bibliography: p45-47*

MAZOUZ, Mohamed
Le Maroc et l'immigration Marocaine en France / Mohamed Mazouz. — [Paris] : Agence de développement des relations interculturelles, 1984. — 69 leaves. — *Includes bibliographical references*

MAZOUZ, Mohamed
Le Maroc et l'immigration marocaine en France / Mohamed Mazouz. — Paris : Agence de Développement des Relations Interculturelles, 1984. — 69 leaves. — *Bibliography: p59-66*

MAZOUZ, Mohamed
La Tunisie et l'immigration Tunisienne en France / Mohamed Mazouz. — [Paris] : Agence de développement des relations interculturelles, 1984. — 48 leaves. — *Includes bibliographical references*

MINCES, Juliette
La génération suivante (les enfants de l'immigration) / Juliette Minces. — Paris : Flammarion, 1986. — 209p

ZEHRAOUI, Ahsène
L'Algerie et l'immigration Algerienne en France / Ahsène Zehraoui, Mohamed Mazouz. — [Paris] : Agence de développement des relations interculturelles, 1984. — 48p. — *Includes bibliographical references*

FRANCE — Emigration and immigration — History

Huguenots in Britain and their French background, 1550-1800 / edited by Irene Scouloudi. — Totowa, N.J. : Barnes & Noble, 1987. — p. cm. — *Includes index*

FRANCE — Emigration and immigration — Statistics

LABAT, Jean-Claude
Projection de la population étrangère résidant en France métropolitaine / Jean-Claude Labat et Joël Dekneudt. — Paris : I.N.S.E.E., 1986. — 41,6,24p. — (Archives et documents / Institut national de le statistique et des études économiques ; no.166)

FRANCE — Ethnic relations

COHEN, Richard I
The burden of conscience : French Jewish leadership during the holocaust / Richard I. Cohen. — Bloomington : Indiana University Press, c1987. — p. cm. — (The Modern Jewish experience). — *Includes index. — Bibliography: p*

FRANCE — Foreign economic relations

NGUYÊN DUY-TÂN, Joële
Le commerce extérieur de la France : environnement international et instruments juridiques / Joële Nguyên Duy-Tân avec la collaboration de Caroline Pignol et Anita Tiraspolsky. — Paris : La Documentation française, c1986. — 143p. — (Notes et études documentaires ; .no4798). — *Bibliography:p.142-143*

FRANCE — Foreign economic relations — Switzerland
WACKERMANN, Gabriel
  Belfort, Colmar, Mulhouse, Bâle, Fribourg-en-Brisgau : un espace économique transfrontalier / Gabriel Wackermann. — [Paris : La Documentation française, 1986]. — 143p. — (Notes et études documentaires ; no.4824). — *Bibliography: p139-142*

FRANCE — Foreign population — Public opinion
SCHOR, Ralph
  L'opinion française et les étrangers en France 1919-1939 / par Ralph Schor. — [Paris] : Publications de la Sorbonne, 1985. — xi,761p. — (Publications de la Sorbonne / Série "France XIXe-XXe siècles ; No.22). — *Bibliography: p745-748*

FRANCE — Foreign population — Statistics
LABAT, Jean-Claude
  Projection de la population étrangère résidant en France métropolitaine / Jean-Claude Labat et Joël Dekneudt. — Paris : I.N.S.E.E., 1986. — 41,6,24p. — (Archives et documents / Institut national de le statistique et des études économiques ; no.166)

FRANCE — Foreign relations
CARROLL, E. Malcolm
  French public opinion and foreign affairs 1870-1914 / by E. Malcolm Carroll. — New York : the Century, 1931. — viii,348p

FRANCE — Foreign relations — Treaties
Droit international et droit français : étude adoptée par la Section du Rapport et des Etudes du Conseil d'Etat le 25 avril 1985 / [réalisée sous la présidence de M. Jean-Jacques de Bresson]. — Paris : La Documentation française, 1986. — 116p. — (Notes et études documentaires ; no.4803)

FRANCE — Foreign relations — 1715-1793
BLACK, Jeremy
  Natural and necessary enemies : Anglo-French relations in the eighteenth century / Jeremy Black. — London : Duckworth, 1986. — [236]p. — *Includes index*

FRANCE — Foreign relations — 1945-1958
BELLINI, James
  An analysis of the effect of the development of French foreign policy on the evolution of the Western Alliance 1948-1954 / James Bellini. — 310 leaves. — PhD (Econ) 1986 LSE

FRANCE — Foreign relations — Algeria
BEN KHEDDA, Bengoucef
  Les accords d'Évian / Bengoucef Ben Khedda. — Alger : Publisud, [1986]. — 119p

LACOUTURE, Jean
  Algérie, la guerre est finie / Jean Lacouture avec la collaboration de Catherine Grönblatt. — Bruxelles : Complexe, [1985]. — 207p

FRANCE — Foreign relations — Germany
WEISENFELD, Ernst
  Welches Deutschland soll es sein? : Frankreich und die deutsche Einheit seit 1945 / Ernst Weisenfeld. — München : Beck, 1986. — 203p. — *Bibliographical notes*

FRANCE — Foreign relations — Germany (West)
WACKERMANN, Gabriel
  Belfort, Colmar, Mulhouse, Bâle, Fribourg-en-Brisgau : un espace économique transfrontalier / Gabriel Wackermann. — [Paris : La Documentation française, 1986]. — 143p. — (Notes et études documentaires ; no.4824). — *Bibliography: p139-142*

FRANCE — Foreign relations — Spain
ACUÑA, Ramón Luis
  Como los dientes de una sierra : (Francia-España de 1975 a 1985, una década) / Ramón Luis Acuña. — Barcelona : Plaza & Janes, 1986. — 300p. — *Bibliography: p [285]-288*

FERNANDEZ DE CASADEVANTE ROMANI, Carlos
  La frontera hispano-francesca y las relaciones de vecindad : (especial refrncia al sector fronterizo del País Vasco) / Carlos Fernandez de Casadevante Romani. — [Bilbao] : Universidad del País Vasco, 1985. — xx,547p. — *Bibliography: p[507]-539*

JENSEN, De Lamar
  Diplomacy and dogmatism : Bernardino de Mendoza and the French Catholic League / De Lamar Jensen. — Cambridge, Mass. : Harvard University Press, 1964. — xii,322p. — *Bibliography: p241-263*

FRANCE — Foreign relations — Turkey
SAAKIAN, R. G.
  Franko-turetskie otnosheniia i Kilikiia v 1918-1923 gg. / R. G. Saakian. — Erevan : Izd-vo AN Armianskoi SSR, 1986. — 281p. — Summary in French. — *Bibliography: p245-272*

FRANCE — Foreign relations — United States
LEFFLER, Melvyn P.
  The elusive quest : the America's pursuit of European stability and French security, 1919-1933 / by Melvyn P. Leffler. — Chapel Hill : University of North Carolina Press, c1979. — xvi, 409 p.. — *Includes index*. — *Bibliography: p. 369-393*

FRANCE — Foreign relations by 1914-1940
CAMERON, Elizabeth R.
  Prologue to appeasement : a study in French foreign policy / by Elizabeth R. Cameron. — Washington : American Council on Public Affairs, 1942. — xii,228p. — *Bibliography: p212-221*

FRANCE — Handbooks, manuals, etc.
L'État de la France et de ses habitants / sous la direction de Jean-Yves Potel. — Paris : Éditions la Découverte, c1985. — 640 p.

FRANCE — History — Consulate and Empire, 1799-1815
LEFEBVRE, Georges
  [Napoléon. English. Selections]. Napoleon : from Tilsit to Waterloo, 1807-1815 / by Georges Lefebvre ; translated from the French by J. E. Anderson. — New York : Columbia University Press, 1969. — viii, 414p. — "Translation of the first three parts of Napoléon...this translation is based on the 5th (1965) ed." — Verso t.p.

FRANCE — History — Revolution — 1789-1793
FURET, François
  La Gauche et la Révolution françoise au milieu du XIXe siècle : Edgar Quinet et la question du Jacobinisme (1865-1870) / François Furet ; textes présentés par Marina Valensise. — [Paris?] : Hachette, 1986. — 317p. — (Librarie du bicentenaire de la Revolution française). — *Includes bibliographic notes*

FRANCE — History — Revolution, 1789-1799 — Causes
PAINE, Thomas
  Rights of man / Thomas Paine ; with a biographical introduction by Philip S. Foner. — Secaucus : Citadel, c1974. — 262p

FRANCE — History — 16th century
CONSTANT, Jean-Marie
  Les Guise / Jean-Marie Constant. — [Paris] : Hachette littérature, c1984. — 266 p.. — *Includes index*. — *Bibliography: p. [235]-244*

FRANCE — History — Wars of the Huguenots, 1562-1598
CONSTANT, Jean-Marie
  Les Guise / Jean-Marie Constant. — [Paris] : Hachette littérature, c1984. — 266 p.. — *Includes index*. — *Bibliography: p. [235]-244*

FRANCE — History — Bourbons, 1589-1789 — Historiography
DOYLE, William
  The Ancien Regime / William Doyle. — Basingstoke : Macmillan, 1986. — ix,62p. — (Studies in European history). — *Bibliography: p52-58*. — *Includes index*

FRANCE — History — 18th century
SHENNAN, J. H.
  France before the revolution / J.H. Shennan. — London : Methuen, 1983. — vii,37p. — (Lancaster pamphlets). — *Bibliography: p37*

FRANCE — History — Revolution, 1789-1792
MURRAY, William James
  The right-wing press in the French Revolution : 1789-92 / William James Murray. — London : Royal Historical Society, 1986, c1985. — viii, 349p. — (Royal Historical Society studies in history series ; no.44). — *Bibliography: p.314-326*

FRANCE — History — Revolution, 1789-1793
CASTRIES, Rene de la Croix, duc de
  Mirabeau ou l'échec du destin / Duc de Castries. — Nouvelle ed.. — Paris : Fayard, 1986. — 595p. — *Bibliography: p581-593*

JOHNSON, Hubert C
  The Midi in revolution : a study of regional political diversity, 1789-1793 / Hubert C. Johnson. — Princeton, N.J. : Princeton University Press, c1986. — viii, 309 p. — *Includes index*. — *Bibliography: p. [281]-292*

FRANCE — History — Revolution, 1789-1794
JORDAN, David P.
  The revolutionary career of Maximilien Robespierre / David P. Jordan. — New York : Free Press, c1985. — xii, 308p. — *Includes index*. — *Bibliography: p.299-304*

FRANCE — History — Revolution, 1789-1797
GREGORY, Desmond
  The ungovernable rock : a history of the Anglo-Corsican Kingdom and its role in Britain's Mediterranean strategy during the Revolutionary War, 1793-1797 / Desmond Gregory. — Rutherford : Fairleigh Dickinson University Press ; London ; Cranbury, NJ : Associated University Presses, c1985. — 211p. — *Bibliography: p202-206*

FRANCE — History — Revolution, 1789-1799
FURET, François
  La revolution française / François Furet [et] Denis Richet. — Paris : Hachette, [1986]. — 544p

SLAVIN, Morris
  The making of an insurrection : Parisian sections and the Gironde / Morris Slavin. — Cambridge, Mass. : Harvard University Press, 1986. — ix, 236 p.. — *Includes index*. — *Bibliography: p. [222]-228*

FRANCE — History — Revolution, 1789-1799 — Biography
SOBOUL, Albert
  Portroits de révolutionnaires / Albert Soboul. — Paris : Messidor/Éditions sociales, 1986. — 313p. — (Bibliotéque du bicentenoire de la Révolution Française 1789-1989 ; 13). — *Includes bibliographicol notes*

FRANCE — History — Revolution, 1789-1799 — Causes
BLUM, Carol
  Rousseau and the republic of virtue : the language of politics in the French Revolution / Carol Blum. — Ithaca : Cornell University Press, 1986. — 302 p.. — *Includes index*. — *Bibliography: p. 283-294*

FRANCE — History — Revolution, 1789-1799 — Dictionaries
Historical dictionary of the French Revolution 1789-1799 / edited by Samuel F. Scott and Barry Rothaus. — Westport, Conn. : Greenwood Press, c1984. — 2v(xvii, 1143p). — *Includes index. — Includes bibliographies*

FRANCE — History — 1789-1815
SUTHERLAND, D. M. G.
France 1789-1815 : revolution and counterrevolution / D.M.G. Sutherland. — London : Collins, c1985. — 493p. — (Fontana history of modern France). — *Bibliography: p.[443]-470*

FRANCE — History — Revolution, 1789-1815
SUTHERLAND, D. M. G.
France 1789-1815 : revolution and counterrevolution / D.M.G. Sutherland. — London : Collins, c1985. — 493p. — (Fontana history of modern France). — *Bibliography: p.[443]-470*

FRANCE — History — Revolution, 1795-1799
SAINT-JUST, Louis Antoine
De la nécessité de déclarer le gouvernement révolutionnaire justquàla paix / Louis Antoine Saint-Just. — [S.l.] : Obsidiane, 1986. — [12p]

FRANCE — History — Consulate and Empire, 1799-1815
LEFEBVRE, Georges
[Napoléon. English. Selections]. Napoleon : from 18 Brumaire to Tilsit, 1799-1807 / by Georges Lefebvre ; translated from the French by Henry F. Stockhold. — New York : Columbia University Press, 1969. — x,337p. — *"Translation of the first 3 parts of Napoleon ... this translation is based on the 5th (1965) ed." — Verso t.p.*

FRANCE — History — Consulate and Empire, 1799-1815 — Dictionaries
Historical dictionary of Napoleonic France, 1799-1815 / edited by Owen Connelly ; Harold T. Parker, Peter W. Becker, and June K. Burton, associate editors ; Janice Seaman Berbin, editorial assistant. — Westport, Conn. : Greenwood Press, 1985. — xiii, 586 p.. — *Includes index. — Bibliography: p. [587]-541*

FRANCE — History — Restoration, 1814-1830 — Dictionaries
Historical dictionary of France from the 1815 restoration to the Second Empire / edited by Edgar Leon Newman. — Westport, Conn. : Greenwood Press, c1986. — p. cm. — *Includes index. — Bibliography: p*

FRANCE — History — Louis Philip, 1830-1848
PINKNEY, David H
Decisive years in France, 1840-1847 / David H. Pinkney. — Princeton, N.J. : Princeton University Press, c1985. — xii, 235p. — *Includes index. — Bibliography: p [201]-229*

FRANCE — History — Louis Philip, 1830-1848 — Dictionaries
Historical dictionary of France from the 1815 restoration to the Second Empire / edited by Edgar Leon Newman. — Westport, Conn. : Greenwood Press, c1986. — p. cm. — *Includes index. — Bibliography: p*

FRANCE — History — Second Republic, 1848-1852 — Dictionaries
Historical dictionary of France from the 1815 restoration to the Second Empire / edited by Edgar Leon Newman. — Westport, Conn. : Greenwood Press, c1986. — p. cm. — *Includes index. — Bibliography: p*

FRANCE — History — 1848-1870
FURET, François
La Gauche et la Révolution françoise au milieu du XIXe siècle : Edgar Quinet et la question du Jacobinisme (1865-1870) / François Furet ; textes présentés par Marina Valensise. — [Paris?] : Hachette, 1986. — 317p. — (Librarie du bicentenaire de la Revolution française). — *Includes bibliographic notes*

FRANCE — History — Second Empire, 1852-1870 — Dictionaries
Historical dictionary of the French Second Empire / edited by William E. Echard. — Westport, Conn. ; London : Greenwood Press, c1985. — xvi, 829p. — *Includes bibliographies and index*

FRANCE — History — Third Republic, 1870-1940
BERGERON, Francis
Les droites dans la rue : nationaux et nationalistes sous la Troisième République / Francis Bergeron et Philippe Vilgier ; préface de Jean-François Chiappe. — [Bouére] : Dominique Martin Morin, 1985. — 175p

MONAT, Christophe
Gaston Alexandre Auguste de Golliffet : "le marquis aux talons rouges" : de La Commune à l'affaire Dreyfus- / Christope Monat. — Paris : Jean-Cyrille Godefroy, 1985. — 214p. — *Cover title: Golliffet: le marquis aux talons rouges. — Bibliography: p208-[209]*

FRANCE — History — Third Republic, 1870-1940 — Dictionaries
Historical dictionary of the Third French Republic, 1870-1940 / Patrick J. Hutton, editor-in-chief ; Amanda S. Bourque and Amy J. Staples, assistant editors. — Westport, Conn. : Greenwood Press, c1986. — 2v(xvi, 1206p). — *Includes index. — Includes bibliographies*

FRANCE — History — 20th century
DANOS, Jacques
[Juin '36. English]. June '36 : class struggle and the popular front in France / Jacques Danos and Marcel Gibelin ; edited by Peter Fysh and Peter Marsden ; translated by Peter Fysh and Christine Bourry. — London ; Chicago : Bookmarks, 1986. — 272p

L'État de la France et de ses habitants / sous la direction de Jean-Yves Potel. — Paris : Éditions la Découverte, c1985. — 640 p.

FRANCE — History — 1914-1940
WARNER, Geoffrey
Pierre Laval and the eclipse of France / by Geoffrey Warner. — London : Eyre and Spottiswoode, 1968. — 461p

FRANCE — History — German occupation, 1940-1945
BLOCH-LAINÉ, François
La France restaurée, 1944-1954 : dialogue sur les choix d'une modernisation / François Bloch-Lainé, Jean Bouvier ; prologue de Jean-Pierre Rioux. — Paris : Fayard, 1986. — 338p

FRANCE — History — German Occupation: 1940-45
Journal Officiel de la Republique Francaise: debats de l'Assemblée consultative provisoire. — Alger : Government Printer, 1944-1945. — *Irregular. — Continued by: Journal Officiel de la Republique Francaise: debats de l'Assemblée Constituante*

FRANCE — History — German occupation, 1940-1945
LOTTMAN, Herbert R.
The people's anger : justice and revenge in post-liberation France / Herbert R. Lottman. — London : Hutchinson, 1986. — 332p,[8]p of plates. — *Includes index*

RIMBAUD, Christiane
Le procès Mendès France / Christiane Rimbaud ; préface de Jean-Denis Bredin. — Paris : Librairie Academique Perrin, 1986. — 216p. — *Bibliography: p215-216*

ROSSITER, Margaret L
Women in the resistance / Margaret L. Rossiter. — New York, U.S.A. : Praeger, 1985. — p. cm. — *Includes index. — Bibliography: p*

WARNER, Geoffrey
Pierre Laval and the eclipse of France / by Geoffrey Warner. — London : Eyre and Spottiswoode, 1968. — 461p

FRANCE — History — 1945-
BLOCH-LAINÉ, François
La France restaurée, 1944-1954 : dialogue sur les choix d'une modernisation / François Bloch-Lainé, Jean Bouvier ; prologue de Jean-Pierre Rioux. — Paris : Fayard, 1986. — 338p

Procès da'près-guerre : "Je suis partout", René Hardy, Orodour-sur-Glane, Oberg et Knochen / présenté et étobli par Jean-Marc Théolleyre. — Paris : Éditions la Découverte, 1985. — 221p

FRANCE — History — 1958-
Mitterrand's France / edited by Sonia Mazey and Michael Newman. — London : Croom Helm, c1987. — [256]p. — *Includes index*

FRANCE — History, Military — 1789-1815
LEFEBVRE, Georges
[Napoléon. English. Selections]. Napoleon : from Tilsit to Waterloo, 1807-1815 / by Georges Lefebvre ; translated from the French by J. E. Anderson. — New York : Columbia University Press, 1969. — viii, 414p. — *"Translation of the first three parts of Napoléon...this translation is based on the 5th (1965) ed." — Verso t.p.*

LEFEBVRE, Georges
[Napoléon. English. Selections]. Napoleon : from 18 Brumaire to Tilsit, 1799-1807 / by Georges Lefebvre ; translated from the French by Henry F. Stockhold. — New York : Columbia University Press, 1969. — x,337p. — *"Translation of the first 3 parts of Napoleon ... this translation is based on the 5th (1965) ed." — Verso t.p.*

FRANCE — Industries
Les consommations d'énergie dans l'industrie. — Paris : Documentation Française, 1982-. — (Traits fondamentaux du système industriel français) (Collection chiffres et documents: Serie industrie). — *Annual*

Formation emploi / Centre d'Études et de Recherches sur les Qualifications. — Paris : La Documentation Française, 1986-. — *Quarterly*

L'industrie et les régions / Ministère de l'Industrie et de la Recherche [et] Service d'Étude des Stratégies et des Statistiques Industrielles. — Paris : Documentation Française, 1981-. — (Traits fondamentaux du système industriel français). — *Annual*

La situation de l'industrie française : synthèse des rapports des groupes de stratégie industrielle. — [Paris] : La Documentation française, [1987]. — 100p

FRANCE — Industries — Statistics
DELATTRE, Michel
Forces et faiblesses des secteurs industriels 1979-1984 / Michel Delattre. — [Paris] : I.N.S.E.E., 1986. — 136p. — (Les collections de l'INSEE. Série E. Entreprises ; no.100). — *Bibliography: p123*

L'implantation étrangère dans l'industrie. — Paris : Documentation Française, 1979-. — (Traits fondamentaux du système industriel français) (Collection chiffres et documents: Serie industrie). — *Annual. — Issuing body varies; France. Service du Traitement de l'Information et des Statistiques Industrielles and France. Service d'Étude des Stratégies et des Statistiques Industrielles*

Premiers resultats: les indices de chiffres d'affaires dans le commerce et les services / Institut National de la Statistique et des Études Économiques. — Paris : INSEE, 1986. — *Monthly*

QUÉLENNEC, Michel
Les statistiques d'entreprises : réalités observées et méthodes d'observation / par Michel Quélennec. — [Paris] : I.N.S.E.E., 1986. — 221p. — (Les collections de l'INSEE. Série E. Entreprises ; no.101). — *Bibliography: p211-212*

FRANCE — Kings and rulers
NELSON, Janet
Politics and ritual in early medieval Europe / Janet L. Nelson. — London : Hambledon, 1985. — [440]p. — (History series ; 42). — *Includes index*

FRANCE — Kings and rulers — Biography
NAPOLÉON I, Emperor of the French
Napoleon's memoirs / edited by Somerset de Chair ; translated by B. O'Meara. — London : Soho, 1986. — [605]p. — *Translated from the French. — Originally published: London : Faber, 1945. — Includes index*

FRANCE — Law and legislation
Table mensuelle du journal officiel de la République Francaise : lois et décrets. — Paris : Journaux Officiels, 1986-. — *Monthly*

FRANCE — Manufactures — Statistics
DEMAILLY, Dominique
Rétropolation 1959-1969 de comptes détaillés des biens et des services / Dominique Demailly, Alain Tranap. — Paris : I.N.S.E.E., 1986. — 71p. — (Archives et documents / Institut national de la statistique et des études économiques ; no.164)

FRANCE — Maps, mental
OSTROWETSKY, Sylvia
L'imaginaire bâtisseur : les villes nouvelles françaises / préface de Louis Marin. — Paris : Librairie des Méridiens, 1983. — viii,345p. — *Bibliography: p331-342*

FRANCE — Military policy
French security policy : from independence to interdependence / edited by Robbin F. Laird. — Boulder ; London : Westview Press, 1986. — xii, 180p. — (Westview special studies in international security). — *Includes index*

FRANCE — National security
French security policy : from independence to interdependence / edited by Robbin F. Laird. — Boulder ; London : Westview Press, 1986. — xii, 180p. — (Westview special studies in international security). — *Includes index*

FRANCE — Nobility — Biography
CONSTANT, Jean-Marie
Les Guise / Jean-Marie Constant. — [Paris] : Hachette littérature, c1984. — 266 p.. — *Includes index. — Bibliography: p. [235]-244*

FRANCE — Nobility — History — 16th century
SCHALK, Ellery
From valor to pedigree : ideas of nobility in France in the sixteenth and seventeenth centuries / by Ellery Schalk. — Princeton, N.J. ; Guildford : Princeton University Press, c1986. — xvii,242p. — *Bibliography: p223-231. — Includes index*

FRANCE — Nobility — History — 17th century
SCHALK, Ellery
From valor to pedigree : ideas of nobility in France in the sixteenth and seventeenth centuries / by Ellery Schalk. — Princeton, N.J. ; Guildford : Princeton University Press, c1986. — xvii,242p. — *Bibliography: p223-231. — Includes index*

FRANCE — Nobility — History — 19th century
HIGGS, David
Nobles in nineteenth-century France : the practice of inegalitarianism / David Higgs. — Baltimore : Johns Hopkins University Press, c1987. — xix, 287 p.. — (The Johns Hopkins University studies in historical and political science ; 105th ser., 1). — *Includes index. — Bibliography: p. 237-240*

FRANCE — Officials and employees
Problèmes actuels de la fonction publique local / Alain Mangerie...[et al.]. — Paris : Librairies Techniques : Groupement de recherches coordonnées sur l'administration locale : Centre national de la recherche scientifique, [ca.1982]. — 210p. — (Collection du GRAL ; no.11) (Etudes et recherches juridiques)

FRANCE — Officials and employees — Classification
Les emplois-types de la fonction publique. — [Paris : La Documentation française, 1986]. — 267p. — (Répertoire français des emplois ; cahier 17)

FRANCE — Officials and employees — Salaries, allowances, etc. — Statistics
Salaires des agents de l'état / Institut National de la Statistique et des Études Économiques. — Paris : I.N.S.É.É., 1982-. — (Collections de l'Insée). — *Annual*

FRANCE — Politics and goverment — 1958-
MASSOT, Jean
La Présidence de la République en France : vingt ans d'élection au suffrage universel 1965-1985 / par Jean Massot. — Paris : La Documentation française, 1986. — 195p. — (Notes et études documentaires ; no.4801). — *Bibliography: p187-189*

FRANCE — Politics and government
DANOS, Jacques
[Juin '36. English]. June '36 : class struggle and the popular front in France / Jacques Danos and Marcel Gibelin ; edited by Peter Fysh and Peter Marsden ; translated by Peter Fysh and Christine Bourry. — London ; Chicago : Bookmarks, 1986. — 272p

GOGUEL, François
La politique en France / François Goguel [et] Alfred Grosser. — Nouv. éd. — Paris : Colin, 1984. — 283 p. — *Bibliography: p279*

Journal officiel de la République Francaise: annexe administrative. — Paris : Government Printer, 1945-1958. — *Irregular. — Continued by: Journal Officiel de la République Francaise: documents administratifs*

Table mensuelle du journal officiel de la République Francaise : lois et décrets. — Paris : Journaux Officiels, 1986-. — *Monthly*

FRANCE — Politics and government — To 987
NELSON, Janet
Politics and ritual in early medieval Europe / Janet L. Nelson. — London : Hambledon, 1985. — [440]p. — (History series ; 42). — *Includes index*

FRANCE — Politics and government — 18th century
KELLY, George Armstrong
Mortal politics in eighteenth-century France / George Kelly Armstrong. — Waterloo, Ontario : University of Waterloo Press, 1986. — xxiii,334p. — *Bibliographical note: p[318]*

FRANCE — Politics and government — 1870-1940
ELWITT, Sanford
The Third Republic defended : bourgeois reform in France, 1880-1914 / Sanford Elwitt. — Baton Rouge : Louisiana State University Press, c1986. — xvi, 304 p.. — *Includes bibliographical references and index*

FRANCE — Politics and government — 20th century
GOGUEL, François
La politique en France / François Goguel et Alfred Grosser. — 4e. ed. — Paris : Colin, 1970. — 365p. — *First published 1981*

HALL, Peter A.
Governing the economy : the politics of state intervention in Britain and France / Peter A. Hall. — Cambridge : Polity, 1986. — 341p. — (Europe and the international order). — *Bibliography: p292-321. — Includes index*

MARTINET, Gilles
Cassandre et les tueurs : cinquante ans d'une histoire française / Gilles Martinet. — Paris : Grasset, [1986]. — iii,269p

PETITFILS, Jean Christian
L'extrême droite en France / Jean Christian Petitfils. — Paris : [Presses Universitaires de France], 1983. — 127p. — (Que sais-je? ; 2118) . — *Bibliography: p126*

FRANCE — Politics and government — 1945-1958
CALLOT, Emile-François
L'action et l'oeuvre politique du Mouvement républicain populaire : un parti politique de la démocratie chrétienne en France / Emile-François Callot. — Paris : Champion ; Genève : Slatkine, 1986. — 388p. — *Bibliography: p[383]*

WINOCK, Michel
La République se meurt, 1956-1958 / Michel Winock. — Nouvelle édition. — [Paris : Seuil, c1985]. — 285p. — (Collection folio/histoire ; 4). — *Publié originellement en Paris par Seuil, 1978*

FRANCE — Politics and government — 1945-
BOURRICAUD, François
Le retour de la droite / François Bourricaud. — Paris : Calmann-Lévy, 1986. — 323p

Géopolitiques des régions françaises / sous la direction de Yves Lacoste ; Yves Lacoste ... [et al.]. — Paris : Fayard, 1986. — 3v. — *Contents: t.1. France septentrionale - t.2. La façade occidentale - t.3. La France du sud-est*

LÉVÊQUE, Jean-Maxime
En première ligne / Jean-Maxime Lévêque. — Paris : Albin Michel, [1986]. — 202p

WILLIAMS, Philip M.
Politics in post-war France : parties and the constitution in the Fourth Republic. — London : Longmans, 1955. — 500p

FRANCE — Politics and government — 1958-
BERGERON, Francis
De Le Pen à Le Pen : une histoire des nationaux et des nationalistes sous la Ve République / Francis Bergeron, Philippe Vilgier ; préface de François Brigneau. — Bouère : Dominique Martin Morin, 1985. — 214p. — *Bibliography: p204-205*

BOISSONADE, Euloge
Jamais deux sans trois?... = ou, l'étonnant destin d'Alain Poher / Euloge Boissonade. — Paris : Editions France-Empire, 1986. — 238p

HAYWARD, Jack Ernest Shalom
Governing France : the one and indivisible republic / Jack Hayward. — 2nd American ed. — New York : W.W. Norton, 1983. — 322 p.. — (Comparative modern governments). — *Rev. ed. of: The one and indivisible French republic. 1973. — Includes index. — Bibliography: p. 301-309*

Paris: May 1986. — [London] : Rebel Press : Dark Star, 1986. — 55p

FRANCE — Politics and government — 1969-
GAUDIN, Jean-Claude
La gauche à l'imparfait / Jean-Claude Gaudin. — Paris : France-Empire, 1985. — 299p

HAMAOUI, Ernest
Le regime politique de la Ve république selon l'éthique pompidolienne : évolution ou révolution? / Ernest Hamaoui. — Paris : Éditions Montchrestian
Tome 2: Les institutions politiques actuelles de la France. — 1971
Fascicule 2: Actualisation au 4 mai 1974 de "le regime politique de la V republique" Paris 1970. — 32p

FRANCE — Politics and government — 1974-1981
LAFONT, Robert
Le dénouement Français / Robert Lafont. — Paris : Pauvert, (1985). — 243p

FRANCE — Politics and government — 1981
LE PEN, Jean-Marie
La France est de retour. — Paris : Carrere/Michel Lafon, [1985]. — 301p

FRANCE — Politics and government — 1981-
DROIT, Michel
Lettre ouverte à ceux qui en ont plus qu'assez du socialisme / Michel Droit. — Paris : Albin Michel, [1985]. — 183p

FABIUS, Laurent
Le coeur du futur / Laurent Fabius. — [Paris] : Calmann-Lévy, 1985. — 263p

LAFONT, Robert
Le dénouement Français / Robert Lafont. — Paris : Pauvert, (1985). — 243p

LEBACQZ, Albert
Journal politique de 1985 : le retour de Raymond Barre / Albert Lebacqz. — Paris : Editions France-Empire, 1986. — 279p

NEMBRINI, Pierre
Le coeur et la raison / Pierre Nembrini. — Paris : Encre, [1985]. — 172p. — *Bibliography : p169*

Regards sur l'actualité / Direction de la Documentation Française. — Paris : La Documentation Française, 1986-. — *10 per year*

Structures gouvernementales et organisation administrative : étude adoptée par la Section du rapport et des études du Conseil d'Etat le 5 décembre 1985 / ...réalisée sous la direction de Bernard Tricot. — Paris : La Documentation français, 1986. — 151p. — (Notes et études documentaires ; no.4818)

TRICOT, Bernard
Les institutions politiques françaises / Bernard Tricot, Rapha"el Hadas-Lebel. — Paris : Presses de la Fondation Nationale des Sciences Politiques, [1985]. — 532p. — *Bibliography: p519-529*

ZIEGLER, Jean
Vive le pouvoir! : ou les délices de la raison d'état / Jean Ziegler. — Paris : Seuil, [1985]. — 281p

FRANCE — Politics and government — 1981- — Biography
Guide du nouveau pouvoir : cabinets ministériels et parlement biographies et adresses des membres du gouvernement[...] / [réalisé sous la direction de Jean-François Doumic, assisté d'Eduardo Olivares]. — [2nd ed.] — Paris : Jean-François Doumic, 1986. — 243p. — (Supplément à la Lettre de la communication ; no.156)

FRANCE — Popular culture — History
MUCHEMBLED, Robert
[Culture populaire et culture des élites dans la France moderne. English]. Popular culture and elite culture in France, 1400-1750 / Robert Muchembled ; translated by Lydia Cochrane. — Baton Rouge : Louisiana State University Press, c1985. — p. cm. — *Translation of: Culture populaire et culture des élites dans la France moderne. — Includes bibliographical references and index*

FRANCE — Population
GUILLOT, Françoise
Recensement général de la population de 1982. — [Paris] : INSEE. — *Sondage au 1/4. — RP 82/8*
Les populations des dom-tom en France métropolitaine / par Françoise Guillot, Solange Hémery et Claude-Valentin Marie. — 1985. — 157p

FRANCE — Population — Classification
FRANCE. Institut national de la statistique et des études économiques
Recensement général de la population de 1982 : guide d'utilisation. — Paris : I.N.S.E.E.
Tome 6: Publications et microfiches : description des tableaux. — [1986]. — 200p

FRANCE — Population — History
BRAUDEL, Fernand
L'identité de la France / Fernand Braudel. — Paris : Arthaud-Flammarion
2: Les hommes et les choses
[1]: [Le nombre et les fluctuations longues]. — 1986. — 221p

FRANCE — Population — Statistical methods
Recensement général de la population de 1982 : guide d'utilisation. — Paris : INSEE, [1986]. — *Cover title*
Tome 5: Chiffrement, saisie, contrôles, redressements, calculs de codes (exploitation-exhaustive). — 162p

FRANCE — Population — Statistics
DINH QUANG CHI
Projection de population totale pour la France / par Dinh Quang Chi et Jean-Claude Labat. — [Paris] : INSEE, 1987. — 93p. — (Les collections de l'INSEE. Série D. Démographic et emploi ; 113)

KERROMES, Armelle
Tableaux normalisés simplifiés par région et département / Armelle Kerromes. — [Paris] : INSEE, 1984. — 273p. — (Archives et documents / Institut National de la Statistique et des Études Économiques ; no.100)

FRANCE — Population, Rural
BRAUDEL, Fernand
L'identité de la France / Fernand Braudel. — Paris : Arthaud-Flammarion
2: Les hommes et les choses
[2]: Une "économie paysanne" jusqu'au XXe siècle. — 1986. — 476p

FRANCE — Presidents
DERFLER, Leslie
President & Parliament : a short history of the French Presidency / Leslie Derfler. — Boca Raton : University Presses of Florida, c1983. — ix, 286 p.. — *"A Florida Atlantic University book.". — Includes index. — Bibliography: p. 273-279*

FRANCE — Race relations
GALLISSOT, René
Misère de l'antiracisme : racisme et identité nationale : le défi de l'immigration / René Gallissot. — Paris : Editions de l'Arcantère, 1985. — 154p

FRANCE — Relations — Germany (West)
WILLIS, F. Roy
France, Germany and the new Europe, 1945—1963 / F. Roy Willis. — Stanford : Stanford University Press ; London : Oxford University Press, 1965. — xiv,397p. — *Bibliography: p373-387*

FRANCE — Relations — Indian Ocean Region
CAMPREDON, Jean-Pierre
France, océan Indien, mer Rouge : études / menées sous la responsabilité de Jean-Pierre Campredon et Jean-Jacques Schweitzer. — Paris : Fondation pour les études de défense nationale, 1986. — 449p. — *Bibliography: p443-445*

FRANCE — Relations — Japan
CALLIES, Albane
France-Japan : confrontation culturelle dans les entreprises mixtes / Albane Callies. — Paris : Librairie des Méridiens, 1986. — 208p. — *Bibliography: p199-206*

FRANCE — Relations — Red Sea
CAMPREDON, Jean-Pierre
France, océan Indien, mer Rouge : études / menées sous la responsabilité de Jean-Pierre Campredon et Jean-Jacques Schweitzer. — Paris : Fondation pour les études de défense nationale, 1986. — 449p. — *Bibliography: p443-445*

FRANCE — Relations — Spain
SERRANO, Carlos
L'enjeu espagnol : PCF et guerre d'Espagne / Carlos Serrano. — Paris : Messidor/Éditions sociales, 1987. — 292p

FRANCE — Relations (general) with Germany
WILLIS, F. Roy
France, Germany and the New Europe, 1945—1967 / F. Roy Willis. — Rev. and expanded ed. — Stanford, Calif. : Stanford University Press ; London : Oxford University Press, 1968. — 431 p

FRANCE — Rural conditions
BRAUDEL, Fernand
L'identité de la France / Fernand Braudel. — Paris : Arthaud-Flammarion
2: Les hommes et les choses
[2]: Une "économie paysanne" jusqu'au XXe siècle. — 1986. — 476p

GROUPE POUR LA FONDATION DE L'UNION DES COMMUNISTES FRANÇAIS (marxiste-léniniste)
Le livre des paysans pauvres : 5 années de travail maoïste dans une campagne française / Groupe pour la fondation de l'Union des communistes de France marxiste-léniniste. — Paris : F. Maspero, 1976. — 302 p.. — (Collection Yenan) (Série Propositions et documents)

LE ROY LADURIE, Emmanuel
The French peasantry 1450-1660 / Emmanuel Le Roy Ladurie ; translated by Alan Sheridan. — Aldershot : Scolar, 1987. — 447p. — *Translation of: Les masses profondes. — Bibliography: p431-436. — Includes index*

FRANCE — Social conditions
Journal Officiel de la Republique Francaise: avis et rapports du Conseil Economique. — Paris : Government Printer, 1948-1959. — *Irregular. — Continued by: Journal Officiel de la Republique: avis et rapports du Conseil Economique et Sociale*

Journal Officiel [de la Republique Francaise]: avis et rapports du Conseil Economique et Sociale. — Paris : Government Printer, 1959-. — *From Jan 1986 on microfiche. — Continues: Journal Officiel de la Republique Francaise: avis et rapports du Conseil Economique*

FRANCE — Social conditions — 19th century
STONE, Judith F.
The search for social peace : reform legislation in France, 1890-1914 / Judith F. Stone. — Albany : State University of New York Press, c1985. — p. cm

FRANCE — Social conditions — 1945-
Géopolitiques des régions françaises / sous la direction de Yves Lacoste ; Yves Lacoste ... [et al.]. — Paris : Fayard, 1986. — 3v. — *Contents: t.1. France septentrionale - t.2. La façade occidentale - t.3. La France du sud-est*

HANLEY, David
Contemporary France : politics and society since 1945 / D.L. Hanley, A.P. Kerr and N.H. Waites. — Rev. ed. — London : Routledge & Kegan Paul, 1984. — xii,372p. — *Previous ed.: 1979. — Includes index*

[Institutions sociales de la France. English]. The Social institutions of France : translations from the first French edition = [Les institutions sociales de la France] / coordinated by Roy Evans with the assistance of Patricia G. Evans. — New York : Gordon and Breach, c1983. — xxii, 802 p.. — : *"Original French work was produced under the direction of Pierre Laroque"--P. v. — Includes bibliographical references*

SAVY, Michel
Atlas des français / Michel Savy, Pierre Beckouche. — [Paris] : Hachette, c1985. — 331p. — (Collection Pluriel). — *Bibliography: p[311-312]*

FRANCE — Social life and customs

DEVLIN, Judith
The superstitious mind : French peasants and the supernatural in the nineteenth century / Judith Devlin. — New Haven, Conn. : Yale University Press, 1987. — p .cm. — *Includes index. — Bibliography: p*

FRANCE — Social life and customs — 1328-1600

MUCHEMBLED, Robert
[Culture populaire et culture des élites dans la France moderne. English]. Popular culture and elite culture in France, 1400-1750 / Robert Muchembled ; translated by Lydia Cochrane. — Baton Rouge : Louisiana State University Press, c1985. — p. cm. — *Translation of: Culture populaire et culture des élites dans la France moderne. — Includes bibliographical references and index*

SCHALK, Ellery
From valor to pedigree : ideas of nobility in France in the sixteenth and seventeenth centuries / by Ellery Schalk. — Princeton, N.J. ; Guildford : Princeton University Press, c1986. — xvii,242p. — *Bibliography: p223-231. — Includes index*

FRANCE — Social life and customs — 17th-18th centuries

MUCHEMBLED, Robert
[Culture populaire et culture des élites dans la France moderne. English]. Popular culture and elite culture in France, 1400-1750 / Robert Muchembled ; translated by Lydia Cochrane. — Baton Rouge : Louisiana State University Press, c1985. — p. cm. — *Translation of: Culture populaire et culture des élites dans la France moderne. — Includes bibliographical references and index*

SCHALK, Ellery
From valor to pedigree : ideas of nobility in France in the sixteenth and seventeenth centuries / by Ellery Schalk. — Princeton, N.J. ; Guildford : Princeton University Press, c1986. — xvii,242p. — *Bibliography: p223-231. — Includes index*

FRANCE — Social policy

ELWITT, Sanford
The Third Republic defended : bourgeois reform in France, 1880-1914 / Sanford Elwitt. — Baton Rouge : Louisiana State University Press, c1986. — xvi, 304 p.. — *Includes bibliographical references and index*

[Institutions sociales de la France. English]. The Social institutions of France : translations from the first French edition = [Les institutions sociales de la France] / coordinated by Roy Evans with the assistance of Patricia G. Evans. — New York : Gordon and Breach, c1983. — xxii, 802 p.. — : *"Original French work was produced under the direction of Pierre Laroque"--P. v. — Includes bibliographical references*

Les politiques sociales transversales : une méthodologie d'évaluation de leurs effets locaux. — Paris : La Documentation Française, 1986. — 178p. — *Président: Jean-Claude Ray*

FRANCE — Statistics — Bibliography

FRANCE. Institut National de la Statistique et des Etudes Economiques
Catalogue / Institut National de la Statistique et des Etudes Economiques. — Paris : INSEE, 1986-. — *Annual*

FRANCE — Statistics, Vital

GUILLOT, Françoise
Recensement général de la population de 1982. — [Paris] : INSEE. — *Sondage au 1/4. — RP 82/8*
Les populations des dom-tom en France métropolitaine / par Françoise Guillot, Solange Hémery et Claude-Valentin Marie. — 1985. — 157p

KERROMES, Armelle
Tableaux normalisés simplifiés par région et département / Armelle Kerromes. — [Paris] : INSEE, 1984. — 273p. — (Archives et documents / Institut National de la Statistique et des Études Économiques ; no.100)

FRANCE — Politics and government

Journal Officiel de la Republique Francaise: documents administratifs. — Paris : Government Printer, 1959-. — *Irregular*

FRANCE — Census, 1982

Recensement général de la population de 1982. — [Paris : Institut national de la statistique et des études économiques, 1985]
Résultats du sondage au 1/4 : population, emploi, ménages, familles, logements
Ville de Paris. — 540p

FRANCE — Foreign relations

COHEN, Samy
La monarchie nucléaire : les Coulisses de la politique étrangère sous la Ve République / Samy Cohen. — Paris : Hachette, [1986]. — 271p

FRANCE — Foreign relations — Great Britain

BLACK, Jeremy
Natural and necessary enemies : Anglo-French relations in the eighteenth century / Jeremy Black. — London : Duckworth, 1986. — [236]p. — *Includes index*

FRANCE. Armée — Biography

BAUMONT, Maurice
Bazaine : les secrets d'un maréchal 1811/1888. — Paris : Imprimere nationale, 1978. — 425p. — (Collection "Personnages"). — *Includes index. — Bibliography: p401-406*

FRANCE. Armée — History — 20th century

DOUGHTY, Robert A
The seeds of disaster : the development of French Army doctrine, 1919-1939 / Robert Allan Doughty. — Hamden, Conn. : Archon Books, 1985. — xi, 232p. — *Includes index. — Bibliography: p.217-226*

FRANCE. Assemblée Consultative Provisoire, [1943-45]

Journal officiel de la Republique Francaise: documents de l'Assemblée Consultative Provisoire. — Paris : Government Printer, 1943-1945. — *Irregular. — Continued by: Journal officiel de la Republique Francaise: documents de l'Assemblée Nationale Constituante. — Nov. 1943-July 1944 published in Alger*

FRANCE. Assemblée de L'Union Francaise, [Dec.1947-58]

Journal Officiel de la Republique Française: debats: Assemblée de L'Union Française. — Paris : Government Printer, 1947-58. — *Irregular*

FRANCE. Assemblée de L'Union Francaise, Dec.1947-58

Journal officiel de la Republique Francaise: documents Assemblée de L'Union Française. — Paris : Government Printer, 1947-1958

FRANCE. Assemblée Nationale — Biography

Guide du nouveau pouvoir : cabinets ministériels et parlement biographies et adresses des membres du gouvernement[...] / [réalisé sous la direction de Jean-François Doumic, assisté d'Eduardo Olivares]. — [2nd ed]. — Paris : Jean-François Doumic, 1986. — 243p. — (Supplément à la Lettre de la communication ; no.156)

FRANCE. Assemblée Nationale — Elections,1876

LOGRE, Bernard
Jozon-Menier : récit d'une campagne électorale : les élections législatives de 1876 dans l'arrondissement de Meaux / Bernard Logre. — Dammarie-les-Lys : Editions Amatteis, 1986. — 111p

FRANCE. Assemblée Nationale Constituante, [1945-46]

Journal officiel de la Republique Francaise: documents de l'Assemblée Nationale Constituante. — Paris : Government Printer, 1945-1946. — *Irregular. — Continues: Journal officiel de la Republique Francaise: documents de l'Assemblée Consultative Provisoire. Continued by: Journal officiel de la Republique Francaise: documents parlementaires: Assemblée Nationale*

FRANCE. Caisse Nationale des Allocations Familiales

Statistiques: prestations de logement / Caisse Nationale des Allocations Familiales. — Paris : C.N.A.F., 1981/1982-. — *Annual*

FRANCE. Conseil Economique

Journal Officiel de la Republique Francaise: avis et rapports du Conseil Economique. — Paris : Government Printer, 1948-1959. — *Irregular. — Continued by: Journal Officiel de la Républiquе: avis et rapports du Conseil Economique et Sociale*

FRANCE. Conseil économique et social

FRAYSSINET, Jean
Le Conseil économique et social / Jean Frayssinet. — Paris : La Documentation française, 1986. — 184p. — (Notes et études documentaires ; no.4807)

FRANCE. Haut Conseil du Secteur Public

FRANCE. Haut Conseil du Secteur Public
Rapport. — Paris : Documentation Française, 1984-. — *Annual*

FRANCE. Institut National de la Statistique et des Etudes Economiques — Bibliography

FRANCE. Institut National de la Statistique et des Etudes Economiques
Catalogue / Institut National de la Statistique et des Etudes Economiques. — Paris : INSEE, 1986-. — *Annual*

FRANCE. Ministère de la Justice — Statistics

Annuaire statistique de la justice / Ministère de la Justice. — Paris : Documentation Française, 1982-. — *Annual*

FRANCE.. Ministère de l'Économie, des Finances et de la Privatisation

FRANCE.. Ministère de l'Économie, des Finances et de la Privatisation
Les notes bleues / Ministère de l'Économie, des Finances et de la Privatisation. — Paris : France. Ministère de l'Économie, des Finances et de la Privatisation, 1986. — *Fortnightly*

FRANCE. Parlement — Biography

Guide du nouveau pouvoir : cabinets ministériels et parlement biographies et adresses des membres du gouvernement[...] / [réalisé sous la direction de Jean-François Doumic, assisté d'Eduardo Olivares]. — [2nd ed]. — Paris : Jean-François Doumic, 1986. — 243p. — (Supplément à la Lettre de la communication ; no.156)

FRANCE. Parlement. Assemblée Constituante

Journal Officiel de la Republique Francaise: debats de l'Assemblée Constituante. — Paris : Government Printer, 1945-1946. — *Continues: Journal Officiel de la Republique Francaise: debats de L'Assemblée Consultative Provisoire. Continued by: Journal Officiel de la Republique Francaise: debats parlementaires: Assemblée Nationale*

FRANCE. Parlement. Assemblée Consultative Provisoire

Journal Officiel de la Republique Francaise: debats de l'Assemblée consultative provisoire. — Alger : Government Printer, 1944-1945. — *Irregular. — Continued by: Journal Officiel de la Republique Francaise: debats de l'Assemblée Constituante*

FRANCE. Parlement. Assemblée Nationale
Journal Officiel de la République Francaise: debats parlementaires: Assemblée Nationale. — Paris, 1946- : Government Printer. — *From 1986 on microfiche.* — *Continues: Journal Officiel de la République Francaise: debats de l'Assemblée Constituante*

FRANCE. Parlement. Senat
Journal officiel de la République Française: débats parlementaires: Sénat. — Paris : Direction des Journaux Officiels, 1958-. — *Irregular*

Journal officiel de la République Française: [documents]: Sénat. — Paris : Government Printer, 1958/59-. — *Irregular.* — *Title varies*

FRANCE. Parlement (Paris) — History
STONE, Bailey
The French parlements and the crisis of the old regime / Bailey Stone. — Chapel Hill ; London : University of North Carolina Press, c1986. — x, 326 p.. — *Includes index.* — *Bibliography: p. [303]-317*

FRANCE. Présidence — Biography
Guide du nouveau pouvoir : cabinets ministériels et parlement biographies et adresses des membres du gouvernement[...] / [réalisé sous la direction de Jean-François Doumic, assisté d'Eduardo Olivares]. — [2nd ed]. — Paris : Jean-François Doumic, 1986. — 243p. — (Supplément à la Lettre de la communication ; no.156)

FRANCE. President
MASSOT, Jean
La Présidence de la République en France : vingt ans d'élection au suffrage universel 1965-1985 / par Jean Massot. — Paris : La Documentation française, 1986. — 195p. — (Notes et études documentaires ; no.4801). — *Bibliography: p187-189*

FRANCE, PUBLIC — Hungary
State budget / Ministry of Finance, Hungary. — Budapest : Ministry of Finance, 1983-. — (Public finance in Hungary). — *Annual*

FRANCE, SOUTHERN — History
JOHNSON, Hubert C
The Midi in revolution : a study of regional political diversity, 1789-1793 / Hubert C. Johnson. — Princeton, N.J. : Princeton University Press, c1986. — viii, 309 p.. — *Includes index.* — *Bibliography: p. [281]-292*

FRANCHISES (RETAIL TRADE)
KACKER, M. P
Transatlantic trends in retailing : takeovers and flow of know-how / Madhav P. Kacker. — Westport, Conn. : Quorum Books, c1985. — p. cm. — *Includes index.* — *Bibliography: p*

FRANCHISES (RETAIL TRADE) — Great Britain
ADAMS, J. N. (John Norman)
Franchising : practice and precedents in business format franchising / John Adams, K.V. Prichard Jones. — 2nd ed. — London : Butterworths, 1987. — xxxvii,409p. — *Previous ed.: 1981.* — *Includes index*

FRANCO BAHAMONDE, FRANCISCO
GARRIGA, Ramón
Franco-Serrano Suñer : un drama político / Ramón Garriga Alemany. — Barcelona : Planeta, 1986. — 209p

SUÁREZ FERNÁNDEZ, Luis
Francisco Franco y su tiempo / Luis Suárez Fernández. — Madrid : Fundación Nacional Francisco Franco, 1984. — 8 v.. — (Azor ; núm. 2). — *Includes indexes.* — *Bibliography: v. 1, p. 37-51*

TUSELL GÓMEZ, Javier
Franco y Mussolini : la política española durante la segunda guerra mundial / Xavier Tusell, Genoveva García Queipo de Llano. — Barcelona : Planeta, 1985. — 299p. — (Espejo de España ; 109). — *Bibliography: p293-296*

FRANCO-GERMAN WAR, 1870-1871
MILLMAN, Richard
British foreign policy and the coming of the Franco-Prussian War / Richard Millman. — Oxford : Clarendon Press, 1965. — 238p

FRANCOISM
CÁMARA VILLAR, Gregorio
Nacional - Catolicismo y escuela : la socialización política del franquismo : 1936-1951 / Gregorio Camara Villar. — [Jaén] : Hesperia, c1984. — 421p. — (Colección "Ciencias sociales"). — *Bibliography:p411-421*

CIERVA, Ricardo de la
Pro y contra Franco : franquismo y antifranquismo / Ricardo de la Cierva [y] Sergio Vilar. — Barcelona : Planeta, 1985. — 279p. — (Espejo de España ; 114)

FERNÁNDEZ, Carlos
Franquismo y transición politica en Galicia : (apuntes para una historia de nuestro pasado reciente) 1939-1979 / Carlos Fernández ; con la colaboración de Carlos Luis Rodríguez. — La Coruña : Ediciós do Castro, 1985. — 476p. — (Documentos para a historia contemporánea de Galicia). — *Bibliography: p469-476*

FERNÁNDEZ, Carlos
Tensiones militares durante el franquismo / Carlos Fernández. — Barcelona : Plaza & Janes Editores, 1985. — 223p. — *Bibliography: p[219]-223*

FERRANDO BADÍA, Juan
El regimen de Franco : un enfoque politico-juridico / Juan Ferrando Badía. — Madrid : Tecnos, 1984. — 302p

JÁUREGUI, Fernando
Crónica del antifranquismo / Fernando Jáuregui, Pedro Vega. — Barcelona : Argos Vergara
2. — 1984. — 428p

SUÁREZ FERNÁNDEZ, Luis
Francisco Franco y su tiempo / Luis Suárez Fernández. — Madrid : Fundación Nacional Francisco Franco, 1984. — 8 v.. — (Azor ; núm. 2). — *Includes indexes.* — *Bibliography: v. 1, p. 37-51*

FRANCOISM — History — Philosophy
MORODO, Raúl
Los orígines ideologicos del franquismo : Acción Española / Raúl Morodo. — Madrid : Alianza, 1985. — 227p. — (Alianza universidad ; 429)

FRANKENTHAL, KÄTE
FRANKENTHAL, Käte
Jüdin, Intellektuelle, Sozialistin : Lebenserinnerungen einer Ärztin in Deutschland und im Exil / Käte Frankenthal ; herausgegeben von Kathleen M. Pearle und Stephan Leibfried. — Frankfurt/Main : Campus, 1985. — 250p

FRANKFURT SCHOOL OF SOCIOLOGY
FAY, Brian
Critical social science : liberation and its limits / Brian Fay. — Ithaca, N.Y. : Cornell University Press, [1987]. — p. cm. — *Includes index.* — *Bibliography: p*

FRANKLIN, BENJAMIN
WRIGHT, Esmond
Franklin of Philadelphia / Esmond Wright. — Cambridge, Mass. : Belknap Press of Harvard University Press, 1986. — p. cm. — *Includes index.* — *Bibliography: p*

FRANKS — France — Kings and rulers
NELSON, Janet
Politics and ritual in early medieval Europe / Janet L. Nelson. — London : Hambledon, 1985. — [440]p. — (History series ; 42). — *Includes index*

FRAUD
Economic crime : programs for future research / Dan Magnusson, editor. — Stockholm : National Council for Crime Prevention, Sweden, 1985. — 156p. — (Report / Brottsforebygganderadet (Sweden) ; no.15)

FRAUD — Canada
EWART, J. Douglas
Criminal fraud / J. Douglas Ewart. — Toronto : Carswell, 1986. — xv, 182 p.. — (Carswell's criminal law series). — *Includes bibliographical references and index*

FRAUD INVESTIGATION
GREAT BRITAIN. Department of Health and Social Security
Evidence by the Department of Health and Social Security to the Royal Commission on Criminal Procedure. — [London : the Department, 1978]. — 13,4p

GREAT BRITAIN. Department of Health and Social Security. Co-ordinating Committee on Abuse
Second report : action taken against social security fraud and abuse from September 1977-December 1978, and work still in hand / by the Coordinating Committee on Abuse. — [London : the Department, 1979]. — 14,3p

FREDERICK II, King of Prussia
GOOCH, G. P.
Frederick the Great : the ruler, the writer, the man. — London : Longmans, 1947. — viii,363p

FREE PORTS AND ZONES — China
China's special economic zones : policies, problems, and prospects / editors, Y.C. Jao , C.K. Leung ; contributors, C.H. Chai ... [et al.]. — Hong Hong ; New York : Oxford University Press, 1986. — x, 249 p.. — *Includes bibliographies and index*

FREE PRESBYTERIAN CHURCH OF ULSTER — History
BRUCE, Steve
God save Ulster : the religion and politics of Paisleyism / Steve Bruce. — Oxford : Clarendon, 1986. — xv,308p. — *Includes index*

FREE THOUGHT — Spain — History
ALVAREZ LÁZARO, Pedro F.
Masoneña y librepensamiento en la España de la Restauración : (aproximación historica) / Pedro F. Alvarez Lázaro. — Madrid : UPCM, 1985. — xxxi,412p. — (Publicaciones de la Universidad Pontificia Comillas. Estudios ; 33). — *Bibliography: p400-4*

FREE TRADE
The Free trade papers / edited by Duncan Cameron. — Toronto : James Lorimer & Company, 1986. — xlix,227p

FREE TRADE AND PROTECTION
The Free trade papers / edited by Duncan Cameron. — Toronto : James Lorimer & Company, 1986. — xlix,227p

GENERAL AGREEMENT ON TARIFFS AND TRADE (Organization)
Text of the General Agreement. — Geneva : the Organization, 1986. — vi,96p

GREAT BRITAIN. Parliament. House of Commons. Library. Research Division
Alternative economic strategies / Christopher Barclay, Paul Hutt. — [London] : the Division, 1980. — 46p. — (Background paper ; no.82). — *Bibliography: p38-46*

GREAT BRITAIN. Parliament. House of Commons. Library. Research Division
The dangers of a world free trade / Christopher Barclay, Alan Sutherland. — [London] : the Division, 1987. — 21p. — (Background paper ; no.201)

GREAT BRITAIN. Parliament. House of Commons. Library. Research Division
Free trade and international GATT negotiations / Christopher Barclay. — [London] : the Division, 1986. — 25p. — (Background paper ; no.180)

GRJEBINE, André
La nouvelle économie internationale : de la crise mondiale au développement autocentré / André Grjebine. — Paris : Presses Universitaires de France, 1980. — 326p

FREE TRADE AND PROTECTION
continuation

Protection and competition in international trade : essays in honour of W.M. Corden / edited by Henryk Kierzkowski. — Oxford : Basil Blackwell, 1987. — [256]p. — *Includes index*

RAYACK, Elton
Not so free to choose : the political economy of Milton Friedman and Ronald Reagan / Elton Rayack. — New York : Praeger, 1987. — x, 215 p.. — *Includes index. — Bibliography: p. 203-208*

The texts of the Tokyo Round Agreements. — Geneva : General Agreement on Tariffs and Trade, 1986. — vii,208p

WONNACOTT, Paul
The United States and Canada : the quest for freer trade : an examination of selected issues / Paul Wonnacott ; with an appendix by John Williamson. — Washington, DC : Institute for International Economics, 1987. — p. cm. — (Policy analyses in international economics ; 16). — *Bibliography: p*

WONNACOTT, R. J.
Selected new developments in international trade theory / R. J. Wonnacott. — Montreal : The Institute for Research on Public Policy/LÍnstitut de recherches politiques, 1984. — xxi,40p. — (Essays in international economics). — *Prefatory material in English and French. — Bibliography: p27-29*

FREE TRADE AND PROTECTION — Congresses

The legal framework for Canada-United States trade / edited by Maureen Irish and Emily F. Carasco. — Toronto : Carswell, 1987. — xxxviii,275p

FREE TRADE AND PROTECTION — Free trade

C. D. HOWE INSTITUTE
Policy harmonization : the effects of a Canadian-American free trade area / C. D. Howe Institute. — Toronto : the Institute, 1986. — xv,164p. — *Includes bibliographical references*

HART, Michael
Some thoughts on Canada-United States sectoral free trade / Michael Hart. — Montreal, Quebec : Institute for Research on Public Policy, c1985. — xiii, 54 p.. — (Essays in international economics). — *Bibliography: p. 43-44*

LAWRENCE, Robert Z.
Saving free trade : a pragmatic approach / Robert Z. Lawrence and Robert E. Litan. — Washington, D.C. : Brookings Institution, 1986. — p. cm. — *Includes bibliographical references and index*

FREE TRADE AND PROTECTION — History — 19th century

FORSTER, Jakob Johann Benjamin
A conjunction of interests : business, politics, and tariffs, 1825-1879 / Ben Forster. — Toronto ; Buffalo : University of Toronto Press, c1986. — vi, 288 p.. — (The State and economic life ; 8). — *Includes index. — Bibliography: p. [259]-276*

FREE TRADE AND PROTECTION — Protection

The new protectionist threat to world welfare / edited by Dominick Salvatore. — new York : Elsevier Science, 1986. — xvi,581p

WALDMANN, Raymond J
Managed trade : the new competition between nations / Raymond J. Waldmann. — Cambridge, Mass. : Ballinger Pub. Co., [1986]. — p. cm. — *Includes index. — Bibliography: p*

FREE TRADE AND PROTECTION — Protection — Case studies

HUFBAUER, Gary Clyde
Trade protection in the United States : thirty-one case studies / Gary Clyde Hufbauer, assisted by Diane T. Berliner, Kimberly Ann Elliott. — Washington, DC : Institute for International Economics, 1985. — p. cm. — *Bibliography: p*

FREE WILL AND DETERMINISM

KANE, R
Free will and values / R. Kane. — Albany : State University of New York Press, c1985. — vii, 229 p.. — (SUNY series in philosophy). — *Includes indexes. — Bibliography: p. 206-218*

FREE WILL AND DETERMINISM — History — 20th century

ABOULAFIA, Mitchell
The mediating self : Mead, Sartre, and self-determination / Mitchell Aboulafia. — New Haven : Yale University Press, c1986. — xvii, 139p. — *Includes index. — Bibliography: p.127-131*

FREEDMEN — Education

RICHARDSON, Joe Martin
Christian reconstruction : the American Missionary Association and Southern Blacks, 1861-1890 / Joe M. Richardson. — Athens : University of Georgia Press, c1986. — ix, 348 p., [16] p. of plates. — *Includes index. — Bibliography: p. 323-335*

FREEDMEN — Religion

RICHARDSON, Joe Martin
Christian reconstruction : the American Missionary Association and Southern Blacks, 1861-1890 / Joe M. Richardson. — Athens : University of Georgia Press, c1986. — ix, 348 p., [16] p. of plates. — *Includes index. — Bibliography: p. 323-335*

FREEDMEN — Georgia

DUNCAN, Russell
Freedom's shore : Tunis Campbell and the Georgia freedmen / by Russell Duncan. — Athens : University of Georgia Press, c1986. — p. cm. — *Includes index. — Bibliography: p*

FREEDOM OF ASSOCIATION

VON PRONDZYNSKI, Ferdinand
Freedom of association and industrial relations : a comparative study / Ferdinand von Prondzynski. — London : Mansell, 1987. — [250]p. — (Studies in labour and social law). — *Includes bibliography and index*

FREEDOM OF ASSOCIATION — Digests

INTERNATIONAL LABOUR OFFICE. Freedom of Association Committee
Freedom of association : digest of decisions and principles of the Freedom of Association Committee of the governing body of the ILO. — 3rd ed. — Geneva : International Labour Office, 1985. — xii, 140 [i.e. 262] p.

FREEDOM OF INFORMATION

GARCIA ARIAS, Ludivina
Report of the Sub-Committee on the free flow of information and people / Ludivina Garcia Arias. — Brussels : North Atlantic Assembly, 1986. — i,24p

MEHRA, Achal
Free flow of information : a new paradigm / Achal Mehra. — New York : Greenwood Press, 1986. — xiii, 225 p.. — (Contributions to the study of mass media and communications ; no. 7). — *Includes index. — Bibliography: p. [209]-214*

FREEDOM OF INFORMATION — Bibliography

GREAT BRITAIN. Civil Service Department. Central Management Library
Public access to government information. — London : the Library, 1977. — 3p. — (Policy science documentation. Bibliography series ; B8)

FREEDOM OF INFORMATION — Legal status, laws, etc. — Great Britain

GREAT BRITAIN. Parliament. House of Commons. Library. Research Division
Freedom of Information Bill [Bill 25, 1980/81] / [Margaret M. Camsell]. — [London] : the Division, 1981. — 12p. — (Reference sheet ; no.81/6). — *Bibliographical references: p12*

FREEDOM OF INFORMATION — Canada

Canada's new access laws : public and personal access to government documents / edited by Donald C. Rowat. — Ottawa : Carleton University, 1983. — x,166p. — *"The essays in this volume were written by [...] graduate students in a special seminar on Canada's new access laws given in the winter term, 1983 [at Carleton University, Ottawa]". — Includes references. — Bibliography: p159-165*

The media, the courts and the Charter / edited by Philip Anisman and Allen M. Linden. — Toronto : Carswell, 1986. — xiv,521p

FREEDOM OF INFORMATION — Colombia

GÓMEZ JARAMILLO, Juan Carlos
El acceso público a la información estatal y el derecho de petición de informaciones / Juan Carlos Gómez Jaramillo. — Bogotá : Facultad de Ciencias Juridicas y Socio-Economicas, Pontificia Universidad Javeriana, 1984. — 115p. — *"Trabajo de Grado para optar al título de Abogado". — Bibliography: p[119-121]*

FREEDOM OF INFORMATION — Great Britain

BIRKINSHAW, Patrick
Open government : freedom of information and local government : a study conducted for the Local Government Legal Society Trust and the Society of Town Clerks' Education and Research Trust / Patrick Birkinshaw. — [London] : Local Government Legal Society Trust in association with the Society of Town Clerks' Education and Research Trust, 1985. — 84p

GREAT BRITAIN. Parliament. House of Commons. Library. Research Division
Official secrets and open government / [H. Rosamund Coates]. — [London] : the Division, 1979. — 32p. — (Reference sheet ; no79/1)

FREEDOM OF INFORMATION — Great Britain — Bibliography

GREAT BRITAIN. Civil Service Department. Central Management Library
Public access to government information : a bibliography. — London : the Library, 1979. — [12]p. — (Policy science documentation. Bibliography series ; B8) (Policy science documentation. Bibliography series ; B25) (Policy science documentation. Bibliography series ; B29). — *Part I, November 1977; Part II, March 1979; Part III, August 1979*

FREEDOM OF INFORMATION — United States

DEMAC, Donna A
Keeping America uninformed : government secrecy in the 1980's / Donna A. Demac ; preface by Ben H. Bagdikian. — New York : Pilgrim Press, c1984. — xii, 180 p.. — *Includes index. — Bibliography: p. 169-174*

MEHRA, Achal
Free flow of information : a new paradigm / Achal Mehra. — New York : Greenwood Press, 1986. — xiii, 225 p.. — (Contributions to the study of mass media and communications ; no. 7). — *Includes index. — Bibliography: p. [209]-214*

FREEDOM OF INFORMATION BILL 1980-81

GREAT BRITAIN. Parliament. House of Commons. Library. Research Division
Freedom of Information Bill [Bill 25, 1980/81] / [Margaret M. Camsell]. — [London] : the Division, 1981. — 12p. — (Reference sheet ; no.81/6). — *Bibliographical references: p12*

FREEDOM OF MOVEMENT — European Economic Community countries

CRAYENCOUR, J.—P. de
The professions in the European Community : towards freedom of movement and mutual recognition of qualifications / J.—P. de Crayencour. — Luxembourg : Office for Official Publications of the European Communities, 1981. — 137p. — (The European perspectives series)

LASOK, Dominik
The professions and services in the European Economic Community / by D. Lasok. — Deventer, The Netherlands ; New York : Kluwer Law and Taxation Publishers, c1986. — p. cm

FREEDOM OF MOVEMENT (INTERNATIONAL LAW)

GARCIA ARIAS, Ludivina
Report of the Sub-Committee on the free flow of information and people / Ludivina Garcia Arias. — Brussels : North Atlantic Assembly, 1986. — i,24p

FREEDOM OF SPEECH — Addresses, essays, lectures

SALISBURY, Harrison Evans
The book enchained / Harrison E. Salisbury. — Washington : Library of Congress, 1984. — 9p. — (The Center for the Book viewpoint series ; 10). — "A lecture sponsored by The Center for the Book in the Library of Congress and the Authors League of America; presented at the Library of Congress September 28, 1983."

FREEDOM OF SPEECH — Australia

Freedom of expression and section 116 of the Broadcasting and Television Act 1942. — Canberra : Australian Government Publishing Service, 1985. — vii,22p. — (Report / Human Rights Commission ; no.16)

FREEDOM OF SPEECH — United States

The First Amendment : the legacy of George Mason / edited by T. Daniel Shumate. — Fairfax : George Mason University Press ; London : Associated University Presses, c1985. — 201 p.. — (The George Mason lectures). — Includes bibliographies and index

PELL, Eve
The big chill : how the Reagan administration, corporate America, and religious conservatives are subverting free speech and the public's right to know / Eve Pell, with research assistance by Seth Rosenfeld. — Boston : Beacon Press, c1984. — x, 269 p.. — Includes index. — Bibliography: p. [251]-254

RICHARDS, David A. J
Toleration and the Constitution / David A.J. Richards. — New York : Oxford University Press, 1986. — p. cm. — Bibliography: p

ROME, Edwin P
Corporate and commercial free speech : first amendment protection of expression in business / Edwin P. Rome and William H. Roberts. — Westport, Conn. : Quorum Books, c1985. — p. cm. — Includes index. — Bibliography: p

SMITH, Donald L.
Zechariah Chafee, Jr., defender of liberty and law / Donald L. Smith. — Cambridge, Mass. : Harvard University Press, 1986. — x, 355 p.. — Includes index. — Bibliography: p. [283]-343

SPITZER, Matthew Laurence
Seven dirty words and six other stories : controlling the content of print and broadcast / Matthew Laurence Spitzer. — New Haven : Yale University Press, 1986. — p. cm. — Includes index

FREEDOM OF THE PRESS

Pressefreiheit / herausgegeben von Jürgen Wilke. — Darmstadt : Wissenschaftliche Buchgesellschaft, 1984. — vii,525p. — (Wege der Forschung ; Bd.625). — Bibliography: p493-521

FREEDOM OF THE PRESS — Canada

The media, the courts and the Charter / edited by Philip Anisman and Allen M. Linden. — Toronto : Carswell, 1986. — xiv,521p

FREEDOM OF THE PRESS — Great Britain

HOLMES, Deborah
Governing the press : media freedom in the U.S. and Great Britain / Deborah Holmes. — Boulder : Westview Press, 1986. — xi, 107 p.. — (A Westview special study). — Includes index. — Bibliography: p. 93-102

FREEDOM OF THE PRESS — India — History

SANKHDHER, Brijendra Mohan
Press, politics, and public opinion in India : dynamics of modernization and social transformation / B.M. Sankhdher ; foreword by Amba Prasad. — New Delhi : Deep & Deep Publications, c1984. — xxiv, 400 p.. — Summary: On the role of the press in India, 1780-1835. — Includes index. — Bibliography: p. [353]-388

FREEDOM OF THE PRESS — Spain — Cádiz (Province) — History — 19th century

LA PARRA LÓPEZ, Emilio
La libertad de prensa en las Cortes de Cádiz / Emilio La Parra López. — Valencia : NAU llibres, 1984. — 130p. — Includes references

FREEDOM OF THE PRESS — Tanzania

KONDE, Hadji
Press freedom in Tanzania / Hadji Konde. — Arusha [Tanzania] : Eastern Africa Publications, 1984. — x, 242 p.

FREEDOM OF THE PRESS — United States

The First Amendment : the legacy of George Mason / edited by T. Daniel Shumate. — Fairfax : George Mason University Press ; London : Associated University Presses, c1985. — 201 p.. — (The George Mason lectures). — Includes bibliographies and index

HOLMES, Deborah
Governing the press : media freedom in the U.S. and Great Britain / Deborah Holmes. — Boulder : Westview Press, 1986. — xi, 107 p.. — (A Westview special study). — Includes index. — Bibliography: p. 93-102

PELL, Eve
The big chill : how the Reagan administration, corporate America, and religious conservatives are subverting free speech and the public's right to know / Eve Pell, with research assistance by Seth Rosenfeld. — Boston : Beacon Press, c1984. — x, 269 p.. — Includes index. — Bibliography: p. [251]-254

FREEMASONRY — United States — History

DEMOTT, Bobby J
Freemasonry in American culture and society / Bobby J. Demott. — Lanham Md. ; London : University Press of America, c1986. — xiv, 346 p.. — Includes bibliographies and index

FREEMASONS — Soviet Union — History — 20th century

BERBEROVA, N.
Liudi i lozhi : russkie masony XX stoletiia / N. Berberova. — New York : Russica Publishers, 1986. — 298p. — Bibliography: p271-285

FREEMASONS — Spain — History

ALVAREZ LÁZARO, Pedro F.
Masonería y librepensamiento en la España de la Restauración : (aproximación historica) / Pedro F. Alvarez Lázaro. — Madrid : UPCM, 1985. — xxxi,412p. — (Publicaciones de la Universidad Pontificia Comillas. Estudios ; 33). — Bibliography: p400-4

GÓMEZ MOLLEDA, María Dolores
La masonería en la crisis española del siglo XX / María Dolores Gómez Molleda. — Madrid : Taurus, 1986. — 537p

FREEMASONS — Spain — Catalonia — History

SÁNCHEZ I FERRÉ, Pere
La lògia lealtad : un exemple de maçoneria catalana (1869-1939) / Pere Sánchez i Ferré. — Barcelona : Editorial Alta Fulla, 1985. — 211p. — (Hores d'Estudi ; 2). — Bibliography: p207-211

FREGE, GOTTLOB

DUMMETT, Michael
The interpretation of Frege's philosophy / Michael Dummett. — London : Duckworth, 1981. — xviii,621p. — Bibliography: p604-612. — Includes index

FREIBURG IM BREISGAU REGION (GERMANY) — Social conditions

SCOTT, Tom, 1947-
Freiburg and the Breisgau : town-country relations in the Age of Reformation and Peasants' War / Tom Scott. — Oxford : Clarendon, 1986. — 265p. — Bibliography: p239-256. — Includes index

FREIE DEMOKRATISCHE PARTEI

JEUTTER, Peter
EWG - Kein Weg nach Europa : [die Haltung der Freien Demokratischen Partei zu den Römischen Verträgen 1957] / Peter Jeutter. — Bonn : Europa Union Verlag, 1985. — 330p. — (Europäische Studien des Instituts für Europäische Politik ; Bd.14). — Bibliography: p299-327

FREIGHT AND FREIGHTAGE — Statistics

Carriage of goods: inland waterways / Statistical Office of the European Communities. — Luxembourg : Office for Official Publications of the European Communities, 1983-. — Annual. — Text in Community languages. — Title varies

Carriage of goods: road / Statistical Office of the European Communities. — Luxembourg : Office for Official Publications of the European Communities, 1983-. — Annual. — Text in Community languages. — Title varies

FREIGHT AND FREIGHTAGE — Canada

Transport of dangerous goods: annual report = Transport des marchandises dangereuses: rapport annuel / Transport Canada. — Ottawa : Transport Canada, 1985/86-. — Annual. — Text in English and French

FREIGHT AND FREIGHTAGE — Great Britain

MACKIE, P. J.
The British transport industry and the European Community : a study of regulation and modal split in the long distance and international freight market / Peter J. Mackie, David Simon and Anthony E. Whiteing. — Aldershot : Gower, c1987. — xvi,184p. — (Institute for Transport Studies ; 3). — Bibliography: p154-159. — Includes index

FREIGHT AND FREIGHTAGE — Ireland

Road freight transport survey / Central Statistics Office, Ireland. — Dublin : Stationary Office, 1984-. — Annual

FREIGHT AND FREIGHTAGE — Nigeria — Kaduna

OGWNDE, Innocent C.
Industrial demand for freight transport in Kaduna State / Innocent C. Ogwunde. — Zaria : Ahmadu Bello University. Centre for Social and Economic Research, 1984. — iv,102p. — (C.S.E.R. research report ; no.11). — Bibliography: p84-86

FRENCH — Czechoslovakia — Slovak Socialist Republic

CHŇOUPEK, Bohuš
Les résistants de la dernière chance : combattants français dans les maquis slovaques, 1944-45 / Bohuš Chňoupek. — Paris : Jacques Grancher, 1986. — 189p

FRENCH — England — History

Huguenots in Britain and their French background, 1550-1800 / edited by Irene Scouloudi. — Totowa, N.J. : Barnes & Noble, 1987. — p. cm. — *Includes index*

FRENCH — Germany — Saarland

LEMPERT, Peter
"Das Saarland den Saarländern!" : die frankophilen Bestrebungen im Saargebiet 1918-1935 / Peter Lempert. — Köln : dme-Verlag, 1985. — 542p. — (Kölner Schriften zur romanischen Kultur ; Bd.3). — *Bibliography: p523-532*

FRENCH — History

KENNETT, Lee
The French armies in the Seven Years' War : a study in military organization and administration / Lee Kennett. — Durham, N.C. : Duke University Press, 1967. — xvi,165p

FRENCH-CANADIAN DRAMA — History and criticism

NARDOCCHIO, Elaine F
Theatre and politics in modern Québec / Elaine F. Nardocchio. — Edmonton, Alta., Canada : University of Alberta Press, 1986. — xii, 157 p.. — *Includes index*. — *Bibliography: p. 133-148*

FRENCH-CANADIANS — New England — History

BRAULT, Gerard J
The French-Canadian heritage in New England / Gerard J. Brault. — Hanover, N.H. ; London : University Press of New England, c1986. — xiii, 282p, 14p of plates. — *Includes index*. — *Bibliography: p 241-264*

FRENCH GUIANA — Census, 1974

ELIE, P.
Recensement général de la population en 1974, départements d'outre-mer : Guyane : tableaux sur la structure démographique / P. Elie et C. Maroger. — [Paris] : INSEE, 1983. — 199p. — (Archives et documents / Institut National de la Statistique et des Études Économiques ; no.66)

FRENCH GUIANA — Population — Statistics

ELIE, P.
Recensement général de la population en 1974, départements d'outre-mer : Guyane : tableaux sur la structure démographique / P. Elie et C. Maroger. — [Paris] : INSEE, 1983. — 199p. — (Archives et documents / Institut National de la Statistique et des Études Économiques ; no.66)

FRENCH GUIANA — Statistics, Vital

ELIE, P.
Recensement général de la population en 1974, départements d'outre-mer : Guyane : tableaux sur la structure démographique / P. Elie et C. Maroger. — [Paris] : INSEE, 1983. — 199p. — (Archives et documents / Institut National de la Statistique et des Études Économiques ; no.66)

FRENCH LANGUAGE — Dictionaires — English

Population terminology = Terminologie de la population = Terminología de población. — Washington, D.C. : The World Bank, 1986. — iii,27p. — (A World Bank glossary)

FRENCH LANGUAGE — Dictionaries

Harrap's business French-English dictionary = dictionnaire anglais-français / edited by Françoise Laurendeau-Collin, Jane Pratt [and] Peter Collin. — London ; Paris : Harrap, 1986. — xiv,224p

FRENCH LANGUAGE — Dictionaries — English

GORSE, Jean Eugène
A World Bank glossary : forestry terms : English-French = Glossaire de la Banque mondiale : terminologie forestière : français-anglais. — Washington, D.C. : World Bank, 1984. — v,42p. — *In English and French*

KETTRIDGE, J. O.
French dictionary : French-English, English-French / compiled by J.O. Kettridge. — Rev. ed / completely revised by Alec Strahan, Wyn Johnson and Sarah Edwards. — London : Routledge & Kegan Paul, 1986. — x,566p. — *Previous ed.: i.e. New rev. ed. published as Kettridge's French-English, English-French dictionary. New York : New American Library, 1984*

FRENCH LANGUAGE — Political aspects — Manitoba — History

DOERN, Russell
The battle over bilingualism : the Manitoba language question 1983-1985 / Russell Deorn. — Winnipeg : Cambridge Publishers, 1985. — 227p

FRENCH LITERATURE — 17th century — History and criticism

VIALA, Alain
Naissance de l'écrivain : sociologie de la littérature à l'âge classique / Alain Viala. — Paris : Minuit, 1985. — 317p. — (Le sens commun)

FRENCH POLYNESIA — Census, 1983

Tableaux normalisés du recensement général de la population : 15 octobre 1983. — [Papeete] : Institut territorial de la statistique

Tableaux normalisés du recensement général de la population : 15 octobre 1983. — [Papeete] : Institut territorial de la statistique Résultats de la commune de Anaa. — [1985?]. — 4p,11 leaves

Tableaux normalisés du recensement général de la population : 15 octobre 1983. — [Papeete] : Institut territorial de la statistique Résultats de la commune de Arue. — [1985?]. — 4p,11 leaves

Tableaux normalisés du recensement général de la population : 15 octobre 1983. — [Papeete] : Institut territorial de la statistique Résultats de la commune de Arutua. — [1985?]. — 4p,ll leaves

Tableaux normalisés du recensement général de la population : 15 octobre 1983. — [Papeete] : Institut territorial de la statistique Résultats de la commune de Faaa. — [1985?]. — 12 leaves

Tableaux normalisés du recensement général de la population : 15 octobre 1983. — [Papeete] : Institut territorial de la statistique Résultats de la commune de Fakarava. — [1985?]. — 4p,ll leaves

Tableaux normalisés du recensement général de la population : 15 octobre 1983. — [Papeete] : Institut territorial de la statistique Résultats de la commune de Fangatau. — [1985?]. — 4p,ll leaves

Tableaux normalisés du recensement général de la population : 15 ocobre 1983. — [Papeete] : Institut territorial de la statistique Résultats de la commune de Fatu Hiva. — [1985?]. — 4p,11 leaves

Tableaux normalisés du recensement général de la population : 15 octobre 1983. — [Papeete] : Institut territorial de la statistique Résultats de la commune de Gambier. — [1985?]. — 4p,ll leaves

Tableaux normalisés du recensement général de la population : 15 octobre 1983. — [Papeete] : Institut territorial de la statistique Résultats de la commune de Hao. — [1985?]. — 4p,ll leaves

Tableaux normalisés du recensement général de la population : 15 octobre 1983. — [Papeete] : Institut territorial de la statistique Résultats de la commune de Hikueru. — [1985?]. — 4p,ll leaves

Tableaux normalisés du recensement général de la population : 15 octobre 1983. — [Papeete] : Institut territorial de la statistique Résultats de la commune de Hitiaa o te ra. — [1985?]. — 4p,11 leaves

Tableaux normalisés du recensement général de la population : 15 octobre 1983. — [Papeete] : Institut territoria de la statistique Résultats de la commune de Hiva Oa. — [1985?]. — 4p,11 leaves

Tableaux normalisés du recensement général de la population : 15 octobre 1983. — [Papeete] : Institut territorial de la statistique Résultats de la commune de Huahine. — [1985?]. — 4p,11 leaves

Tableaux normalisés du recensement général de la population : 15 octobre 1983. — [Papeete] : Institut territorial de la statistique Résultats de la commune de Mahina. — [1985?]. — 15 leaves

Tableaux normalisés du recensement général de la population : 15 octobre 1983. — [Papeete] : Institut territorial de la statistique Résultats de la commune de Makemo. — [1985?]. — 4p,ll leaves

Tableaux normalisés du recensement général de la population : 15 octobre 1983. — [Papeete] : Institut territorial de la statistique Résultats de la commune de Manihi. — [1985?]. — 4p,ll leaves

Tableaux normalisés du recensement général de la population : 15 octobre 1983. — [Papeete] : Institut territorial de la statistique Résultats de la commune de Maupiti. — [1985?]. — 4p,11 leaves

Tableaux normalisés du recensement général de la population : 15 octobre 1983. — [Papeete] : Institut territorial de la statistique Résultats de la commune de Moorea-Maiao. — [1985?]. — 11 leaves

Tableaux normalisés du recensement général de la population : 15 octobre 1983. — [Papeete] : Institut territorial de la statistique Résultats de la commune de Napuka. — [1985?]. — 4p,ll leaves

Tableaux normalisés du recensement général de la population : 15 octobre 1983. — [Papeete] : Institut territorial de la statistique Résultats de la commune de Nuku Hiva. — [1985?]. — 4p,11 leaves

Tableaux normalisés du recensement général de la population : 15 octobre 1983. — [Papeete] : Institut territorial de la statistique Résultats de la commune de Nukutavake. — [1985?]. — 4p,ll leaves

Tableaux normalisés du recensement général de la population : 15 octobre 1983. — [Papeete] : Institut territorial de la statistique Résultats de la commune de Paea. — [1985?]. — 4p,11 leaves

Tableaux normalisés du recensement général de la population : 15 octobre 1983. — [Papeete] : Institut territorial de la statistique Résultats de la commune de Papara. — [1985?]. — 4p,11 leaves

Tableaux normalisés du recensement général de la population : 15 octobre 1983. — [Papeete] : Institut territorial de la statistique Résultats de la commune de Papeete. — [1985?]. — 16 leaves

Tableaux normalisés du recensement général de la population : 15 octobre 1983. — [Papeete] : Institut territorial de la statistique Résultats de la commune de Pirae. — [1985?]. — 4p,11 leaves

Tableaux normalisés du recensement général de la population : 15 octobre 1983. — [Papeete] : Institut territorial de la statistique Résultats de la commune de Punaauia. — [1985?]. — 11 leaves

FRENCH POLYNESIA — Census, 1983
continuation

Tableaux normalisés du recensement général de la population : 15 octobre 1983. — [Papeete : Institut territorial de la statistique Résultats de la commune de Raivavae. — [Papeete : Institut territorial de la statistique. — 4p,11 leaves

Tableaux normalisés du recensement général de la population : 15 octobre 1983. — [Papeete] : Institut territorial de la statistique Résultats de la commune de Rangiroa. — [1985?]. — 4p,ll leaves

Tableaux normalisés du recensement général de la population : 15 octobre 1983. — [Papeete] : Institut territorial de la statistique Résultats de la commune de Rapa. — {1985?]. — 4p,11 leaves

Tableaux normalisés du recensement général de la population : 15 octobre 1983. — [Papeete] : Institut territorial de la statistique Résultats de la commune de Reao. — [1985?]. — 4p,ll leaves

Tableaux normalisés du recensement général de la population : 15 octobre 1983. — [Papeete] : Institut territorial de la statistique Résultats de la commune de Rimatara. — [1985?]. — 4p,11 leaves

Tableaux normalisés du recensement général de la population : 15 octobre 1983. — [Papeete] : Institut territorial de la statistique Résultats de la commune de Rurutu. — [Papeete] : Institut territorial de la statistique. — 4p,11 leaves

Tableaux normalisés du recensement général de la population : 15 octobre 1983. — [Papeete] : Institut territorial de la statistique Résultats de la commune de Tahaa. — [1985?]. — 11 leaves

Tableaux normalisés du recensement général de la population : 15 octobre 1983. — [Papeete] : Institut territorial de la statistique Résultats de la commune de Tahuata. — [1985?]. — 4p,11 leaves

Tableaux normalisés du recensement général de la population : 15 octobre 1983. — [Papeete] : Institut territorial de la statistique Résultats de la commune de Taiarapu-Est. — [1985?]. — 4p,11 leaves

Tableaux normalisés du recensement général de la population : 15 octobre 1983. — [Papeete] : Institut territorial de la statistique Résultats de la commune de Taiarapu-Ouest. — [1985?]. — 4p,11 leaves

Tableaux normalisés du recensement général de la population : 15 octobre 1983. — [Papeete] : Institut territorial de la statistique Résultats de la commune de Takaroa. — [1985?]. — 2p,ll leaves

Tableaux normalisés du recensement général de la population : 15 octobre 1983. — [Papeete] : Institut territorial de la statistique Résultats de la Commune de Taputapuatea. — [1985?]. — 4p,11 leaves

Tableaux normalisés du recensement général de la population : 15 octobre 1983. — [Papeete] : Institut territorial de la statistique Résultats de la commune de Tatakoto. — [1985?]. — 4p,ll leaves

Tableaux normalisés du recensement général de la population : 15 octobre 1983. — [Papeete] : Institut territorial de la statistique Résultats de la commune de Teva i Uta. — [1985?]. — 4p,11 leaves

Tableaux normalisés du recensement général de la population : 15 octobre 1983. — [Papeete] : Institut territorial de la statistique Résultats de la commune de Tumaraa. — [1985?]. — 4p,11 leaves

Tableaux normalisés du recensement général de la population : 15 octobre 1983. — [Papeete] : Institut territorial de la statistique Résultats de la commune de Tureia. — [1985?]. — 4p,ll leaves

Tableaux normalisés du recensement général de la population : 15 octobre 1983. — [Papeete] : Institut territorial de la statistique Résultats de la commune de Ua Huka. — [1985?]. — 4p,11 leaves

Tableaux normalisés du recensement général de la population : 15 octobre 1983. — [Papeete] : Institut territorial de la statistique Résultats de la commune de Ua Pou. — [1985?]. — 4p,11 leaves

Tableaux normalisés du recensement général de la population : 15 octobre 1983. — [Papeeta] : Institut territorial de la statistique Résultats de la commune de Uturoa. — [1985?]. — 4p,11 leaves

Tableaux normalisés du recensement général de la population : 15 octobre 1983. — [Papeete] : Institut territorial de la statistique Résultats de la subdivision administrative des Iles Australes. — [1985?]. — 4p,11 leaves

Tableaux normalisés du recensement général de la population : 15 octobre 1983. — [Papeete] : Institut territorial de la statistique Résultats de la subdivision administrative des Iles Marquises. — [1985?]. — 4p,11 leaves

Tableaux normalisés du recensement général de la population : 15 octobre 1983. — [Papeete] : Institut territorial de la statistique Résultats de la subdivision administrative des Iles Sous le Vent. — [1985?]. — 4p,12 leaves

Tableaux normalisés du recensement général de la population : 15 octobre 1983. — [Papeete] : Institut territorial de la statistique Résultats de la subdivision administrative des Iles Tuamotu-Gambier. — [1985?]. — 4p,12 leaves

Tableaux normalisés du recensement général de la population : 15 octobre 1983. — [Papeete] : Institut territorial de la statistique Résultats de la subdivision adminstrative des Iles du Vent. — [1985?]. — 4p,12 leaves

Tableaux normalisés du recensement général de la population : 15 octobre 1983. — [Papeete] : Institut territorial de la statistique Résultats de la zone rurale de Tahiti. — [1985?]. — 4p,11 leaves

Tableaux normalisés du recensement général de la population : 15 octobre 1983. — [Papeete] : Institut territorial de la statistique Résultats de la zone urbaine de Tahiti. — [1985?]. — 11 leaves

Tableaux normalisés du recensement général de la population : 15 octobre 1983. — [Papeete] : Institut territorial de la statistique Résultats de l'Ile de Raiatea. — [1985?]. — 4p,11 leaves

Tableaux normalisés du recensement général de la population : 15 octobre 1983. — [Papeete] : Institut territorial de la statistique Résultats de l'Ile de Tahiti. — [1985?]. — 12 leaves

Tableaux normalisés du recensement général de la population : 15 octobre 1983. — [Papeete] : Institut territorial de la statistique Résultats des Marquises du Sud. — [1985?]. — 4p,11 leaves

Tableaux normalisés du recensement général de la population : 15 octobre 1983. — [Papeete] : Institut territorial de la statistique Résultats des Tuamotu de l'Ouest. — [1985?]. — 4p,11 leaves

Tableaux normalisés du recensement général de la population : 15 octobre 1983. — [Papeete] : Institut territorial de la statistique Résultats des Tuamotu Nord-Est. — [1985?]. — 4p,12 leaves

Tableaux normalisés du recensement général de la population : 15 octobre 1983. — [Papeete] : Institut territorial de la statistique Rsultats des Marquises du Nord. — [1985?]. — 4p,11 leaves

Tableaux normalisés du recensement général de la popultion : 15 octobre 1983. — [Papeete] : Institut territorial de la statistique Résultats de la commune de Tubuai. — [1985?]. — 4p,11 leaves

FRENCH POLYNESIA — Politics and government

DANIELSSON, Bengt
Poisoned reign : French nuclear colonialism in the Pacific / Bengt Danielsson and Mariè-Thérèse Danielsson. — 2nd rev. ed. — Ringwood, Victoria : Penguin, 1986. — xiv,323p. — *First published in Paris, 1974, under the title "Moruroa Mon Amour"*

FRENCH POLYNESIA — Population — Statistics

Tableaux normalisés du recensement général de la population : 15 octobre 1983. — [Papeete] : Institut territorial de la statistique

Tableaux normalisés du recensement général de la population : 15 octobre 1983. — [Papeete] : Institut territorial de la statistique Résultats de la commune de Huahine. — [1985?]. — 4p,11 leaves

Tableaux normalisés du recensement général de la population : 15 octobre 1983. — [Papeete] : Institut territorial de la statistique Résultats de la commune de Maupiti. — [1985?]. — 4p,11 leaves

Tableaux normalisés du recensement général de la population : 15 octobre 1983. — [Papeete] : Institut territorial de la statistique Résultats de la commune de Tahaa. — [1985?]. — 11 leaves

Tableaux normalisés du recensement général de la population : 15 octobre 1983. — [Papeete] : Institut territorial de la statistique Résultats de la Commune de Taputapuatea. — [1985?]. — 4p,11 leaves

Tableaux normalisés du recensement général de la population : 15 octobre 1983. — [Papeete] : Institut territorial de la statistique Résultats de la commune de Tumaraa. — [1985?]. — 4p,11 leaves

Tableaux normalisés du recensement général de la population : 15 octobre 1983. — [Papeeta] : Institut territorial de la statistique Résultats de la commune de Uturoa. — [1985?]. — 4p,11 leaves

Tableaux normalisés du recensement général de la population : 15 octobre 1983. — [Papeete] : Institut territorial de la statistique Résultats de la subdivision administrative des Iles Australes. — [1985?]. — 4p,11 leaves

Tableaux normalisés du recensement général de la population : 15 octobre 1983. — [Papeete] : Institut territorial de la statistique Résultats de la subdivision administrative des Iles Sous le Vent. — [1985?]. — 4p,12 leaves

Tableaux normalisés du recensement général de la population : 15 octobre 1983. — [Papeete] : Institut territorial de la statistique Résultats de la subdivision adminstrative des Iles du Vent. — [1985?]. — 4p,12 leaves

Tableaux normalisés du recensement général de la population : 15 octobre 1983. — [Papeete] : Institut territorial de la statistique Résultats de l'Ile de Raiatea. — [1985?]. — 4p,11 leaves

FRENTE POPULAR

TUÑON DE LARA, Manuel
Tres claves de la Segunda República : la cuestión agraria, los aparatos del Estado, Frente Popular / Manuel Tuñon de Lara. — Madrid : Alianza Editorial, 1985. — 367p. — *Bibliographies*

FRENTE SANDINISTA DE LIBERACIÓN NACIONAL

HODGES, Donald Clark
 Intellectual foundations of the Nicaraguan revolution / by Donald C. Hodges. — 1st ed. — Austin : University of Texas Press, 1986. — p. cm. — *Includes index.* — *Bibliography: p*

NOLAN, David
 The ideology of the Sandinistas and the Nicaraguan revolution / David Nolan. — Coral Gables, Fla. (P.O. Box 248123, Coral Gables 33124) : Institute of Interamerican Studies, Graduate School of International Studies, University of Miami, c1984. — v, 203 p.. — *Includes index.* — *Bibliography: p. 186-199*

FREUD, SIGMUND. Totem und Tabu

WALLACE, Edwin R
 Freud and anthropology : a history and reappraisal / Edwin R. Wallace, IV. — New York : International Universities Press, c1983. — xi, 306p. — (Psychological issues ; monograph 55). — *Bibliography: p.281-294. Includes index*

FREUD, SIGMUND

FREUD, Sigmund
 Collected papers / Sigmund Freud ; edited by James Strachey ; translated by Joan Riviere. — London : Hogarth Press, 1950. — 5 vols. — *Bibliographies*

MASSON, J. Moussaieff
 The assault on truth : Freud's suppression of the seduction theory / Jeffrey Moussaieff Masson. — New York, N.Y. : Penguin Books, 1985, c1984. — p. cm. — : *Reprint. Originally published: New York : Farrar, Straus, and Giroux, 1984.* — *Includes index.* — *Bibliography: p*

NELSON, Benjamin, ed
 Freud and the 20th century. — New York : Meridian Books, 1957. — 314 p. — (Meridian books, M45). — *Includes bibliography*

ZANUSO, Billa
 The young Freud : the origins of psychoanalysis in late nineteenth-century Viennese culture / Billa Zanuso. — Oxford : Basil Blackwell, 1986. — [v,192]p. — *Translation of: La nascita della psicoanalisi.* — *Includes bibliography and index*

FREY, ROBERT SEITZ

FREY, Robert Seitz
 The imperative of response : the holocaust in human context / Robert Seitz Frey, Nancy Thompson-Frey. — Lanham, MD : University Press of America, c1985. — xix, 165 p.. — *Bibliography: p. 144-164*

FRIEDMAN, MILTON

FRIEDMAN, Milton
 The essence of Friedman / edited by Kurt R. Leube ; foreword by W. Glenn Campbell. — Stanford, Calif. : Hoover Institution Press, 1987. — p. cm. — (Hoover Press publication ; 366). — *Includes index.* — *Bibliography: p*

BELKA, Marek
 Doktryna ekonomiczno-społeczna Miltona Friedmana / Marek Belka. — Warszawa : Państwowe Wydawnictwo Naukowe, 1986. — 387p. — (Ekonomia XX wieku). — *Bibliography: p364-[373]*

DAY, A. C. L.
 Economic strategies : Keynes, Friedman and their disciples / Alan Day. — [London] : Banking World, 1986. — 48p. — *At head of title: Alan Day report*

RAYACK, Elton
 Not so free to choose : the political economy of Milton Friedman and Ronald Reagan / Elton Rayack. — New York : Praeger, 1987. — x, 215 p.. — *Includes index.* — *Bibliography: p. 203-208*

FRIENDLY SOCIETIES — Singapore

CHENG, Lim Keak
 Social change and the Chinese in Singapore : a socio-economic geography with special reference to bang structure / Cheng Lim-Keak. — Singapore : Singapore University Press : National University of Singapore, c1985. — xix, 235 p., [8] p. of plates. — : *Revision of the author's thesis (Ph. D.--University of London, 1979).* — *Includes index.* — *Bibliography: p. 206-228*

FRIENDSHIP

Friendship and social interaction / edited by Valerian J. Derlega and Barbara A. Winstead. — New York : Springer-Verlag, c1986. — p. cm. — (Springer series in social psychology). — *Includes index.* — *Bibliography: p*

FRIENDSHIP — Research

MATTHEWS, Sarah H
 Friendships through the life-course : oral biographies in old age / by Sarah H. Matthews. — Beverly Hills : Sage Publications, c1986. — p. cm. — (Sage library of social research ; v. 161). — *Includes index.* — *Bibliography: p*

FRIENDSHIP — London

WILLMOTT, Peter, 1923-
 Friendship networks and social support / Peter Willmott. — London : Policy Studies Institute, 1987. — vii,115p. — (PSI research report ; no.666). — *Bibliographies*

FRIESLAND (NETHERLANDS) — Economic policy

NETHERLANDS. Stuurgroep Integraal Structuurplan Noorden des Lands
 Het Noorden : een versterkte bevolkingsgroei? Of juist niet! : een bewerking van het rapport Bevolkingsaspecten Noorden des Lands / Samensteller R. Idenburg. — 's-Gravenhage : Staatsuitgeverij, 1974. — 21p

NETHERLANDS. Werkgroep Beleidsdoelstellingen Analyse Noorden
 ISP : integraal structuurplan Noorden des lands : rapport van de Werkgroep Beleidsdoelstellingen Analyse Noorden. — [s-Gravenhage] : the Werkgroep 2. — 1974. — 27p

FRIMODTS FORLAG — History

Frimodts Forlag 100 °ar : 1884-1984. — Fredericia : Frimodt, 1984. — 26p

FRONT LIBÉRATION DE QUÉBEC

LOOMIS, D. G.
 Not much glory : quelling the F.L.Q. / Dan G. Loomis. — Toronto : Deneau, 1984. — 199p

FRONT NATIONAL

DUMONT, Serge
 Le système Le Pen / Serge Dumont, Joseph Lorien, Karl Criton. — Anvers : EPO, 1985. — 336p. — *Bibliography: p334-335*

LE PEN, Jean-Marie
 La France est de retour. — Paris : Carrere/Michel Lafon, [1985]. — 301p

LE PEN, Jean Marie
 Pour la France : programme du Front National / Jean Marie Le Pen. — Paris : Albatros, 1985. — 200p

FRONTIER AND PIONEER LIFE — Oklahoma

THOMPSON, John
 Closing the frontier : radical response in Oklahoma, 1889-1923 / by John Thompson. — 1st ed. — Norman : University of Oklahoma Press, c1986. — xiii, 262 p.. — *Includes index.* — *Bibliography: p. 249-258*

FROZEN GROUND

HARRIS, Stuart A.
 The permafrost environment / Stuart A. Harris. — London : Croom Helm, c1986. — 276p. — (The Croom Helm natural environment. Problems and management series) . — *Bibliography: p235-270.* — *Includes index*

FRUIT — England — London — Marketing

DAVIS, Keith
 London's wholesale fruit and vegetable markets : a survey of the four east London markets / Keith Davis, Tim Catchpole. — [London] : London Research Centre, 1986. — 65p. — (Reviews and studies series ; no.31). — *Re-issue of the Greater London Council's study report of February 1986 with an appendix added giving a detailed analysis of the survey data including comparisons between the markets*

A new site for Covent Garden Market : report on a feasibility study for the Nine Elms area. — [London] : Covent Garden Market Authority, 1964. — 34leaves. — [21]folded leaves

FUEL — Prices — Congresses

INTERNATIONAL ASSOCIATION OF ENERGY ECONOMISTS. North American Meeting (1985 : Philadelphia, Pa.)
 World energy markets : stability or cyclical change? : proceedings, Seventh Annual North American Meeting, International Association of Energy Economists, Philadelphia, Pennsylvania, December 1985 / edited by William F. Thompson and David J. DeAngelo. — Boulder : Westview Press, 1985. — xiii, 690 p. — (Westview special studies in natural resources and energy management). — *Includes bibliographies*

FUEL — Great Britain

NATIONAL COUNCIL FOR ONE PARENT FAMILIES
 Fuel poverty : case-studies from one parent families. — London : National Council for One Parent Families, 1985. — 10p

FUKUSHIMA-KEN (JAPAN) — Social conditions

VLASTOS, Stephen
 Peasant protests and uprisings in Tokugawa Japan / Stephen Vlastos. — Berkeley : University of California Press, c1986. — xii, 184 p.. — *Includes index.* — *Bibliography: p. [169]-179*

FULBRIGHT, J. WILLIAM

BROWN, Eugene
 J. William Fulbright : advice and dissent / Eugene Brown. — Iowa City : University of Iowa Press, c1985. — x, 171p. — *Includes index.* — *Bibliography: p.153-167*

FULHAM (LONDON) — Economic policy

ALLAN, Malcolm
 Creating a local economic development network : a case study of Hammersmith and Fulham / Malcolm Allan, Mike Fenton, Andy Flockhart. — Glasgow : The Planning Exchange, 1985. — iii,82p

FULL EMPLOYMENT POLICIES

ALBEDA, W.
 De crisis van de werkgelegenheid en de verzorgingsstaat : analyse en perspectief / W. Albeda. — Kampen : J. H. Kok, c1984. — 108p

RUTHERFORD, Malcolm
 Has full employment gone forever? : a report on the Ditchley Foundation Conference, held at Ditchley Park, Oxfordshire, April 8-10, 1983. — Oxford : Ditchley Foundation, 1983. — 5p. — (Ditchley conference report ; no.5/1983)

De weg naar volledige werkgelegenheid / W. K. T. van Ginneken ...[et al.] ; Vereniging voor de Staathuishoudkunde. — Leiden : Stenfert Kroese, 1985. — 79p. — (Preadviezen van Vereniging voor de Staathuishoudkunde ; 1985)

WHITING, Edwin
 A guide to unemployment reduction measures / Edwin Whiting. — Basingstoke : Macmillan, 1986. — [280]p. — *Includes index*

FULL EMPLOYMENT POLICIES — Great Britain
BRITTON, Andrew, 1940-
Full employment and the balance of payments / Andrew Britton. — London : Employment Institute, 1987. — 28p. — *At head of title: Employment Institute*

FUNCTIONALISATION (SOCIAL SCIENCES)
FAIA, Michael A.
Dynamic functionalism : strategy and tactics / Michael A. Faia. — Cambridge : Cambridge University Press, 1986. — xiv,187p. — (The Arnold and Caroline Rose monograph series of the American Sociological Association) (ASA rose monograph series). — *Bibliography: p174-184. — Includes index*

FUNCTIONALISM
INGRAM, David
Habermas and the dialectic of reason / David Ingram. — New Haven, CT : Yale University Press, c1987. — xvii, 263p. — *Includes index. — Bibliography: p.243-254*

FUNCTIONALISM (LINGUISTICS)
Social and functional approaches to language and thought / edited by Maya Hickmann ; with a foreword by Jerome Bruner. — Orlando : Academic Press, 1987. — p. cm. — *Includes index*

FUNCTIONALISM (SOCIAL SCIENCES) — Addresses, essays, lectures
RAPPAPORT, Roy A
Ecology, meaning, and religion / Roy A. Rappaport. — Richmond, Calif. : North Atlantic Books, c1979. — xi, 259 p.. — *Includes bibliographical references and index*

FUNCTIONS, CONTINUOUS
MENTZENIOTIS, Dionisios
Three views concerning continuity and infinitesimals : non-standard analysis, topos theory and intuitionism / by Dionisios Mentzeniotis. — 251 leaves. — *PhD (Econ) 1987 LSE. — Leaves 218-234 are appendices*

FUND RAISING — Canada
MARTIN, Samuel A
An essential grace : funding Canada's health care, education, welfare, religion, and culture / by Samuel A. Martin. — Toronto : McClelland and Stewart, c1985. — xvii, 322 p.. — *Includes index*

FUND RAISING — Great Britain
Advertising by charities : a practical guide to raising money by press advertising, direct mail, posters, radio and television appeals and telephone selling / edited by Ken Burnett. — London : Directory of Social Changes, 1986. — vii,152p

Raising money from government / edited by Michael Norton. — 2nd ed. — London : Directory of Social Change, 1985. — [144]p. — *Previous ed.: 1981*

FUNDAMENTALISM — History of doctrines — 20th century
HALSELL, Grace
Prophecy and politics : militant evangelists on the road to nuclear war / Grace Halsell. — Westport, Conn. : Lawrence Hill & Co., c1986. — 210 p.. — *Includes index*

FUNERAL RITES AND CEREMONIES — Ghana
NKETIA, J.H.Kwabena
Funeral dirges of the Akan people / J.H.Nketia. — New York : Negro Universities Press, 1969. — v,296p. — *Reprint of 1955 edition. — Bibliography: p295-296*

FUNERAL RITES AND CEREMONIES, SENUFO (AFRICAN PEOPLE)
GLAZE, Anita J.
Art and death in a Senufo village / Anita J. Glaze. — Bloomington : Indiana University Press, c1981. — xvi, 267 p., [2] leaves of plates. — (Traditional arts of Africa). — *Includes index. — Bibliography: p. [246]-254*

FUR TRADE — Canada — History
NEWMAN, Peter C., 1929-
Company of Adventurers / Peter C. Newman. — Ontario : Viking Penguin
Vol.1. — c1985. — xxiii, 413p. — *Map on lining papers*

FUR TRADE — Soviet Union — History
MARTIN, Janet, 1945-
Treasure of the land of darkness : the fur trade and its significance for medieval Russia / Janet Martin. — Cambridge : Cambridge University Press, 1986. — x,277p. — *Bibliography: p243-266. — Includes*

FURNITURE WORKERS — Great Britain — Recruiting
FURNITURE AND TIMBER INDUSTRY TRAINING BOARD
Education for our industries : a report / by the Furniture and Timber Industry Training Board. — [High Wycombe] : the Board, 1978. — 35p

FUTUNA *See* Wallis and Futuna

FYVEL, T. R.
FYVEL, T. R.
And there my trouble began : uncollected writings, 1945-1985 / T. R. Fyvel. — London : Weidenfeld and Nicolson, 1986. — xii,240p

GABON — History — Dictionaries
GARDINIER, David E
Historical dictionary of Gabon / by David E. Gardinier. — Metuchen, N.J. : Scarecrow Press, 1981. — xxv, 254 p.. — (African historical dictionaries ; no. 30). — *Bibliography: p. 198-254*

GAELIC ATHLETIC ASSOCIATION — History
MANDLE, W. F.
The Gaelic Athletic Association & Irish nationalist politics, 1884-1924 / W.F. Mandle. — London : Christopher Helm, 1987. — xi,240p. — *Bibliography: p225-229. — Includes index*

GAHUKU (PAPUA NEW GUINEA PEOPLE)
READ, Kenneth E
Return to the high valley : coming full circle / Kenneth E. Read. — Berkeley : University of California Press, c1986. — xxi, 269 p., [8] p. of plates. — (Studies in Melanesian anthropology). — *Includes bibliographical references and index*

GAITÁN, JORGÉ ELIÉCER — Assassination
BRAUN, Herbert
The assassination of Gaitán : public life and urban violence in Colombia / Herbert Braun. — Madison, Wis. : University of Wisconsin Press, 1985. — xiii, 282p. — *Includes index. — Bibliography: p.257-271*

GALBRAITH, JOHN KENNETH
GALBRAITH, John Kenneth
A view from the stands : of people, politics, military power, and the arts / John Kenneth Galbraith ; with notes by the author ; arranged and edited by Andrea D. Williams. — Boston : Houghton Mifflin, 1986. — p. cm. — *Includes index*

GALICIA (POLAND AND UKRAINE) — History — Uprising, 1848
KOZIK, Jan
The Ukrainian national movement in Galicia : 1815-1849 / Jan Kozik ; edited with an introduction by Lawrence D. Orton ; translated from the Polish by Andrew Gorski and Lawrence D. Orton. — Edmonton : University of Alberta, Canadian Institute of Ukrainian Studies, 1986. — xx,498p. — (Canadian library in Ukrainian studies). — *Abridged translation of "Ukraiński ruch narodowy w Galicji w latach 1830-1848" (Cracow, 1973) and "Miedzy reakcja a rewolucja" (Warsaw, 1975). — Bibliography: p[451]-471*

GALICIA (POLAND AND UKRAINE) — Politics and government
KOZIK, Jan
The Ukrainian national movement in Galicia : 1815-1849 / Jan Kozik ; edited with an introduction by Lawrence D. Orton ; translated from the Polish by Andrew Gorski and Lawrence D. Orton. — Edmonton : University of Alberta, Canadian Institute of Ukrainian Studies, 1986. — xx,498p. — (Canadian library in Ukrainian studies). — *Abridged translation of "Ukraiński ruch narodowy w Galicji w latach 1830-1848" (Cracow, 1973) and "Miedzy reakcja a rewolucja" (Warsaw, 1975). — Bibliography: p[451]-471*

KOZUB-CIEMBRONIEWICZ, Wiesław
Austria a Polska w konserwatyzmie Antoniego Z. Helcla, 1846-1865 / Wiesław Kozub-Ciembroniewicz. — Kraków : Krajowa Agencja Wydawnicza, 1986. — 215p. — *Summary in German. — Bibliography: p191-[200]*

GALICIA (SPAIN) — Economic conditions
SAAVEDRA, Pegerto
Economía, política y sociedad en Galicia : la provincia de Mondoñedo, 1480-1830 / Pegerto Saavedra. — [Santiago de Compostela] : Xunta de Galicia, 1985. — 700p. — *Bibliography: p685-697*

GALICIA (SPAIN) — Politics and government — 20th century
CASTRO PÉREZ, Xavier
O galeguismo na encrucillada republicana / Xavier Castro. — La Coruña : Editorial Atlántico
Tomo 1. — 1985. — 540p

CASTRO PÉREZ, Xavier
O galeguismo na encrucillada republicana / Xavier Castro. — La coruña : Editorial Atlántico. — *Bibliography: p867-872*
Tomo 2. — 1985. — p545-988

FERNÁNDEZ, Carlos
Franquismo y transición política en Galicia : (apuntes para una historia de nuestro pasado reciente) 1939-1979 / Carlos Fernández ; con la colaboración de Carlos Luis Rodríguez. — La Coruña : Ediciós do Castro, 1985. — 476p. — (Documentos para a historia contemporánea de Galicia). — *Bibliography: p469-476*

GALIEV, MIRSAID SULTAN *See* Sultan Galiev, Mirsaid

GALLIFFET, GASTON ALEXANDRE AUGUSTE DE, 1930-1909
MONAT, Christophe
Gaston Alexandre Auguste de Golliffet : "le marquis aux talons rouges" : de La Commune à l'affaire Dreyfus- / Christope Monat. — Paris : Jean-Cyrille Godefroy, 1985. — 214p. — *Cover title: Golliffet: le marquis aux talons rouges. — Bibliography: p208-[209]*

GÁLVEZ, MANUEL
QUIJADA, Mónica
Manuel Gálvez : 60 años de pensamiento nacionalista / Mónica Quijada. — Buenos Aires : Centro Editor de América Latina, 1985. — 139p. — *Bibliography: p133-139*

GAMBIA — Commerce — Statistics
External trade statistics of the Gambia / Central Statistics Department, Ministry of Economic Planning and Industrial Development, Gambia. — Banjul : Central Statistics Department, 1974/75-. — *Annual*

GAMBIA — Economic ploicy
Five year plan for economic and social development 1975/76-1979/80. — [Banjul : Ministry of Economic Planning and Industrial Development], 1975. — 183p

GAMBIA — Economic policy
Five year plan for economic and social development 1981/82-1985/86. — [Banjul] : Ministry of Economic Planning and Industrial Development, 1983. — 377p

GAMBIA — Economic policy
continuation

Midterm review of the five year plan for economic and social development 1981/82-1985/6. — Banjul : Ministry of Econoomic Planning and Industrial Development, 1983. — 131p. — *Title on front cover: Midterm review of the second five year plan*

GAMBIA — History

REEVE, Henry Fenwick
The Gambia : its history, ancient, medieval and modern together with its geographical, geological, and ethnographical conditions and a description of the birds, beasts and fishes found therein / by Henry Fenwick Reeve. — New York : Negro Universities Press, 1969. — xv,287p. — *Reprint of the 1912 edition*

GAMBIA — History — Dictionaries

GAILEY, Harry A
Historical dictionary of the Gambia / by Harry A. Gailey. — Metuchen, N.J. : Scarecrow Press, 1975. — viii, 172 p.. — (African historical dictionaries ; no. 4). — *Bibliography: p. 142-172*

GAMBIA — Social policy

Five year plan for economic and social development 1975/76-1979/80. — [Banjul : Ministry of Economic Planning and Industrial Development], 1975. — 183p

Five year plan for economic and social development 1981/82-1985/86. — [Banjul] : Ministry of Economic Planning and Industrial Development, 1983. — 377p

Midterm review of the five year plan for economic and social development 1981/82-1985/6. — Banjul : Ministry of Econoomic Planning and Industrial Development, 1983. — 131p. — *Title on front cover: Midterm review of the second five year plan*

GAMBIER ISLANDS — Population — Statistics

Tableaux normalisés du recensement général de la population : 15 octobre 1983. — [Papeete] : Institut territorial de la statistique Résultats de la commune de Gambier. — [1985?]. — 4p,ll leaves

Tableaux normalisés du recensement général de la population : 15 octobre 1983. — [Papeete] : Institut territorial de la statistique Résultats de la subdivision administrative des Iles Tuamotu-Gambier. — [1985?]. — 4p,12 leaves

GAMBLING — Economic aspects — Australia

Gambling in Australia / edited by Geoffrey Caldwell...[et al.]. — Sydney ; London : Croom Helm, c1985. — 288p

GAMBLING — Economic aspects — United States

ABT, Vicki
The business of risk : commercial gambling in mainstream America / Vicki Abt, James F. Smith, Eugene Martin Christiansen. — Lawrence, Kan. : University Press of Kansas, c1985. — p. cm. — *Includes index.* — *Bibliography: p*

GAMBLING — Legal status, laws, etc. — Australia

Gambling in Australia / edited by Geoffrey Caldwell...[et al.]. — Sydney ; London : Croom Helm, c1985. — 288p

GAMBLING — Social aspects — France

DUNKLEY, John
Gambling : a social and moral problem in France, 1685-1792 / John Dunkley. — Oxford : Voltaire Foundation, 1985. — 243p. — (Studies on Voltaire and the eighteenth century ; 235). — *Revision of author's thesis (doctoral) - University of Exeter, 1975*

GAMBLING — Social aspects — United States

ABT, Vicki
The business of risk : commercial gambling in mainstream America / Vicki Abt, James F. Smith, Eugene Martin Christiansen. — Lawrence, Kan. : University Press of Kansas, c1985. — p. cm. — *Includes index.* — *Bibliography: p*

GAMBLING — Australia

Gambling in Australia / edited by Geoffrey Caldwell...[et al.]. — Sydney ; London : Croom Helm, c1985. — 288p

GAMBLING — France — History — 17th century

DUNKLEY, John
Gambling : a social and moral problem in France, 1685-1792 / John Dunkley. — Oxford : Voltaire Foundation, 1985. — 243p. — (Studies on Voltaire and the eighteenth century ; 235). — *Revision of author's thesis (doctoral) - University of Exeter, 1975*

GAMBLING — France — History — 18th century

DUNKLEY, John
Gambling : a social and moral problem in France, 1685-1792 / John Dunkley. — Oxford : Voltaire Foundation, 1985. — 243p. — (Studies on Voltaire and the eighteenth century ; 235). — *Revision of author's thesis (doctoral) - University of Exeter, 1975*

GAMBLING — United States

ABT, Vicki
The business of risk : commercial gambling in mainstream America / Vicki Abt, James F. Smith, Eugene Martin Christiansen. — Lawrence, Kan. : University Press of Kansas, c1985. — p. cm. — *Includes index.* — *Bibliography: p*

GAME THEORY

BINMORE, K. G.
Remodeled rational players / K. G. Binmore. — London : Suntory Toyota International Centre for Economics and Related Disciplines, 1987. — 54p. — (Theoretical economics). — *Bibliography: p[55-56]*

BRAMS, Steven J
Rational politics : decisions, games, and strategy / Steven J. Brams. — Washington, D.C. : CQ Press, c1985. — xiv, 233 p.. — *Bibliography: p. 215-224.* — *Includes index*

Economic organizations as games / edited by Ken Binmore and Partha Dasgupta. — Oxford : Basil Blackwell, 1986. — 219p.. — *Includes bibliography and index*

The Economics of bargaining / edited by Ken Binmore and Partha Dasgupta. — Oxford : Basil Blackwell, 1987. — 260p. — *Includes bibliographies and index*

MCMILLAN, John
Game theory in international economics / John McMillan. — Chur, Switzerland ; New York : Harwood Academic Publishers, c1986. — p. cm. — (Fundamentals of pure and applied economics ; vol. 1. International trade section). — *Includes index.* — *Bibliography: p*

MOULIN, Hervé
89 exercises with solutions from Game theory for the social sciences, 2nd and revised edition / Hervé Moulin. — New York : New York University Press, 1986, c1985. — p. cm. — (Studies in game theory and mathematical economics). — *Includes index*

MOULIN, Hervé
[Théorie des jeux pour l'économie et la politique. English]. Game theory for the social sciences / Hervé Moulin. — 2nd, rev. ed. — New York : New York University Press, 1986, c1985. — p. cm. — (Studies in game theory and mathematical economics). — *Translation of: Théorie des jeux pour l'économie et la politique.* — *Includes index.* — *Bibliography: p*

ORDESHOOK, Peter C.
Game theory and political theory : an introduction / Peter C. Ordeshook. — Cambridge : Cambridge University Press, 1986. — viii,511p. — *Includes index*

GAME THEORY — Congresses

Dynamic games and applications in economics / edited by T.Basar. — Berlin : Springer-Verlag, 1986. — vii,288p. — (Lecture notes in economics and mathematical systems ; 265)

GAMES — History

BELL, J. Bowyer
To play the game : an analysis of sports / J. Bowyer Bell. — New Brunswick, U.S.A. : Transaction Books, c1986. — p. cm. — *Includes index*

GAMKASKLOOF VALLEY, SOUTH AFRICA

DU TOIT, Brian M.
People of the valley : life in an isolated Afrikaner community in South Africa / by Brian M. du Toit ; with an introductory statement by Solon T. Kimball. — Cape Town : Balkema (A. A.), 1974. — 134 p., [8] p. of plates. — *Includes index.* — *Bibliography: p. 126-129*

GAMO (AFRICAN PEOPLE)

ABÉLÈS, Marc
Le lieu du politique / par Marc Abélès. — Paris : Société d'Ethnographie, 1983. — 240p. — (Histoire et Civilisations de l'Afrique Orientale ; 4). — *Bibliography: p237-238*

GAMO (ETHIOPIA) — History

BUREAU, Jacques
Les Gamo d'Ethiopie : étude du système politique / Jacques Bureau. — Paris : Société d'ethnographie, 1981. — 303p. — (Histoire et civilisations de l'Afrique Orientale ; 3). — *Bibliography: p277-299*

GAMO (ETHIOPIA) — Politics and government

BUREAU, Jacques
Les Gamo d'Ethiopie : étude du système politique / Jacques Bureau. — Paris : Société d'ethnographie, 1981. — 303p. — (Histoire et civilisations de l'Afrique Orientale ; 3). — *Bibliography: p277-299*

GANDHI, Mahatma — Bibliography

Mohandas Karamchand Gandhi : a bibliography / a project of the Indian Council of Social Science Research. — New Delhi : Orient Longman, [1974]. — xxii, 379 p.. — (Gandhi bibliography series ; no. 1) (Publication - Indian Council of Social Science Research ; no. 53). — *Includes indexes.* — *"Much preliminary work of compilation of this bibliography was done by the staff of the Gandhi Bibliography Project appointed by the National Committee for Gandhi Centenary."*

GANDHI, INDIRA

SISODIA, Sawai Singh
Foreign policy of India : Indira Gandhi era : with special reference to non-alignment / S. S. Sisodio. — New Delhi : Inter-India Publications, 1985. — 196p. — *Bibliography: p183-189*

SOOD, P.
Indira Gandhi and the constitution : modernisation and development / by P. Sood ; foreword by H.K.L. Bhagat. — New Delhi : Marwah Publications, 1985 [i.e. 1984]. — xxvi, 257 p.. — *Includes index.* — *Bibliography: p. [243]-252*

GANDHI, INDIRA, 1917-1984 — Assassination

SHOURIE, Arun
The assassination and after / by Arun Shourie...[et al.]. — New Delhi : Roli Books, 1985. — 160p

GANDHI, M. K.
COPLEY, Antony
Gandhi : against the tide / Antony Copley. — Oxford : Basil Blackwell, 1987. — v,118p. — (Historical Association studies). — *Bibliography: p107-110. — Includes index*

EDWARDES, Michael, 1923-
The myth of the Mahatma : Gandhi, the British and the Raj / Michael Edwardes. — London : Constable, 1986. — 270p,[24]p of plates. — *Bibliography: p261-262. — Includes index*

GANDHI, M. K.
The moral and political writings of Mahatma Gandhi / edited by Raghavan Iyer. — Oxford : Clarendon
Vol.3: Non-violent resistance and social transformation. — 1987. — xx,641p. —
Bibliography: p625-630. — Includes index

GANGAL, Anurag
New international economic order : a Gandhian perspective / Anurag Gangal. — Delhi : Chanakya Publications, 1985. — 160p. — *Bibliography: p147-157*

HAKSAR, Vinit
Civil disobedience, threats and offers: Gandhi and Rawls : Vinit Haksar. — Delhi : Oxford University Press, 1986. — 58p

PRASAD, Bimal
Gandhi, Nehru & J. P. : studies in leadership / Bimal Prasad. — Delhi : Chanakya Publications, 1985. — 294p. — *Bibliography: p283-287*

GANDHI, MAHATMA
THOMAS, Antony
Mahatma Gandhi and the communal problem / Antony Thomas. — New Delhi : Indian Social Institute, 1983. — 29p. — (Monograph series / Indian Social Institute ; 13). — *Bibliography: p28-29*

GANDHI, MAHATMA — Views on peace
PURI, Rashmi-Sudha
Gandhi on war and peace / Rashmi-Sudha Puri. — New York : Praeger, 1987. — xiv, 244 p.. — *Includes index. — Bibliography: p. 229-238*

GANDHI, MAHATMA — Views on war
PURI, Rashmi-Sudha
Gandhi on war and peace / Rashmi-Sudha Puri. — New York : Praeger, 1987. — xiv, 244 p.. — *Includes index. — Bibliography: p. 229-238*

GANG-WEON DO (KOREA (SOUTH)) — Statistics
1970 population and housing census report (complete). — [Seoul] : Economic Planning Board. — In Korean and English
Vol.12-5: Gang-weon Do. — 1972. — 236p

GARANG, JOHN
GARANG, John
John Garang speaks / by John Garang ; edited and introduced by Mansour Khalid. — London : KPI Limited, 1987. — xiii,147p

GARDEN CITIES — United States
CHRISTENSEN, Carol A
The American garden city and the new towns movement / by Carol A. Christensen. — Ann Arbor, Mich. : UMI Research Press, c1986. — x, 203p. — (Architecture and urban design ; no. 13). — *: Revision of author's thesis (Ph.D)--University of Minnesota, 1977. — Includes index. — Bibliography: p. [179]-190*

GARDEN CITIES — United States — Case studies
CHRISTENSEN, Carol A
The American garden city and the new towns movement / by Carol A. Christensen. — Ann Arbor, Mich. : UMI Research Press, c1986. — x, 203p. — (Architecture and urban design ; no. 13). — *: Revision of author's thesis (Ph.D)--University of Minnesota, 1977. — Includes index. — Bibliography: p. [179]-190*

GARIBALDI, GIUSEPPE
Pages from the Garibaldian epic / edited by Anthony P. Campanella. — Sarasota, Fla. : International Institute of Garibaldian Studies, 1984. — xxv,368p

GARVEY, MARCUS
STEIN, Judith
The world of Marcus Garvey : race and class in modern society / Judith Stein. — Baton Rouge ; London : Louisiana State University Press, c1986. — xii, 294p. — *Includes index. — Bibliography: p.281-284*

GARY (IND.) — Ethnic relations
MOHL, Raymond A
Steel city : urban and ethnic patterns in Gary, Indiana, 1906-1950 / Raymond A. Mohl and Neil Betten. — New York : Holmes & Meier, 1986. — x, 227 p., [16] p. of plates. — *Includes index. — Bibliography: p. 190-218*

GARY (IND.) — History
MOHL, Raymond A
Steel city : urban and ethnic patterns in Gary, Indiana, 1906-1950 / Raymond A. Mohl and Neil Betten. — New York : Holmes & Meier, 1986. — x, 227 p., [16] p. of plates. — *Includes index. — Bibliography: p. 190-218*

GARY (IND.) — Social conditions
MOHL, Raymond A
Steel city : urban and ethnic patterns in Gary, Indiana, 1906-1950 / Raymond A. Mohl and Neil Betten. — New York : Holmes & Meier, 1986. — x, 227 p., [16] p. of plates. — *Includes index. — Bibliography: p. 190-218*

GAS — Law and legislation — Great Britain
GREAT BRITAIN. Parliament. House of Commons. Library. Research Division
The Gas Bill (Bill 13 of 1985/6) / Christopher Barclay, Caroline Gilmour. — [London] : the Division, 1985. — 30p. — (Reference sheet ; no.85/10). — *Bibliography: p28-30*

GREAT BRITAIN. Parliament. House of Commons. Library. Research Division
Oil and Gas (Enterprise) Bill / [B. L. Miller]. — [London] : the Division, 1982. — 17p. — (Reference sheet ; no.82/1). — *Bibliography: p15-17*

GAS — Prices — European Economic Community Countries
Gas prices / Statistical Office of the European Communities. — Luxembourg : Statistical Office of the European Communities, 1984-. — Annual. — *Table headings in European Community languages. — Continues: Gas statistics/Statistical Office of the European Communities*

GAS — Prices — European Economic Community Countries — Statistics
Gas statistics / Statistical Office of the European Communities. — Luxembourg : Statistical Office of the European Communities, 1976-1977. — Annual. — *Table headings in European Community languages. — Continued by: Gas prices/Statistical Office of the European Communities*

GAS BILL 1985-86
GREAT BRITAIN. Parliament. House of Commons. Library. Research Division
The Gas Bill (Bill 13 of 1985/6) / Christopher Barclay, Caroline Gilmour. — [London] : the Division, 1985. — 30p. — (Reference sheet ; no.85/10). — *Bibliography: p28-30*

GAS COMPANIES — England — Lincoln (Lincolnshire) — History
ROBERTS, D. E.
The Lincoln gas undertaking 1828-1949 / prepared for EMGAS by D.E. Roberts. — [Leicester] ([51 DeMontfort) : [East Midlands Gas], [1981]. — 46p. — *Ill on inside covers. — Bibliography: p45-46*

GAS COMPANIES — England — Nottingham (Nottinghamshire) — History
ROBERTS, D. E.
The Nottingham gas undertaking 1818-1949 / prepared for Emgas by D. E. Roberts. — Leicester : East Midlands Gas, 1980. — 54p. — (Studies in East Midlands gas history). — *Bibliography: p53-54*

GAS INDUSTRY
The World gas trade : a resource for the future / edited by Melvin A. Conant. — Boulder, Colo. : Westview Press, 1986. — xiv, 290 p.. — (Westview special studies in natural resources and energy management). — *Bibliography: p. 284-285*

GAS INDUSTRY — Accounting
HEAZLEWOOD, C. T.
Financial accounting and reporting in the oil and gas industry : (a discussion of selected issues including a survey of United Kingdom company practices) / by C. T. Heazlewood. — [S.l.] : Institute of Chartered Accountants in England and Wales, [1987?]. — x,119p. — (Research paper / Institute of Chartered Accountants in England and Wales. Research Board). — *Bibliography: p107-119*

GAS INDUSTRY — Political aspects
BANKS, Ferdinand E.
The political economy of natural gas / Ferdinand E. Banks. — London : Croom Helm, c1987. — [240]p. — (Croom Helm commodity series). — *Includes bibliography and index*

GAS INDUSTRY — Political aspects — Soviet Union
STERN, Jonathan P.
Soviet oil and gas exports to the west : commercial transaction or security threat? / Jonathan P. Stern. — Aldershot : Gower, 1987. — xi,123p. — (Energy papers ; no.21). — *Bibliographical notes*

GAS INDUSTRY — England — Grimsby (Humberside)
ROBERTS, D. E.
The Grimsby gas undertaking 1836-1949 / D. E. Roberts. — Leicester : East Midlands Gas, 1983. — 38p. — (Studies in East Midlands gas history). — *Bibliography: p38*

GAS INDUSTRY — Great Britain
STERN, Jonathan P.
Natural gas in the U.K. : options to 2000 / Jonathan P. Stern. — Aldershot : Gower, c1986. — xvi,75p. — (Energy papers ; no.18)

GAS, NATURAL
OXFORD ENERGY SEMINAR
Natural gas : an international perspective : proceedings of the Oxford Energy Seminar 1982-1985 / edited by Robert Mabro. — Oxford : Oxford University Press for the Oxford Institute for Energy Studies, 1986. — xv,155p. — *Includes index*

GAS, NATURAL — Developing countries — Reserves
FEE, D. A.
Oil and gas databook for ACP countries : with special reference to the ACP countries / Derek Fee. — London : Graham & Trotman, 1985. — 215p

GAS, NATURAL — Political aspects
BANKS, Ferdinand E.
The political economy of natural gas / Ferdinand E. Banks. — London : Croom Helm, c1987. — [240]p. — (Croom Helm commodity series). — *Includes bibliography and index*

GAS, NATURAL — Ecuador — Statistics
Estadistica mensual de hidrocarburos / Direccion Nacional de Hidrocarburos. — Quito : Dpto. de Estadistica e Informacion Hidrocarburifera, 1985-. — *Monthly*

GAS, NATURAL — Great Britain
STERN, Jonathan P.
  Natural gas in the U.K. : options to 2000 / Jonathan P. Stern. — Aldershot : Gower, c1986. — xvi,75p. — (Energy papers ; no.18)

GAS, NATURAL — North Sea
OKLAHOMA. University. Science and Public Policy Program. Technology Assessment Group
  North Sea oil and gas : implications for future United States development / [by] Irvin L. White [and others] A study sponsored by the Council on Environmental Quality. — [1st ed.]. — Norman : University of Oklahoma Press, [c1973]. — xiii, 176 p. — *Includes bibliographical references*

GAUDOIS, JEAN
GANDOIS, Jean
  Mission acier : mon aventure belge / Jean Gandois. — Gembloux : Duculot Perspectives, 1986. — 141p

GAULLE, CHARLES DE
LACOUTURE, Jean
  De Gaulle / Jean Lacouture. — Paris : Le Seuil
  3: Le souverain. — 1986. — 865p. — *Bibliography: p843-[853]*

MESSMER, Pierre
  Les écrits militaires de Charles de Gaulle / Pierre Messmer, Alain Larcan. — Paris : Presses Universitaires de France, 1985. — 592p . — *Bibliography: p[553]-570*

WERTH, Alexander
  De Gaull : a political biography / Alexander Werth. — Harmondsworth : Penguin, 1965. — 391p. — *Bibliography: p379-382*

GAWA (PAPUA NEW GUINEA) — Social life and customs
MUNN, Nancy D.
  The fame of Gawa : a symbolic study of value tranformation in a Massim (Papua New Guinea) society / Nancy D. Munn. — Cambridge : Cambridge University Press, 1987. — xviii,331p. — (The Lewis Henry Morgan lectures ; 1976). — *Bibliography: p317-325. — Includes index*

GAZETTEERS
FISHER, Morris
  Provinces and provincial capitals of the world / compiled by Morris Fisher. — 2nd ed. — Metuchen, N.J. : Scarecrow, 1985. — ix, 248 p. . — *Includes index*

READER'S DIGEST
  Guide to places of the world. — London : Reader's Digest Association, 1987. — 736p

GDAŃSK (POLAND) — History
SCHOLZ, Joachim
  Von Danzig nach Danzig - ein weiter Weg / Joachim Scholz. — Limburg an der Lahn : C. A. Starke, 1985. — 236p

GEBUSI (PAPUA NEW GUINEA PEOPLE) — Rites and ceremonies
KNAUFT, Bruce M
  Good company and violence : sorcery in a lowland New Guinea society / Bruce M. Knauft. — Berkeley : University of California Press, c1985. — p. cm. — *Includes index. — Bibliography: p*

GEBUSI (PAPUA NEW GUINEA PEOPLE) — Social life and customs
KNAUFT, Bruce M
  Good company and violence : sorcery in a lowland New Guinea society / Bruce M. Knauft. — Berkeley : University of California Press, c1985. — p. cm. — *Includes index. — Bibliography: p*

GEMS
CLARK, Grahame
  Symbols of excellence : precious materials as expressions of status / Grahame Clark. — Cambridge : Cambridge University Press, 1986. — [144]p. — *Includes index*

GENE BANKS, PLANT
  Gene banks and the world's food / Donald L. Plucknett ... [et al.]. — Princeton, N.J. : Princeton University Press, c1987. — p. cm. — *Includes index. — Bibliography: p*

GENERAL AGREEMENT ON TARIFFS AND TRADE
GENERAL AGREEMENT ON TARIFFS AND TRADE
  [Documents]. — Geneva : GATT, 1952-. — *Irregular*

GREAT BRITAIN. Parliament. House of Commons. Library. Research Division
  Free trade and international GATT negotiations / Christopher Barclay. — [London] : the Division, 1986. — 25p. — (Background paper ; no.180)

GENERAL AGREEMENT ON TARIFFS AND TRADE (Organization)
  Text of the General Agreement. — Geneva : the Organization, 1986. — vi,96p

GENERAL AGREEMENT ON TARIFFS AND TRADE (1947)
STONE, Frank
  Canada, the GATT and the international trade system / Frank Stone. — Montreal, Quebec : Institute for Research on Public Policy, [1985] c1984. — xix, 236 p.. — (Essays in international economics). — *Bibliography: p. 217-224*

GENERAL ELECTRIC COMPANY
NYE, David E.
  Image worlds : corporate identities at General Electric, 1890-1930 / David E. Nye. — Cambridge, Mass. ; London : MIT Press, c1985. — xiv, 188p, [38]p of plates. — *Includes index. — Bibliography: p.[161]-182*

GENERAL MOTORS CORPORATION
JONES, Bryan D
  The sustaining hand : community leadership and corporate power / Bryan D. Jones and Lynn W. Bachelor with Carter Wilson. — Lawrence, Kan. : University Press of Kansas, c1986. — xii, 247 p.. — (Studies in government and public policy). — *Includes index. — Bibliography: p. 223-239*

GENERAL MOTORS CORPORATION — Management
KUHN, Arthur J
  Organizational cybernetics and business policy : System design for performance control / Arthur J. Kuhn. — University Park : Pennsylvania State University Press, 1986. — p. cm. — *Includes index. — Bibliography: p*

GENERAL MOTORS CORPORATION — Management — History — 20th century
KUHN, Arthur J
  GM passes Ford, 1918-1938 : designing the General Motors performance-control system / Arthur J. Kuhn. — University Park : Pennsylvania State University Press, 1986. — p. cm. — *Includes indexes. — Bibliography: p*

GENERAL THEORY OF EMPLOYMENT, INTEREST AND MONEY
  Keynes's general theory : fifty years on : its relevance and irrelevance to modern time / John Burton...[and others]. — London : Institute of Economic Affairs, 1986. — viii, 159p. — (Hobart paperback ; 24)

GENERAL WILL — History
RILEY, Patrick
  The general will before Rousseau : the transformation of the divine into the civic / Patrick Riley. — Princeton, N.J. : Princeton University Press, c1986. — xvii, 274p. — (Studies in moral, political, and legal philosophy). — *Includes index*

GENERALS — China — Biography
ANSCHEL, Eugene
  Homer Lea, Sun Yat-sen, and the Chinese revolution / by Eugene Anschel. — New York : Praeger, 1984. — xvi, 269 p.. — *Includes index. — Bibliography: p. 253-262*

P'ENG, Te-huai
  [P'eng Te-huai tzu shu. English]. Memoirs of a Chinese marshal : the autobiographical notes of Peng Dehuai (1898-1974) / translated by Zheng Longpu ; English text edited by Sara Grimes. — 1st ed. — Beijing : Foreign Languages Press, 1984. — vi, 523 p., [15] p. of plates. — *Translation of: P'eng Te-huai tzu shu*

GENERALS — Great Britain — Biography
THOMPSON, Neville
  Wellington after Waterloo / Neville Thompson. — London : Routledge & Kegan Paul, 1986. — [320]p. — *Includes index*

GENERALS — Spain — Bibliography
GARRIGA, Ramón
  El general Juan Yagüe : figura clave para conocer nuestra historia / Ramón Garriga. — Barcelona : Planeta, 1985. — 282p

GENERALS — Spain — Biography
INIESTA CANO, Carlos
  Memorias y recuerdos : los años que le vivido en le proceso histórico de España / Carlos Iniesta Cano ; prólogo de Emilio Romero. — Barcelona : Planeta, 1984. — 270p

GENERALS — United States — Biography
BAUER, K. Jack
  Zachary Taylor : soldier, planter, statesman of the old Southwest / K. Jack Bauer. — Baton Rouge : Louisiana State University Press, c1985. — xxiv, 348 p.. — (Southern biography series). — *Includes index. — Bibliography: p. 329-338*

BRENDON, Piers
  Ike, his life and times / Piers Brendon. — 1st ed. — New York : Harper & Row, c1986. — xvi, 478 p., [16] p. of plates. — *Includes index. — Bibliography: p. [461]-462*

BURK, Robert Fredrick
  Dwight D. Eisenhower, hero & politician / Robert F. Burk. — Boston : Twayne Publishers, c1986. — xii, 207 p., [14] p. of plates. — (Twayne's twentieth-century American biography series ; no. 2). — *Includes index. — Bibliography: p. 178-199*

HERSHEY, Lewis Blaine
  Lewis B. Hershey, Mr. Selective Service / George Q. Flynn. — Chapel Hill : University of North Carolina Press, c1985. — p. cm. — *Includes index. — Bibliography: p*

GENERATIVE GRAMMAR
CHOMSKY, Noam
  Barriers / Noam Chomsky. — Cambridge, Mass. : MIT Press, c1986. — p. cm. — (Linguistic inquiry monographs ; 13). — *Includes index. — Bibliography: p*

SELKIRK, Elisabeth O.
  The syntax of words / Elisabeth O. Selkirk. — Cambridge, Mass. : MIT Press, c1982. — x, 136 p.. — (Linguistic inquiry monographs ; 7). — *Bibliography: p. [132]-136*

GENETIC ENGINEERING — Law and legislation — United States
NATIONAL SYMPOSIUM ON GENETICS AND THE LAW (3rd Mass. : 1984 : Boston)
  Genetics and the law III / [proceedings of the Third National Symposium on Genetics and the Law, held April 2-4, 1984, in Boston, Massachusetts] ; [cosponsored by the American Society of Law and Medicine ... et al.] ; edited by Aubrey Milunsky and George J. Annas. — New York ; London : Plenum, c1985. — xix,514p. — *Bibliography: p491-504. — Includes index*

GENETIC ENGINEERING — Organisation for Economic Co-operation and Development countries — Safety measures
  Recombinant DNA safety considerations : safety considerations for industrial, agricultural and environmental applications of organisms derived by recombinant DNA techniques. — Paris : Organisation for Economic Co-operation and Development, 1986. — 69p. — *Includes bibliographical references*

GENIUS
Conceptions of giftedness / edited by Robert J. Sternberg, Janet E. Davidson. — Cambridge : Cambridge University Press, 1986. — x,460p

GENTILE, GIOVANNI
ROMANO, Sergio
Giovanni Gentile : la filosofia al potere / Sergio Romano. — Milano : Bompiani, 1984. — 352p, [32]p of plates

GENTRIFICATION — England — Norfolk
PARSONS, D. J.
Rural gentrification : the influence of rural settlement planning policies / D. J. Parsons. — [Brighton : University of Sussex, 1980]. — 36p. — (University of Sussex Research Papers in Geography)

GENTRIFICATION — England — Nottinghamshire
PARSONS, D. J.
Rural gentrification : the influence of rural settlement planning policies / D. J. Parsons. — [Brighton : University of Sussex, 1980]. — 36p. — (University of Sussex Research Papers in Geography)

GEO A. HORMEL AND CO.
HALSTEAD, Fred
The 1985-86 Hormel meat-packers strike in Austin, Minnesota / Fred Halstead. — New York : Pathfinder Press, 1986. — 44p

GEOGRAPHICAL DISTRIBUTION OF PLANTS AND ANIMALS
CROSBY, Alfred W.
Ecological imperialism : the biological expansion of Europe, 900-1900 / Alfred W. Crosby. — Cambridge : Cambridge University Press, 1986. — xiv,368p,[16]p of plates. — (Studies in environment and history). — Includes index

GEOGRAPHICAL PERCEPTION
GOLD, John R.
An introduction to behavioural geography / John R. Gold. — Oxford : Oxford University Press, 1980. — [9],290p. — Bibliography: p.253-286. — Includes index

GEOGRAPHY
Acta universitatis carolinae: Geographica. — Praha : Univerzita Karlova, 1966-. — Semi-annual

Spectrum of modern geography : essays in memory of Prof. Mohammad Anas / edited by Mohammad Shafi, Mehdi Raza. — New Delhi : Concept Pub. Co., 1986, c1985. — xxvii, 492 p.. — Summary: Festschrift honoring Mohammad Anas, 1925-1983, professor of geography, Aligarh Muslim University; comprises articles mostly in Indian context. — Includes bibliographies and index

GEOGRAPHY — Bibliography
A Geographical bibliography for American libraries / edited by Chauncy D. Harris ... [et al.]. — Washington, D.C. : Association of American Geographers, 1985. — 437p. — "A joint project of the Association of American Geographers and the National Geographic Society.". — Includes index

GEOGRAPHY — Dictionaries
READER'S DIGEST
Guide to places of the world. — London : Reader's Digest Association, 1987. — 736p

GEOGRAPHY — Mathematical models
Integrated models in geography : part IV of models in geography / edited by Richard J. Chorley, Peter Haggett. — London : Methuen, 1969. — c.250p. — (University paperbacks ; 260). — Sections originally published in the editors Models in geography: London: Methuen, 1967

GEOGRAPHY — Mathematics
Quantitative geography : a British view / edited by N. Wrigley and R.J. Bennett. — London : Routledge & Kegan Paul, 1981. — vi,419p. — Includes bibliographies and index

GEOGRAPHY — Methodology
Concepts and techniques in modern geography / Study Group in Quantitative Methods of the Institue of British Geographers. — London : Institute of British Geographers : 1976-. — Irregular

SHESKIN, Ira M.
Survey research for geographers / Ira M. Sheskin. — Washington, DC : Association of American Geographers, 1985. — 112p. — (Resource Publications in geography). — Bibliography: p.105-112

GEOGRAPHY — Philosophy
GOULD, Peter
The geographer at work / Peter Gould. — London : Routledge & Kegan Paul, 1985. — xviii, 351p

GEOGRAPHY — Psychological aspects
The use of psychology in geography : four perspectives / Alistair Fulton...[et al.]. — London : Graduate School of Geography, London School of Economics, 1987. — 77p. — (Geography Discussion Papers / London School of Economics and Political Science. Graduate School of Geography) ; New Series ; No.21). — Bibliography: p74-77

GEOGRAPHY — Social aspects — Great Britain
Changing Britain, changing world : geographical perspectives. — Milton Keynes : Open University Press. — (Social sciences : a second level course) (D 205 ; 8/11). — At head of title: The Open University. — Contents: Unit 8: Urban land use: change and conflict; Chris Hamnett; Unit 9: Housing and social divisions; Linda McDowell; Unit 10: Health care: unequal access; Stephanie Goodenough and Phil Sarre; Unit 11: Review: location and distance; Doreen Massey
Section II: Analysis: aspects of the geography of society
Block 3: Land use and services. — 1985. — 1v.(various pagings)

Changing Britain, changing world : geographical perspectives. — Milton Keynes : Open University Press. — (Social Sciences : a second level course)
Section 3: Synthesis: uniqueness and interdependence of place
Block 5: The changing face of the Isles. — 1985. — 1v (various pagings). — (D205 ; 17/20). — At head title: The Open University. — Contents: Unit 17: Local change in the west of Ireland/Pat Jess - Unit 18: Inner-city decline/Chris Hamnett - Unit 19: Are there two Britains? The North-South divide/Richard Meegan - Unit 20: Regional cultures/Doreen Massey

GEOGRAPHY — Statistical methods
JOHNSTON, R. J.
Multivariate statistical analysis in geography : a primer on the general linear method / R.J. Johnston. — London : Longman, 1978. — xx,280p. — Bibl.: p.272-277. - Index

JOHNSTON, R. J.
Multivariate statistical analysis in geography : a primer on the general linear model / by R.J. Johnston. — London : Longman, 1980. — xx,280p. — Originally published: 1978. — Bibliography: p. 272-277. — Includes index

GEOGRAPHY — Statistical methods — Congresses
Statistical applications in the spatial sciences / editor N. Wrigley. — London : Pion, 1979. — [9],310p. — '[Papers from] a joint conference of the Group [i.e. the Quantitative Methods Study Group of the Institute of British Geographers] with the Royal Statistical Society General Applications Section [which] was held at the University of Bristol in September 1977 ...' - Preface. — Includes bibliographies and index

GEOGRAPHY — Great Britain — Data processing
GREAT BRITAIN. Committee of Enquiry into the Handling of Geographic Information
Handling geographic information : report to the Secretary of State for the Environment of the Committee of Enquiry into the Handling of Geographic Information. — London : H.M.S.O., 1987. — vi,208p. — Chairman: Lord Chorley. — References and bibliography: p125-126,p174

GEOGRAPHY, ECONOMIC
The Spatial impact of technological change / edited by John F. Brotchie, Peter Hall & Peter W. Newton. — London : Croom Helm, c1987. — xxv,460p

Technical change and industrial policy / edited by Keith Chapman and Graham Humphrys. — Oxford : Basil Blackwell, 1987. — 264p. — (Institute of British Geographers special publications ; 19). — Conference papers. — Includes bibliographies and index

WATTS, H. D.
Industrial geography / H.D. Watts. — Harlow : Longman Scientific & Technical, 1987. — xii,260p. — Bibliography: p241-251. — Includes index

GEOGRAPHY, ECONOMIC — Maps
Atlas of the United States : a thematic and comparative approach / [edited by] Jilly Glassborow, Gillian Freeman. — New York : Macmillan : Nomad : Michael W. Dempsey, 1985. — 127p

GEOGRAPHY, HISTORICAL
Historical geography : progress and prospect / edited by Michael Pacione. — London : Croom Helm, c1987. — x,306p. — (Croom Helm progress in geography series). — Includes bibliographies and index

GEOGRAPHY, POLITICAL
AGNEW, John A.
Place and politics : the geographical mediation of state and society / John A. Agnew. — Boston ; London : Allen & Unwin, 1987. — [288]p. — Includes bibliography and index

Changing Britain, changing world : geographical perspectives. — Milton Keynes : Open University Press. — (Social Sciences : a second level course)
Section 2: Analysis: aspects of the geography of society
Block 4: Culture and conflict: views of space, place and nature. — 1985. — 28,27,25,32,24p. — (D205 ; 12/16). — Contents: Unit 12: Whose land?/Doreen Massey - Unit 13: Place and perception/Phil Sarre - Unit 14: Environment and politics in a capitalist society/Andrew Blowers - Unit 15: Environment and politics in a state socialist society/Allan Cochrane - Unit 16: Geopolitics/John Short

International geopolitical analysis : a selection from Hérodote / edited and translated by Pascal Girot and Eleonore Kofman. — London : Croom Helm, c1987. — [256]p. — (Croom Helm series in geography and environment). — Translated from the French. — Includes index

JOO-JOCK, Lim
Territorial power domains, southeast Asia, and China : the geo-strategy of an overarching massif / Lim Joo-Jock. — Singapore : Institute of Southeast Asian Studies, 1984. — 230p. — Bibliography: p215-229

LEY, David
A social geography of the city / David Ley. — New York : Harper & Row, c1983. — xii,449p. — (Harper & Row series in geography). — Bibliography: p.401-441

GEOLOGY — England
EDMONDS, E. A.
South-West England / by E.A. Edmonds, M.C. McKeown, M. Williams ; [for the] Natural Environment Research Council, Institute of Geological Sciences. — 4th ed. / based on previous eds. by H. Dewey. — London : H.M.S.O., 1975. — xi,138p,fold leaf,[3]fold leaves of plates. — (British regional geology). — *Previous ed.: 1969. — Bibliography: p.113-124. — Includes index*

GEOLOGY — Scotland — Midland Valley
CAMERON, I. B.
The Midland Valley of Scotland. — 3rd ed. / by I.B. Cameron and D. Stephenson. — London : HMSO, 1985. — viii, 172p. — (British regional geology). — *At head of title: British Geological Survey, Natural Environment Research Council. — Previous ed.: 1948. — Folded map (col.) in pocket. — Map in back pocket. — Bibliography: p 153-162*

GEOMORPHOLOGY — History
TINKLER, Keith J.
A short history of geomorphology / Keith J. Tinkler. — London : Croom Helm, c1985. — xviii,317p. — *Bibliography: p241-279. — Includes index*

GEOPOLITICS — Asia, Southeastern
JOO-JOCK, Lim
Territorial power domains, southeast Asia, and China : the geo-strategy of an overarching massif / Lim Joo-Jock. — Singapore : Institute of Southeast Asian Studies, 1984. — 230p. — *Bibliography: p215-229*

GEOPOLITICS — Great Britain
Changing Britain, changing world : geographical perspectives. — Milton Keynes : Open University Press. — (Social Sciences : a second level course)
Section 2: Analysis: aspects of the geography of society
Block 4: Culture and conflict: views of space, place and nature. — 1985. — 28,27,25,32,24p. — (D205 ; 12/16). — *Contents: Unit 12: Whose land?/Doreen Massey - Unit 13: Place and perception/Phil Sarre - Unit 14: Environment and politics in a capitalist society/Andrew Blowers - Unit 15: Environment and politics in a state socialist society/Allan Cochrane - Unit 16: Geopolitics/John Short*

GEORGE I, King of Great Britain
MURRAY, John Joseph
George I, the Baltic and the Whig split of 1717 : a study in diplomacy and propaganda / John J. Murray. — London : Routledge and Kegan Paul, 1969. — xv,366p

GEORGIA — Census, 1860
BODE, Frederick A.
Farm tenancy and the census in antebellum Georgia / Frederick A. Bode, Donald E. Ginter. — Athens : University of Georgia Press, c1987. — p. cm. — *Includes index. — Bibliography: p*

GEORGIA — History — 1775-1865
SMITH, Julia Floyd
Slavery and rice culture in low country Georgia, 1750-1860 / Julia Floyd Smith. — Knoxville : University of Tennessee Press, c1985. — p. cm. — *Includes index. — Bibliography: p*

GEORGIA — History — Civil War, 1861-1865
MOHR, Clarence L
On the threshold of freedom : masters and slaves in Civil War Georgia / Clarence L. Mohr. — Athens, Ga. ; London : University of Georgia Press, c1986. — xxi, 397p, 18p of plates. — *Includes index. — Bibliography: p.367-385*

GEORGIA — Politics and government — 1865-1950
DRAGO, Edmund L.
Black politicians and reconstruction in Georgia : a splendid failure / Edmund L. Drago. — Baton Rouge ; London : Louisiana State University Press, c1982. — xii,201p

GEORGIA — Race relations
DRAGO, Edmund L.
Black politicians and reconstruction in Georgia : a splendid failure / Edmund L. Drago. — Baton Rouge ; London : Louisiana State University Press, c1982. — xii,201p

DUNCAN, Russell
Freedom's shore : Tunis Campbell and the Georgia freedmen / by Russell Duncan. — Athens : University of Georgia Press, c1986. — p. cm. — *Includes index. — Bibliography: p*

MOHR, Clarence L
On the threshold of freedom : masters and slaves in Civil War Georgia / Clarence L. Mohr. — Athens, Ga. ; London : University of Georgia Press, c1986. — xxi, 397p, 18p of plates. — *Includes index. — Bibliography: p.367-385*

WALLENSTEIN, Peter
From slave South to New South : public policy in nineteenth-century Georgia / Peter Wallenstein. — Chapel Hill : University of North Caroline Press, c1987. — xii, 284 p.. — (The Fred W. Morrison series in Southern studies). — *Includes index. — Bibliography: p. [257]-272*

GEORGIA — Social life and customs
GREENHOUSE, Carol J.
Praying for justice : faith, order, and community in an American town / Carol J. Greenhouse. — Ithaca : Cornell University Press, 1986. — p. cm. — (Anthropology of contemporary issues). — *Includes index. — Bibliography: p*

GEORGIAN S.S.R. — Economic policy
BURDULI, V. Sh.
Sovershenstvovanie upravlenie ekonomikoi regiona : (na primere Gruzinskoi SSR) / V. Sh. Burduli. — Tbilisi : Metsniereba, 1985. — 200p

GERIATRIC PSYCHIATRY — England — Hampshire
Something to look forward to : an evaluation of a travelling day hospital for elderly mentally ill people / Neil Evans...[et al.]. — Portsmouth : Social Services Research and Intelligence Unit, 1986. — x,254p. — (SSRIU Report ; No.15). — *Bibliography: p[251]-254*

GERMAN AMERICANS — History — Congresses
America and the Germans : an assessment of a three hundred year history / Frank Trommler and Joseph McVeigh, editors. — Philadelphia, Pa. : University of Pennsylvania Press. — *Rev. versions of papers presented at the Tricentennial Conference of German-American History, Politics and Culture, held at the University of Pennsylvania, Philadelphia, Oct.3-6, 1983*
Vol.1: Immigration, language, ethnicity. — 1985. — xxxii,376p

America and the Germans : an assessment of a three hundred year history / Frank Trommler and Joseph McVeigh, editors. — Philadelphia, Pa. : University of Pennsylvania Press. — *Rev. versions of papers presented at the Tricentennial Conference of German-American History, Politics and Culture, held at the University of Pennsylvania, Philadelphia, Oct. 3-6, 1983*
Vol.2: The relationship in the twentieth century. — 1985. — xvii,369p

GERMAN LANGUAGE — Dictionaries — English
Shorter Cambridge-Eichborn German dictionary : business and business law, economics, administration. — Cambridge : Cambridge University Press, 1984. — 2v.

GERMAN LANGUAGE — Grammar — 1950-
TURNER, G. W
German for librarians / by G. W. Turner. Rev. and edited by A. J. A. Vieregg and J. W. Blackwood. — [Palmerston North, N.Z. : Massey University], 1972. — iii, 137 p. — (Massey University. Library series ; no. 5)

GERMAN LANGUAGE — Slang — Dictionaries
HENSCHEID, Eckhard
Dummdeutsch : ein satirisch polemisches Wörterbuch / unter Federführung von Eckhard Henscheid und Mitwirkung von Carl Lierow und Elsemarie Maletzke ; mit Zeichnungen von Chlodwig Poth. — Frankfurt am Main : Fischer Taschenbuch, 1985. — 85p

GERMAN LITERATURE — 20th century — History and criticism
BERLINER COLLOQUIUM ZUR LITERATURPOLITIK IM 'DRITTEN REICH'
"Das war ein Vorspiel nur ..." : Berliner ... / hrsg. [von] Aorst Denkler [und] Eberhard Lämmert. — Berlin : Akademie der Künste Freie Universität Berlin, 1985. — 211 p. — (Schriftenreihe der Akademie der Künste : Bd. 15)

PARKES, K. Stuart
Writers and politics in West Germany / K. Stuart Parkes. — London : Croom Helm, c1986. — 251p. — *Bibliography: p242-246. — Includes index*

GERMAN LITERATURE — Germany (East) — History and criticism — Congresses
INTERNATIONAL SYMPOSIUM ON THE GERMAN DEMOCRATIC REPUBLIC ((7th : 1981 : World Fellowship Center)
Studies in GDR culture and society 2 : proceedings of the Seventh International Symposium on the German Democratic Republic / editorial board, Margy Gerber, chief editor ... [et al.]. — Washington, D.C. : University Press of America, c1982. — iv, 292 p.. — *English and German. — Includes bibliographical references*

GERMAN REUNIFICATION QUESTION (1949-)
BREDOW, Wilfried von
Deutschland : ein Provisorium? / Wilfried von Bredow. — Berlin : Siedler, 1985. — 166p

ERLER, Fritz
The struggle for German reunification / by Fritz Erler. — Bonn : Social-Democratic Party of Germany, [1956?]. — 20p. — *Reprinted from Foreign Affairs, April, 1956*

KLÖNNE, Arno
Zurück zur Nation? : Kontroversen zu deutschen Fragen / Arno Klönne. — Köln : Eugen Diederichs, 1984. — 159p

Nation Deutschland ? / Guido Knapp...[et al.] (Hrsg.) ; mit Beiträagen von Hellmut Diwald... [et al.]. — Paderborn : Ferdinand Schöningh. — (Geschichte, Politik und Massenmedien ; Bd.3)
1: Hambacher Disput. — 1984. — 77p

SCHULZ, Eberhard
Bewegung in der deutsche Frage? : die ausländischen Besorgnisse über die Entwicklung in den beiden deutschen Staaten / Eberhard Schulz, Peter Danylow. — 2e, erw. Auflage. — Bonn : Europa Union, 1985. — iv,224p. — (Arbeitspapiere zur internationalen Politik ; 33)

STEININGER, Rolf
Eine vertane Chance : die Stalin-Note vom 10. März 1952 und die Wiedervereinigung : eine Studie auf der Grundlage unveröffentlichter britischer und amerikanischer Akten / Rolf Steininger. — 2. Aufl.. — Berlin : Dietz, 1985. — 158p. — *Bibliography: p153-156*

GERMAN REUNIFICATION QUESTION (1949-) *continuation*

WEISENFELD, Ernst
Welches Deutschland soll es sein? : Frankreich und die deutsche Einheit seit 1945 / Ernst Weisenfeld. — München : Beck, 1986. — 203p. — *Bibliographical notes*

WETZLAUGK, Udo
Berlin und die deutsche Frage / Udo Wetzlaugk. — Köln : Verlag Wissenschaft und Politik, 1985. — 272p. — *Bibliography: p257-272*

GERMAN REUNIFICATION QUESTION (1949-) — Sources

Dokumente zur Deutschlandpolitik. — Frankfurt : Metzner (for) Bundesministerium für innerdeutsche Beziehungen
Reihe 4: Vom 10. November 1958 bis 30. November 1966 / bearbeitet von Ernst Deuerlein [and others]. — 1971-1981. — 12v. in 22

GERMANS — Argentina

Presencia alemana y austríaca en la Argentina = Deutsche und österreichische Präsenz in Argentina / proyecto y dirección Manrique Zago. — Buenos Aires : Manrique Zago, [1985]. — 220p

GERMANS — Brazil — São Pedro (Rio Grande do Sul)

PINHEIRO, José Feliciano Fernandes, Visconde de São Leopoldo
Anais da província de São Pedro : história da colonização alemã no Rio Grande do Sul / José Feliciano Fernandes Pinheiro, Visconde de São Leopoldo ; introdução de Viana Moog. — 4 edição. — Petrópolis : Vozes ; [Brasília] : Instituto Nacional do Livro, Ministério da Educação e Cultura, 1978. — 250p. — (Dimensões do Brasil ; 9). — *Publicado originalmente em Rio de Janeiro, Regia, 1819-1822, com o título: "Annaes da capitania de S. Pedro*

GERMANS — Canada — History

LEHMANN, Heinz
The German Canadians, 1750-1937 : immigration, settlement & culture / Heinz Lehmann ; translated, edited & introduced by Gerhard P. Bassler. — St. John's, Nfld. : Jesperson Press, 1986. — lxii, 541 p., [24] p. of plates. — *Col. map on lining paper. — One folded col. map in pocket. — Includes index. — Bibliography: p. 459-496*

GERMANS — Hungary

LÁSZLÓ, Lajos
Jégszikrák : (A hazai nemzetiségek életéb"ol) / László Lajos. — [Budapest] : Népszava, 1984. — 177p

GERMANS — Ontario — Renfrew (County) — History

LEE-WHITING, Brenda
Harvest of stones : the German settlement in Renfrew County / Brenda Lee-Whiting. — Toronto ; Buffalo : University of Toronto Press, c1985. — xii, 323 p.. — *Includes index. — Bibliography: p. [301]-314*

GERMANY. Enabling Act 1933

BIESEMANN, Jörg
Das Ermächtigungsgestz als Grundlage der Gesetzgebung im nationalsozialistischen Staat : ein Beitrag zur Stellung des Gesetzes in der Verfassungsgeschichte 1919-1945 / Jörg Biesemann. — Münster : Lit, 1985. — lviii,403p. — (Studien zur Politikwissenschaft ; Bd.13). — *Includes bibliographic notes*

GERMANY — Armed forces — History — Sources

Die geheimen Tagesberichte der deutschen Wehrmachtführung im zweiten Weltkrieg 1939-1945 / herausgegeben...von Kurt Mehner. — Osnabrück : Biblio. — (Veröffentlichungen deutschen Quellenmaterials zum zweiten Weltkrieg ; no.2)
Band 10: 1. März 1944-31. August 1944. — 1985. — 722p,48p of plates

Die geheimen Tagesberichte der deutschen Wehrmachtführung im zweiten Weltkrieg 1939-1945 / herausgegeben von Kurt Mehner. — Osnabrück : Biblio. — (Veröffentlichungen deutschen Quellenmaterials zum zweiten Weltkrieg)
Band 11: 1. September 1944-31. Dezember 1944. — 1984. — 492p,35p of plates

Die geheimen Tagesberichte der deutschen Wehrmachtführung im zweiten Weltkrieg 1939-1945 / herausgegehen...von Kurt Mehner. — Osnabrück : Biblio. — (Veröffentlichungen deutschen Quellenmaterials zum zweiten Weltkrieg)
Band 12: 1. Januar 1945-9. Mai 1945. — 1984. — 611p,35p of plates

GERMANY — Bibliography

German studies: British resources : papers presented at a colloquium at the British Library 25-27 September 1985 : organised in conjunction with the Institute of Germanic Studies of the University of London / edited by David Paisey. — London : British Library, 1986. — xiv,320p. — (British Library occasional papers ; 8)

GERMANY — Biography

FEST, Joachim C.
The face of the Third Reich / Joachim C. Fest ; translated from the German by Michael Bullock. — London : Weidenfeld and Nicolson, 1970. — xiii,402p

GERMANY — Boundaries — Poland

MROCZKO, Marian
Polska myśl zachodnia 1918-1939 : (kształtowanie i upowszechnianie / Marian Mroczko. — Poznań : Instytut Zachodni, 1986. — 429p. — (Dzieje polskiej granicy zachodniej ; 6). — *Summary in English and German. — Bibliography: p352-393*

GERMANY — Colonies

German imperialism in Africa : from the beginnings until the Second World War / edited by Helmuth Stoecker ; translated from the German by Bernd Zöllner. — London : Hurst, 1986. — 446p. — *Translation of: Drang nach Afrika. — Includes bibliography and index*

SCHINZINGER, Francesca
Die Kolonien und das Deutsche Reich : die wirtschaftliche Bedentung der deutschen Besitzungen in 'Ubersee / Francesca Schinzinger. — Stuttgart : Steiner Verlag Wiesbaden, 1984. — 179p. — *Bibliography: p177-179*

GERMANY — Colonies — History

SCHINZINGER, Francesca
Die Kolonien und das Deutsche Reich : die wirtschaftliche Bedentung der deutschen Besitzungen in 'Ubersee / Francesca Schinzinger. — Stuttgart : Steiner Verlag Wiesbaden, 1984. — 179p. — *Bibliography: p177-179*

SCHULTZ-NAUMANN, Joachim
Unter Kaisers Flagge : Deutschlands Schutzgebiete im Pazifik und in China einst und heute / Joachim Schultz-Naumann. — München : Universitasa, 1985. — 351p. — *Bibliography: p333-339*

GERMANY — Constitutional history

KIRCHHEIMER, Otto
Social democracy and the rule of law / Otto Kirchheimer and Franz Neumann ; edited by Keith Tribe ; translated by Leena Tanner and Keith Tribe. — London : Allen & Unwin, 1987. — [224]p. — *Translated from the German. — Includes bibliography and index*

GERMANY — Diplomatic and consular service — History

Das Diplomatische Korps 1871-1945 : Büdinger Forschungen zur Sozialgeschichte 1982 / herausgegeben von Klaus Schwabe. — Boppard am Rhein : Harald Boldt, 1985. — 227p. — (Deutsche Führungsschichten in der Neuzeit ; Bd.16)

GERMANY — Economic conditions

SOMMARIVA, Andrea
German macroeconomic history, 1880-1979 : a study of the effects of economic policy on inflation, currency depreciation and growth / Andrea Sommariva and Giuseppe Tullio ; foreword by Clifford Wymer. — Basingstoke : Macmillan, 1986, c1987. — xx,264p. — *Bibliography: p249-257. — Includes index*

GERMANY — Economic conditions — 19th century

MOSSE, W. E.
Jews in the German economy : the German-Jewish economic élite, 1820-1935 / W.E. Mosse. — Oxford : Clarendon, 1987. — 420p. — *Bibliography: p406-409. — Includes index*

GERMANY — Economic conditions — 20th century

MOSSE, W. E.
Jews in the German economy : the German-Jewish economic élite, 1820-1935 / W.E. Mosse. — Oxford : Clarendon, 1987. — 420p. — *Bibliography: p406-409. — Includes index*

GERMANY — Economic conditions — 1918-1945

KUNZ, Andreas
Civil servants and the politics of inflation in Germany, 1914-1924 / Andreas Kunz. — Berlin ; New York : De Gruyter, 1986. — xix, 427 p.. — (Veröffentlichungen der Historischen Kommission zu Berlin ; Bd. 66) (Beiträge zu Inflation und Wiederaufbau in Deutschland und Europa 1914-1924 ; Bd. 7). — *Includes indexes. — Bibliography: p. [393]-413*

GERMANY — Economic history

MOMMSEN, Wolfgang J.
Britain and Germany 1800 to 1914 : two developmental paths towards industrial society / Wolfgang J. Mommsen. — London : German Historical Institute, London, 1986. — 38p. — (The 1985 Annual lecture / German Historical Institute, London)

GERMANY — Economic policy

SOMMARIVA, Andrea
German macroeconomic history, 1880-1979 : a study of the effects of economic policy on inflation, currency depreciation and growth / Andrea Sommariva and Giuseppe Tullio ; foreword by Clifford Wymer. — Basingstoke : Macmillan, 1986, c1987. — xx,264p. — *Bibliography: p249-257. — Includes index*

GERMANY — Economic policy — 1933-1945

HERBERT, Ulrich
Fremdarbeiter : Politik und Praxis des "Ausländer-Einsatzes" in der Kriegswirtschaft des Dritten Reiches / Ulrich Herbert. — Berlin : J. H. W. Dietz, 1985. — 494p. — *Bibliography: p454-478*

GERMANY — Emigration and immigration — History

Presencia alemana y austríaca en la Argentina = Deutsche und österreichische Präsenz in Argentina / proyecto y dirección Manrique Zago. — Buenos Aires : Manrique Zago, [1985]. — 220p

GERMANY — Ethnic relations

ZIMMERMANN, Mosche
[Vilhelm Mar, "ha-paṭri'arkh shel ha-Anṭishemiyut". English]. Wilhelm Marr, the patriarch of Antisemitism / by Moshe Zimmermann. — New York : Oxford University Press, 1986. — p. cm. — *Translation of: Vilhelm Mar, "ha-paṭri'arkh shel ha-Anṭishemiyut.". — Includes index*

GERMANY — Ethnic relations — Congresses

The Jewish response to German culture : from the enlightenment to the Second World War / edited by Jehuda Reinharz and Walter Schatzberg. — Hanover, NH : Published for Clark University by University Press of New England, 1985. — xii, 362p. — *"Essays based on papers delivered at the International Conference on German Jews, held at Clark University, Worcester, Massachusetts, October 8-11, 1983."*. — *Includes index*

GERMANY — Foreign economic relations — Italy

RASPIN, Angela
The Italian war economy, 1940-1943 : with particular reference to Italian relations with Germany / Angela Raspin. — New York : Garland Pub., 1986. — p. cm. — (Outstanding theses from the London School of Economics and Political Science). — *Thesis (Ph. D.)--London University, 1980.* — *Bibliography: p*

GERMANY — Foreign relations

Deutschland und der Westen : Vorträge und Diskussionsbeiträge des Symposiums zu Ehren von Gordon A. Craig veranstaltet von der Freien Universität Berlin vom 1.-3. Dezember 1983 / herausgegeben von Henning Köhler. — Berlin : Colloquium Verlag, 1984. — 218p. — (Studien zur europäischen Geschichte ; Bd.15). — *Includes three chapters in English*

GERMANY — Foreign relations — Sources — Great Britain

Dokumente zur Deutschlandpolitik. — Frankfurt : Metzner (for) Bundesministerium für immerdeutsche Beziechunqen
Reihe 1: Vom 3. September 1939 bis 8. Mai 1945 / bearbeitet von Rainer A. Blasius [and others]. — 1984-

GERMANY — Foreign relations — Sources — United States

Dokumente zur Deutschlandpolitik. — Frankfurt : Metzner (for) Bundesministerium für immerdeutsche Beziechunqen
Reihe 1: Vom 3. September 1939 bis 8. Mai 1945 / bearbeitet von Rainer A. Blasius [and others]. — 1984-

GERMANY — Foreign relations — 1871-1918

HERWIG, Holger H
Germany's vision of empire in Venezuela, 1871-1914 / Holger H. Herwig. — Princeton, N.J. : Princeton University Press, c1986. — xii, 285 p.. — *Includes index.* — *Bibliography: p. [247]-272*

GERMANY — Foreign relations — 20th century — Addresses, essays, lectures

Aspekte deutscher Aussenpolitik im 20. [i.e. zwanzigsten] Jahrhundert : Aufsätze Hans Rothfels z. Gedächtnis / hrsg. von Wolfgang Benz u. Hermann Graml. — Stuttgart : Deutsche Verlags-Anstalt, 1976. — 304 p.. — *"Schriftenreihe der Vierteljahrshefte für Zeitgeschichte, Sondernummer."*. — *Bibliography of H. Rothfels' works: p. [287]-304.* — *Includes bibliographical references*

GERMANY — Foreign relations — 1918-1933

HIDEN, John
The Baltic states and Weimar Ostpolitik / John Hiden. — Cambridge : Cambridge University Press, 1987. — xi,296p. — *Bibliography: p243-265* — *Includes index*

LEE, Marshall M.
German foreign policy 1917-1933 : continuity or break? / Marshall M. Lee, Wolfgang Michalka. — Leamington Spa : Berg, c1987. — 180p. — *Bibliography : p167-173.* — *Includes index*

STOAKES, Geoffrey
Hitler and the quest for world dominion : Nazi ideology and foreign policy in the 1920s / Geoffrey Stoakes. — Leamington Spa : Berg, 1986. — [304]p. — *Includes bibliography and index*

GERMANY — Foreign relations — 1933-1945

HIDEN, John
The Baltic states and Weimar Ostpolitik / John Hiden. — Cambridge : Cambridge University Press, 1987. — xi,296p. — *Bibliography: p243-265* — *Includes index*

GERMANY — Foreign relations — 1945-

FELDMAN, Lily Gardner
The special relationship between West Germany and Israel / Lily Gardner Feldman. — Boston ; London : Allen & Unwin, 1984. — xix,330p. — *Bibliography: p295-322.* — *Includes index*

Kalter Krieg und Deutsche Frage : Deutschland im Widerstreit der Mächte 1945-1952 / herausgegeben von Josef Foschepoth. — Göttingen : Vandenhoeck und Ruprecht, 1985. — 388p. — (Veröffentlichungen des Deutschen Historischen Instituts London = Publications of the German Historical Insitute London ; Bd.16). — *Bibliograhical notes*

STEININGER, Rolf
Eine vertane Chance : die Stalin-Note vom 10. März 1952 und die Wiedervereinigung : eine Studie auf der Grundlage unveröffentlichter britischer und amerikanischer Akten / Rolf Steininger. — 2. Aufl.. — Berlin : Dietz, 1985. — 158p. — *Bibliography: p153-156*

GERMANY — Foreign relations — Africa

German imperialism in Africa : from the beginnings until the Second World War / edited by Helmuth Stoecker ; translated from the German by Bernd Zöllner. — London : Hurst, 1986. — 446p. — *Translation of: Drang nach Afrika.* — *Includes bibliography and index*

GERMANY — Foreign relations — Baltic States

HIDEN, John
The Baltic states and Weimar Ostpolitik / John Hiden. — Cambridge : Cambridge University Press, 1987. — xi,296p. — *Bibliography: p243-265* — *Includes index*

GERMANY — Foreign relations — Czechoslovakia

KŘEN, Jan
Integration oder Ausgrenzung : Deutsche und Tschechen 1890-1945 / J. Křen, V. Kural [und] D. Brandes ; mit einen Vorwort von Dieter Beyran. — Bremen : Donat und Temmen, 1986. — 156p. — *Bibliographical notes*

GERMANY — Foreign relations — Europe — Addresses, essays, lectures

German nationalism and the European response, 1890-1945 / edited by Carole Fink, Isabel V. Hull, and MacGregor Knox. — 1st ed. — Norman : University of Oklahoma Press, c1985. — xv, 299 p.. — *Includes bibliographical references and index*

GERMANY — Foreign relations — France

WEISENFELD, Ernst
Welches Deutschland soll es sein? : Frankreich und die deutsche Einheit seit 1945 / Ernst Weisenfeld. — München : Beck, 1986. — 203p. — *Bibliographical notes*

GERMANY — Foreign relations — Great Britain

BIRKE, Adolf M.
Britain and Germany : historical patterns of a relationship / Adolf M. Birke. — London : German Historical Institute, 1987. — 40p. — *Bibliography: p33-35*

SCHMIDT, Gustav
The politics and economics of appeasement : British foreign policy in the 1930s / Gustav Schmidt ; translated from the German by Jackie Bennett-Ruete. — Leamington Spa : Berg, c1986. — 435p. — *Translation of: England in der Krise.* — *Bibliography: p394-429.* — *Includes index*

GERMANY — Foreign relations — Japan

German-Japanese relations in the 1930's / edited by Ian Nish. — London : Suntory-Toyota International Centre for Economics and Related Disciplines, 1986. — 49p. — (International studies ; 1986/3)

GERMANY — Foreign relations — Poland

Studia z najnowszej historii niemiec i stosunków polsko-niemieckich / pod redakcją Stanisława Sierpowskiego. — Poznań : Uniwersytet im. Adama Mickiewicza, 1986. — 634p. — (Seria Historia / Uniwersytet im. Adama Mickiewicza w Poznaniu ; Nr.129). — *In Polish or German*

GERMANY — Foreign relations — Silesia, Upper (Poland and Czechoslovakia)

OPITZ, Michael
Schlesien bleibt unser : Deutschlands Kampf um Oberschlesien 1919-1921 / Michael Opitz. — Kiel : Arndt, 1985. — 252p. — *Bibliography: p248-251*

GERMANY — Foreign relations — Soviet Union

LEONHARD, Wolfgang
Der Schock des Hitler-Stalin-Paktes : Grinnerungen aus der Sowjetunion, Westeuropa und USA / Wolfgang Leonhard. — Freiburg im Breisgau : Herder, 1986. — 220p. — *Bibliographical notes*

ZETTERBERG, Seppo
Die Liga der Fremdvölker Russlands 1916-1918 : ein Beitrag zu Deutschlands antirussischem Propagandakreig unter den Fremdvölkern Russlands im ersten Weltkrieg / Seppo Zetterberg. — Helsinki : [Suomen Historiallinen Seura], 1978. — 279p. — (Studia historica veröffentlicht von der Finnischen Historischen Gesellschaft/Suomen Historiallinen Seura/Finska Historiska Samfundet ; vol.8). — *Bibliography: p263-271*

GERMANY — Foreign relations — Spain

RUIZ HOLST, Matthias
Neutralität oder Kriegsbeteiligung? : die deutsch-spanischen Verhandlungen im Jahre 1940 / Matthias Ruiz Holst. — Pfaffenweiler : Centaurus-Verlagsgesellschaft, 1986. — vi,231p. — *Bibliography: p225-231*

GERMANY — Foreign relations — United States

FROHN, Axel
Neutralisierung als Alternative zur Westintegration : die Deutschlandpolitik der Vereinigten Staaten von Amerika 1945-1949 / von Axel Frohn. — Frankfurt : Metzner, 1985. — 170p. — (Dokumente zur Deutschlandpolitik. Beihefte ; Bd.7). — *Bibliography: p145-162*

GERMANY — Foreign relations — United States — Addresses, essays, lectures

FLETCHER, Willard Allen
United States-German relations, past and present / Willard Allen Fletcher, Stephen F. Szabo, Stanley R. Sloan. — Washington : Library of Congress, 1984. — iii,25p. — *Bibliography: p23-25*

GERMANY — Foreign relations — United States — Congresses

America and the Germans : an assessment of a three hundred year history / Frank Trommler and Joseph McVeigh, editors. — Philadelphia, Pa. : University of Pennsylvania Press. — *Rev. versions of papers presented at the Tricentennial Conference of German-American History, Politics and Culture, held at the University of Pennsylvania, Philadelphia, Oct.3-6, 1983*
Vol.1: Immigration, language, ethnicity. — 1985. — xxxii,376p

GERMANY — Foreign relations — United States — Congresses
continuation
America and the Germans : an assessment of a three hundred year history / Frank Trommler and Joseph McVeigh, editors. — Philadelphia, Pa. : University of Pennsylvania Press. — *Rev. versions of papers presented at the Tricentennial Conference of German-American History, Politics and Culture, held at the University of Pennsylvania, Philadelphia, Oct. 3-6, 1983*
Vol.2: The relationship in the twentieth century. — 1985. — xvii,369p

GERMANY — Foreign relations — Venezuela
HERWIG, Holger H
Germany's vision of empire in Venezuela, 1871-1914 / Holger H. Herwig. — Princeton, N.J. : Princeton University Press, c1986. — xii, 285 p.. — *Includes index. — Bibliography: p. [247]-272*

GERMANY — History
FITZGIBBON, Constantine
A concise history of Germany / Constantine FitzGibbon. — London : Thames and Hudson, 1972. — 192p. — *Bibliographyp.181. — Includes index*

GERMANY — History — 20th century
Studia z najnowszej historii niemiec i stosunków polsko-niemieckich / pod redakcją Stanisława Sierpowskiego. — Poznań : Uniwersytet im. Adama Mickiewicza, 1986. — 634p. — (Seria Historia / Uniwersytet im. Adama Mickiewicza w Poznaniu ; Nr.129). — *In Polish or German*

GERMANY — History — 843-1273
FUHRMANN, Horst
Germany in the high Middle Ages c.1050-1200 / Horst Fuhrmann ; translated by Timothy Reuter. — Cambridge : Cambridge University Press, 1986. — vii,209p. — (Cambridge medieval textbooks). — *Translation of: Deutsche Geschichte in hohen Mittelalter. — Includes bibliography and index*

GERMANY — History — To 1517
PRINZ, Friedrich
Grundlagen und Anfänge : Deutschland bis 1056 / Friedrich Prinz. — München : Beck, 1985. — 438p. — (Neue deutsche Geschichte ; Bd 1)

GERMANY — History — 1618-1648
SCHORMANN, Gerhard
Der dreissigjährige Krieg / Gerhard Schormann. — Göttingen : Vandenhoeck & Ruprecht, 1985. — 151p. — *Bibliography: p145-147*

GERMANY — History — 19th century
Deutschland und der Westen : Vorträge und Diskussionsbeiträge des Symposions zu Ehren von Gordon A. Craig veranstaltet von der Freien Universität Berlin vom 1.-3. Dezember 1983 / herausgegeben von Henning Köhler. — Berlin : Colloquium Verlag, 1984. — 218p. — (Studien zur europäischen Geschichte ; Bd.15). — *Includes three chapters in English*

ENGELBERG, Ernst
Bismarck : Urpreusse und Reichsgründer / Ernst Engelberg. — Berlin : Siedler, 1985. — xvi,839p

GERMANY — History — 1871-1918
FISCHER, Fritz
From Kaiserreich to Third Reich : elements of continuity in German history, 1871-1945 / Fritz Fischer ; translated and with an introduction by Roger Fletcher. — London : Allen & Unwin, 1986. — 118p. — *Translation of: Bundnis der Eliten. — Includes index*

GERMANY — History — William II, 1888-1918
DOERRY, Martin
Übergangsmenschen : die Mentalität der Wilhelminer und die Krise des Kaiserreichs / Martin Doerry. — Weinheim : Juventa Verlag, 1986. — 197p. — *Bibliography: p193-197*

GERMANY — History — 20th century
Deutschland und der Westen : Vorträge und Diskussionsbeiträge des Symposions zu Ehren von Gordon A. Craig veranstaltet von der Freien Universität Berlin vom 1.-3. Dezember 1983 / herausgegeben von Henning Köhler. — Berlin : Colloquium Verlag, 1984. — 218p. — (Studien zur europäischen Geschichte ; Bd.15). — *Includes three chapters in English*

FISCHER, Fritz
From Kaiserreich to Third Reich : elements of continuity in German history, 1871-1945 / Fritz Fischer ; translated and with an introduction by Roger Fletcher. — London : Allen & Unwin, 1986. — 118p. — *Translation of: Bundnis der Eliten. — Includes index*

MOELLER, Robert G
German peasants and agrarian politics, 1914-1924 : the Rhineland and Westphalia / Robert G. Moeller. — Chapel Hill ; London : University of North Carolina Press, c1986. — xv, 286p. — *Includes index. — Bibliography: p 241-279*

GERMANY — History — Revolution, 1918 — Sources
The German revolution and the debate on Soviet power : documents, 1918-1919 : preparing the founding congress / edited by John Riddell. — New York : Anchor Foundation, 1986. — xx,540p. — (Communist International in Lenin's time)

GERMANY — History — Allied occupation, 1918-1930 — Bibliography
IMPERIAL WAR MUSEUM. Library
The occupation of the Rhineland 1918-1930. — [London : the library, 1975]. — 4p. — (Booklist / Imperial War Museum ; no.1055)

GERMANY — History — 1918-1933
BOESCH, Hermann
Jugend in der Weimarer Republik : erlebte Zeitgeschichte / Hermann Boesch. — Isenbüttel : Aurora Verlag, 1986. — 495p

KÜHNL, Reinhard
Die Weimarer Republik : Errichtung, Machtstruktur und Zerstörung einer Demokratie / Reinhard Kühnl. — Reinbek bei Hamburg : Rowohlt, 1985. — 281p. — *Bibliography: p269-[281]*

GERMANY — History — 1918-1933 — Bibliography
The Weimar Republic : a historical bibliography. — Santa Barbara, Calif. : ABC-Clio Information Services, 1984. — xii, 265p. — (ABC-Clio research guides ; 9). — *Includes index*

GERMANY — History — Revolution, 1918- — Sources
The German revolution and the debate on Soviet power : documents, 1918-1919 : preparing the founding conference / edited by John Riddell. — New York : Anchor : Distributed by Pathfinder Press, 1986. — xx,540p. — (The Communist International in Lenin's time). — *Bibliography: p528*

GERMANY — History — 1933-1945
Der antifaschistische Widerstandskampf unter Führung der KPD in Mecklenburg 1933 bis 1945 / [Horst Bendig...et al.]. — Berlin : Dietz Verlag, 1985. — 343p

BUCHSTAB, Günter
Verfolgung und Widerstand 1933-1945 : Christliche Demokraten gegen Hitler / Günter Buchstab, Brigitte Kaff, Hans-Otto Kleinmann. — Düsseldorf : Droste Verlag, 1986. — 288p. — *Bibliography: p282-283*

GERMANY — History — 1933-45
HELMERS, Gerrit
"Wenn die Messer blitzen und die Nazis flitzen..." : der Widerstand von Arbeiterjugendcliquen und -banden in der Weimarer Republik und im 'Dritten Reich' / Gerrit Helmers, Alfons Kenkmann. — Lippstadt : Leimeier, c1984. — iv,267p. — *Bibliography: p256-267*

GERMANY — History — 1933-1945
Life in the Third Reich / edited, with an introduction, by Richard Bessel. — Oxford : Oxford University Press, 1987. — [128]p. — *Includes bibliography and index*

PENTZLIN, Heinz
Die Deutschen im Dritten Reich : Nationalsozialisten, Mitläufer, Gegner / Heinz Penzlin. — Stuttgart : Seewald, 1985. — 222p

PEUKERT, Detlev J. K.
Inside Nazi Germany : conformity, opposition and racism in everyday life / Detlev J.K. Peukert ; translated by Richard Deveson. — London : Batsford, 1987. — 288p,20p of plates. — *Translation of: Volksgenossen und Gemeinschaftsfremde. — Bibliography: p278-279. — Includes index*

RABE, Bernd
Die "Sozialistische Front" : Sozialdemokraten gegen den Faschismus 1933-1936 / Bernd Rabe ; [Vortwort: Peter von Oertzen]. — Hanover : Fackelträger-Verlag, 1984. — 120p. — *Includes bibliographic notes*

Recht und Unrecht im Nationalsozialismus / herausgegeben von Peter Salje ; mit Beiträgen von Friedrich Dencker...[et al.]. — Münster : Wissenschaftliche Verlagsgesellschaft Regensberg und Biermann, 1985. — 310p

Der Widerstand gegen den Nazionalsozialismus : die deutsche Gesellschaft und der Widerstand gegen Hitler / herausgegeben von Jürgen Schmädeke und Peter Steinbach ; im Auftrage der Historischen Kommission zu Berlin in Zusammenarbeit mit der Gedenkstätte Deutscher Widerstand. — München : Piper, 1985. — xxxviii,1185p. — (Publikationen der Historischen Kommission zu Berlin). — *[Die Internationale Konferenz zum 40. Jahrestag des 20. Juli 1944, "Die deutsche Gesellschaft und der Widerstand gegen Hitler - eine Bilanz nach 40 Jahren" vom 2-6 Juli 1984 in Berlin]*

GERMANY — History — 1933-1945 — Bibliography
The Third Reich, 1933-1939 : a historical bibliography. — Santa Barbara, Calif ; Oxford : ABC-Clio Information Services, c1984. — xii,239p. — (ABC-Clio research guides ; 10). — *Includes indexes*

The Third Reich at war : a historical bibliography. — Santa Barbara, Calif. : ABC-Clio Information Services, [1984]. — xii, 270 p.. — (ABC-Clio research guides ; 11). — *Includes indexes*

GERMANY — History — 1933-1945 — Maps
FREEMAN, Michael, 1950-
Atlas of Nazi Germany / Michael Freeman ; consulting editor Tim Mason. — London : Croom Helm, c1987. — 205p. — *Bibliography: p195-196. — Includes index*

GERMANY — History — Allied occupation, 1945-
BOTTING, Douglas
In the ruins of the Reich / Douglas Botting. — London : Allen & Unwin, 1985. — viii,248p,[12]p of plates. — *Bibliography: p238-243. — Includes index*

BRÜLLS, Klaus
Neubeginn oder Wiederaufbau? : Gewerkschaftsjugend in der britischen Zone 1945-1950 / Klaus Brülls. — Marburg : Verlag Arbeiterbewegung und Gesellschaftswissenschaft, 1985. — 384p. — (Schriftenreihe der Studiengesellschaft für Sozialgeschichte und Arbeiterbewegung ; Bd.52). — *Bibliography: p349-384*

DASTRUP, Boyd L
Crusade in Nuremberg : military occupation, 1945-1949 / Boyd L. Dastrup. — Westport, Conn. : Greenwood Press, c1985. — p. cm. — (Contributions in military history ; no. 47). — *Includes index. — Bibliography: p*

GERMANY — History — Allied occupation, 1945-
continuation

STÜBER, Gabriele
Der Kampf gegen den Hunger 1945-1950 : der Ernährungslage in der britischen Zone Deutschlands, insbesondere in Schleswig-Holstein und Hamburg / Gabriele Stüber. — Neumunster : Wachholtz, 1984. — 935p. — (Studien zur Wirtschafts- und Sozialgeschichte Schleswig-Holsteins ; Bd.6). — *Bibliography: p824-913*

GERMANY — Intellectual life — Congresses

The Jewish response to German culture : from the enlightenment to the Second World War / edited by Jehuda Reinharz and Walter Schatzberg. — Hanover, NH : Published for Clark University by University Press of New England, 1985. — xii, 362p. — *"Essays based on papers delivered at the International Conference on German Jews, held at Clark University, Worcester, Massachusetts, October 8-11, 1983.".* — *Includes index*

GERMANY — Kings and rulers — Biography

JORDAN, Karl, 1909-ca.1986
Henry the Lion : a biography / Karl Jordan ; translated by P.S. Falla. — Oxford : Clarendon, 1986. — 266p. — *Translation of: Heinrich der Löwe.* — *Bibliography: p227-231.* — *Includes index*

GERMANY — Officials and employees — Political activity — History — 20th century

KUNZ, Andreas
Civil servants and the politics of inflation in Germany, 1914-1924 / Andreas Kunz. — Berlin ; New York : De Gruyter, 1986. — xix, 427 p.. — (Veröffentlichungen der Historischen Kommission zu Berlin ; Bd. 66) (Beiträge zu Inflation und Wiederaufbau in Deutschland und Europa 1914-1924 ; Bd. 7). — *Includes indexes.* — *Bibliography: p. [393]-413*

GERMANY — Politics and government — 1871-1888

GALL, Lothar
Bismarck : the white revolutionary / Lothar Gall ; translated from the German by J.A. Underwood. — London : Allen & Unwin. — *Translation of: Bismarck.* — *Originally published under the title, Bismarck der weiss Revolutionaär, Frankfurt am Main : Ullstein, 1980*
Vol.1: 1815-1871. — 1986. — [640]p. — *Includes bibliography and index*

GERMANY — Politics and government — 1871-1918

PARK, Ho-Leong
Sozialismus und Nationalismus : Grundsatzdiskussionen über Nationalismus, Imperialismus, Militarismus und Krieg in der deutschen Sozialdemokratie vor 1914 / von Ho-Leong Park ; mit einem Vorwort von Wolf-Dieter Narr. — Berlin : Schelzky und Jeep, 1986. — 349p. — *Bibliography: p323-349*

GERMANY — Politics and government — 1871-1933

AUERNHEIMER, Gustav
Genosse Herr Doktor : zur Rolle von Akademikern in der deutschen Sozialdemokratie 1890 bid 1933 / Gustav Auernheimer. — Giessen : Focus-verlag, 1985. — 240p. — *Bibliography: p223-240*

GERMANY — Politics and government — 1871-1933 — Addresses, essays, lectures

German nationalism and the European response, 1890-1945 / edited by Carole Fink, Isabel V. Hull, and MacGregor Knox. — 1st ed. — Norman : University of Oklahoma Press, c1985. — xv, 299 p.. — *Includes bibliographical references and index*

GERMANY — Politics and government — 1888-1918

DOERRY, Martin
Übergangsmenschen : die Mentalität der Wilhelminer und die Krise des Kaiserreichs / Martin Doerry. — Weinheim : Juventa Verlag, 1986. — 197p. — *Bibliography: p193-197*

THOMAS, R. Hinton
Nietzsche in German politics and society, 1890-1918 / R. Hinton Thomas. — Manchester : Manchester University Press, 1983 (1986 [printing]). — [146]p. — *Bibliography: p146.* — *Includes index*

GERMANY — Politics and government — 20th century

MOELLER, Robert G
German peasants and agrarian politics, 1914-1924 : the Rhineland and Westphalia / Robert G. Moeller. — Chapel Hill ; London : University of North Carolina Press, c1986. — xv, 286p. — *Includes index.* — *Bibliography: p 241-279*

GERMANY — Politics and government — 1918-1933

BIESEMANN, Jörg
Das Ermächtigungsgestz als Grundlage der Gesetzgebung im nationalsozialistschen Staat : ein Beitrag zur Stellung des Gesetzes in der Verfassungsgeschichte 1919-1945 / Jörg Biesemann. — Münster : Lit, 1985. — lviii,403p. — (Studien zur Politikwissenschaft ; Bd.13). — *Includes bibliographic notes*

BROSZAT, Martin
Hitler and the collapse of Weimar Germany / Martin Broszat ; translated and with a foreword by V.R. Berghahn. — Leamington Spa : Berg, c1987. — ix,157p. — *Translation of: Die Machtergreifung.* — *Bibliography: p151-153.* — *Includes index*

The Formation of the Nazi constituency, 1919-1933 / edited by Thomas Childers. — London : Croom Helm, c1986. — viii,263p. — *Includes index*

FRYE, Bruce B.
Liberal Democrats in the Weimar Republic : the history of the German Democratic Party and the German State Party / Bruce B. Frye. — Carbondale : Southern Illinois University Press, c1985. — p. cm. — *Includes index.* — *Bibliography: p*

GALLIN, Alice
Midwives to Nazism : university professors in Weimar Germany, 1925-1933 / Alice Gallin. — Macon, Ga. : Mercer, c1986. — viii, 134 p.. — *Includes index.* — *Bibliography: p. [115]-128*

HOLT, Tonie
Germany awake! : the rise of National Socialism 1919-1939 / Tonie and Valmai Holt. — London : Longman, 1986. — vii,124p. — *Includes index*

Keine Stimme dem Radikalismus : Christliche, liberale und konservative Parteien in den Wahlen 1930-1933 / Günter Buchstab...[et al.] (Hrsg.). — Berlin : Colloquium, 1984. — 136p. — *Bibliography: p133-134*

LANG, Jochen von
Der Adjutant : der Mann zwischen Hitler und Himmler / Jochen v. Lang ; unter Mitarbeit von Claus Sibyll. — München : Herbig, 1985. — 428p

MARTENS, Stefan
Hermann Göring : "Erster Paladin des Führers" und "Zweiter Mann im Reich" / Stefan Martens. — Paderborn : Schöningh, 1985. — 405p. — (Sammlung Schöningh zur Geschichte und Gegenwart)

Die nationalsozialistische Machtergreifung / Wolfgang Michalka (Hrsg.). — Paderborn : Schöningh, 1984. — 415p. — *Bibliography: p412-415*

ZITELMANN, Rainer
Hitler : Selbstverständnis eines Revolutionärs / Rainer Zitelmann. — Hamburg ; Leamington Spa : Berg, 1987. — x,485p. — *Bibliography: p467-480*

GERMANY — Politics and government — 1933-1945

BIESEMANN, Jörg
Das Ermächtigungsgestz als Grundlage der Gesetzgebung im nationalsozialistschen Staat : ein Beitrag zur Stellung des Gesetzes in der Verfassungsgeschichte 1919-1945 / Jörg Biesemann. — Münster : Lit, 1985. — lviii,403p. — (Studien zur Politikwissenschaft ; Bd.13). — *Includes bibliographic notes*

DÜRKEFÄLDEN, Karl
"Schreiben, wie es wirklich war-" : Aufzeichnungen Karl Dürkefäldens aus den Jahren 1933-1945 / herausgegeben von Herbert und Sibylle Obenaus. — Hannover : Fackelträger, 1985. — 136p. — *Bibliography: p132-136*

HOLT, Tonie
Germany awake! : the rise of National Socialism 1919-1939 / Tonie and Valmai Holt. — London : Longman, 1986. — vii,124p. — *Includes index*

KERSHAW, Ian
The 'Hitler myth' : image and reality in the Third Reich / Ian Kershaw. — Oxford : Clarendon, 1987. — xii,297p. — *Rev. ed. of: Der Hitler-Mythos. 1980.* — *Bibliography: p277-287.* — *Includes index*

LEHKER, Marianne
Frauen im Nationalsozialismus : wie aus Opfern Handlanger der Täter wurden : eine nötige Trauerarbeit / Marianne Lehker. — Frankfurt : Materialis, 1984. — 132p. — *Bibliography: p123-132*

MARTENS, Stefan
Hermann Göring : "Erster Paladin des Führers" und "Zweiter Mann im Reich" / Stefan Martens. — Paderborn : Schöningh, 1985. — 405p. — (Sammlung Schöningh zur Geschichte und Gegenwart)

MÜLLER, Klaus-Jürgen
The army, politics and society in Germany, 1933-1945 : studies in the army's relation to Nazism / Klaus-Jürgen Müller. — Manchester : Manchester University Press, 1987. — ix,122p. — (War, armed forces and society). — *Translation of: Armee, Politik und Gesellschaft in Deutschland, 1933-1945*

Die nationalsozialistische Machtergreifung / Wolfgang Michalka (Hrsg.). — Paderborn : Schöningh, 1984. — 415p. — *Bibliography: p412-415*

PLANT, Richard
The pink triangle : the Nazi war against homosexuals / Richard Plant. — 1st ed. — New York : H. Holt, c1986. — x, 257 p.. — *"A New Republic book.".* — *Includes index.* — *Bibliography: p. 236-248*

RABE, Bernd
Die "Sozialistische Front" : Sozialdemokraten gegen den Faschismus 1933-1936 / Bernd Rabe ; [Vortwort: Peter von Oertzen]. — Hanover : Fackelträger-Verlag, 1984. — 120p. — *Includes bibliographic notes*

THEWELEIT, Klaus
Male fantasies 1 : women, floods, bodies, history / Klaus Theweleit ; translated by Stephen Conway in collaboration with Erica Carter and Chris Turner ; foreword by Barbara Ehrenreich. — Cambridge : Polity, 1987. — xxii,517p. — *Translation of: Männerphantasien.* — *Includes index*

ZITELMANN, Rainer
Hitler : Selbstverständnis eines Revolutionärs / Rainer Zitelmann. — Hamburg ; Leamington Spa : Berg, 1987. — x,485p. — *Bibliography: p467-480*

GERMANY — Politics and government — 1933-1945 — Addresses, essays, lectures
German nationalism and the European response, 1890-1945 / edited by Carole Fink, Isabel V. Hull, and MacGregor Knox. — 1st ed. — Norman : University of Oklahoma Press, c1985. — xv, 299 p.. — *Includes bibliographical references and index*

GERMANY — Politics and government — 1933-1945 — Bibliography
Bibliographie zur Deutschlandpolitik 1941-1974 / bearbeitet von Marie-Luise Goldbach [and others] ; Redaktion, Albrecht Tyrell. — Frankfurt : Metznev, 1975. — 248p. — (Dokumente zur Deutschlandpolitik. Beihefte ; Bd.1)

GERMANY — Politics and government — 1945-
Kalter Krieg und Deutsche Frage : Deutschland im Widerstreit der Mächte 1945-1952 / herausgegeben von Josef Foschepoth. — Göttingen : Vandenhoeck und Ruprecht, 1985. — 388p. — (Veröffentlichungen des Deutschen Historischen Instituts London = Publications of the German Historical Insitute London ; Bd.16). — *Bibliograhical notes*

NOLTE, Ernst
Deutschland und der kalte Krieg / Ernst Nolte. — München : Piper, 1974. — 755p

SUCKUT, Siegfried
Blockpolitik in der SBZ/DDR 1945-1949 : Die Sitzungsprotokolle des zentralen Einheitsfront-Ausschusses / Siegfried Suckut. — Quellenedition. — Köln : Verlag Wissenschaft und Politik, 1986. — 640p. — (Mannheimer Untersuchungen zu Politik und Geschichte der DDR ; Bd.3). — *Bibliography: p627-632*

GERMANY — Politics and government — 1945- — Bibliography
Bibliographie zur Deutschlandpolitik 1941-1974 / bearbeitet von Marie-Luise Goldbach [and others] ; Redaktion, Albrecht Tyrell. — Frankfurt : Metznev, 1975. — 248p. — (Dokumente zur Deutschlandpolitik. Beihefte ; Bd.1)

GERMANY — Popular culture — History
GROSCHOPP, Horst
Zwischen Bierabend und Bildungsverein : zur Kulturarbeit in der deutschen Arbeiterbewegung vor 1914 / Horst Groschopp. — Berlin : Dietz Verlag, 1985. — 243p

GERMANY — Relations — Soviet Union
AGURSKY, Mikhail
The third Rome : national Bolshevism in the USSR / Mikhail Agursky ; foreword by Leonard Shapiro. — Boulder : Westview Press, 1987. — p. cm. — *Includes index.* — *Bibliography: p*

GERMANY — Relations — Spain
SEMOLINOS ARRIBAS, Mercedes
Hitler y la prensa de la II República Española / Mercedes Semolinos Arribas. — Madrid : Centro de Investigaciones Sociológicas : Siglo Veintiuno de España, [1985]. — vi.,290p

GERMANY — Relations (general) with France
WILLIS, F. Roy
France, Germany and the New Europe, 1945—1967 / F. Roy Willis. — Rev. and expanded ed. — Stanford, Calif. : Stanford University Press ; London : Oxford University Press, 1968. — 431 p

GERMANY — Social conditions
STÜBER, Gabriele
Der Kampf gegen den Hunger 1945-1950 : der Ernährungslage in der britishchen Zone Deutschlands, insbesondere in Schleswig-Holstein und Hamburg / Gabriele Stüber. — Neumunster : Wachholtz, 1984. — 935p. — (Studien zur Wirtschafts- und Sozialgeschichte Schleswig-Holsteins ; Bd.6). — *Bibliography: p824-913*

GERMANY — Social conditions — 1871-1918
GREBING, Helga
Arbeiterbewegung : sozialer Protest und kollektive Interessenvertretung bis 1914 / Helga Grebing. — München : Deutscher Taschenbuch Verlag, 1985. — 204p. — *Bibliography: p175-190*

GERMANY — Social conditions — 1918-1933
KOONZ, Claudia
Mothers in the fatherland : women, the family and Nazi politics / Claudia Koonz. — London : Jonathan Cape, 1987, c1986. — [700]p. — *Originally published: New York : St. Martin's Press, 1986.* — *Includes bibliography and index*

ZITELMANN, Rainer
Hitler : Selbstverständnis eines Revolutionärs / Rainer Zitelmann. — Hamburg ; Leamington Spa : Berg, 1987. — x,485p. — *Bibliography: p467-480*

GERMANY — Social conditions — 1933-1945
KOONZ, Claudia
Mothers in the fatherland : women, the family and Nazi politics / Claudia Koonz. — London : Jonathan Cape, 1987, c1986. — [700]p. — *Originally published: New York : St. Martin's Press, 1986.* — *Includes bibliography and index*

ZITELMANN, Rainer
Hitler : Selbstverständnis eines Revolutionärs / Rainer Zitelmann. — Hamburg ; Leamington Spa : Berg, 1987. — x,485p. — *Bibliography: p467-480*

GERMANY — Social conditions — 1945-
ARDAGH, John
Germany and the Germans / by John Ardagh ; consultant and research assistant: Katharina Schmitz. — London : Hamilton, 1987. — ix,478p. — *Bibliography: p465-467.* — *Includes index*

GERMANY — Social life and customs — 20th century
PEUKERT, Detlev J. K.
Inside Nazi Germany : conformity, opposition and racism in everyday life / Detlev J.K. Peukert ; translated by Richard Deveson. — London : Batsford, 1987. — 288p,20p of plates. — *Translation of: Volksgenossen und Gemeinschaftsfremde.* — *Bibliography: p278-279.* — *Includes index*

GERMANY — Social policy
RITTER, Gerhard A.
Social welfare in Germany and Britain : origins and development / Gerhard A. Ritter ; translated from the German by Kim Traynor. — Leamington Spa : Berg, c1986. — xi,211p. — *Translation of: Sozialversicherung in Deutschland und England.* — *Bibliography: p199-206.* — *Includes index*

GERMANY — Territorial expansion — History
HERWIG, Holger H
Germany's vision of empire in Venezuela, 1871-1914 / Holger H. Herwig. — Princeton, N.J. : Princeton University Press, c1986. — xii, 285 p.. — *Includes index.* — *Bibliography: p.[247]-272*

GERMANY. Heer — Political activity
MÜLLER, Klaus-Jürgen
The army, politics and society in Germany, 1933-1945 : studies in the army's relation to Nazism / Klaus-Jürgen Müller. — Manchester : Manchester University Press, 1987. — ix,122p. — (War, armed forces and society). — *Translation of: Armee, Politik und Gesellschaft in Deutschland, 1933-1945*

GERMANY. Reichstag — Elections, 1930-1933
Keine Stimme dem Radikalismus : Christliche, liberale und konservative Parteien in den Wahlen 1930-1933 / Günter Buchstab...[et al.] (Hrsg.). — Berlin : Colloquium, 1984. — 136p. — *Bibliography: p133-134*

GERMANY (Federal Republic). Bundestag
SCHWENCKE, Olaf
Hoffen lernen : 12 Jahre Politik als Beruf : eine Zwischenbilanz / Olaf Schwencke. — Stuttgart : Radius, 1985. — 105p

GERMANY — Civilization — Congresses
Blacks and German culture : essays / edited by Reinhold Grimm and Jost Hermand. — Madison, Wis. : Published for Monatshefte [by] University of Wisconsin Press, 1986. — vii, 184 p.. — (Monatshefte occasional volumes ; no. 4) . — : *Revised and enlarged papers read at the 15th Wisconsin Workshop, held at the University of Wisconsin-Madison Oct. 5-6, 1984.* — *Includes bibliographies*

GERMANY — Foreign relations — Soviet Union
CARR, Edward Hallett
German-Soviet relations between the two world wars, 1919-1939 / Edward H. Carr. — Baltimore : Johns Hopkins Press, 1951. — 146p

GERMANY (EAST)
CHILDS, David
East Germany. — London : Benn, 1969. — 286p

GERMANY (EAST) — Armed Forces
HOLZWEISSIG, Gunter
Militärwesen in der DDR / von Gunter Holzweissig. — Berlin : Verlag Gebr. Holzapfel, 1985. — 160p. — *Bibliography: p147-148*

GERMANY (EAST) — Bibliography
WALLACE, Ian, 1942-
East Germany : the German Democratic Republic / Ian Wallace, compiler, with the assistance of Douglas Burrington ... [et al.]. — Oxford : Clio, c1987. — xviii,295p. — (World bibliographical series ; v.77). — *Includes index*

GERMANY (EAST) — Congresses
INTERNATIONAL SYMPOSIUM ON THE GERMAN DEMOCRATIC REPUBLIC ((8th : 1982 : World Fellowship Center)
Studies in GDR culture and society 3 : selected papers from the Eighth International Symposium on the German Democratic Republic / editorial board, Margy Gerber, chief editor ... [et al.]. — Lanham : University Press of America, c1983. — vi, 264 p.. — *Rev. versions of papers presented at the symposium held at the World Fellowship Center near Conway, N.H., June 18-25, 1982.* — *Includes bibliographical references*

INTERNATIONAL SYMPOSIUM ON THE GERMAN DEMOCRATIC REPUBLIC (1980 : World Fellowship Center)
Studies in GDR culture and society : proceedings of the sixth International Symposium on the German Democratic Republic / editorial board, Margy Gerber, chief editor ... [et al.]. — Washington, D.C. : University Press of America, c1981. — p. cm. — *Bibliography: p*

GERMANY (EAST) — Economic conditions
The East German economy / edited by Ian Jeffries and Manfred Melzer ; advisory editor Eleonore Breuning ; translations by Eleonore Breuning and Ian Jeffries. — London : Croom Helm, c1987. — 328p. — *Bibliography: p314-322.* — *Includes index*

GERMANY (EAST) — Economic policy
The East German economy / edited by Ian Jeffries and Manfred Melzer ; advisory editor Eleonore Breuning ; translations by Eleonore Breuning and Ian Jeffries. — London : Croom Helm, c1987. — 328p. — *Bibliography: p314-322.* — *Includes index*

GERMANY (EAST) — Foreign relations
BRUNS, Wilhelm
Die Aussenpolitik der DDR / Wilhelm Bruns. — Berlin : Colloquium, 1985. — 86p. — (Beiträge zur Zeitgeschichte ; Bd.16). — *Bibliography: p82-86*

GERMANY (EAST) — Foreign relations — Europe

FREY, Eric G
Division and detente : the Germanies and their alliances / Eric G. Frey. — New York : Praeger, 1987. — xvi, 194 p.. — *Includes index.* — *Bibliography: p. 173-183*

GERMANY (EAST) — Foreign relations — Germany (West)

FREY, Eric G
Division and detente : the Germanies and their alliances / Eric G. Frey. — New York : Praeger, 1987. — xvi, 194 p.. — *Includes index.* — *Bibliography: p. 173-183*

NICLAUSS, Karlheinz
Kontroverse Deutschlandpolitik : die politische Auseinandersetzung in der Bundesrepublik Deutschland über den Grundlagenvertrag mit der DDR / von Karlheinz Niclauss. — Frankfurt : Metzner, 1977. — 135p. — (Dokumente zur Deutschlandpolitik. Beihefte ; Bd.3). — *Bibliography: p133-135*

GERMANY (EAST) — Foreign relations — Germany (West) — History

BUCHHEIM, Hans
Deutschlandpolitik 1949-1972 : der politisch-diplomatische Prozess. — Stuttgart : Deutsche Verlags-Anstalt, 1984. — 179p. — (Schriftenreihe der Vierteljahrshefte für Zeitgeschichte ; Nr.49). — *Bibliography: p175-179*

GERMANY (EAST) — Foreign relations — Poland

Dokumenty i materiały do stosunków Polski z Niemiecką Republiką Demokratyczną / Komitet Redakcyjny: Kazimierz Wajda, Heinz Heitzer...[et al.]. — Wrocław : Ossolineum
T.1: Październik 1949-maj 1955 / opracowali Gerhard Keiderling...[et al.]. — 1986. — xxii,609p

GERMANY (EAST) — Foreign relations — Soviet Union

PHILLIPS, Ann L
Soviet policy toward East Germany reconsidered : the postwar decade / Ann L. Phillips. — Westport, Conn. : Greenwood Press, 1986. — xii, 262 p.. — (Contributions in political science ; no. 142). — *Includes index.* — *Bibliography: p. [233]-256*

GERMANY (EAST) — Government policy — Germany (West) — History

BUCHHEIM, Hans
Deutschlandpolitik 1949-1972 : der politisch-diplomatische Prozess. — Stuttgart : Deutsche Verlags-Anstalt, 1984. — 179p. — (Schriftenreihe der Vierteljahrshefte für Zeitgeschichte ; Nr.49). — *Bibliography: p175-179*

GERMANY (EAST) — Intellectual life — Congresses

NEW HAMPSHIRE SYMPOSIUM ON THE GERMAN DEMOCRATIC REPUBLIC ((9th : 1983 : World Fellowship Center)
Studies in GDR culture and society 4 : selected papers from the Ninth New Hampshire Symposium on the German Democratic Republic / editorial board, Margy Gerber, chief editor ... [et al.]. — Lanham : University Press of America, c1984. — vii, 307 p.. — *Includes bibliographical references*

GERMANY (EAST) — Militia

HOLZWEISSIG, Gunter
Militärwesen in der DDR / von Gunter Holzweissig. — Berlin : Verlag Gebr. Holzapfel, 1985. — 160p. — *Bibliography: p147-148*

GERMANY (EAST) — Politics and government

BRUNS, Wilhelm
Die Aussenpolitik der DDR / Wilhelm Bruns. — Berlin : Colloquium, 1985. — 86p. — (Beiträge zur Zeitgeschichte ; Bd.16). — *Bibliography: p82-86*

GLAESSNER, Gert-Joachim
Bürokratische Herrschaft : Konflikt-bewältigung in der DDR / Gert-Joachim Glaessner. — München : Spendenkonto Projekt, 1986. — 64p. — (Krisen in den Systemen Sowjetischen typs ; Studie nr.13). — *Bibliography: p63-64*

SUCKUT, Siegfried
Blockpolitik in der SBZ/DDR 1945-1949 : Die Sitzungsprotokolle des zentralen Einheitsfront-Ausschusses / Siegfried Suckut. — Quellenedition. — Köln : Verlag Wissenschaft und Politik, 1986. — 640p. — (Mannheimer Untersuchungen zu Politik und Geschichte der DDR ; Bd.3). — *Bibliography: p627-632*

GERMANY (EAST) — Social conditions

HILLE, Barbara
Familie und Sozialisation in der DDR / Barbara Hille. — Opladen : Leske & Budrich, 1985. — 216p. — *Bibliography: p196-216*

OBERTREIS, Gesine
Familienpolitik in der DDR 1945-1980 / Gesine Obertreis. — Opladen : Leske & Budrich, 1986. — v,378p. — (Forschungstexte Wirtschafts- und Sozialwissenschaften ; Bd.17)

Studies in GDR culture and society. — Lanham ; London : University Press of America
6: Selected papers from the Eleventh New Hampshire Symposium on the German Democratic Republic / editorial board Margy Gerber ... [et al.]. — 1987. — [214]p

GERMANY (EAST) — Social conditions — Congresses

INTERNATIONAL SYMPOSIUM ON THE GERMAN DEMOCRATIC REPUBLIC ((7th : 1981 : World Fellowship Center)
Studies in GDR culture and society 2 : proceedings of the Seventh International Symposium on the German Democratic Republic / editorial board, Margy Gerber, chief editor ... [et al.]. — Washington, D.C. : University Press of America, c1982. — iv, 292 p.. — *English and German.* — *Includes bibliographical references*

GERMANY (EAST) — Statistics

Statistical pocket book of the German Democratic Republic / Central Statistical Board. — Berlin : Staatsverlag der Deutschen Demokratischen Republik, 1974-. — *Annual*

GERMANY (FEDERAL REPUBLIC). Bundesregierung

Die Kabinettsprotokolle der Bundesregierung. — Boppard am Rhein : Boldt. — *Bibliography: p359-368*
Bd.1: 1949 / bearbeitet von Ulrich Enders und Konrad Reiser. — [1982]. — 377p

Die Kabinettsprotokolle der Bundesregierung. — Boppard am Rhein : Boldt. — *Bibliography: p933-940*
Bd.2: 1950 / bearbeitet von Ulrich Enders und Konrad Reiser. — [1984]. — viii,962p

Die Kabinettsprotokolle der Bundesregierung. — Boppard am Rhein : Boldt. — *Bibliography: p237-241*
Bd.3: 1950 : Wortprotokolle / bearbeitet von Ulrich Enders und Konrad Reiser. — [1986]. — 250p

GERMANY (FEDERAL REPUBLIC). Deutscher Bundestag

Amtliches Handbuch des Deutschen Bundestages. — [Bonn] : Deutscher Bundestag, 1985-. — *Every Wahlperiode (every four years), plus Ergänzungslieferung (supplements)*

GERMANY (FEDERAL REPUBLIC). Parlamentarischer Rat

Der Parlamentarische Rat 1948-1949 : Akten und Protokolle / herausgegeben für den Deutschen Bundestag von Kurt Georg Wernicke, für das Bundesarchiv von Hans Booms. — Boppard am Rhein : Boldt. — *Bibliography: p441-450*
Band1: Vorgeschichte / bearbeitet von Johannes Volker Wagner. — 1975. — lxxxvii,457p

Der Parlamentarische Rat 1948-1949 : Akten und Protokolle / herausgegeben vom Deutschen Bundestag und vom Bundesarchiv unter Leitung von Kurt G. Wernicke und Hans Booms. — Boppard am Rhein : Boldt. — *Bibliography: p633-651*
Band 2: Der Verfassungskonvent auf Herrenchiemsee / bearbeitet von Peter Bucher. — 1981. — cxxxv,676p

GERMANY (FEDERAL REPUBLIC). Parlamentarischer Rat. Ausschuss für Zuständigkeitsabgrenzung

Der Parlamentarischer Rat 1948-1949 : Akten und Protokolle / herausgegeben vom Deutschen Bundestag und vom Bundesarchiv unter Leitung von Kurt G. Wernicke und Hans Booms. — Boppard am Rhein : Boldt. — *Bibliography: p777-783*
Band 3: Ausschuss für Zuständigkeitsabgrenzung / bearbeitet von Wolfram Werner. — 1986. — xlix,798p

GERMANY (WEST) — Armed Forces — Procurement

COWEN, Regina H. E
Defense procurement in the Federal Republic of Germany : politics and organization / Regina H.E. Cowen. — Boulder, Colo. : Westview Press, 1986. — xvii, 334 p.. — (Westview special studies in military affairs). — *Bibliography: p. 309-334*

GERMANY (WEST) — Commerce — Classification

Gegenüberstellung des Güterverzeichnisses für Produktionsstatistiken (GP) mit dem Warenverzeichnis für die Aussenhandelsstatistik (WA). — Wiesbaden : Statistisches Bundesamt, 1984-. — (Systematische Verzeichnisse). — *Annual*

GERMANY (WEST) — Commerce — Statistics

Foreign trade according to the Standard International Trade Classification (SITC - Rev.II) - special trade / Federal Statistical Office, Wiesbaden. — Wiesbaden : Federal Statistical Office, 1977-

GERMANY (WEST) — Constitutional history — Sources

Der Parlamentarischer Rat 1948-1949 : Akten und Protokolle / herausgegeben vom Deutschen Bundestag und vom Bundesarchiv unter Leitung von Kurt G. Wernicke und Hans Booms. — Boppard am Rhein : Boldt. — *Bibliography: p633-651*
Band 2: Der Verfassungskonvent auf Herrenchiemsee / bearbeitet von Peter Bucher. — 1981. — cxxxv,676p

Der Parlamentarischer Rat 1948-1949 : Akten und Protokolle / herausgegeben vom Deutschen Bundestag und vom Bundesarchiv unter Leitung von Kurt G. Wernicke und Hans Booms. — Boppard am Rhein : Boldt. — *Bibliography: p777-783*
Band 3: Ausschuss für Zuständigkeitsabgrenzung / bearbeitet von Wolfram Werner. — 1986. — xlix,798p

GERMANY (WEST) — Economic conditions

STRASSER, Dietrich
Abschied von den Wunderknaben : die Krise der deutschen Manager und Unternehmer / Dietrich Strasser. — München : C. Bertelsmann, c1985. — 224p. — *Bibliography: p218-220*

GERMANY (WEST) — Economic history

German yearbook on business history / edited by the German Society for Business History, Cologne in cooperation with the Institute for Bank-Historical Research, Frankfurt/Main. — Berlin : Springer-Verlag, 1985-. — *Annual*

GERMANY (WEST) — Economic policy

Grüne Wirtschaftspolitik, machbare Utopien / Frank Beckenbach...[et. al.] ; mit einem Vorwort von Otto Schily. — [Originalausg.]. — Köln : Kiepenheuer und Witsch, 1985. — 363p . — *Bibliographies*

LAMPERT, Heinz
Die Wirtschafts- und Sozialordnung der Bundesrepublik Deutschland / Heinz Lampert. — 8. überarbeitete Auflage. — München : Olzog, 1985. — 323p. — (Geschichte und Staat ; Bd.107/108). — *First published 1965.* — *Includes bibliographies*

GERMANY (WEST) — Economic policy — 1974-

BULMER, Simon
The domestic structure of European community policy-making in West Germany / Simon Bulmer. — New York : Garland, 1986. — 403 p.. — (Outstanding theses from the London School of Economics and Political Science). — Thesis (Ph. D.)--University of London, 1982. — *Bibliography: p. 388-400*

GERMANY (WEST) — Finance

Beteiligungen des Bundes. — Bonn : Verlag Dr. Hans Heger for Bundesminister der Finanzen, 1969-. — *Annual.* — *Supplement to Finanzbericht*

GERMANY (WEST) — Foreign economic relations — France

WACKERMANN, Gabriel
Belfort, Colmar, Mulhouse, Bâle, Fribourg-en-Brisgau : un espace économique transfrontalier / Gabriel Wackermann. — [Paris : La Documentation française, 1986]. — 143p. — (Notes et études documentaires ; no.4824). — *Bibliography: p139-142*

GERMANY (WEST) — Foreign economic relations — Netherlands

WETENSCHAPPELIJKE RAAD VOOR HET REGERINGSBELEID
Faktor Deutschland : zur sensibilitat der Beziehungen zwischen den Niederlanden und der Bundesrepublik / Wissenschaftlicher Rat für die Regierungspolitik der Niederlande. — 's-Gravenhage ; Wiesbaden : Staatsuitgeverij : Steiner, 1984. — 242p. — (Berichte für die Regierung / Wissenschaftlicher Rat für die Regierungspolitik der Niederlande ; 23). — *In German.* — *Includes bibliographical references*

GERMANY (WEST) — Foreign economic relations — Switzerland

WACKERMANN, Gabriel
Belfort, Colmar, Mulhouse, Bâle, Fribourg-en-Brisgau : un espace économique transfrontalier / Gabriel Wackermann. — [Paris : La Documentation française, 1986]. — 143p. — (Notes et études documentaires ; no.4824). — *Bibliography: p139-142*

GERMANY (WEST) — Foreign population

HÜBNER, Irene
"-wie eine zweite Hant" : Ausländerinnen in Deutschland / Irene Hübner. — Weinheim : Beltz, 1985. — 211p. — *Bibliography: p209-210*

KOCH-ARZBERGER, Claudia
Die schwierige Integration : die bundesrepublikanische Gesellschaft und ihre 5 Millionen Ausländer / Claudia Koch-Arzberger. — Opladen : Westdeutscher Verlag, 1985. — 211p. — (Beiträge zur sozialwissenschaften Forschung ; Bd.80). — *Bibliography: p197-211*

GERMANY (WEST) — Foreign relations

Deutschland und der Westen : Vorträge und Diskussionsbeiträge des Symposions zu Ehren von Gordon A. Craig veranstaltet von der Freien Universität Berlin vom 1.-3. Dezember 1983 / herausgegeben von Henning Köhler. — Berlin : Colloquium Verlag, 1984. — 218p. — (Studien zur europäischen Geschichte ; Bd.15). — *Includes three chapters in English*

OBERMEYER, Ute
Das Nein der SPD - eine nene Ära? : SPD und Raketen 1977-1983 / Ute Obermeyer ; mit einem Vorwort von Karl Heinz Hansen. — Marburg : Verlag Arbeiterbewegung und Gesellschaftswissenschaft, 1985. — 170p. — (Schriftenreihe der Studiengesellschaft für sozialgeschichte und Arbeiterbewegung ; Bd.45)

GERMANY (WEST) — Foreign relations — Europe

FREY, Eric G
Division and detente : the Germanies and their alliances / Eric G. Frey. — New York : Praeger, 1987. — xvi, 194 p.. — *Includes index.* — *Bibliography: p. 173-183*

GERMANY (WEST) — Foreign relations — Germany (East)

FREY, Eric G
Division and detente : the Germanies and their alliances / Eric G. Frey. — New York : Praeger, 1987. — xvi, 194 p.. — *Includes index.* — *Bibliography: p. 173-183*

NICLAUSS, Karlheinz
Kontroverse Deutschlandpolitik : die politische Auseinandersetzung in der Bundesrepublik Deutschland über den Grundlagenvertrag mit der DDR / von Karlheinz Niclauss. — Frankfurt : Metzner, 1977. — 135p. — (Dokumente zur Deutschlandpolitik. Beihefte ; Bd.3). — *Bibliography: p133-135*

GERMANY (WEST) — Foreign relations — Germany (East) — History

BUCHHEIM, Hans
Deutschlandpolitik 1949-1972 : der politisch-diplomatische Prozess. — Stuttgart : Deutsche Verlags-Anstalt, 1984. — 179p. — (Schriftenreihe der Vierteljahrshefte für Zeitgeschichte ; Nr.49). — *Bibliography: p175-179*

GERMANY (WEST) — Foreign relations — Israel

FELDMAN, Lily Gardner
The special relationship between West Germany and Israel / Lily Gardner Feldman. — Boston ; London : Allen & Unwin, 1984. — xix,330p. — *Bibliography: p295-322.* — *Includes index*

GERMANY (WEST) — Foreign relations — Middle East

ROLEF, Susan Hattis
The Middle East policy of the Federal Republic of Germany / Susan Hattis Rolef. — Jerusalem : Magnes Press, Hebrew University, 1985. — 79, [1] p.. — (Jerusalem papers on peace problems ; 39). — *Bibliography: p. 76-[80]*

GERMANY (WEST) — Foreign relations — United States — Addresses, essays, lectures

FLETCHER, Willard Allen
United States-German relations, past and present / Willard Allen Fletcher, Stephen F. Szabo, Stanley R. Sloan. — Washington : Library of Congress, 1984. — iii,25p. — *Bibliography: p23-25*

GERMANY (WEST) — Government policy — Germany (East) — History

BUCHHEIM, Hans
Deutschlandpolitik 1949-1972 : der politisch-diplomatische Prozess. — Stuttgart : Deutsche Verlags-Anstalt, 1984. — 179p. — (Schriftenreihe der Vierteljahrshefte für Zeitgeschichte ; Nr.49). — *Bibliography: p175-179*

GERMANY (WEST) — History

Ploetz : die Bundesrepublik Deutschland : Daten, Fakten, Analysen / herausgegeben von Thomas Ellwein und Wolfgang Bruder unter Mitarbeit von Peter Hofelich. — 2e., akt. Auflage. — Freiburg : Ploetz, 1985. — 247p. — *Bibliography: p223-225*

GERMANY (WEST) — Industries

JAPANISCH-DEUTSCHES SYMPOSIUM (1983 : Köln)
Die Arbeitswelt in Japan und in der Bundesrepublik Deutschland : ein Vergleich : Japanisch-Deutsches Symposium am 27./28. Juni 1983 im Japanischen Kulturinstitut in Köln / herausgegeben von Peter Hanau...[et al.]. — Darmstadt : Luchterhand, 1983. — ix,162p.

GERMANY (WEST) — Industries — Classification

Gegenüberstellung des Güterverzeichnisses für Produktionsstatistiken (GP) mit dem Warenverzeichnis für die Aussenhandelsstatistik (WA). — Wiesbaden : Statistisches Bundesamt, 1984-. — (Systematische Verzeichnisse). — *Annual*

GERMANY (WEST) — Manufactures — Classification

GERMANY (Federal Republic). Statistisches Bundesamt
Alphabetisches Güterverzeichnis für Produktionsstatistiken : Ausgabe 1982. — Wiesbaden : the Bundesamt, 1984. — 796p. — (Systematische Verzeichnisse)

GERMANY (Federal Republic). Statistisches Bundesamt
Systematisches Güterverzeichnis für Produktionsstatistiken : Ausgabe 1982. — Wiesbaden : the Bundesamt, 1981. — 528p. — (Systematische Verzeichnisse)

GERMANY (WEST) — Politics and government

ADENAUER, Konrad
Memoirs, 1945-53 / translated by Beate Ruhm von Oppen. — London : Weidenfeld and Nicolson, 1966. — 478p

Beginn in Bonn : Erinnerungen an den ersten Deutschen Bundestag / herausgegeben von Horst Ferdinand ; mit einem Geleitwort des Bundestagspräsidenten. — Freiburg im Breisgan : Herder, 1985. — 155p

BEYME, Klaus von
The political system of the Federal Republic of Germany / Klaus von Beyme. — Aldershot : Gower, 1983. — 209 p

BILLSTEIN, Reinhold
Neubeginn ohne Neuordnung : Dokumente und Materialien zur politischen Weichenstellung in den Westzonen nach 1945 / Reinhold Billstein. — Köln : Pahl-Rugenstein, 1984. — 351p. — *Bibliography: p340-349*

DUDEK, Peter
Entstehung und Entwicklung des Rechtsextremismus in der Bundesrepublik : zur Tradition einer besonderen politischen Kultur / Peter Dudek, Hans-Gerd Jaschke. — Opladen : Westdeutscher Verlag
Bd.2: Dokumente und Materialien. — 1984. — 374p

DUDEK, Peter
Entstehung und Entwicklung des Rechtsextremismus in der Bundesrepublik : zur Tradition einer besonderen politischen Kultur / Peter Dudek, Hans-Gerd Jaschke. — Opladen : Westdeutscher Verlag. — *Bibliography: p [488]-496*
Bd.1. — 1984. — 507p

GREIFFENHAGEN, Martin
Von Potsdam nach Bonn : zehn Kapitol zur politischen Kultur Deutschlands / Martin Greiffenhagen. — München : Piper, 1986. — 246p

HISCOCKS, Richard
Democracy in Western Germany. — London : Oxford University Press, 1957. — ix,324p

GERMANY (WEST) — Politics and government *continuation*

HUHN, Anne
"Einst kommt der Tag der Rache" : die rechtsextreme Herausforderung 1945 bis heute / Anne Huhn; Alwin Meyer. — Freiburg : Dreisam-Verlag, 1986. — 229p

KOELSCHTZKY, Martina
Die Stimme ihrer Herren : Ideologie und Strategie der 'Neuen Rechten' in der Bundesrepublik / Martina Koelschtzky. — Köln : Pahl-Rugenstein, 1986. — 124p. — *Bibliography: p121-124*

MÜLLER-HERMANN, Ernst
Politik der Bewährung im Wandel / Ernst Müller-Hermann. — Stuttgart : Kohlhammer, 1985. — 132p

OBERMEYER, Ute
Das Nein der SPD - eine nene Ära? : SPD und Raketen 1977-1983 / Ute Obermeyer ; mit einem Vorwort von Karl Heinz Hansen. — Marburg : Verlag Arbeiterbewegung und Gesellschaftswissenschaft, 1985. — 170p. — (Schriftenreihe der Studiengesellschaft für sozialgeschichte und Arbeiterbewegung ; Bd.45)

Ploetz : die Bundesrepublik Deutschland : Daten, Fakten, Analysen / herausgegeben von Thomas Ellwein und Wolfgang Bruder unter Mitarbeit von Peter Hofelich. — 2e., akt. Auflage. — Freiburg : Ploetz, 1985. — 247p. — *Bibliography: p223-225*

Das politische System der BRD : Geschichte und Gegenwart / herausgeber Prof. Dr. Karl-Heinz Röder. — Berlin : Staatsverlag der DDR, 1985. — 480p. — (Studien zum politischen System des Imperialismus ; Bd.3)

SALENTIN, Ursula
Elisabeth Schwarzhaupt : erste Ministerin der Bundesrepublik : ein demokratischer Lebensweg / Ursula Salentin. — Freiburg im Breisgan : Herder, 1986. — 126p

SCHWENCKE, Olaf
Hoffen lernen : 12 Jahre Politik als Beruf : eine Zwischenbilanz / Olaf Schwencke. — Stuttgart : Radius, 1985. — 105p

GERMANY (WEST) — Politics and government — Sources

Dokumente zur Deutschlandpolitik. — Frankfurt : Metzner (for) Bundesministerium für innerdeutsche Beziehungen Reihe 4: Vom 10. November 1958 bis 30. November 1966 / bearbeitet von Ernst Deuerlein [and others]. — 1971-1981. — 12v. in 22

Die Kabinettsprotokolle der Bundesregierung. — Boppard am Rhein : Boldt. — *Bibliography: p359-368*
Bd.1: 1949 / bearbeitet von Ulrich Enders und Konrad Reiser. — [1982]. — 377p

Die Kabinettsprotokolle der Bundesregierung. — Boppard am Rhein : Boldt. — *Bibliography: p933-940*
Bd.2: 1950 / bearbeitet von Ulrich Enders und Konrad Reiser. — [1984]. — viii,962p

Die Kabinettsprotokolle der Bundesregierung. — Boppard am Rhein : Boldt. — *Bibliography: p237-241*
Bd.3: 1950 : Wortprotokolle / bearbeitet von Ulrich Enders und Konrad Reiser. — [1986]. — 250p

Der Parlamentarische Rat 1948-1949 : Akten und Protokolle / herausgegeben für den Deutschen Bundestag von Kurt Georg Wernicke, für das Bundesarchiv von Hans Booms. — Boppard am Rhein : Boldt. — *Bibliography: p441-450*
Band1: Vorgeschichte / bearbeitet von Johannes Volker Wagner. — 1975. — lxxxvii,457p

GERMANY (WEST) — Politics and government — 1982-

Bund transparent : Parlament, Regierung, Bundesbehörden; Organisation, Gremien, Anshriften, Namen / [Redaktion: Philipp Eggers, Peter Lichtenberg]. — 3., völlig neubearbeitete Aufl., Ausg.'86. — Bad Honnef : Bock, 1986. — 512p

MENG, Richard
Die sozialdemokratische Wende : Aussenbild und innerer Prozess der SPD 1981-1984 / Richard Meng. — Giessen : Focus, 1985. — 409p. — *Bibliography: p406-409*

SMITH, Gordon, 1927-
Democracy in Western Germany : parties and politics in the Federal Republic / Gordon Smith. — 2nd ed. — Aldershot : Gower, 1982 (1985 [printing]). — ix,229p. — *Previous ed.: London : Heinemann, 1979. — Includes bibliographies and index*

SMITH, Gordon, 1927-
Democracy in Western Germany : parties and politics in the Federal Republic / Gordon Smith. — 3rd ed. — Aldershot : Gower, c1986. — [240]p. — *Previous ed.: London : Heinemann, 1982. — Includes index*

SPD und Grüne : das neue Bündnis? / Wolfram Bickerich (Hg.). — Reinbek bei Hamburg : Rowohlt Taschenbuch Verlag, 1985. — 282p

GERMANY (WEST) — Politics and governmernt

Der Weg der Bundesrepublik : von 1945 bis zur Gegenwart / herausgegeben von Franz Schneider. — München : Beck, 1985. — 255p

GERMANY (WEST) — Relations — France

WILLIS, F. Roy
France, Germany and the new Europe, 1945—1963 / F. Roy Willis. — Stanford : Stanford University Press ; London : Oxford University Press, 1965. — xiv,397p. — *Bibliography: p373-387*

GERMANY (WEST) — Relations — Netherlands

WETENSCHAPPELIJKE RAAD VOOR HET REGERINGSBELEID
Faktor Deutschland : zur sensibilitat der Beziehungen zwischen den Niederlanden und der Bundesrepublik / Wissenschaftlicher Rat für die Regierungspolitik der Niederlande. — 's-Gravenhage ; Wiesbaden : Staatsuitgeverij : Steiner, 1984. — 242p. — (Berichte für die Regierung / Wissenschaftlicher Rat für die Regierungspolitik der Niederlande ; 23). — *In German. — Includes bibliographical references*

GERMANY (WEST) — Social conditions

NAUJECK, Kurt
Die Anfänge des sozialen Netzes 1945-1952 / Kurt Naujeck. — Bielefeld : Kleine, c1984. — 276p. — (Wissenschaftliche Reihe ; Bd.19). — *Dissertation, Universität Düsseldorf, 1983. — Bibliography: p261-267*

GERMANY (WEST) — Social policy

LAMPERT, Heinz
Die Wirtschafts- und Sozialordnung der Bundesrepublik Deutschland / Heinz Lampert. — 8. überarbeitete Auflage. — München : Olzog, 1985. — 323p. — (Geschichte und Staat ; Bd.107/108). — *First published 1965. — Includes bibliographies*

GERMANY (WEST) — Social policy — Statisitcs

GERMANY (FEDERAL REPUBLIC). Statistisches Bundesamt
Sozialleistungen: Reihe S.7: Einmalige Leistungen der Hilfe zum Lebensunterhalt. — Wiesbaden : Statistisches Bundesamt, 1981/81-. — *Annual*

GERMAY (WEST) — Constitution

SCHULZE-FIELITZ, Helmuth
Der informale Verfassungsstaat : aktuelle Beobachtungen des Verfassungslebens der Bundesrepublik Deutschland im Lichte der Verfassungstheorie / von Helmuth Schulze-Fielitz. — Berlin : Duncker & Humblot, [1984]. — 176p. — (Schriften zum öffentlichen Recht ; Bd.475)

GERMENY (FEDERAL REPUBLIC). Bundestag — History

Beginn in Bonn : Erinnerungen an den ersten Deutschen Bundestag / herausgegeben von Horst Ferdinand ; mit einem Geleitwort des Bundestagspräsidenten. — Freiburg im Breisgan : Herder, 1985. — 155p

GERMPLASM RESOURCES, PLANT

Gene banks and the world's food / Donald L. Plucknett ... [et al.]. — Princeton, N.J. : Princeton University Press, c1987. — p. cm. — *Includes index. — Bibliography: p*

GERONTOLOGY

Later life : the social psychology of aging / edited by Victor W. Marshall. — Beverly Hills, Calif. : Sage, c1986. — 352 p.. — *Includes bibliographies and indexes. — Contents: Dominant and emerging paradigms in the social psychology of aging / Victor W. Marshall -- The subjective construction of self and society / Carol D. Ryff -- Socialization in old age--a Meadian perspective / Neena Chappell and Harold L. Orbach -- Some contributions of symbolic interaction to the study of growing old / Don Spence -- A sociological perspective on aging and dying / Victor Marshall -- The old person as stranger / James J. Dowd -- Social networks and social support / Barry Wellman and Alan Hall -- Friendships in old age / Sarah H. Matthews -- The world we forgot / Martin Kohli -- Comparative perspectives on the microsociology of aging / Vern L. Bengtson*

GERONTOLOGY — Addresses, essays, lectures

Handbook of aging and the social sciences / editors, Robert H. Binstock, Ethel Shanas ; with the assistance of associate editors George L. Maddox, George C. Myers, James H. Schulz. — 2nd ed. — New York ; Wokingham : Van Nostrand Reinhold, c1985. — xiv, 809p. — *Includes indexes*

GERONTOLOGY — Bibliography

Bibliographie internationale de gérontologie sociale : sélection commentée par pays = International bibliography of social gerontology : an annotated core list by country / réalisée par Maggy Bieulac. — Paris : Centre International de Gérontologie Sociale, [1982]. — 2(v.)(xxxi,776p). — *Vol. 1: Africa, North America, South America, Asia; Vol.2: Europe, Oceania, U.S.S.R.*

GERONTOLOGY — Congresses

INTERNATIONAL CONFERENCE OF SOCIAL GERONTOLOGY ((8th : 1978 : Mohammedia, Morocco)
Ecology and aging : 8th International Conference of Social Gerontology, Mohammedia, Morocco, 12/16 December 1978. — Paris, France : International Center of Social Gerontology, [1980]. — 440 p.. — *Includes bibliographies*

GERONTOLOGY — Canada

NOVAK, Mark
Successful aging : the myths, realities and future of aging in Canada / Mark Novak. — Ontario : Penguin, 1985. — 368p. — *Bibliography: p[345]-361*

GERONTOLOGY — United States

KAUFMAN, Sharon R
The ageless self : sources of meaning in late life / Sharon R. Kaufman. — Madison, Wis. : University of Wisconsin Press, 1986. — xii, 208 p.. — (Life course studies). — *Includes index. — Bibliography: p. 199-204*

GERONTOLOGY — United States — History

Old age in a bureaucratic society : the elderly, the experts, and the state in American history / edited by David Van Tassel and Peter N. Stearns. — Westport, Conn. : Greenwood Press, c1986. — xx, 259 p.. — (Contributions to the study of aging ; no. 4). — *Includes bibliographies and index*

GEWERKSCHAFT NAHRUNG-GENUSS-GASTSTÄTTEN

BUSCHAK, Willy
Von Menschen, die wie Menschen leben wollten : die Geschichte der Gewerkschaft Nahrung-Genuss-Gaststätten und ihrer Vorläufer / Willy Buschak ; Vorwork: Günter Döding. — Köln : Bund, 1985. — 645p. — *Bibliography: p634-639*

GHANA — Foreign relations

KRAFONA, Kwesi
The Pan-African movement : Ghana's contribution / Kwesi Krafona. — London : Afroworld, 1986. — 85p

GHANA — History — 1957-

PELLOW, Deborah
Ghana : coping with uncertainty / Deborah Pellow and Naomi Chazan. — Boulder, Colo. : Westview ; London : Gower, 1986. — xiv,238p. — (Profiles : nations of contemporary Africa). — *Bibliography: p225-230. — Includes index*

GHANA — Politics and government

SMERTIN, Yuri
Kwame Nkrumah / Yuri Smertin ; translated from the Russian by Sharon McKee. — Moscow : Progress Publishers, 1987. — 312p

GHANA — Population

ENGMANN, E. V. T.
Population of Ghana 1850-1960 / E. V. T. Engmann. — Accra : Ghana Universities Press, 1986. — 300p. — *Bibliography: p292-298*

GHANA — Population — Statistics

GAISIE, S. K.
The proximate determinants of fertility in Ghana / S.K. Gaisie. — Voorburg : International Statistical Institute, 1984. — 63p. — (Scientific reports / World Fertility Survey ; no.53)

The Ghana Fertility Survey, 1979—80 : a summary of findings. — Voorburg : International Statistical Institute, 1983. — 16p. — (World Fertility Survey ; no.39)

GHANA — Population — Statistics — Evaluation

OWUSU, John Y.
Evaluation of the Ghana Fertility Survey 1979-80 / John Y. Owusu. — Voorburg : International Statistical Institute, 1984. — 44p. — (Scientific reports / World Fertility Survey ; no.69)

GHANA — Presidents — Biography

SMERTIN, Yuri
Kwame Nkrumah / Yuri Smertin ; translated from the Russian by Sharon McKee. — Moscow : Progress Publishers, 1987. — 312p

GHANA — Rural conditions

KONINGS, Piet
The State and rural class formation in Ghana : a comparative analysis / Piet Konings. — London : KPI, 1986. — xvi,391p. — *Bibliography: p356-377*

GHANA — Social conditions

ASSIMENG, J. M
Social structure of Ghana : a study in persistence and change / Max Assimeng. — Tema, Ghana : Ghana Pub. Corp., 1981. — x, 201 p.. — *Includes index. — Bibliography: p. 189-197*

GHANDI, M. K.

GANDHI, M. K.
The moral and political writings of Mahatma Gandhi. — Oxford : Clarendon
volume 2: Truth and non-violence / edited by Raghavan Iyer. — 1986. — xxii,678p. — *Bibliography:p659-664*

GHOST DANCE

THORNTON, Russell
We shall live again : the 1870 and 1890 ghost dance movements as demographic revitalization / Russell Thornton. — Cambridge : Cambridge University Press, 1986. — xiii,95p. — (The Arnold and Caroline Rose monograph series of the American Sociology Association). — *Bibliography: p.85-92. — Includes index*

GIBRALTAR — Strategic aspects

CASALDUERO, Francisco
Europa, Gibraltar y la O.T.A.N. / Francisco Casalduero. — Madrid : Dyrsa, 1985. — 114p

GIFTED CHILDREN — Counseling of — Congresses

Identifying and nurturing the gifted : an international perspective / edited by Kurt A. Heller and John F. Feldhusen. — Toronto ; Lewiston, N.Y. : H. Huber, c1986. — p. cm. — *Based on the papers presented at a symposium, held on Aug. 9, 1985, at the 6th World Conference on Gifted and Talented Children, in Hamburg. — Includes indexes. — Bibliography: p*

GIFTED CHILDREN — Identification — Congresses

Identifying and nurturing the gifted : an international perspective / edited by Kurt A. Heller and John F. Feldhusen. — Toronto ; Lewiston, N.Y. : H. Huber, c1986. — p. cm. — *Based on the papers presented at a symposium, held on Aug. 9, 1985, at the 6th World Conference on Gifted and Talented Children, in Hamburg. — Includes indexes. — Bibliography: p*

GIFTED CHILDREN — Psychology

Conceptions of giftedness / edited by Robert J. Sternberg, Janet E. Davidson. — Cambridge : Cambridge University Press, 1986. — x,460p

GILBERT AND ELLICE ISLANDS COLONY

GILBERT AND ELLICE ISLANDS COLONY
Gilbert and Ellice Islands Colony and the Central and Southern Line Islands: annual report. — London : HMSO, 1949-1974. — *Annual. — Continued by: Gilbert Islands: report*

GILBERT ISLANDS

GILBERT ISLANDS
[Report] / Gilbert Islands. — Tarawa : [s.n.], 1975-1976. — *Annual. — Continues: Gilbert and Ellice Islands Colony and the Central and Southern Line Islands: annual report*

GIPSIES — Scotland — Grampian

GRAMPIAN. Regional Council. Social Work Department
Travelling families in Grampian region : report of the travelling peoples' survey unit. — Aberdeen : [the Department], 1985-. — 139p

GIRONDISTS — History

SLAVIN, Morris
The making of an insurrection : Parisian sections and the Gironde / Morris Slavin. — Cambridge, Mass. : Harvard University Press, 1986. — ix, 236 p.. — *Includes index. — Bibliography: p. [222]-228*

GLADSTONE, W. E

The Gladstonian turn of mind : essays presented to J.B. Conacher / edited by Bruce L. Kinzer. — Toronto ; London : University of Toronto Press, c1985. — xv, 294 p.. — *"James Blennerhasset Conacher publications, 1947-84" / compiled by N. Merrill Distad" --p. [265]-271. — Includes bibliographies and index*

GLADSTONE, W. E. (William Ewart)

KNAPLUND, Paul
Gladstone and Britain's imperial policy / Paul Knaplund. — London : Allen and Unwin, 1927. — 256p

LOUGHLIN, James
Gladstone, Home Rule and the Ulster question 1882-93 / James Loughlin. — Dublin : Gill and Macmillan, c1986. — 369p. — *Bibliography: p333-361. — Includes index*

MATTHEW, H. C. G.
Gladstone 1809-1874 / H.C.G. Matthew. — Oxford : Clarendon, 1986. — [230]p,[8]p of plates. — *Includes index*

PARRY, J. P. (Jonathan Philip)
Democracy and religion : Gladstone and the Liberal Party, 1867-1875 / J.P. Parry. — Cambridge : Cambridge University Press, 1986. — xiii,504p. — (Cambridge studies in the history and theory of politics). — *Bibliography: p453-492. — Includes index*

GLAMORGAN — City planning

MID GLAMORGAN. County Council
Position and prospects 1975 : an analysis of the special problems of Mid Glamorgan and their solution / Mid Glamorgan County Council. — Cardiff : Mid Glamorgan County Council
Vol.1. — 1975. — [xi],20p

MID GLAMORGAN. County Council
Position and prospects 1975 : an analysis of the special problems of Mid Glamorgan and their solution / Mid Glamorgan County Council. — Cardiff : Mid Glamorgan County Council
Vol.2. — 1975. — [viii],138,vp

GLASGOW (STRATHCLYDE) — History

Glasgow observed / edited by Simon Berry and Hamish Whyte. — Edinburgh : John Donald, 1987. — x,289p. — *Bibliography: p280-281*

GLASGOW (STRATHCLYDE) — Social conditions

Regenerating the inner city : Glasgow's experience / edited by David Donnison and Alan Middleton. — London : Routledge & Kegan Paul, 1987. — [304]p. — (Geography, environment and planning). — *Includes bibliography and index*

The Working class in Glasgow 1750-1914 / edited by R.A. Cage. — London : Croom Helm, c1987. — xix,203p. — *Bibliography: p188-189. — Includes index*

GLASS MANUFACTURE — European Economic Community countries

COMITÉ PERMANENT DES INDUSTRIES DU VERRE
The glass industry in the European Economic Community / Standing Committee of the EC Glass Industries. — Luxembourg : Office for Official Publications of the European Communities, 1984. — 3microfiches. — (Energy audit ; no.4) (EUR ; 9287). — *Contract no.: XVII/82/464/AR*

GLEISPRACH, WENZESLAUS K.

RABOFSKY, Eduard
Verborgene Wurzeln der NS-Justiz : strafrechtliche Rüstung für zwei Weltkriege / Eduard Rabofsky [und] Gerhard Oberkofler. — Wien : Europa Verlag, 1985. — 261p. — *Bibliography: p251-[262]*

GLENCOE MASSACRE, 1692

HOPKINS, Paul
Glencoe and the end of the Highland war / Paul Hopkins. — Edinburgh : John Donald, 1986. — 543p. — *Bibliography: p.500-509*

GOA (INDIA) — Politics and government

GAITONDE, P. D.
The liberation of Goa : a participant's view of history / P.D. Gaitonde. — London : Hurst, c1987. — xiii,192p,[1]p of plates. — *Bibliography: p182-186. — Includes index*

GODDESSES, GREEK
SPRETNAK, Charlene
Lost goddesses of early Greece : a collection of pre-Hellenic myths / Charlene Spretnak. — New ed. — Boston : Beacon Press, 1984, c1978. — 132 p.. — *Bibliography: p. 129-132.* — *Contents: Gaia — Pandora — Themis — Aphrodite — Triad of the moon : Artemis, Selene, Hecate — Hera — Athena — Demeter and Persephone*

GODWIN, WILLIAM
GODWIN, William
The anarchist writings of William Godwin / edited with an introduction by Peter Marshall. — London : Freedom Press, 1986. — 182p. — *Bibliography: p180-181*

GOFF (Family)
LUKAS, J. Anthony
Common ground : a turbulent decade in the lives of three American Families / J. Anthony Lukas. — New York : Vintage Books, 1986. — xiv,674p. — *Originally published: New York : Random House, 1985*

GOKALP, ZIYA
PARLA, Taha
The social and political thought of Ziya Gokalp, 1876-1924 / by Taha Parla. — Leiden : Brill, 1985. — vi,157p. — (Social, Economic and Political Studies of the Middle East ; 35). — *Bibliography: P149-157*

GOLD INDUSTRY — Russian S.F.S.R. — Siberia, Eastern
KHATYLAEV, M. M.
Rabochie zolotodobyrainshchei promyshlennosti Vostochnoi Sibiri 1921-1937 gg. / M. M. Khatylaev ; otv. redaktor M. N. Khalbaev. — Novosibirsk : Nauka, Sibirskoe otdelenie, 1986. — 171p

GOLD INDUSTRY — South Africa — History
JOHNSON, Paul, 1928-
Consolidated Gold Fields : a centenary portrait / Paul Johnson. — London : Weidenfeld and Nicolson, c1987. — 256p

GOLD MINERS — Russian S.F.S.R. — Siberia, Eastern
KHATYLAEV, M. M.
Rabochie zolotodobyrainshchei promyshlennosti Vostochnoi Sibiri 1921-1937 gg. / M. M. Khatylaev ; otv. redaktor M. N. Khalbaev. — Novosibirsk : Nauka, Sibirskoe otdelenie, 1986. — 171p

GOLD MINES AND MINING — History
KEANE, A. H.
The gold of Ophir : whence brought and by whom? / by A.H.Keane. — New York : Negro Universities Press, 1969. — xviii,244p. — *Originally published in 1901*

GOLD MINES AND MINING — South Africa
COUNTER INFORMATION SERVICES
Consolidated Gold Fields PLC : partner in apartheid / Counter Information Services. — London : Counter Information Services, 1986. — 48p. — *Bibliography: p48*

JEEVES, Alan H.
Migrant labour in South Africa's mining economy : the struggle for the gold mines' labour supply 1890-1920 / Alan H. Jeeves. — Kingston, Canada : McGill-Queen's University Press, 1985. — xiv,323p

GOLD STANDARD
MARCUZZO, Maria Cristina
La teoria del gold standard : Ricardo e il suo tempo / Maria Cristina Marcuzzo, Annalisa Rosselli. — Bologna : Il Mulino, 1986. — 266p . — *Bibliography: p245-255*

GOLD STANDARD — Addresses, essays, lectures
Alternative monetary regimes / edited by Colin D. Campbell and William R. Dougan. — Baltimore : Johns Hopkins University Press, c1986. — xi, 251 p.. — *Includes bibliographies and index*

GOLD STANDARD — History
KUNZ, Diane B.
The battle for Britain's gold standard in 1931 / Diane B. Kunz. — London : Croom Helm, c1987. — viii,207p. — *Bibliography: p194-202.* — *Includes index*

GOLDSTEIN, ISRAEL
GOLDSTEIN, Israel
My world as a Jew : the memoirs of Israel Goldstein. — New York : Herzl Press ; London : Cornwall Books, c1984. — p. cm. — *Includes index*

GOLLANCZ, VICTOR
EDWARDS, Ruth Dudley
Victor Gollancz : a biography / by Ruth Dudley Edwards. — London : Gollancz, 1987. — 782p,[24]p of plates. — *Bibliography: p761-764.* — *Includes index*

GOMPERS, SAMUEL
The Samuel Gompers papers / editor, Stuart B. Kaufman. — Urbana, Ill. : University of Illinois Press
volume 1: The making of a union leader, 1850-86. — 1986. — xxxvi,529p

GOMULKA, WŁADYSŁAW
SYZDEK, Eleonora
Polityczne dylematy Władysława Gomułki / Eleonora Syzdek, Bronisław Syzdek. — Warszawa : Czytelnik, 1985. — 260p. — *Bibliography: p257-[261]*

GOODNESS-OF-FIT TESTS
Goodness-of-fit techniques / edited by Ralph B. D'Agostino, Michael A. Stephens. — New York : M. Dekker, c1986. — p. cm. — (Statistics, textbooks and monographs ; vol. 68) . — *Includes bibliographies and index*

GORBACHEV, M. S.
WALKER, Martin, 1947-
The waking giant : the Soviet Union under Gorbachev / Martin Walker. — London : Joseph, 1986. — xxviii,282p. — *Includes index*

GORBACHEV, M. S.
The results and lessons of Reykjavik : summit meeting in the Icelandic capital October 11-12, 1986 / Mikhail Gorbachev. — Moscow : Novosti Press Agency Publishing House, 1986. — 42p

GORBACHEV, MIKHAIL SERGEEVICH
SCHMIDT-HÄUER, Christian
Gorbachev : the path to power / Christian Schmidt-Häuer ; with an appendix on the Soviet economy by Maria Huber ; edited by John Man ; translated by Ewald Osers and Chris Romberg. — London : I. B. Tauris, 1986. — v,218p

GORBALS (LANARKSHIRE) — Social life and customs
GLASSER, Ralph
Growing up in the Gorbals / Ralph Glasser. — London : Chatto & Windus, 1986. — 207p

GÖRING, HERMANN
MARTENS, Stefan
Hermann Göring : "Erster Paladin des Führers" und "Zweiter Mann im Reich" / Stefan Martens. — Paderborn : Schöningh, 1985. — 405p. — (Sammlung Schöningh zur Geschichte und Gegenwart)

GOR'KII, MAKSIM
TROYAT, Henri
Gorki / Henri Troyat. — Paris : Flammarion, 1986. — 260p. — *Bibliography: p[247]-249*

GOROKA DISTRICT (PAPUA NEW GUINEA) — Economic conditions
SEXTON, Lorraine
Mothers of money, daughters of coffee : the Wok Meri movement / by Lorraine Sexton. — Ann Arbor, Mich. : UMI Research Press, c1986. — p. cm. — (Studies in cultural anthropology ; no. 10). — : *Revision of thesis (Ph. D.)--Temple University, 1980.* — *Includes index.* — *Bibliography: p*

GOROKA DISTRICT (PAPUA NEW GUINEA) — Social conditions
SEXTON, Lorraine
Mothers of money, daughters of coffee : the Wok Meri movement / by Lorraine Sexton. — Ann Arbor, Mich. : UMI Research Press, c1986. — p. cm. — (Studies in cultural anthropology ; no. 10). — : *Revision of thesis (Ph. D.)--Temple University, 1980.* — *Includes index.* — *Bibliography: p*

GOSSAGE, PATRICK
GOSSAGE, Patrick
Close to the charisma : my years between the press and Pierre Elliott Trudeau / Patrick Gossage. — Toronto : McClelland and Stewart, c1986. — 271 p., [16] p. of plates

GOTTWALD, KLEMENT
Klement Gottwald : revolucionař a politik : sborník statí / [redakční rada: Ivan Krempa, Antonín Faltys, Květoslava Volková]. — Praha : Nakladatelství Svoboda, 1986. — 353p

GOVERNESSES — Soviet Union
PATIN, Louise
Journal d'une institutrice française en Russie pendant la révolution, 1917-1919 / Louise Pation ; préface de Geneviève Legras. — Paris : La Table Ronde ; Pontoise : Edijac, 1987. — 249p

GOVERNMENT AND THE PRESS — Australia
Presidents, prime ministers, and the press / edited by Kenneth W. Thompson. — Lanham, MD : University Press of America, c1986. — xii, 85 p.. — (The White Burkett Miller Center series on the presidency and the press). — *"Tenth anniversary volume."*

GOVERNMENT AND THE PRESS — Canada
GOSSAGE, Patrick
Close to the charisma : my years between the press and Pierre Elliott Trudeau / Patrick Gossage. — Toronto : McClelland and Stewart, c1986. — 271 p., [16] p. of plates

GOVERNMENT AND THE PRESS — Great Britain
HOLMES, Deborah
Governing the press : media freedom in the U.S. and Great Britain / Deborah Holmes. — Boulder : Westview Press, 1986. — xi, 107 p.. — (A Westview special study). — *Includes index.* — *Bibliography: p. 93-102*

Presidents, prime ministers, and the press / edited by Kenneth W. Thompson. — Lanham, MD : University Press of America, c1986. — xii, 85 p.. — (The White Burkett Miller Center series on the presidency and the press). — *"Tenth anniversary volume."*

GOVERNMENT AND THE PRESS — India — History
SANKHDHER, Brijendra Mohan
Press, politics, and public opinion in India : dynamics of modernization and social transformation / B.M. Sankhdher ; foreword by Amba Prasad. — New Delhi : Deep & Deep Publications, c1984. — xxiv, 400 p.. — *Summary: On the role of the press in India, 1780-1835.* — *Includes index.* — *Bibliography: p. [353]-388*

GOVERNMENT AND THE PRESS — South Africa
Presidents, prime ministers, and the press / edited by Kenneth W. Thompson. — Lanham, MD : University Press of America, c1986. — xii, 85 p.. — (The White Burkett Miller Center series on the presidency and the press). — *"Tenth anniversary volume."*

GOVERNMENT AND THE PRESS — Tanzania
KONDE, Hadji
Press freedom in Tanzania / Hadji Konde. — Arusha [Tanzania] : Eastern Africa Publications, 1984. — x, 242 p.

GOVERNMENT AND THE PRESS — United States

HOLMES, Deborah
Governing the press : media freedom in the U.S. and Great Britain / Deborah Holmes. — Boulder : Westview Press, 1986. — xi, 107 p.. — (A Westview special study). — Includes index. — Bibliography: p. 93-102

MORGAN, David
The flacks of Washington : government information and the public agenda / David Morgan. — Westport, Conn. : Greenwood Press, c1986. — p. cm. — (Contributions in political science ; no. 137). — Includes index. — Bibliography: p

GOVERNMENT AND THE PRESS — United States — Bibliography

MCKERNS, Joseph P.
News media and public policy : an annotated bibliography / Joseph P. McKerns. — New York : Garland, 1985. — p. cm. — (Public affairs and administration ; vol. 11) (Garland reference library of social science ; vol. 219). — Includes indexes

GOVERNMENT AND THE PRESS — United States — History — 20th century

SPEAR, Joseph C.
Presidents and the press : the Nixon legacy / Joseph C.Spear. — Cambridge, Massachusetts ; London : MIT Press, 1984

STEELE, Richard W
Propaganda in an open society : the Roosevelt administration and the media, 1933-1941 / Richard W. Steele. — Westport, Conn. ; London : Greenwood Press, c1985. — x, 231p. — (Contributions in American history ; no. 111). — Includes index. — Bibliography: p.[213]-224

GOVERNMENT BUSINESS ENTERPRISES — Developing countries — Bibliography

UMEK, Manca
Bibliography of ICPE, 1974-1981. / compiled by Manca Umek and Matjaž Musek, with the assistance of Srihari R. Iyengar. — Ljubljana, Yugoslavia : ICPE, 1982. — 159p. — Includes indexes

GOVERNMENT BUSINESS ENTERPRISES

AHARONI, Yair
The evolution and management of state owned enterprises / Yair Aharoni. — Melrose, MA : Pitman Pub., 1986. — p.cm. — Includes index. — Bibliography: p

AYUB, Mahmood Ali
Public industrial enterprises : determinants of performance / Mahmood Ali Ayub and Sven Olaf Hegstad. — Washington, D.C. : The World Bank, 1986. — xi,77p. — (Industry and finance series ; v.17). — Includes bibliographical references

The Management of interlinkages / edited by Ricardo Acosta Suárez. — Ljubljana, Yugoslavia : International Center for Public Enterprises in Developing Countries, c1985. — 272p. — Includes bibliographies. — Contents: Towards management of interlinkages / Ricardo Acosta Suárez -- Interlinkages / Horacio Boneo -- The management of interlinkages / Praxy J. Fernandes -- Patterns of strategic behaviour and models for strategic planning in state enterprises in some developing countries / M.S.S. El-Namaki -- Some theoretical and operational aspects of interlinkage planning / Aleš Vahčič -- Empirical evaluation of macroeconomic linkages between public and private sectors / Boris Pleskovič and Gustavo Treviño -- Public enterprise interlinkages / Georg Sørensen

GOVERNMENT BUSINESS ENTERPRISES — Accounting — France

CASTILLE, Didier
Les comptes du secteur public concurrentiel séries 1981-1983 / Didier Castille, Denis Cavaud et Pierre Muller. — Paris : I.N.S.E.E., 1985. — 213p. — (Les collections de l'INSEE ; 96)

GOVERNMENT BUSINESS ENTERPRISES — Bibliography

Nationalization or take-over of foreign enterprises : a select bibliography = Nationalisation ou reprise des entreprises étrangères : bibliographie sélective. — New York : United Nations, 1974. — 17p. — ([Document] / United Nations ; ST/LIB/35). — In various languages

GOVERNMENT BUSINESS ENTERPRISES — Congresses

Public financial institutions and their role in development / edited by Ali El Mir. — Ljubljana, Yugoslavia : International Center for Public Enterprises in Developing Countries, 1983. — 257p. — Papers from a meeting organized by the International Center for Public Enterprises in Developing Countries, held in Ljubljana, July 11-15, 1983. — Includes bibliographies. — Contents: The role of public enterprise banks/financial institutions and their relationship with other public enterprises in Pakistan / Zafar Iqbal -- The role of public enterprise banks/financial institutions and their relationship with other public enterprises in India / Manu R. Shroff -- The role of government financial institutions in Japan / Hiromitsu Ishi -- The experience of the National Development Bank of Sri Lanka / R.M.S. Fernando -- Institutional, operational, and financial characteristics of development banking in Latin America / Rommel Acevedo -- The developmental role of OPEC/ARAB funds and international Arab and Islamic banks / Traute Wohlers-Scharf

Seeking the personality of public enterprise : a enquiry into the concept, definition, and classification of public enterprises : report and papers of an expert group meeting held in Tangier, Morocco, 15-19 December, 1980 / edited by Praxy Fernandes and Pavle Sicherl. — Ljubljana : International Center for Public Enterprises in Developing Countries in collaboration with the African Training and Research Centre in Administration for Development (CAFRAD), 1981. — 214p. — Includes bibliographical references

GOVERNMENT BUSINESS ENTERPRISES — Employment — Egypt

EL SALMI, Aly
Public sector management : an analysis of decision-making and employment policies and practices in Egypt / Aly El Salmi. — Geneva : International Labour Office, 1983. — 40p. — (Employment opportunities and equity in Egypt ; no.6). — A technical paper of the ILO/UNDP comprehensive employment strategy mission to Egypt, 1980

HANDOUSSA, Heba Ahmad
Public sector employment and productivity in the Egyptian economy / Heba Ahmad Handoussa. — Geneva : International Labour Office, 1983. — 39p. — (Employment opportunities and equity in Egypt ; no.7). — Includes bibliographical references. — A technical paper of the ILO/UNDP comprehensive employment strategy mission to Egypt, 1980

GOVERNMENT BUSINESS ENTERPRISES — Finance — Congresses

Pricing policy and investment criteria in public enterprises : proceedings of two international workshops / organized by ICPE in collaboration with the United Nations Development Administration Division ; edited by Zia U. Ahmed. — Ljubljana, Yugoslavia : International Center for Public Enterprises in Developing Countries, 1982. — 297p. — Includes bibliographical references

GOVERNMENT BUSINESS ENTERPRISES — Management

RAPP, Lucien
Public multinational enterprises and strategic decision-making / by Lucien Rapp. — Geneva : International Labour Office, 1986. — iv,56p. — (Working paper / Multinational Enterprises Programme ; no.34). — Bibliography: p[51]

GOVERNMENT BUSINESS ENTERPRISES — Price policy — Congresses

Pricing policy and investment criteria in public enterprises : proceedings of two international workshops / organized by ICPE in collaboration with the United Nations Development Administration Division ; edited by Zia U. Ahmed. — Ljubljana, Yugoslavia : International Center for Public Enterprises in Developing Countries, 1982. — 297p. — Includes bibliographical references

GOVERNMENT BUSINESS ENTERPRISES — Africa

Labour-management relations in public enterprises in Africa. — [Geneva] : International Labour Office, [1983]. — 84p. — (Labour-management relations series ; 60)

GOVERNMENT BUSINESS ENTERPRISES — Africa, Sub-Saharan

NELLIS, John R.
Public enterprises in Sub-Saharan Africa / John R. Nellis. — Washington, D.C. : The World Bank, 1986. — 66p. — (World Bank discussion papers ; no.1). — Bibliographical references: p66

GOVERNMENT BUSINESS ENTERPRISES — Developing countries — Case studies

A Casebook of public enterprise studies : diagnostic reviews of selected public enterprises prepared in the course of ICPE OPTIMA programmes in three developing countries / introduced by Praxy Fernandes and Vladimir Kreačić. — Ljubljana, Yugoslavia : International Center for Public Enterprises in Developing Countries, 1982. — 207p. — Includes bibliographical references. — Contents: Somaltex / Praxy Fernandes -- Jowhar Sugar Factory / Ales Vahčič -- The cigarette and match factory / Vladimir Kreačić -- The Foundry and Mechanical Workshop / Zia Uddin Ahmed -- Cyprus Telecommunications Authority / Ales Vahčič ... [et al.] -- The Electricity Authority of Cyprus / Praxy Fernandes, Costakis Panayiotou and John Charalambides -- Air Jamaica / Praxy Fernandes and Marie Slyfield -- Jamaica Railway Corporation / Vladimir Kreačić and Phyllis Green

GOVERNMENT BUSINESS ENTERPRISES — Developing countries — Congresses

Public enterprises and employment in developing countries / edited by W.D. Lakshman. — Ljubljana, Yugoslavia : International Center for Public Enterprises in Developing Countries, c1984. — 182p. — Papers presented at a meeting held in Amman, Jordan in April 1983. — Includes bibliographies. — Contents: The role of public enterprises in employment generation in underdeveloped countries / W.D. Lakshman -- The role of public enterprises in employment in Latin America / Horacio Boneo -- Conflicts between employment and output growth objectives of public enterprises in developing countries / Frances Stewart -- Public enterprise, technology, and employment in less developed countries / Jeffrey James -- Measurement of indirect employment effects of public enterprises in developing countries through social accounting matrices / Aleš Vahčič -- Thoughts about the probable employment conditions of women in public enterprises / Souad N. Barnouti -- Manpower development through public enterprises / Tayseer Abdel Jaber -- Public enterprises as sources of employment for less developed regions in developing countries / Hassan A. El Tayeb

GOVERNMENT BUSINESS ENTERPRISES — Developing countries — Congresses *continuation*

Public financial institutions and their role in development / edited by Ali El Mir. — Ljubljana, Yugoslavia : International Center for Public Enterprises in Developing Countries, 1983. — 257p. — *Papers from a meeting organized by the International Center for Public Enterprises in Developing Countries, held in Ljubljana, July 11-15, 1983. — Includes bibliographies. — Contents: The role of public enterprise banks/financial institutions and their relationship with other public enterprises in Pakistan / Zafar Iqbal -- The role of public enterprise banks/financial institutions and their relationship with other public enterprises in India / Manu R. Shroff -- The role of government financial institutions in Japan / Hiromitsu Ishi -- The experience of the National Development Bank of Sri Lanka / R.M.S. Fernando -- Institutional, operational, and financial characteristics of development banking in Latin America / Rommel Acevedo -- The developmental role of OPEC/ARAB funds and international Arab and Islamic banks / Traute Wohlers-Scharf*

GOVERNMENT BUSINESS ENTERPRISES — Developing countries — Employees — Training of

La gestion de la formation dans les entreprises publiques dans les pays en voie de developpement : compte rendu d'un séminaire international tenu du 3 au 15 mars, 1980 / rédaction: Anton Kukovica et Stane Možina. — Ljubljana : Centre International des Entreprises Publiques dans les Pays en Voie de Développement, 1980. — 240p. — *"Convoque par le Centre International des Entreprises Publiques dans les Pays en Voie de Développement en coopération avec l'Organization des Nations Unies pour le Développement Industriel*

GOVERNMENT BUSINESS ENTERPRISES — Developing countries — Finance

Financing of public enterprises in developing countries : an examination into financial issues affecting the organization and management of public enterprises in developing countries / edited by Praxy Fernandes. — [2nd ed.]. — Ljubljana, Yugoslavia : International Center for Public Enterprises in Developing Countries, 1981. — 148p. — *"Incorporating country studies and conceptual research papers and the findings of an interregional workshop held at Ljubljana, May 22 to 26, 1978 convened by ICPE in collaboration with the UN Division of Public Administration and Finance.". — Includes bibliographical references*

GOVERNMENT BUSINESS ENTERPRISES — Developing countries — Management

Management training and development in public enterprises in developing countries : report and papers of a regional workshop held in Karachi, Pakistan, 5-15 January 1981, convened by ICPE in collaboration with the United Nations Industrial Development Organization and the Pakistan Institute of Management / edited by Irshad H. Khan, Shahiruddin Al[v]i and Stane Možina. — Ljubljana, Yugoslavia : International Center for Public Enterprises in Developing Countries, 1982. — 199p. — *Includes bibliographical references*

GOVERNMENT BUSINESS ENTERPRISES — Egypt — Labor productivity

HANDOUSSA, Heba Ahmad
Public sector employment and productivity in the Egyptian economy / Heba Ahmad Handoussa. — Geneva : International Labour Office, 1983. — 39p. — (Employment opportunities and equity in Egypt ; no.7). — *Includes bibliographical references. — A technical paper of the ILO/UNDP comprehensive employment strategy mission to Egypt, 1980*

GOVERNMENT BUSINESS ENTERPRISES — Egypt — Management

EL SALMI, Aly
Public sector management : an analysis of decision-making and employment policies and practices in Egypt / Aly El Salmi. — Geneva : International Labour Office, 1983. — 40p. — (Employment opportunities and equity in Egypt ; no.6). — *A technical paper of the ILO/UNDP comprehensive employment strategy mission to Egypt, 1980*

GOVERNMENT BUSINESS ENTERPRISES — Europe

PARRIS, Henry
Public enterprise in Western Europe / Henry Parris, Pierre Pestieau and Peter Saynor. — London : Croom Helm, c1987. — viii,197p. — *Bibliography: p191-192. — Includes index*

GOVERNMENT BUSINESS ENTERPRISES — France

FRANCE. Haut Conseil du Secteur Public
Rapport. — Paris : Documentation Française, 1984- . — *Annual*

THOLLON-POMMEROL, V.
Répertoire des entreprises controleés majoritairement par l'état au 31 décembre 1984 / V. Thollon-Pommerol. — [Paris] : I.N.S.E.E., 1986. — 158p. — (Archives et documents / France. Institut national de la statistique et des études économiques ; no.170)

GOVERNMENT BUSINESS ENTERPRISES — Great Britain

PROSSER, Tony
Nationalised industries and public control : legal, constitutional and political issues / Tony Prosser. — Oxford : Blackwell, 1986. — [220]p. — *Includes bibliography and index*

Strategic planning in nationalised industries / edited by John Grieve Smith. — London : Macmillan, 1984. — xvi,268p. — *Includes index*

GOVERNMENT BUSINESS ENTERPRISES — Great Britain — Finance

GREAT BRITAIN. Parliament. House of Commons. Library. Research Division
The financing of nationalised industries / Christopher Barclay. — [London] : the Division, 1979. — 21p. — (Reference sheet ; no79/9)

GREAT BRITAIN. Parliament. House of Commons. Library. Research Division
The financing of nationalised industries / C. R. Barclay. — [London] : the Division, 1980. — 26p. — (Background paper ; no.88). — *Includes bibliographical references*

GREAT BRITAIN. Parliament. House of Commons. Library. Research Division
The financing of nationalised industries / C. R. Barclay. — [New ed.]. — [London] : the Division, 1982. — 21p. — (Background paper ; no.103)

GOVERNMENT BUSINESS ENTERPRISES — India

SURYA PRAKASH
Parliamentary control over public enterprises in India / Surya Prakash. — 1st ed. — Allahabad, India : Chugh Publications, 1985. — 293 p.. — *Includes index. — Bibliography: p. [271]-278*

GOVERNMENT BUSINESS ENTERPRISES — India — Location

KUNDU, Amitabh
Location of public enterprises and regional development / Amitabh Kundu, Girish K. Misra, Rajkishor Meher. — New Delhi : Concept Pub. Co., 1986. — xv, 178 p.. — *Summary: Economic study of the impact of Bharat Heavy Electricals Limited on Bhopal City. — Includes index. — Bibliography: p. [170]-174*

GOVERNMENT BUSINESS ENTERPRISES — India — Orissa — Personnel management

ROY, R. C.
State public enterprises in India : a study of personnel administration / R. C. Roy. — New Delhi : Uppal, 1985. — xx,393p. — *Bibliography: p[353]-380*

GOVERNMENT BUSINESS ENTERPRISES — Pakistan — Statistics

Federal government public sector development programme, 1985-86. — [Islamabad] : Planning Commission, Government of Pakistan, 1985. — xvi,223p

GOVERNMENT BUSINESS ENTERPRISES — Poland — Finance

WERALSKI, Marian
Le développement du système financier des entreprises d'état en Pologne / Marian Weralski. — Warszawa : Panstwowe Wydawnictwo Nankowe, 1963. — 15p. — (Conférences fascicule / Académie Polonaise des Sciences. Centre Scientifique à Paris ; 43)

GOVERNMENT EXECUTIVES — Handbooks, manuals, etc — Bibliography

KORMAN, Richard I
Checklist of government directories, lists, and rosters / compiled by Richard I. Korman. — Westport, CT : Meckler Pub. ; Cambridge, Eng. : Chadwyck-Healey, c1982. — x, 51 p.. — *"The collections of the Library of Congress are the source of the nearly 300 titles cited"--P. x. — Includes index*

GOVERNMENT EXECUTIVES — Training of — Great Britain

Management training needs in DHSS local offices. — [London : Department of Health and Social Security?] 2: HEOs; a joint report to the Department / from Civil Service Department, Personnel Management Research Branch, PM4 Division [and] Department of Health and Social Security, Management Training Centre. — 1978. — 17,[19]p

GOVERNMENT EXECUTIVES — United States

LYNN, Laurence E.
Managing public policy / Laurence E. Lynn, Jr. — Boston : Little, Brown, c1987. — xiv, 282 p.. — (Little, Brown foundations of public management series). — *Includes bibliographies and index*

GOVERNMENT FINANCIAL INSTITUTIONS — Congresses

Public financial institutions and their role in development / edited by Ali El Mir. — Ljubljana, Yugoslavia : International Center for Public Enterprises in Developing Countries, 1983. — 257p. — *Papers from a meeting organized by the International Center for Public Enterprises in Developing Countries, held in Ljubljana, July 11-15, 1983. — Includes bibliographies. — Contents: The role of public enterprise banks/financial institutions and their relationship with other public enterprises in Pakistan / Zafar Iqbal -- The role of public enterprise banks/financial institutions and their relationship with other public enterprises in India / Manu R. Shroff -- The role of government financial institutions in Japan / Hiromitsu Ishi -- The experience of the National Development Bank of Sri Lanka / R.M.S. Fernando -- Institutional, operational, and financial characteristics of development banking in Latin America / Rommel Acevedo -- The developmental role of OPEC/ARAB funds and international Arab and Islamic banks / Traute Wohlers-Scharf*

GOVERNMENT FINANCIAL INSTITUTIONS — Developing countries — Congresses

Public financial institutions and their role in development / edited by Ali El Mir. — Ljubljana, Yugoslavia : International Center for Public Enterprises in Developing Countries, 1983. — 257p. — *Papers from a meeting organized by the International Center for Public Enterprises in Developing Countries, held in Ljubljana, July 11-15, 1983. — Includes bibliographies. — Contents: The role of public enterprise banks/financial institutions and their relationship with other public enterprises in Pakistan / Zafar Iqbal -- The role of public enterprise banks/financial institutions and their relationship with other public enterprises in India / Manu R. Shroff -- The role of government financial institutions in Japan / Hiromitsu Ishi -- The experience of the National Development Bank of Sri Lanka / R.M.S. Fernando -- Institutional, operational, and financial characteristics of development banking in Latin America / Rommel Acevedo -- The developmental role of OPEC/ARAB funds and international Arab and Islamic banks / Traute Wohlers-Scharf*

GOVERNMENT FINANCIAL INSTITUTIONS — India

UPPAL, J. S.
Public financial institutions in India / J.S. Uppal. — Delhi : Macmillan India, 1984. — 111 p.. — *Bibliography: p. [107]-111*

GOVERNMENT INFORMATION

Communicating politics : mass communications and the political process / edited by Peter Golding, Graham Murdock, and Philip Schlesinger. — New York, NY : Holmes & Meier, 1986. — p. cm. — *Bibliography: p223-225. — Bibliography: p*

Public access to government-held information : a comparative symposium / general editor, Norman S. Marsh. — London : Published under the auspices of the British Institute of International & Comparative Law [by] Stevens, 1987. — xxi,342p. — *Includes index*

GOVERNMENT INFORMATION — Legal status, laws, etc. — Great Britain

GREAT BRITAIN. Parliament. House of Commons. Library. Research Division
Freedom of Information Bill [Bill 25, 1980/81] / [Margaret M. Camsell]. — [London] : the Division, 1981. — 12p. — (Reference sheet ; no.81/6). — *Bibliographical references: p12*

GOVERNMENT INFORMATION — Canada

CANADA
Access register / Canada. — Ottawa : Canadian Government Publishing Centre, 1986-. — *Annual*

Canada's new access laws : public and personal access to government documents / edited by Donald C. Rowat. — Ottawa : Carleton University, 1983. — x,166p. — *"The essays in this volume were written by [...] graduate students in a special seminar on Canada's new access laws given in the winter term, 1983 [at Carleton University, Ottawa]". — Includes references. — Bibliography: p159-165*

GOVERNMENT INFORMATION — Colombia

GÓMEZ JARAMILLO, Juan Carlos
El acceso público a la información estatal y el derecho de petición de informaciones / Juan Carlos Gómez Jaramillo. — Bogotá : Facultad de Ciencias Jurídicas y Socio-Economicas, Pontifica Universidad Javeriana, 1984. — 115p. — *"Trabajo de Grado para optar al título de Abogado". — Bibliography: p[119-121]*

GOVERNMENT INFORMATION — Great Britain

GREAT BRITAIN. Parliament. House of Commons. Library. Research Division
Official secrets and open government / [H. Rosamund Coates]. — [London] : the Division, 1979. — 32p. — (Reference sheet ; no79/1)

GOVERNMENT INFORMATION — United States

MORGAN, David
The flacks of Washington : government information and the public agenda / David Morgan. — Westport, Conn. : Greenwood Press, c1986. — p. cm. — (Contributions in political science ; no. 137). — *Includes index. — Bibliography: p*

GOVERNMENT LENDING — United States

BOSWORTH, Barry
The economics of federal credit programs / Barry P. Bosworth, Andrew S. Carron, Elisabeth H. Rhyne. — Washington, D.C. : Brookings Institution, c1987. — xii, 214 p.. — *Includes bibliographical references and index*

GOVERNMENT LIABILITY

HUFFMAN, James
Government liability and disaster mitigation : a comparative study / James Huffman. — London : University Press of America, 1987. — [660]p

GOVERNMENT LIABILITY — United States

LEE, Mark R.
Antitrust law and local government / Mark R. Lee. — Westport, Conn. : Quorum Books, c1985. — p. cm. — *Includes index. — Bibliography: p*

GOVERNMENT OWNERSHIP

RAMANADHAM, V. V.
Studies in public enterprise : from evaluation to privatisation / V.V. Ramanadham. — London : Cass, 1987. — x,221p. — *Includes index*

GOVERNMENT OWNERSHIP — Economic aspects

STIGLITZ, Joseph E.
Economics of the public sector / Joseph E. Stiglitz. — New York ; London : Norton, 1986. — xxiii,509p. — *Bibliography: p577-586*

GOVERNMENT OWNERSHIP — Great Britain

BICKERSTAFFE, Rodney
Privatisation and low pay : the impact of government policies / Rodney Bickerstaffe. — Nottingham : Trent Polytechnic, 1984. — 46p. — *Trent Business School. Open lectures on industrial relations: the changing contours of collective bargaining*

COOMBES, David
State enterprise : business or politics? / David Coombes. — London : Allen and Unwin [for] Political and Economic Planning, 1971. — 3-244p

LABOUR RESEARCH DEPARTMENT
Privatisation : paying the price. — London : LRD Publications, 1987. — 48p

REDWOOD, John
Equity for everyman : new ways to widen ownership / John Redwood. — London : Centre for Policy Studies, 1986. — 39p. — (Policy study ; no.74)

SLOMAN, Martyn
Socialising public ownership / Martin Sloman. — London : Macmillan, 1978

GOVERNMENT OWNERSHIP — Great Britain — Statistics

TRADES UNION CONGRESS
A report on a survey carried out by NOP for the TUC on public ownership. — London : Trades Union Congress, 1986. — 15,[36p]

GOVERNMENT OWNERSHIP — Poland

GOŁĘBIOWSKI, Jerzy
Sektor państwowy w gospodarce Polski międzywojennej / Jerzy Gołębiowski. — Warszawa : Państwowe Wydawnictwo Naukowe, 1985. — 366p. — *Bibliography: p336-[355]*

GOVERNMENT OWNERSHIP — United States — Addresses, essays, lectures

DE ALESSI, Louis
Some economic aspects of government ownership and regulation : essays from Economia pubblica / Louis De Alessi ; with a preface by Armen A. Alchian. — Coral Gables, FL : Law and Economics Center, University of Miami, c1983. — v, 38 p.. — (An LEC occasional paper). — *Essays in this collection originally appeared in Italian in Economia pubblica. — Bibliography: p. 39-40*

GOVERNMENT PAPERWORK — Great Britain

JAMES, Simon, 1952-
The comprehensibility of taxation : a study of taxation and communications / Simon James, Alan Lewis and Frances Allison. — Aldershot : Avebury, c1987. — xiii,314p. — *Includes bibliographies and index*

GOVERNMENT, PRIMITIVE — Ethiopia

The Southern marches of Imperial Ethiopia : essays in history and social anthropology / edited by Donald Donham and Wendy James. — Cambridge : Cambridge University Press, 1986. — xvi,308p. — (African studies series ; 51). — *Bibliography: p295-298. — Includes index*

GOVERNMENT PRODUCTIVITY — United States — Measurement

MUNDEL, Marvin Everett
Improving productivity and effectiveness / Marvin E. Mundel. — Englewood Cliffs, N.J. : Prentice-Hall, c1983. — x,467p. — (Prentice-Hall international series in industrial and systems engineering). — *Includes bibliographical references*

GOVERNMENT PUBLICITY — France

GANNE, Roger
L'administration branchée : premierès expériences dans la Somme et en Ille et Vilaine / Roger Ganne, Dominique Berthet-Diet, Didier Bazzocchi. — [Paris : Documentation française], 1984. — 158p

GOVERNMENT PUBLICITY — Great Britain

GREAT BRITAIN. Department of the Environment
Publication of financial and other information by local authorities : a consultation document. — London : the Department, [1979?]. — 5 leaves

GOVERNMENT PUBLICITY — United States

MORGAN, David
The flacks of Washington : government information and the public agenda / David Morgan. — Westport, Conn. : Greenwood Press, c1986. — p. cm. — (Contributions in political science ; no. 137). — *Includes index. — Bibliography: p*

GOVERNMENT PUBLICITY — United States — Addresses, essays, lectures

Public communication campaigns / edited by Ronald E. Rice and William J. Paisley. — Beverly Hills : Sage Publications, c1981. — p. cm. — Includes indexes. — Bibliography: p. — Contents: Historical and theoretical foundations: Public communication campaigns / William Paisley. Theoretical foundations of campaigns / William McGuire. Mass communicating / Brenda Dervin -- Campaign experiences from the field: Anti-smoking campaigns / Alfred McAlister. Heart disease prevention / Nathan Maccoby and Douglas Solomon. Family planning communication campaigns / Shahnaz Taplin. Communication efforts to prevent wildfires / Troy Kurth, Eugene McNamara, and Donald Hansen. Campaigns to affect energy behavior / Barbara Farhar-Pilgrim and Floyd Shoemaker. Mass media in political campaigns / Steven Chaffee. Mass campaigns in the People's Republic of China / Alan Liu -- Putting theory into practice: Shaping persuasive messages with formative research / Edward Palmer. Evaluation of mass media prevention campaigns / Brian Flay and Thomas Cook. Mass media information campaign effectiveness / Charles Atkin. A social marketing perspective on campaigns / Douglas Solomon

GOVERNMENT PURCHASING — Great Britain — Management

AUDIT COMMISSION FOR LOCAL AUTHORITIES IN ENGLAND AND WALES
Improving supply management in local authorities : a report. — London : H.M.S.O., 1987. — 55p

GOVERNMENT, RESISTANCE TO

ANDERSEN, Alfred F.
Liberating the early American dream : a way to transcend the capitalist/communist dilemma nonviolently / by Alfred F. Andersen. — Ukiah, Calif. : Tom Paine Institute, c1985. — p. cm. — Rev. ed. of: Updating the early American dream. c1984. — Includes index. — Bibliography: p

HAKSAR, Vinit
Civil disobedience, threats and offers: Gandhi and Rawls / Vinit Haksar. — Delhi : Oxford University Press, 1986. — 58p

ZIEGENHAGEN, Eduard A.
The regulation of political conflict / Eduard A. Ziegenhagen. — New York : Praeger, 1986. — xix, 224 p.. — Includes bibliographies and index

GOVERNMENT, RESISTANCE TO — England — London

SAINSBURY, John
Disaffected patriots : London supporters of revolutionary America / John Sainsbury. — Kingston, Ont. : McGill — Queen's University Press, 1987. — xi, 305p. — Bibliography: p.[281]-296

GOVERNMENT SPENDING POLICY — Australia

Public sector expenditure in Australia. — Canberra : Economic Planning Advisory Council, 1985. — v,19p. — (Council paper / Economic Planning Advisory Council ; no.5)

The size of government and economic performance : international comparisons. — Canberra : Economic Planning Advisory Council, 1985. — v,20p. — (Council paper / Economic Planning Advisory Council ; no.4). — Bibliography: p13

GOVERNMENT SPENDING POLICY — Canada

AULD, D. A. L.
Budget reform : should there be a capital budget for the public sector? / D. A. L. Auld. — Toronto : C.D. Howe Institute, 1985. — vi,36p

CARMICHAEL, Edward A
Tackling the federal deficit / Edward A. Carmichael. — Toronto : C.D. Howe Institute, [1984]. — 88 p.. — (Observation ; no. 26). — Includes bibliographical references

GOVERNMENT SPENDING POLICY — Great Britain

GREAT BRITAIN. Parliament. House of Commons. Library. Research Division
Public expenditure and the economy / [Priscilla Baines, Christopher Barclay, Robert Clements]. — [London] : the Division, 1980. — 19p. — (Background paper ; no.75). — Bibliography: p18-19

GOVERNMENT SPENDING POLICY — Pakistan — Statistics

Federal government public sector development programme, 1985-86. — [Islamabad] : Planning Commission, Government of Pakistan, 1985. — xvi,223p

GOVERNMENT SPENDING POLICY — United States

BENNETT, James T
Destroying democracy : how government funds partisan politics / James T. Bennett, Thomas J. DiLorenzo. — Washington, D.C. : Cato Institute, c1985. — xiii, 561 p.. — Includes index. — Bibliography: p. 505-543

LEONARD, Herman B
Checks unbalanced : the quiet side of public spending / Herman B. Leonard. — New York : Basic Books, c1986. — xii, 289 p.. — Includes index. — Bibliography: p. 265-279

GOVERNMENT TRADING — Developing countries

State trading and development : a perspective view of state trading organizations in developing countries as instruments of national development and channels of international cooperation / edited by Praxy Fernandes. — Ljubljana, Yugoslavia : International Center for Public Enterprises in Developing Countries, 1982. — 277p. — Includes bibliographical references

GOVERNMENTAL INVESTIGATIONS — Australia

WILLIAMS, David John Parry
Investigations by administrative agencies / by David John Parry Williams. — Sydney : Law Book Company, 1987. — cxiii,1099p

GOVERNMENTAL INVESTIGATIONS — Canada

ANTHONY, Russell J.
A handbook on the conduct of public inquiries in Canada / Russell J. Anthony and Alastair R. Lucas. — Toronto : Butterworths, 1985. — vii,273p

GOVERNMENTAL INVESTIGATIONS — Great Britain

HUTTON, N. R.
Lay participation in a public local inquiry : a sociological case study / Neil Hutton. — Aldershot : Gower, c1986. — x,203p. — Bibliography: p199-203

GOVERNORS — United States — Election — Case studies

Re-electing the governor : the 1982 elections / edited by Thad L. Beyle. — Lanham [Md.] : University Press of America, c1986. — xli, 336 p.. — "Copublished by arrangement with the Center for the Study of Federalism"--T.p. verso. — Includes bibliographies

GOVERNORS — United States — History

KALLENBACH, Joseph Ernest
American State Governors, 1776-1976 / by Joseph E. Kallenbach and Jessamine S. Kallenbach. — Dobbs Ferry, New York : Oceana Publications, 1977-1982. — 3 v.. — Includes index. — Bibliography: v. 3, p. 611-629. — Contents: v. 1. Electoral and personal data -- v. 2. Biographical data, Alabama-Montana -- v. 3. Biographical data, Nebraska-Wyoming

GOVERNORS GENERAL — Canada — Biography

WOODS, Shirley E.
Her Excellency Jeanne Sauvé / Shirley E. Woods. — Toronto : Macmillan of Canada, 1986. — xii,242p

GRADUATE MANAGEMENT ADMISSION COUNCIL

The official guide to MBA programs, admissions, and careers / Graduate Management Admission Council. — Princeton, N.J. : Graduate Management Admission Council

GRADUATE STUDENTS — Great Britain

The social science PhD : the ESRC inquiry on submission rates / chairman: Graham Winfield. — London : Economic and Social Research Council
Background papers. — 1987. — 232p

The social science PhD : the ESRC inquiry on submission rates / chairman: Graham Winfield. — London : Economic and Social Research Council
The report. — 1987. — 133p

GRAF BROCKDORFF-RANTZAN, ULRICH See Brockdorff-Rantzan, Ulrich, Graf von

GRAHAM, JOHN

MACLENNAN, Ben
A proper degree of terror : John Graham and the Capes Eastern frontier / Ben Maclennan. — Braamfontein : Ravan Press, 1986. — 252p

GRAIN

WEBBER, Alan
Cereals production and policy, 1921-39 : the background to the international trade agreements of the 1930s / Alan Webber. — London : City University, 1987. — 31 leaves. — (Discussion paper series / City University. Centre for Banking and International Finance ; no.59)

GRAIN — Economic aspects — Hungary — Congresses

A magyar buza minösége, ára és értékesítése : a Magyar Közgazdasági Társaság ankétja / contributions by Éber Antal...[et al.]. — Budapest : Gergely R., 1930. — 202p. — (Közgazdasági Könyvtár ; köt.9). — Proceedings of a conference "A magyar buza minösége, ára és értékesítése", [Budapest?], 1929-1930 ????????

GRAIN — Fertilizers and manures

Maximizing the efficiency of fertilizer use by grain crops / Fertilizer and Plant Nutrition Service and Joint FAO/IACA [sic] Division of Isotopes and Radiation Applications of Atomic Energy for Food and Agriculture Development. — Rome : Food and Agriculture Organization of the United Nations, 1980. — 30 p.. — (FAO fertilizer bulletin ; 3). — Bibliography: p. 29

GRAIN — European Economic Community Countries

Agricultural review for Europe. — New York : United Nations, 1983/84-. — Annual. — Continues: Review of the agricultural situation in Europe and Agricultural trade in Europe. — In 6 vols. Vol.I: General review, Vol.II: Agricultural trade, Vol.III: The Grain Market, Vol.IV: The Livestock and meat market, Vol.V: The milk and dairy products market, Vol.VI: The egg market

GRAIN — Soviet Union — Climatic factors

DESAI, Padma
Weather and grain yields in the Soviet Union / Padma Desai. — Washington, D.C. : International Food Policy Research Institute, 1986. — p. cm. — (Research report ; 54). — Bibliography: p

GRAIN TRADE

BUTLER, Nick
The international grain trade : problems and prospects / Nick Butler. — London : Croom Helm for The Royal Institute of International Affairs, c1986. — [192]p. — (Croom Helm Commodity series). — Includes bibliography and index

GRAIN TRADE
continuation
Exports of cereals by source and destination = Exportations de céréales par provenance et destination = Exportaciones de cereales por origen y destino / Food and Agriculture Organization of the United Nations. — Rome : Food and Agriculture Organization of the United Nations, 1983/84-. — *Annual. — Text in English, French and Spanish*

GRAIN TRADE — Australia
AUSTRALIA. Bureau of Agricultural Economics
Coarse grains: situation and outlook. — Canberra : [the Bureau], 1954-1984. — *Annual. — Title varies*

GRAIN TRADE — Baltic States — History
The Baltic grain trade : five essays / edited by Walter Minchinton. — [Exeter] : Association for the History of the Northern Seas, Department of Economic History, University of Exeter, 1985. — 59p

GRAIN TRADE — Developing countries — Forecasting
SARMA, J. S
Cereal feed use in the Third World : past trends and projections to 2000 / J.S Sarma. — Washington, D.C. : International Food Policy Research Institute, c1987. — p. cm. — (Research report ; 57). — *Bibliography: p*

GRAIN TRADE — Soviet Union
LUNDBORG, Per
The economics of export embargo : the case of the US-Soviet grain suspension / Per Lundborg. — London : Croom Helm, c1987. — xi,127p. — *Bibliography: p119-122. — Includes index*

GRAIN TRADE — United States
LUNDBORG, Per
The economics of export embargo : the case of the US-Soviet grain suspension / Per Lundborg. — London : Croom Helm, c1987. — xi,127p. — *Bibliography: p119-122. — Includes index*

GRAMMAR, COMPARATIVE AND GENERAL — Morphology
SELKIRK, Elisabeth O.
The syntax of words / Elisabeth O. Selkirk. — Cambridge, Mass. : MIT Press, c1982. — x, 136 p.. — (Linguistic inquiry monographs ; 7). — *Bibliography: p. [132]-136*

GRAMMAR, COMPARATIVE AND GENERAL — Syntax
SELKIRK, Elisabeth O.
The syntax of words / Elisabeth O. Selkirk. — Cambridge, Mass. : MIT Press, c1982. — x, 136 p. — (Linguistic inquiry monographs ; 7). — *Bibliography: p. [132]-136*

GRAMSCI, ANTONIO
BOCOCK, Robert
Hegemony / Robert Bocock. — Chichester : Ellis Horwood, 1986. — 136p. — *Bibliography: p.[130]-132*

GRAMSCI, Antonio
Selections from cultural writings / Antonio Gramsci ; edited by David Forgacs and Geoffrey Nowell-Smith ; translated by William Boelhower. — London : Lawrence and Wishart, 1985. — xvi,448p

SASSOON, Anne Showstack
Gramsci's politics / Anne Showstack Sassoon. — 2nd ed. — London : Hutchinson Education, 1987. — [261]p. — (Contemporary politics). — *Previous ed.: London : Croom Helm, 1980. — Includes bibliography and index*

GRANADA — History — American invasion, 1983
DAVIDSON, Scott
Grenada : a study in politics and the limits of international law / Scott Davidson. — Aldershot : Avebury, c1987. — xii,196p. *Bibliography: p184-190. — Includes index*

GRAND ALLIANCE, WAR OF THE, 1689-1697 — Diplomatic history
OAKLEY, Stewart P
William III and the northern crowns during the Nine Years War, 1689-1697 / Stewart Philip Oakley. — New York : Garland Pub., 1987. — 504 p. (some folded). — (Outstanding theses from the London School of Economics and Political Science). — *Bibliography: p. 480-501*

GRAND-SÉMINAIRE DE SAINT-SULPICE — History
YOUNG, Brian J.
In its corporate capacity : the Seminary of Montreal as a business institution, 1816-1876 / Brian Young. — Kingston ; Montreal : McGill-Queen's University Press, 1986. — xix,295p. — *Bibliography: p[263]-285*

GRANTS-IN-AID — Council of Europe countries
MEADOWS, W. J.
The response of local authorities to central government incitement to reduce expenditure / by W. J. Meadows. — Strasbourg : Council of Europe, 1986. — 33p. — (Study series local and regional authorities in Europe ; 37). — *Prepared under the guidance of the Committee of Experts on Local and Regional Finance of the Steering Committee for Regional and Municipal Matters*

GRANTS-IN-AID — Great Britain
GREAT BRITAIN. Parliament. House of Commons. Library. Research Division
Local Government Finance (No.2) Bill (Bill 41 of 1981-82) and 1982-83 rate support grant settlement / [Priscilla Baines]. — [London] : the Division, 1982. — 8p. — (Reference sheet ; no.82/2)

GREAT BRITAIN. Parliament. House of Commons. Library. Research Division
The Rate Support Grant settlement 1980 / [Margaret M. Camsell, Rob Clements]. — [London] : the Division, 1981. — 9p. — (Research note ; no.37). — *Bibliography: p9*

GRANTS-IN-AID — United States
PETERSON, Paul E
When federalism works / Paul E. Peterson, Barry G. Rabe, Kenneth K. Wong. — Washington, D.C. : Brookings Institution, c1986. — xvi, 245 p.. — *Includes bibliographical references and index*

GRANTS-IN-AID — Wales
JOINT WORKING PARTY ON A WELSH RATE SUPPORT GRANT SYSTEM
First report of the Joint Working Party on a Welsh Rate Support Grant System. — [Cardiff] ([Cathays Park, Cardiff]) : [Welsh Office], [1977]. — [1],97p

JOINT WORKING PARTY ON A WELSH RATE SUPPORT GRANT SYSTEM
Second report of the Joint Working Party on a Welsh Rate Support Grant System. — [Cardiff] ([Cathays Park, Cardiff]) : Welsh Office, 1978. — [1],106p

GRAPHIC METHODS
CHAPMAN, Myra
Plain figures / Myra Chapman ; in collaboration with Basil Mahon. — London : Her Majesty's Stationery Office, 1986. — 111p. — *At head of title: Cabinet Office (Management and Personnel Office) [and] Civil Service College*

ORE, Oystein
Graphs and their uses / by Oystein Ore. — [New York] : Random House, 1963. — (New mathematical library ; 10)

GRAUE PANTHER
UNRUH, Trude
Aufruf zur Rebellion : Graue Panther machen Geschichte / Trude Unruh. — [Essen] : Klartext Verlag, 1984. — 142p

GREAT BITAIN. MI5 — History — 20th century
WEST, Nigel
Molehunt : the full story of the Soviet spy in MI5 / Nigel West. — London : Weidenfeld and Nicholson, 1987. — 208p. — *Bibliography: p.197-199*

GREAT BRITAIN, Judicial Committee — History
SWINFEN, David B.
Imperial appeal : the debate on the appeal to the Privy Council, 1833-1986 / David B. Swinfen. — Manchester : Manchester University Press, c1987. — viii,268p. — *Bibliography: p255-260. — Includes index*

GREAT BRITAIN. British North America Act, 1867
GREAT BRITAIN. Parliament. House of Commons. Library. International Affairs Section
Patriation of the Canadian constitution / Simon Young. — [London] : the Library, 1980. — 9p. — (Background paper / House of Commons. Library. [Research Division] ; no.84). — *Bibliography: p9*

GREAT BRITAIN. Parliament. House of Commons. Library. International Affairs Section
Patriation of the Canadian constitution / Simon Young. — [London] : the Library, 1981. — 23p. — (Background paper / House of Commons. Library. [Research Division] ; no.96). — *Replaces Background Paper no.84. — Bibliography: p21-23*

GREAT BRITAIN. Building Societies Bill
BUILDING SOCIETIES ASSOCIATION
The Building Societies Bill : BSA commentary. — London : the Association, 1985. — viii,206p

GREAT BRITAIN. Companies Act 1980
PENNINGTON, Robert R.
The Companies Acts 1980 and 1981 : a practitioners' manual / by Robert R. Pennington. — London : Lloyds of London Press, 1983. — lxii,313p. — *Includes index*

GREAT BRITAIN. Companies Act 1981
PENNINGTON, Robert R.
The Companies Acts 1980 and 1981 : a practitioners' manual / by Robert R. Pennington. — London : Lloyds of London Press, 1983. — lxii,313p. — *Includes index*

GREAT BRITAIN. Companies Act 1985
JOHNSON, Barry
Accounting provisions of the Companies Act 1985 / Barry Johnson, Matthew Patient ; legal consultant editor: Mary Arden. — [London : Farringdon], c1985. — xix,908p

RENSHALL, Michael
The Companies Act 1985 : a guide to the accounting and reporting requirements / Michael Renshall, John Aldis. — London : Peat, Marwick, Mitchell, 1985. — xxx,274p. — *Includes index*

GREAT BRITAIN. Consumer Credit Act 1974
GREAT BRITAIN. Department of Prices and Consumer Protection
Consumer Credit Act 1974 : guide on appeals from licensing determinations of the Director General of Fair Trading. — London : the Department, [1976]. — 6p

GREAT BRITAIN. Data Protection Act
GREATER LONDON COUNCIL. Central Computer Service
The Data Protection Act : implications, security, registration, training. — [London : the Council, 1985]. — 50 leaves

GREAT BRITAIN. Data Protection Act 1984
CORNWELL, Roger
Data protection : putting the record straight : the NCCL guide to the Data Protection Act / Roger Cornwell and Marie Staunton. — London : National Council for Civil Liberties, c1985. — 122p. — *Bibliography: p106. — Includes index*

GREAT BRITAIN. Data Protection Act 1984 *continuation*
GULLEFORD, Kenneth
Data protection in practice / Kenneth Gulleford. — London : Butterworths, 1986. — xi,306p. — *Includes index*

GREAT BRITAIN. Financial Services Act 1986
GREAT BRITAIN
[Financial Services Act 1986]. The Financial Services Act 1986 : a guide to the new law / Andrew Whittaker, Geoffrey Morse. — London : Butterworths, 1987. — vii,475p. — *Includes index*

GREAT BRITAIN. Financial Services Act, 1986
A guide to the Financial Services Act 1986 / A.J. Wedgwood ... [et al.]. — London : Financial Training, 1986. — xi,371p. — *Includes index.* — *Includes the text of the Act*

GREAT BRITAIN. Housing Act 1985
ARDEN, Andrew
Homeless persons : the Housing Act 1985 Part III / Andrew Arden. — 2nd ed. — London : Legal Action Group, 1986. — xxiii,200p. — (Law and Practice Guide ; No.5). — *Previous ed.: 1982*

GREAT BRITAIN. Housing (Homeless Persons) Act 1977
RICHARDS, Janet
The Housing (Homeless Persons) Act 1977 : a study in policymaking / Janet Richards. — Bristol : School for Advanced Urban Studies, 1987, c1981. — 95p. — (Working papers / University of Bristol School for Advanced Urban Studies ; 22). — *Bibliography: p90-95*

GREAT BRITAIN. Industry Act 1972
GREAT BRITAIN. Department of Industry
Industry Act 1972 : criteria for assistance to industry. — [London : the Department, 1975]. — 16,3p

GREAT BRITAIN. National Insurance (Industrial Injuries) Act 1946
COLWILL, Jeremy Giles
Capital, labour, and the state : the origins of the National Insurance (Industrial Injuries) Act 1946 / by Jeremy Giles Colwill. — 338 leaves. — PhD (Laws) 1986 LSE

GREAT BRITAIN. Police and Criminal Evidence Act 1984
HARGREAVES, Fiona
A practitioner's guide to the Police and Criminal Evidence Act 1984 / Fiona Hargreaves [and] Howard Levenson. — [London] : Legal Action Group, 1985. — xxviii,429p. — *Contains the text of the act*

GREAT BRITAIN. Police and Criminal Evidence Act, 1984
The Police : powers, procedures and proprieties / edited by John Benyon and Colin Bourn ; with a foreword by Lord Scarman. — Oxford : Pergamon, 1986. — xxiv,334p. — *Bibliography: p299-312.* — *Includes index*

GREAT BRITAIN. Prevention of Terrorism (Temporary Provisions) Act 1974
SCORER, Catherine
The new Prevention of Terrorism Act : the case for repeal. — Updated and expanded 3rd ed., covering the extension of the Act in 1984 to cover 'international terrorism' / Catherine Scorer, Sarah Spencer and Patricia Hewitt. — London : National Council for Civil Liberties, c1985. — 82p. — *Previous ed.: published as The Prevention of Terrorism Act. 1981*

GREAT BRITAIN. Prevention of Terrorism (Temporary Provisions) Act 1976
SCORER, Catherine
The new Prevention of Terrorism Act : the case for repeal. — Updated and expanded 3rd ed., covering the extension of the Act in 1984 to cover 'international terrorism' / Catherine Scorer, Sarah Spencer and Patricia Hewitt. — London : National Council for Civil Liberties, c1985. — 82p. — *Previous ed.: published as The Prevention of Terrorism Act. 1981*

GREAT BRITAIN. Public Health Act 1936
GREAT BRITAIN. Department of the Environment
A consultation paper on the review of the law of statutory nuisance and offensive trades. — London : the Department, [1979?]. — [30]p

GREAT BRITAIN. Public Order Act 1936
THORNTON, Peter, 1946-
We protest : the public order debate / Peter Thornton. — London : National Council for Civil Liberties, 1985. — [96]p

GREAT BRITAIN. Public Order Act, 1986
CARD, Richard
Public order — the new law / Richard Card. — London : Butterworths, 1987. — [170]p. — *Includes index*

GREAT BRITAIN. Public Order Act 1986
THORNTON, Peter, 1946-
Public order law : including the Public Order Act 1986 / Peter Thornton. — London : Financial Training Publications, c1987. — xxi, 226p. — *Bibliography: p.[219]-220.* — *Includes the text of the Public Order Act 1986*

GREAT BRITAIN. Public Utilities Street Works Act 1950
GREAT BRITAIN
Public utilities street works : the government response to the Horne report on the review of the Public Utilities Street Works Act 1950. — London : H.M.S.O., 1986. — 32p. — *At head of title page: Department of Transport*

GREAT BRITAIN. Registered Homes Act 1984
BIGGS, Simon
The Registered Homes Act 1984 : staff training issues / Simon Biggs. — London : Central Council for Education and Training in Social Work, 1986. — 47p. — (CCETSW paper ; 24). — *Bibliographical references: p46-47*

GREAT BRITAIN. Rehabilitation of Offenders Act, 1974
BREED, Bryan
Off the record : an examination of the workings of the Rehabilitation of Offenders Act / Bryan Breed. — London : John Clare, [1987?]. — xvi,171p

GREAT BRITAIN. Transport Act 1978
GREAT BRITAIN. Welsh Office
Transport Act 1978 : public transport planning in non-metropolitan counties. — Cardiff : the Office, 1978. — 10p. — (Circular ; no.78/115)

GREAT BRITAIN. Transport Act 1985
OPEN TECH TRANSPORT PROJECT
Your guide to the 1985 Transport Act / Open Tech Transport Project. — London : Transport Publishing Projects, 1986. — xviii,130p

GREAT BRITAIN. Wages Act 1986
DAVIDSON, Fraser
A guide to the Wages Act 1986 / Fraser P. Davidson. — London : Financial Training, 1986. — [vi],136p. — *Includes the text of the Wages Act 1986*

GREAT BRITAIN
Civil service year book / Great Britain. Civil Service Department. — London : HMSO, 1974-. — Annual. — *Continues British Imperial Calendar and Civil Service List*

HEWISON, Robert
Too much : art and society in the Sixties 1960-75 / Robert Hewison. — London : Methuen, 1986. — [300]p. — *Includes index*

Striking a balance : the role of the Board of Trade 1786-1986 : bicentenary lectures / edited by Susan Foreman. — London : HMSO, 1986. — 76p. — *At head of title: Department of Trade and Industry.* — *Includes bibliographies*

GREAT BRITAIN — Appropriations and expenditures
CHILD POVERTY ACTION GROUP
A budget to unite a divided Britain : memorandum to the Chancellor of the Exchequer from the Child Poverty Action Group. — London : Child Poverty Action Group, 1985. — 9p

CONFEDERATION OF BRITISH INDUSTRY
Building a better Britain. — London : Confederation of British Industry, 1986. — 44p. — (Fabric of the nation ; 3)

CONFEDERATION OF BRITISH INDUSTRY
CBI budget representations to the Chancellor of the Exchequer, 1986. — London : Confederation of British Industry, 1986. — 23p

CONFEDERATION OF BRITISH INDUSTRY
Financing the future : 3rd report of the CBI Working Party on government expenditure. — London : Confederation of British Industry, 1985. — 68p

DAVIES, Phillip L.
Are programme resources related to organizational change? / Dr. Phillip L. Davies and Professor Richard Rose. — Glasgow : University of Strathclyde. Centre for the Study of Public Policy, 1987. — 35p. — (Studies in public policy ; 159)

FLEGMANN, Vilma
Public expenditure and the select committees of the Commons / Vilma Flegmann. — Aldershot : Gower, c1986. — [80]p. — *Includes bibliography and index*

GREAT BRITAIN. Parliament. House of Commons. Library. Research Division
Economic background to the March 1982 budget / Christopher Barclay. — [London] : the Division, 1982. — 26p. — (Background paper ; no.99)

GREAT BRITAIN. Parliament. House of Commons. Library. Research Division
The economic background to the March 1984 Budget / Christopher Barclay. — [London] : the Division, 1984. — 16p. — (Background paper ; no.136)

GREAT BRITAIN. Parliament. House of Commons. Library. Research Division
The economic background to the March 1985 Budget / Christopher Barclay. — [London] : the Division, 1985. — 18p. — (Background paper ; no.165)

GREAT BRITAIN. Parliament. House of Commons. Library. Research Division
Economic forecasts and the March 1980 budget / Christopher Barclay. — [London] : the Division, 1980. — 22p. — (Background paper ; no.78)

GREAT BRITAIN. Parliament. House of Commons. Library. Research Division
Economic forecasts and the March 1981 budget / Christopher Barclay, Paul Hutt. — [London] : the Division, 1981. — 41p. — (Background paper ; no.89)

GREAT BRITAIN. Parliament. House of Commons. Library. Research Division
Economic forecasts and the March 1983 budget / Christopher Barclay. — [London] : the Division, 1983. — 18p. — (Background paper ; no.113)

GREAT BRITAIN. Parliament. House of Commons. Library. Research Division
Public expenditure and the economy / [Priscilla Baines, Christopher Barclay, Robert Clements]. — [London] : the Division, 1980. — 19p. — (Background paper ; no.75). — *Bibliography: p18-19*

MULLARD, Maurice
The politics of public expenditure / Maurice Mullard. — London : Croom Helm, c1987. — 220p. — *Bibliography: p208-220*

GREAT BRITAIN — Appropriations and expenditures *continuation*
PEACOCK, Alan, 1922-
The growth of public expenditure in the United Kingdom / by Alan T. Peacock and Jack Wiseman assisted by Jindrich Veverka. — 2nd rev. ed.. — Allen & Unwin, 1967. — 213p. — (University of York studies in economics ; 1) (University books). — *Previous ed (B62-2055): Oxford U.P. 1962*

GREAT BRITAIN — Appropriations and expentitures
GREAT BRITAIN. Parliament. House of Commons. Library. Research Division
The April 1979 Budget - forcasts made for the Budget debate using the Treasury model / [Liz Spilsbury, Christopher Barclay]. — [London] : the Division, [1979]. — 21p. — (Background paper ; 69)

GREAT BRITAIN — Armed forces — Appropriations and expenditures
GREAT BRITAIN. Parliament. House of Commons. Library. Research Division
Statistics of defence / Robert Clements. — [London] : the Division, 1977. — 21p. — (Background paper ; no.62). — *Bibliography: p20-21*

GREAT BRITAIN — Armed Forces — Colonial forces — History
CLAYTON, Anthony
The British Empire as a superpower, 1919-39 / Anthony Clayton. — Basingstoke : Macmillan, 1986. — xiv,545p. — *Bibliography: p518-537. — Includes index*

GREAT BRITAIN — Armed Forces — History — World War, 1939-1945
GAUNSON, A. B.
The Anglo-French clash in Lebanon and Syria, 1940-45 / A.B. Gaunson. — London : Macmillan, 1986. — xi,233p,[8] of plates. — *Bibliography: p219-225. — Includes index*

GREAT BRITAIN — Bibliography
ISRAEL. Central Office of Information
Best book of the year / edited by Alexander J. Philips. — Gravesend : Alex J. Philip Lodgewood, 1929-. — *Annual*

GREAT BRITAIN — Biography
The Dictionary of national biography. — Oxford : Oxford University Press 1971-1980 : with an index covering the years 1901-1980 in one alphabetical series / edited by Lord Blake and C.S. Nicholls. — 1986. — [1010]pp. — *Includes index*

Handbook of British chronology. — 3rd ed. / edited by E. B. Fryde ... [et al.]. — London : Royal Historical Society, 1986. — xxxix,605p. — (Royal Historical Society guides and handbooks ; no.2). — *Previous ed.: / by Sir Maurice Powicke and E. B. Fryde. 1961. — Bibliography: pxxiii-xxxix*

KEYNES, John Maynard
Essays in biography / John Maynard Keynes. — London : Macmillan, 1933. — x,318p

GREAT BRITAIN — Census, 1981
Britain's workforce : 1981 Census / [prepared by the Office of Population Censuses and Surveys and the Central Office of Information]. — London : HMSO, 1985. — 20p. — (Census guide ; 3)

Census newsletter / Office of Population Censuses and Surveys, Great Britain. — London : Office of Population Censuses and Surveys, 1986-. — *Continues: OPCS monitor*

OPCS monitor: 1981 census / Office of Population Censuses and Surveys, Great Britain. — London : Office of Population Censuses and Surveys, 1978-1986. — *Continued by: Census newsletter*

GREAT BRITAIN — Census, 1981 — Bibliography
GREAT BRITAIN. Office of Population Censuses and Surveys
Guide to 1981 census publications / Office of Population Censuses and Surveys. — Titchfield : the Office. — (Census 1981 user guide 225) England and Wales. — [1985]. — 13p

GREAT BRITAIN — Church history — Sources
COMMISSION FOR BUILDING FIFTY NEW CHURCHES
The Commissions for Building Fifty New Churches : the minute books, 1711-27 : a calendar / edited by M.H.Port. — London : London Record Society, 1986. — xl, 193p. — (London Record Society publications ; v.23)

GREAT BRITAIN — Church history — 19th century
MACHIN, G. I. T.
Politics and the churches in Great Britain 1869 to 1921 / G.I.T. Machin. — Oxford : Clarendon, 1987. — x,376p. — *Bibliography: p332-362. — Includes index*

GREAT BRITAIN — Church history — 20th century
MACHIN, G. I. T.
Politics and the churches in Great Britain 1869 to 1921 / G.I.T. Machin. — Oxford : Clarendon, 1987. — x,376p. — *Bibliography: p332-362. — Includes index*

GREAT BRITAIN — Church history — 19th century
PARRY, J. P. (Jonathan Philip)
Democracy and religion : Gladstone and the Liberal Party, 1867-1875 / J.P. Parry. — Cambridge : Cambridge University Press, 1986. — xiii,504p. — (Cambridge studies in the history and theory of politics). — *Bibliography: p453-492. — Includes index*

GREAT BRITAIN — Civil defence — Bibliography
GREAT BRITAIN. Parliament. House of Commons. Library. Research Division
Civil defence / [J. B. Poole]. — [London] : the Division, 1980. — [15]p. — (Reference sheet ; no.80/9)

GREAT BRITAIN — Civil defense — Bibliography
GREAT BRITAIN. Parliament. House of Commons. Library. Research Division
Civil defence : a new urgency? / [J. B. Poole]. — [London] : the Division, 1981. — 6p. — (Reference sheet ; no.81/4)

GREAT BRITAIN — Civil defense — History — 20th century — Bibliography
IMPERIAL WAR MUSEUM. Library
The Home Guard, 1940-1944. — [London] : the Library, [1951?]. — 23leaves. — ([Booklist / Imperial War Museum Library ; no.1084B])

IMPERIAL WAR MUSEUM. Library
The Home Guard 1940-1944. — [London : the Library, 1972]. — 3p. — (Booklist / Imperial War Museum [Library] ; no.1082)

IMPERIAL WAR MUSEUM. Library
The Home Guard 1940-1944. — [London : the Library, 1975?]. — [1]. — (Booklist / Imperial War Museum [Library] ; 1084A)

GREAT BRITAIN — Civilization — 18th century
CARSWELL, John, 1918-
From revolution to revolution : England 1688-1776 / John Carswell. — London : Routledge and Kegan Paul, 1973. — xxvi,204p. — (Development of English society). — *Bibliographyp.192-196. — Includes index*

GREAT BRITAIN — Climate
Climate in the United Kingdom : a handbook of solar radiation, temperature and other data for thirteen principal cities and towns / edited by John Page and Ralph Lebens for David Bartholomew. — London : H.M.S.O., 1986. — x, 391p. — *Produced for the Energy Technology Support Unit of the Department of Energy. — Bibliography: p.389-391*

GREAT BRITAIN — Colonies
INGHAM, Barbara
Colonialism and peripheral development / Barbara Ingham. — Salford : University of Salford, 1986. — 22p. — (Salford papers in economics ; 86-6)

SIEBERG, Herward
Colonial development : die Grundlegung moderner Entwicklungspolitik durch Grossbritannien 1919-1949 / Herward Sieberg. — Stuttgart : Steiner-Verlag-Wiesbaden, 1985. — xvii,736p. — (Beiträge zur Kolonial- und Überseegeschichte ; Bd.31). — *Bibliography: p710-717*

GREAT BRITAIN — Colonies — Administration — History
GREENE, Jack P.
Peripheries and center : constitutional development in the extended polities of the British Empire and the United States, 1607-1788 / Jack P. Greene. — London : University of Georgia Press, 1987. — [288]p

GREAT BRITAIN — Colonies — Constitutional History
SWINFEN, David B.
Imperial appeal : the debate on the appeal to the Privy Council, 1833-1986 / David B. Swinfen. — Manchester : Manchester University Press, c1987. — viii,268p. — *Bibliography: p255-260. — Includes index*

GREAT BRITAIN — Colonies — Economic conditions
DAVIS, Lance E.
Mammon and the pursuit of empire : the political economy of British imperialism, 1860-1912 / Lance E. Davis and Robert A. Huttenback with the assistance of Susan Gray Davis. — Cambridge : Cambridge University Press, 1986. — x,394p. — (Interdisciplinary perspectives on modern history). — *Bibliography: p365-388. — Includes index*

GREAT BRITAIN — Colonies — History
THORNTON, A. P.
The imperial idea and its enemies : a study in British power / by A.P. Thornton. — 2nd ed. — London : Macmillan, 1985. — [v,392]p. — *Previous ed.: 1959. — Includes index*

GREAT BRITAIN — Colonies — History — 20th century
British imperial policy and decolonization, 1938-64 / [edited by] A.N. Porter and A.J. Stockwell. — Basingstoke : Macmillan. — (Cambridge commonwealth series) Vol.1: 1938-51. — 1987. — xvii,403p. — *Bibliography: p390-393. — Includes index*

GREAT BRITAIN — Colonies — Social policy
SIEBERG, Herward
Colonial development : die Grundlegung moderner Entwicklungspolitik durch Grossbritannien 1919-1949 / Herward Sieberg. — Stuttgart : Steiner-Verlag-Wiesbaden, 1985. — xvii,736p. — (Beiträge zur Kolonial- und Überseegeschichte ; Bd.31). — *Bibliography: p710-717*

GREAT BRITAIN — Colonies — Africa
DARBY, Phillip
Three faces of imperialism : British and American approaches to Asia and Africa, 1870-1970 / Phillip Darby. — New Haven : Yale University Press, 1987. — 267p. — *Includes index. — Bibliography: p.[256]-262*

GREAT BRITAIN — Colonies — Africa — Administration

The British in the Sudan, 1898-1956 : the sweetness and the sorrow / edited by Robert O. Collins and Francis M. Deng. — London : Macmillan in association with St. Antony's College, Oxford, 1984. — xxii,258p,[12]p of plates. — (St. Antony's/Macmillan series). — *Bibliography: p251. — Includes index*

GREAT BRITAIN — Colonies — Asia

DARBY, Phillip
Three faces of imperialism : British and American approaches to Asia and Africa, 1870-1970 / Phillip Darby. — New Haven : Yale University Press, 1987. — 267p. — *Includes index. — Bibliography: p.[256]-262*

GREAT BRITAIN — Colonies — India — Administration — Collected works

STOKES, Eric
The peasant and the Raj : studies in agrarian society and peasant rebellion in colonial India / Eric Stokes. — Cambridge : Cambridge University Press, 1978. — viii,308p. — (Cambridge South Asian studies ; [no.23]). — *Includes index*

GREAT BRITAIN — Commerce

ANDERTON, R.
Modelling the behaviour of export volumes of manufactures : an evaluation of the performance of different measures of international competitiveness / R. Anderton and A. Dunnett. — London : National Institute of Economic and Social Research, 1987. — 30p. — (Discussion paper / National Institute of Economic and Social Research ; no.126)

BEAN, Charles R.
Sterling misalignment and British trade performance / C. Bean. — London : Centre for Labour Economics, London School of Economics, 1987. — 49p. — (Discussion paper / London School of Economics and Political Science. Centre for Labour Economics ; no.288). — *Bibliography: p46-49*

NATIONAL ECONOMIC DEVELOPMENT OFFICE
Trade patterns and industrial change : paper presented by the Director General of NEDO to the National Economic Development Council on 7 March 1984. — London : the Office, 1984. — 79p. — (NEDC papers). — *NEDC: (84) 21*

GREAT BRITAIN — Commerce — Near East

SHIMIZU, Hiroshi
Anglo-Japanese trade rivalry in the Middle East in the inter-war period / by Hiroshi Shimizu. — London : Published for The Middle East Centre, St. Antony's College, Oxford by Ithaca Press, 1986. — [302]p. — (St. Antony's Middle East monographs ; no.17) . — *Includes bibliography and index*

GREAT BRITAIN — Commerce — Statistics

Annual statistical abstract of the U.K. ports industry / British Ports Association. — London : British Ports Association, 1983. — *Annual*

GREAT BRITAIN. Business Statistics Office
Guide to short term statistics of manufacturers' sales. — London : H.M.S.O., 1976. — 28p. — (Business monitor. PQ ; 1001)

Import penetration and export sales ratios for manufacturing industry. — London : HMSO, 1979-. — (Business monitor. MQ ; 12). — *Quarterly*

Overseas trade analysed in terms of industries. — London : HMSO, 1974-. — (Business monitor. MQ ; 10) (Business monitor. M ; 10). — *Quarterly*

Statistics trade through United Kingdom ports / Customs and Excise Department, Great Britain. — London : Customs and Excise Department, 1976-1980. — *Annual*

GREAT BRITAIN — Commerce — Canada

NADEAU, Bertrand
Britain's entry into the European Economic Community and its effect on Canada's agricultural exports / Bertrand Nadeau. — Montreal : The Institute for Research on Public Policy/L'Institut de recherches politiques, 1985. — xx,111p. — (Essays in international economics). — *Foreword and summary in English and French. — Bibliography: p95-100*

GREAT BRITAIN — Commerce — Chile — History — 19th century

MAYO, John
British merchants and Chilean development, 1851-1886 / John Mayo. — Boulder, Colo : Westview Press, 1986. — p. cm. — (Dellplain Latin American studies ; 22). — *Bibliography: p*

GREAT BRITAIN — Commerce — China — History — 19th century

CHINA AND THE RED BARBARIANS: AMERICAN AND BRITISH RELATIONS WITH CHINA IN THE 19TH CENTURY (Symposium : 1972 : London)
China and the red barbarians : [papers read at the Symposium]. — London : National Maritime Museum, 1973. — 26p. — (Maritime monographs and reports ; no.8)

GREAT BRITAIN — Commerce — European Economic Community countries

PERRY, K.
Business in Europe : opportunites for British companies in the EEC / Keith Perry. — London : Heinemann, 1987. — xii,206p. — *Bibliography: p199-200. — Includes index*

GREAT BRITAIN — Commerce — Poland

MIERZWA, Edward Alfred
Anglia a Polska w pierwszej połowie XVII w. / Edward Alfred Mierzwa. — Warszawa : Państwowe Wydawnictwo Naukowe, 1986. — 314p. — *Bibliography: p284-[300]*

GREAT BRITAIN — Commerce — Romania

CERNOVODEANU, Paul
Relațiile comerciale româno-engleze în contextul politicii orientale a Mării Britanii (1803-1878) / Paul Cernovodeanu. — Cluj-Napoca : Editura Dacia, 1986. — 402p. — *English summary*

GREAT BRITAIN — Constitution

Constitutional reform : the quarterly review. — London : Constitutional Reform Centre, 1986-. — *Quarterly*

GREAT BRITAIN. Paliament. House of Commons. Library. Research Division
A bill of rights. — [London] : the Division, 1976. — 10p. — (Background paper ; no.49). — *Bibliography: p9-10*

GREAT BRITAIN — Constitutional history

SDP-LIBERAL ALLIANCE
People in power : why constitutional reform matters to everyone in Britain. — Hebden Bridge : Liberal Party ; London : Social Democratic Party, 1986. — 16p

WASS, Douglas
Policy analysis and constitutional issues : a need for new political institutions? / Sir Douglas Wass, Michael Elliott [and] Anthony Barker. — London : Royal Institute of Public Administration, 1986. — 19p. — *Bibliography: p17*

GREAT BRITAIN — Constitutional law

BAGEHOT, Walter
The English Constitution : With an introd. by R. H. S. Crossman. — Ithaca, N.Y. : Cornell University Press, [1966]. — 310 p. — (Cornell paperbacks, CP-23). — *"First published in 1867."*

DICEY, A. V.
Introduction to the study of the law of the constitution / by A.V. Dicey. — 10th ed. / with an introduction by E.C.S. Wade. — Basingstoke : Macmillan Education, 1959 (1985 [printing]). — cxcviii,534p. — *Previous ed.: London : Macmillan, 1939. — Bibliography: p500-502. — Includes index*

GANZ, Gabriele
Understanding public law / Gabriele Ganz. — London : Fontana, 1987. — 125p. — (Understanding law). — *Bibliography: p117*

GEISSELER, Andrea
Reformbestrebungen im Englischen Verfassungsrecht : Aussicht auf eine Grundrechtskodifizierung in Grossbritannien in naher Zukunft? / Andrea Geisseler. — Frankfurt am Main : Peter Lang, 1985. — xxxii,167p. — (Europäische Hochschulschriften. Reihe 2, Rechtswissenschaft ; Bd.465). — *Bibliography: pvii-xxix*

HARDEN, Ian
The noble lie : the British constitution and the rule of law / Ian Harden and Norman Lewis ; foreword by Sir Douglas Wass. — London : Hutchinson, 1986. — xiii,334p. — (Contemporary politics). — *Bibliography: p313-317. — Includes index*

MUNRO, Colin R.
Studies in constitutional law / Colin R. Munro. — London : Butterworths, 1987. — xviii,220p. — *Includes index*

GREAT BRITAIN — Defenses

Across the divide : Liberal values for defence and disarmament / Simon Hughes [et al.]. — Hebden Bridge : Hebden Royd Publications, 1986. — 60p. — (Liberal challenge ; no.8)

ALTERNATIVE DEFENCE COMMISSION
The politics of alternative defence : a policy for a non-nuclear Britain. — London : Paladin, 1987. — 399p

COKER, Christopher
British defence policy in the 1990's : a guide to the defence debate / by Christopher Coker. — London : Brassey's Defence Publishers, 1987. — xii,186p

HICKEY, Michael
The Spetsnaz threat : can Britain be defended? / Michael Hickey. — London : Alliance Publishers for the Institute for European Defence and Strategic Studies, 1986. — 52p. — (Occasional paper / Institute for European Defence and Strategic Studies ; no.23)

KENNEDY, Gavin
The privatisation of defence supplies / Gavin Kennedy. — Glencorse : David Hume Institute, 1986. — vii,38p. — (Hume paper ; no.5). — *Bibliography: p38*

LABOUR PARTY (Great Britain)
The defence industry : the key seats, industries and regions. — London : Labour Party, 1986. — 41p. — (Special briefing note / Labour Party ; no.2)

LABOUR PARTY (Great Britain)
Labour's defence policy : defending Britain the modern way. — London : Labour Party, 1985. — [6p]. — (Special briefing note / Labour Party ; no.1)

LABOUR PARTY (Great Britain)
Modern Britain in a modern world : the power to defend our country. — London : Labour Party, 1986. — 10p

PRESSLEY, Neville
Uniting for peace : a policy for the nineties / Neville Pressley. — Hebden Bridge : Liberal Party Publications, 1986. — 57p

SMITH, Peter
Real defence : Britain without the bomb / Peter Smith [and] Mike Gapes ; foreword by Joan Ruddock. — Leeds : Independent Labour Publications, 1984. — iii,40p

GREAT BRITAIN — Defenses — Appropriations and expenditures
CHALMERS, Malcolm
Trends in UK defence spending in the 1980's / Malcolm Chalmers. — Bradford : University of Bradford. School of Peace Studies, 1986. — 62p. — (Peace research reports ; no.11)

GREAT BRITAIN — Defenses — Public opinion
Perception and reality : an opinion poll on defence and disarmament / with commentaries by Clive Rose and Peter Blaker. — London : Institute for European Defence and Strategic Studies, 1986. — 35p. — (Occasional paper / Institute for European Defence and Strategic Studies ; no.17)

GREAT BRITAIN — Description and travel — 1971-
Britain : a view from Westminster / edited by Julian Critchley. — Poole, Blandford, 1986. — [224]p. — *Includes index*

GREAT BRITAIN — Diplomatic and consular service — History
WARMAN, Roberta M
The Foreign Office, 1916-1918 : a study of its role and functions / Roberta M. Warman. — New York : Garland Pub., 1986. — 286 p.. — (Outstanding theses from the London School of Economics and Political Science). — *Thesis (Ph. D.)--University of London, 1982. — Bibliography: p. 282-286*

GREAT BRITAIN — Economic condition — 1945
Global restructuring local response / edited by Philip Cooke. — London : Economic and Social Research Council, 1986. — 308p. — *A report commissioned by the Environment and Planning Committee of the ESRC. — Includes bibliographies*

GREAT BRITAIN — Economic conditions
CIAMAGA, Lucjan
Polska-Wielka Brytania : gospodarka, stosunki ekonomiczne / Lucjan Ciamaga. — Warszawa : Państwowe Wydawnictwo Ekonomiczne, 1982. — 359p. — (Polska - RWPG - Świat)

Forecasts for the UK economy : a comparision of independent forecasts / compiled by EB Division, HM Treasury. — London : Treasury, 1986-. — *Monthly*

LAWLESS, Paul
Urban growth and change in Britain : an introduction / Paul Lawless and Frank Brown. — London : Harper & Row, 1986. — 247p. — *Includes bibliographies*

LEE, C. H.
The British economy since 1700: a macroeconomic perspective / C.H. Lee. — Cambridge : Cambridge University Press, 1986. — 297p. — *Bibliography: p279-291. — Includes index*

Local economic development information service. — Glasgow : Planning Exchange, 1986-. — *Monthly*

GREAT BRITAIN — Economic conditions — Addresses, Essays, Lectures
Population and history : from the traditional to the modern world : edited by Robert I. Rotberg and Theodore K. Rabb / guest editors: Roger S. Schofield and E. Anthony Wrigley ; contributors: Michael Anderson ... [et al.]. — Cambridge : Cambridge University Press, 1986. — [iv],219p. — (Studies in interdisciplinary history)

GREAT BRITAIN — Economic conditions — Regional disparities
GREAT BRITAIN, Parliament, House of Commons, Library, Research Division
The devolution question - regional statistics. — [London] : the Division, [1979]. — 28p. — (Background paper ; no.67)

GREAT BRITAIN — Economic conditions — Sources
SMITH, Richard Michael
The Sir Nicholas Bacon collection: sources on English society, 1250-1700 : a catalogue of an exhibition at the Joseph Regenstein Library of the University of Chicago, April-June, 1972 / [prepared by Richard M. Smith. — Chicago : University of Chicago Library, 1972]. — ix, 101 p. — *Bibliography: p. 101*

GREAT BRITAIN — Economic conditions — Statistics
GREAT BRITAIN. Central Statistical Office. Press and Information Service
[Press notices]. — London : Central Statistical Office, 1984-. — *Irregular*

GREAT BRITAIN — Economic conditions — 1760-1860
ROTELLI, Claudio
Le origini della controversia monetaria (1797-1844) / Claudio Rotelli. — Bologna : Il Mulino, 1982. — 258p. — (Saggi ; 236)

GREAT BRITAIN — Economic conditions — 19th century
The Decline of the British economy / [edited by] Bernard Elbaum and William Lazonick. — Oxford : Clarendon, 1986. — vii,310p. — *Includes bibliographies and index*

GAMBLE, Andrew
Britain in decline : economic policy, political strategy and the British state / Andrew Gamble. — 2nd ed. — London : Macmillan, 1985. — [302]p. — *Previous ed.: 1981. — Includes index*

HARBURY, C. D.
An introduction to the UK economy / Colin Harbury, Richard G. Lipsey. — 2nd ed. — London : Pitman, 1986. — x,260p. — *Previous ed.: 1983. — Includes index*

KENNEDY, William P.
Industrial structure, capital markets and origins of British economic decline / William P. Kennedy. — Cambridge : Cambridge University Press, 1987. — [248]p. — *Includes bibliography and index*

MINGAY, G. E.
The transformation of Britain, 1830-1939 / G.E Mingay. — London : Routledge & Kegan Paul, 1986. — xii,231p. — (The Making of Britain, 1066-1939)

SAUL, S. B.
The myth of the Great Depression, 1873-1896 / prepared for the Economic History Society by S.B. Saul. — 2nd ed. — London : Macmillan, 1985. — 85p. — (Studies in economic and social history). — *Previous ed.: 1969. — Bibliography: p73-83. — Includes index*

SKED, Alan
Britain's decline : problems and perspectives / Alan Sked. — Oxford : Basil Blackwell, 1987. — 90p. — (Historical Association studies). — *Bibliography: p84-86. — Includes index*

GREAT BRITAIN — Economic conditions — 20th century
The Decline of the British economy / [edited by] Bernard Elbaum and William Lazonick. — Oxford : Clarendon, 1986. — vii,310p. — *Includes bibliographies and index*

GAMBLE, Andrew
Britain in decline : economic policy, political strategy and the British state / Andrew Gamble. — 2nd ed. — London : Macmillan, 1985. — [302]p. — *Previous ed.: 1981. — Includes index*

HARBURY, C. D.
An introduction to the UK economy / Colin Harbury, Richard G. Lipsey. — 2nd ed. — London : Pitman, 1986. — x,260p. — *Previous ed.: 1983. — Includes index*

HOLLOWAY, Edward
Money matters : a modern pilgrim's economic progress / Edward Holloway. — London : Sherwood Press, 1986. — [vii],198p

KENNEDY, William P.
Industrial structure, capital markets and origins of British economic decline / William P. Kennedy. — Cambridge : Cambridge University Press, 1987. — [248]p. — *Includes bibliography and index*

Managing the UK economy : current controversies / edited by Grahame Thompson, Vivienne Brown and Rosalind Levačić. — Cambridge : Polity, 1987. — xxvii,328p. — *Based on the Open University social sciences course D210 'Introduction to eonomics'. — Includes bibliographies and index*

MINGAY, G. E.
The transformation of Britain, 1830-1939 / G.E Mingay. — London : Routledge & Kegan Paul, 1986. — xii,231p. — (The Making of Britain, 1066-1939)

SKED, Alan
Britain's decline : problems and perspectives / Alan Sked. — Oxford : Basil Blackwell, 1987. — 90p. — (Historical Association studies). — *Bibliography: p84-86. — Includes index*

GREAT BRITAIN — Economic conditions — 1918-1945
BANK OF ENGLAND. Panel of Academic Consultants
The UK economic recovery in the 1930's : papers presented at the Twenty-third Meeting of the Panel of Academic Consultants on 27 January 1984. — London : Bank of England, 1984. — 85p. — *Bibliographies*

CAPIE, Forrest
Explaining monetary changes between the two world wars / Forrest Capie and Ghila Rodrik-Bali. — London : Centre for Banking and International Finance, City University, 1986. — 38p. — (Monetary history discussion paper series ; no.21). — *Bibliography: p35-37*

MILWARD, Alan S.
The economic effects of the two world wars on Britain / prepared for the Economic History Society by Alan S. Milward. — 2nd ed. — Basingstoke : Macmillan Education, 1984 (1987 [printing]). — 86p. — (Studies in economic and social history). — *Previous ed.: 1970. — Bibliography: p78-84. — Includes index*

GREAT BRITAIN — Economic conditions — 1945-
Britain : a view from Westminster / edited by Julian Critchley. — Poole, Blandford, 1986. — [224]p. — *Includes index*

CAIRNCROSS, Frances
Guide to the economy, volume 3 / Frances Cairncross and Phil Keeley. — London : Methuen, 1987. — [176]p. — *Includes bibliographies*

CEPG model of the U.K. economy : technical manual / edited by K. J. Coutts. — 9th ed. — Cambridge : University of Cambridge. Department of Applied Economics, 1984. — 16p

The Changing experience of employment : restructuring and recession / edited by Kate Purcell ... [et al.]. — Basingstoke : Macmillan in association with British Sociological Association, 1986. — [256]p. — (Explorations in sociology ; 22). — *Includes bibliography and index*

Developing the socially useful economy. — London : Centre for Alternative Industrial and Technological Systems, 1984. — 1v.(various pagings)

The Economic revival of modern Britain : the debate between left and right / edited by David Coates, John Hillard. — Aldershot : Gower, c1987. — [320]p. — *Includes bibliography and index*

GREAT BRITAIN — Economic conditions — 1945- *continuation*

GARDNER, Nick
Decade of discontent : the changing British economy since 1973 / Nick Gardner. — Oxford : Basil Blackwell, 1987. — [232]p. — *Includes bibliography and index*

The Geography of de-industrialisation / edited by Ron Martin and Bob Rowthorn. — London : Macmillan, 1986. — xxiii,365p. — (Critical human geography). — *Includes bibliographies and index*

The growing divide : a social audit 1979-1987 / edited by Alan Walker and Carol Walker. — London : Child Poverty Action Group, 1987. — [vi],162p. — (Poverty publication ; no.72)

HENDERSON, Sir Nicholas
Channels and tunnels : reflections on Britain and abroad / Nicholas Henderson. — London : Weidenfeld and Nicolson, 1987. — 166p

MACKAY, Donald Iain
The political economy of North Sea oil / D. I. MacKay & G. A. Mackay. — Boulder, Colo. : Westview Press, 1975. — ix, 193 p. — *Includes bibliographical references and index*

POUNDS, Norman
Success in economic geography / Norman Pounds ; consultant editor Jonathan Edwards. — London : Murray, 1981. — ix,374p. — (Success studybooks). — *Bibliography: p362-366. — Includes index*

PRATTEN, C. F.
Destocking in the recession / Cliff Pratten. — Aldershot : Gower, c1985. — x,147p

ROWTHORN, R. E.
De-industrialization and foreign trade / R.E. Rowthorn, J.R. Wells. — Cambridge : Cambridge University Press, 1987. — xi,422p. — *Bibliography: p411-416. — Includes index*

SARGAN, J. D.
A set of preliminary estimates of a small model of the British economy / J. D. Sargan and G. Weber. — London : Economic and Social Research Council : London School of Economics, 1986. — [48p]. — (ESRC/LSE econometrics project discussion paper ; A.61). — *Bibliography: p42*

SDP/LIBERAL ALLIANCE
Jobs and competitiveness : SDP/Liberal Alliance budget priorities 1986. — London : [the Alliance], 1986. — [6p]

SHORT, John R.
The urban arena : capital, state and community in contemporary Britain / John R. Short. — London : Macmillan, 1984. — viii,202p. — (Critical human geography). — *Bibliography: p185-194. — Includes index*

The south west economy : proceedings of the conference held at Plymouth Polytechnic in May 1985 / edited by Peter Gripaios. — Plymouth : South West Economy Unit, 1985. — 121p

THIRD WORLD FIRST
The underdevelopment of Britain. — [London] : Third World First, 1986. — 13p

GREAT BRITAIN — Economic conditions — 1945- — Addresses, essays, lectures

TOMBS, Sir Francis
Britain, the manufacturer / given by Sir Francis Tombs [at the Hatfield Polytechnic on Wednesday, 11th March 1987]. — Hatfield : Hatfield Polytechnic, [1987]. — 26p. — (The Third Hatfield lecture). — *Third Hatfield lecture*

GREAT BRITAIN — Economic conditions — 1945- — Econometric models

Models of the UK economy : a third review by the ESRC macroeconomic modelling bureau / K.F. Wallis, editor ... [et al.]. — Oxford : Oxford University Press, 1986. — [192]p

GREAT BRITAIN — Economic conditions — 1945- — Regional disparities

GREAT BRITAIN. Parliament. House of Commons. Library. Research Division
Regional policy and the north-south divide / C. R. Barclay. — [London] : the Division, 1987. — 25p. — (Background paper ; no.198). — *Bibliography: p25*

JOHNSTONE, Derrick
Effective economic development : a discussion of local authority organization, management and training / by Derrick Johnstone. — Glasgow : The Planning Exchange, 1985. — 30leaves. — (Occasional paper ; no.19). — *Bibliography: leaves 28-30*

MARSHALL, Michael, 1957-
Long waves of regional development / Michael Marshall. — Basingstoke : Macmillan, 1987. — xv,280p. — (Critical human geography). — *Bibliography: p254-268. — Includes index*

Regional problems, problem regions and public policy in the United Kingdom / edited by P.J. Damesick and P.A. Wood. — Oxford : Clarendon, 1987. — xii,275p. — *Includes bibliographies and index*

GREAT BRITAIN — Economic conditions — 1979-

ALOGOSKOUFIS, George S.
Competitiveness, oil prices and government expenditure in the United Kingdom business cycle / George Alogoskoufis. — London : Centre for Economic Policy Research, 1987. — 28p. — (Discussion paper series / Centre for Economic Policy Research ; no.184). — *Bibliography: p22-23*

CHAMPION, A. G.
In search of Britain's booming towns : an index of local economic performance for Britain / A. G. Champion and A. E. Green. — Newcastle upon Tyne : University of Newcastle upon Tyne. Centre for Urban and Regional Development Studies, 1985. — 47p. — (Discussion paper / University of Newcastle upon Tyne. Centre for Urban and Regional Development Studies ; no.72). — *Bibliography: p39-40*

LABOUR RESEARCH DEPARTMENT
A state of collapse : the UK economy under the Tories. — London : LRD Publications, 1987. — 44p

TUC - LABOUR PARTY LIAISON COMMITTEE
A new partnership : a new Britain. — London : TUC : Labour Party, 1985. — 29p. — (Jobs and industry)

GREAT BRITAIN — Economic history

MOMMSEN, Wolfgang J.
Britain and Germany 1800 to 1914 : two developmental paths towards industrial society / Wolfgang J. Mommsen. — London : German Historical Institute, London, 1986. — 38p. — (The 1985 Annual lecture / German Historical Institute, London)

GREAT BRITAIN — Economic policy

CONFEDERATION OF BRITISH INDUSTRY
CBI budget representations to the Chancellor of the Exchequer, 1986. — London : Confederation of British Industry, 1986. — 23p

CONFEDERATION OF BRITISH INDUSTRY
Planning and working together : report of the Joint Working Party on Planning of the National Development Control Forum and the CBI. — London : Confederation of British Industry, 1986. — 24p

HALL, Peter A.
Governing the economy : the politics of state intervention in Britain and France / Peter A. Hall. — Cambridge : Polity, 1986. — 341p. — (Europe and the international order). — *Bibliography: p292-321. — Includes index*

LABOUR PARTY (Great Britain)
Investing in people. — London : Labour Party, 1986. — [20p]

MARSH, David
On structural power : an empirical test of the structuralist thesis / by David Marsh. — Colchester : Department of Government University of Essex, 1986. — 56 p. — (Essex papers in politics and government ; no. 39)

GREAT BRITAIN — Economic policy — 1918-1945

BANK OF ENGLAND. Panel of Academic Consultants
The UK economic recovery in the 1930's : papers presented at the Twenty-third Meeting of the Panel of Academic Consultants on 27 January 1984. — London : Bank of England, 1984. — 85p. — *Bibliographies*

GREAT BRITAIN — Economic policy — 1945-

ASHDOWN, Paddy
Investing in our future : tackling short-termism in the British economy / Paddy Ashdown [and] Richard Holme. — Hebden Bridge : Hebden Royd Publications, 1986. — 51p. — (Liberal challenge ; no.6). — *Bibliography : p51*

BROWNING, Peter, 1920-
The Treasury and economic policy, 1964-1985 / Peter Browning. — London : Longman, 1986. — [368]p. — *Includes bibliography and index*

CHICK, Martin John
Economic planning, managerial decision-making and the role of fixed capital in the investment in the economic recovery of the United Kingdom, 1945-1955 / Martin John Chick. — 313 leaves. — PhD (Econ) 1986 LSE

CHURCH OF ENGLAND. Industrial and Economic Affairs Committee
Growth, justice and work : the report of the...committee. — London : CIO Publishing, 1985. — 50p

Current controversies in economics / edited by Howard Vane and Terry Caslin. — Oxford : Basil Blackwell, 1987. — xii,319p. — *Includes bibliographies and index*

GREAT BRITAIN. Parliament. House of Commons. Library. Research Division
Regional policy / Christopher Barclay. — [London] : the Division, 1983. — 17p. — (Background paper ; no.131)

GREAT BRITAIN. Parliament. House of Commons. Library. Research Division
Regional policy and the north-south divide / C. R. Barclay. — [London] : the Division, 1987. — 25p. — (Background paper ; no.198). — *Bibliography: p25*

HATTERSLEY, Roy
Economic priorities for a Labour government / Roy Hattersley ; edited and introduced by Doug Jones. — Basingstoke : Macmillan, 1987. — x,198p

HESELTINE, Michael, 1933-
Where there's a will / Michael Heseltine. — London : Hutchinson, 1987. — 312p,[8]p of plates. — *Includes index*

MORISON, Hugh
The regeneration of local economies / Hugh Morison. — Oxford : Clarendon, 1987. — viii,212p. — *Bibliography: p199-205. — Includes index*

The "New right" enlightenment : the spectre that haunts the left : essays by young writers / mustered by Arthur Seldon. — Sevenoaks : E. & L. Books, 1985. — xv,261p. — *Bibliography: p252-261*

Socialist enterprise : reclaiming the economy / by Diana Gilhespy...[et al.]. — Nottingham : New Socialist / Spokesman, 1986. — 230p. — *Bibliography: p.226-229*

GREAT BRITAIN — Economic policy — 1945- *continuation*

TRADES UNION CONGRESS
Urban and regional policy : a discussion document. — [London : National Economic Development Council, 1983]. — 4,32p. — *NEDC: (83)53*

TUC-LABOUR PARTY LIAISON COMMITTEE
People at work : new rights, new responsibilities. — London : TUC : Labour Party, 1986. — 22p. — (Jobs and industry)

WADHWANI, Sushil Baldev
Inflation : real effects and possible cures / by Sushil B. Wadhwani. — 200 leaves. — *PhD (Econ) 1986 LSE*

GREAT BRITAIN — Economic policy — 1945- — Forcasting

GREAT BRITAIN. Parliament. House of Commons. Library. Research Division
The April 1979 Budget - forcasts made for the Budget debate using the Treasury model / [Liz Spilsbury, Christopher Barclay]. — [London] : the Division, [1979]. — 21p. — (Background paper ; 69)

GREAT BRITAIN — Economic policy — 1945- — Forecasting

GREAT BRITAIN. Parliament. House of Commons. Library. Research Division
Economic background to the March 1982 budget / Christopher Barclay. — [London] : the Division, 1982. — 26p. — (Background paper ; no.99)

GREAT BRITAIN. Parliament. House of Commons. Library. Research Division
The economic background to the March 1984 Budget / Christopher Barclay. — [London] : the Division, 1984. — 16p. — (Background paper ; no.136)

GREAT BRITAIN. Parliament. House of Commons. Library. Research Division
The economic background to the March 1985 Budget / Christopher Barclay. — [London] : the Division, 1985. — 18p. — (Background paper ; no.165)

GREAT BRITAIN. Parliament. House of Commons. Library. Research Division
The economic background to the March 1986 budget : oil and the UK economy / Christopher Barclay. — [London] : the Division, 1986. — 13p. — (Background paper ; no.181)

GREAT BRITAIN. Parliament. House of Commons. Library. Research Division
Economic forecasts and the March 1980 budget / Christopher Barclay. — [London] : the Division, 1980. — 22p. — (Background paper ; no.78)

GREAT BRITAIN. Parliament. House of Commons. Library. Research Division
Economic forecasts and the March 1981 budget / Christopher Barclay, Paul Hutt. — [London] : the Division, 1981. — 41p. — (Background paper ; no.89)

GREAT BRITAIN. Parliament. House of Commons. Library. Research Division
Economic forecasts and the March 1983 budget / Christopher Barclay. — [London] : the Division, 1983. — 18p. — (Background paper ; no.113)

GREAT BRITAIN — Economic policy — 1945- — Simulation methods

GREAT BRITAIN. Parliament. House of Commons. Library. Research Division
Ready reckoners on the Treasury Model / Christopher Barclay. — [London] : the Division, 1981. — 26 leaves. — (Background paper ; no.95)

GREAT BRITAIN. Parliament. House of Commons. Library. Research Division
Ready reckoners on the Treasury Model / Christopher Barclay. — [London] : the Division, 1982. — 39p. — (Background paper ; no.108). — *Updates Background Paper no.95*

GREAT BRITAIN. Parliament. House of Commons. Library. Research Division
Ready reckoners on the Treasury Model / Christopher Barclay. — [London] : the Division, 1984. — 21p. — (Background paper ; no.157)

GREAT BRITAIN — Economic policy — 1970-

CONFEDERATION OF BRITISH INDUSTRY
Building a better Britain. — London : Confederation of British Industry, 1986. — 44p. — (Fabric of the nation ; 3)

CONFEDERATION OF BRITISH INDUSTRY
Issues in UK competition policy : a discussion document. — London : Confederation of British Industry, 1986. — 44p. — *Bibliography: p33-35*

GREAT BRITAIN. Parliament. House of Commons. Library. Research Division
Industrial policy / Christopher Barclay. — [London] : the Division, 1984. — 24p. — (Background paper ; no.153)

GREAT BRITAIN — Economic policy — 1979-

LABOUR PARTY (Great Britain)
Investing in Britain : jobs and industry / Labour Party. — London : Labour Party, [1985]. — 23p

GREAT BRITAIN — Emigration and Immigration

GREAT BRITAIN. Commission for Racial Equality
Immigration. — [London : the Commission, 1978]. — 4p. — (Fact sheet / Commission for Racial Equality ; 1). — *First published 1976*

GREAT BRITAIN — Emigration and immigration

JENKINS, Keith
The closed door : a Christian critique of Britain's immigration policies / by Keith Jenkins. — London : British Council of Churches, 1984. — iii,45,[2]p. — *Bibliography: p[2]*

Leaving Britain? : a tax and legal guide for intending emigrants / edited by Tax Haven Review, Technical Services Group. — London : Tax Haven Review, 1976. — 63p

ROSE, E. J. B.
Colour and citizenship : a report on British race relations / E.J.B. Rose ... [et al.]. — London : Oxford University Press for the Institute of Race Relations, 1969. — xxiii,815p. — *Bibliography: p.797-805*

Towards a just immigration policy / edited by Ann Dummett. — London : Cobden Trust, 1986. — [240]p

UNITED KINGDOM IMMIGRANTS ADVISORY SERVICE
Annual report / United Kingdom Immigrants Advisory Service. — London : United Kingdom Immigrants Advisory Service, 1983/84-. — *Annual*

GREAT BRITAIN — Emigration and Immigration

VAN VUGT, William
British emigration during the early 1850's : with special reference to emigration to the USA / by William E. Van Vugt. — 351 leaves. — *PhD (Econ) 1986 LSE. — Leaves 287-322 are appendices*

GREAT BRITAIN — Emigration and immigration — Bibliography

WALKER, Christine
Immigration. — [London] : Home Office Library, 1978. — [2]leaves. — (Reading list / Home Office, Library)

GREAT BRITAIN — Emigration and immigration — Government policy

GREAT BRITAIN. Home Office
Home Secretary's speech to the annual conference of the Race Relations Board in York on Friday, 13th September, 1974. — [London : Home Office, 1974]. — 7leaves

SONDHI, Ranjit
Divided families : British immigration control in the Indian Subcontinent / Ranjit Sondhi. — London : Runnymede Trust, 1987. — 128p

GREAT BRITAIN — Emigration and immigration — History — 18th century

BAILYN, Bernard
Voyagers to the west : a passage in the peopling of America on the eve of the Revolution / Bernard Bailyn with the assistance of Barbara DeWolfe. — London : Tauris, 1987, c1986. — [550]p. — *Originally published: New York : Knopf, 1986. — Includes bibliography and index*

GREAT BRITAIN — Emigration and immigration — History — 19th century

WOOLCOCK, Helen R.
Rights of passage : emigration to Australia in the nineteenth century / Helen R. Woolcock. — London : Tavistock, 1986. — [xv,304]p. — *Includes index*

GREAT BRITAIN — Emigration and immigration — Law and legislation

Immigration and nationality : law and practice. — London : Frank Cass, 1986-. — *Quarterly*

GREAT BRITAIN — Executive departments — Management

ROSE, Richard, 1933-
Ministers and ministries : a functional analysis / Richard Rose. — Oxford : Clarendon, 1987. — [256]p. — *Includes bibliography and index*

GREAT BRITAIN — Foreign economic relations

CIAMAGA, Lucjan
Polska-Wielka Brytania : gospodarka, stosunki ekonomiczne / Lucjan Ciamaga. — Warszawa : Państwowe Wydawnictwo Ekonomiczne, 1982. — 359p. — (Polska - RWPG - Świat)

INGHAM, Barbara
Colonialism and peripheral development / Barbara Ingham. — Salford : University of Salford, 1986. — 22p. — (Salford papers in economics ; 86-6)

GREAT BRITAIN — Foreign economic relations — Australia

MCDOUGALL, F. L.
Letters from a ´secret service agent´ : F. L. McDougall to S. M. Bruce, 1924-1929 / W. J. Hudson and Wendy Way, editors. — Canberra : Australian Government Publishing Service, 1986. — xix,937p

GREAT BRITAIN — Foreign economic relations — Nigeria — History

Britain and Nigeria : exploitation of development? / edited by Toyin Falola. — London : Zed, 1986. — [272]p. — *Includes index*

GREAT BRITAIN — Foreign economic relations — Poland

CIAMAGA, Lucjan
Polska-Wielka Brytania : gospodarka, stosunki ekonomiczne / Lucjan Ciamaga. — Warszawa : Państwowe Wydawnictwo Ekonomiczne, 1982. — 359p. — (Polska - RWPG - Świat)

GREAT BRITAIN — Foreign economic relations — South Africa

LABOUR RESEARCH DEPARTMENT
Profiting from apartheid : Britain's links with South Africa. — London : Labour Research Department, 1986. — 54p

GREAT BRITAIN — Foreign economic relations — Sudan

BADAL, Raphael Koba
Origins of the underdevelopment of the Southern Sudan : British administrative neglect / Raphael Koba Badal. — Khartoum : University of Khartoum. Faculty of Economic and Social Studies. Development Studies and Research Centre, 1983. — 51p. — (Monograph series / University of Khartoum. Faculty of Economic and Social Studies. Development and Research Centre ; no.16)

GREAT BRITAIN — Foreign population — Photograph collections

RACE TODAY COLLECTIVE
The arrivants : a pictorial essay on blacks in Britain. — London : Race Today Publications for Creation for Liberation, 1987. — 112p

GREAT BRITAIN — Foreign relations — Sources

Documents on British policy overseas / edited by Roger Bullen and M. E. Pelly ; assisted by :H. J. Yasamee and G. Bennett. — London : H.M.S.O.. — *Accompanied by microfiches of documents calendared*
Ser. 1: [1945-1950]
Vol. 3: Britain and America : negotiation of the United States loan, 3 August - 7 December, 1945. — 1986. — 453 p.

GREAT BRITAIN — Foreign relations — Sources — Germany

Dokumente zur Deutschlandpolitik. — Frankfurt : Metzner (for) Bundesministerium für innerdeutsche Beziechungen
Reihe 1: Vom 3. September 1939 bis 8. Mai 1945 / bearbeitet von Rainer A. Blasius [and others]. — 1984-

GREAT BRITAIN — Foreign relations — 1689-1702

BARANY, George
The Anglo-Russian entente cordiale of 1697-1698 : Peter I and William III at Utrecht / George Barany. — Boulder : East European Monographs ; New York : Columbia University Press [distributor], 1986. — 101p, plates. — (East European monographs ; no.207)

OAKLEY, Stewart P
William III and the northern crowns during the Nine Years War, 1689-1697 / Stewart Philip Oakley. — New York : Garland Pub., 1987. — 504 p. (some folded). — (Outstanding theses from the London School of Economics and Political Science). — *Bibliography: p. 480-501*

GREAT BRITAIN — Foreign relations — 18th century

BLACK, Jeremy
Natural and necessary enemies : Anglo-French relations in the eighteenth century / Jeremy Black. — London : Duckworth, 1986. — [236]p. — *Includes index*

DORAN, Patrick F
Andrew Mitchell and Anglo-Prussian diplomatic relations during the Seven Years War / Patrick Francis Doran. — [Garland ed.]. — New York : Garland, 1986. — 408 p.. — (Outstanding theses from the London School of Economics and Political Science). — *Bibliography: p. [397]-408*

GREAT BRITAIN — Foreign relations — 1702-1714

GREGG, Edward
The Protestant succession in international politics, 1710-1716 / Edward Gregg. — New York : Garland, 1986. — 456 p.. — (Outstanding theses from the London School of Economics and Political Science). — *Bibliography: p. 417-456*

GREAT BRITAIN — Foreign relations — 1714-1727

GREGG, Edward
The Protestant succession in international politics, 1710-1716 / Edward Gregg. — New York : Garland, 1986. — 456 p.. — (Outstanding theses from the London School of Economics and Political Science). — *Bibliography: p. 417-456*

SMITH, Lawrence Bartlam
Spain and Britain, 1715-1719 : the Jacobite issue / Lawrence Bartlam Smith. — New York : Garland Pub., 1987. — 361 p.. — (Outstanding theses from the London School of Economics and Political Science). — *Thesis (Ph. D.)--University of London. Bibliography: p. 344-361*

GREAT BRITAIN — Foreign relations — 1714-1927

MCKAY, Derek
Allies of convenience : diplomatic relations between Great Britain and Austria, 1714-1719 / Derek McKay. — New York : Garland Pub., 1986. — 378 p.. — (Outstanding theses from the London School of Economics and Political Science). — *Bibliography: p. 350-378*

GREAT BRITAIN — Foreign relations — 19th century

PORTER, Bernard
Britain, Europe and the world 1850-1986 : delusions of grandeur / Bernard Porter. — 2nd ed. — London : Allen & Unwin, 1987. — [xv,184]p. — *Previous ed.: published as Britain, Europe and the world 1850-1982. 1983. — Includes index*

WEBSTER, Sir Charles
The foreign policy of Palmerston, 1830-1841 : Britain, the Liberal movement and the Eastern question / by Sir Charles Webster. — London : Bell, 1951. — 2v

GREAT BRITAIN — Foreign relations — 19th century — Dictionaries

WEIGALL, David
Britain & the world 1815-1986 : a dictionary of international relations / David Weigall ; with editorial assistance from Christopher Catherwood. — London : Batsford, 1987. — 240p

GREAT BRITAIN — Foreign relations — 1837-1901

British documents on foreign affairs - reports and papers from the Foreign Office confidential print / general editors: Kenneth Bourne and D. Cameron Watt. — [Frederick, Md.] : University Publications of America
Part I: From the mid-nineteenth century to the first world war
Series C: North America, 1837-1914 / editor: Kenneth Bourne. — 1986. —

[British imperialism in the nineteenth century]. British imperialism in the 19th century / edited by C.C. Eldridge. — London : Macmillan, 1984. — 214p. — (Problems in focus series)

EDWARDS, E. W.
British diplomacy and finance in China, 1895-1914 / E.W. Edwards. — Oxford : Clarendon, 1987. — 212p. — *Bibliography: p202-208. — Includes index*

WILSON, Keith M.
Empire and continent : studies in British foreign policy from the 1880s to the First World War / Keith M. Wilson. — London : Mansell, 1987. — [225]p. — *Includes index*

GREAT BRITAIN — Foreign relations — 20th century

BORINSKI, Ludwig
Die Rolle der imperialistischen Bewegung in der britischen Weltpolitik von 1900 bis 1940 / Ludwig Borinski. — Göttingen : Vandenhoeck und Ruprecht, 1985. — 19p. — (Berichte aus den Sitzungen der Joachim-Jungius-Gesellschaft der Wissenschaften ; Jg.3, Heft 1)

PORTER, Bernard
Britain, Europe and the world 1850-1986 : delusions of grandeur / Bernard Porter. — 2nd ed. — London : Allen & Unwin, 1987. — [xv,184]p. — *Previous ed.: published as Britain, Europe and the world 1850-1982. 1983. — Includes index*

RYAN, Henry Butterfield
The vision of Anglo-America : the US-UK alliance and the emerging Cold War, 1943-1946 / Henry Butterfield Ryan. — Cambridge : Cambridge University Press, 1987. — [vi,240]p. — *Bibliography: p281-301. — Includes index*

GREAT BRITAIN — Foreign relations — 20th century — Dictionaries

WEIGALL, David
Britain & the world 1815-1986 : a dictionary of international relations / David Weigall ; with editorial assistance from Christopher Catherwood. — London : Batsford, 1987. — 240p

GREAT BRITAIN — Foreign relations — 1901-1910

British documents on foreign affairs - reports and papers from the Foreign Office confidential print / general editors: Kenneth Bourne and D. Cameron Watt. — [Frederick, Md.] : University Publications of America
Part I: From the mid-nineteenth century to the first world war
Series C: North America, 1837-1914 / editor: Kenneth Bourne. — 1986. —

GREAT BRITAIN — Foreign relations — 1901-1936

DOCKRILL, M. L
The formulation of a continental foreign policy by Great Britain, 1908-1912 / Michael Lawrence Dockrill. — New York : Garland, 1986. — 407 p.. — (Outstanding theses from the London School of Economics and Political Science). — *Bibliography: p. 399-407*

EDWARDS, E. W.
British diplomacy and finance in China, 1895-1914 / E.W. Edwards. — Oxford : Clarendon, 1987. — 212p. — *Bibliography: p202-208. — Includes index*

WILSON, Keith M.
Empire and continent : studies in British foreign policy from the 1880s to the First World War / Keith M. Wilson. — London : Mansell, 1987. — [225]p. — *Includes index*

GREAT BRITAIN — Foreign relations — 1910-1936

HARTLEY, Stephen
The Irish question as a problem in British foreign policy, 1914-18 / Stephen Hartley. — Basingstoke : Macmillan in association with King's College, London, 1987. — xi,243p. — (Studies in military and strategic history). — *Bibliography: p228-236. — Includes index*

PETERS, A. R.
Anthony Eden at the Foreign Office, 1931-1938 / A.R. Peters. — Aldershot : Gower, 1986. — viii,402p. — *Bibliography: p383-392. — Includes index*

PRITCHARD, R. John
Far Eastern influences upon British strategy towards the great powers, 1937-1939 / R. John Pritchard. — New York : Garland Pub., 1987. — 328 p.. — (Outstanding theses from the London School of Economics and Political Science). — *Thesis (Ph.D.)--University of London, 1979. — Bibliography: p. 275-328*

SILVERFARB, Daniel
Britain's informal empire in the Middle East : a case study of Iraq, 1929-1941 / Daniel Silverfarb. — New York ; Oxford : Oxford University Press, 1986. — x, 200p. — *Includes index. — Bibliography: p.185-191*

GREAT BRITAIN — Foreign relations — 1936-1945

PETERS, A. R.
Anthony Eden at the Foreign Office, 1931-1938 / A.R. Peters. — Aldershot : Gower, 1986. — viii,402p. — *Bibliography: p383-392. — Includes index*

PRAŻMOWSKA, Anita
Britain, Poland and the Eastern Front, 1939 / Anita Prazmowska. — Cambridge : Cambridge University Press, 1987. — viii,231p. — (Soviet and East European studies). — *Bibliography: p220-224. — Includes index*

SILVERFARB, Daniel
Britain's informal empire in the Middle East : a case study of Iraq, 1929-1941 / Daniel Silverfarb. — New York ; Oxford : Oxford University Press, 1986. — x, 200p. *Includes index. — Bibliography: p.185-191*

GREAT BRITAIN — Foreign relations — 1945-

BEST, Richard A
Co-operation with like-minded peoples : British influences on American security policy, 1945-1949 / Richard A. Best, Jr. — Westport, Conn. : Greenwood Press, 1986. — x, 226 p.. — (Contributions in American history ; no. 116). — *Includes index. — Bibliography: p. [197]-212*

COHEN, Yoel
Media diplomacy : the Foreign Office in the mass communications age / Yoel Cohen. — London : Cass, 1986. — x,197p. — *Bibliography: p184-189. — Includes index*

EDMONDS, Robin
Setting the mould : the United States and Britain 1945-1950 / Robin Edmonds. — Oxford : Clarendon, 1986. — [450]p. — *Includes bibliography and index*

HARBUTT, Fraser J
The iron curtain : Churchill, America, and the origins of the Cold War / Fraser J. Harbutt. — New York ; Oxford : Oxford University Press, 1986. — xiv, 370p. — *Includes index. — Bibliography: p.341-353*

HENDERSON, Sir Nicholas
Channels and tunnels : reflections on Britain and abroad / Nicholas Henderson. — London : Weidenfeld and Nicolson, 1987. — 166p

MOORE, R. J. (Robin James)
Making the new Commonwealth / R.J. Moore. — Oxford : Clarendon, 1987. — [224]p. — *Includes bibliography and index*

The 'Special relationship' : Anglo-American relations since 1945 / edited by Wm. Roger Louis and Hedley Bull. — Oxford : Clarendon, 1986. — [xviii,450]p. — *Includes index*

THATCHER, Margaret
In defence of freedom : speeches on Britain's relations with the world, 1976-1986 / Margaret Thatcher ; introduced by Ronald Butt ; foreword by...Lord Home. — London : Aurum Press, 1986. — 150p

URBAN, George
A case for coherence : assumptions and aims of British foreign policy / George Urban. — London : Centre for Policy Studies, 1986. — 31p. — (Policy study ; no.75)

GREAT BRITAIN — Foreign relations — Africa, Southern

WINDRICH, Elaine
Britain and the politics of Rhodesian independence / Elaine Windrich. — London : Croom Helm, 1978. — 283p. — *Includes index*

GREAT BRITAIN — Foreign relations — Argentina

CERÓN, Sergio
Malvinas : ¿Gesta heroica o derrota vergonzosa? / Sergio Cerón. — Buenos Aires : Editorial Sudamericana, [ca.1984]. — 344p

FERRER VIEYRA, Enrique
Las islas Malvinas y el derecho internacional : los títulos argentinos y británicos, la convención de Nootka, la prescripción adquisitiva, la libre determinación de los pueblos, las Malvinas y la Antártica Argentina / Enrique Ferrer Vieyra. — Buenos Aires : Depalma, 1984. — xvi, 364p. — *Bibliography: p.333-364*

GREAT BRITAIN. Parliament. House of Commons. Library. International Affairs Section
The Falkland Islands and Dependencies / Richard Ware. — [London] : the Library, 1982. — 21p. — (Background paper / House of Commons. Library. [Research Division] ; no.101). — *Updated and expanded version of paper first issued on 5th April 1982*

GREAT BRITAIN — Foreign relations — Asia — History

FREY, Werner
Sir Valentine Chirol : die britische Postition und Politik in Asien 1895-1925. — Zürich : Juris Druck und Verlag, 1976. — viii,255p. — *Dissertation-Universität Zürich, 1975. — Bibliography: p230-255*

GREAT BRITAIN — Foreign relations — Australia

DAY, David
Menzies & Churchill at war : a controversial new account of the 1941 struggle for power / David Day. — North Ryde : Angus & Robertson, 1986. — xii,271p

MCDOUGALL, F. L.
Letters from a 'secret service agent' : F. L. McDougall to S. M. Bruce, 1924-1929 / W. J. Hudson and Wendy Way, editors. — Canberra : Australian Government Publishing Service, 1986. — xix,937p

MARKWELL, D. J.
The Crown and Australia / D. J. Markwell. — London : Australian Studies Centre, 1987. — 26p. — *Trevor Reese Memorial Lecture, 1987. — Bibliography: p25-26*

GREAT BRITAIN — Foreign relations — Austria

MCKAY, Derek
Allies of convenience : diplomatic relations between Great Britain and Austria, 1714-1719 / Derek McKay. — New York : Garland Pub., 1986. — 378 p.. — (Outstanding theses from the London School of Economics and Political Science). — *Bibliography: p. 350-378*

GREAT BRITAIN — Foreign relations — Canada

GREAT BRITAIN. Parliament. House of Commons. Library. International Affairs Section
Patriation of the Canadian constitution / Simon Young. — [London] : the Library, 1980. — 9p. — (Background paper / House of Commons. Library. [Research Division] ; no.84). — *Bibliography: p9*

GREAT BRITAIN. Parliament. House of Commons. Library. International Affairs Section
Patriation of the Canadian constitution / Simon Young. — [London] : the Library, 1981. — 23p. — (Background paper / House of Commons. Library. [Research Division] ; no.96). — *Replaces Background Paper no.84. — Bibliography: p21-23*

GREAT BRITAIN — Foreign relations — China

EDWARDS, E. W.
British diplomacy and finance in China, 1895-1914 / E.W. Edwards. — Oxford : Clarendon, 1987. — 212p. — *Bibliography: p202-208. — Includes index*

JONES, A. Phillip
Britain's search for Chinese cooperation in the First World War / A. Phillip Jones. — New York : Garland, 1986. — p. cm. — (Outstanding theses from the London School of Economics and Political Science). — *Thesis (Ph.D)--University of London, 1976. — Bibliography: p*

GREAT BRITAIN — Foreign relations — Europe

DOCKRILL, M. L
The formulation of a continental foreign policy by Great Britain, 1908-1912 / Michael Lawrence Dockrill. — New York : Garland, 1986. — 407 p.. — (Outstanding theses from the London School of Economics and Political Science). — *Bibliography: p. 399-407*

GREAT BRITAIN — Foreign relations — France

BLACK, Jeremy
Natural and necessary enemies : Anglo-French relations in the eighteenth century / Jeremy Black. — London : Duckworth, 1986. — [236]p. — *Includes index*

GREAT BRITAIN — Foreign relations — Germany

BIRKE, Adolf M.
Britain and Germany : historical patterns of a relationship / Adolf M. Birke. — London : German Historical Institute, 1987. — 40p. — *Bibliography: p33-35*

SCHMIDT, Gustav
The politics and economics of appeasement : British foreign policy in the 1930s / Gustav Schmidt ; translated from the German by Jackie Bennett-Ruete. — Leamington Spa : Berg, c1986. — 435p. — *Translation of: England in der Krise. — Bibliography: p394-429. — Includes index*

GREAT BRITAIN — Foreign relations — Hong Kong

HONG KONG LINK
Hong Kong : towards the future: British responsibilities. — London : Hong Kong Link, 1985. — 12p

Hong Kong towards the future: British responsibilities. — London : Hong Kong Link, 1987. — 12p

WALDEN, John
Excellency, your gap is showing! / John Walden. — [Hong Kong : Corporate Communications], c1983. — 82,72p. — *Text in English and Chinese*

GREAT BRITAIN — Foreign relations — Iceland

HARĐARSON, S. B. Jensdottír
Anglo-Icelandic relations during the First World War / S.B. Jensdottir Hardarson. — New York : Garland Pub., 1986. — 220 p.. — (Outstanding theses from the London School of Economics and Political Science). — *Thesis (M.A.)--London School of Economics and Political Science, 1980. — Includes index. — Bibliography: p. 217-220*

GREAT BRITAIN — Foreign relations — India

HAMID, S. Shahid
Disastrous twilight : a personal record of the partition of India / Shahid Hamid ; with a foreword by Philip Ziegler. — London : Leo Cooper in association with Secker & Warburg, 1986. — xix,364p, 4p of plates

GREAT BRITAIN — Foreign relations — Iraq

HAMDI, Walid M. S.
Rashid Ali al-Gailani and the Nationalist Movement in Iraq 1939-1941 : a political and military study of the British campaign in Iraq and the national revolution of May 1941 / by Walid M. S. Hamdi. — London : Darf, 1987. — x,277p. — *Bibliography: p266-277*

SILVERFARB, Daniel
Britain's informal empire in the Middle East : a case study of Iraq, 1929-1941 / Daniel Silverfarb. — New York ; Oxford : Oxford University Press, 1986. — x, 200p. *Includes index. — Bibliography: p.185-191*

GREAT BRITAIN — Foreign relations — Ireland
Ireland and Britain since 1922 / edited by P.J. Drudy. — Cambridge : Cambridge University Press, 1986. — [200]p. — (Irish studies ; 5). — Includes index

Lest we forget : an Irish record of one year, July 1920-July 1921. — London : Vacher, 1921. — 48p

The slaying of John Downes / issued by Sinn Fein Publicity Department. — Dublin : Republican Publications, 1984. — 30p

GREAT BRITAIN — Foreign relations — Israel
HARON, Miriam Joyce
Palestine and the Anglo-American connection, 1945-1950 / Miriam Joyce Haron. — New York : P. Lang, c1986. — 209 p.. — (American university studies. Series IX. History ; vol. 17). — Includes index. — Bibliography: p. [197]-201

GREAT BRITAIN — Foreign relations — Japan
KIBATA, Yoichi
Anglo-Japanese relations in the 1930s and 1940s / Yoichi Kibata and Antony Adamthwaite ; edited by Ian Nish. — London : Suntory-Toyota International Centre for Economics and Related Disciplines, 1986. — 28p. — (International studies ; 1986/2)

KYOZO, Sato
Japan and Britain at the crossroads, 1939-1945 : a study in the dilemmas of Japanese Diplomacy / Sato Kyozo. — Tokyo : Senshu University Press, 1986. — [xiii],301p. — Bibliography: p[269]-288

PRITCHARD, R. John
Far Eastern influences upon British strategy towards the great powers, 1937-1939 / R. John Pritchard. — New York : Garland Pub., 1987. — 328 p.. — (Outstanding theses from the London School of Economics and Political Science). — Thesis (Ph.D.)--University of London, 1979. — Bibliography: p. 275-328

GREAT BRITAIN — Foreign relations — Near East
SHUCKBURGH, Sir Evelyn
Descent to Suez : diaries, 1951-56 / Evelyn Shuckburgh ; selected for publication by John Charmley. — London : Weidenfeld and Nicolson, 1986. — x,380p,[12]p of plates

GREAT BRITAIN — Foreign relations — Palestine
ZWEIG, Ronald W.
Britain and Palestine during the Second World War / Ronald W. Zweig. — London : Royal Historical Society, 1986, c1985. — ix, 198p. — (Royal Historical Society studies in history series ; no.43). — Bibliography: p.184-190

GREAT BRITAIN — Foreign relations — Poland
MIERZWA, Edward Alfred
Anglia a Polska w pierwszej połowie XVII w. / Edward Alfred Mierzwa. — Warszawa : Pa'nstwowe Wydawnictwo Naukowe, 1986. — 314p. — Bibliography: p284-[300]

PRAŻMOWSKA, Anita
Britain, Poland and the Eastern Front, 1939 / Anita Prazmowska. — Cambridge : Cambridge University Press, 1987. — viii,231p. — (Soviet and East European studies). — Bibliography: p220-224. — Includes index

GREAT BRITAIN — Foreign relations — Prussia (Germany)
DORAN, Patrick F
Andrew Mitchell and Anglo-Prussian diplomatic relations during the Seven Years War / Patrick Francis Doran. — [Garland ed.]. — New York : Garland, 1986. — 408 p.. — (Outstanding theses from the London School of Economics and Political Science). — Bibliography: p. [397]-408

GREAT BRITAIN — Foreign relations — Scandinavia
OAKLEY, Stewart P
William III and the northern crowns during the Nine Years War, 1689-1697 / Stewart Philip Oakley. — New York : Garland Pub., 1987. — 504 p. (some folded). — (Outstanding theses from the London School of Economics and Political Science). — Bibliography: p. 480-501

GREAT BRITAIN — Foreign relations — South Asia
MOORE, R. J. (Robin James)
Making the new Commonwealth / R.J. Moore. — Oxford : Clarendon, 1987. — [224]p. — Includes bibliography and index

GREAT BRITAIN — Foreign relations — Soviet Union
BARANY, George
The Anglo-Russian entente cordiale of 1697-1698 : Peter I and William III at Utrecht / George Barany. — Boulder : East European Monographs ; New York : Columbia University Press [distributor], 1986. — 101p, plates. — (East European monographs ; no.207)

KITCHEN, Martin
British policy towards the Soviet Union during the Second World War / Martin Kitchen. — Basingstoke : Macmillan, 1986. — viii,309p. — Bibliography: p297-309. — Includes index

RYZHIKOV, V. A.
Sovetsko-angliiskie otnosheniia : osnovnye etapy istorii / V. A. Ryzhikov. — Moskva : Mezhdunarodnye otnosheniia, 1987. — 276p

VOLKOV, F. D.
Secrets from Whitehall and Downing Street / Fyodor Volkov. — Moscow : Progress, 1986. — 334p

GREAT BRITAIN — Foreign relations — Spain
MALTBY, William S.
The black legend in England, 1558-1660 / by William Saunders Maltby. — Ann Arbor : University Microfilms, [1986]. — 203p. — Dissertation (PhD)-Duke University, 1966. — Bibliography: p191-202

SMITH, Lawrence Bartlam
Spain and Britain, 1715-1719 : the Jacobite issue / Lawrence Bartlam Smith. — New York : Garland Pub., 1987. — 361 p.. — (Outstanding theses from the London School of Economics and Political Science). — Thesis (Ph. D.)--University of London. — Bibliography: p. 344-361

GREAT BRITAIN — Foreign relations — Turkey
HELLER, Joseph, 1937-
British policy towards the Ottoman Empire 1908-1914 / Joseph Heller. — London : Cass, 1983. — xi,228p. — Bibliography: p214-218. — Includes index

ROBERTSON, John
Turkey and Allied strategy, 1941-1945 / John Robertson. — New York : Garland Pub., 1986. — xvi, 309 p.. — (Outstanding theses from the London School of Economics and Political Science). — : Originally presented as the author's thesis (Ph.D.--University of London, 1982) under title: Anglo-Turkish relations 1941-1945. — Includes index. — Bibliography: p. 272-295

GREAT BRITAIN — Foreign relations — United States
British documents on foreign affairs - reports and papers from the Foreign Office confidential print / general editors: Kenneth Bourne and D. Cameron Watt. — [Frederick, Md.] : University Publications of America
Part I: From the mid-nineteenth century to the first world war
Series C: North America, 1837-1914 / editor: Kenneth Bourne. — 1986. —

DANCHEV, Alex
Very special relationship : Field-Marshall Sir John Dill and the Anglo-American alliance 1941-44 / Alex Danchev. — London : Brassey's Defence, 1986. — xv,201p. — Bibliography: p183-197. — Includes index

EDMONDS, Robin
Setting the mould : the United States and Britain 1945-1950 / Robin Edmonds. — Oxford : Clarendon, 1986. — [450]p. — Includes bibliography and index

HALL, Christopher, 1956-
Britain, America and arms control,1921-37 / Christopher Hall. — Basingstoke : Macmillan, 1987. — vii,295p. — Bibliography: p276-285. — Includes index

HARON, Miriam Joyce
Palestine and the Anglo-American connection, 1945-1950 / Miriam Joyce Haron. — New York : P. Lang, c1986. — 209 p.. — (American university studies. Series IX. History ; vol. 17). — Includes index. — Bibliography: p. [197]-201

HELMREICH, Jonathan E
Gathering rare ores : the diplomacy of uranium acquisition, 1943-1954 / Jonathan E. Helmreich. — Princeton, N.J. : Princeton University Press, c1986. — xiv, 303 p.. — Includes index. — Bibliography: p. 287-291

MASTERSON, William H
Tories and Democrats : British diplomats in the pre-Jacksonian America / by William H. Masterson ; foreword by Frank E. Vandiver. — 1st ed. — College Station : Texas A&M University Press, c1985. — xvi, 280p, [8]p of plates. — Includes index. — Bibliography: p.[259]- 274

RYAN, Henry Butterfield
The vision of Anglo-America : the US-UK alliance and the emerging Cold War, 1943-1946 / Henry Butterfield Ryan. — Cambridge : Cambridge University Press, 1987. — [vi,240]p. — Bibliography: p281-301. — Includes index

The 'Special relationship' : Anglo-American relations since 1945 / edited by Wm. Roger Louis and Hedley Bull. — Oxford : Clarendon, 1986. — [xviii,450]p. — Includes index

THORNE, Christopher
Allies of a kind : the United States, Britain, and the war against Japan, 1941-1945 / Christopher Thorne. — Oxford : Oxford University Press, 1979. — xxii, 772 p. — Includes index. — Bibliography: p. [732]-746

WRIGHT, Oliver
Anglo-American relations : the Atlantic grows wider / Sir Oliver Wright. — London : David Davies Memorial Institute of International Studies, 1986. — 16p. — Annual memorial lecture, 1986

GREAT BRITAIN — Foreign relations — United States — History
SOSIN, Jack M
English America and imperial inconstancy : the rise of provincial autonomy, 1696-1716 / J.M. Sosin. — Lincoln, Neb. ; London : University of Nebraska Press, 1985. — xii, 287p. — Includes index

GREAT BRITAIN — Foreign relations — Vatican City
CHADWICK, Owen
Britain and the Vatican during the Second World War / Owen Chadwick. — Cambridge : Cambridge University Press, 1986. — [ix,644]p. — (The Ford lectures). — Includes bibliography and index

GREAT BRITAIN — Forest policy
NATIONAL FARMERS' UNION
Farming trees : the case for government support for woodland on farms / National Farmers' Union. — London : The Union, 1986

GREAT BRITAIN — Full employment policies
GREAT BRITAIN. Parliament. House of Commons. Library. Research Division
The economics of special employment measures / Christopher Barclay. — [London] : the Division, 1985. — 24p. — (Background paper ; no.160). — *Bibliographical references: p24*

JONES, Russell, 1959-
Wages and employment policy, 1936-1985 / Russell Jones ; with a foreword by Sir Alec Cairncross. — London : Allen & Unwin, 1987. — xvii,175p. — *Bibliography: p160-169. — Includes index*

LAYARD, Richard
How to beat unemployment / Richard Layard with assistance from Andrew Sentance. — Oxford : Oxford University Press, 1986. — 201p. — *Bibliography: p192-197. — Includes index*

NATIONAL ECONOMIC DEVELOPMENT OFFICE
Job generation in areas of high unemployment : memorandum / by the Director General. — [London] : National Economic Development Council, 1985. — 1v (various pagings). — *Bibliography: Annex D. — NEDC: (85) 74*

GREAT BRITAIN — Full employment policies — History — 20th century
The Road to full employment / edited by Sean Glynn, Alan Booth. — London : Allen & Unwin, 1987. — ix,214p. — *Bibliography: p198-210. — Includes index*

GREAT BRITAIN — Full employment policy
TOMLINSON, Jim
Employment policy : the crucial years 1939-1955 / Jim Tomlinson. — Oxford : Clarendon, 1987. — [192]p. — *Includes bibliography and index*

GREAT BRITAIN — Gazetteers
Bartholomew gazetteer of Britain / compiled by Oliver Mason. — Edinburgh : J. Bartholomew, 1977. — xlviii,271p,128p of plates. — *Col. map on lining papers*

GREAT BRITAIN — Government publications
GREAT BRITAIN. Parliament. House of Commons. Public Information Office
Command papers / [C. C. Pond]. — London : the Office, 1983. — 6p. — (Factsheet ; no.19)

GREAT BRITAIN. Parliament. House of Commons. Public Information Office
House of Commons papers / [C. C. Pond]. — London : the Office, [1983]. — 7p. — (Factsheet ; no.20)

HORROCKS, Sidney
The state as publisher : a librarian's guide to the publications of His Majesty's Stationery Office / Sidney Horrocks ; with a foreword by H. G. C. Welch. — London : Library Association, 1952. — 32p. — (Library Association pamphlet ; no.10)

GREAT BRITAIN — Historical geography
REED, Michael, 1930-
The age of exuberance 1550-1700 / Michael Reed. — London : Routledge & Kegan Paul, 1986. — [320]p. — (The Making of Britain, 1066-1939)

GREAT BRITAIN — Historiography
LEVINE, Joseph M
Humanism and history : origins of modern English historiography / Joseph M. Levine. — Ithaca : Cornell University Press, 1987. — 297 p.. — *Includes index. — Bibliography: p. 214-288*

GREAT BRITAIN — History — Chronology — Tables
Handbook of dates for students of English history / edited by C. R. Cheney. — London : Royal Historical Society, 1978. — xviii,164p. — (Royal Historical Society Guides and Handbooks ; no.4)

GREAT BRITAIN — History — Civil War, 1642-1649
Politics, religion and the English Civil War / edited by Brian Manning. — London : Edward Arnold, 1973. — vii,272p. — *Bibliographyp.251-259. — Includes index*

GREAT BRITAIN — History — Handbooks, manuals, etc
Handbook of dates for students of English history / edited by C. R. Cheney. — London : Royal Historical Society, 1978. — xviii,164p. — (Royal Historical Society Guides and Handbooks ; no.4)

GREAT BRITAIN — History — Anglo-Saxon period, 449-1066
HODGKIN, R. H.
A history of the Anglo-Saxons / by R. H. Hodgkin. — 3rd ed. — London : Oxford University Press
Vol.2. — 1952. — xii,[383]-796

STENTON, Sir Frank Merry
Anglo-Saxon England / Sir Frank Merry Stenton. — 3rd ed. — Oxford : Clarendon, 1971. — 765 p. — (Oxford history of England ; 2)

STENTONANGLO-SAXON ENGLAND, F. M., F. M. Stenton
. — 3rd ed. — Oxford : Clarendon Press, 1971. — xli,765p. — *Bibliography: p[688-730]*

GREAT BRITAIN — History — Anglo-Saxon period, 449-1066 — Addresses, essays, lectures
CAMPBELL, James
Essays in Anglo-Saxon history / James Campbell. — London : Hambledon Press, 1986. — xi,240p. — (History series ; 26)

GREAT BRITAIN — History — To 1066
HILLS, Catherine
Blood of the British : from Ice Age to Norman Conquest / Catherine Hills. — London : Philip in association with Channel Four Television Company, 1986. — 255p. — *Bibliography: p248-250. — Includes index*

GREAT BRITAIN — History — Norman period, 1066-1154
HOLLISTER, C. Warren
Monarchy, magnates and institutions in the Anglo-Norman world / C. Warren Hollister. — London : Hambledon, 1985. — [310]p. — (History series ; 43). — *Includes bibliography and index*

MATTHEW, Donald
The Norman Conquest / D. J. A. Matthew. — London : Batsford, 1966. — ix,336p

GREAT BRITAIN — History — Medieval period, 1066-1485
ROWLEY, Trevor
The High Middle Ages, 1200-1540 / Trevor Rowley. — London : Routledge & Kegan Paul, 1986. — [256]p. — (The Making of Britain, 1066-1939). — *Includes bibliography and index*

GREAT BRITAIN — History — Medieval period, 1066-1485 — Addresses, essays, lectures
CAMPBELL, James
Essays in Anglo-Saxon history / James Campbell. — London : Hambledon Press, 1986. — xi,240p. — (History series ; 26)

GREAT BRITAIN — History — Medieval period, 1066-1485 — Sources — Bibliography
BATES, David
A bibliography of Domesday book / David Bates. — Woodbridge : Boydell, 1986, c1985. — xi,166p

GREAT BRITAIN — History — 1154-1399
PAINTER, Sidney
William Marshal : knight-errant, baron and regent of England / by Sidney Painter. — Baltimore : Johns Hopkins, 1933. — xi,305p

GREAT BRITAIN — History — Henry III, 1216-1272 — Sources
ENGLAND. Exchequer
The Great Roll of the Pipe for the fourth year of the reign of King Henry III, Michaelmas 1220 : (Pipe Roll 64) : now first printed from the original in the Public Record Office / with an introduction by B.E. Harris. — London : Pipe Roll Society, 1987. — xviii,307p. — (Publications of the Pipe Roll Society ; v.85. New series ; v.47). — *Latin text, English introduction and notes*

GREAT BRITAIN — History — 14th century
GIVEN-WILSON, Chris
The royal household and the King's affinity : service, politics and finance in England 1360-1413 / Chris Given-Wilson. — New Haven ; London : Yale University Press, 1986. — viii,327p. — *Bibliography: p316-320. — Includes index*

GREAT BRITAIN — History — Henry IV, 1399-1413
GIVEN-WILSON, Chris
The royal household and the King's affinity : service, politics and finance in England 1360-1413 / Chris Given-Wilson. — New Haven ; London : Yale University Press, 1986. — viii,327p. — *Bibliography: p316-320. — Includes index*

GREAT BRITAIN — History — 15th century
KINGSFORD, Charles Lethbridge
Prejudice and promise in XVth century England / Charles Lethbridge Kingsford. — London : Oxford University Press, 1925. — vii,215p

GREAT BRITAIN — History — Edward IV, 1461-1483
ROSS, Charles, 1924-
Edward IV / Charles Derek Ross. — London : Eyre Methuen, 1974. — 479p

GREAT BRITAIN — History — Henry VII, 1485-1509
STOREY, Robin Lindsay
The reign of Henry VII : Robin Lindsay. — London : Blandford Press, 1968. — 243p

GREAT BRITAIN — History — Tudors, 1485-1603
JAMES, Mervyn
Society, politics and culture : studies in early modern England / Mervyn James. — Cambridge : Cambridge University Press, 1986. — vii,485p. — (Past and present publications). — *Includes index*

LEVINE, Mortimer
Tudor dynastic problems, 1460-1571 / Mortimer Levine. — London : Allen and Unwin, 1973. — 191p. — (Historical problems, studies and documents ; 21). — *Includes index*

ROWLEY, Trevor
The High Middle Ages, 1200-1540 / Trevor Rowley. — London : Routledge & Kegan Paul, 1986. — [256]p. — (The Making of Britain, 1066-1939). — *Includes bibliography and index*

ROWSE, A. L.
Court & country : studies in Tudor social history / A.L. Rowse. — Brighton : Harvester, 1987. — x,310p. — *Includes index*

GREAT BRITAIN — History — Elizabeth, 1558-1603
MACCAFFREY, Wallace T
The shaping of the Elizabethan regime / by Wallace MacCaffrey. — Princeton, N.J. : Princeton University Press, 1968. — xiv, 501 p. — *Bibliographical footnotes*

A Spaniard in Elizabethan England : the correspondence of Antonio Perez's exile / [compiled and annotated by] Gustav Ungerer. — London : Tamesis, 1974-1976. — 2v. — *Bibliographies*

GREAT BRITAIN — History — James I, 1603-1625
GALLOWAY, Bruce
The union of England and Scotland : 1603-1608 / Bruce Galloway. — Edinburgh : John Donald, c1986. — vii, 197p. — *Bibliography: p.179-192*

GREAT BRITAIN — History — Stuarts, 1603-1714
KENYON, J. P.
The Stuarts : a study in English kingship / J. P. Kenyon. — London : Batsford, 1958. — 240p

STONE, Lawrence
The causes of the English revolution 1529-1642 / Lawrence Stone. — [2nd ed.]. — London : Ark Paperbacks, 1986. — xv,185p

GREAT BRITAIN — History — Stuarts, 1603-1714 — Sources
Divine right and democracy : an anthology of political writing in Stuart England / edited by David Wootton. — Harmondsworth : Penguin, 1986. — 512p. — (Penguin classics)

GREAT BRITAIN — History — Civil War, 1642-1649
STONE, Lawrence
The causes of the English revolution 1529-1642 / Lawrence Stone. — [2nd ed.]. — London : Ark Paperbacks, 1986. — xv,185p

GREAT BRITAIN — History — Charles II, 1660-1685
OGG, David
England in the reign of Charles II / David Ogg. — Oxford : Clarendon Press
Vol.1. — 1934. — 388p

GREAT BRITAIN — History — 1689-1714 — Sources
The divided society : party conflict in England 1694-1716 / edited by Geoffrey Holmes and W. A. Speck. — London : Arnold, 1967. — xii,179p. — (Documents of modern history)

GREAT BRITAIN — History — 18th century
CARSWELL, John, 1918-
From revolution to revolution : England 1688-1776 / John Carswell. — London : Routledge and Kegan Paul, 1973. — xxvi,204p. — (Development of English society). — *Bibliographyp.192-196. — Includes index*

GREAT BRITAIN — History — George I-II, 1714-1760
PLUMB, J. H.
Sir Robert Walpole / by J. H. Plumb. — London : Cresset
vol.2: The King's minister. — 1960. — xi,363p

GREAT BRITAIN — History — 1714-1837
NEWMAN, Gerald
The rise of English nationalism : a cultural history, 1720-1830 / Gerald Newman. — New York : St. Martin's Press, 1987. — xxiii, 294 p. . — *Includes index. — Bibliography: p. [269]-280*

GREAT BRITAIN — History — 1789-1820
GREEN, Daniel
Great Cobbett : the noblest agitator / Daniel Green. — Oxford : Oxford University Press, 1985. — ix,496p. — *Bibliography: p483-486*

GREAT BRITAIN — History — 1800-1857
GREEN, Daniel
Great Cobbett : the noblest agitator / Daniel Green. — Oxford : Oxford University Press, 1985. — ix,496p. — *Bibliography: p483-486*

GREAT BRITAIN — History — 19th century
WOOD, Anthony, 1923-
Nineteenth century Britain : 1815-1914 / Anthony Wood. — 2nd ed. — Harlow : Longman, 1982. — viii,470p. — *Previous ed: 1960. — Bibliography: p450-456. — Includes index*

GREAT BRITAIN — History — 1837-1901 — Historiography
LEVINE, Philippa
The amateur and the professional : antiquarians, historians and archaeologists in Victorian England, 1838-1886 / Philippa Levine. — Cambridge : Cambridge University Press, 1986. — [220]p. — *Includes bibliography*

GREAT BRITAIN — History — 20th century
MORGAN, Kenneth O.
Labour people : leaders and lieutenants, Hardie to Kinnock / Kenneth O. Morgan. — Oxford : Oxford University Press, 1987. — xii,370p,[16]p of plates. — *Includes bibliography and index*

GREAT BRITAIN — History — 1901-1910
WOOD, Anthony, 1923-
Nineteenth century Britain : 1815-1914 / Anthony Wood. — 2nd ed. — Harlow : Longman, 1982. — viii,470p. — *Previous ed: 1960. — Bibliography: p450-456. — Includes index*

GREAT BRITAIN — History — George V, 1910-1936
BASSETT, R.
[Nineteen thirty-one]. Nineteen thirty-one : political crisis / R. Bassett. — Aldershot : Gower, 1986, c1958. — 464p. — *Originally published: London : Macmillan, 1958. — Includes index*

GREAT BRITAIN — History — George VI, 1936-1952
ROBERTSON, Alex J.
The bleak midwinter : 1947 / Alex J. Robertson. — Manchester : Manchester University Press, 1987. — x,207p. — *Bibliography: p197-199. — Includes index*

GREAT BRITAIN — History — Elizabeth II, 1952-
CLARK, William, 1916-1985
From three worlds : memoirs / William Clark. — London : Sidgwick & Jackson, [1986]. — xi,292p

GREAT BRITAIN — History, Military — Stuarts, 1603-1714
WOOLRYCH, Austin
Soldiers and statesmen : the General Council of the Army and its debates 1647-1648 / Austin Woolrych. — Oxford : Clarendon, 1987. — [250]p. — *Includes bibliography and index*

GREAT BRITAIN — History, Military — 20th century
CLAYTON, Anthony
The British Empire as a superpower, 1919-39 / Anthony Clayton. — Basingstoke : Macmillan, 1986. — xiv,545p. — *Bibliography: p518-537. — Includes index*

COOPER, Malcolm, 19---
The birth of independent air power : British policy in the First World War / Malcolm Cooper. — London : Allen & Unwin, 1986. — xix,169p,[16]p of plates. — *Bibliography: p158-165. — Includes index*

GREAT BRITAIN — Industries
CONFEDERATION OF BRITISH INDUSTRY
Change to succeed : a consultation document. — London : Confederation of British Industry, 1985. — 68p

CONFEDERATION OF BRITISH INDUSTRY
Change to succeed : action now. — London : Confederation of British Industry, 1986. — 23p

CONFEDERATION OF BRITISH INDUSTRY
Late payment of trade debts : questionnaire results. — London : Confederation of British Industry, 1986. — 22p

CONFEDERATION OF BRITISH INDUSTRY
Technical budget representations 1987. — London : Confederation of British Industry, 1986. — 31p

CONFEDERATION OF BRITISH INDUSTRY
Vision 2010 : a preliminary report by the CBI under-35s group. — London : Confederation of British Industry, 1986. — 30p

EVELY, Richard
Concentration in British industry : an empirical study of the structure of industrial production, 1935-51 / Richard Evely and Ian Malcolm David Little. — Cambridge : Cambridge University Press, 1960. — xvi,357p. — (Economic and social studies / National Institute of Economic and Social Research ; no.16)

The Geography of de-industrialisation / edited by Ron Martin and Bob Rowthorn. — London : Macmillan, 1986. — xxiii,365p. — (Critical human geography). — *Includes bibliographies and index*

Global restructuring local response / edited by Philip Cooke. — London : Economic and Social Research Council, 1986. — 308p. — *A report commissioned by the Environment and Planning Committee of the ESRC. — Includes bibliographies*

GREAT BRITAIN. Parliament. House of Commons. Library. Research Division
Industrial policy / Christopher Barclay. — [London] : the Division, 1984. — 24p. — (Background paper ; no.153)

Industrial development guide / compiled by Cambridge Information and Research Services Limited. — 7th ed. — London : Longman, 1985-. — *Annual*

KINNOCK, Neil
Making our way : investing in Britain's future / Neil Kinnock. — Oxford : Basil Blackwell, 1986. — [160]p. — *Includes index*

MATTHEWS, Rob
Managing for success / Rob Matthews. — London : Confederation of British Industry, 1985. — 38p

NATIONAL ECONOMIC DEVELOPMENT OFFICE
Trade patterns and industrial change : paper presented by the Director General of NEDO to the National Economic Development Council on 7 March 1984. — London : the Office, 1984. — 79p. — (NEDC papers). — *NEDC: (84) 21*

NORTHCOTT, Jim
Microelectronics in industry : promise and performance / Jim Northcott. — London : Policy Studies Institute, c1986. — 258p. — (Research report ; 657)

NORTHCOTT, Jim
Promoting innovation 2 : microelectronics consultancy support / Jim Northcott...[et al.]. — London : Policy Studies Institute, 1986. — 181p. — (PSI Research Report ; 662)

Planning for microelectronics in the workplace / edited by Peter J. Senker. — Aldershot : Gower, c1985. — ix,175p. — *Includes bibliographies*

PRATTEN, C. F.
Destocking in the recession / Cliff Pratten. — Aldershot : Gower, c1985. — x,147p

SMITH, A. D.
A current cost accounting measure of the stock of equipment in British manufacturing industry / A. D. Smith. — London : National Institute of Economic and Social Research, 1986. — 25p. — (Discussion paper / National Institute of Economic and Social Research ; no.115)

Software : a vital key to UK competitiveness. — London : H.M.S.O., 1986. — viii,87p. — (An ACARD report). — *At head of title: Cabinet Office, Advisory Council for Applied Research and Development*

GREAT BRITAIN — Industries — Addresses, essays, lectures
TOMBS, Sir Francis
Britain, the manufacturer / given by Sir Francis Tombs [at the Hatfield Polytechnic on Wednesday, 11th March 1987]. — Hatfield : Hatfield Polytechnic, [1987]. — 26p. — (The Third Hatfield lecture). — *Third Hatfield lecture*

GREAT BRITAIN — Industries — Classification
Classified list of manufacturing businesses 1984. — London : Business Statistics Office, 1984. — 6v. — (Business monitor. PO ; 1007). — *Contents: 1. Extraction of minerals and ores; manufacture of metals; mineral products and chemicals - 2. Metal goods and mechanical engineering - 3. Office machinery; data processing equipment; electrical and electronic, transport, instrument engineering; other transport equipment - 4. Food, drink, tobacco - 5. Textile, leather, footwear, clothing, etc. - 6. Timber, furniture, paper, printing, publishing, rubber and plastics; other manufacturing industries*

GREAT BRITAIN — Industries — Energy consumption
LYNK, Edward L.
The demand for energy by U.K. manufacturing industry / Edward L. Lynk. — Oxford : Oxford Institute for Energy Studies, 1985. — 27p. — *Bibliography: p26-27*

GREAT BRITAIN — Industries — Environmental aspects
GREAT BRITAIN. Department of the Environment
A consultation paper on the review of the law of statutory nuisance and offensive trades. — London : the Department, [1979?]. — [30]p

GREAT BRITAIN — Industries — History
ACKRILL, Margaret
Manufacturing industry since 1870 / Margaret Ackrill. — Deddington : Philip Allan, 1987. — [256]p. — (Industrial studies series). — *Includes index*

The Economics of the Industrial Revolution / edited by Joel Mokyr. — London : Allen & Unwin, 1985. — 267p. — *Bibliography: p241-259. — Includes index*

GREAT BRITAIN — Industries — History — Maps
Atlas of industrializing Britain, 1780-1914 / edited by John Langton and R.J. Morris. — London : Methuen, 1986. — 1v.. — *Includes bibliography and index*

GREAT BRITAIN — Industries — Location
Industrial change in the United Kingdom / edited by William F. Lever. — Harlow : Longman Scientific & Technical, 1987. — 272p. — *Includes bibliographies and index*

GREAT BRITAIN — Industries — Power supply
SCHAFFER, I. R.
Combined heat and power and electricity generation in British industry, 1983-1988 : a statistical and economic survey / I. R. Schaffer ; technical consultant, R.W. Clayton. — London : H.M.S.O. [for the Energy Efficiency Office, Dept. of Energy], 1986. — [ca.190]p in various pagings. — (Energy efficiency series ; 5)

GREAT BRITAIN — Industries — Statistics
Business monitor : quarterly statistics. — London : HMSO, 1962-. — (Business monitor. P series) (Business monitor. PQ series). — *Quarterly. — From 1962-1973, statistics were included in the P series. — Contents: Quarterly Statistics of production for selected U.K. industries*

Business monitor : monthly statistics. — London : HMSO, 1962-. — (Business monitor. P series) (Business monitor. PM series). — *Monthly. — From 1962-1973, statistics were included in the P series. — Contents: Monthly statistics of production for selected U.K. industries*

GREAT BRITAIN. Business Statistics Office.
Visit of University Professors (1973 : Newport) [Papers]. — [Newport] : the Office, 1973. — 1v.(various pagings)

MITCHELL, B.
Measuring value added from the census of production / by Dr. B. Mitchell. — [Newport, Gwent?] : Business Statistics Office, 1977. — 9 leaves. — *At haed of title page: "Seminar on value added"*

Report on the census of production. — London : HMSO, 1907-. — (Business monitor. PA series). — *Quinquennial (1907-1968), annual (1970-). — Contents: Annual census of production for selected industries. Includes: introductory notes and summary tables, analyses of production industries, manufacturing units and input/output tables*

GREAT BRITAIN — Industries — Technological innovations
NORTHCOTT, Jim
Robots in British industry : expectations and experience / Jim Northcott with Colin Brown...[et al.]. — London : Policy Studies Institute, 1986. — 215p. — (Research report / Policy Studies Institute ; no.660)

GREAT BRITAIN — Intellectual life — 18th century
SMITH, R. J. (Roger John), 1938-
The Gothic bequest : medieval institutions in British thought, 1688-1863 / R.J. Smith. — Cambridge : Cambridge University Press, 1987. — [240]p. — *Includes bibliography and index*

GREAT BRITAIN — Intellectual life — 19th century
SMITH, R. J. (Roger John), 1938-
The Gothic bequest : medieval institutions in British thought, 1688-1863 / R.J. Smith. — Cambridge : Cambridge University Press, 1987. — [240]p. — *Includes bibliography and index*

YOUNG, Robert M. (Robert Maxwell)
Darwin's metaphor : nature's place in Victorian culture / Robert M. Young. — Cambridge : Cambridge University Press, 1985. — xvii,341p . — *Bibliography: p287-332. — Includes index*

GREAT BRITAIN — Kings and rulers
KENYON, J. P.
The Stuarts : a study in English kingship / J. P. Kenyon. — London : Batsford, 1958. — 240p

NELSON, Janet
Politics and ritual in early medieval Europe / Janet L. Nelson. — London : Hambledon, 1985. — [440]p. — (History series ; 42). — *Includes index*

GREAT BRITAIN — Kings and rulers — Biography
WEINTRAUB, Stanley
Victoria : biography of a queen / Stanley Weintraub. — London : Allen & Unwin, 1987. — [704]p. — *Includes index*

GREAT BRITAIN — Kings and rulers — Succession
GREGG, Edward
The Protestant succession in international politics, 1710-1716 / Edward Gregg. — New York : Garland, 1986. — 456 p.. — (Outstanding theses from the London School of Economics and Political Science). — *Bibliography: p. 417-456*

LEVINE, Mortimer
Tudor dynastic problems, 1460-1571 / Mortimer Levine. — London : Allen and Unwin, 1973. — 191p. — (Historical problems, studies and documents ; 21). — *Includes index*

GREAT BRITAIN — Manufacturers — Accounting
GREAT BRITAIN. Central Statistical Office
Value added and the national accounts. — [London : the Office, 1977]. — 6p. — *"Paper to be presented at seminar on value added: 6 December 1977"*

GREAT BRITAIN — Manufacturers — Employees
CRUM, R. E.
Non—productive activities in U.K. manufacturing industry : a report by the School of Social Studies of the University of East Anglia (Norwich) to the U.K. Department of Industry and the European Economic Community / R. E. Crum [and] G. Gudgin. — Luxembourg : Office for Official Publications of the European Communities, 1977. — ix, 176p. — (Regional policy series ; no.3)

GREAT BRITAIN — Manufactures — Statistics
GREAT BRITAIN. Business Statistics Office
Guide to short term statistics of manufacturers' sales. — London : H.M.S.O., 1976. — 28p. — (Business monitor. PQ ; 1001)

GREAT BRITAIN — Military policy
Choices : nuclear and non-nuclear defence options / assessed by: Peter Carrington...[et al.] ; organized and presented by Oliver Ramsbotham. — London : Brassey's, 1987. — xiv,473p

COKER, Christopher
British defence policy in the 1990's : a guide to the defence debate / by Christopher Coker. — London : Brassey's Defence Publishers, 1987. — xii,186p

CONNOLLY ASSOCIATION. Liverpool Branch. Conference (1985 : Liverpool)
The pollution and militarisation of the Irish Sea. — London : Four Provinces Book Shop, 1985. — 20p. — *Cover title: Irish sea, nuclear cesspool*

COOPER, Malcolm, 19---
The birth of independent air power : British policy in the First World War / Malcolm Cooper. — London : Allen & Unwin, 1986. — xix,169p,[16]p of plates. — *Bibliography: p158-165. — Includes index*

COX, Andrew
Congress, Parliament and defence : the impact of legislative reform on defence accountability in Britain and America / Andrew Cox and Stephen Kirby. — Basingstoke : Macmillan, 1986. — 1v.. — *Includes index*

The Defence equation : British military systems : policy, planning and performance / edited by Martin Edmonds. — London : Brassey's Defence, 1986. — xii,238p

ENNALS, J. R.
Star Wars : a question of initiative / Richard Ennals. — Chichester : Wiley, c1986. — xiv,236p. — *Includes index*

The Geography of defence / edited by Michael Bateman and Raymond Riley. — London : Croom Helm, c1987. — xi,237p. — *'Published on the occasion of the Annual Conference of the Institute of British Geographers, Portsmouth Polytechnic, January 1987.'. — Includes bibliographies and index*

MCINNES, Colin
Trident : the only option? / by Colin McInnes. — London : Brassey's Defence, 1986. — xv,235p. — *Bibliography: p228-231. — Includes index*

PRITCHARD, R. John
Far Eastern influences upon British strategy towards the great powers, 1937-1939 / R. John Pritchard. — New York : Garland Pub., 1987. — 328 p.. — (Outstanding theses from the London School of Economics and Political Science). — *Thesis (Ph.D.)--University of London, 1979. — Bibliography: p. 275-328*

GREAT BRITAIN — Military policy — Bibliography
GREAT BRITAIN. Parliament. House of Commons. Library. Research Division
British defence policy 1980-81 / [J. B. Poole, J. M. Laney]. — [London] : the Division, 1981. — [10]p. — (Reference sheet ; no.81/13)

GREAT BRITAIN. Parliament. House of Commons. Library. Research Division
The future of Britain's strategic nuclear force : the Trident II decision / [J. B. Poole]. — [London] : the Division, 1982. — 5leaves. — (Reference sheet ; no.82/8)

GREAT BRITAIN — Military relations — Japan
PRITCHARD, R. John
Far Eastern influences upon British strategy towards the great powers, 1937-1939 / R. John Pritchard. — New York : Garland Pub., 1987. — 328 p.. — (Outstanding theses from the London School of Economics and Political Science). — Thesis (Ph.D.)--University of London, 1979. — Bibliography: p. 275-328

GREAT BRITAIN — Military relations — United States
BEST, Richard A
Co-operation with like-minded peoples : British influences on American security policy, 1945-1949 / Richard A. Best, Jr. — Westport, Conn. : Greenwood Press, 1986. — x, 226 p.. — (Contributions in American history ; no. 116). — Includes index. — Bibliography: p. [197]-212

GREAT BRITAIN — National Health Service
LIBERAL PARTY
An agenda for action on the NHS : health service priorities for Liberals in government. — Hebden Bridge : Hebden Royd Publications, 1986. — 8p. — (Liberal Party health panel papers ; no.16)

BAINBRIDGE, Sheila
National Health surgical footwear : a survey carried out on behalf of the Department of Health and Social Security ... / Sheila Bainbridge ; [for the] Office of Population Censuses and Surveys, Social Survey Division. — London : H.M.S.O., 1979. — [10],77p

Collaboration in community care : a discussion document. — London : H.M.S.O., 1978. — [6],64p. — *The Working Party on Collaboration between the health and social services in Community Care was the joint creation of the Standing Medical and the Standing Nursing and Midwifery Advisory Committees of the Central Health Services Council, and the Personal Social Services Council'* - Introduction. — Chairman of the working party: Dame Albertine Winner. — Bibliography: p55-59

ELWELL, Hugh
NHS : the road to recovery / Hugh Elwell. — London : Centre for Policy Studies, 1986. — 28p. — (Policy study ; no.78)

GREAT BRITAIN. Department of Health and Social Security. Chief Nursing Officer
Nursing 1974-76 : report. — [London] : the Department, [1977]. — 60p. — Includes bibliographical references. — Includes index

PEARSON, Maggie
Equal opportunities in the NHS : a handbook / by Maggie Pearson. — Leeds : Training in Health and Race, 1985. — 39p

GREAT BRITAIN — National Health Service — Bibliography
ALLBROOKE, Jill C.
Selected references on joint planning and joint finance in the health and social services / compiled by Jill C. Allbrooke. — London : Department of Health and Social Security Library, 1979. — 4p. — (Bibliography series / Department of Health and Social Security Library ; no.B123)

GREAT BRITAIN. Department of Health and Social Security. Library
Selected references on resource allocation 1975-1978. — London : the Library, 1978. — 8p. — (Bibliography series ; no.B116)

PRICE, Claire
National Health Service : major non-official publications and reports / compiled by Claire Price and K. W. Best. — [London?] : Department of Health and Social Security Library, 1976. — 10leaves. — (Bibliography series / Department of Health and Social Security Library ; no.B32)

SHRIGLEY, Sheila M.
National Health Service : major official publications and reports / compiled by Sheila M. Shrigley. — [London] : Department of Health and Social Security Library, 1975. — 8p. — (Bibliography series ; no.B23)

GREAT BRITAIN — National health service — Employees
GREAT BRITAIN. Department of Health and Social Security
McCarthy report "Making Whitley work" : position paper. — [London : the Department], 1978. — 10p

GREAT BRITAIN — National Health Service — Employees
GREAT BRITAIN. Joint DHSS/NHS Manpower Planning and Personnel Information Sub Group
Absence from work : second report of joint DHSS/NHS Sub-Group. — [London] : Department of Health and Social Security, 1977. — 45p. — (Manpower planning and personnel information ; no.2). — Bibliography: p43-44

GREAT BRITAIN. Joint DHSS/NHS Manpower Planning and Personnel Information Sub Group
Leavers (standard measures and classifications) : first report of Joint DHSS/NHS Sub-Group. — [London] : Department of Health and Social Security, 1975. — 9,[15]p. — (Manpower planning and personnel information ; no.1)

GREAT BRITAIN — National Health Service — Employees — Supply and demand
GREAT BRITAIN. Department of Health and Social Security
Staffing of the National Health Service (England) : an analysis of the demand and supply positions in the major staff groups. — [London] : the Department, 1979. — [66]p

GREAT BRITAIN — National Health Service — Equipment and supplies
GREAT BRITAIN. Supply Board Working Group
Report of the Supply Board Working Group. — [London] : Department of Health and Social Security, 1978. — vii,125p

GREAT BRITAIN — National Health Service — Officials and employees
PRICE, C. J.
Selected references on manpower planning in the National Health Service / compiled by C.J. Price. — London : Department of Health and Social Security Library, 1978. — 6p. — (Bibliography series / Department of Health and Social Security Library ; no.B106)

GREAT BRITAIN — National Health Service — Procurement
GREAT BRITAIN. Supply Board Working Group
Report of the Supply Board Working Group. — [London] : Department of Health and Social Security, 1978. — vii,125p

GREAT BRITAIN — National security
COX, Andrew
Congress, Parliament and defence : the impact of legislative reform on defence accountability in Britain and America / Andrew Cox and Stephen Kirby. — Basingstoke : Macmillan, 1986. — 1v.. — Includes index

GREAT BRITAIN. Parliament. House of Commons. Research Division
Security / Barry K. Winetrobe. — [London] : the Division, 1983. — 52p. — (Background paper ; no.114)

GREAT BRITAIN — Nobility — Biography
FIELD, Leslie
Bendor : the golden Duke of Westminster / Leslie Field. — London : Weidenfeld and Nicolson, 1983. — ix,292p,[16]p of plates. — Ill on lining papers. — Bibliography: p273-281. — Includes index

GREAT BRITAIN — Nobility — History
LEWIS, Judith Schneid
In the family way : childbearing in the British aristocracy, 1760-1860 / Judith Schneid Lewis. — New Brunswick, N.J. : Rutgers University Press, c1986. — xi, 313 p.. — Includes index. — Bibliography: p. 291-303

GREAT BRITAIN — Occupations
PAYNE, Geoff
Mobility and change in modern society / Geoff Payne. — Basingstoke : Macmillan, 1987. — xiii,174p. — Bibliography: p155-165. — Includes index

GREAT BRITAIN — Officials and employees
Top jobs in Whitehall : appointments and promotions in the senior civil service / report of an RIPA working group. — London : Royal Institute of Public Administration, 1987. — 76p

GREAT BRITAIN — Officials and employees — Health and hygiene
THOMSON, Sir Daniel
The health of the higher civil service : a report / D. Thomson. — London : Civil Service Department, 1975. — 9p

GREAT BRITAIN — Officials and employees — Statistics
GREAT BRITAIN. Parliament. House of Commons. Library. Research Division
Civil service statistics / Robert Twigger. — [London] : the Division, 1980. — 20p. — (Background paper ; no.85). — Bibliography: p20

GREAT BRITAIN — Officials and employees — Training of — Evaluation
GREAT BRITAIN. Civil Service Department
Evaluation of training in the civil service : a survey. — [London] : the Department, 1977. — 126p. — Bibliography: p126

GREAT BRITAIN — Parliament — Elections, 1983
MCALLISTER, Ian
The nationwide competition for votes : the 1983 British election / Ian McAllister & Richard Rose. — London : Pinter in association with the Centre for the Study of Public Policy, c1984. — viii,257p. — Bibliography: p248-254. — Includes index

GREAT BRITAIN — Political events — 1910-1936
BASSETT, R.
[Nineteen thirty-one]. Nineteen thirty-one : political crisis / R. Bassett. — Aldershot : Gower, 1986, c1958. — 464p. — Originally published: London : Macmillan, 1958. — Includes index

GREAT BRITAIN — Politics and goverment — 1945-
MOLE, Stuart
The decade of realignment : the leadership speeches of David Steel (1976-1986) / by Stuart Mole. — Hebden Bridge : Hebden Royd Publications, [1986]. — 176p

GREAT BRITAIN — Politics and government
BAGEHOT, Walter
The English Constitution : With an introd. by R. H. S. Crossman. — Ithaca, N.Y. : Cornell University Press, [1966]. — 310 p. — (Cornell paperbacks, CP-23). — "First published in 1867."

GREAT BRITAIN — Politics and government *continuation*

Politicheskoe razvitie Velikobritanii i SShA v XVII-XIX vv. : mezhvuzovskii sbornik nauchnykh trudov / [red. kollegiia: G. R. Levin...et al.]. — Leningrad : LGPI im. A. I. Gertsena, 1985. — 104p

GREAT BRITAIN — Politics and government — Addresses, essays, lectures

Politics in Britain and the United States : comparative perspectives / edited by Richard Hodder-Williams and James Ceaser. — Durham : Duke University Press, 1986. — xvi, 232p. — *Includes index. — Contains bibliographies*

GREAT BRITAIN — Politics and government — Bibliography

GREAT BRITAIN. Civil Service Department. Central Management Library
Policy making in the Civil Service. — London : the Library, 1977. — 4p. — (Policy science documentation. Bibliography series ; B10)

GREAT BRITAIN — Politics and government — 449-1066

NELSON, Janet
Politics and ritual in early medieval Europe / Janet L. Nelson. — London : Hambledon, 1985. — [440]p. — (History series ; 42). — *Includes index*

GREAT BRITAIN — Politics and government — 1066-1154

GREEN, Judith A.
The government of England under Henry I / Judith A. Green. — Cambridge : Cambridge University Press, 1986. — [ix,539]p. — (Cambridge studies in medieval life and thought. Fourth series ; 3). — *Includes bibliography and index*

GREAT BRITAIN — Politics and government — 1066-1485

WARREN, W. L.
The governance of Norman and Angevin England 1086-1272 / W.L. Warren. — London : Edward Arnold, 1987. — x,237p. — (The governance of England). — *Includes index*

GREAT BRITAIN — Politics and government — 1399-1485

MYERS, A. R.
Crown, household and Parliament in fifteenth-century England / A.R. Myers ; edited by Cecil H. Clough ; introduction by R.B. Dobson. — London : Hambledon, 1985. — xix,394p,[2]p of plates. — (History series ; 46) ([History series]). — *Includes text in Latin. — Includes index*

GREAT BRITAIN — Politics and government — 1485-1509

MYERS, A. R.
Crown, household and Parliament in fifteenth-century England / A.R. Myers ; edited by Cecil H. Clough ; introduction by R.B. Dobson. — London : Hambledon, 1985. — xix,394p,[2]p of plates. — (History series ; 46) ([History series]). — *Includes text in Latin. — Includes index*

GREAT BRITAIN — Politics and government — 1558-1603

GRAVES, Michael A. R.
Elizabethan parliaments, 1559-1601 / Michael A. R. Graves. — London : Longman, 1987. — v,123p. — (Seminar studies in history). — *Text on inside cover. — Bibliography: p114-118. — Includes index*

KISHLANSKY, Mark A.
Parliamentary selection : social and political choice in early modern England / Mark A. Kishlansky. — Cambridge : Cambridge University Press, 1986. — 1v.. — *Includes bibliography and index*

GREAT BRITAIN — Politics and government — 1603-1649

Faction and Parliament : essays on early Stuart history / edited by Kevin Sharpe. — London : Methuen, 1985, c1978. — [ix,304p. — *Originally published: Oxford : Clarendon, 1978. — Includes index*

THOMPSON, Christopher, 19---
Parliamentary history in the 1620s : in or out of perspective? / by Christopher Thompson. — Wivenhoe : Orchard, c1986. — 26leaves

GREAT BRITAIN — Politics and government — 1603-1714

CLARK, J. C. D.
Revolution and rebellion : state and society in England in the seventeenth and eighteenth centuries / J.C.D. Clark. — Cambridge : Cambridge University Press, 1986. — 1v.

FLETCHER, Anthony J.
Reform in the provinces : the government of Stuart England / Anthony Fletcher. — New Haven : Yale University Press, c1986. — p. cm . — *Includes index. — Bibliography: p*

KENYON, J. P.
Stuart England / J.P. Kenyon. — 2nd ed. — Harmondsworth : Penguin, 1985. — 382p. — (The Pelican history of England ; 6). — *Previous ed.: London : Allen Lane, 1978. — Includes index*

KISHLANSKY, Mark A.
Parliamentary selection : social and political choice in early modern England / Mark A. Kishlansky. — Cambridge : Cambridge University Press, 1986. — 1v.. — *Includes bibliography and index*

Politics and people in revolutionary England : essays in honour of Ivan Roots / edited by Colin Jones, Malyn Newitt and Stephen Roberts. — Oxford : Blackwell, 1986. — xiv,316p. — *Includes index*

ROBERTS, Clayton
Schemes & undertakings : a study of English politics in the seventeenth century / Clayton Roberts. — Columbus : Ohio State University Press, 1985. — xiii, 333p. — *Includes index. — Bibliography: p.299-316*

GREAT BRITAIN — Politics and government — 1625-1649

COPE, Esther S.
Politics without parliaments, 1629-1640 / Esther S. Cope. — London : Allen & Unwin, 1987. — xiii,252p. — *Bibliography : p221-238. — Includes index*

CUST, Richard
The forced loan and English politics : 1626-1628 / Richard Cust. — Oxford : Clarendon, 1987. — [380]p. — *Includes bibliography and index*

GREAT BRITAIN — Politics and government — 1642-1649

Puritanism and liberty : being the army debates (1647-9) from the Clarke manuscripts, with supplementary documents / selected and edited with an introduction by A.S.P. Woodhouse ; new preface by Ivan Roots. — 3rd ed. — London : Dent, 1986. — 506p. — (Everyman's library)

GREAT BRITAIN — Politics and government — 1642-1660

HILL, Christopher, 1912-
The world turned upside down : radical ideas during the English Revolution / Christopher Hill. — Harmondsworth : Penguin, 1975. — 431p. — (Pelican books). — *Originally published: London : Temple Smith, 1972. — Includes index*

ROWSE, A. L.
Reflections on the Puritan Revolution / A.L. Rowse. — London : Methuen, 1986. — [256]p. — *Includes index*

GREAT BRITAIN — Politics and government — 1660-1668

GREAVES, Richard L
Deliver us from evil : the radical underground in Britain, 1660-1663 / Richard L. Greaves. — New York : Oxford University Press, 1986. — x, 291p. — *Includes index. — Includes bibliographical references*

GREAT BRITAIN — Politics and government — 1660-1688

PRALL, Stuart E
The bloodless revolution : England, 1688 / Stuart E. Prall. — Madison, WI : University of Wisconsin Press, 1985, c1972. — xvi, 343p, [8]p of plates. — : *Reprint. Originally published: Garden City, N.Y., 1972. — Includes index. — Bibliography: p.[326]-330*

GREAT BRITAIN — Politics and government — Revolution of 1688

PRALL, Stuart E
The bloodless revolution : England, 1688 / Stuart E. Prall. — Madison, WI : University of Wisconsin Press, 1985, c1972. — xvi, 343p, [8]p of plates. — : *Reprint. Originally published: Garden City, N.Y., 1972. — Includes index. — Bibliography: p.[326]-330*

GREAT BRITAIN — Politics and government — 1689-1702

PRALL, Stuart E
The bloodless revolution : England, 1688 / Stuart E. Prall. — Madison, WI : University of Wisconsin Press, 1985, c1972. — xvi, 343p, [8]p of plates. — : *Reprint. Originally published: Garden City, N.Y., 1972. — Includes index. — Bibliography: p.[326]-330*

GREAT BRITAIN — Politics and government — 1702-1714

GREGG, Edward
The Protestant succession in international politics, 1710-1716 / Edward Gregg. — New York : Garland, 1986. — 456 p. — (Outstanding theses from the London School of Economics and Political Science). — *Bibliography: p. 417-456*

HOLMES, Geoffrey, 1928-
British politics in the age of Anne / Geoffrey Holmes. — 2nd ed. — London : Hambledon, 1985. — [576]p. — *Previous ed.: London : Macmillan, 1967. — Includes bibliography and index*

GREAT BRITAIN — Politics and government — 1714-1727

GREGG, Edward
The Protestant succession in international politics, 1710-1716 / Edward Gregg. — New York : Garland, 1986. — 456 p. — (Outstanding theses from the London School of Economics and Political Science). — *Bibliography: p. 417-456*

MURRAY, John Joseph
George I, the Baltic and the Whig split of 1717 : a study in diplomacy and propaganda / John J. Murray. — London : Routledge and Kegan Paul, 1969. — xv,366p

GREAT BRITAIN — Politics and government — 1714-1760

PLUMB, J. H.
Sir Robert Walpole / by J. H. Plumb. — London : Cresset
vol.2: The King's minister. — 1960. — xi,363p

GREAT BRITAIN — Politics and government — 1714-1820

CLARK, J. C. D.
Revolution and rebellion : state and society in England in the seventeenth and eighteenth centuries / J.C.D. Clark. — Cambridge : Cambridge University Press, 1986. — 1v.

GREAT BRITAIN — Politics and government — 1760-1820

PAINE, Thomas
Rights of man / Thomas Paine ; with a biographical introduction by Philip S. Foner. — Secaucus : Citadel, c1974. — 262p

GREAT BRITAIN — Politics and government — 1800-1837

DINWIDDY, J. R.
From Luddism to the First Reform Bill : reform in England 1810-1832 / J.R. Dinwiddy. — Oxford : Basil Blackwell, 1986. — [96]p. — (Historical Association studies). — *Includes bibliography and index*

MATHER, F. C.
Achilles or Nestor? : the Duke of Wellington in British politics after the great Reform Act / F. C. Mather. — Southampton : University of Southampton, 1986. — 21p. — *A public lecture delivered on 6 February 1986. — Bibliography: p17-21*

WELLINGTON, Arthur Wellesley, Duke of Wellington / ed. by R. J. Olney and Julia Melvin. — London : H.M.S.O.
2: Political correspondence, November 1834 — April 1835. — 1986. — v, 664p. — (Prime Ministers' papers series)

GREAT BRITAIN — Politics and government — 19th century

BRENT, Richard
Liberal Anglican politics : Whiggery, religion and reform, 1830-1841 / Richard Brent. — Oxford : Clarendon, 1987. — 340p. — (Oxford historical monographs). — *Bibliography: p301-330. — Includes index*

COX, Gary W.
The efficient secret : the Cabinet and the development of political parties in Victorian England / Gary W. Cox. — Cambridge : Cambridge University Press, 1987. — [208]p. — (Political economy of institutions and decisions). — *Includes bibliography and index*

OSTROGORSKI, M.
Democracy and the organization of political parties / with a preface by...James Bryce ; edited...by Seymour Martin Lipset. — Chicago : Quadrangle
volume 1: England. — 1964. — lxxxii,350p. — *First published in English in 1902*

Politics and social change in modern Britain : essays presented to A.F. Thompson / editor, P.J. Waller. — Brighton : Harvester, 1987. — xx,236p. — *Includes index*

GREAT BRITAIN — Politics and government — 1837-1901

EDSALL, Nicholas C
Richard Cobden, independent radical / Nicholas C. Edsall. — Cambridge, Mass. ; London : Harvard University Press, 1986. — xiv, 465p. — *Includes index. — Bibliography: p.[429]-433*

GAMBLE, Andrew
Britain in decline : economic policy, political strategy and the British state / Andrew Gamble. — 2nd ed. — London : Macmillan, 1985. — [302]p. — *Previous ed.: 1981. — Includes index*

The Gladstonian turn of mind : essays presented to J.B. Conacher / edited by Bruce L. Kinzer. — Toronto ; London : University of Toronto Press, c1985. — xv, 294 p.. — *"James Blennerhasset Conacher publications, 1947-84 / compiled by N. Merrill Distad" --p. [265]-271. — Includes bibliographies and index*

HINDE, Wendy
Richard Cobden : a Victorian outsider : a biography / by Wendy Hinde. — New Haven : Yale University Press, 1987. — p. cm. — *Includes index. — Bibliography: p*

SPENCER, John Poyntz Spencer, Earl
The red earl : the papers of the fifth Earl Spencer 1835-1910 / edited by Peter Gordon. — Nothampton : Northamptonshire Record Society
Vol.2: 1885-1910. — 1986. — xii, 387p, [9]p of plates. — (The Publications of the Northamptonshire Record Society ; v.34)

WELLINGTON, Arthur Wellesley, Duke of Wellington / ed. by R. J. Olney and Julia Melvin. — London : H.M.S.O.
2: Political correspondence, November 1834 — April 1835. — 1986. — v, 664p. — (Prime Ministers' papers series)

GREAT BRITAIN — Politics and government — 1894-1895

HAMILTON, Sir Edward, 1847-1908
The destruction of Lord Rosebery : from the diary of Sir Edward Hamilton, 1894-1895 / edited with an introductory essay by David Brooks. — London : Historians' Press, [1987?]. — x,290p. — (Sources for modern British history). — *Includes index*

GREAT BRITAIN — Politics and government — 20th century

BORINSKI, Ludwig
Die Rolle der imperialistischen Bewegung in der britischen Weltpolitik von 1900 bis 1940 / Ludwig Borinski. — Göttingen : Vandenhoeck und Ruprecht, 1985. — 19p. — (Berichte aus den Sitzungen der Joachim-Jungius-Gesellschaft der Wissenschaften ; Jg.3, Heft 1)

CAMPBELL, John, 1947-
Nye Bevan and the mirage of British socialism / John Campbell. — London : Weidenfeld and Nicolson, c1987. — 430 p.. — *Bibliography: p.411-417*

GAMBLE, Andrew
Britain in decline : economic policy, political strategy and the British state / Andrew Gamble. — 2nd ed. — London : Macmillan, 1985. — [302]p. — *Previous ed.: 1981. — Includes index*

HALL, Peter A.
Governing the economy : the politics of state intervention in Britain and France / Peter A. Hall. — Cambridge : Polity, 1986. — 341p. — (Europe and the international order). — *Bibliography: p292-321. — Includes index*

JAMES, Robert Rhodes
Anthony Eden / Robert Rhodes James. — London : Weidenfeld and Nicolson, c1986. — xiv,665,[16]p of plates. — *Includes index*

Politics and social change in modern Britain : essays presented to A.F. Thompson / editor, P.J. Waller. — Brighton : Harvester, 1987. — xx,236p. — *Includes index*

GREAT BRITAIN — Politics and government — 1910-1936

GUNN, Paul
British strategy and politics 1914-1918 / Paul Gunn. — Oxford : Oxford University Press, 1965. — 359p

WEBBER, G. C.
The ideology of the British Right, 1918-1939 / G.C. Webber. — London : Croom Helm, c1986. — 185p. — *Bibliography: p166-177. — Includes index*

WOLFE, Joel D
Workers, participation, and democracy : internal politics in the British union movement / Joel D. Wolfe. — Westport, Conn. ; London : Greenwood Press, c1985. — xii, 258p. — (Contributions in political science ; no. 136). — *Includes index. — Bibliography: p.[219]-243*

GREAT BRITAIN — Politics and government — 1936-1945

WEBBER, G. C.
The ideology of the British Right, 1918-1939 / G.C. Webber. — London : Croom Helm, c1986. — 185p. — *Bibliography: p166-177. — Includes index*

GREAT BRITAIN — Politics and government — 1945-

BUTT, Ronald
The unfinished task : the Conservative record in perspective : summer address / Ronald Butt. — London : Centre for Policy Studies, c1986. — 26p

FLETCHER, Eric George Molyneux, Baron
Random reminiscences / of Lord Fletcher of Islington. — London : Bishopsgate Press, 1986. — xii,269p

GREAT BRITAIN — Politics and Government — 1945-

Implementing government policy initiatives : the Thatcher administration, 1979-83 / edited by Peter Jackson. — London : Royal Institute of Public Administration, 1985. — 285 p

GREAT BRITAIN — Politics and government — 1945-

Policy change in government : three case studies / edited by Nicholas Deakin. — London : Royal Institute of Public Administration, 1986. — 91p

SKED, Alan
Post-war Britain : a political history / Alan Sked and Chris Cook. — 2nd ed. — Harmondsworth : Penguin, 1984. — 478p. — (Pelican books). — *Previous ed.: Brighton : Harvester, 1979. — Bibliography: p440-445. — Includes index*

VAN MECHELEN, Denis
Patterns of Parliamentary legislation / by Denis Van Mechelen & Richard Rose. — Aldershot : Gower, c1986. — [100]p. — *Bibliography: p97-100*

GREAT BRITAIN — Politics and government — 1964-1979

The political science of British politics / edited by Jack Hayward and Philip Norton. — Brighton : Wheatsheaf, 1986. — xi, 228p

PRIOR, James
A balance of power / by Jim Prior. — London : Hamilton, 1986. — [288]p,[16]p of plates. — *Includes index*

GREAT BRITAIN — Politics and government — 1964-

BUTLER, David, 1924-
Governing without a majority : dilemmas for hung parliaments in Britain / David Butler. — 2nd ed. — Basingstoke : Macmillan, 1986. — [156]p. — *Previous ed.: London : Collins, 1983. — Includes index*

FATCHETT, Derek
Trade unions and politics in the 1980s : the 1984 act and political funds / Derek Fatchett. — London : Croom Helm, c1987. — 135p. — *Bibliography: p:131-132. — Includes index*

HILL, Michael, 1937-
The state, administration and the individual / Michael Hill. — [London] : Fontana, 1976. — 256p. — (Studies in public administration). — *Bibliography: p.235-249. — Includes index*

The Omega file. — London : Adam Smith Institute
Foreign policy. — 1983. — ii,47 leaves

SHORT, John R.
The urban arena : capital, state and community in contemporary Britain / John R. Short. — London : Macmillan, 1984. — viii,202p. — (Critical human geography). — *Bibliography: p185-194. — Includes index*

GREAT BRITAIN — Politics and government — 1979-

ANWAR, Muhammad
Race and politics : ethnic minorities and the British political system / Muhammad Anwar. — London : Tavistock, 1986. — [x,176]p. — *Includes index*

BLACK, A. M.
The British government is the worst in the world, apart from all the rest / by A.M. Black. — Bromley : Ravensbourne Papers, 1985. — 12 leaves. — (Ravensbourne papers ; no.1). — *Bibliography: p13*

GREAT BRITAIN — Politics and government — 1979- *continuation*

BLUNKETT, David
Democracy in crisis : the town halls respond / David Blunkett and Keith Jackson. — London : Hogarth, 1987. — xv,240p. — (Current affairs). — *Includes index*

CABLE, James, 1920-
Political institutions and issues in Britain / James Cable. — Basingstoke : Macmillan, 1987. — [vii,192]p. — *Includes bibliography and index*

COLE, John, 1927-
The Thatcher years : a decade of revolution in British politics / John Cole. — London : BBC Books, 1987. — viii,216p. — *Bibliography: p [210]*

CREWE, Ivor
Thatcherism : its origins, electoral impact and implications for Down's theory of party strategy / Ivor Crewe and Donald D. Searing. — Colchester : University of Essex. Department of Government, 1986. — [48p]. — (Essex papers in politics and government ; no.37)

GREAT BRITAIN — Politics and Government — 1979-

Developing the socially useful economy. — London : Centre for Alternative Industrial and Technological Systems, 1984. — 1v.(various pagings)

GREAT BRITAIN — Politics and government — 1979-

FRANKEL, Boris
The post-industrial Utopians / Boris Frankel. — Cambridge : Polity, 1987. — xi,303p. — *Includes index*

GILROY, Paul
"There ain't no black in the Union Jack" : the cultural politics of race and nation / Paul Gilroy. — London : Hutchinson, 1987. — 271p . — *Bibliography: p251-266. — Includes index*

Government popularity and the Falklands War : a reassessment / by David Sanders ... [et al.]. — Colchester : Department of Government University of Essex, 1986. — 33 p. — (Essex papers in politics and government ; no.40)

HAMBLETON, Robin
Rethinking policy planning : a study of planning systems linking central and local government / Robin Hambleton. — [Bristol] : University of Bristol, School for Advanced Urban Studies, 1986. — v,189p. — (SAUS study ; no.2). — *Bibliography: p175-189*

HESELTINE, Michael, 1933-
Where there's a will / Michael Heseltine. — London : Hutchinson, 1987. — 312p,[8]p of plates. — *Includes index*

HOGWOOD, Brian W.
From crisis to complacency? : shaping public policy in Britain / Brian W. Hogwood. — Oxford : Oxford University Press, 1987. — 264p. — *Bibliography: p247-256. — Includes index*

HOLME, Richard
The people's kingdom / Richard Holme. — London : Bodley Head, 1987. — x,150p. — *Includes index*

JORDAN, A. G.
British politics and the policy process : an arena approach / A.G. Jordan, J.J. Richardson. — London : Allen & Unwin, 1987. — [366]p. — *Includes bibliography and index*

KILROY-SILK, Robert
Hard Labour : the political diary of Robert Kilroy-Silk. — London : Chatto & Windus, 1986. — 176p

KRIEGER, Joel
Reagan, Thatcher, and the politics of decline / Joel Krieger. — Cambridge : Polity, 1986. — [220]p. — (Europe and the international order) . — *Includes index*

Labour's first hundred days / edited by Ben Pimlott. — London : Fabian Society, 1987. — 34 p. — (Fabian tract ; 519)

Labour's next moves forward / Jeremy Beecham ... [et al.]. — London : Fabian Society, 1987. — 28 p. — (Fabian tract ; 521)

LUNDBERG, Lars-Olof
Thatcher och facket : brittisk fackföreningsrörelse under den konservativa regeringen / Lars-Olof Lundberg. — Stockholm : Tiden, 1984. — 224p. — *Bibliography: p216-218*

MILLER, Charles
Lobbying government : understanding and influencing the corridors of power / Charles Miller. — Oxford : Basil Blackwell, 1987. — [200]p. — *Includes index*

OWEN, David, 1938-
The time has come : partnership for progress / David Owen and David Steel. — London : Weidenfeld and Nicholson, 1987. — 128p

Political culture of modern Britain : studies in memory of Stephen Koss / edited by J.M.W.Bean. — London : Hamilton, 1987. — [224]p

The political science of British politics / edited by Jack Hayward and Philip Norton. — Brighton : Wheatsheaf, 1986. — xi, 228p

PRIOR, James
A balance of power / by Jim Prior. — London : Hamilton, 1986. — [288]p,[16]p of plates. — *Includes index*

Race, government and politics in Britain / edited by Zig Layton-Henry and Paul B. Rich. — Basingstoke : Macmillan, 1986. — [224]p. — *Includes index*

ROSE, Richard, 1933-
A house divided : political administration in Britain today / Professor Richard Rose. — Glasgow : Centre for the Study of Public Policy, University of Strathclyde, 1986. — 62p. — (Studies in public policy ; 158). — *Bibliography: p57-62*

Thatcherism : personality and politics / edited by Kenneth Minogue and Michael Biddiss. — Basingstoke : Macmillan, 1987. — [208]p

Urban political theory and the management of fiscal stress / edited by Michael Goldsmith, Søren Villadsen. — Aldershot : Gower, c1986. — xviii,269p

WALKER, Peter, 1932-
Trust the people : the selected essays and speeches of Peter Walker / edited by Neale Stevenson ; with an introduction by Robert Rhodes James. — London : Collins, 1987. — 206p

WORKERS POWER
The class struggle and the elections : a workers' manifesto. — London : Workers Power, 1987. — 58p

GREAT BRITAIN — Politics and government — 1979- — Addresses, essays, lectures

British politics in perspective / edited by R.L. Borthwick and J.E. Spence. — New York : St. Martin's Press, 1984. — 251 p. — *Includes index. — Bibliography: p. [241]-243*

GREAT BRITAIN — Politics and government — 1837-1901

PARRY, J. P. (Jonathan Philip)
Democracy and religion : Gladstone and the Liberal Party, 1867-1875 / J.P. Parry. — Cambridge : Cambridge University Press, 1986. — xiii,504p. — (Cambridge studies in the history and theory of politics). — *Bibliography: p453-492. — Includes index*

GREAT BRITAIN — Popular culture — History — 20th century

MILES, Peter
Cinema, literature & society : elite and mass culture in interwar Britain / Peter Miles and Malcolm Smith. — London : Croom Helm, c1987. — 271p. — *Bibliography: p257-266. — Includes index*

GREAT BRITAIN — Population

Changing places : Britain's demographic, economic and social complexion / A.G. Champion ... [et al.]. — London : Edward Arnold, 1987. — [192]p. — *Includes bibliography and index*

GREAT BRITAIN. Office of Population Censuses and Surveys
Britain's elderly population : 1981 Census / [prepared by the Office of Population Censuses and Surveys and the Central Office of Information]. — London : HMSO, 1984. — 12p. — (Census guide ; 1)

Measuring socio-demographic change : University of Sussex 9-11 September 1985, conference papers / [conference arranged by] British Society for Population Studies. — [London] : Office of Population Censuses and Surveys, 1985. — vi,114p. — (Occasional paper ; 34)

Variant population projections: population projections by sex and age, with varying fertility assumptions, for Great Britain / Great Britain Office of Population, Censuses and Surveys. — London : Great Britain Office of Population, Censuses and Surveys, 1974-1983. — *Irregular. — Supersedes in part Registrar-General's statistical review of England and Wales*

GREAT BRITAIN — Population — Forecasting

GREAT BRITAIN. Department of the Environment
1983 based estimates of numbers of households in England, the regions, counties, metropolitan districts and London boroughs 1983-2001. — London : the Department, 1986. — vi,58,[11]p. — *Bibliography: Appendix E*

GREAT BRITAIN. Government Actuary
Variant population projections : variant population projections by sex and age for United Kingdom and selected constituent countries from mid 1983 : 1983-2023. — [London : H.M.S.O.], 1986. — vi,17p,. — (Series PP2 / Office of Population Censuses and Surveys ; no.14). — *Microfiches in end pocket*

GREAT BRITAIN — Public lands — Management

GREAT BRITAIN. Department of the Environment
Management of publicly-owned land in urban areas. — [London : the Department, 1976]. — 10 leaves. — *National report: United Kingdom, prepared for the eleventh meeting of the Group on the Urban Environment, Paris, 22nd-25th November, 1976*

GREAT BRITAIN — Race relations

Anti-racism : an assault on education and value / edited by Frank Palmer. — London : Sherwood Press, 1986. — xii,210p

BROCK, John
The basic figures / John Brock. — London : Commission for Racial Equality, 1978. — [2]p. — (Fact paper / Commission for Racial Equality ; 1). — *Written at the request of the Trades Union Advisory Group of the former Community Relations Commission*

GREAT BRITAIN — Race relations
continuation

GILROY, Paul
"There ain't no black in the Union Jack" : the cultural politics of race and nation / Paul Gilroy. — London : Hutchinson, 1987. — 271p. — *Bibliography: p251-266. — Includes index*

GREAT BRITAIN. Commission for Racial Equality
Annual report / Commission for Racial Equality. — London : [the Commission], 1983-. — *Annual*

HEWITT, Roger
White talk black talk : inter-racial friendship and communication amongst adolescents / Roger Hewitt. — Cambridge : Cambridge University Press, 1986. — [264]p. — (Comparative ethnic and race relations). — *Includes bibliography and index*

HOLDEN, Tony
People, churches and multi-racial projects : an account of English Methodism's response to plural Britain / Tony Holden. — London : Division of Social Responsibility, Methodist Church, [1985]. — 151p. — *Bibliography: p142-151*

Race, government and politics in Britain / edited by Zig Layton-Henry and Paul B. Rich. — Basingstoke : Macmillan, 1986. — [224]p. — *Includes index*

Strategies for improving race relations : the Anglo-American experience / edited by John W. Shaw, Peter G. Nordlie, Richard M. Shapiro ; with a preface by Bhiku Parekh. — Manchester : Manchester University Press, c1987. — xiii,226p. — *Includes index*

THAKOORDIN, Jim
Eradicate racism : a murderous crime / Jim Thakoordin and Tony Gilbert. — London : Liberation, 1985. — 28p

GREAT BRITAIN — Race relations — Bibliography

HARRIS, Kevin
Transracial adoption : a bibliography / Kevin Harris. — London : British Agencies for Adoption and Fostering, 1985. — 122p

GREAT BRITAIN — Race relations — History — 20th century

CARTER, Trevor
Shattering illusions : West Indians in British politics / Trevor Carter ; with Jean Coussins. — London : Lawrence and Wishart, 1986. — 158p

GREAT BRITAIN — Relations — Soviet Union

RYLE, Claire
Citizens' diplomacy : a handbook on Anglo-Soviet initiatives / Claire Ryle and Jim Garrison. — London : Merlin, 1986. — 90p

GREAT BRITAIN — Religion — Statistical services

Religion. — Oxford : Published for the Royal Statistical Society and [the] Economic and Social Research Council by Pergamon, 1987. — xiv,621p. — (Reviews of United Kingdom statistical sources ; v.20). — *Includes bibliographies and index. — Contents: Recurrent Christian sources / by L.M. Barley. — Non-recurrent Christian data / by C.D. Field. — Judaism / by B.A. Kosmin. — Other religions / by J.S. Nielsen*

GREAT BRITAIN — Religious life and customs — History — 19th century

MCLEOD, Hugh
Religion and the working class in nineteenth-century Britain / prepared for the Economic History Society by Hugh McLeod. — London : Macmillan, 1984. — 76p. — (Studies in economic and social history). — *Bibliography: p67-72. — Includes index*

GREAT BRITAIN — Road maps

Bartholomew gazetteer of Britain / compiled by Oliver Mason. — Edinburgh : J. Bartholomew, 1977. — xlviii,271p,128p of plates. — *Col. map on lining papers*

GREAT BRITAIN — Roads — Bibliography

WEBB, Sidney
Bibliography of road making and maintenance in Great Britain / by Sidney and Beatrice Webb. — London : Roads Improvement Association, 1906. — 35p

GREAT BRITAIN — Royal household — Finance

GREAT BRITAIN. Parliament. House of Commons. Library. Research Division
The finances of the monarchy. — [London] : the Division, 1975. — [22]p. — (Background paper ; no.45). — *Bibliographical references: p [21]-[22]*

GREAT BRITAIN — Royal Household — Finance

GREAT BRITAIN. Parliament. House of Commons. Library. Research Division
The finances of the monarchy / Paul Hutt. — [London] : the Division, 1980. — 26p. — (Background paper ; no.79). — *Bibliography: p22-24*

GREAT BRITAIN — Rural conditions

LABOUR PARTY (Great Britain)
Labour's charter for rural areas. — London : Labour Party, 1986. — 47p

WILLETT, Rodney
Village ventures : rural communities in action / written for Rural Voice by Rodney Willett. — London : Published in association with Rural Voice by Bedford Square Press/NCVO, 1985. — 44p

GREAT BRITAIN — Rural conditions — Sources

SMITH, Richard Michael
The Sir Nicholas Bacon collection: sources on English society, 1250-1700 : a catalogue of an exhibition at the Joseph Regenstein Library of the University of Chicago, April-June, 1972 / [prepared by Richard M. Smith. — Chicago : University of Chicago Library, 1972]. — ix, 101 p. — *Bibliography: p. 101*

GREAT BRITAIN — Social conditions

Getting into life / edited by Halla Beloff ; afterword by David Hargreaves ; contributions from Michael Billig ... [et al.]. — London : Methuen, 1986. — xii,157p. — *Includes bibliographies and index*

ROYLE, Edward
Modern Britain : a social history 1750-1985 / Edward Royle. — London : Edward Arnold, 1987. — [400]p. — *Includes bibliography and index*

WEBB, Sidney
The sphere of voluntary agencies in the prevention of destitution / by Sidney and Beatrice Webb. — London : National Committee for the Prevention of Destitution, 1911. — 46p

GREAT BRITAIN — Social conditions — Sources

SMITH, Richard Michael
The Sir Nicholas Bacon collection: sources on English society, 1250-1700 : a catalogue of an exhibition at the Joseph Regenstein Library of the University of Chicago, April-June, 1972 / [prepared by Richard M. Smith. — Chicago : University of Chicago Library, 1972]. — ix, 101 p. — *Bibliography: p. 101*

GREAT BRITAIN — Social conditions — 16th century

ROWSE, A. L.
Court & country : studies in Tudor social history / A.L. Rowse. — Brighton : Harvester, 1987. — x,310p. — *Includes index*

GREAT BRITAIN — Social conditions — 18th century

CARSWELL, John, 1918-
From revolution to revolution : England 1688-1776 / John Carswell. — London : Routledge and Kegan Paul, 1973. — xxvi,204p. — (Development of English society). — *Bibliographyp.192-196. — Includes index*

STAFFORD, William
Socialism, radicalism and nostalgia : social criticism in Britain, 1775-1830 / William Stafford. — Cambridge : Cambridge University Press, 1987. — viii,304p. — *Includes index*

GREAT BRITAIN — Social conditions — 19th century

MINGAY, G. E.
The transformation of Britain, 1830-1939 / G.E Mingay. — London : Routledge & Kegan Paul, 1986. — xii,231p. — (The Making of Britain, 1066-1939)

SPRINGHALL, John
Coming of age : adolescence in Britain, 1860-1960 / John Springhall. — Dublin : Gill and Macmillan, c1986. — 270p. — *Bibliography: p250-264. — Includes index*

STAFFORD, William
Socialism, radicalism and nostalgia : social criticism in Britain, 1775-1830 / William Stafford. — Cambridge : Cambridge University Press, 1987. — viii,304p. — *Includes index*

GREAT BRITAIN — Social conditions — 20th century

CONSTANTINE, Stephen
Social conditions in Britain, 1918-1939 / Stephen Constantine. — London : Methuen, 1983. — vii,48p. — (Lancaster pamphlets). — *Bibliography: p47-48*

MINGAY, G. E.
The transformation of Britain, 1830-1939 / G.E Mingay. — London : Routledge & Kegan Paul, 1986. — xii,231p. — (The Making of Britain, 1066-1939)

SPRINGHALL, John
Coming of age : adolescence in Britain, 1860-1960 / John Springhall. — Dublin : Gill and Macmillan, c1986. — 270p. — *Bibliography: p250-264. — Includes index*

War and social change : British society in the Second World War / edited by Harold L. Smith. — Manchester : Manchester University Press, c1986. — [288]p. — *Includes index*

WINTER, J. M.
The Great War and the British people / J.M. Winter. — London : Macmillan, 1986, c1985. — xiv,360p. — *Bibliography: p334-349. — Includes index*

GREAT BRITAIN — Social conditions — 1945-

Britain : a view from Westminster / edited by Julian Critchley. — Poole, Blandford, 1986. — [224]p. — *Includes index*

Changing Britain, changing world : geographical perspectives. — Milton Keynes : Open University Press. — (Social sciences : a second level course) (D 205 ; 8/11). — *At head of title: The Open University. — Contents: Unit 8: Urban land use: change and conflict; Chris Hamnett; Unit 9: Housing and social divisions; Linda McDowell; Unit 10: Health care: unequal access; Stephanie Goodenough and Phil Sarre; Unit 11: Review: location and distance; Doreen Massey Section II: Analysis : aspects of the geography of society Block 3: Land use and services. — 1985. — 1v.(various pagings)*

GREAT BRITAIN — Social conditions — 1945- *continuation*

Changing Britain, changing world : geographical perspectives. — Milton Keynes : Open University Press. — (Social Sciences : a second level course) Section 3: Synthesis: uniqueness and interdependence of place
Block 5: The changing face of the Isles. — 1985. — lv (various pagings). — (D205 ; 17/20). — At head title: The Open University. — Contents: Unit 17: Local change in the west of Ireland/Pat Jess - Unit 18: Inner-city decline/Chris Hamnett - Unit 19: Are there two Britains? The North-South divide/Richard Meegan - Unit 20: Regional cultures/Doreen Massey

CHILD POVERTY ACTION GROUP
Building one nation : memorandum to the Chancellor of the Exchequer. — London : Child Poverty Action Group, 1987. — 16p

FRANKEL, Boris
The post-industrial Utopians / Boris Frankel. — Cambridge : Polity, 1987. — xi,303p. — *Includes index*

FYVEL, T. R.
And there my trouble began : uncollected writings, 1945-1985 / T. R. Fyvel. — London : Weidenfeld and Nicolson, 1986. — xii,240p

GLINGA, Werner
Legacy of empire : a journey through British society / Werner Glinga ; translated by Stephan Paul Jost. — Manchester : Manchester University Press, c1986. — 200p. — *Translation of: Erben des Empire. — Bibliography: p182-192. — Includes index*

The growing divide : a social audit 1979-1987 / edited by Alan Walker and Carol Walker. — London : Child Poverty Action Group, 1987. — [vi],162p. — (Poverty publication ; no.72)

HEWITT, Roger
White talk black talk : inter-racial friendship and communication amongst adolescents / Roger Hewitt. — Cambridge : Cambridge University Press, 1986. — [264]p. — (Comparative ethnic and race relations). — *Includes bibliography and index*

HOLLIDAY, John C.
Land at the centre : choices in a fast changing world / John C. Holliday. — London : Shepheard-Walwyn, 1986. — xiii,241p. — *Includes index*

Political issues in Britain today / edited by Bill Jones. — 2nd ed. — Manchester : Manchester University Press, 1987. — viii,287p. — (Politics today series). — *Previous ed.: 1985. — Includes bibliographies*

Symbolising boundaries : identity and diversity in British cultures / edited by Anthony P. Cohen. — Manchester : Manchester University Press, c1986. — x,189p. — (Anthropological studies of Britain ; no.2). — *Includes index*

GREAT BRITAIN — Social life and customs

DAVIDOFF, Leonore
The best circles : society, etiquette and the Season / Leonore Davidoff ; new introduction by Victoria Glendinning. — London : Cresset Library, 1986, c1973. — xii,127p. — *Originally published: London : Croom Helm, 1974. — Bibliography: p118-120. — Includes index*

GREAT BRITAIN — Social life and customs — 19th century — Bibliography

The Autobiography of the working class : an annotated, critical bibliography / editors John Burnett, David Vincent, David Mayall. — Brighton : Harvester
Vol. 2: 1900-1945. — 1987. — xii,435p. — *Includes index*

GREAT BRITAIN — Social life and customs — 20th century

HARRISON, Tom
Britain by Mass-Observation / arranged and written by Tom Harrison and Charles Madge ; new introduction by Angus Calder. — London : Cresset, 1986. — xv,246p,[6]p of plates. — (The Cresset library). — *Originally published: Harmondsworth : Penguin, 1939*

LEWIS, Peter, 1928-
A people's war / Peter Lewis. — London : Thames Methuen, 1986. — vi,250p. — *Bibliography: p245. — Includes index*

GREAT BRITAIN — Social life and customs — 20th century — Bibliography

The Autobiography of the working class : an annotated, critical bibliography / editors John Burnett, David Vincent, David Mayall. — Brighton : Harvester
Vol. 2: 1900-1945. — 1987. — xii,435p. — *Includes index*

GREAT BRITAIN — Social life and customs — 1945-

GLINGA, Werner
Legacy of empire : a journey through British society / Werner Glinga ; translated by Stephan Paul Jost. — Manchester : Manchester University Press, c1986. — 200p. — *Translation of: Erben des Empire. — Bibliography: p182-192. — Includes index*

LAING, Stuart
Representations of working-class life 1957-1964 / Stuart Laing. — Basingstoke : Macmillan, 1986. — 246p. — *Includes index*

GREAT BRITAIN — Social policy

ATKINSON, A. B.
The welfare state in Britain 1970-1985 : extent and effectiveness / A.B. Atkinson, J. Hills and J. Le Grand. — London : Suntory-Toyota International Centre for Economics and Related Disciplines, 1986. — 64p. — (Discussion paper / Welfare State Programme. Suntory-Toyota International Centre for Economics and Related Disciplines ; no.9). — *Bibliography: p61-64*

BOOTH, Alan
Life on the margins : the politics of mass poverty / Alan Booth. — London : Communist Party, 1985. — 33p

BROWN, Muriel
Introduction to social administration in Britain / Muriel Brown. — 6th ed. — London : Hutchinson, 1985. — 304p. — (Hutchinson university library). — *Previous ed.: 1982. — Includes bibliographies and index*

Challenges to social policy / edited by Richard Berthoud. — Aldershot : Gower, c1985. — x,220p. — *Includes bibliographies and index*

CLARKE, John
Ideologies of welfare : from dreams to disillusion / John Clarke, Allan Cochrane and Carol Smart. — London : Hutchinson, 1987. — 206p. — (The state of welfare). — *Bibliography: p[197]-201*

DEAKIN, Nicholas
The politics of welfare / Nicholas Deakin. — London : Methuen, 1987. — viii,205p. — *Bibliography: p191-197. — Includes index*

EDWARDS, John, 1943-
Positive discrimination, social justice and social policy : moral scrutiny of a policy practice / John Edwards ; foreword by Lord Scarman. — London : Tavistock, 1987. — x,243p. — *Bibliography: p222-235. — Includes index*

The future role of social services departments / John Rea Price [et al.]. — London : Policy Studies Institute, 1987. — 40p

McBRIAR, A. M.
An Edwardian mixed doubles : the Bosanquets versus the Webbs : a study in British social policy 1890-1929 / A.M. McBriar. — Oxford : Clarendon, 1987. — x,407p. — *Bibliography: p381-396. — Includes index*

PASCALL, Gillian
Social policy : a feminist analysis / Gillian Pascall. — London : Tavistock, 1986. — [v,220]p. — *Includes bibliography and index*

PROVIDER MOVEMENT
[Manifesto]. — London : [the Providor Movement], 1984. — 48p

The Research relationship : practice and politics in social policy research / edited by G. Clare Wenger. — London : Allen & Unwin, 1987. — xix,228p. — (Contemporary social research series ; 15). — *Includes bibliographies and index*

RINGEN, Stein
The possibility of politics : a study in the political economy of the welfare state / Stein Ringen. — Oxford : Clarendon, 1987. — x,303p. — *Bibliography: p267-295. — Includes index*

RITTER, Gerhard A.
Social welfare in Germany and Britain : origins and development / Gerhard A. Ritter ; translated from the German by Kim Traynor. — Leamington Spa : Berg, c1986. — xi,211p. — *Translation of: Sozialversicherung in Deutschland und England. — Bibliography: p199-206. — Includes index*

Towards the sensitive bureaucracy : consumers, wlefare, and the new pluralism / editors, Drew Clode, Christopher Parker, Stuart Etherington. — [Brookfield, VT] : Gower Pub., 1986. — p. cm. — *Includes bibliographies and index*

Towards the sensitive bureaucracy : consumers, welfare and the new pluralism / edited by Drew Clode, Christopher Parker, Stuart Etherington. — Aldershot : Gower, c1987. — x,145p. — *Includes bibliographies and index*

WICKS, Malcolm
A future for all : do we need the Welfare State? / Malcolm Wicks. — Harmondsworth : Penguin, 1987. — 301p. — *Bibliography: p.[258]-280*

Women and social policy : a reader / edited by Clare Ungerson. — Basingstoke : Macmillan Education, 1985. — x,278p. — (Women in society). — *Bibliography: p261-274. — Includes index*

GREAT BRITAIN — Social policy — Sources

Critics of capitalism : Victorian reactions to 'political economy' / edited by Elisabeth Jay and Richard Jay. — Cambridge : Cambridge University Press, 1986. — vii,268p. — (Cambridge English prose texts). — *Bibliography: p262-268*

GREAT BRITAIN — Statistical services

MORT, D.
Sources of unofficial UK statistics / compiled by David Mort and Leona Siddall. — Aldershot : Gower, c1985. — x,457p. — *Includes index*

SLATTERY, Martin
Official statistics / Martin Slattery. — London : Tavistock, 1986. — 154p. — (Society now) (Social science paperbacks ; 337). — *Bibliography: p143-148. — Includes index*

GREAT BRITAIN — Statistics

Key data / Central Statistical Office. — London : HMSO, 1986-. — *Annual*

GREAT BRITAIN — Statistics, Medical

Morbidity statistics from general practice. — London : HMSO, 1958-62. — 3v. — (Studies on medical and population subjects ; no.14). — *Contents: Vol.1: General/W. P. D. Logan and A. A. Cushion - v.2: Occupation/W. P. D. Logan - v.3: Disease in general practice/Research Committee of the Council of the College of General Practitioners*

GREAT BRITAIN — Statistics, Medical
continuation

Morbidity statistics from general practice 1981-1982 : third national study. — London : HMSO, 1986. — ix,245p. — *Includes 8 microfiches of morbidity tabulations in pocket on rear cover*

GREAT BRITAIN — Statistics, Vital

BROWNLEE, John
The history of the birth and death rates in England and Wales taken as a whole from 1750 to the present time / John Brownlee. — London : Society of Medical Officers of Health, 1916. — 24p

GREAT BRITAIN. Office of Population Censuses and Surveys
Birth statistics : historical series of statistics from registrations of births in England and Wales, 1837-1983. — London : H.M.S.O., 1987. — x,206p. — (Series FM1 / Office of Population Censuses and Surveys ; no.13)

GREAT BRITAIN. Office of Population Censuses and Surveys
Period and cohort birth order statistics : period analyses for years from 1938-85 and cohort analyses for women born in each year from 1920 (England and Wales). — London : H.M.S.O., 1987. — iii,30p. — (Series FM1 ; no.14). — *7 microfiches in end pocket. — Bibliographical references: p13*

LYONS, N. J.
A summary of investigations into the relationships between standardised mortality ratio and measures of social deprivation, and a consideration of the effect of social deprivation on hospital use / N. J. Lyons. — [London : Department of Health and Social Security, 1977]. — 6leaves

GREAT BRITAIN. Admiralty. Compass Department

FANNING, A. E.
Steady as she goes : a history of the Compass Department of the Admiralty / by A.E. Fanning. — London : H.M.S.O., c1986. — xlv, 462p. — *"The National Maritime Museum...sponsored the writing and publication" - foreword. — Bibliography: p.[445]-446*

GREAT BRITAIN. Army

KITSON, Frank
Warfare as a whole / Frank Kitson. — London : Faber, 1987. — [190]p. — *Includes index*

GREAT BRITAIN. Army — Biography

THOMPSON, Neville
Wellington after Waterloo / Neville Thompson. — London : Routledge & Kegan Paul, 1986. — [320]p. — *Includes index*

GREAT BRITAIN. Army — History — Military life

BRERETON, J. M.
The British soldier : a social history from 1661 to the present day / J.M. Brereton. — London : Bodley Head, 1986. — [288]p. — *Includes index*

GREAT BRITAIN. Army. Cavalry Brigade, 3rd — History

The Army and the Curragh incident / edited by Ian F.W. Beckett. — London : Bodley Head for the Army Records Society, 1986. — [448]p. — *Includes bibliography and index*

GREAT BRITAIN. Army. Home Guard — History — Sources

IMPERIAL WAR MUSEUM. Library
The Home Guard, 1940-1944. — [London] : the Library, [1951?]. — 23leaves. — ([Booklist / Imperial War Museum Library ; no.1084B])

IMPERIAL WAR MUSEUM. Library
The Home Guard 1940-1944. — [London : the Library, 1975?]. — [1]. — (Booklist / Imperial War Museum [Library] ; 1084A)

GREAT BRITAIN. Army. Special Operations Executive — History

GLEES, Anthony
The secrets of the service : British intelligence and Communist subversion 1939-51 / Anthony Glees. — London : Cape, 1987. — 1v.. — *Includes bibliography and index*

GREAT BRITAIN. Board of Trade

Striking a balance : the role of the Board of Trade 1786-1986 : bicentenary lectures / edited by Susan Foreman. — London : HMSO, 1986. — 76p. — *At head of title: Department of Trade and Industry. — Includes bibliographies*

GREAT BRITAIN. Commission for Racial Equality

GREAT BRITAIN. Commission for Racial Equality
Annual report / Commission for Racial Equality. — London : [the Commission], 1983-. — *Annual*

GREAT BRITAIN. Committee of Enforcement Powers of Revenue Departments

GREAT BRITAIN. Board of Inland Revenue
The Inland Revenue and the taxpayer : proposals in response to the recommendations of the Keith Committee on income tax, capital gains tax and corporation tax : a consultative document / Board of Inland Revenue. — London : H.M.S.O., 1986. — 170p

GREAT BRITAIN. Department of Education and Science. Inspectorate of Schools — History

LAWTON, Denis
H M I / Denis Lawton and Peter Gordon. — London : Routledge & Kegan Paul, 1987. — [192]p. — *Includes bibliography and index*

GREAT BRITAIN. Department of Health and Social Security

Statutory sick pay / Department of Health and Social Security. — London : HMSO, 1986-

GREAT BRITAIN. Department of Health and Social Security — Bibliography

SHRIGLEY, Sheila
Selected references on the organisation and functions of the Department of Health and Social Security / compiled by Sheila M. Shrigley and Jill C. Allbrooke. — London : Department of Health and Social Security Library, 1977. — 12p. — (Bibliography series / Department of Health and Social Security Library ; no.B75)

GREAT BRITAIN. Department of Health and Social Security — Management

Management training needs in DHSS local offices. — [London : Department of Health and Social Security?]
2: HEOs; a joint report to the Department / from Civil Service Department, Personnel Management Research Branch, PM4 Division [and] Department of Health and Social Security, Management Training Centre. — 1978. — 17,[19]p

GREAT BRITAIN. Department of Health and Social Security. Library

Annual list of publications / Department of Health and Social Security Library, Great Britain. — London : DHSS, 1978-1979. — *Annual*

GREAT BRITAIN. Department of Health and Social Security. Social Work Service. Development Group

GREAT BRITAIN. Department of Health and Social Security. Social Work Service. Development Group
Some brief notes on the Development Group. — [London] : the Group, 1978. — 3p

GREAT BRITAIN. Department of the Director of Public Prosecutions

MANSFIELD, Graham
The Director of Public Prosecutions : principles and practices for the Crown Prosecutor : an inquiry carried out at the Centre for Criminological Research, University of Oxford / Graham Mansfield and Jill Peay ; foreword by Sir Thomas Hetherington. — London : Tavistock, 1987. — viii,246p. — *Bibliography: p237-241. — Includes index*

GREAT BRITAIN. Department of the Environment. Streamlining the cities

REGIONAL STUDIES ASSOCIATION. National Executive Committee
A response to the government's white paper "Streamlining the cities", Cmnd. 9063 ... / M.R. Bristow, on behalf of the National Executive Committee, Regional Studies Association. — London : R.S.A., 1984. — 23p

GREAT BRITAIN. Department of Trade and Industry

Striking a balance : the role of the Board of Trade 1786-1986 : bicentenary lectures / edited by Susan Foreman. — London : HMSO, 1986. — 76p. — *At head of title: Department of Trade and Industry. — Includes bibliographies*

GREAT BRITAIN. Department of Trade and Industry. Radio Regulatory Division

GREAT BRITAIN. Department of Trade and Industry. Radio Regulatory Division
Annual report / Radio Regulatory Division, Department of Trade and Industry, Great Britain. — London : [the Division], 1985/86-. — *Annual*

GREAT BRITAIN. Foreign and Commonwealth Office

COHEN, Yoel
Media diplomacy : the Foreign Office in the mass communications age / Yoel Cohen. — London : Cass, 1986. — x,197p. — *Bibliography: p184-189. — Includes index*

The Omega file. — London : Adam Smith Institute
Foreign policy. — 1983. — ii,47 leaves

GREAT BRITAIN. Foreign Office — History

British foreign secretaries and foreign policy : from Crimean War to First World War / edited by Keith M. Wilson. — London : Croom Helm, c1987. — v,218p. — *Includes index*

WARMAN, Roberta M
The Foreign Office, 1916-1918 : a study of its role and functions / Roberta M. Warman. — New York : Garland Pub., 1986. — 286 p.. — (Outstanding theses from the London School of Economics and Political Science). — Thesis (Ph. D.)--University of London, 1982. — *Bibliography: p. 282-286*

GREAT BRITAIN. Forensic Science Service

RAMSAY, Malcolm
The effectiveness of the Forensic Science Service / by Malcolm Ramsay. — London : H.M.S.O., 1987. — v,93p. — (Home Office research study ; 92). — *A Home Office Research and Planning Unit report*

GREAT BRITAIN. General Register Office — History

NISSEL, Muriel
People count : a history of the General Register Office / Muriel Nissel : [for the] Office of Population Censuses and Surveys. — London : H.M.S.O., 1987. — 157p. — *Includes index*

GREAT BRITAIN. Government Communications Headquarters

WEST, Nigel
GCHQ : the secret wireless war, 1900-86 / Nigel West. — London : Weidenfeld and Nicolson, c1986. — xviii,294p,[8]p of plates. — *Bibliography: p272-277. — Includes index*

GREAT BRITAIN. Her Majesty's Stationery Office — Officials and employees

DULEWICZ, Victor
Job appraisal reviews in HMSO : an evaluation including a before-and-after study / Victor Dulewicz. — London : Behavioural Sciences Research Division, Civil Service Department, 1976. — [43]p. — (BSRD report ; no.32)

GREAT BRITAIN. Home Office. Review of the Public Order Act 1936 and related legislation

THORNTON, Peter, 1946-
We protest : the public order debate / Peter Thornton. — London : National Council for Civil Liberties, 1985. — [96]p

GREAT BRITAIN. Medicines Commission

Annual report of Medicines Commission, Committee on Safety of Medicines, Veterinary Pruducts Committee, British Pharmacopoeia Commission, Committee on the Review of Medicine, Committee on Dental and Surgical Materials, Committee on Radiation fron Radioactive Medicinal Products. — London : Department of Health and Social Security, 1980-. — Annual

GREAT BRITAIN. National Health Service

CARR-HILL, R. A.
Health status, resource allocation and socio-economic conditions (interim report of health needs research study) / Roy A. Carr-Hill. — rev. ed. — York : University of York. Centre for Health Economics, 1987. — xii,93p. — Bibliography: p86-93

GLENNERSTER, Howard
The nursing management function after Griffiths : a study in the North West Thames Region / Professor Howard Glennerster, Dr. Pat Owens [and] Ms. Angela Kimberley. — London : London School of Economics and Political Science : North West Thames Regional Health Authority, 1986. — 85,viiip.. — Bibliography: p.ix-x

GREAT BRITAIN. National Rivers Authority

GREAT BRITAIN. Department of the Environment
The National Rivers Authority : the government's proposals for a public regulatory body in a privatised water industry. — [London : the Department], 1987. — 42p

GREAT BRITAIN. Office of Population Censuses and Surveys. Social Survey Division

GREAT BRITAIN. Office of Population Censuses and Surveys. Social Survey Division
Annual report / Social Survey Division, Office of Population Censuses and Surveys. — London : OPCS, 1984/85-. — Annual

GREAT BRITAIN. Parliament

CAIN, Bruce E
The personal vote : constituency service and electoral independence / Bruce Cain, John Ferejohn, Morris Fiorina. — Cambridge, Mass. : Harvard University Press, 1986. — p. cm. — Includes index. — Bibliography: p

CLIFFORD, Brendan
Parliamentary despotism : John Hume's aspiration / by Brendan Clifford. — Belfast : Athol, 1986. — 18p

COX, Andrew
Congress, Parliament and defence : the impact of legislative reform on defence accountability in Britain and America / Andrew Cox and Stephen Kirby. — Basingstoke : Macmillan, 1986. — 1v.. — Includes index

GREAT BRITAIN. Parliament — Committees

FLEGMANN, Vilma
Public expenditure and the select committees of the Commons / Vilma Flegmann. — Aldershot : Gower, c1986. — [80]p. — Includes bibliography and index

GREAT BRITAIN. Parliament — Elections

BRADBURY, Farel
The Brecon mandate : portrait of an electorate / Farel Bradbury. — Ross-on-Wye : Hydatum, 1986. — ix,99p. — Subtitle: An analysis of 159,137 replies to the Voice of the People (VP) policy survey by the Electorate at the Parliamentary by-election for the constituency of Brecon and Radnor, 4th July, 1985. — "Voice of the People...Policy Survey" sample form in rear pocket

GREAT BRITAIN. Parliament — Elections — History — Chronology

Chronology of British parliamentary by-elections 1833-1987 / compiled and edited by F.W.S. Craig. — Chichester : Parliamentary Research Services, c1987. — xvi,383p. — Includes index

GREAT BRITAIN. Parliament — Elections — Statistics

GREAT BRITAIN. Parliament. House of Commons. Library. Research Division
By-election results since the General Election of October 1974. — [London] : the Division, 1977. — 9p. — (Background paper ; no.60)

GREAT BRITAIN. Parliament. House of Commons. Public Information Office
Statistical digest of by-election results since the General Election of May 1979 / [Jennifer Tanfield, Robert Clements]. — Rev. ed. — London : the Office, 1983. — 14p. — (Factsheet ; no.16)

GREAT BRITAIN. Parliament — Elections, 1970

BLUMLER, Jay G.
Political communication and the young voter : a panel study, 1970-1971, examining the role of election communication in the political socialisation of first time voters / Jay G. Blumler, Denis McQuail and T. J. Nossiter ; report to the Social Science Research Council, October 1975. — [London : Social Science Research Council, 1975]. — 1v. (various pagings). — Bibliographical references: end of vol.

GREAT BRITAIN. Parliament — Elections, 1974 (February)

BLUMLER, Jay G.
Political communication and the young voter in the general election of February 1974 : a panal study, 1970-1974, examining influences on the political socialisation of young voters between their first and second election campaigns / Jay G. Blumler, Denis McQuail and T. J. Nossiter ; report to the Social Science Research Council, July 1976. — [London : Social Science Research Council, 1976]. — 99 leaves. — Bibliographical references: p98-99

GREAT BRITAIN. Parliament — Elections, 1983

ANWAR, Muhammad
Ethnic minorities and the 1983 General Election : a research report / Muhammad Anwar. — London : Commission for Racial Equality, 1984. — 35p

GUNTER, Barrie
Television coverage of the 1983 general election : audiences, appreciation and public opinion / Barrie Gunter, Michael Svennevig and Mallory Wober. — Aldershot : Gower, c1986. — v,138p. — Bibliography: p134-136

Political communications : the general election campaign of 1983 / edited by Ivor Crewe and Martin Harrop. — Cambridge : Cambridge University Press, 1986. — [342]p. — Includes index

GREAT BRITAIN. Parliament — Elections, 1987

ITN election factbook / edited by Glyn Mathias; political analysis, David Cowling; contributions by Robert Waller...[et al.] ; introduced by Alastair Burnett. — London : Michael O'Mara Books in association with Independent Television News, [1987]. — 240p

TYLER, Rodney
Campaign! : the selling of the Prime Minister / by Rodney Tyler. — London : Grafton, 1987. — 251p

WILSON, Des
Battle for power : [the inside story of the Alliance and the 1987 General Election] / Des Wilson. — London : Sphere, 1987. — xv,326p

GREAT BRITAIN. Parliament — Reform

DINWIDDY, J. R.
From Luddism to the First Reform Bill : reform in England 1810-1832 / J.R. Dinwiddy. — Oxford : Basil Blackwell, 1986. — [96]p. — (Historical Association studies). — Includes bibliography and index

GREAT BRITAIN. Parliament. House of Commons. Abolition of Domestic Rates etc. [Scotland] Bill 1986-87

GREAT BRITAIN. Parliament. House of Commons. Library. Research Division
Abolition of Domestic Rates etc. [Scotland] Bill, Bill 9 of 1986-87 / Barry Winetrobe, Rob Clements. — [London] : the Division, 1986. — 20p. — (Reference sheet ; no.86/16)

GREAT BRITAIN. Parliament. House of Commons. Abortion (Amendment) Bill 1979-80

GREAT BRITAIN. Parliament. House of Commons. Library. Research Division
Abortion (Amendment) Bill 1979/80 (Bill 7 and Bill 110) / [Julia Lourie]. — [London] : the Division, 1980. — 3leaves. — (Reference sheet ; no.80/7)

GREAT BRITAIN. Parliament. House of Commons. Agricultural Marketing Bill 1982-83

GREAT BRITAIN. Parliament. House of Commons. Library. Research Division
Agricultural Marketing Bill (Bill 7 of 1982-83) / [Priscilla Baines]. — [London] : the Division, [1982]. — 8p. — (Reference sheet ; no.82/12)

GREAT BRITAIN. Parliament. House of Commons. Airports Bill 1985-86

GREAT BRITAIN. Parliament. House of Commons. Library. Research Division
Airports Bill (Bill 60 of 1985/86) / Priscilla Baines. — [London] : the Division, 1986. — 31p. — (Reference sheet ; no.86/4). — Bibliographical references: p27-31

GREAT BRITAIN. Parliament. House of Commons. Broadcasting Bill 1979-80

GREAT BRITAIN. Parliament. House of Commons. Library. Research Division
Broadcasting 1980 / [Fiona Poole]. — [London] : the Division, 1980. — 15p. — (Reference sheet ; no.80/8). — Includes bibliographical references

GREAT BRITAIN. Parliament. House of Commons. Chronically Sick and Disabled Persons (Amendment) Bill 1983-84

GREAT BRITAIN. Parliament. House of Commons. Library. Research Division
The Chronically Sick and Disabled Persons (Amendment) Bill (Bill 15, Session 1983/84) / Christine Gillie. — [London] : the Division, 1983. — 13p. — (Reference sheet ; no.83/20). — Bibliographical references: p12-13

GREAT BRITAIN. Parliament. House of Commons. Criminal Justice Bill 1981-82

GREAT BRITAIN. Parliament. House of Commons. Library. Research Division
Criminal Justice Bill 1981-82 [Bill 32] / [Patrick Nealon]. — [London] : the Division, 1982. — 25p. — (Reference sheet ; no.82/3). — Bibliography: p18-25

GREAT BRITAIN. Parliament. House of Commons. Criminal Justice Bill 1986-87

GREAT BRITAIN. Parliament. House of Commons. Library. Research Division
The Criminal Justice Bill 1986/87 [Bill 2] / Mary Baber. — [London] : the Division, 1986. — 23p. — (Reference sheet ; no.86/14). — Bibliographical references: p21-23

GREAT BRITAIN. Parliament. House of Commons. Data Protection Bill 1983-84

GREAT BRITAIN. Parliament. House of Commons. Library. Research Division
Data Protection Bill, Bill 51, 1983-84 / Barry K. Winetrobe. — [London] : the Division, 1984. — 10p. — (Reference sheet ; no.84/1). — *Bibliographical references: p7-10*

GREAT BRITAIN. Parliament. House of Commons. Disabled Persons (Services, Consultation and Representation) Bill 1985-86

GREAT BRITAIN. Parliament. House of Commons. Library. Research Division
Disabled Persons (Services, Consultation and Representation) Bill, session 1985-86 / Christine Gillie. — [London] : the Division, 1986. — 26,xp. — (Reference sheet ; no.86/9). — *Bibliographical references: p22-26*

GREAT BRITAIN. Parliament. House of Commons. Education (Amendment) Bill 1985-86

GREAT BRITAIN. Parliament. House of Commons. Library. Research Division
Education (Amendment) Bill, [Bill 12 of 1985/86] / Kay Andrews. — [London] : the Division, 1985. — 18p. — (Reference sheet ; no.85/8). — *Bibliographical references: p17-18*

GREAT BRITAIN. Parliament. House of Commons. Education Bill 1980-81

GREAT BRITAIN. Parliament. House of Commons. Library. Research Division
Education Bill (Bill 48 of 1980/81) / [Kay Andrews]. — [London] : the Division, 1981. — 20p. — (Reference sheet ; no.81/5). — *Bibliography: p16-20*

GREAT BRITAIN. Parliament. House of Commons. Education (Corporal Punishment) Bill 1984-85

GREAT BRITAIN. Parliament. House of Commons. Library. Research Division
Education (Corporal Punishment) Bill [Bill 57 of 1984/85] / Kay Andrews. — [London] : the Division, 1985. — 25p. — (Reference sheet ; no.85/2). — *Bibliography: p21-25*

GREAT BRITAIN. Parliament. House of Commons. Education (Fees and Awards) Bill 1982-83

GREAT BRITAIN. Parliament. House of Commons. Library. Research Division
Education (Fees and Awards) Bill (Bill 135 of 1982/83) / Kay Andrews. — [London] : the Division, 1983. — 16p. — (Reference sheet ; no.83/9). — *Bibliographical references: p14-16*

GREAT BRITAIN. Parliament. House of Commons. Education (Grants and Awards) Bill 1983-84

GREAT BRITAIN. Parliament. House of Commons. Library. Research Division
The Education (Grants and Awards) Bill [Bill 40 of 1983-84] / Kay Andrews. — [London] : the Division, 1983. — 27p. — (Reference sheet ; no.83/19). — *Bibliographical references: p23-27*

GREAT BRITAIN. Parliament. House of Commons. Education (Scotland) Bill 1980-81

GREAT BRITAIN. Parliament. House of Commons. Library. Research Division
Education (Scotland) Bill, Bill 14 of 1980-81 / [Keith Cuninghame]. — [London] : the Division, 1981. — 13p. — (Reference sheet ; no.81/2). — *Includes bibliographical references*

GREAT BRITAIN. Parliament. House of Commons. Employment Bill 1979-80

GREAT BRITAIN. Parliament. House of Commons. Library. Research Division
Employment Bill (Bill 97, 1979-80) / Celia Nield. — Rev. ed. — [London] : the Division, 1980. — 53p. — (Reference sheet ; no.79/17). — *First Published in 1979. — Includes bibliographical references*

GREAT BRITAIN. Parliament. House of Commons. Employment Bill 1981-82

GREAT BRITAIN. Parliament. House of Commons. Library. Research Division
Employment Bill (Bill 56 1981-82) / Celia Nield. — [London] : the Division, 1982. — 30p. — (Reference sheet ; no.82/5). — *Bibliography: p28-30*

GREAT BRITAIN. Parliament. House of Commons. European Communities (Amendment) Bill 1985-86

GREAT BRITAIN. Parliament. House of Commons. Library c 245.10European Communities (Amendment) Bill (Bill 126 of 1985-86) (Simon Young)
. — [London] : the Library, 1986. — 16p. — (Reference sheet / House of Commons. Library. [Research Division] ; no.86/11). — *Bibliographical references: p15-16*

GREAT BRITAIN. Parliament. House of Commons. Freedom of Information Bill 1980-81

GREAT BRITAIN. Parliament. House of Commons. Library. Research Division
Freedom of Information Bill [Bill 25, 1980/81] / [Margaret M. Camsell]. — [London] : the Division, 1981. — 12p. — (Reference sheet ; no.81/6). — *Bibliographical references: p12*

GREAT BRITAIN. Parliament. House of Commons. Gas Bill 1985-86

GREAT BRITAIN. Parliament. House of Commons. Library. Research Division
The Gas Bill (Bill 13 of 1985/6) / Christopher Barclay, Caroline Gilmour. — [London] : the Division, 1985. — 30p. — (Reference sheet ; no.85/10). — *Bibliography: p28-30*

GREAT BRITAIN. Parliament. House of Commons. Health and Social Security Bill 1983-84

GREAT BRITAIN. Parliament. House of Commons. Library. Research Division
Health and Social Security Bill 1983 / Keith Cuninghame, Julia Lourie, Christine Gillie. — [London] : the Division, 1983. — 50p. — (Reference sheet ; no.83/24). — *Includes bibliographical references*

GREAT BRITAIN. Parliament. House of Commons. Health Services Bill 1979-80

GREAT BRITAIN. Parliament. House of Commons. Library. Research Division
Health Services Bill (Bill 98 of 1979-80) / [Keith Cuninghame]. — [London] : the Division, 1979. — 12p. — (Reference sheet ; no.79/18). — *Bibliography: p9-12*

GREAT BRITAIN. Parliament. House of Commons. Housing and Building Control Bill 1983-84

GREAT BRITAIN. Parliament. House of Commons. Library. Research Division
The Housing and Building Control Bill (Bill 3, session 1983/84) / [Christine Gillie, Barry Winetrobe]. — [London] : the Division, 1983. — 21p. — (Reference sheet ; no.83/10). — *Includes bibliographical references*

GREAT BRITAIN. Parliament. House of Commons. Housing and Planning Bill 1985-86

GREAT BRITAIN. Parliament. House of Commons. Library. Research Division
Housing and Planning Bill (Bill 63 of 1985/86) / Oonagh Gay, Barry Winetrobe, Betty Miller. — [London] : the Division, 1986. — 38p. — (Reference sheet ; no.86/5). — *Bibliographical references: p30-38*

GREAT BRITAIN. Parliament. House of Commons. Housing Defects Bill 1983-84

GREAT BRITAIN. Parliament. House of Commons. Library. Research Division
Housing Defects Bill [Bill 147 session 1983/84] / Oonagh Gay. — [London] : the Division, 1984. — 16p. — (Reference sheet ; no.84/6). — *Bibliographical references: p14-16*

GREAT BRITAIN. Parliament. House of Commons. Iron and Steel Bill 1980-81

GREAT BRITAIN. Parliament. House of Commons. Library. Research Division
The Iron and Steel Bill / Christopher Barclay. — [London] : the Division, 1981. — 9p. — (Reference sheet ; no.81/11). — *Bibliography: p7-9*

GREAT BRITAIN. Parliament. House of Commons. Landlord and Tenant (No.2) Bill 1986-87

GREAT BRITAIN. Parliament. House of Commons. Library. Research Division
Landlord and Tenant (No.2) Bill [Bill 98 of session 1986/87] / Oonagh Gay. — [London] : the Division, 1987. — 26p. — (Reference sheet ; no.87/1). — *Bibliographical references: p24-26*

GREAT BRITAIN. Parliament. House of Commons. Local Government Bill 1984-85

GREAT BRITAIN. Parliament. House of Commons. Library. Research Division
Local Government Bill [Bill 11, 1984/85] / [Barry K. Winetrobe]. — [London] : the Division, 1984. — 27p. — (Reference sheet ; no.84/12). — *Bibliographical references: p25-27*

GREAT BRITAIN. Parliament. House of Commons. Local Government Finance Bill 1981-82

GREAT BRITAIN. Parliament. House of Commons. Library. Research Division
Local Government Finance Bill (Bill 8 of 1981-82) / Priscilla Baines, Robert Clements. — [London] : the Division, 1981. — 21p. — (Reference sheet ; no.81/18)

GREAT BRITAIN. Parliament. House of Commons. Local Government Finance (No.2) Bill 1981-82

GREAT BRITAIN. Parliament. House of Commons. Library. Research Division
Local Government Finance (No.2) Bill (Bill 41 of 1981-82) and 1982-83 rate support grant settlement / [Priscilla Baines]. — [London] : the Division, 1982. — 8p. — (Reference sheet ; no.82/2)

GREAT BRITAIN. Parliament. House of Commons. Local Government (Interim Provisions) Bill 1983-84

GREAT BRITAIN. Parliament. House of Commons. Library. Research Division
Local Government (Interim Provisions) Bill, Bill 145, 1983-84 / Barry K. Winetrobe. — [London] : the Division, 1984. — 20p. — (Reference sheet ; no.84/5). — *Includes bibliographical references*

GREAT BRITAIN. Parliament. House of Commons. London Regional Transport Bill 1983-84

GREAT BRITAIN. Parliament. House of Commons. Library. Research Division
London Regional Transport Bill (Bill 68 of 1983-1984) / [Priscilla Baines]. — [London] : the Division, 1983. — 22p. — (Reference sheet ; no.83/23). — *Bibliographical references: p21-22*

GREAT BRITAIN. Parliament. House of Commons. National Health Service (Amendment) Bill 1985-86

GREAT BRITAIN. Parliament. House of Commons. Library. Research Division
National Health Service (Amendment) Bill [Bill 119 of 1985-86] / Keith Cuninghame, C. J. Gilmour. — [London] : the Division, 1986. — 28p. — (References sheet ; no.86/10). — *Includes bibliographical references*

GREAT BRITAIN. Parliament. House of Commons. Oil and Gas (Enterprise) Bill 1981-82

GREAT BRITAIN. Parliament. House of Commons. Library. Research Division
Oil and Gas (Enterprise) Bill / [B. L. Miller]. — [London] : the Division, 1982. — 17p. — (Reference sheet ; no.82/1). — *Bibliography: p15-17*

GREAT BRITAIN. Parliament. House of Commons. Oil Taxation Bill 1983-84
GREAT BRITAIN. Parliament. House of Commons. Library. Research Division
The Oil Taxation Bill / Timothy Edmonds. — [London] : the Division, 1983. — 6p. — (Reference sheet ; no.83/18)

GREAT BRITAIN. Parliament. House of Commons. Police and Criminal Evidence Bill 1982-83
GREAT BRITAIN. Parliament. House of Commons. Library. Research Division
Police and Criminal Evidence Bill (Bill 16, session 1982-83) / [Patrick Nealon]. — [London] : the Division, [1982]. — 25p. — (Reference sheet ; no.82/17). — Includes bibliographical references

GREAT BRITAIN. Parliament. House of Commons. Police and Criminal Evidence Bill 1983-84
GREAT BRITAIN. Parliament. House of Commons. Library. Research Division
Police and Criminal Evidence Bill, 1983-84 [Bill 44] / [Patrick Nealon]. — [London] : the Division, 1983. — 11p. — (Reference sheet ; no.83/17). — Bibliographical references: p10-11

GREAT BRITAIN. Parliament. House of Commons. Ports (Financial Assistance) Bill 1980-81
GREAT BRITAIN. Parliament. House of Commons. Library. Research Division
Ports (Financial Assistance) Bill / Christopher Barclay, Robert Twigger, Celia Nield. — [London] : the Division, 1981. — 14p. — (Reference sheet ; no.81/12). — Bibliographical references: p14

GREAT BRITAIN. Parliament. House of Commons. Prevention of Terrorism Bill 1983-84
GREAT BRITAIN. Parliament. House of Commons. Library. Research Division
Prevention of Terrorism Bill 1983-4 [Bill 8] / [Patrick Nealon]. — [London] : the Division, [1983]. — 12p. — (Reference sheet ; no.83/13). — Bibliographical references: p8-12

GREAT BRITAIN. Parliament. House of Commons. Public Order Bill 1985-86
GREAT BRITAIN. Parliament. House of Commons. Library. Research Division
Public Order Bill, Bill 40 of 1985-86 / Mary Baber, Jane Fiddick. — [London] : the Division, 1986. — 24p. — (Reference sheet ; no.86/1). — Bibliographical references: p23-24

GREATER LONDON COUNCIL
The control of protest : the new Public Order Bill : the Greater London Council's response, adopted 19 December 1985. — [London : the Council], 1986. — 51p. — (Policing London)

GREAT BRITAIN. Parliament. House of Commons. Rates Bill 1983-84
GREAT BRITAIN. Parliament. House of Commons. Library. Research Division
Rates Bill, Bill 79, 1983-84 / Barry K. Winetrobe. — [London] : the Division, 1984. — 18p. — (Reference sheet ; no.84/3). — Includes bibliographical references

GREAT BRITAIN. Parliament. House of Commons. Rating and Valuation (Amendment) (Scotland) Bill 1983-84
GREAT BRITAIN. Parliament. House of Commons. Library. Research Division
Rating & Valuation (Amendment) (Scotland) Bill, Bill 61 of 1983-84 / [Barry K. Winetrobe]. — [London] : the Division, 1983. — 9p. — (Reference sheet ; no.83/22). — Includes bibliographical references

GREAT BRITAIN. Parliament. House of Commons. Representation of the People Bill 1980-81
GREAT BRITAIN. Parliament. House of Commons. Library. Research Division
Representation of the People Bill [Bill 153 of 1980-81] / [Rosamund Coates]. — [London] : the Division, 1981. — 18p. — (Reference sheet ; no.81/16)

GREAT BRITAIN. Parliament. House of Commons. Shops Bill 1980-81
GREAT BRITAIN. Parliament. House of Commons. Library. Research Division
Shops Bill, Bill 26 (Revised) 80-81 / [Joanna Roll]. — [London] : the Division, [1981]. — 13p. — (Reference sheet ; no.81/7)

GREAT BRITAIN. Parliament. House of Commons. Shops Bill 1985-86
GREAT BRITAIN. Parliament. House of Commons. Library. Research Division
Shops Bill (Bill 94 of 1985-86) / Fiona Poole. — [London] : the Division, 1986. — 23p. — (Reference sheet ; no.86/7). — Bibliographical references: p22-23

GREAT BRITAIN. Parliament. House of Commons. Social Security (Age of Retirement) Bill 1983-84
GREAT BRITAIN. Parliament. House of Commons. Library. Research Division
Social Security (Age of Retirement) Bill 1983/4 [Bill 16] / Julia Lourie. — [London] : the Division, 1983. — 20p. — (Reference sheet ; no.83/21). — Bibliographical references: p15-18

GREAT BRITAIN. Parliament. House of Commons. Social Security and Housing Benefits Bill 1982-83
GREAT BRITAIN. Parliament. House of Commons. Library. Research Division
Social Security and Housing Benefits Bill 1982/83 (Bill 109) / Julia Lourie. — [London] : the Division, 1983. — 23p. — (Reference sheet ; no.83/7). — Bibliographical references: p14-15

GREAT BRITAIN. Parliament. House of Commons. Social Security Bill 1979-80 — Bibliography
GREAT BRITAIN. Parliament. House of Commons. Library. Research Division
Social Security Bill (No.86 of 1979/80) / [Julia Lourie]. — [London] : the Division, 1979. — 5p. — (Reference sheet ; no.79/16)

GREAT BRITAIN. Parliament. House of Commons. Social Security Bill 1980-81
GREAT BRITAIN. Parliament. House of Commons. Library. Research Division
Social Security Bill 1980/81 (Bill 68) / [Julia Lourie]. — [London] : the Division, 1981. — 10p. — (Reference sheet ; no.81/8). — Bibliography: p8-10

GREAT BRITAIN. Parliament. House of Commons. Social Security Bill 1984-85
GREAT BRITAIN. Parliament. House of Commons. Library. Research Division
Social Security Bill 1984/5 [Bill 10] / Julia Lourie. — [London] : the Division, 1984. — 23p. — (Reference sheet ; no.84/11). — Bibliographical references: p18-23

GREAT BRITAIN. Parliament. House of Commons. Social Security Bill 1985-86
GREAT BRITAIN. Parliament. House of Commons. Library. Research Division
Social Security Bill 1985/6 [Bill 59] / Julia Lourie, Christine Gillie. — [London] : the Division, 1986. — 52p. — (Reference sheet ; no.86/3). — Bibliographical references: p46-52

GREAT BRITAIN. Parliament. House of Commons. Social Security (Contributions) Bill 1980-81
GREAT BRITAIN. Parliament. House of Commons. Library. Research Division
Social Security (Contributions) Bill 1980-81 [Bill 4] / [Julia Lourie]. — [London] : the Division, 1980. — 19p. — (Reference sheet ; no.80/16). — Bibliographical references: p17-19

GREAT BRITAIN. Parliament. House of Commons. Social Security (No.2) Bill 1979-80
GREAT BRITAIN. Parliament. House of Commons. Library. Research Division
The Social Security (No.2) Bill 1979/80 (Bill 180) / Julia Lourie, Christine Fretten. — [London] : the Division, 1980. — 13p. — (Reference sheet ; no.80/11). — Bibliography: p10-13

GREAT BRITAIN. Parliament. House of Commons. Teachers' Pay and Conditions Bill 1986-87
GREAT BRITAIN. Parliament. House of Commons. Library. Research Division
The Teachers' Pay and Conditions Bill [Bill 10], session 1986/87 / Christine Gillie, Gillian Allen. — [London] : the Division, 1986. — 24p. — (Reference sheet ; no.86/15). — Bibliographical references: p20-24

GREAT BRITAIN. Parliament. House of Commons. Telecommunications Bill 1982-83
GREAT BRITAIN. Parliament. House of Commons. Library. Research Division
Telecommunications Bill (Bill 15) / Christopher Barclay. — [London] : the Division, 1982. — 12p. — (Reference sheet ; no.82/15). — Bibliography: p11-12

GREAT BRITAIN. Parliament. House of Commons. Telecommunications Bill 1983-84
GREAT BRITAIN. Parliament. House of Commons. Library. Research Division
Telecommunications Bill 1983/84 (Bill 5) / Christopher Barclay. — [London] : the Division, 1983. — 15p. — (Reference sheet ; no.83/11). — Bibliography: p11-13

GREAT BRITAIN. Parliament. House of Commons. Trade Union Bill 1983-84
GREAT BRITAIN. Parliament. House of Commons. Library. Research Division
Trade Union Bill (Bill 43, 1983-84) / Celia Neald. — [London] : the Division, 1983. — 27p. — (Reference sheet ; no.83/16). — Bibliographical references: p26-27

GREAT BRITAIN. Parliament. House of Commons. Transport Bill 1980-81
GREAT BRITAIN. Parliament. House of Commons. Library. Research Division
The Transport Bill 1980-81 / C. R. Barclay. — [London] : the Division, 1981. — 21p. — (Reference sheet ; no.81/1). — Bibliography: p20-21

GREAT BRITAIN. Parliament. House of Commons. Transport Bill 1981-82
GREAT BRITAIN. Parliament. House of Commons. Library. Research Division
Transport Bill (Bill 57 of 1981-82) / [Priscilla Baines]. — [London] : the Division, 1982. — 11p. — (Reference sheet ; no.82/6)

GREAT BRITAIN. Parliament. House of Commons. Transport Bill 1982-83
GREAT BRITAIN. Parliament. House of Commons. Library. Research Division
Transport Bill (Bill 5 of 1982-83) / Priscilla Baines. — [London] : the Division, 1982. — 14p. — (Reference sheet ; no.82/11). — Includes bibliographical references

GREAT BRITAIN. Parliament. House of Commons. Transport Bill 1984-85
GREAT BRITAIN. Parliament. House of Commons. Library. Research Division
Transport Bill, Bill 68 of 1984-85 / Priscilla Baines. — [London] : the Division, 1985. — 34p. — (Reference sheet ; no.85/4). — Includes bibliographical references

GREAT BRITAIN. Parliament. House of Commons. Wages Bill 1985-86
GREAT BRITAIN. Parliament. House of Commons. Library. Research Division
Wages Bill (Bill 70 of 1985-86) / Fiona Poole, Celia Nield. — [London] : the Division, 1986. — 35p. — (Reference sheet ; no.86/6). — Bibliographical references: p33-35

GREAT BRITAIN. Parliament. House of Commons
GREAT BRITAIN. Parliament. House of Commons. Library
Sessional information digest / House of Commons. — London : H.M.S.O., 1983/84-. — Annual. — Index and companion to the Weekly Information Bulletin

GREAT BRITAIN. Parliament. House of Commons *continuation*
NORTON, Philip
The Commons in perspective / Philip Norton. — Oxford : Blackwell, 1985, c1981. — [x,265]p . — *Originally published: Oxford : Robertson, 1981. — Includes bibliography and index*

GREAT BRITAIN. Parliament. House of Commons — Biography
EDSALL, Nicholas C
Richard Cobden, independent radical / Nicholas C. Edsall. — Cambridge, Mass. ; London : Harvard University Press, 1986. — xiv, 465p. — *Includes index. — Bibliography: p.[429]-433*

HINDE, Wendy
Richard Cobden : a Victorian outsider : a biography / by Wendy Hinde. — New Haven : Yale University Press, 1987. — p. cm. — *Includes index. — Bibliography: p*

GREAT BRITAIN. Parliament. House of Commons — Election districts
GREAT BRITAIN. Parliament. House of Commons. Library. Research Division
The Parliamentary Boundary Commissions and the redistribution of seats / H. Rosamund Coates. — [London] : the Division, 1983. — 28p. — (Background paper ; no.111)

WALLER, Robert
The almanac of British politics / Robert Waller. — 3rd ed. — London : Croom Helm, c1987. — [640]p. — *Previous ed.: 1983*

GREAT BRITAIN. Parliament. House of Commons — Elections — History — 17th ceentury
KISHLANSKY, Mark A
Parliamentary selection : social and political choice in early modern England / Mark A. Kishlansky. — Cambridge : Cambridge University Press, 1986. — 1v.. — *Includes bibliography and index*

GREAT BRITAIN. Parliament. House of Commons — History
DENTON, Jeffrey H.
Representatives of the lower clergy in Parliament, 1295-1340 / J.H. Denton and J.P. Dooley. — Woodbridge : Boydell, 1987. — [viii,256]p. — (Royal Historical Society studies in history series ; no.50). — *At foot of t.p.: Royal Historical Society. — Includes bibliography and index*

GREAT BRITAIN. Parliament. House of Commons — History — Bibliography
SEATON, Janet
English constituency histories, 1265-1832 : a guide to printed sources / by Janet Seaton. — London : H.M.S.O., 1986. — xvii, 143p. — (House of Commons Library document ; no.15)

GREAT BRITAIN. Parliament. House of Commons — Qualifications
GREAT BRITAIN. Parliament. House of Commons. Library. Research Division
Representation of the People Bill [Bill 153 of 1980-81] / [Rosamund Coates]. — [London] : the Division, 1981. — 18p. — (Reference sheet ; no.81/16)

GREAT BRITAIN. Parliament. House of Commons — Salaries, pensions, etc.
GREAT BRITAIN. Parliament. House of Commons. Library. Research Division
Members' pay / Rosamund Coates. — [London] : the Division, 1983. — 45p. — (Background paper ; no.124)

GREAT BRITAIN. Parliament. House of Commons. Committee on Welsh Affairs — History
JONES, J. Barry
Parliament and territoriality : the Committee on Welsh Affairs, 1979-1983 / J. Barry Jones and R.A. Wilford. — Cardiff : University of Wales Press, 1986. — [102]p. — *Includes index*

GREAT BRITAIN. Parliament. House of Lords. Agricultural Holdings Bill 1983-84
GREAT BRITAIN. Parliament. House of Commons. Library. Research Division
Agricultural Holdings Bill (HL) Bill 110 of 1983-84 / Priscilla Baines. — [London] : the Division, 1983. — 12p. — (Reference sheet ; no.84/4). — *Bibliographical references: p11-12*

GREAT BRITAIN. Parliament. House of Lords. Contempt of Court Bill 1980-1981
GREAT BRITAIN. Parliament. House of Commons. Library. Research Division
Contempt of Court Bill (Bill 74) / [Patrick Nealon]. — [London] : the Division, 1981. — 22p. — (Reference sheet ; no.81/10). — *Bibliography: p17-22*

GREAT BRITAIN. Parliament. House of Lords. Data Protection Bill 1982-83
GREAT BRITAIN. Parliament. House of Commons. Library. Research Division
Data Protection Bill (HL), Bill 117 of 1982-83 / Barry K. Winetrobe. — [London] : the Division, 1983. — 11p. — (Reference sheet ; no.83/8). — *Bibliographical references: p2-5*

GREAT BRITAIN. Parliament. House of Lords. Education Bill 1985-86
GREAT BRITAIN. Parliament. House of Commons. Library. Research Division
Education Bill (HL) [Bill 87 of 1985-86] / Kay Andrews. — [London] : the Division, 1986. — 37p. — (Reference sheet ; no.86/8). — *Bibliographical references: p31-37*

GREAT BRITAIN. Parliament. House of Lords. Matrimonial and Family Proceedings Bill 1983-84
GREAT BRITAIN. Parliament. House of Commons. Library. Research Division
Matrimonial and Family Proceedings Bill (H.L.) 1983-4 [Bill 96] / [Patrick Nealon]. — [London] : the Division, 1984. — 11p. — (Research note ; no.141)

GREAT BRITAIN. Parliament. House of Lords. Mental Health (Amendment) (Scotland) Bill 1982-83
GREAT BRITAIN. Parliament. House of Commons. Library. Research Division
Mental Health (Amendment) (Scotland) Bill (HL) 1982-83 [Bill 82] / Keith Cuninghame. — [London] : the Division, 1983. — 11p. — (Reference sheet ; no.83/5). — *Bibliographical references: p9-11*

GREAT BRITAIN. Parliament. House of Lords. Mobile Homes Bill 1982-83
GREAT BRITAIN. Parliament. House of Commons. Library. Research Division
The Mobile Homes Bill (H.L.) (Bill 74, session 1982/83) / [Christine Gillie]. — [London] : the Division, 1983. — 13p. — (Reference sheet ; no.83/2). — *Bibliographical references: p12-13*

GREAT BRITAIN. Parliament. House of Lords. National Heritage Bill 1982-83
GREAT BRITAIN. Parliament. House of Commons. Library. Research Division
National Heritage Bill [HL] - Bill 85 of 1982-83 / [Fiona Poole, Barry Winetrobe]. — [London] : the Division, 1983. — 23p. — (Reference sheet ; no.83/4). — *Includes bibliographical references*

GREAT BRITAIN. Parliament. House of Lords. Sex Discrimination Bill 1985-86
GREAT BRITAIN. Parliament. House of Commons. Library. Research Division
Sex Discrimination Bill [HL] (Bill 151 of 1985-86) / Celia Nield. — [London] : the Division, 1986. — 32p. — (Reference sheet ; no.86/12). — *Bibliographical references: p32*

GREAT BRITAIN. Parliament. House of Lords. Select Committee on the European Communities
GREAT BRITAIN. Parliament. House of Lords. Select Committee on the European Communities
Progress of scrutiny / Select Committee on the European Communities. — London : HMSO, 1982-

GREAT BRITAIN. Planning Inspectorate
Chief planning inspector's report / Planning Inspectorate, Great Britain. — Bristol : Planning Inspectorate, 1985-. — *Annual*

GREAT BRITAIN. Resource Allocation Working Party
MAYS, Nicholas
Resource allocation in the Health Service : a review of the methods of the Resource Allocation Working Party / Nicholas Mays, Gwyn Bevan. — London : Bedford Square Press/NCVO, 1987. — 180p. — (Occasional papers on social administration ; 81). — *Bibliography: p161-180*

GREAT BRITAIN. Royal Air Force
COOPER, Malcolm, 19---
The birth of independent air power : British policy in the First World War / Malcolm Cooper. — London : Allen & Unwin, 1986. — xix,169p,[16]p of plates. — *Bibliography: p158-165. — Includes index*

GREAT BRITAIN. Royal Navy — Biography
HUNT, Barry D.
Sailor-scholar : Admiral Sir Herbert Richmond 1871-1946 / Barry D. Hunt. — Waterloo, Ont. : Wilfred Laurier University Press ; Gerrards Cross : distributed by Smythe, c1982. — xii,259p. — *Bibliography: p238-248. — Includes index*

ZIEGLER, Philip
Mountbatten : the official biography / Philip Ziegler. — London : Collins, 1985. — 786p,[48]p of plates. — *Geneal.table on lining papers. — Bibliography: p751-756. — Includes index*

GREAT BRITAIN. Royal Navy — History
DINGMAN, Roger
Power in the Pacific : the origins of naval arms limitation, 1914-1922 / Roger Dingman. — Chicago : University of Chicago Press, 1976. — xiii, 318 p.. — *Includes index. — Bibliography: p. 287-310*

GREAT BRITAIN. Royal Navy — History — 19th century
HAMILTON, W. Mark
The nation and the navy : methods and organization of British navalist propaganda, 1889-1914 / W. Mark Hamilton. — New York : Garland Pub., 1986. — p. cm. — (Outstanding theses from the London School of Economics and Political Science). — *Thesis (Ph.D.)--University of London, 1977. — Bibliography: p*

GREAT BRITAIN. Royal Navy — History — 20th century
HAMILTON, W. Mark
The nation and the navy : methods and organization of British navalist propaganda, 1889-1914 / W. Mark Hamilton. — New York : Garland Pub., 1986. — p. cm. — (Outstanding theses from the London School of Economics and Political Science). — *Thesis (Ph.D.)--University of London, 1977. — Bibliography: p*

GREAT BRITAIN. Royal Navy — Societies, etc
HAMILTON, W. Mark
The nation and the navy : methods and organization of British navalist propaganda, 1889-1914 / W. Mark Hamilton. — New York : Garland Pub., 1986. — p. cm. — (Outstanding theses from the London School of Economics and Political Science). — *Thesis (Ph.D.)--University of London, 1977. — Bibliography: p*

GREAT BRITAIN. Special Operations Executive. Special Training School 103 (Whitby, Ont.)
STAFFORD, David
Camp X / David Stafford. — New York : Dodd, Mead, 1987. — p. cm. — *Includes index. — Bibliography: p*

GREAT BRITAIN. Standing Advisory Committee on Trunk Road Assessment. Urban road appraisal
GREAT BRITAIN. Department of Transport
The government response to the SACTRA report on urban road appraisal / Department of Transport. — London : H.M.S.O., 1986. — 32p

GREAT BRITAIN. Treasury — History — 20th century
BROWNING, Peter, 1920-
The Treasury and economic policy, 1964-1985 / Peter Browning. — London : Longman, 1986. — [368]p. — *Includes bibliography and index*

GREAT BRITAIN — Economic conditions
SIEBERG, Herward
Colonial development : die Grundlegung moderner Entwicklungspolitik durch Grossbritannien 1919-1949 / Herward Sieberg. — Stuttgart : Steiner-Verlag-Wiesbaden, 1985. — xvii,736p. — (Beiträge zur Kolonial- und Überseegeschichte ; Bd.31). — *Bibliography: p710-717*

GREAT BRITAIN — 1970-
GREAT BRITAIN. Parliament. House of Commons. Library. Research Division
Alternative economic strategies / Christopher Barclay, Paul Hutt. — [London] : the Division, 1980. — 46p. — (Background paper ; no.82). — *Bibliography: p38-46*

GREAT BRITIAN — Law and legislation
SDP-LIBERAL ALLIANCE
Government, law and justice : the case for a Ministry of Justice. — Hebden Bridge : Hebden Royd Publications, 1985. — 14p. — (Alliance paper ; no.1)

GREAT BRITIAN — Race relations
GREAT BRITAIN. Commission for Racial Equality
Living in terror : a report on racial violence & harassment in housing. — London : the Commission, 1987. — 53p

GREAT BRITIAN. Parliament. House of Lords. Dentists Bill 1982-83
GREAT BRITAIN. Parliament. House of Commons. Library. Research Division
Dentists Bill (HL) 1982-83 (Bill 90) / Keith Cuninghame. — [London] : the Division, 1983. — 5p. — (Reference sheet ; no.83/6). — *Bibliographical references: p5*

GREAT POWERS
AKZIN, Benjamin
On great powers and superpowers / Benjamin Akzin. — Den Haag : Martinus Nijhoff, [1972]. — p.610-626. — *Offprint of chapter from "Theory and politics/Theorie und Politik: Festschrift zum 70. Geburtstag für Carl Joachim Friedrich", ed. Klaus von Beyme, pub. Nijhoff, 1972*

GREAT WESTERN RAILWAY — History
BOOKER, Frank
The Great Western Railway : a new history / Frank Booker. — 2nd ed. — Newton Abbot : David St. John Thomas, 1985. — 208p,[8]p of plates. — *Previous ed.: 1977. Previous ed.: Newton Abbot : David and Charles, 1977. Bibliography: p201-203. — Includes index*

GREAT WESTERN RAILWAY (GREAT BRITAIN) — History
BOOKER, Frank
The Great Western Railway : a new history / Frank Booker. — 2nd ed. — Newton Abbot : David St. John Thomas, 1985. — 208p,[8]p of plates. — *Previous ed.: 1977. Previous ed.: Newton Abbot : David and Charles, 1977. Bibliography: p201-203. — Includes index*

GREATER LONDON ARTS
Greater London Arts : annual report and accounts. — London : Greater London Arts, 1984/5-. — *Annual*

GREATER LONDON COUNCIL
GREAT BRITAIN. Parliament. House of Commons. Library. Research Division
Local government in the English metropolitan areas / Barry K. Winetrobe. — [London] : the Division, 1984. — 33p. — (Background paper ; no.135). — *Bibliographical references: p28*

GREATER LONDON COUNCIL
The future of London's government : consultation document : GLC research project. — [London : the Council, 1985]. — 23p

GREATER LONDON COUNCIL
London calling : the future of London's government. — [London : the Council, 1985]. — [12]p

GREATER LONDON COUNCIL. Contract Compliance Equal Opportunities Unit
Information pack. — [London : the Council, 1983-85]. — 7pts.

RIDOUTT, Tim
London government reorganisation in 1965 : objectives and outcomes / Tim Ridoutt. — London : North East London Polytechnic. Centre for Institutional Studies, 1984. — 61p. — (Commentary / North East London Polytechnic. Centre for Institutional Studies ; 26)

WESTMINSTER. Finance Department. Policy Unit
Financial effects of GLC abolition : a Westminster briefing paper for industry and commerce. — Westminster : [the Department], 1985. — 8p

GREATER LONDON COUNCIL — History
SOFER, Anne
The London Left takeover / Anne Sofer. — London : J. Caslake, 1987. — 118p. — *Collection of reprinted articles*

GREECE — Census, 1981
GREECE. Ethnikē Statistikē Hypēresia tēs Ellados
Apotelesmata apographēs plethysmoy-katoikion tēs 5ēs Aprilioy 1981 = Résultats du recensement de la population et des habitations effectué 4 avril 1981. — Athēnai : Ethnikē Statistikē Hypēresia tēs Ellados. — *In Greek with French translation of introduction and table headings*
Tomos 3: Oikonomika charakteristika tou plethysmou = Caractéristiques économiques de la population. — 1985. — 2 fascicules. — (A : plēthysmos = population ; 49)

GREECE — Census 1981
GREECE. Ethnikē Statistikē Hypēresia tēs Ellados
Pragmatikos plēthysmos tēs Ellados kata tēn apographē tēs 5 Aprilioy 1981 kata nomous, eparchies, dēmous, koinotētes kai oikismoüs = Population de fait de la Grèce au recensement du 5 avril 1981 par départements, éparchies, communes-dèmes, communes et localités. — Athēnai : Ethnikē Statistikē Hypēresia tēs Ellados, 1982. — 189p. — *In Greek and French*

GREECE — Census, 1981
GREECE. Ethnikē Statistikē Hypēresia tēs Hellados
Apotelesmata apographēs plēthysmoy-katoikiōn tēs 5ē Aprilioy 1981 = Résultats du recensement de la population et des habitations effectúe le 5 avril 1981. — Athēnai : Ethnikē Statistikē Hypēresia tēs Ellados. — *In Greek and French*
Tomos 2: Dēmografika kai koinōnika charakteristika tou plēthysmoy = caractéristiques démographiques et sociales de la population. — 1985. — xl,167p. — (A : plēthysmos = population ; 48)

GREECE — Economic conditions — 1974-
Greece and the EEC : integration and convergence / edited by George N. Yannopoulos. — Basingstoke : Macmillan in association with the Graduate School of European and International Studies, University of Reading, 1986. — xii,178p. — (University of Reading European and international studies). — *Includes bibliographies and index*

GREECE — Foreign relations — Turkey
PHOTIADES, Kostas
The annihilation of the Greeks in Pontus by the Turks / Kostas Photiades. — [S.l.] : Union of the Fighters for the Liberation of the Greek lands seized by Turkey, 1987. — 38p

GREECE — History — Occupation, 1941-1944
HONDROS, John Louis
Occupation and resistance : the Greek agony, 1941-44 / John Louis Hondros. — New York, NY : Pella Pub. Co., 1983. — 340 p.. — *Based on the author's thesis, Vanderbilt University. — Bibliography: p. 305-324*

GREECE — Politics and government — To 146 B.C
STARR, Chester G.
Individual and community : the rise of the polis, 800-500 B.C. / Chester G. Starr. — New York ; Oxford : Oxford University Press, 1986. — x, 133p. — *Includes index. — Bibliography: p.127-130*

WHITEHEAD, David, 19---
The demes of Attica, 508/7-ca. 250 B.C. : a political and social study / by David Whitehead. — Princeton, N.J. : Princeton University Press, c1985. — xxvii,485p. — *Bibliography: p.455-459*

GREECE — Politics and government — 19th century
MCGREW, William W.
Land and revolution in modern Greece, 1800-1881 : the transition in the tenure and exploitation of land from Ottoman rule to independence / William W. McGrew. — [Kent, OH] : Kent State University Press, c1985. — xxii, 339 p.. — *Includes index. — Bibliography: p. [306]-333*

GREECE — Population — Statistics
GREECE. Ethnikē Statistikē Hypēresia tēs Ellados
Apotelesmata apographēs plethysmoy-katoikion tēs 5ēs Aprilioy 1981 = Résultats du recensement de la population et des habitations effectué 4 avril 1981. — Athēnai : Ethnikē Statistikē Hypēresia tēs Ellados. — *In Greek with French translation of introduction and table headings*
Tomos 3: Oikonomika charakteristika tou plethysmou = Caractéristiques économiques de la population. — 1985. — 2 fascicules. — (A : plēthysmos = population ; 49)

GREECE. Ethnikē Statistikē Hypēresia tēs Ellados
Pragmatikos plēthysmos tēs Ellados kata tēn apographē tēs 5 Aprilioy 1981 kata nomous, eparchies, dēmous, koinotētes kai oikismoüs = Population de fait de la Grèce au recensement du 5 avril 1981 par départements, éparchies, communes-dèmes, communes et localités. — Athēnai : Ethnikē Statistikē Hypēresia tēs Ellados, 1982. — 189p. — *In Greek and French*

GREECE. Ethnikē Statistikē Hypēresia tēs Hellados
Apotelesmata apographēs plēthysmoy-katoikiōn tēs 5ē Aprilioy 1981 = Résultats du recensement de la population et des habitations effectúe le 5 avril 1981. — Athēnai : Ethnikē Statistikē Hypēresia tēs Ellados. — *In Greek and French*
Tomos 2: Dēmografika kai koinōnika charakteristika tou plēthysmoy = caractéristiques démographiques et sociales de la population. — 1985. — xl,167p. — (A : plēthysmos = population ; 48)

GREECE — Rural conditions
Gender & power in rural Greece / edited by Jill Dubisch. — Princeton, N.J. : Princeton University Press, c1986. — p. cm. — *Includes index. — Bibliography: p*

GREECE — Social life and customs
Gender & power in rural Greece / edited by Jill Dubisch. — Princeton, N.J. : Princeton University Press, c1986. — p. cm. — *Includes index. — Bibliography: p*

GREEK AMERICANS — Politics and government
HALLEY, Laurence
Ancient affections : ethnic groups and foreign policy / Laurence Halley. — New York : Praeger, 1985. — viii, 180 p.. — *Includes index. — Bibliography: p. 172-174*

GREEK DRAMA (TRAGEDY) — History and criticism
NUSSBAUM, Martha C.
The fragility of goodness : luck and ethics in Greek tragedy and philosophy / Martha C. Nussbaum. — Cambridge : Cambridge University Press, 1986. — xvii,544p. — *Bibliography: p512-525. — Includes index*

GREEK LANGUAGE, MODERN — Dictionaries — English
PRING, J. T.
The Oxford dictionary of modern Greek : English-Greek / compiled by J.T. Pring. — Oxford : Clarendon, 1982. — x,370p

GREEN PARTY
GREEN PARTY
[Manifesto]. — London : Green Party, 1987. — 28p

GREEN REVOLUTION — India
JHA, Nand Kishore
Bank finance & green revolution in India / Nand Kishore Jha. — Delhi : Amar Prakashan, 1985. — xi, 358 p.. — *Bibliography: p. [351]-358*

GREENBELTS
ELSON, Martin J.
Green belts : conflict mediation in the urban fringe / Martin J. Elson. — London : Heinemann, 1986. — xxxi,304p. — *Includes index*

GREENBELTS — England — London
LAND USE CONSULTANTS
London's green belt : a handbook for action / Land Use Consultants Ltd ; for the Countryside Commission and the Sports Council. — [London : Sports Council, 1984]. — 59,[8]p. — *Bibliography: Appendix A*

GREENLAND — Population — Statistics
Befolkningen i Grønland. — København : Ministeriet for Grønland, 1981-. — (Meddelelser fra Statistisk Kontor). — *Annual. — Text in Danish with English translation of table headings*

GREENLAND — Defenses
ARCHER, Clive
Greenland and the Atlantic Alliance / Clive Archer. — Aberdeen : Centre for Defence Studies, 1985. — 66p. — (Centrepieces ; no.7)

GREENLAND — Foreign relations
ARCHER, Clive
Greenland and the Atlantic Alliance / Clive Archer. — Aberdeen : Centre for Defence Studies, 1985. — 66p. — (Centrepieces ; no.7)

GREENLAND — Statistics, Vital
Befolkningen i Grønland pr.1. januar 1981 samt fødsler og dødsfald i 1980. — [København?] : Ministeriet for Grønland, 1982. — 56p. — (Meddelelser fra Statistisk Kontor / Ministeriet for Grønland ; nr.80)

GREENLAND EMIGRATION AND IMMIGRATION — Statistics
Vandringsstatistik 1968-1971. — [København?] : Ministeriet for Grønland. — (Meddelelser fra Statistisk Kontor / Ministeriet for Grønland ; nr.31)
B : Vandringer mellem Grønland og Danmark, mellem Grønland og udlandet, samt et samlet overblik over vandringerne i perioden. — 1973. — 10,7p

GREENWICH (LONDON, ENGLAND) — City planning
GREENWICH. Planning Department
The people's plan : a community-based local plan for the London Borough of Greenwich. — Greenwich : [the Department], 1986. — 314p. — *Includes two maps*

GREG (Family)
ROSE, Mary B.
The Gregs of Quarry Bank Mill : the rise and decline of a family firm, 1750-1914 / Mary B. Rose. — Cambridge : Cambridge University Press, 1987. — [viii,186]p. — *Pbk from Quarry Bank Mill Trust only. — Bibliography: p221*

GREGORY, Sir WILLIAM
JENKINS, Brian
Sir William Gregory of Coole : the biography of an Anglo-Irishman / Brian Jenkins. — Gerrards Cross : Colin Smythe, 1986. — xi, 339p. — *Bibliography: p.323-332*

GRENADA — Economic conditions
Grenada, economic report. — Washington, D.C., U.S.A. : World Bank, c1985. — [xii],90p. — (A World Bank country study)

PRYOR, Frederic L
Revolutionary Grenada : a study in political economy / Frederic L. Pryor. — New York : Praeger, 1986. — xx, 395 p.. — *Includes index. — Bibliography: p. 375-382*

GRENADA — Economic policy
Grenada, economic report. — Washington, D.C., U.S.A. : World Bank, c1985. — [xii],90p. — (A World Bank country study)

PRYOR, Frederic L
Revolutionary Grenada : a study in political economy / Frederic L. Pryor. — New York : Praeger, 1986. — xx, 395 p.. — *Includes index. — Bibliography: p. 375-382*

GRENADA — Foreign relations — United States
DAVIDSON, Scott
Grenada : a study in politics and the limits of international law / Scott Davidson. — Aldershot : Avebury, c1987. — xii,196p. — *Bibliography: p184-190. — Includes index*

GRENADA — Politics and government — 1974-
PRYOR, Frederic L
Revolutionary Grenada : a study in political economy / Frederic L. Pryor. — New York : Praeger, 1986. — xx, 395 p.. — *Includes index. — Bibliography: p. 375-382*

GRENOBLE (FRANCE) — Social conditions
NORBERG, Kathryn
Rich and poor in Grenoble, 1600-1814 / Kathryn Norberg. — Berkeley ; London : University of California Press, c1985. — xii, 366p. — *Includes index. — Bibliography: p.345-352*

GREW, JOSEPH C
HEINRICHS, Waldo H
American ambassador : Joseph C. Grew and the development of the United States diplomatic tradition / Waldo H. Heinrichs, Jr. — New York : Oxford University Press, 1986, c1966. — p. cm. — *Reprint. Originally published: Boston : Little, Brown, 1966. — Includes index. — Bibliography: p*

GRIFFITHS, W. J.
GLENNERSTER, Howard
The nursing management function after Griffiths : a study in the North West Thames Region / Professor Howard Glennerster, Dr. Pat Owens [and] Ms. Angela Kimberley. — London : London School of Economics and Political Science : North West Thames Regional Health Authority, 1986. — 85,viiip.. — *Bibliography: p.ix-x*

GRIMES, SARA
P'ENG, Te-huai
[P'eng Te-huai tzu shu. English]. Memoirs of a Chinese marshal : the autobiographical notes of Peng Dehuai (1898-1974) / translated by Zheng Longpu ; English text edited by Sara Grimes. — 1st ed. — Beijing : Foreign Languages Press, 1984. — vi, 523 p., [15] p. of plates. — *Translation of: P'eng Te-huai tzu shu*

GRIMM, ROBERT
PLATTEN, Fritz
Die Reise Lenins durch Deutschland im plombierten Wagen / Fritz Platten. — Frankfurt am Main : isp, 1985. — 152p. — *First published in 1924*

GROCERY TRADE — Latin America — History — 18th century
KINSBRUNER, Jay
Petty capitalism in Spanish America : the Pulperos of Puebla, Mexico City, Caracas, and Buenos Aires / Jay Kinsbruner. — Boulder, Colo. ; London : Westview Press, 1987. — xxii,159p. — (Dellplain Latin American studies ; no.21). — *Bibliography: p[143]-152*

GROCERY TRADE — Latin America — History — 19th century
KINSBRUNER, Jay
Petty capitalism in Spanish America : the Pulperos of Puebla, Mexico City, Caracas, and Buenos Aires / Jay Kinsbruner. — Boulder, Colo. ; London : Westview Press, 1987. — xxii,159p. — (Dellplain Latin American studies ; no.21). — *Bibliography: p[143]-152*

GRONINGEN (NETHERLANDS: PROVINCE) — Economic policy
NETHERLANDS. Stuurgroep Integraal Structuurplan Noorden des Lands
Het Noorden : een versterkte bevolkingsgroei? Of juist niet! : een bewerking van het rapport Bevolkingsaspecten Noorden des Lands / Samensteller R. Idenburg. — 's-Gravenhage : Staatsuitgeverij, 1974. — 21p

NETHERLANDS. Werkgroep Beleidsdoelstellingen Analyse Noorden
ISP : integraal structuurplan Noorden des lands : rapport van de Werkgroep Beleidsdoelstellingen Analyse Noorden. — [s-Gravenhage] : the Werkgroep 2. — 1974. — 27p

GRØNLAND — Statistics, Vital
Befolkningsprognose for Grønland 1975-2000 : personer født i Grønland. — [København?] : Ministeriet for Grønland, 1975. — 9,[16]p. — (Meddelelser fra Statistisk Kontor / Ministeriet for Grønland ; nr.42)

GROSS NATIONAL PRODUCT
KRAVIS, Irving B.
World product and income : international comparisons of real gross product / Irving B. Kravis, Alan Heston, Robert Summers. — Baltimore : John Hopkins University Press for the World Bank, 1982. — x,388p. — *At head of title: United Nations International Comparison Project, phase III. — Produced by the Statistical Office of the United Nations and the World Bank*

GROSS NATIONAL PRODUCT — Canada
Provincial gross domestic product by industry = Produit intérieur brut provincial par industrie / Statistics Canada, Industry Product Division. — Ottawa : Ministry of Supply and Services, 1982-. — (System of national accounts / Statistics Canada). — *Annual. — Text in English and French*

GROSS NATIONAL PRODUCT — European Economic Community countries — Statistics

STATISTICAL OFFICE OF THE EUROPEAN COMMUNITIES
Quarterly national accounts - ESA = Comptes nationaux trimestriels - SEC / Statistical Office of the European Communities. — Luxembourg : Office des publications officielles des Communautés européennes, 1986-. — *Quarterly*

GROSS NATIONAL PRODUCT — Gambia — Statistics

Estimates of national income at constant prices in The Gambia. — [Banjul] : Central Statistics Department, 1985. — 49p

Sources and methods of estimation of national income at current prices in The Gambia. — [Banjul] : Central Statistics Department, 1985. — 151p

GROSS NATIONAL PRODUCT — Kiribati — Statistics

National accounts, 1972-74 / Gilbert Islands Ministry of Finance, Economics Division. — Bairiki : Government Printing Division, 1977. — 95p. — *Bibliography: p95*

GROSS NATIONAL PRODUCT — Tuvalu — Statistics

National accounts, 1972-74 / Gilbert Islands Ministry of Finance, Economics Division. — Bairiki : Government Printing Division, 1977. — 95p. — *Bibliography: p95*

GROSSMAN, ALLAN

OLIVER, Peter
Unlikely Tory : the life and politics of Allan Grossman / Peter Oliver. — 1st ed. — Toronto, Ont. : L. & O. Dennys, c1985. — xi, 322 p., [8] p. of plates. — *Includes bibliographical references and index*

GROTIUS, HUGO — Congresses

International law and the Grotian heritage : a commemorative colloquium held at The Hague on 8 April 1983 on the occasion of the fourth centenary of the birth of Hugo Grotius / organized by the Interuniversitair Instituut voor Internationaal Recht T.M.C. Asser Instituut in co-operation with the Grotiana Foundation. — The Hague : T.M.C. Asser Instituut, 1985. — xxii,370p

GROUP IDENTITY

ELLIOTT, W. A.
Us and them : a study of group consciousness / W.A. Elliott. — Aberdeen : Aberdeen University Press, 1986. — viii,164p. — *Bibliography˝ p157-159. — Includes index*

TURNER, John C.
Rediscovering the social group : a self-categorization theory / John C. Turner with Michael A. Hogg ... (et al.). — Oxford : Basil Blackwell, 1987. — x,239p. — *Bibliography: p209-232. — Includes index*

GROUP PSYCHOANALYSIS

FREUD, Sigmund
Group psychology and the analysis of the ego / Sigmund Freud ; translated and edited by James Strachey. — London : Hogarth Press, 1959. — x,85p. — *Bibliographies*

GROUP RELATIONS TRAINING

KATZ, Judy H.
White awareness : handbook for anti-racism training / by Judy H. Katz. — 1st ed. — Norman : University of Oklahoma Press, c1978. — x, 211 p.. — *Includes index. — Bibliography: p. 201-205*

GRUNDTVIG, N. F. S.

Grundtvig´s ideas in North America : influences and parallels / edited by Det Danske Selskab/The Danish Institute. — Copenhagen : Det Danske Selskab, 1983. — 173p. — *Bibliography: p167*

GRÜNEN, DIE

Eingriffe im Diesseits : Beiträge zu einer radikalen grünen Realpolitik / herausgegeben von Gabriel Falkenberg und Heiner Kersting. — Essen : Klartext, 1985. — 203p

Die quotierte Hälfte : Frauenpolitik in den grün-alternativen Parteien / herausgegeben von Regina Michalik und Elke A. Richardsen. — Berlin : LitPol, 1985. — 151p

SPD und Grüne : das neue Bündnis? / Wolfram Bickerich (Hg.). — Reinbek bei Hamburg : Rowohlt Taschenbuch Verlag, 1985. — 282p

GRÜNEN, DIE — Economic policy

Grüne Wirtschaftspolitik, machbare Utopien / Frank Beckenbach...[et. al.] ; mit einem Vorwort von Otto Schily. — [Originalausg.]. — Köln : Kiepenheuer und Witsch, 1985. — 363p . — *Bibliographies*

GRÜNEN, DIE

DRÄGER, Klaus
Aus für Grün? : die grüne Orientierungskrise zwischen Anpassung und Systemopposition / Klaus Dräger, Werner Hülsberg. — Frankfurt : ISP, 1986. — 318p

GUADELOUPE — Economic conditions

3 ans de gestion : le bilan 1982-1985. — [Basse-Terre] : Conseil général de la Guadeloupe, [1985]. — [20]p

GUADELOUPE — Economic conditions — Statistics

Recensement général de l´agriculture : 1980-1981 : inventaires par commune et par zone agricole : Guadeloupe. — [Basse-Terre?] : Service départemental de statistique agricole de Guadeloupe, [1984]. — 95p

GUADELOUPE — Economic policy

Les grandes orientations du VII ème plan. — [Basse-Terre?] : Secretariat Général, 1975. — 42p

Rapport du schéma directeur d´aménagement et d´urbanisme. — [Basse-Terre?] : Atelier d´urbanisme et de d´aménagement de la Guadeloupe, [1976?]. — 144p. — *Three maps in end pocket*

Rapport sur les orientations générales du VII ème plan. — [Basse-Terre?] : Conseil Régional, [1975]. — 33 leaves

GUADELOUPE — Politics and government

Règlement intérieur du Conseil Général de la Guadeloupe suivi de la loi du 10 aout 1871 sur les Conseils généraux. — [Basse-Terre?] : Conseil Général, 1951. — 44p

GUADELOUPE — Social conditions

3 ans de gestion : le bilan 1982-1985. — [Basse-Terre] : Conseil général de la Guadeloupe, [1985]. — [20]p

GUADELOUPE — Social policy

Les grandes orientations du VII ème plan. — [Basse-Terre?] : Secretariat Général, 1975. — 42p

Rapport sur les orientations générales du VII ème plan. — [Basse-Terre?] : Conseil Régional, [1975]. — 33 leaves

GUARANTEED ANNUAL INCOME — Great Britain

LENKOWSKY, Leslie
Politics, economics, and welfare reform : the failure of the negative income tax in Britain and the United States / Leslie Lenkowsky. — Lanham, MD : University Press of America ; [Washington, D.C.] : American Enterprise Institute for Public Policy Research, c1986. — vii, 207 p.. — *Bibliography: p. 195-206*

GUARANTEED ANNUAL INCOME — United States

LENKOWSKY, Leslie
Politics, economics, and welfare reform : the failure of the negative income tax in Britain and the United States / Leslie Lenkowsky. — Lanham, MD : University Press of America ; [Washington, D.C.] : American Enterprise Institute for Public Policy Research, c1986. — vii, 207 p.. — *Bibliography: p. 195-206*

GUARDIAN AND WARD — Australia

CARNEY, Terry
Ethical and legal issues in guardianship options for intellectually disadvantaged people / Dr. Terry Carney and Professor Peter Singer. — Canberra : Australian Government Publishing Service, 1986. — ix, 124p. — (Monograph series / Human Rights Commission ; no.2). — *Bibliography: p121-124*

GUARDIAN AND WARD — England

GREAT BRITAIN. Law Commission
Family law : review of child law : wards of court / the Law Commission. — London : H.M.S.O., 1987. — v,86p. — (Working paper / Law Commission ; no.101)

LOWE, N. V.
Wards of court / N. V. Lowe and R. A. H. White. — 2nd ed. — London : Barry Rose, 1986. — xxviii,388p

GUATEMALA — Foreign relations — United States

SCHLESINGER, Stephen C
Bitter fruit : the untold story of the American coup in Guatemala / Stephen Schlesinger and Stephen Kinzer. — 1st ed. — Garden City, N.Y. : Doubleday, 1982. — xv, 320 p., [16] p. of plates. — *Includes index. — Bibliography: p. [293]-305*

GUATEMALA — History — To 1821

LOVELL, William George
Conquest and survival in colonial Guatemala : a historical geography of the Cuchumatán Highlands, 1500-1821 / W. George Lovell. — Kingston : McGill-Queen´s University Press, c1985. — xv, 254 p., [16] p. of plates. — *Includes index. — Bibliography: p. [225]-245*

GUATEMALA — History — Revolution, 1954

SCHLESINGER, Stephen C
Bitter fruit : the untold story of the American coup in Guatemala / Stephen Schlesinger and Stephen Kinzer. — 1st ed. — Garden City, N.Y. : Doubleday, 1982. — xv, 320 p., [16] p. of plates. — *Includes index. — Bibliography: p. [293]-305*

GUATEMALA — Politics and government — 1945-

PAINTER, James
Guatemala : false hope, false freedom : the rich, the poor and the Christian Democrats / James Painter. — London : CIIR, 1987. — xviii,134p. — *Bibliography: p120. — Includes index*

TORIELLO GARRIDO, Guillermo
[La agresión imperialista contra dos revoluciones. English]. A popular history of two revolutions : Guatemala and Nicaragua / Guillermo Toriello Garrido ; translated by Rebecca Schwaner. — San Francisco : Synthesis Publications, 1985. — 58p

GUATEMALA — Social conditions

PAINTER, James
Guatemala : false hope, false freedom : the rich, the poor and the Christian Democrats / James Painter. — London : CIIR, 1987. — xviii,134p. — *Bibliography: p120. — Includes index*

GUAYAQUIL (ECUADOR) — Social conditions
MOSER, Caroline O. N.
Residential level struggle and consciousness : the experiences of poor women in Guayaquil, Ecuador / Caroline O. N. Moser. — London : Development Planning Unit, University College London, 1985. — 36p. — (DPU Gender and Planning Working Paper ; No.1). — *Bibliography: p35-36*

GUERILLAS — Argentina — History — 20th century
OLLIER, Maria Matilde
El fenómeno insurreccional y la cultura política (1969-1973) / Maria Matilde Ollier. — Buenos Aires : Centro Editor de América Latina, 1986. — 141p. — (Biblioteca Política Argentina ; 145). — *Bibliography: p139-141*

GUERRILLA WARFARE — United States — History — 20th century — Bibliography
BEEDE, Benjamin R
Intervention and counterinsurgency : an annotated bibliography of the small wars of the United States, 1898-1984 / Benjamin R. Beede. — New York : Garland Pub., 1985. — xxxviii, 321 p.. — (Wars of the United States ; vol. 5) (Garland reference library of social science ; vol. 251). — *Includes indexes*

GUERRILLAS — Central America
REED, Roger
El Salvador and the crisis in Central America / Roger Reed. — Washington, D.C. : Council for Inter-American Security, c1984. — 59 p.. — *Includes bibliographical references*

GUERRILLAS — Nicaragua — History — 20th century
NOLAN, David
The ideology of the Sandinistas and the Nicaraguan revolution / David Nolan. — Coral Gables, Fla. (P.O. Box 248123, Coral Gables 33124) : Institute of Interamerican Studies, Graduate School of International Studies, University of Miami, c1984. — v, 203 p.. — *Includes index*. — *Bibliography: p. 186-199*

GUERRILLAS — Uruguay
MERCADER, Antonio
Los Tupamaros : estrategia y acción / Antonio Mercader y Jorge de Vera. — Barcelona : Editorial Anagrama, [1986]. — 161p. — (Colección documentos ; 9). — *New edition of 'Tupamaros: estrategia y acción', Montevideo, Editoria Alfa, 1969.*

GUILD SOCIALISM
LUNDH, Christer
Gillesocialismen i England 1912-1923 : inspirationskälla för svensk arbetarrörelse / Christer Lundh. — Lund : Ekonomisk-historiska föreningen, 1982. — 130p. — (Skrifter utgivna av ekonomisk-historiska föreningen ; vol.37). — *Bibliography: p127-130*

GUILDFORD (SURREY) — History
KEE, Robert
Trial and error : the Maguires, the Guildford pub bombings and British justice / Robert Kee. — London : Hamish Hamilton, 1986. — 284p. — *Includes index*

GUILDS — Europe — History
MACKENNEY, Richard
Tradesmen and traders : the world of the guilds in Venice and Europe, c. 1250-c. 1650 / Richard MacKenney. — London : Croom Helm, c1987. — xv,289p. — *Bibliography: p257-277*. — *Includes index*

GUINEA — Bibliography
O'TOOLE, Thomas
Historical dictionary of Guinea (Republic of Guinea/Conakry) / by Thomas E. O'Toole. — Metuchen, N.J. : Scarecrow Press, 1978. — xxiv, 157 p.. — (African historical dictionaries ; no. 16). — *Bibliography: p. 79-157*

GUINEA — History — Dictionaries
O'TOOLE, Thomas
Historical dictionary of Guinea (Republic of Guinea/Conakry) / by Thomas E. O'Toole. — Metuchen, N.J. : Scarecrow Press, 1978. — xxiv, 157 p.. — (African historical dictionaries ; no. 16). — *Bibliography: p. 79-157*

GUINEA-BISSAU — Bibliography
LOBBAN, Richard
Historical dictionary of the Republics of Guinea-Bissau and Cape Verde / Richard Lobban. — Metuchen, N.J. : Scarecrow Press, 1979. — xv, 193 p.. — (African historical dictionaries ; no. 22). — *Bibliography: p. 121-184*

GUINEA BISSAU — Economic conditions — To 1974
GALLI, Rosemary
Guinea Bissau : politics, economics, and society / Rosemary Galli and Jocelyn Jones. — Boulder, Colo. : L. Rienner, 1987. — p. cm. — (Marxist regimes series). — *Includes index*. — *Bibliography: p*

GUINEA BISSAU — Economic conditions — 1974-
GALLI, Rosemary
Guinea Bissau : politics, economics, and society / Rosemary Galli and Jocelyn Jones. — Boulder, Colo. : L. Rienner, 1987. — p. cm. — (Marxist regimes series). — *Includes index*. — *Bibliography: p*

GUINEA-BISSAU — Economic policy
DAVILA, Julio D.
Shelter, poverty and African revolutionary socialism : human settlements in Guinea Bissau / Julio D. Davila. — [London] : International Institute for Environment and Development, 1987. — vi,97p. — *Bibliography: p94-97*

GUINEA-BISSAU — Foreign relations — Portugal
CABRAL, Amilcar
PAIGC : rapport general sur la lutte de liberation nationale / Amilcar Cabral. — Bissau : P.A.I.G.C., 1961. — 38p

GUINEA-BISSAU — History — Dictionaries
LOBBAN, Richard
Historical dictionary of the Republics of Guinea-Bissau and Cape Verde / Richard Lobban. — Metuchen, N.J. : Scarecrow Press, 1979. — xv, 193 p.. — (African historical dictionaries ; no. 22). — *Bibliography: p. 121-184*

GUINEA-BISSAU — Nationalism
CABRAL, Amilcar
PAIGC : rapport general sur la lutte de liberation nationale / Amilcar Cabral. — Bissau : P.A.I.G.C., 1961. — 38p

GUINEA-BISSAU — Politics and government
CABRAL, Vasco
1956-1980 : PAIGC : 24 anos de luta / Vasco Cabral. — Bissau : PAIGC, 1980. — 29p

LOPES, Carlos
Guinea Bissau : from liberation struggle to independent statehood / by Carlos Lopes ; translated by Michael Wolfers. — London : Zed, 1986. — [224]p. — *Translated from the Portuguese*. — *Includes bibliography and index*

GUINEA BISSAU — Politics and government — To 1974
GALLI, Rosemary
Guinea Bissau : politics, economics, and society / Rosemary Galli and Jocelyn Jones. — Boulder, Colo. : L. Rienner, 1987. — p. cm. — (Marxist regimes series). — *Includes index*. — *Bibliography: p*

GUINEA BISSAU — Politics and government — 1974-
GALLI, Rosemary
Guinea Bissau : politics, economics, and society / Rosemary Galli and Jocelyn Jones. — Boulder, Colo. : L. Rienner, 1987. — p. cm. — (Marxist regimes series). — *Includes index*. — *Bibliography: p*

GUINEA BISSAU — Social conditions
GALLI, Rosemary
Guinea Bissau : politics, economics, and society / Rosemary Galli and Jocelyn Jones. — Boulder, Colo. : L. Rienner, 1987. — p. cm. — (Marxist regimes series). — *Includes index*. — *Bibliography: p*

GUINEA-BISSAU — Social policy
DAVILA, Julio D.
Shelter, poverty and African revolutionary socialism : human settlements in Guinea Bissau / Julio D. Davila. — [London] : International Institute for Environment and Development, 1987. — vi,97p. — *Bibliography: p94-97*

GUINNESS GROUP — History
KOCHAN, Nick
The Guinness affair : anatomy of a scandal / Nick Kochan & Hugh Pym. — Bromley : Helm, c1987. — [224]p. — *Includes index*

GUISE, HOUSE OF
CONSTANT, Jean-Marie
Les Guise / Jean-Marie Constant. — [Paris] : Hachette littérature, c1984. — 266 p.. — *Includes index*. — *Bibliography: p. [235]-244*

GUJARAT (INDIA) — Population — Statistics
Census of India 1981. — [Delhi : Controller of Publications]
Series 5: Gujarat. — [1985]

GUJARAT (INDIA) — Rural conditions
HIRWAY, Indira
Abolition of poverty in India : with special reference to target group approach in Gujarat / Indira Hirway. — New Delhi : Vikas Pub. House, c1986. — vi, 284 p. [i.e. 184]. — *Includes bibliographies and index*

GULF COOPERATION COUNCIL
NAKHLEH, Emile A.
The Gulf Cooperation Council : policies, problems, and prospects / Emile A. Nakhleh. — New York : Praeger, 1986. — xviii, 128 p.. — "Praeger special studies. Praeger scientific.". — *Includes index*. — *Bibliography: p. 123-126*

GULF STATES — Relations — Iraq
NONNEMAN, Gerd
Iraq, the Gulf States and the war : a changing relationship 1980-1986 and beyond / Gerd Nonneman. — London : Ithaca Press, 1986. — 216p. — (Exeter Middle East politics ; no.1). — *Bibliography: p203-211*

GUN CONTROL — United States
WRIGHT, James D
Armed and considered dangerous : a survey of felons and their firearms / James D. Wright, Peter H. Rossi. — New York : Aldine de Gruyter, c1986. — xvi, 247 p.. — (Social institutions and social change). — *Includes index*. — *Bibliography: p. 239-242*

GURWITSCH, ARON — Correspondence
SCHÜTZ, Alfred
Briefwechsel 1939-1959 / Alfred Schütz [und] Aron Gurwitsch ; herausgegeben von Richard Grathoff ; mit einer Einleitung von Ludwig Landgrebe. — München : Wilhelm Fink, 1985. — xxxviii,544p. — (Übergänge : Texte und Studien zu Handung, Sprache und Lebenswelt ; Bd.4). — *Bibliography: p531-534*

GUYANA — Economic conditions — 1966-
HOPE, Kempe R
Economic development in the Caribbean / Kempe Ronald Hope. — New York : Praeger, 1986. — xv, 215p. — *Includes bibliographical references and index*

GUYANA — Economic conditions — 1966-
continuation

JEFFREY, Henry B.
Guyana : politics, economics and society : beyond the Burnham era / Henry B. Jeffrey and Colin Baber. — Boulder, Colo. : L. Rienner Publishers, 1986. — viii, 203p. — (Marxist regimes series). — *Includes index.* — *Bibliography: p [187]-191*

GUYANA — Economic policy

KING, K. F. S.
A great future together : the development and employment plan : address / by Dr. K. F. S. King. — [Georgetown? : Ministry of Economic Development?], 1973. — 28p

GUYANA — Politics and government — 1966-

JEFFREY, Henry B.
Guyana : politics, economics and society : beyond the Burnham era / Henry B. Jeffrey and Colin Baber. — Boulder, Colo. : L. Rienner Publishers, 1986. — viii, 203p. — (Marxist regimes series). — *Includes index.* — *Bibliography: p [187]-191*

GUYANA — Population

SINGH, Susheela
Guyana, Jamaica and Trinidad and Tobago : socio—economic differentials in cumulative fertility / Susheela Singh. — Voorburg : International Statistical Institute, 1984. — 89p. — (Scientific reports / World Fertility Survey ; no.57)

GUYANA — Population — Statistics

ABDULAH, Norma
Contraceptive use and fertility in the Commonwealth Caribbean / Norma Abdulah, Jack Harewood. — Voorburg : International Statistical Institute, 1984. — 55p. — (Scientific reports / World Fertility Survey ; no.60)

LIGHTBOURNE, Robert E.
Fertility preferences in Guyana, Jamaica and Trinidad and Tobago, from World Fertility Survey, 1975-77 : a multiple indicator approach / R.E. Lightbourne. — Voorburg : International Statistical Institute, 1984. — 128p. — (Scientific reports / World Fertility Survey ; no.68)

GUYANA — Social policy

KING, K. F. S.
A great future together : the development and employment plan : address / by Dr. K. F. S. King. — [Georgetown? : Ministry of Economic Development?], 1973. — 28p

GUYANA — Statistics, Vital

EBANKS, G. Edward
Infant and child mortality and fertility : Trinidad and Tobago, Guyana and Jamaica / G. Edward Ebanks. — Voorburg : International Statistical Institute, 1985. — 68p. — (Scientific reports / World Fertility Survey ; no.75)

GWYNEDD — Economic policy

Structure plans for Gwynedd : report by the Panel conducting the examination in public. — [Cardiff? : Welsh Office?], 1976. — 95p

GYNECOLOGIST AND PATIENT

FISHER, Sue
In the patient's best interest : women and the politics of medical decisions / Sue Fisher. — New Brunswick, N.J. : Rutgers University Press, c1986. — ix, 214 p.. — *Includes index.* — *Bibliography: p. 195-207*

GYNECOLOGISTS — United States — Interviews

IMBER, Jonathan B.
Abortion and the private practice of medicine / Jonathan B. Imber. — New Haven : Yale University Press, c1986. — xviii, 164 p.. — *Includes index.* — *Bibliography: p. 147-160*

GYNECOLOGY — Decision making

FISHER, Sue
In the patient's best interest : women and the politics of medical decisions / Sue Fisher. — New Brunswick, N.J. : Rutgers University Press, c1986. — ix, 214 p.. — *Includes index.* — *Bibliography: p. 195-207*

GYNECOLOGY, OPERATIVE — Decision making

FISHER, Sue
In the patient's best interest : women and the politics of medical decisions / Sue Fisher. — New Brunswick, N.J. : Rutgers University Press, c1986. — ix, 214 p.. — *Includes index.* — *Bibliography: p. 195-207*

GYPSIES — Bibliography

KENNINGTON, Don
Gypsies and travelling people : a select guide to documentary and organisational sources of information / by Don Kennington. — 3rd ed. — Stamford : Capital Planning Information, 1986. — 59p. — (CPI topicguide ; no.1). — *Previous ed.: 1982.* — *Includes bibliography and index*

GYPSIES — History

HANCOCK, Ian
The Pariah syndrome : an account of Gypsy slavery and persecution / Ian Hancock. — Ann Arbor, Mich. : Karoma, 1987. — xii,175p. — *Bibliography: p163-175*

LIÉGEOIS, Jean-Pierre
Gypsies : an illustrated history / [Jean-Pierre Liégeois] ; [translated by Tony Berrett]. — London : Al Saqi, 1986. — 192p. — *Translation of: Tsiganes.* — *Bibliography: p184-192*

GYPSIES — Information services

KENNINGTON, Don
Gypsies and travelling people : a select guide to documentary and organisational sources of information / by Don Kennington. — 3rd ed. — Stamford : Capital Planning Information, 1986. — 59p. — (CPI topicguide ; no.1). — *Previous ed.: 1982.* — *Includes bibliography and index*

HABERMAS, JÜRGEN. Theorie des kommunikativen Handelns

INGRAM, David
Habermas and the dialectic of reason / David Ingram. — New Haven, CT : Yale University Press, c1987. — xvii, 263p. — *Includes index.* — *Bibliography: p.243-254*

HABERMAS, JÜRGEN

INGRAM, David
Habermas and the dialectic of reason / David Ingram. — New Haven, CT : Yale University Press, c1987. — xvii, 263p. — *Includes index.* — *Bibliography: p.243-254*

HABERMAS, JÜRGEN — Contributions in science

ALFORD, C. Fred
Science and the revenge of nature : Marcuse & Habermas / C. Fred Alford. — Gainesville, FL : University Presses of Florida, c1985. — x, 226 p.. — *Includes index.* — *Bibliography: p. 199-210*

HACIENDAS — Mexico — History — Congresses

Haciendas in central Mexico from late colonial times to the revolution : labour conditions, hacienda management, and its relation to the state / R. Buve, ed. — Amsterdam : Centre for Latin American Research and Documentation, 1984. — 307 p.. — (CEDLA incidentele publicaties ; 28). — *Text in English and Spanish.* — *Contributions from the International Conference of "The Hacienda in Mexican History," held on 10 May 1982 in Amsterdam, organized by the Interunivrsity Centre for Study and Documentation of Latin America.* — *Includes bibliographies*

HACIENDAS — Peru — Cajamarca — History

TAYLOR, Lewis
Estates, freeholders and peasant communities in Cajamarca, 1876-1972 / by Lewis Taylor. — Cambridge : Centre of Latin American Studies, University of Cambridge, 1986. — 45p. — (Working papers / University of Cambridge, Centre of Latin American Studies ; no.42)

HACKNEY (LONDON, ENGLAND) — City planning

HACKNEY. Planning Division
The draft Hackney borough plan. — Hackney : [the Division], 1986. — 114p. — *Cover title: London Borough of Hackney: local plan: consultation draft.* — *Includes folded map in back pocket*

HACKNEY (LONDON, ENGLAND) — Population

HOWES, Eileen
Black and ethic minority population estimates / Eileen Howes. — Hackney : London Borough of Hackney. Research and Intelligence Section. Chief Executive's Office, 1986. — 27p. — (Research note / Hackney. Chief Executive's Office. Research and Intelligence Section ; 10). — *At head of cover title: Research in Hacknry*

HACKNEY (LONDON, ENGLAND) — Social policy

MERRETT, Stephen
The way forward : Haringey's local housing plan 1986-90 / compiled by Stephen Merrett. — London : Haringey Housing Information Unit, 1986. — 58p

TIPLER, Jonathan
Social services committee : review of policy implementation 1985-6 / Jonathan Tipler. — Hackney : London Borough of Hackney. Directorate of Social Services, Research Planning and Development, 1986. — 12p. — (Social service research note / Hackney. Directorate of Social Services. Research. Development and Programming ; 5). — *At head of cover title: Research in Hackney*

HAGUE. Permanent Court of International Justice

Les nouvelles conventions de la Haye : leur application par les juges nationaux. — Dordrecht : Martinus Nijhoff. — *Bibliography: p249-268*
Tome 3: Jurisprudence, situation actuelle, bibliographie / Mathilde Sumampouw. — 1984. — xx,286p

HAILE SELASSIE I, Emperor of Ethiopia

MARCUS, Harold G
Haile Sellassie I : the formative years, 1892-1936 / Harold G. Marcus. — Berkeley : University of California Press, c1986. — p. cm. — *Includes index.* — *Bibliography: p*

HAIN, PETER

HAIN, Peter
A Putney plot? Peter Hain. — Nottingham : Spokesman, 1987. — 158p. — *Includes index*

HAIRDRESSING — Great Britain

A cut below the rest : pay and conditions in hairdressing / Dominic Byrne...[et al.]. — London : Low Pay Unit, 1987. — 38p

HAITI — Economic conditions — 1971 — Statistics

Indicateurs de la conjoncture / Institut Haitien de Statistique et d'Informatique. — Port-au-Prince : Institut Haitien de Statistique et d'Informatique, 1984-. — *Annual*

HAITI — Economic conditions — 1971-

Haiti : public expenditure review. — Washington, D.C. : The World Bank, 1987. — xix,254p. — (A World Bank country study). — *Includes bibliographical references*

HAITI — Economic policy

Haiti : public expenditure review. — Washington, D.C. : The World Bank, 1987. — xix,254p. — (A World Bank country study). — *Includes bibliographical references*

HAITI — History — Revolution, 1791-1804

GARRETT, Mitchell Bennett
The French colonial question 1789-1791 : dealings of the constituent assembly with problems arising from the revolution in the West Indies / by Mitchell Bennett Garrett. — New York : Negro Universities Press, 1970. — iv,167p. — Reprint of 1916 edition. — Bibliography: p[135]-160

HAITI — Politics and government

GARRETT, Mitchell Bennett
The French colonial question 1789-1791 : dealings of the constituent assembly with problems arising from the revolution in the West Indies / by Mitchell Bennett Garrett. — New York : Negro Universities Press, 1970. — iv,167p. — Reprint of 1916 edition. — Bibliography: p[135]-160

HAITI — Population — Statistics

FORTUNAT, F.
Les déterminants proches de la fécondité en Haïti / F. Fortunat. — Voorburg : International Statistical Institute, 1984. — 77p. — (Scientific reports / World Fertility Survey ; no.61)

HAITI — Population — Statistics — Evaluation

TARDIEU, Camille
Evaluation des données de l'Enquête Haïtienne sur la Fécondité / Camille Tardieu. — Voorburg : International Statistical Institute, 1984. — 59p. — (Scientific reports / World Fertility Survey ; no.50)

HAITI — Statistics, Vital

ROUSSEAU, J. A.
La mortalité infantile et juvénile en Haïti / J. A. Rousseau. — Voorburg : International Statistical Institute, 1985. — 23p. — (Scientific reports / World Fertility Survey ; no.82)

HAITIANS — Employment — Dominican Republic

PLANT, Roger
Sugar and modern slavery : a tale of two countries / Roger Plant. — London : Zed, 1987. — [208]p. — Includes bibliography and index

HALFWAY HOUSES

Reassessing community care : (with particular reference to provision for people with mental handicap and for people with mental illness) / edited by Nigel Malin. — London : Croom Helm, c1987. — 354p. — Includes bibliographies and index

HALL, EMMETT M.

GRUENDING, Dennis
Emmett Hall : establishment radical / Dennis Gruending. — Toronto, Canada : Macmillan of Canada, c1985. — ix, 246 p., [16] p. of plates. — Includes index. — Bibliography: p. 231-243

HAMLET

KNIGHTS, L. C.
An approach to 'Hamlet' / L. C. Knights. — London : Chatto & Windus, 1960. — 91 p

HAMMER, ARMAND

HAMMER, Armand
Witness to history / by Armand Hammer with Neil Lyndon. — New York ; London : Simon & Schuster, 1987. — [512]p. — Includes index

HAMMERSMITH AND FULHAM (LONDON, ENGLAND) — Economic conditions

HAMMERSMITH AND FULHAM. Directorate of Development Planning
The long-term unemployed : a study of their characteristics and problems. — Hammersmith : [the Directorate], 1985. — 120p. — (Research report / Hammersmith and Fulham. Directorate of Development Planning ; 71)

HAMMERSMITH AND FULHAM. Unemployment and Economic Development Group
The long-term unemployed : a joint strategy for the support, training and provision of employment opportunities for long-term unemployed adults. — Hammersmith : [the Group], 1985. — 124p

HAMMERSMITH (LONDON) — Economic policy

ALLAN, Malcolm
Creating a local economic development network : a case study of Hammersmith and Fulham / Malcolm Allan, Mike Fenton, Andy Flockhart. — Glasgow : The Planning Exchange, 1985. — iii,82p

HAMMERSMITH (LONDON : ENGLAND)

EMSLEY, Ian
The development of housing associations : with special reference to London and including a case study of the London borough of Hammersmith / Ian Emsley. — New York : Garland Pub., 1986. — 477 p.. — (Outstanding theses from the London School of Economics and Political Science). — : Originally presented as the author's thesis (Ph. D.)--London School of Economics. — Bibliography: p. 464-475

HANDICAPPED

Disasters and the disabled. — New York : United Nations, 1982. — 63p. — Includes bibliographical references

HANDICAPPED — Care and treatment

Caring : experiences of looking after disabled relatives / edited by Anna Briggs and Judith Oliver. — London : Routledge & Kegan Paul, 1985

HANDICAPPED — Education — European Economic Community countries

HANSEN, Jørgen
Teaching and training the handicapped through the new information technology : computeraided special education / Jørgen Hansen. — Luxembourg : Office for Official Publications of the European Communities, 1984. — 119p. — At head of title page: Commission of the European Communities

HANDICAPPED — Employment

Adaptation of jobs and the employment of the disabled. — Geneva : International Labour Office, 1984. — xiii,112p. — Bibliography: p83-86

Employment of disabled persons : manual on selective placement. — Geneva : International Labour Office, 1984. — xv,119p. — Includes bibliographical references

STACE, Sheila
Vocational rehabilitation for women with disabilities / Sheila Stace. — Geneva : International Labour Office, 1986. — viii,38p. — Bibliography: p33-36

HANDICAPPED — Employment — European Economic Community countries

ALBEDA, Wil
Disabled people and their employment / by Wil Albeda ; in co-operation with the European Centre for Work and Society. — Luxembourg : Office for Official Publications of the European Communities, 1985. — 47p. — At head of title page: Commission of the European Communities

CROXEN, Mary
Overview : disability and employment / report by Dr. Mary Croxen. — Luxembourg : Office for Official Publications of the European Communities, 1984. — 1v.(various pagings). — At head of title page: Commission of the European Communities

The economic integration of the disabled : an analysis of measures and trends in member states / research conducted by the Centre de Sociologie du Droit Social, directed by Professor Eliane Vogel-Polsky. — Luxembourg : Office for Official Publications of the European Communities, 1984. — 1v.(various pagings). — At head of title page: Commission of the European Communities

HANDICAPPED — Employment — European Economic Community countries — Statistics

MANGIN, Guy
The handicapped and their employment : statistical study of the situation in the member states of the European Communities / by Guy Mangin. — Luxembourg : Office for Official Publications of the European Communities, 1983. — 226p

ROUAULT, Georges Y.
The handicapped and their employment : a statistical study of the situation in the Member States of the European Communities / by Georges Y. Rouault. — Luxembourg : Office for Official Publications of the European Communities, 1978. — x,214p

HANDICAPPED — Employment — Great Britain

The disabled worker. — [London] : Department of Health and Social Security : Department of Employment, 1978. — 86p. — Includes report of the "Disabled Worker" seminar held at Church House, Westminster on 21st May 1976, p27-81

Quota scheme for the employment of disabled people : working group report on suggestions for improving the scheme's effectiveness. — [Sheffield] : Manpower Services Commission, [1985]. — 102p. — Chairman: B. Swindell. — Bibliographical references: p101-102

SIKKING, Maggi
Co-ops with a difference : worker co-ops for people with special needs / Maggi Sikking. — London : ICOM, 1986. — 65p. — Bibliography: p61-62

HANDICAPPED — Government policy — Great Britain

GREAT BRITAIN. Department of Health and Social Security
Sunningdale Seminar on Disablement : progress report and discussion paper. — [London : the Department, 1978]. — 19p

HANDICAPPED — Government policy — New Brunswick

NEW BRUNSWICK. Cabinet Secretariat
Action plan for the disabled in New Brunswick. — [Fredericton] : the Secretariat, 1985. — 77,10,8,48 leaves

HANDICAPPED — Housing — Denmark

[Oversigt over institutions- og boligforhold for aeldre og handicappede]. Institutions and housing for the elderly and the handicapped in Denmark. — Copenhagen : Housing Committee for Handicapped, 1979. — 23p. — Translation of:Oversigt over institutions- og boligforhold for aeldre og handicappede

HANDICAPPED — Legal status, laws, etc. — European Economic Community countries

The economic integration of the disabled : an analysis of measures and trends in member states / research conducted by the Centre de Sociologie du Droit Social, directed by Professor Eliane Vogel-Polsky. — Luxembourg : Office for Official Publications of the European Communities, 1984. — 1v.(various pagings). — At head of title page: Commission of the European Communities

HANDICAPPED — Legal status, laws, etc. — Great Britain

GREAT BRITAIN. Parliament. House of Commons. Library. Research Division
The Chronically Sick and Disabled Persons (Amendment) Bill (Bill 15, Session 1983/84) / Christine Gillie. — [London] : the Division, 1983. — 13p. — (Reference sheet ; no.83/20). — *Bibliographical references: p12-13*

GREAT BRITAIN. Parliament. House of Commons. Library. Research Division
Disabled Persons (Services, Consultation and Representation) Bill, session 1985-86 / Christine Gillie. — [London] : the Division, 1986. — 26,xp. — (Reference sheet ; no.86/9). — *Bibligraphical references: p22-26*

HANDICAPPED — Pensions — Denmark

Samfundet og invalidepensionisterne. — 2 udg.. — [København] : Socialministeriet, 1971. — 30p

HANDICAPPED — Services for — France — Nomenclature

FRANCE. Comité des Nomenclatures
Etat des nomenclatures applicables aux établissements sanitaires et sociaux : période de validité: exercice 1986 : nomenclatures concernées, catégories d'établissements, statuts juridiques. — [Paris : Ministère des Affaires sociales et de la Solidarité nationale, 1986]. — 105p

HANDICAPPED — Taxation — Australia

The treatment of disabled persons in social security and taxation law. — Canberra : Australian Government Publishing Service, 1986. — viii,149p. — (Occasional paper / Human Rights Commission ; no.11). — *Bibliography: p134-149*

HANDICAPPED — Training of — European Economic Community countries

HANSEN, Jørgen
Teaching and training the handicapped through the new information technology : computeraided special education / Jørgen Hansen. — Luxembourg : Office for Official Publications of the European Communities, 1984. — 119p. — *At head of title page: Commission of the European Communities*

HANDICAPPED — Australia — Legal status, laws, etc.

The treatment of disabled persons in social security and taxation law. — Canberra : Australian Government Publishing Service, 1986. — viii,149p. — (Occasional paper / Human Rights Commission ; no.11). — *Bibliography: p134-149*

HANDICAPPED — Cyprus — Statistics

Census of disabled persons 1982. — [Nicosia] : Department of Statistics and Research, [1983]. — 195p. — (General Social Statistics / Cyprus. Department of Statistics and Research. Series 1 ; Report no.4)

HANDICAPPED — England — Milton Keynes (Buckinghamshire)

HIBBERD, Andrew
A report on the action on disability survey conducted in Milton Keynes by Outset. — London : Outset, 1985. — 48p

HANDICAPPED — European Economic Community countries

The economic integration of the disabled : an analysis of measures and trends in member states / research conducted by the Centre de Sociologie du Droit Social, directed by Professor Eliane Vogel-Polsky. — Luxembourg : Office for Official Publications of the European Communities, 1984. — 1v.(various pagings). — *At head of title page: Commission of the European Communities*

HANDICAPPED — Great Britain — Transportation

MCTAVISH, A. D.
Survey of concessionary bus fares for the elderly, blind and disabled in England and Wales / A. D. McTavish and P. Mullen. — London : Department of Transport, 1977. — 2,21p. — (Local transport note ; 77/1)

HANDICAPPED — India — Dadra and Nagar Haveli — Statistics

Census of India 1981 / S. K. Gandhe, Director of Census Operations, Dadra and Nagar Haveli. — [Delhi : Controller of Publications] Series 27: Dadra & Nagar Haveli. — [1985-]

HANDICAPPED CHILDREN — Education — European Economic Community countries

Special education in the European Community. — Luxembourg : Office for Official Publications of the European Communities, 1978. — 164p. — (Education series / Commission of the European Communities ; no. 11)

HANDICAPPED CHILDREN — Services for — Great Britain

PERSONAL SOCIAL SERVICES COUNCIL. People with Handicaps Group
"Fit for the future" - report of the Committee on Child Health Services : comments. — [London?] : the Group, [1977]. — 10leaves

HANDICRAFT — Taiwan

Handicraft industry on Taiwan, Republic of China. — [Taipei : Ministry of Economic Affairs, 1958]. — [28]p

HANOVER, HOUSE OF

GREGG, Edward
The Protestant succession in international politics, 1710-1716 / Edward Gregg. — New York : Garland, 1986. — 456 p.. — (Outstanding theses from the London School of Economics and Political Science). — *Bibliography: p. 417-456*

HANSA TOWNS

D'HAENENS, Albert
Europe of the North Sea and the Baltic : the world of the Hanse / Albert d'Haenens ; preface by Etienne Davignon. — Antwerp : Fonds Mercator, c1984. — 427p. — *Spine title: The world of the Hanse. — Includes bibliographies*

HANSA TOWNS — History

D'HAENENS, Albert
Europe of the North Sea and the Baltic : the world of the Hanse / Albert d'Haenens ; preface by Etienne Davignon. — Antwerp : Fonds Mercator, c1984. — 427p. — *Spine title: The world of the Hanse. — Includes bibliographies*

HAO (TUAMOTU ISLANDS) — Population — Statistics

Tableaux normalisés du recensement général de la population : 15 octobre 1983. — [Papeete] : Institut territorial de la statistique Résultats de la commune de Hao. — [1985?]. — 4p,ll leaves

HAOUZ (MOROCCO) — Economic conditions

PASCON, Paul
Capitalism and agriculture in the Haouz of Marrakesh / Paul Pascon ; edited with an introduction to the English edition by John R. Hall ; translated by C. Edwin Vaughan and Veronique Ingman. — London : Routledge and Kegan Paul, 1986. — xiv,248p. — *Bibliography: p233-242*

HAPPINESS

ARGYLE, Michael
The psychology of happiness / Michael Argyle. — London : Methuen, 1987. — xv, 256p. — *Bibliography: p.[218]-245*

HARBORS

FRANKEL, Ernst G
Port planning and development / Ernst G. Frankel. — New York : Wiley, [1986]. — p. cm. — "A Wiley-Interscience publication.". — *Includes index. — Bibliography: p*

HARBORS — Design and contruction

Port development : a handbook for planners in developing countries / prepared by the secretariat of UNCTAD. — 2nd ed., rev. and expanded. — New York : United Nations, 1985. — xiv,227p. — ([Document] / United Nations ; TD/B/C.4/175/Rev.1). — *Bibliography: p225-227. — Sales no.: E.84.II.D.1*

HARBORS — Management

Port development : a handbook for planners in developing countries / prepared by the secretariat of UNCTAD. — 2nd ed., rev. and expanded. — New York : United Nations, 1985. — xiv,227p. — ([Document] / United Nations ; TD/B/C.4/175/Rev.1). — *Bibliography: p225-227. — Sales no.: E.84.II.D.1*

HARBORS — Maps

Lloyd's maritime atlas of world ports and shipping places / editors, A.K.C. Beresford, H.W. Dobson, C. Holmes. — 15th ed. — Colchester : Lloyd's of London Press, 1986. — [144]p. — *Previous ed.: 1983. — Includes bibliography and index*

HARBORS — Planning

FRANKEL, Ernst G
Port planning and development / Ernst G. Frankel. — New York : Wiley, [1986]. — p. cm. — "A Wiley-Interscience publication.". — *Includes index. — Bibliography: p*

HARBORS — Canada — Finance

CANADA. Transport Canada
Annual report : public harbours and port facilities : report on financial operations = Rapport annuel : ports et installations de port publics : rapport sur les opérations financières / Transport Canada. — Ottawa : Transport Canada, 1984/85-. — *Annual. — Text in English and French*

HARBORS — Developing countries

Port development : a handbook for planners in developing countries / prepared by the secretariat of UNCTAD. — 2nd ed., rev. and expanded. — New York : United Nations, 1985. — xiv,227p. — ([Document] / United Nations ; TD/B/C.4/175/Rev.1). — *Bibliography: p225-227. — Sales no.: E.84.II.D.1*

HARBORS — France — Normandy

HAUTE-NORMANDIE (FRANCE). Comité économique et sociale
Un projet portuaire régional : adopté par le Comité économique et social de Haute-Normandie au cours de sa séance du 23 novembre 1984 / sur le rapport de Robert Gireme, Dominique Gambier. — [Rouen] : Comité économique et social, [1985]. — 157 [22]p. — *Cover title*

HARBORS — Great Britain — Finance — Law and legislation

GREAT BRITAIN. Parliament. House of Commons. Library. Research Division
Ports (Financial Assistance) Bill / Christopher Barclay, Robert Twigger, Celia Nield. — [London] : the Division, 1981. — 14p. — (Reference sheet ; no.81/12). — *Bibliographical references: p14*

HARD-CORE UNEMPLOYED — France

FRANCE. Agence nationale pour l'emploi. Division des Etudes
Les demandeurs d'emploi de longue durée : analyse d'une population. — [Paris : Agence nationale pour l'emploi, 1983. — 2v. — *Vol.2 contains annexes*

HARD-CORE UNEMPLOYED — United States
MAHARIDGE, Dale
  Journey to nowhere : the saga of the new underclass / by Dale Maharidge ; photographs by Michael Williamson. — Garden City, N.Y. : Doubleday, 1984. — p. cm. *"Dolphin book."*

HARDINGE, HENRY HARDINGE, Viscount
HARDINGE, Henry Hardinge, Viscount
  The letters of the first Viscount Hardinge of Lahore to Lady Hardinge and Sir Walter and Lady James, 1844-1847 / Bawa Satinder Singh, editor. — London : Royal Historical Society, 1986. — [300]p. — (Camden Fourth series : v.32). — *Includes bibliography and index*

HARE KRISHNAS — Psychology
POLING, Tommy H
  The Hare Krishna character type : a study of the sensate personality / Tommy H. Poling & J. Frank Kenney. — Lewiston N.Y. : E. Mellen Press, c1986. — 184 p.. — (Studies in religion and society ; v. 15). — *Bibliography: p.178-184*

HAREM
ALLOULA, Malek
  [Harem colonial. English]. The colonial harem / Malek Alloula ; translation by Myrna Godzich and Wlad Godzich ; introduction by Barbara Harlow. — Minneapolis : University of Minnesota Press, c1986. — xxii, 135 p.. — (Theory and history of literature ; v. 21). — *Translation of: Le harem colonial.* — *Bibliography: p. 135*

HARINGEY (LONDON, ENGLAND) — Industries
HARINGEY TOWN PLANNING SERVICE
  Industrial land needs study : policy background paper. — Haringey : Haringey Town Planning Service, 1986. — 12p. — (Planning working note / Haringey Town Planning Service ; 16)

HARINGEY (LONDON, ENGLAND) — Population — Statistics
HARINGEY TOWN PLANNING SERVICE
  1981 : census word digest. — Haringey : London Borough of Haringey. — (Planning working paper / Haringey Town Planning Service ; 7)
  1: a summary of the 1981 small area statistics (100%) word data. — 1982. — [64p]

HARINGEY TOWN PLANNING SERVICE
  1981 census ward digest. — Haringey : London Borough of Haringey. — (Planning working paper / Haringey Town Planning Service ; 8)
  2: A summary of the 1981 small area statistics (10%) ward data. — 1982. — [44p]

HARINGEY (LONDON, ENGLAND) — Social conditions
HARINGEY TOWN PLANNING SERVICE
  Community profile. — Haringey : London Borough of Haringey, 1982. — in 13 parts

HARLAND AND WOLFF — Northern Ireland — Belfast — History
MOSS, Michael S.
  Shipbuilders to the world : 125 years of Harland and Wolff, Belfast, 1861-1986 / Michael Moss and John R. Hume. — Belfast : Blackstaff, 1986. — xvii,601p,[10]p of plates. — *Bibliography: p502-505.* — *Includes index*

HARRIMAN, EDWARD HENRY
MERCER, Lloyd J
  E.H. Harriman, master railroader / Lloyd J. Mercer. — Boston, Mass. : Twayne Publishers, c1985. — p. cm. — (The Evolution of American business). — *Includes index.* — *Bibliography: p*

HARRIS, CHAUNCY DENNISON
  World patterns of modern urban change : essays in honor of Chauncy D. Harris / edited by Michael P. Conzen. — Chicago : University of Chicago, Dept. of Geography, 1985. — p. cm. — (Research paper / the University of Chicago, Department of Geography ; no. 217-218). — *Includes index*

HARROW (LONDON, ENGLAND) — Social conditions
  The tenant census / M. Wright. — Harrow : Department of Housing, 1986. — [8]p

HART, H. L. A.
  Issues in contemporary legal philosophy : the influence of H.L.A. Hart / edited by Ruth Gavison. — Oxford : Clarendon, 1987. — [368]p. — *Includes bibliography and index*

HARVARD INSTITUTE FOR INTERNATIONAL DEVELOPMENT
MASON, Edward Sagendorph
  The Harvard Institute for International Development and its antecedents / Edward S. Mason. — [Cambridge, Mass.] : Harvard Institute for International Development, Harvard University ; Lanham, MD : University Press of America, c1986. — x, 97 p.. — *Bibliography: p. 74-78*

HARVARD UNIVERSITY — Presidents — Biography
SMITH, Richard Norton
  The Harvard century : the making of a university to a nation / Richard Norton Smith. — New York : Simon and Schuster, c1986. — 397 p., [8] p. of plates. — *Includes index.* — *Bibliography: p. 340-377*

HASINA, SHEIKH
HASINA, Sheikh
  Address by Sheikh Hasina, President, Bangladesh Awami League at the inaugural session of Awami League's National Council on 1 January 1987. — London : Radical Asia Publications, 1987. — 16p

HASKALAH — Congresses
  Toward modernity : the European Jewish model / edited by Jacob Katz. — New Brunswick, N.J. : Transaction, Inc., c1986. — p. cm. — *Includes bibliographies and index*

HAULTIN, PIERRE
DROZ, E.
  Complément à la bibliographie de Pierre Haultin / E. Droz. — Genève : E. Droz, 1961. — p.375-394. — (Bibliothèque d'humanisme et renaissance. travaux et documents ; Tome 23). — *Offprint*

HAUTES-PYRÉNÉES (FRANCE)
  Les départements français. — Paris : La Documentation française, 1985. — (Notes et études documentaires ; no.4799)
  65: Les départments français 4h Hautes-Pyrénées, Midi-Pyrénées / Robert Boure [et al.]. — 118p

HAVEL, VÁCLAV
  Václav Havel, or, Living in truth : twenty-two essays published on the occasion of the award of the Erasmus Prize to Václav Havel / edited by Jan Vladislav. — London : Faber, 1987. — xix,315p. — *Translation from various European languages*

HAVERING (LONDON, ENGLAND) — History
MCINTOSH, Marjorie Keniston
  Autonomy and community : the Royal Manor of Havering, 1200-1500 / Marjorie Keniston McIntosh. — Cambridge : Cambridge University Press, 1986. — [460]p. — (Cambridge studies in medieval life and thought. Fourth series). — *Includes bibliography and index*

HAWAII — Economic conditions
HAWKINS, Richard Adrian
  Economic diversification in the American Pacific Territory of Hawai'i, 1893-1941 / Richard Adrian Hawkins. — 576 leaves. — PhD (Econ) 1986 LSE. — Leaves 547-576 are appendices

HAWAII — Economic conditions — 1959-
  The political economy of Hawaii / Gerard Sullivan, Gary Hawes, guest editors. — Honolulu : University of Hawaii Press, 1985. — xii,216p. — *Special issue of Social Processes in Hawaii, vol.31, 1984-5.* — *Bibliographies*

HAWAII — Kings and rulers — Religious aspects
VALERI, Valerio
  Kingship and sacrifice : ritual and society in ancient Hawaii / Valerio Valeri ; translated by Paula Wissing. — Chicago : University of Chicago Press, 1985. — p. cm. — *Translated from the French.* — *Includes index.* — *Bibliography: p*

HAWAII — Politics and government — 1959-
  The political economy of Hawaii / Gerard Sullivan, Gary Hawes, guest editors. — Honolulu : University of Hawaii Press, 1985. — xii,216p. — *Special issue of Social Processes in Hawaii, vol.31, 1984-5.* — *Bibliographies*

HAWAII — Religion
VALERI, Valerio
  Kingship and sacrifice : ritual and society in ancient Hawaii / Valerio Valeri ; translated by Paula Wissing. — Chicago : University of Chicago Press, 1985. — p. cm. — *Translated from the French.* — *Includes index.* — *Bibliography: p*

HAWAII — Social conditions
  The political economy of Hawaii / Gerard Sullivan, Gary Hawes, guest editors. — Honolulu : University of Hawaii Press, 1985. — xii,216p. — *Special issue of Social Processes in Hawaii, vol.31, 1984-5.* — *Bibliographies*

HAWAII — Social life and customs
VALERI, Valerio
  Kingship and sacrifice : ritual and society in ancient Hawaii / Valerio Valeri ; translated by Paula Wissing. — Chicago : University of Chicago Press, 1985. — p. cm. — *Translated from the French.* — *Includes index.* — *Bibliography: p*

HAWKS, ESTHER HILL
HAWKS, Esther Hill
  A woman doctor's Civil War : Esther Hill Hawks' diary / edited with a foreword and afterword by Gerald Schwartz. — 1st ed. — Columbia, S.C. : University of South Carolina Press, c1984. — p. cm. — *Bibliography: p283-288.* — *Bibliography: p*

HAWKS NEST TUNNEL (W. VA.)
CHERNIACK, Martin
  The Hawk's Nest incident : America's worst industrial disaster / Martin Cherniack ; foreword by Phillip Landrigan and Anthony Robbins. — New Haven : Yale University Press, c1986. — x, 194p, [16]p of plates. — *Includes index.* — *Bibliography: p.184-188*

HAWLEY GROUP PLC
SERVICES TO COMMUNITY ACTION AND TRADE UNIONS
  Hawley Group PLC Cleaning up? / researched by Services to Community Action and Trade Unions and Hillingdon Trade Union Support Unit. — London : SCAT Publications, 1986. — [8]p

HAYEK, F. A.
HANNES H. GISSURARSON
  Hayek's conservative liberalism / Hannes H. Gissurarson. — New York : Garland Pub., 1987. — 222 p.. — (Political theory and political philosophy). — *Originally presented as the author's thesis (Ph. D.--Oxford University, 1985).* — *Includes index.* — *Bibliography: p. 206-220*

HAZARDOUS SUBSTANCES — Accidents
SCHUCK, Peter H
  Agent Orange on trial : mass toxic disasters in the courts / Peter H. Schuck. — Cambridge, Mass. : Belknap Press of Harvard University Press, 1986. — ix, 347 p.. — *Includes index.* — *Bibliography: p. [301]-335*

HAZARDOUS SUBSTANCES — Packaging — Law and legislation — Great Britain

GREAT BRITAIN. Health and Safety Commission
Proposals for packaging and labelling of dangerous substances (amendment) regulations. — London : H.M.S.O., 1980. — 10p. — (Consultative document / Health and Safety Commission)

HAZARDOUS SUBSTANCES — Great Britain

GREAT BRITAIN INTERDEPARTMENTAL COMMITTEE ON THE REDEVELOPMENT OF CONTAMINATED LAND
Progress report of the Interdepartmental Committee on the Redevelopment of Contaminated Land, 1979. — [London : Department of the Environment, 1979]. — [12]. — *Bibliographical references: p[11]*. — ICRCL 19/79

HAZARDOUS WASTE SITES — Hygienic aspects — United States — Statistics

GOULD, Jay M
Quality of life in American neighborhoods : levels of affluence, toxic waste, and cancer mortality in residential Zip code areas / Jay M. Gould ; edited by Alice Tepper Marlin. — Boulder : Westview Press, 1986. — ix, 402 p.. — *"Published in cooperation with the Council on Economic Priorities."*

HAZARDOUS WASTE SITES — Location

CHATTERJI, Manas
Hazardous materials disposal : siting and management / edited by Manas Chatterji. — Aldershot : Avebury, c1987. — 331p. — *Includes bibliography*

HAZARDOUS WASTE SITES — Management

CHATTERJI, Manas
Hazardous materials disposal : siting and management / edited by Manas Chatterji. — Aldershot : Avebury, c1987. — 331p. — *Includes bibliography*

HAZARDOUS WASTES

CHATTERJI, Manas
Hazardous materials disposal : siting and management / edited by Manas Chatterji. — Aldershot : Avebury, c1987. — 331p. — *Includes bibliography*

GREAT BRITAIN. Central Directorate of Environmental Protection
Monitoring waste : the duty of care : the Government's response to the eleventh report of the Royal Commission on Environmental Pollution / Central Directorate of Environmental Protection, Department of the Environment. — London : H.M.S.O., 1986. — (Pollution paper ; no.24)

HAZARDOUS WASTES — Organisation for Economic Co-operation and Development countries

YAKOWITZ, Harvey
Fate of small quantities of hazardous waste. — [Paris] : OECD, 1986. — 100p. — (OECD environment monographs ; no.6). — *Includes bibliographical references*

HAZLETON (PA.) — Population

AURAND, Harold W
Population change and social continuity : ten years in a coal town / Harold W. Aurand. — Selinsgrove [Pa.] : Susquehanna University Press ; London : Associated University Presses, c1986. — 139 p.. — *Includes index*. — *Bibliography: p. 131-134*

HAZLETON (PA.) — Social conditions

AURAND, Harold W
Population change and social continuity : ten years in a coal town / Harold W. Aurand. — Selinsgrove [Pa.] : Susquehanna University Press ; London : Associated University Presses, c1986. — 139 p.. — *Includes index*. — *Bibliography: p. 131-134*

HEADS OF HOUSEHOLDS — England — Statistics

1981 census of population : household and family headship in the London boroughs and the counties of south east England / prepared in the Intelligence Unit by Bill Armstrong. — [London] : Greater London Council, 1985. — 1v (various pagings). — (Statistical series / Greater London Council ; no.45)

HEADS OF HOUSEHOLDS — England — London — Statistics

1981 census of population : household and family headship in the London boroughs and the counties of south east England / prepared in the Intelligence Unit by Bill Armstrong. — [London] : Greater London Council, 1985. — 1v (various pagings). — (Statistical series / Greater London Council ; no.45)

HEADS OF HOUSEHOLDS — France — Statistics

TAFFIN, Claude
Le patrimoine de logements en 1978 / Claude Taffin. — Paris : I.N.S.E.E., 1986. — 103p. — (Archives et documents / Institut national de la statistique et des études économiques ; no.154). — *Bibliographical references: p103*

HEADS OF HOUSEHOLDS — Poland

LINK, Krzysztof
Społeczno-ekonomiczne czynniki tworzenia gospodarstw domowych / Krzysztof Link. — Warszawa : Szkoła Główna Planowania i Statystyki, 1986. — 155p. — (Kształtowanie procesów demograficznych a rozwój społeczno-gospodarczy Polski) (Monografie i opracowania / Szkoła Główna Planowania i Statystyki). — *Contents and summary in English and Russian*

HEADS OF STATE — Handbooks, manuals stc.

TRUHART, Peter
Regents of nations : systematic chronology of states and their political representives in past and present : a biographical reference book = Regenten der Nationen : systematische Chronologie die Sraaten und ihrer politischen Repräsentanten in Vergangenheit und Gegenwart : ein biographisches Nachgeschlagewerk / Peter Truhart. — München : K.G. Saur. — *Headings in English and German*
Pt.3
1: Mittel-, Ost-, Nord-, Süd-, Südosteuropa. — 1986. — xii,2280-3357

HEADS OF STATE — Health and hygiene

PARK, Bert Edward
The impact of illness on world leaders / Bert Edward Park. — Philadelphia : University of Pennsylvania Press, 1986. — p. cm. — *Includes bibliographies and index*

HEADS OF STATE — China — Biography

MAO, Zedong
The writings of Mao Zedong, 1949-1976 / edited by Michael Y.M. Kau, John K. Leung. — Armonk, N.Y. ; London : M.E. Sharpe. — *Translated from the Chinese*
Vol.1: September 1949-December 1955. — c1986. — xli,771p. — *Bibliography: p755-771*

HEADS OF STATE — Cuba — Biography

BOURNE, Peter G.
[Fidel : una biografia de Fidel Castro. English]. Castro : a biography of Fidel Castro / Peter Bourne. — London : Macmillan, 1987, c1986. — xii,332,[17]p of plates. — *Originally published: New York : Dodd, Mead, 1986.* — *Bibliography: p319-322*. — *Includes index*

GONZALEZ, Edward
Castro, Cuba, and the world / Edward Gonzalez, David Ronfeldt. — Santa Monica, CA. : Rand, 1986. — xx, 133 p. — *"June 1986."*. — *"R-3420."*. — *Includes bibliographical references*

HEADS OF STATE — Germany — Biography

WAGENER, Otto
Hitler : memoirs of a confidant / edited by Henry Ashby Turner, Jr. ; translated by Ruth Hein. — New Haven ; London : Yale University Press, c1985. — xxvi,333p,[14]p of plates. — *Translation of: Hitler aus nächster Nähe*. — *Author: Otto Wagener*. — *Includes index*

HEADS OF STATE — Soviet Union — Biography

CAMERON, Kenneth Neill
Stalin : Man of contradiction / Kenneth Neill Cameron. — Toronto : NC Press Limited, 1987. — 190p. — *Bibliography: p181-184*

HEADS OF STATE — Soviet Union — Succession

COLTON, Timothy J.
The dilemma of reform in the Soviet Union / Timothy J. Colton. — Rev. and expanded ed. — New York : Council of Foreign relations, 1986. — p. cm. — *Includes index*

HEALING — Thailand

GOLOMB, Louis
An anthropology of curing in multiethnic Thailand / Louis Golomb. — Urbana : University of Illinois Press, c1985. — p. cm. — (Illinois studies in anthropology ; no. 15). — *Includes index*. — *Bibliography: p*

HEALTH

A Diet of reason : sense and nonsense in the healthy eating debate / edtited by Digby Anderson. — [London] : Social Affairs Unit, c1986. — 150p

HO, Teresa J.
Measuring health as a component of living standards / Teresa J. Ho. — Washington, D.C., U.S.A. : World Bank, c1982 ((1985 printing)). — 58p. — (LSMS working papers ; no.15) (LSMS working papers ; no. 15). — *Bibliography: p56-58*

HEALTH — Addresses, essays, lectures

Imperialism, health and medicine / edited by Vicente Navarro. — Farmingdale,N.Y. : Baywood, 1981. — 282p. — (Policy, politics, health and medicine). — *Collection of essays*

HEALTH — Moral and ethical aspects

GRIFFIN, James, 1933-
Well-being : its meaning, measurement and moral importance / James Griffin. — Oxford : Clarendon, 1986. — xii,412p. — *Bibliography: p391-402*. — *Includes index*

HEALTH — United States

GINZBERG, Eli
Local health policy in action : the Municipal Health Services Program / Eli Ginzberg, Edith Davis, Miriam Ostow. — Totowa, N.J. : Rowman & Allanheld, c1985. — xiv, 136 p.. — (LandMark studies). — *Includes bibliographies and index*

HEALTH AND RACE — England

Racial equality and good practice maternity care : a report of two workshops held in Bradford organised by Training in Health and Race and the Centre for Ethnic Minorities Health Studies / compiled by Maggie Pearson ; Health Education Council and National Extension College for Training in Health and Race. — London : Training in Health and Race, 1985. — 37p. — *Bibliographical references: p36-37*

HEALTH AND SOCIAL SECURITY BILL 1983-84

GREAT BRITAIN. Parliament. House of Commons. Library. Research Division
Health and Social Security Bill 1983 / Keith Cuninghame, Julia Lourie, Christine Gillie. — [London] : the Division, 1983. — 50p. — (Reference sheet ; no.83/24). — *Includes bibliographical references*

HEALTH ATTITUDES
CALNAN, Michael
Health and illness : the lay perspective / Michael Calnan. — London : Tavistock, 1987. — [192]p. — *Includes index*

HEALTH ATTITUDES — Great Britain
WHITEHEAD, Margaret
The health divide : inequalities in health in the 1980's / Margaret Whitehead. — London : Health Education Council, 1987. — iv,119p

HEALTH BEHAVIOR
CALNAN, Michael
Health and illness : the lay perspective / Michael Calnan. — London : Tavistock, 1987. — [192]p. — *Includes index*

HEALTH BEHAVIOR — Congresses
RUSSELL, Louise B
Evaluating preventive care : report on a workshop / Louise B. Russell. — Washington, D.C. : Brookings Institution, c1987. — p. cm. — (Studies in social economics). — *Workshop held May 8-9, 1986, and sponsored by the Brookings Institution. — Includes index. — Bibliography: p*

HEALTH EDUCATION — Political aspects — Great Britain
The Politics of health education : raising the issues / edited by Sue Rodmell & Alison Watt. — London : Routledge & Kegan Paul, 1986. — x,241p. — *Bibliography: p224-235. — Includes index*

HEALTH EDUCATION — Europe
Self-help and health in Europe : new approaches in health care / edited by Stephen Hatch and Ilona Kickbusch. — Copenhagen : WHO Regional Office for Europe, 1983

HEALTH EDUCATION — Wales
WORKING PARTY ON HEALTH EDUCATION IN WALES
Report of a Working Party on health education in Wales. — [S.L.] : Welsh General Medical Services Committee, 1978. — [14]leaves. — *Chairman: D. Hubert Jones. — Bibliographical references: p[13]*

HEALTH FACILITIES — Albania
CIKULI, Zisa
Health service in the Peoples Socialist Republic of Albania / Zisa Cikuli. — Tirana : 8 Nentori Publishing House, 1984. — 88p

HEALTH FACILITIES — England
TOWNSEND, Peter
Inequalities in health in the northern region : an interim report / Peter Townsend, Peter Phillimore [and] Alastair Beattie. — Bristol : University of Bristol ; Newcastle upon Tyne : Northern Regional Health Authority, 1986. — 252p. — *Bibliography: p245-252*

HEALTH FACILITIES — France — Nomenclature
FRANCE. Comité des Nomenclatures
Etat des nomenclatures applicables aux établissements sanitaires et sociaux : période de validité: exercice 1986 : nomenclatures concernées, catégories d'établissements, statuts juridiques. — [Paris : Ministère des Affaires sociales et de la Solidarité nationale, 1986]. — 105p

HEALTH FACILITIES — Greenland
Sundhedstilstanden i Grønland : Landslaegens °arsberetning = the state of health in Greenland: annual report from the Chief Medical Officer in Greenland / Ministeriet for Grønland, Denmark. — København : Ministeriet for Grønland, 1982-. — *Annual. — Text in Danish with English summary and table headings*

HEALTH FACILITIES — Namibia
A nation in peril : health in apartheid Namibia. — London : International Defence and Aid Fund, 1985. — 40p. — (Fact paper on Southern Africa ; no.13)

HEALTH FACILITIES — South Africa
SOUTH AFRICA
White paper on the report of the Commission of Inquiry into Health Services (The Browne Report). — [Pretoria : Government Printer, 1986]. — 46p. — *In English and Afrikaans*

HEALTH FACILITIES — Sweden
DODD, John
Swedish hospitals and health services : notes and impressions / John Dodd. — Bristol : British Hospitals Contributory Schemes Association, 1950. — 42p

HEALTH FACILITIES, PROPRIETARY — Great Britain — Surveys
LAING, William
Private health care, 1985 / William Laing. — London : Office of Health Economics, [1985]. — 55 p.

HEALTH INSURANCE FOR AGED AND DISABLED, TITLE 18 — history
FEIN, Rashi
Medical care, medical costs : the search for a health insurance policy / Rashi Fein. — Cambridge, Mass. : Harvard University Press, 1986. — viii, 240 p.. — *Includes index*

HEALTH MAINTENANCE ORGANIZATIONS — Great Britain
GREAT BRITAIN. Parliament. House of Commons. Library. Research Division
Health maintenance organisations : the future for British health care? / Keith Cuninghame. — [London] : the Division, 1986. — 16p. — (Background paper ; no.191). — *Bibliography: p15-16*

HEALTH MAINTENANCE ORGANIZATIONS — United States
GREAT BRITAIN. Parliament. House of Commons. Library. Research Division
Health maintenance organisations : the future for British health care? / Keith Cuninghame. — [London] : the Division, 1986. — 16p. — (Background paper ; no.191). — *Bibliography: p15-16*

HEALTH PLANNING — Africa
Towards a philosophy of health work in the African region. — Brazzaville : Regional Office for Africa, World Health Organization, 1970. — 38p. — (AFRO technical papers ; no.1). — *Includes bibliographical references*

HEALTH PLANNING
Health manpower planning : principles, methods, issues / edited by T. L. Hall and A. Mejía. — Geneva : World Health Organization, ; [Albany, N.Y. : distributed by WHO Publications Centre USA], 1978. — 311p. — *Includes bibliographical references*

The international journal of health planning and management. — Chichester : John Wiley, 1985-. — *Quarterly*

Investigating practices in health manpower planning : report on country case study. — Copenhagen : World Health Organization, 1986. — 41p

HEALTH PLANNING — Africa
An integrated concept of the public health services in the African region / Contributors, B. Adjou-Moumouni...[et al.]. — Brazzaville : Regional Office for Africa, World Health Organization, 1970. — 108p. — (AFRO technical papers ; no.2). — *Includes bibliographies*

WORLD HEALTH ORGANIZATION. Regional Committee for Africa
National health planning : its value and methods of preparation ; The place of public health in the economy of the African countries ; The principles and methods of evaluation of national health. — Brazzaville : Regional Office for Africa, World Health Organization, 1974. — 150p. — (AFRO technical papers ; no.7). — *Includes bibliographies. — Background papers for the technical discussions of the 18th, 19th and the 20th sessions of the Regional Committee for Africa*

WORLD HEALTH ORGANIZATION. Regional Experts Meeting on Health Manpower Development (1977 : Brazzaville)
Health manpower development : the problems of the health team : report / of a WHO Regional Experts Meeting on Health Manpower Development. — Brazzaville : Regional Office for Africa, World Health Organization, 1977. — [viii]13p. — (AFRO technical report series ; no.4). — *Includes bibliographical references*

HEALTH PLANNING — Denmark
DENMARK. Sundhedsprioriteringsudvalget
Extract from the report on the Committee of Health Priorities. — Copenhagen : Ministry of the Interior, 1981. — 87p

Redegørelse ´84 om social- og sundhedsplanlaegning 1984-88. — [København] : Socialstyrelsen, 1984. — 177p

HEALTH PLANNING — Developing countries
MACH, E. P
Planning the finances of the health sector : a manual for developing countries / by E.P. Mach, B. Abel-Smith. — Geneva : World Health Organization, 1983. — 124p. — *Bibliography: p105-106*

HEALTH PLANNING — England
OXFORD REGIONAL HEALTH AUTHORITY
The strategic plan in outline to 1991 : for discussion and development. — [Oxford] : the Authority, 1978. — 121,[16]p

HEALTH PLANNING — Europe — Methodology
Health projections in Europe : Methods and applications. — Copenhagen : World Health Organization, Regional Office for Europe, 1986. — xxi,306p. — *Includes bibliographical references*

HEALTH PLANNING — Great Britain
GREAT BRITAIN. Department of Health and Social Security
Option appraisal : a guide for the National Health Service. — London : H.M.S.O., 1987. — 42p. — *Bibliography: p41-42*

Investigating practices in health manpower planning : report on country case study. — Copenhagen : World Health Organization, 1986. — 41p

HEALTH PLANNING — Nepal
JUSTICE, Judith
Policies, plans, and people : culture and health development in Nepal / Judith Justice. — Berkeley : University of California Press, c1986. — p. cm. — (Comparative studies of health systems and medical care). — *Includes index. — Bibliography: p*

HEALTH PLANNING — Wales
GREAT BRITAIN. Welsh Office. Health and Social Work Department
Joint planning - health and local authorities : joint financing of personal social services projects. — Cardiff : the Office, 1977. — 4,4p. — (Health circular ; WHC (77)21)

HEALTH POLICY
Mobilizing against AIDS : the unfinished story of a virus / Institute of Medicine, National Academy of Sciences ; Eve K. Nichols, writer. — Cambridge, Mass. : Harvard University Press, 1986. — x, 212 p.. — *Drawn from the 1985 Annual Meeting of the Institute of Medicine. — Includes index. — Bibliography: p. 189-190*

HEALTH POLICY — Congresses
Systèmes de santé, pouvoirs publics et financeurs : qui contrôle quoi? : communications présentés au Colloque sur les politiques de santé étrangères...25 et 26 mars 1985. — [Paris : La Documentation française, 1987]. — 407p

HEALTH POLICY — economics — United States
FUCHS, Victor R
The health economy / Victor R. Fuchs. — Cambridge, Mass. ; London : Harvard University Press, 1986. — viii, 401p. — *Includes index. — Bibliography: p.385-386*

HEALTH POLICY — history — Great Britain
HOLLINGSWORTH, J. Rogers
A political economy of medicine : Great Britain and the United States / J. Rogers Hollingsworth. — Baltimore : Johns Hopkins University Press, c1986. — xix, 312 p.. — *Includes index. — Bibliography: p. 275-303*

HEALTH POLICY — trends — United States
CALIFANO, Joseph A.
America's health care revolution : who lives? who dies? who pays? / Joseph A. Califano, Jr. — 1st ed. — New York : Random House, c1986. — x, 241 p.. — *Includes index. — Bibliography: p. [227]-230*

HEALTH POLICY — trends — United States — congresses
CORNELL UNIVERSITY MEDICAL COLLEGE CONFERENCE ON HEALTH POLICY (1985 : New York, N.Y.)
The U.S. health care system : a look to the 1990s / Cornell University Medical College Conference on Health Policy, March 7-8, 1985, New York City ; Eli Ginzberg, editor. — Totowa, N.J. : Rowman & Allanheld, 1985. — x, 133 p.. — (Conservation of human resources series ; 26) (Land Mark studies). — *Includes index. — Bibliography: p. 115-123*

HEALTH POLICY — United States
GINZBERG, Eli
Local health policy in action : the Municipal Health Services Program / Eli Ginzberg, Edith Davis, Miriam Ostow. — Totowa, N.J. : Rowman & Allanheld, c1985. — xiv, 136 p.. — (LandMark studies). — *Includes bibliographies and index*

HEALTH RESORTS, WATERING PLACES, ETC. — Norway
KROHN-HOLM, Jan W.
Farriskildene i Larvik gjennem 150 °ar / Jan W. Krohn-Holm. — Larvik : Utgitt av Farris, 1971. — 165p

HEALTH RESORTS, WATERING PLACES, ETC. — Soviet Union
POLTORANOV, V. V.
Zdravnitsy profsoiuzov SSSR : kurorty, sanatorii, pansionaty, doma otdykha / V. V. Poltoranov, S. Ia. Slutskii ; pod redaktsiei I. I. Kozlova. — Izd. 6-e, perer. i dop.. — Moskva : Profizdat, 1986. — 700p

HEALTH RISK ASSESSMENT — Congresses
Hazards : technology and fairness / National Academy of Engineering. — Washington, D.C. : National Academy Press, 1986. — viii, 225 p.. — (Series on technology and social priorities). — *Consists of papers based on the Symposium on Hazards: Technology and Fairness, held June 3-4, 1985. — Includes bibliographies and index*

HEALTH RISK ASSESSMENT — Government policy — United States — History
RUSHEFSKY, Mark R.
Making cancer policy / Mark R. Rushefsky. — Albany : State University of New York Press, c1986. — xiii, 257 p.. — (SUNY series in public administration in the 1980s). — *Includes index. — Bibliography: p. 225-245*

HEALTH SERVICES — economics — United States
FUCHS, Victor R
The health economy / Victor R. Fuchs. — Cambridge, Mass. ; London : Harvard University Press, 1986. — viii, 401p. — *Includes index. — Bibliography: p.385-386*

GINZBERG, Eli
From health dollars to health services : New York City, 1965-1985 / Eli Ginzberg and the Conservation of Human Resources staff. — Totowa, N.J. : Rowman & Allanheld, c1986. — xii, 163 p.. — ([Conservation of human resources series ; 25]) (Land Mark studies). — *First series from jacket. — Includes index. — Bibliography: p. [155]*

HEALTH SERVICES — organization & administration
SCHAEFER, Morris
Designing and using procedure in health and human services / by Morris Schaefer. — Beverly Hills : Sage Publications, c1985. — p. cm. — (Sage human services guides ; 39)

HEALTH SERVICES — Nepal
JUSTICE, Judith
Policies, plans, and people : culture and health development in Nepal / Judith Justice. — Berkeley : University of California Press, c1986. — p. cm. — (Comparative studies of health systems and medical care). — *Includes index. — Bibliography: p*

HEALTH SERVICES ADMINISTRATION
SCHAEFER, Morris
Designing and using procedure in health and human services / by Morris Schaefer. — Beverly Hills : Sage Publications, c1985. — p. cm. — (Sage human services guides ; 39)

HEALTH SERVICES ADMINISTRATION — England — London
DOWNEY, Peter
Accountability and democracy in London's health services / Peter Downey ; for the Health Panel of the Greater London Council. — [London : Greater London Council, 1986]. — 32p

HEALTH SERVICES ADMINISTRATION — France
Une décentralisation du système de santé. — [Paris] : La Documentation française, 1986. — 161p

HEALTH SERVICES ADMINISTRATION — Great Britain
GREAT BRITAIN. Welsh Office. Health and Social Work Department
Health services management : model standing orders for area health authorities. — Cardiff : the Office, 1976. — 3,11p. — ([Health circular] ; WHC (76)25)

HAM, Christopher
Managing health services : health authority members in search of a role / Christopher Ham. — Bristol : School for Advanced Urban Studies, c1986. — 138 p. — (SAUS study ; no.3)

HEALTH SERVICES ADMINISTRATION — Great Britain — Case studies
HAYWOOD, Stuart
District health authorities in action two years on : a progress report / Stuart C. Haywood and Wendy Ranade. — Birmingham : University of Birmingham, Health Services Management Centre, 1985. — 127,[29]p,[12] leaves of plates

HEALTH SERVICES ADMINISTRATION — Wales — Statistics
Key statistical indicators for National Health Service management in Wales = Dangosyddion ystadegol allweddol i reolaeth y Gwasanaeth lechyd Gwladol yng Nghymru / Welsh Office. — Cardiff : Economic and Statistical Services Division, Welsh Office, 1983-. — *Annual*

HEALTH SERVICES BILL 1979-80
GREAT BRITAIN. Parliament. House of Commons. Library. Research Division
Health Services Bill (Bill 98 of 1979-80) / [Keith Cuninghame]. — [London] : the Division, 1979. — 12p. — (Reference sheet ; no.79/18). — *Bibliography: p9-12*

HEALTH STATUS INDICATORS
HO, Teresa J.
Measuring health as a component of living standards / Teresa J. Ho. — Washington, D.C., U.S.A. : World Bank, c1982 ((1985 printing)). — 58p. — (LSMS working papers ; no.15) (LSMS working papers ; no. 15). — *Bibliography: p56-58*

HEALTH STATUS INDICATORS — Developing countries
MARTORELL, Reynaldo
Nutrition and health status indicators : suggestions for surveys of the standard of living in developing countries / Reynaldo Martorell. — Washington, D.C., U.S.A. : World Bank, Development Research Center, c1981. — 97p. — (LSMS working papers ; no.13). — *"February 1982.". — Bibliography: p91-97*

HEALTH SURVEYS
HO, Teresa J.
Measuring health as a component of living standards / Teresa J. Ho. — Washington, D.C., U.S.A. : World Bank, c1982 ((1985 printing)). — 58p. — (LSMS working papers ; no.15) (LSMS working papers ; no. 15). — *Bibliography: p56-58*

HEALTH SURVEYS — Great Britain
LAING, William
Private health care, 1985 / William Laing. — London : Office of Health Economics, [1985]. — 55 p.

HEARING AIDS
SYMPOSIUM ON ARTIFICIAL AUDITORY STIMULATION (1982 : Erlangen)
Discussions on artificial auditory stimulation : symposium 29 September - 2 October 1982, Erlangen, Federal Republic of Germany / edited by W. D. Keidel, P. Finkenzeller. — Luxembourg : Office for Official Publications of the European Communities, 1984. — ix,182p. — (EUR ; 8980). — *Series title: Medicine. — Bibliography: p155-179*

HEAT
MACH, Ernst
[Principien der Wärmelehre. English]. Principles of the theory of heat : historically and critically elucidated / Ernst Mach ; with an introduction by Martin J. Klein ; edited by Brian McGuinness. — Dordrecht ; Lancaster : D. Reidel, ç1986. — xxii, 456p. — (Vienna circle collection ; v. 17). — *Translation of: Die Principien der Wärmelehre. — Includes indexes*

HEBREW LANGUAGE
Readings in the sociology of Jewish languages / edited by Joshua A. Fishman. — Leiden : E. J. Brill, 1985. — xii,298p. — (Contributions to the sociology of Jewish languages ; Vol.1)

HEDGING (FINANCE)
KOBOLD, Klaus
Interest rate futures markets and capital market theory : theoretical concepts and empirical evidence / Klaus Kobold. — Berlin ; New York : W. de Gruyte, 1986. — p. cm. — (Series D--Economcis =Economique ; 1)

WELLER, Paul
The influence of technology and demand conditions on futures prices and hedging / Paul Weller and Makoto Yano. — Coventry : University of Warwick. Department of Economics, 1987. — 23p. — (Warwick economic research papers ; no.283). — *Bibliography: p24*

HEGEL, GEORG WILHELM FRIEDRICH
GASCOIGNE, Robert
Religion, rationality, and community : sacred and secular in the thought of Hegel and his critics / by Robert Gascoigne. — The Hague ; Boston : M. Nijhoff, 1985. — xiv, 308p. — (International archives of the history of ideas ; 105). — *Bibliography: p.271-277*

HEGEL, GEORG WILHELM FRIEDRICH *continuation*
GOTTFRIED, Paul
The search for historical meaning : Hegel and the postwar American right / Paul Edward Gottfried. — DeKalb, Ill. : Northern Illinois University Press, 1986. — xv, 178 p.. — *Includes index.* — *Bibliography: p. [163]-170*

Hegel's critique of Kant / edited by Stephen Priest. — Oxford : Clarendon, 1986. — [ix,240]p. — *Includes index*

PEPERZAK, Adriaan Theodoor
Philosophy and politics : a commentary on the preface to Hegel's Philosophy of right / Adriaan Th. Peperzak. — Dordrecht ; Boston : M. Nijhoff ; Norwell, MA, USA : Distributors for the U.S. and Canada, Kluwer Academic, 1987. — x, 144 p.. — (Archives internationales d'histoire des idées =International archives of the history of ideas ; 113). — *Bibliography: p. [141]-144*

HEGEL, GEORG WILHELM FRIEDRICH — Contributions in theory of knowledge
ROCKMORE, Tom
Hegel's circular epistemology / Tom Rockmore. — Bloomington : Indiana University Press, c1986. — xv, 202p. — (Studies in phenomenology and existential philosophy). — *Includes index.* — *Includes bibliographical references*

HEGEL, GEORG WILHELM FRIEDRICH — Influence
ARTHUR, C. J.
Dialectics of Labour : Marx and his relation to Hegel / C.J. Arthur. — Oxford : Basil Blackwell, 1986. — 182p. — *Bibliography: p174-179.* — *Includes index*

HEGEL, GEORG WILHELM FRIEDRICH — Metaphysics
HOULGATE, Stephen
Hegel, Nietzsche and the criticism of metaphysics / Stephen Houlgate. — Cambridge : Cambridge University Press, 1986. — [320]p. — *Bibliography: p451-469.* — *Includes index*

HEIDEGGER, MARTIN
SCHÜRMANN, Reiner
[Principe d'anarchie. English]. Heidegger on being and acting : from principles to anarchy / Reiner Schürmann ; translated from the French by Christine-Marie Gros in collaboration with the author. — Bloomington : Indiana University Press, c1986. — 406p. — (Studies in phenomenology and existential philosophy). — *Translation of: Le principe d'anarchie.* — *Includes indexes.* — *Bibliography: p.305-309; 387-391*

HEJAZ — History
OCHSENWALD, William
Religion, society, and the state in Arabia : the Hijaz under Ottoman control, 1840-1908 / William Ochsenwald. — Columbus : Ohio State University Press, 1984. — xiii, 241p. — *Includes index.* — *Bibliography: p.[229]-234*

HELCEL, ANTONI ZYGMUNT
KOZUB-CIEMBRONIEWICZ, Wiesław
Austria a Polska w konserwatyzmie Antoniego Z. Helcla, 1846-1865 / Wiesław Kozub-Ciembroniewicz. — Kraków : Krajowa Agencja Wydawnicza, 1986. — 215p. — *Summary in German.* — *Bibliography: p191-[200]*

HELMS, JESSE
FURGURSON, Ernest B.
Hard right : the rise of Jesse Helms / by Ernest B. Furgurson. — 1st ed. — New York : Norton, c1986. — p. cm

SNIDER, William D
Hunt and Helms : North Carolina chooses a Senator / by William D. Snider. — Chapel Hill : University of North Carolina Press, c1985. — p. cm. — *Includes index*

HELSINKI CONSULTATIONS
HELSINKI CONSULTATIONS
Final recommendations of the Helsinki consultations. — Helsinki, 1973. — 6 language versions separately paginated. — *Text of the Helsinki Consultations' recommendations on the holding of the Conference on Security and Co-operation in Europe given in each language version in the order: German, English, Spanish, French, Italian and Russian*

HENDERSON, Sir NICHOLAS
HENDERSON, Sir Nicholas
Channels and tunnels : reflections on Britain and abroad / Nicholas Henderson. — London : Weidenfeld and Nicolson, 1987. — 166p

HENDERSON (LA.) — Social conditions
ESMAN, Marjorie R
Henderson, Louisiana : cultural adaptation in a Cajun community / by Marjorie R. Esman. — New York : Holt, Rinehart, and Winston, c1985. — xv, 137 p.. — (Case studies in cultural anthropology). — *Includes index.* — *Bibliography: p. 133-134*

HENDERSON (LA.) — Social life and customs
ESMAN, Marjorie R
Henderson, Louisiana : cultural adaptation in a Cajun community / by Marjorie R. Esman. — New York : Holt, Rinehart, and Winston, c1985. — xv, 137 p.. — (Case studies in cultural anthropology). — *Includes index.* — *Bibliography: p. 133-134*

HENEQUEN INDUSTRY — Mexico — Yucatán — History
BRANNON, Jeffery
Agrarian reform & public enterprise in Mexico : the political economy of Yucatán's henequen industry / Jeffery Brannon, Eric N. Baklanoff ; a foreword by Edward H. Moseley. — Tuscaloosa, Ala. : University of Alabama Press, c1987. — xv, 237 p.. — *Includes index.* — *Bibliography: p. 220-230*

HENRY VIII, King of England
SCARISBRICK, J. J.
Henry VIII / J.J. Scarisbrick. — Harmondsworth : Penguin, 1971. — 715p. — (Pelican biographies). — *Originally published, London: Eyre and Spottiswoode, 1968.* — *bibl p678-690*

HENRY, Duke of Saxony and Bavaria
JORDAN, Karl, 1909-ca.1986
Henry the Lion : a biography / Karl Jordan ; translated by P.S. Falla. — Oxford : Clarendon, 1986. — 266p. — *Translation of: Heinrich der Löwe.* — *Bibliography: p227-231.* — *Includes index*

HERBERG, WILL
AUSMUS, Harry J.
Will Herberg, from right to right / by Harry J. Ausmus ; with a foreword by Martin E. Marty. — Chapel Hill : University of North Carolina Press, c1987. — p. cm. — (Studies in religion). — *Includes index.* — *Bibliography: p*

HEREDITY, HUMAN
KEVLES, Daniel J.
In the name of eugenics : genetics and the uses of human heredity / Daniel Jo Kevles. — Harmondsworth : Penguin, 1986. — x,426p. — (Pelican books). — *Previously published: New York : Knopf, 1986*

HEREROS — Psychology
POEWE, Karla O
The Namibian Herero : a history of their psychosocial disintegration and survival / by Karla Poewe. — Lewiston, N.Y., USA : E. Mellen Press, [1985]. — 364 p.. — (African studies ; v. 1). — *Includes index.* — *Bibliography: p. [359]-364*

HEREROS — Social conditions
POEWE, Karla O
The Namibian Herero : a history of their psychosocial disintegration and survival / by Karla Poewe. — Lewiston, N.Y., USA : E. Mellen Press, [1985]. — 364 p.. — (African studies ; v. 1). — *Includes index.* — *Bibliography: p. [359]-364*

HERMENEUTICS
WALZER, Michael
Interpretation and social criticism / Michael Walzer. — Cambridge, Mass. : Harvard University Press, 1987. — viii, 96 p.. — (The Tanner lectures on human values). — *Includes bibliographical references and index*

HEROES — Mexico
O'MALLEY, Ilene V
The myth of the revolution : hero cults and the institutionalization of the Mexican State, 1920-1940 / Ilene V. O'Malley. — New York : Greenwood Press, 1986. — xii, 199 p.. — (Contributions to the study of world history ; no. 1). — *Includes index.* — *Bibliography: p.[179]-194*

HEROIN HABIT
ROBERTSON, Roy
Heroin, AIDS and society / Roy Robertson. — London : Hodder and Stoughton, 1987. — 133p. — *Bibliography: p124-128.* — *Includes index*

HEROIN HABIT — England, Northern
PEARSON, Geoffrey
Young people and heroin : an examination of heroin use in the North of England : a report to the Health Education Council / by Geoffrey Pearson, Mark Gilman, Shirley McIver. — Aldershot : Gower, c1987. — [72]p. — *Includes bibliography*

HEROIN HABIT — Great Britain
STEWART, Tam
The heroin users / Tam Stewart. — London : Pandora, 1987. — xii,240p. — *Bibliography: p234-235.* — *Includes index*

HEROINES — India
LEBRA-CHAPMAN, Joyce
The Rani of Jhansi : a study in female heroism in India / Joyce Lebra-Chapman. — Honolulu : University of Hawaii Press, c1986. — xii, 199 p., [2] leaves of plates. — *Includes index.* — *Bibliography: p. [185]-193*

HERRIOT, EDOUARD
BRUGAS, Jacques
Edouard Herriot / Jacques Brugas. — Roanne : Horvath, 1985. — 143p. — *Bibliography: p141-142*

HERSHEY, LEWIS BLAINE
HERSHEY, Lewis Blaine
Lewis B. Hershey, Mr. Selective Service / George Q. Flynn. — Chapel Hill : University of North Carolina Press, c1985. — p. cm. — *Includes index.* — *Bibliography: p*

HESSE-KASSEL (GERMANY) — History
INGRAO, Charles W.
The Hessian mercenary state : ideas, institutions and reform under Frederick II, 1760-1785 / Charles W. Ingrao. — Cambridge : Cambridge University Press, 1987. — 1v.. — *Includes bibliography and index*

HEYDRICH, REINHARD — Biography
DESCHNER, Günther
Reinhard Heydrich : Statthalter der totalen Macht / Günther Deschner. — 3. aktualisierte Aufl.. — München : Edition Meyster, 1986. — 368p. — *Bibliography: p354-360*

HEYWORTH OF OXTON, GEOFFREY
HEYWORTH, Baron
Geoffrey Heyworth : Baron Heyworth of Oxton : a memoir. — [London] ([PO Box 68, Unilever Hse., Blackfriars, EC4P 4BQ]) : [Unilever], c1985. — 71p

HIERARCHIES — Fiji
TOREN, Christina Camden
Symbolic space and the construction of hierarchy : an anthropological and cognitive development study in a Fijian village / by Christina Toren. — 523 leaves. — *PhD (Arts) 1986 LSE.* — *Leaves 432-512 are appendices*

HIGH SCHOOL GRADUATES — Employment — O.E.C.D. countries

ORGANISATION FOR ECONOMIC CO-OPERATION AND DEVELOPMENT
Entry of young people into working life : general report / [Organisation for Economic Co-operation and Development]. — Paris : O.E.C.D. ; [London] : [H.M.S.O.], 1977. — 106p. — *Bibliography: p.103-106*

HIGH SCHOOL STUDENTS — South Arica

DU TOIT, Brian M.
Drug use and South African students / by Brian M. Du Toit. — [Athens] : Ohio University Center for International Studies, Africa Program, 1978. — 127 p. — (Papers in international studies : Africa series ; no. 35). — *Bibliography: p. 126-127*

HIGH SPEED GROUND TRANSPORTATION

POTTER, Stephen
On the right lines? : the limits of technological innovation / Stephen Potter. — New York : St. Martin's Press, 1987. — viii, 208 p.. — *Includes index. — Bibliography: p. [201]-204*

HIGH TECHNOLOGY — Government policy — United States

CAHILL, Kevin
Trade wars : the high-technology scandal of the 1980's / Kevin Cahill. — London : W.H. Allen, 1986. — [176]p

HIGH TECHNOLOGY — Social aspects

LYON, David, 1948-
The silicon society / David Lyon. — Tring : Lion, 1986. — 127p. — (London lectures in contemporary Christianity ; 1985). — *Includes index*

HIGH TECHNOLOGY INDUSTRIES

The Development of high technology industries : an international survey / edited by Michael J. Breheny and Ronald McQuaid. — London : Croom Helm, c1987. — 363p. — *Includes index*

HIGH TECHNOLOGY INDUSTRIES — Government ownership — Brazil

RAMAMURTI, Ravi
State-owned enterprises in high technology industries : studies in India and Brazil / Ravi Ramamurti. — London : Praeger, 1987. — xii,306p. — *Bibliography: p289-294. — Includes index*

HIGH TECHNOLOGY INDUSTRIES — Government ownership — India

RAMAMURTI, Ravi
State-owned enterprises in high technology industries : studies in India and Brazil / Ravi Ramamurti. — London : Praeger, 1987. — xii,306p. — *Bibliography: p289-294. — Includes index*

HIGH TECHNOLOGY INDUSTRIES — Government policy — Case studies

National policies for developing high technology industries : international comparisons / edited by Francis W. Rushing and Carole Ganz Brown. — Boulder, Colo. : Westview Press, c1986. — xiv, 247 p.. — (Westview special studies in science, technology, and public policy). — *Includes bibliographies*

HIGH TECHNOLOGY INDUSTRIES — Government policy — Japan

Japan's high technology industries : lessons and limitations of industrial policy / edited by Hugh Patrick, with the assistance of Larry Meissner. — Seattle, WA : University of Washington Press, c1986. — p. cm. — "Sponsored by the Committee on Japanese Economic Studies"--T.p. verso. — *Includes bibliographies and index. — Contents: Japanese high technology industrial policy in comparative context / Hugh Patrick -- Regime characteristics of Japanese industrial policy / Daniel I. Okimoto -- Industrial policy and factor markets : biotechnology in Japan and the United States / Gary Saxonhouse -- Japan's industrial policy for high technology industries / Ken-ichi Imai -- Joint research and antitrust : Japanese vs. American strategies / Kozo Yamamura -- Technology in transition / Yasusuke Murakami -- Japanese high technology policy : what lessons for the United States? / George Eads and Richard Nelson*

HIGH TECHNOLOGY INDUSTRIES — Government policy — Pennsylvania

ALLEN, David N
Nurturing advanced technology enterprises : emerging issues in state and local economic development policy / David N. Allen and Victor Levine. — New York : Praeger, 1986. — xvi, 268 p.. — *Includes index. — Bibliography: p. 239-262*

HIGH TECHNOLOGY INDUSTRIES — Government policy — United States

Japan's high technology industries : lessons and limitations of industrial policy / edited by Hugh Patrick, with the assistance of Larry Meissner. — Seattle, WA : University of Washington Press, c1986. — p. cm. — "Sponsored by the Committee on Japanese Economic Studies"--T.p. verso. — *Includes bibliographies and index. — Contents: Japanese high technology industrial policy in comparative context / Hugh Patrick -- Regime characteristics of Japanese industrial policy / Daniel I. Okimoto -- Industrial policy and factor markets : biotechnology in Japan and the United States / Gary Saxonhouse -- Japan's industrial policy for high technology industries / Ken-ichi Imai -- Joint research and antitrust : Japanese vs. American strategies / Kozo Yamamura -- Technology in transition / Yasusuke Murakami -- Japanese high technology policy : what lessons for the United States? / George Eads and Richard Nelson*

HIGH TECHNOLOGY INDUSTRIES — Germany (West)

SCHMIDT, Karlheinz
Der Traum vom deutschen Silicon Valley / Karlheinz Schmidt. — Landsberg am Lech : Verlag Moderne Industrie, 1985. — 225p. — *Bibliography: p211*

HIGH TECHNOLOGY INDUSTRIES — United States

CAHILL, Kevin
Trade wars : the high-technology scandal of the 1980's / Kevin Cahill. — London : W.H. Allen, 1986. — [176]p

MARKUSEN, Ann R
High tech America : the what, how, where, and why of the sunrise industries / Ann Markusen, Peter Hall, Amy Glasmeier. — Boston : Allen & Unwin, 1986. — p. cm. — *Includes index. — Bibliography: p*

HIGH TECHNOLOGY INDUSTRIES — Wales — Wrexham Region (Denbighshire)

CLWYD. Science and Technology Working Party
Opportunities for high technology industries in South East Clwyd : report of the Science and Technology Working Party = Agoriadau ar gyfer diwydiannau uwch-dechnoleg yn Ne-ddwyrain Clwyd : adroddiad y Gweithgor Gwyddoniaeth a Thechnoleg. — [Mold] : [Clwyd County Council], 1984. — x,55p

HIGHER EDUCATION AND STATE — England

GREAT BRITAIN. Department of Education and Science
Higher education in England outside the Universities : policy, funding and management : a consultative document issued by the Secretary of State for Education and Science. — [London] : the Department, 1981. — 14p

HIGHER EDUCATION AND STATE — Europe

CERYCH, Ladislav
Great expectations and mixed performance : the implementation of higher education reforms in Europe / Ladislav Cerych and Paul Sabatier. — Stoke-on-Trent : Trentham Books, 1986. — xx,276p

HIGHER EDUCATION AND STATE — Great Britain

GREAT BRITAIN. Parliament. House of Commons. Library. Research Division
The future of higher education / Kay Andrews. — [London] : the Division, 1984. — 25p. — (Reference sheet ; no.84/9). — *Bibliography: p21-24*

HIGHER EDUCATION AND STATE — India

GHOSH, Suresh Chandra
Indian nationalism : a case study for the first university reform by the British Raj / Suresh Chandra Ghosh. — New Delhi : Vikas Pub. House, c1985. — 195 p.. — 89-9. — *Includes index. — Bibliography: p. [182]-189*

HIGHER EDUCATION AND STATE — United States

Policy controversies in higher education / edited by Samuel K. Gove and Thomas M. Stauffer ; prepared under the auspices of the Policy Studies Organization. — New York : Greenwood Press, 1986. — xi, 274 p.. — (Contributions to the study of education ; no. 19). — *Includes index. — Bibliography: p. [261]-264*

HIGHER EDUCATION OF WOMEN — Great Britain

STONEY, Sheila M.
Further opportunities in focus : a study of bridging courses for women / by Sheila M. Stoney and Margaret I. Reid. — [London] ([39 York Rd., SE1 7PH]) : Further Education Curriculum Review and Development Unit, 1980. — vi,158p. — (Project report / Further Education Curriculum Review and Development Unit ; P.R.5). — *Bibliography: p149-158*

HIGHLANDS (SCOTLAND) — Description and travel

CLOSE-BROOKS, Joanna
The Highlands / Joanna Close-Brooks. — Edinburgh : H.M.S.O., 1986. — 184p. — (Exploring Scotland's heritage). — *At foot of t.p.: Royal Commission on the Ancient and Historical Monuments of Scotland. — Bibliography: p.179-180*

HIGHLANDS (SCOTLAND) — Rural conditions

ALEXANDER, K. J. W.
Rural renewal : experience in the Highlands and Islands / Sir Kenneth Alexander. — Cambridge : University of Cambridge, Department of Land Economy, 1984. — 26p. — (The Denman lecture ; 1984)

HIGHWAY DEPARTMENTS — Great Britain

AUDIT COMMISSION FOR LOCAL AUTHORITIES IN ENGLAND AND WALES
Improving highways agency arrangements between counties and districts : an interim report. — London : H.M.S.O., 1987. — 80p

HIGHWAY PLANNING — Great Britain

GREAT BRITAIN. Department of Transport
The government response to the SACTRA report on urban road appraisal / Department of Transport. — London : H.M.S.O., 1986. — 32p

HIKUERU (TUAMOTU ISLANDS) — Population — Statistics
Tableaux normalisés du recensement général de la population : 15 octobre 1983. — [Papeete] : Institut territorial de la statistique Résultats de la commune de Hikueru. — [1985?]. — 4p,ll leaves

HILL FARMING — Philippines — Mindoro
LOPEZ-GONZAGA, Violeta
Peasants in the hills : a study of the dynamics of social change among the Buhid swidden cultivators in the Philippines / Violeta Lopez-Gonzaga. — Quezon City, Philippines : University of the Philippines Press, 1983. — xiv,226p. — *Bibliography: p[211]-219*

HILLINGDON (LONDON, ENGLAND) — Social policy
HILLINGDON
Report of the review panel of the London Borough of Hillingdon Area Review Committee on Child Abuse into the death of Heidi Koseda. — Hillingdon : [the Council], 1986. — 66p

HIMACHAL PRADESH (INDIA) — Statistics
Statistical abstract of Himachal Pradesh / Directorate of Economics and Statistics, Himachal Pradesh. — Simla : Directorate of Economics and Statistics, 1981-. — *Annual*

HINDI LANGUAGE — Political aspects
EKBOTE, Gopalrao
A nation without a national language / by Gopalrao Ekbote. — Hyderabad : Hindi Prachar Sabha, 1984. — 258 p.. — *Bibliography: p. [256]-258*

HINDUISM — Congresses
INTERNATIONAL CONFERENCE ON HINDUISM (1983 : Barrytown, N.Y.)
In search of Hinduism / edited by Cromwell Crawford. — Barrytown, N.Y. : Unification Theological Seminary, 1986. — xl,181p. — *Bibliographical notes*

HINDUISM — Great Britain — History
Hinduism in Great Britain : the perpetuation of religion in an alien cultural milieu / edited by Richard Burghart. — London : Tavistock, 1987. — [288]p. — *Includes bibliography and index*

HINDUISM — Sri Lanka — Rituals
TANAKA, Masakazu
Sacrifice and divine power : Hindu temple rituals and village festivals in a fishing village, Sri Lanka / by Masakazu Tanaka. — 562 leaves. — PhD (Econ) 1986 LSE. — *Leaves 477-536 are appendices*

HIRSCHMAN, ALBERT O
Development, democracy, and the art of trespassing : essays in honor of Albert O. Hirschman / edited by Alejandro Foxley, Michael S. McPherson, and Guillermo O'Donnell. — Notre Dame, Ind. : Published for the Helen Kellogg Institute for International Studies by University of Notre Dame Press, c1986. — vii, 379 p.. — *Bibliography: p. 375-379*

HISPANIC AMERICANS — Economic conditions — Addresses, essays, lectures
Hispanics in the U.S. economy / edited by George J. Borjas, Marta Tienda. — Orlando : Academic Press, 1985. — p. cm. — *Includes index.* — *Bibliography: p*

HISPANIC AMERICANS — Employment — Addresses, essays, lectures
Hispanics in the U.S. economy / edited by George J. Borjas, Marta Tienda. — Orlando : Academic Press, 1985. — p. cm. — *Includes index.* — *Bibliography: p*

HISPANIC AMERICANS — History
GANN, Lewis H.
The Hispanics in the United States : a history / L.H. Gann, Peter J. Duignan. — Boulder : Westview Press, 1986. — p. cm. — *Includes index.* — *Bibliography: p*

HISPANIC AMERICANS — History Bibliography
Latinos in the United States : a historical bibliography / Albert M. Camarillo, editor. — Santa Barbara, Calif. : ABC-Clio, [1986]. — p. cm. — (ABC-Clio research guides). — *Includes index*

HISPANIC AMERICANS — Social conditions — Addresses, essays, lectures
Hispanics in the U.S. economy / edited by George J. Borjas, Marta Tienda. — Orlando : Academic Press, 1985. — p. cm. — *Includes index.* — *Bibliography: p*

HISTORIAL MATERIALISM
Istoricheskii materializm kak metodologiia poznaniia i preobrazovaniia obshchestvennoi zhizni / otv. redaktor V. V. Denisov. — Moskva : Nauka, 1987. — 283p

HISTORIANS — Canada
BERGER, Carl
The writing of Canadian history : aspects of English-Canadian historical writing since 1900 / Carl Berger. — 2nd ed. — Toronto : University of Toronto Press, 1986. — x,364p. — *Bibliographical note and references: p [320]-352*

HISTORIANS — Canada — Biography
FRANCIS, R. Douglas
Frank H. Underhill : intellectual provocateur / R. Douglas Francis. — Toronto : University of Toronto Press, 1986. — x,219p. — *Notes: p [183]-206*

HISTORIANS — France
WALCH, Jean
Les maîtres de l'histoire 1815-1850 : Augustin Thierry, Mignet, Guizot, Thiers, Michelet, Edgard Quinet / Jean Walch. — Paris : Champion ; Genève : Slatkine, 1986. — 307p. — *Bibliography: p[265]-293*

HISTORIANS — Poland — Biography
TOPOLSKI, Jerzy
O nowy model historii : Jan Rutkowski (1886-1949) / Jerzy Topolski. — Warszawa : Państwowe Wydawnictwo Naukowe, 1986. — 310p

HISTORIANS — Soviet Union — Biography
CHISTIAKOVA, E. V.
Mikhail Nikolaevich Tikhomirov (1893-1965) / E. V. Chistiakova ; otv. redaktor V. I. Buganov. — Moskva : Nauka, 1987. — 157p. — (Nauchnye biografii)

HISTORIANS — United States — Biography
BAKER, Susan Stout
Radical beginnings : Richard Hofstadter and the 1930s / Susan Stout Baker. — Westport, Conn. ; London : Greenwood Press, 1985. — xxi, 268p. — (Contributions in American history ; no. 112). — *Includes index.* — *Bibliography: p.[253]-259*

WOODWARD, C. Vann
Thinking back : the perils of writing history / C. Vann Woodward. — Baton Rouge ; London : Louisiana State University Press, c1986. — x, 158p. — *Includes index.* — *Bibliography: p 147-151*

HISTORIC BUILDINGS — Law and legislation — Great Britain
GREAT BRITAIN. Parliament. House of Commons. Library. Research Division
National Heritage Bill [HL] - Bill 85 of 1982-83 / [Fiona Poole, Barry Winetrobe]. — [London] : the Division, 1983. — 23p. — (Reference sheet ; no.83/4). — *Includes bibliographical references*

HISTORIC BUILDINGS — Great Britain — Conservation and restoration
GREAT BRITAIN. Parliament. House of Commons. Library. Research Division
Town and country planning : conservation and European Architectural Heritage Year 1975. — [London] : the Division, [1975]. — 18 leaves. — (Background paper ; no.46). — *Bibliographical references: leaf 18*

HISTORIC BUILDINGS — Scotland — Fife
WALKER, Bruce
Exploring Scotland's heritage : Fife and Tayside / Bruce Walker and Graham Ritchie. — Edinburgh : H.M.S.O., 1987. — 202p. — (Exploring Scotland's heritage). — *At foot of t.p.: The Royal Commission on the Ancient and Historical Monuments of Scotland.* — *Bibliography: p.196-197*

HISTORIC BUILDINGS — Scotland — Tayside
WALKER, Bruce
Exploring Scotland's heritage : Fife and Tayside / Bruce Walker and Graham Ritchie. — Edinburgh : H.M.S.O., 1987. — 202p. — (Exploring Scotland's heritage). — *At foot of t.p.: The Royal Commission on the Ancient and Historical Monuments of Scotland.* — *Bibliography: p.196-197*

HISTORIC BUILDINGS — United States — Conservation and restoration
STAHL, Frederick A.
A guide to the maintenance, repair, and alteration of historic buildings / Frederick A. Stahl. — New York : Van Nostrand Reinhold, c1984. — 185 p.. — *Includes index*

HISTORIC BUILDINGS — United States — Maintenance and repair
STAHL, Frederick A.
A guide to the maintenance, repair, and alteration of historic buildings / Frederick A. Stahl. — New York : Van Nostrand Reinhold, c1984. — 185 p.. — *Includes index*

HISTORIC SITES — Great Britain — Conservation and restoration
GREAT BRITAIN. Department of the Environment
Proposals to amend the laws relating to ancient monuments : a consultative document. — [London] : the Department, [1976?]. — 24,2p

HISTORICAL LINGUISTICS — Congresses
INTERNATIONAL CONFERENCE ON HISTORICAL LINGUISTICS (1979 : Stanford University)
Papers from the 4th International Conference on Historical Linguistics / ed. by Elizabeth Closs Traugott, Rebecca Labrum & Susan Shepherd. — Amsterdam : Benjamins, 1980. — ix, 437 p.. — (Amsterdam studies in the theory and history of linguistic science. Series 4, Current issues in linguistic theory ; v.14). — *Includes bibliographies and indexes*

HISTORICAL MATERIALISM
CHAGIN, B. A.
Istoricheskii materializm v SSSR v perekhodnyi period 1917-1936 gg. : istoriko-sotsiologicheskii ocherk / B. A. Chagin, V. I. Klushin ; otv. redaktor A. A. Fedoseev. — Moskva : Nauka, 1986. — 439p

SAYER, Derek
The violence of abstraction : the analytic foundations of historical materialism / Derek Sayer. — Oxford : Basil Blackwell, 1987. — [192]p. — *Includes bibliography and index*

HISTORICAL RESEARCH
Bulletin of the Institute of Historical Research. — London : Longmans, Green and Co., 1923-1986. — *3 per year.* — *Continued by: Historical research: the bulletin of the Institute of Historical Research*

Historical research : the bulletin of the Institute of Historical Research. — London : Blackwell, 1987-. — *3 per year.* — *Continues: Bulletin of the Institute of Historical Research*

HISTORIOGRAPHY

Approaches to history : a symposium / edited by Herbert Patrick Reginald Finsberg. — London : Routledge and Kegan Paul, 1962. — 221p

COHEN, Sande
Historical culture : on the recoding of an academic discipline / Sande Cohen. — Berkeley : University of California Press, c1986. — ix, 354 p.. — Includes indexes. — Bibliography: p. 333-344

ENGELS, Friedrich
The role of force in history : a study of Bismarck's policy of blood and iron / translated by Jack Cohen; edited and with an introduction by Ernst Wangermann. — London : Lawrence and Wishart, 1968. — 108p

FINLEY, M. I.
The use and abuse of history / M.I. Finley. — London : Hogarth, 1986, c1975. — [256]p. — Originally published: London : Chatto & Windus, 1975. — Includes index

GARDINER, Patrick Lancaster
The nature of historical explanation / Patrick Lancaster Gardiner. — London : Oxford University Press, 1965. — vii,142p

Knowing and telling history : the Anglo-Saxon debate / edited by F. R. Ankersmit. — Middletown, Conn. : Wesleyan University, 1986. — 100p. — (History and theory ; Beiheft 25)

STANFORD, Michael, 1923-
The nature of historical knowledge / Michael Stanford. — Oxford : Basil Blackwell, 1986. — vii,196p. — Includes index

HISTORIOGRAPHY — Data processing

History and computing / edited by Peter Denley and Deian Hopkin. — Manchester : Manchester University Press, c1987. — [224]p. — Includes bibliography and index

HISTORIOGRAPHY — Dictionaries

RITTER, Harry
Dictionary of concepts in history / Harry Ritter. — Westport, Conn. : Greenwood Press, c1986. — p. cm. — (Reference sources for the social sciences and humanities ; no. 3). — Includes index. — Bibliography: p

HISTORIOGRAPHY — Dictionaries and encyclopedias

Dictionnaire des sciences historiques / publié sous la direction de André Burguière. — Paris : Presses Universitaires de France, 1986. — ix,693p

HISTORIOGRAPHY — Czechoslavakia

Independent historiography in Czechoslavakia. — Page 1 reads: "Presented to the 16th International Congress of Historical Sciences, Stuttgart, 25th August-1st September 1985" 2. — [Prague : s.n.]. — 1985. — 247p

HISTORIOGRAPHY — France

WALCH, Jean
Les maîtres de l'histoire 1815-1850 : Augustin Thierry, Mignet, Guizot, Thiers, Michelet, Edgard Quinet / Jean Walch. — Paris : Champion ; Genève : Slatkine, 1986. — 307p. — Bibliography: p[265]-293

HISTORIOGRAPHY — Great Britain — History

LEVINE, Joseph M
Humanism and history : origins of modern English historiography / Joseph M. Levine. — Ithaca : Cornell University Press, 1987. — 297 p.. — Includes index. — Bibliography: p. 214-288

HISTORIOGRAPHY — Spain

CIRUJANO MARÍN, Paloma
Historiografía y nacionalismo español (1834-1868) / Paloma Cirujano Marín, Teresa Elorriaga Planes, Juan Sisinio Pérez Garzón. — Madrid : Centro de Estudios Históricos, Consejo Superior de Investigaciones Científicas, 1985. — xi,206p. — (Monografías / Consejo Superior de Investigaciones Científicas, Centro de Estudios Históricos ; 2)

HISTORY

ARIÈS, Philippe
Le temps de l'histoire / Philippe Ariès ; préface de Roger Chartier. — Paris : Seuil, [1986]. — 255p

HISTORY — Abstracts — Periodicals — Bibliography

HENIGE, David P
Serial bibliographies and abstracts in history : an annotated guide / compiled by David Henige. — Westport, Conn. ; London : Greenwood Press, c1986. — xiv, 220p. — (Bibliographies and indexes in world history ; no. 2). — Includes index

HISTORY — Bibliography — Periodicals — Bibliography

HENIGE, David P
Serial bibliographies and abstracts in history : an annotated guide / compiled by David Henige. — Westport, Conn. ; London : Greenwood Press, c1986. — xiv, 220p. — (Bibliographies and indexes in world history ; no. 2). — Includes index

HISTORY — Methodology

STANFORD, Michael, 1923-
The nature of historical knowledge / Michael Stanford. — Oxford : Basil Blackwell, 1986. — vii,196p. — Includes index

HISTORY — Philosophy

BOOTH, William James
Interpreting the world : Kant's philosophy of history and politics / William James Booth. — Toronto ; London : University of Toronto Press, c1986. — xxviii, 189p. — Includes index. — Includes bibliographical references

CARR, Edward Hallett
What is history? : the George Macaulay Trevelyan lectures delivered in the University of Cambridge January-March 1961 / by E.H. Carr. — 2nd ed. / edited by R.W. Davies. — Basingstoke : Macmillan, 1986. — xlvi,154p. — Previous ed.: 1961. — Includes index

COHEN, Sande
Historical culture : on the recoding of an academic discipline / Sande Cohen. — Berkeley : University of California Press, c1986. — ix, 354 p.. — Includes indexes. — Bibliography: p. 333-344

RICKERT, Heinrich
The limits of concept formation in natural science : a logical introduction to the historical sciences / Heinrich Rickert. — Abridged ed. / edited and translated by Guy Oakes. — Cambridge : Cambridge University Press, 1986. — xxxii,240p. — (Texts in German philosophy). — Translation of: Die Grenzen der naturwissenschaftlichen Begriffsbildung. — Includes index

HISTORY — Philosophy — Addresses, essays, lectures

MEYERHOFF, Hans, ed
The philosophy of history in our time : an anthology selected, and with an introd. and commentary / by Hans Meyerhoff. — [1st ed.]. — Garden City, N.Y. : Doubleday, 1959. — 350 p. — (Doubleday anchor books, A164)

HISTORY — Statistical methods

FLOUD, Roderick
An introduction to quantitative methods for historians. — 2nd ed. — London : Methuen, Oct. 1979. — [200]p. — Previous ed.: 1973

HISTORY — Study and teaching

BEATTIE, Alan
History in peril : may parents preserve it / Alan Beattie. — London : Centre for Policy Studies, 1987. — 37p. — (C.P.S. Education Quartet ; part 1). — Bibliography: p36-37

HISTORY — Study and teaching (Higher) — England — History — 19th century

SLEE, Peter R. H.
Learning and a liberal education : the study of modern history in the Universities of Oxford, Cambridge and Manchester, 1800-1914 / Peter R.H. Slee. — Manchester : Manchester University Press, c1986. — [200]p. — Includes bibliography and index

HISTORY — Study and teaching (Secondary) — England — London

INNER LONDON EDUCATION AUTHORITY. Inspectorate
History and social sciences at secondary level. — [London : the Authority] Part 2: History. — [1982]. — 90p. — Bibliography: p86-89

HISTORY, MODERN

Bulletin trimestriel / Institut d'Histoire du Temps Present. — Paris : Institut d'Histoire du Temps Present, 1986-. — Quarterly

Cahiers de l'Institut d'Histoire du Temps Present. — Paris : Institut d'Histoire du Temps Present, 1985-. — Irregular

LASKI, Harold Joseph
Reflections on the revolution of our time / Harold Joseph Laski. — London : Allen and Unwin, 1943. — 367p

ROBERTSON, R. T.
The making of the modern world : an introductory history / R.T. Robertson. — London : Zed, 1986. — [256]p. — Includes bibliography and index

HISTORY, MODERN — 20th century

CHAMBERS, Frank Pentland
This age of conflict : the Western world-1914 to the present / Frank Pentland Chambers. — 3rd ed. — New York : Harcourt, 1943. — xiii,880p. — Bibliographies

PARK, Bert Edward
The impact of illness on world leaders / Bert Edward Park. — Philadelphia : University of Pennsylvania Press, 1986. — p. cm. — Includes bibliographies and index

STOESSINGER, John G.
Why nations go to war / John G. Stoessinger. — 4th ed. — Basingstoke : Macmillan Education, 1987, c1985. — xiii,221p. — Previous ed.: New York : St. Martin's, 1982. — Includes bibliographies

WATT, Donald Cameron
A history of the world in the twentieth century / D.C. Watt, Frank Spencer, Neville Brown. — London : Hodder and Stoughton, 1967. — 864p. — Maps on lining papers. — Includes bibliographical references

HISTORY, MODERN — 1945-

BERRIDGE, G. R.
International politics : states, power and conflict since 1945 / G.R. Berridge. — Brighton : Wheatsheaf, 1987. — xii,228p. — Includes index

CALVOCORESSI, Peter
World politics since 1945 / Peter Calvocoressi. — 5th ed. — London : Longman, 1987. — [564]p. — Previous ed.: 1982. — Includes index

Documents in communist affairs. — Brighton : Wheatsheaf 1985 / edited by Bogdan Szajkowski. — 1986. — [352]p

MORTIMER, Edward
Roosevelt's children : tomorrow's world leaders and their world / by Edward Mortimer. — London : Hamilton, 1987. — xxiii,422p. — Includes index

HISTORY, MODERN — 1945-
continuation

The World order : socialist perspectives / edited by Ray Bush, Gordon Johnston and David Coates. — Cambridge : Polity, 1987. — [280]p. — *Includes index*

HISTORY OF MEDICINE

Western diseases, their emergence and prevention / edited by H. C. Trowell, D. P. Burkitt ; foreword by John R. K. Robson. — Cambridge, Mass. : Harvard University Press, 1981. — xix, 456 p.. — *Includes bibliographies and index*

HITIAA O TE RA (TAHITI : REGION) — Population — Statistics

Tableaux normalisés du recensement général de la population : 15 octobre 1983. — [Papeete] : Institut territorial de la statistique Résultats de la commune de Hitiaa o te ra. — [1985?]. — 4p,11 leaves

HITLER, Adolf

BULLOCK, Alan Bullock, Baron
Hitler : a study in tyranny / by Alan Bullock. — Rev. ed. — London : Hamlyn, 1973. — 848p

HITLER, ADOLF

DAIM, Wilfried
Der Mann, der Hitler die Ideen gab : die sektiererischen Grundlagen des Nationalsozialismus / Wilfried Daim. — 2e, erw. und verb. Aufl. — Wien : Hermann Böhlau, 1985. — 316p. — (Böhlaus zeitgeschichtliche Bibliothek ; Bd.4). — *First published 1958*

Die nationalsozialistische Machtergreifung / Wolfgang Michalka (Hrsg.). — Paderborn : Schöningh, 1984. — 415p. — *Bibliography: p412-415*

WAGENER, Otto
Hitler : memoirs of a confidant / edited by Henry Ashby Turner, Jr. ; translated by Ruth Hein. — New Haven ; London : Yale University Press, c1985. — xxvi,333p,[14]p of plates. — *Translation of: Hitler aus nächster Nähe. — Author: Otto Wagener. — Includes index*

HITLER, ADOLF — Diaries — Forgeries

BAHNSEN, Uwe
Der "Stern" - Prozess : Heidemann und Kujau vor Gericht / Uwe Bahnsen. — Mainz : v. Hase und Kochler, 1986. — 192p

BISSINGER, Manfred
Hitlers Sternstunde : Kujau, Heidemann und die Millionen / Manfred Bissinger. — Hamburg : Rasch und Röhring, 1984. — 238p

HITLER, ADOLF — Political and social views

ZITELMANN, Rainer
Hitler : Selbstverständnis eines Revolutionärs / Rainer Zitelmann. — Hamburg ; Leamington Spa : Berg, 1987. — x,485p. — *Bibliography: p467-480*

HITLER, ADOLF — Views on foreign relations

STOAKES, Geoffrey
Hitler and the quest for world dominion : Nazi ideology and foreign policy in the 1920s / Geoffrey Stoakes. — Leamington Spa : Berg, 1986. — [304]p. — *Includes bibliography and index*

HIVA OA (MARQUESAS ISLANDS) — Population — statistics

Tableaux normalisés du recensement général de la population : 15 octobre 1983. — [Papeete] : Institut territoria de la statistique Résultats de la commune de Hiva Oa. — [1985?]. — 4p,11 leaves

HIZB AL-BA'TH AL-'ARABĪ AL-ISHTIRĀKI (SYRIA)

ROBERTS, David, 19---
The Ba'th and the creation of modern Syria / David Roberts. — London : Croom Helm, c1987. — 182p. — *Bibliography: p167-169. — Includes index*

HJØRRING (DENMARK) — Economic conditions

Analyse af Hjørring og Thisted amter. — København : Boligministeriets kommitterede i byplansager, 1960. — 60p. — *Cover title: Hjørring og Thisted amter*

HMONG (ASIAN PEOPLE) — Thailand, Northern

TAPP, Nicholas
The Hmong of Thailand : opium people of the Golden Triangle / Nicholas Tapp. — London : Anti-Slavery Society, 1986. — 72p. — (Indigenous peoples and development series. report no.4). — *Bibliography: p69-70*

HOBBES, THOMAS. Contributions in political science

KAVKA, Gregory S.
Hobbesian moral and political theory / Gregory S. Kavka. — Princeton, N.J. : Princeton University Press, c1986. — xviii, 460p. — (Studies in moral, political, and legal philosophy). — *Includes index. — Includes bibliographical references*

HOBBES, THOMAS. Leviathan

JOHNSTON, David
The rhetoric of Leviathan : Thomas Hobbes and the politics of cultural transformation / David Johnston. — Princeton, N.J. : Princeton University Press, c1986. — xx, 234 p.. — (Studies in moral, political, and legal philosophy). — *Includes index. — Bibliography: p. 219-227*

KAVKA, Gregory S.
Hobbesian moral and political theory / Gregory S. Kavka. — Princeton, N.J. : Princeton University Press, c1986. — xviii, 460p. — (Studies in moral, political, and legal philosophy). — *Includes index. — Includes bibliographical references*

HOBBES, THOMAS

ROGOW, Arnold A
Thomas Hobbes : radical in the service of reaction / Arnold A. Rogow. — New York ; London : W.W. Norton, c1986. — 287p. — *Includes index. — Bibliography: p.275-277*

SORELL, Tom
Hobbes / Tom Sorell. — London : Routledge & Kegan Paul, 1986. — 163p. — (The arguments of the philosophers). — *Includes index. — Bibliography: p.155-157*

HOBBES, THOMAS — Contributions in political science

JOHNSTON, David
The rhetoric of Leviathan : Thomas Hobbes and the politics of cultural transformation / David Johnston. — Princeton, N.J. : Princeton University Press, c1986. — xx, 234 p.. — (Studies in moral, political, and legal philosophy). — *Includes index. — Bibliography: p. 219-227*

HOBBES, THOMAS — Ethics

KAVKA, Gregory S.
Hobbesian moral and political theory / Gregory S. Kavka. — Princeton, N.J. : Princeton University Press, c1986. — xviii, 460p. — (Studies in moral, political, and legal philosophy). — *Includes index. — Includes bibliographical references*

HOBBES, THOMAS — Political science

HAMPTON, Jean
Hobbes and the social contract tradition / Jean Hampton. — Cambridge : Cambridge University Press, 1986. — xii,299p. — *Bibliography: p285-291. — Includes index*

HOBHOUSE, EMILY — Correspondence

HOBHOUSE, Emily
Boer war letters / edited by Rykie Van Reenen. — Cape Town : Human and Rousseau, 1984. — 557p. — *Bibliography: p543-546*

HOECHST (Firm) — History

Geschichte der Farbwerke Hoechst und der chemischen Industrie in Deutschland : ein Lesebuch aus der Arbeiterbildung. — Offenbach : Verlag 2000, c1984. — 176p. — *Bibliography: p174-176*

HOELZ, MAX — Biography

GEBHARDT, Manfred
Max Hoelz : Wege und Irrwege eines Revolutionärs : Biografie / von Manfred Gebhardt. — 2., durchgesehene Aufl.. — Berlin : Verlag Neves Leben, 1985, c1983. — [336]p. — *Bibliography: p333-[334]*

HOFER, ANDREAS

EYCK, F. Gunther
Loyal rebels : Andreas Hofer and the Tyrolean uprising of 1809 / F. Gunther Eyck. — Lanham, MD : University Press of America, c1986. — xvii, 278 p., [1] p. of plates. — *Includes index. — Bibliography: p. 255-266*

HOFSTADTER, RICHARD

BAKER, Susan Stout
Radical beginnings : Richard Hofstadter and the 1930s / Susan Stout Baker. — Westport, Conn. ; London : Greenwood Press, 1985. — xxi, 268p. — (Contributions in American history ; no. 112). — *Includes index. — Bibliography: p.[253]-259*

HOLCH, KNUD Ø.

HOLCH, Mogens
K.Ø. Holch : landets sidste kgl. borgmester / Mogens Holch. — København : Dansk Historisk Håndbogsforlag, c1986. — 200p. — *Bibliography: p193*

HOLDEN, ISAAC

HONEYMAN, Katrina
Technology and enterprise : Isaac Holden and the mechanisation of woolcombing in France, 1848-1914 / Katrina Honeyman and Jordan Goodman. — Aldershot : Scolar [for] the Pasold Research Fund, 1986. — ix,121p,[4]p of plates. — (Pasold studies in textile history ; 6)

HOLIDAYS WITH PAY ACT, 1971

The Holidays with Pay Act, 1971. — [Copenhagen : Ministry of Labour?], 1971. — 8 leaves

HOLISM

Liberating theory / by Michael Albert ... [et al.]. — 1st ed. — Boston, MA. : South End Press, c1986. — 197 p.. — *Bibliography: p. 195-197*

HOLLOWAY, EDWARD — Biography

HOLLOWAY, Edward
Money matters : a modern pilgrim's economic progress / Edward Holloway. — London : Sherwood Press, 1986. — [vii],198p

HOLOCAUST (CHRISTIAN THEOLOGY)

FREY, Robert Seitz
The imperative of response : the holocaust in human context / Robert Seitz Frey, Nancy Thompson-Frey. — Lanham, MD : University Press of America, c1985. — xix, 165 p.. — *Bibliography: p. 144-164*

HOLOCAUST, JEWISH (1939-1945)

BISS, Andreas
Wir hielten die Vernichtung an : der Kampf gegen die "Endlösung" 1944 / Andreas Biss ; mit einer Nachbemerkung von Hans Dieter Heilmann. — Herbstein : März Verlag, 1985. — 403p

HOLOCAUST, JEWISH (1939-1945)
continuation

CASTRO, Fidel
Fidel Castro habla a los trabajadores de América Latina sobre la deuda externa : diálogo sostenido con los delegados de la Conferencia Sindical de los Trabajadores de América Latina y el Caribe sobre la Deuda Externa, durante la sesión de clausura del evento, el jueves 18 de julio de 1985. — Buenos Aires : Editorial Anteo, 1985. — 102 p.

FRANCQ, Henri G.
Hitler's holocaust : a fact of history / Henri G. Francq. — Vancouver : New Star Books, 1986. — 255p. — *Bibliography: p249-252*

GILBERT, Martin
The Macmillan atlas of the Holocaust / Martin Gilbert. — Scales differ. — New York, N.Y. : Da Capo Press, [1984], c1982. — 1 atlas (256 p.). — (A Da Capo paperback). — : *Reprint: Originally published: New York : Macmillan, 1982. — Includes index. — Bibliography: p. 246-254*

Der Mord an den Juden im Zweiten Weltkrieg : Entschlussbildung und Verwicklichung / herausgegeben von Eberhard Jäckel und Jürgen Rohwer. — Stuttgart : Deutsche Verlags-Anstalt, 1985. — 252p

HOLOCAUST, JEWISH (1939-1945) — Addresses, essays, lectures

Genocide, critical issues of the Holocaust : a companion to the film, Genocide / edited by Alex Grobman and Daniel Landes ; associate editor, Sybil Milton. — 1st ed. — Los Angeles, Calif. : Simon Weisenthal Center ; Chappaqua, N.Y. : Rossel Books, 1983. — viii, 501 p.. — *Includes bibliographies and index*

HOLOCAUST, JEWISH (1939-1945) — Anniversaries, etc — Addresses, essays, lectures

Bitburg in moral and political perspective / edited by Geoffrey H. Hartman. — Bloomington : Indiana University Press, c1986. — xvi, 284 p.. — *Bibliography: p. [281]-282*

HOLOCAUST, JEWISH (1939-1945) — Bibliography

CARGAS, Harry J
The Holocaust : an annotated bibliography / Harry James Cargas. — 2nd ed. — Chicago : American Library Association, 1985. — viii, 196 p.. — *Includes indexes*

EDELHEIT, Abraham J
Bibliography on Holocaust literature / Abraham J. Edelheit, Hershel Edelheit. — Boulder : Westview Press, 1986. — xxxvi, 842 p.. — *Includes index*

HOLOCAUST, JEWISH (1939-1945) — Causes

The Persisting question : sociological perspectives and social contexts of modern antisemitism / edited by Helen Fein. — Berlin ; New York : De Gruyter, 1987. — p. cm. — (Current research on antisemitism ; v. 1)

HOLOCAUST, JEWISH (1939-1945) — Congresses

The Holocaust in Hungary : forty years later / edited by Randolph L. Braham and Bela Vago. — New York : Institute of Holocaust Studies of the City University of New York, and Institute of Holocaust Studies of the University of Haifa : Columbia University Press [distributor], 1985. — xv,235p. — (East European monographs ; no.190) (Holocaust studies series). — '... an outgrowth of two international conferences held in 1984....'

HOLOCAUST, JEWISH (1939-1945) — Maps

GILBERT, Martin
The Macmillan atlas of the Holocaust / Martin Gilbert. — Scales differ. — New York, N.Y. : Da Capo Press, [1984], c1982. — 1 atlas (256 p.). — (A Da Capo paperback). — : *Reprint: Originally published: New York : Macmillan, 1982. — Includes index. — Bibliography: p. 246-254*

HOLOCAUST, JEWISH (1939-1945) — Moral and ethical aspects

FREY, Robert Seitz
The imperative of response : the holocaust in human context / Robert Seitz Frey, Nancy Thompson-Frey. — Lanham, MD : University Press of America, c1985. — xix, 165 p.. — *Bibliography: p. 144-164*

HOLOCAUST, JEWISH (1939-1945) — Psychological aspects

BETTELHEIM, Bruno
The informed heart / Bruno Bettelheim. — Harmondsworth : Penguin, 1986. — xix, 309p

HOLOCAUST, JEWISH (1939-1945) — Public opinion — Addresses, essays, lectures

Bitburg in moral and political perspective / edited by Geoffrey H. Hartman. — Bloomington : Indiana University Press, c1986. — xvi, 284 p.. — *Bibliography: p. [281]-282*

HOLOCAUST, JEWISH (1939-1945) — France

COHEN, Richard I
The burden of conscience : French Jewish leadership during the holocaust / Richard I. Cohen. — Bloomington : Indiana University Press, c1987. — p. cm. — (The Modern Jewish experience). — *Includes index. — Bibliography: p*

KLARSFELD, Serge
Vichy-Auschwitz : le rôle de Vichy dans la solution finale de la question juive en France / Serge Klarsfeld. — Paris : Fayard [2]: 1943-1944. — 1985. — 408p

HOLOCAUST, JEWISH (1939-1945) — Italy

ZUCCOTTI, Susan
The Italians and the Holocaust : persecution, rescue and survival / Susan Zuccotti. — London : Halban, 1987. — xviii,334p,[8]p of plates. — *Includes index*

HOLOCAUST (JEWISH THEOLOGY)

FREY, Robert Seitz
The imperative of response : the holocaust in human context / Robert Seitz Frey, Nancy Thompson-Frey. — Lanham, MD : University Press of America, c1985. — xix, 165 p.. — *Bibliography: p. 144-164*

HOLY ROMAN EMPIRE — Kings and rulers — Biography

BEALES, Derek
Joseph II / Derek Beales. — Cambridge : Cambridge University Press
1: In the shadow of Maria Theresa, 1741-1780. — 1987. — [940]p. — *Includes bibliography and index*

EVANS, R. J. W.
Rudolf II and his world : a study in intellectual history 1576-1612 / by R.J.W. Evans. — Oxford : Clarendon, 1984, c1973. — xv,323,[16]p. — *Originally published: 1973. — Bibliography: p299-310. — Includes index*

HOME AND SCHOOL — European Economic Community countries

MACBETH, Alastair
The child between : a report on school-family relations in the countries of the European Community / Dr. Alastair Macbeth. — Luxembourg : Office for Official Publications of the European Communities, 1984. — 236p. — (Education series / Commission of the European Communities ; no.13)

HOME CARE SERVICES — Great Britain

AUDIT COMMISSION FOR LOCAL AUTHORITIES IN ENGLAND AND WALES
Making a reality of community care : a report. — London : H.M.S.O., 1986. — 131p. — *Bibliographical references: p79-81*

HOME CARE SERVICES — Netherlands — Statistics

Cliëntenonderzoek gezinsverzorging 1980. — 's-Gravenhage : Staatsvitgeverij, 1985. — 51p. — *Title on back cover: Clients of home help services 1980*

HOME ECONOMICS

CHABAUD-RYCHTER, Danielle
Espace et temps du travail domestique / Danielle Chabaud-Rychter, Dominique Fongeyrollas-Schwebel [et] Françoise Southounax. — Paris : Libraries des Méridiens, 1985. — 156p

CONTRIBUTIONS TO HUMAN RESOURCES RESEARCH: A MULTI-DISCIPLINARY SYMPOSIUM (1986 : St. Louis)
Human resources research, 1887-1987 : proceedings / ; edited by Ruth E. Deacon and Wallace E. Huffman. — Ames, Iowa : Iowa State University. College of Home Economics, 1986. — xiii,263p. — *Includes bibliographies*

HOME ECONOMICS — Bangladesh

KABEER, Naila
The functions of children in the household economy and levels of fertility : a case study of a village in Bangladesh / Naila Kabeer. — 311 leaves. — *PhD (Econ) 1986 LSE. — Leaves 260-301 are appendices*

HOME ECONOMICS — Bulgaria — Accounting — Statistics

BULGARIA, 10, Komitet za sotsialna informatsiia pri Ministerskiia Suvet
Biudzheti na domakinstvata v NR Bulgaria (1965-1984g.). — Sofiia : Komitet za sotsialna information, 1985. — 233p

HOME ECONOMICS — Finland — Accounting

Kotitaloustiedustelu 1981 = Hushållsbudgetundersökningen 1981. — Helsinki : Tilastokeskus
Osa 3: Laatuselvitys = Del 3: Kvalitetsutredning. — 1986. — 127p. — (Tilastollisia tiedonantoja = Statistical surveys ; no.71). — *In Finnish and Swedish*

MARJOMAA, Pertti
Väestökehitys ja kotitalouks n kulutusmenot = Demografic [sic] development and household consumption expenditure. — Helsinki : Tilastokeskus, 1982. — 57p. — (Tutkimuksia / Finland. Tilastokeskus ; no.79). — *Bibliography: p56-57*

HOME ECONOMICS — Hong Kong — Accounting — Statistics

Report of the household expenditure survey, 1984-85. — Hong Kong : Census and Statistics Department, 1986. — viii,153p. — *Cover title: Report on the household expenditure survey, 1984-85*

HOME ECONOMICS — Nepal — Accounting — Statistics

Report on household budget survey Kathmandu : mid-April 1973-mid-April 1974. — Kathmandu : Nepal Rastra Bank, 1976. — 81p

HOME ECONOMICS — Netherlands — Accounting

De leefsituatie van de Nederlandse bevolking 1983. — 's-Gravenhage : Staatsuitgeverij. — *Title on back cover: Well-being of the population in the Netherlands 1983: financial strength of one and two income households. — Bibliography: p31-32*
De draagkracht van één- en tweeverdieners. — 1986. — 32p

HOME GUARD *See* Great Britain. Army. Home Guard

HOME LABOR — Germany — History

FRANZOI, Barbara
At the very least she pays the rent : women and German industrialization 1871-1914 / Barbara Franzoi. — Westport, Conn. ; London : Greenwood Press, 1985. — xii, 206p, 10p of plates. — (Contributions in women's studies ; no.57). — *Bibliography: p.[187]-199*

HOME LABOR — Great Britian
HAKIM, C.
Employers' use of outwork : a study using the 1980 Workplace industrial relations survey and the 1981 National survey of homeworking / by Catherine Hakim. — [London] : Department of Employment, 1985. — 107p. — (Research paper / Department of Employment ; no.44). — *Bibliography: p.104-107*

HOME OWNERSHIP — Government policy — Great Britain
BALL, Michael
Home ownership : a suitable case for reform / Michael Ball. — London : Shelter, 1986. — 70p

HOME OWNERSHIP — Great Britain
FORREST, Ray
A foot on the ladder? : an evaluation of low cost home ownership initiatives / Ray Forrest, Stewart Lansley, Alan Murie. — Bristol : University of Bristol School for Advanced Urban Studies, c1984. — 150p. — (Working paper ; no.41)

HOME RULE (IRELAND)
LOUGHLIN, James
Gladstone, Home Rule and the Ulster question 1882-93 / James Loughlin. — Dublin : Gill and Macmillan, c1986. — 369p. — *Bibliography: p333-361. — Includes index*

HOME RULE (IRELAND) — History — Sources
MCMINN, J. R. B.
Against the tide : a calendar of the papers of Rev. J. B Armour, Irish Presbyterian minister and Home Ruler, 1869-1914. — Belfast : PRONI, 1985. — lxii,225p

HOMELANDS (SOUTH AFRICA)
UNTERHALTER, Elaine
Forced removal : the division, segregation and control of the people of South Africa / Elaine Unterhalter. — London : International Defence and Aid Fund for Southern Africa, 1987. — viii,177p,[8]p of plates. — *Bibliography: p156-167. — Includes index*

HOMELANDS (SOUTH AFRICA) — Constitutional law
The Constitutions of Transkei, Bophuthatswana, Venda, and Ciskei / editors M.P. Vorster, M. Wiechers, D.J. van Vuuren ; contributors G.N. Barrie ... [et al.]. — Durban : Butterworths, 1985. — 269 p.. — *Includes bibliographical references and indexes*

HOMELESS MEN — England — Gloucester (Gloucestershire)
COWEN, Harry
The hidden homeless : a report of a survey on homelessness and housing amongst single young Blacks in Gloucester / Harry Cowen with Richard Lording. — Gloucester (15 Brunswick Rd, Gloucester GL1 1HG) : Gloucester Community Relations Council, 1982. — 54p

HOMELESS PERSONS — Legal status, laws, etc. — Great Britain
ARDEN, Andrew
Homeless persons : the Housing Act 1985 Part III / Andrew Arden. — 2nd ed. — London : Legal Action Group, 1986. — xxiii,200p. — (Law and Practice Guide ; No.5). — *Previous ed.: 1982*

HOMELESS PERSONS — Great Britain
SAUNDERS, Barbara
Homeless young people in Britain : the contribution of the voluntary sector / written for ERICA and DSU by Barbara Saunders ; with cartoons by Peter Kneebone. — London : published in association with ERICA and DSU by Bedford Square Press NCVO, 1986. — iv,108p. — *Bibliography: p108*

HOMELESS WOMEN — England — Gloucester (Gloucestershire)
COWEN, Harry
The hidden homeless : a report of a survey on homelessness and housing amongst single young Blacks in Gloucester / Harry Cowen with Richard Lording. — Gloucester (15 Brunswick Rd, Gloucester GL1 1HG) : Gloucester Community Relations Council, 1982. — 54p

HOMELESS YOUTH — Great Britain
LUPTON, Carol
Moving out : older teenagers leaving residential care / Carol Lupton. — Portmouth : Social Services Research and Intelligence Unit, 1985. — 206p. — (SSRIU Report ; no.12)

HOMELESSNESS — Government policy — Great Britain
CONWAY, Jean
Bed and breakfast : slum housing of the eighties / Jean Conway and Peter Kemp. — London : SHAC, c1985. — 54p. — (SHAC policy paper ; 7)

HOMELESSNESS — Government policy — London metropolitan area
TUCKLEY, Will
Temporary accommodation - counting the cost : the 1985 GLC survey of the use of temporary accommodation for homeless households in London / [... by Will Tuckley and Debra Levison ...]. — London : Greater London Council, 1986. — 64p. — (GLC housing research & policy report ; no.4). — *Title from cover*

HOMELESSNESS — Law and legislation — Great Britain
ARDEN, Andrew
Homeless persons : the Housing Act 1985 Part III / Andrew Arden. — 2nd ed. — London : Legal Action Group, 1986. — xxiii,200p. — (Law and Practice Guide ; No.5). — *Previous ed.: 1982*

HOMELESSNESS — England — London
GREATER LONDON COUNCIL. Controller of Housing and Technical Services
The use of temporary accommodaion by homeless families in London. — [London] : the Council, 1984. — 17,[9]p. — *Cover title : Temporary accommodation : long term problem*

GREATER LONDON COUNCIL. Housing Department
Temporary accommodation and homeless households. — [London] : the Council, 1985. — 26 leaves

It's the limit : an exposé of pricing in London's B and B land. — London : CHAR, 1986. — 40p

LONDON HOUSING RESEARCH GROUP
The homeless in Brent and Lewisham : a report. — [London : Greater London Council, 1983]. — 14 leaves

LOWE, Clare
Outside the Act : a study of young single homeless people in the London borough of Southwark / Clare Lowe. — Southwark : Southwark Housing Departmnt. Research and Development Group, 1986. — 54p. — *At head of title: Southwark housing*

SINGLE HOMELESSNESS IN LONDON WORKING PARTY
Single homelessness in London 1986 : a report. — London : Greater London Council, 1986. — 54p. — *A joint GLC and London Boroughs Working Party. — Bibliography: p54*

HOMELESSNESS — Great Britain
CONWAY, Jean
Bed and breakfast : slum housing of the eighties / Jean Conway and Peter Kemp. — London : SHAC, c1985. — 54p. — (SHAC policy paper ; 7)

INSTITUTE OF HOUSING. Vacant Properties Working Party
The key to empty housing. — London : Institute of Housing, 1986. — 63p. — (Professional practice series / Institute of Housing ; no.5)

HOMELESSNESS — Great Britain — Government policy
RICHARDS, Janet
The Housing (Homeless Persons) Act 1977 : a study in policymaking / Janet Richards. — Bristol : School for Advanced Urban Studies, 1987, c1981. — 95p. — (Working papers / University of Bristol School for Advanced Urban Studies ; 22). — *Bibliography: p90-95*

HOMELESSNESS — London
Homelessness in London : a statement and recommendations by the Research Team : submitted to the Greater London Council in March 1986 / John Greve ... [et al.]. — Bristol : University of Bristol, School for Advanced Urban Studies, 1986. — 39p. — (Working paper / University of Bristol, School for Advanced Urban Studies ; 60). — *Study commissioned from the University of Leeds, University of Birmingham and the University of Bristol*

HOMELESSNESS — New York (State) — History — 20th century
CROUSE, Joan M.
The homeless transient in the Great Depression : New York State, 1929-1941 / Joan M. Crouse. — Albany, N.Y. : State University of New York Press, c1986. — xii, 319 p., [8] p. of plates. — : *Revision of thesis (doctoral)--State University of New York at Buffalo. — Includes index. — Bibliography: p. 296-306*

HOMELESSNESS — Scotland
BRITAIN, Amanda
Joint initiatives : a guide to special projects between welfare and housing agencies / Amanda Britain, Hector Currie and Fiona Philipson. — Edinburgh : Scottish Council for Single Homeless, 1986. — 85p. — *Bibliography: p85*

HOMELESSNESS — United States
REDBURN, F. Stevens
Responding to America's homeless : public policy alternatives / F. Stevens Redburn and Terry F. Buss. — New York : Praeger, 1986. — xvi, 154 p.. — *Includes index. — Bibliography: p. 142-148*

HOMESITES — Government policy — Great Britain
RYDIN, Yvonne
Housing land policy / Yvonne Rydin. — Aldershot : Gower, c1986. — xii,153p. — *Bibliography: p136-150. — Includes index*

HOMICIDE — Great Britain — Statistics
GREAT BRITAIN. Parliament. House of Commons. Library. Research Division
Homicide statistics / Robert Clements. — [London] : the Division, 1982. — 23p. — (Background paper ; no.102)

GREAT BRITAIN. Parliament. House of Commons. Library. Research Division
Homicide statistics / Robert Clements. — [London] : the Division, 1983. — 22p. — (Background paper ; no.123). — *Update of Background Paper no.102. — Bibliography: p8-9*

GREAT BRITAIN. Parliament. House of Commons. Library. Research Division
Homicide statistics / Robert Clements. — [London] : the Division, 1984. — 23p. — (Background paper ; no.139). — *Updates Background Paper no.123. — Bibliography: p8-9*

GREAT BRITAIN. Parliament. House of Commons. Library. Research Division
Homicide statistics / Robert Clements. — [London] : the Division, 1987. — 26p. — (Background paper ; no.197). — *Updates Background Paper no.139. — Bibliography: p9-10*

HOMICIDE — Great Britain — Statistics
continuation
GREAT BRITAIN. Parliament. House of Commons. Library. Research Division
Statistics of murder / [Rob Clements]. — [London] : the Division, [1979]. — 14p. — (Background paper ; no.71). — *Select bibliography: p14*

HOMICIDE — Kentucky — History
MONTELL, William Lynwood
Killings : folk justice in the Upper South / William Lynwood Montell. — Lexington, KY : University Press of Kentucky, 1986. — p. cm. — *Includes index. — Bibliography: p*

HOMICIDE — Tennesee — History
MONTELL, William Lynwood
Killings : folk justice in the Upper South / William Lynwood Montell. — Lexington, KY : University Press of Kentucky, 1986. — p. cm. — *Includes index. — Bibliography: p*

HOMOSEXUALITY
CARPENTER, Edward, 1844-1929
Selected writings / Edward Carpenter. — London : GMP. — (Gay modern classics) Vol.1: Sex / with an introduction by Nöel Grieg. — 1984. — 318p. — *Includes index*

GREEN, Richard
The "sissy boy syndrome" and the development of homosexuality / Richard Green. — New Haven : Yale University Press, c1987. — x, 416 p.. — *Includes index. — Bibliography: p. 399-409*

HOMOSEXUALITY — Bibliography
CRAWFORD, William
Homosexuality in Canada : a bibliography / compiled by William Crawford. — 2nd ed. — Toronto, Ont., Canada : Canadian Gay Archives, c1984. — viii, 378 columns. — (Canadian Gay Archives publication ; no. 9). — : *Previous ed.: Homosexuality in Canada : a bibliography / compiled by Alex Spence. 1979. — Includes index*

HOMOSEXUALITY — Law and legislation — Germany
PLANT, Richard
The pink triangle : the Nazi war against homosexuals / Richard Plant. — 1st ed. — New York : H. Holt, c1986. — x, 257 p.. — "A New Republic book.". — *Includes index. — Bibliography: p. 236-248*

HOMOSEXUALITY — Law and legislation — Great Britain
GREASLEY, Phil
Gay men at work : a report on discrimination against gay men in employment in London / by Phil Greasley ; contributions from: Matt Williams...[et al.]. — [London?] : Lesbian and Gay Employment Rights, 1986. — vi,104p. — *Bibliography: p103-104*

HOMOSEXUALITY — Canada
KINSMAN, Gary
The regulation of desire : sexuality in Canada / Gary Kinsman. — Montréal ; New York : Black Rose Books, 1987. — 233p. — *Includes references*

HOMOSEXUALITY — Canada — Bibliography
CRAWFORD, William
Homosexuality in Canada : a bibliography / compiled by William Crawford. — 2nd ed. — Toronto, Ont., Canada : Canadian Gay Archives, c1984. — viii, 378 columns. — (Canadian Gay Archives publication ; no. 9). — : *Previous ed.: Homosexuality in Canada : a bibliography / compiled by Alex Spence. 1979. — Includes index*

HOMOSEXUALITY, MALE — Cross-cultural studies
WHITAM, Frederick L
Male homosexuality in four societies : Brazil, Guatemala, the Philippines, and the United States / Frederick L. Whitam and Robin M. Mathy ; foreword by Milton Diamond. — New York : Praeger, 1985. — p. cm. — *Includes indexes. — Bibliography: p*

HOMOSEXUALITY, MALE — Germany — History — 20th century
PLANT, Richard
The pink triangle : the Nazi war against homosexuals / Richard Plant. — 1st ed. — New York : H. Holt, c1986. — x, 257 p.. — "A New Republic book.". — *Includes index. — Bibliography: p. 236-248*

HOMOSEXUALITY, MALE — Papua New Guinea
HERDT, Gilbert H.
Sambia : ritual and gender in New Guinea / by Gilbert H. Herdt. — New York : Holt, Rinehart and Winston, 1986. — p. cm. — (Case studies in cultural anthropology). — *Includes index. — Bibliography: p*

HOMOSEXUALS — Great Britain
FITZPATRICK, Michael
The truth about the Aids panic / Michael Fitzpatrick, Don Milligan. — London : Junius, 1987. — 66p. — *Bibliography: p65-66*

HOMOSEXUALS — United States — Political activity
PATTON, Cindy
Sex & germs : the politics of AIDS / Cindy Patton. — 1st ed. — Boston : South End Press, c1985. — 182 p.. — *Includes index. — Bibliography: p. 175-178*

HOMOSEXUALS, MALE — Employment — England — London
GREASLEY, Phil
Gay men at work : a report on discrimination against gay men in employment in London / by Phil Greasley ; contributions from: Matt Williams...[et al.]. — [London?] : Lesbian and Gay Employment Rights, 1986. — vi,104p. — *Bibliography: p103-104*

HONDURANS — Scotland
SHERWWOD, Marika
The British Honduran forestry unit in Scotland 1941-43 / Marika Sherwwod. — London : One Caribbean, 1982. — 51p. — *Bibliography: p.51*

HONDURAS — Economic conditions — 1918-
Honduras confronts its future : contending perspectives on critical issues / edited by Mark B. Rosenberg and Philip L. Shepherd. — Boulder, Colo. : L. Rienner Publishers, 1986. — xii, 268p. — *Essays first presented at "Honduras: An International Dialogue", in Miami, Fla., December 1984. — Includes bibliographical references and index*

HONDURAS — Foreign relations
Honduras confronts its future : contending perspectives on critical issues / edited by Mark B. Rosenberg and Philip L. Shepherd. — Boulder, Colo. : L. Rienner Publishers, 1986. — xii, 268p. — *Essays first presented at "Honduras: An International Dialogue", in Miami, Fla., December 1984. — Includes bibliographical references and index*

HONDURAS — Politics and government — 1982-
Honduras confronts its future : contending perspectives on critical issues / edited by Mark B. Rosenberg and Philip L. Shepherd. — Boulder, Colo. : L. Rienner Publishers, 1986. — xii, 268p. — *Essays first presented at "Honduras: An International Dialogue", in Miami, Fla., December 1984. — Includes bibliographical references and index*

HONG KONG — Census, 1976
Statistical experimentation for household surveys : two case studies of Hong Kong / Christiaan Grootaert ... [et al.]. — Washington, D.C. : World Bank, 1982. — 66p. — (LSMS working papers ; no.20). — *Cover title. — Bibliography: p65-66*

HONG KONG — Census, 1986
Hong Kong 1986 by-census : District Board district tabulations. — Hong Kong : Census and Statistics Department, [1987]. — 19Parts

Hong Kong 1986 by-census : District Board Constituency Area summary tables. — Hong Kong : Census and Statistics Department, [1987]. — xv,330p. — *With three maps in end pockets*

Hong Kong 1986 by-census : District Board district summary tables. — Hong Kong : Census and Statistics Department, [1987]. — xi,35p. — *With 3 maps in end-pocket*

Hong Kong 1986 by-census : tertiary planning unit summary tables : Hong Kong Island. — Hong Kong : Census and Statistics Department, [1987]. — xiii,140p. — *Has map in end pocket*

Hong Kong 1986 by-census : tertiary planning unit summary tables / Kowloon and New Kowloon. — Hong Kong : Census and Statistics Department, [1987]. — xiii,152p. — *Has map in end pocket*

Hong Kong 1986 by-census : tertiary planning unit summary tables / new territories. — Hong Kong : Census and Statistics Department, [1987]. — xiii,268p. — *Has two maps in end pocket*

HONG KONG — Description and travel
A Geography of Hong Kong / editors T.N. Chiu, C.L. So. — 2nd ed. / contributors P. Catt ... [et al.]. — Hong Kong ; Oxford : Oxford University Press, 1986. — [400]p. — *Previous ed.: 1983. — Includes bibliography and index*

HONG KONG — Economic conditions
Hong Kong in transition / editor Joseph Y.S. Cheng ; contributors Albert H.Y. Chen ... [et al.]. — Hong Kong ; Oxford : Oxford University Press, 1986. — xvi,457p. — *Includes bibliographies and index*

KELLY, Ian
Hong Kong : a political-geographic analysis / Ian Kelly. — Basingstoke : Macmillan, 1987. — xiv,191p. — *Bibliography: p172-181. — Includes index*

LIU, Siu-kai
Society and politics in Hong Kong / Lau Siu-kai. — Hong Kong : Chinese University Press ; New York : St. Martin's Press, 1983. — x, 205 p.. — *Includes index. — Bibliography: p. [191]-201*

Long-term economic and agricultural commodity projections for Hong Kong, 1970, 1975, and 1980. — Jerusalem : Publications Services Division of the Israel Program for Scientific Translations for the U.S. Department of Agriculture, 1969. — xiv,248p. — *Contents: A contract study...for the United States Department of Agriculture under the principal research directorship of Anthony M. Tang*

HONG KONG — Economic conditions — Statistics
Hong Kong 1986 by-census : District Board Constituency Area summary tables. — Hong Kong : Census and Statistics Department, [1987]. — xv,330p. — *With three maps in end pockets*

Hong Kong 1986 by-census : tertiary planning unit summary tables : Hong Kong Island. — Hong Kong : Census and Statistics Department, [1987]. — xiii,140p. — *Has map in end pocket*

Hong Kong 1986 by-census : tertiary planning unit summary tables / Kowloon and New Kowloon. — Hong Kong : Census and Statistics Department, [1987]. — xiii,152p. — *Has map in end pocket*

Hong Kong 1986 by-census : tertiary planning unit summary tables / new territories. — Hong Kong : Census and Statistics Department, [1987]. — xiii,268p. — *Has two maps in end pocket*

HONG KONG — Economic policy
The Political economy of the new Asian industrialism / edited by Frederic C. Deyo. — Ithaca, N.Y. : Cornell University Press, 1987. — 252 p.. — (Cornell studies in political economy). — Includes bibliographies and index. — Contents: Export-oriented industrializing states in the capitalist world system / Richard E. Barrett and Soomi Chin -- The origins and development of the Northeast Asian political economy / Bruce Cumings -- State and foreign capital in the East Asian NICs / Stephan Haggard and Tun-jen Cheng -- Political institutions and economic performance / Chalmers Johnson -- The interplay of state, social class, and world system in East Asian development / Hagen Koo -- State and labor / Frederic C. Deyo -- Class, state, and dependence in East Asia / Peter Evans -- Coalitions, institutions, and linkage sequencing toward a strategic capacity model of East Asian development / Frederic C. Deyo

HONG KONG — Foreign relations — Great Britain
HONG KONG LINK
Hong Kong : towards the future: British responsibilities. — London : Hong Kong Link, 1985. — 12p

Hong Kong towards the future: British responsibilities. — London : Hong Kong Link, 1987. — 12p

WALDEN, John
Excellency, your gap is showing! / John Walden. — [Hong Kong : Corporate Communications], c1983. — 82,72p. — *Text in English and Chinese*

HONG KONG — Languages
GIBBONS, John, 1946-
Code-mixing and code choice : a Hong Kong case study / John Gibbons. — Clevedon : Multilingual Matters, c1987. — [184]p. — (Multilingual matters ; 27). — *Includes bibliography and index*

HONG KONG — Politics and government
HONG KONG LINK
Hong Kong : towards the future: British responsibilities. — London : Hong Kong Link, 1985. — 12p

Hong Kong towards the future: British responsibilities. — London : Hong Kong Link, 1987. — 12p

KELLY, Ian
Hong Kong : a political-geographic analysis / Ian Kelly. — Basingstoke : Macmillan, 1987. — xiv,191p. — *Bibliography: p172-181. — Includes index*

LIU, Siu-kai
Society and politics in Hong Kong / Lau Siu-kai. — Hong Kong : Chinese University Press ; New York : St. Martin's Press, 1983. — x, 205 p.. — *Includes index. — Bibliography: p. [191]-201*

MINERS, Norman
The government and politics of Hong Kong / Norman Miners. — 4th ed. — Hong Kong ; Oxford : Oxford University Press, 1986. — [320]p. — *Previous ed.: 1981. — Includes bibliography and index*

WALDEN, John
Excellency, your gap is showing! / John Walden. — [Hong Kong : Corporate Communications], c1983. — 82,72p. — *Text in English and Chinese*

HONG KONG — Population — Statistics
Hong Kong 1986 by-census : District Board district tabulations. — Hong Kong : Census and Statistics Department, [1987]. — 19Parts

Hong Kong 1986 by-census : District Board Constituency Area summary tables. — Hong Kong : Census and Statistics Department, [1987]. — xv,330p. — *With three maps in end pockets*

Hong Kong 1986 by-census : District Board district summary tables. — Hong Kong : Census and Statistics Department, [1987]. — xi,35p. — *With 3 maps in end-pocket*

Hong Kong 1986 by-census : tertiary planning unit summary tables : Hong Kong Island. — Hong Kong : Census and Statistics Department, [1987]. — xiii,140p. — *Has map in end pocket*

Hong Kong 1986 by-census : tertiary planning unit summary tables / Kowloon and New Kowloon. — Hong Kong : Census and Statistics Department, [1987]. — xiii,152p. — *Has map in end pocket*

Hong Kong 1986 by-census : tertiary planning unit summary tables / new territories. — Hong Kong : Census and Statistics Department, [1987]. — xiii,268p. — *Has two maps in end pocket*

HONG KONG — Social conditions
Hong Kong in transition / editor Joseph Y.S. Cheng ; contributors Albert H.Y. Chen ... [et al.]. — Hong Kong ; Oxford : Oxford University Press, 1986. — xvi,457p. — *Includes bibliographies and index*

LIU, Siu-kai
Society and politics in Hong Kong / Lau Siu-kai. — Hong Kong : Chinese University Press ; New York : St. Martin's Press, 1983. — x, 205 p.. — *Includes index. — Bibliography: p. [191]-201*

WARD, Barbara E.
Through other eyes : essays in understanding 'conscious models' : mostly in Hong Kong / Barbara E. Ward. — Hong Kong : Chinese University Press ; Boulder : Westview, 1985. — xvi,280p

HONG KONG — Social conditions — Statistics
Hong Kong 1986 by-census : District Board Constituency Area summary tables. — Hong Kong : Census and Statistics Department, [1987]. — xv,330p. — *With three maps in end pockets*

Social data collected by the General Household Survey. — Hong Kong : Census and Statistics Department, [1984]. — 103p. — (Special topics / Census and Statistics Department, Hong Kong ; Report 2)

HONG KONG — Social conditions — Addresses, essays, lectures
Social life and development in Hong Kong / edited by Ambrose Y.C. King and Rance P.L. Lee. — Hong Kong : Chinese University Press, c1981. — xxv, 366 p.. — *"Papers ... from research sponsored by the Social Research Centre of the Chinese University of Hong Kong"--P. v. — Bibliography: p. [325]-366*

HONG KONG — Social policy
The Common welfare : Hong Kong's social services / edited by John F. Jones. — Hong Kong : Chinese University Press ; Manila, Philippines : United Nations Social Welfare and Development Centre for Asia and the Pacific, c1981. — xix, 148 p.. — *Includes index. — Bibliography: p. [131]-146*

HONG KONG ISLAND (HONG KONG) — Statistics
Hong Kong 1986 by-census : tertiary planning unit summary tables : Hong Kong Island. — Hong Kong : Census and Statistics Department, [1987]. — xiii,140p. — *Has map in end pocket*

HONGKONG TRAMWAYS LIMITED
Hongkong Tramways Ltd : analysis of individual workers reactions to management policies and techniques. — [S.l.] : [S.n.], 1960. — 33 leaves

HONK KONG — Social conditions — Statistics
Social data collected by the General Household Survey. — Hong Kong : Census and Statistics Department, [1985]. — 77p. — (Special topics ; Report 3)

HOOKER, RICHARD, 1553 or 4-1600
D'ENTRÈVES, A. P.
The medieval contribution to political thought : Thomas Aquinas, Marsilius of Padua, Richard Hooker / by Alexander Passerin D'Entreves. — New York : Humanities, 1959. — viii,148p. — *On spine: Medieval contributions to political thought. — Originally published: Oxford University Press, 1939*

HOOVER, HERBERT — Views on race relations
LISIO, Donald J
Hoover, Blacks, and lily-whites : a study of Southern strategies / Donald J. Lisio. — Chapel Hill ; London : University of North Carolina Press, c1985. — xxii, 373p. — (The Fred W. Morrison series in Southern studies). — *Includes index. — Bibliography: p.357-364*

HOOVER INSTITUTION ON WAR, REVOLUTION, AND PEACE
The Library of the Hoover Institution on War, Revolution, and Peace / edited by Peter Duignan. — Stanford, Calif. : Hoover Institution, Stanford University, 1985. — p. cm . — *Bibliography: p*

HOOVER INSTITUTION ON WAR, REVOLUTION, AND PEACE — Catalogs
HOOVER INSTITUTION ON WAR, REVOLUTION, AND PEACE
Unofficial documents of the Democracy Movement in Communist China, 1978-1981 = : Chung-kuo min chu yun tung tzu liao : a checklist of Chinese materials in the Hoover Institution on War, Revolution and Peace / compiled by I-mu. — Stanford, Calif. : East Asian Collection, Hoover Institution, 1986. — viii, 100 p.. — (Hoover Press bibliographical series ; 67). — *English and Chinese*

HORKHEIMER, MAX
Max Horkheimer heute : Werk und Wirkung / herausgegeben von Alfred Schmidt und Norbert Altwicker. — Frankfurt am Main : Fischer, 1986. — 399p. — *Bibliography: p372-379*

HORNE, MICHAEL R.. Review of the Public Utilities Street Works Act 1950
GREAT BRITAIN
Public utilities street works : the government response to the Horne report on the review of the Public Utilities Street Works Act 1950. — London : H.M.S.O., 1986. — 32p. — *At head of title page: Department of Transport*

HORNEY, KAREN
WESTCOTT, Marcia
The feminist legacy of Karen Horney / Marcia Westkott. — New Haven : Yale University Press, c1986. — p. cm. — *Includes index. — Bibliography: p*

HORROR FILMS
GREAT BRITAIN. Parliament. House of Commons. Library. Research Division
"Video nasties" : a background to the Video Recordings Bill, 1983-84 / [Jane Fiddick]. — [London] : the Division, 1983. — 29p. — (Background paper ; no.130)

HORTICULTURAL PRODUCTS INDUSTRY — Europe, Southern — Congresses
Horticultural trade of the expanded European Community : implications for Mediterranean countries / edited by Malcolm D. Bale. — Washington, D.C., U.S.A. : World Bank, 1986. — x,274p. — (A World Bank symposium). — *Based on symposiums held Oct. 1984 at the World Bank of Wahington, D.C. and at the Food and Agriculture Organization in Rome, Italy*

HORTICULTURAL PRODUCTS INDUSTRY — European Economic Community countries — Congresses
Horticultural trade of the expanded European Community : implications for Mediterranean countries / edited by Malcolm D. Bale. — Washington, D.C., U.S.A. : World Bank, 1986. — x,274p. — (A World Bank symposium). — *Based on symposiums held Oct. 1984 at the World Bank of Wahington, D.C. and at the Food and Agriculture Organization in Rome, Italy*

HORTICULTURAL PRODUCTS INDUSTRY — Mediterranean Region — Congresses
Horticultural trade of the expanded European Community : implications for Mediterranean countries / edited by Malcolm D. Bale. — Washington, D.C., U.S.A. : World Bank, 1986. — x,274p. — (A World Bank symposium). — *Based on symposiums held Oct. 1984 at the World Bank of Wahington, D.C. and at the Food and Agriculture Organization in Rome, Italy*

HORTICULTURE — Bibliography
DAVID LUBIN MEMORIAL LIBRARY
FAO documentation : plant production and protection : 1979-1983 = Documentation de la FAO : production et protection des végétaux : 1979-1983 = Documentacion de la FAO : produccion y proteccion de plantas : 1979-1983. — Rome : Food and Agriculture Organization, 1985. — 112,13,34,12p. — *In English with introductions also in French and Spanish*

HOSIERY INDUSTRY — Great Britain — History — 19th century
ERICKSON, Charlotte
British industrialists : steel and hosiery 1850-1950 / Charlotte Erickson. — Aldershot : Gower in association with he London School of Economics and Political Science, c1986. — xxi,276p. — *Originally published: Cambridge : Cambridge University Press, 1959.* — *Bibliography: p248-257.* — *Includes index*

HOSIERY INDUSTRY — Great Britain — History — 20th century
ERICKSON, Charlotte
British industrialists : steel and hosiery 1850-1950 / Charlotte Erickson. — Aldershot : Gower in association with he London School of Economics and Political Science, c1986. — xxi,276p. — *Originally published: Cambridge : Cambridge University Press, 1959.* — *Bibliography: p248-257.* — *Includes index*

HOSPITAL CARE
FLEMMING, Carol
The other side of medical care / Carol Flemming ; illustrated by Gillian Symonds. — Basingstoke : Macmillan, 1986. — xii,113p. — (The new approaches to care series)

HOSPITAL UTILIZATION — Length of stay — United States
Swing beds : assessing flexible health care in rural communities / edited by Joshua M. Wiener. — Washington, D.C. : Brookings Institution, 1987. — 140p. — (Brookings dialogues on public policy). — *Papers presented at a conference at the Brookings Institution. February 24, 1986*

HOSPITALS — Administration — Australia — Political aspects
DICKENSON, Mary
Hospitals and politics : the Australian Hospital Association 1946-86 / Mary Dickenson and Catherine Mason. — Deakin, A.C.T. : The Association, 1986. — 144p. — *Notes and references p133-138*

HOSPITALS — Finance — Australia
DICKENSON, Mary
Hospitals and politics : the Australian Hospital Association 1946-86 / Mary Dickenson and Catherine Mason. — Deakin, A.C.T. : The Association, 1986. — 144p. — *Notes and references p133-138*

HOSPITALS — Management and regulation — United States
Swing beds : assessing flexible health care in rural communities / edited by Joshua M. Wiener. — Washington, D.C. : Brookings Institution, 1987. — 140p. — (Brookings dialogues on public policy). — *Papers presented at a conference at the Brookings Institution. February 24, 1986*

HOSPITALS — Australia — Finance
LEVY, V. M.
Financial management of hospitals / by V. M. Levy. — 3rd ed. — Sydney : The Law Book Company Ltd, 1986. — xxii,510p

HOSPITALS — Canada
O'MALLEY, Martin
Hospital : life and death in a major medical centre / Martin O'Halley. — Toronto : Macmillan of Canada, 1986. — xv,239p

HOSPITALS — Canada — Statistics
Annual return of hospitals: hospital indicators = Rapport annuel des hôpitaux: indicateurs des hôpitaux / Statistics Canada. — Ottawa : Minister of Supply and Services, Canada, 1982/83-. — *Annual.* — *Text in English and French*

HOSPITALS — Denmark — Statistics
CHRISTENSEN, Sven Collatz
Befolkningens forbrug af sygehusydelser 1966-1978 / Sven Collatz Christensen, Jørgen Jørgensen og Lene Sørensen. — [København] : Sundhedsstyrelsen, 1981. — 128p. — (Medicinalstatistiske meddelelser / Sundhedsstyrelsen ; 1981:1)

HOSPITALS — England
NORTH-EAST METROPOLITAN REGIONAL HOSPITAL BOARD
NEMET 1948-1974 : a record of progress in the North East Metropolitan Region. — [London : the Board, ca.1974]. — 28p

HOSPITALS — England — London — After care
Policies, practices and projects : hospital discharge and aftercare initiatives in London. — London (54 Knatchbull Road, SE5 9QY) : Age Concern Greater London, 1985. — 34p. — *Cover title.* — *At head of title: ACGL Health Forum.* — *Bibliography: p31-32*

HOSPITALS — England — London — History
RIVETT, Geoffrey
The development of the London hospital system 1823-1982 / Geoffrey Rivett. — London : King Edward's Hospital Fund for London, c1986. — 423p. — (King's fund historical series ; no.4)

HOSPITALS — Finland
200 years of Finnish hospitals : addresses and articles on the anniversary published by the WHO Committee for Finland. — Helsinki : the Committee, 1958. — 20p

HOSPITALS — France — Statistics
RUHLMANN, O.
Les hôpitaux publics : résultats nationaux de la statistique H80 sur l'exercice 83 (France métropolitaine) / O. Ruhlmann, V. Massinon. — [Paris] : Ministère des Affaires sociales et de la Solidarité nationale, Service des Statistiques, des Etudes et des Systèmes d'Information, 1985. — 67p. — (Solidarité santé. Cahiers statistiques ; 6)

HOSPITALS — Great Britain — Admission and discharge
Administrative arrangements : admissions policy - establishing a policy for controlling admissions / [Department of Health and Social Security, Central Management Services]. — London : H.M.S.O., 1977. — [3]p. — (Notes on good practices ; 1)

GREAT BRITAIN. Parliament. House of Commons. Library. Research Division
Hospital waiting lists / Keith Cuningham, Richard Cracknell. — [London] : the Division, 1987. — 26p. — (Background paper ; no.195). — *Bibliography: p25-26*

HOSPITALS — Great Britain — Waiting lists
YATES, John, 1943 Nov.15-
Why are we waiting? : an analysis of hospital waiting-lists / John Yates. — Oxford : Oxford University Press, 1987. — iv,90p. — *Includes index*

HOSPITALS — London — Hackney
Access to hospitals in the City and Hackney Health Authority, London : a report / prepared by the M.Phil. (Town Planning) students. — [London] : Bartlett School of Architecture and Planning, 1985. — 39p. — (Town Planning discussion paper ; no.43). — *"The original report has been rewritten and extended by David Banister" -p.1*

HOSPITALS — Scotland — Edinburgh (Lothian) — History — 18th century
RISSE, Guenter B.
Hospital life in Enlightenment Scotland : care and teaching at the Royal Infirmary of Edinburgh / Guenter B. Risse. — Cambridge : Cambridge University Press, 1986. — xiv,450p. — (Cambridge history of medicine). — *Includes index*

HOSPITALS — South Australia — Administration
SOUTH AUSTRALIA. Enquiry into Hospital Services in South Australia
Report of the Enquiry into Hospital Services in South Australia. — Adelaide : [South Australian Health Commission], 1983. — xix,456p. — *Bibliography: p451-454.* — *Chairman: Sidney Sax*

HOSPITALS — Sweden
DODD, John
Swedish hospitals and health services : notes and impressions / John Dodd. — Bristol : British Hospitals Contributory Schemes Association, 1950. — 42p

HOSPITALS — Wales — Personnel management
CRICHTON, Anne
Disappointed expectations? : Report on a survey of professional and technical staff in the hospital service in Wales 1963 / [by] Anne Crichton [and] Marion P. Crawford. — [Whitchurch : Glamorgan] Welsh Hospital Board, Welsh Staff Advisory Committee, [1964]. — 110 p. — *Includes bibliographical references*

HOSPITALS — Wales — Staff
CRICHTON, Anne
Disappointed expectations? : Report on a survey of professional and technical staff in the hospital service in Wales 1963 / [by] Anne Crichton [and] Marion P. Crawford. — [Whitchurch : Glamorgan] Welsh Hospital Board, Welsh Staff Advisory Committee, [1964]. — 110 p. — *Includes bibliographical references*

HOSPITALS, MOBILE
INTERNATIONAL MEETING ON MOBILE DISASTER UNITS (1984 : Geneva)
Final report. — Geneva : United Nations, 1984. — 68p

INTERNATIONAL MEETING ON MOBILE SISASTER UNITS (1982 : Geneva)
Final report. — Geneva : United Nations, 1982. — ii,18,8,5p

Something to look forward to : an evaluation of a travelling day hospital for elderly mentally ill people / Neil Evans...[et al.]. — Portsmouth : Social Services Research and Intelligence Unit, 1986. — x,254p. — (SSRIU Report ; No.15). — *Bibliography: p[251]-254*

HOSPITALS, PROPRIETARY — England — South East — Planning

MOHAN, John
Spatial aspects and planning implications of private hospital developments in South East England, 1976-84 / John Mohan. — London (7/15 Gresse St., W1P 1PA) : Geography Department, Birkbeck College, [1984]. — vi,65p. — (Occasional paper / Geography Department)

HOSPITALS, PUBLIC — Australia

DICKENSON, Mary
Hospitals and politics : the Australian Hospital Association 1946-86 / Mary Dickenson and Catherine Mason. — Deakin, A.C.T. : The Association, 1986. — 144p. — Notes and references p133-138

HOSTAGES — Iran

RYAN, Paul B
The Iranian rescue mission : why it failed / by Paul B. Ryan. — Annapolis, Md. : Naval Institute Press, c1985. — xiii, 185p. — Includes index. — Bibliography: p [177]-180

HOSTAGES — United States

RYAN, Paul B
The Iranian rescue mission : why it failed / by Paul B. Ryan. — Annapolis, Md. : Naval Institute Press, c1985. — xiii, 185p. — Includes index. — Bibliography: p [177]-180

HOTELS, TAVERNS, ETC — Employees — Bermuda

Report on the employment of all workers and housing of non-Bermudians in the hotel industry / Statistical Department, Ministry of Finance, Bermuda. — Hamilton : Ministry of Finance, Statistical Department, 1985-. — Quarterly

HOTELS, TAVERNS, ETC. — Employees — Great Britain

Waiting for change? : working in hotel and catering / edited by Dominic Byrne. — London : Low Pay Unit, 1986. — v,66p. — (Low pay pamphlet ; no.42). — Bibliography: p65-86

HOTELS, TAVERNS, ETC. — England — West Country

FRANKLIN, Adrian
Pub drinking and the licensed trade : a study of drinking cultures and local community in two areas of south west England / Adrian Franklin. — Bristol : University of Bristol, School for Advanced Urban Studies, 1985. — 64p. — (Occasional paper / School for Advanced Urban Studies ; 21)

HOTELS, TAVERNS, ETC. — Great Britain — Employees — Statistics

HOTEL AND CATERING INDUSTRY TRAINING BOARD
Manpower in the hotel and catering industry. — [Wembley] : the Board, [ca.1977]. — 47p

HOTELS, TAVERNS, ETC. — Netherlands — Statistics

Vierde algemene bedrijfstelling, 1978. — 's-Gravenhage : Staatsuitgeverij
d.2: Algemene sectorale gegevens. — 1985
C: hotels, restaurants, cafés e.d.. — 61p

HOTELS, TAVERNS, ETC. — Singapore — Statistics

Report on the censuses of wholesale trade, retail trade, restaurants and hotels, 1983. — Singapore : Department of Statistics, 1986. — iv,231p

HOTHAM, Sir CHARLES

ROBERTS, Shirley
Charles Hotham : a biography / Shirley Roberts. — Carlton : Melbourne University Press ; Ashford : HB Sales [distributor], 1985. — xi,201p. — Bibliography: p193-195. — Includes index

HOTU MATÚ'A, Easter Island Chief

BARTHEL, Thomas S.
[Achte Land. English]. The eighth land : the Polynesian discovery and settlement of Easter Island / Thomas S. Barthel ; translated for the German by Anneliese Martin. — Honolulu : University Press of Hawaii, c1978. — xi, 372 p.. — Translation of Das achte Land. — Includes index. — Bibliography: p. [357]-362

HOURS OF LABOR

ÅBERG, Yngve
The impact of working hours and other factors on production and employment / Yngve Åberg. — Aldershot : Gower, 1987. — [173]p. — Includes bibliography

HART, Robert A.
Working time and employment / Robert A. Hart. — Boston ; London : Allen & Unwin, 1987. — [224]p. — Includes bibliography and index

INTERNATIONAL LABOUR COFERENCE (70th : 1984 : Geneva). Committee of Exports on the Application of Conventions and Recommendations
General survey of the reports relating to the Reduction of Hours of Work Recommendation (no.116), the Weekly Rest (Industry) Convention (no.14), the Weekly Rest (Commerce and Offices) Convention (no.106) and Recommendation (no.103), and the Holidays with Pay Convention (Revised) (no.132). — Geneva : International Labor Office. — Cover title: Working time : reduction of hours of work, weekly rest and holidays with pay
Report III
Part 4B. — 1984. — ix,171p

LABOUR RESEARCH DEPARTMENT
Shift work and unsocial hours : a negotiators' guide. — London : Labour Research Department, 1987. — 48p

METCALF, David
Cutting work time as a cure for unemployment / David Metcalf. — Buckingham : University of Buckingham. Employment Research Centre, 1987. — 32p. — (Occasional papers in employment studies (University of Buckingham. Employment Research Centre) ; no.6)

HOURS OF LABOR — Bibliography

Annotated bibliography on working time. — Geneva : International Labour Office, 1986. — v,100p

HOURS OF LABOR — Flexible

Flexibility and jobs : myths and realities : (a research report of the European Trade Union Institute) / (prepared by John Evans, Rafael Nedzynski and Gosta Karlsson). — Brussels : ETUI, [1985]. — 157p

HOURS OF LABOR — Societies, etc. — Directories

Conditions of work and quality of working life : a directory of institutions / edited by Linda Stoddart. — 2nd ed. — Geneva : International Labour Office, 1986. — xxi,306

HOURS OF LABOR — Statistics — Sources

Statistical sources and methods. — Geneva : International Labour Office
V.2: Employment, wages and hours of work (establishment surveys). — 1987. — vii,241p. — Includes bibliographical references. — A technical guide to series published in the Bulletin of Labour Statistics and the Year Book of Labour Statistics

HOURS OF LABOR — Cyprus — Statistics

Statistics of wages, salaries and hours of work / Department of Statistics and Research, Ministry of Finance. — Nicosia : Department of Statistics and Research, 1984-. — Annual

HOURS OF LABOR — European Economic Community countries — Statistics

Working time statistics : methods and measurement in the European Community / study carried out by David Marsden ... [et al.]. — Luxembourg : Office for Official Publications of the European Communities, 1984. — 128p

HOURS OF LABOR — Germany

STEINISCH, Irmgard
Arbeitszeitverkürzung und sozialer Wandel : der Kampf um die Achtstundenschicht in der deutschen und amerikanischen Eisen- und Stahlindustrie 1880-1929 / Irmgard Steinisch. — Berlin : de Gruyter, 1986. — xiv,640p. — (Veröffentlichungen der Historischen Kommission zu Berlin ; Bd.65) (Beiträge zu Inflation und Wiederaufbau in Deutschland und Europa 1914-1924 ; Bd.6). — Bibliography: p577-620

HOURS OF LABOR — Great Britain

Flexible patterns of work / edited by Chris Curson. — London : Institute of Personnel Management, 1986. — 1v.. — Includes bibliography and index

HOURS OF LABOR — Japan

NIHON RŌDŌ KYŌKAI
Wages and hours of work. — [Rev. ed]. — Tokyo : Japan Institute of Labour, 1984. — 36p. — (Japanese industrial relations series ; 3)

HOURS OF LABOR — Québec (Province)

ACOCA, Viviane
Le partage du travail : problématique et possibilités d'application dans la fonction publique du Québec / Viviane Acoca ; avec la collaboration de Jean-François Manègre. — Quebec : Ministère de la main-d'oeuvre et de la sécurité du revenu, 1985. — xiv,254p. — Includes bibliographical references

HOURS OF LABOR — Sri Lanka — Statistics

Sample survey of earnings, hours of work : June, 1980. — 8th ed. — Colombo : Department of Labour, 1983. — xi,41p

HOURS OF LABOR — United States

STEINISCH, Irmgard
Arbeitszeitverkürzung und sozialer Wandel : der Kampf um die Achtstundenschicht in der deutschen und amerikanischen Eisen- und Stahlindustrie 1880-1929 / Irmgard Steinisch. — Berlin : de Gruyter, 1986. — xiv,640p. — (Veröffentlichungen der Historischen Kommission zu Berlin ; Bd.65) (Beiträge zu Inflation und Wiederaufbau in Deutschland und Europa 1914-1924 ; Bd.6). — Bibliography: p577-620

HOURS OF LABOR, FLEXIBLE

Flexible Arbeitszeit gegen starre Sozialsysteme / Günter Buttler...[et al.] (Hrsg.). — Baden-Baden : Namos, 1986. — 254p. — (Soziale Ordnungspolitik). — With English summary

HOUSE BUYING — Decision-making — Great Britain

BALL, Michael
Home ownership : a suitable case for reform / Michael Ball. — London : Shelter, 1986. — 70p

HOUSE BUYING — Law and legislation — Great Britain

HAWKE, Neil
The right to buy in rural areas : an investigation of section 19 of the Housing Act 1980 / Neil Hawke. — Leicester : Leicester Polytechnic. School of Law, 1985. — 33p. — (Research monographs / Leicester Polytechnic. School of Law)

HOUSE BUYING — Great Britain

FORREST, Ray
Monitoring the right to buy, 1980-1982 / Ray Forrest, Alan Murie. — Bristol : University of Bristol, School for Advanced Urban Studies, 1984. — 85p. — (Working paper / University of Bristol, School for Advanced Urban Studies ; no.40)

HOLMANS, A. E.
Flows of funds associated with house purchase for owner-occupation in the United Kingdom 1977-1984 and equity withdrawal from house purchase finance / A. E. Holmans. — London : Departments of the Environment and Transport, 1986. — 128p. — (Government Economic Service working paper ; no.92)

HOUSE CONSTRUCTION — Congresses

INTERNATIONAL CONFERENCE ON LOW COST HOUSING FOR DEVELOPING COUNTRIES (1984 : Central Building Research Institute)
International Conference on Low Cost Housing for Developing Countries / [sponsored by] Central Building Research Institute, Roorkee ; co-sponsors, Union Ministry of Works & Housing ... [et al.]. — Meerut : Sarita Prakashan, [1985?]. — 2V. — Cover title: Proceedings, International Conference on Low Cost Housing for Developing Countries, November 12-17, 1984. — Includes bibliographies

HOUSEHOLD ELECTRONICS

From television to home computer : the future of consumer electronics / edited by Angus Robertson. — Poole : Blandford Press, 1979. — x,323p. — Includes index

HOUSEHOLD SURVEYS — Africa

BOOKER, William
Household survey experience in Africa / William Booker, Parmeet Singh, Landing Savane. — Washington, D.C., U.S.A. : World Bank, 1985 printing, c1980. — 54p. — (LSMS working papers ; no.6) (LSMS working papers ; no. 6). — Includes bibliographical references

HOUSEHOLD SURVEYS — Asia

VISARIA, Pravin M
Poverty and living standards in Asia : an overview of the main results and lessons of selected household surveys / Pravin Visaria assisted by Shyamalendu Pal. — Washington, D.C., U.S.A. — World Bank, 1986 printing, c1980. — xii,224p. — (LSMS working papers ; no.2). — Includes bibliographical references

HOUSEHOLD SURVEYS — Developing countries

ABDUL WAHAB, Mohammed
Income and expenditure surveys in developing countries : sample design and execution / Mohammed Abdul Wahab. — Washington, D.C., U.S.A. : World Bank, 1985 printing, c1980. — 126p. — (LSMS working papers ; no.9) (LSMS working papers ; no. 9). — Bibliography: p. 124-216

MARTORELL, Reynaldo
Nutrition and health status indicators : suggestions for surveys of the standard of living in developing countries / Reynaldo Martorell. — Washington, D.C., U.S.A. : World Bank, Development Research Center, c1981. — 97p. — (LSMS working papers ; no.13). — "February 1982.". — Bibliography: p91-97

HOUSEHOLD SURVEYS — Developing countries — Case studies

SCOTT, Christopher
Conducting surveys in developing countries : practical problems and experience in Brazil, Malaysia, and the Philippines / Christopher Scott, Paulo T.A. de Andre, Ramesh Chander. — Washington, D.C., U.S.A. : World Bank, 1986 printing, c1980. — 113p. — (LSMS working papers ; no.5). — Includes bibliographical references

HOUSEHOLD SURVEYS — Developing countries — Congresses

SAUNDERS, Christopher Thomas
Reflections on the LSMS group meeting / Christopher Saunders, Christiaan Grootaert. — Washington, D.C., U.S.A. : World Bank, 1985 printing, c1980. — 76p. — (LSMS working papers ; no.10) (LSMS working papers ; no. 10). — Includes bibliographical references

HOUSEHOLD SURVEYS — Hong Kong

Statistical experimentation for household surveys : two case studies of Hong Kong / Christiaan Grootaert ... [et al.]. — Washington, D.C. : World Bank, 1982. — 66p. — (LSMS working papers ; no.20). — Cover title. — Bibliography: p65-66

HOUSEHOLD SURVEYS — Ivory Coast

AINSWORTH, Martha
The Côte d'Ivoire living standards survey / Martha Ainsworth and Juan Muñoz. — Washington, D.C. : The World Bank, 1986. — vii,43p. — (LSMS working papers ; no.26)

GROOTAERT, Christian
Measuring and analyzing levels of living in developing countries : an annotated questionnaire / Christian Grootaert. — Washington, D.C. : The World Bank, 1986. — x,139p. — (LSMS working papers ; no.24)

HOUSEHOLD SURVEYS — Netherlands — Methodology

NETHERLANDS. Centraal Bureau voor de Statistiek
Werknemersbudgetonderzoek 1974-75. — s-Gravenhage : Staatsuitgeverij. — Contents list in English. — Title on back cover: Workers' budget survey 1974-75. Part 5. Methodology. Appendix 1. Instruments and instructions for data collection
deel 5: Methodologie
bijlage 1: Enquêtedocumenten. — 1980. — 187p

NETHERLANDS. Centraal Bureau voor de Statistiek
Werknemersbudgetonderzoek, 1974-75. — s-Gravenhage : Staatsuitgeverij, 1980. — Contents list in English. — Title on back cover: Workers' budget survey 1974-75. Part 5. Methodology. — Bibliography: p86
deel 5: Methodologie. — 86p

HOUSEHOLD SURVEYS — Sri Lanka

DEATON, Angus
Three essays on a Sri Lanka household survey / Angus Deaton. — Washington, D.C., U.S.A. : World Bank, 1985 printing, c1981. — [iv],87p. — (LSMS working papers ; no.11). — Bibliographical references: p85-87

HOUSEHOLD SURVEYS — Thailand

PEJARANONDA, Chintana
Household structure and factor affecting size of household. — [Bangkok] : National Statistical Office, 1985. — 32p. — (1980 population and housing census. Subject report ; no.6). — In English and Thai. — Cover title

HOUSEHOLDS — Economics aspects

CONTRIBUTIONS TO HUMAN RESOURCES RESEARCH: A MULTI-DISCIPLINARY SYMPOSIUM (1986 : St. Louis)
Human resources research, 1887-1987 : proceedings / ; edited by Ruth E. Deacon and Wallace E. Huffman. — Ames, Iowa : Iowa State University. College of Home Economics, 1986. — xiii,263p. — Includes bibliographies

HOUSEHOLDS — Africa, Sub-Saharan

Understanding Africa's rural households and farming systems / [edited by] Joyce Lewinger Moock. — Boulder : Westview Press, 1986. — p. cm. — (Westview special studies on Africa). — Bibliography: p

HOUSEHOLDS — Brazil — São Paulo (State) — History

KUZNESOF, Elizabeth Anne
Household economy and urban development : São Paulo, 1765 to 1836 / Elizabeth Anne Kuznesof. — Boulder ; London : Westview Press, 1986. — xvii, 216p. — (Dellplain Latin American studies ; 18). — Includes index. — Bibliography: p199-211

HOUSEHOLDS — Canada

FALLIS, George
Housing economics / George Fallis. — Toronto ; Boston : Butterworths, c1985. — 241 p.. — Includes index. — Bibliography: p. [221]-231

HOUSEHOLDS — England — Statistics

TODD, J. E.
Changing the definition of a household : a study based on the 1981 Labour Force Survey in England to estimate the effect on housing data of a change in the definition of a household / Jean Todd, David Griffiths ; [for the] Office of Population Censuses and Surveys, Social Survey Division. — London : H.M.S.O., 1986. — viii,43p. — Social Survey no.: SS1182

HOUSEHOLDS — Europe — History

HERLIHY, David
Medieval households / David Herlihy. — Cambridge, Mass. ; London : Harvard University Press, 1985. — vii, 227p. — (Studies in cultural history). — Includes index. — Bibliography: p.[161]-177

HOUSEHOLDS — European Economic Community countries — Statistics

Economic and social features of households in the member states of the European Community / Comitato italiano per lo studio dei problemi della populazione, Roma. — Luxembourg : Statistical Office of the European Communities, 1982. — 91p. — Nora Federici, coordinator

HOUSEHOLDS — Finland — Statistics — Methodolgy

HJERPPE, Reino
Development of a household data base in Finland / Reino Hjerppe, Olavi E. Niitamo, Aino Salomäki. — Helsinki : Tilastokeskus, 1984. — 18p. — (Tutkimuksia / Finland. Tilastokeskus ; no.107)

HOUSEHOLDS — France

Les revenus des ménages 1960-1984 : rapport de synthese / ...établi sous la direction de Alain Foulon. — Paris : La Documentation française, [1986]. — 132p. — (Documents du centre d'étude des revenus et des coûts ; no.80 numéro spécial)

HOUSEHOLDS — Great Britain — Forecasting

GREAT BRITAIN. Department of the Environment
1983 based estimates of numbers of households in England, the regions, counties, metropolitan districts and London boroughs 1983-2001. — London : the Department, 1986. — vi,58,[11]p. — Bibliography: Appendix E

HOUSEHOLDS — Hong Kong — Statistics

Report of the household expenditure survey, 1984-85. — Hong Kong : Census and Statistics Department, 1986. — viii,153p. — Cover title: Report on the household expenditure survey, 1984-85

HOUSEHOLDS — Israel — Statistics

Demographic characteristics of households. — Jerusalem : Central Bureau of Statistics. — (1983 Census of Population and Housing Publications ; No.8). — In English and Hebrew
Data from the complete enumeration. — 1986. — xli,251p

Population and households : provisional results. — Jerusalem : Central Bureau of Statistics, 1983. — xxxix,91p. — (1983 census of population and housing publications ; no.1). — In Hebrew and English

HOUSEHOLDS — Italy — Economic aspects

LECALDANO SASSO LA TERZA, E.
Households' saving and the real rate of interest : the Italian experience, 1970-1983 / E. Lecaldano Sasso la Terza, G. Marotta, R. S. Masera. — [Roma] : Banca d'Italia, 1985. — 33p , addenda. — (Temi di discussione ; 47) (Servizio studi della Banca d'Italia). — *Bibliography: p32-33*

HOUSEHOLDS — Ivory Coast

GROOTAERT, Christiaan
The demand for urban housing in the Ivory Coast / Christiaan Grootaert and Jean-Luc Dubois. — Washington, D.C. : The World Bank, 1986. — viii,70p. — (LSMS working papers ; no.25). — *Bibliographical references: p68-70*

HOUSEHOLDS — Nigeria — Statistics

National integrated survey of households (Nish): report of rural agricultural sample survey / Agricultural Survey Unit, Nigeria. — Lagos : Agricultural Survey Unit, 1981/82-. — *Annual*

HOUSEHOLDS — Pakistan

IRFAN, Mohammad
Poverty and household demographic behaviour in Pakistan : insights from PLM survey 1979 / Mohammad Irfan. — Islamabad : Pakistan Institute of Development Economics, 1986. — 57p. — (Studies in population, labour force and migration project report ; no.11). — *Bibliography: p[58-59]*

HOUSEWIVES

CHABAUD-RYCHTER, Danielle
Espace et temps du travail domestique / Danielle Chabaud-Rychter, Dominique Fongeyrollas-Schwebel [et] Françoise Southounax. — Paris : Libraries des Méridiens, 1985. — 156p

HOUSEWIVES — United States — History

OGDEN, Annegret S
The great American housewife : from helpmate to wage earner, 1776-1986 / Annegret S. Ogden. — Westport, Conn. : Greenwood Press, 1986. — xxiii, 256 p.. — (Contributions in women's studies ; no. 61). — *Includes index. — Bibliography: p. [241]-247*

HOUSING

Housing studies. — Harlow : Longman, 1986-. — *Quarterly*

HOUSING — Finance

Tax policies and urban housing markets. — Paris : Organisation for Economic Co-operation and Development, 1986. — 113p. — *At head of cover: OECD urban affairs programme*

HOUSING — Korea (South) — Statistics

1970 population and housing census report (complete). — [Seoul] : Economic Planning Board. — *In Korean and English*
Vol.12-3: Busan City. — 1972. — 126p

HOUSING — Law and legislation — England

ARDEN, Andrew
Manual of housing law / by Andrew Arden. — 3rd ed. — London : Sweet & Maxwell, 1986. — [275]p. — *Previous ed.: 1983. — Includes index*

HOUSING — Law and legislation — Great Britain

GREAT BRITAIN. Parliament. House of Commons. Library. Research Division
Housing and Planning Bill (Bill 63 of 1985/86) / Oonagh Gay, Barry Winetrobe, Betty Miller. — [London] : the Division, 1986. — 38p. — (Reference sheet ; no.86/5). — *Bibliographical references: p30-38*

HOUSING — Law and legislation — Northern Ireland

HADDEN, Tom
Northern Ireland housing law : the public and private rented sectors / by T.B. Hadden and W.D. Trimble. — Belfast : SLS Legal Publications, 1986. — xxxvi,323p. — *Includes bibliographical references and index*

HOUSING — Montserrat — Statistics

Preliminary data of the 1980 Commonwealth Caribbean population census, May 12, 1980. — [Plymouth?] : Government of Montserrat Statistics Office, 1980. — iv,26p,iv,23p. — *Contents: Part 1. Household and housing information - part 2. Age distribution and economic activity data*

HOUSING — Taxation — Organisation for Economic Co-operation and Development countries

Tax policies and urban housing markets. — Paris : Organisation for Economic Co-operation and Development, 1986. — 113p. — *At head of cover: OECD urban affairs programme*

HOUSING — Argentina — Statistics

INSTITUTO NACIONAL DE ESTADISTICA Y CENSOS (Argentina)
Censo nacional de poblacion y vivienda 1980 : serie C : vivienda. — Buenos Aires : the Instituto, [1981-]. — 3v

HOUSING — Australia — Western Australia

WESTERN AUSTRALIA. Commonwealth Bureau of Census and Statistics. Western Australian Office
Building and housing. — Perth : [Office], 1968/9-. — *Annual. — Supercedes in part its Statistical register of Western Australia: part 12. Retail prices, wages, employment and miscellaneous*

HOUSING — Austria — Statistics

AUSTRIA. Statistisches Zentralamt
Häuser- und Wohnungszählung 1981. — Wien : Statistisches Zentralamt
Gebäude- und Wohnungen ohne Wohnbevölkerung. — 1986. — xxi,166p. — (Beiträge zur österreichischen Statistik ; Heft 640/12)

Umweltbedingungen des Wohnens: Ergebnisse des Mikrozensus / Statistisches Zentralamt, Austria. — Wien : Statistisches Zentralamt, 1976-. — (Beiträge zur Österreichischen Statistik). — *Irregular*

HOUSING — Barbados — Statistics

Commonwealth Caribbean population census 1970 : Barbados : preliminary bulletin : housing. — St. Michael : Barbados Statistical Service, 1972. — iii,17p

HOUSING — Belgium — Statistics

Recensement de la population et des logements au 1er mars 1981. — Bruxelles : Institut national de statistique. — *Cover title*
t.2: Royaume, régions, provinces et arrondissements. — [1986]. — 378p

HOUSING — Botswana — Statistics

1981 population and housing census : guide to the villages and towns of Botswana. — Gaborone : Central Statistics Office, [1983]. — 1 vol.(various pagings)

1981 population and housing census : census administrative/technical report and national statistical tables. — Gaborone : Central Statistics Office, [1983]. — 1 vol. (various pagings)

BOTSWANA. Presidential Commission on Housing Policy in Botswana
Report of the Presidential Commission on Housing Policy in Botswana. — Gaborone : Government Printer, 1981. — 67p

HOUSING — Brazil — Salvador

PINHO, Jose Antonio Gomes de
Housing provision and labour reproduction in peripheral capitalism : the case of Salvador, Brazil / Jose Antonio Gomes de Pinho. — 430 leaves, [3] leaves of plates. — *PhD (Econ) 1986 LSE*

HOUSING — Canada

FALLIS, George
Housing economics / George Fallis. — Toronto ; Boston : Butterworths, c1985. — 241 p.. — *Includes index. — Bibliography: p. [221]-231*

HOUSING — Cape Verde — Statistics

1° recenseamento geral da populacão e habitacáo-1980. — Praia : Direccão de Recenseamento e Inqueritos
Vol.4: Habitação. — 1983. — 177p

HOUSING — Colombia — Finance

UPAC a theory converted into a successful reality : Colombian system of savings and housing. — Bogota : Instituto Colombiano de Ahorro y Vivienda, 1986. — [40p]

HOUSING — Comoros — Statistics

Recensement général de la population et de l'habitat 15 septembre 1980. — Moroni : Direction de la Statistique. — *On front cover: Bureau Central de Recensement*
vol.3: Analyse des resultats du recensement d l'habitat et tableaux. — 1984. — 26p

HOUSING — Costa Rica — Statistics

Censo de vivienda 1984. — San José : Ministerio de Gobernacion y Policia, 1986. — xxxiii,335p

COSTA RICA. Dirección General de Estadística y Censos
Encuesta de hogares por muestreo : zonas urbanas de Costa Rica, julio de 1967 a junio de 1968. — [San José] : the Dirección, 1970. — 75p

HOUSING — Cyprus — Statistics

CYPRUS. Department of Statistics and Research
Census of housing 1982. — [Nicosia] : Department of Statistics and Research
Vol.2: Nicosia district. — [1984]. — 333p. — (Housing statistics / Department of Statistics and Research. Series 1 ; Report no.3)

CYPRUS. Department of Statistics and Research
Census of housing 1982. — [Nicosia] : Department of Statistics and Research
Vol.3: Limassol district. — [1985]. — 331p. — (Housing statistics / Department of Statistics and Research. Series 1 ; Report no.4)

CYPRUS. Department of Statistics and Research
Census of housing 1982. — [Nicosia] : Department of Statistics and Research
Vol.4: Larnaca and Famagusta districts. — [1985]. — 407p. — (Housing census / Cyprus. Department of Statistics and Research. Series 1 ; Report no.5)

CYPRUS. Department of Statistics and Research
Census of housing 1982. — [Nicosia] : Department of Statistics and Research
Vol.5: Paphos district. — [1985]. — 327p. — (Housing census / Cyprus. Department of Statistics and Research. Series 1 ; Report no.6)

CYPRUS. Department Statistics and Research
Census of housing 1982. — [Nicosia] : Department of Statistics and Research
Vol.1: All districts. — [1984]. — 412p. — (Housing statistics / Department of Statistics and Research. Series 1 ; Report no.2)

HOUSING — Denmark

JØRGENSEN, Jørgen
Betonbørn / Jørgen Jørgensen. — Aarhus : Modtryk, 1978. — 94p

HOUSING — Developing countries

LINDEN, J. J. van der
The sites and services approach reviewed : solution or stopgap to the Third World housing shortage? / Jan van der Linden. — Aldershot : Gower, c1986. — xi,178p. — *Bibliography: p143-178*

HOUSING — Developing countries — Congresses

INTERNATIONAL CONFERENCE ON LOW COST HOUSING FOR DEVELOPING COUNTRIES (1984 : Central Building Research Institute)
International Conference on Low Cost Housing for Developing Countries / [sponsored by] Central Building Research Institute, Roorkee ; co-sponsors, Union Ministry of Works & Housing ... [et al.]. — Meerut : Sarita Prakashan, [1985?]. — 2V. — *Cover title: Proceedings, International Conference on Low Cost Housing for Developing Countries, November 12-17, 1984. — Includes bibliographies*

HOUSING — Egypt — Statistics

1976 population and housing census : total republic. — Cairo : Central Agency for Public Mobilisation and Statistics
Vol. 1. — 1980. — 478p

HOUSING — England — Societies, etc.

HOUSING CORPORATION. Corporate Planning Unit
The Housing Corporation's programme in England, 1979/80 : a consultation paper. — [London : the Corporation, 1978]. — [16]p

HOUSING CORPORATION. Corporate Planning Unit
Programme in England 1979/80. — [London : the Corporation, 1979]. — 4p

HOUSING — England — Brighton

BENNETT, Matthew
Housing in Brighton / Matthew Bennett. — Brighton (Education Development Building, Falmer, Brighton BN1 9RG) : Centre for Continuing Education, University of Sussex, 1977. — [2],iii,50[i.e.51],[1]p. — (Occasional papers / University of Sussex. Centre for Continuing Education ; no.7)

HOUSING — England — Hertfordshire

MCNAMARA, Paul
Restraint policy and development interests : housing in Dacorum and North Hertfordshire / by Paul McNamara. — [Oxford : Oxford Polytechnic, Dept. of Town Planning], 1982. — iii,75p. — (Working paper / Oxford Polytechnic, Dept. of Town Planning ; no.76). — *Cover title: Housing in Dacorum & North Hertfordshire : restraint policy & development interests. — "... the eighth working paper forming part of an SSRC sponsored study entitled "Land release and development in areas of restraint" - p.i*

HOUSING — England — Liverpool (Merseyside)

LIVERPOOL
Liverpool's population. — Liverpool : [the Council]. — 1986
1: Population, social, and housing stock, changes and trends 1971-1991. — 56p

HOUSING — England — London

The Docklands housing needs survey, 1985 : the report of a survey of Newham, Southwark and Tower Hamlets / (report written by Hal Pawson with the assistance of Will Tuckley and other staff in the Housing Group of the London Research Centre). — [London] : London Research Centre
Technical volume. — 1986. — 83p. — (Reviews and studies series ; no.32). — *Bibliographical references: p80-83*

SULLIVAN, Anne
Co-ordinating special needs housing in London : a borough-by-borough survey / [written by Anne Sullivan] ; [edited by Vera Joscelyne]. — 2nd ed. — London : CHAR, the Housing Campaign for Single People in association with Special Needs Housing Advisory Service and the London Special Needs Housing Group. — 50p. — *Previous ed.: 198-?*

HOUSING — England — London — History

EMSLEY, Ian
The development of housing associations : with special reference to London and including a case study of the London borough of Hammersmith / Ian Emsley. — New York : Garland Pub., 1986. — 477 p.. — (Outstanding theses from the London School of Economics and Political Science). — : *Originally presented as the author's thesis (Ph. D.)--London School of Economics. — Bibliography: p. 464-475*

WOHL, Anthony S
The eternal slum : housing and social policy in Victorian London / Anthony S. Wohl. — Montreal : McGill-Queen's University Press, 1977. — xxiv, 386 p., [8] leaves of plates. — (Studies in urban history ; 5). — *"A note on sources": p. 341-355. — Includes index*

HOUSING — England — London — Statistics

EBANI, Rafaella
London Borough of Camden "private sector housing register statistics 1986" / Rafaella Ebani [and] David Mullins. — Camden : Housing Department. Policy and Information Unit, 1986. — 23p. — (Policy and information paper / Camden. Housing Department. Policy and Information Unit ; 6/86)

Greater London housing statistics / Greater London Council, Housing Department, Policy and Resources Branch. — London : Greater London Council, 1984. — (GLC housing abstract)

HOUSING — England — Sheffield (South Yorkshire)

HENRION, Emma
Housing information needs : the results of an information needs survey carried out in the City of Sheffield Housing Department / Emma Henrion and Linda White. — 2nd ed. — Sheffield : Housing Department, 1987. — 51p

HOUSING — England — Southampton (Hampshire) — History

Dilapidated housing and housing policy in Southampton 1890-1914 / edited, with an introduction, by Martin Doughty. — Southampton : Southampton University Press, 1986. — xxxvi,119p. — (Southampton Records Series ; v.29)

HOUSING — England — West Midlands

WEST MIDLAND REGIONAL STUDY
A developing strategy for the West Midlands : report of the West Midland Regional Study : 1971, Technical appendix 2: housing study. — Birmingham : West Midland Regional Study, 1971. — 49,[78]p. — *Includes folded maps*

HOUSING — Equatorial Guinea — Statistics

Censos nacionales : I de población y I de vivienda - 4 al 17 de Julio de 1983 : resultados provisionales. — Malabo : Dirección General de Estadística, 1983. — 8p

HOUSING — Europe

SEMINAR ON THE RELATIONSHIP BETWEEN HOUSING AND THE NATIONAL ECONOMY (1982 : Prague)
Relationship between housing and the national economy : synthesis report on the Seminar held in Prague (Czechoslovakia) 10-14 May 1982 / prepared by the Research Institute for Building and Architecture (VUVA), Czechoslovakia. — New York : United Nations, 1985. — vi,60p. — ([Document] / United Nations ; ECE/HBP/56). — *Sales no.: E.85.II.E.16*

HOUSING — Finland — Statistics

PUTKONEN, Carita
Confidence study : population and housing census 1980 : measurement and processing errors / Carita Putkonen. — Helsinki : Tilastokeskus, 1984. — 90p. — (Tutkimuksia / Finland. Tilastokeskus ; no.99)

PUTKONEN, Carita
Luotettavuustutkimus : vaestö- ja och bostadsräkningen 1980 / Carita Putkonen. — Helsinki : Tilastokeskus. — (Tutkimuksia / Finland. Tilastokeskus ; no.99). — *Summary in Swedish*
Osa 1: Selvitys mittaus- ja käsittelyvirheistä = Del 1: Utredning av mätfel och bearbetningsfel. — 1983. — 212p

PUTKONEN, Carita
Luotettavuustutkimus : vaesto- ja asuntolaskenta 1980 / Carita Putkonen. — Helsinki : Tilastokeskus. — (Tutkimuksia / Finland. Tilastokeskus ; no.100)
Osa 2: Peittävyysselvitys. — 1984. — 69p

HOUSING — FRance

HEUGAS-DARRASPEN, Henri
Le logement en France et son financement / Henri Heugas-Darraspen. — Paris : La Documentation Française, 1985. — 143p. — (Notes et études documentaires ; no.4794). — *Bibliography: p142*

HOUSING — France — Finance

HEUGAS-DARRASPEN, Henri
Le logement en France et son financement / Henri Heugas-Darraspen. — Paris : La Documentation Française, 1985. — 143p. — (Notes et études documentaires ; no.4794). — *Bibliography: p142*

HOUSING — France — Statistics

Statistiques: prestations de logement / Caisse Nationale des Allocations Familiales. — Paris : C.N.A.F., 1981/1982-. — *Annual*

TAFFIN, Claude
Le patrimoine de logements en 1978 / Claude Taffin. — Paris : I.N.S.E.E., 1986. — 103p. — (Archives et documents / Institut national de la statistique et des études économiques ; no.154). — *Bibliographical references: p103*

HOUSING — Great Britain

BOLEAT, Mark
Housing in Britain / Mark Boleat. — London : The Building Societies Association, 1986. — 40p

SHELTER campaign news. — London : SHELTER, 1987-. — *Quarterly*

WARD, Colin
When we build again : lets have housing that works! / Colin Ward. — London : Pluto, 1985. — 127p

HOUSING — Great Britain — Finance

BOLÉAT, Mark
The mortgage market / Mark Boléat and Adrian Coles : theory and practice of housing finance. — London : Allen & Unwin, 1987. — [192]p. — (Studies in financial institutions and markets ; 3). — *Includes bibliography and index*

GOSS, Sue
What price housing? : a review of housing subsidies and proposals for reform / Sue Goss [and] Stewart Lansley ; revised by Peter Kemp. — rev. ed. — London : SHAC, 1984. — 39p

GREAT BRITAIN. Parliament. House of Commons. Library. Research Division
Housing investment programmes / Oonagh Gay. — [London] : the Division, 1984. — 27p. — (Background paper ; no.147)

GREAT BRITAIN. Parliament. House of Commons. Library. Research Division
Housing investment programmes and capital receipts / Oonagh Gay. — [London] : the Division, 1985. — 38p. — (Background paper ; no.162)

LANSLEY, Stewart
Housing finance : new policies for Labour / Stewart Lansley. — London : Labour Housing Group, [1986]. — 20p

HOUSING — Great Britain — Finance
continuation

WALKER, Andrew
Housing taxation : owner-occupation and the reform of housing finance / Andrew Walker. — London : Catholic Housing Aid Society, c1986. — 99 p. — (CHAS occasional paper ; 9). — *Bibliography: p96-99*

WARBURTON, Matthew
Housing finance : the case for reform / Matthew Warburton. — London : Catholic Housing Aid Society, 1983. — 95p. — (CHAS occasional papers ; 8). — *Bibliography: p93-95*

HOUSING — Great Britain — History

EMSLEY, Ian
The development of housing associations : with special reference to London and including a case study of the London borough of Hammersmith / Ian Emsley. — New York : Garland Pub., 1986. — 477 p.. — (Outstanding theses from the London School of Economics and Political Science). — : *Originally presented as the author's thesis (Ph. D.)--London School of Economics. — Bibliography: p. 464-475*

HOUSING — Great Britain — Law and legislation

NATIONAL FEDERATION OF HOUSING ASSOCIATIONS
Housing legislation : a guide to the consolidated Acts / National Federation of Housing Associations. — London : The Federation, 1986. — vii,45p

HOUSING — Great Britain — Social aspects

BRITISH ASSOCIATION OF SOCIAL WORKERS
Housing and social work : the BASW green paper : a consultative report. — Birmingham : British Association of Social Workers, 1985. — v,79p

HOUSING — Great Britain — Statistics

Local area housing statistics / Nationwide Building Society. — London : Nationwide Building Society, 1985-. — *Annual*

NATIONWIDE BUILDING SOCIETY
House prices / Nationwide Building Society. — London : Nationwide Building Society. — *Quarterly*

HOUSING — Great Britain — Statistics — Bibliography

CLINTON, Alan
Housing statistics : a guide to sources / Alan Clinton. — London : Institute of Housing/Centre for Urban and Regional Studies, 1986. — xxiv,156p. — (Professional Practice Series / Institute of Housing ; no.8)

HOUSING — Hungary — Statistics

Lakasstatisztikai evkonyv = Yearbook of housing statistics / Kozponti Statisztikai Hivatal. — Budapest : Kozponti Statisztikai Hivatal, 1983-. — *Annual. — Table headings in Hungarian, English and Russian*

HOUSING — Hungary — Budapest

25 [ie. huszonöt] éve az állami építöiparban a 100 éves Budapestért 1948-1973 / Kisvári János, and 43 sz. állami építöipari vállalat. — Budapest : Révai Nyomda, [1973?]. — 119p

HOUSING — India — Dadra and Nagar Haveli — Statistics

Census of India 1981 / S. K. Gandhe, Director of Census Operations, Dadra and Nagar Haveli. — [Delhi : Controller of Publications] Series 27: Dadra & Nagar Haveli. — [1985-]

HOUSING — Ireland — Statistics

Census of population of Ireland 1981 / compiled by the Central Statistics Office. — Dublin : Stationery Office
Vol.8: Housing. — 1986. — xix,337p. — *"The statistics herein relate to the population of Ireland exclusive of Northern Ireland*

HOUSING — Israel — Statistics

Housing conditions and possession of household equipment. — Jerusalem : Central Bureau of Statistics. — (1983 Census of Population and Housing Publications ; No.9). — *In English and Hebrew*
Data from the sample enumeration. — 1986. — lxix,133p

HOUSING — Ivory Coast

GROOTAERT, Christiaan
The demand for urban housing in the Ivory Coast / Christiaan Grootaert and Jean-Luc Dubois. — Washington, D.C. : The World Bank, 1986. — viii,70p. — (LSMS working papers ; no.25). — *Bibliographical references: p68-70*

HOUSING — Japan — Statistics

JAPAN. Statistics Bureau
1983 housing survey of Japan. — [Tokyo] : the Bureau
Vol.1: Results for whole Japan
Part 1: Characteristics of dwellings. — [1985]. — xxxv,769,56p. — *Text in Japanese and English*

JAPAN. Statistics Bureau
1983 housing survey of Japan. — [Tokyo] : the Bureau
Vol.1: Results for whole Japan
Part 2: Residential conditions. — 1985. — xxxv,565,56p. — *Text in Japanese and English*

HOUSING — Korea (South) — Finance

STRUYK, Raymond J
Finance and housing quality in two developing countries : Korea and the Philippines / Raymond J. Struyk, Margery Austin Turner. — Lanham, MD : University Press of America ; Washington, D.C. : Urban Institute Press, c1986. — xix, 146 p.. — *Bibliography: p. 135-138*

HOUSING — Korea (South) — Statisitics

1970 population and housing census report (complete). — [Seoul] : Economic Planning Board. — *In Korean and English*
Vol.12-12: Jeju Do. — 1972. — 120p

HOUSING — Korea (South — Statistics

1970 population and housing census report. — [Seoul] : Bureau of Statistics, Economic Planning Board. — *In Korean and English*
Vol.2: 10% sample survey. — [Seoul] : Bureau of Statistics, Economic Planning Board. — *In Korean and English*
Vol.4-4: Housing. — 1973. — 219p

HOUSING — Korea (South) — Statistics

1970 population and housing census report (complete). — [Seoul] : Economic Planning Board. — *In Korean and English*
Vol.12-5: Gang-weon Do. — 1972. — 236p

1970 population and housing census report (complete). — [Seou] : Economic Planning Board. — *In Korean and English*
Vol.12-6: Chungcheong Bug Do. — 1972. — 202p

1970 population and housing census report (complete). — [Seoul] : Economic Planning Board. — *In Korean and English*
Vol.12-7: Chungcheong Nam Do. — 1972. — 126p

1970 population and housing census report (complete). — [Seoul] : Economic Planning Board. — *In Korean and English*
Vol.12-8: Jeonra Bug Do. — 1972. — 250p

1970 population and housing census report (complete). — [Seoul] : Economic Planning Board. — *In Korean and English*
Vol.12-9: Jeonra Nam Do. — 1972. — 354p

HOUSING — London metropolitan area — Societies, etc.

CAMPAIGN FOR HOMES IN CENTRAL LONDON
Priced out of town : the problems for housing associations working in central London / Campaign for Homes in Central London. — London : CHICL, 1986. — 34p

HOUSING — Malaysia — Statistics

Banci penduduk dan perumahan Malaysia 1980 = Population and housing census of Malaysia 1980. — Kuala Lumpur : Department of Statistics. — *Text in Malay and English*
Laporan am banci perumahan = General report of the housing census. — 1983. — 2v

HOUSING — Malaysia — Sabah — Statistics

Banci penduduk dan perumahan Malaysia 1980 = Population and housing census of Malaysia 1980. — Kuala Lumpur : Department of Statistics. — *Text in Malay and English*
Laporan perumahan negeri = State housing report

HOUSING — Malaysia — Selangor — Statistics

Banci penduduk dan perumahan Malaysia 1980 = Population and housing census of Malaysia 1980. — Kuala Lumpur : Department of Statistics. — *Text in Malay and English*
Laporan perumahan negeri = State housing report
Selangor. — 1984. — 232p. — 1map

HOUSING — Malaysia — Wilayah Persekutuan — Statistics

Banci penduduk dan perumahan Malaysia 1980 = Population and housing census of Malaysia 1980. — Kuala Lumpur : Department of Statistics. — *Text in Malay and English*
Laporan perumahan negeri = State housing report
Wilayah Persekutuan. — 1984. — 54p. — 1map

HOUSING — Mauritius — Statistics

1983 housing and population census of Mauritius. — [Rose Hill] : Central Statistical Office, 1984-85. — 6v

1983 housing and population census of Mauritius : analysis report. — Rose Hill : Central Statistical Office
vol. 3: Households and housing needs: estimates and implications : (Island of Mauritius). — 1986. — 67p

1983 Housing and population census of Mauritius. — Rose Hill : Central Statistical Office
Analysis report
Volume 1: Evaluation of data. — 1985. — 76p

HOUSING — Mexico — Statistics

MEXICO. Subcomisión de Programación de la Vivienda
Construcción de vivienda de interés social 1974. — [México] : the Subcomisión, [ca.1974]. — 24p

HOUSING — Netherlands — Mathematical models

LIEROP, Wal van
Spatial interaction modelling and residential choice analysis / Wal Van Lierop. — Aldershot : Gower, c1986. — [290]p. — *Includes bibliography and index*

HOUSING — New Zealand

POOL, Ian
Population and social trends : implications for New Zealand housing / Ian Pool... for the National Housing Commission. — Wellington : National Housing Commission, 1986. — x,175p . — *Bibliographical references: p155-161*

HOUSING — Norway — Statistics

NORWAY
Folke- og bustadteljing 1980 = Population and housing census 1980. — Oslo : Statistisk Sentralbyrå. — (Norges offisielle statistikk ; B588). — *Text in Norwegian and English. — Previous volumes entitled 'Folke- og boligtelling 1980'*
Hefte 4: Hovudtal 1960, 1970 og 1980 = Main results 1960, 1970 and 1980. — 1986. — 114p

HOUSING — Panama — Statistics
Censos nacionales de 1980 : octavo censo de poblacion, cuarto censo de vivienda, 11 de mayo de 1980. — [Panama] : Dirección de Estadística y Censo
Volumen 7: Sectores censales de los distritos de Panama, San Miguelito y Colon. — 1986. — vii,196p

PANAMA. Dirección de Estadística y Censo
Censos nacionales de 1980 : octavo censo de población, cuarto censo de vivienda, 11 de mayo de 1980. — [Panamá] : the Dirección, [1984-]

HOUSING — Philippines — Finance
STRUYK, Raymond J
Finance and housing quality in two developing countries : Korea and the Philippines / Raymond J. Struyk, Margery Austin Turner. — Lanham, MD : University Press of America ; Washington, D.C. : Urban Institute Press, c1986. — xix, 146 p.. — *Bibliography: p. 135-138*

HOUSING — San Marino — Statistics
1° censimento generale edilizio : 30 novembre 1976. — San Marino : Ufficio Statale di Statistica, 1978. — 2v

HOUSING — Scotland
ROBERTSON, G.
Housing tenure and labour mobility in Scotland / G. Robertson. — Edinburgh (New St Andrew's House, St James Centre, Edinburgh) : Economics and Statistics Unit, Scottish Economic Planning Department, 1979. — 47p,[1]leaf of plates. — (ESU discussion paper ; no.4). — *Bibliography: p47*

SHUCKSMITH, Mark
Scotland's rural housing : a forgotten problem / Mark Shucksmith. — [Edinburgh] : Rural Forum, 1984. — 45p. — (Rural Forum discussion paper)

HOUSING — Scotland — Dumfries and Galloway
DUMFRIES AND GALLOWAY. Regional Council
Structure plan : report of survey : population, employment and housing (revised). — Dumfries : [the Regional Council], 1979. — 105p

HOUSING — Scotland — Strathclyde — Glasgow
Inquiry into housing in Glasgow. — Glasgow : Glasgow District Council, 1986. — 67p

HOUSING — Sri Lanka — Statistics
Sri Lanka census of population and housing 1981 : district report. — [Colombo] : Department of Census and Statistics, [1984-85]. — 1v (in 24 parts)

HOUSING — Sweden — Finance — Statistics
Låneobjektsstatistik = Statistics of government housing loan projects / Statistiska Centralbyrån, Sweden. — Stockholm : Statistiska Centralbyrån, 1985-. — Annual. — *Text in Swedish with English translation of table headings. — Various sub-titles. — In various parts*

HOUSING — Sweden — Statistics
Låneobjektsstatistik = Statistics of government housing loan projects / Statistiska Centralbyrån, Sweden. — Stockholm : Statistiska Centralbyrån, 1985-. — Annual. — *Text in Swedish with English translation of table headings. — Various sub-titles. — In various parts*

HOUSING — United States
STERNLIEB, George
Patterns of development / by George Sternlieb. — New Brunswick, N.J. : Center for Urban Policy Research, c1986. — p. cm. — *Includes index. — Bibliography: p*

HOUSING — United States — Addresses, essays, lectures
The Urban predicament / edited by William Gorham, Nathan Glazer. — Washington : Urban Institute, c1976. — 363 p.. — *Includes bibliographical references and index*

HOUSING — United States — Finance
Housing and the new financial markets / edited by Richard L. Florida. — New Brunswick, N.J. : Center for Urban Policy Research, c1986. — xviii, 482 p.. — *Includes index. — Bibliography: p. 469-472*

HOUSING — United States — Forecasting
BURNS, Leland Smith
The future of housing markets : a new appraisal / Leland S. Burns and Leo Grebler. — New York : Plenum Press, c1986. — p. cm. — (Environment, development, and public policy. Cities and development). — *Includes index. — Bibliography: p*

HOUSING — United States — History
HAYS, R. Allen
The federal government and urban housing : ideology and change in public policy / R. Allen Hays. — Albany : State University of New York Press, c1985. — xvi, 297 p.. — (SUNY series in urban public policy). — *Includes index. — Bibliography: p. 267-287*

HOUSING — Wales — Clwyd
CLWYD. County Council
Clwyd county structure plan : public participation seminar : housing : report of proceedings. — Mold : [the Council], 1975. — 33p

CLWYD. County Council
Clwyd county structure plan : report of survey. — Mold [the Council]. — 1978. — *Includes folded maps*
Technical appendix: population, housing and settlements. — 64p

HOUSING — Washington, D.C — Addresses, essays, lectures
The Urban predicament / edited by William Gorham, Nathan Glazer. — Washington : Urban Institute, c1976. — xix, 363 p.. — *Includes bibliographical references and index*

HOUSING AND BUILDING CONTROL BILL 1983-84
GREAT BRITAIN. Parliament. House of Commons. Library. Research Division
The Housing and Building Control Bill (Bill 3, session 1983/84) / [Christine Gillie, Barry Winetrobe]. — [London] : the Division, 1983. — 21p. — (Reference sheet ; no.83/10). — *Includes bibliographical references*

HOUSING AND PLANNING BILL 1985-86
GREAT BRITAIN. Parliament. House of Commons. Library. Research Division
Housing and Planning Bill (Bill 63 of 1985/86) / Oonagh Gay, Barry Winetrobe, Betty Miller. — [London] : the Division, 1986. — 38p. — (Reference sheet ; no.86/5). — *Bibliographical references: p30-38*

HOUSING ASSOCIATION MOVEMENT
See National Federation of Housing Associations

HOUSING AUTHORITIES — Great Britain — Employees
LEEVERS, Kate
Women at work in housing / Kate Leevers ; with illustrations by Candy Walker. — London : HERA, 1986. — 32p

HOUSING AUTHORITIES — Scotland
GREAT BRITAIN. Scottish Development Department
Housing development, layout, roads and services / Scottish Development Department. — [Edinburgh] : H.M.S.O, 1977. — [117]p. — (Scottish housing handbook ; 3)

GREAT BRITAIN. Scottish Development Department
Scottish housing handbook / Scottish Development Department. — [Edinburgh] : H.M.S.O
1: Assessing housing need : a manual of guidance. — 1977. — [2],106p,fold leaf. — *Bibliography: p.100-101. — Includes index*

HOUSING, COOPERATIVE — Law and legislation — England
ALDER, John
Housing association law / by John Alder and Christopher R. Handy. — London : Sweet & Maxwell, 1987. — xlii,330p. — *Bibliography: p313-314. — Includes index*

HOUSING, COOPERATIVE — Britain
HILLS, John
The voluntary sector in housing : the role of British housing associations / John Hills. — London : Suntory-Toyota International Centre for Economics and Related Disciplines, 1987. — 41p. — (Welfare State Programme ; no.20) (Discussion paper / Welfare State Programme. Suntory-Toyota International Centre for Economics and Related Disciplines. London School of Economics ; no.20). — *Bibliography: p41*

HOUSING, COOPERATIVE — Great Britain
LEEVERS, Kate
Women at work in housing / Kate Leevers ; with illustrations by Candy Walker. — London : HERA, 1986. — 32p

HOUSING, COOPERATIVE — Great Britain — Finance
HILLS, John
When is a grant not a grant? : the current system of Housing Association finance / John Hills. — London : London School of Economics, 1987. — 113p. — (Welfare State Programme ; no.13) (Discussion paper / Welfare State Programme ; Suntory Toyota International Centre for Economics and Related Disciplines ; London School of Economics ; no.13). — *Bibliography: p111-113*

HOUSING, COOPERATIVE — Great Britain — History
EMSLEY, Ian
The development of housing associations : with special reference to London and including a case study of the London borough of Hammersmith / Ian Emsley. — New York : Garland Pub., 1986. — 477 p.. — (Outstanding theses from the London School of Economics and Political Science). — : *Originally presented as the author's thesis (Ph. D.)--London School of Economics. — Bibliography: p. 464-475*

HOUSING DEFECTS BILL 1983-84
GREAT BRITAIN. Parliament. House of Commons. Library. Research Division
Housing Defects Bill [Bill 147 session 1983/84] / Oonagh Gay. — [London] : the Division, 1984. — 16p. — (Reference sheet ; no.84/6). — *Bibliographical references: p14-16*

HOUSING DEVELOPMENT
LEICESTER POLYTECHNIC. School of Land and Building Studies. Research Unit
Land for residential development : available or not available? / SLABS Research Unit. — Leicester : School of Land and Building Studies, Leicester Polytechnic, 1984. — iv,55 leaves. — (Housing land in urban areas ; Working paper no.1)

HOUSING DEVELOPMENT — England — Leicester (Leicestershire)
LEICESTER POLYTECHNIC. School of Land and Building Studies. Research Unit
Interviews with representatives of parties involved in residential development within the Leicester urban area / SLABS Research Unit. — Leicester : School of Land and Building Studies, Leicester Polytechnic, 1984. — 61 leaves. — (Housing land in urban areas ; Working paper no.3)

HOUSING DEVELOPMENT — England — Leicester (Leicestershire) — Case studies

LEICESTER POLYTECHNIC. School of Land and Building Studies. Research Unit
Land for residential development in the Leicester urban area : site specific case studies / SLABS Research Unit. — Leicester : School of Land and Building Studies, Leicester Polytechnic, 1984. — v,97 leaves. — (Housing land in urban areas ; Working paper no.4)

HOUSING DEVELOPMENT — England — Leicestershire

LEICESTER POLYTECHNIC. School of Land and Building Studies. Research Unit
Development planning in Leicestershire : policies and problems / SLABS Research Unit. — Leicester : School of Land and Building Studies, Leicester Polytechnic, 1984. — iii,51 leaves. — (Housing land in urban areas ; Working paper no.2)

HOUSING DEVELOPMENT — Hungary — Budapest

25 [ie. huszonöt] éve az állami építöiparban a 100 éves Budapestért 1948-1973 / Kisvári János, and 43 sz. állami építöipari vállalat. — Budapest : Révai Nyomda, [1973?]. — 119p

HOUSING DEVELOPMENT — United States

The Housing outlook, 1980-1990 / William C. Apgar, Jr. ... [et al.]. — New York : Praeger, 1985. — p. cm. — Includes index. — Bibliography: p

HOUSING FORECASTING — United States

The Housing outlook, 1980-1990 / William C. Apgar, Jr. ... [et al.]. — New York : Praeger, 1985. — p. cm. — Includes index. — Bibliography: p

HOUSING MANAGEMENT — Great Britain

MATTHEWS, Alison
Management cooperatives : the early stages / Alison Matthews. — London : H.M.S.O., 1981. — iv,34p. — At head of cover title: Department of the Environment

MINFORD, Patrick
The housing morass : regulation, immobility and unemployment : an economic analysis of the consequences of government regulation, with proposals to restore the market in rented housing / Patrick Minford, Michael Peel and Paul Ashton. — London : Institute of Economic Affairs, 1987. — 162p. — (Hobart paperback ; 25). — Bibliography: p157-162

HOUSING POLICY

MOSER, Caroline O. N.
Housing policy and women : towards a gender aware approach : draft document commissioned by United Nations Centre for Human Settlements. — London : Development Planning Unit, Bartlett School of Architecture and Planning, University College, 1985. — 37p. — (DPU gender and planning working paper ; no.7). — Bibliography: p35-37

HOUSING POLICY — Australia

BURKE, Terry
A roof over their heads : housing issues and families in Australia / Terry Burke, Linda Hancock, Peter Newton. — Melbourne : Institute of Family Studies, 1984. — 178p. — (Institute of Family Studies Monograph ; no.4). — Bibliography: p165-174

HOUSING POLICY — Botswana

BOTSWANA. Presidential Commission on Housing Policy in Botswana
Report of the Presidential Commission on Housing Policy in Botswana. — Gaborone : Government Printer, 1981. — 67p

HOUSING POLICY — Canada

FALLIS, George
Housing economics / George Fallis. — Toronto ; Boston : Butterworths, c1985. — 241 p.. — Includes index. — Bibliography: p. [221]-231

HOUSING POLICY — England — Bedfordshire

Land committed for housing development / Bedfordshire. County Council. — Bedford : Bedfordshire County Council, 1984-. — Annual

HOUSING POLICY — England — Birmingham (West Midlands)

BIRMINGHAM. Environmental Health Department
HMO's : a new initiative : tackling the problems of houses in multiple occupation in Birmingham's inner city. — Birmingham : [the Department], 1986. — 8p. — (Urban renewal)

THOMAS, Andrew D.
Managing houses in multiple occupation : a preliminary report on Birmingham's Housing Action Team / Andrew D. Thomas. — Birmingham : Environmental Health Department, 1986. — 64p. — (Urban renewal)

HOUSING POLICY — England — Kent

KENT. County Planning Department
Housing land supply in Kent 1985-1991 / [prepared by the County Planning Department on behalf of the Kent Planning Officers Group]. — Maidstone : [the Department], 1986. — [28p]

HOUSING POLICY — England — Liverpool (Merseyside)

COUCH, Chris
Housing trends in Liverpool / Chris Couch and Sue Wynne ; prepared by the Urban Policy Studies Unit, Liverpool Polytechnic for Liverpool Council for Voluntary Service. — Liverpool : Liverpool Council for Voluntary Service, 1986. — 47p

HOUSING POLICY — England — London

CAMDEN. Housing Department. Policy and Information Unit
London Borough of Camden : organisation of the housing department. — Camden : [the Unit], 1987. — 36p. — (Policy and information paper / Camden. Housing Department. Policy and Information Unit)

COUNTER INFORMATION SERVICES
London's recurrent crisis. — 2nd ed. — [London] : Counter Information Services, 1973. — 45 leaves

GLC PLANNING FOR HOUSING CONFERENCE (1985 : London)
The future of planning : planning for housing. — [London : Greater London Council], 1985. — 49p

GREATER LONDON COUNCIL
Housing 1983/5. — [London : the Council, 1985]. — 36p

Home truths : an investigation into Westminster City Council's housing policies. — London : Paddington Federation of Tennants and Residents Associations, 1977. — 67p

It's the limit : an exposé of pricing in London's B and B land. — London : CHAR, 1986. — 40p

MERRETT, Stephen
The way forward : Haringey's local housing plan 1986-90 / compiled by Stephen Merrett. — London : Haringey Housing Information Unit, 1986. — 58p

Women and housing policy : reports submitted to the GLC Housing and Women's Committees. — London : Greater London Council, 1986. — 100p. — (GLC housing research and policy report ; no.3). — Research commissioned and coordinated by GLC Housing Department Policy and Resources Branch, Policy Division

HOUSING POLICY — England — London — History

WOHL, Anthony S
The eternal slum : housing and social policy in Victorian London / Anthony S. Wohl. — Montreal : McGill-Queen's University Press, 1977. — xxiv, 386 p., [8] leaves of plates. — (Studies in urban history ; 5). — "A note on sources": p. 341-355. — Includes index

HOUSING POLICY — England — Manchester (Greater Manchester)

MANCHESTER. City Council
Housing defects in Manchester. — Manchester : [the Council], 1986. — [50p]

HOUSING POLICY — England — Sheffield (South Yorkshire)

GOODCHILD, Barry
New housing in the city : a case study of the inner-area of Sheffield / Barry Goodchild, Helen Duckworth [and] Anne Simmonite. — Sheffield : Sheffield City Polytechnic, Department of Education Services, 1984. — 48p

HOMES AND JOBS CONFERENCE (1986 : Sheffield)
Building for our future needs : homes and jobs. — Sheffield : Sheffield City Council, 1986. — 64p. — Includes information pack in seven sections

HOUSING POLICY — England — Southampton (Hampshire) — History

Dilapidated housing and housing policy in Southampton 1890-1914 / edited, with an introduction, by Martin Doughty. — Southampton : Southampton University Press, 1986. — xxxvi,119p. — (Southampton Records Series ; v.29)

HOUSING POLICY — Europe

HOGLUND, David J.
Housing for the elderly : privacy and independence / J. David Hoglund. — New York : Van Nostrand Reinhold, c1985. — p. cm. — Includes index. — Bibliography: p

HOUSING POLICY — Great Britain

BALL, Michael
Home ownership : a suitable case for reform / Michael Ball. — London : Shelter, 1986. — 70p

BARLOW, John Robert
Central-local government relations : the role of finance in influencing local policy making in education and housing in England : with special reference to the period 1974-1982 / John Robert Barlow. — 459 leaves. — PhD (Econ) 1986 LSE

BOLEAT, Mark
Housing in Britain / Mark Boleat. — London : The Building Societies Association, 1986. — 40p

DAVIES, J. G.
Asian housing in Britain / J. G. Davies. — London : Social Affairs Unit, — 23p. — (Research reports / Social Affairs Unit ; 6). — Bibliography: p19

FORREST, Ray
Monitoring the right to buy, 1980-1982 / Ray Forrest, Alan Murie. — Bristol : University of Bristol, School for Advanced Urban Studies, 1984. — 85p. — (Working paper / University of Bristol, School for Advanced Urban Studies ; no.40)

GREAT BRITAIN. Department of the Environment
Shared ownership : a new choice for tenants : Minister's speech to Shelter conference, 27 July 1979 / John Stanley. — London : the Department, 1979. — 36p

HOUSING POLICY — Great Britain
continuation

GREAT BRITAIN. Department of the Environment
United Kingdom memorandum on current trends and policies in the fields of housing, building and planning during the year 1975. — [London] : the Department, [1976]. — ii,28p. — *Prepared for the thirty-seventh session of the Committee on Housing, Building and Planning, United Nations Economic Commission for Europe*

INSTITUTE OF HOUSING. Vacant Properties Working Party
The key to empty housing. — London : Institute of Housing, 1986. — 63p. — (Professional practice series / Institute of Housing ; no.5)

LABOUR HOUSING GROUP
Homelessness : a plan for action. — Waltham Cross : Labour Housing Group, 1985. — 58p

LABOUR PARTY (Great Britain)
The new Tory housing plans. — London : Labour Party, 1987. — 9p. — (Information paper)

MCKECHNIE, Sheila
Homes above all : housing in Britain: the facts, the failures, the future / Sheila McKechnie [and] Des Wilson. — London : Shelter, 1986. — 64p

RYDIN, Yvonne
Housing land policy / Yvonne Rydin. — Aldershot : Gower, c1986. — xii,153p. — *Bibliography: p136-150. — Includes index*

SHELTER
Housing manifesto : SHELTER's plan for action : October 1974 election edition. — London : SHELTER, 1974. — 17p

HOUSING POLICY — Great Britain — History

EMSLEY, Ian
The development of housing associations : with special reference to London and including a case study of the London borough of Hammersmith / Ian Emsley. — New York : Garland Pub., 1986. — 477 p.. — (Outstanding theses from the London School of Economics and Political Science). — : *Originally presented as the author's thesis (Ph. D.)--London School of Economics. — Bibliography: p. 464-475*

HOLMANS, A. E.
Housing policy in Britain : a history / A.E. Holmans. — London : Croom Helm, c1987. — 489p. — *Includes index*

HOUSING POLICY — Great Britain — History — 20th century

DAUNTON, M. J.
A property-owning democracy? : housing in Britain / M. J. Daunton. — London : Faber and Faber, 1987. — xi,148p. — (Historical handbooks). — *Bibliography: p133-141*

HOUSING POLICY — Guinea-Bissau

DAVILA, Julio D.
Shelter, poverty and African revolutionary socialism : human settlements in Guinea Bissau / Julio D. Davila. — [London] : International Institute for Environment and Development, 1987. — vi,97p. — *Bibliography: p94-97*

HOUSING POLICY — Malaysia

INSTITUTE OF STRATEGIC AND INTERNATIONAL STUDIES CONFERENCE ON HOUSING (1986 : Kuala Lumpur)
The government plan on 80,000 low-cost houses : plan, obstacles and remedies; and how the private sector can contribute and benefit. — Kuala Lumpur : Institute of Stategic and International Studies, 1986. — 46p. — *Cover title: Target 80,000: Malaysia's special low-cost housing scheme*

HOUSING POLICY — Northern Ireland

BRETT, C. E. B.
Housing a divided community / C. E. B. Brett. — Dublin : Institute of Public Administration in association with Institute of Irish Studies, Queen's University of Belfast, 1986. — xi,171p. — *Bibliography: p152-3*

HOUSING POLICY — Scotland

GREAT BRITAIN. Scottish Development Department
Housing development, layout, roads and services / Scottish Development Department. — [Edinburgh] : H.M.S.O., 1977. — [117]p. — (Scottish housing handbook ; 3)

GREAT BRITAIN. Scottish Development Department
Scottish housing handbook / Scottish Development Department. — [Edinburgh] : H.M.S.O
1: Assessing housing need : a manual of guidance. — 1977. — [2],106p,fold leaf. — *Bibliography: p.100-101. — Includes index*

HOUSING POLICY — Scotland — Edinburgh

Short changed ? : a study of housing trends in central Edinburgh. — Edinburgh : Planning Study Group : Shelter, 1984. — 25p

HOUSING POLICY — United States

BELL, Robert
The culture of policy deliberations / Robert Bell. — New Brunswick, N.J. : Rutgers University Press, c1985. — viii, 264 p.. — *Includes index. — Bibliography: p. 227-253*

BURNS, Leland Smith
The future of housing markets : a new appraisal / Leland S. Burns and Leo Grebler. — New York : Plenum Press, c1986. — p. cm. — (Environment, development, and public policy. Cities and development). — *Includes index. — Bibliography: p*

Housing America's poor / edited by Peter D. Salins. — Chapel Hill : University of North Carolina Press, c1987. — p. cm. — (Urban and regional policy and development studies). — *Includes index*

Housing and the new financial markets / edited by Richard L. Florida. — New Brunswick, N.J. : Center for Urban Policy Research, c1986. — xviii, 482 p.. — *Includes index. — Bibliography: p. 469-472*

Housing desegregation and federal policy / edited by John M. Goering. — Chapel Hill : University of North Carolina Press, c1986. — x, 343 p.. — (Urban and regional policy and development studies). — *Includes bibliographies and index*

HOUSING POLICY — United States — History

HAYS, R. Allen
The federal government and urban housing : ideology and change in public policy / R. Allen Hays. — Albany : State University of New York Press, c1985. — xvi, 297 p.. — (SUNY series in urban public policy). — *Includes index. — Bibliography: p. 267-287*

HOUSING POLICY — Wales — West Glamorgan

WEST GLAMORGAN. County Council
People and homes : what are the issues?. — Swansea : [the Council], 1976. — 37p

HOUSING REHABILITATION

Maintenance and modernisation of urban housing. — Paris : Organisation for Economic Co-operation and Development, 1986. — 88p. — *At head of cover: OECD urban affairs programme*

HOUSING REHABILITATION — Finance — Law and legislation — Great Britain

GREAT BRITAIN. Parliament. House of Commons. Library. Research Division
Housing Defects Bill [Bill 147 session 1983/84] / Oonagh Gay. — [London] : the Division, 1984. — 16p. — (Reference sheet ; no.84/6). — *Bibliographical references: p14-16*

HOUSING REHABILITATION — Government policy — Great Britain

GREAT BRITAIN. Parliament. House of Commons. Library. Research Division
Improvement policies for private housing / Oonagh Gay. — [London] : the Division, 1985. — 47p. — (Background paper ; no.169)

HOUSING REHABILITATION — England

GREAT BRITAIN. Department of the Environment. Yorkshire and Humberside Regional Office
General improvement areas. — [Leeds] : the Office, 1971. — 33,[7]p

HOUSING REHABILITATION — England — London

LONDON HOUSING RESEARCH GROUP
Avoiding the bulldozer : the renewal of London's private housing. — [London : Greater London Council], 1983. — 63p. — *Bibliography: p62-63*

HOUSING REHABILITATION — England — Newcastle-upon-Tyne (Tyne and Wear)

BENWELL GROVE RESIDENTS ASSOCIATION DEVELOPMENT GROUP
Compulsory improvment notices don't work : further report from the B.G.R.A. Development Group. — Newcastle on Tyne : the Group, 1976. — 5 leaves

HOUSING REHABILITATION — England — Newcastle-upon-Tyne (Tyne and Wear)

BENWELL GROVE RESIDENTS ASSOCIATION DEVELOPMENT GROUP
G.I.A.s - left to rot? : report by the Benwell Grove Residents Association Development Group, November 1975. — Newcastle on Tyne : the Group, 1975. — [6]p

HOUSING REHABILITATION — European Economic Community countries

Employment and housing renovation in Europe / by Euro—Construct. — Luxembourg : Office for Official Publications of the European Communities, 1986. — 89p. — *At head of title: Commission of the European Communities*

HOUSING SUBSIDIES — Great Britain

Benefits : a housing and supplementary benefits guide for single people without a permanent home : incorporating: Desperate measures, the DHSS supplementary benefit regulations for board and lodging : currency: April 1987 to April 1988 / [written and published by CHAR]. — 1987/1988 ed. — London : CHAR, 1987. — xv,200p. — *Previous ed.: 1986. — Includes index*

HOUSING SUBSIDIES — United States

HAMMOND, Claire Holton
The benefits of subsidized housing programs : an intertemporal approach / Claire Holton Hammond. — Cambridge : Cambridge University Press, 1987. — 1v. — *Includes bibliography and index*

HOUSING SURVEYS

Principles and recommendations for population and housing censuses. — New York : United Nations, 1980. — xiv,330p. — (Statistical papers / United Nations, Statistical Office. Series M ; no.67) ([Document] (United Nations) ; ST/ESA/STAT/SER.M/67). — *Sales no.: E.80.XVII.8*

HOUSING SURVEYS — England — London
The Docklands housing needs survey, 1985 : the report of a survey of Newham, Southwark and Tower Hamlets / (report written by Hal Pawson with the assistance of Will Tuckley and other staff in the Housing Group of the London Research Centre). — [London] : London Research Centre
Technical volume. — 1986. — 83p. — (Reviews and studies series ; no.32). — *Bibliographical references: p80-83*

HOUSING SURVEYS — Great Britain
THOMAS, Andrew, 1950-
The 1985 physical and social survey of houses in multiple occupation in England and Wales / Andrew D. Thomas with Alan Hedges. — London : H.M.S.O., 1986. — vi,163p. — *Carried out for the Dept. of the Environment*

HOVAS — History
BLOCH, Maurice
From blessing to violence : history and ideology in the circumcision ritual of the Merina of Madagascar / Maurice Bloch. — Cambridge : Cambridge University Press, 1986. — x,214p. — (Cambridge studies in social anthropology ; 61). — *Bibliography: p200-205*

HOVAS — Rites and ceremonies
BLOCH, Maurice
From blessing to violence : history and ideology in the circumcision ritual of the Merina of Madagascar / Maurice Bloch. — Cambridge : Cambridge University Press, 1986. — x,214p. — (Cambridge studies in social anthropology ; 61). — *Bibliography: p200-205*

HOWMAN, H. R. G.
HOWMAN, H. R. G.
H.R.G. Howman on provincialisation in Rhodesia, 1968-1969 : and rational and irrational elements / edited by G.C. Passmore. — Cambridge : African Studies Centre, [1986]. — xxvii,65p. — (Cambridge African occasional papers ; 4)

HSÜAN-T'UNG *See* Pu Yi, Emperor of China

HUA (PAPUA NEW GUINEA PEOPLE) — Religion
MEIGS, Anna S.
Food, sex, and pollution : a New Guinea religion / Anna S. Meigs. — New Brunswick, N.J. : Rutgers University Press, c1984. — xix, 196 p.. — : *Revision of thesis (Ph. D.)--University of Pennsylvania. — Includes index. — Bibliography: p. 181-187*

HUA (PAPUA NEW GUINEA PEOPLE) — Sexual behavior
MEIGS, Anna S.
Food, sex, and pollution : a New Guinea religion / Anna S. Meigs. — New Brunswick, N.J. : Rutgers University Press, c1984. — xix, 196 p.. — : *Revision of thesis (Ph. D.)--University of Pennsylvania. — Includes index. — Bibliography: p. 181-187*

HUAHINE (SOCIETY ISLANDS) — Population — Statistics
Tableaux normalisés du recensement général de la population : 15 octobre 1983. — [Papeete] : Institut territorial de la statistique
Résultats de la commune de Huahine. — [1985?]. — 4p,11 leaves

HUDSON'S BAY COMPANY — History
NEWMAN, Peter C., 1929-
Company of Adventurers / Peter C. Newman. — Ontario : Viking Penguin
Vol.1. — c1985. — xxiii, 413p. — *Map on lining papers*

HUGUENOTS — Canada — History — 18th century
BOSHER, J. F.
The Canada merchants 1713-1763 / J.F. Bosher. — Oxford : Clarendon, 1987. — viii,234p. — *Includes index*

HUGUENOTS — England — History
Huguenots in Britain and their French background, 1550-1800 / edited by Irene Scouloudi. — Totowa, N.J. : Barnes & Noble, 1987. — p. cm. — *Includes index*

HUGUENOTS — France — History
Huguenots in Britain and their French background, 1550-1800 / edited by Irene Scouloudi. — Totowa, N.J. : Barnes & Noble, 1987. — p. cm. — *Includes index*

HUMAN BEHAVIOR
GOLD, John R.
An introduction to behavioural geography / John R. Gold. — Oxford : Oxford University Press, 1980. — [9],290p. — *Bibliography: p.253-286. — Includes index*

GOLLEDGE, Reginald G.
Analytical behavioural geography / Reginald G. Golledge and Robert J. Stimson. — London : Croom Helm, c1987. — 245p. — (Croom Helm series in geography and environment). — *Bibliography: p315-337. — Includes index*

Human behavior and environment: advances in theory and research. — New York ; London : Plenum Press, 1980-. — *Annual*

Information and behavior. — New Brunswick ; Oxford : Transaction Books. — *Bibliographies*
volume 1 / edited by Brent D. Ruben. — 1985. — xxiv,521p

HUMAN BEHAVIOR — Mathematical models
SIMON, Herbert A.
Models of man : social and rational : mathematical essays on rational human behavior in a social setting / Herbert A. Simon. — New York ; London : John Wiley, 1957 (1967 repr.). — xiv,287p

HUMAN BIOLOGY — Social aspects
Essays in human sociobiology / edited by Jan Wind. — London : Academic Press. — *"This volume is a slightly adapted reprint of the Journal of Human Evolution 13/1 (1984)"*
Vol.1 / contributions by R. Cliquet...[et al.]. — 1985. — 164p

Essays in human sociobiology. — Brussels : Vrije Universiteit, Pleinlaan 2. — (V. U. B. Study series ; 26). — *Includes references*
Vol.2 / edited by Jan Wind and Vernon Reynolds. — 1986. — xv,253p

HUMAN CAPITAL — Congresses
GENEVA CONFERENCE ON THE VALUE OF LIFE AND SAFETY (1981)
The value of life and safety : proceedings of a conference held by the "Geneva Association" : collection of papers presented at the Geneva Conference on the Value of Life and Safety held at the University of Geneva, 30th, 31st March and 1st April 1981 / edited by M.W. Jones-Lee. — Amsterdam ; New York : North-Holland Pub. Co. ; New York, N.Y. : Sole distributors for the U.S.A. and Canada, Elsevier Science Pub. Co., 1982. — xvii, 309 p.. — *Bibliography: p. xi*

HUMAN CAPITOL
CONTRIBUTIONS TO HUMAN RESOURCES RESEARCH: A MULTI-DISCIPLINARY SYMPOSIUM (1986 : St. Louis)
Human resources research, 1887-1987 : proceedings / ; edited by Ruth E. Deacon and Wallace E. Huffman. — Ames, Iowa : Iowa State University. College of Home Economics, 1986. — xiii,263p. — *Includes bibliographies*

HUMAN DEVELOPMENT — Congresses
Development in adolescence : psychological, social, and biological aspects / [edited by] W. Everaerd ... [et al.]. — Boston ; Lancaster : Nijhoff, c1983. — x, 254 p.. — *Based on a postgraduate course for medical practitioners, held in Leiden, Nov. 1981, which was entitled, Adolescence: psychological, social, and biological aspects. — Includes bibliographical references and index*

HUMAN ECOLOGY
BIDWELL, Charles E
The organization and its ecosystem : a theory of structuring in organizations / by Charles E. Bidwell, John D. Kasarda. — Greenwich, Conn. : JAI Press, c1985. — xxiv, 248 p. — (Monographs in organizational behavior and industrial relations ; v. 2). — *Includes indexes. — Bibliography: p. 229-236*

BOOKCHIN, Murray
The modern crisis / Murray Bookchin. — Philadelphia : New Society Publishers, 1986. — xi,167p. — *Published in cooperation with Institute for Social Ecology, Rochester, Vermont*

CROSBY, Alfred W.
Ecological imperialism : the biological expansion of Europe, 900-1900 / Alfred W. Crosby. — Cambridge : Cambridge University Press, 1986. — xiv,368p,[16]p of plates. — (Studies in environment and history). — *Includes index*

HALL, Charles A. S
Energy and resource quality : the ecology of the economic process / Charles A.S. Hall, Cutler J. Cleveland, Robert Kaufmann. — New York : Wiley, c1986. — xxi, 577 p.. — (Environmental science and technology). — *"A Wiley-Interscience publication.". — Includes index. — Bibliography: p. 535-568*

INGOLD, Tim
The appropriation of nature : essays on human ecology and social relations. — Manchester : Manchester University Press, c1986. — ix,287p. — (Themes in social anthropology). — *Includes bibliographies and index*

LEE, James A.
The environment, public health, and human ecology : considerations for economic development / James A. Lee. — Baltimore : Johns Hopkins University Press for the World Bank, 1985. — x,288p. — *Bibliography: p233-288*

LEY, David
A social geography of the city / David Ley. — New York : Harper & Row, c1983. — xii,449p. — (Harper & Row series in geography). — *Bibliography: p.401-441*

MCHALE, John
The ecological context. — New York : G. Braziller, [1970]. — 188 p. — *Bibliography: p. 175-188*

SALE, Kirkpatrick
Dwellers in the land : the bioregional vision / Kirkpatrick Sale. — San Francisco : Sierra Club Books, c1985. — x, 217 p.. — *Includes index. — Bibliography: p. 193-207*

HUMAN ECOLOGY — Addresses, essays, lectures
RAPPAPORT, Roy A
Ecology, meaning, and religion / Roy A. Rappaport. — Richmond, Calif. : North Atlantic Books, c1979. — xi, 259 p.. — *Includes bibliographical references and index*

HUMAN ECOLOGY — Congresses
INTERNATIONAL CONFERENCE OF SOCIAL GERONTOLOGY ((8th : 1978 : Mohammedia, Morocco)
Ecology and aging : 8th International Conference of Social Gerontology, Mohammedia, Morocco, 12/16 December 1978. — Paris, France : International Center of Social Gerontology, [1980]. — 440 p.. — *Includes bibliographies*

HUMAN ECOLOGY — Economic aspects
DUMONT, René
Les raisons de la colère, ou L'utopie et les Verts / René Dumont ; avec Charlotte Paquet. — Paris : Éditions Entente, 1986. — 137p. — *Bibliography: p135-137*

HUMAN ECOLOGY — Moral and ethical aspects

TAYLOR, Paul W
Respect for nature : a theory of environmental ethics / Paul W. Taylor. — Princeton, N.J. : Princeton University Press, c1986. — p. cm. — (Studies in moral, political, and legal philosophy). — Includes index. — Bibliography: p

HUMAN ECOLOGY — Moral and ethical aspects — Congresses

Religion and environmental crisis / edited by Eugene C. Hargrove. — Athens : University of Georgia Press, c1986. — p. cm. — Papers presented at a colloquium held at the University of Denver made possible by a grant from the Phillips Foundation of Minneapolis through the University Denver's Center for Judaic Studies. — Bibliography: p. — Contents: Introduction / Freddedick Ferré -- Pan / J. Donald Hughes -- A native American environmental ethic / Gerard Reed -- The earth is the Lord's / Jonathan Helfand -- Christian ecotheology and the Old Testament / Susan Power Bratton -- A biblical perspective on nonhuman organisms / Martin LeBar -- Taoism and the foundations of environmental ethics / Po-keung Ip -- On the ethics of man's interaction with the environment / Iqtidar H. Zaidi -- Roman Catholic teaching and environmental ethics in Latin America / Sophie Jakowska -- Christian realism and environmental ethics / Robert H. Ayers -- Christian existence in a world of limits / John B. Cobb -- Christianity and the need for new vision / Jay McDaniel

HUMAN ECOLOGY — Public opinion

GRAY, David B
Ecological beliefs and behaviors : assessment and change / David B. Gray, in collaboration with Richard J. Borden and Russell H. Weigel ; foreword by Riley E. Dunlap. — Westport, Conn. : Greenwood Press, c1985. — p. cm. — (Contributions in psychology ; no. 4). — Includes index. — Bibliography: p

HUMAN ECOLOGY — Religious aspects — Congresses

Religion and environmental crisis / edited by Eugene C. Hargrove. — Athens : University of Georgia Press, c1986. — p. cm. — Papers presented at a colloquium held at the University of Denver made possible by a grant from the Phillips Foundation of Minneapolis through the University Denver's Center for Judaic Studies. — Bibliography: p. — Contents: Introduction / Freddedick Ferré -- Pan / J. Donald Hughes -- A native American environmental ethic / Gerard Reed -- The earth is the Lord's / Jonathan Helfand -- Christian ecotheology and the Old Testament / Susan Power Bratton -- A biblical perspective on nonhuman organisms / Martin LeBar -- Taoism and the foundations of environmental ethics / Po-keung Ip -- On the ethics of man's interaction with the environment / Iqtidar H. Zaidi -- Roman Catholic teaching and environmental ethics in Latin America / Sophie Jakowska -- Christian realism and environmental ethics / Robert H. Ayers -- Christian existence in a world of limits / John B. Cobb -- Christianity and the need for new vision / Jay McDaniel

HUMAN ECOLOGY — Social aspects

DUMONT, René
Les raisons de la colère, ou L'utopie et les Verts / René Dumont ; avec Charlotte Paquet. — Paris : Éditions Entente, 1986. — 137p. — Bibliography: p135-137

HUMAN ECOLOGY — Statistics — Bibliography

Directory of environment statistics. — New York : United Nations, 1983. — v,305p. — (Statistical papers / United Nations, Statistical Office. Series M ; no.75) ([Document] (United Nations) ; ST/ESA/STAT/SER.M/75). — Sales no.: E.83.XVII.12

HUMAN ECOLOGY — Indonesia

DONNER, Wolf
Land use and environment in Indonesia / Wolf Donner ; photography by Erika Donner. — London : Published in association with the Institute of Asian Affairs, Hamburg by Hurst, 1987. — xix,368p. — Bibliography: p336-363. — Include index

HUMAN ECOLOGY — Southwest, New

BOWDEN, Charles
Blue desert / Charles Bowden. — Tucson : University of Arizona Press, c1986. — 175 p.

HUMAN ECOLOGY — United States

BOWDEN, Charles
Blue desert / Charles Bowden. — Tucson : University of Arizona Press, c1986. — 175 p.

LOGAN, John R.
Urban fortunes : the political economy of place / John R. Logan, Harvey L. Molotch. — Berkeley, CA : University of California Press, 1987. — p. cm. — Includes index. — Bibliography: p

The Social ecology of crime / edited by James M. Byrne and Robert J. Sampson. — New York : Springer-Verlag, c1986. — p. cm. — (Research in criminology). — Includes index. — Bibliography: p

HUMAN ENGINEERING

MEISTER, David
Behavioral analysis and measurement methods / David Meister. — New York : Wiley, c1985. — xiii, 509 p.. — "A Wiley-Interscience publication.". — Includes bibliographies and index

NICKERSON, Raymond S
Using computers : human factors in information systems / Raymond S. Nickerson. — Cambridge, Mass. ; London : MIT Press, c1986. — xiv, 434p. — "A Bradford book."

User centered system design : new perspectives on human-computer interaction / edited by Donald A. Norman, Stephen W. Draper. — Hillsdale, N.J. ; London : Lawrence Erlbaum Associates, 1986. — xiii, 526p. — Includes index. — Bibliography: p.[499]-512

WEST EUROPEAN CONFERENCE ON THE PSYCHOLOGY OF WORK AND ORGANIZATION (1985 : Aachen, Germany)
The psychology of work and organization : current trends and issues : selected and edited proceedings of the West European Conference on the Psychology of Work and Organization, Aachen, F.R.G., 1-3 April, 1985 / edited by G. Debus and H.-W. Schroiff. — Amsterdam ; New York : North Holland ; New York, N.Y., U.S.A. : Sole distributors for the U.S.A. and Canada, Elsevier Science Pub. Co., 1986. — xi, 407 p.. — Includes bibliographies and indexes

HUMAN EVOLUTION

INGOLD, Tim
Evolution and social life / Tim Ingold. — Cambridge : Cambridge University Press, 1986. — xv,431p. — (Themes in the social sciences). — Bibliography: p399-417. — Includes index

HUMAN EXPERIMENTATION IN MEDICINE — Law and legislation

COWEN, Zelman
Reflections on medicine, biotechnology, and the law / Sir Zelman Cowen. — [Lincoln, NE] : University of Nebraska College of Law : Distributed by the University of Nebraska Press, 1986, c1985. — p. cm. — "Eleventh in the series of Roscoe Pound lectures at the University of Nebraska College of Law"--Foreword

HUMAN GENETICS — Law and legislation — United States

NATIONAL SYMPOSIUM ON GENETICS AND THE LAW (3rd Mass. : 1984 : Boston)
Genetics and the law III / [proceedings of the Third National Symposium on Genetics and the Law, held April 2-4, 1984, in Boston, Massachusetts] ; [cosponsored by the American Society of Law and Medicine ... [et al.] ; edited by Aubrey Milunsky and George J. Annas. — New York ; London : Plenum, c1985. — xix,514p. — Bibliography: p491-504. — Includes index

HUMAN INFORMATION PROCESSING

Applications of cognitive psychology : problem solving, education, and computing / edited by Dale E. Berger, Kathy Pezdek, William P. Banks. — Hillsdale, N.J. : L. Erlbaum Associates, 1987. — xii, 235 p.. — Includes bibliographies and indexes

LEWICKI, Paweł
Nonconscious social information processing / Paweł Lewicki. — Orlando : Academic Press, 1986. — p. cm. — Includes bibliographical references and index

LINDSAY, Peter H.
Human information processing : An introduction to psychology / Peter H. Lindsay and Donald A. Norman. — 2d ed. — New York : Academic Press, c1977. — xxiii, 777 p. — Includes indexes. — Bibliography: p. [734]-762

MCCLELLAND, James L.
Parallel distributed processing : explorations in the microstructure of cognition. — Cambridge, Mass. : MIT Press. — (Computational models of cognition and perception)
Vol.2: Psychological and biological models / James L. McClelland, David E. Rumelhart and the PDP Research Group. — 1986. — xii,611p. — Bibliography: p[553]-579

PAIVIO, Allan
Mental representations : a dual coding approach / Allan Paivio. — New York : Oxford University Press ; Oxford : Clarendon Press, 1986. — x, 322p. — (Oxford psychology series ; no. 9). — Includes index. — Bibliography: p.277-305

RUMELHART, David E.
Parallel distributed processing : explorations in the microstructure of cognition. — Cambridge, Mass. ; London : MIT Press. — (Computational models of cognition and perception) (A Bradford book)
Vol.1: Foundations / David E. Rumelhart, James L. McClelland and the PDP Research Group ; Chisato Asanuma ... [et al.]. — c1986. — xx,547p. — Bibliography: p507-516. — Includes index

SOWA, John F.
Conceptual structures : information processing in mind and machine / John F. Sowa. — Reading, Mass. ; London : Addison-Wesley, 1984. — (The Systems programming series)

HUMAN POPULATION GENETICS — Philosophy

JACQUARD, Albert
[Au péril de la science?. English]. Endangered by science? / Albert Jacquard ; translated by Margaret M. Moriarty. — New York : Columbia University Press, 1985. — p. cm. — Translation of: Au péril de la science?. — Includes index

HUMAN POPULATION GENETICS — Social aspects

JACQUARD, Albert
[Au péril de la science?. English]. Endangered by science? / Albert Jacquard ; translated by Margaret M. Moriarty. — New York : Columbia University Press, 1985. — p. cm. — Translation of: Au péril de la science?. — Includes index

HUMAN POPULATION GENETICS — Wales
Genetic and population studies in Wales / edited by Peter S. Harper and Eric Sunderland. — Cardiff : University of Wales Press, 1986. — vii,432p. — *Includes index*

HUMAN REPRODUCTION — Moral and ethical aspects
OVERALL, Christine
Ethics and human reproduction : a feminist analysis / Christine Overall. — Boston [Mass.] ; London : Allen & Unwin, 1987. — [224]p. — *Includes bibliography and index*

HUMAN REPRODUCTION — Political aspects
COREA, Gena
The mother machine : reproductive technologies from artificial insemination to artificial wombs / Gena Corea. — 1st ed. — New York : Harper & Row, c1985. — p. cm. — *Includes index. — Bibliography: p*

HUMAN REPRODUCTION — Social aspects
Reproductive technologies : gender, motherhood and medicine / edited by Michelle Stanworth. — Cambridge : Polity in association with Blackwell, 1987. — [220]p. — (Feminist perspectives). — *Includes bibliography and index*

HUMAN REPRODUCTION — Social aspects — Cross-cultural studies
BETZIG, L. L
Despotism and differential reproduction : a Darwinian view of history / L.L. Betzig. — New York : Aldine Pub., 1986. — p. cm. — *Bibliography: p*

HUMAN REPRODUCTION — Great Britain — Statistics
MCDOWALL, M. E.
Occupational reproductive epidemiology : the use of routinely collected statistics in England and Wales 1980-82 / M. E. McDowall, Medical Statistics Division, Office of Population Censuses and Surveys. — London : H.M.S.O., 1985. — iii,77p. — (Studies on medical and population subjects ; no.50). — *Bibliographical references: p76-77*

HUMAN SETTLEMENTS
PACIONE, Michael
Rural geography / Michael Pacione. — London : Harper & Row, 1984. — 384p. — *Includes bibliographies and index*

HUMAN SETTLEMENTS — Societies, etc. — Directories
GREAT BRITAIN. Department of the Environment
British services overseas. — [London] : the Department, 1976. — 15p. — *A contribution by the United Kingdom to the United Nations Conference on Human Settlements, 1976, Vancouver*

HUMAN SETTLEMENTS — Guinea-Bissau
DAVILA, Julio D.
Shelter, poverty and African revolutionary socialism : human settlements in Guinea Bissau / Julio D. Davila. — [London] : International Institute for Environment and Development, 1987. — vi,97p. — *Bibliography: p94-97*

HUMAN TERRITORIALITY
SACK, Robert David
Human territoriality : its theory and history / Robert David Sack. — Cambridge : Cambridge University Press, 1986. — [ix,315]p. — (Cambridge studies in historical geography ; 7)

HUMANISM — Knowledge, Theory of
KAIN, Philip J.
Marx' method, epistemology, and humanism : a study in the development of his thought / Philip J. Kain. — Dordrecht ; Boston : D. Reidel ; Hingham, MA, U.S.A. : Sold and distributed in the U.S.A. and Canada by Kluwer Academic Publishers, c1986. — x, 197 p.. — (Sovietica ; v. 48). — *Includes index. — Bibliography: p. 176-184*

HUMANISM — Great Britain
LEVINE, Joseph M
Humanism and history : origins of modern English historiography / Joseph M. Levine. — Ithaca : Cornell University Press, 1987. — 297 p.. — *Includes index. — Bibliography: p. 214-288*

HUMANITIES
Current research in Britain: the humanities. — Boston Spa : British Library Lending Division, 1985-. — *Annual*

HUMANITIES — Information services — Great Britain
KATZEN, May
Recent initiatives in communication in the humanities / M. Katzen and S.M. Howley. — London : British Library Research & Development Department, 1984. — xii,125p. — (Library and information research report ; 11)

KATZEN, May
Technology and communication in the humanities : training and services in universities and polytechnics in the UK / M. Katzen. — London : British Library, c1985. — x,121p. — (Library and information research report ; 32)

HUMANITIES — Information services — United States
KATZEN, May
Recent initiatives in communication in the humanities / M. Katzen and S.M. Howley. — London : British Library Research & Development Department, 1984. — xii,125p. — (Library and information research report ; 11)

HUMANITIES — Scholarships, fellowships, etc. — Great Britain
BRITISH ACADEMY
Guide to awards in the humanities and social sciences, 1986-87. — London : British Academy, 1986. — 27p

HUMANITIES — China
New directions in the social sciences and humanities in China / edited by Michael B. Yahuda. — Basingstoke : Macmillan, 1987. — xxi,169p. — *Includes index*

HUMANITIES — Great Britain — Research grants
BRITISH ACADEMY
Guide to awards in the humanities and social sciences, 1986-87. — London : British Academy, 1986. — 27p

HUMBER RIVER VALLEY (ONT.) — Economic conditions
FISHER, Sidney T.
The merchant-millers of the Humber Valley : a study of the early economy of Canada / Sidney Thomson Fisher. — Toronto : NC Press, 1985. — xxiii,188p

HUMBER RIVER VALLEY (ONT.) — History
FISHER, Sidney T.
The merchant-millers of the Humber Valley : a study of the early economy of Canada / Sidney Thomson Fisher. — Toronto : NC Press, 1985. — xxiii,188p

HUME, DAVID
WILSON, Fred
Laws and other worlds : a Humean account of laws and counterfactuals / Fred Wilson. — Dordrecht ; Lancaster : Reidel, c1986. — xv, 328 p.. — (The University of Western Ontario series in philosophy of science ; v. 31). — *Includes index. — Bibliography: p. 315-321*

HUME, DAVID, 1711-1776
FLEW, Antony
David Hume : philosopher of moral science / Antony Flew. — Oxford : Basil Blackwell, 1986. — [220]p. — *Includes index*

PASSMORE, John
Hume's intentions / John Arthur Passmore. — Cambridge : Cambridge University Press, 1952. — ix,164p

HUNAN PROVINCE (CHINA) — Population — History
PERDUE, Peter C.
Exhausting the earth : state and peasant in Hunan, 1500-1850 / Peter C. Perdue. — Cambridge, Mass. : Council on East Asian Studies, Harvard University : Distributed by Harvard University Press, 1987. — p. cm. — (Harvard East Asian monographs ; 1987). — *Includes index. — Bibliography: p*

HUNGARIAN LITERATURE — 20th century
FÜLEP, Lajos
A magyarság pusztulása / Fülep Lajos. — Budapest : Magvető Kiadó, 1984. — 65p. — (Gondolkodó Magyarok)

HUNGARIAN WORKER' PARTY *See* Magyar Dolgozók Pártja

HUNGARY — Bibliography
KABDEBO, Thomas
Hungary / Thomas Kabdebo. — Oxford : Clio Press, 1980. — lvi,280p. — (The world bibliographical series ; vol.15). — *Includes index*

HUNGARY — Census — 1984
HUNGARY. Központi Statisztikai Hivatal
Az 1984. évi mikrocenzus f"obb eredményei. — Budapest : KSH, 1985. — 75p

HUNGARY — Census,1984
Data of the 1984 Hungarian microcensus. — Budapest : Hungarian Central Statistical Office, 1986. — 158p

HUNGARY — Commerce — Bibliography
KONJUNKTÚRA-ÉS PIACKUTATÓ INTÉZET. Kulkereskedelmi Információs Központ
Register of papers and publications prepared in the Institute for Economic and Market Research in 1986 / edited by Judith Trébits ; translated by Márta Lempert. — Budapest : Institute for Economic and Market Research, 1987. — 42p

HUNGARY — Commercial policy
KARDOS, Péter
Külföldi licencek a magyar gazdaságban / Kardos Péter , Szatmári Tamás. — Budapest : Közgazdasági és Jogi Könyvkiadó, 1984. — 204p. — *Bibliography: p201-[205]*

HUNGARY — Economic conditions
An economic geography of Hungary / edited by Tivadar Bernat. — Budapest : Akademiai Kiado, 1985. — 450p. — *Translated from the Hungarian by I. Veges and P. A. Compton. — Col. maps on end papers*

FELLNER, Frigyes
Ausztria és Magyarország nemzeti jövedelme / Fellner Frigyes. — Budapest : Magyar Tudományos Akadémia, 1916. — 152p. — (Értekezések a philosophia és társadalmi tudományok köréb"ol ; köt.1 ; sz.8)

FELLNER, Frigyes
A nemzetközi fizetési mérleg és alakulása Magyarországon / a Magyar Tudományos Akadémia megbízásából irta Fellner Frigyes. — Budapest : Politzer-féle Könyvkiadóvállalat, 1908. — 181p. — (Magyar Közgazdasági Könyvtár ; Köt.5)

HOÓS, János
Az új növekedési pálya feltételei és követelményei / Hoós János. — Budapest : Közgazdasági és Jogi könyvkiadó, 1985. — 227p. — *Bibliography: p[229]*

MÉREY, Klára T.
Dél-Dunántúl iparának története a kapitalizmus idején / T. Mérey Klára. — Budapest : Akadémiai Kiadó, 1985. — 289p

HUNGARY — Economic conditions
continuation

SZÁDECZKY-KARDOSS, Tibor
A magyarországi pénzintézetek fejl"odése / írta Szádeczky-Kardoss Tibor. — Budapest : [Pallas részvénytársaság nyomdája], 1928. — vii,212p. — (Közgazdasági Könyvtár ; köt.4)

HUNGARY — Economic conditions — 1918-1945

DOMÁNY, Gyula
Az önáló jegybank felállítása / írta Domány Gyula. — Budapest : Benkö Gyula Könyvkereskedése, 1918. — 45p

FELLNER, Frigyes
Csonka-Magyarország nemzeti jövedelme / írta Fellner Frigyes. — Budapest : Magyar Tudományos Akadémia, 1930. — 107p

FELLNER, Frigyes
Csonka-Magyarország nemzeti vagyona / írta Fellner Frigyes. — Budapest : Magyar Tudományos Akadémia, 1929. — 94p

MAGYARORSZÁG KÖZÉPEURÓPAI IUTÉZETE. Conference (Budapest : 1936)
A dunai államok valutarendezése / Magyarország Középeurópa Intézete ; [contributions by] Hantos Elemér...[et al.]. — Budapest : Szeged Városi Nyomda, 1936. — 72p

HUNGARY — Economic conditions — 1945-

NYITRAI, Ferencné
A magyar gazdaság negyven eve / Nyitrai Ferencné. — Budapest : Kossuth K"onyukiadó, 1985. — 385p. — *Bibliography: p385*

HUNGARY — Economic conditions — 1968-

Az 1983. évi iparstatisztikai világprogram adatai : Magyarország = Results of the 1983 World Programme of Industrial Statistics : Hungary. — Budapest : Központi Statisztikai Hivatal, 1986. — 289p. — *In Hungarian and English*

HUNGARY, Központi Statisztikai Hivatal
Report of the Hungarian Statistical Office on the fulfilment of the 1975 plan and the development of the national economy. — Budapest : the Office, 1976. — 18p

HUNGARY. Központi Statisztikai Hivatal
Report of the Central Statistical Office on the fulfilment of the 1978-year plan and on the development of the national economy. — [Budapest] : the Office, [1979]. — 15p

HUNGARY. Központi Statisztikai Hivatal
Report of the Hungarian Statistical Office on the economic development and plan-fulfilment in 1972. — Budapest : the Office, 1973. — 14p

Hungary today. — Budapest : Central Statistical Office, 1985. — 199p

HUNGARY — Economic policy — 1945-

NYITRAI, Ferencné
A magyar gazdaság negyven eve / Nyitrai Ferencné. — Budapest : Kossuth K"onyukiadó, 1985. — 385p. — *Bibliography: p385*

HUNGARY — Economic policy — 1968

HUNGARY. Központi Statisztikai Hivatal
Report of the Hungarian Statistical Office on the economic development and plan-fulfilment in 1972. — Budapest : the Office, 1973. — 14p

HUNGARY — Economic policy — 1968-

FLAKIERSKI, Henryk
Economic reform & income distribution : a case study of Hungary and Poland / by Henryk Flakierski. — Armonk, N.Y. : M.E. Sharpe, c1986. — xi, 194 p... — *"Published simultaneously as vol. XXIV, no. 1-2, of Eastern European economics"--Verso t.p. — Bibliography: p. 165-194*

HUNGARY, Központi Statisztikai Hivatal
Report of the Hungarian Statistical Office on the fulfilment of the 1975 plan and the development of the national economy. — Budapest : the Office, 1976. — 18p

HUNGARY. Központi Statisztikai Hivatal
Report of the Central Statistical Office on the fulfilment of the 1978-year plan and on the development of the national economy. — [Budapest] : the Office, [1979]. — 15p

KASPER, Egon F.
Ungarn : Lebenskünstler auf der Suche nach der kleinen Freiheit / Egon F. Kasper. — München : printul, 1986. — xiip,p9-213

Koncepció és kritika : vita Liska Tibor "szocialista vállalkozási szektor" javaslatáról / szerkesztette síklaky István. — Budapest : Magvető kiadó, [1985]. — 387p. — (Gyorsuló idő)

PONGRÁCZ, László
A kereseti arányok távlati fejlesztése / Pongrácz László. — Budapest : Közgazdasági és Jogi Könyvkiadó, 1975. — 211p. — *Bibliography: p205-211*

HUNGARY — Ethnic relations

LÁSZLÓ, Lajos
Jégszikrák : (A hazai nemzetiségek életéb"ol) / László Lajos. — [Budapest] : Népszava, 1984. — 177p

HUNGARY — Foreign economic relations — European Economic Community countries

HEDRI, Gabriella
A Közös Piac és a magyar export / Hedri Gabriella. — Budapest : Közgazdasági és Jogi könyvkiadó, 1970. — 178p. — *Bibliography: p173-174*

HUNGARY — Foreign economic relations — Romania

SCHAFARIK BRUNNER, Wladimir
Rom'ania szerepe h'aborus gazdálkodásunkban / 'irta Schafarik Brunner Wladimir. — Budapest : Sylvester irodalmi 'es nyomdai intézet R.T., 1935. — 137p. — (Közgazdas'agi Könyut'ar ; Köt.9)

HUNGARY — Foreign population

LÁSZLÓ, Lajos
Jégszikrák : (A hazai nemzetiségek életéb"ol) / László Lajos. — [Budapest] : Népszava, 1984. — 177p

HUNGARY — Foreign relations

LOSONCZI, Pál
Erösödö népi-nemzeti egység, békés egymás mellett élés : válogatott beszédek, cikkek 1960-1984 / Losonczi. — Budapest : Kossuth Könyvkiadó, 1984. — 325p

HUNGARY — Foreign relations — 1945-

Questions of international law. — Dordrecht : Nijhoff ; Budapest : Akadémiai Kiadó volume 3: Hungarian perspectives / edited by Hanna Bokor-Szegö. — 1986. — 274p

HUNGARY — Foreign relations — Soviet Union

GATI, Charles
Hungary and the Soviet bloc / by Charles Gati. — Durham [N.C.] : Duke University Press, 1986. — 244 p.. — *Includes index. — Bibliography: p. [233]-237*

HUNGARY — History — German occupation, 1944-1945

The liberation of Hungary 1944-1945 : selected documents / [Introduction by Gyula Kállai, documents selected and explanatory texts written by Béla Estisf translated by Károly Ravasz]. — Budapest : Corvina, 1975. — 185p

HUNGARY — History — Revolution, 1918-1919

NEMES, Dezső
Kun Béla politikai életútjáról / Nemes Dezső. — [Budapest] : Kossuth Könyvkiadó, 1985. — 186p

HUNGARY — History — 1867-1918

GALÁNTAI, József
A Habsburg-monarchia alkonya : osztrák-magyar dualizmus 1867-1918 / Galántai József. — [Budapest] : Kossuth Könyvkiadó, 1985. — 386p. — *References: p367-[387]*

HUNGARY — History — 1918-1945

PINTÉR, István
Hungarian anti-fascism and resistance, 1941-1945 / by István Pintér. — Budapest : Akadémiai Kiadó, 1986. — 234p

VARGYAI, Gyula
Sisak és cilinder : a katonai vezetés és a politika magyarországon a második világháború elöestéjén / Vargyai Gyula. — Budapest : Kozmosz Könyvek, 1984. — 191p. — (Az én világom)

HUNGARY — History — 1945-

SZABÓ, Bálint
Az "ötvenes évek" : elmélet és politika a szocialista építés elso" időszakában Magyarországon 1948-1957 / Szabó Bálint. — Budapest : Kossuth Könyvkiadó, 1986. — 432p . — *References: p397-[433]*

HUNGARY — History — Revolution, 1956

BERECZ, János
1956 counter-revolution in Hungary : words and weapons / János Berecz ; translated by István Buttkay ; translation revised by Charles Coutts. — Budapest : Akadémiai Kiadó, 1986. — 223p. — *Translated from the second, enlarged and revised edition of 'Ellenforradalom tollal és fegyverrel 1956', Budapest, Kossuth, 1981*

GADNEY, Reg
Cry Hungary! : uprising 1956 / by Reg Gadney ; introduction by George Mikes. — 1st American ed. — New York : Atheneum, 1986. — p. cm. — *Includes index*

GERÉB, Sándor
Az ellenforradalom utóvédharca : 1956 november-1957 március / Geréb Sándor-Hajdú Pál. — Budapest : Kossuth Könyvkiadó, 1986. — 231p. — *References: p225-[230]*

HUNGARY — History — Revolution, 1956 — Personal narratives

KOPÁCSI, Sándor
[Au nom de la classe ouvrière. English]. "In the name of the working class" : the inside story of the Hungarian Revolution / Sándor Kopácsi ; translated by Daniel and Judy Stoffman ; with a foreword by George Jonas. — 1st ed. — New York : Grove Press, 1987, c1986. — p. cm. — *Translation of: Au nom de la classe ouvrière. — Bibliography: p*

HUNGARY — Industries

MÉREY, Klára T.
Dél-Dunántúl iparának története a kapitalizmus idején / T. Mérey Klára. — Budapest : Akadémiai Kiadó, 1985. — 289p

HUNGARY — Industries — Statistics

Az 1983. évi iparstatisztikai világprogram adatai : Magyarország = Results of the 1983 World Programme of Industrial Statistics : Hungary. — Budapest : Központi Statisztikai Hivatal, 1986. — 289p. — *In Hungarian and English*

HUNGARY — Intellectual life

HERNÁDI, Miklós
Olyan amilyen? : körkép új kultúránkról / Hernádi Miklós. — Budapest : Kozmosz Könyvek, 1984. — 285p. — (Az én világom)

HUNGARY — Politics and government — 1918-1945

VARGYAI, Gyula
Sisak és cilinder : a katonai vezetés és a politika magyarországon a második világháború elöestéjén / Vargyai Gyula. — Budapest : Kozmosz Könyvek, 1984. — 191p. — (Az én világom)

HUNGARY — Politics and government — 1945-

KÁDÁR, János
Béke, f̋uggetlenség, honvédelem : beszédek és cikkek 1957-1985 / Kádár János. — Budapest : Zrínyi Katonai Kiadó, 1985. — 342p

KAPLAN, Karel
The overcoming of the regime crisis after Stalin's death in Czechoslovakia, Poland and Hungary / Karel Kaplan. — Munchen : Projekt 'Crises in Soviet-type systems', 1986. — 119p. — (Research project Crises in Soviet-type systems ; Study no.11)

Politics and public administration in Hungary / edited by György Szoboszlai. — Budapest : Akadémiai Kiadó, 1985. — x,485p. — *Translated from the Hungarian.* — *Includes amended text of the Constitution of the Hungarian People's Republic: p427-484*

SZABÓ, Bálint
Az "ötvenes évek" : elmélet és politika a szocialista építés elso" idoszakában Magyarországon 1948-1957 / Szabó Bálint. — Budapest : Kossuth Könyvkiadó, 1986. — 432p . — *References: p397-[433]*

HUNGARY — Popular culture

HERNÁDI, Miklós
Olyan amilyen? : körkép új kultúránkról / Hernádi Miklós. — Budapest : Kozmosz Könyvek, 1984. — 285p. — (Az én világom)

HUNGARY — Population

An economic geography of Hungary / edited by Tivadar Bernat. — Budapest : Akademiai Kiado, 1985. — 450p. — *Translated from the Hungarian by I. Veges and P. A. Compton.* — *Col. maps on end papers*

FÜLEP, Lajos
A magyarság pusztulása / Fülep Lajos. — Budapest : Magvető Kiadó, 1984. — 65p. — (Gondolkodó Magyarok)

HUNGARY. Központi Statisztikai Hivatal
Az 1984. évi mikrocenzus f̋obb eredményei. — Budapest : KSH, 1985. — 75p

HUNGARY — Population — Statistics

Data of the 1984 Hungarian microcensus. — Budapest : Hungarian Central Statistical Office, 1986. — 158p

The population of Hungary. — Budapest : Hungarian Central Statistical Office, 1984. — 30p

Summary of the 1986 fertility surveys. — Budapest : Central Statistical Office, 1987. — 21p

HUNGARY — Relations — Romania — History

PĂCURARIU, Mircea
Politica statului ungar față de Biserica românească din Transilvania în perioada dualismului (1867-1918) / Mircea Păcurariu. — Sibiu : Editura Institutului Biblic și de Misiune al Bisericii Ortodoxe Române, 1986. — 301p

HUNGARY — Social conditions — 1968-

Hungary today. — Budapest : Central Statistical Office, 1985. — 199p

HUNGARY — Statistics

Lakasstatisztikai evkonyv = Yearbook of housing statistics / Kozponti Statisztikai Hivatal. — Budapest : Kozponti Statisztikai Hivatal, 1983-. — *Annual.* — *Table headings in Hungarian, English and Russian*

HUNGARY — Ethnic relations — Congresses

The Holocaust in Hungary : forty years later / edited by Randolph L. Braham and Bela Vago. — New York : Institute of Holocaust Studies of the City University of New York, and Institute of Holocaust Studies of the University of Haifa : Columbia University Press [distributor], 1985. — xv,235p. — (East European monographs ; no.190) (Holocaust studies series). — *'... an outgrowth of two international conferences held in 1984....'*

HUNGER

Ending hunger : an idea whose time has come / the Hunger Project. — New York ; Eastbourne : Praeger, 1985. — 430p. — (Praeger special studies). — *Bibliography: p413-417.* — *Includes index*

HUNGER STRIKES — Northern Ireland

BERESFORD, David
Ten men dead : the story of the 1981 Irish hunger strike / David Beresford. — London : Grafton, 1987. — 432p

HUNT, JAMES B.

SNIDER, William D
Hunt and Helms : North Carolina chooses a Senator / by William D. Snider. — Chapel Hill : University of North Carolina Press, c1985. — p. cm. — *Includes index*

HUNTING — Congresses

Resource managers : North American and Australian hunter-gatherers / edited by Nancy M. Williams and Eugene S. Hunn. — Canberra : Australian Institute of Aboriginal Studies, 1982. — xii,267p. — (AAAS selected symposia series). — *Based on a symposium of the American Association for the Advancement of Science 1980.* — *Bibliography at end of each paper*

HUNTING — Finland — Accounting

MÄKELÄ, Pekka
Kansantalouden tilinpito : maa-, metsä- ja kalatalous sekä metsästys kansantalouden tilinpidossa = National accounts : agriculture, forestry, fishing and hunting in national accounts. — Helsinki : Tilastokeskus, 1980. — 126p. — (Tutkimuksia / Finland. Tilastokeskus ; no.61). — *Summary and table headings in English and Swedish*

HUNTING AND GATHERING SOCIETIES

INGOLD, Tim
The appropriation of nature : essays on human ecology and social relations. — Manchester : Manchester University Press, c1986. — ix,287p. — (Themes in social anthropology). — *Includes bibliographies and index*

TESTART, Alain
Les chasseurs-cueilleurs, ou l'origine des inégalités / Alain Testart. — Paris : Société d'ethnographie, 1982. — 254p. — (Mémoires de la Société d'ethnographie ; 26). — *Bibliography: p227-247*

TESTART, Alain
Essai sur les fondements de la division sexuelle du travail chez les chasseurs-cueilleurs / Alain Testart. — Paris : École des Hautes Études en Sciences Sociales, 1986. — 102p. — (Cahiers de l'homme : ethnologie, géographie, linguistique. nouvelle série ; 25). — *Bibliography: p91-99*

ḤUSAYNĪ, AMĪN, Grand Mufti of Jerusalem

TAGGAR, Yehuda
The Mufti of Jerusalem and Palestine : Arab politics, 1930-1937 / Yehuda Taggar. — New York : Garland, 1986, c1987. — 472 p.. — (Outstanding theses from the London School of Economics and Political Science). — *Thesis (Ph. D.)--University of London, 1973.* — *Bibliography: p. 466-472*

HUSBAND AND WIFE

RAPOPORT, Rhona
Dual-career families re-examined : new integrations of work & family / Rhona & Robert N. Rapoport. — New York : Harper & Row, 1977, c1976. — 382 p. — (Harper colophon books ; CN 521). — *Sequel to the author's Dual-career families.* — *Bibliography: p. [373]-382*

HUSBAND AND WIFE — Taxation — Great Britain

ATKINSON, A. B.
Taxation of husband and wife in the UK and changes in the tax-benefit system / A. B. Atkinson and H. Sutherland. — [London : London School of Economics and Political Science], 1987. — 42p. — (Taxation, incentives and the distribution of income ; no.104). — *Economic and Social Research Council programme.* — *Bibliographical references: p42*

HUSBAND AND WIFE — United States

WEITZMAN, Lenore J
The marriage contract : spouses, lovers and the law / Lenore J. Weitzman. — New York : Free Press, c1981. — p. cm. — *Includes index*

HUSBANDS — Addresses, essays, lectures

Men in families / edited by Robert A. Lewis and Robert E. Salt. — Beverly Hills : Sage Publications, c1985. — p. cm. — (Sage focus editions ; v. 76). — *Includes bibliographical references*

HUTTERITE BRETHREN

PETER, Karl A.
The dynamics of Hutterite Society : an analytical approach / Karl A. Peter. — Edmonton : University of Alberta Press, 1987. — xxiii,232p. — *Bibliography: p229-232*

HUTTERITE BRETHREN — Social conditions

PETER, Karl A.
The dynamics of Hutterite Society : an analytical approach / Karl A. Peter. — Edmonton : University of Alberta Press, 1987. — xxiii,232p. — *Bibliography: p229-232*

HYDERABAD (INDIA : STATE) — History

BHASKARA RAO, V.
Agrarian and industrial relations in Hyderabad State / V. Bhaskara Rao. — New Delhi : Associated Pub. House, c1985. — xi, 179 p.. — *Includes index.* — *Bibliography: p. [169]-173*

HYDROELECTRIC POWER PLANTS — Economic aspects — Latin America

INSTITUTE FOR LATIN AMERICAN INTEGRATION
Obras hidroelectricas binacionales en America Latina. — [Buenos Aires] : the Institute, Banco Interamericano de Desarollo, 1985. — vii,385p

HYDROELECTRIC POWER PLANTS — Québec (Province)

BOURASSA, Robert
Power from the north / Robert Bourassa ; with a foreword by James Schlesinger. — Scarborough, Ontario : Prentice-Hall, 1985. — x,181p

HYDROELETRIC POWER PLANTS — Peru — Mantaro River Valley

CORPORACIÓN DE ENERGÍA ELÉTRICA DEL MANTARO
Proyecto del Mantaro Y estado de su ejecución al 31 de enero de 1966. — Lima : the Corporación, 1966. — [9]p

HYDROGRAPHIC SURVEYING — Congresses

INTERNATIONAL CONFERENCE ON SHIP SAFETY AND MARINE SURVEYING (1986 : Malmo, Sweden)
International Conference on Ship Safety and Marine Surveying : [proceedings] / [organized by] the Nautical Institute and the World Maritime University, Malmo, Sweden, 8-9 May 1986. — London : Nautical Institute, 1986. — 158p

HYDROLOGY
WARD, Roy Charles
Principles of hydrology / R. C. Ward. — 2d ed. — London ; New York : McGraw-Hill, [1975]. — xvi, 367 p. — *Includes bibliographies and index*

HYSTERECTOMY
STOKES, Naomi Miller
The castrated woman : what your doctor won't tell you about hysterectomy / Naomi Miller Stokes. — New York : F. Watts, 1986. — 206 p.. — *Includes index. — Bibliography: p. 187-200*

HYSTERECTOMY — Patients — Interviews
STOKES, Naomi Miller
The castrated woman : what your doctor won't tell you about hysterectomy / Naomi Miller Stokes. — New York : F. Watts, 1986. — 206 p.. — *Includes index. — Bibliography: p. 187-200*

HYSTERECTOMY — Psychological aspects
STOKES, Naomi Miller
The castrated woman : what your doctor won't tell you about hysterectomy / Naomi Miller Stokes. — New York : F. Watts, 1986. — 206 p.. — *Includes index. — Bibliography: p. 187-200*

IACOCCA, LEE
ABODAHER, David
Iacocca / David Abodaher. — London : W.H. Allen, 1986. — 276p,[8]p of plates. — (A Star book). — *Originally published: New York : Macmillan, 1982*

IBÁRRURI, DOLORES
IBÁRRURI, Dolores
Memorias de Dolores Ibárruri : Pasionaria: La Lucha y la vida / Dolores Ibárruri. — Barcelona : Planeta, 1985. — 763p. — *Contents: El único camino, Me faltaba España*

Pasionaria : memoria grafica / [coordinación, textos y selección: Andreu Claret Serra]. — Madrid : [Ediciones PCE], 1985. — 160p

IBM DISK OPERATING SYSTEM VERSION 3.20
IBM disk operating system version 3.20 : [operating guide]. — Portsmouth : IBM United Kingdom, 1986. — [3 pamphlets in one box]. — *Contents: Quick reference card - User's Guide - Reference*

IBM PERSONAL COMPUTER
BERRY, Paul
Operating the IBM PC networks / Paul Berry. — Berkeley : Sybex, c1986. — xvii, 363 p.. — *Includes index. — Bibliography: p. [343]-344*

LASSELLE, Joan
The abc's of the IBM PC / Joan Lasselle, Carol Ramsay. — 1st ed. — Berkeley : Sybex, 1984. — xi, 143 p.. — *Includes index. — Bibliography: p. 122-128*

IBM PERSONAL COMPUTER — Programming
LEMONE, Karen A
Assembly language and systems programming for the IBM personal computer / by Karen A. Lemone. — Boston : Little, Brown, 1985. — p. cm. — (The Little, Brown microcomputer bookshelf). — *Includes index*

ROLLINS, Dan
IBM-PC 8088 MACRO Assembler programming / Dan Rollins. — New York ; Macmillan ; London : Collier Macmillan, c1985. — xxiii,435p. — *Includes index*

IBN SA'UD, 'ABD AL-'AZ IZ IBN 'ABD AR-RAHM AN, King of Saudia Arabia
GOLDBERG, Jacob
The foreign policy of Saudi Arabia : the formative years, 1902-1918 / Jacob Goldberg. — Cambridge, Mass. : London : Harvard University Press, 1986. — viii,231p. — (Harvard Middle Eastern ; 19). — *Includes index*

ICELAND — Economic conditions
MAGNÚSSON, Magnús S.
Iceland in transition : labour and socio-economic change before 1940 / Magnús S. Magnússon. — Lund : Ekonomisk-Historiska Föreningen i Lund, 1985. — 306p. — (Skrifter Utgivna av Ekonomisk-Historiska Föreningen i Lund ; Vol.45). — *Bibliography: p289-303*

ICELAND — Foreign relations — Great Britain
HARDARSON, S. B. Jensdottír
Anglo-Icelandic relations during the First World War / S.B. Jensdottir Hardarson. — New York : Garland Pub., 1986. — 220 p.. — (Outstanding theses from the London School of Economics and Political Science). — *Thesis (M.A.)--London School of Economics and Political Science, 1980. — Includes index. — Bibliography: p. 217-220*

ICELAND — Social conditions
MAGNÚSSON, Magnús S.
Iceland in transition : labour and socio-economic change before 1940 / Magnús S. Magnússon. — Lund : Ekonomisk-Historiska Föreningen i Lund, 1985. — 306p. — (Skrifter Utgivna av Ekonomisk-Historiska Föreningen i Lund ; Vol.45). — *Bibliography: p289-303*

IDAHO — Economic conditions
FAHEY, John
The inland empire, unfolding years, 1879-1929 / John Fahey. — Seattle : University of Washington Press, c1986. — p. cm. — *Includes index. — Bibliography: p*

IDAHO — Social conditions
FAHEY, John
The inland empire, unfolding years, 1879-1929 / John Fahey. — Seattle : University of Washington Press, c1986. — p. cm. — *Includes index. — Bibliography: p*

IDENTIFICATION CARDS — Australia
AUSTRALIA. Parliament. Joint Select Committee on an Australia Card
Report of the Joint Select Committee of an Australia Card. — Canberra : Australian Government Publishing Service, 1986. — xxiv,324p. — *Includes bibliographical references*

IDENTIFICATION CARDS — United States
EATON, Joseph W
Card-carrying Americans : privacy, security, and the national ID card debate / Joseph W. Eaton. — Totowa, NJ : Rowman &Allanheld, 1986. — p. cm. — *Includes index*

IDENTITY
MORRIS, Thomas V.
Understanding identity statements / Thomas V. Morris. — Aberdeen : Aberdeen University Press, 1984. — xv,152p. — () (Scots philosophical monographs ; no.5). — *Bibliography: p147-152*

IDENTITY (PSYCHOLOGY)
WESTCOTT, Marcia
The feminist legacy of Karen Horney / Marcia Westkott. — New Haven : Yale University Press, c1986. — p. cm. — *Includes index. — Bibliography: p*

IDENTITY (PSYCHOLOGY) — Social aspects
BREAKWELL, Glynis M.
Coping with threatened identities / Glynis M. Breakwell. — London : Methuen, 1986. — [232]p. — *Includes index*

IDENTITY (PSYCHOLOGY) IN CHILDREN — Great Britain
WILSON, Anne, 19---
'Mixed race' children : a study of identity / Anne Wilson. — London : Allen & Unwin, 1987. — [172]p. — *Includes bibliography and index*

IDEOLOGY
BOCOCK, Robert
Hegemony / Robert Bocock. — Chichester : Ellis Horwood, 1986. — 136p. — *Bibliography: p.[130]-132*

GLUCK, Carol
Japan's modern myths : ideology in the late Meiji period / Carol Gluck. — Princeton, N.J. : Princeton University Press, c1985. — xi, 407p, [8]p of plates. — *Includes index. — Bibliography: p 287-311*

GRADER, Sheila Lillian
The problem of ideology and international relations / by Sheila Grader. — 271 leaves. — *PhD (Econ) 1986 LSE*

GRAY, John, 1948 Nov.5-
Liberalism / John Gray. — Milton Keynes : Open University Press, 1986. — xi,106p. — (Concepts in the social sciences). — *Bibliography: p100-101. — Includes index*

HAGOPIAN, Mark N.
Ideals and ideologies of modern politics / Mark Hagopian. — New York ; Longman, c1985. — viii,263p. — *Includes bibliographies and index*

Ideology and national competitiveness : an analysis of nine countries / edited by George C. Lodge and Ezra F. Vogel. — Boston, Mass. : Harvard Business School Press, c1987. — x, 350 p.. — *Includes index. — Bibliography: p. 327-342*

MCLELLAN, David
Ideology / David McLellan. — Milton Keynes : Open University Press, 1986. — [112]p. — (Concepts in the social sciences). — *Includes bibliography and index*

MINOGUE, Kenneth R.
Alien powers : the pure theory of ideology / Kenneth Minogue. — London : Weidenfeld & Nicolson, c1985. — vi,255p. — *Includes index*

MORISHIMA, Michio
Ideology and economic activity / Michio Morishima. — London : Suntory-Toyota International Centre for Economics and Related Disciplines, 1986. — 38p. — (Japanese studies). — *Bibliography: p37-38*

STEINBERGER, Peter J.
Ideology and the urban crisis / Peter J. Steinberger. — Albany : State University of New York Press, c1985. — ix, 175 p.. — (SUNY series in urban public policy). — *Includes index. — Bibliography: p. 163-170*

IDEOLOGY — Addresses, essays, lectures
Professions and professional ideologies in America / edited by Gerald L. Geison. — Chapel Hill : University of North Carolina Press, c1983. — x, 147 p.. — *Includes bibliographical references and index*

IDEOLOGY — History
RICŒUR, Paul
Lectures on ideology and utopia / Paul Ricoeur ; edited by George H. Taylor. — New York : Columbia University Press, 1986. — xxxvi, 353 p.. — *Includes index. — Bibliography: p. [329]-337*

IG DRUCK UND PAPIER
HEINE, Werner
Ein Tabu fällt : Kampf der Drucker um Arbeitszeitverkürzung und Lohnstruktur / Werner Heine ; mit einem Vorwort von Erwin Ferlemann. — Köln : Bund-Verlag, 1986. — 159p

IG METALL
BAHNMÜLLER, Reinhard
Der Streik : Tarifkonflikt um Arbeitszeitverkürzung in der Metallindustrie 1984 / Reinhard Bahnmüller. — Hamburg : VSA-Verlag, 1985. — 204p. — *Bibliography: p202-204*

IGBO (AFRICAN PEOPLE) — Rites and ceremonies
OTTENBERG, Simon
Masked rituals of Afikpo, the context of an African art : [published in connection with an exhibition shown at the Henry Art Gallery, University of Washington, May 24-June 21, 1975]. — Seattle : Published for the Henry Art Gallery by the University of Washington Press, [1975]. — 229 p., [8] leaves of plates. — (Index of art in the Pacific Northwest ; no. 9). — *Includes index.* — *Bibliography: p. 223-225*

IGBO (AFRICAN PEOPLE) — Nigeria
AMADIUME, Ifi
Afrikan matriarchal foundations : the Igbo case / Ifi Amadiume. — London : Karnak House, 1987. — [120]p. — *Includes bibliography*

IGLESIAS, PABLO
Pablo Iglesias : el socialismo en España. — Barcelona : Anthropos, 1985. — 192p. — *Numero extraordinario 6 de "Anthropos: boletín de información y documentación", No.45-46-47, 1985*

ILE-DE-FRANCE (FRANCE) — Industries — Statistics
Système d'observation de l'appareil productif de l'Ile-de-France. — Paris : Institut d'aménagement et d'urbanisme de la région d'Ile-de-France, 1984. — 60 leaves

ILLAWARRA (N.S.W. : REGION) — Economic conditions
JOHNSTONE, Helen
Older unemployed people in the Illawarra Region, New South Wales / Helen Johnstone. — Woden, ACT : Department of Social Security, 1986. — 14 leaves. — (Background/discussion paper / Social Security Review ; no.7). — *Bibliographical references: p14*

ILLUSTRATION OF BOOKS
NATIONAL BOOK DEVELOPMENT COUNCIL OF SINGAPORE
Report : training seminar on book design and illustration 1980 / National Book Development Council of Singapore. — Singapore : the Council, c1980. — 51p

IMAGERY (PSYCHOLOGY)
Imagery / edited by Ned Block. — Cambridge, Mass. ; London : MIT Press, c1981. — 261p. — (A Bradford book). — *Bibliography: p247-258.* — *Includes index*

KOSSLYN, Stephen Michael
Image and mind / Stephen Michael Kosslyn. — Cambridge, Mass. : Harvard University Press, 1980. — p. cm. — *Includes index.* — *Bibliography: p*

PAIVIO, Allan
Mental representations : a dual coding approach / Allan Paivio. — New York : Oxford University Press ; Oxford : Clarendon Press, 1986. — x, 322p. — (Oxford psychology series ; no. 9). — *Includes index.* — *Bibliography: p.277-305*

IMAGINARY CONVERSATIONS
MYERS, David B.
Marx and Nietzsche : the reminiscences and transcripts of a nineteenth century journalist / David B. Myers. — Lanham, MD : University Press of America, c1986. — xviii, 168 p.. — *Spine title: Marx & Nietzsche.* — *Bibliography: p. 164-167*

IMAGINATION
BEIDELMAN, T. O
Moral imagination in Kaguru modes of thought / T.O. Beidelman. — Bloomington : Indiana University Press, c1986. — xiii, 231 p.. — (African systems of thought). — *Includes index.* — *Bibliography: p. [216]-224*

IMMUNITIES OF FOREIGN STATES
LEWIS, Charles J.
State and diplomatic immunity / by Charles J. Lewis. — 2nd ed. — London : Lloyd's of London, 1985. — [xxvi,250]p. — *Previous ed.: 1980.* — *Includes index*

IMPERIAL CHEMICAL INDUSTRIES — History
KENNEDY, Carol
ICI : the company that changed our lives / Carol Kennedy. — London : Hutchinson, 1986. — xii,209p,[20]p of plates(some col.). — *Includes bibliography and index*

IMPERIALISM
BERBEROGLU, Berch
The international of capital : imperialism and capitalist development on a world scale / Berch Berberoglu. — New York : Praeger, 1987. — p. cm. — *Bibliography: p*

BORINSKI, Ludwig
Die Rolle der imperialistischen Bewegung in der britischen Weltpolitik von 1900 bis 1940 / Ludwig Borinski. — Göttingen : Vandenhoeck und Ruprecht, 1985. — 19p. — (Berichte aus den Sitzungen der Joachim-Jungius-Gesellschaft der Wissenschaften ; Jg.3, Heft 1)

[British imperialism in the nineteenth century]. British imperialism in the 19th century / edited by C.C. Eldridge. — London : Macmillan, 1984. — 214p. — (Problems in focus series)

DARBY, Phillip
Three faces of imperialism : British and American approaches to Asia and Africa, 1870-1970 / Phillip Darby. — New Haven : Yale University Press, 1987. — 267p. — *Includes index.* — *Bibliography: p.[256]-262*

GEYER, Dietrich
Russian imperialism : the interaction of domestic and foreign policy, 1860-1914 / Dietrich Geyer ; translated from the German by Bruce Little. — Leamington Spa : Berg, 1987. — [368]p. — *Translation of: Der russische Imperialismus.* — *Includes bibliography and index*

HERMAN, Edward S.
The real terror network : terrorism in fact and propaganda / Edward S. Herman. — Montréal : Black Rose, 1985. — ix,252p. — *Includes bibliographical notes*

SOUZA, George Bryan
The survival of empire : Portuguese trade and society in China and the South China Sea, 1630-1754 / George Bryan Souza. — Cambridge : Cambridge University Press, 1986. — xx,282p. — *Bibliography: p262-275.* — *Includes index*

UNION OF SOVIET SOCIALIST REPUBLICS. Ministerstvo inostrannykh del
SSSR v bor'be protiv kolonializma i neokolonializma, 1960-mart 1986 gg. : dokumenty i materialy / red. kollegiia: A. A. Gromyko...[et al.]. — Moskva : Politizdat. — V dvukh tomakh
T.1: (1960-1981 gg.). — 1986. — 542p

UNION OF SOVIET SOCIALIST REPUBLICS. Ministerstvo inostrannykh del
SSSR v bor'be protiv kolonializma i neokolonializma, 1960-mart 1986 gg. : dokumenty i materialy / red. kollegiia: A. A. Gromyko...[et al.]. — Moskva : Politizdat. — V dvukh tomakh
T.2: (1981-mart 1986 gg.). — 1986. — 431p

IMPERIALISM — Addresses, essays, lectures
Imperialism, health and medicine / edited by Vicente Navarro. — Farmingdale,N.Y. : Baywood, 1981. — 282p. — (Policy, politics, health and medicine). — *Collection of essays*

IMPERIALISM — Economic aspects — Soviet Union
The Costs and benefits of the Soviet empire, 1981-1983 / Charles Wolf, Jr. ... [et al.]. — Santa Monica, CA : Rand, [1986]. — xv, 46 p.. — *"Prepared for the Director of Net Assessment, Office of the Secretary of Defense.".* — *"August 1986.".* — *"R-3419-NA.".* — *Includes bibliographical references*

IMPERIALISM — History
Britain and Nigeria : exploitation of development? / edited by Toyin Falola. — London : Zed, 1986. — [272]p. — *Includes index*

DAVIS, Lance E.
Mammon and the pursuit of empire : the political economy of British imperialism, 1860-1912 / Lance E. Davis and Robert A. Huttenback with the assistance of Susan Gray Davis. — Cambridge : Cambridge University Press, 1986. — x,394p. — (Interdisciplinary perspectives on modern history). — *Bibliography: p365-388.* — *Includes index*

IMPERIALISM IN LITERATURE
HARLOW, Barbara
Resistance literature / Barbara Harlow. — New York ; London : Methuen, 1987. — xx,234p. — *Bibliography: p217-226.* — *Includes index*

IMPERIALIZM: KAK VYSSHAIA STADIIA KAPITALIZMA
Lenin and imperialism : an appraisal of theories and contemporary reality / edited by Prabhat Patnaik. — London : Sangam Books, 1986. — 414p

IMPORT QUOTAS — Great Britain
GREAT BRITAIN. Parliament. House of Commons. Library. Research Division
Import controls / [Priscilla Baines, Christopher Barclay, Elizabeth Spilsbury]. — [London] : the Division, 1979. — 28p. — (Background paper ; no.70). — *Bibliography: p27-28*

IMPORT QUOTAS — Taiwan
YIN, K. Y.
A review of existing foreign exchange and trade control policy and technique / K. Y. Yin. — [Taipei : Foreign Exchange and Trade Control, 1959. — 34p

IMPRISONMENT — Congress
INTERNATIONAL CONFERENCE ON PRISON ABOLITION (2nd : 1985 : Amsterdam)
Abolitionism : towards a non-repressive approach to crime : proceedings of the Second International Conference on Prison Abolition, Amsterdam, 1985 / edited by Herman Bianchi, René van Swaaningen. — Amsterdam : Free University Press, 1986. — 247p

INCAS
MÉTRAUX, Alfred
The history of the Incas / Alfred Métraux ; translated from the French by George Ordish. — New York : Schocken Books, 1970. — 205p

INCAS — Politics and government
SALOMON, Frank
Native lords of Quito in the age of the Incas : the political economy of north Andean chiefdoms / Frank Salomon. — Cambridge : Cambridge University Press, 1986. — xviii,274p. — (Cambridge studies in social anthropology ; no.59)

INCAS — Social conditions — Addresses, essays, lectures
Anthropological history of Andean politics / edited by John V. Murra, Nathan Wachtel and Jacques Revel. — Cambridge : Cambridge University Press, 1986. — x,383p. — *Translation of Anthropologie historique des sociétés andines, a special double issue of Annales ; v.33, nos. 5-6 (1978)*

INCENTIVES IN INDUSTRY
ARNE RYDE SYMPOSIUM (8th : 1985 : Frostavallen)
Incentives and economic systems : proceedings of the Eighth Arne Ryde Symposium, Frostavallen, 26-27 August 1985 / edited by Stefan Hedlund. — London : Croom Helm, c1987. — 372p. — *Includes index*

INCENTIVES IN INDUSTRY — European Economic Community countries

The promotion of the small and medium—sized enterprises : opinion. — Brussels : Economic and Social Committee of the European Communities, 1982. — iii, 70p

INCENTIVES IN INDUSTRY — Great Britain

BEENSTOCK, Michael
Work, welfare and taxation : a study of labour supply incentives in the UK / Michael Beenstock and associates. — London : Allen & Unwin, 1987. — xi,275p. — *Bibliography : p268-271. — Includes index*

INCENTIVES IN INDUSTRY — Hungary

FALUS-SZIKRA, Katalin
The system of incomes and incentives in Hungary / Katalin Falus-Szikra. — Budapest : Akadémiai Kiadó, 1985. — xiii,317p. — *Translated from Hungarian*

INCENTIVES IN INDUSTRY — Soviet Union

KUNEL'SKII, L. E.
Povyshenie effektivnosti truda v promyshlennosti / L. E. Kunel'skii. — Moskva : Ekonomika, 1987. — 254p

INCENTIVES IN INDUSTRY — United States

HENEMAN, Robert L.
Pay for performance : exploring the merit system / by Robert L. Heneman. — New York ; Oxford : Pergamon, c1984. — 64p. — (Work in America Institute studies in productivity ; 38). — *Bibliography: p57-64*

INCEST

MAISCH, Herbert
Incest / Herbert Maisch ; translated by Colin Bearne. — London : Deutsch, 1973. — 252p. — *First published in German under the title "Inzest". — Bibliography: p233-244*

NELSON, Sarah
Incest : fact and myth / Sarah Nelson. — 2nd rev. ed. — Edinburgh : Stramullion, 1987. — 128p. — *Previous ed.: 1982. — Bibliography: p122-128*

RUSSELL, Diana E. H
The secret trauma : incest in the lives of girls and women / Diana E.H. Russell. — New York : Basic Books, c1986. — xviii, 426 p.. — *Includes index. — Bibliography: p. [413]-417*

INCEST — Cross-cultural studies

ARENS, W.
The original sin : incest and its meaning / W. Arens. — New York : Oxford University Press, 1986. — xiii, 190 p.. — *Includes index. — Bibliography: p. 171-186*

INCEST — United States

RUSSELL, Diana E. H
The secret trauma : incest in the lives of girls and women / Diana E.H. Russell. — New York : Basic Books, c1986. — xviii, 426 p.. — *Includes index. — Bibliography: p. [413]-417*

TWITCHELL, James B.
Forbidden partners : the incest taboo in modern culture / James B. Twitchell. — New York : Columbia University Press, 1986. — p. cm. — *Includes index. — Bibliography: p*

INCEST IN ART

TWITCHELL, James B.
Forbidden partners : the incest taboo in modern culture / James B. Twitchell. — New York : Columbia University Press, 1986. — p. cm. — *Includes index. — Bibliography: p*

INCEST IN LITERATURE

TWITCHELL, James B.
Forbidden partners : the incest taboo in modern culture / James B. Twitchell. — New York : Columbia University Press, 1986. — p. cm. — *Includes index. — Bibliography: p*

INCEST IN POPULAR CULTURE — United States

TWITCHELL, James B.
Forbidden partners : the incest taboo in modern culture / James B. Twitchell. — New York : Columbia University Press, 1986. — p. cm. — *Includes index. — Bibliography: p*

INCEST VICTIMS — Case studies

MASSON, J. Moussaieff
The assault on truth : Freud's suppression of the seduction theory / Jeffrey Moussaieff Masson. — New York, N.Y. : Penguin Books, 1985, c1984. — p. cm. — : Reprint. Originally published: New York : Farrar, Straus, and Giroux, 1984. — *Includes index. — Bibliography: p*

INCEST VICTIMS — United States — Psychology

RUSSELL, Diana E. H
The secret trauma : incest in the lives of girls and women / Diana E.H. Russell. — New York : Basic Books, c1986. — xviii, 426 p.. — *Includes index. — Bibliography: p. [413]-417*

INCOME

DEATON, Angus
The measurement of welfare : theory and practical guidelines / Angus Deaton. — Washington, D.C., U.S.A. : World Bank, 1985 printing, c1980. — 82p. — (LSMS working papers ; no.7) (LSMS working papers ; no. 7). — *Bibliographical references: p79-82*

Introduction to economics. — Milton Keynes : Open University Press. — (Social Sciences : a second level course)
Block 5: Income and wealth. — 1985. — [26],29p. — (D210 ; 18-19). — *At head of title: The Open University. — Contents: Unit 18: Redistribution and the fiscal system/prepared for the course team by Julian Le Grand - Unit 19: income and wealth in the USSR/prepared for the course team by Alastair McAuley*

INCOME — Government policy — India

PRAKASH, Om
Guided incomes policy / Om Prakash. — New Delhi : Sterling, c1983. — vi, 214 p.. — *Includes bibliographical references and index*

INCOME — Mathematical models

COE, David T.
International investment-income determination in INTERLINK : models for 23 OECD countries and six non-OECD regions / by David T. Coe, Richard Herd. — Paris : OECD, 1987. — iii,47p. — (Working papers / OECD Department of Economics and Statistics ; no.45). — *Bibliographical references: p47*

INCOME — Statistics

Incomes from work : between equity and efficiency. — Geneva : International Labour Office, 1987. — viii,169p. — (World labour report ; 3). — *Bibliography: p165-169*

INCOME — Asia

VISARIA, Pravin M
Poverty and living standards in Asia : an overview of the main results and lessons of selected household surveys / Pravin Visaria assisted by Shyamalendu Pal. — Washington, D.C., U.S.A. : World Bank, 1986 printing, c1980. — xii,224p. — (LSMS working papers ; no.2). — *Includes bibliographical references*

INCOME — Australia — Statistics

MOORF, Jim
Trends in the disposable incomes of Australian families : 1964-65 to 1985-86 / Jim Moore and Peter Whiteford. — Woden, ACT : Department of Social Security, 1986. — vii,102p. — (Background/discussion paper / Social Security Review ; no.11) (Research paper / Development Division, Department of Social Security ; no.31). — *Bibliographical references: p35-37*

INCOME — Bahamas — Statistics

Commonwealth of the Bahama Islands : report of the 1980 census of population. — Nassau : Ministry of Finance
V.2: Economic activity and income. — [1986]. — xlvi,673p

INCOME — Denmark

DENMARK. Socialindkomstudvalg
Socialindkomstens gennemførelse og virkninger : redegørelse / fra det faste socialindkomstudvalg. — [København : Socialindkomstudvalg], 1981. — 2v. — *Includes supplementary material in separate volume*

INCOME — Egypt

EL-ISSAWY, Ibrahim H.
Employment inadequacy in Egypt / Ibrahim H. El-Issawy. — Geneva : International Labour Office, 1983. — 32p. — (Employment opportunities and equity in Egypt ; no.3). — *Bibliographical references: p29-32. — A technical paper of the ILO/UNDP comprehensive employment strategy mission to Egypt, 1980*

INCOME — France

Les agriculteurs et leurs revenus. — Paris : La Documentation française. — (Documents du Centre d'Étude des Revenus et des Coûts ; no.78)
1: Familles et exploitations agricoles / ...réalisée par Yves Chassard [et al.]. — 1985. — 108p

Les agriculteurs et leurs revenus. — Paris : La Documentation française. — (Documents du Centre d'Étude des Revenus et des Coûts ; no.79)
2: Composition et emploi des revenus / ...réalisée par Yves Chassard [et al.]. — 1986. — 130p

Constat de l'évolution récente des revenus en France 1982-1985 / ...réalisée sous la direction de Jean-Etienne Chapron et Jean-Jacques Malpot. — Paris : La Documentation française, 1986. — 183p. — (Documents du Centre d'étude des revenus et des coûts ; no.82)

Les revenus des ménages 1960-1984 : rapport de synthèse / ...établi sous la direction de Alain Foulon. — Paris : La Documentation française, [1986]. — 132p. — (Documents du centre d'étude des revenus et des coûts ; no.80 numéro spécial)

INCOME — Great Britain

GREAT BRITAIN. Parliament. House of Commons. Library. Research Division
The impact of the 1982 budget on individual incomes and real income movements since 1979 / Jennifer Tanfield. — [London] : the Division, 1982. — 22p. — (Background paper ; no.100)

GREAT BRITAIN. Parliament. House of Commons. Library. Research Division
The impact of the 1983 Budget on individual incomes and real income movements since 1979 / Jennifer Tanfield. — [London] : the Division, 1983. — 22p. — (Background paper ; no.115)

INCOME — Great Britain — Statistical methods

ROTHMAN, James
The development of an income surrogate : report of a research contract prepared for the Department of the Environment (Statistics Planning and Regional) / by James Rothman. — [London] : Department of the Environment, 1977. — 40,[16]p

ROTHMAN, James
Further development of an income surrogate : report of a research contract prepared for the Department of the Environment (Statistics, Planning and Regional) / by James Rothman. — [London] : Department of the Environment, 1979. — ii,32 leaves

INCOME — Great Britain — Statistics
GREAT BRITAIN. Department of Health and Social Security
Low income families - 1983 : estimated numbers of families and persons with incomes at various levels relative to supplementary benefit level analysed by family type and economic status. — [London] : the Department, 1986. — [12]p

INCOME — Hungary
FALUS-SZIKRA, Katalin
The system of incomes and incentives in Hungary / Katalin Falus-Szikra. — Budapest : Akadémiai Kiadó, 1985. — xiii,317p. — *Translated from Hungarian*

INCOME — Japan — Statistics
JAPAN. Statistics Bureau
1984 national survey of family income and expenditure. — [Tokyo] : Statistics Bureau, [1985-1987]. — *Text in Japanese and English*

INCOME — Northeastern States — Forecasting
Method for the initial superdistrict projections of Northeast Corridor population, employment and income / by Robert Crow...[et al.]. — [Washington, D.C.] : U.S. Department of Commerce, 1966. — 45p. — (Northeast Corridor Transportation Project technical paper ; no.6)

INCOME — Norway — Statistics
Lønninger og inntekter 1982 = Wages, salaries and income 1982. — Oslo : Statistisk Sentralbyrå, 1985. — 96p. — (Norges offisielle statistikk ; B536). — *In Norwegian and English*

INCOME DISTRIBUTION
CONGRÈS DE LA C.S.C. (26th : 1975 : Bruxelles)
Pour une répartition équitable des revenus. — Bruxelles : Éditions C.S.C., 1975. — 160p

DAVIDMANN, M.
Community leadership and management. — Stanmore : Social Organisation. — *Bibliography: p21*
4: Work and pay: incomes and differentials: employer, employee and community. — 1986. — 21 leaves

Introduction to economics. — Milton Keynes : Open University Press. — (Social Sciences : a second level course)
Block 5: Income and wealth. — 1985. — [26],29p. — (D210 ; 18-19). — *At head of title: The Open University. — Contents: Unit 18: Redistribution and the fiscal system/prepared for the course team by Julian Le Grand - Unit 19: income and wealth in the USSR/prepared for the course team by Alastair McAuley*

LE GRAND, Julian
On researching the distributional consequences of public policies / Julian Le Grand. — London : Welfare State Programme. Suntory-Toyota International Centre for Economics and Related Disciplines, 1986. — 47p. — (Discussion paper / Welfare State Programme. Suntory-Toyota International Centre for Economics and Related Disciplines ; no.6). — *Bibliography: p47*

INCOME DISTRIBUTION — Addresses, essays, lectures
The Collection and analysis of economic and consumer behavior data : in memory of Robert Ferber / edited by Seymour Sudman and Mary A. Spaeth. — Champaign, Ill. : Bureau of Economic and Business Research & Survey Research Laboratory, University of Illinois, c1984. — x, 406 p.. — *Includes bibliographies*

Macroeconomic conflict and social institutions / edited by Shlomo Maital, Irwin Lipnowski. — Cambridge, Mass. : Ballinger Pub. Co., 1985. — p. cm. — *Chiefly papers originating from a session on "Income policy as a social institution," at the American Economic Association's 95th Annual Meeting in New York, Dec. 28-30, 1982. — Includes bibliographies and index*

INCOME DISTRIBUTION — Congresses
International comparisons of the distribution of household wealth / edited by Edward N. Wolff. — Oxford : Clarendon, 1987. — xii,283p. — *Includes bibliographies and index*

INCOME DISTRIBUTION — Data processing
COWELL, F. A.
Analysis of income distribution using microcomputer technology / F. A. Cowell. — London : London School of Economics and Political Science, 1987. — 31p. — (Information technology). — *Bibliography: p27-28*

INCOME DISTRIBUTION — Government policy
RINGEN, Stein
The possibility of politics : a study in the political economy of the welfare state / Stein Ringen. — Oxford : Clarendon, 1987. — x,303p. — *Bibliography: p267-295. — Includes index*

INCOME DISTRIBUTION — Mathematical models
COWELL, F. A.
Poverty measures, inequality and decomposability / F. A. Cowell. — [London : London School of Economics and Political Science], 1987. — 28p. — (Taxation, incentives and the distribution of income ; no.99). — Economic and Social Research Council programme. — *Bibliographical references: p27-28*

INCOME DISTRIBUTION — Statistical methods
MEHRAN, Farhad
Employment data for the measurement of living standards / Farhad Mehran. — Washington, D.C., U.S.A. : World Bank, 1985 printing, c1980. — 14p. — (LSMS working papers ; no.8) (LSMS working papers ; no. 8). — *Includes bibliographical references*

INCOME DISTRIBUTION — Statistics
National accounts statistics : compendium of income distribution statistics. — New York : United Nations, 1985. — v,552p. — (Statistical papers / United Nations, Statistical Office. Series M ; no.79) ([Document] / United Nations ; ST/ESA/STAT/SER.M/79). — *Sales no.: E.85.XVII.6*

A survey of national sources of income distribution statistics (first report). — New York : United Nations, 1981. — vi,385p. — (Statistical papers / United Nations, Statistical Office. Series M ; no.72) ([Document] (United Nations) ; ST/ESA/STAT/SER.M/72). — *Sales no.: E.81.XVII.7*

INCOME DISTRIBUTION — Statistics — Bibliography
A survey of national sources of income distribution statistics (first report). — New York : United Nations, 1981. — vi,385p. — (Statistical papers / United Nations, Statistical Office. Series M ; no.72) ([Document] (United Nations) ; ST/ESA/STAT/SER.M/72). — *Sales no.: E.81.XVII.7*

INCOME DISTRIBUTION — Denmark
DENMARK. Socialindkomstudvalg
Socialindkomstens gennemførelse og virkninger : redegørelse / fra det faste socialindkomstudvalg. — [København : Socialindkomstudvalg], 1981. — 2v. — *Includes supplementary material in separate volume*

Udviklingen i den personlige indkomstfordeling for erhvervsaktive 1970-1976. — [København] : Lavindkomstkommissionen, 1979. — 177p. — (Delrapport / Lavindkomstkommissionen ; 1)

INCOME DISTRIBUTION — Developing countries
Capitalism and equality in the Third World / edited by Peter L. Berger. — Lanham, MD : Hamilton Press ; [Washington, D.C.] : Institute for Educational Affairs, <1987- >. — p. cm. — *Bibliography: p. — Contents: -- v. 2. Modern capitalism*

Fund-supported programs, fiscal policy, and income distribution : a study / by the Fiscal Affairs Department of the International Monetary Fund. — Washington, D.C. : International Monetary Fund, 1986. — v,58p. — (Occasional paper / International Monetary Fund ; no.46). — *Bibliographical references: p54-58*

INCOME DISTRIBUTION — Developing countries — Addresses, essays, lectures
Work, income, and inequality : payments systems in the Third World / edited by Frances Stewart. — New York : St. Martin's Press, 1983. — x, 333 p.. — *Includes bibliographical references and index*

INCOME DISTRIBUTION — Developing countries — Case studies
BHATIA, D. P
Inter-class distribution and growth of net national product in a developing economy : a case study of India during the sixties / D.P. Bhatia ; foreword by M. Mukherjee. — New Delhi : Concept Pub. Co., 1986, c1985. — xviii, 221 p.. — : *Originally presented as the author's thesis (Ph. D.--University of Delhi). — Includes index. — Bibliography: p. [208]-217*

INCOME DISTRIBUTION — Egypt
HANSEN, Best
Employment opportunities and equity in a changing economy : Egypt in the 1980s : a labour market approach : report of an inter-agency team financed by the United Nations Development Programme and organised by the International Labour Office / Bent Hansen, Samir Radwan. — Geneva : International Labour Office, 1982. — xviii,292p. — (A WEP study). — *Includes bibliographical references*

INCOME DISTRIBUTION — Great Britain
HUGHES, John, 1927-
Nowt for nowt? or who got what, when? / John Hughes. — Nottingham : Institute for Workers Control, 1986. — 14p

LABOUR RESEARCH DEPARTMENT
The widening gap : rich and poor today. — London : Labour Research Department, 1987. — 44p

RAINWATER, Lee
Income packaging in the welfare state : a comparative study of family income / Lee Rainwater, Martin Rein, and Joseph Schwartz. — New York : Oxford University Press, 1986. — p. cm. — *Includes index. — Bibliography: p*

STARK, Thomas
Income and wealth in the 1980's / Thomas Stark. — London : Fabian Society, 1987. — 67 leaves. — (Working group papers / Fabian Society)

TZANNATOS, Z.
A general equilibrium model of discrimination and its effect on incomes / Z. Tzannatos. — London : Centre for Labour Economics, London School of Economics, 1986. — 28p. — (Discussion paper / London School of Economics and Political Science. Centre for Labour Economics ; no.244). — *Bibliography: p26-28*

INCOME DISTRIBUTION — Hungary
FALUS-SZIKRA, Katalin
The system of incomes and incentives in Hungary / Katalin Falus-Szikra. — Budapest : Akadémiai Kiadó, 1985. — xiii,317p. — *Translated from Hungarian*

FLAKIERSKI, Henryk
Economic reform & income distribution : a case study of Hungary and Poland / by Henryk Flakierski. — Armonk, N.Y. : M.E. Sharpe, c1986. — xi, 194 p.. — *"Published simultaneously as vol. XXIV, no. 1-2, of Eastern European economics"--Verso t.p. — Bibliography: p. 165-194*

INCOME DISTRIBUTION — Hungary
continuation

PONGRÁCZ, László
A kereseti arányok távlati fejlesztése / Pongrácz László. — Budapest : Közgazdasági és Jogi Könyvkiadó, 1975. — 211p. — *Bibliography: p205-211*

INCOME DISTRIBUTION — India — Case studies

BHATIA, D. P
Inter-class distribution and growth of net national product in a developing economy : a case study of India during the sixties / D.P. Bhatia ; foreword by M. Mukherjee. — New Delhi : Concept Pub. Co., 1986, c1985. — xviii, 221 p.. — : *Originally presented as the author's thesis (Ph. D.--University of Delhi). — Includes index. — Bibliography: p. [208]-217*

INCOME DISTRIBUTION — India — Punjab

WESTLEY, John Richard
Agriculture and equitable growth : the case of Punjab-Haryana / John R. Westley. — Boulder : Westview Press, 1986. — p. cm. — (Westview special studies in agriculture science and policy). — *Includes index. — Bibliography: p*

INCOME DISTRIBUTION — Indonesia — Jawa Tengah

HART, Gillian Patricia
Power, labor, and livelihood : processes of change in rural Java / Gillian Hart. — Berkeley : University of California Press, c1986. — xvi, 228 p.. — *Includes index. — Bibliography: p. 213-222*

INCOME DISTRIBUTION — Kenya

COLLIER, Paul
Labour and poverty in Kenya, 1900-1980 / Paul Collier and Deepak Lal. — Oxford : Clarendon, 1986. — xii,296p

INCOME DISTRIBUTION — Latin America

MUSGROVE, Philip
The ECIEL study of household income and consumption in urban Latin America : an analytical history / Philip Musgrove. — Washington, D.C. : World Bank, Development Research Center, 1982, c1981. — 72p. — (LSMS working papers ; no.12). — *Bibliography: p67-72*

INCOME DISTRIBUTION — Nepal

Employment, income distribution, and consumption patterns in Nepal : results of a survey conducted by the National Planning Commission, Nepal, March-July 1977. — Kathmandu, Nepal : His Majesty's Govt., National Planning Commission Secretariat, 1983. — xiv,122p. — *Cover title: A survey of employment, income distribution, and consumption patterns in Nepal*

INCOME DISTRIBUTION — Netherlands — Statistics

NETHERLANDS. Centraal Bureau voor de Statistiek
De personele inkomensverdeling 1979 : verdelingen in inkomensklassen en 10%-groepen : inkomens van gehuwde vrouwen : inkomensbestanddelen. — s-Gravenhage : Staatsuitgeverij, 1984. — 187p. — *Title on back cover: Distribution of personal income 1979: distribution to size-classes of income and 10%-groups: income of married women: components of income*

INCOME DISTRIBUTION — Poland

FLAKIERSKI, Henryk
Economic reform & income distribution : a case study of Hungary and Poland / by Henryk Flakierski. — Armonk, N.Y. : M.E. Sharpe, c1986. — xi, 194 p.. — *"Published simultaneously as vol. XXIV, no. 1-2, of Eastern European economics"--Verso t.p. — Bibliography: p. 165-194*

INCOME DISTRIBUTION — Sweden

RAINWATER, Lee
Income packaging in the welfare state : a comparative study of family income / Lee Rainwater, Martin Rein, and Joseph Schwartz. — New York : Oxford University Press, 1986. — p. cm. — *Includes index. — Bibliography: p*

INCOME DISTRIBUTION — United States

RAINWATER, Lee
Income packaging in the welfare state : a comparative study of family income / Lee Rainwater, Martin Rein, and Joseph Schwartz. — New York : Oxford University Press, 1986. — p. cm. — *Includes index. — Bibliography: p*

INCOME DISTRIBUTION — Uruguay

GONZÁLEZ GARCÍA, José I.
La segmentación del mercado del credito y sus impactos sobre la distribución del ingreso / José I. González. — Montevideo : Centro Interdisciplinario de Estudios sobre el Desarollo Uruguay, 1984. — 123p. — (Serie Investigaciones / Centro Interdisciplinario de Estudios sobre el Desarollo Uruguay ; no.18). — *Bibliography: p89-92*

INCOME MAINTENANCE PROGRAMS

ATKINSON, A. B.
Income maintenance and social insurance : a survey / A. B. Atkinson. — London : Suntory-Toyota International Centre for Economics and Related Disciplines, London School of Economics, 1985. — 234p. — (Welfare State Programme ; no.5). — *Bibliography: p205-234*

GRIFFITHS, Bob
Overseas countries' maintenance provisions / Bob Griffiths, Shelley Cooper and Neil McVicar. — Woden, ACT : Department of Social Security, 1986. — [45]p. — (Background/discussion paper / Social Security Review ; no.13). — *Bibliography: p[40-41]*

INCOME MAINTENANCE PROGRAMS — Mathematical models

COWELL, F. A.
Welfare benefits and the economics of takeup / F. A. Cowell. — [London : London School of Economics and Political Science], 1986. — 28p. — (Taxation, incentives and the distribution of income ; no.89). — *Economic and Social Research Council programme. — Bibliography: p25*

INCOME MAINTENANCE PROGRAMS — Australia

CASS
Income support for families with children / Bettina Cass. — Canberra : Australian Government Publishing Service, 1986. — xiii,126p. — (Issues paper / Social Security Review ; no.1). — *Bibliography: p115-120*

INCOME MAINTENANCE PROGRAMS — Canada — Statistics

Monthly statistics: income security programs = Statistiques mensuelles: programmes de la sécurité du revenu. / Health and Welfare Canada. — Ottawa : Health and Welfare Canada, 1985-. — *Annual. — Text in English and French. — From April 1987 this publication incorporates Canada Pension Statistical Bulletin and Canada. Department of Health and Welfare. Income Security Programs Branch. Research notes*

INCOME MAINTENANCE PROGRAMS — Great Britain

Benefits : a housing and supplementary benefits guide for single people without a permanent home : incorporating: Desperate measures, the DHSS supplementary benefit regulations for board and lodging : currency: April 1987 to April 1988 / [written and published by CHAR]. — 1987/1988 ed. — London : CHAR, 1987. — xv,200p. — *Previous ed.: 1986. — Includes index*

Desperate measures : the DHSS supplementary benefit regulations for board and lodging. — [Rev. and updated]. — London : CHAR, 1985. — 49p

INCOME MAINTENANCE PROGRAMS — Ireland

IRELAND. Commission on Social Welfare
Report of the Commission on Social Welfare. — Dublin : Stationery Office, 1986. — xiv,530p. — *Chairman: John Curry*

INCOME TAX

BAYE, Michael R.
Consumer behavior, cost of living measures, and the income tax / Michael R. Baye, Dan A. Black. — Berlin ; New York : Springer-Verlag, c1986. — 119 p.. — (Lecture notes in economics and mathematical systems ; 276). — *Bibliography: p. [112]-119*

BEAN, Charles R.
Budget deficits, interest rates and the incentive effects of income tax cuts / C. R. Bean and S. V. Wijnbergen. — London : Centre for Labour Economics, London School of Economics, 1987. — 37p. — (Discussion paper / London School of Economics and Political Science. Centre for Labour Economics ; no.270)

INCOME TAX — Foreign income

ARNOLD, Brian J
The taxation of controlled foreign corporations : an international comparison / Brian J. Arnold. — Toronto, Ont. : Canadian Tax Foundation, c1986. — xxiii, 816. — (Canadian tax paper ; no. 78). — *Includes index. — Bibliography: p. 797-811*

INCOME TAX — Law and legislation — Australia

RYAN, K. W.
Manual of the law of income tax in Australia / by K. W. Ryan and and G.W. O'Grady. — 6th ed. — Sydney : Law Book Company, 1985. — xxvi,360p

INCOME TAX — Law and legislation — Canada

SCACE, Arthur R. A
The income tax law of Canada / Arthur R.A. Scace and Douglas S. Ewens ; contributors, Robert A. Brown ... [et al.]. — 5th ed. — [Agincourt, Ont. : Published for the Law Society of Upper Canada by] Carswell Legal Publications, 1983. — xxx, 610 p.. — *Includes bibliographical references and index*

INCOME TAX — Law and legislation — United States

A Citizen's guide to the new tax reforms : fair tax, simple tax, flat tax / Joseph A. Pechman, editor. — Totowa, N.J. : Rowman & Allanheld, 1985. — p. cm. — *Includes index*

INCOME TAX — Mathematical models

KING, Mervyn A.
The empirical analysis of tax reforms / Mervyn A. King. — [London : London School of Economics and Political Science], 1986. — 51p. — (Taxation, incentives and the distribution of income ; no.96). — *Economic and Social Research Council programme. — Paper presented to the Symposium on Empirical Public Finance at the Fifth World Congress of the Econometric Society, MIT, 1985. — Bibliographical references: p44-47*

INCOME TAX — Political aspects — United States — History

WITTE, John F
The politics and development of the federal income tax / John F. Witte. — Madison, Wis. : University of Wisconsin Press, 1985. — p. cm . — *Includes index. — Bibliography: p*

INCOME TAX — Australia

NORMAN, Neville R.
The economics of personal tax escalation in Australia / Neville R. Norman. — Sydney ; London : Published for Committee for Economic Development of Australia by Allen & Unwin, 1985. — [xii,181]p. — *Bibliography: p164-166. — Includes index*

INCOME TAX — Great Britain
ATKINSON, A. B.
Taxation of husband and wife in the UK and changes in the tax-benefit system / A. B. Atkinson and H. Sutherland. — [London : London School of Economics and Political Science], 1987. — 42p. — (Taxation, incentives and the distribution of income ; no.104). — *Economic and Social Research Council programme. — Bibliographical references: p42*

BENNETT, Robert J.
Local income tax in Britain : a reappraisal of theory and practice / Robert J. Bennett. — London : Association of Metropolitan Authorities, 1987. — 28p. — *Paper presented at AMA seminar on "Local income tax", AMA, London, 29th January 1987*

GREAT BRITAIN. Board of Inland Revenue
PAYE - possible future developments : a review by the Inland Revenue of the Pay As You Earn system and of possible alternative methods of collecting tax from wages and salaries. — [London] : the Board, 1979. — 50p

GREAT BRITAIN. Parliament. House of Commons. Library. Research Division
Income tax : problems & possibilities / Timothy Edmonds. — [London] : the Division, 1986. — 37p. — (Background paper ; no.178)

SUTHERLAND, H.
Modelling the SDP tax/benefit scheme / Holly Sutherland. — [London : London School of Economics and Political Science], 1986. — 25p. — (Taxation, incentives and the distribution of income ; no.101). — *Economic and Social Research Council programme. — Bibliographical references: p25*

INCOME TAX — Nigeria — Law
OLA, Christopher S.
Nigerian income tax law and practice : incorporating income tax laws relating to personal income tax law, partnership tax law, companies income tax law, petroleum profits tax law, capital gains tax law, capital transfer tax law and guidelines to a tax system under the presidential system of government with accountancy and decided cases illustrations and a supplement (1985) / C.S. Ola. — London : Macmillan, 1985. — xxvi,566p. — *Includes index*

INCOME TAX — Peru
PERU
[Decreto supremo no.287-68-HC]. Income tax, real estate ownership value and stock assets : Supreme decree no.287-68-HC. — [Lima : Presidencia?, 1968]. — 106leaves. — *Translation from Spanish into English*

INCOME TAX — Québec (Province)
White paper on the personal tax and transfer systems / [prepared by the Ministère des finances ; edited by the Direction générale de publications gouvernementales]. — Québec : Le Ministere, 1984. — 380p. — *Cover title. — Inclues index. — Includes index*

INCOME TAX — United States
Tax reform and U.S. economy / papers by Henry J. Aaron...[et al.] ; edited by Joseph A. Pechman. — Washington, D.C. : Brookings Institution, 1987. — 107p. — (Brookings dialogues on public policy). — *Papers presented at a conference at the Brookings institution, December 2, 1986*

TEPLITZ, Paul V
Alternative tax proposals : how the numbers add up / Paul V. Teplitz, Stephen H. Brooks. — Lexington, Mass. : Lexington Books, c1986. — xii, 131 p.. — *Includes bibliographies and index*

INCOME TAX — United States — Addresses, essays, lectures
Examination of basic weaknesses of income as the major federal tax base / edited by Richard W. Lindholm. — New York : Praeger, 1986. — xv, 320 p.. — *Includes bibliographies and index*

INCOME TAX — United States — History
WITTE, John F
The politics and development of the federal income tax / John F. Witte. — Madison, Wis. : University of Wisconsin Press, 1985. — p. cm . — *Includes index. — Bibliography: p*

INDECENT ASSAULT — England — History
CLARK, Anna
Women's silence, men's violence : sexual assault in England 1770-1845 / Anna Clark. — London : Pandora Press, 1987. — viii,180p. — *Bibliography: p168-175*

INDECENT ASSAULT — South Australia
Sexual assault in South Australia. — [Adelaide] : Office of Crime Statistics, 1983. — iii,74 leaves. — (Research report / Office of Crime Statistics ; no.1). — *Bibliographical references: p73-74*

INDENTURED SERVANTS — Mauritius
MIÈGE, Jean-Louis
Indentured labour in the Indian Ocean and the particular case of Mauritius / Jean-Louis Miège. — Leiden : Centre for the History of European Expansion, 1986. — 62p. — (Intercontinenta ; no.5)

INDEPENDENT BROADCASTING AUTHORITY
Airwaves: the quarterly journal of the IBA. — London : Independent Broadcasting Authority, 1985/6-. — *Quarterly*

INDEPENDENT COMMISSION AGAINST CORRUPTION
LETHBRIDGE, H. J.
Hard graft in Hong Kong : scandal; corruption; the ICAC / H. J. Lethbridge. — Hong Kong ; Oxford : Oxford University Press, 1985. — viii,247p. *Bibliography: p232-243*

INDEPENDENT LABOUR PARTY — Biography
BROWN, Gordon, 1951-
Maxton / by Gordon Brown. — Edinburgh : Mainstream, 1986. — 335p,[8]p of plates. — *Includes index*

INDEXING
HEEKS, Richard
Personal bibliographic indexes and their computerisation / Richard Heeks. — London : published by Taylor Graham on behalf of the Primary Communications Research Centre, University of Leicester, c1986. — 189p. — *Bibliography: p185-189*

INDIA — Biography — Directories
India Who's Who 1986. — New Delhi : LNFA Publications, 1986. — 216p

INDIA — Boundaries — China
BANERJEE, D. K.
Sino-Indian border dispute / D. K. Banerjee. — New Delhi : Intellectual Publishing House, 1985. — xii,116p. — *Bibliography: p[110]-112*

LU, Chih H
The Sino-Indian border dispute : a legal study / Chih H. Lu. — New York : Greenwood Press, 1986. — x, 143 p.. — (Contributions in political science ; no. 139). — *Includes index. — Bibliography: p. [125]-134*

INDIA — Census — Statistics
Census of India 1981. — [Delhi : Controller of Publications]
Series 5: Gujarat. — [1985]

INDIA — Census, 1981
Census of India 1981. — [Delhi : Controller of Publications]
Series II: Madhya Pradesh. — [1984]

Census of India 1981. — [Delhi : Controller of Publications]
Series 13: Manipur. — [1985-]

INDIA — Census 1981
Census of India 1981. — [Delhi : Controller of Publications]
Series 14: Meghalaya. — [1985-]

INDIA — Census, 1981
Census of India 1981. — [Delhi : Controller of Publications]
Series 15: Nagaland. — [1985-]

Census of India 1981. — [Delhi : Controller of Publications]
Series 21: Tripura. — [1985]

Census of India 1981. — [Delhi : Controller of Publications]
Series 23: West Bengal / S. N. Ghosh, Director of Census Operations, West Bengal. — [1984]

Census of India 1981 / B. K. Singh, Director of Census Operations. — [Delhi : Controller of Publications]
Series 24: Andaman and Nicobar Islands. — [1985-]

Census of India 1981. — [Delhi : Controller of Publications]
Series 25: Arunachal Pradesh. — [1985]

Census of India 1981. — [New Delhi : Controller of Publications
Series 26: Chandigarh / Ardaman Singh, Director of Census Operations, Chandigarh. — 1985-]. —

Census of India 1981 / S. K. Gandhe, Director of Census Operations, Dadra and Nagar Haveli. — [Delhi : Controller of Publications]
Series 27: Dadra & Nagar Haveli. — [1985-]

Census of India 1981 / P. L. Samy, Director of Census Operations, Pondicherry. — [New Delhi : Controller of Publications]
Series 32: Pondicherry. — [1985-]

Census of India 1981. — New Delhi : Registrar General and Census Commissioner, India, Ministry of Home Affairs
Tabulation plan. — [1980]. — 266p

INDIA — Commerce
SINGH, Deo Raj
Pattern of foreign trade and planning in India / Deo Raj Singh. — New Delhi : Criterion Publications : Distributed by Deep & Deep Publications, 1985. — xii, 419 p.. — *Includes index. — Bibliography: p. [395]-414*

INDIA — Commerce — History
AGARWALA, P. N
The history of Indian business : a complete account of trade exchanges from 3000 B.C. to the present day / P.N. Agarwala. — New Delhi : Vikas, c1985. — xvi, 604 p.. — *Includes index. — Bibliography: p. [573]-588*

INDIA — Commercial policy
SINGH, Deo Raj
Pattern of foreign trade and planning in India / Deo Raj Singh. — New Delhi : Criterion Publications : Distributed by Deep & Deep Publications, 1985. — xii, 419 p.. — *Includes index. — Bibliography: p. [395]-414*

INDIA — Constitutional history
BARUA, B. P.
Politics and constitution-making in India and Pakistan / B. P. Barua ; foreword by Hugh Tinker. — New Delhi : Deep and Deep Publications, 1984. — 216p. — *Bibliography: p201-213*

INDIA — Constitutional law
CHOUDHARY, Valmiki
President and the Indian Constitution / Valmiki Choudhary. — New Delhi : Allied Publishers, 1985. — x, 379 p.. — 60-9. — *Includes index*

KRISHNAPURAM, R. Mohan
Sovereignty of Parliament in India / R. Mohan Krishnapuram ; foreword by J. M. L. Sinha. — New Delhi : Deep & Deep, 1985. — 214p. — *Bibliography: p[211]-212*

INDIA — Constitutional law
continuation

SOOD, P.
Indira Gandhi and the constitution : modernisation and development / by P. Sood ; foreword by H.K.L. Bhagat. — New Delhi : Marwah Publications, 1985 [i.e. 1984]. — xxvi, 257 p.. — *Includes index. — Bibliography: p. [243]-252*

VARADACHARI, V.K.
President in the Indian constitution / V. K. Varadachari. — New Delhi : Deep and Deep Publications, 1985. — 188p. — *Bibliography: p185-186*

INDIA — Economic conditions

KAMBLE, J. R.
Pursuit of equality in Indian history / J. R. Kamble. — New Delhi : National Publishing House, 1985. — xi,414p. — *Bibliography: p386-394*

MADDISON, Angus
Class structure and economic growth : India and Pakistan since the Moghuls. — New York : Norton, [1972, c1971]. — 181 p. — *Bibliography: p. 173-176*

SIVAYYA, K. V.
Indian industrial economy / K. V. Sivayya and V. B. M. Das. — 4th rev. ed. — New Delhi : S. Chand, 1980. — 506p. — *Bibliography: p502-506*

SRIVASTAVA, A. K.
Integrated rural development programme in India : policy and administration / A. K. Srivastava. — New Delhi : Deep and Deep Publications, 1986. — 272p. — *Bibliography: p262-270*

INDIA — Economic conditions — Addresses, essays, lectures

Economy, society & politics in modern India / edited by D.N. Panigrahi. — New Delhi : Vikas, c1985. — x, 487 p.. — *"Issued under the auspices of Nehru Memorial Museum and Library.". — Includes bibliographies and index*

INDIA — Economic conditions — Bibliography

Artha Suchi: an index to Indian economic literature / National Council of Applied Economic Research, New Delhi. — New Delhi : National Council of Applied Economic Research, 1984-. — *Quarterly*

INDIA — Economic conditions — Maps

DHURANDHER, K. P.
An atlas of assets and liabilities of Indian rural households / K. P. Dhurandher. — New Delhi : Vikas, 1985. — 180p. — *Contains 107 black and white maps*

INDIA — Economic conditions — Statistics

INDIA. Central Statistical Organisation
Basic statistics relating to the Indian economy, 1950-51 to 1975-76. — [New Delhi] : Central Statistical Organisation, [1977]. — 153p

National accounts statistics / Central Statistical Organisation, India. — New Delhi : Central Statistical Organisation, 1982-. — *Annual*

INDIA — Economic conditions — 1947-

BIRLA INSTITUTE OF SCIENTIFIC RESEARCH. Economic Research Division
Capital and technological progress in the Indian economy, 1950/51 - 1980/81. — New Delhi : Radiant Publishers, 1985. — xvi,198p. — *Bibliography: p192-198*

CHAUDHURI, Pramit
The Indian economy : poverty and development / Pramit Chaudhuri. — New York : St. Martin's Press, 1979. — ix, 279 p.. — *Includes indexes. — Bibliography: p. [259]-274*

Essays on economic progress and welfare : in honour of I.G. Patel / edited by S. Guhan and Manu Shroff. — Delhi ; New York : Oxford University Press, 1986. — xvi, 330 p., [1] leaf of plates. — *Includes bibliographies and index*

NAGPAL, R. L.
Indian economy : probelms [sic] & prospects / R.L. Nagpal. — Delhi : B.R. Pub. Corp. ; New Delhi : Distributed by D.K. Publishers' Distributors, 1985. — vii, 332 p.. — *Includes index*

POITEVIN, Guy
Inde : le developpement, une impasse / Guy Poitevin [et] Hema Rairkar. — Paris : L'Harmattan, 1985. — 247p

UNIVERSITY OF TEXAS. Center for Asian Studies. Symposium (1985 : Austin)
India 2000 : The next fifteen years : the papers of a symposium... / James R. Roach, editor. — Riverdale : Riverdale Company, [1986]. — xxi,228p. — *Includes bibliographic notes*

INDIA — Economic conditions — 1947- — Addresses, essays, lectures

DUBASHI, Jay.
Snakes and ladders : the development game / Jay Dubashi. — New Delhi : Allied, 1985. — xii, 299 p.. — *Includes index*

INDIA — Economic conditions — 1947- — Mathematical models

KRISHNAMURTY, K.
Macroeconomic modelling of the Indian economy : studies on inflation and growth / K. Krishnamurty and V. Pandit ; foreword by Lawrence R. Klein. — Delhi : Hindustan Publishing Corporation, 1985. — xii,159. — *Bibliography: p152-156*

INDIA — Economic policy

BAGCHI, Amiya Kumar
Private investment in India, 1900-1939 / Amiya Kumar Bagchi. — London : Cambridge University Press, 1972. — xi,482p. — (Cambridge South Asian studies ; 10). — *Bibliographyp.445-469. — Includes index*

BHARADWAJ, Krishna
Classical political economy and rise to dominance of supply and demand theories / Krishna Bharadwaj. — 2nd rev. ed. — London : Sangain Books, 1986. — viii,88p

CHAUDHARY, Shobha Kant
Planning and employment trends in Indai / S. K. Chaudhary. — New Delhi : Deep and Deep Publications, 1987. — 300p. — *Bibliography: p290-298*

CHAUDHURI, Pramit
The Indian economy : poverty and development / Pramit Chaudhuri. — New York : St. Martin's Press, 1979. — ix, 279 p.. — *Includes indexes. — Bibliography: p. [259]-274*

DOGRA, Bharat
IMF conditionality and its social costs : case study of India / Bharat Dogra. — New Delhi : Indian Social Institute, 1984. — 30p. — (Monograph series / Indian Social Institute ; 15)

GOWDA, K. Venkatagiri
India's seventh five year plan, 1985-90 : between the blades of growth scissors / K. Venkatagiri Gowda. — Bangalore : World View Publications, 1986. — 28p. — (World view monograph series ; 2)

INDIA. Planning Commission
The seventh five year plan 1985-90. — New Delhi : the Commission, 1985
v.2: Perspective, objectives, strategy, macro-dimensions and resources. — 78p

INDIA. Planning Commission
The seventh five year plan 1985-90. — New Delhi : Planning Commission, 1985
v.2: Sectoral programmes of development. — 421p

INDIAN NATIONAL CONGRESS
A tryst with destiny : a study of economic policy resolutions of INC passed during the last 100 years / edited by A. Moin Zaidi. — New Delhi : Publication Dept, Indian Institute of Applied Political Research, 1985. — 436 p.. — *Includes index*

Population, poverty, and hope. — New Delhi : Uppal, c1983. — xvii, 564 p.. — *"Under the auspices of the Centre for Policy Research and Family Planning Foundation."*

PRAKASH, Om
Guided incomes policy / Om Prakash. — New Delhi : Sterling, c1983. — vi, 214 p.. — *Includes bibliographical references and index*

INDIA — Economic policy — 1947-

BIRLA INSTITUTE OF SCIENTIFIC RESEARCH. Economic Research Division
Capital and technological progress in the Indian economy, 1950/51 - 1980/81. — New Delhi : Radiant Publishers, 1985. — xvi,198p. — *Bibliography: p192-198*

CHAKRAVARTY, Sukhamoy
Development planning : the Indian experience / Sukhamoy Chakravarty. — Oxford : Clarendon, 1987. — [128]p. — *Includes index*

Essays on economic progress and welfare : in honour of I.G. Patel / edited by S. Guhan and Manu Shroff. — Delhi ; New York : Oxford University Press, 1986. — xvi, 330 p., [1] leaf of plates. — *Includes bibliographies and index*

India's economic policies / editor J. N. Mongia. — 2nd ed.. — New Delhi : Allied Publishers, 1984. — 990p. — *Previous edition: 1980. — Includes bibliographies*

SINGH, Charan
India's economic policy ; the Gandhian blueprints / Charan Singh. — New Delhi ; Vikas Pub. House, c1978 [i.e.1977]. — vii, 127 p.. — *Includes bibliographical references*

Studies in Indian planning and economic policy / edited by R. K. Sinha. — New Delhi : Deep & Deep, 1984. — 472p. — *Bibliography: p [466]-468*

TICKNER, J. Ann
Self-reliance versus power politics : the American and Indian experience in building nation states / J. Ann Tickner. — New York : Columbia University Press, 1987. — xi, 282 p.. — (The Political economy of international change). — *Includes index. — Bibliography: p. [231]-267*

INDIA — Economic policy — 1947- — Addresses, essays, lectures

India's economic development strategies, 1951-2000 A.D. / J.N. Mongia, editor. — Dordrecht ; Boston : D. Reidel Pub. Co. ; Higham, MA : Distributors for the U.S.A. and Canada, Kluwer Academic Publishers, c1985. — li, 774 p., [16] p. of plates. — *Includes index*

INDIA — Economic policy — 1974-

BAJAJ, J. L
Rural poverty : issues and option / J.L. Bajaj, C. Shastri ; foreword, T.S. Papola. — Lucknow : Print House (India), c1985. — 252 p.. — *Includes bibliographies and index*

INDIA — Economic policy — 1980-

BHATTACHARYA, Sib Nath
Strategy for economic development in agricultural, industrial and tertiary sectors in different Indian states / Sib Nath Bhattacharya. — New Delhi : Metropolitan, 1985. — xvi,244p. — *Bibliography: p[225]-244*

MISHRA, D. K.
Public debt and economic development in India / D.K. Mishra. — Lucknow : Print House (India), c1985. — xii, 552 p.. — *Includes bibliographical references and index*

SEN, Pradip K
Deficit financing and development planning / Pradip K. Sen. — New Delhi : Criterion Publications ; Distributed by Deep & Deep Publications, 1985. — xvi, 341 p.. — *Includes index. — Bibliography: p. [319]-338*

INDIA — Economic policy — 1980- — Congresses

Seventh Plan and development of weaker sections : questions, challenges, and alternatives / edited by Jose Kananaikil. — New Delhi : Indian Social Institute, c1985. — xv, 188 p.. — *Includes index. — Bibliography: p. [171]-186*

INDIA — Economic policy — 1980- — Econometric models

MANOHAR RAO, M. J
Filtering and control of macroeconomic systems : a control system incorporating the Kalman filter for the Indian economy / M.J. Manohar Rao. — Amsterdam ; New York : North-Holland ; New York, N.Y., U.S.A. : Sole distributors for the U.S.A. and Canada, Elsevier Science Pub. Co., 1987. — p. cm. — (Contributions to economic analysis ; 160). — *Includes indexes. — Bibliography: p*

INDIA — Exiles

FRIES, Yvonne
The undesirables : the expatriation of the Tamil people "of recent Indian origin" from the plantations in Sri Lanka to India / Yvonne Fries, Thomas Bibin. — Calcutta : K P Bagchi, 1984. — 253 p.. — *Bibliography: p [248]-253*

INDIA — Foreign economic relations

SALVI, P. G
India in world affairs / P.G. Salvi ; foreword by T.N. Kaul. — Delhi : B.R. Pub. Corp. ; New Delhi : Distributed by D.K. Publishers' Distributors, 1985. — viii, 174 p.. — 60-9. — *Includes index*

INDIA — Foreign relations

AGARWAL, Sushila
Super powers and the Third World / Sushila Agarwal. — Jaipur, India : Aalekh, 1985. — ii,151p

APPADORAI, A
India's foreign policy and relations / A. Appadorai and M.S. Rajan. — New Delhi : South Asian Publishers, c1985. — x, 709 p.. — *Includes index. — Bibliography: p. [676]-688*

KUMAR, Vijay
India and Sri Lanka-China Relations (1948-84) / Vijay Kumar. — New Delhi : Uppal Publishing House, 1986. — 196p. — *Bibliography: p181-187*

NOORANI, Abdul Gafoor Abdul Majeed
India, the superpowers and the neighbours : essays in foreign policy / A.G. Noorani. — New Delhi : South Asian Publishers, c1985. — viii, 273 p.

SALVI, P. G
India in world affairs / P.G. Salvi ; foreword by T.N. Kaul. — Delhi : B.R. Pub. Corp. ; New Delhi : Distributed by D.K. Publishers' Distributors, 1985. — viii, 174 p.. — 60-9. — *Includes index*

SISODIA, Sawai Singh
Foreign policy of India : Indira Gandhi era : with special reference to non-alignment / S. S. Sisodio. — New Delhi : Inter-India Publications, 1985. — 196p. — *Bibliography: p183-189*

INDIA — Foreign relations — Great Britain

HAMID, S. Shahid
Disastrous twilight : a personal record of the partition of India / Shahid Hamid ; with a foreword by Philip Ziegler. — London : Leo Cooper in association with Secker & Warburg, 1986. — xix,364p, 4p of plates

INDIA — Foreign relations — Nepal

HUSAIN, Asad
Conflict in Asia : a case study of Nepal / Asad Husain, Asifa Anwar ; foreword by Q. Ahmad. — New Delhi : Classical Publications, 1979. — x, 88 p.. — *Includes bibliographical references and index*

INDIA — Foreign relations — Pakistan

SEMINAR ON INDO-PAK RELATIONS (1984 : New Delhi)
Studies in Indo-Pak relations : papers presented at the seminar on Indo-Pak relations by the Indian Centre for Regional Affairs, New Delhi, 24-25 April, 1984 / edited by V. D. Chopra ; with a sum-up by P. N. Haksar. — New Delhi : Patriot [for the Indian Centre for Regional Affairs], 1984. — xxxii,299p

INDIA — Foreign relations — Soviet Union

KIDWAI, M. Saleem
Indo-Soviet relations / M. Saleem Kidwai. — New Delhi, India : Rima Pub. House, 1985. — vi, 144 p.. — *: Revision of the author's thesis (Ph. D.--Aligarh Muslim University). — Includes index. — Bibliography: p. [127]-141*

SINGH, S. Nihal
The yogi and the bear : story of Indo-Soviet relations / S. Nihal Singh. — London : Mansell, 1986. — [328]p

INDIA — Foreign relations — Tibet

LAMB, Alastair
British India and Tibet, 1766-1910 / Alastair Lamb. — 2nd ed. — London : Routledge and Kegan Paul, 1986. — xiv,353p. — *Bibliography: p323-338*

INDIA — Foreign relations — United States — History

CHOPRA, V. D.
Pentagon shadow over India / V. D. Chopra ; with an introduction by T. N. Kaul. — New Delhi : Patriot Publishers, 1985. — xvi,223p

INDIA — Government publications (State Governments) — Bibliograpahy

SINGH, Mohinder
State governments publications in India 1947-1982 / Mohinder Singh. — Delhi : Academic Publications. — (Academic Series in Library and Information Science ; 3). — *Vol.1 of two volumes*
Vol.1. — 1985. — 323p

INDIA — Government publications (State governments) — Bibliography

SINGH, Mohinder
State governments publications in India 1947-1982 / Mohinder Singh. — Delhi : Academic publications. — (Academic Series in Library and Information Science ; 3). — *Vol.2 of two volumes*
Vol.2. — 1985. — [335]-659p

INDIA — Governors

GEHLOT, N. S.
State governors in India : trends and issues / N. S. Ghelot [i.e. Gehlot]. — New Delhi : Gitanjali, 1985. — x,388p. — *Bibliography: p367-382*

INDIA — Governors — Biography

HARDINGE, Henry Hardinge, Viscount
The letters of the first Viscount Hardinge of Lahore to Lady Hardinge and Sir Walter and Lady James, 1844-1847 / Bawa Satinder Singh, editor. — London : Royal Historical Society, 1986. — [300]p. — (Camden Fourth series : v.32). — *Includes bibliography and index*

INDIA — History

KAMBLE, J. R.
Pursuit of equality in Indian history / J. R. Kamble. — New Delhi : National Publishing House, 1985. — xi,414p. — *Bibliography: p386-394*

INDIA — History — Sepoy Rebellion, 1857-1858

LEBRA-CHAPMAN, Joyce
The Rani of Jhansi : a study in female heroism in India / Joyce Lebra-Chapman. — Honolulu : University of Hawaii Press, c1986. — xii, 199 p., [2] leaves of plates. — *Includes index. — Bibliography: p. [185]-193*

INDIA — History — 19th century — Addresses, essays, lectures

Writings on South Asian history and society / edited by Ranajit Guha. — Delhi ; New York : Oxford University Press, 1984. — x, 327 p.. — (Subalterm studies ; 3). — *: "Revised versions of papers read at the First Subaltern Studies Conference on 'Subaltern and Elite in South Asian History and Society', held in November 1982 under the auspices of the South Asian History Section of the Research School of Pacific Studies, Australian National University, Canberra"--11th prelim. p. — Includes bibliographical references and index*

INDIA — History — Sepoy Rebellion, 1857-1858

Two colonial empires : the Java War, 1825-30, and the Indian "mutiny" of 1857-59 / edited by C.A. Bayly, D.H.A. Kolff. — Dordrecht ; Boston : M. Nijhoff, 1986. — p. cm. — (Comparative studies in overseas history ; v. 6). — *Includes index*

INDIA — History — 20th century

COPLEY, Antony
Gandhi : against the tide / Antony Copley. — Oxford : Basil Blackwell, 1987. — v,118p. — (Historical Association studies). — *Bibliography: p107-110. — Includes index*

HAMID, S. Shahid
Disastrous twilight : a personal record of the partition of India / Shahid Hamid ; with a foreword by Philip Ziegler. — London : Leo Cooper in association with Secker & Warburg, 1986. — xix,364p, 4p of plates

HYDRICK, Blair
Guide to confidential U.S. State Department central files : India : internal affairs, 1945-1949. — Frederick, MD : University Publications of America, Inc., 1986. — *Contents: U.S. State Department documents in the National Archives*
Part 1: Political, government, and national defense affairs : decimal numbers 845.0-845.3 / compiled by Blair Hydrick. — 1986. — 23microfilms

NEHRU, Jawaharlal
Jawaharlal Nehru : la promesse tenue / avant-propos de Rajiv Gandhi... ; anthologie traduite et présentée par Monique Morazé avec la collaboration de Georges Frémont. — Paris : Editions de l'Harmattan, 1986. — 344p

INDIA — History — 20th Century

NEHRU, Jawaharlal
Selected works of Jawaharlal Nehru. — New Delhi : Jawaharlal Nehru Memorial Fund Series 2
Vol.3. — 1985. — 521p

INDIA — History — 20th century — Addresses, essays, lectures

Writings on South Asian history and society / edited by Ranajit Guha. — Delhi ; New York : Oxford University Press, 1984. — x, 327 p.. — (Subaltern studies ; 3). — *: "Revised versions of papers read at the First Subaltern Studies Conference on 'Subaltern and Elite in South Asian History and Society', held in November 1982 under the auspices of the South Asian History Section of the Research School of Pacific Studies, Australian National University, Canberra"--11th prelim. p. — Includes bibliographical references and index*

INDIA — History — 1947-

BANG, Thakurdas
Whither India / by Thakurdas Bang. — Rajghat, Varanasi : Sarva Seva Sangh Prakashan, 1985. — 200p

INDIA. Parliament. Lok Sabha
Parliament of India : the seventh Lok Sabha 1980-84 : a study. — New Delhi : Lok Sabha Secretariat, 1985. — 221p [31]p of plates

INDIA — Imprints

INDIA OFFICE LIBRARY AND RECORDS
Publications proscribed by the Government of India : a catalogue of the collections in the India Office Library and Records and the Department of Oriental Manuscripts and Printed Books, British Library Reference Division / edited by Graham Shaw and Mary Lloyd. — London : British Library, 1985. — [224]p. — *Includes index*

INDIA — Industries

BAGCHI, Amiya Kumar
Private investment in India, 1900-1939 / Amiya Kumar Bagchi. — London : Cambridge University Press, 1972. — xi,482p. — (Cambridge South Asian studies ; 10). — *Bibliographyp.445-469. — Includes index*

LALL, Sanjaya
Learning to industrialize : the acquisition of technological capability by India / Sanjaya Lall. — Basingstoke : Macmillan, 1987. — [280]p. — *Includes index*

SIVAYYA, K. V.
Indian industrial economy / K. V. Sivayya and V. B. M. Das. — 4th rev. ed. — New Delhi : S. Chand, 1980. — 506p. — *Bibliography: p502-506*

INDIA — Industries — History

AGARWALA, P. N
The history of Indian business : a complete account of trade exchanges from 3000 B.C. to the present day / P.N. Agarwala. — New Delhi : Vikas, c1985. — xvi, 604 p.. — *Includes index. — Bibliography: p. [573]-588*

INDIA — Industries — Statistics

Directory manufacturing establishments survey 1978-79 : summary results for central sample. — New Delhi : Central Statistical Organisation, Ministry of Planning, [1984?]. — iv,136p

INDIA — Military policy

HABIBULLAH, E
Compulsions of Indian security : a plea for geographic and demographic defence / E. Habibullah and B.K. Narayan. — New Delhi : ABC Pub. House, 1984. — viii, 192 p.. — *Includes index*

Pakistan's bomb : a documentary study / [compiled by] Sreedhar ; introduction by K. Subrahmanyam. — New Delhi : ABC Pub. House, 1986. — xviii, 331 p.. — *Includes index. — Bibliography: p. [310]-316*

THOMAS, Raju G. C
Indian security policy / Raju G.C. Thomas. — Princeton, N.J. : Princeton University Press, c1986. — p cm. — *"Written under the auspices of the Center for International and Strategic Affairs, University of California, Los Angeles.". — Includes index*

INDIA — National security

HABIBULLAH, E
Compulsions of Indian security : a plea for geographic and demographic defence / E. Habibullah and B.K. Narayan. — New Delhi : ABC Pub. House, 1984. — viii, 192 p.. — *Includes index*

THOMAS, Raju G. C
Indian security policy / Raju G.C. Thomas. — Princeton, N.J. : Princeton University Press, c1986. — p cm. — *"Written under the auspices of the Center for International and Strategic Affairs, University of California, Los Angeles.". — Includes index*

INDIA — Nonalignment

SISODIA, Sawai Singh
Foreign policy of India : Indira Gandhi era : with special reference to non-alignment / S. S. Sisodio. — New Delhi : Inter-India Publications, 1985. — 196p. — *Bibliography: p183-189*

INDIA — Politics and government

GAUTAM, Om P.
The Indian National Congress : an analytical biography / Om P. Gautam. — Delhi : B. R. Publishing Corporation, 1985. — 400p. — *Bibliography: p368-389*

NARAYAN, Jayaprakash
Towards total revolution / Jayaprakash Narayan ; edited with an introduction by Brahmanand. — Richmond, Surrey : Richmond Publishing Co., 1978. — 4v.(cli,268p;[7],307p;[7],193p;[7],226p). — *In slip case. — Bibliography(4p.). — Includes index. — Vol.1: Search for an ideology; Vol.2: Politics in India; Vol.3: India and her problems; Vol.4: Total revolution*

PRASAD, Bimal
Gandhi, Nehru & J. P. : studies in leadership / Bimal Prasad. — Delhi : Chanakya Publications, 1985. — 294p. — *Bibliography: p283-287*

SHARMA, P. D.
Police and political order in India / P. D. Sharma. — New Delhi : Research Publications, 1984. — ix,292p

SISODIA, Sawai Singh
Foreign policy of India : Indira Gandhi era : with special reference to non-alignment / S. S. Sisodio. — New Delhi : Inter-India Publications, 1985. — 196p. — *Bibliography: p183-189*

Times of India. — Bombay : Times of India, 1986-. — *Monthly*

INDIA — Politics and government — 1765-1947

HUSAIN, Syed Anwar
Administration of India (1858-1924) / Syed Anwar Husain. — Delhi : Seema Publications, 1985. — xxviii,323p. — *Bibliography: p [297]-314*

KAUR, Manmohan
Manmohan Kaur. — New Delhi : Sterling, 1985. — 282p. — *Bibliography: p[253]-263*

INDIA — Politics and government — 1765-1947 — Addresses, essays, lectures

Economy, society & politics in modern India / edited by D.N. Panigrahi. — New Delhi : Vikas, c1985. — x, 487 p.. — *"Issued under the auspices of Nehru Memorial Museum and Library.". — Includes bibliographies and index*

INDIA — Politics and government — 19th century

HARDINGE, Henry Hardinge, Viscount
The letters of the first Viscount Hardinge of Lahore to Lady Hardinge and Sir Walter and Lady James, 1844-1847 / Bawa Satinder Singh, editor. — London : Royal Historical Society, 1986. — [300]p. — (Camden Fourth series : v.32). — *Includes bibliography and index*

INDIA — Politics and government — 1857-1919

CHATTERJI, Rakhahari
Working class and the nationalist movement in India : the critical years / Rakhahari Chatterji. — New Delhi : South Asian Publishers, c1984. — ix, 215 p. — *Includes bibliographical references and index*

MAHAJAN, Sneh
Imperialist strategy and moderate politics : Indian legislature at work, 1909-1920 / Sneh Mahajan. — 1st ed. — Delhi : Chanakya Publications, [1983], c1982. — 316 p., [1] folded leaf of plate. — : *Revision of the author's thesis (Ph. D.--University of Delhi). — Includes index. — Bibliography: p. [302]-310*

INDIA — Politics and government — 1857-1919 — Sources

A Century of state craft in India : a study of the political resolutions of INC adopted during the last 100 years / edited by A. Moin Zaidi. — New Delhi : Publication Dept., Indian Institute of Applied Political Research, 1985. — 504 p.. — *Includes index*

INDIA — Politics and government — 20th century

Inde : l'un et le multiple / Jean-A. Bernard ...[et al.]. — Paris : Le Centre des Hautes Études sur l'Afrique et l'Asie Modernes, 1986. — 226p. — (Publications de CHEAM ; 8). — *Summaries in English. — Includes bibliographical references*

SESHADRI, K
Studies in Indian polity / Kandadai Seshadri. — New Delhi : Uppal Pub. House, c1986. — vi, 267 p.. — *Includes bibliographies and index*

INDIA — Politics and government — 20th century — Bibliography

INDIA OFFICE LIBRARY AND RECORDS
Publications proscribed by the Government of India : a catalogue of the collections in the India Office Library and Records and the Department of Oriental Manuscripts and Printed Books, British Library Reference Division / edited by Graham Shaw and Mary Lloyd. — London : British Library, 1985. — [224]p. — *Includes index*

INDIA — Politics and government — 1919-1947

BAKSHI, S. R
Swaraj Party and the Indian National Congress / S.R. Bakshi. — New Delhi : Vikas Pub. House, c1985. — vi, 200 p.. — *Bibliography: p [191]-195. — Bibliography: p. [191]-195*

CHATTERJI, Rakhahari
Working class and the nationalist movement in India : the critical years / Rakhahari Chatterji. — New Delhi : South Asian Publishers, c1984. — ix, 215 p.. — *Includes bibliographical references and index*

CHOUDHURY, Veena
Indian nationalism and external forces, 1920-47 / Veena Choudhury. — Delhi : Capital Pub. House, 1985. — xii, 234 p.. — *Includes index. — Bibliography: p. [210]-228*

HAMID, S. Shahid
Disastrous twilight : a personal record of the partition of India / Shahid Hamid ; with a foreword by Philip Ziegler. — London : Leo Cooper in association with Secker & Warburg, 1986. — xix,364p, 4p of plates

HYDRICK, Blair
Guide to confidential U.S. State Department central files : India : internal affairs, 1945-1949. — Frederick, MD : University Publications of America, Inc., 1986. — *Contents: U.S. State Department documents in the National Archives*
Part 1: Political, government, and national defense affairs : decimal numbers 845.0-845.3 / compiled by Blair Hydrick. — 1986. — 23microfilms

POTTER, David, 1931 Nov. 3-
India's political administrators 1919-1983 / David C. Potter. — Oxford : Clarendon, 1986. — xv,289p. — *Bibliography: p253-277. — Includes index*

PRASAD, Rajendra
Dr. Rajendra Prasad : correspondence and select documents / edited by Valmiki Choudhary. — New Delhi : Allied Publishers
Vol.2: (1938). — 1984. — 446p

PRASAD, Rajendra
Dr. Rajendra Prasad : correspondence and select documents / edited by Valmiki Choudhary. — New Delhi : Allied Publishers
Vol.3: (January to July 1939). — 1984. — 444p

PRASAD, Rajendra
Dr. Rajendra Prasad : correspondence and select documents / edited by Valmiki Choudhary. — New Delhi : Allied Publishers
Vol.4: (August to December 1939). — 1985. — 302p

PRASAD, Rajendra
Dr. Rajendra Prasad : correspondence and select documents / edited by Valmiki Choudhary. — New Delhi : Allied Publishers
Vol.5: (1940 to 1942). — 1986. — 374p

INDIA — Politics and government — 1919-1947 *continuation*

PRASAD, Rajendra
Dr. Rajendra Prasad : correspondence and select documents / edited by Valmiki Choudhary. — New Delhi : Allied Publishers
Vol.6: (1945 to 1946). — 1986. — 358p

PRASAD, Rajendra
Dr. Rajendra Prasad : correspondence and select documents / edited by Valmiki Choudhary. — New Delhi : Allied Publishers
Vol.7: (1947). — 1987. — 534p

INDIA — Politics and government — 1919-1947 — Sources

A Century of state craft in India : a study of the political resolutions of INC adopted during the last 100 years / edited by A. Moin Zaidi. — New Delhi : Publication Dept., Indian Institute of Applied Political Research, 1985. — 504 p.. — Includes index

Sources on national movement / edited by V.N. Datta & S.C. Mittal. — New Delhi : Allied Publishers : Indian Council of Historical Research, 1985-. — v. <1- >. — *Includes bibliographical references and index. — Contents: v. 1. Protests, disturbances, and defiance, January 1919 to September 1920*

Towards freedom, 1937-47 / chief editor, P.N. Chopra. — New Delhi : Indian Council of Historical Research, 1985-. — v. <1 >. — *Includes index. — Contents: v. 1. Experiment with provincial autonomy, 1 January-31 December 1937*

INDIA — Politics and government — 1945-

PANDEY, Sachchidanand
Naxal violence : a socio-political study / Sachchidanand Pandey. — Delhi : Chanakya Publications, 1985. — vi,156p. — *Bibliography: p144-153*

INDIA — Politics and government — 1947-

BRASS, Paul R.
Caste, faction and party in Indian politics / Paul R. Brass. — Delhi : Chanakya Publications
Vol.2: Election studies. — 1985. — 325p

INDIA. Parliament. Lok Sabha
Parliament of India : the seventh Lok Sabha 1980-84 : a study. — New Delhi : Lok Sabha Secretariat, 1985. — 221p [31]p of plates

MISRA, B. B.
Government and bureaucracy in India, 1947-1976 / B. B. Misra. — Delhi ; Oxford : Oxford University Press, 1986. — 416 p

NARAIN, Udai
Parliamentary control of public administration in India / Udai Narain. — Allahabad : Chugh, 1981. — xiv,484p. — *Thesis (D. Litt.)-University of Lucknow, 1980. — Bibliography: p[447]-477*

NEHRU, Jawaharlal
Letters to chief ministers, 1947-1964 / Jawaharlal Nehru ; general editor, G. Parthasarathi. — Delhi : Distributed by Oxford University Press, 1985-. — v. <1 >. — *"A project of the Jawaharlal Nehru Memorial Fund"--T.p. verso. — Includes index. — Contents: v. 1. 1947-1949*

OSTERGAARD, Geoffrey
Nonviolent revolution in India / Geoffrey Ostergaard. — Sevagram : J.P. Amrit Kosh ; New Delhi : Gandhi Peace Foundation, c1985. — xxiii, 419 p.. — *"Silver jubliee publication of the Gandhi Peace Foundation."--T.p. verso. — Includes index. — Bibliography: p. [370]-406*

SADASIVAN, S. N
Party and democracy in India / S. N. Sadasivan. — New Delhi : Tata McGraw-Hill, c1977. — xv, 537 p.. — *A revision of the author's thesis, University of Poona. — Includes index. — Bibliography: p. [495]-512*

SOOD, P.
Indira Gandhi and the constitution : modernisation and development / by P. Sood ; foreword by H.K.L. Bhagat. — New Delhi : Marwah Publications, 1985 [i.e. 1984]. — xxvi, 257 p.. — *Includes index. — Bibliography: p. [243]-252*

TICKNER, J. Ann
Self-reliance versus power politics : the American and Indian experience in building nation states / J. Ann Tickner. — New York : Columbia University Press, 1987. — xi, 282 p.. — (The Political economy of international change). — *Includes index. — Bibliography: p. [231]-267*

INDIA — Politics and government — 1977-

GUPTA, R. L.
Electoral politics in India / R. L. Gupta. — Delhi : Discovery, 1985. — xv,175p. — *Bibliography: p[161]-170*

HARDGRAVE, Robert L.
India : government and politics in a developing nation / Robert L. Hardgrave, Stanley A. Kochanek. — 4th ed. — New York ; London : Harcourt Brace Jovanovich, 1986. — xii,395p. — *Bibliographies*

RAGHAVULU, C. V
Organizational conflict in Indian government organizations / C.V. Raghavulu. — Delhi : Academic Publications, c1984. — xiv, 139 p.. — : *Revision of the author's thesis (Ph. D.--University of Illinois, 1976). — Includes index. — Bibliography: p. [125]-133*

SHOURIE, Arun
The assassination and after / by Arun Shourie...[et al.]. — New Delhi : Roli Books, 1985. — 160p

UNIVERSITY OF TEXAS. Center for Asian Studies. Symposium (1985 : Austin)
India 2000 : The next fifteen years : the papers of a symposium... / James R. Roach, editor. — Riverdale : Riverdale Company, [1986]. — xxi,228p. — *Includes bibliographic notes*

Violation of democratic rights in India / editor,A. R. Desai. — London : Sangam volume 1. — 1986. — 624p

INDIA — Population

Contributions to Indian geography. — New Delhi : Heritage
Vol.6: Population geography / editors K. V. Sundaram, Sudesh Nangia. — 1985. — 400p. — *Contains bibliographies*

KANGAS, Georgia Lee
Population dilemma : India's struggle for survival / Georgia Lee Kangas. — New Delhi : Arnold-Heinemann, 1985. — 152 p.. — *Bibliography: p. [146]-150*

SUKHWAL, B. L.
India : economic resource base and contemporary political patterns / B.L. Sukhwal. — 1st ed. — New York : Envoy Press, 1987. — viii, 200 p.. — *Includes index. — Bibliography: p. [189]-192*

INDIA — Population — Bibliography

DESAI, Prasannavadan B
Annotated and classified bibliography of Indian demography / editors, P.B. Desai, R.P. Tyagi. — Bombay : Popular Prakashan, 1985. — xii, 509 p.. — *"A project sponsored by the Indian Council of Social Science Research, New Delhi.". — Includes index*

Population and family planning in India : a select bibliography / compiled and edited by G. C. Kendadamath. — Gurgaon : Indian Documentation Service, 1985. — xxii,162p

INDIA — Population — Statistics

Census of India 1981. — [New Delhi : Controller of Publications
Series 26: Chandigarh / Ardaman Singh, Director of Census Operations, Chandigarh. — 1985-].

Census of India 1981. — New Delhi : Registrar General and Census Commissioner, India, Ministry of Home Affairs
Tabulation plan. — [1980]. — 266p

INDIA — Population policy

Population, poverty, and hope. — New Delhi : Uppal, c1983. — xvii, 564 p.. — *"Under the auspices of the Centre for Policy Research and Family Planning Foundation."*

INDIA — Population, Rural

SRIVASTAVA, A. K.
Integrated rural development programme in India : policy and administration / A. K. Srivastava. — New Delhi : Deep and Deep Publications, 1986. — 272p. — *Bibliography: p262-270*

INDIA — President

VARADACHARI, V.K.
President in the Indian constitution / V. K. Varadachari. — New Delhi : Deep and Deep Publications, 1985. — 188p. — *Bibliography: p185-186*

INDIA — Presidents — Correspondence

PRASAD, Rajendra
Dr. Rajendra Prasad : correspondence and select documents / edited by Valmiki Choudhary. — New Delhi : Allied Publishers
Vol.2: (1938). — 1984. — 446p

PRASAD, Rajendra
Dr. Rajendra Prasad : correspondence and select documents / edited by Valmiki Choudhary. — New Delhi : Allied Publishers
Vol.3: (January to July 1939). — 1984. — 444p

PRASAD, Rajendra
Dr. Rajendra Prasad : correspondence and select documents / edited by Valmiki Choudhary. — New Delhi : Allied Publishers
Vol.4: (August to December 1939). — 1985. — 302p

PRASAD, Rajendra
Dr. Rajendra Prasad : correspondence and select documents / edited by Valmiki Choudhary. — New Delhi : Allied Publishers
Vol.5: (1940 to 1942). — 1986. — 374p

PRASAD, Rajendra
Dr. Rajendra Prasad : correspondence and select documents / edited by Valmiki Choudhary. — New Delhi : Allied Publishers
Vol.6: (1945 to 1946). — 1986. — 358p

PRASAD, Rajendra
Dr. Rajendra Prasad : correspondence and select documents / edited by Valmiki Choudhary. — New Delhi : Allied Publishers
Vol.7: (1947). — 1987. — 534p

INDIA — Relations — China

BINDRA, S. S
India and her neighbours : a study of political, economic, and cultural relations, and interactions / S.S. Bindra. — New Delhi : Deep & Deep, c1984. — 404 p.. — *Includes index. — Bibliography: p. [364]-398*

INDIA — Relations — Japan

NARASIMHA MURTHY, P. A
India and Japan : dimensions of their relations : historical and political / P.A. Narasimha Murthy. — New Delhi : ABC Pub. House, 1986. — viii, 431 p.. — *Companion volume to: India and Japan : dimensions of their relations : documents. — Includes index. — Bibliography: p. [425]-426*

INDIA — Relations — South Asia

BINDRA, S. S
India and her neighbours : a study of political, economic, and cultural relations, and interactions / S.S. Bindra. — New Delhi : Deep & Deep, c1984. — 404 p.. — *Includes index. — Bibliography: p. [364]-398*

INDIA — Relations — Soviet Union
Studies in Indo-Soviet relations / P.N. Haksar ... [et al.] ; V.D. Chopra, editor. — New Delhi : Published by Patriot Publishers on behalf of Indian Centre for Regional Affairs, 1986. — 288 p.. — *Includes bibliographical references and index*

INDIA — Relations — Sri Lanka
VAIDIKA, Vedapratapa
Ethnic crisis in Sri Lanka : India's options / V.P. Vaidik. — 1st ed. — New Delhi, India : National, 1986. — viii, 239 p.. — *Includes index. — Bibliography: p. [221]-231*

INDIA — Religion — History
WITZ, Cornelia
Religionspolitik in Britisch-Indien 1793-1813 : christliches Sendungsbewusstsein und Achtung hinduistischer Tradition im Widerstreit / von Cornelia Witz. — Stuttgart : Steiner Verlag Wiesbaden, 1985. — viii,137p. — (Beiträge zur Südasienforschung ; Bd.98). — *Summary and conclusion in English. — Bibliography: p117-127*

INDIA — Rural conditions
Agrarian struggles in India after independence / edited by A. R. Desai. — Delhi : Oxford University Press, 1986. — xxvi,666p

DREZE, Jean
Labour contracts in rural India : theories and evidence / Jean Dreze and Anindita Mukherjee. — London : Suntory Toyota International Centre for Economics and Related Disciplines, 1987. — 43p. — (Development research programme / London School of Economics and Political Science. Suntory Toyota International Centre for Economics and Related Disciplines ; no.7). — *Bibliography: p[44-49]*

HIRWAY, Indira
Abolition of poverty in India : with special reference to target group approach in Gujarat / Indira Hirway. — New Delhi : Vikas Pub. House, c1986. — vi, 284 p. [i.e. 184]. — *Includes bibliographies and index*

OOMMEN, T. K.
Social transformation in rural India : mobilization and state intervention / T.K. Oommen. — Delhi : Vikas, c1984. — xx, 326 p.. — *Includes bibliographies and index*

The Peasant movement today / Sunil Sahasrabudhey. — New Delhi : Ashish Pub. House, 1986. — xix, 224 p.. — *English and Hindi. — "Under the auspices of Gandhian Institute of Studies, Rajghat, Varanasi"--T.p. verso. — Includes bibliographies and index*

SRIVASTAVA, A. K.
Integrated rural development programme in India : policy and administration / A. K. Srivastava. — New Delhi : Deep and Deep Publications, 1986. — 272p. — *Bibliography: p262-270*

INDIA — Rural conditions — Collected works
STOKES, Eric
The peasant and the Raj : studies in agrarian society and peasant rebellion in colonial India / Eric Stokes. — Cambridge : Cambridge University Press, 1978. — viii,308p. — (Cambridge South Asian studies ; [no.23]). — *Includes index*

INDIA — Rural conditions — Maps
DHURANDHER, K. P.
An atlas of assets and liabilities of Indian rural households / K. P. Dhurandher. — New Delhi : Vikas, 1985. — 180p. — *Contains 107 black and white maps*

INDIA — Scheduled tribes
PRAKASH, Om
Caste Hindu and scheduled caste children in rural India / Om Prakash and Arun K. Sen. — New Delhi : Ess Ess Publications, 1985. — xiv, 184 p.. — *Spine title: Hindu caste and scheduled caste children in rural India. — Includes index. — Bibliography: p. [155]-182*

Struggle for status / edited by Prakash N. Pimpley, Satish K. Sharma. — Delhi : B.R. Pub. Corp. ; New Delhi : D.K. Publishers' Distributors, 1985. — xii, 232 p.. — *Includes bibliographies and index*

VIDYARTHI, Lalita Prasad
The tribal culture of India / L. P. Vidyarthi, B. K. Rai. — 2nd ed. — New Delhi : Concept Publishing, 1985. — 488p. — *Previous ed: 1976. — Includes bibliographical references*

INDIA — Scheduled tribes — Economic conditions — Bibliography
SHARMA, Rajendra Narayan
Tribes and tribal development : a select bibliography / edited by R.N. Sharma, Santosh Bakshi. — New Delhi : Uppal, c1984. — 489 p.. — *Includes index*

INDIA — Scheduled tribes — Government policy — Bibliography
SHARMA, Rajendra Narayan
Tribes and tribal development : a select bibliography / edited by R.N. Sharma, Santosh Bakshi. — New Delhi : Uppal, c1984. — 489 p.. — *Includes index*

INDIA — Social conditions
KAMBLE, J. R.
Pursuit of equality in Indian history / J. R. Kamble. — New Delhi : National Publishing House, 1985. — xi,414p. — *Bibliography: p386-394*

MADDISON, Angus
Class structure and economic growth : India and Pakistan since the Moghuls. — New York : Norton, [1972, c1971]. — 181 p. — *Bibliography: p. 173-176*

SRIVASTAVA, A. K.
Integrated rural development programme in India : policy and administration / A. K. Srivastava. — New Delhi : Deep and Deep Publications, 1986. — 272p. — *Bibliography: p262-270*

INDIA — Social conditions — Addresses, essays, lectures
Economy, society & politics in modern India / edited by D.N. Panigrahi. — New Delhi : Vikas, c1985. — x, 487 p.. — *"Issued under the auspices of Nehru Memorial Museum and Library.". — Includes bibliographies and index*

INDIA — Social conditions — Statistics
INDIA. Central Statistical Organisation
Basic statistics relating to the Indian economy, 1950-51 to 1975-76. — [New Delhi] : Central Statistical Organisation, [1977]. — 153p

INDIA — Social conditions — 20th century
RAJ BALA
Trends in urbanisation in India, 1901-1981 / Raj Bala. — Jaipur : Rawat Publication, 1986. — xxvi, 231 p.. — *Based on the author's thesis (Ph. D.--Panjab University, Chandigarh). — Includes index. — Bibliography: p. [202]-226*

INDIA — Social conditions — 1945-
PANDEY, Sachchidanand
Naxal violence : a socio-political study / Sachchidanand Pandey. — Delhi : Chanakya Publications, 1985. — vi,156p. — *Bibliography: p144-153*

INDIA — Social conditions — 1947-
UNIVERSITY OF TEXAS. Center for Asian Studies. Symposium (1985 : Austin)
India 2000 : The next fifteen years : the papers of a symposium... / James R. Roach, editor. — Riverdale : Riverdale Company, [1986]. — xxi,228p. — *Includes bibliographic notes*

INDIA — Social life and customs
FÜRER-HAIMENDORF, Christoph von
Tribal populations and cultures of the Indian subcontinent / by C. Von Fürer-Haimendorf. — Leiden : E.J. Brill, 1985. — vi, 182 p.. — (Handbuch der Orientalistik. Zweite Abteilung. Indien ; 7. Bd). — *Includes bibliographies and index*

KURUP, Ayyappan Madhava
Continuity and change in a little community : a study of the Bharias of Patalkot in Madhya Pradesh / A. M. Kurup. — New Delhi : Concept Publishing, 1985. — 140p. — *Includes references*

UNIVERSITY OF TEXAS. Center for Asian Studies. Symposium (1985 : Austin)
India 2000 : The next fifteen years : the papers of a symposium... / James R. Roach, editor. — Riverdale : Riverdale Company, [1986]. — xxi,228p. — *Includes bibliographic notes*

INDIA — Social policy
INDIA. Planning Commission
The seventh five year plan 1985-90. — New Delhi : the Commission, 1985
v.2: Perspective, objectives, strategy, macro-dimensions and resources. — 78p

INDIA. Planning Commission
The seventh five year plan 1985-90. — New Delhi : Planning Commission, 1985
v.2: Sectoral programmes of development. — 421p

INDIAN NATIONAL CONGRESS
A tryst with destiny : a study of economic policy resolutions of INC passed during the last 100 years / edited by A. Moin Zaidi. — New Delhi : Publication Dept., Indian Institute of Applied Political Research, 1985. — 436 p.. — *Includes index*

SHARMA, K. M.
Social assistance in India / K. M. Sharma. — Delhi : Macmillan Co. of India, 1976. — x,119p. — *Revision of author's thesis, University of Allahabad. — Bibliography: p [109]-114*

INDIA — Social policy — Congresses
Seventh Plan and development of weaker sections : questions, challenges, and alternatives / edited by Jose Kananaikil. — New Delhi : Indian Social Institute, c1985. — xv, 188 p.. — *Includes index. — Bibliography: p. [171]-186*

INDIA — Statistics
INDIA. Central Statistical Organisation
Basic statistics relating to the Indian economy, 1950-51 to 1975-76. — [New Delhi] : Central Statistical Organisation, [1977]. — 153p

INDIA — Karnataka — Population
PRABHAKARA, N. R
Population growth and unemployment in India / N.R. Prabhakara, M.N. Usha. — New Delhi : Ashish Pub. House, 1986. — ix, 102 p.. — *Includes index. — Bibliography: p. 97-99*

INDIA — West Bengal — Scheduled tribes
Census of India 1981. — [Delhi : Controller of Publications]
Series 23: West Bengal / S. N. Ghosh, Director of Census Operations, West Bengal. — [1984]

INDIA. Imperial Legislative Council
MAHAJAN, Sneh
Imperialist strategy and moderate politics : Indian legislature at work, 1909-1920 / Sneh Mahajan. — 1st ed. — Delhi : Chanakya Publications, [1983], c1982. — 316 p., [1] folded leaf of plate. — *: Revision of the author's thesis (Ph. D.--University of Delhi). — Includes index. — Bibliography: p. [302]-310*

INDIA. Parliament
NARAIN, Udai
Parliamentary control of public administration in India / Udai Narain. — Allahabad : Chugh, 1981. — xiv,484p. — *Thesis (D. Litt.)-University of Lucknow, 1980. — Bibliography: p[447]-477*

INDIA. Parliament. Lok Sabha
INDIA. Parliament. Lok Sabha
Parliament of India : the seventh Lok Sabha 1980-84 : a study. — New Delhi : Lok Sabha Secretariat, 1985. — 221p [31]p of plates

INDIA. Parliament. Lok Sabha — Speaker
GEHLOT, N. S.
Office of the speaker in India / N.S. Gehlot. — New Delhi : Deep & Deep Publications, c1985. — 211 p.. — *Includes index.* — *Bibliography: p. [205]-209*

INDIA — Statistics
INDIA. Central Statistical Organisation
Economic census 1980 : all-India report. — [New Delhi] : Central Statistical Organisation, [1985]. — 101p

INDIA FOREIGN RELATIONS
REID, Escott
Hungary and Suez 1956 : a view from New Delhi / Escott Reid. — Oakville [Ontario] : Mosaic Press, 1986. — 163p

INDIA, NORTHEASTERN — Economic policy — Congresses
Northeast region : problems and prospects of development / edited by B.L. Abbi. — Chandigarh : Centre for Research in Rural and Industrial Development, 1984. — 361 p.. — *Includes bibliographical references*

INDIA, NORTHEASTERN — Ethnic relations — Congresses
Northeast region : problems and prospects of development / edited by B.L. Abbi. — Chandigarh : Centre for Research in Rural and Industrial Development, 1984. — 361 p.. — *Includes bibliographical references*

INDIA, NORTHEASTERN — Politics and government — Congresses
Northeast region : problems and prospects of development / edited by B.L. Abbi. — Chandigarh : Centre for Research in Rural and Industrial Development, 1984. — 361 p.. — *Includes bibliographical references*

INDIAN NATIONAL CONGRESS
BAKSHI, S. R
Swaraj Party and the Indian National Congress / S.R. Bakshi. — New Delhi : Vikas Pub. House, c1985. — vi, 200 p.. — *Bibliography: p [191j-195.* — *Bibliography: p. [191]-195*

GAUTAM, Om P.
The Indian National Congress : an analytical biography / Om P. Gautam. — Delhi : B. R. Publishing Corporation, 1985. — 400p. — *Bibliography: p368-389*

INDIAN NATIONAL CONGRESS
A tryst with destiny : a study of economic policy resolutions of INC passed during the last 100 years / edited by A. Moin Zaidi. — New Delhi : Publication Dept., Indian Institute of Applied Political Research, 1985. — 436 p.. — *Includes index*

Not by a class war : a study of Congress policy on land reforms during the last 100 years / edited by A. Moin Zaidi. — New Delhi : Indian Institute of Applied Political Research, 1985. — 176p

INDIAN NATIONAL CONGRESS — History
Aloud & straight : frank talks at party meetings / [edited by] A. Moin Zaidi. — New Delhi : Indian Institute of Applied Political Research, 1984. — 358 p.. — *"A verbatim account of major controversial debates inside the Congress Party during the last 100 years.".* — *Includes index*

SAXENA, Vinod Kumar
Muslims and the Indian National Congress (1885-1924) / Vinod Kumar Saxena. — Delhi : Discovery, 1985. — ix,258p. — *Bibliography: p [233]-252*

INDIAN NATIONAL CONGRESS — History — Sources
A Century of state craft in India : a study of the political resolutions of INC adopted during the last 100 years / edited by A. Moin Zaidi. — New Delhi : Publication Dept., Indian Institute of Applied Political Research, 1985. — 504 p.. — *Includes index*

Congress and the minorities : preserving national cohesion : a study of Congress policy towards minorities during the last 100 years / edited by A. Moin Zaidi ; with a foreword by Indira Gandhi. — New Delhi : Publication Dept., Indian Institute of Applied Political Research, 1984. — xvi, 288 p.. — *"Compiled and edited under the auspices of the Minorities' Cell, All India Congress Committee (I).".* — *Includes index*

INDIAN OCEAN — Strategic aspects
RAIS, Rasul B.
The Indian Ocean and the superpowers : economic, political and strategic perspectives / Rasul B. Rais. — London : Croom Helm, c1986. — 215p. — *Bibliography: p194-298.* — *Includes index*

INDIAN OCEAN REGION — Politics and government
Indian Ocean : conflict & regional cooperation. — New Delhi : ABC Pub. House, 1986. — xix, 239 p.. — *Editor: Akhtar Majeed.* — *Bibliography: p. [231]-239*

INDIAN OCEAN REGION — Relations — France
CAMPREDON, Jean-Pierre
France, océan Indien, mer Rouge : études / menées sous la responsabilité de Jean-Pierre Campredon et Jean-Jacques Schweitzer. — Paris : Fondation pour les études de défense nationale, 1986. — 449p. — *Bibliography: p443-445*

INDIAN OCEAN REGION — Strategic aspects
ALLEN, Philip M
Security and nationalism in the Indian Ocean : lessons from the Latin Quarter Islands / Philip M. Allen. — Boulder, Colo. : Westview Press, 1986. — p. cm. — (Westview special studies in international relations). — *Includes index.* — *Bibliography: p*

INDIANA — Politics and government
VANDERMEER, Philip R.
The Hoosier politician : officeholding and political culture in Indiana, 1896-1920 / Philip R. VanderMeer. — Urbana : University of Illinois Press, c1985. — p. cm. — *Includes index.* — *Bibliography: p*

INDIANS OF CENTRAL AMERICA — Guatemala — History
LOVELL, William George
Conquest and survival in colonial Guatemala : a historical geography of the Cuchumatán Highlands, 1500-1821 / W. George Lovell. — Kingston : McGill-Queen's University Press, c1985. — xv, 254 p., [16] p. of plates. — *Includes index.* — *Bibliography: p. [225]-245*

INDIANS OF CENTRAL AMERICA — Nicaragua — Cultural assimilation
NEWSON, Linda A
Indian survival in colonial Nicaragua / by Linda A. Newson. — 1st ed. — Norman [OK] : University of Oklahoma Press, c1987. — xiv, 466 p.. — (The Civilization of the American Indian series ; v. 175). — *Includes index.* — *Bibliography: p. 429-447*

INDIANS OF CENTRAL AMERICAN — Nicaragua — History
NEWSON, Linda A
Indian survival in colonial Nicaragua / by Linda A. Newson. — 1st ed. — Norman [OK] : University of Oklahoma Press, c1987. — xiv, 466 p.. — (The Civilization of the American Indian series ; v. 175). — *Includes index.* — *Bibliography: p. 429-447*

INDIANS OF MEXICO — Government relations
MCGUIRE, Thomas R
Politics and ethnicity on the Río Yaqui : Potam revisited / Thomas R. McGuire. — Tucson : University of Arizona Press, c1986. — xiv, 186p. — (Profmex monograph series ; 1). — *Includes index.* — *Bibliography: p.165-178*

INDIANS OF MEXICO — Rites and ceremonies
EL GUINDI, Fadwa
The myth of ritual : a native's ethnography of Zapotec life-crisis rituals / Fadwa El Guindi, with the collaboration of Abel Hernández Jiménez. — Tucson : University of Arizona Press, c1986. — xvii, 147p. — *Includes index.* — *Bibliography: p.125-139*

INDIANS OF MEXICO — Women
CHIÑAS, Beverly
The Isthmus Zapotecs : women's roles in cultural context / Beverly Chiñas. — Prospect Heights, Ill. : Waveland Press, 1983. — ix,129p . — *First published in 1973.* — *Bibliography: p128-129*

INDIANS OF MEXICO — Mexico, Valley of — Economic conditions
HASSIG, Ross
Trade, tribute, and transportation : the sixteenth-century political economy of the Valley of Mexico / by Ross Hassig. — Norman : University of Oklahoma Press, c1985. — xvi, 364p. — (Civilization of the American Indian series ; v. 171). — *Includes index.* — *Bibliography: p 319-350*

INDIANS OF MEXICO — Sonora (State) — Ethnic identity
MCGUIRE, Thomas R
Politics and ethnicity on the Río Yaqui : Potam revisited / Thomas R. McGuire. — Tucson : University of Arizona Press, c1986. — xiv, 186p. — (Profmex monograph series ; 1). — *Includes index.* — *Bibliography: p.165-178*

INDIANS OF MEXICO — Sonora (State) — Water rights
MCGUIRE, Thomas R
Politics and ethnicity on the Río Yaqui : Potam revisited / Thomas R. McGuire. — Tucson : University of Arizona Press, c1986. — xiv, 186p. — (Profmex monograph series ; 1). — *Includes index.* — *Bibliography: p.165-178*

INDIANS OF NORTH AMERICA — Biography
Indian lives : essays on nineteenth- and twentieth-century Native American leaders / edited by L.G. Moses and Raymond Wilson. — 1st ed. — Albuquerque : University of New Mexico Press, c1985. — 227p. — *Includes index.* — *Bibliography: p.[215]-216*

INDIANS OF NORTH AMERICA — Courts
DELORIA, Vine
American Indians, American justice / by Vine Deloria, Jr. and Clifford M. Lytle. — 1st ed. — Austin : University of Texas Press, 1983. — xiii, 262 p.. — *Includes indexes.* — *Bibliography: p. [247]-249*

INDIANS OF NORTH AMERICA — Crime
MCKECHNIE, Gail
Native North Americans : crime, conflict and criminal justice : a research bibliography / prepared by Gail McKechnie. — 3rd ed. — [Burnaby] : Northern Conference Resource Centre, 1986. — 156p (loose-leaf)

INDIANS OF NORTH AMERICA — Cultural assimilation — History
BOLT, Christine
American Indian policy and American reform : case studies of the campaign to assimilate the American Indians / Christine Bolt. — London : Allen & Unwin, 1987. — [xii,288]p. — *Includes bibliography and index*

INDIANS OF NORTH AMERICA — Government relations
Indian lives : essays on nineteenth- and twentieth-century Native American leaders / edited by L.G. Moses and Raymond Wilson. — 1st ed. — Albuquerque : University of New Mexico Press, c1985. — 227p. — *Includes index.* — *Bibliography: p.[215]-216*

**INDIANS OF NORTH AMERICA —
Government relations** *continuation*

MINER, H. Craig
The end of Indian Kansas : a study of cultural revolution, 1854-1871 / H. Craig Miner and William E. Unrau. — Lawrence : Regents Press of Kansas, c1978. — xiii, 179 p., [4] leaves of plates. — Includes index. — Bibliography: p. 167-173

**INDIANS OF NORTH AMERICA —
Government relations — Addresses, essays, lectures**

PRUCHA, Francis Paul
The Indians in American society : from the revolutionary war to the present / Francis Paul Prucha. — Berkeley ; London : University of California Press, c1985. — ix, 127p. — (Quantum books). — Essays presented as the Gasson lectures at Boston College on Nov. 30, 1983, Mar. 14, 1984, Nov. 7, 1984, and Mar. 13, 1985. — Includes bibliographical references and index. — Bibliography: p. [105]-117. — Contents: Paternalism -- Dependency -- Indian rights -- Self-determination

**INDIANS OF NORTH AMERICA —
Government relations — History**

BOLT, Christine
American Indian policy and American reform : case studies of the campaign to assimilate the American Indians / Christine Bolt. — London : Allen & Unwin, 1987. — [xii,288]p. — Includes bibliography and index

**INDIANS OF NORTH AMERICA —
Government relations — 1934-**

DRINNON, Richard
Keeper of concentration camps : Dillon S. Myer and American racism / Richard Drinnon. — Berkeley : University of California Press, c1987. — xxviii, 339 p.. — Includes index. — Bibliography: p. 271-324

HAUPTMAN, Laurence M
The Iroquois struggle for survival : World War II to red power / Laurence M. Hauptman. — 1st ed. — Syracuse, N.Y. : Syracuse University Press, 1986. — xiii, 328p. — (An Iroquois book). — Includes index. — Bibliography: p. 285-313

**INDIANS OF NORTH AMERICA —
History — 20th century**

HAUPTMAN, Laurence M
The Iroquois struggle for survival : World War II to red power / Laurence M. Hauptman. — 1st ed. — Syracuse, N.Y. : Syracuse University Press, 1986. — xiii, 328p. — (An Iroquois book). — Includes index. — Bibliography: p. 285-313

**INDIANS OF NORTH AMERICA —
Hunting — Congresses**

Resource managers : North American and Australian hunter-gatherers / edited by Nancy M. Williams and Eugene S. Hunn. — Canberra : Australian Institute of Aboriginal Studies, 1982. — xiv,267p. — (AAAS selected symposia series). — Based on a symposium of the American Association for the Advancement of Science 1980. — Bibliography at end of each paper

**INDIANS OF NORTH AMERICA —
Juvenile delinquency**

MCKECHNIE, Gail
Native North Americans : crime, conflict and criminal justice : a research bibliography / prepared by Gail McKechnie. — 3rd ed. — [Burnaby] : Northern Conference Resource Centre, 1986. — 156p (loose-leaf)

**INDIANS OF NORTH AMERICA —
Legal status, laws, etc**

DELORIA, Vine
American Indians, American justice / by Vine Deloria, Jr. and Clifford M. Lytle. — 1st ed. — Austin : University of Texas Press, 1983. — xiii, 262 p.. — Includes indexes. — Bibliography: p. [247]-249

**INDIANS OF NORTH AMERICA —
Legal status, laws, etc — History**

WILKINSON, Charles F.
American Indians, time, and the law : native societies in a modern constitutional democracy / Charles F. Wilkinson. — New Haven ; London : Yale University Press, c1987. — xi, 225 p.. — "Supreme Court cases in Indian law during the modern era": p. 123-132. — Includes index. — Bibliography: p. 133-219

**INDIANS OF NORTH AMERICA —
Population**

THORNTON, Russell
We shall live again : the 1870 and 1890 ghost dance movements as demographic revitalization / Russell Thornton. — Cambridge : Cambridge University Press, 1986. — xiii,95p. — (The Arnold and Caroline Rose monograph series of the American Sociology Association). — Bibliography: p85-92. — Includes index

**INDIANS OF NORTH AMERICA —
Social conditions**

MCKECHNIE, Gail
Native North Americans : crime, conflict and criminal justice : a research bibliography / prepared by Gail McKechnie. — 3rd ed. — [Burnaby] : Northern Conference Resource Centre, 1986. — 156p (loose-leaf)

**INDIANS OF NORTH AMERICA —
Statistics**

A catalogue of statistical data in the Program Reference Centre = Catalogue de données Statistiques du Centre de référence du Programme / Indian and Northern Affairs Canada. — Ottawa : Minister of Indian Affairs and Northern Development, 1985-. — Annual. — Text in English and French

**INDIANS OF NORTH AMERICA —
Alaska — Claims**

BERGER, Thomas R
Village journey : the report of the Alaska Native Review Commission / by Thomas R. Berger. — New York : Hill and Wang, c1985. — p. cm

**INDIANS OF NORTH AMERICA —
Alaska — Economic conditions —
Addresses, essays, lectures**

Contemporary Alaskan native economies / edited by Steve J. Langdon. — Lanham, MD : University Press of America, c1986. — ix, 183 p.. — Includes bibliographies. — Contents: Economic growth and development strategies for rural Alaska / Bradford H. Tuck and Lee Huskey -- Subsistence as an economic system in Alaska / Thomas D. Lonner -- Contradictions in Alaskan native economy and society / Steve J. Langdon -- Limited entry policy and impacts on Bristol Bay fishermen / J. Anthony Koslow -- The Cape Romanzoff project / Dean F. Olson -- The Pribilof Island Aleuts / Michael K. Orbach and Beverly Holmes -- The economic efficiency of food production in a western Alaska Eskimo population / Robert J. Wolfe -- Subsistence and the North Slope Inupiat / John A. Kruse -- Subsistence beluga whale hunting in Alaska / Kerry D. Feldman -- Traditional subsistence activities and systems of exchange among the Nelson Island Yup'ik / Ann Fienup-Riordan

**INDIANS OF NORTH AMERICA —
Alaska — Government relations**

BERGER, Thomas R
Village journey : the report of the Alaska Native Review Commission / by Thomas R. Berger. — New York : Hill and Wang, c1985. — p. cm

**INDIANS OF NORTH AMERICA —
Alaska — Land tenure**

BERGER, Thomas R
Village journey : the report of the Alaska Native Review Commission / by Thomas R. Berger. — New York : Hill and Wang, c1985. — p. cm

**INDIANS OF NORTH AMERICA —
Canada**

CANADA. Parliament. House of Commons. Standing Committee on Aboriginal Affairs and Northern Development
Minutes of proceedings and evidence... = Procès verbaux et témoignages. — Ottawa : Government Printer, 1986-. — Continues: Canada. Parliament. House of Commons. Standing Committee on Indian Affairs and Northern Development. Minutes of proceedings and evidence...

CANADA. Parliament. House of Commons. Standing Committee on Indian Affairs and Northern Development
Minutes of proceedings and evidence... = Procès-verbaux et témoignages.... — Ottawa : Government Printer, 1968-1986. — Irregular. — Continued by: Canada. Parliament. House of Commons. Standing Committee on Aboriginal Affairs and Northern Development

**INDIANS OF NORTH AMERICA —
Canada — Civil rights**

SCHWARTZ, Bryan
First principles : constitutional reform with respect to the aboriginal peoples of Canada, 1982-1984 / Bryan Schwartz. — Kingston, Ont., Canada : Institute of Intergovernmental relations, Queen's University, [1985]. — xiv, 292 p.. — (Aboriginal peoples and constitutional reform. Background paper ; no. 6). — Errata slip inserted. — Bibliography: p. 287-292

**INDIANS OF NORTH AMERICA —
Canada — Constitutional law**

The Quest for justice : aboriginal peoples and aboriginal rights / edited by Menno Boldt and J. Anthony Long in association with Leroy Little Bear. — Toronto ; Buffalo : University of Toronto Press, c1985. — viii, 406 p.. — Bibliography: p. [381]-403

**INDIANS OF NORTH AMERICA —
Canada — Councils — Bibliography**

PETERS, Evelyn J.
Aboriginal self-government in Canada : a bibliography 1986 / Evelyn J. Peters. — Kingston, Ont. : Queens University Institute of Intergovernmental Relations, 1986. — ix,112p. — (Aboriginal peoples and constitutional reform). — English text with French summary

**INDIANS OF NORTH AMERICA —
Canada — First contact with Occidental civilization**

TRIGGER, Bruce G.
Natives and newcomers : Canada's "Heroic age" reconsidered / Bruce G. Trigger. — Manchester : Manchester University Press, 1986. — xiii, 430p

**INDIANS OF NORTH AMERICA —
Canada — Government relations**

Indigenous peoples and the nation-state : 'fourth world' politics in Canada, Australia, and Norway / edited by Noel Dyck. — St. John's, Nfld., Canada : Institute of Social and Economic Research, Memorial University of Newfoundland, c1985. — 263 p.. — (Social and economic papers ; no. 14). — Bibliography: 242-259

ROBINSON, Eric
The infested blanket : Canada's constitution, genocide of Indian nations / Eric Robinson and Henry Bird Quinney. — Winnipeg, Man. : Queenston House Pub., c1985. — xxiv, 168 p.

**INDIANS OF NORTH AMERICA —
Canada — Government relations —
Bibliography**

PETERS, Evelyn J.
Aboriginal self-government in Canada : a bibliography 1986 / Evelyn J. Peters. — Kingston, Ont. : Queens University Institute of Intergovernmental Relations, 1986. — ix,112p. — (Aboriginal peoples and constitutional reform). — English text with French summary

INDIANS OF NORTH AMERICA — Canada — History

TRIGGER, Bruce G.
Natives and newcomers : Canada's "Heroic age" reconsidered / Bruce G. Trigger. — Manchester : Manchester University Press, 1986. — xiii, 430p

INDIANS OF NORTH AMERICA — Canada — Legal status, laws, etc.

HAWLEY, Donna Lea
The Indian Act annotated / by Donna Lea Hawley. — 2nd ed. — Toronto : Carswell, 1986. — xvii,103p

INDIANS OF NORTH AMERICA — Canada — Legal status, laws, etc

The Quest for justice : aboriginal peoples and aboriginal rights / edited by Menno Boldt and J. Anthony Long in association with Leroy Little Bear. — Toronto ; Buffalo : University of Toronto Press, c1985. — viii, 406 p.. — *Bibliography: p. [381]-403*

ROBINSON, Eric
The infested blanket : Canada's constitution, genocide of Indian nations / Eric Robinson and Henry Bird Quinney. — Winnipeg, Man. : Queenston House Pub., c1985. — xxiv, 168 p.

INDIANS OF NORTH AMERICA — Canada — Mixed bloods — Addresses, essays, lectures

The New peoples : being and becoming métis in North America / edited by Jacqueline Peterson, Jennifer S.H. Brown. — Lincoln : University of Nebraska Press, c1985. — xvi, 266 p., 16 p. of plates. — (Manitoba studies in native history ; 1). — *Includes bibliographies and index*

INDIANS OF NORTH AMERICA — Canada — Mixed bloods — History — Addresses, essays, lectures

The New peoples : being and becoming métis in North America / edited by Jacqueline Peterson, Jennifer S.H. Brown. — Lincoln : University of Nebraska Press, c1985. — xvi, 266 p., 16 p. of plates. — (Manitoba studies in native history ; 1). — *Includes bibliographies and index*

INDIANS OF NORTH AMERICA — Canada — Treaties

ROBINSON, Eric
The infested blanket : Canada's constitution, genocide of Indian nations / Eric Robinson and Henry Bird Quinney. — Winnipeg, Man. : Queenston House Pub., c1985. — xxiv, 168 p.

INDIANS OF NORTH AMERICA — Great Plains — History — 20th century — Addresses, essays, lectures

The Plains Indians of the twentieth century / edited and with an introduction by Peter Iverson. — Norman ; London : University of Oklahoma Press, c1985. — ix, 277p. — *Includes bibliographical references and index*

INDIANS OF NORTH AMERICA — Kansas — History

MINER, H. Craig
The end of Indian Kansas : a study of cultural revolution, 1854-1871 / H. Craig Miner and William E. Unrau. — Lawrence : Regents Press of Kansas, c1978. — xiii, 179 p., [4] leaves of plates. — *Includes index.* — *Bibliography: p. 167-173*

INDIANS OF NORTH AMERICA — Kansas — Land tenure

MINER, H. Craig
The end of Indian Kansas : a study of cultural revolution, 1854-1871 / H. Craig Miner and William E. Unrau. — Lawrence : Regents Press of Kansas, c1978. — xiii, 179 p., [4] leaves of plates. — *Includes index.* — *Bibliography: p. 167-173*

INDIANS OF NORTH AMERICA — Northwestern States — Government relations

Indians, superintendents, and councils : northwestern Indian policy, 1850-1855 / edited by Clifford E. Trafzer. — Lanham, MD : University Press of America, c1986. — xi, 173 p.. — *Includes index.* — *Bibliography: p. 137-161*

INDIANS OF NORTH AMERICA — Northwestern States — Legal status, laws, etc

Indians, superintendents, and councils : northwestern Indian policy, 1850-1855 / edited by Clifford E. Trafzer. — Lanham, MD : University Press of America, c1986. — xi, 173 p.. — *Includes index.* — *Bibliography: p. 137-161*

INDIANS OF NORTH AMERICA — Northwestern States — Treaties

Indians, superintendents, and councils : northwestern Indian policy, 1850-1855 / edited by Clifford E. Trafzer. — Lanham, MD : University Press of America, c1986. — xi, 173 p.. — *Includes index.* — *Bibliography: p. 137-161*

INDIANS OF NORTH AMERICA — South Dakota — Social life and customs

POWERS, Marla N
Oglala women : myth, ritual, and reality / Marla N. Powers. — Chicago ; London : University of Chicago Press, c1986. — xv, 241 p., [16] p. of plates. — (Women in culture and society). — *Includes index.* — *Bibliography: p. 223-233*

INDIANS OF NORTH AMERICA — South Dakota — Women

POWERS, Marla N
Oglala women : myth, ritual, and reality / Marla N. Powers. — Chicago ; London : University of Chicago Press, c1986. — xv, 241 p., [16] p. of plates. — (Women in culture and society). — *Includes index.* — *Bibliography: p. 223-233*

INDIANS OF NORTH AMERICA — Southwest, New — Art

WITHERSPOON, Gary
Language and art in the Navajo universe / Gary Witherspoon. — Ann Arbor : University of Michigan Press, c1977. — xviii, 214 p., [2] leaves of plates. — *Includes index.* — *Bibliography: p. 207-210*

INDIANS OF NORTH AMERICA — Southwest, New — Economic conditions

WEISS, Lawrence David
The development of capitalism in the Navajo nation : a political-economic history / by Lawrence David Weiss. — Minneapolis : MEP Publications, c1984. — 180 p.. — (Studies in Marxism ; vol. 15). — *Includes index.* — *Bibliography: p. 159-175*

INDIANS OF NORTH AMERICA — Southwest, New — Philosophy

WITHERSPOON, Gary
Language and art in the Navajo universe / Gary Witherspoon. — Ann Arbor : University of Michigan Press, c1977. — xviii, 214 p., [2] leaves of plates. — *Includes index.* — *Bibliography: p. 207-210*

INDIANS OF SOUTH AMERICA — Congresses

INSTITUTO INTERNACIONAL DE HISTORIA DEL DERECHO INDIANO. Congreso (6 : [1984] : Valladolid)
Estructuras, gobierno y agentes de la administración en la América española : siglos XVI, XVII y XVIII : trabajos del VI Congreso del Instituto Internacional de Historia del Derecho Indiano en homenaje al Dr. Alfonso García-Gallo. — Valladolid : [Instituto de Cooperación Iberoamericana, Seminario Americanista de la Universidad de Valladolid], 1984. — 533p. — (Serie americanista "Bernal" ; vol.17)

INDIANS OF SOUTH AMERICA — Ethics

SANTOS GRANERO, Fernando
The power of love : the moral use of knowledge amongst the Amuesha of Central Peru / Fernando Santos Granero. — 395 leaves. — *PhD (Econ) 1986 LSE.* — *Leaves 374-384 are appendices*

INDIANS OF SOUTH AMERICA — Amazon Valley

MEGGERS, Betty Jane
Amazonia: man and culture in a counterfeit paradise / [by] Betty J. Meggers. — Chicago : Aldine, Atherton, [1971]. — viii, 182 p. — (Worlds of man). — *Bibliography: p. 169-173*

INDIANS OF SOUTH AMERICA — Andes region — Addresses, essays, lectures

Anthropological history of Andean politics / edited by John V. Murra, Nathan Wachtel and Jacques Revel. — Cambridge : Cambridge University Press, 1986. — x,383p. — *Translation of Anthropologie historique des sociétés andines, a special double issue of Annales ; v.33, nos. 5-6 (1978)*

INDIANS OF SOUTH AMERICA — Bolivia — Government relations

COLE, Jeffrey A
The Potosí mita, 1573-1700 : compulsory Indian labor in the Andes / Jeffrey A. Cole. — Stanford, Calif. : Stanford University Press, 1985. — xi, 206p. — *Includes index.* — *Bibliography: p.187-196*

INDIANS OF SOUTH AMERICA — Bolivia — Potosí (Dept.) — Employment — History

COLE, Jeffrey A
The Potosí mita, 1573-1700 : compulsory Indian labor in the Andes / Jeffrey A. Cole. — Stanford, Calif. : Stanford University Press, 1985. — xi, 206p. — *Includes index.* — *Bibliography: p.187-196*

INDIANS OF SOUTH AMERICA — Brazil — Sexual behavior

GREGOR, Thomas
Anxious pleasures : the sexual lives of an Amazonian people / Thomas Gregor. — Chicago : University of Chicago Press, 1985. — xii, 223 p.. — *Includes index.* — *Bibliography: p. [211]-216*

INDIANS OF SOUTH AMERICA — Brazil — Social life and customs

MURPHY, Yolanda
Women of the forest / Yolanda Murphy and Robert F. Murphy. — 2nd ed. — New York : Columbia University Press, 1985. — xvi, 262 p. . — *Includes index.* — *Bibliography: p. [259]-260*

INDIANS OF SOUTH AMERICA — Brazil — Women

MURPHY, Yolanda
Women of the forest / Yolanda Murphy and Robert F. Murphy. — 2nd ed. — New York : Columbia University Press, 1985. — xvi, 262 p. . — *Includes index.* — *Bibliography: p. [259]-260*

INDIANS OF SOUTH AMERICA — Ecuador — Quito region — Economic conditions

SALOMON, Frank
Native lords of Quito in the age of the Incas : the political economy of north Andean chiefdoms / Frank Salomon. — Cambridge : Cambridge University Press, 1986. — xviii,274p. — (Cambridge studies in social anthropology ; no.59)

INDIANS OF SOUTH AMERICA — Ecuador — Quito region — Politics and government

SALOMON, Frank
Native lords of Quito in the age of the Incas : the political economy of north Andean chiefdoms / Frank Salomon. — Cambridge : Cambridge University Press, 1986. — xviii,274p. — (Cambridge studies in social anthropology ; no.59)

INDIANS OF SOUTH AMERICA — Paraguay — Economic conditions
RENSHAW, Jonathan Charles
The economy and economic morality of the Indians of the Paraguayan Chaco / Jonathan Charles Renshaw. — 369 leaves. — PhD (Econ) 1986 LSE. — Leaves 337-356 are appendices

INDIANS OF SOUTH AMERICA — Paraguay — Social conditions
RENSHAW, Jonathan Charles
The economy and economic morality of the Indians of the Paraguayan Chaco / Jonathan Charles Renshaw. — 369 leaves. — PhD (Econ) 1986 LSE. — Leaves 337-356 are appendices

INDIANS OF SOUTH AMERICA — Peru — Ethnobotany
BROWN, Michael
Tsewa's gift : magic and meaning in an Amazonian society / Michael F. Brown. — Washington, D.C. : Smithsonian Institution Press, 1985. — p. cm. — (Smithsonian series in ethnographic inquiry). — Includes index. — Bibliography: p

INDIANS OF SOUTH AMERICA — Peru — Magic
BROWN, Michael
Tsewa's gift : magic and meaning in an Amazonian society / Michael F. Brown. — Washington, D.C. : Smithsonian Institution Press, 1985. — p. cm. — (Smithsonian series in ethnographic inquiry). — Includes index. — Bibliography: p

INDIANS OF SOUTH AMERICA — Peru — Religion and mythology
BROWN, Michael
Tsewa's gift : magic and meaning in an Amazonian society / Michael F. Brown. — Washington, D.C. : Smithsonian Institution Press, 1985. — p. cm. — (Smithsonian series in ethnographic inquiry). — Includes index. — Bibliography: p

INDIANS OF THE WEST INDIES — Government relations
HULME, Peter
Colonial encounters : Europe and the native Caribbean, 1492-1797 / Peter Hulme. — London : Methuen, 1986. — xv,348p. — Includes index. — Bibliography: p329-348

INDIANS OF THE WEST INDIES — Saint Vincent — Folklore
GULLICK, C. J. M. R.
Myths of a minority : the changing traditions of the Vincentian Caribs / C. J. M. R. Gullick. — Assen : Van Gorcum, 1985. — 211p. — (Studies of developing countries ; 30). — Bibliography: p196-211

INDIANS, TREATMENT OF — Latin America
CASAS, Bartolomé de las
Brevísima relación de la destrucción de las Indias / Bartolomé de las Casas. — [Madrid] : Anjana, [ca.1983]. — 104p. — Publicado originalmente en 1552

INDIANS, TREATMENT OF — Nicaragua — History
NEWSON, Linda A
Indian survival in colonial Nicaragua / by Linda A. Newson. — 1st ed. — Norman [OK] : University of Oklahoma Press, c1987. — xiv, 466 p.. — (The Civilization of the American Indian series ; v. 175). — Includes index. — Bibliography: p. 429-447

INDIVIDUALISM
BERTELSON, David
Snowflakes and snowdrifts : individualism and sexuality in America / David Bertelson. — Lanham, MD : University Press of America, c1986. — ix, 282 p.. — Includes index. — Bibliography: p. 255-275

Ideology and national competitiveness : an analysis of nine countries / edited by George C. Lodge and Ezra F. Vogel. — Boston, Mass. : Harvard Business School Press, c1987. — x, 350 p.. — Includes index. — Bibliography: p. 327-342

INDIVIDUALISM — Addresses, essays, lectures
Freedom, feminism, and the state : an overview of individualist feminism / edited by Wendy McElroy ; foreword by Lewis Perry. — Washington, D.C. : Cato Institute, c1982. — xi, 357 p.. — Includes index. — Bibliography: p. 349-352

Reconstructing individualism : autonomy, individuality, and the self in Western thought / edited by Thomas C. Heller, Morton Sosna, and David E. Wellbery. — Stanford, Calif. : Stanford University Press, 1986. — xiv, 365p. — Includes index. — Includes bibliographical references

INDIVIDUALISM — History
DUMONT, Louis
[Essais sur l'individualisme. English]. Essays on individualism : modern ideology in anthropological perspective / Louis Dumont. — Chicago : University of Chicago Press, 1986. — p. cm. — Enl. translation of: Essais sur l'individualisme. — Includes index. — Bibliography: p

INDIVIDUALITY — Addresses, essays, lectures
Reconstructing individualism : autonomy, individuality, and the self in Western thought / edited by Thomas C. Heller, Morton Sosna, and David E. Wellbery. — Stanford, Calif. : Stanford University Press, 1986. — xiv, 365p. — Includes index. — Includes bibliographical references

INDOCHINA — Emigration and immigration
HOO KHOA, Le
Les réfugié set immigrés originaires de la péninsule Indochinoise / Le Huu Khoa. — [Paris] : Agence de développement des relations interculturelles, 1984. — 54 leaves. — Bibliography: p40-51

INDOCHINA — Foreign relations — Australia
ROSS, Estelle
Australia, the Indochina problem, and the derecognition of the Pol Pot regime / Estelle Ross. — Nathan, Australia : Centre for the Study of Australian-Asian Relations, School of Modern Asian Studies, Griffith University, [1984]. — iii, 65 p.. — (Research paper ; no. 28). — "September 1984.". — Bibliography: p. 64-65

INDOCHINA — Foreign relations — China
CHANG, Pao-min
Kampuchea between China and Vietnam / Chang Pao-min. — Singapore : Singapore University Press, National University of Singapore, c1985. — xi, 204 p.. — Includes bibliographical references and index

INDOCHINA — Foreign relations — United States
SARAVANAMUTTU, Paikiasothy
The influence of an idea on foreign policy : the case of domino theory in American foreign policy in Indochina, 1945-56 / P. Saravanamuttu. — 348 leaves. — PhD (Econ) 1986 LSE

INDOCHINESE — France
HOO KHOA, Le
Les réfugié set immigrés originaires de la péninsule Indochinoise / Le Huu Khoa. — [Paris] : Agence de développement des relations interculturelles, 1984. — 54 leaves. — Bibliography: p40-51

INDOCHINESE WAR, 1946-1954 — United States
GIBBONS, William Conrad
The U.S. government and the Vietnam war : executive and legislative roles and relationships / William Conrad Gibbons ; with a new preface by the author. — Princeton, N.J. : Princeton University Press, [1986-. — p. cm. — "Prepared for the Committee on Foreign Relations, United States Senate, by the Congressional Research Service, Library of Congress.". — : "Originally published by the U.S. Government Printing Office in April 1984"--T.p. verso. — Includes bibliographical references and indexes. — Contents: pt. 1. 1945-1960 -- pt. 2. 1961-1964

INDONESIA — Constitutional law
INTERNATIONAL COMMISSION OF JURISTS
Indonesia and the rule of law : twenty years of 'New Order' government : a study / prepared by the International Commission of Jurists and the Netherlands Institute of Human Rights ; edited by Hans Thoolen. — London : Pinter, 1987. — xii,208p. — Includes index

INDONESIA — Economic conditions — 1945- — Statistics
Sistem neraca sosial ekonomi Indonesia, 1975 = Social accounting matrix Indonesia, 1975. — Jakarta : Biro Pusat Statistik. — Tables in Indonesian with list of tables in English
Vol.2. — [1983]. — xx,311 leaves

Social accounting matrix Indonesia, 1975. — Jakarta : Biro Pusat Statistik. — Bibliography: p101-105
Vol.1. — [1982]. — v,105p

INDONESIA — Foreign relations — Netherlands — Sources
Officiële beschieden betreffende de Nederlands-Indonesische betrekkingen 1945-1950 / vitgegeven door P. J. Drooglever en M. J. B. Schouten. — s-Gravenhage : Nijhoff
Deel 13: 20 februari-4juni 1948. — 1986. — xxvii,878p. — (Rijks geschiedkundige publicatiën. Kleine serie ; 61)

INDONESIA — Foreign relations — Papua New Guinea
HARRIS, Stephen V.
Indonesia, Papua New Guinea and Australia : the Irian Jaya Problem of 1984 / Stephen V. Harris and Colin Brown. — Nathan : Centre for the Study of Australian-Asian Relations, Griffith University, 1980. — 83p. — (Australia-Asia papers ; no.29)

INDONESIA — History — Java War, 1825-1830
Two colonial empires : the Java War, 1825-30, and the Indian "mutiny" of 1857-59 / edited by C.A. Bayly, D.H.A. Kolff. — Dordrecht ; Boston : M. Nijhoff, 1986. — p. cm. — (Comparative studies in overseas history ; v. 6). — Includes index

INDONESIA — History — Revolution, 1945-1949
Regional dynamics of the Indonesian Revolution : unity from diversity / edited by Audrey R. Kahin. — Honolulu : University of Hawaii Press, c1985. — xi, 306 p.. — Includes bibliographies and index

INDONESIA — History, Local
Regional dynamics of the Indonesian Revolution : unity from diversity / edited by Audrey R. Kahin. — Honolulu : University of Hawaii Press, c1985. — xi, 306 p.. — Includes bibliographies and index

INDONESIA — Military policy
JENKINS, David
Suharto and his generals : Indonesian military politics 1975-1983 / David Jenkins. — Ithaca (N.Y.) : Cornell Modern Indonesia Project. Southeast Asia Program, 1984. — xiii,280p. — (Monograph series / Cornell Modern Indonesia Project ; no.64)

INDONESIA — Politics and government

Indonesia / Department of Information, Directorate of Foreign Information Services, Indonesia. — Jakarta : Directorate of Foreign Information Services. Department of Information, 1986-. — *Annual*

JENKINS, David
Suharto and his generals : Indonesian military politics 1975-1983 / David Jenkins. — Ithaca (N.Y.) : Cornell Modern Indonesia Project. Southeast Asia Program, 1984. — xiii,280p. — (Monograph series / Cornell Modern Indonesia Project ; no.64)

INDONESIA — Population — Statistics — Forecasting

Proyeksi penduduk Indonesia : 1976-2001. — Jakarta : Biro Pusat Statistik, 1978. — 12 leaves

INDONESIA — Social conditions

KING, Victor T.
The Maloh of West Kalimantan : an ethnographic study of social inequality and social change among an Indonesian Borneo people / Victor T. King. — Dordrecht : Foris Publications, 1985. — viii,252p. — (Verhandelingen van het Koninklijk Instituut voor Taal-, Land-en Volkenkunde ; 108). — *Bibliography: p232-243*

INDONESIA — Social conditions — Statistics

Indikator kesejahteraan rakyat = Welfare indicators / Biro Pusat Statistik, Indonesia. — Jakarta : Biro Pusat Statistik, Indonesia, 1983-

Sistem neraca sosial ekonomi Indonesia, 1975 = Social accounting matrix Indonesia, 1975. — Jakarta : Biro Pusat Statistik. — *Tables in Indonesian with list of tables in English*
Vol.2. — [1983]. — xx,311 leaves

Social accounting matrix Indonesia, 1975. — Jakarta : Biro Pusat Statistik. — *Bibliography: p101-105*
Vol.1. — [1982]. — v,105p

INDUCTION (LOGIC)

Induction : processes of inference, learning, and discovery / John H. Holland ... [et al.]. — Cambridge, Mass. : MIT Press, c1986. — xvi, 385p. — (Computational models of cognition and perception). — *Includes index. — Bibliography: p.357-372*

ROSENKRANTZ, Roger D.
Foundations and applications of inductive probability / R.D. Rosenkrantz. — Atascadero, Calif. : Ridgeview Publishing Co., 1981

INDUSTRIAL ACCIDENTS

LABOUR RESEARCH DEPARTMENT
Repetitive strain injury at work : a preventable disease. — London : Labour Research Department, 1987. — 40p

LEWIS, Richard, 19---
Compensation for industrial injury : a guide to the revised scheme of benefits for work accidents and diseases / by Richard Lewis. — Abingdon : Professional Books, 1987. — 359p

INDUSTRIAL ACCIDENTS — Costs

ANDREONI, Diego
The cost of occupational accidents and diseases / Diego Andreoni. — Geneva : International Labour Office, 1986. — viii, 142p. — (Occupational safety and health series ; no.54). — *Bibliography: p135-142*

INDUSTRIAL ACCIDENTS — Legal status, laws, etc. — Great Britain

COLWILL, Jeremy Giles
Capital, labour, and the state : the origins of the National Insurance (Industrial Injuries) Act 1946 / by Jeremy Giles Colwill. — 338 leaves. — *PhD (Laws) 1986 LSE*

INDUSTRIAL ACCIDENTS — Australia — Tasmania — Statistics

TASMANIA. Bureau of census and Statistics. Tasmanian Office
Industrial accident statistics. — Hobart : [the Office], 1969/70-1980/81. — *Annual*

INDUSTRIAL ACCIDENTS — Great Britain

GLENDON, A. I.
A study of 1700 accidents on the Youth Opportunities Programme / A.I. Glendon, A. R. Hale. — [Sheffield] : Manpower Services Commission, 1985. — 1v. (various pagings)

INDUSTRIAL ACCIDENTS — United States — Case studies

CHERNIACK, Martin
The Hawk's Nest incident : America's worst industrial disaster / Martin Cherniack ; foreword by Phillip Landrigan and Anthony Robbins. — New Haven : Yale University Press, c1986. — x, 194p, [16]p of plates. — *Includes index. — Bibliography: p.184-188*

INDUSTRIAL ARTS — Study and teaching — Evaluation

HUNTING, Gordon
Evaluating vocational training programs : a practical guide / Gordon Hunting, Manuel Zymelman, Martin Godfrey. — Washington, D.C. : The World Bank, 1986. — vii,96p

INDUSTRIAL BUILDINGS — Economic aspects — Great Britain

FOTHERGILL, Stephen
Property and industrial development / Stephen Fothergill, Sarah Monk, Martin Perry. — London : Hutchinson, 1987. — 187p. — (The Built environment series). — *Bibliography: p177-180. — Includes index*

INDUSTRIAL BUILDINGS — Great Britain

JACKSON, Annabel
Managing workspaces : prepared for the Department of the Environment / by Annabel Jackson, Daphne Mair and Rupert Nabarro, Land and Urban Analysis Ltd.. — London : H.M.S.O., 1987. — 133p. — (Case studies of good practice in urban regeneration). — *Commissioned by the Inner Cities Directorate of the Department of the Environment. — Bibliography: p132*

URBED (URBAN AND ECONOMIC DEVELOPMENT) LTD.
Re-using redundant buildings : prepared for the Department of the Environment / by URBED (Urban and Economic Development) Ltd.. — London : H.M.S.O., 1987. — 115p. — (Case studies of good practice in urban regeneration). — *Commissioned by the Inner Cities Directorate of the Department of the Environment*

INDUSTRIAL CAPACITY — Finance — Mathematical models

ERLENKOTTER, Donald
Preinvestment planning for capacity expansion : a multi-location dynamic model / Donald Erlenkotter. — New Delhi : United States of America Agency for International Development, 1969. — x,223p. — *Bibliographical references: p218-223*

INDUSTRIAL CONCENTRATION — France — Statistics

MONFORT, Jean Alain
La concentration des activités économiques : les établissements, les entreprises et les groupes / Jean Alain Monfort, Laurent Vassille. — Paris : Institut national de la statistique et des études économiques, 1985. — 171p. — (Les collections de l'INSEE. Série E ; no.98)

INDUSTRIAL CONCENTRATION — Great Britain — Statistics

Acquisitions and mergers of industrial and commercial companies. — London : HMSO, 1974-. — (Business monitor. MQ ; 7) (Business monitor. M ; 7). — *Quarterly*

INDUSTRIAL CONCENTRATION — United States

ADAMS, Walter
The bigness complex : industry, labor, and government in the American economy / Walter Adams and James W. Brock. — 1st ed. — New York : Pantheon Books, 1986. — xiii, 426 p.. — *Includes indexes. — Bibliography: p. 381-413*

BAIN, Joe Staten
Industrial organization : a treatise / by Joe S. Bain, P. David Qualls. — Greenwich, Conn. : JAI Press, c1987. — 2 v.. — (Monographs in organizational behavior and industrial relations ; v. 6). — *Includes bibliographies and index*

INDUSTRIAL DESIGN COORDINATION

KIRBY, John
Creating the library identity : a manual of design / John Kirby. — Aldershot : Gower, c1985. — ix,140p. — (A Grafton book). — *Fiche in pocket. — "Copyright freesheets" in pocket. — Bibliography: p137-138. — Includes index*

INDUSTRIAL DEVELOPMENT BANK OF INDIA

SINGH, Vimal Shankar
Development banking in India / Vimal Shankar Singh. — New Delhi : Deep & Deep Publications, c1985. — 376 p.. — *Includes index. — Bibliography: p. [371]-374*

INDUSTRIAL DEVELOPMENT PROJECTS — Australia

Review of the Industries Assistance Commission. — Canberra : Australian Government Publishing Service
Vol.2: Submissions to the review
Pt.1. — 1984. — 1v (various pagings)

Review of the Industries Assistance Commission. — Canberra : Australian Government Publishing Service
Vol.3: Submissions to the review
Pt.2. — 1984. — 1v (various pagings)

INDUSTRIAL DEVELOPMENT PROJECTS — Greece

APOSTOLOPOULOS, Yannis N.
Maritime industrial area : a new investment concept for shipping and industry / Yannis N. Apostolopoulos. — Athens : Development Division, Hellenic Industrial Development Bank, 1984. — 135p. — *Bibliography: p133-135*

INDUSTRIAL DISTRICTS — Law and legislation — Colombia

COLOMBIA
[Laws, etc]. Decreto no. 2613 (Diciembre 14 de 1976), por el cual se adoptan medidas de estímulo a la organización de parques industriales. — Bogotá : Departamento Nacional de Planeación, Unidad de Desarrollo Regional y Urbano, División de Estudios Regionales, 1976. — 7leaves

INDUSTRIAL EQUIPMENT — Netherlands — Statistics

Bijdragen tot de statistieken betreffende de kapitaalgoederenvoorraal 1985. — 's-Gravenhage : Staatsuitgeverij, 1986. — 66p. — *Contents list and summary in English. — Title on back cover: Contributions to the statistics on stocks of capital goods 1985*

INDUSTRIAL EQUIPMENT INDUSTRY — Developing countries

The capital goods sector in developing countries : technology issues and policy options : study / by the UNCTAD secretariat. — New York : United Nations, 1985. — xxiv,183p. — ([Document] / United Nations ; UNCTAD/TT/78). — *Sales no.: E.85.II.D.4*

INDUSTRIAL HYGIENE

ANDREONI, Diego
The cost of occupational accidents and diseases / Diego Andreoni. — Geneva : International Labour Office, 1986. — viii, 142p. — (Occupational safety and health series ; no.54). — *Bibliography: p135-142*

INDUSTRIAL HYGIENE — Bibliography
PANTRY, Sheila
Health and safety : a guide to sources of information / compiled by Sheila Pantry. — 2nd rev. ed. — Edinburgh : Capital Planning Information, 1985. — 103p.in various pagings. — (CPI information reviews ; no.6).
Previous ed.: 1983. — Includes bibliography and index

INDUSTRIAL HYGIENE — Government — India
SUFRIN, Sidney C.
Bhopal, its setting, responsibility, and challenge / Sidney C. Surfin. — Delhi : Ajanta Publications : Distributors, Ajanta Books International, 1985. — 98 p.. — *60-9*

INDUSTRIAL HYGIENE — Law and legislation — Denmark
The Occupational Safety, Health and Welfare (General) Act, 1968. — [Copenhagen : Ministry of Labour], 1968. — 49 leaves. — *Promulgated by the Ministry of Labour on 4th July 1968*

INDUSTRIAL HYGIENE — Moral and ethical aspects
The Environment of the workplace and human values / editor, Sheldon W. Samuels. — New York : Liss, c1986. — vii, 118 p.. — *Published also as the American journal of industrial medicine, v. 9, no. 1, 1986. — Conference cosponsored by the Labor Policy Institute and the Marshall-Wythe School of Law at the College of William and Mary, May 20-22, 1982. — Includes bibliographical references and index*

INDUSTRIAL HYGIENE — Societies, etc. — Directories
Conditions of work and quality of working life : a directory of institutions / edited by Linda Stoddart. — 2nd ed. — Geneva : International Labour Office, 1986. — xxi,306

INDUSTRIAL HYGIENE — Denmark
Bedriftssundhedstjenesten og virksomhederne : rapport nr.4 fra BST-undersøgelsen / Hans Dankert...[et al.]. — København : Socialforskningsinstituttet : Institut for Arbejdsmiljø ved Danmarks Tekniske Højskole, 1986. — 189p. — (Publikation / Socialforskningsinstituttet ; 152). — *Bibliography: p185-186*

NORD-LARSEN, Mogens
Bedriftssundhedstjenesten i udvikling 1982-1985 : rapport nr.3 fra BST-undersøgelsen. — København : Socialforskningsinstituttet : Institut for Arbejdsmiljø ved Danmarks Tekniske Højskole, 1986. — 188p. — (Publikation / Socialforskningsinstituttet ; 151)

INDUSTRIAL HYGIENE — Great Britain
Employee participation in health and safety : the impact of the legislative provisions : first report of a survey of thirty organisations / undertaken by Brenda Barrett, Richard Howells, Philip James. — [London] : Middlesex Polytechnic, Business School, 1985. — [230]p. — *Bibliography: p277-279*

INDUSTRIAL HYGIENE — Norway — Management — Employee participation
LEWIS, Gary A.
News from somewhere : connecting health and freedom at the workplace / Gary A. Lewis. — New York : Greenwood Press, 1986. — xii, 213 p.. — (Contributions in political science ; no. 151). — *Includes index. — Bibliography: p. [185]-195*

INDUSTRIAL HYGIENE — Spain — History — 19th century
MONLAU, Pere Felip
Condiciones de vida y trabajo obrero en España a mediados del siglo XIX / Pere Felip Monlau y Joaquim Salarich ; estudio preliminar y notas críticas a cargo de Antoni Jutglar. — Barcelona : Anthropos, 1984. — 290p. — (Historia, ideas y textos ; 6). — *Reprint of "Higiene industrial" by P. F. Monlau (Madrid, 1856) and "Higiene del tejedor" by J. Salarich (Vich, 1858)*

INDUSTRIAL HYGIENE — United States
The language of risk : conflicting perspectives on occupational health / edited by Dorothy Nelkin. — Beverly Hills : Sage Publications, c1985. — p. cm. — (Sage Focus edition ; v. 71). — *Includes bibliographies and index*

INDUSTRIAL HYGIENE — United States — History — 20th century
Dying for work : workers' safety and health in twentieth-century America / edited by David Rosner and Gerald Markowitz. — Bloomington : Indiana University Press, c1987. — xx, 234 p.. — *Includes index. — Bibliography: p. 224-225*

INDUSTRIAL LAWS AND LEGISLATION — Congresses
Law and economics and the economics of legal regulation / edited by J.-Matthias Graf v.d. Schulenburg, Göran Skogh. — Dordrecht ; Boston : M. Nijhoff, 1986. — p. cm. — (International studies in economics and econometrics ; 13). — *"Selected papers of a conference of the International Institute of Management Wissenschaftszentum Berlin.". — Includes index. — Contents: Law and economics and the economics of legal regulation / Göran Skogh -- Efficiency, equity, and inalienability / Susan Rose-Ackerman -- Negotiated settlement / Gordon Tullock -- Economic efficiency and the common law / Peter H. Aranson -- Default risk and the optimal pricing of court enforcement services / Hugh Gravelle -- Transaction cost and communincation / Michael Hutter -- Regulatory measures to enforce quality production of self-employed professinals / J.-Matthias Graf v.d. Schulenburg -- Controlling insider trading in Europe and America / David D. Haddock, Jonathan R. Macey -- The regulatin of shop opening hours in the United Kingdom / Susan M. Jaffer, John A. Kay Belgian public policy towards the retailing trade / Roger Van den Bergh -- Assessing the effectiveness of economic efficiency of an E.E.C. pollution control directive / John Ashworth, Ivy Papps, David J. Storey*

INDUSTRIAL LAWS AND LEGISLATION — Africa
OCRAN, Tawia Modibo
Law in aid of development : issues in legal theory, institution building, and economic development in Africa / Tawia Modibo Ocran. — Tema, Ghana : Ghana Pub. Corp., 1978. — xii, 247 p.. — *Includes bibliographical references*

INDUSTRIAL LAWS AND LEGISLATION — Ecuador
ECUADOR
[Laws, etc.]. Leyes de fomento : industrial, pequeña industria y artesanía, parques industriales. — Quito : Corporación de Estudios y Publicaciones, 1976. — [66]p

INDUSTRIAL LAWS AND LEGISLATION — India — History
MARATHE, Shared S.
Regulation and development : India´s experience of controls over industry / Shared S. Marathe ; under the auspices of the Centre for Policy Research. — New Delhi ; Beverly Hills : Sage Publications, 1986. — p. cm. — *Includes index. — Bibliography: p*

INDUSTRIAL LAWS AND LEGISLATION — United States — History
BINDLER, Norman
The conservative court, 1910-1930 / by Norman Bindler. — Port Washington, N.Y. : Associated Faculty Press, 1986. — p. cm. — (The Supreme Court in American life series). — *Includes index. — Bibliography: p*

INDUSTRIAL MANAGEMENT
ABDULLAEVA, K. Sh.
Planirovanie i ekonomicheskoe stimulirovanie v sisteme upravleniia proizvodstvom : (opyt i rezul'taty eksperimental'nykh issledovanii) / K. Sh. Abdullaeva, E. G. Krushel', V. A. Galushkin. — Frunze : Ilim, 1983. — 162p. — *Bibliography: p154-[161]*

DOWNS, George W
The search for government efficiency : from hubris to helplessness / George W. Downs, Patrick D. Larkey. — 1st ed. — Philadelphia : Temple University Press, c1986. — viii, 273 p.. — *Includes bibliographies*

Organizing industrial development / editor, Rolf H. Wolff. — Berlin ; New York : W. de Gruyter, 1986. — p. cm. — (De Gruyter studies in organization ; 7). — *Includes index. — Bibliography: p*

URWICK, Lyndall Fownes
The elements of administration / by L. Urwick. — 2nd ed. — London : Pitman, 1951. — 132p. — *Bibliography: p[12]*

INDUSTRIAL MANAGEMENT — Dictionaries
HUCZYNSKI, Andrzej
Encyclopedia of organizational change methods / Andrzej Huczynski. — Aldershot : Gower, c1987. — xxvi,344p. — *Bibliography: p341-344. — Includes index*

INDUSTRIAL MANAGEMENT — Belgium — Case studies
GANDOIS, Jean
Mission acier : mon aventure belge / Jean Gandois. — Gembloux : Duculot Perspectives, 1986. — 141p

INDUSTRIAL MANAGEMENT — Developing countries
SAEED, Syed Mumtaz
Managerial challenge in the Third World / by Syed Mumtaz Saeed. — New York : Praeger, 1986. — p. cm. — *Includes index. — Bibliography: p*

INDUSTRIAL MANAGEMENT — Europe
SERVAN-SCHREIBER, J. J.
The American challenge / J. J. Servan-Schreiber ; translated from the French by Ronald Steel ; with a foreword by Arthur Schlesinger, Jr.. — New York : Atheneum, 1979. — 254p. — *Originally published as Le défi américain, by Denöel, 1967*

INDUSTRIAL MANAGEMENT — Europe, Eastern
Organizatsiia obucheniia khoziaistvennykh rukovoditelei : opyt sotsialisticheskikh stran / pod redaktsiei F. M. Rusinova, T. V. Burgeevoi. — Moskva : Ekonomika, 1986. — 255p

INDUSTRIAL MANAGEMENT — France
MAURICE, Marc
The social foundations of industrial power : a comparison of France and Germany / Marc Maurice, François Sellier, and Jean-Jacques Silvestre ; translated by Arthur Goldhammer. — Cambridge, Mass ; London : MIT Press, c1986. — xi, 292p. — *Translation of: Politique d'éducation et organisation industrielle en France et en Allemagne. — Includes index*

INDUSTRIAL MANAGEMENT — Germany (West)
JAPANISCH-DEUTSCHES SYMPOSIUM (1983 : Köln)
Die Arbeitswelt in Japan und in der Bundesrepublik Deutschland : ein Vergleich : Japanisch-Deutsches Symposium am 27./28. Juni 1983 im Japanischen Kulturinstitut in Köln / herausgegeben von Peter Hanau...[et al.]. — Darmstadt : Luchterhand, 1983. — ix,162p

MAURICE, Marc
The social foundations of industrial power : a comparison of France and Germany / Marc Maurice, François Sellier, and Jean-Jacques Silvestre ; translated by Arthur Goldhammer. — Cambridge, Mass ; London : MIT Press, c1986. — xi, 292p. — *Translation of: Politique d'éducation et organisation industrielle en France et en Allemagne. — Includes index*

INDUSTRIAL MANAGEMENT — Great Britain
ANTHONY, P. D.
The foundation of management / P.D. Anthony. — London : Tavistock, 1986. — 211p. — (Social science paperbacks ; no.324). — Bibliography: p200-205. — Includes index

INDUSTRIAL MANAGEMENT — Great Britain — Case studies
ADAMSON, Ian
Sinclair and the sunrise technology : the deconstruction of a myth / Ian Adamson and Richard Kennedy. — Harmondsworth : Penguin, 1986. — 262p

CONFEDERATION OF BRITISH INDUSTRY
Managing change : the organisation of work / CBI. — London : Confederation of British Industry, 1985. — 99p

LESSEM, Ronnie
Enterprise development / Ronnie Lessem. — Aldershot : Gower, c1986. — x,190p. — Includes bibliography

INDUSTRIAL MANAGEMENT — Great Britain — Employee participation
TOWERS, Brian
Worker-directors in private manufacturing industry in Great Britain. — [London] : Department of Employment, 1987. — 34p. — (Research paper / Department of Employment ; no.29). — Bibliography: p33-34

INDUSTRIAL MANAGEMENT — India — Employee participation
VISHNU GOPAL
Industrial democracy in India : a sociological study of workers' participation in management / by Vishnu Gopal. — Allahabad, India : Chugh, c1984. — xxviii, 535 p.. — : Revision of the author's thesis (Ph. D.--Banaras Hindu University, 1983) under the title: Workers' participation in management : a sociological study of the new scheme of shop and the joint councils. — Includes index. — Bibliography: p. [501]-526

INDUSTRIAL MANAGEMENT — Japan
JAPANISCH-DEUTSCHES SYMPOSIUM (1983 : Köln)
Die Arbeitswelt in Japan und in der Bundesrepublik Deutschland : ein Vergleich : Japanisch-Deutsches Symposium am 27./28. Juni 1983 im Japanischen Kulturinstitut in Köln / herausgegeben von Peter Hanau...[et al.]. — Darmstadt : Luchterhand, 1983. — ix,162p

MATSUMOTO, Kogi
Organizing for higher productivity : an analysis of Japanese systems and practices / Koji Matsumoto. — Tokyo : Asian Productivity Organization, 1982. — 75p. — Includes bibliographical references

[Nichi-Bei kigyō no keiei hikaku. English]. Strategic vs. evolutionary management : a U.S.-Japan comparison of strategy and organization / Tadao Kagono ... [et al.] ; in collaboration with Shiori Sakamoto, Johhny K. Johansson. — Amsterdam ; New York : North-Holland ; New York : Sole distributors for the U.S.A. and Canada, Elsevier Science Pub. Co., 1985. — p. cm. — (Advanced series in management ; v. 10). — Translation of: Nichi-Bei kigyō no keiei hikaku

ODAKA, Kunio
Japanese management : a forward-looking analysis / Kunio Odaka. — Tokyo : Asian Productivity Organization, 1986. — v,85p. — Includes bibliographical references

SETHI, S. Prakash
The false promise of the Japanese miracle : illusion and realities of the Japanese management system / S. Prakash Sethi, Nobuaki Namiki, Carl L. Swanson. — Boston : Pitman, c1984. — xxi, 361 p.. — (Pitman series in business and public policy). — Includes indexes. — Bibliography: p. 321-340

INDUSTRIAL MANAGEMENT — Northwest, Pacific — Employee participation — Case studies
GREENBERG, Edward S.
Workplace democracy : the political effects of participation / Edward S. Greenberg. — Ithaca : Cornell University Press, 1986. — p. cm. — Includes index. — Bibliography: p

INDUSTRIAL MANAGEMENT — Romania — Employee representation
BABE, Alecsandru
Mecanismul autogestiunii în unitătile economice / Alecsandru Babe. — Bucureşti : Editura Politică, 1986. — 303p. — Table of contents in English, French, German and Russian

INDUSTRIAL MANAGEMENT — South Africa
NEL, P. S
Worker representation in practice in South Africa / P.S. Nel and P.H. van Rooyen. — Pretoria : Academica, 1985. — 170 p.. — Bibliography: p. 166-170

INDUSTRIAL MANAGEMENT — Soviet Union
KULISH, N. E.
Upravlenie agro-promyshlennymi obʺedineniiami v usloviiakh integrirovannoi ekonomiki / N. E. Kulish. — Kiev ; Odessa : Vyshcha Shkola, 1985. — 174p. — (Voprosy agropromyshlennoi integratsii). — Bibliography: p168-[173]

Organizatsiia obucheniia khoziaistvennykh rukovoditelei : opyt sotsialisticheskikh stran / pod redaktsiei F. M. Rusinova, T. V. Burgeevoi. — Moskva : Ekonomika, 1986. — 255p

Rezervy povysheniia effektivnosti proizvodstva / [A. N. Zolotarev...et al.]. — Kiev : Naukova dumka, 1983. — 200p. — Bibliography: p196-[201]

INDUSTRIAL MANAGEMENT — Soviet Union — Dictionaries
Upravlenie ekonomiki : [slovar-spravochnik] : osnovnye poniatiia i kategoriia / pod redaktsiei R. A. Belousova i A. Z. Selezneva. — Moskva : Ekonomika, 1986. — 302p

INDUSTRIAL MANAGEMENT — Soviet Union — Mathematical models
Perspektivnoe otraslevoe planirovanie : ekonomiko-matematicheskie metody i modeli / otv. redaktor A. G. Aganbegian. — Novosibirsk : Nauka, Sibirskoe otdelenie, 1986. — 355p. — Bibliography: p350-[356]

INDUSTRIAL MANAGEMENT — United States
[Nichi-Bei kigyō no keiei hikaku. English]. Strategic vs. evolutionary management : a U.S.-Japan comparison of strategy and organization / Tadao Kagono ... [et al.] ; in collaboration with Shiori Sakamoto, Johhny K. Johansson. — Amsterdam ; New York : North-Holland ; New York : Sole distributors for the U.S.A. and Canada, Elsevier Science Pub. Co., 1985. — p. cm. — (Advanced series in management ; v. 10). — Translation of: Nichi-Bei kigyō no keiei hikaku

PETERS, Thomas J
A passion for excellence : the leadership difference / Tom Peters, Nancy Austin. — Warner books ed. — New York, N.Y. : Warner Books, 1986, c1985. — p. cm. — : Reprint. Originally published: New York : Random House, c1985. — Includes index. — Bibliography: p

SERVAN-SCHREIBER, J. J.
The American challenge / J. J. Servan-Schreiber ; translated from the French by Ronald Steel ; with a foreword by Arthur Schlesinger, Jr.. — New York : Atheneum, 1979. — 254p. — Originally published as Le défi américain, by Denöel, 1967

SETHI, S. Prakash
The false promise of the Japanese miracle : illusion and realities of the Japanese management system / S. Prakash Sethi, Nobuaki Namiki, Carl L. Swanson. — Boston : Pitman, c1984. — xxi, 361 p.. — (Pitman series in business and public policy). — Includes indexes. — Bibliography: p. 321-340

Views from the top : establishing the foundation for the future of business / edited by Jerome M. Rosow. — London : Sphere, 1987. — xv,[208]p. — Originally published: Facts on File, 1985

INDUSTRIAL MANAGEMENT — United States — Case studies
JURAVICH, Tom
Chaos on the shop floor : a worker's view of quality, productivity, and management / by Tom Juravich. — Philadelphia : Temple University Press, 1985. — ix, 160 p.. — (Labor and social change). — Includes index. — Bibliography: p. 153-160

INDUSTRIAL MANAGEMENT — United States — Case Studies
Productivity and quality through people : practices of well-managed companies / edited by Y.K. Shetty and Vernon M. Buehler ; foreword by John A. Young. — Westport, Conn. : Quorum Books, 1985. — xvi, 351 p.. — Includes index. — Bibliography: p. [329]-340

INDUSTRIAL MANAGEMENT — United States — Employee participation
Teamwork, joint labor-management programs in America / edited by Jerome M. Rosow. — New York : Pergamon Press, c1986. — xvi, 199 p.. — (Pergamon Press/Work in America Institute series). — Includes bibliographies and index

INDUSTRIAL MARKETING
CHISNALL, Peter M.
Strategic industrial marketing / Peter M. Chisnall. — Englewood Cliffs ; London : Prentice Hall International, c1985. — xiv,352p. — Includes index

INDUSTRIAL MARKETING — Research — Germany (West)
Industrial marketing : a German-American perspective / edited by Klaus Backhaus and David T. Wilson. — Berlin ; New York : Springer-Verlag, 1986. — viii,373p

INDUSTRIAL MARKETING — Research — United States
Industrial marketing : a German-American perspective / edited by Klaus Backhaus and David T. Wilson. — Berlin ; New York : Springer-Verlag, 1986. — viii,373p

INDUSTRIAL ORGANIZATION
ALVESSON, Mats
[Organisationsteori och teknokratiskt medvetande. English]. Organization theory and technocratic consciousness : rationality, ideology, and quality of work / Mats Alvesson. — Berlin ; New York : W. De Gruyter, 1987. — p. cm. — (De Gruyter studies in organization ; 8). — Translation of: Organisationsteori och teknokratiskt medvetande. — Includes index. — Bibliography: p

BIDWELL, Charles E
The organization and its ecosystem : a theory of structuring in organizations / by Charles E. Bidwell, John D. Kasarda. — Greenwich, Conn. : JAI Press, c1985. — xxiv, 248 p.. — (Monographs in organizational behavior and industrial relations ; v. 2). — Includes indexes. — Bibliography: p. 229-236

International review of industrial and organizational psychology. — Chichester : John Wiley, 1986-. — Annual

REID, Gavin C
Theories of industrial organization / Gavin C. Reid. — Oxford : Basil Blackwell, 1987. — [256]p. — Includes bibliography and index

INDUSTRIAL ORGANIZATION
continuation

TIROLE, Jean
Concurrence imparfaite / Jean Tirole. — Paris : Economica, c1985. — 133p. — (Economie et statistiques avencées)

WHITE, G. C.
Redesign of work organisations - its impact on supervisors / Geoff White. — London : Work Research Unit, 1983. — 10p. — (WRU occasional paper ; 26). — *At head of title page: Advisory, Conciliation and Arbitration Service.* — *Bibliographical references: p9-10*

INDUSTRIAL ORGANIZATION — Case studies

LORSCH, Jay William, comp
Organization planning; cases and concepts / Edited by Jay W. Lorsch [and] Paul R. Lawrence. — Homewood, Ill. : R. D. Irwin, inc., 1972. — x, 341 p. — (The Irwin-Dorsey series in behavioral science). — *Bibliography: p. 73-74*

INDUSTRIAL ORGANIZATION — Congresses

Mainstreams in industrial organization / edited by H.W. de Jong, W.G. Shepherd. — Dordrecht ; Boston : Kluwer Academic Publishers, 1986. — 2 v. (x, 465 p.). — (Studies in industrial organization ; 6). — *Essays and part of the discussions presented at a conference held Aug. 21-23, 1985 at the University of Amsterdam. — Bibliography: p. 463-465. — Contents: bk. 1. Theory and international aspects -- bk. 2. Policies, antitrust, deregulation, and industrial*

INDUSTRIAL ORGANIZATION — History

LITTLER, Craig R.
The development of the labour process in capitalist societies : a comparative study of the transformation of work organization in Britain, Japan and the USA / Craig R. Littler. — Aldershot : Gower, 1986, c1982. — [240]p. — *Originally published: London : Heinemann Educational, 1982*

INDUSTRIAL ORGANIZATION — Germany (West)

GRANT, Wyn
Why employer organisation matters : a comparative analysis of business association activity in Britain and West Germany / Wyn Grant. — Coventry : University of Warwick, 1986. — 29p. — (Working paper / University of Warwick ; no.42). — *Bibliography: p28-29*

JAPANISCH-DEUTSCHES SYMPOSIUM (1983 : Köln)
Die Arbeitswelt in Japan und in der Bundesrepublik Deutschland : ein Vergleich : Japanisch-Deutsches Symposium am 27./28. Juni 1983 im Japanischen Kulturinstitut in Köln / herausgegeben von Peter Hanau...[et al.]. — Darmstadt : Luchterhand, 1983. — ix,162p

INDUSTRIAL ORGANIZATION — Great Britain

GRANT, Wyn
Why employer organisation matters : a comparative analysis of business association activity in Britain and West Germany / Wyn Grant. — Coventry : University of Warwick, 1986. — 29p. — (Working paper / University of Warwick ; no.42). — *Bibliography: p28-29*

NATIONAL ECONOMIC DEVELOPMENT OFFICE
Changing working patterns and practices : memorandum / by the Director General. — [London] : National Economic Development Council, 1985. — 1pamphlet (various pagings). — *NEDC: (85) 84*

INDUSTRIAL ORGANIZATION — Japan

JAPANISCH-DEUTSCHES SYMPOSIUM (1983 : Köln)
Die Arbeitswelt in Japan und in der Bundesrepublik Deutschland : ein Vergleich : Japanisch-Deutsches Symposium am 27./28. Juni 1983 im Japanischen Kulturinstitut in Köln / herausgegeben von Peter Hanau...[et al.]. — Darmstadt : Luchterhand, 1983. — ix,162p

MATSUMOTO, Kogi
Organizing for higher productivity : an analysis of Japanese systems and practices / Koji Matsumoto. — Tokyo : Asian Productivity Organization, 1982. — 75p. — *Includes bibliographical references*

[Nichi-Bei kigyō no keiei hikaku. English]. Strategic vs. evolutionary management : a U.S.-Japan comparison of strategy and organization / Tadao Kagono ... [et al.] ; in collaboration with Shiori Sakamoto, Johhny K. Johansson. — Amsterdam ; New York : North-Holland ; New York : Sole distributors for the U.S.A. and Canada, Elsevier Science Pub. Co., 1985. — p. cm. — (Advanced series in management ; v. 10). — *Translation of: Nichi-Bei kigyō no keiei hikaku*

SELL, R. G.
Work organisation and attitudes in some Japanese factories : a report of a study tour / Reg Sell. — London : Work Research Unit, 1983. — 62p. — *At head of title page: Advisory, Conciliation and Arbitration Service.* — *Bibliographical references: p45*

INDUSTRIAL ORGANIZATION — Japan — Case studies

ROHLEN, Thomas P
For harmony and strength : Japanese white-collar organization in anthropological perspective / Thomas P. Rohlen. — Berkeley : University of California Press, [1974]. — 285 p., [4] leaves of plates. — *Includes index.* — *Bibliography: p. [271]-280*

INDUSTRIAL ORGANIZATION — Soviet Union

KHRUSHCHEV, A. T.
Geografiia promyshlennosti SSSR / A. T. Khrushchev. — 3-e izd., perer. i dop.. — Moskva : Mysl', 1986. — 415p

Planirovanie razmeshcheniia proizvoditel'nykh sil SSSR : osushchestvlenie politiki KPSS na etapakh sotsialisticheskogo stroitel'stva / [red. kollegiia: V. P. Mozhin...et al.]. — Moskva : Ekonomika
Ch.2: Planirovanie razmeshcheniia proizvoditel'nykh sil na etape razvitogo sotsializma. — 1986. — 382p

ZASTAVNYI, F. D.
Sovershenstvovanie territorial'noi organizatsii proizvoditel'nykh sil : teoriia, metody, praktika / F. D. Zastavnyi ; otv. redaktor N. T. Agafonov. — Leningrad : Nauka, Leningradskoe otdelenie, 1986. — 139p

INDUSTRIAL ORGANIZATION — Ukraine

Planovoe upravlenie ekonomikoi razvitogo sotsializma / redaktsionnaia kollegiia: A. S. Emel'ianov...[et al.]. — Kiev : Naukova dumka . — *V piati tomakh*
T.5: Otraslevye problemy planovogo razvitiia ekonomiki respubliki / otv. redaktor A. S. Emel'ianov. — 1986. — 403p. — *Bibliography: p299-[302]*

INDUSTRIAL ORGANIZATION — United States

BAIN, Joe Staten
Industrial organization : a treatise / by Joe S. Bain, P. David Qualls. — Greenwich, Conn. : JAI Press, c1987. — 2 v. — (Monographs in organizational behavior and industrial relations ; v. 6). — *Includes bibliographies and index*

[Nichi-Bei kigyō no keiei hikaku. English]. Strategic vs. evolutionary management : a U.S.-Japan comparison of strategy and organization / Tadao Kagono ... [et al.] ; in collaboration with Shiori Sakamoto, Johhny K. Johansson. — Amsterdam ; New York : North-Holland ; New York : Sole distributors for the U.S.A. and Canada, Elsevier Science Pub. Co., 1985. — p. cm. — (Advanced series in management ; v. 10). — *Translation of: Nichi-Bei kigyō no keiei hikaku*

INDUSTRIAL ORGANIZATION (ECONOMIC THEORY)

BAIN, Joe Staten
Industrial organization : a treatise / by Joe S. Bain, P. David Qualls. — Greenwich, Conn. : JAI Press, c1987. — 2 v. — (Monographs in organizational behavior and industrial relations ; v. 6). — *Includes bibliographies and index*

BOLTON, Patrick
The role of contracts in industrial organisation theory / by Patrick Bolton. — 182 leaves. — *PhD (Econ) 1986 LSE*

The Economics of the firm / edited by Roger Clarke and Tony McGuinness. — Oxford : Basil Blackwell, 1987. — 190p. — *Bibliography : p174-185.* — *Includes index*

HERRERO-DELGADO, Maria Jose
A strategic bargaining approach to market institutions / by Maria-Jose Herrero-Delgado. — 152 leaves. — *PhD (Econ) 1985 LSE*

JACQUEMIN, Alexis
The new industrial organization : market forces and strategic behaviour / Alexis Jacquemin ; translated by Fatemeh Mehta. — Oxford : Clarendon, 1987. — xii. — *Translation of: Sélection et pouvoir dans la nouvelle économie industrielle.* — *Includes bibliographies and index*

New developments in the analysis of market structure : proceedings of a conference held by the International Economic Association in Ottawa, Canada / edited by Joseph E. Stiglitz and G. Frank Mathewson. — Basingstoke : Macmillan, 1986. — xxiv,559p. — *Includes bibliographies and index*

Strategic behaviour and industrial competition / edited by D.J. Morris ... [et al.]. — Oxford : Clarendon, 1986. — 243p. — (Oxford economic papers. New series ; v.38, suppl). — *Includes bibliographies*

INDUSTRIAL ORGANIZATION (ECONOMIC THEORY) — Mathematical models

BOWRING, Joseph
Competition in a dual economy / Joseph Bowring. — Princeton, N.J. : Princeton University Press, c1986. — p. cm. — *Includes index.* — *Bibliography: p*

INDUSTRIAL PROCUREMENT — Contracts and specifications

Procurement of goods. — [Washington, D.C.? : World Bank?], 1983. — iii,44p. — (Sample bidding documents)

INDUSTRIAL PRODUCTIVITY — Congresses

The Global economy : divergent perspectives on economic change / edited by Edward W. Gondolf, Irwin M. Marcus, and James P. Dougherty. — Boulder : Westview Press, 1986. — xvii, 212 p.. — (Westview special studies in international economics and business). — *"Essays ... drawn from a conference on 'Industry and society' at Indiana University of Pennsylvania"--Acknowledgments*

Technology and human productivity : challenges for the future / edited by John W. Murphy and John T. Pardeck. — New York : Quorum Books, 1986. — xx, 236 p.. — *"Result of the proceedings of the conference titled 'Technology and human productivity: myth or reality,' held at Arkansas State University, April 12-13, 1985"--Foreword.* — *Includes index.* — *Bibliography: p. [225]-228*

INDUSTRIAL PRODUCTIVITY — Mathematical models

Measurement issues and behavior of productivity variables / edited by Ali Dogramaci. — Boston : Kluwer Nijhoff ; Hingham, MA, USA : Distributors for the United States and Canada, Kluwer Academic Publishers, c1986. — ix, 262 p.. — (Studies in productivity analysis). — *Includes bibliographies and indexes*

INDUSTRIAL PRODUCTIVITY — Measurement — Computer programs

MUNDEL, Marvin Everett
Measuring total productivity in manufacturing organizations : algorithms and P-C programs / Marvin E. Mundel. — Tokyo, Japan : Asian Productivity Organization, c1986. — iv[i.e.vi], 155p. — *Includes index*

INDUSTRIAL PRODUCTIVITY — Measurement — Data processing

MUNDEL, Marvin Everett
Measuring total productivity in manufacturing organizations : algorithms and P-C programs / Marvin E. Mundel. — Tokyo, Japan : Asian Productivity Organization, c1986. — iv[i.e.vi], 155p. — *Includes index*

INDUSTRIAL PRODUCTIVITY — Australia

Structured chaos : the process of productivity advance / Richard Blandy...[et al.]. — Melbourne ; Oxford : Oxford University Press, 1985. — viii,111p. — *Published in conjunction with the Australian Productivity Council and the National Institute of Labour Studies. — Bibliography: p101-107*

INDUSTRIAL PRODUCTIVITY — Communist countries

Ekonomiia vremeni i effektivnost' sotsialisticheskogo proizvodstva / pod redaktsiei M. S. Atlas, A. G. Griaznovoi. — Moskva : Ekonomika, 1986. — 237p

INDUSTRIAL PRODUCTIVITY — Great Britain — History — 20th century

DAVIES, S. W.
Britain's productivity gap / Stephen Davies, Richard E. Caves. — Cambridge : Cambridge University Press, 1987. — xiv,131p. — (Occasional papers / The National Institute of Economic and Social Research ; 40). — *Bibliography: p122-127. — Includes index*

INDUSTRIAL PRODUCTIVITY — Norway

HALVORSEN, Ragnar
Lønnsomhetskrav : Strategi for lønnsom vekst sett fra Dyno Industrier A.S' side / Ragnar Halvorsen. — Bergen : Norges handelshøyskole, 1985. — 34p. — (Kristofer Lehmkuhl Forelesning ; 1985)

INDUSTRIAL PRODUCTIVITY — Soviet Union

PAPENOV, K. V.
Rezervy obshchestvennogo proizvodstva : (voprosy teorii i praktiki) / K. V. Papenov. — Moskva : Izd-vo Moskovskogo universiteta, 1985. — 143p

INDUSTRIAL PRODUCTIVITY — United States — Case studies

Productivity and quality through people : practices of well-managed companies / edited by Y.K. Shetty and Vernon M. Buehler ; foreword by John A. Young. — Westport, Conn. : Quorum Books, 1985. — xvi, 351 p.. — *Includes index. — Bibliography: p.[329]-340*

INDUSTRIAL PRODUCTIVITY — United States — History — 20th century

DAVIES, S. W.
Britain's productivity gap / Stephen Davies, Richard E. Caves. — Cambridge : Cambridge University Press, 1987. — xiv,131p. — (Occasional papers / The National Institute of Economic and Social Research ; 40). — *Bibliography: p122-127. — Includes index*

INDUSTRIAL PRODUCTIVITY — United States — Measurement

MUNDEL, Marvin Everett
Improving productivity and effectiveness / Marvin E. Mundel. — Englewood Cliffs, N.J. : Prentice-Hall, c1983. — x,467p. — (Prentice-Hall international series in industrial and systems engineering). — *Includes bibliographical references*

INDUSTRIAL PROMOTION — Australia

Review of the Industries Assistance Commission. — Canberra : Australian Government Publishing Service
Vol.2: Submissions to the review
Pt.1. — 1984. — 1v (various pagings)

Review of the Industries Assistance Commission. — Canberra : Australian Government Publishing Service
Vol.3: Submissions to the review
Pt.2. — 1984. — 1v (various pagings)

INDUSTRIAL PROMOTION — Australia — Tasmania

TASMANIAN DEVELOPMENT AUTHORITY
Review of operations / Tasmanian Development Authority. — Hobart : the Authority, 1984/5-. — Annual

INDUSTRIAL PROMOTION — Developing countries

GREAT BRITAIN. Overseas Development Administration. Economic Planning Staff
Project handbook : small-scale enterprises. — [London] : the Adminstration, [1979]. — 10leaves. — *Bibliography: leaf[10]*

INDUSTRIAL PROMOTION — England

DEVELOPMENT COMMISSION FOR RURAL ENGLAND
Action for rural enterprise : a guide to the assistance available to business in rural areas of England from the government and other agencies. — [London : the Commission, 1987]. — 29p. — *One of five publications in folder entitled Farming and rural enterprise*

JURUE
Evaluation of industrial and commercial improvement areas / JURUE ; [for the] Department of the Environment. — London : H.M.S.O., 1986. — vi,51p. — *At head of cover title: Inner Cities Research Programme. — Commissioned by the Inner Cities Directorate of the Department of the Environment. — Bibliographical references: p51*

INDUSTRIAL PROMOTION — European Economic Community countries

CLAYTON, M.
Study into EC-wide criteria for the identification of new technology based enterprises / M. Clayton, T. Mitchell. — Luxemburg : Office for Official Publications of the European Communities, 1984. — iv,174p. — (EUR ; 8926). — *Includes bibliographical references*

INDUSTRIAL PROMOTION — Morocco

Morocco : industrial incentives and export promotion. — Washington, D.C., U.S.A. : World Bank, c1984. — Lxxvii,219p. — (A World Bank country study). — *Report prepared by an economic mission that visited Morocco in Sept. 1982 composed of Bela Balassa and others. — Summaries in French and Spanish. — Includes bibliographical references*

INDUSTRIAL PROMOTION — Northern Ireland

INDUSTRIAL DEVELOPMENT BOARD FOR NORTHERN IRELAND
Encouraging enterprise : a medium term strategy for 1985-1990. — Belfast : H.M.S.O., 1985. — 39p

INDUSTRIAL PROMOTION — Pennsylvania

ALLEN, David N
Nurturing advanced technology enterprises : emerging issues in state and local economic development policy / David N. Allen and Victor Levine. — New York : Praeger, 1986. — xvi, 268 p.. — *Includes index. — Bibliography: p. 239-262*

INDUSTRIAL PROMOTION — Scotland

GREAT BRITAIN. Scottish Office
Rural Scotland. — [Edinburgh : the Office, 1987]. — 28p. — *One of five publications in folder entitled Farming and rural enterprise*

INDUSTRIAL PROMOTION — Wales

Action for rural enterprise in Wales / Manpower Services Commission, Mid Wales Development, Wales Tourist Board, Welsh Development Agency. — [Cardiff? : Welsh Development Agency?, 1987]. — 17,19p. — *In English and Welsh. — One of five publications in folder entitled Farming and rural enterprise*

INDUSTRIAL PROPERTY

LADAS, Stephen Pericles
Patents, trademarks, and related rights : national and international protection / Stephen P. Ladas. — Cambridge (Mass.) : Harvard U.P., 1975. — 3v

INDUSTRIAL PROPERTY — European Economic Community countries

La Integración de España en la Comunidad Económica Europea, en materia de propiedad industrial (su problemática). — [Madrid] : Montecorvo, 1979. — 460 p.. — *At head of title: Colegio Universitario de Estudios Financieros. — In French and Spanish. — Title on spine: Integración en la C.E.E. y propiedad industrial*

INDUSTRIAL PROPERTY — Korea (South)

Business laws in Korea : investment, taxation, and industrial property / Chan-jin Kim, editor. — Seoul, Korea : Panmun Book Co., 1982. — xii, 799 p.. — *Includes bibliographical references*

INDUSTRIAL PROPERTY — Spain

La Integración de España en la Comunidad Económica Europea, en materia de propiedad industrial (su problemática). — [Madrid] : Montecorvo, 1979. — 460 p.. — *At head of title: Colegio Universitario de Estudios Financieros. — In French and Spanish. — Title on spine: Integración en la C.E.E. y propiedad industrial*

INDUSTRIAL PROPERTY (INTERNATIONAL LAW)

LADAS, Stephen Pericles
Patents, trademarks, and related rights : national and international protection / Stephen P. Ladas. — Cambridge (Mass.) : Harvard U.P., 1975. — 3v

INDUSTRIAL RELATIONS

Conciliation services : structures, functions and techniques. — Geneva : International Labour Office, 1983. — 141p. — (Labour-management relations series ; 62)

EDWARDS, P. K.
Conflict at work : a materialist analysis of workplace relations / P.K. Edwards. — Oxford : Basil Blackwell, 1986. — [300]p. — (Warwick studies in industrial relations). — *Includes bibliography and index*

FOX, Alan
Man mismanagement / Alan Fox. — London : Hutchinson, 1974. — 178p. — (Industry in action)

Incomes from work : between equity and efficiency. — Geneva : International Labour Office, 1987. — viii,169p. — (World labour report ; 3). — *Bibliography: p165-169*

INDUSTRIAL RELATIONS
continuation

Industrial relations in a new age / Clark Kerr, Paul D. Staudohar, editors. — 1st ed. — San Francisco : Jossey-Bass, 1986. — xx, 419 p.. — (The Jossey-Bass management series). — *Includes bibliographies and indexes*

International and comparative industrial relations : a study of developed market economies / edited by Greg J. Bamber and Russell D. Lansbury. — London : Allen & Unwin, c1987. — xvi,289p. — *Includes bibliographies and index*

JACKSON-COX, Jacqueline
Strategies, issues and events in industrial relations : disclosure of information in context / Jacqueline Jackson-Cox, John McQueeney, John E.M. Thirkell. — London : Routledge & Kegan Paul, 1987. — [216]p. — *Includes bibliography and index*

MARGINSON, Paul
Labour and the modern corporation : mutual interest or control? / Paul Marginson. — Coventry : University of Warwick. School of Industrial and Business Studies. Industrial Relations Research Unit, 1985. — 15 leaves. — (Warwick papers in industrial relations ; no.9). — *Bibliography: p15*

PARKER, Mike
Inside the circle : a union guide to quality of work life / by Mike Parker. — Boston, MA : South End Press, c1985. — p. cm. — *Includes index.* — *Bibliography: p*

RICHARDSON, John Henry
An introduction to the study of industrial relations / John Henry Richardson. — London : Allen and Unwin, 1956. — 442p

SALAMON, M. W.
Industrial relations : theory and practice / Michael Salamon. — Englewood Cliffs, N.J. ; London : Prentice-Hall International, c1987. — xiv,577p. — *Includes bibliographies and index*

Working papers / Princeton University, Industrial Relations Section. — Princeton : Princeton University, 1986-. — *Irregular*

INDUSTRIAL RELATIONS — Bibliography
INFIR: : information in industrial relations / Middlesex Polytechnic Library Services. — Enfield : Middlesex Polytechnic, 1987-. — *6 per year*

INDUSTRIAL RELATIONS — Congresses
Economic and social partnership and incomes policy = : Pacto social e política de rendimentos / edited by Aníbal A. Cavaco Silva. — Lisboa : Faculdade de Ciências Humanas da Universidade Católica Portuguesa, c1984. — 304 p.. — *English, French, and Portuguese.* — *Papers and comemntary presented at the Conference on "Economic and Social Partnership and Incomes Policy" organized by the Austrian Embassy in Portugal and the Faculty of Social Sciences of the Portuguese Catholic University, held Mar. 15-16, 1983, in Lisbon.* — *Includes bibliographical references*

INDUSTRIAL RELATIONS — Dictionaries
ROBERTS, Harold Selig
[Dictionary of industrial relations]. Roberts' Dictionary of industrial relations / Harold S. Roberts. — 3rd ed. / prepared by Industrial Relations Center, University of Hawaii at Manoa. — Washington, D.C. : Bureau of National Affairs, c1986. — xxi, 811 p.. — *Bibliography: p. 803-809*

INDUSTRIAL RELATIONS — Economic aspects — Great Britain
FOGARTY, Michael P.
Trade Unions and British industrial development / Michael Fogarty with Douglas Brooks. — London : Policy Studies Institute, 1986. — 184p. — (Research report / Policy Studies Institute ; [no.658]). — *Bibliographical references*

INDUSTRIAL RELATIONS — History — Addresses, essays, lectures
Technological change and workers' movements / edited by Melvyn Dubofsky. — Beverly Hills : Sage Publications, c1985. — p. cm. — (Explorations in the world-economy ; v. 4). — : *"Originally presented at the Third U.S.-U.S.S.R. Colloquium on World Labor and Social Change held at the State University of New York at Binghamton in January 1983"--Introd*

INDUSTRIAL RELATIONS — Legal status laws, etc.
Selected basic agreements and joint declarations on labour-management relations. — Geneva : International Labour Office, 1983. — iv,299p. — (Labour-management relations series ; 63)

INDUSTRIAL RELATIONS — Africa
Labour-management relations in public enterprises in Africa. — [Geneva] : International Labour Office, [1983]. — 84p. — (Labour-management relations series ; 60)

SYMPOSIUM ON THE DEVELOPMENT OF SOUND LABOUR RELATIONS IN ENGLISH-SPEAKING AFRICAN COUNTRIES (1982 : Nairobi)
Labour-relations in Africa : English-speaking countries : proceedings of and documents submitted to a Symposium (Nairobi, 22-26 November 1982). — Geneva : International Labour Office, 1983. — v,159p. — (Labour-management relations series ; 64)

INDUSTRIAL RELATIONS — Asia — Congresses
ASIAN REGIONAL CONFERENCE ON INDUSTRIAL RELATIONS (6th : 1975 : Tokyo)
Foreign investment and labor in Asian countries : proceedings of the 1975 Asian Regional Conference on Industrial Relations, Tokyo, Japan, 1975. — [Tokyo] : Japan Institute of Labour, [1976]. — iii, 240 p.. — *Held March 17-20, 1975; co-sponsored by the Japan Institute of Labour and the Japan Industrial Relations Research Association.* — *Includes bibliographical References*

INDUSTRIAL RELATIONS — Australia
DEERY, S.
Australian industrial relations / S.Deery, D.Plowman. — 2nd ed.. — Sydney ; London : McGraw-Hill, 1985. — *Previous ed: 1980*

INDUSTRIAL RELATIONS — Austria
TOMANDL, Theodor
Social partnership : the Austrian system of industrial relations and social insurance / Theodor Tomandl, Karl Fuerboeck. — Ithaca, NY : ILR Press, New York State School of Industrial and Labor Relations, Cornell University, c1986. — viii, 165 p.. — (Cornell international industrial and labor relations report ; no. 12). — *Includes index.* — *Bibliography: p. 157-159*

The trade union situation and industrial relations in Austria : report of an ILO mission. — Geneva : International Labour Office, 1986. — xiii,107p. — *Includes bibliographical references*

INDUSTRIAL RELATIONS — British Columbia — Vancouver — History
Working lives : Vancouver 1886-1986 / The Working Lives Collective. — Vancouver : New Star Books, 1985. — 211p. — *References: p202-208*

INDUSTRIAL RELATIONS — Canada
SIMMONS, C. Gordon
Labour relations law in the public sector : cases, materials and commentary / by C. Gordon Simmons and Kenneth P. Swan. — Kingston, Ontario : Industrial Relations Centre, Queen's University, 1982. — xviii,422p

WELLS, Don
Soft sell : "quality of life" programs and the productivity race / by Don Wells. — Ottawa : Canadian Centre for Policy Alternatives, 1986. — xi,97p

INDUSTRIAL RELATIONS — Canada — History
On the job : confronting the labour process in Canada / edited by Craig Heron and Robert Storey. — Kingston : McGill-Queen's University Press, c1986. — xiv, 360 p.. — *Includes bibliographies and index*

INDUSTRIAL RELATIONS — Colombia — Case studies
SAVAGE, Charles H
Sons of the machine : case studies of social change in the workplace / Charles H. Savage and George F.F. Lombard. — Cambridge, Mass : MIT Press, c1986. — xvi, 313 p., [17] pages of plates. — (MIT Press series on organization studies ; 7). — *Includes index.* — *Bibliography: p. 283-291*

INDUSTRIAL RELATIONS — Denmark
Industrial relations in Denmark : basic collective agreements and laws on labour desputes. — Copenhagen : Socialt Tidsskrift, 1947. — 32p. — *Edited and published under the auspices of Socialt Tidsskrift journal*

INDUSTRIAL RELATIONS — Denmark — Bibliography
Bibliography of foreign-language literature on industrial relations and social services in Denmark. — København : Arbejds- og socialministeriernes bibliotek, 1975. — 28 leaves

INDUSTRIAL RELATIONS — England — History — 20th century
MORRIS, Timothy
Innovations in banking : business strategies and employee relations / Timothy Morris. — London : Croom Helm, c1986. — 137p. — *Bibliography: p128-132.* — *Includes index*

INDUSTRIAL RELATIONS — Europe
WEST EUROPEAN CONFERENCE ON THE PSYCHOLOGY OF WORK AND ORGANIZATION (1985 : Aachen, Germany)
The psychology of work and organization : current trends and issues : selected and edited proceedings of the West European Conference on the Psychology of Work and Organization, Aachen, F.R.G., 1-3 April, 1985 / edited by G. Debus and H.-W. Schroiff. — Amsterdam ; New York : North Holland ; New York, N.Y., U.S.A. : Sole distributors for the U.S.A. and Canada, Elsevier Science Pub. Co., 1986. — xi, 407 p.. — *Includes bibliographies and indexes*

INDUSTRIAL RELATIONS — European Economic Community countries
The prevention and settlement of industrial conflict in the Community member states. — Luxembourg : Office for Official Publications of the European Communities, 1984. — 162,16p. — *At head of title page: Commission of the European Communities*

INDUSTRIAL RELATIONS — France
ERBÈS-SEGUIN, Sabine
Syndicats et relations de travail dans la vie économique française / Sabine Erbès-Seguin. — Lille : Presses Universitaires de Lille, 1985. — 137p. — *Bibliography: p135-137*

INDUSTRIAL RELATIONS — Great Britain
ANTHONY, Peter
The conduct of industrial relations / P.D. Anthony. — London : Institute of Personnel Management, 1977. — vi,327p. — *Bibliography: p.322-327*

BICKERSTAFFE, Rodney
Privatisation and low pay : the impact of government policies / Rodney Bickerstaffe. — Nottingham : Trent Polytechnic, 1984. — 46p. — *Trent Business School. Open lectures on industrial relations: the changing contours of collective bargaining*

INDUSTRIAL RELATIONS — Great Britain *continuation*

FARNHAM, David
Understanding industrial relations / David Farnham, John Pimlott. — 3rd ed. — London : Holt, Rinehart and Winston, 1986. — xx,392p. — *Previous ed.: London : Cassell, 1983.* — *Bibliography: p379-383.* — *Includes index*

FERRY, Alex
Bargaining : 1984 and beyond / Alex Ferry. — Nottingham : Trent Polytechnic, 1984. — 39p. — *Trent Business School. Open lectures on industrial relations: the changing contours of collective bargaining*

FOGARTY, Michael P.
Trade Unions and British industrial development / Michael Fogarty with Douglas Brooks. — London : Policy Studies Institute, 1986. — 184p. — (Research report / Policy Studies Institute ; [no.658]). — *Bibliographical references*

GREAT BRITAIN. Parliament. House of Commons. Library. Research Division
Labour relations legislation / [Celia Nield]. — [London] : the Division, 1979. — 6p. — (Background paper ; no.65)

MILLWARD, Neil
British workplace industrial relations 1980-1984 : the DE/PSI/ESRC/ACAS surveys / Neil Millward and Mark Stevens. — Aldershot : Gower, c1986. — xxi,341p. — *Includes index*

PEGGE, Tony
U.K. management - union relations - Japanese style / Tony Pegge. — Nottingham : Trent Polytechnic, 1984. — 50p. — *Trent Business School. Open lectures on industrial relations: the changing contours of collective bargaining*

ROOTS, Paul
Do companies get the trade unions they deserve? / Paul Roots. — Nottingham : Trent Polytechnic, 1984. — 57p. — *Trent Business School. Open lectures on industrial relations: the changing contours of collective bargaining*

TUC HEALTH SERVICES COMMITTEE
Improving industrial relations in the National Health Service : a report / by the TUC Health Services Committee. — London (Congress House, Great Russell St., WC1B 3LS) : Trades Union Congress, 1981. — 254p

WILLMAN, Paul
New technology and industrial relations : a review of the literature / Paul Willman. — [London] : Department of Employment, [1987]. — 55p. — (Research paper ; no.56). — *Bibliographical references: p49-53*

INDUSTRIAL RELATIONS — Great Britain — Dictionaries

JONES, Jack, 1913-
A-Z of trade unionism and industrial relations / Jack Jones and Max Morris. — London : Sphere Books, 1986. — xii,355p

INDUSTRIAL RELATIONS — Great Britain — Effect of technological innovations on

DANIEL, W. W.
Workplace industrial relations and technical change / W.W. Daniel. — London : Pinter in association with Policy Studies Institute, 1987. — [14],312p. — *Includes index*

INDUSTRIAL RELATIONS — Great Britain — History

A History of British industrial relations. — Brighton : Harvester
Vol.2: 1914-1939 / edited by Chris Wrigley. — 1987. — vii,328p. — *Includes index*

INDUSTRIAL RELATIONS — Great Britain — Law and legislation

LABOUR RESEARCH DEPARTMENT
Employment law under the Tories. — London : LRD Publications, 1986. — 38p

INDUSTRIAL RELATIONS — Hungary

The trade union situation and industrial relations in Hungary : report of an ILO mission. — Geneva : International Labour Office, 1984. — x,100p. — *Includes bibliographical references*

INDUSTRIAL RELATIONS — India

ASDHIR, Vijay
Industrial relations in India : settlement of industrial disputes / Vijay Asdhir. — New Delhi : Deep and Deep Publications, 1987. — 376p. — *Bibliography: p369-374*

FERNANDES, Walter
Trade-unions and industrial relations in India / Walter Fernandes. — New Delhi : Indian Social Institute, 1984. — 43p. — (Monograph series / Indian Social Institute ; 20)

VISHNU GOPAL
Industrial democracy in India : a sociological study of workers' participation in management / by Vishnu Gopal. — Allahabad, India : Chugh, c1984. — xxviii, 535 p.. — : *Revision of the author's thesis (Ph. D.--Banaras Hindu University, 1983) under the title: Workers' participation in management : a sociological study of the new scheme of shop and the joint councils.* — *Includes index.* — *Bibliography: p. [501]-526*

INDUSTRIAL RELATIONS — India — History

RAMANUJAM, G.
Indian labour movement / G. Ramanujam. — New Delhi : Sterling Publishers, c1986. — xvi, 423 p.. — *Includes bibliographical references and index*

INDUSTRIAL RELATIONS — Indonesia — Java — History

INGLESON, John
In search of justice : workers and unions in colonial Java, 1908-1926 / John Ingleson. — Singapore ; New York : Oxford University Press, 1986. — xiii, 342 p., [1] p. of plates. — (Southeast Asia publications series / Asian Studies Association of Australia ; no. 12). — *Includes index.* — *Bibliography: p. [327]-337*

INDUSTRIAL RELATIONS — Japan

FUJITA, Yoshitaka
Employee benefits and industrial relations / Yoshitaka Fujita. — Tokyo : Japan Institute of Labour, 1984. — 47p. — (Japanese industrial relations series ; 12)

INTERNATIONAL LABOUR OFFICE
Labour relations and development : country studies on Japan, the Philippines, Singapore and Sri Lanka / International Labour Office. — Geneva : I.L.O., 1982. — (Labour-management relations series ; 59)

PEGGE, Tony
U.K. management - union relations - Japanese style / Tony Pegge. — Nottingham : Trent Polytechnic, 1984. — 50p. — *Trent Business School. Open lectures on industrial relations: the changing contours of collective bargaining*

TAIRA, Koji
Economic development & the labour market in Japan / Koji Taira. — New York ; London (70 Great Russell St., W.C.1) : Columbia University Press, 1970. — xix,282p. — (Studies / Columbia University. East Asian Institute). — *bibl p267-273*

INDUSTRIAL RELATIONS — New York (State) — Albany — History — 19th century

GREENBERG, Brian
Worker and community : response to industrialization in a nineteenth-century American city, Albany, New York, 1850-1884 / Brian Greenberg. — Albany : State University of New York Press, c1985. — ix, 227 p.. — (SUNY series in American social history). — *Maps on endpapers.* — *Includes index.* — *Bibliography: p. 211-220*

INDUSTRIAL RELATIONS — New Zealand

Industrial relations in transport : proceedings of a seminar / edited by Kevin Hince. — Wellington : Victoria University of Wellington. Industrial Relations Centre : Chartered Institute of Transport in New Zealand, 1985. — 55p

Rights and responsibilities in industrial relations / edited by C. J. Knox and R. J. Taylor. — Wellington : New Zealand Institute of Public Administration, 1979. — 125p. — (Studies in public administration ; no.24)

INDUSTRIAL RELATIONS — Norway

The trade union situation and industrial relations in Norway : report of an ILO mission. — Geneva : International Labour Office, 1984. — x,90p. — *Includes bibliographical references*

INDUSTRIAL RELATIONS — Philippines

INTERNATIONAL LABOUR OFFICE
Labour relations and development : country studies on Japan, the Philippines, Singapore and Sri Lanka / International Labour Office. — Geneva : I.L.O., 1982. — (Labour-management relations series ; 59)

INDUSTRIAL RELATIONS — Singapore

INTERNATIONAL LABOUR OFFICE
Labour relations and development : country studies on Japan, the Philippines, Singapore and Sri Lanka / International Labour Office. — Geneva : I.L.O., 1982. — (Labour-management relations series ; 59)

INDUSTRIAL RELATIONS — South Africa

Labour relations in southern Africa : proceedings of and documents submitted to a seminar (Gaborone, 2-4 December 1981). — Geneva : International Labour Office, 1982. — (Labour-management relations series ; 61)

NEL, P. S
Worker representation in practice in South Africa / P.S. Nel and P.H. van Rooyen. — Pretoria : Academica, 1985. — 170 p.. — *Bibliography: p. 166-170*

INDUSTRIAL RELATIONS — Spain

The trade union situation and industrial relations in Spain : report of an ILO mission. — Geneva : International Labour Office, 1985. — xiii,138p. — *Includes bibliographical references*

INDUSTRIAL RELATIONS — Sri Lanka

INTERNATIONAL LABOUR OFFICE
Labour relations and development : country studies on Japan, the Philippines, Singapore and Sri Lanka / International Labour Office. — Geneva : I.L.O., 1982. — (Labour-management relations series ; 59)

INDUSTRIAL RELATIONS — Turkey

SHABON, Anwar
The political, economic, and labor climate in Turkey / by Anwar M. Shabon and Isik U. Zeytinoglu. — Philadelphia, Pa., U.S.A. : Industrial Research Unit, Wharton School, University of Pennsylvania, c1985. — xiii, 277 p.. — (Multinational industrial relations series. No. 10. European studies ; 10b). — *Includes index*

INDUSTRIAL RELATIONS — United States — Addresses, essays, lectures

Teamwork, joint labor-management programs in America / edited by Jerome M. Rosow. — New York : Pergamon Press, c1986. — xvi, 199 p.. — (Pergamon Press/Work in America Institute series). — *Includes bibliographies and index*

INDUSTRIAL RELATIONS — United States — History — 20th century

JEFFERYS, Steve
Management and managed : fifty years of crisis at Chrysler / Steve Jefferys. — Cambridge : Cambridge University Press, 1986. — xiv,290p. — *Bibliography: p275-282.* — *Includes index*

INDUSTRIAL RELATIONS — United States — History — 20th century
continuation

KOCHAN, Thomas A
The transformation of American industrial relations / Thomas A. Kochan, Harry C. Katz, Robert B. McKersie. — New York : Basic Books, c1986. — viii, 287 p.. — *Includes index. — Bibliography: p. 254-273*

INDUSTRIAL RELATIONS — Yugoslavia
The trade union situation and industrial relations in Yugoslavia. — Geneva : International Labour Office, 1985. — xii,104p. — *Includes bibliographical references*

INDUSTRIAL SAFETY
ANDREONI, Diego
The cost of occupational accidents and diseases / Diego Andreoni. — Geneva : International Labour Office, 1986. — viii, 142p. — (Occupational safety and health series ; no.54). — *Bibliography: p135-142*

INDUSTRIAL SAFETY — Bibliography
PANTRY, Sheila
Health and safety : a guide to sources of information / compiled by Sheila Pantry. — 2nd rev. ed. — Edinburgh : Capital Planning Information, 1985. — 103p.in various pagings. — (CPI information reviews ; no.6). — *Previous ed.: 1983. — Includes bibliography and index*

INDUSTRIAL SAFETY — Law and legislation — Denmark
The Occupational Safety, Health and Welfare (General) Act, 1968. — [Copenhagen : Ministry of Labour], 1968. — 49 leaves. — *Promulgated by the Ministry of Labour on 4th July 1968*

INDUSTRIAL SAFETY — Europe — Congresses
Work and health in the 1980s : experiences of direct workers' participation in occupational health / Sebastiano Bagnara, Raffaello Misiti, Helmut Wintersberger, eds. — Berlin : Edition Sigma, c1985. — 384 p.. — *"Wissenschaftszentrum Berlin, International Institute for Comparative Social Research/Labor Policy"--Cover. — Includes bibliographies*

INDUSTRIAL SAFETY — Great Britain
Employee participation in health and safety : the impact of the legislative provisions : first report of a survey of thirty organisations / undertaken by Brenda Barrett, Richard Howells, Philip James. — [London] : Middlesex Polytechnic, Business School, 1985. — [230]p. — *Bibliography: p277-279*

Inspecting industry: pollution and safety : report and annexes / commissioned jointly by the Secretary of State for the Environment and for Employment. — London : H.M.S.O., 1986. — 110p. — (Efficiency scrutiny report)

INDUSTRIAL SAFETY — United States
The language of risk : conflicting perspectives on occupational health / edited by Dorothy Nelkin. — Beverly Hills : Sage Publications, c1985. — p. cm. — (Sage Focus edition ; v. 71). — *Includes bibliographies and index*

INDUSTRIAL SITES — Great Britain
PERRY, Martin
Small factories and economic development / Martin Perry. — Aldershot : Gower, c1986. — [245]p. — *Includes bibliography*

INDUSTRIAL SOCIOLOGY
ALVESSON, Mats
[Organisationsteori och teknokratiskt medvetande. English]. Organization theory and technocratic consciousness : rationality, ideology, and quality of work / Mats Alvesson. — Berlin ; New York : W. De Gruyter, 1986. — p. cm. — (De Gruyter studies in organization ; 8). — *Translation of: Organisationsteori och teknokratiskt medvetande. — Includes index. — Bibliography: p*

Confrontation, class consciousness, and the labor process : studies in proletarian class formation / edited by Michael Hanagan and Charles Stephenson. — Westport, Conn. ; London : Greenwood Press, 1986. — viii, 261p. — (Contributions in labor studies ; no. 18). — *Includes index. — Bibliography: p.[241]-253*

FRANCIS, Arthur
New technology at work / Arthur Francis. — Oxford : Clarendon, 1986. — [224]p

OPEN UNIVERSITY
Work and society. — Milton Keynes : Open University Press. — (DE325. Block 1, Units 5-7). — *Cover title: Industrial societies* Block 2: The organization of industrial societies / Kenneth Thompson...[et al.]. — 1985. — 65p

ROHLEN, Thomas P
For harmony and strength : Japanese white-collar organization in anthropological perspective / Thomas P. Rohlen. — Berkeley : University of California Press, [1974]. — 285 p., [4] leaves of plates. — *Includes index. — Bibliography: p. [271]-280*

SALAMAN, Graeme
Working / Graeme Salaman. — Chichester : Ellis Horwood, 1986. — [128]p. — (Key ideas) . — *Includes bibliography and index*

Work, employment and society / British Sociological Association. — London : British Sociological Association, 1987-. — *Quarterly*

INDUSTRIAL SOCIOLOGY — Canada
Work in the Canadian context : continuity despite change / [edited by] Katherina L. P. Lundy and Barbara Warme. — 2nd ed.. — Toronto ; Vancouver : Butterworths, 1986. — xvii,369p. — *Includes bibliographical references*

INDUSTRIAL SOCIOLOGY — Canada — History
On the job : confronting the labour process in Canada / edited by Craig Heron and Robert Storey. — Kingston : McGill-Queen's University Press, c1986. — xiv, 360 p.. — *Includes bibliographies and index*

INDUSTRIAL SOCIOLOGY — Colombia — Case studies
SAVAGE, Charles H
Sons of the machine : case studies of social change in the workplace / Charles H. Savage and George F.F. Lombard. — Cambridge, Mass : MIT Press, c1986. — xvi, 313 p., [17] pages of plates. — (MIT Press series on organization studies ; 7). — *Includes index. — Bibliography: p. 283-291*

INDUSTRIAL SOCIOLOGY — Europe, Eastern
MATEJKO, Alexander J
Comparative work systems : ideologies and reality in Eastern Europe / Alexander J. Matejko. — New York : Praeger, 1985. — p. cm. — *Includes index. — Bibliography: p*

INDUSTRIAL SOCIOLOGY — France
Industrial sociology : work in the French tradition / edited by Michael Rose ; translated by Alan Raybould. — London : Sage, 1987. — [224]p. — *Translation of: Le travail et sa sociologie. — Includes bibliography and index*

INDUSTRIAL SOCIOLOGY — Great Britain
GLOVER, Ian A
Engineers in Britain : a sociological study of the engineering dimension / Ian A. Glover, Michael P. Kelly. — London : Allen & Unwin, 1987. — [288]p. — *Includes bibliography and indexes*

HARRIS, Rosemary, 1930-
Power and powerlessness in industry : an analysis of the social relations of production / Rosemary Harris. — London : Tavistock, 1987. — viii,245p. — *Bibliography: p238-239. — Includes index*

INDUSTRIAL SOCIOLOGY — United States
SILVER, Marc L.
Under construction : work and alienation in the building trades / Marc L. Silver. — Albany : State University of New York Press, c1986. — xi, 251 p.. — (SUNY series in the sociology of work). — *Includes indexes. — Bibliography: p. 229-242*

INDUSTRIAL SOCIOLOGY — United States — Addresses, essays, lectures
Becoming a worker / edited by Kathryn M. Borman. — Norwood, N.J. : Ablex Pub. Co., 1986. — p. cm. — *Based on a symposium held in October 1983 at the Ohio State University. — Includes index. — Bibliography: p*

INDUSTRIAL SOCIOLOGY — United States — History
STEPHENSON, Charles
Life and labor : dimensions of American working-class history / by Charles Stephenson and Robert Asher. — Albany : State University of New York Press, c1986. — p. cm. — (American labor history series). — *Includes index*

INDUSTRIAL STATISTICS
Handbook of industrial statistics = Manuel de statistiques industrielles / United Nations Industrial Development Organization. — Vienna : UNIDO, 1986-. — *Annual. — Text in English and French*

Industry and development: global report / United Nations Industrial Development Organization. — Vienna : United Nations Industrial Development Organisation, 1985-. — *Annual*

Recommendations for the 1983 World Programme of Industrial Statistics. — New York : United Nations. — (Statistical papers / United Nations, Statistical Office. Series M ; no.71 (part 1)) ([Document] (United Nations) ; ST/ESA/STAT.M/71 (part 1))
Pt.1: General statistical objectives. — 1981. — iv,59p. — *Includes bibliographical references. — Sales no.: E.81.XII.11*

Recommendations for the 1983 World Programme of Industrial Statistics. — New York : United Nations. — (Statistical papers / United Natins, Statistical Office. Series M ; no.71 (part 2)) ([Document] / United Nations ; ST/ESA/STAT/SER.M/71 (part 2))
Pt.2: Organization and conduct of industrial censuses. — 1981. — v,125p. — *Includes bibliographical references. — Sales no.: E.81.XVII.12*

INDUSTRIAL STATISTICS — Bibliography
Bibliography of industrial and distributive-trade statistics. — New York : United Nations, 1981. — iv,149p. — (Statistical papers / United Nations, Statistical Office. Series M ; no.36, Rev. 5) ([Document] (United Nations) ; ST/ESA/STAT/SER.M/36,Rev.5). — *Sales no.: E.81.XVII.5*

INDUSTRIAL STATISTICS — Standards
International recommendations for industrial statistics. — New York : United Nations, 1983. — iv,61p. — (Statistical papers / United Nations, Statistical Office. Series M ; no.48,rev.1) ([Document] / United Nations ; ST/ESA/STAT/SER.M/48/Rev.1). — *Bibliographical references: p59-61. — Sales no.: E.83.XVII.8*

INDUSTRIAL TOXICOLOGY — India — Bhopal
SUFRIN, Sidney C.
Bhopal, its setting, responsibility, and challenge / Sidney C. Surfin. — Delhi : Ajanta Publications : Distributors, Ajanta Books International, 1985. — 98 p.. — *60-9*

INDUSTRIAL WORKERS OF THE WORLD — Bibliography

MILES, Dione
Something in common : an IWW bibliography / compiled by Dione Miles. — Detroit : Wayne State University Press, 1986. — 560 p.. — *On cover: Archives of Labor and Urban Affairs, Walter P. Reuther Library, Wayne State University.* — *Includes index*

INDUSTRIALISTS — Great Britain — History — 19th century

ERICKSON, Charlotte
British industrialists : steel and hosiery 1850-1950 / Charlotte Erickson. — Aldershot : Gower in association with he London School of Economics and Political Science, c1986. — xxi,276p. — *Originally published: Cambridge : Cambridge University Press, 1959.* — *Bibliography: p248-257.* — *Includes index*

INDUSTRIALISTS — Great Britain — History — 20th century

ERICKSON, Charlotte
British industrialists : steel and hosiery 1850-1950 / Charlotte Erickson. — Aldershot : Gower in association with he London School of Economics and Political Science, c1986. — xxi,276p. — *Originally published: Cambridge : Cambridge University Press, 1959.* — *Bibliography: p248-257.* — *Includes index*

INDUSTRIALISTS — Mexico

STORY, Dale
Industry, the state, and public policy in Mexico / by Dale Story. — Austin : University of Texas Press, 1986. — xii, 275p. — (Latin American monographs / Institute of Latin American Studies, the University of Texas at Austin ; no. 66). — *Includes index.* — *Bibliography: p*

INDUSTRIALISTS — United States — Biography

WANG, An
Lessons, an autobiography / An Wang ; with Eugene Linden. — Reading, Mass. : Addison-Wesley, 1986. — p. cm. — *Includes index*

INDUSTRIALIZATION

CHENERY, Hollis Burnley
Industrialization and growth : a comparative study / Hollis Chenery, Sherman Robinson, Moshe Syrquin. — New York : Published for the World Bank [by] Oxford University Press, c1986. — x,387p. — *Bibliographical references: p361-377.* — *Bibliography: p*

Industrial change in advanced economies / edited by F.E. Ian Hamilton. — London : Croom Helm, c1987. — 319p. — *Includes bibliographies and index*

Industry and development : global report 1986. — Vienna : United Nations Industrial Development Organization, 1986. — xxiii,330p. — (Document ; ID/343). — *Bibliography: p143-145.* — *Document no.ID/343; Sales no. E.86.II.B.5*

LAVOIE, Don
National economic planning : what is left? / Don Lavoie. — Cambridge, Mass. : Ballinger Pub. Co., c1985. — xii, 291 p.. — *Includes index.* — *Bibliography: p. 267-279*

LUTTRELL, William L
Post-capitalist industrialization : planning economic independence in Tanzania / William L. Luttrell. — New York : Praeger, 1986. — xv, 189 p.. — *Includes index.* — *Bibliography: p. 181-184*

Transnational corporations in South East Asia and the Pacific. — Sydney : Transnational Corporations Research Project, University of Sydney
vol.7: Transnational corporations and export-oriented industrialization / Ernst Utrecht, editor. — 1985. — 273p

INDUSTRIALIZATION — Addresses, essays, lectures

Industrialization and development : a Third World perspective / Pradip K. Ghosh, editor ; foreword by Subbiah Kannappan. — Westport, Conn. : Greenwood Press, c1984. — xxviii, 566 p.. — (International development resource books ; no. 1). — *"Prepared under the auspices of the Center for Advanced Study of International Development, Michigan State University.".* — *Includes indexes.* — *Bibliography: p. [381]-516*

INDUSTRIALIZATION — Bibliography

UNITED NATIONS. Industrial Development Organization
Index to documents issued by the Committee for Industrial Development, Centre for Industrial Development and Division for Industrial Development from inception to end of 1966. — New York : United Nations Industrial Development Organization, 1967. — v,114p. — (Document / United Nations ; ID/SER.G/1). — *United Nations document no.ID/SER.G/1*

INDUSTRIALIZATION — History — Addresses, essays, lectures

Technological change and workers' movements / edited by Melvyn Dubofsky. — Beverly Hills : Sage Publications, c1985. — p. cm. — (Explorations in the world-economy ; v. 4). — : *"Originally presented at the Third U.S.-U.S.S.R. Colloquium on World Labor and Social Change held at the State University of New York at Binghamton in January 1983"--Introd*

INDUSTRIES — Germany (West) — Statistics

Ergebnisse für Wirtschaftsbereiche (Branchenblättev) : 1960 bis 1985. — Stuttgart : Statistisches Bundesamt, [1987]. — 444p. — (Volkswirtschaftliche Gesamtrechnungen. Reihe S ; 9). — *Text in German with contents list and list of characteristics in English*

INDUSTRIES, LOCATION OF — Great Britain

KEEBLE, David
Industrial location and planning in the United Kingdom / David Keeble. — London : Methuen, 1976. — [8],317p. — *Bibliography: p.290-305.* — *Includes index*

SHORTLAND, Susan M.
Managing relocation / Susan M. Shortland. — London : Macmillan, 1987. — [256]p. — (Industrial relations in practice). — *Includes bibliography and index*

INDUSTRIES, SIZE OF

EVELY, Richard
Concentration in British industry : an empirical study of the structure of industrial production, 1935-51 / Richard Evely and Ian Malcolm David Little. — Cambridge : Cambridge University Press, 1960. — xvi,357p. — (Econonic and social studies / National Institute of Economic and Social Research ; no.16)

INDUSTRIES, SIZE OF — United States

ADAMS, Walter
The bigness complex : industry, labor, and government in the American economy / Walter Adams and James W. Brock. — 1st ed. — New York : Pantheon Books, 1986. — xiii, 426 p.. — *Includes indexes.* — *Bibliography: p. 381-413*

INDUSTRY

BALLANCE, Robert H.
International industry and business : structural change, industrial policy and industry strategies / Robert H. Ballance. — London : Allen & Unwin, 1987. — [220]p. — *Includes bibliography and index*

Industrie mondiale : la compétitivité à tout prix / sous la direction de Michel Fouquin. — [Paris : Economica, 1986]. — xxiv,332p

International capitalism and industrial restructuring : a critical analysis / edited by Richard Peet. — Boston ; London : Allen & Unwin, 1987. — [224]p. — *Includes bibliography and index*

RAY, George
The diffusion of mature technologies / George F. Ray. — Cambridge : Cambridge University Press, 1984. — ix,96p. — (Occasional papers / National Institute of Economic and Social Research ; 36)

The Spatial impact of technological change / edited by John F. Brotchie, Peter Hall & Peter W. Newton. — London : Croom Helm, c1987. — xxv,460p

Technical change and industrial policy / edited by Keith Chapman and Graham Humphrys. — Oxford : Basil Blackwell, 1987. — 264p. — (Institute of British Geographers special publications ; 19). — *Conference papers.* — *Includes bibliographies and index*

INDUSTRY — Directories — Bibliography

SCIENCE REFERENCE AND INFORMATION SERVICE
Trade directory information in journals / Business Information Service. — 6th ed. — London : Science Reference and Information Service, 1986. — 50p. — *Previous ed.: 1985*

INDUSTRY — Location

Changing Britain, changing world : geographical perspectives. — Milton Keynes : Open University Press. — (Social services : a second level course) (D205; Units 4-7). — *At head of title: Open University*
Section 2: Analysis: aspects of the geography of society
Block 2: Industry and resources / Piers Blaikie...[et al.]. — 1985. — *Various pagings*

CHAPMAN, Keith
Industrial location : principles and policies / Keith Chapman and David Walker. — Oxford : Basil Blackwell, 1987. — 305p. — *Includes bibliography and index*

Location theory / Jean Jaskold Gabszewicz ... [et. al.]. — Chur, Switzerland ; New York : Harwood Academic Publishers, c1986. — vii, 190 p.. — (Fundamentals of pure and applied economics ; v. 5Regional and urban economics section). — *Includes bibliographies and index*

SPENCE, Nigel
Notes to accompany the John Löschian landscapes / Nigel Spence and John Metcalfe. — London : University of London Audio-Visual Centre, 1975. — 20p

WATTS, H. D.
Industrial geography / H.D. Watts. — Harlow : Longman Scientific & Technical, 1987. — xii,260p. — *Bibliography: p241-251.* — *Includes index*

INDUSTRY — Power supply

HALL, Charles A. S
Energy and resource quality : the ecology of the economic process / Charles A.S. Hall, Cutler J. Cleveland, Robert Kaufmann. — New York : Wiley, c1986. — xxi, 577 p.. — (Environmental science and technology). — *"A Wiley-Interscience publication.".* — *Includes index.* — *Bibliography: p. 535-568*

INDUSTRY — Social apsects

HOSELITZ, Berthold Frank
Sociological aspects of economic growth / Berthold Frank Hoselitz. — Glencoe, Ill. : Free Press, [1960]. — vii,250p

INDUSTRY — Social aspects

Corporate social responsibility : contemporary viewpoints / Suzanne Robitaille Ontiveros, editor ; foreword by Joan L. Bavaria. — Santa Barbara, Calif. : ABC-CLIO, c1986. — xv, 229 p.. — (The Dynamic organization series). — *Includes indexes*

INDUSTRY — Social aspects
continuation

DAVIDMANN, M.
Social responsibility, profits and social accountability, incidents, disasters and catastrophes, the world-wide struggle for social accountability, community aims and community leadership / M. Davidmann. — [Stanmore] : Social Organisation Ltd., [c1981]. — 57leaves. — (Community leadership and management)

GRAY, Rob
Corporate social reporting : accounting and accountability / Rob Gray, Dave Owen, Keith Maunders. — Englewood Cliffs ; London : Prentice-Hall International, c1987. — xi,224p. — *Bibliography: p206-220.* — *Includes index*

INDUSTRY — Social aspects — England

WIENER, Martin J.
English culture and the decline of the industrial spirit, 1850-1980 / Martin J. Wiener. — Harmondsworth : Penguin, 1985. — xi,217p. — (Pelican book)

INDUSTRY — Social aspects — Great Britain

BRADLEY, Ian, 1950-
Enlightened entrepreneurs / Ian Campbell Bradley. — London : Weidenfeld and Nicolson, 1987. — xii, 207p, 12p of plates. — *Bibliography: p202*

INDUSTRY — Social aspects — India

SURESH KUMAR
Social mobility in industrializing society / Suresh Kumar. — Jaipur : Rawat Publications, 1986. — x, 188 p.. — *Includes bibliographies and index*

INDUSTRY — Social aspects — United States

BRUYN, Severyn T.
The field of social investment / Severyn T. Bruyn. — Cambridge : Cambridge University Press, 1987. — [560]p. — (The Arnold and Caroline Rose monograph series of the American Sociological Association). — *Bibliography: p556*

Patterns of power : an introductory study of corporate control for the members of the Securities and Exchange Commission. — [Hampton, Va.] (532 Settlers Landing Rd., P.O. Box 302, Hampton 23669) : Foundation for the Study of Philanthropy, c1982. — 3, ii-v, 151 leaves. — *Includes index.* — *Bibliography: leaves 135-140*

INDUSTRY — Social aspects — United States — Case studies

Productivity and quality through people : practices of well-managed companies / edited by Y.K. Shetty and Vernon M. Buehler ; foreword by John A. Young. — Westport, Conn. : Quorum Books, 1985. — xvi, 351 p.. — *Includes index.* — *Bibliography: p. [329]-340*

INDUSTRY ACT 1972

GREAT BRITAIN. Department of Industry
Industry Act 1972 : criteria for assistance to industry. — [London : the Department, 1975]. — 16,3p

INDUSTRY AND EDUCATION — Australia

DWYER, Peter
Confronting school and work : youth and class cultures in Australia / Peter Dwyer, Bruce Wilson, and Roger Woock. — Sydney ; Boston : G. Allen & Unwin, 1984. — 175 p. — (Studies in the society ; 23). — *Includes index.* — *Bibliography: p. [166]-173*

INDUSTRY AND EDUCATION — Great Britain

FURNITURE AND TIMBER INDUSTRY TRAINING BOARD
Education for our industries : a report / by the Furniture and Timber Industry Training Board. — [High Wycombe] : the Board, 1978. — 35p

INDUSTRY AND EDUCATION — United States

Schooling in social context : qualitative studies / edited by George W. Noblit, William T. Pink. — Norwood, N.J. : Ablex Pub. Corp., c1987. — xviii, 332 p.. — *Includes bibliographies and indexes*

INDUSTRY AND STATE

BUICK, Adam
State capitalism : the wages system under new management / Adam Buick and John Crump. — Basingstoke : Macmillan, 1986. — ix,165p. — *Bibliography: p154-158.* — *Includes index*

Comparative government-industry relations : Western Europe, United States and Japan / edited by Stephen Wilks and Maurice Wright. — Oxford : Clarendon, 1987. — [224]p. — (Government-industry relations ; 1). — *Includes index*

Industrial policies for growth and competitiveness. — Lexington, Mass : Lexington Books. — (The Wharton econometric studies series. Industrial policy studies)
[Volume 1]: An economic perspective / edited by F. Gerard Adams, Lawrence R. Klein. — c1983. — viii,434p

Industrial policy : structural dynamics / edited by Bodo B. Gemper. — Hamburg : Verlag Weltarchiv, 1985. — x, 208 p.. — (A Publication of the HWWA-Institut für Wirtschaftsforschung-Hamburg and the Unabhängiges Institut für Rechts-, Sozial- und Wirtschaftswissenschaften e. V). — *Includes bibliographies and indexes*

JACOBSON, Staffan
Electronics and industrial policy : the case of computer-controlled lathes / Staffan Jacobson. — London : Allen & Unwin, 1986. — xx,252p. — (World industry studies ; 5). — *Bibliography: p241-248.* — *Includes index*

LOVETT, William Anthony
World trade rivalry : trade equity and competing industrial policies / William A. Lovett. — Lexington, Mass. : Lexington Books, c1987. — p. cm. — *Includes index.* — *Bibliography: p*

Organizing industrial development / editor, Rolf H. Wolff. — Berlin ; New York : W. de Gruyter, 1986. — p. cm. — (De Gruyter studies in organization ; 7). — *Includes index.* — *Bibliography: p*

STIGLER, George J.
The regularities of regulation / George J. Stigler. — Glencorse : David Hume Institute, 1986. — vi,12p. — (Hume occasional paper ; no.3). — *Bibliography: p11*

TICKNER, J. Ann
Self-reliance versus power politics : the American and Indian experience in building nation states / J. Ann Tickner. — New York : Columbia University Press, 1987. — xi, 282 p.. — (The Political economy of international change). — *Includes index.* — *Bibliography: p. [231]-267*

INDUSTRY AND STATE — Case studies

National policies for developing high technology industries : international comparisons / edited by Francis W. Rushing and Carole Ganz Brown. — Boulder, Colo. : Westview Press, c1986. — xiv, 247 p.. — (Westview special studies in science, technology, and public policy). — *Includes bibliographies*

States versus markets in the world-system / edited by Peter Evans, Dietrich Rueschemeyer, Evelyne Huber Stephens. — Beverly Hills, Calif. : Sage Publications, c1985. — 295 p.. — (Political economy of the world-system annuals ; v. 8). — *Includes bibliographies*

INDUSTRY AND STATE — Congresses

Mainstreams in industrial organization / edited by H.W. de Jong, W.G. Shepherd. — Dordrecht ; Boston : Kluwer Academic Publishers, 1986. — 2 v. (x, 465 p.). — (Studies in industrial organization ; 6). — *Essays and part of the discussions presented at a conference held Aug. 21-23, 1985 at the University of Amsterdam. Bibliography: p. 463-465.* — *Contents: bk. 1. Theory and international aspects -- bk. 2. Policies, antitrust, deregulation, and industrial*

Theories of business-government relations / edited by V. V. Murray. — Toronto : Trans-Canada Press, 1985. — 381p. — *Papers presented at a conference held at York University, May 1984, sponsored by the Max Bell Business-Government Studies Programme*

INDUSTRY AND STATE — Australia

TERRY, Chris
Australian microeconomics : policies and industry cases / Chris Terry, Ross Jones, Richard Braddock. — 2nd ed. — Sydney : Prentice-Hall of Australia, c1985. — xi, 362 p.. — *Includes bibliographies*

INDUSTRY AND STATE — Brazil

GOMES, Gustavo Maia
The roots of state intervention in the Brazilian economy / Gustavo Maia Gomes. — New York : Praeger, 1986. — xvii, 376 p.. — *Includes indexes.* — *Bibliography: p. 353-367*

INDUSTRY AND STATE — Canada

CLARK-JONES, Melissa
A staple state : Canadian industrial resources in cold war / Melissa Clark-Jones. — Toronto : University of Toronto Press, 1987. — ix,260p. — (The State and economic life ; no.10). — *Bibliographical notes: p[225]-252*

GILLIES, James
Facing reality : consultation, consensus and making economic policy for the 21st century / James M. Gillies. — Montreal : The Institute for Research on Public Policy/L'Institut de recherches politiques, 1986. — xxxviii,221p. — *Bibliography: p199-221*

STANBURY, W. T.
Business-government relations in Canada : grappling with Leviathan / W. T. Stanbury. — Toronto : Methuen, 1986. — xx,678p. — *Bibliography: p599-667*

INDUSTRY AND STATE — Canada — Congresses

Theories of business-government relations / edited by V. V. Murray. — Toronto : Trans-Canada Press, 1985. — 381p. — *Papers presented at a conference held at York University, May 1984, sponsored by the Max Bell Business-Government Studies Programme*

INDUSTRY AND STATE — Canada — History — 19th century

FORSTER, Jakob Johann Benjamin
A conjunction of interests : business, politics, and tariffs, 1825-1879 / Ben Forster. — Toronto ; Buffalo : University of Toronto Press, c1986. — vi, 288 p.. — (The State and economic life ; 8). — *Includes index.* — *Bibliography: p. [259]-276*

INDUSTRY AND STATE — Colombia

HELMSING, A. H. J.
Firms, farms, and the state in Colombia : a study of rural, urban, and regional dimensions of change / A.H.J. Helmsing. — Boston : Allen & Unwin, 1986. — xix, 297 p.. — *Includes index.* — *Bibliography: p. 275-288*

INDUSTRY AND STATE — Communist countries

Intensifikatsiia i effektivnost' sotsialisticheskogo vosproizvodstva / [redkol.: A. Braun...et al.]. — Moskva : Politizdat, 1986. — 350p

INDUSTRY AND STATE — East Asia — Congresses
The 21st Century, the Asian century? / Takeshi Ishida ... [et al.] ; Sung-Jo Park (Hg.). — Berlin : EXpress Edition, c1985. — 140 p.. — Includes bibliographical references

INDUSTRY AND STATE — Europe
HIBBS, Douglas A.
The political economy of industrial democracies / Douglas A. Hibbs, Jr. — Cambridge, Mass. ; London : Harvard University Press, 1987. — viii, 327 p.. — Includes bibliographical references and index

UDIS, Bernard
The challenge to European industrial policy : redirecting military spending / Bernard Udis. — Boulder : Westview Press, 1986. — p. cm. — (Westview special studies in international economics). — Includes index

INDUSTRY AND STATE — Europe — History — 20th century
Managing industrial change in Western Europe / edited by François Duchêne and Geoffrey Shepherd. — London : Pinter, 1987. — xii,247p. — Includes bibliographies and index

INDUSTRY AND STATE — European Economic Community countries
A Competitive future for Europe? : towards a new European industrial policy / edited by P.R. Beije ... [et al.]. — London : Croom Helm, c1987. — 324p

INDUSTRY AND STATE — European Economic Community countries — Directories
LOVASZ, J.
Incentives for industrial research, development and innovation : directory of direct and indirect public measures for promoting industrial research, development and innovation in the member states of the European Communities. — 2nd ed. / compiled for the Commission of the European Communities by J. Lovasz assisted by P. McCann. — London : Kogan Page, 1986. — [470]p. — Previous ed.: 1985

INDUSTRY AND STATE — France
CHALANDON, Albin
Quitte ou double / Albin Chalandon. — Paris : Grasset, [1986]. — 317p

French industrial policy : its practice and implications / William James Adams, Christian Stoffaës, editors. — Washington, D.C. : Brookings Institution, c1986. — p. cm. — Includes bibliographies and index

INDUSTRY AND STATE — France — History — 20th century
GODFREY, John F.
Capitalism at war : industrial policy and bureaucracy in France, 1914-1918 / John F. Godfrey ; with a foreword by Jay Winter. — Leamington Spa : Berg, 1987. — xiv,313p. — Bibliography: p301-309. — Includes index

INDUSTRY AND STATE — Great Britain
CONFEDERATION OF BRITISH INDUSTRY
Building a better Britain. — London : Confederation of British Industry, 1986. — 44p. — (Fabric of the nation ; 3)

GORMAN, Teresa
Business still burdened : more regulations for the scrapheap / Teresa Gorman. — London : Centre for Policy Studies, 1986. — 43p. — (Policy study ; no.76). — Bibliography: p38-39

GRANT, Wyn
Business and politics in Britain / Wyn Grant with Jane Sargent. — Basingstoke : Macmillan, 1987. — [288]p. — Includes bibliography and index

GREAT BRITAIN. Department of Industry
Industry Act 1972 : criteria for assistance to industry. — [London : the Department, 1975]. — 16,3p

GREAT BRITAIN. Parliament. House of Commons. Library. Research Division
Industrial policy / Christopher Barclay. — [London] : the Division, 1984. — 24p. — (Background paper ; no.153)

Industrial change in the United Kingdom / edited by William F. Lever. — Harlow : Longman Scientific & Technical, 1987. — 272p . — Includes bibliographies and index

UTTON, M. A.
The economics of regulating industry / M.A. Utton. — Oxford : Basil Blackwell, 1986. — [288]p. — Includes bibliography and index

INDUSTRY AND STATE — India
HANDA, Jagdish
The economic behaviour of industrial corporations : an econometric study of four Indian industries / Jagdish Handa, Chandra Prakash Khetan, Ramesh R. Waghmare. — Delhi : Macmillan India, 1985. — xii, 123 p.. — 74-9. — Bibliography: p. [119]-123

MALYAROV, O. V.
The role of the state in the socio-economic structure of India / O. V. Malyanov. — New Delhi : Vikas, 1983. — 463p. — Bibliography: p445-459

INDUSTRY AND STATE — India — History
MARATHE, Shared S.
Regulation and development : India's experience of controls over industry / Shared S. Marathe ; under the auspices of the Centre for Policy Research. — New Delhi ; Beverly Hills : Sage Publications, 1986. — p. cm. — Includes index. — Bibliography: p

INDUSTRY AND STATE — India — Hyderabad (State) — History
BHASKARA RAO, V.
Agrarian and industrial relations in Hyderabad State / V. Bhaskara Rao. — New Delhi : Associated Pub. House, c1985. — xi, 179 p.. — Includes index. — Bibliography: p. [169]-173

INDUSTRY AND STATE — Japan
DORE, R. P.
Structural adjustment in Japan, 1970-82 / R. P. Dore ; with contributions by K. Taira. — Geneva : International Labour Office, 1986. — xii,189p. — (Employment, adjustment and industrialisation ; 1). — Bibliography: p [183]-189

GREAT BRITAIN. Parliament. House of Commons. Library. Research Division
Industrial policy and the Japanese economic miracle / C. R. Barclay. — [London] : the Division, 1986. — 26p. — (Background paper ; no.190). — Bibliography: p26

INDUSTRY AND STATE — Korea (South)
Korea : managing the industrial transition. — Washington, D.C. : The World Bank V.1: The conduct of industrial policy. — 1987. — xiv,182p. — (A World Bank Country study) . — Includes bibliographical references

Korea : Managing the Industrial Transition. — Washington, D.C. : The World Bank V.2: Selected topics and case studies. — 1987. — x,225p. — (A World Bank Country study). — Bibliography: p218-225

INDUSTRY AND STATE — Mexico
Industrial strategy and planning in Mexico and the United States / edited by Sidney Weintraub. — Boulder, Colo. : Westview Press, 1986. — xiv, 279 p.. — (Westview special studies in international economics and business) . — Includes bibliographies and index. — Contents: Industrial policy in the United States / William Diebold -- The new industrialization strategy in Mexico for the eighties / René Villarreal Arrambide -- Industrial strategy in the United States and the impact on Mexico / Sidney Weintraub -- The petrochemical industry in Mexico / Francisco Barnés de Castro, Lars Christianson -- The Mexican iron and steel industry / Gerardo M. Bueno, Gustavo S. Cortés, Rafael R. Rubio -- Steel in transition / Robert Crandall -- The U.S. motor vehicle industry / Neil D. Schuster -- Industry on the northern border of Mexico / José Luis Fernández, Jesús Tamayo -- Industry on the southern border of the United States / Jerry R. Ladman -- A United States view / Clark Reynolds -- A Mexican view / Francisco Javier Alejo

STORY, Dale
Industry, the state, and public policy in Mexico / by Dale Story. — Austin : University of Texas Press, 1986. — xii, 275p. — (Latin American monographs / Institute of Latin American Studies, the University of Texas at Austin ; no. 66). — Includes index. — Bibliography: p

INDUSTRY AND STATE — Mexico — History — 19th century
WALKER, David W
Kinship, business, and politics : the Martínez del Río family in Mexico, 1824-1867 / by David W. Walker. — 1st ed. — Austin : University of Texas Press, 1986. — x, 278 p.. — (Latin American monographs / Institute of Latin American Studies, University of Texas at Austin ; no.70). — Includes index. — Bibliography: p. [259]-267

INDUSTRY AND STATE — Organisation for Economic Co-operation and Development countries
Structural adjustment and economic performance : synthesis report. — Paris : Organisation for Economic Co-operation and Development, 1987. — 39p

INDUSTRY AND STATE — Pakistan
PAKISTAN. Ministry of Industries
Industrial policy statement. — Islamabad : the Ministry, 1984. — 32p

INDUSTRY AND STATE — Panama
Panama : structural change and growth prospects. — Washington, D.C., U.S.A. : World Bank, 1985. — xxv,307p. — (A World Bank country study). — "Report no. 5236-PAN.". — "February 28, 1985."

INDUSTRY AND STATE — Pennsylvania
ALLEN, David N
Nurturing advanced technology enterprises : emerging issues in state and local economic development policy / David N. Allen and Victor Levine. — New York : Praeger, 1986. — xvi, 268 p.. — Includes index. — Bibliography: p. 239-262

INDUSTRY AND STATE — Poland — History
MAGIERSKA, Anna
Przywrócić Polsce : przemysł na Ziemiach Odzyskanych 1945-1946. — Warszawa : Państwowe Wydawnictwo Naukowe, 1986. — 467p. — Bibliography: p439-[451]

INDUSTRY AND STATE — Soviet Union
HOFFMANN, Erik P.
Technocratic socialism : the Soviet Union in the advanced industrial era / Erik P. Hoffmann and Robbin F. Laird. — Durham : Duke University Press, 1985. — 228p. — (Duke Press policy studies). — Includes index. — Bibliography: p.[201]-225

INDUSTRY AND STATE — Soviet Union
continuation
Planirovanie razmeshcheniia proizvoditel'nykh sil SSSR : osushchestvlenie politiki KPSS na etapakh sotsialisticheskogo stroitel'stva / [red. kollegiia: V. P. Mozhin...et al.]. — Moskva : Ekonomika
Ch.2: Planirovanie razmeshcheniia proizvoditel'nykh sil na etape razvitogo sotsializma. — 1986. — 382p

INDUSTRY AND STATE — Spain
BRAÑA, Javier
El Estadio y el cambio tecnológico en la industrialización tardía : un analisis del caso español / Javier Braña, Mikel Buesa, Jose Molero. — México ; Madrid : Fondo de Cultura Económica, 1984. — 380p. — *Bibliography: p345-375*

La empresa española ante la CEE / selección de textos y coordinación Eduardo Bueno Campos. — Madrid : Instituto de Estudios Económicos, 1984. — xxvii,184p. — *Revista del Instituto de Estudios Económicos, 1984, No.2*

MARAVALL, Fernando
Economía y política industrial en España / Fernando Maravall. — Madrid : Ediciones Pirámide, 1987. — 231p. — *Bibliographies*

INDUSTRY AND STATE — Sudan
AFFAN, Bodour O. Abu
Industrial policies and industrialization in the Sudan / Bodour Osman Abu Affan. — Khartoum : University of Khartoum, 1985. — 180p. — (Graduate college publications / University of Khartoum ; no.16).
Bibliography: p174-180

INDUSTRY AND STATE — Tanzania
LUTTRELL, William L
Post-capitalist industrialization : planning economic independence in Tanzania / William L. Luttrell. — New York : Praeger, 1986. — xv, 189 p.. — *Includes index. — Bibliography: p. 181-184*

SKARSTEIN, Rune
Industrial development in Tanzania : some critical issues / Rune Skarstein, Sammuel M. Wangwe. — Uppsala : Scandinavian Institute of African Studies ; Dar es Salaam : Tanzania Publishing House, 1986. — [xii],291p. — *Bibliography: p275-291*

INDUSTRY AND STATE — Ukraine
SOKOLOV, V. N.
Kursom na sotsialisticheskuiu industrializatsiiu / V. N. Sokolov. — Kiev : Vyshcha shkola, 1985. — 158p. — *Bibliography: p154-[159]*

INDUSTRY AND STATE — United States
CAHILL, Kevin
Trade wars : the high-technology scandal of the 1980's / Kevin Cahill. — London : W.H. Allen, 1986. — [176]p

French industrial policy : its practice and implications / William James Adams, Christian Stoffaës, editors. — Washington, D.C. : Brookings Institution, c1986. — p. cm. — *Includes bibliographies and index*

GRAY, H. Peter
International trade, employment and structural adjustment : the United States / H. Peter Gray, Thomas Pugel and Ingo Walter. — Geneva : International Labour Office, 1986. — x,108p. — (Employment, adjustment and industrialisation ; 3). — *Includes bibliographical references*

HIBBS, Douglas A.
The political economy of industrial democracies / Douglas A. Hibbs, Jr. — Cambridge, Mass. ; London : Harvard University Press, 1987. — viii, 327 p.. — *Includes bibliographical references and index*

Industrial strategy and planning in Mexico and the United States / edited by Sidney Weintraub. — Boulder, Colo. : Westview Press, 1986. — xiv, 279 p.. — (Westview special studies in international economics and business) . — *Includes bibliographies and index. — Contents: Industrial policy in the United States / William Diebold -- The new industrialization strategy in Mexico for the eighties / René Villarreal Arrambide -- Industrial strategy in the United States and the impact on Mexico / Sidney Weintraub -- The petrochemical industry in Mexico / Francisco Barnés de Castro, Lars Christianson -- The Mexican iron and steel industry / Gerardo M. Bueno, Gustavo S. Cortés, Rafael R. Rubio -- Steel in transition / Robert Crandall -- The U.S. motor vehicle industry / Neil D. Schuster -- Industry on the northern border of Mexico / José Luis Fernández, Jesús Tamayo -- Industry on the southern border of the United States / Jerry R. Ladman -- A United States view / Clark Reynolds -- A Mexican view / Francisco Javier Alejo*

KARLSSON, Svante
Oil and the world order : American foreign oil policy / Svante Karlsson. — Leamington Spa : Berg, 1986. — 308p. — *Bibliography: p293-297. — Includes index*

ZEGVELD, Walter
SDI and industrial technology policy : threat or opportunity? / Walter Zegveld and Christien Enzing. — London : Pinter, 1987. — 186p. — *Includes bibliographies and index*

INDUSTRY AND STATE — United States — Addresses, essays, lectures
DE ALESSI, Louis
Some economic aspects of government ownership and regulation : essays from Economia pubblica / Louis De Alessi ; with a preface by Armen A. Alchian. — Coral Gables, FL : Law and Economics Center, University of Miami, c1983. — v, 38 p.. — (An LEC occasional paper). — *Essays in this collection originally appeared in Italian in Economia pubblica. — Bibliography: p. 39-40*

INDUSTRY AND STATE — United States — History
PAINTER, David S.
Private power and public policy : multinational oil corporations and United States foreign policy 1941-1954 / David S. Painter. — London : Tauris, 1986. — [300]p. — *Includes bibliography and index*

INDUSTRY AND STATES — Europe
The Politicisation of business in western Europe / edited by M.C.P.M. van Schendelen and R.J. Jackson. — London : Croom Helm, c1987. — 185p. — *Includes bibliographies and index*

INFANT
STERN, Daniel N
The interpersonal world of the infant : a view from psychoanalysis annd developmental psychology / Daniel N. Stern. — New York : Basic Books, c1985. — x, 304p. — *Includes index. — Bibliography: p.278-294*

INFANT — popular works
RESTAK, Richard M.
The infant mind / Richard M. Restak. — 1st ed. — Garden City, N.Y. : Doubleday, 1986. — xi, 274 p.. — *Includes index. — Bibliography: p. [255]-264*

INFANT PSYCHOLOGY
RESTAK, Richard M.
The infant mind / Richard M. Restak. — 1st ed. — Garden City, N.Y. : Doubleday, 1986. — xi, 274 p.. — *Includes index. — Bibliography: p. [255]-264*

STERN, Daniel N
The interpersonal world of the infant : a view from psychoanalysis annd developmental psychology / Daniel N. Stern. — New York : Basic Books, c1985. — x, 304p. — *Includes index. — Bibliography: p.278-294*

INFANTS — Development
RESTAK, Richard M.
The infant mind / Richard M. Restak. — 1st ed. — Garden City, N.Y. : Doubleday, 1986. — xi, 274 p.. — *Includes index. — Bibliography: p. [255]-264*

INFANTS — Mortality — Social aspects — Bangladesh
AL—KABIR, Ahmed
Effects of community factors on infant and child mortality in rural Bangladesh / Ahmed Al—Kabir. — Voorburg : International Statistical Institute, 1984. — 33p. — (Scientific reports / World Fertility Survey ; no.56)

INFANTS — Mortality — Statistical methods
COCHRANE, Susan Hill
Procedures for collecting and analyzing mortality data in LSMS / Susan H. Cochrane, William D. Kalsbeek, Jeremiah M. Sullivan. — Washington, D.C. : World Bank, Development Research Dept., 1982, c1981. — 148p. — (LSMS working papers ; no.16). — *Bibliography: p64-69*

INFANTS — Nutrition — History
FILDES, Valerie A.
Breasts, bottles and babies : a history of infant feeding / by Valerie A. Fildes. — Edinburgh : Edinburgh University Press, c1986. — xxviii,462p. — *Includes bibliographies and index*

INFANTS — Ecuador — Mortality
BORJA M., Eduardo
Factores determinantes de una mortalidad prematura en Ecuador / Eduardo Borja M.. — Voorburg : International Statistical Institute, 1985. — 31p. — (Scientific reports / World Fertility Survey ; no.74)

INFANTS — Great Britain — Mortality
GREAT BRITAIN. Working Party on Infant and Perinatal Mortality and Morbidity
Report. — [London] : Department of Health and Social Security, 1977. — 7,[12] leaves. — *Includes bibliographical references*

INFANTS — Great Britain — Nutrition
PANEL ON CHILD NUTRITION. Working Party on Infant Feeding
Present day practice in infant feeding: 1980 : report. — Rev. ed. — London : H.M.S.O., 1983. — x,50p. — (Report on health and social subjects ; 20). — *First published 1980. — Bibliographical references: p40-50*

INFANTS — Guyana — Mortality
EBANKS, G. Edward
Infant and child mortality and fertility : Trinidad and Tobago, Guyana and Jamaica / G. Edward Ebanks. — Voorburg : International Statistical Institute, 1985. — 68p. — (Scientific reports / World Fertility Survey ; no.75)

INFANTS — Haiti — Mortality — Statistics
ROUSSEAU, J. A.
La mortalité infantile et juvénile en Haïti / J. A. Rousseau. — Voorburg : International Statistical Institute, 1985. — 23p. — (Scientific reports / World Fertility Survey ; no.82)

INFANTS — Italy — Mortality — Statistics
ITALY. Istituto Centrale di Statistica
Recenti livelli e caratteristiche della mortalità infantile in Italia : analisi delle informazioni e proposte di miglioramento. — [Roma] : Istituto Centrale di Statistica, 1983. — 102p. — (Collana di informazioni. Anno 7 ; 4)

INFANTS — Jamaica — Mortality
EBANKS, G. Edward
Infant and child mortality and fertility : Trinidad and Tobago, Guyana and Jamaica / G. Edward Ebanks. — Voorburg : International Statistical Institute, 1985. — 68p. — (Scientific reports / World Fertility Survey ; no.75)

INFANTS — Syria — Mortality — Statistics

Pregnancy follow-up study in Syria : 1976-1979. — [Damascus] : Central Bureau of Statistics, 1984. — 90p

VAIDYANATHAN, K. E.
Estimation of infant and child mortality in Syria from the 1970 Census data / K. E. Vaidyanathan. — Damascus : Central Bureau of Statistics, 1976. — 17p. — (Syrian Population Studies Series ; No.2)

INFANTS — Thailand — Mortality — Statistics

The survey of population change, 1974-76 : special report on fertility, nuptiality and infant mortality measures. — Bangkok : National Statistical Office, [1979]. — 81p. — *Contents: Estimating fertility in Thailand from information on children ever born/Kenneth Hill - Some indirect estimates of fertility and infant mortality.../Arjun L. Adlakha and Chintana Pejaranonda - Marriage pattern/Chinatana Pejaranonda*

INFANTS — Trinidad and Tobago — Mortality

EBANKS, G. Edward
Infant and child mortality and fertility : Trinidad and Tobago, Guyana and Jamaica / G. Edward Ebanks. — Voorburg : International Statistical Institute, 1985. — 68p. — (Scientific reports / World Fertility Survey ; no.75)

INFANTS — Mortality — Bibliography

HILL, Allan G.
A review of materials and methods for the study of infant and child mortality in Africa / Allan G. Hill and Georgia L. Kaufmann. — London : London School of Hygiene and Tropical Medicine, Centre for Population Studies, 1987. — 38p. — (CPS research paper ; 87-1)

INFANTS (NEWBORN) — Diseases — Treatment — Government policy — Congresses

Euthanasia and the newborn : conflicts regarding saving lives / edited by Richard M. McMillan, H. Tristram Engelhardt, Jr., and Stuart F. Spicker. — Dordrecht ; Boston : D. Reidel Pub. Co. ; Norwell, MA, U.S.A. : Sold and distributed in the U.S.A. and Canada by Kluwer Academic Publishers, c1987. — p. cm. — (Philosophy and medicine ; v. 24). — *Based on a symposium entitled "Conflicts with Newborns: Saving Lives, Scarce Resources, and Euthanasis," held May 10-12, 1984, at the Mercer University School of Medicine, Macon, Ga. — Includes bibliographies and index*

INFANTS (NEWBORN) — Diseases — Treatment — Moral and ethical aspects — Congresses

Euthanasia and the newborn : conflicts regarding saving lives / edited by Richard M. McMillan, H. Tristram Engelhardt, Jr., and Stuart F. Spicker. — Dordrecht ; Boston : D. Reidel Pub. Co. ; Norwell, MA, U.S.A. : Sold and distributed in the U.S.A. and Canada by Kluwer Academic Publishers, c1987. — p. cm. — (Philosophy and medicine ; v. 24). — *Based on a symposium entitled "Conflicts with Newborns: Saving Lives, Scarce Resources, and Euthanasis," held May 10-12, 1984, at the Mercer University School of Medicine, Macon, Ga. — Includes bibliographies and index*

INFANTS (NEWBORN) — Great Britain — Statistics

MCDOWALL, M. E.
Occupational reproductive epidemiology : the use of routinely collected statistics in England and Wales 1980-82 / M. E. McDowall, Medical Statistics Division, Office of Population Censuses and Surveys. — London : H.M.S.O., 1985. — iii,77p. — (Studies on medical and population subjects ; no.50). — *Bibliographical references: p76-77*

INFERENCE

Induction : processes of inference, learning, and discovery / John H. Holland ... [et al.]. — Cambridge, Mass. : MIT Press, c1986. — xvi, 385p. — (Computational models of cognition and perception). — *Includes index. — Bibliography: p.357-372*

INFERENCE (LOGIC)

FORREST, Peter
The dynamics of belief : a normative logic / Peter Forrest. — Oxford : Basil Blackwell, 1986. — vii,213p. — (Philosophical theory). — *Bibliography: p199-202. — Includes index*

INFLATION — Developing countries

KAPUR, Basant K.
Studies in inflationary dynamics : financial repression and financial liberalization in less developed countries / Basant K. Kapur. — Singapore : Singapore University Press, 1986. — xviii,146p. — *Bibliography: p142-146*

INFLATION (FINANCE)

CAPIE, Forrest
Conditions in which very rapid inflation has appeared / Forrest Capie. — London : City University, 1985. — 64p. — (Discussion paper series ; no.20). — *Bibliography: p58-64*

DESAI, Meghnad
Money, inflation and unemployment : an econometric model of the Keynes effect / M. Desai and G. Weber. — London : Economic and Social Research Council : London School of Economics, 1986. — [77p]. — (ESRC/LSE econometrics project discussion paper ; A.59). — *Bibliography: p[69.71]*

DORNBUSCH, Rudiger
Inflation, exchange rates, and stabilization / Rudiger Dornbusch. — Princeton, N.J. : International Finance Section, Dept. of Economics, Princeton University, 1986. — p. cm. — (Essays in international finance ; no. 165 (Oct. 1986)). — *Bibliography: p*

HOLTHAM, G. H.
Wealth and inflation effects in the aggregate consumption function / by G. H. Holtham, H. Kato. — [Paris] : OECD, 1986. — 37p. — (Working papers / OECD Department of Economics and Statistics ; no.35). — *Bibliographical references: p19*

Inflation, trade and taxes : essays in honor of Alice Bourneuf / edited by David A. Belsley...[et al.]. — Columbus : Ohio State University Press, 1976. — 252p

LEMAIRE, Bruno
Mystères de L ínflation : valeurs et prix en économie de marché / Bruno Lemaire. — Gif sur Yvette, France : Frontières, [1985]. — 222p

PLOEG, Frederick van der
Capital accumulation, inflation and long-run conflict in international objectives / F. van der Ploeg. — London : Centre for Labour Economics, London School of Economics, 1986. — 29p. — (Discussion paper / London School of Economics and Political Science. Centre for Labour Economics ; no.250). — *Bibliography: p28-29*

INFLATION (FINANCE) — Effect of energy costs on — Mathematical models

Macroeconomics [i.e. Macroeconimic] impacts of energy shocks / edited by Bert G. Hickman, Hillard G. Huntington, and James L. Sweeney. — Amsterdam ; New York : North-Holland ; New York, N.Y., U.S.A. : Sole distributors for the U.S.A. and Canada, Elsevier Science Pub. Co., 1987. — xvi, 331 p.. — (Contributions to economic analysis ; 163). — *Includes bibliographical references*

INFLATION (FINANCE) — Social aspects

GILBERT, Michael
Inflation and social conflict : a sociology of economic life in advanced societies / Michael Gilbert. — Brighton : Wheatsheaf, 1986. — xii,260p. — *Bibliography: p239-253. — Includes index*

INFLATION (FINANCE) — Social aspects — Germany — History — 20th century

KUNZ, Andreas
Civil servants and the politics of inflation in Germany, 1914-1924 / Andreas Kunz. — Berlin ; New York : De Gruyter, 1986. — xix, 427 p.. — (Veröffentlichungen der Historischen Kommission zu Berlin ; Bd. 66) (Beiträge zu Inflation und Wiederaufbau in Deutschland und Europa 1914-1924 ; Bd. 7). — *Includes indexes. — Bibliography: p. [393]-413*

INFLATION (FINANCE) — Yugoslavia

JOVANOVIĆ, Batrić
Kosovo, inflacija, socijalne razlike : istupanja u Skupštini SFRJ, 1982-85 / Batrić Jovanović. — Beograd : [Partizanska knjiga], 1985. — 331p. — (Sučeljavanja)

INFLATION (FINANCE) — Belgium

FÉDÉRATION DES ENTREPRISES DE BELGIQUE
La FEB et l ínflation. — Bruxelles : Fédération des Entreprises, 1974. — 7p

INFLATION (FINANCE) — Canada

Un modele de l'inflation au Canada / Pierre Fortin [et al.]. — Montreal : Université de Montréal Departement des Sciences Economiques, 1976. — 22p. — (Cahier / Université de Montréal. Departement des Sciences Economiques ; no.7602). — *Bibliography: p22*

INFLATION (FINANCE) — Developing countries

NBAGUI, Sambwa Pida
L'inflation dans les pays en voie de developpement : conférence donnée par Monsieur Sambwa Pida Nbagui. — Bruxelles : Société Royale d'Économie Politique de Belgique, 1972. — 38p

INFLATION (FINANCE) — Great Britain

WADHWANI, Sushil Baldev
Inflation : real effects and possible cures / by Sushil B. Wadhwani. — 200 leaves. — *PhD (Econ) 1986 LSE*

INFLATION (FINANCE) — Great Britain — Measurement

GREAT BRITAIN. Parliament. House of Commons. Library. Research Division
The measurement of inflation / R. Twigger. — [London] : the Division, 1982. — 12p. — (Background paper ; no.105). — *Bibliography: p12*

GREAT BRITAIN. Parliament. House of Commons. Library. Research Division
The measurement of inflation / Robert Twigger. — [London] : the Division, 1983. — 12p. — (Background paper ; no.120). — *June 1983 version*

GREAT BRITAIN. Parliament. House of Commons. Library. Research Division
The measurement of inflation / Robert Twigger. — [London] : the Division, 1983. — 12p. — (Background paper ; no.129). — *November 1983 version. — Bibliography: p12*

GREAT BRITAIN. Parliament. House of Commons. Library. Research Division
The measurement of inflation / Robert Twigger. — [London] : the Division, 1984. — 12p. — (Background paper ; no.142). — *June 1984 version. — Bibliography: p12*

GREAT BRITAIN. Parliament. House of Commons. Library. Research Division
The measurement of inflation / Robert Twigger. — [London] : the Division, 1985. — 12p. — (Background paper ; no.171). — *June 1985 version. — Bibliography: p12*

GREAT BRITAIN. Parliament. House of Commons. Library. Research Division
The measurement of inflation / Robert Twigger. — [London] : the Division, 1986. — 12p. — (Background paper ; no.182). — *May 1986 version. — Bibliography: p12*

INFLATION (FINANCE) — Great Britain — Measurement
continuation

GREAT BRITAIN. Parliament. House of Commons. Library. Research Division
The measurement of inflation / Robert Twigger. — May 1987 version. — [London] : the Division, 1987. — 13p. — (Background paper ; no.199). — *Bibliography: p14*

INFLATION (FINANCE) — Peru
REBOLLEDO SOBERÓN, Luis
Insuficiencia de ahorro y financiamiento por la inflación / Luis Rebolledo Soberón. — [Lima] : Ministerio de Economía y Finanzas, Dirección General de Asuntos Financieros, 1974. — 16leaves

INFLATION (FINANCE) — Spain
MARTÍNEZ MÉNDEZ, Pedro
Los gastos financieros y los resultados empresariales en condiciones de inflación / Pedro Martínez Méndez. — [Madrid] : Banco de España, 1986. — 134p. — (Estudios económicos / Banco de España, Servicio de Estudios ; no.39). — *Bibliography: p129-131*

INFLATION (FINANCE) — Switzerland
LINDER, Wolf
Inflation législative? : une recherche sur l'évolution quantitative du droit suisse / Wolf Linder, Stefan Schwager [et] Fabrizio Comandini. — Lausanne : Institut de hautes études en administration publique, 1985. — 109p. — (Recherches sur le secteur public suisse ; 1)

INFLATION (FINANCE) — United States
FINANCIAL ACCOUNTING STANDARDS BOARD
Statement of financial accounting standards. — Stamford, Conn. : Financial Accounting Standards Board
No.89: Financial reporting and changing prices. — 1986. — 81p

GOLDSCHMIDT, Yaaqov
The impact of inflation of financial activity in business, with applications to the U.S. farming sector / Yaaqov Goldschmidt, Leon Sashua, Jimmye S. Hillman. — Totowa, N.J. : Rowman & Allanheld, 1986. — p. cm. — *Includes index. — Bibliography: p*

INFLUENCE (PSYCHOLOGY)
HOLLANDER, Edwin Paul
Leadership dynamics : a practical guide to effective relationships / Edwin P. Hollander. — New York : Free Press, c1978. — xii, 212 p.. — *Includes indexes. — Bibliography: p. 185-201*

INFLUENZA
CLIFF, A. D.
Spatial aspects of influenza epidemics / A. D. Cliff, P. Haggett, J. K. Ord. — London : Pion, 1986. — [xii],280p. — *Bibliography: p[269]-275*

INFORMAL SECTOR (ECONOMICS)
ROSS, David P
From the roots up : economic development as if community mattered / David P. Ross and Peter J. Usher ; with a foreword by George McRobie. — Croton-on-Hudson, N.Y. : Bootstrap Press, c1986. — xviii, 173 p.. — *Bibliography: p. 167-172*

The Unofficial economy : consequences and perspectives in different economic systems / edited by Sergio Alessandrini and Bruno Dallago. — Aldershot : Gower, c1987. — 345p . — *Conference proceedings. — Includes bibliographies*

INFORMAL SECTOR (ECONOMICS) — Egypt
ABDEL-FADIL, Mahmoud
Informal sector employment in Egypt / Mahmoud Abdel-Fadil. — Geneva : International Labour Office, 1983. — viii,39p. — (Employment opportunities and equity in Egypt ; no.1). — *Bibliographical references: p35-39. — A technical paper of the ILO/UNDP comprehensive employment strategy mission to Egypt, 1980*

INFORMAL SECTOR (ECONOMICS) — France
ADAIR, Philippe
L'economie informelle : (figures et discours) / Philippe Adair. — Paris : Anthropos, [1985]. — 180p. — *Bibliography: p161-171*

INFORMATION NETWORKS
ANDREWS, David
Th hidden manager : communication technology and information networks in business organisations / David Andrews and John Kent. — London : Taylor Graham, 1986. — 90p

HILTZ, Starr Roxanne
The network nation : human communication via computer / Starr Roxanne Hiltz, Murray Turoff ; with forewords by Suzanne Keller and Herbert R.J. Grosch. — Reading, Mass. ; London : Addison-Wesley, 1978. — xxxv,528 [i.e.536]p. — *Text on lining paper. — Bibliography(21p.). — Includes index*

Network user (incorporating Network). — London : British Telecommunications, 1986-. — *Quarterly*

INFORMATION NETWORKS — Directories
Encyclopedia of information systems and services / edited by John Schmittroth, Jr. ; Amy F. Lucas and Annette Novallo, associate editors ; Kathleen Young Marcaccio, contributing editor. — 6th ed. — Detroit, Mich. : Gale Research Co., c1985-. — v. <1 >. — *At head of title: 1985-86. — Includes indexes. — Contents: v. 1. International volume*

INFORMATION RESOURCES MANAGEMENT
New methods and techniques for information management / editor: Mary Feeney. — London : Taylor Graham on behalf of the Primary Communications Research Centre, 1986. — iv,364p. — (Scholarly communications guide). — *Bibliographies*

INFORMATION RESOURCES MANAGEMENT — Security measures
BASKERVILLE, Richard Lee
Implications of office automation on information systems security / Richard Lee Baskerville. — 403 leaves. — *PhD (Econ) 1986 LSE. — Leaves 371-403 are appendices*

INFORMATION RETRIEVAL
New methods and techniques for information management / editor: Mary Feeney. — London : Taylor Graham on behalf of the Primary Communications Research Centre, 1986. — iv,364p. — (Scholarly communications guide). — *Bibliographies*

INFORMATION SCIENCE
Annual review of information science and technology / American Society for Information Science. — White Plains, N.Y. : Knowledge Industry Publications, 1985-. — *Annual. — vol.7 published by American Society for Information Science*

Information and behavior. — New Brunswick ; Oxford : Transaction Books. — *Bibliographies* volume 1 / edited by Brent D. Ruben. — 1985. — xxiv,521p

Information and communication technologies : social science research and training. — London : Economic and Social Research Council. — *At head of title: A report by the ESRC Programme on Information and Communication Technologies*
Vol 2: National directory / edited by Robin E. Mansell ; assisted by Barbara J. Richards. — 1986

Information comes of age : proceedings of the annual conference of the Institute of Information Scientists, University of Kent at Canterbury, July 1984 / edited by Charles Oppenheim. — London : Rossendale, c1984. — 126p

Information technology and information use : towards a unified view of information and information technology / edited by Peter Ingwersen, Leif Kajberg [and] Annelise Mark Pejtersen. — London : Taylor Graham, 1986. — 194p. — *Includes Bibliographies*

MELODY, William H.
Information and communication technologies : social science research and training. — London : Economic and Social Research Council. — *At head of title: A report by the ESRC Programme on Information and Communication Technologies*
Vol 1: An over-view of research / William H. Melody, Robin E. Mansell. — 1986

New methods and techniques for information management / editor: Mary Feeney. — London : Taylor Graham on behalf of the Primary Communications Research Centre, 1986. — iv,364p. — (Scholarly communications guide). — *Bibliographies*

Oxford surveys in information technology. — Oxford : Oxford University Press, 1984-. — *Annual*

INFORMATION SCIENCE — Economic aspects — Organisation for Economic Co-operation and Development countries
KIMBEL, Dieter
Information technology and economic prospects / [Dieter Kimbel, Paul Stoneman]. — Paris : OECD, 1987. — 221p. — (Information, computer, communications policy ; 12). — *Bibliography: p219-220*

INFORMATION SCIENCE — Social aspects
CLEVELAND, Harlan
The knowledge executive : leadership in an information society / by Harlan Cleveland. — 1st ed. — New York : Dutton, c1985. — p. cm . — *"A Truman Talley Book.". — Includes index. — Bibliography: p*

INFORMATION SCIENCE — Great Britain
The World of books and information : essays in honour of Lord Dainton / edited by Maurice Line. — London : British Library, 1987. — [256]p. — *Includes bibliography*

INFORMATION SERVICES
International journal of information management. — Guildford : Butterworth Scientific, 1986-. — *Quarterly. — Continues: Social science information studies*

INFORMATION SERVICES — Cost control
ROBERTS, Stephen A.
Cost management for library and information services / Stephen A. Roberts. — London : Butterworths, 1985. — 181 p

INFORMATION SERVICES — Directories
Encyclopedia of information systems and services / edited by John Schmittroth, Jr. ; Amy F. Lucas and Annette Novallo, associate editors ; Kathleen Young Marcaccio, contributing editor. — 6th ed. — Detroit, Mich. : Gale Research Co., c1985-. — v. <1 >. — *At head of title: 1985-86. — Includes indexes. — Contents: v. 1. International volume*

INFORMATION SERVICES — Economic aspects — Organisation for Economic Co-operation and Development countries
Information computer communications policy. — Paris : Organisation for Economic Co-operation and Development. — *Includes bibliographical references*
11: Trends in the information economy. — 1986. — 42p

INFORMATION SERVICES — Finance
ROBERTS, Stephen A.
Cost management for library and information services / Stephen A. Roberts. — London : Butterworths, 1985. — 181 p

INFORMATION SERVICES — Legal status, laws, etc. — Peru

PERU
[Laws, etc]. Ley orgánica del Sistema Nacional de Información. — Lima : [Oficina Central de Información, Oficina de Relaciones Públicas, ca.1975]. — 38p

INFORMATION SERVICES — Management

CLEVELAND, Harlan
The knowledge executive : leadership in an information society / by Harlan Cleveland. — 1st ed. — New York : Dutton, c1985. — p. cm . — *"A Truman Talley Book."*. — *Includes index. — Bibliography: p*

Information management : from strategies to action / edited by Blaise Cronin. — London : Aslib, 1985. — [196]p. — *Includes bibliography*

ROBERTS, Stephen A.
Cost management for library and information services / Stephen A. Roberts. — London : Butterworths, 1985. — 181 p

INFORMATION SERVICES — Australia

Australian and New Zealand studies : papers presented at a colloquium at the British Library 7-9 February 1984 / edited by Patricia McLaren-Turner. — London : The Library, 1985. — [232]p. — (British Library occasional papers ; 4)

BLOOMFIELD, Valerie
Resources for Australian and New Zealand studies : a guide to library holdings in the United Kingdom / Valerie Bloomfield. — London : Australian Studies Centre, 1986. — xvi,284p. — *Bibliography: p264. — Includes index*

Design for diversity : library services for higher education and research in Australia / edited by Harrison Bryan and Gordon Greenwood. — St. Lucia [Aus.] : University of Queensland Press, c1977. — xvi, 790 p., [11] p. of plates. — *Distributed by Prentice-Hall International, Hemel Hempstead, Eng. — Includes index. — Bibliography: p. [713]-740*

INFORMATION SERVICES — Canada

Canadian studies : papers presented at a colloquium at the British Library, 17-19 August 1983 / edited by Patricia McLaren-Turner. — London : British Library, 1984. — vii,210p,[8]p of plates. — (British Library occasional papers ; 1). — *Includes bibliographies*

INFORMATION SERVICES — Great Britain

LIBRARY AND INFORMATION SERVICES COUNCIL
Joint enterprise : roles and relationships of the public and private sectors in the provision of library and information services / [report of Library and Information Services Council and British Library Research and Development Department Working Party]. — London : H.M.S.O., 1987. — vii, 49p. — (Library information series ; no.16). — *On cover: Office of Arts and Libraries*

INFORMATION SERVICES — New Zealand

Australian and New Zealand studies : papers presented at a colloquium at the British Library 7-9 February 1984 / edited by Patricia McLaren-Turner. — London : The Library, 1985. — [232]p. — (British Library occasional papers ; 4)

BLOOMFIELD, Valerie
Resources for Australian and New Zealand studies : a guide to library holdings in the United Kingdom / Valerie Bloomfield. — London : Australian Studies Centre, 1986. — xvi,284p. — *Bibliography: p264. — Includes index*

INFORMATION SERVICES — South Asia

South Asian studies : papers presented at a colloquium 24-26 April 1985 / edited by Albertine Gaur. — London : British Library, 1986. — xvi,327p. — (British library occasional papers ; 7)

INFORMATION SERVICES — United States — Statistics

RUBIN, Michael Rogers
The knowledge industry in the United States, 1960-1980 / Michael Rogers Rubin and Mary Taylor Huber with Elizabeth Lloyd Taylor. — Princeton, N.J. : Princeton University Press, c1986. — p. cm. — *Includes index*

INFORMATION SERVICES AND STATE

SAUVANT, Karl P
International transactions in services : the politics of transborder data flows / Karl P. Sauvant. — Boulder : Westview Press, 1986. — p. cm. — (The Atwater series on the world information economy) (Westview special studies in international economics and business)

INFORMATION SERVICES AND STATE — Legal status, laws, etc. — Peru

PERU
[Decreto ley no.21099]. Ley orgánica de la Agencia de Publicidad del Estado : decreto ley no.21099. — [Lima : Presidencia?, 1975]. — 9leaves

INFORMATION SERVICES AND STATE — Peru

PERU
[Laws, etc]. Ley orgánica del Sistema Nacional de Información. — Lima : [Oficina Central de Información, Oficina de Relaciones Públicas, ca.1975]. — 38p

INFORMATION SERVICES EMPLOYEES — Great Britain

CONNOR, Helen
Information technology manpower into the 1990's / Helen Connor and Richard Pearson. — Falmer : Institute of Manpower Studies, University of Sussex, 1986. — xxiv,206p. — *Bibliography: p197-199*

CONNOR, Helen
The labour market for IT postgraduates / by Helen Connor and Richard Pearson. — Brighton : Institute of Manpower Studies, 1986. — vi,108p. — (IMS report ; No.118)

INFORMATION STORAGE AND RETRIEVAL SYSTEMS

BEHAN, Kate
Understanding information technology : text, readings, and cases / Kate Behan, Diana Holmes. — Englewood Cliffs, N.J. : Prentice-Hall, c1986. — xiv, 493 p.. — *Includes bibliographies and indexes*

Database: the magazine of database reference and review. — Western (CT) : Online, Inc, 1986. — *6 times per year*

DELAPIERRE, Michel
L'informatique du Nord au Sud : un complexe industriel transnationalisé / Michel Delapierre, Jean-Benoît Zimmermann. — Paris : La Documentation française, 1986. — 143p. — (Notes et études documentaires ; no.4809)

FORSYTH, Richard
Machine learning : applications in expert systems and information retrieval / R. Forsyth and R. Rada. — Chichester : Ellis Horwood, 1986. — 277p. — (Ellis Horwood series in artificial intelligence). — *Text on lining papers. — Bibliography: p264-273. — Includes index*

GOLDSMITH, G.
Online searching made simple : a microcomputer interface for inexperienced users / G. Goldsmith and P.W. Williams. — London : British Library, c1986. — ix,113p. — (Library and information research report ; 41)

GREAT BRITAIN. Parliament. House of Commons. Library. Research Division
The UK information technology industry / C. R. Barclay. — [London] : the Division, 1987. — 33p. — (Background paper ; no.194). — *Bibliography: p33*

Handbook of information technology and office systems / edited by A.E. Cawkell. — Amsterdam ; New York : North-Holland ; New York, N.Y., U.S.A. : Sole distributors for the U.S.A. and Canada, Elsevier Science Pub. Co., 1986. — x, 996 p.. — *Includes bibliographies and index*

HEEKS, Richard
Personal bibliographic indexes and their computerisation / Richard Heeks. — London : published by Taylor Graham on behalf of the Primary Communications Research Centre, University of Leicester, c1986. — 189p. — *Bibliography: p185-189*

HENDLEY, Tony
CD-Rom and optical publishing systems : an assessment of the impact of optical read only memory systems on the information industry and a comparison between them and traditional paper, microfilm and on-line publishing systems / Tony Hendley. — Hatfield : Cimtech, 1987. — 151p. — (Cimtech publication ; 26) (British National Bibliography Research Fund report ; no.25)

HENDLEY, Tony
Videodiscs, compact discs and digital optical disk systems : an introduction to the technologies and the systems and their potential for information storage, retrieval and dissemination / by Tony Hendley. — Hatfield : Cimtech, 1985

Human factors of information technology in the office / edited by Bruce Christie. — Chichester : Wiley, c1985. — ix,352p. — (Wiley series in information processing). — *Bibliography: p326-340. — Includes index*

Information technology & people : designing for the future / edited by Frank Blackler and David Oborne. — Leicester : British Psychological Society, 1987. — 262 p

NATIONAL ECONOMIC DEVELOPMENT COUNCIL. Economic Development Committee for the Information Technology Industry. Long-Term Perspectives Group
I T futures...it can work : an optimistic view of the long-term potential of information technology for Britain. — London : [H.M.S.O.], 1987. — xiv,171p. — *Chairman: Alan Benjamin. — Includes bibliographical references*

New methods and techniques for information management / editor: Mary Feeney. — London : Taylor Graham on behalf of the Primary Communications Research Centre, 1986. — iv,364p. — (Scholarly communications guide). — *Bibliographies*

Online: the magazine of online information systems. — Weston : On-Line, Inc., 1986-. — *6 times a year*

Oxford surveys in information technology. — Oxford : Oxford University Press, 1984-. — *Annual*

TEXT RETRIEVAL '85 CONFERENCE
Integrating text with non-text : a picture is worth IK words / edited by Robert Kimberley : proceedings of the Institute of Information Scientists Text Retrieval '85 Conference. — London : Taylor Graham, 1986. — 120p

WEBSTER, Frank
Information technology : a luddite analysis / Frank Webster Kevin Robins. — Norwood, N.J. : Ablex Pub. Corp., 1986. — x,387p.. — (Communication and information science). — *Bibliography: p.349-375. — Bibliography: p*

INFORMATION STORAGE AND RETRIEVAL SYSTEMS *continuation*
WOOD-HARPER, A. T.
Information systems definition : the multiview approach / A.T. Wood-Harper, Lyn Antill and D.E. Avison. — Oxford : Blackwell Scientific, 1985. — 167p. — (Computer Science texts). — *Includes bibliographies and index*

INFORMATION STORAGE AND RETRIEVAL SYSTEMS — Addresses, essays, lectures
Trends in information systems : an anthology of papers from conferences of the IFIP Technical Committee 8 "Information Systems" to commemorate their tenth anniversary / edited by B. Langefors, A.A. Verrijn-Stuart, G. Bracchi. — Amsterdam ; New York : North-Holland ; New York : Sole distributors for the U.S.A. and Canada Elsevier Science Pub. Co., 1986. — xv, 469 p.. — *Includes bibliographies*

INFORMATION STORAGE AND RETRIEVAL SYSTEMS — Archival material
CENTRAL COMPUTER AND TELECOMMUNICATIONS AGENCY
Data storage on optical disk : an experiment. — London : H.M.S.O., 1986. — 26p. — (Information technology in the civil service. IT series ; no.13)

INFORMATION STORAGE AND RETRIEVAL SYSTEMS — Business
FOSTER, Allan
Online business sourcebook / by Allan Foster and Gerry Smith. — Hartlepool : Headland, 1985. — 1v.(looseleaf). — *Includes index*

INFORMATION STORAGE AND RETRIEVAL SYSTEMS — Directories
Encyclopedia of information systems and services / edited by John Schmittroth, Jr. ; Amy F. Lucas and Annette Novallo, associate editors ; Kathleen Young Marcaccio, contributing editor. — 6th ed. — Detroit, Mich. : Gale Research Co., c1985-. — v. <1 >. — At head of title: 1985-86. — *Includes indexes.* — Contents: v. 1. International volume

INFORMATION STORAGE AND RETRIEVAL SYSTEMS — Evaluation
Information retrieval experiment / edited by Karen Sparck Jones. — London : Butterworths, 1981. — viii,352p. — *Bibliography: p330-342. — Includes index*

INFORMATION STORAGE AND RETRIEVAL SYSTEMS — Geography
GREAT BRITAIN. Committee of Enquiry into the Handling of Geographic Information
Handling geographic information : report to the Secretary of State for the Environment of the Committee of Enquiry into the Handling of Geographic Information. — London : H.M.S.O., 1987. — vi,208p. — Chairman: Lord Chorley. — *References and bibliography: p125-126,p174*

INFORMATION STORAGE AND RETRIEVAL SYSTEMS — Humanities — Congresses
INTERNATIONAL CONFERENCE ON DATABASES IN THE HUMANITIES AND SOCIAL SCIENCES (4th : 1983 : New Brunswick, N.J.)
The International Conference on Databases in the Humanities and Social Sciences 1983 / edited by Robert F. Allen. — Osprey, Fla. : Paradigm Press, 1985. — 434p. — Cover title: *Databases in the humanities and social sciences*. — *Bibliographical references*

INFORMATION STORAGE AND RETRIEVAL SYSTEMS — Labor supply
CONNOR, Helen
Information technology manpower into the 1990's / Helen Connor and Richard Pearson. — Falmer : Institute of Manpower Studies, University of Sussex, 1986. — xxiv,206p. — *Bibliography: p197-199*

INFORMATION STORAGE AND RETRIEVAL SYSTEMS — Law
INTERNATIONAL CONFERENCE ON "LOGIC, INFORMATICS, LAW" (2nd : 1985 : Florence, Italy)
Automated analysis of legal texts : logic, informatics, law : edited versions of selected papers from the Second International Conference on "Logic, Informatics, Law,"Florence, Italy, September 1985 / edited by Antonio A. Martino, Fiorenza Socci Natali ; editorial assistant, Simona Binazzi. — Amsterdam ; New York : North-Holland ; New York, N.Y., U.S.A. : Sole distributors for the U.S.A. and Canada, Elsevier Science Pub. Co., 1986. — xxii, 938 p.. — *Includes bibliographies and index*

INFORMATION STORAGE AND RETRIEVAL SYSTEMS — Law — Bibliography
Applications of computer technology to law : a selected bibliography (1969-1981) for British lawyers / Society for Computers and Law. — Milton, Oxon. : the Society, 1982. — 60p

INFORMATION STORAGE AND RETRIEVAL SYSTEMS — Law — Europe
SYMPOSIUM ON LEGAL DATA PROCESSING IN EUROPE (8th : 1985 : Luxembourg)
Access to legal data bases in Europe : reports presented at the Symposium. — Strasbourg : Council of Europe, 1986. — 226p

INFORMATION STORAGE AND RETRIEVAL SYSTEMS — Law — Europe — Public opinion
LLOYD, Michael Gordon
Legal databases in Europe : user attitudes and supplier strategies / Michael Lloyd. — Amsterdam ; New York : North-Holland ; New York, N.Y., U.S.A. : Sole distributors for the U.S.A. and Canada, Elsevier Science Pub. Co., c1986. — xiii, 218 p.. — At head of title: *Commission of the European Communities.* — "Report no. EUR 10439 of the Commission of the European Communities"--T.p. verso. — *Bibliography: p.205*

INFORMATION STORAGE AND RETRIEVAL SYSTEMS — Law — Great Britain
Applications of computer technology to law : a selected bibliography (1969-1981) for British lawyers / Society for Computers and Law. — Milton, Oxon. : the Society, 1982. — 60p

INFORMATION STORAGE AND RETRIEVAL SYSTEMS — Management
FOSTER, Allan
Online business sourcebook / by Allan Foster and Gerry Smith. — Hartlepool : Headland, 1985. — 1v.(looseleaf). — *Includes index*

INFORMATION STORAGE AND RETRIEVAL SYSTEMS — Names, Geographical — Code numbers
Standard country or area codes for statistical use. — Rev.2. — New York : United Nations, 1982. — vii,23p. — (Statistical papers / United Nations, Statistical Office. Series M ; no.49,Rev.2) [Document] / United Nations ; ST/ESA/STAT/SER.M/49/Rev.2). — *Includes Bibliographical references*. — Sales: E.82.XVII.8

INFORMATION STORAGE AND RETRIEVAL SYSTEMS — Social aspects
FORESTER, Tom
High-tech society : the story of the information technology revolution / Tom Forester. — Oxford : Basil Blackwell, 1987. — viii,311p. — *Bibliography: p290-296.* — *Includes index*

Pour une informatique consciente : réflexions sur l'enjeu humain et l'impact socio-culturel de l'informatique / Michel Bassand...[et al.] ; textes rassemblés par Pierre-Gerard Fontolliet dans le cadre d'un cours de l'Université populaire de Lausanne. — Lausanne : Presses polytechniques romandes, [1985]. — 208p

INFORMATION STORAGE AND RETRIEVAL SYSTEMS — Social aspects — Great Britain — Forecasting
IT futures surveyed : a study of informed opinion concerning the long-term implications of information technology for society / a report prepared by John Bessant...[et al.] for the Long-Term Perspectives Group of the Information Technology Economic Development Committee. — London : National Economic Development Office, 1986. — x,92p

INFORMATION STORAGE AND RETRIEVAL SYSTEMS — Social sciences — Congresses
INTERNATIONAL CONFERENCE ON DATABASES IN THE HUMANITIES AND SOCIAL SCIENCES (4th : 1983 : New Brunswick, N.J.)
The International Conference on Databases in the Humanities and Social Sciences 1983 / edited by Robert F. Allen. — Osprey, Fla. : Paradigm Press, 1985. — 434p. — Cover title: *Databases in the humanities and social sciences*. — *Bibliographical references*

INFORMATION STORAGE AND RETRIEVAL SYSTEMS — Technological innovations
BENIGER, James R
The control revolution : technological and economic origins of the information society / James R. Beniger. — Cambridge, Mass. : Harvard University Press, 1986. — x, 493 p.. — *Includes index.* — *Bibliography: p. [439]-476*

INFORMATION STORAGE AND RETRIEVAL SYSTEMS — Technology — Great Britain
CONNOR, Helen
Information technology manpower into the 1990's / Helen Connor and Richard Pearson. — Falmer : Institute of Manpower Studies, University of Sussex, 1986. — xxiv,206p. — *Bibliography: p197-199*

INFORMATION STORAGE AND RETRIEVAL SYSTEMS — Experiments
Information retrieval experiment / edited by Karen Sparck Jones. — London : Butterworths, 1981. — viii,352p. — *Bibliography: p330-342. — Includes index*

INFORMATION STORAGE AND RETRIEVAL SYSTEMS — Great Britain — Labor supply
CONNOR, Helen
The labour market for IT postgraduates / by Helen Connor and Richard Pearson. — Brighton : Institute of Manpower Studies, 1986. — vi,108p. — (IMS report ; No.118)

INFORMATION STORAGE AND RETRIEVAL SYSTEMS — Portugal — Congresses
CONGRESO HISPANO-LUSO DE INFORMÁTICA (1st : 1971 : Madrid)
Actas del 1er Congreso Hispano-Luso de informática / [organizador del Congreso CITEMA]. — Madrid : CITEMA, 1971. — 439p

INFORMATION STORAGE AND RETRIEVAL SYSTEMS — Spain — Congresses
CONGRESO HISPANO-LUSO DE INFORMÁTICA (1st : 1971 : Madrid)
Actas del 1er Congreso Hispano-Luso de informática / [organizador del Congreso CITEMA]. — Madrid : CITEMA, 1971. — 439p

INFORMATION THEORY — Statistical methods
KRIPPENDORFF, Klaus
Information theory : structural models for qualitative data / Klaus Krippendorff. — Beverly Hills ; London : Sage, c1986. — 96 p. — (Quantitative applications in the social sciences ; 62)

INFORMATION THEORY IN BIOLOGY — Data processing
SAMPSON, Jeffrey R.
Biological information processing : current theory and computer simulation / Jeffrey R. Sampson. — New York ; Chichester : Wiley, c1984. — xvii,310p. — *Bibliography: p287-292.* — *Includes index*

INFRASTRUCTURE (ECONOMICS)
DIEWERT, W. E
The measurement of the economic benefits of infrastructure services / Walter E. Diewert. — Berlin ; New York : Springer-Verlag, c1986. — 202 p.. — (Lecture notes in economics and mathematical systems ; 278). — *Bibliography: p. [191]-202*

INFRASTRUCTURE (ECONOMICS) — Saint Lucia
St. Lucia : economic performance and prospects. — Washington, D.C., U.S.A. : World Bank, 1985. — [xi],99p. — (World Bank country study). — *"Based on the findings of a World Bank mission to St. Lucia in February 1985"--Pref*

INFRASTRUCTURE (ECONOMICS) — Saint Vincent and the Grenadines
St. Vincent and the Grenadines : economic situations and selected development issues. — Washington, D.C., U.S.A. : World Bank, 1985. — xiii,108p. — (World Bank country study)

INFRASTRUCTURE (ECONOMICS) — Soviet Union
ORESHIN, V. P.
Planirovanie proizvodstvennoi infrastruktury : kompleksnyi podkhod / V. P. Oreshin. — Moskva : Ekonomika, 1986. — 143p. — *Bibliography: p140-142*

INFRASTRUCTURE (ECONOMICS) — Spain — Vizcaya
Los grandes problemas infraestructurales de Bizkaia / [realizado por] Jon Imanol Azua Mendía...[et al.]. — Bilbao : Diputación Foral de Vizcaya, 1983-. — v. <1 >

INGESTION DISORDERS
Fed up and hungry : women, oppression and food / Marilyn Lawrence (editor) ; with a foreword by Susie Orbach. — London : Women's Press, 1987. — 236p

INHERITANCE AND SUCCESSION — France
Droit civil. — Paris : Dalloz. — (Précis Dalloz)
Les successions, les libéralités / François Terré, Yves Lequette. — 1983. — xxx,986p. — *Bibliography: p.30. - Includes index*

INIESTA CANO, CARLOS
INIESTA CANO, Carlos
Memorias y recuerdos : los años que le vivido en le proceso histórico de España / Carlos Iniesta Cano ; prólogo de Emilio Romero. — Barcelona : Planeta, 1984. — 270p

INITIATION RITES — Papua New Guinea
HERDT, Gilbert H.
Sambia : ritual and gender in New Guinea / by Gilbert H. Herdt. — New York : Holt, Rinehart and Winston, 1986. — p. cm. — (Case studies in cultural anthropology). — *Includes index. — Bibliography: p*

INJUNCTIONS — England
OUGH, Richard N.
The Mareva injunction and Anton Piller order : practice and precedents / by Richard N. Ough. — London : Butterworths, 1987. — xxii,175p. — *Includes index*

INLAND NAVIGATION — Government policy — Great Britain
BRITISH WATERWAYS BOARD
Government observations on the fourth report of the Select Committee on Nationalised Industries : a memorandum. — [London] : the Board, 1978. — 6p

INLAND WATERWAYS AMENITY ADVISORY COUNCIL
Comments on "The water industry in England and Wales: the next steps", Government White Paper Command 6876, submitted to the House of Commons Select Committee on Nationalised Industries. — [London] : the Council, [1977]. — 22p

INLAND NAVIGATION — History
HADFIELD, Charles, 1909-
World canals : inland navigation past and present / Charles Hadfield. — Newton Abbot : David & Charles, c1986. — 432p. — *Includes index*

INLAND NAVIGATION — Great Britain — Management
BRITISH WATERWAYS BOARD
Government observations on the fourth report of the Select Committee on Nationalised Industries : a memorandum. — [London] : the Board, 1978. — 6p

INLAND NAVIGATION — Great Britain — Recreational use
GREAT BRITAIN. Countryside Commission
Memorandum to Secretaries of State for Environment and for Wales on the future organisation of water and sewage services. — [Cheltenham] : the Commission, 1972. — 9p

INLAND REVENUE STAFF FEDERATION
Assessment : newspaper of the Inland Revenue Staff Federation. — London : Inland Revenue Staff Federation, 1985-. — *Monthly*

INLAND WATER TRANSPORTATION — Statistics — European Economic Community countries
Carriage of goods by inland waterways. — Luxembourg : Office for Official Publications of the European Communities, 1985. — *Text in Community languages*
1983. — xxx,170p

INLAND WATER TRANSPORTATION — Statistics
Carriage of goods: inland waterways / Statistical Office of the European Communities. — Luxembourg : Office for Official Publications of the European Communities, 1983-. — *Annual. — Text in Community languages. — Title varies*

INLAND WATER TRANSPORTATION — Europe — Congresses
ROUND TABLE ON TRANSPORT ECONOMICS (49th : 1980 : Paris)
Competitive position and future of inland waterway transport : report of the forty-ninth Round Table on Transport Economics held in Paris on 31st January and 1st February 1980. — Paris : European Conference of Ministers of Transport, 1980. — 97p. — *Bibliography: p75-76*

INMATES OF INSTITUTIONS — Great Britain
BREARLEY, C. Paul
Admission to residential care / Paul Brearley, with Penny Gutridge ... [et al.]. — London : Tavistock Publications, 1980. — xi,225p. — (Residential social work). — *Bibliography: p206-216. — Includes index*

INNER LONDON EDUCATION AUTHORITY
CAMDEN COMMITTEE FOR COMMUNITY RELATIONS
ILEA's anti-racist policy : what is it, what it will do, how it should work : a guide for Camden parents and community groups. — London : Camden Committee for Community Relations, 1984. — 29p

INPUT-OUTPUT ANALYSIS
HEWINGS, Geoffrey J. D.
Regional input-output analysis / Geoffrey J.D. Hewings. — Beverly Hills, CA : Sage Publications, c1985. — 95p. — (Scientific geography series ; v. 6). — *Bibliography: p90-95*

LEONTIEF, Wassily W.
Input-output economics / Wassily Leontief. — 2nd ed. — New York : Oxford University Press, c1985. — xii, 436p

INPUT-OUTPUT TABLES — Denmark — Mathematical models
Input-output system i ADAM : Danmarks Statistiks økonomiske model / redigeret af J. Asger Olsen. — [København] : Danmarks Statistik, 1985. — 240p. — (Arbejdsnotat / Danmarks Statistik ; nr.19)

INPUT-OUTPUT TABLES — Developing countries
Input-output tables for developing countries. — New York : United Nations. — (Document ; ID/325). — *UN document no.ID/325; Sales no. E.84.II.B.6*
Vol.1. — 1985. — ix,299p

Input-output tables for developing countries. — New York : United Nations. — (Document ; ID/325/Add.1). — *UN document no. ID/325/Add.1; Sales no. E.85.II.B.6*
Vol.2. — 1985. — ix,316p

INPUT-OUTPUT TABLES — European Economic Community countries
DURU, Gérard
Structures productives européennes : analyse prétopologique des phénomènes de dépendance interindustrielle / Gérard Duru, Michel Mougeot, Jean-Paul Auray. — Paris : Editions du Centre national de la recherche scientifique, 1982. — 327 p.. — *On cover: Centre national de la recherche scientifique, Centre régional de publication Lyon. — Bibliography: p. 320-325*

INPUT-OUTPUT TABLES — Ghana
SINGAL, M. S.
Input-output table of Ghana 1968. — Accra : Central Bureau of Statistics, 1973. — 20p

INPUT-OUTPUT TABLES — Ghana — Methodolgy
SINGAL, M. S.
Input-output table of Ghana 1968. — Accra : Central Bureau of Statistics, 1973. — 20p

INPUT-OUTPUT TABLES — Indonesia
Input-output table Indonesia, 1980. — Jakarta : Biro Pusat Statistik, 1984. — 2v. — *Vol. 1 in English, vol. 2 in Indonesian. — Title of volume 2: Tabel input-output Indonesia, 1980*

INPUT-OUTPUT TABLES — Italy
ITALY. Istituto Centrale di Statistica
Tavola intersettoriale dell'economia italiana per l'anno 1975. — Roma : Istituto Centrale di Statistica, 1981. — 254p. — (Bollettino mensile di statistica. Supplemento ; 1981 n.7)

ITALY. Istituto Centrale di Statistica
Tavola intersettoriale dell'economia italiana per l'anno 1978 : versione a 84 branche. — Roma : Istituto Centrale di Statistica, 1983. — 206p. — (Bollettino mensile di statistica. Supplemento ; 1983 n.21)

INPUT-OUTPUT TABLES — Switzerland
SWITZERLAND. Office fédéral de la statistique
Die laufenden Einnahmen und Ausgaben des Staates nach Bund, Kantonen und Gemeinden, 1951-1982 : eine Analyse der Daten der nationalen Buchhaltung der Schweiz = Les recettes et les dépenses courantes de l'Etat-confédération, cantons et communes-de 1951 à 1982 : analyse des données des comptes nationaux de la Suisse. — Bern : Office fédéral de la statistique, 1984. — 46p. — (Beiträge zur schweizerischen Statistik = Contributions à la statistique suisse ; Heft 118). — *In German and French*

INPUT-OUTPUT TABLES — United States
LEONTIEF, Wassily W.
Input-output economics / Wassily Leontief. — 2nd ed. — New York : Oxford University Press, c1985. — xii, 436p

INQUISITION — Europe
Inquisition and society in early modern Europe / edited and translated by Stephen Haliczer. — London : Croom Helm, c1987. — 196p. — *Includes index*

INQUISITION — Spain — Congresses
SIMPOSIO INTERNACIONAL "LA INQUISICIÓN ESPAÑOLA Y LA MENTALIDAD INQUISITORIAL" (1983 : New York)
Inquisición española y mentalidad inquisitorial : ponencias del Simposio Internacional sobre Inquisición, Nueva York, abril de 1983 / Angel Alcalá y otros. — Barcelona : Ariel, [1984]. — 618p. — (Ariel - historia)

INSANE — Commitment and detention — Great Britain
GOSTIN, Larry
Institutions observed : towards a new concept of secure provision in mental health / Larry Gostin. — London : King Edward's Hospital Fund for London, 1986. — 179p. — *Bibliography: p165-172*

INSANE — Commitment and detention — Great Britain — History
UNSWORTH, Clive
The politics of mental health legislation / Clive Unsworth. — Oxford : Clarendon, 1987. — [384]p. — *Includes bibliography and index*

INSANE — Commitment and detention — Netherlands
BRAND-KOOLEN, M. J. M.
"At the government's pleasure" : trends and developments in the compulsory treatment of mentally disturbed offender in the Netherlands / Dr. Maria J. M. Brand-Koolen. — The Hague : Research and Documentation Centre, Ministry of Justice, 1986. — 18p. — ([Report, papers, articles] ; 91). — *Bibliography: p16-18*

INSANE, CRIMINAL AND DANGEROUS — England
Secure provision : a review of special services for the mentally ill and mentally handicapped in England and Wales / edited by Larry Gostin. — London : Tavistock, 1985. — [vii,300]p. — *Includes bibliography and index*

INSANE, CRIMINAL AND DANGEROUS — Netherlands
BRAND-KOOLEN, M. J. M.
"At the government's pleasure" : trends and developments in the compulsory treatment of mentally disturbed offender in the Netherlands / Dr. Maria J. M. Brand-Koolen. — The Hague : Research and Documentation Centre, Ministry of Justice, 1986. — 18p. — ([Report, papers, articles] ; 91). — *Bibliography: p16-18*

INSANITY — Jurisprudence — Council of Europe countries
COUNCIL OF EUROPE. Criminological Colloquium (7th : 1985)
Studies on criminal responsibility and psychiatric treatment of mentally ill offenders : reports presented to the seventh Criminological Colloquium (1985). — Strasbourg : Council of Europe, 1986. — 103p. — (Collected studies in criminological research ; v.24) (Legal affairs). — *On cover: European Committee on Crime Problems*

INSIDER TRADING IN SECURITIES — Law and legislation — Australia
ANISMAN, Philip
Insider trading legislation for Australia : an outline of the issues and alternatives / Philip Anisman. — Canberra : Australian Government Publishing Service, 1986. — xi,132p. — *An issues paper prepared for the Working Party on Insider Trading of the National Companies and Securities Commission*

INSTALMENT PLAN — Great Britain — Statistics
Instalment credit business of finance houses. — London : HMSO, 1974-78. — (Business monitor. SD ; 6) (Business monitor. SDM ; 6). — *Monthly. — Continued by: Credit business of finance houses and other specialist consumer credit grantors*

Instalment credit business of retailers. — London : HMSO, 1974-1979. — (Business monitor. SD ; 8). — *Monthly. — Continued by: Consumer credit business of retailers*

INSTITUTE OF CHARTERED ACCOUNTANTS IN ENGLAND AND WALES. Current cost accounting
MALLINSON, Derek
Understanding current cost accounting : a guide for those preparing and using financial statements / by Derek Mallinson. — London : Butterworth, 1980. — xviii,428p. — *Includes: Current cost accounting / Institute of Chartered Accountants in England and Wales - Guidance notes on SSAP 16, current cost accounting / Accounting Standards Committee*

INSTITUTE OF CHARTERED ACCOUNTANTS IN ENGLAND AND WALES
MARGERISON, Tom
The making of a profession / Tom Margerison. — London : Institute of Chartered Accountants in England and Wales, 1980. — 43p

INSTITUTE OF COST AND MANAGEMENT ACCOUNTANTS — History
BANYARD, C. W.
The Institute of Cost and Management Accountants : a history / C. W. Banyard. — London : ICMA, 1985. — 104p

INSTITUTE OF PUBLIC ADMINISTRATION (Dublin, Dublin, Ireland)
INSTITUTE OF PUBLIC ADMINISTRATION (Dublin, Ireland)
Annual report / Institute of Public Administration, [Eire]. — Dublin : The Institute, 1984-. — *Annual. — In English and Irish*

INSTITUTE OF SOUTHEAST ASIAN STUDIES. Southeast Asian Studies Program
Government and politics of Thailand / edited by Somsakdi Xuto. — Singapore ; Oxford : University Press, 1987. — xii,243p. — *Bibliography: p[217]-229*

INSTITUTIONAL CARE
ATHERTON, James S.
Professional supervision in group care : a contract-based approach / James S. Atherton. — London : Tavistock Publications, 1986. — [192]p. — (Residential social work). — *Includes index*

INSTITUTIONAL CARE — Great Britain
AUDIT COMMISSION FOR LOCAL AUTHORITIES IN ENGLAND AND WALES
Making a reality of community care : a report. — London : H.M.S.O., 1986. — 131p. — *Bibliographical references: p79-81*

BIGGS, Simon
The Registered Homes Act 1984 : staff training issues / Simon Biggs. — London : Central Council for Education and Training in Social Work, 1986. — 47p. — (CCETSW paper ; 24). — *Bibliographical references: p46-47*

BREARLEY, C. Paul
Admission to residential care / Paul Brearley, with Penny Gutridge ... [et al.]. — London : Tavistock Publications, 1980. — xi,225p. — (Residential social work). — *Bibliography: p206-216. — Includes index*

ERNST & WHINNEY
Survey of private and voluntary residential and nursing homes for the Department of Health and Social Security / Ernst & Whinney. — [London : Department of Health and Social Security], 1986. — 1v. (various pagings)

SOCIAL CARE ASSOCIATION
The Bonnington report : residential services : the next ten years & trends and developments in residential services. — Surbiton : SCA Publications, 1984. — 77p

STEIN, Mike
Leaving care / Mike Stein and Kate Carey. — Oxford : Blackwell, 1986. — [192]p. — (The Practice of social work ; 14). — *Includes index*

INSTITUTIONAL CARE — Great Britain — Finance
Public support for residential care : report of a joint central and local government working party. — [London] : Department of Health and Social Security, 1987. — 124p. — *Chairman: Joan Firth*

INSTITUTIONAL ECONOMICS — Addresses, essays, lectures
Macroeconomic conflict and social institutions / edited by Shlomo Maital, Irwin Lipnowski. — Cambridge, Mass. : Ballinger Pub. Co., 1985. — p. cm. — *Chiefly papers originating from a session on "Income policy as a social institution," at the American Economic Association's 95th Annual Meeting in New York, Dec. 28-30, 1982. — Includes bibliographies and index*

INSTITUTIONAL MARKET
HERRERO-DELGADO, Maria Jose
A strategic bargaining approach to market institutions / by Maria-Jose Herrero-Delgado. — 152 leaves. — *PhD (Econ) 1985 LSE*

INSTITUTO MEXICANO DEL SEGURO SOCIAL. Unidad de Promoción Voluntaria
INSTITUTO MEXICANO DEL SEGURO SOCIAL. Unidad de Promoción Voluntaria
Memoria de actividades 1977-1982 = Activities report 1977-1982. — [México] : la Unidad, 1982. — [34p]. — *Text in Spanish and English*

INSTITUTO NACIONAL DE ADMINISTRACIÓN PÚBLICA (Peru) — Legal status, laws, etc
PERU
[Laws, etc.]. Ley orgánica [del Instituto Nacional de Administración Pública] : Decreto-ley no.20316. — [Lima] : Instituto Nacional de Administración Pública, [ca.1973]. — 25p

INSTITUTO NACIONAL DE PREVISIÓN (Spain) — History
SAMANIEGO BONEU, Mercedes
La elite dirigente del Instituto Nacional de Previsión : un equipo plurideológico durante la II República / Mercedes Samaniego Boneu. — Salamanca : Departamento de Historia Contemporánea, Universidad de Salamanca, 1984. — 57p. — (Temas científicos, literarios e históricos ; 50) (Estudios y documentos / Departamento de Historia Contemporánea, Universidad de Salamanca ; 2)

INSURANCE — Economic aspects
The insurance industry in economic development / Bernard Wasow and Raymond D. Hill, editors. — New York : New York University Press, c1986. — p. cm. — *Includes bibliographies and index*

INSURANCE — Finance
Insurance mathematics and economics. — Amsterdam : North Holland, 1986-. — *Quarterly*

INSURANCE — Mathematics
Insurance mathematics and economics. — Amsterdam : North Holland, 1986-. — *Quarterly*

INSURANCE — State supervision
The Economics of insurance regulation : a cross-national study / edited by Jörg Finsinger and Mark V. Pauly. — Basingstoke : Macmillan, 1986. — [256]p. — *Includes index*

INSURANCE — Austria — Statistics
Versicherungsstatistik: Veröffentlichungen des Bundesministeriums für Finanzen betreffend die Vertragsversicherung / Bundesministeriums für Finanzen, Austria. — Wien : Bundesministeriums für Finanzen, 1984-. — *Annual*

INSURANCE — Developing countries
The insurance industry in economic development / Bernard Wasow and Raymond D. Hill, editors. — New York : New York University Press, c1986. — p. cm. — Includes bibliographies and index

INSURANCE — England — London
DAVISON, Ian Hay
A view of the Room : Lloyd's : change and disclosure / Ian Hay Davison. — London : Weidenfeld and Nicolson, 1987. — x, 238p. — Bibliography: p.209-212

INSURANCE — European Economic Community countries
AARONOVICH, Sam
The insurance industry in the countries of the EEC : structure, conduct and performance / by Sam Aaronovitch, Peter Samson. — Luxembourg : Office for Official Publications of the European Communities, 1985. — 233p. — At head of title page: Commission of the European Communities

INSURANCE — Great Britain — Statistics
Insurance business statistics. — London : HMSO, 1977-. — (Business monitor. MA ; 16). — Annual

INSURANCE — Netherlands — Statistics
Vierde algemene bedrijfstelling, 1978. — 's-Gravenhage : Staatsuitgeverij. — Rear cover title: Fourth general economic census, 1978: volume 2, part E: banking, insurance and services
d. 2: Algemene sectorale gegevens E: bank- en verzekeringswezen; dienstverlening. — 1985. — 107p

INSURANCE — Organisation for Economic Co-operation and Development countries — Statistics
Statistics on insurance : comparative tables of insurance statistics for 1983. — Paris : Organisation for Economic Co-operation and Development, 1986. — 40p

INSURANCE — Turkey — Statistics
TURKEY. Ba g-Kur
Istatistik yilli gi / Ba g-Kur, Turkey. — Ankara : Ba g-Kur, 1980-. — Annual. — Text in Turkish and English

INSURANCE, ACCIDENT — Denmark
Arbejdsskadeforsikringen beretning for årene 1980 og 1981. — [København] : Sikringsstyrelsen, 1982. — 53p. — (Sikringsstyrelsens undersøgelser ; nr.7)

Beretning fra Sikringsstyrelsen : arbejdsskadeforsikringen for årene 1977,1978 og 1979. — København : [Sikringsstyrelsen], 1980. — 150p

INSURANCE, ACCIDENT — Switzerland
SWITZERLAND. Commission d'experts chargée d'examiner la revision de l'assurance-accidents
Rapport de la commission d'experts chargée d'examiner la revision de l'assurance-accidents : du 14 septembre 1973. — Berne : the Commission, 1973. — ix,223p

INSURANCE COMPANIES — Employees — Great Britain
HAFEEZ, Tariq
Race and recruitment in the insurance sector / Tariq Hafeez. — London : London Boroughs Grant Scheme, 1987. — 26p. — Bibliography: p26

INSURANCE COMPANIES — European Economic Community countries
AARONOVICH, Sam
The insurance industry in the countries of the EEC : structure, conduct and performance / by Sam Aaronovitch, Peter Samson. — Luxembourg : Office for Official Publications of the European Communities, 1985. — 233p. — At head of title page: Commission of the European Communities

INSURANCE COMPANIES — Great Britain — Finance
BOYD, Stewart C.
Minet Holdings plc, W. M. D. Underwriting Agencies Limited : investigation under Section 165 (1) (b) of the Companies Act 1948 : interim report / S. C. Boyd, P. W. G. DuBuisson, inspectors appointed by the Secretary of State for Trade and Industry. — London : H.M.S.O., 1986. — 88p

INSURANCE COMPANIES — Great Britain — Investments — Statistics
Insurance companies' and pension funds' investment. — London : HMSO, 1970-. — (Business monitor. MQ ; 5) (Business monitor. M ; 5). — Quarterly

INSURANCE COMPANIES — Netherlands
Financiële gegevens schadeverzekeringsmaatschappijen 1981-1983. — 's-Gravenhage : Staatsuvitgeverij, 1985. — 43p. — Summary and table headings in English. — Title on back cover: Financial data of non-life insurance companies 1981-1983

INSURANCE COMPANIES — United States — Employees — Supply and demand — Forecasting
The Impact of office automation on clerical employment, 1985-2000 : forecasting techniques and plausible futures in banking and insurance / J. David Roessner ... [et al.]. — Westport, Conn. : Quorum Books, c1986. — p. cm. — Includes index. — Bibliography: p

INSURANCE COMPANIES — United States — Investments — History
PRITCHETT, B. Michael
Financing growth : a financial history of American life insurance through 1900 / B. Michael Pritchett. — Philadelphia : S.S. Huebner Foundation for Insurance Education, Wharton School, University of Pennsylvania ; Homewood, Ill. : Distributed by R.D. Irwin, c1985. — xvi, 90 p.. — (S.S. Huebner Foundation monograph series ; no. 13). — Includes index. — Bibliography: p. 79-88

INSURANCE, CREDIT
LEVITSKY, Jacob
Credit guarantee schemes for small and medium enterprises / Jacob Levitsky and Ranga N. Prasad. — Washington, D.C. : The World Bank, 1987. — vi,91p. — (Industry and finance series ; v.19) (World Bank technical paper ; no.58). — Bibliography: p89-91

INSURANCE, DISABILITY — Denmark
Revalidering- og pensionsnaevnenes afgørelser i førtidspensionssager 1.april 1976 til 31 december 1978 : redegørelse fra sikringsstyrelsen. — [København] : Sikringsstyrelsen, 1980. — 106p. — (Sikringsstyrelsens undersøgelser ; nr.5). — Includes bibliographical references

INSURANCE, DISABILITY — Denmark — Statistics
Afsluttende statistik fra invalideforsikringsretten og førtidspensionsudvalget. — [København] : Sikringsstyrelsen, 1978. — 60p. — (Sikringsstyrelsens undersøgelser ; nr3). — Cover tittle. — Includes bibliographical references

INSURANCE, FIRE — Great Britain
SMITH, A. D.
The feasibility of fire insurance measures of capital stock / A. D. Smith. — London : National Institute of Economic and Social Research, 1986. — 25p. — (Discussion paper / National Institute of Economic and Social Research ; no.116)

INSURANCE, FIRE — Great Britain — Policies
JENKINS, D. T.
Indexes of the fire insurance policies of the Sun Fire Office and the Royal Exchange Assurance 1775-1787 : [an introduction]. — London : Economic and Social Research Council, 1986. — 35p. — Bibliography: p32-35

ROYAL EXCHANGE ASSURANCE
Fire policies 1775-1787. — London : Economic and Social Research Council, 1986. — 10microfiches

SUN FIRE OFFICE
Fire policies 1775-1787. — London : Economic and Social Research Council, [1986]. — 24microfiches

INSURANCE, HEALTH
INTERNATIONAL SOCIAL SECURITY ASSOCIATION
Volume and cost of sickness benefits in kind and cash (1967-1970). — Geneva : International Social Security Association
Part 1: National analyses: report of the Permanent Committee on Medical Care and Sickness Insurance. — 1973. — iv,209p

INSURANCE, HEALTH — history — United States
FEIN, Rashi
Medical care, medical costs : the search for a health insurance policy / Rashi Fein. — Cambridge, Mass. : Harvard University Press, 1986. — viii, 240 p.. — Includes index

INSURANCE, HEALTH — Law and legislation — Great Britain
JOYCE, Josephine
Tolley's guide to Statutory Sick Pay : implementing and operating SSP in practice / Josephine Joyce with assistance from Veronica Cowan ; consultant: Erich Suter. — 2nd ed. — Croydon : Tolley, 1986. — x,93p

INSURANCE, HEALTH — Law and legislation — India
BHATNAGAR, Deepak
State and labour welfare in India : an appraisal of the ESI scheme / Deepak Bhatnagar. — New Delhi : Deep & Deep Publications, c1985. — 256 p.. — Includes index. — Bibliography: p. [254]

INSURANCE, HEALTH — Social aspects — United States
RUSHING, William A
Social functions and economic aspects of health insurance / William A. Rushing. — Boston : Kluwer-Nijhoff Pub. ; Norwell, Mass., USA : Distributors for the U.S. and Canada, Kluwer Academic, c1986. — vii, 226 p.. — (Huebner international series on risk, insurance, and economic security). — Includes bibliographies and index

INSURANCE, HEALTH — Canada
Canada Health Act: annual report = Loi canadienne sur la santé: rapport annuel / Health and Welfare Canada. — Ottawa : Health and Welfare Canada, 1984/5-. — Annual. — In English and French

INSURANCE, HEALTH — Canada — History
NAYLOR, C. David
Private practice, public payment : Canadian medicine and the politics of health insurance, 1911-1966 / C. David Naylor. — Kingston ; Montreal : McGill-Queen's University Press, 1986. — xii,324p. — Notes: p[259]-303

INSURANCE, HEALTH — Denmark
Sygesikringen 1973/74 og 1974/75. — [København] : Sikringsstyrelsen, 1977. — 45p. — (Sikringsstyrelsens undersøgelser ; nr.1)

INSURANCE, HEALTH — Great Britain
PROPPER, Carol
An econometric estimation of the demand for private health insurance in the U.K. / Carol Propper. — York : University of York. Centre for Health Economics, 1987. — 42p. — (Discussion paper / University of York. Centre for Health Economics ; 24). — Bibliography: p36-37

INSURANCE, HEALTH — India
BHATNAGAR, Deepak
State and labour welfare in India : an appraisal of the ESI scheme / Deepak Bhatnagar. — New Delhi : Deep & Deep Publications, c1985. — 256 p.. — *Includes index. Bibliography: p. [254]*

INSURANCE, HEALTH — United States
FEIN, Rashi
Medical care, medical costs : the search for a health insurance policy / Rashi Fein. — Cambridge, Mass. : Harvard University Press, 1986. — viii, 240 p.. — *Includes index*

RUSHING, William A
Social functions and economic aspects of health insurance / William A. Rushing. — Boston : Kluwer-Nijhoff Pub. ; Norwell, Mass., USA : Distributors for the U.S. and Canada, Kluwer Academic, c1986. — vii, 226 p.. — (Huebner international series on risk, insurance, and economic security). — *Includes bibliographies and index*

VALDEZ, Robert Otto Burciaga
The effects of cost sharing on the health of children / Robert Otto Burciaga Valdez. — Santa Monica, CA : Rand, 1986. — xiv, 117 p.. — (Health insurance experiment series). — "March 1986.". — "R-3270-HHS.". — *Bibliography: p. 109-117*

INSURANCE LAW — Great Britain
New foundations for insurance law / edited by F.D. Rose. — London : Stevens, 1987. — xvii,106p. — (Current legal problems). — *Includes index*

INSURANCE LAW — United States
ABRAHAM, Kenneth S.
Distributing risk : insurance, legal theory, and public policy / Kenneth S. Abraham. — New Haven : Yale University Press, c1986. — p. cm . — *Includes index. — Bibliography: p*

INSURANCE LIFE
Continuous mortality investigation reports / compiled by the Continuous Mortality Investigation Committee of the Institute and Faculty of Actuaries. — London : Institute of Actuaries and Faculty of Actuaries, 1973-. — *Annual*

INSURANCE, LIFE — Rates and tables — Mathematical models
NEILL, Alistair
Life contingencies / by Alistair Neill. — London : Heinemann for the Institute of Actuaries and the Faculty of Actuaries, 1977. — xi,452p. — *Bibliography: p.448. — Includes index*

INSURANCE, LIFE — Netherlands — Statistics
Financiële gegevens Levensverzekeringsmaatschappijen / Central Bureau voor de Statistiek, Netherlands. — 's-gravenhage : Staatsuitgeverij, 1982-. — *Annual*

INSURANCE, LIFE — Organisation for Economic Co-operation and Development countries
ORGANISATION FOR ECONOMIC CO-OPERATION AND DEVELOPMENT. Committee on Consumer Policy
Consumers and life insurance : report / by the OECD Committee on Consumer Policy. — Paris : OECD, 1987. — 79p. — *Bibliographical references: p76-79*

INSURANCE, LIFE — United States — History
PRITCHETT, B. Michael
Financing growth : a financial history of American life insurance through 1900 / B. Michael Pritchett. — Philadelphia : S.S. Huebner Foundation for Insurance Education, Wharton School, University of Pennsylvania ; Homewood, Ill. : Distributed by R.D. Irwin, c1985. — xvi, 90 p.. — (S.S. Huebner Foundation monograph series ; no. 13). — *Includes index. — Bibliography: p. 79-88*

INSURANCE, MALPRACTICE — United States
DANZON, Patricia M.
Medical malpractice : theory, evidence and public policy / Patricia M. Danzon. — Cambridge, Mass. ; London : Harvard University Press, 1985. — vi,264p. — *Bibliography: p231-238. — Includes index*

INSURANCE, MARINE — Law and legislation — Great Britain
TEMPLEMAN, F.
Templeman on marine insurance : its principles and practice. — 6th ed. / R.J. Lambeth. — London : Pitman, c1986. — [608]p. — *Previous ed.: 1981. — Includes index*

INSURANCE, SOCIAL
ATKINSON, A. B.
Social insurance and income maintenance / A. B. Atkinson. — London : Welfare State Programme. Suntory-Toyota International Centre for Economics and Related Disciplines, 1986. — 32p. — (Discussion paper / Welfare State Programme. Suntory-Toyota International Centre for Economics and Related Disciplines ; no.11). — *Bibliography: p30-32*

INSURANCE, UNEMPLOYMENT
ATKINSON, A. B.
Income maintenance and social insurance : a survey / A. B. Atkinson. — London : Suntory-Toyota International Centre for Economics and Related Disciplines, London School of Economics, 1985. — 234p. — (Welfare State Programme ; no.5). — *Bibliography: p205-234*

INSURANCE, UNEMPLOYMENT — Denmark
The Employment Service and Unemployment Insurance Act, 1970, as amended. — [Copenhagen : Ministry of Labour?], 1970. — 35p

INSURANCE, UNEMPLOYMENT — Great Britain
FEDERATION OF CLAIMANTS UNIONS
On the dole : a claimants union guide for the unemployed. — London : Federation of Claimants Unions, 1985. — 37p

INSURANCE, UNEMPLOYMENT — United States
VROMAN, Wayne
The funding crisis in state unemployment insurance / Wayne Vroman. — Kalamazoo, MI : Upjohn Institute for Employment Research, 1986. — xi, 199 p.. — *Bibliography: p. 197-199*

INTEGRATED WATER DEVELOPMENT — Political aspects — Africa
COLLOQUE DE LA SORBONNE "PARTICIPATION PAYSANNE ET DÉVELOPPEMENT AGRICOLE: L'EXEMPLE DES POLITIQUES DE L'EAU EN AFRIQUE" (1983 : Paris)
Les politiques de l'eau en Afrique : développement agricole et participation paysanne / actes du Colloque de la Sorbonne (organise par le) Centre d'Études Juridiques et Politiques du Monde Africain sous la direction de Gérard Conac, Claudette Savonnet-Guyot [et] Françoise Conac. — Paris : Economica, 1985. — 767p

COLLOQUE DE LA SORBONNE "PARTICIPATION PAYSANNE ET DÉVELOPPEMENT AGRICOLE: L'EXEMPLE DES POLITIQUES DE L'EAU EN AFRIQUE" (1983 : Paris)
Les politiques de l'eau en Afrique : développement agricole et participation paysanne / actes du Colloque de la Sorbonne (organise par le) Centre d'Études Juridiques et Politiques du Monde Africai sous la direction de Gérard Conac, Claudette Savonnet-Guyot [et] Françoise Conac. — Paris : Economica, 1985. — 767p

INTEL 8086 (COMPUTER)
MORSE, Stephen P
The 8086/8088 primer : an introduction to their architecture, system design, and programming / Stephen P. Morse. — 2nd ed. — Rochelle Park, N.J. : Hayden Book Co., c1982. — 276 p.. — : *Previous ed. published as: The 8086 primer. c1980. — Includes index. — Bibliography: p. 258-259*

INTEL 8088 (COMPUTER)
MORSE, Stephen P
The 8086/8088 primer : an introduction to their architecture, system design, and programming / Stephen P. Morse. — 2nd ed. — Rochelle Park, N.J. : Hayden Book Co., c1982. — 276 p.. — : *Previous ed. published as: The 8086 primer. c1980. — Includes index. — Bibliography: p. 258-259*

INTELLECT
BARON, Jonathan
Rationality and intelligence / Jonathan Baron. — Cambridge : Cambridge University Press, 1985. — 299p

CARRUTHERS, Peter
Introducing persons : theories and arguments in the philosophy of mind / Peter Carruthers. — London : Croom Helm, c1986. — [256]p

GUNDERSON, Keith
Mentality and machines / Keith Gunderson. — 2nd ed. — London : Croom Helm, 1985. — xxii,260p. — *Bibliography: p[249]-255*

HOFSTADTER, Douglas R.
Metamagical themas : questioning for the essence of mind and pattern : [an interlocked collection of literary, scientific and artistic studies] / Douglas R. Hofstadter. — Harmondsworth : Penguin, 1986, c1985. — xxviii,852p. — *Originally published: Basic Books, 1985. — Bibliography: p802-819*

Practical intelligence : nature and origins of competence in the everyday world / edited by Robert J. Sternberg and Richard K. Wagner. — Cambridge : Cambridge University Press, 1986. — 1v.. — *Includes index*

INTELLECT — Addresses, essays, lectures
Minds, machines and evolution : philosophical studies / edited by Christopher Hookway. — Cambridge : Cambridge University Press, 1984. — xi,177p. — *Includes bibliographies and index*

INTELLECT — Genetic aspects
SCHIFF, Michel
Education and class : the irrelevance of IQ genetic studies / Michel Schiff, Richard Lewontin with contributions from A. Dumaret ... [et al.]. — Oxford : Clarendon, 1986. — xxiii,243p. — (Oxford science publications). — *Bibliography: p228-236 Includes index*

INTELLECTUAL COOPERATION
AILES, Catherine P.
Cooperation in science and technology : an evaluation of the U.S.-Soviet agreement / Catherine P. Ailes and Arthur E. Pardee. — Boulder : Westview, 1986. — xxiii,334p

INTELLECTUAL PROPERTY — Great Britain — Statistical services
BOSWORTH, Derek L.
Intellectual property rights / by Derek L. Bosworth. — Oxford : Published for the Royal Statistical Society and Economic and Social Research Council by Pergamon, 1986. — [300] p. — (Reviews of United Kingdom statistical sources ; v.19). — *Includes index*

INTELLECTUALS — Political activity — Addresses, essays, lectures
Intellectuals in politics / edited by Nissan Oren. — Jerusalem : Magnes Press, Hebrew University, 1984. — 106 p. — *Includes bibliographies*

INTELLECTUALS — Algeria — Biography
BULHAN, Hussein Abdilahi
Frantz Fanon and the psychology of oppression / Hussein Abdilahi Bulhan. — New York ; London : Plenum Press, c1985. — xiii, 299p. — (PATH in psychology). — *Includes index.* — *Includes bibliographical references*

INTELLECTUALS — Canada
OWRAM, Doug
The government generation : Canadian intellectuals and the state 1900-1945 / Doug Owram. — Toronto ; London : University of Toronto Press, 1986. — 402p

INTELLECTUALS — China
SCHWARCZ, Vera
The Chinese enlightenment : intellectuals and the legacy of the May Fourth movement of 1919 / Vera Schwarcz. — Berkeley : University of California Press, c1986. — xvi, 393 p.. — *Includes index.* — *Bibliography: p. 358-375*

INTELLECTUALS — Germany — History
ALFRED WEBER-KONGRESS (1st : 1984 : Heidelberg)
Alfred Weber als Politiker und Gelehrter : die Referate des Ersten Alfred Weber-Kongresses... / Eberhard Demm (Hrsg.). — Stuttgart : Steiner Verlag Wiesbaden, 1986. — 218p. — *Bibliography: p[205]-218*

INTELLECTUALS — Mexico
CAMP, Roderic Ai
Intellectuals and the state in twentieth-century Mexico / by Roderic A. Camp. — Austin : University of Texas Press, 1985. — ix, 279p. — (Latin American monographs ; no. 65). — *Includes index.* — *Bibliography: p.[233]-265*

INTELLECTUALS — New York (N.Y.) — History — 20th century
COONEY, Terry A
The rise of the New York Intellectuals : Partisan review and its circle / Terry A. Cooney. — Madison, Wis. : University of Wisconsin Press, 1986. — xi, 350p. — (History of American thought and culture). — *Includes index.* — *Bibliography: p.331-333*

WALD, Alan M.
The New York intellectuals : the rise and decline of the anti-Stalinist left from the 1930s to the 1980s / by Alan M. Wald. — Chapel Hill : University of North Carolina Press, c1987. — p. cm. — *Includes index.* — *Bibliography: p*

INTELLECTUALS — Soviet Union — Political activity
BURBANK, Jane
Intelligentsia and revolution : Russian views of Bolshevism, 1917-1922 / Jane Burbank. — New York : Oxford University Press, 1986. — viii, 340 p.. — *Includes index.* — *Bibliography: p. 315-326*

INTELLECTUALS — Soviet Union — Sociological aspects
Sotsial'noe razvitie sovetskoi intelligentsii / otv. redaktor R. G. Ianovskii. — Moskva : Nauka, 1986. — 335p

INTELLIGENCE LEVELS — Social aspects
SCHIFF, Michel
Education and class : the irrelevance of IQ genetic studies / Michel Schiff, Richard Lewontin with contributions from A. Dumaret ... [et al.]. — Oxford : Clarendon, 1986. — xxiii,243p. — (Oxford science publications). — *Bibliography: p228-236 Includes index*

INTELLIGENCE OFFICERS — Great Britain — Biography
HOWARTH, Patrick
Intelligence chief extraordinary : the life of the ninth Duke of Portland / Patrick Howarth. — London : Bodley Head, c1986. — 256p,[4]p of plates. — *Bibliography: p244-245.* — *Includes index*

INTELLIGENCE SERVICE
Intelligence and national security. — London : Frank Cass, 1986-. — *3 per year*

INTELLIGENCE SERVICE — International cooperation
LITTLETON, James
Target nation : Canada and the western intelligence network / James Littleton. — 1st ed. — Toronto, Canada : L. & O. Dennys : CBC Enterprises, c1986. — viii, 228 p.. — *Includes index.* — *Bibliography: p. 209-220*

INTELLIGENCE SERVICE — Canada — History — 20th century
LITTLETON, James
Target nation : Canada and the western intelligence network / James Littleton. — 1st ed. — Toronto, Canada : L. & O. Dennys : CBC Enterprises, c1986. — viii, 228 p.. — *Includes index.* — *Bibliography: p. 209-220*

INTELLIGENCE SERVICE — France
WOLTON, Thierry
Le KGB en France / Thierry Wolton. — Paris : Grasset, [1986]. — 310p

INTELLIGENCE SERVICE — Great Britain
LIBERAL PARTY WORKING GROUP ON THE INTELLIGENCE SERVICES
Liberty and security : report of the Liberal Party Working Group on the Intelligence Services. — Hebden Bridge : Hebden Royd Publications, 1986. — 28p

REEVE, Gillian
Offence of the realm : how peace campaigners get bugged / Gillian Reeve [and] Joan Smith. — London : CND Publications, 1986. — 44p

WEST, Nigel
Molehunt : the full story of the Soviet spy in MI5 / Nigel West. — London : Weidenfeld and Nicholson, 1987. — 208p. — *Bibliography: p.197-199*

INTELLIGENCE SERVICE — Great Britain — History — 20th century
SINCLAIR, Andrew
The red and the blue : intelligence, treason and the universities / Andrew Sinclair. — London : Weidenfeld and Nicolson, 1986. — 179p. — *Bibliography: p162-168.* — *Includes index*

INTELLIGENCE SERVICE — Soviet Union
WOLTON, Thierry
Le KGB en France / Thierry Wolton. — Paris : Grasset, [1986]. — 310p

INTELLIGENCE SERVICE — United States
British and American approaches to intelligence / edited by K. G. Robertson. — Basingstoke : Macmillan, 1987. — xii,281p. — (RUSI defence studies series). — *Includes index*

FREEDMAN, Lawrence
US intelligence and the Soviet strategic threat / Lawrence Freedman. — 2nd ed. — London : Macmillan, 1986. — [288]p. — *Previous ed.: 1977.* — *Includes bibliography and index*

INTER-AMERICAN COMMISSION ON HUMAN RIGHTS
Handbook of existing rules pertaining to human rights in the inter-American system / Inter-American Commission on Human Rights. — Washington, D.C. : Organization of American States, 1977-. — *Biennial.* — *Title varies*

INTER-AMERICAN COURT OF HUMAN RIGHTS
INTER-AMERICAN COURT OF HUMAN RIGHTS
Serie A: Fallos y opiniones = Series A: Judgments and opinions / Inter-American Court of Human Rights. — ; San José, Costa Rica : Secretariat of the Court, 1982-. — *Annual.* — *Text in Spanish and English*

INTER-AMERICAN COURT OF HUMAN RIGHTS
Serie B: Memorias, argumentos orales y documentos = Series B: Pleadings, oral arguments and documents / Inter-American Court of Human Rights. — San José, Costa Rica : Secretariat of the Court, 1983-. — *Annual.* — *Text in Spanish and English*

INTER-LIBRARY LOANS — Great Britain
WHITE, Brenda
Interlending in the United Kingdom 1985 : a survey of interlibrary document transactions / Brenda White. — London : British Library, 1986. — [xii,84]p. — (Library and information research report ; 44)

INTERACTIVE COMPUTER SYSTEMS
BLEND-5 : the computer human factors journal / journal editors: B. Shackel, J. Florentin, P. Wright ... ; this report was collated and edited by David J. Pullinger and produced with the help of Wendy Buckland. — London : British Library, c1986. — xi,221p. — (Library and information research report ; 47). — *Includes bibliographies*

GOLDSMITH, G.
Online searching made simple : a microcomputer interface for inexperienced users / G. Goldsmith and P.W. Williams. — London : British Library, c1986. — ix,113p. — (Library and information research report ; 41)

PULLINGER, D. J.
BLEND-4 : user-system interaction / D.J. Pullinger with B. Shackel ... [et al.]. — [London] : British Library, c1985. — xi,76p. — (Library and information research report ; 45). — *Bibliography: p67-69*

ROGERS, Everett M
Communication technology / Everett M. Rogers. — New York : Free Press, c1986. — p. cm. — (Series in communication technology and society). — *Includes index.* — *Bibliography: p*

SHNEIDERMAN, Ben
Designing interactive computer systems / Ben Shneiderman. — Reading, Mass. : Addison-Wesley, 1986. — p. cm. — *Includes indexes.* — *Bibliography: p*

User centered system design : new perspectives on human-computer interaction / edited by Donald A. Norman, Stephen W. Draper. — Hillsdale, N.J. ; London : Lawrence Erlbaum Associates, 1986. — xiii, 526p. — *Includes index.* — *Bibliography: p.[499]-512*

WINFIELD, Ian
Human resources and computing / Ian Winfield. — London : Heinemann, 1986. — [256]p

INTERACTIVE VIDEO
ROGERS, Everett M
Communication technology / Everett M. Rogers. — New York : Free Press, c1986. — p. cm. — (Series in communication technology and society). — *Includes index.* — *Bibliography: p*

INTERCULTURAL COMMUNICATION
Communication and Latin American society : trends in critical research, 1960-1985 / edited by Rita Atwood and Emile McAnany. — Madison, Wis. : University of Wisconsin Press, 1986. — p. cm. — (Studies in communication and society). — Includes bibliographies and index. — Contents: Assessing critical mass communication scholarship in the Americas / Rita Atwood -- Seminal ideas in Latin American critical communication research in its historical context / Cristina Schwarz and Oscar Jaramillo -- Transnational communication and culture / Rafael Roncagliolo -- Transnational communication and Brazilian culture / Carlos Eduardo Lins Da Silva -- Means of communication and construction of hegemony / Javier Esteinou Madrid -- Transnational advertising / Noreene Janus -- Commercial television as an educational and political institution / Alberto Montoya Martín Del Campo and Maria Antonieta Rebeil Corella -- Trends in alternative communication research in Latin America / Maximo Simpson Grinberg -- Alternative communication, solidarity, and development in the face of transnational expansion / Fernando Reyes Matta

Discourse among cultures : strategies in world Englishes / edited by Larry E. Smith. — Hemel Hempstead : Prentice-Hall International, 1987. — 1v.. — (English in the international context series). — Includes bibliography and index

SIEGEL, James T.
Solo in the new order : language and hierarchy in an Indonesian city / James T. Siegel. — Princeton, N.J. : Princeton University Press, c1986. — p. cm. — Includes index. — Bibliography: p

INTERCULTURAL COMMUNICATION — Congresses
The Communication of ideas / edited by J.S. Yadava, Vinayshil Gautam. — New Delhi : Concept, 1980, c1978. — xx, 276 p.. — (Xth ICAES series ; no. 3). — Selection of papers presented at the 10th International Congress of Anthropological and Ethnological Sciences held at New Delhi, 1978. — Includes bibliographies and index

Foreign languages and international trade : a global perspective / edited by Samia I. Spencer. — Athens : University of Georgia Press, c1987. — xxiv, 255 p.. — Collection of papers derived from an international symposium held in the spring of 1983, sponsored by the Committee for the Humanities in Alabama and Auburn University. — Includes bibliographies

INTERCULTURAL EDUCATION — Great Britain
Anti-racism : an assault on education and value / edited by Frank Palmer. — London : Sherwood Press, 1986. — xii,210p

INTERDISCIPLINARY APPROACH IN EDUCATION
Feminist scholarship : challenge, discovery, and impact / Ellen Carol DuBois ... [et al.]. — Urbana : University of Illinois Press, c1985. — p. cm. — Includes index. — Bibliography: p

INTERDISCIPLINARY APPROACH TO KNOWLEDGE
Feminist scholarship : challenge, discovery, and impact / Ellen Carol DuBois ... [et al.]. — Urbana : University of Illinois Press, c1985. — p. cm. — Includes index. — Bibliography: p

INTEREST
DONALD, David William Alexander
Compound interest and annuities-certain / David William Donald. — Cambridge : Cambridge University Press, 1963. — 300p

INTEREST AND USURY — Europe
MICOSSI, Stefano
Can Europeans control their interest rates? / Stefano Micossi and Tommaso Padoa-Schioppa. — Bruxelles : Centre for European Policy Studies, 1984. — 40p. — (CEPS papers ; no.17)

INTEREST RATE FUTURES
Compensation for compulsory purchase : papers from a conference organized by the Law Society, the Bar Council and the Royal Institution of Chartered Surveyors. — London : Sweet and Maxwell, 1975. — 53p. — (Journal of planning and environment law occasional papers)

KOBOLD, Klaus
Interest rate futures markets and capital market theory : theoretical concepts and empirical evidence / Klaus Kobold. — Berlin ; New York : W. de Gruyte, 1986. — p. cm. — (Series D--Economcis =Economique ; 1)

INTEREST RATES
BEAN, Charles R.
Budget deficits, interest rates and the incentive effects of income tax cuts / C. R. Bean and S. V. Wijnbergen. — London : Centre for Labour Economics, London School of Economics, 1987. — 37p. — (Discussion paper / London School of Economics and Political Science. Centre for Labour Econcmics ; no.270)

KNEESHAW, J. T.
International interest rate relationships : policy choices and constraints / by J. T. Kneeshaw and P. Van den Bergh. — Basle : Bank For International Settlements, 1985. — 67p. — (BIS economic papers ; no.13)

INTEREST RATES — Government policy — Developing countries
HANSON, James A.
Interest rate policies in selected developing countries 1970-82 / James A. Hanson and Craig R. Neal. — Washington, D.C. : The World Bank, 1986. — xviii,139p. — Bibliographical references: p137-139

INTEREST RATES — Developing countries
HANSON, James A.
High interest rates, spreads, and the costs of intermediation : two studies / James A. Hanson and Roberto de Rezende Rocha. — Washington, D.C. : The World Bank, 1986. — x,82p. — (Industry and finance series ; v.18). — Bibliographical refernces: p79-82

INTEREST RATES — Italy
LECALDANO SASSO LA TERZA, E.
Households' saving and the real rate of interest : the Italian experience, 1970-1983 / E. Lecaldano Sasso la Terza, G. Marotta, R. S. Masera. — [Roma] : Banca d'Italia, 1985. — 33p , addenda. — (Temi di discussione ; 47) (Servizio studi della Banca d'Italia). — Bibliography: p32-33

INTEREST RATES — United States
BENOÎT, J. Pierre V
United States interest rates and the interest rate dilemma for the developing world / J. Pierre V. Benoît. — Westport, Conn. : Quorum Books, 1986. — xviii, 230 p.. — Includes index. — Bibliography: p. [215]-219

Responses to deregulation : retail deposit pricing from 1983 through 1985 / Patrick I. Mahoney...[et al.]. — Washington, D. C. : Board of Governors of the Federal Reserve System, 1987. — 29p. — (Staff study / Board of Governors of the Federal Reserve System ; 151). — Includes bibliographical references

INTERGENERATIONAL RELATIONS
GREENE, Roberta
Social work with the aged and their families / Roberta Greene. — New York : Aldine de Gruyter, c1986. — p. cm. — Includes index. — Bibliography: p

INTERGENERATIONAL RELATIONS — Congresses
Life-span developmental psychology : intergenerational relations / edited by Nancy Datan, Anita L. Greene, Hayne W. Reese. — Hillsdale, N.J. ; London : Lawrence Erlbaum Associates, 1986. — xiii, 280p. — Proceedings of the Ninth West Virginia University Conference on Life-Span Developmental Psychology held in Morgantown on May 10-12, 1984. — Includes bibliographies and index

INTERGOVERNMENTAL FISCAL RELATIONS — Great Britain
BARLOW, John Robert
Central-local government relations : the role of finance in influencing local policy making in education and housing in England : with special reference to the period 1974-1982 / John Robert Barlow. — 459 leaves. — PhD (Econ) 1986 LSE

STEWART, John, 1929-
The dilemma of central-local relations / J. D. Stewart. — Cambridge : University of Cambridge. Department of Land Economy, 1981. — 19p. — The Denman Lecture, 1981

INTERGOVERNMENTAL FISCAL RELATIONS — India
LAKSHMINATH, A
Union state financial relations / by A. Lakshminath and A.P. Shrivastava. — 1st ed. — Nagpur : Wadhwa, 1985. — x, 97 p.. — Includes index. — Bibliography: p. [96]-97

INTERGOVERNMENTAL FISCAL RELATIONS — Nigeria
ASHWE, Chiichii
Fiscal federalism in Nigeria / Chiichii Ashwe. — Canberra : The Australian National University of Canberra, Centre for Research on Federal Financial Relations, 1986. — xi,140p. — (Research monograph / Australian National University. Centre for Research on Federal Financial Relations ; no.46). — Bibliography: p112-125

INTERGOVERNMENTAL FISCAL RELATIONS — Switzerland
Les relations financières entre le Jura Sud et l'État de Berne. — [s.l.] : [s.n.], 1975. — 36p

INTERGOVERNMENTAL FISCAL RELATIONS — United States
KIMMICH, Madeleine H
America's children, who cares? : growing needs and declining assistance in the Reagan era / Madeleine H. Kimmich. — Washington, D.C. : Urban Institute Press, c1985. — xvii 112 p.. — (The Changing domestic priorities series). — Includes bibliographical references

PETERSON, Paul E
When federalism works / Paul E. Peterson, Barry G. Rabe, Kenneth K. Wong. — Washington, D.C. : Brookings Institution, c1986. — xvi, 245 p.. — Includes bibliographical references and index

State politics and the new federalism : readings and commentary / edited by Marilyn Gittell. — New York : Longman, c1986. — xv, 544 p.. — Includes index. — Bibliography: p. 533-535

INTERLOCKING DIRECTORATES — Scotland — History — 20th century
SCOTT, John, 1949-
Multiple directors in top Scottish companies. — [Rev. version] / John Scott. — [Leicester] ([c/o Dept of Sociology, University of Leicester, Leicester LE1 7RH]) : J. Scott, [1983]. — 75p. — 'Working paper for the Company Analysis Project 1982'. — Previous ed.: published as Multiple directors in top Scottish companies 1904-1956. 1980

INTERMEDIATION (FINANCE)
BRYANT, Ralph C.
International financial intermediation / Ralph C. Bryant. — Washington, D.C. : Brookings Institution, c1987. — p. cm. — (Studies in international economics). — Includes index. — Bibliography: p

INTERNAL REVENUE — Australia — Statistics
AUSTRALIA. Commonwealth Bureau of Census and Statistics
Trade and customs amd excise revenue of the Commonwealth of Australia. — Melbourne : [the Bureau], 1903/4-1920/21. — Annual. — Title varies. — Continued by Australia. Commonwealth Bureau of Census and Statistics. Overseas trade

INTERNAL SECURITY — Great Britain

GREAT BRITAIN. Parliament. House of Commons. Research Division
Security / Barry K. Winetrobe. — [London] : the Division, 1983. — 52p. — (Background paper ; no.114)

INTERNAL SECURITY — United States — History

BIGEL, Alan I.
The Supreme Court on emergency powers, foreign affairs, and protection of civil liberties, 1935-1975 / Alan I. Bigel. — Lanham, MD : University Press of America, c1986. — xv, 211 p.. — : Originally presented as the author's thesis (doctoral--New School for Social Research). — Includes indexes. — Bibliography: p. 194-203

INTERNATIONAL ACCOUNTING STANDARDS COMMITTEE

INTERNATIONAL ACCOUNTING STANDARDS COMMITTEE
Objectives and procedures. — London : International Accounting Standards Committee, 1985. — [28p]

INTERNATIONAL AGENCIES

The All-in-one guide to European-Atlantic organisations (intergovernmental and supporting voluntary bodies) : what they are, what they do, and where to get further information. Plus a specially prepared chronology 1945-1984. — 10th ed., rev. and enlarged. — Exeter (7 Cathedral Close, Exeter, EX1 1E2, Devon) : European-Atlantic Movement (TEAM), 1984. — 32p. — Cover title. — Previous ed.: 1976

GORDENKER, Leon
Refugees in international politics / Leon Gordenker. — London : Croom Helm, c1987. — 227p. — (The Croom Helm United Nations and its agencies series). — Bibliography: p215-220. — Includes index

WILLIAMS, Douglas, 1917-
The specialized agencies and the United Nations : the system in crisis / Douglas Williams ; with a foreword by Sir Anthony Parsons. — London : Hurst in association with the David Davies Memorial Institute of International Studies, London, c1987. — xvi,279p. — Bibliography: p271-274. — Includes index

INTERNATIONAL AGENCIES — Addresses, essays, lectures

MORGENSTERN, Felice
Legal problems of international organizations / by Felice Morgenstern. — Cambridge : Grotius Publications, 1986. — xiv,147p. — (Hersch Lauterpacht memorial lectures). — At head of title: University of Cambridge Research Centre for International Law. — Includes bibliographical references and index

INTERNATIONAL AGENCIES — Administration

AMERASINGHE, C. F.
Index of decisions of international administrative tribunals / C. F. Amerasinghe, D. Bellinger. — 2nd ed. — Washington, D. C. : International Bank for Reconstruction and Development, 1985. — vi,149p. — Cover title. — Previous ed: 1981

INTERNATIONAL AGENCIES — Bibliography

ATHERTON, Alexine L
International organizations : a guide to information sources / Alexine L. Atherton. — Detroit : Gale Research Co., c1976. — xxviii, 350 p.. — (International relations information guide series ; v. 1) (Gale information guide library). — Includes indexes

KLECKNER, Simone-Marie
Public international law and international organization : international law bibliography / prepared by Simone-Marie Kleckner. — New York : Oceana Publications, 1984. — vi,99p. — (A collection of bibliographic and research resources)

Public international law and international organizations : a basic selective bibliography. — New York : United Nations, 1982. — ([Document] / United Nations ; ST/LIB/38). — In various languages. — Prepared by the Dag Hammarskjöld Library

INTERNATIONAL AGENCIES — Bibliography — Catalogs

COMMISSION OF THE EUROPEAN COMMUNITIES. Library
List of additions to the Library : supplement. — [Luxembourg : Office for Official Publications of the European Communities] 1982/1: Publications of international organisations (EC excluded) received by the Library 1978-1981. — 1982. — vp,461 columns . — In Community languages

INTERNATIONAL AGENCIES — Foreign relations — Treaties — Bibliography

A select bibliography on the law of treaties between states and international organizations or between international organizations. — New York : United Nations, 1985. — iii,33p. — ([Document] / United Nations ; ST/LIB/SER.B/36). — In various languages. — Prepared by the Dag Hammerskjöld Library

INTERNATIONAL AGENCIES — officials and employees

AMERASINGHE, C. F.
Index of decisions of international administrative tribunals / C. F. Amerasinghe, D. Bellinger. — 2nd ed. — Washington, D. C. : International Bank for Reconstruction and Development, 1985. — vi,149p. — Cover title. — Previous ed: 1981

INTERNATIONAL AND MUNICIPAL LAW — European Economic Community countries

AUDRETSCH, H. A. H.
Supervision in European Community law : observance by the member states of their treaty obligations : a treatise on international and supra-national supervision / H.A.H. Audretsch. — 2nd rev. ed. — Amsterdam ; Oxford : North-Holland, 1986. — xix,782p. — Previous ed.: 1978. — Bibliography: p.591-613. - Includes index

INTERNATIONAL BANK FOR RECONSTRUCTION AND DEVELOPMENT

List of recent periodical articles / Joint library, International Monetary Fund and International Bank for Reconstruction and Development. — Washington, D.C. : International Monetary Fund : International Bank for Reconstruction and Development, 1978-. — Monthly

INTERNATIONAL BUSINES ENTERPRISES — Eployees — Effect of technological innovations on

LALL, Sanjaya
Technological change, employment generation and multinationals : a case study of a foreign firm and a local multinational in India / by Sanjaya Lall. — Geneva : International Labour Office, 1983. — iii,72p. — (Multinational Enterprises Programme working papers. Research on employment effects of multinational enterprises ; no.27)

INTERNATIONAL BUSINESS ENTERPRISES

Meeting the corporate challenge / [edited by John Cavanagh...[et al]] : a handbook on corporate campaigns. — Amsterdam : Transnationals Information Exchange, 1985. — 77p. — (TIE Report ; 18/19)

British multinationals : origins, management and performance / edited by Geoffrey Jones. — Aldershot : Gower, c1986. — [200]p. — (Business history series). — Includes index

CALLIES, Albane
France-Japan : confrontation culturelle dans les entreprises mixtes / Albane Callies. — Paris : Librairie des Méridiens, 1986. — 208p. — Bibliography: p199-206

CASSON, Mark
The firm and the market : studies on multinational enterprise and the scope of the firm / Mark Casson. — Oxford : Basil Blackwell, 1987. — 1v.. — Includes bibliography and index

CATEORA, Philip R
International marketing / Philip R. Cateora. — 6th ed. — Homewood, Ill. : Irwin, 1987. — xvii, 839 p.. — Includes index. — Bibliography: p. 801-805

CLEGG, Jeremy
Multinational enterprise and world competition : a comparative study of the USA, Japan, the UK, Sweden and West Germany / Jeremy Clegg ; foreword by John H. Dunning. — Basingstoke : Macmillan in association with the Graduate School of European and International Studies, University of Reading, 1987. — xiv,206p. — (University of Reading European and international studies). — Bibliography: p194-202. — Includes index

Competition in global industries / edited by Michael E. Porter. — Boston, Mass. : Harvard Business School Press, c1986. — x, 581 p.. — (Research colloquium / Harvard Business School). — Includes bibliographies and index

The Economics of market dominance / edited by Donald Hay and John Vickers. — Oxford : Basil Blackwell, 1987. — 172p. — Conference papers. — Includes bibliographies and index

HILDEBRAND, Karl-Gustav
Expansion, crisis, reconstruction 1917-1939 / Karl-Gustav Hildebrand ; translation by Michael Callow. — Stockholm : Liber Forlag, 1985. — 496p. — (The Swedish Match Company, 1917-1939. studies in business internationalisation). — Bibliography: p473-484

The industrial relations practices of multi-plant foreign owned firms : submission to the House of Commons Select Committee on Employment / John Purcell...[et al.]. — Coventry : University of Warwick. School of Industrial and Business Studies. Industrial Relations Research Unit, 1986. — 17 leaves. — (Warwick papers in industrial relations ; no.13)

International accounting and transnational decisions / edited by S.J. Gray. — London ; Boston : Butterworth, 1983. — 500p. — Includes bibliographical references. — Includes index

MACCHARLES, Donald C.
Trade among multinationals : intra-industry trade and national competitiveness / Donald C. MacCharles. — London : Croom Helm, c1987. — xiv,207p. — (The Croom Helm series in international business). — Bibliography: p190-194 — Includes index

Multinationals, governments and international technology transfer / edited by A.E. Safarian and Gilles Y. Bertin. — London : Croom Helm, c1987. — [240]p. — (Croom Helm series in international business). — Includes bibliography and index

Multinationals of the south : new actors in the international economy / edited by Khushi M. Khan. — London : Pinter, 1986. — xi,250p. — Includes index

RIGONI, Raymond
Les multinationales de la pharmacie : polémiques, perceptions et paradoxes / Raymond Rigoni, Adrian Griffiths, William Laing. — Genève : Institut de Recherche et d'Information sur les Multinationales, [1985]. — 123p. — (Dossiers de l'Institut de Recherche et d'Information sur les Multinationales ; No.5). — Bibliography: p121-123

Survey of multinational enterprises. — [Luxembourg : Office for Official Publications of the European Communities]
V.1. — 1976. — 57p. — Bibliography: p55-57

INTERNATIONAL BUSINESS ENTERPRISES
continuation

VOZNESENSKAIA, N. N.
Smeshannye predpriiatiia kak forma mezhdunarodnogo ekonomicheskogo sotrudnichestva / N. N. Voznesenskaia ; otv. redaktor A. A. Rubanov. — Moskva : Nauka, 1986. — 181p

INTERNATIONAL BUSINESS ENTERPRISES — Accounting

BELKAOUI, Ahmed
International accounting : issues and solutions / Ahmed Belkaoui. — Westport, Conn. : Quorum Books, 1985. — xiv, 364 p.. — *Includes bibliographies and index*

CHOI, Frederick D. S.
International accounting / Frederick D.S. Choi, Gerhard G. Mueller. — Englewood Cliffs, N.J. : Prentice-Hall, c1984. — xvi, 525 p.. — *Rev. ed. of: An introduction to multinational accounting. c1978. — Includes bibliographies and index*

Managerial accounting and analysis in multinational enterprises / editors, H. Peter Holzer, Hanns-Martin W. Schoenfeld. — Berlin ; New York : W. de Gruyter, 1986, c1985. — p. cm. — *Bibliography: p[253]-257. — Bibliography: p*

INTERNATIONAL BUSINESS ENTERPRISES — Employees

Social and labour practices of multinational enterprises in the textiles, clothing, and footwear industries. — Geneva : International Labour Office, 1984. — xii,184p. — *Includes bibliographies*

INTERNATIONAL BUSINESS ENTERPRISES — Employment

GERSHENBERG, Irving
Multinational enterprises, transfer of managerial know-how, technology choice and employment of Kenya / Irving Gershenberg. — Geneva : International Labour Office, 1983. — iii,33p. — (Multinational Enterprises Programme working papers. Research on employment effects of multinational enterprises ; no.28). — *Bibliography: p29*

Multinational enterprises : information and consultation concerning their manpower plans. — Geneva : International Labour Office, 1985. — xii,195p

INTERNATIONAL BUSINESS ENTERPRISES — Employment — Developing countries

LALL, Sanjaya
The indirect employment effects of multinational enterprises in developing countries / by Sanjaya Lall. — Geneva : International Labour Office, 1979. — (Multinational Enterprises Programme working papers ; no.3)

INTERNATIONAL BUSINESS ENTERPRISES — Employment — Germany (West)

OLLE, Werner
The development of employment in multinational enterprises in the Federal Republic of Germany : results of a new survey (1974-1982) / by Werner Olle. — Geneva : International Labour Office, 1985. — 68p. — (Working paper / Multinational Enterprises Programme ; no.33). — *Bibliography: p62-63*

INTERNATIONAL BUSINESS ENTERPRISES — Employment — India

LALL, Sanjaya
Technological change, employment generation and multinationals : a case study of a foreign firm and a local multinational in India / by Sanjaya Lall. — Geneva : International Labour Office, 1983. — iii,72p. — (Multinational Enterprises Programme working papers. Research on employment effects of multinational enterprises ; no.27)

INTERNATIONAL BUSINESS ENTERPRISES — Employment — Liberia

IYANDA, Olukunle
Multinationals and employment in a West African sub-region : Liberia and Sierra Leone / by Olukunde Iyanda. — Geneva : International Labour Office, 1984. — iv,49p. — (Multinational Enterprises Programme working papers. Research on employment effects of multinational enterprises ; no.29). — *Bibliographical references: p37-39*

INTERNATIONAL BUSINESS ENTERPRISES — Employment — Sierra Leone

IYANDA, Olukunle
Multinationals and employment in a West African sub-region : Liberia and Sierra Leone / by Olukunde Iyanda. — Geneva : International Labour Office, 1984. — iv,49p. — (Multinational Enterprises Programme working papers. Research on employment effects of multinational enterprises ; no.29). — *Bibliographical references: p37-39*

INTERNATIONAL BUSINESS ENTERPRISES — Finance

ABDULLAH, Fuad A.
Financial management for the multinational firm / Fuad A. Abdullah. — Prentice-Hall International ed. — Englewood Cliffs ; London : Prentice-Hall, 1987. — xiii,594p. — *Bibliographies*

KETTELL, Brian
The finance of international business / Brian Kettell. — London : Graham & Trotman, 1979. — xviii,275p. — *Bibliography: p261-267. — Includes index*

LEVI, Maurice D.
International finance : financial management and the international economy / Maurice Levi. — New York : McGraw-Hill, c1983. — xvii, 460p. — (McGraw-Hill series in finance). — *Includes bibliographies and indexes*

SHAPIRO, Alan C
Multinational financial management / Alan C. Shapiro. — 2nd ed. — Boston ; London : Allyn and Bacon, c1986. — xv, 672p. — *Includes bibliographies and index*

SIEGEL, Michael H
Foreign exchange risk and direct foreign investment / by Michael H. Siegel. — Ann Arbor, Mich. : UMI Research Press, c1983. — vi, 97 p.. — (Research for business decisions ; no. 60). — *Includes index. — Bibliography: p. [89]-92*

INTERNATIONAL BUSINESS ENTERPRISES — Finance — Addresses, essays, lectures

International financial management : theory and application / edited by Donald R. Lessard. — 2nd ed. — New York : Wiley, c1985. — xi, 594 p.. — *Includes bibliographies and indexes*

INTERNATIONAL BUSINESS ENTERPRISES — Government ownership — Bibliography

Nationalization or take-over of foreign enterprises : a select bibliography = Nationalisation ou reprise des entreprises étrangères : bibliographie sélective. — New York : United Nations, 1974. — 17p. — ([Document] / United Nations ; ST/LIB/35). — *In various languages*

INTERNATIONAL BUSINESS ENTERPRISES — Government policy — Colombia

WALLACE, Brian F
Ownership and development : a comparison of domestic and foreign firms in Colombian manufacturing / by Brian F. Wallace. — Athens, Ohio : Ohio University Center for International Studies, 1987. — p. cm. — (Monographs in international studies. Latin America series ; no. 12). — *Bibliography: p*

INTERNATIONAL BUSINESS ENTERPRISES — History — 19th century

JONES, Charles A.
International business in the nineteenth century : the rise and fall of a cosmopolitan bourgeoisie / Charles A. Jones. — Brighton : Wheatsheaf, 1987. — xi,260p. — *Includes index*

INTERNATIONAL BUSINESS ENTERPRISES — Law and legislation — Developing countries

ACQUAAH, Kwamena
International regulation of transnational corporations : the new reality / Kwamena Acquaah. — New York : Praeger, 1986. — xx, 213 p.. — : *Revision of the author's thesis (Ph. D.)--New York University. — Includes index. — Bibliography: p. 195-208*

INTERNATIONAL BUSINESS ENTERPRISES — Law and legislation — Ghana

Essays from the Ghana-Valco renegotiations, 1982-85 / edited by Fui S. Tsikata. — [Accra] : Ghana Publishing Corporation, 1986. — viii,163p. — *Bibliographies*

INTERNATIONAL BUSINESS ENTERPRISES — Management

BROOKE, Michael Z.
International management : a review of strategies and operations / Michael Z. Brooke. — London : Hutchinson, 1986. — xvii,323p. — *Bibliography: p309-311. — Includes index*

European approaches to international management / Klaus Macharzina and Wolfgang H.Staehle. — Berlin : Walter de Gruyter, 1986

GHERTMAN, Michel
Decision-making regarding restructuring in multinational enterprises / by Michel Ghertman. — Geneva : International Labour Office, 1986. — 69p. — (Working paper / Multinational Enterprises Programme ; no.39). — *Includes bibliographical references*

RAPP, Lucien
Public multinational enterprises and strategic decision-making / by Lucien Rapp. — Geneva : International Labour Office, 1986. — iv,56p. — (Working paper / Multinational Enterprises Programme ; no.34). — *Bibliography: p[51]*

INTERNATIONAL BUSINESS ENTERPRISES — Management — Environmental aspects — Developing countries

Multinational corporations, environment, and the Third World : business matters / edited by Charles S. Pearson. — Durham, NC : Duke University Press, 1987. — xvi, 295 p.. — (Duke Press policy studies). — *"A World Resources Institute book.". — Based on an international meeting held in 1984 and sponsored by the World Resources Institute. — Includes index. — Bibliography: p. 261-284*

INTERNATIONAL BUSINESS ENTERPRISES — Moral and ethical aspects — Congresses

NATIONAL CONFERENCE ON BUSINESS ETHICS (1985 : Waltham, Mass.)
Ethics and the multinational enterprise : proceedings of the Sixth National Conference on Business Ethics, October 10 and 11, 1985 / sponsored by Center for Business Ethics, Bentley College, Waltham, Massachusetts ; edited by W. Michael Hoffman, Ann E. Lange, David A. Fedo. — Lanham, MD : University Press of America, c1986. — xlix, 530 p.. — *Includes bibliographies*

INTERNATIONAL BUSINESS ENTERPRISES — Personnel management

Multinational enterprises : information and consultation concerning their manpower plans. — Geneva : International Labour Office, 1985. — xii,195p

INTERNATIONAL BUSINESS ENTERPRISES — Personnel management
continuation

Social and labour practices of multinational enterprises in the textiles, clothing, and footwear industries. — Geneva : International Labour Office, 1984. — xii,184p. — *Includes bibliographies*

ZEIRA, Yoran
Personnel decision-making in wholly-owned foreign subsidiaries and in international joint ventures / Yoran Zeira and Oded Shenkar. — Geneva : International Labour Office, 1986. — 43p. — (Multinational Enterprises Programme working paper ; no.45). — *Bibliographical references: p[35]-36*

INTERNATIONAL BUSINESS ENTERPRISES — Reorganization

CASSON, Mark
International divestment and restructuring decisions (with special reference to the motor industry) / by Mark Casson. — Geneva : International Labour Office, 1986. — 46p. — (Working paper / Multinational Enterprises Programme ; no.40). — *Bibliography: p[38]-39*

GHERTMAN, Michel
Decision-making regarding restructuring in multinational enterprises / by Michel Ghertman. — Geneva : International Labour Office, 1986. — 69p. — (Working paper / Multinational Enterprises Programme ; no.39). — *Includes bibliographical references*

INTERNATIONAL BUSINESS ENTERPRISES — Safety measures

INTERNATIONAL LABOUR OFFICE
Safety and health practices of multinational enterprises. — Geneva : I.L.O., 1984. — viii,90p

INTERNATIONAL BUSINESS ENTERPRISES — Social aspects

Social and labour practices of multinational enterprises in the textiles, clothing, and footwear industries. — Geneva : International Labour Office, 1984. — xii,184p. — *Includes bibliographies*

INTERNATIONAL BUSINESS ENTERPRISES — Taxation — Law and legislation

Cross-border transactions between related companies : a summary of tax rules / edited by William R. Lawlor. — Deventer, The Netherlands ; Boston : Kluwer Law and Taxation Publishers, c1985. — p. cm. — *Derived from an international tax planning symposium in New York sponsored by Ernst & Whinney. — "Current to January 1985"--Foreword*

INTERNATIONAL BUSINESS ENTERPRISES — Argentina

SOURROUILLE, Juan V.
Transnacionalización y política económica en la Argentina / Juan V. Sourrouille, Bernardo P. Kosacoff, Jorge Lucangeli. — [Buenos Aires] : Bibliotecas Universitarias, Centro Editor de América Latina : Centro de Economía Transnacional, c1985. — 164p. — (Economía). — *Bibliography: p161-164*

UNITED NATIONS. Economic Commission for Latin America
Internacionalización de empresas y tecnología de origen argentino / Eduardo R. Ablin...[et al.]. — Buenos Aires : CEPAL : EUDEBA, c1985. — 331p

INTERNATIONAL BUSINESS ENTERPRISES — Australia

TSOKHAS, Kosmas
Beyond dependence : companies, labour processes and Australian mining / Kosmas Tsokhas. — Melbourne : Oxford University Press, 1986. — 291p. — *Bibliography: p [273]-281*

INTERNATIONAL BUSINESS ENTERPRISES — Canada

SAFARIAN, A. E
Foreign direct investment : a survey of Canadian research / A.E. Safarian. — Montreal, Québec : Institute for Research on Public Policy, c1985. — xv, 83 p.. — (Essays in international economics). — *Summary in French. — Bibliography: p. 53-[72]*

INTERNATIONAL BUSINESS ENTERPRISES — Caribbean Area

LONG, Frank
Employment effects of multinational enterprises in export processing zones in the Caribbean : a joint ILO/UNCTC research project / by Frank Long. — Geneva : International Labour Office, 1986. — 82p. — *Includes bibliographical references*

INTERNATIONAL BUSINESS ENTERPRISES — Developing countries

BORNSCHIER, Volker
Transnational corporations and underdevelopment / Volker Bornschier, Christopher Chase-Dunn. — New York : Praeger, 1985. — p. cm. — *Includes index. — Bibliography: p*

Investing in development : new roles for private capital? / Theodore H. Moran, editor ; Joseph M. Grieco ... [et al., contributors]. — New Brunswick (USA) : Transaction Books, c1985. — p. cm. — (U.S.-Third World policy perspectives ; no. 6)

Transnational corporations in South East Asia and the Pacific. — Sydney : Transnational Corporations Research Project, University of Sydney
vol.7: Transnational corporations and export-oriented industrialization / Ernst Utrecht, editor. — 1985. — 273p

INTERNATIONAL BUSINESS ENTERPRISES — Germany (West)

Multinationale Konzerne in der Bundesrepublik Deutschland / herausgegeben von Peter H. Mettler. — Frankfurt am Main : Haag und Herchen, 1985. — xii,103,48p. — (Arnoldshainer Schriften zur Interdisziplinären Ökonomie ; Bd.9). — *Bibliography: pA33-A48*

INTERNATIONAL BUSINESS ENTERPRISES — Ghana

Essays from the Ghana-Valco renegotiations, 1982-85 / edited by Fui S. Tsikata. — [Accra] : Ghana Publishing Corporation, 1986. — viii,163p. — *Bibliographies*

INTERNATIONAL BUSINESS ENTERPRISES — Great Britain — Management

DUNNING, John. H.
Decision-making structures in US and Japanese manufacturing offiliates in the UK : some similarities and contrasts / John H. Dunning. — Geneva : International Labour Office, 1986. — 28p. — (Working paper / Multinational Enterprises Programme ; no.41)

YOUNG, Stephen
Decision-making in foreign-owned multinational subsidiaries in the United Kingdom / by Stephen Young, Neil Hood and James Hamill. — Geneva : International Labour Office, 1985. — iv,66p. — (Working paper / Multinational Enterprises Programme ; no.35). — *Includes bibliographical references*

INTERNATIONAL BUSINESS ENTERPRISES — Kenya

GERSHENBERG, Irving
Multinational enterprises, transfer of managerial know-how, technology choice and employment of Kenya / Irving Gershenberg. — Geneva : International Labour Office, 1983. — iii,33p. — (Multinational Enterprises Programme working papers. Research on employment effects of multinational enterprises ; no.28). — *Bibliography: p29*

Readings on the multinational corporation in Kenya / edited by Raphael Kaplinsky. — Nairobi ; Oxford : Oxford University Press, 1978. — x,316p. — *Bibliography: p.308-313. — Includes index*

INTERNATIONAL BUSINESS ENTERPRISES — Latin America

Transnacionalización y desarrollo nacional en América Latina / compilador: Luciano Tomassini. — [Buenos Aires] : Grupo Editor Latinoamericano, c1984. — 291p. — (Colección estudios internacionales ; volumen 6)

INTERNATIONAL BUSINESS ENTERPRISES — Latin America — History

CLAYTON, Lawrence A
Grace : W.R. Grace & Co., the formative years, 1850-1930 / Lawrence A. Clayton. — Ottawa, Ill. : Jameson Books, c1985. — xiii, 403 p., [35] p. of plates. — *Includes index. — Bibliography: p. 387-394*

INTERNATIONAL BUSINESS ENTERPRISES — Namibia

Activities of transnational corporations in South Africa and Namibia and the responsibilities of home countries with respect to their operations in this area. — New York : United Nations, 1986. — iii,59p. — ([Document] / United Nations ; ST/CTC/84). — *Bibliographical references. — Sales no.: E.85.II.A.16*

UNITED NATIONS COUNCIL FOR NAMIBIA
Report on the activities of foreign economic interests operating in Namibia : report of Standing Committee II / Chairman: Mr Ali Sarwar Naqvi (Pakistan). — Vienna : United Nations, 1986. — 39p. — *Annexes I and II list transnational corporations with interests in South Africa or Namibia. Annex III-map of Namibia showing principal mines and minerals. — U.N. document A/CONF.138/7 and A/AC.131/203*

INTERNATIONAL BUSINESS ENTERPRISES — Nigeria

BIERSTEKER, Thomas J
Multinationals, the state, and control of the Nigerian economy / Thomas J. Biersteker. — Princeton, N.J. : Princeton University Press, c1987. — p. cm. — *Includes index. — Bibliography: p*

INTERNATIONAL BUSINESS ENTERPRISES — Peru — History

CLAYTON, Lawrence A
Grace : W.R. Grace & Co., the formative years, 1850-1930 / Lawrence A. Clayton. — Ottawa, Ill. : Jameson Books, c1985. — xiii, 403 p., [35] p. of plates. — *Includes index. — Bibliography: p. 387-394*

INTERNATIONAL BUSINESS ENTERPRISES — Poland

GARLAND, John S
Industrial cooperation between Poland and the West / by John Garland. — Ann Arbor, Mich. : UMI Research Press, c1985. — p. cm. — (Research for business decisions ; no. 71). — *: Originally presented as the author's thesis (Indiana University, 1982). — Includes index. — Bibliography: p*

INTERNATIONAL BUSINESS ENTERPRISES — South Africa

Activities of transnational corporations in South Africa and Namibia and the responsibilities of home countries with respect to their operations in this area. — New York : United Nations, 1986. — iii,59p. — ([Document] / United Nations ; ST/CTC/84). — *Bibliographical references. — Sales no.: E.85.II.A.16*

SEIDMAN, Ann
The roots of crisis in Southern Africa / Ann Seidman. — Trenton, N.J. : Africa World Press, 1985. — xvii,209p. — (Impact audit ; No.4). — *Bibliography: p175-180*

INTERNATIONAL BUSINESS ENTERPRISES — United States
GORDON, Sara L.
Foreign multinational investment in the United States : struggle for industrial Supremacy / Sara L. Gordon and Francis A. Lees. — New York ; London : Quorum, 1986. — xviii,289p. — Bibliography: p269-277. — Includes index

INTERNATIONAL BUSINESS ENTERPRISES — Yugoslavia
ARTISIEN, Patrick F. R.
Joint ventures in Yugoslav industry / Patrick F.R. Artisien. — Aldershot : Gower, c1985. — [xv,240]p. — Bibliography: p210-218. — Includes index

INTERNATIONAL BUSINESS MACHINES CORPORATION — History
DELAMARTER, Richard Thomas
Big Blue : IBM's use and abuse of power / Richard Thomas DeLamarter. — London : Macmillan, 1987, c1986. — [412]p. — Originally published: New York : Dodd, Mead, 1986. — Includes index

MERCER, David
IBM : how the world's most successful corporation is managed / David Mercer. — London : Kogan Page, 1987. — 306p. — Bibliography: p299. — Includes index

INTERNATIONAL CLEARING — Finland
HIRVENSAL O, Inkeri
Suomen ja SNTL : n välinen clearing-maksujärjestelmë / Inkeri Hirvensal o. — Helsinki : Suomen Pankki, 1979. — 125p. — (Suomen Pankin julkaisuja ; Sarji A: 49). — Bibliography: p[105]-107

INTERNATIONAL CLEARING — Soviet Union
HIRVENSAL O, Inkeri
Suomen ja SNTL : n välinen clearing-maksujärjestelmë / Inkeri Hirvensal o. — Helsinki : Suomen Pankki, 1979. — 125p. — (Suomen Pankin julkaisuja ; Sarji A: 49). — Bibliography: p[105]-107

INTERNATIONAL COMMITTEE OF THE RED CROSS — Greece — Political activity
SIEGRIST, Roland
The protection of political detainees : the International Committee of the Red Cross in Greece 1967-1971 / Roland Siegrist. — Montreux : Editions Corbaz, 1985. — 171p. — Bibliography: p[157]-171

INTERNATIONAL CONVENTION FOR THE SAFETY OF LIFE AT SEA (1974). Protocols, amendments, etc.
[International Convention for the Safety of Life at Sea (1974). Protocols, amendments, etc.]. Consolidated text of the 1974 SOLAS Convention, the 1978 SOLAS Protocol, the 1981 and 1983 SOLAS amendments. — London : International Maritime Organization, 1986. — vii,439p

INTERNATIONAL CONVENTION RELATING TO THE LIMITATION OF THE LIABILITY OF OWNERS OF SEA-GOING SHIPS
GRIGGS, Patrick
Limitation of liability for maritime claims / by Patrick Griggs and Richard Williams. — London : Lloyd's, 1986. — [122]p

INTERNATIONAL COOPERATION
JUSTICE, Judith
Policies, plans, and people : culture and health development in Nepal / Judith Justice. — Berkeley : University of California Press, c1986. — p. cm — (Comparative studies of health systems and medical care). — Includes index. — Bibliography: p

The international law of development : basic documents / compiled and edited by A. Peter Mutharika. — Dobbs Ferry, N.Y. : Oceana Vol.4. — 1979. — vii.1999-2620p

The Third World and the world economic system / V.R. Panchamukhi ... [et al.]. — New Delhi : Radiant Publishers ; Atlantic Highlands, N.J. : Distributed in the U.S.A. by Humanities Press, 1986. — viii, 309 p.. — Includes bibliographies

VYSOTSKII, A. F.
Morskoi regionalism : (mezhdunarodno-pravovye problemy regional'nogo sotrudnichestva gosudarstv) / A. F. Vysotskii. — Kiev : Naukova dumka, 1986. — 193p

INTERNATIONAL COOPERATION — Communist countries
Nauchno-tekhnicheskii progress i sotrudnichestvo stran SEV / pod redaktsiei O. A. Chukanova, G. M. Kharakhash'iana, Iu. F. Kormnova. — Moskva : Mezhdunarodnye otnosheniia, 1973. — 205p

Nauchno-tekhnicheskoe sotrudnichestvo stran SEV : spravochnik / pod redaktsiei O. A. Chukanova. — Moskva : Ekonomika, 1986. — 287p

INTERNATIONAL COOPERATION — Persian Gulf Region
NAKHLEH, Emile A.
The Gulf Cooperation Council : policies, problems, and prospects / Emile A. Nakhleh. — New York : Praeger, 1986. — xviii, 128 p.. — "Praeger special studies. Praeger scientific.". — Includes index. — Bibliography: p. 123-126

INTERNATIONAL COURT OF JUSTICE
INTERNATIONAL COURT OF JUSTICE
[Judgements]. Military and paramilitary activities in and against Nicaragua : (Nicaragua v. United States of America). Merits. 27 June 1986 = Activités militaires et paramilitaires au Nicaragua c. Etats-Unis d'America. Fond. 27 June 1986. — New York : United Nations, 1986. — 142 bis. — U.N. Security Council document S/18221 conveying the judgment of the Court at the request of the Permanent Representative of Nicaragua to the United Nations

PROTT, Lyndel V.
The latent power of culture and the international judge / by Lyndell [i.e. Lyndel] V. Prott. — Abingdon : Professional, 1979. — xxi,250p. — Bibliography: p235-244. — Includes index

ROSENNE, Shabtai
The International Court of Justice : an essay in political and legal theory / Shabtai Rosenne. — Leyden : Sijthoff, 1957. — xxiv,592p

INTERNATIONAL COURTS
AMERASINGHE, C. F.
Index of decisions of international administrative tribunals / C. F. Amerasinghe, D. Bellinger. — 2nd ed. — Washington, D. C. : International Bank for Reconstruction and Development, 1985. — vi,149p. — Cover title. — Previous ed: 1981

JENNINGS, Robert Yewdall
International courts and international politics / Robert Yewdall Jennings. — Hull : Hull University Press, 1986. — 17p. — Josephine Onoh Memorial Lecture

INTERNATIONAL COVENANT ON ECONOMIC, SOCIAL, AND CULTURAL RIGHTS
MOWER, A. Glenn
International cooperation for social justice : global and regional protection of economic/social rights / A. Glenn Mower, Jr. — Westport, Conn. : Greenwood Press, c1985. — p. cm. — (Studies in human rights ; no. 6). — Includes index. — Bibliography: p

INTERNATIONAL CROPS RESEARCH INSTITUTE FOR THE SEMI-ARID TROPICS
MAHAPATRA, Ishwar Chandra
India and the international crops research institute for the semi-arid tropics : a study of their collaboration in agricultural research / Ishwar Chandra Mahapatre, Dev Raj Bhumbla, Shriniwas Dattatraya Bokil. — Washington, D.C. : The World Bank, 1986. — x,48p. — (Study paper / Consultative group on International Agricultural Research ; no.18)

INTERNATIONAL DEVELOPMENT ASSOCIATION
INTERNATIONAL DEVELOPMENT ASSOCIATION
General conditions applicable to development credit agreements. — |[Washington, D.C.?] : the Association, 1980. — iii,12p

INTERNATIONAL DEVELOPMENT ASSOCIATION — Legal status, laws, etc.
INTERNATIONAL DEVELOPMENT ASSOCIATION
By-laws : as amended through March 2, 1981. — Washington, D.C. : the Association, 1981. — 2p

INTERNATIONAL DIVISION OF LABOR
Changing Britain, changing world : geographical perspectives. — Milton Keynes : Open University Press. — (Social sciences : a second level course) (D205; Units 21-25). — At head of title : Open University
Section 3: Synthesis: uniqueness and interdependence of place
Block 6: Uneven development and the world order / John Allen...[et al.]. — 1985. — Various pagings

Kuba v mezhdunarodnom sotsialisticheskom razdelenii truda / otv. redaktor M. A. Manasov. — Moskva : Nauka, 1986. — 146p

INTERNATIONAL DIVISION OF LABOR — Congresses
The Americas in the new international division of labor / edited by Steven E. Sanderson. — New York, N.Y. : Holmes & Meier, 1985. — p. cm. — Includes index. — Bibliography: p

INTERNATIONAL DRINKING WATER SUPPLY AND SANITATION DECADE, 1981-1990 — Statistics
The International Drinking Water Supply and Sanitation Decade : review of national baseline data (as at 31 December 1980). — Geneva : World Health Organization, 1984. — 169p. — (WHO offset publication ; no.85)

INTERNATIONAL ECONOMIC INTEGRATION
CARL, Beverly May
Economic integration among developing nations : law and policy / Beverly May Carl. — New York : Praeger, 1986. — xx, 285 p.. — "Praeger special studies. Praeger scientific.". — Includes bibliographies and index

INTERNATIONAL ECONOMIC RELATIONS
ACQUAAH, Kwamena
International regulation of transnational corporations : the new reality / Kwamena Acquaah. — New York : Praeger, 1986. — xx, 213 p.. — : Revision of the author's thesis (Ph. D.)--New York University. — Includes index. — Bibliography: p. 195-208

ADAMS, Patricia
In the name of progress : the underside of foreign aid / Patricia Adams and Lawrence Solomon. — Toronto, Canada : Energy Probe Research Foundation, 1985. — 229 p.. — "An energy probe project.". — Includes index. — Bibliography: p. 168-214

BANKS, Ferdinand E.
The political economy of natural gas / Ferdinand E. Banks. — London : Croom Helm, c1987. — [240]p. — (Croom Helm commodity series). — Includes bibliography and index

INTERNATIONAL ECONOMIC RELATIONS
continuation

BERBEROGLU, Berch
The international of capital : imperialism and capitalist development on a world scale / Berch Berberoglu. — New York : Praeger, 1987. — p. cm. — *Bibliography: p*

BOLLECKER-STERN, Brigitte
Droit économique / Brigitte Bollecker-Stern, Maurice Dahan, Lazare Kopelmanas. — Paris : Pedone, 1978. — 166p. — (Cours et travaux / Institut des hautes études internationales de Paris)

BORNER, Silvio
Internationalization of industry : an assessment in the light of a small open economy (Switzerland) / Silvio Borner. — Berlin ; New York : Springer-Verlag, c1986. — p. cm. — *Bibliography: p*

BULAJIĆ, Milan
Principles of international development law : progressive development of the principles of international law relating to the new international economic order / Milan Bulajić. — Dordrecht, Netherlands ; Boston : Martinus Nijhoff Publishers, 1986. — 403p. — *Bibliography: p.359-366*

CASTRO, Fidel
Fidel Castro : nothing can stop the course of history / interview by Jeffrey M. Elliot and Mervyn M. Dymally. — New York ; London : Pathfinder Press, 1986. — 258p

CHICHILNISKY, Graciela
The evolving international economy / Graciela Chichilnisky, Geoffrey Heal. — Cambridge : Cambridge University Press, 1987. — [176]p. — *Includes index*

CLAUSEN, A. W
The development challenge of the eighties : A.W. Clausen at the World Bank : major policy addresses, 1981-1986. — Washington, D.C., U.S.A. : The Bank, 1986. — p. cm

CLAUSEN, A. W.
The development challenge of the eighties : A. W. Clausen at the World Bank : major policy addresses, 1981-1986 / A. W. Clausen. — Washington, D.C. : The World Bank, 1986. — xxvii,496p. — *Contents: Addresses to various bodies by A. W. Clausen, ex-President of the World Bank*

CZEPURKO, Aleksander
Świat a gospodarka Polski. — Warszawa : Książka i Wiedza, 1986. — 191p

DOMÁNY, Gyula
Nemzetközi pénzügyi kapcsolatok / irta Domány Gyula. — Budapest : Grill-féle udvari könyvkereskedés kiadása, 1936. — 36p. — *Bibliography: p[35]-36*

EMMANUEL, Arghiri
La dynamique des inégalités / Arghiri Emmanuel ; préface de Serge Latouche. — Paris : Anthropos, [1985]. — 284p

The Export-Import Bank at fifty : the international environment and the institution's role / edited by Rita M. Rodriguez. — Lexington, Mass. : Lexington Books, c1987. — xii, 206 p.. — *Includes bibliographies and index*

FELLNER, Frigyes
A nemzetközi fizetési mérleg és alakulása Magyarországon / a Magyar Tudományos Akadémia megbízásából irta Fellner Frigyes. — Budapest : Politzer-féle Könyvkiadóvállalat, 1908. — 181p. — (Magyar Közgazdasági Könyvtár ; Köt.5)

FEUER, Guy
Droit international du développement / Guy Feuer [et] Hervé Cassan. — Paris : Dalloz, 1985. — xxx,644p.

GALTUNG, Johan
The North/South debate : technology, basic human needs and the new international economic order / Johan Galtung. — New York : Institute for World Order, 1980. — 50p. — (World Order Models Project working paper ; no.12)

GANDOLFO, Giancarlo
International economics / Giancarlo Gandolfo. — Berlin ; New York : Springer-Verlag, c1986. — p. cm

GANGAL, Anurag
New international economic order : a Gandhian perspective / Anurag Gangal. — Delhi : Chanakya Publications, 1985. — 160p. — *Bibliography: p147-157*

GOUREVITCH, Peter Alexis
Politics in hard times : comparative responses to international economic crises / Peter Gourevitch. — Ithaca : Cornell University Press, 1986. — p. cm. — (Cornell studies in political economy). — *Includes index*

GREAT BRITAIN. Parliament. House of Commons. Library. Research Division
The U.S. budget deficit and its consequences for the world / Christopher Barclay. — [London] : the Division, 1984. — 17p. — (Background paper ; no.145)

GRJEBINE, André
La nouvelle économie internationale : de la crise mondiale au développement autocentré / André Grjebine. — Paris : Presses Universitaires de France, 1980. — 326p

HENNING, C. Randall
Macroeconomic diplomacy in the 1980s : domestic politics and international conflict among the United States, Japan, and Europe / C. Randall Henning. — London : Croom Helm for the Atlantic Institute for International Affairs, c1987. — [96]p. — (Atlantic paper ; no.65)

HOLLY, Daniel
L'Unesco : le tiers-monde et l'économie mondiale / Daniel A. Holly. — Montréal : Presses de l'Université de Montréal ; Genève : Institute Universitaire de Hautes Études Internationales, 1981. — 176p. — *Bibliography: p161-172*

INGHAM, Barbara
Colonialism and peripheral development / Barbara Ingham. — Salford : University of Salford, 1986. — 22p. — (Salford papers in economics ; 86-6)

International trade and exchange rates in the late eighties / edited by Theo Peeters, Peter Praet and Paul Reding. — Amsterdam : North-Holland ; Bruxelles : Université de Bruxelles, 1985. — xii,418p

KIDRON, Michael
The book of business, money and power / Michael Kidron and Ronald Segal. — London : Pluto Projects, 1987. — 187p

KNEESHAW, J. T.
International interest rate relationships : policy choices and constraints / by J. T. Kneeshaw and P. Van den Bergh. — Basle : Bank For International Settlements, 1985. — 67p. — (BIS economic papers ; no.13)

LEVINE, Paul
Does international macroeconomic policy co-ordinate pay and is it sustainable : a two-country analysis / Paul Levine and David Currie. — London : National Institute of Economic and Social Research, 1986. — 43p. — (Discussion paper / National Institute of Economic and Social Research ; no.113). — *Bibliography: p42-43*

LOWENFELD, Andreas F.
International economic law. — New York : Matthew Bender
Vol.1: International private trade / Andreas F. Lowenfeld. — 2nd ed. — 1981. — xi,183,177,7,8p. — *Includes Documents Supplement*

LOWENFELD, Andreas F.
International economic law. — New York : Matthew Bender
Vol.2: International private investment / Andreas F. Lowenfeld. — 1982. — xi,207,355,2,12p. — *Includes Documents Supplement*

LOWENFELD, Andreas F.
International economic law. — New York : Matthew Bender
Vol.3: Trade controls for political ends / Andreas F. Lowenfeld. — 2nd ed. — 1983. — x,621,910,5,21p. — *Includes Documents Supplement*

LOWENFELD, Andreas F.
International economic law. — New York : Matthew Bender
Vol.4: The international monetary system / Andreas F. Lowenfeld. — 2nd ed. — 1984. — xvi,404,473,4,17p. — *Includes Documents Supplement*

LOWENFELD, Andreas F.
International economic law. — New York : Matthew Bender
Vol.6: Public controls on international trade / Andreas F. Lowenfeld. — 2nd ed. — 1983. — xvii,457,775,4,22p. — *Includes Documents Supplement*

MCNAMARA, Robert S.
Economic interdependance and global poverty : the challenge of our time / Robert S. McNamara. — Durham, N.C. : Published by the Commission for International Justice and Peace of the Bishops' Conference of England and Wales, 1983. — 15p. — *First Barbara Ward Memorial Lecture*

NEU, C. R
Surprises in the international economy : toward an agenda for planning and research / C.R. Neu, Donald Putnam Henry. — Santa Monica, CA : Rand, [1986]. — xiii, 74 p.. — "June 1986.". — "R-3401."

The new protectionist threat to world welfare / edited by Dominick Salvatore. — new York : Elsevier Science, 1986. — xvi,581p

OGNEV, A. P.
Ekonomicheskie otnosheniia Vostok-Zapad v 80-e gody : novye iavleniia, problemy, perspektivy / A. P. Ognev ; otv. redaktor V. N. Shenaev. — Moskva : Nauka, 1986. — 220p

OSMOVA, M. N.
New international economic relations : realities and problems / Markiana Osmova ; translated from the Russian by Boris Lunkov. — Moscow : Novosti Press Agency, 1986. — 76p. — (Socialism and the global problems of today)

PASZYNSKI, Marian
International organizations, economic security and normalization of east-west economic relations / Marian Paszynski. — Warsaw : Foreign Trade Research Institute, 1986. — 29p

PLOEG, Frederick van der
Capital accumulation, inflation and long-run conflict in international objectives / F. van der Ploeg. — London : Centre for Labour Economics, London School of Economics, 1986. — 29p. — (Discussion paper / London School of Economics and Political Science. Centre for Labour Economics ; no.250). — *Bibliography: p28-29*

POOL, John Charles
The ABCs of international finance : understanding the trade and debt crisis / John Charles Pool, Steve Stamos. — Lexington, Mass. : Lexington Books, c1987. — xii, 138 p.. — *Includes index. — Bibliography: p. [131]-132*

Positive sum : improving North-South relations / edited by I. William Zartman. — New Brunswick, N.J. : Transaction Books, c1986. — p. cm. — *Includes bibliographies*

INTERNATIONAL ECONOMIC RELATIONS
continuation

RAMPHAL, Shridath S.
For the South, a time to think / Shridath S. Ramphal. — London : Third World Foundation, 1986. — 18p. — (Third World Foundation monograph ; 16)

REGAN, Colm
75:25, Ireland in an unequal world / by Colm Regan, with Pauline Eccles ... [et al.]. — Dublin, Ireland : Development Education Commission of CONGOOD, c1984. — 208 p.

Research in international business and international relations. — Greenwich, Conn. : Jai Press, 1986. — *Annual*

STEVENS, Christopher, 1948-
The new Lome convention : implications for Europe's third world policy / Christopher Stevens. — Bruxelles : Centre for European Policy Studies, 1984. — 39p. — (CEPS papers ; no.16)

TILLINGHAST, David R.
International economic law. — New York : Matthew Bender
Vol.5: Tax aspects of international transactions / David R. Tillinghast. — 2nd ed. — 1984. — xv,473,177,12,10p. — *Bibliography*

TINBERGEN, Jan
L'Europe et le nouvel ordre economique international / Jan Tinbergen. — Bruxelles : Fondation Paul-Henri Spaak, 1977. — 23p

TWOSE, Nigel
Cultivating hunger : an Oxfam study of food, power and poverty / Nigel Twose. — Oxford : Oxfam, 1984. — 48p. — *Bibliography: p46-47*

VANDAMME, J
La politique de la concurrence dans la C.E.E. / J.A. Van Damme. — Kortrijk, Belgique : UGA, [1980]. — 658 p., [1] leaf of plates. — (Cours / Centre international d'études et de recherches européennes ; 1977). — At head of title: Institut universitaire international, Luxembourg. — *Bibliography: p. 589-658*

VOZNESENSKAIA, N. N.
Smeshannye predpriiatiia kak forma mezhdunarodnogo ekonomicheskogo sotrudnichestva / N. N. Voznesenskaia ; otv. redaktor A. A. Rubanov. — Moskva : Nauka, 1986. — 181p

WOOLCOCK, Stephen
Interdependence in the post-multilateral era : trends in U.S.- European trade relations / Stephen Woolcock, Jeffrey Hart and Hans van der Ven. — Lanham,MD : Havard University Center for International Affairs : University Press of America, 1985. — xxv,138p

INTERNATIONAL ECONOMIC RELATIONS — Addresses, essays, lectures

Dependency theory and the return of high politics / edited by Mary Ann Tétreault and Charles Frederick Abel. — New York : Greenwood Press, 1986. — xii, 270 p.. — (Contributions in political science ; no. 140). — *Includes index.* — *Bibliography: p. [255]-260*

Strategic trade policy and the new international economics / edited by Paul R. Krugman. — Cambridge, Mass ; London : MIT Press, c1986. — 313p. — *Includes bibliographies and index*

INTERNATIONAL ECONOMIC RELATIONS — Bibliography

UNCTAD 1963-1983 : bibliography = CNUCED 1963-1983 : bibliographie. — Geneva : United Nations Library, 1983. — ii,81p. — (Publications / United Nations Library. Series C. special bibliographies, repertoires and indexes ; no.4 = Publications / Nations Unie, Bibliothèque. Serie C. Bibliographies speciales, repertoires et index ; no.4)

INTERNATIONAL ECONOMIC RELATIONS — Congresses

The Global economy : divergent perspectives on economic change / edited by Edward W. Gondolf, Irwin M. Marcus, and James P. Dougherty. — Boulder : Westview Press, 1986. — xvii, 212 p.. — (Westview special studies in international economics and business). — "Essays ... drawn from a conference on 'Industry and society' at Indiana University of Pennsylvania"--Acknowledgments

IAEE CONFERENCE ((7th : 1985 : Bonn, Germany)
Energy and economy, global interdependences : papers of the plenary sessions of the 1985 International Conference of the International Association of Energy Economists (IAEE) and its German Chapter, the Gesellschaft für Energiewissenschaft und Energiepolitik (GEE) / Mark Baier (Hrsg.). — Köln : Verlag TÜV Rheinland, c1986. — 183 p.. — *Includes bibliographies*

Production and trade in services : policies and their underlying factors bearing upon international service transactions : report / by the UNCTAD secretariat. — New York : United Nations, 1985. — vii,64p. — At head of title: United Nations Conference on Trade and Development, Geneva. — "TD/B/941/Rev.1"--T.p. verso. — "United Nations publication sales no. E.84.II.D.2"--T.p. verso. — *Includes bibliographical references*

SOCIÉTE FRANÇAISE POUR LE DROIT INTERNATIONAL. Colloque (19e : 1985 : Nice)
Les nations unies et le droit international économique : [actes du colloque]. — Paris : A. Pedone, 1986. — vii,383p

INTERNATIONAL ECONOMIC RELATIONS — History — 20th century

KARLSSON, Svante
Oil and the world order : American foreign oil policy / Svante Karlsson. — Leamington Spa : Berg, 1986. — 308p. — *Bibliography: p293-297.* — *Includes index*

INTERNATIONAL ECONOMIC RELATIONS — Law and legislation

UNITED NATIONS. Secretary General
Progressive development of the principles and norms of international law relating to the new international economic order : report of the Secretary-General : Addendum. — New York : United Nations, 1984. — Docment contains study by UNITAR entitled: Analytical study [on the progressive development of the principles and norms of international law relating to the new international economic order] prepared by Dr. Georges Abi-Saab. — U.N. document A/39/504/Add.1

INTERNATIONAL ECONOMIC RELATIONS — Mathematical models

MCMILLAN, John
Game theory in international economics / John McMillan. — Chur, Switzerland ; New York : Harwood Academic Publishers, 1986. — p. cm. — (Fundamentals of pure and applied economics ; vol. 1. International trade section). — *Includes index.* — *Bibliography: p*

The U.S. economy in an interdependent world : a multicountry model / Guy V.G. Stevens ... [et al.]. — Washington, D.C. : Board of Governors of the Federal Reserve System : Copies obtained from Publications Services, Board of Governors of the Federal Reserve System, 1984. — x,590p. — *Includes bibliographical references and indexes*

INTERNATIONAL ECONOMIC RELATIONS — Mathematical models — Congresses

International macroeconomic modelling for policy decisions / edited by P. Artus and O. Guvenen in collaboration with F. Gagey. — Dordrecht ; Boston : M. Nijhoff, c1986. — viii, 269 p.. — (Advanced studies in theoretical and applied econometrics ; v. 5). — "Based on an international conference organised by the Applied Econometric Association (AEA) ... which was held in Brussels at the Commission of the European Communities in December 1983"--Pref. — *Includes bibliographies and index*

INTERNATIONAL ECONOMIC RELATIONS — Research

Research in international business and finance: a research annual. — Greenwich, Conn. : Jai Press, 1979-. — *Irregular*

INTERNATIONAL EDUCATION

ATLANTISCHE COMMISSIE
De school en het buitenlands beleéd. — Den Haag : Atlantische Commissie, 1969. — *Bibliography: p[27-28]*
7: Bestaat er een Atlantische Wereld?. — 26, [2] leaves

INTERNATIONAL FEDERATION FOR INFORMATION PROCESSING. Technical Committee for Information Systems

Trends in information systems : an anthology of papers from conferences of the IFIP Technical Committee 8 "Information Systems" to commemorate their tenth anniversary / edited by B. Langefors, A.A. Verrijn-Stuart, G. Bracchi. — Amsterdam ; New York : North-Holland ; New York : Sole distributors for the U.S.A. and Canada Elsevier Science Pub. Co., 1986. — xv, 469 p.. — *Includes bibliographies*

INTERNATIONAL FEDERATION OF LIBRARY ASSOCIATIONS — Bibliography

CAMBIO, Edward P.
The International Federation of Library Associations : a selected list of references / compiled by Edward P. Cambio. — Washington, D. C. : Library of Congress, 1974. — 14p. — *Supt. of Docs. no.:LC2.2:In8/2*

INTERNATIONAL FINANCE

ABDULLAH, Fuad A.
Financial management for the multinational firm / Fuad A. Abdullah. — Prentice-Hall International ed. — Englewood Cliffs ; London : Prentice-Hall, 1987. — xiii,594p. — *Bibliographies*

ALIBER, Robert Z
The international money game / Robert Z. Aliber. — 5th ed., rev. — New York : Basic Books, c1987. — p. cm. — *Includes index*

AYLING, D. E.
The internationalisation of stockmarkets : the trend towards greater foreign borrowing and investment / D.E. Ayling. — Aldershot : Gower, c1986. — [200]p. — (Gower Studies in finance and investment ; 1). — *Includes bibliography*

BRYANT, Ralph C.
International financial intermediation / Ralph C. Bryant. — Washington, D.C. : Brookings Institution, c1987. — p. cm. — (Studies in international economics). — *Includes index.* — *Bibliography: p*

COLLIN, Fernand
La hautise des réserves monétaires / Fernand Collin. — Siena : [Note Economidie], 1973. — 36-45p

COOPER, Richard N
The international monetary system : essays in world economics / Richard N. Cooper. — Cambridge, Mass. : MIT Press, c1987. — p. cm. — *Includes bibliographies and index*

INTERNATIONAL FINANCE
continuation

CROCKETT, Andrew
Strengthening the international monetary system : exchange rates, surveillance, and objective indicators / by Andrew Crockett and Morris Goldstein. — Washington, D. C. : International Monetary Fund, 1987. — vii,84p. — (Occasional paper / International Monetary Fund ; no.50). — *Bibliographical references: p83-84*

CUDDINGTON, John T
Capital flight : estimates, issues, and explanations / John T. Cuddington. — Princeton, N.J. : International Finance Section, Dept. of Economics, Princeton University, c1986. — 44 p.. — (Princeton studies in international finance ; no. 58 (Dec. 1986). — *Bibliography: p. 39-40*

DE VRIES, Margaret Garritsen
Balance of payments adjustment, 1945 to 1986 : the IMF experience / Margaret Garritsen de Vries. — Washington, D.C. : International Monetary Fund, 1987. — xi,336p. — *Bibliography: p310-322*

DEHOVE, M.
Le système monétaire international / M. Dehove, J. Mathis. — [Paris] : Dunod, 1986. — 271p. — *Bibliography: p266-267*

EICHENGREEN, Barry
Hegemonic stability theories of the international monetary system / Barry Eichengreen. — London : Centre for Economic Policy Research, 1987. — 76p. — (Discussion paper series / Centre for Economic Policy Research ; no.193). — *Bibliography: p69-76*

FRIEDMAN, Irving Sigmund
Toward world prosperity : reshaping the global money system / by Irving S. Friedman. — Lexington, Mass. : Lexington Books, c1987. — xiii, 317 p.. — *Includes index. — Bibliography: p. [295]-296*

FUKAO, Mitsuhiro
Internationalisation of financial markets : some implications for macroeconomic policy and for the allocation of capital / by Mitsuhiro Fukao and Masaharu Hanazaki. — [Paris] : OECD, 1986. — 97p. — (Working papers / OECD Department of Economics and Statistics ; no.37). — *Bibliographical references: p36-40*

GANDOLFO, Giancarlo
International economics / Giancarlo Gandolfo. — Berlin ; New York : Springer-Verlag, c1986. — p. cm

GREAT BRITAIN. Parliament. House of Commons. Library. Research Division
The international monetary system and the world debt crisis / Christopher Barclay. — [London] : the Division, 1983. — 18p. — (Background paper ; no.126)

GUTTENTAG, Jack M.
Disaster myopia in international banking / Jack M. Guttentag and Richard J. Herring. — Princeton, N.J. : Princeton University. Department of Economics. International Finance Section, 1986. — 40p. — (Essays in international finance ; no.164). — *Bibliography: p34-*

International borrowing : negotiating and structuring international debt transactions / Daniel D. Bradlow, editor. — 2nd ed. — Washington, D.C. : International Law Institute, c1986. — 499p. — (International negotiation and development : sourcebooks on policy and practice ; 1)

International capital markets : development and prospects / by Maxwell Watson...[et al.]. — Washington, D. C. : International Monetary Fund, 1986. — ix,152p. — (World economic and financial surveys). — *Includes Bibliographical references*

INTERNATIONAL MONETARY FUND
Documents relating to the Second Amendment of the Articles of Agreement of the International Monetary Fund. — Washington, D.C. : the Fund, 1980-86. — 2v (in 6 parts). — *Contents: V.1: Documents - v.2: Minutes - Index (1986)*

INTERNATIONAL MONETARY FUND. Board of Governors. Committee on Reform of the International Monetary System and Related Issues
International monetary reform : documents of the Committee of Twenty. — Washington, D.C. : the Fund, 1974. — viii,253p. — *Includes the Report to the Board of Governors, Outline of Reform and accompanying Annexes, Reports of Technical groups, and related documents*

International monetary problems and supply-side economics : essays in honour of Lorie Tarshis / edited by Jon S. Cohen and G.C. Harcourt. — Basingstoke : Macmillan, 1986. — viii,162p. — *Includes bibliographies and index*

JOHNSTON, R. B.
Theories of the growth of the Euro—currency market : a review of the Euro—currency deposit multiplier / by R. B. Johnston. — Basle : Bank for International Settlements, 1981. — 52p. — (BIS economic papers ; no.4)

KAMBATA, Dara
The practice of multinational banking : macro-policy issues and key international concepts / Dara M. Khambata. — Westport, Conn. : Quorum Books, c1986. — p. cm. — *Includes bibliographies and index*

KASHIWAGI, Yusuke
The emergence of global finanace / Yusuke Kashiwagi. — Washington, D.C. : George Washington University, 1986. — 20p. — *The 1986 Per Jacobsson Lecture*

KIDRON, Michael
The book of business, money and power / Michael Kidron and Ronald Segal. — London : Pluto Projects, 1987. — 187p

KINDLEBERGER, Charles P.
International capital movements : based on the Marshall Lectures given at the University of Cambridge 1985 / Charles P. Kindleberger. — Cambridge : Cambridge University Press, 1987. — 1v. — *Includes bibliography and index*

LEVI, Maurice D.
International finance : financial management and the international economy / Maurice Levi. — New York : McGraw-Hill, c1983. — xvii, 460p. — (McGraw-Hill series in finance). — *Includes bibliographies and indexes*

LOFTUS, Martin L.
The International Monetary Fund, 1965-1967 : a selected bibliography / Martin L. Loftus. — [Washington, D.C. : International Monetary Fund], 1968. — p.143-195. — *Reprinted from the March 1968 issue of the International Monetary Fund staff papers*

LOFTUS, Martin L.
The International Monetary Fund, 1968-1971 : a selected bibliography / Martin L. Loftus. — [Washington, D.C. : International Monetary Fund], 1972. — p.174-258. — *Reprinted from the March 1972 issue of the International Monetary Fund staff papers*

MBIYE, Tshiunza
La douce negligence et les crises actuelles / Tshiunza Mbiye. — Kinshasa : "Zaire-Afrique", 1975. — 40p

MILLER, Morris
Coping is not enough! : the international debt crisis and the roles of the World Bank and International Monetary Fund / Morris Miller. — Homewood, Ill. : Dow Jones-Irwin, c1986. — xiii, 268 p.. — *Includes bibliographical references and index*

Monetary disorder : opinion. — Brussels : Economic and Social Committee, 1978. — iv,98p

PASCALLON, Pierre
Le système monétaire international : théorie et réalité / Pierre Pascallon. — 1e éd rev. et augm.. — Paris : Editions de l'Epargne, 1983. — 542p. — *Bibliography: p[491]-532*

PLOEG, Frederick van der
International policy coordination in interdependent monetary economies / F. van der Ploeg. — London : Centre for Labour Economics. London School of Economics, 1987. — 24p. — (Discussion paper / London School of Economics and Political Science. Centre for Labour Economics ; no.278). — *Bibliography: p22-24*

POOL, John Charles
The ABCs of international finance : understanding the trade and debt crisis / John Charles Pool, Steve Stamos. — Lexington, Mass. : Lexington Books, c1987. — xii, 138 p.. — *Includes index. — Bibliography: p. [131]-132*

Problems of international money, 1972-85 / edited by Michael Posner. — Washington. D.C. ; London : International Monetary Fund : Overseas Development Institute, 1986. — ix,191p. — *Papers presented at a seminar organized by the International Monetary Fund and the Overseas Development Institute in London in March 1985*

The role of the SDR in the international monetary system : studies by the Research and Treasurer's Departments of the International Monetary Fund. — Washington, D. C. : International Monetary Fund, 1987. — vii,62p. — (Occasional paper / International Monetary Fund ; no.51). — *Bibliography: p60-62*

ROOSA, Robert V.
The United States and Japan in the international monetary system 1946-1985 / Robert V. Roosa. — New York : Group of Thirty, 1986. — ii,75p. — (Occasional papers / Group of Thirty ; no.21)

SCAMMELL, W. M.
The stability of the international monetary system / W.M. Scammell. — Basingstoke : Macmillan Education, 1987. — vii,162p. — *Includes index*

Threats to international financial stability / edited by Richard Portes and Alexander K. Swoboda. — Cambridge : Cambridge University Press, 1987. — xviii,307p. — *Conference proceedings. — Includes bibliographies and index*

WACHTEL, Howard M
The money mandarins : the making of a new supranational economic order / Howard M. Wachtel. — 1st ed. — New York : Pantheon Books, c1986. — xvi, 254 p.. — *Includes index. — Bibliography: p. [227]-245*

WACHTEL, Howard M.
The politics of international money / Howard M. Wachtel. — Amsterdam : Transnational Institute, 1987. — 47p. — (Transnational issues ; 2)

INTERNATIONAL FINANCE — Bibliography

LOFTUS, Martin L.
The International Monetary Fund, 1962-1965 : a selected bibliography / Martin L. Loftus. — [Washington,D.C. : International Monetary Fund], 1965. — p.470-524. — *Reprinted from the November 1965 issue of the International Monetary Fund staff papers*

INTERNATIONAL FINANCE — Congresses

The international monetary system : forty years after Bretton Woods : proceedings of a conference held at Bretton Woods, New Hampshire, May 1984 / sponsored by: Federal Reserve Bank of Boston. — Boston, Mass. : Federal Reserve Bank of Boston, 1984. — 275p. — (Conference series / Federal Reserve Bank of Boston ; No.28)

SEMINÁRIO "AJUSTAMENTO E CRESCIMENTO NA ACTUAL CONJUNTURA ECONÓMICA MUNDIAL" (1985 : Estoril)
Ajustamento e crescimento na actual conjuntura económica mundial / editado por José de Silva Lopes. — Washington, D.C. : International Monetary Fund, 1985. — xi,200p. — *Includes bibliographical references*

INTERNATIONAL FINANCE — History — 20th century

BROWN, Brendan
The flight of international capital : a contemporary history / Brendan Brown. — London : Croom Helm, c1987. — xiv,447p. — *Bibliography: p421-428. — Includes index*

INTERNATIONAL FINANCE — Law and legislation

LOWENFELD, Andreas F.
International economic law. — New York : Matthew Bender
Vol.4: The international monetary system / Andreas F. Lowenfeld. — 2nd ed. — 1984. — xvi,404,473,4,17p. — *Includes Documents Supplement*

INTERNATIONAL FINANCE — Moral and ethical aspects

The Political morality of the International Monetary Fund / edited by Robert J. Myers. — New Brunswick, U.S.A. : Transaction Books, c1985. — 184p. — (Ethics and foreign policy ; v. 3). — *"Published for the Garnegie Council on Ethics & International Affairs.". — Includes index*

INTERNATIONAL FINANCE — Research

Research in international business and finance: a research annual. — Greenwich, Conn. : Jai Press, 1979-. — *Irregular*

INTERNATIONAL FINANCE CORPORATION — Legal status, laws, etc.

INTERNATIONAL FINANCE CORPORATION
Articles of agreement of the International Finance Corporation : as amended by resolutions effective September 21, 1961 and September 1, 1965. — Washington, D.C. : the Corporation, 1979. — 13p

INTERNATIONAL FINANCE CORPORATION
By-laws of the International Finance Corporation : as amended through February 18, 1980. — Washington, D.C. : the Corporation, 1980. — 4p

INTERNATIONAL LABOR ACTIVITIES

MAHLEIN, Leonhard
Gewerkschaften international : im Spannungsfeld zwischen Ost und West : aus eigener Sicht / Leonhard Mahlein. — Frankfurt am Main : Nachrichten-Verlags-Gesellschaft, 1984. — 205p. — *Bibliography: p9*

INTERNATIONAL LABOUR CONFERENCE — Rules and practice

INTERNATIONAL LABOUR ORGANISATION
[Constitution (1963)]. Constitution of the International Labour Organisation and standing orders of the International Labour Conference = Constitution de l'Organisation internationale du Travail et réglement de la Conférence internationale du Travail. — Geneva : International Labour Office, 1963. — 82,82p. — *In English and French. — Opposite pages bear duplicate numbering*

INTERNATIONAL LABOUR ORGANISATION

Constitution of the International Labour Organisation and standing orders of the International Labour Conference = Constitution de l'Organisation internationale du Travail et règlement de la Conférence internationale du Travail. — Geneva : International Labour Office, 1977. — 86,86p. — *In English and French. — Opposite pages bear duplicate numbering*

INTERNATIONAL LABOUR ORGANISATION

Constitution of the International Labour Organisation and standing orders of the International Labour Conference = Constitution de l'Organisation internationale du Travail et règlement de la Conférence internationale du Travail. — Geneva : International Labour Office, 1986. — 84,84p. — *In English and French. — Opposite pages bear duplicate numbering*

INTERNATIONAL LABOUR OFFICE

Working conditions and environment : a worker's education manual. — Geneva : International Labour Office, 1983. — vi, 81 p., [6] p. of plates. — *"A selection of recommended ILO publications and documents": p. 75. — "ILO films and film strips": p. 76*

INTERNATIONAL LABOUR ORGANISATION

Labour information data base / International Labour Organisation. — London : International Labour Office, 1985-. — *Irregular*

INTERNATIONAL LABOUR ORGANISATION — Constitution

INTERNATIONAL LABOUR ORGANISATION
[Constitution (1963)]. Constitution of the International Labour Organisation and standing orders of the International Labour Conference = Constitution de l'Organisation internationale du Travail et réglement de la Conférence internationale du Travail. — Geneva : International Labour Office, 1963. — 82,82p. — *In English and French. — Opposite pages bear duplicate numbering*

INTERNATIONAL LABOUR ORGANISATION
Constitution of the International Labour Organisation and standing orders of the International Labour Conference = Constitution de l'Organisation internationale du Travail et règlement de la Conférence internationale du Travail. — Geneva : International Labour Office, 1977. — 86,86p. — *In English and French. — Opposite pages bear duplicate numbering*

INTERNATIONAL LABOUR ORGANISATION
Constitution of the International Labour Organisation and standing orders of the International Labour Conference = Constitution de l'Organisation internationale du Travail et règlement de la Conférence internationale du Travail. — Geneva : International Labour Office, 1986. — 84,84p. — *In English and French. — Opposite pages bear duplicate numbering*

INTERNATIONAL LABOUR ORGANISATION. Jobs and Skills Programme for Africa

JASPA bulletin / Jobs and Skills Programme for Africa, International Labour Organisation. — Addis Ababa : ILO. Jobs and Skills Programme for Africa, 1984-. — *Quarterly*

INTERNATIONAL LABOUR ORGANIZATION — History

JOSHI, Preeta
International Labour Organization and its impact on India / Preeta Joshi. — Delhi : B.R. Pub. Corp. ; New Delhi : Distributed by D.K. Publishers' Distributors, 1985. — viii, 158 p.. — *Includes index. — Bibliography: p. [147]-151*

INTERNATIONAL LAW

AKEHURST, Michael
A modern introduction to international law / Michael Akehurst. — 6th ed. — London : Allen & Unwin, 1987. — [320]p. — *Previous ed.: 1984. — Includes index*

CASSESE, Antonio
International law in a divided world / Antonio Cassese. — Oxford : Clarendon, 1986. — [xiii,420]p. — *Includes bibliography and index*

D'AMATO, Anthony A
International law : prospect and process / by Anthony D'Amato. — Dobbs Ferry, N.Y. : Transnational Publishers, c1987. — vi, 250 p.. — *Includes bibliographical references and index*

DELUPIS, Ingrid
International law and the independent state / Ingrid Detter De Lupis. — 2nd ed. — Aldershot : Gower, 1987. — xxvi,252p. — *Previous ed.: 1974. — Includes index*

DELUPIS, Ingrid Detter
The concept of international law / by Ingrid Detter De Lupis. — Stockholm : Norstedts Förlag, 1987. — 145p. — *Bibliography: p [137]-145*

DORSEY, Gray L
Beyond the United Nations : changing discourse in international politics and law / Gray L. Dorsey. — Lanham ; London : University Press of America, c1986. — xi, 111p. — (Exxon Education Foundation series on rhetoric and political discourse ; v. 5). — *Bibliography: p. 103-111. — Bibliography: p.103-111*

Droit international et droit français : étude adoptée par la Section du Rapport et des Etudes du Conseil d'Etat le 25 avril 1985 / [réalisée sous la présidence de M. Jean-Jacques de Bresson]. — Paris : La Documentation française, 1986. — 116p. — (Notes et études documentaires ; no.4803)

GRAY, Christine D.
Judicial remedies in international law / Christine D. Gray. — Oxford : Clarendon Press, 1987. — [300]p. — (Oxford monographs in international law). — *Includes bibliography and index*

HIGGINS, Rosalyn
Conflict of interests : international law in a divided world. — Bodley Head, 1965. — 170p.,19cm. — (Background books)

International law : a textbook / edited by G. I. Tunkin. — Moscow : Progress, 1986. — 546p

International maritime law conventions / [compiled by] Maharaj Nagendra Singh. — [Updated ed.] / foreword by C.P. Srivastava. — London : Stevens, 1983. — 4v.(xxvii,,3305p). — (British shipping laws). — *Previous ed.: published in 1v. as International conventions of maritime shipping. 1973. — Includes index*

LANG, Daniel George
Foreign policy in the early republic : the law of nations and the balance of power / Daniel George Lang. — Baton Rouge : Louisiana State University Press, c1985. — 175 p.. — (Political traditions in foreign policy series). — *Includes index. — Bibliography: p. 165-170*

LAUTERPACHT, Sir Hersch
Private law sources and analogies on international law / with special reference to international arbitration. — [Hamden, Conn.] : Archon Books, 1970. — xxiv, 326 p. — *Reprint of the 1927 ed. — Bibliography: p. 307-312*

MANKABADY, Samir
The International Maritime Organization / Samir Mankkabady. — [2nd ed.]. — London : Croom Helm. — *Previous ed.: published in 1 vol. 1984*
Vol.1: International shipping rules. — c1986. — xxi,450p. — *Includes index*

INTERNATIONAL LAW
continuation

Osnovy sovremennogo pravoporiadka v Mirovom okeane / otv. redaktory A. P. Movchan, A. Iankov. — Moskva : Nauka, 1986. — 295p. — (Mirovoi okean i mezhdunarodnoe pravo)

Questions of international law. — Dordrecht : Nijhoff ; Budapest : Akadémiai Kiadó volume 3: Hungarian perspectives / edited by Hanna Bokor-Szegö. — 1986. — 274p

SCHWARZENBERGER, Georg
International law as applied by international courts and tribunals / by Georg Schwarzenberger. — London : Stevens. — (International law ; v.1)
[Vol.]1: [General principles]. — 3rd ed. — 1957. — xlviii, 808p

SCHWARZENBERGER, Georg
International law as applied by international courts and tribunals / by Georg Schwarzenberger. — London : Stevens
Vol.2: The law of armed conflict. — 1968. — lv, 881p

SCHWARZENBERGER, Georg
International law as applied by international courts and tribunals / by Georg Schwarzenberger. — London : Stevens
Vol.3: International constitutional law : fundamentals, the United Nations, related agencies. — 1976. — lii,680p. — *Volume III has grown out of part seven of the first and second editions of "International Law as Applied by International Courts and Tribunals"* - Preface. — Bibliography: p.607-661. — *Includes index*

SCHWARZENBERGER, Georg
International law as applied by international courts and tribunals / by Georg Schwarzenberger. — London : Stevens
Vol.4: International judicial law. — 1986. — lxx,899p. — *Bibliography: p823-888. — Includes index*

SHAW, Malcolm N.
International law / Malcolm N. Shaw. — 2nd ed. — Cambridge : Grotius, 1986. — [635]p. — *Previous ed.: 1977?. — Includes index*

SUGANAMI, Hidemi
Domestic analogy in proposals for world order, 1814-1945 : the transfer of legal and political principles from the domestic to the international sphere in thought on international law and relations / Hidemi Suganami. — 356 leaves. — PhD (Econ) 1986 LSE

UNITED NATIONS. Secretary General
Progressive development of the principles and norms of international law relating to the new international economic order : report of the Secretary-General : Addendum. — New York : United Nations, 1984. — Docment contains study by UNITAR entitled: Analytical study *[on the progressive development of the principles and norms of international law relating to the new international economic order]* prepared by Dr. Georges Abi-Saab. — U.N. document A/39/504/Add.1

INTERNATIONAL LAW — Addresses, essays, lectures

Principles of international law concerning friendly relations and cooperation / edited by Milan Šahović. — Belgrade : Institute of International Politics and Economics ; Dobbs Ferry, N.Y. : Oceana Publications, 1972. — 450 p. — *Rev. translation of Kodifikacija pŗincipa miroljubive i aktivne koegzistencije. — Includes bibliographical references*

INTERNATIONAL LAW — Bibliography

A collection of bibliographic and research resources : international law bibliography. — New York : Oceana Publications, 1984-. — 1vol.(loose-leaf)

KLECKNER, Simone-Marie
Public international law and international organization : international law bibliography / prepared by Simone-Marie Kleckner. — New York : Oceana Publications, 1984. — vi,99p. — (A collection of bibliographic and research resources)

Public international law and international organizations : a basic selective bibliography. — New York : United Nations, 1982. — ([Document] / United Nations ; ST/LIB/38). — *In various languages. — Prepared by the Dag Hammarskjöld Library*

A select bibliography on the law of treaties between states and international organizations or between international organizations. — New York : United Nations, 1985. — iii,33p. — ([Document] / United Nations ; ST/LIB/SER.B/36). — *In various languages. — Prepared by the Dag Hammerskjöld Library*

INTERNATIONAL LAW — Codification

ROSENEE, Shabtai
League of Nations Conference for the Codification of International Law (1930) / edited, with an introd. by Shabtai Rosenne. — Dobbs Ferry, N.Y. : Oceana Publications, 1975. — 4 v. (lvi, 1661 p.. — *"A continuation of the present writer's republication of the minutes and reports of the Committee of Experts for the Progressive Codification of International Law ... Volumes 1 and 2 of the present publication contain the reports prepared by the Preparatory Committee constituting the bases of discussion at the Codification Conference of 1930. Volumes 3 and 4 contain the official records of the conference itself."*

INTERNATIONAL LAW — Congresses

International law and the Grotian heritage : a commemorative colloquium held at The Hague on 8 April 1983 on the occasion of the fourth centenary of the birth of Hugo Grotius / organized by the Interuniversitair Instituut voor Internationaal Recht T.M.C. Asser Instituut in co-operation with the Grotiana Foundation. — The Hague : T.M.C. Asser Instituut, 1985. — xxii,370p

SOCIÉTE FRANÇAISE POUR LE DROIT INTERNATIONAL. Colloque (19e : 1985 : Nice)
Les nations unies et le droit international économique : [actes du colloque]. — Paris : A. Pedone, 1986. — vii,383p

INTERNATIONAL LAW — Dictionaries

PARRY, Clive
The encyclopaedic dictionary of international law / [compiled by] Parry and Grant ; general editors, Clive Parry ... [et al.] with assistance from some members of the Scottish Group of International Lawyers. — Dobbs Ferry, N.Y. : Oceana Publications, 1985. — p. cm

INTERNATIONAL LAW — Sources

International organization and integration : annotated basic doucments of international organizations and arrangements / selected by Louis B. Sohn. — Student ed. — Dordrecht [Netherlands] ; Boston : Nijhoff ; Norwell, MA, USA : Distributors for the U.S. and Canada, Kluwer Academic Publishers, 1986. — xxviii, 1082 p.. — *Based on the five-volume set International organization and integration. — Includes index*

INTERNATIONAL LAW — Study and teaching

LACHS, Manfred
The teacher in international law : teachings and teaching / Manfred Lachs. — Rev. 2nd ed. — Dordrecht ; Boston : M. Nijhoff, 1986. — p. cm. — *Includes index. — Bibliography: p*

INTERNATIONAL LAW — China

Selected articles from Chinese yearbook of international law / edited by Chinese Society of International Law. — Beijing : China Translation & Publishing Corporation, 1983. — vi,308p

INTERNATIONAL LAW — Developing countries

ANAND, R. P
International law and the developing countries : confrontation or cooperation? / R.P. Anand. — Dordrecht ; Boston : M. Nijhoff, 1987. — p. cm. — *Includes index*

INTERNATIONAL LAW — Developing countries — Bibliography

The Third world and international law : selected bibliography, 1955-1982 / United Nations Library, Geneva = Le Tiers monde et le droit international : bibliographie sélective, 1955-1982 / Nations Unies, Bibliothèque, Genève. — Geneva : United Nations Library, 1983. — 100p. — (Publications / United Nations Library, Geneva. Series C, Special bibliographies, repertoires, and indexes =Publications / Nations Unies, Bibliothèque, Genève. Série C, Bibliographies spéciales, répertoires, et index ; no. 5). — *Includes indexes*

INTERNATIONAL LAW (ISLAMIC LAW) — Congresses

COLLOQUE FRANCO-PAKISTANAIS (4e : 1984 : Paris)
L'Islam dans les relations internationales : actes du IVe Colloque franco-pakistanais, Paris, 14-15 mai 1984. — [Aix-en-Provence] : Édisud, 1986. — 181p. — *Contributions in English and French*

INTERNATIONAL LIBRARIANSHIP — Addresses, essays, lectures

BOORSTIN, Daniel J.
The invisible world : libraries and the myth of cultural exchange / Daniel J. Boorstin. — Washington, D. C. : Library of Congress, 1985. — 14p. — (The Center for the Book viewpoint series ; no.15). — *"Remarks at the IFLA General Conference, August 19, 1985"*

INTERNATIONAL MONETARY FUND

BIRD, Graham, 1947-
International financial policy and economic development : a disaggregated approach / Graham Bird. — Basingstoke : Macmillan, 1987. — xvi,348p. — *Bibliography: p338-343. — Includes index*

DE VRIES, Margaret Garritsen
Balance of payments adjustment, 1945 to 1986 : the IMF experience / Margaret Garritsen de Vries. — Washington, D.C. : International Monetary Fund, 1987. — xi,336p. — *Bibliography: p310-322*

DOGRA, Bharat
IMF conditionality and its social costs : case study of India / Bharat Dogra. — New Delhi : Indian Social Institute, 1984. — 30p. — (Monograph series / Indian Social Institute ; 15)

GOLD, Joseph, 1912-
The Fund Agreement in the courts. — Washington, D.C. : International Monetary Fund
Vol.3: Further studies in jurisprudence involving the Articles of Agreement of the International Monetary Fund / by Joseph Gold. — 1986. — xvi,841p. — *Includes bibliographical references*

GYLFASON, Thorvaldur
Credit policy and economic activity in developing countries with IMF stabilization programs / Thorvaldur Gylfason. — Princeton, N.J. : International Finance Section, Dept. of Economics, Princeton University, 1987. — p. cm. — (Princeton studies in international finance ; no. 60 (August 1987)). — *Bibliography: p*

The IMF and stabilisation : developing country experiences / directed and edited by Tony Killick ; contributors : Graham Bird ... [et al.]. — London : Gower in association with the Overseas Development Institute, c1984. — viii,216p. — *Originally published: London : Heinemann Educational in association with the Overseas Development Institute, 1984. — Includes bibliographies*

INTERNATIONAL MONETARY FUND
continuation

INTERNATIONAL MONETARY FUND.
Board of Governors. Committee on Reform of the International Monetary System and Related Issues
International monetary reform : documents of the Committee of Twenty. — Washington, D.C. : the Fund, 1974. — viii,253p. — *Includes the Report to the Board of Governors, Outline of Reform and accompanying Annexes, Reports of Technical groups, and related documents*

List of recent periodical articles / Joint library, International Monetary Fund and International Bank for Reconstruction and Development. — Washington, D.C. : International Monetary Fund : International Bank for Reconstruction and Development, 1978-. — *Monthly*

MILLER, Morris
Coping is not enough! : the international debt crisis and the roles of the World Bank and International Monetary Fund / Morris Miller. — Homewood, Ill. : Dow Jones-Irwin, c1986. — xiii, 268 p.. — *Includes bibliographical references and index*

The Quest for economic stabilisation : the IMF and the Third World / directed and edited by Tony Killick ; contributors Graham Bird ... [et al.]. — Aldershot : Gower in association with the Overseas Development Institute, 1985, c1984. — [xii,352]p. — *Originally published: London : Heinemann, 1984. — Bibliography: p321-331. — Includes index*

SPRAOS, John
IMF conditionality : ineffectual, inefficient, mistargeted / John Spraos. — Princeton, N.J. : International Finance Section, Dept. of Economics, Princeton University, 1986. — p. cm. — (Essays in international finance ; no. 166 (Dec. 1986)). — *Bibliography: p*

INTERNATIONAL MONETARY FUND — Bibliography

INTERNATIONAL MONETARY FUND
Publications catalog / International Monetary Fund. — Washington, D.C. : International Monetary Fund, 1980-. — *Annual. — Title varies*

LOFTUS, Martin L.
The International Monetary Fund, 1962-1965 : a selected bibliography / Martin L. Loftus. — [Washington,D.C. : International Monetary Fund], 1965. — p.470-524. — *Reprinted from the November 1965 issue of the International Monetary Fund staff papers*

LOFTUS, Martin L.
The International Monetary Fund, 1965-1967 : a selected bibliography / Martin L. Loftus. — [Washington, D.C. : International Monetary Fund], 1968. — p.143-195. — *Reprinted from the March 1968 issue of the International Monetary Fund staff papers*

LOFTUS, Martin L.
The International Monetary Fund, 1968-1971 : a selected bibliography / Martin L. Loftus. — [Washington, D.C. : International Monetary Fund], 1972. — p.174-258. — *Reprinted from the March 1972 issue of the International Monetary Fund staff papers*

INTERNATIONAL MONETARY FUND — Legal status, laws, etc.

INTERNATIONAL MONETARY FUND
Documents relating to the Second Amendment of the Articles of Agreement of the International Monetary Fund. — Washington, D.C. : the Fund, 1980-86. — 2v (in 6 parts). — *Contents: V.1: Documents - v.2: Minutes - Index (1986)*

INTERNATIONAL MONETARY FUND — Developing countries

CARVOUNIS, Chris C
The foreign debt/national development conflict : external adjustment and internal disorder in the developing nations / Chris C. Carvounis. — New York : Quorum Books, 1986. — xxiii, 243 p.. — *Includes index. — Bibliography: p.[223]-235*

INTERNATIONAL MONETARY FUND — Jamaica

LOONEY, Robert E
The Jamaican economy in the 1980's : economic decline and structural adjustment / Robert Looney. — Boulder, Colo. : Westview Press, 1986. — xiii, 257p. — (A Westview special study). — *Includes bibliographical references and index*

INTERNATIONAL MONETARY FUND — Nigeria — Bibliography

COKER, Q. F.
IMF and Nigeria : a selected bibliography / Q. F. Coker. — [S.l.] : Nigerian Institute of International Affairs, 1985. — iii,94p

INTERNATIONAL MONETARY FUND — Peru

SCHEETZ, Thomas Edward
Peru and the International Monetary Fund / Thomas Scheetz. — Pittsburgh, PA : University of Pittsburgh Press, c1986. — xi, 257 p.. — (Pitt Latin American series). — *Includes index. — Bibliography: p. 251-254*

INTERNATIONAL MONETARY FUND

Fund-supported programs, fiscal policy, and income distribution : a study / by the Fiscal Affairs Department of the International Monetary Fund. — Washington, D.C. : International Monetary Fund, 1986. — v,58p. — (Occasional paper / International Monetary Fund ; no.46). — *Bibliographical references: p54-58*

The Political morality of the International Monetary Fund / edited by Robert J. Myers. — New Brunswick, U.S.A. : Transaction Books, c1985. — 184p. — (Ethics and foreign policy ; v. 3). — *"Published for the Carnegie Council on Ethics & International Affairs.". — Includes index*

INTERNATIONAL MONETARY FUND — Finance

GOLD, Joseph
Relations between banks' loan agreements and IMF stand-by arrangements / Sir Joseph Gold. — London : Euromoney Publications Ltd., 1983. — 28-35p. — *Reprinted from: International Financial Law Review, September 1983*

INTERNATIONAL MONETARY FUND — History

DE VRIES, Margaret Garritsen
The IMF in a changing world, 1945-85 / Margaret Garritsen de Vries. — Washington, D.C. : International Monetary Fund, 1986. — x,226p. — *Bibliography: p226*

INTERNATIONAL NORTH PACIFIC FISHERIES COMMISSION — History

JACKSON, Roy I.
Ocean forum : an interpretative history of the International North Pacific Fisheries Commission / Roy Jackson, William F. Royce. — Fareham : Fishing News, c1986. — 240p. — *Ill on lining papers. — Bibliography: p227-231. — Includes index*

INTERNATIONAL OFFENSES

International criminal law / edited by M. Cherif Bassiouni. — Dobbs Ferry, N.Y. : Transnational Publishers
Vol.1: Crimes. — 1986. — xix,581p

International criminal law / edited by M. Cherif Bassiouni. — Dobbs Ferry, N.Y. : Transnational Publishers
Vol.2: Procedure. — 1986. — xvii,552p

International criminal law / edited by M. Cherif Bassiouni. — Dobbs Ferry, N.Y. : Transnational Publishers
Vol.3: Enforcement. — 1987. — xvii,313p

Terrorism and international order / Lawrence Freedman...[et al.]. — London : Routledge and Kegan Paul, 1986. — [vii], [112]p. — (Chatham House special paper). — *Bibliographical notes*

INTERNATIONAL OFFICIALS AND EMPLOYEES — Biography

CLARK, William, 1916-1985
From three worlds : memoirs / William Clark. — London : Sidgwick & Jackson, [1986]. — xi,292p

INTERNATIONAL ORGANIZATION

DILLOWAY, James
Is world order evolving? : an adventure into human potential / by James Dilloway. — Oxford : Pergamon, 1986. — [220]p. — (Systems science and world order library). — *Includes index*

International development policies : review of the activities of international organisations / Commonwealth Secretariat. — London : Commonwealth Secretariat, 1983. — *Quarterly*

MCKINLAY, R. D.
Global problems and world order / R. D. McKinlay and R. Little. — London : Pinter, 1986. — 292p. — *Includes index*

Negotiating world order : the artisanship and architecture of global diplomacy / edited by Alan K. Henrikson ; with essays by Gamani Corea ... [et al.]. — Wilmington, Del. : Scholarly Resources, 1986. — xxx, 265 p.. — *Includes bibliographies and index*

Les organisations internationales entre l'innovation et la stagnation / Gérard Blanc...[et al.] ; textes rassemblés par Nicolas Jéquier et préfacés par Franz Muheim. — Lausanne : Presses polytechniques romandes, [1985]. — 271p

Prognosen für Europa : die siebziger Jahre zwischen Ost und West. — Opladen : Leske Verlag, 1968. — 140p

ROCHE, Douglas
United Nations : divided world / Douglas Roche. — Toronto : NC Press, 1984. — 152p. — *Bibliography: p[151]-152p*

INTERNATIONAL ORGANIZATION — Addresses, essays, lectures

Conflict in world society : a new perspective on international relations / edited by Michael Banks ; foreword by Herbert Kelman. — New York : St. Martin's Press, 1984. — xx, 234 p.. — *Essays written in honor of John Burton. — Includes indexes. — Bibliography: p. [209]-225*

INTERNATIONAL ORGANIZATION — History

MURPHY, Cornelius F
The search for world order : a study of thought and action / by Cornelius F. Murphy, Jr. — Dordrecht ; Boston : M. Nijhoff ; Hingham, MA, USA : [Distributor] for the U.S. and Canada, Kluwer Academic Publishers, 1985. — xiii, 192 p.. — (Developments in international law ; 9). — *Includes bibliographical references and index*

INTERNATIONAL RELATIONS

AKINJIDE, R. O. A.
Mercenarism and international law / Chief R. O. A. Akinjide. — [s.l.] : [s.n.], 1986. — 13p. — *Lecture delivered at the International Law Seminar, Palais des nations, Geneva, on 27.5.1986*

As China sees the world : perception of Chinese scholars / edited by Harish Kapur. — London : Pinter, 1987. — [300]p. — *Includes index*

INTERNATIONAL RELATIONS
continuation

BOBROW, Davis B.
International relations : new approaches / Davis B. Bobrow. — New York : Free Press, [1972]. — 95p

BOGNÁR, J.
Politique internationale, securité européenne et coopération ecónomique (faits, rapports de forces et possibilités en été 1972) / J. Bognár. — Budapest : Conseil Scientifique Hongrois D'Économie Mondiale, 1972. — 18p. — (Tendances dans l'économie mondiale ; no.9)

BURTON, John Wear
International relations : a general theory. — Cambridge U.P, 1965. — 288p.,23cm

CHAN, Steve
Issues in international relations : a view from Africa / Stephen Chan. — Basingstoke : Macmillan, 1987. — [224]p. — *Includes bibliography and index*

CONFERENCE ON FOREIGN ASPECTS OF UNITED STATES NATIONAL SECURITY (1958 : Washington, D.C.)
Foreign aspects of U.S. national security : conference report and proceedings. — Washington, D.C. : Committee for International Economic Growth, 1958. — 120p

CONFERENCE ON SECURITY AND CO-OPERATION IN EUROPE. Stage I (1973 : Helsinki)
Verbatim records : July 3-7, 1973 : Private sessions. — [Helsinki], 1973. — Various paginations. — *Restricted distribution documents*
CSCE/I/CM/PV.1-CSCE/I/CM/PV.7

DORSEY, Gray L
Beyond the United Nations : changing discourse in international politics and law / Gray L. Dorsey. — Lanham ; London : University Press of America, c1986. — xi, 111p. — (Exxon Education Foundation series on rhetoric and political discourse ; v. 5). — *Bibliography: p. 103-111. — Bibliography: p.103-111*

East Asia, the West and international security : prospects for peace. — London : International Institute for Strategic Studies. — (Adelphi papers ; 217) (IISS annual conference papers)
Part 2. — 1987. — 80p

East Asia, the West and international security : proposals for peace. — London : International Institute for Strategic Studies. — (Adelphi papers ; 218) (IISS annual conference papers)
Part 3. — 1987. — 78p

East Asia, the west and international security: prospects for peace. — London : International Institute for Strategic Studies. — (Adelphi papers ; 216). — *Papers resented to the 28th IISS Annual Conference held in Kyoto, Japan from 8th to 11th September 1986*
Part 1. — 1987. — 84p

Exploring long cycles / edited by George Modelski. — Boulder : Rienner ; London : Pinter, 1987. — x,277p. — (Long cycles: studies in international relations ; v.1). — *Bibliography: p249-272. — Includes index*

Foreign policy implementation / edited by Steve Smith, Michael Clarke. — London : Allen & Unwin, 1985. — 195p. — *Bibliography: p181-190. — Includes index*

Foreign policy in world politics / Roy C. Macridis, editor ; contributing authors, Robert J. Art ... [et al.]. — 6th ed. — Englewood Cliffs ; London : Prentice-Hall, c1985. — xxi,442p. — *Previous ed.: 1976. — Includes bibliographies and index*

Foreign policy in world politics ; Roy C. Macridis, editor ; contributing authors, Robert J. Art ... [et al.]. — 6th ed. — Englewood Cliffs, N.J. : Prentice-Hall, c1985. — p. cm. — *Includes bibliographies and index*

HALLE, Louis Joseph
History, philosophy, and foreign relations : background for the making of foreign policy / Louis J. Halle ; with a preface by Kenneth W. Thompson. — Lanham : University Press of America ; [s.l.] : The White Burkett Miller Center of Public Affairs, University of Virginia, c1987. — xii, 404 p.. — (Papers on presidential transitions and foreign policy ; v. 7). — *Includes bibliographies*

HERRMANN, Richard K.
Perceptions and behavior in Soviet foreign policy / Richard K. Herrmann. — Pittsburgh, Pa. : University of Pittsburgh Press, c1985. — xxi, 266 p.. — (Pitt series in policy and institutional studies) (Series in Russian and East European studies ; no. 7). — *Includes index. — Bibliography: p. 249-261*

HERZ, Martin Florian
Making the world a less dangerous place : lessons learned from a career in diplomacy / Martin F. Herz. — Washington, D.C. : Georgetown University. Iinstitute for Study of Diplomacy, 1981. — iv,27p. — *Fifth Oscar Iden lecture*

HIGGINS, Rosalyn
Conflict of interests : international law in a divided world. — Bodley Head, 1965. — 170p.,19cm. — (Background books)

HOFFMANN, Stanley
Janus and Minerva : essays in the theory and practice of international politics / Stanley Hoffmann. — Boulder : Westview Press, 1987. — xiv, 457 p.. — *Includes bibliographies*

HOFFMANN, Stanley
The state of war : essays on the theory and practice of international politics / Stanley Hoffmann. — London : Pall Mall Press, 1965. — xi,276p

IBRÜGGER, Lothar
General report on East-West scientific co-operation, the Chernobyl accident, and nuclear waste / Lothar Ibrügger. — Brussels : North Atlantic Assembly, 1986. — ii,33p

International conflict and national public policy issues / Stuart Oskamp; editor. — Beverly Hills : Sage, 1985. — 312p. — (Applied social psychology annual ; 6). — *Bibliographies*

Korean journal of international studies / Korean Institute of International Studies. — Seoul : Korean Institute of International Studies, 1985-. — *Quarterly*

KROMBACH, Hayo Benedikt Ernst Désiré
Scientific and philosophical thought about the discourse of international relations in the 20th century : a hermeneutic inquiry into the implications of the idea of nuclear war / Hayo Benedikt Ernst Désiré Krombach. — 606 leaves. — *PhD (Econ) 1986 LSE*

LIDER, Julian
Correlation of forces : an analysis of Marxist-Leninist concepts / Julian Lider. — Aldershot : Gower, c1986. — vii,384p. — (Swedish studies in international relations). — *Bibliography: p347-372. — Includes index*

MCNAMARA, Robert S.
Blundering into disaster : surviving the first century of the nuclear age / by Robert McNamara. — London : Bloomsbury, 1987. — [194]p. — *Originally published: New York : Pantheon Books, 1986*

MERLE, Marcel
The sociology of international relations / Marcel Merle ; translated from the French by Dorothy Parkin. — Leamington Spa : Berg, c1987. — 430p. — *Translation of: Sociologie des relations internationales. — Bibliography: p421-424. — Includes index*

Military strategy and the origins of the First World War / edited by Steven E. Miller. — Princeton, N.J. : Princeton University Press, 1985. — 186p. — (An International security reader). — *"The contents of this book were first published in International security" - verso t.p.*

Negotiating world order : the artisanship and architecture of global diplomacy / edited by Alan K. Henrikson ; with essays by Gamani Corea ... [et al.]. — Wilmington, Del. : Scholarly Resources, 1986. — xxx, 265 p.. — *Includes bibliographies and index*

Les nouvelles conventions de la Haye : leur application par les juges nationaux. — Dordrecht : Martinus Nijhoff. — *Bibliography: p249-268*
Tome 3: Jurisprudence, situation actuelle, bibliographie / Mathilde Sumampouw. — 1984. — xx,286p

Papers on presidential transitions and foreign policy. — Lanham, MD : University Press of America, <c1986- >. — v. <1-3 >. — *Includes bibliographies. — Contents: v. 1. History and current issues / edited by Kenneth W. Thompson -- v. 2. Problems and prospects / edited by Kenneth W. Thompson -- v. 3. Political transitions and foreign affairs in Britain and France / edited with a preface by Frederick C. Mosher*

Political change and foreign policies / edited by Gavin Boyd and Gerald W. Hopple. — London : Pinter, 1987. — [280]p. — *Includes index*

Power and policy : doctrine, the alliance and arms control. — London : International Institute for Strategic Studies. — (IISS annual conference papers)
Part 1. — 1986. — 72p. — (Adelphi papers ; 205)

Power and policy : doctrine, the alliance and arms control. — London : International Institute for Strategic Studies. — (IISS annual conference papers)
Part 2. — 1986. — 78p. — (Adelphi papers ; 206)

Power and policy : doctrine, the alliance and arms control. — London : International Institute for Strategic Studies. — (IISS annual conference papers)
Part 3. — 1986. — 76p. — (Adelphi papers ; 207)

SCRUTON, Roger
World studies : education or indoctrination / Roger Scruton. — London : Institute for European Defence and Strategic Studies, 1985. — 69p. — (Occasional paper / Institute for European Defence and Strategic Studies ; no.15)

SEGAL, Gerald
The guide to the world today / Gerald Segal. — London : Smith & Schuster, 1987. — [300]p . — *Includes bibliography and index*

SOROOS, Marvin S.
Beyond sovereignty : the challenge of global policy / by M rvin S. Soroos. — Columbia : University of South Carolina Press, c1986. — x, 388 p.. — (Studies in international relations). — *Includes bibliographies and index*

STOCKTON, Paul
Strategic stability between the super-powers / Paul Stockton. — London : International Institute for Strategic Studies, 1986. — 90p. — (Adelphi papers ; 213)

SUGANAMI, Hidemi
Domestic analogy in proposals for world order, 1814-1945 : the transfer of legal and political principles from the domestic to the international sphere in thought on international law and relations / Hidemi Suganami. — 356 leaves. — *PhD (Econ) 1986 LSE*

INTERNATIONAL RELATIONS
continuation
Technology and international relations / edited by Otto Hieronymi ; with contributions by Michel Barjon ... [et al.]. — Basingstoke : Macmillan, 1987. — 194p

URQUHART, Brian
The United Nations and international law: : the Rede Lecture / Brian Urquhart. — Cambridge : Cambridge University Press, 1985. — 20p

WINDASS, Stan
The rite of war / by Stan Windass. — London : Brassey's, 1986. — viii,132p

INTERNATIONAL RELATIONS — Addresses, essays, lectures
Conflict in world society : a new perspective on international relations / edited by Michael Banks ; foreword by Herbert Kelman. — New York : St. Martin's Press, 1984. — xx, 234 p.. — *Essays written in honor of John Burton. — Includes indexes. — Bibliography: p. [209]-225*

Dependency theory and the return of high politics / edited by Mary Ann Tétreault and Charles Frederick Abel. — New York : Greenwood Press, 1986. — xii, 270 p.. — (Contributions in political science ; no. 140). — *Includes index. — Bibliography: p. [255]-260*

Neorealism and its critics / Robert O. Keohane, editor. — New York : Columbia University Press, c1986. — p. cm. — (The Political economy of international change). — *Includes index. — Bibliography: p. — Contents: Realism, neorealism, and the study of world politics / Robert O. Keohane -- Laws and theories / Kenneth N. Waltz -- Reductionist and systemic theories / Kenneth N. Waltz -- Political structures / Kenneth N. Waltz -- Anarchic orders and balances of power / Kenneth N. Waltz -- Continuity and transformation in the world polity / John Gerard Ruggie -- Theory of world politics / Robert O. Keohane -- Social forces, states, and world orders / Robert W. Cox -- The poverty of neorealism / Richard K. Ashley -- The richness of the tradition of political realism / Robert G. Gilpin -- Reflections on theory of international politics / Kenneth N. Waltz*

INTERNATIONAL RELATIONS — Congresses
CONFERENCE ON SECURITY AND CO-OPERATION IN EUROPE
Final Act. — Helsinki : 1975. — 397p [viii]. — *Text also available in English in British Parliamentary Papers, Command Paper Cmnd 6198. — Text of the Final Act is given in German, English, Spanish, French, Italian and Russian, the English text being between pages 73 and 135*

CONFERENCE ON SECURITY AND CO-OPERATION IN EUROPE. Stage I (1973 : Helsinki)
Documents. — [Helsinki], 1973. — *Restricted distribution documents CSCE/I/1-CSCE/I/30*

CONFERENCE ON SECURITY AND CO-OPERATION IN EUROPE. Stage I (1973 : Helsinki)
Verbatim records : July 3-7, 1973 : Open sessions. — [Helsinki], 1973. — various paginations. — *Restricted distribution documents CSCE/I/PV.1-CSCE/I/PV.8*

CONFERENCE ON SECURITY AND CO-OPERATION IN EUROPE. Stage III (1975 : Helsinki)
Verbatim records and documents. — [Helsinki], 1975. — Various paginations. — *Restricted distribution documents CSCE/III/PV.1-CSCE/III/PV.7 and CSCE/III/1 and CSCE/III/2*

CONFERENCE SUR LA SECURITÉ ET LA COOPERATION EN EUROPE. Phase I (1973 : Helsinki)
Liste des participants. — Helsinki, 1973. — 39p

CONFERENCE SUR LA SECURITÉ ET LA COOPERATION EN EUROPE. Phase III (1975 : Helsinki)
Liste des participants. — Helsinki, 1975. — 74p

HELSINKI CONSULTATIONS
Final recommendations of the Helsinki consultations. — Helsinki, 1973. — 6 language versions separately paginated. — *Text of the Helsinki Consultations' recommendations on the holding of the Conference on Security and Co-operation in Europe given in each language version in the order: German, English, Spanish, French, Italian and Russian*

INTERNATIONAL RELATIONS — Methodology
New directions in the study of foreign policy / edited by Charles F. Hermann, Charles W. Kegley, Jr., James N. Rosenau. — London : Allen & Unwin, 1987, c1986. — [450]p. — *Includes bibliography and index*

INTERNATIONAL RELATIONS — Moral and ethical aspects
Ethics and international relations / edited by Anthony Ellis. — Manchester : Manchester University Press in association with the Fulbright Commission, c1986. — xiii,232p. — (Fulbright papers ; v.2). — *Conference proceedings. — Includes index*

INTERNATIONAL RELATIONS — Philosophy
CARLSNAES, Walter
Ideology and foreign policy : problems of comparative conceptualization / Walter Carlsnaes. — Oxford : Basil Blackwell, 1986. — [224]p. — *Includes bibliography and index*

INTERNATIONAL RELATIONS — Psychological aspects
Image and reality in world politics / edited by John Carleton Farrell and Asa P. Smith. — New York : Columbia Univesity Press, [1967]. — xi,140p

INTERNATIONAL RELATIONS — Research
BRECHER, Michael
Crisis and change in world politics / Michael Brecher, Patrick James. — Boulder : Westview Press, 1986. — p. cm. — *Includes index. — Bibliography: p*

Foreign policy analysis / edited by Richard L. Merritt. — Lexington, Mass. : Lexington Books, c1975. — viii, 164 p.. — (Policy Studies Organization series ; 9). — *Includes bibliographies and index*

MORGAN, Patrick M.
Theories and approaches to international politics : what are we to think? / Patrick M. Morgan. — 4th ed. — New Brunswick, N.J. : Transaction Books, c1987. — xi, 308 p.. — *Includes bibliographies and index*

New directions in the study of foreign policy / edited by Charles F. Hermann, Charles W. Kegley, Jr., James N. Rosenau. — London : Allen & Unwin, 1987, c1986. — [450]p. — *Includes bibliography and index*

Role theory and foreign policy analysis / edited by Stephen G. Walker. — Durham [N.C.] : Duke University Press, 1987. — xvi, 304 p.. — (Duke Press policy studies). — *Includes index. — Bibliography: p. 290-300*

ZAGARE, Frank C
The dynamics of deterrence / Frank C. Zagare. — Chicago : University of Chicago Press, 1987. — p. cm. — *Includes index. — Bibliography: p*

INTERNATIONAL RELATIONS — Research — Congresses
Communication and interaction in global politics / edited by Claudio Cioffi-Revilla, Richard L. Merritt, Dina A. Zinnes. — Beverly Hills : Sage Publications, c1985. — p. cm. — (Advances in political science ; v. 5). — *Includes index*

INTERNATIONAL RELATIONS — Study and teaching
WILKINSON, David O.
Comparative foreign relations : framework and methods / David O. Wilkinson. — Belmont, Calif. : Dickenson, 1969. — 191p

INTERNATIONAL RELATIONS — Yearbooks
Sage international yearbook of foreign policy studies. — Beverley Hills (Calif.) ; London : Sage Publications, 1973-1983. — *Annual*

INTERNATIONAL SOCIETY FOR KRISHNA CONSCIOUSNESS — United States
ROCHFORD, E. Burke
Hare Krishna in America / E. Burke Rochford, Jr. — New Brunswick, N.J. : Rutgers University Press, c1985. — xiv, 324p. — *Includes index. — Bibliography: p.305-318*

INTERNATIONAL SOCIETY OF KRISHNA CONSCIOUSNESS
POLING, Tommy H
The Hare Krishna character type : a study of the sensate personality / Tommy H. Poling & J. Frank Kenney. — Lewiston N.Y. : E. Mellen Press, c1986. — 184 p. — (Studies in religion and society ; v. 15). — *Bibliography: p.178-184*

INTERNATIONAL TRANSPORT WORKERS' FEDERATION — Archives
BALDWIN, Nicholas
The International Transport Workers' Federation archive / by Nicholas Baldwin ; with a preface by Volker Berghahn ; edited by Richard Storey. — Coventry : University of Warwick, 1985. — 46p. — (Occasional publications / University of Warwick Library ; no.13)

INTERNATIONAL WOMEN'S DECADE, 1976-1985
FRASER, Arvonne S
The U.N. Decade for Women : documents and dialogue / Arvonne S. Fraser. — Boulder : Westview Press, 1987. — p. cm. — (Westview special studies on women in contemporary society)

INTERNATIONAL WORKERS ASSOCIATION
INTERNATIONAL WORKERS ASSOCIATION
Principles, aims and statutes / International Workers Association. — [Sydney] : Monty Miller Press, 1983. — 16p. — (Rebel worker pamphlet ; 2)

INTERNATIONALISTS — Biography
KUEHL, Warren F.
Biographical dictionary of internationalists / edited by Warren F. Kuehl. — Westport, Conn. : Greenwood Press, 1983. — xvi, 934 p.. — *Includes bibliographies and index*

INTERNAYIONAL BUSINESS ENTERPRISES — Management
GERSHENBERG, Irving
Multinational enterprises, transfer of managerial know-how, technology choice and employment of Kenya / Irving Gershenberg. — Geneva : International Labour Office, 1983. — iii,33p. — (Multinational Enterprises Programme working papers. Research on employment effects of multinational enterprises ; no.28). — *Bibliography: p29*

INTERPERSONAL ATTRACTION
Friendship and social interaction / edited by Valerian J. Derlega and Barbara A. Winstead. — New York : Springer-Verlag, c1986. — p. cm. — (Springer series in social psychology). — *Includes index. — Bibliography: p*

PERPER, Timothy
Sex signals : the biology of love / Timothy Perper. — Philadelphia : ISI Press, c1985. — xvi, 323 p.. — *Includes index. — Bibliography: p. 296-314*

INTERPERSONAL COMMUNICATION

Communication by children and adults : social, cognitive and strategic processes / edited by Howard E. Sypher, James L. Applegate. — Beverly Hills ; London : Sage, c1984. — 328p. — (Sage series In interpersonal communication ; v.5). — *Includes index*

Handbook of interpersonal communication / edited by Mark L. Knapp and Gerald R. Miller. — Beverly Hills, Calif. : Sage Publications, c1985. — 768p. — *Includes bibliographies and indexes*

ROSS, Percy
Ask for the moon--and get it! : the secret to getting what you want by knowing how to ask / Percy Ross with Dick Samson. — New York : Putnam, c1987. — 219 p.

Talk and social organisation / edited by Graham Button and John R.E. Lee. — Clevedon : Multilingual Matters, c1987. — 335p. — (Intercommunication ; 1). — *Bibliography: p323-327.* — *Includes index*

INTERPERSONAL COMMUNICATION — Addresses, essays, lectures

Inter/media : interpersonal communication in a media world / edited by Gary Gumpert and Robert Cathcart. — 3rd ed. — New York : Oxford University Press, 1986. — ix, 666 p.. — *Bibliography: p. 649-666*

INTERPERSONAL COMMUNICATION IN CHILDREN

Communication by children and adults : social, cognitive and strategic processes / edited by Howard E. Sypher, James L. Applegate. — Beverley Hills ; London : Sage, c1984. — 328p. — (Sage series In interpersonal communication ; v.5). — *Includes index*

INTERPERSONAL CONFLICT — Congresses

Experimental social dilemmas / Henk A.M. Wilke, Dave M. Messick, Christel G. Rutte, eds. — Frankfurt am Main ; New York : P. Lang, c1986. — vi, 234 p.. — (Psychologie des Entscheidungsverhaltens und des Konfliktes =Psychology of decisions and conflict ; Bd. 3). — Papers were presented at a conference held at the University of Groningen in the spring of 1984. — *Includes bibliographies*

INTERPERSONAL CONFLICT — Papua New Guinea

GELBER, Marilyn G
Gender and society in the New Guinea Highlands : an anthropological perspective on antagonism toward women / Marilyn G. Gelber. — Boulder : Westview Press, 1986. — xi, 180 p.. — (Women in cross-cultural perspective). — *Includes index.* — *Bibliography: p. [159]-175*

INTERPERSONAL RELATIONS

ABRAMSON, Jane B
Mothermania : a psychological study of mother-daughter conflict / Jane B. Abramson. — Lexington, Mass. : Lexington Books, c1987. — p. cm. — *Includes index.* — *Bibliography: p*

BERENSON, F. M.
Understanding persons : personal and impersonal relationships / F.M. Berenson. — Brighton : Harvester, 1981. — 198p. — (Harvester studies in philosophy ; 22). — *Bibliography: p191-193.* — *Includes index*

BREAKWELL, Glynis M.
Coping with threatened identities / Glynis M. Breakwell. — London : Methuen, 1986. — [232]p. — *Includes index*

Intimate relationships : development, dynamics, and deterioration / edited by Daniel Perlman, Steve Duck. — Beverly Hills : Sage Publications, c1987. — 320 p.. — (Sage focus editions ; v. 80). — *Includes bibliographies and index*

LEARY, Mark R
Social psychology and dysfunctional behavior : origins, diagnosis, and treatment / Mark R. Leary and Rowland S. Miller. — New York : Springer-Verlag, c1986. — xiii, 262 p.. — (Springer series in social psychology). — *Includes indexes.* — *Bibliography: p. [203]-244*

LUHMANN, Niklas
Love as passion : the codification of intimacy / Niklas Luhmann ; translated by Jeremy Gaines and Doris L. Jones. — Cambridge : Polity, 1986. — 247p. — (Social and political theory). — Translation of: Leibe als Passion. — *Includes index*

MATTHEWS, Sarah H
Friendships through the life-course : oral biographies in old age / by Sarah H. Matthews. — Beverly Hills : Sage Publications, c1986. — p. cm. — (Sage library of social research ; v. 161). — *Includes index.* — *Bibliography: p*

MATTINSON, Janet
The reflection process in casework supervision / Janet Mattinson. — [London] : Institute of Marital Studies, The Tavistock Institute of Human Relations : Distributed by Research Publications Services, 1975. — 149p

PIN, Emile Jean
The pleasure of your company : a socio-psychological analysis of modern sociability / Emile Jean Pin ; in collaboration with Jamie Turndorf. — New York : Praeger, 1985. — p. cm. — *Includes indexes.* — *Bibliography: p*

The Social construction of emotions / edited by Rom Harré. — Oxford : Basil Blackwell, 1986. — viii,316p. — *Includes bibliographies and index*

THIBAUT, John W
The social psychology of groups / John W. Thibaut and Harold H. Kelley ; with a new introduction by the authors. — New Brunswick, U.S.A. : Transaction Books, 1985. — p. cm. — : *Reprint. Originally published:* New York : Wiley, 1959. — *Includes index.* — *Bibliography: p*

INTERPERSONAL RELATIONS — Addresses, essays, lectures

Inter/media : interpersonal communication in a media world / edited by Gary Gumpert and Robert Cathcart. — 3rd ed. — New York : Oxford University Press, 1986. — ix, 666 p.. — *Bibliography: p. 649-666*

INTERPERSONAL RELATIONS IN CHILDREN

Attachment in social networks : contributions to the Bowlby-Ainsworth attachment theory / edited by Louis W.C. Tavecchio and Marinus H. van IJzendoorn. — Amsterdam ; New York : North-Holland ; New York, N.Y., U.S.A. : Sole distributors for the U.S.A. and Canada, Elsevier Science Pub. Co., 1987. — xx, 483 p.. — (Advances in psychology ; 44). — *Includes bibliographies and indexes*

INTERRACIAL ADOPTION — Government policy — Great Britain

DALE, David
Denying homes to black children : Britain's new race adoption policies / David Dale. — London : Social Affairs Unit, [1987]. — 45p. — (Research report ; 8)

INTERSTATE BANKING — United States — Congresses

Interstate banking : strategies for a new era : conference proceedings / sponsored by Federal Reserve Bank of Atlanta. — Westport, Conn. : Quorum Books, 1985. — xxvi, 260 p.. — *Includes index.* — *Bibliography: p. [251]-256*

INTERVENTION (INTERNATIONAL LAW)

DAVIDSON, Scott
Grenada : a study in politics and the limits of international law / Scott Davidson. — Aldershot : Avebury, c1987. — xii,196p. — *Bibliography: p184-190.* — *Includes index*

DUNÉR, Bertil, 1942-
Military intervention in civil wars : the 1970s / Bertil Dunér. — Aldershot : Gower, c1985. — xiii,197p. — (Swedish studies in international relations ; 14). — *Bibliography: p173-191.* — *Includes index*

INTERVIEWING

Interviewing in educational research / Janet Powney ... [et al.]. — London : Routledge & Kegan Paul, 1987. — [210]p. — (Routledge education books). — *Includes bibliography and index*

KADUSHIN, Alfred
The social work interview / Alfred Kadushin. — 2nd ed. — New York : Columbia University Press, 1983. — 423 p.. — *Includes index.* — *Bibliography: p. [403]-416*

MAPLE, Frank F
Dynamic interviewing : an introduction to counseling / by Frank F. Maple. — Beverly Hills ; London : Sage Publications, c1985. — 174p. — (Sage Human services guides ; 41). — *Bibliography: p 173-174*

MISHLER, Elliot George
Research interviewing : context and narrative / Elliot G. Mishler. — Cambridge, Mass. : Harvard University Press, 1986. — xi, 189 p.. — *Includes index.* — *Bibliography: p. [171]-185*

INTERVIEWING IN DEMOGRAPHY

WOOLF, Myra
The reliability of fertility data obtained from pregnancy histories / Myra Woolf ; [for the] Office of Population Censuses and Surveys. — London : H.M.S.O., 1979. — [4],16p. — (Studies on medical and population subjects ; no.40). — *Bibliography: p.16*

INTERVIEWING IN ETHNOLOGY

WERNER, Oswald
Systematic fieldwork / Oswald Werner, G. Mark Schoepfle. — Newbury Park [Calif.] ; London : Sage
Vol.1: Foundations of ethnography and interviewing. — 1987. — 416p. — *Bibliography: p395-406*

INTERVIEWS — Nicaragua

[Contra. English]. The Contras : interviews with anti-Sandinistas / [edited] Dieter Eich and Carlos Rincón. — San Francisco : Synthesis Publications, c1985. — iv, 193 p.. — Translation of: La contra

ZWERLING, Philip
Nicaragua : a new kind of revolution / Philip Zwerling & Connie Martin. — Westport, Conn. : L. Hill, 1985. — xii, 251p

INTIMACY (PSYCHOLOGY)

Intimate relationships : development, dynamics, and deterioration / edited by Daniel Perlman, Steve Duck. — Beverly Hills : Sage Publications, c1987. — 320 p.. — (Sage focus editions ; v. 80). — *Includes bibliographies and index*

PERPER, Timothy
Sex signals : the biology of love / Timothy Perper. — Philadelphia : ISI Press, c1985. — xvi, 323 p.. — *Includes index.* — *Bibliography: p. 296-314*

INTRINSIC MOTIVATION

DECI, Edward L
Intrinsic motivation and self-determination in human behavior / Edward L. Deci and Richard M. Ryan. — New York ; London : Plenum, c1985. — xv, 371 p.. — (Perspectives in social psychology). — *Includes indexes.* — *Bibliography: p. 335-358*

INVENTIONS — England

Innovation and labour during British industrialisation : a celebration of the life and work of Harry Dutton, 1947-1984. — Cambridge : Huntington, [1985]. — 92p. — *Bibliography: p90*

INVENTORIES
ALPERN, S.
Inventories as an information-gathering device / Steve Alpern and Dennis J. Snower. — London : Suntory Toyota International Centre for Economics and Related Disciplines, 1987. — 37p. — (Theoretical economics ; 87/151). — Bibliography: p37

INVENTORS — Great Britain — Biography
WILSON, A. Gordon
Walter Wilson : portrait of an inventor / A Grodon Wilson ; edited by Rodney Dale. — London : Duckworth, 1986. — 173p

INVESTIGATION OF THE POSSIBLE INCREASED INCIDENCE OF CANCER IN WEST CUMBRIA
GREAT BRITAIN. Committee on Medical Aspects of Radiation in the Environment
First report : the implications of the new data on the releases from Sellafield in the 1950s for the conclusions of the report on the investigation of the possible increased incidence of cancer in West Cumbria / chairman: M. Bobrow. — London : H.M.S.O., 1986. — 42p. — Bibliographical references: p25-26

INVESTMENT ANALYSIS
TAYLOR, Stephen, 1954-
Modelling financial time series / Stephen Taylor. — Chichester : Wiley, c1986. — xvi,268p. — Bibliography: p256-261. — Includes index

INVESTMENT ANALYSIS — Great Britain
BALLARDIE
Tolley's tax efficient personal investments : [a detailed explanatory guide to tax efficient investments for the individual] / [Patricia Ballardie] ; [edited by David Marks]. — Croydon, Surrey : Tolley, 1986. — ix,103p

INVESTMENT BANKING
FERRIS, Paul
Gentlemen of fortune : the world's merchant and investment bankers / Paul Ferris. — London : Weidenfeld & Nicolson, 1984. — 260p. — Includes index

INVESTMENT BANKING — Colombia
Colombia, the investment banking system and related issues in the financial sector. — Washington, D.C., U.S.A. : World Bank, c1985. — xl,82p. — (A World Bank country study). — Preface and summary in English and Spanish. — Includes bibliographical references

INVESTMENT BANKING — Developing countries
WELLONS, Phillip
Banks and specialised financial intermediaries in development / by Phillip Wellons, Dimitri Germidis and Bianca Glavanis. — Paris : Organisation for Economic Co—operation and Development, 1986. — 150p. — (Development Centre studies). — Bibliography: p131-133

INVESTMENT OF PUBLIC FUNDS — Soviet Union
Rol' finansov v sotsial'no-ekonomicheskom razvitii strany / pod redaktsiei G. V. Bazarovoi. — Moskva : Finansy i statistika, 1986. — 230p

INVESTMENT TRUSTS — Great Britain
GREAT BRITAIN. Department of Trade and Industry
The regulation of authorised unit trust schemes : a consultative document on the proposed regulations for unit trust schemes authorised under the Financial Services Bill / Department of Trade and Industry. — London : HMSO, 1986. — [viii].74p

INVESTMENTS
DAVIS, E. P.
Portfolio behaviour of the non-financial private sectors in the major economies / by E. P. Davies. — Basle : Bank for International Settlements, 1986. — 140p. — (BIS economic papers ; no.17). — Bibliographical references: p136-139

GOFF, T. G.
Theory and practice of investment / T.G. Goff. — 5th ed. — London : Heinemann, 1986. — 1v.. — Previous ed.: 1982. — Includes index

HAYES, Douglas Anderson
Investments : analysis and management / Douglas A. Hayes. — New York : Macmillan, 1961. — x,598p

HAYES, Douglas Anderson
Investments : analysis and management / Douglas A. Hayes. — 2nd ed. — New York : Macmillan, 1966. — x,501p

PRECIOUS, Mark
Rational expectations, non-market clearing and investment theory / Mark Precious. — Oxford : Clarendon, 1987. — vi,167p. — Bibliography: p161-163. — Includes index

SHILLER, Robert J.
Survey evidence of diffusion of interest among institutional investors / Robert J. Shiller, John Pound. — Cambridge, MA : NBER, 1986. — 25p. — (NBER working paper series ; no.1851) . — Bibliography: p24-25

WARD, Sue
Socially responsible investment / by Sue Ward. — London : Directory of Social Change in association with EIRIS, 1986. — x,197p. — Bibliography: p195-196

INVESTMENTS — Accounting
RAPPAPORT, Alfred
Creating shareholder value : the new standard for business performance / Alfred Rappaport. — New York : Free Press ; London : Collier Macmillan, c1986. — xv, 270 p.. — Includes index. — Bibliography: p. 241-257

INVESTMENTS — Decision making
PENCE, Christine Cope
How venture capitalists make investment decisions / by Christine Cope Pence. — Ann Arbor, Mich. : UMI Research Press, c1982. — x, 138 p.. — (Research for business decisions ; no. 53). — : A revision of the author's thesis, University of California, Irvine, 1981. — Includes index. — Bibliography: p. [133]-135

INVESTMENTS — Law and legislation — Taiwan
Enforcement rules of the Statute for Encouragement of Investment : promulgated on January 11, 1961. — Taipei : Industrial Development and Investment Center, [1961]. — iv,57p

Investment laws of the Republic of China. — 2nd ed. — [Taipei : Industrial Development and Investment Center, 1961]. — ii,67p

INVESTMENTS — Mathematical models
BÜTTLER, Hans-Jürgen
Estimation of disequilibrium models / Hans-Jürg Büttler, Gertrude Frei, Bernd Schips. — Berlin ; New York : Springer-Verlag, c1986. — p. cm. — (Lecture notes in economics and mathematical systems ; 279). — Includes bibliographies

LEAPE, Jonathan
Taxes and transaction costs in asset market equilibrium / Jonathan Leape. — Rev. ed. — [London : London School of Economics and Political Science], 1986. — 34p. — (Taxation, incentives and the distribution of income ; no.97). — Economic and Social Research Council programme. — Bibliographical references: p33-34

INVESTMENTS — Social aspects — United States
BRUYN, Severyn T.
The field of social investment / Severyn T. Bruyn. — Cambridge : Cambridge University Press, 1987. — [560]p. — (The Arnold and Caroline Rose monograph series of the American Sociological Association). — Bibliography: p556

INVESTMENTS — Taxation — Finland
KOSKENKYLÄ, Heikki
Investment behaviour and market imperfections with an application to the Finnish corporate sector / Heikki Koskenkylä. — Helsinki : Bank of Finland, 1985. — 65p. — Bibliography: p52-65

INVESTMENTS — Australia
Business investment and the capital stock. — Canberra : Economic Planning Advisory Council, 1986. — v,27p. — (Council paper / Economic Planning Advisory Council ; no.10). — Bibliographical references: p25

INVESTMENTS — Bolivia
Bolivia : agricultural pricing and investment policies. — Washington, D.C., U.S.A. : World Bank, c1984. — xlii,130p. — (A World Bank country study). — Summaries in French and Spanish. — Includes bibliographical references

INVESTMENTS — Canada
HUNTER, W. T.
Canadian financial markets / W. T. Hunter. — Peterborough, Canada : Broadview Press, 1986. — 193p. — Includes references

INVESTMENTS — Denmark — Statistics
STETKAER, Karsten
Beregningen af erhvervsfordelte investeringer i nationalregnskabet 1966-81 / Karsten Stetkaer. — [København] : Danmarks Statistik, 1986. — 130p. — (Arbejdsnotat / Danmarks Statistik ; nr.14)

INVESTMENTS — Developing countries
MITSOTAKI, Alexandra Gourdain
Public development finance corporations : their role in the new forms of investment in developing countries / by Alexandra Gourdain Mitsotaki. — [Paris] : Development Centre of the Organisation for Economic Co-operation and Development, [1986]. — 40p. — (Development Centre papers). — Bibliographical references: p.39-40

TURTIAINEN, Turto
Investment and finance in agricultural service cooperatives / Turto Turtiainen and J. D. Von Pischke. — Washington, D. C. : The World Bank, 1986. — x,173p. — (World Bank technical paper ; no.50). — Bibliography: p120-122

WELLONS, Phillip
Banks and specialised financial intermediaries in development / by Phillip Wellons, Dimitri Germidis and Bianca Glavanis. — Paris : Organisation for Economic Co—operation and Development, 1986. — 150p. — (Development Centre studies). — Bibliography: p131-133

INVESTMENTS — Dominica
Dominica, priorities and prospects for development. — Washington, D.C., U.S.A. : World Bank, c1985. — [xiv],105p. — (World Bank country study)

INVESTMENTS — European Economic Community countries
Comparative follow—up and evaluation of current employment measures / by Centre de Recherche "Travail et Société", Paris, France... [et al.]. — Luxembourg : Office for Official Publications of the European Communities, 1985. — vi, 221p. — (Programme of research and actions on the development of the labour market). — At head of title: Commission of the European Communities

INVESTMENTS — Finland
KOSKENKYLÄ, Heikki
Investment behaviour and market imperfections with an application to the Finnish corporate sector / Heikki Koskenkylä. — Helsinki : Bank of Finland, 1985. — 65p. — Bibliography: p52-65

INVESTMENTS — Great Britain

ASHDOWN, Paddy
Investing in our future : tackling short-termism in the British economy / Paddy Ashdown [and] Richard Holme. — Hebden Bridge : Hebden Royd Publications, 1986. — 51p. — (Liberal challenge ; no.6). — *Bibliography : p51*

The City and the Empire. — London : Institute of Commonwealth Studies. — (Collected seminar papers (University of London. Institute of Commonwealth Studies) ; no.36)
vol.2. — 1987. — 142p

LABOUR PARTY (Great Britain)
Investing in Britain : jobs and industry / Labour Party. — London : Labour Party, [1985]. — 23p

INVESTMENTS — Great Britain — Mathematical models

BLAKE, David Peter Courtney
The characteristics model of portfolio behaviour : with reference to United Kingdom private sector pension funds 1963-1978 / by David Peter Courtney Blake. — 322 leaves. — *PhD (Econ) 1987 LSE*

KELLY, Christopher
Factor prices in the Treasury model / Christopher Kelly, David Owen. — London : HM Treasury, 1985. — 81p. — (Government Economic Service working paper ; no.83) (Treasury working paper ; no.37). — *Bibliographical references: p73-74*

INVESTMENTS — Great Britain — Statistics

Insurance companies' and pension funds' investment. — London : HMSO, 1970-. — (Business monitor. MQ ; 5) (Business monitor. M ; 5). — *Quarterly*

Overseas transactions. — London : HMSO, 1968-. — (Business monitor. MA ; 4) (Business monitor. M ; 4). — *Annual. — Has occasional supplement: Census of overseas assets*

INVESTMENTS — India

BAGCHI, Amiya Kumar
Private investment in India, 1900-1939 / Amiya Kumar Bagchi. — London : Cambridge University Press, 1972. — xi,482p. — (Cambridge South Asian studies ; 10). — *Bibliographyp.445-469. — Includes index*

INVESTMENTS — Japan

Private sector fixed investment : recent trends and views on future inducement. — Tokyo : Bank of Japan. Research and Statistics Department, 1987. — 21p. — (Special paper / Bank of Japan. Research and Statistics Department ; no.143)

INVESTMENTS — Organisation for Economic Co-operation and Development countries

CHAN-LEE, James H.
Pure profit rates and Tobin's q in nine OECD countries / by James H. Chan-Lee. — [Paris] : OECD, 1986. — 41p. — (Working papers / OECD. Department of Economics and Statistics ; no.34). — *Bibliographical references: p.39-41*

INVESTMENTS — Puerto Rico — History

DIETZ, James L.
Economic history of Puerto Rico : institutional change and capitalist development / James L. Dietz. — Princeton, N.J. : Princeton University Press, c1986. — xxiii, 337p, [11]p of plates. — *Includes index. — Bibliography: p.[311]-326*

INVESTMENTS — United States

DYCKMAN, Thomas R.
Efficient capital markets and accounting : a critical analysis. — 2nd ed. / Thomas R. Dyckman, Dale Morse. — Englewood Cliffs ; London : Prentice-Hall, c1986. — xiv,129p. — (Prentice-Hall contemporary topics in accounting series). — *Previous ed.: 1975. — Bibliography: p92-105. — Includes index*

INVESTMENTS, AMERICAN

KACKER, M. P
Transatlantic trends in retailing : takeovers and flow of know-how / Madhav P. Kacker. — Westport, Conn. : Quorum Books, c1985. — p. cm. — *Includes index. — Bibliography: p*

INVESTMENTS, AMERICAN — Social aspects

BRUYN, Severyn T.
The field of social investment / Severyn T. Bruyn. — Cambridge : Cambridge University Press, 1987. — [560]p. — (The Arnold and Caroline Rose monograph series of the American Sociological Association). — *Bibliography: p556*

INVESTMENTS, AMERICAN — Europe

SERVAN-SCHREIBER, J. J.
The American challenge / J. J. Servan-Schreiber ; translated from the French by Ronald Steel ; with a foreword by Arthur Schlesinger, Jr.. — New York : Atheneum, 1979. — 254p. — *Originally published as Le défi américain, by Denöel, 1967*

INVESTMENTS, AMERICAN — South Africa

SEIDMAN, Ann
The roots of crisis in Southern Africa / Ann Seidman. — Trenton, N.J. : Africa World Press, 1985. — xvii,209p. — (Impact audit ; No.4). — *Bibliography: p175-180*

INVESTMENTS, BRAZILIAN

New forms of overseas investment by developing countries : the case of India, Korea and Brazil / edited by Charles Oman. — Paris : Development Centre of the Organisation for Economic Co-operation and Development, 1986. — 183p. — (Development Centre papers) . — *Bibliography: p166*

INVESTMENTS, BRITISH — Argentina

MÍGUEZ, Eduardo José
Las tierras de los ingleses en la Argentina (1870-1914) / Eduardo José Míguez. — [Buenos Aires] : Editorial de Belgrano, 1985. — 348p. — "El presente libro es una traducción y adaptación de mi tesis doctoral, titulada 'British interests in Argentine Land Development, 1870-1914. A study of British investment in Argentina', defendida en la Universidad de Oxford en abril de 1981.". — *Bibliography: p[331]-342*

INVESTMENTS, BRITISH — South Africa

LABOUR RESEARCH DEPARTMENT
Profiting from apartheid : Britain's links with South Africa. — London : Labour Research Department, 1986. — 54p

INVESTMENTS, DUTCH

NIEUWKERK, Marius van
The Netherlands international direct investment position / Marius van Nieuwkerk and Robert P. Sparling. — Dordrecht : Nijhoff [for] Nederlandsche Bank, 1985. — 135p. — (Monetary Monographs ; No.4). — *Bibliography: p134-135*

INVESTMENTS, FOREIGN

BORNER, Silvio
Internationalization of industry : an assessment in the light of a small open economy (Switzerland) / Silvio Borner. — Berlin ; New York : Springer-Verlag, c1986. — p. cm. — *Bibliography: p*

HANER, F. T
Country risk assessment : theory and worldwide practice / F.T. Haner and John S. Ewing. — New York : Praeger, 1985. — p. cm . — *Includes index. — Bibliography: p*

SIEGEL, Michael H
Foreign exchange risk and direct foreign investment / by Michael H. Siegel. — Ann Arbor, Mich. : UMI Research Press, c1983. — vi, 97 p.. — (Research for business decisions ; no. 60). — *Includes index. — Bibliography: p. [89]-92*

INVESTMENTS, FOREIGN — Accounting

INTERNATIONAL ACCOUNTING STANDARDS COMMITTEE
Proposed statement : consolidated financial statements and accounting for investments in subsidiaries. — London : International Accounting Standards Committee, 1987. — [12p]. — (Exposure draft ; 30)

INVESTMENTS, FOREIGN — Addresses, essays, lectures

International financial management : theory and application / edited by Donald R. Lessard. — 2nd ed. — New York : Wiley, c1985. — xi, 594 p.. — *Includes bibliographies and indexes*

INVESTMENTS, FOREIGN — Government policy — Colombia

WALLACE, Brian F
Ownership and development : a comparison of domestic and foreign firms in Colombian manufacturing / by Brian F. Wallace. — Athens, Ohio : Ohio University Center for International Studies, 1987. — p. cm. — (Monographs in international studies. Latin America series ; no. 12). — *Bibliography: p*

INVESTMENTS, FOREIGN — Government policy — Mexico

CAMPILLO SÁINZ, José
Tesis de México sobre inversiones extranjeras / [José Campillo Sáinz]. — [México : Subsecretaría de Industria y Comercio, ca.1972]. — 18p

INVESTMENTS, FOREIGN — Law and legislation

LOWENFELD, Andreas F.
International economic law. — New York : Matthew Bender
Vol.2: International private investment / Andreas F. Lowenfeld. — 2nd ed. — 1982. — xi,207,355,2,12p. — *Includes Documents Supplement*

INVESTMENTS, FOREIGN — Law and legislation — Developing countries

DE LUPIS, Ingrid Detter
Finance and protection of investments in developing countries / Ingrid Detter De Lupis. — 2nd ed. — Aldershot : Gower, 1987. — xvii,183p. — *Previous ed.: 1973. — Includes index*

INVESTMENTS, FOREIGN — Law and legislation — Korea (South)

Business laws in Korea : investment, taxation, and industrial property / Chan-jin Kim, editor. — Seoul, Korea : Panmun Book Co., 1982. — xii, 799 p.. — *Includes bibliographical references*

INVESTMENTS, FOREIGN — Mathematical models

COE, David T.
International investment-income determination in INTERLINK : models for 23 OECD countries and six non-OECD regions / by David T. Coe, Richard Herd. — Paris : OECD, 1987. — iii,47p. — (Working papers / OECD Department of Economics and Statistics ; no.45). — *Bibliographical references: p47*

INVESTMENTS, FOREIGN — Statistics

DUNNING, John H.
IRM directory of statistics of international investment and production / John Dunning and John Cantwell with the assistance of Paz E. Tolentino and Faith Province. — [Basingstoke] : Macmillan Reference, 1987. — xix,820p

INVESTMENTS, FOREIGN — Asia

External financing by developing Asian countries : present situation and future outlook. — Tokyo : Bank of Japan. Research and Statistics Department, 1986. — 24p. — (Special paper / Bank of Japan. Research and Statistics Department ; no.138)

INVESTMENTS, FOREIGN — Asia, Southeastern
SKULLY, Michael T
Merchant banking in ASEAN : a regional examination of its development and operations / Michael T. Skully. — rev. ed. — Singapore ; Oxford : Oxford University Press, 1986. — viii,204p

INVESTMENTS, FOREIGN — Canada
Balance of payments : Canada's international investment position = Balance des paiements : le bilan canadien des investissements internationaux / Statistics Canada. — Ottawa : Statistics Canada, 1982/85-. — Annual. — Text in English and French

SAFARIAN, A. E
Foreign direct investment : a survey of Canadian research / A.E. Safarian. — Montreal, Québec : Institute for Research on Public Policy, c1985. — xv, 83 p.. — (Essays in international economics). — Summary in French. — Bibliography: p. 53-[72]

INVESTMENTS, FOREIGN — Canada, Western — History — Bibliography
OSTRYE, Anne T.
Foreign investment in the American and Canadian West, 1870-1914 : an annotated bibliography / by Anne T. Ostrye. — Metuchen, N.J. ; London : Scarecrow Press, 1986. — vii, 192p. — Includes indexes

INVESTMENTS, FOREIGN — Canada, Western — History — Sources
OSTRYE, Anne T.
Foreign investment in the American and Canadian West, 1870-1914 : an annotated bibliography / by Anne T. Ostrye. — Metuchen, N.J. ; London : Scarecrow Press, 1986. — vii, 192p. — Includes indexes

INVESTMENTS, FOREIGN — Communist countries
MCMILLAN, Carl H.
Multinationals from the Second World : growth of foreign investment by Soviet and East European enterprises / Carl H. McMillan. — London : Macmillan for the Trade Policy Research Centre, 1987. — xvii,220p. — Bibliography: p203-210. — Includes index

INVESTMENTS, FOREIGN — Developing countries
BAUM, Warren C
Investing in development : lessons of World Bank experience / Warren C. Baum and Stokes M. Tolbert. — New York : Published for the World Bank [by] Oxford University Press, c1985. — p. cm. — Includes index

BORNSCHIER, Volker
Transnational corporations and underdevelopment / Volker Bornschier, Christopher Chase-Dunn. — New York : Praeger, 1985. — p. cm. — Includes index. — Bibliography: p

Investing in development : new roles for private capital? / Theodore H. Moran, editor ; Joseph M. Grieco ... [et al., contributors]. — New Brunswick (USA) : Transaction Books, c1985. — p. cm. — (U.S.-Third World policy perspectives ; no. 6)

New forms of overseas investment by developing countries : the case of India, Korea and Brazil / edited by Charles Oman. — Paris : Development Centre of the Organisation for Economic Co-operation and Development, 1986. — 183p. — (Development Centre papers) . — Bibliography: p166

Recent trends in international direct investment. — Paris : Organisation for Economic Co-operation and Development, 1987. — 213p. — (International investment and multinational enterprises). — Bibliographical references: p51-54

INVESTMENTS, FOREIGN — Ecuador
In versiones extranjeras en el Ecuador. — Quito : Superintendencia de Bancos, 1981-. — Annual

INVESTMENTS, FOREIGN — France — Statistics
L'implantation étrangère dans l'industrie. — Paris : Documentation Française, 1979-. — (Traits fondamentaux du système industriel français) (Collection chiffres et documents: Serie industrie). — Annual. — Issuing body varies; France. Service du Traitement de l'Information et des Statistiques Industrielles and France. Service d'Étude des Stratégies et des Statistiques Industrielles

INVESTMENTS, FOREIGN — Great Britain
GREAT BRITAIN. Parliament. House of Commons. Library. Research Division
Foreign involvement in United Kingdom industry / Christopher Barclay. — [London] : the Library, 1986. — 25p. — (Background paper ; no.186). — Bibliography: p25

INVESTMENTS, FOREIGN — Great Britain — Statistics
Overseas transactions. — London : HMSO, 1968-. — (Business monitor. MA ; 4) (Business monitor. M ; 4). — Annual. — Has occasional supplement: Census of overseas assets

INVESTMENTS, FOREIGN — Mexico
CAMPILLO SÁINZ, José
Tesis de México sobre inversiones extranjeras / [José Campillo Sáinz]. — [México : Subsecretaría de Industria y Comercio, ca.1972]. — 18p

INVESTMENTS, FOREIGN — Nigeria
BIERSTEKER, Thomas J
Multinationals, the state, and control of the Nigerian economy / Thomas J. Biersteker. — Princeton, N.J. : Princeton University Press, c1987. — p. cm. — Includes index. — Bibliography: p

INVESTMENTS, FOREIGN — Organisation for Economic Co-operation and Development countries
Recent trends in international direct investment. — Paris : Organisation for Economic Co-operation and Development, 1987. — 213p. — (International investment and multinational enterprises). — Bibliographical references: p51-54

INVESTMENTS, FOREIGN — Taiwan
Facts for investors in Taiwan. — [Taipei] : Industrial Development Commission, 1958. — ii,60p

INVESTMENTS, FOREIGN — United States
GORDON, Sara L.
Foreign multinational investment in the United States : struggle for industrial Supremacy / Sara L. Gordon and Francis A. Lees. — New York ; London : Quorum, 1986. — xviii,289p. — Bibliography: p269-277. — Includes index

KACKER, M. P
Transatlantic trends in retailing : takeovers and flow of know-how / Madhav P. Kacker. — Westport, Conn. : Quorum Books, c1985. — p. cm. — Includes index. — Bibliography: p

INVESTMENTS, FOREIGN — West (U.S.) — History — Bibliography
OSTRYE, Anne T.
Foreign investment in the American and Canadian West, 1870-1914 : an annotated bibliography / by Anne T. Ostrye. — Metuchen, N.J. ; London : Scarecrow Press, 1986. — vii, 192p. — Includes indexes

INVESTMENTS, FOREIGN — West (U.S.) — History — Sources
OSTRYE, Anne T.
Foreign investment in the American and Canadian West, 1870-1914 : an annotated bibliography / by Anne T. Ostrye. — Metuchen, N.J. ; London : Scarecrow Press, 1986. — vii, 192p. — Includes indexes

INVESTMENTS, FOREIGN — Yugoslavia
ARTISIEN, Patrick F. R.
Joint ventures in Yugoslav industry / Patrick F.R. Artisien. — Aldershot : Gower, c1985. — [xv,240]p. — Bibliography: p210-218. — Includes index

INVESTMENTS, FOREIGN AND EMPLOYMENT — Australia
TSOKHAS, Kosmas
Beyond dependence : companies, labour processes and Australian mining / Kosmas Tsokhas. — Melbourne : Oxford University Press, 1986. — 291p. — Bibliography: p [273]-281

INVESTMENTS, FOREIGN (INTERNATIONAL LAW)
DE LUPIS, Ingrid Detter
Finance and protection of investments in developing countries / Ingrid Detter De Lupis. — 2nd ed. — Aldershot : Gower, 1987. — xvii,183p. — Previous ed.: 1973. — Includes index

INVESTMENTS, INDIAN
New forms of overseas investment by developing countries : the case of India, Korea and Brazil / edited by Charles Oman. — Paris : Development Centre of the Organisation for Economic Co-operation and Development, 1986. — 183p. — (Development Centre papers) . — Bibliography: p166

INVESTMENTS, IRANIAN — United States
HULBERT, Mark
Interlock : the untold story of American banks, oil interests, the Shah's money, debts and the astounding connections between them / Mark Hulbert. — New York : Richardson and Snyder, 1982. — 272p

INVESTMENTS, JAPANESE — European Economic Community countries
The Internationalization of Japanese business : European and Japanese perspectives / edited by Malcolm Trevor. — Boulder : Westview Press, 1986. — p. cm

INVESTMENTS, JAPANESE — United States
YOSHIDA, Mamoru
Japanese direct manufacturing investment in the United States / Mamoru Yoshida. — New York : Praeger, 1987. — xiv, 220 p.. — : Originally presented as the author's thesis (doctoral--University of Miami). — Includes index. — Bibliography: p. 209-216

INVESTMENTS, KOREAN
New forms of overseas investment by developing countries : the case of India, Korea and Brazil / edited by Charles Oman. — Paris : Development Centre of the Organisation for Economic Co-operation and Development, 1986. — 183p. — (Development Centre papers) . — Bibliography: p166

INVISIBLE ITEMS OF TRADE
KAKABADSE, Mario A.
International trade in services : prospects for liberalisation in the 1990s / Mario A. Kakabadse. — London : Croom Helm for the Atlantic Institute for International Affairs, c1987. — [80]p. — (Atlantic paper ; no.64)

IRAN
Iran / Middle East Research Institute, University of Pennsylvania. — London : Croom Helm, c1985. — 181p. — (MERI report)

IRAN — Bibliography
GHANI, Cyrus
Iran and the West : a critical bibliography / Cyrus Ghani. — London : Kegan Paul International, 1987. — viii,967p

IRAN — Boundaries — Iraq
SCHOFIELD, Richard N.
Evolution of the Shatt al-'Arab boundary dispute / by Richard N. Schofield. — Wisbech : Middle East and North African Studies Press, 1986. — viii,111p. — Bibliography: p87-94

IRAN — Economic conditions
Economic report and balance sheet / Bank Markazi Jomhouri, Islami Iran. — Tehran : Bank Markazi Jomhouri Islami Iran, 1981-. — Annual. — Continues: Annual report and balance sheet

IRAN — Economic conditions — Addresses, essays, lectures
ISSAWI, Charles
The economic history of Iran, 1800-1914 / edited by Charles Issawi. — Chicago ; London : University of Chicago Press, 1971. — xvii,405p. — (Publications / University of Chicago. Center for Middle Eastern Studies ; no.8). — Bibliographyp.391-399. — Includes index

IRAN — Economic conditions — 1945
Islamic Republic of Iran. — Berne : Embassy of the Islamic Republic of Iran, [1986?]. — 160p. — 1map

IRAN — Economic conditions — 1945- — Case studies
GOODELL, Grace E
The elementary structures of political life : rural development in Pahlavi Iran / Grace E. Goodell. — New York : Oxford University Press, 1986. — vii, 362 p.. — Includes index. — Bibliography: p. 345-350

IRAN — Ethnic relations — Congresses
The State, religion, and ethnic politics : Afghanistan, Iran, and Pakistan / edited by Ali Banuazizi and Myron Weiner. — 1st ed. — [Syracuse, N.Y.] : Syracuse University Press, 1986. — xi, 390 p.. — (Contemporary issues in the Middle East). — "Sponsored by the Joint Committee on the Near and Middle East and the Committee on South Asia of the American Council of Learned Societies and the Social Science Research Council.". — Includes bibliographies and index

IRAN — Foreign relations — 1979-
RAMAZANI, Rouhollan K.
Revolutionary Iran : challenge and response in the Middle East / R.K. Ramazani. — Baltimore : Johns Hopkins University Press, c1986. — xv, 311 p.. — Includes index. — Bibliography: p. 295-302

IRAN — Foreign relations — Iraq
GREAT BRITAIN. Parliament. House of Commons. Library. International Affairs Section
The Gulf War / Richard Ware. — [London] : the Library, 1984. — 16p. — (Background paper / House of Commons. Library. [Research Division] ; no.137)

GREAT BRITAIN. Parliament. House of Commons. Library. Research Division
The war between Iraq and Iran / Richard Ware. — [London] : the Division, 1985. — 20p. — (Background paper ; no.163). — Bibliography: p19-20

KARSH, Efraim
The Iran-Iraq war : a military analysis / Efraim Karsh. — London : International Institute for Strategic Studies, 1987. — 72p. — (Adelphi papers ; 220)

KING, Ralph
The Iran-Iraq war : the political implications / Ralph King. — London : International Institute for Strategic Studies, 1987. — 76p. — (Adelphi papers ; 219)

IRAN — Foreign relations — Middle East
RAMAZANI, Rouhollan K.
Revolutionary Iran : challenge and response in the Middle East / R.K. Ramazani. — Baltimore : Johns Hopkins University Press, c1986. — xv, 311 p.. — Includes index. — Bibliography: p. 295-302

IRAN — Foreign relations — Soviet Union
VOLODARSKII, M. I.
Sovety i ikh iuzhnye sosedi Iran i Afganistan (1917-1933) / M. I. Volodarskii ; predislovie S. Mogilevskogo. — London : Overseas Publications Interchange, 1985. — 241p. — Bibliography: p235

IRAN — Foreign relations — United States
HULBERT, Mark
Interlock : the untold story of American banks, oil interests, the Shah's money, debts and the astounding connections between them / Mark Hulbert. — New York : Richardson and Snyder, 1982. — 272p

HUYSER, Robert E.
Mission to Tehran / by Robert E. Huyser ; introduction by Alexander M. Haig. — London : Deutsch, 1986. — [320]p. — Includes index

RYAN, Paul B
The Iranian rescue mission : why it failed / by Paul B. Ryan. — Annapolis, Md. : Naval Institute Press, c1985. — xiii, 185p. — Includes index. — Bibliography: p [177]-180

IRAN — History — Qajar dynasty, 1779-1925
BECK, Lois
The Qashqa'i of Iran / Lois Beck. — New Haven ; London : Yale University Press, c1986. — xvi, 384p, [24]p of plates. — Includes index. — Bibliography: p.353-367

IRAN — History — 20th century
BECK, Lois
The Qashqa'i of Iran / Lois Beck. — New Haven ; London : Yale University Press, c1986. — xvi, 384p, [24]p of plates. — Includes index. — Bibliography: p.353-367

Twentieth century Iran / selected by Hossein Amirsadeghi ; assisted by R.W. Ferrier ; introduction by Sir Denis Wright. — London : Heinemann, 1977. — xv,299p,[8]p of plates. — Includes index

IRAN — History — Revolution, 1979
Shi'ism, resistance and revolution / edited by Martin Kramer. — London : Mansell, 1987. — [352]p. — Conference proceedings. — Includes index

IRAN — Politics and government — 1941-1979
AFKHAMI, Gholam R
The Iranian revolution : thanatos on a national scale / Gholam R. Afkhami. — Washington, DC : Middle East Institute, 1985. — x, 276 p.. — Includes index. — Bibliography: p. 259-268

BAYAT, Assef
Workers and revolution in Iran : a Third World experience of workers' control / Assef Bayat. — London : Zed, 1987. — 227p. — Bibliography: p208-222. — Includes index

IRAN — Politics and government — 1941-1979 — Case studies
GOODELL, Grace E
The elementary structures of political life : rural development in Pahlavi Iran / Grace E. Goodell. — New York : Oxford University Press, 1986. — vii, 362 p.. — Includes index. — Bibliography: p. 345-350

IRAN — Politics and government — 1979
Islamic Republic of Iran. — Berne : Embassy of the Islamic Republic of Iran, [1986?]. — 160p. — 1map

IRAN — Politics and government — 1979-
AFKHAMI, Gholam R
The Iranian revolution : thanatos on a national scale / Gholam R. Afkhami. — Washington, DC : Middle East Institute, 1985. — x, 276 p.. — Includes index. — Bibliography: p. 259-268

HIRO, Dilip
Iran under the Ayatollahs / Dilip Hiro. — [Repr.] with corrections and new postscript. — London : Routledge & Kegan Paul, 1987. — xv,438p. — Originally published: 1985. — Bibliography: p418-420 — Includes index

HUYSER, Robert E.
Mission to Tehran / by Robert E. Huyser ; introduction by Alexander M. Haig. — London : Deutsch, 1986. — [320]p. — Includes index

IRAN — Politics and government — 1979- — Congresses
The State, religion, and ethnic politics : Afghanistan, Iran, and Pakistan / edited by Ali Banuazizi and Myron Weiner. — 1st ed. — [Syracuse, N.Y.] : Syracuse University Press, 1986. — xi, 390 p.. — (Contemporary issues in the Middle East). — "Sponsored by the Joint Committee on the Near and Middle East and the Committee on South Asia of the American Council of Learned Societies and the Social Science Research Council.". — Includes bibliographies and index

IRAN — Relations — Soviet Union
NISSMAN, David B.
The Soviet Union and Iranian Azerbaijan : the use of nationalism for political penetration / David B. Nissman. — Boulder, Colo. : Westview Press, 1987. — ix,123p. — (Westview special studies on the Soviet Union and Eastern Europe). — Bibliography: p109-113

IRAN — Social conditions
LIMBERT, John W.
Iran : at war with history / John W. Limbert. — Boulder, Colo. : Westview ; London : Croom Helm, 1987. — xviii,186p. — (Profiles : nations of the contemporary Middle East). — Bibliography: p168-174. — Includes index

IRAN — Social life and customs
BEEMAN, William O
Language, status, and power in Iran / William O. Beeman. — Bloomington : Indiana University Press, c1986. — xx, 255 p.. — (Advances in semiotics). — Includes indexes. — Bibliography: p. 213-235

Women and the family in Iran / edited by Asghar Fathi. — Leiden : E. J. Brill, 1985. — 239p. — (Social, economic and political studies of the Middle East ; v.38)

IRAN-CONTRA AFFAIR, 1985-
UNITED STATES. President. President's Special Review Board
The Tower Commission report : the full text of the President's Special Review Board : John Tower, chairman; Edmund Muskie and Brent Scowcroft, members / introduction by R. W. Apple. — [New York] : Bantam Books : Times Books : 1987. — xix,550p

IRAN HOSTAGE CRISIS, 1979-1981
HOLMES, Deborah
Governing the press : media freedom in the U.S. and Great Britain / Deborah Holmes. — Boulder : Westview Press, 1986. — xi, 107 p.. — (A Westview special study). — Includes index. — Bibliography: p. 93-102

RYAN, Paul B
The Iranian rescue mission : why it failed / by Paul B. Ryan. — Annapolis, Md. : Naval Institute Press, c1985. — xiii, 185p. — Includes index. — Bibliography: p [177]-180

IRAN-IRAQ WAR, 1980- See Iraqi-Iranian Conflict, 1980-

IRAQ — Armed Forces — Political activity
SIMON, Reeva S
Iraq between the two world wars : the creation and implementation of a nationalist ideology / Reeva S. Simon. — New York : Columbia University Press, 1986. — xv, 233p. — Includes index. — Bibliography: p.[211]-227

IRAQ — Boundaries — Iran
SCHOFIELD, Richard N.
Evolution of the Shatt al-'Arab boundary dispute / by Richard N. Schofield. — Wisbech : Middle East and North African Studies Press, 1986. — viii,111p. — Bibliography: p87-94

IRAQ — Foreign relations — Great Britain
HAMDI, Walid M. S.
Rashid Ali al-Gailani and the Nationalist Movement in Iraq 1939-1941 : a political and military study of the British campaign in Iraq and the national revolution of May 1941 / by Walid M. S. Hamdi. — London : Darf, 1987. — x,277p. — Bibliography: p266-277

IRAQ — Foreign relations — Great Britain
continuation

SILVERFARB, Daniel
Britain's informal empire in the Middle East : a case study of Iraq, 1929-1941 / Daniel Silverfarb. — New York ; Oxford : Oxford University Press, 1986. — x, 200p. — *Includes index.* — *Bibliography: p.185-191*

IRAQ — Foreign relations — Iran

GREAT BRITAIN. Parliament. House of Commons. Library. International Affairs Section
The Gulf War / Richard Ware. — [London] : the Library, 1984. — 16p. — (Background paper / House of Commons. Library. [Research Division] ; no.137)

GREAT BRITAIN. Parliament. House of Commons. Library. Research Division
The war between Iraq and Iran / Richard Ware. — [London] : the Division, 1985. — 20p. — (Background paper ; no.163). — *Bibliography: p19-20*

KARSH, Efraim
The Iran-Iraq war : a military analysis / Efraim Karsh. — London : International Institute for Strategic Studies, 1987. — 72p. — (Adelphi papers ; 220)

KING, Ralph
The Iran-Iraq war : the political implications / Ralph King. — London : International Institute for Strategic Studies, 1987. — 76p. — (Adelphi papers ; 219)

IRAQ — History — Hashemite Kingdom, 1921-1958

SILVERFARB, Daniel
Britain's informal empire in the Middle East : a case study of Iraq, 1929-1941 / Daniel Silverfarb. — New York ; Oxford : Oxford University Press, 1986. — x, 200p. — *Includes index.* — *Bibliography: p.185-191*

SIMON, Reeva S
Iraq between the two world wars : the creation and implementation of a nationalist ideology / Reeva S. Simon. — New York : Columbia University Press, 1986. — xv, 233p. — *Includes index.* — *Bibliography: p.[211]-227*

IRAQ — History — 1921-

SHIKARA, Ahmad Abdul Razzaq
Iraqi politics 1921-41 : the interaction between domestic politics and foreign policy / Ahmed Abdul Razzaq Shikara. — London : Laam, 1987. — [240]p. — *Includes index*

IRAQ — Politics and government

BATATU, Hanna
The old social classes and the revolutionary movements of Iraq : a study of Iraq's old landed and commercial classes and of its Communists, Ba'thists, and Free Officers / Hanna Batatu. — Princeton, N.J. : Princeton University Press, c1978. — xxiv, 1283 p., [8] leaves of plates. — (Princeton studies on the Near East). — *Includes indexes.* — *Bibliography: p. [1231]-1252*

HAMDI, Walid M. S.
Rashid Ali al-Gailani and the Nationalist Movement in Iraq 1939-1941 : a political and military study of the British campaign in Iraq and the national revolution of May 1941 / by Walid M. S. Hamdi. — London : Darf, 1987. — x,277p. — *Bibliography: p266-277*

SHIKARA, Ahmad Abdul Razzaq
Iraqi politics 1921-41 : the interaction between domestic politics and foreign policy / Ahmed Abdul Razzaq Shikara. — London : Laam, 1987. — [240]p. — *Includes index*

IRAQ — Relations — Gulf States

NONNEMAN, Gerd
Iraq, the Gulf States and the war : a changing relationship 1980-1986 and beyond / Gerd Nonneman. — London : Ithaca Press, 1986. — 216p. — (Exeter Middle East politics ; no.1). — *Bibliography: p203-211*

IRAQI-IRANIAN CONFLICT, 1980-

GREAT BRITAIN. Parliament. House of Commons. Library. International Affairs Section
The Gulf War / Richard Ware. — [London] : the Library, 1984. — 16p. — (Background paper / House of Commons. Library. [Research Division] ; no.137)

GREAT BRITAIN. Parliament. House of Commons. Library. International Affairs Section
The Gulf War : an end in sight? / Richard Ware. — [London] : the Library, 1987. — 23p. — (Background paper / House of Commons. Library. [Research Division] ; no.193). — *Bibliographical references: p22-23*

GREAT BRITAIN. Parliament. House of Commons. Library. Research Division
The war between Iraq and Iran / Richard Ware. — [London] : the Division, 1985. — 20p. — (Background paper ; no.163). — *Bibliography: p19-20*

IRAQI-IRANIAN CONFLICT, 1980

NONNEMAN, Gerd
Iraq, the Gulf States and the war : a changing relationship 1980-1986 and beyond / Gerd Nonneman. — London : Ithaca Press, 1986. — 216p. — (Exeter Middle East politics ; no.1). — *Bibliography: p203-211*

IRELAND — Appropriations and expenditures

Comprehensive public expenditure programmes. — Dublin : Stationery Office, 1985-. — *Annual*

IRELAND — Appropriations and expenditures — Congresses

Public expenditure : the key issues / edited by John Bristow and Declan McDonagh. — Dublin, Ireland : Institute of Public Administration, 1986. — 138 p.. — *Proceedings of National Conference on Public Expenditure: the Key Issues, held Nov. 1985 in Dublin, organized by the Institute.* — *Includes bibliographies.* — *Contents: Public expenditure and public debt / Vito Tanzi -- The political economy of public expenditure / Alan Peacock -- Public employment and public expenditure / Richard Rose -- Public expenditure and the bureaucracy / Peter Jackson -- An Irish overview / Alan Dukes*

IRELAND — Bibliography

SHANNON, Michael Owen
Irish Republic / Michael Owen Shannon, compiler. — Oxford : Clio, c1986. — xxiv,405p. — (World bibliographical series ; v.69). — *Includes index*

IRELAND — Census, 1981

Census of population of Ireland 1981 / compiled by the Central Statistics Office. — Dublin : Stationery Office
Vol.8: Housing. — 1986. — xix,337p. — *"The statistics herein relate to the population of Ireland exclusive of Northern Ireland*

IRELAND. Central Statistics Office
Census of population of Ireland 1981. — Dublin : Stationery Office. — *"The statistics herein relate to the population of Ireland exclusive of Northern Ireland"*
Part 1: Usual residence and migrationPart 2: Birthplaces
Volume 9. — 1986. — xxi,199p

IRELAND — Census, 1986

Census of population of Ireland 1986 / compiled by the Central Statistics Office. — Dublin : Stationery Office
Preliminary report. — 1986. — xiii,15p. — *"The statistics herein relate to the population of Ireland exclusive of Northern Ireland*

IRELAND — Commerce — History — Congresses

FRANCO-IRISH SEMINAR OF SOCIAL AND ECONOMIC HISTORIANS (4th : 1984 : Trinity College Dublin)
Cities and merchants : French and Irish perspectives on urban development, 1500-1900 : proceedings of the fourth Franco-Irish Seminar of Social and Economic Historians / edited by P. Butel and L. M. Cullen. — Dublin : Department of Modern History, Trinity College Dublin, 1986. — 259p. — *English and French text.* — *Maps on lining papers*

IRELAND — Description and travel — 1801-1900

GROUSSET, Paschal
Ireland's disease : the English in Ireland 1887 / Paschal Grousset ; with an introduction by Constance Ramillon Conner. — Belfast, Northern Ireland ; Dover, N.H. : Blackstaff Press, 1986. — p. cm. — : *Reprint. Originally published: London ; New York : G. Routledge, 1888.* — *Includes index*

IRELAND — Directories

Ireland: a directory. — Dublin : Institute of Public Administration, 1986-. — *Annual*

IRELAND — Economic conditions

Natives and newcomers : essays on the making of Irish colonial society, 1534-1641 / Ciaran Brady and Raymond Gillespie, editors. — Dublin : Irish Academic, c1986. — 259p. — *Bibliography: p239-248.* — *Includes index*

Who owns Ireland, who owns you?. — Dublin : Women in Community Publishing Course in conjunction with Attic, 1985. — 160p. — *Bibliography: p150.* — *Includes index*

IRELAND — Economic conditions — 1949- — Econometric models

HENRY, E. W.
Multisector modelling of the Irish economy : with special reference to employment projections / E. W. Henry. — Dublin : Economic and Social Research Institute, 1986. — 169p. — (Paper / Economic and Social Research Institute ; 128)

IRELAND — Economic conditions — 1949-

BARRY, Ursula
Lifting the lid : handbook of facts and information on Ireland / Ursula Barry. — Dublin : Attic Press, 1986. — 144p. — *Bibliographies*

IRELAND — Economic policy

Innovation policy : Ireland. — Paris : Organisation for Economic Co-operation and Development, 1987. — 75p. — *Bibliographical references: p55*

IRELAND — Emigration and immigration — History

GALLAGHER, Tom, 1954-
Glasgow : the uneasy peace : religious tension in modern Scotland, 1819-1914 / Tom Gallagher. — Manchester : Manchester University Press, c1987. — ix,382p. — *Bibliography: p357-366.* — *Includes index*

IRELAND — Foreign economic relations

REGAN, Colm
75:25, Ireland in an unequal world / by Colm Regan, with Pauline Eccles ... [et al.]. — Dublin, Ireland : Development Education Commission of CONGOOD, c1984. — 208 p.

IRELAND — Foreign relations — Great Britain

Ireland and Britain since 1922 / edited by P.J. Drudy. — Cambridge : Cambridge University Press, 1986. — [200]p. — (Irish studies ; 5). — *Includes index*

Lest we forget : an Irish record of one year, July 1920-July 1921. — London : Vacher, 1921. — 48p

The slaying of John Downes / issued by Sinn Fein Publicity Department. — Dublin : Republican Publications, 1984. — 30p

IRELAND — Handbooks, manuals, etc.
Who owns Ireland, who owns you?. — Dublin : Women in Community Publishing Course in conjunction with Attic, 1985. — 160p. — *Bibliography: p150. — Includes index*

IRELAND — History
Ireland and Irish-Australia : studies in cultural and political history / edited by Oliver MacDonagh and W.F. Mandle. — London : Croom Helm, c1986. — x,293p. — *Includes index*

A New history of Ireland. — Oxford : Clarendon
2: Medieval Ireland 1169-1534 / edited by Art Cosgrove. — 1987. — lxii,982p,[48]p of plates. — *Bibliography: p827-941. — Includes index*

IRELAND — History — 16th century
Natives and newcomers : essays on the making of Irish colonial society, 1534-1641 / Ciaran Brady and Raymond Gillespie, editors. — Dublin : Irish Academic, c1986. — 259p. — *Bibliography: p239-248. — Includes index*

IRELAND — History — 17th century
Natives and newcomers : essays on the making of Irish colonial society, 1534-1641 / Ciaran Brady and Raymond Gillespie, editors. — Dublin : Irish Academic, c1986. — 259p. — *Bibliography: p239-248. — Includes index*

IRELAND — History — 1837-1901
GAILEY, Andrew
Ireland and the death of kindness : the experience of constructive unionism 1890-1905 / Andrew Gailey. — Cork : Cork University Press, 1987. — xiv,345p. — (Studies in Irish history). — *Bibliography: p323-336. — Includes index*

Reactions to Irish nationalism, 1865-1914 / edited by Alan O'Day. — London : Hambledon, 1987. — [400]p. — *Includes index*

IRELAND — History — 1837-1901 — Quotations
Phrases make history here : a century of Irish political quotations, 1886-1986 / [compiled by] Conor O'Clery. — Dublin : O'Brien Press, 1986. — 229p. — *Includes index*

IRELAND — History — 20th century — Quotations
Phrases make history here : a century of Irish political quotations, 1886-1986 / [compiled by] Conor O'Clery. — Dublin : O'Brien Press, 1986. — 229p. — *Includes index*

IRELAND — History — 1901-1910
GAILEY, Andrew
Ireland and the death of kindness : the experience of constructive unionism 1890-1905 / Andrew Gailey. — Cork : Cork University Press, 1987. — xiv,345p. — (Studies in Irish history). — *Bibliography: p323-336. — Includes index*

Reactions to Irish nationalism, 1865-1914 / edited by Alan O'Day. — London : Hambledon, 1987. — [400]p. — *Includes index*

IRELAND — History — 1910-1921
HARTLEY, Stephen
The Irish question as a problem in British foreign policy, 1914-18 / Stephen Hartley. — Basingstoke : Macmillan in association with King's College, London, 1987. — xi,243p. — (Studies in military and strategic history). — *Bibliography: p228-236. — Includes index*

Ireland and the First World War / [a collection of essays compiled by Trinity History Workshop] edited by David Fitzpatrick. — Dublin : Trinity History Workshop, 1986. — x,108p

Reactions to Irish nationalism, 1865-1914 / edited by Alan O'Day. — London : Hambledon, 1987. — [400]p. — *Includes index*

IRELAND — History — 1910-1921 — Bibliography
IMPERIAL WAR MUSEUM. Library
Ireland 1914-1921 : a selected list of references. — [London : the Library, 1966]. — . — (Booklist / Imperial War Museum [Library] ; no.1241)

IMPERIAL WAR MUSEUM. Library
Ireland 1914-1921. — [London : the Library, 1973]. — [1]p. — (Booklist / Imperial War Museum [Library] ; no.1241A)

IRELAND — History — Civil War, 1922-1923
BLAKE, Frances M.
The Irish civil war 1922-1923 and what it still means for the Irish people / by Frances M. Blake. — London : Information on Ireland, 1986. — [72]p

IRELAND — History — 1922-
The years of the great test / edited by Francis MacManus. — Cork : Published in collaboration with Radio Telefís Eireann by the Mercier Press, 1978,c1967. — 183p. — (The Thomas Davis lecture series)

IRELAND — Nobility — History
Marriage in Ireland / edited by Art Cosgrove. — Dublin : College, 1985. — 160p. — *Bibliography: p151-156. — Includes index*

IRELAND — Occupations — Forecasting
HENRY, E. W.
Multisector modelling of the Irish economy : with special reference to employment projections / E. W. Henry. — Dublin : Economic and Social Research Institute, 1986. — 169p. — (Paper / Economic and Social Research Institute ; 128)

IRELAND — Politics and government
IRISH CONFERENCE OF HISTORIANS (16th : 1983 : Maynooth)
Radicals, rebels & establishments : papers read before the Irish Confernce of Historians, Maynooth, 16-19 June 1983 / Ciaran Brady ... [et al.] ; edited by Patrick J. Corish. — Belfast : Appletree, 1985. — 237p. — (Historical studies ; 15)

Irish political review. — Dublin : Irish Political Review, 1986-. — *Monthly. — Continues the Communist and the Irish communist*

Irish political studies: yearbook of the Political Studies Association of Ireland. — Galway : PSAI Press. Social Sciences Research Centre. University College, 1986-. — *Annual*

IRELAND — Politics and government — 1172-1603
Natives and newcomers : essays on the making of Irish colonial society, 1534-1641 / Ciaran Brady and Raymond Gillespie, editors. — Dublin : Irish Academic, c1986. — 259p. — *Bibliography: p239-248. — Includes index*

IRELAND — Politics and government — 19th century
LOUGHLIN, James
Gladstone, Home Rule and the Ulster question 1882-93 / James Loughlin. — Dublin : Gill and Macmillan, c1986. — 369p. — *Bibliography: p333-361. — Includes index*

IRELAND — Politics and government — 1837-1901
Phrases make history here : a century of Irish political quotations, 1886-1986 / [compiled by] Conor O'Clery. — Dublin : O'Brien Press, 1986. — 229p. — *Includes index*

IRELAND — Politics and government — 20th century
LOUGHLIN, James
Gladstone, Home Rule and the Ulster question 1882-93 / James Loughlin. — Dublin : Gill and Macmillan, c1986. — 369p. — *Bibliography: p333-361. — Includes index*

IRELAND — Politics and government — 20th century — Quotations
Phrases make history here : a century of Irish political quotations, 1886-1986 / [compiled by] Conor O'Clery. — Dublin : O'Brien Press, 1986. — 229p. — *Includes index*

IRELAND — Politics and government — 1901-1910
CONNOLLY, James
The words of James Connolly / edited by James Connolly Heron. — Cork : Mercier, 1986. — 136p

IRELAND — Politics and government — 1910-1921
CONNOLLY, James
The words of James Connolly / edited by James Connolly Heron. — Cork : Mercier, 1986. — 136p

IRELAND — Politics and government — 1922-1949
BLAKE, Frances M.
The Irish civil war 1922-1923 and what it still means for the Irish people / by Frances M. Blake. — London : Information on Ireland, 1986. — [72]p

The years of the great test / edited by Francis MacManus. — Cork : Published in collaboration with Radio Telefís Eireann by the Mercier Press, 1978,c1967. — 183p. — (The Thomas Davis lecture series)

IRELAND — Politics and government — 1949-
ADAMS, Gerry
The politics of Irish freedom / Gerry Adams. — Dingle : Brandon, 1986. — [192]p

BARRY, Ursula
Lifting the lid : handbook of facts and information on Ireland / Ursula Barry. — Dublin : Attic Press, 1986. — 144p. — *Bibliographies*

Ireland in the contemporary world : essays in honour of Garret FitzGerald / edited by James Dooge. — Dublin : Gill and Macmillan, 1986. — [viii],160p

O'BYRNES, Stephen
Hiding behind a face : Fine Gael under Fitzgerald / Stephen O'Byrnes. — Dublin : Gill and Macmillan, 1986. — 330p

Politics and society in contemporary Ireland / [edited by] Brian Girvin, Roland Sturm. — Aldershot : Gower, 1986. — [x,209]p. — *Bibliography: p180-200*

IRELAND — Population — Statistics
IRELAND. Central Statistics Office
Census of population of Ireland 1981. — Dublin : Stationery Office. — *"The statistics herein relate to the population of Ireland exclusive of Northern Ireland"*
Part 1: Usual residence and migrationPart 2: Birthplaces
Volume 9. — 1986. — xxi,199p

IRELAND — Religious life and customs
CONNOLLY, Sean
Religion and society in nineteenth century Ireland / Sean Connolly. — Dundalk : Dundalgan Press, 1985. — 69p. — (Studies in Irish economic and social history ; 3). — *Bibliography: p62-69*

INGLIS, Tom
Moral monopoly : the Catholic Church in modern Irish society / Tom Inglis. — Dublin : Gill and Macmillan, c1987. — 251p. — *Includes index*

IRELAND — Rural conditions
Rural landscapes and communities : essays presented to Desmond McCourt / edited by Colin Thomas. — Blackrock : Irish Academic Press, c1986. — 256p. — *Includes index*

IRELAND — Rural conditions — Congresses

The future of the Irish rural landscape : papers presented at a conference organised by the Dept. of Geography, Trinity College, Dublin and the Irish Planning Institute held at Trinity College, Dublin, 19th March 1985 / edited by F.H.A. Aalen. — Dublin : Trinity College, 1985. — iv,201p

IRELAND — Social conditions

BARRY, Ursula
Lifting the lid : handbook of facts and information on Ireland / Ursula Barry. — Dublin : Attic Press, 1986. — 144p. — *Bibliographies*

GROUSSET, Paschal
Ireland's disease : the English in Ireland 1887 / Paschal Grousset ; with an introduction by Constance Ramillon Conner. — Belfast, Northern Ireland ; Dover, N.H. : Blackstaff Press, 1986. — p. cm. — : *Reprint. Originally published: London ; New York : G. Routledge, 1888.* — *Includes index*

HAUGHEY, Charles
The spirit of the nation : the speeches and statements of Charles J. Haughey (1957-1986) / edited by Martin Mansergh ; photographs collated by Fionnuala O'Kelly. — Cork : Mercier, c1986. — xlii,1216p,[36]p of plates. — *Includes index*

Ireland : a sociological profile / edited by: Patrick Clancy ... [et al.]. — Dublin : Institute of Public Administration in association with The Sociological Association of Ireland, 1986. — viii,434p. — *Includes bibliographies and index*

Ireland in transition / edited by Kieran A. Kennedy. — Cork : Published in collaboration with Radio Telefís Éireann by Mercier, 1986. — 178p. — (The Thomas Davis lecture series). — *Includes bibliographies and index*

Natives and newcomers : essays on the making of Irish colonial society, 1534-1641 / Ciaran Brady and Raymond Gillespie, editors. — Dublin : Irish Academic, c1986. — 259p. — *Bibliography: p239-248.* — *Includes index*

Who owns Ireland, who owns you?. — Dublin : Women in Community Publishing Course in conjunction with Attic, 1985. — 160p. — *Bibliography: p150.* — *Includes index*

IRELAND — Social conditions — Statistics

Statistical information on social welfare services / Department of Social Welfare, Ireland. — Dublin : Stationery Office, 1985-. — *Annual*

IRELAND — Social life and customs — 19th century

GROUSSET, Paschal
Ireland's disease : the English in Ireland 1887 / Paschal Grousset ; with an introduction by Constance Ramillon Conner. — Belfast, Northern Ireland ; Dover, N.H. : Blackstaff Press, 1986. — p. cm. — : *Reprint. Originally published: London ; New York : G. Routledge, 1888.* — *Includes index*

IRELAND — Statistics, Vital

Quarterly report on births, deaths and marriages and on certain infectious diseases / Central Statistics Office, Ireland. — Dublin : Central Statistics Office, 1875-1985. — *Quarterly.* — *Continued by: Quarterly report on vital statistics*

Quarterly report on vital statistics / Ireland Central Statistics Office. — Dublin : Central Statistics Office, 1985-. — *Quarterly.* — *Continues: Quarterly report on births, deaths and marriage and on certain infectious diseases*

IRELAND — Voting registers — Analysis

KEOGH, Gary
A statistical analysis of the Irish electoral register and its use for population estimation and sample surveys / Gary Keogh and Brendan J. Whelan. — Dublin, Ireland : Economic and Social Research Institute, 1986. — 126p. — (Papers / Economic and Social Research Institute ; 130). — *Bibliography: p99-100*

IRELAND. Department of Labour

IRELAND. Department of Labour
Annual report / Department of Labour, Ireland. — Dublin : Stationary Office, 1984-. — *Annual*

IRELAND. Garda Síochána

DOHERTY, Frank
The Stalker affair / Frank Doherty. — Cork : Mercier, c1986. — 90p

IRELAND. Oireachtas. Dail. Committee on Public Expenditure

IRELAND. Oireachtas. Dail. Committee on Public Expenditure
Annual progress report / Committee on Public Expenditure, Ireland. — Dublin : Stationery Office, 1986-. — *Annual*

IRELAND. Select Committee on Statutory Instruments

IRELAND. Select Committee on Statutory Instruments
Report / Select Committee on Statutory Instruments, Ireland. — Dublin : Stationary Office, 1978-. — *Irregular.* — *Text in English and Gaelic*

IRIAN JAYA (INDONESIA) — Politics and government

HARRIS, Stephen V.
Indonesia, Papua New Guinea and Australia : the Irian Jaya Problem of 1984 / Stephen V. Harris and Colin Brown. — Nathan : Centre for the Study of Australian-Asian Relations, Griffith University, 1980. — 83p. — (Australia-Asia papers ; no.29)

IRISH — Attitudes

O'HALLORAN, Clare
Partition and the limits of Irish nationalism : an ideology under stress / Clare O'Halloran. — Dublin : Gill and Macmillan, [c1987]. — xviii,234p. — *Bibliography: p233-240*

IRISH — Australia — History

Australia and Ireland 1788-1988 : bicentenary essays / edited by Colm Kiernan. — Dublin : Gill and Macmillan, c1986. — xviii,309p. — *Includes index*

IRISH — Great Britain — History — Bibliography

HARTIGAN, Maureen
The history of the Irish in Britain : a bibliography / [compiled by Maureen Hartigan]. — London : Irish in Britain History Centre, 1986. — 85p. — *Includes index*

IRISH — Scotland — Strathclyde — History

GALLAGHER, Tom, 1954-
Glasgow : the uneasy peace : religious tension in modern Scotland, 1819-1914 / Tom Gallagher. — Manchester : Manchester University Press, c1987. — ix,382p. — *Bibliography: p357-366.* — *Includes index*

IRISH — United States

CRONIN, Sean
The Transport Workers Union of America : the Irish connection / Sean Cronin. — Dublin : Labour History Workshop, 1984. — 22 leaves

IRISH AMERICANS — History — Addresses, essays, lectures

From Paddy to Studs : Irish-American communities in the turn of the century era, 1880 to 1920 / edited by Timothy J. Meagher. — Westport, Conn. ; London : Greenwood Press, 1986. — xiv, 202 p.. — (Contributions in ethnic studies ; no. 13). — *Includes index.* — *Bibliography: p. [189]-194*

IRISH AMERICANS — Public opinion — History — 19th century

KNOBEL, Dale T.
Paddy and the republic : ethnicity and nationality in antebellum America / by Dale T. Knobel. — 1st ed. — Middletown, Conn. : Wesleyan University Press, Scranton, Pa. : Distributed by Harper & Row c1986. — p. cm. — *Includes index.* — *Bibliography: p*

IRISH AMERICANS — Social conditions — Addresses, essays, lectures

From Paddy to Studs : Irish-American communities in the turn of the century era, 1880 to 1920 / edited by Timothy J. Meagher. — Westport, Conn. ; London : Greenwood Press, 1986. — xiv, 202 p.. — (Contributions in ethnic studies ; no. 13). — *Includes index.* — *Bibliography: p. [189]-194*

IRISH REPUBLICAN ARMY — Biography

RYAN, Meda
Liam Lynch : the real chief / Meda Ryan. — Cork : Mercier, c1986. — 192p. — *Includes index*

IRISH UNIFICATION QUESTION

GAILEY, Andrew
Ireland and the death of kindness : the experience of constructive unionism 1890-1905 / Andrew Gailey. — Cork : Cork University Press, 1987. — xiv,345p. — (Studies in Irish history). — *Bibliography: p323-336.* — *Includes index*

IRISH UNIFICATION QUESTION — Public opinion

O'HALLORAN, Clare
Partition and the limits of Irish nationalism : an ideology under stress / Clare O'Halloran. — Dublin : Gill and Macmillan, [c1987]. — xviii,234p. — *Bibliography: p233-240*

IRON AND STEEL BILL 1980-81

GREAT BRITAIN. Parliament. House of Commons. Library. Research Division
The Iron and Steel Bill / Christopher Barclay. — [London] : the Division, 1981. — 9p. — (Reference sheet ; no.81/11). — *Bibliography: p7-9*

IRON AND STEEL WORKERS — Employment

INTERNATIONAL LABOUR ORGANISATION. Iron and Steel Committee (11th Session : 1986)
Productivity improvement and its effects on the level of employment and working conditions in the iron and steel industry. — Geneva : International Labour Office, 1986. — ii,66p. — *At head of title: Report III, International Labour Organisation, Sectoral Activities Programme.* — *Includes bibliographical references*

IRON AND STEEL WORKERS — Labor productivity

INTERNATIONAL LABOUR ORGANISATION. Iron and Steel Committee (11th Session : 1986)
Productivity improvement and its effects on the level of employment and working conditions in the iron and steel industry. — Geneva : International Labour Office, 1986. — ii,66p. — *At head of title: Report III, International Labour Organisation, Sectoral Activities Programme.* — *Includes bibliographical references*

IRON AND STEEL WORKERS — Great Britain

INDUSTRIAL TRAINING SERVICE
Supervision - now and then : a report of a research study into the role and training of supervisors in the iron and steel industry carried out by Industrial Training Service on behalf of the Iron and Steel Industry Training Board. — [London] ([190 Fleet St., EC4A 2AH]) : [Iron and Steel Industry Training Board], [1980]. — 19p

IRON AND STEELWORKERS — Germany

YANA, Hisashi
Hüttenarbeiter im Dritten Reich : die Betriebsverhältnisse und soziale Lage bei der Guteheffnungshütte Aktienverein und der Fried. Krupp AG 1936 bis 1939 / Hisashi Yana. — Stuttgart : Steiner Verlag Wiesbaden, 1986. — xii,193p. — (Zeitschrift für Unternehmensgeschichte ; Beiheft 34). — Bibliography: p[184]-193

IRON-FOUNDING — Economic aspects

BHAT, B. A.
Choice of technique in iron founding / B.A. Bhat and C.C. Prendergast. — Edinburgh : Scottish Academic Press, 1984. — xiv,110p. — (David Livingstone Institute series on choice of technique in developing countries ; v.8). — Bibliography: p104-105. — Includes index

IRON INDUSTRY AND TRADE

BHAT, B. A.
Choice of technique in iron founding / B.A. Bhat and C.C. Prendergast. — Edinburgh : Scottish Academic Press, 1984. — xiv,110p. — (David Livingstone Institute series on choice of technique in developing countries ; v.8). — Bibliography: p104-105. — Includes index

IRON INDUSTRY AND TRADE — Forecasting

FRANZ, Juergen
Iron ore : global prospects for the industry, 1985-95 / Juergen Franz, Bo Stenberg, and John Strongman. — Washington, D.C. : The World Bank, 1986. — xvi,57p. — (Industry and finance series ; v.12). — Includes bibliographical references

IRON INDUSTRY AND TRADE — Government policy — Europe

MÉNY, Yves
La crise de la sidérurgie européenne 1974-1984 / Yves Mény et Vincent Wright ; avec la collaboration de Patrick A. Messerlin... [et al.]. — [Paris] : Presses universitaires de France, [1985]. — 306p

IRON INDUSTRY AND TRADE — Canada

Metallurgical works in Canada : primary iron and steel = L'activité métallurgique au Canada : fer et acier de première fusion / Energy, Mines and Resources Canada. — Ottawa : Energy, Mines and Resources Canada, 1986-. — Annual. — Text in English and French

IRON INDUSTRY AND TRADE — Finland

ERIKSSON, Gösta A.
Finnish and Swedish iron export to England in the 18th and 19th centuries with an excursus / Gösta A. Eriksson. — °Abo : °Abo Akademis, 1987. — 43p. — (Meddelanden fr°an Ekonomisk-Statsveten skapliga Fakulteten vid °Abo Akademi ; Ser.A.:239). — Bibliography: p42-43

IRON INDUSTRY AND TRADE — France — Lorraine

GENDARME, René
Les coulées du futur : sidérurgie lorraine / René Gendarme. — Nancy : Presses Universitaires de Nancy ; Metz : Editions Serpenoise, 1985. — 314p

IRON INDUSTRY AND TRADE — India

KRISHNA MOORTHY, K.
Engineering change : India's iron and steel / K. Krishna Moorthy. — Indiranagar : Technology Books, 1984. — 434p. — Includes bibliographic notes

IRON INDUSTRY AND TRADE — Spain — Basque provinces — History

GONZÁLEZ PORTILLA, Manuel
La siderurgia vasca (1880-1901) : nuevas tecnologías, empresarios y Política económica / Manuel González Portilla. — Bilbao : Servicio Editorial Universidad del País Vasco, 1985. — 345p

IRON INDUSTRY AND TRADE — Sweden

ERIKSSON, Gösta A.
Finnish and Swedish iron export to England in the 18th and 19th centuries with an excursus / Gösta A. Eriksson. — °Abo : °Abo Akademis, 1987. — 43p. — (Meddelanden fr°an Ekonomisk-Statsveten skapliga Fakulteten vid °Abo Akademi ; Ser.A.:239). — Bibliography: p42-43

IRON INDUSTRY AND TRADE — Wales, South — History — 18th century

ATKINSON, Mick
The growth and decline of the South Wales iron industry 1760-1880 : an industrial history / Michael Atkinson and Colin Baber. — Cardif : University of Wales Press, 1987. — 101p. — At head of title: University of Wales. Board of Celtic Studies. — Includes index

IRON INDUSTRY AND TRADE — Wales, South — History — 19th century

ATKINSON, Mick
The growth and decline of the South Wales iron industry 1760-1880 : an industrial history / Michael Atkinson and Colin Baber. — Cardif : University of Wales Press, 1987. — 101p. — At head of title: University of Wales. Board of Celtic Studies. — Includes index

IROQUOIS INDIANS — Government relations

HAUPTMAN, Laurence M
The Iroquois struggle for survival : World War II to red power / Laurence M. Hauptman. — 1st ed. — Syracuse, N.Y. : Syracuse University Press, 1986. — xiii, 328p. — (An Iroquois book). — Includes index. — Bibliography: p. 285-313

IROQUOIS INDIANS — History

HAUPTMAN, Laurence M
The Iroquois struggle for survival : World War II to red power / Laurence M. Hauptman. — 1st ed. — Syracuse, N.Y. : Syracuse University Press, 1986. — xiii, 328p. — (An Iroquois book). — Includes index. — Bibliography: p. 285-313

IRRELIGION — History

TURNER, James
Without God, without creed : the origins of unbelief in America / James Turner. — Baltimore : Johns Hopkins University Press, c1985. — p. cm. — Includes index. — Bibliography: p

IRRELIGION — United States — History

TURNER, James
Without God, without creed : the origins of unbelief in America / James Turner. — Baltimore : Johns Hopkins University Press, c1985. — p. cm. — Includes index. — Bibliography: p

IRRIGATION — Economic aspects

BOTTRALL, Anthony
Managing large irrigation schemes : a problem of political economy / Anthony Bottrall. — London : Overseas Development Institute,, 1985. — 81p. — (Occasional paper / Overseas Development Institute Agricultural Adminstration Unit ; 5)

IRRIGATION — History — Congresses

Irrigation civilizations : a comparative study : a symposium on method and result in cross-cultural regularities / [by] Julian H. Steward ... [et al.]. — Westport, Conn. : Greenwood Press, [1981]. — v, 78 p.. — : Reprint. Originally published: Washington, D.C. : Social Science Section, Dept. of Cultural Affairs, Pan American Union, 1955. (Social science monographs ; 1). — Includes bibliographies. — Contents: Introduction / by Julian H. Steward -- Developmental stages in ancient Mesopotamia / by Robert M. Adams -- Development of civilization on the coast of Peru / by Donald Collier -- The agricultural bases of urban civilization in Mesoamerica / by Angel Palerm -- Developmental aspects of hydraulic societies / by Karl A. Wittfogel -- Discussion: symposium on irrigation civilizations / by Ralph L. Beals -- Some implications of the symposium / by Julian H. Steward

Irrigation's impact on society / collaborating authors, Robert McC. Adams ... [et al.] ; editors, Theodore E. Downing and McGuire Gibson. — Tucson : University of Arizona Press, 1974. — xi, 181 p.. — (Anthropological papers of the University of Arizona ; no. 25). — Papers from a symposium presented at the 1972 meeting of the Southwestern Anthropological Association, Long Beach, Calif. — Includes bibliographies and index

IRRIGATION — Management

BOTTRALL, Anthony
Managing large irrigation schemes : a problem of political economy / Anthony Bottrall. — London : Overseas Development Institute,, 1985. — 81p. — (Occasional paper / Overseas Development Institute Agricultural Adminstration Unit ; 5)

IRRIGATION — Social aspects — Congresses

Irrigation's impact on society / collaborating authors, Robert McC. Adams ... [et al.] ; editors, Theodore E. Downing and McGuire Gibson. — Tucson : University of Arizona Press, 1974. — xi, 181 p.. — (Anthropological papers of the University of Arizona ; no. 25). — Papers from a symposium presented at the 1972 meeting of the Southwestern Anthropological Association, Long Beach, Calif. — Includes bibliographies and index

IRRIGATION — Philippines — Pampanga River Project — Management

NG, Ronald
Monitoring systems and irrigation management : an experience from the Philippines / Ronald Ng and Francis Lethem. — Washington, D.C. : World Bank, 1983. — xvii,145p. — (Monitoring and evaluation case studies series)

IRRIGATION — Sudan

SØRBØ, Gunnar M.
Tenants and nomads in Eastern Sudan : a study of economic adaptations in the New Halfa Scheme / Gunnar M. Sørbø. — Uppsala : Scandinavian Institute of African Studies, 1985. — 159p

IRRIGATION — Thailand

PLUSQUELLEC, Herve L.
Irrigation design and management : experience in Thailand and its general applicability / Herve L. Plusquellec and Thomas Wickham. — Washington, D.C. : The World Bank, 1985. — x,76p. — (World Bank technical paper ; no.40). — Includes bibliographical references

IRRIGATION ENGINEERING — Thailand

PLUSQUELLEC, Herve L.
Irrigation design and management : experience in Thailand and its general applicability / Herve L. Plusquellec and Thomas Wickham. — Washington, D.C. : The World Bank, 1985. — x,76p. — (World Bank technical paper ; no.40). — Includes bibliographical references

ISHIBASHI, TANZAN
NOLTE, Sharon H
Liberalism in modern Japan : Ishibashi Tanzan and his teachers, 1905-1960 / Sharon H. Nolte. — Berkeley : University of California Press, c1987. — xii, 378 p.. — *Includes index.* — *Bibliography: p. 343-370*

ISKON *See* International Society for Krishna Consciousness

ISKRA
SHARAPOV, Ia. Sh.
Iz iskry-plamia : (V. I. Lenin i kazanskie bol'sheviki / Ia. Sh. Sharapov. — Kazan' : Tatarskoe knizhnoe izd-vo, 1985. — 255p. — (Leniniana Sovetskoi Tatarii ; T.2)

ISLAM
AYOUB, Mahmoud M.
Islam and the Third Universal Theory : the religious thought of Mu'ammar al-Qadhdhafi / Mahmoud M. Ayoub. — London : KPI, 1987. — 155p. — *Bibliography: p148-150*

BARBULESCO, Luc
L'Islam en questions : vingt-quatre écrivains arabes répondent / Luc Barbulesco et Philippe Cardinal. — Paris : Bernard Grasset, [1986]. — 280p

NIEUWENHUIJZE, C. A. O. van
The lifestyles of Islam : recourse to classicism, need of realism / by C. A. O. van Nieuwenhuijze. — Leiden : E. J. Brill, 1985. — 255p. — (Social, economic and political studies of the Middle East ; Vol.37)

ROY, Manabendra Nath
The historical role of Islam / M. N. Roy. — Delhi : Ajanta Books, 1939. — 91p

RUTHVEN, Malise
Islam in the world / Malise Ruthven. — Harmondsworth : Penguin, 1984. — 400p. — (A Pelican book). — *Bibliography: p.[376]-378.* — *Includes index*

ISLAM — Biography
SULAIMAN, Ibraheem
A revolution in history : the jihad of Usman Dan Fodio / Ibraheem Sulaiman ; with a foreword by Shehu Usman M. Bugaje. — London : Mansell, 1986. — [208]p. — (East-West University Islamic studies)

ISLAM — Congresses
COLLOQUE FRANCO-PAKISTANAIS (4e : 1984 : Paris)
L'Islam dans les relations internationales : actes du IVe Colloque franco-pakistanais, Paris, 14-15 mai 1984. — [Aix-en-Provence] : Édisud, 1986. — 181p. — *Contributions in English and French*

ISLAM — History
CRONE, Patricia
Meccan trade and the rise of Islam / Patricia Crone. — Princeton, N.J. : Princeton University Press, c1986. — vii, 300p. — *Includes index.* — *Bibliography: p.271-291*

ISLAM — Political aspects
PISCATORI, James P.
Islam in a world of nation-states / James P. Piscatori. — Cambridge : Cambridge University Press in association with the Royal Institute of International Affairs, 1986. — viii,193p. — *Includes index*

ISLAM — 20th century
DEKMEJIAN, R. Hrair
Islam in revolution : fundamentalism in the Arab world / R. Hrair Dekmejian. — 1st ed. — Syracuse, N.Y. : Syracuse University Press, 1985. — p. cm. — *Includes index.* — *Bibliography: p*

Revolt against modernity : Muslim zealots and the West / Michael Youssef. — Leiden : Brill, 1985. — 189p. — (Social, economic and political studies of the Middle East ; v. 39). — *Bibliography: p182-184*

YOUSSEF, Michael
Revolt against modernity : Muslim zealots and the West / Michael Youssef. — Leiden : Brill, 1985. — 189p. — (Social, economic and political studies of the Middle East ; v.39). — *Bibliography: p182-184*

ISLAM — Arab countries — History
DEKMEJIAN, R. Hrair
Islam in revolution : fundamentalism in the Arab world / R. Hrair Dekmejian. — 1st ed. — Syracuse, N.Y. : Syracuse University Press, 1985. — p. cm. — *Includes index.* — *Bibliography: p*

ISLAM — Indonesia
TAMARA, M. Nasir
Indonesia in the wake of Islam : 1965-1985 / M. Nasir Tamara. — Kuala Lumpur : Institute of Strategic and International Studies, 1986. — 35p

ISLAM — Senegal
MAGASSOUBA, Moriba
L'Islam au Sénégal : demain les mollahs? : la "question" musulmane et les partis politiques au Sénégal de 1946 à nos jours. — Paris : Editions Karthala, 1985. — 219p

ISLAM AND POLITICS
Islam and the political economy of meaning : comparative studies of Muslim discourse / edited by William R. Roff. — London : Croom Helm, c1987. — 295p. — *Includes bibliographies and index*

Radicalismes Islamiques / publié sous la direction de Olivier Carré et Paul Dumont. — Paris : Editions L'Harmattan. — *Includes bibliographic notes*
v.1: Iran, Liban,Turquie. — 1985. — 256p

Radicalismes Islamiques / publié sous la direction de Olivier Carré et Paul Dumont. — Paris : Editions L'Harmattan. — *Includes bibliographies*
v.2: Maroc, Pakistan, Inde, Yougoslavie, Mali. — 1986. — 181p

ISLAM AND POLITICS — Afghanistan
ROY, Oliver
Islam and resistance in Afghanistan / Olivier Roy. — Cambridge : Cambridge University Press, c1986. — vi,253p. — (Cambridge Middle East library). — *Translation of: L'Afghanistan.* — *Bibliography: p243-249.* — *Includes index*

ISLAM AND POLITICS — Libya
WORLD ISLAMIC CALL SOCIETY
God is great. — Rome : World Islamic Call Society, 1986. — [36p]

ISLAM AND POLITICS — Near East
The Islamic impulse / edited by Barbara Freyer Stowasser. — London : Croom Helm in association with Center for Contemporary Arab Studies, Georgetown University, c1987. — 329p. — *Conference proceedings.* — *Includes index*

Shi'ism, resistance and revolution / edited by Martin Kramer. — London : Mansell, 1987. — [352]p. — *Conference proceedings.* — *Includes index*

TAHERI, Amir
Holy terror : The inside story of Islamic terrorism / Amir Taheri. — London : Hutchinson, 1987. — 313p. — *Spine title: Holy terror: Islamic terrorism and the West.* — *Bibliography: p[295]-301*

ISLAM AND POLITICS — Pakistan
AHMED, Ishtiaq
The concept of an Islamic state : an analysis of the ideological controversy in Pakistan / Ishtiaq Ahmed. — Stockholm : University of Stockholm, 1985. — vii, 255p. — (Stockholm studies in politics ; 28). — *Doctoral dissertation - University of Stockholm, 1985.* — *Bibliography: p.249-255*

ISLAM AND POLITICS — Turkey
TOPRAK, Binnaz
Islam and political development in Turkey / by Binnaz Toprak. — Leiden : Brill, 1981. — 164 p. — (Social, economic and political studies of the Middle East ; v. 32)

ISLAM AND SOCIAL PROBLEMS
The black book : the true political philosophy of Malcolm X (El Hajj Malik el Shabazz / edited and compiled by Y. N. Kly. — Ottawa ; Atlanta : Clarity Press, 1986. — viii,91p. — *Bibliography: p89-91*

ISLAM AND STATE
CHARNAY, Jean Paul
L'Islam et la guerre : de la guerre juste à la révolution sainte / Jean Paul Charnay. — Paris : Fayard, 1986. — 354p. — *Bibliography: p [341]-342*

ISLAM AND STATE — Afghanistan — Congresses
The State, religion, and ethnic politics : Afghanistan, Iran, and Pakistan / edited by Ali Banuazizi and Myron Weiner. — 1st ed. — [Syracuse, N.Y.] : Syracuse University Press, 1986. — xi, 390 p.. — (Contemporary issues in the Middle East). — *"Sponsored by the Joint Committee on the Near and Middle East and the Committee on South Asia of the American Council of Learned Societies and the Social Science Research Council.".* — *Includes bibliographies and index*

ISLAM AND STATE — Iran — Congresses
The State, religion, and ethnic politics : Afghanistan, Iran, and Pakistan / edited by Ali Banuazizi and Myron Weiner. — 1st ed. — [Syracuse, N.Y.] : Syracuse University Press, 1986. — xi, 390 p.. — (Contemporary issues in the Middle East). — *"Sponsored by the Joint Committee on the Near and Middle East and the Committee on South Asia of the American Council of Learned Societies and the Social Science Research Council.".* — *Includes bibliographies and index*

ISLAM AND STATE — Pakistan
AHMED, Ishtiaq
The concept of an Islamic state : an analysis of the ideological controversy in Pakistan / Ishtiaq Ahmed. — Stockholm : University of Stockholm, 1985. — vii, 255p. — (Stockholm studies in politics ; 28). — *Doctoral dissertation - University of Stockholm, 1985.* — *Bibliography: p.249-255*

ISLAM AND STATE — Pakistan — Congresses
The State, religion, and ethnic politics : Afghanistan, Iran, and Pakistan / edited by Ali Banuazizi and Myron Weiner. — 1st ed. — [Syracuse, N.Y.] : Syracuse University Press, 1986. — xi, 390 p.. — (Contemporary issues in the Middle East). — *"Sponsored by the Joint Committee on the Near and Middle East and the Committee on South Asia of the American Council of Learned Societies and the Social Science Research Council.".* — *Includes bibliographies and index*

ISLAM AND WORLD POLITICS
PISCATORI, James P
International relations of the Asian Muslim states / by James Piscatori. — Lanham [Md.] : University Press of America ; New York : The Asia Society, c1986. — ix, 41 p.. — *Bibliography: p. 39*

ISLAMIC COUNTRIES — Economic integration
MOINUDDIN, Hasan
The Charter of the Islamic Conference and legal framework of economic co-operation among its member states : a study of the charter, the General Agreement for Economic, Technical and Commercial Co-operation and the Agreement for Promotion, Protection and Guarantee of Investments among Member States of the OIC / Hasan Moinuddin. — Oxford : Clarendon, 1987. — xx,322p. — *Bibliography: p297-313.* — *Includes index*

ISLAMIC COUNTRIES — Foreign relations — Congresses
COLLOQUE FRANCO-PAKISTANAIS (4e : 1984 : Paris)
L'Islam dans les relations internationales : actes du IVe Colloque franco-pakistanais, Paris, 14-15 mai 1984. — [Aix-en-Provence] : Édisud, 1986. — 181p. — *Contributions in English and French*

ISLAMIC COUNTRIES — Relations
PISCATORI, James P
International relations of the Asian Muslim states / by James Piscatori. — Lanham [Md.] : University Press of America ; New York : The Asia Society, c1986. — ix, 41 p.. — *Bibliography: p. 39*

ISLAMIC COUNTRIES
ROY, Manabendra Nath
The historical role of Islam / M. N. Roy. — Delhi : Ajanta Books, 1939. — 91p

ISLAMIC COUNTRIES — History
Issues in the Islamic movement, 1983-84 (1403-04) / edited by Kalim Siddidqui. — London : Open Press, 1985. — 417 p

ISLAMIC LAW
MOINUDDIN, Hasan
The Charter of the Islamic Conference and legal framework of economic co-operation among its member states : a study of the charter, the General Agreement for Economic, Technical and Commercial Co-operation and the Agreement for Promotion, Protection and Guarantee of Investments among Member States of the OIC / Hasan Moinuddin. — Oxford : Clarendon, 1987. — xx,322p. — *Bibliography: p297-313. — Includes index*

ISLAMIC LAW — History
A'ZAMĪ, Muḥammad Muṣṭafá
On Schacht's Origins of Muhammadan jurisprudence / M. Mustafa Al-Azami. — New York : Wiley, c1986. — p. cm. — *Includes index. — Bibliography: p*

ISLAMIC LAW — Social aspects
AL-DIN AL-MUNADJDJID, Salah
Le concept de justice sociale en Islam, ou la société islamique à l'ombre de la justice / Salah al-Din al-Munadjdjid ; traduit de l'arabe et annoté par Mohammed Hadj Sadok. — Paris : Publisud, c1982. — 143p. — *Publié originellement en Beyrouth, 1969, sous le titre: "Dar al-kitab al-Djadid"*

ISLANDS — Scotland — Rural conditions
ALEXANDER, K. J. W.
Rural renewal : experience in the Highlands and Islands / Sir Kenneth Alexander. — Cambridge : University of Cambridge, Department of Land Economy, 1984. — 26p. — (The Denman lecture ; 1984)

ISLINGTON (LONDON, ENGLAND) — Economic conditions
ISLINGTON. Council
Putting Islington back to work : a major job creation initiative by Islington Council. — Islington : [the Council], 1987. — 32p

ISLINGTON (LONDON, ENGLAND) — Economic policy
ISLINGTON. Council
Making the most of your abilities : a training plan for Islington. — Islington : [the Council], 1987. — 69p

ISRAEL
Israel / Middle East Research Institute, University of Pennsylvania. — London : Croom Helm, c1985. — 180p. — (MERI report)

ISRAEL — Armed forces — History
SCHIFF, Zeév
A history of the Israeli army : 1874 to present / Zeév Schiff. — London : Sidgwick & Jackson, 1987. — viii,274p

ISRAEL — Census, 1983
Demographic characteristics of households. — Jerusalem : Central Bureau of Statistics. — (1983 Census of Population and Housing Publications ; No.8). — *In English and Hebrew*
Data from the complete enumeration. — 1986. — xli,251p

Demographic characteristics of the population. — Jerusalem : Central Bureau of Statistics. — (1983 Census of Population and Housing Publications ; No.7). — *In English and Hebrew*
National data from the complete enumeration. — 1985. — xxxiv,175p

The geographical-statistical division of urban localities in Israel : 1983. — Jerusalem : Central Bureau of Statistics, 1985. — 1v. (various pagings). — 71maps. — (1983 Census of Population and Housing Publications ; No.2) . — *In English and Hebrew*

Housing conditions and possession of household equipment. — Jerusalem : Central Bureau of Statistics. — (1983 Census of Population and Housing Publications ; No.9). — *In English and Hebrew*
Data from the sample enumeration. — 1986. — lxix,133p

List of localities. — Jerusalem : Central Bureau of Statistics. — (1983 Census of Population and Housing Publications ; No.6). — *In English and Hebrew*
Geographical information and population : 1948; 1961; 1972; 1983. — 1985. — xxiii,211p

Localities. — Jerusalem : Central Bureau of Statistics. — *In Enlish and Hebrew*
Population and households
Demographic characteristics from the complete enumeration, by locality. — 1984. — xxiii,561p. — (1983 Census of Population and Housing Publications ; No.3)

Localities (2,000 inhabitants and more) and statistical areas. — Jerusalem : Central Bureau of Statistics. — *In English and Hebrew*
Population and households
Socio-economic characteristics from the sample enumeration. — 1985. — lxi,553p. — (1983 Census of Population and Housing Publications ; No.5)

Localities and statistical areas. — Jerusalem : Central Bureau of Statistics. — *In English and Hebrew*
Population and households
Demographic characteristics from the complete enumeration, by statistical area. — 1985. — xliii,677p. — (1983 Census of Population and Housing Publications ; No.4)

Population and households : provisional results. — Jerusalem : Central Bureau of Statistics, 1983. — xxxix,91p. — (1983 census of population and housing publications ; no.1). — *In Hebrew and English*

ISRAEL — Defenses
SHALEV, Ariyeh
[Ḳav haganah bi-Yehudah uva-Shomron. English]. The West Bank : line of defense / by Aryeh Shalev ; with a historical supplement by Mordechai Gichon. — New York : Praeger, 1985. — p. cm. — *"A JCSS book.". — Translation of: Ḳay haganah bi-Yehudah uva-Shomron. — Includes index. — Bibliography: p*

Study on Israeli nuclear armament. — New York : United Nations, 1982. — vii,22p. — (Disarmament. study series ; 6) ([Document] / United Nations ; A/36/431). — *Includes bibliographical references. — Sales no.: E.82.IX.2*

ISRAEL — Economic conditions
SUSSMAN, Zvi
Israel's economy : performance, problems and policies / Zvi Sussman. — London : Institute of Jewish Affairs ; Tel Aviv : Jacob Levinson Center of the Israel-Diaspora Institute, 1986. — xii,21p

ZAKAI, Dan
Economic development in Judea-Samaria and the Gaza District 1981-82 / Dan Zakai. — Jerusalem : Bank of Israel. Research Department, 1985. — 69p. — *Bibliography: p69*

ISRAEL — Economic policy
SHARKANSKY, Ira
The political economy of Israel / Ira Sharkansky. — New Brunswick, N.J., U.S.A. : Transaction Books, c1987. — p. cm. — *Includes index*

SUSSMAN, Zvi
Israel's economy : performance, problems and policies / Zvi Sussman. — London : Institute of Jewish Affairs ; Tel Aviv : Jacob Levinson Center of the Israel-Diaspora Institute, 1986. — xii,21p

ISRAEL — Foreign opinion, American
GILBOA, Eytan
American public opinion toward Israel and the Arab-Israeli conflict / Eytan Gilboa. — Lexington, Mass. : Lexington Books, c1987. — xvi, 366 p.. — *Includes index. — Bibliography: p. [337]-347*

ISRAEL — Foreign relations
AL-ABID, Ibrahim
Militarisme, racisme et expansionnisme : trois aspects fondamentaux de l'état israélien / Ibrahim Al-Abid. — Beyrouth : Organisation de Libération Palestinienne. Centre de Recherches, 1970. — 62p. — (Essais sur la Palestine ; no.16)

Israel, the Middle East and the great powers : studies in the contemporary history and politics of the Middle East and the Arab-Israel conflict / edited by Israel Stockman-Shomron. — [Jerusalem] : Shikmona Publishing Co., 1984. — 389p

SEMENIUK, V. A.
Sovremennyi sionizm : kursom politicheskikh i voennykh avantiur / V. A. Semeniuk. — Minsk : Belarus', 1986. — 236p

ISRAEL — Foreign relations — Addresses, essays, lectures
HERZOG, Yaacov
A people that dwells alone : speeches and writings of Yaacov Herzog / edited by Misha Louvish. — London : Weidenfeld and Nicolson, 1975. — 283p. — *Includes index*

ISRAEL — Foreign relations — Germany (West)
FELDMAN, Lily Gardner
The special relationship between West Germany and Israel / Lily Gardner Feldman. — Boston ; London : Allen & Unwin, 1984. — xix,330p. — *Bibliography: p295-322. — Includes index*

ISRAEL — Foreign relations — Great Britain
HARON, Miriam Joyce
Palestine and the Anglo-American connection, 1945-1950 / Miriam Joyce Haron. — New York : P. Lang, c1986. — 209 p.. — (American university studies. Series IX. History ; vol. 17). — *Includes index. — Bibliography: p. [197]-201*

ISRAEL — Foreign relations — United States
Dynamics of dependence : U.S.-Israeli relations / edited by Gabriel Sheffer. — Boulder, Colo. : Westview Press, 1987. — x, 210 p. — (Studies in international politics). — *Includes bibliographies and index*

HARON, Miriam Joyce
Palestine and the Anglo-American connection, 1945-1950 / Miriam Joyce Haron. — New York : P. Lang, c1986. — 209 p.. — (American university studies. Series IX. History ; vol. 17). — *Includes index. — Bibliography: p. [197]-201*

ISRAEL — Foreign relations — United States *continuation*

ROSE, John
Israel : the hijack state : America's watchdog in the Middle East / John Rose. — London : Bookmarks, 1986. — 78p

ISRAEL — History, Military

SCHIFF, Zeév
A history of the Israeli army : 1874 to present / Zeév Schiff. — London : Sidgwick & Jackson, 1987. — viii,274p

YANIV, A
Deterrence without the bomb : the politics of Israeli strategy / Avner Yaniv. — Lexington, Mass. : Lexington Books, 1986, c1987. — x, 324p. — *Includes index.* — *Bibliography: p.[304]-313*

ISRAEL — Military policy

AL-ABID, Ibrahim
Militarisme, racisme et expansionnisme : trois aspects fondamentaux de l'état israélien / Ibrahim Al-Abid. — Beyrouth : Organisation de Libération Palestinienne. Centre de Recherches, 1970. — 62p. — (Essais sur la Palestine ; no.16)

Study on Israeli nuclear armament. — New York : United Nations, 1982. — vii,22p. — (Disarmament. study series ; 6) ([Document] / United Nations ; A/36/431). — *Includes bibliographical references.* — Sales no.: E.82.IX.2

YANIV, A
Deterrence without the bomb : the politics of Israeli strategy / Avner Yaniv. — Lexington, Mass. : Lexington Books, 1986, c1987. — x, 324p. — *Includes index.* — *Bibliography: p.[304]-313*

ISRAEL — Military relations — United States

HALSELL, Grace
Prophecy and politics : militant evangelists on the road to nuclear war / Grace Halsell. — Westport, Conn. : Lawrence Hill & Co., c1986. — 210 p.. — *Includes index*

ISRAEL — Politics and government

AL-ABID, Ibrahim
Militarisme, racisme et expansionnisme : trois aspects fondamentaux de l'état israélien / Ibrahim Al-Abid. — Beyrouth : Organisation de Libération Palestinienne. Centre de Recherches, 1970. — 62p. — (Essais sur la Palestine ; no.16)

ARIAN, Alan
Politics in Israel : the second generation / Asher Arian. — Chatham, N.J. : Chatham House, c1985. — p. cm. — *Includes index.* — *Bibliography: p*

Israel faces the future / edited by Bernard Reich and Gershon R. Kieval. — New York : Praeger, 1986. — viii, 229 p.. — "Derived from a conference held in Washington, D.C., in January 1985"--P. viii. — *Includes index.* — *Bibliography: p. 207-211*

JANSEN, Michael
Dissonance in Zion / Michael Jansen. — London : Zed, 1987. — xvi,140p. — *Includes index*

MERGUI, Raphael
Israel's ayatollahs : Meir Kahane and the far right in Israel / Raphael Mergui & Philippe Simonnot. — London : Saqi, 1987. — [176]p. — Translation of: Meir Kahane: le Rabbin qui fait peur aux Juifs. — *Includes index*

SAGER, Samuel
The parliamentary system of Israel / Samuel Sager ; with a foreword by Abba Eban. — Syracuse, N.Y. : Syracuse University Press, 1985. — p. cm. — *Bibliography: p237-243.* — *Bibliography: p*

ISRAEL — Politics and government — Addresses, essays, lectures

Cross-currents in Israeli culture and politics / edited by Myron J. Aronoff. — New Brunswick, N.J. : Transaction Books, c1984. — 115 p.. — (Political anthropology ; v. 4). — *Includes bibliographies and index*

ISRAEL — Politics and government — 1948-

COHEN, Mitchell
Zion and state : nation, class and the shaping of modern Israel / Mitchell Cohen. — Oxford : Basil Blackwell, 1987. — [288]p. — *Includes bibliography and index*

ISRAEL — Population — Statistics

Demographic characteristics of households. — Jerusalem : Central Bureau of Statistics. — (1983 Census of Population and Housing Publications ; No.8). — *In English and Hebrew*
Data from the complete enumeration. — 1986. — xli,251p

Demographic characteristics of the population. — Jerusalem : Central Bureau of Statistics. — (1983 Census of Population and Housing Publications ; No.7). — *In English and Hebrew*
National data from the complete enumeration. — 1985. — xxxiv,175p

The geographical-statistical division of urban localities in Israel : 1983. — Jerusalem : Central Bureau of Statistics, 1985. — 1v. (various pagings). — 71maps. — (1983 Census of Population and Housing Publications ; No.2). — *In English and Hebrew*

Housing conditions and possession of household equipment. — Jerusalem : Central Bureau of Statistics. — (1983 Census of Population and Housing Publications ; No.9). — *In English and Hebrew*
Data from the sample enumeration. — 1986. — lxix,133p

List of localities. — Jerusalem : Central Bureau of Statistics. — (1983 Census of Population and Housing Publications ; No.6). — *In English and Hebrew*
Geographical information and population : 1948; 1961; 1972; 1983. — 1985. — xxiii,211p

Localities. — Jerusalem : Central Bureau of Statistics. — *In Enlish and Hebrew*
Population and households
Demographic characteristics from the complete enumeration, by locality. — 1984. — xxiii,561p. — *(1983 Census of Population and Housing Publications ; No.3)*

Localities (2,000 inhabitants and more) and statistical areas. — Jerusalem : Central Bureau of Statistics. — *In English and Hebrew*
Population and households
Socio-economic characteristics from the sample enumeration. — 1985. — lxi,553p. — *(1983 Census of Population and Housing Publications ; No.5)*

Localities and statistical areas. — Jerusalem : Central Bureau of Statistics. — *In English and Hebrew*
Population and households
Demographic characteristics from the complete enumeration, by statistical area. — 1985. — xliii,677p. — *(1983 Census of Population and Housing Publications ; No.4)*

Population and households : provisional results. — Jerusalem : Central Bureau of Statistics, 1983. — xxxix,91p. — (1983 census of population and housing publications ; no.1). — *In Hebrew and English*

ISRAEL — Presidents — Biography

ROSE, Norman
Chaim Weizmann : a biography / Norman Rose. — London : Weidenfeld and Nicolson, 1986. — xiv,520p. — *Bibliography: p.463-470*

ISRAEL — Social conditions — Statistics

BERMAN, Yitzchak
Social profile of cities and towns in Israel / Yitzchak Berman. — [Jerusalem] : Ministry of Labour and Social Affairs, 1978. — xix,142p. — *In English and Hebrew*

BERMAN, Yitzchak
Social profile of cities and towns in Israel. — [Jerusalem] : Ministry of Social Welfare. — *In Hebrew and English*
Pt.2 / Yitzchak Berman. — 1977. — xviii,162p

ISRAEL — Statistics, Vital

Mortality of adult jews in Israel 1950-1967 / E. Peritz, F. Dreyfuss, H. S. Halevi, U. O. Schmelz. — Jerusalem : Central Bureau of Statistics, 1973. — 226p. — (Special Series / Israel. Central Bureau of Statistics ; No.409)

ISRAEL — Yearbooks

Government yearbook / Central Office of Information, Israel. — Jerusalem : Central Office of Information, 1950-. — *Annual*

ISRAEL. Keneset

SAGER, Samuel
The parliamentary system of Israel / Samuel Sager ; with a foreword by Abba Eban. — Syracuse, N.Y. : Syracuse University Press, 1985. — p. cm. — *Bibliography: p237-243.* — *Bibliography: p*

ISRAEL. Keneset — Elections, 1981 — Addresses, essays, lectures

Israel at the polls, 1981 : a study of the Knesset elections / edited by Howard R. Penniman and Daniel J. Elazar. — Washington : American Enterprise Institute for Public Policy Research ; Bloomington : Indiana University Press, c1986. — xiii, 280 p.. — (Jewish political and social studies). — *Includes bibliographies and index*

ISRAEL. National Insurance Institute

ISRAEL. National Insurance Institute
Annual survey / National Insurance Institute, Israel. — Jerusalem : National Insurance Institute. Bureau of Research and Planning, 1983-. — *Annual*

ISRAEL AND THE DIASPORA — Addresses, essays, lectures

HERZOG, Yaacov
A people that dwells alone : speeches and writings of Yaacov Herzog / edited by Misha Louvish. — London : Weidenfeld and Nicolson, 1975. — 283p. — *Includes index*

ISRAEL-ARAB BORDER CONFLICTS — 1949-

Israel, the Middle East and the great powers : studies in the contemporary history and politics of the Middle East and the Arab-Israel conflict / edited by Israel Stockman-Shomron. — [Jerusalem] : Shikmona Publishing Co., 1984. — 389p

ISRAEL-ARAB BORDER CONFLICTS, 1949-

GAINSBOROUGH, J. R.
The Arab-Israeli conflict : a politico-legal analysis / J.R. Gainsborough. — Aldershot : Gower, c1986 (1987 [printing]). — xxxv,345p. — *Bibliography: p319-334.* — *Includes index*

GREAT BRITAIN. Parliament. House of Commons. Library. International Affairs Section
Middle East peace plans and negotiations / Richard Ware. — [London] : the Library, 1983. — 17p. — (Background paper / House of Commons. Library. [Research Division] ; no.121). — *Bibliography: p13*

KARSH, Efraim
The cautious bear : Soviet military engagement in Middle East wars in the post-1967 era / Ephraim [i.e. Efraim] Karsh. — Jerusalem, Israel : Published for the Jaffee Center for Strategic Studies by the Jerusalem Post ; Boulder, Colo. : Westview Press, c1985. — 97 p.. — (JCSS study ; no. 3). — *Bibliography: p. 91-97*

ISRAEL-ARAB BORDER CONFLICTS, 1949- — Lebanon
GREAT BRITAIN. Parliament. House of Commons. Library. International Affairs Section
The Lebanon / Richard Ware. — [London] : the Library, 1983. — 15p. — (Background paper / House of Commons. Library. [Research Division] ; no.127). — *Bibliography: p14*

ISRAEL-ARAB WAR, 1948-1949
GAINSBOROUGH, J. R.
The Arab-Israeli conflict : a politico-legal analysis / J.R. Gainsborough. — Aldershot : Gower, c1986 (1987 [printing]). — xxxv,345p. — *Bibliography: p319-334. — Includes index*

ISRAEL-ARAB WAR, 1967 — Diplomatic history
EL-FARRA, Muhammad
Years of no decision / Muhammad El-Farra. — London : KPI, 1987. — xi,222p

ISRAEL-ARAB WAR, 1967 — Occupied territories
SHEHADEH, Raja
Occupier's law : a study of Israeli practices in the West Bank and Gaza / by Raja Shehadeh. — Washington, DC : Institute for Palestine Studies, 1985. — p. cm. — *Bibliography: p*

ISRAELIS — Psychology
ELON, Amos
The Israelis : founders and sons / Amos Elon. — New York : Penguin, 1983. — xiv, 359 p.. — : *Previously published: New York : Holt, Rinehart, and Winston, 1971. — Includes index. — Bibliography: p. 336-348*

ITALIAN AMERICAN WOMEN — Folklore
MATHIAS, Elizabeth
Italian folktales in America : the verbal art of an immigrant woman / Elizabeth Mathias and Richard Raspa ; foreword by Roger D. Abrahams. — Detroit : Wayne State University Press, 1985. — p. cm. — (Wayne State University Folklore Archive study series). — *Includes 22 tales as told by Clementina Todesco. — Includes indexes. — Bibliography: p*

ITALIAN AMERICAN WOMEN — New York (N.Y.) — History
EWEN, Elizabeth
Immigrant women in the land of dollars : life and culture on the Lower East Side, 1890-1925 / Elizabeth Ewen. — New York : Monthly Review Press, 1985. — p. cm. — (New feminist library)

ITALIAN AMERICANS — Folklore
MATHIAS, Elizabeth
Italian folktales in America : the verbal art of an immigrant woman / Elizabeth Mathias and Richard Raspa ; foreword by Roger D. Abrahams. — Detroit : Wayne State University Press, 1985. — p. cm. — (Wayne State University Folklore Archive study series). — *Includes 22 tales as told by Clementina Todesco. — Includes indexes. — Bibliography: p*

ITALIAN AMERICANS — New Jersey — History
STARR, Dennis J.
The Italians of New Jersey : a historical introduction and bibliography / Dennis J. Starr. — Newark : New Jersey Historical Society, 1985. — ii,130p

ITALIAN AMERICANS — New Jersey — History — Bibliography
STARR, Dennis J.
The Italians of New Jersey : a historical introduction and bibliography / Dennis J. Starr. — Newark : New Jersey Historical Society, 1985. — ii,130p

ITALIANS — Foreign countries — Bibliography
BRIANI, Vittorio
Italian immigrants abroad : a bibliography on the Italian experience outside Italy in Europe, the Americas, Australia, and Africa = Emigrazione e lavoro italiano all'estero : repertorio bibliografico / by Vittorio Briani ; edited and with a new introd. and supplemental bibliography by Francesco Cordasco. — Detroit : B. Ethridge Books, c1979. — xlix, 229 p.. — *Edition of 1967 published under title: Emigrazione e lavoro italiano all'estero. — Includes indexes*

ITALIANS — Argentina — History — 19th century
La inmigración Italiana en la Argentina / Fernando Devoto, Gianfausto Rosoli (compiladores). — Buenos Aires : Editorial Biblos, 1985. — 270p

ITALIANS — Switzerland
FEDERAZIONE COLONIE LIBERE ITALIANE IN SVIZZERA
"Passaporti, prego!" : ricordi e testimonianze di emigrati italiani / Federazione colonie libere italiane in Svizzera ; [Tullio Agelli...et al.]. — Zurigo : Federazione colonie libere italiane in Svizzera, 1985. — 210p

ITALIANS IN FOREIGN COUNTRIES
FEDERAZIONE COLONIE LIBERE ITALIANE IN SVIZZERA
"Passaporti, prego!" : ricordi e testimonianze di emigrati italiani / Federazione colonie libere italiane in Svizzera ; [Tullio Agelli...et al.]. — Zurigo : Federazione colonie libere italiane in Svizzera, 1985. — 210p

ITALY — Census, 1981
12 censimento generale della popolazione 25 ottobre 1981. — Roma : Istituto Centrale di Statistica
vol.2: Dati sulle caratteristiche strutturali della popolazione e della abitazioni
t.2: fascicoli regionali. — 1983-1984. — 20v

12 censimento generale della popolazione 25 ottobre 1981. — Roma : Istituto Centrale di Statistica. — 1984-
vol.3: Popolazione delle frazioni geografiche e delle località abitate dei comuni
Fascicoli regionali. — 20v

12 censimento generale della popolazione 25 ottobre 1981. — Roma : Istituto Centrale di Statistica. — 1983
Dati sulle caratteristiche strutturali della popolazione e delle abitazioni
Campione al 2% dei fogli di famiglia : dati provvisori. — 119p

12 censimento generale della popolazione 25 ottobre 1981. — Roma : Istituto Centrale di Statistica
Popolazione legale dei comuni. — 1983. — 225p

ITALY — Civilization — 1559-1789
BURKE, Peter
The historical anthropology of early modern Italy : essays on perception and communication / Peter Burke. — Cambridge : Cambridge University Press, 1987. — [304]p. — *Includes bibliography and index*

ITALY — Economic conditions
Contributi alla ricerca economica: servizio studi della Banca d'Italia. — Roma : Banca d'Italia, 1972-1976. — *Annual*

Contributi all'analisi economica del Servizio Studi / Banca d'Italia. — [Rome] : Banca d'Italia, 1985

WOOLF, S. J
A history of Italy, 1700-1860 : the social constraints of political change / Stuart Woolf. — New York : Methuen, 1986, c1979. — p. cm. — *Includes index. — Bibliography: p*

ITALY — Economic conditions — 1870-1918
JONES, Simon Mark
Domestic factors in Italian intervention in the First World War / Simon Mark Jones. — New York : Garland, 1986. — 292 p. — (Outstanding theses from the London School of Economics and Political Science). — *Thesis (Ph.D.)--London School of Economics and Political Science. — Bibliography: p. 275-292*

ITALY — Economic conditions — 1945-
Industrializzazione senza fratture / a cura di Giorgio Fuà e Carlo Zacchia. — Bologna : Il Mulino, 1983. — 334p

KING, Russell
Italy / Russell King. — London : Harper & Row, 1987. — x,222p. — (Western Europe : economic and social studies). — *Bibliography: p203-212. — Includes index*

LECALDANO SASSO LA TERZA, E.
Households' saving and the real rate of interest : the Italian experience, 1970-1983 / E. Lecaldano Sasso la Terza, G. Marotta, R. S. Masera. — [Roma] : Banca d'Italia, 1985. — 33p . addenda. — (Temi di discussione ; 47) (Servizio studi della Banca d'Italia). — *Bibliography: p32-33*

ITALY — Economic policy
RASPIN, Angela
The Italian war economy, 1940-1943 : with particular reference to Italian relations with Germany / Angela Raspin. — New York : Garland Pub., 1986. — p. cm. — (Outstanding theses from the London School of Economics and Political Science). — *Thesis (Ph. D.)--London University, 1980. — Bibliography: p*

ITALY — Elections
Italy at the polls, 1983 : a study of the national elections / edited by Howard R. Penniman. — Durham, NC : Duke University Press, 1987. — p. cm. — (At the polls). — *"An American Enterprise Institute book.". — Includes index. — Bibliography: p*

ITALY — Emigration and immigration — Bibliography
BRIANI, Vittorio
Italian immigrants abroad : a bibliography on the Italian experience outside Italy in Europe, the Americas, Australia, and Africa = Emigrazione e lavoro italiano all'estero : repertorio bibliografico / by Vittorio Briani ; edited and with a new introd. and supplemental bibliography by Francesco Cordasco. — Detroit : B. Ethridge Books, c1979. — xlix, 229 p.. — *Edition of 1967 published under title: Emigrazione e lavoro italiano all'estero. — Includes indexes*

ITALY — Foreign economic relations — Germany
RASPIN, Angela
The Italian war economy, 1940-1943 : with particular reference to Italian relations with Germany / Angela Raspin. — New York : Garland Pub., 1986. — p. cm. — (Outstanding theses from the London School of Economics and Political Science). — *Thesis (Ph. D.)--London University, 1980. — Bibliography: p*

ITALY — Foreign relations — 1870-1915
JONES, Simon Mark
Domestic factors in Italian intervention in the First World War / Simon Mark Jones. — New York : Garland, 1986. — 292 p. — (Outstanding theses from the London School of Economics and Political Science). — *Thesis (Ph.D.)--London School of Economics and Political Science. — Bibliography: p. 275-292*

ITALY — Foreign relations — 1922-1945
AGA ROSSI, Elena
L'Italia nella sconfitta : politica interna e situazione internazionale durante la seconda guerra mondiale / Elena Aga-Rossi ; introduzione di Renzo De Felice. — Napoli : Edizioni scientifiche italiane, c1985. — 485 p.. — (Biblioteca storica ; 4). — *Includes bibliographical references and index*

ITALY — Foreign relations — 1945-

BRECCIA, Alfredo
L'Italia e la difesa dell'Europa : alle origini del "Piano Pleven" / Alfredo Breccia. — Roma : Istituto di Studi Europei A. de Gasperi, 1984. — 274p. — *Bibliography: p257-261*

ITALY — Foreign relations — Egypt

La frontière occidentale de l'Egypte : accord Italo-Egyptien du 6 Décembre 1925. — Le Caire : Ministère des Affaires Étrangères, 1927. — 22p. — (Documents réservés ; no.1)

ITALY — Foreign relations — Poland

KIENIEWICZ, Stefan
L'Italie et l'insurrection polonaise de 1863 / Stefan Kieniewicz. — Wroclaw : Accademia Polacca Delle Scienze, 1975. — 20p

ITALY — Foreign relations — Spain

SAZ CAMPOS, Ismael
Mussolini contra la II República : hostilidad, conspiraciones, intervención (1931-1936) / Ismael Saz. — Valencia : Edicions Alfons el Magnànim, Institució Valenciana d'Estudis i Investigació, 1986. — 265p. — *Bibliography: p [255]-265*

TUSELL GÓMEZ, Javier
Franco y Mussolini : la política española durante la segunda guerra mundial / Xavier Tusell, Genoveva García Queipo de Llano. — Barcelona : Planeta, 1985. — 299p. — (Espejo de España ; 109). — *Bibliography: p293-296*

ITALY — Foreign relations — United States

AGA ROSSI, Elena
L'Italia nella sconfitta : politica interna e situazione internazionale durante la seconda guerra mondiale / Elena Aga-Rossi ; introduzione di Renzo De Felice. — Napoli : Edizioni scientifiche italiane, c1985. — 485 p.. — (Biblioteca storica ; 4). — *Includes bibliographical references and index*

ITALY — Foreign relations — Yugoslavia

PAVLOWITCH, Stevan K.
"Il caso Mirošević" : lèxpulsion du ministre de Yougoslavie au Vatican par le gouvernement fasciste en 1941 / Stevan K. Pavlowitch. — Thessaloniki : [s.n.], 1978. — p107-137. — *Offprint from Balkan Studies*

ITALY — History — 1559-1789

CARPANETTO, Dino
Italy in the age of reason : 1685-1789 / Dino Carpanetto and Giuseppe Ricuperati ; translated by Caroline Higgitt. — London : Longman, 1987. — x,357p. — (Longman history of Italy ; v.5). — *Translated from the Italian. — Includes index*

ITALY — History — 18th century

WOOLF, S. J
A history of Italy, 1700-1860 : the social constraints of political change / Stuart Woolf. — New York : Methuen, 1986, c1979. — p. cm. — *Includes index. — Bibliography: p*

ITALY — History — 19th century

WOOLF, S. J
A history of Italy, 1700-1860 : the social constraints of political change / Stuart Woolf. — New York : Methuen, 1986, c1979. — p. cm. — *Includes index. — Bibliography: p*

ITALY — History — 1849-1870

GOOCH, John
The unification of Italy / John Gooch. — London : Methuen, 1986. — 1v.. — (Lancaster pamphlets). — *Includes bibliography*

ITALY — History — 1914-1945

Rethinking Italian Fascism : capitalism, populism and culture / edited by David Forgacs. — London : Lawrence and Wishart, [1986]. — xxi,209p

ITALY — History — 1945-

SASSOON, Donald
Contemporary Italy : politics, economy and society since 1945 / Donald Sassoon. — London : Longman, 1986. — [320]p. — *Includes bibliography and index*

ITALY — Industries

Industrializzazione senza fratture / a cura di Giorgio Fuà e Carlo Zacchia. — Bologna : Il Mulino, 1983. — 334p

ITALY — Industries — Statistics

ITALY. Istituto Centrale di Statistica
6 censimento generale dell'industria, del commercio, dei servizi e dell'artigianato 26 ottobre 1981. — Roma : the Istituto
vol.3: Atti del censimento. — 1985. — 264p

ITALY. Istituto Centrale di Statistica
Tavola intersettoriale dell'economia italiana per l'anno 1975. — Roma : Istituto Centrale di Statistica, 1981. — 254p. — (Bollettino mensile di statistica. Supplemento ; 1981 n.7)

ITALY. Istituto Centrale di Statistica
Tavola intersettoriale dell'economia italiana per l'anno 1978 : versione a 84 branche. — Roma : Istituto Centrale di Statistica, 1983. — 206p. — (Bollettino mensile di statistica. Supplemento ; 1983 n.21)

ITALY — Politics and government — 1922-1945

AGA ROSSI, Elena
L'Italia nella sconfitta : politica interna e situazione internazionale durante la seconda guerra mondiale / Elena Aga-Rossi ; introduzione di Renzo De Felice. — Napoli : Edizioni scientifiche italiane, c1985. — 485 p.. — (Biblioteca storica ; 4). — *Includes bibliographical references and index*

Rethinking Italian Fascism : capitalism, populism and culture / edited by David Forgacs. — London : Lawrence and Wishart, [1986]. — xxi,209p

ITALY — Politics and government — 1922-1945 — Sources

AGA ROSSI, Elena
L'Italia nella sconfitta : politica interna e situazione internazionale durante la seconda guerra mondiale / Elena Aga-Rossi ; introduzione di Renzo De Felice. — Napoli : Edizioni scientifiche italiane, c1985. — 485 p.. — (Biblioteca storica ; 4). — *Includes bibliographical references and index*

ITALY — Politics and government — 1945-

BRECCIA, Alfredo
L'Italia e la difesa dell'Europa : alle origini del "Piano Pleven" / Alfredo Breccia. — Roma : Istituto di Studi Europei A. de Gasperi, 1984. — 274p. — *Bibliography: p257-261*

Italy at the polls, 1979 : a study of the parliamentary elections / [edited by Howard R. Penniman]. — Washington, D.C. : American Enterprise Institute for Public Policy Research, c1981. — xiv, 335 p.. — (At the polls) (AEI studies ; 321) (Studies in political and social processes). — *Includes bibliographical references and index*

Il sistema politico Italiano / a cura di Gianfranco Pasquino. — Roma-Bari : Laterza, 1985. — ix,461p. — *Bibliography:pix*

SPOTTS, Frederic
Italy : a difficult democracy : a survey of Italian politics / Frederic Spotts, Theodor Wieser. — Cambridge : Cambridge University Press, 1986. — [352]p. — *Includes index*

ITALY — Politics and government — 1976-

Italian politics, a review / edited by Robert Leonardi and Raffaella Y. Nanetti. — London : Pinter
Vol.1. — 1986. — [200]p. — *Includes index*

Italy at the polls, 1983 : a study of the national elections / edited by Howard R. Penniman. — Durham, NC : Duke University Press, 1987. — p. cm. — (At the polls). — *"An American Enterprise Institute book."*. — *Includes index. — Bibliography: p*

WAGNER-PACIFICI, Robin Erica
The Moro morality play : terrorism as social drama / Robin Erica Wagner-Pacifici. — Chicago : The University of Chicago Press, c1986. — p. cm. — *Includes index. — Bibliography: p*

ITALY — Population — Statistics

12 censimento generale della popolazione 25 ottobre 1981. — Roma : Istituto Centrale di Statistica
vol.2: Dati sulle caratteristiche strutturali della popolazione e della abitazioni
t.2: fascicoli regionali. — 1983-1984. — 20v

12 censimento generale della popolazione 25 ottobre 1981. — Roma : Istituto Centrale di Statistica. — 1984-
vol.3: Popolazione delle frazioni geografiche e delle località abitate dei comuni
Fascicoli regionali. — 20v

12 censimento generale della popolazione 25 ottobre 1981. — Roma : Istituto Centrale di Statistica. — 1983
Dati sulle caratteristiche strutturali della popolazione e delle abitazioni
Campione al 2% dei fogli di famiglia : dati provvisori. — 119p

12 censimento generale della popolazione 25 ottobre 1981. — Roma : Istituto Centrale di Statistica
Popolazione legale dei comuni. — 1983. — 225p

Fertility Survey in Italy, 1979 : a summary of findings. — Voorburg : International Statistical Institute, 1982. — 20p. — (World Fertility Survey ; no.37)

ITALY. Istituto Centrale di Statistica
Forze di lavoro e flussi di popolazione anni 1979 e 1980. — Roma : Istituto Centrale di Statistica, 1981. — 149p. — (Bollettino mensile di statistica. Supplemento ; 1981 n.15)

ITALY — Social conditions

WOOLF, S. J
A history of Italy, 1700-1860 : the social constraints of political change / Stuart Woolf. — New York : Methuen, 1986, c1979. — p. cm. — *Includes index. — Bibliography: p*

ITALY. Parlamento — Elections

Italy at the polls, 1979 : a study of the parliamentary elections / [edited by Howard R. Penniman]. — Washington, D.C. : American Enterprise Institute for Public Policy Research, c1981. — xiv, 335 p.. — (At the polls) (AEI studies ; 321) (Studies in political and social processes). — *Includes bibliographical references and index*

IVORY COAST — Cencus, 1975

Recensement général de la population 1975. — Abidjan : Direction de la Statistique
La population de la Côte d'Ivoire. — 1981. — 58p

IVORY COAST — Census, 1975

Recensement général de la population 1975. — Abidjan : Direction de la Statistique
Vol. 1: Département d'Abidjan, Agglomération du Grand Abidjan : Résultats definitifs. — 1978. — 280p

Recensement général de la population 1975. — Abidjan : Direction de la Statistique
Département d'Abengourou : résultats définitifs. — 1977. — 1v. (various pagings)

Recensement général de la population 1975. — Abidjan : Direction de la Statistique
Quelques données globales : résultats définitifs. — 1979. — 85p

Recensement général de la population 1975. — Abidjan : Direction de la Statistique
Région FRAR Sud-Ouest : résultats définitifs. — 1981. — 121p

IVORY COAST — Commerce — Statistics

Bilan du commerce exterieur ivoirien / Direction de la Statistique, Ivory Coast. — [S.l.] : [the Direction], 1982-. — *Annual*

IVORY COAST — Constitution
IVORY COAST
La Constitution. — [Abidjan] : [s.n.], [1986?]. — 16p. — (Codes et Lois Usuelles de Côte d'Ivoire). — *Introduction by Albert Aggrey*

IVORY COAST — Economic conditions — Statistics
Statistiques economiques ivoiriennes / Chambre d'Industrie de Côte D'Ivoire. — Abidjan-Plateau : Chambre d'Industrie de Côte d'Ivoire, 1982-. — *Annual*

IVORY COAST — Economic policy
Plan quinquennal de développement économique, social et culturel 1971-1975 : édition résumée. — [Abidjan] : Ministère du plan, 1971. — 52p

IVORY COAST — Population — Statistics
AHONZO, Etienne
Population de la Côte d'Ivoire : analyse des donnés démographiques disponibles / Etienne Ahonzo, Bernard Barrère, Pierre Kopylov. — Abidjan : Ministère de l'Economie et des finances, 1984. — 324p

Enquête démographique à passages répétés 1978-79 : résultats définitifs : méthodologie, structure, mortalité fécondité. — [Abidjan] : Ministère du Plan et de l'Industrie, [1981?]. — 270p

Recensement général de la population 1975. — Abidjan : Direction de la Statistique Département d'Abengourou : résultats définitifs. — 1977. — 1v. (various pagings)

Recensement général de la population 1975. — Abidjan : Direction de la Statistique La population de la Côte d'Ivoire. — 1981. — 58p

Recensement général de la population 1975. — Abidjan : Direction de la Statistique Quelques données globales : résultats définitifs. — 1979. — 85p

Recensement général de la population 1975. — Abidjan : Direction de la Statistique Région FRAR Sud-Ouest : résultats définitifs. — 1981. — 121p

IVORY COAST — Population — Statistics — Evaluation
SOMBO, N'cho
Enquête Ivoirienne sur la fecondité, 1980-81 : rapport d'évaluation / N'cho Sombo. — Voorburg : International Statistical Institute, 1985. — 63p. — (Scientific reports / World Fertility Survey ; no.79)

IVORY COAST — Social policy
Plan quinquennal de développement économique, social et culturel 1971-1975 : édition résumée. — [Abidjan] : Ministère du plan, 1971. — 52p

IVORY COAST — Statistics, vital
Enquête démographique à passages répétés 1978-79 : résultats définitifs : méthodologie, structure, mortalité fécondité. — [Abidjan] : Ministère du Plan et de l'Industrie, [1981?]. — 270p

JACA (SPAIN) — History
AZPÍROZ PASCUAL, José María
La sublevación de Jaca / José María Aspíroz Pascual, Fernando Elboj Broto. — Zaragoza : Guara, 1984. — 180p. — (Colección básica aragonesa ; 43). — *Bibliography: p[170]-174*

JACKSON, ANDREW
BELOHLAVEK, John M
Let the eagle soar! : The foreign policy of Andrew Jackson / John M. Belohlavek. — Lincoln : University of Nebraska Press, c1985. — x, 328 p.. — *Includes index.* — *Bibliography: p. [309]-318*

JACKSON, Andrew
The papers of Andrew Jackson. — Knoxville, Tenn. : University of Tennessee Press Vol.2: 1804-1813 / Harold D. Moser, Sharon Macpherson, editors. — 1984. — xxvii,634p

Jacksonian democracy / [edited by] James L. Bugg, Jr., Peter C. Stewart. — 2nd ed. — Lanham, Md. ; London : University Press of America, 1986. — 166p. — ; *Reprint. Originally published: 2nd ed. Hinsdale, Ill. : Dryden Press, c1976.* — *Bibliography: p.[160]-166*

JACKSON, HENRY M — Views on national security
Staying the course : Henry M. Jackson and national security / edited by Dorothy Fosdick. — Seattle : University of Washington Press, c1987. — p. cm

JACKSON, JESSE
COLLINS, Sheila D
From melting pot to rainbow coalition : the future of race in American politics / Sheila D. Collins. — New York : Monthly Review Press, 1986. — p. cm. — *Includes index.* — *Bibliography: p*

LANDESS, Tom
Jesse Jackson and the politics of race / Thomas H. Landess, Richard M. Quinn. — Ottawa, Ill. : Jameson Books, c1985. — 269p. — *Includes index*

JACKSON STRUCTURED PROGRAMMING
CAMERON, John R.
JSP & JSD : the Jackson approach to software development / John R. Cameron. — New York : IEEE Computer Society Press, 1983. — (A monograph in the Computer Society Press series)

JACOBINS — France
FURET, François
La Gauche et la Révolution françoise au milieu du XIXe siècle : Edgar Quinet et la question du Jacobinisme (1865-1870) / François Furet ; textes présentés par Marina Valensise. — [Paris?] : Hachette, 1986. — 317p. — (Librarie du bicentenaire de la Revolution française). — *Includes bibliographic notes*

JACOBITE REBELLION, 1715
SMITH, Lawrence Bartlam
Spain and Britain, 1715-1719 : the Jacobite issue / Lawrence Bartlam Smith. — New York : Garland Pub., 1987. — 361 p.. — (Outstanding theses from the London School of Economics and Political Science). — *Thesis (Ph. D.)--University of London.* — *Bibliography: p. 344-361*

JACOBITE REBELLION, 1719
SMITH, Lawrence Bartlam
Spain and Britain, 1715-1719 : the Jacobite issue / Lawrence Bartlam Smith. — New York : Garland Pub., 1987. — 361 p.. — (Outstanding theses from the London School of Economics and Political Science). — *Thesis (Ph. D.)--University of London.* — *Bibliography: p. 344-361*

JACOBITE REBELLION, 1745-1746
YOUNGSON, A. J.
The prince and the pretender : a study in the writing of history / A.J. Youngson. — London : Croom Helm, c1985. — vii,270p. — *Includes index*

JACOBITES
SMITH, Lawrence Bartlam
Spain and Britain, 1715-1719 : the Jacobite issue / Lawrence Bartlam Smith. — New York : Garland Pub., 1987. — 361 p.. — (Outstanding theses from the London School of Economics and Political Science). — *Thesis (Ph. D.)--University of London.* — *Bibliography: p. 344-361*

JAHANZEB, MIANGUL, Wali of Swat — Bibliography
JAHANZEB, Miangul, Wali of Swat
The last Wali of Swat : an autobiography / as told to Fredrik Barth. — Oslo : Universitetsforlaget : Distributed world-wide excluding Scandinavia by Oxford University Press, c1985. — 199p, 8p of plates. — *Bibliography:p.191-192*

JAILS — Social aspects — California — Case studies
IRWIN, John
The jail : managing the underclass in American society / John Irwin. — Berkeley : University of California Press, c1985. — xvi, 148 p.. — *Includes index.* — *Bibliography: p. 135-139*

JAKOBSON, MAX
JAKOBSON, Max
Trettioåttonde våningen : hågkomster och anteckningar 1965-1971 / Max Jakobson ; översättning av Henrik von Bonsdorff. — Helsinki : Holger Schildts, 1983. — 351p. — *Translated into Swedish from Finnish. Originally published Helsinki Keuruu, 1983*

JALISCO (MEXICO) — Governors
VALLARTA, Ignacio Luis
Vallarta en la reforma / prólogo y selección: Moisés González Navarro. — México, D.F. : Universidad Nacional Autónoma de México, 1956. — xxxv,232p. — (Biblioteca del estudiante Universitario ; 76)

JAMAICA — Census, 1970
Jamaica : population census 1970. — Kingston : Department of Statistics. — (Commonwealth Caribbean population census 1970) Vol.2
Pt.E: Economic activity
Bk.4: By sex, ethnic origin, etc.. — [1978]. — 309p

JAMAICA — Economic conditions
HOPE, Kempe R
Economic development in the Caribbean / Kempe Ronald Hope. — New York : Praeger, 1986. — xv, 215p. — *Includes bibliographical references and index*

LOONEY, Robert E
The Jamaican economy in the 1980's : economic decline and structural adjustment / Robert Looney. — Boulder, Colo. : Westview Press, 1986. — xiii, 257p. — (A Westview special study). — *Includes bibliographical references and index*

MANLEY, Michael
Up the down escalator : development and the international economy : a Jamaican case study / Michael Manley. — London : Andre Deutsch, 1987. — xv,332p

JAMAICA — Economic conditions — Statistics
Jamaica : population census 1970. — Kingston : Department of Statistics. — (Commonwealth Caribbean population census 1970) Vol.2
Pt.E: Economic activity
Bk.4: By sex, ethnic origin, etc.. — [1978]. — 309p

JAMAICA — Economic policy
LOONEY, Robert E
The Jamaican economy in the 1980's : economic decline and structural adjustment / Robert Looney. — Boulder, Colo. : Westview Press, 1986. — xiii, 257p. — (A Westview special study). — *Includes bibliographical references and index*

MANLEY, Michael
Up the down escalator : development and the international economy : a Jamaican case study / Michael Manley. — London : Andre Deutsch, 1987. — xv,332p

JAMAICA — Population
SINGH, Susheela
Guyana, Jamaica and Trinidad and Tobago : socio—economic differentials in cumulative fertility / Susheela Singh. — Voorburg : International Statistical Institute, 1984. — 89p. — (Scientific reports / World Fertility Survey ; no.57)

JAMAICA — Population — Statistics
ABDULAH, Norma
Contraceptive use and fertility in the Commonwealth Caribbean / Norma Abdulah, Jack Harewood. — Voorburg : International Statistical Institute, 1984. — 55p. — (Scientific reports / World Fertility Survey ; no.60)

JAMAICA — Population — Statistics
continuation

LIGHTBOURNE, Robert E.
Fertility preferences in Guyana, Jamaica and Trinidad and Tobago, from World Fertility Survey, 1975-77 : a multiple indicator approach / R.E. Lightbourne. — Voorburg : International Statistical Institute, 1984. — 128p. — (Scientific reports / World Fertility Survey ; no.68)

JAMAICA — Statistics, Vital

EBANKS, G. Edward
Infant and child mortality and fertility : Trinidad and Tobago, Guyana and Jamaica / G. Edward Ebanks. — Voorburg : International Statistical Institute, 1985. — 68p. — (Scientific reports / World Fertility Survey ; no.75)

JAMES, HENRY — Authorship

ANESKO, Michael
"Friction with the market" : Henry James and the profession of authorship / Michael Anesko. — New York : Oxford University Press, 1986. — xii, 258 p.. — *Includes index. — Bibliography: p. 245-249*

JAMES, HENRY — Criticism and interpretation

ANESKO, Michael
"Friction with the market" : Henry James and the profession of authorship / Michael Anesko. — New York : Oxford University Press, 1986. — xii, 258 p.. — *Includes index. — Bibliography: p. 245-249*

JAMES, WILLIAM

MYERS, Gerald E
William James, his life and thought / Gerald E. Myers. — New Haven : Yale University Press, c1986. — xxi, 628p, [16]p of plates. — *Includes index. — Includes bibliographical references*

JAMMU AND KASHMIR (INDIA) — Kings and rulers — Biography

KARAN SINGH, Sadar-i-Riyasat of Jammu and Kashmir
Heir apparent : an autobiography / Karan Singh. — New Delhi : Oxford University Press, 1982. — xi,171p. — *Vol.1 of two volume autobiography; vol.2 has title 'Sadar-i-Riyasat'*

KARAN SINGH, Sadar-i-Riyasat of Jammu and Kashmir
Sadar-i-Riyasat : an autobiography [1953-1967] / Karan Singh. — New Delhi : Oxford University Press, 1985. — xi,168p. — *Vol.2 of two volume autobiography; Vol.1 has title 'Heir apparent'*

JAMMU AND KASHMIR (INDIA) — Politics and government

KARAN SINGH, Sadar-i-Riyasat of Jammu and Kashmir
Heir apparent : an autobiography / Karan Singh. — New Delhi : Oxford University Press, 1982. — xi,171p. — *Vol.1 of two volume autobiography; vol.2 has title 'Sadar-i-Riyasat'*

KARAN SINGH, Sadar-i-Riyasat of Jammu and Kashmir
Sadar-i-Riyasat : an autobiography [1953-1967] / Karan Singh. — New Delhi : Oxford University Press, 1985. — xi,168p. — *Vol.2 of two volume autobiography; Vol.1 has title 'Heir apparent'*

JAPAN — Bibliography

DOWER, John W.
Japanese history & culture from ancient to modern times : seven basic bibliographies / John W. Dower. — Manchester : Manchester University Press, c1986. — vi,232p

JAPAN — Census, 1980

[1980 population census of Japan]. Population of Japan : final report of the 1980 population census / Statistics Bureau. — [Tokyo] : Statistics Bureau, [1985]. — 59,360p. — *Text in Japanese*

1980 population census of Japan / Statistics Bureau. — [Tokyo] : Statistics Bureau Vol.7: Results of special tabulation Part 1: Industry and occupation (one percent sample tabulation). — [1984]. — xx,171,[12]p. — *Text in Japanese and English*

1980 population census of Japan / Statistics Bureau. — [Tokyo] : Statistics Bureau Vol.7: Results of special tabulation Part 2: Internal migration for three major metropolitan areas (out-migrants from main cities). — [1984]. — 1v (various pagings). — *Text in Japanese and English*

JAPAN — Civilization

Europe interprets Japan / edited by Gordon Daniels. — Tenterden : Paul Norbury Publications, 1984. — xi,279p. — *Papers presented at the Third International Japanese Studies Conference, the Hague, 20 to 23 September 1982*

VARLEY, H. Paul
Japanese culture / H. Paul Varley. — 3rd ed. — Honolulu : University of Hawaii Press, c1984. — 331 p.. — *Includes index. — Bibliography: p. [319]-322*

JAPAN — Civilization — 1945-

DALE, Peter N.
The myth of Japanese uniqueness / Peter N. Dale. — London : Croom Helm, c1986. — [240]p. — (The Nissan Institute/Croom Helm Japanese studies series). — *Includes index*

TSURUMI, Shunsuke
A cultural history of postwar Japan 1945-1980 / Shunsuke Tsurumi. — London : KPI, 1987. — xi,174p. — *Bibliography: p134-164*

JAPAN — Colonies — History

BEASLEY, W. G.
Japanese imperialism, 1894-1945 / W.G. Beasley. — Oxford : Oxford University Press, 1987. — [280]p. — *Includes bibliography and index*

JAPAN — Commerce

FUJIWARA, Sadao
Foreign trade, investment and industrial imperialism in postwar Japan, 1951-1985 / Sadao Fujiwara. — Yamaguchi : Economic Society of Yamaguchi University, 1986. — 62p. — (Paper series / Economic Society of Yamaguchi University ; no.3)

JAPAN — Commerce — Near East

SHIMIZU, Hiroshi
Anglo-Japanese trade rivalry in the Middle East in the inter-war period / by Hiroshi Shimizu. — London : Published for The Middle East Centre, St. Antony's College, Oxford by Ithaca Press, 1986. — [302]p. — (St. Antony's Middle East monographs ; no.17) . — *Includes bibliography and index*

JAPAN — Commerce — Canada

WRIGHT, Richard W.
Japanese business in Canada : the elusive alliance / Richard W. Wright. — Montreal : The Institute for Research on Public Policy/L'Institut de recherches politiques, 1984. — xxxi,110p. — *Summary in French and English. — Bibliography: p99-100*

JAPAN — Commerce — Europe

MOORHOUSE, James, 1924-
Righting the balance : a new agenda for Euro-Japanese trade / James Moorhouse and Anthony Teasdale. — London : Conservative Political Centre, 1987. — 87p

JAPAN — Commerce — United States

MCCREARY, Don R
Japanese-U.S. business negotiations : a cross-cultural study / Don R. McCreary. — New York : Praeger, 1986. — viii, 121 p.. — *"Praeger special studies. Praeger scientific.". — Includes index. — Bibliography: p. 109-115*

WONNACOTT, Ronald J
Aggressive U.S. reciprocity evaluated with a new analytical approach to trade conflicts / R.J. Wonnacott. — Montreal, Quebec : Institute for Research on Public Policy, c1984. — xxi, 68 p.. — (Essays in international economics). — *Bibliography: p. 57-58*

JAPAN — Commercial policy

MOORHOUSE, James, 1924-
Righting the balance : a new agenda for Euro-Japanese trade / James Moorhouse and Anthony Teasdale. — London : Conservative Political Centre, 1987. — 87p

JAPAN — Constitutional history

Democratizing Japan : the allied occupation / edited by Robert E. Ward and Sakamoto Yoshikazu. — Honolulu : University of Hawaii Press, c1987. — xv, 456 p., [1] folded leaf of plates. — *One leaf of plates in pocket. — Based on papers presented at a conference sponsored by both the Japan Society for the Promotion of Science and the Joint Committee on Japanese Studies of the American Council of Learned Societies and the Social Science Research Council with support from the National Endowment for the Humanities. — Includes bibliographies and index*

JAPAN — Economic conditions

BANK OF JAPAN. Research and Statistics Department
Recent business fluctuations and future tasks. — Tokyo : Bank of Japan. Research and Statistics Department, 1986. — 22p

FUJIWARA, Sadao
Foreign trade, investment and industrial imperialism in postwar Japan, 1951-1985 / Sadao Fujiwara. — Yamaguchi : Economic Society of Yamaguchi University, 1986. — 62p. — (Paper series / Economic Society of Yamaguchi University ; no.3)

Quarterly economic outlook / Bank of Japan. Research and Statistics Department. — Tokyo : Bank of Japan. Research and Statistics Department, 1986-. — *Quarterly*

The state and economic enterprise in Japan : essays in the political economy of growth / edited by William W. Lockwood. — Princeton : Princeton University Press, c1965. — x,753p

White paper on Japanese economy / Economic Planning Agency, Japan. — Tokyo : Business Intercommunications, 1986-. — *Annual*

JAPAN — Economic conditions — Statistics

BANK OF JAPAN. Research and Statistics Department
Hundred-year statistics of the Japanese economy. — [Tokyo] : Statistics Department, Bank of Japan, 1966. — 617p. — *Accompanied by 2 supplements in box*

JAPAN — Economic conditions — To 1868

HANLEY, Susan B.
Economic and demographic change in preindustrial Japan, 1600-1868 / by Susan B. Hanley and Kozo Yamamura. — Princeton, N.J. ; Guildford : Princeton University Press, c1977. — xiii, 409 p. — *Includes index. — Bibliography: p. 387-403*

MINAMI, Ryōshin
The economic development of Japan : a quantative study / Ryōshin Minami ; translated by Ralph Thompson and Ryōshin Minami with assistance from David Merriman. — Basingstoke : Macmillan, 1986. — xxvi,487p. — (Studies in the modern Japanese economy). — *Translated from the Japanese. — Bibliography: p460-477. — Includes index*

JAPAN — Economic conditions — 1868-1918

NORMAN, E. Herbert
Japan's emergence as a modern state : political and economic problems of the Meiji period. — Westport, Conn. : Greenwood Press, [1973, c1940]. — xvi, 254 p. — *Reprint of the ed. published by International Secretariat, Institute of Pacific Relations, New York, in series: I. P. R. inquiry series. — Bibliography: p. 211-242*

JAPAN — Economic conditions — 1868-1945

MACPHERSON, W. J.
The economic development of Japan c. 1868-1941 / prepared for the Economic History Society by W.J. Macpherson. — Basingstoke : Macmillan, 1987. — [96]p. — (Studies in economic and social history). — *Includes bibliography and index*

JAPAN — Economic conditions — 1868-

MINAMI, Ryōshin
The economic development of Japan : a quantative study / Ryōshin Minami ; translated by Ralph Thompson and Ryōshin Minami with assistance from David Merriman. — Basingstoke : Macmillan, 1986. — xxvi,487p. — (Studies in the modern Japanese economy). — *Translated from the Japanese. — Bibliography: p460-477. — Includes index*

YOSHIHARA, Kunio
Japanese economic development : a short introduction / Yoshihara Kunio. — 2nd ed. — Tokyo ; Oxford : Oxford University Press, 1986. — xii,205p. — *Bibliography: p[195]-201*

JAPAN — Economic conditions — 1918-1945

BARNHART, Michael A.
Japan prepares for total war : the search for economic security, 1919-1941 / Michael A. Barnhart. — Ithaca : Cornell University Press, 1987. — 290 p.. — (Cornell studies in security affairs). — *Includes index. — Bibliography: p. 275-282*

COHEN, Jerome Bernard
Japan's economy in war and reconstruction / by Jerome B. Cohen. With a foreword by Sir George Sansom. Issued under the auspices of the International Secretariat, Institute of Pacific Relations. — Westport, Conn. : Greenwood Press, [1973, c1949]. — xix, 545 p. — *Reprint of the ed., originally presented as the author's thesis under title: The Japanese war economy, 1937-1945, and published by the University of Minnesota Press, Minneapolis. — Includes bibliographical references*

HOSTON, Germaine A.
Marxism and the crisis of development in prewar Japan / Germaine A. Hoston. — Princeton, N.J. : Princeton University Press, c1986. — xviii, 401 p.. — *Includes index. — Bibliography: p. 357-386*

Japan and world depression : then and now : essays in memory of E.F. Penrose / edited by Ronald Dore and Radha Sinha with assistance from Mari Sako. — Basingstoke : Macmillan, 1987. — xxiv,208p. — *Includes index*

JAPAN — Economic conditions — 1945-

Adjustment of the Japanese economy under the strong Yen. — Tokyo : Bank of Japan. Research and Statistics Department, 1987. — 46p. — (Special paper / Bank of Japan. Research and Statistics Department ; no.149)

COHEN, Jerome Bernard
Japan's economy in war and reconstruction / by Jerome B. Cohen. With a foreword by Sir George Sansom. Issued under the auspices of the International Secretariat, Institute of Pacific Relations. — Westport, Conn. : Greenwood Press, [1973, c1949]. — xix, 545 p. — *Reprint of the ed., originally presented as the author's thesis under title: The Japanese war economy, 1937-1945, and published by the University of Minnesota Press, Minneapolis. — Includes bibliographical references*

DORE, Ronald
Flexible rigidities : industrial policy and structural adjustment in the Japanese economy 1970-80 / Ronald Dore. — London : Athlone, 1986. — [240]p. — *Includes bibliography and index*

DORE, Ronald
Taking Japan seriously : a Confucian perspective on leading economic issues / Ronald Dore. — London : Athlone, 1987. — [272]p. — *Includes bibliography and index*

GREAT BRITAIN. Parliament. House of Commons. Library. Research Division
Industrial policy and the Japanese economic miracle / C. R. Barclay. — [London] : the Division, 1986. — 26p. — (Background paper ; no.190). — *Bibliography: p26*

Japan and world depression : then and now : essays in memory of E.F. Penrose / edited by Ronald Dore and Radha Sinha with assistance from Mari Sako. — Basingstoke : Macmillan, 1987. — xxiv,208p. — *Includes index*

SUMITA, Satoshi
Address to the fortieth annual convention of Federation of Bankers' Associations of Japan / Satoshi Sumita. — Tokyo : Bank of Japan. Research and Statistics Department, 1986. — 6p. — (Special paper / Bank of Japan. Research and Statistics Department ; no.140)

WORONOFF, Jon
The Japan syndrome : symptoms, ailments, and remedies / Jon Woronoff. — New Brunswick (U.S.A.) : Transaction Books, c1986. — 230 p.. — *Includes index. — Bibliography: p. [225]-226*

JAPAN — Economic history

Japanese yearbook on business history / Japan Business History Institute. — [Tokyo] : Japan Business History Institute, 1984-. — *Annual*

MORISHIMA, Michio
A historical transformation from feudalism to 'capitalism' / Michio Morishima. — London : London School of Economics and Political Science. Suntory Toyota International Centre for Economics and Related Disciplines, 1986. — 58p. — (Japanese studies)

JAPAN — Economic policy

BARNHART, Michael A.
Japan prepares for total war : the search for economic security, 1919-1941 / Michael A. Barnhart. — Ithaca : Cornell University Press, 1987. — 290 p.. — (Cornell studies in security affairs). — *Includes index. — Bibliography: p. 275-282*

DORE, R. P.
Structural adjustment in Japan, 1970-82 / R. P. Dore ; with contributions by K. Taira. — Geneva : International Labour Office, 1986. — xii,189p. — (Employment, adjustment and industrialisation ; 1). — *Bibliography: p [183]-189*

Europe interprets Japan / edited by Gordon Daniels. — Tenterden : Paul Norbury Publications, 1984. — xi,279p. — *Papers presented at the Third International Japanese Studies Conference, the Hague, 20 to 23 September 1982*

NORMAN, E. Herbert
Japan's emergence as a modern state : political and economic problems of the Meiji period. — Westport, Conn. : Greenwood Press, [1973, c1940]. — xvi, 254 p. — *Reprint of the ed. published by International Secretariat, Institute of Pacific Relations, New York, in series: I. P. R. inquiry series. — Bibliography: p. 211-242*

The Sun also sets : lessons in 'looking East' / editor, Jomo. — 2nd ed., rev. & expanded. — Kuala Lumpur : INSAN, 1985. — xvi, 415 p.. — *Includes bibliographies*

YOSHIHARA, Kunio
Japanese economic development : a short introduction / Yoshihara Kunio. — 2nd ed. — Tokyo ; Oxford : Oxford University Press, 1986. — xii,205p. — *Bibliography: p[195]-201*

JAPAN — Economic policy — 1945- — Congresses

Japan and the United States today : exchange rates, macroeconomic policies, and financial market innovations / Hugh T. Patrick, Ryuichiro Tachi, editors. — New York : Center on Japanese Economy and Business, Columbia University, 1986, c1987. — vii, 234 p.. — *Papers presented at a conference held in New York, June 4-5, 1986, sponsored by the Center on Japanese Economy and Business at the Graduate School of Business, Columbia University, and the Institute of Fiscal and Monetary Policy of the Japanese Ministry of Finance, together with the Foundation for Advanced Information and Research, Japan. — Includes bibliographies*

JAPAN — Foreign economic relations

Japan and world depression : then and now : essays in memory of E.F. Penrose / edited by Ronald Dore and Radha Sinha with assistance from Mari Sako. — Basingstoke : Macmillan, 1987. — xxiv,208p. — *Includes index*

ROOSA, Robert V.
The United States and Japan in the international monetary system 1946-1985 / Robert V. Roosa. — New York : Group of Thirty, 1986. — ii,75p. — (Occasional papers / Group of Thirty ; no.21)

JAPAN — Foreign economic relations — Africa

MOSS, Joanna
Emerging Japanese economic influence in Africa : implications for the United States / Joanna Moss & John Ravenhill. — Berkeley : Institute of International Studies, University of California, c1985. — xi, 150 p.. — (Policy papers in international affairs ; no. 21). — *Includes index. — Bibliography: p. 139-143*

JAPAN — Foreign economic relations — Malaysia

The Sun also sets : lessons in 'looking East' / editor, Jomo. — 2nd ed., rev. & expanded. — Kuala Lumpur : INSAN, 1985. — xvi, 415 p.. — *Includes bibliographies*

JAPAN — Foreign economic relations — United States — Congresses

Japan and the United States today : exchange rates, macroeconomic policies, and financial market innovations / Hugh T. Patrick, Ryuichiro Tachi, editors. — New York : Center on Japanese Economy and Business, Columbia University, 1986, c1987. — vii, 234 p.. — *Papers presented at a conference held in New York, June 4-5, 1986, sponsored by the Center on Japanese Economy and Business at the Graduate School of Business, Columbia University, and the Institute of Fiscal and Monetary Policy of the Japanese Ministry of Finance, together with the Foundation for Advanced Information and Research, Japan. — Includes bibliographies*

Law and trade issues of the Japanese economy : American and Japanese perspectives / edited by Gary R. Saxonhouse and Kozo Yamamura. — Seattle : University of Washington Press ; [Tokyo] : University of Tokyo Press, c1986. — xx, 290 p.. — *Based on a workshop held in Sept. 1983, sponsored by the Committee on Japanese Economic Studies. — Includes bibliographies and index*

JAPAN — Foreign opinion, British

YOKOYAMA, Toshio
Japan in the Victorian mind : a study of stereotyped images of a nation, 1850-80 / Toshio Yokoyama. — London : Macmillan, 1987. — xxiii,233p,[16]p of plates. — (St Antony's/Macmillan series). — *Bibliography: p208-219. — Includes index*

JAPAN — Foreign relations — 1868-1912

BEASLEY, W. G.
Japanese imperialism, 1894-1945 / W.G. Beasley. — Oxford : Oxford University Press, 1987. — [280]p. — *Includes bibliography and index*

JAPAN — Foreign relations — 1912-1945

BEASLEY, W. G.
Japanese imperialism, 1894-1945 / W.G. Beasley. — Oxford : Oxford University Press, 1987. — [280]p. — *Includes bibliography and index*

IRIYE, Akira
The origins of the Second World War in Asia and the Pacific / Akira Iriye. — London : Longman, 1987. — 1v.. — (Origins of modern wars). — *Includes bibliography and index*

KYOZO, Sato
Japan and Britain at the crossroads, 1939-1945 : a study in the dilemmas of Japanese Diplomacy / Sato Kyozo. — Tokyo : Senshu University Press, 1986. — [xiii],301p. — *Bibliography: p[269]-288*

JAPAN — Foreign relations — 1945-

Europe and Japan : changing relationships since 1945 / edited by Gordon Daniels and Reinhard Drifte. — Ashford : Norbury, 1985. — 1v.. — *Includes index*

JAPAN — Foreign relations — Europe

Europe and Japan : changing relationships since 1945 / edited by Gordon Daniels and Reinhard Drifte. — Ashford : Norbury, 1985. — 1v.. — *Includes index*

JAPAN — Foreign relations — Germany

German-Japanese relations in the 1930's / edited by Ian Nish. — London : Suntory-Toyota International Centre for Economics and Related Disciplines, 1986. — 49p. — (International studies ; 1986/3)

JAPAN — Foreign relations — Great Britain

KIBATA, Yoichi
Anglo-Japanese relations in the 1930s and 1940s / Yoichi Kibata and Antony Adamthwaite ; edited by Ian Nish. — London : Suntory-Toyota International Centre for Economics and Related Disciplines, 1986. — 28p. — (International studies ; 1986/2)

KYOZO, Sato
Japan and Britain at the crossroads, 1939-1945 : a study in the dilemmas of Japanese Diplomacy / Sato Kyozo. — Tokyo : Senshu University Press, 1986. — [xiii],301p. — *Bibliography: p[269]-288*

PRITCHARD, R. John
Far Eastern influences upon British strategy towards the great powers, 1937-1939 / R. John Pritchard. — New York : Garland Pub., 1987. — 328 p.. — (Outstanding theses from the London School of Economics and Political Science). — Thesis (Ph.D)--University of London, 1979. — *Bibliography: p. 275-328*

JAPAN — Foreign relations — New Zealand

KAY, Robin
The ANZUS Pact and the Treaty of Peace with Japan / [compiled and] edited by Robin Kay. — Wellington : Historical Publications Branch, Department of Internal Affairs, 1985. — lxx,1268p. — (Documents on New Zealand external relations ; v.3). — *Includes bibliographical references*

JAPAN — Foreign relations — United States

HEINRICHS, Waldo H
American ambassador : Joseph C. Grew and the development of the United States diplomatic tradition / Waldo H. Heinrichs, Jr. — New York : Oxford University Press, 1986, c1966. — p. cm. — : Reprint. Originally published: Boston : Little, Brown, 1966. — *Includes index. — Bibliography: p*

KUSANO, Atsushi
Two Nixon shocks and Japan-U.S. relations / Atsushi Kusano. — Princeton, N.J. : Princeton University. Woodrow Wilson School of Public and International Affairs, 1987. — 46p. — (Research monograph / Princeton University. Woodrow Wilson School of Public and International Affairs ; no.50)

LIBAL, Michael
Japans Weg in den Krieg : die Aussenpolitik der Kabinette Konoye 1940/1941 : Michael Libal. — Düsseldorf : Droste, [1971]. — 261p

TOKINOYA, Atsushi
The Japan—US alliance : a Japanese perspective / Atsushi Tokinoya. — London : International Institute for Strategic Studies, 1986. — 47p. — (Adelphi papers ; 212)

JAPAN — History — Tokigawa period, 1600-1868

JANNETTA, Ann Bowman
Epidemics and mortality in early modern Japan / Ann Bowman Jannetta. — Princeton, N.J. : Princeton University Press, c1986. — p. cm. — *Includes index. — Bibliography: p*

JAPAN — History — Tokugawa period, 1600-1868 — Addresses, essays, lectures

Studies in the institutional history of Early Modern Japan / edited by John W. Hall and Marius B. Jansen ; with an introduction by Joseph R. Strayer ; contributors [include] Harumi Befu [and nine others]. — Princeton, N.J. : Princeton University Press, 1968. — x, 396p

JAPAN — History — 1787-1868

KOSCHMANN, J. Victor
The Mito ideology : discourse, reform, and insurrection in late Tokugawa Japan, 1790-1864 / J. Victor Koschmann. — Berkeley : University of California Press, c1987. — p. cm. — "This volume is sponsored by the Center for Japanese Studies, University of California, Berkeley.". — *Includes index. — Bibliography: p*

JAPAN — History — 19th century

Japan in transition, from Tokugawa to Meiji / edited by Marius B. Jansen and Gilbert Rozman. — Princeton, N.J. : Princeton University Press, c1986. — ix, 485 p.. — *Spine title: Japan in transition. — Includes bibliographical references and index*

JAPAN — History — Meiji period, 1868-1912

Japan in transition, from Tokugawa to Meiji / edited by Marius B. Jansen and Gilbert Rozman. — Princeton, N.J. : Princeton University Press, c1986. — ix, 485 p.. — *Spine title: Japan in transition. — Includes bibliographical references and index*

JAPAN — History — 1868-1945

GLUCK, Carol
Japan's modern myths : ideology in the late Meiji period / Carol Gluck. — Princeton, N.J. : Princeton University Press, c1985. — xi, 407p, [8]p of plates. — *Includes index. — Bibliography: p 287-311*

JAPAN — History — 1868-

HUNTER, Janet
Concise dictionary of modern Japanese history / compiled by Janet Hunter. — Berkeley ; London : University of California Press, c1984. — xiv,347p. — *Includes index*

Japan examined : perspectives on modern Japanese history / edited by Harry Wray and Hilary Conroy. — Honolulu : University of Hawaii Press, c1983. — x, 411p. — *Bibliography: p.391-399*

JAPAN — History — 1868- — Historiography

Japan examined : perspectives on modern Japanese history / edited by Harry Wray and Hilary Conroy. — Honolulu : University of Hawaii Press, c1983. — x, 411p. — *Bibliography: p.391-399*

JAPAN — History — 20th century

Europe interprets Japan / edited by Gordon Daniels. — Tenterden : Paul Norbury Publications, 1984. — xi,279p. — *Papers presented at the Third International Japanese Studies Conference, the Hague, 20 to 23 September 1982*

MIYAMOTO, Kenji
Selected works / Kenji Miyamoto. — Tokyo : Japan Press Service, 1985. — v,560p

JAPAN — History — Taishō period, 1912-1926

NOLTE, Sharon H
Liberalism in modern Japan : Ishibashi Tanzan and his teachers, 1905-1960 / Sharon H. Nolte. — Berkeley : University of California Press, c1987. — xii, 378 p.. — *Includes index. — Bibliography: p. 343-370*

JAPAN — History — 1912-1945

BARNHART, Michael A.
Japan prepares for total war : the search for economic security, 1919-1941 / Michael A. Barnhart. — Ithaca : Cornell University Press, 1987. — 290 p.. — (Cornell studies in security affairs). — *Includes index. — Bibliography: p. 275-282*

THORNE, Christopher
Allies of a kind : the United States, Britain, and the war against Japan, 1941-1945 / Christopher Thorne. — Oxford : Oxford University Press, 1979. — xxii, 772 p. — *Includes index. — Bibliography: p. [732]-746*

JAPAN — History — Allied occupation, 1945-1952

Democratizing Japan : the allied occupation / edited by Robert E. Ward and Sakamoto Yoshikazu. — Honolulu : University of Hawaii Press, c1987. — xv, 456 p., [1] folded leaf of plates. — *One leaf of plates in pocket. — Based on papers presented at a conference sponsored by both the Japan Society for the Promotion of Science and the Joint Committee on Japanese Studies of the American Council of Learned Societies and the Social Science Research Council with support from the National Endowment for the Humanities. — Includes bibliographies and index*

PARK, Sung-Jo
U.S. labor policy in postwar Japan / Sung-Jo Park. — [Berlin] : Express Edition, [c1985]. — 157 p.. — (Reihe Horizonte Asiens). — *Bibliography: p. 152-157*

JAPAN — History, Military

HOYT, Edwin P.
Japan's war : the great Pacific conflict 1853-1952 / Edwin P. Hoyt. — London : Hutchinson, 1987, c1986. — x,514p,[24]pof plates. — *Originally published: New York : McGraw-Hill, 1986*

JAPAN — History, Military — 1945-

HARRIES, Meirion
Sheathing the sword : the demilitarisation of Japan / by Meirion and Susie Harries. — London : Hamilton, 1987. — xxxiv,364p,[8]p of plates. — *Includes index*

JAPAN — Industries

Aspects of the relationship between agriculture and industrialisation in Japan / edited by Janet Hunter. — London : Suntory-Toyota International Centre for Economics and Related Disciplines, 1986. — 51p. — (International Studies ; 1986/4)

FUJIWARA, Sadao
Foreign trade, investment and industrial imperialism in postwar Japan, 1951-1985 / Sadao Fujiwara. — Yamaguchi : Economic Society of Yamaguchi University, 1986. — 62p. — (Paper series / Economic Society of Yamaguchi University ; no.3)

GREAT BRITAIN. Parliament. House of Commons. Library. Research Division
Industrial policy and the Japanese economic miracle / C. R. Barclay. — [London] : the Division, 1986. — 26p. — (Background paper ; no.190). — *Bibliography: p26*

Japanese yearbook on business history / Japan Business History Institute. — [Tokyo] : Japan Business History Institute, 1984-. — *Annual*

JAPAN — Industries
continuation

JAPANISCH-DEUTSCHES SYMPOSIUM (1983 : Köln)
Die Arbeitswelt in Japan und in der Bundesrepublik Deutschland : ein Vergleich : Japanisch-Deutsches Symposium am 27./28. Juni 1983 im Japanischen Kulturinstitut in Köln / herausgegeben von Peter Hanau...[et al.]. — Darmstadt : Luchterhand, 1983. — ix,162p

The state and economic enterprise in Japan : essays in the political economy of growth / edited by William W. Lockwood. — Princeton : Princeton University Press, c1965. — x,753p

JAPAN — Industries — Reorganization

DORE, R. P.
Structural adjustment in Japan, 1970-82 / R. P. Dore ; with contributions by K. Taira. — Geneva : International Labour Office, 1986. — xii,189p. — (Employment, adjustment and industrialisation ; 1). — *Bibliography: p [183]-189*

JAPAN — Industries — 1945-

WORONOFF, Jon
The Japan syndrome : symptoms, ailments, and remedies / Jon Woronoff. — New Brunswick (U.S.A.) : Transaction Books, c1986. — 230 p.. — *Includes index. — Bibliography: p. [225]-226*

JAPAN — Intellectual life — 20th century

NOLTE, Sharon H
Liberalism in modern Japan : Ishibashi Tanzan and his teachers, 1905-1960 / Sharon H. Nolte. — Berkeley : University of California Press, c1987. — xii, 378 p.. — *Includes index. — Bibliography: p. 343-370*

JAPAN — Military policy

HOYT, Edwin P.
Japan's war : the great Pacific conflict 1853-1952 / Edwin P. Hoyt. — London : Hutchinson, 1987, c1986. — x,514p,[24]pof plates. — *Originally published: New York : McGraw-Hill, 1986*

JAPAN — Military relations — Great Britain

PRITCHARD, R. John
Far Eastern influences upon British strategy towards the great powers, 1937-1939 / R. John Pritchard. — New York : Garland Pub., 1987. — 328 p.. — (Outstanding theses from the London School of Economics and Political Science). — *Thesis (Ph.D.)--University of London, 1979. — Bibliography: p. 275-328*

JAPAN — National security

BARNHART, Michael A.
Japan prepares for total war : the search for economic security, 1919-1941 / Michael A. Barnhart. — Ithaca : Cornell University Press, 1987. — 290 p.. — (Cornell studies in security affairs). — *Includes index. — Bibliography: p. 275-282*

JAPAN — Occupations — Statistics

1980 population census of Japan / Statistics Bureau. — [Tokyo] : Statistics Bureau
Vol.7: Results of special tabulation
Part 1: Industry and occupation (one percent sample tabulation). — [1984]. — xx,171,[12]p. — *Text in Japanese and English*

JAPAN — Politics and government — 1868-1912

NORMAN, E. Herbert
Japan's emergence as a modern state : political and economic problems of the Meiji period. — Westport, Conn. : Greenwood Press, [1973, c1940]. — xvi, 254 p. — *Reprint of the ed. published by International Secretariat, Institute of Pacific Relations, New York, in series: I. P. R. inquiry series. — Bibliography: p. 211-242*

JAPAN — Politics and government — 1926-1945

FÄLT, Olavi K
Fascism, militarism, or Japanism? : the interpretation of the crisis years of 1930-1941 in the Japanese English-language press / Olavi K. Fält ; [translated by Malcolm Hicks]. — Rovaniemi : Pohjois-Suomen Historiallinen Yhdistys : Societas Historica Finlandiae Septentrionalis, 1985. — 150 p.. — (Studia historica septentrionalia ; 8). — *Includes index. — Bibliography: p. 146-148*

HOSTON, Germaine A.
Marxism and the crisis of development in prewar Japan / Germaine A. Hoston. — Princeton, N.J. : Princeton University Press, c1986. — xviii, 401 p... — *Includes index. Bibliography: p. 357-386*

JAPAN — Politics and government — 1945-

BAERWALD, Hans H.
Party politics in Japan / Hans Baerwald. — Boston ; London : Allen & Unwin, 1986. — xiv,204p. — *Bibliography: p193-196. Includes index*

Democracy in contemporary Japan / edited by Gavan McCormack & Yoshio Sugimoto. — Armonk, N.Y. ; London : M.E. Sharpe, 1987. — 1v.

Democratizing Japan : the allied occupation / edited by Robert E. Ward and Sakamoto Yoshikazu. — Honolulu : University of Hawaii Press, c1987. — xv, 456 p., [1] folded leaf of plates. — *One leaf of plates in pocket. — Based on papers presented at a conference sponsored by both the Japan Society for the Promotion of Science and the Joint Committee on Japanese Studies of the American Council of Learned Societies and the Social Science Research Council with support from the National Endowment for the Humanities. — Includes bibliographies and index*

JAPAN — Population

[1980 population census of Japan]. Population of Japan : final report of the 1980 population census / Statistics Bureau. — [Tokyo] : Statistics Bureau, [1985]. — 59,360p. — *Text in Japanese*

JAPAN — Population — History

HANLEY, Susan B.
Economic and demographic change in preindustrial Japan, 1600-1868 / by Susan B. Hanley and Kozo Yamamura. — Princeton, N.J. ; Guildford : Princeton University Press, c1977. — xiii, 409 p. — *Includes index. — Bibliography: p. 387-403*

JAPAN — Population — Statistics

Population of Japan. — Tokyo : Statistics Bureau, 1986. — 124p

JAPAN — Relations — France

CALLIES, Albane
France-Japan : confrontation culturelle dans les entreprises mixtes / Albane Callies. — Paris : Librairie des Méridiens, 1986. — 208p. — *Bibliography: p199-206*

JAPAN — Relations — India

NARASIMHA MURTHY, P. A
India and Japan : dimensions of their relations : historical and political / P.A. Narasimha Murthy. — New Delhi : ABC Pub. House, 1986. — viii, 431 p.. — *Companion volume to: India and Japan : dimensions of their relations : documents. — Includes index. — Bibliography: p. [425]-426*

JAPAN — Relations — Middle East — Congresses

Japan and the Middle East in alliance politics / edited by Ronald A. Morse. — Washington, D.C. : Asia Program, International Security Studies Program, Wilson Center ; Lanham, MD : University Press of America, c1986. — 124 p. — (Conference report / Wilson Center) . — *Papers presented at a conference held at the Wilson Center on Nov. 16, 1984; co-sponsored by the Asia and the International Security Studies Programs of the Wilson Center. — Includes bibliographies*

JAPAN — Rural conditions

FUKUTAKE, Tadashi
[Nihon no nōson. English]. Rural society in Japan / Tadashi Fukutake ; translated by the staff of the Japan Interpreter. — Tokyo : University of Tokyo Press, c1980. — xii, 218 p. . — *Translation of: Nihon no nōson. 2nd ed., 1978. — Includes index*

WASWO, Ann
Japanese landlords : the decline of a rural elite / Ann Waswo. — Berkeley ; London : University of California Press, 1977. — viii,152p. — *Bibliography: p.141-149. — Includes index*

JAPAN — Social conditions — 1600-1868

BIX, Herbert P
Peasant protest in Japan, 1590-1884 / Herbert P. Bix. — New Haven [Conn.] : Yale University Press, c1986. — p. cm. — *Includes index. — Bibliography: p*

VLASTOS, Stephen
Peasant protests and uprisings in Tokugawa Japan / Stephen Vlastos. — Berkeley : University of California Press, c1986. — xii, 184 p.. — *Includes index. — Bibliography: p. [169]-179*

JAPAN — Social conditions — 1868-1912

Japan in transition, from Tokugawa to Meiji / edited by Marius B. Jansen and Gilbert Rozman. — Princeton, N.J. : Princeton University Press, c1986. — ix, 485 p... — *Spine title: Japan in transition. — Includes bibliographical references and index*

JAPAN — Social conditions — 1945-

HENDRY, Joy
Understanding Japanese society / Joy Hendry. — London : Croom Helm, c1987. — 218p. — *Includes bibliographies and index*

ROHLEN, Thomas P
For harmony and strength : Japanese white-collar organization in anthropological perspective / Thomas P. Rohlen. — Berkeley : University of California Press, [1974]. — 285 p., [4] leaves of plates. — *Includes index. — Bibliography: p. [271]-280*

TSURUMI, Shunsuke
A cultural history of postwar Japan 1945-1980 / Shunsuke Tsurumi. — London : KPI, 1987. — xi,174p. — *Bibliography: p134-164*

UPHAM, Frank K
Law and social change in postwar Japan / Frank K. Upham. — Cambridge, Mass. : Harvard University Press, 1987. — p. cm. — *Includes index*

JAPAN — Social conditions — 1945- — Statistics

JAPAN. Statistics Bureau
Statistical indicators on social life. — [Tokyo] : the Bureau, 1984. — xiii,621p. — *Text in Japanese and English*

JAPAN — Social life and customs

EKKEN, Kaibara Atsunobu
The way of contentment ; and Women and wisdom of Japan [Greater learning for women] / Kaibara Ekken ; translated from the Japanese by Ken Hoshino. — Washington, D.C. : University Publications of America, 1979. — 124,64p. — (Studies in Japanese history and civilization). — *At head of title: Wisdom of the East. — Reprint the way of contentment (London: John Murray, 1913) and Women and wisdom of Japan [Greater learning for women] (London: John Murray, 1905)*

MOERAN, Brian
Okubo diary : portrait of a Japanese valley / Brian Moeren. — Stanford, Calif. : Stanford University, 1985. — p. cm. — *Bibliography: p*

JAPAN. Kaigun — History

DINGMAN, Roger
Power in the Pacific : the origins of naval arms limitation, 1914-1922 / Roger Dingman. — Chicago : University of Chicago Press, 1976. — xiii, 318 p.. — *Includes index. — Bibliography: p. 287-310*

JAPANESE AMERICANS — Civil rights
COLLINS, Donald E
Native American aliens : renunciation of citizenship by Japanese Americans during World War II / Donald E. Collins. — Westport, Conn. : Greenwood Press, c1985. — p. cm. — (Contributions in legal studies ; no. 32). — Includes index. — Bibliography: p

JAPANESE AMERICANS — Cultural assimilation
LYMAN, Stanford M
Chinatown and Little Tokyo : power, conflict, and community among Chinese and Japanese immigrants to America / Stanford Morris Lyman. — Millwood, N.Y. : Associated Faculty Press, c1986. — xiv, 282 p.. — (Minority structures and race and ethnic relations series). — Bibliography: p. 255-272

JAPANESE AMERICANS — Evacuation and relocation, 1942-1945
COLLINS, Donald E
Native American aliens : renunciation of citizenship by Japanese Americans during World War II / Donald E. Collins. — Westport, Conn. : Greenwood Press, c1985. — p. cm. — (Contributions in legal studies ; no. 32). — Includes index. — Bibliography: p

JAPANESE AMERICANS — Evacuation and relocation, 1942-1945 — Congresses
Japanese Americans, from relocation to redress / edited by Roger Daniels, Sandra C. Taylor, and Harry H.L. Kitano ; contributions by Leonard J. Arrington ... [et al.]. — Salt Lake City, Utah : University of Utah Press, c1986. — xxi, 216 p. — Based on the International Conference on Relocation and Redress held in Salt Lake City in March 1983. — Includes bibliographies

JAPANESE AMERICANS — Legal status, laws, etc
COLLINS, Donald E
Native American aliens : renunciation of citizenship by Japanese Americans during World War II / Donald E. Collins. — Westport, Conn. : Greenwood Press, c1985. — p. cm. — (Contributions in legal studies ; no. 32). — Includes index. — Bibliography: p

JAPANESE AMERICANS — Evacuation and relocation, 1942-1945
DRINNON, Richard
Keeper of concentration camps : Dillon S. Myer and American racism / Richard Drinnon. — Berkeley : University of California Press, c1987. — xxviii, 339 p.. — Includes index. — Bibliography: p. 271-324

JAPANESE COMMUNIST PARTY See
Nihon Kyosanto

JAPANESE IN CANADA
WARD, W. Peter
The Japanese in Canada / W. Peter Ward. — Ottawa : Canadian Historical Association, 1982. — 21p. — (Canada's ethnic groups. booklet ; no. 3)

JAPANESE LANGUAGE — Dictionaries
MITSUBISHI SHŌJI KABUSHIKI KAISHA
Japanese business language : an essential dictionary / compiled by the Mitsubishi Corporation ; introduction by Kaori O'Connor. — London : KPI ; London : Routledge and Kegan Paul, 1987. — xiii,221p

JAPANESE LITERATURE — Meiji period, 1868-1912 — translations into English
Modern Japanese literature : an anthology / compiled and edited by Donald Keene. — New York : Grove Press, Inc., 1956. — 440p. — (Grove Press Eastern literature and philosophy books). — Bibliography: p[439]-440

JAPANESE LITERATURE — 20th century — translations into English
Modern Japanese literature : an anthology / compiled and edited by Donald Keene. — New York : Grove Press, Inc., 1956. — 440p. — (Grove Press Eastern literature and philosophy books). — Bibliography: p[439]-440

JAPANESE STUDIES — Europe
Europe interprets Japan / edited by Gordon Daniels. — Tenterden : Paul Norbury Publications, 1984. — xi,279p. — Papers presented at the Third International Japanese Studies Conference, the Hague, 20 to 23 September 1982

JAVA (INDONESIA) — History
INGLESON, John
In search of justice : workers and unions in colonial Java, 1908-1926 / John Ingleson. — Singapore ; New York : Oxford University Press, 1986. — xiii, 342 p., [1] p. of plates. — (Southeast Asia publications series / Asian Studies Association of Australia ; no. 12). — Includes index. — Bibliography: p. [327]-337

JAVANESE LANGUAGE — Social aspects
SIEGEL, James T.
Solo in the new order : language and hierarchy in an Indonesian city / James T. Siegel. — Princeton, N.J. : Princeton University Press, c1986. — p. cm. — Includes index. — Bibliography: p

JAWA TENGAH (INDONESIA) — Rural conditions
HART, Gillian Patricia
Power, labor, and livelihood : processes of change in rural Java / Gillian Hart. — Berkeley : University of California Press, c1986. — xvi, 228 p. — Includes index. — Bibliography: p. 213-222

JEJU DO (KOREA (SOUTH)) — Statistics
1970 population and housing census report (complete). — [Seoul] : Economic Planning Board. — In Korean and English
Vol.12-12: Jeju Do. — 1972. — 120p

JENKINS, DAFYDD — Bibliography
Lawyers and laymen / edited by T.M. Charles-Edwards, Morfydd E. Owen and D. B. Walters. — Cardiff : University of Wales Press, 1986. — 394,[1]p of plates. — Includes two papers in Welsh. — Festschrift in honour of Professor Dafydd Jenkins. — Bibliography: p355-368. — Includes index

JEONRA BUG DO (KOREA(SOUTH)) — Statistics
1970 population and housing census report (complete). — [Seoul] : Economic Planning Board. — In Korean and English
Vol.12-8: Jeonra Bug Do. — 1972. — 250p

JEONRA NAM DO (KOREA (SOUTH)) — Statistics
1970 population and housing census report (complete). — [Seoul] : Economic Planning Board. — In Korean and English
Vol.12-9: Jeonra Nam Do. — 1972. — 354p

JEROME, JAMES
JEROME, James
Mr. Speaker / James Jerome. — Toronto, Ont. : McClelland and Stewart, c1985. — 175 p., [8] p. of plates. — Includes index

JERUSALEM — History
GILBERT, Martin
Jerusalem : rebirth of a city / Martin Gilbert. — London : Chatto & Windus, 1985. — [viii,224]p. — Includes bibliography and index

JERUSALEM — International status
MALLISON, W. Thomas
The Palestine problem in international law and world order / W. Thomas Mallison and Sally V. Mallison. — London : Longman, 1986. — xvi,564p

JERUSALEM — Politics and government
BENVENISTI, Meron
Conflicts and contradictions / Meron Benvenisti. — 1st ed. — New York : Villard Books, 1986. — xii, 210 p.. — Includes index

JESUS CHRIST — Political and social views
YODER, John Howard
The politics of Jesus : vicit agnus noster / John H. Yoder. — Grand Rapids, Mioch : Eerdmans, 1972. — 260p

JEVONS, WILLIAM STANLEY — Addresses, essays, lectures
SHAW, George Bernard
Bernard Shaw & Karl Marx : a symposium, 1884-1889. — Folcroft, Pa. : Folcroft Library Editions, 1977. — ix, 200 p., [1] fold. leaf of plates. — Reprint of the 1930 ed. printed for Random House by R. W. Ellis, The Georgian Press, New York

JEWISH-ARAB RELATIONS
AVNERY, Uri
My friend, the enemy / Uri Avnery. — London : Zed, 1985. — [336]p. — Includes index

BENVENISTI, Meron
Conflicts and contradictions / Meron Benvenisti. — 1st ed. — New York : Villard Books, 1986. — xii, 210 p.. — Includes index

ELON, Amos
The Israelis : founders and sons / Amos Elon. — New York : Penguin, 1983. — xiv, 359 p.. — : Previously published: New York : Holt, Rinehart, and Winston, 1971. — Includes index. — Bibliography: p. 336-348

Israel, the Middle East and the great powers : studies in the contemporary history and politics of the Middle East and the Arab-Israel conflict / edited by Israel Stockman-Shomron. — [Jerusalem] : Shikmona Publishing Co., 1984. — 389p

MILLER, Aaron David
The Arab states and the Palestine question : between ideology and self-interest / Aaron David Miller ; foreword by Alfred A. Atherton. — New York : Praeger Published with the Center for Strategic and International Studies, Georgetown University, Washington, D.C., c1986. — p. cm. — (The Washington papers ; 120). — "Praeger special studies. Praeger scientific."

TURKI, Fawaz
The Disinherited : journal of a Palestinian exile. — 2nd Modern Reader pbk. ed. — New York ; london : [Modern Reader], 1974, c1972. — Originally published in 1972. — Bibliographical references

WHITFIELD, David
A land with people : a report from occupied Palestine / David Whitfield. — London : Morning Star, 1986. — 56p

JEWISH-ARAB RELATIONS — Public opinion
Public opinion and the Palestine question / edited by Elia Zureik and Fouad Moughrabi. — London : Croom Helm, c1987. — 206p. — Includes index

JEWISH-ARAB RELATIONS — To 1917
GORNI, Yosef
Zionism and the Arabs 1882-1948 : a study of ideology / Yosef Gorny. — Oxford : Clarendon, 1987. — x,342p. — Translation of: Ha-She' elah ha-'Arvit veha-be 'ayah ha-Yehundit. — Bibliography: p326-330. — Includes index

JEWISH-ARAB RELATIONS — 1917-1949
BLACK, Ian
Zionism and the Arabs, 1936-1939 / Ian Black. — New York : Garland, 1986. — 435 p.. — (Outstanding theses from the London School of Economics and Political Science). — Thesis (Ph. D.)--University of London, 1978. — Bibliography: p. 426-435

GORNI, Yosef
Zionism and the Arabs 1882-1948 : a study of ideology / Yosef Gorny. — Oxford : Clarendon, 1987. — x,342p. — Translation of: Ha-She' elah ha-'Arvit veha-be 'ayah ha-Yehundit. — Bibliography: p326-330. — Includes index

PALUMBO, Michael
The Palestinian catastrophe : the 1948 expulsion of a people from their homeland / Michael Palumbo. — London : Faber, 1987. — xix,233p. — Includes index

JEWISH-ARAB RELATIONS — 1917-1949
continuation

TAGGAR, Yehuda
The Mufti of Jerusalem and Palestine : Arab politics, 1930-1937 / Yehuda Taggar. — New York : Garland, 1986, c1987. — 472 p.. — (Outstanding theses from the London School of Economics and Political Science). — Thesis (Ph. D.)--University of London, 1973. — *Bibliography: p. 466-472*

JEWISH-ARAB RELATIONS — 1917-

TEVETH, Shabtai
Ben-Gurion and the Palestinian Arabs : from peace to war / Shabtai Teveth. — Oxford : Oxford University Press, 1985. — x,234p

JEWISH-ARAB RELATIONS — 1949-

EL-FARRA, Muhammad
Years of no decision / Muhammad El-Farra. — London : KPI, 1987. — xi,222p

MALLISON, W. Thomas
The Palestine problem in international law and world order / W. Thomas Mallison and Sally V. Mallison. — London : Longman, 1986. — xvi,564p

JEWISH-ARAB RELATIONS — 1949- — Public opinion

GILBOA, Eytan
American public opinion toward Israel and the Arab-Israeli conflict / Eytan Gilboa. — Lexington, Mass. : Lexington Books, c1987. — xvi, 366 p.. — *Includes index. — Bibliography: p. [337]-347*

JEWISH-ARAB RELATIONS — 1967-1973

MISHAL, Shaul
The PLO under 'Arafat : between gun and olive branch / Shaul Mishal. — New Haven ; London : Yale University Press, c1986. — xiv, 190p. — *Includes index*

JEWISH-ARAB RELATIONS — 1973-

GREAT BRITAIN. Parliament. House of Commons. Library. International Affairs Section
The search for peace and stability in the Middle East / Richard Ware. — [London] : the Library, 1986. — 23p. — (Background paper / House of Commons. Library. [Research Division] ; no.187)

GREAT BRITAIN. Parliament. House of Commons. Library. International Affairs Section
Western Europe and the Palestinian question / Richard War. — [London] : the Library, 1981. — 29p. — (Background paper / House of Commons. Library. [Research Division] ; no.94). — *Bibliography: p24*

INSTITUT FRANÇAIS DE POLÉMOLOGIE
La conflit israélo-arabe. — Paris : La Documentation française. — (Notes et études documentaires ; no.4792)
t 2: 1974-1984. — 1985. — 141p

KREISKY, Bruno
Das Nahostproblem : Reden, Interviews, Kommentare / Bruno Kreisky ; [Claudia Reinhardt (Hrsgn)] ; [mit einem Vorwort von Olof Palme]. — Wien : Europaverlag, 1985. — 262p

MISHAL, Shaul
The PLO under 'Arafat : between gun and olive branch / Shaul Mishal. — New Haven ; London : Yale University Press, c1986. — xiv, 190p. — *Includes index*

JEWISH-ARAB RELATIONS — 1973- — Study and teaching (Higher) — Israel

GORDON, Hayim
Dance, dialogue, and despair : existentialist philosophy and education for peace in Isreal / Haim Gordon. — University, Ala. : University of Alabama Press, c1986. — xvii, 250 p.. — (Judaic studies series). — *Includes index. — Bibliographical essay: p. 240-244*

JEWISH BANKERS — Biography

ATTALI, Jacques
A man of influence : Sir Siegmund Warburg 1902-82 / Jacques Attali ; translated by Barbara Ellis. — London : Weidenfeld and Nicholson, 1986. — vii,346p. — *Translation of: Un homme d'influence*

JEWISH CHILDREN — Israel

Between two worlds : children from the Soviet Union in Israel / edited by Tamar Ruth Horowitz. — Lanham [Md.] : University Press of America, c1986. — vi, 233 p.. — *Includes bibliographies*

JEWISH COLLEGE TEACHERS — Connecticut — New Haven — History

OREN, Dan A.
Joining the club : a history of Jews and Yale / Dan A. Oren. — New Haven : Yale University Press, c1985. — xiv, 440 p.. — (The Yale scene. University series ; 4). — *Published in cooperation with the American Jewish Archives. — Includes index. — Bibliography: p. 397-423*

JEWISH CRIMINALS — New York (State) — Brooklyn — Case studies

ROSNER, Lydia S
The Soviet way of crime : beating the system in the Soviet Union and the U.S.A. / Lydia S. Rosner. — South Hadley, Mass. : Bergin & Garvey Publishers, 1986. — xvii, 140 p.. — *Includes bibliographies and index*

JEWISH CRIMINALS — Soviet Union

EVEL'SON, Evgeniia
Sudebnye protsessy po ekonomicheskim delam v SSSR (shestidesiatye gody) / Evgeniia Evel'son. — London : Overseas Publications Interchange, 1986. — 370p. — *Published in conjunction with the Soviet and East European Research Centre of the Hebrew University, Jerusalem. — Bibliography: p365-370*

JEWISH FAMILIES — Bibliography

SCHLESINGER, Benjamin
Jewish family issues : a resource guide / Benjamin Schlesinger. — New York : Garland, 1987. — xvi, 144 p.. — (Garland library of sociology ; v. 10) (Garland reference library of social science ; v. 385). — *Includes index*

JEWISH LAW

QUINT, Emanuel B.
Jewish jurisprudence : its sources and modern applications / Emanuel B. Quint and Neil S. Hecht. — Chur : Harwood Academic Publishers
Vol.2. — 1986. — xvii,237p

JEWISH TRADE-UNIONS — France — Paris

GREEN, Nancy L
The Pletzl of Paris : Jewish immigrant workers in the "belle epoque" / Nancy L. Green. — New York : Holmes & Meier, 1986. — ix, 270 p.. — *Includes index. — Bibliography: p. 249-263*

JEWS

Commentary / American Jewish Committee. — New York : American Jewish Committee, 1987-. — *Monthly*

JEWS — Cultural assimilation — Congresses

Toward modernity : the European Jewish model / edited by Jacob Katz. — New Brunswick, N.J. : Transaction, Inc., c1986. — p. cm. — *Includes bibliographies and index*

JEWS — Education — Connecticut — New Haven — History

OREN, Dan A.
Joining the club : a history of Jews and Yale / Dan A. Oren. — New Haven : Yale University Press, c1985. — xiv, 440 p.. — (The Yale scene. University series ; 4). — *Published in cooperation with the American Jewish Archives. — Includes index. — Bibliography: p. 397-423*

JEWS — Education — Europe, Eastern — History

BRUMBERG, Stephan F
Going to America, going to school : the Jewish immigrant public school encounter in turn-of-the-century New York City / Stephan F. Brumberg. — New York : Praeger, 1986. — xiii, 282 p.. — *Includes bibliographies and indexes*

JEWS — History

HALEVI, Ilan
A history of the Jews, ancient and modern / Ilan Halevi ; translated by A.M. Berrett. — London : Zed, 1987. — [272]p. — *Translation of: Question Juive, la tribu, la loi, l'espace. — Includes index*

JEWS — History — Atlases

GILBERT, Martin
Jewish history atlas / Martin Gilbert ; cartography by Arthur Banks and Terry Bicknell. — 3rd ed. — London : Weidenfeld and Nicolson, 1985. — 124,[4]p. — *Bibliography: 4 pages following p124*

JEWS — History — 1789-1945 — Congresses

Toward modernity : the European Jewish model / edited by Jacob Katz. — New Brunswick, N.J. : Transaction, Inc., c1986. — p. cm. — *Includes bibliographies and index*

JEWS — History — 1945-

Hopes & realities 1945-1985 : papers delivered at a conference held by the Institute of Jewish Affairs in London on 5 May 1985 to commemorate the fortieth anniversary of VE Day / edited by William Frankel. — London : Institute of Jewish Affairs, 1986. — 77p

JEWS — Languages

Readings in the sociology of Jewish languages / edited by Joshua A. Fishman. — Leiden : E. J. Brill, 1985. — xii,298p. — (Contributions to the sociology of Jewish languages ; Vol.1)

JEWS — Politics and government

Comparative Jewish politics. — [Ramat Gan] : Bar-Ilan University Press. — (Bar-Ilan departmental researches)
Vol.2: Conflict and consensus in Jewish political life / edited by Stuart A. Cohen and Eliezer Don-Yehiya. — 1986. — 218p

JEWS — Public opinion — History — 19th century

COWEN, Anne
Victorian Jews through British eyes / Anne and Roger Cowen. — Oxford : published for the Littman Library by Oxford University Press, 1986. — xxviii,196p. — (The Littman library of Jewish civilization). — *Includes index*

JEWS — Social conditions — Bibliography

SCHLESINGER, Benjamin
Jewish family issues : a resource guide / Benjamin Schlesinger. — New York : Garland, 1987. — xvi, 144 p.. — (Garland library of sociology ; v. 10) (Garland reference library of social science ; v. 385). — *Includes index*

JEWS — Argentina — Persecutions

SENKMAN, Leonardo
El antisemitismo en la Argentina / Leonardo Senkman. — Buenos Aires : Centro Editor de América Latina. — (Biblioteca Política Argentina ; 146)
t.1. — 1986. — 128p

SENKMAN, Leonardo
El antisemitismo en la Argentina / Leonard Senkman. — Buenos Aires : Centro Editor de América Latina. — (Biblioteca Política Argentina ; 149). — *Bibliography: p233-235*
t.2. — 1986. — 129-250p

JEWS — Austria — Biography
SICHROVSKY, Peter
[Wir wissen nicht was morgen wird, wir wissen wohl was gestern war. English]. Strangers in their own land : young Jews in Germany and Austria today / Peter Sichrovsky ; translated by Jean Steinberg. — New York : Basic Books, c1986. — ix, 165 p.. — *Translation of: Wir wissen nicht was morgen wird, wir wissen wohl was gestern war*

JEWS — California — Los Angeles — Cultural assimilation
SANDBERG, Neil C
Jewish life in Los Angeles : a window to tomorrow / Neil C. Sandberg. — Lanham [MD] : University Press of America, c1986. — p. cm. — *Includes index*. — *Bibliography: p*

JEWS — California — Los Angeles — Identify
SANDBERG, Neil C
Jewish life in Los Angeles : a window to tomorrow / Neil C. Sandberg. — Lanham [MD] : University Press of America, c1986. — p. cm. — *Includes index*. — *Bibliography: p*

JEWS — Cananda
VIGOD, Bernard L.
The Jews in Canada / Bernard L.Vigod. — Ottawa : Canadian Historical Association, 1984. — 19p. — (Canada's ethnic groups. booklet ; no.7)

JEWS — Ethiopia
Coming home : the story of Ethiopian Jewry. — London : Britain-Israel Public Affairs Committee : Spiro Institute for the Study of Jewish History and Culture, 1985. — 13p

JEWS — France
WILSON, Nelly
Bernard-Lazare : l'antisémitisme, l'affaire Dreyfus, et la recherche de l'identité juive / Nelly Wilson ; traduit de l'anglais par Christiane et Douglas Gallagher. — Paris : Albin Michel, [1985]. — 461p. — *Bibliography: p435-450*

JEWS — France — Persecutions
COHEN, Richard I
The burden of conscience : French Jewish leadership during the holocaust / Richard I. Cohen. — Bloomington : Indiana University Press, c1987. — p. cm. — (The Modern Jewish experience). — *Includes index*. — *Bibliography: p*

KLARSFELD, Serge
Vichy-Auschwitz : le rôle de Vichy dans la solution finale de la question juive en France / Serge Klarsfeld. — Paris : Fayard [2]: 1943-1944. — 1985. — 408p

JEWS — France — Politics and government
COHEN, Richard I
The burden of conscience : French Jewish leadership during the holocaust / Richard I. Cohen. — Bloomington : Indiana University Press, c1987. — p. cm. — (The Modern Jewish experience). — *Includes index*. — *Bibliography: p*

JEWS — France — Paris
GREEN, Nancy L
The Pletzl of Paris : Jewish immigrant workers in the "belle epoque" / Nancy L. Green. — New York : Holmes & Meier, 1986. — ix, 270 p.. — *Includes index*. — *Bibliography: p. 249-263*

JEWS — Germany — History
FRIEDMANN, Friedrich Georg
Hannah Arendt : eine deutsche Jüdin im Zeitalter des Totalitarismus / Friedrich Georg Friedmann. — München : Piper, 1985. — 160p

MOSSE, W. E.
Jews in the German economy : the German-Jewish economic élite, 1820-1935 / W.E. Mosse. — Oxford : Clarendon, 1987. — 420p. — *Bibliography: p406-409*. — *Includes index*

JEWS — Germany — Intellectual life — Congresses
The Jewish response to German culture : from the enlightenment to the Second World War / edited by Jehuda Reinharz and Walter Schatzberg. — Hanover, NH : Published for Clark University by University Press of New England, 1985. — xii, 362p. — *"Essays based on papers delivered at the International Conference on German Jews, held at Clark University, Worcester, Massachusetts, October 8-11, 1983."*. — *Includes index*

JEWS — Germany (West) — Biography
SICHROVSKY, Peter
[Wir wissen nicht was morgen wird, wir wissen wohl was gestern war. English]. Strangers in their own land : young Jews in Germany and Austria today / Peter Sichrovsky ; translated by Jean Steinberg. — New York : Basic Books, c1986. — ix, 165 p.. — *Translation of: Wir wissen nicht was morgen wird, wir wissen wohl was gestern war*

JEWS — Great Britain
T. A. C. : bulletin of the Trades Advisory Council. — London : Trades Advisory Council, 1942-. — *Monthly*

JEWS — Great Britain — History — 1789-1945
COWEN, Anne
Victorian Jews through British eyes / Anne and Roger Cowen. — Oxford : published for the Littman Library by Oxford University Press, 1986. — xxviii,196p. — (The Littman library of Jewish civilization). — *Includes index*

JEWS — Great Britain — Social conditions
COWEN, Anne
Victorian Jews through British eyes / Anne and Roger Cowen. — Oxford : published for the Littman Library by Oxford University Press, 1986. — xxviii,196p. — (The Littman library of Jewish civilization). — *Includes index*

WATERMAN, Stanley
British Jewry in the eighties : a statistical and geographical guide / by Stanley Waterman and Barry Kosmin. — London : Board of Deputies of British Jews Research Unit, 1986. — 56p

JEWS — Hungary — History
The tragedy of Hungarian Jewry : essays, documents, depositions / edited by Randolph L. Braham. — Boulder, Colo. : Social Science Monographs ; New York : Institute for Holocaust Studies of the City University of New York, 1986. — viii,328p. — (Holocaust studies series) (East European monographs ; no.208)

JEWS — Hungary — Persecutions — Congresses
The Holocaust in Hungary : forty years later / edited by Randolph L. Braham and Bela Vago. — New York : Institute of Holocaust Studies of the City University of New York, and Institute of Holocaust Studies of the University of Haifa : Columbia University Press [distributor], 1985. — xv,235p. — (East European monographs ; no.190) (Holocaust studies series). — *'... an outgrowth of two international conferences held in 1984....'*

JEWS — Italy — Persecutions
ZUCCOTTI, Susan
The Italians and the Holocaust : persecution, rescue and survival / Susan Zuccotti. — London : Halban, 1987. — xviii,334p,[8]p of plates. — *Includes index*

JEWS — Lithuania — Vilnius — Addresses, essays, lectures
KAHAN, Arcadius
Essays in Jewish social and economic history / Arcadius Kahan ; edited by Roger Weiss ; with an introduction by Jonathan Frankel. — Chicago : University of Chicago Press, 1986. — xx, 208 p.. — *Includes bibliographical references and index*

JEWS — Palestine — Economic conditions
BERNSTEIN, Deborah
The struggle for equality : urban women workers in pre-state Israeli society / by Deborah Bernstein. — New York : Praeger, 1986. — p. cm. — *"Praeger special studies. Praeger scientific."*. — *Includes index*. — *Bibliography: p*

JEWS — Palestine — History
SHAVIT, Yaacov
The new Hebrew nation : a study in Israeli heresy and fantasy / Yaacov Shavit. — London : Cass, 1987. — xv,192p. — *Bibliography: p164-174*. — *Includes index*

JEWS — Palestine — History — 19th century
BLUMBERG, Arnold
Zion before Zionism, 1838-1880 / Arnold Blumberg. — 1st ed. — Syracuse, N.Y. : Syracuse University Press, 1985. — xv, 235p. — *Includes index*. — *Bibliography: p.207-221*

JEWS — Poland
CONFERENCE ON POLES AND JEWS: MYTH AND REALITY IN THE HISTORICAL CONTEXT (1983 : Columbia University)
Proceedings of the Conference on Poles and Jews--Myth and Reality in the Historical Context, held at Columbia University, March 6-10, 1983 / editorial staff, John Micgiel, Robert Scott, H.B. Segel. — New York : Institute on East Central Europe, Columbia University, 1986. — vi, 562 p.. — *Cover title: Poles and Jews*. — *"Sponsored by the Institute on East Central Europe, Columbia University, in collaboration with the Center for Israel and Jewish Studies, Columbia University"--Cover*. — *Includes bibliographies*

GRYNBERG, Michał
Żydowska spółdzielczość prazy w Polsce w latach 1945-1949 / Michał Grynberg. — Warszawa : Państwowe Wydawnictwo Naukowe, 1986. — 183p. — *Bibliography: p174-176*

JEWS — Poland — Bibliography
LERSKI, Jerzy J
Jewish-Polish coexistence, 1772-1939 : a topical bibliography / compiled by George J. Lerski and Halina T. Lerski ; foreword by Lucjan Dobroszycki. — New York : Greenwood Press, 1986. — xiv, 230 p.. — (Bibliographies and indexes in world history ; no. 5). — *Includes index*

JEWS — Poland — History
The Jews in Poland / edited by Chimen Abramsky, Maciej Jachimczyk and Antony Polansky. — Oxford : Blackwell, 1986. — vi,264p. — *Conference papers*. — *Includes index*

Polin : a journal of Polish-Jewish studies. — Oxford : Basil Blackwell for the Institute for Polish-Jewish Studies, 1986

JEWS — Soviet Union
EVEL'SON, Evgeniia
Sudebnye protsessy po ekonomicheskim delam v SSSR (shestidesiatye gody) / Evgeniia Evel'son. — London : Overseas Publications Interchange, 1986. — 370p. — *Published in conjunction with the Soviet and East European Research Centre of the Hebrew University, Jerusalem*. — *Bibliography: p365-370*

SARFATI, Georges Elia
La nation captive sur la question juive soviétique / Georges Elia Sarfati. — Paris : Nouvelle Cité, 1985. — 298p

JEWS — Soviet Union — Economic conditions — Addresses, essays, lectures
KAHAN, Arcadius
Essays in Jewish social and economic history / Arcadius Kahan ; edited by Roger Weiss ; with an introduction by Jonathan Frankel. — Chicago : University of Chicago Press, 1986. — xx, 208 p.. — *Includes bibliographical references and index*

JEWS — Soviet Union — History — 18th century
KLIER, John
Russia gathers her Jews : the origins of the "Jewish question" in Russia, 1772-1825 / John Doyle Klier. — DeKalb, Ill. : Northern Illinois University Press, 1986. — xxiv, 236p. — *Map on lining papers. — Includes index. — Bibliography: p. [213]-223*

JEWS — Soviet Union — History — 19th century
KLIER, John
Russia gathers her Jews : the origins of the "Jewish question" in Russia, 1772-1825 / John Doyle Klier. — DeKalb, Ill. : Northern Illinois University Press, 1986. — xxiv, 236p. — *Map on lining papers. — Includes index. — Bibliography: p. [213]-223*

JEWS — Soviet Union — Identity — Addresses, essays, lectures
KAHAN, Arcadius
Essays in Jewish social and economic history / Arcadius Kahan ; edited by Roger Weiss ; with an introduction by Jonathan Frankel. — Chicago : University of Chicago Press, 1986. — xx, 208 p.. — *Includes bibliographical references and index*

JEWS — Soviet Union — Social conditions
The Position of Soviet Jewry 1983-86 : report on the implementation of the Helsinki Final Act since the Madrid Follow-Up Conference. — London : Published on behalf of the International Council of the World Conference on Soviet Jewry in co-operation with the Jewish communities concerned [by] Institute of Jewish Affairs, 1986. — [72]p

ROTHCHILD, Sylvia
A special legacy : an oral history of Soviet Jewish emigrés in the United States / by Sylvia Rothchild. — New York : Simon and Schuster, c1985. — p. cm. — *Includes index*

JEWS — United States
BRENNER, Lenni
Jews in America today / Lenni Brenner. — London : Al Saqi, 1986. — [320]p. — *Includes bibliography and index*

Commentary / American Jewish Committee. — New York : American Jewish Committee, 1987-. — *Monthly*

JEWS — United States — Abstracts
The Jewish experience in America : a historical bibliography. — Santa Barbara, Calif. ; Oxford : ABC-Clio, 1983. — vi,190p. — *"Compiled from the periodicals database of the American Bibliographical Center by editors at ABC-Clio Information Services"*

JEWS — United States — Attitudes toward Israel
GILBOA, Eytan
American public opinion toward Israel and the Arab-Israeli conflict / Eytan Gilboa. — Lexington, Mass. : Lexington Books, c1987. — xvi, 366 p.. — *Includes index. — Bibliography: p. [337]-347*

JEWS — United States — Biography
AUSMUS, Harry J.
Will Herberg, from right to right / by Harry J. Ausmus ; with a foreword by Martin E. Marty. — Chapel Hill : University of North Carolina Press, c1987. — p. cm. — (Studies in religion). — *Includes index. — Bibliography: p*

JEWS — United States — Economic conditions — Addresses, essays, lectures
KAHAN, Arcadius
Essays in Jewish social and economic history / Arcadius Kahan ; edited by Roger Weiss ; with an introduction by Jonathan Frankel. — Chicago : University of Chicago Press, 1986. — xx, 208 p.. — *Includes bibliographical references and index*

JEWS — United States — History
BRENNER, Lenni
Jews in America today / Lenni Brenner. — London : Al Saqi, 1986. — [320]p. — *Includes bibliography and index*

JEWS — United States — Intellectual life
OREN, Dan A.
Joining the club : a history of Jews and Yale / Dan A. Oren. — New Haven : Yale University Press, c1985. — xiv, 440 p.. — (The Yale scene. University series ; 4). — *Published in cooperation with the American Jewish Archives. — Includes index. — Bibliography: p. 397-423*

JEWS — United States — Politics and government — History
CASTRO, Fidel
Fidel Castro habla a los trabajadores de América Latina sobre la deuda externa : diálogo sostenido con los delegados a la Conferencia Sindical de los Trabajadores de América Latina y el Caribe sobre la Deuda Externa, durante la sesión de clausura del evento, el jueves 18 de julio de 1985. — Buenos Aires : Editorial Anteo, 1985. — 102 p.

JEWS — United States — Social conditions
MAYER, Egon
Love and tradition : marriage between Jews and Christians / Egon Mayer. — New York : Plenum Press, c1985. — p. cm. — *Includes index. — Bibliography: p*

ROSENWAIKE, Ira
On the edge of greatness : a portrait of American Jewry in the early national period / Ira Rosenwaike. — [Cincinnati] : American Jewish Archives, c1985. — xvi, 189 p.. — (Publications of the American Jewish Archives ; no. 14). — *Bibliography: p. 171-189*

JEWS — Yemen — History
AHRONI, Reuben
Yemenite Jewry : origins, culture and literature / Reuben Ahroni. — Bloomington : Indiana University Press, 1986. — x,227. — (Jewish literature and culture). — *Bibliography: p [204]-220*

JEWS, EAST EUROPEAN — Education — New York (N.Y.) — History
BRUMBERG, Stephan F
Going to America, going to school : the Jewish immigrant public school encounter in turn-of-the-century New York City / Stephan F. Brumberg. — New York : Praeger, 1986. — xiii, 282 p.. — *Includes bibliographies and indexes*

JEWS, EAST EUROPEAN — France — Paris
GREEN, Nancy L
The Pletzl of Paris : Jewish immigrant workers in the "belle epoque" / Nancy L. Green. — New York : Holmes & Meier, 1986. — ix, 270 p.. — *Includes index. — Bibliography: p. 249-263*

JEWS, EAST EUROPEAN — United States — Economic conditions — Addresses, essays, lectures
KAHAN, Arcadius
Essays in Jewish social and economic history / Arcadius Kahan ; edited by Roger Weiss ; with an introduction by Jonathan Frankel. — Chicago : University of Chicago Press, 1986. — xx, 208 p.. — *Includes bibliographical references and index*

JEWS, GERMAN — Netherlands
MOORE, Bob
Refugees from Nazi Germany in the Netherlands, 1933-1940 / by Bob Moore. — Dordrecht ; Boston : M. Nijhoff, 1986. — xiv, 241 p.. — (Studies in social history ; 9). — *Includes index. — Bibliography: p. 221-233*

JEWS IN ART
COWEN, Anne
Victorian Jews through British eyes / Anne and Roger Cowen. — Oxford : published for the Littman Library by Oxford University Press, 1986. — xxviii,196p. — (The Littman library of Jewish civilization). — *Includes index*

JEWS, RUSSIAN — Education — New York (N.Y.) — History
BRUMBERG, Stephan F
Going to America, going to school : the Jewish immigrant public school encounter in turn-of-the-century New York City / Stephan F. Brumberg. — New York : Praeger, 1986. — xiii, 282 p.. — *Includes bibliographies and indexes*

JEWS, RUSSIAN — Israel — Cultural assimilation
Between two worlds : children from the Soviet Union in Israel / edited by Tamar Ruth Horowitz. — Lanham [Md.] : University Press of America, c1986. — vi, 233 p.. — *Includes bibliographies*

JEWS, RUSSIAN — United States
ROTHCHILD, Sylvia
A special legacy : an oral history of Soviet Jewish emigrés in the United States / by Sylvia Rothchild. — New York : Simon and Schuster, c1985. — p. cm. — *Includes index*

JIHAD
CHARNAY, Jean Paul
L'Islam et la guerre : de la guerre juste à la révolution sainte / Jean Paul Charnay. — Paris : Fayard, 1986. — 354p. — *Bibliography: p [341]-342*

JIYŪ MINSHUTŌ
HVEBENAR, Ronald J.
The Japanese party system : from one-party rule to coalition government / Ronald J. Hrebenar with contributions by Peter Berton ... [et al.]. — Boulder, Colo. : Westview Press, 1986. — xviii, 330 p.. — *Includes bibliographies and index*

JOB ANALYSIS
DULEWICZ, Victor
Job appraisal reviews in HMSO : an evaluation including a before-and-after study / Victor Dulewicz. — London : Behavioural Sciences Research Division, Civil Service Department, 1976. — [43]p. — (BSRD report ; no.32)

GREAT BRITAIN. Civil Service Department. Staff Inspection and Evaluation Branch
Staff inspection in the civil service : an instrument of manpower control and an aid to management efficiency. — London : the Department, 1975. — 10p

PUBLIC ADMINISTRATION SERVICE
Introduction and administration of position classification and pay plans / [prepared for the United Nations Secretariat by the Public Administration Service]. — New York : United Nations, 1976. — xxxiii, 159 p. — ([Document - United Nations] ; ST/ESA/ser.E/5). — *"United Nations publication. Sales no. E.77.II.H.1.". — Bibliography: p. 155-159*

JOB EVALUATION
ELIZUR, Dov
Systematic job evaluation and comparable worth / Dov Elizur. — Aldershot : Gower, c1987. — xxiv,290p. — *Bibliography: p217-244. — Includes index*

Job evaluation. — Geneva : International Labour Office, 1986. — xi,203p. — *Includes bibliographical references*

JOB EVALUATION — Great Britain
GHOBADIAN, Abby
Job evaluation and equal pay / Abby Ghobadian, Michael White, Policy Studies Institute. — [London] : Department of Employment, [1986]. — 177p. — (Research paper / Department of Employment ; no.58)

JOB EVALUATION — Ontario
Report on job evaluation systems in the Ontario public sector. — Kingston, Ont. : Queen's University at Kingston. Industrial Relations Centre, 1986. — 68p. — (Research and current issues series / Queen's University at Kingston. Industrial Relations Centre ; no.47)

JOB HUNTING — Great Britain
CONWAY, Jean
A job to move : the housing problems of job seekers / by Jean Conway & Evan Ramsay. — London : SHAC, 1986. — 64p. — (SHAC research report ; 8)

JOB SATISFACTION
DAVIDMANN, M.
Community leadership and management / M. Davidmann. — Stanmore : Social Organisation 6: The will to work: remuneration, job satisfaction and motivation: what people strive to achieve: struggle for independence and good life. — 1986. — 24p

JOB SATISFACTION — Great Britain
CLOTHING AND ALLIED PRODUCTS INDUSTRY TRAINING BOARD
The aspirations of female shop-floor workers : a report of the survey undertaken by Board staff. — [Leeds] : the Board, c1979. — 109p

JOB SHARING — Québec (Province)
ACOCA, Viviane
Le partage du travail : problématique et possibilités d'application dans la fonction publique du Québec / Viviane Acoca ; avec la collaboration de Jean-François Manègre. — Québec : Ministère de la main-d'oeuvre et de la sécurité du revenu, 1985. — xiv,254p. — *Includes bibliographical references*

JOB STRESS — United States
CHERNISS, Cary
Staff burnout : job stress in the human services / Cary Cherniss. — Beverly Hills ; London : Sage, 1980. — 199p. — (Sage studies in community mental health ; 2). — *Bibliography: p193-197*

JOB VACANCIES
MCKEE, William L
Where the jobs are : identification and analysis of local employment opportunities / William L. McKee, Richard C. Froeschle. — Kalamazoo, MI : W.E. Upjohn Institute for Employment Research, c1985. — xii, 175 p.

ROPER, S.
The economics of job vacancies / Stephen Roper. — London : Centre for Labour Economics, London School of Economics, 1986. — 58p. — (Discussion paper / London School of Economics and Political Science. Centre for Labour Economics ; no.252). — *Bibliography: p53-58*

JOB VACANCIES — Information services
MCKEE, William L
Where the jobs are : identification and analysis of local employment opportunities / William L. McKee, Richard C. Froeschle. — Kalamazoo, MI : W.E. Upjohn Institute for Employment Research, c1985. — xii, 175 p.

JOB VACANCIES — England — Cleveland
CLEVELAND. Planning Department
Employment trends and forecasts. — Middlesbrough : [the] Department, 1983. — 20,[12]p. — (Monitoring note report / Cleveland Planning Department ; no.234)

CLEVELAND. Planning Department
Employment trends and forecasts. — Middlesbrough : [the Department], 1987. — [6]p. — (Monitoring note / Cleveland. Planning Department ; 87/2)

JOB VACANCIES — England — Sheffield (South Yorkshire)
HOMES AND JOBS CONFERENCE (1986 : Sheffield)
Building for our future needs : homes and jobs. — Sheffield : Sheffield City Council, 1986. — 64p. — *Includes information pack in seven sections*

JOB VACANCIES — Great Britain
HART, P. E.
Job generation and size of firm / P. E. Hart. — London : National Institute of Economic and Social Research, 1987. — 24p. — (Discussion paper / National Institute of Economic and Social Research ; no.125). — *Bibliography: p22*

JACKMAN, Richard
A job guarantee for long-term unemployed people / Richard Jackman. — London : Employment Institute, 1986. — 67p

MICHAEL, I. M.
Employment creation in the US and UK : an econometric comparison / I. M. Michael. — London : Bank of England, 1986. — 74p. — (Discussion paper / Bank of England ; no.27). — *Bibliography: p71-74*

TAYLOR, Cyril
Employment examined : the Right approach to more jobs / Cyril Taylor. — London : Centre for Policy Studies, 1986. — 44p. — (Policy study ; no.77)

TODD, Graham
Job creation in the UK : a national survey of local models / by Graham Todd. — London : Economist Publications ; Paris : OECD, 1986. — 98p. — (Sepcial report / Economist Intelligence Unit ; no.1075)

JOB VACANCIES — Kenya
HUGHES, Rees
Higher education and employment in Kenya : a liberal interpretation of the literature / Rees Hughes [and] James Gituro Wahome. — Nairobi : University of Nairobi. Institute for Development Studies, 1985. — 34p. — (Working paper / University of Nairobi. Institute for Development Studies ; no.426). — *Bibliography: p[35-36]*

JOB VACANCIES — United States
MICHAEL, I. M.
Employment creation in the US and UK : an econometric comparison / I. M. Michael. — London : Bank of England, 1986. — 74p. — (Discussion paper / Bank of England ; no.27). — *Bibliography: p71-74*

JOB VACANCIES — Wales — Clwyd
CLWYD. County Council
Clwyd county structure plan : public participation seminar : employment : report of proceedings. — Mold : [the Council], 1975. — 24p

JOHANNESBURG (SOUTH AFRICA) — Buildings, structures, etc
BARRY, Margaret
Magnates and mansions : Johannesburg, 1886-1914 / Margaret Barry and Nimmo Law. — Johannesburg : Lowry : Thorold's Africana Books [distributor], 1985. — 162 p.. — *Includes index. — Bibliography: p. 151-152*

JOHANNESBURG (SOUTH AFRICA) — History
APPELGRYN, M. S.
Johannesburg : origins and early management 1886-1899 / M. S. Appelgryn. — Pretoria : University of South Africa, 1984. — viii,144p. — *Bibliography: p130-135*

BARRY, Margaret
Magnates and mansions : Johannesburg, 1886-1914 / Margaret Barry and Nimmo Law. — Johannesburg : Lowry : Thorold's Africana Books [distributor], 1985. — 162 p.. — *Includes index. — Bibliography: p. 151-152*

KENNEDY, Brian Ernest
A tale of two mining cities : Johannesburg and Broken Hill 1885-1925 / Brian Kennedy. — Johannesburg : Ad. Donker, 1984. — xiii,146p. — *Bibliography: p136-142*

JOHANNESBURG (SOUTH AFRICA) — Race relations — History
KENNEDY, Brian Ernest
A tale of two mining cities : Johannesburg and Broken Hill 1885-1925 / Brian Kennedy. — Johannesburg : Ad. Donker, 1984. — xiii,146p. — *Bibliography: p136-142*

JOHN LEWIS PARTNERSHIP
BRADLEY, Keith
Profit sharing in the retail trade sector : the relative performance of the John Lewis partnership / K. Bradley and S. Estrin. — London : Centre for Labour Economics, London School of Economics, 1987. — 30p. — (Discussion paper / London School of Economics and Political Science. Centre for Labour Economics ; no.279). — *Bibliography: p20-21*

BRADLEY, Keith
The success story of the John Lewis Partnership : a study of comparative performance : a research report / prepared by Keith Bradley and Saul Estrin for Partnership Research Ltd.. — London : [Partnership Research Ltd.], 1986. — 29 leaves

JOHN SUMMERS & SONS
REDHEAD, Brian
The Summers of Shotton / Brian Redhead & Sheila Gooddie. — London : Hodder and Stoughton, 1987. — 160p. — *Map on lining papers. — Bibliography: p156. — Includes index*

JOHNSEN AND JORGENSEN LTD
Johnsen and Jorgensen 1884-1984. — London : Johnsen and Jorgensen, 1984. — 81p

JOHNSON, HUGH S
OHL, John Kennedy
Hugh S. Johnson and the New Deal / John Kennedy Ohl. — Dekalb, Ill. : Northern Illinois University Press, 1985. — xi, 374p. — *Includes index. — Bibliography: p.[345]-359*

JOHNSON, LYNDON B.
The Johnson Presidency : twenty intimate perspectives of Lyndon B. Johnson / edited by Kenneth W. Thompson. — Lanham ; London : University Press of America, c1987. — [310]p. — (Portraits of American presidents ; 5)

JOHNSON, LYNDON B
MCFEELEY, Neil
Appointment of judges, the Johnson presidency / by Neil D. McFeeley. — 1st ed. — Austin : University of Texas Press, 1987. — p. cm. — (An Administrative history of the Johnson presidency series). — *Includes index*

JOHNSTON, DONALD J.
JOHNSTON, Donald J
Up the hill / Donald Johnston. — Montréal : Optimum, c1986. — vii, 304 p.. — *Includes index. — Bibliography: p. 289-295*

JOINT ADVENTURES — Yugoslavia
ARTISIEN, Patrick F. R.
Joint ventures in Yugoslav industry / Patrick F.R. Artisien. — Aldershot : Gower, c1985. — [xv,240]p. — *Bibliography: p210-218. — Includes index*

JOINT VENTURES
VOZNESENSKAIA, N. N.
Smeshannye predpriiatiia kak forma mezhdunarodnogo ekonomicheskogo sotrudnichestva / N. N. Voznesenskaia ; otv. redaktor A. A. Rubanov. — Moskva : Nauka, 1986. — 181p

JOINT VENTURES — Personnel management
ZEIRA, Yoran
Personnel decision-making in wholly-owned foreign subsidiaries and in international joint ventures / Yoran Zeira and Oded Shenkar. — Geneva : International Labour Office, 1986. — 43p. — (Multinational Enterprises Programme working paper ; no.45). — *Bibliographical references: p[35]-36*

JOINT VENTURES — Europe
TURNER, Louis
Industrial collaboration with Japan / Louis Turner ; with a foreword by Hiroshi Takeuchi, in association with Ayako Asakura ... [et al.]. — London : Routledge & Kegan Paul, [for the] Royal Institute of International Affairs, 1987. — 118p. — (Chatham House papers ; no.34)

JOINT VENTURES — Japan
TURNER, Louis
Industrial collaboration with Japan / Louis Turner ; with a foreword by Hiroshi Takeuchi, in association with Ayako Asakura ... [et al.]. — London : Routledge & Kegan Paul, [for the] Royal Institute of International Affairs, 1987. — 118p. — (Chatham House papers ; no.34)

JOINT VENTURES — Poland
GARLAND, John S
Industrial cooperation between Poland and the West / by John Garland. — Ann Arbor, Mich. : UMI Research Press, c1985. — p. cm. — (Research for business decisions ; no. 71). — : Originally presented as the author's thesis (Indiana University, 1982). — Includes index. — Bibliography: p

JOINT VENTURES — United States
TURNER, Louis
Industrial collaboration with Japan / Louis Turner ; with a foreword by Hiroshi Takeuchi, in association with Ayako Asakura ... [et al.]. — London : Routledge & Kegan Paul, [for the] Royal Institute of International Affairs, 1987. — 118p. — (Chatham House papers ; no.34)

JONS (PERIODICAL)
LEDESMA RAMOS, Ramiro
Escritos políticos : JONS, 1933-1934 / Ramiro Ledesma Ramos. — Madrid : Trinidad Ledesma Ramos, 1985. — 239,[35]p

JONSSON, Family
JONSSON, Karl
Sågverksarbetare i österled : liv och leverne kring det svenska sågverket i Kovda / berättet av Karl Jonsson och nedtecknat av Linnéa Jonsson. — 2:a upplagan. — [s.l. : s.n.], 1981. — 136p. — Bibliography: p135-136

JORDAN — Economic conditions
The Economic development of Jordan / edited by Bichara Khader and Adnan Badran ; with an address by His Royal Highness Crown Prince Hassan. — London : Croom Helm, c1987. — 246p. — Conference papers

JORDAN — Population — Statistics — Evaluation
ABDEL-AZIZ, Abdallah
Evaluation of the Jordan Fertility Survey 1976 / Abdallah Abdel-Aziz. — Voorburg : International Statistical Institute, 1983. — 31p. — (Scientific reports / World Fertility Survey ; no. 42)

JORDAN — Social conditions
LEWIS, Norman N.
Nomads and settlers in Syria and Jordan, 1800-1980 / Norman N. Lewis. — Cambridge : Cambridge University Press, 1987. — xvii,249p. — (Cambridge Middle East library). — Bibliography: p238-244. — Includes index

JORDAN — Statistics, Vital
BLACKER, J. G. C.
Mortality levels and trends in Jordan estimated from the results of the 1976 fertility survey / J. G. C. Blacker, Allan G. Hill, Kath A. Moser. — Voorburg : International Statistical Institute, 1983. — 35p. — (Scientific reports / World Fertility Survey ; no.47)

JOSEPH II, Holy Roman Emperor
BEALES, Derek
Joseph II / Derek Beales. — Cambridge : Cambridge University Press
1: In the shadow of Maria Theresa, 1741-1780. — 1987. — [940]p. — Includes bibliography and index

JOSEPH, MICHAEL, 1897-1958
JOSEPH, Richard, 1940-
Michael Joseph : master of words / Richard Joseph ; with a prologue by Monica Dickens. — Southampton : Ashford, 1986. — xviii,238p. — Geneal. table on lining papers. — Bibliography: p217-229. — Includes index

JOURNALISM
IFJ information / International Federation of Journalists. — Brussels : International Federation of Journalists, 1959-. — Annual

JOURNALISM — Authorship
BORN, Roscoe C
The suspended sentence : a guide for writers / Roscoe C. Born. — New York : Scribner, c1986. — x, 214 p.. — Includes index

JOURNALISM — Moral and ethical aspects
Responsible journalism / edited by Deni Elliott. — Beverly Hills, Calif. : Sage Publications, c1986. — 187 p.. — (Sage focus editions ; 83). — Includes index. — Bibliography: p. 167-179

JOURNALISM — Political aspects
PICARD, Robert G
The press and the decline of democracy : the democratic socialist response in public policy / Robert G. Picard. — Westport, Conn. ; London : Greenwood Press, 1985. — 173p. — (Contributions to the study of mass media and communications ; no. 4). — Includes index. — Bibliography: p [153]-168

Scientists and journalists : reporting science as news / edited by Sharon M. Friedman, Sharon Dunwoody, Carol L. Rogers. — New York : Free Press ; London : Collier Macmillan, c1986. — p. cm. — (AAAS issues in science and technology series). — Includes index

TATARYN, Lloyd
The pundits : power, politics & the press / Lloyd Tataryn. — Toronto, Canada : Deneau, 1985. — 198 p.. — Includes index. — Bibliography: p. 181-191

JOURNALISM — Political aspects — Mexico
SECANELLA, Petra María
El periodismo político en México / Petra Ma. Secanella. — [Barcelona] : Mitre, 1983. — 202p. — (Textos de periodismo). — Bibliography: p181-199

JOURNALISM — Political aspects — United States
PARENTI, Michael
Inventing reality : the politics of the mass media / Michael Parenti. — New York : St. Martin's Press, c1986. — xiii, 258 p.. — Includes bibliographies and index

JOURNALISM — Social aspects — Great Britain — History
The Press in English society from the seventeenth to nineteenth centuries / edited by Michael Harris and Alan Lee. — Rutherford : Fairleigh Dickinson University Press ; London ; Cranbury, NJ : Associated University Presses, c1986. — 261 p.. — Includes index. — Bibliography: p. 249-250

JOURNALISM — Germany (East)
BLAUM, Verena
Ideologie und Fachkompetenz : das journalistische Berafsbild in der DDR / Verena Blaum. — [Köln : Verlag Wissenschaft und Politik, 1985]. — 156p. — (Bibliothek Wissenschaft und Politik ; Bd.34). — Bibliography: p151-156

JOURNALISM — Soviet Union — History
EMEL'IANOV, N. P.
"Otechestvennye zapiski" N. A. Nekrasova i M. E. Saltykova-Shchedrina (1868-1884) / N. P. Emel'ianov. — Leningrad : Khudozhestvennaia literatura, Leningradskoe otdelenie, 1986. — 333p

JOURNALISM — United States — Objectivity
PARENTI, Michael
Inventing reality : the politics of the mass media / Michael Parenti. — New York : St. Martin's Press, c1986. — xiii, 258 p.. — Includes bibliographies and index

JOURNALISM, MILITARY
MERCER, Derrik
The fog of war : the media on the battlefield / by Derrik Mercer, Geoff Mungham, Kevin Williams ; foreword by Sir Tom Hopkinson. — London : Heinemann, 1987. — xvi,413p

JOURNALISM, SCIENTIFIC
Scientists and journalists : reporting science as news / edited by Sharon M. Friedman, Sharon Dunwoody, Carol L. Rogers. — New York : Free Press ; London : Collier Macmillan, c1986. — p. cm. — (AAAS issues in science and technology series). — Includes index

JOURNALISTIC ETHICS
COMBER, Mary Anne
The newsmongers : how the media distort the political news / Mary Anne Comber and Robert S. Mayne. — Toronto : McClelland and Stewart, 1986. — 178p. — Bibliography: p177-178

Responsible journalism / edited by Deni Elliott. — Beverly Hills, Calif. : Sage Publications, c1986. — 187 p.. — (Sage focus editions ; 83). — Includes index. — Bibliography: p. 167-179

JOURNALISTS — Legal status, laws, etc — Ecuador
ECUADOR
[Laws, etc]. Ley de ejercicio profesional del periodista : registro oficial no.900, martes 30 de septiembre de 1975, decreto no.799-B. — Quito : Secretaría Nacional de Información Pública, 1975. — 23p

JOURNALISTS — Brazil — Biography
LACOMBE, Américo Jacobina
À sombra de Rui Barbosa / Américo Jacobina Lacombe. — [São Paulo] : Companhia Editora Nacional ; [Brasília : Instituto Nacional do Livro, MEC, 1978]. — x,226p. — (Brasiliana ; volume 365)

JOURNALISTS — Czechoslovakia — Biography
ŠIŠKA, Miroslav
Publicista Andrej Siracky : Miroslav Šiška. — Praha : Vydavatelství Novinař, 1986. — 248,19p

JOURNALISTS — France — Biography
BUSI, Frederick
The pope of antisemitism : the career and legacy of Edouard-Adolphe Drumont / Frederick Busi. — Lanham ; London : University Press of America, 1987. — [242]p. — Includes bibliography and index

JOURNALISTS — Germany — Biography
AUSTERMANN, Anton
Kurt Tucholsky : der Journalist und sein Publikum / Anton Austermann. — München : Piper, 1985. — 202p. — (Serie Piper ; Bd.5214)

JOURNALISTS — Great Britain
FYVEL, T. R.
And there my trouble began : uncollected writings, 1945-1985 / T. R. Fyvel. — London : Weidenfeld and Nicolson, 1986. — xii,240p

JOURNALISTS — Great Britain — Biography
CLARK, William, 1916-1985
From three worlds : memoirs / William Clark. — London : Sidgwick & Jackson, [1986]. — xi,292p

FREY, Werner
Sir Valentine Chirol : die britische Postition und Politik in Asien 1895-1925. — Zürich : Juris Druck und Verlag, 1976. — viii,255p. — Dissertation-Universität Zürich, 1975. — Bibliography: p230-255

JOURNALISTS — Great Britain — Biography *continuation*
HUBBACK, David
No ordinary press baron : a life of Walter Layton / David Hubback. — London : Weidenfeld and Nicolson, c1985. — [240]p. — *Includes index*

JOURNALISTS — Ohio — Biography
CEBULA, James E.
James M. Cox : journalist and politician / James E. Cebula. — New York : Garland, 1985. — 181 p.. — (Modern American history). — *Includes index*. — *Bibliography: p. 171-173*

JOURNALISTS — United States
Outstanding international press reporting : Pulitzer Prize winning articles in foreign correspondence / editor Heinz-Dietrich Fischer. — Berlin ; New York : Walter de Gruyter
Vol.1: 1928-1945, from the consequences of World War I to the end of World War II. — 1984. — liii,368p

Outstanding international press reporting : Pulitzer Prize winning articles in foreign correspondence / editor Heinz-Dietrich Fischer. — Berlin ; New York : Walter de Gruyter
Vol.2: 1946-1962, from the end of World War II to the various stations of the Cold War. — 1985. — lxvii,304p

Outstanding international press reporting : Pulitzer Prize winning articles in foreign correspondence / editor Heinz-Dietrich Fischer. — Berlin ; New York : Walter de Gruyter
Vol.3: 1963-1977, from the escalation of the Vietnam war to the East Asian refugee problems. — 1986. — lxxii,309p

WEAVER, David H
The American journalist : a portrait of U.S. news people and their work / David H. Weaver and G. Cleveland Wilhoit. — Bloomington : Indiana University Press, c1986. — viii, 216 p.. — *Includes index*. — *Bibliography: p. 205-211*

JOURNALISTS — United States — Biography
ROVERE, Richard Halworth
Final reports : personal reflections on politics and history in our time / Richard Rovere ; foreword by Arthur M. Schlesinger, Jr. — Middletown, Conn. : Wesleyan University Press ; Scranton, Pa. : Distributed by Harper & Row, 1986, c1984. — xviii, 244 p.. — (Wesleyan paperback). — *Includes index*

J.P. MORGAN & CO — History
CAROSSO, Vincent P
The Morgans : private international bankers 1854-1913 / Vincent P. Carosso ; with the assistance of Rose C. Carosso. — Cambridge, Mass. ; London : Harvard University Press, 1987. — xvi, 888p, [12]p of plates. — (Harvard studies in business history ; 38). — *Includes index*. — *Bibliography: p.649-653*

J.P. STEVENS & CO — Case studies
DOUGLAS, Sara U
Labor's new voice : unions and the mass media / by Sara U. Douglas. — Norwood, N.J. : Ablex, 1986. — p. cm. — (Communication and information science). — *Includes index*. — *Bibliography: p*

JUAN CARLOS I, King of Spain
NOURRY, Philippe
Juan Carlos : un roi pour les républicains / Philippe Nourry. — 2e éd.. — Paris : Le Centurion, 1986. — 430p

JUDAISM — History
DE LANGE, Nicholas
Judaism / Nicholas de Lange. — Oxford : Oxford University Press, 1986. — viii,156p. — (OPUS). — *Includes bibliography and index*

JUDAISM — Germany — History — Congresses
The Jewish response to German culture : from the enlightenment to the Second World War / edited by Jehuda Reinharz and Walter Schatzberg. — Hanover, NH : Published for Clark University by University Press of New England, 1985. — xii, 362p. — *"Essays based on papers delivered at the International Conference on German Jews, held at Clark University, Worcester, Massachusetts, October 8-11, 1983."*. — *Includes index*

JUDAISM — Yemen — History
AHRONI, Reuben
Yemenite Jewry : origins, culture and literature / Reuben Ahroni. — Bloomington : Indiana University Press, 1986. — x,227. — (Jewish literature and culture). — *Bibliography: p [204]-220*

JUDAISM AND POLITICS — History
Comparative Jewish politics. — [Ramat Gan] : Bar-Ilan University Press. — (Bar-Ilan departmental researches)
Vol.2: Conflict and consensus in Jewish political life / edited by Stuart A. Cohen and Eliezer Don-Yehiya. — 1986. — 218p

JUDAISM AND SOCIAL PROBLEMS
SACKS, Jonathan
Wealth and poverty : a Jewish analysis / Jonathan Sacks. — London : Social Affairs Unit, 1985. — 23p

JUDGE-MADE LAW — United States — History
WOLFE, Christopher
The rise of modern judicial review : from constitutional interpretation to judge-made law / Christopher Wolfe. — New York : Basic Books, c1986. — ix, 392 p.. — ([Basic series in American government]). — *Series statement from jacket*. — *Includes indexes*. — *Bibliography: p. 357-380*

JUDGEMENT — Congresses
Human judgment and decision processes / edited by Martin F. Kaplan, Steven Schwartz. — New York ; London : Academic Press, 1975. — xiii,325p. — (Academic Press series in cognition and perception). — *This volume ... grew out of a 3 day conference held at Northern Illinois University in October 1974' - Preface*. — *Includes bibliographies and index*

JUDGEMENTS, CRIMINAL — France — Statistics
BAILLON, Denis
Les condemnations 1979 à 1982 / Denis Baillon. — Paris : Ministerè de la justice, [1985]. — 209p. — (Statistique annuelle / France. Ministerè de la justice ; 1)

JUDGEMENTS, FOREIGN — Asia
CAFFREY, Bradford A.
International jurisdiction and the recognition and enforcement of foreign judgements in the LAWASIA region : a comparative study of the laws of eleven Asian countries inter-se and with the E.E.C. countries / Bradford A. Caffrey. — Sydney : CCH Australia, 1985. — xxxii,407p. — *Cover title: Enforcement of foreign judgements*

JUDGEMENTS, FOREIGN — European Economic Community countries
CAFFREY, Bradford A.
International jurisdiction and the recognition and enforcement of foreign judgements in the LAWASIA region : a comparative study of the laws of eleven Asian countries inter-se and with the E.E.C. countries / Bradford A. Caffrey. — Sydney : CCH Australia, 1985. — xxxii,407p. — *Cover title: Enforcement of foreign judgements*

JUDGES
The magistrate / Journal of the Magistrates' Association. — London : Journal of the Magistrates' Association, 1921-. — *Monthly*

PROTT, Lyndel V.
The latent power of culture and the international judge / by Lyndell [i.e. Lyndel] V. Prott. — Abingdon : Professional, 1979. — xxi,250p. — *Bibliography: p235-244*. — *Includes index*

JUDGES — Canada — Biography
BATTEN, Jack
Judges / Jack Batten. — Toronto : Macmillan of Canada, 1986. — xv,335p

GRUENDING, Dennis
Emmett Hall : establishment radical / Dennis Gruending. — Toronto, Canada : Macmillan of Canada, c1985. — ix, 246 p., [16] p. of plates. — *Includes index*. — *Bibliography: p. 231-243*

JUDGES — Developing countries
The Role of the judiciary in plural societies / edited by Neelan Tiruchelvam and Radhika Coomaraswamy. — London : Pinter, 1987. — xxi,193p. — *Includes index*

JUDGES — England
MCCLUSKEY, John Herbert McCluskey, Baron
Law, justice and democracy / Lord McCluskey. — London : Sweet & Maxwell, 1987. — 116p. — *Includes index*

PANNICK, David
Judges / David Pannick. — Oxford : Oxford University Press, 1987. — [224]p. — *Includes index*

JUDGES — England — History
PORT, Sir John
The notebook of Sir John Port / edited for the Selden Society by J. H. Baker. — London : Selden Society, 1986. — lvii,217p. — (Publications of the Selden Society ; 102)

JUDGES — France — History
BLUCHE, François
Les magistrats du Parlement de Paris au XVIIIe siècle / préface d'Emmanuel Le Roy Ladurie. — [nouv. éd]. — Paris : Economica, 1986. — xiii,481p. — *1er ed : 1961*. — *Bibliography: p399-426*

JUDGES — Great Britain — Directories
Hazell's guide to the judiciary and the courts. With, The Holborn Law Society's list of barristers by chambers. — 1986. — Henley-on-Thames : Hazell & Co., 1986. — 314p

JUDGES — Scotland — Biography
WHEATLEY, John Wheatley, Lord
One man's judgement : an autobiography / Lord Wheatley. — London : Butterworths, 1987. — [220]p. — *Includes index*

JUDGES — Spain
BASTIDA, Francisco J.
Jueces y franquismo : el pensamiento político del Tribunal Supremo en la dictadura / prólogo de J. A. González Casanova. — Barcelona : Editorial Ariel, 1986. — 205p

JUDGES — United States — Appointment, qualifications, tenure, etc
MCFEELEY, Neil
Appointment of judges, the Johnson presidency / by Neil D. McFeeley. — 1st ed. — Austin : University of Texas Press, 1987. — p. cm. — (An Administrative history of the Johnson presidency series). — *Includes index*

TRIBE, Laurence H
God save this honorable court : how the choice of justices can change our lives / Laurence H. Tribe. — 1st ed. — New York : Random House, c1985. — p. cm. — *Includes index*

JUDGES — United States — Biography
BINDLER, Norman
The conservative court, 1910-1930 / by Norman Bindler. — Port Washington, N.Y. : Associated Faculty Press, 1986. — p. cm. — (The Supreme Court in American life series). — *Includes index*. — *Bibliography: p*

JUDGES — United States — Biography
continuation

NEWMYER, R. Kent
Supreme Court Justice Joseph Story : statesman of the Old Republic / R. Kent Newmyer. — Chapel Hill : University of North Carolina Press, c1985. — p. cm. — (Studies in legal history). — Includes index. — Bibliography: p

JUDGES — United States — History — Addresses, essays, lectures

Professions and professional ideologies in America / edited by Gerald L. Geison. — Chapel Hill : University of North Carolina Press, c1983. — x, 147 p.. — *Includes bibliographical references and index*

JUDGMENT

Judgment and decision making : an interdisciplinary reader / edited by Hal R. Arkes, Kenneth R. Hammond. — Cambridge : Cambridge University Press, 1986. — xiv,818p. — *Bibliography: p739-799*. — *Includes index*

Judgmental forecasting / edited by George Wright and Peter Ayton. — Chichester : Wiley, c1987. — ix,293p. — *Includes bibliographies and index*

JUDICIAL ASSISTANCE — Asia

CAFFREY, Bradford A.
International jurisdiction and the recognition and enforcement of foreign judgements in the LAWASIA region : a comparative study of the laws of eleven Asian countries inter-se and with the E.E.C. countries / Bradford A. Caffrey. — Sydney : CCH Australia, 1985. — xxxii,407p. — *Cover title: Enforcement of foreign judgements*

JUDICIAL ASSISTANCE — European Economic Community countries

CAFFREY, Bradford A.
International jurisdiction and the recognition and enforcement of foreign judgements in the LAWASIA region : a comparative study of the laws of eleven Asian countries inter-se and with the E.E.C. countries / Bradford A. Caffrey. — Sydney : CCH Australia, 1985. — xxxii,407p. — *Cover title: Enforcement of foreign judgements*

JUDICIAL OPINIONS — United States

SCHWARTZ, Bernard
The unpublished opinions of the Warren court / Bernard Schwartz. — New York : Oxford University Press, 1985. — p. cm

JUDICIAL POWER — United States — History

ORTH, John V
The judicial power of the United States : the eleventh amendment in American history / John V. Orth. — New York : Oxford University Press, 1986. — p. cm. — *Includes index*. — *Bibliography: p*

JUDICIAL PROCESS

ABRAHAM, Henry Julian
The judicial process : an introductory analysis of the courts of the United States, England, and France / Henry J. Abraham. — 5th ed. — New York : Oxford University Press, 1985. — p. cm. — *Includes indexes*. — *Bibliography: p*

JUDICIAL PROCESS — Data processing

INTERNATIONAL CONFERENCE ON "LOGIC, INFORMATICS, LAW" (2nd : 1985 : Florence, Italy)
Automated analysis of legal texts : logic, informatics, law : edited versions of selected papers from the Second International Conference on "Logic, Informatics, Law,"Florence, Italy, September 1985 / edited by Antonio A. Martino, Fiorenza Socci Natali ; editorial assistant, Simona Binazzi. — Amsterdam ; New York : North-Holland ; New York, N.Y., U.S.A. : Sole distributors for the U.S.A. and Canada, Elsevier Science Pub. Co., 1986. — xxii, 938 p.. — *Includes bibliographies and index*

JUDICIAL PROCESS — Social aspects — United States

CLARK, Gordon L
Judges and the cities : interpreting local autonomy / Gordon L. Clark. — Chicago : University of Chicago Press, c1985. — xv, 247 p.. — *Includes index*. — *Bibliography: p. 231-242*

JUDICIAL PROCESS — European Economic Community countries

RASMUSSEN, Hjalte
On law and policy in the European Court of Justice : a comparative study in judicial policymaking / by Hjalte Rasmussen. — Dordrecht ; Boston : M. Nijhoff ; Hingham, MA, USA : Distributors, for the U.S. and Canada, Kluwer Academic Publishers, 1986. — xxv, 555 p.. — *Summary in Danish*. — *Thesis (doctoral)--University of Copenhagen, 1985*. — *Includes bibliographies and indexes*

VOLCANSEK, Mary L.
Judicial politics in Europe : an impact analysis / Mary L. Volcansek. — New York : P. Lang, c1986. — xi, 325 p.. — (American university studies. Series X, Political science ; vol. 7). — *Includes index*. — *Bibliography: p. [295]-313*

JUDICIAL PROCESS — Spain

BASTIDA, Francisco J.
Jueces y franquismo : el pensamiento político del Tribunal Supremo en la dictadura / prólogo de J. A. González Casanova. — Barcelona : Editorial Ariel, 1986. — 205p

JUDICIAL PROCESS — United States

PROVINE, Doris Marie
Judging credentials : nonlawyer judges and the politics of professionalism / Doris Marie Provine. — Chicago : University of Chicago Press, 1986. — xvii, 248 p.. — *Includes index*. — *Bibliography: p. 201-240*

JUDICIAL REVIEW

ANTIEAU, Chester James
Adjudicating constitutional issues / Chester James Antieau. — London : Oceana Publications, 1985. — xxviii,441p

Judicial review of administrative action in the 1980's : problems and prospects : papers presented at a Conference held by the Legal Research Foundation Inc. at the University of Auckland on 20 and 21 February 1986 / edited by Michael Taggart ; with a foreword by Lord Wilberforce. — Auckland : Oxford University Press, in association with the Legal Research Foundation Inc, 1986. — xx,208p

JUDICIAL REVIEW — European Economic Community countries — Addresses, essays, lectures

MACKENZIE STUART, Alexander John Mackenzie Stuart, Lord
Control of power within the European Communities : being the presidential address of Lord Mackenzie Stuart, president of the Holdsworth Club of the Faculty of Law in the University of Birmingham, 1985-1986. — Birmingham : Holdsworth Club of the University of Birmingham, 1986. — 18p. — (The Holdsworth Club)

JUDICIAL REVIEW — United Satates

BICKEL, Alexander M.
The least dangerous branch : the Supreme Court at the bar of politics / Alexander M. Bickel. — 2nd ed. / with a new foreword by Harry H. Wellington. — New Haven ; London : Yale University Press, c1986. — xii,303p. — *Previous ed.: Indianapolis : Bobbs-Merrill, 1962*. — *Includes index*

JUDICIAL REVIEW — United States — History

KACZOROWSKI, Robert J
The politics of judicial interpretation : the federal courts, Department of Justice and civil rights, 1866-1876 / by Robert J. Kaczorowski. — Dobbs Ferry, N.Y. : Oceana Publications, 1985. — xiv, 241 p.. — (New York University School of Law series in legal history). — "New York University School of Law, Linden studies in legal history.". — *Includes bibliographies and index*

WOLFE, Christopher
The rise of modern judicial review : from constitutional interpretation to judge-made law / Christopher Wolfe. — New York : Basic Books, c1986. — ix, 392 p.. — ([Basic series in American government]). — *Series statement from jacket*. — *Includes indexes*. — *Bibliography: p. 357-380*

JUDICIAL REVIEW OF ADMINISTRATIVE ACTS — Australia

SHARPE, Jennifer M.
The Administrative Appeals Tribunal and policy review / by Jennifer M. Sharpe. — Sydney : The Law Book Company Limited, 1986. — xxvi,232p

JUDICIAL REVIEW OF ADMINISTRATIVE ACTS — Canada

ANTHONY, Russell J.
A handbook on the conduct of public inquiries in Canada / Russell J. Anthony and Alastair R. Lucas. — Toronto : Butterworths, 1985. — vii,273p

JUDICIAL REVIEW OF ADMINISTRATIVE ACTS — Great Britain

EMERY, C. T.
Judicial review : legal limits of official power / by C.T. Emery and B. Smythe ; foreword by Sir Gordon Slynn. — London : Sweet & Maxwell, 1986. — xxxi,330p. — *Includes index*

LEGOMSKY, Stephen H.
Immigration and the judiciary : law and politics in Britain and America / Stephen H. Legomsky. — Oxford : Clarendon, 1987. — xxxix,345p. — *Bibliography: p327-345*

JUDICIAL REVIEW OF ADMINISTRATIVE ACTS — Scotland

ST. CLAIR, John
Judicial review in Scotland / John St. Clair, Neil F. Davidson. — Edinburgh : W. Green, 1986. — xxi,94p. — *Includes index*

JUDICIAL REVIEW OF ADMINISTRATIVE ACTS — United States

LEGOMSKY, Stephen H.
Immigration and the judiciary : law and politics in Britain and America / Stephen H. Legomsky. — Oxford : Clarendon, 1987. — xxxix,345p. — *Bibliography: p327-345*

JUNG, C. G.

JAFFE, Aniela
The myth of meaning in the work of C. G. Jung / Aniela Jaffe ; translated [from the German] by R. F. C. Hull. — Zürich : Daimon, [1984]. — 186p. — *Bibliography: p179-186*

JUNG, C. G — Interviews

BENNET, E. A
Meetings with Jung : conversations recorded during the years 1946-1961 / by E.A. Bennet. — Zürich : Daimon, c1985. — 125 p.. — *Includes bibliographical references*

JUNGLE ECOLOGY

CAUFIELD, Catherine
In the rainforest / Catherine Caufield. — London : Picador, 1986, c1984. — ix,304p. — *Originally published: London : Heinemann, 1985*. — *Bibliography: p281-285*. — *Includes index*

JUNIOR MINISTERS (POLITICAL SCIENCE) — Great Britain — History

THEAKSTON, Kevin
Junior ministers in British government / Kevin Theakston. — Oxford : Basil Blackwell, 1987. — [256]p. — *Includes index*

JUNTAS DE OFENSIVA NACIONAL-SINDICALISTA

LEDESMA RAMOS, Ramiro
Escritos politicos : JONS, 1933-1934 / Ramiro Ledesma Ramos. — Madrid : Trinidad Ledesma Ramos, 1985. — 239,[35]p

JURA (SWITZERLAND) — History — Autonomy and independence movements
JENKINS, John R. G.
Jura separatism in Switzerland / John R.G. Jenkins. — Oxford : Clarendon, 1986. — xv,221p,[4]p of plates. — (Oxford research studies in geography). — *Bibliography: p201-215. — Includes index*

JURISDICTION — America
Anuario juridico interamericano = Inter-American juridical yearbook / Organizacion de los Estados Americanos. — Washington, D.C. : Organization of American States, 1949-1957. — *Annual. — Text in English and Spanish. — 1949-1957 issuing body entitled Pan-American Union*

JURISDICTION — United States — History
ORTH, John V
The judicial power of the United States : the eleventh amendment in American history / John V. Orth. — New York : Oxford University Press, 1986. — p. cm. — *Includes index. — Bibliography: p*

JURISPRUDENCE
ATIAS, Christian
Epistémologie juridique / Christian Atias. — 1re éd. — Paris : Presses universitaires de France, c1985. — 222 p.. — (Collection Droit fondamental. Droit politique et théorique). — *Includes bibliographies and indexes*

DWORKIN, Ronald
A matter of principle / Ronald Dworkin. — Cambridge, Mass. ; London : Harvard University Press, 1985. — 425p

LAUTERPACHT, Sir Hersch
Private law sources and analogies on international law / with special reference to international arbitration. — [Hamden, Conn.] : Archon Books, 1970. — xxiv, 326 p. — *Reprint of the 1927 ed. — Bibliography: p. 307-312*

MACCORMICK, Neil
An institutional theory of law : new approaches to legal positivism / Neil MacCormick and Ota Weinberger. — Dordrecht[Holland] ; Lancaster : Reidel, c1986. — xiv, 229p. — (Law and philosophy library)

Oxford essays in jurisprudence : third series / edited by John Eekelaar and John Bell. — Oxford : Clarendon, 1987. — 267p. — *Includes index*

JURISPRUDENCE — Addresses, essays, lectures
Essays in legal theory : a collaborated work / edited by D.J. Galligan ; editorial advisers Colin Howard and Michael Crommelin. — Melbourne : Melbourne University Press, 1984. — viii,256p

The philosophy of law / edited by R.M. Dworkin. — Oxford : Oxford University Press, 1977. — [9],177p. — (Oxford readings in philosophy). — *Bibliography: p.173-176. — Includes index*

JURISPRUDENCE — History
MCCOUBREY, H.
The development of naturalist legal theory / H. McCoubrey. — London : Croom Helm, c1987. — xxii,210p. — *Includes index*

JURISPRUDENCE — Russia — History
WALICKI, Andrzej
Legal philosophies of Russian liberalism / Andrzej Walicki. — Oxford : Clarendon, 1987. — [480]p. — *Includes index*

JURISPRUDENCE — Russia — Philosophy
WALICKI, Andrzej
Legal philosophies of Russian liberalism / Andrzej Walicki. — Oxford : Clarendon, 1987. — [480]p. — *Includes index*

JURY — Spain
SORIANO, Ramón
El nuevo jurado español / Ramón Soriano. — Barcelona : Ariel, 1985. — 157p

JURY — United States
HANS, Valerie P
Judging the jury / Valerie P. Hans and Neil Vidmar. — New York : Plenum Press, c1986. — 285 p.. — *Includes indexes. — Bibliography: p. 253-272*

HASTIE, Reid
Inside the jury / Reid Hastie, Steven D. Penrod, Nancy Pennington. — Cambridge, Mass. : Harvard University Press, 1983. — 277 p.. — *Includes indexes. — Bibliography: p. 247-266*

JUST WAR DOCTRINE
TEICHMAN, Jenny
Pacifism and the just war : a study in applied philosophy / Jenny Teichman. — Oxford : Basil Blackwell, 1986. — [128]p. — *Bibliography: p130. — Includes index*

JUSTICE
DAY, J. P.
Liberty and justice / J.P. Day. — London : Croom Helm, c1987. — 232p. — *Includes index*

Fondements d'une théorie de la justice : essais critiques sur la philosophie politique de John Rawls / publiés sous la direction de Jean Ladrière et Philippe Van Parijs. — Louvain-la-Neuve : Institut Supérieur de Philosophie, 1984. — x,275p. — (Essais philosophiques). — *Bibliography: p260-266*

HAYEK, F. A.
Law, legislation and liberty : a new statement of the liberal principles of justice and political economy / F.A. Hayek. — London : Routledge & Kegan Paul, 1982. — xxi,180,191,244p. — *Originally published in 3 vols.. — Includes index*

Justice : views from the social sciences / edited by Ronald L. Cohen. — New York : Plenum Press, c1986. — p. cm. — (Critical issues in social justice). — *Includes bibliographies and index*

JUSTICE — Addresses, essays, lectures
PERELMAN, Chaïm
Justice, law, and argument : essays on moral and legal reasoning / Ch. Perelman ; with an intod. by Harold J. Berman. — Dordrecht, Holland ; Boston : D. Reidel Pub. Co. ; Hingham, MA : sold and distributed in the U.S.A. and Canada by Kluwer Boston, c1980. — xiii,181p. — (Synthese library ; 142). — *Chapters translated into English by various persons. — Includes bibliographical references and index*

JUSTICE, ADMINISTRATION OF
DAMAŠKA, Mirjan R.
The faces of justice and state authority : a comparative approach to the legal process / Mirjan R. Damaška. — New Haven : Yale University Press, c1986. — xi, 247 p.. — *Includes bibliographical references and index*

JUSTICE, ADMINISTRATION OF — Canada
The social dimensions of law / Neil Boyd...[et al.]. — Scarborough, Ontario : Prentice-Hall Canada Inc., [1986]. — xii,259p. — *Includes references*

JUSTICE, ADMINISTRATION OF — Canada — Public opinion — Congresses
Law in a cynical society? : Opinion and law in the 1980's : papers presented at a conference held in 1982 at the University of Manitoba / edited by Dale Gibson [and] Janet K. Baldwin. — Calgary : Carswell Legal Publications, 1985. — xviii,464p

JUSTICE, ADMINISTRATION OF — England
EDDEY, K. J.
The English legal system / by Keith J. Eddey. — 4th ed. — London : Sweet & Maxwell, 1987. — xv,196p. — (Concise college texts). — *Previous ed.: 1982. — Bibliography: p189-190. — Includes index*

PICKLES, James
Straight from the bench / James Pickles. — London : Phoenix House, 1987. — [240]p. — *Includes index*

SELDON, Arthur
Law and lawyers in perspective / Arthur Seldon. — Harmondsworth : Penguin, 1987. — 170p

JUSTICE, ADMINISTRATION OF — Japan — History
UPHAM, Frank K
Law and social change in postwar Japan / Frank K. Upham. — Cambridge, Mass. : Harvard University Press, 1987. — p. cm. — *Includes index*

JUSTICE, ADMINISTRATION OF — New Zealand
ROBSON, J. L.
Sacred cows and rogue elephants : policy development in the New Zealand Justice Department / J. L. Robson. — Wellington : Government Printing Office, 1987. — xii,296p. — *Bibliographical references: p[285]-292*

JUSTICE, ADMINISTRATION OF — Ontario — History
ROMNEY, Paul
Mr. Attorney : the Attorney General for Ontario in court, cabinet and legislature 1791-1899 / Paul Romney. — Toronto : Published for The Osgoode Society by University of Toronto Press, 1986. — xiii,396p. — *Notes: p[337]-381*

JUSTICE, ADMINISTRATION OF — Spain
RUIZ, José
La justicia en España / José Ruiz. — Madrid : Ediciones Libertarias, [1985]. — 287p. — (Colección Pluma Rota)

JUSTICE, ADMINISTRATION OF — Sri Lanka
TIRUCHELVAM, Neelan
The ideology of popular justice in Sri Lanka : a socio-legal inquiry / Neelan Tiruchelvam. — New Delhi : Vikas, 1984. — 215p. — *Bibliography: p[207]-210*

JUSTICE, ADMINISTRATION OF — United States
ESTREICHER, Samuel
Redefining the Supreme Court's role : a theory of managing the federal judicial process / Samuel Estreicher and John Sexton. — New Haven : Yale University Press, c1986. — p. cm . — *Includes index. — Bibliography: p*

FRIEDMAN, Lawrence M.
Total justice / Lawrence M. Friedman. — New York : Russell Sage Foundation, c1985. — ix, 166 p.. — *"75th anniversary series"--Jacket. — Includes bibliographies and index*

JUSTICE, ADMINSTRATION OF — Germany — History — 20th century
RABOFSKY, Eduard
Verborgene Wurzeln der NS-Justiz : strafrechtliche Rüstung für zwei Weltkriege / Eduard Rabofsky [und] Gerhard Oberkofler. — Wien : Europa Verlag, 1985. — 261p. — *Bibliography: p251-[262]*

JUSTICE AND POLITICS — Spain
RUIZ, José
La justicia en España / José Ruiz. — Madrid : Ediciones Libertarias, [1985]. — 287p. — (Colección Pluma Rota)

JUSTICE (PHILOSOPHY)
HELLER, Agnes
Beyond justice / Agnes Heller. — Oxford : Basil Blackwell, 1987. — [352]p. — *Includes bibliography and index*

JACKSON, M. W.
Matters of justice / M.W. Jackson. — London : Croom Helm, c1986. — 181p. — *Bibliography: p170-180. — Includes index*

SANDEL, Michael J.
Liberalism and the limits of justice / Michael J. Sandel. — Cambridge : Cambridge University Press, 1982. — ix,191p. — *Bibliography: p184-186. — Includes index*

JUSTICES ACT
NAFFIN, Ngaire
Domestic violence and the law : a study of S.99 of the Justices Act (S. A.) / by Naffin. — [Adelaide] : Women's Adviser's Office, Department of the Premier and Cabinet, 1985. — iv,iii,170p. — *Includes bibliographical references*

JUSTICES OF THE PEACE — England
BANKOWSKI, Zenon
Lay justice? / Z.K. Bankowski, N.R. Hutton and J.J. McManus. — Edinburgh : T. & T. Clark, 1987. — xi,187p. — *Includes index*

JUSTICES OF THE PEACE — Great Britain
GREAT BRITAIN. Law Commission
Criminal law : binding over - the issues / The Law Commission. — London : H.M.S.O., 1987. — vi,113p. — (Working paper / The Law Commission ; no.103)

JUSTICES OF THE PEACE — Scotland
BANKOWSKI, Zenon
Lay justice? / Z.K. Bankowski, N.R. Hutton and J.J. McManus. — Edinburgh : T. & T. Clark, 1987. — xi,187p. — *Includes index*

JUSTIFICATION
SCHNÜBBE, Otto
Paul Tillich und seine Bedeutung für den Protestantismus heute : das Prinzip der Rechtfertigung im theologischen, philosophischen und politischen Denken Paul Tillichs / Otto Schnübbe. — Hannover : Lutherhaus, 1985. — 288p

JUSTIFICATION (THEORY OF KNOWLEDGE)
MOSER, Paul K.
Empirical justification / Paul K. Moser. — Dordrecht ; Boston : D. Reidel Pub. Co. ; Hingham MA, U.S.A. : Sold and distributed in the U.S.A. and Canada by Kluwer Boston, c1985. — x, 263p. — (Philosophical studies series in philosophy ; v. 34). — *Includes indexes*

JUTE INDUSTRY — Forecasting
THIGPEN, M. Elton
World demand prospects for jute / M. Elton Thigpen, Paula Marongiu and Saidur R. Lasker. — Washington, D. C. : The World Bank, 1987. — vi,178p. — (World Bank staff commodity working papers ; no.16). — *"A joint study by the Commodities and Trade Division of the Food and Agriculture Organization of the United Nations and the Commodity Studies and Projections Division of the World Bank"*

JUTE INDUSTRY — Bangladesh
AKIYAMA, Takamasa
Jute supply response in Bangladesh / Takamasa Akiyama. — Washington, D.C. : The World Bank, 1985. — vi,39p. — (World Bank staff commodity working papers ; no.13). — *Bibliographical references: p38-39*

JUVENILE CORRECTIONS
STUMPHAUZER, Jerome S
Helping delinquents change : a treatment manual of social learning approaches / Jerome S. Stumphauzer. — New York : Haworth Press, c1986. — p. cm. — *"Published also as v. 8, no. 1/2 of the Child & youth services.". — Includes index. — Bibliography: p*

JUVENILE CORRECTIONS — Legal status, laws, etc — Great Britain
GREAT BRITAIN. Parliament. House of Commons. Library. Research Division
Criminal Justice Bill 1981-82 [Bill 32] / [Patrick Nealon]. — [London] : the Division, 1982. — 25p. — (Reference sheet ; no.82/3). — *Bibliography: p18-25*

JUVENILE CORRECTIONS — England — History — 20th century
BAILEY, Victor
Delinquency and citizenship : reclaiming the young offender, 1914-1948 / Victor Bailey. — Oxford : Clarendon, 1987. — viii,352p. — *Bibliography: p331-341. — Includes index*

JUVENILE CORRECTIONS — France — Statistics
FRANCE. Direction de l'éducation surveillée. Bureau des études et programmes - K4
Bilan statistique de l'évolution de l'activité des juridictions de la jeunesse 1976-1984 et de l'incarcération des mineurs 1976-1985 : France métropolitaine, départements et territoires d'outre-mer. — [Paris] : Ministère de la Justice, [1986?]. — 39p

JUVENILE CORRECTIONS — Massachusetts
MILLER, Alden D
Delinquency and community : creating opportunities and controls / Alden D. Miller, Lloyd E. Ohlin. — Beverly Hills : Sage Publications, c1985. — 208 p.. — *Includes bibliographies*

JUVENILE CORRECTIONS — Netherlands
JUNGER-TAS, J.
New trends in Dutch juvenile justice : alternative sanctions / J. Junger-Tas. — The Hague : Research and Documentation Centre, Ministry of Justice, 1985. — 23p. — ([Reports, papers, articles] ; 83). — *Includes bibliographical references*

JUVENILE COURTS — England — London
TIPLER, Jonathan
Is justice colour blind? : a study of the impact of race in the juvenile justice system in Hackney / Jonathan Tipler. — Hackney : London Borough of Hackney. Directorate of Social Services. Research, Development and Programming, 1985. — 25p. — (Social services research note / Hackney. Directorate of Social Services. Research, Development and Programming ; 6). — *At head of cover title: Research in Hackney*

TIPLER, Jonathan
Juvenile justice in Hackney / Jonathan Tipler. — Hackney : Directorate of Social Services. Research, Development and Programming, 1985. — 31p. — *At head of cover title: Research in Hackney*

JUVENILE COURTS — France — Statistics
FRANCE. Direction de l'éducation surveillée. Bureau des études et programmes - K4
Bilan statistique de l'évolution de l'activité des juridictions de la jeunesse 1976-1984 et de l'incarcération des mineurs 1976-1985 : France métropolitaine, départements et territoires d'outre-mer. — [Paris] : Ministère de la Justice, [1986?]. — 39p

JUVENILE COURTS — United States
BORTNER, M. A.
Inside a juvenile court : the tarnished ideal of individualized justice / M.A. Bortner. — New York : New York University Press, 1982. — vii, 283 p.. — *Includes index. — Bibliography: p. [271]-279*

JUVENILE DELINQUENCY
Ecologic-biochemical approaches to treatment of delinquents and criminals / edited by Leonard J. Hippchen. — New York : Van Nostrand Reinhold Co., c1978. — xx,396p. — *Bibliography: p389-392. — Bibliography: p. 389-392*

HIRSCHI, Travis
Causes of delinquency / Travis Hirschi. — Berkeley ; London : University of California Press, 1969. — 309p. — *Bibliography: p. 301-303*

MCGURK, Barry J.
The relationship between Lanyon's Psychological Screening Inventory and indices of juvenile delinquency / Barry J. McGurk and Rick Evans. — London : Home Office, Prison Department, Directorate of Psychological Services, 1977. — 8p. — (DPS report. Series 1 ; no.10). — *Bibliography: p7-8*

JUVENILE DELINQUENCY — Prevention
CRIMINOLOGICAL RESEARCH CONFERENCE (14th : 1980)
Prevention of juvenile delinquency : the rôle of institutions of socialisation in a changing society : reports presented to the fourteenth Criminological Research Conference, 1980. — Strasbourg : Council of Europe, 1982. — 141p. — (Collected studies in criminological research ; v.19). — *On cover: European Committee on Crime Problems*

STUMPHAUZER, Jerome S
Helping delinquents change : a treatment manual of social learning approaches / Jerome S. Stumphauzer. — New York : Haworth Press, c1986. — p. cm. — *"Published also as v. 8, no. 1/2 of the Child & youth services.". — Includes index. — Bibliography: p*

JUVENILE DELINQUENCY — Research
RESEARCH WORKSHOP ON PERSPECTIVES IN ACTION-ORIENTED RESEARCH: YOUTH, CRIME AND JUVENILE JUSTICE (1985 : Milan)
Action-oriented research on youth crime : an international perspective / edited by Ugljesa Zvekić. — Rome : United Nations Social Defence Research Institute, 1986. — 275p. — (Publication / United Nations Social Defence Research Institute ; no.27). — *Bibliography: p235-270. — Research workshop on perspectives in action-oriented research: youth, crime and juvenile justice held in the framework of the Seventh United Nations Congress on the Prevention of Crime and the Treatment of Offenders, Milan*

JUVENILE DELINQUENCY — Canada
WEST, W. Gordon
Young offenders and the state : a Canadian perspective on delinquency / W. Gordon West. — Toronto : Butterworths, 1984. — xviii,269p. — *Bibliography: p237-260*

JUVENILE DELINQUENCY — Denmark
BALVIG, Flemming
Ungdomskriminalitet i en forstadskommune / af Flemming Balvig. — [København] : Det Kriminalpraeventive Råd, [1984]. — 188p

JUVENILE DELINQUENCY — England — Durham (Durham)
Challenge alternative to care and custody project. — Durham : Durham Training and Enterprise, 1987. — 4p

The Challenge report : intensive I. T. in Durham. — Durham : Dragon Enterprises, 1985. — 16p

JUVENILE DELINQUENCY — Great Britain — Bibliography
SHRIGLEY, Sheila
Selected references on soccer hooliganism / compiled by Sheila M. Shrigley. — London : Department of Health and Social Security Library, 1979. — 4p. — (Bibliography series / Department of Health and Social Security Library ; no.B122)

JUVENILE DELINQUENCY — Massachusetts
MILLER, Alden D
Delinquency and community : creating opportunities and controls / Alden D. Miller, Lloyd E. Ohlin. — Beverly Hills : Sage Publications, c1985. — 208 p.. — *Includes bibliographies*

JUVENILE DELINQUENCY — Netherlands

Democratie en geweld : probleemanalyse naar aanleiding van de gebeurtenissen in Amsterdam op 30 april 1980. — 's-Gravenhage : Staatsuitgeverij, 1980. — 32 p.. — (Rapporten aan de regering ; 20). — *Prepared by the Wetenschappelijke Raad voor het Regeringsbeleid. — Includes bibliographical references*

JUNGER-TAS, J.
Young immigrants in the Netherlands and their contacts with the police / Josine Junger-Tas. — The Hague : Research and Documentation Centre, Ministry of Justice, 1985. — 21p. — ([Reports, papers, articles] ; 85a). — *Bibliography: p21*

JUNGER-TAS, Josine
Juvenile delinquency II : the impact of judicial intervention / Josine Junger-Tas, Marianne Junger. — The Hague : : Research and Documentation Centre, Ministry of Justice, 1985. — 67p. — ([Reports, papers, articles] ; 82). — *Includes bibliographical references*

JUVENILE DELINQUENCY — South Australia

MESCHEMBERG, H.
Juvenile offenders in South Australia 1972-1973 : a sociological pilot study / H. Meschemberg. — Adelaide : South Australian Department for Community Welfare, 1974. — 36p. — *Bibliography: p36*

JUVENILE DELINQUENCY — United States

BORTNER, M. A.
Inside a juvenile court : the tarnished ideal of individualized justice / M.A. Bortner. — New York : New York University Press, 1982. — vii, 283 p.. — *Includes index. — Bibliography: p. [271]-279*

SCHWENDINGER, Herman
Adolescent subcultures and delinquency / Herman Schwendinger and Julia Siegel Schwendinger. — Research ed. — New York ; Eastbourne : Praeger, 1985. — xvi,524p. — *Bibliography: p497-511. — Includes index*

SHIREMAN, Charles H
Rehabilitating juvenile justice / Charles H. Shireman and Frederic G. Reamer. — New york : Columbia University Press, 1986. — ix, 188 p.. — *Includes index. — Bibliography: p. [173]-184*

JUVENILE DELINQUENCY — United States — Public opinion

GILBERT, James Burkhart
A cycle of outrage : juvenile delinquency and mass media in the 1950s / James Gilbert. — New York ; Oxford : Oxford University Press, 1986. — vi, 258p, [6]p of plates. — *Includes bibliographical references and index. — Bibliography: p*

JUVENILE DELINQUENTS

DUSSICH, John P. J.
New perspectives in control theory : social coping of youth under supervision / John P. J. Dussich. — Köln : Carl Heymanns Verlag, c1985. — 306,liip. — (Interdisziplinäre Beiträge zur kriminologischen Forschung ; Band 11). — *Text in English, with German summary. — Bibliography: p281-306*

JUVENILE DELINQUENTS — Training of — Great Britain

CROW, Iain
Youth training and young offenders / Iain Crow, Paul Richardson, National Association for the Care and Resettlement of Offenders. — [Sheffield] : Manpower Services Commission, [1985]. — 28p. — (Research & development ; no.24)

JUVENILE DELINQUENTS — Great Britain

CAWSON, Pat
Young offenders in care / Pat Cawson. — [London] : Department of Health and Social Security, Social Research Branch, 1978. — iii,38p. — *Bibliography: p23*

JUVENILE DELINQUENTS — Great Britain — Alcohol use

FULLER, J. R.
Alcohol abuse and the treatment of young offenders : a progress report / J. R. Fuller. — London : Home Office, Prison Department, Directorate of Psychological Services, 1979. — 41p. — (DPS report. Series 1 ; no.13). — *Bibliographical references: p25*

JUVENILE DELINQUENTS — South Australia — Services for

SOUTH AUSTRALIA. Department for Community Welfare
The services of the Department for the care of the young offender, the support of the family, the protection of the community. — [Adelaide] : the Department, 1975. — 36 leaves

JUVENILE DETENTION HOMES — Australia

ASHER, Geoff
Custody and control : the social worlds of imprisoned youth / Geoff Asher. — Sydney ; London : Allen & Unwin, 1986. — [x,180]p. — (Studies in society ; 31). — *Includes bibliography and index*

JUVENILE DETENTION HOMES — England — Management

GREAT BRITAIN. Department of Health and Social Security. Social Work Service. Development Group
Management of community homes with education on the premises : (a discussion document). — [London] : the Department, 1977. — 152p. — *Joint project involving DHSS Social Work Service Development Group/London Region, London Boroughs Children's Regional Planning Committee (Area 8) and associated local authorities and voluntary associations*

JUVENILE DETENTION HOMES — England — Derbyshire

Report of a seminar on community homes at Digby Hall, Leicester on June 30 - July 1 1975. — [London] : Department of Health and Social Security, [1975]. — 41p. — *At head of title: Social Work Service Development Group and East Midlands Region in collaboration with the social services departments of Derbyshire and Lincolnshire*

JUVENILE DETENTION HOMES — England — Isle of Wight

From approved school to community home : a Development Group exercise 15th - 17th October 1973 at Eastmore House, Isle of Wight County Council Social Services Department. — [London] : Department of Health and Social Security, [1973]. — [54]p. — *At head of title: Social Work Service Development Group and London Region South*

From approved school to community home : Eastmore House : report of a one day follow up exercise at Eastmore House, Isle of Wight County Council Social Services Department, on 7th January 1975. — [London : Department of Health and Social Security, 1975]. — 24p. — *At head of title: Social Work Service Development Group and Southern Region*

JUVENILE DETENTION HOMES — England — Lincolnshire

Report of a seminar on community homes at Digby Hall, Leicester on June 30 - July 1 1975. — [London] : Department of Health and Social Security, [1975]. — 41p. — *At head of title: Social Work Service Development Group and East Midlands Region in collaboration with the social services departments of Derbyshire and Lincolnshire*

JUVENILE DETENTION HOMES — England — London

"Approved school to community home" : St. Christopher's, Hillingdon : report of a Development Group Seminar October 4th-6th, 1973. — [London] : Department of Health and Social Security, [1973]. — 76p. — *At head of title: Social Work Service, Development Group. — Includes bibliographical references*

JUVENILE DETENTION HOMES — Great Britain

SPEIRS, Sheila
Neighbourhood borstals : interim papers on their evaluation / by Sheila Speirs and David Grayson ; with preface and summary by Vernon Holloway. — London : Directorate of Psychological Services, Prison Department, 1977. — 1v. (various pagings). — (DPS report. Series 1 ; no.11). — *Includes bibliographical references*

JUVENILE JUSTICE, ADMINISTRATION OF

PRISON REFORM TRUST
Comparisons in juvenile justice. — [London] : Prison Reform Trust, 1987. — 8p. — (Juvenile justice project ; report no.1)

JUVENILE JUSTICE, ADMINISTRATION OF — England

MORRIS, Allison
Understanding juvenile justice / Allison Morris Henri Giller. — London : Croom Helm, c1987. — 287p

Panel services for offenders : comparative studies of England and Poland 1984/85 / edited by Thelma Wilson. — Aldershot : Avebury, c1987. — ix,103p. — *Bibliography: p96-103*

JUVENILE JUSTICE, ADMINISTRATION OF — Great Britain

BURNEY, Elizabeth
Sentencing young people : what went wrong with the Criminal Justice Act 1982 / Elizabeth Burney. — Aldershot : Gower, c1985. — 120p

GRAHAM, Finlay
Young persons remanded in custody : can the numbers safely be reduced? / F. Graham. — London : Home Office, Prison Department, Directorate of Psychological Services, 1979. — 17p. — (DPS report. Series 1 ; no.14). — *Bibliography: p17*

JUVENILE JUSTICE, ADMINISTRATION OF — Poland

Panel services for offenders : comparative studies of England and Poland 1984/85 / edited by Thelma Wilson. — Aldershot : Avebury, c1987. — ix,103p. — *Bibliography: p96-103*

JUVENILE JUSTICE, ADMINISTRATION OF — United States

SHIREMAN, Charles H
Rehabilitating juvenile justice / Charles H. Shireman and Frederic G. Reamer. — New york : Columbia University Press, 1986. — ix, 188 p.. — *Includes index. — Bibliography: p. [173]-184*

JUVENILE PAROLE

DUSSICH, John P. J.
New perspectives in control theory : social coping of youth under supervision / John P. J. Dussich. — Köln : Carl Heymanns Verlag, c1985. — 306,liip. — (Interdisziplinäre Beiträge zur kriminologischen Forschung ; Band 11). — *Text in English, with German summary. — Bibliography: p281-306*

KAFIRS (KAFIRISTAN)

ROBERTSON, Sir George Scott, b.1852
The Kafirs of the Hindu-Kush / by Sir George Scott Robertson ; illustrated by A.D. McCormick. — [1st] ed. reprinted / with an introduction by Louis Dupree. — Karachi ; London : Oxford University Press, 1974. — xxviii,vii-xx,667p,[2]fold leaves of plate. — (Oxford in Asia historical reprints from Pakistan). — *Facsimile reprint of: 1st ed., London : Lawrence and Bullen, 1896. — Includes index*

KAGURU (AFRICAN PEOPLE)

BEIDELMAN, T. O
Moral imagination in Kaguru modes of thought / T.O. Beidelman. — Bloomington : Indiana University Press, c1986. — xiii, 231 p. — (African systems of thought). — *Includes index. — Bibliography: p. [216]-224*

KALECKI, MICHAŁ
KRIESLER, Peter
Kalecki's microanalysis : the development of Kalecki's analysis of pricing and distribution / Peter Kriesler. — Cambridge : Cambridge University Press, 1987. — [140]p. — Includes bibliography and index

KAMPUCHEA — Foreign relations — Asia, Southeastern
PARIBATRA, Sukhumbhand
Kampuchea without delusion / Sukhumbhand Paribatra. — Kuala Lumpur : Institute of Strategic and International Studies, 1986. — 27p. — (ISIS ASEAN series)

KAMUNISTYCHNAIA PARTIYA BELARUSI — History — Sources
Kommunisticheskaia partiia Belorussii v resoliutsiiakh i resheniiakh s"ezdov i plenumov Tsk / [pod obshchei redaktsiei: G. G. Bartoshevicha...et al.]. — Minsk : Belarus' T.5: 1956-1965. — 1986. — 597p

KAMUNISTYCHNAIA PARTYIA BELARUSI — History — Sources
Kommunisticheskaia partiia Belorussii v rezoliutsiiakh i resheniiakh s"ezdov i plenumov TsK / [pod obshchei redaktsiei G. G. Bartoshevicha...et al.]. — Minsk : Belarus' T.4: 1945-1955. — 1986. — 615p

KANATCHIKOV, S
KANATCHIKOV, S
[Iz istorii moego bytiīa. English]. A radical worker in Tsarist Russia : the autobiography of Semën Ivanovich Kanatchikov / translated and edited by Reginald E. Zelnik. — Stanford, Calif. : Stanford University Press, 1986. — xxx, 472p, [3]p of plates. — Translation of: Iz istorii moego bytiīa

KANSAS — History
MINER, H. Craig
The end of Indian Kansas : a study of cultural revolution, 1854-1871 / H. Craig Miner and William E. Unrau. — Lawrence : Regents Press of Kansas, c1978. — xiii, 179 p., [4] leaves of plates. — Includes index. — Bibliography: p. 167-173

KANSAS CITY (MO.) — Politics and government
SHARP, Elaine B
Citizen demand-making in the urban context / Elaine B. Sharp. — University, AL : University of Alabama Press, c1986. — p. cm. — Includes index. — Bibliography: p

KANT, IMMANUEL
GULYGA, Arsenii Vladimirovich
Emmanuel Kant, une vie / Arsenij Goulyga ; Cat. Is this correct (2 spellings)? ; traduction de Jean-Marie Vaysse. suivi de En quel sens sommes-nous tous Kantiens? / par Jean-Marie Vaysse. — Paris : Aubier, [1985]. — 349p

KANT, IMMANUEL. Metaphysische Anfangsgründe der Naturwissenschaft
Kant's philosophy of physical science : Metaphysische Anfangsgründe der Naturwissenschaft, 1786-1986 / edited by Robert E. Butts. — Dordrecht ; Lancaster : Reidel, c1986. — xii, 363p. — (The University of Western Ontario series in philosophy of science ; v. 33). — Includes index. — Includes bibliographies

KANT, IMMANUEL
BOOTH, William James
Interpreting the world : Kant's philosophy of history and politics / William James Booth. — Toronto ; London : University of Toronto Press, c1986. — xxviii, 189p. — Includes index. — Includes bibliographical references

Hegel's critique of Kant / edited by Stephen Priest. — Oxford : Clarendon, 1986. — [ix,240]p. — Includes index

STUCKENBERG, J. H. W
The life of Immanuel Kant / by J.H.W. Stuckenberg ; with a new preface by Rolf George. — Lanham, MD : University Press of America, 1986. — xiv, 474 p.. — : Reprint. Originally published: London : Macmillan, 1882. — Bibliography: p. [451]-474

KANT, IMMANUEL — Ethics
EVANS, Peter
An examination of politics and morality in Kant's theory / by Peter Evans. — 216 leaves. — PhD (Econ) 1986 LSE

KANT, IMMANUEL — Metaphysics
KANT, Immanuel
Prolegomena to any future metaphysics that will be able to present itself as a science / Immanuel Kant ; a translation from the German based on the original editions with an introduction and notes by P. Gray Lucas. — Manchester : Manchester University Press, 1953. — (Philosophical classics)

KANT, IMMANUEL — Political science
EVANS, Peter
An examination of politics and morality in Kant's theory / by Peter Evans. — 216 leaves. — PhD (Econ) 1986 LSE

KAPITAL
FOLEY, Duncan K
Understanding capital : Marx's economic theory / Duncan K. Foley. — Cambridge, Mass. ; London : Harvard University Press, 1986. — viii, 183p. — Includes index. — Bibliography: p.[177]-180

KARAN SINGH, Sadar-i-Riyasat of Jammu and Kashmir
KARAN SINGH, Sadar-i-Riyasat of Jammu and Kashmir
Heir apparent : an autobiography / Karan Singh. — New Delhi : Oxford University Press, 1982. — xi,171p. — Vol.1 of two volume autobiography; vol.2 has title 'Sadar-i-Riyasat'

KARAN SINGH, Sadar-i-Riyasat of Jammu and Kashmir
Sadar-i-Riyasat : an autobiography [1953-1967] / Karan Singh. — New Delhi : Oxford University Press, 1985. — xi,168p. — Vol.2 of two volume autobiography; Vol.1 has title 'Heir apparent'

KARDELJ, EDVARD
Socijalistički savez radnog naroda u razvoju socijalističkog samoupravnog društva / redakcioni odbor: Ilija Globačnik...[et al.]. — Beograd : Izdavački centar Komunist ; Ljubljana : Jugoslovenski centar za teoriju i praksu samoupravljanja "Edvard Kardelj", [1986]. — 902p. — U zborniku objavljuju se saopštenja i diskusije sa naučnog skupa, 26. i 27. januara 1984 godine u okviru Teorijskih rasprava "Misao i revolucionarno delo Edvarda Kardelja". — Summaries in Serbian, Croat, Macedonian, Hungarian, Albanian and English

KARST (YUGOSLAVIA AND ITALY) — Economic conditions
DAVIS, James C
Rise from want : a peasant family in the machine age / James C. Davis. — Philadelphia : University of Pennsylvania Press, 1986. — xv, 165 p.. — Includes index. — Bibliography: p. [153]-161

KARST (YUGOSLAVIA AND ITALY) — Social conditions
DAVIS, James C
Rise from want : a peasant family in the machine age / James C. Davis. — Philadelphia : University of Pennsylvania Press, 1986. — xv, 165 p.. — Includes index. — Bibliography: p. [153]-161

KASHKAI TRIBE
BECK, Lois
The Qashqa'i of Iran / Lois Beck. — New Haven ; London : Yale University Press, c1986. — xvi, 384p, [24]p of plates. — Includes index. — Bibliography: p.353-367

KASPRZAK, MARCIN
PATERCZYK, Zygmunt
Marcin Kasprzak i jego "sprawa" : anatomia funkcjonowania niesłusznego oskarżenia / Zygmunt Paterczyk. — Warszawa : Państwowe Wydawnictwo Naukowe, 1985. — 351p. — (Biblioteka kroniki Wielkopolski). — Bibliography: p335-[340]

KAUTSKY, KARL
GEARY, Dick
Karl Kautsky / Dick Geary. — Manchester : Manchester University Press, c1987. — viii,146p. — (Lives of the left). — Bibliography: p132-140. — Includes index

KAWAI, EIJIRŌ
HIRSI, Atsuko
Individualism and socialism : Kawai Eijirō's life and thought (1891-1944) / Atsuko Hirai. — Cambridge, Mass. : Council on East Asian Studies, Harvard University : Distributed by Harvard University Press, 1986. — p. cm. — (Harvard East Asian monographs ; 127). — Includes index. — Bibliography: p

KAZAKH S.S.R. — History — Revolution of 1905
Revoliustiia 1905-1907 gg. v Srednem Azii i Kazakhstane / [B. V. Lunin...et al.; otv. redaktor Kh. Z. Ziiaev]. — Tashkent : "Fan" Uzbekskoi SSR, 1985. — 206p

Revoliutsiia 1905-1907 gg. v Srednei Azii i Kazakhstane / [B. V. Lunin...et al.; otv. red. Kh. Z. Ziiaev]. — Tashkent : "Fan" Uzbekskoi SSR, 1985. — 206p

KAZAKH S.S.R. — History — Revolution, 1917-1921
GRIGOR'EV, V. K.
Razgrom melkoburzhuaznoi kontrrevoliutsii v Kazakhstane (1920-1922 gg.) / V. K. Grigor'ev. — Alma-Ata : Kazakhstan, 1984. — 174p

KAZAKH S.S.R. — Population
BEKMAKHANOVA, N. E.
Mnogonatsional'noe naselenie Kazakhstana i Kirgizii v epokhu kapitalizma : (60-e gody XIX v.-1917g.) / N. E. Bekmakhanova ; otv. redaktor V. M. Kabuzan. — Moskva : Nauka, 1986. — 242p

KELANTAN — Population — Statistics
Banci penduduk dan perumahan Malaysia 1980 = Population and housing census of Malaysia 1980. — Kuala Lumpur : Department of Statistics. — Text in Malay and English State population report

KENNEDY, JOHN F. (John Fitzgerald)
BORCH, Herbert von
John F. Kennedy : Amerikas unerfüllte Hoffnung / Herbert von Borch. — München : Piper, 1986. — 169p. — Bibliography: p163-164

KENT — Social policy
KENT. Social Services Department
Helping the community to care : Kent County Council Social services. — Maidstone : [the Department], 1987. — 42p. — At head of title: Kent Care

KENTUCKY — Rural conditions
MONTELL, William Lynwood
Killings : folk justice in the Upper South / William Lynwood Montell. — Lexington, KY : University Press of Kentucky, 1986. — p. cm. — Includes index. — Bibliography: p

KENYA — Bibliography
A guide to government monographs, reports and research works. — Nairobi : Kenya National Archives, 1984. — 157p

KENYA — Constitution
KENYA
[Constitution (1969)]. The Constitution of Kenya. — [Nairobi] : [s.n.], [1969]. — 79p

KENYA — Economic policy

Development plan 1984-1988. — Nairobi : Government Printer, 1983. — 225p. — *Preface by The Minister for Finance and Planning*

GHAI, Dharam Pal
Planning for basic needs in Kenya : performance, policies and prospects / Dharam Ghai, Martin Godfrey [and] Franklyn Lisk. — Geneva : International Labour Office, 1979. — x, 166p

KENYA — Government Publications — Bibliography

A guide to government monographs, reports and research works. — Nairobi : Kenya National Archives, 1984. — 157p

KENYA — History — Dictionaries

OGOT, Bethwell A
Historical dictionary of Kenya / by Bethwell A. Ogot. — Metuchen, N.J. : Scarecrow Press, 1981. — xvii, 279 p.. — (African historical dictionaries ; no. 29). — *Bibliography: p. 219-276*

KENYA — History — 1895-1963

TRZEBINSKI, Errol
The Kenya pioneers / by Errol Trzebinski. — London : Heinemann, 1985. — xiii, 240p, [16]p of plates. — *Bibliography: p.[227]-229*

KENYA — Officials and employees — Salaries, allowances, etc

KENYA. Civil Service Salaries Review Committee
Report of the Civil Service Committee, 1985 : Presented to His Excellency the President July, 1985. — Nairobi : Government Printer, 1985. — 130p. — *Chairman: T.C.J. Ramtu*

KENYA — Politics and government

MOI, Daniel T. arap
Kenya African nationalism : Nyayo philosophy and principles / Daniel T. arap Moi. — London : Macmillan, 1986. — xvi,192p

KENYA — Population

FRANK, Odile
An interpretation of fertility and population policy in Kenya / Odile Frank [and] Geoffrey McNicoll. — New York : Population Council, 1987. — 49p. — (Working papers / Population Council. Center for Policy Studies ; no.131). — *Bibliography: p42-46*

KENYA — Race relations

KANOGO, Tabitha
Squatters and the roots of Mau Mau / Tabitha Kanogo. — London : Currey, 1987. — [224]p. — (East African studies). — *Includes bibliography and index*

KENYA — Rural conditions

Approaches to rural-urban development : proceedings of a workshop organised by the Institute for Development Studies, University of Nairobi, 22 May 1985 / edited by Hugh E. Evans [and] George M. Ruigu. — Nairobi : University of Nairobi. Institute for Development, 1985. — 40p. — (Occasional paper / University of Nairobi. Institute for Development Studies ; no.46)

KENYA — Rural conditions — Statistics

Data dictionary for the integrated rural surveys 1976-79. — Nairobi : Central Bureau of Statistics, 1982. — 135p

KENYA — Social policy

Development plan 1984-1988. — Nairobi : Government Printer, 1983. — 225p. — *Preface by The Minister for Finance and Planning*

GHAI, Dharam Pal
Planning for basic needs in Kenya : performance, policies and prospects / Dharam Ghai, Martin Godfrey [and] Franklyn Lisk. — Geneva : International Labour Office, 1979. — x, 166p

KERENSKY, ALEKSANDR FYODOROVICH

ABRAHAM, Richard
Alexander Kerensky : the first love of the revolution / Richard Abraham. — New York : Columbia University Press, 1987. — xiii, 503p, [32]p of plates. — *Includes index. — Includes bibliographical references*

KERN, ALFRED

RIEDL-EHRENBERG, Renate
Alfred Kern (1850-1893) : Edouard Sandoz (1853-1928) : Gründer der Sandoz AG, Basel / Renate Riedl-Ehrenberg. — Zürich : Verein für wirtschaftshistorische Studien, 1986. — 90p. — (Schweizer Pioniere der Wirtschaft und Technik ; 44). — *Bibliography: p84*

KEWA (PAPUA NEW GUINEA PEOPLE) — Folklore

LEROY, John D.
Fabricated world : an interpretation of Kewa tales / John LeRoy. — Vancouver : University of British Columbia Press, 1985. — xii, 319 p.. — *Includes index. — Bibliography: p. [304]-311*

KEYNES

DESAI, Meghnad
Money, inflation and unemployment : an econometric model of the Keynes effect / M. Desai and G. Weber. — London : Economic and Social Research Council : London School of Economics, 1986. — [77p]. — (ESRC/LSE econometrics project discussion paper ; A.59). — *Bibliography: p[69.71]*

KEYNES, JOHN MAYNARD. General theory of employment, interest and money

Keynes's general theory : fifty years on : its relevance and irrelevance to modern time / John Burton...[and others]. — London : Institute of Economic Affairs, 1986. — viii, 159p. — (Hobart paperback ; 24)

KEYNES, JOHN MAYNARD

DAY, A. C. L.
Economic strategies : Keynes, Friedman and their disciples / Alan Day. — [London] : Banking World, 1986. — 48p. — *At head of title: Alan Day report*

FLETCHER, Gordon A. (Gordon Alan)
The Keynesian revolution and its critics : issues of theory and policy for the monetary production economy / Gordon A. Fletcher. — Basingstoke : Macmillan, 1987. — xxiii,348p. — *Includes index*

KEYNES SEMINAR (7th : 1985 : University of Kent at Canterbury)
Keynes and economic development : the Seventh Keynes Seminar Hold at the University of Kent at Canterbury, 1985 / edited by A.P. Thirlwall. — Basingstoke : Macmillan, 1987. — x,186p. — *Includes bibliographies and index*

STEWART, Michael, 1933-
Keynes and after / Michael Stewart. — 3rd ed. — Harmondsworth : Penguin, 1986. — 230p. — (Pelican books). — *Previous ed.: 1972*

YOUNG, Warren
Interpreting Mr. Keynes : the IS-LM enigma / Warren L. Young. — Cambridge : Polity, 1987. — xii,218p. — *Bibliography: p203-212. — Includes index*

KEYNES, JOHN MAYNARD — Congresses

Marx, Schumpeter, and Keynes : a centenary celebration of dissent / Suzanne W. Helburn and David F. Bramhall, editors. — Armonk, N.Y. : M.E. Sharpe, c1986. — xii, 343 p.. — *Papers presented at a symposium held Apr. 20-22, 1983 at the University of Colorado at Denver. — Includes bibliographies*

KEYNESIAN ECONOMICS

DAY, A. C. L.
Economic strategies : Keynes, Friedman and their disciples / Alan Day. — [London] : Banking World, 1986. — 48p. — *At head of title: Alan Day report*

FLETCHER, Gordon A. (Gordon Alan)
The Keynesian revolution and its critics : issues of theory and policy for the monetary production economy / Gordon A. Fletcher. — Basingstoke : Macmillan, 1987. — xxiii,348p. — *Includes index*

HSIEH, Ching-Yao
A search for synthesis in economic theory / by Ching-Yao Hsieh and Stephen L. Mangum. — Armonk, N.Y. : M.E. Sharpe, c1986. — p. cm. — *Bibliography: p*

KEYNES SEMINAR (7th : 1985 : University of Kent at Canterbury)
Keynes and economic development : the Seventh Keynes Seminar Hold at the University of Kent at Canterbury, 1985 / edited by A.P. Thirlwall. — Basingstoke : Macmillan, 1987. — x,186p. — *Includes bibliographies and index*

Prices, quantities and expectations : Keynes and macroeconomics in the fifty years since the publication of the General theory / edited by P.J.N. Sinclair. — Oxford : Clarendon, 1987. — xxiv,487p. — *Includes index*

STEWART, Michael, 1933-
Keynes and after / Michael Stewart. — 3rd ed. — Harmondsworth : Penguin, 1986. — 230p. — (Pelican books). — *Previous ed.: 1972*

YOUNG, Warren
Interpreting Mr. Keynes : the IS-LM enigma / Warren L. Young. — Cambridge : Polity, 1987. — xii,218p. — *Bibliography: p203-212. — Includes index*

KHARLAMOV, N. M.

KHARLAMOV, N. M.
Difficult mission : war memoirs / N. Kharlamov. — Moscow : Progress, 1986. — 228p

KHRUSHCHEV, N.

KHRUSHCHEV, N.
For victory in peaceful competition with capitalism : with a special preface written for the English edition / Nikita S. Khrushchev. — London : Hutchinson, 1960. — 784p

KIBBUTZIM

BLASI, Joseph R
The communal experience of the kibbutz / Joseph Blasi. — New Brunswick, U.S.A : Transaction Books, c1986. — viii, 210 p.. — *Includes index. — Bibliography: p. 190-204*

KILLINGHOLME (HUMBERSIDE) — Economic policy

Killingholme: development potential : the final report. — Newcastle upon Tyne : Coopers and Lybrand Associates, 1986. — [216p]

KINGS AND RULERS

GIVEN-WILSON, Chris
The royal household and the King's affinity : service, politics and finance in England 1360-1413 / Chris Given-Wilson. — New Haven ; London : Yale University Press, 1986. — viii,327p. — *Bibliography: p316-320. — Includes index*

KINGS AND RULERS (IN RELIGION, FOLK-LORE, ETC.)

BRITISH MUSEUM
Divine kingship in Africa / William Fagg. — London : British Museum, 1970. — 60p. — *'...[catalogue of an exhibition of] the British Museum's entire Benin collection...' - Preface and dedication. — bibl p60*

KINMEN (TAIWAN) — Economic conditions

LIN, Si-dang
Land reform on Kinmen / by Lin Si-dang and Lin Li. — Taipei : Chinese-American Joint Commission on Rural Reconstruction, 1958. — [iii],66p

KINSHIP
SEGALEN, Martine
Historical anthropology of the family / Martine Segalen ; translated by J.C. Whitehouse and Sarah Matthews. — Cambridge : Cambridge University Press, 1986. — x,328p. — (Themes in the social sciences). — Translation of: Sociologie de la famille. — Includes bibliographies and index

YOUNG, Michael, 1915-
Family and kinship in East London / Michael Young & Peter Willmott. — London : Routledge & Kegan Paul, 1986. — xxxi,234p. — (Reports of the Institute of Community Studies). — Originally published in 1957, reprinted with a new introduction 1986

KINSHIP — China — History — Addresses, essays, lectures
Kinship organization in late imperial China, 1000-1940 / edited by Patricia Buckley Ebrey and James L. Watson. — Berkeley : University of California Press, c1986. — p. cm. — (Studies on China ; 5). — Includes index. — Bibliography: p

KINSHIP — England — History
WOLFRAM, Sybil
In-laws and outlaws : kinship and marriage in England / Sybil Wolfram. — London : Croom Helm, c1987. — [240]p. — Bibliography: p295-331

KINSHIP — Europe — History
LYNCH, Joseph H.
Godparents and kinship in early medieval Europe / Joseph H. Lynch. — Princeton, N.J. : Princeton University Press, 1986. — xiv, 378 p.. — Includes index. — Bibliography: p. [340]-369

KINSHIP — India — Bengal
DASGUPTA, Satadal
Caste, kinship and community : social system of a Bengal caste / Satadal Dasgupta. — London : Sangam Books Ltd., 1986. — xii,291p. — Bibliography: p[283]-286

KINSHIP — India — Tirunelveli District
FANSELOW, Frank Sylvester
Trade, kinship and Islamisation : a comparative study of the social and economic organisation of Muslim and Hindu traders in Tirunelveli district, South India / by Frank Sylvester Fanselow. — 306 leaves. — PhD (Econ) 1986 LSE

KINSHIP — Indonesia — Mamboru
NEEDHAM, Rodney
Mamboru : history and structure in a domain of Northwestern Sumba / Rodney Needham. — Oxford : Clarendon, 1987. — xxv,202p,[6]p of plates. — Bibliography: p194-200. — Includes index

KINSHIP — North Carolina
BEAVER, Patricia D
Rural community in the Appalachian South / Patricia Duane Beaver. — Lexington, KY : University Press of Kentucky, c1996. — p. cm. — Includes index. — Bibliography: p

KINSHIP — Soviet Union
KOLLMANN, Nancy Shields
Kinship and politics : the making of the Muscovite political system, 1345-1547 / Nancy Shields Kollmann. — Stanford, Calif. : Stanford University Press, 1987. — x, 324 p.. — Includes index. — Bibliography: p. [289]-308

KINSHIP — Spain — Barcelona — History
MCDONOGH, Gary W
Good families of Barcelona : a social history of power in the industrial era / Gary Wray McDonogh. — Princeton, N.J. : Princeton University Press, c1986. — xiv, 262 p.. — Includes index. — Bibliography: p. [227]-251

KINSHIP — West Bank
ATA, Ibrahim Wade
The West Bank Palestinian family / Ibrahim Wade Ata. — London : KPI, 1986. — xiii,166p. — Bibliography: p152-160

KIRGHIZ S.S.R. — Population
BEKMAKHANOVA, N. E.
Mnogonatsional´noe naselenie Kazakhstana i Kirgizii v epokhu kapitalizma : (60-e gody XIX v.-1917g.) / N. E. Bekmakhanova ; otv. redaktor V. M. Kabuzan. — Moskva : Nauka, 1986. — 242p

KIRIBATI — Economic policy
Development plan : 1973-1976 : first annual review. — Tarawa : Government Printing Works, [1973?]. — iii,132p

Third development plan review. — Bairiki : Government Printing Division, 1977. — v,126p

Third development plan revised project list and expenditure, 1973-1976. — Bairiki : Government Printing Division, [1977?]. — 38p

KIRIBATI — Social ploicy
Development plan : 1973-1976 : first annual review. — Tarawa : Government Printing Works, [1973?]. — iii,132p

KIRIBATI — Social policy
Third development plan review. — Bairiki : Government Printing Division, 1977. — v,126p

Third development plan revised project list and expenditure, 1973-1976. — Bairiki : Government Printing Division, [1977?]. — 38p

KIRIWINIAN LANGUAGE
SENFT, Gunter
Kilivila : the language of the Trobriand islanders / Gunter Senft. — Berlin ; New York : Mouton de Gruyter, c1986. — p. cm. — (Mouton grammar library ; 3). — Bibliography: p

KIROV, S. M.
Kirov i vremia / [sostaviteli : M. I. Bugaeva, D. L. Shumskii; redaktsionnaia kollegiia : V. I. Bokovnia...et al.]. — Leningrad : Lenizdat, 1986. — 316p

KISSINGER, HENRY A.
STRONG, Robert J.
Bureaucracy and statesmanship : Henry Kissinger and the making of American foreign policy / Robert J. Strong. — Lanham ; London : University Press of America, c1987. — [124]p. — Includes bibliography

KITCHENS — Manufactures
STEEDMAN, Hilary
Machinery, production organization and skills : kitchen manufacture in Britain and Germany / Hilary Steedman and Karin Wagner. — London : National Institute of Economic and Social Research, 1985. — 22p. — (Discussion paper / National Institute of Economic and Social Research ; no.117)

KITH AND KIDS
JONES, Ann, 1946-
Two-to-One : a Kith and Kids community project / by Ann Jones ; preface by Albert Kushlick. — London (14 Talacre Rd, NW5 3PE) : Inter-Action Imprint, 1986. — 48p. — (Handbooks / Inter-Action Advisory Service)

KITSON, NORMA
KITSON, Norma
Where sixpence lives / Norma Kitson. — London : Hogarth, 1987, c1986. — 326p,[16]p of plates. — (Current affairs)

KLEIN, MELANIE
KLEIN, Melanie
The selected Melanie Klein / edited by Juliet Mitchell. — Harmondsworth : Penguin, 1986. — 256p. — Bibliography: p.[242]-245

KLEIVAN, HELGE
Native power : the quest for autonomy and nationhood of indigenous peoples / edited by Jens Brøsted ... [et al.]. — Bergen : Universitetsforlaget, c1985. — 350 p.. — Festschrift in memory of Helge Kleivan (1924-1983). — Includes bibliographies. — "Bibliography of Helge Kleivan": p. [341]-348

KLIMENT, GUSTAV
KODEŠ, Jiří
Gustav Kliment / Jiří Kodeš. — Praha : Práce, 1986. — 187p

KNOWLEDGE, SOCIOLOGY OF — Addresses, essays, lectures
Religion and the sociology of knowledge : modernization and pluralism in Christian thought and structure / edited by Barbara Hargrove. — New York : E. Mellen Press, c1984. — 402 p.. — (Studies in religion and society ; v. 8). — Includes bibliographies

KNOWLEDGE, THEORY OF
ARBIB, Michael A.
The construction of reality / Michael A. Arbib and Mary B. Hesse. — Cambridge : Cambridge University Press, 1986. — xii,286p. — Bibliography: p268-275. — Includes index

BOOTH, William James
Interpreting the world : Kant's philosophy of history and politics / William James Booth. — Toronto ; London : University of Toronto Press, c1986. — xxviii, 189p. — Includes index. — Includes bibliographical references

HABERMAS, Jürgen
Knowledge and human interests / Jürgen Habermas ; translated by Jeremy J. Shapiro. — Cambridge : Polity, 1987. — [392]p. — Translation of: Erkenntnis und Interesse. — Originally published: London : Heinemann Educational, 1972

LEVI, Isaac
Hard choices : decision making under unresolved conflict / Isaac Levi. — Cambridge : Cambridge University Press, 1986. — [272]p. — Includes bibliography

NEWELL, R. W.
Objectivity, empiricism and truth / R.W. Newell. — London : Routledge & Kegan Paul, 1986. — x,124p. — (Studies in philosophical psychology). — Includes index

WATKINS, John W. N
Science and scepticism / John Watkins. — Princeton, N.J. : Princeton University Press, c1984. — xvii, 387 p.. — Includes indexes. — Bibliography: p. 356-380

KNOWLEDGE, THEORY OF — Congresses
Metatheory in social science : pluralisms and subjectivities / edited by Donald W. Fiske and Richard A. Shweder. — Chicago : University of Chicago Press, 1986. — x, 390 p.. — (Chicago original paperbacks). — Proceedings of a conference on "Potentialities for Knowledge in Social Science," held at the University of Chicago, Sept. 11-14, 1983. — Includes indexes. — Bibliography: p. 371-377

KNOWLEDGE, THEORY OF — History — 20th century
KITCHENER, Richard F.
Piaget's theory of knowledge : genetic epistemology and scientific reason / Richard F. Kitchener. — New Haven [Conn.] ; London : Yale University Press, c1986. — [288]p. — Includes bibliography and index

KOESTLER, ARTHUR — Archives — Catalogs
The Koestler Archive in Edinburgh University Library : a checklist. — Edinburgh : Edinburgh University Library, 1987. — [95]p

KOMITET OSVOBOZHDENIIA NARODOV ROSSI — History
ANDREYEV, Catherine
Vlasov and the Russian Liberation Movement : Soviet reality and émigré theories / Catherine Andreyev. — Cambridge : Cambridge University Press, 1987. — xiv,251p. — (Soviet and East European studies). — Bibliography: p224-239. — Includes index

KOMMUNISTICHESKAIA PARTIIA SOVETSKAIA SOIUZA — Biography — Directories

HELF, Gavin
A biographical directory of Soviet regional party leaders / compiled by Gavin Helf. — Munich : Radio Liberty Research, RFE/RL Part 1: RSFSR oblasts, krais, and ASSRs. — 1987. — 90p

KOMMUNISTICHESKAIA PARTIIA SOVETSKOGO SOIUZA

DOROSHENKO, V. S.
Bor'ba KPSS za mezhdunarodnuiu razriadku i nesostoiatel'nost' burzhuaznykh fal'sifikatsii / V. S. Doroshenko. — Kiev : Vyshcha shkola, 1985. — 204p. — *Bibliography: p202-[205]*

KOMMUNISTICHESKAĨÃ PARTIÏÃ SOVETSKOGO SOĨUZA

HILL, Ronald J.
The Soviet Communist Party / Ronald J. Hill, Peter Frank. — 3rd ed. — Boston ; London : Allen & Unwin, 1986. — [196]p. — *Previous ed.: 1983. — Bibliography: p154-165. — Includes index*

KOMMUNISTICHESKAIA PARTIIA SOVETSKOGO SOIUZA

Internatsional'noe sotrudnichestvo KPSS i BKP : istoriia i sovremennost' / pod obshchei redaktsiei A. G. Egorova (SSSR) i D. Elazara (NRB). — Moskva : Politizdat, 1985. — 415p

KPSS - organizator bratskoi druzhby narodov SSSR / [redaktsionnaia kollegiia: V. A. Smyshliaev...et al.]. — Leningrad : Izd-vo Leningradskogo universiteta, 1973. — 153p. — (Uchenie zapiski kafedr obshchestvennykh nauk vuzov Leningrada. Istoriia KPSS ; vyp.13)

KOMMUNISTICHESKAIA PARTIIA SOVETSKOGO SOIUZA — Congresses

KOMMUNISTICHESKAIA PARTIIA SOVETSKOGO SOIUZA. S"ezd (27-oi : 1986)
Materialy XXVII S"ezda Kommunisticheskoi partii Sovetskogo Soiuza. — Moskva : Politizdat, 1986. — 351p

KOMMUNISTICHESKAIA PARTIIA SOVETSKOGO SOIUZA. S"ezd (27-oi : 1986)
XXVII s"ezd Kommunisticheskaia partiia Sovetskogo Soiuza, 25 fevralia-6 marta 1986 goda : stenograficheskii otchet. — Moskva : Politizdat
3. — 1986. — 589p

KOMMUNISTICHESKAIA PARTIIA SOVETSKOGO SOIUZA. S"ezd (27-oi : 1986)
XXVII s"ezd Kommunisticheskoi partii Sovetskogo Soiuza, 25 fevralia-6 marta 1986 goda : stenograficheskii otchet. — Moskva : Politizdat
1. — 1986. — 654p

KOMMUNISTICHESKAIA PARTIIA SOVETSKOGO SOIUZA. S"ezd (27-oi : 1986)
XXVII s"ezd Kommunisticheskoi partii Sovetskogo Soiuza, 25 fevralia-6 marta 1986 goda : stenograficheskii otchet. — Moskva : Politizdat
2. — 1986. — 320p

KOMMUNISTICHESKAĨÃ PARTIÏÃ SOVETSKOGO SOĨUZA — History

AVIDAR, Yosef
[Yehasim ben ha-miflagah le-ven ha-tsava bi-Verit ha-Mo'atsot, 1953 'ad 1964. English]. The party and the army in the Soviet Union / Yosef Avidar. — University Park : Pennsylvania State University Press, 1985. — p. cm. — *Translation of: ha-Yehasim ben ha-miflagah le-ven ha-tsava bi-Verit ha-Mo'atsot, 1953 'ad 1964. — Includes index. — Bibliography: p*

KOMMUNISTICHESKAIA PARTIIA SOVETSKOGO SOIUZA — History

Ispytannyi avangard mass / [red. kollegiia: V. A. Smyshliaev...et al.]. — Leningrad : Izd-vo Leningradskogo universiteta, 1975. — 199p. — (Uchenye zapiski kafedr obshchestvennykh nauk vuzov Leningrada. Istoriia KPSS ; vyp.15)

MOREKHINA, G. G.
Partiinoe stroitel'stvo v period Velikoi Otechestvennoi voiny Sovetskogo Soiuza 1941-1945 / G. G. Morekhina. — Moskva : Politizdat, 1986. — 391p

Voennye organizatsii partii bol'shevikov v 1917 godu / otv. redaktor Iu. I. Korablev. — Moskva : Nauka, 1986. — 253p

KOMMUNISTICHESKAIA PARTIIA SOVETSKOGO SOIUZA — History — Sources

Kommunisticheskaia partiia Sovetskogo Soiuza v rezoliutsiiakh i resheniiakh s"ezdov, konferentsii i plenumov TsK (1898-1986). — Izd. 9-e, dop. i isprav.. — Moskva : Politizdat. — *At head of title: Institut marksizma-leninizma pri TsK KPSS*
T.10: 1961-1965. — 1986. — 493p

Kommunisticheskaia partiia Sovetskogo Soiuza v rezoliutsiiakh i resheniiakh s"ezdov, konferentsii i plenumov TsK (1898-1986). — Izd. 9-e, dop. i isprav.. — Moskva : Politizdat. — *At head of title: Institut marksizma-leninizma pri TsK KPSS*
T.11: 1966-1970. — 1986. — 573p

KOMMUNISTICHESKAIA PARTIIA SOVETSKOGO SOIUZA — Membership

IATSKOV, V. Ia.
Kadrovaia politika KPSS : opyt i problemy / V. Ia. Iatskov. — Moskva : Mysl', 1986. — 315p

ZHUKOVA, L. N.
Deiatel'nost' KPSS po uluchsheniiu kachestvennogo sostava partii (1945-nachalo 1950-kh godov) : na materialakh Leningradskoi partiinoi organizatsii / L. N. Zhukova. — Leningrad : Izd-vo Leningradskogo universiteta, 1987. — 150p

KOMMUNISTICHESKAIA PARTIIA SOVETSKOGO SOIUZA — Party work

Problemy partiinogo i gosudarstvennogo stroitel'stva / Akademiia obschestvennykh nauk pri TSK KPSS. — Moskva : Akademiia obschestvennykh nauk pri TSK KPSS, 1982-. — *Annual*

KOMMUNISTICHESKAIA PARTIIA SOVETSKOGO SOIUZA — Party work — Dictionaries

Slovar' po partiinomu stroitel'stvu / [redaktor-sostavitel' I. A. Shvets]. — Moskva : Politizdat, 1987. — 365p

KOMMUNISTICHESKAIA PARTIIA SOVETSKOGO SOIUZA. Tsentral'nyi komitet. Politbiuro

LAIRD, Roy D.
The Politburo : demographic trends, Gorbachev, and the future / Roy D. Laird. — Boulder, Colo. : Westview Press, 1986. — xv,198p. — (Westview special studies on the Soviet Union and Eastern Europe). — *Bibliography: p187-189*

KOMMUNISTISCHE PARTEI DEUTSCHLANDS

KARL, Frank D.
Die K-Gruppen : Kommunist. Bund Westdeutschland, Kommunist. Partei Deutschlands, Kommunist. Partei Deutschlands/Marxisten-Leninisten: Entwicklung, Ideologie, Programmes / Frank D. Karl ; hrsg. von d. Friedrich-Ebert-Stiftung. — 1. Aufl. — Bonn-Bad Godesberg : Verlag Neue Gesellschaft, 1976. — 126 p. — (Reihe praktische Demokratie). — *"Veröffentlichungen der K-Gruppen": p. 123-125. — Bibliography: p. 126*

KOMMUNISTISCHE PARTEI DEUTSCHLANDS

Der Sieg des Faschismus in Deutschland und seine Lehren für unseren gegenwärtigen Kampf / herausgegeben vom Zentralkomitee der Kommunistischen Partei Deutschlands. — Berlin : [KPD], [1945?]. — 21p. — (Vortragsdisposition ; Nr.1)

KOMMUNISTISCHE PARTEI DEUTSCHLANDS — History

Der antifaschistische Widerstandskampf unter Führung der KPD in Mecklenburg 1933 bis 1945 / [Horst Bendig...et al.]. — Berlin : Dietz Verlag, 1985. — 343p

KPD und Staatsfrage : Staats- und rechtstheoretisches Erbe in der Politik der KPD von 1919 bis 1945 / Herausgeber: Karl-Heinz Schöneburg. — Berlin : Staatsverlag der Deutschen Demokratischen Republik, 1986. — 152p

KOMMUNISTISCHE PARTEI DEUTSCHLANDS (MARXISTEN-LENINISTEN)

KARL, Frank D.
Die K-Gruppen : Kommunist. Bund Westdeutschland, Kommunist. Partei Deutschlands, Kommunist. Partei Deutschlands/Marxisten-Leninisten: Entwicklung, Ideologie, Programmes / Frank D. Karl ; hrsg. von d. Friedrich-Ebert-Stiftung. — 1. Aufl. — Bonn-Bad Godesberg : Verlag Neue Gesellschaft, 1976. — 126 p. — (Reihe praktische Demokratie). — *"Veröffentlichungen der K-Gruppen": p. 123-125. — Bibliography: p. 126*

KOMMUNISTISCHER BUND WESTDEUTSCHLAND

KARL, Frank D.
Die K-Gruppen : Kommunist. Bund Westdeutschland, Kommunist. Partei Deutschlands, Kommunist. Partei Deutschlands/Marxisten-Leninisten: Entwicklung, Ideologie, Programmes / Frank D. Karl ; hrsg. von d. Friedrich-Ebert-Stiftung. — 1. Aufl. — Bonn-Bad Godesberg : Verlag Neue Gesellschaft, 1976. — 126 p. — (Reihe praktische Demokratie). — *"Veröffentlichungen der K-Gruppen": p. 123-125. — Bibliography: p. 126*

KOMUNISTIČKA PARTIJA CRNE GORE — History

KOVAČEVI'C, Branislav
Komunistička partija Crne Gore 1945-1952. godine / Branislav Kovačevi'c. — Titograd : NIO "Univerzitetska riječ", 1986. — 524p

KOMUNISTYCHNA PARTIIA UKRAINY — Party work

PETLIAK, F. A.
Partiinoe rukovodstvo Sovetami na Ukraine v gody Velikoi Otechestvennoi voiny (1941-1945) / F. A. Petliak. — Kiev : Vyshcha shkola, 1986. — 181p

KOMUNISTYCZNA PARTIA POLSKI — History

Komunistyczna Partia Polski (1918-1938) : zarys historii / Antoni Czubiński. — Warszawa : Wydawnictwa Szkolne i Pedagogiczne, 1985. — 283p. — *Bibliography: p275-[281]*

KONDRAT'EV, N. D

MAGER, N. H
The Kondratieff waves / Nathan H. Mager. — New York : Praeger, 1987. — viii, 247 p.. — *"Praeger special studies. Praeger scientific.". — Includes index. — Bibliography: p. 241-247*

KONJUNKTÚRA-ÉS PIACKUTATÓ INTÉZET. Kulkereskedelmi Információs Kospont — Bibliography

KONJUNKTÚRA-ÉS PIACKUTATÓ INTÉZET. Kulkereskedelmi Információs Központ
Register of papers and publications prepared in the Institute for Economic and Market Research in 1986 / edited by Judith Trébits ; translated by Márta Lempert. — Budapest : Institute for Economic and Market Research, 1987. — 42p

KONSERVATIVE FOLKEPARTI (Denmark)

KONSERVATIVE FOLKEPARTI (Denmark)
En fremtid i frihed : det konservative folkepartis program : ditto partiprogram er vedtaget på Det konservative folkepartis landsråd i Herning i September 1981 / Det konservative folkeparti. — København : Det konservative folkeparti, 1981. — 64p

KOPÁCSI, SÁNDOR

KOPÁCSI, Sándor
[Au nom de la classe ouvrière. English]. "In the name of the working class" : the inside story of the Hungarian Revolution / Sándor Kopácsi ; translated by Daniel and Judy Stoffman ; with a foreword by George Jonas. — 1st ed. — New York : Grove Press, 1987, c1986. — p. cm. — Translation of: Au nom de la classe ouvrière. — Bibliography: p

KORAN — Commentaries

AYOUB, Mahmoud
The Qur'an and its interpreters / Mahmoud Ayoub. — Albany : State University of New York Press, c1984-. — v. <1- >. — Includes bibliographies and index

KOREA — Civilization — Addresses, essays, lectures

Folk culture in Korea / edited by International Cultural Foundation ; general editor Chun Shin-yong. — Popular ed. — Seoul : Si-sa-yong-o-sa Publishers, Inc., 1982. — 138p. — (Korean culture series ; 4)

KOREA — Economic conditions — 1945-

KIM, Kyong-Dong
Man and society in Korea's economic growth : sociological studies / Kyong-Dong Kim. — 3rd ed. — Seoul : Seoul National University Press, 1985. — 216p. — (Korean Studies Series ; No.1)

KOREA — Foreign relations — 1864-1910

KIM, Jang-Soo
Korea und der 'Westen' von 1860 bis 1900 : die Beziehungen Koreas zu den europäischen Grossmächten, mit besonderer Berücksichtigung der Beziehungen zum Deutschen Reich / Jang-Soo Kim. — Frankfurt am Main : Lang, 1986. — 216p. — (Europäische Hochschulschriften. Reihe 3, Geschichte und ihre Hilfswissenschaften ; Bd.298). — Bibliography: p158-173

KOREA — Foreign relations — United States

MATRAY, James Irving
The reluctant crusade : American foreign policy in Korea, 1941-1950 / James Irving Matray. — Honolulu : University of Hawaii Press, c1985. — xii, 351 p.. — Includes index. — Bibliography: p.[319]-330

KOREA — Foreign relations — United States — Congresses

One hundred years of Korean-American relations, 1882-1982 / edited by Yur-Bok Lee and Wayne Patterson. — University, Ala. : University of Alabama Press, c1986. — x, 188p . — Based on papers presented at the annual meeting of the American Historical Association or that of the Association for Asian Studies in 1982. — Includes index. — Bibliography: p.163-181

KOREA — History — 1864-

KIM, Jang-Soo
Korea und der 'Westen' von 1860 bis 1900 : die Beziehungen Koreas zu den europäischen Grossmächten, mit besonderer Berücksichtigung der Beziehungen zum Deutschen Reich / Jang-Soo Kim. — Frankfurt am Main : Lang, 1986. — 216p. — (Europäische Hochschulschriften. Reihe 3, Geschichte und ihre Hilfswissenschaften ; Bd.298). — Bibliography: p158-173

KOREA — History — Japanese occupation, 1910-1945 — Congresses

CONFERENCE ON KOREA (3d : 1970 : Western Michigan University)
Korea under Japanese colonial rule : studies of the policy and techniques of Japanese colonialism : [proceedings of the Conference on Korea, November 12-14, 1970] / edited with introd. by Andrew C. Nahm. — [Kalamazoo] : Center for Korean Studies, Institute of International and Area Studies, Western Michigan University, 1973. — 290 p.. — (Korean studies series ; 2). — Includes bibliographical references and index

KOREA — History — Allied occupation, 1945-1948

Aspects of the Korean War / Peter Lowe [et al.]. — London : Suntory Toyota International Centre for Economics and Related Disciplines, 1987. — 54p. — (International studies)

KOREA — History — War and intervention, 1950-1953 — Bibliography

IMPERIAL WAR MUSEUM. Library
The war in Korea, 1950-1953 : a list of selected references. — [London] : the Library. — (Booklist / Imperial War Museum Library ; no.1229A)
Section 1: Books and pamphlets. — [196-]. — 9p

IMPERIAL WAR MUSEUM. Library
The war in Korea, 1950-1953 : a list of selected references. — [London] : the Library
Section 2: Periodical articles. — [196-]. — 11p — (Booklist ; no.1229B)

KOREA — Politics and government

PAE, Sung M
Testing democratic theories in Korea / Sung M. Pae. — Lanham, MD : University Press of America, c1986. — xvii, 300 p.. — Includes index. — Bibliography: p. [281]-289

KOREA — Popular culture — Addresses, essays, lectures

Folk culture in Korea / edited by International Cultural Foundation ; general editor Chun Shin-yong. — Popular ed. — Seoul : Si-sa-yong-o-sa Publishers, Inc., 1982. — 138p. — (Korean culture series ; 4)

KOREA — Rural conditions — Addresses, essays, lectures

LEE, Man-Gap
Sociology and social change in Korea / by Man-Gap Lee. — [Seoul] : Seoul National University Press, c1982. — v, 336 p.. — Includes bibliographical references and index

KOREA — Social conditions — Addresses, essays, lectures

LEE, Man-Gap
Sociology and social change in Korea / by Man-Gap Lee. — [Seoul] : Seoul National University Press, c1982. — v, 336 p.. — Includes bibliographical references and index

KOREA — Social conditions — 1945-

KIM, Kyong-Dong
Man and society in Korea's economic growth : sociological studies / Kyong-Dong Kim. — 3rd ed. — Seoul : Seoul National University Press, 1985. — 216p. — (Korean Studies Series ; No.1)

KOREA (NORTH) — Defenses

The Changing balance : South and North Korean capabilities for long-term military competition / Charles Wolf, Jr. ... [et al.]. — Santa Monica, CA : Rand, [1985]. — xv, 70 p.. — "Prepared for the Director of Net Assessment, Office of the Secretary of Defense.". — "December, 1985.". — "R-3305/1-NA.". — Includes bibliographical references

KOREA (NORTH) — Foreign relations

BRIDGES, Brian
Korea and the West / Brian Bridges. — London : Routledge and Kegan Paul, 1986. — [ix],101p. — (Chatham House Papers ; 33)

KOREA (NORTH) — Foreign relations — Korea (South)

The communist invasion of the Republic of Korea. — London : United States Information Service, 1950. — v,36p

KOREA (NORTH) — Military policy

SNEIDER, Richard L.
The political and social capabilities of north and south Korea for the long-term military competition / Richard L. Sneider. — Santa Monica (Calif.) : Rand, 1985. — ix,47p. — Bibliography: p47

KOREA (NORTH) — Politics and government

BRIDGES, Brian
Korea and the West / Brian Bridges. — London : Routledge and Kegan Paul, 1986. — [ix],101p. — (Chatham House Papers ; 33)

SNEIDER, Richard L.
The political and social capabilities of north and south Korea for the long-term military competition / Richard L. Sneider. — Santa Monica (Calif.) : Rand, 1985. — ix,47p. — Bibliography: p47

KOREA (SOUTH) — Census, 1970

1970 population and housing census report. — [Seoul] : Bureau of Statistics, Economic Planning Board. — In Korea and English Vol. 2: 10% sample survey
Vol 4-1: Economic activity. — 1973. — 391p

1970 population and housing census report. — [Seoul] Bureau of Statistics, Economic Planninfg Board. — In Korean and English Vol.2: 10% sample survey. — [Seoul] Bureau of Statistics, Economic Planninfg Board. — In Korean and English
Vol.4-2: Fertility. — 1973. — 258p

1970 population and housing census report. — [Seoul] : Bureau of Statistics, Economic Planning Board. — In Korean and English Vol.2: 10% sample survey
Vol.4-3: Internal migration. — 1973. — 217p

KOREA (SOUTH — Census, 1970

1970 population and housing census report. — [Seoul] : Bureau of Statistics, Economic Planning Board. — In Korean and English Vol.2: 10% sample survey. — [Seoul] : Bureau of Statistics, Economic Planning Board. — In Korean and English
Vol.4-4: Housing. — 1973. — 219p

KOREA (SOUTH) — Census. 1970

1970 population and housing census report (complete). — [Seoul] : Economic Planning Board. — In Korean and English
Vol.12-3: Busan City. — 1972. — 126p

KOREA (SOUTH) — Census, 1970

1970 population and housing census report (complete). — [Seoul] : Economic Planning Board. — In Korean and English
Vol.12-5: Gang-weon Do. — 1972. — 236p

1970 population and housing census report (complete). — [Seoul] : Economic Planning Board. — In Korean and English
Vol.12-6: Chungcheong Bug Do. — 1972. — 202p

1970 population and housing census report (complete). — [Seoul] : Economic Planning Board. — In Korean and English
Vol.12-7: Chungcheong Nam Do. — 1972. — 126p

1970 population and housing census report (complete). — [Seoul] : Economic Planning Board. — In Korean and English
Vol.12-8: Jeonra Bug Do. — 1972. — 250p

1970 population and housing census report (complete). — [Seoul] : Economic Planning Board. — In Korean and English
Vol.12-9: Jeonra Nam Do. — 1972. — 354p

1970 population and housing census report (complete). — [Seoul] : Economic Planning Board. — In Korean and English
Vol.12-12: Jeju Do. — 1972. — 120p

KOREA (SOUTH) — Commercial policy

INTERNATIONAL BANK FOR RECONSTRUCTION AND DEVELOPMENT
Korea : development in a global context. — Washington, D.C., U.S.A. : World Bank, c1984. — xlii,241p. — (A World Bank country study). — *Bibliographical references: p221-241*

Korea : managing the industrial transition. — Washington, D.C. : The World Bank
V.1: The conduct of industrial policy. — 1987. — xiv,182p. — (A World Bank Country study). — *Includes bibliographical references*

Korea : Managing the Industrial Transition. — Washington, D.C. : The World Bank
V.2: Selected topics and case studies. — 1987. — x,225p. — (A World Bank Country study). — *Bibliography: p218-225*

KOREA (SOUTH) — Defenses

The Changing balance : South and North Korean capabilities for long-term military competition / Charles Wolf, Jr. ... [et al.]. — Santa Monica, CA : Rand, [1985]. — xv, 70 p.. — *"Prepared for the Director of Net Assessment, Office of the Secretary of Defense."*. — *"December, 1985."*. — *"R-3305/1-NA."*. — *Includes bibliographical references*

KOREA (SOUTH) — Economic conditions — 1960-

1970 population and housing census report. — [Seoul] : Bureau of Statistics, Economic Planning Board. — *In Korean and English*
Vol. 2: 10% sample survey
Vol 4-1: Economic activity. — 1973. — 391p

The Changing balance : South and North Korean capabilities for long-term military competition / Charles Wolf, Jr. ... [et al.]. — Santa Monica, CA : Rand, [1985]. — xv, 70 p.. — *"Prepared for the Director of Net Assessment, Office of the Secretary of Defense."*. — *"December, 1985."*. — *"R-3305/1-NA."*. — *Includes bibliographical references*

INTERNATIONAL BANK FOR RECONSTRUCTION AND DEVELOPMENT
Korea : development in a global context. — Washington, D.C., U.S.A. : World Bank, c1984. — xlii,241p. — (A World Bank country study). — *Bibliographical references: p221-241*

KIM, Kwang Suk
Sources of economic growth in Korea, 1963-1982 / Kim Kwang-suk, Park Joon-kyung. — Seoul, Korea : Korea Development Institute, 1985. — xx, 217 p.. — *Includes bibliographical references and index*

Models of development : a comparative study of economic growth in South Korea and Taiwan / edited by Lawrence J. Lau. — San Francisco, Calif. : ICS Press, Institute for Contemporary Studies, c1986. — xv, 217 p.. — *Includes index*. — *Bibliography: p. 203-208*

KOREA (SOUTH) — Economic policy

INTERNATIONAL BANK FOR RECONSTRUCTION AND DEVELOPMENT
Korea : development in a global context. — Washington, D.C., U.S.A. : World Bank, c1984. — xlii,241p. — (A World Bank country study). — *Bibliographical references: p221-241*

Korea : managing the industrial transition. — Washington, D.C. : The World Bank
V.1: The conduct of industrial policy. — 1987. — xiv,182p. — (A World Bank Country study). — *Includes bibliographical references*

Korea : Managing the Industrial Transition. — Washington, D.C. : The World Bank
V.2: Selected topics and case studies. — 1987. — x,225p. — (A World Bank Country study). — *Bibliography: p218-225*

The Political economy of the new Asian industrialism / edited by Frederic C. Deyo. — Ithaca, N.Y. : Cornell University Press, 1987. — 252 p.. — (Cornell studies in political economy). — *Includes bibliographies and index*. — Contents: Export-oriented industrializing states in the capitalist world system / Richard E. Barrett and Soomi Chin -- The origins and development of the Northeast Asian political economy / Bruce Cumings -- State and foreign capital in the East Asian NICs / Stephan Haggard and Tun-jen Cheng -- Political institutions and economic performance / Chalmers Johnson -- The interplay of state, social class, and world system in East Asian development / Hagen Koo -- State and labor / Frederic C. Deyo -- Class, state, and dependence in East Asia / Peter Evans -- Coalitions, institutions, and linkage sequencing toward a strategic capacity model of East Asian development / Frederic C. Deyo

KOREA (SOUTH) — Economic policy — 1960-

Models of development : a comparative study of economic growth in South Korea and Taiwan / edited by Lawrence J. Lau. — San Francisco, Calif. : ICS Press, Institute for Contemporary Studies, c1986. — xv, 217 p.. — *Includes index*. — *Bibliography: p. 203-208*

KOREA (SOUTH) — Foreign relations

BRIDGES, Brian
Korea and the West / Brian Bridges. — London : Routledge and Kegan Paul, 1986. — [ix],101p. — (Chatham House Papers ; 33)

KOREA (SOUTH) — Foreign relations — Korea (North)

The communist invasion of the Republic of Korea. — London : United States Information Service, 1950. — v,36p

KOREA (SOUTH) — Foreign relations — United States

MOON, Changjoo
The balance of power in Asia and U.S.-Korea relations = : [Asia ŭi seryŏk kyunhyŏng kwa Han-Mi kwan'gye] / Changjoo Moon. — Seoul, Korea : Gimm-Young Press ; Maple Shade, N.J. : Distributive Office for the U.S.A., Gimm-Young Co., c1983. — 386 p.. — *English and Korean*. — *Includes bibliographical references*

KOREA (SOUTH) — Military policy

SNEIDER, Richard L.
The political and social capabilities of north and south Korea for the long-term military competition / Richard L. Sneider. — Santa Monica (Calif.) : Rand, 1985. — ix,47p. — *Bibliography: p47*

KOREA (SOUTH) — National security

YI, Sang-u
Security and unification of Korea / Sang-Woo Rhee. — Seoul, Korea : Sogang University Press, [1983]. — viii, 398 p.. — *Includes bibliographical references and indexes*

KOREA (SOUTH) — Politics and government

BRIDGES, Brian
Korea and the West / Brian Bridges. — London : Routledge and Kegan Paul, 1986. — [ix],101p. — (Chatham House Papers ; 33)

PAE, Sung M
Testing democratic theories in Korea / Sung M. Pae. — Lanham, MD : University Press of America, c1986. — xvii, 300 p.. — *Includes index*. — *Bibliography: p. [281]-289*

KOREA (SOUTH) — Politics and government — 1945-1948

MATRAY, James Irving
The reluctant crusade : American foreign policy in Korea, 1941-1950 / James Irving Matray. — Honolulu : University of Hawaii Press, c1985. — xii, 351 p.. — *Includes index*. — *Bibliography: p.[319]-330*

KOREA (SOUTH) — Politics and government — 1948-1960

MATRAY, James Irving
The reluctant crusade : American foreign policy in Korea, 1941-1950 / James Irving Matray. — Honolulu : University of Hawaii Press, c1985. — xii, 351 p.. — *Includes index*. — *Bibliography: p.[319]-330*

KOREA (SOUTH) — Politics and government — 1960-

SNEIDER, Richard L.
The political and social capabilities of north and south Korea for the long-term military competition / Richard L. Sneider. — Santa Monica (Calif.) : Rand, 1985. — ix,47p. — *Bibliography: p47*

KOREA (SOUTH) — Population — Statistics

1970 population and housing census report (complete). — [Seoul] : Economic Planning Board. — *In Korean and English*
Vol.12-3: Busan City. — 1972. — 126p

1970 population and housing census report (complete). — [Seoul] : Economic Planning Board. — *In Korean and English*
Vol.12-5: Gang-weon Do. — 1972. — 236p

1970 population and housing census report (complete). — [Seoul] : Economic Planning Board. — *In Korean and English*
Vol.12-6: Chungcheong Bug Do. — 1972. — 202p

1970 population and housing census report (complete). — [Seoul] : Economic Planning Board. — *In Korean and English*
Vol.12-7: Chungcheong Nam Do. — 1972. — 126p

1970 population and housing census report (complete). — [Seoul] : Economic Planning Board. — *In Korean and English*
Vol.12-8: Jeonra Bug Do. — 1972. — 250p

1970 population and housing census report (complete). — [Seoul] : Economic Planning Board. — *In Korean and English*
Vol.12-9: Jeonra Nam Do. — 1972. — 354p

1970 population and housing census report (complete). — [Seoul] : Economic Planning Board. — *In Korean and English*
Vol.12-12: Jeju Do. — 1972. — 120p

KOREAN AIR LINES INCIDENT, 1983

HERSH, Seymour M
"The target is destroyed" : what really happened to flight 007 and what America knew about it / Seymour Hersh. — 1st ed. — New York : Random House, c1986. — p. cm. — *Includes index*. — *Bibliography: p*

KOREAN REUNIFICATION QUESTION (1945)-

South-north dialogue in Korea / International Cultural Society of Korea. — Seoul : International Cultural Society of Korea, 1986-. — *Irregular*

KOREAN REUNIFICATION QUESTION (1945-)

YI, Sang-u
Security and unification of Korea / Sang-Woo Rhee. — Seoul, Korea : Sogang University Press, [1983]. — viii, 398 p.. — *Includes bibliographical references and indexes*

KOREAN WAR, 1950-1953

The communist invasion of the Republic of Korea. — London : United States Information Service, 1950. — v,36p

MACDONALD, C. A.
Korea : the war before Vietnam / Callum A. Macdonald. — Basingstoke : Macmillan, 1986. — xx,330p,[16]p of plates. — *Bibliography: p310-31*. — *Includes index*

KOSEDA, HEIDI
HILLINGDON
Report of the review panel of the London Borough of Hillingdon Area Review Committee on Child Abuse into the death of Heidi Koseda. — Hillingdon : [the Council], 1986. — 66p

KOSOVA (YUGOSLAVIA) — Politics and government
The status of a republic for Kosova is a just demand: article of the newspaper "Zëri i popullit", organ of the CC of the PLA, May 17, 1981. — Tirana : 8 Nentori Publishing House, 1981. — 54p

KOSOVO (SERBIA) — Constitutional law
RAJOVIĆ, Radošin
Autonomiji Kosova : istorijsko-pravna studija / Radošin Rajović. — Beograd : Ekonomika, 1985. — 583p. — *Summary in English and Russian.* — *Bibliography: p553-560*

KOSOVO (SERBIA) — History
RAJOVIĆ, Radošin
Autonomiji Kosova : istorijsko-pravna studija / Radošin Rajović. — Beograd : Ekonomika, 1985. — 583p. — *Summary in English and Russian.* — *Bibliography: p553-560*

KOSOVO (SERBIA) — Politics and government
JOVANOVIĆ, Batrić
Kosovo, inflacija, socijalne razlike : istupanja u Skupštini SFRJ, 1982-85 / Batrić Jovanović. — Beograd : [Partizanska knjiga], 1985. — 331p. — (Sučeljavanja)

VUKOVI'C, Ilija
Autonomaštvo i separatizam na Kosovu / Ilija Vukovi'c. — Beograd : Nova Knjiga, 1985. — 238p

KOWLOON (HONG KONG) — Statistics
Hong Kong 1986 by-census : tertiary planning unit summary tables / Kowloon and New Kowloon. — Hong Kong : Census and Statistics Department, [1987]. — xiii,152p. — *Has map in end pocket*

KRISTELIGT FOLKEPARTI (Denmark)
Kristeligt Folkeparti, 1970-1980 / [redaktion, Ebbe Jensen]. — [København] : Kristeligt Folkeparti, 1980. — 48p

KUBEL, ALFRED
RENZSCH, Wolfgang
Alfred Kubel : 30 Jahre Politik für Niedersachsen : eine politische Biographie / Wolfgang Renzsch. — Bonn : Neue Gesellschaft, 1985. — 232p. — *Bibliography: p222-229*

KUCZYNSKI, JÜRGEN
Ein Gespräch mit Jürgen Kuczynski über Arbeiterklasse, Alltag, Geschichte, Kultur und vor allem über Krieg und Frieden [/ Frank Deppe...et al.]. — Marburg : Verlag Arbeiterbewegung und Gesellschaftswissenschaft, 1984. — 141p. — (Schriftenreihe der Studiengesellschaft für Sozialgeschichte und Arbeiterbewegung ; Bd.48)

KUN, BÉLA
NEMES, Dezső
Kun Béla politikai életútjáról / Nemes Dezső. — [Budapest] : Kossuth Könyvkiadó, 1985. — 186p

KUOMINTANG
MAKHMUTKHODZHAEV, M. Kh.
Natsional'naia politika gomin'dana (1927-1937) / M. Kh. Makhmutkhodshaev. — Moskva : Nauka (IVL), 1986. — 124p. — *Table of contents in English.* — *Bibliography: p116-[125]*

KURDS — Civil rights
MCDOWALL, David
The Kurds / by David McDowall. — New ed. — London : Minority Rights Group, 1985. — 32p. — (Report / Minority Rights Group ; no. 23). — *Previous ed.: by Martin Short and Anthony McDermott. 1981.* — *Bibliography: p.24*

KUWAIT — Economic conditions — Econometric models
MOOSA, Imad A.
An econometric model of Kuwait's monetary sector / Imad A. Moosa. — Safat : Industrial Bank of Kuwait, 1986. — 143p. — (The IBK Papers ; no.22). — *Bibliography: p134-140*

KWAIO (MELANESIAN PEOPLE) — Religion
KEESING, Roger M.
Kwaio religion : the living and the dead in a Solomon Island society / Roger M. Keesing. — New York : Columbia University Press, 1982. — xi, 257p. — *Includes index.* — *Bibliography: p.[249]-253*

KWOMA (PAPUAN PEOPLE) — Social life and customs
BOWDEN, Ross
Yena : art and ceremony in a Sepik society / Ross Bowden ; with a foreword by Rodney Needham. — Oxford : Pitt Rivers Museum, 1983. — xii,179p, 32 plates. — (Monograph / Pitt Rivers Museum ; 3)

LA RIOJA (SPAIN) — History
HERNÁNDEZ GARCÍA, Antonio
La represión en La Rioja durante la Guerra Civil / Antonio Hernández García. — Logroño : A. Hernández García, 1984. — 3v

LA TOUR, CHARLES DE ST. ETIENNE
MACDONALD, M. A.
Fortune and La Tour : the civil war in Acadia / M. A. MacDonald. — Toronto : Methuen, 1986. — xii,228p. — *Bibliography: p219-224*

LABOR AND LABORING CLASSES
Confrontation, class consciousness, and the labor process : studies in proletarian class formation / edited by Michael Hanagan and Charles Stephenson. — Westport, Conn. ; London : Greenwood Press, c1986. — viii, 261p. — (Contributions in labor studies ; no. 18). — *Includes index.* — *Bibliography: p.[241]-253*

Journal of labor research. — Fairfax, VA : Department of Economics, George Mason University, 1986-. — *Quarterly*

Labor essays. — Blackburn, Victoria : Done Communications on behalf of the Australian Labor Party (Victorian Branch), 1981-. — *Annual*

RINEHART, James W.
The tyranny of work : alienation and the labour process / James W. Rinehart ; with the assistance of Seymour Faber. — 2nd ed. — Toronto : Harcourt Brace Jovanovich, 1987. — x,226p. — *Bibliography: p[211]-222*

Science, technology and the labour process : Marxist studies / edited by Les Levidow and Bob Young. — London : Free Association Books
Vol.2. — 1985. — v,232p. — *Includes bibliographies*

Working conditions and environment : a worker's education manual. — Geneva : International Labour Office, 1983. — vi, 81 p., [6] p. of plates. — *"A selection of recommended ILO publications and documents": p. 75.* — *"ILO films and film strips": p. 76*

LABOR AND LABORING CLASSES — Attitudes
WILLMAN, Paul
Technological change, collective bargaining, and industrial efficiency / Paul Willman. — Oxford : Clarendon, 1986. — [xvii.264]p. — *Includes index*

LABOR AND LABORING CLASSES — Dwellings — Brazil — Salvador
PINHO, Jose Antonio Gomes de
Housing provision and labour reproduction in peripheral capitalism : the case of Salvador, Brazil / Jose Antonio Gomes de Pinho. — 430 leaves, [3] leaves of plates. — *PhD (Econ) 1986 LSE*

LABOR AND LABORING CLASSES — Dwellings — Great Britain — History
GASKELL, S. Martin
Model housing : from the Great Exhibition to the Festival of Britain / S. Martin Gaskell. — London : Mansell, 1986, c1987. — x,180p. — (Studies in history, planning and the environment) (An Alexandrine Press book). — *Bibliography: p163-173.* — *Includes index*

LABOR AND LABORING CLASSES — Education
SEMINAR ON EDUCATION, DEVELOPMENT AND SOCIAL TRANSFORMATION (982)
[Proceedings of the] seminar...jointly organized by the National Institute of Research, Gaborone, Botswana [and] the Foundation of Education with Production, Gaborone, Botswana. — Gaborone : National Institute of Research : Foundation for Education with Production, [1982]. — 233p

LABOR AND LABORING CLASSES — Education — Australia
DWYER, Peter
Confronting school and work : youth and class cultures in Australia / Peter Dwyer, Bruce Wilson, and Roger Woock. — Sydney ; Boston : G. Allen & Unwin, 1984. — 175 p.. — (Studies in the society ; 23). — *Includes index.* — *Bibliography: p. [166]-173*

Human capital and productivity growth. — Canberra : Economic Planning Advisory Council, 1986. — v,43p. — (Council paper / Economic Planning Advisory Council ; no.15). — *Bibliographical references: p40-41*

LABOR AND LABORING CLASSES — Education — England — Liverpool (Merseyside)
EDWARDS, Judith
Working class adult education in Liverpool : a radical approach : an evaluation of Second Chance to Learn / Judith Edwards. — Manchester : University of Manchester Centre for Adult and Higher Education, 1986. — (Manchester monographs ; 25)

LABOR AND LABORING CLASSES — Education — Finland
The Workers' Institutes and other Free Institutes of Finland. — Helsinki : Board of Schools, 1924. — 18p

LABOR AND LABORING CLASSES — Education — Germany — History
GROSCHOPP, Horst
Zwischen Bierabend und Bildungsverein : zur Kulturarbeit in der deutschen Arbeiterbewegung vor 1914 / Horst Groschopp. — Berlin : Dietz Verlag, 1985. — 243p

LABOR AND LABORING CLASSES — History — Addresses, essays, lectures
Proletarians and protest : the roots of class formation in an industrializing world / edited by Michael Hanagan and Charles Stephenson. — New York : Greenwood Press, 1986. — viii, 250 p.. — (Contributions in labor studies ; no. 17). — *Includes index.* — *Bibliography: p. [231]-241*

LABOR AND LABORING CLASSES — History — 20th century
The international working-class movement : problems of history and theory / General editorial committee: B. N. Ponomarev...[et al.]. — Moscow : Progress
Vol.5: The builder of socialism and fighter against fascism / Editorial board: S. S. Salychev...[et al.]. — 1985. — 757p

LABOR AND LABORING CLASSES — Moral and ethical aspects

The Environment of the workplace and human values / editor, Sheldon W. Samuels. — New York : Liss, c1986. — vii, 118 p.. — *Published also as the American journal of industrial medicine, v. 9, no. 1, 1986. — Conference cosponsored by the Labor Policy Institute and the Marshall-Wythe School of Law at the College of William and Mary, May 20-22, 1982. — Includes bibliographical references and index*

LABOR AND LABORING CLASSES — Political activity

DENIS, Serge
Syndicats, parti des travailleurs et parti ouvrier révolutionnaire / Serge Denis. — Montreal : Presses Socialistes Internationales, 1976. — 61p. — (Documents du Groupe socialiste des travailleurs du Québec ; 1)

LABOR AND LABORING CLASSES — Social aspects — Soviet Union

SOKOLOV, A. K.
Rabochii klass i revoliutsionnye izmeneniia v sotsial'noi strukture obshchestva / A. K. Sokolov. — Moskva : Izd-vo Moskovskogo universiteta, 1987. — 226p

LABOR AND LABORING CLASSES — Argentina — History

BILSKY, Edgardo J.
La F.O.R.A. y el movimiento obrero (1900-1910) / Edgardo J. Bilsky. — Buenos Aires : Centro Editor de América Latina. — (Biblioteca Política Argentina ; 97). — *Bibliographic notes: p97-108*
t.1. — 1985. — 108p

BILSKY, Edgardo J.
La F.O.R.A. y el movimiento obrero (1900-1910) / Edgardo J. Bilsky. — Buenos Aires : Centro Editor de América Latina. — (Biblioteca Política Argentina ; 98)
t.2. — 1985. — 109-243p

LABOR AND LABORING CLASSES — America — Congresses

The Americas in the new international division of labor / edited by Steven E. Sanderson. — New York, N.Y. : Holmes & Meier, 1985. — p. cm. — *Includes index. — Bibliography: p*

LABOR AND LABORING CLASSES — Argentina

GARCÍA COSTA, Victor O.
El Obrero : selección de textos / Victor O. García Costa. — Buenos Aires : Centro Editor de América Latina, 1985. — 107p. — (Biblioteca Política Argentina ; 121)

MASCALI, Humberto
Desocupación y conflictos laborales en el campo argentino (1940-1965) / Humberto Mascali. — Buenos Aires : Centro Editor de América Latina, 1986. — 127p. — (Biblioteca Política Argentina ; 139). — *Bibliography: p121-127*

LABOR AND LABORING CLASSES — Argentina — History

FERNÁNDEZ, Arturo
Ideologías de los grupos dirigentes sindicales / Arturo Fernández. — Buenos Aires : Centro Editor de América Latina. — (Biblioteca Política Argentina ; 144). — *Bibliography: p141-143*
t.2: (1966-1973). — 1986. — 143p

FERNÁNDEZ, Arturo
Las prácticas sociales del sindicalismo (1976-1982) / Arturo Fernández. — Buenos Aires : Centro Editor de América Latina, 1985. — 145p. — (Biblioteca Política Argentina ; 113). — *Bibliography: p143-144*

ISUANI, Ernesto A.
Los orígenes conflictivos de la seguridad social argentina / Ernesto A. Isuani. — Buenos Aires : Centro Editor de América Latina, 1985. — 140p. — (Biblioteca Política Argentina ; 129). — *Bibliography: p137-140*

LOZZA, Arturo Marcos
Tiempo de huelgas : los apasionados relatos del campesino y ferroviario Florindo Moretti sobre aquellas épocas de fundaciones, luchas y serenatas / Arturo Marcos Lozza. — Buenos Aires : Editorial Anteo, 1985. — 299p. — *Bibliography: p293-294*

MUNCK, Ronnie
Argentina : from anarchism to Peronism / Ronaldo Munck, Ricardo Falcon, Bernardo Galitelli ; edited and translated by Ronaldo Munck. — London : Zed, 1987. — [272]p. — *Includes bibliography and index*

LABOR AND LABORING CLASSES — Argentina — History — 19th century

FALCÓN, Ricardo
Los orígenes del movimiento obrero (1857-1899) / Ricardo Falcón. — Buenos Aires : Centro Editor de América Latina, c1984. — 129p. — (Biblioteca política argentina ; 53). — *Includes bibliographical references*

LABOR AND LABORING CLASSES — Argentina — History — 20th century

BIALET-MASSÉ, Juan
Informe sobre el estados de las clases obreras argentinas a comienzos del siglo / Juan Bialet-Massé. — Buenos Aires : Centro Editor de América Latina. — (Biblioteca Política Argentina ; 116)
t.2: [selección]. — 1985. — 159-297p

LABOR AND LABORING CLASSES — Argentina — Political activity — History

BIALET-MASSÉ, Juan
Informe sobre el estados de las clases obreras argentinas a comienzos del siglo / Juan Bialet-Massé. — Buenos Aires : Centro Editor de América Latina. — (Biblioteca Política Argentina ; 116)
t.2: [selección]. — 1985. — 159-297p

LABOR AND LABORING CLASSES — Australia — History

BURGMANN, Verity
'In our time' : socialism and the rise of Labor, 1885-1905 / Verity Burgmann. — Sydney ; London : Allen & Unwin, 1985. — [ix,240]p. — *Bibliography: p213-226. — Includes index*

LABOR AND LABORING CLASSES — Australia — Tasmania

TASMANIA. Commonwealth Bureau of Census and Statistics. Tasmanian Office
Labour, wages and prices. — Hobart : [the Office], 1970/71-1980/81. — *Annual*

LABOR AND LABORING CLASSES — Austria

MAGAZINER, Alfred
Die Bahnbrecher : aus der Geschichte der Arbeiterbewegung / Alfred Magaziner. — Wien : Europaverlag, c1985. — 189p

LABOR AND LABORING CLASSES — British Columbia — History

Fighting heritage : highlights of the 1930s struggle for jobs and militant unionism in British Columbia / edited by Sean Griffin. — Vancouver : Tribune Publishing Company, [1985]. — 159p

LABOR AND LABORING CLASSES — British Columbia — Vancouver — History

Working lives : Vancouver 1886-1986 / The Working Lives Collective. — Vancouver : New Star Books, 1985. — 211p. — *References: p202-208*

LABOR AND LABORING CLASSES — Bulgaria

Kharakteristika na bŭlgarskoto naselenie : trudovi vŭzmozhnosti i realizatsiia : pod obshchata redaktsiia Minko Minkov. — Sofiia : Dŭrzhavno izd-vo nauka i izkustvo, 1984. — 483p. — *Summary in Russian and French*

LABOR AND LABORING CLASSES — Canada

CHEN, Mervin Yaotsu
Work in the changing Canadian society / Mervin Y.T. Chen, Thomas G. Regan. — Toronto : Butterworths, c1985. — xiv, 289 p.. — *Includes index. — Bibliography: p. [245]-286*

RINEHART, James W.
The tyranny of work : alienation and the labour process / James W. Rinehart ; with the assistance of Seymour Faber. — 2nd ed. — Toronto : Harcourt Brace Jovanovich, 1987. — x,226p. — *Bibliography: p[211]-222*

Work in the Canadian context : continuity despite change / [edited by] Katherina L. P. Lundy and Barbara Warme. — 2nd ed.. — Toronto ; Vancouver : Butterworths, 1986. — xvii,369p. — *Includes bibliographical references*

LABOR AND LABORING CLASSES — Canada — Bibliography

LAPERRIÈRE, René
Bibliographie du droit du travail canadien et québécois 1964-1983 / René Laperrière. — Cowansville (Quebec) : Éditions Yvon Blais, 1984. — xv,70p

LABOR AND LABORING CLASSES — Canada — History

Canadian labour history : selected readings / edited by David J. Bercuson. — Toronto : Copp Clark Pitman, 1987. — 276p. — (New Canadian readings). — *Bibliography: p273-276*

Lectures in Canadian labour and working-class history / edited by W. J. C. Cherwinski and Gregory S. Kealey. — St. John's Newfoundland : Committee on Canadian Labour History, Department of History, Memorial University of Newfoundland, 1985. — 198p

On the job : confronting the labour process in Canada / edited by Craig Heron and Robert Storey. — Kingston : McGill-Queen's University Press, c1986. — xiv, 360 p.. — *Includes bibliographies and index*

LABOR AND LABORING CLASSES — Canada — Atlantic Provinces

FORSEY, Eugene Albert
Perspectives on the Atlantic Canadian Labour Movement and the working-class experience / Eugene A. Forsey, J. Albert Richardson, Gregory S. Kealey. — New Brunswick : Centre for Canadian Studies, Mount Allison University, 1985. — 62p. — (Winthrop Pickard Bell Lectures in Maritime Studies ; 4)

LABOR AND LABORING CLASSES — Chicago (Illinois) — History

REPIN, Anatoly
Haymarket heritage : on centenary of Chicago events in May 1886 / Anatoly Repin. — [S.l.] : [s.n.], 1986. — 13p

LABOR AND LABORING CLASSES — Colombia — Bogota

MOHAN, Rakesh
Work, wages, and welfare in a developing, metropolis : some consequences of growth in Bogotá, Colombia / by Rakesh Mohan. — Washington, D.C. : World Bank, 1986. — xi,403p. — *Bibliographical references: p382-395*

LABOR AND LABORING CLASSES — Colombia — Cali

MOHAN, Rakesh
Work, wages, and welfare in a developing, metropolis : some consequences of growth in Bogotá, Colombia / by Rakesh Mohan. — Washington, D.C. : World Bank, 1986. — xi,403p. — *Bibliographical references: p382-395*

LABOR AND LABORING CLASSES — Denmark

PETERSEN, Jens Peter Østerby
Arbeijderne og krisen : forholdet mellem AOF's arbejderuddannelse, reformismen og arbejderbevidstheden i 30 'erne / Jens Peter Østerby Petersen & Jens Skovholm. — København : Litteratur & Samfund, 1978. — 240p. — *Bibliography: p237-239*

LABOR AND LABORING CLASSES — Denmark — Political activity

PETERSEN, Jens Peter Østerby
Arbeijderne og krisen : forholdet mellem AOF's arbejderuddannelse, reformismen og arbejderbevidstheden i 30 'erne / Jens Peter Østerby Petersen & Jens Skovholm. — København : Litteratur & Samfund, 1978. — 240p. — *Bibliography: p237-239*

LABOR AND LABORING CLASSES — Egypt — Political activity

GOLDBERG, Ellis
Tinker, tailor, and textile worker : class and politics in Egypt, 1930-1952 / Ellis Goldberg. — Berkeley : University of California Press, 1986. — p. cm. — *Includes index.* — *Bibliography: p*

LABOR AND LABORING CLASSES — England

REID, Robert, 1933-
Land of lost content : the Luddite revolt, 1812 / Robert Reid. — London : Heinemann, 1986. — viii, 333p, [5]p of plates. — *Bibliography: p.315-320*

LABOR AND LABORING CLASSES — England — History

Innovation and labour during British industrialisation : a celebration of the life and work of Harry Dutton, 1947-1984. — Cambridge : Huntington, [1985]. — 92p. — *Bibliography: p90*

THOMPSON, E. P.
The making of the English working class / by E.P. Thompson. — London : Gollancz, 1980. — 958p. — *Originally published: 1963.* — *Includes index*

LABOR AND LABORING CLASSES — England — Coventry — History

Life and labour in a twentieth century city : the experience of Coventry / edited by Bill Lancaster and Tony Mason. — Coventry : Cryfield Press, Centre for the Study of Social History, University of Warwick, [1986?]. — 372p

LABOR AND LABORING CLASSES — England — London

TOWER HAMLETS. Planning Department. Directorate of Development
Workers in Tower Hamlets. — Tower Hamlets : [the Directorate], 1986. — 42 leaves. — *At head of title: Planning research and information*

LABOR AND LABORING CLASSES — England — Oldham, Lancs. — History

FOSTER, John, 1940-
Class struggle and the Industrial Revolution : early industrial capitalism in three English towns / John Foster ; with a foreword by E.J. Hobsbawm. — London : Weidenfeld and Nicolson, 1974. — xiii,346p. — *Bibliography: p.337-338.* — *Includes index*

LABOR AND LABORING CLASSES — England — West Country — Alcohol use

FRANKLIN, Adrian
Pub drinking and the licensed trade : a study of drinking cultures and local community in two areas of south west England / Adrian Franklin. — Bristol : University of Bristol, School for Advanced Urban Studies, 1985. — 64p. — (Occasional paper / School for Advanced Urban Studies ; 21)

LABOR AND LABORING CLASSES — Europe — History

LIEBERMAN, Sima
Labor movements and labor thought : Spain, France, Germany, and the United States / Sima Lieberman. — New York ; Eastbourne : Praeger, 1986. — ix, 288p. — *Includes bibliographies and index*

LINDER, Marc
European labor aristocracies : trade unionism, the hierarchy of skill, and the stratification of the manual working class before the First World War / Marc Linder. — Frankfurt : Campus, 1985. — 343 p.. — *Includes bibliographical references*

LABOR AND LABORING CLASSES — Europe — History — 20th century

KIRBY, D. G. (David Gordon)
War, peace and revolution : international socialism at the crossroads 1914-1918 / David Kirby. — Aldershot : Gower, c1986. — ix,310p. — *Bibliography: p284-301.* — *Includes index*

LABOR AND LABORING CLASSES — Europe, Eastern

MATEJKO, Alexander J
Comparative work systems : ideologies and reality in Eastern Europe / Alexander J. Matejko. — New York : Praeger, 1985. — p. cm. — *Includes index.* — *Bibliography: p*

LABOR AND LABORING CLASSES — France

MAURICE, Marc
The social foundations of industrial power : a comparison of France and Germany / Marc Maurice, François Sellier, and Jean-Jacques Silvestre ; translated by Arthur Goldhammer. — Cambridge, Mass ; London : MIT Press, c1986. — xi, 292p. — *Translation of: Politique d'éducation et organisation industrielle en France et en Allemagne.* — *Includes index*

LABOR AND LABORING CLASSES — France — History — 19th century

Working-class formation : nineteenth-century patterns in Western Europe and the United States / edited by Ira Katznelson and Aristide R. Zolberg. — Princeton, N.J. : Princeton University Press, c1986. — viii, 470p. — *Includes index*

LABOR AND LABORING CLASSES — France — Ladrecht — Language (New words, slang, etc)

GARDÈS-METTRAY, Françoise
Parole ouvrière : autour de Ladrecht / Françoise Gardès-Mattray et Jacques Bres ; péface [sic] d'Henri Krasucki. — Paris : Messidor/Editions Sociales, [1986]. — 307p

LABOR AND LABORING CLASSES — Germany — History

ABENDROTH, Wolfgang
Die Aktualität der Arbeiterbewegung : Beiträge zu ihrer Theorie und Geschichte / Wolfgang Abendroth ; herausgegeben von Joachim Perels. — Frankfurt am Main : Suhrkamp, 1985. — 225p. — *Bibliography: p225-[226]*

Die Arbeiter : Lebensformen, Alltag und Kultur von der Frühindustrialisierung bis zum "Wirtschaftswunder" / herausgegeben von Wolfgang Ruppert. — München : Beck, 1986. — 512p. — *Bibliography: p499-510*

BREUILLY, John
Joachim Friedrich Martens (1806-1877) und die deutsche Arbeiterbewegung / John Breuilly, Wieland Sachse. — Göttingen : Otto Schwartz, 1984. — (xviii),489p. — (Göttinger Beiträge zur Wirtschafts- und Sozialgeschichte ; Bd.8). — *Bibliography: p469-485*

BUSCHAK, Willy
Von Menschen, die wie Menschen leben wollten : die Geschichte der Gewerkschaft Nahrung-Genuss-Gaststätten und ihrer Vorläufer / Willy Buschak ; Vorwork: Günter Döding. — Köln : Bund, 1985. — 645p. — *Bibliography: p634-639*

GREBING, Helga
Arbeiterbewegung : sozialer Protest und kollektive Interessenvertretung bis 1914 / Helga Grebing. — München : Deutscher Taschenbuch Verlag, 1985. — 204p. — *Bibliography: p175-190*

GREBING, Helga
Arbeiterbewegung und politische Moral : Aufsätze, Kommentare und Berichte zur Geschichte und Theorie der deutschen Arbeiterbewegung / Helga Grebing. — Göttingen : SOVEC, 1985. — 293p. — *Bibliography: p286-289*

HERBERT, Ulrich
Fremdarbeiter : Politik und Praxis des "Ausländer-Einsatzes" in der Kriegswirtschaft des Dritten Reiches / Ulrich Herbert. — Berlin : J. H. W. Dietz, 1985. — 494p. — *Bibliography: p454-478*

LABOR AND LABORING CLASSES — Germany — History — 19th century

Working-class formation : nineteenth-century patterns in Western Europe and the United States / edited by Ira Katznelson and Aristide R. Zolberg. — Princeton, N.J. : Princeton University Press, c1986. — viii, 470p. — *Includes index*

LABOR AND LABORING CLASSES — Germany — Political activity

GREBING, Helga
Arbeiterbewegung und politische Moral : Aufsätze, Kommentare und Berichte zur Geschichte und Theorie der deutschen Arbeiterbewegung / Helga Grebing. — Göttingen : SOVEC, 1985. — 293p. — *Bibliography: p286-289*

LABOR AND LABORING CLASSES — Germany — Political activity — History

GREBING, Helga
Arbeiterbewegung : sozialer Protest und kollektive Interessenvertretung bis 1914 / Helga Grebing. — München : Deutscher Taschenbuch Verlag, 1985. — 204p. — *Bibliography: p175-190*

LABOR AND LABORING CLASSES — Germany — Social conditions

Die Arbeiter : Lebensformen, Alltag und Kultur von der Frühindustrialisierung bis zum "Wirtschaftswunder" / herausgegeben von Wolfgang Ruppert. — München : Beck, 1986. — 512p. — *Bibliography: p499-510*

LABOR AND LABORING CLASSES — Germany (West)

MAURICE, Marc
The social foundations of industrial power : a comparison of France and Germany / Marc Maurice, François Sellier, and Jean-Jacques Silvestre ; translated by Arthur Goldhammer. — Cambridge, Mass ; London : MIT Press, c1986. — xi, 292p. — *Translation of: Politique d'éducation et organisation industrielle en France et en Allemagne.* — *Includes index*

LABOR AND LABORING CLASSES — Great Britain

ADVISORY, CONCILIATION AND ARBITRATION SERVICE
Developments in harmonisation. — [London : the Service], 1982. — 15p. — (Discussion paper ; no.1). — *Includes Bibliographical references*

BLACK WORKERS' PLANNING GROUP
Black workers in the north west : a report of a conference held on 3rd November 1984. — Manchester : Black Workers' Planning Group, 1984. — 19p

LABOR AND LABORING CLASSES — Great Britain — History

GORNY, Joseph
The British Labour movement and Zionism 1917-1948 / Joseph Gorny. — London : Cass, 1983. — xvi,251p. — *Bibliography: p239-242.* — *Includes index*

LABOR AND LABORING CLASSES — Great Britain — History
continuation

LINDER, Marc
European labor aristocracies : trade unionism, the hierarchy of skill, and the stratification of the manual working class before the First World War / Marc Linder. — Frankfurt : Campus, 1985. — 343 p.. — *Includes bibliographical references*

RAMDIN, Ron
The making of the black working class in Britain / Ron Ramdin. — Aldershot, Gower, c1987. — x,626p. — *Bibliography: p559-605. — Includes index*

LABOR AND LABORING CLASSES — Great Britain — History — Bibliography

The Autobiography of the working class : an annotated, critical bibliography / editors John Burnett, David Vincent, David Mayall. — Brighton : Harvester
Vol. 2: 1900-1945. — 1987. — xii,435p. — *Includes index*

LABOR AND LABORING CLASSES — Great Britain — History — 19th century

MCLEOD, Hugh
Religion and the working class in nineteenth-century Britain / prepared for the Economic History Society by Hugh McLeod. — London : Macmillan, 1984. — 76p. — (Studies in economic and social history). — *Bibliography: p67-72. — Includes index*

LABOR AND LABORING CLASSES — Great Britain — Law and legislation

MATHER, Graham
The future of labour law : two views / Graham Mather and Lord McCarthy. — Coventry : University of Warwick. School of Industrial and Business Studies. Industrial Relations Research Unit, 1987. — 31p. — (Warwick papers in industrial relations)

LABOR AND LABORING CLASSES — Iceland

MAGNÚSSON, Magnús S.
Iceland in transition : labour and socio-economic change before 1940 / Magnús S. Magnússon. — Lund : Ekonomisk-Historiska Föreningen i Lund, 1985. — 306p. — (Skrifter Utgivna av Ekonomisk-Historiska Föreningen i Lund ; Vol.45). — *Bibliography: p289-303*

LABOR AND LABORING CLASSES — India

AZIZ, Abdul
Labour problems of a developing economy / Abdul Aziz. — New Delhi : Ashish Pub. House, c1984. — viii, 157 p.. — *Includes bibliographical references and index*

JOSHI, P. C.
Marxism and social revolution in India and other essays / P. C. Joshi. — New Delhi : Patriot Publishers, 1986. — xiv,227p

LABOR AND LABORING CLASSES — India — History

JOSHI, Preeta
International Labour Organization and its impact on India / Preeta Joshi. — Delhi : B.R. Pub. Corp. ; New Delhi : Distributed by D.K. Publishers' Distributors, 1985. — viii, 158 p.. — *Includes index. — Bibliography: p. [147]-[151]*

LABOR AND LABORING CLASSES — India — Political activity

CHATTERJI, Rakhahari
Working class and the nationalist movement in India : the critical years / Rakhahari Chatterji. — New Delhi : South Asian Publishers, c1984. — ix, 215 p.. — *Includes bibliographical references and index*

LABOR AND LABORING CLASSES — India — Statistics

INDIA. Labour Bureau
Labour Bureau's labour : master reference book on labour statistics 1984. — Shinla : Labour Bureau, Ministry of Labour and Rehabilitation, 1984. — 471p

LABOR AND LABORING CLASSES — India — Hyderabad (State) — History

BHASKARA RAO, V.
Agrarian and industrial relations in Hyderabad State / V. Bhaskara Rao. — New Delhi : Associated Pub. House, c1985. — xi, 179 p.. — *Includes index. — Bibliography: p. [169]-173*

LABOR AND LABORING CLASSES — India — Manipur — Statistics

Census of India 1981. — [Delhi : Controller of Publications]
Series 13: Manipur. — [1985-]

LABOR AND LABORING CLASSES — Iran

BAYAT, Assef
Workers and revolution in Iran : a Third World experience of workers' control / Assef Bayat. — London : Zed, 1987. — 227p. — *Bibliography: p208-222. — Includes index*

LABOR AND LABORING CLASSES — Iran — Political activity

ORGANIZATION OF REVOLUTIONARY WORKERS OF IRAN
Resolutions on Working Class Party, United Workers Front, United Democratic Anti-Imperialist Front. — Aliozadi : Organization of Revolutionary Workers of Iran, 1987. — 20p

LABOR AND LABORING CLASSES — Italy — Turin — History — 20th century

PASSERINI, Luisa
Fascism in popular memory : the cultural experience of the Turin working class / Luisa Passerini ; translated by Bob Lumley and Jude Bloomfield. — Cambridge : Cambridge University Press, 1987. — x,244p. — (Studies in modern capitalism = Etudes sur le capitalisme moderne). — *Translation of: Torino operaia e Fascismo. — Includes index*

LABOR AND LABORING CLASSES — Japan — Statistics

Japanese working life profile : statistical aspects. — Tokyo : Japan Institute of Labor, 1985. — 80p

LABOR AND LABORING CLASSES — Louisiana — History

COOK, Bernard A
Louisiana labor from slavery to "right-to-work" / Bernard A. Cook, James R. Watson. — Lanham : University Press of America, c1985. — p. cm

LABOR AND LABORING CLASSES — Mexico — History

La clase obrera en la historia de México. — México : Siglo Veintiuno
11: Del avilacamachismo al alemanismo (1940-1952) / Jorge Basurto. — 1984. — 291p

LABOR AND LABORING CLASSES — Moldavian S.S.R.

SHORNIKOV, P. M.
Promyshlennost' i rabochii klass Moldavskoi SSR v gody Velikoi Otechestvennoi voiny / P. M. Shornikov ; otv. redaktor I. E. Levit. — Kishinev : Shtiintsa, 1986. — 148p. — *Brief summary in English and French*

LABOR AND LABORING CLASSES — Namibia

Working under South African occupation : labour in Namibia. — London : International Defence and Aid Fund for Southern Africa, 1987. — 56p. — (Fact paper on Southern Africa ; no.14). — *Bibliography: p47-48*

LABOR AND LABORING CLASSES — Netherlands

Vernieuwingen in het arbeidsbestel. — 's-Gravenhage : Staatsuitgeverij, 1981. — 350p. — (Rapporten aan de regering ; 21). — *Prepared by the Wetenschappelijke Raad voor het Regeringsbeleid. — Includes bibliographical references*

LABOR AND LABORING CLASSES — New York (State) — Albany — History — 19th century

GREENBERG, Brian
Worker and community : response to industrialization in a nineteenth-century American city, Albany, New York, 1850-1884 / Brian Greenberg. — Albany : State University of New York Press, c1985. — ix, 227 p.. — (SUNY series in American social history). — *Maps on endpapers. — Includes index. — Bibliography: p. 211-220*

LABOR AND LABORING CLASSES — Nigeria, Northern — History

LUBECK, Paul M.
Islam and urban labor in Northern Nigeria : the making of a Muslim working class / Paul M. Lubeck. — Cambridge : Cambridge Univesity Press, 1986. — [368]p. — (African studies series ; 52). — *Includes bibliography and index*

LABOR AND LABORING CLASSES — Peru

TOVAR, Teresa
Velasquismo y movimiento popular : otra historia prohibida / Teresa Tovar. — Lima : Centro de Estudios y Promoción del Desarrollo, 1985. — 399p. — *Bibliography: p395-399*

LABOR AND LABORING CLASSES — Poland

KOZŁOWSKI, Czesław
Tradycje polskiego ruchu robotniczego / Czesław Kozłowski. — Warszawa : Książka i Wiedza, 1986. — 119p. — *Bibliography: p119*

LABOR AND LABORING CLASSES — Poland — History

Historia polskiego ruchu robotniczego / pod ogólną redakcją Mariana Orzechowskiego. — Warszawa : Książka i Wiedza
1: Do 1890 / pod redakcją Ryszarda Kołodziejczyka. — 1985. — 418p

STANKIEWICZ, Zbigniew
Kwestia chłopska w okresie narodzin polskiego ruchu robotniczego / Zbigniew Stankiewicz. — Warszawa : Ludowa Spółdzielnia Wydawnicza, 1985. — 329p. — *Bibliography: p305-[314]*

LABOR AND LABORING CLASSES — Poland — Łódź

W dymach czarnych budzi się Łódź : z dziejów łódzkiego ruchu robotniczego 1882-1948 / [Alina Barszczewska-Krupa...et al.]. — Łódź : Wydawnictwo Łódzkie, 1985. — 507p

LABOR AND LABORING CLASSES — Russian S.F.S.R. — Gor'kii

Rabochii klass i nauchno-tekhnicheskii progress / otv. redaktor G. V. Osipov. — Moskva : Nauka, 1986. — 187p

LABOR AND LABORING CLASSES — Russian S.F.S.R. — Moscow — Political activity

IONOV, I. N.
Profsoiuzy rabochikh Moskvy v revoliutsii 1905-1907 gg. / I. N. Ionov ; otv. redaktor A. M. Sinitsyn. — Moskva : Nauka, 1986. — 166p

LABOR AND LABORING CLASSES — Russian S.F.S.R. — Siberia

Rabochii klass Sibiri 1961-1980 gg. / [redkollegiia: E. V. Vasil'evskaia, I. I. Komogortsev...et al.]. — Novosibirsk : Nauka, Sibirskoe otdelenie, 1986. — 355p. — (Istoriia rabochego klassa Sibiri)

LABOR AND LABORING CLASSES — Russian S.F.S.R. — Siberia — Historiography

VOLCHENKO, A. V.
Ocherki istoriografii rabochego klassa Sibiri 1917-1937 gg. / A. V. Volchenko, A. S. Moskovskii ; otv. redaktor I. M. Savitskii. — Novosibirsk : Nauka, Sibirskoe otdelenie, 1986. — 159p

LABOR AND LABORING CLASSES — Scotland — History

MACDOUGALL, Ian
Labour in Scotland : a pictorial history from the eighteenth century to the present / Ian MacDougall. — Edinburgh : Mainstream, 1985. — 270p. — *Bibliography: p[271]*

LABOR AND LABORING CLASSES — Scotland — Glasgow (Strathclyde) — History

The Working class in Glasgow 1750-1914 / edited by R.A. Cage. — London : Croom Helm, c1987. — xix,203p. — *Bibliography: p188-189. — Includes index*

LABOR AND LABORING CLASSES — South Africa — History

CALLINICOS, Luli
A people's history of South Africa. — Johannesburg : Ravan Press
Vol.2: Working life, 1886-1940 : factories, townships and popular culture on the Rand. — 1987. — 263p

LABOR AND LABORING CLASSES — South America — History

BERGQUIST, Charles W
Labor in Latin America : comparative essays on Chile, Argentina, Venezuela, and Colombia / Charles Bergquist. — Stanford, Calif. : Stanford University Press, 1986. — xiv, 397p. — *Includes index. — Includes bibliographical references*

LABOR AND LABORING CLASSES — Soviet Union

Rabochii klass i nauchno-tekhnicheskii progress / otv. redaktor G. V. Osipov. — Moskva : Nauka, 1986. — 187p

SHISHKINA, I. M.
Partiia i rabochii klass v sotsialisticheskom obshchestve : izmyshleniia sovetologov i deistvitel'nost' / I. M. Shishkina. — Leningrad : Lenizdat, 1986. — 260p

VIOLA, Lynne
The best sons of the fatherland : workers in the vanguard of soviet collectivization / Lynne Viola. — New York : Oxford University Press, 1987. — p. cm. — *Includes index. — Bibliography: p*

LABOR AND LABORING CLASSES — Soviet Union — Biography

KANATCHIKOV, S
[Iz istorii moego bytiia. English]. A radical worker in Tsarist Russia : the autobiography of Semën Ivanovich Kanatchikov / translated and edited by Reginald E. Zelnik. — Stanford, Calif. : Stanford University Press, 1986. — xxx, 472p, [3]p of plates. — *Translation of: Iz istorii moego bytiia*

LABOR AND LABORING CLASSES — Soviet Union — Historiography

Velikii Oktiabr' i ukreplenie edinstva Sovetskogo obshchestva / [otv. redaktor: A. I. Vdovin]. — Moskva : Izd-vo Moskovskogo universiteta, 1987. — 384p. — (Voprosy metodologii i istorii istoricheskoi nauki ; vyp.5)

LABOR AND LABORING CLASSES — Soviet Union — History

IVANOVA, N. A.
Struktura rabochego klassa Rossii 1910-1914 / N. A. Ivanova ; otv. redaktor S. V. Tiutiukin. — Moskva : Nauka, 1987. — 280p

SOKOLOV, A. K.
Rabochii klass i revoliutsionnye izmeneniia v sotsial'noi strukture obshchestva / A. K. Sokolov. — Moskva : Izd-vo Moskovskogo universiteta, 1987. — 226p

LABOR AND LABORING CLASSES — Soviet Union — Political activity

IVANOVA, N. A.
Struktura rabochego klassa Rossii 1910-1914 / N. A. Ivanova ; otv. redaktor S. V. Tiutiukin. — Moskva : Nauka, 1987. — 280p

PETROVA, N. K.
Obshchestvenno-politicheskii oblik sovetskoi rabochei molodezhi [70-e gody] / N. K. Petrova ; otv. redaktor V. E. Poletaev. — Moskva : Nauka, 1986. — 157p

LABOR AND LABORING CLASSES — Soviet Union, Northern

Sotsial'nye problemy truda u narodnostei Severa / otv. redaktor V. I Boiko. — Novosibirsk : Nauka, Sibirskoe otdelenie, 1986. — 213p. — (Sotsial'noe i ekonomicheskoe razvitie narodnostei Severa)

LABOR AND LABORING CLASSES — Spain

GÁMIR, Luis
Contra el paro y la crisis en España / Luis Gamir. — Barcelona : Planeta, 1985. — 330p

SÁNCHEZ CREUS, Fernando
Estudio socio-laboral de la empresa española : segundo análisis / estudio dirigido por Fernando Sánchez Creus y Emilio Arevalo Eizaguirre. — [Madrid] : Asociación para el Progreso de la Dirección, 1983. — 259p

LABOR AND LABORING CLASSES — Spain — Bibliography

LAMBERET, Renée
Movimientos obreros y socialistas : (cronologia y bibliografia) : España 1700-1939 : libros y folletos / Renée Lamberet, Luis Moreno Herrero. — [2a ed]. — Madrid : Júcar. — (Crónica general de España ; 37). — *First ed. published Paris, 1953*
T.1
Vol.1: 1700-1788. — 1985. — xlvii,467p

LABOR AND LABORING CLASSES — Spain — History — 19th century

MONLAU, Pere Felip
Condiciones de vida y trabajo obrero en España a mediados del siglo XIX / Pere Felip Monlau y Joaquim Salarich ; estudio preliminar y notas críticas a cargo de Antoni Jutglar. — Barcelona : Anthropos, 1984. — 290p. — (Historia, ideas y textos ; 6). — *Reprint of "Higiene industrial" by P. F. Monlau (Madrid, 1856) and "Higiene del tejedor" by J. Salarich (Vich, 1858)*

LABOR AND LABORING CLASSES — Spain — Statistics

Estadistica de regulacion de empleo / Ministerio de Trabajo y Seguridad Social, Spain. — Madrid : Ministerio de Trabajo y Seguridad Social. Servicio de Publicaciones, 1984-. — *Quarterly*

LABOR AND LABORING CLASSES — Spain — Andalusia — History

Seis estudios sobre el proletariado andaluz (1868-1939) / R. Rodriguez Aguilera...[et al.]. — Córdoba : Excmo. Ayuntamiento de Córdoba, Delegación de Cultura, 1984. — 247p

LABOR AND LABORING CLASSES — Spain — Asturias — History — 20th century

SHUBERT, Adrian
Hacia la revolución : orígenes sociales del movimiento obrero en Asturias, 1860-1934 / Adrian Shubert ; traducción castellana de Agueda Palacios Honorato. — Barcelona : Crítica, 1984. — 235p. — *Bibliography: p [215]-223*

LABOR AND LABORING CLASSES — Spain — Cantabria — History — 20th century

ARGOS VILLAR, José Carlos
El movimiento obrero en Cantabria (1955-1977) / José Carlos Argos Villar, José Emilio Gómez Díaz ; prólogo de J.R. Saiz Viadero. — [Santander?] : J.E. Gómez Díaz, [1982?]. — 227 p.. — (Puntal libros)

LABOR AND LABORING CLASSES — Spain — Madrid — History — 20th century

JULIÁ DÍAZ, Santos
Madrid, 1931-1934 : de la fiesta popular a la lucha de clases / por Santos Juliá Díaz. — Madrid : Siglo Veintiuno, 1984. — 509p

LABOR AND LABORING CLASSES — Spain — Seville — History

MACARRO VERA, José Manuel
La utopia revolucionaria : Sevilla en la Segunda Republica / José Manuel Macarro Vera. — Sevilla : Monte de Piedad y Caja de Ahorros de Sevilla, 1985. — 518p

LABOR AND LABORING CLASSES — Spain — Valladolid

PRADO MOURA, Angel de
El movimiento obrero en Valladolid durante la II República (1931-1936) / Angel de Prado Moura. — Valladolid : Junta de Castilla y Leon, 1985. — 234p. — *Bibliography: p231-232*

LABOR AND LABORING CLASSES — Spain — Vitoria — History

RIVERA BLANCO, Antonio
Situación y comportamiento de la clase obrera en Vitoria (1900-1915) / Antonio Rivera Blanco. — [Bibao] : Servicio Editorial, Universidad del Vasco, [1985]. — 195p

LABOR AND LABORING CLASSES — Sweden

Towards a democratic rationality : making the case for Swedish labour / [edited by] John Fry. — Aldershot : Gower, c1986. — xi,281p. — *Bibliography: p271-281*

LABOR AND LABORING CLASSES — Ukraine — History

SKRYPNIK, N. A.
Leninskaia partiia v bor'be za edinstvo rabochego klassa : (na materialakh Ukrainy) / N. A. Skrypnik. — Kiev : Vyshcha shkola, 1985. — 150p. — *Bibliography: p143-150*

LABOR AND LABORING CLASSES — United States

Ethnicity and the work force / Winston A. Van Horne [and] Thomas V. Tonnesen; editors. — Milwaukee : University of Wisconsin System American Ethnic Studies Coordination Committee/Urban Corridor Consortium, 1985. — xi,222p. — (Ethnicity and public policy ; vol.4). — *Bibliographies*

LABOR AND LABORING CLASSES — United States — Attitudes

The language of risk : conflicting perspectives on occupational health / edited by Dorothy Nelkin. — Beverly Hills : Sage Publications, c1985. — p. cm. — (Sage Focus edition ; v. 71). — *Includes bibliographies and index*

LABOR AND LABORING CLASSES — United States — History

FORM, William Humbert
Divided we stand : working-class stratification in America / William Form. — Urbana : University of Illinois Press, c1985. — p. cm. — *Includes index. — Bibliography: p*

LIEBERMAN, Sima
Labor movements and labor thought : Spain, France, Germany, and the United States / Sima Lieberman. — New York ; Eastbourne : Praeger, 1986. — ix, 288p. — *Includes bibliographies and index*

LABOR AND LABORING CLASSES — United States — History
continuation

STEPHENSON, Charles
Life and labor : dimensions of American working-class history / by Charles Stephenson and Robert Asher. — Albany : State University of New York Press, c1986. — p. cm. — (American labor history series). — *Includes index*

LABOR AND LABORING CLASSES — United States — History — Sources

The Samuel Gompers papers / editor, Stuart B. Kaufman. — Urbana, Ill. : University of Illinois Press
volume 1: The making of a union leader, 1850-86. — 1986. — xxxvi,529p

LABOR AND LABORING CLASSES — United States — History — 19th century

Working-class formation : nineteenth-century patterns in Western Europe and the United States / edited by Ira Katznelson and Aristide R. Zolberg. — Princeton, N.J. : Princeton University Press, c1986. — viii, 470p. — *Includes index*

LABOR AND LABORING CLASSES — United States — 1914-

BERNSTEIN, Irving
A caring society : the New Deal, the worker, and the Great Depression : a history of the American worker, 1933-1941 / Irving Bernstein. — Boston : Houghton Mifflin, 1985. — 338 p., [24] p. of plates. — *Includes index.* — *Bibliography: p. 309-326*

LABOR AND LABORING CLASSES IN ART

LAING, Stuart
Representations of working-class life 1957-1964 / Stuart Laing. — Basingstoke : Macmillan, 1986. — 246p. — *Includes index*

LABOR AND LABORING CLASSES IN LITERATURE

LAING, Stuart
Representations of working-class life 1957-1964 / Stuart Laing. — Basingstoke : Macmillan, 1986. — 246p. — *Includes index*

LABOR CAMPS — Canada

BROWN, Lorne
When freedom was lost : the unemployed, the agitator, and the state / Lorne Brown. — Montréal : Black Rose Books, 1987. — 208p. — *Includes bibliographic references*

LABOR CONTRACT

AZARIADIS, Costas
Human capital and self-enforcing contracts / Costas Azariadis. — Coventry : University of Warwick. Department of Economics, 1987. — 44p. — (Warwick economic research papers ; no.281). — *Bibliography: p42-44*

OSWALD, A. J.
Efficient contracts are on the labour demand curve: theory and facts / A. Oswald. — London : Centre for Labour Economics, London School of Economics, 1987. — 44p. — (Discussion paper / London School of Economics and Political Science. Centre for Labour Economics ; no.284). — *Bibliography: p40-44*

LABOR CONTRACT — Economic aspects

OSWALD, A. J.
New research on the economics of trade unions and labour contracts / A. Oswald. — London : Centre for Labour Economics, London School of Economics, 1986. — 34p. — (Discussion paper / London School of Economics and Political Science. Centre for Labour Economics ; no.261). — *Bibliography: p20-34*

LABOR CONTRACT — Graphic methods

OSWALD, A. J.
Efficient contracts are on the labour demand curve : theory and facts / Andrew J. Oswald. — Princeton : Industrial Relations Section, Princeton University, 1984. — 43p. — (Working Paper / Princeton University. Industrial Relations Section ; 178). — *Bibliography: leaves 33-36*

LABOR CONTRACT — Great Britain

JULYAN, Alan J.
Service agreements / . — 5th ed. / Alan Julyan. — London : Longman, c1986. — xxiii,215p. — (Longman practitioner series). — *Previous ed.: / by Trevor Aldridge, 1982.* — *Includes index*

SUTER, Erich
Contracts at work / Erich Suter. — London : Institute of Personnel Management, 1982. — x,276p. — *Includes index*

LABOR COSTS

Flexibility in the labour market : the current debate : a technical report / Organisation for Economic Co—operation and Development. — Paris : Organisation for Economic Co—operation and Development, 1986. — 146p

TACHIBANAKI, Toshiaki
Non-wage labour costs : their rationale and economic effect / Toshiaki Tachibanaki. — London : Suntory International Centre for Economics and Related Disciplines, 1987. — 63p. — (Welfare State Programme ; no.19) (Discussion paper / Welfare State Programme Suntory-Toyota International Centre for Economics and Related Disciplines. ; no.19). — *Bibliography: p59-63*

LABOR COSTS — France

Les coûts de la main d'oeuvre dans l'industrie, les commerces, les banques et les assurances / Institut National de la Statistique et des Études Économiques, France. — Paris : Institut, National de la Statistique et des Études Économiques, 1981-. — (Collections de l'Insée). — *Irregular*

LABOR COSTS — Great Britain

Fringe benefits, labour costs and social security / edited by Graham L Reid and Donald J. Robertson. — London : Allen and Unwin, 1965. — 336p

LABOR COSTS — Peru — Statistics

PERU. Dirección de Planificación Estadística
Indices de precios de materiales de construcción e indices de costo de mano de obra, noviembre 1975. — Lima : the Dirección, [1976]. — 9p. — (Serie de indices de precios al por mayor). — *Cover title: Materiales de construcción y costo de mano de obra*

LABOR COURTS — Great Britain

LEONARD, Alice M.
Pyrrhic victories : winning sex discrimination and equal pay cases in the industrial tribunals, 1980-84 / Alice M. Leonard. — London : H.M.S.O., 1987. — 55p. — (Research series / Equal Opportunities Commission)

LABOR DISPUTES

EDWARDS, P. K.
Conflict at work : a materialist analysis of workplace relations / P.K. Edwards. — Oxford : Basil Blackwell, 1986. — [300]p. — (Warwick studies in industrial relations). — *Includes bibliography and index*

LABOR DISPUTES — Law and legislation

The strike / [Angarita Barón Ciro...et al.]. — Milano : Giuffrè, 1987. — xvi,554p. — (Inchieste di diritto comparato / M. Rotondi ; 9). — *Contributions by various authors in English, Italian, French, Spanish, German or Portuguese*

LABOR DISPUTES — European Economic Community countries

The prevention and settlement of industrial conflict in the Community member states. — Luxembourg : Office for Official Publications of the European Communities, 1984. — 162,16p. — *At head of title page: Commission of the European Communities*

LABOR DISPUTES — Germany (West)

Krisenpolitik und Belegschaftsverhalten : Metallarbeiter zwischen Gegenwehr und Unterwerfung / Norbert Kubach...[et al.]. — Hamburg : VSA-Verlag, 1985. — 155p. — *Bibliography: p154-155*

LABOR DISPUTES — Great Britain

WALSH, Kenneth
The measurement of industrial disputes in selected industries : the report of a research study financed by the Leverhulme Trust / Kenneth Walsh. — Brighton : Institute of Manpower Studies, 1986. — x,205p. — (IMS report ; No.125). — *Bibliography: p204-206*

LABOR DISPUTES — India

ASDHIR, Vijay
Industrial relations in India : settlement of industrial disputes / Vijay Asdhir. — New Delhi : Deep and Deep Publications, 1987. — 376p. — *Bibliography: p369-374*

LABOR ECONOMICS

Confrontation, class consciousness, and the labor process : studies in proletarian class formation / edited by Michael Hanagan and Charles Stephenson. — Westport, Conn. ; London : Greenwood Press, c1986. — viii, 261p. — (Contributions in labor studies ; no. 18). — *Includes index.* — *Bibliography: p.[241]-253*

Current research in labor economics / Walter Fogel (editor). — Los Angeles : Institute of Industrial Relations, University of California, 1984. — viii,159p. — (Monograph and Research series / Institute of Industrial Relations, University of California, Los Angeles ; 38)

Economics of labor in industrial society / Clark Kerr, Paul D. Staudohar, editors. — 1st ed. — San Francisco, Calif. : Jorsey-Bass, c1986. — p. cm. — (The Jossey-Bass management series). — *Includes bibliographies and indexes*

Handbook of labor economics / edited by Orley Ashenfelter and Richard Layard. — Amsterdam ; New York ; North-Holland ; New York, N.Y., U.S.A. : Sole distributors for the U.S.A. and Canada, Elsevier Science Pub. Co., 1986-. — p. cm. — (Handbooks in economics ; 5). — *Includes bibliographies*

Journal of labor research. — Fairfax, VA : Department of Economics, George Mason University, 1986-. — *Quarterly*

MILES, Robert
Capitalism and unfree labour : anomaly or necessity? / Robert Miles. — London : Tavistock, 1987. — [viii,272]p. — *Includes bibliography and index*

LABOR LAW AND LEGISLATION — Canada

SIMMONS, C. Gordon
Labour relations law in the public sector : cases, materials and commentary / by C. Gordon Simmons and Kenneth P. Swan. — Kingston, Ontario : Industrial Relations Centre, Queen's University, 1982. — xviii,422p

LABOR LAWS AND LEAGISLATION — Canada

ARTHURS, H. W.
Labour law and industrial relations in Canada / by H.W. Arthurs, D.D. Carter, H.J. Glasbeek. — 2nd ed. — Deventer ; London : Kluwer Law and Taxation, 1984. — 316p. — *Previous ed: 1981.* — *Includes index*

LABOR LAWS AND LEGISLATION

Labour law research in twelve countries / editor: Sten Edlund. — Stockholm : Arbetarskyddsfonden + Arbetslivscentrum, 1986. — 296p

LABOR LAWS AND LEGISLATION — Addresses, essays, lectures

Fifty years of labour law and social security : studies at the occasion of the fiftiest [sic] anniversary of the chair in sociaal recht at the Rijksuniversiteit Leiden, the Netherlands. — Deventer ; London : Kluwer, 1986. — viii,166p . — Authors listed on cover as: M.G. Rood ... [et al.]

LABOR LAWS AND LEGISLATION — Australia

O'DEA, Raymond
O'Dea's Industrial relations in Australia : fourth edition / by Luigi M. B. Lamprati. — [4th ed]. — Wiley : Brisbane, 1984. — xvi,304p . — Bibliography: p297-301

SMITH, Douglas W.
Trade union law in Australia : the legal status of Australian trade unions / Douglas W. Smith and Donald W. Rawson ; with a foreward by J. E. Isaac. — 2nd ed. — Sydney : Butterworths, 1985. — xvii,204p

LABOR LAWS AND LEGISLATION — Canada

FOISY, Claude H.
Canada Labour Relations Board policies and procedures / Claude H. Foisy, Daniel E. Lavery and Luc Martineau. — Toronto ; Vancouver : Butterworths, 1986. — li,553p

LABOR LAWS AND LEGISLATION — Europe — History

The Making of labour law in Europe : a comparative study of nine countries up to 1945 / edited by Bob Hepple. — London : Mansell, 1986. — xiv,412p. — (Studies in labour and social law). — Bibliography: p387-401. — Includes index

LABOR LAWS AND LEGISLATION — France

FRANCE
Code de travail, 1986 / [realisée par Bernard Teyssié]. — Paris : LITEC, 1986. — xl,2014p

FRANCE
[Code du travail]. Code du travail. — 47e éd. — Paris : Dalloz, 1985. — viii,1766,2p. — (Petits codes Dalloz). — Previous ed.: 1984. — Includes index

SACHS-DURAND, Corinne
Les seuils d'effectif en droit du travail / par Corinne Sachs-Durand ; préface de Hélène Sinay. — Paris : Librairie Générale de Droit et de Jurisprudence, 1985. — 314p. — (Bibliothèque d'Ouvrages de Droit Social ; Tome 23). — Bibliography: p275-290

Le travail : marchés, règles, conventions / Robert Salais et Laurent Thévenot, éds.. — Paris : INSEE, [1986]. — 370p

LABOR LAWS AND LEGISLATION — Great Britain

BOWERS, John
A practical approach to employment law / John Bowers. — 2nd ed. — London : Financial Training, 1986. — liv,385p

Butterworths employment law handbook / edited by Peter Wallington. — 4th ed. — London : Butterworths, 1987. — xxx,892,14p

Comparative labour law : Anglo-Soviet perspectives / edited by W.E. Butler, B.A. Hepple, Alan C. Neal. — Aldershot : Gower in conjunction with the International journal of comparative labour law and industrial relations, c1987. — xii,219p. — Conference proceedings. — Bibliography: p217-219

Freedom and fairness : empowering people at work / edited by Ken Coates ; with contributions from Stephen Bodington...[et al.] ; foreword by John Prescott. — Nottingham : Spokesman for the Institute for Workers' Control, 1986. — 157p

GREAT BRITAIN. Parliament. House of Commons. Library. Research Division
Emergency powers / [J. B. Poole]. — [London] : the Division, [1979]. — 7p. — (Background paper ; no.66)

GREAT BRITAIN. Parliament. House of Commons. Library. Research Division
Employment Bill (Bill 56 1981-82) / Celia Nield. — [London] : the Division, 1982. — 30p. — (Reference sheet ; no.82/5). — Bibliography: p28-30

GREAT BRITAIN. Parliament. House of Commons. Library. Research Division
Labour relations legislation / [Celia Nield]. — [London] : the Division, 1979. — 6p. — (Background paper ; no.65)

LABOUR RESEARCH DEPARTMENT
Employment law under the Tories. — London : LRD Publications, 1986. — 38p

LEWIS, David, 1949-
Essentials of employment law / David Lewis. — 2nd ed. — London : Institute of Personnel Management, 1986. — xxiii,265p. — Previous ed.: 1983. — Bibliography: p256-257. — Includes index

TITMAN, Barry
Titman & Camp, individual employment law / Barry Titman, Peter Camp. — 2nd ed. — London : Sweet & Maxwell, 1986. — xxv,240p. — Previous ed.: published as Dismissal and taxation of employees. London : Butterworth, 1982. — Includes index

WEDDERBURN OF CHARLTON, Kenneth William Wedderburn, Baron
The worker and the law / Lord Wedderburn. — 3rd ed. — Harmondsworth : Penguin, 1986. — xiv,1026p. — (A Pelican book). — Previous ed.: 1971. — Includes index

WHINCUP, Michael
Modern employment law : a guide to job security and safety / Michael Whincup. — 5th ed. — London : Heinemann, 1986. — l,354p. — Previous ed.: 1983. — With Appendix 1 (29p). — Includes index

LABOR LAWS AND LEGISLATION — Iran — History — 20th century

FLOOR, Willem
Labour unions, law and conditions in Iran (1900-1941) / by Willem Floor. — Durham City (South End House, South Road, Durham City, DH1 3TG) : Centre for Middle Eastern and Islamic Studies, University of Durham, c1985. — 124p. — (Occasional paper series ; no.26 (1985)). — Bibliography: p119-124

LABOR LAWS AND LEGISLATION — Nigeria

EMIOLA, Akintunde
Nigerian labour law / by Akintunde Emiola. — 2nd ed. — Ibadan : Ibadan University Press, 1982. — xxxviii,599p. — Previous ed.: 1979. — Bibliography: p.599. - Includes index

UVIEGHARA, E. E
Trade union law in Nigeria / by E. E. Uvieghara. — Benin City, Nigeria : Ethiope Pub. Co., 1976. — xxxiii, 248 p.. — (Ethiope law series ; no. 4). — Includes index

LABOR LAWS AND LEGISLATION — Singapore

Butterworths handbook of Singapore employment law. — 2nd ed. — Singapore : Butterworths, 1986. — xii,775p

LABOR LAWS AND LEGISLATION — South Africa

SWANEPOEL, J. P. A.
Introduction to labour law / by J. P. A. Swanepoel ; translated by M. Euijen. — 2nd ed.. — Johannesburg : McGraw-Hill, 1986. — 252,18p. — Accompanied by supplement issued in 1987

LABOR LAWS AND LEGISLATION — Soviet Union

Comparative labour law : Anglo-Soviet perspectives / edited by W.E. Butler, B.A. Hepple, Alan C. Neal. — Aldershot : Gower in conjunction with the International journal of comparative labour law and industrial relations, c1987. — xii,219p. — Conference proceedings. — Bibliography: p217-219

LABOR LAWS AND LEGISLATION — Turkey

SHABON, Anwar
The political, economic, and labor climate in Turkey / by Anwar M. Shabon and Isik U. Zeytinoglu. — Philadelphia, Pa., U.S.A. : Industrial Research Unit, Wharton School, University of Pennsylvania, c1985. — xiii, 277 p.. — (Multinational industrial relations series. No. 10. European studies ; 10b). — Includes index

LABOR LAWS AND LEGISLATION — United States

FLANAGAN, Robert J
Labor relations and the litigation explosion / Robert J. Flanagan. — Washington, D.C. : Brookings Institution, c1987. — p. cm. — Includes index

GOULD, William B
Strikes, dispute procedures, and arbitration : essays on labor law / William B. Gould IV. — Westport, Conn. : Greenwood Press, c1985. — p. cm. — (Contributions in American studies ; no. 82). — Includes index. — Bibliography: p

LABOR LAWS AND LEGISLATION, INTERNATIONAL

Selected international labour conventions and recommendations. — Bangkok : International Labour Organisation, 1984. — xv,216p. — (Labour administration training material ; TM.1). — At head of title: Labour administration training material

Selected international labour conventions and recommendations. — Bangkok : International Labour Organisation. — (Labour administration training material ; TM.2). — At head of title: Labour administration training material
Vol.2. — 1985. — iv,205p

LABOR LAWS AND LEGISLATIONOFF. PUBNS. — European Economic Community countries 986

The stage reached in aligning labour legislation in the European Community : documentation. — Brussels : Economic and Social Committee, 1978. — xi,33,12p

LABOR MARKET

Die Arbeitsgesellschaft zwischen Sachgesetzlichkeit und Ethik / Anton Rauscher (Hrsg.). — Köln : J. P. Bachem, 1985. — 174p. — (Mönchengladbacher Gespräche ; Bd.6) (Veröffentlichungen der Kathelischen Sozialwissenschaftlichen Zentralstelle Mönchengladbach)

WALSH, Kenneth
Accessing local labour market information : a brief guide to needs and sources / Kenneth Walsh. — Brighton : Institute of Manpower Studies. University of Sussex, 1986. — vi,22p. — (IMS report ; no.122)

LABOR MARKET — Great Britain

MACKIE, D. J.
A three sector model of earnings behaviour / D. J. Mackie. — London : Bank of England, 1987. — 71p. — (Discussion papers / Bank of England. Technical series ; no.16). — Bibliography: p68-71

LABOR MOBILITY
Flexibility in the labour market : the current debate : a technical report / Organisation for Economic Co—operation and Development. — Paris : Organisation for Economic Co—operation and Development, 1986. — 146p

LABOR MOBILITY — Australia
Relocation assistance scheme : review of operational statistics, October 1976 to September 1980. — Canberra : Australian Government Publishing Service, 1983. — vii,38p. — (Research report / Bureau of Labour Market Research ; no.1). — *Bibliographical references: p38*

LABOR MOBILITY — Denmark
BACH, Henning Bjerregaard
Lønmodtageres geografiske mobilitet / Henning Bjerregaard Bach. — København : Socialforskningsinstituttet, 1987. — 120p. — (Publikation / Socialforskningsinstituttet ; 162). — *Bibliography: p113-114*

LABOR MOBILITY — France
MAURICE, Marc
The social foundations of industrial power : a comparison of France and Germany / Marc Maurice, François Sellier, and Jean-Jacques Silvestre ; translated by Arthur Goldhammer. — Cambridge, Mass ; London : MIT Press, c1986. — xi, 292p. — *Translation of: Politique d'éducation et organisation industrielle en France et en Allemagne.* — Includes index

LABOR MOBILITY — Germany (West)
MAURICE, Marc
The social foundations of industrial power : a comparison of France and Germany / Marc Maurice, François Sellier, and Jean-Jacques Silvestre ; translated by Arthur Goldhammer. — Cambridge, Mass ; London : MIT Press, c1986. — xi, 292p. — *Translation of: Politique d'éducation et organisation industrielle en France et en Allemagne.* — Includes index

LABOR MOBILITY — Great Britain
CONWAY, Jean
A job to move : the housing problems of job seekers / by Jean Conway & Evan Ramsay. — London : SHAC, 1986. — 64p. — (SHAC research report ; 8)

DEX, Shirley
Women's occupational mobility : a lifetime perspective / Shirley Dex. — London : Macmillan, 1987. — xii,157p. — *Bibliography: p148-154.* — Includes index

PAYNE, Geoff
Employment and opportunity / Geoff Payne. — London : Macmillan, 1987. — xii,215p. — *Bibliography: p199-205.* — Includes index

STANDING, Guy
Unemployment and labour market flexibilty : the United Kingdom / Guy Standing. — Geneva : International Labour Office, 1986. — xi,147p. — *Including bibliographical references*

LABOR MOBILITY — India — Bombay
RAMACHANDRAN, P
Some aspects of labour mobility in Bombay City / [by] P. Ramachandran. — Bombay : Somaiya Publications, [1974]. — vi, 139 p. — (Tata Institute of Social Sciences series, no. 30). — *Includes bibliographical references*

LABOR MOBILITY — Organisation for Economic Co-operation and Development countries
Labour market flexibility : report / by a high-level group of experts to the Secretary. — Paris : OECD, 1986. — 23p

LABOR MOBILITY — Scotland
ROBERTSON, G.
Housing tenure and labour mobility in Scotland / G. Robertson. — Edinburgh (New St Andrew's House, St James Centre, Edinburgh) : Economics and Statistics Unit, Scottish Economic Planning Department, 1979. — 47p,[1]leaf of plates. — (ESU discussion paper ; no.4). — *Bibliography: p47*

LABOR MOBILITY — Soviet Union
VERSHININA, T. N.
Vzaimosviaz' tekuchesti i proizvodstvennoi adaptatsii rabochikh / T. N. Vershinina ; otv. redaktor Z. V. Kupriianova. — Novosibirsk : Nauka, Sibirskoe otdelenie, 1986. — 164p

LABOR MOBILITY — Sudan — Statistics
EL BESHIR, Z. A.
Sudanese labour mobility : a statistical investigation / Z. A. El Beshir and Siddig M. Ahmed. — Khartoum : University of Khartoum. Faculty of Economic and Social Studies. Development Studies and Research Centre, 1978. — 87p. — (Monograph series / University of Khartoum. Faculty of Economic and Social Studies. Development Studies and Research Centre ; no.9)

LABOR POLICY
Working conditions and environment : a worker's education manual. — Geneva : International Labour Office, 1983. — vi, 81 p., [6] p. of plates. — *"A selection of recommended ILO publications and documents": p. 75.* — *"ILO films and film strips": p. 76*

LABOR POLICY — Canal Zone — History — 20th century
CONNIFF, Michael L
Black labor on a white canal : Panama, 1904-1981 / Michael L. Conniff. — Pittsburgh : University of Pittsburgh Press, 1985. — p. cm. — *Includes index.* — *Bibliography: p*

LABOR POLICY — Egypt
HANSEN, Best
Employment opportunities and equity in a changing economy : Egypt in the 1980s : a labour market approach : report of an inter-agency team financed by the United Nations Development Programme and organised by the International Labour Office / Bent Hansen, Samir Radwan. — Geneva : International Labour Office, 1982. — xviii,292p. — (A WEP study). — *Includes bibliographical references*

LABOR POLICY — Europe, Eastern
Employment policies in the Soviet Union and Eastern Europe / edited by Jan Adam. — 2nd rev. ed. — Basingstoke : Macmillan, 1987. — xviii,224p. — *Previous ed.: 1982.* — Includes index

LABOR POLICY — Great Britain — History — 20th century
JONES, Russell, 1959-
Wages and employment policy, 1936-1985 / Russell Jones ; with a foreword by Sir Alec Cairncross. — London : Allen & Unwin, 1987. — xvii,175p. — *Bibliography: p160-169.* — Includes index

TOMLINSON, Jim
Employment policy : the crucial years 1939-1955 / Jim Tomlinson. — Oxford : Clarendon, 1987. — [192]p. — *Includes bibliography and index*

LABOR POLICY — India
AZIZ, Abdul
Labour problems of a developing economy / Abdul Aziz. — New Delhi : Ashish Pub. House, c1984. — viii, 157 p.. — *Includes bibliographical references and index*

LABOR POLICY — Japan — History
PARK, Sung-Jo
U.S. labor policy in postwar Japan / Sung-Jo Park. — [Berlin] : Express Edition, [c1985]. — 157 p.. — (Reihe Horizonte Asiens). — *Bibliography: p. 152-157*

LABOR POLICY — Netherlands
Vernieuwingen in het arbeidsbestel. — 's-Gravenhage : Staatsuitgeverij, 1981. — 350p. — (Rapporten aan de regering ; 21). — *Prepared by the Wetenschappelijke Raad voor het Regeringsbeleid.* — Includes bibliographical references

LABOR POLICY — Soviet Union
Employment policies in the Soviet Union and Eastern Europe / edited by Jan Adam. — 2nd rev. ed. — Basingstoke : Macmillan, 1987. — xviii,224p. — *Previous ed.: 1982.* — Includes index

LABOR POLICY — United States
VALE, Vivian
Labour in American politics / Vivian Vale. — London : Routledge and K. Paul, 1971. — [6],172p. — *Originally published, New York: Barnes & Noble, 1971.* — bibl p161-166

LABOR POLICY — United States — History
BERNSTEIN, Irving
A caring society : the New Deal, the worker, and the Great Depression : a history of the American worker, 1933-1941 / Irving Bernstein. — Boston : Houghton Mifflin, 1985. — 338 p., [24] p. of plates. — *Includes index.* — *Bibliography: p. 309-326*

LABOR POLICY — United States — History — 20th century
CONNIFF, Michael L
Black labor on a white canal : Panama, 1904-1981 / Michael L. Conniff. — Pittsburgh : University of Pittsburgh Press, 1985. — p. cm. — *Includes index.* — *Bibliography: p*

KOCHAN, Thomas A
The transformation of American industrial relations / Thomas A. Kochan, Harry C. Katz, Robert B. McKersie. — New York : Basic Books, c1986. — viii, 287 p.. — *Includes index.* — *Bibliography: p. 254-273*

LABOR PRODUCTIVITY
ÅBERG, Yngve
The impact of working hours and other factors on production and employment / Yngve Åberg. — Aldershot : Gower, 1987. — [173]p. — *Includes bibliography*

Flexibility and jobs : myths and realities : (a research report of the European Trade Union Institute) / (prepared by John Evans, Rafael Nedzynski and Gosta Karlsson). — Brussels : ETUI, [1985]. — 157p

LABOR PRODUCTIVITY — Australia
Human capital and productivity growth. — Canberra : Economic Planning Advisory Council, 1986. — v,43p. — (Council paper / Economic Planning Advisory Council ; no.15). — *Bibliographical references: p40-41*

Structured chaos : the process of productivity advance / Richard Blandy...[et al.]. — Melbourne ; Oxford : Oxford University Press, 1985. — viii,111p. — *Published in conjunction with the Australian Productivity Council and the National Institute of Labour Studies.* — *Bibliography: p101-107*

LABOR PRODUCTIVITY — Australia — Measurement
The measurement and implications of productivity growth : proceedings of a workshop, 22-23 November 1984, Canberra / edited by Peter Scherer with Tracey Malone. — Canberra : Australian Government Publishing Service, 1986. — xi,290p. — (Monograph series / Bureau of Labour Market Research ; no.14). — *Includes bibliographical references*

LABOR PRODUCTIVITY — Canada
WELLS, Don
Soft sell : "quality of life" programs and the productivity race / by Don Wells. — Ottawa : Canadian Centre for Policy Alternatives, 1986. — xi,97p

LABOR PRODUCTIVITY — Papua New Guinea
labour productivity and industrial growth. — [Port Moresby?] : Department of Labour and Industry, 1982. — 12p,[142]leaves. — (Information paper / Department of Labour and Industry ; no.1-82)

LABOR PRODUCTIVITY — Soviet Union

KOSTIN, L. A.
Povyshenie effektivnosti truda v novykh usloviiakh khoziaistvovaniia / L. A. Kostin. — Moskva : Mysl', 1971. — 287p

KUNEL'SKII, L. E.
Povyshenie effektivnosti truda v promyshlennosti / L. E. Kunel'skii. — Moskva : Ekonomika, 1987. — 254p

Soviet policies on labour productivity and trade unions : a report based on Russian publications. — London : Labour Information Office, United States Information Service, [1958?]. — 5p

Vosproizvodstvo naseleniia i trudovykh resursov v usloviiakh razvitogo sotsializma / redaktsionnaia kollegiia: V. S. Steshenko...[et al.]. — Kiev : Naukova dumka. — V 4-kh tomakh
T.4: Povyshenie effektivnosti obshchestvennogo truda / otv. redaktor: D. P. Boginiia. — 1986. — 334p

LABOR SUPPLY

ÅBERG, Yngve
The impact of working hours and other factors on production and employment / Yngve Åberg. — Aldershot : Gower, 1987. — [173]p. — Includes bibliography

ANDREWS, Martyn
A disaggregated disequilibrium model of the labour market / Martyn Andrews and Stephen Nickell. — London : Centre for Labour Economics, London School of Economics, 1986. — 35p. — (Discussion paper / London School of Economics and Political Science. Centre for Labour Economics ; no.251). — Bibliography: p27-29

Automation and industrial workers : a fifteen nation study. — Oxford : Pergamon
Vol.2 / edited by Frank Adler ... [et al.] for the European Coordination Centre for Research and Documentation in Social Sciences. — 1986. — 2v.(xxiv,866p). — Vol.2 has sub-title: A cross-national comparison of fifteen countries

CARRUTH, Alan
On union preferences and labour market models : insiders and outsiders / A. A. Carruth [and] A. J. Oswald. — London : Centre for Labour Economics, London School of Economics, 1986. — 30p. — (Discussion paper / London School of Economics and Political Science. Centre for Labour Economics ; no.256)

Flexibility in labour markets / edited by Roger Tarling. — London : Academic, 1987. — xiv,345p. — Includes bibliographies

Flexibility in the labour market : the current debate : a technical report / Organisation for Economic Co—operation and Development. — Paris : Organisation for Economic Co—operation and Development, 1986. — 146p

HART, Robert A.
Working time and employment / Robert A. Hart. — Boston ; London : Allen & Unwin, 1987. — [224]p. — Includes bibliography and index

Manpower and social affairs. — Paris : OECD, [1986?]. — 1Portfolio (various pagings). — Contents: Reprints taken from various issues of the OECD Observer

OPEN UNIVERSITY
Work and society. — Milton Keynes : Open University Press. — (D325; block 3; units 8-12) . — Social sciences: a third level sociology course. — At head of title: The Open University
Block 3: Labour : processes and control. — 1985. — 137p. — Contents: Units 8-12

OSWALD, A. J.
Efficient contracts are on the labour demand curve: theory and facts / A. Oswald. — London : Centre for Labour Economics, London School of Economics, 1987. — 44p. — (Discussion paper / London School of Economics and Political Science. Centre for Labour Economics ; no.284). — Bibliography: p40-44

Staff studies for the World Economic Outlook / by the Research Department of the International Monetary Fund. — Washington, D. C. : International Monetary Fund, 1986. — xi,195p. — (World economic and financial surveys). — Includes bibliographical references. — Contents: Differences in employment behaviour among industrial countries/Charles Adams, Paul R. Fenton and Flemming Larsen - Labor markets, external developments, and unemployment in developing countries/Omotunde E.G. Johnson - Velocity of money and the practice of monetary targeting/Peter Isard and Liliana Rojas-Suarez - Effects of exchange rate changes in industrial countries/James M. Boughton, et al. - Transmission of economic influences from industrial to developing countries/David Goldsbrough and Iqbal Zaidi

Unemployment and the structure of labor markets / edited by Kevin Lang and Jonathan S. Leonard. — Oxford : Blackwell, 1987. — vi,253p. — Bibliography: p234-243. — Includes index

WORSWICK, G. D. N.
Real wages and employment / G. D. N. Worswick [and] R. Gansden. — London : National Institute of Economic and Social Research, 1986. — 53p. — (Discussion paper / National Institute of Economic and Social Research ; no.122). — Bibliography: p[52-53]

LABOR SUPPLY — Addresses, essays, lectures

Employment, outlook and insights : a collection of essays on industrialised market-economy countries / edited by David H. Freedman. — Geneva : International Labour Office, 1979. — 148 p.. — Includes bibliographical references

LABOR SUPPLY — Effect of technological innovations on

HELD, Daniel
Marché de l'emploi : entreprises et régions / Daniel Held et Denis Maillat. — [Lausanne] : Presses Polytechniques Romandes, 1984. — 205p. — (Collection "villes, régions et sociétés")

LEACH, Donald
Future employment & technological change / Donald Leach and Howard Wagstaff with Anne-Marie Bostyn, Colin Pritchard and Daniel Wright. — London : Kogan Page, 1986. — 264p. — Includes index

LABOR SUPPLY — Effect of technological innovations on — Congresses

INTERNATIONAL SYMPOSIUM ON TECHNOLOGICAL CHANGE AND EMPLOYMENT: URBAN AND REGIONAL DIMENSIONS (1985 : Zandvoort, Netherlands)
Technological change, employment, and spatial dynamics : proceedings of an International Symposium on Technological Change and Employment: Urban and Regional Dimensions, held at Zandvoort, the Netherlands, April 1-3, 1985 / edited by Peter Nijkamp. — Berlin ; New York : Springer-Verlag, c1986. — vii, 466 p.. — (Lecture notes in economics and mathematical systems ; 270). — Includes bibliographies

LABOR SUPPLY — Government policy — Peru

PERU. Servicio del Empleo y Recursos Humanos Junta Nacional de Mano de Obra. — [Lima : the Servicio, ca.1970]. — [12p]

LABOR SUPPLY — Great Britain — Statistics

MCILWEE, Terry
Personnel management in context : the late 1980s, statistics supplement / Terry McIlwee. — 2nd ed. — Kings Ripton : Elm, 1986. — [60]p. — Previous ed.: 1983

LABOR SUPPLY — Mathematical models

BÜTTLER, Hans-Jürgen
Estimation of disequilibrium models / Hans-Jürg Büttler, Gertrude Frei, Bernd Schips. — Berlin ; New York : Springer-Verlag, c1986. — p. cm. — (Lecture notes in economics and mathematical systems ; 279). — Includes bibliographies

LABOR SUPPLY — Regional disparities

HELD, Daniel
Marché de l'emploi : entreprises et régions / Daniel Held et Denis Maillat. — [Lausanne] : Presses Polytechniques Romandes, 1984. — 205p. — (Collection "villes, régions et sociétés")

LABOR SUPPLY — Research — Bibliography

Bibliography of published research of the World Employment Programme. — 5th ed. — Geneva : International Labour Office, 1984. — vi,151p

Bibliography of published research of the World Employment Programme. — 6th ed. — Geneva : International Labour Office, 1986. — vii,177p. — Includes supplement

World Employment Programme : research in retrospect and prospect. — Geneva : International Labour Office, 1976. — 278p. — Bibliography: p245-273

LABOR SUPPLY — Statistical methods

GROOTAERT, Christiaan
The labor market and social accounting : a framework of data presentation / Christiaan Grootaert. — Washington, D.C. : World Bank, c1982 ((1985 printing)). — 36p. — (LSMS working papers ; no.17) (LSMS working papers ; no. 17). — Bibliographical references: p36

GROOTAERT, Christiaan
The role of employment and earnings in analyzing levels of living / Christiaan Grootaert. — Washington D.C. : The World Bank, 1986. — xiv,278p. — (LSMS working papers ; no.27). — Bibliographical references: p269-278

MEHRAN, Farhad
Employment data for the measurement of living standards / Farhad Mehran. — Washington, D.C., U.S.A. : World Bank, 1985 printing, c1980. — 14p. — (LSMS working papers ; no.8) (LSMS working papers ; no. 8). — Includes bibliographical references

LABOR SUPPLY — Statistics

Economically active population : estimates and projections : 1950-2025 = Evaluations et projections de la population active : 1950-2025 = Estimaciones y proyecciones de la población económicamente activa : 1950-2025. — 3rd ed. — Geneva : International Labour Office
V.4: Northern America, Europe, Oceania and USSR. — 1986. — xxvi,177p. — Introduction and table headings in English, French and Spanish

Economically active population : estimates and projections : 1950-2025 = Evaluations et projections de la population active : 1950-2025 = Estimaciones y proyecciones de la población económicamente activa : 1950-2025. — 3rd ed. — Geneva : International Labour Office
V.5: World summary. — 1986. — xxvi,132p. — Introductions and table headings in English, French and Spanish

Incomes from work : between equity and efficiency. — Geneva : International Labour Office, 1987. — viii,169p. — (World labour report ; 3). — Bibliography: p165-169

LABOR SUPPLY — Statistics — Sources
Statistical sources and methods. — Geneva : International Labour Office
V.2: Employment, wages and hours of work (establishment surveys). — 1987. — vii,241p. — *Includes bibliographical references.* — *A technical guide to series published in the Bulletin of Labour Statistics and the Year Book of Labour Statistics*

LABOR SUPPLY — Africa
The Challenge of employment : and basic needs in Africa : essays in honour of Shyam B. L. Nigam and to mark the tenth anniversary of JASPA. — Nairobi : Oxford University Press, 1986. — xii,379p. — *Includes bibliographical references*

LABOR SUPPLY — Africa — Statistics
Economically active population : estimates and projections : 1950-2025 = Evaluations et projections de la population active : 1950-2025 = Estimaciones y proyecciones de la población económicamente activa : 1950-2025. — 3rd ed. — Geneva : International Labour Office
V.2: Africa. — 1986. — xxvi,210p. — *Introduction and table headings in English, French and Spanish*

LABOR SUPPLY — Alsace (France) — Statistics
FRANCE. Institut national de la statistique et études économiques. Direction régionale de Strasbourg
De la population active à l'emploi : des résultats pour 108 agglomérations, 1968-1975. — Strasbourg : INSEE, [1984?]. — 45p. — (Documents pour l'Alsace)

LABOR SUPPLY — Asia — Statistics
Economically active population : estimates and projections : 1950-2025 = Evaluations et projections de la population active : 1950-2025 = Estimaciones y proyecciones de la población económicamente activa : 1950-2025. — 3rd ed. — Geneva : International Labour Office
V.1: Asia. — 1986. — xxvi,176p. — *Introduction and table headings in English, French and Spanish*

LABOR SUPPLY — Australia
Labour force status and other characteristics of sole parents : 1974-1985. — Woden, ACT : Department of Social Security, 1986. — 33p. — (Background paper / Social Security Review ; no.8)

The medium-term international outlook : an economic, technological and sectoral analysis. — Canberra : Economic Planning Advisory Council, 1986. — v,37p. — (Council paper / Economic Planning Advisory Council ; no.1). — *Bibliography: p36-37*

Trends in the labour market. — Canberra : Economic Planning Advisory Council, 1986. — v,31p. — (Council paper / Economic Planning Advisory Council ; no.21). — *Bibliographical references: p29*

Unemployment and the labour market : anatomy of the problem. — Canberra : Australian Government Publishing Service, 1986. — xv,243p. — (Research report / Bureau of Labour Market Research ; no.9). — *Bibliographical references: p225-243*

Who's in the labour force? : a study of labour force participation. — Canberra : Australian Government Publishing Service, 1985. — xviii,197p. — (Research report / Bureau of Labour Market Research ; no.7). — *Bibliographical references: p189-197*

LABOR SUPPLY — Australia — Longitudinal studies
The first wave of the Australian longitudinal survey : facts and figures about young CES registrants / Jan Muir...[et al.]. — Canberra : Australian Government Publishing Service, 1986. — xxi,220p. — (Monograph series / Bureau of Labour Market Research ; no.12). — *Bibliographical references: p219-220*

LABOR SUPPLY — Australia — Methodology
The measurement and implications of productivity growth : proceedings of a workshop, 22-23 November 1984, Canberra / edited by Peter Scherer with Tracey Malone. — Canberra : Australian Government Publishing Service, 1986. — xi,290p. — (Monograph series / Bureau of Labour Market Research ; no.14). — *Includes bibliographical references*

LABOR SUPPLY — Belgium — Statistics
BELGIUM. Direction de l'étude des problèmes du travail
Estimation de la population active belge au 30 juin des années 1970-1984 : nouvelle série N.A.C.E. = Raming van de Belgische beroepsbevolking op 30 juni der jaren 1970-1984 : nieuwe reeks N.A.C.E.. — [Bruxelles] : Direction de l'étude des problèmes de travail, 1986. — [47] leaves. — *In French and Flemish*

Recensement de la population et des logements au 1er mars 81. — Bruxelles : Institut national de statistique
Résultats généraux
Population active. — 1986. — 305p

LABOR SUPPLY — Botswana — Statistics
Labour force survey 1984-85. — Gaborone : Central Statistics Office, [1986]. — 122p

LABOR SUPPLY — Brazil
HOFFMANN, Helga
Desemprego e subemprego no Brasil / Helga Hoffmann. — São Paulo : Editora Ática, 1977. — 183 p.. — (Ensaios ; 24). — : *Originally presented as the author's thesis, Universidade de São Paulo.* — *Bibliography: p. [175]-183*

LABOR SUPPLY — Brazil — Salvador
PINHO, Jose Antonio Gomes de
Housing provision and labour reproduction in peripheral capitalism : the case of Salvador, Brazil / Jose Antonio Gomes de Pinho. — 430 leaves, [3] leaves of plates. — *PhD (Econ) 1986 LSE*

LABOR SUPPLY — Bulgaria
Kharakteristika na bŭlgarskoto naselenie : trudovi vŭzmozhnosti i realizatsiia : pod obshchata redaktsiia Minko Minkov. — Sofiia : Dŭrzhavno izd-vo nauka i izkustvo, 1984. — 483p. — *Summary in Russian and French*

LABOR SUPPLY — Cape Verde
1° recenseamento geral da popula,áo e habitaçáo. — Praia : Direcçáo de Recenseamentos e Inqueritos
Vol.3: Populaçáo activa. — 1983. — 401p

LABOR SUPPLY — Caribbean Area
LONG, Frank
Employment effects of multinational enterprises in export processing zones in the Caribbean : a joint ILO/UNCTC research project / by Frank Long. — Geneva : International Labour Office, 1986. — 82p. — *Includes bibliographical references*

LABOR SUPPLY — Costa Rica — Statistics
COSTA RICA. Dirección General de Estadística y Censos
Encuesta de hogares por muestreo : zonas urbanas de Costa Rica, julio de 1967 a junio de 1968. — [San José] : the Dirección, 1970. — 75p

LABOR SUPPLY — Cyprus
HOUSE, William J.
Labour market segmentation and sex discrimination in Cyprus : some empirical evidence / by William J. House. — [Nicosia] : Department of Statistics and Research, [1985]. — v,39p

LABOR SUPPLY — Cyprus — Statistics
HOUSE, William J.
Wage structure, manpower analysis and the market in Cyprus / by William J. House. — [Nicosia] : Department of Statistics and Research, [1984]. — 78p. — *Bibliography: p77-78*

Labour statistics report / Department of Statistics and Research, Cyprus. — Nicosia : Department of Statistics and Research, 1982-. — *Annual*

LABOR SUPPLY — Denmark
The Employment Service and Unemployment Insurance Act, 1970, as amended. — [Copenhagen : Ministry of Labour?], 1970. — 35p

ROSDAHL, Anders
Arbejdsgiveres arbejdskrafteftersporgsel : ansaettelses processer i industrivirksomheder / Anders Rosdahl. — København : Socialforskningsinstituttet, 1986. — 240p. — (Publikation / Socialforskningsinstituttet ; 156). — *Bibliography: p237*

LABOR SUPPLY — Developing countries
NEWELL, A.
Wages and employment in the O.E.C.D. countries / A. Newell and J. S. V. Symons. — London : Centre of Labour Economics, London School of Economics, 1985. — 60p. — (Discussion paper / London School of Economics and Political Science. Centre for Labour Economics ; no.219). — *Bibliography: p59-60*

Population growth and economic development : issues and evidence / edited by D. Gale Johnson and Ronald D. Lee. — Madison, Wis. : University of Wisconsin Press, 1987. — xiii, 702 p.. — (Social demography). — *"Working Group on Population Growth and Economic Development; Committee on Population, Commission on Behavioral and Social Sciences and Education, National Research Council.".* — *Includes bibliographies and index*

LABOR SUPPLY — Egypt
HANSEN, Best
Employment opportunities and equity in a changing economy : Egypt in the 1980s : a labour market approach : report of an inter-agency team financed by the United Nations Development Programme and organised by the International Labour Office / Bent Hansen, Samir Radwan. — Geneva : International Labour Office, 1982. — xviii,292p. — (A WEP study). — *Includes bibliographical references*

LABOR SUPPLY — England — Avon
Economic review : an analysis of the main characteristics and trends that are shaping the structure and future prospects for employment and the workforce in Avon / Planning Department, Avon County Council. — Bristol : County of Avon Public Relations and Publicity Department, 1985. — 44p. — *Cover title*

LABOR SUPPLY — England — Bristol (Avon)
BODDY, Martin
Sunbelt city? : a study of economic change in Britain's M4 growth corridor / Martin Boddy, John Lovering and Keith Bassett. — Oxford : Clarendon Press, 1986. — vii,235p. — (Inner Cities Research Programme series ; 3). — *Bibliography: p221-226.* — *Includes index*

LABOR SUPPLY — England — Cheshire
WALSH, Kenneth
The mid-Cheshire labour market : trends and prospects / Kenneth Walsh, Stephen Bevan. — Brighton : Institute of Manpower Studies, 1986. — 210p. — (IMS report ; No.116)

LABOR SUPPLY — England — London
BUCK, N. H.
The London employment problem / Nick Buck, Ian Gordon and Ken Young, with John Ermisch and Liz Mills. — Oxford : Clarendon Press, 1986. — xvi,213p. — (Inner Cities Research Programme series ; 5). — *Bibliography: p199-205.* — *Includes index*

LABOR SUPPLY — Europe

Labour supply and migration in Europe : demographic dimensions 1950-1975 and prospects / prepared by the Secretariat of the Economic Commission for Europe. — New York : United Nations, 1979. — xi,332p. — *"Economic survey of Europe in 1977: part II"*. — *Sales no.: E.78.II.E.20*

METCALF, David
Labour market flexibility and jobs : a survey of evidence from OECD countries with special reference to Great Britain and Europe / D. Metcalf. — London : Centre for Labour Economics, London School of Economics, 1986. — 40p. — (Discussion paper / London School of Economics and Political Science. Centre for Labour Economics ; no.254)

LABOR SUPPLY — European Economic Community countries

GREAT BRITAIN. Parliament. House of Commons. Library. Research Division
Why the USA creates new jobs and why Europe does not / Christopher Barclay. — [London] : the Division, 1985. — 25p. — (Background paper ; no.170)

LABOR SUPPLY — European Economic Community countries — Statistics

WALSH, Kenneth
Handbook of international manpower market comparisons / [compiled by] Institute of Manpower Studies ; Kenneth Walsh and Adrian King. — New York : New York University Press, c1986. — 318 p.

LABOR SUPPLY — Finland — Statistics

FINLAND. Tilastokeskus
Työvoimatiedustelu : Työvoimatiedastelun tuloksia vaosilta 1959-1975 = Labour force survey : Results of the labour force survey from the years 1959-1975. — Helsinki : Tilastokeskus, 1978. — 54p. — (Tilastollisia tiedonantoja = Statistical surveys ; no.61). — *In Finnish, Swedish and English*

LABOR SUPPLY — France

HELD, Daniel
Marché de l'emploi : entreprises et régions / Daniel Held et Denis Maillat. — [Lausanne] : Presses Polytechniques Romandes, 1984. — 205p. — (Collection "villes, régions et sociétés")

SACHS-DURAND, Corinne
Les seuils d'effectif en droit du travail / par Corinne Sachs-Durand ; préface de Hélène Sinay. — Paris : Librairie Générale de Droit et de Jurisprudence, 1985. — 314p. — (Bibliothèque d'Ouvrages de Droit Social ; Tome 23). — *Bibliography: p275-290*

LABOR SUPPLY — France — Statistics

Données statistiques sur les zones d'emploi. — Paris : I.N.S.E.E., 1986. — 92p. — (Archives et documents / Institut national de la statistique et des études économiques ; no.162)

MARC, Nicole
Projection de population active disponible 1985-2010 / Nicole Marc et Olivier Marchand. — [Paris] : INSEE, 1987. — 51p. — (Les collections de l'INSEE. Série D. Demographic et emploi ; no.118)

Les zones d'emploi : indicateurs socio-économiques. — Paris : Délégation a l'aménagement du territoire et a l'action régionale, 1986. — 59p

LABOR SUPPLY — France — Ile-de-France — Statistics

LEMAHIEU, Marcel
Dynamique et structure de l'emploi en Ile de France / Marcel Lemahieu, Ariel Pecher. — [Paris : the Direction], 1986. — 77 leaves

LABOR SUPPLY — Germany (West)

OLLE, Werner
The development of employment in multinational enterprises in the Federal Republic of Germany : results of a new survey (1974-1982) / by Werner Olle. — Geneva : International Labour Office, 1985. — 68p. — (Working paper / Multinational Enterprises Programme ; no.33). — *Bibliography: p62-63*

LABOR SUPPLY — Great Britain

ATKINSON, John
New forms of work organisation / by John Atkinson and Nigel Meager. — Brighton : Institute of Manpower Studies, 1986. — iv,181p. — (IMS report ; No.121)

BLANCHFLOWER, D. G.
Internal and external influences upon pay settlements : new survey evidence / D. G. Blanchflower and A. J. Oswald. — London : Centre for Labour Economics, London School of Economics, 1987. — 16p. — (Discussion paper / London School of Economics and Political Science. Centre for Labour Economics ; no.275). — *Bibliography: p15-16*

The Changing experience of employment : restructuring and recession / edited by Kate Purcell ... [et al.]. — Basingstoke : Macmillan in association with British Sociological Association, 1986. — [256]p. — (Explorations in sociology ; 22). — *Includes bibliography and index*

CHISHOLM, Michael
The changing pattern of employment : regional specialisation and industrial localisation in Britain / Michael Chisholm and Jim Oeppen. — London : Croom Helm, 1973. — 127p. — *Bibliography: p.121-124. — Includes index*

Education for capability / edited for the RSA (the Royal Society for the Encouragement of Arts, Manufactures and Commerce) by Tyrrell Burgess. — Windsor : NFER-Nelson, 1985. — ix,201p

GREENAWAY, David
Boosting employment by import controls? / D. Greenaway [and] G. K. Shaw. — Buckingham : University of Buckingham. Employment Research Centre, 1986. — 30p. — (Occasional papers in employment studies / University of Buckingham. Employment Research Centre ; no.5). — *Bibliography: p27-29*

LAYARD, Richard
The performance of the British labour market / R. Layard and S. Nickell. — London : Centre for Labour Economics, London School of Economics, 1986. — 128p. — (Discussion paper / London School of Economics and Political Science. Centre for Labour Economics ; no.249). — *Expanded version of chapter in The performance of the British economy / edited by R. Dornbusch and R. Layard. — Bibliography: p122-128*

Measurement issues and behavior of productivity variables / edited by Ali Dogramaci. — Boston : Kluwer Nijhoff ; Hingham, MA, USA : Distributors for the United States and Canada, Kluwer Academic Publishers, c1986. — ix, 262 p.. — (Studies in productivity analysis). — *Includes bibliographies and indexes*

METCALF, David
Labour market flexibility and jobs : a survey of evidence from OECD countries with special reference to Great Britain and Europe / D. Metcalf. — London : Centre for Labour Economics, London School of Economics, 1986. — 40p. — (Discussion paper / London School of Economics and Political Science. Centre for Labour Economics ; no.254)

NATIONAL ECONOMIC DEVELOPMENT OFFICE
Changing working patterns and practices : memorandum / by the Director General. — [London] : National Economic Development Council, 1985. — 1pamphlet (various pagings). — *NEDC: (85) 84*

PARRY, Richard
Public employment in Britain and Germany / Richard Parry and Klaus-Dieter Schmidt. — Glasgow : University of Strathclyde. Centre for the Study of Public Policy, 1987. — 41p. — (Studies in public policy ; 157). — *Bibliography: p25-26*

STANDING, Guy
Unemployment and labour market flexibilty : the United Kingdom / Guy Standing. — Geneva : International Labour Office, 1986. — xi,147p. — *Including bibliographical references*

WILSON, Thomas, 1916-
Unemployment and the labour market / Tom Wilson ; with a commentary by Geoffrey E. Wood. — London : Institute of Economic Affairs, 1987. — 70p. — (Occasional paper / Institute of Economic Affairs ; 75)

LABOR SUPPLY — Great Britain — Effect of automation on

NATIONAL CONFERENCE AND EXHIBITION ON COMPUTERS IN PERSONNEL (5th : 1986)
Computers in personnel : from potential to performance; published in association with CIP 86, the Fifth National Conference and Exhibition on Computers in Personnel, 8-10 July 1986 / edited by Terry Page. — Brighton : Institute of Manpower Studies, University of Sussex ; London : Institute of Personnel Management, 1986. — 105p. — (IMS Report ; No.120)

LABOR SUPPLY — Great Britain — Effect of technological innovations on

FREEMAN, Christopher
Engineering and vehicles / Christopher Freeman, Daniel R. Jones ; edited by Christopher Freeman. — Aldershot : Gower, c1985. — xvii,199p. — (Technological trends and employment ; 4)

Technical change and full employment / edited by Christopher Freeman and Luc Soete. — Oxford : Basil Blackwell, 1987. — [280]p. — *Includes bibliography and index*

LABOR SUPPLY — Great Britain — History — 20th century

Changing places : Britain's demographic, economic and social complexion / A.G. Champion ... [et al.]. — London : Edward Arnold, 1987. — [192]p. — *Includes bibliography and index*

LABOR SUPPLY — Great Britain — Statistical services

Employment statistics : sources and definitions. — London (Caxton House, Tothill Street, London SW1H 9NF) : Department of Employment, 1985. — [156]p

LABOR SUPPLY — Great Britain — Statistics

Britain's workforce : 1981 Census / [prepared by the Office of Population Censuses and Surveys and the Central Office of Information]. — London : HMSO, 1985. — 20p. — (Census guide ; 3)

LABOR SUPPLY — India

CHAUDHARY, Shobha Kant
Planning and employment trends in Indai / S. K. Chaudhary. — New Delhi : Deep and Deep Publications, 1987. — 300p. — *Bibliography: p290-298*

LABOR SUPPLY — India — Statistics

INDIA. Labour Bureau
Labour Bureau's labour : master reference book on labour statistics 1984. — Shinla : Labour Bureau, Ministry of Labour and Rehabilitation, 1984. — 471p

LABOR SUPPLY — India — Karnataka

PRABHAKARA, N. R
Population growth and unemployment in India / N.R. Prabhakara, M.N. Usha. — New Delhi : Ashish Pub. House, 1986. — ix, 102 p.. — *Includes index. — Bibliography: p. 97-99*

LABOR SUPPLY — Ireland — Statistics

IRELAND. Central Statistics Office
Labour force survey 1985. — Dublin : Stationery Office
First results. — 1986. — 48p

LABOR SUPPLY — Italy — Statistics

ITALY. Istituto Centrale di Statistica
Forze di lavoro e flussi di popolazione anni 1979 e 1980. — Roma : Istituto Centrale di Statistica, 1981. — 149p. — (Bollettino mensile di statistica. Supplemento ; 1981 n.15)

LABOR SUPPLY — Jamaica — Statistics

Jamaica : population census 1970. — Kingston : Department of Statistics. — (Commonwealth Caribbean population census 1970)
Vol.2
Pt.E: Economic activity
Bk.4: By sex, ethnic origin, etc.. — [1978]. — 309p

LABOR SUPPLY — Japan — Statistics

1980 population census of Japan / Statistics Bureau. — [Tokyo] : Statistics Bureau
Vol.7: Results of special tabulation
Part 1: Industry and occupation (one percent sample tabulation). — [1984]. — xx,171,[12]p. — Text in Japanese and English

Japanese working life profile : statistical aspects. — Tokyo : Japan Institute of Labor, 1985. — 80p

WALSH, Kenneth
Handbook of international manpower market comparisons / [compiled by] Institute of Manpower Studies ; Kenneth Walsh and Adrian King. — New York : New York University Press, c1986. — 318 p.

LABOR SUPPLY — Jordan — Statistics

[Manpower Survey 1983]. — [Amman : Dept of Statistics, 1983]. — 2v. (various pagings). — *In Arabic with English table headings*

LABOR SUPPLY — Kenya

COLLIER, Paul
Labour and poverty in Kenya, 1900-1980 / Paul Collier and Deepak Lal. — Oxford : Clarendon, 1986. — xii,296p

LABOR SUPPLY — Korea (South) — Statistics

1970 population and housing census report. — [Seoul] : Bureau of Statistics, Economic Planning Board. — *In Korea and English*
Vol. 2: 10% sample survey
Vol 4-1: Economic activity. — 1973. — 391p

LABOR SUPPLY — Latin America — Statistics

Economically active population : estimates and projections : 1950-2025 = Evaluations et projections de la population active : 1950-2025 = Estimaciones y proyecciones de la población económicamente activa : 1950-2025. — 3rd ed. — Geneva : International Labour Office
V.3: Latin America. — 1986. — xxvi,132p. — *Introduction and table headings in English, French and Spanish*

LABOR SUPPLY — London

Services and employment growth in London, 1971-91 / James Simmie ... [et al.]. — London : Bartlett School of Architecture and Planning, 1985. — 32p. — (Town planning discussion paper ; no.45)

LABOR SUPPLY — Mexico

GREGORY, Peter
The myth of market failure : employment and the labor market in Mexico / Peter Gregory. — Baltimore : Johns Hopkins University Press for the World Bank, 1986. — viii,299p. — *Bibliography: p281-291*

LABOR SUPPLY — Nepal

Employment, income distribution, and consumption patterns in Nepal : results of a survey conducted by the National Planning Commission, Nepal, March-July 1977. — Kathmandu, Nepal : His Majesty's Govt., National Planning Commission Secretariat, 1983. — xiv,122p. — *Cover title: A survey of employment, income distribution, and consumption patterns in Nepal*

PANT, Yadav Prasad
Population growth and employment opportunities in Nepal / Y.P. Pant. — New Delhi : Oxford & IBH, c1983. — viii, 131 p.. — *Includes index. — Bibliography: p.[124]-126*

LABOR SUPPLY — Netherlands

Vernieuwingen in het arbeidsbestel. — 's-Gravenhage : Staatsuitgeverij, 1981. — 350p. — (Rapporten aan de regering ; 21). — *Prepared by the Wetenschappelijke Raad voor het Regeringsbeleid. — Includes bibliographical references*

LABOR SUPPLY — Netherlands — Statistics

NETHERLANDS. Centraal Bureau voor de Statistiek
Arbeidskrachtentelling 1981. — s-Gravenhage : Staatsuitgeverij. — *Title on back cover: Labour force sample survey 1981: part 1: method, population and labour force, employment and unemployment*
Deel 1: Methode, bevolking en beroepsbevolking, werkzame personen en werklozen. — 1985. — 233p

Regionale beroeps-bevolking 1971-1980. — 's-Gravenhage : Staatsuitgeverij, 1983. — 215p. — *Title on back cover: Labour force by region 1971-1980*

Statistiek werkzame personen / Centraal Bureau de Statistiek, Netherlands. — 's-gravenhage : Staatsuitgeverij, 1984-. — Annual

LABOR SUPPLY — Nigeria — Statistics

Federal Office of Statistics for National Manpower Board and Federal Ministry of Employment, Labour and Productivity. — Lagos : Federal Office of Statistics
Preliminary report. — 1984. — 45p. — *Survey module of the National Intergrated Survey of Households (NISH of the Federal Office of Statistics*

LABOR SUPPLY — Northeastern States

CROW, Robert Thomas
Description of projections of natural population increase and labor force / by Robert Thomas Crow. — [Washington, D.C.] : U.S. Department of Commerce, 1965. — [15]p. — (Northeast Corridor Transportation Project technical paper ; no.1). — *Bibliography: p [14-15]*

LABOR SUPPLY — Northeastern States — Forecasting

Method for the initial superdistrict projections of Northeast Corridor population, employment and income / by Robert Crow...[et al.]. — [Washington, D.C.] : U.S. Department of Commerce, 1966. — 45p. — (Northeast Corridor Transportation Project technical paper ; no.6)

LABOR SUPPLY — Organisation for Economic Co-operation and Development countries

Employment and unemployment : some issues and facts. — [Paris] : OECD, 1986. — 20p. — *Includes bibliographical references. — Contents: Background paper for OECD meeting of the Manpower and Social Affairs Committee at ministerial level*

Labour market flexibility : report / by a high-level group of experts to the Secretary. — Paris : OECD, 1986. — 23p

The role of large firms in local job creation. — [Paris] : Organisation for Economic Co-operation and Development, 1986. — 31p. — (Local initiatives for employment creation)

LABOR SUPPLY — Panama

Panama : structural change and growth prospects. — Washington, D.C., U.S.A. : World Bank, 1985. — xxv,307p. — (A World Bank country study). — *"Report no. 5236-PAN.". — "February 28, 1985."*

LABOR SUPPLY — Portugal

EUROFI (U.K.) LIMITED
Portugal / compiled by Eurofi (U.K.) Limited. — Northill : Eurofi (U.K.), 1986. — 139p. — (European Business Reports / Eurofi (U.K.) Limited). — *Bibliography: p137-139*

LABOR SUPPLY — Québec (Province) — Effect of technological innovations on

BENOIT, Carmelle
L'incidence de la machine a traitement de textes sur l'emploi et le travail / Carmelle Benoit, Alfred Cossette, Prisco Cardillo ; en collaboration avec Réal Morrissette, Emmanuel Nyahoho. — Québec : Ministère du travail : Ministère de la main-d'oeuvre et de la sécurité du revenu, 1984. — xxi,249p. — *Bibliographical references: p243-249*

LABOR SUPPLY — Québec (Province) — Statistics

Surplus et pénuries de main-d'oeuvre au Québec pour 1986 : diagnostiques par groupe professionel et par région. — Québec : Ministére de la main-d'oeuvre et la sécurité du revenu, 1985. — 215p. — *Includes bibliographical references*

LABOR SUPPLY — Réunion — Statistics

DOMENACH, Hervé
L'emploi à la Réunion / Hervé Domenach, Jean-Pierre Guengant. — Ste Clotilde : Institut National de la Statistique et des Etudes Economiques Service Régional de la Réunion, 1984. — 242p. — (Les dossiers de l'économie réunionnaise ; No. 5)

LABOR SUPPLY — San Marino — Statistics

1° censimento dell'industria e delle forze di lavoro : 10 luglio 1979. — San Marino : Ufficio Statale di Statistica, 1980. — xv,342 leaves

5° censimento generale popolazione : 30 novembre 1976. — San Marino : Ufficio Statale di Statistica, 1979. — xiii,200 leaves

LABOR SUPPLY — Scotland — Clydeside (Strathclyde)

The city in transition : policies and agencies for the economic regeneration of Clydeside / edited by William Lever and Chris Moore. — Oxford : Clarendon Press, 1986. — xvi,173p. — (Inner Cities Research Programme series ; 4). — *Bibliography: p163-167. — Includes index*

LABOR SUPPLY — Singapore

LIM, Linda
Trade, employment and industrialisation in Singapore / Linda Lim and Pang Eng Fong. — Geneva : International Labour Office, 1986. — xi,110p. — *Includes bibliographical references*

LABOR SUPPLY — Southern Africa

TIMAEUS, Ian
Labour circulation, marriage and fertility in Southern Africa / Ian Timaeus and Wendy Graham. — London : London School of Hygiene and Tropical Medicine. Centre for Population Studies, 1986. — 30p. — (CPS research paper ; no.86-2). — *Bibliography: p24-30*

LABOR SUPPLY — Soviet Union

ALYMOV, A. N.
Sbalansirovannost' narodno-khoziaistvennogo razvitiia : (regional'nye i otraslevye problemy) / A. N. Alymov, F. D. Zastavnyi, D. K. Preiger. — Kiev : Naukova dumka, 1986. — 221p. — (Ekonomika razvitogo sotsializma). — *Bibliography: p218-[222]*

LABOR SUPPLY — Soviet Union
continuation

KOSTIN, L. A.
Povyshenie effektivnosti truda v novykh usloviiakh khoziaistvovaniia / L. A. Kostin. — Moskva : Mysl', 1971. — 287p

LANE, David
Soviet labour and the ethic of communism : full employment and the labour process in the USSR / David Lane. — Brighton : Wheatsheaf Books, 1987. — viii, 246p

PAPENOV, K. V.
Rezervy obshchestvennogo proizvodstva : (voprosy teorii i praktiki) / K. V. Papenov. — Moskva : Izd-vo Moskovskogo universiteta, 1985. — 143p

ROMANENKOVA, G. M.
Trudovye resursy krupnogo goroda / G. M. Romanenkova ; pod redaktsiei V. R. Polozova. — Leningrad : Nauka, Leningradskoe otdelenie, 1986. — 159p

Trudovye resursy : problemy sbalansirovannogo raspredeleniia / [V. V. Onikienko...et al.]. — Kiev : Naukova dumka, 1986. — 245p

Vosproizvodstvo naseleniia i trudovykh resursov u usloviiakh razvitogo sotsializma / redaktsionnaia kollegiia: V. S. Steshenko. — Kiev : Naukova dumka. — V 4-kh tomakh
T.2: Formirovanie i raspredelenie trudovykh resursov / otv. redaktor I. N. Nazimov. — 1985. — 278p

Vosproizvodstvo naseleniia i trudovykh resursov v usloviiakh razvitogo sotsializma / redaktsionnaia kollegiia: V. S. Steshenko...[et al.]. — Kiev : Naukova dumka. — V 4-kh tomakh
T.1: Razvitie naseleniia i ego trudovogo potentsiala / otv. redaktor V. S. Steshenko. — 1985. — 318p

Vosproizvodstvo naseleniia i trudovykh resursov v usloviiakh razvitogo sotsializma / redaktsionnaia kollegiia: V. S. Steshenko...[et al.]. — Kiev : Naukova dumka. — V 4-kh tomakh
T.3: Sotsial'no-ekonomicheskie problemy effektivnogo ispol'zovaniia trudovykh resursov regiona / otv. redaktor M. I. Dolishnii. — 1986. — 262p

Vosproizvodstvo naseleniia i trudovykh resursov v usloviiakh razvitogo sotsializma / redaktsionnaia kollegiia: V. S. Steshenko...[et al.]. — Kiev : Naukova dumka. — V 4-kh tomakh
T.4: Povyshenie effektivnosti obshchestvennogo truda / otv. redaktor: D. P. Boginiia. — 1986. — 334p

LABOR SUPPLY — Spain

EUROFI (U.K.) LIMITED
Spain / compiled by Eurofi (U.K.) Limited. — Northill : Eurofi (U.K.), 1986. — 173p. — (European Business Reports / Eurofi (U.K.) Limited). — *Bibliography: p171-173*

LABOR SUPPLY — Sri Lanka — Statistics

Employment survey 1981-82. — Colombo : Department of Labour, 1984. — vi,55p

LABOR SUPPLY — Sweden

Arbetsmarknadsverket / Arbetsmarknadsstyrelsen, Sweden. — Stockholm : Arbetsmarknadsstyrelsen, 1975-. — *Annual.* — *Continues: Berattelse om verksamheten- . Continued by: The Swedish labour market*

Arsberattelse avseende verksamheten / Arbetsmarknadsstyrelsen, Sweden. — Stockholm : Arbetsmarknadsstyrelsen, 1948-1973/74. — *Annual.* — *Continued by: Berattelse om verksamheten*

Berattelse om verksamheten / Arbetsmarknadsstyrelsen, Sweden. — Stockholm : Arbetsmarknadsstyrelsen, 1974/75. — *Annual.* — *Continues: Arsberattelse avseende verksamheten- . Continued by: Arbetsmarknadsverket*

The Swedish labour market : annual report by the National Labour Market Board. — Stockholm : Arbetsmarknadsstyrelsen, 1984/85- . *Annual.* — *Continues: Arbetsmarknadsverket*

LABOR SUPPLY — Sweden — History — 20th century

AXELSSON, Roger
Den svenska arbetsmarknadspolitiken under 1900-talet / Roger Axelsson, Karl-Gustaf Löfgren, Lars-Gunnar Nilsson. — 3e. rev. upplagen. — Stockholm : Prisma, 1985. — 200p. — *First published 1979.* — *Bibliography: p191-196*

LABOR SUPPLY — Thailand — Statistics

Population by detailed classification of industry : 1980 population and housing census : whole kingdom and Bangkok metropolis. — [Bangkok] : National Statistical Office, [1985?]. — 144p. — *In English and Thai.* — *Cover title*

Population by detailed clssification [i.e. classification] of occupation : 1980 population and housing census : whole kingdom and Bangkok metropolis. — [Bangkok] : National Statistical Office, [1985?]. — 120p. — *In English and Thai*

LABOR SUPPLY — Togo — Statistics

Recensement général de la population et de l'habitat 9-22 novembre 1981. — [Lomé] : Bureau Central du Recensement
vol.3: Activités economiques
tome 1: Résultats globaux: ensemble du pays: urbain et rural et ville de Lomé : résultats définitifs. — 1985. — 246p

LABOR SUPPLY — Tonga — Statistics

Industrial employment and output survey, January 1980. — [Nuku'alofa : Statistics Department], 1980. — 12p

Survey of employment and output in the manufacturing sector, 1979. — [Nuku'alofa : Statistics Department], 1979. — 14p

LABOR SUPPLY — Trinidad and Tobago — Statistics

CSSP labour force : by sex. — Port of Spain : Central Statistical Office. — (Continuous sample survey of population / Trinidad and Tobago. Publication ; no.54). — *Contents: Rounds 32,34,35,36,37*
LF2-19: Area, education, attainment, hours worked, size of establishment. — 1983. — xii

CSSP labour force : by sex. — Port of Spain : Central Statistical Office. — (Continuous sample survey of population / Trinidad and Tobago. Publication ; no.55). — *Contents: Rounds 32,34,35,36,37*
LFI-23: Age, industry, occupation, type of worker. — 1983. — xii,17p

LABOR SUPPLY — Ukraine

ALYMOV, A. N.
Sbalansirovannost' narodno-khoziaistvennogo razvitiia : (regional'nye i otraslevye problemy) / A. N. Alymov, F. D. Zastavnyi, D. K. Preiger. — Kiev : Naukova dumka, 1986. — 221p. — (Ekonomika razvitogo sotsializma). — *Bibliography: p218-[222]*

LABOR SUPPLY — United States

GREAT BRITAIN. Parliament. House of Commons. Library. Research Division
Why the USA creates new jobs and why Europe does not / Christopher Barclay. — [London] : the Division, 1985. — 25p. — (Background paper ; no.170)

NICKELL, Stephen
The real wage-employment relationship in the United States / S. J. Nickell and J. S. V. Symons. — London : Centre for Labour Economics, London School of Economics, 1986. — 22p. — (Discussion paper / London School of Economics and Political Science. Centre for Labour Economics ; no.264). — *Bibliography: p18-19*

LABOR SUPPLY — United States — Effect of technological innovations on

GINZBERG, Eli
Technology and employment : concepts and clarifications / Eli Ginzberg, Thierry J. Noyelle, and Thomas M. Stanback, Jr. — Boulder : Westview Press, 1986. — xi, 111 p.. — (Conservation of Human Resources studies in the new economy). — *Includes bibliographies and index*

HOWARD, Robert
Brave new workplace / Robert Howard. — New York : Penguin Books, 1986, c1985. — p. cm. — "Elisabeth Sifton books.". — *Includes index*

LABOR SUPPLY — United States — Statistics

WALSH, Kenneth
Handbook of international manpower market comparisons / [compiled by] Institute of Manpower Studies ; Kenneth Walsh and Adrian King. — New York : New York University Press, c1986. — 318 p.

LABOR SUPPLY — Wales

SADLER, Peter G.
The Welsh social accounts 1968 : a labour dimension / Peter Sadler, Richard Jarvis. — [Cardiff ([Crown Building, Cathays Park, Cardiff CF1 3NQ]) : Welsh Council, 1979. — ix,38,7m[15]p. — *Bibliography: p.36-37*

LABOR SUPPLY — Wales — Clwyd

CLWYD. County Council
Clwyd county structure plan : public participation seminar : employment : report of proceedings. — Mold : [the Council], 1975. — 24p

LABOR SUPPLYOFF. PUBNS. — European Economic Community countries 986

STOREY, David J.
Job creation in small and medium sized enterprises / by David J. Storey. — Luxembourg : Office for Official Publications of the European Communities. — *At head of title: Commission of the European Communities*
Vol.1: Summary report; Issues for research and policy; United Kingdom; Italy : main report. — 1987. — 215p. — (Programme of research and actions on the development of the labour market)

STOREY, David J.
Job creation in small and medium sized enterprises / by David J. Storey, Steven G. Johnson. — Luxembourg : Office for Official Publications of the European Communities. — *At head of title: Commission of the European Communities*
Vol.2: Federal Republic of Germany; France; Netherlands; Belgium; Luxembourg : main report. — 1987. — 216—486p. — (Programme of research and actions on the development of the labour market)

STOREY, David J.
Job creation in small and medium sized enterprises / by David J.Storey, StevenG. Johnson. — Luxembourg : Office for Official Publications of the European Communities. — *At head of title: Commission of the European Communities*
Vol.3: Spain, Ireland, Denmark, Greece, Portugal : main report. — 1987. — 488-663p. — (Programme of research and actions on the development of the labour market)

LABOR THEORY OF VALUE
ROEMER, John E
Value, exploitation, and class / John E. Roemer. — Chur, Switzerland ; New York : Horwood Academic Publishers, c1986. — p. cm. — (Fundamentals of pure and applied economics ; vol. 4. Marxian economics section). — Includes index. — Bibliography: p

LABOR TURNOVER — Great Britain
GREAT BRITAIN. Joint DHSS/NHS Manpower Planning and Personnel Information Sub Group
Leavers (standard measures and classifications) : first report of Joint DHSS/NHS Sub-Group. — [London] : Department of Health and Social Security, 1975. — 9,[15]p. — (Manpower planning and personnel information ; no.1)

WEISBERG, Jacob
Labour turnover : a case study of early quits in British Rail / by Jacob Weisberg. — 333 leaves . — PhD (Econ) 1986 LSE. — Leaves 272-300 are appendices

LABOR TURNOVER — Russian S.F.S.R. — Siberia
MOZYREVA, T. A.
Tekuchest' i stabilizatsiia inzhenernotekhnicheskikh rabotnikov na predpriiatiiakh Sibiri / T. A. Mozyreva ; otv. redaktor E. G. Antosenkov. — Novosibirsk : Nauka, Sibirskoe otdelenie, 1986. — 156p

LABOR TURNOVER — Soviet Union
VERSHININA, T. N.
Vzaimosviaz' tekuchesti i proizvodstvennoi adaptatsii rabochikh / T. N. Vershinina ; otv. redaktor Z. V. Kupriianova. — Novosibirsk : Nauka, Sibirskoe otdelenie, 1986. — 164p

LABOR UND LABORING CLASSES — Germany — History
DEUTSCHE GEWERKSCHAFTSKONGRESS (10 : 1919 : Nürnberg)
Zur Sozialisierungsfrage : die Arbeitgemeinschaft der industriellen und gewerklichen Arbeitgeber und Arbeitnehmer Deutschlands : Vier Referate / erstattet auf dem Zehnten Deutschen Gewerkschaftskongress zu Nürnberg. — Berlin : Verlag des "Allgemeinen Deutschen Gewerkschaftsbundes", 1919. — 68p. — Sonderabdruck aus dem Protokoll der Verhandlungen des Zehnten Deutschen Gewerkschaftskongresses, abgehalten in der Zeit vom 30. Juni bis 5. Juli zu Nürnberg

LABORATORY ANIMALS
CHALLIS, David
Case management in community care : an evaluated experiment in the home care of the elderly / David Challis & Bleddyn Davies. — Aldershot : Gower, c1986. — xvi,289p. — Bibliography: p268-281. — Includes index

STRATMANN, G. C.
Animal experiments and their alternatives / G. C. Stratmann, C. J. Stratmann and C. L. Paxton. — Braunton : Merlin Books, 1987. — 64p. — Bibliographies

LABOUR CAMPAIGN FOR ELECTORAL REFORM
BENJAMIN, Richard
Socialism and modern democratic techniques / Richard Benjamin. — Guildford : Labour Campaign for Electoral Reform, 1987. — 12p

LABOUR CONTRACT — India
DREZE, Jean
Labour contracts in rural India : theories and evidence / Jean Dreze and Anindita Mukherjee. — London : Suntory Toyota International Centre for Economics and Related Disciplines, 1987. — 43p. — (Development research programme / London School of Economics and Political Science. Suntory Toyota International Centre for Economics and Related Disciplines ; no.7). — Bibliography: p[44-49]

LABOUR-MANAGEMENT COMMITTEES — Hungary — History
RÁCZ, János
Az üzemi bizottságok a magyar demokratikus átalakulásban (1944-1948) / Rácz János. — Budapest : Akadémiai Kiadó, 1971. — 159p

LABOUR PARTY, Great Britain — History
MORGAN, Kenneth O.
Labour people : leaders and lieutenants, Hardie to Kinnock / Kenneth O. Morgan. — Oxford : Oxford University Press, 1987. — xii,370p,[16]p of plates. — Includes bibliography and index

LABOUR PARTY (Great Britain)
BOWEN, Jonathan Mark
Labour left policy formulation and Labour Party politics in Britain, 1931-1940 / Jonathan Mark Bowen. — 412 leaves. — PhD (Econ) 1986 LSE

Education, the Labour Party and the election campaign : the principles of the Labour Party's 1988 Education Act. — London : Socialist Educational Association, 1987. — 12p

ELDERGILL, Anselm
Woman's lot : political purdah and the Labour Party / Anselm Eldergill. — Nottingham : Institute of Workers' Control, 1987. — 38p. — (IWC pamphlet ; no.89)

HALLAS, Duncan
The Labour Party : myth and reality / Duncan Hallas. — 3rd ed. — London : Socialist Workers Party, 1986. — 38p. — A Socialist Workers Party pamphlet

HATTERSLEY, Roy
Economic priorities for a Labour government / Roy Hattersley ; edited and introduced by Doug Jones. — Basingstoke : Macmillan, 1987. — x,198p

HEFFER, Eric
Labour's future : socialist or SDP mark 2? / Eric S. Heffer. — London : Verso, 1986. — xiii,159p

HOWE, Darcus
Black sections in the Labour Party / Darcus Howe. — London : Race Today Publications, 1985. — 16p

LABOUR PARTY (Great Britain)
At your service! : Labour's charter for better local services. — London : Labour Party, 1986. — 15p

LABOUR PARTY (Great Britain)
The best of health : charter for the family health service. — London : Labour Party, 1986. — 15p

LABOUR PARTY (Great Britain)
The defence industry : the key seats, industries and regions. — London : Labour Party, 1986. — 41p. — (Special briefing note / Labour Party ; no.2)

LABOUR PARTY (Great Britain)
Health for all : a charter on preventive health. — London : Labour Party, 1986. — 16p

LABOUR PARTY (Great Britain)
How to fight local elections. — London : Labour Party, 1985. — 72p

LABOUR PARTY (Great Britain)
Investing in people. — London : Labour Party, 1986. — [20p]

LABOUR PARTY (Great Britain)
Labour's charter for consumers. — London : Labour Party, 1986. — 27p. — (Labour's Jobs and Industry campaign)

LABOUR PARTY (Great Britain)
Labour's charter for rural areas. — London : Labour Party, 1986. — 47p

LABOUR PARTY (Great Britain)
Labour's defence policy : defending Britain the modern way. — London : Labour Party, 1985. — [6p]. — (Special briefing note / Labour Party ; no.1)

LABOUR PARTY (Great Britain)
Modern Britain in a modern world : the power to defend our country. — London : Labour Party, 1986. — 10p

LABOUR PARTY (Great Britain)
Statements to conference. — London : Labour Party, 1986. — 55p

LABOUR PARTY (Great Britain). National Executive Committee
Labour's ministry for women : N.E.C. discussion document. — London : Labour Party, 1986. — 35p

The Labour Party : personnel, policies and performance. — London : Conservative Research Department, 1987. — 23p

Labour's first hundred days / edited by Ben Pimlott. — London : Fabian Society, 1987. — 34 p. — (Fabian tract ; 519)

Labour's next moves forward / Jeremy Beecham ... [et al.]. — London : Fabian Society, 1987. — 28 p. — (Fabian tract ; 521)

LANSLEY, Stewart
Housing finance : new policies for Labour / Stewart Lansley. — London : Labour Housing Group, [1986]. — 20p

MANN, John
Labour and youth : the missing generation / John Mann [and] Phil Woolas. — London : Fabian Society, 1986. — 19 p. — (Fabian tract ; 515)

MULGAN, Geoff
Saturday night or Sunday morning? : from arts to industry : new forms of cultural policy / by Geoff Mulgan and Ken Worpole. — London : Comedia, 1986. — 132p. — Bibliography: p133

Red-print for ruin : the Labour left in local government. — London : Conservative Research Department, 1986. — 14p

SHIPLEY, Peter
More than Militant : the future of the Labour left / Peter Shipley. — London : Conservative Political Centre, 1986. — 24p

THAMES VALLEY ANARCHISTS
Vote Labour and still die horribly. — Reading : Thames Valley Anarchists, 1986. — [8p]

TUC-LABOUR PARTY LIAISON COMMITTEE
Low pay : policies and priorities. — London : TUC : Labour Party, 1986. — 26p. — (Jobs and industry)

TUC-LABOUR PARTY LIAISON COMMITTEE
People at work : new rights, new responsibilities. — London : TUC : Labour Party, 1986. — 22p. — (Jobs and industry)

WAINWRIGHT, Hilary
Labour : a tale of two parties / Hilary Wainwright. — London : Hogarth, 1987. — ix,338p. — (A Tigerstripe book). — Includes index

Working together : common action for one world. — Nottingham : Spokesman, 1986. — 17p. — (Spokesman pamphlet ; no.86). — Contents: Common action in a common cause: speech to the 1986 Annual Conference of the Labour Party/Neil Kinnock-. A global challenge: speech to the Labour Party Conference/Willy Brandt

LABOUR PARTY (Great Britain) — Biography
MORGAN, Kenneth O.
Labour people : leaders and lieutenants, Hardie to Kinnock / Kenneth O. Morgan. — Oxford : Oxford University Press, 1987. — xii,370p,[16] of plates. — *Includes bibliography and index*

LABOUR PARTY (Great Britain) — Decision making
WOLFE, Joel D
Workers, participation, and democracy : internal politics in the British union movement / Joel D. Wolfe. — Westport, Conn. ; London : Greenwood Press, c1985. — xii, 258p. — (Contributions in political science ; no. 136). — *Includes index. — Bibliography: p.[219]-243*

LABOUR PARTY (Great Britain) — History
CAMPBELL, John, 1947-
Nye Bevan and the mirage of British socialism / John Campbell. — London : Weidenfeld and Nicolson, c1987. — 430 p.. — *Bibliography: p.411-417*

SOUTH, Raymond
Heights and depths : Labour in Windsor / Raymond South. — [Windsor] ([5 St. Andrew's Avenue, Windsor]) : R. South, 1985. — 72p. — *Includes index*

TAYLOR, Andrew, 1954-
The trade unions and the Labour Party / Andrew Taylor. — London : Croom Helm, c1987. — 320p. — *Bibliography: p298-306. — Includes index*

LABOUR PARTY (Great Britain). Deptford Constituency Labour Party
ACKERS, Helen Louise
Racism and political marginalisation in the metropolis : the relationship between black people and the Labour Party in London / Louise Ackers. — 280 leaves. — *Labour Party leaflet and 'Anti-racism action sheets' are in end pocket. — PhD (Econ) 1986 LSE. — Leaves 240-261 are appendices*

LABOUR PARTY (Ireland)
HORGAN, John
Labour : the price of power / John Horgan. — Dublin : Gill and Macmillan, 1986. — 191p

LABOUR PARTY (GREAT BRITAIN)
LABOUR PARTY (Great Britain)
Investing in Britain : jobs and industry / Labour Party. — London : Labour Party, [1985]. — 23p

LABOUR SUPPLY — Egypt
EL-ISSAWY, Ibrahim H.
Labour force, employment and unemployment / Ibrahim H. El-Issawy. — Geneva : International Labour Office, 1983. — ix,80p. — (Employment opportunities and equity in Egypt ; no.4). — *Bibliographical references: p52-56. — A technical paper of the ILO/UNDP comprehensive employment strategy mission to Egypt, 1980*

LABOUR SUPPLY — England — London
GREATER LONDON COUNCIL
The London labour plan. — London : Greater London Council, 1986. — 552p

LABOUR SUPPLY — Great Britain
Global restructuring local response / edited by Philip Cooke. — London : Economic and Social Research Council, 1986. — 308p. — *A report commissioned by the Environment and Planning Committee of the ESRC. — Includes bibliographies*

TRINDER, C.
Unemployment and labour supply in National Institute Model 8 / C. Trinder [and] R. Biswas. — London : National Institute of Economic and Social Research, 1986. — 36p. — (Discussion paper / National Institute of Economic and Social Research ; no.112). — *Bibliography: p36*

LABOUR SUPPLY — Malaysia
Industrialisation and labour force processes : a case study of peninsular Malaysia / T. G. McGee...[et al.] ; with a preface by H. C. Brookfield and a postscript by Benjamin Higgins. — Canberra : Australian National University, 1986. — xviii,244p. — (Research papers on development in East Java and West Malaysia ; No.1). — *Bibliography: p223-238*

LABOUR SUPPLY — New Zealand — Statistics
New Zealand tables of working life, 1971. — Wellington : Department of Statistics, 1977. — 23p. — (Statistical bulletin / Department of Statistics, New Zealand. Miscellaneous series ; 2)

LABOUR SUPPLY — Réunion — Statistics
VERGOZ, Luce
Structure des emplois à la Réunion en 1981 (dans les établissements de plus de 10 salariés). — Ste Clotilde : Institute National de la Statistique et des Etudes Économiques, Service Régional de la Réunion, [1984]. — 165p. — (Dossiers de l'économie réunionnaise ; No. 3)

LADRECHT (FRANCE) — Social conditions
GARDÈS-METTRAY, Françoise
Parole ouvrière : autour de Ladrecht / Françoise Gardès-Mattray et Jacques Bres ; péface [sic] d'Henri Krasucki. — Paris : Messidor/Éditions Sociales, [1986]. — 307p

LADRECHT (FRANCE) — Coal Miners' Strike, 1981-1982
GARDÈS-METTRAY, Françoise
Parole ouvrière : autour de Ladrecht / Françoise Gardès-Mattray et Jacques Bres ; péface [sic] d'Henri Krasucki. — Paris : Messidor/Éditions Sociales, [1986]. — 307p

LAGOS (NIGERIA) — Social conditions
BARNES, Sandra T.
Patrons and power : creating a political community in metropolitan Lagos / Sandra T. Barnes. — Manchester : Manchester University Press, c1986. — [336]p. — (International African library ; v.1). — *Includes bibliography and index*

LAISSEZ-FAIRE
BRUNHOFF, Suzanne de
L'heure du marché : critique du libéralisme / Suzanne de Brunhoff. — Paris : P.U.F., [1986]. — 154p

GIERSCH, Herbert
Liberalisation for faster economic growth : internal and external measures required... / Herbert Giersch. — London : Institute of Economic Affairs for the Wincott Foundation, 1986. — 32p. — (Occasional paper / Institute of Economic Affairs ; 74). — *"Seventeenth Wincott memorial lecture, delivered at the Royal Society of Arts on Thursday, 16 October 1986"*

GREEN, David G
The new conservatism : the counter-revolution in political, economic, and social thought / David G. Green. — New York : St. Martin's Press, 1987. — xi, 238 p.. — *Includes index. — Bibliography: p. 221-232*

Industrial policy : structural dynamics / edited by Bodo B. Gemper. — Hamburg : Verlag Weltarchiv, 1985. — x, 208 p.. — (A Publication of the HWWA-Institut für Wirtschaftsforschung-Hamburg and the Unabhängiges Institut für Rechts-, Sozial- und Wirtschaftswissenschaften e. V). — *Includes bibliographies and indexes*

LEE, Dwight R
Regulating government : a preface to constitutional economics / Dwight R. Lee, Richard B. McKenzie. — Lexington, Mass. : Lexington Books, c1987. — xiv, 192 p.. — *Includes bibliographical references and index*

NEWELL, A.
Corporatism, the laissez-faire and the rise in unemployment / A. Newell and J. S. V. Symons. — London : Centre for Labour Economics, London School of Economics, 1986. — 62p. — (Discussion paper / London School of Economics and Political Science. Centre for Labour Economics ; no.260). — *Bibliography: p60-62*

PFEIFFER, Lucien
Libre entreprise et socialismes. — Paris : Nouvelle Société des Éditions Encre, 1986. — 192p

RAYACK, Elton
Not so free to choose : the political economy of Milton Friedman and Ronald Reagan / Elton Rayack. — New York : Praeger, 1987. — x, 215 p.. — *Includes index. — Bibliography: p. 203-208*

SUGDEN, Robert
The economics of rights, co-operation and welfare / Robert Sugden. — Oxford : Basil Blackwell, 1986. — [224]p. — *Includes index*

LAISSEZ-FAIRE — Congresses
The Dynamics of market economies / edited by Richard H. Day and Gunnar Eliasson. — New York : North Holland Pub. Co. ; New York, N.Y. : Sole distributors for the U.S.A. and Canada, Elsevier Science Pub. Co., 1985. — p. cm. — *"Papers and discussion of a conference on the dynamics of decentralized, market economies held at the Grand Hotel, Saltsjöbaden near Stockholm, August 29-31, 1983 ... sponsored by the Marcus Wallenberg Foundation for International Cooperation in Science"--P*

LAISSEZ-FAIRE — History
NELSON, John R.
Liberty and property : political economy and policymaking in the new nation, 1789-1812 / John R. Nelson, Jr. — Baltimore : Johns Hopkins University Press, c1987. — p. cm. — (The Johns Hopkins University studies in historical and political science ; 105th ser., 2). — *Bibliography: p*

LAISZEZ-FAIRE
WITTMANN, Walter
How social is the market economy? / Walter Wittmann. — London : Centre for Research into Communist Economics, 1985. — 50p. — (Understanding economic systems ; 2). — *Bibliography: p49*

LAKSHMI BAI, Rani of Jhansi
LEBRA-CHAPMAN, Joyce
The Rani of Jhansi : a study in female heroism in India / Joyce Lebra-Chapman. — Honolulu : University of Hawaii Press, c1986. — xii, 199 p., [2] leaves of plates. — *Includes index. — Bibliography: p. [185]-193*

LAMBETH (LONDON, ENGLAND) — City planning
LAMBETH
Lambeth local plan : Lambeth council's response to the inspector's report on the public local inquiry. — Lambeth : [the Council], 1986. — 133p

LAMBETH
Lambeth local plan July 1984 : inspector's report on the public local inquiry, October 1985. — Lambeth : [the Council], 1986. — 56p

LAMBETH (LONDON, ENGLAND) — Economic conditions
LAMBETH
Revised Lambeth local plan : written statement and schedule of proposals (incorporating all changes proposed to the 1984 plan). — Lambeth : [the Council], 1986. — 184p. — *Includes folded map*

LAMBETH (LONDON, ENGLAND) — Economic policy
LAMBETH
The case for Lambeth. — Lambeth : [the Council], 1986. — [16p]

LAMBETH (LONDON, ENGLAND) — Economic policy
continuation

LAMBETH
Rate-capping and Lambeth : a public consultation document. — Lambeth : [the Council], 1986. — 10p

LAMBETH (LONDON, ENGLAND) — Social policy

LAMBETH
The case for Lambeth. — Lambeth : [the Council], 1986. — [16p]

LANCASHIRE — Bibliography

Local studies in Lancashire : the Lancashire Library : a guide to resources. — [Lancaster] : [Lancashire County Council], 1986. — iii,171p

LANCASHIRE — Social conditions

WALTON, John K.
Lancashire : a social history, 1558-1939 / John K. Walton. — Manchester : Manchester University Press, 1987. — x,406p,[12]p of plates. — *Includes index*

LANCASHIRE ASSOCIATION OF TRADES COUNCILS

HIGNEY, Clare
' — Not a bed of roses' : an arts development officer in the trade union movement / by Clare Higney. — London : Calouste Gulbenkian Foundation, 1985. — 51p

LAND

THRALL, Grant Ian
Land use and urban form : the consumption theory of land rent / Grant Ian Thrall. — New York ; London : Methuen, 1987. — xvi,239p. — *Bibliography: p233-236. — Includes index*

LAND — Australia

AUSTRALIA. Commonwealth Bureau of Census and Statistics
Agricultural land use, improvements and labour. — Canberra : [the Bureau], 1979/80-1980/81. — *Annual*

LAND — Czechoslovakia

JELEČEK, Leoš
Zemědělství a půdní fond v Čechách ve 2. polovině 19. století / Leoš Jeleček. — Praha : Academia, 1985. — 283p. — *Summary in English and Russian. — Bibliography: p262-273*

LAND — Great Britain

NATIONAL COUNCIL FOR CIVIL LIBERTIES
Stonehenge : a report into the civil liberties implications of the events relating to the convoys of summer 1985 and 1986. — London : National Council for Civil Liberties, 1986. — 43p

LAND — Kazakh S.S.R.

KOVAL'SKII, S. L.
Osvoenie tselinnykh zemel' v Kazakhstane : (istoriko-partiinyi aspekt) / S. L. Koval'skii, Kh. M. Madanov. — Alma-Ata : "Nauka" Kazakhskoi SSR, 1986. — 223p. — *Bibliography: p214-[222]*

LAND COMPANIES — Argentina

MÍGUEZ, Eduardo José
Las tierras de los ingleses en la Argentina (1870-1914) / Eduardo José Míguez. — [Buenos Aires] : Editorial de Belgrano, 1985. — 348p. — *"El presente libro es una traducción y adaptación de mi tesis doctoral, titulada 'British interests in Argentine Land Development, 1870-1914. A study of British investment in Argentina', defendida en la Universidad de Oxford en abril de 1981.". — Bibliography: p[331]-342*

LAND REFORM — Law and legislation — Ecuador

ECUADOR
[Laws, etc.]. Ley de reforma agraria y colonización : decreto supremo no.1480. — Quito : [Presidencia], 1964. — 107p

ECUADOR
[Laws, etc.]. Reforma agraria, ley y reglamento. — Quito : Ministerio de Agricultura y Ganadería, 1974. — 128p

LAND REFORM — Law and legislation — Peru

PERU
[Laws, etc]. Texto único de la ley de reforma agraria. — [Lima : Empresa Editora del Diario Oficial "El Peruano", ca.1970]. — 66p

LAND REFORM — Botswana

Land reform in the making : tradition, public policy and ideology in Botswana / edited by Richard P. Werbner. — London : Rex Collings, 1982. — xv,162p

LAND REFORM — Great Britain

SHOARD, Marion
This land is our land / Marion Shoard. — London : Grafton, 1987. — 592p

LAND REFORM — India

HAQUE, T
Agrarian reforms and institutional changes in India / T. Haque, A.S. Sirohi. — New Delhi : Concept Pub. Co., 1986, c1985. — xvi, 268 p.. — *Includes index. — Bibliography: p. [249]-262*

LAND REFORM — India — Government policy

KOHLI, Atul
The state and poverty in India : the politics of reform / Atul Kohli. — Cambridge : Cambridge University Press, 1987. — x,262p. — (Cambridge South Asian studies ; no.37). — *Bibliography: p245-254. — Includes index*

LAND REFORM — India — History

Not by a class war : a study of Congress policy on land reforms during the last 100 years / edited by A. Moin Zaidi. — New Delhi : Indian Institute of Applied Political Research, 1985. — 176p

LAND REFORM — Kenya — Case studies

GLAZIER, Jack
Land and the uses of tradition among the Mbere of Kenya / Jack Glazier. — Lanham : University Press of America, c1985. — xiii, 334 p.. — *Includes index. — Bibliography: p. 315-330*

LAND REFORM — Mexico — Yucatán — History

BRANNON, Jeffery
Agrarian reform & public enterprise in Mexico : the political economy of Yucatán's henequen industry / Jeffery Brannon, Eric N. Baklanoff ; a foreword by Edward H. Moseley. — Tuscaloosa, Ala. : University of Alabama Press, c1987. — xv, 237 p.. — *Includes index. — Bibliography: p. 220-230*

LAND REFORM — Peru

PERU. Ministerio de Agricultura
Así marcha la reforma agraria / DPDRA. — [Lima : the Ministerio, 1971]. — 26Leaves

PERU. Dirección de Difusión de la Reforma Agraria
Del latifundio a la cooperativa. — [Lima] : the Dirección, [ca.1970]. — 48p

LAND SETTLEMENT — Nigeria — Kainji Reservoir Region

OYEDIPE, F. P. A
Adjustment to resettlement : a study of the resettled peoples in the Kainji Lake basin / F.P.A. Oyedipe. — Ibadan : University Press, 1983. — xvi, 167 p.. — *Includes bibliographical references and index*

LAND SETTLEMENT — Oregon — History

GIBSON, James R
Farming the frontier : the agricultural opening of the Oregon country, 1786-1846 / James R. Gibson. — Seattle : University of Washington Press, c1985. — 265 p. — *Maps on lining papers. — Includes index. — Bibliography: p. [215]-226*

LAND SETTLEMENT — Prairie Provinces — History

KEYWAN, Zonia
Greater than kings / text by Zonia Keywan ; photographs by Martin Coles. — Montreal : Clio Editions, 1986. — 165p. — *Originally published: Montreal : Harvest House, 1977*

LAND SETTLEMENT — Zimbabwe — Statistics

1985 census of resettlement schemes : crops, fertilizer, equipment and persons on normal intensive and accelerated schemes and model B-Co-operatives (by scheme / Co-operative. — Harare : Central Statistical Office, [1986?]. — 316p

LAND TENURE — Law and legislation — Ecuador

ECUADOR
[Laws, etc.]. Ley de tierras baldias y colonización : decreto supremo no.2172. — Quito : [Presidencia], 1964. — 40p

LAND TENURE — Law and legislation — Hong Kong

CRUDEN, Gordon N.
Land compensation and valuation law in Hong Kong / Gordon N. Cruden. — Singapore : Butterworths, 1986. — xxxii,476p

LAND TENURE — Law and legislation — Peru

PERU
[Laws, etc.]. Texto único de la ley de reforma agraria. — [Lima : Empresa Editora del Diario Oficial "El Peruano", ca.1970]. — 66p

LAND TENURE — Political aspects — England — Wimborne (Dorset)

NICOLSON, I. F.
The mystery of Crichel Down / I.F. Nicolson. — Oxford : Clarendon, 1986. — [344]p. — *Includes bibliography and index*

LAND TENURE — Political aspects — India

WINK, André
Land and sovereignty in India : agrarian society and politics under the eighteenth-century Maratha Svarājya / André Wink. — Cambridge : Cambridge University Press, 1986. — [590]p. — (University of Cambridge oriental publications ; no.36). — *Bibliography: p565-584. — Includes index*

LAND TENURE — Political aspects — Ireland

GEARY, Laurence M.
The plan of campaign, 1886-1891 / Laurence M. Geary. — Cork : Cork University Press, 1986. — viii,226p. — *Bibliography: p212-219. — Includes index*

PARNELL, Anna
Tale of a great sham / by Anna Parnell ; edited with an introduction by Dana Hearne. — Dublin : Arlen House, 1986. — [400]p. — *Includes bibliography*

LAND TENURE — Appalachian Region

Who owns Appalachia? : landownership and its impact / the Appalachian Land Ownership Task Force ; with an introduction by Charles C. Geisler. — Lexington, Ky. : University Press of Kentucky, c1983. — xxxii, 235 p.. — *Map on lining papers. — Includes bibliographies and index*

LAND TENURE — Colombia — History

LEGRAND, Catherine
Frontier expansion and peasant protest in Colombia, 1850-1936 / Catherine LeGrand. — 1st ed. — Albuquerque : University of New Mexico Press, c1986. — xviii, 302p. — *Includes index. — Bibliography: p.267-289*

LAND TENURE — Great Britain

SHOARD, Marion
This land is our land / Marion Shoard. — London : Grafton, 1987. — 592p

LAND TENURE — Greece — History — 19th century

MCGREW, William W.
Land and revolution in modern Greece, 1800-1881 : the transition in the tenure and exploitation of land from Ottoman rule to independence / William W. McGrew. — [Kent, OH] : Kent State University Press, c1985. — xxii, 339 p.. — *Includes index. — Bibliography: p. [306]-333*

LAND TENURE — India

Agrarian struggles in India after independence / edited by A. R. Desai. — Delhi : Oxford University Press, 1986. — xxvi,666p

LAND TENURE — India — History — 18th century

WINK, André
Land and sovereignty in India : agrarian society and politics under the eighteenth-century Maratha Svarājya / André Wink. — Cambridge : Cambridge University Press, 1986. — [590]p. — (University of Cambridge oriental publications ; no.36). — *Bibliography: p565-584. — Includes index*

LAND TENURE — Ireland — History — 19th century

GEARY, Laurence M.
The plan of campaign, 1886-1891 / Laurence M. Geary. — Cork : Cork University Press, 1986. — viii,226p. — *Bibliography: p212-219. — Includes index*

PARNELL, Anna
Tale of a great sham / by Anna Parnell ; edited with an introduction by Dana Hearne. — Dublin : Arlen House, 1986. — [400]p. — *Includes bibliography*

LAND TENURE — Ivory Coast

GROOTAERT, Christiaan
The demand for urban housing in the Ivory Coast / Christiaan Grootaert and Jean-Luc Dubois. — Washington, D.C. : The World Bank, 1986. — viii,70p. — (LSMS working papers ; no.25). — *Bibliographical references: p68-70*

LAND TENURE — Japan — History

SMETHURST, Richard J
Agricultural development and tenancy disputes in Japan, 1870-1940 / Richard J. Smethurst. — Princeton, N.J. : Princeton University Press, c1986. — xii, 472 p.. — *Includes index. — Bibliography: p. 437-450*

WASWO, Ann
Japanese landlords : the decline of a rural elite / Ann Waswo. — Berkeley ; London : University of California Press, 1977. — viii,152p. — *Bibliography: p.141-149. — Includes index*

LAND TENURE — Peru

PERU, Ministerio de Agricultura
Así marcha la reforma agraria / DPDRA. — [Lima : the Ministerio, 1971]. — 26Leaves

PERU. Dirección de Difusión de la Reforma Agraria
Del latifundio a la cooperativa. — [Lima] : the Dirección, [ca.1970]. — 48p

LAND TENURE — Peru — Cajamarca — History

TAYLOR, Lewis
Estates, freeholders and peasant communities in Cajamarca, 1876-1972 / by Lewis Taylor. — Cambridge : Centre of Latin American Studies, University of Cambridge, 1986. — 45p. — (Working papers / University of Cambridge, Centre of Latin American Studies ; no.42)

LAND TENURE — Poland — History

STANKIEWICZ, Zbigniew
Kwestia chłopska w okresie narodzin polskiego ruchu robotniczego / Zbigniew Stankiewicz. — Warszawa : Ludowa Spółdzielnia Wydawnicza, 1985. — 329p. — *Bibliography: p305-[314]*

LAND TENURE — Singapore — Law

RICQUIER, W. J. M.
Land law / W. J. M. Ricquier. — Singapore : Butterworths, 1985. — xxiv,236p. — (Singapore law series)

LAND TENURE — Soviet Union — History

SIMONOVA, M. S.
Krizis agrarnoi politiki tsarizma nakanune pervoi rossiiskoi revoliutsii / M. S. Simonova ; otv. redaktor A. M. Anfimov. — Moskva : Nauka, 1987. — 252p

VOROB'EV, V. M.
Russkoe feodal'noe zemlevladenie ot "smutnogo vremeni" do kanuna petrovskikh reform / V. M. Vorob'ev, A. Ia. Degtiarev ; otv. redaktor A. L. Shapiro. — Leningrad : Izd-vo Leningradskogo universiteta, 1986. — 197p

LAND TENURE — Soviet Union — History — 17th century

MILOV, L. V.
Tendentsii agrarnogo razvitiia Rossii pervoi poloviny XVII stoletiia : istoriografiia, komp'iuter i metody issledovaniia / L. V. Milov, M. B. Bulgakov, I. M. Garskova. — Moskva : Izd-vo Moskovskogo universiteta, 1986. — 299p

LAND TENURE — Spain — History — 20th century

TUÑON DE LARA, Manuel
Tres claves de la Segunda República : la cuestión agraria, los aparatos del Estado, Frente Popular / Manuel Tuñon de Lara. — Madrid : Alianza Editorial, 1985. — 367p. — *Bibliographies*

LAND TENURE — Taiwan

Land-to-the-tiller. — [Taipei : Joint Commission on Rural Reconstruction, 1955]. — 12p

LAND TENURE — Taiwan — Kinmen

LIN, Si-dang
Land reform on Kinmen / by Lin Si-dang and Lin Li. — Taipei : Chinese-American Joint Commission on Rural Reconstruction, 1958. — [iii],66p

LAND TENURE — Transcaucasia — History

AVALIANI, S. L.
Krest'ianskii vopros v Zakavkaz'e / S. L. Avaliani ; podgotovka k izdaniiu G. N. Margiani ; vstupitel'nye stat'i G. N. Margiani i G. I. Megrelishrili. — Tbilisi : Metsniereba. — *Vols.1-3 published in Odessa, 1912-1914; vol.4 published in Tbilisi, 1920*
T.5 (dopolnitel'nyi). — 1986. — 120p

LAND TITLES — Registration and transfer — England

GREAT BRITAIN. Law Commission
Transfer of land : the rule in Bain v. Fothergill / The Law Commission. — London : H.M.S.O., 1986. — iv,49p. — (Working paper / Law Commission ; no. 98) — *Includes bibliographical references*

LAND USE

BLAIKIE, Piers M.
Land degradation and society / Piers Blaikie and Harold Brookfield ; with contributions by Bryant Allen ... [et al.]. — London : Methuen, 1987. — xxiv,296p. — *Bibliography: p251-284. — Includes index*

LAND USE — Dictionaries — Polyglot

LOGIE, Gordon
Glossary of land resources : English-French-Italian-Dutch-German-Swedish / Gordon Logie. — Amsterdam ; New York : Elsevier, 1984. — xxvii, 303 p.. — (International planning glossaries ; 4). — *Includes indexes. — Bibliography: p. 299-300*

LAND USE — Environmental aspects — Kenya

YEAGER, Rodger
Wildlife, wild death : land use and survival in eastern Africa / Rodger Yeager, Norman N. Miller. — Albany, NY : State University of New York Press in association with the African-Caribbean Institute, 1986. — p. cm. — *Includes index. — Bibliography: p*

LAND USE — Environmental aspects — Tanzania

YEAGER, Rodger
Wildlife, wild death : land use and survival in eastern Africa / Rodger Yeager, Norman N. Miller. — Albany, NY : State University of New York Press in association with the African-Caribbean Institute, 1986. — p. cm. — *Includes index. — Bibliography: p*

LAND USE — Government policy — Great Britain

GREAT BRITAIN. Department of the Environment
The United Kingdom's community land scheme. — [London] : the Department, 1976. — [4]. — (Planning in the United Kingdom). — *Prepared for the United Nations Conference on Human Settlements, 1976, Vancouver*

LAND USE — Planning

Disaster prevention and mitigation : a compendium of current knowledge. — New York : United Nations
V.5: Land use aspects. — 1977. — vii,68p. — *Bibliography: p67-68. — "UNDRO/22/76 VOL.V"*

LAND USE — Planning — Case studies

International handbook on land use planning / edited by Nicholas N. Patricios. — Westport, Conn. : Greenwood Press, c1986. — p. cm. — *Includes index. — Bibliography: p*

LAND USE — Planning — Dictionaries, Polyglot

LOGIE, Gordon
Glossary of planning and development : English-French-Italian-Dutch-German-Swedish / Gordon Logie. — Amsterdam ; Oxford : Elsevier, 1986. — xxv,254p. — (International planning glossaries ; 5). — *Text in English and various other European languages. — Bibliography: p251-252*

LAND USE — Social aspects — Great Britain

HOLLIDAY, John C.
Land at the centre : choices in a fast changing world / John C. Holliday. — London : Shepheard-Walwyn, 1986. — xiii,241p. — *Includes index*

LAND USE — Barbados — Planning

Physical development plan for Barbados. — [Bridgetown?] : Town and Country Development Planning Office, 1970. — vii,134p

LAND USE — Bermuda

The Bermuda development plan 1983 : planning statement. — Hamilton : Department of Planning, 1983. — 77p

LAND USE — China — History

CHAO, Kang
Man and land in Chinese history : an economic analysis / Kang Chao. — Stanford, Calif. : Stanford University Press, 1986. — xii, 268 p.. — *Includes index. — Bibliography: p. 255-263*

LAND USE — England — Bedfordshire

Land committed for housing development / Bedfordshire. County Council. — Bedford : Bedfordshire County Council, 1984-. — *Annual*

LAND USE — England — Kent

KENT. County Planning Department
Housing land supply in Kent 1985-1991 / [prepared by the County Planning Department on behalf of the Kent Planning Officers Group]. — Maidstone : [the Department], 1986. — [28p]

LAND USE — England — Killingholme (Humberside)
Killingholme: development potential : the final report. — Newcastle upon Tyne : Coopers and Lybrand Associates, 1986. — [216p]

LAND USE — Great Britain
SHOARD, Marion
This land is our land / Marion Shoard. — London : Grafton, 1987. — 592p

LAND USE — Great Britain — Planning
AMBROSE, Peter
Whatever happened to planning? / Peter Ambrose. — London : Methuen, 1986. — [224]p. — *Includes bibliography and index*

RATCLIFFE, John
Land acquisition and disposal / by John Ratcliffe ; ...commissioned and funded by the Social Science Research Council. — Edinburgh : Capital Planning Information, 1982. — 65p. — (SSRC/CPI planning reviews ; no.3)

LAND USE — Greece — History — 19th century
MCGREW, William W.
Land and revolution in modern Greece, 1800-1881 : the transition in the tenure and exploitation of land from Ottoman rule to independence / William W. McGrew. — [Kent, OH] : Kent State University Press, c1985. — xxii, 339 p.. — *Includes index. — Bibliography: p. [306]-333*

LAND USE — Indonesia — History
DONNER, Wolf
Land use and environment in Indonesia / Wolf Donner ; photography by Erika Donner. — London : Published in association with the Institute of Asian Affairs, Hamburg by Hurst, 1987. — xix,368p. — *Bibliography: p336-363. — Include index*

LAND USE — Nepal
JAIN, S. C.
Nepal : the land question / S. C. Jain. — Indore : Profulla Jain for Development Publishers, 1985. — iv,80p

LAND USE — Netherlands
Aag Bijdragen. — Wageningen : Afdeling Agarische Geschiedenis, 1962-. — *Irregular*

LAND USE — Scotland
SINCLAIR, John
A feeling for the land / John Sinclair [and] Berkeley Heppel. — London : BB Communications, 1986. — 119p

LAND USE — South Africa
TATZ, Colin Martin
Shadow and substance in South Africa : a study in land and franchise policies affecting Africans, 1910-1960 / Colin Tatz. — Pietermaritzburg : University of Natal Press, 1962. — vi,238p

LAND USE — Wales — Flintshire
FLINTSHIRE. County Planning Department
Derelict land report. — Mold : [the Department], 1973. — 61p. — *Includes folded maps*

LAND USE — Wales — West Glamorgan
WEST GLAMORGAN. County Council
Our derelict land problem : what are the issues?. — Swansea : [the Council], 1975. — 27p

LAND USE, RURAL
LEICESTER POLYTECHNIC. School of Land and Building Studies. Research Unit
Land for residential development : available or not available? / SLABS Research Unit. — Leicester : School of Land and Building Studies, Leicester Polytechnic, 1984. — iv,55 leaves. — (Housing land in urban areas ; Working paper no.1)

LAND USE, RURAL — Environmental aspects — Developing countries
Lands at risk in the Third World : local-level perspectives / edited by Peter D. Little and Michael M. Horowitz with A. Endre Nyerges ; foreword by Gilbert F. White. — Boulder : Westview Press, 1987. — xiii, 416 p.. — (Monographs in development anthropology). — *Includes bibliographies and index*

LAND USE, RURAL — Appalachian Region
Who owns Appalachia? : landownership and its impact / the Appalachian Land Ownership Task Force ; with an introduction by Charles C. Geisler. — Lexington, Ky. : University Press of Kentucky, c1983. — xxxii, 235 p.. — *Map on lining papers. — Includes bibliographies and index*

LAND USE, RURAL — China — Hunan Province — History
PERDUE, Peter C.
Exhausting the earth : state and peasant in Hunan, 1500-1850 / Peter C. Perdue. — Cambridge, Mass. : Council on East Asian Studies, Harvard University : Distributed by Harvard University Press, 1987. — p. cm. — (Harvard East Asian monographs ; 1987). — *Includes index. — Bibliography: p*

LAND USE, RURAL — Colombia
HELMSING, A. H. J.
Firms, farms, and the state in Colombia : a study of rural, urban, and regional dimensions of change / A.H.J. Helmsing. — Boston : Allen & Unwin, 1986. — xix, 297 p.. — *Includes index. — Bibliography: p. 275-288*

LAND USE, RURAL — England — Bedfordshire
HOWE, Jonathan
Bedfordshire new agricultural landscape project. — [Bedford] : Bedfordshire County Planning Department, 1987. — 36p

LAND USE, RURAL — England — Leicester (Leicestershire) — Case studies
LEICESTER POLYTECHNIC. School of Land and Building Studies. Research Unit
Land for residential development in the Leicester urban area : site specific case studies / SLABS Research Unit. — Leicester : School of Land and Building Studies, Leicester Polytechnic, 1984. — v,97 leaves. — (Housing land in urban areas ; Working paper no.4)

LAND USE, RURAL — Fiji
BROOKFIELD, Harold Chillingworth
Land, cane and coconuts : papers on the rural economy of Fiji / H. C. Brookfield, F. Ellis, R. G. Ward. — Canberra [A.C.T.] : Australian National University, 1985. — 251p. — (Australian National University Department of Human Geography Publication ; HG/17). — *Includes bibliographies*

LAND USE, RURAL — France
Valeur et rentabilité des biens fonciers agricoles / [par Jean-Jacques Malpot [et al.]]. — [Paris] : La Documentation française, 1985. — 162p. — (Documents du Centre dÉtude des Revenus et des Coûts ; no.74)

LAND USE, RURAL — Great Britain
The Future of the British rural landscape / edited by Douglas Lockhart and Brian Ilbery. — Norwich : Geo, 1987. — xiv,223p. — *Includes bibliographies*

LAND USE, RURAL — Ireland — Congresses
The future of the Irish rural landscape : papers presented at a conference organised by the Dept. of Geography, Trinity College, Dublin and the Irish Planning Institute held at Trinity College, Dublin, 19th March 1985 / edited by F.H.A. Aalen. — Dublin : Trinity College, 1985. — iv,201p

LAND USE, RURAL — Southern States
HEALY, Robert G
Competition for land in the American South : agriculture, human settlement, and the environment / Robert G. Healy. — Washington, D.C. : Conservation Foundation, c1985. — xxxii, 333 p.. — *Includes bibliographies and index*

LAND USE, RURAL — Wales — West Glamorgan
WEST GLAMORGAN. County Council
Our countryside : what are the issues?. — Swansea : [the Council], 1975. — 31p

LAND USE, URBAN
Location theory / Jean Jaskold Gabszewicz ... [et al.]. — Chur, Switzerland ; New York : Harwood Academic Publishers, c1986. — vii, 190 p.. — (Fundamentals of pure and applied economics ; v. 5Regional and urban economics section). — *Includes bibliographies and index*

THRALL, Grant Ian
Land use and urban form : the consumption theory of land rent / Grant Ian Thrall. — New York ; London : Methuen, 1987. — xvi,239p. — *Bibliography: p233-236. — Includes index*

LAND USE, URBAN — England — London
COUNTER INFORMATION SERVICES
London's recurrent crisis. — 2nd ed. — [London] : Counter Information Services, 1973. — 45 leaves

HARINGEY TOWN PLANNING SERVICE
Industrial land needs study : policy background paper. — Haringey : Haringey Town Planning Service, 1986. — 12p. — (Planning working note / Haringey Town Planning Service ; 16)

LONDON STRATEGIC POLICY UNIT. Planning Policy Group
Land for industry : the need for industrial land in London until 1990. — London : [the Group], 1987. — 28p. — *Bibliography: p28*

LAND USE, URBAN — Great Britain
GREAT BRITAIN. Department of the Environment
Management of publicly-owned land in urban areas. — [London : the Department, 1976]. — 10 leaves. — *National report: United Kingdom, prepared for the eleventh meeting of the Group on the Urban Environment, Paris, 22nd-25th November, 1976*

HARVEY, J.
Urban land economics : the economics of real property / Jack Harvey. — Fully rev. 2nd ed. — Basingstoke : Macmillan Education, 1987. — xiv,408p. — *Previous ed: published as Economics of real property. 1981. — Bibliography: p387-391. — Includes index*

LAND VALUE TAXATION — England — History
Land and property : the English land tax 1692-1832 / edited by Michael Turner and Dennis Mills. — Gloucester : Alan Sutton, 1986. — xiii,239p. — *Includes index*

LAND VALUE TAXATION — France
Valeur et rentabilité des biens fonciers agricoles / [par Jean-Jacques Malpot [et al.]]. — [Paris] : La Documentation française, 1985. — 162p. — (Documents du Centre dÉtude des Revenus et des Coûts ; no.74)

LANDER, J. R. — Bibliography
Aspects of late medieval government and society : essays presented to J.R. Lander / edited by J. G. Rowe. — Toronto ; London : published in association with the University of Western Ontario by University of Toronto Press, 1986. — xx,276p

LANDFORMS
SELBY, M. J.
Earth's changing surface : an introduction to geomorphology / M.J. Selby. — Oxford : Clarendon, 1985. — [xxvii,480]p. — *Includes bibliography and index*

LANDLORD AND TENANT — Great Britain

LUBA, Jan
Repairs : Tenant's rights / Jan Luba. — London : Legal Action Group, 1986. — xxxii,127p. — (Law and Practice Guide ; No.12)

LANDLORD AND TENANT — England

GREAT BRITAIN. Law Commission
Landlord and tenant : compensation for tenants' improvements / The Law Commission. — London : H.M.S.O., 1987. — iv,104p. — (Working paper / Law Commission ; no.102)

LANDLORD AND TENANT — England — London

GREATER LONDON COUNCIL
'They who pay the piper...' : evidence submitted by the Greater London Council to the Committee of Inquiry into the Management of Privately Owned Blocks of Flats. — [London] : the Council, 1984. — 27p

GREATER LONDON COUNCIL. Controller of Housing and Technical Services
Relationship breakdown : the implications for local authority tenancies and the impact of the 1980 Housing Act / report by Controller of Housing and Technical Services. — [London : the Council], 1985. — 12 leaves

TUCKLEY, Will
Relationship breakdown and local authority tenancies / survey designed and carried out by Jill Barelli and Lesley Roberts; survey analysed and report written by Will Tuckley, Policy Division, GLC Housing Department. — [London] : Greater London Council, [1985]. — ii,23p. — *Bibliographical references: p19. — A GLC survey of London housing authorities' policies toward relationship breakdown among tenants in local authority housing*

LANDLORD AND TENANT — Great Britain

GREAT BRITAIN. Parliament. House of Commons. Library. Research Division
Landlord and Tenant (No.2) Bill [Bill 98 of session 1986/87] / Oonagh Gay. — [London] : the Division, 1987. — 26p. — (Reference sheet ; no.87/1). — *Bibliographical references: p24-26*

MINFORD, Patrick
The housing morass : regulation, immobility and unemployment : an economic analysis of the consequences of government regulation, with proposals to restore the market in rented housing / Patrick Minford, Michael Peel and Paul Ashton. — London : Institute of Economic Affairs, 1987. — 162p. — (Hobart paperback ; 25). — *Bibliography: p157-162*

PROPHET, John
Fair rents : a practical guide to the law relating to the rents of residential tenancies including the work of rent officers, rent assessment committees and rent tribunals / by John Prophet. — 3rd ed. — London : Shaw and Sons, 1985. — xxxi,243p

LANDLORD AND TENANT — Northern Ireland

DOWLING, J.A.
Ejectment for non-payment of rent / by J. A. Dowling ; with a supplement for the Republic of Ireland by G. McCormack. — Belfast : Faculty of Law, the Queen's University of Belfast, 1986. — xvii,84p

LANDLORD AND TENANT (NO.2) BILL 1986-87

GREAT BRITAIN. Parliament. House of Commons. Library. Research Division
Landlord and Tenant (No.2) Bill [Bill 98 of session 1986/87] / Oonagh Gay. — [London] : the Division, 1987. — 26p. — (Reference sheet ; no.87/1). — *Bibliographical references: p24-26*

LANDOWNERS — Mexico — History — Congresses

Haciendas in central Mexico from late colonial times to the revolution : labour conditions, hacienda management, and its relation to the state / R. Buve, ed. — Amsterdam : Centre for Latin American Research and Documentation, 1984. — 307 p.. — (CEDLA incidentele publicaties ; 28). — *Text in English and Spanish. — Contributions from the International Conference of "The Hacienda in Mexican History," held on 10 May 1982 in Amsterdam, organized by the Interunivrsity Centre for Study and Documentation of Latin America. — Includes bibliographies*

LANDSCAPE

Landscape meanings and values / edited by Edmund C. Penning-Rowsell, and David Lowenthal. — London : Allen & Unwin, 1986. — [160]p. — *Conference proceedings. — Includes bibliography and index*

LANDSCAPE — Ireland — Congresses

The future of the Irish rural landscape : papers presented at a conference organised by the Dept. of Geography, Trinity College, Dublin and the Irish Planning Institute held at Trinity College, Dublin, 19th March 1985 / edited by F.H.A. Aalen. — Dublin : Trinity College, 1985. — iv,201p

LANDSCAPE ARCHITECTURE — History — 19th century

RELPH, Edward
The modern urban landscape / Edward Relph. — London : Croom Helm, c1987. — 279p. — *Bibliography: p268-273. — Includes index*

LANDSCAPE ARCHITECTURE — History — 20th century

RELPH, Edward
The modern urban landscape / Edward Relph. — London : Croom Helm, c1987. — 279p. — *Bibliography: p268-273. — Includes index*

LANDSCAPE PROTECTION — Great Britain

MACEWEN, Ann
Greenprints for the countryside? : the story of Britain's national parks / Ann and Malcolm MacEwen. — London : Allen & Unwin, 1987. — [224]p. — *Includes bibliography and index*

LANGE, OSKAR

ZARĘBA, Janusz
Reforma w testamencie : rzecz o Oskarze Langem / Janusz Zaręba. — Warszawa : Młodziezowa Agencja Wydawnicza, 1985. — 230p

LANGUAGE

GREENE, Judith
Language understanding : a cognitive approach / Judith Greene. — Milton Keynes : Open University, 1986. — 158p. — (Open guides to psychology). — *Includes index. — Bibliography: p.153-155*

LANGUAGE ACQUISITION

CORRÊA, Letícia Maria Sicuro
On the comprehension of relative clauses : a developmental study with reference to Portuguese / Letícia Maria Sicuro Corrêa. — 291 leaves. — *PhD (Arts) 1986 LSE*

GARDNER, R. C.
Social psychology and second language learning : the role of attitudes and motivation / R.C. Gardner. — London : Edward Arnold, 1985. — [256]p. — (The Social psychology of language ; 4). — *Includes index*

Language socialization across cultures / edited by Bambi B. Schieffelin and Elinor Ochs. — Cambridge : Cambridge University Press, 1986. — 1v.. — (Studies in the social and cultural foundations of language ; 3). — *Includes index*

LEE, David
Language, children, and society : an introduction to linguistics and language development / David Lee. — New York, N.Y. : New York University Press, 1986. — p. cm. — *Includes index. — Bibliography: p*

NELSON, Katherine
Making sense : the acquisition of shared meaning / Katherine Nelson. — Orlando [Fla.] : Academic Press, 1985. — p. cm. — *Includes index*

Social and functional approaches to language and thought / edited by Maya Hickmann ; with a foreword by Jerome Bruner. — Orlando : Academic Press, 1987. — p. cm. — *Includes index*

LANGUAGE ACQUISITION — Congresses

INTERNATIONAL CONGRESS FOR THE STUDY OF CHILD LANGUAGE ((2nd : 1981 : Vancouver, B.C.)
Proceedings of the Second International Congress for the Study of Child Language. — Washington, D.C. : University Press of America
Vol.1 / edited by Carolyn Echols Johnson, Carol Larson Thew. — c1982. — ix, 604p. — *Includes bibliographies*

LANGUAGE AND CULTURE

Cultural models in language and thought / edited by Dorothy Holland, Naomi Quinn. — Cambridge : Cambridge University Press, 1987. — xii,400p

LANGUAGE AND CULTURE — Mali

CALAME-GRIAULE, Geneviève
[Ethnologie et langage. English]. Words and the Dogon world / Geneviève Calame-Griaule ; translated from the French by Deirdre LaPin. — Philadelphia : Institute for the Study of Human Issues, 1985. — p. cm. — (Translations in folklore studies). — *Translation of: Ethnologie et language. — Bibliography: p*

LANGUAGE AND EDUCATION

Language and education in multilingual settings / edited by Bernard Spolsky. — Clevedon : Multilingual Matters, 1986. — vii,200p. — (Multilingual matters ; 25)

LANGUAGE AND LANGUAGES

CHOMSKY, Noam
Knowledge of language : its nature, origins, and use / Noam Chomsky. — New York : Praeger, 1985. — xxix, 307p. — (Convergence). — *Includes index. — Bibliography: p.288-296*

Doing cross-national research. — Birmingham : Aston Modern Languages Club. — (Cross-national research papers). — *Bibliographies*
3: Language and culture in cross-national research / edited by Linda Hantrais [and] Steen Mangen. — 1987. — x,62p

LANGUAGE AND LANGUAGES — Study and teaching

GARDNER, R. C.
Social psychology and second language learning : the role of attitudes and motivation / R.C. Gardner. — London : Edward Arnold, 1985. — [256]p. — (The Social psychology of language ; 4). — *Includes index*

LANGUAGE AND LANGUAGES — Study and teaching — Congresses

Foreign languages and international trade : a global perspective / edited by Samia I. Spencer. — Athens : University of Georgia Press, c1987. — xxiv, 255 p.. — *Collection of papers derived from an international symposium held in the spring of 1983, sponsored by the Committee for the Humanities in Alabama and Auburn University. — Includes bibliographies*

LANGUAGE AND LANGUAGES — Study and teaching — United States

MÜLLER, Kurt E
Language competence : implications for national security / Kurt E. Müller. — New York : Published with the Center for Strategic and International Studies, Georgetown University, Washington, D.C. by Praeger, 1986. — p. cm. — (The Washington papers ; 119). — *Bibliography: p*

LANGUAGE AND LANGUAGES — Vocational guidance — Congresses
Foreign languages and international trade : a global perspective / edited by Samia I. Spencer. — Athens : University of Georgia Press, c1987. — xxiv, 255 p.. — *Collection of papers derived from an international symposium held in the spring of 1983, sponsored by the Committee for the Humanities in Alabama and Auburn University. — Includes bibliographies*

LANGUAGE AWARENESS
INTERNATIONAL CONGRESS FOR THE STUDY OF CHILD LANGUAGE (2nd : 1981 : Vancouver)
Proceedings of the Second International Congress for the Study of Child Language. — Lanham ; London : University Press of America
Vol.2 / edited by Carol Larson Thew, Carolyn Echols Johnson. — c1984. — viii,520p. — *Includes bibliographies*

LANGUAGE PLANNING
Language and education in multilingual settings / edited by Bernard Spolsky. — Clevedon : Multilingual Matters, 1986. — vii,200p. — (Multilingual matters ; 25)

LANGUAGE PLANNING — Wales
COUNCIL FOR THE WELSH LANGUAGE
Dyfodol i'r iaith Gymraeg = A future for the Welsh language : adroddiad i'r Gwir Anrhydeddus John Morris Q.C., A.S., Ysgrifennydd Gwladol Cymru = a report to the Right Hon. John Morris Q.C., M.P., Secretary of State for Wales / Cyngor yr Iaith Gymraeg = Council for the Welsh Language. — Caerdydd [i.e. Cardiff] : H.M.S.O., 1978. — vii,78p. — *Parallel Welsh and English text*

LANGUAGE POLICY
Language and education in multilingual settings / edited by Bernard Spolsky. — Clevedon : Multilingual Matters, 1986. — vii,200p. — (Multilingual matters ; 25)

LANGUAGE POLICY — India
EKBOTE, Gopalrao
A nation without a national language / by Gopalrao Ekbote. — Hyderabad : Hindi Prachar Sabha, 1984. — 258 p.. — *Bibliography: p. [256]-258*

LANGUAGE POLICY — Manitoba — History
DOERN, Russell
The battle over bilingualism : the Manitoba language question 1983-1985 / Russell Deorn. — Winnipeg : Cambridge Publishers, 1985. — 227p

LANGUAGE, TRUTH AND LOGIC
Fact, science and morality : essays on A.J. Ayer's Language, truth and logic / edited by Graham Macdonald and Crispin Wright. — Oxford : Basil Blackwell, 1986. — 314p. — *Includes bibliographies and index*

LANGUAGES — Philosophy
DEVITT, Michael
Language and reality : an introduction to the philosophy of language / Michael Devitt and Kim Sterelny. — Oxford : Basil Blackwell, 1987. — xii,274p. — *Bibliography: p256-267. — Includes index*

Language and politics / edited by Michael J. Shapiro. — New York : New York University Press, 1984. — 261p. — (Readings in social and political theory)

LOAR, Brian
Mind and meaning / Brian Loar. — Cambridge : Cambridge University Press, 1981. — xi,268p. — (Cambridge studies in philosophy). — *Bibliography: p261-263. — Includes index*

MÁRKUS, György
Language and production : a critique of the paradigms / by Gyorgy Markus. — Dordrecht ; Boston : D. Reidel Pub. Co. ; Hingham, MA, U.S.A. : Kluwer Academic Publishers [distributor], c1986. — p. cm. — (Boston studies in the philosophy of science ; v. 96). — *Includes indexes. — Bibliography: p*

QUINE, W. V
Word and object / W. V. Quine. — [Cambridge] : Technology Press of the Massachusetts Institute of Technology, [1960]. — 294 p. — (Studies in communication). — *Includes bibliographies*

LANGUAGES — Political aspects
Language and politics / edited by Michael J. Shapiro. — New York : New York University Press, 1984. — 261p. — (Readings in social and political theory)

LAPONCE, J. A.
Languages and their territories / J. A. Laponce ; translated from the French by Anthony Martin-Sperry. — Toronto : University of Toronto Press, 1987. — x,265p. — *Bibliography: p[211]-249*

LANHEZES (PORTUGAL) — Population — History
BRETTELL, Caroline
Men who migrate, women who wait : population and history in a Portuguese parish / Caroline B. Brettell. — Princeton, N.J. : Princeton University Press, c1986. — xv, 329 p., [8] p. of plates. — *Includes index. — Bibliography: p. [299]-319*

LANZ VON LIEBENFELS, JÖRG
DAIM, Wilfried
Der Mann, der Hitler die Ideen gab : die sektiererischen Grundlagen des Nationalsozialismus / Wilfried Daim. — 2e, erw. und verb. Aufl. — Wien : Hermann Böhlau, 1985. — 316p. — (Böhlaus zeitgeschichtliche Bibliothek ; Bd.4). — *First published 1958*

LAOS — History — 1975-
STUART-FOX, Martin
Laos : politics, economics and society / Martin Stuart-Fox. — London : Pinter, 1986. — xxiv,220p. — (Marxist regimes series). — *Bibliography: p205-209. — Includes index*

LAOS — Politics and government
STUART-FOX, Martin
Laos : politics, economics and society / Martin Stuart-Fox. — London : Pinter, 1986. — xxiv,220p. — (Marxist regimes series). — *Bibliography: p205-209. — Includes index*

LAPLACE TRANSFORMATION
SPIEGEL, Murray R.
Schaum's outline of theory and problems of Laplace transforms / by Murray R. Spiegel. — New York : Schaum, [1965]. — 261 p

LAPPS — Norway
Indigenous peoples and the nation-state : 'fourth world' politics in Canada, Australia, and Norway / edited by Noel Dyck. — St. John's, Nfld., Canada : Institute of Social and Economic Research, Memorial University of Newfoundland, c1985. — 263 p.. — (Social and economic papers ; no. 14). — *Bibliography: 242-259*

LARKIN, J.
O'RIORDAN, Manus
Larkinism in perspective : from communism to evolutionary socialism / Manus O'Riordan. — Dublin : Labour History Workshop, 1983. — 20 leaves

LARVIK (NORWAY) — Industries
KROHN-HOLM, Jan W.
Farriskildene i Larvik gjennem 150 år / Jan W. Krohn-Holm. — Larvik : Utgitt av Farris, 1971. — 165p

LASSALLE, FERDINAND — Biography
FRIEDERICI, Hans Jürgen
Ferinand Lassalle : eine politische Biographie / Hans Jürgen Friederici. — Berlin : Dietz, 1985. — 240p

LATCHKEY CHILDREN — United States
GROLLMAN, Earl A
The working parent dilemma : how to balance the responsibilities of children and careers / Earl A. Grollman and Gerri L. Sweder. — 1st ed. — Boston : Beacon Press, 1986. — xv, 190 p.. — *Includes index. — Bibliography: p. 181-185*

LATENT VARIABLES
BARTHOLOMEW, David J.
Latent variable models and factor analysis / D.J. Bartholomew. — London : Griffin, 1987. — x,193p. — (Monograph ; no.40). — *Bibliography: p178-187. — Includes index*

LATIN AMERICA
South America, Central America and the Caribbean: survey and directory of the countries of the region. — London : Europa Publications, 1986-. — *Annual*

LATIN AMERICA — Appropriations and expenditures
PFEFFERMANN, Guy P.
Public expenditure in Latin America : effects on poverty / Guy Pfeffermann. — Washington, D.C. : The World Bank, 1987. — 38p. — (World Bank discussion papers ; no.5). — *Includes bibliographical references*

LATIN AMERICA — Armed Forces — Addresses, essays, lectures
The Latin American military institution / edited by Robert Wesson. — New York : Praeger, 1986. — xiii, 234p. — *"Published with the support of the Hoover Institution, Stamford University, Stamford, California" - t.p.. — Includes bibliographical notes and index*

LATIN AMERICA — Armed Forces — Appropriations and expenditures
LOONEY, Robert E
The political economy of Latin American defense expenditures : case studies of Venezuela and Argentina / Robert E. Looney. — Lexington, Mass. : Lexington Books, c1986. — xxii, 325 p.. — *Includes index. — Bibliography: p. [309]-314*

LATIN AMERICA — Armed Forces — Political activity
BLACK, Jan Knippers
Sentinels of empire : United States and Latin American militarism / Jan Knippers Black. — Westport, Conn. : Greenwood Press, 1986. — xix, 240p. — (Contributions in political science ; no. 144). — *Includes index. — Bibliography: p.[221]-236*

LATIN AMERICA — Armed Forces — Political activity — History — 20th century
Armies and politics in Latin America / edited by Abraham F. Lowenthal and J. Samuel Fitch. — Rev. ed. — New York : Holmes & Meier Publishers, 1986. — p. cm. — *Includes index. — Bibliography: p*

LATIN AMERICA — Census — Handbooks, manuals, etc
GOYER, Doreen S.
The handbook of national population censuses : Latin America and the Caribbean, North America, and Oceania / Doreen S. Goyer and Eliane Domschke. — Westport, Conn. : Greenwood Press, 1983. — xii, 711 p.. — *Includes index. — Bibliography: p. 28-30*

LATIN AMERICA — Church history — Addresses, essays, lectures
Religion and political conflict in Latin America / edited by Daniel H. Levine. — Chapel Hill : University of North Carolina Press, c1986. — xiii, 266p. — *Includes index. — Bibliography: p.257-260*

LATIN AMERICA — Civilization

RANGEL, Carlos
[Del buen salvaje al buen revolucionario. English]. The Latin Americans : their love-hate relationship with the United States / Carlos Rangel. — Rev. ed. with a new introduction by the author. — New Brunswick, N.J. (U.S.A.) : Transaction Books, c1987. — p. cm. — *Includes bibliographical references and index*

LATIN AMERICA — Civilization — 1948- — Congresses

INSTITUTO DE COOPERACIÓN IBEROAMERICANA. Encuentro (1983 : Madrid)
Iberoamérica : Encuentro en la democracia. — Madrid : Cultura Hispánica, c1983. — 516p

LATIN AMERICA — Commerce

Commodity export prospects of Latin America / Inter-American Development Bank. — Washington, D.C. : Inter-American Development Bank, 1986-. — *Annual*

INSTITUTE FOR LATIN AMERICAN INTEGRATION
El proceso de integración en América Latina en 1984. — [Buenos Aires] : the Institute : Banco Interamericano de Desarrollo, [1985]. — xi,418p

LATIN AMERICA — Commerce — Bibliography

Business information sources of Latin America and the Caribbean. — Washington, D.C. : Organization of American States, General Secretariat, Columbus Memorial Library, 1982. — v, 60 p.. — (Documentation and information series ; no. 5). — *"Compiled by Ellen G. Schaffer"--P. v. — "OEA/SG/0.1/IV/III.5."*

LATIN AMERICA — Commerce — Information services

Business information sources of Latin America and the Caribbean. — Washington, D.C. : Organization of American States, General Secretariat, Columbus Memorial Library, 1982. — v, 60 p.. — (Documentation and information series ; no. 5). — *"Compiled by Ellen G. Schaffer"--P. v. — "OEA/SG/0.1/IV/III.5."*

LATIN AMERICA — Commerce — Spain

ALONSO, Jose A.
Efectos de la adhesión de España a la CEE sobre las exportaciones de Iberoamerica / Jose A. Alonso, Vicente Donoso. — Madrid : Ediciones Cultura Hispanica, 1983. — 316p. — *Bibliography: p305-310*

ALONSO, Jose Antonio
La empresa exportadora español frente a Iberoamerica y la CEE / Jose Antonio Alonso, Vicente Donoso. — Madrid : Ediciones Cultura Hispanica del Instituto de Cooperación Iberoamericana, 1985. — xiii,263p. — *Bibliography: p193-199*

LATIN AMERICA — Commercial policy

BALASSA, Bela A
Toward renewed economic growth in Latin America / Bela Balassa ... [et al.]. — Washington, DC : Institute for International Economics, 1986. — p. cm. — *Bibliography: p*

Economic reform and stabilization in Latin America / edited by Michael Connolly, Claudio González-Vega. — New York : Praeger, [1987]. — xxiii, 348 p.. — *"Second Dominican Republic Conference on Trade and Financial Liberalization in Latin America held in Santo Domingo, March 22-24, 1985"--P. iii. — Includes bibliographies*

LATIN AMERICA — Congresses

CANADIAN ASSOCIATION FOR LATIN AMERICAN AND CARIBBEAN STUDIES. Conference (1983 : Ottawa)
Latin America and the Caribbean : geopolitics, development and culture : conference proceedings / edited by Arch R. M. Ritter. — Ottawa : CALACS, 1984. — viii,355p. — *Includes chapters in French and Spanish. — Conference cosponsored by the Ontario Cooperative Program for Latin American and Caribbean Studies*

LATIN AMERICA — Defenses

LOONEY, Robert E
The political economy of Latin American defense expenditures : case studies of Venezuela and Argentina / Robert E. Looney. — Lexington, Mass. : Lexington Books, c1986. — xxii, 325 p.. — *Includes index. — Bibliography: p. [309]-314*

LATIN AMERICA — Dependency on foreign countries — Addresses, essays, lectures

Promise of development : theories of change in Latin America / edited by Peter F. Klarén and Thomas J. Bossert. — Boulder, Colo. : Westview Press, 1986. — xiii, 350p. — *Includes index. — Includes bibliographical references*

LATIN AMERICA — Description and travel — Bibliography

WELCH, Thomas L
Travel accounts and descriptions of Latin America and the Caribbean, 1800-1920 : a selected bibliography / compiled by Thomas L. Welch and Myriam Figueras ; with a foreword by Val T. McComie. — Washington, D.C. : Columbus Memorial Library, Organization of American States, 1982. — v, 293 p.. — (Documentation and information series ; no. 6). — *"OEA/SG/0.1/IV/III.6"--Half t.p. — Includes index*

LATIN AMERICA — Economic conditions

FURTADO, Celso
Economic development of Latin America : historical background and contemporary problems / Celso Furtado ; translated [from the Portuguese] by Suzette Macedo. — 2nd ed. — Cambridge : Cambridge University Press, 1976. — xviii,317p. — (Cambridge Latin American studies ; 8). — *Translation of: 'Formação econômica da América Latina'. 2.ed. Rio de Janeiro : Lia, 1970. - Previous English ed.: 1970. — Bibliography: p.305-312. — Includes index*

GRIFFITH-JONES, Stephany
Debt and development crises in Latin America : the end of an illusion / Stephany Griffith-Jones and Osvaldo Sunkel. — Oxford : Clarendon, 1986. — xii,201p. — *Includes index*

Latin American debt and the adjustment crisis / edited by Rosemary Thorp and Laurence Whitehead. — Basingstoke : Macmillan in association with St Antony's College, Oxford, 1987. — xv,359p. — (St Antony's/Macmillan series). — *Includes bibliographies and index*

SZLAJFER, Henryk
Nineteenth century Latin America : two models of capitalism / Henryk Szlajfer. — Warsaw : Polish Academy of Sciences. Center for Studies on Non-European Countries, 1984. — 50p

LATIN AMERICA — Economic conditions — 1945-

BARRETT, Jeffrey W
Impulse to revolution in Latin America / by Jeffrey W. Barrett. — New York : Praeger, 1985. — ix, 357p. — (Praeger special studies)

CHILCOTE, Ronald H
Latin America : capitalist and socialist perspectives of development and underdevelopment / Ronald H. Chilcote and Joel C. Edelstein. — Boulder ; London : Westview Press, 1986. — xv, 175p. — (Latin American perspectives series ; no. 3). — *"This is a complete revision and expansion of our introduction to Latin America : the struggle with dependency and beyond, published in 1974"--Pref. — Includes index. — Bibliography: p.153-164*

Developing Latin America : a modernization perspective / Pradip K. Ghosh, editor ; foreword by Gamani Corea. — Westport, Conn. : Greenwood Press, c1984. — xvi, 416p. — (International development resource books ; no. 19). — *Includes index*

Economic reform and stabilization in Latin America / edited by Michael Connolly, Claudio González-Vega. — New York : Praeger, [1987]. — xxiii, 348 p.. — *"Second Dominican Republic Conference on Trade and Financial Liberalization in Latin America held in Santo Domingo, March 22-24, 1985"--P. iii. — Includes bibliographies*

Economically active population : estimates and projections : 1950-2025 = Evaluations et projections de la population active : 1950-2025 = Estimaciones y proyecciones de la población económicamente activa : 1950-2025. — 3rd ed. — Geneva : International Labour Office
V.3: Latin America. — 1986. — xxvi,132p. — *Introduction and table headings in English, French and Spanish*

Poverty in Latin America : the impact of depression. — Washington, D.C. : The World Bank, 1986. — 25p

Transnacionalización y desarrollo nacional en América Latina / compilador: Luciano Tomassini. — [Buenos Aires] : Grupo Editor Latinoamericano, c1984. — 291p. — (Colección estudios internacionales ; volumen 6)

WIARDA, Howard J.
Latin America at the crossroads : debt, development, and the future / Howard J. Wiarda. — Boulder, Colo. : Westview Press ; Washington, D.C. : American Enterprise Institute for Public Policy Research, 1987. — xiii, 114 p.. — *Includes index. — Bibliography: p. 99-105*

LATIN AMERICA — Economic conditions — 1945- — Addresses, essays, lectures

Promise of development : theories of change in Latin America / edited by Peter F. Klarén and Thomas J. Bossert. — Boulder, Colo. : Westview Press, 1986. — xiii, 350p. — *Includes index. — Includes bibliographical references*

LATIN AMERICA — Economic conditions — 1945- — Bibliography

Business information sources of Latin America and the Caribbean. — Washington, D.C. : Organization of American States, General Secretariat, Columbus Memorial Library, 1982. — v, 60 p.. — (Documentation and information series ; no. 5). — *"Compiled by Ellen G. Schaffer"--P. v. — "OEA/SG/0.1/IV/III.5."*

Developing Latin America : a modernization perspective / Pradip K. Ghosh, editor ; foreword by Gamani Corea. — Westport, Conn. : Greenwood Press, c1984. — xvi, 416p. — (International development resource books ; no. 19). — *Includes index*

LATIN AMERICA — Economic conditions — 1945- — Congresses

INSTITUTO DE COOPERACIÓN IBEROAMERICANA. Encuentro (1983 : Madrid)
Iberoamérica : Encuentro en la democracia. — Madrid : Cultura Hispánica, c1983. — 516p

LATIN AMERICA — Economic conditions — 1945- — Information services

Business information sources of Latin America and the Caribbean. — Washington, D.C. : Organization of American States, General Secretariat, Columbus Memorial Library, 1982. — v, 60 p.. — (Documentation and information series ; no. 5). — "Compiled by Ellen G. Schaffer"--P. v. — "OEA/SG/0.1/IV/III.5."

LATIN AMERICA — Economic integration

INSTITUTE FOR LATIN AMERICAN INTEGRATION
El proceso de integración en América Latina en 1984. — [Buenos Aires] : the Institute : Banco Interamericano de Desarrollo, [1985]. — xi,418p

Regional integration : the Latin American experience / edited by Altaf Gauhar. — London : Third World Foundation, 1985. — [220]p. — Includes index

LATIN AMERICA — Economic policy

BALASSA, Bela A
Toward renewed economic growth in Latin America / Bela Balassa ... [et al.]. — Washington, DC : Institute for International Economics, 1986. — p. cm. — Bibliography: p

Developing Latin America : a modernization perspective / Pradip K. Ghosh, editor ; foreword by Gamani Corea. — Westport, Conn. : Greenwood Press, c1984. — xvi, 416p. — (International development resource books ; no. 19). — Includes index

SLOAN, John W
Public policy in Latin America : a comparative study / John W. Sloan. — Pittsburgh, Pa. : University of Pittsburgh Press, c1984. — xii, 276 p.. — (Pitt Latin American series) (Pitt series in policy and institutional studies). — Includes index. — Bibliography: p. 253-270

LATIN AMERICA — Emigration and immigration

PILDAIN SALAZAR, María Pilar
Ir a América : la emigración vasca a América (Guipúzcoa 1840-1870) / María Pilar Pildain Salazar. — San Sebastián : Donostia, 1984. — xii,245p. — (Monografías / Grupo Doctor Camino de Historia de San Sebastián ; 22). Bibliography: p82-83

LATIN AMERICA — Emigration and immigration — History

MÖRNER, Magnus
Adventurers and proletarians : the story of migrants in Latin America / Magnus Mörner with the collaboration of Harold Sims. — Pittsburgh, PA : University of Pittsburgh Press ; [Paris, France] : Unesco, 1985. — p. cm. — (Pitt Latin American series). — Includes index. — Bibliography: p

LATIN AMERICA — Foreign economic relations — Europe — Bibliography

Trade relations between Latin America and Europe = Les relations commerciales entre l'Amérique Latine et l'Europe. — Geneva : United Nations Library, 1978. — 57p

LATIN AMERICA — Foreign economic relations — United States

CLAYTON, Lawrence A
Grace : W.R. Grace & Co., the formative years, 1850-1930 / Lawrence A. Clayton. — Ottawa, Ill. : Jameson Books, c1985. — xiii, 403 p., [35] p. of plates. — Includes index. — Bibliography: p. 387-394

The United States and Latin America in the 1980s : contending perspectives on a decade of crisis / Kevin J. Middlebrook and Carlos Rico, editors. — Pittsburgh, PA : University of Pittsburgh Press, 1985. — xii, 648p. — (Pitt Latin American series). — Includes index

LATIN AMERICA — Foreign relations — 1948-

Entre la autonomía y la subordinación : política exterior de los países latinoamericanos / compiladores: Heraldo Muñoz y Joseph Tulchin. — Buenos aires : Grupo Editor Latinoamericano, 1984. — 2v. — (Colección Estudios Internacionales)

The Latin American policies of U.S. allies : balancing global interests and regional concerns / edited by William Perry and Peter Wehner. — New York : Praeger, 1985. — xvii, 185p. — Includes bibliographical notes and index

Soviet-Latin American relations in the 1980s / edited by Augusto Varas. — Boulder : Westview Press, 1987. — p. cm. — (Westview special studies on Latin America and the Caribbean)

LATIN AMERICA — Foreign relations — Soviet Union — Congresses

The Red orchestra : instruments of Soviet policy in Latin America and the Caribbean / Dennis L. Bark, editor. — Stanford, Calif. : Hoover Institution Press, Stanford University, c1986. — ix, 139p. — Includes bibliographies and index

LATIN AMERICA — Foreign relations — United States

BLACK, Jan Knippers
Sentinels of empire : United States and Latin American militarism / Jan Knippers Black. — Westport, Conn. : Greenwood Press, 1986. — xix, 240p. — (Contributions in political science ; no. 144). — Includes index. — Bibliography: p.[221]-236

BLAISIER, Cole
The hovering giant : U.S. responses to revolutionary change in Latin America / Cole Blasier. — Rev. ed. — Pittsburgh, Pa. : University of Pittsburgh Press, 1985. — xxi, 339 p.. — (Pitt Latin American series). Includes index. — Bibliography: p. 307-334

Cono sur / Facultad Latinoamericana de Ciencias Sociales. — Santiago : Facultad Latinoamericana de Ciencias Sociales, 1987-. 6 per year

Dominant powers and subordinate states : the United States in Latin America and the Soviet Union in Eastern Europe / edited by Jan F. Triska. — Durham, [N.C.] : Duke University Press, 1986. — xi, 504 p.. — (Duke Press policy studies). — Includes index. — Bibliography: p. [471]-498

GILDERHUS, Mark T
Pan American visions : Woodrow Wilson and regional integration in the western hemisphere, 1913-1921 / Mark T. Gilderhus. — Tucson : University of Arizona Press, c1986. — p. cm. — Includes index. — Bibliography: p

KRYZANEK, Michael J
U.S.-Latin American relations / Michael J. Kryzanek. — New York : Praeger, 1985. — xxx, 242p. — Bibliography: p.227-234

Latin American views of U.S. policy / edited by Robert G. Wesson, Heraldo Munoz. — New York : Praeger, 1986. — vii, 153p. — (Praeger special studies)

LOWENTHAL, Abraham F
Partners in conflict, the United States and Latin America / Abraham F. Lowenthal. — Baltimore, Md. : Johns Hopkins University Press, c1987. — xi, 240 p.. — Includes index. — Bibliography: p. 201-235

The United States and Latin America in the 1980s : contending perspectives on a decade of crisis / Kevin J. Middlebrook and Carlos Rico, editors. — Pittsburgh, PA : University of Pittsburgh Press, 1985. — xii, 648p. — (Pitt Latin American series). — Includes index

WIARDA, Howard J.
Population, internal unrest, and U.S. security in Latin America / Howard J. Wiarda and Iêda Siqueira Wiarda. — Amherst : University of Massachusetts at Amherst, 1986. — 50p. — (Program in Latin American studies. Occasional papers series ; no.18)

LATIN AMERICA — History

The Cambridge history of Latin America. — Cambridge : Cambridge University Press Vol.4: c.1870-1930 / edited by Leslie Bethell. — 1986. — [704]p. — Includes bibliographies and index

LATIN AMERICA — History — Archival resources

Guide des sources de l'histoire de l'Amérique latine et des Antilles dans les archives françaises. — Paris : Archives nationales, 1984. — 711p

LATIN AMERICA — History — Wars of Independence, 1806-1830

LYNCH, John
The Spanish American revolutions, 1808-1826 / John Lynch. — 2nd ed. — New York : W.W. Norton, c1986. — p. cm. — (Revolutions in the modern world). — Includes index. — Bibliography: p

LATIN AMERICA — Library resources — England — London

UNIVERSITY OF LONDON. Library Resources Co-ordinating Committee. Latin American Subject Sub-committee
Select guide to Latin American library resources in London. — 3rd ed. — [London] : the Sub-committee, 1985. — 12p

LATIN AMERICA — Manufactures

Technology generation in Latin American manufacturing industries : theory and case-studies concerning its nature, magnitude and consequences / edited by Jorge M. Katz. — Basingstoke : Macmillan, 1987. — x,549p. — Includes index

LATIN AMERICA — Military relations — United States

BLACK, Jan Knippers
Sentinels of empire : United States and Latin American militarism / Jan Knippers Black. — Westport, Conn. : Greenwood Press, 1986. — xix, 240p. — (Contributions in political science ; no. 144). — Includes index. — Bibliography: p.[221]-236

SCHOULTZ, Lars
National security and United States policy toward Latin America / Lars Schoultz. — Princeton, N.J. : Princeton University Press, c1987. — xx, 377 p.. — Includes index. — Bibliography: p. 331-365

LATIN AMERICA — Politics and government

ANGLADE, Christian
Sources of legitimacy in Latin America : the mechanisms of consensus in exclusionary societies / by Christian Anglade. — Colchester : Department of Government University of Essex, 1986. — 53 p. — (Essex papers in politics and government ; no.38)

Cuadernos de nuestra America. — La Habana : Centro de Estudios Sobre America, 1985-. — Semi-annual

DI TELLA, Torcuato S.
Sociología de los procesos políticos : una perspectiva latinoamericana / Torcuato S. Di Tella. — [Buenos Aires] : Grupo Editor Latinoamericano, 1985. — 428p. — (Colección estudios políticos y sociales ; volumen 2). — Bibliography: p[423-428]

RANGEL, Carlos
[Del buen salvaje al buen revolucionario. English]. The Latin Americans : their love-hate relationship with the United States / Carlos Rangel. — Rev. ed. with a new introduction by the author. — New Brunswick, N.J. (U.S.A.) : Transaction Books, c1987. — p. cm. — Includes bibliographical references and index

LATIN AMERICA — Politics and government — To 1830 — Congresses

INSTITUTO INTERNACIONAL DE HISTORIA DEL DERECHO INDIANO. Congreso (6 : [1984] : Valladolid)
Estructuras, gobierno y agentes de la administración en la América española : siglos XVI, XVII y XVIII : trabajos del VI Congreso del Instituto Internacional de Historia del Derecho Indiano en homenaje al Dr. Alfonso Garćia-Gallo. — Valladolid : [Instituto de Cooperación Iberoamericana, Seminario Americanista de la Universidad de Valladolid], 1984. — 533p. — (Serie americanista "Bernal" ; vol.17)

LATIN AMERICA — Politics and government — 1945- — Addresses, essays, lectures

Promise of development : theories of change in Latin America / edited by Peter F. Klarén and Thomas J. Bossert. — Boulder, Colo. : Westview Press, 1986. — xiii, 350p. — *Includes index. — Includes bibliographical references*

LATIN AMERICA — Politics and government — 1948 — Addresses, essays, lectures

Religion and political conflict in Latin America / edited by Daniel H. Levine. — Chapel Hill : University of North Carolina Press, c1986. — xiii, 266p. — *Includes index. — Bibliography: p.257-260*

LATIN AMERICA — Politics and government — 1948-

Armies and politics in Latin America / edited by Abraham F. Lowenthal and J. Samuel Fitch. — Rev. ed. — New York : Holmes & Meier Publishers, 1986. — p. cm. — *Includes index. — Bibliography: p*

BALASSA, Bela A
Toward renewed economic growth in Latin America / Bela Balassa ... [et al.]. — Washington, DC : Institute for International Economics, 1986. — p. cm. — *Bibliography: p*

Latin American political movements / edited by Ciarán Ó Maoláin. — Harlow : Longman, 1985. — [200]p

New social movements and the state in Latin America / David Slater (ed.). — [Amsterdam] : CEDLA ; Cinnaminson, N.J., U.S.A. : Distributed by FORIS Publications USA, c1985. — 295 p. — (Latin American studies ; 29). — *Papers from a CEDLA workshop held in Oct. 1983. — Includes bibliographies. — Contents: Social movements and a recasting of the political / D. Slater -- New social movements and the plurality of the social / E. Laclau -- Identity / T. Evers -- The pathways to encounter / L. Kowarick -- Base communities and urban social movements / N. Vink -- Urban social movements in Latin America / E. Henry -- The Peruvian state and regional crises / D. Slater -- The impact of sendero luminoso on regional and national politics in Peru / V. Gianotten ... [et al.] -- Social movements and revolution / J.L. Coraggio / Mobilisation without emancipation? / M. Molyneux -- Popular movement to "mass organization" / R. Reddock*

SLOAN, John W
Public policy in Latin America : a comparative study / John W. Sloan. — Pittsburgh, Pa. : University of Pittsburgh Press, c1984. — xii, 276 p.. — (Pitt Latin American series) (Pitt series in policy and institutional studies). — *Includes index. — Bibliography: p. 253-270*

WIARDA, Howard J.
Latin America at the crossroads : debt, development, and the future / Howard J. Wiarda. — Boulder, Colo. : Westview Press ; Washington, D.C. : American Enterprise Institute for Public Policy Research, 1987. — xiii, 114 p.. — *Includes index. — Bibliography: p. 99-105*

LATIN AMERICA — Politics and government — 1948- — Bibliography

SNYDER, Frederick E
Latin American society and legal culture : a bibliography / compiled by Frederick E. Synder. — Westport, Conn. ; London : Greenwood Press, 1985. — xiv, 188p. — (Bibliographies and indexes in law and political science ; no. 5). — *Includes index*

LATIN AMERICA — Politics and government — 1948- — Congresses

INSTITUTO DE COOPERACIÓN IBEROAMERICANA. Encuentro (1983 : Madrid)
Iberoamérica : Encuentro en la democracia. — Madrid : Cultura Hispánica, c1983. — 516p

LATIN AMERICA — Politics and government — 1948- — Philosophy

BARRETT, Jeffrey W
Impulse to revolution in Latin America / by Jeffrey W. Barrett. — New York : Praeger, 1985. — ix, 357p. — (Praeger special studies)

LATIN AMERICA — Population

Population growth in Latin America and U.S. national security / edited by John Saunders. — Boston ; London : Allen & Unwin, 1986. — xxvii,305p. — *Includes bibliographies and index*

WIARDA, Howard J.
Population, internal unrest, and U.S. security in Latin America / Howard J. Wiarda and Iêda Siqueira Wiarda. — Amherst : University of Massachusetts at Amherst, 1986. — 50p. — (Program in Latin American studies. Occasional papers series ; no.18)

LATIN AMERICA — Population — Statistics

Economically active population : estimates and projections : 1950-2025 = Evaluations et projections de la population active : 1950-2025 = Estimaciones y proyecciones de la población económicamente activa : 1950-2025. — 3rd ed. — Geneva : International Labour Office V.3: Latin America. — 1986. — xxvi,132p. — *Introduction and table headings in English, French and Spanish*

LATIN AMERICA — Population — Statistics — Methodology

TORRADO, Susana
La familia como unidad de análisis en censos y encuestas de hogares : metodología actual y prospectiva en América Latina / Susana Torrado. — Buenos Aires : Ediciones CEUR, 1983. — xv,277p. — *Bibliography: p271-273*

LATIN AMERICA — Relations — Soviet Union

Soviet-Latin American relations in the 1980s / edited by Augusto Varas. — Boulder : Westview Press, 1987. — p. cm. — (Westview special studies on Latin America and the Caribbean)

LATIN AMERICA — Relations — Spain

The Iberian-Latin American connection : implications for U.S. foreign policy / edited by Howard J. Wiarda. — Boulder, Colo. ; London : Westview Press ; Washington, D.C. : American Enterprise Institute, 1986. — xiii,482p. — (Westview special studies on Latin America and the Caribbean). — *Bibliographical notes*

LATIN AMERICA — Relations — United States

The Iberian-Latin American connection : implications for U.S. foreign policy / edited by Howard J. Wiarda. — Boulder, Colo. ; London : Westview Press ; Washington, D.C. : American Enterprise Institute, 1986. — xiii,482p. — (Westview special studies on Latin America and the Caribbean). — *Bibliographical notes*

RANGEL, Carlos
[Del buen salvaje al buen revolucionario. English]. The Latin Americans : their love-hate relationship with the United States / Carlos Rangel. — Rev. ed. with a new introduction by the author. — New Brunswick, N.J. (U.S.A.) : Transaction Books, c1987. — p. cm. — *Includes bibliographical references and index*

LATIN AMERICA — Social conditions — 1945-

BARRETT, Jeffrey W
Impulse to revolution in Latin America / by Jeffrey W. Barrett. — New York : Praeger, 1985. — ix, 357p. — (Praeger special studies)

CHILCOTE, Ronald H
Latin America : capitalist and socialist perspectives of development and underdevelopment / Ronald H. Chilcote and Joel C. Edelstein. — Boulder ; London : Westview Press, 1986. — xv, 175p. — (Latin American perspectives series ; no. 3). — *"This is a complete revision and expansion of our introduction to Latin America : the struggle with dependency and beyond, published in 1974"--Pref. — Includes index. — Bibliography: p.153-164*

Latin America / edited by Eduardo P. Archetti, Paul Cammack and Bryan Roberts. — Basingstoke : Macmillan Education, 1987. — xxiii,357p. — (Sociology of 'developing societies'). — *Bibliography: p345-355. — Includes index*

New social movements and the state in Latin America / David Slater (ed.). — [Amsterdam] : CEDLA ; Cinnaminson, N.J., U.S.A. : Distributed by FORIS Publications USA, c1985. — 295 p.. — (Latin American studies ; 29). — *Papers from a CEDLA workshop held in Oct. 1983. — Includes bibliographies. — Contents: Social movements and a recasting of the political / D. Slater -- New social movements and the plurality of the social / E. Laclau -- Identity / T. Evers -- The pathways to encounter / L. Kowarick -- Base communities and urban social movements / N. Vink -- Urban social movements in Latin America / E. Henry -- The Peruvian state and regional crises / D. Slater -- The impact of sendero luminoso on regional and national politics in Peru / V. Gianotten ... [et al.] -- Social movements and revolution / J.L. Coraggio / Mobilisation without emancipation? / M. Molyneux -- Popular movement to "mass organization" / R. Reddock*

Poverty in Latin America : the impact of depression. — Washington, D.C. : The World Bank, 1986. — 25p

WIARDA, Howard J.
Latin America at the crossroads : debt, development, and the future / Howard J. Wiarda. — Boulder, Colo. : Westview Press ; Washington, D.C. : American Enterprise Institute for Public Policy Research, 1987. — xiii, 114 p.. — *Includes index. — Bibliography: p. 99-105*

LATIN AMERICA — Social conditions — 1945- — Congresses

INSTITUTO DE COOPERACIÓN IBEROAMERICANA. Encuentro (1983 : Madrid)
Iberoamérica : Encuentro en la democracia. — Madrid : Cultura Hispánica, c1983. — 516p

LATIN AMERICA — Strategic aspects

SCHOULTZ, Lars
National security and United States policy toward Latin America / Lars Schoultz. — Princeton, N.J. : Princeton University Press, c1987. — xx, 377 p.. — *Includes index. — Bibliography: p. 331-365*

LATIN AMERICA — Yearbooks
Jahrbuch Asien - Afrika - Lateinamerika : Bilanz und Chronik des Jahres 1985 / L. Rathmann [hrsg.]. — Berlin : VEB Deutscher Verlag der Wissenschaften, 1986. — 329p. — *Table of contents in German, Russian, English, French and Spanish. — "Im Auftrag des Zentralen Rates für Asien-, Afrika-, und Lateinamerikawissenschaften in der DDR". — Bibliography: p[296]-326*

LATIN AMERICAN — Relations — Spain
SABSAY, Fernando Leónidas
La sociedad argentina : España y el Rió de la Plata / Fernando L. Sabsay. — Buenos Aires : Ediciones Macchi, [1984]. — 288p. — (Colección Ciencas Economicas). — *Bibliography: p[287]-288*

LATVIA — Economic conditions — Statistics
Latvijas PSR tautas saimnieciba / Centrala statistikas parvalde, Latvijas. — Riga : Avots, 1983-. — *Annual*

LAUNDRESSES — England — History
MALCOLMSON, Patricia E.
English laundresses : a social history, 1850-1930 / Patricia E. Malcolmson. — Urbana : University of Illinois Press, c1986. — xv, 220 p.. — (The Working class in European history). — *Includes index. — Bibliography: p. [164]-209*

LAUNDRESSES — England — Social conditions
MALCOLMSON, Patricia E.
English laundresses : a social history, 1850-1930 / Patricia E. Malcolmson. — Urbana : University of Illinois Press, c1986. — xv, 220 p.. — (The Working class in European history). — *Includes index. — Bibliography: p. [164]-209*

LAUNDRY WORKERS — England — History
MALCOLMSON, Patricia E.
English laundresses : a social history, 1850-1930 / Patricia E. Malcolmson. — Urbana : University of Illinois Press, c1986. — xv, 220 p.. — (The Working class in European history). — *Includes index. — Bibliography: p. [164]-209*

LAVAL, PIERRE
WARNER, Geoffrey
Pierre Laval and the eclipse of France / by Geoffrey Warner. — London : Eyre and Spottiswoode, 1968. — 461p

LAW
Denning law journal. — Buckingham : University of Buckingham, 1986

Essays in memory of Professor F.H. Lawson / edited by Peter Wallington, Robert M. Merkin. — London : Butterworths, 1986. — [ix,200]p. — *Includes index*

GOODRICH, Peter
Reading the law : a critical introduction to legal method and techniques / Peter Goodrich. — Oxford : Basil Blackwell, 1986. — ix,229p. — *Includes bibliographies and index*

Osaka University law review. — Osaka : Osaka University. Faculty of law, 1985-. — *Annual*

SINGH, Chhatrapati
Law from anarchy to Utopia : an exposition of the logical, epistemological and ontological foundations of the idea of law, by an inquiry into the nature of legal propositions and the basis of legal authority / Chhatrapati Singh. — Delhi ; Oxford : Oxford University Press, 1986. — xxi,299p. — *Bibliography: p278-292. — Includes index*

LAW — Addresses, essays, lectures
Fiat iustitia : essays in memory of Oliver Deneys Schreiner / edited by Ellison Kahn. — Cape Town : Published for School of Law, University of the Witwatersrand, Johannesburg by Juta, 1983. — xxii,405p. — *Includes bibliographical references*

LAW — Bibliography
Legal research in the United Kingdom 1905-84 : a classified list of legal theses and dissertations successfully completed for postgraduate degrees awarded by universities and polytechnics in the United Kingdom from 1905-1984 / Institute of Advanced Legal Studies. — London : The Institute, [1986]. — xxx, ca. 300p. — *Supersedes: List of legal research topics completed and approved since about 1935. - 2nd ed. - 1961; and, Supplement 1961-July 1966. — Supplemented by: List of current legal research topics. — Includes indexes*

LAW — Congresses
Law and economics and the economics of legal regulation / edited by J.-Matthias Graf v.d. Schulenburg, Göran Skogh. — Dordrecht ; Boston : M. Nijhoff, 1986. — p. cm. — (International studies in economics and econometrics ; 13). — *"Selected papers of a conference of the International Institute of Management Wissenschaftszentum Berlin.". — Includes index. — Contents: Law and economics and the economics of legal regulation / Göran Skogh -- Efficiency, equity, and inalienability / Susan Rose-Ackerman -- Negotiated settlement / Gordon Tullock -- Economic efficiency and the common law / Peter H. Aranson -- Default risk and the optimal pricing of court enforcement services / Hugh Gravelle -- Transaction cost and communincation / Michael Hutter -- Regulatory measures to enforce quality production of self-employed professinals / J.-Matthias Graf v.d. Schulenburg -- Controlling insider trading in Europe and America / David D. Haddock, Jonathan R. Macey -- The regulatin of shop opening hours in the United Kingdom / Susan M. Jaffer, John A. Kay Belgian public policy towards the retailing trade / Roger Van den Bergh -- Assessing the effectiveness of economic efficiency of an E.E.C. pollution control directive / John Ashworth, Ivy Papps, David J. Storey*

LAW — Dictionaries
BESELER, Dora von
Law dictionary : technical dictionary of the Anglo-Americal legal terminology including commercial and political terms : English-German / von Beseler/Jacobs-Wüstefeld. — 4th rev. and enl. ed. / by Barbara Wüstefeld (nee Jacobs). — Berlin ; New York : W. de Gruyter, 1986. — p. cm

DIETL, Clara-Erika
Wörterbuch für Rechts, Wirtschaft und Politik : mit erläuternden und rechtsvergleichenden Kommentaren. — 4., völlig n. bearbeitete und erw. Aufl.. — München : Beck ; New York : Bender
T.1: Englisch-Deutsch: einschliesslich der Besonderheiten des amerikanischen Sprachgebrauchs / von Clara-Erika Dietl, Anneliese A. Moss, Egon Lorenz ; unter Mitarbeit von Wiebke Buxbaum. — 1987. — lxxi,911p. — *English and German text. — Title on added title page : Dictionary of legal, commercial and political terms*

SAMYN, O.
Dictionnaire des terms juridiques / O. Samyn, P. Simonetta, C. Sogno. — Paris : Editions de Vecchi, 1986. — 328p

LAW — Economic aspects
Contract and organization : legal analysis in the light of economic and social theory / edited by Terence Daintith and Gunther Teubner. — Berlin ; New York : W. de Gruyter, 1986. — p. cm. — (Series A--Law =Droit ; 5). — *Includes index. — Bibliography: p*

VELJANOVSKI, Cento G.
The new law-and-economics : a research review / C.G. Veljanovski. — Oxford : Centre for Socio-Legal Studies, 1982. — xi,169p. — *Bibliography: p.144-169*

LAW — Interpretation and construction
AARNIO, Aulis
The rational as reasonable : a treatise on legal justification / Aulis Aarnio. — Dordrecht ; Lancaster : D. Reidel, c1987. — xix, 276p. — (Law and philosophy library). — *Includes index. — Bibliography: p 261-271*

CROSS, Sir Rupert
Statutory interpretation / by the late Sir Rupert Cross. — 2nd ed. / by John Bell and Sir George Engle. — London : Butterworths, 1987. — [200]p. — *Previous ed.: 1976. — Includes index*

LAW — Language
GOODRICH, Peter
Legal discourse : studies in linguistics, rhetoric and legal analysis / Peter Goodrich. — London : Macmillan, 1987. — x,266p. — (Language, discourse, society series). — *Bibliography: p247-258. — Includes index*

WHITE, James Boyd
Heracles' bow : essays on the rhetoric and poetics of law / by James Boyd White. — Madison, Wis. : University of Wisconsin Press, 1985. — p. cm. — (Rhetoric of the human sciences). — *Includes index*

WHITE, James Boyd
The legal imagination / James Boyd White. — Abridged ed. — Chicago : University of Chicago Press, 1985. — p. cm

LAW — Methodology
AARNIO, Aulis
The rational as reasonable : a treatise on legal justification / Aulis Aarnio. — Dordrecht ; Lancaster : D. Reidel, c1987. — xix, 276p. — (Law and philosophy library). — *Includes index. — Bibliography: p 261-271*

Dilemmas of law in the welfare state / edited by Gunther Teubner. — Berlin : W. de Gruyter, 1986. — viii,341p. — (Series A, Law / European University Institute ; 3). — *Includes bibliographies and index*

LAW — Methodology — Addresses, essays, lectures
PERELMAN, Chaïm
Justice, law, and argument : essays on moral and legal reasoning / Ch. Perelman ; with an intod. by Harold J. Berman. — Dordrecht, Holland ; Boston : D. Reidel Pub. Co. ; Hingham, MA : sold and distributed in the U.S.A. and Canada by Kluwer Boston, c1980. — xiii,181p. — (Synthese library ; 142). — *Chapters translated into English by various persons. — Includes bibliographical references and index*

LAW — Methodology — Data processing
INTERNATIONAL CONFERENCE ON "LOGIC, INFORMATICS, LAW" (2nd : 1985 : Florence, Italy)
Automated analysis of legal texts : logic, informatics, law : edited versions of selected papers from the Second International Conference on "Logic, Informatics, Law,"Florence, Italy, September 1985 / edited by Antonio A. Martino, Fiorenza Socci Natali ; editorial assistant, Simona Binazzi. — Amsterdam ; New York : North-Holland ; New York, N.Y., U.S.A. : Sole distributors for the U.S.A. and Canada, Elsevier Science Pub. Co., 1986. — xxii, 938 p.. — *Includes bibliographies and index*

LAW — Philosophy
Authority revisited / edited by J. Roland Pennock and John W. Chapman. — New York : New York University Press, 1987. — xii, 344 p.. — (Nomos ; 29). — *Includes bibliographies and index*

BEYLEVELD, Deryck
Law as a moral judgment / Deryck Beyleveld, Roger Brownsword. — London : Sweet & Maxwell, 1986. — xxix,483p. — *Bibliography: p457-462. — Includes index*

LAW — Philosophy
continuation

BLOCH, Ernst
[Naturrecht und menschliche Würde. English].
Natural law and human dignity / Ernst Bloch ; translated by Dennis J. Schmidt. — Cambridge, Mass. ; London : MIT Press, c1986. — xxx, 323p. — (Studies in contemporary German social thought). — *Translation of: Naturrecht und menschliche Würde. — Includes index*

DWORKIN, Ronald
A matter of principle / Ronald Dworkin. — Cambridge, Mass. ; London : Harvard University Press, 1985. — 425p

GREENAWALT, R. Kent
Conflicts of law and morality / Kent Greenawalt. — New York : Oxford University Press ; Oxford : Clarendon Press, 1987. — xii, 383p. — (Clarendon law series). — *Includes index*

LAPENNA, Ivo
State and law : Soviet and Yugoslav theory. — Athlone P, 1964. — 135p.,23cm. — (Papers in Soviet and East European law, economics and politics ; no. 1)

Liberty, equality, and law : selected Tanner lectures on moral philosophy / John Rawls ... [et al.] ; Sterling M. McMurrin, editor. — Salt Lake City : University of Utah Press, 1987. — x, 205 p.. — *Includes bibliographical references and index. — Contents: The basic liberties and their priority / John Rawls -- Is liberty possible? / Charles Fried -- Equality of what? / Amartya Sen -- Ethics, law, and the exercise of self-command / Thomas C. Schelling*

MACCORMICK, Neil
An institutional theory of law : new approaches to legal positivism / Neil MacCormick and Ota Weinberger. — Dordrecht[Holland] ; Lancaster : Reidel, c1986. — xiv, 229p. — (Law and philosophy library)

PEPERZAK, Adriaan Theodoor
Philosophy and politics : a commentary on the preface to Hegel's Philosophy of right / Adriaan Th. Peperzak. — Dordrecht ; Boston : M. Nijhoff ; Norwell, MA, USA : Distributors for the U.S. and Canada, Kluwer Academic, 1987. — x, 144 p.. — (Archives internationales d'histoire des idées =International archives of the history of ideas ; 113). — *Bibliography: p. [141]-144*

Philosophy and law / edited by Jules Coleman & Ellen Frankel Paul. — Oxford : Basil Blackwell for the Social Philosophy and Policy Center, Bowling Green State University, 1987. — 234p

POSTEMA, Gerald J.
Bentham and the common law tradition / Gerald J. Postema. — Oxford : Clarendon, 1986. — xvi, 490p. — (Clarendon law series). — *Bibliography: p465-476. — Includes indexes*

UNGER, Roberto Mangabeira
The critical legal studies movement / Roberto Mangabeira Unger. — Cambridge, Mass. : Harvard University Press, 1986. — 128 p.. — *Includes index. — Bibliography: p. [121]-122*

VINING, Joseph
The authoritative and the authoritarian / Joseph Vining. — Chicago : University of Chicago Press, 1986. — xiii, 261 p.. — *Includes indexes. — Bibliography: p. 239-242*

WHITE, James Boyd
Heracles' bow : essays on the rhetoric and poetics of law / by James Boyd White. — Madison, Wis. : University of Wisconsin Press, 1985. — p. cm. — (Rhetoric of the human sciences). — *Includes index*

LAW — Philosophy — Addresses, essays, lectures

PERELMAN, Chaïm
Justice, law, and argument : essays on moral and legal reasoning / Ch. Perelman ; with an intod. by Harold J. Berman. — Dordrecht, Holland ; Boston : D. Reidel Pub. Co. ; Hingham, MA : sold and distributed in the U.S.A. and Canada by Kluwer Boston, c1980. — xiii,181p. — (Synthese library ; 142). — *Chapters translated into English by various persons. — Includes bibliographical references and index*

LAW — Philosphy

HONORÉ, Tony
Making law bind : essays legal and philosophical / Tony Honoré. — Oxford : Clarendon, 1987. — [288]p. — *Includes index*

LAW — Quotations

A Dictionary of legal quotations / compiled and edited by Simon James and Chantal Stebbings. — London : Croom Helm, c1987. — [250]p. — *Includes indexes*

LAW — Sociological aspects

REHBINDER, Manfred
Die Begründung der Rechtssoziologie durch Eugen Ehrlich / von Manfred Rehbinder. — 2nd ed. — Berlin : Duncker and Humblot, [1986]. — 147p. — (Schriftenreihe zur Rechtssoziologie und Rechtstatschenforschung ; Bd.6). — *Bibliography: p143-147*

LAW — Study and teaching — Egypt

SULTANIA SCHOOL OF LAW
Syllabus of the course of study. — Cairo : Ministry of Justice, 1919. — [26]p. — *In English and Arabic*

LAW — Study and teaching — England

The Observer book of moots / edited by Paul Dobson and Barry Fitzpatrick. — London : Sweet & Maxwell, 1986. — 123p

LAW — Study and teaching — Great Britain

How to study law / Anthony Bradney ... [et al.]. — London : Sweet & Maxwell, 1986. — 237p

LAW — Study and teaching — Latin America — Bibliography

SNYDER, Frederick E.
Latin-American legal studies : a guide to basic research / Frederick Snyder. — Cambridge, Mass. : Harvard Law School, 1983. — iv,45p

LAW — Afghanistan

KAMALI, Mohammad Hashim
Law in Afghanistan : a study of the Constitutions, matrimonial law and judiciary / by Mohammad Hashim Kamali. — Leiden : E. J. Brill, 1985. — viii,265p. — (Social, economic and political studies of the Middle East ; Vol.36). — *Bibliography: p[254]-259*

LAW — Africa

OCRAN, Tawia Modibo
Law in aid of development : issues in legal theory, institution building, and economic development in Africa / Tawia Modibo Ocran. — Tema, Ghana : Ghana Pub. Corp., 1978. — xii, 247 p.. — *Includes bibliographical references*

LAW — Asia

Asian indigenous law in interaction with received law / edited by Masaji Chiba. — London : KPI, 1986. — xiii,416p

LAW — Canada

GALL, Gerald L
The Canadian legal system / Gerald L. Gall. — 2nd ed. — Toronto : Carswell, 1983. — xxiv, 348 p.. — *"With Chapter 8, The Quebec legal system, by Mr. Justice Paul Reeves of the Quebec Superior Court.". — Includes bibliographical references and index*

LAW — Canada — Public opinion — Congresses

Law in a cynical society? : Opinion and law in the 1980's : papers presented at a conference held in 1982 at the University of Manitoba / edited by Dale Gibson [and] Janet K. Baldwin. — Calgary : Carswell Legal Publications, 1985. — xviii,464p

LAW — Canada, Northern — History and criticism

Law and justice in a new land : essays in Western Canadian legal history / edited by Louis A. Knafla. — Toronto : Carswell, 1986. — xv,379p. — *Based on papers originally presented at the first Western Canadian Legal History Conference, held at the University of Calgary, April 25-27, 1984. — Bibliography: p [333]-354*

LAW — Canada, Western — History and criticism

Law and justice in a new land : essays in Western Canadian legal history / edited by Louis A. Knafla. — Toronto : Carswell, 1986. — xv,379p. — *Based on papers originally presented at the first Western Canadian Legal History Conference, held at the University of Calgary, April 25-27, 1984. — Bibliography: p [333]-354*

LAW — Developing countries

The international law of development : basic documents / compiled and edited by A. Peter Mutharika. — Dobbs Ferry, N.Y. : Oceana Vol.1. — 1978. — x,646p

The international law of development : basic documents / compiled and edited by A. Peter Mutharika. — Dobbs Ferry, N.Y. : Oceana Vol.2. — 1978. — vii,647-1303p

The international law of development : basic documents / compiled and edited by A. Peter Mutharika. — Dobbs Ferry, N.Y. : Oceana Vol.3. — 1979. — vii,1305-1997p

The international law of development : basic documents / compiled and edited by A. Peter Mutharika. — Dobbs Ferry, N.Y. : Oceana Vol.4. — 1979. — vii.1999-2620p

The international law of development : basic documents / compiled and edited by A. Peter Mutharika. — Dobbs Ferry, N.Y. : Oceana Vol.5. — 1985. — xiii,708p

LAW — England

ATIYAH, P. S.
Pragmatism and theory in English law / by P.S. Atiyah. — London : Stevens & Sons under the auspices of the Hamlyn Trust, 1987. — 193p. — (The Hamlyn lectures ; 39). — *Includes index*

EDDEY, K. J.
The English legal system / by Keith J. Eddey. — 4th ed. — London : Sweet & Maxwell, 1987. — xv,196p. — (Concise college texts). — *Previous ed.: 1982. — Bibliography: p189-190. — Includes index*

GIFFORD, Anthony Maurice Gifford, Baron
Where's the justice ? : a manifesto of law reform / Tony Gifford. — Harmondsworth : Penguin, 1986. — 126p. — (A Penguin special)

PICKLES, James
Straight from the bench / James Pickles. — London : Phoenix House, 1987. — [240]p. — *Includes index*

SELDON, Arthur
Law and lawyers in perspective / Arthur Seldon. — Harmondsworth : Penguin, 1987. — 170p

SMITH, Kenneth, 1910-1966
Smith and Keenan's English law. — 8th ed. / Denis Keenan. — London : Pitman, 1986. — [viii,888]p. — *Previous ed.: published as English law. 1982. — Includes index*

LAW — England *continuation*

ZANDER, Michael
Cases and materials on the English legal system / Michael Zander. — 4th ed. — London : Weidenfeld and Nicolson, 1984. — xxx,631p. — (Law in context). — *Previous ed.: 1980. — Bibliography: p.xxviii-xxx. - Includes index*

LAW — England — History

CHAMBERS, Sir Robert, 1737-1803
A course of lectures on the English law : delivered at the University of Oxford, 1767-1773 / by Sir Robert Chambers and composed in association with Samuel Johnson ; edited by Thomas M. Curley. — Oxford : Clarendon Press
Vol.1. — 1986. — xix,483p

CHAMBERS, Sir Robert, 1737-1803
A course of lectures on the English law : delivered at the University of Oxford, 1767-1773 / by Sir Robert Chambers and composed in association with Samuel Johnson ; edited by Thomas M. Curley. — Oxford : Clarendon Press
Vol.2. — 1986. — xv,445p

LAW — England — History and criticism

Lawyers and laymen / edited by T.M. Charles-Edwards, Morfydd E. Owen and D. B. Walters. — Cardiff : University of Wales Press, 1986. — 394,[1]p of plates. — *Includes two papers in Welsh. — Festschrift in honour of Professor Dafydd Jenkins. — Bibliography: p355-368. — Includes index*

LAW — Europe — Bibliography

SYMPOSIUM ON LEGAL DATA PROCESSING IN EUROPE (8th : 1985 : Luxembourg)
Access to legal data bases in Europe : reports presented at the Symposium. — Strasbourg : Council of Europe, 1986. — 226p

LAW — European Communities countries

Thirty years of Community law / Commission of the European Communities. — Luxembourg : Office for Official Publications of the European Communities, 1983. — xxiv,498p. — (The European perspectives series)

LAW — European Economic Community

MANGAS MARTÍN, Araceli
Derecho comunitario europeo y derecho español / Araceli Mangas Martín. — Madrid : Tecnos, 1986. — 302p. — *Bibliography: p [289]-302*

LAW — European Economic Community countries

Basic Community laws / edited by Bernard Rudden and Derrick Wyatt. — 2nd ed. — Oxford : Clarendon, 1986. — xvi,407p.. — *Previous ed.: 1980*

BURROWS, F.
Free movement in European Community law / F. Burrows. — Oxford : Clarendon, 1987. — xxxvii,346p. — *Bibliography: xxxvii — Includes index*

COURT OF JUSTICE OF THE EUROPEAN COMMUNITIES
Digest of case-law relating to the European Communities: A series: judgements of the Courts of Justice of the European Communities excluding cases connected with the European civil service and cases on the Convention of 27 September 1968 on Jurisdiction and the Enforcement of Judgements in Civil and Commercial Matters. — Luxembourg : Office for Official Publications of the European Communities, 1983-

Information on the Court of Justice of the European Communities. — Luxembourg : Information Office, Court of Justice of the European Communities, 1977-1982. — *Quarterly*

Integration through law : Europe and the American federal experience / series under the general editorship of Mauro Cappelletti, Monica Seccombe, Joseph Weiler. — Berlin ; New York : W. de Gruyter, 1985- <1987 >. — < v. 1-3; in 5 >. — (Series A, Law / European University Institute =Series A, Droit / Institut Universitaire Européen ; 2.1- <2.3 >). — *Includes bibliographical references and indexes. — Contents: v. 1. Methods, tools, and institutions. bk. 1. A political, legal, and economic overview. bk. 2. Political organs, integration techniques, and judicial process. bk. 3. Forces and potential for a European identity -- v. 2. Environmental protection policy / by Eckard Rehbinder and Richard Stewart -- v. 3. Consumer law, common markets, and Federalism in Europe and the United States / by Thierry Bourgoignie and David Trubek (with Louise Trubek and Denis Stingl)*

Integration through law : Europe and the American federal experience / under the general editorship of Mauro Cappelletti, Monica Seccombe [and] Joseph Weiler. — Berlin : Walter de Gruyter
Vol. 1: Methods, tools and institutions / edited by Mauro Cappelletti, Monica Seccombe [and] Joseph Weiler
Bk.1: A political, legal and economic overview. — 1986, c1985. — xc,616p. — (Series A. Law ; 2.1.1). — *Bibliographical notes*

Integration through law : Europe and the American federal experience / under the general editorship of Mauro Cappelletti, Monica Seccombe [and] Joseph Weiler. — Berlin : Walter de Gruyter
Vol.3: Consumer law, common markets and federalism in Europe and the United States / by Thierry Bourgoignie and David Trubek ; (with Louise Trubek and Denis Stingl). — 1987, c1986. — xxiii,271p. — (Series A. Law / European University Institute ; 2.3). *Bibliographical references*

MUÑOZ MACHADO, Santiago
El Estado, el derecho interno y la Comunidad Europea / Santiago Muñoz Machado. — Madrid : Editorial Civitas, 1986. — 300p. — *Bibliography: p[291]-300*

Official journal of the European Communities : Directory of Community legislation in force and other acts of the Community institutions / Commission of the European Communities. — Luxembourg : Office for Official Publications of the European Communities, 1984-. — *Annual. — Continues: Register of current community legal instruments. — Published as 2 separate volumes*

Official journal of the European Communities : Directory of Community legislation in force. — Luxembourg : Office for Official Publications of the European Communities, 1984-. — *Published in annual volumes with supplements. — Continues: Register of current community legal instruments*

LAW — European Economic Community Countries

Register of current Community legal instruments. — Luxembourg : Office for Official Publications of the European Communities, 1980-1983. — *Continued by: Official journal of the European Communities: Directory of Community legislation in force*

LAW — European Economic Community countries

Synopsis of case-law: the EEC convention of 27 September 1968 on jurisdiction and the enforcement of judgements in civil and commercial matters. — Luxembourg : Documentation Branch, Court of Justice, 1977. — *Annual. — Continued by: Digest of case-law relating to the European Communities: Series D*

WYATT, Derrick
The substantive law of the EEC / by Derrick Wyatt and Alan Dashwood. — 2nd ed. — London : Sweet & Maxwell, 1987. — [450]p. — *Previous ed.: 1980. — Includes index*

LAW — European Economic Community Countries — Bibliography — Catalogs

LIBRARY
Recent publications on the European Communities received by the Library : supplement. — [Luxembourg : Office for Official Publications of the European Communities]
1985/4: Bibliography on European Community law. — 1985. — 576,18 columns. — *In Community languages*

LAW — Finland — Addresses, essays, lectures

The Finnish legal system / edited by Jaakko Uotila ; translated by Leena Lehto. — 2nd completely rev. ed. — Helsinki : Finnish Lawyers Pub. Co., 1985. — 254p

LAW — Finland — Bibliography

REINIKAINEN, Veikko
Litterature sur le droit finlandais publiée entre 1860 et 1956 en langues française, allemande et anglaise = Die deutsch-, Englisch-, und französischsprachige literatur über finnisches recht von 1860-1956 = English, French and German literature on Finnish law in 1860-1956. — Helsinki : [Eduskunnan Kirjasto], 1957. — 179p. — (Julkaisuja / Eduskunnan Kirjaston ; 2). — *In English, French and German*

LAW — France

Droit international et droit français : étude adoptée par la Section du Rapport et des Etudes du Conseil d'Etat le 25 avril 1985 / [réalisée sous la présidence de M. Jean-Jacques de Bresson]. — Paris : La Documentation française, 1986. — 116p. — (Notes et études documentaires ; no.4803)

Journal Officiel de la République Francaise: Lois et decrets. — Paris : Government Printer, 1937-. — *From 1986 on microfiche. — Several issues weekly. — July 1940-Sept 1944 published in Vichy (Allier). — File includes supplements*

LAW — France — Dictionaries

SAMYN, O.
Dictionnaire des terms juridiques / O. Samyn, P. Simonetta, C. Sogno. — Paris : Editions de Vecchi, 1986. — 328p

LAW — Germany — History

Recht und Unrecht im Nationalsozialismus / herausgegeben von Peter Salje ; mit Beiträgen von Friedrich Dencker...[et al.]. — Münster : Wissenschaftliche Verlagsgesellschaft Regensberg und Biermann, 1985. — 310p

LAW — Germany — History — 20th century

RABOFSKY, Eduard
Verborgene Wurzeln der NS-Justiz : strafrechtliche Rüstung für zwei Weltkriege / Eduard Rabofsky [und] Gerhard Oberkofler. — Wien : Europa Verlag, 1985. — 261p. — *Bibliography: p251-[262]*

LAW — Germany (West) — Bibliography

LANSKY, Ralph
Grundliteratur Recht : Bundesrepublik Deutschland : eine Auswahlbibliographie = Basic literature on law : Federal Republic of Germany : a selective bibliography / Ralph Lansky. — 3rd rev. ed. — München : J. Schweitzer, 1984. — xvii,172p. — *Previous ed.: 1978. — Includes index*

LAW — Great Britain

Is it in force: a guide to the commencement of statutes passed / prepared by Butterworths. — London : Butterworths. — *Annual*

LEWIS, Charles J.
State and diplomatic immunity / by Charles J. Lewis. — 2nd ed. — London : Lloyd's of London, 1985. — [xxvi,250]p. — *Previous ed.: 1980. — Includes index*

The road to reform : thoughts for a third term / edited by Christopher Frazer. — London : Conservative Political Centre, 1987. — 52p

LAW — Greece — Athens
GARNER, Richard
Law & society in classical Athens / Richard Garner. — London : Croom Helm, c1987. — viii,161p. — *Bibliography: p145-151.* — *Includes index*

LAW — India — Public opinion
INDRAYAN, N. K
Law and public opinion in India / N.K. Indrayan. — New Delhi : Deep & Deep Publications, c1985. — 311 p.. — *Includes index.* — *Bibliography: p. [302]-308*

LAW — Korea (South)
Business laws in Korea : investment, taxation, and industrial property / Chan-jin Kim, editor. — Seoul, Korea : Panmun Book Co., 1982. — xii, 799 p.. — *Includes bibliographical references*

LAW — Latin America — Bibliography
SNYDER, Frederick E.
Latin-American legal studies : a guide to basic research / Frederick Snyder. — Cambridge, Mass. : Harvard Law School, 1983. — iv,45p

SNYDER, Frederick E
Latin American society and legal culture : a bibliography / compiled by Frederick E. Synder. — Westport, Conn. ; London : Greenwood Press, 1985. — xiv, 188p. — (Bibliographies and indexes in law and political science ; no. 5). — *Includes index*

LAW — Netherlands
De delegatiebepalingen in het wetsontwerp venootschapsbelasting 1960 : Stenografisch verslag van de lezing, gehouden door de Heer Dr. D. Brüll, en het hierop gevolgde debat in de vergadering van 20 februari 1965 = Rapport inzake het ontwerpsuccessiewet 1964, uitgebracht door de commissie voor de successiebelasting : Stenografisch verslag van het debat over dit rapport in de vergadering van 20 februari 1965. — Alphen aan den Rijn : Samsom, 1965. — 51p. — (Geschriften van de Vereniging voor Belastingswetenschap ; nr.114)

JEUKENS, H. J. M.
Recht en politiek : enige aantekeningen bij een advies van de Hoge Raad / H. J. M. Jeukens. — Alphen aan den Rijn : Samsom, 1971. — 23p. — *Rede uitgesproken bij de drieënveertigste herdenking van de dies natalis van de Katholieke Hogeschool ite Tilburg op vrijdag 20 november 1970*

NETHERLANDS. Ministerie van Justitie. Wetenschappelijk Onderzoek-en Dokumentatie Centrum
Constitution, justice. — [The Hague : Research and Documentation Centre, Ministry of Justice, 1986?]. — 66p. — *Contents: State administration, justice.* — *Reprint of 1972 edition*

LAW — Netherlands — Addresses, essays, lectures
Sociology of law and legal anthropology in the Dutch speaking countries / J. van Houtte, editor. — Dordrecht ; Boston : M. Nijhoff Publishers, 1985. — p. cm. — (Nijhoff law specials). — *Bibliography of 'The sociology of law in Dutch-speaking countries': p67-102.* — *Bibliography of 'Current legal anthropology in the Netherlands': p149-162*

LAW — Russian S.F.S.R. — Moscow
MOSCOW (R.S.F.S.R). Sovet deputatov trudiashchikhsia
Sobranie postanovlenii i rasporiazhenii Moskovskogo Soveta Rabochikh i Krasnoarmeiskikh Deputatov, Nos.1-46 : (1 May 1918-30 September 1919). — Moskva : Izd. Iuridicheskogo Otdela, 1918-1919. — (Rare printed material relating to Moscow, 1887-1923)

LAW — Scotland — Dictionaries
The Laws of Scotland : Stair memorial encyclopaedia. — Edinburgh : Law Society of Scotland. — *Includes index*
Vol.1. — 1986. — [650]p

LAW — South Africa
HUND, John
Legal ideology and politics in South Africa : a social science approach / by John Hund and Hendrik W. van der Merwe. — 1st ed. — Lanham, MD : University Press of America ; Rondebosch, South Africa : Centre for Intergroup Studies, c1986. — 132 p.. — *Includes index.* — *Bibliography: p. 122-126*

LAW — South Africa — Addresses, essays, lectures
Fiat iustitia : essays in memory of Oliver Deneys Schreiner / edited by Ellison Kahn. — Cape Town : Published for School of Law, University of the Witwatersrand, Johannesburg by Juta, 1983. — xxii,405p. — *Includes bibliographical references*

LAW — Soviet Union
LAPENNA, Ivo
State and law : Soviet and Yugoslav theory. — Athlone P, 1964. — 135p.,23cm. — (Papers in Soviet and East European law, economics and politics ; no. 1)

Opublikovanie normativnykh aktov / otv. redaktor A. S. Pigolkin. — Moskva : Iuridicheskaia literatura, 1978. — 167p

RUSSIA (RSFSR)
[Laws, etc (1920-1921)]. Dekrety sovetskoi vlasti. — Moskva : Politzdat
t.12: Dekabr´ 1920g.- ianvar´ 1921g.. — 1986. — 427p

Soviet law and economy / edited by Olimpiad S. Ioffe and Mark W. Janis. — Dordrecht : Martinus Nijhoff, 1987. — xii,335p. — (Law in Eastern Europe ; no.32)

LAW — Spain
MANGAS MARTÍN, Araceli
Derecho comunitario europeo y derecho español / Araceli Mangas Martín. — Madrid : Tecnos, 1986. — 302p. — *Bibliography: p [289]-302*

LAW — Spain — Autonomous communities
MUÑOZ MACHADO, Santiago
Derecho publico de las comunidades autonomas / Santiago Muñoz Machado. — Madrid : Editorial Civitas
1. — 1982. — 634p

MUÑOZ MACHADO, Santiago
Derecho publico de las comunidades autonomas / Santiago Muñoz Machado. — Madrid : Editorial Civitas
2. — 1982. — 471p

El sistema juridico de las comunidades autonomas / Eliseo Aja...[et al.]. — Madrid : Tecnos, 1985. — 476p. — *Bibliograhies*

VANDELLI, Luciano
El ordenamiento español de las comunidades autónomas / Luciano Vandelli ; prologo de Eduardo García de Enterria ; traducción española; Fernando Lopez Ramón, Pablo Lucas Murillo de la Cueva. — Madrid : Instituto de Estudios de Administración Local, 1982. — 431p. — *Bibliography: p415-431*

LAW — Spain — History and criticism
TUSELL GOMEZ, Javier
La derecha española contemporánea : sus orígenes: el maurismo / Javier Tusell, Juan Avilés. — Madrid : Espasa Calpe, 1986. — 376p. — *Bibliography: p371-376*

LAW — Sparta (Ancient city)
MACDOWELL, D. M.
Spartan law / by Douglas M. MacDowell. — Edinburgh : Scottish Academic, c1986. — xiii,182p. — (Scottish classical studies ; 1). — *Bibliography: pix-xiii.* — *Includes index*

LAW — Sri Lanka — Language
COORAY, L. J. M
Changing the language of the law : the Sri Lanka experience / L. J. Mark Cooray. — Québec : Presses de l'Université Laval, 1985. — 183p. — (Travaux du Centre international de recherche sur le bilinguisme ; A-20)

LAW — United States
Integration through law : Europe and the American federal experience / series under the general editorship of Mauro Cappelletti, Monica Seccombe, Joseph Weiler. — Berlin ; New York : W. de Gruyter, 1985-<1987 >. — < v. 1-3; in 5 > . — (Series A, Law / European University Institute =Series A, Droit / Institut Universitaire Européen ; 2.1-<2.3 >). — *Includes bibliographical references and indexes.* — *Contents: v. 1. Methods, tools, and institutions. bk. 1. A political, legal, and economic overview. bk. 2. Political organs, integration techniques, and judicial process. bk. 3. Forces and potential for a European identity -- v. 2. Environmental protection policy / by Eckard Rehbinder and Richard Stewart -- v. 3. Consumer law, common markets, and Federalism in Europe and the United States / by Thierry Bourgoignie and David Trubek (with Louise Trubek and Denis Stingl)*

Integration through law : Europe and the American federal experience / under the general editorship of Mauro Cappelletti, Monica Seccombe [and] Joseph Weiler. — Berlin : Walter de Gruyter
Vol. 1: Methods, tools and institutions / edited by Mauro Cappelletti, Monica Seccombe [and] Joseph Weiler
Bk.1: A political, legal and economic overview. — 1986, c1985. — xc,616p. — (Series A. Law ; 2.1.1). — *Bibliographical notes*

Integration through law : Europe and the American federal experience / under the general editorship of Mauro Cappelletti, Monica Seccombe [and] Joseph Weiler. — Berlin : Walter de Gruyter
Vol.3: Consumer law, common markets and federalism in Europe and the United States / by Thierry Bourgoignie and David Trubek ; (with Louise Trubek and Denis Stingl). — 1987, c1986. — xxiii,271p. — (Series A. Law / European University Institute ; 2.3). — *Bibliographical references*

POSNER, Richard A.
Economic analysis of law. — 3rd ed. — Boston : Little, Brown and Company, c1986. — xxi,666p

SCHEINGOLD, Stuart A
The politics of rights : lawyers, public policy, and political change / Stuart A. Scheingold. — New Haven : Yale University Press, 1974. — xiv, 224 p.. — *Includes bibliographical references and index*

LAW — United States — Methodology
NAGEL, Stuart S.
Law, policy, and optimizing analysis / Stuart S. Nagel. — New York : Quorum Books, 1986. — xix, 328 p.. — *Includes indexes.* — *Bibliography: p. [313]-320*

LAW — Wales — History and criticism
Lawyers and laymen / edited by T.M. Charles-Edwards, Morfydd E. Owen and D. B. Walters. — Cardiff : University of Wales Press, 1986. — 394,[1]p of plates. — *Includes two papers in Welsh.* — *Festschrift in honour of Professor Dafydd Jenkins.* — *Bibliography: p355-368.* — *Includes index*

LAW — Yemen
AMIN, S. H.
Law and justice in contemporary Yemen : the People's Democratic Republic of Yemen and the Yemen Arab Republic by S.H. Amin. — Glasgow : Royston, 1987. — v,159p. — *Bibliography: p129-140.* — *Includes index*

LAW — Yugoslavia
LAPENNA, Ivo
State and law : Soviet and Yugoslav theory. — Athlone P, 1964. — 135p.,23cm. — (Papers in Soviet and East European law, economics and politics ; no. 1)

LAW — Zambia
Law in Zambia / Muna Ndulo, ed. — Nairobi, Kenya : East African Pub. House, 1984. — 308 p.. — *Includes bibliographies*

LAW AND ETHICS

GREENAWALT, R. Kent
Conflicts of law and morality / Kent Greenawalt. — New York : Oxford University Press ; Oxford : Clarendon Press, 1987. — xii, 383p. — (Clarendon law series). — *Includes index*

LEE, Simon, 19---
Law and morals : Warnock, Gillick and beyond / Simon Lee. — Oxford : Oxford University Press, 1986. — [144]p. — *Includes bibliography and index*

Liberty, equality, and law : selected Tanner lectures on moral philosophy / John Rawls ... [et al.] ; Sterling M. McMurrin, editor. — Salt Lake City : University of Utah Press, 1987. — x, 205 p.. — *Includes bibliographical references and index*. — Contents: The basic liberties and their priority / John Rawls -- Is liberty possible? / Charles Fried -- Equality of what? / Amartya Sen -- Ethics, law, and the exercise of self-command / Thomas C. Schelling

VEATCH, Henry B.
Human rights : fact or fancy? / Henry B. Veatch. — Baton Rouge : Louisiana State University Press, c1985. — xi, 258p. — *Includes index.* — *Bibliography: p.251-253*

LAW AND ETHICS — Addresses, essays, lectures

PERELMAN, Chaïm
Justice, law, and argument : essays on moral and legal reasoning / Ch. Perelman ; with an intod. by Harold J. Berman. — Dordrecht, Holland ; Boston : D. Reidel Pub. Co. ; Hingham, MA : sold and distributed in the U.S.A. and Canada by Kluwer Boston, c1980. — xiii,181p. — (Synthese library ; 142). — *Chapters translated into English by various persons.* — *Includes bibliographical references and index*

WARNOCK, Mary
Morality and the law : some problems / by Baroness Warnock. — [Cardiff] : University College Cardiff, 1986. — 16 p. — *"The third Lord Morris Memorial Lecture delivered at Cardiff on 21st November 1986 ..."*

LAW AND POLITICS

DAMAŠKA, Mirjan R.
The faces of justice and state authority : a comparative approach to the legal process / Mirjan R. Damaška. — New Haven : Yale University Press, c1986. — xi, 247 p.. — *Includes bibliographical references and index*

DWORKIN, Ronald
A matter of principle / Ronald Dworkin. — Cambridge, Mass. ; London : Harvard University Press, 1985. — 425p

HUND, John
Legal ideology and politics in South Africa : a social science approach / by John Hund and Hendrik W. van der Merwe. — 1st ed. — Lanham, MD : University Press of America ; Rondebosch, South Africa : Centre for Intergroup Studies, c1986. — 132 p.. — *Includes index.* — *Bibliography: p. 122-126*

JEUKENS, H. J. M.
Recht en politiek : enige aantekeningen bij een advies van de Hoge Raad / H. J. M. Jeukens. — Alphen aan den Rijn : Samsom, 1971. — 23p. — *Rede uitgesproken bij de drieënveertigste herdenking van de dies natalis van de Katholieke Hogeschool ite Tilburg op vrijdag 20 november 1970*

Law and politics : readings in legal and political thought / edited with introduction and essay by Shadia B. Drury ; associate editor Rainer Knopff. — Calgary : Detselig Enterprises, c1980. — 270p. — *Bibliography: p [267]-270*

Public law and politics / edited by Carol Harlow. — London : Sweet & Maxwell, 1986. — [250]p. — *Includes index*

SCHEINGOLD, Stuart A
The politics of rights : lawyers, public policy, and political change / Stuart A. Scheingold. — New Haven : Yale University Press, 1974. — xiv, 224 p.. — *Includes bibliographical references and index*

LAW AND SOCIALISM

LAPENNA, Ivo
State and law : Soviet and Yugoslav theory. — Athlone P, 1964. — 135p.,23cm. — (Papers in Soviet and East European law, economics and politics ; no. 1)

LAW, ASHANTI

RATTRAY, R. S.
Ashanti law and constitution / R. S. Rattray. — Oxford : Clarendon, 1929. — xx,420p

LAW, CHAGA (AFRICAN PEOPLE)

MOORE, Sally Falk
Social facts and fabrications : "customary" law on Kilimanjaro, 1880-1980 / Sally Falk Moore. — Cambridge : Cambridge University Press, 1986. — xvi,397p. — (The Lewis Henry Morgan Lectures ; 1981). — *Bibliography: p376-384.* — *Includes index*

LAW ENFORCEMENT

International criminal law / edited by M. Cherif Bassiouni. — Dobbs Ferry, N.Y. : Transnational Publishers
Vol.3: Enforcement. — 1987. — xvii,313p

KLOCKARS, Carl B
The idea of police / by Carl Klockars. — Beverly Hills, Calif. : Sage Publications, c1985. — p. cm. — (Law and criminal justice series ; v. 2). — *Includes index*

LAW, GREEK

GARNER, Richard
Law & society in classical Athens / Richard Garner. — London : Croom Helm, c1987. — viii,161p. — *Bibliography: p145-151.* — *Includes index*

LAW LIBRARIES

The law librarian: bulletin of the British and Irish Association of Law Librarians. — London : Published for the British and Irish Association of Law Librarians by Sweet and Maxwell, 1986-. — *3 per year*

Manual of law librarianship : the use and organization of legal literature / edited by Elizabeth M. Moys. — 2nd ed. — Aldershot : Gower, for the British and Irish Association of Law Librarians, c1987. — xxxv,915p. — *Previous ed.: London : Deutsch, 1976.* — *Bibliography: p802-891.* — *Includes index*

LAW LIBRARIES — Great Britain — Directories

Directory of law libraries in the British Isles. — 2nd ed. / edited by Christine Miskin. — [Yeovil] : Legal Library Publishing & Distribution Service for the British and Irish Association of Law Librarians, 1984. — 1v. — *Includes index*

LAW OF THE SEA *See* Maritime law

LAW PUBLISHING — Ireland

Law publishing and legal information : small jurisdictions of the British Isles / edited by William Twining and Jennifer Uglow. — London : Sweet & Maxwell, 1981. — 181p. — *Bibliography: p150-178.* — *Includes index*

LAW PUBLISHING — Isle of Man

Law publishing and legal information : small jurisdictions of the British Isles / edited by William Twining and Jennifer Uglow. — London : Sweet & Maxwell, 1981. — 181p. — *Bibliography: p150-178.* — *Includes index*

LAW PUBLISHING — Scotland

Law publishing and legal information : small jurisdictions of the British Isles / edited by William Twining and Jennifer Uglow. — London : Sweet & Maxwell, 1981. — 181p. — *Bibliography: p150-178.* — *Includes index*

LAW REFORM — Australia

HURLBURT, William H.
Law reform commissions in the United Kingdom, Australia and Canada / by William H. Hurlburt. — Edmonton : Juriliber, c1986. — vii,514p. — *Bibliography: p.498-514*

LAW REFORM — Canada

HURLBURT, William H.
Law reform commissions in the United Kingdom, Australia and Canada / by William H. Hurlburt. — Edmonton : Juriliber, c1986. — vii,514p. — *Bibliography: p.498-514*

LAW REFORM — Great Britain

HURLBURT, William H.
Law reform commissions in the United Kingdom, Australia and Canada / by William H. Hurlburt. — Edmonton : Juriliber, c1986. — vii,514p. — *Bibliography: p.498-514*

LAW REFORM — New Zealand

ROBSON, J. L.
Sacred cows and rogue elephants : policy development in the New Zealand Justice Department / J. L. Robson. — Wellington : Government Printing Office, 1987. — xii,296p. — *Bibliographical references: p[285]-292*

LAW REFORM — Northern Ireland — History

GREER, S. C.
Abolishing the Diplock courts : the case for restoring jury trial to scheduled offences in Northern Ireland / S.C. Greer, A. White. — London : Cobden Trust, c1986. — x,133p. — *Includes index*

LAW REPORTS, DIGESTS, ETC. — England — History

PORT, Sir John
The notebook of Sir John Port / edited for the Selden Society by J. H. Baker. — London : Selden Society, 1986. — lvii,217p. — (Publications of the Selden Society ; 102)

LAW REPORTS, DIGESTS, ETC. — Soviet Union

UNION OF SOVIET SOCIALIST REPUBLICS. Verkhovnyi sud
Sbornik postanovlenii Plenuma i opredelenii Kollegii Verkhovnogo suda SSSR po ugolovnym delam, 1971-1979 / [sostaviteli: E. A. Smolentsev (otv. redaktor)...et al.]. — Moskva : Izd-vo "Izvestiia Sovetov narodnykh deputatov SSSR, 1981. — 992p

LAW TEACHERS — United States — Biography

SMITH, Donald L.
Zechariah Chafee, Jr., defender of liberty and law / Donald L. Smith. — Cambridge, Mass. : Harvard University Press, 1986. — x, 355 p.. — *Includes index.* — *Bibliography: p. [283]-343*

LAWYERS — Brazil — Biography

LACOMBE, Américo Jacobina
À sombra de Rui Barbosa / Américo Jacobina Lacombe. — [São Paulo] : Companhia Editora Nacional ; [Brasília : Instituto Nacional do Livro, MEC, 1978]. — x,226p. — (Brasiliana ; volume 365)

LAWYERS — Denmark

Advokaterhvervet : struktur, tasker og indtjening. — København : Monopoltilsynet, 1982. — 47p

LAWYERS — Denmark — Fees

Advokaterhvervet : struktur, tasker og indtjening. — København : Monopoltilsynet, 1982. — 47p

LAWYERS — England

REEVES, Peter, 19---
Are two legal professions necessary? / Peter Reeves. — London : Waterlow, 1986. — xiii,175p. — (Legal and social policy library). — *Bibliography: p145-171.* — *Includes index*

LAWYERS — England — History — 16th century

PREST, Wilfrid R.
The rise of the barristers : a social history of the English bar, 1590-1640 / Wilfrid R. Prest. — Oxford : Clarendon, 1986. — [xii,440]p. — Includes index

LAWYERS — England — History — 17th century

PREST, Wilfrid R.
The rise of the barristers : a social history of the English bar, 1590-1640 / Wilfrid R. Prest. — Oxford : Clarendon, 1986. — [xii,440]p. — Includes index

LAWYERS — Great Britain — Directories

Hazell's guide to the judiciary and the courts. With, The Holborn Law Society's list of barristers by chambers. — 1986. — Henley-on-Thames : Hazell & Co., 1986. — 314p

LAWYERS — Ireland — Biography

Daniel O'Connell : portrait of a radical / edited by Kevin B. Nowlan and Maurice R. O'Connell. — Belfast : Appletree Press, 1984. — 120p. — (The Thomas Davis lectures)

LAWYERS — Mississippi — Biography

MAY, Robert E
John A. Quitman : Old South crusader / Robert E. May. — Baton Rouge : Louisiana State University Press, c1985. — p. cm. — (Southern biography series). — Includes index. — Bibliography: p

LAWYERS — United States

SCHEINGOLD, Stuart A
The politics of rights : lawyers, public policy, and political change / Stuart A. Scheingold. — New Haven : Yale University Press, 1974. — xiv, 224 p.. — Includes bibliographical references and index

LAWYERS — United States — History — Addresses, essays, lectures

Professions and professional ideologies in America / edited by Gerald L. Geison. — Chapel Hill : University of North Carolina Press, c1983. — x, 147 p.. — Includes bibliographical references and index

LAY JUDGES — United States

PROVINE, Doris Marie
Judging credentials : nonlawyer judges and the politics of professionalism / Doris Marie Provine. — Chicago : University of Chicago Press, 1986. — xvii, 248 p.. — Includes index. — Bibliography: p. 201-240

LAYOFF SYSTEMS — Case studies

Workforce reductions in undertakings : policies and measures for the protection of redundant workers in seven industrialised market economy countries / edited by Edward Yemin. — Geneva : International Labour Office, 1982. — 214p

LAYOFF SYSTEMS — England — Stoke-on-Trent (Staffordshire)

Re-employment experiences of redundant Michelin workers / L. Fishman [et al.]. — Keele : University of Keele, 1986. — 187p. — Bibliography: p147-148

LAYTON, WALTER

HUBBACK, David
No ordinary press baron : a life of Walter Layton / David Hubback. — London : Weidenfeld and Nicolson, c1985. — [240]p. — Includes index

LAZARE, BERNARD

WILSON, Nelly
Bernard-Lazare : l'antisémitisme, l'affaire Dreyfus, et la recherche de l'identité juive / Nelly Wilson ; traduit de l'anglais par Christiane et Douglas Gallagher. — Paris : Albin Michel, [1985]. — 461p. — Bibliography: p435-450

LE PEN, JEAN MARIE

BERGERON, Francis
De Le Pen à Le Pen : une histoire des nationaux et des nationalistes sous la Ve République / Francis Bergeron, Philippe Vilgier ; préface de François Brigneau. — Bouère : Dominique Martin Morin, 1985. — 214p. — Bibliography: p204-205

DUMONT, Serge
Le système Le Pen / Serge Dumont, Joseph Lorien, Karl Criton. — Anvers : EPO, 1985. — 336p. — Bibliography: p334-335

LE PEN, JEAN-MARIE

LE PEN, Jean-Marie
La France est de retour. — Paris : Carrere/Michel Lafon, [1985]. — 301p

LEA, HOMER

ANSCHEL, Eugene
Homer Lea, Sun Yat-sen, and the Chinese revolution / by Eugene Anschel. — New York : Praeger, 1984. — xvi, 269 p. — Includes index. — Bibliography: p. 253-262

LEAD — Environmental aspects — Great Britain

HOOPER, Lisa
The regulation of lead levels in petrol / by Lisa Hooper. — Colchester : Department of Government University of Essex, 1987. — 27 p. — (Essex papers in politics and government ; no.36)

LEAD MINES AND MINING — Wales — Cardiganshire — Statistics

BURT, Roger, 1942-
The mines of Cardiganshire : metalliferous and associated minerals 1845-1913 / Roger Burt, Peter Waite, Ray Burnley. — Exeter : Department of Economic History, University of Exeter, in association with the Northern Mine Research Society, [1985]. — xxviii, 92p

LEAD POISONING — Law and legislation — Great Britain

HOOPER, Lisa
The regulation of lead levels in petrol / by Lisa Hooper. — Colchester : Department of Government University of Essex, 1987. — 27 p. — (Essex papers in politics and government ; no.36)

LEADERSHIP

BASS, Bernard M
Leadership and performance beyond expectations / Bernard M. Bass. — New York : Free Press ; London : Collier Macmillan, c1985. — p. cm. — Includes indexes. — Bibliography: p

BURNS, James MacGregor
Leadership / James MacGregor Burns. — New York ; London : Harper & Row, 1979, c1978. — ix, 530p. — (Harper torchbooks)

Charisma, history, and social structure / edited by Ronald M. Glassman and William H. Swatos, Jr. — New York : Greenwood Press, 1986. — viii, 240 p.. — (Contributions in sociology ; no. 58). — Includes index. — Bibliography: p. [223]-232. — Contents: Introduction / Ronald M. Glassman and William H. Swatos, Jr. -- On the interpretation and misinterpretation of the concept of charismatic leadership. Bureaucracy and charisma : a philosophy of history / H.H. Gerth and C. Wright Mills. Reflections on charismatic leadership / Reinhard Bendix. Charisma and modernity : the use and abuse of a concept / Joseph Bensman and Michael Givant. Charisma and illegitimate authority / Richard S. Bell -- Charisma and religion. Charismatic Calvinism : forging a missing link / William H. Swatos, Jr. Hasidism and Moonism : charisma in the counterculture / Alan L. Berger. Against Satan : charisma and tradition in Iran / Michael S. Kimmel and Rahmat Tavakol -- The fate of charisma in the modern world. Manufactured charisma and legitimacy / Ronald M. Glassman. The disenchantment of charisma : on revolution in a rationalized world / William H. Swatos, Jr. Hitler's dictatorial charisma / Arthur Schweitzer. The historic fate of the charisma of r

China's provincial leaders 1949-1985 / editor David S.G. Goodman. — Cardiff : University College Cardiff Press. — (Studies on East Asia) Vol.1: Directory. — 1986. — [xii,298]p. — Includes index

CLEVELAND, Harlan
The knowledge executive : leadership in an information society / by Harlan Cleveland. — 1st ed. — New York : Dutton, c1985. — p. cm . — "A Truman Talley Book.". — Includes index. — Bibliography: p

FINE, Doris R
When leadership fails : desegregation and demoralization in the San Francisco schools / Doris R. Fine. — New Brunswick, U.S.A. : Transaction Books, c1986. — ix, 222 p.. — (Observations in education). — Includes bibliographical references and index

HOLLANDER, Edwin Paul
Leadership dynamics : a practical guide to effective relationships / Edwin P. Hollander. — New York : Free Press, c1978. — xii, 212 p.. — Includes indexes. — Bibliography: p. 185-201

Leaders and followers : challenges for the future / edited by Trudy Heller, Jon Van Til, Louis A. Zurcher. — Greenwich, Conn. : JAI Press, c1986. — xiv, 279 p.. — (Contemporary studies in applied behavioral science ; v. 4). — Includes bibliographies and index

SCHEIN, Edgar H
Organizational culture and leadership : a dynamic view / Edgar H. Schein. — 1st ed. — San Franciso : Jossey-Bass Publishers, c1985. — p. cm. — (A Joint publication in the Jossey-Bass management series and the Jossey-Bass social and behavioral science series) . — Includes index. — Bibliography: p

LEADERSHIP — Addresses, essays, lectures

Human systems development / [edited by] Robert Tannenbaum, Newton Margulies, Fred Massarik, and associates. — 1st ed. — San Francisco : Jossey-Bass Publishers, 1985. — xxxi, 605 p.. — (The Jossey-Bass management series) (The Jossey-Bass social and behavioral science series). — Includes bibliographies and indexes

LEADERSHIP — Congresses

Changing conceptions of leadership / edited by Carl F. Graumann and Serge Moscovici. — New York : Springer-Verlag, c1986. — p. cm. — (Springer series in social psychology). — Based on contributions from symposia held by the Study Group on Historical Change in Social Psychology. — Includes index. — Bibliography: p

LEADERSHIP — History — Congresses

Changing conceptions of leadership / edited by Carl F. Graumann and Serge Moscovici. — New York : Springer-Verlag, c1986. — p. cm. — (Springer series in social psychology). — *Based on contributions from symposia held by the Study Group on Historical Change in Social Psychology*. — *Includes index*. — *Bibliography: p*

LEADERSHIP — India — Case studies

SOOD, Santosh
Trade union leadership in India : a case study / Santoosh Sood. — New Delhi : Deep & Deep, 1984. — 262p. — *Bibliography: p [249]-258*

LEAGUE OF WOMEN VOTERS (U.S.)

FOWLER, Robert Booth
Carrie Catt : feminist politician / Robert Booth Fowler. — Boston : Northeastern University Press, c1986. — xx, 226 p.. — *Includes index*. — *Bibliography: p. 201-218*

LEARNING

Thinking and learning skills / edited by Judith W. Segal, Susan F. Chipman, Robert Glaser. — Hillsdale, N.J. ; London : Erlbaum Volume 1: Relating instruction to research. — 1985. — xii,554p

Thinking and learning skills / edited by Susan F. Chipman, Judith W. Segal, Robert Glaser. — Hillsdale, N.J. ; London : Erlbaum Volume 2: Research and open questions. — 1985. — xii,639p

LEARNING AND SCHOLARSHIP — Data processing

PFAFFENBERGER, Bryan
The scholar's personal computing handbook : a practical guide / Bryan Pfaffenberger. — Boston : Little, Brown, c1986. — xiii, 359 p.. — (The Little, Brown microcomputer bookshelf). — *Includes bibliographies and index*

LEARNING AND SCHOLARSHIP — California — Stanford — Case studies

KATCHADOURIAN, Herant A
Careerism and intellectualism among college students / Herant A. Katchadourian, John Boli ; with the assistance of Nancy Olsen, Raymond F. Bacchetti, Sally Mahoney. — 1st ed. — San Francisco : Jossey-Bass Publishers, 1985. — xxvi, 324 p.. — (The Jossey-Bass higher education series). — *Includes indexes*. — *Bibliography: p. 311-316*

LEARNING AND SCHOLARSHIP — United States — Statistics

RUBIN, Michael Rogers
The knowledge industry in the United States, 1960-1980 / Michael Rogers Rubin and Mary Taylor Huber with Elizabeth Lloyd Taylor. — Princeton, N.J. : Princeton University Press, c1986. — p. cm. — *Includes index*

LEARNING DISABILITIES

BRYAN, Tanis H.
Understanding learning disabilities / Tanis H. Bryan [and] James H. Bryan. — 3rd ed. — Palo Alto, Calif. : Mayfield Publishing Company, 1986. — xii,442p

MCGUINNESS, Diane
When children don't learn : understanding the biology and psychology of learning disabilities / Diane McGuinness. — New York : Basic Books, c1985. — x, 310p. — *Includes index*. — *Bibliography: p.277-295*

LEARNING DISABILITIES — United States — History

CARRIER, James G
Learning disability : social class and the construction of inequality in American education / James G. Carrier. — New York : Greenwood Press, c1986. — xiii, 154 p.. — (Contributions to the study of education ; no. 18). — *Includes index*. — *Bibliography: p. [137]-149*

LEARNING, PSYCHOLOGY OF

Induction : processes of inference, learning, and discovery / John H. Holland ... [et al.]. — Cambridge, Mass. : MIT Press, c1986. — xvi, 385p. — (Computational models of cognition and perception). — *Includes index*. *Bibliography: p.357-372*

JEHU, Derek
Learning theory and social work / Derek Jehu. — London : Routledge and Kegan Paul, 1967. — viii,139p. — *Bibliography: p122-136*. *Includes index*

NATO CONFERENCE ON THE ACQUISITION OF SYMBOLIC SKILLS (1982 : University of Keele)
The acquisition of symbolic skills / [proceedings of a NATO Conference on the Acquisition of Symbolic Skills, held July 5-10, 1982, at the University of Keele, Keele, England] ; edited by Don Rogers and John A. Sloboda. — New York ; London : Published in cooperation with NATO Scientific Affairs Division [by] Plenum, c1983. — xii,623p. — (NATO conference series. III, Human factors ; v.22). — *Includes bibliographies and index*

ROGERS, Carl R
Freedom to learn for the 80's / Carl R. Rogers ; with special contributions by Julie Ann Allender ... [et al.]. — Columbus, Ohio : C.E. Merrill Pub. Co., c1983. — viii, 312 p.. — Rev. ed. of: Freedom to learn. 1969. — *Includes bibliographies and index*

SMITH, Robert M. (Robert McCaughan)
Learning how to learn : applied theory for adults / Robert M. Smith. — Milton Keynes : Open University Press, 1983, c1982 (1984 [printing]). — 200p. — *Originally published: Chicago : Follet, 1982*. — *Bibliography: p183-194*. — *Includes index*

TIZARD, Barbara
Young children learning : talking and thinking at home and at school / Barbara Tizard and Martin Hughes. — London : Fontana, 1984. — 286p

LEARNING, PSYCHOLOGY OF — Congresses

Constraints on learning : limitations and predispositions, based on a conference sponsored by St John's College, Cambridge, England / edited by R.A. Hinde and J. Stevenson-Hinde. — London : Academic Press, 1973. — xv,488p. — *'The conference was held in ... [St John's] College between April 4th and 7th, 1972' - Preface*. — *Includes bibliographies and index*

LEASES — Accounting

Statement of financial accounting standards. — Stanford, Conn. : Financial Accounting Standards Board. — (Financial accounting series)
no.91: Accounting for non refundable fees and costs associated with originating or acquiring loans and initial direct costs of leases: an amendment of FASB Statements No.13, 60, and 65 and a rescission of FASB Statement No.17. — 1986. — 49p

LEAST DEVELOPED COUNTRIES *See* Developing countries

LEATHER INDUSTRY AND TRADE — Mexico

MEXICO. Dirección General de Economía Agrícola
El comportamiento de la producción y consumo de cuero de bovino en el país. — [México] : la Dirección, 1982. — 28p

LEBANON — Foreign relations — Near East

NASRALLAH, Fida Bahige
The Lebanese crisis : historical roots and contemporary international forces, 1958-1983 / Fida Bahige Nasrallah. — 407 leaves. — PhD (Econ) 1986 LSE

SAYEGH, Raymond
Les conflits dans les zones de crise : le Proche-Orient et le Liban : essai de polémologie, de géopolitique et de sociologie / Raymond Sayegh. — Cousset, Switzerland : Delval, 1986. — 260p. — *Bibliography: p259-260*

LEBANON — Foreign relations — Syria

WEINBERGER, Naomi Joy
Syrian intervention in Lebanon : the 1975-76 civil war / Naomi Joy Weinberger. — New York : Oxford University Press, 1986. — ix, 367 p.. — *Includes index*. — *Bibliography: p. [339]-348*

LEBANON — History

GREAT BRITAIN. Parliament. House of Commons. Library. International Affairs Section
The Lebanon / Richard Ware. — [London] : the Library, 1983. — 15p. — (Background paper / House of Commons. Library. [Research Division] ; no.127). — *Bibliography: p14*

LEBANON — History — Israeli intervention, 1982-

GREAT BRITAIN. Parliament. House of Commons. Library. International Affairs Section
The Lebanon / Richard Ware. — [London] : the Library, 1983. — 15p. — (Background paper / House of Commons. Library. [Research Division] ; no.127). — *Bibliography: p14*

GREAT BRITAIN. Parliament. House of Commons. Library. International Affairs Section
Middle East peace plans and negotiations / Richard Ware. — [London] : the Library, 1983. — 17p. — (Background paper / House of Commons. Library. [Research Division] ; no.121). — *Bibliography: p13*

LEBANON — History — French occupation, 1918-1946

GORIA, Wade R.
Sovereignty and leadership in Lebanon, 1943-1976 / Wade R. Goria. — London : Ithaca, 1985. — 286p. — *Bibliography: p253-270*. — *Includes index*

LEBANON — History — 1946-

CORM, Georges
Géopolitique du conflit libanais : étude historique et sociologique / Georges Corm. — Paris : Éditions la Découverte, 1986. — 260p

GORIA, Wade R.
Sovereignty and leadership in Lebanon, 1943-1976 / Wade R. Goria. — London : Ithaca, 1985. — 286p. — *Bibliography: p253-270*. — *Includes index*

NASRALLAH, Fida Bahige
The Lebanese crisis : historical roots and contemporary international forces, 1958-1983 / Fida Bahige Nasrallah. — 407 leaves. — PhD (Econ) 1986 LSE

LEBANON — History — Civil War, 1975-1976

WEINBERGER, Naomi Joy
Syrian intervention in Lebanon : the 1975-76 civil war / Naomi Joy Weinberger. — New York : Oxford University Press, 1986. — ix, 367 p.. — *Includes index*. — *Bibliography: p. [339]-348*

LEBANON — History — Israeli intervention, 1982-

KHALIDI, Rashid
Under siege : P.L.O. decisionmaking during the 1982 war / Rashid Khalidi. — New York : Columbia University Press, 1985. — p. cm. — *Includes index*. — *Bibliography: p*

SARASTE, Leena
For Palestine / by Leena Saraste. — London : Zed, 1985. — [96]p. — *Translation of: Rakkaani, Palestiina*. — *Includes bibliography*

LEBANON — Politics and government — 1946-
CORM, Georges
Géopolitique du conflit libanais : étude historique et sociologique / Georges Corm. — Paris : Editions la Découverte, 1986. — 260p

LEBANON — Politics and government — 1975-
EVRON, Yair
War and intervention in Lebanon : the Israeli-Syrian deterrence dialogue / Yair Evron. — London : Croom Helm, 1987. — x,246p. — *Bibliography: p230-236. — Includes index*

LEBANON — History — Israeli intervention, 1982-
INSTITUT FRANÇAIS DE POLÉMOLOGIE
La conflit israélo-arabe. — Paris : La Documentation française. — (Notes et études documentaires ; no.4792)
t 2: 1974-1984. — 1985. — 141p

LEBERGOTT, STANLEY
Quantity & quiddity : essays in U.S. economic history / Peter Kilby, editor ; Jeremy Atack ... [et al.]. — 1st ed. — Middletown, Conn. : Wesleyan University Press ; Scranton, Pa. : Distributed by Harper & Row, c1987. — xxiii, 423 p.. — *Papers presented at a symposium in honor of Stanley Lebergott, Mar. 28th and 29th, 1985. "Selected publications of Stanley Lebergott": p. 399-405. — Includes bibliographical references and index*

LECLERC, EDOUARD
CHAVANE, Laurence
Le phénomène Leclerc : de Landerneau à l'an 2000 / Laurence Chavane. — Paris : Plon, 1986. — 253p

LECLERC, MICHEL-EDOUARD
CHAVANE, Laurence
Le phénomène Leclerc : de Landerneau à l'an 2000 / Laurence Chavane. — Paris : Plon, 1986. — 253p

LECTURES AND LECTURING — United States — History — 19th century — Addresses, essays, lectures
Professions and professional ideologies in America / edited by Gerald L. Geison. — Chapel Hill : University of North Carolina Press, c1983. — x, 147 p.. — *Includes bibliographical references and index*

LEDESMA RAMOS, RAMIRO
LEDESMA RAMOS, Ramiro
Escritos politicos : JONS, 1933-1934 / Ramiro Ledesma Ramos. — Madrid : Trinidad Ledesma Ramos, 1985. — 239,[35]p

LEDESMA RAMOS, Ramiro
Escritos politicos : La Conquista del Estado, 1931 / Ramiro Ledesma Ramos. — Madrid : Trinidad Ledesma Ramos, 1986. — 329p

LEEWARD ISLANDS (SOCIETY ISLANDS) — Population — Statistics
Tableaux normalisés du recensement général de la population : 15 octobre 1983. — [Papeete] : Institut territorial de la statistique
Résultats de la subdivision administrative des Iles Sous le Vent. — [1985?]. — 4p,12 leaves

LEGA NAZIONALE DELLE COOPERATIVE E MUTUE — History
EARLE, John, 1921-
The Italian cooperative movement : a portrait of the Lega Nazionale delle Cooperative e Mutue / John Earle. — London : Allen & Unwin, 1986. — [224]p. — *Includes index*

LEGAL AID — Directories
International directory of legal aid / edited by Judy Lane and Simon Hillyard. — London : International Bar Association : Sweet & Maxwell, 1985. — 244p

LEGAL AID — Handbooks, manuals, etc.
International directory of legal aid / edited by Judy Lane and Simon Hillyard. — London : International Bar Association : Sweet & Maxwell, 1985. — 244p

LEGAL AID — Australia
HARKINS, Joseph P.
Inquiry into Aboriginal legal aid. — Canberra : Australian Government Publishing Service
V.1: General issues / Jodseph P. Harkins. — 1986. — lvii,160p

HARKINS, Joseph P.
Inquiry into Aboriginal legal aid. — Canberra : Australian Government Publishing Service
V.2: Legal aid in the states and territories / Joseph P. Harkins. — 1986. — xii,642p

HARKINS, Joseph P.
Inquiry into Aboriginal legal aid. — Canberra : Australian Government Publishing Service
V.3: Appendixes / Joseph P. Harkins. — 1986. — iii,486p

LEGAL AID — England — Greater Manchester
GENN, Hazel
Meeting legal needs? : an evaluation of a scheme for personal injury victims / Hazel Genn. — Oxford : SSRC Centre for Socio-Legal Studies, 1982. — ix,69p. — *A report commissioned by the Greater Manchester Legal Services Committee*

LEGAL AID — Great Britain
Legal aid : efficiency scrutiny / [report of a scrutiny team to the Lord Chancellor]. — [London] : Lord Chancellor's Department, 1986. — 2v (in 1)

LEGAL AID — Great Britain — Handbooks, manuals, etc.
LAW SOCIETY
Legal aid handbook 1986 / prepared by the Law Society. — 7th ed. — London : HMSO, 1986. — v,460p

LEGAL ASSISTANCE TO CHILDREN — Canada
SAMMON, William J.
Advocacy in child welfare cases : a practitioner's guide / William J. Sammon. — Toronto, Canada : Carswell Co., 1985. — xvii, 191 p.. — *Includes bibliographical references and indexes*

LEGAL COMPOSITION
WHITE, James Boyd
The legal imagination / James Boyd White. — Abridged ed. — Chicago : University of Chicago Press, 1985. — p. cm

LEGAL DEPOSIT (OF BOOKS, ETC.) — Great Britain
PINION, Catherine F.
Legal deposit of non-book materials / Catherine F. Pinion. — London : British Library, 1986. — 1v.. — (Library and information research report ; 49). — *Includes bibliography*

LEGAL POSITIVISM
MACCORMICK, Neil
An institutional theory of law : new approaches to legal positivism / Neil MacCormick and Ota Weinberger. — Dordrecht[Holland] ; Lancaster : Reidel, c1986. — xiv, 229p. — (Law and philosophy library)

LEGAL RESEARCH — Europe — Data processing — Public opinion
LLOYD, Michael Gordon
Legal databases in Europe : user attitudes and supplier strategies / Michael Lloyd. — Amsterdam ; New York : North-Holland ; New York, N.Y., U.S.A. : Sole distributors for the U.S.A. and Canada, Elsevier Science Pub. Co., c1986. — xiii, 218 p.. — *At head of title: Commission of the European Communities. — "Report no. EUR 10439 of the Commission of the European Communities"--T.p. verso. — Bibliography: p.205*

LEGAL RESEARCH — France
SZLADITS, Charles
Guide to foreign legal materials / by Charles Szladits and Claire M. Germain. — 2nd rev. ed. — Dobbs Ferry, N.Y. : Published for the Parker School of Foreign and Comparative Law, Columbia University in the City of New York by Oceana Publications. — (Parker School studies in foreign and comparative law). — *Includes bibliographical references and indexes*
French. — c1985. — xi, 205 p.

LEGAL RESEARCH — Great Britain
Legal research in the United Kingdom 1905-84 : a classified list of legal theses and dissertations successfully completed for postgraduate degrees awarded by universities and polytechnics in the United Kingdom from 1905-1984 / Institute of Advanced Legal Studies. — London : The Institute, [1986]. — xxx, ca. 300p. — *Supersedes: List of legal research topics completed and approved since about 1935. - 2nd ed. - 1961; and, Supplement 1961-July 1966. — Supplemented by: List of current legal research topics. — Includes indexes*

LEGAL SERVICES — Canada — Economic aspects
Lawyers and the consumer interest : regulating the market for legal services / edited by Robert G. Evans, Michael J. Trebilcock. — Toronto ; London : Butterworths, 1982. — xxiii,459p. — (Studies in law and economics ; 2). — *Includes bibliographical references*

LEGAL SERVICES — Great Britain
Public interest law / edited by Jeremy Cooper and Rajeev Dhavan. — Oxford : Basil Blackwell, 1986. — xviii,482p.. — *Includes index*

LEGAL TENDER — Hungary
FELLNER, Frigyes
A valuta rendezése Magyarországon : különös tekintettel a készpénzfizetések megkezdésére / a Magyar Tudományos Akadémia megbízásából írta Fellner Frigyes. — Budapest : Grill Károley Könyvkiadó-vállalat, 1911. — 287p. — (Magyar Közgazdasági Könyvtár ; köt.6)

LEGENDS — Australia — Victoria
MASSOLA, Aldo
Bunjil's cave : myths, legends and superstitions of the aborigines of south-east Australia / Photographs by John Gollings. — [Melbourne] : Lansdowne Press, [1968]. — xvi, 208 p. — *Bibliography: p. [203]-205*

LEGENDS — India — History and criticism
LEBRA-CHAPMAN, Joyce
The Rani of Jhansi : a study in female heroism in India / Joyce Lebra-Chapman. — Honolulu : University of Hawaii Press, c1986. — xii, 199 p., [2] leaves of plates. — *Includes index. — Bibliography: p. [185]-193*

LEGISLATION — Great Britain — History — 16th century
ELTON, G. R.
The Parliament of England, 1559-1581 / G.R. Elton. — Cambridge : Cambridge University Press, 1986. — [411]p. — *Includes index*

LEGISLATION — Great Britain — History — 20th century
VAN MECHELEN, Denis
Patterns of Parliamentary legislation / by Denis Van Mechelen & Richard Rose. — Aldershot : Gower, c1986. — [100]p. — *Bibliography: p97-100*

LEGISLATION — Soviet Union
Opublikovanie normativnykh aktov / otv. redaktor A. S. Pigolkin. — Moskva : Iuridicheskaia literatura, 1978. — 167p

LEGISLATIVE BODIES
Parliaments of the world : a comparative reference compendium. — 2nd ed. / prepared by the International Centre for Parliamentary Documentation of the Inter-Parliamentary Union. — Aldershot : Gower, c1986. — 2v.(1422p). — Previous ed.: published in 1 vol. London : Macmillan, 1976. — Includes index

LEGISLATIVE BODIES — Addresses, essays, lectures
Handbook of legislative research / edited by Gerhard Loewenberg, Samuel C. Patterson, Malcolm E. Jewell. — Cambridge, Mass. : Harvard University Press, 1985. — x, 810 p.. — Includes bibliographies and index

LEGISLATIVE BODIES — Bibliography
INTERNATIONAL CENTRE FOR PARLIAMENTARY DOCUMENTATION
World-wide bibliography on parliaments = Bibliographie des institutions parlementaires dans le monde. — Genève : International Centre for Parliamentary Documentation. — (Reports and documents / Inter-Parliamentary Union ; no.13)
Vol.4: 1983-1985. — 1986. — x,421,viip

LEGISLATIVE BODIES — Great Britain — Reform
DINWIDDY, J. R.
From Luddism to the First Reform Bill : reform in England 1810-1832 / J.R. Dinwiddy. — Oxford : Basil Blackwell, 1986. — [96]p. — (Historical Association studies). — Includes bibliography and index

LEGISLATIVE BODIES — India
INDIA. Parliament. Lok Sabha
Parliament of India : the seventh Lok Sabha 1980-84 : a study. — New Delhi : Lok Sabha Secretariat, 1985. — 221p [31]p of plates

LEGISLATIVE BODIES — India — Privileges and immunities
ARORA, Ranjana
Parliamentary privileges in India : Jawaharlal Nehru to Indira Gandhi / Ranjana Arora. — New Delhi : Deep & Deep Publications, c1986. — 268 p.. — Includes index. — Bibliography: p. [260]-265

LEGISLATIVE BODIES — United States — States — Ethics — Addresses, essays, lectures
Representation and responsibility : exploring legislative ethics / edited by Bruce Jennings and Daniel Callahan. — New York : Plenum Press, 1985. — p. cm. — (Hastings Center series in ethics). — Includes index. — Bibliography: p

LEGISLATIVE OVERSIGHT — India
SURYA PRAKASH
Parliamentary control over public enterprises in India / Surya Prakash. — 1st ed. — Allahabad, India : Chugh Publications, 1985. — 293 p.. — Includes index. — Bibliography: p. [271]-278

LEGISLATIVE POWER — France — History
DERFLER, Leslie
President & Parliament : a short history of the French Presidency / Leslie Derfler. — Boca Raton : University Presses of Florida, c1983. — ix, 286 p.. — "A Florida Atlantic University book.". — Includes index. — Bibliography: p. 273-279

LEGISLATIVE POWER — India
KRISHNAPURAM, R. Mohan
Sovereignty of Parliament in India / R. Mohan Krishnapuram ; foreword by J. M. L. Sinha. — New Delhi : Deep & Deep, 1985. — 214p. — Bibliography: p[211]-212

LEGISLATIVE POWER — United States
MERRY, Henry J
The constitutional system : the group character of the elected institutions / Henry J. Merry. — New York : Praeger, 1986. — x, 215 p.. — Includes bibliographies and index

The President, the Congress, and foreign policy / [foreword by] Edmund S. Muskie, Kenneth Rush ; Kenneth W. Thompson [rapporteur]. — Lanham : University Press of America, c1986. — xv, 311 p.. — "A joint policy project of the Association of Former Members of Congress and the Atlantic Council of the United States. — Includes bibliographies

LEGISLATORS — Addresses, essays, lectures
Handbook of legislative research / edited by Gerhard Loewenberg, Samuel C. Patterson, Malcolm E. Jewell. — Cambridge, Mass. : Harvard University Press, 1985. — x, 810 p.. — Includes bibliographies and index

LEGISLATORS — Canada — Biography
BROCK, Peter Jeffry
William Rees Brock, 1836-1917 : paradise regained : an odyssey in Canadian business / by Peter Jeffry Brock. — Toronto : National Press, 1984. — 382p

JEROME, James
Mr. Speaker / James Jerome. — Toronto, Ont. : McClelland and Stewart, c1985. — 175 p., [8] p. of plates. — Includes index

PICKERSGILL, J. W.
The road back : by a Liberal in opposition / J. W. Pickersgill. — Toronto : University of Toronto Press, 1986. — 320p

LEGISLATORS — France — Lower Normandy
BOIVIN, Michel
Députés de Basse-Normandie : les élections législatives sous la cinquième république / Michel Boivin. — Paris : Paradigme, 1986. — 249p

LEGISLATORS — Great Britain
CAIN, Bruce E
The personal vote : constituency service and electoral independence / Bruce Cain, John Ferejohn, Morris Fiorina. — Cambridge, Mass. : Harvard University Press, 1986. — p. cm. — Includes index. — Bibliography: p

LEGISLATORS — Great Britain — Biography
EDSALL, Nicholas C
Richard Cobden, independent radical / Nicholas C. Edsall. — Cambridge, Mass. ; London : Harvard University Press, 1986. — xiv, 465p. — Includes index. — Bibliography: p.[429]-433

HINDE, Wendy
Richard Cobden : a Victorian outsider : a biography / by Wendy Hinde. — New Haven : Yale University Press, 1987. — p. cm. — Includes index. — Bibliography: p

LEGISLATORS — Great Britain — History
DENTON, Jeffrey H.
Representatives of the lower clergy in Parliament, 1295-1340 / J.H. Denton and J.P. Dooley. — Woodbridge : Boydell, 1987. — [viii,256]p. — (Royal Historical Society studies in history series ; no.50). — At foot of t.p.: Royal Historical Society. — Includes bibliography and index

LEGISLATORS — United States
CAIN, Bruce E
The personal vote : constituency service and electoral independence / Bruce Cain, John Ferejohn, Morris Fiorina. — Cambridge, Mass. : Harvard University Press, 1986. — p. cm. — Includes index. — Bibliography: p

LEGISLATORS — United States — Biography
BROWN, Eugene
J. William Fulbright : advice and dissent / Eugene Brown. — Iowa City : University of Iowa Press, c1985. — x, 171p. — Includes index. — Bibliography: p.153-167

FERRARO, Geraldine
Ferraro, my story / Geraldine A. Ferraro, with Linda Bird Francke. — Toronto ; New York : Bantam Books, 1985. — 340 p., [24] p. of plates. — Includes index

FURGURSON, Ernest B.
Hard right : the rise of Jesse Helms / by Ernest B. Furgurson. — 1st ed. — New York : Norton, c1986. — p. cm

MAY, Robert E
John A. Quitman : Old South crusader / Robert E. May. — Baton Rouge : Louisiana State University Press, c1985. — p. cm. — (Southern biography series). — Includes index. — Bibliography: p

MORGAN, Chester M
Redneck liberal : Theodore G. Bilbo and the New Deal / Chester M. Morgan. — Baton Rouge : Louisiana State University Press, c1985. — p. cm. — Includes index. — Bibliography: p

RICHARDS, Leonard L
The life and times of Congressman John Quincy Adams / Leonard L. Richards. — New York : Oxford University Press, 1986. — viii, 245 p.. — Includes index. — Bibliography: p. 205-238

LEGISLATORS — United States — History — 19th century
SHIELDS, Johanna Nicol
The line of duty : maverick congressmen and the development of American political culture, 1836-1860 / Johanna Nicol Shields. — Westport, Conn. : Greenwood Press, c1985. — p. cm. — (Contributions in American studies ; no. 80). — Includes index. — Bibliography: p

LEGITIMACY OF GOVERNMENTS
CONNOLLY, William E
Politics and ambiguity / William E. Connolly. — Madison, Wis. : University of Wisconsin Press, 1987. — xiii, 168 p.. — (Rhetoric of the human sciences). — Includes bibliographical references and index

LEGITIMACY OF GOVERNMENTS — Asia
PYE, Lucian W.
Asian power and politics : the cultural dimensions of authority / Lucian W. Pye with Mary W. Pye. — Cambridge, Mass. : Belknap Press, 1985. — p. cm. — Includes index. — Bibliography: p

LEGITIMACY OF GOVERNMENTS — United States — History
ROHR, John A
To run a constitution : the legitimacy of the administrative state / John A. Rohr. — Lawrence, Kan. : University Press of Kansas, c1986. — xv, 272 p.. — (Studies in government and public policy). — Includes index. — Bibliography: p. 215-264

LEHMAN BROTHERS
AULETTA, Ken
Greed and glory on Wall Street : the fall of the house of Lehman / Ken Auletta. — Harmondsworth : Penguin Books, 1986. — xi,253p

LEHMANN, E. L
A Festschrift for Erich L. Lehmann in honor of his sixty-fifth birthday / editors, Peter J. Bickel, Kjell A. Doksum, J.L. Hodges, Jr. — Belmont, Calif. : Wadsworth International Group, c1983. — vii, 461 p.. — (Wadsworth statistics/probability series). — Bibliography of works by E.L. Lehmann: p. [456]-461. — Includes bibliographies

LEIBNIZ, GOTTFRIED WILHELM
AITON, E. J.
Leibniz : a biography / E.J. Aiton. — Bristol : Hilger, c1985. — xiv,370p. — Bibliography: p354-360. — Includes index

LEICESTER (LEICESTERSHIRE) — City planning
LEICESTER POLYTECHNIC. School of Land and Building Studies. Research Unit
Development planning in Leicestershire : policies and problems / SLABS Research Unit. — Leicester : School of Land and Building Studies, Leicester Polytechnic, 1984. — iii,51 leaves. — (Housing land in urban areas ; Working paper no.2)

LEISURE
Management of work and personal life : problems and opportunities / edited by Mary Dean Lee and Rabindra N. Kanungo. — New York, N.Y. : Praeger, 1984. — p. cm. — Includes index. — Bibliography: p

MARTIN, William H.
A new view of leisure : rethinking our priorities / W. H. Martin [and] S. Mason. — Maastricht : European Centre for Work and Society, 1985. — 39p. — (Work and Social change ; 16). — Bibliography: p39

LEISURE — Economic aspects — Great Britain
COUNTRYSIDE RECREATION RESEARCH ADVISORY GROUP CONFERENCE (1985 : Oxford)
Countryside leisure and jobs : proceedings of the...Conference, Oxford Polytechnic, September 18-19, 1985 / edited by Hilary Talbot-Ponsonby. — Bristol : Countryside Recreation Research Advisory Group, 1985. — 161p

LEISURE — Social aspects — Great Britain
HOGGETT, Paul
Organising around enthusiasms : patterns of matual aid in leisure / by Paul Hoggett and Jeff Bishop. — London : Comedia, 1986. — 132p

Sport, leisure and social relations / edited by John Horne, David Jary and Alan Tomlinson. — London : Routledge and Kegan Paul, 1987. — (Sociological review monograph ; 33)

VEAL, A. J.
Leisure and the future / A.J. Veal. — London : Allen & Unwin, 1987. — [224]p. — (Leisure and recreation studies ; 4). — Includes bibliography and index

LEISURE — Finland — Statistics
FINLAND. Tilastokeskus
Kulttuaritilasto : Tilastotietoja taiteesta, tiedonvälityksestä, vapaa-ajasta, urheilusta ja nuorisotoiminnasta vuosilta 1930-1977 = Cutlural statistics : Statistical information on arts, communication, leisure, sports and youth activities in 1930-1977. — Helsinki : Tilastokeskus, 1978. — 256p. — (Tilastollisia tiedonantoja = Statistical surveys ; no.60). — In Finnish, Swedish and English

FINLAND. Tilastokeskus
Kulttuuritilasto 1981 : Tilastotietoja taiteesta, tiedonvälityksestä, vapaa-ajasta, urheilusta ja nuorisotojmninasta = Cultural statistics 1981 : Statistical information on arts, communication, leisure, sports and youth activities. — Helsinki : Tilastokeskus, 1984. — 683p. — (Tilastollisia tiedonantoja = Statistical surveys ; no.73). — In Finnish, Swedish and English

LEISURE — Great Britain
Leisure provision and people's needs / Michael Dower...[et al.]. — London : H.M.S.O., 1981. — viii,152p. — Main report on Stage II of the study of Leisure Provision and Human Need undertaken for the Department of the Environment by the Institute of Family and Environmental Research and Dartington Amenity Research Trust. — Bibliography: p.149-152

LEISURE — Norway — Statistics
Kulturstatistikk 1985 = Cultural statistics 1985. — Oslo : Statistisk Sentralbyrå, 1986. — 187p. — (Norges offisielle statistikk ; B589). — In Norwegian and English

LENIN, V. I.. Imperializm: kak vysshaia stadiia kapitalizma
Lenin and imperialism : an appraisal of theories and contemporary reality / edited by Prabhat Patnaik. — London : Sangam Books, 1986. — 414p

LENIN, V. I.
Leninskii sbornik / Institut Marksizma-Leninizma pri TSK KPSS. — Moskva : Politizdat, 1924-. — Irregular

Perepiska V. I. Lenina i rukovodimykh im uchrezhdenii RSDRP s partiinymi organizatsiiami 1905-1907 gg. : sbornik dokumentov. V piati tomakh. — Moskva : Mysl'
t.3: iiul'-avgust 1905 g.
Kn.1 / red. kollegiia D. I. Antoniuk...[et al.]. — 1986. — 368p

Perepiska V. I. Lenina i rukovodimykh im uchrezhdenii RSDRP s partiinymi organizatsiiami 1905-1907 gg. : sbornik dokumentov. V piati tomakh. — Moskva : Mysl'
t.3: iiul'-avgust 1905 g.
Kn.2 / red. kollegiia D. I. Antoniuk...[et al.]. — 1986. — 420p

PLATTEN, Fritz
Die Reise Lenins durch Deutschland im plombierten Wagen / Fritz Platten. — Frankfurt am Main : isp, 1985. — 152p. — First published in 1924

SHARAPOV, Ia. Sh.
Iz iskry-plamia : (V. I. Lenin i kazanskie bol'sheviki / Ia. Sh. Sharapov. — Kazan' : Tatarskoe knizhnoe izd-vo, 1985. — 255p. — (Leniniana Sovetskoi Tatarii ; T.2)

Voenno-teoreticheskoe nasledie V. I. Lenina i problemy sovremennoi voiny / pod redaksiei A. S. Milovidova. — Moskva : Voennoe izd-vo, 1987. — 359p

WILLIAMS, Robert Chadwell
The other Bolsheviks : Lenin and his critics, 1904-1914 / Robert C. Williams. — Bloomington : Indiana University Press, c1986. — 233 p.. — Includes index. — Bibliography: p. 222-228

LENIN, V. I. — Bibliography
Leniniana : bibliograficheskii ukazatel' proizvedenii V. I. Lenina i literatury o nem / [red. kollegiia: D. I. Antoniuk...et al.]. — Moskva : Kniga
T.7: Proizvedeniia V. I. Lenina i literatura o nikh, 1972-1976. — 1986. — 519p

LENINGRAD (R.S.F.S.R.) — History — Revolution, 1917-1921
IVANOV, N. Ia.
Velikii Oktiabr' v Petrograde : istoricheskii ocherk / N. Ia. Ivanov. — Leningrad : Lenizdat, 1957. — 333p

LENINGRAD (R.S.F.S.R.) — Politics and government
Krushenie tsarizma : vospominaniiā uchastnikov revoliutsionnogo dvizheniia v Petrograde (1907 g.- fevral' 1917 g.) / sostaviteli: R. Sh. Ganelin, V. A. Ulanov ; nauchnyi redaktor L. M. Spirin. — Leningrad : Lenizdat, 1986. — 429p. — (Biblioteka revoliutsionnykh memuarov "Iz iskry vozgoritsia plamia")

Leningradskii Sovet v gody Grazhdanskoi voiny i sotsialisticheskogo stroitel'stva 1917-1937 gg. : sbornik statei / [redaktsionnaia kollegiia: M. P. Iroshnikov...et al.]. — Leningrad : Nauka, Leningradskoe otdelenie, 1986. — 258p

ROSSIISKAIA SOTSIAL-DEMOKRATICHESKAIA RABOCHAIA PARTIIA. Peterburgskii komitet
Peterburgskii komitet RSDRP : protokoly i materialy zasedanii. Iiul' 1902-fevral' 1917 / [sbornik podgotovili: T. P. Bondarevskaia, T. A. Abrosimova, E. T. Leikina]. — Leningrad : Lenizdat, 1986. — 588p

LENINGRAD (R.S.F.S.R.) — Siege, 1941-1944
SALISBURY, Harrison E.
The 900 days : the siege of Leningrad / Harrison E. Salisbury ; new introduction by the author. — London : Papermac, 1986, c1969. — 635p,[16]p of plates. — Originally published: New York : Harper & Row, 1969. — Bibliography: p585-610. — Includes index

LENINGRAD (R.S.F.S.R.) — Politics and government
KRUCHKOVSKAIA, V. M.
Tsentral'naia gorodskaia duma Petrograda v 1917 g. / V. M. Kruchkovskaia ; otv. redaktor O. N. Znamenskii. — Leningrad : Nauka, Leningradskoe otdelenie, 1986. — 138p

LERDO DE TEJADA, SEBASTIÁN
KNAPP, Averill
The life of Sebastián Lerdo de Tejada 1823-1889 : a study of influence and obscurity / by Frank Averill Knapp. — Reprint ed.. — New York : Greenwood Press, 1968. — ix,292p. — Bibliography: p269-280

LERIDA (SPAIN) — Politics and government
MIR, Conxita
Lleida (1890-1936) : caciquisme polític i lluita electoral / Conxita Mir. — Barcelona : Publicaciones de l'Abadia de Montserrat, 1985. — 778p. — Maps in end pocket. — Bibliography: p[753]-760

LEROUX, PIERRE
LE BRAS-CHOPARD, Armelle
De l'égalité dans la différence : le socialisme de Pierre Leroux / Armelle Le Bras-Chopard. — [Paris] : Presses de la Fondation nationale des sciences politiques, 1986. — 460p. — Bibliography: p[435]-455

LERROUX, ALEJANDRO
CULLA I CLARÀ, Joan B.
El republicanisme lerrouxista a Catalunya (1901-1923) / per Joan B. Culla i Clarà. — Barcelona : Curial, 1986. — 493p. — (Documents de cultura ; 19). — Bibliography: p[465]-478

LESAGE, JEAN
THOMSON, Dale C
Jean Lesage & the quiet revolution / Dale C. Thomson. — Toronto, Canada : MacMillan of Canada, c1984. — x, 501 p., [16] p. of plates. — Includes bibliographical references and index

LESBIAN MOTHERS — Legal status, laws, etc. — England
Lesbian mothers's legal handbook / Rights of Women Lesbian Custody Group. — London : Women's, 1986. — [214]p. — Includes bibliography and index

LESBIANISM — France — Paris — History
VAN CASSELAER, Catherine
Lot's wife : lesbian Paris, 1890-1914 / Catherine van Casselaer. — Liverpool : Janus, 1986. — 176p. — Bibliography: p173-176

LESOTHO — Foreign relations — South Africa
Massacre at Maseru : South African aggression against Lesotho. — London : International Defence and Aid Fund, 1985. — 36p. — (Fact paper on Southern Africa ; no.12)

LESOTHO — History — Dictionaries
HALIBURTON, Gordon MacKay
Historical dictionary of Lesotho / by Gordon Haliburton. — Metuchen, N.J. : Scarecrow Press, 1977. — xxxv, 223 p.. — (African historical dictionaries ; no. 10). — Bibliography: p. 185-223

LESOTHO — Population — Statistics
MOROJELE, C. M. H.
Basutoland village population lists / C. M. H. Morojele. — Maseni : Agricultural Department, 1960

LESOTHO — Population — Statistics — Evaluation
TIMAEUS, Ian
Evaluation of the Lesotho Fertility Survey 1977 / Ian Timaeus, K. Balasubramanian. — Voorburg : International Statistical Institute, 1984. — 39p. — (Scientific reports / World Fertility Survey ; no.58)

LETTERS OF CREDIT — United States
HARFIELD, Henry
Letters of credit / Henry Harfield. — Philadelphia, Pa. : American Law Institute-American Bar Association Committee on Continuing Professional Education, c1979 ((1981 printing)). — xvii, 167 p.. — (Uniform commercial code/practice handbook ; 5 (1979)) . — Includes indexes

LETTERS ROGATORY — Canada
ZUMBAKIS, S. Paul
Soviet evidence in North American courts : an analysis of problems and concerns with reliance on communist source evidence in alleged war criminal trials / S. Paul Zumbakis. — Toronto : Canadians for Justice, 1986. — 168p

LETTERS ROGATORY — Soviet Union
ZUMBAKIS, S. Paul
Soviet evidence in North American courts : an analysis of problems and concerns with reliance on communist source evidence in alleged war criminal trials / S. Paul Zumbakis. — Toronto : Canadians for Justice, 1986. — 168p

LETTERS ROGATORY — United States
ZUMBAKIS, S. Paul
Soviet evidence in North American courts : an analysis of problems and concerns with reliance on communist source evidence in alleged war criminal trials / S. Paul Zumbakis. — Toronto : Canadians for Justice, 1986. — 168p

LÉVÊQUE, JEAN-MAXIME
LÉVÊQUE, Jean-Maxime
En première ligne / Jean-Maxime Lévêque. — Paris : Albin Michel, [1986]. — 202p

LEVIATHAN
JOHNSTON, David
The rhetoric of Leviathan : Thomas Hobbes and the politics of cultural transformation / David Johnston. — Princeton, N.J. : Princeton University Press, c1986. — xx, 234 p.. — (Studies in moral, political, and legal philosophy). — Includes index. — Bibliography: p. 219-227

KAVKA, Gregory S.
Hobbesian moral and political theory / Gregory S. Kavka. — Princeton, N.J. : Princeton University Press, c1986. — xviii, 460p. — (Studies in moral, political, and legal philosophy). — Includes index. — Includes bibliographical references

LEVY, LEONARD WILIAMS
Essays on the making of the Constitution / edited by Leonard W. Levy. — 2nd ed. — New York : Oxford University Press, 1987. — p. cm — Bibliography: p

LEWISHAM (LONDON, ENGLAND) — Economic conditions
LEWISHAM
Getting Lewisham back to work : Lewisham council's contribution to reducing unemployment in the borough. — Lewisham : [the Council], 1987. — 20p

LIABILITY FOR MARINE ACCIDENTS
The Limitation of shipowners' liability : the new law. — London : Sweet & Maxwell, 1986. — xxv,378p. — Includes index

MANKABADY, Samir
The International Maritime Organisation / Samir Mankabady. — [2nd ed.]. — London : Croom Helm. — Previous ed.: published in 1 vol. 1984
Vol.2: Accidents at sea. — c1987. — xxvii,452p. — Includes index

LIABILITY (LAW) — England
HARLOW, Carol
Understanding tort law : Carol Harlow. — London : Fontana, 1987. — 160p. — (Understanding law) (Understanding law). — Bibliography: p147-151

LIBEL AND SLANDER — England — Cases
HOOPER, David, 1949-
Public scandal, odium and contempt : an investigation of recent libel cases / David Hooper. — [Sevenoaks] : Coronet, 1986, c1984. — x,229p. — Originally published: London : Secker & Warburg, 1984. — Bibliography: p221-222. — Includes index

LIBEL AND SLANDER — Ireland
MCDONALD, Marc
Irish law of defamation / Marc McDonald ; with a foreword by Thomas A. Finlay. — Dublin : Round Hall in association with Irish Academic Press, c1987. — xx,304p. — Includes index

LIBEL AND SLANDER — United States — Cases
SMOLLA, Rodney A
Suing the press / Rodney A. Smolla. — New York : Oxford University Press, 1986. — p. cm . — Includes index. — Bibliography: p. — Contents: The thinning American skin -- The trials of Martin Luther King : the New York times case -- From chasing Communists to fighting Lillian Hellman : the libel suit as guerilla warfare -- Ariel Sharon v. Time magazine : the libel suit as politcal forum, international style -- "I read it in the Enquirer -- Carol Burnett and Henry Kissinger!" : the Carol Burnett case -- Jackie Onassis, Elizabeth Taylor, Clint Eastwood, and Mohammed Ali--of public personality and private property -- From "touching" to "missing" : libel arising from fiction and docudrama -- Of Vanessa Williams and Jerry Falwell : the contributions of Penthouse to the First Amendment -- Mobil Oil meets the Washington Post : can investigative journalism ever be objective? -- Westmoreland v. CBS : litigating the symbols and lessons of Vietnam -- "I'm okay but you're sued."

LIBERAL PARTY
HOWE, Geoffrey Sir
Partnership for paralysis : Liberal and SDP policies examined / Sir Geoffrey Howe. — London : Conservative Political Centre, 1987. — 14p

JOHNSON, Elizabeth
Liberal Party handbook. — 1986-87 edition. — 51p

LIBERAL PARTY
An agenda for action on the NHS : health service priorities for Liberals in government. — Hebden Bridge : Hebden Royd Publications, 1986. — 8p. — (Liberal Party health panel papers ; no.16)

LIBERAL PARTY
For a future thats safe : the Liberal alternative to nuclear power : the campaign pact. — London : Liberal Party, 1986. — [36p]

LIBERAL PARTY
Freedom in sickness and in health. — Hebden Bridge : Liberal Party Publications, 1986. — 20p. — (Liberal Party health panel papers ; no.18)

LIBERAL PARTY WORKING GROUP ON THE INTELLIGENCE SERVICES
Liberty and security : report of the Liberal Party Working Group on the Intelligence Services. — Hebden Bridge : Hebden Royd Publications, 1986. — 28p

MOLE, Stuart
The decade of realignment : the leadership speeches of David Steel (1976-1986) / by Stuart Mole. — Hebden Bridge : Hebden Royd Publications, [1986]. — 176p

New outlook. — London : New Outlook Publishing, 1961-1978. — Monthly. — Sub-title varies. — Continued by: The Radical Quarterly

Promoting greater involvement : Report of the Commission of Inquiry into ethnic minority involvement in the Liberal Party. — Hebden Bridge : Hebden Royd Publications on behalf of the Liberal Party and the Commission of Enquiry into Ethnic Minority Involvement in the Liberal Party, 1986. — 59p

The radical quarterly. — Hebden Bridge : Hedben Royd Publications, 1986-. — Quarterly. — Continues: New Outlook

SDP/LIBERAL ALLIANCE
The essential investment : Liberal/SDP Alliance Policies for Education. — Hebden Bridge : Hebden Royd Publications, [1987]. — [12 leaves]

SDP-LIBERAL ALLIANCE
People in power : why constitutional reform matters to everyone in Britain. — Hebden Bridge : Liberal Party ; London : Social Democratic Party, 1986. — 16p

LIBERAL PARTY — Finance
LIBERAL PARTY
Fundraising by direct mail. — Hebden Bridge : Hebden Royd Publications, 1987. — 24p. — (Liberal fundraising ; Booklet no.1)

LIBERAL PARTY — History
BRENT, Richard
Liberal Anglican politics : Whiggery, religion and reform, 1830-1841 / Richard Brent. — Oxford : Clarendon, 1987. — 340p. — (Oxford historical monographs). — Bibliography: p301-330. — Includes index

LIBERAL PARTY — History — 19th century
PARRY, J. P. (Jonathan Philip)
Democracy and religion : Gladstone and the Liberal Party, 1867-1875 / J.P. Parry. — Cambridge : Cambridge University Press, 1986. — xiii,504p. — (Cambridge studies in the history and theory of politics). — Bibliography: p453-492. — Includes index

LIBERAL PARTY. SDP Liberal Alliance
See SDP Liberal Alliance

LIBERAL PARTY — History — 19th century
PARRY, J. P. (Jonathan Philip)
Democracy and religion : Gladstone and the Liberal Party, 1867-1875 / J.P. Parry. — Cambridge : Cambridge University Press, 1986. — xiii,504p. — (Cambridge studies in the history and theory of politics). — Bibliography: p453-492. — Includes index

LIBERAL PARTY (CANADA)
ROBERTS, John
Agenda for Canada : towards a new liberalism / John Roberts. — 1st ed. — Toronto, Ont., Canada : Lester & Orpen Dennys, c1985. — 239 p.. — Bibliography: p. 237-239

LIBERAL PARTY OF CANADA
DAVEY, Keith
The rainmaker : a passion for politics / Keith Davey. — Toronto : Stoddart, 1986. — xii,383p

LIBERAL PARTY OF CANADA — Biography
MACLAREN, Roy
Honourable mentions : the uncommon diary of an M.P. / Roy MacLaren. — Toronto : Deneau, 1986. — 226p

PICKERSGILL, J. W.
The road back : by a Liberal in opposition / J. W. Pickersgill. — Toronto : University of Toronto Press, 1986. — 320p

LIBERAL SDP ALLIANCE See SDP Liberal Alliance

LIBERALISM

BARRY, Norman P.
On classical liberalism and libertarianism / Norman P. Barry. — Basingstoke : Macmillan, c1986. — [240]p. — *Includes index*

BOESCHE, Roger
The strange liberalism of Alexis de Tocqueville / Roger Boesche. — Ithaca, N.Y. ; London : Cornell University Press, 1987. — 288p. — *Includes index. — Bibliography: p.267-281*

BRUNHOFF, Suzanne de
L'heure du marché : critique du libéralisme / Suzanne de Brunhoff. — Paris : P.U.F., [1986]. — 154p

GRAHAM, David, 19---
The new enlightenment : the rebirth of liberalism / David Graham and Peter Clarke. — London : Macmillan in association with Channel Four Television Co., 1986. — xii,180p. — *Bibliography: p173-174. — Includes index*

GREEN, David G.
The new right : the counter-revolution in political, economic and social thought / David G. Green. — Brighton : Wheatsheaf, 1987. — xi,238p. — *Bibliography: p221-232. — Includes index*

LÉVÊQUE, Jean-Maxime
En première ligne / Jean-Maxime Lévêque. — Paris : Albin Michel, [1986]. — 202p

Marxism and liberalism / edited by Ellen Frankel Paul ... [et al.]. — Oxford : Basil Blackwell for the Social Philosophy and Policy Center, Bowling Green State University, 1986. — xii,223p

PACHER-THEINBURG, Regina
The concept of consent and its role in liberal democratic theory / by Regina Pacher-Theinburg. — 201 leaves. — *PhD (Econ) 1986 LSE*

LIBERALISM — Brazil — History — 19th century

COSTA, Emília Viotti da
[Da monarquia à república. English]. The Brazilian Empire : myths and histories / Emilia Viotti da Costa. — Chicago ; London : University of Chicago Press, 1985. — xxv, 287p. — *: Revised translation of: Da monarquia à república. — Includes index. — Bibliographical notes: p.249-278*

LIBERALISM — Canada

MANZER, Ronald A
Public policies and political development in Canada / Ronald Manzer. — Toronto ; Buffalo : University of Toronto Press, c1985. — x, 240 p.. — *Includes index. — Bibliography: p. [191]-228*

ROBERTS, John
Agenda for Canada : towards a new liberalism / John Roberts. — 1st ed. — Toronto, Ont., Canada : Lester & Orpen Dennys, c1985. — 239 p.. — *Bibliography: p. 237-239*

LIBERALISM — England — History — 19th century

BRENT, Richard
Liberal Anglican politics : Whiggery, religion and reform, 1830-1841 / Richard Brent. — Oxford : Clarendon, 1987. — 340p. — (Oxford historical monographs). — *Bibliography: p301-330. — Includes index*

LIBERALISM — Germany — History

FRYE, Bruce B.
Liberal Democrats in the Weimar Republic : the history of the German Democratic Party and the German State Party / Bruce B. Frye. — Carbondale : Southern Illinois University Press, c1985. — p. cm. — *Includes index. — Bibliography: p*

LIBERALISM — Japan

NOLTE, Sharon H
Liberalism in modern Japan : Ishibashi Tanzan and his teachers, 1905-1960 / Sharon H. Nolte. — Berkeley : University of California Press, c1987. — xii, 378 p.. — *Includes index. — Bibliography: p. 343-370*

LIBERALISM — Japan — History

HIRSI, Atsuko
Individualism and socialism : Kawai Eijirō's life and thought (1891-1944) / Atssuko Hirai. — Cambridge, Mass. : Council on East Asian Studies, Harvard University : Distributed by Harvard University Press, 1986. — p. cm. — (Harvard East Asian monographs ; 127). — *Includes index. — Bibliography: p*

LIBERALISM — Poland — History

JASZCZUK, Andrzej
Spór pozytywistów z konserwatystami o przysałość Polski 1870-1903 / Andrzej Jaszczuk. — Warszawa : Państwowe Wydawnictwo Naukowe, 1986. — 292p. — (Polska XIX i XX wieku : dzieje społeczne)

LIBERALISM — South Africa — Congresses

South Africa, a chance for liberalism? : papers presented during a seminar of the Friedrich Naumann Foundation in December 1983. — 1. Aufl. — Sankt Augustin [Germany] : Liberal Verlag, 1985. — vi, 407 p.. — (Schriften der Friedrich-Naumann-Stiftung. Liberale Texte). — *Includes bibliographies*

LIBERALISM — Soviet Union — History

GALAI, Shmuel
The liberation movement in Russia, 1900-1905 / Shmuel Galai. — Cambridge : Cambridge University Press, 1973. — x,325p. — (Soviet and East European Studies). — *Bibliography: p277-315*

LIBERALISM — Spain — History

GUTIÉRREZ LLORET, Rosa Ana
Republicanos y liberales : la revolución de 1868 y la I.a República en Alicante / Rosa Ana Gutiérrez Lloret. — Alicante : Instituto Juan Gil-Albert, 1985. — 188p. — *Bibliography: p175-185*

LIBERALISM — Switzerland

PARTI LIBÉRAL SUISSE
Pour une politique libérale de la santé : rapport d'une commission d'étude du Parti libéral suisse. — Berne : Parti Libéral Suisse, 1977. — 15p

LIBERALISM — United States

GREEN, David G
The new conservatism : the counter-revolution in political, economic, and social thought / David G. Green. — New York : St. Martin's Press, 1987. — xi, 238 p.. — *Includes index. — Bibliography: p. 221-232*

MCCANN, Michael W.
Taking reform seriously : perspectives on public interest liberalism / Michael W. McCann. — Ithaca : Cornell University Press, 1986. — 345 p.. — *Includes index. — Bibliography: p. 321-335*

LIBERALISM — United States — History

NELSON, John R.
Liberty and property : political economy and policymaking in the new nation, 1789-1812 / John R. Nelson, Jr. — Baltimore : Johns Hopkins University Press, c1987. — p. cm. — (The Johns Hopkins University studies in historical and political science ; 105th ser., 2). — *Bibliography: p*

LIBERALISM — United States — History — 20th century

SEIDEMAN, David
The New republic : a voice of modern liberalism / by David Seideman. — New York : Praeger, 1986. — xv, 205 p.. — *Includes index. — Bibliography: p. [195]-200*

TOBIN, Eugene M
Organize or perish : America's independent progressives, 1913-1933 / Eurgene M. Tobin. — Westport, Conn. ; London : Greenwood Press, c1986. — xiv, 279p. — (Contributions in American history ; no. 114). — *Includes index. — Bibliography: p [251]-260*

LIBERATION THEOLOGY

BERRYMAN, Phillip
Liberation theology : essential facts about the revolutionary movement in Latin America and beyond / Phillip Berryman. — London : Tauris, 1987. — [224]p. — *Includes bibliography and index*

LIBERIA — Foreign relations

FAHNBULLEH, H. Boima
The diplomacy of prejudice : Liberia in international politics, 1945-1970 / H. Boima Fahnbulleh. — New York : Vantage Press, 1985. — 234p. — *Bibliography: p225-234*

LIBERIA — History — Dictionaries

DUNN, D. Elwood
Historical dictionary of Liberia / by D. Elwood Dunn & Svend E. Holsoe. — Metuchen, N.J. : Scarecrow Press, 1985. — xx, 274 p.. — (African historical dictionaries ; no. 38). — *Includes index. — Bibliography: p. 193-240*

LIBERIA — Politics and government

LIEBENOW, J. Gus
Liberia : the quest for democracy / J. Gus Liebenow. — Bloomington : Indiana University Press, c1987. — xiii, 336 p.. — *Includes index. — Bibliography: p. [317]-330*

LIBERTARIANISM — United States

GREEN, David G
The new conservatism : the counter-revolution in political, economic, and social thought / David G. Green. — New York : St. Martin's Press, 1987. — xi, 238 p.. — *Includes index. — Bibliography: p. 221-232*

LIBERTARIONISM

BARRY, Norman P.
On classical liberalism and libertarianism / Norman P. Barry. — Basingstoke : Macmillan, c1986. — [240]p. — *Includes index*

LIBERTY

MERKEL, Bernard
The concept of freedom and the development of Sartre's early political thought / Bernard Merkel. — New York : Garland Pub., 1987. — p. cm. — (Political theory and political philosophy). — *Thesis (Ph. D.)--University of Reading, 1984. — Bibliography: p*

BOESCHE, Roger
The strange liberalism of Alexis de Tocqueville / Roger Boesche. — Ithaca, N.Y. ; London : Cornell University Press, 1987. — 288p. — *Includes index. — Bibliography: p.267-281*

DAY, J. P.
Liberty and justice / J.P. Day. — London : Croom Helm, c1987. — 232p. — *Includes index*

FAY, Brian
Critical social science : liberation and its limits / Brian Fay. — Ithaca, N.Y. : Cornell University Press, [1987]. — p. cm. — *Includes index. — Bibliography: p*

FLATHMAN, Richard E
The philosophy and politics of freedom / Richard E. Flathman. — Chicago : University of Chicago Press, c1987. — x, 360 p.. — (A Chicago original paperback). — *Includes index. — Bibliography: p. 349-356*

HAYEK, F. A.
Law, legislation and liberty : a new statement of the liberal principles of justice and political economy / F.A. Hayek. — London : Routledge & Kegan Paul, 1982. — xxi,180,191,244p. — *Originally published in 3 vols.. — Includes index*

LIBERTY *continuation*
Liberty, equality, and law : selected Tanner lectures on moral philosophy / John Rawls ... [et al.] ; Sterling M. McMurrin, editor. — Salt Lake City : University of Utah Press, 1987. — x, 205 p.. — *Includes bibliographical references and index. — Contents: The basic liberties and their priority / John Rawls -- Is liberty possible? / Charles Fried -- Equality of what? / Amartya Sen -- Ethics, law, and the exercise of self-command / Thomas C. Schelling*

LINDLEY, Richard
Autonomy / Richard Lindley. — Basingstoke : Macmillan, 1986. — x,198p. — (Issues in political theory). — *Bibliography: p192-195. — Includes index*

Lives, liberties and the public good : new essays in political theory for Maurice Cranston / edited by George Feaver and Frederick Rosen. — Basingstoke : Macmillan in association with the London School of Economics and Political Science, 1987. — ix,272p. — *Bibliography: p259-266. — Includes index*

MADISON, Gary Brent
The logic of liberty / G. B. Madison. — New York ; London : Greenwood, 1986. — xiv,293p. — (Contributions in philosophy ; 30). — *Bibliography: p281-288. — Includes index*

MILL, John Stuart
On liberty / John Stuart Mill ; edited with an introduction by Gertrude Himmelfarb. — Harmondsworth : Penguin, 1982 (1985 [printing]). — 186p. — (Penguin classics). — *Originally published: London : Parker, 1859*

NORMAN, Richard
Free and equal : a philosophical examination of political values / Richard Norman. — Oxford : Clarendon, 1987. — [192]p. — *Includes index*

PACHER-THEINBURG, Regina
The concept of consent and its role in liberal democratic theory / by Regina Pacher-Theinburg. — 201 leaves. — *PhD (Econ) 1986 LSE*

SANDEL, Michael J.
Liberalism and the limits of justice / Michael J. Sandel. — Cambridge : Cambridge University Press, 1982. — ix,191p. — *Bibliography: p184-186. — Includes index*

STRAWSON, Galen
Freedom and belief / Galen Strawson. — Oxford : Clarendon, 1986. — xiv,339p. — *Bibliography: p333-336. — Includes index*

SUGDEN, Robert
The economics of rights, co-operation and welfare / Robert Sugden. — Oxford : Basil Blackwell, 1986. — [224]p. — *Includes index*

LIBERTY — History
KAMMEN, Michael G
Spheres of liberty : changing perceptions of liberty in American culture / Michael Kammen. — Madison, Wis. : University of Wisconsin Press, 1986. — xiv, 191 p.. — (The Curti lectures ; 1985). — *Includes bibliographical references and index. — Contents: Liberty, authority, and property in early America -- Ordered liberty and law in nineteenth-century America -- Liberty, justice, and equality in twentieth-century America -- Notes on liberty in American iconography*

LIBERTY — Philosophy
FLATHMAN, Richard E
The philosophy and politics of freedom / Richard E. Flathman. — Chicago : University of Chicago Press, c1987. — x, 360 p.. — (A Chicago original paperback). — *Includes index. — Bibliography: p. 349-356*

LIBERTY OF THE PRESS — Hungary
TÁNCSICS, Mihály
Sajtószabadságról nézetei egy rabnak / Táncsics Mihály. — Budapest : Magvető Kiadó, 1984. — 97p. — (Gondolkodó Magyarok)

LIBRARIANS
AMERICAN COUNCIL OF LEARNED SOCIETIES. Joint Committee on Soviet Studies. Subcommittee on Bibliography, Information Retrieval and Documentation
International directory of librarians and library specialists in the Slavic and East European field / prepared under the auspices of the Subcommittee on Bibliography,Information Retrieval and Documentation of the Joint Committee on Soviet Studies of the American Council of Learned Societies and the Social Science Research Council. — New York : American Council of Learned Societies, 1985. — 58p

LIBRARIES
KIRBY, John
Creating the library identity : a manual of design / John Kirby. — Aldershot : Gower, c1985. — ix,140p. — (A Grafton book). — *Fiche in pocket. — "Copyright freesheets" in pocket. — Bibliography: p137-138. — Includes index*

LIBRARIES — Automation
CORBIN, John Boyd
Managing the library automation project / John Corbin. — [Phoenix, AZ] : Oryx Press, 1985. — vi, 274 p.. — *Includes index. — Bibliography: p. [261]-267*

GOSLING, Jane
SWALCAP : a guide for librarians and systems managers / Jane Gosling. — Aldershot : Gower, c1987. — 129 p

LIBRARIES — Cost control
ROBERTS, Stephen A.
Cost management for library and information services / Stephen A. Roberts. — London : Butterworths, 1985. — 181 p

LIBRARIES — Handbooks
REED, Jeffrey G.
Library use : a handbook for psychology / Jeffrey G. Reed and Pam M. Baxter. — Washington, DC : American Psychological Association, c1983. — 137 p.. — *Includes bibliographies and index*

LIBRARIES — Special collections — Government publications
HERNON, Peter
GPO's depository library program : a descriptive analysis / by Peter Hernon, Charles R. McClure, Gary R. Purcell. — Norwood, N.J. : Ablex Pub. Corp., 1985. — p. cm. — *Includes index. — Bibliography: p*

LIBRARIES — Asia, Southeastern
SOUTH-EAST ASIA LIBRARY GROUP
Newsletter / South-East Asia Library Group. — Hull : South-East Asia Library Group, 1982-. — *Biennial*

LIBRARIES — Europe — Automation
EUROPEAN CONFERENCE ON LIBRARY AUTOMATION (1986 : Harrogate)
European Conference on Library Automation : 11-12 September 1986, Harrogate, England : proceedings of the conference / organised and sponsored jointly by the Library Association and CLSI. — London : The Association, 1987. — vii,84p. — (LA conference proceedings series in Library automation ; 5)

LIBRARIES — Europe — Special collections — China
MA, John T.
Chinese collections in western Europe : survey of their technical and readers' service / John T. Ma. — Zug : Inter Documentation Company, 1985. — 90p. — (Bibliotheca Asiatica ; 18)

LIBRARIES — Great Britain
EDMONDS, Diana J.
Current library cooperation and co-ordination : an investigation / by Diana J. Edmonds. — London : HMSO, 1986. — v, 49p. — (Library information series ; no.15)

LIBRARIES — Great Britain — Directories
Libraries in the United Kingdom and the Republic of Ireland, 1986 / edited by Ann Harrold. — London : Library Association, 1986. — vii,166p

LIBRARIES — Great Britain — Security measures
ANDERSON, Hazel
Planning manual for disaster control in Scottish libraries & record offices / Hazel Anderson, John E. McIntyre. — Edinburgh : National Library of Scotland, 1985. — 75p. — *Bibliography: p71-72. — Includes index*

LIBRARIES — Great Britian
LIBRARY AND INFORMATION SERVICES COUNCIL
Joint enterprise : roles and relationships of the public and private sectors in the provision of library and information services / [report of Library and Information Services Council and British Library Research and Development Department Working Party]. — London : H.M.S.O., 1987. — vii, 49p. — (Library information series ; no.16). — *On cover: Office of Arts and Libraries*

LIBRARIES — London (England)
UNIVERSITY OF LONDON
Guide to the library resources of the University of London / compiled by Kenneth Garside. — [London] : University of London, Library Resources Co-ordinating Committee, 1983. — vii,179p. — *Includes index*

LIBRARIES AND THE PHYSICALLY HANDICAPPED
CRADDOCK, Peter
The public library and blind people : a survey and review of current practice / Peter Craddock. — London : British Library, c1985. — xv,106p. — (Library and information research report ; 36). — *Bibliography: p92-102*

LIBRARIES, DEPOSITORY — Great Britain
PINION, Catherine F.
Legal deposit of non-book materials / Catherine F. Pinion. — London : British Library, 1986. — 1v.. — (Library and information research report ; 49). — *Includes bibliography*

LIBRARIES, DEPOSITORY — United States
HERNON, Peter
GPO's depository library program : a descriptive analysis / by Peter Hernon, Charles R. McClure, Gary R. Purcell. — Norwood, N.J. : Ablex Pub. Corp., 1985. — p. cm. — *Includes index. — Bibliography: p*

LIBRARIES, UNIVERSITY AND COLLEGE — Administration
JOINT ANNUAL STUDY CONFERENCE OF THE COLLEGES OF FURTHER AND HIGHER EDUCATION GROUP AND THE EDUCATION LIBRARIANS GROUP OF THE LIBRARY ASSOCIATION (1985 : Chester)
Management issues in university libraries : proceedings of the Joint Annual Study Conference of the Colleges of Further and Higher Education Group and the Education Librarians Group of the Library Association, 1-4 April 1985 / edited by Tim Lomas. — London : Rossendale, c1986. — 84p

LIBRARIES, UNIVERSITY AND COLLEGE — Evaluation — Statistical methods
KANTOR, Paul B
Objective performance measures for academic and research libraries / by Paul B. Kantor. — Washington, D.C. : Association of Research Libraries, 1984. — viii, 76 p., [13] leaves. — *Bibliography: p. 75-76*

LIBRARIES, UNIVERSITY AND COLLEGE — Australia

Design for diversity : library services for higher education and research in Australia / edited by Harrison Bryan and Gordon Greenwood. — St. Lucia [Aus.] : University of Queensland Press, c1977. — xvi, 790 p., [11] p. of plates. — *Distributed by Prentice-Hall International, Hemel Hempstead, Eng. — Includes index. — Bibliography: p. [713]-740*

LIBRARIES, UNIVERSITY AND COLLEGE — Great Britain

British journal of academic librarianship. — London : Taylor Graham, 1986-. — *3 per year*

LIBRARIES, UNIVERSITY AND COLLEGE — Great Britain — Acquisitions

SPILLER, David
Book selection : an introduction to principles and practice / David Spiller ; with an introduction by Brian Baumfield. — 4th ed. — London : Bingley, 1986. — ix,235p. — *Previous ed.: 1980. — Bibliography: p206-223. — Includes index*

LIBRARY ADMINISTRATION

ROBERTS, Stephen A.
Cost management for library and information services / Stephen A. Roberts. — London : Butterworths, 1985. — 181 p

LIBRARY COOPERATION — Great Britain

EDMONDS, Diana J.
Current library cooperation and co-ordination : an investigation / by Diana J. Edmonds. — London : HMSO, 1986. — v, 49p. — (Library information series ; no.15)

LIBRARY AND INFORMATION SERVICES COUNCIL
The future development of libraries and information services : progress through planning and partnership : report by the Library and Information Services Council, Office of Arts and Libraries. — London : HMSO, 1986. — (Library information series ; no.14)

LIBRARY EMPLOYEES — Training of

Guidelines for training in libraries. — London : Library Association
2: The evaluation of staff training / A. Conyers. — 2nd ed. — 1986. — 40p. — *Previous ed.: published as: Evaluation. 1980. — Bibliography: p24*

LIBRARY FINANCE

CUMMINGS, Martin M.
The economics of research libraries / Martin Marc Cummings. — Washington, D.C. : Council on Library Resources, 1986. — p. cm. — *"User fees and library economics : a selected, annotated bibliography / Jane A. Rosenberg": p. — Includes bibliographies and index*

ROBERTS, Stephen A.
Cost management for library and information services / Stephen A. Roberts. — London : Butterworths, 1985. — 181 p

LIBRARY FINES AND FEES

CUMMINGS, Martin M.
The economics of research libraries / Martin Marc Cummings. — Washington, D.C. : Council on Library Resources, 1986. — p. cm. — *"User fees and library economics : a selected, annotated bibliography / Jane A. Rosenberg": p. — Includes bibliographies and index*

LIBRARY ORIENTATION

LUTZKER, Marilyn
Criminal justice research in libraries : strategies and resources / Marilyn Lutzker and Eleanor Ferrall ; foreword by Edward Sagarin. — Westport, Conn. : Greenwood Press, c1986. — p. cm. — *Includes indexes*

LIBRARY PERSONNEL MANAGEMENT

Personnel issues in reference services / edited by Bill Katz and Ruth A. Fraley. — New York : Haworth Press, c1986. — xvi, 200 p.. — *Includes bibliographies*

LIBRARY PERSONNEL MANAGEMENT — Great Britain

WEBB, Sylvia P.
Personal development in information work / Sylvia P. Webb. — London : Aslib, 1986. — [128]p. — *Includes index*

LIBRARY PUBLICATIONS

Library publishing : report of a seminar held at the British Library, 11-13 April 1983 / edited by David Way. — London : British Library, 1985. — 80p. — (British Library occasional papers ; 2)

LIBRARY RESOURCES — Great Britain — Statistics

The scope for automatic data processing in the British Library. — Lancaster : Library Research Unit, University of Lancaster. — *Photocopy of unpublished paper*
Supporting paper N: Nationsal catalogue coverage study / Library Research Unit, University of Lancaster. — 1971. — 26 leaves

LIBRARY SCIENCE — Bibliography

CAMBIO, Edward P.
The International Federation of Library Associations : a selected list of references / compiled by Edward P. Cambio. — Washington, D. C. : Library of Congress, 1974. — 14p. — *Supt. of Docs. no.:LC2.2:In8/2*

LIBRARY SCIENCE — Terminology

TURNER, G. W
German for librarians / by G. W. Turner. Rev. and edited by A. J. A. Vieregg and J. W. Blackwood. — [Palmerston North, N.Z. : Massey University], 1972. — iii, 137 p. — (Massey University. Library series ; no. 5)

LIBRARY SCIENCE — Vocational guidance — Great Britain

JOHNSON, Iam M.
The library school leavers handbooks / by Ian M. Johnson. — London : Association of Assistant Librarians, 1987. — 51p

LIBRARY SCIENCE — Great Britain

The World of books and information : essays in honour of Lord Dainton / edited by Maurice Line. — London : British Library, 1987. — [256]p. — *Includes bibliography*

LIBRARY STATISTICS

KANTOR, Paul B
Objective performance measures for academic and research libraries / by Paul B. Kantor. — Washington, D.C. : Association of Research Libraries, 1984. — viii, 76 p., [13] leaves. — *Bibliography: p. 75-76*

MACDOUGALL, A. F.
Statistical series in library and information services : current provision and future potential / A. F. MacDougall. — Oxford : Elsevier International Bulletins, 1985. — 59p. — (EIB report series ; no.9) (British Library R and D report ; 5865)

LIBRARY SURVEYS

KANTOR, Paul B
Objective performance measures for academic and research libraries / by Paul B. Kantor. — Washington, D.C. : Association of Research Libraries, 1984. — viii, 76 p., [13] leaves. — *Bibliography: p. 75-76*

LIBYA — Dictionaries and encyclopedias

HAHN, Lorna
Historical dictionary of Libya / by Lorna Hahn with the assistance of Maureen Muirragui. — Metuchen, N.J. : Scarecrow Press, 1981. — xiii, 116 p.. — (African historical dictionaries ; no. 33). — *Bibliography: p. 85-108*

LIBYA — Economic conditions

The Economic development of Libya / edited by Bichara Khader and Bashir El-Wifati. — London : Croom Helm, c1987. — 250p. — *Bibliography: p228-249*

Planning and development in modern Libya / edited by M. M. Burn, S. M. Ghanem and K. S. McLachlan. — London ; Wisbech : Society for Libyan Studies : Middle East and North African Studies Press, 1985. — x,234p. — *Includes bibliographic references*

LIBYA — Economic policy

Planning and development in modern Libya / edited by M. M. Burn, S. M. Ghanem and K. S. McLachlan. — London ; Wisbech : Society for Libyan Studies : Middle East and North African Studies Press, 1985. — x,234p. — *Includes bibliographic references*

Summary of the socio-economic transformation plan 1390-1394 F.D.P. 1981-1985 A.D.. — [Tripoli] : Secretariat of Planning, [1981]. — 60p

LIBYA — Foreign relations — Soviet Union

SHVEDOV, A. A.
Sovetsko-liviiskie otnosheniia / A. Shvedov, V. Rumiantsev. — Moskva : Progress, 1986. — 186p

LIBYA — Foreign relations — United States

MCCORMICK, Bob
Libya : the truth behind the bombings / Bob McCormick. — London : Straight Left, 1987. — 12p

Mad dogs : the US raids on Libya / edited by Mary Kaldor and Paul Anderson ; introduction by Mary Kaldor. — London : Pluto in association with European Nuclear Disarmament, 1986. — 172p

WORLD ISLAMIC CALL SOCIETY
God is great. — Rome : World Islamic Call Society, 1986. — [36p]

LIBYA — History

BEARMAN, Jonathan
Qadhafi´s Libya / Jonathan Bearman ; foreword by Claudia Wright. — London : Zed, 1986. — [320]p

HARRIS, Lillian Craig
Libya : Qadhafi´s revolution and the modern state / Lillian Craig Harris. — Boulder, Colo. : Westview ; London : Croom Helm, 1986. — xviii,157p. — (Profiles : nations of the contemporary Middle East). — *Bibliography: p139-144. — Includes index*

LIBYA — Politics and government

ANDERSON, Lisa
The state and social transformation in Tunisia and Libya, 1830-1980 / Lisa Anderson. — Princeton, N.J. : Princeton University Press, c1986. — xxiv, 325 p.. — (Princeton studies on the Near East). — *Includes index. — Bibliography: p. 295-311*

LIBYA — Rural conditions

ANDERSON, Lisa
The state and social transformation in Tunisia and Libya, 1830-1980 / Lisa Anderson. — Princeton, N.J. : Princeton University Press, c1986. — xxiv, 325 p.. — (Princeton studies on the Near East). — *Includes index. — Bibliography: p. 295-311*

LIBYA — Social policy

Planning and development in modern Libya / edited by M. M. Burn, S. M. Ghanem and K. S. McLachlan. — London ; Wisbech : Society for Libyan Studies : Middle East and North African Studies Press, 1985. — x,234p. — *Includes bibliographic references*

Summary of the socio-economic transformation plan 1390-1394 F.D.P. 1981-1985 A.D.. — [Tripoli] : Secretariat of Planning, [1981]. — 60p

LICENSES — Hungary
KARDOS, Péter
Külföldi licencek a magyar gazdaságban / Kardos Péter , Szatmári Tamás. — Budapest : Közgazdasági és Jogi Könyvkiadó, 1984. — 204p. — *Bibliography: p201-[205]*

LIDDELL, HENRY. c.1673-1717 — Correspondence
LIDDELL, Henry
The Letters of Henry Liddell to William Cotesworth / edited by J. M. Ellis. — [Durham?] : Surtees Society, 1987. — xvi,293p. — (Publications of the Surtees Society ; v.197)

LIECHTENSTEIN — Biography
Who's who in Switzerland including the Principality of Liechtenstein 1986-1987. — Geneva : Nagel, 1986. — 564p

LIETUVOS KOMMUNISTA PARTYA
LOIKO, I. I.
Za podėm i intensifikatsiiu sel'skogo khoziaistva : (opyt rukovodstva Kompartii Litvy otrasl'iu v 1952-1970 gg.) / I. Loiko. — Vil'nius : Mintis, 1986. — 214p

LIFE — Economic aspects — Congresses
GENEVA CONFERENCE ON THE VALUE OF LIFE AND SAFETY (1981)
The value of life and safety : proceedings of a conference held by the "Geneva Association" : collection of papers presented at the Geneva Conference on the Value of Life and Safety held at the University of Geneva, 30th, 31st March and 1st April 1981 / edited by M.W. Jones-Lee. — Amsterdam ; New York : North-Holland Pub. Co. ; New York, N.Y. : Sole distributors for the U.S.A. and Canada, Elsevier Science Pub. Co., 1982. — xvii, 309 p.. — *Bibliography: p. xi*

LIFE CHANGE EVENTS
Social support, life events, and depression / edited by Nan Lin, Alfred Dean, and Walter M. Ensel. — New York : Academic Press, 1986. — p. cm. — *Includes index*

LIFE CYCLE, HUMAN
DESPLANQUES, Guy
Cycle de vie et milieu social / Guy Desplanques. — Paris : INSEE, 1987. — 272p. — (Les collections de l'INSEE. Série D. Démographie et emploi ; no.117)

Family demography : methods and their application / editors John Bongaarts, Thomas K. Burch and Kenneth W. Wachter. — Oxford : Clarendon, 1987. — viii,365p. — (International studies in demography ; 2). — *Conference papers.* — *Includes bibliographies and index*

MATTHEWS, Sarah H
Friendships through the life-course : oral biographies in old age / by Sarah H. Matthews. — Beverly Hills : Sage Publications, c1986. — p. cm. — (Sage library of social research ; v. 161). — *Includes index.* — *Bibliography: p*

LIFE CYCLE, HUMAN — Handbooks, manuals, etc
Handbook of marriage and the family / edited by Marvin B. Sussman and Suzanne K. Steinmetz. — New York : Plenum Press, c1986. — p. cm. — *Includes bibliographical references and index*

LIFE EXPECTANCY — Great Britain
MELINEK, S. J.
Loss of life expectancy due to fire / by S. J. Melinek. — Borehamwood : Fire Research Station, 1973. — 12p. — (Fire research note ; no.978). — *Bibliographical references: p6*

LIFE SKILLS — Study and teaching — Great Britain — History
Studies in social education / edited and introduced by Frank Booton. — Hove : Benfield
Vol.1: Work with youth 1863-1896. — 1985. — 1v.

LIFE SPAN, PRODUCTIVE — Japan — Statistics
Japanese working life profile : statistical aspects. — Tokyo : Japan Institute of Labor, 1985. — 80p

LIFE SPAN, PRODUCTIVE — New Zealand — Statistics
New Zealand tables of working life, 1971. — Wellington : Department of Statistics, 1977. — 23p. — (Statistical bulletin / Department of Statistics, New Zealand. Miscellaneous series ; 2)

LIFE STYLE
Family, self, and society : emerging issues, alternatives, and interventions / edited by Douglas B. Gutknecht, Edgar W. Butler. — 2nd ed. — Lanham ; New York ; London : University Press of America, 1985. — xii,373p. — *Includes bibliographies*

LIFESPAN, PRODUCTIVE
BOSANQUET, Nicholas
A generation in limbo : government, the economy and the 55-65 age group in Britain / Nick Bosanquet. — London : Public Policy Centre, 1987. — xiii,49p. — *Bibliography: p48-49*

LIGA DER FREMDVÖLKER RUSSLANDS
ZETTERBERG, Seppo
Die Liga der Fremdvölker Russlands 1916-1918 : ein Beitrag zu Deutschlands antirussischem Propagandakreig unter den Fremdvölkern Russlands im ersten Weltkrieg / Seppo Zetterberg. — Helsinki : [Suomen Historiallinen Seura], 1978. — 279p. — (Studia historica veröffentlicht von der Finnischen Historischen Gesellschaft/Suomen Historiallinen Seura/Finska Historiska Samfundet ; vol.8). — *Bibliography: p263-271*

LIMA (PERU) — Population
PERU. Dirección Nacional de Estadística y Censos. Unidad de Análisis Demográfico
Encuesta de inmigración de Lima Metropolitana : Tercer informe. — Lima : the Dirección, 1968. — ii,53p. — ([Publicación] / Dirección Nacional de Estadística y Censos ; no.3)

LIMITED LIABILITY
PINEUS, Kaj
International maritime law : limited liability in collision cases / Kaj Pineus and Hans Georg Röhreke. — London : Lloyd's of London Press, 1984. — iv,23p

LIMITED LIABILITY — Austria
The Austrian law on companies with limited liability, as of January 1, 1984, with excerpted provisions of other relevant laws and annotations / editor Julie Goldberg. — Deventer ; Antwerp : Kluwer Law and Taxation Publishers, c1985. — 122p. — (Series on international corporate law ; 1). — *Bibliography: p122*

LINCOLN, ABRAHAM
FEHRENBACHER, Don Edward
Lincoln in text and context : collected essays / Don E. Fehrenbacher. — Stanford, Calif. : Stanford University Press, 1987. — p. cm. — *Includes index.* — *Bibliography: p*

LINCOLN, ABRAHAM — Addresses, essays, lectures
Abraham Lincoln and the American political tradition / edited by John L. Thomas. — Amherst : University of Massachusetts Press, 1986. — 162 p.. — *"The essays in this volume were presented in briefer form as papers at a conference on "Lincoln and the American Political Tradition" held at Brown University, June 7-9, 1984, and sponsored by the university's John Hay Library and the Lincoln Group of Boston."--Acknowledgements.* — *Includes bibliographies*

LINCOLN (LINCOLNSHIRE) — Industries — History
ROBERTS, D. E.
The Lincoln gas undertaking 1828-1949 / prepared for EMGAS by D.E. Roberts. — [Leicester] ([51 DeMontfort) : [East Midlands Gas], [1981]. — 46p. — *Ill on inside covers.* — *Bibliography: p45-46*

LINE AND STAFF ORGANIZATION
WHITE, Jonathan Peter
Roles of boundary-spanning individuals in decision-making involving organization-environment communication / by Jonathan Peter White. — 318 leaves. — *PhD (Econ) 1986 LSE.* — *Leaves 289-318 are appendices*

LINEAR MODELS (STATISTICS)
Statistical methods of model building. — Chichester : Wiley. — (Wiley series in probability and mathematical statistics)
Vol.1: Statistical inference in linear models / edited by Helga Bunke and Olaf Bunke ; translated by John Bibby and Michal Basch. — c1986. — 614p. — *Translation of: Statistische Inferenz für lineare Parameter.* — *Includes index*

LINEAR PROGRAMMING
DAVIDSON, James
Cointegration in linear dynamic systems / James Davidson. — London : Suntory-Toyota International Centre for Economics and Related Disciplines, 1986. — 46p. — (Econometrics). — *Bibliography: p45-46*

HEADY, Earl O.
Linear programming methods / Earl O. Heady and Wilfred V. Candler. — Ames : Iowa State University Press, 1958. — ix,597p

KLEIN HANEVELD, Willem K.
Duality in stochastic linear and dynamic programming / Willem K. Klein Haneveld. — Berlin ; New York : Springer-Verlag, c1986. — p. cm. — (Lecture notes in economics and mathematical systems ; 274). — *Includes bibliographies and index*

LINGUISTIC MINORITIES — Education
CHURCHILL, Stacy
The education of linguistic and cultural minorities in the OECD countries / Stacy Churchill. — Clevedon : Multilingual Matters, c1986. — [170]p. — (Multilingual matters ; 13) . — *Bibliography: p166-169.* — *Includes index*

LINGUISTIC MINORITIES — England — London
Languages in London / compiled by Euan Reid, Greg Smith and Anna Morawska. — London : University of London. Institute of Education. Community Languages and Education Project, 1985. — 124p. — (CLE/LMP working paper ; no.12). — *Bibliography: p84*

LINGUISTIC MINORITIES — India
EKBOTE, Gopalrao
A nation without a national language / by Gopalrao Ekbote. — Hyderabad : Hindi Prachar Sabha, 1984. — 258 p.. — *Bibliography: p. [256]-258*

LINGUISTICS
AKMAJIAN, Adrian
Linguistics, an introduction to language and communication / Adrian Akmajian, Richard A. Demers, Robert M. Harnish. — 2nd ed. — Cambridge, Mass. ; London : MIT Press, c1984. — xvi, 547 p.. — *Includes bibliographies and index*

KRISTEVA, Julia
The Kristeva reader / Julia Kristeva ; edited by Toril Moi. — Oxford : Basil Blackwell, 1986. — vii,327p. — *Translation of the French.* — *Includes index*

LEE, David
Language, children, and society : an introduction to linguistics and language development / David Lee. — New York, N.Y. : New York University Press, 1986. — p. cm. — *Includes index.* — *Bibliography: p*

LINGUISTICS *continuation*

PATEMAN, Trevor
Language in mind and language in society : studies in Linguistic reproduction / Trevor Pateman. — Oxford : Clarendon, c1987. — xiii,194p. — *Includes bibliography and index*

LINGUISTICS — Data processing

Readings in knowledge representation / edited by Ronald J. Brachman and Hector J. Levesque. — [Los Altos, Calif.] : M. Kaufmann Publishers, 1985. — p. cm. — *Includes index.* — *Bibliography: p*

LINGUISTICS — History

The Figural and the literal : problems of language in the history of science and philosophy, 1630-1800 / edited by Andrew E. Benjamin, Geoffrey N. Cantor and John R.R. Christie. — Manchester : Manchester University Press, c1987. — 229p. — *Conference papers*

LINGUISTICS — History — 19th century

AMSTERDAMSKA, Olga
Schools of thought : the development of linguistics from Bopp to Saussure / Olga Amsterdamska. — Dordrecht ; Boston : D. Reidel Pub. Co. ; Norwell, MA, U.S.A. : Sold and distributed in the U.S.A. and Canada by Kluwer Academic Publishers, c1987. — x, 320 p.. — (Sociology of the sciences monographs). — *Includes index.* — *Bibliography: p. 301-313*

LINGUISTICS — History — 20th century

AMSTERDAMSKA, Olga
Schools of thought : the development of linguistics from Bopp to Saussure / Olga Amsterdamska. — Dordrecht ; Boston : D. Reidel Pub. Co. ; Norwell, MA, U.S.A. : Sold and distributed in the U.S.A. and Canada by Kluwer Academic Publishers, c1987. — x, 320 p.. — (Sociology of the sciences monographs). — *Includes index.* — *Bibliography: p. 301-313*

LINGUISTICS — Periodicals — Bibliography

UNIVERSITY OF LONDON. Library Resources Co-ordinating Committee. Linguistics Subject Sub-Committee
Current holdings of linguistics periodicals in the libraries of the University of London and other London institutions. — 2nd ed. — London : the Committee, 1986. — 53p

LIQUIDATION

RAAD VOOR HET MIDDEN- EN KLEINBEDRIJF
Beroepskenmerken en bedrijfsbeëindiging : raaport inzake de beroepspositie, de beroepsgeschiedenis en de beëindigingsmotieven van ondernemers die bedrijfsbeëindigingshulp bij de Stichting Ontwikkeling en Sanering voor het Midden- en Kleinbedrijf hebben anngevraagd. — 's-Gravenhage : Raad voor het Midden- en Kleinbedrijf, 1969. — 60p. — *Summaries in French, German and English*

LIQUIDATION — England

FRIEZE, Steven A.
Compulsory winding up procedure / Steven A. Frieze. — 2nd ed. — London : Longman, c1987. — xvii,117p. — (Longman practice notes ; 77). — *Previous ed.: 1983.* — *Includes index*

LIQUIDATION — Netherlands

RAAD VOOR HET MIDDEN- EN KLEINBEDRIJF
Beroepskenmerken en bedrijfsbeëindiging : raaport inzake de beroepspositie, de beroepsgeschiedenis en de beëindigingsmotieven van ondernemers die bedrijfsbeëindigingshulp bij het Midden- en Kleinbedrijf hebben anngevraagd. — 's-Gravenhage : Raad voor het Midden- en Kleinbedrijf, 1969. — 60p. — *Summaries in French, German and English*

LIQUIDITY (ECONOMICS)

JOHNSTON, R. B.
The demand for liquidity aggregates by the UK personal sector / R. B. Johnston. — London : HM Treasury, 1985. — 45p. — (Government Economic Service working paper ; no.81) (Treasury working paper ; no.36). — *Bibliographical references: p39-41*

LIQUOR LAWS — Great Britain

Where Erroll went wrong on liquor licensing : a critque of the report of the departmental committee on liquor licensing (H.M.S.O. Cmnd. 5154). — London : Institute of Psychiatry. Addiction Research Unit, 1973. — 64p

LISP (COMPUTER PROGRAM LANGUAGE)

WILENSKY, Robert
LISPcraft / Robert Wilensky. — 2nd ed. — New York : W.W. Norton, 1987. — p. cm

LIST, FRIEDRICH

HENDERSON, W. O.
Friedrich List : economist and visionary 1789-1846 / W.O. Henderson. — London : Cass, 1983. — xi,288p,[5]p of plates. — *Bibliography: p262-273.* — *Includes index*

LISTENING

Language for hearers / edited by Graham McGregor. — Oxford : Pergamon, 1986. — [vii, 235]p. — (Language & communication library ; v.8). — *Includes index*

LISTENING COMPREHENSION TESTS

VOSS, Bernd
Slips of the ear : investigations into the speech perception behaviour of German speakers of English / Bernd Voss. — Tübingen : G. Narr, c1984. — 184 p.. — (Tübinger Beiträge zur Linguistik ; 254). — *Bibliography: p. 126-134*

LITERACY

Literacy, society, and schooling : a reader / edited by Suzanne de Castell, Allan Luke, Kieran Egan. — Cambridge : Cambridge University Press, 1986. — xiv,336p. — *Conference proceedings.* — *Includes bibliographies and indexes*

LITERACY — Social aspects

Literacy, society, and schooling : a reader / edited by Suzanne de Castell, Allan Luke, Kieran Egan. — Cambridge : Cambridge University Press, 1986. — xiv,336p. — *Conference proceedings.* — *Includes bibliographies and indexes*

LITERACY — Social aspects — England — History — 19th century

STEPHENS, W. B.
Education, literacy and society, 1830-70 : the geography of diversity in provincial England / W.B. Stephens. — Manchester : Manchester University Press, c1987. — xii,386p. — *Includes index*

LITERACY — Social aspects — Europe — History — 19th century

MAYNES, Mary Jo
Schooling in Western Europe : a social history / Mary Jo Maynes. — Albany : State University of New York, 1985. — p. cm. — *Includes index.* — *Bibliography: p*

LITERACY — Cuba — History — 20th century

MACDONALD, Theodore H
Making a new people : education in revolutionary Cuba / Theodore MacDonald. — Vancouver : New Star Books, c1985. — 248 p.. — *Includes index.* — *Bibliography: p. 242-245*

LITERACY — Developing countries

BOWERS, John
Communication and rural development / by John Bowers. — London : Commonwealth Secretariat, 1970. — 17p. — *At head of title page: Commonwealth Conference on Education in Rural Areas.* — *CRE(70)B/3 and C/5*

LITERACY — European Economic Community countries

Literacy training in Europe : a comparative analysis of the most effective and innovatory literacy schemes being implemented in member states by the authorities or private agents / report produced by the International Movement Aide à toute détresse fourth world. — Luxembourg : Office for Official Publications of the European Communities, 1985. — 156p. — *At head of title: Commission of the European Communities*

LITERACY — Nicaragua

ARNOVE, Robert F
Education and revolution in Nicaragua / Robert F. Arnove. — New York : Praeger, 1986. — xii, 160 p.. — (Praeger special studies series in comparative education). — "Praeger special studies. Praeger scientific.". — *Includes index.* — *Bibliography: p. 145-153*

LITERACY — Pakistan — Statistics

Literacy profile of Pakistan : 1951-1981 / edited by Syed Firasat Ali Kazi. — Islamabad : Literacy and Mass Education Commission : 1984. — (Statistical series ; no.1)

LITERACY — Soviet Union — History

BROOKS, Jeffrey
When Russia learned to read : literacy and popular literature, 1861-1917 / Jeffrey Brooks. — Princeton, N.J. : Princeton University Press, c1985. — xxii, 450 p.. — *Includes index.* — *Bibliography: p. 415-435*

LITERARY FORGERIES AND MYSTIFICATIONS

BAHNSEN, Uwe
Der "Stern" - Prozess : Heidemann und Kujau vor Gericht / Uwe Bahnsen. — Mainz : v. Hase und Kochler, 1986. — 192p

BISSINGER, Manfred
Hitlers Sternstunde : Kujau, Heidemann und die Millionen / Manfred Bissinger. — Hamburg : Rasch und Röhring, 1984. — 238p

LITERARY LANDMARKS

BLYTHE, Ronald
Divine landscapes / Ronald Blythe ; illustrated with photographs by Edwin Smith. — [Harmondsworth] : Viking, 1986. — 253p. — *Bibliography: p248-250.* — *Includes index*

LITERATURE — Directories

The International authors and writers who's who / editorial director Ernest Kay. — 10th ed. — Cambridge : International Biographical Centre, 1986. — 879p

LITERATURE — Philosophy

FOULKES, A. P.
Literature and propaganda / A.P. Foulkes. — London : Methuen, 1983. — viii,124p. — (New accents). — *Bibliography: p109-119.* — *Includes index*

LITERATURE — Women authors

Wall tappings : an anthology of writings by women prisoners / [compiled] by Judith A. Scheffler. — Boston : Northeastern University Press, c1986. — p. cm. — *Bibliography: p*

LITERATURE AND SOCIETY — France

VIALA, Alain
Naissance de l'écrivain : sociologie de la littérature à l'âge classique / Alain Viala. — Paris : Minuit, 1985. — 317p. — (Le sens commun)

LITERATURE AND SOCIETY — Great Britain — History — 20th century

MILES, Peter
Cinema, literature & society : elite and mass culture in interwar Britain / Peter Miles and Malcolm Smith. — London : Croom Helm, c1987. — 271p. — *Bibliography: p257-266.* — *Includes index*

LITERATURE AND STATE
BERLINER COLLOQUIUM ZUR LITERATURPOLITIK IM 'DRITTEN REICH'
"Das war ein Vorspiel nur ..." : Berliner ... / hrsg. [von] Aorst Denkler [und] Eberhard Lämmert. — Berlin : Akademie der Künste Freie Universität Berlin, 1985. — 211 p. — (Schriftenreihe der Akademie der Künste : Bd. 15)

LITERATURE, MODERN — 20th century — translations from Japanese
Modern Japanese literature : an anthology / compiled and edited by Donald Keene. — New York : Grove Press, Inc., 1956. — 440p. — (Grove Press Eastern literature and philosophy books). — *Bibliography: p[439]-440*

LITHUANIANS — Canada
DANYS, Matilda
D. P. [Displaced Persons] : Lithuanian immigration to Canada after the second world war / Matilda Danys. — Toronto : Multicultural History Society of Ontario, 1986. — 365p. — (Studies in ethnic and immigration history). — *Bibliography: p[352]-353*

LIVERPOOL COMMUNITY ORGANISATIONS COMMITTEE
CLAY, Dave
Voluntary issues: a conference review / compiled by Dave Clay, Mike Walsh [and] Hilary Jones. — Liverpool : Liverpool Community Organisations Committee, 1985. — 8p

LIVERPOOL (MERSEYSIDE) — Politics and government
LIVERPOOL BLACK CAUCUS
The racial politics of Militant in Liverpool : the black community's struggle for participation in local politics 1980-1986. — Liverpool : Merseyside Area Profile Group : Runnymede Trust, 1986. — 144p. — *Bibliography: p139-142*

MILITANT
Marxism on trial : defend the Liverpool socialists. — London : Militant Publications, 1986. — 32p

LIVERPOOL (MERSEYSIDE) — Population
LIVERPOOL
Liverpool's population. — Liverpool : [the Council]. — 1986
1: Population, social, and housing stock, changes and trends 1971-1991. — 56p

LIVERPOOL (MERSEYSIDE) — Race relations
LIVERPOOL BLACK CAUCUS
The racial politics of Militant in Liverpool : the black community's struggle for participation in local politics 1980-1986. — Liverpool : Merseyside Area Profile Group : Runnymede Trust, 1986. — 144p. — *Bibliography: p139-142*

LIVERPOOL (MERSEYSIDE) — Social conditions
COONEY, Anthony
The sources of poverty : the causes of poverty in Liverpool in general and Toxteth in particular during the decade (1900-1910) of the Royal Commission on the Poor Law and Relief of Distress / Anthony Cooney. — Liverpool : Gild of St. George, 1984. — 77p. — *Bibliography: p77*

LIVESTOCK — Genetics — History
RUSSELL, Nicholas
Like engend'ring like : heredity and animal breeding in early modern England / Nicholas Russell. — Cambridge : Cambridge University Press, 1986. — [280]p. — *Includes bibliography and index*

LIVESTOCK — Australia — Statistics
AUSTRALIA. Commomwealth Bureau of Census and Statistics
A summary of live-stock statistics, Australia. — Canberra : [the Bureau], 1951-52. — *Annual. — Continued by: Statistical bulletin: livestock numbers, Australia*

AUSTRALIA. Commonwealth Bureau of Census and Statistics
Livestock statistics, Australia. — Canberra : [the Bureau], 1974-1980/81. — *Irregular. — Title varies. — Continues: Statistical bulletin: Livestock numbers Australia*

AUSTRALIA. Commonwealth Bureau of Census and Statistics
Statistical bulletin: livestock numbers, Australia / Commonwealth Bureau of Census and Statistics, Australia. — Canberra : [the Bureau], 1953-1970. — *Irregular. — Continues: A summary of live-stock statistics, Australia continued by Livestock statistics, Australia*

LIVESTOCK — China
China, the livestock sector. — Washington, D.C., U.S.A. : World Bank, 1987. — [xx], 195p. — (A World Bank country study). — *Includes bibliographical references*

LIVESTOCK — England — Breeding — History
RUSSELL, Nicholas
Like engend'ring like : heredity and animal breeding in early modern England / Nicholas Russell. — Cambridge : Cambridge University Press, 1986. — [280]p. — *Includes bibliography and index*

LIVESTOCK — European Economic Community Countries
Agricultural review for Europe. — New York : United Nations, 1983/84-. — *Annual. — Continues: Review of the agricultural situation in Europe and Agricultural trade in Europe. — In 6 vols. Vol.I: General review, Vol.II: Agricultural trade, Vol.III: The Grain Market, Vol.IV: The Livestock and meat market, Vol.V: The milk and dairy products market, Vol.VI: The egg market*

LIVESTOCK — India — Statistics
INDIA. Ministry of Agriculture and Irrigation. Directorate of Economics and Statistics
Indian livestock census. — [New Delhi] : Ministry of Agriculture and Irrigation, Directorate of Economics and Statistics
vol.2: Detailed tables. — [1976?]. — 3v.

INDIA. Ministry of Agriculture and Irrigation. Directorate of Economics and Statistics
Indian livestock census 1977. — [New Delhi] : the Directorate
V.1: Summary tables. — [1984]. — xxiv,219p

LIVESTOCK — Latin America
JARVIS, Lovell S.
Livestock development in Latin America / Lovell S. Jarvis. — Washington, D.C. : The World Bank, 1986. — x,214p. — *Bibliography: p200-207*

LIVESTOCK PRODUCTIVITY — Africa — Statistics
SOCIÉTÉ D'ÉTUDES POUR LE DÉVELOPPEMENT ÉCONOMIQUE ET SOCIAL (FRANCE)
Recueil statistique de la production animale. — [Paris] : Ministère de la coopération, [1975]. — 1201p

LIVING ALONE — United States
RUBINSTEIN, Robert L
Singular paths : old men living alone / Robert L. Rubinstein. — New York : Columbia University Press, 1986. — viii, 265 p.. — (Columbia studies of social gerontology and aging). — *Includes index. — Bibliography: p. [257]-261*

LIVINGSTONE, KEN
CARVEL, John
Citizen Ken / John Carvel. — Rev. and enl. ed. — London : Hogarth, 1987. — 267p. — (Current affairs). — *Previous ed.: London : Chatto & Windus, 1984. — Includes index*

LLOYD GEORGE, DAVID
GILBERT, Bentley B.
David Lloyd George : a political life / Bentley Briakerhoff Gilbert. — London : Batsford
The architect of change, 1863-1912. — 1987. — 546p,[8]p of plates. — *Bibliography: p529-536. — Includes index*

LLOYD'S OF LONDON
DAVISON, Ian Hay
A view of the Room : Lloyd's : change and disclosure / Ian Hay Davison. — London : Weidenfeld and Nicolson, 1987. — x, 238p. — *Bibliography: p.209-212*

MACVE, Richard
A survey of Lloyd's syndicate accounts : financial reporting at Lloyd's in 1985 / Richard Macve. — Englewood Cliffs ; London : Prentice Hall International in association with The Institute of Chartered Accountants in England and Wales, 1986. — xxv,263p. — (Research studies in accounting). — *Bibliography: p261-262. — Includes index*

LOANS — Europe
A guide to European Community grants and loans 1986/87 : for commerce, industry, local authorities, academic and research institutions / compiled by Gay Scott. — 7th ed. — Newbury : Eurofi (UK), 1986. — 1v.(loose-leaf)

LOANS — European Economic Community countries — Directories
SCOTT, Gay
A guide to European Community grants and loans, 1985/86 for commerce, industry, local authorities, academic and research institutions / compiled by Gay Scott. — 6th ed : Northill, Beds. : Eurofi, 1985. — 1v(loose-leaf)

LOANS — United States — Government guaranty
BOSWORTH, Barry
The economics of federal credit programs / Barry P. Bosworth, Andrew S. Carron, Elisabeth H. Rhyne. — Washington, D.C. : Brookings Institution, c1987. — xii, 214 p.. — *Includes bibliographical references and index*

LOANS, AMERICAN — Developing countries
BENOÎT, J. Pierre V
United States interest rates and the interest rate dilemma for the developing world / J. Pierre V. Benoît. — Westport, Conn. : Quorum Books, 1986. — xviii, 230 p.. — *Includes index. — Bibliography: p. [215]-219*

LOANS, FOREIGN
CONNOLLY, Michael B
International trade and lending / Michael B. Connolly. — New York, NY, USA : Praeger, 1985. — xi, 131 p.. — *Includes bibliographies and index*

CRAWFORD, Vincent P.
International lending, long-term credit relationships, and dynamic contract theory / Vincent P. Crawford. — Princeton, N.J. : International Finance Section, Dept. of Economics, Princeton University, 1987. — p. cm. — (Princeton studies in international finance ; no. 59 (March 1987)). — *Bibliography: p*

International borrowing : negotiating and structuring international debt transactions / Daniel D. Bradlow, editor. — 2nd ed. — Washington, D.C. : International Law Institute, c1986. — 499p. — (International negotiation and development : sourcebooks on policy and practice ; 1)

International capital markets : development and prospects / by Maxwell Watson...[et al.]. — Washington, D. C. : International Monetary Fund, 1986. — ix,152p. — (World economic and financial surveys). — *Includes Bibliographical references*

SPRAOS, John
IMF conditionality : ineffectual, inefficient, mistargeted / John Spraos. — Princeton, N.J. : International Finance Section, Dept. of Economics, Princeton University 1986. — p. cm. — (Essays in international finance ; no. 166 (Dec. 1986)). — *Bibliography: p*

LOANS, FOREIGN *continuation*
WELLONS, Philip A
Passing the buck : banks, governments, and Third World debt / Philip A. Wellons. — Boston, Mass. : Harvard Business School Press, c1987. — xiv, 342 p.. — *Includes bibliographical references and index*

LOANS, FOREIGN — Asia
PAL, Mahendra
World Bank and the Third World countries of Asia : (with special reference to India) / Mahendra Pal. — New Delhi : National, 1985. — x,407p. — *Bibliography: p[379]-389*

LOANS, FOREIGN — Contracts and specifications
GOLD, Joseph
Relations between banks' loan agreements and IMF stand-by arrangements / Sir Joseph Gold. — London : Euromoney Publications Ltd., 1983. — 28-35p. — *Reprinted from: International Financial Law Review, September 1983*

INTERNATIONAL DEVELOPMENT ASSOCIATION
General conditions applicable to development credit agreements. — [[Washington, D.C.?] : the Association, 1980. — iii,12p

WORLD BANK
General conditions applicable to loan and guarantee agreements. — [Washington, D.C.] : the Bank, 1974. — iii,18p. — *At head of title page: International Bank for Reconstruction and Development*

WORLD BANK
Loan regulations no.3 : applicable to loans made by the Bank to member governments : dated February 15, 1961 as amended February 9, 1967. — [Washington, D.C.?] : the Bank, 1967. — iv,35p

WORLD BANK
Loan regulations no.4 : applicable to loans made by the Bank to borrowers other than member governments : dated Februrary 15, 1961 as amended February 9, 1967. — [Washington, D.C.?] : the Bank, 1967. — iv,40p

LOANS, FOREIGN — Dictionaries — Polyglot
Borrowing and lending terminology : English-French-Spanish = Terminologie des emprunts et des prêts : Français-anglais-espagnol = Terminología de empréstitos y prśetamos : Español-inglés-francés. — Washington, D.C. : The World Bank, 1984. — vii,56p. — (A World Bank glossary). — *In English, French and Spanish*

LOANS, FOREIGN — Africa, West
Croissance et ajustement : les problèmes de l'Afrique de l'Ouest / préparée par Patrick Guillaumont. — Paris : Economica, 1985. — 248p. — *Includes bibliographies*

LOANS, FOREIGN — Brazil
BATISTA JUNIOR, Paulo Nogueira
International financial flows to Brazil since the late 1960s : an analysis of debt expansion and payments problems / Paulo Nogueira Batista. — Washington, D.C. : The World Bank, 1987. — vi,66p. — (World Bank discussion papers ; 7). — *Bibliographical references: p59-66*

LOANS, FOREIGN — Developing countries
CHITALE, V. P
India and Euro-currency markets / V.P. Chitale. — New Delhi : Economic and Scientific Research Foundation, [1984]. — viii, 150 p.. — *Includes bibliographical references*

LEVITSKY, Jacob
World Bank lending to small enterprises : a review / Jacob Levitsky. — Washington, D.C. : The World Bank, 1986. — viii,53p. — (Industry and finance series ; v.16). — *Includes bibliographical references*

VENUGOPAL REDDY, Y
World Bank, borrowers' perspectives / Y. Venugopal Reddy. — New Delhi : Sterling Publishers, c1985. — x, 143 p.. — *Includes index*

WELLONS, Philip A
Passing the buck : banks, governments, and Third World debt / Philip A. Wellons. — Boston, Mass. : Harvard Business School Press, c1987. — xiv, 342 p.. — *Includes bibliographical references and index*

LOANS, FOREIGN — India
CHITALE, V. P
India and Euro-currency markets / V.P. Chitale. — New Delhi : Economic and Scientific Research Foundation, [1984]. — viii, 150 p.. — *Includes bibliographical references*

LOANS, FOREIGN — Jamaica
LOONEY, Robert E
The Jamaican economy in the 1980's : economic decline and structural adjustment / Robert Looney. — Boulder, Colo. : Westview Press, 1986. — xiii, 257p. — (A Westview special study). — *Includes bibliographical references and index*

LOANS, FOREIGN — Nigeria
RANDLE, J. K.
The natives are friendly? / by J. K. Randle. — Winchester : Hambleside, 1986. — x,297p

LOANS, FOREIGN — Peru
SCHEETZ, Thomas Edward
Peru and the International Monetary Fund / Thomas Scheetz. — Pittsburgh, PA : University of Pittsburgh Press, c1986. — xi, 257 p.. — (Pitt Latin American series). — *Includes index. — Bibliography: p. 251-254*

LOBBYING — Canada
MALVERN, Paul
Persuaders : influence peddling, lobbying and political corruption in Canada / Paul Malvern. — Toronto ; London : Methuen, 1985. — 350p . — *Includes bibliographical notes*

LOBBYING — Great Britain
MILLER, Charles
Lobbying government : understanding and influencing the corridors of power / Charles Miller. — Oxford : Basil Blackwell, 1987. — [200]p. — *Includes index*

LOBBYING — Great Britain — Handbooks, manuals, etc.
CONFEDERATION OF BRITISH INDUSTRY
Working with politicians / CBI. — London : Confederation of British Industry, 1985. — 135p. — *Includes supplement of updating information, May 1986*

LOBBYING — United States
DORAN, Charles F
Canada and Congress : lobbying in Washington / by Charles F. Dòran, Joel J. Sokolsky. — Halifax, N.S., Canada : Centre for Foreign Policy Studies, Dalhousie University, 1985. — vi, 257 p.. — *Includes bibliographies*

PERTSCHUK, Michael
Giantkillers / by Michael Pertschuk. — New York : Norton, c1986. — p. cm. — *Includes index*

LOBBYING — United States — Case studies
HALLEY, Laurence
Ancient affections : ethnic groups and foreign policy / Laurence Halley. — New York : Praeger, 1985. — viii, 180 p.. — *Includes index. — Bibliography: p. 172-174*

LOBBYISTS — United States
PERTSCHUK, Michael
Giantkillers / by Michael Pertschuk. — New York : Norton, c1986. — p. cm. — *Includes index*

LOCAL AREA NETWORKS (COMPUTER NETWORKS)
BERRY, Paul
Operating the IBM PC networks / Paul Berry. — Berkeley : Sybex, c1986. — xvii, 363 p.. — *Includes index. — Bibliography: p. [343]-344*

COLLIER, Mel
Local area networks : the implications for library and information science / Mel Collier. — [London] : British Library, c1984. — vii,41p. — (Library and information research report ; 19)

Local network technology / [edited by] William Stallings. — 2nd ed. — Washington, D.C. : IEEE CS Press ; Amsterdam : North Holland, 1985. — vii,429p. — *Bibliography: p415-426*

Localnet '86 : proceedings of the conference held in San Francisco, November 1986. — London : Online, 1986. — [250]p

LOCAL AREA NETWORKS (COMPUTER NETWORKS) — Congresses
IFIP WG 7.3 INTERNATIONAL SEMINAR ON COMPUTER NETWORKING AND PERFORMANCE EVALUATION (1985 : Tokyo, Japan)
Computer networking and performance evaluation : proceedings of the IFIP WG 7.3 International Seminar on Computer Networking and Performance Evaluation, 18-20 September 1985, Tokyo, Japan / edited by T. Hasegawa, H. Takagi, Y. Takahashi. — Amsterdam ; New York : North-Holland ; New York, N.Y., U.S.A. : Sole distributors for the U.S.A. and Canada, Elsevier Science Pub. Co., 1986. — p. cm

LOCAL BUDGETS — Great Britain
GREAT BRITAIN. Parliament. House of Commons. Library. Research Division
Local rates and budgets : Liverpool and beyond / Barry K. Winetrobe. — [London] : the Division, 1984. — 22p. — (Background paper ; no.143). — *Includes bibliographical references*

LOCAL ELECTIONS — England — Statistics
GREAT BRITAIN. Parliament. House of Commons. Library. Research Division
The English county council elections of 2 May 1985 : voting by party, county and constituency / Robert Clements. — [London] : the Division, 1985. — 47p. — (Background paper ; no.172)

RALLINGS, Colin
The 1987 metropolitan borough council election results : a statistical digest / Colin Rallings and Michael Thrasher. — [Plymouth] : Centre for the Study of Local Elections, Plymouth Polytechnic, [1987]. — 224,[128]p

LOCAL ELECTIONS — Scotland — Statistics
BOCHEL, J. M.
The Scottish regional elections 1986 : results and statistics / J. M. Bochel and D. T. Denver. — Dundee : Election Studies, 1986. — i,55p

LOCAL FINANCE — Accounting
COUNCIL OF EUROPE. Committee of Experts on Local and Regional Finance
Local authority accounting in Europe : report / prepared by the Committee of Experts on Local and Regional Finance of the Steering Committee for Regional and Municipal Matters. — Strasbourg : Council of Europe, 1985. — 120p. — (Study series local and regional authorities in Europe ; 33)

LOCAL FINANCE — Law and legislation — Great Britain
GREAT BRITAIN. Parliament. House of Commons. Library. Research Division
Local Government Finance Bill (Bill 8 of 1981-82) / Priscilla Baines, Robert Clements. — [London] : the Division, 1981. — 21p. — (Reference sheet ; no.81/18)

LOCAL FINANCE — Law and legislation — Great Britain
continuation

GREAT BRITAIN. Parliament. House of Commons. Library. Research Division
Local Government Finance (No.2) Bill (Bill 41 of 1981-82) and 1982-83 rate support grant settlement / [Priscilla Baines]. — [London] : the Division, 1982. — 8p. — (Reference sheet ; no.82/2)

GREAT BRITAIN. Parliament. House of Commons. Library. Research Division
Rates Bill, Bill 79, 1983-84 / Barry K. Winetrobe. — [London] : the Division, 1984. — 18p. — (Reference sheet ; no.84/3). — *Includes bibliographical references*

LOCAL FINANCE — Law and legislation — Scotland

GREAT BRITAIN. Parliament. House of Commons. Library. Research Division
Abolition of Domestic Rates etc. [Scotland] Bill, Bill 9 of 1986-87 / Barry Winetrobe, Rob Clements. — [London] : the Division, 1986. 20p. — (Reference sheet ; no.86/16)

GREAT BRITAIN. Parliament. House of Commons. Library. Research Division
Rating & Valuation (Amendment) (Scotland) Bill, Bill 61 of 1983-84 / [Barry K. Winetrobe]. — [London] : the Division, 1983. — 9p. — (Reference sheet ; no.83/22). — *Includes bibliographical references*

LOCAL FINANCE — Mathematical models — Congresses

Measuring local government expenditure needs : the Copenhagen workshop. — Paris : Organisation for Economic Co-operation and Development, c1981. — 353p. — (OECD urban management studies ; 4). — *Bibliography: p340-346. — Includes indexes*

LOCAL FINANCE — Statistical methods — Congresses

Measuring local government expenditure needs : the Copenhagen workshop. — Paris : Organisation for Economic Co-operation and Development, c1981. — 353p. — (OECD urban management studies ; 4). — *Bibliography: p340-346. — Includes indexes*

LOCAL FINANCE — Appalachian Region

Who owns Appalachia? : landownership and its impact / the Appalachian Land Ownership Task Force ; with an introduction by Charles C. Geisler. — Lexington, Ky. : University Press of Kentucky, c1983. — xxxii, 235 p.. — *Map on lining papers. — Includes bibliographies and index*

LOCAL FINANCE — Australia

HOWARD, John
Local government revenue raising : report to the National Inquiry into Local Government Finance. — [Queanbeyan? : National Inquiry into Local Government Finance?], 1985. — 4,171 leaves. — *Includes bibliographical references*

NATIONAL INQUIRY INTO LOCAL GOVERNMENT FINANCE (Australia)
Report / National Inquiry into Local Government Finance. — Canberra : Australian Government Publishing Service, 1985. — xxxvi,482p. — *Bibliographical references: p399-419*

SITLINGTON
Local government functions : an investigation of changes in patterns of expenditure in local government from 1971-1981 / J. A. Sitlington. — 1985 ; Queanbeyan : National Inquiry into Local Government Finance. — viii,183 leaves. — *Bibliographical references: p182-183*

LOCAL FINANCE — Canary Islands

Contabilidad regional de Canarias / Consejería de Economía ye Comercio, Gobierno de Canarias. — Las Palmas : Gobierno de Canarias. Consejería de Economía y Comercio,, 1985-. — *Annual*

LOCAL FINANCE — Council of Europe countries

KELLY, Graham
Financial resources for local and regional authorities : report / prepared under the guidance of the Committee of Experts on Local and Regional Finance of the Steering Committee for Regional and Municipal Matters by G. Kelly. — Strasbourg : Council of Europe, 1985. — 79p. — (Study series local and regional authorities in Europe ; 34)

MEADOWS, W. J.
The response of local authorities to central government incitement to reduce expenditure / by W. J. Meadows. — Strasbourg : Council of Europe, 1986. — 33p. — (Study series local and regional authorities in Europe ; 37). — *Prepared under the guidance of the Committee of Experts on Local and Regional Finance of the Steering Committee for Regional and Municipal Matters*

LOCAL FINANCE — Denmark — Copenhagen — Statistics

Københavnernes indkomster 1980-1983. — [København : Københavns Statistiske Kontor, 1985]. — 98p. — (Undersøgelser fra Københavns Statistiske Kontor ; nr.23)

LOCAL FINANCE — England — London

LAMBETH
Rate-capping and Lambeth : a public consultation document. — Lambeth : [the Council], 1986. — 10p

LONDON RESIDUARY BODY
Budget / London Residuary Body. — London : London Residuary Body, 1986/87-. — *Annual. — Continues: Annual report and accounts/London Residuary Body*

WESTMINSTER. Finance Department. Policy Unit
Financial effects of GLC abolition : a Westminster briefing paper for industry and commerce. — Westminster : [the Department], 1985. — 8p

LOCAL FINANCE — Europe

KELLY, Graham
Financial apportionment and equalisation / report prepared under the guidance of the members of the Committee of Experts on Local and Regional Finance by Graham Kelly. — Strasbourg : Council of Europe, 1981. — 95p. — (Study series local and regional authorities in Europe ; study no.24). — *Up-dated and expanded version of: Financial structures of local and regional authorities in Europe. - Vol. 2. - 1976. - (Study series local and regional authorities in Europe ; no. 13)*

LOCAL FINANCE — France — Statistics

DONNELLIER, Jean-Christophe
Les comptes régionaux des adminstrations publiques locales de 1962 à 1981 Quettier. — [Paris] : I.N.S.E.E., 1986. — 69p. — (Archives et documents / France. Institut national de la statistique et des études économiques ; no.179)

LOCAL FINANCE — Great Britain

BANHAM, John
"On local accountability" / John Banham. — London : National Association of Local Councils, 1986. — 17p. — *Lord Merthyr Memorial Lecture*

BENNETT, Robert J.
Local income tax in Britain : a reappraisal of theory and practice / Robert J. Bennett. — London : Association of Metropolitan Authorities, 1987. — 28p. — *Paper presented at AMA seminar on "Local income tax", AMA, London, 29th January 1987*

BLOOMFIELD, John
Local authority capital spending : controls and consequences / John Bloomfield. — London : North East London Polytechnic and Essex County Council. Anglian Regional Management Centre, 1986. — 42p. — (Commentary series / North East London Polytechnic ; 30). — *Bibliography: p[44-45]*

Capital financing in local authorities : a Working Party report. — [London] : Audit Commission for Local Authorities in England and Wales, 1986. — 32p. — *Leader of the Working Party: Jeff Pipe*

GREAT BRITAIN. Parliament. House of Commons. Library. Research Division
Local rates and budgets : Liverpool and beyond / Barry K. Winetrobe. — [London] : the Division, 1984. — 22p. — (Background paper ; no.143). — *Includes bibliographical references*

GREAT BRITAIN. Parliament. House of Commons. Library. Research Division
The Rate Support Grant settlement 1980 / [Margaret M. Camsell, Rob Clements]. — [London] : the Division, 1981. — 9p. — (Research note ; no.37). — *Bibliography: p9*

GREAT BRITAIN. Parliament. House of Commons. Library. Research Division
The rating system / Margaret M. Camsell, Robert Clements. — [London] : the Division, 1980. — 22p. — (Background paper ; no.80). — *Bibliography: p19*

HEPWORTH, N. P.
The finance of local government / by N.P. Hepworth. — 7th ed. — London : Allen & Unwin, 1984. — xvi,349p. — (The New local government series ; no.6). — *Previous ed.: 1980. — Bibliography: p335-339. — Includes index*

KAY, J. A.
The future of local government finance / John Kay. — Cambridge (19 Silver Street, Cambridge, CB3 9EP) : University of Cambridge, Dept. of Land Economy, c1983. — 17p. — (The Denman lecture ; 1983)

OPPENHEIM, Carey
A feudal levy : a response to the Green Paper on paying for local government / Carey Oppenheim. — London : Child Poverty Action Group, 1986. — 18p

STRATHCLYDE. Regional Council
Excerpt from minutes of meeting of Policy and Resources Committee (Augmented) of 3rd April 1986, as approved by the Regional Council at their meeting on 30th April 1986. — Glasgow : [the Council]
2: Green paper "Paying for local government". — 1986. — 6p

TRAVERS, Tony
The politics of local government finance / Tony Travers. — London : Allen & Unwin, 1986. — xii,241p. — (The New Local government series ; no.27). — *Includes index*

LOCAL FINANCE — Great Britain — Auditing

AUDIT COMMISSION FOR LOCAL AUTHORITIES IN ENGLAND AND WALES
Competitiveness and contracting out of local authorities' services. — [London : H.M.S.O.], 1987. — 7p. — (Occasional papers ; no.3)

AUDIT COMMISSION FOR LOCAL AUTHORITIES IN ENGLAND AND WALES
Improving cash flow management in local government : a report. — London : H.M.S.O., 1986. — 80p

AUDIT COMMISSION FOR LOCAL AUTHORITIES IN ENGLAND AND WALES
Improving supply management in local authorities : a report. — London : H.M.S.O., 1987. — 55p

LOCAL FINANCE — Iceland — Statistics

ICELAND. Hagstofa
Sveitarsjóðareikningar 1953-62 = Communal finance 1953-62. — Reykjavík : Hagstofa Íslands, 1967. — 57p. — (Hagskýrslur Íslands ; 2,37). — *Text in Icelandic, with headings in English*

ICELAND. Hagstofa
Sveitarsjóðareikningar 1963-65 = Communal finance 1963-65. — Reykjavík : Hagstofa Íslands, 1968. — 93p. — (Hagskýrslur Íslands ; 2,44). — *Text in Icelandic, with headings in English*

LOCAL FINANCE — Iceland — Statistics
continuation

ICELAND. Hagstofa
Sveitarsjóðareikningar 1966-68 = Communal finance 1966-68. — Reykjavík : Hagstofa Íslands, 1970. — 93p. — (Hagskýrslur Íslands ; 2,48). — *Text in Icelandic, with headings in English*

ICELAND. Hagstofa
Sveitarsjóðareikningar 1969-71 = Communal finance 1969-71. — Reykjavík : Hagstofa Íslands, 1974. — 95p. — (Hagskýrslur Íslands ; 2,56). — *Text in Icelandic, with headings in English*

LOCAL FINANCE — Illinois

CHICOINE, David L
Governmental structure and local public finance / David L. Chicoine, Norman Walzer. — Boston, Mass. : Oelgeschlager, Gunn & Hain, c1985. — xi, 235 p.. — *Includes bibliographies and index*

LOCAL FINANCE — Japan — Tokyo

The fiscal outlook for the metropolis of Tokyo. — Tokyo : Tokyo Metropolitan Government, 1986. — viii,143p. — (TMG municipal library ; no.21)

LOCAL FINANCE — Northern Ireland

District councils summary of statements of accounts / Department of the Environment for Northern Ireland. — Belfast : HMSO, 1985-. — *Annual*

LOCAL FINANCE — Scotland — Dumfries and Galloway

DUMFRIES AND GALLOWAY. Regional Council
Structure plan : report of survey : finance (revised). — Dumfries : [the Regional Council], 1979. — 15p

DUNFRIES AND GALLOWAY. Regional Council
Structure plan : report of survey : finance. — Dumfries : [the Regional Council], 1978. — 15p

LOCAL FINANCE — Switzerland — Berne

Les relations financières entre le Jura Sud et l'État de Berne. — [s.l.] : [s.n.], 1975. — 36p

LOCAL FINANCE — Switzerland — Jura Sud

Les relations financières entre le Jura Sud et l'État de Berne. — [s.l.] : [s.n.], 1975. — 36p

LOCAL FINANCE — United States

Studies in state and local public finance / edited by Harvey S. Rosen. — Chicago : University of Chicago Press, c1986. — ix, 236 p.. — (A National Bureau of Economic Research project report). — *Includes bibliographies and indexes*

LOCAL FINANCE — Zambia — Statistics

District councils revenue and capital estimates / Government of the Republic of Zambia. — Lusaka : Government Printer, 1983-. — *Annual*

LOCAL GOVERNMENT — Information services — Europe

BERGQVIST, Sven-Runo
Information and communication about municipal affairs : the use of various means for informing citizens to facilitate their participation / report prepared by Sven-Runo Bergqvist, consultant, with the assistance of the Secretariat of the Steering Committee for Regional and Municipal Matters. — Strasbourg : Council of Europe, 1979. — iii,191p. — (Study series local and regional authorities in Europe ; study no. 17)

LOCAL GOVERNMENT — Information services — Great Britain

GAITS, G. M.
An overview of information systems developments in UK local authorities / G. M. Gaits. — London : Department of the Environment, 1973. — 14leaves. — (PDPS3 planning techniques paper ; 73/9). — *Paper given at the Third European Symposium on Urban Data Management, 24-27 April, Paris*

GREAT BRITAIN. Department of the Environment
Publication of financial and other information by local authorities : a consultation document. — London : the Department, [1979?]. — 5 leaves

LOCAL GOVERNMENT — Information services — Great Britain — Bibliography

ROBINSON, Mary
Local authority information sources : a guide to publications, databases and services / compiled by Mary Robinson. — London : SCOOP Publications. Information Services Group of the Library Association, 1986. — 78p

LOCAL GOVERNMENT — Law and legislation — Spain

GARCÍA-ESCUDERO MARQUEZ, Piedad
El nuevo régimen local español : estudio sistemático de la Ley 7/1985 de 2 de abril, reguladora de las bases del régimen local / Piedad García-Escudero Marquez, Benigno Pendás García ; prólogo de Fernando Sainz Moreno. — Barcelona : Praxis, 1985. — xii,564p. — *Bibliographies*

GONZALEZ PEREZ, Jesus
Régimen jurídico de la Administración local / Jesus Gonzalez Perez. — Madrid : Abella, 1985. — 867p

VANDELLI, Luciano
El ordenamiento español de las comunidades autónomas / Luciano Vandelli ; prologo de Eduardo García de Enterria ; traducción española: Fernando Lopez Ramón, Pablo Lucas Murillo de la Cueva. — Madrid : Instituto de Estudios de Administración Local, 1982. — 431p. — *Bibliography: p415-431*

LOCAL GOVERNMENT — Law and legislation — United States

LEE, Mark R.
Antitrust law and local government / Mark R. Lee. — Westport, Conn. : Quorum Books, c1985. — p. cm. — *Includes index.* — *Bibliography: p*

LOCAL GOVERNMENT — Planning

MOFFITT, Leonard C
Strategic management : public planning at local level / by Leonard C. Moffitt. — Greenwich, Conn. : JAI Press, [1984]. — xvi, 273 p.. — (Contemporary studies in economic and financial analysis ; v. 45). — *Includes bibliographies and indexes*

LOCAL GOVERNMENT — Research — Great Britain — Registers

UNIVERSITY OF BIRMINGHAM. Institute of Local Government Studies
INLOGOV register of local government research 1987 / editor: E. M. Davies ; prepared in association with the Library of the Departments of Environment and Transport. — Birmingham : The Institute, 1987. — 1v (various pagings)

LOCAL GOVERNMENT — Social aspects — France

Les politiques sociales transversales : une méthodologie d'évaluation de leurs effets locaux. — Paris : La Documentation Française, 1986. — 178p. — *Président: Jean-Claude Ray*

LOCAL GOVERNMENT — Alabama

MARTIN, David L
Alabama's state and local governments / David L. Martin. — 2nd ed. — University, Ala. : University of Alabama Press, c1985. — xii, 230 p.. — *Includes bibliographies and index*

LOCAL GOVERNMENT — Alberta

MASSON, Jack K
Alberta's local governments and their politics / Jack Masson. — Edmonton, Alta., Canada : Pica Pica Press, 1985. — xiii, 397 p.. — (Local government series). — *Includes indexes.* — *Bibliography: p. 369-381*

LOCAL GOVERNMENT — Argentina

DROMI, José Roberto
Administración territorial y economiá : (la provincia, la región y el municipio en Argentina / José Roberto Dromi. — Madrid : Instituto de Estudios de Administración Local, 1983. — 423p. — (Autores Hispanoamericanos de Derecho Público)

LOCAL GOVERNMENT — Australia — Brisbane (Qld.) — History

COLE, John R.
Shaping a city : Greater Brisbane 1925-1985 / by John R. Cole. — Eagle Farm (Qld.) : William Brooks Queensland, 1984. — 416p. — *Bibliography: p411-416*

LOCAL GOVERNMENT — Bangladesh

RAHMAN, Atiur
Rural power structure : a study of the local level leaders in Bangladesh / Atiur Rahman. — Dacca : Papri Publishers, 1981. — viii,63p. — *Bibliography: p59-63*

LOCAL GOVERNMENT — British Columbia — Statistics

Statistics relating to regional and municipal governments in British Columbia / Ministry of Municipal Affairs, British Columbia. — [Victoria] : Ministry of Municipal Affairs, 1982-. — *Annual*

LOCAL GOVERNMENT — Colombia

COLOMBIA. División de Asistencia Técnica Departamental y Municipal
Regiones para la descentralización adminstrativa. — Bogotá : the División. — (Documento / Departamento Nacional de Planeación, Unidad de Desarrollo Regional y Urbano, División de Asistencia Técnica Departamental y Municipal ; 76/3)
Parte 2: Anexo - aspectos metodológicos. — 1976. — 23,16leaves

COLOMBIA. División de Asistencia Técnica Departamental y Municipal
Regiones para la descentralización adminstrativa. — Bogotá : the División. — (Documento / Departamento Nacional de Planeación, Unidad de Desarrollo Regional y Urbano, División de Asistencia Técnica Departamental y Municipal ; 76/3)
Parte 1. — 1976. — 24leaves

LOCAL GOVERNMENT — Council of Europe countries — Management

KELLY, Graham
Management structures in local and regional government : report / prepared under the guidance of the Committee of Experts on Management in Local and Regional Government of the Steering Committee for Regional and Municipal Matters by G. Kelly. — Strasbourg : Council of Europe, 1985. — 54p. — (Study series local and regional authorities in Europe ; 32)

LOCAL GOVERNMENT — Denmark — State supervision

Urban political theory and the management of fiscal stress / edited by Michael Goldsmith, Søren Villadsen. — Aldershot : Gower, c1986. — xviii,269p

LOCAL GOVERNMENT — Egypt

ADAMS, Richard H
Development and social change in rural Egypt / Richard H. Adams, Jr. — 1st ed. — Syracuse, N.Y. : Syracuse University Press, 1986. — xii, 231 p.. — (Contemporary issues in the Middle East). — : *Revision of the author's thesis (Ph. D.)--University of California, Berkeley, 1981.* — *Includes index.* — *Bibliography: p. 213-224*

LOCAL GOVERNMENT — England

KNOWLES, Raymond S. B.
The law and practice of local authority meetings / Raymond S.B. Knowles. — [Rev. and substantially expanded ed.]. — Cambridge : ICSA Publishing, 1987. — [312]p. — *Previous ed.: published as The law and practice relating to local authority meetings. Chichester : Rose, 1978. — Includes index*

LLOYD, Philip L.
Services administration by local authorities / Philip L. Lloyd. — Cambridge : ICSA, 1985. — [320]p. — *Includes bibliography and index*

LOCAL GOVERNMENT — Europe

Decentralisation of local government at neighbourhood level / ... prepared by the Secretariat of the Steering Committee for Regional and Municipal Matters with the assistance of Sven-Runo Bergqvist. — Strasbourg : Council of Europe, 1981. — 30p. — (Study series local and regional authorities in Europe ; study no. 27)

Functional decentralisation at local and regional level / report prepared by the Steering Committee for Regional and Municipal Matters. — Strasbourg : Council of Europe, 1981. — i,29p. (Study series local and regional authorities in Europe ; study no. 26)

LOCAL GOVERNMENT — Europe — Citizen participation

BERGQVIST, Sven-Runo
Information and communication about municipal affairs : the use of various means for informing citizens to facilitate their participation / report prepared by Sven-Runo Bergqvist, consultant, with the assistance of the Secretariat of the Steering Committee for Regional and Municipal Matters. — Strasbourg : Council of Europe, 1979. — iii,191p. — (Study series local and regional authorities in Europe ; study no. 17)

Methods of consulting citizens on municipal affairs. — Strasbourg : Council of Europe, 1979. — iii,43p. — (Study series local and regional authorities in Europe ; study no. 18). — *"Prepared by the Secretariat of the Steering Committee for Regional and Municipal Matters with the assistance of two consultants, Mr. Bart (France) and Mr. Couchepin (Switzerland)"*

LOCAL GOVERNMENT — Europe — Congresses

The reforms of local and regional authorities in Europe : theory, practice and critical appraisal : colloquy organised by the Council of Europe, Linz, 5-6 November 1981. — Strasbourg : Council of Europe, 1983. — 220p. — (Study series local and regional authorities in Europe ; 28). — *Bibliography: p.181-182*

LOCAL GOVERNMENT — Europe — Data processing

DURIAUD, Serge
Final report on the operation of national organisations concerned with the co-ordination of computer use in local government / by Serge Duriaud under the guidance of the Committee of Experts on Local and Regional Management. — Strasbourg : Council of Europe, 1980. — iii,39p. — (Study series local and regional authorities in Europe ; study no. 20)

GAITS, G.
Survey of computing in European local and regional authorities / ... prepared under the guidelines of the Committee of Experts on Management in Local and Regional Government by G.Gaits. — Strasbourg : Council of Europe, 1981. — iii,61p. — (Study series local and regional authorities in Europe ; 23)

LOCAL GOVERNMENT — France

Problèmes actuels de la fonction publique local / Alain Mangerie...[et al.]. — Paris : Librairies Techniques : Groupement de recherches coordonnées sur l'administration locale : Centre national de la recherche scientifique, [ca.1982]. — 210p. — (Collection du GRAL ; no.11) (Etudes et recherches juridiques)

LOCAL GOVERNMENT — France — Data processing

L'informatisation des collectivités locales : rapport au premier ministre / Gérard Saumade. — Paris : La Documentation Française, 1985. — 195p. — (Collection des rapports officiels)

LOCAL GOVERNMENT — Germany (West)

GUNLICKS, Arthur B.
Local government in the German federal system / Arthur B. Gunlicks. — Durham : Duke University Press, 1986. — p. cm. — (Duke Press policy studies). — *Includes index. — Bibliography: p*

LOCAL GOVERNMENT — Great Britain

ASCHER, Kate Julie
Contracting out in local authorities and the NHS : developments under the Conservative governments 1979-1985 / Kate J. Ascher. — 378 leaves. — *PhD (Econ) 1986 LSE. Leaves 333-350 are appendices*

AUDIT COMMISSION FOR LOCAL AUTHORITIES IN ENGLAND AND WALES
Improving highways agency arrangements between counties and districts : an interim report. — London : H.M.S.O., 1987. — 80p

BANHAM, John
"On local accountability" / John Banham. — London : National Association of Local Councils, 1986. — 17p. — *Lord Merthyr Memorial Lecture*

BIRKINSHAW, Patrick
Open government : freedom of information and local government : a study conducted for the Local Government Legal Society Trust and the Society of Town Clerks' Education and Research Trust / Patrick Birkinshaw. — [London] : Local Government Legal Society Trust in association with the Society of Town Clerks' Education and Research Trust, 1985. — 84p

BLUNKETT, David
Democracy in crisis : the town halls respond / David Blunkett and Keith Jackson. — London : Hogarth, 1987. — xv,240p. — (Current affairs). — *Includes index*

BYRNE, A.
Local government in Britain : everyone' guide to how it all works / Tony Byrne. — 4th ed. — Harmondsworth : Penguin, c1986. — xxii, 401p. — (Pelican books). — *Bibliography: p.[334]-346*

ELCOCK, Howard
Local government : politicians, professionals and the public in local authorities / Howard Elcock ; with a chapter by Michael Wheaton. — 2nd ed. — London : Methuen, 1986. — xi,338p. — *Previous ed.: 1982. — Includes index*

FRIEND, John Kimball
Local government and strategic choice : an operational research approach to the processes of public planning / J. K. Friend and W. N. Jessop. — 2d ed. — Oxford ; New York : Pergamon Press, 1977. — xxvi, 304 p., [1] leaf of plates (fold.). — (Urban and regional planning series ; v. 14) (Pergamon international library of science, technology, engineering and social studies). — *Includes index. — Bibliography: p. 297-298*

GREAT BRITAIN. Department of the Environment
Local authority direct labourconsultation paper. — [London : the Department, 1979?]. — 7 leaves

GREAT BRITAIN. Working Party on Direct Labour Organisations
Final report. — [London] : Department of the Environment, 1978. — 98p

JOHNSTONE, Derrick
Effective economic development : a discussion of local authority organization, management and training / by Derrick Johnstone. — Glasgow : The Planning Exchange, 1985. — 30leaves. — (Occasional paper ; no.19). — *Bibliography: leaves 28-30*

LABOUR PARTY (Great Britain)
At your service! : Labour's charter for better local services. — London : Labour Party, 1986. — 15p

LABOUR PARTY (Great Britain)
How to fight local elections. — London : Labour Party, 1985. — 72p

Red-print for ruin : the Labour left in local government. — London : Conservative Research Department, 1986. — 14p

RIDOUTT, Tim
Local government reorganisation in England 1974 / Tim Ridoutt. — London : N.E. London Polytechnic and Essex County Council. Anglian Regional Management Centre, 1984. — 45p. — (Commentary series / North East London Polytechnic ; 27). — *Bibliography: p [46-50]*

SMITH, Stephen, 19---
Local taxes and local government / Stephen Smith and Duncan Squire. — London : Institute for Fiscal Studies : Distributed by Woodhead-Faulkner, c1987. — 80p. — (IFS report series ; no.25). — *Bibliography: p.77-79*

STEWART, John, 1929 Mar. 19-
The new management of local government / John Stewart. — London : Allen & Unwin for the Institute of Local Government Studies, University of Birmingham, 1986. — [224]p. — *Includes bibliography and index*

TYLDESLEY, David
Gaining momentum : an analysis of the role and performance of local authorities in nature conservation / David Tyldesley. — Oxford : Published by Pisces Publications ... for the British Association of Nature Conservationists, 1986. — 96p. — *Report commissioned by the British Association of Nature Conservationists and sponsored by the World Wildlife Fund*

YOUNG, Ken, 1943-
The race relations adviser in local government / Ken Young and Pat Gay. — London : Local Authorities Race Relations Information Exchange, 1986. — 38p

LOCAL GOVERNMENT — Great Britain — Data processing

BARRAS, Richard
The adoption and impact of information technology in UK local Government / Richard Barras, Julia Swann. — London : Technical Change Centre, 1985. — 73p. — *Text on inside covers. — Bibliography: p72-73*

GAITS, G. M.
An overview of information systems developments in UK local authorities / G. M. Gaits. — London : Department of the Environment, 1973. — 14leaves. — (PDPS3 planning techniques paper ; 73/9). — *Paper given at the Third European Symposium on Urban Data Management, 24-27 April, Paris*

LOCAL GOVERNMENT — Great Britain — Data processing — Auditing

AUDIT COMMISSION FOR LOCAL AUTHORITIES IN ENGLAND AND WALES
Computing in local government : an audit survey. — [London] : the Commission, 1986. — 74p

LOCAL GOVERNMENT — Great Britain — History — 17th century
FLETCHER, Anthony J.
Reform in the provinces : the government of Stuart England / Anthony Fletcher. — New Haven : Yale University Press, c1986. — p. cm. — *Includes index. — Bibliography: p*

LOCAL GOVERNMENT — Great Britain — History — 20th century
COOKE, George
Education committees / George Cooke and Peter Gosden. — Harlow : Councils and Education, 1986. — x,166p. — *Includes index*

LOCAL GOVERNMENT — Great Britain — Management
AUDIT COMMISSION FOR LOCAL AUTHORITIES IN ENGLAND AND WALES
Performance review in local government : a handbook for auditors and local authorities. — London : H.M.S.O., 1986. — 8booklets in ring binder. — *Includes bibliographies*

LOCAL GOVERNMENT — Great Britain — Research — Bibliography
INLOGOV register of local government research 1986 / edited by E. M. Davies. — Birmingham : Institute of Local Government Studies, University of Birmingham, 191986. — Various pagings

LOCAL GOVERNMENT — Great Britain — State supervision
LAFFIN, Martin
Professionalism and policy : the role of the professions in the central-local government relationship / Martin Laffin. — Aldershot : Gower, c1986. — vii,228p

Legality and local politics / Lee Bridges ... [et al.]. — Aldershot : Gower, c1987. — [154]p

STEWART, John, 1929-
The dilemma of central-local relations / J. D. Stewart. — Cambridge : University of Cambridge. Department of Land Economy, 1981. — 19p. — *The Denman Lecture, 1981*

Urban political theory and the management of fiscal stress / edited by Michael Goldsmith, Søren Villadsen. — Aldershot : Gower, c1986. — xviii,269p

LOCAL GOVERNMENT — Greece — Attikí
WHITEHEAD, David, 19---
The demes of Attica, 508/7-ca. 250 B.C. : a political and social study / by David Whitehead. — Princeton, N.J. : Princeton University Press, c1985. — xxvii,485p. — *Bibliography: p.455-459*

LOCAL GOVERNMENT — Illinois
CHICOINE, David L
Governmental structure and local public finance / David L. Chicoine, Norman Walzer. — Boston, Mass. : Oelgeschlager, Gunn & Hain, c1985. — xi, 235 p. — *Includes bibliographies and index*

LOCAL GOVERNMENT — Mexico
FRIEDRICH, Paul
The princes of Naranja : an essay in anthrohistorical method / by Paul Friedrich. — 1st ed. — Austin : University of Texas Press, 1986. — p. cm. — *Bibliography: p*

LOCAL GOVERNMENT — Nigeria — East-Central State — Congresses
SEMINAR ON DIVISIONAL ADMINISTRATION, INSTITUTE OF ADMINISTRATION (1971)
A new system of local government : government by the community in the East Central State of Nigeria : a report of the Seminar on Divisional Administration held at the Institute of Administration Enugu, 24th-26th February, 1971 / edited by G. A. Odenigwe, assisted by C. E. Emezi, H. N. Nwosu. — Enugu, Nigeria : Nwamife, 1977. — xxi, 298, [112] p.. — *Includes bibliographical references*

LOCAL GOVERNMENT — Norway
Bypolitikk i Norge : historie, planlegging, styring, framtid / redigert av Harald Baldersheim. — Oslo : Gyldendal, 1983. — 215p. — *Bibliography: p203-216*

LOCAL GOVERNMENT — Pakistan
Local government in Pakistan. — [Islamabad? : Directorate of Films and Publications?, 1984]. — [27p]

LOCAL GOVERNMENT — Russian S.F.S.R. — Moscow
MOSCOW (R.S.F.S.R.). Sovet deputatov trudiasnchikhsia
Sobranie postanovlenii i rasporiazhenii Moskovskogo Soveta Rabochikh i Krasnoarmeiskikh Deputatov, Nos.1-46 : (1 May 1918-30 September 1919). — Moskva : Izd. Iuridicheskogo Otdela, 1918-1919. — (Rare printed material relating to Moscow, 1887-1923)

MOSCOW (R.S.F.S.R.: Guberniia). Ispolnitel'nyi komitet
Otchet o deiatel'nosti Moskovskogo Gubernskogo Ispolnitel'nogo Komiteta i Gubernskogo Ekonomicheskogo Soveshchaniia s 1/X 1922g.-po 1/X1923g.. — Moskva : Tip. Administrativnago Otdela M.S. im M. I. Rogova. — (Rare printed material relating to Moscow, 1887-1923)
Vyp.1: Otchet Gubispolkoma / (sostavlen pod redaktsiei Organiz. - Instr. otd. M.S.R.,K. i K.D.). — 1924. — 649p

LOCAL GOVERNMENT — Scotland
MONIES, George
Local government in Scotland / George Monies. — Edinburgh : W. Green, 1985. — x,88p. — *Bibliography: pix-x*

LOCAL GOVERNMENT — Soviet Union
ROSS, Cameron, 19---
Local government in the Soviet Union : problems of implementation and control / Cameron Ross. — London : Croom Helm, c1987. — [272]p. — *Includes bibliography*

LOCAL GOVERNMENT — Spain
MORELL OCAÑA, Luis
La administración local / Luis Morell Ocaña. — [Madrid] : Tecnos, c1984. — 180p. — (Temas clave de la constitución española). — *Bibliograpy: p179-180*

LOCAL GOVERNMENT — Spain — Madrid
Madrid, Comunidad autónoma metropolitana / [equipo dirigido por] E. García de Enterría. — Madrid : Instituto de Estudios Económicos, 1983. — 482p. — (Colección Estudios / Instituto de Estudios Económicos)

LOCAL GOVERNMENT — Sudan
EL-ARIFI, Salih Abdalla
Local government and local participation in rural development in the Sudan / Salih Abdalla El-Arifi. — Khartoum : University of Khartoum. Faculty of Economic and Social Studies. Development Studies and Research Centre, 1978. — 34p. — (Monograph series / University of Khartoum. Faculty of Economic and Social Studies. Development Studies and Research Centre ; no.10). — *Bibliography: p29-34*

LOCAL GOVERNMENT — United States
CLARK, Gordon L
Judges and the cities : interpreting local autonomy / Gordon L. Clark. — Chicago : University of Chicago Press, c1985. — xv, 247 p.. — *Includes index. — Bibliography: p. 231-242*

State politics and the new federalism : readings and commentary / edited by Marilyn Gittell. — New York : Longman, c1986. — xv, 544 p.. — *Includes index. — Bibliography: p. 533-535*

LOCAL GOVERNMENT — Wales
GREAT BRITAIN. Welsh Office
The Local Government Area Changes Regulations 1976 (S.I.no.246). — Cardiff : the Office, 1976. — 5p. — (Circular ; no.76/43)

LOCAL GOVERNMENT BILL 1984-85
GREAT BRITAIN. Parliament. House of Commons. Library. Research Division
Local Government Bill [Bill 11, 1984/85] / [Barry K. Winetrobe]. — [London] : the Division, 1984. — 27p. — (Reference sheet ; no.84/12). — *Bibliographical references: p25-27*

LOCAL GOVERNMENT FINANCE BILL 1981-82
GREAT BRITAIN. Parliament. House of Commons. Library. Research Division
Local Government Finance Bill (Bill 8 of 1981-82) / Priscilla Baines, Robert Clements. — [London] : the Division, 1981. — 21p. — (Reference sheet ; no.81/18)

LOCAL GOVERNMENT FINANCE (NO.2) BILL 1981-82
GREAT BRITAIN. Parliament. House of Commons. Library. Research Division
Local Government Finance (No.2) Bill (Bill 41 of 1981-82) and 1982-83 rate support grant settlement / [Priscilla Baines]. — [London] : the Division, 1982. — 8p. — (Reference sheet ; no.82/2)

LOCAL GOVERNMENT (INTERIM PROVISIONS) BILL 1983-84
GREAT BRITAIN. Parliament. House of Commons. Library. Research Division
Local Government (Interim Provisions) Bill, Bill 145, 1983-84 / Barry K. Winetrobe. — [London] : the Division, 1984. — 20p. — (Reference sheet ; no.84/5). — *Includes bibliographical references*

LOCAL OFFICIALS AND EMPLOYEES
RAHMAN, Nasreen
Council non-manual workers and low pay / Nasreen Rahman. — London : Low Pay Unit, 1986. — 32p. — (Low pay pamphlet ; no.41)

LOCAL OFFICIALS AND EMPLOYEES — England
BOYNTON, Sir John, 1918-
Job at the top : the chief executive in local government / Sir John Boynton. — Harlow : Longman, 1986. — [160]p. — *Includes index*

LONDON AND METROPOLITAN GOVERNMENT STAFF COMMISSION
Report of the London and Metropolitan Government Staff Commission. — London : H.M.S.O., 1987. — v,144p. — *Chairman: Sir Philip Woodfield*

LOCAL OFFICIALS AND EMPLOYEES — France
DOLIQUE, Robert
Les effectifs des collectivités territoriales au 31 décembre 1983 / Robert Dolique, Dominique Quarré, Brigitte Rabin. — Paris : I.N.S.E.E., 1986. — 164p. — (Archives et documents / France. Institut national de la statistique et des études économiques ; no.155)

LOCAL OFFICIALS AND EMPLOYEES — Great Britain — History
DIX, Bernard
Serving the public : building the union : the history of the National Union of Public Employees / Bernard Dix and Stephen Williams. — London : Lawrence and Wishart
Volume 1: The forerunners, 1889-1928. — 1987. — 238p. — *Bibliography: p229-231*

LOCAL OFFICIALS AND EMPLOYEES — United States — Salaries, allowances, etc — Congresses
Public sector payrolls / edited by David A. Wise. — Chicago : University of Chicago Press, 1987. — ix, 327 p.. — (A National Bureau of Economic Research project report). — *Papers presented at a conference held in Williamsburg, Va., Nov. 15-17, 1984. — Includes bibliographies and indexes*

LOCAL TAXATION — Great Britain
MIDWINTER, Arthur F.
Rates reform : issues, arguments and evidence / by Arthur Midwinter. — Edinburgh : Mainstream, 1987. — [192]p. — *Includes bibliography and index*

LOCAL TAXATION — Great Britain
continuation

SMITH, Stephen, 19---
Local taxes and local government / Stephen Smith and Duncan Squire. — London : Institute for Fiscal Studies : Distributed by Woodhead-Faulkner, c1987. — 80p. — (IFS report series ; no.25). — *Bibliography: p.77-79*

LOCAL TRANSIT

ARMSTRONG-WRIGHT, Alan
Urban transit systems : guidelines for examining options / Alan Armstrong-Wright. — Washington, D.C. : The World Bank, 1986. — xii,77p. — (World Bank technical paper ; no.52) (Urban transport series). — *Bibliography: p77*

LOCAL TRANSIT — Finance — Law and legislation — England

GREAT BRITAIN. Parliament. House of Commons. Library. Research Division
Transport Bill (Bill 5 of 1982-83) / Priscilla Baines. — [London] : the Division, 1982. — 14p. — (Reference sheet ; no.82/11). — *Includes bibliographical references*

LOCAL TRANSIT — Statistics

International statistical handbook of public transport = Recueil international de statistiques des transports publics = Internationales Statistik-Handbuch für den öffentlichen Verkehr / by Lee H. Rogers, compiler/editor in collaboration with UITP Documentation Centre. — Bruxelles, Belgique : International Union of Public Transport, c1985. — 3 v. (1645 p.). — *Cover title: UITP handbook of public transport = Recueil UITP des transports publics = UITP-Handbuch für öffentlichen Verkehr*

LOCAL TRANSIT — Asia, Southeastern

RIMMER, Peter J.
Rikisha to rapid transport : urban public transport systems and policy in southeast Asia / Peter J. Rimmer. — Sydney ; Oxford : Pergamon, 1986. — xxvi,387p. — *Bibliography: p333-371*

LOCAL TRANSIT — England — Fares

GREAT BRITAIN. Parliament. House of Commons. Library. Research Division
Transport Bill (Bill 5 of 1982-83) / Priscilla Baines. — [London] : the Division, 1982. — 14p. — (Reference sheet ; no.82/11). — *Includes bibliographical references*

LOCKE, ALAIN LEROY

WASHINGTON, Johnny
Alain Locke and philosophy : a quest for cultural pluralism / Johnny Washington. — Westport, Conn. : Greenwood Press, c1986. — p. cm. — (Contributions in Afro-American and African studies ; no. 94). — *Includes index. — Bibliography: p*

LOCKE, JOHN, 1632-1704

ASHCRAFT, Richard
Locke's Two treatises of government / Richard Ashcraft. — London : Allen & Unwin, 1987. — [420]p. — (Unwin critical library). — *Includes bibliography and index*

CRANSTON, Maurice
John Locke : a biography / Maurice Cranston. — Oxford : Oxford University Press, 1985, c1957. — [ix,512]p. — *Originally published: London : Longmans, Green, 1957. — Includes bibliography and index*

LOCKE, JOHN, 1632-1704 — Bibliography

ATTIG, John C.
The works of John Locke : a comprehensive bibliography from the seventeenth century to the present / compiled by John C. Attig. — Westport, Conn. : Greenwood Press, c1985. — xx, 185p. — (Bibliographies and indexes in philosophy ; no. 1). — *Includes indexes*

LOCKHEED AIRCRAFT CORPORATION

PIERCE, Christine
How to solve the Lockheed case / Christine Pierce. — Bowling Green, OH : Social Philosophy and Policy Center ; New Brunswick, USA : Transaction Books, 1986. — 41 p. — (Original papers / Social Philosophy and Policy Center ; no. 5). — *Bibliography: p. 37-41*

LOCKNEVI (SWEDEN) — History

MILLER, Roger
Social change in 19th-century Swedish agrarian society / Roger Miller, Torvald Gerger. — Stockholm : Almqvist & Wiksell International, 1985. — 130p. — (Acta universitatis Stockholmiensis. Stockholm studies in human geography ; 5) (Stockholm studies in human geography ; 5)

LODGING-HOUSES — Great Britain

CONWAY, Jean
Bed and breakfast : slum housing of the eighties / Jean Conway and Peter Kemp. — London : SHAC, c1985. — 54p. — (SHAC policy paper ; 7)

ŁÓDŹ (POLAND) — History

W dymach czarnych budzi się Łódź : z dziejów łódzkiego ruchu robotniczego 1882-1948 / [Alina Barszczewska-Krupa...et al.]. — Łódź : Wydawnictwo Łódzkie, 1985. — 507p

ŁÓDŹ (POLAND) — Industries — Location

KOTER, Marek
Geneza układu przestrzennego Łodzi przemysłowej / Marek Koter. — Warszawa : Państwowe Wydawnictwo Naukowe, 1969. — 134p. — (Prace geograficzne / Polska Akademia Nauk. Instytut Geografii ; Nr.79). — *Summary in Russian and English. — Bibliography: p118-[121]*

ŁÓDZ (POLAND) — Politics and government

SAMUŚ, Paweł
Dzieje SDKPiL w Łódzi 1893-1918 / Paweł Samuś. — Łódz : Wydawnictwo Łódzkie, 1984. — 288p. — *Bibliography: p281-[289]*

LOFTHOUSE, GEOFF — Biography

LOFTHOUSE, Geoff
A very miner MP / by Geoff Lofthouse ; Foreword by Viscount Tonypandy. — Pontefract : Yorkshire Arts Circus, 1986. — 127p

LOGIC

Policy analysis and deductive reasoning / edited by Gordon Tullock, Richard E. Wagner. — Lexington, Mass. : D.C. Heath ; Farnborough, Hants. ([1 Westmead, Farnborough, Hants. GU14 7RU]) : [Distributed by] Teakfield, 1978. — xii,207p. — (Policy Studies Organization series ; 15). — *Based on symposia coordinated by the Policy Studies Organization. - 'Lexington Books'. — Includes index*

QUINE, W. V.
Methods of logic / by Willard van Orman Quine. — London : Routledge & Kegan Paul, 1952. — xix,264p

LOGIC — Addresses, essays, lectures

QUINE, W. V
From a logical point of view : 9 logico-philosophical essays / Willard Van Orman Quine [with a new foreword by the author]. — 2d ed., rev. — Cambridge, Mass. : Harvard University Press, c1980. — xii, 184 p.. — *Includes index. — Bibliography: p. 171-178*

LOGIC, SYMBOLIC AND MATHEMATICAL

NATO CONFERENCE ON THE ACQUISITION OF SYMBOLIC SKILLS (1982 : University of Keele)
The acquisition of symbolic skills / [proceedings of a NATO Conference on the Acquisition of Symbolic Skills, held July 5-10, 1982, at the University of Keele, Keele, England] ; edited by Don Rogers and John A. Sloboda. — New York ; London : Published in cooperation with NATO Scientific Affairs Division [by] Plenum, c1983. — xii,623p. — (NATO conference series. III, Human factors ; v.22). — *Includes bibliographies and index*

QUINE, W. V
Word and object / W. V. Quine. — [Cambridge] : Technology Press of the Massachusetts Institute of Technology, [1960]. — 294 p. — (Studies in communication). — *Includes bibliographies*

LOKEREN (BELGIUM) — Economic conditions

VERSTEGEN, Vedastus
Lokeren onder de Franse overheersing / Vedastus Verstegen. — Hasselt : Provinciale Bibliothek, 1971. — (Mededelingen van het Centrum voor Studie van de Boerenkrijg ; 79) 11: De finantiële toestand. — 72p

LOKEREN (BELGIUM) — History

VERSTEGEN, Vedastus
Lokeren onder de Franse overheersing / Vedastus Verstegen. — Hasselt : Provinciale Bibliothek, 1971. — (Mededelingen van het Centrum voor Studie van de Boerenkrijg ; 79) 11: De finantiële toestand. — 72p

LOME CONVENTION

STEVENS, Christopher, 1948-
The new Lome convention : implications for Europe's third world policy / Christopher Stevens. — Bruxelles : Centre for European Policy Studies, 1984. — 39p. — (CEPS papers ; no.16)

LOMÉ CONVENTION

SABLÉ, Victor
La politique de coopération régionale entre les DOM-TOM et les États ACP : rapport au Premier ministre / Victor Sablé. — [Paris : La Documentation française, 1987]. — 237p. — (Collection des rapports officiels)

LONDON — History

GEORGE, Mary Dorothy
London life in the XVIIIth century / by M. Dorothy George. — London : Kegan Paul, Trench & Trubner, 1925. — xi,452p. — *Bibliography: p431-439*

LONDON — Social conditions

GEORGE, Mary Dorothy
London life in the XVIIIth century / by M. Dorothy George. — London : Kegan Paul, Trench & Trubner, 1925. — xi,452p. — *Bibliography: p431-439*

LONDON — Social policy — History

WOHL, Anthony S
The eternal slum : housing and social policy in Victorian London / Anthony S. Wohl. — Montreal : McGill-Queen's University Press, 1977. — xxiv, 386 p., [8] leaves of plates. — (Studies in urban history ; 5). — *"A note on sources": p. 341-355. — Includes index*

LONDON CHAMBER OF COMMERCE AND INDUSTRY

Periodicals holding list / Research and Information Department, London Chamber of Commerce and Industry. — London : LCCI, 1985-

LONDON (ENGLAND) — Airports

BRITISH AIRPORTS AUTHORITY
Heathrow airport-London : master development plan report, March 1976. — [London : the Authority], 1976. — 18p

LONDON (ENGLAND) — Airports
continuation

GREAT BRITAIN. Parliament. House of Commons. Library. Research Division
Third London airport / [Christopher Barclay]. — [London] : the Division, 1980. — 10p. — (Reference sheet ; no.80/3). — *Bibliography: p8-10*

LONDON (ENGLAND) — Buildings, structures, etc

GREEN, Shirley
Who owns London ? / Shirley Green. — London : Weidenfeld and Nicolson, c1986. — 224p

LONDON (ENGLAND) — Census, 1981

London's ethnic population : census statistics from the 1981 census / prepared in the Intelligence Unit by Maryse Hodgson. — [London] : Greater London Council, 1985. — 82p. — (Statistical series / Greater London Council ; no.44). — *Bibliography: p82*

LONDON (ENGLAND) — City planning

CITY OF LONDON. Department of Architecture and Planning
City of London local plan : written statement and proposals map. — London : [the Department], 1986. — 226p. — *Includes modifications to the revised plan*

GLC PLANNING FOR HOUSING CONFERENCE (1985 : London)
The future of planning : planning for housing. — [London : Greater London Council], 1985. — 49p

GLC PLANNING FOR LAND CONFERENCE (1985 : London)
The future of planning : planning for land. — [London : Greater London Council], 1985. — 52p

GREATER LONDON COUNCIL
The future of London : alterations to the Greater London development plan. — [London : the Council], 1983. — 220,[20]p

GREATER LONDON COUNCIL
The future of London's government : discussion document : options for planning : GLC research project. — [London : the Council, 1985]. — 48,ixp. — *Bibliographical references: pii-iv*

LONDON (ENGLAND) — Civil defense

GLAWARS COMMISSION
London under attack : the report of the Glawars Commission / commissioners: Anne Ehrlich...[et al.]; rapporteur: Robin Clarke. — [London : Greater London Council, 1986]. — 426p. — *Includes bibliographical references*

LONDON (ENGLAND) — Docks, wharves, etc

ROGER TYM AND PARTNERS
The potential for future docks use of the Royals : report for the Greater London Council. — [London : Greater London Council], 1983. — 1v (various pagings)

LONDON (ENGLAND) — Dwellings

GREATER LONDON COUNCIL
'They who pay the piper...' : evidence submitted by the Greater London Council to the Committee of Inquiry into the Management of Privately Owned Blocks of Flats. — [London] : the Council, 1984. — 27p

LONDON (ENGLAND) — Economic conditions

BUCK, N. H.
The London employment problem / Nick Buck, Ian Gordon and Ken Young, with John Ermisch and Liz Mills. — Oxford : Clarendon Press, 1986. — xvi,213p. — (Inner Cities Research Programme series ; 5). — *Bibliography: p199-205. — Includes index*

MCMULLAN, John L.
The canting crew : London's criminal underworld, 1550-1700 / John L. McMullan. — New Brunswick, N.J. : Rutgers University Press, c1984. — ix, 226 p.. — (Crime, law, and deviance series). — *Includes index. — Bibliography: p. 197-213*

LONDON (ENGLAND) — Economic conditions — Statistics

GREATER LONDON COUNCIL
Comparative economic and financial statistics on London and the rest of England. — [Rev. ed]. — [London] : the Council, 1986. — 1v.(unpaged). — (Statistical series ; no.49)

Regional trends in the south east: the south east regional monitor / London and South East Regional Planning Conference. — London : London and South East Regional Planning Conference, 1983/4-. — *Annual*

LONDON (ENGLAND) — Economic policy

BUCK, N. H.
The London employment problem / Nick Buck, Ian Gordon and Ken Young, with John Ermisch and Liz Mills. — Oxford : Clarendon Press, 1986. — xvi,213p. — (Inner Cities Research Programme series ; 5). — *Bibliography: p199-205. — Includes index*

GREATER LONDON COUNCIL
The London labour plan. — London : Greater London Council, 1986. — 552p

The London Labour plan : black workers. — London : London Strategic Policy Unit, 1986. — 51p. — *Bibliography: p49*

The London Labour plan : education and training. — London : London Strategic Policy Unit, 1986. — 77p. — *Bibliography: p75*

The London Labour plan : the state and the labour market. — London : London Strategic Policy Unit, 1986. — 61p. — *Bibliography: p59*

LONDON (ENGLAND) — Full employment policies

GREATER LONDON COUNCIL
The London labour plan. — London : Greater London Council, 1986. — 552p

LONDON (ENGLAND) — Harbor

ROGER TYM AND PARTNERS
The potential for future docks use of the Royals : report for the Greater London Council. — [London : Greater London Council], 1983. — 1v (various pagings)

LONDON (ENGLAND) — History — 18th century

SAINSBURY, John
Disaffected patriots : London supporters of revolutionary America / John Sainsbury. — Kingston, Ont. : McGill — Queen's University Press, 1987. — xi, 305p. — *Bibliography: p.[281]-296*

LONDON (ENGLAND) — History — 1800-1950

MACK, Joanna
London at war / Joanna Mack and Steve Humphries. — London : Sidgwick & Jackson, 1985. — 176p. — (The making of modern London ; 1939-1945)

LONDON (ENGLAND) — History — 20th century

HUMPHRIES, Steve
The making of modern London, 1945-1985 / Steve Humphries and John Taylor. — London : Sidgwick & Jackson, 1986. — 172p. — *Bibliography: p.[169]-170*

LONDON (ENGLAND) — Languages

Languages in London / compiled by Euan Reid, Greg Smith and Anna Morawska. — London : University of London. Institute of Education. Community Languages and Education Project, 1985. — 124p. — (CLE/LMP working paper ; no.12). — *Bibliography: p84*

LONDON (ENGLAND) — Markets

DAVIS, Keith
London's wholesale fruit and vegetable markets : a survey of the four east London markets / Keith Davis, Tim Catchpole. — [London] : London Research Centre, 1986. — 65p. — (Reviews and studies series ; no.31). — *Re-issue of the Greater London Council's study report of February 1986 with an appendix added giving a detailed analysis of the survey data including comparisons between the markets*

A new site for Covent Garden Market : report on a feasibility study for the Nine Elms area. — [London] : Covent Garden Market Authority, 1964. — 34leaves. — [21]folded leaves

LONDON (ENGLAND) — Office buildings

GREATER LONDON COUNCIL
Survey of office firms and establishments. — [London] : the Council
Report No. 2: Preliminary findings on employment, use of floorspace and location. — 1986. — 16p

GREATER LONDON COUNCIL
Survey of office firms and establishments. — [London] : the Council
Report No. 3: New technology analysis: preliminary findings. — 1986. — 17p

GREATER LONDON COUNCIL
Survey of office firms and establishments. — [London] : the Council
Report No.1: Background to the design and implementation of the survey. — 1986. — 14p

LONDON (ENGLAND) — Politics and government

AUDIT COMMISSION FOR LOCAL AUTHORITIES IN ENGLAND AND WALES
The management of London's authorities : preventing the breakdown of services. — [London : H.M.S.O.], 1987. — 16p. — (Occasional papers ; no.2)

GREATER LONDON COUNCIL
The future of London's government : consultation document : GLC research project. — [London : the Council, 1985]. — 23p

GREATER LONDON COUNCIL
The future of London's government : discussion document : options for planning : GLC research project. — [London : the Council, 1985]. — 48,ixp. — *Bibliographical references: pii-iv*

GREATER LONDON COUNCIL
London calling : the future of London's government. — [London : the Council, 1985]. — [12]p

GREGORY, Sarah
Decentralisation in London / Sarah Gregory. — [London] : Greater London Council, 1985. — 52p. — (Reviews and studies series / Greater London Council ; no.26)

RIDOUTT, Tim
London government reorganisation in 1965 : objectives and outcomes / Tim Ridoutt. — London : North East London Polytechnic. Centre for Institutional Studies, 1984. — 61p. — (Commentary / North East London Polytechnic. Centre for Institutional Studies ; 26)

SOFER, Anne
The London Left takeover / Anne Sofer. — London : J. Caslake, 1987. — 118p. — *Collection of reprinted articles*

LONDON (ENGLAND) — Politics and government — Legal status, laws, etc.

GREAT BRITAIN. Parliament. House of Commons. Library. Research Division
Local Government Bill [Bill 11, 1984/85] / [Barry K. Winetrobe]. — [London] : the Division, 1984. — 27p. — (Reference sheet ; no.84/12). — *Bibliographical references: p25-27*

LONDON (ENGLAND) — Politics and government — Legal status, laws, etc

GREAT BRITAIN. Parliament. House of Commons. Library. Research Division
Local Government (Interim Provisions) Bill, Bill 145, 1983-84 / Barry K. Winetrobe. — [London] : the Division, 1984. — 20p. — (Reference sheet ; no.84/5). — *Includes bibliographical references*

LONDON (ENGLAND) — Population

HOLLIS, John
The 1985 round of demographic projections for Greater London / prepared in the GLC Intelligence Unit by John Hollis, Carole Hills and Ian Longhurst. — [London] : Greater London Council, 1986. — 1v.(various pagings). — (Statistical series / Greater London Council ; no.52). — *Bibliographical references: p22*

LANDAU, Nick
Statistics of London's ethnic minorities, 1979 and 1981 / computed and written in the Intelligence Unit by Nick Landau. — [London] : Greater London Council, 1986. — ii,142p. — (Statistical series / Greater London Council ; no.40). — *Bibliography : p135*

London's ethnic population : census statistics from the 1981 census / prepared in the Intelligence Unit by Maryse Hodgson. — [London] : Greater London Council, 1985. — 82p. — (Statistical series / Greater London Council ; no.44). — *Bibliography: p82*

LONDON (ENGLAND) — Race relations

DEUTSCH, Francis
Street crime in London 1981 / Francis Deutsch. — London : Commission for Racial Equality, 1982. — 12p

GREAT BRITAIN. Commission for Racial Equality
The Antwerp Arms Public House : report of a formal investigation. — London : the Commission, 1979. — 13p

PRASHAR, Usha
Routes or roadblocks? : consulting minority communities in London Boroughs / Usha Prashar and Sh an Nicholas. — London : Runnymede Trust, 1986. — 64p

LONDON (ENGLAND) — Recreational facilities

Leisure provision and people's needs / Michael Dower...[et al.]. — London : H.M.S.O., 1981. — viii,152p. — *Main report on Stage II of the study of Leisure Provision and Human Need undertaken for the Department of the Environment by the Institute of Family and Environmental Research and Dartington Amenity Research Trust. — Bibliography: p.149-152*

LONDON (ENGLAND) — Schools

INNER LONDON EDUCATION AUTHORITY. Research and Statistics Branch
The junior school project. — [London : the Authority]. — *Bibliographical references: p139-143*
Part C: Understanding school effectiveness. — [1986]. — 143,122p

INNER LONDON EDUCATION AUTHORITY. Research and Statistics Branch
The junior school project. — [London : the Authority]. — *Bibliographical references: p77-81*
Part A: Pupils' progress and development. — [1986]. — 81p

INNER LONDON EDUCATION AUTHORITY. Research and Statistics Branch
The junior school project. — [London : the Authority]. — *Bibliographical references: p225-228*
Part B: Differences between junior schools. — [1986]. — 228p

INNER LONDON EDUCATION AUTHORITY. Research and Statistics Branch
The junior school project. — [London : the Authority]
Technical appendices. — [1986]. — 247p

LONDON (ENGLAND) — Social conditions

BOULTON, J. P.
Neighbourhood and society : a London suburb in the seventeenth century / J.P. Boulton. — Cambridge : Cambridge University Press, 1987. — [352]p. — (Cambridge studies in population, economy and society in past time ; 5). — *Includes bibliography and index*

DICKENS, Charles, 1812-1870
A December vision : his social journalism / Charles Dickens ; edited by Neil Philip and Victor Neuburg. — London : Collins, 1986. — 160p. — *Bibliography: p157-158. — Includes index*

LONDON (ENGLAND) — Social conditions — Statistics

Regional trends in the south east: the south east regional monitor / London and South East Regional Planning Conference. — London : London and South East Regional Planning Conference, 1983/4-. — *Annual*

WALTERS, Stuart
The scale of London's problems / Stuart Walters. — [London] : Greater London Council, 1986. — 10p. — (Reviews and studies series / Greater London Council ; no.29)

LONDON (ENGLAND) — Social conditions — 20th century

HUMPHRIES, Steve
The making of modern London, 1945-1985 / Steve Humphries and John Taylor. — London : Sidgwick & Jackson, 1986. — 172p. — *Bibliography: p.[169]-170*

LONDON (ENGLAND) — Social life and customs — 19th century

SHONFIELD, Zuzanna
The precariously privileged : a medical man's family in Victorian London / Zuzanna Shonfield. — Oxford : Oxford University Press, 1987. — [320]p. — *Includes index*

LONDON (ENGLAND) — Statistics, Vital

HILLS, Carole
Greater London lifetables, 1979-82 / prepared in the Intelligence Unit by Carole Hills and John Hollis. — [London] : Greater London Council, 1986. — [113]p. — (Statistical series / Greater London Council ; no.50). — *Bibliographical references: p17*

HILLS, Carole
London borough fertility rates, 1981 / Carole Hills. — [London] : London Research Centre, 1986. — iii,12,[66]p. — (Statistical series ; no.54). — *Bibliographical references: p12*

LONDON (ENGLAND) — Transit systems

LONDON REGIONAL TRANSPORT
Annual report and accounts. — London : London Regional Transport, 1984/5. — *Annual. — Continues: London Transport Executive : Annual report and accounts*

LONDON TRANSPORT
Docklands rail study 1981. — London : London Transport
Appendices to main report. — 1981. — 1v (various pagings)

LONDON TRANSPORT
Docklands rail study 1981. — London : London Transport
Main report. — 1981. — 43p

LONDON TRANSPORT EXECUTIVE
Annual report and accounts. — London : London Transport Executive, 1970-1983. — *Annual. — Continued by: London Regional Transport : Annual report and accounts*

LONDON (ENGLAND) — Transit systems — Law and legislation

GREAT BRITAIN. Parliament. House of Commons. Library. Research Division
London Regional Transport Bill (Bill 68 of 1983-1984) / [Priscilla Baines]. — [London] : the Division, 1983. — 22p. — (Reference sheet ; no.83/23). — *Bibliographical references: p21-22*

LONDON METROPOLITAN AREA — Manufactures

Monitoring manufacturing employment change in London, 1976-1978 / Roger Leigh ... [et al.]. — [London] : Middlesex Polytechnic, London Industry and Employment Research Group
Vol.1: The implications for local economic policy. — [1983?]. — xv,216p

Monitoring manufacturing employment change in London, 1976-1981 / Roger Leigh ... [et al.]. — [London] : Middlesex Polytechnic, London Industry and Employment Research Group
Vol.2: Industrial Sector Studies. — [1983]. — 150p

LONDON METROPOLITAN AREA — Politics and government

FOLEY, Donald Leslie
Governing the London region : reorganization and planning in the 1960's / Donald L. Foley. — Berkeley ; London : University of California Press for the Institute of Governmental Studies, 1972. — xiv,223p. — (Publications / Franklin K. Lane Memorial Fund). — *Includes index*

LONDON REGIONAL TRANSPORT

LONDON REGIONAL TRANSPORT
Annual report and accounts. — London : London Regional Transport, 1984/5. — *Annual. — Continues: London Transport Executive : Annual report and accounts*

LONDON REGIONAL TRANSPORT — Legal status, laws, etc.

GREAT BRITAIN. Parliament. House of Commons. Library. Research Division
London Regional Transport Bill (Bill 68 of 1983-1984) / [Priscilla Baines]. — [London] : the Division, 1983. — 22p. — (Reference sheet ; no.83/23). — *Bibliographical references: p21-22*

LONDON REGIONAL TRANSPORT BILL 1983-84

GREAT BRITAIN. Parliament. House of Commons. Library. Research Division
London Regional Transport Bill (Bill 68 of 1983-1984) / [Priscilla Baines]. — [London] : the Division, 1983. — 22p. — (Reference sheet ; no.83/23). — *Bibliographical references: p21-22*

LONDON RESIDUARY BODY

LONDON RESIDUARY BODY
Budget / London Residuary Body. — London : London Residuary Body, 1986/87-. — *Annual. — Continues: Annual report and accounts/London Residuary Body*

LONDON REVIEW OF BOOKS — Indexes

London review of books: index. — London : London Review of Books, 1979/80-. — *Annual*

LONDON SCHOOL ECONOMICS AND POLITICAL SCIENCE

L.S.E. quarterly. — Oxford : Blackwell, 1987-. — *Quarterly*

LONDON SCHOOL OF ECONOMICS AND POLITICAL SCIENCE — Fiction

RUFF, Ivan
Dead reckoning / Ivan Ruff. — London : Heinemann, 1987. — 229p. — *Spy novel written by former LSE student, with some of the plot taking place in and around the LSE*

LONDON SCHOOL OF ECONOMICS AND POLITICAL SCIENCE — Students

YETTRAM, Pamela June
Contrary imaginations : causes and consequences of left wing ideology among student activists in the mid-seventies / by Pamela J. Yettram. — 511 leaves. — *PhD (Econ) 1986 LSE. — Leaves 457-486 are appendices*

LONDON SCHOOL OF ECONOMICS AND POLITICAL SCIENCE. Centre for Labour Economics
LONDON SCHOOL OF ECONOMICS AND POLITICAL SCIENCE. Centre for Labour Economics
Review of the year's work, 1985-86. — London : Centre for Labour Economics, London School of Economics, 1986. — 30p. — (Discussion paper / London School of Economics and Political Science. Centre for Labour Economics ; no.263)

LONDON TRANSPORT — Legal status, laws, etc.
GREAT BRITAIN. Parliament. House of Commons. Library. Research Division
London Regional Transport Bill (Bill 68 of 1983-1984) / [Priscilla Baines]. — [London] : the Division, 1983. — 22p. — (Reference sheet ; no.83/23). — *Bibliographical references: p21-22*

LONDON TRANSPORT EXECUTIVE
LONDON TRANSPORT EXECUTIVE
Annual report and accounts. — London : London Transport Executive, 1970-1983. — Annual. — *Continued by: London Regional Transport : Annual report and accounts*

LONDONDERRY, ROBERT STEWARD, 2nd Marquis of
KISSINGER, Henry A.
A world restored / Henry A. Kissinger. — Gloucester, Man. : Peter Smith, 1973. — xi,354p. — *Originally published, Houghton Mifflin, 1957. — Bibliography: p333-346*

LONDONDERRY (NORTHERN IRELAND) — History
CURL, James Stevens
The Londonderry Plantation 1609-1914 : the history, architecture, and planning of the estates of the City of London and its Livery Companies in Ulster / James Stevens Curl. — Chichester : Phillimore, 1986. — xxiii,503p. — *Bibliography: p484-492*

LONELINESS
RUBINSTEIN, Robert L
Singular paths : old men living alone / Robert L. Rubinstein. — New York : Columbia University Press, 1986. — viii, 265 p.. — (Columbia studies of social gerontology and aging). — *Includes index. — Bibliography: p.[257]-261*

LONERGAN, BERNARD J. F — Congresses
Religion and culture : essays in honor of Bernard Lonergan, S.J. / edited by Timothy P. Fallon and Philip Boo Riley. — Albany, NY : State University of New York Press, c1987. — x, 395 p.. — *Papers from the International Lonergan Symposium on Religion and Culture, held in March, 1984, at the University of Santa Clara. — Includes bibliographies and index*

LONG, HUEY PIERCE
LONG, Huey Pierce
Kingfish to America, share our wealth : selected senatorial papers of Huey P. Long / edited and with an introduction by Henry M. Christman. — New York : Schocken Books, 1985. — xvi, 145 p.. — *Includes index*

LONG-TERM CARE OF THE SICK — Moral and ethical aspects — Congresses
Ethics and critical care medicine / edited by John C. Moskop and Loretta Kopelman. — Dordrecht ; Lancaster : D. Reidel, c1985. — xx, 236p. — (Philosophy and medicine ; v. 19). — *Based on papers presented at a symposium held at East Carolina University School of Medicine in Greenville, N.C. on Mar. 17-19, 1983; sponsored by the East Carolina University School of Medicine and others. — Includes bibliographies and index*

LONG WAVES (ECONOMICS)
BOOTH, Douglas E
Regional long waves, uneven growth, and the cooperative alternative / Douglas E. Booth. — New York : Praeger, 1987. — 121 p.. — *Includes index. — Bibliography: p. 109-115*

KLEINKNECHT, Alfred
Innovation patterns in crisis and prosperity : Schumpeter's long cycle reconsidered / Alfred Kleinknecht ; foreword by Jan Tinbergen. — Basingstoke : Macmillan, 1987. — xviii,235p. — *Bibliography: p221-229. — Includes index*

Long waves in the world economy. — London : Pinter, Apr.1984. — [252]p. — *Originally published: London : Butterworths, 1983*

MAGER, N. H
The Kondratieff waves / Nathan H. Mager. — New York : Praeger, 1987. — viii, 247 p.. — *"Praeger special studies. Praeger scientific.". — Includes index. — Bibliography: p. 241-247*

LONG WAVES (ECONOMICS) — Great Britain
MARSHALL, Michael, 1957-
Long waves of regional development / Michael Marshall. — Basingstoke : Macmillan, 1987. — xv,280p. — (Critical human geography). — *Bibliography: p254-268. — Includes index*

LONGEVITY — Georgian S.S.R. — Abkhazian A.S.S.R.
Sredi dolgozhitelei Abkhazii / [otv. redaktory: Sh. D. Inal-ipa, V. D. Kozlov]. — Tbilisi : Metsniereba, 1987. — 129p

LORRAINE (FRANCE) — Industries
GENDARME, René
Les coulées du futur : sidérurgie lorraine / René Gendarme. — Nancy : Presses Universitaires de Nancy ; Metz : Editions Serpenoise, 1985. — 314p

LOS ANGELES (CALIF.) — Ethnic relations
SANDBERG, Neil C
Jewish life in Los Angeles : a window to tomorrow / Neil C. Sandberg. — Lanham [MD] : University Press of America, c1986. — p. cm. — *Includes index. — Bibliography: p*

LOTUS 1-2-3 (COMPUTER PROGRAM)
GILBERT, Chris
The ABC's of 1-2-3 / Chris Gilbert and Laurie Williams. — Berkeley : Sybex, [1985]. — 227p

HOSKIN, Robert E.
Financial accounting with Lotus 1-2-3 / Robert E. Hoskin, Resa A. Labbe. — Englewood Cliffs, N.J. : Prentice-Hall, c1986. — p. cm. — *Includes index*

JORGENSEN, Carolyn
Mastering 1-2-3 / Carolyn Jorgensen. — Berkeley : Sybex, 1986. — 466p

MCLAUGHLIN, Hugh S
Financial management with Lotus 1-2-3 / Hugh S. McLaughlin, J. Russell Boulding. — Englewood Cliffs, N.J. : Prentice-Hall, c1986. — p. cm. — *On t.p. the circled symbol "R" is superscript following "Lotus" and "1-2-3" in the title. — Includes bibliographies and index*

SIMPSON, Alan
Simpson's 1-2-3 macro Library / Alan Simpson. — Berkeley : Sybex, [1986]. — 298p

LOUGHEED, PETER
WOOD, David G.
The Lougheed legacy / David G. Wood. — Toronto, Ont., Canada : Key Porter Books, c1985. — v, 250 p., [16] p. of plates. — *Includes index*

LOVE
LUHMANN, Niklas
Love as passion : the codification of intimacy / Niklas Luhmann ; translated by Jeremy Gaines and Doris L. Jones. — Cambridge : Polity, 1986. — 247p. — (Social and political theory). — *Translation of: Leibe als Passion. — Includes index*

LOVE — Psychological aspects
GAYLIN, Willard
Rediscovering love / Willard Gaylin. — New York, N.Y., U.S.A. : Viking, 1986. — 288 p.. — *Includes index. — Bibliography: p. 263-271*

LOWER SAVONY (GERMANY) — Statistics
Niedersächsen... das Jahr in Zahlen / Niedersächsisches Landesverwaltungsamt. — Hannover : Niedersächsisches Landesverwaltungsamt, 1984-. — *Annual*

LOWER SAXONY (GERMANY) — Politics and government
RENZSCH, Wolfgang
Alfred Kubel : 30 Jahre Politik für Niedersachsen : eine politische Biographie / Wolfgang Renzsch. — Bonn : Neue Gesellschaft, 1985. — 232p. — *Bibliography: p222-229*

:LOYALTY — security programs, 1947-
BEHRSTOCK, Julian
The eighth case : troubled times at the United Nations / Julian Behrstock. — Lanham : University Press of America, c1987. — p. cm. — *Includes bibliographical references and index*

LOZI (AFRICAN PEOPLE) — Social life and customs
STIRKE, D. E. C. R.
Barotseland : eight years among the Barotse / by D. W. Stirke ; with an introductory chapter by Sir Harry Johnston. — New York : Negro Universities Press, 1969. — xii,135p. — *Reprint of 1922 edition*

LUCKNOW (INDIA) — Buildings, structures, etc.
LLEWELLYN-JONES, Rosie
A fatal friendship : the Nawabs, the British and the city of Lucknow / Rosie Llewellyn-Jones. — Delhi ; Oxford : Oxford University Press, c1985. — xii,284p,[12]p of plates. — *Bibliography: p269-276. — Includes index*

LUDDITES
DINWIDDY, J. R.
From Luddism to the First Reform Bill : reform in England 1810-1832 / J.R. Dinwiddy. — Oxford : Basil Blackwell, 1986. — [96]p. — (Historical Association studies). — *Includes bibliography and index*

REID, Robert, 1933-
Land of lost content : the Luddite revolt, 1812 / Robert Reid. — London : Heinemann, 1986. — viii, 333p, [5]p of plates. — *Bibliography: p.315-320*

LUKÁCS, GYÖRGY
Revolutionäres Denken : Georg Lukács : eine Einführung in Leben und Werk / herausgegeben und eingeleitet von Frank Benseler. — Darmstadt : Luchterhand, 1984. — 327p. — *Bibliography: p309-324*

SZIKLAI, László
Proletárforradalom után : Lukács György marxista fejlődése 1930-1945 / Sziklai László. — [Budapest] : Kossuth Könyvkiadó, 1986. — 361p. — *References: p331-[362]*

ZOLTAI, Dénes
Egy írástudó visszatér : Lukács György 1945 utáni munkásságáról / Zoltai Dénes. — [Budapest] : Kossuth Könyvkiadó, 1985. — 249p. — *Notes and references: p231-248*

LUMBER TRADE — Soviet Union
JONSSON, Karl
Sågverksarbetare i österled : liv och leverne kring det svenska sågverket i Kovda / berättat av Karl Jonsson och nedtecknat av Linnéa Jonsson. — 2:a upplagan. — [s.l. : s.n.], 1981. — 136p. — *Bibliography: p135-136*

LUNDA, NORTHERN (AFRICAN PEOPLE)
PALMEIRIM, Maria Manuela Mestre Marques
The sterile mother : aspects of court symbolism among the Lunda of Mwant Yaav (Aruund) / Manuela M. Palmeirim. — 128 leaves. — *MPhil (Econ) 1986 LSE*

LUNGS — Dust diseases
HAMILTON, R. J.
Industrial hygiene in mines : a synthesis report on research supported by the Commission during the period 1977/82 / R. J. Hamilton. — Luxembourg : Office for Official Publications of the European Communities, 1985. — xii,95p. — (EUR ; 9253). — *Cover title. — Series title: Industrial health and safety. — Bibliographical references: p88-94. — Contract no.: V/E/4-1380(20928) of 9/3/1982*

LURISTAN (IRAN) — Social conditions
BLACK-MICHAUD, Jacob
Sheep and land : the economics of power in a tribal society / Jacob Black-Michaud. — Cambridge : Cambridge University Press, 1986. — xiv,231p. — (Collection production pastorale et société ; 4). — *English text with foreword in French. — Bibliography: p218-225. — Includes index*

LUTHERAN CHURCH — Soviet Union
KAHLE, Wilhelm
Die lutherischen Kirchen und Gemeinden in der Sowjetunion : seit 1938/1940 / Wilhelm Kahle. — Gütersloh : Gütersloher Verlagshaus Mohn, 1985. — 279p. — (Die lutherische Kirche, Geschichte und Gestalten ; Bd.8). — *Bibliography: p264-269*

LUTTE OUVRIÈRE
AVENAS, Denise
"Lutte ouvrière" et la révolution mondiale / Denise Avenas. — Paris : François Maspero, 1971. — 45p. — (Série "Marx ou crève" ; 3) (Cahiers rouges)

LUXEMBOURG — Description and travel
GREAT BRITAIN. Civil Service Department
Luxembourg briefing. — [London : the Department, 1973]. — 7leaves

LUXEMBOURG — Economic conditions
ALS, Georges
Luxembourg historic, geographic and economic profile / by Georges Als. — Luxembourg : Information and Press Service, [1976]. — 98p

LUXEMBOURG — Social conditions
ALS, Georges
Luxembourg historic, geographic and economic profile / by Georges Als. — Luxembourg : Information and Press Service, [1976]. — 98p

GREAT BRITAIN. Civil Service Department
Luxembourg briefing. — [London : the Department, 1973]. — 7leaves

LUXEMBOURG — Statistics
Le Grand-Duché de Luxembourg en chiffres : 1983. — Luxembourg : Service Central de la Statistique et des Études Économiques, 1983. — 1folding booklet

LUXEMBOURG — Statistics — Bibliography
Répertoire analytique des publications statistiques et économiques du 19e siècle à ce jour. — 8th ed. — Luxembourg : Service central de la statistique et des études économiques, 1986. — ix,168p. — (Collection "Définitions et méthodes" ; no.3)

LUXEMBOURG (BELGIUM) — Emigration and immigration — Statistics
MAGNETTE, Gérard
Les migrations alternantes dans la province de Luxembourg : approche statistique / Gérard Magnette. — Arlon : Fondation Universitaire Luxembourgeoise, 1976. — 56p. — (Serie "Notes de Recherche" / Fondation Universitaire Luxembourgeoise ; 7)

LUXEMBOURG CONFERENCE ON THE COMMUNITY PATENT — 1975

LUXEMBURG, ROSA
ETTINGER, Elżbieta
Rosa Luxemburg : a life / Elżbieta Ettinger. — London : Harrap, 1987. — xv, 286p, [24]p of plates

LYNCH, LIAM
RYAN, Meda
Liam Lynch : the real chief / Meda Ryan. — Cork : Mercier, c1986. — 192p. — *Includes index*

LYNDON BAINES JOHNSON LIBRARY
The Johnson years / edited by Robert A. Divine. — Lawrence, Kan. : University Press of Kansas, 1987-. — v. <1 >. — *Includes index. — Contents: v. 1. Foreign policy, the Great Society, and the White House*

LYSERGIC ACID DIETHYLAMIDE
LEE, Martin A
Acid dreams : the CIA, LSD, and the sixties rebellion / by Martin A. Lee and Bruce Shlain. — 1st Grove Press ed. — New York : Grove Press, 1986. — xxi, 343p, [12] p of plates. — *Includes index. — Bibliography: p.320-329*

M. D. P. See Magyar Dolgozók Pártja

MCCARTHY, JOSEPH
EWALD, William Bragg
McCarthyism and consensus / William Bragg Ewald, Jr. — Lanham [Md.] : University Press of America, c1986. — viii, 68 p.. — (The Credibility of institution, policies and leadership ; v. 13). — *"Co-published by arrangement with the White Burkett Miller Center of Public Affairs, University of Virginia"--T.p. verso. — Contents: Rotunda lecture: "McCarthyism revisited" / William Bragg Ewald, Jr. -- Miller Center discussion: "McCarthyism and consensus."*

MACDONALD, JAMES RAMSAY
MORGAN, Austen
J. Ramsay MacDonald / Austen Morgan. — Manchester : Manchester University Press, c1987. — 276p. — (Lives of the left). — *Includes index*

MCDONALD'S CORPORATION — History
LOVE, John F.
McDonald's : behind the arches / John F. Love. — London : Bantam, 1987, c1986. — [556]p. — *Originally published: New York : Bantam, 1986. — Includes index*

MACDOUGALL, DONALD
MACDOUGALL, Donald
Don and mandarin : memoirs of an economist / Donald MacDougall. — London : Murray, 1987. — [312]p. — *Includes index*

MCDOUGALL, F. L.
MCDOUGALL, F. L.
Letters from a 'secret service agent' : F. L. McDougall to S. M. Bruce, 1924-1929 / W. J. Hudson and Wendy Way, editors. — Canberra : Australian Government Publishing Service, 1986. — xix,937p

MACEO, ANTONIO
FRANCO, José Luciano
La vida heroica y ejemplar de Antonio Maceo (Cronología) / por José L. Franco. — La Habana : Comisión Nacional de la Academia de Ciencias, Instituto de Historia, 1963. — 117p

MCGILL UNIVERSITY — History
SHORE, Marlene
The science of social redemption : McGill, the Chicago School, and the origins of social research in Canada. — Toronto : University of Toronto Press, 1987. — xviii,340p. — *Bibliographical notes: p[275]-324*

MACHINE LEARNING
Induction : processes of inference, learning, and discovery / John H. Holland ... [et al.]. — Cambridge, Mass. : MIT Press, c1986. — xvi, 385p. — (Computational models of cognition and perception). — *Includes index. — Bibliography: p.357-372*

Machine learning : an artificial intelligence approach / contributing authors, John Anderson ... [et al.] ; editors, Ryszard S. Michalski, Jaime G. Carbonell, Tom M. Mitchell. — Los Altos, Calif. : Morgan Kaufmann, 1986, c1983. — p. cm. — : Reprint. Originally published: Palo Alto, Calif. : Tioga Pub. Co., c1983. — *Includes index. — Bibliography: p*

MACHINE-TOOL INDUSTRY — Technological innovations — Government policy
JACOBSON, Staffan
Electronics and industrial policy : the case of computer-controlled lathes / Staffan Jacobson. — London : Allen & Unwin, 1986. — xx,252p. — (World industry studies ; 5). — *Bibliography: p241-248. — Includes index*

MACHINE-TOOL INDUSTRY — Developing countries
The capital goods sector in developing countries : technology issues and policy options : study / by the UNCTAD secretariat. — New York : United Nations, 1985. — xxiv,183p. — ([Document] / United Nations ; UNCTAD/TT/78). — *Sales no.: E.85.II.D.4*

MACHINE TRANSLATING
INTERNATIONAL CONFERENCE ON TRANSLATING (7th : 1985 : London)
Translating and the computer : 7th International Conference on Translating / edited by Catriona Picken. — London : Aslib Publications, 1986. — [200]p

MACHINERY — Trade and manufacture
Machinery and economic development / edited by Martin Fransman. — Basingstoke : Macmillan, 1986. — xvii,274p. — *Includes bibliographies and index*

MACHINERY IN INDUSTRY
Automation and industrial workers : a fifteen nation study. — Oxford : Pergamon Vol.2 / edited by Frank Adler ... [et al.] for the European Coordination Centre for Research and Documentation in Social Sciences. — 1986. — 2v.(xxiv,866p). — *Vol.2 has sub-title: A cross-national comparison of fifteen countries*

MACHINERY INDUSTRY — Developing countries
The capital goods sector in developing countries : technology issues and policy options : study / by the UNCTAD secretariat. — New York : United Nations, 1985. — xxiv,183p. — ([Document] / United Nations ; UNCTAD/TT/78). — *Sales no.: E.85.II.D.4*

MACIEL, MERVYN — Biography
MACIEL, Mervyn
Bwana Karani / Mervyn Maciel ; with foreword by Sir Richard Turnbull. — Braunton : Merlin, 1985. — 262p

MACLAREN, ROY, 1934-
MACLAREN, Roy
Honourable mentions : the uncommon diary of an M.P. / Roy MacLaren. — Toronto : Deneau, 1986. — 226p

MACROECONOMICS
BENASSY, Jean-Pascal
Macroeconomics : an introduction to the Non-Walrasian approach / Jean-Pascal Benassy. — Orlando : Academic Press, 1986. — p. cm. — (Economic theory, econometrics, and mathematical economics). — *Includes index. — Bibliography: p*

BHADURI, Amit
Macroeconomics : the dynamics of commodity production / Amit Bhaduri. — Basingstoke : Macmillan, 1986. — xii,278p. — (Radical economics). — *Bibliography: p259-263. — Includes index*

BHANDARI, Jagdeep S
Studies in international macroeconomics / Jagdeep S. Bhandari. — New York : Praeger, 1986. — p. cm. — *Includes index*

MACROECONOMICS *continuation*

BIRD, Graham, 1947-
International macroeconomics : theory, policy and applications / Graham Bird. — Basingstoke : Macmillan, 1987. — [256]p

BRUNO, Michael
Economics of worldwide stagflation / Michael Bruno and Jeffrey D. Sachs. — Cambridge, Mass. : Harvard University Press, 1985. — 315p. — *Includes index. — Bibliography: p.[297]-310*

DORNBUSCH, Rudiger
Macroeconomics / Rudiger Dornbusch, Stanley Fischer. — 4th ed. — New York ; London : McGraw-Hill, c1987. — xiv,798p. — *Previous ed.: 1984. — Tables on lining papers. — Includes index*

FELDERER, B
[Makroökonomik und neue Makroökonomik. English]. Macroeconomics and new macroeconomics / Bernhard Felderer, Stefan Homburg. — Berlin ; New York : Springer-Verlag, c1986. — p. cm. — *Translation of: Makroökonomik und neue Makroökonomik. 2nd corr. ed. 1985. — Includes indexes. — Bibliography: p*

FOSTER, John, 1947-
Evolutionary macroeconomics / John Foster. — London : Allen & Unwin, 1987. — [xii,280]p. — *Includes bibliography and index*

FROYEN, Richard T
Macroeconomics : theories and policies / Richard T. Froyen. — 2nd ed. — New York : Macmillan ; London : Collier Macmillan, c1986. — xxiv, 661p. — *Includes bibliographical references*

HEILBRONER, Robert L
Understanding macroeconomics / Robert L. Heilbroner, James K. Galbraith. — Rev. 8th ed. — Englewood Cliffs, NJ : Prentice-Hall, c1987. — xi, 484 p. — *Includes index*

HENNING, C. Randall
Macroeconomic diplomacy in the 1980s : domestic politics and international conflict among the United States, Japan, and Europe / C. Randall Henning. — London : Croom Helm for the Atlantic Institute for International Affairs, c1987. — [96]p. — (Atlantic paper ; no.65)

HOLLAND, Stuart
The global economy : from meso to macroeconomics / Stuart Holland. — London : Weidenfeld and Nicolson, c1987. — x, 443p. — *Bibliography: p.[424]-434*

LEVINE, Paul
Does international macroeconomic policy co-ordinate pay and is it sustainable : a two-country analysis / Paul Levine and David Currie. — London : National Institute of Economic and Social Research, 1986. — 43p. — (Discussion paper / National Institute of Economic and Social Research ; no.113). — *Bibliography: p42-43*

Macroeconomics annual / National Bureau of Economic Research. — Cambridge, Mass. ; London : MIT Press, 1986-. — *Annual*

MANOHAR RAO, M. J
Filtering and control of macroeconomic systems : a control system incorporating the Kalman filter for the Indian economy / M.J. Manohar Rao. — Amsterdam ; New York : North-Holland ; New York, N.Y., U.S.A. : Sole distributors for the U.S.A. and Canada, Elsevier Science Pub. Co., 1987. — p. cm. — (Contributions to economic analysis ; 160). — *Includes indexes. — Bibliography: p*

SOMMARIVA, Andrea
German macroeconomic history, 1880-1979 : a study of the effects of economic policy on inflation, currency depreciation and growth / Andrea Sommariva and Giuseppe Tullio ; foreword by Clifford Wymer. — Basingstoke : Macmillan, 1986, c1987. — xx,264p. — *Bibliography: p249-257. — Includes index*

WHITELEY, Paul
Political control of the macroeconomy : the political economy of public policy making / by Paul Whiteley. — London : Sage, 1986. — 212p. — *Bibliogrpahy: p191-201. — Includes index*

MACROECONOMICS — Addresses, essays, lectures

Macroeconomic conflict and social institutions / edited by Shlomo Maital, Irwin Lipnowski. — Cambridge, Mass. : Ballinger Pub. Co., 1985. — p. cm. — *Chiefly papers originating from a session on "Income policy as a social institution," at the American Economic Association's 95th Annual Meeting in New York, Dec. 28-30, 1982. — Includes bibliographies and index*

MACROECONOMICS — Computer programs

RICHARDSON, Pete
Recent developments in OECD's international macroeconomic model / by Pete Richardson. — [Paris] : OECD, 1987. — iv,31p. — (Working papers / OECD Department of Economics and Statistics ; no.46). — *Bibliographical references:p30-31*

RICHARDSON, Pete
A review of the simulation properties of OECD's INTERLINK model / by Pete Richardson. — [Paris] : OECD, 1987. — iv,67p. — (Working papers / OECD Department of Economics and Statistics ; no.47). — *Bibliographical references: p55*

MACROECONOMICS — Econometric models — Congresses

Developments of control theory for economic analysis / Carlo Carraro and Domenico Sartore, editors. — Dordrecht ; Boston : M. Nijhoff, 1987. — p. cm. — (Advanced studies in theoretical and applied econometrics ; v. 7). — *"Proceedings of the Conference on "Economic Policy and Control Theory" which was held at the University of Venice (Italy) on 27 January-1 February 1985"--Pref*

MACROECONOMICS — Mathematical models

Macroeconomics [i.e. Macroeconimic] impacts of energy shocks / edited by Bert G. Hickman, Hillard G. Huntington, and James L. Sweeney. — Amsterdam ; New York : North-Holland ; New York, N.Y., U.S.A. : Sole distributors for the U.S.A. and Canada, Elsevier Science Pub. Co., 1987. — xvi, 331 p.. — (Contributions to economic analysis ; 163). — *Includes bibliographical references*

SARGENT, Thomas J
Dynamic macroeconomic theory / Thomas J. Sargent. — Cambridge, Mass. : Harvard University Press, 1987. — xii, 369 p.. — *Includes bibliographies and index*

MACROECONOMICS — Mathematical models — Congresses

Competition, instability, and nonlinear cycles : proceedings of an international conference, New School for Social Research, New York, USA, March 1985 / edited by Willi Semmler. — Berlin ; New York : Springer-Verlag, c1986. — p. cm. — (Lecture notes in economics and mathematical systems ; 275)

MACSWINEY, MARY

FALLON, Charlotte H.
Soul of fire : a biography of Mary MacSwiney / Charlotte H. Fallon. — Cork : Mercier, c1986. — 207p. — *Bibliography: p204-207*

MACWRITE (COMPUTER PROGRAM) — Handbooks, manuals, etc.

APPLE COMPUTER, INC.
Macintosh MacWrite / Apple Computer ; written by Lynnea Johnson. — Cupertino, Calif. : Apple Computer, 1984. — 143p

MADAGASCAR — Description and travel

MAUDE, Francis Cornwallis
Five years in Madagascar : with notes on the military situation / by Francis Cornwallis Maude. — New York : Negro Universities Press, 1969. — 285p. — *Reprint of 1985 edition*

MADAGASCAR — History

MAUDE, Francis Cornwallis
Five years in Madagascar : with notes on the military situation / by Francis Cornwallis Maude. — New York : Negro Universities Press, 1969. — 285p. — *Reprint of 1985 edition*

MADAGASCAR — History — Revolution, 1947

TRONCHON, Jacques
L'insurrection malgache de 1947 : essai d'interprétation historique / Jacques Tronchon. — Fianarantsoa, Madagascar : Editions Ambozontany Fianarantsoa ; Paris : Editions-Diffusion Karthala, 1986. — 399p

MADAGASCAR — Politics and government — 1960

CHAIGNEAU, Pascal
Rivalités politiques et socialisme a Madagascar / Pascal Chaigneau. — Paris : Le Centre des Hautes Études sur l'Afrique et l'Asie Modernes, 1986. — 263p. — (Publicatioms du CHEAM ; 6). — *Bibliography: p255-263*

MADHYA PRADESH (INDIA) — Population — Statistics

Census of India 1981. — [Delhi : Controller of Publications]
Series II: Madhya Pradesh. — [1984]

MADRID OFFICE EUROPEAN COMMUNITIES

Comunidad Europea / Commission of the European Communities. — Madrid : Comisión de las Comunidades Europeas. Oficina de Madrid, 1986-. — *Monthly*

MADRID (SPAIN) — Census, 1981

Censo de población de 1981 de los municipios de menos de 50,000 habitantes de la Comunidad de Madrid. — Madrid : Consejería de Economía y Hacienda
Vol.1: Características de la población total. — [1985]. — 309p. — (Documentación y estadísticas)

MADRID (SPAIN) — History

MONTÓN, Juan Carlos
La revolución armada del Dos de Mayo en Madrid / Juan Carlos Montón. — Madrid : Istmo, 1983. — 332p,[4]leaves of plates. — *Bibliography: p.323-329*

MADRID (SPAIN) — Politics and government

Madrid, Comunidad autónoma metropolitana / [equipo dirigido por] E. García de Enterría. — Madrid : Instituto de Estudios Económicos, 1983. — 482p. — (Colección Estudios / Instituto de Estudios Económicos)

MADRID (SPAIN) — Population — Statistics

Censo de población de 1981 de los municipios de menos de 50,000 habitantes de la Comunidad de Madrid. — Madrid : Consejería de Economía y Hacienda
Vol.1: Características de la población total. — [1985]. — 309p. — (Documentación y estadísticas)

MAFETENG (LESOTHO) — Economic conditions — Statistics

FOSA, N.
Mafeteng data bank : analysis and tables. — [Maseru] : Ministry of Cooperatives and Rural Development, 1982. — 88p. — (Assistance to rural development ; LES/77/026)

MAFETENG (LESOTHO) — Social conditions — Statistics

FOSA, N.
Mafeteng data bank : analysis and tables. — [Maseru] : Ministry of Cooperatives and Rural Development, 1982. — 88p. — (Assistance to rural development ; LES/77/026)

MAFIA — Italy — History

ARLACCHI, Pino
Mafia business : the Mafia ethic and the spirit of capitalism / Pino Arlacchi ; translated by Martin Ryle. — London : Verso, 1986. — xix,239p

MAGARS — Commerce

FISHER, James F
Trans-Himalayan traders : economy, society, and culture in northwest Nepal / James F. Fisher. — Berkeley : University of California Press, c1986. — xiv, 232 p., [8] p. of plates. — Includes index. — Bibliography: p. 219-223

MAGARS — Economic conditions

FISHER, James F
Trans-Himalayan traders : economy, society, and culture in northwest Nepal / James F. Fisher. — Berkeley : University of California Press, c1986. — xiv, 232 p., [8] p. of plates. — Includes index. — Bibliography: p. 219-223

MAGIC — Africa, Central

EVANS-PRITCHARD, Sir Edward Evan
Witchcraft, oracles and magic among the Azande / Sir Edward Evans-Pritchard ; with a foreword by C. G. Seligman. — Oxford : Clarendon Press, 1937. — 558p

MAGISTRATES' ASSOCIATION

Annual report / Magistrates' Association. — London : Magistrates' Association, 1985/86-. — Annual

MAGOMERO (MALAWI) — History

WHITE, Landeg
Magomero : portrait of an African village / Landeg White. — Cambridge : Cambridge University Press, 1987. — &f 1. — Includes index

MAGOMERO (MALAWI) — Social life and customs

WHITE, Landeg
Magomero : portrait of an African village / Landeg White. — Cambridge : Cambridge University Press, 1987. — &f 1. — Includes index

MAGYAR DOLGOZÓK PÁRTJA — History

SZABÓ, Bálint
Az "ötvenes évek" : elmélet és politika a szocialista építés elso" időszakában Magyarországon 1948-1957 / Szabó Bálint. — Budapest : Kossuth Könyvkiadó, 1986. — 432p . — References: p397-[433]

MAGYAR SZOCIALISTA MUNKÁSPÁRT

BERECZ, János
Folyamatosság és megújulás az MSZMP politikájában / Berecz János. — Budapest : Kossuth Könyvkiadó, 1985. — 128p

MAGYAR SZOCIALISTA MUNKÁSPÁRT — Congresses

MAGYAR SZOCIALISTA MUNKÁSPÁRT. Kongresszus (13th : 1985 : Budapest)
A Magyar Szocialista Munkáspárt XIII. Kongresszusa : 1985. március 25-28. — [Budapest] : Kossuth Könyvkiadó, 1985. — 229p

MAHARASHTRA (INDIA) — Economic conditions — Statistics

Maharashtra's economy in figures / Directorate of Economics and Statistics, Maharashtra. — Bombay : Directorate of Economics and Statistics, 1983-. — Annual

MAHINA (TAHITI) — Population — Statistics

Tableaux normalisés du recensement général de la population : 15 octobre 1983. — [Papeete] : Institut territorial de la statistique
Résultats de la commune de Mahina. — [1985?]. — 15 leaves

MAIAO (SOCIETY ISLANDS) — Population — Statistics

Tableaux normalisés du recensement général de la population : 15 octobre 1983. — [Papeete] : Institut territorial de la statistique
Résultats de la commune de Moorea-Maiao. — [1985?]. — 11 leaves

MAJOK, DENG

DENG, Francis Mading
The man called Deng Majok : a biography of power, polygyny, and change / Francis Mading Deng. — New Haven : Yale University Press, c1986. — p. cm. — Includes index

MAKEMO (TUAMOTU ISLANDS) — Population — Statistics

Tableaux normalisés du recensement général de la population : 15 octobre 1983. — [Papeete] : Institut territorial de la statistique
Résultats de la commune de Makemo. — [1985?]. — 4p,ll leaves

MALAGA (SPAIN) — History — Civil War, 1936-1939

NADAL SANCHEZ, Antonio
Guerra civil en Málaga / Antonio Nadal. — Málaga : Arguval, 1984. — 474p

MALAGA (SPAIN) — Politics and government

ARCAS CUBERO, Fernando
El republicanismo malagueño durante la Restauración (1875-1923) / Fernando Arcas Cubero. — Cordoba : Ayuntamiento Cordoba, 1985. — 600p. — Bibliography: p585-593

MALAWI — History — Dictionaries

CROSBY, C. A
Historical dictionary of Malawi / by Cynthia A. Crosby. — Metuchen, N.J. : Scarecrow Press, 1980. — xxxvi, 169 p.. — (African historical dictionaries ; no. 25). — Bibliography: p. 119-169

MALAWI — Politics and government — 1964-

MTEWA, Mekki
Malawi democratic theory and public policy : a preface / by Mekki Mtewa. — Cambridge, Mass. : Schenkman Pub. Co., 1986. — p. cm. — Includes index. — Bibliography: p

MALAYA — Economic conditions

SUNDARAM, Jomo Kwame
A question of class : capital, the state and uneven development in Malaya / Jomo Kwame Sundaram. — Singapore : Oxford University Press, 1986. — xxiii,360p. — (East Asian Social Science Monographs). — Bibliography: p331-354

MALAYA — Social conditions

SUNDARAM, Jomo Kwame
A question of class : capital, the state and uneven development in Malaya / Jomo Kwame Sundaram. — Singapore : Oxford University Press, 1986. — xxiii,360p. — (East Asian Social Science Monographs). — Bibliography: p331-354

MALAYSIA — Census, 1980

Banci penduduk dan perumahan Malaysia 1980 = Population and housing census of Malaysia 1980. — Kuala Lumpur : Department of Statistics. — Text in Malay and English
State population report

Banci penduduk dan perumahan Malaysia 1980 = Population and housing census of Malaysia 1980. — Kuala Lumpur : Department of Statistics. — Text in Malay and English
Laporan am banci perumahan = General report of the housing census. — 1983. — 2v

Banci penduduk dan perumahan Malaysia 1980 = Population and housing census of Malaysia 1980. — Kuala Lumpur : Department of Statistics. — Text in Malay and English
Laporan penduduk negeri = State population report

Banci penduduk dan perumahan Malaysia 1980 = Population and housing census of Malaysia 1980. — Kuala Lumpur : Department of Statistics. — Text in Malay and English
Laporan penduduk negeri = State population report
Perak. — 1984. — 599p. — 1map

Banci penduduk dan perumahan Malaysia 1980 = Population and housing census of Malaysia 1980. — Kuala Lumpur : Department of Statistics. — Text in Malay and English
Laporan penduduk negeri = State population report
Perlis. — 1984. — 555p

Banci penduduk dan perumahan Malaysia 1980 = Population and housing census of Malaysia 1980. — Kuala Lumpur : Department of Statistics. — Text in Malay and English
Laporan penduduk negeri = State population report
Sarawak. — 1980. — 2v. — 1map in v.2

Banci penduduk dan perumahan Malaysia 1980 = Population and housing census of Malaysia 1980. — Kuala Lumpur : Department of Statistics. — Text in Malay and English
Laporan penduduk negeri = State population report
Selangor. — 1983. — 599p. — 1map

Banci penduduk dan perumahan Malaysia 1980 = Population and housing census of Malaysia 1980. — Kuala Lumpur : Department of Statistics. — Text in Malay and English
Laporan penduduk negeri = State population report
Wilayah Persekutuan. — 1983. — 297p. — 1map

Banci penduduk dan perumahan Malaysia 1980 = Population and housing census of Malaysia 1980. — Kuala Lumpur : Department of Statistics. — Text in Malay and English
Laporan perumahan negeri = State housing report

Banci penduduk dan perumahan Malaysia 1980 = Population and housing census of Malaysia 1980. — Kuala Lumpur : Department of Statistics. — Text in Malay and English
Laporan perumahan negeri = State housing report
Selangor. — 1984. — 232p. — 1map

Banci penduduk dan perumahan Malaysia 1980 = Population and housing census of Malaysia 1980. — Kuala Lumpur : Department of Statistics. — Text in Malay and English
Laporan perumahan negeri = State housing report
Wilayah Persekutuan. — 1984. — 54p. — 1map

MALAYSIA — Constitutional law

The constitution of Malaysia : further perspectives and developments : essays in honour of Tun Mohamed Suffian / edited by F.A. Trindade and H.P. Lee. — Singapore ; Oxford : Oxford University Press, 1986. — xix,275p. — Includes bibliographical references and index

MALAYSIA — Economic conditions

AIKEN, S. Robert
Development and environment in peninsular Malaysia / S. Robert Aiken...[et al.]. — Singapore ; New York : McGraw-Hill International, 1982. — xx,310p. — (McGraw-Hill Southeast Asia series). — Bibliography: p283-301

KAUR, Amarjit
Bridge and barrier : transport and communications in colonial Malaya 1870-1957 / Amarjit Kaur. — Oxford : Oxford University Press, 1985. — 235p

MALAYSIA — Economic policy
AIKEN, S. Robert
Development and environment in peninsular Malaysia / S. Robert Aiken...[et al.]. — Singapore ; New York : McGraw-Hill International, 1982. — xx,310p. — (McGraw-Hill Southeast Asia series). — *Bibliography: p283-301*

The Sun also sets : lessons in 'looking East' / editor, Jomo. — 2nd ed., rev. & expanded. — Kuala Lumpur : INSAN, 1985. — xvi, 415 p.. — *Includes bibliographies*

MALAYSIA — Foreign economic relations — Japan
The Sun also sets : lessons in 'looking East' / editor, Jomo. — 2nd ed., rev. & expanded. — Kuala Lumpur : INSAN, 1985. — xvi, 415 p.. — *Includes bibliographies*

MALAYSIA — Foreign relations
ABDULLAH AHMAD, Datuk
Tengku Abdul Rahman and Malaysia's foreign policy, 1963-1970 / Dato' Abdullah Ahmad. — Kuala Lumpur : Berita Publishing, 1985. — ix, 182 p.. — *Includes index. — Bibliography: 157-167*

MALAYSIA — Industries
Industrialisation and labour force processes : a case study of peninsular Malaysia / T. G. McGee...[et al.] ; with a preface by H. C. Brookfield and a postscript by Benjamin Higgins. — Canberra : Australian National University, 1986. — xviii,244p. — (Research papers on development in East Java and West Malaysia ; No.1). — *Bibliography: p223-238*

MALAYSIA — Politics and government
ISIS CONFERENCE ON NATIONAL INTEGRATION (1st : 1985 : Kuala Lumpur)
The bonding of a nation : federalism and territorial integration in Malaysia : proceedings of the first ISIS Conference.... — Kuala Lumpur : Institute of Strategic and International Studies, 1986. — v,131p

Malaysia : last chance for a new beginning? : a report for CSCS by a South-East Asian Observer. — London : Centre for Security and Conflict Studies, 1987. — 26p. — (Conflict studies ; no.195)

Malaysian digest. — Kuala Lumpur : External Information Division of the Ministry of Foreign Affairs, 1984-. — *Monthly*

MALAYSIA — Bibliography
BROWN, Ian, 1947-
Malaysia / Ian Brown, Rajeswary Ampalavanar, compilers. — Oxford : Clio, c1986. — xxxv,308p,[23]leaves. — (World bibliographical series ; v.12). — *Includes index*

MALI — Census, 1976
Recensement Général de la Population décembre 1976. — Bamako : Bureau Central de Recensement
vol.3: Répertoire de villages : résultats définitifs. — 1980. — 166p

MALI — Economic policy
LECAILLON, Jacques
Economic policies and agricultural performance : the case of Mali, 1960-1983 / by Jacques Lecaillon and Christian Morrisson. — Paris : Development Centre of the Organisation for Economic Co-operation and Development, 1986. — 174p. — (Development Centre papers) . — *Bibliography: p155-157*

MALI — History — Dictionaries
IMPERATO, Pascal James
Historical dictionary of Mali / by Pascal James Imperato. — 2nd ed. — Metuchen, N.J. : Scarecrow Press, 1986. — p. cm. — (African historical dictionaries ; no. 11). — *Bibliography: p*

MALI — Population — Statistics
Recensement Général de la Population décembre 1976. — Bamako : Bureau Central de Recensement
vol.3: Répertoire de villages : résultats définitifs. — 1980. — 166p

MALMÖ (SWEDEN) — City planning
General plan för Malmö / verkställd på stadsingenjörskontoret av Martin Weibull. — Malmö : Stadsingenjörskontoret
Del 2: Inventering av näringsliv och allmänna institutioner. — 1952. — 353,41p

MALNUTRITION — Latin America
KANBUR, S. M. Ravi
Malnutrition and poverty in Latin America / S. M. Ravi Kanbur. — Coventry : University of Warwick. Department of Economics, 1987. — 62p. — (Warwick economic research papers ; no.278). — *Bibliography: p59-62*

MALOHS (BORNEAN PEOPLE)
KING, Victor T.
The Maloh of West Kalimantan : an ethnographic study of social inequality and social change among an Indonesian Borneo people / Victor T. King. — Dordrecht : Foris Publications, 1985. — viii,252p. — (Verhandelingen van het Koninklijk Instituut voor Taal-, Land-en Volkenkunde ; 108). — *Bibliography: p232-243*

MALPRACTICE — Trends — United States — Legislation
WERTHMANN, Barbara
Medical malpractice law : how medicine is changing the law / Barbara Werthmann. — Lexington, Mass. : LexingtonBooks, c1984. — xii, 268 p.. — *Includes indexes*

MALPRACTICE — England
JACKSON, Rupert M.
Professional negligence / by Rupert M. Jackson and John L. Powell. — 2nd ed. — London : Sweet & Maxwell, 1987. — xlvii,472p . — *2nd ed. — Previous ed.: 1982. — Includes index*

MALTHUS, T. R.
Thomas Robert Malthus : critical assessments / edited by John Cunningham Wood. — London : Croom Helm, c1986. — 4v.([2000]p). — (The Croom Helm critical assessments of leading economists)

WINCH, Donald
Malthus / Donald Winch. — Oxford : Oxford University Press, 1987. — [144]p. — (Past masters). — *Includes bibliography and index*

MALTHUSIANISM
NJOKU, John E. Eberegbulam
Malthusianism, an African dilemma : hunger, drought, and starvation in Africa / by John E. Eberegbulam Njoku. — Metuchen, N.J. : Scarecrow Press, 1986. — xxix, 181 p.. — *Bibliography: p. [163]-181*

MAMBAI (INDONESIAN PEOPLE) — Rites and ceremonies
TRAUBE, Elizabeth G
Cosmology and social life : ritual exchange among the Mambai of East Timor / Elizabeth G. Traube. — Chicago : University of Chicago Press, 1986. — xxiii, 289 p.. — *Includes index. — Bibliography: p. 275-279*

MAMBORU (INDONESIA) — Social life and customs
NEEDHAM, Rodney
Mamboru : history and structure in a domain of Northwestern Sumba / Rodney Needham. — Oxford : Clarendon, 1987. — xxv,202p,[6]p of plates. — *Bibliography: p194-200. — Includes index*

MAN, HENDRIK DE
BRÉLAZ, Michel
Henri de Man : une autre idée du socialisme / Michel Brélaz. — Genève : Antipodes, 1985. — 814p. — *Bibliography: p739-790*

MAN
BERRY, Christopher J.
Human nature / Christopher J. Berry. — Basingstoke : Macmillan, 1986. — xiv,162p. — (Issues in political theory). — *Bibliography: p145-155. Includes index*

MAN — History
LANGFORD, Peter
Modern philosophies of human nature : their emergence from Christian thought / Peter Langford. — Dordrecht ; Lancaster : Nijhoff, 1986. — 265p. — (Martinus Nijhoff philosophy library ; v. 15). — *Includes bibliographies and index*

MAN — Influence of environment
GRAY, David B
Ecological beliefs and behaviors : assessment and change / David B. Gray, in collaboration with Richard J. Borden and Russell H. Weigel ; foreword by Riley E. Dunlap. — Westport, Conn. : Greenwood Press, c1985. — p. cm. — (Contributions in psychology ; no. 4). — *Includes index. — Bibliography: p*

Human behavior and environment: advances in theory and research. — New York ; London : Plenum Press, 1980-. — *Annual*

MINGAY, G. E.
The transformation of Britain, 1830-1939 / G.E Mingay. — London : Routledge & Kegan Paul, 1986. — xii,231p. — (The Making of Britain, 1066-1939)

MAN — Influence on nature
INTERNATIONAL LABOUR ORGANIZATION. Identification and Programming Mission to the Republic of the Sudan (1985)
After the famine : a programme of action to strengthen the survival strategies of affected populations / report of the ILO Identification and Programming Mission to the Republic of the Sudan, September 1985. — Geneva : ILO, c1986. — xi,309p

SEYMOUR, John, 1914-
Far from paradise : the story of man's impact on the environment / John Seymour, Herbert Girardet. — London : BBC, 1986. — 216p, 50p of plates. — *Bibliography: p.214-216*

TIMBERLAKE, Lloyd
Only one earth : living for the future / Lloyd Timberlake. — London : BBC : Earthscan, 1987. — 168p. — *Bibliography: p160-161*

MAN — Influence on nature — China
Learning from China? : development and environment in Third World countries / edited by Bernhard Glaeser. — London : Allen & Unwin, 1987. — xvii,282p,[8]p of plates. — *Conference papers. — Includes bibliographies and index*

MAN — Influence on nature — Developing countries
Learning from China? : development and environment in Third World countries / edited by Bernhard Glaeser. — London : Allen & Unwin, 1987. — xvii,282p,[8]p of plates. — *Conference papers. — Includes bibliographies and index*

MAN — Machine systems
Information technology & people : designing for the future / edited by Frank Blackler and David Oborne. — Leicester : British Psychological Society, 1987. — 262 p

MAN — Migrations
CLARK, W. A. V.
Human migration / W. A. V. Clark. — Beverly Hills ; London : Sage Publications, 1986. — 96p. — (Scientific geography series ; v.7)

MAN (CHRISTIAN THEOLOGY) — History of doctrines
LANGFORD, Peter
Modern philosophies of human nature : their emergence from Christian thought / Peter Langford. — Dordrecht ; Lancaster : Nijhoff, 1986. — 265p. — (Martinus Nijhoff philosophy library ; v. 15). — *Includes bibliographies and index*

MAN-MACHINE SYSTEMS

Applications of cognitive psychology : problem solving, education, and computing / edited by Dale E. Berger, Kathy Pezdek, William P. Banks. — Hillsdale, N.J. : L. Erlbaum Associates, 1987. — xii, 235 p.. — *Includes bibliographies and indexes*

BLEND-5 : the computer human factors journal / journal editors: B. Shackel, J. Florentin, P. Wright ... ; this report was collated and edited by David J. Pullinger and produced with the help of Wendy Buckland. — London : British Library, c1986. — xi,221p. — (Library and information research report ; 47). — *Includes bibliographies*

BRITISH COMPUTER SOCIETY. Human Computer Interaction Specialist Group. Conference (2nd : 1986 : University of York) People and computers : designing for usability : proceedings of the Second Conference of the British Computer Society, Human Computer Interaction Specialist Group, University of York, 23-26 September 1986 / edited by M.D. Harrison, A.F. Monk. — Cambridge : Cambridge University Press on behalf of the British Computer Society, 1986. — xiii,650p. — (The British Computer Society Workshop series). — *Bibliography: p615-644*. — *Includes index*

CHI '85 CONFERENCE (San Francisco) Human factors in computing systems II : proceedings of the CHI '85 conference held San Francisco, C.A., U.S.A., 14-18 April 1985, sponsored by the association for Computing Machinery's Special Interest Group on Computer and Human Interaction (ACH/SIGCHI) in cooperation with the Human Factors Society edited by Lorraine Borman and Bill Curtis. — Amsterdam ; Oxford : North-Holland, 1985. — vii,231p. — *Includes index*

Designing for human-computer communication / edited by M.E. Sime and M.J. Coombs. — London : Academic Press, 1983. — x,338p. — (Computers and people). — *Includes bibliographies and index*

New technology and human error / edited by Jens Rasmussen, Keith Duncan, and Jacques Leplat. — Chichester : Wiley, c1986. — xvi,354p. — (New technologies and work). — *Includes bibliographies and index*

PULLINGER, D. J.
BLEND-4 : user-system interaction / D.J. Pullinger with B. Shackel ... [et al.]. — [London] : British Library c1985. — xi,76p. — (Library and information research report ; 45). — *Bibliography: p67-69*

WINFIELD, Ian
Human resources and computing / Ian Winfield. — London : Heinemann, 1986. — [256]p

MANAGEMENT

DAUDI, Philippe
Power in the organisation : the discourse of power in managerial praxis / Philippe Daudi. — Oxford : Blackwell, 1986. — [250]p. — *Translation of: Makt, diskurs ach handling*. — *Includes bibliography and index*

DAVIDMANN, M.
Community leadership and management. — Stanmore : Social Organisation. — *Bibliography: p21*
4: Work and pay: incomes and differentials: employer, employee and community. — 1986. — 21 leaves

DAVIDMANN, M.
Community leadership and management / M. Davidmann. — Stanmore : Social Organisation
6: The will to work: remuneration, job satisfaction and motivation: what people strive to achieve: struggle for independence and good life. — 1986. — 24p

DONALD, Archibald Gordon
Management, information and systems / by Archie Donald. — 2nd ed. — Oxford : Pergamon, 1979. — xiii,253p. — (Pergamon international library). — *Previous ed.: 1967.* — *Bibliography: p.246-249*. — *Includes index*

DRUCKER, Peter F.
The frontiers of management : where tomorrow's decisions are being shaped today / Peter F. Drucker. — London : Heinemann, 1987, c1986. — xi,368p. — *Originally published: New York : Dutton, 1986*. — *Includes index*

GLUECK, William F
Strategic management and business policy / William F. Glueck, Lawrence R. Jauch. — 2nd ed. — New York : McGraw-Hill, c1984. — xiii, 447 p.. — (McGraw-Hill series in management). — *Includes bibliographical references and index*

GOLEMBIEWSKI, Robert T.
Humanizing public relations : perspectives on doing better-than-average when average ain't at all bad / Robert T. Golembiewski. — Mt. Airy, Md. : Lomond, 1985. — viii,377

HAYES, Roger
Corporate revolution : new strategies for executive leadership / Roger Hayes and Reginald Watts. — London : Heinemann, 1986. — 246p. — *Includes index*

Issues: the PA journal for management. — London : PA Corporate Headquarters, 1986-

JAY, Antony
Management and Machiavelli / by Antony Jay. — Rev. ed. — London : Hutchinson Business, 1987. — 245p. — *Previous ed.: London : Hodder & Stoughton, 1967*. — *Includes index*

KANTER, Rosabeth Moss
The change masters / Rosabeth Moss Kanter. — London : Allen & Unwin, 1984, c1983. — 432p. — *Originally published: New York : Simon and Schuster, 1983*. — *Includes index*

MCFARLAND, Dalton E
The managerial imperative : the age of macromanagement / Dalton E. McFarland. — Cambridge, Mass. : Ballinger, c1986. — xxiv, 369 p.. — *Includes bibliographies and index*

Managing in different cultures / edited by Pat Joynt and Malcolm Warner. — Oslo : Universitets forlaget AS, [1985]. — 226p

MATTHEWS, Rob
Managing for success / Rob Matthews. — London : Confederation of British Industry, 1985. — 38p

METCALFE, Beverly Alban
The effects of socialisation on women's management careers : a review / Beverly Alban Metcalfe. — Bradford : MCB University Press, 1985. — 50p. — (Management bibliographies and reviews ; ol.2,no.3). — *Bibliography: p42-50*

MORVILLE, Pierre
Les nouvelles politiques sociales du patronat / Pierre Morville. — Paris : La Découverte, 1985. — 127p. — *Bibliography: p124-125*

New directions in management science / edited by Michael C. Jackson, Paul Keys. — Aldershot : Gower, c1987. — xv,166p. — *Includes index*

SCHERMERHORN, John R.
Managing organizational behavior / John R. Schermerhorn, James G. Hunt, Richard N. Osborn. — 2nd ed. — New York ; Chichester : Wiley, c1985. — 1v.(various pagings). — (Wiley series in management). — *Previous ed.: 1982*. — *Includes index*

URWICK, Lyndall Fownes
The elements of administration / by L. Urwick. — 2nd ed. — London : Pitman, 1951. — 132p. — *Bibliography: p[12]*

WEICK, Karl E.
The social psychology of organizing / Karl E. Weick. — 2nd ed. — Reading, Mass. ; London : Addison-Wesley, c1979. — ix,294p. — (Topics in social psychology). — *Previous ed.: 1969*. — *Bibliography: p265-283*. — *Includes index*

WOODCOCK, Mike
Team development manual / Mike Woodcock. — Aldershot : Gower, 1984, c1979. — [200]p. — *Bibliography: p210-213*

Working paper / Alfred P. Sloan School of Management, Massachusetts Institute of Technology. — Massachusetts : Massachusetts Institute of Technology, 1986-

MANAGEMENT — Case studies

JONES, Roger
The carpetmakers / Roger Jones, Chris Lakin. — London : McGraw-Hill, 1978

MANAGEMENT — Data processing

CHAMPINE, George A.
Distributed computer systems : impact on management, design, and analysis / George A. Champine with Ronald D. Coop, Russell C. Heinselman. — Amsterdam ; Oxford : North-Holland, 1980. — xvi,380p. — *Bibliography: p341-369*. — *Includes index*

Managers, micros and mainframes : integrating systems for end-users / edited by Matthias Jarke. — Chichester : Wiley, c1986. — x,302p. — (John Wiley information systems series). — *Bibliography: p285-294*. — *Includes index*

The Rise of managerial computing : the best of the Center for Information Systems Research, Sloan School of Management, Massachusetts Institute of Technology / edited by John F. Rockart and Christine V. Bullen. — Homewood, Ill. : Dow Jones-Irwin, c1986. — xxvii, 443 p.. — *Includes bibliographies and index*

MANAGEMENT — Data processing — Addresses, essays, lectures

BJØRN-ANDERSEN, Niels
Managing computer impact : an international study of management and organizations / by Niels Bjørn-Andersen, Ken Eason, Daniel Robey. — Norwood, N.J. : Ablex, 1986. — viii, 248p. — *Includes index*. — *Bibliography: p.233-239*

MANAGEMENT — Employee participation

LEWIS, Gary A.
News from somewhere : connecting health and freedom at the workplace / Gary A. Lewis. — New York : Greenwood Press, 1986. — xii, 213 p.. — (Contributions in political science ; no. 151). — *Includes index*. — *Bibliography: p. [185]-195*

PERU. Dirección nacional de Personal. Programa Participación de los TAP
Nueva política de incentivos para los trabajadores de la administración pública. — [Lima] : la Dirección, [197-?]. — 35p. — *Documento de trabajo*. — *Bibliography: p[35]*

ROTHSCHILD, Joyce
The cooperative workplace : potentials and dilemmas of organizational democracy and participation / Joyce Rothschild, J. Allen Whitt. — Cambridge : Cambridge University Press, 1986. — viii,221p. — (The Arnold and Caroline Rose Monograph series of the American Sociological Association). — *Bibliography: p201-211*. — *Includes index*

Die Unternehmung in der demokratischen Gesellschaft = : The business corporation in the democratic society / herausgegeben von Wolfgang Dorow. — Berlin ; New York : W. de Gruyter, 1987. — xiii, 390 p.. — "Günter Dlugos zum 65. Geburtstagegewidmet.". — *English and German*. — *Includes bibliographies*

Workers' participation : a voice in decisions, 1981-85 / edited by Jacques Monat and Hedva Sarfati. — Geneva : International Labour Office, 1986. — 284p

MANAGEMENT — Employee participation — Bibliography
ELECTRICITY COUNCIL. Intelligence Section
Employee participation : list of references 1967-April 1975. — London : the Section, [1975]. — 5p. — (Bibliographies / Electricity Council, Intelligence Section ; B104)

MANAGEMENT — Social aspects
Managing the labour process / edited by David Knights and Hugh Willmott. — Aldershot : Gower, c1986. — [200]p. — *Conference papers. — Includes index*

MANAGEMENT — Study and teaching — Developing countries
Management training and development in public enterprises in developing countries : report and papers of a regional workshop held in Karachi, Pakistan, 5-15 January 1981, convened by ICPE in collaboration with the United Nations Industrial Development Organization and the Pakistan Institute of Management / edited by Irshad H. Khan, Shahiruddin Al[v]i and Stane Možina. — Ljubljana, Yugoslavia : International Center for Public Enterprises in Developing Countries, 1982. — 199p. — *Includes bibliographical references*

MANAGEMENT — Study and teaching — European Economic Community countries
EUROPEAN FOUNDATION FOR MANAGEMENT DEVELOPMENT
Management education in the European community / by European Foundation for Management Development. — Brussels : Commission of the European Communities ; [Washington, D.C : sold by European Communities Information Service], 1978. — 68 p. — (Education series ; no. 4) (Studies collection - Commission of the European Communities)

MANAGEMENT — Study and teaching — France
KESLER, Jean-François
L'E.N.A., La société, l'Etat / Jean-François Kesler. — [Paris] : Berger-Levrault, c1985. — 584p. — (L'administration nouvelle). — *Bibliography: p577-[584]*

MANAGEMENT — Study and teaching — Great Britain
BOND, Michael
Able to manage : a national survey of the progress and performance of part-time DMS students / Michael Bond. — [Poole] : Dorset Institute of Higher Education, 1987. — v,68p. — *This report is based on the findings of the survey, carried out by Michael Bond and Rita Austin, formerly Registrar for Development Services, CNAA. — Bibliography: p28*

MANAGEMENT — Australia — Employee participation
Future directions in the democratisation of work in Australia / Reg Cole...[et al.]. — Canberra : Australian Government Publishing Service, 1985. — viii,136p. — (Employee participation research report ; no.5). — *Contains 12 microfiche in end pocket. — Bibliography: p125-136*

SEMINAR ON INDUSTRIAL DEMOCRACY AND EMPLOYEE PARTICIPATION (1984 : Melbourne)
Industrial Democracy and employee participation. — Canberra : Australian Government Publishing Service, 1985. — ix,272p. — *Proceedings of a seminar held by the Federal Government in conjunction with the National Labour Consultative Council's Committee on Employee Participation*

MANAGEMENT — China
BATTAT, Joseph Y
Management in post-Mao China : an insider's view / by Joseph Y. Battat. — Ann Arbor, Mich. : UMI Research Press, c1986. — xiii, 182 p.. — (Research for business decisions ; no. 76). — *Includes index. — Bibliography: p. [173]-176*

Management reforms in China / edited by Malcolm Warner. — London : Pinter, 1987. — [200]p. — *Includes index*

MANAGEMENT — Costa Rica — Employee participation
Workers' self-management and participation in developing countries : national reports. — Ljubljana : International Center for Public Enterprises in Developing Countries. — *In Spanish and English. — Bibliography: p335. — Contents: Analysis de las formas autogestionarias en Costa Rica/Hermán Mora Corrales - Experiences of workers' participation in Sri Lanka/M. Somasundram - Industrial participatory democracy in Zambia/John F. Kalombo*
vol.3: Costa Rica, Sri Lanka, Zambia. — 1985. — 351p

MANAGEMENT — Developing countries — Employee participation
Workers' self-management and participation in developing countries : national reports. — Ljubljana : International Center for Public Enterprises in Developing Countries. — *In Spanish and English. — Bibliography: p335. — Contents: Analysis de las formas autogestionarias en Costa Rica/Hermán Mora Corrales - Experiences of workers' participation in Sri Lanka/M. Somasundram - Industrial participatory democracy in Zambia/John F. Kalombo*
vol.3: Costa Rica, Sri Lanka, Zambia. — 1985. — 351p

MANAGEMENT — England
LLOYD, Philip L.
Services administration by local authorities / Philip L. Lloyd. — Cambridge : ICSA, 1985. — [320]p. — *Includes bibliography and index*

MANAGEMENT — Europe
TREVOR, Malcolm
The Japanese management development system : generalists and specialists in Japanese companies abroad / Malcolm Trevor, Jochen Schendel and Bernhard Wilpert. — London : Pinter, 1986. — 278p. — *Bibliography: p268-273. — Includes index*

MANAGEMENT — Germany (West)
STRASSER, Dietrich
Abschied von den Wunderknaben : die Krise der deutschen Manager und Unternehmer / Dietrich Strasser. — München : C. Bertelsmann, c1985. — 224p. — *Bibliography: p218-220*

MANAGEMENT — Great Britain — Employee participation
GREAT BRITAIN. Parliament. House of Commons. Library. Research Division
Worker participation. — [London] : the Division, [1975]. — 22p. — (Background paper ; no.30). — *Bibliography: p15-22*

GREAT BRITAIN. Parliament. House of Commons. Library. Research Division
Worker participation in the public sector. — [London] : the Division, 1977. — 17p. — (Reference sheet ; no.77/13). — *Bibliography:p13-17*

LOVERIDGE, Ray
Codetermination, communication and control in the workplace : a study of participation in four Midlands companies / by Ray Loveridge, Paul Lloyd and Geoffrey Broad. — London : Department of Employment, [1986]. — 79p. — (Research paper / Department of Employment ; no.54)

MANAGEMENT — Hungary — Employee participation — History
RÁCZ, János
Az üzemi bizottságok a magyar demokratikus átalakulásban (1944-1948) / Rácz János. — Budapest : Akadémiai Kiadó, 1971. — 159p

MANAGEMENT — Ireland — Employee participation
IRELAND. Advisory Committee on Worker Participation
Report of the Advisory Committee on Worker Participation. — Dublin : Stationery Office, 1986. — 108p. — *Chairman: T. Morrissey*

MANAGEMENT — Japan
The Internationalization of Japanese business : European and Japanese perspectives / edited by Malcolm Trevor. — Boulder : Westview Press, 1986. — p. cm

MATSUMOTO, Kogi
Organizing for higher productivity : an analysis of Japanese systems and practices / Koji Matsumoto. — Tokyo : Asian Productivity Organization, 1982. — 75p. — *Includes bibliographical references*

ODAKA, Kunio
Japanese management : a forward-looking analysis / Kunio Odaka. — Tokyo : Asian Productivity Organization, 1986. — v,85p. — *Includes bibliographical references*

TREVOR, Malcolm
The Japanese management development system : generalists and specialists in Japanese companies abroad / Malcolm Trevor, Jochen Schendel and Bernhard Wilpert. — London : Pinter, 1986. — 278p. — *Bibliography: p268-273. — Includes index*

MANAGEMENT — Japan — Employee participation — History
PARK, Sung-Jo
U.S. labor policy in postwar Japan / Sung-Jo Park. — [Berlin] : Express Edition, [c1985]. — 157 p.. — (Reihe Horizonte Asiens). — *Bibliography: p. 152-157*

MANAGEMENT — Norway — Employee participation
LEWIS, Gary A.
News from somewhere : connecting health and freedom at the workplace / Gary A. Lewis. — New York : Greenwood Press, 1986. — xii, 213 p. — (Contributions in political science ; no. 151). — *Includes index. — Bibliography: p. [185]-195*

MANAGEMENT — Romania — Employee representation
BABE, Alecsandru
Mecanismul autogestiunii în unitățile economice / Alecsandru Babe. — București : Editura Politică, 1986. — 303p. — *Table of contents in English, French, German and Russian*

MANAGEMENT — Sri Lanka — Employee participation
Workers' self-management and participation in developing countries : national reports. — Ljubljana : International Center for Public Enterprises in Developing Countries. — *In Spanish and English. — Bibliography: p335. — Contents: Analysis de las formas autogestionarias en Costa Rica/Hermán Mora Corrales - Experiences of workers' participation in Sri Lanka/M. Somasundram - Industrial participatory democracy in Zambia/John F. Kalombo*
vol.3: Costa Rica, Sri Lanka, Zambia. — 1985. — 351p

MANAGEMENT — Zambia — Employee participation
Workers' self-management and participation in developing countries : national reports. — Ljubljana : International Center for Public Enterprises in Developing Countries. — *In Spanish and English. — Bibliography: p335. — Contents: Analysis de las formas autogestionarias en Costa Rica/Hermán Mora Corrales - Experiences of workers' participation in Sri Lanka/M. Somasundram - Industrial participatory democracy in Zambia/John F. Kalombo*
vol.3: Costa Rica, Sri Lanka, Zambia. — 1985. — 351p

MANAGEMENT BUYOUTS — Great Britain
WRIGHT, Michael, 1952-
Spicer & Pegler's management buy-outs / Mike Wright, John Coyne and Adam Mills. — Cambridge : Woodhead-Faulkner, 1987. — [160]p. — *Includes index*

MANAGEMENT BY OBJECTIVES
HONGO, Takanobu
[Mokuhyō kanri no shinkō. English].
Management by objectives : a Japanese experience / by Takanobu Hongo. — Tokyo : Asian Productivity Organization, 1980. — viii,86p. — *Translation of: Mokuhyō kanri no shinkō*

MANAGEMENT BY OBJECTIVES — Evaluation
HUMPHREY, P. B.
The development of a methodology for the evaluation of management by objectives in the British civil service / P. B. Humphrey, M. C. Davey, N. M. Hardinge. — [London?] : Civil Service Department, Behavioural Sciences Research Division, 1974. — 66p. — (BSRD report ; no. 17). — *Bibliography: p65-66*

MANAGEMENT INFORMATION SYSTEMS
DAVIS, Gordon B.
Management information systems : conceptual foundations, structure, and development. — 2nd ed. / Gordon B. Davis, Margrethe H. Olson. — New York ; London : McGraw-Hill, c1984. — ix,693p. — (McGraw-Hill series in management information systems). — *Previous ed.: 1974. — Includes bibliographies and index*

FEDERICO, Pat-Anthony
Management information systems and organizational behavior / Pat-Anthony Federico with the assistance of Kim E. Brun and Douglas B. McCalla. — 2nd ed. — New York ; Eastbourne : Praeger, 1985. — ix,221p. — *Bibliography: p191-221. — Includes index*

Management information systems : the technology challenge / edited by Nigel Piercy. — New York : Nichols, 1986. — p. cm. — *Includes index*

Managers, micros and mainframes : integrating systems for end-users / edited by Matthias Jarke. — Chichester : Wiley, c1986. — x,302p. — (John Wiley information systems series). — *Bibliography: p285-294. — Includes index*

MIS quarterly: management information systems / sponsored jointly by the Society for Information Management and Management Information Systems Research Centre of the University of Minnesota. — Chicago : Society for Information Management ; Minnesota : Society for Management Information Systems Research Centre of the University of Minnesota, 1986-. — *Quarterly*

MURDICK, Robert G.
MIS : concepts and design. — 2nd ed, Robert G. Murdick with John C. Munison. — Englewood Cliffs ; London : Prentice-Hall, c1986. — xii,691p. — *Previous ed.: 1980. — Includes bibliographies and index*

The Rise of managerial computing : the best of the Center for Information Systems Research, Sloan School of Management, Massachusetts Institute of Technology / edited by John F. Rockart and Christine V. Bullen. — Homewood, Ill. : Dow Jones-Irwin, c1986. — xxvii, 443 p.. — *Includes bibliographies and index*

STEVENS, John M
Information systems and public management / by John M. Stevens. — New York : Praeger, 1985. — p. cm. — *Includes index. — Bibliography: p*

WELDON, Jay-Louise
Data base administration / Jay-Louise Weldon. — New York ; London : Plenum, c1981. — xii,250p. — (Applications of modern technology in business). — *Includes index*

WILKINSON, Joseph W
Information systems for accounting and management : concepts, applications, and technology / Joseph W. Wilkinson, Dan C. Kneer. — Englewood Cliffs, N.J. : Prentice-Hall, c1987. — x, 338 p.. — *Includes bibliographies*

MANAGEMENT INFORMATION SYSTEMS — Data processing
BLOKDIJK, André
Planning and design of information systems / André Blokdijk, Paul Blokdijk. — London : Academic, 1987. — xxiii,578p

MANAGEMENT INFORMATION SYSTEMS — Design and construction
CONNOR, Denis
Information system specification and design road map / Denis Connor. — Englewood Cliffs : Prentice-Hall, 1985. — xix, 236p

MANAGEMENT INFORMATION SYSTEMS — Evaluation
SEGURA, Edilberto L.
Guidelines for evaluating the management information systems of industrial enterprises / Edilberto L. Segura. — Washington, D. C. : The World Bank, 1985. — xviii,109p. — (World Bank technical paper ; no.47)

MANAGEMENT INFORMATION SYSTEMS — Great Britain
BENNETT, Richard, 19---
Preliminary survey of business databases in the UK : final report on the study January-April 1983 : report to the British Library Research and Development Department on Project SI/CT/96 / Richard Bennett. — Edinburgh : Capital Planning Information, [1983?]. — 35leaves. — (British Library R & D report ; 5766). — *Bibliography: leaf 32-33*

MANAGEMENT SCIENCE
Delivery of urban services : with a view towards applications in management science and operations research / edited by Arthur J. Swersey, Edward J. Ignall. — Amsterdam ; New York : North-Holland ; New York, NY, U.S.A. : Sole distributors for the U.S.A. and Canada, Elsevier Science Pub. Co., 1986. — vi, 274 p.. — (TIMS studies in the management science ; v. 22). — *Includes bibliographies*

MANAGERIAL ACCOUNTING
HEITGER, Lester E
Managerial accounting / Lester E. Heitger, Serge Matulich. — 2nd ed. — New York : McGraw-Hill, 1986, c1980. — xx, 956p. — *Includes index*

Managerial accounting and analysis in multinational enterprises / editors, H. Peter Holzer, Hanns-Martin W. Schoenfeld. — Berlin ; New York : W. de Gruyter, 1986, c1985. — p. cm. — *Bibliography: p[253]-257. — Bibliography: p*

OTLEY, David T.
Accounting control and organizational behaviour / David T. Otley. — London : Heinemann, 1987. — *Includes bibliography and index*

Research and current issues in management accounting / edited by Michael Bromwich and Anthony G. Hopwood. — London : Pitman, 1986. — 236p. — *Includes bibliographies*

MANAGERIAL ACCOUNTING — History
JOHNSON, H. Thomas
Relevance lost : the rise and fall of management accounting / H. Thomas Johnson and Robert S. Kaplan. — Boston, Mass. : Harvard Business School Press, c1987. — p. cm. — *Includes bibliographical references and index*

MANAGERIAL ACCOUNTING — United States — History
JOHNSON, H. Thomas
Relevance lost : the rise and fall of management accounting / H. Thomas Johnson and Robert S. Kaplan. — Boston, Mass. : Harvard Business School Press, c1987. — p. cm. — *Includes bibliographical references and index*

MANAGERIAL ECONOMICS
The Economic nature of the firm : a reader / edited by Louis Putterman with the assistance of Randy Kroszner. — Cambridge : Cambridge University Press, 1986. — x,371p. — *Bibliography: p356-371*

The Economics of the firm / edited by Roger Clarke and Tony McGuinness. — Oxford : Basil Blackwell, 1987. — 190p. — *Bibliography : p174-185. — Includes index*

Organizational economics : toward a new paradigm for understanding and studying organizations / Jay B. Barney and William G. Ouchi, editors. — 1st ed. — San Francisco, Calif. : Jossey-Bass, c1986. — p. cm. — (The Jossey-Bass management series) (The Jossey-Bass social and behavioral science series) . — *Includes index. — Bibliography: p*

MANAGERIAL ECONOMICS — Congresses
Mainstreams in industrial organization / edited by H.W. de Jong, W.G. Shepherd. — Dordrecht ; Boston : Kluwer Academic Publishers, 1986. — 2 v. (x, 465 p.). — (Studies in industrial organization ; 6). — *Essays and part of the discussions presented at a conference held Aug. 21-23, 1985 at the University of Amsterdam. — Bibliography: p. 463-465. — Contents: bk. 1. Theory and international aspects -- bk. 2. Policies, antitrust, deregulation, and industrial*

MANAGERIAL ECONOMICS — Canada
NEAVE, Edwin H.
Canada's financial system : a managerial approach / Edwin H. Neave, Jacques Préfontaine. — Toronto : Methuen, 1987. — ix,414p. — *Includes references*

MANAYUNK (PHILADELPHIA, PA.)
SHELTON, Cynthia J.
The mills of Manayunk : industrialization and social conflict in the Philadelphia region, 1787-1837 / Cynthia J. Shelton. — Baltimore : Johns Hopkins University Press, c1986. — xii, 227 p.. — (Studies in industry and society ; 5). — : *Revision of thesis (Ph. D.)--UCLA, 1982. — Includes index. — Bibliography: p. 211-215*

MANCHESTER (GREATER MANCHESTER) — Economic conditions
MANCHESTER. City Council
Poverty in Manchester. — Manchester : [the Council], 1986. — 22p

MANCHESTER SHIP CANAL COMPANY
MANCHESTER SHIP CANAL COMPANY
Annual report and accounts / Manchester Ship Canal Company. — Manchester : Manchester Ship Canal Company, 1944-. — *Annual. — Title varies*

MANCHURIA (CHINA) — History
LEVINE, Steven I
Anvil of victory : the Communist revolution in Manchuria, 1945-1948 / Steven I. Levine. — New York : Columbia University Press, 1987. — p. cm. — (Studies of the East Asian Institute, Columbia University). — *Based on the author's thesis (Ph.D.)--Harvard University. — Includes index. — Bibliography: p*

MANDELA, WINNIE
MANDELA, Winnie
Part of my soul / Winnie Mandela ; edited by Anne Benjamin and adapted by Mary Benson. — Harmondsworth : Penguin, 1985. — 164p

MANDEVILLE, BERNARD
SCHNEIDER, Louis
Paradox and society : the work of Bernard Mandeville / Louis Schneider ; editorial foreword by Jay Weinstein. — New Brunswick, N.J. : Transaction Books, c1986. — p. cm. — *Includes index. — Bibliography: p*

MANGANESE — Metallurgy
Analysis of processing technology for manganese modules / United Nations Ocean Economics and Technology Branch. — London : Published in cooperation with the United Nations by Graham & Trotman, 1986. — 97p. — (Seabed minerals series ; v.3). — *Includes index*

MANGANESE MINES AND MINING, SUBMARINE
Analysis of exploration and mining technology for manganese nodules / United Nations Ocean Economics and Technology Branch. — London : Published in co-operation with the United Nations by Graham & Trotman, 1984. — ix,140p. — (Seabed minerals series ; v.2). — *Bibliography: p111-132. — Includes index*

MANGANESE NODULES
Analysis of exploration and mining technology for manganese nodules / United Nations Ocean Economics and Technology Branch. — London : Published in co-operation with the United Nations by Graham & Trotman, 1984. — ix,140p. — (Seabed minerals series ; v.2). — *Bibliography: p111-132. — Includes index*

Analysis of processing technology for manganese modules / United Nations Ocean Economics and Technology Branch. — London : Published in cooperation with the United Nations by Graham & Trotman, 1986. — 97p. — (Seabed minerals series ; v.3). — *Includes index*

Assessment of manganese nodule resources : the data and the methodologies / United Nations Ocean Economics and Technology Branch. — London : Published in co-operation with the United Nations by Graham & Trotman, 1982. — x,79p. — (Seabed minerals series ; v.1). — *Includes index*

MANGOLIA — Economic conditions — Statistics
Narodnoe khoziaistvo MNR za 60 let = National economy of the MPR for 60 years / Central Statistical Board of the MPR. — Ulaanbaatar : Central Statistical Board of the MPR, 1984-. — *Irregular. — In English and Russian*

MANGYANS
LOPEZ-GONZAGA, Violeta
Peasants in the hills : a study of the dynamics of social change among the Buhid swidden cultivators in the Philippines / Violeta Lopez-Gonzaga. — Quezon City, Philippines : University of the Philippines Press, 1983. — xiv,226p. — *Bibliography: p[211]-219*

MANIHI (TUAMOTU ISLANDS) — Population — Statistics
Tableaux normalisés du recensement général de la population : 15 octobre 1983. — [Papeete] : Institut territorial de la statistique Résultats de la commune de Manihi. — [1985?]. — 4p,ll leaves

MANIPUR (INDIA) — Population — Statistics
Census of India 1981. — [Delhi : Controller of Publications]
Series 13: Manipur. — [1985-]

MANITOBA — Politics and government
DOERN, Russell
The battle over bilingualism : the Manitoba language question 1983-1985 / Russell Deorn. — Winnipeg : Cambridge Publishers, 1985. — 227p

MANITOBA. Department of Industry, Trade and Technology
MANITOBA. Department of Industry, Trade and Technology
Annual report / Department of Industry, Trade and Technology, Manitoba. — Winnipeg : [the Department], 1983/84-. — *Annual*

MANITOBA LABOUR
MANITOBA LABOUR
Annual report / Manitoba Labour. — Winnipeg : Manitoba Labour, 1984-. — *Continues: Manitoba. Department of Labour and Employment Services. Annual report*

MANNERHEIM, CARL
MANNERHEIM, Carl
The memoirs of Marshal Mannerheim [/ Carl Mannerheim] ; translated by Count Eric Lewenhaupt. — London : Cassell, 1953. — xi,540p

MANNERHEIM, CARL GUSTAF EMIL, Frihene
JÄGERSKIÖLD, Stig
Mannerheim : Marshal of Finland / Stig Jägerskiöld. — London : Hurst, c1986. — x,210p,[8]p of plates. — *Translation of: Gustaf Mannerheim 1867-1951. — Bibliography: p200-202. — Includes index*

MANNERHEIM, CARL GUSTAF EMIL, Friherre
JÄGERSKIÖLD, Stig
Gustaf Mannerheim 1867-1951 / Stig Jägerskiöld. — Helsingfors : Schildts, 1983. — 235p. — *Bibliography: p235*

JÄGERSKIÖLD, Stig
Gustaf Mannerheim 1918 / Stig Jägerskiöld. — [Stockholm?] : Bonniers, 1967. — 411p. — *Bibliography: p399-402*

MANNERHEIM, CARL GUSTAF EMIL, friherre
WARNER, Oliver
Marshal Mannerheim and the Finns / Oliver Warner. — London : Weidenfeld and Nicholson, 1967. — 232p

MANORS — England — Essex — History
MCINTOSH, Marjorie Keniston
Autonomy and community : the Royal Manor of Havering, 1200-1500 / Marjorie Keniston McIntosh. — Cambridge : Cambridge University Press, 1986. — [460]p. — (Cambridge studies in medieval life and thought. Fourth series). — *Includes bibliography and index*

MANOUCHIAN, MISSAK
ROBRIEUX, Phillippe
Låffaire Manouchian : vie et mort dùn héros communiste / Philippe Robrieux. — Paris : Fazard, [1986]. — 434p

MANPOWER — Cyprus — Statistics
HOUSE, William J.
Wage structure, manpower analysis and the market in Cyprus / by William J. House. — [Nicosia] : Department of Statistics and Research, [1984]. — 78p. — *Bibliography: p77-78*

MANPOWER — Jordan — Statistics
[Manpower Survey 1983]. — [Amman : Dept of Statistics, 1983]. — 2v. (various pagings). — *In Arabic with English table headings*

MANPOWER — United States
BINKIN, Martin
Military technology and defense manpower / Martin Binkin. — Washington, D.C. : Brookings Institution, 1986. — p. cm. — (Studies in defense policy). — *Includes index*

MANPOWER PLANNING — Mathematical models
BARTHOLOMEW, David J.
Statistical techniques for manpower planning / David J. Bartholomew and Andrew F. Forbes. — Chichester : Wiley, 1979. — xiii,288p. — (Wiley series in probability and mathematical statistics). — *Bibliography: p.273-282. — Includes index*

MANPOWER PLANNING — Statistical methods
BARTHOLOMEW, David J.
Statistical techniques for manpower planning / David J. Bartholomew and Andrew F. Forbes. — Chichester : Wiley, 1979. — xiii,288p. — (Wiley series in probability and mathematical statistics). — *Bibliography: p.273-282. — Includes index*

MANPOWER PLANNING — Denmark
ROSDAHL, Anders
Arbejdsgiveres arbejdskrafteftersporgsel : ansaettelses processer i industrivirksomheder / Anders Rosdahl. — Kobenhavn : Socialforskningsinstituttet, 1986. — 240p. — (Publikation / Socialforskningsinstituttet ; 156). — *Bibliography: p237*

MANPOWER PLANNING — Great Britain
INSTITUTE OF MANPOWER STUDIES
Changing working patterns : how companies achieve flexibility to meet new needs / prepared by the Institute of Manpower Studies for the National Economic Development Office in association with the Department of Employment. — London : National Economic Development Office, 1986. — v,120p. — *Researchers: John Atkinson and Nigel Meager. — Bibliography: p86-88*

LONG, A. F.
Health manpower : planning, production and management / Andrew F. Long and Geoffrey Mercer in collaboration with Fiona Brooks ... [et al.]. — London : Croom Helm, c1987. — [288]p. — *Bibliography: p247-265. — Includes index*

MANPOWER PLANNING — Great Britain — Bibliography
PRICE, C. J.
Selected references on manpower planning in the National Health Service / compiled by C.J. Price. — London : Department of Health and Social Security Library, 1978. — 6p. — (Bibliography series / Department of Health and Social Security Library ; no.B106)

MANPOWER PLANNING — United States — Addresses, essays, lectures
GINZBERG, Eli
Understanding human resources : perspectives, people, and policy / Eli Ginzberg. — Lanham, MD : University Press of America ; Cambridge, MA : Abt Books, c1985. — xvii, 744 p. — *Includes index. — Bibliography: p. 697-703*

MANPOWER POLICY
Health manpower planning : principles, methods, issues / edited by T. L. Hall and A. Mejía. — Geneva : World Health Organization ; [Albany, N.Y. : distributed by WHO Publications Centre USA], 1978. — 311p. — *Includes bibliographical references*

KINSEY, B. H.
Creating rural employment / B.H. Kinsey. — London : Croom Helm, c1987. — [11],116p. — *Bibliography: p107-112. — Includes index*

MCGILL, David
Personnel led planning : supply side influences on manpower targets / David McGill [and] Wendy Hirsh. — Brighton : University of Sussex. Institute of Manpower Studies, 1986. — iv,16p. — (IMS report ; no.119)

Manpower and social affairs. — Paris : OECD, [1986?]. — 1Portfolio (various pagings). — *Contents: Reprints taken from various issues of the OECD Observer*

PICKAVANCE, Rachel
Employee utilisation and deployment / Rachel Pickavance. — Brighton : Institute of Manpower Studies, University of Sussex, 1985. — iv,32p. — (IMS report ; no.115)

MANPOWER POLICY — Congresses

Medical specialization in relation to health needs : report on a WHO meeting : Abano Terme, Italy, 22-25 October 1984. — Copenhagen : World Health Organization, 1986. — 67p. — *Summary in French, German, and Russian. — Bibliography: p42*

MANPOWER POLICY — Models

BRYANT-MOLE, Michael
Information needs for manpower supply models / Michael Bryant-Mole. — Brighton : Institute of Manpower Studies. University of Sussex, 1986. — vi,32p. — (IMS report ; no.126)

MANPOWER POLICY — Australia

Community Employment Program : the first year. — Canberra : Australian Government Publishing Service, 1984. — ix,101p

MANPOWER POLICY — Australia — Methodology

The measurement and implications of productivity growth : proceedings of a workshop, 22-23 November 1984, Canberra / edited by Peter Scherer with Tracey Malone. — Canberra : Australian Government Publishing Service, 1986. — xi,290p. — (Monograph series / Bureau of Labour Market Research ; no.14). — *Includes bibliographical references*

MANPOWER POLICY — Brazil

PASSARINHO, Jarbas G.
Discurso... na 51a. sessão da Conferência Internacional do Trabalho (Genebra - 1967) / Jarbas Passarinho. — [Brasília] : Ministério do Trabalho e Previdência Social, Serviço de Documentação, Seção de Publicação, 1967. — 6p

MANPOWER POLICY — Developing countries

Major stages and steps in energy manpower analysis : a practical framework. — Geneva : International Labour Office, 1986. — viii,80p. — *Bibliographical references: p[74]-80*

MANPOWER POLICY — Egypt

HANSEN, Best
Employment opportunities and equity in a changing economy : Egypt in the 1980s : a labour market approach : report of an inter-agency team financed by the United Nations Development Programme and organised by the International Labour Office / Bent Hansen, Samir Radwan. — Geneva : International Labour Office, 1982. — xviii,292p. — (A WEP study). — *Includes bibliographical references*

MANPOWER POLICY — England — Cleveland

CLEVELAND. Planning Department
Employment trends and forecasts. — Middlesbrough : [the] Department, 1983. — 20,[12]p. — (Monitoring note report / Cleveland Planning Department ; no.234)

CLEVELAND. Planning Department
Employment trends and forecasts. — Middlesbrough : [the Department], 1987. — [6] p. — (Monitoring note / Cleveland. Planning Department ; 87/2)

MANPOWER POLICY — England — London

GREATER LONDON COUNCIL
The London labour plan. — London : Greater London Council, 1986. — 552p

ISLINGTON. Council
Putting Islington back to work : a major job creation initiative by Islington Council. — Islington : [the Council], 1987. — 32p

LEWISHAM
Getting Lewisham back to work : Lewisham council's contribution to reducing unemployment in the borough. — Lewisham : [the Council], 1987. — 20p

The London Labour plan : the state and the labour market. — London : London Strategic Policy Unit, 1986. — 61p. — *Bibliography: p59*

TOWER HAMLETS. Planning Department. Directorate of Development
Workers in Tower Hamlets. — Tower Hamlets : [the Directorate], 1986. — 42 leaves. — *At head of title: Planning research and information*

MANPOWER POLICY — England — Sheffield (South Yorkshire)

SHEFFIELD. Department of Employment and Economic Development
Sheffield : working it out : an outline employment plan for Sheffield. — Sheffield : [the Department] and Central Policy Unit, 1987. — 28p

MANPOWER POLICY — England — Stoke-on-Trent (Staffordshire)

Re-employment experiences of redundant Michelin workers / L. Fishman [et al.]. — Keele : University of Keele, 1986. — 187p. — *Bibliography: p147-148*

MANPOWER POLICY — England — Surrey

SURREY. County Planning Department
Employment and commuting in Surrey 1971-1981. — [Kingston upon Thames] : The [Department], 1985. — [93 leaves]. — (Technical report / Surrey. County Planning Department ; no.1/85). — *Bound with Structure plan monitoring: Employment and commercial data*

SURREY. County Planning Department
Structure plan monitoring : employment and commercial data. — [Kingston upon Thames] : [the Department], 1985. — [25 leaves]. — (Technical report / Surrey. County Planning Department ; no.5/85). — *Bound with Employment and commuting in Surrey*

MANPOWER POLICY — Europe — Congresses

Medical specialization in relation to health needs : report on a WHO meeting : Abano Terme, Italy, 22-25 October 1984. — Copenhagen : World Health Organization, 1986. — 67p. — *Summary in French, German, and Russian. — Bibliography: p42*

MANPOWER POLICY — European Economic Community countries

BUIREN, Shirley van
The quantitative and qualitative significance of the emergence of local initiatives for employment creation / by Shirley van Buiren. — Luxembourg : Office for Official Publications of the European Communities, 1986. — iii,141p. — (Programme of research and actions on the development of the labour market). — *At head of title: Commission of the European Communities*

Comparative follow—up and evaluation of current employment measures / by Centre de Recherche "Travail et Société", Paris, France... [et al.]. — Luxembourg : Office for Official Publications of the European Communities, 1985. — vi, 221p. — (Programme of research and actions on the development of the labour market). — *At head of title: Commission of the European Communities*

Local employment initiatives : report on a series of local consultations held in European Countries 1982—1983 : main report / by the Centre for Employment Initiatives, London. — Luxembourg : Office for Official Publications of the European Communities, 1985. — 159p. — (Programme of research and actions on the development of the labour market). — *At head of title: Commission of the European Communities*

Local employment initiatives : an evaluation of support agencies / by Centre for Research on European Women - CREW, Brussels. — Luxembourg : Office for Official Publications of the European Communities, 1985. — 356p. — (Programme of Research and Actions on the Development of the Labour Market). — *At head of title: Commission of the European Communities*

Local employment initiatives : a manual on intermediary and support organisations : main report / by The Centre for Employment Initiatives, London. — Luxembourg : Office for Official Publications of the European Communities, 1985. — 90p. — (Programme of research and actions on the development of the labour market). — *At head of title: Commission of the European Communities*

MANPOWER POLICY — France

Gestion de l'emploi et développement de l'entreprise / rapport pour la Délégation á l'Emploi sous la direction de Renaud Sainsaulieu, avec la collaboration de Nicole Monod et Dominique Thierry. — [Paris : La Documentation française, 1987]. — 182p. — (Document travail emploi). — *Bibliography: p181-182*

SACHS-DURAND, Corinne
Les seuils d'effectif en droit du travail / par Corinne Sachs-Durand ; préface de Hélène Sinay. — Paris : Librairie Générale de Droit et de Jurisprudence, 1985. — 314p. — (Bibliothèque d'Ouvrages de Droit Social ; Tome 23). — *Bibliography: p275-290*

MANPOWER POLICY — France — Statistics

Emploi par region / Institut National de la Statistique et des Études Économiques, Paris. — Paris : Institut National de la Statistique et des Études Économiques, 1983-. — (Archives et documents / France. Institut National de la Statistique et des Études Économiques). — *Annual. — Continues: Emploi salarié par region*

Emploi salarié par region / Institut National de la Statistique et des Études Économiques, Paris. — Paris : Institut National de la Statistique et de Études Economiques, 1970-1982. — (Archives et documents / France. Institut National de la Statistique et des Études Economiques). — *Annual. — Continued by Emploi par region*

MANPOWER POLICY — Great Britain

BUIREN, Shirley van
The quantitative and qualitative significance of the emergence of local initiatives for employment creation / by Shirley van Buiren. — Luxembourg : Office for Official Publications of the European Communities, 1986. — iii,141p. — (Programme of research and actions on the development of the labour market). — *At head of title: Commission of the European Communities*

GREAT BRITAIN. Parliament. House of Commons. Library. Research Division
The economics of special employment measures / Christopher Barclay. — [London] : the Division, 1985. — 24p. — (Background paper ; no.160). — *Bibliographical references: p24*

LAYARD, Richard
How to beat unemployment / Richard Layard with assistance from Andrew Sentance. — Oxford : Oxford University Press, 1986. — 201p. — *Bibliography: p192-197. — Includes index*

Local employment initiatives : local enterprise agencies in Great Britain : a study of their impact, operational lessons and policy implications / by Community Initiatives Research Trust (CIRT) Liverpool. — Luxembourg : Office for Official Publications of the European Communities, 1985. — iv, 61p. — (Programme of research and action on the development of the labour market). — *At head of title: Commission of the European Communities*

MANPOWER POLICY — India
CHAUDHARY, Shobha Kant
Planning and employment trends in Indai / S. K. Chaudhary. — New Delhi : Deep and Deep Publications, 1987. — 300p. — *Bibliography: p290-298*

MANPOWER POLICY — Nigeria
OJO, Folayan
Nigerian universities and high level manpower development / by Folayan Ojo. — Lagos : Lagos University Press, 1985. — 135p. — *Bibliography: p126-135*

MANPOWER POLICY — Northern Ireland — Statistics
DMS gazette / Department of Manpower Services, Northern Ireland. — Belfast : Department of Manpower Services, 1978-1979. — *Irregular*

MANPOWER POLICY — Québec (Province)
FÉDÉRATION DES TRAVAILLEURS DU QUÉBEC. Congrès (13th : 1973 : Montréal)
La politique de main dòeuvre : le Québec dàbord. — Québec : Fédération des Travailleurs du Québec, 1973. — 23p. — (Document économique / Fédération des Travailleurs du Québec ; 1)

MANPOWER POLICY — Soviet Union
KUNEL'SKII, L. E.
Povyshenie effektivnosti truda v promyshlennosti / L. E. Kunel'skii. — Moskva : Ekonomika, 1987. — 254p

Vosproizvodstvo naseleniia i trudovykh resursov v usloviiakh razvitogo sotsializma / redaktsionnaia kollegiia V. S. Steshenko...[et al.]. — Kiev : Naukova dumka. — *V 4-kh tomakh*
T.3: Sotsial'no-ekonomicheskie problemy effektivnogo ispol'zovaniia trudovykh resursov regiona / otv. redaktor M. I. Dolishnii. — 1986. — 262p

MANPOWER POLICY — Sweden — History — 20th century
AXELSSON, Roger
Den svenska arbetsmarknadspolitiken under 1900-talet / Roger Axelsson, Karl-Gustaf Löfgren, Lars-Gunnar Nilsson. — 3e. rev. upplagen. — Stockholm : Prisma, 1985. — 200p. — *First published 1979.* — *Bibliography: p191-196*

MANPOWER POLICY — United States
LATIMORE, James
Weeding out the target population : the law of accountability in a manpower program / James Latimore. — Westport, Conn. : Greenwood Press, 1985. — x, 176 p.. — (Contributions in sociology ; no. 54). — *Includes index.* — *Bibliography: p. [173]-174*

MANPOWER POLICY — United States — Addresses, essays, lectures
GINZBERG, Eli
Understanding human resources : perspectives, people, and policy / Eli Ginzberg. — Lanham, MD : University Press of America ; Cambridge, MA : Abt Books, c1985. — xvii, 744 p.. — *Includes index.* — *Bibliography: p. 697-703*

MANPOWER POLICY — Wales — West Glamorgan
WEST GLAMORGAN, County Council
Jobs today - and tomorrow? : what are the issues?. — Swansea : [the Council], 1976. — 43p

MANPOWER POLICY, RURAL — France — Statistics
RÉGNIER, Élisabeth
La pluriactivité en agriculture en 1981 / Élisabeth Régnier. — Paris : I.N.S.E.E., 1986. — 77p. — (Archives et documents / Institut national de la statistique et des études économiques)

MANPOWER SERVICES COMMISSION
THOMSON, Alastair
A users̀ guide to the Manpower Services Commission / Alastair Thomson and Hilary Rosenberg. — London : Kogan Page, 1986. — 332 p. — (10.1 Great Britain)

MANUFACTURES — Finland — Accounting
JESKANEN-SUNDSTRÖM, Heli
Kansantalouden tilinpito : teollinen toiminta kansantalouden tilinpidossa = National accounts : manufacturing and related industries in national accounts / Heli Jeskanen-Sundström. — Helsinki : Tilastokeskus, 1982. — 52p. — (Tutkimuksia / Finland. Tilastokeskus ; no.74). — *In Finish with English summary*

MANUS PROVINCE (PAPUA NEW GUINEA) — Population — Statistics
1980 national population census : final figures : provincial summary : Manus Province. — Port Moresby : National Statistical Office, 1985. — iii,96p

MANUSCRIPT PREPARATION (AUTHORSHIP) — Handbooks, manuals, etc
Chicago guide to preparing electronic manuscripts for authors and publishers. — Chicago : University of Chicago Press, 1986. — xi, 143p. — (Chicago guides to writing, editing, and publishing). — *Includes index.* — *Bibliography: p 131*

MANUSCRIPTS — Soviet Union — Bibliography
Vospominaniia i dnevniki XVIII-XX vv. : ukazatel' rukopisei / redaktsiia i predislovie S. V. Zhitomirskoi. — Moskva : Kniga, 1976. — 619p

MANUSCRIPTS, AMERICAN — United States — Catalogs
BURTON, Dennis A.
A guide to manuscripts in the Presidential Libraries / compiled and edited by Dennis A. Burton, James B. Rhoads, Raymond W. Smock. — College Park, Md. : Research Materials Corp., 1985. — p. cm. — *Includes index*

MAO, ZEDONG
MAO, Zedong
The writings of Mao Zedong, 1949-1976 / edited by Michael Y.M. Kau, John K. Leung. — Armonk, N.Y. ; London : M.E. Sharpe. — *Translated from the Chinese*
Vol.1: September 1949-December 1955. — c1986. — xli,771p. — *Bibliography: p755-771*

MAORIS — Social conditions
BALLARA, Angela
Proud to be white? : a survey of Pakeha prejudice in New Zealand / Angela Ballara. — Auckland, N.Z. : Heinemann ; Portland, OR : Exclusive distributor, ISBS, 1986. — x, 205 p.. — *Includes index.* — *Bibliography: p. 194-199*

MAORIS
BELICH, James
The New Zealand wars and the Victorian interpretation of racial conflict / James Belich. — Auckland : Auckland University Press, 1986. — 396p

MAORIS — Education — Case studies
HARKER, Richard K
Education as cultural artifact : studies in Maori and Aboriginal education / R.K. Harker & K.R. McConnochie. — Palmerston North, N.Z. : Dunmore Press ; Sydney, N.S.W. : Distributed in Australia by Hedley Australia, 1985. — 198 p.. — *Includes index.* — *Bibliography: p. [183]-192*

MAORIS — Government relations
LEVINE, Stephen I.
Maori political perspectives / Stephen Levine, Raj Vasil. — Auckland : Hutchinson of New Zealand, 1985. — 206p. — *Bibliography: p205-206*

SIMPSON, Tony, 19-
Te riri Pakeha : the white man´s anger / Tony Simpson. — Auckland ; London : Hodder and Stoughton, 1986. — 272p. — *Bibliography: p260-262*

MAORIS — History
BINNEY, Judith
Ngā Mōrehu : the survivors / Judith Binney and Gillian Chaplin. — Auckland ; Oxford : Oxford University Press, 1986. — 218p. — *Bibliography: p212-215*

MAORIS — Land tenure
SIMPSON, Tony, 19-
Te riri Pakeha : the white man´s anger / Tony Simpson. — Auckland ; London : Hodder and Stoughton, 1986. — 272p. — *Bibliography: p260-262*

MAORIS — Social conditions
BINNEY, Judith
Ngā Mōrehu : the survivors / Judith Binney and Gillian Chaplin. — Auckland ; Oxford : Oxford University Press, 1986. — 218p. — *Bibliography: p212-215*

MAPS
SCOTT, David
Mental imagery and the process of visualisation in map reading / David Scott. — London : London School of Economics. Graduate School of Geography, 1986. — 84p. — (Geography discussion papers / London School of Economics and Political Science. Graduate School of Geography. New series ; no.16). — *Bibliography: p76-84*

UNWIN, David J.
Introductory spatial analysis / David Unwin. — London : Methuen, 1981. — xii,212p. — *Includes bibliographies and index*

MARBURG (GERMANY) — Politics and government
KOSHAR, Rudy
Social life, local politics, and Nazism : Marburg, 1880-1935 / Rudy Koshar. — Chapel Hill ; London : University of North Carolina Press, c1986. — xviii, 395p. — *Includes index.* — *Bibliography: p.[361]-382*

MARBURG (GERMANY) — Social life and customs
KOSHAR, Rudy
Social life, local politics, and Nazism : Marburg, 1880-1935 / Rudy Koshar. — Chapel Hill ; London : University of North Carolina Press, c1986. — xviii, 395p. — *Includes index.* — *Bibliography: p.[361]-382*

MARCEL, GABRIEL
PLOURDE, Simonne
Vocabulaire philosophique de Gabriel Marcel / Simonne Plourde en collaboration avec Jeanne Parain-Vial, Abbé Marcel Belay, René Davignon ; avec une préface de Paul Ricoeur. — Montréal : Bellarmin, [1985]. — 583p. — (Collection Recherches. nouvelle série ; 6). — *Bibliography: p563-566*

MARCHLEWSKI, JULIAN BALTAZAR
MICHTA, Norbert
Julian Marchlewski / Norbert Michta. — Warszawa : Iskry, 1979. — 113p. — (Współczesne zyciorysy Polaków)

MARCOS, FERDINAND E
Crisis in the Philippines : the Marcos era and beyond / edited by John Bresnan. — Princeton, NJ : Princeton University Press, c1986. — xiv, 284p. — *Includes index.* — *Bibliography: p.[259]-267*

MARCUSE, HERBERT. Eros and civilization
ROTH, Roland
Rebellische Subjektivität : Herbert Marcuse und die neuen Protestbewegungen / Roland Roth. — Frankfurt : Campus, 1985. — 338p. — *Bibliography: p325-338*

MARCUSE, HERBERT. One-dimensional man
ROTH, Roland
Rebellische Subjektivität : Herbert Marcuse und die neuen Protestbewegungen / Roland Roth. — Frankfurt : Campus, 1985. — 338p. — *Bibliography: p325-338*

MARCUSE, HERBERT
LANGERBEIN, Berthold
Roman und Revolte : zur Grundlegung der ästhetischen Theorie Herbert Marcuses und ihrer Stellung in seinem politisch-anthropologischen Denken / Berthold Langerbein. — Pfaffenweiler : Centaurus, 1985. — 115p. — (Reihe Sprach- und Literaturwissenschaft ; Bd.3)

ROTH, Roland
Rebellische Subjektivität : Herbert Marcuse und die neuen Protestbewegungen / Roland Roth. — Frankfurt : Campus, 1985. — 338p. — *Bibliography: p325-338*

MARCUSE, HERBERT — Contributions in science
ALFORD, C. Fred
Science and the revenge of nature : Marcuse & Habermas / C. Fred Alford. — Gainesville, FL : University Presses of Florida, c1985. — x, 226 p.. — *Includes index.* — *Bibliography: p. 199-210*

MARCUSE, HERBERT — Criticism and interpretation
ROTH, Roland
Rebellische Subjektivität : Herbert Marcuse und die neuen Protestbewegungen / Roland Roth. — Frankfurt : Campus, 1985. — 338p. — *Bibliography: p325-338*

MARCUSE, HERBERT, 1898-
MARTINEAU, Alain
Herbert Marcuseś utopia / by Alain Martineau. — Montreal : Harvest House, 1986. — 156p

MARGINALITY, SOCIAL
HOFFMANN, Helga
Desemprego e subemprego no Brasil / Helga Hoffmann. — São Paulo : Editora Ática, 1977. — 183 p.. — (Ensaios ; 24). — *: Originally presented as the author's thesis, Universidade de São Paulo.* — *Bibliography: p. [175]-183*

MARGINALITY, SOCIAL — France
LAGRÉE, Jean-Charles
La galère : marginalisations juvéniles et collectivités locales / par Jean-Charles Lagrée et Paula Lew-Foi. — Paris : Centre National de la Recherche Scientifique, 1985. — 280p

MARGINALITY, SOCIAL — Germany (West)
Marginalisierung im Sozialstaat : Beiträge aus Grossbritannien und der Bundesrepublik / Autorengruppe Fulda, Portsmouth, Sheffield ; Friedrich Blahusch...[et al.]. — Marburg : Verlag Arbeiterbewegung und Gesellschaftswissenschaft, 1986. — 197p

MARGINALITY, SOCIAL — Great Britain
Marginalisierung im Sozialstaat : Beiträge aus Grossbritannien und der Bundesrepublik / Autorengruppe Fulda, Portsmouth, Sheffield ; Friedrich Blahusch...[et al.]. — Marburg : Verlag Arbeiterbewegung und Gesellschaftswissenschaft, 1986. — 197p

MARGINALITY, SOCIAL — Peru — Lima
BUNSTER, Ximena
Sellers and servants : working women in Lima, Peru / Ximena Bunster, Elsa M. Chaney ; photos by Ellan Young. — New York : Praeger, 1985. — x, 258p. — *Includes index.* — *Bibliography: p.235-246*

MARIHUANA — Addresses, essays, lectures
Teen drug use / edited by George Beschner, Alfred S. Friedman. — Lexington, Mass. : Lexington Books, c1986. — x, 243 p.. — *Includes bibliographies and index*

MARINE ACCIDENTS — Legal aspects, laws, etc.
MANKABADY, Samir
The International Maritime Organisation / Samir Mankabady. — [2nd ed.]. — London : Croom Helm. — *Previous ed.: published in 1 vol. 1984*
Vol.2: Accidents at sea. — c1987. — xxvii,452p. — *Includes index*

MARINE MINERAL RESOURCES
FORD, Glyn
The future for ocean technology / Glyn Ford, Chris Niblett and Lindsay Walker. — London : Pinter, 1987. — xii,139p.. — (The Future for science and technology series). — *Bibliography: p133-135.* — *Includes index*

WEST GLAMORGAN. County Council
The Celtic sea - oil and gas? : what are the issues?. — Swansea : [the Council], 1975. — v,26p

MARINE MINERAL RESOURCES — Law and legislation — Congresses
LAW OF THE SEA INSTITUTE. Conference (16th : 1982 : Halifax, N.S.)
The law of the sea and ocean industry : new opportunities and restraints : proceedings, Sixteenth Annual Conference / co-sponsored by the Dalhousie Ocean Studies Programme, June 21-24, 1982, Halifax, Nova Scotia ; edited by Douglas M. Johnston and Norman G. Letalik. — Honolulu : Law of the Sea Institute, University of Hawaii, c1983. — p. cm. — (Sea grant cooperative report ; UNIHI-SEAGRANT-CR-83-02). — *Bibliography: p*

MARINE MINERAL RESOURCES — South Pacific Ocean
Sedimentation and mineral deposits in the southwestern Pacific Ocean / edited by D.S. Cronan. — London : Academic, 1986. — ix,344p. — (Ocean science, resources and technology). — *Bibliography: p307-337.* — *Includes index*

MARINE POLLUTION
Aquatic environment monitoring report / Directorate of Fisheries Research, Ministry of Agriculture Fisheries and Food, Great Britain. — London : Ministry of Agriculture Fisheries and Food. Directorate of Fisheries Research, 1983-. — *Annual*

MARINE POLLUTION — Government policy — European Economic Community countries
The Oslo and Paris Commissions : the first decade. — London : Oslo and Paris Commissions, c1984. — x,377p. — *Contains summaries of the presentations prepared by all contracting parties of the Olso and Paris Conventions*

MARINE POLLUTION — Law and legislation
AMIN, S. H.
Marine pollution in international and Middle Eastern law / by Sayed Hassan Amin ; foreword by John P. Grant. — Glasgow : Royston, 1986. — 138p. — *Bibliography: p119-135.* — *Includes index*

MARINE POLLUTION — Legal status, laws, etc.
The law of the sea : pollution by dumping : legislative history of Articles 1, paragraph 1 (5), 210 and 216 of the United Nations Convention on the Law of the Sea. — New York : United Nations, 1985. — V,77p. — *Sales no.: E.85.V.12*

MARINE POLLUTIONOFF. PUBNS. — Prevention 986
Prevention of marine pollution : 2 opinions. — Brussels : Economic and Social Committee, 1981. — ii,65p

MARINE RESOURCES
Aquatic environment monitoring report / Directorate of Fisheries Research, Ministry of Agriculture Fisheries and Food, Great Britain. — London : Ministry of Agriculture Fisheries and Food. Directorate of Fisheries Research, 1983-. — *Annual*

EXCLUSIVE ECONOMIC ZONES - RESOURCES, OPPORTUNITIES AND THE LEGAL REGIME (Conference : 1986 : London)
Exclusive economic zones - resources, opportunities and the legal regime : proceedings of an international conference (Exclusive Economic Zones - Resources, Opportunities and the Legal Regime) / organized by the Society for Underwater Technology ; sponsored by the Society for Underwater Technology, the Royal Geographical Society and the Royal Institution of Chartered Surveyors and held in London, UK, 20 May 1986. — London : Graham & Trotman, 1986. — vii,187p. — (Advances in underwater technology and offshore engineering ; v.8). — *Includes bibliographies*

INTERNATIONAL CENTRE FOR OCEAN DEVELOPMENT
Introduction to marine affairs : [a] marine affairs course [organized by the Centre] held at the World Maritime University, November 23-28, 1986, Malmö, Sweden. — Halifax : International Centre for Ocean Development, 1986. — 419p. — *Bibliographies*

MARINE RESOURCES — Economic aspects
Marine resource economics. — New York : Taylor and Francis, 1986-. — *Quarterly*

MARINE RESOURCES — British Virgin Islands
Management and utilization of the marine resources of the British Virgin Islands : a study conducted by the Dalhousie Ocean Studies Programme on behalf of the Government of the British Virgin Islands with funding from the Special Programs Division of the Canadian International Development Agency (CIDA). — Halifax, N.S. [Nova Scotia] : Dalhousie Ocean Studies Programme, Dalhousie University, 1985. — xi,125p

MARINE RESOURCES — Caribbean Area — Management
Ocean use and resource development and management in the eastern Caribbean : proceedings of a seminar held in Basseterre, St.Kitts, West Indies, 7-9 June 1983. — Halifax, N.S. : Dalhousie Ocean Studies Programme, 1984. — xxii,219p

MARINE RESOURCES CONSERVATION
The New order of the ocean : the advent of a managed environment / edited by Giulio Pontecorvo. — New York : Columbia University Press, 1986. — p. cm. — *Includes bibliographies and index*

MARINE RESOURCES CONSERVATION — Law and legislation
LAW OF THE SEA INSTITUTE. Conference (1984 : San Francisco, Calif.)LAW OF THE SEA INSTITUTE. Conference (18th : 1984 : San Francisco, Calif.)

The developing order of the oceans : proceedings / Law of the Sea Institute Eighteenth Annual Conference ; co-sponsored by the University of San Francisco, October 24-27, 1984, San Francisco ; edited by Robert B. Krueger, Stefan A. Riesenfeld. — Honolulu : Law of the Sea Institute, William S. Richardson School of Law, University of Hawaii, 1986. — p. cm. — (Sea grant cooperative report ; UNIHI-SEAGRANT-CR-85-03). — *Includes bibliographies*

The New order of the ocean : the advent of a managed environment / edited by Giulio Pontecorvo. — New York : Columbia University Press, 1986. — p. cm. — *Includes bibliographies and index*

MARINE RESOURCES CONSERVATION — Law and legislation — Great Britain
CLARK, R. B.
The waters around the British Isles : their conflicting uses : report of a study group of the David Davies Memorial Institute of International Studies / R.B. Clark. — Oxford : Clarendon, 1987. — xvi,386p. — *Includes index*

MARINE RESURCES AND STATE — Caribbean Area
Ocean use and resource development and management in the eastern Caribbean : proceedings of a seminar held in Basseterre, St.Kitts, West Indies, 7-9 June 1983. — Halifax, N.S. : Dalhousie Ocean Studies Programme, 1984. — xxii,219p

MARINE SCIENCES
INTERNATIONAL CENTRE FOR OCEAN DEVELOPMENT
Introduction to marine affairs : [a] marine affairs course [organized by the Centre] held at the World Maritime University, November 23-28, 1986, Malmö, Sweden. — Halifax : International Centre for Ocean Development, 1986. — 419p. — *Bibliographies*

MARING (NEW GUINEA PEOPLE) — Addresses, essays, lectures
RAPPAPORT, Roy A
Ecology, meaning, and religion / Roy A. Rappaport. — Richmond, Calif. : North Atlantic Books, c1979. — xi, 259 p.. — *Includes bibliographical references and index*

MARITAL PROPERTY — History
Marriage and property / edited by Elizabeth M. Craik ; foreword by J. Steven Watson. — Aberdeen : Aberdeen University Press, 1984. — vi,192p. — *Includes bibliographies and index*

MARITAL PROPERTY — Australia
Matrimonial property law. — Sydney : Law Reform Commission, 1985. — 105p. — (Discussion paper / Law Reform Commission ; no.22). — *Includes bibliographical references*

MARITAL PROPERTY — England
DUCKWORTH, Peter
Matrimonial property and finance / Peter Duckworth. — 3rd ed. — London : Longman, 1986. — 2v. — *Vol.2 will be revised and updated annually*

MARITAL PSYCHOTHERAPY
CLULOW, Christopher F.
Marital therapy : an inside view / Christopher F. Clulow in collaboration with Lynne Cudmore. — Aberdeen : Aberdeen University Press, 1985. — [108]p

MARITAL STATUS — Bahamas — Statistics
Commonwealth of the Bahama Islands : report of the 1980 census of population. — Nassau : Ministry of Finance
V.4: Fertility and union status. — [1986]. — xxv,396p

MARITIME LAW
Aktual'nye pravovye problemy ispol'zovaniia Mirovogo okeana : sbornik nauchnykh trudov / pod redaktsiei A. L. Kolodkina, V. A. Musina. — Moskva : Transport, 1986. — 144p. — *At head of title: Ministerstvo morskogo flota SSSR*

Carriage of goods by sea / edited by Peter Koh Soon Kwang. — Singapore : Butterworths, 1986. — xviii,198p

DEGENHARDT, Henry W.
Maritime affairs : a world handbook : a reference guide to maritime organizations, conventions and disputes and to the international politics of the sea / compiled and written by Henry W. Degenhard ; editorial consultant, Brian Meredith ; general editor, Alan J. Day. — Harlow : Longman, c1985. — viii,412p. — (A Keesing's reference publication). — *Bibliography: p385-390. — Includes index*

International maritime law conventions / [compiled by] Mahararj Nagendra Singh. — [Updated ed.] / foreword by C.P. Srivastava. — London : Stevens, 1983. — 4v.(xxvii,,3305p). — (British shipping laws). — *Previous ed.: published in 1v. as International conventions of maritime shipping. 1973. — Includes index*

The law of the sea : master file containing references to official documents of the Third United Nations Conference on the Law of the Sea. — New York : United Nations, 1985. — xiii,176p. — *Sales no.: E.85.V.9*

The law of the sea : multilateral treaties relevant to the United Nations Convention on the Law of the Sea. — New York : United Nations, 1985. — ix,108p. — *Sales no.: E.85.V.11*

The law of the sea : pollution by dumping : legislative history of Articles 1, paragraph 1 (5), 210 and 216 of the United Nations Convention on the Law of the Sea. — New York : United Nations, 1985. — V,77p. — *Sales no.: E.85.V.12*

The law of the sea : being a series of articles first published in Acta Juridica 1986 / editorial board: T. W. Bennett...[et al.]. — Cape Town : Juta, 1986. — ix,226p. — *Published under the auspices of the Faculty of Law, University of Cape Town*

The law of the sea : national legislation on the exclusive economic zone, the economic zone and the exclusive fishery zone. — New York : United Nations, 1986. — xv,337p

The law of the sea : current developments in state practice. — New York : United Nations, 1987. — viii,225p

Law of the sea bulletin. — New York : United Nations, 1983-. — *Irregular*

LAW OF THE SEA INSTITUTE. Conference (1984 : San Francisco, Calif.)LAW OF THE SEA INSTITUTE. Conference (18th : 1984 : San Francisco, Calif.)
The developing order of the oceans : proceedings / Law of the Sea Institute Eighteenth Annual Conference ; co-sponsored by the University of San Francisco, October 24-27, 1984, San Francisco ; edited by Robert B. Krueger, Stefan A. Riesenfeld. — Honolulu : Law of the Sea Institute, William S. Richardson School of Law, University of Hawaii, 1986. — p. cm. — (Sea grant cooperative report ; UNIHI-SEAGRANT-CR-85-03). — *Includes bibliographies*

MANKABADY, Samir
The International Maritime Organisation / Samir Mankabady. — [2nd ed.]. — London : Croom Helm. — *Previous ed.: published in 1 vol. 1984*
Vol.2: Accidents at sea. — c1987. — xxvii,452p. — *Includes index*

MANKABADY, Samir
The International Maritime Organization / Samir Mankkabady. — [2nd ed.]. — London : Croom Helm. — *Previous ed.: published in 1 vol. 1984*
Vol.1: International shipping rules. — c1986. — xxi,450p. — *Includes index*

Morskoe pravo i mezhdunarodnoe sudokhodstvo na sovremennom etape : sbornik nauchnykh trudov / pod redaktsiei A. L. Kolodkina. — Moskva : Transport, 1986. — 174p. — *At head of title: Ministerstvo morskogo flota SSSR*

The New order of the ocean : the advent of a managed environment / edited by Giulio Pontecorvo. — New York : Columbia University Press, 1986. — p. cm. — *Includes bibliographies and index*

Osnovy sovremennogo pravoporiadka v Mirovom okeane / otv. redaktory A. P. Movchan, A. Iankov. — Moskva : Nauka, 1986. — 295p. — (Mirovoi okean i mezhdunarodnoe pravo)

SANGER, Clyde
Ordering the oceans : the making of the law of the sea / Clyde Sanger. — London : Zed, 1986. — xii,225p. — *Includes index*

VYSOTSKII, A. F.
Morskoi regionalism : (mezhdunarodno-pravovye problemy regional'nogo sotrudnichestva gosudarstv) / A. F. Vysotskii. — Kiev : Naukova dumka, 1986. — 193p

WARD, David
The law of the sea : a choice between anarchy and order / David Ward. — London : World Development Movement, 1984. — vi,55p

MARITIME LAW — Bibliography
KUDEJ, Blanka
The new law of the sea : international law bibliography / prepared by: Blanka Kudej. — New York ; London : Oceana Publications, 1984. — vi,156p. — (A collection of bibliographic and research resources). — *Specially prepared for the Law of the Sea Conference*

The law of the sea : a select bibliography. — New York : United Nations, 1987. — vi,84p. — (Document / United Nations ; LOS/LIB/2) . — *Sales no.: E.87.V.2*

MARITIME LAW — Congresses
LAW OF THE SEA INSTITUTE. Conference (16th : 1982 : Halifax, N.S.)
The law of the sea and ocean industry : new opportunities and restraints : proceedings, Sixteenth Annual Conference / co-sponsored by the Dalhousie Ocean Studies Programme, June 21-24, 1982, Halifax, Nova Scotia ; edited by Douglas M. Johnston and Norman G. Letalik. — Honolulu : Law of the Sea Institute, University of Hawaii, c1983. — p. cm. — (Sea grant cooperative report ; UNIHI-SEAGRANT-CR-83-02). — *Bibliography: p*

UNITED NATIONS. Conference on the Law of the Sea (3rd : 1973-1982 : New York, etc.)
Official records / third United Nations Conference on the Law of the Sea. — New York : United Nations, 1975-. — 28cm

MARITIME LAW — Sources
New directions in the law of the sea : new series / compiled and edited by Kenneth R. Simmonds ; with the collaboration of specialist consulting editors. — London : Oceana, 1983-. — v(looseleaf)

MARITIME LAW — Artic Ocean — Congresses
LAW OF THE SEA INSTITUTE. Workshop (1981 : Mackinac Island, Michigan)
Artic Ocean issues in the 1980's : proceedings, Law of the Sea Institute, University of Hawaii, and Dalhousie Ocean Studies Programme, Dalhousie University ... Workshop, June 10-12, 1981, Mackinac Island, Michigan / edited by Douglas M. Johnston. — Honolulu : The Institute, 1982. — iii,60p

MARITIME LAW — Asia, Southeastern
VALENCIA, Mark J.
South-East Asian seas : oil under troubled waters : hydrocarbon potential, jurisdictional issues, and international relations / Mark J. Valencia. — Oxford ; New York : Oxford University Press, 1985. — xiv,155p. — (Natural Resources of South-East Asia). — *Bibliography: p137-146*

MARITIME LAW — Caribbean Area
Ocean use and resource development and management in the eastern Caribbean : proceedings of a seminar held in Basseterre, St.Kitts, West Indies, 7-9 June 1983. — Halifax, N.S. : Dalhousie Ocean Studies Programme, 1984. — xxii,219p

MARITIME LAW — Caribbean Area — Congresses

Maritime issues in the Caribbean / edited by Farrokh Jhabvala. — Miami : University Presses of Florida, 1983. — xii,130p. — *Proceedings of a conference held at Florida International University 13 April 1981*

MARITIME LAW — East Asia

PARK, Choon-ho
East Asia and the law of the sea / by Choon-ho Park. — [Seoul, Korea] : Seoul National University Press, c1983. — 445 p.. — (International studies series ; no. 5). — *Bibliography: p. 425-445*

MARITIME LAW — England

HILL, Christopher, 19---
Maritime law / Christopher Hill. — 2nd ed. — London : Lloyds of London, 1985. — [400]p. — *Previous ed.: London : Pitman, 1981. — Includes index*

MARITIME LAW — Great Britain

IVAMY, E. R. Handy
Encyclopedia of shipping law sources (U.K.) / by E.R. Hardy Ivamy. — London : Lloyds of London Press, 1985. — v.(loose-leaf). — *Periodically updated by service guides*

MARITIME LAW — Malaysia

Malaysia and the United Nations Conference on the Law of the Sea : selected documents / edited by Hamzah Ahmad. — [Kuala Lumpur : s.n.], 1983. — v,319p. — *Cover title: Malaysia and the law of the sea*

MARITIME LAW — South Africa

The law of the sea : being a series of articles first published in Acta Juridica 1986 / editorial board: T. W. Bennett...[et al.]. — Cape Town : Juta, 1986. — ix,226p. — *Published under the auspices of the Faculty of Law, University of Cape Town*

MARITIME LAW — Soviet Union

Aktual'nye pravovye problemy ispol'zovaniia Mirovogo okeana : sbornik nauchnykh trudov / pod redaktsiei A. L. Kolodkina, V. A. Musina. — Moskva : Transport, 1986. — 144p. — *At head of title: Ministerstvo morskogo flota SSSR*

MARITIME LAW — United States

JUDA, Lawrence
The UNCTAD Liner Code : United States maritime policy at the crossroads / Lawrence Juda. — Boulder, Colo. : Westview Press, 1983. — xiv, 234 p.. — (A Westview replica edition). — *"Appendix 1: The Convention on a Code of Conduct for Liner Conferences, and the Resolutions adopted by the United Nations Conference of Plenipotentiaries": p. 169-207. — Includes index. — Bibliography: p. 215-229*

MARITIME PROVINCES — History

MACDONALD, M. A.
Fortune and La Tour : the civil war in Acadia / M. A. MacDonald. — Toronto : Methuen, 1986. — xii,228p. — *Bibliography: p219-224*

MARITIME PROVINCES — Industries — History

ACHESON, T. W.
Industrialization and underdevelopment in the Maritimes, 1880-1930 / T. W. Acheson, David Frank, James D. Frost ; introduction by David Frank. — Toronto : Garamond Press, 1985. — 86p. — *Articles reprinted from: Acadiensis. — Includes references*

MARKET SEGMENTATION

WEINSTEIN, Art
Market segmentation : using demographics, psychographics, and other segmentation techniques to uncover and exploit new markets / Art Weinstein. — Chicago, Ill. : Probus Pub. Co., c1987. — xii, 296 p.. — *Includes index. — Bibliography: p. 286-288*

MARKET SURVEYS

GREAT BRITAIN. Ministry of Agriculture, Fisheries and Food
Survey of consumer attitudes to food additives. — London : HMSO
Vol.1: Reports prepared for the Ministry of Agriculture, Fisheries and Food, Food Science Division / by Research Surveys of Great Britain Limited. — c1987. — 51p

GREAT BRITAIN. Ministry of Agriculture, Fisheries and Food
Survey of consumer attitudes to food additives. — London : HMSO
Vol.2: Reports prepared for the Ministry of Agriculture, Fisheries and Food, Food Science Division : computer tabulations of fieldwork questionnaires conducted by Research Surveys of Great Britain, 10 to 13 July 1986. — c1987. — various paging

MARKET SURVEYS — Canada

LESSER, Barry
Computer communications and the mass market in Canada / Barry Lesser, Louis Vagianos. — Montreal, Quebec : Institute for Research on Public Policy, c1985. — xxiii, 163 p.. — *Includes bibliographies*

MARKETING

DICKENS, R. R.
International comparison of asset market volatility : a further application of the ARCH model / R.R.Dickens. — London : Bank of England, 1987. — 48p. — (Discussion papers / Bank of England. Technical series ; no.15). — *Bibliography: p47-48*

IRELAND, Norman J.
Product differentiation and non-price competition / Norman Ireland. — Oxford : Basil Blackwell, 1987. — 1v.. — *Includes bibliography and index*

SHAW, Stephen
Airline marketing and management / Stephen Shaw. — 2nd ed. — London : Pitman, 1985. — 296p. — *2nd ed. of "Air transport: a marketing perspective" (1982)*

World food marketing systems / edited by Erdener Kaynak. — London : Butterworth, 1986. — [320]p. — *Includes bibliography and index*

MARKETING — Congresses

INTERNATIONAL CONFERENCE ON BUSINESS HISTORY (7th : 1981 : Fuji Education Center)
Development of mass marketing : the automobile and retailing industries : proceedings of the Fuji Conference / edited by Akio Okochi, Koichi Shimokawa. — Tokyo : University of Tokyo Press, 1981. — xiii,308p. — *Includes references*

MARKETING — Decision making

HERRERO-DELGADO, Maria Jose
A strategic bargaining approach to market institutions / by Maria-Jose Herrero-Delgado. — 152 leaves. — *PhD (Econ) 1985 LSE*

MARKETING — Management

KINNEAR, Thomas C.
Marketing research : an applied approach / Thomas C. Kinnear, James R. Taylor. — 2nd ed. — New York : McGraw-Hill, c1983. — xviii, 698 p.. — (McGraw-Hill series in marketing). — *Includes bibliographies and indexes*

MARKETING — Management — Social aspects

Marketing management technology as a social process / edited by George Fisk. — New York : Praeger, 1986. — xvi, 301 p.. — *"Significant issues ... analyzed by purpose of publications of Reavis Cox compared to papers in this book"--P. xii. — Includes bibliographies and index*

MARKETING — Social aspects

Marketing management technology as a social process / edited by George Fisk. — New York : Praeger, 1986. — xvi, 301 p.. — *"Significant issues ... analyzed by purpose of publications of Reavis Cox compared to papers in this book"--P. xii. — Includes bibliographies and index*

MARKETING — Developing countries

KAYNAK, Erdener
Marketing and economic development / by Erdener Kaynak. — New York : Praeger, 1986. — xxii, 200 p.. — *Includes index. — Bibliography: p. 180-193*

MARKETING — Great Britain

WATKINS, Trevor
Marketing financial services / by Trevor Watkins and Mike Wright. — London : Butterworths, 1986. — ix,170p. — *Bibliography: p159-163. — Includes index*

MARKETING — Great Britain — History

Markets and bagmen : studies in the history of marketing and British industrial performance 1830-1939 / edited by R.P.T. Davenport-Hines. — Aldershot : Gower, c1986. — xii,204p. — ([Business history series]). — *Includes index*

MARKETING — United States — Decision making

LENT, Rebecca J.
Uncertainty, market disequilibrium and the firm's decision process : applications to the Pacific salmon market / Rebecca J. Lent. — Corvallis, Or. : Sea Grant College Program, Oregon State University, [1984]. — vii,109p. — *Bibliography: p94-97*

MARKETING CHANNELS — Congresses

Marketing channels : relationships and performance / [edited by] Luca Pellegrini, Srinivas K. Reddy. — Lexington, Mass. : Lexington Books, c1986. — xiii, 209p. — (The Advances in retailing series). — *"Some of the papers presented at the Third International Conference on Distribution held at Angera, Italy, on April 19 and 20, 1985, sponsored by the Centro di studi sul commercio of the Università Bocconi, Milan, and the Institute of Retail Management, New York University"--Pref. — Includes index*

MARKETING RESEARCH

CHISNALL, Peter M.
Marketing research / Peter M. Chisnall. — 3rd ed. — London : McGraw-Hill, c1986. — [312] p. — (McGraw-Hill marketing series). — *Previous ed.: 1981. — Includes index*

Consumer market research handbook / editors, Robert M. Worcester, John Downham. — 3rd rev. and enl. ed. — Amsterdam ; New York : North-Holland ; New York, N.Y., U.S.A. : Sole distributors for the U.S.A. and Canada, Elsevier Science Pub. Co., 1986. — ix, 840 p.. — *Includes index. — Bibliography: p. 773-801*

GREEN, Paul E
Research for marketing decisions / Paul E. Green, Donald S. Tull. — 4th ed. — Englewood Cliffs, N.J. : Prentice-Hall, c1978. — xiii, 673 p.. — (Prentice-Hall international series in management). — *Includes index. — Bibliography: p.645-658*

KINNEAR, Thomas C.
Marketing research : an applied approach / Thomas C. Kinnear, James R. Taylor. — 2nd ed. — New York : McGraw-Hill, c1983. — xviii, 698 p.. — (McGraw-Hill series in marketing). — *Includes bibliographies and indexes*

MAHATOO, Winston H
The dynamics of consumer behavior / Winston H. Mahatoo. — Toronto ; New York : J. Wiley, c1985. — xix, 428 p.. — *Includes bibliographies and index*

MARKETING RESEARCH — Addresses, essays, lectures
Perspectives on methodology in consumer research / [edited] by David Brinberg, Richard J. Lutz. — New York : Springer-Verlag, c1986. — p. cm. — *Includes bibliographies and indexes*

MARKETING RESEARCH — Case studies
Applied marketing and social research / edited by Ute Bradley. — New York ; London : Van Nostrand Reinhold, c1982. — xiii,314p. — *Includes bibliographies*

MARKETING RESEARCH — Great Britain — Case studies
Applied marketing and social research / edited by Ute Bradley. — New York ; London : Van Nostrand Reinhold, c1982. — xiii,314p. — *Includes bibliographies*

MARKETS
SHAKED, Avner
Opting out : bazaars versus "hi-tech" markets / Avner Shaked. — London : Suntory Toyota International Centre for Economics and Related Disciplines, 1987. — 16p. — (Theoretical economics ; 87/159). — *Bibliography: p16*

MARKETS — India — Tirunelveli District
FANSELOW, Frank Sylvester
Trade, kinship and Islamisation : a comparative study of the social and economic organisation of Muslim and Hindu traders in Tirunelveli district, South India / by Frank Sylvester Fanselow. — 306 leaves. — *PhD (Econ) 1986 LSE*

MARKS & SPENCER (Firm)
SIEFF, Marcus Joseph, Baron Sieff of Brimpton
Don't ask the price : memoirs of the president of Marks & Spencer / Marcus Sieff. — London : Weidenfeld and Nicolson, c1986. — 260p, 8p of plates

MARQUESAS ISLANDS — Population — Statistics
Tableaux normalisés du recensement général de la population : 15 octobre 1983. — [Papeete] : Institut territorial de la statistique Résultats de la commune de Nuku Hiva. — [1985?]. — 4p,11 leaves

Tableaux normalisés du recensement général de la population : 15 octobre 1983. — [Papeete] : Institut territorial de la statistique Résultats de la commune de Tahuata. — [1985?]. — 4p,11 leaves

Tableaux normalisés du recensement général de la population : 15 octobre 1983. — [Papeete] : Institut territorial de la statistique Résultats de la commune de Ua Huka. — [1985?]. — 4p,11 leaves

Tableaux normalisés du recensement général de la population : 15 octobre 1983. — [Papeete] : Institut territorial de la statistique Résultats de la subdivision administrative des Iles Marquises. — [1985?]. — 4p,11 leaves

Tableaux normalisés du recensement général de la population : 15 octobre 1983. — [Papeete] : Institut territorial de la statistique Résultats des Marquises du Sud. — [1985?]. — 4p,11 leaves

Tableaux normalisés du recensement général de la population : 15 octobre 1983. — [Papeete] : Institut territorial de la statistique Résultats des Marquises du Nord. — [1985?]. — 4p,11 leaves

MARR, WILHELM
ZIMMERMANN, Mosche
[Vilhelm Mar, "ha-paṭri'arkh shel ha-Anṭishemiyut". English]. Wilhelm Marr, the patriarch of Antisemitism / by Moshe Zimmermann. — New York : Oxford University Press, 1986. — p. cm. — *Translation of: Vilhelm Mar, "ha-paṭri'arkh shel ha-Anṭishemiyut.". — Includes index*

MARRIAGE
CARPENTER, Edward, 1844-1929
Selected writings / Edward Carpenter. — London : GMP. — (Gay modern classics) Vol.1: Sex / with an introduction by Nöel Grieg. — 1984. — 318p. — *Includes index*

MURSTEIN, Bernard I
Paths to marriage / by Bernard I. Murstein. — Beverly Hills, Calif. : Sage Publications, c1986. — p. cm. — (Family studies text series ; v. 5). — *Includes index*

SEGALEN, Martine
Historical anthropology of the family / Martine Segalen ; translated by J.C. Whitehouse and Sarah Matthews. — Cambridge : Cambridge University Press, 1986. — x,328p. — (Themes in the social sciences). — *Translation of: Sociologie de la famille. — Includes bibliographies and index*

MARRIAGE — Handbooks, manuals, etc
Handbook of marriage and the family / edited by Marvin B. Sussman and Suzanne K. Steinmetz. — New York : Plenum Press, c1986. — p. cm. — *Includes bibliographical references and index*

MARRIAGE — Religious aspects — Judaism
MAYER, Egon
Love and tradition : marriage between Jews and Christians / Egon Mayer. — New York : Plenum Press, c1985. — p. cm. — *Includes index. — Bibliography: p*

MARRIAGE — Religious aspects — Unification Church
GRACE, James H
Sex and marriage in the Unification movement : a sociological study / James H. Grace ; with a preface by Mac Linscott Ricketts. — New York : E. Mellen Press, c1985. — 284 p.. — (Studies in religion and society ; v. 13). — *Bibliography: p. [275]-284*

MARRIAGE — Developing countries — Statistics
ZOUGHLAMI, Younès
The demographic characteristics of household populations / Younès Zoughlami, Diana Allsopp. — Voorburg : International Statistical Institute, 1985. — 82p. — (Comparative studies / World Fertility Survey ; no.45). — *Bibliographical references: p31*

MARRIAGE — England — History
WOLFRAM, Sybil
In-laws and outlaws : kinship and marriage in England / Sybil Wolfram. — London : Croom Helm, c1987. — [240]p. — *Bibliography: p295-331*

MARRIAGE — France — Statistics
DESPLANQUES, Guy
Recensement général de la population de 1982. — [Paris] : INSEE. — *Bibliography: p55. — RP 82/7*
Principaux résultats de l'enquête sur les familles : nuptialité et fécondité : France métropolitaine / par Guy Desplanques. — 1985. — 136p

MARRIAGE — Great Britain — History
GILLIS, John R.
For better, for worse : British marriages, 1600 to the present / John R. Gillis. — New York ; Oxford : Oxford University Press, 1985. — 417 p.

MARRIAGE — Ireland — History
Marriage in Ireland / edited by Art Cosgrove. — Dublin : College, 1985. — 160p. — *Bibliography: p151-156. — Includes index*

MARRIAGE — Pakistan
MAHMOOD, Naushin
Nuptiality patterns in Pakistan / Naushin Mahmood [and] Syed Mubashir Ali. — Islamabad : Pakistan Institute of Development Economics, 1986. — 36,[3]p. — (Studies in population, labour force and migration project report ; no.2). — *Bibliography: p.[37-39]*

MARRIAGE — Portugal — Lanhezes — History
BRETTELL, Caroline
Men who migrate, women who wait : population and history in a Portuguese parish / Caroline B. Brettell. — Princeton, N.J. : Princeton University Press, c1986. — xv, 329 p., [8] p. of plates. — *Includes index. — Bibliography: p. [299]-319*

MARRIAGE — Southern Africa
TIMAEUS, Ian
Labour circulation, marriage and fertility in Southern Africa / Ian Timaeus and Wendy Graham. — London : London School of Hygiene and Tropical Medicine. Centre for Population Studies, 1986. — 30p. — (CPS research paper ; no.86-2). — *Bibliography: p24-30*

MARRIAGE — Thailand — Statistics
The survey of population change, 1974-76 : special report on fertility, nuptiality and infant mortality measures. — Bangkok : National Statistical Office, [1979]. — 81p. — *Contents: Estimating fertility in Thailand from information on children ever born/Kenneth Hill - Some indirect estimates of fertility and infant mortality.../Arjun L. Adlakha and Chintana Pejaranonda - Marriage pattern/Chinatana Pejaranonda*

MARRIAGE — Trinidad and Tobago
Marriages and divorces report, 1979-1983. — [Port of Spain] : Central Statistical Office, 1985. — v,19p

MARRIAGE — United States
RICHARDSON, Laurel Walum
The new other woman : contemporary single women in affairs with married men / Laurel Richardson. — New York : Free Press ; London : Collier Macmillan, c1985. — p. cm. — *Includes index. — Bibliography: p*

MARRIAGE — United States — Addresses, essays, lectures
Current controversies in marriage and family studies / edited by Harold Feldman & Margaret Feldman. — Beverly Hill : Sage Publications, c1985. — p. cm

MARRIAGE COUNSELING
CLULOW, Christopher F.
Marital therapy : an inside view / Christopher F. Clulow in collaboration with Lynne Cudmore. — Aberdeen : Aberdeen University Press, 1985. — [108]p

MARRIAGE COUNSELLING
Marital relationship as a focus for casework : [report of proceedings of a conference]. — London : Institute of Marital Studies, 1962. — 60p

MATTINSON, Janet
The reflection process in casework supervision / Janet Mattinson. — [London] : Institute of Marital Studies, The Tavistock Institute of Human Relations : Distributed by Research Publications Services, 1975. — 149p

MARRIAGE CUSTOMS AND RITES — Social aspects
BRIDGWOOD, Ann
Marriage, honour and property : Turkish Cypriots in North London / Ann Bridgwood. — 486 leaves. — *Only 1 set of photographs deposited. — PhD (Econ) 1986 LSE. — Photographs are shelved with thesis. — Leaves 452-477 are appendices*

MARRIAGE CUSTOMS AND RITES — England — History
WRIGLEY, E. A.
The local and the general in population history : the sixteenth Harte lecture, delivered in the University of Exeter on 13 May 1983 / by E.A. Wrigley. — [Exeter] : University of Exeter, 1985. — 19p

MARRIAGE (ISLAMIC LAW) — Afghanistan
KAMALI, Mohammad Hashim
Law in Afghanistan : a study of the Constitutions, matrimonial law and judiciary / by Mohammad Hashim Kamali. — Leiden : E. J. Brill, 1985. — viii,265p. — (Social, economic and political studies of the Middle East ; Vol.36). — Bibliography: p[254]-259

MARRIAGE LAW — Australia
Matrimonial property law. — Sydney : Law Reform Commission, 1985. — 105p. — (Discussion paper / Law Reform Commission ; no.22). — Includes bibliographical references

MARRIAGE, MIXED — United States
MAYER, Egon
Love and tradition : marriage between Jews and Christians / Egon Mayer. — New York : Plenum Press, c1985. — p. cm. — Includes index. — Bibliography: p

MARRIED PEOPLE — Employment — Canada
HARPELL, Cindy
An analysis of dual-earner families in Canada / Cindy Harpell. — Kingston, Ont., Canada : Industrial Relations Centre, Queen's University at Kingston, 1985. — 48 p.. — (School of Industrial Relations research essay series ; no. 2). — Bibliography: p. 47-48

MARRIED PEOPLE — Employment — United States
HERTZ, Rosanna
More equal than others : women and men in dual-career marriages / Rosanna Hertz. — Berkeley : University of California Press, c1986. — p. cm. — Includes index. — Bibliography: p

MARRIED PEOPLE — Psychology
Intimate relationships : development, dynamics, and deterioration / edited by Daniel Perlman, Steve Duck. — Beverly Hills : Sage Publications, c1987. — 320 p.. — (Sage focus editions ; v. 80). — Includes bibliographies and index

MARRIED WOMEN — United States — Case studies
OSTRANDER, Susan A
Women of the upper class / Susan A. Ostrander. — Philadelphia : Temple University Press, 1984. — x, 183 p.. — (Women in the political economy). — Bibliography: p. 175-183

MARRIED WOMEN — United States — History
SALMON, Marylynn
Women and the law of property in early America / Marylynn Salmon. — Chapel Hill ; London : University of North Carolina Press, c1986. — xvii, 267 p.. — (Studies in legal history). — Based on the author's thesis (Ph. D.). — Includes indexes. — Bibliography: p. 239-251

MARSHAL, WILLIAM
PAINTER, Sidney
William Marshal : knight-errant, baron and regent of England / by Sidney Painter. — Baltimore : Johns Hopkins, 1933. — xi,305p

MARSHALL, ALFRED, 1842-1924 — Contributions in economics
REISMAN, David
The economics of Alfred Marshall / David Reisman ; foreword by G.L.S. Shackle. — London : Macmillan, 1986. — [384]p. — Includes index

MARSHALL PLAN, 1948-1952
HOGAN, Michael J., 1943-
The Marshall Plan : America, Britain, and the reconstruction of Western Europe, 1947-1952 / Michael J. Hogan. — Cambridge : Cambridge University Press, 1987. — xiv,482p. — Bibliography: p446-463. — Includes index

MARSHALS — France — Biography
BAUMONT, Maurice
Bazaine : les secrets d'un maréchal 1811/1888. — Paris : Imprimere nationale, 1978. — 425p. — (Collection "Personnages"). — Includes index. — Bibliography: p401-406

MARSHALS — Great Britain — Biography
HARDINGE, Henry Hardinge, Viscount
The letters of the first Viscount Hardinge of Lahore to Lady Hardinge and Sir Walter and Lady James, 1844-1847 / Bawa Satinder Singh, editor. — London : Royal Historical Society, 1986. — [300]p. — (Camden Fourth series : v.32). — Includes bibliography and index

MARSILIUS, of Padua
D'ENTRÈVES, A. P.
The medieval contribution to political thought : Thomas Aquinas, Marsilius of Padua, Richard Hooker / by Alexander Passerin D'Entreves. — New York : Humanities, 1959. — viii,148p. — On spine: Medieval contributions to political thought. — Originally published: Oxford University Press, 1939

MARTENS, JOACHIM FRIEDRICH
BREUILLY, John
Joachim Friedrich Martens (1806-1877) und die deutsche Arbeiterbewegung / John Breuilly, Wieland Sachse. — Göttingen : Otto Schwartz, 1984. — (xviii),489p. — (Göttinger Beiträge zur Wirtschafts- und Sozialgeschichte ; Bd.8). — Bibliography: p469-485

MARTIAL LAW — Gaza Strip
SHEHADEH, Raja
Occupier's law : a study of Israeli practices in the West Bank and Gaza / by Raja Shehadeh. — Washington, DC : Institute for Palestine Studies, 1985. — p. cm. — Bibliography: p

MARTIAL LAW — West Bank
SHEHADEH, Raja
Occupier's law : a study of Israeli practices in the West Bank and Gaza / by Raja Shehadeh. — Washington, DC : Institute for Palestine Studies, 1985. — p. cm. — Bibliography: p

MARTIN, ANNE
HOWARD, Anne Bail
The long campaign : a biography of Anne Martin / Anne Bail Howard. — Reno, Nevada : University of Nevada Press, c1985. — p. cm. — (Nevada studies in history and political science ; no. 20). — Includes index. — Bibliography: p

MARTÍNEZ DEL RÍO (Family)
WALKER, David W
Kinship, business, and politics : the Martínez del Río family in Mexico, 1824-1867 / by David W. Walker. — 1st ed. — Austin : University of Texas Press, 1986. — x, 278 p.. — (Latin American monographs / Institute of Latin American Studies, University of Texas at Austin ; no.70). — Includes index. — Bibliography: p. [259]-267

MARX, KARL. Das kapital — Addresses, essays, lectures
SHAW, George Bernard
Bernard Shaw & Karl Marx : a symposium, 1884-1889. — Folcroft, Pa. : Folcroft Library Editions, 1977. — ix, 200 p., [1] fold. leaf of plates. — Reprint of the 1930 ed. printed for Random House by R. W. Ellis, The Georgian Press, New York

MARX, KARL. Kapital
FOLEY, Duncan K
Understanding capital : Marx's economic theory / Duncan K. Foley. — Cambridge, Mass. ; London : Harvard University Press, 1986. — viii, 183p. — Includes index. — Bibliography: p.[177]-180

MARX, KARL
AVINERI, Shlomo
The social and political thought of Karl Marx / Shlomo Avineri. — Cambridge : Cambridge University Press, 1970. — viii,268p. — Bibliography: p259-264

BARKER, Jeffrey H.
Individualism and community : the state in Marx and early anarchism / Jeffrey H. Barker. — New York : Greenwood Press, 1986. — xiv, 235 p.. — (Contributions in political science ; no. 143). — Includes index. — Bibliography: p. [221]-229

GORDON, David
Critics of Marxism / David Gordon. — Bowling Green, Ohio : Social Philosophy and Policy Center ; New Brunswick, USA : Transaction Books, 1986. — 57 p.. — (Original papers ; no. 6). — Bibliography: p. 49-57

MÁRKUS, György
Language and production : a critique of the paradigms / by Gyorgy Markus. — Dordrecht ; Boston : D. Reidel Pub. Co. ; Hingham, MA, U.S.A. : Kluwer Academic Publishers [distributor], c1986. — p. cm. — (Boston studies in the philosophy of science ; v. 96). — Includes indexes. — Bibliography: p

MYERS, David B.
Marx and Nietzsche : the reminiscences and transcripts of a nineteenth century journalist / David B. Myers. — Lanham, MD : University Press of America, c1986. — xviii, 168 p.. — Spine title: Marx & Nietzsche. — Bibliography: p. 164-167

SCHWALBE, Michael L.
The psychosocial consequences of natural and alienated labor / Michael L. Schwalbe. — Albany, N.Y. : State University of New York Press, c1986. — ix, 233 p.. — (SUNY series in the sociology of work). — Includes index. — Bibliography: p. 215-227

MARX, KARL — Bibliography
DRAPER, Hal
The Marx-Engels register : a complete bibliography of Marx and Engels' individual writings / by Hal Draper with the assistance of the Center for Socialist History. — New York : Schocken Books, 1985. — xxx, 271 p.. — (Marx-Engels cyclopedia ; v. 2). — Includes index

MARX, KARL — Chronology
DRAPER, Hal
The Marx-Engels chronicle : a day-by-day chronology of Marx and Engels' life and activity / by Hal Draper ; with the assistance of the Center for Socialist History. — New York : Schocken Books, 1985. — xxii, 297 p.. — (The Marx-Engels cyclopedia ; v. 1)

MARX, KARL — Congresses
Marx, Schumpeter, and Keynes : a centenary celebration of dissent / Suzanne W. Helburn and David F. Bramhall, editors. — Armonk, N.Y. : M.E. Sharpe, c1986. — xii, 343 p.. — Papers presented at a symposium held Apr. 20-22, 1983 at the University of Colorado at Denver. — Includes bibliographies

MARX, KARL — Language — Glossaries, etc
DRAPER, Hal
The Marx-Engels glossary : glossary to the chronicle and register, annd index to the glossary / by Hal Draper ; with the assistance of the Center for Socialist History. — New York : Schocken Books, 1986. — xx, 249 p.. — (The Marx-Engels encyclopedia ; v. 3). — Includes index

MARX, KARL, 1818-1833
LUNDKVIST, Anders
Introduktion til metoden: Kapitalen / Anders Lundkvist. — ºArhus : Modtryk, 1975. — 77p. — (Til kritikken af den politiske økonomi ; 2). — Bibliography: p74-77

MARX, KARL, 1818-1883
ARTHUR, C. J.
Dialectics of Labour : Marx and his relation to Hegel / C.J. Arthur. — Oxford : Basil Blackwell, 1986. — 182p. — Bibliography: p174-179. — Includes index

MARX, KARL, 1818-1883 *continuation*

CONWAY, David
A farewell to Marx : an outline and appraisal of his theories / David Conway. — Harmondsworth : Penguin, 1987. — 230p. — (Pelican books). — *Bibliography: p.221-224*

DÄMPFLING, Björn
Die Marxsche Theorie der Grundrente : eine kritische Studie / Björn Dämpfling. — Hamburg : VSA-Verlag, 1985. — 161p. — *Bibliography: p154-161*

ELSTER, Jon
An introduction to Karl Marx / Jon Elster. — Cambridge : Cambridge University Press, 1986. — vii,200p. — *Includes bibliographies*

KAIN, Philip J.
Marx' method, epistemology, and humanism : a study in the development of his thought / Philip J. Kain. — Dordrecht ; Boston : D. Reidel ; Hingham, MA, U.S.A. : Sold and distributed in the U.S.A. and Canada by Kluwer Academic Publishers, c1986. — x, 197 p.. — (Sovietica ; v. 48). — *Includes index. Bibliography: p. 176-184*

LOVE, Nancy Sue
Marx, Nietzsche, and modernity / Nancy S. Love. — New York : Columbia University Press, 1986. — xii, 264 p.. — *Includes index. — Bibliography: p. [243]-255*

MARX, Karl, 1818-1883
[Collected works]. Werke, Artikel, Entwurfe : Juli 1851 bis Dezember 1852 / Karl Marx, Friedrich Engels ; [Bearbeitung des Bandes: Martin Hundt...et al.]. — Berlin : Dietz, 1985. — 2v. — (Karl Marx Friedrich Engels Gesamtausgabe (MEGA). 1 Abt. ; Bd.11)

Marx i Sverige : 100 år med Marx i svensk historia, vetenskap och politik / redigerad ar Lars Vikström. — Stockholm : Arbetarkultur, 1983. — 258p. — (Teori & praxis ; 6)

Marx refuted : the verdict of history / edited by Ronald Duncan and Colin Wilson. — Bath : Ashgrove Press, 1987. — 284p

Marxismus, Ideologie, Politik : Krise des Marxismus oder Krise des "Arguments"? / herausgegeben von Hans Heinz Holz, Thomas Metscher, Josef Schleifstein, Robert Steigerwald ; mit Beiträgen von Karl-Heinz Brown...[et al.]. — Frankfurt am Main : Verlag Marxistische Blätter, 1984. — 318p. — *Includes bibliographical notes*

Marx...ou pas? : réflexions sur un centenaire / Denis Woronoff...[et al.]. — Paris : Etudes et documentation internationales, 1986. — 340p

MÉSZÁROS, István
Philosophy, ideology and social science : essays in negation and affirmation / István Mészáros. — Brighton : Harvester, 1986. — [272]p

MÜLLER, Manfred
Auf dem Wege zum "Kapital" : zur Entwicklung des Kapitalbegriffs von Marx in den Jahren 1857-1863 / Manfred Müller. — Berlin : Das Europäische Buch, 1978. — 160p. — *With folded chart. — Bibliography: p152-160*

PAGE, Leslie R.
Karl Marx and the critical examination of his works / Leslie R. Page. — London : Freedom Association, 1987. — [150]p. — *Includes index*

POTIER, Jean-Pierre
Lectures italiennes de Marx : les conflits d'interpretation chez les économistes et les philosophes, 1883-1983 / Jean-Pierre Potier. — Lyon : Presses Universitaires de Lyon, 1986. — 500p. — *Bibliography: p471-492*

SCHWARZCHILD, Leopold
The red Prussian : the life and legend of Karl Marx / Leopold Schwarzschild ; with an introduction by Antony Flew. — London : Pickwick Books, 1986. — 382p. — *Translated from the German by Margaret Wing. — First published in Great Britain in 1948*

MARX, KARL, 1818-1883 — Contributions in economics

Karl Marx's economics : critical assessments / edited by John Cunningham Wood. — London : Croom Helm, c1987. — 4v.. — (The Croom Helm critical assessments of leading economists). — *In slip case*

MARX, KARL, 1818-1883 — Dictionaries

Dictionnaire critique du marxisme / Georges Labica et Gérard Bensussan; directeurs de la production. — 2nd ed. — Paris : Presses Universitaires de France, 1985. — xi,1240p

MARX, KARL, 1818-1883 — Dictionaries, indexes, etc.

CARVER, Terrell
The Marx dictionary / Terrell Carver. — Cambridge : Polity in association with Blackwell, 1986. — [220]p. — *Includes bibliography and index*

MARXIAN ECONOMICS

BERG, Hermann von
Marxismus-Leninismus : das Elend der halb deutschen, halb russischen Ideologie. — 2., überarbeitete Aufl.. — Köln : Bund-Verlag, 1987. — 320p

BUZUEV, A. V.
Political economy : a beginner's course / Buzuev, A. [and] Buzuev, V. ; translated from the Russian by Jane Sayer. — Moscow : Progress, 1986. — 342p

CONWAY, David
A farewell to Marx : an outline and appraisal of his theories / David Conway. — Harmondsworth : Penguin, 1987. — 230p. — (Pelican books). — *Bibliography: p.221-224*

DÄMPFLING, Björn
Die Marxsche Theorie der Grundrente : eine kritische Studie / Björn Dämpfling. — Hamburg : VSA-Verlag, 1985. — 161p. — *Bibliography: p154-161*

Essays in the political economy of Australian capitalism / edited by E. L. Wheelwright and Ken Buckley. — Sydney : Australia & New Zealand Book Company vol.5. — 1983. — 304p

FOLEY, Duncan K
Money, accumulation, and crisis / Duncan K. Foley. — Chur, Switzerland ; New York : Harwood Academic Publishers, c1986. — 60 p.. — (Fundamentals of pure and applied economics ; vol. 2Marxian economics section). — *Includes index. — Bibliography: p. 55-58*

FOLEY, Duncan K
Understanding capital : Marx's economic theory / Duncan K. Foley. — Cambridge, Mass. ; London : Harvard University Press, 1986. — viii, 183p. — *Includes index. — Bibliography: p.[177]-180*

FOSTER, John Bellamy
The theory of monopoly capitalism : an elaboration of Marxian political economy / John Bellamy Foster. — New York : Monthly Review Press, c1986. — 280 p.. — *Includes index. — Bibliography: p. 225-263*

Karl Marx's economics : critical assessments / edited by John Cunningham Wood. — London : Croom Helm, c1987. — 4v.. — (The Croom Helm critical assessments of leading economists). — *In slip case*

LUNDKVIST, Anders
Introduktion til metoden: Kapitalen / Anders Lundkvist. — °Arhus : Modtryk, 1975. — 77p. — (Til kritikken af den politiske økonomi ; 2). — *Bibliography: p74-77*

MCKEOWN, Kieran
Marxist political economy and Marxist urban sociology : a review and elaboration of recent developments / Kieran McKeown. — Basingstoke : Macmillan, 1987. — [256]p. — *Includes bibliography and index*

MARSH, David

On structural power : an empirical test of the structuralist thesis / by David Marsh. — Colchester : Department of Government University of Essex, 1986. — 56 p. — (Essex papers in politics and government ; no. 39)

Marxismus, Ideologie, Politik : Krise des Marxismus oder Krise des "Arguments"? / herausgegeben von Hans Heinz Holz, Thomas Metscher, Josef Schleifstein, Robert Steigerwald ; mit Beiträgen von Karl-Heinz Brown...[et al.]. — Frankfurt am Main : Verlag Marxistische Blätter, 1984. — 318p. — *Includes bibliographical notes*

MÜLLER, Manfred
Auf dem Wege zum "Kapital" : zur Entwicklung des Kapitalbegriffs von Marx in den Jahren 1857-1863 / Manfred Müller. — Berlin : Das Europäische Buch, 1978. — 160p. — *With folded chart. — Bibliography: p152-160*

PACK, Spencer J
Reconstructing Marxian economics : Marx based upon a Sraffian commodity theory of value / by Spencer J. Pack. — New York : Praeger, 1985. — p. cm. — *Includes index. — Bibliography: p*

PALKIN, Iu. I.
Ekonomicheskie zakony i ekonomicheskaia politika KPSS / Iu. I. Palkin, P. S. Eshchenko. — Kiev : Vishcha shkola, 1985. — 245p

POLIAKOV, R. I.
Obobshchestvlenie proizvodstva v usloviiakh razvitogo sotsializma / R. I. Poliakov. — Leningrad : Izd-vo Leningradskogo universiteta, 1984. — 222p

Political economy : socialism / under the general editorship of G. A. Kozlov. — Moscow : Progress Publishers, 1977. — 493p

POPOV, Iu. N.
Essays in political economy / Yuri Popov ; [translated from the Russion by Yuri Sdobnikov]. — Moscow : Progress Publishers. — (Progress guides to the social sciences) [1]: Imperialism and developing countries. — 1984. — 292p

Rethinking socialist economics : a new agenda for Britain / edited by Peter Nolan and Suzanne Paine. — Cambridge : Polity, 1986. — [300]p

ROEMER, John E
Value, exploitation, and class / John E. Roemer. — Chur, Switzerland ; New York : Harwood Academic Publishers, c1986. — p. cm. — (Fundamentals of pure and applied economics ; vol. 4. Marxian economics section). — *Includes index. — Bibliography: p*

ROLAND, Gérard
La valeur d'usage chez Karl Marx / Gérard Roland. — Bruxelles : Université de Bruxelles, [1985]. — 200p. — *Bibliography: p191-196*

THANH-HUNG, Nguyen
Zur Theorie der vorkapitalistischen Produktionsweisen bei K. Marx und F. Engels : dargestellt anhand der Probleme der "asiatischen Produktionsweise" / Nguyen Thanh-Hung. — Gaiganz : Politladen, 1975. — 119p. — (Politladen Typoskript ; 9). — *Bibliography: p110-119*

MARXIAN ECONOMICS — History and criticism

DOZEKAL, Egbert
Von der 'Rekonstruktion' der Marxschen Theorie zur 'Krise des Marxismus' : Darstellung und Kritik eines Diskussionsprozesses in der Bundesrepublik von 1967 bis 1984 / Egbert Dozekal. — Köln : Pahl-Rugenstein, 1985. — 301p. — (Pahl-Rugenstein Hochschulschriften Gesellschafts- und Naturwissenschaften ; 204). — *Bibliography: p294-301*

MARXIAN HISTORIOGRAPHY — Soviet Union
CHAGIN, B. A.
Istoricheskii materializm v SSSR v perekhodnyi period 1917-1936 gg. : istoriko-sotsiologicheskii ocherk / B. A. Chagin, V. I. Klushin ; otv. redaktor A. A. Fedoseev. — Moskva : Nauka, 1986. — 439p

MARXIAN SCHOOL OF SOCIOLOGY
ARTHUR, C. J.
Dialectics of Labour : Marx and his relation to Hegel / C.J. Arthur. — Oxford : Basil Blackwell, 1986. — 182p. — *Bibliography: p174-179. — Includes index*

LIAZOS, Alexander
Sociology : a liberating perspective / Alezander Liazos. — London : Allyn and Bacon, 1985. — xviii,461p. — *Bibliography: p[415]-444*

MCKEOWN, Kieran
Marxist political economy and Marxist urban sociology : a review and elaboration of recent developments / Kieran McKeown. — Basingstoke : Macmillan, 1987. — [256]p. — *Includes bibliography and index*

MÉSZÁROS, István
Philosophy, ideology and social science : essays in negation and affirmation / István Mészáros. — Brighton : Harvester, 1986. — [272]p

MARXIST ECONOMICS
O'CONNOR, James
The meaning of crisis : a theoretical introduction / James O'Connor. — Oxford : Basil Blackwell, 1987. — [192]p v,197p. — *Includes index*

MARXIST THEORY AND SOCIAL SCIENCES
MCKEOWN, Kieran
Marxist political economy and Marxist urban sociology : a review and elaboration of recent developments / Kieran McKeown. — Basingstoke : Macmillan, 1987. — [256]p. — *Includes bibliography and index*

MARY, Blessed Virgin, Saint — Apparitions and miracles
CARROLL, Michael P.
The cult of the Virgin Mary : psychological origins / Michael P. Carroll. — Princeton, N.J. : Princeton University Press, 1986. — xv, 253 p.. — *Includes index. — Bibliography: p. 227-248*

MARY, Blessed Virgin, Saint — Cult
CARROLL, Michael P.
The cult of the Virgin Mary : psychological origins / Michael P. Carroll. — Princeton, N.J. : Princeton University Press, 1986. — xv, 253 p.. — *Includes index. — Bibliography: p. 227-248*

MASARYK, TOMAS GARRIGUE
PECHÁČEK, Jaroslav
Masaryk - Beneš -Hrad : Masarykovy dopisi Benešovi / Jaroslav Pecháček. — München : České Slovo, 1984. — 182p

MASCULINITY (PSYCHOLOGY)
ELSHTAIN, Jean Bethke
Meditations on modern political thought : masculine/feminine themes from Luther to Arendt / Jean Bethke Elshtain. — New York : Praeger, 1986. — p. cm. — *Includes index. — Bibliography: p*

HEARN, Jeff
The gender of oppression : men, masculinity and the critique of Marxism / Jeff Hearn. — Brighton : Wheatsheaf, 1987. — [224]p. — *Includes bibliography and index*

MASCULINITY (PSYCHOLOGY) — Papua New Guinea
HERDT, Gilbert H.
Sambia : ritual and gender in New Guinea / by Gilbert H. Herdt. — New York : Holt, Rinehart and Winston, 1986. — p. cm. — (Case studies in cultural anthropology). — *Includes index. — Bibliography: p*

MASDEU, JUAN FRANCISCO — Contributions in historiography
MANTELLI, Roberto
The political, religious, and historiographical ideas of Juan Francisco Masdeu, S.J., 1744-1817 / Roberto Mantelli. — New York : Garland, 1987. — p. cm. — (Political theory and political philosophy). — *Thesis (Ph. D.)--University of London, 1978. — Bibliography: p*

MASDEU, JUAN FRANCISCO — Contributions in political science
MANTELLI, Roberto
The political, religious, and historiographical ideas of Juan Francisco Masdeu, S.J., 1744-1817 / Roberto Mantelli. — New York : Garland, 1987. — p. cm. — (Political theory and political philosophy). — *Thesis (Ph. D.)--University of London, 1978. — Bibliography: p*

MASHONALAND (ZIMBABWE) — Economic conditions — Statistics
Zimbabwe National Household Survey Capability Programme. — Harare : Central Statisical Office
Report number 1: Report on demographic socio-economic survey
Communal lands of Mashonaland Central Province 1983/84. — [1984]. — 18p

MASHONALAND (ZIMBABWE) — Population — Statistics
Zimbabwe National Household Survey Capability Programme. — Harare : Central Statisical Office
Report number 1: Report on demographic socio-economic survey
Communal lands of Mashonaland Central Province 1983/84. — [1984]. — 18p

MASHONALAND (ZIMBABWE) — Social conditions — Statistics
Zimbabwe National Household Survey Capability Programme. — Harare : Central Statisical Office
Report number 1: Report on demographic socio-economic survey
Communal lands of Mashonaland Central Province 1983/84. — [1984]. — 18p

MASKS (SCULPTURE) — Nigeria
OTTENBERG, Simon
Masked rituals of Afikpo, the context of an African art : [published in connection with an exhibition shown at the Henry Art Gallery, University of Washington, May 24-June 21, 1975]. — Seattle : Published for the Henry Art Gallery by the University of Washington Press, [1975]. — 229 p., [8] leaves of plates. — (Index of art in the Pacific Northwest ; no. 9). — *Includes index. — Bibliography: p. 223-225*

MASON, GEORGE
The First Amendment : the legacy of George Mason / edited by T. Daniel Shumate. — Fairfax : George Mason University Press ; London : Associated University Presses, c1985. — 201 p.. — (The George Mason lectures). — *Includes bibliographies and index*

MASS MEDIA — United States — History
KIRBY, Jack Temple
Media-made Dixie : the South in the American imagination / Jack Temple Kirby. — Rev. ed. — Athens : University of Georgia Press, c1986. — p. cm. — *Includes index. — Bibliography: p*

MASS MEDIA
Documentary and the mass media / editor, John Corner. — London : Edward Arnold, 1986. — [192]p. — (Stratford-upon-Avon studies. Second series). — *Includes index*

MCLUHAN, Marshall
Understanding media : the extensions of man / Marshall McLuhan ; Marshall McLuhan. — London : ARK, 1987. — 359 p

POSTMAN, Neil
Amusing ourselves to death : public discourse in the age of show business / Neil Postman. — London : Heinemann, 1986. — viii, 184p

TAN, Alexis S
Mass communication theories and research / Alexis S. Tan. — 2nd ed. — New York : Wiley, c1985. — p. cm. — *Includes index*

MASS MEDIA — Addresses, essays, lectures
Inter/media : interpersonal communication in a media world / edited by Gary Gumpert and Robert Cathcart. — 3rd ed. — New York : Oxford University Press, 1986. — ix, 666 p.. — *Bibliography: p. 649-666*

MASS MEDIA — Audiences — Research — Addresses, essays, lectures
Media gratifications research : current perspectives / edited by Karl Erik Rosengren, Lawrence A. Wenner, Philip Palmgreen. — Beverly Hills, Calif. : Sage Publications, c1985. — p. cm. — *Bibliography: p*

MASS MEDIA — Censorship
MERCER, Derrik
The fog of war : the media on the battlefield / by Derrik Mercer, Geoff Mungham, Kevin Williams ; foreword by Sir Tom Hopkinson. — London : Heinemann, 1987. — xvi,413p

MASS MEDIA — Economic aspects — Australia
BROWN, Allan G
Commercial media in Australia : economics, ownership, technology, and regulation / Allan Brown. — St. Lucia ; New York : University of Queensland Press, 1986. — xii, 240 p.. — (University of Queensland Press scholars' library). — *Includes index. — Bibliography: p. [226]-240*

MASS MEDIA — Influence
Impacts and influences : essays on media power in the twentieth century / edited by James Curran, Anthony Smith and Pauline Wingate. — London : Methuen, 1987. — [350]p. — *Includes index*

MASS MEDIA — Law and legislation — Australia
BROWN, Allan G
Commercial media in Australia : economics, ownership, technology, and regulation / Allan Brown. — St. Lucia ; New York : University of Queensland Press, 1986. — xii, 240 p.. — (University of Queensland Press scholars' library). — *Includes index. — Bibliography: p. [226]-240*

MASS MEDIA — Law and legislation — United States — Digests
BENSMAN, Marvin R.
Broadcast regulation : selected cases and decisions / Marvin R. Bensman. — 2nd ed. — Lanham, MD : University Press of America, c1985. — v, 192 p.. — *Includes index*

MASS MEDIA — Methodology
BERGER, Arthur Asa
Media analysis techniques / Arthur Asa Berger. — Beverly Hills : Sage Publications, c1982. — 160 p.. — (The Sage commtext series ; v. 10). — *Bibliography: p. 158-159*

MASS MEDIA — Moral and ethical aspects
Maincurrents in mass communications / [compiled by] Warren K. Agee, Phillip H. Ault, Edwin Emery. — New York : Harper & Row, c1986. — xiv, 457 p.. — *Rev. ed. of: Perspectives on mass communications. c1982. — Includes bibliographical references and index*

MASS MEDIA — Political aspects
Communicating politics : mass communications and the political process / edited by Peter Golding, Graham Murdock, and Philip Schlesinger. — New York, NY : Holmes & Meier, 1986. — p. cm. — *Bibliography: p223-225. — Bibliography: p*

Political communication research : approaches, studies, assessments / edited by David L. Paletz. — Norwood, N.J. : Ablex Pub. Corp., c1987. — xii, 276 p.. — (Communication and information science). — *Includes bibliographies and indexes*

MASS MEDIA — Political aspects — Italy
WAGNER-PACIFICI, Robin Erica
The Moro morality play : terrorism as social drama / Robin Erica Wagner-Pacifici. — Chicago : The University of Chicago Press, c1986. — p. cm. — *Includes index. Bibliography: p*

MASS MEDIA — Political aspects — Canada
FRIZZELL, Alan
The Canadian general election of 1984 : politicians, parties, press and polls / Alan Frizzell, Anthony Westell ; with contributions by Nick Hills, Jeffrey Simpson, and Val Sears. — Ottawa : Carleton University Press, 1985. — vii,139p

MASS MEDIA — Political aspects — Great Britain
The Media in British politics / edited by Jean Seaton and Ben Pimlott. — Aldershot : Gower, c1987. — xviii,266p. — *Includes index*

Political communications : the general election campaign of 1983 / edited by Ivor Crewe and Martin Harrop. — Cambridge : Cambridge University Press, 1986. — [342]p. — *Includes index*

MASS MEDIA — Psychological aspects
WINETT, Richard A
Information and behavior : systems of influence / Richard A. Winett. — Hillsdale, N.J. : L. Erlbaum Associates, 1986, c1985. — p. cm. — *Includes index*

MASS MEDIA — Psychological aspects — Addresses, essays, lectures
Mass media and political thought : an information-processing approach / edited by Sidney Kraus, Richard M. Perloff. — Beverly Hills : Sage Publications, c1985. — 350 p.. — *Includes bibliographies and index*

MASS MEDIA — Social aspects
DUTTON, Brian, 19---
The media / Brian Dutton. — London : Longman, 1986. — 106p. — (Sociology in focus series). — *Bibliography: p102-104. — Includes index*

Media, culture and society : a critical reader / edited by Richard Collins ... [et al.]. — London : Sage, c1986. — 346p. — *Includes bibliographies and index*

WINETT, Richard A
Information and behavior : systems of influence / Richard A. Winett. — Hillsdale, N.J. : L. Erlbaum Associates, 1986, c1985. — p. cm. — *Includes index*

MASS MEDIA — Social aspects — Great Britain
WARNOCK, Mary
The social responsibility of the broadcasting media / Mary Warnock. — Liverpool : Liverpool University Press, 1985. — 17p. — (Eleanor Rathbone Memorial Lectures ; no.30)

MASS MEDIA — Social aspects — Great Britain — History — 20th century
Impacts and influences : essays on media power in the twentieth century / edited by James Curran, Anthony Smith and Pauline Wingate. — London : Methuen, 1987. — [350]p. — *Includes index*

MASS MEDIA — Social aspects — Italy
WAGNER-PACIFICI, Robin Erica
The Moro morality play : terrorism as social drama / Robin Erica Wagner-Pacifici. — Chicago : The University of Chicago Press, c1986. — p. cm. — *Includes index. Bibliography: p*

MASS MEDIA — Social aspects — United States
Maincurrents in mass communications / [compiled by] Warren K. Agee, Phillip H. Ault, Edwin Emery. — New York : Harper & Row, c1986. — xiv, 457 p.. — *Rev. ed. of: Perspectives on mass communications. c1982. — Includes bibliographical references and index*

MASS MEDIA — Social aspects — United States — Addresses, essays, lectures
The Media, social science, and social policy for children / Eli A. Rubinstein and Jane D. Brown, editors. — Norwood, N.J. : Ablex Pub. Corp., 1985. — xv, 240 p.. — (Child and family policy ; v. 5). — *Includes bibliographies and indexes*

Public communication campaigns / edited by Ronald E. Rice and William J. Paisley. — Beverly Hills : Sage Publications, c1981. — p. cm. — *Includes indexes. — Bibliography: p. — Contents: Historical and theoretical foundations: Public communication campaigns / William Paisley. Theoretical foundations of campaigns / William McGuire. Mass communicating / Brenda Dervin -- Campaign experiences from the field: Anti-smoking campaigns / Alfred McAlister. Heart disease prevention / Nathan Maccoby and Douglas Solomon. Family planning communication campaigns / Shahnaz Taplin. Communication efforts to prevent wildfires / Troy Kurth, Eugene McNamara, and Donald Hansen. Campaigns to affect energy behavior / Barbara Farhar-Pilgrim and Floyd Shoemaker. Mass media in political campaigns / Steven Chaffee. Mass campaigns in the People's Republic of China / Alan Liu -- Putting theory into practice: Shaping persuasive messages with formative research / Edward Palmer. Evaluation of mass media prevention campaigns / Brian Flay and Thomas Cook. Mass media information campaign effectiveness / Charles Atkin. A social marketing perspective on campaigns / Douglas Solomon*

MASS MEDIA — Study and teaching
MASTERMAN, Len
Teaching the media / by Len Masterman. — London : Comedia, 1985. — xiv,341p. — (Comedia series ; no.26)

MASS MEDIA — Australia — Technological innovations
BROWN, Allan G
Commercial media in Australia : economics, ownership, technology, and regulation / Allan Brown. — St. Lucia ; New York : University of Queensland Press, 1986. — xii, 240 p.. — (University of Queensland Press scholars' library). — *Includes index. — Bibliography: p. [226]-240*

MASS MEDIA — Canada
The media, the courts and the Charter / edited by Philip Anisman and Allen M. Linden. — Toronto : Carswell, 1986. — xiv,521p

WEIMANN, Gabriel
Hate on trial : thr media public opinion in Canada / Gabriel Weimann and Conrad Winn. — Oakville, Ontario : Mosaic Press, 1986. — 201p. — *Includes references*

MASS MEDIA — Canada — Influence
COMBER, Mary Anne
The newsmongers : how the media distort the political news / Mary Anne Comber and Robert S. Mayne. — Toronto : McClelland and Stewart, 1986. — 178p. — *Bibliography: p177-178*

MASS MEDIA — Europe — Bibliography
Mass communications in western Europe : an annotated bibliography = Communication de masse en Europe occidentale : une bibliographie annotée / edited by George Wedell, George-Michael Luyken and Rosemary Leonard ; with a contribution from UNESCO. — Manchester : European Institute for the Media, University of Manchester, [1985]. — xiii,327p. — (Media Monograph ; No.6)

MASS MEDIA — Great Britain
Bending reality : the state of the media / edited by James Curran ... [et al.]. — London : Pluto in association with the Campaign for Press and Broadcasting Freedom, 1986. — 242p

COHEN, Yoel
Media diplomacy : the Foreign Office in the mass communications age / Yoel Cohen. — London : Cass, 1986. — x,197p. — *Bibliography: p184-189. — Includes index*

MASS MEDIA — Great Britain — History — 20th century
ADAMS, Valerie, 1950-
The media and the Falklands campaign / Valerie Adams. — Basingstoke : Macmillan, 1986. — x,224p. — *Bibliography: p214-217. — Includes index*

MASS MEDIA — Québec (Province) — Statistics
Rapport statistique sur les médias Québécois. — Québec : Ministère des communications, 1986. — x,140p. — *Bibliography: p139-140*

MASS MEDIA — Syria — Damascus
Radio listening and exposure to other mass media in Damascus, Syria. — [Washington, D.C.] : United States Information Agency, 1965. — iv,21p. — R-122-65

MASS MEDIA — United States — History — 20th century
BROOKEMAN, Christopher
American culture and society since the 1930s / Christopher Brookeman. — 1st American ed. — New York : Schocken Books, 1984. — xv, 241 p., [8] p. of plates. — *Includes index. — Bibliography: p. 227-233*

MASS MEDIA — United States — Technological innovations
Maincurrents in mass communications / [compiled by] Warren K. Agee, Phillip H. Ault, Edwin Emery. — New York : Harper & Row, c1986. — xiv, 457 p.. — *Rev. ed. of: Perspectives on mass communications. c1982. — Includes bibliographical references and index*

MASS MEDIA — West Bank
SHINAR, Dov
Palestinian voices : communication and nation building in the West Bank / Dov Shinar. — Boulder, Colo. : L. Rienner, 1987. — xi, 211 p. . — *Includes index. — Bibliography: p. 201-202*

MASS MEDIA AND THE ARTS — United States
LYNES, Russell
The lively audience : a social history of American visual and performing arts, 1890-1950 / Russell Lynes. — 1st ed. — New York ; London : Harper and Row, c1985. — x, 489p. — *Includes index. — Bibliography: p.[463]-472*

MASS MEDIA IN EDUCATION
Media, knowledge and power : a reader / edited by Oliver Boyd-Barrett and Peter Braham. — London : Croom Helm in association with the Open University, c1987. — 483p. — *Includes index*

MASS MEDIA POLICY
MERCER, Derrik
The fog of war : the media on the battlefield / by Derrik Mercer, Geoff Mungham, Kevin Williams ; foreword by Sir Tom Hopkinson. — London : Heinemann, 1987. — xvi,413p

MASS MEDIA POLICY — Australia
BROWN, Allan G
Commercial media in Australia : economics, ownership, technology, and regulation / Allan Brown. — St. Lucia ; New York : University of Queensland Press, 1986. — xii, 240 p.. — (University of Queensland Press scholars' library). — *Includes index. — Bibliography: p. [226]-240*

MASS MEDIA SURVEYS
WEDELL, George
Media in competition : the future of print and electronic media in 22 countries / George Wedell and Georg-Michael Luyken ; with contributions by Alberto Cavallari...[et al.]. — Manchester : European Institute for the Media, 1986. — 173p. — (Euromedia Indicator ; No.1). — Includes summaries in French and German

MASS MURDER — United States — Psychological aspects — Case studies
LEYTON, Elliott
Compulsive killers : the story of modern multiple murder / Elliott Leyton. — New York : Washington Mews Books, 1986. — 318 p.. — Bibliography: p. 312-318

MASSEY, VINCENT
BISSELL, Claude
The imperial Canadian : Vincent Massey in office / Claude Bissell. — Toronto ; London : University of Toronto Press, c1986. — xii, 361p, [23]p of plates. — Sequel to: Young Vincent Massey

MATCH INDUSTRY — Sweden — History
HILDEBRAND, Karl-Gustav
Expansion, crisis, reconstruction 1917-1939 / Karl-Gustav Hildebrand ; translation by Michael Callow. — Stockholm : Liber Forlag, 1985. — 496p. — (The Swedish Match Company, 1917-1939. studies in business internationalisation). — Bibliography: p473-484

MATE SELECTION
MURSTEIN, Bernard I
Paths to marriage / by Bernard I. Murstein. — Beverly Hills, Calif. : Sage Publications, c1986. — p. cm. — (Family studies text series ; v. 5). — Includes index

MATERIALISM
MÁRKUS, György
Language and production : a critique of the paradigms / by Gyorgy Markus. — Dordrecht ; Boston : D. Reidel Pub. Co. ; Hingham, MA, U.S.A. : Kluwer Academic Publishers [distributor], c1986. — p. cm. — (Boston studies in the philosophy of science ; v. 96). — Includes indexes. — Bibliography: p

MATERNAL AGE
MERCER, Ramona Thieme
First-time motherhood : experiences from teens to forties / Ramona T. Mercer. — New York : Springer Pub. Co., c1986. — xv, 384 p.. — Includes index. — Bibliography: p. 357-374

MATERNAL AND INFANT WELFARE — Great Britain
FAMILY POLICY STUDIES CENTRE
Dear mother?: maternity payments. — London : Family Policy Studies Centre, 1986. — 13p

MATERNAL HEALTH SERVICES — Developing countries
HERZ, Barbara
The safe motherhood initiative : proposals for action / Barbara Herz, Anthony R. Measham. — Washington, D.C. : The World Bank, 1987. — x,52p. — (World Bank discussion papers ; no.9). — Bibliography: p52

MATERNAL HEALTH SERVICES — England
Racial equality and good practice maternity care : a report of two workshops held in Bradford organised by Training in Health and Race and the Centre for Ethnic Minorities Health Studies / compiled by Maggie Pearson ; Health Education Council and National Extension College for Training in Health and Race. — London : Training in Health and Race, 1985. — 37p — Bibliographical references: p36-37

MATERNITY LEAVE
NATIONAL COUNCIL FOR ONE PARENT FAMILIES
Time-off for child care : evidence to the House of Lords on the European Commission's proposed directive on parental leave and leave for family reasons. — London : National Council for One Parent Families, 1984. — 24p

MATERNITY LEAVE — Great Britain
GREAT BRITAIN. Equal Opportunities Commission
Response to the DHSS consultative document 'A fresh look at maternity benefits'. — Manchester : the Commission, 1980. — 15p

MATFORS PAPPERSBRUK
TÖRNER, Pär
[Matforsrapporten. English]. The Matfors report : experimental activities with changed organization at SCA-Matfors : final report from the reference group / Pär Törner. — Stockholm : Swedish Employers' Confederation, Technical department, 1976. — 107 p.

MATHABANE, MARK
MATHABANE, Mark
Kaffir boy : growing out of apartheid / Mark Mathabane. — London : Pan, 1987. — xii,354p

MATHEMATICAL ABILITY — Great Britain
SMITH, Stuart
Separate tables? : an investigation into single-sex setting in mathematics / Stuart Smith. — London : H.M.S.O., 1986. — (Research series / Equal Opportunities Commission)

MATHEMATICAL ANALYSIS
BAUMOL, William J.
Economic theory and operations analysis / William J. Baumol. — 4th ed. — Englewood Cliffs, N.J : Prentice-Hall, c1977. — xxi, 695 p. — (Prentice-Hall international series in management). — Includes bibliographies and index

MATHEMATICAL MODELS
LAING, Gordon J.
Building scientific models / Gordon J. Laing. — Aldershot : Published in association with the London School of Economics and Political Science by Gower, c1986. — xiii,416p. — Includes index

MATHEMATICAL OPTIMIZATION
BENARD, Jean
Economie publique / Jean Benard. — Paris : Economica, c1985. — 430p. — (Collection "Economie"). — Bibliography: p[401]-414

SENGUPTA, Jatikumar
Stochastic optimization and economic models / Jati K. Sengupta. — Dordrecht ; Boston : D. Reidel ; Norwell, MA, U.S.A. : Sold and distributed in the U.S.A. and Canada by Kluwer Academic, c1986. — x, 373 p.. — (Theory and decision library. Series B. Mathematical and statistical methods). — Includes bibliographies and indexes

MATHEMATICAL OPTIMIZATION — Congresses
UNIVERSITY OF CALIFORNIA, IRVINE, CONFERENCE ON POLITICAL ECONOMY ((2nd : 1983)
Information pooling and group decision making : proceedings of the Second University of California, Irvine, Conference on Political Economy / edited by Bernard Grofman, Guillermo Owen. — Greenwich, Conn. : JAI Press, c1986. — xii, 279 p.. — (Decision research ; v. 2). — Includes index. — Bibliography: p. 231-264

MATHEMATICAL PHYSICS — History
JUNGNICKEL, Christa
Intellectual mastery of nature / Christa Jungnickel and Russell McCormmach. — Chicago : University of Chicago Press, c1986-. — v. < 1 >. — Includes index. — Bibliography: v. 1, p. 311-338. — Contents: v. 1. The torch of mathematics, 1800-1870

MATHEMATICAL STATISTICS
Bayesian inference and decision techniques : essays in honor of Bruno de Finetti / edited by Prem K. Croel [and] Arnold Zellner. — Amsterdam : North Holland, 1986. — 496p. — (Studies in Bayesian econometrics and statistics ; 6)

BEAUMONT, G. P.
Probability and random variables / G.P. Beaumont. — Chichester : Ellis Horwood, 1986. — 345p. — (Ellis Horwood series in mathematics and its applications). — Text on lining papers. — Includes index

CLARKE, G. M.
A basic course in statistics / G.M. Clarke and D. Cooke. — 2nd ed. — London : Edward Arnold, 1983. — xvi,421p. — Previous ed.: 1978. — Bibliography: p391. — Includes index

DACUNHA-CASTELLE, Didier
[Probabilités et statistiques. English]. Probability and statistics / Didier Dacunha-Castelle, Marie Duflo ; translated by David McHale. — New York : Springer-Verlag, c1986-. — p. cm. — 2 vols. — Translation of: Probabilités et statistiques. — Includes index. — Bibliography: v. 1, p

KENDALL, Sir Maurice
Kendall's advanced theory of statistics / originally by Sir Maurice Kendall. — 5th ed / by Alan Stuart and J. Keith Ord. — London : Griffin. — Previous ed.: 1977. — Bibliography: p556-579. — Includes index
Vol.1: Distribution theory. — 1987. — xvi,604p

KYBURG, Henry E.
The logical foundations of statistical inference / by Henry E. Kyburg. — Dordrecht ; Boston : Reidel, 1974. — ix, 427 p.. — (Synthese library ; vol.65). — Includes bibliographical references and index

LINDGREN, Bernard W.
Statistical theory / Bernard W. Lindgren. — 3rd ed. — New York : Macmillan ; London : Collier Macmillan, 1976. — xv,614p. — Previous ed.: 1968. — Bibliography: p.569-570. — Includes index

MOOD, Alexander M.
Introduction to the theory of statistics / Alexander M. Mood, Franklin A. Graybill [and] Duane C. Boes. — 3rd ed. — New York ; London : McGraw-Hill, 1974. — 564 p. — (McGraw-Hill series in probability and statistics). — Previous ed. by A.M. Mood and F.A. Graybill : New York ; London : McGraw-Hill, 1963

SILVEY, S. D.
Statistical inference / S.D. Silvey. — [1st ed.], reprinted with corrections. — London : Chapman and Hall, 1975. — 3-192p. — (Monographs on applied probability and statistics). — Originally published: Harmondsworth : Penguin, 1970. — Bibliography: p.189-190. — Includes index

Statistical science: a review journal of the institute of mathematical statistics. — Hayward, Calif., : Institute of Mathematical Statistics, 1986-. — Quarterly

MATHEMATICAL STATISTICS — Addresses, essays, lectures
A Festschrift for Erich L. Lehmann in honor of his sixty-fifth birthday / editors, Peter J. Bickel, Kjell A. Doksum, J.L. Hodges, Jr. — Belmont, Calif. : Wadsworth International Group, c1983. — vii, 461 p.. — (Wadsworth statistics/probability series). — Bibliography of works by E.L. Lehmann: p. [456]-461. — Includes bibliographies

MATHEMATICAL STATISTICS — Collected works
KIEFER, Jack
[Works. 1984]. Jack Carl Kiefer collected papers / edited by Lawrence D. Brown ... [et al.]. — New York : Springer-Verlag, c1985-c1986. — 4 v.. — "Published with the co-operation of the Institute of Mathematical Statistics.". — Includes bibliographies. — Contents: 1. Statistical inference and probability, 1951-1963 -- 2. Statistical inference and probability, 1964-1984 -- 3. Design of experiments -- [4] Supplementary volume

MATHEMATICAL STATISTICS — Dictionaries
Encyclopedia of statistical sciences / [editors-in-chief Samuel Kotz, Norman L. Johnson] ; [associate editor Campbell B. Read]. — New York ; Chichester : Wiley
Vol.6: Multivariate analysis to Plackett and Burman designs. — c1985. — x,758p. — Includes bibliographies

MATHEMATICS
BUDNICK, Frank S.
Applied mathematics : for business, economics, and the social sciences / Frank S. Budnick. — 2nd ed. — New York ; London : McGraw-Hill, c1983. — xviii,769,[67]p. — Previous ed.: 1979. — Text on lining papers. — Includes index

MATHEMATICS — Collected works
MAGIROS, Demetrios G
[Selections. 1985]. Selected papers of Demetrios C. Magiros : applied mathematics, nonlinear mechanics, and dynamical systems analysis / edited by S.G. Tzafestas. — Dordrecht, Holland : D. Reidel Pub. Co. ; Hingham, MA, U.S.A. : Sold and distributed in the U.S.A. and Canada by Kluwer Academic Publishers, c1985. — xv, 518 p.. — "Published on behalf of the Greek Mathematical Society.". — Bibliography: p. 511-518

MATHEMATICS — Computer-assisted instruction
PAPERT, Saymour
Mindstorms : children, computers, and powerful ideas / Seymour Papert. — New York : Basic Books ; Brighton, Sussex : Harvester Press, c1980. — p. cm. — (Harvester studies in cognitive science ; 14). — Includes bibliographical references and index

MATHEMATICS — Dictionaries
[Iwanami sūgaku jiten. English]. Encyclopedic dictionary of mathematics / by the Mathematical Society of Japan ; edited by Kiyosi Itô. — 3rd ed. — Cambridge, Mass. : MIT Press, c1986. — p. cm. — Translation of: Iwanami sūgaku jiten. — Includes bibliographies and indexes

MATHEMATICS — History
SHANKER, S. G.
Wittgenstein and the turning point in the philosophy of mathematics / S. G. Shanker. — London : Croom Helm, c1986. — [320]p. — Includes bibliography and index

MATHEMATICS — Indexes
CMCI compumath citation index. — Philadelphia : Institute for Scientific Information, 1985. — Annual

MATHEMATICS — Popular works
STEWART, Ian, 1945-
The problems of mathematics / Ian Stewart. — Oxford : Oxford University Press, 1987. — [224]p. — (OPUS). — Bibliography: p235-246. — Includes index

MATHEMATICS — 1961-
LIAL, Margaret L
Mathematics with applications in the management, natural, and social sciences / Margaret L. Lial, Charles D. Miller. — 3rd ed. — Glenview, Ill. : Scott, Foresman, c1983. — 690 p.. — Includes bibliographical references and index

MATLAB (BANGLADESH) — Population — Statistics
BECKER, Stan
A validation study of backward and forward pregnancy histories in Matlab, Bangladesh / Stan Becker, Simeen Mahmud. — Voorburg : International Statistical Institute, 1984. — 37p. — (Scientific reports / World Fertility Survey ; no.52)

MATRIARCHY — Caribbean Area
ABBAS, Ibrahim
The proximate determinants of fertility in North Sudan / Ibrahim Abbas, I. Kalule—Sabiti. — Voorburg : International Statistical Institute, 1985. — 35p. — (Scientific reports / World Fertility Survey ; no.73)

MATRIARCHY — Nigeria
AMADIUME, Ifi
Afrikan matriarchal foundations : the Igbo case / Ifi Amadiume. — London : Karnak House, 1987. — [120]p. — Includes bibliography

MATRICES
BRADLEY, Ian
Matrices and society / Ian Bradley and Ronald L. Meek. — Princeton, N.J. : Princeton University Press, 1986. — p. cm. — Bibliography: p

MATRIMONIAL ACTIONS — England
JACKSON, Joseph
Jackson's matrimonial finance and taxation. — 4th ed. / by Joseph Jackson and D.T.A. Davies. — London : Butterworths, 1986. — 1v. . — Previous ed.: 1980. — Includes index

MATRIMONIAL AND FAMILY PROCEEDINGS BILL 1983-84
GREAT BRITAIN. Parliament. House of Commons. Library. Research Division
Matrimonial and Family Proceedings Bill (H.L.) 1983-4 [Bill 96] / [Patrick Nealon]. — [London] : the Division, 1984. — 11p. — (Research note ; no.141)

MATRIX INVERSION
CHUANG, Min Hwei
A sparse matrix implementation of the simplex method : its application to a class of combinatorial optimization problems / by Chuang Min Hwei. — 210 leaves. — PhD (Econ) 1986 LSE

MATTEI, ENRICO
BAZZOLI, Luigi
Il miracolo Mattei / Luigi Bazzoli & Riccardo Renzi. — Milano : Rizzoli, 1984. — 258p. — Bibliography: p251-2

MAU MAU — History
KANOGO, Tabitha
Squatters and the roots of Mau Mau / Tabitha Kanogo. — London : Currey, 1987. — [224]p. — (East African studies). — Includes bibliography and index

MAUPITI (SOCIETY ISLANDS) — Population — Statistics
Tableaux normalisés du recensement général de la population : 15 octobre 1983. — [Papeete] : Institut territorial de la statistique
Résultats de la commune de Maupiti. — [1985?]. — 4p,11 leaves

MAURA Y MONTANER, ANTONIO
TUSELL GOMEZ, Javier
La derecha española contemporánea : sus orígenes: el maurismo / Javier Tusell, Juan Avilés. — Madrid : Espasa Calpe, 1986. — 376p. — Bibliography: p371-376

MAURÍN, JOAQUÍN
MONREAL, Antoni
El pensamiento político de Joaquín Maurín / Antoni Monreal. — [Barcelona] : Península, [1984]. — 204p. — (Historia, ciencia sociedad ; 190)

MAURITANIA — History — Dictionaries
GERTEINY, Alfred G
Historical dictionary of Mauritania / by Alfred G. Gerteiny. — Metuchen, N.J. : Scarecrow Press, 1981. — xv, 98 p.. — (African historical dictionaries ; no. 31). — Bibliography: p. 83-98

MAURITIUS — Census, 1983
1983 housing and population census of Mauritius. — [Rose Hill] : Central Statistical Office, 1984-85. — 6v

1983 housing and population census of Mauritius : analysis report. — Rose Hill : Central Statistical Office
vol.2: Education: characteristics, prospects and some implications : (Island of Mauritius). — 1986. — 57p

1983 housing and population census of Mauritius : analysis report. — Rose Hill : Central Statistical Office
vol. 3: Households and housing needs: estimates and implications : (Island of Mauritius). — 1986. — 67p

1983 Housing and population census of Mauritius. — Rose Hill : Central Statistical Office
Analysis report
Volume 1: Evaluation of data. — 1985. — 76p

MAURITIUS — History — Dictionaries
RIVIÈRE, Lindsay
Historical dictionary of Mauritius / by Lindsay Riviere. — Metuchen, N.J. : Scarecrow Press, 1982. — xxxiv, 172 p.. — (African historical dictionaries ; no. 34). — Bibliography: p. 141-172

MAURITIUS — Population — Statistics
1983 housing and population census of Mauritius : analysis report. — Rose Hill : Central Statistical Office
vol.2: Education: characteristics, prospects and some implications : (Island of Mauritius). — 1986. — 57p

1983 housing and population census of Mauritius : analysis report. — Rose Hill : Central Statistical Office
vol. 3: Households and housing needs: estimates and implications : (Island of Mauritius). — 1986. — 67p

1983 Housing and population census of Mauritius. — Rose Hill : Central Statistical Office
Analysis report
Volume 1: Evaluation of data. — 1985. — 76p

MAURRAS, CHARLES
FESSARD DE FOUCAULT, Bertrand
Charles Maurras et le socialisme / Bertrand Fessard de Foucault. — [Paris : Royaliste, ca.1984]. — 296p. — (Collection lys rouge). — Bibliography: p290

MAUS, HEINZ — Bibliography
KAESTNER, Jürgen
Personalbibliographie Heinz Maus (1911-1978) : ein Beitrag zur Geschichte der deutschen Soziologie / Jürgen Kaestner. — Berlin : Wissenschaftlicher Autoren-Verlag (WAV), 1984. — 80p

MAUSS, MARCEL
LÉVI-STRAUSS, Claude
Introduction to the work of Marcel Mauss / Claude Lévi-Strauss ; translated by Felicity Baker. — London : Routledge & Kegan Paul, 1987. — [50]p. — Translation of: Introduction à l'œuvre de Marcel Mauss. — Includes bibliography and index

MAXIMA AND MINIMNA
TIKHOMIROV, V. M.
Fundamental principles of the theory of extremal problems / by Vladimir M. Tikhomirov ; translated by Bernd Luderer. — Chichester : Wiley, 1986. — 136p. — Translation of: Grundprinzien der Theorie der Extremalaufgaben. — Bibliography: p127-132. — Includes index

MAXIMOFF, GREGORI PETROVICH
MAXIMOFF, Gregory Petrovich
"My social credo" / G. P. Maximoff. — Sydney : Monty Miller Press, 1983. — 15p. — (Rebel worker pamphlet ; 3). — Translated into English by H. Frank it appeared in the book Constructive Anarchism by Maximoff, published by the 'Maximoff Memorial Publishing Committee'

MAXTON, JAMES
BROWN, Gordon, 1951-
Maxton / by Gordon Brown. — Edinburgh : Mainstream, 1986. — 335p,[8]p of plates. — Includes index

MAXWELL, ROBERT, 1923-
Malice in Wonderland : Robert Maxwell v. Private Eye / reported by John Jackson ; introduced and with an epilogue by Robert Maxwell ; edited by Joe Haines and Peter Donnelly ; cartoons by Charles Griffin and David Langdon. — London : Macdonald, 1986. — 191p

MAY, SOMETH
MAY, Someth
Cambodian witness : the autobiography of Someth May / edited and with an introduction by James Fenton. — London : Faber, 1986. — [300]p

MAY DAY (LABOR HOLIDAY) — United States — History
FONER, Philip S.
May Day : a short history of the international workers' holiday 1886-1986 / by Philip S. Foner. — New York : International Publishers, 1986. — 184p

MAYDAY
REPIN, Anatoly
Haymarket heritage : on centenary of Chicago events in May 1886 / Anatoly Repin. — [S.l.] : [s.n.], 1986. — 13p

MAYER, HENRY — Bibliography
GOOT, Murray
Henry Mayer's "Immortal works" : scholarly, semi-scholarly and nor very scholarly at all : a descriptive bibliography, with index, 1940-1985 / Murray Goot. — Canberra, A.C.T. : Australian National University for the Australasian Political Studies Association, 1986. — 245p

MAYORS — United States
FERMAN, Barbara
Governing the ungovernable city : political skill, leadership, and the modern mayor / Barbara Ferman. — Philadelphia : Temple University Press, 1985. — p. cm. — Includes index. — Bibliography: p

MBERE (AFRICAN PEOPLE) — Land tenure
GLAZIER, Jack
Land and the uses of tradition among the Mbere of Kenya / Jack Glazier. — Lanham : University Press of America, c1985. — xiii, 334 p.. — Includes index. — Bibliography: p. 315-330

MBERE (AFRICAN PEOPLE) — Social conditions
GLAZIER, Jack
Land and the uses of tradition among the Mbere of Kenya / Jack Glazier. — Lanham : University Press of America, c1985. — xiii, 334 p.. — Includes index. — Bibliography: p. 315-330

MEAD, GEORGE HERBERT
BALDWIN, John D.
George Herbert Mead : a unifying theory for sociology / by John D. Baldwin. — Beverly Hills, Calif. : Sage Publications, c1986. — 168p. — (Masters of social theory ; v. 6). — Includes index. — Bibliography: p.165-168

MEAD, GEORGE HERBERT, 1863-1931
ABOULAFIA, Mitchell
The mediating self : Mead, Sartre, and self-determination / Mitchell Aboulafia. — New Haven : Yale University Press, c1986. — xvii, 139p. — Includes index. — Bibliography: p.127-131

MEANING (PHILOSOPHY)
ALLAN, Keith
Linguistic meaning / Keith Allan. — London ; New York : Routledge & Kegan Paul, 1986. — 2v.

DESCOMBES, Vincent
Objects of all sorts : a philosophical grammar / Vincent Descombes ; translated by Lorna Scott-Fox and Jeremy Harding. — Oxford : Basil Blackwell, 1986. — [350]p. — Translation of: Grammaire d'objets en tous genres

MEANING (PSYCHOLOGY)
JAFFE, Aniela
The myth of meaning in the work of C. G. Jung / Aniela Jaffe ; translated [from the German] by R. F. C. Hull. — Zürich : Daimon, [1984]. — 186p. — Bibliography: p179-186

NELSON, Katherine
Making sense : the acquisition of shared meaning / Katherine Nelson. — Orlando [Fla.] : Academic Press, 1985. — p. cm. — Includes index

WAGNER, Roy
Symbols that stand for themselves / Roy Wagner. — Chicago : University of Chicago Press, 1986. — p. cm. — Sequel to: The invention of culture. — Includes index. — Bibliography: p

MEAT INDUSTRY AND TRADE — Statistics
Meat balances in OECD countries = Bilans de la viande dans les pays de l'OCDE / Organisation for Economic Co-operation and Development. — Paris : OECD, 1986-. — Irregular. — text in English and French

MEAT INDUSTRY AND TRADE — Australia
AUSTRALIA. Bureau of Agricultural Economics
Meat: situation and outlook. — Canberra : [the Bureau], 1972-1980. — Annual. — Continues: Australia. Bureau of Agricultural Economics: Beef situation and Mutton and Lamb situation

MECCA (SAUDI ARABIA) — Commerce — History
CRONE, Patricia
Meccan trade and the rise of Islam / Patricia Crone. — Princeton, N.J. : Princeton University Press, c1986. — vii, 300p. — Includes index. — Bibliography: p.271-291

MECHANICAL ENGINEERS — Germany — Biography
THOMAS, Donald E.
Diesel : technology and society in industrial Germany / Donald E. Thomas, Jr. — Tuscaloosa, Ala. : University of Alabama Press, c1987. — xii, 279 p.. — Includes index. — Bibliography: p. 262-267

MEDIATION
MOORE, Christopher W.
The mediation process : practical strategies for resolving conflict / Christopher W. Moore. — 1st ed. — San Francisco : Jossey-Bass, 1986. — p. cm. — (The Jossey-Bass social and behavioral science series). — Includes index. — Bibliography: p

MEDIATION — Delaware
BEER, Jennifer E.
Peacemaking in your neighborhood : reflections on an experiment in community mediation / Jennifer E. Beer ; foreword by Elise Boulding. — Philadelphia, Pa. : New Society, 1986. — [viii],245p. — Bibliography: p[235]-245

MEDIATION AND CONCILIATION, INDUSTRIAL
Conciliation services : structures, functions and techniques. — Geneva : International Labour Office, 1983. — 141p. — (Labour-management relations series ; 62)

MAGGIOLO, Walter A.
Techniques of mediation / by Walter A. Maggiolo. — New York : Oceana Publications, c1985. — xviii, 458 p.. — Includes index. — Bibliography: p. 319-333

MEDIATION AND CONCILIATION, INDUSTRIAL — European Economic Community countries
The prevention and settlement of industrial conflict in the Community member states. — Luxembourg : Office for Official Publications of the European Communities, 1984. — 162,16p. — At head of title page: Commission of the European Communities

MEDIATION AND CONCILIATION, INDUSTRIAL — Great Britain
GRAHAM, Cosmo
The role of ACAS conciliation in equal pay and sex discrimination cases / Cosmo Graham, Norman Lewis ; [for the] Equal Opportunities in Commission. — Manchester : Equal Opportunities Commission, 1985. — 70p. — Bibliographical references: p69-70

MEDIATION AND CONCILIATION, INDUSTRIAL — United States
MAGGIOLO, Walter A.
Techniques of mediation / by Walter A. Maggiolo. — New York : Oceana Publications, c1985. — xviii, 458 p.. — Includes index. — Bibliography: p. 319-333

MEDIATION, INTERNATIONAL
ASSEFA, Hizkias
Mediation of civil wars / Hizkias Assefa. — Boulder, Colo. : Westview Press, 1986. — p. cm. — (Westview special studies in peace, conflict, and conflict resolution). — Includes index. — Bibliography: p

CURLE, Adam
In the middle : non-official mediation in violent situations / Adam Curle. — Leamington Spa : Berg, 1986. — [56]p. — (Bradford peace studies papers. New series ; no.1). — Includes bibliography

MEDICAID
SORKIN, Alan L
Health care and the changing economic environment / Alan L. Sorkin. — Lexington, Mass. : Lexington Books, c1986. — xiv, 161 p.. — Includes bibliographies and index

MEDICAID — United States
FEIN, Rashi
Medical care, medical costs : the search for a health insurance policy / Rashi Fein. — Cambridge, Mass. : Harvard University Press, 1986. — viii, 240 p.. — Includes index

MEDICAL ANTHROPOLOGY — Thailand
GOLOMB, Louis
An anthropology of curing in multiethnic Thailand / Louis Golomb. — Urbana : University of Illinois Press, c1985. — p. cm. — (Illinois studies in anthropology ; no. 15). — Includes index. — Bibliography: p

MEDICAL ASSISTANCE, SWISS — Nepal
ACHARD, Thomas
Primary health care in the hills of Nepal / Thomas Achard. — Kathmandu, Nepal : Integrated Hill Development Project, HMG/SATA, 1983. — 105p. — Bibliography: p104-105

MEDICAL ASSISTANCE, TITLE 19 — history
FEIN, Rashi
Medical care, medical costs : the search for a health insurance policy / Rashi Fein. — Cambridge, Mass. : Harvard University Press, 1986. — viii, 240 p.. — Includes index

MEDICAL CARE

HERZLICH, Claudine
Health and illness : a social psychological analysis / Claudine Herzlich ; translated [from the French] by Douglas Graham. — London : Academic Press [for] the European Association of Experimental Social Psychology, 1973. — xvi,159p. — (European monographs in social psychology ; 5). — *Translation of: 'Santé et maladie'. Paris : Mouton, 1970. — Bibliography: p.151-154. — Includes index*

LE GRAND, Julian
An international comparison of inequalities in health / Julian Le Grand. — London : Suntory-Toyota International Centre for Economics and Related Disciplines, 1987. — 31p. — (Welfare State Programme ; no.16). — *Bibliography: p30-31*

Public and private health services : complementarities and conflicts / edited by A.J. Culyer and Bengt Jönsson. — Oxford, Basil Blackwell, 1986. — 242p. — *Includes bibliographies and index*

MEDICAL CARE — Congresses

Good health at low cost : proceedings of a conference held at the Bellagio Conference Center, Bellagio, Italy, April 29-May 3, 1985, sponsored by the Rockefeller Foundation / editors: Scott B. Halstead, Julia A. Walsh, Kenneth S. Warren. — New York : Rockefeller Foundation, 1985. — 248p

MEDICAL CARE — Cost effectiveness

MCGUIRE, Alistair
The economics of health care : an introductory text / Alistair McGuire, John Henderson and Gavin Mooney. — London : Routledge & Kegan Paul, 1988. — x,286p. — (International library of economics). — *Bibliography: p261-279. — Includes index*

MEDICAL CARE — Cost effectiveness — Congresses

The Price of health / edited by George J. Agich and Charles E. Begley. — Dordrecht ; Boston : D. Reidel Pub. Co. ; Hingham, MA, U.S.A. : Sold and distributed in the U.S.A. and Canada by Kluwer Academic Publishers, c1987. — p. cm. — (Philosophy and medicine ; v. 21). — *Based on a conference entitled "The price of health: economics and ethics in medicine," held at the School of Public Health, University of Texas Health Science Center, Houston, Tex., June 24-26, 1985. — Includes bibliographies and index*

MEDICAL CARE — Cross-cultural studies

GRIFFITH, Ben
Banking on sickness : commercial medicine in Britain and the USA / Ben Griffith, Steve Iliffe and Geof Rayner. — London : Lawrence and Wishart, 1987. — 287p

MEDICAL CARE — Economic aspects — Great Britain

GRIFFITH, Ben
Banking on sickness : commercial medicine in Britain and the USA / Ben Griffith, Steve Iliffe and Geof Rayner. — London : Lawrence and Wishart, 1987. — 287p

MEDICAL CARE — Economic aspects — United States

GRIFFITH, Ben
Banking on sickness : commercial medicine in Britain and the USA / Ben Griffith, Steve Iliffe and Geof Rayner. — London : Lawrence and Wishart, 1987. — 287p

MEDICAL CARE — Social aspects

Health and disease : a reader / edited by Nick Black ... [et al.]. — Milton Keynes : Open University Press, c1984. — xii,371p. — *Includes bibliographies and index*

MEDICAL CARE — Africa — Addresses, essays, lectures

Biomedical lectures / Contributors; A. Quenum...[et al.]. — Brazzaville : Regional Office for Africa, World Health Organization, 1972. — 83p. — (AFRO technical papers ; no.4). — *Cover title: 1970-1971 series. — Includes bibliographies*

Biomedical lectures / Contributors; P. Correa...[et al.]. — Brazzaville : Regional Office for Africa, World Health Organization, 1975. — 69p. — (AFRO technical papers ; no.11). — *Cover title: 1970-1973 series. — Includes bibliographical references*

Biomedical lectures / Contributors; A. M. Wright...[et al.]. — Brazzaville : Regional Office for Africa, World Health Organization, 1978. — 53p. — (AFRO technical papers ; no.13). — *Cover title: 1976-1977 series. — Includes bibliographical references*

MEDICAL CARE — Albania

CIKULI, Zisa
Health service in the People's Socialist Republic of Albania / Zisa Cikuli. — Tirana : 8 Nentori Publishing House, 1984. — 88p

MEDICAL CARE — Canada

Health and Canadian society : sociological perspectives / [edited by David] Coburn...[et al.]. — 2nd ed. — [Markham, Ontario] : Fitzhenry & Whiteside, 1987. — vii,670p. — *Includes references*

Medicare at maturity : achievements, lessons & challenges / edited by Robert G. Evans and Greg L. Stoddart. — Calgary : University of Calgary Press, 1986. — xiii,480p. — *Taken from the Proceedings of the Health Policy Conference on Canada's National Health Care System : 1984 : Banff Centre, School of Management (Alberta)*

MEDICAL CARE — Canada — Finance

WHITFIELD, Dexter
Private health care dossier : fines, failures and illegal practices in North America : the implications for health care in Britain / Dexter Whitfield. — London : NUPE/SCAT, 1985. — 18p

MEDICAL CARE — China

China, the health sector / Dean T. Jamison ... [et al.]. — Washington, D.C., U.S.A. : World Bank, 1984. — xl,190p. — (A World Bank country study). — *Six folded maps tipped in. — Includes bibliographical references*

MEDICAL CARE — Denmark

National Health Security Act, 1975. — Copenhagen : Ministry of Social Affairs, [1975]. — 14 leaves

The Public Health Security Act, 1971. — [Copenhagen : Sundhedsstyrelsen?], 1971. — 15 leaves

MEDICAL CARE — Developing countries — Finance

AKIN, John S.
Financing health services in developing countries / [prepared by John Akin, Nancy Birdsall and David de Ferranti]. — Washington, D.C. : The World Bank, 1987. — vi,93p. — *Bibliography: p85-93*

MEDICAL CARE — Developing countries — Finance — Evaluation

MACH, E. P
Planning the finances of the health sector : a manual for developing countries / by E.P. Mach, B. Abel-Smith. — Geneva : World Health Organization, 1983. — 124p. — *Bibliography: p105-106*

MEDICAL CARE — England

GREAT BRITAIN. Department of Health and Social Security
Priorities for health and personal social services in England : a consultative document / Department of Health and Social Security. — London : H.M.S.O., 1976. — iv,83p

TOWNSEND, Peter
Inequalities in health in the northern region : an interim report / Peter Townsend, Peter Phillimore [and] Alastair Beattie. — Bristol : University of Bristol ; Newcastle upon Tyne : Northern Regional Health Authority, 1986. — 252p. — *Bibliography: p245-252*

MEDICAL CARE — Europe — Needs assessment

Health projections in Europe : Methods and applications. — Copenhagen : World Health Organization, Regional Office for Europe, 1986. — xxi,306p. — *Includes bibliographical references*

MEDICAL CARE — European Economic Community countries — Cost control

ABEL-SMITH, Brian
Cost containment in health care : the experience of 12 European countries 1977-83 / by Brian Abel-Smith. — Luxembourg : Office for Official Publications of the European Communities, 1984. — 148p

MEDICAL CARE — European Economic Community countries — Finance

ABEL-SMITH, Brian
Cost containment in health care : the experience of 12 European countries 1977-83 / by Brian Abel-Smith. — Luxembourg : Office for Official Publications of the European Communities, 1984. — 148p

MEDICAL CARE — France — Nomenclature

FRANCE. Ministerè des Affaires Sociales et de la Solidarité Nationale. Service des Statistiques, des Etudes et des Systèmes d'Information
Nomenclatures applicables aux unités de production des éstablissements sanitaires, sociaux et médico-sociaux et aux prestations qui y sont servies : période de validité: exercice 1986. — [Paris] : Ministère des Affaires Sociales et de la Solidarité Nationale, SESI, 1986. — 194p. — (Solidarité santé. Cahiers statistiques ; no.7 bis)

MEDICAL CARE — France — Utilization — Statistics

CHARRAUD, Alain
Disparités de consommation médicale : enquête santé 1980-1981 / par Alain Charraud et Pierre Mormiche. — [Paris] : I.N.S.E.E., 1986. — 135p. — (Les collections de l'INSEE. Série M. Ménages ; no.118)

MEDICAL CARE — Great Britain

CARR-HILL, R. A.
Health status, resource allocation and socio-economic conditions (interim report of health needs research study) / Roy A. Carr-Hill. — rev. ed. — York : University of York. Centre for Health Economics, 1987. — xii,93p. — *Bibliography: p86-93*

CULYER, A. J.
Health service ills : the wrong economic medicine / A. J. Culyer. — York : University of York, Centre for Health Economics, 1986. — 13p. — (Discussion paper / University of York. Centre for Health Economics ; 16)

EYLES, John
The geography of the national health : an essay in welfare geography / John Eyles. — London : Croom Helm, c1987. — [256]p. — *Includes bibliography and index*

GREAT BRITAIN. Working Party on Under-Doctored Areas
Draft report. — [London : Department of Health and Social Security], 1979. — [11]p

ILSLEY, Raymond
Measurement of inequality in health / Raymond Ilsley and Julian Le Grand. — London : Suntory Toyota International Centre for Economics and Related Disciplines, 1987. — 29p. — (Welfare State Programme ; no.12). — *Bibliography: p[32-33]*

LABOUR PARTY (Great Britain)
The best of health : charter for the family health service. — London : Labour Party, 1986. — 15p

LIBERAL PARTY
Freedom in sickness and in health. — Hebden Bridge : Liberal Party Publications, 1986. — 20p. — (Liberal Party health panel papers ; no.18)

MEDICAL CARE — Great Britain
continuation

LIBERAL PARTY
Health care in the inner cities. — Hebden Bridge : Hebden Royd Publications, 1986. — 12p. — (Liberal Party Health panel papers ; no.15)

MEDICAL CARE — Great Britain — Bibliography

PRICE, C. J.
Selected references on health care in inner cities (1974-1978) / compiled by C. J. Price. — London : Department of Health and Social Security Library, 1979. — 3p. — (Bibliography series / Department of Health and Social Security Library ; no.B121)

MEDICAL CARE — Great Britain — Citizen participation

RICHARDSON, Ann
Promoting health through participation : experience of groups for patient participation in general practice / Ann Richardson [and] Caroline Bray. — London : Policy Studies Institute, 1987. — 78p. — (Research report / Policy Studies Institute ; 659). — *Bibliography: p77-78*

MEDICAL CARE — Great Britain — Finance

WHITFIELD, Dexter
Private health care dossier : fines, failures and illegal practices in North America : the implications for health care in Britain / Dexter Whitfield. — London : NUPE/SCAT, 1985. — 18p

MEDICAL CARE — Great Britain — History

HOLLINGSWORTH, J. Rogers
A political economy of medicine : Great Britain and the United States / J. Rogers Hollingsworth. — Baltimore : Johns Hopkins University Press, c1986. — xix, 312 p.. — *Includes index. — Bibliography: p. 275-303*

MEDICAL CARE — Great Britain — Statistics

STATISTICS USERS CONFERENCE (1980)
Health statistics in Britain : proceedings of the 1980 Statistics Users Conference; arranged by the Society for Social Medicine on behalf of the Standing Committee of Statistics Users. — Newcastle upon Tyne : University of Newcastle upon Tyne. Health Care Research Unit, 1980. — [96]p

MEDICAL CARE — Ireland

DELAP, Ruth
The development of public policy for the medical care of the physically ill in Ireland, 1900-1970 / by Ruth Delap. — 425 leaves. — *PhD (Econ) 1986 LSE*

MEDICAL CARE — New York (N.Y.) — History

GINZBERG, Eli
From health dollars to health services : New York City, 1965-1985 / Eli Ginzberg and the Conservation of Human Resources staff. — Totowa, N.J. : Rowman & Allanheld, c1986. — xii, 163 p.. — ([Conservation of human resources series ; 25]) (Land Mark studies). — *First series from jacket. — Includes index. — Bibliography: p. [155]*

MEDICAL CARE — Scotland — History — 20th century

Improving the common weal : aspects of Scottish health services 1900-1984 / edited by Gordon McLachlan. — [Edinburgh] : Edinburgh University Press for the Nuffield Provincial Hospitals Trust, c1987. — xviii,635p . — *Includes index*

MEDICAL CARE — Switzerland

PARTI LIBÉRAL SUISSE
Pour une politique libérale de la santé : rapport dúne commission d´étude du Parti libéral suisse. — Berne : Parti Libéral Suisse, 1977. — 15p

MEDICAL CARE — Tanzania — History

TURSHEN, Meredeth
The political ecology of disease in Tanzania / Meredeth Turshen. — New Brunswick, N.J. : Rutgers University Press, c1984. — xiv, 259 p., [2] leaves of plates. — *Includes index. — Bibliography: p. 211-239*

MEDICAL CARE — United States

GINZBERG, Eli
American medicine : the power shift / Eli Ginzberg. — Totowa, N.J. : Rowman & Allanheld, 1985. — xv, 207 p.. — *Includes index. — Bibliography: p. [194]-199*

MEDICAL CARE — United States — Congresses

CORNELL UNIVERSITY MEDICAL COLLEGE CONFERENCE ON HEALTH POLICY (1985 : New York, N.Y.)
The U.S. health care system : a look to the 1990s / Cornell University Medical College Conference on Health Policy, March 7-8, 1985, New York City ; Eli Ginzberg, editor. — Totowa, N.J. : Rowman & Allanheld, 1985. — x, 133 p.. — (Conservation of human resources series ; 26) (Land Mark studies). — *Includes index. — Bibliography: p. 115-123*

MEDICAL CARE — United States — Cost effectiveness

CALIFANO, Joseph A.
America's health care revolution : who lives? who dies? who pays? / Joseph A. Califano, Jr. — 1st ed. — New York : Random House, c1986. — x, 241 p.. — *Includes index. — Bibliography: p. [227]-230*

MEDICAL CARE — United States — Finance

JONES, Tom, 1946-
Money medics and management : the English and American systems compared / Tom Jones, Colin Kerr. — London : Certified Accountants Educational Trust, c1986. — [120]p. — *Bibliography: p99. — Includes index*

WHITFIELD, Dexter
Private health care dossier : fines, failures and illegal practices in North America : the implications for health care in Britain / Dexter Whitfield. — London : NUPE/SCAT, 1985. — 18p

MEDICAL CARE — United States — History

HOLLINGSWORTH, J. Rogers
A political economy of medicine : Great Britain and the United States / J. Rogers Hollingsworth. — Baltimore : Johns Hopkins University Press, c1986. — xix, 312 p.. — *Includes index. — Bibliography: p. 275-303*

MEDICAL CARE — Wales

A review of the health services - Wales 1974-75. — [Cardiff : Welsh Office, 1975?]. — 63leaves

MEDICAL CARE, COST OF — Organisation for Economic Co-operation and Development countries — Statistics

SCHIEBER, George J.
Financing and delivering health care : a comparative analysis of OECD countries / [George J. Schieber]. — Paris : Organisation for Economic Co-operation and Development, 1987. — 101p. — (Social policy studies / Organisation for Economic Co-operation and Development ; no.4). — *Includes bibliographical references*

MEDICAL CARE, COST OF — United States

CALIFANO, Joseph A.
America's health care revolution : who lives? who dies? who pays? / Joseph A. Califano, Jr. — 1st ed. — New York : Random House, c1986. — x, 241 p.. — *Includes index. — Bibliography: p. [227]-230*

FEIN, Rashi
Medical care, medical costs : the search for a health insurance policy / Rashi Fein. — Cambridge, Mass. : Harvard University Press, 1986. — viii, 240 p.. — *Includes index*

MEDICAL CENTERS — Government policy — England — Lancashire

LANCASHIRE AREA HEALTH AUTHORITY
Health centres : policy on provision, staffing, charges and allied matters / [D. S. Parken]. — [S.l.] : the Authority, [1976]. — 11p

MEDICAL CENTERS — London (England) — Peckham

PEARSE, Innes H.
The Peckham experiment : a study of the living structure of society / by Innes H. Pearse [and] Lucy H. Crocker. — Edinburgh : Scottish Academic Press, 1985. — xxx,333p. — *First published by Allen and Unwin in 1943*

MEDICAL ECONOMICS

CULLIS, John G
The economics of health : an introduction / John G. Cullis & Peter A. West. — New York : New York University Press, 1979. — ix, 309 p.. — *Includes bibliographical references and indexes*

DRUMMOND, M. F.
Methods for the economic evaluation of health care programmes / Michael F. Drummond, Greg L. Stoddart, George W. Torrance. — Oxford : Oxford University Press, 1987. — x,182p. — (Oxford medical publications). — *Includes bibliographies and index*

EVANS, Robert G.
Strained mercy : the economics of Canadian health care / Robert G. Evans. — Toronto : Butterworths, c1984. — xvi, 390 p.. — *Includes index. — Bibliography: p. 355-363*

GRIFFITH, Ben
Banking on sickness : commercial medicine in Britain and the USA / Ben Griffith, Steve Iliffe and Geof Rayner. — London : Lawrence and Wishart, 1987. — 287p

Health economics : prospects for the future / edited by George Teeling Smith. — London : Croom Helm, c1987. — x,278p. — *Includes bibliographies and index*

JACOBS, Philip
The economics of health and medical care / Philip Jacobs. — 2nd ed. — Rockville, Md. : Aspen Publishers, c1986. — p. cm. — *Includes index. — Bibliography: p*

Journal of health economics. — Amsterdam : North-Holland, 1986-. — *3 times per year*

MCGUIRE, Alistair
The economics of health care : an introductory text / Alistair McGuire, John Henderson and Gavin Mooney. — London : Routledge & Kegan Paul, 1988. — x,286p. — (International library of economics). — *Bibliography: p261-279. — Includes index*

MEDICAL ECONOMICS — Addresses, essays, lectures

FUCHS, Victor R
The health economy / Victor R. Fuchs. — Cambridge, Mass. ; London : Harvard University Press, 1986. — viii, 401p. — *Includes index. — Bibliography: p.385-386*

MEDICAL ECONOMICS — Moral and ethical aspects — Congresses

The Price of health / edited by George J. Agich and Charles E. Begley. — Dordrecht ; Boston : D. Reidel Pub. Co. ; Hingham, MA, U.S.A. : Sold and distributed in the U.S.A. and Canada by Kluwer Academic Publishers, c1987. — p. cm. — (Philosophy and medicine ; v. 21). — *Based on a conference entitled "The price of health: economics and ethics in medicine," held at the School of Public Health, University of Texas Health Science Center, Houston, Tex., June 24-26, 1985. — Includes bibliographies and index*

MEDICAL ECONOMICS — Canada

EVANS, Robert G.
Strained mercy : the economics of Canadian health care / Robert G. Evans. — Toronto : Butterworths, c1984. — xvi, 390 p.. — *Includes index. — Bibliography: p. 355-363*

MEDICAL ECONOMICS — Great Britain
CULYER, A. J.
Health service ills : the wrong economic medicine / A. J. Culyer. — York : University of York, Centre for Health Economics, 1986. — 13p. — (Discussion paper / University of York. Centre for Health Economics ; 16)

MEDICAL ECONOMICS — New York (N.Y.) — History
GINZBERG, Eli
From health dollars to health services : New York City, 1965-1985 / Eli Ginzberg and the Conservation of Human Resources staff. — Totowa, N.J. : Rowman & Allanheld, c1986. — xii, 163 p.. — ([Conservation of human resources series ; 25]) (Land Mark studies). — First series from jacket. — Includes index. — Bibliography: p. [155]

MEDICAL ECONOMICS — Scotland
GREAT BRITAIN. Working Party on Revenue Resource Allocation
Scottish Health Authorities Revenue Equalisation (SHARE) : report of the Working Party on Revenue Resource Allocation. — Edinburgh : H.M.S.O., 1977. — 95p

MEDICAL ECONOMICS — Tanzania — History
TURSHEN, Meredeth
The political ecology of disease in Tanzania / Meredeth Turshen. — New Brunswick, N.J. : Rutgers University Press, c1984. — xiv, 259 p., [2] leaves of plates. — Includes index. — Bibliography: p. 211-239

MEDICAL ECONOMICS — United States
GINZBERG, Eli
American medicine : the power shift / Eli Ginzberg. — Totowa, N.J. : Rowman & Allanheld, 1985. — xv, 207 p.. — Includes index. — Bibliography: p. [194]-199

JACOBS, Philip
The economics of health and medical care / Philip Jacobs. — 2nd ed. — Rockville, Md. : Aspen Publishers, c1986. — p. cm. — Includes index. — Bibliography: p

SORKIN, Alan L
Health care and the changing economic environment / Alan L. Sorkin. — Lexington, Mass. : Lexington Books, c1986. — xiv, 161 p.. — Includes bibliographies and index

MEDICAL ECONOMICS — Wales
GREAT BRITAIN. Steering Committee on Resource Allocations in Wales
The distribution of resources to health authorities in Wales : third report. — [Cardiff] : Welsh Office, 1979. — 43p

GREAT BRITAIN. Steering Committee on Resource Allocations in Wales
The distribution of resources to health authorities in Wales : fourth report. — [Cardiff] : Welsh Office, 1979. — 44p

Morbidity and its relationship to resource allocation / edited by Sir John Brotherston. — [Cardiff ([Crown Building, Cathays Park, Cardiff CF1 3NQ]) : Welsh Office, [1978]. — [1],vii,97p. — 'Papers and proceedings of a workshop held at the Hill Residential College, Abergavenny, Gwent on Tuesday 24 and Wednesday 25 January 1978' - p.i

MEDICAL EDUCATION — Social aspects — United States
BECKER, Howard Saul
Boys in white : student culture in medical school / Howard S. Becker ... [et al.]. — New Brunswick, N.J. : Transaction Books, 1977, c1961. — xiv, 456 p.. — Reprint of the ed. published by University of Chicago Press, Chicago

MEDICAL EDUCATION — Africa
Health progress in Africa : 1968-1973. — Brazzaville : Regional Office for Africa, World Health Organization, 1973. — 110p. — (AFRO technical papers ; no.6). — Includes bibliographical references

LUTWAMA, J. S.
The place of public health education in programmes for the training of health team personnel / by Professor J. S. Lutwama. — Brazzaville : Regional Office for Africa, World Health Organization, 1971. — 44p. — (AFRO technical papers ; no.3). — Bibliographical references: p31. — Background paper for the technical discussions of the 21st session of the Regional Committee

QUENUM, Comlan A. A.
The health development of African communities : ten years of reflexion / Comlan A. A. Quenum. — Brazzaville : Regional Office for Africa, World Health Organization, 1979. — 283p. — (AFRO technical papers ; no.15). — Includes bibliographical references

MEDICAL EDUCATION — Africa — Addresses, essays, lectures
Biomedical lectures / Contributors; A. Quenum...[et al.]. — Brazzaville : Regional Office for Africa, World Health Organization, 1972. — 83p. — (AFRO technical papers ; no.4). — Cover title: 1970-1971 series. — Includes bibliographies

Biomedical lectures / Contributors; P. Correa...[et al.]. — Brazzaville : Regional Office for Africa, World Health Organization, 1975. — 69p. — (AFRO technical papers ; no.11). — Cover title: 1970-1973 series. — Includes bibliographical references

Biomedical lectures / Contributors; A. M. Wright...[et al.]. — Brazzaville : Regional Office for Africa, World Health Organization, 1978. — 53p. — (AFRO technical papers ; no.13). — Cover title: 1976-1977 series. — Includes bibliographical references

MEDICAL EDUCATION — England
UNIVERSITY OF LONDON. Working Party on Medical & Dental Teaching Resources
London Medical education— a new framework / report of a Working Party on Medical & Dental Teaching Resources ; Chairman, the Lord Flowers. — [London] : University of London, 1980. — 79p

MEDICAL ETHICS
BLISS, Brian Peter
Aims and motives in clinical medicine : a practical approach to medical ethics / B.P. Bliss, A.G. Johnson. — London ([42 Camden Rd, Tunbridge Wells, Kent TN1 2QD]) : Pitman Medical, 1975. — viii,188p. — Includes index

ENGELHARDT, H. Tristram
The foundations of bioethics / by H. Tristram Engelhardt, Jr. — New York : Oxford University Press, 1986. — p. cm. — Includes bibliographies and index

FRANCE
Éthique et recherche biomédicale : rapport 1985. — [Paris] : Documentation française, [1986]. — 170p

GILLON, Raanan
Philosophical medical ethics / Raanan Gillon. — Chichester : Wiley, c1986. — 1v.. — Includes index

JORDAN, Shannon M
Decision making for incompetent persons : the law and morality of who shall decide / by Shannon M. Jordan. — Springfield, Ill., U.S.A. : C.C. Thomas, c1985. — xxvii, 142 p.. — Includes index. — Bibliography: p. 135-138

MEDICAL ETHICS — Congresses
Ethics and critical care medicine / edited by John C. Moskop and Loretta Kopelman. — Dordrecht ; Lancaster : D. Reidel, c1985. — xx, 236p. — (Philosophy and medicine ; v. 19). — Based on papers presented at a symposium held at East Carolina University School of Medicine in Greenville, N.C. on Mar. 17-19, 1983; sponsored by the East Carolina University School of Medicine and others. — Includes bibliographies and index

The Price of health / edited by George J. Agich and Charles E. Begley. — Dordrecht ; Boston : D. Reidel Pub. Co. ; Hingham, MA, U.S.A. : Sold and distributed in the U.S.A. and Canada by Kluwer Academic Publishers, c1987. — p. cm. — (Philosophy and medicine ; v. 21). — Based on a conference entitled "The price of health: economics and ethics in medicine," held at the School of Public Health, University of Texas Health Science Center, Houston, Tex., June 24-26, 1985. — Includes bibliographies and index

MEDICAL GEOGRAPHY
Western diseases, their emergence and prevention / edited by H. C. Trowell, D. P. Burkitt ; foreword by John R. K. Robson. — Cambridge, Mass. : Harvard University Press, 1981. — xix, 456 p.. — Includes bibliographies and index

MEDICAL GEOGRAPHY — Great Britain
EYLES, John
The geography of the national health : an essay in welfare geography / John Eyles. — London : Croom Helm, c1987. — [256]p. — Includes bibliography and index

MEDICAL INNOVATIONS — Social aspects
Reproductive technologies : gender, motherhood and medicine / edited by Michelle Stanworth. — Cambridge : Polity in association with Blackwell, 1987. — [220]p. — (Feminist perspectives). — Includes bibliography and index

MEDICAL LAWS AND LEGISLATION — Canada — History
HAMOWY, Ronald
Canadian medicine : a study in restricted entry / Ronald Hamowy. — Vancouver : Fraser Institute, 1984. — xxii,394p

MEDICAL LAWS AND LEGISLATION — Commonwealth of Nations
PAXMAN, John M.
The use of paramedicals for primary health in the Commonwealth : a survey of medical-legal issues and alternatives / John M. Paxman and Francis M. Shattock and N.R.E. Fendall. — London : Commonwealth Secretariat, 1979. — 129p

MEDICAL LAWS AND LEGISLATION — England
BRAZIER, Margaret
Medicine, patients and the law / Margaret Brazier. — Harmondsworth : Penguin, 1987. — xxiii,375p. — (Pelican books)

GREAT BRITAIN
Sweet & Maxwell's encyclopedia of health services and medical law. — London : Sweet & Maxwell, 1987. — 1v.(looseleaf). — Includes index

MASON, J. K.
Law and medical ethics / J.K. Mason, R.A. McCall Smith. — 2nd ed. — London : Butterworths, 1987. — [345]p. — Previous ed.: 1983. — Includes index

MEDICAL LAWS AND LEGISLATION — Great Britain — Dictionaries
MASON, J. K.
Butterworths medico-legal encyclopaedia / J.K. Mason, R.A. McCall Smith. — London : Butterworths, 1987. — 650p. — Includes index

MEDICAL ONCOLOGY — United States — legislation
RUSHEFSKY, Mark R.
Making cancer policy / Mark R. Rushefsky. — Albany : State University of New York Press, c1986. — xiii, 257 p.. — (SUNY series in public administration in the 1980s). — Includes index. — Bibliography: p. 225-245

MEDICAL PERSONNEL

Health manpower planning : principles, methods, issues / edited by T. L. Hall and A. Mejía. — Geneva : World Health Organization, ; [Albany, N.Y. : distributed by WHO Publications Centre USA], 1978. — 311p. — *Includes bibliographical references*

Investigating practices in health manpower planning : report on country case study. — Copenhagen : World Health Organization, 1986. — 41p

MEDICAL PERSONNEL — Malpractice — Economic aspects — United States

DANZON, Patricia M.
Medical malpractice : theory, evidence and public policy / Patricia M. Danzon. — Cambridge, Mass. ; London : Harvard University Press, 1985. — vi,264p. — *Bibliography: p231-238. — Includes index*

MEDICAL PERSONNEL — Malpractice — United States

WERTHMANN, Barbara
Medical malpractice law : how medicine is changing the law / Barbara Werthmann. — Lexington, Mass. : LexingtonBooks, c1984. — xii, 268 p.. — *Includes indexes*

MEDICAL PERSONNEL — Great Britain — Bibliography

PRICE, C. J.
Selected references on manpower planning in the National Health Service / compiled by C.J. Price. — London : Department of Health and Social Security Library, 1978. — 6p. — (Bibliography series / Department of Health and Social Security Library ; no.B106)

MEDICAL PERSONNEL — Great Britain — Supply and demand

GREAT BRITAIN. Department of Health and Social Security
Staffing of the National Health Service (England) : an analysis of the demand and supply positions in the major staff groups. — [London} : the Department, 1979. — [66]p

LONG, A. F.
Health manpower : planning, production and management / Andrew F. Long and Geoffrey Mercer in collaboration with Fiona Brooks ... [et al.]. — London : Croom Helm, c1987. — [288]p. — *Bibliography: p247-265. — Includes index*

MEDICAL PERSONNEL — South Africa — Statistics

Sensus van ge nee shere en tan dartse = census of medical practitioners and dentists / Central Statistical Services, South Africa. — Pretoria : Government Printer, 1979-. — *Annual. — Text in Afrikaans and English*

MEDICAL PERSONNEL — United States

GINZBERG, Eli
American medicine : the power shift / Eli Ginzberg. — Totowa, N.J. : Rowman & Allanheld, 1985. — xv, 207 p.. — *Includes index. — Bibliography: p. [194]-199*

MEDICAL POLICY

Epidemiology and health policy / edited by Sol Levine and Abraham M. Lilienfeld. — New York ; London : Tavistock, 1987. — xvi,301p. — (Contemporary issues in health, medicine, and social policy). — *Includes bibliographies and index*

MEDICAL POLICY — Addresses, essays, lectures

FUCHS, Victor R
The health economy / Victor R. Fuchs. — Cambridge, Mass. ; London : Harvard University Press, 1986. — viii, 401p. — *Includes index. — Bibliography: p.385-386*

MEDICAL POLICY — Social aspects

Applications of social science to clinical medicine and health policy / edited by Linda H. Aiken and David Mechanic. — New Brunswick, N.J. : Rutgers University Press, c1986. — p. cm. — *Sponsored by the Medical Sociology Section of the American Sociological Association*

MEDICAL POLICY — Social aspects — Congresses

Current health policy issues and alternatives : an applied social science perspective / Carole E. Hill, editor. — Athens [Georgia] ; London : University of Georgia Press, 1986. — vi,212p. — (Southern Anthropological Proceedings ; no.19). — *Bibliography: p[195]-209*

MEDICAL POLICY — Social aspects — United States

Applications of social science to clinical medicine and health policy / edited by Linda H. Aiken and David Mechanic. — New Brunswick, N.J. : Rutgers University Press, c1986. — p. cm. — *Sponsored by the Medical Sociology Section of the American Sociological Association*

Current health policy issues and alternatives : an applied social science perspective / Carole E. Hill, editor. — Athens [Georgia] ; London : University of Georgia Press, 1986. — vi,212p. — (Southern Anthropological Proceedings ; no.19). — *Bibliography: p[195]-209*

MEDICAL POLICY — Australia

DICKENSON, Mary
Hospitals and politics : the Australian Hospital Association 1946-86 / Mary Dickenson and Catherine Mason. — Deakin, A.C.T. : The Association, 1986. — 144p. — *Notes and references p133-138*

MEDICAL POLICY — Canada — History — 20th century

NAYLOR, C. David
Private practice, public payment : Canadian medicine and the politics of health insurance, 1911-1966 / C. David Naylor. — Kingston ; Montreal : McGill-Queen's University Press, 1986. — xii,324p. — *Notes: p[259]-303*

MEDICAL POLICY — Developing countries

AKIN, John S.
Financing health services in developing countries / [prepared by John Akin, Nancy Birdsall and David de Ferranti]. — Washington, D.C. : The World Bank, 1987. — vi,93p. — *Bibliography: p85-93*

INSTITUT NATIONAL D'ETUDES DÉMOGRAPHIQUES
Health policy, social policy and mortality prospects : proceedings of a seminar at Paris, France, February 28-March 4, 1983 / edited by Jacques Vallin and Alan D. Lopez. — [Liège] : Ordina, 1985. — 557p. — *Bibliographies*

MEDICAL POLICY — Europe

INSTITUT NATIONAL D'ETUDES DÉMOGRAPHIQUES
Health policy, social policy and mortality prospects : proceedings of a seminar at Paris, France, February 28-March 4, 1983 / edited by Jacques Vallin and Alan D. Lopez. — [Liège] : Ordina, 1985. — 557p. — *Bibliographies*

MEDICAL POLICY — Great Britain

GRIFFITH, Ben
Banking on sickness : commercial medicine in Britain and the USA / Ben Griffith, Steve Iliffe and Geof Rayner. — London : Lawrence and Wishart, 1987. — 287p

MEDICAL POLICY — Great Britain — History

HOLLINGSWORTH, J. Rogers
A political economy of medicine : Great Britain and the United States / J. Rogers Hollingsworth. — Baltimore : Johns Hopkins University Press, c1986. — xix, 312 p.. — *Includes index. — Bibliography: p. 275-303*

MEDICAL POLICY — Ireland

DELAP, Ruth
The development of public policy for the medical care of the physically ill in Ireland, 1900-1970 / by Ruth Delap. — 425 leaves. — *PhD (Econ) 1986 LSE*

MEDICAL POLICY — Nepal

JUSTICE, Judith
Policies, plans, and people : culture and health development in Nepal / Judith Justice. — Berkeley : University of California Press, c1986. — p. cm. — (Comparative studies of health systems and medical care). — *Includes index. — Bibliography: p*

MEDICAL POLICY — North America

INSTITUT NATIONAL D'ETUDES DÉMOGRAPHIQUES
Health policy, social policy and mortality prospects : proceedings of a seminar at Paris, France, February 28-March 4, 1983 / edited by Jacques Vallin and Alan D. Lopez. — [Liège] : Ordina, 1985. — 557p. — *Bibliographies*

MEDICAL POLICY — Tanzania — History

TURSHEN, Meredeth
The political ecology of disease in Tanzania / Meredeth Turshen. — New Brunswick, N.J. : Rutgers University Press, c1984. — xiv, 259 p., [2] leaves of plates. — *Includes index. — Bibliography: p. 211-239*

MEDICAL POLICY — United States — Congresses

CORNELL UNIVERSITY MEDICAL COLLEGE CONFERENCE ON HEALTH POLICY (1985 : New York, N.Y.)
The U.S. health care system : a look to the 1990s / Cornell University Medical College Conference on Health Policy, March 7-8, 1985, New York City ; Eli Ginzberg, editor. — Totowa, N.J. : Rowman & Allanheld, 1985. — x, 133 p.. — (Conservation of human resources series ; 26) (Land Mark studies). — *Includes index. — Bibliography: p. 115-123*

MEDICAL POLICY — United States — History

HOLLINGSWORTH, J. Rogers
A political economy of medicine : Great Britain and the United States / J. Rogers Hollingsworth. — Baltimore : Johns Hopkins University Press, c1986. — xix, 312 p.. — *Includes index. — Bibliography: p. 275-303*

RUSHEFSKY, Mark R.
Making cancer policy / Mark R. Rushefsky. — Albany : State University of New York Press, c1986. — xiii, 257 p.. — (SUNY series in public administration in the 1980s). — *Includes index. — Bibliography: p. 225-245*

MEDICAL RECORDS

LIBERAL PARTY
Access by patients to health care records. — Hebden Bridge : Hebden Royd Publications, 1986. — 15p. — (Liberal Party panel health papers ; no.14)

MEDICAL RESEARCH

DOLLERY, Colin Terence
The end of an age of optimism : medical science in retrospect and prospect / Colin Dollery. — London (3 Prince Albert Rd, NW1 7SP) : Nuffield Provincial Hospitals Trust, 1978. — viii,95p. — (The Rock Carling Fellowship ; 1978)

MEDICAL SOCIAL WORK

RUSHTON, Andrée
Social work and health care / Andrée Rushton and Penny Davies. — London : Heinemann Educational, 1984. — 103 p. — (Community care practice handbooks ; 16)

MEDICAL SOCIAL WORK — France — Nomenclature

FRANCE. Ministerè des Affaires Sociales et de la Solidarité Nationale. Service des Statistiques, des Etudes et des Systèmes d'Information
Nomenclatures applicables aux unités de production des établissements sanitaires, sociaux et médico-sociaux et aux prestations qui y sont servies : période de validité: exercice 1986. — [Paris] : Ministère des Affaires Sociales et de la Solidarité Nationale, SESI, 1986. — 194p. — (Solidarité santé. Cahiers statistiques ; no.7 bis)

MEDICAL STUDENTS — United States

BECKER, Howard Saul
Boys in white : student culture in medical school / Howard S. Becker ... [et al.]. — New Brunswick, N.J. : Transaction Books, 1977, c1961. — xiv, 456 p.. — *Reprint of the ed. published by University of Chicago Press, Chicago*

MEDICAL SUPPLIES — Great Britain

GREAT BRITAIN. Supply Board Working Group
Report of the Supply Board Working Group. — [London] : Department of Health and Social Security, 1978. — vii,125p

MEDICAL TECHNOLOGY

JENNETT, Bryan
High technology medicine : benefits and burdens / Bryan Jennett. — New ed. — Oxford : Oxford University Press, 1986. — xii,317p. — (Oxford medical publications). — *Previous ed.: London : Nuffield Provincial Hospitals Trust, 1984. — Includes index*

The Machine at the bedside : strategies for using technology in patient care / edited by Stanley Joel Reiser, Michael Anbar. — Cambridge : Cambridge University Press, 1984. — xviii,363p. — *Includes bibliographies and index*

MEDICARE

SORKIN, Alan L
Health care and the changing economic environment / Alan L. Sorkin. — Lexington, Mass. : Lexington Books, c1986. — xiv, 161 p.. — *Includes bibliographies and index*

MEDICARE — United States

FEIN, Rashi
Medical care, medical costs : the search for a health insurance policy / Rashi Fein. — Cambridge, Mass. : Harvard University Press, 1986. — viii, 240 p.. — *Includes index*

MEDICINE

BENNET, Glin
The wound and the doctor : healing, technology and power in modern medicine / Glin Bennet. — London : Secker & Warburg, 1987. — [320]p. — *Includes index*

Medical science and the advancement of world health / edited by Robert Lanza. — New York : Praeger, 1985. — p. cm. — *Includes index*

MEDICINE — Addresses, essays, lectures

Imperialism, health and medicine / edited by Vicente Navarro. — Farmingdale,N.Y. : Baywood, 1981. — 282p. — (Policy, politics, health and medicine). — *Collection of essays*

MEDICINE — Decision making — Moral and ethical aspects

JORDAN, Shannon M
Decision making for incompetent persons : the law and morality of who shall decide / by Shannon M. Jordan. — Springfield, Ill., U.S.A. : C.C. Thomas, c1985. — xxvii, 142 p. — *Includes index. — Bibliography: p. 135-138*

MEDICINE — History

MCKEOWN, Thomas
The modern rise of population / Thomas McKeown. — London : Edward Arnold, 1976. — [5],168p. — *Includes index*

MEDICINE — History — 18th century

Medical fringe and medical orthodoxy 1750-1850 / edited by W.F. Bynum and Roy Porter. — London : Croom Helm, c1987. — 274p. — (Wellcome Institute series in the history of medicine)

MEDICINE — History — 19th century

Medical fringe and medical orthodoxy 1750-1850 / edited by W.F. Bynum and Roy Porter. — London : Croom Helm, c1987. — 274p. — (Wellcome Institute series in the history of medicine)

MEDICINE — Political aspects — Great Britain

WATKINS, Steve
Medicine and labour : the politics of a profession / Steve Watkins. — London : Lawrence and Wishart, 1987. — 272p

MEDICINE — Research

FRANCE
Éthique et recherche biomédicale : rapport 1985. — [Paris] : Documentation française, [1986]. — 170p

MEDICINE — Research — Social aspects — Addresses, essays, lectures

Medical science and the advancement of world health / edited by Robert Lanza. — New York : Praeger, 1985. — p. cm. — *Includes index*

MEDICINE — Research — Great Britain — Endowments

HALL, A. Rupert
Physic and philanthropy : a history of the Wellcome Trust 1936-1986 / A.R. Hall and B.A. Bembridge ; with a foreword by Sir David Steel. — Cambridge : Cambridge University Press, 1986. — xii,479p. — *Includes index*

MEDICINE — Specialties and specialists — Congresses

Medical specialization in relation to health needs : report on a WHO meeting : Abano Terme, Italy, 22-25 October 1984. — Copenhagen : World Health Organization, 1986. — 67p. — *Summary in French, German, and Russian. — Bibliography: p42*

MEDICINE — Specialties and specialists — Europe — Congresses

Medical specialization in relation to health needs : report on a WHO meeting : Abano Terme, Italy, 22-25 October 1984. — Copenhagen : World Health Organization, 1986. — 67p. — *Summary in French, German, and Russian. — Bibliography: p42*

MEDICINE — Study and teaching

WORLD HEALTH ORGANIZATION. Regional Office for Europe
Training in family planning for health personnel : report on a W.H.O. meeting, Paris, 6-11 July 1981 / World Health Organization, Regional Office for Europe. — Copenhagen : World Health Organization, 1985. — 99p. — (Public health in Europe ; 20)

MEDICINE — Canada — History — 20th century

NAYLOR, C. David
Private practice, public payment : Canadian medicine and the politics of health insurance, 1911-1966 / C. David Naylor. — Kingston ; Montreal : McGill-Queen's University Press, 1986. — xii,324p. — *Notes: p[259]-303*

MEDICINE — England

STEVENS, Rosemary
Medical practice in modern England : the impact of specialization in state medicine / Rosemary Stevens. — New Haven : Yale University Press, 1966

MEDICINE — Great Britain

GREAT BRITAIN. Working Party on Fortification of Food with Vitamin D
Rickets and osteomalacia / report of the Working Party on Fortification of Food with Vitamin D. Committee on Medical Aspects of Food Policy. — London : H.M.S.O., 1980. — xii,66p. — (Report on health and social subjects ; 19). — *At head of title: Department of Health and Social Security. — Bibliography: p54-66*

MEDICINE, CHINESE — Philosophy

UNSCHULD, Paul U
Medicine in China : a history of ideas / Paul U. Unschuld. — Berkeley : University of California Press, c1985. — xi, 423 p.. — (Comparative studies of health systems and medical care). — *Includes index. — Bibliography: p. 391-404*

MEDICINE, MAGIC, MYSTIC, AND SPAGIRIC — Thailand

GOLOMB, Louis
An anthropology of curing in multiethnic Thailand / Louis Golomb. — Urbana : University of Illinois Press, c1985. — p. cm. — (Illinois studies in anthropology ; no. 15). — *Includes index. — Bibliography: p*

MEDICINE, PREVENTIVE

HARPER, Andrew C
The health of populations : an introduction / Andrew C. Harper. — New York : Springer Pub. Co., c1986. — xvii, 222 p.. — *Includes index. — Bibliography: p. 199-216*

LABOUR PARTY (Great Britain)
Health for all : a charter on preventive health. — London : Labour Party, 1986. — 16p

MEDICINE, PREVENTIVE — Cost effectiveness — Congresses

RUSSELL, Louise B
Evaluating preventive care : report on a workshop / Louise B. Russell. — Washington, D.C. : Brookings Institution, c1987. — p. cm. — (Studies in social economics). — *Workshop held May 8-9, 1986, and sponsored by the Brookings Institution. — Includes index. — Bibliography: p*

MEDICINE, STATE — England

STEVENS, Rosemary
Medical practice in modern England : the impact of specialization in state medicine / Rosemary Stevens. — New Haven : Yale University Press, 1966

MEDICINE, STATE — European Economic Community countries

ABEL-SMITH, Brian
Cost containment in health care : the experience of 12 European countries 1977-83 / by Brian Abel-Smith. — Luxembourg : Office for Official Publications of the European Communities, 1984. — 148p

MEDICINE, STATE — Great Britain — Bibliography

ALLBROOKE, Jill C.
Selected references on joint planning and joint finance in the health and social services / compiled by Jill C. Allbrooke. — London : Department of Health and Social Security Library, 1979. — 4p. — (Bibliography series / Department of Health and Social Security Library ; no.B123)

GREAT BRITAIN. Department of Health and Social Security. Library
Selected references on resource allocation 1975-1978. — London : the Library, 1978. — 8p. — (Bibliography series ; no.B116)

MEDICINE, STATE — Northern Ireland

GREAT BRITAIN. Working Group on Revenue Resource Allocations to Health and Social Services Boards in Northern Ireland
Proposals for the allocation of revenue resources for health and personal social services (PARR) : report. — [Belfast] : the Department, 1978. — [76]p

MEDIEVALISM — Great Britain — History
SMITH, R. J. (Roger John), 1938-
The Gothic bequest : medieval institutions in British thought, 1688-1863 / R.J. Smith. — Cambridge : Cambridge University Press, 1987. — [240]p. — *Includes bibliography and index*

MEDITERRANEAN REGION — Defenses
SNYDER, Jed C
Defending the fringe : NATO, the Mediterranean, and the Gulf / Jed C. Snyder. — Boulder : Westview Press, 1986. — p. cm. — (SAIS papers in international affairs ; no. 11). — *Includes index*

MEDITERRANEAN REGION — History — 16th century
BRAUDEL, Fernand
La Méditerranée et le monde méditerranéen à l'époque de Philippe II / Fernand Braudel. — [6e ed]. — Paris : Armand Colin
Tome 1. — [1986]. — 587p

BRAUDEL, Fernand
La Méditerranée et le monde méditerranéen à l'époque de Philippe II / Fernand Braudel. — Paris : Armand Colin. — *Bibliography: p523-578*
Tome 2. — [1986]. — 627p

MEDITERRANEAN REGION — Politics and government
Jeux de Go en Méditerranee orientale / Olivier Da Lage...[and others]. — [Paris] : Fondation pour les études de défense nationale, [1986]. — 184p. — *Bibliography: p183-184*

MEGHALAYA (INDIA) — Population — Statistics
Census of India 1981. — [Delhi : Controller of Publications]
Series 14: Meghalaya. — [1985-]

MEHINACU INDIANS — Sexual behavior
GREGOR, Thomas
Anxious pleasures : the sexual lives of an Amazonian people / Thomas Gregor. — Chicago : University of Chicago Press, 1985. — xii, 223 p.. — *Includes index. — Bibliography: p. [211]-216*

MEKEO (PAPUA NEW GUINEA PEOPLE)
MUSKO, Mark S.
Quadripartite structures : categories, relations and homologies in Bush Mekeo culture / Mark S. Musko. — Cambridge : Cambridge University Press, 1985. — xiii,298p — *Bibliography: p278-288. — Includes index*

MELANESIA
Melanesia : beyond diversity / R. J. May and Hank Nelson, editors. — Canberra : Research School of Pacific Studies, The Australian National University, 1982. — 2v.. — *Includes references*

MELANESIA — Social life and custome
EPSTEIN, A. L.
The experience of shame in Melanesia : an essay on the anthropology of affect / by A.L. Epstein. — London : Royal Anthropological Institute, 1984. — iv,58p. — (Occasional paper / Royal Anthropological Institute of Great Britain and Ireland ; no.40)

MELBOURNE (VIC.) — Dwellings — History
LOGAN, William Stewart
The gentrification of inner Melbourne : a political geography of inner city housing / William Stewart Logan. — St Lucia ; London : University of Queensland Press, 1985. — xxxiii,328p. — (The University of Queensland Press scholars' library). — *Bibliography: p305-315. — Includes index*

MEMORIAL UNIVERSITY OF NEWFOUNDLAND. Institute of Social and Economic Research
HOUSE, J. D.
The challenge of oil : Newfoundland's quest for controlled development / J. D. House. — St. John's, Newfoundland : Institute of Social and Economic Research, Memorial University of Newfoundland, [1985]. — xv,329p. — (Social and economic studies / Memorial University of Newfoundland Institute of Social and Economic Research ; no.30). — *Notes and references: p[313]-326*

MEMORY
BADDELEY, Alan D.
The psychology of memory / Alan D. Baddeley. — London : Harper & Row, 1985, c1976. — xvii,430p. — (Basic topics in cognition series). — *Originally published: 1976. — Bibliography: p379-413. — Includes index*

BADDELEY, Alan D.
Working memory / Alan Baddeley. — Oxford : Clarendon, 1986. — xi,289p. — (Oxford psychology series ; no.11) (Oxford science publications). — *Bibliography: p260-278. — Includes index*

Induction : processes of inference, learning, and discovery / John H. Holland ... [et al.]. — Cambridge, Mass. : MIT Press, c1986. — xvi, 385p. — (Computational models of cognition and perception). — *Includes index. — Bibliography: p.357-372*

KOSSLYN, Stephen Michael
Image and mind / Stephen Michael Kosslyn. — Cambridge, Mass. : Harvard University Press, 1980. — p. cm. — *Includes index. — Bibliography: p*

PERSPECTIVES ON MEMORY RESEARCH (Conference : 1977 : University of Uppsala)
Perspectives on memory research : essays in honor of Uppsala University's 500th anniversary / edited by Lars-Göran Nilsson. — Hillsdale : Erlbaum ; New York ; London : Distributed by Wiley, 1979. — xiii,400p. — 'This conference on "Perspectives on Memory Research" was held at the University of Uppsala, June 20-24, 1977' - Preface. — *Includes bibliographies and index*

MEN
ROWAN, John
The horned god : feminism and men as wounding and healing / John Rowan. — London : Routledge & Kegan Paul, 1987. — xi,155p. — *Bibliography: Includes p143-150. — index*

MENDÈS FRANCE, PIERRE
RIMBAUD, Christiane
Le procès Mendès France / Christiane Rimbaud ; préface de Jean-Denis Bredin. — Paris : Librairie Academique Perrin, 1986. — 216p. — *Bibliography: p215-216*

MENDOZA, BERNARDINO DE
JENSEN, De Lamar
Diplomacy and dogmatism : Bernardino de Mendoza and the French Catholic League / De Lamar Jensen. — Cambridge, Mass. : Harvard University Press, 1964. — xii,322p. — *Bibliography: p241-263*

MENNONITES — Case studies
NAFZIGER, E. Wayne
Entrepreneurship, equity, and economic development / by E. Wayne Nafziger. — Greenwich, Conn. : JAI Press, c1986. — p. cm. — (Contemporary studies in economic and financial analysis ; v. 53). — *Includes index. — Bibliography: p*

MENTAL HEALTH — Cross-cultural studies
ROHNER, Ronald P
The warmth dimension : foundations of parental acceptance-rejection theory / Ronald P. Rohner. — Beverly Hills [Calif.] : Sage Publications, c1986. — 248 p.. — (New perspectives on family). — *Includes index. — Bibliography: p. 214-236*

MENTAL HEALTH — Social aspects
Social support, life events, and depression / edited by Nan Lin, Alfred Dean, and Walter M. Ensel. — New York : Academic Press, 1986. — p. cm. — *Includes index*

MENTAL HEALTH — Social aspects — Bibliography
BIEGEL, David E
Social networks and mental health : an annotated bibliography / David E. Biegel, Ellen McCardle, Susan Mendelson ; foreword by Stephen E. Goldston. — Beverly Hills, Calif. : Sage Publications, [1985]. — 391 p.. — *Includes indexes*

MENTAL HEALTH — China — Congresses
Chinese culture and mental health / edited by Wen-Shing Tseng, David Y.H. Wu. — Orlando : Academic Press, 1985. — xxiii, 412 p.. — *Derived from a conference held in Hawaii, Mar. 1-6, 1982, and sponsored by the Culture Learning Institute of the East-West Center, the Dept. of Psychiatry, University of Hawaii School of Medicine, and the Queen's Medical Center in Honolulu. — Includes bibliographies and index*

MENTAL HEALTH — England — History
SHOWALTER, Elaine
The female malady : women, madness, and culture in England, 1830-1980 / Elaine Showalter. — New York : Pantheon Books, 1986. — p. cm. — *Includes index. — Bibliography: p*

MENTAL HEALTH (AMENDMENT) (SCOTLAND) BILL 1982-83
GREAT BRITAIN. Parliament. House of Commons. Library. Research Division
Mental Health (Amendment) (Scotland) Bill (HL) 1982-83 (Bill 82) / Keith Cuninghame. — [London] : the Division, 1983. — 11p. — (Reference sheet ; no.83/5). — *Bibliographical references: p9-11*

MENTAL HEALTH FACILITIES — Denmark — Utilization — Statistics
DREYER, Karen
Befolkningens forbrug af psykiatriske sengepladser : en analyse i henhold til bopael pr. 1 April 1976 = Utilization of psychiatric beds : an analysis according to residence per April 1st, 1976 / Karen Dreyer og Annalise Dupont. — København : Sundhedsstyrelsen, [1978]. — 56p. — (Medicinalstatistiske meddelelser ; 1978:2). — *Summary and table headings in English. — Bibliography: p36-37*

MENTAL HEALTH LAWS — Australia
CARNEY, Terry
Ethical and legal issues in guardianship options for intellectually disadvantaged people / Dr. Terry Carney and Professor Peter Singer. — Canberra : Australian Government Publishing Service, 1986. — ix, 124p. — (Monograph series / Human Rights Commission ; no.2). — *Bibliography: p121-124*

MENTAL HEALTH LAWS — Great Britain
BEAN, Philip
Mental disorder and legal control / Philip Bean. — Cambridge : Cambridge University Press, 1986. — [304]p. — *Includes bibliographical references and index*

MENTAL HEALTH LAWS — Great Britain — History
UNSWORTH, Clive
The politics of mental health legislation / Clive Unsworth. — Oxford : Clarendon, 1987. — [384]p. — *Includes bibliography and index*

MENTAL HEALTH LAWS — Scotland
GREAT BRITAIN. Parliament. House of Commons. Library. Research Division
Mental Health (Amendment) (Scotland) Bill (HL) 1982-83 (Bill 82) / Keith Cuninghame. — [London] : the Division, 1983. — 11p. — (Reference sheet ; no.83/5). — *Bibliographical references: p9-11*

MENTAL HEALTH PLANNING — Great Britain
The provision of mental health services in Britain : the way ahead / edited by Greg Wilkinson, Hugh Freeman. — London : Gaskell, 1986. — xi,197p. — *Includes bibliographic references*

MENTAL HEALTH PLANNING — United States — Addresses, essays, lectures
The Organization of mental health services : societal and community systems / edited by W. Richard Scott and Bruce L. Black. — Beverly Hills, Calif. : Sage Publications, c1986. — 311 p.. — (Sage focus editions ; v. 78). — *Includes bibliographies*

MENTAL HEALTH SERVICES — Great Britain
GREAT BRITAIN. Department of Health and Social Security
Mental handicap : progress, problems and priorities : a review of mental handicap services in England since the 1971 white paper "Better services for the mentally handicapped". — London : H.M.S.O., 1987. — 105 p

The provision of mental health services in Britain : the way ahead / edited by Greg Wilkinson, Hugh Freeman. — London : Gaskell, 1986. — xi,197p. — *Includes bibliographic references*

TURNER, Paul
A summary of trends affecting provision and requirement of mental illness resources / P. Turner. — [London : Department of Health and Social Security], 1977. — [15]leaves

MENTAL HEALTH SERVICES — Great Britain — Bibliography
SHRIGLEY, Sheila
Selected references on mental health services / compiled by Sheila M. Shrigley. — London : Department of Health and Social Security Library, 1977. — 12p. — (Bibliography series / Department of Health and Social Security Library ; no.B72)

MENTAL ILLNESS
MILES, Agnes
The mentally ill in contemporary society : a sociological introduction / Agnes Miles. — 2nd ed. — Oxford : Basil Blackwell, 1987. — x,229p. — *Previous ed.: Oxford : Robertson, 1981.* — *Bibliography: p211-224. — Includes index*

ROTH, Martin, 1917-
The reality of mental illness / Martin Roth & Jerome Kroll. — Cambridge : Cambridge University Press, 1986. — viii,128p

MENTAL ILLNESS — Diagnosis
Risk in intellectual and psychosocial development / edited by Dale C. Farran, James D. McKinney. — Orlando [FL] : Academic Press, 1986. — xii, 331 p.. — (Developmental psychology series). — *Includes bibliographies and indexes*

MENTAL ILLNESS — Social aspects
LEARY, Mark R
Social psychology and dysfunctional behavior : origins, diagnosis, and treatment / Mark R. Leary and Rowland S. Miller. — New York : Springer-Verlag, c1986. — xiii, 262 p.. — (Springer series in social psychology). — *Includes indexes. — Bibliography: p. [203]-244*

MENTAL ILLNESS — England — History
SHOWALTER, Elaine
The female malady : women, madness, and culture in England, 1830-1980 / Elaine Showalter. — New York : Pantheon Books, 1986. — p. cm. — *Includes index. — Bibliography: p*

MENTAL ILLNESS — France
RIPA, Yannick
La ronde des folles : femme, folie et enfermement au XIXe siècle, (1838-1870) / Yannick Ripa. — Paris : Aubier, 1986. — 216p

MENTAL ILLNESS — Great Britain — Diagnosis
RACK, Philip
Race, culture, and mental disorder / Philip Rack ; foreword by G. Morris Carstairs. — London : Tavistock, 1982. — xiii,305p. — *Bibliography: p273-292. — Includes index*

MENTAL ILLNESS IN LITERATURE
SHOWALTER, Elaine
The female malady : women, madness, and culture in England, 1830-1980 / Elaine Showalter. — New York : Pantheon Books, 1986. — p. cm. — *Includes index. — Bibliography: p*

MENTAL RETARDATION — Diagnosis
Risk in intellectual and psychosocial development / edited by Dale C. Farran, James D. McKinney. — Orlando [FL] : Academic Press, 1986. — xii, 331 p.. — (Developmental psychology series). — *Includes bibliographies and indexes*

MENTAL RETARDATION — Social aspects
BOGDAN, Robert
Inside out : the social meaning of mental retardation / Robert Bogdan and Steven J. Taylor. — Toronto ; Buffalo : University of Toronto Press, c1982. — xiv, 231 p.. — *Bibliography: p. [227]-231*

MENTALLY HANDICAPPED — Abuse of
MORLOK, Karl
Wo bringt ihr uns hin? : "Geheime Reichssache" Grafeneck / Karl Morlok. — Stuttgart : Quell, 1985. — 96p. — *Bibliography: p96*

MENTALLY HANDICAPPED — Care and treatment
Supporting people with a mental handicap in ordinary housing : good practice guide. — Worcester : Joint Research and Information Unit, 1986. — 18p. — *Bibliography: p18*

MENTALLY HANDICAPPED — Case studies
BOGDAN, Robert
Inside out : the social meaning of mental retardation / Robert Bogdan and Steven J. Taylor. — Toronto ; Buffalo : University of Toronto Press, c1982. — xiv, 231 p.. — *Bibliography: p. [227]-231*

MENTALLY HANDICAPPED — Civil rights — Australia
CARNEY, Terry
Ethical and legal issues in guardianship options for intellectually disadvantaged people / Dr. Terry Carney and Professor Peter Singer. — Canberra : Australian Government Publishing Service, 1986. — ix, 124p. — (Monograph series / Human Rights Commission ; no.2). — *Bibliography: p121-124*

MENTALLY HANDICAPPED — Institutional care — England — London — Statistics
Profile of mental handicap services in London / London Health Planning Consortium. — [London] ([Alexander Fleming House, Elephant & Castle, SE1 6BY]) : [Department of Health and Social Security], 1981. — [28]p

MENTALLY HANDICAPPED — Medical care — Moral and ethical aspects
JORDAN, Shannon M
Decision making for incompetent persons : the law and morality of who shall decide / by Shannon M. Jordan. — Springfield, Ill., U.S.A. : C.C. Thomas, c1985. — xxvii, 142 p.. — *Includes index. — Bibliography: p. 135-138*

MENTALLY HANDICAPPED — Services for — Great Britain
MIND
Services for mentally handicapped people : MIND's evidence to the Royal Commission on the NHS / [MIND]. — [London] : MIND, 1977. — vi,88p

MENTALLY HANDICAPPED — Training of — Wales
The role and function of adult training centres... : report of the special interest seminars held at Llandudno in November and December 1975 / Welsh Office Social Work Service. — [Cardiff] : The Service, [1981]. — 74p. — *Cover title*

MENTALLY HANDICAPPED — England — Gateshead (Tyne and Wear)
FENWICK, J.
Mental handicap and special needs in Gateshead : a research study amongst 350 families / J. Fenwick [and] Graham Lythe. — Gateshead : Gateshead Metropolitan Borough Council, 1985. — 152p

MENTALLY HANDICAPPED — England — London
BLIGH, John
Report on survey of people with mental handicaps in the City and Hackney health district / John Bligh [and] Marjorie Letchford. — Hackney : Directorate of Social Services Research, Development and Programming, 1985. — [56p]. — *At head of cover title: Research in Hackney*

MENTALLY HANDICAPPED — Great Britain
CUBBON, J. E.
A national survey of registers of mentally handicapped people : main report / J. E. Cubbon [and] N. A. Malin. — Sheffield : Sheffield City Polytechnic, 1985. — 110,[48]p. — *Bibliography: p106-110*

MENTALLY HANDICAPPED — Wales — Statistics
GREAT BRITAIN. Welsh Office
Census of patients in mental handicap hospitals and units in Wales, 31 August 1979. — [Cardiff] : the Office, [1979]. — [119]p

MENTALLY HANDICAPPED CHILDREN — United States — Family relationships
MORONEY, Robert
Shared responsibility : families and social policy / Robert M. Moroney. — New York : Aldine Pub. Co., c1986. — xi, 218 p.. — *Includes index. — Bibliography: p. 177-211*

MENTALLY ILL — Care and treatment — England — History
DIGBY, Anne
Madness, morality and medicine : a study of the York Retreat, 1796-1914 / Anne Digby. — Cambridge : Cambridge University Press, 1985. — xvi,323p. — (Cambridge history of medicine)

MENTALLY ILL — Care and treatment — England — Shropshire
BERNARD, Miriam
Shropshire's demonstration development district project : a joint Health Authority/Social Services Department initiative for care of the elderly mentally ill / Miriam Bernard. — Shrewsbury : Shropshire Health Authority/Shropshire County Council Social Services Department, 1985. — vii,75p. — *Bibliography: p64-66*

MENTALLY ILL — Care and treatment — Great Britain
KAY, Adah
Discharged to the community : a review of housing and support in London for people leaving psychiatric care / Adah Kay and Charlie Legg. — London : Good Practices in Mental Health, 1986. — vi,91p. — *"Original research funded by the Greater London Council". — Bibliography: p89-91*

MENTALLY ILL — Care and treatment — Ireland — History
ROBINS, Joseph
Fools and mad : a history of the insane in Ireland / Joseph Robins. — 255p, [17]p of plates. — *ill on lining papers. — Bibliography: p208-229. — Includes index*

MENTALLY ILL — Civil rights
HEGINBOTHAM, Chris
The rights of mentally ill people / Chris Heginbotham. — London : Minority Rights Group, 1987. — 12p. — (Minority Rights Group report ; no.74)

MENTALLY ILL — Housing — Great Britain
KAY, Adah
Discharged to the community : a review of housing and support in London for people leaving psychiatric care / Adah Kay and Charlie Legg. — London : Good Practices in Mental Health, 1986. — vi,91p. — "Original research funded by the Greater London Council". — Bibliography: p89-91

MENTALLY ILL — Institutional care — Great Britain
GOSTIN, Larry
Institutions observed : towards a new concept of secure provision in mental health / Larry Gostin. — London : King Edward's Hospital Fund for London, 1986. — 179p. — Bibliography: p165-172

MENTALLY ILL — Rehabilitation
Reassessing community care : (with particular reference to provision for people with mental handicap and for people with mental illness) / edited by Nigel Malin. — London : Croom Helm, c1987. — 354p. — Includes bibliographies and index

MENTALLY ILL — Rehabilitation — Great Britain
KAY, Adah
Discharged to the community : a review of housing and support in London for people leaving psychiatric care / Adah Kay and Charlie Legg. — London : Good Practices in Mental Health, 1986. — vi,91p. — "Original research funded by the Greater London Council". — Bibliography: p89-91

MENTALLY ILL — Services for — United States
BURT, Martha R
Testing the social safety net : the impact of changes in support programs during the Reagan administration / Martha R. Burt, Karen J. Pittman. — Washington, D.C. : Urban Institute Press, c1985. — xix, 183 p.. — (The Changing domestic priorities series). — Includes bibliographical references

MENTALLY ILL — Great Britain — Home care
NORMAN, A. J.
Severe dementia : the provision of longstay care / Alison Norman. — London : Centre for Policy on Ageing, 1987. — xxiv,275p. — (Policy Studies in Ageing ; No.7)

MENTALLY ILL — Wales — Statistics
GREAT BRITAIN. Welsh Office
Census of patients in mental illness hospitals and units in Wales, 31 August 1979. — [Cardiff] : the Office, [1979]. — [111]p

MENZIES, Sir ROBERT, 1894-1978
DAY, David
Menzies & Churchill at war : a controversial new account of the 1941 struggle for power / David Day. — North Ryde : Angus & Robertson, 1986. — xii,271p

MERCANTILE SYSTEM — History
EKELUND, Robert B
Mercantilism as a rent-seeking society : economic regulation in historical perspective / by Robert B. Ekelund and Robert D. Tollison. — 1st ed. — College Station, Tex. : Texas A&M University Press, 1981. — xiii, 169 p.. — (Texas A & M University economics series ; no. 5). — Includes index. — Bibliography: p. [157]-164

MERCENARY TROOPS
AKINJIDE, R. O. A.
Mercenarism and international law / Chief R. O. A. Akinjide. — [s.l.] : [s.n.], 1986. — 13p. — Lecture delivered at the International Law Seminar, Palais des nations, Geneva, on 27.5.1986

MERCHANT BANKS
FERRIS, Paul
Gentlemen of fortune : the world's merchant and investment bankers / Paul Ferris. — London : Weidenfeld & Nicolson, 1984. — 260p. — Includes index

MERCHANT BANKS — Germany — Hamburg
ANDRESEN, Bruno W. F.
Mit Stehpult und Tintenfass : Erinnerungen aus dem Kontor einer Hamburger Merchant-Bank / Bruno W. F. Andresen. — Hamburg : Christians, 1984. — 239p

MERCHANT MARINE
Prospects of demand for containerships in the second half of the 1980s. — Tokyo : Japan Maritime Research Institute, 1986. — 58p. — (Jamri report ; no.18)

MERCHANT MARINE — Management
MARCUS, Henry S.
Marine transportation management / Henry S. Marcus. — London : Croom Helm, c1987. — 322p

MERCHANT MARINE — Safety measures — Congresses
INTERNATIONAL CONFERENCE ON SHIP SAFETY AND MARINE SURVEYING (1986 : Malmo, Sweden)
International Conference on Ship Safety and Marine Surveying : [proceedings] / [organized by] the Nautical Institute and the World Maritime University, Malmo, Sweden, 8-9 May 1986. — London : Nautical Institute, 1986. — 158p

MERCHANT MARINE — Australia
AUSTRALIA. Bureau of Transport Economics. Seminar on Australia's Liner Shipping (1986 : Sydney)
Papers and proceedings. — Canberra : Australian Government Publishing Service, 1986. — viii,277p

MERCHANT MARINE — Europe — History
BERRIDGE, G. R.
The politics of the South Africa run : European Shipping and Pretoria / G.R. Berridge. — Oxford : Clarendon, 1987. — [298]p. — Includes bibliography and index

MERCHANT MARINE — South Africa — History
BERRIDGE, G. R.
The politics of the South Africa run : European Shipping and Pretoria / G.R. Berridge. — Oxford : Clarendon, 1987. — [298]p. — Includes bibliography and index

MERCHANT MARINE — Soviet Union
LONG, D. M.
The Soviet merchant fleet : its growth, strategy, strength and weaknesses 1920-1999 : a special report / by D.M. Long. — London : Lloyd's of London Press, 1986. — [164]p. — Includes bibliography

MERCHANT SEAMEN — Canada
GREEN, Jim
Against the tide : the story of the Canadian Seamen's Union / Jim Green. — Toronto : Progress Books, 1986. — 324p. — Bibliography: p297-316

MERCHANT SEAMEN — Canada — History
KAPLAN, William
Everything that floats : Pat Sullivan, Hal Banks, and the Seamen's Unions of Canada / William Kaplan. — Toronto : University of Toronto Press, 1987. — xii,241p. — Bibliography: p[227]-231

MERCHANT SEAMEN — Pacific States — History
SCHWARTZ, Stephen
Brotherhood of the sea : a history of the Sailors' Union of the Pacific, 1885-1985 / by Stephen Schwartz ; foreword by Paul Dempster, preface by John F. Henning, introduction by Karl Kortum. — San Francisco, CA : Sailors' Union of the Pacific ; New Brunswick, USA : Distributed by Transaction Books, c1986. — p. cm. — Includes index

MERCHANT SHIPS — Great Britain — Statistics
Nationality of vessels in United Kingdom seaborne trade. — London : HMSO, 1973-. — (Business monitor. MA ; 8) (Business monitor. M ; 8). — Annual

MERCHANTS — Canada — History — 18th century
BOSHER, J. F.
The Canada merchants 1713-1763 / J.F. Bosher. — Oxford : Clarendon, 1987. — viii,234p. — Includes index

MERCHANTS — China — History
MANN, Susan
Local merchants and the Chinese bureaucracy, 1750-1950 / Susan Mann. — Stanford, Calif. : Stanford University Press, 1987. — viii, 278 p.. — Includes index. — Bibliography: p. [255]-267

MERCHANTS — New Zealand — Auckland — Biography
STONE, R. C. J.
Young Logan Campbell / R.C.J. Stone. — [Auckland] : Auckland University Press ; [Oxford] : Oxford University Press, 1982. — 287p,[24]p of plates. — Bibliography: p273-280. — Includes index

MERCHANTS, FOREIGN — Chile — History — 19th century
MAYO, John
British merchants and Chilean development, 1851-1886 / John Mayo. — Boulder, Colo : Westview Press, 1986. — p. cm. — (Dellplain Latin American studies ; 22). — Bibliography: p

MERINO SHEEP — History
GARRAN, J. C.
Merinos, myths and Macarthurs : Australian graziers and their sheep, 1788-1900 / J. C. Garran and L. White. — Rushcutters Bay, N.S.W. : Australian National University Press, 1985. — xv,288p. — Bibliography: p[261]-270

MERRHEIM, ALPHONSE
PAPAYANIS, Nicholas
Alphonse Merrheim : the emergence of reformism in revolutionary syndicalism, 1871-1925 / by Nicholas Papayanis. — Dordrecht ; Lancaster : Nijhoff, 1985. — xx,184p. — (Studies in social history ; 8). — Bibliography: p169. — Includes index

MERRIAM, CHARLES E.
SIMON, Herbert A.
Charles E. Merriam and the "Chicago School" of political science / Herbert A. Simon. — Urbana, Ill. : Department of Political Science. University of Illinois at Urbana-Champaign, 1987. — 11p. — Edmund Jones James lecture. — Bibliography: p11

MESSIANISM
RODRÍGUEZ, Pepe
Esclavos de un mesías : sectas y lavado de cerebro / Pepe Rodríguez. — Barcelona : Elfos, 1984. — 277p. — (Temas de actualidad). — Bibliography: p[276]-277

MESSIANISM — Comparative studies

AHLBERG, Sture
  Messianic movements : a comparative analysis of the Sabbatians, the People's Temple, and the Unification Church / by Sture Ahlberg. — Stockholm : Almqvist & Wiksell International, 1986. — 128 p.. — (Acta Universitatis Stockholmiensis. Stockholm studies in comparative religion ; 26). — *Continuation of author's thesis (doctoral--Stockholm, 1977) originally presented as: Messianism in the State of Israel. — Includes indexes. — Bibliography: p. 118-122*

METAL TRADE

  Primary commodities : market developments and outlook / by the Commodities Division of the Research Department. — Washington, D.C. : International Monetary Fund, 1986. — vii,74p. — (World economic and financial surveys)

METAL TRADE — Employees — Effect of technological innovations on

SCHMIDTCHEN, Gerhard
  Neue Technik neue Arbeitsmoral : eine sozialpsychologische Untersuchung über Motivation in der Metallindustrie / Gerhard Schmidtchen. — Köln : Deutscher Instituts-Verlag, 1984. — 382p

METAL-WORKERS — Germany (West)

  Krisenpolitik und Belegschaftsverhalten : Metallarbeiter zwischen Gegenwehr und Unterwerfung / Norbert Kubach...[et al.]. — Hamburg : VSA-Verlag, 1985. — 155p. — *Bibliography: p154-155*

SCHMIDTCHEN, Gerhard
  Neue Technik neue Arbeitsmoral : eine sozialpsychologische Untersuchung über Motivation in der Metallindustrie / Gerhard Schmidtchen. — Köln : Deutscher Instituts-Verlag, 1984. — 382p

METAL-WORKERS' STRIKE, U.S., 1935 — History

SUGGS, George G.
  Union busting in the Tri-State : the Oklahoma, Kansas, and Missouri metal workers' strike of 1935 / by George G. Suggs, Jr. — Norman : University of Oklahoma Press, c1986. — xiv, 282 p.. — *Includes index. — Bibliography: p. [231]-260*

METALS — Miscellanea

ELIADE, Mircea
  [Forgerons et alchimistes. English]. The forge and the crucible / Mircea Eliade ; translated from the French by Stephen Corrin. — 2d ed. — Chicago : University of Chicago Press, 1978. — 238 p.. — *Subtitle on cover: The origins and structures of alchemy. — Translation of Forgerons et alchimistes. — Includes bibliographical references and index*

METALS — Religious aspects

ELIADE, Mircea
  [Forgerons et alchimistes. English]. The forge and the crucible / Mircea Eliade ; translated from the French by Stephen Corrin. — 2d ed. — Chicago : University of Chicago Press, 1978. — 238 p.. — *Subtitle on cover: The origins and structures of alchemy. — Translation of Forgerons et alchimistes. — Includes bibliographical references and index*

METAPHOR

COOPER, David, 1942-
  Metaphor / David Cooper. — Oxford : Blackwell, 1986. — [240]p. — (Aristotelian Society series)

METAPHYSICS

CARR, Brian
  Metaphysics : an introduction / Brian Carr. — Basingstoke : Macmillan, 1987. — [256]p.. — (Modern introductions to philosophy). — *Includes bibliography and index*

KANT, Immanuel
  Prolegomena to any future metaphysics that will be able to present itself as a science / Immanuel Kant ; a translation from the German based on the original editions with an introduction and notes by P. Gray Lucas. — Manchester : Manchester University Press, 1953. — (Philosophical classics)

METAPHYSISCHE ANFANGSGRÜNDE DER NATURWISSENSCHAFT

  Kant's philosophy of physical science : Metaphysische Anfangsgründe der Naturwissenschaft, 1786-1986 / edited by Robert E. Butts. — Dordrecht ; Lancaster : Reidel, c1986. — xii, 363p. — (The University of Western Ontario series in philosophy of science ; v. 33). — *Includes index. — Includes bibliographies*

MÉTAYER SYSTEM

CHEUNG, Steven N. S.
  The theory of share tenancy, with special application to Asian agriculture and the first phase of Taiwan land reform / by Steven N. S. Cheung. — Chicago ; London : University of Chicago P, 1969. — xv,188p. — *bibl p175-182*

MÉTAYER SYSTEM — Africa

ROBERTSON, A. F.
  The dynamics of productive relationships : African share contracts in comparative perspective / A.F. Robertson. — Cambridge : Cambridge University Press, 1987. — [341]p. — *Includes bibliography and index*

METEOROLOGY

  Disaster prevention and mitigation : a compendium of current knowledge. — New York : United Nations
  V.4: Meteorological aspects. — 1978. — viii,96p. — *Bibliography: p95-96. — "UNDRO/22/76 VOL.IV"*

METHADONE MAINTENANCE — Denmark

WINSLØW, Jacob Hilden
  Stofmisbrug, kriminalitet og metadon / Jacob Hilden Winsløw og Peter Ege. — [København] : Alkohol- og Narkotikarådet, 1984. — 95p. — (Alkohol- og Narkotikarådets skriftserie ; 2). — *Summary in English. — Bibliography: p93-95*

METHODISM

WALTON, Heather
  A tree god planted : black people in British methodism / Heather Walton, Robin Ward and Mark Johnson. — London : Ethic Minorities in Methodism Working Group, 1985. — v,73p. — *Bibliography: p73*

METHYL ISOCYANATE — Environemental aspects — India — Bhopal

SUFRIN, Sidney C.
  Bhopal, its setting, responsibility, and challenge / Sidney C. Surfin. — Delhi : Ajanta Publications : Distributors, Ajanta Books International, 1985. — 98 p.. — *60-9*

METROPOLITAN AREAS — Congresses

  The Future of the metropolis : Berlin, London, Paris, New York : economic aspects / editors, Hans-Jürgen Ewers, John B. Goddard, and Horst Matzerath. — Berlin ; New York : W. de Gruyter, 1986. — xi, 484 p.. — *"Presents the papers of an international conference ... held at the Technical University Berlin in October 1984"--Pref. — Includes bibliographies*

METROPOLITAN AREAS — Asia

SIVARAMAKRISHNAN, K. C.
  Metropolitan management : the Asian experience / K. C. Sivaramakrishnan and Leslie Green. — New York : Oxford University Press for the Economic Development Institute of the World Bank, 1986. — xiv,290p. — (EDI series in economic development). — *Includes bibliographical references*

METROPOLITAN AREAS — Canada — Congresses

  The Metropolis : proceedings of a conference in honour of Hans Blumenfeld, University of Toronto, November 4-5, 1983 / edited by John R. Hitchcock, Anne McMaster, with the assistance of Judith Kjellberg. — [Toronto] : Dept. of Geography and Centre for Urban and Community Studies, University of Toronto, c1985. — 249 p.. — *"The writings of Hans Blumenfeld": p. 241-249. — Includes bibliographies*

METROPOLITAN AREAS — Middle West

  The Metropolitan Midwest : policy problems and prospects for change / edited by Barry Checkoway and Carl V. Patton. — Urbana : University of Illinois Press, c1985. — 309 p.. — *Includes bibliographies*

METROPOLITAN AREAS — Middle West — Case studies

ELAZAR, Daniel Judah
  Cities of the prairie revisited : the closing of the metropolitan frontier / Daniel J. Elazar with Rozann Rothman ... [et al.]. — Lincoln : University of Nebraska Press, c1986. — 288 p.. — *Sequel to: Cities of the prairie. — Includes index. — Bibliography: p. [269]-276*

METROPOLITAN AREAS — Sunbelt States

ABBOTT, Carl
  The new urban America : growth and politics in Sunbelt cities / Carl Abbott. — Rev. ed. — Chapel Hill : University of North Carolina Press, c1987. — p. cm. — *Includes index. — Bibliography: p*

METROPOLITAN AREAS — United States — Congresses

  The Metropolis : proceedings of a conference in honour of Hans Blumenfeld, University of Toronto, November 4-5, 1983 / edited by John R. Hitchcock, Anne McMaster, with the assistance of Judith Kjellberg. — [Toronto] : Dept. of Geography and Centre for Urban and Community Studies, University of Toronto, c1985. — 249 p.. — *"The writings of Hans Blumenfeld": p. 241-249. — Includes bibliographies*

METROPOLITAN GOVERNMENT — Legal status, laws, etc. — England

GREAT BRITAIN. Parliament. House of Commons. Library. Research Division
  Local Government Bill [Bill 11, 1984/85] / [Barry K. Winetrobe]. — [London] : the Division, 1984. — 27p. — (Reference sheet ; no.84/12). — *Bibliographical references: p25-27*

METROPOLITAN GOVERNMENT — Legal status, laws, etc — England

GREAT BRITAIN. Parliament. House of Commons. Library. Research Division
  Local Government (Interim Provisions) Bill, Bill 145, 1983-84 / Barry K. Winetrobe. — [London] : the Division, 1984. — 20p. — (Reference sheet ; no.84/5). — *Includes bibliographical references*

METROPOLITAN GOVERNMENT — Asia

SIVARAMAKRISHNAN, K. C.
  Metropolitan management : the Asian experience / K. C. Sivaramakrishnan and Leslie Green. — New York : Oxford University Press for the Economic Development Institute of the World Bank, 1986. — xiv,290p. — (EDI series in economic development). — *Includes bibliographical references*

METROPOLITAN GOVERNMENT — Australia — Addresses, essays, lectures

  Australian urban politics : critical perspectives / edited by John Halligan and Chris Paris, with the assistance of Jan Wells. — Melbourne, Australia : Longman Cheshire, 1984. — xi, 247 p.. — (Australian studies). — *Includes index. — Bibliography: p. [222]-249*

METROPOLITAN GOVERNMENT — England

GREAT BRITAIN. Parliament. House of Commons. Library. Research Division
Local government in the English metropolitan areas / Barry K. Winetrobe. — [London] : the Division, 1984. — 33p. — (Background paper ; no.135). — *Bibliographical references: p28*

METROPOLITAN GOVERNMENT — England — Bibliography

GREAT BRITAIN. Parliament. House of Commons. Library. Research Division
"Streamlining the cities" : responses to the government's proposals / [Barry K. Winetrobe]. — [London] : the Division, 1984. — 4p. — (Reference sheet ; no.84/8)

METROPOLITAN GOVERNMENT — Great Britain

REGIONAL STUDIES ASSOCIATION. National Executive Committee
A response to the government's white paper "Streamlining the cities", Cmnd. 9063 ... / M.R. Bristow, on behalf of the National Executive Committee, Regional Studies Association. — London : R.S.A., 1984. — 23p

METROPOLITAN GOVERNMENT — Middle West — Case studies

ELAZAR, Daniel Judah
Cities of the prairie revisited : the closing of the metropolitan frontier / Daniel J. Elazar with Rozann Rothman ... [et al.]. — Lincoln : University of Nebraska Press, c1986. — 288 p.. — *Sequel to: Cities of the prairie. — Includes index. — Bibliography: p. [269]-276*

METROPOLITAN POLICE

GREATER LONDON COUNCIL. Police Committee
Policing London : collected reports of the GLC Police Committee. — [London : the Council, 1986]. — 136p

GREATER LONDON COUNCIL. Police Committee Support Unit
Guide to the Met. — [London] : the Council, 1986. — 88p

METTERNICH, CLEMENS, Fürst von

BERTIER DE SAUVIGNY, Guillaume de
Metternich / Guillaume de Bertier de Sauvigny. — Paris : Fayard, 1986. — 535p

KISSINGER, Henry A.
A world restored / Henry A. Kissinger. — Gloucester, Man. : Peter Smith, 1973. — xi,354p. — *Originally published, Houghton Mifflin, 1957. — Bibliography: p333-346*

MEXICAN AMERICAN AGRICULTURAL LABORERS — Employment — California, Northern

GONZALEZ, Juan L
Mexican and Mexican American farm workers : the California agricultural industry / Juan L. Gonzalez, Jr. — New York : Praeger, c1985. — p. cm. — *Includes index*

MEXICAN AMERICAN AGRICULTURAL LABORERS — California, Northern — Economic conditions

GONZALEZ, Juan L
Mexican and Mexican American farm workers : the California agricultural industry / Juan L. Gonzalez, Jr. — New York : Praeger, c1985. — p. cm. — *Includes index*

MEXICAN-AMERICAN BORDER REGION — Industries

Industrial strategy and planning in Mexico and the United States / edited by Sidney Weintraub. — Boulder, Colo. : Westview Press, 1986. — xiv, 279 p.. — (Westview special studies in international economics and business) . — *Includes bibliographies and index. — Contents: Industrial policy in the United States / William Diebold -- The new industrialization strategy in Mexico for the eighties / René Villarreal Arrambide -- Industrial strategy in the United States and the impact on Mexico / Sidney Weintraub -- The petrochemical industry in Mexico / Francisco Barnés de Castro, Lars Christianson -- The Mexican iron and steel industry / Gerardo M. Bueno, Gustavo S. Cortés, Rafael R. Rubio -- Steel in transition / Robert Crandall -- The U.S. motor vehicle industry / Neil D. Schuster -- Industry on the northern border of Mexico / José Luis Fernández, Jesús Tamayo -- Industry on the southern border of the United States / Jerry R. Ladman -- A United States view / Clark Reynolds -- A Mexican view / Francisco Javier Alejo*

MEXICAN AMERICAN LEADERSHIP — Politics and government

HAMMERBACK, John C
A war of words : Chicano protest in the 1960s and 1970s / John C. Hammerback, Richard J. Jensen, and Jose Angel Gutierrez. — Westport, Conn. ; London : Greenwood Press, 1985. — x, 187p. — (Contributions in ethnic studies ; no. 12). — *Includes index. — Bibliography: p.[173]-178*

MEXICAN AMERICANS — Congresses

Missions in conflict : essays on U.S.-Mexican relations and Chicano culture / Renate von Bardeleben (managing editor). — Tübingen : Narr, 1986. — xxi,304p. — *Collection of essays first presented at First International Symposium on Chicano Culture, 1984, Mainz*

MEXICAN AMERICANS — Economic conditions

MIRANDÉ, Alfredo
The Chicano experience : an alternative perspective / Alfredo Mirandé. — Notre Dame, Ind. : University of Notre Dame Press, c1985. — ix, 271p. — *Includes index. — Bibliography: p.249-267*

MEXICAN AMERICANS — Education — Texas — History — 20th century

SAN MIGUEL, Guadalupe
"Let all of them take heed" : Mexican Americans and the campaign for educational equality in Texas, 1910-1981 / by Guadalupe San Miguel, Jr. — 1st ed. — Austin : University of Texas Press, 1987. — p. cm. — (Mexican American monograph ; 11). — *Includes index. — Bibliography: p*

MEXICAN AMERICANS — Politics and government

HAMMERBACK, John C
A war of words : Chicano protest in the 1960s and 1970s / John C. Hammerback, Richard J. Jensen, and Jose Angel Gutierrez. — Westport, Conn. ; London : Greenwood Press, 1985. — x, 187p. — (Contributions in ethnic studies ; no. 12). — *Includes index. — Bibliography: p.[173]-178*

MEXICAN AMERICANS — Politics and suffrage

MOSQUEDA, Lawrence J.
Chicanos, Catholicism and political ideology / Lawrence J. Mosqueda. — Lanham ; London : University Press of America, c1986. — vii,219p . — *Bibliography: p199-213. — Includes index*

MEXICAN AMERICANS — Social conditions

MIRANDÉ, Alfredo
The Chicano experience : an alternative perspective / Alfredo Mirandé. — Notre Dame, Ind. : University of Notre Dame Press, c1985. — ix, 271p. — *Includes index. — Bibliography: p.249-267*

MEXICAN AMERICANS — Arizona — Tucson — History

SHERIDAN, Thomas E
Los Tucsonenses : the Mexican community in Tucson, 1854-1941 / Thomas E. Sheridan. — Tucson : University of Arizona Press, c1986. — xiv, 327 p., [28] p. of plates. — *Includes index. — Bibliography: p. 303-314*

MEXICAN AMERICANS — Illinois — Chicago — Ethnic identity

PADILLA, Felix M
Latino ethnic consciousness : the case of Mexican Americans and Puerto Ricans in Chicago / Felix M. Padilla. — Notre Dame, Ind. : University of Notre Dame Press, c1985. — ix, 187 p.. — *Includes index. — Bibliography: p. 173-183*

MEXICAN AMERICANS — Texas — History — 19th century

MONTEJANO, David
Anglos and Mexicans in the making of Texas, 1836-1986 / by David Montejano. — 1st ed. — Austin : University of Texas Press, 1987. — p. cm. — *Includes index. — Bibliography: p*

MEXICANS — Employment — California, Northern

GONZALEZ, Juan L
Mexican and Mexican American farm workers : the California agricultural industry / Juan L. Gonzalez, Jr. — New York : Praeger, c1985. — p. cm. — *Includes index*

MEXICANS — California, Northern — Economic conditions

GONZALEZ, Juan L
Mexican and Mexican American farm workers : the California agricultural industry / Juan L. Gonzalez, Jr. — New York : Praeger, c1985. — p. cm. — *Includes index*

MEXICO — Commerce — History — 19th century

WALKER, David W
Kinship, business, and politics : the Martínez del Río family in Mexico, 1824-1867 / by David W. Walker. — 1st ed. — Austin : University of Texas Press, 1986. — x, 278 p.. — (Latin American monographs / Institute of Latin American Studies, University of Texas at Austin ; no.70). — *Includes index. — Bibliography: p. [259]-267*

MEXICO — Description and travel

COXSEDGE, Joan
Thank God for the revolution : a journey through Central America / Joan Coxsedge ; foreword by Noam Chomsky. — Sydney ; London : Pluto Press, 1986. — xiv,175p

MEXICO — Description and travel — 1951-1980

BASSOLS BATALLA, Angel
El Noroeste de México : un estudio geográfico-económico / Angel Bassols Batalla ; colaboraron Guadalupe Alvarez Z., Arturo Ortiz Wadgymar. — México : Universidad Nacional Autónoma de México, 1972. — 622p. — *Bibliography: p603-611*

MEXICO — Dictionaries and encyclopedias

BRIGGS, Donald C.
Historical dictionary of Mexico / by Donald C. Briggs and Marvin Alisky. — Metuchen ; London : Scarecrow, 1981. — xiv,259p. — (Latin American historical dictionaries ; no.21). — *Bibliography: p237-259*

MEXICO — Economic conditions — 1918-

BASSOLS BATALLA, Angel
El Noroeste de México : un estudio geográfico-económico / Angel Bassols Batalla ; colaboraron Guadalupe Alvarez Z., Arturo Ortiz Wadgymar. — México : Universidad Nacional Autónoma de México, 1972. — 622p. — *Bibliography: p603-611*

CARDENAS, Lázaro
Condiciones económicas de México / Lázaro Cardenas. — México : [Departamento Autónomo de Prensa y Publicidad], 1937. — 13p

MEXICO — Economic conditions — 1918-
continuation
MARTÍNEZ LE CLAINCHE, Roberto
Mexico : elementos para el estudio estructural de su economía / Roberto Martínez Le Clainche. — México : U.N.A.M., Institute de Investigaciones Económicas, 1972. — 136p. — *Bibliography: p131-134*

MEXICO — Economic conditions — 1970-
MEXICO. Comisión Nacional Tripartita
Confrontación sobre problemas económicos : Museo Nacional de Antropología, 5 de junio, 1973. — [México] : Dirección General de Documentación e Informe Presidencial, [1973]. — 61p. — (Cuadernos de documentación. Serie documentos ; num.6)

RIDING, Alan
Distant neighbors : a portrait of the Mexicans / Alan Riding. — 1st ed. — New York : Knopf, 1985, c1984. — xii, 385 p.. — *Includes index. — Bibliography: p. [373]-375*

MEXICO — Economic policy
ECHEVERRÍA, Luis
Equilibrio y justicia social / Luis Echeverría Alvarez. Política laboral y desarrollo nacional / Porfirio Muñoz Ledo. — [México : s.n., ca.1973]. — 16p. — (Testimonios de política social). — *Separata de "Reseña Laboral" no.1*

ECHEVERRÍA, Luis
Una filosofía social mexicana / Luis Echeverría Alvarez. Un proyecto nacional de desarrollo / Porfirio Muñoz Ledo. — [México : s.n., ca.1973]. — 12p. — (Testimonios de política social). — *Separata de "Reseña Laboral" no.2*

LEIBY, John S.
Colonial bureaucrats and the Mexican economy : growth of a patrimonial state, 1763-1821 / John S. Leiby. — New York : P. Lang, c1986. — xvii, 252 p.. — (American university studies. Series IX. History ; vol. 13). — *Bibliography: p. [239]-252*

MARTÍNEZ LE CLAINCHE, Roberto
Mexico : elementos para el estudio estructural de su economía / Roberto Martínez Le Clainche. — México : U.N.A.M., Institute de Investigaciones Económicas, 1972. — 136p. — *Bibliography: p131-134*

MEXICO — Economic policy — 1970-
MEXICO. Comisión Nacional Tripartita
Confrontación sobre problemas económicos : Museo Nacional de Antropología, 5 de junio, 1973. — [México] : Dirección General de Documentación e Informe Presidencial, [1973]. — 61p. — (Cuadernos de documentación. Serie documentos ; num.6)

MEXICO — Emigration and immigration
GREGORY, Peter
The myth of market failure : employment and the labor market in Mexico / Peter Gregory. — Baltimore : Johns Hopkins University Press for the World Bank, 1986. — viii,299p. — *Bibliography: p281-291*

MEXICO — Foreign economic relations — European Economic Community countries
The European Economic Community and Mexico / editors, Peter Coffey and Miguel S. Wionczek. — Dordrecht ; Boston : M. Nijhoff, 1987. — p. cm. — (Euro-Latin American relations - the Omagua series). — *Includes index*

MEXICO — Foreign relations — United States
VÁZQUEZ, Josefina Zoraida
The United States and Mexico / Josefina Zoraida Vázquez and Lorenzo Meyer. — Chicago : University of Chicago Press, 1985. — xiii, 220p. — (The United States and the world. foreign perspectives). — *Includes index. — Bibliography: p.199-207*

MEXICO — History — Spanish Colony, 1540-1810
LEIBY, John S.
Colonial bureaucrats and the Mexican economy : growth of a patrimonial state, 1763-1821 / John S. Leiby. — New York : P. Lang, c1986. — xvii, 252 p.. — (American university studies. Series IX. History ; vol. 13). — *Bibliography: p. [239]-252*

MEXICO — History — 1810-
KNAPP, Averill
The life of Sebastián Lerdo de Tejada 1823-1889 : a study of influence and obscurity / by Frank Averill Knapp. — Reprint ed.. — New York : Greenwood Press, 1968. — ix,292p. — *Bibliography: p269-280*

MEXICO — History — 1821-1861
GREEN, Stanley C
The Mexican Republic : the first decade, 1823-1832 / Stanley C. Green. — Pittsburgh, PA : University of Pittsburgh Press, 1986. — p. cm. — (Pitt Latin American series). — *Includes index. — Bibliography: p*

MEXICO — History — 1910-1946
O'MALLEY, Ilene V
The myth of the revolution : hero cults and the institutionalization of the Mexican State, 1920-1940 / Ilene V. O'Malley. — New York : Greenwood Press, 1986. — xii, 199 p.. — (Contributions to the study of world history ; no. 1). — *Includes index. — Bibliography: p.[179]-194*

MEXICO — Industries — Case studies
Industrial strategy and planning in Mexico and the United States / edited by Sidney Weintraub. — Boulder, Colo. : Westview Press, 1986. — xiv, 279 p.. — (Westview special studies in international economics and business) . — *Includes bibliographies and index. — Contents: Industrial policy in the United States / William Diebold -- The new industrialization strategy in Mexico for the eighties / René Villarreal Arrambide -- Industrial strategy in the United States and the impact on Mexico / Sidney Weintraub -- The petrochemical industry in Mexico / Francisco Barnés de Castro, Lars Christianson -- The Mexican iron and steel industry / Gerardo M. Bueno, Gustavo S. Cortés, Rafael R. Rubio -- Steel in transition / Robert Crandall -- The U.S. motor vehicle industry / Neil D. Schuster -- Industry on the northern border of Mexico / José Luis Fernández, Jesús Tamayo -- Industry on the southern border of the United States / Jerry R. Ladman -- A United States view / Clark Reynolds -- A Mexican view / Francisco Javier Alejo*

MEXICO — Officials and employees
MEXICO. Secretaría de Relaciones Exteriores
Funcionarios de la Secretaría de Relaciones desde el año de 1821 a 1940. — México : the Secretaría, 1940. — 205p

MEXICO — Politics and government — 1810-
WALKER, David W
Kinship, business, and politics : the Martínez del Río family in Mexico, 1824-1867 / by David W. Walker. — 1st ed. — Austin : University of Texas Press, 1986. — x, 278 p.. — (Latin American monographs / Institute of Latin American Studies, University of Texas at Austin ; no.70). — *Includes index. — Bibliography: p. [259]-267*

MEXICO — Politics and government — 20th century
CAMP, Roderic Ai
Intellectuals and the state in twentieth-century Mexico / by Roderic A. Camp. — Austin : University of Texas Press, 1985. — ix, 279p. — (Latin American monographs ; no. 65). — *Includes index. — Bibliography: p.[233]-265*

LEVY, Daniel C
Mexico : paradoxes of stability and change / by Daniel Levy, Gabriel Székely. — 2nd ed., rev. and updated. — Boulder : Westview Press, 1986. — p. cm. — (Westview profiles. Nations of contemporary Latin America). — *Includes index*

MEXICO — Politics and government — 1946-
DE ROUFFIGNAC, Ann Elizabeth Lucas
The contemporary peasantry in Mexico : a class analysis / by Ann Elizabeth Lucas de Rouffignac. — New York : Praeger, 1985. — xix, 203p. — *Includes index. — Bibliography: p[186]-196*

MEXICO — Politics and government — 1970-
Mexico's political stability : the next five years / edited by Roderic A. Camp. — Boulder : Westview Press, 1986. — ix, 279 p. — (Westview special studies on Latin America and the Caribbean). — *Includes bibliographies and index. — Contents: Overview / Roderic A. Camp -- The political consequences of changing socialization patterns / Daniel C. Levy -- How will economic recovery be managed? / William P. Glade -- Distributional and sectoral problems in the New Economic Policy / William P. Glade -- Leadership and change, Intellectuals and technocrats in Mexico / Peter H. Smith -- The impact of major groups on policy-making trends in government-business relations in Mexico / John Bailey -- The evolution of the Mexican military and its implications for civil-military relations / Edward J. Williams -- What explains the decline of the PRI and will it continue? / John Bailey -- Potential strengths of the political opposition and what it means to the PRI / Roderic A. Camp -- The implications of the border for Mexican-United States relations / Edward J. Williams -- The implications of Central American conflicts for Mexican politics / Daniel C. Levy*

RIDING, Alan
Distant neighbors : a portrait of the Mexicans / Alan Riding. — 1st ed. — New York : Knopf, 1985, c1984. — xii, 385 p.. — *Includes index. — Bibliography: p. [373]-375*

MEXICO — Presidents
La clase obrera en la historia de México. — México : Siglo Veintiuno
11: Del avilacamachismo al alemanismo (1940-1952) / Jorge Basurto. — 1984. — 291p

MEXICO — Presidents — Biography
KNAPP, Averill
The life of Sebastián Lerdo de Tejada 1823-1889 : a study of influence and obscurity / by Frank Averill Knapp. — Reprint ed.. — New York : Greenwood Press, 1968. — ix,292p. — *Bibliography: p269-280*

MEXICO — Relations — United States — Congresses
Missions in conflict : essays on U.S.-Mexican relations and Chicano culture / Renate von Bardeleben (managing editor). — Tübingen : Narr, 1986. — xxi,304p. — *Collection of essays first presented at First International Symposium on Chicano Culture, 1984, Mainz*

MEXICO — Rural conditions
TUTINO, John
From insurrection to revolution in Mexico : social bases of agrarian violence, 1750-1940 / John Tutino. — Princeton, N.J. : Princeton University Press, c1986. — xx, 425 p.. — *Includes index. — Bibliography: p. [399]-417*

MEXICO — Social conditions
Pouvoirs et contre-pouvoirs dans la culture mexicaine / Louis Panabière, coordinateur. — Paris : CNRS, 1985. — 160p. — (Amérique latine-pays ibériques). — *Bibliography: p161*

VALLARTA, Ignacio Luis
Vallarta en la reforma / prólogo y selección: Moisés González Navarro. — México, D.F. : Universidad Nacional Autónoma de México, 1956. — xxxv,232p. — (Biblioteca del estudiante Universitario ; 76)

MEXICO — Social conditions — 1970-
RIDING, Alan
Distant neighbors : a portrait of the Mexicans / Alan Riding. — 1st ed. — New York : Knopf, 1985, c1984. — xii, 385 p.. — *Includes index. — Bibliography: p. [373]-375*

MEXICO — Social policy
ECHEVERRÍA, Luis
Equilibrio y justicia social / Luis Echeverría Alvarez. Política laboral y desarrollo nacional / Porfirio Muñoz Ledo. — [México : s.n., ca.1973]. — 16p. — (Testimonios de política social). — *Separata de "Reseña Laboral" no.1*

ECHEVERRÍA, Luis
Una filosofía social mexicana / Luis Echeverría Alvarez. Un proyecto nacional de desarrollo / Porfirio Muñoz Ledo. — [México : s.n., ca.1973]. — 12p. — (Testimonios de política social). — *Separata de "Reseña Laboral" no.2*

MEXICO. Comisión Federal de Electricidad
Energy efficiency and conservation in Mexico : perspectives on efficiency and conservation policies / edited by Oscar Guzmán, Antonio Yúnez-Naude, Miguel S. Wionczek. — Boulder, Colo. : Westview Press, 1986. — p. cm. — (Westview special studies on Latin America and the Caribbean). — *Bibliography: p*

MEXICO. Secretaría de Relaciones Exteriores — Officials and employees
MEXICO. Secretaría de Relaciones Exteriores
Funcionarios de la Secretaría de Relaciones desde el año de 1821 a 1940. — México : the Secretaría, 1940. — 205p

MEXICO, VALLEY OF (MEXICO) — Economic conditions
HASSIG, Ross
Trade, tribute, and transportation : the sixteenth-century political economy of the Valley of Mexico / by Ross Hassig. — Norman : University of Oklahoma Press, c1985. — xvi, 364p. — (Civilization of the American Indian series ; v. 171). — *Includes index. — Bibliography: p 319-350*

MICHAEL HENLEY AND SON — History
VILLE, Simon P.
English shipowning during the industrial revolution : Michael Henley and Son, London shipowners, 1770-1830 / Simon P. Ville. — Manchester : Manchester University Press, c1987. — [224]p. — *Includes bibliography and index*

MICHIGAN — Industries — Location — Case studies
JONES, Bryan D
The sustaining hand : community leadership and corporate power / Bryan D. Jones and Lynn W. Bachelor with Carter Wilson. — Lawrence, Kan. : University Press of Kansas, c1986. — xii, 247 p.. — (Studies in government and public policy). — *Includes index. — Bibliography: p. 223-239*

MICHNIK, ADAM — Addresses, essays, lectures
MICHNIK, Adam
Letters from prison and other essays / Adam Michnik ; translated by Maya Latynski ; foreword by Czeslaw Milosz ; introduction by Jonathan Schell. — Berkeley ; London : University of Calif. Press, c1985. — xlii, 354p. — *Translated from Polish*

MICROCOMPUTERS
BESSANT, J. R.
Microprocessors in production processes / John Bessant. — London : Policy Studies Institute, 1982. — 134p. — (P.S.I. ; no.609)

BHASKAR, Krish
The impact of microprocessors on the small accounting practice / K.N. Bhaskar and B.C. Williams. — Englewood Cliffs, N.J. ; London : Prentice-Hall in association with the Institute of Chartered Accountants in England & Wales, c1986. — xvi,167p. — (Research studies in accounting). — *Bibliography: p143-162. — Includes index*

BRIGHTMAN, Richard W
Using computers in an information age / Richard W. Brightman, Jeffrey M. Dimsdale. — Albany, N.Y. : Delmar Publishers, c1986. — p. cm. — *Includes index. — Bibliography: p*

BUGG, Phillip W
Microcomputers in the corporate environment / Phillip W. Bugg. — Englewood Cliffs, N.J. : Prentice-Hall, c1986. — xv, 192 p.. — *Includes index*

CORNFORD, Tony
Designing a computer workstation for researchers in the quantitative social sciences / Tony Cornford, Brian Hayes. — [London : London School of Economics and Political Science], 1986. — 19p. — (Taxation, incentives and the distribution of income ; no.93). — *Economic and Social Research Council programme. — Bibliographical references: p19*

GARSON, G. David
Academic microcomputing : a resource guide / G. David Garson. — Beverly Hills : Sage Publications, c1987. — 175 p.. — *Includes bibliographies*

MADRON, Thomas W.
Using microcomputers in research / Thomas Wm Madron, C. Neal Tate [and] Robert G. Brookshire. — Beverly Hills ; London : Sage, 1985. — 87 p. — (Quantitative applications in the social sciences ; 52)

Micros in practice : report of an appraisal of GP microcomputer systems / sponsored jointly by the Department of Health and Social Security and the Joint Computer Policy Group. — London : H.M.S.O., 1986. — ii,130, [34]p. — *'User survey ... carried out by a team from the Department of General Practice at Exeter University' — preface*

PFAFFENBERGER, Bryan
The scholar's personal computing handbook : a practical guide / Bryan Pfaffenberger. — Boston : Little, Brown, c1986. — xiii, 359 p.. — (The Little, Brown microcomputer bookshelf). — *Includes bibliographies and index*

MICROCOMPUTERS — Congresses
CONFERENCE "OR MODELS ON MICROCOMPUTERS" (1985 : Lisbon, Portugal)
OR models on microcomputers : proceedings of the Conference "OR Models on Microcomputers" held in Lisbon, Portugal, 25-27 September, 1985 / edited by J.D. Coelho and L.V. Tavares. — Amsterdam ; New York : North-Holland ; New York, N.Y. : Sole distributors for the U.S.A. and Canada, Elsevier Science Pub. Co., 1986. — p. cm

Impacts of microcomputers on operations research : proceedings of a symposium sponsored by the Computer Science Technical Section of the Operations Research Society of America, held on March 20-22, 1985, at the University of Colorado at Denver, Denver, Colorado, U.S.A. / editors, Saul I. Gass ... [et a.]. — New York : North-Holland, c1986. — viii, 255 p.. — (Publications in operations research series ; v. 5). — *Papers presented at the Symposium on Impacts of Microcomputers on Operations Research. — Includes bibliographies and index*

MICROCOMPUTERS — Design and construction
WRAY, William C
What every engineer should know about microcomputer systems design and debugging / Bill Wray and Bill Crawford. — New York, N.Y. : M. Dekker, c1984. — ix, 183 p.. — (What every engineer should know ; v. 12). — *Includes index*

MICROCOMPUTERS — Library applications
BURTON, Paul F.
The librarian's guide to microcomputers for information management / Paul F. Burton and J. Howard Petrie. — Wokingham : Van Nostrand Reinhold, 1986. — vii,271p. — *New ed. — Previous ed.: published as Introducing microcomputers. 1984. — Bibliography: p253-264. — Includes index*

MICROCOMPUTERS — Programming
WRAY, William C
What every engineer should know about microcomputer systems design and debugging / Bill Wray and Bill Crawford. — New York, N.Y. : M. Dekker, c1984. — ix, 183 p.. — (What every engineer should know ; v. 12). — *Includes index*

MICROECONOMICS
BAUMOL, William J.
Economic theory and operations analysis / William J. Baumol. — 4th ed. — Englewood Cliffs, N.J : Prentice-Hall, c1977. — xxi, 695 p. — (Prentice-Hall international series in management). — *Includes bibliographies and index*

BENASSY, Jean-Pascal
Macroeconomics : an introduction to the Non-Walrasian approach / Jean-Pascal Benassy. — Orlando : Academic Press, 1986. — p. cm. — (Economic theory, econometrics, and mathematical economics). — *Includes index. — Bibliography: p*

CHACHOLIADES, Miltiades
Microeconomics / Miltiades Chacholiades. — New York : Macmillan ; London : Collier Macmillan, c1986. — xvii, 629p. — *Includes bibliographies and index*

COWELL, F. A.
Microeconomic principles / Frank A. Cowell. — Oxford : Philip Allan, 1986. — lx,413p. — *Includes index*

The Economic nature of the firm : a reader / edited by Louis Putterman with the assistance of Randy Kroszner. — Cambridge : Cambridge University Press, 1986. — x,371p. — *Bibliography: p356-371*

HEY, John D.
Uncertainty in microeconomics / John D. Hey. — Oxford : Martin Robertson, 1979. — ix,261p. — *Bibliography: p.243-253. — Includes index*

KING, David N.
Microeconomics : an introduction to theory and applications / David King, Ronald Shone. — London : Edward Arnold, 1987. — xi,224p. — *Includes index*

LYONS, Brian
Canadian microeconomics : problems and policies / Brian Lyons. — 3rd ed. — Scarborough, Ontario : Prentice-Hall Canada, 1987. — xvi,388p

TERRY, Chris
Australian microeconomics : policies and industry cases / Chris Terry, Ross Jones, Richard Braddock. — 2nd ed. — Sydney : Prentice-Hall of Australia, c1985. — xi, 362 p.. — *Includes bibliographies*

ZAMAGNI, Stefano
Microeconomic theory : an introduction / Stefano Zamagni. — Oxford : Basil Blackwell, 1986. — [480]p. — *Translation of: Economia politica. — Includes bibliography and index*

MICROECONOMICS — Addresses, essays, lectures
Microeconomic theory / edited by Larry Samuelson. — Boston : Kluwer-Nijhoff Pub. ; Hingham, MA, U.S.A. : Distributors for the United States and Canada, Kluwer Academic Publishers, c1986. — xv, 278 p.. — (Recent economic thought series). — *Includes bibliographies and index*

MICROECONOMICS — Mathematical models
RASHID, Salim
Economies with many agents : an approach using nonstandard analysis / Salim Rashid. — Baltimore : Johns Hopkins University Press, c1987. — xii, 160 p.. — *Includes indexes. — Bibliography: p. [149]-156*

MICROELECTRONICS

NATIONAL ECONOMIC DEVELOPMENT COUNCIL. Economic Development Committee for the Information Technology Industry. Long-Term Perspectives Group
I T futures...it can work : an optimistic view of the long-term potential of information technology for Britain. — London : [H.M.S.O.], 1987. — xiv,171p. — *Chairman: Alan Benjamin. — Includes bibliographical references*

MICROELECTRONICS — Economic aspects

WHITE, G. C.
Redesign of work organisations - its impact on supervisors / Geoff White. — London : Work Research Unit, 1983. — 10p. — (WRU occasional paper ; 26). — *At head of title page: Advisory, Conciliation and Arbitration Service. — Bibliographical references: p9-10*

MICROELECTRONICS — Economic aspects — Great Britain

NORTHCOTT, Jim
Microelectronics in industry : promise and performance / Jim Northcott. — London : Policy Studies Institute, c1986. — 258p. — (Research report ; 657)

NORTHCOTT, Jim
Promoting innovation 2 : microelectronics consultancy support / Jim Northcott...[et al.]. — London : Policy Studies Institute, 1986. — 181p. — (PSI Research Report ; 662)

Planning for microelectronics in the workplace / edited by Peter J. Senker. — Aldershot : Gower, c1985. — ix,175p. — *Includes bibliographies*

MICROELECTRONICS — Popular works

MIMS, Forrest M
Siliconnections : coming of age in the electronic era / Forrest M. Mims, III. — New York : McGraw-Hill, c1986. — viii, 208 p.. — *Includes index*

MICROELECTRONICS — Social aspects

NATIONAL RESEARCH COUNCIL (U.S.). Committee on Women's Employment and Related Social Issues. Panel on Technology and Women's Employment
Computer chips and paper clips : technology and women's employment / Heidi I. Hartmann, Robert E. Kraut, and Louise A. Tilly, editors ; Panel on Technology and Women's Employment, Committee on Women's Employment and Related Social Issues, Commission on Behavioral and Social Sciences and Education, National Research Council. — Washington, D.C. : National Academy Press, 1986-1987. — 2 v.. — *Includes bibliographies and index. — Contents: v. 1. [without special title] -- v. 2. Case studies and policy perspectives / Heidi I. Hartmann, editor*

MICROELECTRONICS — Social aspects — Great Britain — Forecasting

IT futures surveyed : a study of informed opinion concerning the long-term implications of information technology for society / a report prepared by John Bessant...[et al.] for the Long-Term Perspectives Group of the Information Technology Economic Development Committee. — London : National Economic Development Office, 1986. — x,92p

MICROELECTRONICS — Social aspects — United States

GINZBERG, Eli
Technology and employment : concepts and clarifications / Eli Ginzberg, Thierry J. Noyelle, and Thomas M. Stanback, Jr. — Boulder : Westview Press, 1986. — xi, 111 p.. — (Conservation of Human Resources studies in the new economy). — *Includes bibliographies and index*

MICROELECTRONICS — Great Britain

INFORMATION TECHNOLOGY ADVISORY PANEL
Learning to live with IT : an overview of the potential of information technology for education and training. — London : H.M.S.O., 1986. — 44p

WILLMAN, Paul
New technology and industrial relations : a review of the literature / Paul Willman. — [London] : Department of Employment, [1987]. — 55p. — (Research paper ; no.56). — *Bibliographical references: p49-53*

MICROELECTRONICS CONSULTANCY SUPPORT

NORTHCOTT, Jim
Promoting innovation 2 : microelectronics consultancy support / Jim Northcott...[et al.]. — London : Policy Studies Institute, 1986. — 181p. — (PSI Research Report ; 662)

MICROELECTRONICS INDUSTRY — Government policy — North Carolina — Addresses, essays, lectures

High hopes for high tech : microelectronics policy in North Carolina / edited by Dale Whittington. — Chapel Hill : University of Carolina Press, c1985. — p. cm. — (Urban and regional policy and development studies). — *Includes index*

MICROELECTRONICS INDUSTRY — California — Santa Clara County

MALONE, Michael S.
The big score : the billion dollar story of Silicon Valley / by Michael S. Malone. — 1st ed. — Garden City, N.Y. : Doubleday, 1985. — p. cm. — *Includes index. — Bibliography: p*

MICROELECTRONICS INDUSTRY — Great Britain

ADAMSON, Ian
Sinclair and the sunrise technology : the deconstruction of a myth / Ian Adamson and Richard Kennedy. — Harmondsworth : Penguin, 1986. — 262p

GREAT BRITAIN. Parliament. House of Commons. Library. Research Division
The UK information technology industry / C. R. Barclay. — [London] : the Division, 1987. — 33p. — (Background paper ; no.194). — *Bibliography: p33*

MICROPHOTOGRAPHY

WELLS, Rosemary, 19---
Newsplan : report of the pilot project in the south-west / Rosemary Wells. — London : British Library, c1986. — x,218p. — (Library and information research report ; 38). — *Two microfiches (11x15cm) in pocket*

MIDDLE AGED WOMEN — United States — Employment

Midlife women at work : a fifteen-year perspective / edited by Lois Banfill Shaw. — Lexington, Mass. : Lexington Books, c1986. — xi, 142 p.. — *Based on data from the National Longitudinal Surveys of Labor Market Experience of Mature Women begun in 1967 by the Ohio State University Center for Human Resource Research. — Includes bibliographies and index*

MIDDLE AGED WOMEN — United States — Social conditions

Midlife women at work : a fifteen-year perspective / edited by Lois Banfill Shaw. — Lexington, Mass. : Lexington Books, c1986. — xi, 142 p.. — *Based on data from the National Longitudinal Surveys of Labor Market Experience of Mature Women begun in 1967 by the Ohio State University Center for Human Resource Research. — Includes bibliographies and index*

MIDDLE AGES — History

HERLIHY, David
Medieval households / David Herlihy. — Cambridge, Mass. ; London : Harvard University Press, 1985. — vii, 227p. — (Studies in cultural history). — *Includes index. Bibliography: p.[161]-177*

STAFFORD, Pauline
Queens, concubines, and dowagers : the king's wife in the early Middle Ages / Pauline Stafford. — Athens, Ga. : University of Georgia Press, c1983. — xiii, 248 p.. — *Includes index. — Bibliography: p. 211-226*

MIDDLE CLASSES — History

GOODIN, Robert E.
Not only the poor : the middle classes and the welfare state / Robert E. Goodin, Julian Le Grand with John Dryzek ... [et al.]. — London : Allen & Unwin, 1987. — [288]p. — *Includes bibliography and index*

MIDDLE CLASSES — Australia

GOODIN, Robert E.
The middle class infiltration of the welfare state : some evidence from Australia / Robert E. Goodin and Julian Le Grand. — London : Welfare State Programme. Suntory-Toyota International Centre for Economics and Related Disciplines, 1986. — 29p. — (Discussion paper / Welfare State Programme. Suntory-Toyota International Centre for Economics and Related Disciplines ; no.10). — *Bibliography: p27-29*

MIDDLE CLASSES — California — Santa Monica — Case studies

KANN, Mark E
Middle class radicalism in Santa Monica / Mark E. Kann. — Philadelphia : Temple University Press, 1986. — xiv, 322 p.. — *Includes index. — Bibliography: p. [289]-314*

MIDDLE CLASSES — England — History

DAVIDOFF, Leonore
Family fortunes : men and women of the English middle class 1780-1850 / Leonore Davidoff and Catherine Hall. — London : Hutchinson, 1987. — 576p. — *Bibliography: p542-559. — Includes index*

MIDDLE CLASSES — England — London — History — 19th century

SHONFIELD, Zuzanna
The precariously privileged : a medical man's family in Victorian London / Zuzanna Shonfield. — Oxford : Oxford University Press, 1987. — [320]p. — *Includes index*

MIDDLE CLASSES — Europe — Conduct of life

MOSSE, George L
Nationalism and sexuality : respectability and abnormal sexuality in modern Europe / George L. Mosse. — 1st ed. — New York : H. Fertig, 1985. — viii, 232 p., [10] p. of plates. — *Includes index. — Bibliography: p. 195-223*

MIDDLE CLASSES — Germany (West) — Marburg — Political activity

KOSHAR, Rudy
Social life, local politics, and Nazism : Marburg, 1880-1935 / Rudy Koshar. — Chapel Hill ; London : University of North Carolina Press, c1986. — xviii, 395p. — *Includes index. — Bibliography: p.[361]-382*

MIDDLE CLASSES — Great Britain

LE GRAND, Julian
The middle classes and the welfare state / Julian Le Grand and David Winter. — London : Welfare State Programme. Suntory-Toyota International Centre for Economics and Related Disciplines, 1987. — 52p. — (Discussion paper / Welfare State Programme. Suntory-Toyota International Centre for Economics and Related Disciplines ; no.14). — *Bibliography: p51-52*

MIDDLE CLASSES — Poland — History

KOŁODZIEJCZYK, Ryszard
Burżuazja polska w XIX i XX wieku : szkice historyczne / Ryszard Kołodziejczyk. — Warszawa : Państwowy Instytut Wydawniczy, 1979. — 215p

MIDDLE CLASSES — Rhode Island — Providence — History
GILKESON, John S.
Middle-class Providence, 1820-1940 / John S. Gilkeson, Jr. — Princeton, N.J. : Princeton University Press, c1986. — ix, 380 p.. — *Includes index. — Bibliography: p. [357]-369*

MIDDLE CLASSES — Spain — Political activity
La revolución burguesa en España : actas del Coloquio hispano-alemán celebrado en Leipzig los dias 17 y 18 de noviembre de 1983 / edición e introducción de Alberto Gil Novales. — Madrid : Universidad Complutense, 1985. — 291p

MIDDLE CLASSES — Spain — Castellón de la Plana — History — 19th century
MARTÍ, Manuel
Cossieros i anticossieros : burgesia i política local, Castelló de la Plana, 1875-1891 / Manuel Martí. — [Castelló] : Diputació Provincial de Castelló, 1985. — 333 p.. — (Col·lecció universitària). — *: Originally presented as the author's thesis (llicenciatura--Universitat de València, 1984) under the title: Burgesia i política local, Castelló de la Plana, 1875-1891. — Bibliography: p. 323-333*

MIDDLE CLASSES — Spain — Catalonia
JUTGLAR, Antoni
[Els burgesos catalans. Spanish]. Historia crítica de la burguesía en Cataluña / Antoni Jutglar. — Edición ampliada. — [Barcelona] : Anthropos, [1984]. — 554p. — (Historia, ideas y textos ; 8). — *Publicado originalmente en catalán por Editorial Norfeu, Barcelona, 1966. — Con un "Prólogo para no catalanes" y "Unas últimas reflexiones: en turno a unas posibles claves para la comprensión de la burguesía catalana actual"*

MUNIESA, Bernat
La burguesía catalana ante la II República española / Bernat Muniesa ; prólogo de Antoni Jutglar. — Barcelona : Anthropos. — (Historia, ideas y textos ; 10)
1: "Il trovatore" frente a Wotan. — 1985. — 321p

MUNIESA, Bernat
La burguesía catalana ante la II República española (1931-1936) / Bernat Muniesa. — Barcelona : Anthropos. — (Historia, ideas y textos ; 12)
2: El triunfo de Wagner sobre Verdi. — 1986. — 262p

MIDDLE CLASSES — United States
BENSMAN, Joseph
American society : the welfare state & beyond / Joseph Bensman & Arthur J. Vidich. — Rev. — South Hadley, Mass. : Bergin & Garvey Publishers, 1986. — p. cm. — *: Previous ed. published as: The new American society. 1971. — Includes index. — Bibliography: p*

MIDDLE EAST — Economic conditions
The Middle East : from transition to development / edited by Sami G. Hajjar. — Leiden : E.J. Brill, 1985. — 158 p.. — (International studies in sociology and social anthropology ; v. 41). — *Includes bibliographies and index. — Contents: Introduction: The Middle East, from transition to development / Sami G. Hajjar -- Middle East oil and economic development / Abbas Alnasrawi -- Spatial aspects of demographic change in the Arab world / Basheer K. Nijim -- Modernization and political development in the Middle East / J. Leo Cefkin -- The so-called Renaissance of Islam / Antonie Wessels -- Education and political development in the Middle East / Nancy W. Jabbra and Joseph G. Jabbra -- The processes of administrative change in the Arab Middle East / Zaki R. Gosheh -- Leadership, ideology, and development in the Middle East / Bashir Khadra -- Development and the evolving foreign policy orientations of Middle East regimes -- Between Lebanon and the Gulf / David B. Capitanchik*

MIDDLE EAST — Foreign relations — Germany (West)
ROLEF, Susan Hattis
The Middle East policy of the Federal Republic of Germany / Susan Hattis Rolef. — Jerusalem : Magnes Press, Hebrew University, 1985. — 79, [1] p.. — (Jerusalem papers on peace problems ; 39). — *Bibliography: p. 76-[80]*

MIDDLE EAST — Foreign relations — Iran
RAMAZANI, Rouhollah K.
Revolutionary Iran : challenge and response in the Middle East / R.K. Ramazani. — Baltimore : Johns Hopkins University Press, c1986. — xv, 311 p.. — *Includes index. — Bibliography: p. 295-302*

MIDDLE EAST — Foreign relations — United States
NOVIK, Nimrod
Encounter with reality : Reagan and the Middle East during the first term / Nimrod Novik. — Jerusalem, Israel : Jerusalem Post ; Boulder, Colo. : Westview Press, c1985. — 106 p.. — (JCSS study ; no. 1). — *Bibliography: p. 99-106*

MIDDLE EAST — Politics and government
The Government and politics of the Middle East and North Africa / edited by David E. Long and Bernard Reich. — Boulder, Colo. : Westview Press, 1980. — xiv, 480 p.. — *Includes bibliographies and index*

Israel, the Middle East and the great powers : studies in the contemporary history and politics of the Middle East and the Arab-Israel conflict / edited by Israel Stockman-Shomron. — [Jerusalem] : Shikmona Publishing Co., 1984. — 389p

The Middle East : from transition to development / edited by Sami G. Hajjar. — Leiden : E.J. Brill, 1985. — 158 p.. — (International studies in sociology and social anthropology ; v. 41). — *Includes bibliographies and index. — Contents: Introduction: The Middle East, from transition to development / Sami G. Hajjar -- Middle East oil and economic development / Abbas Alnasrawi -- Spatial aspects of demographic change in the Arab world / Basheer K. Nijim -- Modernization and political development in the Middle East / J. Leo Cefkin -- The so-called Renaissance of Islam / Antonie Wessels -- Education and political development in the Middle East / Nancy W. Jabbra and Joseph G. Jabbra -- The processes of administrative change in the Arab Middle East / Zaki R. Gosheh -- Leadership, ideology, and development in the Middle East / Bashir Khadra -- Development and the evolving foreign policy orientations of Middle East regimes -- Between Lebanon and the Gulf / David B. Capitanchik*

MIDDLE EAST — Politics and government — 1945-
KREISKY, Bruno
Das Nahostproblem : Reden, Interviews, Kommentare / Bruno Kreisky ; [Claudia Reinhardt (Hrsgn)] ; [mit einem Vorwort von Olof Palme]. — Wien : Europaverlag, 1985. — 262p

RAMAZANI, Rouhollah K.
Revolutionary Iran : challenge and response in the Middle East / R.K. Ramazani. — Baltimore : Johns Hopkins University Press, c1986. — xv, 311 p.. — *Includes index. — Bibliography: p. 295-302*

MIDDLE EAST — Relations
KREISKY, Bruno
Das Nahostproblem : Reden, Interviews, Kommentare / Bruno Kreisky ; [Claudia Reinhardt (Hrsgn)] ; [mit einem Vorwort von Olof Palme]. — Wien : Europaverlag, 1985. — 262p

MIDDLE EAST — Relations — Japan — Congresses
Japan and the Middle East in alliance politics / edited by Ronald A. Morse. — Washington, D.C. : Asia Program, International Security Studies Program, Wilson Center ; Lanham, MD : University Press of America, c1986. — 124 p.. — (Conference report / Wilson Center) . — *Papers presented at a conference held at the Wilson Center on Nov. 16, 1984; co-sponsored by the Asia and the International Security Studies Programs of the Wilson Center. — Includes bibliographies*

MIDDLE EAST — Social conditions
GERBER, Haim
The social origins of the modern Middle East / Haim Gerber. — Boulder, Colo. : Rienner ; London : Mansell, 1987. — vii,221p. — *Bibliography: p213-215. — Includes index*

The Middle East : from transition to development / edited by Sami G. Hajjar. — Leiden : E.J. Brill, 1985. — 158 p.. — (International studies in sociology and social anthropology ; v. 41). — *Includes bibliographies and index. — Contents: Introduction: The Middle East, from transition to development / Sami G. Hajjar -- Middle East oil and economic development / Abbas Alnasrawi -- Spatial aspects of demographic change in the Arab world / Basheer K. Nijim -- Modernization and political development in the Middle East / J. Leo Cefkin -- The so-called Renaissance of Islam / Antonie Wessels -- Education and political development in the Middle East / Nancy W. Jabbra and Joseph G. Jabbra -- The processes of administrative change in the Arab Middle East / Zaki R. Gosheh -- Leadership, ideology, and development in the Middle East / Bashir Khadra -- Development and the evolving foreign policy orientations of Middle East regimes -- Between Lebanon and the Gulf / David B. Capitanchik*

MIDDLE WEST — Race relations
The ethnic frontier : essays in the history of group survival in Chicago and the Midwest / edited by Melvin G. Holli and Peter d'A. Jones. — Grand Rapids : Eerdmans, c1977. — 422p. — *Includes bibliographical references and index*

MIDDLESEX — History
MIDDLESEX VICTORIA COUNTY HISTORY COUNCIL
The Middlesex Victoria County History Council 1955-1984 : an account of its work and a guide to the contents of Volumes I-VIII of the Middlesex History / [I. W. Davies, Chairman]. — London : University of London Institute of Historical Research, 1984. — 29p

MIDLAND BANK GROUP — History
HOLMES, A. R.
Midland : 150 years of banking business / A.R. Holmes & Edwin Green. — London : B.T. Batsford, 1986. — xvi, 352p, 41p of plates

MIDLANDS (ENGLAND) — Industries — History — Bibliography
GREENWOOD, John, 1940-
The industrial archaeology and industrial history of the English Midlands : a bibliography / by John Greenwood. — Cranfield : Kewdale, 1987. — 410p. — *Includes index*

MIGRANT AGRICULTURAL LABORERS — Kenya — History — 20th century
KANOGO, Tabitha
Squatters and the roots of Mau Mau / Tabitha Kanogo. — London : Currey, 1987. — [224]p. — (East African studies). — *Includes bibliography and index*

MIGRANT LABOR
GERHARDT, Paul
The people trade : an IBT study guide / Paul Gerhardt, Stuart Howard [and] Pratibha Parmar. — London : International Broadcasting Trust, 1985. — 64p

MIGRANT LABOR — Health and hygiene — United States

JOHNSTON, Helen L.
Health for the nation's harvesters : a history of the Migrant Health Program in its economic and social setting / Helen L. Johnston. — Farmington Hills, Mich. : National Migrant Worker Council, 1985. — 252p. — *Bibliography: p[193]-206*

MIGRANT LABOR — Legal status, laws, etc. — Europe — Congresses

Situation juridique et sociale des travailleurs migrants en Europe : conference internationale / organisée par l'Association Internationale des Juristes Démocrates. — Bruxelles : Association Internationale des Juristes Democrates, 1977. — 224p

MIGRANT LABOR — Medical care — Europe

CONSULTATIVE GROUP ON ETHNIC MINORITIES (1983 : The Hague)
Migration and health : towards an understanding of the health care needs of ethnic minorities : proceedings of a Consultative Group on Ethnic Minorities, The Hague, Netherlands 28-30 November 1983 / edited by M. Colledge, H. A. van Geuns and P. -G. Svensson. — Copenhagen : World Health Organization, Regional Office for Europe, 1986. — vii,203p. — *Includes bibliographical references*

MIGRANT LABOR — Medical care — United States

JOHNSTON, Helen L.
Health for the nation's harvesters : a history of the Migrant Health Program in its economic and social setting / Helen L. Johnston. — Farmington Hills, Mich. : National Migrant Worker Council, 1985. — 252p. — *Bibliography: p[193]-206*

MIGRANT LABOR — America — Congresses

The Americas in the new international division of labor / edited by Steven E. Sanderson. — New York, N.Y. : Holmes & Meier, 1985. — p. cm. — *Includes index.* — *Bibliography: p*

MIGRANT LABOR — Europe — History

LUCASSEN, Jan
Migrant labour in Europe, 1600-1900 : the drift to the North Sea / Jan Lucassen ; translated by Donald A. Bloch. — London : Croom Helm, c1987. — 339p,[16]p of plates. — *Bibliography: p312-327.* — *Includes index*

MIGRANT LABOR — European Economic Community countries

The children of migrant workers. — Luxembourg : Office for Official Publications of the European Communities, 1977. — 53p. — (Education series / Commission of the European Communities ; no.1)

MIGRANT LABOR — France

Travail et frontière : le cas franco-genevois / Claude Raffestin [et al.]. — Genève : Université de Genève. Département de Géographie, 1971. — 79p

MIGRANT LABOR — Panama Canal (Panama)

CONNIFF, Michael L
Black labor on a white canal : Panama, 1904-1981 / Michael L. Conniff. — Pittsburgh : University of Pittsburgh Press, 1985. — p. cm . — *Includes index.* — *Bibliography: p*

MIGRANT LABOR — Switzerland — Geneva

Travail et frontière : le cas franco-genevois / Claude Raffestin [et al.]. — Genève : Université de Genève. Département de Géographie, 1971. — 79p

MIGRANT LABORERS — Soviet Union — History

TUDORIANU, N. L.
Ocherki rossiiskoi trudovoi emigratsii perioda imperializma : (v Germaniiu, Skandinavskie strany i SShA) / N. L. Tudorianu ; otv. redaktor E. M. Shchagin. — Kishinev : Shtiintsa, 1986. — 309p

MIGRANT LABOUR — Scotland

SHERWWOD, Marika
The British Honduran forestry unit in Scotland 1941-43 / Marika Sherwwod. — London : One Caribbean, 1982. — 51p. — *Bibliography: p.51*

MIGRANT LABOUR — South Africa

JEEVES, Alan H.
Migrant labour in South Africa's mining economy : the struggle for the gold mines' labour supply 1890-1920 / Alan H. Jeeves. — Kingston, Canada : McGill-Queen's University Press, 1985. — xiv,323p

MIGRATION ACT 1958

Human rights and the Migration Act 1985. — Canberra : Australian Government Publishing Service, 1985. — xiv,211p. — (Report / Human Rights Commission ; no.13)

MIGRATION, INTERNAL — Case studies

Migration and settlement : a multiregional comparative study / edited by Andrei Rogers and Frans J. Willekens. — Dordrecht ; Lancaster : Reidel, 1986. — xiii, 496p. — (The Geojournal library). — *Bibliography: p.475-489*

MIGRATION, INTERNAL — Cross-cultural studies

Migration and settlement : a multiregional comparative study / edited by Andrei Rogers and Frans J. Willekens. — Dordrecht ; Lancaster : Reidel, 1986. — xiii, 496p. — (The Geojournal library). — *Bibliography: p.475-489*

MIGRATION, INTERNAL — Developing countries — Research

BILSBORROW, Richard E.
Migration surveys in low income countries : guidelines for survey and questionnaire design : a study prepared for the International Labour Organisation within the framework of the World Employment Programme with the financial support of the United Nations Fund for Population Activities / Richard E. Bilsborrow, A.S. Oberai and Guy Standing. — London : Croom Helm, c1984. — 552p. — *Bibliography: p499-535.* — *Includes index*

MIGRATION, INTERNAL — Economic aspects — Portugal — History

CHANEY, Rick
Regional emigration and remittances in underdeveloped countries : the Portugese experience / by Rick Chaney. — New York : Praeger, 1986. — p. cm. — *Includes index.* — *Bibliography: p*

MIGRATION, INTERNAL — History — Congresses

Migration across time and nations : population mobility in historical contexts / edited by Ira Glazier and Luigi De Rosa. — New York ; London : Holmes & Meier, c1986. — viii, 384p . — *Papers presented at a session of the Eighth International Congress on Economic History held in Budapest in 1982.* — *Contains bibliographies*

MIGRATION, INTERNAL — Measurement — Methodology

Methods of measuring internal migration. — New York : United Nations, 1970. — x,72p. — (Manuals on methods of estimating population ; Manual 6) (Population studies / Department of Economic and Social Affairs ; no.47) ([Document] ; ST/SOA/Series A/47). — *Sales no.E.70.XIII.3*

MIGRATION, INTERNAL — Africa

Afrika zwischen Subsistenzökonomie und Imperialismus / Georg Elwert, Roland Felt (hg.) ; [mit Beiträgen von C. Meillassoux...[et al.]]. — Frankfurt/Main : Campus, 1982. — 295p. — *Bibliographies*

MIGRATION, INTERNAL — Asia, Southeastern — Congresses

Urbanization and migration in ASEAN development / edited by Philip M. Hauser, Daniel B. Suits, Naohiro Ogawa. — Tokyo : National Institute for Research Advancement, 1985. — xiv,496p. — *Papers presented at Conference on Migration and Development in ASEAN in 1984.* — *Bibliographies*

MIGRATION, INTERNAL — Australia

NEILSON ASSOCIATES PTY. LTD.
Internal migration. — Canberra : Australian Government Publishing Service, 1986. — 91p. — (Studies in adult migrant education). — *Written for the Adult Migrant Education Program 1984-85 Research Program.* — *Bibliography: p87-91*

MIGRATION, INTERNAL — Bahamas — Statistics

Commonwealth of the Bahama Islands : report of the 1980 census of population. — Nassau : Ministry of Finance
V.3: Migration. — [1986]. — xxxxi,804p

MIGRATION, INTERNAL — Bolivia — Santa Cruz (Dept.)

STEARMAN, Allyn MacLean
Camba and Kolla : migration and development in Santa Cruz, Bolivia / Allyn MacLean Stearman. — Orlando : University of Central Florida Press, c1985. — xi, 227p. — *Includes index.* — *Bibliography: p 211-217*

MIGRATION, INTERNAL — Botswana — Statistics

Final report of the National Migration Study. — Gaborone : Central Statistics Office
vol.3: Migration in Botswana : patterns, causes and consequences. — 1982. — 960p

MIGRATION, INTERNAL — Comoros — Statistics

Recensement général de la population et de l'habitat 15 Septembre 1980. — Moroni : Direction de la Statistique. — *On front cover: Bureau Central de Recensement*
vol.1: Caracteristiques demographiques et movements de la population. — 1984. — 149p

MIGRATION, INTERNAL — Egypt — Statistics

1976 Population and housing census : total Republic. — Cairo : Central Agency for Public Mobilisation and Statistics
Vol. 2: Fertility and internal migration and movement of workers and students. — 1980. — 440p

MIGRATION, INTERNAL — England — Surrey

The National Health Service Central Register as an indicator of recent migration trends in Surrey. — [Kingston upon Thames] ([County Hall, Penrhyn Rd., Kingston upon Thames KT1 2DT]) : County Planning Department, Surrey County Council, 1985. — 14leaves. — (Technical report ; no.4/85). — *Cover title*

MIGRATION, INTERNAL — Europe

Labour supply and migration in Europe : demographic dimensions 1950-1975 and prospects / prepared by the Secretariat of the Economic Commission for Europe. — New York : United Nations, 1979. — xi,332p. — *"Economic survey of Europe in 1977: part II".* — *Sales no.: E.78.II.E.20*

MIGRATION, INTERNAL — Greenland — Statistics

Vandringsstatistik 1968-1971. — [København?] : Ministeriet for Grønland. — (Meddelelser fra Statistisk Kontor / Ministeriet for Grønland ; nr.30)
A.: Vandringer internt i Grønland. — 1973. — 12,9,6p

MIGRATION, INTERNAL — India — Andaman and Nicobar Islands — Statistics

Census of India 1981 / B. K. Singh, Director of Census Operations. — [Delhi : Controller of Publications]
Series 24: Andaman and Nicobar Islands. — [1985-]

MIGRATION, INTERNAL — India — Arunachal Pradesh — Statistics
Census of India 1981. — [Delhi : Controller of Publications]
Series 25: Arunachal Pradesh. — [1985]

MIGRATION, INTERNAL — India — Chandigarh
Census of India 1981. — [New Delhi : Controller of Publications
Series 26: Chandigarh / Ardaman Singh, Director of Census Operations, Chandigarh. — 1985-]. —

MIGRATION, INTERNAL — India — Dadra and Nagar Haveli — Statistics
Census of India 1981 / S. K. Gandhe, Director of Census Operations, Dadra and Nagar Haveli. — [Delhi : Controller of Publications]
Series 27: Dadra & Nagar Haveli. — [1985-]

MIGRATION, INTERNAL — India — Pondicherry — Statistics
Census of India 1981 / P. L. Samy, Director of Census Operations, Pondicherry. — [New Delhi : Controller of Publications]
Series 32: Pondicherry. — [1985-]

MIGRATION, INTERNAL — Japan — Statistics
1980 population census of Japan / Statistics Bureau. — [Tokyo] : Statistics Bureau
Vol.7: Results of special tabulation
Part 2: Internal migration for three major metropolitan areas (out-migrants from main cities). — [1984]. — 1v (various pagings). — Text in Japanese and English

MIGRATION INTERNAL — Korea (South)
1970 population and housing census report. — [Seoul] : Bureau of Statistics, Economic Planning Board. — *In Korean and English*
Vol.2: 10% sample survey
Vol.4-3: Internal migration. — 1973. — 217p

MIGRATION, INTERNAL — Korea (South)
LEE, On-Jook
Urban-to-rural return migration in Korea / Lee On-Jook. — [Seoul] : Seoul National University Press, c1980. — xii, 182 p.. — "A publication of the Population and Development Studies Center.". — *Includes indexes.* — *Bibliography: p. 169-174*

MIGRATION, INTERNAL — Latin America — History
MÖRNER, Magnus
Adventurers and proletarians : the story of migrants in Latin America / Magnus Mörner with the collaboration of Harold Sims. — Pittsburgh, PA : University of Pittsburgh Press ; [Paris, France] : Unesco, 1985. — p. cm. — (Pitt Latin American series). — *Includes index.* — *Bibliography: p*

MIGRATION, INTERNAL — Mexico
GREGORY, Peter
The myth of market failure : employment and the labor market in Mexico / Peter Gregory. — Baltimore : Johns Hopkins University Press for the World Bank, 1986. — viii,299p. — *Bibliography: p281-291*

MIGRATION, INTERNAL — Morocco
NAJIB, Ali Ben Salah
Migration of labour and the transformation of the economy of the Wedimoon region in Morocco / Ali Ben Salah Najib. — Uppsala : Uppsala University, 1986. — xii,206p. — (Geografiska regionstudier ; nr.17). — *English text with a summary in French.* — *Doctoral dissertation at Uppsala University, 1986.* — *Bibliography: p199-206*

MIGRATION, INTERNAL — Nigeria — Kainji Reservoir Region
OYEDIPE, F. P. A
Adjustment to resettlement : a study of the resettled peoples in the Kainji Lake basin / F.P.A. Oyedipe. — Ibadan : University Press, 1983. — xvi, 167 p.. — *Includes bibliographical references and index*

MIGRATION, INTERNAL — Pakistan
IRFAN, Mohammad
Migration patterns in Pakistan : preliminary results from the PLM survey, 1979 / Mohammad Irfan, Lionel Demery [and] Ghulam Mohammad Arif. — Islamabad : Pakistan Institute of Development Economics, 1986. — 61,vi leaves. — (Studies in population, labour force and migration project report ; no.6). — *Bibliography: p[vii]*

MIGRATION, INTERNAL — Pennsylvania — Hazleton
AURAND, Harold W
Population change and social continuity : ten years in a coal town / Harold W. Aurand. — Selinsgrove [Pa.] : Susquehanna University Press ; London : Associated University Presses, c1986. — 139 p.. — *Includes index.* — *Bibliography: p. 131-134*

MIGRATION, INTERNAL — Peru
PERU. Dirección Nacional de Estadística y Censos. Unidad de Análisis Demográfico
Encuesta de inmigración de Lima Metropolitana : Tercer informe. — Lima : the Dirección, 1968. — ii,53p. — ([Publicación] / Dirección Nacional de Estadística y Censos ; no.3)

MIGRATION, INTERNAL — Poland
OCHOCKI, Andrzej
Wpływ migracji na rozmieszczenie zasobów pracy w latach 1970-1983 / Andrzej Ochocki. — Warszawa : Szkoła Główna Planowania i Statystyki, 1986. — 155p. — (Kształtowanie procesów demograficznych a rozwój społeczno-gospodarczy Polski) (Monografie i opracowania / Szkoła Główna Planowania i Statystyki ; 221/8). — *Summary and contents in English and Russian*

Studia nad migracjami i przemianami systemu osadniczego w Polsce : opracowanie zbiorowe / pod redakcją Kazimierza Dziewońskiego i Piotra Korcellego. — Wrocław : Ossolineum, 1981. — 267p. — (Prace geograficzne / Polska Akademia Nauk. Instytut Geografii i Przestrzennego Zagospodarowania ; Nr.140). — *Summaries in Russian and English.* — *Bibliographies*

MIGRATION, INTERNAL — Spain
CANDEL, Francesc
Els altres catalans vint anys després / Francesc Candel ; pròleg d'Oriol Badia. — Barcelona : edicions 62, [1985]. — 281p. — (Llibres a l'abast ; 210)

MIGRATION, INTERNAL — Thailand
GOLDSTEIN, Sidney
Migration in Thailand : a twenty-five-year review / Sidney Goldstein and Alice Goldstein. — Honolulu, Hawaii : East-West Center, [1986]. — vii, 54 p.. — (Papers of the East-West Population Institute ; no. 100). — *Expanded version of a paper presented at the annual meeting of thePopulation Association of America, Boston, March 1985.* — *"July 1986.".* — *Bibliography: p. 51-54*

MIGRATION, INTERNAL — Togo — Statistics
Recensement général de la population et de l'habitat 9-22 novembre 1981. — [Lomé] : Bureau Central du Recensement
vol.4: Mouvements naturels: migrations : résultats définitifs. — 1985. — 252p

MIGRATION, INTERNAL — United States
MORALES, Julio
Puerto Rican poverty and migration : we just had to try elsewhere / Julio Morales. — New York : Praeger, 1986. — xvii, 253p. — *Includes index.* — *Bibliography: p.225-245*

MIGRATION, INTERNATIONAL — India — Statistics
Census of India 1981. — [Delhi : Controller of Publications]
Series 5: Gujarat. — [1985]

MILITARISM — Germany
PARK, Ho-Leong
Sozialismus und Nationalismus : Grundsatzdiskussionen über Nationalismus, Imperialismus, Militarismus und Krieg in der deutschen Sozialdemokratie vor 1914 / von Ho-Leong Park ; mit einem Vorwort von Wolf-Dieter Narr. — Berlin : Schelzky und Jeep, 1986. — 349p. — *Bibliography: p323-349*

MILITARISM — Japan — History — 20th century
HARRIES, Meirion
Sheathing the sword : the demilitarisation of Japan / by Meirion and Susie Harries. — London : Hamilton, 1987. — xxxiv,364p,[8]p of plates. — *Includes index*

MILITARISM — Spain — History
LLEIXÀ, Joaquim
Cien años de militarismo en España : funciones estatales confiadas al Ejército en la Restauración y el franquismo / Joaquim Lleixà. — Barcelona : Editorial Anagrama, 1986. — 217p

MILITARY ART AND SCIENCE
BELLAMY, Chris
The future of land warfare / Chris Bellamy. — London : Croom Helm, c1987. — [320]p. — *Includes index*

SHEEHAN, Michael
The Economist pocket guide to defence / Michael Sheehan and James H. Wyllie. — Oxford : Basil Blackwell, 1986. — 269p. — *Bibliography: p269*

MILITARY ART AND SCIENCE — History
DELBRÜCK, Hans
History of the art of war : within the framework of political history / by Hans Delbrück ; translated from the German by Walter J. Renfroe, Jr. — Westport, Conn. ; London : Greenwood. — 1985. — *Translation of: Geschichte der Kriegskunst in Rahmen der politschen Geschichte.* — *Includes index*
Vol.4: The modern era. — xi,487p. — (Contributions in military history ; no.39)

FERRILL, Arther
The fall of the Roman Empire : the military explanation / Arther Ferrill. — London : Thames and Hudson, c1986. — 192p. — *Bibliography: p.182-187*

MCNEILL, William Hardy
The pursuit of power : technology, armed force, and society since A.D. 1000 / William H. McNeill. — Chicago : University of Chicago Press, 1982. — x, 405 p.. — *Includes bibliographical references and index*

Makers of modern strategy from Machiavelli to the nuclear age / edited by Peter Paret with the collaboration of Gordon A. Craig and Felix Gilbert. — Oxford : Clarendon, 1986. — [944]p. — *Includes index*

MILITARY ART AND SCIENCE — History — 19th century
Clausewitz and modern strategy / edited by Michael I. Handel. — London : Cass, 1986. — [320]p. — (Journal of strategic studies ; 9, no.1 & 2). — *Includes index*

MILITARY ART AND SCIENCE — Europe — History
HALE, J. R.
Renaissance war studies / J.R. Hale. — London : Hambledon, c1983. — x,524p,[90]p of plates. — (History series ; v.11). — *Includes text in Italian.* — *Includes index*

MILITARY ART AND SCIENCE — France
MESSMER, Pierre
Les écrits militaires de Charles de Gaulle / Pierre Messmer, Alain Larcan. — Paris : Presses Universitaires de France, 1985. — 592p . — *Bibliography: p[553]-570*

MILITARY ART AND SCIENCE — France — History — 20th century
DOUGHTY, Robert A
The seeds of disaster : the development of French Army doctrine, 1919-1939 / Robert Allan Doughty. — Hamden, Conn. : Archon Books, 1985. — xi, 232p. — *Includes index. — Bibliography: p.217-226*

MILITARY ART AND SCIENCE — Soviet Union
Voenno-teoreticheskoe nasledie V. I. Lenina i problemy sovremennoi voiny / pod redaksiei A. S. Milovidova. — Moskva : Voennoe izd-vo, 1987. — 359p

MILITARY ART AND SCIENCE — United States — History
HIGGINBOTHAM, Don
George Washington and the American military tradition / Don Higginbotham. — Athens : University of Georgia Press, c1985. — xii, 170 p.. — (Mercer University Lamar memorial lectures ; no. 27). — *Includes index. — Bibliography: p. [139]-161*

MILITARY ASSISTANCE
NEUMAN, Stephanie G
Military assistance in recent wars : the dominance of the superpowers / Stephanie Neuman ; foreword by Ernest Graves. — New York : Praeger, 1986. — p. cm. — (The Washington papers ; 122). — *"Published with the Center for Strategic and International Studies, Georgetown University, Washington, D.C.". — "Praeger special studies. Praeger scientific."*

MILITARY ASSISTANCE, AMERICAN — Middle East
ULFKOTTE, Udo K.
Interessenspezifische Nahostpolitik der Grossmächte im Nahen Osten 1948-1979 : sowjetische, amerikanische, französische und britische Waffenexporte... / Udo K. Ulfkotte. — Frankfurt am Main : Haag und Herchen, 1984. — iv,253p. — *Bibliography: p245-253*

MILITARY ASSISTANCE, AMERICAN — Turkey
HALLEY, Laurence
Ancient affections : ethnic groups and foreign policy / Laurence Halley. — New York : Praeger, 1985. — viii, 180 p.. — *Includes index. — Bibliography: p. 172-174*

MILITARY ASSISTANCE, AMERICAN — Turkey — History — 20th century
CAMPANY, Richard C
Turkey and the United States : the arms embargo period / Richard C. Campany, Jr. — New York : Praeger, 1986. — p. cm. — *Includes index. — Bibliography: p*

MILITARY ASSISTANCE, BRITISH — Middle East
ULFKOTTE, Udo K.
Interessenspezifische Nahostpolitik der Grossmächte im Nahen Osten 1948-1979 : sowjetische, amerikanische, französische und britische Waffenexporte... / Udo K. Ulfkotte. — Frankfurt am Main : Haag und Herchen, 1984. — iv,253p. — *Bibliography: p245-253*

MILITARY ASSISTANCE, FRENCH — Middle East
ULFKOTTE, Udo K.
Interessenspezifische Nahostpolitik der Grossmächte im Nahen Osten 1948-1979 : sowjetische, amerikanische, französische und britische Waffenexporte... / Udo K. Ulfkotte. — Frankfurt am Main : Haag und Herchen, 1984. — iv,253p. — *Bibliography: p245-253*

MILITARY ASSISTANCE, RUSSIAN — Middle East
ULFKOTTE, Udo K.
Interessenspezifische Nahostpolitik der Grossmächte im Nahen Osten 1948-1979 : sowjetische, amerikanische, französische und britische Waffenexporte... / Udo K. Ulfkotte. — Frankfurt am Main : Haag und Herchen, 1984. — iv,253p. — *Bibliography: p245-253*

MILITARY BASES, AMERICAN — Great Britain — History
DUKE, Simon
U.S. defence bases in the United Kingdom : a matter for joint decision? / Simon Duke ; foreword by Margaret Gowing. — Basingstoke : Macmillan in association with St. Antony's College, Oxford, 1987. — xx,261p. — (St. Antony's/Macmillan series). — *Bibliography: p243-254. — Includes index*

MILITARY GEOGRAPHY — Great Britain
The Geography of defence / edited by Michael Bateman and Raymond Riley. — London : Croom Helm, c1987. — xi,237p. — *'Published on the occasion of the Annual Conference of the Institute of British Geographers, Portsmouth Polytechnic, January 1987.'. — Includes bibliographies and index*

MILITARY GOVERNMENT — Germany (West) — Nuremberg
DASTRUP, Boyd L
Crusade in Nuremberg : military occupation, 1945-1949 / Boyd L. Dastrup. — Westport, Conn. : Greenwood Press, c1985. — p. cm. — (Contributions in military history ; no. 47). — *Includes index. — Bibliography: p*

MILITARY GOVERNMENT — Latin America — History — 20th century
Armies and politics in Latin America / edited by Abraham F. Lowenthal and J. Samuel Fitch. — Rev. ed. — New York : Holmes & Meier Publishers, 1986. — p. cm. — *Includes index. — Bibliography: p*

MILITARY HISTORY, MEDIEVAL
MCNEILL, William Hardy
The pursuit of power : technology, armed force, and society since A.D. 1000 / William H. McNeill. — Chicago : University of Chicago Press, 1982. — x, 405 p.. — *Includes bibliographical references and index*

MILITARY HISTORY, MODERN
MCNEILL, William Hardy
The pursuit of power : technology, armed force, and society since A.D. 1000 / William H. McNeill. — Chicago : University of Chicago Press, 1982. — x, 405 p.. — *Includes bibliographical references and index*

MILITARY HISTORY, MODERN — 18th century — Congresses
Adapting to conditions : war and society in the eighteenth century / edited by Maarten Ultee. — University, AL : University of Alabama Press, c1986. — viii, 197p. — *Includes index*

MILITARY HISTORY, MODERN — 20th century
BETTS, Richard K.
Nuclear blackmail and nuclear balance / Richard K. Betts. — Washington, D.C. : Brookings Institution, c1987. — p. cm. — *Includes bibliographical references and index*

JOES, Anthony James
From the barrel of a gun : armies and revolutions / Anthony J. Joes. — Washington, D.C. : Pergamon-Brassey's, 1986. — p. cm. — *Includes index. — Bibliography: p*

LIDER, Julian
Origins and development of West German military thought. — Aldershot : Gower. — (Swedish studies in international relations ; 16) Vol.1: 1949-1966 / Julian Lider. — c1986. — ix,433p

NEUMAN, Stephanie G
Military assistance in recent wars : the dominance of the superpowers / Stephanie Neuman ; foreword by Ernest Graves. — New York : Praeger, 1986. — p. cm. — (The Washington papers ; 122). — *"Published with the Center for Strategic and International Studies, Georgetown University, Washington, D.C.". — "Praeger special studies. Praeger scientific."*

Escalation and intervention : multilateral security and its alternatives / edited by Arthur R. Day and Michael W. Doyle. — Boulder, Colo. : Westview ; London : Mansell, 1986. — x,181p. — (Westview special studies in international security). — *Published in cooperation with the United Nations Association of the United States of America. — Includes index*

MILITARY INTELLIGENCE — Canada
STAFFORD, David
Camp X / David Stafford. — New York : Dodd, Mead, 1987. — p. cm. — *Includes index. — Bibliography: p*

MILITARY PLANNING — Europe
CHARLES, Daniel
Nuclear planning in NATO : pitfalls of first use / Daniel Charles. — Cambridge, Mass. : Ballinger Pub. Co., c1987. — xv, 177 p.. — *"A Federation of American Scientists book.". — Includes bibliographies and index*

MILITARY PLANNING — Germany — History — 20th century
LIDER, Julian
Origins and development of West German military thought. — Aldershot : Gower. — (Swedish studies in international relations ; 16) Vol.1: 1949-1966 / Julian Lider. — c1986. — ix,433p

MILITARY POLICY
CONNELL, Jon
The new Maginot Line / Jon Connell. — London : Secker & Warburg, 1986. — [224]p. — *Includes bibliography and index*

DEMILLE, Dianne
Challenges to deterrence : doctrines, technologies and public concerns : a conference report / Dianne DeMille. — Ottawa : Canadian Institute for International Peace and Security, 1985. — iv,69p. — (Report / Canadian Institute for International Peace and Security ; no.2)

GOŁĄB, Zdzisław
Wojna a system obronny państwa / Zdzisław Gołąb. — Warszawa : Wydawnictwo Ministerstwa Obrony Narodowej, 1984. — 312p. — *Bibliography: p[311]-312*

Sicherheit für Westeuropa : alternative Sicherheits- und Militärpolitik / "Generale für Frieden und Abrüstung". — Hamburg : Rasch und Röhring, 1985. — 223p

WINDASS, Stan
The rite of war / by Stan Windass. — London : Brassey's, 1986. — viii,132p

MILITARY SERVICE, COMPULSORY — Great Britain — History — 20th century
ADAMS, R. J. Q.
The conscription controversy in Great Britain, 1900-18 / R.J.Q. Adams and Philip P. Poirier. — Basingstoke : Macmillan, 1987. — [288]p. — *Includes index*

ROYLE, Trevor
The best years of their lives : the National Service experience 1945-63 / Trevor Royle. — London : Joseph, c1986. — xvii,288p,[16]p of plates. — *Bibliography: p268-271. — Includes index*

MILITARY SERVICE, COMPULSORY — United States
DANZIG, Richard
National service : what would it mean? / Richard Danzig, Peter Szanton. — Lexington, Mass. : Lexington Books, c1986. — xii, 307 p.. — *Includes index. — Bibliography: p. [281]-298*

MILITARY SERVICE, COMPULSORY — United States — Draft resisters
KOHN, Stephen M
Jailed for peace : the history of American draft law violators, 1658-1985 / Stephen M. Kohn. — Westport, Conn. : Greenwood Press, 1986. — xii, 169 p.. — (Contributions in military studies ; no. 49). — *Includes index. — Bibliography: p. [145]-158*

MILITARY SERVICE, COMPULSORY — United States — History — 20th century
HERSHEY, Lewis Blaine
Lewis B. Hershey, Mr. Selective Service / George Q. Flynn. — Chapel Hill : University of North Carolina Press, c1985. — p. cm. — Includes index. — Bibliography: p

MILK, HUMAN
PANEL ON CHILD NUTRITION. Working Party on Human Milk Banks
The collection and storage of human milk : report. — London : H.M.S.O., 1981. — viii,37p. — (Report on health and social subjects ; 22). — Bibliographical references: p33-37

MILK TRADE — European Economic Community Countries
Agricultural review for Europe. — New York : United Nations, 1983/84-. — Annual. — Continues: Review of the agricultural situation in Europe and Agricultural trade in Europe. — In 6 vols. Vol.I: General review, Vol.II: Agricultural trade, Vol.III: The Grain Market, Vol.IV: The Livestock and meat market, Vol.V: The milk and dairy products market, Vol.VI: The egg market

MILL, JOHN STUART
MILL, John Stuart
Newspaper writings / by John Stuart Mill ; edited by Ann P. Robson and John M. Robson. — Toronto : University of Toronto Press ; London : Routledge & Kegan Paul 1: December 1822 - July 1831. — 1986. — cxvii,333p. — (Collected works of John Stuart Mill ; v.22)

MILL, John Stuart
Newspaper writings / by John Stuart Mill ; edited by Ann P. Robson and John M. Robson. — Toronto : University of Toronto Press ; London : Routledge & Kegan Paul 2: August 1831 - October 1834. — 1986. — ix,335-751p. — (Collected works of John Stuart Mill ; v.23)

MILL, John Stuart
Newspaper writings / by John Stuart Mill ; edited by Ann P. Robson and John M. Robson. — Toronto : University of Toronto Press ; London : Routledge & Kegan Paul 3: January 1835 - June 1847. — 1986. — vii,753-1088p. — (Collected works of John Stuart Mill ; v.24)

MILL, John Stuart
Newspaper writings / by John Stuart Mill ; edited by Ann P. Robson and John M. Robson. — Toronto : University of Toronto Press ; London : Routledge & Kegan Paul 4: December 1847 - July 1873. — 1986. — vii,1089-1526p. — (Collected works of John Stuart Mill ; v.25)

STEPHEN, Sir Leslie
The English utilitarians / by Sir Leslie Stephen. — London : Duckworth Vol.3: John Stuart Mill. — 1900

MILL, JOHN STUART — Economics
John Stuart Mill critical assessments / edited by John Cunningham Wood. — London : Croom Helm, 1986, c1987. — 4v. — (The Croom Helm critical assessments of leading economists)

MILL, JOHN STUART, 1806-1873
GLASSMAN, Peter J.
J.S. Mill : the evolution of a genius / by Peter Glassman. — Gainesville : University of Florida Press, c1985. — xvi, 188p. — Includes index. — Bibliography: p.181-185

MILLENIALISM — United States — History — 18th century
BLOCH, Ruth H.
Visionary republic : millennial themes in American thought, 1756-1800 / Ruth H. Bloch. — Cambridge : Cambridge University Press, 1985. — xvi,291p

MILLENNIALISM — Indians — New Harmony
TAYLOR, Anne, 1932-
Visions of harmony : a study of nineteenth-century millenarianism / Anne Taylor. — Oxford : Clarendon, 1987. — 285p,[8]p of plates. — Bibliography: p269-275. — Includes index

MILLENNIALISM IN LITERATURE
HOLSTUN, James
A rational millennium : Puritan utopias of seventeenth-century England and America / James Holstun. — New York : Oxford University Press, 1987. — p. cm. — Includes index. — Bibliography: p

MILLIONAIRES — Great Britain — Biography
KAY, William
Tycoons : where they came from and how they made it / William Kay. — London : Pan, 1986. — 208p

MILTON KEYNES (BUCKINGHAMSHIRE : DISTRICT)
BISHOP, Jeff
Milton Keynes - the best of both worlds? : public and professional views of a new city / Jeff Bishop. — Bristol : School for Advanced Urban Studies, 1986. — 189p. — (Occasional paper / University of Bristol, School for Advanced Urban Studies ; 24). — Bibliography: p.177-189

MIND AND BODY
CARRUTHERS, Peter
Introducing persons : theories and arguments in the philosophy of mind / Peter Carruthers. — London : Croom Helm, c1986. — [256]p

MIND-BRAIN IDENTITY THEORY
CHURCHLAND, Patricia Smith
Neurophilosophy : toward a unified science of the mind-brain / Patricia Smith Churchland. — Cambridge, Mass. ; London : MIT Press, 1986. — xi, 546p., [1] leaf of plates. — (Computational models of cognition and perception). — "A Bradford book.". — Bibliography: p[491]-523. — Includes index

MINE DUSTS
HAMILTON, R. J.
Industrial hygiene in mines : a synthesis report on research supported by the Commission during the period 1977/82 / R. J. Hamilton. — Luxembourg : Office for Official Publications of the European Communities, 1985. — xii,95p. — (EUR ; 9253). — Cover title. — Series title: Industrial health and safety. — Bibliographical references: p88-94. — Contract no.: V/E/4-1380(20928) of 9/3/1982

MINE SANITATION
HAMILTON, R. J.
Industrial hygiene in mines : a synthesis report on research supported by the Commission during the period 1977/82 / R. J. Hamilton. — Luxembourg : Office for Official Publications of the European Communities, 1985. — xii,95p. — (EUR ; 9253). — Cover title. — Series title: Industrial health and safety. — Bibliographical references: p88-94. — Contract no.: V/E/4-1380(20928) of 9/3/1982

MINERAL INDUSTRIES
MIKESELL, Raymond F.
New patterns of world mineral development / by Raymond F. Mikesell. — Washington ; London : British-North American Committee, 1979. — Sponsored by British-North American Research Association (U.K.), National Planning Association (U.S.A.), C.D. Howe Research Institute (Canada)

Primary commodities : market developments and outlook / by the Commodities Division of the Research Department. — Washington, D.C. : International Monetary Fund, 1986. — vii,74p. — (World economic and financial surveys)

MINERAL INDUSTRIES — Economic aspects — South Africa
ANDOR, Lydia Eve
South Africa's chrome, manganese, platinum and vanadium : foreign views on the mineral dependency issue 1970-1984 : a select and annotated bibliography / L. E. Andor. — Braamfontein, [R.S.A.] : South African Institute of International Affairs, 1985. — 222p. — (South African Institute of International Affairs Bibliographical Series ; No.13)

MINERAL INDUSTRIES — Finance
Negotiation and drafting of mining development agreements : an inter-regional workshop arranged by the United Nations. — London : Mining Journal Books, 1976

MINERAL INDUSTRIES — Government policy — Canada
YUDELMAN, David
Canadian mineral policy, past and present : the ambiguous legacy / David Yudelman. — Kingston, Ontario : Centre for Resource Studies, Queen's University, 1985. — xii,176p. — (Monographs / Queens University (Kingston, Ontario) ; Centre for Resource Studies). — Bibliography: p156-162

YUDELMAN, David
Mining and the MacDonald Commission : the state of the industry in the mid-1980s / David Yudelman. — [Kingston, Ont.] : Centre for Resource Studies, Queen's University, c1985. — x, 106 p.. — (Working paper / Centre for Resource Studies ; no. 34). — Bibliography: p. 99-106

MINERAL INDUSTRIES — government policy — Canada — History
YUDELMAN, David
Canadian mineral policy, past and present : the ambiguous legacy / David Yudelman. — Kingston, Ontario : Centre for Resource Studies, Queen's University, 1985. — xii,176p. — (Monographs / Queens University (Kingston, Ontario) ; Centre for Resource Studies). — Bibliography: p156-162

MINERAL INDUSTRIES — Taxation — Appalachian Region
Who owns Appalachia? : landownership and its impact / the Appalachian Land Ownership Task Force ; with an introduction by Charles C. Geisler. — Lexington, Ky. : University Press of Kentucky, c1983. — xxxii, 235 p.. — Map on lining papers. — Includes bibliographies and index

MINERAL INDUSTRIES — Asia, Southeastern
The Pacific challenge in international business / edited by W. Chan Kim and Philip K.Y. Young ; with a foreword by Vern Terpstra. — Ann Arbor, Mich. : UMI Research Press, 1987. — viii, 342 p.. — (Research for business decisions ; no. 72). — Includes bibliographies and index

MINERAL INDUSTRIES — Australia
Mining and Australia / edited by W.H.Richmond and P.C.Sharma. — St Lucia ; London : University of Queensland Press, 1983

TSOKHAS, Kosmas
Beyond dependence : companies, labour processes and Australian mining / Kosmas Tsokhas. — Melbourne : Oxford University Press, 1986. — 291p. — Bibliography: p [273]-281

MINERAL INDUSTRIES — Canada
Mining communities : hard lessons for the future : proceedings of the twelfth CRS policy discussion seminar, Kingston, Ontario, September 27-29, 1983. — [Kingston, Ont.] : [Centre for Resource Studies, Queen's University], 1984. — v,205p. — (Proceedings / Centre for Resource Studies, Queen's University ; no.14)

MINERAL INDUSTRIES — Developing countries
NWOKE, Chibuzo
Third World minerals and global pricing : a new theory / Chibuzo Nwoke. — London : Zed, 1987. — [272]p. — Includes bibliography and index

MINERAL INDUSTRIES — East Asia
The Pacific challenge in international business / edited by W. Chan Kim and Philip K.Y. Young ; with a foreword by Vern Terpstra. — Ann Arbor, Mich. : UMI Research Press, 1987. — viii, 342 p.. — (Research for business decisions ; no. 72). — Includes bibliographies and index

MINERAL INDUSTRIES — Great Britain — Statistics
Minerals. — London : HMSO, 1974/75-. — (Business monitor. PA ; 1007). — Annual. — Some years include provisional results

MINERAL INDUSTRIES — South Africa — Statistics
Industrial minerals / Department of Mines, South Africa. — Pretoria : Department of Mines, 1935-1957. — Quarterly. — Continued by: Minerals

Mineral production and sales statistics = Mineraal produksie-en verkoopstatistieke / Minerals Bureau, Department of Mineral and Energy Affairs, South Africa. — Braamfontein : Minerals Bureau, 1987-. — Monthly. — Text in English and Afrikaans. — Continues in part : Minerals : quarterly information circular

Minerals : quarterly information circular / Department of Mines, South Africa. — Pretoria : Department of Mines, 1958-1981. — Quarterly. — Continues: Industrial minerals. Continued in part by Mineral production and sales statistics

MINERAL INDUSTRIES — Spain — History — 19th century
FLORES CABALLERO, Manuel
Rio Tinto : la fiebre minera del XIX / Manuel Flores Caballero. — Huelva : Instituto de Estudios Onubenses "Padre Marchena" : Excma, Diputación Provincial, 1983. — 218p. — Bibliography: p211-218

MINERAL INDUSTRIES — Spain — Almería — History
SÁNCHEZ PICÓN, Andrés
La minería del Levante almeriense 1838-1930 : especulación, industrialización y colonización económica / Andrés Sánchez Picón. — Almería : Cajal, c1983. — 307p. — (Biblioteca de temas almerienses. Serie monografías ; 7). — Publicado con la colaboración económica del Monte de Piedad y Caja de Ahorros de Almería. — Bibliography: p297-307

MINERAL INDUSTRIES — Spain — Murcia (Province) — History
VILAR, Juan Bautista
La minería murciana contemporánea (1840-1930) / Juan Bta. Vilar, Pedro Ma. Egea Bruno ; con la colaboración de Diego Victoria Moreno. — Murcia : [Caja de Ahorros de Murcia : Departamento de Historia Moderna y Contemporánea, Universidad de Murcia], 1985. — 368p. — Bibliography: p[359-368]

MINERAL INDUSTRIES — Wales — Cardiganshire — Statistics
BURT, Roger, 1942-
The mines of Cardiganshire : metalliferous and associated minerals 1845-1913 / Roger Burt, Peter Waite, Ray Burnley. — Exeter : Department of Economic History, University of Exeter, in association with the Northern Mine Research Society, [1985]. — xxviii, 92p

MINERAL INDUSTRIES — Wales — Flintshire
FLINTSHIRE. County Council
Flintshire mineral workings report. — Mold : [the Council], 1973. — 30p

MINERAL INDUSTRY — South Africa
SOUTH AFRICA. Department of Mineral and Energy Affairs. Minerals Bureau
Directory / Minerals Bureau, Department of Mineral and Energy Affairs, South Africa. — Braamfontein : Minerals Bureau, 1984-. — Annual

MINERAL WATERS — Norway
KROHN-HOLM, Jan W.
Farriskildene i Larvik gjennem 150 år / Jan W. Krohn-Holm. — Larvik : Utgitt av Farris, 1971. — 165p

MINERS — Australia — Broken Hill (N.S.W.)
KENNEDY, Brian Ernest
A tale of two mining cities : Johannesburg and Broken Hill 1885-1925 / Brian Kennedy. — Johannesburg : Ad. Donker, 1984. — xiii,146p. — Bibliography: p136-142

MINERS — Great Britain — Social life and customs
PARKER, Tony
Red Hill : a mining community / Tony Parker. — London : Heinemann, 1986. — [xi],196p. — Bibliography: p[191]-192

MINERS — South Africa — Johannesburg
KENNEDY, Brian Ernest
A tale of two mining cities : Johannesburg and Broken Hill 1885-1925 / Brian Kennedy. — Johannesburg : Ad. Donker, 1984. — xiii,146p. — Bibliography: p136-142

MINES AND MINERAL RESOURCES — Bibliography
STEENBLIK, Ronald P.
A guide to the periodic literature on energy and mineral resources available in London libraries / by Ronald P. Steenblik. — Rev. ed.. — [London?] : LSE International Resources Programme, 1986. — 27 leaves

MINES AND MINERAL RESOURCES — Commerce — South Africa
ANDOR, Lydia Eve
South Africa's chrome, manganese, platinum and vanadium : foreign views on the mineral dependency issue 1970-1984 : a select and annotated bibliography / L. E. Andor. — Braamfontein, [R.S.A.] : South African Institute of International Affairs, 1985. — 222p. — (South African Institute of International Affairs Bibliographical Series ; No.13)

MINES AND MINERAL RESOURCES — Information services — England — London
STEENBLIK, Ronald P.
A guide to the periodic literature on energy and mineral resources available in London libraries / by Ronald P. Steenblik. — Rev. ed.. — [London?] : LSE International Resources Programme, 1986. — 27 leaves

MINES AND MINERAL RESOURCES — Taxation
GOSS, Christopher
Petroleum and mining taxation : handbook on a method for equitable sharing of profits and risk / Christopher Goss. — Aldershot : Gower, c1986. — xiv,69p. — (Energy papers ; no.19)

MINES AND MINERAL RESOURCES — Union lists
STEENBLIK, Ronald P.
A guide to the periodic literature on energy and mineral resources available in London libraries / by Ronald P. Steenblik. — Rev. ed.. — [London?] : LSE International Resources Programme, 1986. — 27 leaves

MINES AND MINERAL RESOURCES — British Columbia
Exploration in British Columbia / Ministry of Energy, Mines and Petroleum Resources. — Victoria : Ministry of Energy, Mines and Petroleum Resources, 1982

MINES AND MINERAL RESOURCES — Great Britain
Minerals. — London : HMSO, 1974/75-. — (Business monitor. PA ; 1007). — Annual. — Some years include provisional results

MINES AND MINERAL RESOURCES — Netherlands — Statistics
Vierde algemene bedrijfstelling, 1978. — 's-Gravenhage : Staatsuitgeverij. — Rear cover title: Fourth general economic census, 1978: volume 2, part A: mining and quarrying, manufacturing, public utilities, construction and installation on construction projects
d.2: Algemene sectorale gegevens
A: Delfstoffenwinning, industrie, openbare nutsbedrijven, bouwnijverheid en bouwinstallatie. — 1985. — 87p

MINES AND MINERAL RESOURCES — Ontario — History
NEWELL, Dianne
Technology on the frontier : mining in old Ontario / Dianne Newell. — Vancouver : University of British Columbia Press, 1986. — 220 p.. — Based on author's thesis (Ph. D.--University of Western Ontario, 1981) under title: Technological change in a new and developing country. — Includes indexes. — Bibliography: p. [185]-205

SMITH, Philip
Harvest from the rock : a history of mining in Ontario / Philip Smith. — Toronto, Ont., Canada : MacMillan of Canada, c1986. — 346 p., [24] p. of plates. — "Published with the co-operation of the Ontario Ministry of Northern Development and Mines.". — Maps on lining papers. — Includes index. — Bibliography: p. 336-338

MINES AND MINERAL RESOURCES — Tanzania
KIMAMBO, R. H.
Mining and mineral prospects in Tanzania / R.H.N.Kimambo. — Dar es Salaam : Eastern Africa Publications Limited, 1984. — v,250p

MINES AND MINERAL RESOURCES — United States
CAMERON, Eugene N
At the crossroads : the mineral problems of the United States / Eugene N. Cameron. — New York : Wiley, c1986. — p. cm. — Includes indexes

MINES AND MINERAL RESOURCES — Wales — Clwyd
CLWYD. Council
Clwyd county structure plan : public participatiuon seminar : minerals : report of proceedings. — Mold : [the Council], 1975. — 30p

MINES AND MINERAL RESOURCES — Wales — West Glamorgan
WEST GLAMORGAN. County Council
Minerals : what are the issues?. — Swansea : [the Council], 1975. — iii,27p

MINET HOLDINGS
BOYD, Stewart C.
Minet Holdings plc, W. M. D. Underwriting Agencies Limited : investigation under Section 165 (1) (b) of the Companies Act 1948 : interim report / S. C. Boyd, P. W. G. DuBuisson, inspectors appointed by the Secretary of State for Trade and Industry. — London : H.M.S.O., 1986. — 88p

MINIMUM WAGE — Great Britain
BROSNAN, Peter
Cheap labour : Britain's false economy : the costs of a low wage economy versus a national minimum wage / Peter Brosnan and Frank Wilkinson. — London : Low Pay Unit, 1987. — 44p

MINING DISTRICTS — Canada
Mining communities : hard lessons for the future : proceedings of the twelfth CRS policy discussion seminar, Kingston, Ontario, September 27-29, 1983. — [Kingston, Ont.] : [Centre for Resource Studies, Queen's University], 1984. — v,205p. — (Proceedings / Centre for Resource Studies, Queen's University ; no.14)

MINING DISTRICTS — Great Britain — Social conditions
PARKER, Tony
Red Hill : a mining community / Tony Parker. — London : Heinemann, 1986. — [xi],196p. — *Bibliography: p[191]-192*

MINING ENGINEERING — Ontario — History
NEWELL, Dianne
Technology on the frontier : mining in old Ontario / Dianne Newell. — Vancouver : University of British Columbia Press, 1986. — 220 p.. — *Based on author's thesis (Ph. D.--University of Western Ontario, 1981) under title: Technological change in a new and developing country. — Includes indexes. — Bibliography: p. [185]-205*

MINING ENGINEERS — Great Britain — Biography
KENNEDY, K. H.
Mining tsar : the life and times of Leslie Urquhart / K.H. Kennedy. — Sydney ; London : Allen & Unwin, 1986. — [276]p. — *Bibliography: p346-351. — Includes index*

MINING LAW — Antarctic regions
MYHRE, Jeffrey D
The Antarctic Treaty system : politics, law, and diplomacy / Jeffrey D. Myhre. — Boulder : Westview Press, 1986. — p. cm. — (Westview special studies in international relations). — *Includes index. — Bibliography: p*

MINING LAW — United States
LESHY, John D
The mining law : a study in perpetual motion / John D. Leshy. — Washington, D.C. : Resources for the Future, Inc., [1986]. — p. cm. — *Includes index. — Bibliography: p*

MINISTERIAL RESPONSIBILITY — Great Britain — Bibliography
GREAT BRITAIN. Civil Service Department. Central Management Library
Ministerial responsibility. — London : the Library, 1977. — 3p. — (Policy science documentation. Bibliography series ; B9)

MINITAB (COMPUTER SYSTEM)
MINITAB, INC.
Primer : an introduction to Minitab Data Analysis Software Release 5.1. — State College, Pa. : Minitab, 1986. — 40p

MINNEAPOLIS (MINN.) — Social life and customs
The Bohemian Flats / compiled by the workers of the Writers' Program of the Work Projects Administration in the State of Minnesota ; with an introduction by Thaddeus Radzilowsky. — St. Paul : Minnesota Historical Society Press, 1986. — p. cm. — (Borealis books). — : *Reprint. Originally published: Minneapolis : University of Minnesota Press, 1941. With new introd. and index. — Bibliography: p[189]-203*

MINORITIES
Diversité culturelle : société industrielle état national. — Paris : l'Harmattan, 1984. — 268p

THORNBERRY, Patrick
Monorities and human rights law / Dr. Patrick Thornberry. — London : Minority Rights Group, 1987. — 19p. — (Minority Rights Group report ; no.73). — *Bibliography: p19*

MINORITIES — Civil rights
DENCH, Geoff
Minorities in the open society : prisoners of ambivalence / Geoff Dench. — London : Routledge & Kegan Paul, 1986. — vii, 275p. — *Bibliography: p.262-268*

MINORITIES — Civil rights — Canada
Minorities and the Canadian state / edited by Neil Nevitte and Allan Kornberg. — Oakville ; New York : Mosaic Press ; New York, N.Y., U.S.A. : Flatiron Book Distributors, 1985. — 324 p.. — *Includes bibliographies and indexes*

MINORITIES — Dictionaries and encyclopedias
CARATINI, Roger
La force des faibles : encyclopédie mondiale des minorités / Roger Caratini. — Paris : Larousse, [1986]. — 399p. — *Bibliography: p370-382*

MINORITIES — Education
Multicultural education : the interminable debate / edited by Sohan Modgil ... [et al.]. — London : Falmer, 1986. — 240p. — *Includes bibliographies and index*

MINORITIES — Education — Government policy — Great Britain
MULLARD, Chris
Process, problem, and prognosis : a survey of local education authorities' multicultural education policies and practices / [Chris Mullard, Lemah Bonnick, Birthe King]. — London : Race Relations Policy and Practice Research Unit. — (Working paper ; 3)
Pt. One: The multicultural process. — 1984. — ii,133p

MINORITIES — Education — Denmark — Case studies
BYRAM, Michael
Minority education and ethnic survival : case study of a German school in Denmark / Michael S. Byram. — Clevedon : Multilingual Matters, c1986. — [192]p. — (Multilingual matters ; 20). — *Bibliography: p187-190. — Includes index*

MINORITIES — Education — England
Survey of organisation in multi-racial schools. — London : Commission for Racial Equality, 1977. — [3]p. — *Summary of Organisation in multi-racial schools, by H .E .R. Townsend and E .M .Britain. — Reprint from Education & community relations, November 1972*

MINORITIES — Education — Great Britain
Chinese children. — London : Commission for Racial Equality, 1980. — [2]p. — *Summary of work by Brian Jackson and Anne Garvey. — Reprint from Education & community relations, November, 1974*

GREAT BRITAIN. Committee of Inquiry into the Education of Children from Ethnic Minority Groups
Education for all : the report of the Committee of Inquiry into the Education of Children from Ethnic Minority Groups ... March 1985 / Chairman Lord Swann. — London : H.M.S.O., 1985. — (Cmnd. ; 9453)

Select Committee calls for action on multi-racial education. — London : Commission for Racial Equality, 1977. — 3p. — *Summary of report by Select Committee on Race Relations and Immigration, session 1972-1973. — Reprint from Education & community relations, October 1973*

Sikh children in Britain. — London : Commission for Racial Equality, 1977. — [1]p. — *Summary of work with same title by Alan G. James. — Reprint from Education & community relations, October 1974*

MINORITIES — Education — Great Britain — Language arts
Mother tongue teaching in school and community : an HMI enquiry in four LEAs. — London : H.M.S.O, 1984. — 25p. — *At head of title: Department of Education and Science*

MINORITIES — Education — Organisation for Economic Co-operation and Development countries
Multicultural education. — Paris : Organisation for Economic Co-operation and Development, 1987. — 349p. — *Includes bibliographies*

MINORITIES — Education — United States
PRASZAŁOWICZ, Dorota
Amerykańska etniczna szkoła parafialna : studium porównawcze frzech wybranych odmian instytucji / Dorota Praszałowicz. — Wrocław : Ossolineum, 1986. — 226p. — (Biblioteka polonijna ; 15). — *Summaries in English*

MINORITIES — Education (Higher) — Israel
ANABTAWI, Samir N.
Palestinian higher education in the West Bank and Gaza : a critical assessment / Samir N. Anabtawi. — London : KPI, 1986. — 94p

MINORITIES — Education (Secondary) — England — Coventry (West Midlands)
School and community in Coventry. — London : Commission for Racial Equality, [1980?]. — [2]p. — *Reprint from Education & community relations, December 1974*

MINORITIES — Education (Secondary) — Great Britain
EALING COMMUNITY RELATIONS COUNCIL. Education Committee
Race relations & the secondary school curriculum : a statement of minimum requirements. — London : Commission for Racial Equality on behalf of Ealing CRC, 1980. — [2]p

MINORITIES — Employment — Great Britain
BLACK WORKERS' PLANNING GROUP
Black workers in the north west : a report of a conference held on 3rd November 1984. — Manchester : Black Workers' Planning Group, 1984. — 19p

GREAT BRITAIN. Commission for Racial Equality
Employment. — Rev. ed. — London : the Commission, 1981, 1981. — 4p. — (Fact sheet / Commission for Racial Equality ; 3). — *First published 1976*

HAFEEZ, Tariq
Race and recruitment in the insurance sector / Tariq Hafeez. — London : London Boroughs Grant Scheme, 1987. — 26p. — *Bibliography: p26*

ROBERTS, Celia
The language barrier in employment / Celia Roberts. — London : Commission for Racial Equality, 1978. — 4p. — (Fact paper / Commission for Racial Equality ; 4). — *Written at the request of the Trades Union Advisory Group of the former Community Relations Commission*

MINORITIES — Government policy — Canada
Minorities and the Canadian state / edited by Neil Nevitte and Allan Kornberg. — Oakville ; New York : Mosaic Press ; New York, N.Y., U.S.A. : Flatiron Book Distributors, 1985. — 324 p.. — *Includes bibliographies and indexes*

MINORITIES — Health and hygiene — England
WANDSWORTH COUNCIL FOR COMMUNITY RELATIONS
Asians & the health service : a directory of measures implemented by area health authorities to meet the needs of the Asian community. — London : Commission for Racial Equality for Wandsworth Council for Community Relations, 1978. — iv,30p

MINORITIES — Health and hygiene — England — London
DONOVAN, Jenny
  We don't buy sickness, it just comes : health, illness and health care in the lives of black people in London / Jenny Donovan. — Aldershot : Gower, c1986. — [306]p. — *Includes bibliography*

MINORITIES — Housing — Government policy — United States
  Race, ethnicity, and minority housing in the United States / edited by Jamshid A. Momeni ; foreword by Joe T. Darden. — New York : Greenwood Press, 1986. — xxv, 224 p.. — (Contributions in ethnic studies ; no. 16). — *Includes index. — Bibliography: p. [217]-220*

MINORITIES — Housing — England
HENDERSON, Jeff
  Race, class and state housing : inequality and the allocation of public housing in Britain / Jeff Henderson and Valerie Karn. — Aldershot : Gower, c1987. — xxiii,331p. — (Studies in urban and regional policy ; 4). — *Bibliography: p313-320. — Includes index*

MINORITIES — Housing — England — Bedford (Bedfordshire)
SKELLINGTON, R.
  The housing of minority groups in Bedford : a descriptive account / R. Skellington. — [Milton Keynes] : Open University. Faculty of Social Sciences. Urban Research Group, 1978. — 42p. — (Occasional paper / Open University . Faculty of Social Sciences. Urban Research Group ; no.1)

MINORITIES — Housing — England — Gloucester (Gloucestershire)
COWEN, Harry
  The hidden homeless : a report of a survey on homelessness and housing amongst single young Blacks in Gloucester / Harry Cowen with Richard Lording. — Gloucester (15 Brunswick Rd, Gloucester GL1 1HG) : Gloucester Community Relations Council, 1982. — 54p

MINORITIES — Housing — England — Leeds (West Yorkshire)
  Colour & rehousing - a study of redevelopment in Leeds. — London : Commission for Racial Equality, 1978. — [1]p. — (Research summary / Commission for Racial Equality ; 1). — *First published by the Community Relations Commission; summary of work with same title by Christopher Duke*

MINORITIES — Housing — Great Britain
  Constraints on immigrant housing choice. — London : Commission for Racial Equality, 1978. — [2]p. — (Research summary / Commission for Racial Equality ; 2). — *Summary of an unpublished report by Stuart Hatch, 1971; summary first published by the Community Relations Commission*

GREAT BRITAIN. Commission for Racial Equality
  Housing. — Rev. ed. — London : the Commission, 1978. — [2]p. — (Fact sheet / Commission for Racial Equality ; 2). — *First published 1976*

GRIFFIN, Jenny
  Joint mortages : a discussion paper / prepared by Jenny Griffin. — London : Commission for Racial Equality, 1978. — 2p. — *First published by the Community Relations Commission, 1975*

  Housing & communication with ethnic minorities : report on one-day seminar for London Housing Aid Centre managers, 20 May 1975. — London : Commission for Racial Equality, 1978. — 4p. — *First published by the Community Relations Commission, 1975. — With report of Working Group on Housing and Race Relations: Local authority housing, by Jenny Griffin*

  New perspectives on race and housing in Britain / edited by Susan J. Smith and John Mercer. — [Glasgow] : Centre for Housing Research, 1987. — 247p. — (Studies in housing ; no.2). — *Bibliographies*

PETTIT, Michael
  Housing centres and the Asian community / Michael Pettit. — London : Commission for Racial Equality, 1978. — [2]p. — *First published by the Community Relations Commission, 1975*

  Racial minorities & public housing. — London : Commission for Racial Equality, 1978. — [2]p. — (Research summary / Commission for Racial Equality ; 4). — *Summary of work by David J. Smith and Anne Whalley, published by P.E.P., 1975*

MINORITIES — Housing — Great Britian
GREAT BRITAIN. Commission for Racial Equality
  Living in terror : a report on racial violence & harassment in housing. — London : the Commission, 1987. — 53p

MINORITIES — Housing — London metropolitan area — Tower Hamlets
PHILLIPS, Deborah
  What price equality? : a report on the allocation of GLC housing in Tower Hamlets / by Deborah Phillips. — London : Greater London Council, 1986. — 83p. — (GLC housing research and policy report ; no.9). — *Title from cover*

MINORITIES — Housing — United States
  Race, ethnicity, and minority housing in the United States / edited by Jamshid A. Momeni ; foreword by Joe T. Darden. — New York : Greenwood Press, 1986. — xxv, 224 p.. — (Contributions in ethnic studies ; no. 16). — *Includes index. — Bibliography: p. [217]-220*

MINORITIES — Legal status, laws, etc
  Minorities in national and international laws / edited by Satish Chandra. — New Delhi : Deep & Deep Publications, c1985. — 376 p.. — *Includes index. — Bibliography: p. [372]-373*

MINORITIES — Medical care — England
  Racial equality and good practice maternity care : a report of two workshops held in Bradford organised by Training in Health and Race and the Centre for Ethnic Minorities Health Studies / compiled by Maggie Pearson ; Health Education Council and National Extension College for Training in Health and Race. — London : Training in Health and Race, 1985. — 37p. — *Bibliographical references: p36-37*

MINORITIES — Medical care — Great Britain
  Providing effective health care in a multiracial society : a checklist for looking at local issues / Health Education Council/National Extension College for Training in Health and Race. — 2nd ed. — London : Training in Health and Race, 1984. — iii,18p. — *Cover title. — Previous ed.: 1984. — Bibliography: p15*

MINORITIES — Mental health services — Great Britain
RACK, Philip
  Race, culture, and mental disorder / Philip Rack ; foreword by G. Morris Carstairs. — London : Tavistock, 1982. — xiii,305p. — *Bibliography: p273-292. — Includes index*

MINORITIES — Political activity — Case studies
  Competitive ethnic relations / edited by Susan Olzak, Joane Nagel. — Orlando : Academic Press, 1986. — ix, 252 p.. — *Includes bibliographies and index*

MINORITIES — Belgium
IRVING, Ronald Eckford Mill
  Flemings and Walloons of Belgium / Ronald Eckford Mill Irving. — London : Minority Rights Group, 1980. — (Report / Minority Rights Group ; 46)

MINORITIES — Canada
  Canada : the state of the Federation 1985 / edited by Peter M. Leslie. — Kingston, Ontario : Queen's University (Kingston, Ont.), Institute of Intergovernmental Relations, 1985. — v,225p. — *Includes references*

  Ethnic Canada : identities and inequalities / [edited by] Leo Driedger. — Toronto : Copp Clark Pitman, 1987. — v,442p. — *Bibliography: p408-433*

MINORITIES — Canada — Employment
COSPER, Ronald L.
  Ethnicity and occupation in Atlantic Canada : the social and economic implications of cultural diversity / Ronald L. Cosper. — Halifax : International Education Centre, 1984. — 47p. — (Ethnic heritage series ; vol.10). — *Bibliography: p46-47*

MINORITIES — China
MAKHMUTKHODZHAEV, M. Kh.
  Natsional'naia politika gomin'dana (1927-1937) / M. Kh. Makhmutkhodshaev. — Moskva : Nauka (IVL), 1986. — 124p. — *Table of contents in English. — Bibliography: p116-[125]*

MINORITIES — England
ROSE, E. J. B.
  Colour and citizenship : a report on British race relations / E.J.B. Rose ... [et al.]. — London : Oxford University Press for the Institute of Race Relations, 1969. — xxiii,815p. — *Bibliography: p.797-805*

MINORITIES — England — Bristol (Avon) — Socioeconomic status
FENTON, Steve
  Race, health and welfare : Afro-Caribbean and South Asian people in central Bristol : health and social services : based on interviews with middle-aged and elderly West Indians, South Asians, and UK born white residents of four central wards / C.S. Fenton ; researchers Steve Fenton ... [et al.]. — [Bristol] : [University of Bristol, Dept. of Sociology], [1985?]. — x,101p. — *Cover title. — Bibliography: p102-103*

MINORITIES — England — Coventry (West Midlands) — Statistics
MCCHESNEY, N. P.
  A statistical digest of ethnic minority population / N. P. McChesney, M. Z. Hassan [and] F. Prevc. — Coventry : Department of Economic Development and Planning. Forward Planning Division, 1986. — 50p. — (Coventry-trends)

MINORITIES — England — London
HOWES, Eileen
  Black and ethic minority population estimates / Eileen Howes. — Hackney : London Borough of Hackney. Research and Intelligence Section. Chief Executive's Office, 1986. — 27p. — (Research note / Hackney. Chief Executive's Office. Research and Intelligence Section ; 10). — *At head of cover title: Research in Hacknry*

PRASHAR, Usha
  Routes or roadblocks? : consulting minority communities in London Boroughs / Usha Prashar and Sh˜an Nicholas. — London : Runnymede Trust, 1986. — 64p

MINORITIES — England — London — Statistics
LANDAU, Nick
  Statistics of London's ethnic minorities, 1979 and 1981 / computed and written in the Intelligence Unit by Nick Landau. — [London] : Greater London Council, 1986. — ii,142p. — (Statistical series / Greater London Council ; no.40). — *Bibliography : p135*

  London's ethnic population : census statistics from the 1981 census / prepared in the Intelligence Unit by Maryse Hodgson. — [London] : Greater London Council, 1985. — 82p. — (Statistical series / Greater London Council ; no.44). — *Bibliography: p82*

MINORITIES — Europe — History
MOORE, R. I.
The formation of a persecuting society : power and deviance in Western Europe, 950-1250 / R.I. Moore. — Oxford : Basil Blackwell, 1987. — [192]p. — *Includes bibliography and index*

MINORITIES — Great Britain
BROCK, John
The basic figures / John Brock. — London : Commission for Racial Equality, 1978. — [2]p. — (Fact paper / Commission for Racial Equality ; 1). — *Written at the request of the Trades Union Advisory Group of the former Community Relations Commission*

EVANS, Roy
Racial justice : an SDP approach to equal opportunities / Roy Evans and Dr Francis Bridger. — London : SDP Open Forum Committee, 1985. — 38p. — (SDP Open Forum ; no.12)

The facts of racial disadvantage: a national survey : summary. — London : Commission for Racial Equality, 1980. — [2]p. — *Summary of report by David J. Smith. — Original report published by P.E.P., 1976*

MINORITIES — Great Britain — History
RAMDIN, Ron
The making of the black working class in Britain / Ron Ramdin. — Aldershot, Gower, c1987. — x,626p. — *Bibliography: p559-605. — Includes index*

MINORITIES — Great Britain — Languages
ROBERTS, Celia
The language barrier in employment / Celia Roberts. — London : Commission for Racial Equality, 1978. — 4p. — (Fact paper / Commission for Racial Equality ; 4). — *Written at the request of the Trades Union Advisory Group of the former Community Relations Commission*

MINORITIES — Great Britain — Photograph collections
RACE TODAY COLLECTIVE
The arrivants : a pictorial essay on blacks in Britain. — London : Race Today Publications for Creation for Liberation, 1987. — 112p

MINORITIES — Great Britain — Political activity
ANWAR, Muhammad
Ethnic minorities and the 1983 General Election : a research report / Muhammad Anwar. — London : Commission for Racial Equality, 1984. — 35p

ANWAR, Muhammad
Race and politics : ethnic minorities and the British political system / Muhammad Anwar. — London : Tavistock, 1986. — [x,176]p. — *Includes index*

Promoting greater involvement : Report of the Commission of Inquiry into ethnic minority involvement in the Liberal Party. — Hebden Bridge : Hebden Royd Publications on behalf of the Liberal Party and the Commission of Enquiry into Ethnic Minority Involvement in the Liberal Party, 1986. — 59p

MINORITIES — Great Britain — Services for
Third World impact / edited by Arif Ali. — 7th ed. — London : Hansib, 1986. — 272p

MINORITIES — Great Britain — Social conditions
Third World impact / edited by Arif Ali. — 7th ed. — London : Hansib, 1986. — 272p

MINORITIES — Great Britain — Statistics
DEMUTH, Clare
Immigration - numbers and dispersal / Clare Demuth. — London : Commission for Racial Equality, 1978. — 4p. — (Fact paper / Commission for Racial Equality ; 2). — *Written at the request of the Trades Union Advisory Group of the former Community Relations Commission. — Bibliography: p[4]*

MINORITIES — India — History — Sources
Congress and the minorities : preserving national cohesion : a study of Congress policy towards minorities during the last 100 years / edited by A. Moin Zaidi ; with a foreword by Indira Gandhi. — New Delhi : Publication Dept., Indian Institute of Applied Political Research, 1984. — xvi, 288 p.. — ″Compiled and edited under the auspices of the Minorities' Cell, All India Congress Committee (I).″. — *Includes index*

MINORITIES — Indiana — Gary — History — 20th century
MOHL, Raymond A
Steel city : urban and ethnic patterns in Gary, Indiana, 1906-1950 / Raymond A. Mohl and Neil Betten. — New York : Holmes & Meier, 1986. — x, 227 p., [16] p. of plates. — *Includes index. — Bibliography: p. 190-218*

MINORITIES — Iran
MCDOWALL, David
The Kurds / by David McDowall. — New ed. — London : Minority Rights Group, 1985. — 32p. — (Report / Minority Rights Group ; no. 23). — *Previous ed.: by Martin Short and Anthony McDermott. 1981. — Bibliography: p.24*

MINORITIES — Iraq
MCDOWALL, David
The Kurds / by David McDowall. — New ed. — London : Minority Rights Group, 1985. — 32p. — (Report / Minority Rights Group ; no. 23). — *Previous ed.: by Martin Short and Anthony McDermott. 1981. — Bibliography: p.24*

MINORITIES — Israel
EISENSTADT, S. N.
The development of the ethnic problem in Israeli society : observations and suggestions for research / S. N. Eisenstadt. — Jerusalem : Jerusalem Institute for Israel Studies, 1986. — 45p. — (Jerusalem Institute for Israel Studies ; no.17)

MINORITIES — Kenya
ALILA, Patrick O.
Kenya′s parliamentary elections : ethnic politics in two rural constituencies in Nyanza / Patrick O. Alila. — Nairobi : University of Nairobi. Institute for Development Studies, 1986. — 37p. — (Discussion paper / University of Nairobi. Institute for Development Studies ; no.282)

MINORITIES — Middle West — History
The ethnic frontier : essays in the history of group survival in Chicago and the Midwest / edited by Melvin G. Holli and Peter d′A. Jones. — Grand Rapids : Eerdmans, c1977. — 422p. — *Includes bibliographical references and index*

MINORITIES — Middle West (U.S.) — History
The ethnic frontier : essays in the history of group survival in Chicago and the Midwest / edited by Melvin G. Holli and Peter d′A. Jones. — Grand Rapids : Eerdmans, c1977. — 422p. — *Includes bibliographical references and index*

MINORITIES — Poland
TOMASZEWSKI, Jerzy
Rzeczpospolita wielu narodów / Jerzy Tomaszewski. — Warszawa : Czytelnik, 1985. — 285

MINORITIES — South Africa — Civil rights
South Africa : a plural society in transition / editors, D.J. van Vuuren ... [et al.]. — Durban ; Stoneham, MA : Butterworths, c1985. — 510 p.. — *Includes bibliographies and index*

MINORITIES — Soviet Union
TSAMERIAN, I. P.
Natsional'nye otsosheniia v SSSR / I. P. Tsamerian. — Moskva : Mysl', 1987. — 181p

MINORITIES — Soviet Union — Historiography
Natsional'nye otnosheniia v SSSR v trudakh uchenykh soiuznykh respublik / otv. redaktor V. P. Sherstobitov. — Moskva : Nauka, 1986. — 348p. — (Natsional'nye otnosheniia v sovremennuiu epokhu)

MINORITIES — United States
CARLSON, Robert A.
The Americanization syndrome : a quest for conformity / Robert A. Carlson. — [Rev. and updated ed.]. — London : Croom Helm, c1987. — 197p. — (Croom Helm series on theory and practice of adult education in North America). — *Previous ed.: published as the quest for conformity. New York : London : Wiley, 1975. — Includes index*

Ethnicity and the work force / Winston A. Van Horne [and] Thomas V. Tonnesen; editors. — Milwaukee : University of Wisconsin System American Ethnic Studies Coordination Committee/Urban Corridor Consortium, 1985. — xi,222p. — (Ethnicity and public policy ; vol.4). — *Bibliographies*

HAGEMAN, Mary J
Police-community relations / Mary Jeannette Hageman. — Beverly Hills, Calif. : Sage Publications, c1985. — 157p. — (Law and criminal justice series ; v. 6). — *Bibliography: p149-154*

PARRILLO, Vincent N.
Strangers to these shores : race and ethnic relations in the United States / Vincent N. Parrillo. — 2nd ed. — New York ; Chichester : Wiley, c1985. — xix,547p. — *Previous ed.: Boston [Mass.]; London : Houghton Mifflin, 1980. — Includes bibliographies and index*

MINORITIES — United States — Addresses, essays, lectures
Making it in America : the role of ethnicity in business enterprise, education, and work choices / edited by M. Mark Stolarik and Murray Friedman. — Lewisburg [Pa.] : Bucknell University Press ; London : Associated University Presses, c1986. — 143 p. . — *Includes bibliographies and index. — Contents: Ethnicity and business enterprise / Ivan Light, Randall M. Miller ; comments, Kenneth L. Kusmer -- Ethnicity and education / David Hogan, Mark Hutter ; comments, Henry N. Drewry -- Ethnicity and the world of work / Milton Cantor, Dennis Clark ; comments, Arthur B. Shostak -- Making it in America--and in the world / Michael Novak -- Conclusion / M. Mark Stolarik*

A melting pot or a nation of minorities / [by] Robert L. Payton...[et al.] ; edited by W. Lawson Taitte ; with an introduction by Andrew R. Cecil. — Dallas : University of Texas, 1986. — 205p. — (Andrew R. Cecil Lectures on Moral Values in a Free Society ; vol.7)

MINORITIES — United States — Political activity — Case studies
HALLEY, Laurence
Ancient affections : ethnic groups and foreign policy / Laurence Halley. — New York : Praeger, 1985. — viii, 180 p.. — *Includes index. — Bibliography: p. 172-174*

MINORITIES — United States — Psychology — Case studies
PERRY, Ronald W.
Minority citizens in disasters / Ronald W. Perry, Alvin H. Mushkatel. — London : University of Georgia Press, 1987. — [224]p

MINORITIES — Venezuela — Political activity
ARROYO TALAVERA, Eduardo
Elections and negotiation : the limits of democracy in Venezuela / Eduardo Arroyo Talavera. — [New York, N.Y.] : Garland Pub., 1986. — 450 p.. — (Outstanding theses from the London School of Economics and Political Science). — *Spine title: The limites of democracy in Venezuela, 1958-1981. — Thesis (Ph. D.)--University of London, 1983. — Bibliography: p. 421-450*

MINORITIES IN MEDICINE — Great Britain
PEARSON, Maggie
Equal opportunities in the NHS : a handbook / by Maggie Pearson. — Leeds : Training in Health and Race, 1985. — 39p

MINORITY AGED — England — London — Societies and clubs
ACKERS, Louise
The provision of clubs for elderly people from ethnic minorities / prepared in the Social Studies Group of the Director General's Department by Louise Ackers and Kevin Grimwade. — [London] : Greater London Council, 1986. — 50p. — (Reviews and studies series / Greater London Council ; no.28). — *Bibliography: p49-50*

MINORITY BUSINESS ENTERPRISES — United States — Addresses, essays, lectures
Making it in America : the role of ethnicity in business enterprise, education, and work choices / edited by M. Mark Stolarik and Murray Friedman. — Lewisburg [Pa.] : Bucknell University Press ; London : Associated University Presses, c1986. — 143 p. . — *Includes bibliographies and index. — Contents: Ethnicity and business enterprise / Ivan Light, Randall M. Miller ; comments, Kenneth L. Kusmer -- Ethnicity and education / David Hogan, Mark Hutter ; comments, Henry N. Drewry -- Ethnicity and the world of work / Milton Cantor, Dennis Clark ; comments, Arthur B. Shostak -- Making it in America--and in the world / Michael Novak -- Conclusion / M. Mark Stolarik*

MIRABEAU, GABRIEL-HONORE DE RIQUETTI, Comte de
CASTRIES, Rene de la Croix, duc de
Mirabeau ou l'échec du destin / Duc de Castries. — Nouvelle ed.. — Paris : Fayard, 1986. — 595p. — *Bibliography: p581-593*

MISES, LUDWIG VON
EDWARDS, James Rolph
The economist of the country : Ludwig von Mises in the history of monetary thought / by James Rolph Edwards. — New York : Carlton Press, 1985. — 143p. — *Bibliography: p137-143*

MISSING PERSONS
Disappeared! : technique of terror : a report / for the Independent Commission on International Humanitarian Issues ; preface by Simone Veil. — London : Zed, 1986. — [112]p

MISSIONARIES — Asia — Biography
DAVY, Yvonne
Trail of peril : the story of Joseph Wolff / Yvonne Davy. — Washington, D.C. : Review and Herald Pub. Association, c1984. — 94 p.

MISSIONARIES — Germany — Biography
DAVY, Yvonne
Trail of peril : the story of Joseph Wolff / Yvonne Davy. — Washington, D.C. : Review and Herald Pub. Association, c1984. — 94 p.

MISSIONARIES — Middle East — Biography
DAVY, Yvonne
Trail of peril : the story of Joseph Wolff / Yvonne Davy. — Washington, D.C. : Review and Herald Pub. Association, c1984. — 94 p.

MISSIONARIES — South Africa — Biography
ROSS, Andrew, 19---
John Philip (1775-1851) : missions, race and politics in South Africa / Andrew Ross. — Aberdeen : Aberdeen University Press, 1986. — ix,249p. — *Bibliography: p240-242. — Includes index*

MISSIONS — Asia
DAVY, Yvonne
Trail of peril : the story of Joseph Wolff / Yvonne Davy. — Washington, D.C. : Review and Herald Pub. Association, c1984. — 94 p.

MISSIONS — Middle East
DAVY, Yvonne
Trail of peril : the story of Joseph Wolff / Yvonne Davy. — Washington, D.C. : Review and Herald Pub. Association, c1984. — 94 p.

MISSIONS — South Africa — Educational work — History
CHRISTIE, Pam
The right to learn : the struggle for education in South Africa / prepared for Sached by Pam Christie. — Braamfontein, South Africa : Ravan Press ; Johannesburg, South Africa : Sached Trust, [1985]. — 272 p.. — (A People's college book). — *Includes bibliographies*

MISSIONS, MEDICAL — Nepal
ACHARD, Thomas
Primary health care in the hills of Nepal / Thomas Achard. — Kathmandu, Nepal : Integrated Hill Development Project, HMG/SATA, 1983. — 105p. — *Bibliography: p104-105*

MISSIONS, NORWEGIAN — Africa — History
Norwegian missions in African history. — Oslo : Norwegian University Press ; Oxford : Oxford University Press [distributor]
Vol.1: South Africa 1845-1906 / edited by Jarle Simensen. — c1986. — 280p. — *Includes index*

Norwegian missions in African history. — Oslo : Norwegian University Press ; Oxford : Oxford University Press [distributor]. — *Includes index*
Vol.2: Madagascar / edited by Finn Fuglestad and Jarle Simensen. — c1986. — 155p

MISSIONS TO AFRO-AMERICANS
RICHARDSON, Joe Martin
Christian reconstruction : the American Missionary Association and Southern Blacks, 1861-1890 / Joe M. Richardson. — Athens : University of Georgia Press, c1986. — ix, 348 p., [16] p. of plates. — *Includes index. — Bibliography: p. 323-335*

MISSIONS TO BURIATS — History — 19th century
BAWDEN, C. R.
Shamans, lamas and evangelicals : the English missionaries in Siberia / C.R. Bawden. — London : Routledge & Kegan Paul, 1985. — xviii,382p24p of plates. — *Bibliography: p359-366. — Includes index*

MISSIONS TO JEWS — History — 19th century
DAVY, Yvonne
Trail of peril : the story of Joseph Wolff / Yvonne Davy. — Washington, D.C. : Review and Herald Pub. Association, c1984. — 94 p.

MISSIONS TO MUSLIMS — History — 19th century
DAVY, Yvonne
Trail of peril : the story of Joseph Wolff / Yvonne Davy. — Washington, D.C. : Review and Herald Pub. Association, c1984. — 94 p.

MISSISSIPPI — Governors — Biography
MAY, Robert E
John A. Quitman : Old South crusader / Robert E. May. — Baton Rouge : Louisiana State University Press, c1985. — p. cm. — (Southern biography series). — *Includes index. — Bibliography: p*

MISSISSIPPI — Politics and government — To 1865
MAY, Robert E
John A. Quitman : Old South crusader / Robert E. May. — Baton Rouge : Louisiana State University Press, c1985. — p. cm. — (Southern biography series). — *Includes index. — Bibliography: p*

MISSISSIPPI — Politics and government — 1865-1950
MORGAN, Chester M
Redneck liberal : Theodore G. Bilbo and the New Deal / Chester M. Morgan. — Baton Rouge : Louisiana State University Press, c1985. — p. cm. — *Includes index. — Bibliography: p*

MISSOURI — Politics and government
CHEN, Stephen C. S.
Missouri in the federal system / Stephen C.S. Chen. — Lanham ; London : University Press of America, 1987. — [240]p. — *Includes bibliography and index*

MISTRESSES — United States
RICHARDSON, Laurel Walum
The new other woman : contemporary single women in affairs with married men / Laurel Richardson. — New York : Free Press ; London : Collier Macmillan, c1985. — p. cm. — *Includes index. — Bibliography: p*

MITCHELL, ANDREW
DORAN, Patrick F
Andrew Mitchell and Anglo-Prussian diplomatic relations during the Seven Years War / Patrick Francis Doran. — [Garland ed.]. — New York : Garland, 1986. — 408 p.. — (Outstanding theses from the London School of Economics and Political Science). — *Bibliography: p. [397]-408*

MITO-HAN (JAPAN) — History
KOSCHMANN, J. Victor
The Mito ideology : discourse, reform, and insurrection in late Tokugawa Japan, 1790-1864 / J. Victor Koschmann. — Berkeley : University of California Press, c1987. — p. cm. — "This volume is sponsored by the Center for Japanese Studies, University of California, Berkeley.". — *Includes index. — Bibliography: p*

MITOGAKU
KOSCHMANN, J. Victor
The Mito ideology : discourse, reform, and insurrection in late Tokugawa Japan, 1790-1864 / J. Victor Koschmann. — Berkeley : University of California Press, c1987. — p. cm. — "This volume is sponsored by the Center for Japanese Studies, University of California, Berkeley.". — *Includes index. — Bibliography: p*

MITTERRAND, FRANÇOIS
NAY, Catherine
Le Noir et le Rouge : ou l'histoire d'une ambition / Catherine Nay. — [Paris] : Grasset, 1984. — 536p. — *Bibliographie: p535-6*

MIYAMOTO, KENJI
MIYAMOTO, Kenji
Selected works / Kenji Miyamoto. — Tokyo : Japan Press Service, 1985. — v,560p

MŁYNARSKI, FELIKS
SUŁKOWSKA, Wanda
Koncepcje społeczno-ekonomiczne i działalność Feliksa Młynarskiego / Wanda Sułkowska. — Wrocław Ossolineum, 1985. — 104p. — (Prace Komisji Nauk Ekonomicznch / Polska Akademia Nauk. Oddział w Krakowie ; Nr13) . — *Summary in French and English. — Bibliography: p[96]-99*

MOBILE (ALA.) — Economic conditions
AMOS, Harriet E.
Cotton City : urban development in antebellum Mobile / Harriet E. Amos. — University, Ala. : University of Alabama Press, c1985. — xvi, 311 p.. — *Includes index. — Bibliography: p. 287-297*

MOBILE (ALA.) — History — 19th century
AMOS, Harriet E.
Cotton City : urban development in antebellum Mobile / Harriet E. Amos. — University, Ala. : University of Alabama Press, c1985. — xvi, 311 p.. — *Includes index. — Bibliography: p. 287-297*

MOBILE HOMES — Law and legislation — Great Britain
GREAT BRITAIN. Parliament. House of Commons. Library. Research Division
The Mobile Homes Bill (H.L.) (Bill 74, session 1982/83) / [Christine Gillie]. — [London] : the Division, 1983. — 13p. — (Reference sheet ; no.83/2). — *Bibliographical references: p12-13*

MOBILE HOMES — Great Britain — Handbooks, manuals, etc.
Ideal home / Jon Preston...[et al.]. — Survival edition. — [London? : Suspect : Hooligan, 1986]. — [127p]

MOBILE HOMES BILL 1982-83
GREAT BRITAIN. Parliament. House of Commons. Library. Research Division
The Mobile Homes Bill (H.L.) (Bill 74, session 1982/83) / [Christine Gillie]. — [London] : the Division, 1983. — 13p. — (Reference sheet ; no.83/2). — *Bibliographical references: p12-13*

MOBILE POST OFFICES — Great Britain
JOHNSON, Peter, 1949-
The British travelling post office / Peter Johnson. — London : Ian Allen, c1985. — 104p. — *Bibliography: p.104*

MODELS, PSYCHOLOGICAL
RYBASH, John M
Adult cognition and aging : developmental changes in processing, knowing and thinking / John M. Rybash, William J. Hoyer, Paul A. Roodin. — New York : Pergamon Press, c1986. — x, 194 p.. — (Pergamon general psychology series ; 139) (Pergamon international library of science, technology, engineering, and social studies). — *Includes indexes.* — *Bibliography: p. 165-185*

MODERNISM — Catholic Church
KURTZ, Lester R
The politics of heresy : the modernist crisis in Roman Catholicism / Lester R. Kurtz. — Berkeley : University of California Press, c1986. — xii, 267 p.. — *Includes index.* — *Bibliography: p. [229]-254*

MODIGLIANI, FRANCO. The contribution of intergenerational transfer to total wealth
KOTLIKOFF, Laurence J.
The contribution of intergenerational transfers to total wealth : a reply / Laurence J. Kotkikoff, Lawrence H. Summers. — Cambridge, Mass. : NBER, 1986. — 24p. — (NBER working paper series ; no.1827). — *Bibliography: p22-24*

MOERAN, BRIAN
MOERAN, Brian
Okubo diary : portrait of a Japanese valley / Brian Moeren. — Stanford, Calif. : Stanford University, 1985. — p. cm. — *Bibliography: p*

MOHAMMED REZA PAHLAVI, Shah of Iran
HULBERT, Mark
Interlock : the untold story of American banks, oil interests, the Shah's money, debts and the astounding connections between them / Mark Hulbert. — New York : Richardson and Snyder, 1982. — 272p

MOLDAVIA — Politics and government
IOVVA, I. F.
Peredovaia Rossiia i obshchestvenno-politicheskoe dvizhenie v Moldavii : (pervaia polovina XIX v.) / I. F Iovva ; otv. redaktor S. S. Volk. — Kishinev : Shtiintsa, 1986. — 256p. — *Brief summary in English and French*

MOLDAVIA — Relations — Soviet Union
IOVVA, I. F.
Peredovaia Rossiia i obshchestvenno-politicheskoe dvizhenie v Moldavii : (pervaia polovina XIX v.) / I. F Iovva ; otv. redaktor S. S. Volk. — Kishinev : Shtiintsa, 1986. — 256p. — *Brief summary in English and French*

MOLDAVIAN S.S.R. — Economic conditions
Narodnokhoziaistvennyi kompleks Moldavii / [redkollegiia: S. E. Chertan...et al.]. — Kishinev : Shtiintsa, 1986. — 153p

MOLDAVIAN S.S.R. — Economic conditions — Statistics
Narodnoe khoziaistvo Moldavskoi SSR / Tsentral'noe statistichekoe upravlenie, Moldavian S.S.R.. — Kishinev : Statistika, 1984-. — *Annual*

MOLDAVIAN S.S.R. — Industries
SHORNIKOV, P. M.
Promyshlennost' i rabochii klass Moldavskoi SSR v gody Velikoi Otechestvennoi voiny / P. M. Shornikov ; otv. redaktor I. E. Levit. — Kishinev : Shtiintsa, 1986. — 148p. — *Brief summary in English and French*

MONACO — Population
Recensement général de la Population 1982. — [Monte Carlo] : Service des Statistiques et des Etudes Économiques, 1982. — [58] leaves

MONACO — Statistics, Vital
Recensement général de la Population 1982. — [Monte Carlo] : Service des Statistiques et des Etudes Économiques, 1982. — [58] leaves

MONARCHY
Les monarchies : [essais par] Michel Antoine...[et al.] / sous la direction de Emmanuel Le Roy Ladurie. — Paris : Presses Universitaires de France, 1986. — 328p

MONARCHY, BRITISH — Finance
GREAT BRITAIN. Parliament. House of Commons. Library. Research Division
The finances of the monarchy. — [London] : the Division, 1975. — [22]p. — (Background paper ; no.45). — *Bibliographical references: p [21]-[22]*

GREAT BRITAIN. Parliament. House of Commons. Library. Research Division
The finances of the monarchy / Paul Hutt. — [London] : the Division, 1980. — 26p. — (Background paper ; no.79). — *Bibliography: p22-24*

MONASTERIES — Great Britain
SMITH, R. A. L.
Canterbury Cathedral priory : a study in monastic administration / Reginald Anthony Lenden Smith. — Cambridge : Cambridge University Press, 1943. — 237p

MONDOÑEDO (SPAIN) — Economic conditions
SAAVEDRA, Pegerto
Economía, politica y sociedad en Galicia : la provincia de Mondoñedo, 1480-1830 / Pegerto Saavedra. — [Santiago de Compostela] : Xunta de Galicia, 1985. — 700p. — *Bibliography: p685-697*

MONETARY POLICY
ALOGOSKOUFIS, George S.
Monetary policy and the informational implications of the Phillips curve in an open economy / George Alogoskoufis. — London : Centre for Economic Policy Research, 1987. — v,30p. — (Discussion paper series / Centre for Economic Policy Research ; no.183). — *Bibliography: p29*

ANDERSEN, Palle S.
The stability of money demand functions : an alternative approach / by Palle S. Andersen. — Basle : Bank for International Settlements, 1985. — 72p. — (BIS economic papers ; no.14)

ARESTIS, P.
Post-Keynesian theory of money, credit and finance / Philip Arestis. — London : Thames Polytechnic, 1987. — 23p. — (Thames papers in political economy). — *Bibliography: p20-22*

CLINTON, Kevin
Monetary policy in the second half of the 1980's : how much room for manoeuvre? / by Kevin Clinton and Jean-Claide Chouraqui. — Paris : OECD, 1987. — 68p. — (Working papers / OECD Department of Economics and Statistics ; no.39). — *Bibliographical references: p61-68*

CROCKETT, Andrew
Strengthening the international monetary system : exchange rates, surveillance, and objective indicators / by Andrew Crockett and Morris Goldstein. — Washington, D. C. : International Monetary Fund, 1987. — vii,84p. — (Occasional paper / International Monetary Fund ; no.50). — *Bibliographical references: p83-84*

DELIVANIS, D. J.
La rareté et la forme de la réévaluation en fonction des possibilités de l'imposer ou de l'éviter / D. J. Delivanis. — [S.l.] : [S.l.], 1973. — 376-394

DELIVANIS, D. J.
Les repercussions de la réévaluation sur les conditions monétaires, sur la balance des paiements et sur les termes d'échange / D. J. Delivanis. — Athens ; Freiburg : Ch. Katsikalis, 1973. — 579-594p. — *Festschrift für Pan J. Zepos*

DENNIS, Geoffrey E. J.
Monetary aggregates and economic activity : evidence from five industrial countries / by Geoffrey E. J. Dennis. — Basle : Bank for International Settlements, 1983. — 70p. — (BIS economic papers ; no.7)

DESAI, Meghnad
Money, inflation and unemployment : an econometric model of the Keynes effect / M. Desai and G. Weber. — London : Economic and Social Research Council : London School of Economics, 1986. — [77p]. — (ESRC/LSE econometrics project discussion paper ; A.59). — *Bibliography: p[69.71]*

FRIEDMAN, Milton
The essence of Friedman / edited by Kurt R. Leube ; foreword by W. Glenn Campbell. — Stanford, Calif. : Hoover Institution Press, 1987. — p. cm. — (Hoover Press publication ; 366). — *Includes index.* — *Bibliography: p*

LAMFALUSSY, Alexandre
"Rules versus discretion : an essay on monetary policy in an inflationary environment / by Alexandre Lamfalussy. — Basle : Bank for International Settlements, 1981. — 50p. — (BIS economic papers ; no.3)

MCCLAM, Warren D.
Adjustment performance of open economies : some international comparisons / by W. D. McClam and P. S. Andersen. — Basle : Bank for International Settlements, 1983. — 100p. — (BIS economic papers ; no.10)

MCCLAM, Warren D.
US monetary aggregates, income velocity and the euro-dollar market / by Warren D. McClam. — Basle : Bank for International Settlements, 1980. — 43p. — (BIS economic papers ; no.2)

MACESICH, George
Monetary policy and rational expectations / George Macesich. — New York : Praeger, 1987. — x, 154 p.. — *Includes index.* — *Bibliography: p. [139]-147*

MARINI, Giancarlo
Monetary and fiscal policy in an optimizing model with capital accumulation and finite lives / G. Marini [and] F. van der Ploeg. — London : Centre for Labour Economics, London School of Economics, 1987. — 28p. — (Discussion paper / London School of Economics and Political Science. Centre for Labour Economics ; no.277). — *Bibliography: p27-28*

MONETARY POLICY
continuation

Monetary and exchange rate policy / edited by Donald R. Hodgman and Geoffrey E. Wood. — London : Macmillan in association with Centre for Banking and International Finance, the City University Business School, 1987. — xv,223p. — (Studies in banking and international finance). — *Includes bibliographies and index*

NELL, Edward J.
On monetary circulation and the rate of exploitation / Edward Nell. — London : Thames Polytechnic, 1986. — 36p. — (Thames papers in political economy)

PLOEG, Frederick van der
International policy coordination in interdependent monetary economies / F. van der Ploeg. — London : Centre for Labour Economics. London School of Economics, 1987. — 24p. — (Discussion paper / London School of Economics and Political Science. Centre for Labour Economics ; no.278). — *Bibliography: p22-24*

Staff studies for the World Economic Outlook / by the Research Department of the International Monetary Fund. — Washington, D. C. : International Monetary Fund, 1986. — xi,195p. — (World economic and financial surveys). — *Includes bibliographical references.* — *Contents: Differences in employment behaviour among industrial countries/Charles Adams, Paul R. Fenton and Flemming Larsen - Labor markets, external developments, and unemployment in developing countries/Omotunde E.G. Johnson - Velocity of money and the practice of monetary targeting/Peter Isard and Liliana Rojas-Suarez - Effects of exchange rate changes in industrial countries/James M. Boughton, et al. - Transmission of economic influences from industrial to developing countries/David Goldsbrough and Iqbal Zaidi*

MONETARY POLICY — Addresses, essays, lectures

Alternative monetary regimes / edited by Colin D. Campbell and William R. Dougan. — Baltimore : Johns Hopkins University Press, c1986. — xi, 251 p.. — *Includes bibliographies and index*

MONETARY POLICY — Bibliography

GOEHLERT, Robert
Policy studies on the money supply : a selected bibliography / Robert Goehlert. — Monticello, Ill. : Vance Bibliographies, [1983]. — 7 p.. — (Public administration series--bibliography ; P 1312). — *Cover title.* — *"October, 1983."*

MONETARY POLICY — Congresses

The Monetary versus fiscal policy debate : lessons from two decades / edited by R.W. Hafer. — Totowa, N.J. : Rowman & Allanheld, 1986. — 171 p.. — *Papers presented at the ninth annual economic policy conference held Oct. 12-13, 1984, sponsored by the Federal Reserve Bank of St. Louis.* — *Includes bibliographies and index*

MONETARY POLICY — History

SMITH, David
The rise and fall of monetarism / David Smith. — Harmondsworth : Penguin, 1987. — 186p. — *Bibliography: p177-179*

MONETARY POLICY — Mathematical models

CLEMENZ, Gerhard
Credit markets with asymmetric information / Gerhard Clemenz. — Berlin ; New York : Springer-Verlag, c1986. — viii, 212 p.. — (Lecture notes in economics and mathematical systems ; 272). — *Bibliography: p. [204]-212*

GRANDMONT, Jean-Michel
Money and value : a reconsideration of classical and neoclassical monetary theories / Jean-Michel Grandmont. — Cambridge [Cambridgeshire] ; New York : Cambridge University Press, 1983. — xii,199p. — (Econometric Society monographs in pure theory ; no. 5). — *Includes index.* — *Bibliography: p193-195*

MONETARY POLICY — Argentina — History — 20th century

FASANO-FILHO, Ugo
Currency substitution and liberalization : the case of Argentina / Ugo Fasano-Filho. — Aldershot : Gower, c1986. — xi,194p. — *Bibliography: p184-194*

MONETARY POLICY — Australia — History

BUTLIN, S. J.
The Australian monetary system : 1851 to 1914 / S. J. Butlin. — [s.l.] : Judith F. Butlin, 1986. — 404p

MONETARY POLICY — Canada

Fiscal and monetary policy / John Sargent, research coordinator. — Toronto : University of Toronto Press, 1986. — xviii,339p

BARRADOS, John P.
A key to the Canadian economy / John P. Barrados. — Lanham, MD : University Press of America, c1966. — p. cm. — *Includes index*

MONETARY POLICY — Chile

EDWARDS, Sebastián
Monetarism and liberalization : the Chilean experiment / Sebastian Edwards and Alejandra Cox Edwards. — Cambridge, MA : Ballinger Pub. Co., c1987. — xxi, 233 p. — *Includes index.* — *Bibliography: p. 211-226*

MONETARY POLICY — Developing countries

ATTANASIO, O.
Output and employment effects of countercyclical policy : empirical evidence for OECD countries / O. Attanasio and G. Marini. — London : Centre for Labour Economics, London School of Economics, 1986. — 26p. — (Discussion paper / London School of Economics and Political Science. Centre for Labour Economics ; no.248). — *Bibliography: p23-26*

MONETARY POLICY — France

NERE, J.
Le problème du mur d'argent : les crises du franc (1924-1926) / J. Nere. — Paris : La Pensée Universelle, 1985. — 159p

MONETARY POLICY — Great Britain

GREAT BRITAIN. Parliament. House of Commons. Library. Research Division
Monetary policy and monetarism / [Christopher Barclay]. — [London] : the Division, [1979]. — 20p. — (Background paper ; no.72). — *Bibliography: p19-20*

MONETARY POLICY — Great Britain — History

Monetarism in the United Kingdom / edited by Brian Griffiths and Geoffrey E. Wood. — London : Macmillan in association with Centre for Banking and International Finance, 1984. — vi,305p. — *Includes bibliographies and index*

MONETARY POLICY — Great Britain — History — 20th century

KUNZ, Diane B.
The battle for Britain's gold standard in 1931 / Diane B. Kunz. — London : Croom Helm, c1987. — viii,207p. — *Bibliography: p194-202.* — *Includes index*

MONETARY POLICY — Hungary

IVÁN, Miklós
A Koronátol az aranypengöig : a pénzválság bonctana / írta Iván Miklós. — Budapest : Gergely R., 1934. — 104p

MONETARY POLICY — India

MUKHERJEE, Amitava
The proximate determinants of money stock in a developing economy (1951-52 to 1979-80) / Amitava Mukherjee. — Calcutta : Firma KLM, 1981. — 128p. — *Bibliography: p122-128*

MONETARY POLICY — Japan

YOSHITOMI, Masaru
Japan as capital exporter and the world economy / Masaru Yoshitomi. — New York : Group of Thirty, 1986. — 32p. — (Occasional papers / Group of Thirty ; no.18)

MONETARY POLICY — Korea (South)

Korea : managing the industrial transition. — Washington, D.C. : The World Bank
V.1: The conduct of industrial policy. — 1987. — xiv,182p. — (A World Bank Country study) . — *Includes bibliographical references*

Korea : Managing the Industrial Transition. — Washington, D.C. : The World Bank
V.2: Selected topics and case studies. — 1987. — x,225p. — (A World Bank Country study). — *Bibliography: p218-225*

MONETARY POLICY — Latin America

Economic reform and stabilization in Latin America / edited by Michael Connolly, Claudio González-Vega. — New York : Praeger, [1987]. — xxiii, 348 p.. — *"Second Dominican Republic Conference on Trade and Financial Liberalization in Latin America held in Santo Domingo, March 22-24, 1985"--P. iii.* — *Includes bibliographies*

MONETARY POLICY — Papua New Guinea

GARNAUT, Ross
Exchange rate and macro-economic policy in independent Papua New Guinea / Ross Garnaut and Paul Baxter in consultation with Anne O. Krueger. — Canberra, Australia : Development Studies Centre, Australian National University, 1984. — xiv, 173 p.. — (Pacific research monograph ; no. 10). — *Includes bibliographical references*

MONETARY POLICY — Southern Cone of South America

RAMOS, Joseph R
Neoconservative economics in the southern cone of Latin America, 1973-1983 / Joseph Ramos. — Baltimore : Johns Hopkins University Press, c1986. — xviii, 200p. — (The Johns Hopkins studies in development). — *Includes index.* — *Bibliography: p.185-191*

MONETARY POLICY — Switzerland

GENBERG, Hans
External influences on the Swiss economy under fixed and flexible exchange rates / Hans Genberg and Alexander K. Swoboda. — Grüsch : Rüegger, c1985. — ii, 182 p.. — (Schweizerisches Institut für Aussenwirtschafts-, Struktur- und Regionalforschung an der Hochschule St. Gallen ; Bd. 10). — *Bibliography: p. 178-182*

MONETARY POLICY — United States

Central bankers, bureaucratic incentives, and monetary policy / editors, Eugenia Froedge Toma, Mark Toma. — Dordrecht ; Boston : Martinus Nijhoff, 1987. — p. cm. — (Financial and monetary policy studies ; v. 13)

MALKIN, Lawrence
The national debt / Lawrence Malkin. — 1st ed. — New York : Holt, c1987. — ix, 309 p.. — *Includes index.* — *Bibliography: p. 277-298*

ROUSSEAS, Stephen
Post Keynesian monetary economics / Stephen Rousseas. — London : Macmillan, 1986. — [144]p

Seasonal adjustment of the monetary aggregates : report of the Committee of Experts on Seasonal Adjustment Techniques / Board of Governor of the Federal Reserve System. — Washington : The Board, 1981. — 55p

MONETARY POLICY — United States
continuation

WACHTEL, Howard M
The money mandarins : the making of a new supranational economic order / Howard M. Wachtel. — 1st ed. — New York : Pantheon Books, c1986. — xvi, 254 p.. — *Includes index.* — *Bibliography: p. [227]-245*

MONETARY POLICYOFF. PUBNS. — European Economic Community countries 986

Monetary disorder : opinion. — Brussels : Economic and Social Committee, 1978. — iv,98p

MONETARY REFORMERS — Great Britain — Biography

HOLLOWAY, Edward
Money matters : a modern pilgrim's economic progress / Edward Holloway. — London : Sherwood Press, 1986. — [vii],198p

MONEY

ANDERSEN, Palle S.
The stability of money demand functions : an alternative approach / by Palle S. Andersen. — Basle : Bank for International Settlements, 1985. — 72p. — (BIS economic papers ; no.14)

AUERBACH, Robert D
Money, banking, and financial markets / Robert D. Auerbach. — 2nd ed. — New York : Macmillan ; London : Collier Macmillan, c1985. — xvii, 650, 17 p.. — *Includes bibliographies and index*

Compensation for compulsory purchase : papers from a conference organized by the Law Society, the Bar Council and the Royal Institution of Chartered Surveyors. — London : Sweet and Maxwell, 1975. — 53p. — (Journal of planning and environment law occasional papers)

JOHNSTON, R. B.
Theories of the growth of the Euro—currency market : a review of the Euro—currency deposit multiplier / by R. B. Johnston. — Basle : Bank for International Settlements, 1981. — 52p. — (BIS economic papers ; no.4)

LAMFALUSSY, Alexandre
"Rules versus discretion : an essay on monetary policy in an inflationary environment / by Alexandre Lamfalussy. — Basle : Bank for International Settlements, 1981. — 50p. — (BIS economic papers ; no.3)

MCCLAM, Warren D.
US monetary aggregates, income velocity and the euro-dollar market / by Warren D. McClam. — Basle : Bank for International Settlements, 1980. — 43p. — (BIS economic papers ; no.2)

Monetary theory and economic institutions : proceedings of a conference held by the International Economic Association at Fiesole, Florence, Italy / edited by Marcello de Cecco and Jean-Paul Fitoussi. — Basingstoke : Macmillan, 1987. — ix,349p. — *Includes index*

Production, circulation et monnaie / [par] R. Arena...[et al.] ; introduction: R. Arena, A. Graziani [et] post-face: J. Kregel. — Paris : Presses Universitaires de France, 1985. — 435p. — (Travaux et Recherches du Laboratoire Associé No.301. C.N.R.S.-Université de Nice). — *"Le présent ouvrage est né d'une rencontre...organisée par le L.A.T.A.P.S.E.S. (UA CNRS N°301), les 1 er et 2 février 1984 à l'Université de Nice".* — *Bibliograhie: p428-430*

The Reconstruction of international monetary arrangements / edited by Robert Z. Aliber. — Basingstoke : Macmillan, 1987. — vii,330p. — *Includes bibliographies and index*

WACHTEL, Howard M.
The politics of international money / Howard M. Wachtel. — Amsterdam : Transnational Institute, 1987. — 47p. — (Transnational issues ; 2)

MONEY — Economic aspects — Europe

REDDY, William M.
Money and Liberty in modern Europe : a critique of historical understanding / William M. Reddy. — Cambridge : Cambridge University Press, 1987. — xii,264p. — *Includes index*

MONEY — History

EDWARDS, James Rolph
The economist of the country : Ludwig von Mises in the history of monetary thought / by James Rolph Edwards. — New York : Carlton Press, 1985. — 143p. — *Bibliography: p137-143*

MONEY — Mathematical models

GRANDMONT, Jean-Michel
Money and value : a reconsideration of classical and neoclassical monetary theories / Jean-Michel Grandmont. — Cambridge [Cambridgeshire] ; New York : Cambridge University Press, 1983. — xii,199p. — (Econometric Society monographs in pure theory ; no. 5). — *Includes index.* — *Bibliography: p193-195*

MONEY — Social aspects — Europe

REDDY, William M.
Money and Liberty in modern Europe : a critique of historical understanding / William M. Reddy. — Cambridge : Cambridge University Press, 1987. — xii,264p. — *Includes index*

MONEY — Australia

BUTLIN, S. J.
The Australian monetary system : 1851 to 1914 / S. J. Butlin. — [s.l.] : Judith F. Butlin, 1986. — 404p

MONEY — Canada

HUNTER, W. T.
Canadian financial markets / W. T. Hunter. — Peterborough, Canada : Broadview Press, 1986. — 193p. — *Includes references*

MONEY — Chile — Statistics

MAMALAKIS, Markos
Historical statistics of Chile / compiled by Markos J. Mamalakis. — Westport, Conn. : Greenwood Press
vol.5: Money, banking, and financial services. — 1985. — xcii,532p

MONEY — Europe — History

DAY, John, 1924-
The medieval market economy / John Day. — Oxford : Basil Blackwell, 1987. — [288]p. — *Includes bibliography and index*

MONEY — Europe — History — 18th century

REDDY, William M.
Money and Liberty in modern Europe : a critique of historical understanding / William M. Reddy. — Cambridge : Cambridge University Press, 1987. — xii,264p. — *Includes index*

MONEY — Europe — History — 19th century

REDDY, William M.
Money and Liberty in modern Europe : a critique of historical understanding / William M. Reddy. — Cambridge : Cambridge University Press, 1987. — xii,264p. — *Includes index*

MONEY — European Economic Community countries

ALLEN, Polly Reynolds
The ECU : birth of a new currency / Polly Reynolds Allen. — New York : Group of Thirty, 1986. — 68p. — (Occasional papers / Group of Thirty ; no.20). — *Bibliography: p55-59*

COFFEY, Peter
The European monetary system--past, present, and future / by Peter Coffey. — 2nd rev. ed. — Dordrecht ; Boston : M. Nijhoff ; Hingham, MA, USA : Distributors for the U.S. and Canada, Kluwer Academic, 1987. — p. cm. — *Includes bibliographical references and index*

The European Monetary System : recent developments / by Horst Ungerer...[et al.]. — Washington, D. C. : International Monetary Fund, 1986. — vii,75p. — (Occasional paper / International Monetary Fund ; no.48). — *Bibliography: p74-75*

MONEY — European Economic Community countries — Bibliography — Catalogs

COMMISSION OF THE EUROPEAN COMMUNITIES. Library
Recent publications on the European Communities received by the Library : supplement. — [Luxembourg : Office for Official Publications of the European Communities]
1985/1: Bibliography on monetary and financial matters. — 1985. — 750,54 columns. — *In Community languages*

MONEY — France

BANQUE DE FRANCE
La Banque de France et la monnaie. — 4th ed. — [Paris] : Banque de France, [1986]. — 208p

MONEY — France — Statistics

Communique de la Banque de France. — Paris : Banque de France. Direction Générale des Études. — *Monthly*

MONEY — Great Britain — History

ROTELLI, Claudio
Le origini della controversia monetaria (1797-1844) / Claudio Rotelli. — Bologna : Il Mulino, 1982. — 258p. — (Saggi ; 236)

MONEY — Great Britain — History — 20th century

CAPIE, Forrest
Explaining monetary changes between the two world wars / Forrest Capie and Ghila Rodrik-Bali. — London : Centre for Banking and International Finance, City University, 1986. — 38p. — (Monetary history discussion paper series ; no.21). — *Bibliography: p35-37*

MONEY — Hungary

DOMÁNY, Gyula
Az önáló jegybank felállítása / írta Domány Gyula. — Budapest : Benkö Gyula Könyvkereskedése, 1918. — 45p

IVÁN, Miklós
A Koronától az aranypengöig : a pénzválság bonctana / írta Iván Miklós. — Budapest : Gergely R., 1934. — 104p

MONEY — Malaysia

LEE, Sheng-yi
The monetary and banking development of Singapore and Malaysia / Lee Shen-yi. — 2nd ed. — [Singapore] : Singapore University Press, 1986. — 298p

MONEY — Peru

SUSANO LUCERO, Reynaldo
La evolución monetaria en el Perú en la decada del 60, una aproximación cuantitativa / [Reynaldo Susano Lucero]. — [Lima] : Ministerio de Economía y finanzas, Dirección General de Asuntos Financieros, Area de Estudios Financieros, Dirección de Investigación y Desarrollo Financiero, 1974. — 21leaves

MONEY — Singapore

LEE, Sheng-yi
The monetary and banking development of Singapore and Malaysia / Lee Shen-yi. — 2nd ed. — [Singapore] : Singapore University Press, 1986. — 298p

MONEY — Soviet Union — Bibliography

DREMINA, Z. E.
Finansy, denği i kredit SSSR : bibliograficheskii ukazatel' 1976-1985 gg. / [sostaviteli: Z. E. Dremina, A. V. Golousenko, G. M. Klimova; otv. redaktor V. S. Kulikov]. — Moskva : Finansy i statistika, 1986. — 287p

MONEY — Swaziland
RUSSELL, Margo
Beyond remittances : the redistribution of cash in Swazi society / Margo Russell. — Kwaluseni : Kwaluseni Campus, 1984. — 35p. — (Research paper / University of Swaziland. Social Science Research Unit ; no.2). — *Bibliography: p34-36*

MONEY — United States — Statistics
Banking and monetary statistics : 1914-1941. — Washington, D.C. : Board of Governors of the Federal Reserve System, 1976. — 682p

BOARD OF GOVERNORS OF THE FEDERAL RESERVE SYSTEM (U.S.)
Banking and monetary statistics, 1941-1970. — Washington : Board of Governors of the Federal Reserve System, 1976. — vii,1168p

MONEY MARKET
EDEY, Malcolm Lawrence
Volatility and informational efficiency in international currency markets / Malcolm Lawrence Edey. — 170 leaves. — *PhD (Econ) 1986 LSE*

MONEY MARKET — History — 20th century
BROWN, Brendan
The flight of international capital : a contemporary history / Brendan Brown. — London : Croom Helm, c1987. — xiv,447p. — *Bibliography: p421-428. — Includes index*

MONEY MARKET — Australia
CAREW, Edna
Fast money 2 : the money market in Australia / Edna Carew. — Sydney ; London : Allen & Unwin, 1985. — 249p. — *Bibliography: p245. — Includes index*

MONEY MARKET — Canada
HUNTER, W. T.
Canadian financial markets / W. T. Hunter. — Peterborough, Canada : Broadview Press, 1986. — 193p. — *Includes references*

MONEY MARKET — Japan
FELDMAN, Robert Alan
Japanese financial markets : deficits, dilemmas, and deregulation / Robert Alan Feldman. — Cambridge, Mass. : MIT Press, c1986. — p. cm. — *Includes index. — Bibliography: p*

MONEY MARKET — United States
Responses to deregulation : retail deposit pricing from 1983 through 1985 / Patrick I. Mahoney...[et al.]. — Washington, D. C. : Board of Governors of the Federal Reserve System, 1987. — 29p. — (Staff study / Board of Governors of the Federal Reserve System ; 151). — *Includes bibliographical references*

MONEY SUPPLY — Bibliography
GOEHLERT, Robert
Policy studies on the money supply : a selected bibliography / Robert Goehlert. — Monticello, Ill. : Vance Bibliographies, [1983]. — 7 p.. — (Public administration series--bibliography ; P 1312). — *Cover title. — "October, 1983."*

MONEY SUPPLY — Government policy — Great Britain
GREAT BRITAIN. Parliament. House of Commons. Library. Research Division
Control of the money supply / Christopher Barclay, Paul Hutt. — [London] : the Division, 1980. — 26p. — (Background paper ; no.83). — *Bibliography: p24-26*

MONEY SUPPLY — Spain
MAULEÓN, Ignacio
Los activos de caja y la oferta de dinero / Ignacio Mauleón, José Pérez y Beatriz Sanz. — [Madrid] : Banco de España, 1986. — 109p. — (Estudios económicos / Banco de España, Servicio de Estudios ; no.40)

MONEY SUPPLY — United States
Seasonal adjustment of the monetary aggregates : report of the Committee of Experts on Seasonal Adjustment Techniques / Board of Governor of the Federal Reserve System. — Washington : The Board, 1981. — 55p

MONGOLIA (MONGOLIAN PEOPLE'S REPUBLIC)
SANDERS, Alan J. K.
Mongolia : politics, economics and society / Alan J.K. Sanders. — London : Pinter, 1987. — xxi,179p. — (Marxist regimes series). — *Bibliography: p155-168. — Includes index*

MONOPOLIES
TIROLE, Jean
Concurrence imparfaite / Jean Tirole. — Paris : Economica, c1985. — 133p. — (Economie et statistiques avencées)

MONOPOLIES — United States
Breaking up Bell : essays on industrial organisation and regulation / [a CERA research study] ; edited by David S. Evans ; with contributions by Robert Bornholz ... [et al.]. — New York ; Oxford : North-Holland, c1983. — xiv,298p. — *Bibliography: p283-291. — Includes index*

MONTAGNARDS — History
SLAVIN, Morris
The making of an insurrection : Parisian sections and the Gironde / Morris Slavin. — Cambridge, Mass. : Harvard University Press, 1986. — ix, 236 p.. — *Includes index. — Bibliography: p. [222]-228*

MONTAGNE, ROBERT
Regards sur le Maroc : actualité de Robert Montagne. — Paris : CHEAM, 1986. — 239p. — (Publications du CHEAM ; 9). — *Bibliography: p233-239. — Contents: La vie sociale et politique des Berberes/Robert Montagne - The Berbers: their social and political organisation /Ernest Gellner, David Seddon - Robert Montagne et les structures politiques du Maroc pre-colonial/Mohamed Berdouzi*

MONTENEGRO
KOVAČEVI'C, Branislav
Komministička partija Crne Gore 1945-1952. godine / Branislav Kovačevi'c. — Titograd : NIO "Univerzitetska riječ", 1986. — 524p

MONTESQUIEU, CHARLES DE SECONDAT, Baron de
VOLPILHAC-AUGER, Catherine
Tacite et Montesquieu / Catherine Volpilhac-Auger. — Oxford : Voltaire Foundation, 1985. — vii,202p. — (Studies on Voltaire and the eighteenth century ; 232). — *Bibliography: p.193-198*

MONTRÉAL METROPOLITAN AREA (QUÉBEC) — Languages — Political aspects
SANCTON, Andrew
Governing the Island of Montreal : language differences and metropolitan politics / Andrew Sancton. — Berkeley : University of California Press, c1985. — xxxviii, 213 p.. — (Lane studies in regional government) (A Publication of the Franklin K. Lane Memorial Fund, Institute of Governmental Studies, University of California, Berkeley). — *"Published for the Institute of Governmental Studies and the Institute of International Studies, University of California, Berkeley.". — Includes bibliographical references and index*

MONTRÉAL METROPOLITAN AREA (QUÉBEC) — Politics and government
SANCTON, Andrew
Governing the Island of Montreal : language differences and metropolitan politics / Andrew Sancton. — Berkeley : University of California Press, c1985. — xxxviii, 213 p.. — (Lane studies in regional government) (A Publication of the Franklin K. Lane Memorial Fund, Institute of Governmental Studies, University of California, Berkeley). — *"Published for the Institute of Governmental Studies and the Institute of International Studies, University of California, Berkeley.". — Includes bibliographical references and index*

MONTREAL (QUEBEC) — City planning
DIVAY, Gérard
Les promoteurs d'habitation dans la région de Montréal : présentation partielle et préliminaire / Gérard Divay et Luc Hurtubise. — Quebec : Université du Quebec. Institut National de la Recherche Scientifique, 1972. — 41 leaves. — (Notes de recherche / INRS Urbanisation ; no.1)

MONTSERRAT — Census, 1980
Preliminary data of the 1980 Commonwealth Caribbean population census, May 12, 1980. — [Plymouth?] : Government of Montserrat Statistics Office, 1980. — iv,26p,iv,23p. — *Contents: Part 1. Household and housing information - part 2. Age distribution and economic activity data*

MONTSERRAT — Economic conditions — Statistics
Preliminary data of the 1980 Commonwealth Caribbean population census, May 12, 1980. — [Plymouth?] : Government of Montserrat Statistics Office, 1980. — iv,26p,iv,23p. — *Contents: Part 1. Household and housing information - part 2. Age distribution and economic activity data*

MONTSERRAT — Population — Statistics
Preliminary data of the 1980 Commonwealth Caribbean population census, May 12, 1980. — [Plymouth?] : Government of Montserrat Statistics Office, 1980. — iv,26p,iv,23p. — *Contents: Part 1. Household and housing information - part 2. Age distribution and economic activity data*

MONUMENTS — Law and legislation — Great Britain
GREAT BRITAIN. Department of the Environment
Proposals to amend the laws relating to ancient monuments : a consultative document. — [London] : the Department, [1976?]. — 24,2p

GREAT BRITAIN. Parliament. House of Commons. Library. Research Division
National Heritage Bill [HL] - Bill 85 of 1982-83 / [Fiona Poole, Barry Winetrobe]. — [London] : the Division, 1983. — 23p. — (Reference sheet ; no.83/4). — *Includes bibliographical references*

MOOREA (SOCIETY ISLANDS) — Population — Statistics
Tableaux normalisés du recensement général de la population : 15 octobre 1983. — [Papeete] : Institut territorial de la statistique Résultats de la commune de Moorea-Maiao. — [1985?]. — 11 leaves

MOOT COURTS
The Observer book of moots / edited by Paul Dobson and Barry Fitzpatrick. — London : Sweet & Maxwell, 1986. — 123p

MORAL CONDITIONS
DWORKIN, Andrea
Pornography : men possessing women / Andrea Dworkin. — London : Women's Press, 1981. — 304p. — *Originally published: New York : Perigee, 1981. — Bibliography: p239-285. — Includes index*

MORAL DEVELOPMENT — Addresses, essays, lectures
[Moralisches Urteilen und soziale Umwelt. English]. Moral development and the social environment : studies in the philosophy and psychology of moral judgment and education / edited by Georg Lind, Hans A. Hartmann, and Roland Wakenhut ; general editor and translator, Thomas E. Wren. — Chicago, Ill. : Precedent Pub., c1985. — xvii, 327 p.. — (Precedent studies in ethics and the moral sciences). — *Rev. translation of: Moralisches Urteilen und soziale Umwelt. — Includes indexes. — Bibliography: p. [299]-318*

MORAL EDUCATION — United States
The Hidden curriculum and moral education : deception or discovery? / edited by Henry Giroux and David Purpel. — Berkeley, Calif. : McCutchan Pub. Corp., c1983. — x, 425 p.. — *Includes bibliographical references*

MORBIDITY
HO, Teresa J.
Measuring health as a component of living standards / Teresa J. Ho. — Washington, D.C., U.S.A. : World Bank, c1982 ((1985 printing)). — 58p. — (LSMS working papers ; no.15) (LSMS working papers ; no. 15). — *Bibliography: p56-58*

MORELOS (MEXICO) — Moral conditions — Case studies
ROMANUCCI-ROSS, Lola
Conflict, violence, and morality in a Mexican village / Lola Romanucci-Ross ; with a new afterword. — University of Chicago Press ed. — Chicago : University of Chicago Press, 1986. — ix, 222 p.. — : *Reprint. Originally published: Palo Alto, Calif. : National Press Books, 1973. — Bibliography: p. 218-222*

MORELOS (MEXICO) — Social conditions — Case studies
ROMANUCCI-ROSS, Lola
Conflict, violence, and morality in a Mexican village / Lola Romanucci-Ross ; with a new afterword. — University of Chicago Press ed. — Chicago : University of Chicago Press, 1986. — ix, 222 p.. — : *Reprint. Originally published: Palo Alto, Calif. : National Press Books, 1973. — Bibliography: p. 218-222*

MORGAN, J. PIERPONT
CAROSSO, Vincent P
The Morgans : private international bankers 1854-1913 / Vincent P. Carosso ; with the assistance of Rose C. Carosso. — Cambridge, Mass. ; London : Harvard University Press, 1987. — xvi, 888p, [12]p of plates. — *Includes index. — Bibliography: p.649-653*

MORGAN, JUNIUS SPENCER
CAROSSO, Vincent P
The Morgans : private international bankers 1854-1913 / Vincent P. Carosso ; with the assistance of Rose C. Carosso. — Cambridge, Mass. ; London : Harvard University Press, 1987. — xvi, 888p, [12]p of plates. — *Includes index. — Bibliography: p.649-653*

MORITA, AKIO
MORITA, Akio
Made in Japan : Akio Morita and Sony / Akio Morita with Edwin M. Reingold and Mitsuko Shimomura. — London : Collins, 1987. — viii,309p,[8]p of plates. — *Includes index*

MORO, ALDO — Kidnapping, 1978
WAGNER-PACIFICI, Robin Erica
The Moro morality play : terrorism as social drama / Robin Erica Wagner-Pacifici. — Chicago : The University of Chicago Press, c1986. — p. cm. — *Includes index. — Bibliography: p*

MOROBE PROVINCE (PAPUA NEW GUINEA) — Population — Statistics
1980 national population census : final figures : provincial summary : Morobe Province. — Port Moresby : National Statistical Office, 1985. — iii,172p

MOROCCANS — France
MAZOUZ, Mohamed
Le Maroc et l'immigration Marocaine en France / Mohamed Mazouz. — [Paris] : Agence de développement des relations interculturelles, 1984. — 69 leaves. — *Includes bibliographical references*

MAZOUZ, Mohamed
Le Maroc et l'immigration marocaine en France / Mohamed Mazouz. — Paris : Agence de Développement des Relations Interculturelles, 1984. — 69 leaves. — *Bibliography: p59-66*

MOROCCANS — Germany (West) — Social conditions
PLÜCKEN-OPOLKA, Renate
Zur sozialen Lage marokkanischer Familien in der Bundesrepublik Deutschland / Renate Plücken-Opolka ; herausgegeben von Arbeiterwohlfahrt Kreisverband Düsseldorf e.V.. — Berlin : EXpress Edition, 1985. — iv,136p. — *Bibliography: p133-136*

MOROCCO — Dictionaries and encyclopedias
SPENCER, William
Historical dictionary of Morocco / by William Spencer. — Metuchen, N.J. : Scarecrow Press, 1980. — p. cm. — (African historical dictionaries ; no. 24). — *Bibliography: p*

MOROCCO — Economic conditions
NAJIB, Ali Ben Salah
Migration of labour and the transformation of the economy of the Wedimoon region in Morocco / Ali Ben Salah Najib. — Uppsala : Uppsala University, 1986. — xii,206p. — (Geografiska regionstudier ; nr.17). — *English text with a summary in French. — Doctoral dissertation at Uppsala University, 1986. — Bibliography: p199-206*

MOROCCO — Economic conditions — Statistics
Caractéristiques socio-économiques de la population d'après le recensement général de la population et de l'habitat de 1982 : niveau national : sondage au 1/20e. — Rabat : Direction de la Statistique, 1984. — 185p

Statistiques sur les etablissements economiques / Direction de la Statistique, Ministere du Plan, de la Formation des Cadres et de la Formation Professionnelle, Morocco. — Charii Maa Al Ainain-Haut-Agdal : Ministere du Plan, Direction de la Statistique, 1983-. — *Annual*

MOROCCO — Emigration and immigration
MAZOUZ, Mohamed
Le Maroc et l'immigration Marocaine en France / Mohamed Mazouz. — [Paris] : Agence de développement des relations interculturelles, 1984. — 69 leaves. — *Includes bibliographical references*

MAZOUZ, Mohamed
Le Maroc et l'immigration marocaine en France / Mohamed Mazouz. — Paris : Agence de Développement des Relations Interculturelles, 1984. — 69 leaves. — *Bibliography: p59-66*

MOROCCO — Foreign Relations — United States
KAMIL, Leo
Fueling the fire : U.S. policy and the Western Sahara conflict / Leo Kamil. — Trenton, New Jersey : Red Sea Press, 1987. — 104p. — *Distributed in the UK by Spokesman, Nottingham. — Bibliography: p93-96. — Appendices give text of 1983 OAU peace plan: 1985 U.N. General Assembly resolution: and 1979 Algiers peace treaty between the Polisario Front and the Republic of Mauretania*

MOROCCO — History — Dictionaries
SPENCER, William
Historical dictionary of Morocco / by William Spencer. — Metuchen, N.J. : Scarecrow Press, 1980. — p. cm. — (African historical dictionaries ; no. 24). — *Bibliography: p*

MOROCCO — History — 20th century
COMALADA, Angel
España: el ocaso de un parlamento. 1921-1923 / Angel Comalada. — Barcelona : Ediciones Península, 1985. — 172p. — (Temas de historia y política contemporánea ; 18). — *Bibliography: p167-172*

PORCH, Douglas
The conquest of Morocco / Douglas Porch. — London : Cape, 1986, c1982. — xii,335p. — *Originally published: New York : Knopf, 1983. — Bibliography: p317-320. — Includes index*

MOROCCO — Manufactures
Morocco : industrial incentives and export promotion. — Washington, D.C., U.S.A. : World Bank, c1984. — Lxxvii,219p. — (A World Bank country study). — *Report prepared by an economic mission that visited Morocco in Sept. 1982 composed of Bela Balassa and others. — Summaries in French and Spanish. — Includes bibliographical references*

MOROCCO — Politics and government
Regards sur le Maroc : actualité de Robert Montagne. — Paris : CHEAM, 1986. — 239p. — (Publications du CHEAM ; 9). — *Bibliography: p233-239. — Contents: La vie sociale et politique des Berberes/Robert Montagne - The Berbers: their social and political organisation /Ernest Gellner, David Seddon - Robert Montagne et les structures politiques du Maroc pre-colonial/Mohamed Berdouzi*

MOROCCO — Population — Statistics
Caractéristiques socio-économiques de la population d'après le recensement général de la population et de l'habitat de 1982 : niveau national : sondage au 1/20e. — Rabat : Direction de la Statistique, 1984. — 185p

MOROCCO — Relations — Spain
COMALADA, Angel
España: el ocaso de un parlamento. 1921-1923 / Angel Comalada. — Barcelona : Ediciones Península, 1985. — 172p. — (Temas de historia y política contemporánea ; 18). — *Bibliography: p167-172*

MOROCCO — Social conditions — Statistics
Caractéristiques socio-économiques de la population d'après le recensement général de la population et de l'habitat de 1982 : niveau national : sondage au 1/20e. — Rabat : Direction de la Statistique, 1984. — 185p

MOROCCO — Social life and customs
DWYER, Kevin
Moroccan dialogues : anthropology in question / Kevin Dwyer. — Baltimore : Johns Hopkins University Press, c1982. — xxvii, 297 p.. — *Includes dialogues between Kevin Dwyer and Faqir Muhammad. — Includes index. — Bibliography: p. 289-292*

HART, David
The Ait ´Atta of Southern Morocco : daily life and recent history / by David Hart. — Wisbech : Menas Press, 1984. — xxviii,219p

MOROCCO. Ministere du Plan, de la Formation des Cadres et de la Formation Professionnelle
Statistiques sur les etablissements economiques / Direction de la Statistique, Ministere du Plan, de la Formation des Cadres et de la Formation Professionnelle, Morocco. — Charii Maa Al Ainain-Haut-Agdal : Ministere du Plan, Direction de la Statistique, 1983-. — *Annual*

MORRIS, WILLIAM — Influence
BORIS, Eileen
Art and labor : Ruskin, Morris, and the craftsman ideal in America / Eileen Boris. — Philadelphia : Temple University Press, 1986. — xviii, 261 p.. — (American civilization). — *Includes index. — Bibliography: p. 195-247*

MORTALITY
BROWNLEE, John
The history of the birth and death rates in England and Wales taken as a whole from 1750 to the present time / John Brownlee. — London : Society of Medical Officers of Health, 1916. — 24p

Continuous mortality investigation reports / compiled by the Continuous Mortality Investigation Committee of the Institute and Faculty of Actuaries. — London : Institute of Actuaries and Faculty of Actuaries, 1973-. — *Annual*

MORTALITY *continuation*

KITAGAWA, Evelyn Mae
Differential mortality in the United States : a study in socioeconomic epidemiology / [by] Evelyn M. Kitagawa and Philip M. Hauser. — Cambridge, Mass. : Harvard University Press, 1973. — xx, 255 p. — (Vital and health statistics monographs). — *Bibliography: p. 248-251*

MORTALITY — Addresses, essays, lectures

Fertility and mortality : theory, methodology, and empirical issues / edited by K. Mahadevan with P.J. Reddy & D.A. Naidu. — New Delhi ; Beverly Hills ; London : Sage Publications, 1986. — 351p. — *Includes bibliographies*

MORTALITY — History — Congresses

Pre-industrial population change : the mortality decline and short-term population movements / edited by Tommy Bengtsson, Gunnar Fridlizius and Rolf Ohlsson. — Stockholm : Almqvist and Wiksell, 1984. — 419p. — *Conference papers*

MORTALITY — Social aspects — Great Britain

LYONS, N. J.
A summary of investigations into the relationships between standardised mortality ratio and measures of social deprivation, and a consideration of the effect of social deprivation on hospital use / N. J. Lyons. — [London : Department of Health and Social Security, 1977]. — 6leaves

MORTALITY — Statistical methods

BRASS, William
Advances in methods for estimating fertility and mortality from limted and defective data / William Brass. — London : London School of Hygiene and Tropical Medicine, Centre for Population Studies, 1985. — 103p. — (Occasional publication / Centre for Population Studies, London School of Hygiene and Tropical Medicine)

COCHRANE, Susan Hill
Procedures for collecting and analyzing mortality data in LSMS / Susan H. Cochrane, William D. Kalsbeek, Jeremiah M. Sullivan. — Washington, D.C. : World Bank, Development Research Dept., 1982, c1981. — 148p. — (LSMS working papers ; no.16). — *Bibliography: p64-69*

Indirect techniques for demographic estimation. — New York : United Nations, 1983. — xxv,304p. — (Population studies / Department of International Economic and Social Affairs ; no. 81). — *At head of title: Manual X. — "A collaboration of the Population Division of the Department of International Economic and Social Affairs of the United Nations Secretariat with the Committee on Population and Demography of the National Research Council, United States National Academy of Sciences.". — "ST/ESA/SER.A/81.". — "United Nations publication, sales no. E.83.XIII.2"--T.p. verso. — Includes bibliographical references*

MORTALITY — Statistical methods — Congresses

UNITED NATIONS/WORLD HEALTH ORGANIZATION WORKING GROUP ON DATA BASES FOR MEASUREMENT OF LEVELS, TRENDS, AND DIFFERENTIALS IN MORTALITY. Meeting (1981 : Bangkok, Thailand)
Data bases for mortality measurement : papers of the Meeting of the United Nations/World Health Organization Working Group on Data Bases for Measurement of Levels, Trends, and Differentials in Mortality, Bangkok, 20-23 October 1981. — New York : United Nations, 1984. — x,164p. — (Population studies / Department of International Economic and Social Affairs ; no. 84). — *"ST/ESA/SER.A/84".--Verso t.p. — "United Nations publication, sales no. E.83.XIII.3"--Verso t.p. — Bibliography: p159-164*

MORTALITY — Tables

NAMBOODIRI, N. Krishnan
Life table techniques and their applications / Krishnan Namboodiri, C.M. Suchindran. — Orlando [Fla.] : Academic Press, 1987. — xii, 275 p.. — (Studies in population). — *Includes indexes. — Bibliography: p. 243-262*

MORTALITY — Australia

YOUNG, Christabel
Selection and survival : immigrant mortality in Australia / Dr. Christabel Young. — Canberra : Australian Government Publishing Service, 1986. — xiii,251p. — *Bibliography: p132-150*

MORTALITY — Cyprus — Statistics

AGATHANGELOU, Alecos
Mortality in Cyprus / by Alecos Agathangelou. — [Nicosia] : Department of Statistics and Research, [1985]. — 56p. — (Population statistics / Department of Statistics and Research. Series 3 ; Report no.5). — *Bibliography: p55-56*

MORTALITY — Denmark — Statistics

JUEL, Knud
Dødelighedsindeks for kommuner og amter 1971-80 = Age-standardized mortality index for Danish municipalities and countries 1971-80. — [København : Dansk Institut for Klinisk Epidemiologi, 1984]. — 156p. — (Vitalstatistik ; 1984:7:1). — *Includes summary and table headings in English. — Bibliography: p.116-118*

Regionale dødelighedsforskelle i Danmark 1971-79. — København : Danmarks Statistik, 1983. — 136p. — (Statistiske Undersøgelser ; nr.39)

MORTALITY — Developing countries

INSTITUT NATIONAL D'ETUDES DÉMOGRAPHIQUES
Health policy, social policy and mortality prospects : proceedings of a seminar at Paris, France, February 28-March 4, 1983 / edited by Jacques Vallin and Alan D. Lopez. — [Liège] : Ordina, 1985. — 557p. — *Bibliographies*

MORTALITY — England — Cleveland

CLEVELAND. County Council. Research and Intelligence Unit
Mortality in Cleveland. — [Middlesbrough] : [the Unit], 1986. — 13 leaves. — (Information note / Cleveland. County Council. Research and Intelligence Unit ; 299)

MORTALITY — England — London — Tables

HILLS, Carole
Greater London lifetables, 1979-82 / prepared in the Intelligence Unit by Carole Hills and John Hollis. — [London] : Greater London Council, 1986. — [113]p. — (Statistical series / Greater London Council ; no.50). — *Bibliographical references: p17*

MORTALITY — Europe

LYNGE, Elsebeth
Socio-economic differences in mortality in Europe : newly emerging trends in mortality / Elsebeth Lynge. — Strasbourg : Council of Europe, 1984. — 89p. — (Population studies / Council of Europe ; no.9)

MORTALITY — Finland — Tables

KOLARI, Risto
Kuolleisuus : kohorttikuolleisuus Suomessa v:sta 1851 lähtien = Mortality : cohort mortality in Finland from 1851 / Risto Kolari. — Helsinka : Tilastokeskus, 1980. — 94p. — (Tutkimuksia / Finland. Tilastokeskus ; no.57). — *Summary and table headings in English*

MORTALITY — Israel — Statistics

Mortality of adult jews in Israel 1950-1967 / E. Peritz, F. Dreyfuss, H. S. Halevi, U. O. Schmelz. — Jerusalem : Central Bureau of Statistics, 1973. — 226p. — (Special Series / Israel. Central Bureau of Statistics ; No.409)

MORTALITY — Japan — History

JANNETTA, Ann Bowman
Epidemics and mortality in early modern Japan / Ann Bowman Jannetta. — Princeton, N.J. : Princeton University Press, c1986. — p. cm. — *Includes index. — Bibliography: p*

MORTALITY — Jordan — Statistics

BLACKER, J. G. C.
Mortality levels and trends in Jordan estimated from the results of the 1976 fertility survey / J. G. C. Blacker, Allan G. Hill, Kath A. Moser. — Voorburg : International Statistical Institute, 1983. — 35p. — (Scientific reports / World Fertility Survey ; no.47)

MORTALITY — Lesotho

TIMAEUS, Ian
Mortality in Lesotho : a study of levels, trends and differentials based on retrospective survey data / Ian Timaeus. — Voorburg : International Statistical Institute, 1984. — 53p. — (Scientific reports / World Fertility Survey ; no.59)

MORTALITY — Netherlands — Tables

Overlevingstafels naar burgerlijke staat 1976-1980. — 's-Gravenhage : Staatsuitgeverij, 1984. — 103p. — *Preface, summary and table headings in English. — Title on back cover: Life tables by marital status, 1976-1980*

Sterftetafels voor Nederland afgeleid uit waarnemingen over de periode 1976-1980. — 's-Gravenhage : Staatsuitgeverij, 1983. — 59p. — *Summary and table headings in English. — Title on back cover: Life tables for the Netherlands 1976-1980*

MORTALITY — Peru — Statistics

MOSER, Kath
Levels and trends in child and adult mortality in Peru / Kath Moser. — Voorburg : International Statistical Institute, 1985. — 42p. — (Scientific reports / World Fertility Survey ; no.77)

MORTALITY — South Asia

CAIN, Mead
Consequences of reproductive failure : dependence, mobility, and mortality among the elderly in rural South Asia / Mead Cain. — New York : Population Council, 1985. — 30p. — (Working papers / Population Council. Center for Policy Studies ; no.119)

MORTALITY — United States — Statistics

ROSENWAIKE, Ira
The extreme aged in America : a portrait of an expanding population / Ira Rosenwaike, with the assistance of Barbara Logue. — Westport, Conn. ; London : Greenwood Press, 1985. — xix, 253 p.. — (Contributions to the study of aging ; no. 3). — *Includes index. — Bibliography: p. [229]-241*

MORTALITY AND RACE — Australia

YOUNG, Christabel
Selection and survival : immigrant mortality in Australia / Dr. Christabel Young. — Canberra : Australian Government Publishing Service, 1986. — xiii,251p. — *Bibliography: p132-150*

MORTALITY AND RACE — Israel — Statistics

Mortality of adult jews in Israel 1950-1967 / E. Peritz, F. Dreyfuss, H. S. Halevi, U. O. Schmelz. — Jerusalem : Central Bureau of Statistics, 1973. — 226p. — (Special Series / Israel. Central Bureau of Statistics ; No.409)

MORTGAGE LOANS — Great Britain

BOLÉAT, Mark
The mortgage market / Mark Boléat and Adrian Coles : theory and practice of housing finance. — London : Allen & Unwin, 1987. — [192]p. — (Studies in financial institutions and markets ; 3). — *Includes bibliography and index*

GRIFFIN, Jenny
Joint mortages : a discussion paper / prepared by Jenny Griffin. — London : Commission for Racial Equality, 1978. — 2p. — *First published by the Community Relations Commission, 1975*

MORTGAGE LOANS — Great Britain
continuation

HOLMANS, A. E.
Flows of funds associated with house purchase for owner-occupation in the United Kingdom 1977-1984 and equity withdrawal from house purchase finance / A. E. Holmans. — London : Departments of the Environment and Transport, 1986. — 128p. — (Government Economic Service working paper ; no.92)

MEEN, Geoffrey Peter
Some aspects of mortgage market liberalisation in the United Kingdom : an econometric analysis / by Geoffrey P. Meen. — 323 leaves. — PhD (Econ) 1986 LSE. — Leaves 287-304 are appendices

MORTGAGE LOANS — United States

Housing and the new financial markets / edited by Richard L. Florida. — New Brunswick, N.J. : Center for Urban Policy Research, c1986. — xviii, 482 p.. — *Includes index. — Bibliography: p. 469-472*

MORTGAGES — England

GREAT BRITAIN. Law Commission
Land mortgages / the Law Commission. — London : HMSO, 1986. — xv,254,[48]p. — (Working paper / Law Commission ; no.99)

MOSCA, GAETANO, 1858-1941 — Contributions in political science

ALBERTONI, Ettore A.
Mosca and the theory of elitism / Ettore A. Albertoni ; translated by Paul Goodrick. — Oxford : Basil Blackwell, 1987. — xvii,194p. — *Translation of: Dottrina della classe politica e teoria delle elites. — Bibliography: p186-191. — Includes index*

MOSCOW (R.S.F.S.R.) — Economic conditions

BRITISH LIBRARY OF POLITICAL AND ECONOMIC SCIENCE
Rare printed material relating to Moscow, 1887-1923 : contents of the microfilm. — Hebdon Bridge, W. Yorks. : Altair Publishing, [1987]. — 35p

SAUSHKIN, Iu. G.
Moskva sredi gorodov mira : ekonomiko-geograficheskoe issledovanie / Iu. G. Saushkin, V. G. Glushkova. — Moskva : Mysl', 1983. — 282p

MOSCOW (R.S.F.S.R.) — History — Revolution of 1905

IONOV, I. N.
Profsoiuzy rabochikh Moskvy v revoliutsii 1905-1907 gg. / I. N. Ionov ; otv. redaktor A. M. Sinitsyn. — Moskva : Nauka, 1986. — 166p

MOSCOW (R.S.F.S.R.) — History — 1925-1953

Nezabyvaemye 30-e : vospominaniia veteranov partii-moskvichei / [sostavitel': N. B. Ivushkin]. — Moskva : Moskovskii rabochii, 1986. — 303p

MOSCOW (R.S.F.S.R.) — Politics and government

BRITISH LIBRARY OF POLITICAL AND ECONOMIC SCIENCE
Rare printed material relating to Moscow, 1887-1923 : contents of the microfilm. — Hebdon Bridge, W. Yorks. : Altair Publishing, [1987]. — 35p

MOSCOW (R.S.F.S.R.). Sovet deputatov trudiashchikhsia. Ispolnitel'nyi komitet
Otchet Ispolnitel'nogo Komiteta Moskovskogo Soveta R.K. i K.D. 2-mu Ob"edinennomu Guberns komu S"ezdu Sovetov za iiun'-noiabr' 1920g. — Moscow : [s.n.], 1920. — 624p. — (Rare printed material relating to Moscow 1887-1923)

MOSCOW (R.S.F.S.R.) — Statistics

BRITISH LIBRARY OF POLITICAL AND ECONOMIC SCIENCE
Rare printed material relating to Moscow, 1887-1923 : contents of the microfilm. — Hebdon Bridge, W. Yorks. : Altair Publishing, [1987]. — 35p

MOSCOW (R.S.F.S.R.). Gorodskaia uprava. Statisticheskii otdelenie
Statisticheskii atlas goroda Moskvy : ploshchad' Moskvy, naselenie i zaniatiia. — Moskva : Moskovskaia Gorodskara Tip., 1887. — 31p,26maps. — (Rare printed material relating to Moscow, 1887-1923)

MOSCOW (R.S.F.S.R.). Gorodskaia uprava. Statisticheskoe otdelenie
Atlas statistique de la ville de Moscou : territoire et population : explication des diagrammes et des cartogrammes. — Moscou : Typ. Ferd. Neubürger, 1890. — 16p. — (Rare printed material relating to Moscow, 1887-1923). — *In French*

MOSCOW (R.S.F.S.R.). Sovet deputatov trudiashchikhsia. Statisticheskii otdel
Statisticheskii ezhegodnik g. Moskvy i Moskovskii gubernii, 1914-1923 = Annuaire statistique de la ville et gouvernement de Moscou, 1914-1923. — Moskva : Izd. Statisticheskogo Otdela Moskovskogo Soveta. — (Rare printed material relating to Moscow, 1887-1923)
Vyp.1: Sel'skokhoziaistvennyi obzor Moskovskoi gubernii za 1916-1923 gg.. — 1925. — xii,288p

MOSCOW (R.S.F.S.R.: GUBERNIIA) — Economic conditions

MOSCOW (R.S.F.S.R.: Guberniia). Gubernskoe ekonomicheskoe soveshchanie
Otchet Moskovskogo Gubernskogo Ekonomicheskogo Soveshchaniia na 1 aprelia 1923 g.. — Moskva : [s.n.]. — (Rare printed materials relating to Moscow, 1887-1923)
Vyp.1. — 1923. — 185p

MOSCOW (R.S.F.S.R.: Guberniia). Gubernskoe ekonomicheskoe soveshchanie
Otchet Moskovskogo Gubernskogo Ekonomicheskogo Soveshchaniia na 1-e aprelia 1922 g.. — Moskva : [s.n], 1922. — 256p. — (Rare printed material relating to Moscow, 1887-1923). — *At head of title: Moskovskii Sovet Rabochikh, Krest'ianskikh i Krasnoarmeiskikh Deputatov*

MOSCOW (R.S.F.S.R.: Guberniia). Gubernskoe ekonomicheskoe soveshchanie
Otchet Moskovskogo gubernskogo Ekonomicheskogo Soveshchaniia na 1-e oktiabria 1921g. / sostavlen Moskovskim Statisticheskim Otdelom pod redaktsiei L. B. Kameneva. — Moskva : 14-ia Gos.tip., 1921. — 315p. — (Rare printed material relating to Moscow, 1887-1923). — *At head of title: Moskovskii Sovet Rabochikh, Krest'ianskikh i Krasnoarmeiskikh Deputatov*

MOSCOW (R.S.F.S.R.: Guberniia). Ispolnitel'nyi komitet
Otchet o deiatel'nosti Moskovskogo Gubernskogo Ispolnitel'nogo Komiteta i Gubernskogo Ekonomicheskogo Soveshchaniia, Ianvar' - Sentiabr' 1922 g.. — Moskva : [s.n.]. — (Rare printed material relating to Moscow, 1887-1923)
Vyp.2: Otchet Gubekoso na 1-e oktiabria 1922 g.. — 1922. — 203p

MOSCOW (R.S.F.S.R.: Guberniia). Ispolnitel'nyi komitet
Otchet o deiatel'nosti Moskovskogo Gubernskogo Ispolnitel'nogo Komiteta i Gubernskogo Ekonomicheskogo Soveshchaniia. S 1 oktiabria 1922 g. po 1 oktiabria 1923 g.. — Moskva : [s.n.]. — (Rare printed material relating to Moscow, 1887-1923)
Vyp.2: Otchet Gubekoso na 1-e oktiabria 1923 g.. — 1924. — 145p

MOSCOW (R.S.F.S.R.: GUBERNIIA) — Politics and government

MOSCOW (R.S.F.S.R.: Guberniia). Ispolnitel'nyi komitet
Otchet o deiatel'nosti Moskovskogo Gubernskogo Ispolnitel'nogo Komiteta i Gubernskogo Ekonomicheskogo Soveshchaniia s 1/X 1922g.-po 1/X1923g.. — Moskva : Tip. Administrativnago Otdela M.S. im M. I. Rogova. — (Rare printed material relating to Moscow, 1887-1923)
Vyp.1: Otchet Gubispolkoma / (sostavlen pod redaktsiei Organiz. - Instr. otd. M.S.R.,K. i K.D.). — 1924. — 649p

MOSQUITO INDIANS — Civil rights

INTER-AMERICAN COMMISSION ON HUMAN RIGHTS
Informe sobre la situacion de los derechos humanos de un sector de la poblacion Nicaragüense de origen Miskito y resolucion sobre el procedimiento de solucion amistosa sobre la situacion de los derechos humanos de un sector de la poblacion Nicaragüense de origen Miskito. — Washington, D.C. : Secretaría General, Organización de los Estados Americanos, 1984. — ii,150p. — *Includes bibliographical references.* — OEA/Ser.L/V/II.62 doc.10 rev.3 and doc.26

INTER-AMERICAN COMMISSION ON HUMAN RIGHTS
Report on the situation of human rights of a segment of the Nicaraguan population of Miskito origin and resolution on the friendly settlement procedure regarding the human rights situation of a segment of the Nicaraguan population of Miskito origin. — Washington, D.C. : General Secretariat, Organization of American States, 1984. — 142p. — *English translation of: Informe sobre la situacion de los derechos humanos de un sector de la poblacion Nicaragüense de origen Miskito.... — Includes bibliographical references.* — OEA/Ser.L/V/II.62 doc.10 rev. 3 and doc.26

MOTHER AND CHILD

SCARR, Sandra
Mother care/ other care : [the child-care dilemma for women and children] / Sandra Scarr and Judy Dunn. — 2nd ed. — Harmondsworth : Penguin, 1987. — 239p. — *Originally published: New York: Basic Books, 1984. — Bibliography: [p221]-229*

MOTHER-CHILD RELATIONS

MERCER, Ramona Thieme
First-time motherhood : experiences from teens to forties / Ramona T. Mercer. — New York : Springer Pub. Co., c1986. — xv, 384 p.. — *Includes index. — Bibliography: p. 357-374*

MOTHERHOOD — Psychological aspects

MERCER, Ramona Thieme
First-time motherhood : experiences from teens to forties / Ramona T. Mercer. — New York : Springer Pub. Co., c1986. — xv, 384 p.. — *Includes index. — Bibliography: p. 357-374*

MOTHERHOOD — Developing countries

HERZ, Barbara
The safe motherhood initiative : proposals for action / Barbara Herz, Anthony R. Measham. — Washington, D.C. : The World Bank, 1987. — x,52p. — (World Bank discussion papers ; no.9). — *Bibliography: p52*

MOTHERHOOD — Great Britain — History

LEWIS, Judith Schneid
In the family way : childbearing in the British aristocracy, 1760-1860 / Judith Schneid Lewis. — New Brunswick, N.J. : Rutgers University Press, c1986. — xi, 313 p.. — *Includes index. — Bibliography: p. 291-303*

MOTHERS

OAKLEY, Ann
From here to maternity : becoming a mother / Ann Oakley. — Harmondsworth : Penguin, 1986. — 328p

MOTHERS — Attitudes
MAYALL, Berry
Keeping children healthy : the role of mothers and professionals / Berry Mayall. — London ; Boston : Allen & Unwin, 1986. — xiv,258p. — *Bibliography: p[251]-258*

MOTHERS — Employment
Childcare and equal opportunities : some policy perspectives : papers delivered at a workshop organised by the Equal Opportunities Commission / edited by Bronwen Cohen and Karen Clarke. — London : H.M.S.O., 1986. — 87p. — *Includes bibliographical references*

MOTHERS — Employment — France
EUVRARD, Françoise
Mères de famille : coûts et revenus de lâctivité professionnelle / [étude...réalisée par Françoise Euvrard...Marie-Gabrielle David et Kristof Starzek. — [Paris] : Centre dÊtude des Revenus et des Coûts, 1985. — 163p. — (Documents du Centre dÊtude des Revenus et des Coûts ; no.75)

MOTHERS — Employment — United States
FALLOWS, Deborah
A mother's work / Deborah Fallows. — Boston : Houghton-Mifflin, 1985. — p. cm. — "A Richard Todd book"--

LUBIN, Aasta S
Managing success : high-echelon careers and motherhood / Aasta S. Lubin. — New York : Columbia University Press, 1987. — p. cm. — *Includes index.* — *Bibliography: p*

MOTHERS — Employment — United States — History
OGDEN, Annegret S
The great American housewife : from helpmate to wage earner, 1776-1986 / Annegret S. Ogden. — Westport, Conn. : Greenwood Press, 1986. — xxiii, 256 p.. — (Contributions in women's studies ; no. 61). — *Includes index.* — *Bibliography: p. [241]-247*

MOTHERS — Legal status, laws, etc — United States
CHESLER, Phyllis
Mothers on trial : the battle for children and custody / Phyllis Chesler. — New York : McGraw-Hill Book Co., c1986. — xviii, 651 p.. — *Bibliography: p. 457-621.* — *Includes index*

MOTHERS — Mortality — England
GREAT BRITAIN. Department of Health and Social Security
Report on confidential enquiries into maternal deaths in England and Wales : 1976-1978 / Department of Health and Social Security ; by John Tomkinson ... [et al.]. — London : H.M.S.O., 1982. — vii,179p. — (Report on health and social subjects / Great Britain. Department of Health and Social Security ; 26)

GREAT BRITAIN. Department of Health and Social Security
Report on confidential enquiries into maternal deaths in England and Wales : 1979-1981 / Alexander C. Turnbull ... [et al.]. — London : H.M.S.O., 1986. — vii,147p. — (Report on health and social subjects / Great Britain. Department of Health and Social Security ; 29)

MOTHERS — psychology
MERCER, Ramona Thieme
First-time motherhood : experiences from teens to forties / Ramona T. Mercer. — New York : Springer Pub. Co., c1986. — xv, 384 p.. — *Includes index.* — *Bibliography: p. 357-374*

MOTHERS — Developing countries — Mortality — Prevention
HERZ, Barbara
The safe motherhood initiative : proposals for action / Barbara Herz, Anthony R. Measham. — Washington, D.C. : The World Bank, 1987. — x,52p. — (World Bank discussion papers ; no.9). — *Bibliography: p52*

MOTHERS — Great Britain — Attitudes — History
LEWIS, Judith Schneid
In the family way : childbearing in the British aristocracy, 1760-1860 / Judith Schneid Lewis. — New Brunswick, N.J. : Rutgers University Press, c1986. — xi, 313 p.. — *Includes index.* — *Bibliography: p. 291-303*

MOTHERS — Great Britain — Interviews
MAYALL, Berry
Keeping children healthy : the role of mothers and professionals / Berry Mayall. — London ; Boston : Allen & Unwin, 1986. — xiv,258p. — *Bibliography: p[251]-258*

MOTHERS AND DAUGHTERS — Cross-cultural studies
WODAK, Ruth
The language of love and guilt : mother-daughter relationships from a cross-cultural perspective / Ruth Wodak, Muriel Schulz. — Amsterdam ; Philadelphia : J. Benjamins, 1986. — xiv, 253 p.. — *Includes indexes.* — *Bibliography: p. [220]-247*

MOTHERS AND DAUGHTERS — United States
ABRAMSON, Jane B
Mothermania : a psychological study of mother-daughter conflict / Jane B. Abramson. — Lexington, Mass. : Lexington Books, c1987. — p. cm. — *Includes index.* — *Bibliography: p*

MOTIVATION (PSYCHOLOGY)
TOATES, Frederick M.
Motivational systems / Frederick Toates. — Cambridge : Cambridge University Press, 1986. — xii,188p. — (Problems in the behavioural sciences ; 4). — *Bibliography: p172-185.* — *Includes index*

MOTIVATION RESEARCH (MARKETING) — Addresses, essays, lectures
Perspectives on methodology in consumer research / [edited by David Brinberg, Richard J. Lutz. — New York : Springer-Verlag, c1986. — p. cm. — *Includes bibliographies and indexes*

MOTOR BUS TERMINALS — England — London
STEER, DAVIES AND GLEAVE LTD.
London coach terminals : phase IV study: final report. — Richmond : Steer, Davies and Gleave Ltd., 1986. — vi,144 leaves

STEER DAVIES AND GLEAVE LTD
London coach terminals : phase 111 study: interim report. — Richmond : Steer Davies and Gleave Ltd., 1986. — v,56 leaves

STEER DAVIES AND GLEAVE LTD.
Study into coach terminal facilities in London : phase two report / prepared by Steer Davies and Gleave Ltd., Transportation Planning Consultancy for London Regional Transport. — Richmond : Steer Davies and Gleave Ltd., 1986. — iv,51,[6]p

MOULIN, JEAN — Congresses
Jean Moulin et le Conseil national de la Résistance : études et témoignages / sous la direction de François Bédarida et Jean-Pierre Azéma ; textes de Daniel Cordier ; interventions de C. Andrieu ... [et al.]. — Paris : Institut d'histoire du temps présent, Editions du Centre national de la recherche scientifique, 1983. — 192 p.. — "Journée d'études sur le Conseil national de la Résistance, Sorbonne, 9 juin 1983"--P. [5]. — *Bibliography: p. 133-180*

MOUNTBATTEN, LOUIS MOUNTBATTEN, Earl
ZIEGLER, Philip
Mountbatten : the official biography / Philip Ziegler. — London : Collins, 1985. — 786p,[48]p of plates. — *Geneal.table on lining papers.* — *Bibliography: p751-756.* — *Includes index*

MOUVEMENT RÉPUBLICAIN POPULAIRE
CALLOT, Emile-François
L'action et l'oeuvre politique du Mouvement républicain populaire : un parti politique de la démocratie chrétienne en France / Emile-François Callot. — Paris : Champion ; Genève : Slatkine, 1986. — 388p. — *Bibliography: p[383]*

MOVEMENT, PSYCHOLOGY OF
Human motor behavior : an introduction / edited by J.A. Scott Kelso. — Hillsdale, N.J. ; London : L. Erlbaum, 1982. — xi,307p. — *Includes bibliographies and indexes*

MOVIMENTO POPULAR DE LIBERTACAO DE ANGOLA
KHAZANOV, A. M.
Agostinho Neto / A. M. Khazanov ; translated from the Russian by Cynthia Carlile. — Moscow : Progress Publishers, 1986. — 302p

MOVING-PICTURE INDUSTRY — Legal status, laws, etc. — Peru
PERU
[Decreto ley 21244]. Ley orgánica de la Empresa de Cinematografía. — [Lima : Presidencia?, 197-]. — 10leaves

MOVING-PICTURE INDUSTRY — Legal status, laws, etc — Peru
PERU
[Laws, etc]. Junta de Supervigilancia de Películas y su reglamento. — Lima : Oficina Central de Información, 1974. — 25p

MOVING-PICTURE THEATRERS — Great Britain — Statistics
Cinemas. — London : HMSO, 1969-. — (Business monitor. MA ; 2) (Business monitor. M ; 2). — *Annual*

MOVING-PICTURES — Censorship — Great Britain
GREAT BRITAIN. Parliament. House of Commons. Library. Research Division
"Video nasties" : a background to the Video Recordings Bill, 1983-84 / [Jane Fiddick]. — [London] : the Division, 1983. — 29p. — (Background paper ; no.130)

MOVING PICTURES — Political aspects — Great Britain
HOGENKAMP, Bert
Deadly parallels : film and the Left in Britain 1929-1939 / Bert Hogenkamp. — London : Lawrence and Wishart, 1986. — 240p. — *Filmography: p215-231.* — *Bibliography: p232-233*

MOVING-PICTURES — Social aspects
DYER, Richard
Heavenly bodies : film stars and society / Richard Dyer. — Basingstoke : Macmillan, 1986. — xi,208p. — (British Film Institute cinema series). — *Bibliography: p195-202.* — *Includes index*

JARVIE, I. C
Movies and society / I.C. Jarvie. — New York : Garland Pub., 1986, c1970. — xix, 394 p.. — (Cinema classics). — : *Reprint. Originally published: New York : Basic Books, 1970.* — *Includes indexes.* — *Bibliography: p. 229-366*

MOVING-PICTURES, AMERICAN — Social aspects — Great Britain
SWANN, Paul
The Hollywood feature film in postwar Britain / Paul Swann. — London : Croom Helm, c1987. — 168p,[8]p of plates. — (Croom Helm studies on film, television and the media). — *Bibliography: p155-163.* — *Includes index*

MOVING PICTURES AND CHILDREN
BJÖRKQVIST, Kaj
Violent films, anxiety and aggression : experimental studies of the effect of violent films on the level of anxiety and aggressiveness in children / Kaj Björkqvist. — Helsinki : Societas Scientiarum Fennica, 1985. — 75p. — (Commentationes Scientarum Socialium ; 30). — *Bibliography: p71-75*

MOVING PICTURES, CHILEAN — Political aspects
Chilean cinema / edited and introduced by Michael Chanan. — London : British Film Institute, 1976. — [7],102p. — *Bibliography: p.100-120. — List of films: p.97-99*

MOVING PICTURES, DOCUMENTARY — Great Britain — History and criticism
HOGENKAMP, Bert
Deadly parallels : film and the Left in Britain 1929-1939 / Bert Hogenkamp. — London : Lawrence and Wishart, 1986. — 240p. — *Filmography: p215-231. — Bibliography: p232-233*

MOVING-PICTURES IN PROPAGANDA — Great Britain — History
REEVES, Nicholas
Official British film propaganda during the First World War / published in association with the Imperial War Museum ; Nicholas Reeves. — London : Croom Helm, c1986. — xiii,288p,[8]p of plates. — *List of films: p261-271. — Bibliography: p271-278. — Includes index*

MOZAMBIQUE. Treaties, etc. South Africa (1984 Mar. 16)
Confrontation and liberation in southern Africa : regional directions after the Nkomati Accord / edited by Ibrahim S. R. Msabaha and Timothy M. Shaw. — Boulder, Colo : Westview Press, 1987. — xii, 315 p., [1] leaf of plates. — (Westview special studies on Africa). — *Bibliography: p. [307]-315*

MS-DOS (COMPUTER OPERATING SYSTEM) — Handbooks, manuals, etc.
MICROSOFT CORPORATION
Learning DOS : interactive guide to the PC Operating System : handbook / Microsoft Corporation. — [United States] : Microsoft Corporation, 1986. — ii,34p. — *"For IBM Personal Computers and compatibles"*

MUGGING — England — London
DEUTSCH, Francis
Street crime in London 1981 / Francis Deutsch. — London : Commission for Racial Equality, 1982. — 12p

MUHAMMAD, FAQIR
DWYER, Kevin
Moroccan dialogues : anthropology in question / Kevin Dwyer. — Baltimore : Johns Hopkins University Press, c1982. — xxvii, 297 p.. — *Includes dialogues between Kevin Dwyer and Faqir Muhammad. — Includes index. — Bibliography: p. 289-292*

MUHAMMED, MURTALA
BABATOPE, Ebenezer
Murtala Muhammed : a leader betrayed (a study in Buhari's tryanny) / Ebenezer Babatope. — Enugu : Roy & Ezete, 1986. — xiii,138p

MULDOON, ROBERT
GOULD, John
The Muldoon years : an essay on New Zealand's recent economic growth / John Gould. — Auckland ; London : Hodder and Stoughton, 1985. — 87p

MULELE, PIERRE
MARTENS, Ludo
Pierre Mulele : ou la seconde vie de Patrice Lumumba / Ludo Martens. — [Antwerp] : Editions EPO, 1985. — 384p. — *Bibliography: p363-365*

MULRONEY, BRIAN
GRANATSTEIN, J. L
Sacred trust? : Brian Mulroney and the Conservative Party in power / by J.L. Granatstein, David Bercuson, William Young. — 1st ed. — Toronto, Canada : Doubleday Canada ; Garden City, N.Y. : Doubleday, 1986. — p. cm. — *Includes index*

MULTICULTURALISM — Canada
Ethnic Canada : identities and inequalities / [edited by] Leo Driedger. — Toronto : Copp Clark Pitman, 1987. — v,442p. — *Bibliography: p408-433*

MULTILINGUALISM
Language and education in multilingual settings / edited by Bernard Spolsky. — Clevedon : Multilingual Matters, 1986. — vii,200p. — (Multilingual matters ; 25)

LAPONCE, J. A.
Languages and their territories / J. A. Laponce ; translated from the French by Anthony Martin-Sperry. — Toronto : University of Toronto Press, 1987. — x,265p. — *Bibliography: p[211]-249*

MULTILINGUALISM — Belgium
MCRAE, Kenneth D.
Conflict and compromise in multilingual societies : Belgium / Kenneth D.McRae. — Waterloo, Ont. : Wilfrid Laurier University Press, 1986. — xiv, 387p

MULTIPLE COMPARISONS (STATISTICS)
KLOCKARS, Alan J.
Multiple comparisons / Alan J. Klockars, Gilbert Sax. — Beverly Hills, Calif. ; London : Sage Publications, 1986. — 87p. — (Quantitative applications in the social sciences ; 61) (Sage University paper)

MULTIPLE IMPUTATION (STATISTICS)
RUBIN, Donald B
Multiple imputation for nonresponse in surveys / Donald B. Rubin. — New York : Wiley, c1987. — p. cm. — (Wiley series in probability and mathematical statistics. Applied probability and statistics). — *Includes index. — Bibliography: p*

MULTIVARIATE ANALYSIS
JOHNSTON, R. J.
Multivariate statistical analysis in geography : a primer on the general linear method / R.J. Johnston. — London : Longman, 1978. — xx,280p. — *Bibl.: p.272-277. - Index*

JOHNSTON, R. J.
Multivariate statistical analysis in geography : a primer on the general linear model / by R.J. Johnston. — London : Longman, 1980. — xx,280p. — *Originally published: 1978. — Bibliography: p. 272-277. — Includes index*

MANLY, Bryan F. J.
Multivariate statistical methods : a primer / Bryan F.J. Manly. — London : Chapman and Hall, 1986. — [150]p. — *Includes bibliographies and index*

TABACHNICK, Barbara G.
Using multivariate statistics / Barbara G. Tabachnick, Linda S. Fidell. — New York ; London : Harper & Row, c1983. — xviii,509p. — *Bibliography: p489-495. — Includes index*

MUNAZZAMAT AL-TAḤRĪR AL-FILASṬĪNĪYAH
KHALIDI, Rashid
Under siege : P.L.O. decisionmaking during the 1982 war / Rashid Khalidi. — New York : Columbia University Press, 1985. — p. cm. — *Includes index. — Bibliography: p*

MUNAZZAMAT AL-TAḤRĪR AL FILASṬĪNĪYAH
MISHAL, Shaul
The PLO under 'Arafat : between gun and olive branch / Shaul Mishal. — New Haven ; London : Yale University Press, c1986. — xiv, 190p. — *Includes index*

MUNDURUCU INDIANS — Social life and customs
MURPHY, Yolanda
Women of the forest / Yolanda Murphy and Robert F. Murphy. — 2nd ed. — New York : Columbia University Press, 1985. — xvi, 262 p.. — *Includes index. — Bibliography: p. [259]-260*

MUNDURUCU INDIANS — Women
MURPHY, Yolanda
Women of the forest / Yolanda Murphy and Robert F. Murphy. — 2nd ed. — New York : Columbia University Press, 1985. — xvi, 262 p.. — *Includes index. — Bibliography: p. [259]-260*

MUNICH FOUR-POWER AGREEMENT, 1938
NESVADBA, František
Proč nezahřměla děla / František Nesvadba. — [Praha] : Naše vojsko, 1986. — 397p. — (Živá minulost ; sv.85). — *Bibliography: p389-394*

MUNICH (GERMANY) — History
DUMBACH, Annette E
Shattering the German night : the story of the White Rose / by Annette E. Dumbach and Jud Newborn. — 1st ed. — Boston : Little, Brown, c1986. — xi, 259 p.. — *Includes index. — Bibliography: p. 243-247*

MUNICIPAL CORPORATIONS — Canada
MAKUCH, Stanley M
Canadian municipal and planning law / Stanley M. Makuch. — Toronto, Canada : Carswell Co., 1983. — xxxiii, 325 p.. — *Includes bibliographical references and index*

MUNICIPAL CORPORATIONS — Finland
GRÖNHOLM, Christoffer
Kommunal självstyrelse och demokrati i Finland (inklusive en presentation av femkommunsundersökningen 1982) / Christoffer Grönholm. — Helsinki : Schildt, 1983. — 243p. — *Bibliography: p238-243*

MUNICIPAL FINANCE
RUTHERFORD, B. A.
Financial reporting in the public sector / B.A. Rutherford. — London : Butterworths, c1983. — xvi,257p. — *Includes bibliographies and index*

MUNICIPAL FINANCE — Addresses, essays, lectures
Strengthening urban management : international perspectives and issues / edited by Thomas L. Blair. — New York : Plenum Press, c1985. — p. cm. — (Urban innovation abroad). — *"Published in cooperation with the International Union of Local Authorities, The Hague, Netherlands.". — Includes indexes. — Bibliography: p*

MUNICIPAL FINANCE — Iceland — Statistics
ICELAND. Hagstofa
Sveitarsjóðareikningar 1953-62 = Communal finance 1953-62. — Reykjavík : Hagstofa Íslands, 1967. — 57p. — (Hagskýrslur Íslands ; 2,37). — *Text in Icelandic, with headings in English*

ICELAND. Hagstofa
Sveitarsjóðareikningar 1963-65 = Communal finance 1963-65. — Reykjavík : Hagstofa Íslands, 1968. — 93p. — (Hagskýrslur Íslands ; 2,44). — *Text in Icelandic, with headings in English*

ICELAND. Hagstofa
Sveitarsjóðareikningar 1966-68 = Communal finance 1966-68. — Reykjavík : Hagstofa Íslands, 1970. — 93p. — (Hagskýrslur Íslands ; 2,48). — *Text in Icelandic, with headings in English*

ICELAND. Hagstofa
Sveitarsjóðareikningar 1969-71 = Communal finance 1969-71. — Reykjavík : Hagstofa Íslands, 1974. — 95p. — (Hagskýrslur Íslands ; 2,56). — *Text in Icelandic, with headings in English*

MUNICIPAL FINANCE — Mexico — Mexico (State)
MEXICO (Mexico: State). Dirección General de Hacienda
Informática municipal. — Toluca : the Dirección, [ca.1975]. — 93p

MUNICIPAL FINANCE — United States — Addresses, essays, lectures

Crisis and constraint in municipal finance : local fiscal prospects in a period of uncertainty / edited by James H. Carr. — New Brunswick, N.J. : Center for Urban Policy Research, c1984. — xxv, 424 p.. — *Includes index. — Bibliography: p. 392-417*

MUNICIPAL GOVERNMENT — Addresses, essays, lectures

Strengthening urban management : international perspectives and issues / edited by Thomas L. Blair. — New York : Plenum Press, c1985. — p. cm. — (Urban innovation abroad). — *"Published in cooperation with the International Union of Local Authorities, The Hague, Netherlands.". — Includes indexes. — Bibliography: p*

MUNICIPAL GOVERNMENT — Congresses

Pouvoir local et urbanisme : Colloque de Lyon - 16-17 Octobre 1980 / Christian Barbier...[et al.]. — Lyon : Université Lyon II, U.E.R. Sciences juridiques, Centre de recherches sur les institutions publiques : Presses universitaires de Lyon, 1981. — 170p

MUNICIPAL GOVERNMENT — Alberta

MASSON, Jack K
Alberta's local governments and their politics / Jack Masson. — Edmonton, Alta., Canada : Pica Pica Press, 1985. — xiii, 397 p.. — (Local government series). — *Includes indexes. — Bibliography: p. 369-381*

MUNICIPAL GOVERNMENT — Australia — Addresses, essays, lectures

Australian urban politics : critical perspectives / edited by John Halligan and Chris Paris, with the assistance of Jan Wells. — Melbourne, Australia : Longman Cheshire, 1984. — xi, 247 p.. — (Australian studies). — *Includes index. — Bibliography: p. [222]-249*

MUNICIPAL GOVERNMENT — Australia — Tasmania — Statistics

TASMANIA. Commonwealth Bureau of Census and Statistics
Compendium of municpal statistics. — Hobart : [the bureau], 1957-1982. — *Irregular*

MUNICIPAL GOVERNMENT — Belgium

CAUWENBERGHE, Jean-Claude van
Rendre la ville aux citoyens : réflexions sur la participation des citoyens à la gestion de leur cité / Jean-Claude van Cauwenberghe ; préface de Emile Henry. — [Paris] : F. Nathan ; Bruxelles : Labor, cl1980. — 155 p.. — *Includes bibliographical references*

MUNICIPAL GOVERNMENT — British Columbia — Statistics

Statistics relating to regional and municipal governments in British Columbia / Ministry of Municipal Affairs, British Columbia. — [Victoria] : Ministry of Municipal Affairs, 1982-. — *Annual*

MUNICIPAL GOVERNMENT — Denmark

Urban political theory and the management of fiscal stress / edited by Michael Goldsmith, Søren Villadsen. — Aldershot : Gower, c1986. — xviii,269p

MUNICIPAL GOVERNMENT — Great Britain

HAMPTON, William
Local government and urban politics / William Hampton. — Harlow : Longman, 1987. — [320]p. — *Includes bibliography and index*

Urban political theory and the management of fiscal stress / edited by Michael Goldsmith, Søren Villadsen. — Aldershot : Gower, c1986. — xviii,269p

MUNICIPAL GOVERNMENT — Middle West — Case studies

ELAZAR, Daniel Judah
Cities of the prairie revisited : the closing of the metropolitan frontier / Daniel J. Elazar with Rozann Rothman ... [et al.]. — Lincoln : University of Nebraska Press, c1986. — 288 p.. — *Sequel to: Cities of the prairie. — Includes index. — Bibliography: p. [269]-276*

MUNICIPAL GOVERNMENT — Organisation for Economic Co-operation and Development countries

Managing and financing urban services. — Paris : Organisation for Economic Co-operation and Development, 1987. — 94p. — *Bibliography: p77*

MUNICIPAL GOVERNMENT — Russian S.F.S.R. — Leningrad

KRUCHKOVSKAIA, V. M.
Tsentral'naia gorodskaia duma Petrograda v 1917 g. / V. M. Kruchkovskaia ; otv. redaktor O. N. Znamenskii. — Leningrad : Nauka, Leningradskoe otdelenie, 1986. — 138p

MUNICIPAL GOVERNMENT — South Africa

Umkhanyiseli. — Goodwood : Western Cape Development Board, 1986-. — *Monthly*

MUNICIPAL GOVERNMENT — Spain — Barcelona

MASSANA, Carme
Indústria, ciutat i propietat : política econòmica i propietat urbana a l'àrea de Barcelona (1901-1939) / Carme Massana. — Barcelona : Curial, 1985. — 431p. — (Biblioteca de cultura catalana ; 57)

MUNICIPAL GOVERNMENT — United States

ABNEY, Glenn
The politics of state and city administration / Glenn Abney and Thomas P. Lauth. — Albany, N.Y. : State University of New York Press, c1986. — p cm. — (SUNY series in public administration in the 1980's). — *Includes index*

FERMAN, Barbara
Governing the ungovernable city : political skill, leadership, and the modern mayor / Barbara Ferman. — Philadelphia : Temple University Press, 1985. — p. cm. — *Includes index. — Bibliography: p*

MUNICIPAL GOVERNMENT — United States — Case studies

CLAVEL, Pierre
The progressive city : planning and participation, 1969-1984 / Pierre Clavel. — New Brunswick, N.J. : Rutgers University Press, c1986. — xviii, 262 p.. — *Includes index. — Bibliography: p. [241]-255*

SHARP, Elaine B
Citizen demand-making in the urban context / Elaine B. Sharp. — University, AL : University of Alabama Press, c1986. — p. cm. — *Includes index. — Bibliography: p*

MUNICIPAL GOVERNMENT — Zambia — Lusaka

PASTEUR, D.
Management for the absorption of newcomers in Lusaka / D. Pasteur. — Norwich : Geo Books ; Birmingham : Development Administration Group, Institute of Local Government Studies, University of Birmingham, [ca.1976]. — 98p. — (Papers in the administration of development ; no.2)

MUNICIPAL HEALTH SERVICES PROGRAM (U.S.)

GINZBERG, Eli
Local health policy in action : the Municipal Health Services Program / Eli Ginzberg, Edith Davis, Miriam Ostow. — Totowa, N.J. : Rowman & Allanheld, c1985. — xiv, 136 p.. — (LandMark studies). — *Includes bibliographies and index*

MUNICIPAL OWNERSHIP — United States — History

SCHAP, David
Municipal ownership in the electric utility industry : a centennial view / David Schap. — New York : Praeger, 1986. — xiii, 128 p.. — *"Praeger special studies. Praeger scientific.". — Includes index. — Bibliography: p. 117-126*

MUNICIPAL SERVICES

Delivery of urban services : with a view towards applications in management science and operations research / edited by Arthur J. Swersey, Edward J. Ignall. — Amsterdam ; New York : North-Holland ; New York, NY, U.S.A. : Sole distributors for the U.S.A. and Canada, Elsevier Science Pub. Co., 1986. — vi, 274 p.. — (TIMS studies in the management science ; v. 22). — *Includes bibliographies*

MUNICIPAL SERVICES — Addresses, essays, lectures

Strengthening urban management : international perspectives and issues / edited by Thomas L. Blair. — New York : Plenum Press, c1985. — p. cm. — (Urban innovation abroad). — *"Published in cooperation with the International Union of Local Authorities, The Hague, Netherlands.". — Includes indexes. — Bibliography: p*

MUNICIPAL SERVICES — France — Paris region

PINÇON-CHARLOT, Monique
Ségrégation urbaine : classes sociales et équipements collectifs en région parisienne / Monique Pinçon-Charlot, Edmond Preteceille, Paul Rendu. — Paris : Editions Anthropos, 1986. — 291p. — *Bibliography: p[230]-238*

MUNICIPAL SERVICES — Great Britain

DAY, Patricia, 19---
Accountabilities : five public services / Patricia Day, Rudolf Klein. — London : Tavistock, 1987. — 259p. — (Social science paperbacks). — *Includes index*

Decentralisation and democracy : localising public services / edited by Paul Hoggett, Robin Hambleton. — Bristol : University of Bristol, School for Advanced Urban Studies, c1987. — 269p. — (Occasional paper ; no.28). — *Bibliography: p267-269*

NATIONAL UNION OF PUBLIC EMPLOYEES
A NUPE handbook for good local services : 'better services'. — [London] : NUPE, 1987. — 34p

MUNICIPAL SERVICES — Illinois — Finance

CHICOINE, David L
Governmental structure and local public finance / David L. Chicoine, Norman Walzer. — Boston, Mass. : Oelgeschlager, Gunn & Hain, c1985. — xi, 235 p.. — *Includes bibliographies and index*

MUNICIPAL SERVICES — Mexico

RAMOS G., Sergio
Urbanización y servicios públicos en México / Sergio Ramos G.. — México D.F. : Universidad Nacional Autónoma de México, Instituto de Investigaciones Sociales, 1972. — 192p

MUNICIPAL WATER SUPPLY — Developing Countries — Planning

Community piped water supply systems in developing countries : a planning manual / Daniel A. Okun and Walter R. Ernst. — Washington, D.C. : The World Bank, 1987. — x,249p. — (World Bank technical paper ; no.60). — *Bibliography: p212-222*

MUNITIONS

BRZOSKA, Michael
Arms transfers to the Third World, 1971-85 / Michael Brzoska and Thomas Ohlson. — Oxford : Oxford University Press, 1987. — [440]. — *Written for the Stockholm International Peace Research Institute. — Includes bibliography and index*

MUNITIONS *continuation*

The Economics of military expenditures : military expenditures, economic growth and fluctuations : proceedings of a conference held by the International Economic Association in Paris, France / edited by Christian Schmidt. — Basingstoke : Macmillan, 1987. — xxiii,391p. — *Includes bibliographies and index*

NEUMAN, Stephanie G
Military assistance in recent wars : the dominance of the superpowers / Stephanie Neuman ; foreword by Ernest Graves. — New York : Praeger, 1986. — p. cm. — (The Washington papers ; 122). — *"Published with the Center for Strategic and International Studies, Georgetown University, Washington, D.C.". — "Praeger special studies. Praeger scientific."*

MUNITIONS — International cooperation
MOODIE, Frank T. J
Defense technology and the Atlantic Alliance : competition or collaboration? / Frank T. J. Bray. Michael Moodie. — Cambridge, Mass : Institute for Foreign Policy Analysis, 1977. — vi, 42 p.. — (Foreign policy report). — *Includes bibliographical references*

MUNITIONS — Political aspects — Canada
REGEHR, Ernie
Arms Canada : the deadly business of military exports. — Toronto : James Lorimer & Co., 1987. — xx,273p. — *References: p[243]-261*

MUNITIONS — Canada
REGEHR, Ernie
Arms Canada : the deadly business of military exports. — Toronto : James Lorimer & Co., 1987. — xx,273p. — *References: p[243]-261*

MUNITIONS — Developing countries
BRZOSKA, Michael
Arms transfers to the Third World, 1971-85 / Michael Brzoska and Thomas Ohlson. — Oxford : Oxford University Press, 1987. — [440]p. — *Written for the Stockholm International Peace Research Institute. — Includes bibliography and index*

MUNITIONS — Europe
FALTAS, Sami
Arms markets and armament policy : the changing structure of naval industries in Western Europe / by S. Faltas. — Dordrecht, Netherlands ; Boston : M. Nijhoff ; Norwell, MA, USA : Distributors for the U.S. and Canada, Kluwer Academic Publishers, 1986. — 417 p.. — (Studies in industrial organization ; v. 7). — *: Originally presented as the author's thesis (doctoral)--Free University, Amsterdam. — Bibliography: p. [358]-370*

MUNITIONS — Great Britain
LABOUR PARTY (Great Britain)
The defence industry : the key seats, industries and regions. — London : Labour Party, 1986. — 41p. — (Special briefing note / Labour Party ; no.2)

MUNITIONS — Japan
DRIFTE, Reinhard
Arms production in Japan : the military applications of civilian technology / Reinhard Drifte. — Boulder, Colo. : Westview Press, 1986". — p. cm. — (Westview special studies on East Asia). — *Includes index*

MUNITIONS — Netherlands
MEIJS, Marcel
Wapenproduktie en werkgelegenheid : onderzoek naar konversiemogelijkheden bij Van der Giessen de Noord en NWM De Kruithoorn / Marcel Meijs, Jan Prins. — Nijmegen : Studiecentrum voor Vredesvraagstukken. — 349p

MUNITIONS — Sweden
THORSSON, Inga
In pursuit of disarmament : conversion from military to civil production in Sweden / by Inga Thorsson. — Stockholm : [Liber] Vol 1A: Background, facts and analyses. — 1984. — 347p. — *Bibliography: p345-347*

THORSSON, Inga
In pursuit of disarmament : conversion from military to civil production in Sweden / by Inga Thorsson. — Stockholm : [Liber] Vol 1B: Summary, appraisals and recommendations. — 1984. — 66p

MUNITIONS — United States — History — 19th century — Addresses, essays, lectures
Military enterprise and technological change : perspectives on the American experience / edited by Merritt Roe Smith. — Cambridge, Mass. : MIT Press, c1985. — 391 p.. — *Includes bibliographical references and index*

MUNITIONS — United States — History — 20th century — Addresses, essays, lectures
Military enterprise and technological change : perspectives on the American experience / edited by Merritt Roe Smith. — Cambridge, Mass. : MIT Press, c1985. — 391 p.. — *Includes bibliographical references and index*

MURCIA (SPAIN : PROVINCE) — Politics and government — 1975-
HERNÁNDEZ, Felipe Julián
La transición política en Murcia : crónica del proceso autonómico / Felipe Julián Hernández. — Murcia : Ediciones Mediterraneo, 1984. — 509p. — (Colección: El molino y la noria)

MURDER — England, Northern
WARD JOUVE, Nicole
"The streetcleaner : the Yorkshire Ripper case on trial / Nicole Ward Jouve. — London : Boyars, 1986. — 231p

MURDER — Great Britain — Statistics
GREAT BRITAIN. Parliament. House of Commons. Library. Research Division
Homicide statistics / Robert Clements. — [London] : the Division, 1982. — 23p. — (Background paper ; no.102)

GREAT BRITAIN. Parliament. House of Commons. Library. Research Division
Homicide statistics / Robert Clements. — [London] : the Division, 1983. — 22p. — (Background paper ; no.123). — *Update of Background Paper no.102. — Bibliography: p8-9*

GREAT BRITAIN. Parliament. House of Commons. Library. Research Division
Homicide statistics / Robert Clements. — [London] : the Division, 1984. — 23p. — (Background paper ; no.139). — *Updates Background Paper no.123. — Bibliography: p8-9*

GREAT BRITAIN. Parliament. House of Commons. Library. Research Division
Homicide statistics / Robert Clements. — [London] : the Division, 1987. — 26p. — (Background paper ; no.197). — *Updates Background Paper no.139. — Bibliography: p9-10*

GREAT BRITAIN. Parliament. House of Commons. Library. Research Division
Statistics of murder / [Rob Clements]. — [London] : the Division, [1979]. — 14p. — (Background paper ; no.71). — *Select bibliography: p14*

MŪSÁ, SALĀMAH
EGGER, Vernon
A Fabian in Egypt : Salāmah Mūsá and the rise of the professional classes in Egypt, 1909-1939 / Vernon Egger. — Lanham, MD : University Press of America, c1986. — xvi, 255 p.. — *Includes index. — Bibliography: p. 237-252*

MUSEUMS — Law and legislation — Great Britain
GREAT BRITAIN. Parliament. House of Commons. Library. Research Division
National Heritage Bill [HL] - Bill 85 of 1982-83 / [Fiona Poole, Barry Winetrobe]. — [London] : the Division, 1983. — 23p. — (Reference sheet ; no.83/4). — *Includes bibliographical references*

MUSEUMS — Pakistan
Visitors to museums, historical places and archaeological sites : annual report / Ministry of Culture and Tourism, Pakistan. — Islamabad : Ministry of Culture and Tourism, 1983-. — *Annual*

MUSEUMS — Scotland
SCOTTISH MUSEUMS COUNCIL
Museums are for people. — Edinburgh : H.M.S.O., 1985. — 99p

MUSIC — Publishing — Canada
SANDERSON, Paul
Musicians and the law in Canada / by Paul Sanderson. — [Toronto] : Carswell, 1985. — xxxi,258p

MUSIC, POPULAR (SONGS, ETC.) — United States
Cultural change in the United States since World War II / edited by Maurice Gonnand, Sergio Perosa, Christopher W.E. Bigsby ; with contributions from Zoltan Abadi-Nagy...[et al.]. — Amsterdam : Free University Press, 1986. — 102p. — (European contributions to American studies ; 9). — *Includes bibliographies*

MUSIC TRADE — Canada
SANDERSON, Paul
Musicians and the law in Canada / by Paul Sanderson. — [Toronto] : Carswell, 1985. — xxxi,258p

MUSICIANS — Legal status, laws, etc. — Canada
SANDERSON, Paul
Musicians and the law in Canada / by Paul Sanderson. — [Toronto] : Carswell, 1985. — xxxi,258p

MUSLIMS — India — Political activity
SAXENA, Vinod Kumar
Muslims and the Indian National Congress (1885-1924) / Vinod Kumar Saxena. — Delhi : Discovery, 1985. — ix,258p. — *Bibliography: p [233]-252*

MUSLIMS — India — Assam
DEV, Bimal J.
Assam Muslims : politics & cohesion / Bimal J. Dev, Dilip K. Lahiri. — Delhi, India : Mittal Publications : Distributed by Mittal Publishers' Distributors, 1985. — 220 p.. — *Includes bibliographies and index*

MUSLIMS — India — Tirunelveli District
FANSELOW, Frank Sylvester
Trade, kinship and Islamisation : a comparative study of the social and economic organisation of Muslim and Hindu traders in Tirunelveli district, South India / by Frank Sylvester Fanselow. — 306 leaves. — PhD (Econ) 1986 LSE

MUSLIMS — Lebanon — Beirut — Political activity — History
JOHNSON, Michael
Class & client in Beirut : the Sunni Muslim community and the Lebanese state, 1840-1985 / Michael Johnson. — London : Ithaca, c1986. — xvii,243p. — *Includes index*

MUSLIMS — Lebanon — Beirut — Social conditions
JOHNSON, Michael
Class & client in Beirut : the Sunni Muslim community and the Lebanese state, 1840-1985 / Michael Johnson. — London : Ithaca, c1986. — xvii,243p. — *Includes index*

MUSLIMS — Nigeria, Northern — History
LUBECK, Paul M.
Islam and urban labor in Northern Nigeria : the making of a Muslim working class / Paul M. Lubeck. — Cambridge : Cambridge Univesity Press, 1986. — [368]p. — (African studies series ; 52). — *Includes bibliography and index*

MUSLIMS — Soviet Union
AKINER, Shirin
Islamic peoples of the Soviet Union : (with an appendix on the non-Muslim Turkic peoples of the Soviet Union) : an historical and statistical handbook / Shirin Akiner. — 2nd ed. — London : KPI, 1986. — xiii,462p

BENNIGSEN, Alexandre
Muslims of the Soviet empire : a guide / Alexandre Bennigsen, S. Enders Wimbush. — London : C. Hurst, 1985. — xvi,294p. — *Bibliography: p251-278*

MUSLIMS — Soviet Union — Political activity
BENNIGSEN, Alexandre
Sultan Galiev, le père de la révolution tiers-mondiste / Alexandre Bennigsen, Chantal Lemercier-Quelquejay. — Paris : Fayard, 1986. — 305p. — (Les inconnus de l'histoire)

MUSSOLINI, BENITO
SAZ CAMPOS, Ismael
Mussolini contra la II República : hostilidad, conspiraciones, intervención (1931-1936) / Ismael Saz. — Valencia : Edicions Alfons el Magnànim, Institució Valenciana d'Estudis i Investigació, 1986. — 265p. — *Bibliography: p [255]-265*

TUSELL GÓMEZ, Javier
Franco y Mussolini : la política española durante la segunda guerra mundial / Xavier Tusell, Genoveva García Queipo de Llano. — Barcelona : Planeta, 1985. — 299p. — (Espejo de España ; 109). — *Bibliography: p293-296*

MYER, DILLON S
DRINNON, Richard
Keeper of concentration camps : Dillon S. Myer and American racism / Richard Drinnon. — Berkeley : University of California Press, c1987. — xxviii, 339 p.. — *Includes index. — Bibliography: p. 271-324*

MYRDAL, GUNNAR. American dilemma
SOUTHERN, David W
Gunnar Myrdal and Black-white relations : the use and abuse of An American dilemma, 1944-1969 / David W. Southern. — Baton Rouge : Louisiana State University Press, c1987. — xviii, 341 p.. — *Includes index. — Bibliography: p. 311-330*

MYSORE REGION — Population, Rural
PARTHASARATHY, Jakka
Rural population in Indian urban setting / by Jakka Parthasarathy. — Delhi : B.R. Pub. Corp. ; New Delhi, India : Distributed by D.K. Publishers' Distributors, 1984. — xv, 272 p., [10] p. of plates. — : Revision of author's thesis (Ph. D.--Mysore University, 1982). — *Includes index. — Bibliography: p. [249]-268*

MYSORE REGION (INDIA) — Rural conditions
PARTHASARATHY, Jakka
Rural population in Indian urban setting / by Jakka Parthasarathy. — Delhi : B.R. Pub. Corp. ; New Delhi, India : Distributed by D.K. Publishers' Distributors, 1984. — xv, 272 p., [10] p. of plates. — : Revision of author's thesis (Ph. D.--Mysore University, 1982). — *Includes index. — Bibliography: p. [249]-268*

MYTHOLOGY, AFRICAN
PALMEIRIM, Maria Manuela Mestre Marques
The sterile mother : aspects of court symbolism among the Lunda of Mwant Yaav (Aruund) / Manuela M. Palmeirim. — 128 leaves. — MPhil (Econ) 1986 LSE

MYTHOLOGY, GREEK
SPRETNAK, Charlene
Lost goddesses of early Greece : a collection of pre-Hellenic myths / Charlene Spretnak. — New ed. — Boston : Beacon Press, 1984, c1978. — 132 p.. — *Bibliography: p. 129-132*. — Contents: Gaia -- Pandora -- Themis -- Aphrodite -- Triad of the moon : Artemis, Selene, Hecate -- Hera -- Athena -- Demeter and Persephone

NACIONAL FINANCIERA, S.A. (Mexico)
RAMÍREZ, Miguel D
Development banking in Mexico : the case of the Nacional Financiera, S.A. / Miguel D. Ramírez. — New York : Praeger, 1985. — xix, 228p. — *Includes index. — Bibliography: p.215-221*

NAGALAND (INDIA) — Population — Statistics
Census of India 1981. — [Delhi : Controller of Publications]
Series 15: Nagaland. — [1985-]

NALGO ACTION GROUP
NALGO action news / NALGO Action Group. — London : NALGO Action Group, 1971-1976. — Bimonthly

NAMBIA — Foreign economic relations
BARCLAYS SHADOW BOARD
Barclays Shadow report 1986. — London : End loans to South Africa, 1986. — 18p

NAMES, GEOGRAPHICAL — Australia
MASSOLA, Aldo
Aboriginal place names of south-east Australia and their meanings. — [Melbourne] : Lansdowne, [1968]. — 62 p. — *Bibliography: p. 57-62*

NAMES, GEOGRAPHICAL — England — Scandinavian
Place-name evidence for the Anglo-Saxon invasion and Scandinavian settlements : eight studies / collected by Kenneth Cameron ; introduction by Margaret Gelling. — [Nottingham] ([c/o School of English Studies, The University, Nottingham NG7 2RD]) : English Place-Name Society, 1975. — [3],v,171p. — Cover title

NAMES, GEOGRAPHYCAL — England — Anglo-Saxon
Place-name evidence for the Anglo-Saxon invasion and Scandinavian settlements : eight studies / collected by Kenneth Cameron ; introduction by Margaret Gelling. — [Nottingham] ([c/o School of English Studies, The University, Nottingham NG7 2RD]) : English Place-Name Society, 1975. — [3],v,171p. — Cover title

NAMIBIA — Economic conditions
SMITH, Susanna
Namibia : a violation of trust : an Oxfam report on international responsibility for poverty in Namibia / Susanna Smith. — Oxford : Oxfam, 1986. — 99p. — *Bibliography: p99*

NAMIBIA — Foreign economic relations
UNITED NATIONS COUNCIL FOR NAMIBIA
Report on the activities of foreign economic interests operating in Namibia : report of Standing Committee II / Chairman: Mr Ali Sarwar Naqvi (Pakistan). — Vienna : United Nations, 1986. — 39p. — *Annexes I and II list transnational corporations with interests in South Africa or Namibia. Annex III-map of Namibia showing principal mines and minerals. — U.N. document A/CONF.138/7 and A/AC.131/203*

NAMIBIA — International status
GREAT BRITAIN. Parliament. House of Commons. Library. International Affairs Section
Namibia : the persistence of a colonial dispute / Chris Bowlby. — [London] : the Library, 1986. — 28p. — (Background paper / House of Commons. Library. [Research Division] ; no.185). — *Bibliography: p26-27*

NAMIBIA — Politics and government
ATKINSON, David
"Bloody confrontation or constructive compromise?" / David Atkinson, Paul Howell and Sir Fergus Montgomery. — Strasbourg : European Parliament, 1986. — i,13p

EMMETT, Tony
Popular resistance in Namibia, 1920-1925 / Tony Emmett. — Johannesburg : African Studies Institute, 1984. — 43 leaves

Namibia now. — London : Namibia Office, 1986-. — *Irregular*

Towards Namibian independence : prospects for development and cooperation. — Montreal : Centre d'information et de documentation sur le Mozambique et l'Afrique australe, 1984. — 72p. — *Bibliography: p72*

NAMIBIA — Politics and government — 1946-
GREAT BRITAIN. Parliament. House of Commons. Library. International Affairs Section
Namibia : the persistence of a colonial dispute / Chris Bowlby. — [London] : the Library, 1986. — 28p. — (Background paper / House of Commons. Library. [Research Division] ; no.185). — *Bibliography: p26-27*

NAMIBIA — Social conditions
POEWE, Karla O
The Namibian Herero : a history of their psychosocial disintegration and survival / by Karla Poewe. — Lewiston, N.Y., USA : E. Mellen Press, [1985]. — 364 p. — (African studies ; v. 1). — *Includes index. — Bibliography: p. [359]-364*

NAMIBIA — Economic conditions
UNITED NATIONS COUNCIL FOR NAMIBIA
Report on the activities of foreign economic interests operating in Namibia : report of Standing Committee II / Chairman: Mr Ali Sarwar Naqvi (Pakistan). — Vienna : United Nations, 1986. — 39p. — *Annexes I and II list transnational corporations with interests in South Africa or Namibia. Annex III-map of Namibia showing principal mines and minerals. — U.N. document A/CONF.138/7 and A/AC.131/203*

NANTUCKET (MASS.) — Politics and government
BYERS, Edward
The "Nation of Nantucket" : society and politics in an early American commercial center, 1660-1820 / Edward Byers. — Boston : Northeastern University Press, c1987. — p. cm. — (New England studies). — *Includes index. — Bibliography: p*

NANTUCKET (MASS.) — Social conditions
BYERS, Edward
The "Nation of Nantucket" : society and politics in an early American commercial center, 1660-1820 / Edward Byers. — Boston : Northeastern University Press, c1987. — p. cm. — (New England studies). — *Includes index. — Bibliography: p*

NAPOLÉON I, Emperor of the French
LEFEBVRE, Georges
[Napoléon. English. Selections]. Napoleon : from Tilsit to Waterloo, 1807-1815 / by Georges Lefebvre ; translated from the French by J. E. Anderson. — New York : Columbia University Press, 1969. — viii, 414p. — *"Translation of the first three parts of Napoléon...this translation is based on the 5th (1965) ed." — Verso t.p.*

NAPOLÉON I, Emperor of the French
Napoleon's memoirs / edited by Somerset de Chair ; translated by B. O'Meara. — London : Soho, 1986. — [605]p. — *Translated from the French. — Originally published: London : Faber, 1945. — Includes index*

NAPOLEON I, Emperor of the French — Biography
LEFEBVRE, Georges
[Napoléon. English. Selections]. Napoleon : from 18 Brumaire to Tilsit, 1799-1807 / by Georges Lefebvre ; translated from the French by Henry F. Stockhold. — New York : Columbia University Press, 1969. — x,337p. — *"Translation of the first 3 parts of Napoleon ... this translation is based on the 5th (1965) ed." — Verso t.p.*

NAPUKA (TUAMOTU ISLANDS) — Population — Statistics

Tableaux normalisés du recensement général de la population : 15 octobre 1983. — [Papeete] : Institut territorial de la statistique Résultats de la commune de Napuka. — [1985?]. — 4p,ll leaves

NARAYAN, JAYAPRAKASH

PRASAD, Bimal
Gandhi, Nehru & J. P. : studies in leadership / Bimal Prasad. — Delhi : Chanakya Publications, 1985. — 294p. — *Bibliography: p283-287*

NARCOTIC ADDICTS — Legal status, laws, etc — Australia

CARNEY, Terry
Drug users and the law in Australia : from crime control to welfare / by T. Carney ; with a foreword by Dr. Neal Blewett. — Sydney : Law Book Company, 1987. — lxi,390p. — *Bibliography: pxxxvii-xlvii*

NARCOTIC ADDICTS — Rehabilitation — Australia

CARNEY, Terry
Drug users and the law in Australia : from crime control to welfare / by T. Carney ; with a foreword by Dr. Neal Blewett. — Sydney : Law Book Company, 1987. — lxi,390p. — *Bibliography: pxxxvii-xlvii*

NARCOTIC ADDICTS — Rehabilitation — England — Portsmouth

POWELL, Jackie
Commitment to change : a study of Alpha House[,] a rehabilitation unit for drug users / Jackie Powell[,] Diane Goldrick [and] Robin Lovelock. — Portsmouth : Social Services Research and Intelligence Unit, 1986. — vi,281p. — (SSRIU Report ; no.14)

NARCOTIC ADDICTS — Rehabilitation — Great Britain

ADVISORY COUNCIL ON THE MISUSE OF DRUGS. Treatment and Rehabilitation Working Group
First interim report. — [London] : Department of Health and Social Security, 1977. — 18p

NARCOTIC ADDICTS — Great Britain — Social aspects

BLACKWELL, Judith Catherine Stephenson
A study of opiate users in the U.K. who do not pursue a social career of long term dependent use / by Judith Catherine Stephenson Blackwell. — 402 leaves. — *PhD (Econ) 1986 LSE. — Leaves 300-387 are appendices*

NARCOTIC HABIT

PLANT, Martin A.
Drugs in perspective / Martin A. Plant. — London : Hodder and Stoughton, 1987. — xii,176p. — *Originally published: Sevenoaks : Teach Yourself Books, 1981. — Bibliography: p157-169. — Includes index*

NARCOTIC HABIT — Treatment

PORTER, L.
The law and treatment of drug- and alcohol-dependent persons : a comparative study of existing legislation / by L. Porter, A. E. Arif, W. J. Curran. — Geneva : World Health Organization, 1986. — 216p. — *Bibliography: p209-216*

NARCOTIC HABIT — Netherlands

RELEASE (Den Haag)
Verslag van de aktiviteiten over de jaren 1972 en 1973 / Release Den Haag. — [Den Haag : Release, 1974]. — 136p

NARCOTIC LAWS

PORTER, L.
The law and treatment of drug- and alcohol-dependent persons : a comparative study of existing legislation / by L. Porter, A. E. Arif, W. J. Curran. — Geneva : World Health Organization, 1986. — 216p. — *Bibliography: p209-216*

NARCOTIC LAWS — United States — Addresses, essays, lectures

Teen drug use / edited by George Beschner, Alfred S. Friedman. — Lexington, Mass. : Lexington Books, c1986. — x, 243 p.. — *Includes bibliographies and index*

NARCOTICS AND CRIME — Denmark

WINSLØW, Jacob Hilden
Stofmisbrug, kriminalitet og metadon / Jacob Hilden Winsløw og Peter Ege. — [København] : Alkohol- og Narkotikarådet, 1984. — 95p. — (Alkohol- og Narkotikarådets skriftserie ; 2). — *Summary in English. — Bibliography: p93-95*

NARCOTICS, CONTROL OF — Canada

The Steel drug : cocaine in perspective / Patricia G. Erickson ... [et al.]. — Lexington, Mass. : Lexington Books, c1987. — xviii, 169 p.. — *Includes index. — Bibliography: p. [151]-159*

NARCOTICS, CONTROL OF — Scandinavia

Drugs and drug control / edited by Per Stangeland. — Oslo : Norwegian University Press ; Oxford : Oxford University Press [distributor], c1987. — 132p. — (Scandinavian studies in criminology ; v.8). — *Includes bibliographies*

NARCOTICS, CONTROL OF — United States

The Steel drug : cocaine in perspective / Patricia G. Erickson ... [et al.]. — Lexington, Mass. : Lexington Books, c1987. — xviii, 169 p.. — *Includes index. — Bibliography: p. [151]-159*

WISOTSKY, Steven
Breaking the impasse in the war on drugs / Steven Wisotsky ; foreword by Thomas Szasz. — New York : Greenwood Press, 1986. — xxiv, 279 p.. — (Contributions in political science ; no. 159). — *Includes index. — Bibliography: p. [263]-271*

NASSER, GAMAL ABDEL

STEPHENS, Robert
Nasser : a political biography / Robert Stephens. — London : Allen Lane, 1971. — 635p

NATAL (SOUTH AFRICA)

ROBBINS, David
Inside the last outpost / David Robbins, Wyndham Hartley. — 1st ed. — Pietermaritzburg [South Africa] : Shuter & Shooter, 1985. — 198 p.. — *Bibliography: p. 196-198*

NATAL (SOUTH AFRICA) — Economic conditions

Enterprise and exploitation in a Victorian colony : aspects of the economic and social history of colonial Natal / edited by Bill Guest and John M. Sellers. — Pietermaritzburg : University of Natal Press, 1985. — xiv,362p. — *Includes bibliographical references*

NATAL (SOUTH AFRICA) — History — 1843-1893

Enterprise and exploitation in a Victorian colony : aspects of the economic and social history of colonial Natal / edited by Bill Guest and John M. Sellers. — Pietermaritzburg : University of Natal Press, 1985. — xiv,362p. — *Includes bibliographical references*

NATAL (SOUTH AFRICA) — History — 1893-1910

Enterprise and exploitation in a Victorian colony : aspects of the economic and social history of colonial Natal / edited by Bill Guest and John M. Sellers. — Pietermaritzburg : University of Natal Press, 1985. — xiv,362p. — *Includes bibliographical references*

NATAL (SOUTH AFRICA) — Social conditions

Enterprise and exploitation in a Victorian colony : aspects of the economic and social history of colonial Natal / edited by Bill Guest and John M. Sellers. — Pietermaritzburg : University of Natal Press, 1985. — xiv,362p. — *Includes bibliographical references*

NATIONAL ACADEMY OF PEACE AND CONFLICT RESOLUTION

SMITH, Charles Duryea
The Hundred percent challenge : building a national institute of peace : a platform for planning, policy, and programming / edited by Charles Duryea Smith. — 1st ed. — Cabin John, MD : Seven Locks Press, 1985. — p. cm. — *Includes bibliographies and index*

NATIONAL AND LOCAL GOVERNMENT OFFICERS' ASSOCIATION

NALGO action news / NALGO Action Group. — London : NALGO Action Group, 1971-1976. — *Bimonthly*

NALGO news / National and Local Government Officers' Association. — London : NALGO, 1984-. — *Weekly*

NATIONAL AND LOCAL GOVERNMENT OFFICERS ASSOCIATION

Public service / National and Local Government Officers Association. — London : NALGO, 1967-. — *Monthly*

NATIONAL ASSOCIATION FOR THE ADVANCEMENT OF COLORED PEOPLE — History

TUSHNET, Mark V.
Segregated schools and legal strategy : the NAACP's capaign against segregated education, 1925-1950 / Mark Tushnet. — Chapel Hill : University of North Carolina Press, c1987. — p. cm. — *Includes index. — Bibliography: p*

NATIONAL ASSOCIATIONS OF ACCOUNTANTS

COST ACCOUNTING FOR THE '90S: THE CHALLENGE OF TECHNOLOGICAL CHANGE (Conference : 1986 : Boston)
Cost accounting for the '90s.... — Montvale, N.J. : National Association of Accountants, 1986. — v,164p

NATIONAL BUILDING SOCIETY

NATIONWIDE BUILDING SOCIETY
Background bulletin / Nationwide Building Society. — London : Nationwide Building Society, 1987-. — *Annual*

NATIONAL BUREAU OF ECONOMIC RESEARCH

FABRICANT, Solomon
NBER : toward a firmer basis of economic policy : the founding of the National Bureau of Economic Research / Solomon Fabricant. — Cambridge, Mass. : NBER, 1984. — 39p

NATIONAL CAPITAL DISTRICT (PAPUA NEW GUINEA) — Population — Statistics

1980 national population census : final figures : provincial summary : National Capital District. — Port Moresby : National Statistical Office, 1985. — iii,87p

NATIONAL CHARACTERISTICS, AFRICAN

MAZRUI, Ali A.
The Africans : a triple heritage / Ali A. Mazrui. — London : BBC Publications, 1986. — 336p

NATIONAL CHARACTERISTICS, AMERICAN

The American character and the formation of United States foreign policy / edited by Michael P. Hamilton. — Grand Rapids, Mich. : W.B. Eerdmans Pub. Co., c1986. — p. cm. — *Contents: Formative events from Columbus to World War I / Marcus Cunliffe, Robert L. Beisner -- The modern age / John L. Gaddis, Charles M. Lichenstein -- Religious influences on United States foreign policy / Robert N. Bellah, Earl H. Brill -- Profits at what costs? / Richard J. Barnet, Dale R. Weigel -- Ethnicity and race as factors in the formation of United States foreign policy / Elliot P. Skinner -- The American character and the formation of United States foreign policy / McGeorge Bundy, Alton Frye*

HELLMANN, John
The American myth and the legacy of Vietnam / John Hellmann. — New York : Columbia University Press, 1986. — xiv, 241p. — *Includes bibliographical references and index. — Bibliography: p. [225]-233*

NATIONAL CHARACTERISTICS, CANADIAN

HILLER, Harry H.
Canadian society : a macro analysis / Harry H. Hiller. — Scarborough, Ont. : Prentice-Hall Canada, c1986. — x, 245 p.. — *Includes index. — Bibliography: p. 234-241*

MOL, Hans
Faith and fragility : religion and identity in Canada / Hans Mol. — Burlington, Ont., Canada : Trinity Press, c1985. — viii, 354 p.. — *Includes index. — Bibliography: p. 301-338*

NATIONAL CHARACTERISTICS, CHINESE

The Psychology of the Chinese people / editor, Michael Harris Bond ; contributors, Michael Harris Bond ... [et al.]. — Hong Kong ; New York : Oxford University Press, 1986. — xii, 354 p.. — *Includes index. — Bibliography: p. [296]-351*

NATIONAL CHARACTERISTICS, CHINESE — Congresses

Chinese culture and mental health / edited by Wen-Shing Tseng, David Y.H. Wu. — Orlando : Academic Press, 1985. — xxiii, 412 p.. — *Derived from a conference held in Hawaii, Mar. 1-6, 1982, and sponsored by the Culture Learning Institute of the East-West Center, the Dept. of Psychiatry, University of Hawaii School of Medicine, and the Queen's Medical Center in Honolulu. — Includes bibliographies and index*

NATIONAL CHARACTERISTICS, ENGLISH

NEWMAN, Gerald
The rise of English nationalism : a cultural history, 1720-1830 / Gerald Newman. — New York : St. Martin's Press, 1987. — xxiii, 294 p. . — *Includes index. — Bibliography: p. [269]-280*

NATIONAL CHARACTERISTICS, ISRAELI

ELON, Amos
The Israelis : founders and sons / Amos Elon. — New York : Penguin, 1983. — xiv, 359 p.. — *: Previously published: New York : Holt, Rinehart, and Winston, 1971. — Includes index. — Bibliography: p. 336-348*

NATIONAL CHARACTERISTICS, JAPANESE

Japanese culture and behavior : selected readings / edited by Takie Sugiyama Lebra and William P. Lebra. — 2nd ed. — Honolulu : University of Hawaii Press, c1986. — p. cm. — *Includes index. — Bibliography: p*

NATIONAL CHARACTERISTICS, JAPANESE — Addresses, essays, lectures

LEBRA, Takie Sugiyama
Japanese culture and behavior : selected readings / edited by Takie Sugiyama Lebra and William P. Lebra. — Honolulu : University Press of Hawaii, [1974]. — xi, 459 p.. — *"An East-West Center book.". — Includes bibliographical references*

NATIONAL CHARACTERISTICS, LATIN AMERICAN

BARRETT, Jeffrey W
Impulse to revolution in Latin America / by Jeffrey W. Barrett. — New York : Praeger, 1985. — ix, 357p. — (Praeger special studies)

NATIONAL CHARACTERISTICS, MEXICAN

O'MALLEY, Ilene V
The myth of the revolution : hero cults and the institutionalization of the Mexican State, 1920-1940 / Ilene V. O'Malley. — New York : Greenwood Press, 1986. — xii, 199 p.. — (Contributions to the study of world history ; no. 1). — *Includes index. — Bibliography: p.[179]-194*

NATIONAL CHARACTERISTICS, SPANISH

CROW, John Armstrong
Spain : the root and the flower : an interpretation of Spain and the Spanish people / John A. Crow. — 3rd ed., expanded and updated. — Berkeley : University of California Press, c1985. — x, 455 p.. — *Includes index. — Bibliography: p. 435-439*

NATIONAL COAL BOARD

NATIONAL COAL BOARD
Coal consumers' councils : statement by the National Coal Board at the inaugural meetings. — [London : the Board, 1947]. — 19p

NATIONAL COMMUNICATIONS UNION

National Communications Union journal. — London : NCU, 1985-. — *Monthly. — Continues: POEU Journal*

NATIONAL COUNCIL FOR CIVIL LIBERTIES — History

SCAFFARDI, Sylvia
Fire under the carpet : working for civil liberties in the thirties / Sylvia Scaffardi. — London : Lawrence and Wishart, 1986. — 208p

NATIONAL DISTRICT DEVELOPMENT CONFERENCE

NATIONAL DISTRICT DEVELOPMENT CONFERENCE (5th : 1978 : Gaborone)
A record of proceedings and actions. — Gaborone : Ministry of Local Government and Lands, 1978. — 88p

NATIONAL DISTRICT DEVELOPMENT CONFERENCE (7th : 1979 : Gaborone)
[Report]. — Gaborone : Ministry of Local Government and Lands, [1979]. — 279p

NATIONAL FEDERATION OF HOUSING ASSOCIATIONS

HILLS, John
When is a grant not a grant? : the current system of Housing Association finance / John Hills. — London : London School of Economics, 1987. — 113p. — (Welfare State Programme ; no.13) (Discussion paper / Welfare State Programme ; Suntory Toyota International Centre for Economics and Related Disciplines ; London School of Economics ; no.13). — *Bibliography: p111-113*

NATIONAL FREIGHT CORPORATION — Government policy

GREAT BRITAIN. Department of Transport
Proposals for the National Freight Corporation : (policy document). — [London : the Department, 1979]. — 3p

NATIONAL FRONT

EREIRA, Mark
The National Front in Islington : an anti fascist pamphlet / Mark Ereira. — London : Community Education Trust, 1985. — 29p

NATIONAL GIRO

NATIONAL GIRO
Evidence to the Committee to Review the Functioning of Financial Institutions. — [London?] : National Giro, 1977. — 29p

NATIONAL HEALTH SECURITY ACT, 1975

National Health Security Act, 1975. — Copenhagen : Ministry of Social Affairs, [1975]. — 14 leaves

NATIONAL HEALTH SERVICE (Great Britain)

ASCHER, Kate Julie
Contracting out in local authorities and the NHS : developments under the Conservative governments 1979-1985 / Kate J. Ascher. — 378 leaves. — *PhD (Econ) 1986 LSE. — Leaves 333-350 are appendices*

DOWNEY, Peter
Accountability and democracy in London's health services / Peter Downey ; for the Health Panel of the Greater London Council. — [London : Greater London Council, 1986]. — 32p

GREAT BRITAIN. Parliament. House of Commons. Library. Research Division
Hospital waiting lists / Keith Cuninghame, Richard Cracknell. — [London] : the Division, 1987. — 26p. — (Background paper ; no.195). — *Bibliography: p25-26*

HAM, Christopher
Managing health services : health authority members in search of a role / Christopher Ham. — Bristol : School for Advanced Urban Studies, c1986. — 138 p. — (SAUS study ; no.3)

A review of the health services - Wales 1974-75. — [Cardiff : Welsh Office, 1975?]. — 63leaves

NATIONAL HEALTH SERVICE (Great Britain) — Administration

GREAT BRITAIN. Steering Committee on Resource Allocations in Wales
The distribution of resources to health authorities in Wales : third report. — [Cardiff] : Welsh Office, 1979. — 43p

GREAT BRITAIN. Steering Committee on Resource Allocations in Wales
The distribution of resources to health authorities in Wales : fourth report. — [Cardiff] : Welsh Office, 1979. — 44p

GREAT BRITAIN. Welsh Office. Health and Social Work Department
Health services management : model standing orders for area health authorities. — Cardiff : the Office, 1976. — 3,11p. — ([Health circular] ; WHC (76)25)

GREAT BRITAIN. Working Party on Revenue Resource Allocation
Scottish Health Authorities Revenue Equalisation (SHARE) : report of the Working Party on Revenue Resource Allocation. — Edinburgh : H.M.S.O., 1977. — 95p

Morbidity and its relationship to resource allocation / edited by Sir John Brotherston. — [Cardiff] ([Crown Building, Cathays Park, Cardiff CF1 3NQ]) : Welsh Office, [1978]. — [1],vii,97p. — *'Papers and proceedings of a workshop held at the Hill Residential College, Abergavenny, Gwent on Tuesday 24 and Wednesday 25 January 1978' - p.i*

NATIONAL HEALTH SERVICE (Great Britain) — Finance

GREAT BRITAIN. Parliament. House of Commons. Library. Research Division
Health maintenance organisations : the future for British health care? / Keith Cuninghame. — [London] : the Division, 1986. — 16p. — (Background paper ; no.191). — *Bibliography: p15-16*

GREAT BRITAIN. Parliament. House of Commons. Library. Research Division
National Health Service finance / Keith Cuninghame. — [London] : the Division, 1986. — 26p. — (Background paper ; no.188). — *Bibliography: p25-26*

NATIONAL HEALTH SERVICE (Great Britain) — Legal status, laws, etc.

GREAT BRITAIN. Parliament. House of Commons. Library. Research Division
Health and Social Security Bill 1983 / Keith Cuninghame, Julia Lourie, Christine Gillie. — [London] : the Division, 1983. — 50p. — (Reference sheet ; no.83/24). — *Includes bibliographical references*

GREAT BRITAIN. Parliament. House of Commons. Library. Research Division
Health Services Bill (Bill 98 of 1979-80) / [Keith Cuninghame]. — [London] : the Division, 1979. — 12p. — (Reference sheet ; no.79/18). — *Bibliography: p9-12*

GREAT BRITAIN. Parliament. House of Commons. Library. Research Division
National Health Service (Amendment) Bill [Bill 119 of 1985-86] / Keith Cuninghame, C. J. Gilmour. — [London] : the Division, 1986. — 28p. — (References sheet ; no.86/10). — *Includes bibliographical references*

NATIONAL HEALTH SERVICE (Great Britain) — Statistics

Key statistical indicators for National Health Service management in Wales = Dangosyddion ystadegol allweddol i reolaeth y Gwasanaeth lechyd Gwladol yng Nghymru / Welsh Office. — Cardiff : Economic and Statistical Services Division, Welsh Office, 1983-. — *Annual*

NATIONAL HEALTH SERVICE (AMENDMENT) BILL 1985-86

GREAT BRITAIN. Parliament. House of Commons. Library. Research Division
National Health Service (Amendment) Bill [Bill 119 of 1985-86] / Keith Cuninghame, C. J. Gilmour. — [London] : the Division, 1986. — 28p. — (References sheet ; no.86/10). — *Includes bibliographical references*

NATIONAL HEALTH SERVICE (GREAT BRITAIN) — Management

GREAT BRITAIN. Department of Health and Social Security
Option appraisal : a guide for the National Health Service. — London : H.M.S.O., 1987. — 42p. — *Bibliography: p41-42*

NATIONAL HEALTH SERVICE (GREAT BRITAIN)

BAINBRIDGE, Sheila
National Health surgical footwear : a survey carried out on behalf of the Department of Health and Social Security ... / Sheila Bainbridge ; [for the] Office of Population Censuses and Surveys, Social Survey Division. — London : H.M.S.O., 1979. — [10],77p

HAYNES, Robin M.
The geography of health services in Britain / Robin Haynes. — London : Croom Helm, c1987. — [272]p. — *Includes bibliography and index*

Providing effective health care in a multiracial society : a checklist for looking at local issues / Health Education Council/National Extension College for Training in Health and Race. — 2nd ed. — London : Training in Health and Race, 1984. — iii,18p. — *Cover title. — Previous ed.: 1984. — Bibliography: p15*

TUC HEALTH SERVICES COMMITTEE
Improving industrial relations in the National Health Service : a report / by the TUC Health Services Committee. — London (Congress House, Great Russell St., WC1B 3LS) : Trades Union Congress, 1981. — 254p

NATIONAL HEALTH SERVICE (GREAT BRITAIN) — Appropriations and expenditures

JONES, Tom, 1946-
Money medics and management : the English and American systems compared / Tom Jones, Colin Kerr. — London : Certified Accountants Educational Trust, c1986. — [120]p. — *Bibliography: p99. — Includes index*

NATIONAL HEALTH SERVICE (GREAT BRITAIN) — Finance

MAYS, Nicholas
Resource allocation in the Health Service : a review of the methods of the Resource Allocation Working Party / Nicholas Mays, Gwyn Bevan. — London : Bedford Square Press/NCVO, 1987. — 180p. — (Occasional papers on social administration ; 81). — *Bibliography: p161-180*

NATIONAL HERITAGE BILL 1982-83

GREAT BRITAIN. Parliament. House of Commons. Library. Research Division
National Heritage Bill [HL] - Bill 85 of 1982-83 / [Fiona Poole, Barry Winetrobe]. — [London] : the Division, 1983. — 23p. — (Reference sheet ; no.83/4). — *Includes bibliographical references*

NATIONAL INCOME

KRAVIS, Irving B.
World product and income : international comparisons of real gross product / Irving B. Kravis, Alan Heston, Robert Summers. — Baltimore : John Hopkins University Press for the World Bank, 1982. — x,388p. — *At head of title: United Nations International Comparison Project, phase III. — Produced by the Statistical Office of the United Nations and the World Bank*

SMITH, Stephen
The shadow economy in Britain and Germany : based on a comparative research project undertaken by the Institute for Fiscal Studies, London, and the Institut für Angewandte Wirtschaftforschung Tübingen / Stephen Smith and Susanne Wied-Nebbeling. — London : Anglo-German Foundation for the Study of Industrial Society, c1986. — 102 p

NATIONAL INCOME — Accounting

UNITED NATIONS
National accounts statistics : government accounts and tables / United Nations. — New York : United Nations, 1982-. — *Annual*

NATIONAL INCOME — Accounting — Congresses

COLLOQUE DE COMPTABILITÉ NATIONALE (1st : 1984)
Etudes de comptabilité nationale / Edith Archambault, Oleg Arkhipoff (éds.) ; préface, Edmond Malinvaud. — Paris : Economica, [1986]. — xiii,391p

NATIONAL INCOME — Accounting — Canada

Provincial gross domestic product by industry = Produit intérieur brut provincial par industrie / Statistics Canada, Industry Product Division. — Ottawa : Ministry of Supply and Services, 1982-. — (System of national accounts / Statistics Canada). — *Annual. — Text in English and French*

NATIONAL INCOME — Australia

MARZOUK, G. A.
National income and flow of funds accounts : 1959-60 to 1983-84 / G. A. Marzouk. — Sydney : Australian Professional Publications, 1987. — vii,[66p]

NATIONAL INCOME — Austria

FELLNER, Frigyes
Ausztria és Magyarország nemzeti jövedelme / Fellner Frigyes. — Budapest : Magyar Tudományos Akadémia, 1916. — 152p. — (Értekezések a philosophia és társadalmi tudományok köréb″ol ; köt.1 ; sz.8)

NATIONAL INCOME — Burkina Faso — Accounting

Comptes nationaux du Burkina Faso / Institut National de la Statistique et de la Demographie. — Ouagadougou : Institut National de la Statistique et de la Demographie, 1983-. — *Annual*

NATIONAL INCOME — Chile — Accounting

Cuentas nacionales de Chile = national accounts of Chile / Banco Central de Chile. — Santiago : Banco Central de Chile, 1960/83-. — *Annual*

NATIONAL INCOME — Denmark — Accounting

STETKAER, Karsten
Beregningen af erhvervsfordelte investeringer i nationalregnskabet 1966-81 / Karsten Stetkaer. — [København] : Danmarks Statistik, 1986. — 130p. — (Arbejdsnotat / Danmarks Statistik ; nr.14)

NATIONAL INCOME — Developing countries — Case studies

BHATIA, D. P
Inter-class distribution and growth of net national product in a developing economy : a case study of India during the sixties / D.P. Bhatia ; foreword by M. Mukherjee. — New Delhi : Concept Pub. Co., 1986, c1985. — xviii, 221 p.. — *: Originally presented as the author's thesis (Ph. D.--University of Delhi). — Includes index. — Bibliography: p. [208]-217*

NATIONAL INCOME — Finland — Accounting

BROAS, Raili
Kansantalouden tilinpito : yritykset kansantalouden tilinpidossa = National accounts : enterprises in national accounts / Raili Broas. — Helsinki : Tilastokeskus, 1982. — 59p. — (Tutkimuksia / Finland. Tilastokeskus ; no.72)

HAMUNEN, Eeva
Kansantalouden tilinpito : liikenne kansantalouden tilinpidossa = National accounts : transport and communication in national accounts / Eeva Hamunen. — Helsinki : Tilastokeskus, 1982. — 77p. — (Tutkimuksia / Finland. Tilastokeskus ; no.85). — *In Finnish and English*

JESKANEN-SUNDSTRÖM, Heli
Kansantalouden tilinpito : teollinen toiminta kansantalouden tilinpidossa = National accounts : manufacturing and related industries in national accounts / Heli Jeskanen-Sundström. — Helsinki : Tilastokeskus, 1982. — 52p. — (Tutkimuksia / Finland. Tilastokeskus ; no.74). — *In Finish with English summary*

Kansantalouden tilinpito : pääomakanta vuosina 1965-1977 / Vihavainen [and others]. — Helsinka : Tilastokeskus, 1980. — 98p. — (Tutkimuksia / Finland. Tilastokeskus ; no.58). — *Bibliography: p98*

LEPPÄNEN, Veli-Jukka
Kansantalouden tilinpito : rakennustoiminta kansantalouden tilinpidossa = National accounts : construction in national accounts / Veli-Jukka Leppänen, Henry Takala. — Helsinki : Tilastokeskus, 1982. — 109p. — (Tutkimuksia / Finland. Tilastokeskus ; no.73). — *In Finnish with English summary and table headings*

NATIONAL INCOME — Finland — Accounting *continuation*

MÄKELÄ, Pekka
Kansantalouden tilinpito : maa-, metsä- ja kalatalous sekä metsästys kansantalounden tilinpidossa = National accounts : agriculture, forestry, fishing and hunting in national accounts. — Helsinki : Tilastokeskus, 1980. — 126p. — (Tutkimuksia / Finland. Tilastokeskus ; no.61). — *Summary and table headings in English and Swedish*

PIETILÄ, Juha
Statens inkomster och utgifter länsvis 1978 / Juha Pietilä, Aku Alanen. — Helsinki : Tilastokeskus, 1981. — 83p. — (Tutkimuksia / Finland. Tilastokeskus ; no.69)

RITVANEN, Kari
Kansantalouden tilinpito : voittoa tavoittelemattomat yhteisöt kansantalouden tilinpidossa = National accounts : non-profit institutions in national accounts / Kari Ritvanen. — Helsinki : Tilastokeskus, 1982. — 67p. — (Tutkimuksia / Finland. Tilastokeskus ; no.77)

SÖDER, Leena
Kansantalouden tilinpito : kotitaloudet kansantalouden tilinpidossa = National accounts : households in national accounts / Leena Söder. — Helsinki : Tilastokeskus, 1984. — 102p. — (Tutkimuksia / Finland. Tilastokeskus ; no.109). — *Bibliography: p94-98*

UOTILA, Lauri
Kansantalouden tilinpito : neljännesvuosittainen kansantalouden tilinpito = National accounts : quarterly national accounts / Uotila, Leppä, Katajala. — Helsinki : Tilastokeskus, 1980. — 55p. — (Tutkimusksia / Finland. Tilastokeskus ; no.62). — *Summary in English*

NATIONAL INCOME — France — Accounting

BLANC, Patrick
Les comptes régionaux des ménages de 1973 à 1980 / Patrick Blanc et Maryse Vaillard. — [Paris] : I.N.S.E.E., 1986. — 83p. — (Archives et documents / France. Institut national de la statistique et des études économiques ; no.180)

Cinq études de comptabilité nationale : contributions françaises á la session de IARIW 1985. — Paris : I.N.S.E.E., 1985. — 219p. — (Archives et documents / France. Institut national de la statistique et des études économiques ; no.145)

FRANCE. Institut national de la statistique et des études économiques
Les comptes nationaux trimestriels : séries longues 1963-1984. — [Paris] : I.N.S.E.E., 1985. — 252p. — (Archives et documents / France. Institut national de la statistique et des études économiques ; no.136). — *Cover title.* — *Bibliography: p11*

NATIONAL INCOME — Gambia — Accounting

Estimates of national income at constant prices in The Gambia. — [Banjul] : Central Statistics Department, 1985. — 49p

Sources and methods of estimation of national income at current prices in The Gambia. — [Banjul] : Central Statistics Department, 1985. — 151p

NATIONAL INCOME — Germany (West) — Accounting

GERMANY (Federal Republic). Statistisches Bundesamt
Lange Reihen 1950 bis 1984. — Wiesbaden : the Bundesamt, 1985. — 133p. — (Volkswirtschaftliche Gesamtrechnungen. Reihe S ; 7)

NATIONAL INCOME — Germany (West) — Statistics

GERMANY (Federal Republic). Statistisches Bundesamt
Revidierte Reihen ab 1950. — Stuttgart : W. Kohlhammer ; Wiesbaden : Statistisches Bundesamt, 1972. — 123p. — (Volkswirtschaftliche Gesamtrechnungen. Reihe 3 ; Sonderbeiträge)

NATIONAL INCOME — Great Britain — Accounting

GREAT BRITAIN. Central Statistical Office
Value added and the national accounts. — [London : the Office, 1977]. — 6p. — *"Paper to be presented at seminar on value added: 6 December 1977"*

NATIONAL INCOME — Hungary

FELLNER, Frigyes
Ausztria és Magyarország nemzeti jövedelme / Fellner Frigyes. — Budapest : Magyar Tudományos Akadémia, 1916. — 152p. — (Értekezések a philosophia és társadalmi tudományok köréb"ol ; köt.1 ; sz.8)

FELLNER, Frigyes
Csonka-Magyarország nemzeti jövedelme / írta Fellner Frigyes. — Budapest : Magyar Tudományos Akadémia, 1930. — 107p

NATIONAL INCOME — India — Accounting — Statistics

National accounts statistics / Central Statistical Organisation, India. — New Delhi : Central Statistical Organisation, 1982-. — *Annual*

NATIONAL INCOME — India — Case studies

BHATIA, D. P
Inter-class distribution and growth of net national product in a developing economy : a case study of India during the sixties / D.P. Bhatia ; foreword by M. Mukherjee. — New Delhi : Concept Pub. Co., 1986, c1985. — xviii, 221 p.. — : *Originally presented as the author's thesis (Ph. D.--University of Delhi).* — *Includes index.* — *Bibliography: p. [208]-217*

NATIONAL INCOME — Indonesia

Pendapatan nasional Indonesia 1979-1983 (tabel-tabel pokok) = National income of Indonesia 1979-1983 (main tables) / Biro Pusat Statistik. — Jakarta : Biro Pusat Statistik, 1984-. — *Annual.* — *Text in English and Indonesian*

NATIONAL INCOME — Japan — Accounting — Nomenclature — Translations into English

KEIZAI KENKYŪJO, TOKYO. National Income Division
Comparison of Japanese and English item-name of Annual report on national accounts. — [Tokyo] : Economic Research Institute, 1979. — 66 leaves. — *In Japanese and English*

NATIONAL INCOME — Kiribati — Accounting

National accounts, 1972-74 / Gilbert Islands Ministry of Finance, Economics Division. — Bairiki : Government Printing Division, 1977. — 95p. — *Bibliography: p95*

NATIONAL INCOME — Switzerland — Accounting

SWITZERLAND. Office fédéral de la statistique
Die laufenden Einnahmen und Ausgaben des Staates nach Bund, Kantonen und Gemeinden, 1951-1982 : eine Analyse der Daten der nationalen Buchhaltung der Schweiz = Les recettes et les dépenses courantes de l'Etat-confédération, cantons et communes-de 1951 à 1982 : analyse des données des comptes nationaux de la Suisse. — Bern : Office fédéral de la statistique, 1984. — 46p. — (Beiträge zur schweizerischen Statistik = Contributions à la statistique suisse ; Heft 118). — *In German and French*

NATIONAL INCOME — Tanzania — Accounting — Methodolgy

National accounts of Tanzania 1976-1984 : sources and methods. — Dar es Salaam : Bureau of Statistics, 1985. — 35p

NATIONAL INCOME — Tuvalu — Accounting

National accounts, 1972-74 / Gilbert Islands Ministry of Finance, Economics Division. — Bairiki : Government Printing Division, 1977. — 95p. — *Bibliography: p95*

NATIONAL INQUIRY INTO LOCAL GOVERNMENT FINANCE (Australia)

HOWARD, John
Local government revenue raising : report to the National Inquiry into Local Government Finance. — [Queanbeyan? : National Inquiry into Local Government Finance?], 1985. — 4,171 leaves. — *Includes bibliographical references*

NATIONAL INQUIRY INTO LOCAL GOVERNMENT FINANCE (Australia)

Report / National Inquiry into Local Government Finance. — Canberra : Australian Government Publishing Service, 1985. — xxxvi,482p. — *Bibliographical references: p399-419*

SITLINGTON
Local government functions : an investigation of changes in patterns of expenditure in local government from 1971-1981 / J. A. Sitlington. — 1985 ; Queanbeyan : National Inquiry into Local Government Finance. — viii,183 leaves. — *Bibliographical references: p182-183*

NATIONAL INSTITUTE OF PUBLIC AFFAIRS (U.S.)

UNITED STATES CIVIL SERVICE COMMISSION. Bureau of Training
A study of the career education awards program of the National Institute of Public Affairs. — Washington, 1967. — v,173p. — *Bibliography: p170-173*

NATIONAL LIBERATION MOVEMENTS — Africa, Southern

Confrontation and liberation in southern Africa : regional directions after the Nkomati Accord / edited by Ibrahim S. R. Msabaha and Timothy M. Shaw. — Boulder, Colo : Westview Press, 1987. — xii, 315 p., [1] leaf of plates. — (Westview special studies on Africa). — *Bibliography: p. [307]-315*

NATIONAL LIBERATION MOVEMENTS — Ethiopia

HENZE, Paul B.
Rebels and separatists in Ethiopia : regional resistance to a Marxist regime / Paul Henze. — Santa Monica, CA : Rand, [1986]. — xv, 98 p.. — *"Prepared for the Office of the Under Secretary of Defense for Policy.".* — *"R-3347-USDP.".* — *"December 1985.".* — *Bibliography: p. 95-98*

NATIONAL PARKS AND RESERVES — Government policy — Great Britain

MACEWEN, Ann
Greenprints for the countryside? : the story of Britain's national parks / Ann and Malcolm MacEwen. — London : Allen & Unwin, 1987. — [224]p. — *Includes bibliography and index*

NATIONAL PARKS AND RESERVES — England — Broads

GREAT BRITAIN. Countryside Commission
The Broads : consultation paper. — [Cheltenham?] : the Commission, [1976]. — 4p

NATIONAL PARKS AND RESERVES — Great Britain

COUNCIL FOR NATIONAL PARKS
50 years for national parks. — London : Council for National Parks, 1986. — 32p

MACEWEN, Ann
Greenprints for the countryside? : the story of Britain's national parks / Ann and Malcolm MacEwen. — London : Allen & Unwin, 1987. — [224]p. — *Includes bibliography and index*

NATIONAL SECURITY

Intelligence and national security. — London : Frank Cass, 1986-. — *3 per year*

NATIONAL SECURITY
continuation

LEONARD, Ellis P
[Orthopedic surgery of the dog and cat].
Leonard's Orthopedic surgery of the dog and cat. — 3rd ed. / J.W. Alexander. — Philadelphia : Saunders, 1985. — ix, 242 p.. — *Includes bibliographies and index*

STERN, Jonathan P.
Soviet oil and gas exports to the west : commercial transaction or security threat? / Jonathan P. Stern. — Aldershot : Gower, 1987. — xi,123p. — (Energy papers ; no.21). — *Bibliographical notes*

NATIONAL SERVICE — United States

DANZIG, Richard
National service : what would it mean? / Richard Danzig, Peter Szanton. — Lexington, Mass. : Lexington Books, c1986. — xii, 307 p.. — *Includes index. — Bibliography: p. [281]-298*

NATIONAL SOCIALISM

BOCK, Gisela
Zwangssterilisation im Nationalsozialismus : Studien zur Rassenpolitik und Frauenpolitik / Gisela Bock. — Opladen : Westdeutscher Verlag, 1986. — 494p. — *Bibliography: p469-492*

DAIM, Wilfried
Der Mann, der Hitler die Ideen gab : die sektiererischen Grundlagen des Nationalsozialismus / Wilfried Daim. — 2e, erw. und verb. Aufl. — Wien : Hermann Böhlau, 1985. — 316p. — (Böhlaus zeitgeschichtliche Bibliothek ; Bd.4). — *First published 1958*

DÜRKEFÄLDEN, Karl
"Schreiben, wie es wirklich war-" : Aufzeichnungen Karl Dürkefäldens aus den Jahren 1933-1945 / herausgegeben von Herbert und Sibylle Obenaus. — Hannover : Fackelträger, 1985. — 136p. — *Bibliography: p132-136*

FEST, Joachim C.
The face of the Third Reich / Joachim C. Fest ; translated from the German by Michael Bullock. — London : Weidenfeld and Nicolson, 1970. — xiii,402p

KOSHAR, Rudy
Social life, local politics, and Nazism : Marburg, 1880-1935 / Rudy Koshar. — Chapel Hill ; London : University of North Carolina Press, c1986. — xviii, 395p. — *Includes index. — Bibliography: p.[361]-382*

Die nationalsozialistische Machtergreifung / Wolfgang Michalka (Hrsg.). — Paderborn : Schöningh, 1984. — 415p. — *Bibliography: p412-415*

PENTZLIN, Heinz
Die Deutschen im Dritten Reich : Nationalsozialisten, Mitläufer, Gegner / Heinz Penzlin. — Stuttgart : Seewald, 1985. — 222p

RABOFSKY, Eduard
Verborgene Wurzeln der NS-Justiz : strafrechtliche Rüstung für zwei Weltkriege / Eduard Rabofsky [und] Gerhard Oberkofler. — Wien : Europa Verlag, 1985. — 261p. — *Bibliography: p251-[262]*

SEMOLINOS ARRIBAS, Mercedes
Hitler y la prensa de la II República Española / Mercedes Semolinos Arribas. — Madrid : Centro de Investigaciones Sociológicas : Siglo Veintiuno de España, [1985]. — vi.,290p

STOAKES, Geoffrey
Hitler and the quest for world dominion : Nazi ideology and foreign policy in the 1920s / Geoffrey Stoakes. — Leamington Spa : Berg, 1986. — [304]p. *Includes bibliography and index*

Der Widerstand gegen den Nazionalsozialismus : die deutsche Gesellschaft und der Widerstand gegen Hitler / herausgegeben von Jürgen Schmädeke und Peter Steinbach ; im Auftrage der Historische Kommission zu Berlin in Zusammenarbeit mit der Gedenkstätte Deutscher Widerstand. — München : Piper, 1985. — xxxviii,1185p. — (Publikationen der Historischen Kommission zu Berlin). — *[Die Internationale Konferenz zum 40. Jahrestag des 20. Juli 1944, "Die deutsche Gesellschaft und der Widerstand gegen Hitler - eine Bilanz nach 40 Jahren" vom 2-6 Juli 1984 in Berlin]*

ZITELMANN, Rainer
Hitler : Selbstverständnis eines Revolutionärs / Rainer Zitelmann. — Hamburg ; Leamington Spa : Berg, 1987. — x,485p. — *Bibliography: p467-480*

NATIONAL SOCIALISM — History

The Formation of the Nazi constituency, 1919-1933 / edited by Thomas Childers. — London : Croom Helm, c1986. — viii,263p. — *Includes index*

Recht und Unrecht im Nationalsozialismus / herausgegeben von Peter Salje ; mit Beiträgen von Friedrich Dencker...[et al.]. — Münster : Wissenschaftliche Verlagsgesellschaft Regensberg und Biermann, 1985. — 310p

NATIONAL SOCIALISM — Law and legislation

Recht und Unrecht im Nationalsozialismus / herausgegeben von Peter Salje ; mit Beiträgen von Friedrich Dencker...[et al.]. — Münster : Wissenschaftliche Verlagsgesellschaft Regensberg und Biermann, 1985. — 310p

NATIONAL SOCIALISM — Germany

KOMMUNISTISCHE PARTEI DEUTSCHLANDS
Der Sieg des Faschismus in Deutschland und seine Lehren für unseren gegenwärtigen Kampf / herausgegeben vom Zentralkomitee der Kommunistischen Partei Deutschlands. — Berlin : [KPD], [1945?]. — 21p. — (Vortragsdisposition ; Nr.1)

NATIONAL SOCIALISM AND EDUCATION — History

WEBER, R. G. S.
The German student corps in the Third Reich / R.G.S. Weber. — Basingstoke : Macmillan, 1986. — ix,209p. — *Bibliography: p196-202. — Includes index*

NATIONAL SOCIALISM AND EDUCATION — History — 20th century

GALLIN, Alice
Midwives to Nazism : university professors in Weimar Germany, 1925-1933 / Alice Gallin. — Macon, Ga. : Mercer, c1986. — viii, 134 p.. — *Includes index. — Bibliography: p.[115]-128*

NATIONAL SOCIALISTS — Germany (West)

FRIEDRICH, Jörg
Die Kalte Amnestie : NS-Täter in der Bundesrepublik / Jörg Friedrich. — Frankfurt am Main : Fischer Taschenbuch Verlag, 1984. — 431p. — *Bibliographical notes*

NATIONAL STATE

DORSEY, Gray L
Beyond the United Nations : changing discourse in international politics and law / Gray L. Dorsey. — Lanham ; London : University Press of America, c1986. — xi, 111p. — (Exxon Education Foundation series on rhetoric and political discourse ; v. 5). — *Bibliography: p. 103-111. — Bibliography: p.103-111*

NATIONAL UNION OF MINEWORKERS

NATIONAL UNION OF MINEWORKERS
Miners United for peace. — London : National Union of Mineworkers, 1987. — [22p]. — (Campaign briefing ; 3)

NATIONAL UNION OF PUBLIC EMPLOYEES

NATIONAL UNION OF PUBLIC EMPLOYEES
A NUPE handbook for good local services : 'better services'. — [London] : NUPE, 1987. — 34p

NATIONAL UNION OF PUBLIC EMPLOYEES — History

DIX, Bernard
Serving the public : building the union : the history of the National Union of Public Employees / Bernard Dix and Stephen Williams. — London : Lawrence and Wishart Volume 1: The forerunners, 1889-1928. — 1987. — 238p. — *Bibliography: p229-231*

NATIONAL UNION OF RAILWAYMEN. Darlington Branch — History

CORNFORTH, Wilson
The long hard road : (the story of Darlington railwaymen and the struggle for social justice) / by Wilson Cornforth. — Darlington (6 Starmer Crescent, Darlington) : D. Cornforth, c1985. — 120p

NATIONAL UNION OF TEACHERS

MARKS, John, 1934-
London's schools : when even the Communist Party gives up! / John Marks. — London : Aims of Industry, 1985. — 6p

NATIONAL UNION PUBLIC EMPLOYEES

NATIONAL UNION OF PUBLIC EMPLOYEES
The report of the Race Equality Working Party. — London : NUPE, 1985. — 56p

NATIONAL WAGES COUNCIL (Singapore)

LIM, Chong-Yah
Economic restructuring in Singapore / Lim Chong-Yah. — Singapore : Federal Publications, 1984. — v,117p. — *Bibliography: p109*

NATIONAL WOMAN'S PARTY — History

LUNARDINI, Christine A.
From equal suffrage to equal rights : Alice Paul and the National Woman's Party, 1910-1928 / Christine A. Lunardini. — New York : New York University Press, 1986. — xx, 230 p.. — (The American social experience series ; 5). — *Includes index. — Bibliography: p. [206]-220*

NATIONALISM

BERKI, R. N.
State, class, nation / R. N. Berki. — Hull : Hull University Press, 1986. — 20p

BLAS GUERRERO, Andrés de
Nacionalismo e ideologías políticas contemporáneas / Andrés de Blas Guerrero. — Madrid : Espasa-Calpe, 1984. — 178p. — (Ideas e instituciones). — *Bibliography: p [129]-168*

BONANNO, Alfredo M.
Anarchism and the national liberation struggle / Alfredo M. Bonanno ; [translated from the Italian]. — Port Glasgow (c/o 83 Langoide Terrace, Port Glasgow [Renfrewshire]) : Bratach Dubh Publications, 1978. — 16,[4]p. — (Anarchist pamphlets ; no.1). — *This translation originally published: 1976*

FANON, Frantz
The wretched of the earth / Frantz Fanon ; translated from the French by Constance Farrington. — London : MacGibbon and Kee, 1965. — 255p

GROUPE LIBERTAIRE LOUISE MICHEL
Des luttes de liberation nationale : à l'anarchisme. — Paris : Editions La Rue, 1985. — 55p

NATIONALISM
continuation

MACESICH, George
Economic nationalism and stability / by George Macesich. — New York : Praeger, 1985. — p. cm. — *Includes bibliographies and index*

Nationalism and modernity : a Mediterranean perspective / edited by Joseph Alpher. — New York : Praeger, 1986. — vii, 143 p.. — *At head of title: Reuben Hecht Chair of Zionism and Jewish Political Thought. — "University of Haifa.". — Outgrowth of two seminars held at the University of Haifa in 1984 and 1985. — Includes bibliographies and index. — Contents: Introduction / Joseph Alpher -- State, nation, and religion / Hugh Seton-Watson -- State, nation, and religion in Islam / Bernard Lewis -- Will Israel ever become a nation? / Joseph Agassi -- Power or spirit : Jewish political thought in interbellum Europe / Paul Mendes-Flohr -- Zionism, marginalism, and cosmopolitan centralism / Dan V. Segre -- The international information revolution / Harlan Cleveland -- Language and nation : the Italian case / Sergio Romano -- Language and nation : the case of Arabic / Emmanuel Sivan -- Language conflict and national identity : a semiotic approach / Itamar Even-Zohar*

The Sociobiology of ethnocentrism : evolutionary dimensions of xenophobia, discrimination, racism and nationalism / edited by Vernon Reynolds, Vincent Falger and Ian Vine. — London : Croom Helm, c1987. — xx,327p. — *Bibliography: p274-314. — Includes index*

NATIONALISM — History
MCNEILL, William H.
Polyethnicity and national unity in world history / William H. McNeill. — Toronto ; London : University of Toronto Press, 1986. — vii, 85p. — (The Donald G. Creighton lectures ; 1985)

NATIONALISM — Arab countries
Pan-Arabism and Arab nationalism : the continuing debate / edited by Tawfic E. Farah ; foreword by James A. Bill. — Boulder : Westview Press, 1987. — xvi, 208 p.. — *Includes bibliographies and index*

NATIONALISM — Argentina — History
QUIJADA, Mónica
Manuel Gálvez : 60 años de pensamiento nacionalista / Mónica Quijada. — Buenos Aires : Centro Editor de América Latina, 1985. — 139p. — *Bibliography: p133-139*

NATIONALISM — Canada
HILLER, Harry H.
Canadian society : a macro analysis / Harry H. Hiller. — Scarborough, Ont. : Prentice-Hall Canada, c1986. — x, 245 p.. — *Includes index. — Bibliography: p. 234-241*

National politics and community in Canada / edited by R. Kenneth Carty and W. Peter Ward. — Vancouver : University of British Columbia Press, 1986. — 200 p.. — *Includes bibliographical references. — Contents: Canada as political community / R. Kenneth Carty & W. Peter Ward -- The Origins of Canadian politics and John A. Macdonald / Gordon Stewart -- Networks and associations and the nationalizing of sentiment in English Canada / Margaret Prang -- The Making of a Canadian political citizenship / R. Kenneth Carty & W. Peter Ward -- National political parties and the growth of the national political community / David E. Smith -- Leadership conventions and the development of the national political community in Canada / John C. Courtney -- Ceremonial politics / Christopher Armstrong -- Becoming Canadians / P.B. Waite -- Managing the periphery / Donald E. Blake -- The "French lieutenant" in Ottawa / John English*

NATIONALISM — China
MAKHMUTKHODZHAEV, M. Kh.
Natsional'naia politika gomin'dana (1927-1937) / M. Kh. Makhmutkhodshaev. — Moskva : Nauka (IVL), 1986. — 124p. — *Table of contents in English. — Bibliography: p116-[125]*

NATIONALISM — Czechoslovakia
FLORIA, B. N.
Rossiia i cheshskoe vosstanie protiv Gabsburgov / B. N. Floria ; otv. redaktor A. S. Myl'nikov. — Moskva : Nauka, 1986. — 206p

NATIONALISM — Developing countries
CHATTERJEE, Partha
Nationalist thought and the colonial world : a derivative discourse? / Partha Chatterjee. — London : Zed for the United Nations University, 1986. — viii,181p. — (Third World books). — *Bibliography: p172-176. — Includes index*

NATIONALISM — Egypt
GERSHONI, I
Egypt, Islam, and the Arabs : the search for Egyptian nationhood, 1900-1930 / Israel Gershoni and James P. Jankowski. — New York : Oxford University Press, 1986, c1987. — xviii, 346 p.. — (Studies in Middle Eastern history). — *"In cooperation with the Dayan Center and the Shiloah Institute for Middle Eastern and African Studies, Tel Aviv University.". — Includes index. — Bibliography: p. 326-335*

NATIONALISM — England — History
NEWMAN, Gerald
The rise of English nationalism : a cultural history, 1720-1830 / Gerald Newman. — New York : St. Martin's Press, 1987. — xxiii, 294 p. . — *Includes index. — Bibliography: p. [269]-280*

NATIONALISM — France
BERGERON, Francis
De Le Pen à Le Pen : une histoire des nationaux et des nationalistes sous la Ve République / Francis Bergeron, Philippe Vilgier ; préface de François Brigneau. — Bouère : Dominique Martin Morin, 1985. — 214p. — *Bibliography: p204-205*

BERGERON, Francis
Les droites dans la rue : nationaux et nationalistes sous la Troisiéme République / Francis Bergeron et Philippe Vilgier ; préface de Jean-François Chiappe. — [Bouére] : Dominique Martin Morin, 1985. — 175p

DUMONT, Serge
Le système Le Pen / Serge Dumont, Joseph Lorien, Karl Criton. — Anvers : EPO, 1985. — 336p. — *Bibliography: p334-335*

LE PEN, Jean Marie
Pour la France : programme du Front National / Jean Marie Le Pen. — Paris : Albatros, 1985. — 200p

NATIONALISM — France — Brittany — History — 20th century
FRELAUT, Bertrand
Les nationalistes bretons de 1939 à 1945 / Bertrand Frelaut. — [n.p] : Editions Beltan, 1985. — 236p

NATIONALISM — Germany
PARK, Ho-Leong
Sozialismus und Nationalismus : Grundsatzdiskussionen über Nationalismus, Imperialismus, Militarismus und Krieg in der deutschen Sozialdemokratie vor 1914 / von Ho-Leong Park ; mit einem Vorwort von Wolf-Dieter Narr. — Berlin : Schelzky und Jeep, 1986. — 349p. — *Bibliography: p323-349*

NATIONALISM — Germany — Addresses, essays, lectures
German nationalism and the European response, 1890-1945 / edited by Carole Fink, Isabel V. Hull, and MacGregor Knox. — 1st ed. — Norman : University of Oklahoma Press, c1985. — xv, 299 p.. — *Includes bibliographical references and index*

NATIONALISM — India — History
CHATTERJI, Rakahari
Working class and the nationalist movement in India : the critical years / Rakhahari Chatterji. — New Delhi : South Asian Publishers, c1984. — ix, 215 p.. — *Includes bibliographical references and index*

CHOUDHURY, Veena
Indian nationalism and external forces, 1920-47 / Veena Choudhury. — Delhi : Capital Pub. House, 1985. — xii, 234 p.. — *Includes index. — Bibliography: p. [210]-228*

NATIONALISM — India — History — Sources
Sources on national movement / edited by V.N. Datta & S.C. Mittal. — New Delhi : Allied Publishers : Indian Council of Historical Research, 1985-. — v. <1- >. — *Includes bibliographical references and index. — Contents: v. 1. Protests, disturbances, and defiance, January 1919 to September 1920*

NATIONALISM — India — Punjab — History
MOHAN, Kamlesh
Militant nationalism in the Punjab 1919-1935 / by Kamlesh Mohan. — New Delhi : Manohar, 1985. — x,447p. — *Bibliography: p[398]-432*

NATIONALISM — Iraq — History
SIMON, Reeva S
Iraq between the two world wars : the creation and implementation of a nationalist ideology / Reeva S. Simon. — New York : Columbia University Press, 1986. — xv, 233p. — *Includes index. — Bibliography: p.[211]-227*

NATIONALISM — Ireland — History
BEW, Paul
Conflict and conciliation in Ireland, 1890-1910 : Parnellites and radical agrarians / Paul Bew. — Oxford : Clarendon, 1987. — [325]p. — *Includes bibliography and index*

HUTCHINSON, John, 1949-
The dynamics of cultural nationalism : the Gaelic revival and the creation of the Irish nation state / John Hutchinson. — London : Allen & Unwin, 1987. — [272]p. — *Includes bibliography and index*

MANDLE, W. F.
The Gaelic Athletic Association & Irish nationalist politics, 1884-1924 / W.F. Mandle. — London : Christopher Helm, 1987. — xi,240p. — *Bibliography: p225-229. — Includes index*

NATIONALISM — Islamic countries
The Impact of nationalism on the Muslim world / edited by M. Ghayasuddin. — London : Open Press, 1986. — [200]p. — *Conference papers*

NATIONALISM — Kenya
MOI, Daniel T. arap
Kenya African nationalism : Nyayo philosophy and principles / Daniel T. arap Moi. — London : Macmillan, 1986. — xvi,192p

NATIONALISM — Northern Ireland
SEE, Katherine O'Sullivan
First world nationalisms : class and ethnic politics in Northern Ireland and Quebec / Katherine O'Sullivan See. — Chicago : University of Chicago Press, 1986. — p. cm. — *Includes index. — Bibliography: p*

NATIONALISM — Québec (Province)
SEE, Katherine O'Sullivan
First world nationalisms : class and ethnic politics in Northern Ireland and Quebec / Katherine O'Sullivan See. — Chicago : University of Chicago Press, 1986. — p. cm. — *Includes index. — Bibliography: p*

NATIONALISM — Singapore
CHEW, Sock Foon
Ethnicity and nationality in Singapore / by Chew Sock Foon. — Athens, Ohio : Ohio University Center for International Studies, Center for Southeast Asian Studies, 1987. — xv, 229 p.. — (Monographs in international studies. Southeast Asia series ; no. 78). — *Bibliography: p. 213-229*

NATIONALISM — South Africa — History — 20th century
The Politics of race, class and nationalism in twentieth century South Africa / edited by Shula Marks and Stanley Trapido. — Harlow : Longman, 1987. — 1v.. — *Includes index*

NATIONALISM — Soviet Union
KPSS - organizator bratskoi druzhby narodov SSSR / [redaktsionnaia kollegiia: V. A. Smyshliaev...et al.]. — Leningrad : Izd-vo Leningradskogo universiteta, 1973. — 153p. — (Uchenie zapiski kafedr obshchestvennykh nauk vuzov Leningrada. Istoriia KPSS ; vyp.13)

NATIONALISM — Spain
Estructuras sociales y cuestión nacional en España / Francesc Hernández y Francesc Mercadé, compiladores ; prologo de Salvador Giner. — Barcelona : Ariel, 1986. — 512p

Nacionalismo y regionalismo en España : (el horizonte político-institucional, económico, social, cultural e internacional de nuestro tiempo) : seminario en conmemoración del 28 de Febrero / presentación por Manuel Melero Muñoz. — Cordoba : Diputación Provincial de Cordoba, 1984. — 303p

SOLÉ TURA, Jordi
Nacionalidades y nacionalismos en España : autonomías, federalismo, autodeterminación / Jordi Solé Tura. — Madrid : Alianza Editorial, 1985. — 233p. — *Bibliography: p227-233*

NATIONALISM — Spain — History — 19th century
CIRUJANO MARÍN, Paloma
Historiografía y nacionalismo español (1834-1868) / Paloma Cirujano Marín, Teresa Elorriaga Planes, Juan Sisinio Pérez Garzón. — Madrid : Centro de Estudios Históricos, Consejo Superior de Investigaciones Científicas, 1985. — xi,206p. — (Monografías / Consejo Superior de Investigaciones Científicas, Centro de Estudios Históricos ; 2)

NATIONALISM — Spain — Basque Provinces
GRANJA, José Luis de la
Nacionalismo y II República en el País Vasco : estatutos de autonomía, partidos y elecciones : historia de Acción Nacionalista Vasca: 1930-1936 / por José Luis de la Granja Sainz. — Madrid : Centro de Investigaciones Sociologicas : Siglo vientiuno de España, 1986. — xxiv,687p. — *Bibliography: p[641]-659*

GURRUCHAGA, Ander
El código nacionalista vasco durante el franquismo / Ander Gurruchaga ; prólogo de Alfonso Pérez-Agote. — Barcelona : Anthropos, 1985. — 456p. — *Bibliography: p439-456*

NATIONALISM — Spain — Basque Provinces — Congresses
COLOQUIO VASCO-CATALÁN DE HISTORIA (1 : 1982 : Sitges, Spain)
Industrialización y nacionalismo : análisis comparativos / edición a cargo de Manuel González Portilla, Jordi Maluquer de Motes, Borja de Riquer Permanyer. — Bellaterra : Servicio de Publicaciones de la Universidad Autónoma de Barcelona, 1985. — 610p. — *In Spanish, with some papers in Catalan*

NATIONALISM — Spain — Catalonia
CAMPALANS, Rafael
Catalanisme i socialisme : el debat de 1923 / R. Campalans i A. Fabri i Ribas ; edició a cura de Jesús M. Rodés. — [Barcelona] : La Magrana, [1985]. — xliv,114p. — (Biblioteca dels clàssics del nacionalisme català ; 10). — *Iniciativa conjunta d'Edicions de la Magrana i de la Diputació de Barcelona*

NIN, Andres
Socialisme i nacionalisme (1912-1934) : escrits republicans, socialistes i comunistes / Andreu Nin ; edició a cura de Pelai Pagès. — Barcelona : Edicions de la Magrana, 1985. — li,191p. — (Biblioteca dels Clàssics del Nacionalisme Catalá ; 11). — *Bibliography: p [xlv] - xlvii*

NATIONALISM — Spain — Catalonia — Congresses
COLOQUIO VASCO-CATALÁN DE HISTORIA (1 : 1982 : Sitges, Spain)
Industrialización y nacionalismo : análisis comparativos / edición a cargo de Manuel González Portilla, Jordi Maluquer de Motes, Borja de Riquer Permanyer. — Bellaterra : Servicio de Publicaciones de la Universidad Autónoma de Barcelona, 1985. — 610p. — *In Spanish, with some papers in Catalan*

FIGUERES, Josep M.
El primer Congrés Catalanista i Valentí Almirall : materials per a l'estudi dels orígens del catalanisme / Josep M. Figueres. — [Barcelona] : Generalitat de Catalunya, Departament de la Presidència, 1985. — 282p. — *Bibliography: p267-280*

NATIONALISM — Spain — Catalonia — History
FERRER I GIRONÈS, Francesc
La persecució pólitica de la llengua catalana : història de les mesures preses contra el seu ús des de la Nova Planta fins avui / Francesc Ferrer i Gironès. — Barcelona : Edicions 62, 1985. — 309p. — *Bibliography: p[295]-300*

NATIONALISM — Spain — Galacia — History
CASTRO PÉREZ, Xavier
O galeguismo na encrucillada republicana / Xavier Castro. — La Coruña : Editorial Atlántico
Tomo 1. — 1985. — 540p

NATIONALISM — Spain — Galicia — History
CASTRO PÉREZ, Xavier
O galeguismo na encrucillada republicana / Xavier Castro. — La coruña : Editorial Atlántico. — *Bibliography: p867-872*
Tomo 2. — 1985. — p545-988

NATIONALISM — Spain — Valencia
ALCARAZ RAMOS, Manuel
Cuestión nacional y autonomía Valenciana / Manuel Alcaraz Ramos. — Alicante : Instituto Juan Gil-Albert, 1985. — 221p. — *Bibliography: p15-221*

NATIONALISM — Sudan — History
HASABU, Afaf Abdel Majid Abu
Factional conflict in the Sudanese nationalist movement 1918-1948 / Araf [sic.] Abdel Majid Abu Hasabu. — Khartoum : Graduate College, University of Khartoum, 1985. — 179p. — (Graduate College publications / University of Khartoum ; no.12). — *Bibliography: p174-179*

NATIONALISM — Thailand
DHIRAVEGIN, Likhit
Nationalism and the state in Thailand / Likhit Dhiravegin. — Bangkok : Thammasat University. Faculty of Political Science. Research Center, 1985. — 32p. — (Monograph series / Thammasat University ; .no8)

NATIONALISM — Yugoslavia
Savez komunista u borbi protiv antisocijalističkih delovanja i antikomunističkih ideologija / redakcioni odbor David Atlagić...[et al.]. — Beograd : Izdavački centar Komunist, 1986. — viii,555p

NATIONALISM AND EDUCATION — Germany — History — 20th century
GALLIN, Alice
Midwives to Nazism : university professors in Weimar Germany, 1925-1933 / Alice Gallin. — Macon, Ga. : Mercer, c1986. — viii, 134 p.. — *Includes index.* — *Bibliography: p. [115]-128*

NATIONALISM AND EDUCATION — India
GHOSH, Suresh Chandra
Indian nationalism : a case study for the first university reform by the British Raj / Suresh Chandra Ghosh. — New Delhi : Vikas Pub. House, c1985. — 195 p.. — 89-9. — *Includes index.* — *Bibliography: p. [182]-189*

NATIONALISM AND SOCIALISM — Soviet Union
TSAMERIAN, I. P.
Natsional'nye otsosheniia v SSSR / I. P. Tsamerian. — Moskva : Mysl', 1987. — 181p

NATIONALISM AND SOCIALISM — Soviet Union — History
AGURSKY, Mikhail
The third Rome : national Bolshevism in the USSR / Mikhail Agursky ; foreword by Leonard Shapiro. — Boulder : Westview Press, 1987. — p. cm. — *Includes index.* — *Bibliography: p*

NATIONALISTS — France — Biography
BUSI, Frederick
The pope of antisemitism : the career and legacy of Edouard-Adolphe Drumont / Frederick Busi. — Lanham ; London : University Press of America, 1987. — [242]p. — *Includes bibliography and index*

NATIONALISTS — India — Biography
COPLEY, Antony
Gandhi : against the tide / Antony Copley. — Oxford : Basil Blackwell, 1987. — v,118p. — (Historical Association studies). — *Bibliography: p107-110.* — *Includes index*

NATIONALISTS — Indonesia — Biography
Toward a glorius Indonesia : reminiscences and observations of Dr. Soetomo / edited, annotated, and introduced by Paul W. van der Veur ; translated by Suharni Soemarmo and Paul W. van der Veur. — Athens, Ohio : Ohio University, Center for International Studies, 1987. — p. cm. — (Monographs in international studies. Southeast Asia series ; no. 81). — *Translation of Dr. Soetomo's Kenang-kenangan; Poespita mantja nagara; and, Poespa-rinontjé*

NATIONALISTS — Ireland — Biography
FALLON, Charlotte H.
Soul of fire : a biography of Mary MacSwiney / Charlotte H. Fallon. — Cork : Mercier, c1986. — 207p. — *Bibliography: p204-207*

NATIONALSOZIALISTISCHE DEUTSCHE ARBEITER-PARTEI. Sturmabteilung — History
REICHE, Eric G.
The development of the SA in Nürnberg, 1922-1934 / Eric G. Reiche. — Cambridge : Cambridge University Press, 1986. — xviii,314p

NATIONWIDE BUILDING SOCIETY
Local area housing statistics / Nationwide Building Society. — London : Nationwide Building Society, 1985-. — *Annual*

NATIONWIDE BUILDING SOCIETY
House prices / Nationwide Building Society. — London : Nationwide Building Society. — *Quarterly*

NATIVE RACES
Indigenous peoples and the nation-state : 'fourth world' politics in Canada, Australia, and Norway / edited by Noel Dyck. — St. John's, Nfld., Canada : Institute of Social and Economic Research, Memorial University of Newfoundland, c1985. — 263 p.. — (Social and economic papers ; no. 14). — *Bibliography: 242-259*

KIERNAN, V. G
The lords of human kind : black man, yellow man, and white man in an age of empire / V.G. Kiernan. — Columbia University Press morningside ed. — New York : Columbia University Press, 1987, c1969. — 336p, [16]p of plates. — : Reprint. Originally published: Boston : Little, Brown, 1969. — *Includes bibliographical references*

Native power : the quest for autonomy and nationhood of indigenous peoples / edited by Jens Brøsted...[et al.]. — Bergen : Universitetsforlaget As, 1985. — 350p. — *Includes bibliography of Helge Kleivan: p.342-348*

NATIVE RACES — Addresses, essays, lectures

Native power : the quest for autonomy and nationhood of indigenous peoples / edited by Jens Brøsted ... [et al.]. — Bergen : Universitetsforlaget, c1985. — 350 p.. — *Festschrift in memory of Helge Kleivan (1924-1983). — Includes bibliographies. — "Bibliography of Helge Kleivan": p. [341]-348*

NATIVISM — History — 19th century

KNOBEL, Dale T.
Paddy and the republic : ethnicity and nationality in antebellum America / by Dale T. Knobel. — 1st ed. — Middletown, Conn. : Wesleyan University Press ; Scranton, Pa. : Distributed by Harper & Row, c1986. — p. cm. — *Includes index. — Bibliography: p*

NATURAL DISASTERS — Prevention

Disaster prevention and mitigation : a compendium of current knowledge. — Geneva : New York
V.1: Volcanological aspects. — 1976. — iv,38p. — *Bibliographical references: p33-38. "UNDRO/28/75"*

Disaster prevention and mitigation : a compendium of current knowledge. — New York : United Nations
V.2: Hydrological aspects. — 1976. — viii,100p. — *Bibliography: p98-100. — "UNDRO/22/76"*

Disaster prevention and mitigation : a compendium of current knowledge. — New York : United Nations
V.3: Seismological aspects. — 1978. — viii,127p. — *Bibliography: p122-127. "UNDRO/22/76 VOL.III"*

Disaster prevention and mitigation : a compendium of current knowledge. — New York : United Nations
V.4: Meteorological aspects. — 1978. — viii,96p. — *Bibliography: p95-96. "UNDRO/22/76 VOL.IV"*

Disaster prevention and mitigation : a compendium of current knowledge. — New York : United Nations
V.7: Economic aspects. — 1979. — vii,73p. — *Bibliography: p69-73. — "UNDRO/22/76 Vol.VII"*

Disaster prevention and mitigation : a compendium of current knowledge. — New York : United Nations
V.9: Legal aspects. — 1980. — viii,67p. — *Bibliography: p65-67. "UNDRO/22/76 VOL.IX"*

Disaster prevention and mitigation : a compendium of current knowledge. — New York : United Nations
V.11: Preparedness aspects. — 1984. — vi,218p. — *Includes bibliograpical references. UNDRO/22/76 Vol.XI*

NATURAL DISASTERS — Prevention — Public relations

Disaster prevention and mitigation : a compendium of current knowledge. — New York : United Nations
V.10: Public information aspects. — 1979. — ix,142p. — *Bibliography: p137-142. "UNDRO/22/76 Vol.X"*

NATURAL ENVIRONMENT RESEARCH COUNCIL

NATURAL ENVIRONMENT RESEARCH COUNCIL. Working Party on Committee Structure
Report of the Wansbrough-Jones Working Party on Committee Structure. — [London : the Council], 1970. — 22,[11]leaves

NATURAL HISTORY — Gambia

REEVE, Henry Fenwick
The Gambia : its history, ancient, medieval and modern together with its geographical, geological, and ethnographical conditions and a description of the birds, beasts and fishes found therein / by Henry Fenwick Reeve. — New York : Negro Universities Press, 1969. — xv,287p. — *Reprint of the 1912 edition*

NATURAL LAW

BLOCH, Ernst
[Naturrecht und menschliche Würde. English]. Natural law and human dignity / Ernst Bloch ; translated by Dennis J. Schmidt. — Cambridge, Mass. ; London : MIT Press, c1986. — xxx, 323p. — (Studies in contemporary German social thought). — *Translation of: Naturrecht und menschliche Würde. — Includes index*

BUDZISZEWSKI, J.
The resurrection of nature : political theory and the human character / J. Budziszewski. — Ithaca : Cornell University Press, 1986. — 218 p.. — *Includes index. — Bibliography: p. 205-212*

Law and politics : readings in legal and political thought / edited with introduction and essay by Shadia B. Drury ; associate editor Rainer Knopff. — Calgary : Detselig Enterprises, c1980. — 270p. — *Bibliography: p [267]-270*

VEATCH, Henry B.
Human rights : fact or fancy? / Henry B. Veatch. — Baton Rouge : Louisiana State University Press, c1985. — xi, 258p. — *Includes index. — Bibliography: p.251-253*

NATURAL RESOURCES

Changing Britain, changing world : geographical perspectives. — Milton Keynes : Open University Press. — (Social services : a second level course) (D205; Units 4-7). — *At head of title: Open University*
Section 2: Analysis: aspects of the geography of society
Block 2: Industry and resources / Piers Blaikie...[et al.]. — 1985. — Various pagings

HARTWICK, John M
The economics of natural resource use / John Hartwick, Nancy Olewiler. — New York, NY : Harper & Row, c1986. — p. cm. — *Includes bibliographies*

Natural resources economics and policy applications : essays in honor of James A. Crutchfield / edited by Edward Miles, Robert Pealy, and Robert Stokes ; foreword by Brewster C. Denny. — Seattle : Institute for Marine Studies of the University of Washington : Distributed by the University of Washington Press, c1986. — p. cm. — (Public policy issues in resource management). — *Includes index. — Bibliography: p*

Natural resources forum / United Nations. Department of Technical Co-operation and Development. — London : Graham and Trotman for the United Nations, 1985-. — *Quarterly*

Resources policy. — Guildford : Butterworth, 1986-. — *Quarterly*

World resources / World Resources Institute and the International Institute for Environment and Development. — New York : World Resources Institute ; Washington, D.C. : International Institute for Environment and Development, 1986-. — *Annual*

NATURAL RESOURCES — Addresses, essays, lectures

Natural resource economics : policy problems and contemporary analysis / edited by Daniel W. Bromley. — Hingham, MA, USA : Kluwer-Nijhoff : Distributors for the U.S. and Canada, Kluwer Academic Publishers, c1986. — xiv, 234 p.. — (Recent economic thought series). — *Includes index. — Bibliography: p. 226-229*

NATURAL RESOURCES — Economic aspects — Canada

ANDERSON, F. J.
Natural resources in Canada : economic theory and policy / F. J. Anderson. — Toronto ; London : Methuen, 1985. — ix,301p. — *Bibliography: p286-295*

NATURAL RESOURCES — Government policy

HARF, James E.
The politics of global resources : population, food, energy and environment / James E. Harf and B. Thomas Trout. — Durham : Duke University Press, 1986. — xviii, 314p. — *Bibliography: p.[304]-309*

NATURAL RESOURCES — Government policy — Canada

ANDERSON, F. J.
Natural resources in Canada : economic theory and policy / F. J. Anderson. — Toronto ; London : Methuen, 1985. — ix,301p. — *Bibliography: p286-295*

NATURAL RESOURCES — Government policy — India

SUKHWAL, B. L.
India : economic resource base and contemporary political patterns / B.L. Sukhwal. — 1st ed. — New York : Envoy Press, 1987. — viii, 200 p.. — *Includes index. — Bibliography: p. [189]-192*

NATURAL RESOURCES — Government policy — United States

CLARKE, Jeanne Nienaber
Staking out the terrain : power differentials among natural resource management agencies / Jeanne Nienaber Clarke, Daniel McCool. — Albany : State University of New York Press, c1985. — p. cm. — (SUNY series in environmental public policy). — *Includes index. — Bibliography: p*

NATURAL RESOURCES — Law and legislation

ARSANJANI, Mahnoush H
International regulation of internal resources : a study of law and policy / Mahnoush H. Arsanjani. — Charlottesville : University Press of Virginia, 1981. — 558 p.. — (Virginia legal studies). — *Includes bibliographical references and index*

NATURAL RESOURCES — Law and legislation — Antarctic regions — Congresses

Antarctic challenge II : conflicting interests, cooperation, environmental protection, economic development : proceedings of an inter-disciplinary symposium, September 27th-21st, 1985 / organized by the Institut für Internationales Recht an der Universität Kiel and the Alfred-Wegener-Institut für Polar- und Meeresforschung, Bremerhaven; edited by Rüdiger Wolfrum, assistant editors: Klaus Bockslaff and Ingrid L. Jahn. — Berlin : Duncker & Humblot, 1986. — 465p. — (Veröffentlichungen des Instituts für Internationales Recht an der Universität Kiel ; 95)

NATURAL RESOURCES — Law and legislation — Canada

MEEKISON, J. Peter
Origins and meanings of Section 92A : the 1982 Constitutional Amendment on Resources / J. Peter Meekison, Roy J. Romanow [and] William D. Moull. — Montreal : Institute for Research on Public Policy/L'Institut de Recherches Politiques, 1985. — xxii,77p

NATURAL RESOURCES — Management

Information and natural resources. — Paris : Organisation for Economic Co-operation and Development, 1986. — 95p. — *Includes bibliographical references*

NATURAL RESOURCES — Political aspects

HARF, James E.
The politics of global resources : population, food, energy and environment / James E. Harf and B. Thomas Trout. — Durham : Duke University Press, 1986. — xviii, 314p. — *Bibliography: p.[304]-309*

NATURAL RESOURCES — Remote sensing

Terrain analysis and remote sensing / edited by John R.G. Townshend. — London : Allen & Unwin, 1981. — xiii,232p,[2]p of plates. — Includes bibliographies and index

NATURAL RESOURCES — Antarctic regions — Congresses

Antarctic challenge II : conflicting interests, cooperation, environmental protection, economic development : proceedings of an inter-disciplinary symposium, September 27th-21st, 1985 / organized by the Institut für Internationales Recht an der Universität Kiel and the Alfred-Wegener-Institut für Polar- und Meeresforschung, Bremerhaven; edited by Rüdiger Wolfrum, assistant editors: Klaus Bockslaff and Ingrid L. Jahn. — Berlin : Duncker & Humblot, 1986. — 465p. — (Veröffentlichungen des Instituts für Internationales Recht an der Universität Kiel ; 95)

NATURAL RESOURCES — Asia, Southeastern — Congresses

Southeast Asia, an emerging center of world influence? : economic and resource considerations / edited by Wayne Raymond and K. Mulliner. — Athens : Ohio University Center for International Studies, 1977. — vii, 136 p. — (Papers in international studies : Southeast Asia series ; no. 42). — Papers presented at a symposium on May 7-8, 1976 at Ohio University, Athens, hosted by the Southeast Asia Studies Program. — Includes bibliographical references

NATURAL RESOURCES — Australia — Maps

Atlas of Australian resources. Third series. — Canberra : Division of National Mapping, 1986 Vol.4: Climate. — 60p

NATURAL RESOURCES — Developing countries

Population growth and economic development : issues and evidence / edited by D. Gale Johnson and Ronald D. Lee. — Madison, Wis. : University of Wisconsin Press, 1987. — xiii, 702 p.. — (Social demography). — "Working Group on Population Growth and Economic Development; Committee on Population, Commission on Behavioral and Social Sciences and Education, National Research Council.". — Includes bibliographies and index

NATURAL RESOURCES — Developing countries — Management

Multinational corporations, environment, and the Third World : business matters / edited by Charles S. Pearson. — Durham, NC : Duke University Press, 1987. — xvi, 295 p.. — (Duke Press policy studies). — "A World Resources Institute book.". — Based on an international meeting held in 1984 and sponsored by the World Resources Institute. — Includes index. — Bibliography: p. 261-284

NATURAL RESOURCES — France — Statistics

FRANCE. Commission interministérielle des comptes du patrimoine naturel
Les comptes du patrimoine naturel. — [Paris] : I.N.S.E.E., 1986. — 552p. — (Les collections de l'INSEE. Série C. Comptes et planification ; nos.137-138). — Bibliography: p524-533

NATURAL RESOURCES — Great Britain

DAVIS, John, 1923-
As though people mattered : a prospect for Britain / John Davis and Alan Bollard. — London : Intermediate Technology Publications, 1986. — xv, 184p

NATURAL RESOURCES — India

SUKHWAL, B. L.
India : economic resource base and contemporary political patterns / B.L. Sukhwal. — 1st ed. — New York : Envoy Press, 1987. — viii, 200 p.. — Includes index. — Bibliography: p. [189]-192

NATURAL RESOURCES — India — Andhra Pradesh — Maps

Planning atlas of Andhra Pradesh / sponsors, Department of Finance & Planning, Government of Andhra Pradesh [and] Pilot Map Production Plant (C.S.T. & M.P.), Survey of India, Hyderabad [and] Department of Geography, Osmania University, Hyderabad. — Scales differ ; (E 77°--E 85°/N 20°--N 13°). — [S.l. : s.n.]. — Editor: Afzal Mohammad. — "Andhra Pradesh Planning Atlas Project (Supplement) 1978-1980"--Page following verso t.p. — "Reg. no. 1200 PPE '79 (P.M.P. 34 -- 1: = 2,500,000) 520 '79-80"--Verso t.p. — "Based upon Survey of India maps, with the permission of the Surveyor general of India"--Verso t.p. — : "Revised maps ... mostly pertain to socio-economic characteristics"--Foreword. — Contents: Location & administrative divisions -- Land use -- Economic characteristics -- Socio-economic infrastructure
Supplement. — c1980 (Hyderabad, A.P. : Print. Group of the Pilot Map Production Plant, Survey of India). — 1 atlas (xxi p., 40 leaves of plates)

NATURAL RESOURCES — Malaysia

AIKEN, S. Robert
Development and environment in peninsular Malaysia / S. Robert Aiken...[et al.]. — Singapore ; New York : McGraw-Hill International, 1982. — xx,310p. — (McGraw-Hill Southeast Asia series). — Bibliography: p283-301

NATURAL RESOURCES — United States

Resources / Resources for the Future. — Washington, D.C. : Resources for the Future, 1986-. — Quarterly

NATURAL RESOURCES — United States — Management

NOTHDURFT, William E
Renewing America : natural resource assets and state economic development / William E. Nothdurft. — Washington, D.C. : Council of State Planning Agencies, c1984. — xii, 198 p.. — (Studies in renewable resource policy). — Includes index. — Bibliography: p. 181-189

NATURAL SELECTION

DAWKINS, Richard
The blind watchmaker / Richard Dawkins. — Harlow : Longman Scientific & Technical, 1986. — [336]p. — Includes bibliography and index

NATURALISM

LINCOLN, Yvonna S
Naturalistic inquiry / Yvonna S. Lincoln, Egon G. Guba. — Beverly Hills, Calif. : Sage Publications, c1984. — 416p. — Includes index. — Bibliography: p.393-408

SELLARS, Wilfrid
Naturalism and ontology / Wilfrid Sellars. — Reseda, Calif. : Ridgeview, 1979. — viii, 182p. — A revised and expanded version of the John Dewey lectures given at the University of Chicago in May 1974

NATURALISTS — England — Biography

GRUBER, Howard E
Darwin on man : a psychological study of scientific creativity / Howard E. Gruber ; foreword to the 1st ed. by Jean Piaget. — 2d ed. — Chicago : University of Chicago Press, 1981. — xxvii, 310 p.. — First ed., published in 1974, entered under title: Darwin on man. — Includes bibliographical references and index

NATURE

WILLEY, Basil
The eighteenth century background studies on the idea of nature in the thought of the period / Basil Willey. — London : Chatto & Windus, 1940. — viii,302p

NATURE (AESTHETICS)

Landscape meanings and values / edited by Edmund C. Penning-Rowsell, and David Lowenthal. — London : Allen & Unwin, 1986. — [160]p. — Conference proceedings. — Includes bibliography and index

NATURE AND NURTURE

SCHIFF, Michel
Education and class : the irrelevance of IQ genetic studies / Michel Schiff, Richard Lewontin with contributions from A. Dumaret ... [et al.]. — Oxford : Clarendon, 1986. — xxiii,243p. — (Oxford science publications). — Bibliography: p228-236 Includes index

NATURE CONSERVATION — England — Somerset

NATURE CONSERVANCY COUNCIL. South West Region
The Somerset wetlands project : report by a working party. — [S.l.] : the Council, 1977. — 22leaves. — Cover title: The Somerset wetlands project; a consultation paper

NATURE CONSERVANCY COUNCIL. South West Region
The Somerset wetlands project : summary of responses to the consultation paper. — [s.l.] : the Council, 1978. — 16p

NATURE CONSERVATION — France

SMITH, Malcolm
Agriculture and nature conservation in conflict : the less favoured areas of France and the UK / by Malcolm Smith. — Langholm : The Arkleton Trust, 1985. — viii,110p. — Bibliography: p105-106

NATURE CONSERVATION — Great Britain

ADAMS, W. M.
Nature's place : conservation sites and countryside change / W.M. Adams. — London : Allen & Unwin, 1986. — [160p]. — Includes bibliography and index

NATURE CONSERVANCY COUNCIL
Nature conservation in Great Britain : summary of objectives and strategy / Nature Conservancy Council. — Shrewsbury : NCC, 1984

NATURE CONSERVANCY COUNCIL
Nature conservation in Great Britain / Nature Conservancy Council. — Shrewsbury : NCC, 1984

SMITH, Malcolm
Agriculture and nature conservation in conflict : the less favoured areas of France and the UK / by Malcolm Smith. — Langholm : The Arkleton Trust, 1985. — viii,110p. — Bibliography: p105-106

TYLDESLEY, David
Gaining momentum : an analysis of the role and performance of local authorities in nature conservation / David Tyldesley. — Oxford : Published by Pisces Publications ... for the British Association of Nature Conservationists, 1986. — 96p. — Report commisioned by the British Association of Nature Conservationists and sponsored by the World Wildlife Fund

NATURE CONSERVATION — Law and legislation — Great Britain

ADAMS, W. M.
Nature's place : conservation sites and countryside change / W.M. Adams. — London : Allen & Unwin, 1986. — [160p]. — Includes bibliography and index

NATURE CONSERVATION — Wales — West Glamorgan

WEST GLAMORGAN. County Council
Our countryside : what are the issues?. — Swansea : [the Council], 1975. — 31p

NAVAHO INDIANS — Art

WITHERSPOON, Gary
Language and art in the Navajo universe / Gary Witherspoon. — Ann Arbor : University of Michigan Press, c1977. — xviii, 214 p., [2] leaves of plates. — Includes index. — Bibliography: p. 207-210

NAVAHO INDIANS — Philosophy
WITHERSPOON, Gary
Language and art in the Navajo universe / Gary Witherspoon. — Ann Arbor : University of Michigan Press, c1977. — xviii, 214 p., [2] leaves of plates. — Includes index. — Bibliography: p. 207-210

NAVAHO LANGUAGE
WITHERSPOON, Gary
Language and art in the Navajo universe / Gary Witherspoon. — Ann Arbor : University of Michigan Press, c1977. — xviii, 214 p., [2] leaves of plates. — Includes index. — Bibliography: p. 207-210

NAVAJO INDIANS — Economic conditions
WEISS, Lawrence David
The development of capitalism in the Navajo nation : a political-economic history / by Lawrence David Weiss. — Minneapolis : MEP Publications, c1984. — 180 p. — (Studies in Marxism ; vol. 15). — Includes index. — Bibliography: p. 159-175

NAVAL ART AND SCIENCE — History
DELBRÜCK, Hans
History of the art of war : within the framework of political history / by Hans Delbrück ; translated from the German by Walter J. Renfroe, Jr. — Westport, Conn. ; London : Greenwood. — 1985. — Translation of: Geschichte der Kriegskunst in Rahmen der politschen Geschichte. — Includes index Vol.4: The modern era. — xi,487p. — (Contributions in military history ; no.39)

NAVAL HISTORIANS — Great Britain — Biography
HUNT, Barry D.
Sailor-scholar : Admiral Sir Herbert Richmond 1871-1946 / Barry D. Hunt. — Waterloo, Ont. : Wilfred Laurier University Press ; Gerrards Cross : distributed by Smythe, c1982. — xii,259p. — Bibliography: p238-248. — Includes index

NAVIGATION — Channel Islands — History
A people of the sea : the maritime history of the Channel Islands / edited by A.G. Jamieson. — London : Methuen, 1986. — xxxvi, 528p, [41]p of plates (some col.). — Includes index. — Bibliography: p.[482]-502

NAVIGATION — United States — Bibliography
KINNELL, Susan K
American maritime history : a bibliography / Susan K. Kinnell, Susanne R. Ontiveros, editors. — Santa Barbara, Calif. : ABC-Clio, c1986. — x, 260 p. — (ABC-Clio research guides ; 17). — Includes indexes

NAXALITE MOVEMENT
PANDEY, Sachchidanand
Naxal violence : a socio-political study / Sachchidanand Pandey. — Delhi : Chanakya Publications, 1985. — vi,156p. — Bibliography: p144-153

SAMANTA, Amiya K.
Left extremist movement in West Bengal : an experiment in armed agrarian struggle / Amiya K. Samanta. — Calcutta : Firma KLM, 1984. — x,361p. — Bibliography: 329-348

NEAR EAST — Boundaries
BAYLSON, Joshua C.
Territorial allocation by imperial rivalry : the human legacy in the Near East / by Joshua C. Baylson. — Chicago, Ill. : University of Chicago, Dept. of Geography, 1987. — p. cm. — (Research paper / The University of Chicago, Department of Geography ; no. 221). — Includes index. — Bibliography: p

NEAR EAST — Commerce
Middle Eastern exports : problems and prospects / edited by Rodney Wilson. — [Durham] : University of Durham Centre for Middle Eastern and Islamic Studies, c1986. — 119p. — (Occasional papers series ; no.29)

NEAR EAST — Commerce — Great Britain
SHIMIZU, Hiroshi
Anglo-Japanese trade rivalry in the Middle East in the inter-war period / by Hiroshi Shimizu. — London : Published for The Middle East Centre, St. Antony's College, Oxford by Ithaca Press, 1986. — [302]p. — (St. Antony's Middle East monographs ; no.17) . — Includes bibliography and index

NEAR EAST — Commerce — Japan
SHIMIZU, Hiroshi
Anglo-Japanese trade rivalry in the Middle East in the inter-war period / by Hiroshi Shimizu. — London : Published for The Middle East Centre, St. Antony's College, Oxford by Ithaca Press, 1986. — [302]p. — (St. Antony's Middle East monographs ; no.17) . — Includes bibliography and index

NEAR EAST — Economic policy
Food, states, and peasants : analyses of the agrarian question in the Middle East / edited by Alan Richards. — Boulder : Westview Press, 1986. — p. cm. — (Westview special studies on the Middle East). — Includes index

NEAR EAST — Emigration and immigration
ABBASI, Nasreen
Socio-economic effects of international migration on the families left behind / Nasreen Abbasi [and] Mohammad Irfan. — Islamabad : Pakistan Institute of Development Economics, 1986. — 42p. — (Studies in population, labour force and migration project report ; no.7)

SARMAD, Khwaja
Pakistani migration to the Middle East countries / Khwaja Sarmad. — Islamabad : Pakistan Institute of Development Economics, 1985. — 48p. — (Studies in population, labour force and migration project report ; no.9). — Bibliography: p48-49

NEAR EAST — Foreign relations
ISMAEL, Tareq Y
International relations of the contemporary Middle East : a study in world politics / Tareq Y. Ismael. — 1st ed. — Syracuse, N.Y. : Syracuse University Press, 1986. — p. cm. — (Contemporary issues in the Middle East). — Includes index. — Bibliography: p

The Powers in the Middle East : the ultimate strategic arena / edited by Bernard Reich. — New York : Praeger, 1986. — p. cm. — Includes index. — Bibliography: p

NEAR EAST — Foreign relations — Europe
GREAT BRITAIN. Parliament. House of Commons. Library. International Affairs Section
Western Europe and the Palestinian question / Richard War. — [London] : the Library, 1981. — 29p. — (Background paper / House of Commons. Library. [Research Division] ; no.94). — Bibliography: p24

NEAR EAST — Foreign relations — Great Britain
SHUCKBURGH, Sir Evelyn
Descent to Suez : diaries, 1951-56 / Evelyn Shuckburgh ; selected for publication by John Charmley. — London : Weidenfeld and Nicolson, 1986. — x,380p,[12]p of plates

NEAR EAST — Foreign relations — Lebanon
NASRALLAH, Fida Bahige
The Lebanese crisis : historical roots and contemporary international forces, 1958-1983 / Fida Bahige Nasrallah. — 407 leaves. — PhD (Econ) 1986 LSE

SAYEGH, Raymond
Les conflits dans les zones de crise : le Proche-Orient et le Liban : essai de polémologie, de géopolitique et de sociologie / Raymond Sayegh. — Cousset, Switzerland : Delval, 1986. — 260p. — Bibliography: p259-260

NEAR EAST — Foreign relations — Soviet Union
Soviet-American relations with Pakistan, Iran and Afghanistan / edited by Hafeez Malik. — Basingstoke : Macmillan, 1986. — [480]p. — Includes index

NEAR EAST — Foreign relations — United States
CHADDA, Maya
Paradox of power : the United States in Southwest Asia, 1973-1984 / Maya Chadda ; foreword by Afaf Mansot. — Santa Barbara, Calif. : ABC-CLIO, c1986. — xvi, 278 p.. — Includes index. — Bibliography: p. 259-265

LATTER, Richard
The making of American foreign policy in the Middle East, 1945-1948 / Richard Latter. — New York : Garland, 1986. — 463 p.. — (Outstanding theses from the London School of Economics and Political Science). — Thesis (Ph. D.)--University of London, 1976. — Bibliography: p. 457-463

Soviet-American relations with Pakistan, Iran and Afghanistan / edited by Hafeez Malik. — Basingstoke : Macmillan, 1986. — [480]p. — Includes index

STIVERS, William
America's confrontation with revolutionary change in the Middle East 1948-83 / William Stivers. — London : Macmillan, 1986. — [208]p. — Includes index

NEAR EAST — Historical geography
BAYLSON, Joshua C.
Territorial allocation by imperial rivalry : the human legacy in the Near East / by Joshua C. Baylson. — Chicago, Ill. : University of Chicago, Dept. of Geography, 1987. — p. cm. — (Research paper / The University of Chicago, Department of Geography ; no. 221). — Includes index. — Bibliography: p

NEAR EAST — History — 20th century
BAYLSON, Joshua C.
Territorial allocation by imperial rivalry : the human legacy in the Near East / by Joshua C. Baylson. — Chicago, Ill. : University of Chicago, Dept. of Geography, 1987. — p. cm. — (Research paper / The University of Chicago, Department of Geography ; no. 221). — Includes index. — Bibliography: p

NEAR EAST — Military relations — Soviet Union
KARSH, Efraim
The cautious bear : Soviet military engagement in Middle East wars in the post-1967 era / Ephraim [i.e. Efraim] Karsh. — Jerusalem, Israel : Published for the Jaffee Center for Strategic Studies by the Jerusalem Post ; Boulder, Colo. : Westview Press, c1985. — 97 p.. — (JCSS study ; no. 3). — Bibliography: p. 91-97

NEAR EAST — Nationalism
Nationalism and modernity : a Mediterranean perspective / edited by Joseph Alpher. — New York : Praeger, 1986. — vii, 143 p. — At head of title: Reuben Hecht Chair of Zionism and Jewish Political Thought. — "University of Haifa.". — Outgrowth of two seminars held at the University of Haifa in 1984 and 1985. — Includes bibliographies and index. — Contents: Introduction / Joseph Alpher -- State, nation, and religion / Hugh Seton-Watson -- State, nation, and religion in Islam / Bernard Lewis -- Will Israel ever become a nation? / Joseph Agassi -- Power or spirit : Jewish political thought in interbellum Europe / Paul Mendes-Flohr -- Zionism, marginality, and cosmopolitan centralism / Dan V. Segre -- The international information revolution / Harlan Cleveland -- Language and nation : the Italian case / Sergio Romano -- Language and nation : the case of Arabic / Emmanuel Sivan -- Language conflict and national identity : a semiotic approach / Itamar Even-Zohar

NEAR EAST — Politics and government

KLIEMAN, Aaron S.
Israel, Jordan, Palestine : the search for a durable peace / Aaron S. Klieman. — Beverly Hills ; London : Sage Publications for the Center for Strategic and International Studies, 1981. — 96p. — (Washington papers ; 83). — *Bibliography: p95-96*

Merip reports / Middle East Research and Information Project. — New York : Middle East Research and Information Project, 1976-. — *Monthly*

National and international politics in the Middle East : essays in honour of Elie Kedourie / edited by Edward Ingram. — London : Cass, 1986. — xviii,284p. — *Includes index*

Nonviolent struggle in the Middle East. — Santa Cruz, Calif. : New Society Publishers, 1983. — 39p. — *Contents: The Druze of the Golan: a case of nonviolent resistance/ R. Scott Kennedy - Nonviolent resistance: a strategy for the occupied territories/ Mubarak E. Awad*

TAHERI, Amir
Holy terror : The inside story of Islamic terrorism / Amir Taheri. — London : Hutchinson, 1987. — 313p. — *Spine title: Holy terror: Islamic terrorism and the West. — Bibliography: p[295]-301*

NEAR EAST — Politics and government — 1945-

GREAT BRITAIN. Parliament. House of Commons. Library. International Affairs Section
The search for peace and stability in the Middle East / Richard Ware. — [London] : the Library, 1986. — 23p. — (Background paper / House of Commons. Library. [Research Division] ; no.187)

ISMAEL, Tareq Y
International relations of the contemporary Middle East : a study in world politics / Tareq Y. Ismael. — 1st ed. — Syracuse, N.Y. : Syracuse University Press, 1986. — p. cm. — (Contemporary issues in the Middle East). — *Includes index. — Bibliography: p*

MILLER, Aaron David
The Arab states and the Palestine question : between ideology and self-interest / Aaron David Miller ; foreword by Alfred A. Atherton. — New York : Praeger Published with the Center for Strategic and International Studies, Georgetown University, Washington, D.C., c1986. — p. cm. — (The Washington papers ; 120). — *"Praeger special studies. Praeger scientific."*

The Powers in the Middle East : the ultimate strategic arena / edited by Bernard Reich. — New York : Praeger, 1986. — p. cm. — *Includes index. — Bibliography: p*

Shi'ism, resistance and revolution / edited by Martin Kramer. — London : Mansell, 1987. — [352]p. — *Conference proceedings. — Includes index*

NEAR EAST — Social conditions

Forbidden agendas : intolerance and defiance in the Middle East / selected and introduced by Jon Rothschild. — London : Al Saqi Books ; London : Zed Press [distributor], 1984. — 400p. — *" The articles in this anthology were first published in the journal 'Khamsin' 1976-83"*

NEAR EAST — Statistics — Bibliography

BLEANEY, C. H.
Official publications on the Middle East : a selective guide to the statistical sources / C. H. Bleaney. — [London] : Middle East Libraries Committee, 1985. — 31p. — (Middle East Libraries Committee research guides ; 1)

NEAR EAST — Strategic aspects

MEIR, Shemuel
Strategic implications of the new oil reality / Shemuel Meir. — Boulder : Westview Press for Jaffee Center for Strategic Studies, Tel Aviv University, 1986. — 107p. — (JCSS study ; No.4)

NEGATIVE INCOME TAX — Great Britain

LENKOWSKY, Leslie
Politics, economics, and welfare reform : the failure of the negative income tax in Britain and the United States / Leslie Lenkowsky. — Lanham, MD : University Press of America ; [Washington, D.C.] : American Enterprise Institute for Public Policy Research, c1986. — vii, 207 p.. — *Bibliography: p. 195-206*

NEGATIVE INCOME TAX — United States

LENKOWSKY, Leslie
Politics, economics, and welfare reform : the failure of the negative income tax in Britain and the United States / Leslie Lenkowsky. — Lanham, MD : University Press of America ; [Washington, D.C.] : American Enterprise Institute for Public Policy Research, c1986. — vii, 207 p.. — *Bibliography: p. 195-206*

NEGLIGENCE — England

JACKSON, Rupert M.
Professional negligence / by Rupert M. Jackson and John L. Powell. — 2nd ed. — London : Sweet & Maxwell, 1987. — xlvii,472p. — 2nd ed. — *Previous ed.: 1982. — Includes index*

NEGOTIATION — Mathematical models

The Economics of bargaining / edited by Ken Binmore and Partha Dasgupta. — Oxford : Basil Blackwell, 1987. — 260p. — *Includes bibliographies and index*

NEGOTIATION — Psychological aspects

PRUITT, Dean G.
The effect of time pressure, time elapsed, and the opponent's concession rate on behavior in negotiation / by Dean G. Pruitt and Julie Latané Drews. — Buffalo, N.Y. : State University of New York, Department of Psychology, 1967. — 40 leaves. — (Technical report / State University of New York, Department of Psychology ; no.3). — *Spine title: Behavior in negotiation*

NEGOTIATION IN BUSINESS — Japan

MCCREARY, Don R
Japanese-U.S. business negotiations : a cross-cultural study / Don R. McCreary. — New York : Praeger, 1986. — viii, 121 p.. — *"Praeger special studies. Praeger scientific.". — Includes index. — Bibliography: p. 109-115*

NEGOTIATION IN BUSINESS — United States

MCCREARY, Don R
Japanese-U.S. business negotiations : a cross-cultural study / Don R. McCreary. — New York : Praeger, 1986. — viii, 121 p.. — *"Praeger special studies. Praeger scientific.". — Includes index. — Bibliography: p. 109-115*

NEGOTIORUM GESTIO — South Africa — History

VAN ZYL, D. H.
Negotiorum gestio in South African law : an historical and comparative analysis / by D. H. Van Zyl. — Durban ; London : Butterworths, 1985. — viii,238p. — *Bibliography: p202-233*

NEGROES — Addresses, essays, lectures

BLAUNER, Robert
Racial oppression in America / Robert Blauner. — New York ; London : Harper and Row, 1972. — x,309p. — *Includes index*

NEHRU, JAWAHARLAL

NEHRU, Jawaharlal
Jawaharlal Nehru : an anthology / edited by Sarvepalli Gopal. — Delhi ; Oxford : Oxford University Press, 1983. — xxi,662p. — *Includes index*

NEHRU, Jawaharlal
Jawaharlal Nehru : la promesse tenue / avant-propos de Rajiv Gandhi... ; anthologie traduite et présentée par Monique Morazé avec la collaboration de Georges Frémont. — Paris : Editions de l'Harmattan, 1986. — 344p

NEHRU, Jawaharlal
Selected works of Jawaharlal Nehru. — New Delhi : Jawaharlal Nehru Memorial Fund Series 2
Vol.3. — 1985. — 521p

PRASAD, Bimal
Gandhi, Nehru & J. P. : studies in leadership / Bimal Prasad. —, Delhi : Chanakya Publications, 1985. — 294p. — *Bibliography: p283-287*

NEHRU, JAWAHARLAL — Correspondence

NEHRU, Jawaharlal
Letters to chief ministers, 1947-1964 / Jawaharlal Nehru ; general editor, G. Parthasarathi. — Delhi : Distributed by Oxford University Press, 1985-. — v. <1 >. — *"A project of the Jawaharlal Nehru Memorial Fund"--T.p. verso. — Includes index. — Contents: v. 1. 1947-1949*

NEIGHBORHOOD — Michigan — Detroit — Case studies

HUCKFELDT, R. Robert
Politics in context : assimilation and conflict in urban neighborhoods / Robert Huckfeldt. — New York : Agathon Press, c1986. — viii, 191 p.. — *Includes index. — Bibliography: p. 177-185*

NEIGHBORHOOD — New York (State) — Buffalo — Case studies

HUCKFELDT, R. Robert
Politics in context : assimilation and conflict in urban neighborhoods / Robert Huckfeldt. — New York : Agathon Press, c1986. — viii, 191 p.. — *Includes index. — Bibliography: p. 177-185*

NEIGHBORHOOD — United States

VARADY, David P
Neighborhood upgrading : a realistic assessment / David P. Varady. — Albany : State University of New York Press, c1986. — p. cm. — (SUNY series on urban public policy). — *Includes index. — Bibliography: p*

NEIGHBORHOOD — United States — Case studies

WILLIAMS, Michael R.
Neighborhood organizations : seeds of a new urban life / Michael R. Williams. — Westport, Conn. : Greenwood Press, 1985. — xiii, 278 p.. — (Contributions in political science ; no. 131). — *Includes index. — Bibliography: p. [261]-269*

NEIGHBORHOOD GOVERNMENT — Ohio — Cincinnati

THOMAS, John Clayton
Between citizen and city : neighborhood organizations and urban politics in Cincinnati / John Clayton Thomas. — Lawrence : University Press of Kansas, c1986. — xii, 196 p.. — (Studies in government and public policy). — *Includes index. — Bibliography: p. 179-188*

NEIGHBORHOOD GOVERNMENT — United States

ZIMMERMAN, Joseph Francis
Participatory democracy : populism revived / Joseph F. Zimmerman. — New York : Praeger, 1986. — xi, 229 p.. — *Bibliography: p. 185-221*

NEIGHBORHOOD JUSTICE CENTERS — Delaware

BEER, Jennifer E.
Peacemaking in your neighborhood : reflections on an experiment in community mediation / Jennifer E. Beer ; foreword by Elise Boulding. — Philadelphia, Pa. : New Society, 1986. — [viii],245p. — *Bibliography: p[235]-245*

NEIGHBORHOOD JUSTICE CENTERS — United States
HARRINGTON, Christine B
Shadow justice : the ideology and institutionalization of alternatives to court / Christine B. Harrington. — Westport, Conn. : Greenwood Press, c1985. — p. cm. — (Contributions in political science ; no. 133). — Includes index. — Bibliography: p

NEIGHBORLINESS — London
WILLMOTT, Peter, 1923-
Friendship networks and social support / Peter Willmott. — London : Policy Studies Institute, 1987. — vii,115p. — (PSI research report ; no.666). — Bibliographies

NEKRASOV, N. A.
EMEL'IANOV, N. P.
"Otechestvennye zapiski" N. A. Nekrasova i M. E. Saltykova-Shchedrina (1868-1884) / N. P. Emel'ianov. — Leningrad : Khudozhestvennaia literatura, Leningradskoe otdelenie, 1986. — 333p

NEOCLASSICAL SCHOOL OF ECONOMICS
BRIDEL, Pascal
Cambridge monetary thought : the development of saving-investment analysis from Marshall to Keynes / Pascal Bridel. — Basingstoke : Macmillan, 1987. — x,227p. — (Studies in political economy). — Bibliography: p212-221. — Includes index

Current controversies in economics / edited by Howard Vane and Terry Caslin. — Oxford : Basil Blackwell, 1987. — xii,319p. — Includes bibliographies and index

HSIEH, Ching-Yao
A search for synthesis in economic theory / by Ching-Yao Hsieh and Stephen L. Mangum. — Armonk, N.Y. : M.E. Sharpe, c1986. — p. cm. — Bibliography: p

NEOPLASMS — history
RUSHEFSKY, Mark R.
Making cancer policy / Mark R. Rushefsky. — Albany : State University of New York Press, c1986. — xiii, 257 p.. — (SUNY series in public administration in the 1980s). — Includes index. — Bibliography: p. 225-245

NEPAL — Census, 1981
Intercensal changes of some key census variables : Nepal 1952/54-81. — Kathmandu : Central Bureau of Statistics, [1985]. — [vii],127p. — Presented at "Data Users' Meeting" held in Kathmandu, 4-5 March, 1985. — Bibliographical references: p124

Intercensal changes of some key census variables : Nepal 1952/54-81. — Kathmandu : Central Bureau of Statistics Vol.2. — [1986]. — [iv],p.129-183p

Population census-1981 : Nepal. — Kathmandu : Central Bureau of Statistics, 1984. — 4v in 10 parts. — Contents: Vol.1 Development region, zones and district tables - v.2. Geographic region tables - v.3. Urban area tables - v.4. Household characteristics tables

NEPAL — Economic conditions
POUDYAL, Sriram
Impact of foreign aid on Nepal's development / Sriram Poudyal. — Kathmandu : Tribhuvan University. Centre for Economic Development and Administration, 1983. — 58p. — Bibliography: p[59]

NEPAL — Economic conditions — Statistics
Census of manufacturing establishments : Nepal : 1981-1982. — Kathmandu : Central Bureau of Statistics, [1985]. — iii,83p

NEPAL — Economic policy
AMATYA, Daman B
Nepal's fiscal issues : new challenges / D.B. Amatya. — New Delhi : Sterling Publishers, c1986. — xiv, 205 p. — Includes index. — Bibliography: p. [192]-202

Basic principles of the seventh plan, 1985-1990. — Kathmandu : National Planning Commission, 1984. — 75p. — Unofficial translation from original Nepali text

JHA, Hari Bansh
Resource mobilisation and economic development in Nepal during the plan period / by Hari Bansh Jha. — Allahabad : Kitab Mahal, 1984. — xiv,199p. — Revision of author's thesis (PhD: University of Bihar). — Bibliography: p[184]-199

Policy approaches to development issues : a review of Nepal's relation with ESCAP along with policy statements of Nepalese delegations since its thirteenth session / edited by Rabindra K. Shakya. — Kathmandu : National Planning Commission Secretariat, 1983. — [iv],68p

The seventh plan : 1985-1990. — [Kathmandu] : National Planning Commission, 1985. — ix,919p

SVEJNAR, Jan
Economic policies and agricultural performance : the case of Nepal, 1960-1982 / Jan Svejnar and Erik Thorbecke. — Paris : Development Centre of the Organisation for Economic Co-operation and Development, 1986. — 167p. — (Development Centre papers). — Bibliography: p129-131

NEPAL — Economic policy — Bibliography
Population and development in Nepal : an annotated bibliography / edited by Prabha Thacker. — Kathmandu : National Commission on Population, 1984. — vii,99p

NEPAL — Foreign relations — China
HUSAIN, Asad
Conflict in Asia : a case study of Nepal / Asad Husain, Asifa Anwar ; foreword by Q. Ahmad. — New Delhi : Classical Publications, 1979. — x, 88 p.. — Includes bibliographical references and index

NEPAL — Foreign relations — India
HUSAIN, Asad
Conflict in Asia : a case study of Nepal / Asad Husain, Asifa Anwar ; foreword by Q. Ahmad. — New Delhi : Classical Publications, 1979. — x, 88 p.. — Includes bibliographical references and index

NEPAL — Industries
MAHAT, R. S
Capital market, financial flows, and industrial finance in Nepal / R.S. Mahat. — 1st ed. — Lalitpur : Sajha Prakashan, 1981. — xvi, 350 p.. — Bibliography: p. 335-346

NEPAL — Industries — Statistics
Census of manufacturing establishments : Nepal : 1981-1982. — Kathmandu : Central Bureau of Statistics, [1985]. — iii,83p

NEPAL — Politics and government
SHARAN, Parmatma
Government and politics of Nepal / by P. Sharan. — 1st. ed. — New Delhi : Metropolitan, 1983 [i.e. 1982]. — viii, 149 p.. — Includes bibliographical references

NEPAL — Population
PANT, Yadav Prasad
Population growth and employment opportunities in Nepal / Y.P. Pant. — New Delhi : Oxford & IBH, c1983. — viii, 131 p.. — Includes index. — Bibliography: p. [124]-126

NEPAL — Population — Bibliography
Population and development in Nepal : an annotated bibliography / edited by Prabha Thacker. — Kathmandu : National Commission on Population, 1984. — vii,99p

NEPAL — Population — Statistics
Intercensal changes of some key census variables : Nepal 1952/54-81. — Kathmandu : Central Bureau of Statistics, [1985]. — [vii],127p. — Presented at "Data Users' Meeting" held in Kathmandu, 4-5 March, 1985. — Bibliographical references: p124

Intercensal changes of some key census variables : Nepal 1952/54-81. — Kathmandu : Central Bureau of Statistics Vol.2. — [1986]. — [iv],p.129-183p

Population census-1981 : Nepal. — Kathmandu : Central Bureau of Statistics, 1984. — 4v in 10 parts. — Contents: Vol.1 Development region, zones and district tables - v.2. Geographic region tables - v.3. Urban area tables - v.4. Household characteristics tables

NEPAL — Social policy
Basic principles of the seventh plan, 1985-1990. — Kathmandu : National Planning Commission, 1984. — 75p. — Unofficial translation from original Nepali text

The seventh plan : 1985-1990. — [Kathmandu] : National Planning Commission, 1985. — ix,919p

NEPAL — Statistics
NEPAL. Central Bureau of Statistics
Statistical pocket book: Nepal. — Kathmandu : [the Bureau], 1984-. — Irregular

NEPAL — Economic policy
GURUNG, Harka B
Nepal, dimensions of development / Harka Gurung. — Kathmandu : Sahayogi Press, 1984. — 275 p.. — Includes index. — Bibliography: p. [257]-269

NERVOUS SYSTEM — Illnesses
PARK, Bert Edward
The impact of illness on world leaders / Bert Edward Park. — Philadelphia : University of Pennsylvania Press, 1986. — p. cm. — Includes bibliographies and index

NETHERLANDS — Bibliography
KREWSON, Margrit B.
The Netherlands : a selective bibliography of reference works / Margrit B. Krewson. — Washington, D.C. : Library of Congress, 1986. — vii,42p. — Supt. of Docs. no.: LC 1.12/2:N38

NETHERLANDS — Constitution
NETHERLANDS. Ministerie van Justitie. Wetenschappelijk Onderzoek-en Dokumentatie Centrum
Constitution, justice. — [The Hague : Research and Documentation Centre, Ministry of Justice, 1986?]. — 66p. — Contents: State administration, justice. — Reprint of 1972 edition

NETHERLANDS — Constitutional law
NETHERLANDS. Ministerie van Justitie. Wetenschappelijk Onderzoek-en Dokumentatie Centrum
Constitution, justice. — [The Hague : Research and Documentation Centre, Ministry of Justice, 1986?]. — 66p. — Contents: State administration, justice. — Reprint of 1972 edition

NETHERLANDS — Economic conditions — 1945-
Macht : versslagboek van het congres politiek-economisch netwerk in Nederland gehouden woensdag 19 januari 1972 in de tweede kamer. — [s.l.] : De Nieuwe Linie, [1972]. — 80p

A profile of Dutch economic geography / edited by Marc de Smidt and Egbert Wever. — Assen : Van Gorcum, 1984. — ix,201p. — Includes bibliographies

WETENSCHAPPELIJKE RAAD VOOR HET REGERINGSBELEID
A policy-oriented survey of the future : towards a better perspective : summary of the twenty-fifth report to the government. — The Hague : Netherlands Scientific Council for Government Policy, [1983?]. — 80p. — English translation of: Beleidsgerichte toekomstverkenning: een verruiming van perspectief. — Bibliography: p76-80

NETHERLANDS — Economic conditions — 1945- — Statistics

De produktie-structuur van de Nederlandse volkshuishouding. — 's-Gravenhage : Staatsuitgeverij. — *Title on back cover: The production structure of the Netherlands' economy: Part 8: Production structure and aspects of selective growth*
Deel 8: Produktiestructuur en Jacetten van selectieve groei. — 's-Gravenhage : Staatsuitgeverij. — 73p. — *Title on back cover: The production structure of the Netherlands' economy: Part 8: Production structure and aspects of selective growth*

Vierde algemene bedrijfstelling 1978. — 's-Gravenhage : Staatsuitgeverij. — *Title on back cover: Fourth general economic census 1978: volume 3: part C: results of West Netherlands*
C: Landsdeel west. — 1986
d.3: Algemene regionale gegevens. — 118p

Vierde algemene bedrijfstelling 1978. — 's-Gravenhage : Staatsuitgeverij. — *Title on back cover: Fourth general economic census 1978: volume 3: part D: results of Southwest and South Netherlands*
D: Landsdelen zuidwest en zuid. — 1986
d.3: Algemene regionale gegevens. — 110p

Vierde algemene bedrijfstelling, 1978. — 's-Gravenhage : Staatsuigeverij. — *Rear cover title: Fourth general economic census, 1978: volume 3, general results by region*
d.3: Algemene regionale gegevens. — 1985. — 186p

NETHERLANDS — Economic conditions — 1945- — Statistics — Methodology

Vierde algemene bedrijfstelling, 1978. — 's-Gravenhage : Staatsuitgeverij. — *In Dutch with contents list and summary in English. — Rear cover title: Fourth general economic census, 1978: volume 1: methodological introduction*
d.1: Methodologische inleiding. — 1985. — 106p

NETHERLANDS — Economic policy

Macht : versslagboek van het congres politiek-economisch netwerk in Nederland gehouden woensdag 19 januari 1972 in de tweede kamer. — [s.l.] : De Nieuwe Linie, [1972]. — 80p

WETENSCHAPPELIJKE RAAD VOOR HET REGERINGSBELEID
A policy-oriented survey of the future : towards a better perspective : summary of the twenty-fifth report to the government. — The Hague : Netherlands Scientific Council for Government Policy, [1983?]. — 80p. — *English translation of: Beleidsgerichte toekomstverkenning: een verruiming van perspectief. — Bibliography: p76-80*

NETHERLANDS — Emigration and immigration

BRAND-KOOLEN, M. J. M.
Migrants in detention / Maria Brand-Koolen. — The Hague : : Research and Documentation Centre, Ministry of Justice, 1985. — [32]p. — ([Reports, papers, articles] ; 81). — *Bibliography: p27-29*

JUNGER-TAS, J.
Young immigrants in the Netherlands and their contacts with the police / Josine Junger-Tas. — The Hague : Research and Documentation Centre, Ministry of Justice, 1985. — 21p. — ([Reports, papers, articles] ; 85a). — *Bibliography: p21*

WETENSCHAPPELIJKE RAAD VOOR HET REGERINGSBELEID
Buitenlandse invloeden op Nedeland : internationale migratie. — 's-Gravenhage : Staatsuitgeverij, 1976. — 39p. — (Rapporten aan de Regering / Wetenschappelijke Raad voor het Regeringsbeleid ; 7). — *Includes bibliographical references*

NETHERLANDS — Ethnic relations

MOORE, Bob
Refugees from Nazi Germany in the Netherlands, 1933-1940 / by Bob Moore. — Dordrecht ; Boston : M. Nijhoff, 1986. — xiv, 241 p.. — (Studies in social history ; 9). — *Includes index. — Bibliography: p. 221-233*

NETHERLANDS — Foreign economic relations — Germany (West)

WETENSCHAPPELIJKE RAAD VOOR HET REGERINGSBELEID
Faktor Deutschland : zur sensibilitat der Beziehungen zwischen den Niederlanden und der Bundesrepublik / Wissenschaftlicher Rat für die Regierungspolitik der Niederlande. — 's-Gravenhage ; Wiesbaden : Staatsuitgeverij : Steiner, 1984. — 242p. — (Berichte für die Regierung / Wissenschaftlicher Rat für die Regierungspolitik der Niederlande ; 23). — *In German. — Includes bibliographical references*

NETHERLANDS — Foreign relations — History

GEUS, P. B. R. de
De Nieuw-Guinea kwestie : aspecten van buitenlands beleid en militaire macht / P. B. R. de Geus. — Leiden : Martinus Nijhoff, 1984. — 249p. — *Bibliography: p242-245*

NETHERLANDS — Foreign relations — Brazil

STRAATEN, Harald S. van der
Brazil - a destiny : Dutch contacts through the ages. — The Hague : Government Publishing Office, 1984. — 164p. — (Ethnological serie "Verre naasten naderbij"). — *Bibliography: p163-164*

NETHERLANDS — Foreign relations — Indonesia — Sources

Officiële beschieden betreffende de Nederlands-Indonesische betrekkingen 1945-1950 / vitgegeven door P. J. Drooglever en M. J. B. Schouten. — s-Gravenhage : Nijhoff
Deel 13: 20 februari-4juni 1948. — 1986. — xxvii,878p. — (Rijks geschiedkundige publicatiën. Kleine serie ; 61)

NETHERLANDS — History — 1648-1795

SCHAMA, Simon, 1945-
The embarrassment of riches : an interpretation of Dutch culture in the golden age / Simon Schama. — London : Collins, 1987. — xiii,698p. — *Bibliography: p655-670. — Includes index*

NETHERLANDS — Industries — Statistics

De Produktie-structuur van de Nederlandse volkshuishouding / Centraal Bureau voor de Statistiek, Netherlands. — Voorburg : Centraal Bureau voor de Statistiek, 1960-. — *Irregular Annual from 1983*

NETHERLANDS — Manufactures — Statistics

Vierde algemene bedrijfstelling, 1978. — 's-Gravenhage : Staatsuitgeverij. — *Rear cover title: Fourth general economic census, 1978: volume 2, part A: mining and quarrying, manufacturing, public utilities, construction and installation on construction projects*
d.2: Algemene sectorale gegevens
A: Delfstoffenwinning, industrie, openbare nutsbedrijven, bouwnijverheid en bouwinstallatie. — 1985. — 87p

NETHERLANDS — Maps

Atlas van Nederland / Stichting wetenschappelijke Atlas van Nederland. — [2e uitg.]. — 's-Gravenhage : Staatsuitgeverij, 1984

NETHERLANDS — Politics and government — 1945-

Macht : versslagboek van het congres politiek-economisch netwerk in Nederland gehouden woensdag 19 januari 1972 in de tweede kamer. — [s.l.] : De Nieuwe Linie, [1972]. — 80p

PARTIJ VAN DE ARBEID
Verkiezingsprogramma van de Partij van de Arbeid voor de Tweede Kamerverkiezingen op 25 mei 1977. — [Amsterdam] : PvdA, 1977. — 94p. — *Cover-title : Voorwaarts...*

NETHERLANDS — Population — Forecasting

WETENSCHAPPELIJKE RAAD VOOR HET REGERINGSBELEID
Bevolkingprognoses. — 's-Gravenhage : Staatsuitgeverij, 1974. — [36]p. — (Rapporten aan de Regering / Wetenschappelijke Raad voor het Regeringsbeleid ; 5)

NETHERLANDS — Population — Statistics

Bevolking der gemeenden van Nederland. — Utrecht : Centraal Bureau voor de Statistik, 1944-. — *Annual*

NETHERLANDS — Population policy

NETHERLANDS. Stuurgroep Integraal Structuurplan Noorden des Lands
Het Noorden : een versterkte bevolkingsgroei? Of juist niet! : een bewerking van het rapport Bevolkingsaspecten Noorden des Lands / Samensteller R. Idenburg. — 's-Gravenhage : Staatsuitgeverij, 1974. — 21p

NETHERLANDS. Werkgroep Beleidsdoelstellingen Analyse Noorden
ISP : integraal structuurplan Noorden des lands : rapport van de Werkgroep Beleidsdoelstellingen Analyse Noorden. — [s-Gravenhage] : the Werkgroep
2. — 1974. — 27p

NETHERLANDS — Relations — Germany (West)

WETENSCHAPPELIJKE RAAD VOOR HET REGERINGSBELEID
Faktor Deutschland : zur sensibilitat der Beziehungen zwischen den Niederlanden und der Bundesrepublik / Wissenschaftlicher Rat für die Regierungspolitik der Niederlande. — 's-Gravenhage ; Wiesbaden : Staatsuitgeverij : Steiner, 1984. — 242p. — (Berichte für die Regierung / Wissenschaftlicher Rat für die Regierungspolitik der Niederlande ; 23). — *In German. — Includes bibliographical references*

NETHERLANDS — Social conditions

De Nederlandse verzorgingsstaat : terugblik en vooruitzien / onder redactie van W. S. P. Fortuyn ; met een ten geleide van L. de Graaf. — Deventer : Kluwer, 1983. — 178p

NETHERLANDS — Social conditions — 1945-

LOO, Hans van der
Een wenkend perspectief? : nieuwe sociale bewegingen en culturele veranderingen / Hans van der Loo, Erik Snel en Bart van Steenbergen. — Amersfoort : De Horstink, 1984. — 247p. — (Strategieën). — *Bibliography: p234-247*

NETHERLANDS — Social policy

De Nederlandse verzorgingsstaat : terugblik en vooruitzien / onder redactie van W. S. P. Fortuyn ; met een ten geleide van L. de Graaf. — Deventer : Kluwer, 1983. — 178p

NETHERLANDS — Statistical services

Netherlands official statistics / Netherlands Central Bureau of Statistics. — Voorburg/Heerlen : Netherlands Central Bureau of Statistics, 1986-. — *Quarterly*

NETHERLANDS — Statistics

Netherlands official statistics / Netherlands Central Bureau of Statistics. — Voorburg/Heerlen : Netherlands Central Bureau of Statistics, 1986-. — *Quarterly*

Statistiek werkzame personen / Centraal Bureau de Statistiek, Netherlands. — 's-gravenhage : Staatsuitgeverij, 1984-. — *Annual*

NETHERLANDS. Centraal Bureau voor de Statistiek

De Produktie-structuur van de Nederlandse volkshuishouding / Centraal Bureau voor de Statistiek, Netherlands. — Voorburg : Centraal Bureau voor de Statistiek, 1960-. — *Irregular Annual from 1983*

NETHERLANDS. Werkgroep Beleidsdoelstellingen Analyse Noorden

NETHERLANDS. Werkgroep Beleidsdoelstellingen Analyse Noorden ISP : integraal structuurplan Noorden des lands : rapport van de Werkgroep Beleidsdoelstellingen Analyse Noorden. — [s-Gravenhage] : the Werkgroep 2. — 1974. — 27p

NETHERLANDS. Werkgroep Bevolkingsaspecten Noorden des Lands

NETHERLANDS. Stuurgroep Integraal Structuurplan Noorden des Lands Het Noorden : een versterkte bevolkingsgroei? Of juist niet! : een bewerking van het rapport Bevolkingsaspecten Noorden des Lands / Samensteller R. Idenburg. — 's-Gravenhage : Staatsuitgeverij, 1974. — 21p

NETHERLANDS ANTILLES — Dictionaries and encyclopedias

GASTMANN, Albert L
Historical dictionary of the French and Netherlands Antilles / by Albert Gastmann. — Metuchen, N.J. : Scarecrow Press, 1978. — viii, 162 p.. — (Latin American historical dictionaries ; no. 18). — *Includes bibliographies*

NETO, AGOSTINHO — Biography

KHAZANOV, A. M.
Agostinho Neto / A. M. Khazanov ; translated from the Russian by Cynthia Carlile. — Moscow : Progress Publishers, 1986. — 302p

NETTLER, GWYNN — Congresses

Critique and explanation : essays in honor of Gwynne Nettler / edited by Timothy F. Hartnagel and Robert A. Silverman. — New Brunswick, U.S.A. : Transaction Books, c1986. — vii, 215 p.. — *Bibliography: p. 187-214*

NETWORK ANALYSIS — Transportation

MOSLER, Karl C.
Continuous location of transportation networks / K. C. Mosler. — Berlin ; London : Sringer-Verlag, 1987. — 158p. — *Bibliography: p143-153*

NEURASTHENIA — psychology

KLEINMAN, Arthur
Social origins of distress and disease : depression, neurasthenia, and pain in modern China / Arthur Kleinman. — New Haven : Yale University Press, c1986. — xii, 264 p.. — *Includes index. — Bibliography: p. 241-254*

NEURASTHENIA — Somatization — China

KLEINMAN, Arthur
Social origins of distress and disease : depression, neurasthenia, and pain in modern China / Arthur Kleinman. — New Haven : Yale University Press, c1986. — xii, 264 p.. — *Includes index. — Bibliography: p. 241-254*

NEUROLINGUISTICS

The Cognitive neuropsychology of language / edited by Max Coltheart, Giuseppe Sartori, Remo Job. — London : Erlbaum, c1987. — xiii,416p. — *Includes bibliographies and index*

NEUROLOGY — Philosophy

CHURCHLAND, Patricia Smith
Neurophilosophy : toward a unified science of the mind-brain / Patricia Smith Churchland. — Cambridge, Mass. ; London : MIT Press, 1986. — xi, 546p., [1] leaf of plates. — (Computational models of cognition and perception). — "A Bradford book.". — *Bibliography: p[491]-523. — Includes index*

NEUROPSYCHOLOGY

ARBIB, Michael A
In search of the person : philosophical explorations in cognitive science / Michael A. Arbib. — Amherst : University of Massachusetts, 1985. — xii, 156 p.. — *Includes index. — Bibliography: p. [137]-149*

NEUROPSYCHOLOGY — Philosophy

CHURCHLAND, Patricia Smith
Neurophilosophy : toward a unified science of the mind-brain / Patricia Smith Churchland. — Cambridge, Mass. ; London : MIT Press, 1986. — xi, 546p., [1] leaf of plates. — (Computational models of cognition and perception). — "A Bradford book.". — *Bibliography: p[491]-523. — Includes index*

NEUROSES

FREUD, Sigmund
[Übersicht der Übertragungsneurosen. English]. A phylogenetic fantasy : overview of the transference neuroses / Sigmund Freud ; edited and with an essay by Ilse Grubrich-Simitis ; translated by Axel Hoffer and Peter T. Hoffer. — Cambridge, Mass. : Belknap Press of Harvard University Press, 1987. — p. cm. — *Translation of: Übersicht der Übertragungsneurosen. — Bibliography: p*

WALLACE, Edwin R
Freud and anthropology : a history and reappraisal / Edwin R. Wallace, IV. — New York : International Universities Press, c1983. — xi, 306p. (Psychological issues ; monograph 55). — *Bibliography: p.281-294. — Includes index*

NEVADA — Politics and government

HOWARD, Anne Bail
The long campaign : a biography of Anne Martin / Anne Bail Howard. — Reno, Nevada : University of Nevada Press, c1985. — p. cm. — (Nevada studies in history and political science ; no. 20). — *Includes index. — Bibliography: p*

NEW BRUNSWICK — Commerce — Statistics

New Brunswick exports by commodity : 1970-1976. — [Fredericton?] : Office of the Economic Advisor, 1977. — ii,29 leaves

NEW BRUNSWICK. Department of Education — History

NEW BRUNSWICK. Department of Education
Two centuries of educational progress in New Brunswick : 1784-1984 = Deux siècles de progrès en éducation au Nouveau-Brunswick : 1784-1984. — [Moncton?] : the Department, [1985?]. — 30,30p. — *In English and French. — Bibliography: p30*

NEW BRUNSWICK. Legislative Assembly — Rules and practice

NEW BRUNSWICK. Legislative Assembly
Speakers' rulings : 1784-1984 = Décisions des orateurs : 1784-1984. — Fredericton : Office of the Clerk, Legislative Assembly, 1985. — 321,358p

NEW BUSINESS ENTERPRISES

SMILOR, Raymond W
The new business incubator : linking talent, technology, capital, and know-how / Raymond W. Smilor, Michael Doud Gill, Jr. — Lexington, Mass. : Lexington Books, c1986. — xiii, 199 p.. — *Includes index. — Bibliography: p. [183]-187*

NEW CALEDONIA — Economic conditions

Bulletin de conjoncture : Nouvelle Calédonie / Institut Territorial de la Statistique et des Études Économiques. — Nouméa : Institut Territorial de la Statistique et des Études Économiques, 1986-. — *Quarterly*

NEW CALEDONIA — Economic conditions — Statistics

Recensement général de l'agriculture 1983-1984. — Nouméa : Direction territoriale de la statistique et des études économiques t.1: Inventaires communaux. — [1986]. — 141,8p. — (Notes et documents / Direction territoriale de la statistique et des études économiques ; no.36-37)

Recensement général de l'agriculture 1983-1984. — Nouméa : Direction territoriale de la statistique et des études économiques. t.1 ter: Inventaires par région. — [1985]. — 29p. — (Notes et documents / Direction territoriale de la statistique et des études économiques ; no.38 Bis)

Recensement général de l'agriculture 1983-1984. — Nouméa : Institut territoriale de la statistique et des études économiques t.2: Résultats
Pt.1: Exploitations agricoles et productions animales. — [1986]. — 91p. — (Notes et documents / Institut territoriale de la statistique et des études économiques ; no.40)

NEW CALEDONIA — Population — Statistics

PORCHER, Robert
La population de la Nouvelle-Caledonie : résultats de l'année 1978 : estimation au 1er janvier 1980 : projections pour 1985 / par Robert Porcher et Laurance Villageois. — [Noumea?] : Service de la Statistique, 1980. — 67p. — (Notes et documents / Service de la Statistique ; no.4)

NEW DEAL, 1933-1939

LEUCHTENBURG, William Edward
Franklin D. Roosevelt and the New Deal, 1932-1940. — [1st ed.]. — New York : Harper & Row, [1963]. — 393 p. — (The New American Nation series). — *Includes bibliography*

MORGAN, Chester M
Redneck liberal : Theodore G. Bilbo and the New Deal / Chester M. Morgan. — Baton Rouge : Louisiana State University Press, c1985. — p. cm. — *Includes index. — Bibliography: p*

OHL, John Kennedy
Hugh S. Johnson and the New Deal / John Kennedy Ohl. — Dekalb, Ill. : Northern Illinois University Press, 1985. — xi, 374p. — *Includes index. — Bibliography: p.[345]-359*

NEW DEAL, 1933-1939 — Dictionaries

Historical dictionary of the new deal : from inauguration to preparation for war / edited by James S. Olson. — Westport, Conn. ; London : Greenwood Press, c1985. — viii, 611p. — *Includes index. — Bibliography: p.563-575*

NEW DEMOCRATIC PARTY

BRADLEY, Michael Anderson
Crisis of clarity : the New Democratic Party and the quest for the Holy Grail / by Michael Bradley. — Toronto : Summerhill Press ; Don Mills, Ont. : Distributed in Canada by Collier Macmillan Canada, c1985. — 222, [2] p.. — *Bibliography: p. 222-[224]*

NEW DEMOCRATIC PARTY — History — Congresses

"Building the Co-operative Commonwealth" : essays on the Democratic Socialist tradition in Canada / edited by J. William Brennan. — Regina : University of Regina, Canadian Plains Research Center, 1985. — xiii,255p. — (Canadian Plains proceedings ; 13). — "Based on papers delivered at the Regina Conference, June 23-25, 1983, commemorating the 50th anniversary of the Regina Manifesto". — *Includes references*

NEW DIRECTIONS FOR NEW BRUNSWICK: A CONFERENCE FOR WOMEN (Memramcook : 1974)
"NEW DIRECTIONS FOR NEW BRUNSWICK": A CONFERENCE FOR WOMEN (Memramcook : 1974)
A report on new directions for New Brunswick : a conference for women. — [Memramcook? : the Conference, [1974?]. — 3,3 leaves. — *Headings for workshops also given in French*

NEW ENGLAND — Church history
COHEN, Charles Lloyd
God's caress : the psychology of Puritan religious experience / Charles Lloyd Cohen. — New York : Oxford University Press, 1986. — p. cm. — *Includes index. — Bibliography: p*

NEW ENGLAND — Commerce — Canada
Trade and investment across the northeast boundary : Quebec, the Atlantic provinces, and New England / edited by William D. Shipman. — Montreal : The Institute for Research on Public Policy/L'Institute de Recherches Politique 260.01/1, 1986. — xxi,315p

NEW ENGLAND — History
BRAULT, Gerard J
The French-Canadian heritage in New England / Gerard J. Brault. — Hanover, N.H. ; London : University Press of New England, c1986. — xiii, 282p, 14p of plates. — *Includes index. — Bibliography: p 241-264*

NEW ENGLAND — History — Colonial period, ca. 1600-1775 — Congresses
Seventeenth-century New England : a conference / held by the Colonial Society of Massachusetts, June 18 and 19, 1982. — Boston : The Society ; [S.l.] : Distributed by the University Press of Virginia, 1984. — xx, 340 p., [16] p. of plates. — *Includes bibliographical references and index*

NEW GUINEA — History
GEUS, P. B. R. de
De Nieuw-Guinea kwestie : aspecten van buitenlands beleid en militaire macht / P. B. R. de Geus. — Leiden : Martinus Nijhoff, 1984. — 249p. — *Bibliography: p242-245*

NEW HALFA AGRICULTURAL PRODUCTION SCHEME
SØRBØ, Gunnar M.
Tenants and nomads in Eastern Sudan : a study of economic adaptations in the New Halfa Scheme / Gunnar M. Sørbø. — Uppsala : Scandinavian Institute of African Studies, 1985. — 159p

NEW HALFA (SUDAN) — Economic conditions
SÖRBÖ, Gunnar M.
How to survive development : the story of New Halfa / Gunnar M. Sörbö. — Khartoum : University of Khartoum. Faculty of Economic and Social Studies. Development Studies and Research Centre, 1977. — 52p. — (Monograph series / University of Khartoum. Faculty of Economic and Social Studies. Development Studies and Research Centre ; no.6). — *Bibliography: p[2]*

NEW HARMONY (IND.) — History — 19th century
TAYLOR, Anne, 1932-
Visions of harmony : a study of nineteenth-century millenarianism / Anne Taylor. — Oxford : Clarendon, 1987. — 285p,[8]p of plates. — *Bibliography: p269-275. — Includes index*

NEW IRELAND PROVINCE (PAPUA NEW GUINEA) — Population — Statistics
1980 national population census : final figures : provincial summary : New Ireland Province. — Port Moresby : National Statistical Office, 1986. — iii,118p

NEW JERSEY — History
STARR, Dennis J.
The Italians of New Jersey : a historical introduction and bibliography / Dennis J. Starr. — Newark : New Jersey Historical Society, 1985. — ii,130p

NEW JERSEY — History — Bibliography
STARR, Dennis J.
The Italians of New Jersey : a historical introduction and bibliography / Dennis J. Starr. — Newark : New Jersey Historical Society, 1985. — ii,130p

NEW KOWLOON (HONG KONG) — Statistics
Hong Kong 1986 by-census : tertiary planning unit summary tables / Kowloon and New Kowloon. — Hong Kong : Census and Statistics Department, [1987]. — xiii,152p. — *Has map in end pocket*

NEW PRODUCTS
FLESHER, Dale L
The new-product decision / by Dale L. Flesher, Tonya K. Flesher, and Gerald U. Skelly. — New York, NY : National Association of Accountants ; Hamilton, Ont., Canada : Society of Management Accountants of Canada, c1984. — vii, 150 p.. — *Bibliography: p. 147-150*

NEW REPUBLIC (NEW YORK, N.Y.)
SEIDEMAN, David
The New republic : a voice of modern liberalism / by David Seideman. — New York : Praeger, 1986. — xv, 205 p.. — *Includes index. — Bibliography: p. [195]-200*

NEW SCHOOL FOR SOCIAL RESEARCH (NEW YORK, N.Y.) — History
RUTKOFF, Peter M.
New School : a history of the New School for Social Research / Peter M. Rutkoff, William B. Scott. — New York : Free Press ; London : Collier Macmillan, c1986. — xiv, 314p, [16]p of plates. — *Includes bibliographical references and index*

NEW SOUTH WALES — Civilization — 1788-1900
DIXON, Robert
The course of empire : neo-classical culture in New South Wales 1788-1860 / Robert Dixon. — Melbourne : Oxford University Press, 1986. — x,213p. — *Bibliography and picture sources: p201-208*

NEW SOUTH WALES — Governors — Biography
FLETCHER, Brian, 1931-
Ralph Darling : a governor maligned / Brian H. Fletcher. — Melbourne ; Oxford : Oxford University Press, 1984. — xxi,473p. — *Ill on lining papers. — Bibliography: p441-467. — Includes index*

NEW SOUTH WALES — History — 1788-1851
The diaries and letters of G. T. W. B. Boyes. — Melbourne ; Auckland : Oxford University Press. — *Bibliography: p647-657*
vol.1: 1820-1832 / edited by Peter Chapman. — 1985. — xxvi,692p

NEW SOUTH WALES — Politics and government — 1976-
The Wran model : electoral politics in New South Wales 1981 and 1984 / edited by Ernie Chaples, Helen Nelson [and] Ken Turner. — Melbourne : Oxford University Press, 1985. — vi,289p

NEW SOUTH WALES. Australian Bureau of Statistics. New South Wales Office
NEW SOUTH WALES. Australian Bureau of Statistics. New South Wales Office
Schools. — Sydney : [the Office], 1981-. — Annual. — *Continues in part New South Wales. Commonwelath Bureau of Census and Statistics. New South Wales. Education*

NEW SOUTH WALES. Commonwealth Bureau of Census and Statistics. New South Wales Office
NEW SOUTH WALES. Commonwealth Bureau of Census and Statistics. New South Wales Office
Building. — Sydney : [the Bureau], 1958-1979/80. — Annual. — *Supercedes in part 'Social condition' in the bound volume Statistical register*

NEW SOUTH WALES. Commonwealth Bureau of Census and Statistics. New South Wales Office
Education / New South Wales Office, Commonwealth Bureau of Census and Statistics. — Sydney : [the Office], 1976-1980. — Annual. — *Continued by New South Wales. Australian Bureau of Statistics. New South Wales Office. Schools*

NEW TERRITORIES (HONG KONG) — Statistics
Hong Kong 1986 by-census : tertiary planning unit summary tables / new territories. — Hong Kong : Census and Statistics Department, [1987]. — xiii,268p. — *Has two maps in end pocket*

NEW TOWNS
RAMSAY, Anthony
Planning new towns : a review of ideas, policies, plans and programmes relating to new towns together with a guide to relevant documents and organisations / compiled by Anthony Ramsay. — Edinburgh : Capital Planning Information Limited, 1985. — 33p. — (CPI topicguides ; no.6). — *Bibliography: p.19-31*

NEW TOWNS — Government policy — Great Britain
GREAT BRITAIN. Department of the Environment
The role of government in new urban developments in the United Kingdom. — [London] : the Department, 1976. — [8]p. — (Planning in the United Kingdom). — *Paper prepared for the United Nations Conference on Human Settlements, 1976, Vancouver*

NEW TOWNS — England — Essex
LUCAS, Peter
Basildon : birth of a city : background to the development of Basildon New Town (Essex) / Peter Lucas. — Basildon : Peter Lucas, 1986. — 222p

NEW TOWNS — France
OSTROWETSKY, Sylvia
L'imaginaire bâtisseur : les villes nouvelles françaises / préface de Louis Marin. — Paris : Librairie des Méridiens, 1983. — viii,345p. — *Bibliography: p331-342*

NEW TOWNS — Great Britain
BISHOP, Jeff
Milton Keynes - the best of both worlds? : public and professional views of a new city / Jeff Bishop. — Bristol : School for Advanced Urban Studies, 1986. — 189p. — (Occasional paper / University of Bristol, School for Advanced Urban Studies ; 24). — *Bibliography: p.177-189*

DUPREE, Harry
Urban transportation : the new town solution / Harry Dupree. — Aldershot : Gower, c1987. — xxii,267p,[18]p of plates. — *Bibliography: p253-256. — Includes index*

NEW TOWNS — United States
CHRISTENSEN, Carol A
The American garden city and the new towns movement / by Carol A. Christensen. — Ann Arbor, Mich. : UMI Research Press, c1986. — x, 203p. — (Architecture and urban design ; no. 13). — : *Revision of author's thesis (Ph.D.)--University of Minnesota, 1977. — Includes index. — Bibliography: p. [179]-190*

NEW WAVE MUSIC — California — History and criticism

Hardcore California : a history of punk and new wave / Peter Belsito, Bob Davis. — Berkeley, CA : Last Gasp of San Francisco, c1983. — 128 p.. — *Contents: Los Angeles / text by Craig Lee and Shreader -- San Francisco / text by Peter Belsito*

NEW YORK (N.Y.) — Biography

EWEN, Elizabeth
Immigrant women in the land of dollars : life and culture on the Lower East Side, 1890-1925 / Elizabeth Ewen. — New York : Monthly Review Press, 1985. — p. cm. — (New feminist library)

NEW YORK (N.Y.) — Commerce

HEFFER, Jean
Le port de New York et le commerce extérieur américain 1860-1900 / Jean Heffer. — Paris : Université de Paris 1, Panthéon-Sorbonne, 1986. — ii,568p. — (Publications de la Sorbonne. Série internationale ; 25)

NEW YORK (N.Y.) — Economic conditions

HEFFER, Jean
Le port de New York et le commerce extérieur américain 1860-1900 / Jean Heffer. — Paris : Université de Paris 1, Panthéon-Sorbonne, 1986. — ii,568p. — (Publications de la Sorbonne. Série internationale ; 25)

NEW YORK (N.Y.) — Economic conditions — Econometric models

DRENNAN, Matthew P.
Modeling metropolitan economies for forecasting and policy analysis / Matthew P. Drennan. — New York : New York University Press, 1985. — p. cm. — *Includes index. — Bibliography: p*

NEW YORK (N.Y.) — Emigration and immigration

WALDINGER, Roger David
Through the eye of the needle : immigrants and enterprise in New York's garment trades / Roger D. Waldinger. — New York : New York University Press, 1986. — p. cm. — *Includes index. — Bibliography: p*

NEW YORK (N.Y.) — Social life and customs

EWEN, Elizabeth
Immigrant women in the land of dollars : life and culture on the Lower East Side, 1890-1925 / Elizabeth Ewen. — New York : Monthly Review Press, 1985. — p. cm. — (New feminist library)

NEW YORK (STATE) — Emigration and immigration — Case studies

ROSNER, Lydia S
The Soviet way of crime : beating the system in the Soviet Union and the U.S.A. / Lydia S. Rosner. — South Hadley, Mass. : Bergin & Garvey Publishers, 1986. — xvii, 140 p.. — *Includes bibliographies and index*

NEW YORK (STATE) — History — Colonial period, ca. 1600-1775

RINK, Oliver A.
Holland on the Hudson : an economic and social history of Dutch New York / Oliver A. Rink. — Ithaca, N.Y. : Cornell University Press ; Cooperstown, N.Y. : New York State Historical Association, 1986. — p. cm. — *Includes index. — Bibliography: p*

NEW YORK (STATE) — Politics and government — 1865-1950

WESSER, Robert F
A response to progressivism : the Democratic Party and New York politics, 1902-1918 / Robert F. Wesser. — New York : New York University Press, c1986. — p. cm. — *Includes index. — Bibliography: p*

NEW YORK UNIVERSITY — Students — Case studies

EXUM, William H.
Paradoxes of protest : black student activism in a White university / William H. Exum. — Philadelphia : Temple University Press, 1985. — p. cm. — *Includes index. — Bibliography: p*

NEW ZEALAND — Bibliography

Australian and New Zealand studies : papers presented at a colloquium at the British Library 7-9 February 1984 / edited by Patricia McLaren-Turner. — London : The Library, 1985. — [232]p. — (British Library occasional papers ; 4)

BLOOMFIELD, Valerie
Resources for Australian and New Zealand studies : a guide to library holdings in the United Kingdom / Valerie Bloomfield. — London : Australian Studies Centre, 1986. — xvi,284p. — *Bibliography: p264. — Includes index*

NEW ZEALAND — Commerce — Australia

NEW ZEALAND. Ministry of Foreign Affairs
CER : the Australia and New Zealand closer economic relations trade agreement. — Wellington : the Ministry, 1986. — 22p. — (Information bulletin ; no.15)

NEW ZEALAND — Economic conditions

CLEMENTS, R. T.
The Reserve Bank econometric model of the New Zealand economy : model XI / R. T. Clements, C. D. Hansen [and] M. J. Hames. — Wellington : Reserve Bank of New Zealand, 1986. — 62p. — (Research paper / Reserve Bank of New Zealand ; no.40)

NEW ZEALAND — Economic conditions — 1945-

GOULD, John
The Muldoon years : an essay on New Zealand's recent economic growth / John Gould. — Auckland ; London : Hodder and Stoughton, 1985. — 87p

NEW ZEALAND — Economic policy — Mathematical models

SEMINAR ON ECONOMIC MODELLING IN NEW ZEALAND (1984 : Wellington)
Economic modelling in New Zealand : proceedings of a seminar sponsored by the New Zealand Planning Council, Wellington, December 1984 / edited by Brian Silverstone and Graeme Wells. — Wellington : New Zealand Planning Council, 1986. — viii,131p. — *Includes bibliographical references*

Towards 1995 : patterns of national and sectoral development. — Wellington : New Zealand Planning Council, 1986. — ii,86p. — (Planning paper / New Zealand Planning Council ; no.26). — *Includes bibliographical references*

NEW ZEALAND — Emigration and immigration — Government policy

NEW ZEALAND. Immigration Division
Immigration and New Zealand : a statement of current immigration policy. — Wellington : the Division, 1986. — ii,23,2p

NEW ZEALAND — Foreign relations

NEW ZEALAND. Ministry of Foreign Affairs
Perspectives of New Zealand's foreign policy. — Wellington : the Ministry, 1986. — 54p. — *Cover title: Perspectives on New Zealand's foreign policy*

NEW ZEALAND — Foreign relations — ASEAN

NEW ZEALAND. Ministry of Foreign Affairs
ASEAN and New Zealand. — Wellington : the Ministry, 1986. — 31p. — (Information bulletin ; no.17)

NEW ZEALAND — Foreign relations — 1945-

FOREIGN POLICY SCHOOL (20th : 1985 : Otago)
New directions in New Zealand foreign policy / Twentieth Foreign Policy School... ; edited by Hyam Gold. — Auckland : Benton Ross, 1985. — 154p

NEW ZEALAND — Foreign relations — Australia — Sources

KAY, Robin
The Australian-New Zealand agreement 1944 / edited by Robin Kay. — Wellington : Historical Publications Branch, 1972. — xxxvi, 297 p. — (Documents on New Zealand external relations ; v. 1). — *Includes the Agreement establishing the South Pacific Commission. — Includes bibliographical footnotes*

NEW ZEALAND — Foreign relations — Japan

KAY, Robin
The ANZUS Pact and the Treaty of Peace with Japan / [compiled and] edited by Robin Kay. — Wellington : Historical Publications Branch, Department of Internal Affairs, 1985. — lxx,1268p. — (Documents on New Zealand external relations ; v.3). — *Includes bibliographical references*

NEW ZEALAND — Foreign relations — Oceania

NEW ZEALAND. Ministry of Foreign Affairs
The South Pacific Forum. — Wellington : the Ministry, 1986. — 12p. — (Information bulletin ; no.16)

NEW ZEALAND — History — 1843-1870

BELICH, James
The New Zealand wars and the Victorian interpretation of racial conflict / James Belich. — Auckland : Auckland University Press, 1986. — 396p

NEW ZEALAND — History — 1870-

DALZIEL, Raewyn
Julius Vogel : business politician / by Raewyn Dalziel. — Auckland : Auckland University Press, 1986. — 368p

NEW ZEALAND — Military policy

The Anzac connection / edited by Desmond Ball. — Sydney ; London ; Boston : George Allen & Unwin, 1985. — xvi,169p

NEW ZEALAND. Ministry of Foreign Affairs
Disarmament and arms control. — Wellington : the Ministry, 1986. — 45p. — (Information bulletin ; no.18)

NEW ZEALAND — Military relations

KAY, Robin
The ANZUS Pact and the Treaty of Peace with Japan / [compiled and] edited by Robin Kay. — Wellington : Historical Publications Branch, Department of Internal Affairs, 1985. — lxx,1268p. — (Documents on New Zealand external relations ; v.3). — *Includes bibliographical references*

NEW ZEALAND — Parliament — Membership — Biography

Biographies of members of the New Zealand Parliament. — Wellington : Ministry of Foreign Affairs, 1984. — 79p. — (Special bulletin / Ministry of Foreign Affairs ; 1984/5)

NEW ZEALAND — Politics and government

DALZIEL, Raewyn
Julius Vogel : business politician / by Raewyn Dalziel. — Auckland : Auckland University Press, 1986. — 368p

New Zealand politics in perspective / edited by Hyam Gold. — Auckland : Longman Paul, 1985. — x,357p. — *Bibliographies*

SPOONLEY, P.
The politics of nostalgia : racism and the Extreme Right in New Zealand / Paul Spoonley. — Palmerston North : Dunmore Press, 1987. — 318p. — *Bibliography: p267-279*

NEW ZEALAND — Politics and government — 1972-
FOREIGN POLICY SCHOOL (20th : 1985 : Otago)
New directions in New Zealand foreign policy / Twentieth Foreign Policy School... ; edited by Hyam Gold. — Auckland : Benton Ross, 1985. — 154p

NEW ZEALAND — Politics and Government — 1972-
GOULD, John
The Muldoon years : an essay on New Zealand's recent economic growth / John Gould. — Auckland ; London : Hodder and Stoughton, 1985. — 87p

NEW ZEALAND — Politics and government — 1972-
WARING, Marilyn
Women, politics and power / essays by Marilyn Waring. — Wellington : Allen and Unwin New Zealand, [1985]. — 121p

NEW ZEALAND — Population
POOL, Ian
Population and social trends : implications for New Zealand housing / Ian Pool... for the National Housing Commission. — Wellington : National Housing Commission, 1986. — x,175p. — Bibliographical references: p155-161

NEW ZEALAND — Population — Statistics
BROWN, P. G.
An investigation of official ethnic statistics / P. G. Brown. — Wellington : Department of Statistics, 1983. — . — (Occasional paper / Department of Statistics ; no.5). — Bibliographical references: p70-71

NEW ZEALAND — Race relations
BALLARA, Angela
Proud to be white? : a survey of Pakeha prejudice in New Zealand / Angela Ballara. — Auckland, N.Z. : Heinemann ; Portland, OR : Exclusive distributor, ISBS, 1986. — x, 205 p.. — Includes index. — Bibliography: p. 194-199

SIMPSON, Tony, 19-
Te riri Pakeha : the white man's anger / Tony Simpson. — Auckland ; London : Hodder and Stoughton, 1986. — 272p. — Bibliography: p260-262

NEW ZEALAND — Race relations — Political aspects
SPOONLEY, P.
The politics of nostalgia : racism and the Extreme Right in New Zealand / Paul Spoonley. — Palmerston North : Dunmore Press, 1987. — 318p. — Bibliography: p267-279

NEW ZEALAND — Social conditions
POOL, Ian
Population and social trends : implications for New Zealand housing / Ian Pool... for the National Housing Commission. — Wellington : National Housing Commission, 1986. — x,175p. — Bibliographical references: p155-161

NEW ZEALAND — Statistics
New Zealand males and females : a statistical comparison. — Wellington : Department of Statistics, 1977. — 43p. — (Statistical bulletin / Department of Statistics, New Zealand. Miscellaneous series ; 1)

NEW ZEALAND — Study and teaching — Great Britain — Directories
BLOOMFIELD, Valerie
Resources for Australian and New Zealand studies : a guide to library holdings in the United Kingdom / Valerie Bloomfield. — London : Australian Studies Centre, 1986. — xvi,284p. — Bibliography: p264. — Includes index

NEW ZEALAND — Yearbooks
New Zealand official yearbook. — Wellington : Department of Statistics, 1892-. — Annual

NEW ZEALAND. Department of Justice
ROBSON, J. L.
Sacred cows and rogue elephants : policy development in the New Zealand Justice Department / J. L. Robson. — Wellington : Government Printing Office, 1987. — xii,296p. — Bibliographical references: p[285]-292

NEWFOUNDLAND — Annexation to Canada
MACKENZIE, David Clark
Inside the Atlantic Triangle : Canada and the entrance of Newfoundland into confederation, 1939-1949 / David MacKenzie. — Toronto ; Buffalo : University of Toronto Press, c1986. — xi, 285 p.. — Includes index. — Bibliography: p. [263]-273

NEWFOUNDLAND — Appropriations and expenditures
Mid-year financial report / Government of Newfoundland and Labrador. — [St. John's : Department of Finance], 1983/84-. — Annual

NEWFOUNDLAND — Commerce — History — 19th century
RYAN, Shannon
Fish out of water : the Newfoundland saltfish trade 1814-1914 / Shannon Ryan. — St. John's (Nfld.) : Breakwater, 1986. — 320p,[24]p of plates. — (Newfoundland history series ; 2). — Bibliography: p301-310

NEWFOUNDLAND — History
MACKENZIE, David Clark
Inside the Atlantic Triangle : Canada and the entrance of Newfoundland into confederation, 1939-1949 / David MacKenzie. — Toronto ; Buffalo : University of Toronto Press, c1986. — xi, 285 p.. — Includes index. — Bibliography: p. [263]-273

NEWFOUNDLAND — Relations — Canada
MACKENZIE, David Clark
Inside the Atlantic Triangle : Canada and the entrance of Newfoundland into confederation, 1939-1949 / David MacKenzie. — Toronto ; Buffalo : University of Toronto Press, c1986. — xi, 285 p.. — Includes index. — Bibliography: p. [263]-273

NEWFOUNDLAND — Social conditions
SIDER, Gerald M.
Culture and class in anthropology and history : a Newfoundland illustration / Gerald M. Sider. — Cambridge : Cambridge University Press, 1986. — xi, 205p, [8] p of plates. — (Cambridge studies in social anthropology ; 60). — Bibliography: p.195-200

NEWFOUNDLAND — Statistics
NEWFOUNDLAND. Treasury Board. Budgeting Division
Estimates. — [S.1.] : [the Division], 1985/6. — Annual

NEWFOUNDLAND. House of Assembly. Public accounts committee
NEWFOUNDLAND. House of Assembly. Public accounts committee
Report of the public accounts committee of the House of Assembly. — [St.John's] : the Committee, 1982-. — Annual

NEWFOUNDLAND. Treasury Board. Budgeting Division — Statistics
NEWFOUNDLAND. Treasury Board. Budgeting Division
Estimates. — [S.1.] : [the Division], 1985/6. — Annual

NEWFOUNDLAND. Workmen's Compensation Board
NEWFOUNDLAND. Workmen's Compensation Board
Report / Workmen's Compensation Board, Newfoundland. — St Johns : [the Board], 1951-1983. — Annual. — 1964-1977 issuing body entitled: Newfoundland and Labrador. Workmen's Compensation Board. 1978-1983 issuing body entitled: Newfoundland and Labrador. Workers' Compensation Board. — Continued by: Newfoundland and Labrador. Workers' Compensation Commission

NEWFOUNDLAND AND LABRADOR. Worker's Compensation Commission
NEWFOUNDLAND AND LABRADOR. Worker's Compensation Commission
Annual report / Worker's Compensation Commission, Newfoundland and Labrador. — St Johns : [the Commission], 1984-. — Annual. — Continues: Newfoundland. Workmen's Compensation Board Report

NEWFOUNDLAND AND LABRADOR FEDERATION OF LABOUR
GILLESPIE, Bill
A class act : an illustrated history of the labour movement in Newfoundland and Labrador / Bill Gillespie. — St. John's, Newfoundland : The Newfoundland Federation and Labrador Federation of Labour, 1986. — 148p. — Bibliography: p141-148

NEWFOUNDLAND FISHERMEN, FOOD AND ALLIED WORKERS — History
INGLIS, Gordon
More than just a union : the story of the NFFAWU / Gordon Inglis. — St. John's, Nfld. : Jesperson Press, 1985. — 331 p., [8] p. of plates. — Includes index. — Bibliography: p. [317]-323

NEWHAM (LONDON, ENGLAND) — Population
NEWHAM
Beckton survey of population 1985. — Newham : [the Council], 1985. — 127p. — Includes sample survey form

NEWS AGENCIES — Great Britain
COHEN, Yoel
Media diplomacy : the Foreign Office in the mass communications age / Yoel Cohen. — London : Cass, 1986. — x,197p. — Bibliography: p184-189. — Includes index

NEWS INTERNATIONAL
NATIONAL COUNCIL FOR CIVIL LIBERTIES
No way in Wapping : the effect of the policing of the News International dispute on Wapping residents. — London : National Council for Civil Liberties, 1986. — 40p

NEWS INTERNATIONAL STRIKE, GREAT BRITAIN, 1986
LONDON STRATEGIC POLICY UNIT. Police Monitoring and Research Group
Policing Wapping : and account of the dispute 1986/7. — London : London Strategic Policy Unit, 1987-. — 47p. — (Briefing paper / London Strategic Policy Unit. Police Monitoring and Research Group ; no.3)

MELVERN, Linda
The end of the street / Linda Melvern. — London : Methuen, 1986. — 1v.. — Includes index

Picket. — London : Picket, 1986-1987. — Written and printed by two NGA members during the News International Strike 1986/87. — Weekly

Wapping post. — London : Wapping Post, 1986-1987. — Irregular

NEWSPAPER PUBLISHING — Great Britain
GOODHART, David
Eddie Shah and the newspaper revolution / David Goodhart and Patrick Wintour. — Sevenoaks : Coronet, 1986. — 1v.

NEWSPAPERS
A handlist of selected newspaper holdings, national, region and foreign, in London's public libraries. — 7th ed. — Croydon : Croydon Public Libraries, 1986. — 16p

NEWSPAPERS
continuation

WEDELL, George
Media in competition : the future of print and electronic media in 22 countries / George Wedell and Georg-Michael Luyken ; with contributions by Alberto Cavallari...[et al.]. — Manchester : European Institute for the Media, 1986. — 173p. — (Euromedia Indicator ; No.1). — *Includes summaries in French and German*

NEWSPAPERS — History

Journal of newspaper and periodical history. — London : Journal of Newspaper and Periodical History, 1984-. — *3 times per year*

NEWSPAPERS — Sections, columns, etc

TATARYN, Lloyd
The pundits : power, politics & the press / Lloyd Tataryn. — Toronto, Canada : Deneau, 1985. — 198 p.. — *Includes index. Bibliography: p. 181-191*

NEWSPAPERS — Argentina

GARCÍA COSTA, Victor O.
El Obrero : selección de textos / Victor O. García Costa. — Buenos Aires : Centro Editor de América Latina, 1985. — 107p. — (Biblioteca Política Argentina ; 121)

NEWSPAPERS — Great Britain

BAISTOW, Tom
Fourth-rate estate : an anatomy of Fleet Street / by Tom Baistow. — London : Comedia, 1985. — iv,115p. — (Comedia series ; 28). — *Bibliography: p112. — Includes index*

NEWSPAPERS ON MICROFILM

WELLS, Rosemary, 19---
Newsplan : report of the pilot project in the south-west / Rosemary Wells. — London : British Library, c1986. — x,218p. — (Library and information research report ; 38). — *Two microfiches (11x15cm) in pocket*

NEWTON, Sir ISAAC

GJERTSEN, Derek
The Newton handbook / Derek Gjertsen. — London : Routledge & Kegan Paul, 1986. — xiv,665p

NICARAGUA — Church history

O'SHAUGHNESSY, Laura Nuzzi
The church and revolution in Nicaragua / Laura Nuzzi O'Shaughnessy & Luis H. Serra. — Athens, Ohio : Ohio University, Center for International Studies, Latin America Studies Program, 1986, c1985. — p. cm. — (Monographs in international studies. Latin America series ; no. 11). — *Bibliography: p*

ZWERLING, Philip
Nicaragua : a new kind of revolution / Philip Zwerling & Connie Martin. — Westport, Conn. : L. Hill, 1985. — xii, 251p

NICARAGUA — Description and travel

COXSEDGE, Joan
Thank God for the revolution : a journey through Central America / Joan Coxsedge ; foreword by Noam Chomsky. — Sydney ; London : Pluto Press, 1986. — xiv,175p

NICARAGUA — Economic conditions

MELROSE, Dianna
Nicaragua : the threat of a good example? / by Dianna Melrose. — Oxford : Oxfam, 1985. — 68p

NICARAGUA — Economic conditions — 1979-

The political economy of revolutionary Nicaragua / edited by Rose J. Spalding. — Boston, Mass. ; London : Allen & Unwin, 1987. — xii,255p. — (Thematic studies in Latin America). — *Includes index*

VILAS, Carlos M.
The Sandinista revolution : national liberation and social transformation in Central America / Carlos M. Vilas ; translated by Judy Butler. — New York : Monthly Review Press ; Berkeley, Calif. : Centre for the Study of the Americans, 1986. — 317p. — *Originally published as 'Perfiles de la revolución Sandinista: Liberación nacional y transformaciones sociales en Centroamérica' by Editorial Legasa, Madrid. — Bibliography: p293-307*

NICARAGUA — Foreign economic relations — Communist countries

BERRIOS, Ruben
Economic relations between Nicaragua and the socialist countries / Ruben Berrios. — Washington, D.C. : Latin American Program of the Woodrow Wilson International Center for Scholars, 1985. — 23p. — (Working papers / Woodrow Wilson International Center for Scholars. Latin American Program ; 166)

NICARAGUA — Foreign relations — 1979-

VANDERLAAN, Mary B
Revolution and foreign policy in Nicaragua / Mary B. Vanderlaan. — Boulder : Westview Press, 1986. — xiii, 404p. — (Westview special studies on Latin America and the Caribbean). — *Includes index. — Bibliography: p.387-395*

NICARAGUA — Foreign relations — United States

BERMANN, Karl
Under the big stick : Nicaragua and the United States since 1848 / by Karl Bermann. — Boston : South End Press, c1986. — ix, 339 p., [2] p. of plates. — *Includes index. — Bibliography: p. [303]-329*

GROSSMAN, Karl
Nicaragua, America's new Vietnam? / text and photos by Karl Grossman. — Sag Harbor, N.Y. : Permanent Press, c1984. — 228 p.. — *Bibliography: p. 227-228*

Reagan versus the Sandinistas : the undeclared war on Nicaragua / edited by Thomas W. Walker. — Boulder : Westview Press, 1986. — p. cm. — *Includes index*

ROBINSON, William I.
David and Goliath : Washington's war against Nicaragua / William I. Robinson and Kent W. Norsworthy. — London : Zed, 1987. — [272]p. — *Includes bibliography and index*

NICARAGUA — History

ALEN LASCANO, Luis C
Yrigoyen, Sandino y el panamericanismo / Luis C. Alen Lascano. — Buenos Aires : Centro Editor de América Latina, 1986. — 138p. — (Biblioteca Política Argentina ; 131). — *Bibliography: p138*

NICARAGUA — History — 1909-1937

HODGES, Donald Clark
Intellectual foundations of the Nicaraguan revolution / by Donald C. Hodges. — 1st ed. — Austin : University of Texas Press, 1986. — p. cm. — *Includes index. — Bibliography: p*

NICARAGUA — History — 1937-1979

HODGES, Donald Clark
Intellectual foundations of the Nicaraguan revolution / by Donald C. Hodges. — 1st ed. — Austin : University of Texas Press, 1986. — p. cm. — *Includes index. — Bibliography: p*

NICARAGUA — History — Revolution, 1979

NOLAN, David
The ideology of the Sandinistas and the Nicaraguan revolution / David Nolan. — Coral Gables, Fla. (P.O. Box 248123, Coral Gables 33124) : Institute of Interamerican Studies, Graduate School of International Studies, University of Miami, c1984. — v, 203 p.. — *Includes index. — Bibliography: p. 186-199*

La revolución en Nicaragua : liberación nacional, democracia popular y transformación económica / Richard Harris y Carlos M. Vilas compiladores. — México D. F. : Ediciones Era, 1985. — 351p

ROOPER, Alison
Fragile victory : Nicaraguan community at war / Alison Rooper. — London : Weidenfeld and Nicolson, 1987. — xx,229p. — *Bibliography: p [228]-229*

VILAS, Carlos M.
The Sandinista revolution : national liberation and social transformation in Central America / Carlos M. Vilas ; translated by Judy Butler. — New York : Monthly Review Press ; Berkeley, Calif. : Centre for the Study of the Americans, 1986. — 317p. — *Originally published as 'Perfiles de la revolución Sandinista: Liberación nacional y transformaciones sociales en Centroamérica' by Editorial Legasa, Madrid. — Bibliography: p293-307*

NICARAGUA — History — Revolution, 1979 — Influence

Brigadista : harvest and war in Nicaragua / edited by Jeffrey Jones. — New York : Praeger, 1986. — xxviii, 227p. — *Includes index*

HODGES, Donald Clark
Intellectual foundations of the Nicaraguan revolution / by Donald C. Hodges. — 1st ed. — Austin : University of Texas Press, 1986. — p. cm. — *Includes index. — Bibliography: p*

NICARAGUA — History — 1979-

PERALES, Iosu
Nicaragua, valientemente libre / Iosu Perales. — Madrid : Revolución, 1984. — 174p. — *Contiene entrevists con Tomás Borge*

VILAS, Carlos M.
The Sandinista revolution : national liberation and social transformation in Central America / Carlos M. Vilas ; translated by Judy Butler. — New York : Monthly Review Press ; Berkeley, Calif. : Centre for the Study of the Americans, 1986. — 317p. — *Originally published as 'Perfiles de la revolución Sandinista: Liberación nacional y transformaciones sociales en Centroamérica' by Editorial Legasa, Madrid. — Bibliography: p293-307*

ZWERLING, Philip
Nicaragua : a new kind of revolution / Philip Zwerling & Connie Martin. — Westport, Conn. : L. Hill, 1985. — xii, 251p

NICARAGUA — Military relations — United States

DICKEY, Christopher
With the Contras : a reporter in the wilds of Nicaragua / Christopher Dickey. — New York : Simon and Schuster, c1985. — 327 p., [9] p. of plates. — *Includes index. — Bibliography: p. 273-315*

INTERNATIONAL COURT OF JUSTICE
[Judgements]. Military and paramilitary activities in and against Nicaragua : (Nicaragua v. United States of America). Merits. 27 June 1986 = Activités militaires et paramilitaires au Nicaragua c. Etats-Unis d'America. Fond. 27 June 1986. — New York : United Nations, 1986. — 142 bis. — *U.N. Security Council document S/18221 conveying the judgment of the Court at the request of the Permanent Representative of Nicaragua to the United Nations*

NICARAGUA — Politics and government

WEISSBERG, Arnold
Nicaragua : an introduction to the Sandinista revolution: the opening years / Arnold Weissberg. — New York : Pathfinder Press, 1987. — 45p

NICARAGUA — Politics and government — 1937-1979

NOLAN, David
The ideology of the Sandinistas and the Nicaraguan revolution / David Nolan. — Coral Gables, Fla. (P.O. Box 248123, Coral Gables 33124) : Institute of Interamerican Studies, Graduate School of International Studies, University of Miami, c1984. — v, 203 p.. — *Includes index. — Bibliography: p. 186-199*

NICARAGUA — Politics and government — 1937-1979 *continuation*

La revolución en Nicaragua : liberación nacional, democracia popular y transformación económica / Richard Harris y Carlos M. Vilas compiladores. — México D. F. : Ediciones Era, 1985. — 351p

NICARAGUA — Politics and government — 1970-

ARNOVE, Robert F
Education and revolution in Nicaragua / Robert F. Arnove. — New York : Praeger, 1986. — xii, 160 p.. — (Praeger special studies series in comparative education). — "Praeger special studies. Praeger scientific.". — *Includes index. — Bibliography: p. 145-153*

NICARAGUA — Politics and government — 1979-

BRADSTOCK, Andrew
Saints and Sandinistas : the Catholic Church in Nicaragua and its response to the revolution / Andrew Bradstock. — London : Epworth, 1987. — [96]p. — *Includes bibliography*

CABESTRERO, Teófilo
Blood of the innocent : victims of the Contras' war in Nicaragua / Teófilo Cabestrero ; translated from the Spanish by Robert R. Barr. — Maryknoll : Orbis ; London : Catholic Institute for International Relations, c1985. — vii,104p. — *Translation of: Nicaragua*

CATHOLIC INSTITUTE FOR INTERNATIONAL RELATIONS
Nicaragua. — London : Catholic Institute for International Relations, 1986. — 26p

COLBURN, Forrest D
Post-revolutionary Nicaragua : state, class, and the dilemmas of agrarian policy / Forrest D. Colburn. — Berkeley : University of California Press, c1986. — xi, 145p. — *Includes index. — Bibliography: p.133-138*

[Contra. English]. The Contras : interviews with anti-Sandinistas / [edited] Dieter Eich and Carlos Rincón. — San Francisco : Synthesis Publications, c1985. — iv, 193 p.. — *Translation of: La contra*

COXSEDGE, Joan
Thank God for the revolution : a journey through Central America / Joan Coxsedge ; foreword by Noam Chomsky. — Sydney ; London : Pluto Press, 1986. — xiv,175p

DICKEY, Christopher
With the Contras : a reporter in the wilds of Nicaragua / Christopher Dickey. — New York : Simon and Schuster, c1985. — 327 p., [9] p. of plates. — *Includes index. — Bibliography: p. 273-315*

EICH, Dieter
La Contra : der Krieg gegen Nicaragua / Dieter Eich, Carlos Rincon. — Hamburg : Konkret-Literatur, [1984?]. — 192p

GROSSMAN, Karl
Nicaragua, America's new Vietnam? / text and photos by Karl Grossman. — Sag Harbor, N.Y. : Permanent Press, c1984. — 228 p.. — *Bibliography: p. 227-228*

Nicaragua : pueblo y cultura : papers given at Trinity and All Saints' College 9-10 November 1984 / edited by Rob Rix. — Leeds : Trinity All and Saints' College, 1984. — 130p

O'SHAUGHNESSY, Laura Nuzzi
The church and revolution in Nicaragua / Laura Nuzzi O'Shaughnessy & Luis H. Serra. — Athens, Ohio : Ohio University, Center for International Studies, Latin America Studies Program, 1986, c1985. — p. cm. — (Monographs in international studies. Latin America series ; no. 11). — *Bibliography: p*

PERALES, Iosu
Nicaragua, valientemente libre / Iosu Perales. — Madrid : Revolución, 1984. — 174p. — *Contiene entrevists con Tomás Borge*

The political economy of revolutionary Nicaragua / edited by Rose J. Spalding. — Boston, Mass. ; London : Allen & Unwin, 1987. — xii,255p. — (Thematic studies in Latin America). — *Includes index*

Reagan versus the Sandinistas : the undeclared war on Nicaragua / edited by Thomas W. Walker. — Boulder : Westview Press, 1986. — p. cm. — *Includes index*

La revolución en Nicaragua : liberación nacional, democracia popular y transformación económica / Richard Harris y Carlos M. Vilas compiladores. — México D. F. : Ediciones Era, 1985. — 351p

ROBINSON, William I.
David and Goliath : Washington's war against Nicaragua / William I. Robinson and Kent W. Norsworthy. — London : Zed, 1987. — [272]p. — *Includes bibliography and index*

TORIELLO GARRIDO, Guillermo
[La agresión imperialista contra dos revoluciones. English]. A popular history of two revolutions : Guatemala and Nicaragua / Guillermo Toriello Garrido ; translated by Rebecca Schwaner. — San Francisco : Synthesis Publications, 1985. — 58p

NICARAGUA — Rural conditions

COLBURN, Forrest D
Post-revolutionary Nicaragua : state, class, and the dilemmas of agrarian policy / Forrest D. Colburn. — Berkeley : University of California Press, c1986. — xi, 145p. — *Includes index. — Bibliography: p.133-138*

NICARAGUA — Social conditions

MELROSE, Dianna
Nicaragua : the threat of a good example? / by Dianna Melrose. — Oxford : Oxfam, 1985. — 68p

NICARAGUA — Social conditions — 1979-

EVERETT, Melissa
Bearing witness, building bridges : interviews with North Americans living and working in Nicaragua / Melissa Everett ; photographs: Michael Kopec. — Philadelphia, Pa. : New Society, 1986. — xviii,169p

VILAS, Carlos M.
The Sandinista revolution : national liberation and social transformation in Central America / Carlos M. Vilas ; translated by Judy Butler. — New York : Monthly Review Press ; Berkeley, Calif. : Centre for the Study of the Americans, 1986. — 317p. — *Originally published as 'Perfiles de la revolución Sandinista: Liberación nacional y transformaciones sociales en Centroamérica' by Editorial Legasa, Madrid. — Bibliography: p293-307*

NICKEL INDUSTRY — Indonesia — Saroako

ROBINSON, Kathryn May
Stepchildren of progress : the political economy of development in an Indonesian mining town / Kathryn May Robinson. — Albany, N.Y. : State University of New York Press, c1986. — xvi, 315 p.. — (SUNY series in the anthropology of work). — *Originally presented as the author's thesis (Ph.D.)--Australian National University, 1983. — Includes index. — Bibliography: p. 295-307*

NIETZSCHE, FRIEDRICH

LOVE, Nancy Sue
Marx, Nietzsche, and modernity / Nancy S. Love. — New York : Columbia University Press, 1986. — xii, 264 p.. — *Includes index. — Bibliography: p. [243]-255*

NIETZSCHE, FRIEDRICH — History and criticism

HEIDEGGER, Martin
Nietzsche / Martin Heidegger. — San Francisco ; London : Harper and Row Vol.3: The will to power as knowledge and as metaphysics / edited, with notes and an analysis, by David Farrell Krell ; translated from the German by Joan Stambaugh, David Farrell Krell and Frank A. Capuzzi. — 1987. — xiii,288p. — *Heidegger's German text originally published in 'Nietzsche', Erster Band, Zweiter Band, Verlag Günther Neske, Pfullingen, 1961. — Includes bibliographical references*

NIETZSCHE, FRIEDRICH — Influence

THOMAS, R. Hinton
Nietzsche in German politics and society, 1890-1918 / R. Hinton Thomas. — Manchester : Manchester University Press, 1983 (1986 [printing]). — [146]p. — *Bibliography: p146. — Includes index*

NIETZSCHE, FRIEDRICH — Metaphysics

HOULGATE, Stephen
Hegel, Nietzsche and the criticism of metaphysics / Stephen Houlgate. — Cambridge : Cambridge University Press, 1986. — [320]p. — *Bibliography: p451-469. — Includes index*

NIETZSCHE, FRIEDRICH WILHELM

BERGMANN, Peter
Nietzsche, "the last antipolitical German" / Peter Bergmann. — Bloomington : Indiana University Press, c1987. — 239 p.. — *Includes index. — Bibliography: p. [220]-231*

MYERS, David B.
Marx and Nietzsche : the reminiscences and transcripts of a nineteenth century journalist / David B. Myers. — Lanham, MD : University Press of America, c1986. — xviii, 168 p.. — *Spine title: Marx & Nietzsche. — Bibliography: p. 164-167*

NIÈVRE (FRANCE) — Economic conditions

FRANCE. Comité départemental d'expansion économique et de productivité de la Nièvre
La Nièvre ... : pour un aménagement rural concerté / Comité départemental d'expansion économique et de productivité de la Nièvre, Direction departementale de l'agriculture de la Nièvre. — [Nevers?] : Le Comité, [1971?]. — 65p

NIÈVRE (FRANCE) — Social conditions

FRANCE. Comité départemental d'expansion économique et de productivité de la Nièvre
La Nièvre ... : pour un aménagement rural concerté / Comité départemental d'expansion économique et de productivité de la Nièvre, Direction departementale de l'agriculture de la Nièvre. — [Nevers?] : Le Comité, [1971?]. — 65p

NIGAM, SHYAM B. L.

The Challenge of employment : and basic needs in Africa : essays in honour of Shyam B. L. Nigam and to mark the tenth anniversary of JASPA. — Nairobi : Oxford University Press, 1986. — xii,379p. — *Includes bibliographical references*

NIGER — History — Dictionaries

DECALO, Samuel
Historical dictionary of Niger / by Samuel Decalo. — Metuchen, N.J. : Scarecrow Press, 1979. — xvii, 358 p.. — (African historical dictionaries ; no. 20). — *Bibliography: p. 243-358*

NIGER — Statistics

NIGER. Ministere du Plan. Direction de la Statistique et des Comptes Nationaux
Annuaire statistique / Direction de la Statistique et des Comptes Nationaux, Ministere du Plan, Niger. — [S.l.] : Ministere du Plan. Direction de la Statistique et des Comptes Nationaux, 1978/1979-. — *Annual*

NIGERIA — Appropriations and expenditures
Recurrent and capital estimate of the government of the Federal Republic of Nigeria. — Lagos : Federal Government Press, 1981-. — *Annual*

NIGERIA — Commercial policy
OYEJIDE, T. Ademola
The effects of trade and exchange rate policies on agriculture in Nigeria / T. Ademola Oyejide. — Washington, D.C. : International Food Policy Research Institute, 1986. — p. cm. — (Research report ; 55). — *Bibliography: p*

NIGERIA — Economic conditions — History — To 1960
Britain and Nigeria : exploitation of development? / edited by Toyin Falola. — London : Zed, 1986. — [272]p. — *Includes index*

NIGERIA — Economic conditions — Statistics
Economic and social statistics bulletin / Federal Office of Statistics, Nigeria. — Lagos : Federal Office of Statistics, 1984-. — *Annual. — Title varies*

Nigeria's principal economic and financial indicators 1970-1977. — [Lagos] : Central Bank of Nigeria, [1978]. — 12p

NIGERIA — Economic conditions — 1960-
OLAYIWOLA, Peter O.
Petroleum and structural change in a developing country : the case of Nigeria / Peter O. Olayiwola. — New York ; London : Praeger, 1987, c1986. — [224]p. — *Includes bibliography and index*

NIGERIA — Economic conditions — 1970-
OLOFIN, S. O.
Modelling Nigeria's economic development / by S. O. Olofin ; with contributions by S. O. Olayide...[et al.]. — Ibadan : Ibadan University Press for Centre for Econometric and Allied Research, University of Ibadan, 1985. — xxi,316p

NIGERIA — Economic policy
BIERSTEKER, Thomas J
Multinationals, the state, and control of the Nigerian economy / Thomas J. Biersteker. — Princeton, N.J. : Princeton University Press, c1987. — p. cm. — *Includes index. — Bibliography: p*

FADAHUNSI, Akin
The development process and technology : a case for a resources based development strategy in Nigeria / Akin Fadahunsi. — Uppsala : Scandinavian Institute of African Studies, 1986. — 41p. — (Research report / Scandinavian Institute of African Studies ; no.77). — *Bibliographies*

OLAYIWOLA, Peter O.
Petroleum and structural change in a developing country : the case of Nigeria / Peter O. Olayiwola. — New York ; London : Praeger, 1987, c1986. — [224]p. — *Includes bibliography and index*

ONU, C. Ogbonnaya
Technology and national development : the Nigerian state / by C. Ogbonnaya Onu. — Aba : Aduco Nigeria, [1985?]. — x,189p

OYEJIDE, T. Ademola
The effects of trade and exchange rate policies on agriculture in Nigeria / T. Ademola Oyejide. — Washington, D.C. : International Food Policy Research Institute, 1986. — p. cm. — (Research report ; 55). — *Bibliography: p*

State, oil, and agriculture in Nigeria / Michael Watts, editor. — Berkeley : Institute of International Studies, University of California, c1987. — xiv, 327 p.. — (Research series ; no. 66). — *Includes index. — Bibliography: p. 297-317*

NIGERIA — Economic policy — 1970-
BIERSTEKER, Thomas J
Multinationals, the state, and control of the Nigerian economy / Thomas J. Biersteker. — Princeton, N.J. : Princeton University Press, c1987. — p. cm. — *Includes index. — Bibliography: p*

RANDLE, J. K.
The natives are friendly? / by J. K. Randle. — Winchester : Hambleside, 1986. — x,297p

NIGERIA — Foreign economic relations — Bibliography
COKER, Q. F.
IMF and Nigeria : a selected bibliography / Q. F. Coker. — [S.l.] : Nigerian Institute of International Affairs, 1985. — iii,94p

NIGERIA — Foreign economic relations — Great Britain — History
Britain and Nigeria : exploitation of development? / edited by Toyin Falola. — London : Zed, 1986. — [272]p. — *Includes index*

NIGERIA — Foreign relations — United States
ATE, Bassey E
Decolonization and dependence : the development of Nigerian-U.S. relations / Bassey E. Ate. — Boulder, Colo. : Westview Press, 1985. — p. cm. — (Westview special studies on Africa). — *Includes index. — Bibliography: p*

NIGERIA — History — Dictionaries
OYEWOLE, A
Historical dictionary of Nigeria / by A. Oyewole. — Metuchen, N.J. : Scarecrow Press, 1987. — xvii, 391 p.. — (African historical dictionaries ; no. 40). — *Bibliography: p. [347]-384*

NIGERIA — History — Civil War, 1967-1970
ODOGWU, Bernard
No place to hide : crises and conflicts inside Biafra / by Bernard Odogwu. — Enugu : Fourth Dimension Publishing, 1985. — 271p

NIGERIA — History — Coup d'état, 1983
IKOKU, S. G
Nigeria's fourth coup d'etat : options for modern statehood / by S.G. Ikoku. — Enugu, Nigeria : Fourth Dimension Publishers, 1985. — iii, 182 p.. — *Includes index*

NIGERIA — Industries — Statistics
Industrial survey of Nigeria 1980-1983. — Lagos : Federal Office of Statistics, [1986?]. — 62p

NIGERIA — Manufactures — Statistics
Industrial survey of Nigeria 1980-1983. — Lagos : Federal Office of Statistics, [1986?]. — 62p

NIGERIA — Politics and government
BABATOPE, Ebenezer
Murtala Muhammed : a leader betrayed (a study in Buhari's tryanny) / Ebenezer Babatope. — Enugu : Roy & Ezete, 1986. — xiii,138p

JONES, G. I. (Gwilym Iwan)
Annual reports of the Bende Division, South Eastern Nigeria, 1905-1912 : with a commentary by G.I. Jones. — Cambridge : African Studies Centre, University of Cambridge, 1986. — iv,99p. — (Cambridge African occasional papers ; no.2). — *Two maps on folded leaves in pocket*

NWANKWO, Arthur A.
Civilianized soldiers : army-civilian government for Nigeria / Arthur A. Nwankwo. — Enugu : Fourth Dimension Publications, 1984. — iv,70p

NIGERIA — Politics and government — To 1960
CALLAWAY, Helen
Gender, culture and empire : European women in colonial Nigeria / Helen Callaway. — Basingstoke : Macmillan in association with St. Antony's College, Oxford, 1987. — xiv,278p. — (St. Antony's/Macmillan series). — *Bibliography: p252-266. — Includes index*

SCHÄRER, Therese
Das Nigerian Youth Movement : eine Untersuchung zur Politisierung der afrikanischen Bildungsschicht vor dem Zweiten Weltkrieg / Therese Schärer. — Bern : Lang, 1986. — xiii,376,76p. — (Europäische Hochschulschriften. Reihe 31, Politikwissenschaft ; Bd.89). — *Bibliography: pA/67-A/76*

NIGERIA — Politics and government — 1979-1983
IKOKU, S. G
Nigeria's fourth coup d'etat : options for modern statehood / by S.G. Ikoku. — Enugu, Nigeria : Fourth Dimension Publishers, 1985. — iii, 182 p.. — *Includes index*

NIGERIA — Politics and government — 1979-
OYOUBAIRE, Sam Egite
Federalism in Nigeria : a study in the development of the Nigerian state / Sam Egite Oyoubaire. — London : Macmillan, 1985. — xx,306p. — (Contemporary African issues series). — *Bibliography: p285-294. — Includes index*

NIGERIA — Population
OLUSANYA, P. O.
Nigeria's demographic delusion : a critical examination of the census controversy / P. O. Olusanya. — Lagos : University of Lagos, 1980. — 41p

NIGERIA — Population — Statistics
Federal Office of Statistics for National Manpower Board and Federal Ministry of Employment, Labour and Productivity. — Lagos : Federal Office of Statistics Preliminary report. — 1984. — 45p. — *Survey module of the National Intergrated Survey of Households (NISH of the Federal Office of Statistics*

Mid-year population projections by States 1963-2000. — Lagos : National Population Bureau, 1984. — 3 leaves

NIGERIA — Population — Statistics — Evaluation
MORAH, Benson C.
Evaluation of the Nigeria Fertility Survey 1981-2 / Benson C. Morah. — Voorburg : International Statistical Institute, 1985. — 57p. — (Scientific reports / World Fertility Survey ; no.80)

NIGERIA — Presidents — Election — 1979
ADAMU, Haroun
Nigeria : the meaning of the presidential system : 1979 General Elections / Haroun Adamu, Alaba Ogunsanwo. — Kano, Nigeria : Triumph Pub. Co., [1982?]. — x, 267 p.

NIGERIA — Relations — United States
Nigerian opinion on selected national and international issues : (World Survey III series). — [Washington, D.C.] : United States Information Agency, 1966. — xi,42p. — *R-32-66*

NIGERIA — Rural conditions — Statistics
National integrated survey of households (Nish): report of rural agricultural sample survey / Agricultural Survey Unit, Nigeria. — Lagos : Agricultural Survey Unit, 1981/82-. — *Annual*

NIGERIA — Social conditions — Statistics
Economic and social statistics bulletin / Federal Office of Statistics, Nigeria. — Lagos : Federal Office of Statistics, 1984-. — *Annual. — Title varies*

NIGERIA — Social conditions — 1960-
Social change in Nigeria / edited by Simi Afonja and Tola Olu Pearce. — Harlow : Longman, 1986, c1984. — 261p. — *Includes bibliographies and index*

NIGERIA. Industrial Research Council of Nigeria
Annual report and income and expenditure account / Industrial Research Council of Nigeria. — Ikeja : Industrial Research Council of Nigeria, 1973-. — *Annual report*

NIGERIA, NORTHERN. Public Service Commission
NIGERIA, NORTHERN. Public Service Commission
Report / Public Service Commission, Northern Region Nigeria. — Kaduna : Government Printer, 1958-1963. — *Annual*

NIGERIAN YOUTH MOVEMENT
SCHÄRER, Therese
Das Nigerian Youth Movement : eine Untersuchung zur Politisierung der afrikanischen Bildungsschicht vor dem Zweiten Weltkrieg / Therese Schärer. — Bern : Lang, 1986. — xiii,376,76p. — (Europäische Hochschulschriften. Reihe 31, Politikwissenschaft ; Bd.89). — *Bibliography: pA/67-A/76*

NIGERIANS — Attitudes
Nigerian opinion on selected national and international issues : (World Survey III series). — [Washington, D.C.] : United States Information Agency, 1966. — xi,42p. — *R-32-66*

Nigerian university student views on national and international issues. — [Washington, D.C.] : United States Information Agency, 1966. — viii,35p. — *R-44-66*

NIGERIANS — Relations — United States
Nigerian university student views on national and international issues. — [Washington, D.C.] : United States Information Agency, 1966. — viii,35p. — *R-44-66*

NIGHT WORK — Bibliography
Annotated bibliography on working time. — Geneva : International Labour Office, 1986. — v,100p

NIHON KYOSANTO — History — 20th century
[Nihon Kyosanto no rokujunen. English].
Sixty-year history of Japanese Communist Party / Central Committee, Japanese Communist Party. — Tokyo : Japan Press Service, 1984. — 714 p.. — *Translation of: Nihon Kyōsantō no rokujūnen. 1982*

NIKOLAEV, E. B.
NIKOLAEV, E. B.
Predavshie Gippokrata = The betrayal of Hippocrates / Evgenii Nikolaev. — London : Overseas Publications Interchange, 1984. — 324p

NIKOLAEV, LEV NIKOLAEVICH — Journeys — Afghanistan
NIKOLAEV, Lev Nikolaevich
Afghanistan : between the past and the future / Lev Nikolayev ; translated from the Russian by Vic Schneierson. — Moskva : Progress Publishers, c1986. — 206 p.. — *Title on t.p. verso: Afghanistan--mezhdu proshlym i budushchim*

NIN, ANDRES
NIN, Andres
Socialisme i nacionalisme (1912-1934) : escrits republicans, socialistes i comunistes / Andreu Nin ; edició a cura de Pelai Pagès. — Barcelona : Edicions de la Magrana, 1985. — li,191p. — (Biblioteca dels Clàssics del Nacionalisme Català ; 11). — *Bibliography: p [xlv] - xlvii*

NINETEEN FORTY-SEVEN, A.D.
ROBERTSON, Alex J.
The bleak midwinter : 1947 / Alex J. Robertson. — Manchester : Manchester University Press, 1987. — x,207p. — *Bibliography: p197-199. — Includes index*

NITRATES
GREAT BRITAIN. Central Directorate of Environmental Protection
Nitrate in water : a report of the Nitrate Coordination Group / Central Directorate of Environmental Protection, Department of the Environment. — London : H.M.S.O., 1986. — (Pollution paper ; no.26)

NITROGEN
SHELDRICK, William F.
World nitrogen survey / William F. Sheldrick. — Washington, D.C. : The World Bank, 1987. — xxv,227p. — (Industry and finance series ; v20) (World Bank technical paper ; no.59). — *Includes bibliographical references*

NITROGEN INDUSTRIES
SHELDRICK, William F.
World nitrogen survey / William F. Sheldrick. — Washington, D.C. : The World Bank, 1987. — xxv,227p. — (Industry and finance series ; v20) (World Bank technical paper ; no.59). — *Includes bibliographical references*

NIXON, RICHARD
SPEAR, Joseph C.
Presidents and the press : the Nixon legacy / Joseph C.Spear. — Cambridge, Massachusetts ; London : MIT Press, 1984

NIXON, RICHARD M
AMBROSE, Stephen E
Nixon : the education of a politician, 1913-1962 / Stephen E. Ambrose. — New York : Simon and Schuster, c1987. — 752 p., [16] p. of plates. — *Includes index. — Bibliography: p. 717-721*

SCHURMANN, Franz
The foreign politics of Richard Nixon : the grand design / Franz Schurmann. — Berkeley, CA : Institute of International Studies, University of California, Berkeley, 1986. — p. cm. — (Research series ; no. 65). — *Includes index. — Bibliography: p*

NIXON, RICHARD M — Views on public television
STONE, David M.
Nixon and the politics of public television / David M. Stone. — New York : Garland Pub., 1985. — xxi, 370p. — (Modern American history). — *Bibliography: p[342]-360*

NKRUMAH, KWAME
SMERTIN, Yuri
Kwame Nkrumah / Yuri Smertin ; translated from the Russian by Sharon McKee. — Moscow : Progress Publishers, 1987. — 312p

NO-STRIKE CLAUSE — Great Britain
BURROWS, Giles
No-strike agreements and pendulum arbitration / Giles Burrows. — London : Institute of Personnel Management, 1986. — [88]p. — *Includes bibliography*

NOBEL PRIZES — Biography
Lives of the laureates / edited by William Breit and Roger W. Spencer. — Cambridge, Mass. : MIT Press, c1986. — p. cm. — *Bibliography: p*

NOBILITY — Europe — History
The Gentry and lesser nobility in late medieval Europe / edited by Michael Jones and R.L. Storey. — Gloucester : Sutton, 1986. — [192]p

NOISE — Physiological aspects
LOEB, Michel
Noise and human efficiency / by Michel Loeb. — Chichester : Wiley, c1986. — xiv,269p. — (Wiley series on studies in human performance). — *Bibliography: p222-253. — Includes index*

NOISE — Psychological aspects
LOEB, Michel
Noise and human efficiency / by Michel Loeb. — Chichester : Wiley, c1986. — xiv,269p. — (Wiley series on studies in human performance). — *Bibliography: p222-253. — Includes index*

NOISE CONTROL — Organisation for Economic Co-operation and Development countries
Fighting noise : strengthening noise abatement policies. — Paris : Organisation for Economic Co-operation and Development, 1986. — 145p. — *Includes bibliographical references*

NOMADS — Jordan — History
LEWIS, Norman N.
Nomads and settlers in Syria and Jordan, 1800-1980 / Norman N. Lewis. — Cambridge : Cambridge University Press, 1987. — xvii,249p. — (Cambridge Middle East library). — *Bibliography: p238-244. — Includes index*

NOMADS — Oman — Dhofar
JANZEN, Jörg
[Normaden Dhofars/Sultanat Oman. English].
Nomads in the Sultanate of Oman : tradition and development in Dhofar / Jörg Janzen. — Boulder : Westview Press, 1986. — xxiii, 315 p.. — (Westview special studies on the Middle East). — *Translation of: Die Nomaden Dhofars/Sultanat Oman. — Bibliography: p. 299-315*

NOMADS — Sahel — Congresses
COLLOQUIUM ON THE EFFECTS OF DROUGHT ON THE PRODUCTIVE STRATEGIES OF SUDANO-SAHELIAN HERDSMEN AND FARMERS (1975 : Université de Niamey)
Report / Colloquium on the Effects of Drought on the Productive Strategies of Sudano-Sahelian Herdsmen and Farmers ; edited by Michael M. Horowitz. — Binghamton, N.Y. : Institute for Development Anthropology, [1976]. — xiii, 96 p.. — *Cover title*

NOMADS — Sudan
SØRBØ, Gunnar M.
Tenants and nomads in Eastern Sudan : a study of economic adaptations in the New Halfa Scheme / Gunnar M. Sørbø. — Uppsala : Scandinavian Institute of African Studies, 1985. — 159p

NOMADS — Syria — History
LEWIS, Norman N.
Nomads and settlers in Syria and Jordan, 1800-1980 / Norman N. Lewis. — Cambridge : Cambridge University Press, 1987. — xvii,249p. — (Cambridge Middle East library). — *Bibliography: p238-244. — Includes index*

NON-ALIGNED MOVEMENT — History
SINGHAM, A. W.
Non-alignment in an age of alignments / by A.W. Singham and Shirley Hune ; with a preface by Nathan Shamuyarira. — London : Zed, 1986. — [352]p. — *Includes bibliography and index*

NON-FORMAL EDUCATION — Addresses, essays, lectures
Alternative routes to formal education : distance teaching for school equivalency / edited by Hilary Perraton. — Baltimore : Johns Hopkins University Press for the World Bank, 1982. — xiii,329p. — *Includes bibliographical references*

NON-VIOLENCE
GANDHI, M. K.
The moral and political writings of Mahatma Gandhi. — Oxford : Clarendon
volume 2: Truth and non-violence / edited by Raghavan Iyer. — 1986. — xxii,678p. — *Bibliography:p659-664*

NON-WAGE PAYMENTS
TACHIBANAKI, Toshiaki
Non-wage labour costs : their rationale and economic effect / Toshiaki Tachibanaki. — London : Suntory International Centre for Economics and Related Disciplines, 1987. — 63p. — (Welfare State Programme ; no.19) (Discussion paper / Welfare State Programme Suntory-Toyota International Centre for Economics and Related Disciplines. ; no.19). — Bibliography: p59-63

NONALIGNMENT
SENGUPTA, Jyoti
Non-alignment : search for a destination / Jyoti Sengupta. — Calcutta : Naya Prokash, 1979. — xxii,208p

NONALIGNMENT — Bibliography
Non-alignment : a select bibliography = nonalignment bibliographie sélective. — New York : United Nations, 1975. — 39p. — ([Document] / United Nations ; ST/LIB/SER.B/18). — In various languages

NONLINEAR MECHANICS — Collected works
MAGIROS, Demetrios G
[Selections. 1985]. Selected papers of Demetrios C. Magiros : applied mathematics, nonlinear mechanics, and dynamical systems analysis / edited by S.G. Tzafestas. — Dordrecht, Holland : D. Reidel Pub. Co. ; Hingham, MA, U.S.A. : Sold and distributed in the U.S.A. and Canada by Kluwer Academic Publishers, c1985. — xv, 518 p.. — "Published on behalf of the Greek Mathematical Society.". — Bibliography: p. 511-518

NONPARAMETRIC STATISTICS
SILVERMAN, B. W.
Density estimation for statistics and data analysis / B.W. Silverman. — London : Chapman and Hall, 1986. — [200]p. — (Monographs on statistics and applied probability). — Includes bibliography and index

NONRENEWABLE NATURAL RESOURCES — Econometric models
SCHÄFER, Martin
Resource extraction and market structure / Martin Schäfer. — Berlin ; New York : Springer-Verlag, 1986. — 154p. — (Lecture notes in economics and mathematical systems ; 263). — Bibliography: p[150]-151

NONVERBAL COMMUNICATION
ARGYLE, Michael
Bodily communication / Michael Argyle. — London : Methuen, 1975. — ix,403p,[8]p of plates. — Includes bibliographies and index

JOSEPH, Nathan
Uniforms and nonuniforms : communication through clothing / Nathan Joseph. — New York : Greenwood Press, 1986. — vi, 248 p.. — (Contributions in sociology ; no. 61). — Includes index. — Bibliography: p. [221]-238

NONVERBAL COMMUNICATION (PSYCHOLOGY)
PAIVIO, Allan
Mental representations : a dual coding approach / Allan Paivio. — New York : Oxford University Press ; Oxford : Clarendon Press, 1986. — x, 322p. — (Oxford psychology series ; no. 9). — Includes index. — Bibliography: p.277-305

NONVIOLENCE
ALBERT, David H.
People power : applying nonviolence theory / David H. Albert. — Philadelphia : New Society Publishers, 1985. — 64p. — Bibliography: p60-62

ANDERSEN, Alfred F.
Liberating the early American dream : a way to transcend the capitalist/communist dilemma nonviolently / by Alfred F. Andersen. — Ukiah, Calif. : Tom Paine Institute, c1985. — p. cm. — Rev. ed. of: Updating the early American dream. c1984. — Includes index. — Bibliography: p

¡ Basta! : no mandate for war : a pledge of resistance handbook / by the Emergency Response Network ; edited by Ken Butigan, Terry Messman-Rucker, and Marie Pastrick. — Philadelphia : New Society, 1986. — 83,ivp. — Bibliography: pi-iv

Nonviolent struggle in the Middle East. — Santa Cruz, Calif. : New Society Publishers, 1983. — 39p. — Contents: The Druze of the Golan: a case of nonviolent resistance/ R. Scott Kennedy - Nonviolent resistance: a strategy for the occupied territories/ Mubarak E. Awad

NORFOLK — Population
NORFOLK. Department of Planning and Property
1981 census characteristics of county council electoral divisions. — Norwich : [the Department], 1986. — 21p

NORGES KOMMUNISTISKE PARTIE
LORENZ, Einhart
Det er ingen sak å få partiet lite : NKP 1923-1931 / Einhart Lorenz. — Olso : Pax, 1983. — 301p. — Bibliography: p280-287

NORMAN, E. HERBERT
BARROS, James
No sense of evil : espionage, the case of Herbert Norman / James Barros. — Toronto : Deneau, 1986. — xi,259p

NORMANDY (FRANCE) — Population — Statistics
DEZELLUS, André
La démographie en Haute-Normandie / présenté par André Dezellus. — [Rouen] : Comité économique et social de Haute-Normandie, [1986]. — 83,[43]p. — Cover title

NORMANTON (WEST YORKSHIRE) — Civic improvement
GREAT BRITAIN. Department of the Environment. Yorkshire and Humberside Regional Office
A study of the environment in Normanton. — [Leeds] : the Office, 1972. — 51leaves

NORTH AFRICANS — France
COLLOQUE "DES ÉTRANGERS QUI FONT AUSSI LA FRANCE"
Les Nord-Africains en France / ouvrage réalisé sous la direction de Magali Morsy. — Paris : CHEAM, 1984. — 200p. — (Publications du CHEAM ; 3). — Includes bibliographical references

NORTH AMERICA — Air defenses, Military — History
LINDSEY, George
The strategic defence of North America / George R. Lindsey. — [Toronto, Ont., Canada] : Canadian Institute of Strategic Studies, [c1986]. — 40 p.. — (Issues in strategy). — Bibliography: p. 40

NORTH AMERICA — Census — Handbooks, manuals, etc
GOYER, Doreen S.
The handbook of national population censuses : Latin America and the Caribbean, North America, and Oceania / Doreen S. Goyer and Eliane Domschke. — Westport, Conn. : Greenwood Press, 1983. — xii, 711 p.. — Includes index. — Bibliography: p. 28-30

NORTH AMERICA — Economic conditions
Long-term factors in American economic growth / edited by Stanley L. Engerman and Robert E. Gallman. — Chicago : University of Chicago Press, 1986. — p. cm. — (Studies in income and wealth ; v. 51). — Includes indexes

NORTH AMERICA — Economic integration — Congresses
The Integration question : political economy and public policy in Canada and North America / edited by Jon H. Pammett and Brian W. Tomlin. — Don Mills, Ont. ; Reading, Mass. : Addison-Wesley Publishers, c1984. — 262 p.. — : Revised papers of the Conference on Integration and Fragmentation in Canada and North America held March, 1982 at Carleton University, and sponsored by the Carleton Dept. of Political Science in cooperation with Norman Paterson School of International Affairs. — Includes bibliographies and index

NORTH ATLANTIC ASSEMBLY
BRUMTER, Christian
The North Atlantic Asembly / Christian Brumter. — Dordrecht ; Boston : M. Nijhoff, 1986. — xi, 223p

NORTH ATLANTIC ASSEMBLY. Civilian Affairs Committee
CLARK, David
General report on NATO's public relations problems / David Clark. — Brussels : North Atlantic Assembly, 1986. — iii,43p

GARCIA ARIAS, Ludivina
Report of the Sub-Committee on the free flow of information and people / Ludivina Garcia Arias. — Brussels : North Atlantic Assembly, 1986. — i,24p

SKARSTEIN, Inger-Lise
Interim report of the Sub-Committee on Public Information / Inger-Lise Skarstein. — Brussels : North Atlantic Assembly, 1986. — ii,25p

NORTH ATLANTIC ASSEMBLY. Economic Committee
SIMONIS, Heide
Final report of the Sub-Committee on Economic Co-operation / Heide Simonis. — Brussels : North Atlantic Assembly, 1986. — vi,31p

WARTENBERG, Ludolf-Georg von
General report on the economics of Atlantic security / Ludolf-Georg von Wartenberg. — Brussels : North Atlantic Assembly, 1986. — ii,36p

NORTH ATLANTIC ASSEMBLY. Military Committee
PETERSEN, Peter
Interim report of the Sub-Committee on Defence Co-operation / Peter Petersen. — Brussels : North Atlantic Assembly, 1986. — iv,28p

VOIGT, Karsten
Interim report of the Sub-Committee on conventional defence : new strategies and operational concepts / Karsten Voigt. — Brussels : North Atlantic Assembly, 1986. — iv,33p

WAART, Jules de
General report on Alliance security / Jules de Waart. — Brussels : North Atlantic Assembly, 1986. — iii,52p

NORTH ATLANTIC ASSEMBLY. Political Committee
BOUVARD, Loïc
Final report of the Sub-Committee on the Southern Region / Loïc Bouvard. — Brussels : North Atlantic Assembly, 1986. — ii,25p

GEORGE, Bruce
General report on Alliance political developments / Bruce George. — Brussels : North Atlantic Assembly, 1986. — ii,45p

HERRERO RODRIGUEZ DE MINON, Miguel
Final report of the Sub-Committee on Out-of-Area Security Challenges to the Alliance / Miguel Herrero Rodriguez de Minon. — Brussels : North Atlantic Assembly, 1986. — i,47p

NORTH ATLANTIC ASSEMBLY. Scientific and Technical Committee

BANKS, Robert
Special report on the exploitation of space / Robert Banks. — Brussels : North Atlantic Assembly, 1986. — ii,31p

IBRÜGGER, Lothar
General report on East-West scientific co-operation, the Chernobyl accident, and nuclear waste / Lothar Ibrügger. — Brussels : North Atlantic Assembly, 1986. — ii,33p

IBRÜGGER, Lothar
General report on strategic defence : technology issues / Lothar Ibrügger. — Brussels : North Atlantic Assembly, 1986. — ii,30p

STRUICK VAN BEMMELEN, Ton
Interim report of the Sub-Committee on Advanced Technology and Technology Transfer / Ton Struick van Bemmelen. — Brussels : North Atlantic Assembly, 1986. — ii,33p

NORTH ATLANTIC ASSEMBLY. Special Committee on Nuclear Strategy and Arms Control

CARTWRIGHT, John
Interim report [of the Special Committee on Nuclear Strategy and Arms Control] / John Cartwright. — Brussels : North Atlantic Assembly, 1986. — iii,67p

NORTH ATLANTIC TREATY, 1949

ATLANTISCHE COMMISSIE
De school en het buitenlands beleéd. — Den Haag : Atlantische Commissie, 1969. — Bibliography: p[27-28]
7: Bestaat er een Atlantische Wereld?. — 26, [2] leaves

NORTH ATLANTIC TREATY ORGANIZATION

ARCHER, Clive
Greenland and the Atlantic Alliance / Clive Archer. — Aberdeen : Centre for Defence Studies, 1985. — 66p. — (Centrepieces ; no.7)

AUSLAND, John C.
Nordic security and the great powers / John C. Ausland. — Boulder, Colo. ; London : Westview Press, 1986. — xiii,197p

BELLINI, James
An analysis of the effect of the development of French foreign policy on the evolution of the Western Alliance 1948-1954 / James Bellini. — 310 leaves. — PhD (Econ) 1986 LSE

CAMPANY, Richard C
Turkey and the United States : the arms embargo period / Richard C. Campany, Jr. — New York : Praeger, 1986. — p. cm. — Includes index. — Bibliography: p

Choices : nuclear and non-nuclear defence options / assessed by: Peter Carrington...[et al.] ; organized and presented by Oliver Ramsbotham. — London : Brassey's, 1987. — xiv,473p

CLARK, David
General report on NATO's public relations problems / David Clark. — Brussels : North Atlantic Assembly, 1986. — iii,43p

Dealignment : a new foreign policy perspective / edited by Mary Kaldor and Richard Falk with the assistance of Gerard Holden. — Oxford : Basil Blackwell, 1987. — viii,265p. — Includes index

DEAN, Jonathan
Watershed in Europe : dismantling the East-West military confrontation / Jonathan Dean. — Lexington, Mass. : Lexington Books, 1986, c1987. — p. cm. — Includes index

Doctrine, the Alliance and arms control / edited by Robert O'Neill. — Basingstoke : Macmillan in association with International Institute for Strategic Studies, 1986. — 232p. — (International Institute for Strategic Studies conference papers). — Includes index

DOUGHERTY, James E.
Eurocommunism and the Atlantic Alliance / James E. Dougherty and Diane K. Pfaltzgraff. — Cambridge, Mass : Institute for Foreign Policy Analysis, 1977. — xiv, 66 p. — (Special Report - Institute for Foreign Policy Analysis). — Includes bibliographical references

Evolving European defense policies / edited by Catherine M. Kelleher and Gale A. Mattox. — Lexington, Mass. : Lexington Books, c1987. — p. cm. — Includes index

FARINGDON, Hugh
Confrontation : the strategic geography of NATO and the Warsaw Pact / Hugh Faringdon. — London : Routledge & Kegan Paul, 1986. — [352]p. — Includes bibliography and index

GEORGE, Bruce
General report on Alliance political developments / Bruce George. — Brussels : North Atlantic Assembly, 1986. — ii,45p

GOETZE, Bernd A
Security in Europe : a crisis of confidence / Bernd A. Goetze. — New York : Praeger, 1984. — p. cm. — Includes index. — Bibliography: p

HERRERO RODRIGUEZ DE MINON, Miguel
Final report of the Sub-Committee on Out-of-Area Security Challenges to the Alliance / Miguel Herrero Rodriguez de Minon. — Brussels : North Atlantic Assembly, 1986. — i,47p

HUITFELDT, Tønne
NATO's northern security / Tønne Huitfeldt. — London : Institute for the Study of Conflict, 1986. — 24p. — (Conflict studies ; no.191)

JOCKEL, Joseph T
Canada and collective security : odd man out / Joseph T. Jockel, Joel J. Sokolsky ; foreword by John G.H. Halstead. — New York : Praeger, 1986. — xv, 118 p.. — (The Washington papers ; 121). — "Published with the Center for Strategic and International Studies, Georgetown University, Washington, D.C.". — Bibliography: p. 117-118

KRAUSS, Melvyn B
How NATO weakens the West / Melvyn Krauss. — New York : Simon and Schuster, c1986. — 271 p.. — Includes index. — Bibliography: p. 254-262

LANGER, Peter H.
Transatlantic discord and NATO's crisis of cohesion / Peter H. Langer. — Washington, D.C. : Pergamon-Brassey's, 1986. — p. cm. — (Foreign policy report). — "A publication of the Institute for Foreign Policy Analysis, Inc.". — Bibliography: p

The Military buildup in the high North : American and Nordic perspectives / edited by Sverre Jervell and Kare Nyblom. — Lanham ; London : Center for International Affairs, Harvard University and University Press of America, c1986. — xiii,159p

MÜLLER, Harald
Strategic defences : the end of the Alliance strategy? / Harald Müller. — Brussels : Centre for European Policy Studies, 1987. — 52p. — (CEPS papers ; no.32). — Bibliography: p46-52

OLDAG, Andreas
Allianzpolitische Konflikte in der NATO : die sicherheitspolitischen Interessen der USA und Westeuropas zu Beginn der 80er Jahre / Andreas Oldag. — Baden-Baden : Nomos Verlagsgesellschaft, 1985. — vi,185p. — (Darstellungen zur internationalen Politik und Entwicklungspolitik ; 15). — Bibliography: p169-185

PRESSLEY, Neville
Uniting for peace : a policy for the nineties / Neville Pressley. — Hebden Bridge : Liberal Party Publications, 1986. — 57p

RUBIO GARCÍA, Leandro
España y la O.T.A.N. / Leandro Rubio García. — [Zaragoza] : Caja de Ahorros de Zaragoza, Aragón y Rioja, [ca.1982]. — 78p. — (Serie papeles diversos / Caja de Ahorros de Zaragoza, Aragón y Rioja)

SKARSTEIN, Inger-Lise
Interim report of the Sub-Committee on Public Information / Inger-Lise Skarstein. — Brussels : North Atlantic Assembly, 1986. — ii,25p

SNYDER, Jed C
Defending the fringe : NATO, the Mediterranean, and the Gulf / Jed C. Snyder. — Boulder : Westview Press, 1986. — p. cm. . — (SAIS papers in international affairs ; no. 11). — Includes index

WAART, Jules de
General report on Alliance security / Jules de Waart. — Brussels : North Atlantic Assembly, 1986. — iii,52p

WARTENBERG, Ludolf-Georg von
General report on the economics of Atlantic security / Ludolf-Georg von Wartenberg. — Brussels : North Atlantic Assembly, 1986. — ii,36p

NORTH ATLANTIC TREATY ORGANIZATION — Addresses, essays, lectures

Continuity of discord : crises and responses in the Atlantic community / edited by Robert J. Jackson. — New York : Praeger, 1985. — p. cm

NATO in the 1980s : challenges and responses / edited by Linda P. Brady and Joyce P. Kaufman. — New York : Praeger, 1985. — p. cm. — Includes index

NORTH ATLANTIC TREATY ORGANIZATION — Armed Forces

CHARLES, Daniel
Nuclear planning in NATO : pitfalls of first use / Daniel Charles. — Cambridge, Mass. : Ballinger Pub. Co., c1987. — xv, 177 p.. — "A Federation of American Scientists book.". — Includes bibliographies and index

Emerging technologies and military doctrines : a political assessment / edited by Frank Barnaby and Marlies ter Borg. — Basingstoke : Macmillan, 1986. — xxi,328p. — Includes index

NORTH ATLANTIC TREATY ORGANIZATION — Armed Forces — Procurement

MOODIE, Frank T. J
Defense technology and the Atlantic Alliance : competition or collaboration? / Frank T. J. Bray. Michael Moodie. — Cambridge, Mass : Institute for Foreign Policy Analysis, 1977. — vi, 42 p.. — (Foreign policy report). — Includes bibliographical references

NORTH ATLANTIC TREATY ORGANIZATION — Armed Forces — Weapons systems

MOODIE, Frank T. J
Defense technology and the Atlantic Alliance : competition or collaboration? / Frank T. J. Bray. Michael Moodie. — Cambridge, Mass : Institute for Foreign Policy Analysis, 1977. — vi, 42 p.. — (Foreign policy report). — Includes bibliographical references

NORTH ATLANTIC TREATY ORGANIZATION — Congresses

ATLANTISCHE COMMISSIE. International Round Table Conference (1985 : Hague, Netherlands)
The future of European defence : proceedings of the Second International Round Table Conference of the Netherlands Atlantic Commission on May 24 and 25, 1985 / Frans Bletz and Rio Praaning [editors]. — Dordrecht ; Boston : M. Nijhoff, 1986. — p. cm

NORTH ATLANTIC TREATY ORGANIZATION — Congresses
continuation
Security in the North : Nordic and superpower perceptions : papers / presented to a seminar on "The North and the superpowers : mutual security policy perceptions" on March 16, 1983 ; edited by Bo Huldt and Atis Lejins. — Stockholm : Swedish Institute of International Affairs, [1984]. — vii, 78 p.. — (Conference papers / the Swedish Institute of International Affairs ; 5, 1984). — *Includes bibliographies.* — *Contents: Perceptions in international politics and national security / Christer Jönsson -- Nordic perceptions of the great powers and Nordic security / Kari Möttölä -- The USA and security in the Nordic countries / Svein Melby -- Soviet perceptions of Nordic security problems / Bjarne Nörretranders -- The big powers and Nordic security / Sverre Lodgaard*

NORTH ATLANTIC TREATY ORGANIZATION — History
CYR, Arthur
  US foreign policy and European security / Arthur Cyr. — London : Macmillan, 1987. — vii,156p. — *Includes index*

NORTH ATLANTIC TREATY ORGANIZATION — Great Britain
RICHEY, George
  Britain's strategic role in NATO / George Richey ; foreword by Gerald Frost. — Basingstoke : Macmillan, 1986. — x,173p. — *Includes index*

NORTH ATLANTIC TREATY ORGANIZATION — Spain
ARROJO, Pedro
  OTAN : debate directo / Pedro Arrojo. — Zaragoza : Centro de Documentación por la Paz yel Desarme, [1984]. — 32p

CASALDUERO, Francisco
  Europa, Gibraltar y la O.T.A.N. / Francisco Casalduero. — Madrid : Dyrsa, 1985. — 114p

España, Europa, occidente : una política integrada de seguridad / textos de: José María de Areilza...[et al.] ; editado por: Bernhard Hagemeyer...[et al.]. — Madrid : Distribución y Comunicación, 1984. — 177p. — *Papers presented at an international colloquium organized by the Konrad Adenauer Stiftung in Madrid, 26-28 October, 1983*

España y la OTAN : textos y documentos / edición preparada por Celestino del Arenal y Francisco Aldecoa. — Madrid : Tecnos, 1986. — 492p. — (Colección Relaciones exteriores de España)

NORTH CAROLINA — Economic conditions
WOOD, Phillip J.
  Southern capitalism : the political economy of North Carolina, 1880-1980 / Phillip J. Wood. — Durham, N.C. : Duke University Press, 1986. — xi, 272 p.. — *Includes index.* — *Bibliography: p. [250]-267*

NORTH CAROLINA — Economic policy
WOOD, Phillip J.
  Southern capitalism : the political economy of North Carolina, 1880-1980 / Phillip J. Wood. — Durham, N.C. : Duke University Press, 1986. — xi, 272 p.. — *Includes index.* — *Bibliography: p. [250]-267*

NORTH CAROLINA — Industries — History
WOOD, Phillip J.
  Southern capitalism : the political economy of North Carolina, 1880-1980 / Phillip J. Wood. — Durham, N.C. : Duke University Press, 1986. — xi, 272 p.. — *Includes index.* — *Bibliography: p. [250]-267*

NORTH CAROLINA — Politics and government — 1951-
SNIDER, William D
  Hunt and Helms : North Carolina chooses a Senator / by William D. Snider. — Chapel Hill : University of North Carolina Press, c1985. — p. cm. — *Includes index*

NORTH CAROLINA — Rural conditions
BEAVER, Patricia D
  Rural community in the Appalachian South / Patricia Duane Beaver. — Lexington, KY : University Press of Kentucky, c1996. — p. cm. — *Includes index.* — *Bibliography: p*

NORTH-EAST ATLANTIC FISHERIES COMMISSION
NORTH-EAST ATLANTIC FISHERIES COMMISSION
  Report of the annual meeting. — London : Office of the Commission, 1982-. — *Annual*

NORTH-EAST METROPOLITAN REGIONAL HOSPITAL BOARD
NORTH-EAST METROPOLITAN REGIONAL HOSPITAL BOARD
  NEMET 1948-1974 : a record of progress in the North East Metropolitan Region. — [London : the Board, ca.1974]. — 28p

NORTH-WEST TERRITORIES — Economic conditions
CANADA. Parliament. House of Commons. Standing Committee on Aboriginal Affairs and Northern Development
  Minutes of proceedings and evidence... = Procès verbaux et témoignages. — Ottawa : Government Printer, 1986-. — *Continues: Canada. Parliament. House of Commons. Standing Committee on Indian Affairs and Northern Development. Minutes of proceedings and evidence...*

NORTH WEST TERRITORIES — Economic Conditions
CANADA. Parliament. House of Commons. Standing Committee on Indian Affairs and Northern Development
  Minutes of proceedings and evidence... = Procès-verbaux et témoignages.... — Ottawa : Government Printer, 1968-1986. — *Irregular.* — *Continued by: Canada. Parliament. House of Commons. Standing Committee on Aboriginal Affairs and Northern Development*

NORTH WEST THAMES REGIONAL HEALTH AUTHORITY
GLENNERSTER, Howard
  The nursing management function after Griffiths : a study in the North West Thames Region / Professor Howard Glennerster, Dr. Pat Owens [and] Ms. Angela Kimberley. — London : London School of Economics and Political Science : North West Thames Regional Health Authority, 1986. — 85,viiip.. — *Bibliography: p.ix-x*

NORTH YORKSHIRE — Civil defense
NORTH YORKSHIRE. County Council
  County war plan : Part 1. — Northallerton : [the Council], 1981. — 15[4]p

NORTHAMPTON GAS-LIGHT COMPANY — History
EAST MIDLANDS GAS
  The Northampton gas undertaking 1823-1949 / prepared for Emgas by D.E. Roberts, J.H. Frisby. — Leicester (De Montfort St., Leicester) : East Midlands Gas, 1980. — 38p. — (Studies in East Midlands gas history). — *Bibliography: p38*

NORTHEASTERN STATES — Economic conditions
GLANCY, David M.
  Description of the area system for the Northeast Corridor Transportation Project / by David M. Glancy. — [Washington, D.C.] : U.S. Department of Commerce, 1965. — [16],7 leaves. — (Northeast Corridor Transportation Project technical paper ; no.2)

NORTHEASTERN STATES — Population — Forecasting
Method for the initial superdistrict projections of Northeast Corridor population, employment and income / by Robert Crow...[et al.]. — [Washington, D.C.] : U.S. Department of Commerce, 1966. — 45p. — (Northeast Corridor Transportation Project technical paper ; no.6)

NORTHEASTERN STATES — Population — Statistics
CROW, Robert Thomas
  Description of projections of natural population increase and labor force / by Robert Thomas Crow. — [Washington, D.C.] : U.S. Department of Commerce, 1965. — [15]p. — (Northeast Corridor Transportation Project technical paper ; no.1). — *Bibliography: p [14-15]*

NORTHEN IRELAND — Politics and government
GIBBON, Peter
  The origins of Ulster Unionism : the formation of popular Protestant politics and ideology in nineteenth-century Ireland / Peter Gibbon. — Manchester : Manchester University Press, 1975. — viii,163p. — *Bibliography: p.147-152.* — *Includes index*

NORTHERN IRELAND — Bibliography
INFORMATION ON IRELAND
  A resources guide to the north of Ireland. — London : Information on Ireland, 1985. — 30p

NORTHERN IRELAND — Church history
BRUCE, Steve
  God save Ulster : the religion and politics of Paisleyism / Steve Bruce. — Oxford : Clarendon, 1986. — xv,308p. — *Includes index*

NORTHERN IRELAND — Ethnic relations
SEE, Katherine O'Sullivan
  First world nationalisms : class and ethnic politics in Northern Ireland and Quebec / Katherine O'Sullivan See. — Chicago : University of Chicago Press, 1986. — p. cm. — *Includes index.* — *Bibliography: p*

NORTHERN IRELAND — Foreign opinion
O'HALLORAN, Clare
  Partition and the limits of Irish nationalism : an ideology under stress / Clare O'Halloran. — Dublin : Gill and Macmillan, c[1987]. — xviii,234p. — *Bibliography: p233-240*

NORTHERN IRELAND — History
DOUMITT, Donald P.
  Conflict in Northern Ireland : the history, the problem, and the challenge / Donald P. Doumitt. — New York : P. Lang, c1985. — 247 p.. — (American university studies. Series IX. History ; vol. 5). — *Bibliography: p. 233-247*

GRØNLUND ANDERSEN, Steen
  Northern Ireland et samfund i konflikt / Steen Grønlund Andersen, Jørgen Vestergaard Jacobsen. — Herning : Systime, 1984. — 128p. — *Includes chapters in English.* — *Bibliography: p126*

RIDDELL, Patrick
  Fire over Ulster / by Patrick Riddell. — London : Hamilton, 1970. — xiv,208p. — *bibl p207-208*

NORTHERN IRELAND — History — Autonomy and independence movements
SEE, Katherine O'Sullivan
  First world nationalisms : class and ethnic politics in Northern Ireland and Quebec / Katherine O'Sullivan See. — Chicago : University of Chicago Press, 1986. — p. cm. — *Includes index.* — *Bibliography: p*

NORTHERN IRELAND — History — Sources
MCMINN, J. R. B.
  Against the tide : a calendar of the papers of Rev. J. B Armour, Irish Presbyterian minister and Home Ruler, 1869-1914. — Belfast : PRONI, 1985. — lxii,225p

NORTHERN IRELAND — History — 1969-

SHANNON, William V.
A quiet broker? : a way out of the Irish conflict / by William V. Shannon. — New York : Priory Press, 1985. — vi, 52p. — (A Twentieth Century Fund paper)

NORTHERN IRELAND — Politics and government

DOUMITT, Donald P.
Conflict in Northern Ireland : the history, the problem, and the challenge / Donald P. Doumitt. — New York : P. Lang, c1985. — 247 p. — (American university studies. Series IX. History ; vol. 5). — *Bibliography: p. 233-247*

JENKINS, Richard, 1952-
The sectarian divide in Northern Ireland today / Richard Jenkins, Hastings Donnan [and] Graham McFarlane. — London : Royal Anthropological Institute of Great Britain and Ireland, 1986. — 37p. — (Occasional paper / Royal Anthropological Institute of Great Britain and Ireland ; no.41). — *Bibliography: p36-37*

KENNY, Anthony
The road to Hillsborough : the shaping of the Anglo-Irish agreement / by Anthony Kenny. — Oxford : Pergamon, 1986. — xi,141p

MACDONALD, Michael, 19---
Children of wrath : political violence in Northern Ireland / Michael MacDonald. — Cambridge : Pality, 1986. — [220]p. — *Includes index*

Northern Ireland : the historical background to the present situation : four papers read at a meeting of the Graduates' Fellowship Historians' Study Group. — Leicester : UCCF Associates for the Historians' Study Group, 1972. — [36]p

RIDDELL, Patrick
Fire over Ulster / by Patrick Riddell. — London : Hamilton, 1970. — xiv,208p. — *bibl p207-208*

The slaying of John Downes / issued by Sinn Fein Publicity Department. — Dublin : Republican Publications, 1984. — 30p

STEVENS, David
Facing up to Northern Ireland / David Stevens and Brian Lennon. — Dublin : Irish Messenger Publications, 1985. — 30p

NORTHERN IRELAND — Politics and government — Addresses, essays, lectures

Ireland's terrorist dilemma / [edited by] Yonah Alexander and Alan O'Day. — Dordrecht [Netherlands] ; Lancaster : M. Nijhoff, 1986. — 279p. — (International studies on terrorism ; v. 2). — *Bibliography: p.261-277*

NORTHERN IRELAND — Politics and government — Pictorial works

KILLEN, John
John Bull's famous circus : Ulster history through the postcard, 1905-1985 / John Killen. — Dublin : O'Brien, 1985. — 160p

NORTHERN IRELAND — Politics and government — 1969-

BERESFORD, David
Ten men dead : the story of the 1981 Irish hunger strike / David Beresford. — London : Grafton, 1987. — 432p

BEW, Paul
The British state and the Ulster crisis : from Wilson to Thatcher / Paul Bew and Henry Patterson. — London : Verso, 1985. — [152]p. — *Includes index*

BRUCE, Steve
God save Ulster : the religion and politics of Paisleyism / Steve Bruce. — Oxford : Clarendon, 1986. — xv,308p. — *Includes index*

DARBY, John
Intimidation and the control of conflict in Northern Ireland / John Darby. — Dublin : Gill and Macmillan, c1986. — ix,187p. — *Bibliography: p175-178. — Includes index*

FERGUSON, Bob
Television on history : representations of Ireland / Bob Ferguson. — 2nd ed. — London : Department of English and Media Studies, University of London Institute of Education in association with Comedia, 1985. — iv,27p. — (Media analysis paper ; 5). — *Previous ed.: 198-?*

GRØNLUND ANDERSEN, Steen
Northern Ireland et samfund i konflikt / Steen Grønlund Andersen, Jørgen Vestergaard Jacobsen. — Herning : Systime, 1984. — 128p. — *Includes chapters in English. — Bibliography: p126*

MORRISON, Danny
The Hillsborough Agreement : the text of the Bobby Sands commemorative lecture in Twinbrook, Belfast on Sunday 4th May 1986 / Danny Morrison. — Belfast : Republican Publications, 1986. — 23p

NEVIN, Vera E.
Dear Mr. Whitelaw / Vera E. Nevin. — Belfast : Ulster Educational Press, 1987. — 28p

Northern Ireland : a challenge to theology / Enda McDonagh [et al.]. — Edinburgh : University of Edinburgh. Centre for Theology and Public Issues, 1987. — 67p. — (Occasional paper / University of Edinburgh. Centre for Theology and Public Issues ; no12)

SHANNON, William V.
A quiet broker? : a way out of the Irish conflict / by William V. Shannon. — New York : Priory Press, 1985. — vi, 52p. — (A Twentieth Century Fund paper)

The third force / Joanna McMinn [et al.]. — Rathcoole : Hand to Mouth Press, 1986. — 48p

NORTHERN IRELAND — Religion

Northern Ireland : a challenge to theology / Enda McDonagh [et al.]. — Edinburgh : University of Edinburgh. Centre for Theology and Public Issues, 1987. — 67p. — (Occasional paper / University of Edinburgh. Centre for Theology and Public Issues ; no12)

NORTHERN IRELAND — Social conditions

DOUMITT, Donald P.
Conflict in Northern Ireland : the history, the problem, and the challenge / Donald P. Doumitt. — New York : P. Lang, c1985. — 247 p.. — (American university studies. Series IX. History ; vol. 5). — *Bibliography: p. 233-247*

GRØNLUND ANDERSEN, Steen
Northern Ireland et samfund i konflikt / Steen Grønlund Andersen, Jørgen Vestergaard Jacobsen. — Herning : Systime, 1984. — 128p. — *Includes chapters in English. — Bibliography: p126*

The third force / Joanna McMinn [et al.]. — Rathcoole : Hand to Mouth Press, 1986. — 48p

NORTHERN IRELAND — politics and government

BOYLE, Kevin
Law and state : the case of Northern Ireland / by Kevin Boyle, Tom Hadden, Paddy Hillyard. — London : Robertson, 1975. — x,194p. — (Law in society series)

NORTHERN TERRITORY — Economic conditions

DONOVAN, P. F
At the other end of Australia : the commonwealth and the Northern Territory, 1911-1978 / P.F. Donovan. — St. Lucia ; New York : University of Queensland Press ; Lawrence, Mass. : Distributed in the U.S.A. and Canada by Technical Impex Corp., 1984. — xv, 277 p.. — *Includes index. — Bibliography: p. [258]-267*

NORTHERN TERRITORY (AUSTRALIA) — History

DONOVAN, P. F
At the other end of Australia : the commonwealth and the Northern Territory, 1911-1978 / P.F. Donovan. — St. Lucia ; New York : University of Queensland Press ; Lawrence, Mass. : Distributed in the U.S.A. and Canada by Technical Impex Corp., 1984. — xv, 277 p.. — *Includes index. — Bibliography: p. [258]-267*

NORTHERN TERRITORY (AUSTRALIA) — Politics and government

DONOVAN, P. F
At the other end of Australia : the commonwealth and the Northern Territory, 1911-1978 / P.F. Donovan. — St. Lucia ; New York : University of Queensland Press ; Lawrence, Mass. : Distributed in the U.S.A. and Canada by Technical Impex Corp., 1984. — xv, 277 p.. — *Includes index. — Bibliography: p. [258]-267*

NORTHMEN

Place-name evidence for the Anglo-Saxon invasion and Scandinavian settlements : eight studies / collected by Kenneth Cameron ; introduction by Margaret Gelling. — [Nottingham] ([c/o School of English Studies, The University, Nottingham NG7 2RD]) : English Place-Name Society, 1975. — [3],v,171p. — *Cover title*

NORTHUMBERLAND — Bibliography — Union lists

Durham and Northumberland / county editor F.W.D. Manders. — London : British Library, c1982. — xvi,65p. — (Bibliography of British newspapers). — *"The bibliography of British newspapers is edited by the Reference Special and Information Section of the Library Association". — Includes index*

NORTHWEST, CANADIAN — History

MORRISON, William R
Showing the flag : the Mounted Police and Canadian sovereignty in the north, 1894-1925 / William R. Morrison. — Vancouver : University of British Columbia Press, 1985. — xix, 220 p., [16] p. of plates. — *Includes index. — Bibliography: p. [209]-216*

NEWMAN, Peter C., 1929-
Company of Adventurers / Peter C. Newman. — Ontario : Viking Penguin
Vol.1. — c1985. — xxiii, 413p. — *Map on lining papers*

RIEL, Louis
[[Works]]. The collected writings of Louis Riel = Les ecrits complets de Louis Riel / Louis Riel ; general editor George F. G. Stanley. — Edmonton : University of Alberta Press. — *Text in English and French*
Vol.1: 29 December 1861 - 7 December 1875 / editor Raymond Huel. — 1985. — 546p. — *Bibliography and index in Vol.5*

RIEL, Louis
[[Works]]. The collected writings of Louis Riel = Les ecrits complets de Louis Riel / Louis Riel ; general editor George F. G. Stanley. — Edmonton : University of Alberta Press. — *Text in English and French*
Vol.2: 8 December 1875 - 4 June 1884 / editor Gilles Martel. — 1985. — 482p. — *Bibliography and index in Vol.5*

NORTHWEST, CANADIAN — History
continuation

RIEL, Louis
[[Works]]. The collected writings of Louis Riel = Les ecrits complets de Louis Riel / Louis Riel ; general editor George F. G. Stanley. — Edmonton : University of Alberta Press. — *Text in English and French*
Vol.3: 5 June 1884 - 16November 1885 / editor Thomas Flanagan. — Edmonton : University of Alberta Press. — 637p. — *Text in English and French*

RIEL, Louis
[[Works]]. The collected writings of Louis Riel = Les ecrits complets de Louis Riel / Louis Riel ; general editor George F. G. Stanley. — Edmonton : University of Alberta Press. — *Text in English and French*
Vol.4: Poetry / editor Glen Campbell. — 1985. — 544p. — *Bibliography and index in Vol.5*

RIEL, Louis
[[Works]]. The collected writings of Louis Riel = Les ecrits complets de Louis Riel / Louis Riel ; general editor George F. G. Stanley. — Edmonton : University of Alberta Press. — *Text in English and French*
Vol.5: Reference / editors George F. G. Stanley, Thomas Flanagan, Claude Rocan. — 1985. — 360p. — *Contains bibliography, p131-205 and biographical index, p207-360*

NORTHWEST, CANADIAN — Politics and government
ROBERTSON, Gordon
Northern Provinces : a mistaken goal / Gordon Robertson. — Montréal : Institute for Research on Public Policy, 1985. — 77p

NORWAY — Census, 1980
NORWAY
Folke- og bustadteljing 1980 = Population and housing census 1980. — Oslo : Statistisk Sentralbyrå. — (Norges offisielle statistikk ; B588). — *Text in Norwegian and English. Previous volumes entitled 'Folke- og boligtelling 1980'*
Hefte 4: Hovudtal 1960, 1970 og 1980 = Main results 1960, 1970 and 1980. — 1986. — 114p

NORWAY — Economic conditions
BERGH, Trond
Vitenskap og politikk : linjer i norsk sosialøkonomi gjennom 150 år / Trond Bergh og Tore J. Hanisch. — Oslo : Aschehoug, 1984. — 269p

Norge fra u-land til i-land : vekst og utviklingslinjer 1830-1980 / Trond Bergh...[et al.]. — Oslo : Gyldendal, 1983. — 253p. — *Bibliography: p241-254*

NORWAY — Economic conditions — Statistics
NORWAY. Statistik Sentralbyrå
Kvartalsvis hasjonalregnskap = quarterly national accounts / Statistik Sentralbyrå, Norway. — Oslo : Statistik Sentralbyrå, 1978-. — *Annual*

NORWAY — Economic conditions — 1945-
NORENG, Øjstein
Olje-Norge : det bevisstlose eksperiment / Øystein Noreng. — Oslo : Aschehoug, 1984. — 167p

NORWAY — Economic policy
GALENSON, Walter
A welfare state strikes oil : the Norwegian experience / Walter Galenson. — Lanham, MD : University Press of America, c1986. — vii, 128 p.. — *Includes index. — Bibliography: p. 117-123*

Norwegian long-term programme 1986-1989. — [Oslo] : Royal Norwegian Ministry of Finance, [1985?]. — 367p. — (Report to the Storting (1984-85) ; no.83). — *Translation of: Langtidsprogrammet 1986-1989*

NORWAY — Foreign relations — 1945-
Norwegian foreign policy in the 1980s / edited by Johan Jørgen Holst. — Oslo : Norwegian University Press, 1985. — 176p. — (Norwegian foreign policy studies ; no.51)

NORWAY — Officials and employees — Salaries, allowances, etc. — Statistics
Lønnsstatistikk statens embets-og tjenestemenn = Wage statistics - central government employees / Norway. Statistisk Sentralbyrå. — Oslo : Statistisk Sentralbyrå, 1969-. — *Annual. — Text in Norwegian and English. — 1975-1981 entitled: Lønns-og sysselsettingsstatistikk statens embets-og tjenestemenn: Wage and employment statistics for central government employees*

NORWAY — Politics and government — 1905-
BJØRGUM, Jorunn
Venstre og kriseforliket : landbrukspolitikk og parlamentarisk spill 1934-1935 / Jorunn Bjørgum. — 2. utgave. — Oslo : Universitetsforlaget, 1978. — 191p. — *First published 1970. — Bibliography: p164*

LORENZ, Einhart
Det er ingen sak å få partiet lite : NKP 1923-1931 / Einhart Lorenz. — Olso : Pax, 1983. — 301p. — *Bibliography: p280-287*

Venstres hundre år / Ottar Grepstad, Jostein Nerbøvik (red.). — Oslo : Gyldendal Norsk Forlag, 1984. — 304p

NORWAY — Politics and government — 1945-
Bypolitikk i Norge : historie, planlegging, styring, framtid / redigert av Harald Baldersheim. — Oslo : Gyldendal, 1983. — 215p. — *Bibliography: p203-216*

Norwegian foreign policy in the 1980s / edited by Johan Jørgen Holst. — Oslo : Norwegian University Press, 1985. — 176p. — (Norwegian foreign policy studies ; no.51)

Styrk fagbevegelsens kampkraft : faglig studiebok fra AKP (m-l). — Oslo : Forlaget Oktober, 1975. — 205p

NORWAY — Population — Forecasting
Framskriving av folkernengden 1985-2050 : regionale tall = Population projections 1985-2050 : regional figures. — Oslo : Statistisk Sentralbyrå, 1986. — 212p. — (Norges offisielle statistikk ; B583). — *In Norwegian and English*

NORWAY — Population — Statistics
NORWAY
Folke- og bustadteljing 1980 = Population and housing census 1980. — Oslo : Statistisk Sentralbyrå. — (Norges offisielle statistikk ; B588). — *Text in Norwegian and English. — Previous volumes entitled 'Folke- og boligtelling 1980'*
Hefte 4: Hovudtal 1960, 1970 og 1980 = Main results 1960, 1970 and 1980. — 1986. — 114p

NORWAY — Social conditions
SEIP, Anne-Lise
Sosialhjelpstaten blir til : norsk sosialpolitikk 1740-1920 / Anne-Lise Seip. — Oslo : Gyldendal, 1984. — 353p. — *Bibliography: p330-349*

NORWAY — Social conditions — 1945-
Styrk fagbevegelsens kampkraft : faglig studiebok fra AKP (m-l). — Oslo : Forlaget Oktober, 1975. — 205p

NORWAY — Social policy
Norwegian long-term programme 1986-1989. — [Oslo] : Royal Norwegian Ministry of Finance, [1985?]. — 367p. — (Report to the Storting (1984-85) ; no.83). — *Translation of: Langtidsprogrammet 1986-1989*

SEIP, Anne-Lise
Sosialhjelpstaten blir til : norsk sosialpolitikk 1740-1920 / Anne-Lise Seip. — Oslo : Gyldendal, 1984. — 353p. — *Bibliography: p330-349*

NORWEGIAN ESSAYS
BJØRNEBOE, Jens
Politi og anarki : essays / Jens Bjørneboe. — 4. opplag. — Oslo : Pax, 1986. — 372p. — *First published 1975*

NORWEGIAN LANGUAGE — Dictionaries — English
HAUGEN, Einar
Norwegian-English dictionary : a pronouncing and translating dictionary of modern Norwegian (Bokmål and Nynorsk), with a historical and grammatical introduction = Norsk-Engelsk Ordbok / Einar Haugen. — 3rd ed. — Bergen : Universitetsforlaget, 1984. — 506p

NORWEGIAN LANGUAGE — Social aspects
LARSON, Karen A.
Learning without lessons : socialization and language change in Norway / Karen A. Larson. — Lanham, Md. ; London : University Press of America, c1985. — x,133p. — *Bibliography: p121-130. — Includes index*

NOTTINGHAM (NOTTINGHAMSHIRE) — Industries — History
ROBERTS, D. E.
The Nottingham gas undertaking 1818-1949 / prepared for Emgas by D. E. Roberts. — Leicester : East Midlands Gas, 1980. — 54p. — (Studies in East Midlands gas history). — *Bibliography: p53-54*

NOVOSELENGINSK (R.S.F.S.R.) — Church history
BAWDEN, C. R.
Shamans, lamas and evangelicals : the English missionaries in Siberia / C.R. Bawden. — London : Routledge & Kegan Paul, 1985. — xviii,382p24p of plates. — *Bibliography: p359-366. — Includes index*

NOWLAN, GEORGE CLYDE, 1898-1965
CONRAD, Margaret
George Nowlan : Maritime Conservative in national politics / Margaret Conrad. — Toronto : University of Toronto Press, 1986. — xviii,357p. — *Notes: p[309]-343*

NUCLEAR ARMS CONTROL
Arms and disarmament : SIPRI findings / edited by Marek Thee. — Oxford : Oxford University Press, 1986. — 491p. — *Includes index*

Arms control and the arms race : readings from Scientific American / with introductions by Bruce Russett, Fred Chernoff. — New York : W.H. Freeman, c1985. — viii, 229 p.. — *Includes index. — Bibliography: p. [217]-222*

BROWN, Edward Duncan
Arms control in hydrospace: legal aspects. — Washington : Woodrow Wilson International Center for Scholars, 1971. — 131p. — (Oceans series ; 301). — *Includes bibliographical references*

GOODIN, Robert E.
Mood matching and arms control / by Robert E. Goodin. — Colchester : Department of Government University of Essex, 1987. — 27 p. — (Essex papers in politics and government ; no. 41)

INTERNATIONAL SYMPOSIUM ON STRUGGLE FOR PREVENTING NUCLEAR WAR AND ELIMINATING NUCLEAR WEAPONS (1985 : Tokyo)
Struggle for preventing nuclear war and eliminating nuclear weapons : [papers presented at the Symposium]. — Tokyo : Japan Press Service, 1985. — vii,555p

LEWIS, William Hubert
The prevention of nuclear war : an American approach / William H. Lewis. — Boston, Mass. : Oelgeschlager, Gunn & Hain Publishers, c1986. — viii,103p. — *Includes bibliographies. — Sales no. E.85.xv.RR/32*

NUCLEAR ARMS CONTROL — Congresses
International security and arms control / edited by Ellen Propper Mickiewicz and Roman Kolkowicz. — New York : Praeger, 1986. — xii, 171 p.. — *Includes index*

NUCLEAR ARMS CONTROL — Verification

SCRIBNER, Richard A
The verification challenge : problems and promise of strategic nuclear arms control verification / Richard A. Scribner, Theodore J. Ralston, William D. Metz. — Boston : Birkhäuser, c1985. — xiv, 249 p.. — "A project of the Committee on Science, Arms Control, and National Security of the American Association for the Advancement of Science in cooperation with the Center for International Security and Arms Control, Stanford University.". — Includes index. — Bibliography: p. [231]-239

NUCLEAR ARMS CONTROL — Verification — Congresses

Arms control verification : the technologies that make it possible / edited by Kosta Tsipis, David W. Hafemeister, and Penny Janeway. — Washington : Pergamon-Brassey's International Defense Publishers, c1986. — xvi, 419 p.. — "Published in cooperation with the Program in Science and Technology for International Security, Massachusetts Institute of Technology.". — Papers presented at a conference held at M.I.T., Feb. 1984. — Includes bibliographies and index

NUCLEAR ARMS CONTROL — Europe

DEAN, Jonathan
Watershed in Europe : dismantling the East-West military confrontation / Jonathan Dean. — Lexington, Mass. : Lexington Books, 1986, c1987. — p. cm. — Includes index

A European non-proliferation policy : prospects and problems / edited by Harald Müller. — Oxford : Clarendon, 1987. — [450]p. — Includes index

NUCLEAR ARMS CONTROL — Soviet Union

FREEDMAN, Lawrence
Arms control : management or reform? / Lawrence Freedman. — London : Routledge & Kegan Paul, 1986. — 102p. — (Chatham House papers ; 31)

The Race for security : arms and arms control in the Reagan years / edited by Robert Travis Scott. — Lexington, Mass. : Lexington Books, c1987. — p. cm. — Includes index

NUCLEAR ARMS CONTROL — United States

FREEDMAN, Lawrence
Arms control : management or reform? / Lawrence Freedman. — London : Routledge & Kegan Paul, 1986. — 102p. — (Chatham House papers ; 31)

The Race for security : arms and arms control in the Reagan years / edited by Robert Travis Scott. — Lexington, Mass. : Lexington Books, c1987. — p. cm. — Includes index

NUCLEAR DISARMAMENT

Apocalypse no : an Australian guide to the arms race and the peace movement / edited by Rachel Sharp. — Sydney : Pluto Press in association with Rosa Research Associates, 1984. — 294 p.. — Includes bibliographies and index

Arms and disarmament : SIPRI findings / edited by Marek Thee. — Oxford : Oxford University Press, 1986. — 491p. — Includes index

FEHÉR, Ferenc
Doomsday or deterrence / by Ferenc Feher and Agnes Heller. — Armonk, N.Y. : M.E. Sharpe, Inc, c1986. — p. cm

GORBACHEV, M. S.
Speech given by the General Secretary of the Central Committee of the Communist Party of the Soviet Union (CPSU), M. S. Gorbachev, on Soviet television [following the Reykjavik Summit]. — New York : United Nations, 1986. — Distributed by the Secretary General of the U.N. as an official document of the General Assembly and Security Council at the request of the Deputy Head of the U.S.S.R. delegation to the Forty First session of the General Assembly

INTERNATIONAL SYMPOSIUM ON STRUGGLE FOR PREVENTING NUCLEAR WAR AND ELIMINATING NUCLEAR WEAPONS (1985 : Tokyo)
Struggle for preventing nuclear war and eliminating nuclear weapons : [papers presented at the Symposium]. — Tokyo : Japan Press Service, 1985. — vii,555p

LOEB, Paul Rogat
Hope in hard times : America's peace movement and the Reagan era / by Paul Rogat Loeb. — Lexington, Mass. : Lexington Books, [1986], c1987. — ix, 322 p.. — Includes index. — Bibliography: p. [305]-306

ROUSSOPOULOS, Dimitrios I
The coming of World War Three / Dimitrios I. Roussopoulos. — Montréal ; Buffalo : Black Rose Books, c1986-. — v. <1 >. — Includes bibliographies. — Contents: v. 1. From protest to resistance : the international war system

Status of multilateral arms regulation and disarmament agreements. — New York : United Nations, 1978. — iv,144p. — At head of title: Department of Political and Security Council Affairs, United Nations Centre for Disarmament. — "Special supplement to The United Nations disarmament yearbook volume II, 1977.". — "United Nations publication: sales no. E.78.IX.2."

Status of multilateral arms regulation and disarmament agreements. — 2nd ed., 1982. — New York : United Nations, 1983. — iv,176p. — At head of t.p.: United Nations. Department for Disarmament Affairs. — Sales no.

SUTER, Keith D.
The Australian campaign for a Ministry for Peace / Keith D. Suter. — [Sydney] : United Nations Association of Australia, 1984. — iv,153p. — Notes and references: p145-153

TOWLE, Philip
Protest and perish : a critique of unilateralism / by Philip Towle, Iain Elliot and Gerald Frost. — [London] : Alliance Publishers for the Institute for European Defence and Strategic Studies, 1982. — 121p

ZAGARE, Frank C
The dynamics of deterrence / Frank C. Zagare. — Chicago : University of Chicago Press, 1987. — p. cm. — Includes index. — Bibliography: p

NUCLEAR DISARMAMENT — Addresses, essays, lectures

We are ordinary women : a chronicle of the Puget Sound Women's Peace Camp / by Peace Camp participants. — 1st ed. — Seattle : Seal Press, 1985. — p. cm

NUCLEAR DISARMAMENT — History

The United Nations and disarmament, 1945-1985 / United Nations Department for Disarmament Affairs. — New York : United Nations, 1985. — x, 166 p.. — "United Nations publication sales no. E.85.IX.6"--T.p. verso

NUCLEAR DISARMAMENT — Great Britain — Political activity

MERCER, Paul
'Peace' of the dead : the truth behind the nuclear disarmaments / Paul Mercer ; foreword by Lord Chalfont. — London : Policy Research Publications, 1986. — 465p. — Bibliography: p[422]-438

NUCLEAR DISARMAMENT — United States

LEWIS, William Hubert
The prevention of nuclear war : an American approach / William H. Lewis. — Boston, Mass. : Oelgeschlager, Gunn & Hain Publishers, c1986. — viii,103p. — Includes bibliographies. — Sales no. E.85.xv.RR/32

NUCLEAR DISARMAMENT — United States — History

KATZ, Milton S.
Ban the bomb : a history of SANE, the Committee for a Sane Nuclear Policy, 1957-1985 / Milton S. Katz ; foreword by Benjamin Spock. — Westport, Conn. : Greenwood Press, c1986. — p. cm. — (Contributions in political science ; no. 147). — Includes index. — Bibliography: p

NUCLEAR ENERGY

COOK, Judith
Red alert : the worldwide dangers of nuclear power / Judith Cook. — London : New English Library, 1986. — [256]p. — Includes bibliography and index

HA, Young-Sun
Nuclear proliferation, world order and Korea / by Young-Sun Ha. — [Seoul] : Seoul National University Press, [1983]. — xii,208p. — Bibliography: p183-199

NUCLEAR ENERGY — Bibliography

CHESTER, Kerry
Nuclear energy and the nuclear industry : a guide to selected literature and sources of information / compiled by Kerry Chester. — 2nd ed. — London : Science Reference and Information Service, 1986. — [44]p. — Previous ed.: 1982

NUCLEAR ENERGY — Government policy — United States

COMMITTEE FOR ECONOMIC DEVELOPMENT
Nuclear energy and national security : a statement on national policy / by the Research and Policy Committee of the Committee for Economic Development. — Washington : Committee for Economic Development, 1976. — 80 p.

NUCLEAR ENERGY — Government policy — United States — History

HELMREICH, Jonathan E
Gathering rare ores : the diplomacy of uranium acquisition, 1943-1954 / Jonathan E. Helmreich. — Princeton, N.J. : Princeton University Press, c1986. — xiv, 303 p.. — Includes index. — Bibliography: p. 287-291

NUCLEAR ENERGY — Political aspects

Nuclear power in crisis : politics and planning for the nuclear state / edited by Andrew Blowers and David Pepper. — London : Croom Helm, c1987. — 327p. — Includes bibliographies and index

NUCLEAR ENERGY — Religious aspects — Christianity

HODGSON, Peter
Nuclear power / Peter Hodgson. — Oxford : Oxford University Press, 1985. — 47p. — (Studies in Christianity and science). — Bibliography: p46-47

NUCLEAR ENERGY — Great Britain

WATT COMMITTEE ON ENERGY
Nuclear energy : a professional assessment / Watt Committee on Energy. — London : The Committee, 1984. — (Report ; no.13)

NUCLEAR ENERGY — Korea (South)

HA, Young-Sun
Nuclear proliferation, world order and Korea / by Young-Sun Ha. — [Seoul] : Seoul National University Press, [1983]. — xii,208p. — Bibliography: p183-199

NUCLEAR ENERGY — Pakistan

KAPUR, Ashok
Pakistan's nuclear development / Ashok Kapur. — London : Croom Helm, c1987. — [320]p. — Includes index

NUCLEAR ENERGY — Yugoslavia

ILIĆ, Zdravko
Balkanski atomski soko : bezbednosne, ekonomske, moralne i ekološke posledice gradnje atomskih elektrana / Zdravko Ilić. — Beograd : "Četvrti Jul", 1986. — 184p

NUCLEAR FACILITIES — Environmental aspects — Great Britain — Statistics

Cancer incidence and mortality in the vicinity of nuclear installations England and Wales 1959-80 / P. J. Cook-Mozaffari...[et al.] ; [for the] Office of Population Censuses and Surveys. — London : H.M.S.O., 1987. — xiii,280p. — 27microfiches in end pocket. — (Studies on medical and population subjects ; no.51). — *Bibliographical references: p266-274*

NUCLEAR FACILITIES — Mexico — Location

TREVIÑO, R.
Estudio para la localización de un centro nuclear en México / R. Trevino...[et al.]. — México : Comisión Nacional de Energía Nuclear, 1964. — 365-380p. — ([Publicación] / Comisión Nacional de Energía Nuclear ; num.161). — *In Spanish with summaries in English, French, and Russian. — Reprint from: "Siting of power reactors and nuclear research centres", published by the International Atomic Energy Agency, Vienna, 1963*

NUCLEAR INDUSTRY

COOK, Judith
Red alert : the worldwide dangers of nuclear power / Judith Cook. — London : New English Library, 1986. — [256]p. — *Includes bibliography and index*

NUCLEAR INDUSTRY — Government policy

The Nuclear suppliers and nonproliferation : international policy choices / edited by Rodney W. Jones ... [et al.]. — Lexington, Mass. : Lexington Books, c1985. — p. cm. — *Papers from a seminar sponsored by the Georgetown University Center for Strategic and International Studies and other organizations and held June 28-29, 1984 in Washington, D.C. — Includes index*

NUCLEAR INDUSTRY — Government policy — Case studies

Nuclear power in crisis : politics and planning for the nuclear state / edited by Andrew Blowers and David Pepper. — New York : Nichols Pub. Co., 1987. — p. cm. — *Includes index*

NUCLEAR INDUSTRY — Government policy — Great Britain

Nuclear power in crisis : politics and planning for the nuclear state / edited by Andrew Blowers and David Pepper. — New York : Nichols Pub. Co., 1987. — p. cm. — *Includes index*

NUCLEAR INDUSTRY — Political aspects — History

HELMREICH, Jonathan E
Gathering rare ores : the diplomacy of uranium acquisition, 1943-1954 / Jonathan E. Helmreich. — Princeton, N.J. : Princeton University Press, c1986. — xiv, 303 p.. — *Includes index. Bibliography: p. 287-291*

NUCLEAR INDUSTRY — Australia

AUSTRALIAN SCIENCE AND TECHNOLOGY COUNCIL
Nuclear science and technology in Australia : a report to the Prime Minister / by the Australian Science and Technology Council (ASTEC). — Canberra : Australian Government Publishing Service, 1985. — viii,80p. — *Includes bibliographical references*

NUCLEAR INDUSTRY — Canada

FINCH, Ron
Exporting danger : a history of the Canadian nuclear energy export programme / Ron Finch. — Montreal ; Buffalo, N.Y. : Black Rose Books, 1986. — 236p. — *Bibliography: p216-229*

NUCLEAR INDUSTRY — Germany, West

ILIĆ, Zdravko
Balkanski atomski soko : bezbednosne, ekonomske, moralne i ekološke posledice gradnje atomskih elektrana / Zdravko Ilić. — Beograd : "Četvrti Jul", 1986. — 184p

NUCLEAR INDUSTRY — Germany (West)

WOLF, Heinz Georg
Der Schrott von morgen : zum Stand der Atomwirtschaft in der Bundesrepublik / Heinz Georg Wolf. — München : Deutscher Taschenbuch Verlag, 1985. — 147p. — *Bibliography: p147*

NUCLEAR INDUSTRY — Great Britain

WATT COMMITTEE ON ENERGY
Nuclear energy : a professional assessment / Watt Committee on Energy. — London : The Committee, 1984. — (Report ; no.13)

NUCLEAR INDUSTRY — Great Britain — Accidents — Economic aspects

NECTOUX, Francois
Accidents will happen... : an inquiry into the economic and social consequences of a nuclear accident at Sizewell 'B' / Francois Nectoux, William Cannell. — London : Earth Resources Research : Friends of the Earth Trust, 1984. — 109p

NUCLEAR INDUSTRY — Great Britain — Accidents — Social aspects

NECTOUX, Francois
Accidents will happen... : an inquiry into the economic and social consequences of a nuclear accident at Sizewell 'B' / Francois Nectoux, William Cannell. — London : Earth Resources Research : Friends of the Earth Trust, 1984. — 109p

NUCLEAR INDUSTRY — Soviet Union — Safety measures

MARPLES, David R.
Chernobyl and nuclear power in the USSR / David R. Marples. — Basingstoke : Macmillan in association with Canadian Institute of Ukrainian Studies, University of Alberta, 1987, c1986. — xii,228p. — *Originally published: New York : St. Martin's in association with Canadian Institute of Ukrainian Studies, University of Alberta, 1986. — Bibliography: p197-201. — Includes index*

NUCLEAR INDUSTRY — United States

COMMITTEE FOR ECONOMIC DEVELOPMENT
Nuclear energy and national security : a statement on national policy / by the Research and Policy Committee of the Committee for Economic Development. — Washington : Committee for Economic Development, 1976. — 80 p.

NUCLEAR NONPROLIFERATION

FINCH, Ron
Exporting danger : a history of the Canadian nuclear energy export programme / Ron Finch. — Montreal ; Buffalo, N.Y. : Black Rose Books, 1986. — 236p. — *Bibliography: p216-229*

HA, Young-Sun
Nuclear proliferation, world order and Korea / by Young-Sun Ha. — [Seoul] : Seoul National University Press, [1983]. — xii,208p. — *Bibliography: p183-199*

Limiting nuclear proliferation / edited by Jed C. Snyder and Samuel F. Wells, Jr. — Cambridge, Mass. : Ballinger Pub. Co., c1985. — xxxvii, 363 p.. — *Includes bibliographies and index*

MÜLLER, Harald
Nuclear proliferation : facing reality / Harald Müller. European security and the role of arms control / Johan Jørgen Holst. — Bruxelles : Centre for European Policy Studies, 1984. — 68p. — (CEPS papers ; no.14/15)

Nuclear non-proliferation and global security / edited by David B. Dewitt. — London : Croom Helm, c1987. — x,283p. — *Conference proceedings. — Includes index*

The Nuclear suppliers and nonproliferation : international policy choices / edited by Rodney W. Jones ... [et al.]. — Lexington, Mass. : Lexington Books, c1985. — p. cm. — *Papers from a seminar sponsored by the Georgetown University Center for Strategic and International Studies and other organizations and held June 28-29, 1984 in Washington, D.C. — Includes index*

NUCLEAR PHYSICS — Research — Australia

AUSTRALIAN SCIENCE AND TECHNOLOGY COUNCIL
Nuclear science and technology in Australia : a report to the Prime Minister / by the Australian Science and Technology Council (ASTEC). — Canberra : Australian Government Publishing Service, 1985. — viii,80p. — *Includes bibliographical references*

NUCLEAR POWER PLANTS — Accidents — Mathematical models

International comparison study on reactor accident consequence modeling : summary report to CSNI / by an NEA group of experts. — Paris : Nuclear Energy Agency, 1984. — 110p. — *Bibliographical references: p73-76*

NUCLEAR POWER PLANTS — Decommissioning

Decommissioning of nuclear facilities : feasibility, needs and costs : report by an Expert Group. — [Paris] : Nuclear Energy Agency, 1986. — 84p. — *Includes bibliographical references*

NUCLEAR POWER PLANTS — Environment aspects — England — Cumbria

GREAT BRITAIN. Committee on Medical Aspects of Radiation in the Environment
First report : the implications of the new data on the releases from Sellafield in the 1950s for the conclusions of the report on the investigation of the possible increased incidence of cancer in West Cumbria / chairman: M. Bobrow. — London : H.M.S.O., 1986. — 42p. — *Bibliographical references: p25-26*

NUCLEAR POWER PLANTS — Environmental aspects — England — Cumbria

Public local inquiry into an application by British Nuclear Fuels Limited, referred to the Secretary of State under Section 35 of the Town and Country Planning Act 1971, for planning permission to establish a plant for reprocessing irradiated oxide nuclear fuels and support site services at Windscale and Calder Works, Sellafield, Cumbria; before the Hon. Mr Justice Parker (the Inspector), Sir Edward Pochin and Sir Frederick Warner (Assessors), at the Civic Hall, Whitehaven, Cumbria, on 14th June 1977 and succeeding days [to 4th November 1977] : transcript of proceedings. — [London : Department of the Environment, 1979]. — 144microfishes. — *At head of title: Town and Country Planning Act 1971. — Transcripts prepared by J. L. Harpham Ltd., Official Shorthand Writers, Sheffield; filmed August 1979*

SOUTHGATE, Mark
Windscale inquiry : index to the transcripts of the hearings held before Mr Justice Parker / compiled by Mark Southgate. — London : Department of Energy, 1978. — 4microfiches. — *At head of title: Departments of Industry, Trade and Prices and Consumer Protection Common Services: Libraries. — Comprises index of counsel, witnesses and representatives and subject index*

NUCLEAR POWER PLANTS — Environmental aspects — England — Suffolk

Sizewell B public inquiry before Sir Frank Layfield (the Inspector) at The Maltings, Snape, Suffolk, 26 July 1982-7 March 1985 : transcript of proceedings. — [London : Department of Energy, 1985]. — 339microfiches. — *At head of title: Electric Lighting Act 1909 (as amended), Electricity Act 1957, Town and Country Planning Act 1971; Electricity Generating Stations and Overhead Lines (Inquiries Procedure) Rules 1981. — Transcripts prepared by J. L. Harpham Ltd., Official Shorthand Writers, Sheffield; filmed October 1985*

NUCLEAR POWER PLANTS — Environmental aspects — Great Britain

Report on radioactive discharges, associated environmental monitoring and personal radiation doses resulting from operation of CEGB nuclear sites / Central Electricity Generating Board, Health and Safety Department. — London : CEGB, 1976-. — *Annual. — Title varies*

NUCLEAR POWER PLANTS — Environmental aspects — Spain

SANZ, Benito
Centrales nucleares en España : el parón nuclear / Benito Sanz. — [Valencia?] : Torres, c1984. — 509p. — (Debates y testimonios ; 6)

NUCLEAR POWER PLANTS — England — Sizewell (Suffolk)

Power tomorrow : Sizewell B : the Central Electricity Generating Board's case / compiled by Geoffrey Greenhalgh. — London : Kogan Page, [1986]. — 229p. — *Summary and re-presentation of the Central Electricity Generating Board's submissions to the Sizewell B inquiry. — Includes index*

NUCLEAR POWER PLANTS — England — Suffolk

LAYFIELD, Sir Frank
Sizewell B public inquiry : report on applications by the Central Electricity Generating Board for consent for the construction of a pressurised water reactor and a direction that planning permission be deemed to be granted for that development : inquiry 11 January 1983-7 March 1985, presented to the Secretary of State for Energy on 5 December 1986 / Inspector: Sir Frank Layfield; Assessors: J. M. Alexander...[et al.]. — London : H.M.S.O., 1987. — 8v.. — *Summary of conclusions and recommendations issued separately. — Includes bibliographical references. — Includes index (in vol.8)*

LAYFIELD, Sir Frank
Sizewell B public inquiry : summary of conclusions and recommendations from the Inspector's report on the Central Electricity Generating Board's application for consent for the construction of a pressurised water reactor at Sizewell, Suffolk, together with chapters 2,47,90,104,108,109, of that report, being the concluding chapters referred to in that summary / Inspector: Sir Frank Layfield; Assessors: J. M. Alexander...[et al.]. — London : H.M.S.O., 1987. — 1v. (various pagings). — *Report presented to the Secretary of State for Energy on 5 December 1986*

NUCLEAR POWER PLANTS — Spain

SANZ, Benito
Centrales nucleares en España : el parón nuclear / Benito Sanz. — [Valencia?] : Torres, c1984. — 509p. — (Debates y testimonios ; 6)

NUCLEAR POWER PLANTS — Ukraine — Chernobyl

GILLON, Luc
Le nucléaire en question : (après l'accident de Tchernobyl) / Luc Gillon ; préface d'André L. Jaumotte. — [Gembloux] : Duculot, 1986. — vii,251p

NUCLEAR POWER PLANTS — Ukraine — Chernobyl — Accidents

KAFKA, Peter
Tschernobyl : die Informationslüge : Anleitung zum Volkszorn / Peter Kafka, Jürgen König, Wolfgang Limmer. — München : Schneekluth, 1986. — [176]p

NUCLEAR POWER PLANTS — United States — Safety measures

ADATO, Michelle
Safety second : the NRC and America's nuclear power plants / The Union of Concerned Scientists ; contributors, Michelle Adato, principal author, James MacKenzie, Robert Pollard, Ellyn Weiss. — Bloomington : Indiana University Press, c1987. — 194 p.. — *Includes index. — Bibliography: p. [164]-187*

NUCLEAR POWER PLANTS — Washington (State) — Design and construction — Costs

SUGAI, Wayne H
Nuclear power and ratepayer protest : the Washington Public Power Supply System / Wayne H. Sugai. — Boulder : Westview Press, 1987. — p. cm. — (Westview special studies in public policy and public systems management). — *Bibliography: p*

NUCLEAR POWER PLANTS — Yugoslavia

ILIĆ, Zdravko
Balkanski atomski soko : bezbednosne, ekonomske, moralne i ekološke posledice gradnje atomskih elektrana / Zdravko Ilić. — Beograd : "Četvrti Jul", 1986. — 184p

NUCLEAR REACTORS — England — West Cumbria

Investigation of the possible increased incidence of cancer in West Cumbria : report of the independent advisory group / chairman Sir Douglas Black. — London : H.M.S.O., 1984. — 103p

NUCLEAR TERRORISM — United States

HOFFMAN, Bruce
Terrorism in the United States and the potential threat to nuclear facilities / Bruce Hoffman ; prepared for the U.S. Department of Energy. — Santa Monica, CA : Rand, [1986]. — ix, 56 p.. — *"R-3351-DOE.". — "January 1986.". — Bibliography: p. 55-56*

NUCLEAR WARFARE

Apocalypse no : an Australian guide to the arms race and the peace movement / edited by Rachel Sharp. — Sydney : Pluto Press in association with Rosa Research Associates, 1984. — 294 p.. — *Includes bibliographies and index*

BETTS, Richard K.
Nuclear blackmail and nuclear balance / Richard K. Betts. — Washington, D.C. : Brookings Institution, c1987. — p. cm. — *Includes bibliographical references and index*

CHARLTON, Michael
From deterrence to defence : the inside story of strategic policy / Michael Charlton. — Cambridge, Mass. : Harvard University Press, 1987, c1986. — p. cm. — *Based on the author's BBC radio series, The Star wars history. — Includes index*

First and final war : a basic information manual on the effects of nuclear war applied to Australasia / edited by David Blair. — [Melbourne] : Oxford University Press, 1986. — 80p. — *Bibliography: p76-79*

HALSELL, Grace
Prophecy and politics : militant evangelists on the road to nuclear war / Grace Halsell. — Westport, Conn. : Lawrence Hill & Co., c1986. — 210 p.. — *Includes index*

HAYES, Peter
American lake : nuclear peril in the Pacific / Peter Hayes, Lyuba Zarsky, Walden Bello. — Harmondsworth : Penguin, 1987. — xiv, 529p. — *First published by Penguin in Australia in 1986*

KATU, Michio
To win a nuclear war : the Pentagon's secret strategy / Michio Katu and Daniel Axelrod ; with an introduction by Daniel Ellsberg. — Boston : Southend ; London : Zed, 1986. — [350]p

KNELMAN, Fred H
Reagan, God, and the bomb : from myth to policy in the nuclear arms race / F.H. Knelman. — Toronto, Ont. : McClelland and Stewart, c1985. — vii, 343 p.. — *Bibliography: p. 313-330*

KROMBACH, Hayo Benedikt Ernst Désiré
Scientific and philosophical thought about the discourse of international relations in the 20th century : a hermeneutic inquiry into the implications of the idea of nuclear war / Hayo Benedikt Ernst Désiré Krombach. — 606 leaves. — *PhD (Econ) 1986 LSE*

The Logic of nuclear terror Roman Kolkowicz, editor. — Boston, Mass. ; London : Published under the auspices of the University of California Project on Politics and War [by] Allen & Unwin, c1987. — xi,289p. — *Includes index*

Managing nuclear operations / Ashton B. Carter, John D. Steinbruner, Charles A. Zraket, editors. — Washington, D.C. : Brookings Institution, c1987. — xxii, 751 p.. — *A study jointly sponsored by the Brookings Institution and the Center for Science and International Affairs at Harvard University. — Includes bibliographical references and index*

REDNER, Harry
Anatomy of the world : the impact of the atom on Australia and the world / Harry Redner, Jill Redner. — [Melbourne?] : Fontana/Collins, 1983. — 368p. — *Includes chronology (1945-1981): p331-345*

Space weapons and international security / edited by Bhupendra Jasani. — Oxford : Oxford University Press, 1986. — xvi,366p. — *Written for the Stockholm International Peace Research Institute. — Bibliography: p353-354 Includes index*

STRATHCLYDE. Regional Council
Freedom from fear : nuclear weapons and nuclear war / Strathclyde Regional Council, City & Glasgow District Council. — [Glasgow?] : Strathclyde Regional Council, 1984. — 30p

NUCLEAR WARFARE — Congresses

Nuclear deterrence--new risks, new opportunities / edited by Catherine Kelleher, Frank J. Kerr, and George Quester. — Washington : Pergamon-Brassey's International Defense Publishers, 1986. — p. cm. — *: Revision of papers, presented at a conference which was convened by the University of Maryland's International Security Project in Sept. 1984 at College Park, Md*

NUCLEAR WARFARE — Dictionaries

GREEN, Jonathon
The A-Z of nuclear jargon / Jonathon Green. — London : Routledge & Kegan Paul, 1986. — [224]p. — *Includes bibliography*

NUCLEAR WARFARE — Moral and ethical aspects

CHILD, James W.
Nuclear war : the moral dimension / James W. Child. — Bowling Green, OH : Social Philosophy & Policy Center, Bowling Green State University, 1986. — p. cm. — (Studies in social philosophy & policy ; no. 6). — *Bibliography: p*

Ethics & European security / edited by Barrie Paskins. — London : Croom Helm, c1986. — 199p. — *Includes index*

FINNIS, J. M.
Nuclear deterrence, morality and realism / John Finnis, Joseph M. Boyle, Jr., Germain Grisez. — Oxford : Clarendon, 1987. — xv,429p. — *Bibliography: p391-411. — Includes index*

NUCLEAR WARFARE — Psychological aspects

Psychology and the prevention of nuclear war / edited by Ralph K. White. — New York ; London : University Press, 1986. — xxvi,591p. — Bibliography: p569-571. — Includes index

NUCLEAR WARFARE — Religious aspects — Christianity

HARRIES, Richard, 1936-
Christianity and war in a nuclear age / by Richard Harries. — London : Mowbray, 1986. — 170p. — (Mowbray Christian studies series)

NUCLEAR WARFARE — Social aspects — Australia

First and final war : a basic information manual on the effects of nuclear war applied to Australasia / edited by David Blair. — [Melbourne] : Oxford University Press, 1986. — 80p. — Bibliography: p76-79

NUCLEAR-WEAPON-FREE ZONES

LAWYERS FOR NUCLEAR DISARMAMENT
Nuclear free zones. — 2nd ed.. — London : Lawyers for Nuclear Disarmament, 1984. — 30p. — (Working paper / Lawyers for Nuclear Disarmament ; no.1)

Nuclear-free zones / edited by David Pitt and Gordon Thompson. — London : Croom Helm, 1987. — [192]p

NUCLEAR-WEAPON-FREE ZONES — Great Britain — Planning

Environmental and health powers in nuclear free zones. — [London] : Lawyers for Nuclear Disarmament, [1984]. — 64p. — (Working paper ; no.2). — Cover title. — Bibliography: p60-62

NUCLEAR-WEAPON-FREE ZONES — Indian Ocean Region — Congresses

WORKSHOP ON THE INDIAN OCEAN AS A ZONE OF PEACE (1985 : Dacca, Bangladesh)
The Indian Ocean as a zone of peace : Workshop on the Indian Ocean as a Zone of Peace, Dhaka, People People's Republic of Bangladesh, November 23-25, 1985. — Dordrecht ; Boston : Martinus Nijhoff ; New York : International Peace Academy, 1986. — p. cm. — Sponsored and organized by the Bangladesh Institute of International and Strategic Studies in association with the International Peace Academy

NUCLEAR WEAPONS

BARNABY, Frank
What on earth is Star Wars? : a guide to the Strategic Defence Initiative / Frank Barnaby. — London : Fourth Estate, 1986. — [184]p. — Includes bibliography and index

First and final war : a basic information manual on the effects of nuclear war applied to Australasia / edited by David Blair. — [Melbourne] : Oxford University Press, 1986. — 80p. — Bibliography: p76-79

MALCOLMSON, Robert W
Nuclear fallacies : how we have been misguided since Hiroshima / Robert W. Malcolmson. — Kingston : McGill-Queen's University Press, c1985. — xi, 152 p.. — Includes index. — Bibliography: p. [117]-127

The Race for security : arms and arms control in the Reagan years / edited by Robert Travis Scott. — Lexington, Mass. : Lexington Books, c1987. — p. cm. — Includes index

REDNER, Harry
Anatomy of the world : the impact of the atom on Australia and the world / Harry Redner, Jill Redner. — [Melbourne?] : Fontana/Collins, 1983. — 368p. — Includes chronology (1945-1981): p331-345

NUCLEAR WEAPONS — Government policy

KENNAN, George F.
George Kennan on NATO, nuclear war and the Soviet threat / edited, with an extended introductory essay by Phil Braithwaite. — Evesham : West Midlands CND Sales, c1985. — 48p. — (Spokesman pamphlet ; no.84). — Cover title. — Text on inside covers

NUCLEAR WEAPONS — Government policy — Great Britain

Choices : nuclear and non-nuclear defence options / assessed by: Peter Carrington...[et al.] ; organized and presented by Oliver Ramsbotham. — London : Brassey's, 1987. — xiv,473p

NUCLEAR WEAPONS — Government policy — Soviet Union

SHENFIELD, Stephen
The nuclear predicament : explorations in Soviet ideology / Stephen Shenfield. — London : [for] The Royal Institute of International Affairs [by] Routledge & Kegan Paul, 1987. — [96]p. — (Chatham House papers ; 37)

NUCLEAR WEAPONS — History

MCNAMARA, Robert S.
Blundering into disaster : surviving the first century of the nuclear age / by Robert McNamara. — London : Bloomsbury, 1987. — [194]p. — Originally published: New York : Pantheon Books, 1986

NUCLEAR WEAPONS — Political aspects

MIALL, Hugh
Nuclear weapons : who's in charge? / Hugh Miall ; foreword by Scilla McLean. — Basingstoke : Macmillan in association with the Oxford Research Group, 1987. — xi,167p. — Includes index

NUCLEAR WEAPONS — Religious aspects — Christianity

Ethics and defence : power and responsibility in the nuclear age / edited by Howard Davis. — Oxford : Basil Blackwell, 1986. — x,296p. — Bibliography: p277-287. — Includes index

NUCLEAR WEAPONS — Research — Great Britain — History

SIMPSON, John, 1943-
The independent nuclear state : the United States, Britain and the military atom / John Simpson. — 2nd ed. — Basingstoke : Macmillan, 1986. — xxxix,341p. — Previous ed.: 1983. — Bibliography: p313-322. — Includes index

NUCLEAR WEAPONS — Testing

ARNOLD, Lorna
A very special relationship : British atomic weapon trials in Australia / Lorna Arnold. — London : H.M.S.O., 1987. — xvii, 323p, 8p of plates

NUCLEAR WEAPONS — Europe

CHARLES, Daniel
Nuclear planning in NATO : pitfalls of first use / Daniel Charles. — Cambridge, Mass. : Ballinger Pub. Co., c1987. — xv, 177 p.. — "A Federation of American Scientists book.". — Includes bibliographies and index

PROBLEMS DE SEGURIDAD EUROPEA Y DESPLIEGUE DE SISTEMAS DE ALCANCE MEDIO (1984 : Madrid)
Problemas de seguridad europea y despliegue de sistemas de alcance medio : simposio internacional celebrado en el Auditorio del Ministerio de Hacienda, Madrid, mayo de 1984. — [Madrid] : Instituto de Cuestiones Internacionales : Fundación Friedrich Ebert, c1984. — 303p

NUCLEAR WEAPONS — Great Britain

Ethics and defence : power and responsibility in the nuclear age / edited by Howard Davis. — Oxford : Basil Blackwell, 1986. — x,296p. — Bibliography: p277-287. — Includes index

NUCLEAR WEAPONS — Great Britain — Testing

AUSTRALIA. Royal Commission into British Nuclear Tests in Australia
The report of the Royal Commission into British Nuclear Tests in Australia. — Canberra : Australian Government Publishing Service, 1985. — 2v. — President: J. R. McClelland. — Includes bibliography

AUSTRALIA. Royal Commission into British Nuclear Tests in Australia
The report of the Royal Commission into British Nuclear Tests in Australia : conclusions and recommendations. — Canberra : Australian Government Publishing Service, 1985. — 32p. — President: J. R. McClelland

NUCLEAR WEAPONS — Korea (South)

HA, Young-Sun
Nuclear proliferation, world order and Korea / by Young-Sun Ha. — [Seoul] : Seoul National University Press, [1983]. — xii,208p. — Bibliography: p183-199

NUCLEAR WEAPONS — Pakistan

Pakistan's bomb : a documentary study / [compiled by] Sreedhar ; introduction by K. Subrahmanyam. — New Delhi : ABC Pub. House, 1986. — xviii, 331 p.. — Includes index. — Bibliography: p. [310]-316

NUCLEAR WEAPONS — Soviet Union

TRITTEN, James John
Soviet naval forces and nuclear warfare : weapons, employment, and policy / James J. Tritten. — Boulder, Colo. : Westview Press, 1986. — xiii, 282 p.. — (Westview special studies in military affairs). — : Revision of the author's thesis (University of Southern California, 1984) under the title: The strategic employment of the Soviet Navy in a nuclear war. — Includes bibliographies and index

NUCLEAR WEAPONS — United States

The deadly connection : nuclear war and U.S. intervention / [articles and speeches on behalf of the] New England Regional Office of the American Friends Service Committee edited by Joseph Gerson ; forward by Thomas J. Gumbleton. — Philadelphia : New Society Publishers, 1986. — xi,253p

ZUCKERMAN, Solly Zuckerman, Baron
Star wars in a nuclear world / Lord Zuckerman. — London : Kimber, 1986. — 226p. — Includes index

NUCLEAR WEAPONS — United States — Safety measures

HOFFMAN, Bruce
Terrorism in the United States and the potential threat to nuclear facilities / Bruce Hoffman ; prepared for the U.S. Department of Energy. — Santa Monica, CA : Rand, [1986]. — ix, 56 p.. — "R-3351-DOE.". — "January 1986.". — Bibliography: p. 55-56

NUCLEAR WEAPONS TESTING VICTIMS — Australia

AUSTRALIA. Royal Commission into British Nuclear Tests in Australia
The report of the Royal Commission into British Nuclear Tests in Australia. — Canberra : Australian Government Publishing Service, 1985. — 2v. — President: J. R. McClelland. — Includes bibliography

AUSTRALIA. Royal Commission into British Nuclear Tests in Australia
The report of the Royal Commission into British Nuclear Tests in Australia : conclusions and recommendations. — Canberra : Australian Government Publishing Service, 1985. — 32p. — President: J. R. McClelland

NUDE IN ART — Addresses, essays, lectures

The Female body in western culture : contemporary perspectives / Susan Rubin Suleiman, editor. — Cambridge, Mass. : Harvard University Press, 1986. — p. cm. — Includes bibliographies

NUISANCES — Legal status, laws, etc — Great Britain
GREAT BRITAIN. Department of the Environment
A consultation paper on the review of the law of statutory nuisance and offensive trades. — London : the Department, [1979?]. — [30]p

NUKU HIVA (MARQUESAS ISLANDS) — Population — Statistics
Tableaux normalisés du recensement général de la population : 15 octobre 1983. — [Papeete] : Institut territorial de la statistique
Résultats de la commune de Nuku Hiva. — [1985?]. — 4p,11 leaves

NUKUTAVAKE (TUAMOTU ISLANDS) — Population — Statistics
Tableaux normalisés du recensement général de la population : 15 octobre 1983. — [Papeete] : Institut territorial de la statistique
Résultats de la commune de Nukutavake. — [1985?]. — 4p,ll leaves

NULLIFICATION
ELLIS, Richard E
The Union at risk : Jacksonian democracy, states´ rights, and the nullification crisis / Richard E. Ellis. — New York : Oxford University Press, 1987. — p. cm. — *Includes index*

NÚÑEZ, RAFAEL, 1825-1894
PARK, James William
Rafael Núñez and the politics of Colombian regionalism, 1863-1886 / James William Park. — ; Baton Rouge ; London : Louisiana State University Press, c1985. — xii, 304p. — *Includes index. — Bibliography: p.[279]-296*

NUREMBERG (GERMANY) — Politics and government
DASTRUP, Boyd L
Crusade in Nuremberg : military occupation, 1945-1949 / Boyd L. Dastrup. — Westport, Conn. : Greenwood Press, c1985. — p. cm. — (Contributions in military history ; no. 47). — *Includes index. — Bibliography: p*

NUREMBERG (GERMANY (WEST)) — Politics and government
REICHE, Eric G.
The development of the SA in Nürnberg, 1922-1934 / Eric G. Reiche. — Cambridge : Cambridge University Press, 1986. — xviii,314p

NURSERY SCHOOLS — Great Britain
Untying the apron strings : anti-sexist provision for the under-fives / edited by Naima Browne and Pauline France. — Milton Keynes : Open University Press, 1986. — xii,175p. — (Gender and education). — *Bibliography: p162-168. — Includes index*

NURSERY SCHOOLS — Wales — Languages
Y gymraeg mewn addysg feithrin = The Welsh language in nursery education. — Cardiff : HMSO, 1975. — [34]p. — *In English and Welsh*

NURSES — In-service training — Great Britain
MARTIN, Lyn
The role of status of the clinical teacher : with special reference to policy for the education of nurses / by Lyn Martin. — 512 leaves. — *PhD (Econ) 1986 LSE. — 22 leaves are appendices*

NURSES AND NURSING — Great Britain
CLAY, Trevor
Nurses : power and politics / Trevor Clay in association with Alison Dunn and Neil Stewart. — London : Heinemann Medical, 1987. — 165p. — *Contains bibliographies*

NURSING — Political aspects — Great Britain
Political issues in nursing : past, present and future / edited by Rosemary White. — Chichester : Wiley
Vol.2. — c1986. — [xi,150]p. — *Includes index*

NURSING — Study and teaching — Great Britain
MARTIN, Lyn
The role of status of the clinical teacher : with special reference to policy for the education of nurses / by Lyn Martin. — 512 leaves. — *PhD (Econ) 1986 LSE. — 22 leaves are appendices*

NURSING — Great Britain
GREAT BRITAIN. Department of Health and Social Security. Chief Nursing Officer
Nursing 1974-76 : report. — [London] : the Department, [1977]. — 60p. — *Includes bibliographical references. — Includes index*

NURSING HOMES — England — Sheffield (South Yorkshire)
BENNETT, D.
Review of residents and routines in elderly persons homes in Sheffield / D. Bennett, R. Browne [and] M. Oldfield. — Sheffield : Family and Community Services Department, 1982. — 69p. — (Report / Sheffield. Family and Community Services Department ; no.13). — *At head of title: Research and Information*

NURSING SERVICE ADMINISTRATION — Political aspects — Great Britain
CLAY, Trevor
Nurses : power and politics / Trevor Clay in association with Alison Dunn and Neil Stewart. — London : Heinemann Medical, 1987. — 165p. — *Contains bibliographies*

Political issues in nursing : past, present and future / edited by Rosemary White. — Chichester : Wiley
Vol.2. — c1986. — [xi,150]p. — *Includes index*

NUTRITION
A Diet of reason : sense and nonsense in the healthy eating debate / edtited by Digby Anderson. — [London] : Social Affairs Unit, c1986. — 150p

WHEELOCK, Verner
The food revolution / J. Verner Wheelock. — Marlow, Bucks : Chalcombe Publications, c1986. — viii,119p

NUTRITION — Great Britain
Nutritional aspects of bread and flour / report of the Panel on Bread, Flour and other Cereal Products, Committee on Medical Aspects of Food Policy. — London : H.M.S.O., 1981. — x,64p. — (Report on health and social subjects ; 23). — *At head of title: Department of Health and Social Security. — Bibliography: p55-64*

NUTRITION POLICY — Africa, sub-Saharan — Addresses, essays, lectures
Food in sub-Saharan Africa / edited by Art Hansen and Della E. McMillan. — Boulder,Colo. : Lynne Rienner, 1986. — xvi,410p. — (Food in Africa series)

NUTRITION POLICY — Canada
FORBES, James D.
Institutions and influence groups in Canadian farm and food policy / J. D. Forbes. — Toronto : Institute of Public Administration of Canada, 1985. — 131p. — (Monographs on Canadian public administration ; no.10). — *Includes bibliographical references*

NUTRITION POLICY — Developing countries
Food policy : integrating supply, distribution, and consumption / edited by J. Price Gittinger, Joanne Leslie, Caroline Hoisington. — Baltimore : Johns Hopkins University Press for the World Bank, 1987. — xiv,567p. — (EDI series in economic development). — *Bibliography: p509-555*

NUTRITION SURVEYS
FOOD AND AGRICULTURE ORGANIZATION
Review of food consumption surveys = Recueil d´enquêtes sur la consommation alimentaire = Recopilacion de encuestas de consumo de alimentos. — Rome : F.A.O., [1958]

FOOD AND AGRICULTURE ORGANIZATION
Review of food consumption surveys 1985 : household food consumption by economic groups. — Rome : F.A.O., 1986. — xxiv,212p. — (FAO Food and Nutrition Paper ; no.35)

NUTRITION SURVEYS — China
PIAZZA, Alan Lee
Food consumption and nutritional status in the P.R.C. / Alan Piazza. — Boulder : Westview Press, 1986. — p. cm. — (Westview special studies on China). — *Bibliography: p*

NUTRITION SURVEYS — Developing countries
MARTORELL, Reynaldo
Nutrition and health status indicators : suggestions for surveys of the standard of living in developing countries / Reynaldo Martorell. — Washington, D.C., U.S.A. : World Bank, Development Research Center, c1981. — 97p. — (LSMS working papers ; no.13). — *"February 1982.". — Bibliography: p91-97*

NUTRITIONALLY INDUCED DISEASES — Epidemiology
Western diseases, their emergence and prevention / edited by H. C. Trowell, D. P. Burkitt ; foreword by John R. K. Robson. — Cambridge, Mass. : Harvard University Press, 1981. — xix, 456 p.. — *Includes bibliographies and index*

NUTRITIONALLY INDUCED DISEASES — United States
SILVERSTEIN, Brett
Fed up : the food forces that make you fat, sick, and poor / by Brett Silverstein. — Boston, MA : South End Press, c1984. — 160 p.. — *Bibliography: p. 149-160*

NYERERE, JULIUS K
YILMA MAKONNEN
The Nyerere doctrine of state succession : Dar es Salaam to Vienna / Yilma Makonnen. — Arusha ; New York : Eastern Africa Publications, 1985. — p. cm. — *Includes bibliographies and index*

OAKLAND (CALIF.) — Politics and government
STARLING, Jay D
Municipal coping strategies : "as soon as the dust settles" / Jay D. Starling. — Beverly Hills, Calif. : Sage Publications, c1986. — 295 p.. — (Managing information ; v. 7). — *Bibliography: p. 291-294*

OBESITY — Social aspects — United States — History
SCHWARTZ, Hillel
Never satisified : a cultural history of diets, fantasies, and fat / Hillel Schwartz. — New York : Free Press ; London : Collier Macmillan, c1986. — p. cm. — *Bibliography: p*

OBÓZ ZJEDNOCZENIA NARODOWEGO
MAJCHROWSKI, Jacek
Silni, zwarci, gotowi : myśl polityczna Obozu Zjednoczenia Narodowego / Jacek Majchrowski. — Warszawa : Państwowe Wydawnictwo Naukowe, 1985. — 215,xvip. — *Bibliography: p202-[211]*

OBRERO, EL (NEWSPAPER)
GARCÍA COSTA, Victor O.
El Obrero : selección de textos / Victor O. García Costa. — Buenos Aires : Centro Editor de América Latina, 1985. — 107p. — (Biblioteca Política Argentina ; 121)

OBSTETRICIANS — United States — Interviews
IMBER, Jonathan B.
Abortion and the private practice of medicine / Jonathan B. Imber. — New Haven : Yale University Press, c1986. — xviii, 164 p.. — *Includes index. — Bibliography: p. 147-160*

OBSTETRICS
SAVAGE, Wendy
A Savage enquiry : who controls childbirth? / Wendy Savage. — London : Virago, 1986. — xvii,189p,[8]p of plates

OBSTETRICS — Decision making
IMBER, Jonathan B.
Abortion and the private practice of medicine / Jonathan B. Imber. — New Haven : Yale University Press, c1986. — xviii, 164 p.. — *Includes index. — Bibliography: p. 147-160*

OCCULT SCIENCES — France — History — 19th century
DEVLIN, Judith
The superstitious mind : French peasants and the supernatural in the nineteenth century / Judith Devlin. — New Haven, Conn. : Yale University Press, 1987. — p .cm. — *Includes index. — Bibliography: p*

OCCUPATIONAL DISEASES — Costs
ANDREONI, Diego
The cost of occupational accidents and diseases / Diego Andreoni. — Geneva : International Labour Office, 1986. — viii, 142p. — (Occupational safety and health series ; no.54). — *Bibliography: p135-142*

OCCUPATIONAL DISEASES — Epidemiology
Epidemiology of occupational health / edited by M. Karvonen and M.I. Mikheev. — Copenhagen : World Health Organization, Regional Office for Europe, 1986. — ix,392p. — (WHO regional publications. European series ; no.20). — *Includes bibliographies*

OCCUPATIONAL DISEASES — Great Britain — Statistics
MCDOWALL, M. E.
Occupational reproductive epidemiology : the use of routinely collected statistics in England and Wales 1980-82 / M. E. McDowall, Medical Statistics Division, Office of Population Censuses and Surveys. — London : H.M.S.O., 1985. — iii,77p. — (Studies on medical and population subjects ; no.50). — *Bibliographical references: p76-77*

OCCUPATIONAL MOBILITY — Great Britain
CONWAY, Jean
A job to move : the housing problems of job seekers / by Jean Conway & Evan Ramsay. — London : SHAC, 1986. — 64p. — (SHAC research report ; 8)

OCCUPATIONAL MOBILITY — South Africa
SCHNEIER, Steffen
Occupational mobility among Blacks in South Africa / Steffen Schneier. — Cape Town : Southern Africa Labour and Development Research Unit, [1983]. — vi, 219 p.. — (Saldru working paper ; no. 58). "November 1983.". — *Bibliography: p. 214-219*

OCCUPATIONAL MORTALITY — Finland — Statistics
SAULI, Hannele
Kuolleisuus : ammatti ja kuolleisuus 1971-75 = Mortality : occupational mortality in 1971-75 / Hannele Sauli. — Helsinki : Tilastokeskus, 1979. — 156p. — *Summary and table headings in English*

OCCUPATIONAL PRESTIGE — United States
BOSE, Christine E
Jobs and gender : a study of occupational prestige / by Christine E. Bose. — New York : Praeger, 1985. — p. cm. — *Includes index. — Bibliography: p*

OCCUPATIONAL SAFETY, HEALTH AND WELFARE (GENERAL) ACT, 1968
The Occupational Safety, Health and Welfare (General) Act, 1968. — [Copenhagen : Ministry of Labour], 1968. — 49 leaves. — *Promulgated by the Ministry of Labour on 4th July 1968*

OCCUPATIONAL TRAINING
HAYES, Chris
Research and development to improve education and training effectiveness : report prepared at the request of the Manpower Services Commission / Chris Hayes, Alan Anderson, Nickie Fonda, Institute of Manpower Studies. — [Sheffield : Manpower Services Commission, 1985]. — vi,95p

OCCUPATIONAL TRAINING — Government policy
Youth, unemployment and training : a collection of national perspectives / edited by Rob Fiddy. — London : Falmer, 1985. — 247 p. — (Politics and education series)

OCCUPATIONAL TRAINING — Bangladesh
CRACKNELL, Basil E.
A review of the ODM's training cooperation with Bangladesh / B. E. Cracknell, R. Stoneman, R. B. W. Haines. — London : Manpower Planning Unit, Ministry of Overseas Development with the cooperation of the British Council, London and Dacca, 1977. — 14p

OCCUPATIONAL TRAINING — Developing countries — Bibliography
CORVALÁN-VÁSQUEZ, Oscar E.
Youth employment and training in developing countries : an annotated bibliography / Oscar Corvalán-Vásquez. — Geneva : International Labour Office, 1984. — vii,172p. — *Includes indexes*

OCCUPATIONAL TRAINING — Developing countries — Evaluation
CRUISE O'BRIEN, Rita
Third country training : an evaluation / Rita Cruise O'Brien, Jake Jacobs. — London : Ministry of Overseas Development, 1977. — [75]p

OCCUPATIONAL TRAINING — France
STEEDMAN, Hilary
Vocational training in France and Britain : office work / Hilary Steedman. — London : National Institute of Economic and Social Research, 1986. — 23p. — (Discussion paper / National Institute of Economic and Social Research ; no.114)

OCCUPATIONAL TRAINING — Great Britain
DUNCAN, K. D.
Task analysis, learning and the nature of transfer / K.D. Duncan, C.J. Kelly. — Sheffield : Manpower Services Commission, Training Division, 1983. — 29p. — (MSC training studies)

FORD, Kathy
Student supervision / Kathy Ford and Alan Jones. — Basingstoke : Macmillan Education, 1987. — x,162p. — (Practical social work). — *Bibliography: p154-157. — Includes index*

HAYES, Chris
Research and development to improve education and training effectiveness : report prepared at the request of the Manpower Services Commission / Chris Hayes, Alan Anderson, Nickie Fonda, Institute of Manpower Studies. — [Sheffield : Manpower Services Commission, 1985]. — vi,95p

STEEDMAN, Hilary
Vocational training in France and Britain : office work / Hilary Steedman. — London : National Institute of Economic and Social Research, 1986. — 23p. — (Discussion paper / National Institute of Economic and Social Research ; no.114)

WOLF, Alison
Work based learning : trainee assessment by supervisors / Alison Wolf, Ruth Silver. — [Sheffield] : Manpower Services Commission, [1986]. — 35p. — (Research & development ; no.33). — *Bibliographical references: p34-35*

OCCUPATIONAL TRAINING — Great Britain — Evaluation
CRACKNELL, Basil E.
An evaluation of the training received by Bangladesh study fellows in the UK / B. E. Cracknell, R. Stoneman, R. B. W. Haines. — London : Manpower Planning Unit, Ministry of Overseas Development with the co-operation of the British Council, London & Dacca, 1977. — 31p

OCCUPATIONAL TRAINING — Sri Lanka
ODM's training cooperation with Sri Lanka : report of a mission to Sri Lanka, 12-23 October 1977 / B.E. Cracknell...[et al.]. — London : Manpower Planning Unit, Ministry of Overseas Development ; Colombo : British Council, 1977. — 48p

OCCUPATIONAL TRAINING — Thailand
CRACKNELL, Basil E.
ODM's training co-operation with Thailand : report of a visit to Thailand, 4-12 October 1977 / B.E. Cracknell and R. Stoneman. — London : Manpower Planning Unit, Ministry of Overseas Development, 1977. — 13,[6]p

OCCUPATIONAL TRAINING FOR WOMEN — Germany (West) — Case studies
GÄRTNER, Hans J.
Efforts to equalize opportunities for young women : case studies on the impact of new technologies on the vocational training for technicians / Hans J. Gärtner, Rainald von Gizycki ; Korreferent: Camilla Krebsbach-Gnath. — Luxembourg : Office for Official Publications of the European Communities, 1984. — xiii, 105p. — *At head of title page: Commission of the European Communities*

OCCUPATIONAL TRAINING FOR WOMEN — Great Britain — Case studies
GÄRTNER, Hans J.
Efforts to equalize opportunities for young women : case studies on the impact of new technologies on the vocational training for technicians / Hans J. Gärtner, Rainald von Gizycki ; Korreferent: Camilla Krebsbach-Gnath. — Luxembourg : Office for Official Publications of the European Communities, 1984. — xiii, 105p. — *At head of title page: Commission of the European Communities*

OCCUPATIONS
CAPLOW, Theodore
The sociology of work / by Theodore Caplow. — Westport, Conn. : Greenwood Press, 1978, c1954. — viii, 330 p.. — *Reprint of the ed. published by University of Minnesota Press, Minneapolis. — Includes index. — Bibliography: p. 303-322*

OCCUPATIONS — Classification
PUBLIC ADMINISTRATION SERVICE
Introduction and administration of position classification and pay plans / [prepared for the United Nations Secretariat by the Public Administration Service]. — New York : United Nations, 1976. — xxxiii, 159 p. — ([Document - United Nations] ; ST/ESA/ser.E/5). — *"United Nations publication. Sales no. E.77.II.H.1.". — Bibliography: p. 155-159*

SKREDE, Kari
Sosialøkonomisk klassifisering av yrker i Norge, 1960 / Kari Skrede. — [s.l.] : Institutt for anvendt sosialvitenskapelig forskning, 1971. — (ii),66p. — (INAS report ; no.71-1)

OCCUPATIONS — Moral and ethical aspects
TONG, Rosemarie
Ethics in policy analysis / Rosemarie Tong. — Englewood Cliffs, NJ : Prentice-Hall, c1986. — p. cm. — (Occupational ethics series). — *Includes bibliographies and index*

OCCUPATIONS — Netherlands — Classification
NETHERLANDS. Centraal Bureau voor de Statistiek
Beroepenclassificatie 1984. — Voorburg : Centraal Bureau voor de Statistiek, 1984. — 42p. — *Title on back cover: Classification of occupations 1984*

OCEAN
Ocean yearbook / International Ocean Institute. — Chicago ; London : University of Chicago Press, 1978-. — *Annual*

OCEAN BOTTOM (MARITIME LAW)
BROWN, Edward Duncan
Arms control in hydrospace: legal aspects. — Washington : Woodrow Wilson International Center for Scholars, 1971. — 131p. — (Oceans series ; 301). — *Includes bibliographical references*

KRONMILLER, Theodore G.
The lawfulness of deep seabed mining / Theodore G. Kronmiller. — London : Oceana Vol.1. — 1980. — xix,521

KRONMILLER, Theodore G.
The lawfulness of deep seabed mining / Theodore G. Kronmiller. — London : Oceana Vol.2. — 1980. — iii,460p. — *Bibliography: p5-38*

KRONMILLER, Theodore G.
The lawfulness of deep seabed mining / Theodore G. Kronmiller [and] G. Wayne Smith. — London : Oceana Vol.3. — 1981. — xi,556p

LAW OF THE SEA INSTITUTE. Conference (1984 : San Francisco, Calif.)LAW OF THE SEA INSTITUTE. Conference (18th : 1984 : San Francisco, Calif.)

The developing order of the oceans : proceedings / Law of the Sea Institute Eighteenth Annual Conference ; co-sponsored by the University of San Francisco, October 24-27, 1984, San Francisco ; edited by Robert B. Krueger, Stefan A. Riesenfeld. — Honolulu : Law of the Sea Institute, William S. Richardson School of Law, University of Hawaii, 1986. — p. cm. — (Sea grant cooperative report ; UNIHI-SEAGRANT-CR-85-03). — *Includes bibliographies*

OCEAN ENERGY RESOURCES
FORD, Glyn
The future for ocean technology / Glyn Ford, Chris Niblett and Lindsay Walker. — London : Pinter, 1987. — xii,139p.. — (The Future for science and technology series). — *Bibliography: p133-135. — Includes index*

OCEAN ENGINEERING
FORD, Glyn
The future for ocean technology / Glyn Ford, Chris Niblett and Lindsay Walker. — London : Pinter, 1987. — xii,139p.. — (The Future for science and technology series). — *Bibliography: p133-135. — Includes index*

OCEAN LINERS
JANSSON, Jan Owen
Liner shipping economics / J.O. Jansson and D. Shneerson. — London : Chapman and Hall, 1987. — x,299p. — *Bibliography: p289-292. — Includes index*

OCEAN MINING
Deepsea mining : selected papers from a series of seminars held at the Massachusetts Institute of Technology in December 1978 and January 1979 / edited by Judith T. Kildow. — Cambridge, Mass ; London : MIT, 1980. — x, 251p

OCEAN MINING — Law and legislation
KRONMILLER, Theodore G.
The lawfulness of deep seabed mining / Theodore G. Kronmiller. — London : Oceana Vol.1. — 1980. — xix,521

KRONMILLER, Theodore G.
The lawfulness of deep seabed mining / Theodore G. Kronmiller. — London : Oceana Vol.2. — 1980. — iii,460p. — *Bibliography: p5-38*

KRONMILLER, Theodore G.
The lawfulness of deep seabed mining / Theodore G. Kronmiller [and] G. Wayne Smith. — London : Oceana Vol.3. — 1981. — xi,556p

OCEANIA — Bibliography
FRY, Gerald W.
Pacific Basin and Oceania / Gerald W. Fry, Rufino Mauricio. — Oxford : Clio, c1987. — xxxvi,468p. — (World bibliographical series ; 70). — *Includes index*

OCEANIA — Census — Handbooks, manuals, etc
GOYER, Doreen S.
The handbook of national population censuses : Latin America and the Caribbean, North America, and Oceania / Doreen S. Goyer and Eliane Domschke. — Westport, Conn. : Greenwood Press, 1983. — xii, 711 p.. — *Includes index. — Bibliography: p. 28-30*

OCEANIA — Economic conditions
Economically active population : estimates and projections : 1950-2025 = Evaluations et projections de la population active : 1950-2025 = Estimaciones y proyecciones de la población económicamente activa : 1950-2025. — 3rd ed. — Geneva : International Labour Office V.4: Northern America, Europe, Oceania and USSR. — 1986. — xxvi,177p. — *Introduction and table headings in English, French and Spanish*

OCEANIA — Foreign relations — New Zealand
NEW ZEALAND. Ministry of Foreign Affairs
The South Pacific Forum. — Wellington : the Ministry, 1986. — 12p. — (Information bulletin ; no.16)

OCEANIA — Social life and customs
Aging and its transformations : moving toward death in pacific societies / edited by Dorothy Ayers Counts, David R. Counts. — Lanham, MD : University Press of America, c1985. — 336 p., [2] p. of plates. — (ASAO monograph ; no. 10). — *"Co-published by arrangement with the Association for Social Anthropology in Oceania"--T.p. verso. — Includes index. — Bibliography: p. [275]-313*

OCEANIA — Yearbooks
Pacific Islands year book / editor: John Carter. — 15th ed. — Sydney ; New York : Pacific Publications, 1984. — 557p. — *Includes one folded map of the Pacific Islands in end-pocket*

OCEANOGRAPHY
INTERNATIONAL CENTRE FOR OCEAN DEVELOPMENT
Introduction to marine affairs : [a] marine affairs course [organized by the Centre] held at the World Maritime University, November 23-28, 1986, Malmö, Sweden. — Halifax : International Centre for Ocean Development, 1986. — 419p. — *Bibliographies*

Ocean yearbook / International Ocean Institute. — Chicago ; London : University of Chicago Press, 1978-. — *Annual*

OCHOLLO (ETHIOPIA) — Economic conditions
ABÉLÈS, Marc
Le lieu du politique / par Marc Abéles. — Paris : Société d'Ethnographie, 1983. — 240p. — (Histoire et Civilisations de l'Afrique Orientale ; 4). — *Bibliography: p237-238*

OCHOLLO (ETHIOPIA) — Politics and government
ABÉLÈS, Marc
Le lieu du politique / par Marc Abéles. — Paris : Société d'Ethnographie, 1983. — 240p. — (Histoire et Civilisations de l'Afrique Orientale ; 4). — *Bibliography: p237-238*

OCHOLLO (ETHIOPIA) — Social conditions
ABÉLÈS, Marc
Le lieu du politique / par Marc Abéles. — Paris : Société d'Ethnographie, 1983. — 240p. — (Histoire et Civilisations de l'Afrique Orientale ; 4). — *Bibliography: p237-238*

O'CONNELL, DANIEL
Daniel O'Connell : portrait of a radical / edited by Kevin B. Nowlan and Maurice R. O'Connell. — Belfast : Appletree Press, 1984. — 120p. — (The Thomas Davis lectures)

ODENSE (DENMARK) — Civic improvement
DENMARK
Forslag til byudviklingsplan for Odense-Egnen : betaenkning afgivet af byudviklingsudvalget for Odense-Egnen. — Odense : [Fyens Stiftsbogtrykkeri], 1951. — 32p. — *Maps in end-pocket*

ODENSE (DENMARK) — Social conditions
PLATZ, Merete
Laengst muligt i eget hjem... : en undersøgelse blandt aeldre i Odense. — København : Socialforskningsinstituttet, 1987. — 138p. — (Publikation / Socialforskningsinstituttet ; 157). — *Bibliography: p132-134*

ODESSA (UKRAINE) — History
HERLIHY, Patricia
Odessa : a history, 1794-1914 / Patricia Herlihy. — Cambridge, Mass. : Distributed by Harvard University Press for the Harvard Ukrainian Research Institute, c1986. — xiv, 411 p., [8] p. of plates. — (Monograph series / Harvard Ukrainian Research Institute). — *Includes index. — Bibliography: p. [361]-394*

ODORS — Social aspects — France
CORBIN, Alain
The foul and the fragrant : odor and the French social imagination / Alain Corbin. — Leamington Spa : Berg, 1986. — vii,307p. — *Translation of: Le miasme et la jonquille. — Includes index*

OFFENSES AGAINST PROPERTY — Prussia — History
BLASIUS, Dirk
Bürgerliche Gesellschaft und Kriminalität : zur Sozialgeschichte Preussens im Vormärz / Dirk Blasius. — Göttingen : Vandenhoeck und Ruprecht, 1976. — 203 p. — (Kritische Studien zur Geschichtswissenschaft ; Bd. 22). — *Includes index. — Habilitationsschrift--Düsseldorf. — Bibliography: p. 186-198*

OFFICE EQUIPMENT AND SUPPLIES
ARMOUR, Hazel
New technology in the office environment / Hazel Armour. — Aldershot : Gower, c1986. — viii, 138p. — *Bibliography: p.128-138*

PERLIN, Neil
Business technology for managers : an office automation handbook / Neil Perlin. — White Plains, N.Y. : Knowledge Industry Publications, c1985. — v, 206 p.. — *Includes index. — Bibliography: p. 197-200*

OFFICE MANAGEMENT
LONG, Richard J.
New office information technology : human and managerial implications / Richard J. Long. — London : Croom Helm, c1987. — xi,333p. — *Bibliography: p306-327. — Includes index*

OFFICE PRACTICE — Automation
ARMOUR, Hazel
New technology in the office environment / Hazel Armour. — Aldershot : Gower, c1986. — viii, 138p. — *Bibliography: p.128-138*

BASKERVILLE, Richard Lee
Implications of office automation on information systems security / Richard Lee Baskerville. — 403 leaves. — *PhD (Econ) 1986 LSE. — Leaves 371-403 are appendices*

OFFICE PRACTICE — Automation
continuation

CHALUDE, Monique
Office automation and work for women / Monique Chalude ; scientific direction: Marcel Bolle de Bal. — Luxembourg : Office for Official Publications of the European Communities, 1984. — ii, F, 135p. — *At head of title page: Commission of the European Communities*

FREEMAN, Harvey A.
Office automation systems / Harvey A. Freeman, Kenneth J. Thurber. — 2nd ed. — Washington : IEEE Computer Society Press [for] IEEE Computer Society, [1986]. — viii,313p. — (Tutorial). — *Variant title: Tutorial : Office automation systems. — Bibliographies*

GREATER LONDON COUNCIL
Survey of office firms and establishments. — [London] : the Council
Report No. 3: New technology analysis: preliminary findings. — 1986. — 17p

Handbook of information technology and office systems / edited by A.E. Cawkell. — Amsterdam ; New York : North-Holland ; New York, N.Y., U.S.A. : Sole distributors for the U.S.A. and Canada, Elsevier Science Pub. Co., 1986. — x, 996 p.. — *Includes bibliographies and index*

HIRSCHHEIM, R. A.
Office automation : concepts, technologies and issues / R.A. Hirschheim. — Wokingham : Addison-Wesley, c1985. — xv,294p. — (International computer science series). — *Includes bibliographies and index*

Human factors of information technology in the office / edited by Bruce Christie. — Chichester : Wiley, c1985. — ix,352p. — (Wiley series in information processing). — *Bibliography: p326-340. — Includes index*

The Impact of office automation on clerical employment, 1985-2000 : forecasting techniques and plausible futures in banking and insurance / J. David Roessner ... [et al.]. — Westport, Conn. : Quorum Books, c1986. — p. cm. — *Includes index. — Bibliography: p*

KLEINSCHROD, Walter A
Critical issues in office automation / Walter A. Kleinschrod. — New York ; London : McGraw-Hill, c1986. — xiv, 223p. — *Includes index. — Bibliography: p 205-212*

LONG, Richard J.
New office information technology : human and managerial implications / Richard J. Long. — London : Croom Helm, c1987. — xi,333p. — *Bibliography: p306-327. — Includes index*

NATIONAL RESEARCH COUNCIL (U.S.). Committee on Women's Employment and Related Social Issues. Panel on Technology and Women's Employment
Computer chips and paper clips : technology and women's employment / Heidi I. Hartmann, Robert E. Kraut, and Louise A. Tilly, editors ; Panel on Technology and Women's Employment, Committee on Women's Employment and Related Social Issues, Commission on Behavioral and Social Sciences and Education, National Research Council. — Washington, D.C. : National Academy Press, 1986-1987. — 2 v.. — *Includes bibliographies and index. — Contents: v. 1. [without special title] -- v. 2. Case studies and policy perspectives / Heidi I. Hartmann, editor*

PERLIN, Neil
Business technology for managers : an office automation handbook / Neil Perlin. — White Plains, N.Y. : Knowledge Industry Publications, c1985. — v, 206 p.. — *Includes index. — Bibliography: p. 197-200*

WILSON, Thomas D.
Office automation and information services : final report on a study of current developments / T.D. Wilson. — Wetherby : British Library Lending Division, 1985. — vi,75p. — (Library and information research report ; 31)

OFFICE PRACTICE — Automation — Congresses

Technology and the transformation of white-collar work / edited by Robert E. Kraut. — Hillsdale, N.J. : L. Erlbaum Associates, c1987. — x,281p. — *Presented at a conference sponsored by Bell Communications Research, June 1984. — Includes bibliography and indexes*

OFFICE PRACTICE — Automation — Psychological aspects

GRANDJEAN, E.
Ergonomics in computerized offices / Etienne Grandjean. — London : Taylor & Francis, 1987. — [225]p. — *Includes bibliography and index*

OFFICE PRACTICES — Automation — Periodicals

Advances in office automation. — Vol.1. — Chichester : Wiley, Sept.1984. — [300]p. — (Wiley Heyden advances in EDP management)

OFFICES — Location — Government policy — Great Britain — History

MANNERS, Gerald
Office policy in Britain : a review / Gerald Manners and Diana Morris. — Norwich : Geo, 1986. — [164]p. — *Includes index*

OFFICES — Location — England — London

GREATER LONDON COUNCIL
Survey of office firms and establishments. — [London] : the Council
Report No. 2: Preliminary findings on employment, use of floorspace and location. — 1986. — 16p

OFFICIAL JOURNAL OF THE EUROPEAN COMMUNITIES — Handbooks, manuals, etc.

PAU, Giancarlo
The Official Journal : a guide / prepared by Giancarlo Pau. — [s.l.] : Association of EDC Librarians, [1984?]. — 6p. — (European Communities information ; no.7)

OFFICIAL SECRETS

Public access to government-held information : a comparative symposium / general editor, Norman S. Marsh. — London : Published under the auspices of the British Institute of International & Comparative Law [by] Stevens, 1987. — xxi,342p. — *Includes index*

OFFICIAL SECRETS — Great Britain

GREAT BRITAIN. Parliament. House of Commons. Library. Research Division
Official secrets and open government / [H. Rosamund Coates]. — [London] : the Division, 1979. — 32p. — (Reference sheet ; no79/1)

HOOPER, David, 1949-
Official secrets : the use and abuse of the Act / David Hooper. — London : Secker & Warburg, 1987. — ix,348p. — *Bibliography: p329-334. — Includes index*

Open government : a study of the prospects of open government within the limitations of the British political system / edited by Richard A. Chapman and Michael Hunt. — London : Croom Helm, c1987. — 194p. — *Conference papers. — Includes index*

THORNTON, Peter, 1946-
The civil liberties of the Zircon affair : Peter Thornton. — London : National Council for Civil Liberties, 1987. — 23p

OFFICIAL SECRETS — Soviet Union

KAFKA, Peter
Tschernobyl : die Informationslüge : Anleitung zum Volkszorn / Peter Kafka, Jürgen König, Wolfgang Limmer. — München : Schneekluth, 1986. — [176]p

OFFICIAL SECRETS — United States

DEMAC, Donna A
Keeping America uninformed : government secrecy in the 1980's / Donna A. Demac ; preface by Ben H. Bagdikian. — New York : Pilgrim Press, c1984. — xii, 180 p.. — *Includes index. — Bibliography: p. 169-174*

OFFSHORE GAS INDUSTRY — Government policy — United States

Offshore lands : oil and gas leasing and conservation on the outer continental shelf / Walter J. Mead ... [et al.] ; foreword by Stephen L. McDonald. — San Francisco, Calif. : Pacific Institute for Public Policy Research, c1985. — xxviii, 169 p.. — (Pacific studies in public policy). — *Includes index. — Bibliography: p. 157-162*

OFFSHORE GAS INDUSTRY — Great Britain — Security measures

GREAT BRITAIN. Parliament. House of Commons. Library. Research Division
Offshore tapestry. — [London] : the Division, [1975]. — 35p. — (Background paper ; no.41). — *Bibliographical references: p34-35*

OFFSHORE GAS INDUSTRY — North Sea

LOVEGROVE, Martin
Lovegrove's guide to Britain's North Sea oil and gas / Martin Lovegrove. — 2nd ed. — Cambridge : Energy Publications, 1983. — xii,237p. — *Previous ed.: 1981*

OFFSHORE OIL FIELD EQUIPMENT INDUSTRY — Great Britain

FORREST, K. P.
The Venezuelan oil industry : the move offshore and opportunities this presents for UK industry / [K. P. Forrest]. — [Glasgow : Department of Energy, Offshore Supplies Office?, 1978]. — 9p

GREGORY, P.
World offshore markets : can Britain compete? / P. Gregory, I.H. McNicoll, L. Moar. — London : Eastlord, 1986. — [200]p. — *Includes bibliography*

OFFSHORE OIL INDUSTRY — Government policy — Canada

HOUSE, J. D.
The challenge of oil : Newfoundland's quest for controlled development / J. D. House. — St. John's, Newfoundland : Institute of Social and Economic Research, Memorial University of Newfoundland, [1985]. — xv,329p. — (Social and economic studies / Memorial University of Newfoundland Institute of Social and Economic Research ; no.30). — *Notes and references: p[313]-326*

OFFSHORE OIL INDUSTRY — Government policy — Soviet Union

BERGESEN, Helge Ole
Soviet oil and security interests in the Barents Sea / Helge Ole Bergesen, Arild Moe and Willy Østreng. — London : Pinter, 1987. — xv,144p. — *At head of title: Fridtjof Nansen Institute. — Includes index*

OFFSHORE OIL INDUSTRY — Government policy — United States

Offshore lands : oil and gas leasing and conservation on the outer continental shelf / Walter J. Mead ... [et al.] ; foreword by Stephen L. McDonald. — San Francisco, Calif. : Pacific Institute for Public Policy Research, c1985. — xxviii, 169 p.. — (Pacific studies in public policy). — *Includes index. — Bibliography: p. 157-162*

OFFSHORE OIL INDUSTRY — Taxation — Great Britain

ROWLAND, Chris
The economics of North Sea oil taxation / Chris Rowland and Danny Hann. — London : Macmillan, 1987. — [200]p. — *Includes index*

OFFSHORE OIL INDUSTRY — Asia, Southeastern

VALENCIA, Mark J.
South-East Asian seas : oil under troubled waters : hydrocarbon potential, jurisdictional issues, and international relations / Mark J. Valencia. — Oxford ; New York : Oxford University Press, 1985. — xiv,155p. — (Natural Resources of South-East Asia). — *Bibliography: p137-146*

OFFSHORE OIL INDUSTRY — Barents Sea

BERGESEN, Helge Ole
Soviet oil and security interests in the Barents Sea / Helge Ole Bergesen, Arild Moe and Willy Østreng. — London : Pinter, 1987. — xv,144p. — *At head of title: Fridtjof Nansen Institute.* — *Includes index*

OFFSHORE OIL INDUSTRY — Great Britain — Security measures

GREAT BRITAIN. Parliament. House of Commons. Library. Research Division
Offshore tapestry. — [London] : the Division, [1975]. — 35p. — (Background paper ; no.41). — *Bibliographical references: p34-35*

OFFSHORE OIL INDUSTRY — Newfoundland

HOUSE, J. D.
The challenge of oil : Newfoundland's quest for controlled development / J. D. House. — St. John's, Newfoundland : Institute of Social and Economic Research, Memorial University of Newfoundland, [1985]. — xv,329p. — (Social and economic studies / Memorial University of Newfoundland Institute of Social and Economic Research ; no.30). — *Notes and references: p[313]-326*

OFFSHORE OIL INDUSTRY — North Sea

LOVEGROVE, Martin
Lovegrove's guide to Britain's North Sea oil and gas / Martin Lovegrove. — 2nd ed. — Cambridge : Energy Publications, 1983. — xii,237p. — *Previous ed.: 1981*

ROWLAND, Chris
The economics of North Sea oil taxation / Chris Rowland and Danny Hann. — London : Macmillan, 1987. — [200]p. — *Includes index*

OFFSHORE OIL INDUSTRY — Venezuela — Equipment and supplies

FORREST, K. P.
The Venezuelan oil industry : the move offshore and opportunities this presents for UK industry / [K. P. Forrest]. — [Glasgow : Department of Energy, Offshore Supplies Office?, 1978]. — 9p

OFFSHORE PETROLEUM INDUSTRY — Environmental aspects — Georges Bank

MACLEISH, William H.
Oil and water : the struggle for Georges Bank / by William H. MacLeish. — 1st ed. — Boston : Atlantic Monthly Press, c1985. — 304 p.. — *Includes index*

OGAREV, N. P.

MERVAUD, Michel
Socialisme et liberté : la pensée et l'action de Nicolas Ogarev (1813-1877) / Michel Mervaud. — Rouen : Publications de l'Université de Rouen ; Paris : Institut d'études slaves, 1984. — 596p. — (Publications de l'Université de Rouen ; no.97) (Collection historique / Institut d'études slaves ; 31). — *Bibliography: p [545]-566*

OGLALA INDIANS — Social life and customs

POWERS, Marla N
Oglala women : myth, ritual, and reality / Marla N. Powers. — Chicago ; London : University of Chicago Press, c1986. — xv, 241 p., [16] p. of plates. — (Women in culture and society). — *Includes index.* — *Bibliography: p. 223-233*

OGLALA INDIANS — Women

POWERS, Marla N
Oglala women : myth, ritual, and reality / Marla N. Powers. — Chicago ; London : University of Chicago Press, c1986. — xv, 241 p., [16] p. of plates. — (Women in culture and society). — *Includes index.* — *Bibliography: p. 223-233*

OHIO — Economic conditions — Congresses

Structural change in an urban industrial region : the northeastern Ohio case / edited by David L. McKee, Richard E. Bennett. — New York : Praeger, 1987. — ix, 255 p.. — *Includes index.* — *Bibliography: p. 245-250*

OHIO — Economic policy — Congresses

Structural change in an urban industrial region : the northeastern Ohio case / edited by David L. McKee, Richard E. Bennett. — New York : Praeger, 1987. — ix, 255 p.. — *Includes index.* — *Bibliography: p. 245-250*

OHIO — Governors — Biography

CEBULA, James E.
James M. Cox : journalist and politician / James E. Cebula. — New York : Garland, 1985. — 181 p.. — (Modern American history) . — *Includes index.* — *Bibliography: p. 171-173*

OHIO — Politics and government — 1787-1865

CAYTON, Andrew R. L
The frontier republic : ideology and politics in the Ohio Country, 1780-1825 / Andrew R.L. Cayton. — Kent, Ohio : Kent State University Press, c1986. — xii, 197 p.. — *Includes index.* — *Bibliography: p. [179]-186*

OHIO — Politics and government — 1865-1950

CEBULA, James E.
James M. Cox : journalist and politician / James E. Cebula. — New York : Garland, 1985. — 181 p.. — (Modern American history) . — *Includes index.* — *Bibliography: p. 171-173*

OIL AND GAS (ENTERPRISE) BILL 1981-82

GREAT BRITAIN. Parliament. House of Commons. Library. Research Division
Oil and Gas (Enterprise) Bill / [B. L. Miller]. — [London] : the Division, 1982. — 17p. — (Reference sheet ; no.82/1). — *Bibliography: p15-17*

OIL AND GAS LEASES — Canada

BALLEM, John Bishop
The oil and gas lease in Canada / John Bishop Ballem. — 2nd ed. — Toronto : University of Toronto Press, 1985. — xii,363p

OIL AND GAS LEASES — United States

Offshore lands : oil and gas leasing and conservation on the outer continental shelf / Walter J. Mead ... [et al.] ; foreword by Stephen L. McDonald. — San Francisco, Calif. : Pacific Institute for Public Policy Research, c1985. — xxviii, 169 p.. — (Pacific studies in public policy). — *Includes index.* — *Bibliography: p. 157-162*

OIL FIELDS — Oklahoma — Osage County

WILSON, Terry P.
The underground reservation : Osage oil / Terry P. Wilson. — Lincoln : University of Nebraska Press, c1985. — xiv, 263 p.. — *Includes index.* — *Bibliography: p. 237-249*

OIL INDUSTRIES — Prices

SALMOND, Alex
The oil price collapse : some effects on the Scottish economy / Alex Salmond [and] Jim Walker. — Edinburgh : Royal Bank of Scotland, 1986. — [7p]

OIL POLLUTION OF THE SEA — Prevention — History

PRITCHARD, Sonia Zaide
Oil pollution control / Sonia Zaide Pritchard. — London : Croom Helm, c1987. — x,231p. — *Includes index*

OIL SPILLS — Great Britain

GREAT BRITAIN. Department of Trade
The Tarpenbek incident. — London : the Department, 1979. — 31p

OIL TAXATION BILL 1983-84

GREAT BRITAIN. Parliament. House of Commons. Library. Research Division
The Oil Taxation Bill / Timothy Edmonds. — [London] : the Division, 1983. — 6p. — (Reference sheet ; no.83/18)

OIL WELL DRILLING, SUBMARINE

WEST GLAMORGAN. County Council
The Celtic sea - oil and gas? : what are the issues?. — Swansea : [the Council], 1975. — v,26p

OKLAHOMA — History

THOMPSON, John
Closing the frontier : radical response in Oklahoma, 1889-1923 / by John Thompson. — 1st ed. — Norman : University of Oklahoma Press, c1986. — xiii, 262 p.. — *Includes index.* — *Bibliography: p. 249-258*

OLD AGE

FORD, Janet, 1944-
Sixty years on : women talk about old age / Janet Ford and Ruth Sinclair. — London : Women's, 1987. — 168p

SULLEROT, Evelyne
L'âge de travailler / Evelyne Sullerot. — [Paris] : Fayard, 1986. — 224p

OLD AGE — Bibliography

New literature on old age: a guide to new publications, courses and conferences on ageing / Centre for Policy on Ageing. — London : Centre for Policy on Ageing, 1986-. — *Bi-monthly*

OLD AGE — Social aspects

Later life : the social psychology of aging / edited by Victor W. Marshall. — Beverly Hills, Calif. : Sage, c1986. — 352 p.. — *Includes bibliographies and indexes. — Contents: Dominant and emerging paradigms in the social psychology of aging / Victor W. Marshall -- The subjective construction of self and society / Carol D. Ryff -- Socialization in old age--a Meadian perspective / Neena Chappell and Harold L. Orbach -- Some contributions of symbolic interaction to the study of growing old / Don Spence -- A sociological perspective on aging and dying / Victor Marshall -- The old person as stranger / James J. Dowd -- Social networks and social support / Barry Wellman and Alan Hall -- Friendships in old age / Sarah H. Matthews -- The world we forgot / Martin Kohli -- Comparative perspectives on the microsociology of aging / Vern L. Bengtson*

OLD AGE — Georgian S.S.R. — Abkhazian A.S.S.R.

Sredi dolgozhitelei Abkhazii / [otv. redaktory: Sh. D. Inal-ipa, V. D. Kozlov]. — Tbilisi : Metsniereba, 1987. — 129p

OLD AGE ASSISTANCE — Australia

CROMPTON, Cathy
Too old for a job, too young for a pension? : income support for older people out of work / Cathy Crompton. — Canberra : Australian Government Publishing Service, 1986. — x,69p. — (Issues paper / Social Security Review ; no.2). — *Bibliography: p67-69*

OLD AGE ASSISTANCE — France — Nomenclature
FRANCE. Comité des Nomenclatures
Etat des nomenclatures applicables aux établissements sanitaires et sociaux : période de validité: exercice 1986 : nomenclatures concernées, catégories d'établissements, statuts juridiques. — [Paris : Ministère des Affaires sociales et de la Solidarité nationale, 1986]. — 105p

OLD AGE HOMES — Australia — History — 20th century
PARKER, R. A.
The elderly and residential care : Australian lessons for Britain / R.A. Parker. — Aldershot : Gower, c1987. — 128p. — *Bibliography: p118-120. — Includes index*

OLD AGE HOMES — England — London
GREAT BRITAIN. Department of Health and Social Security. Social Work Service. London Region
Residential care for the elderly in London : a study. — [London] : the Department, 1979. — iii,77,[20]p. — *Bibliography: appendix, p[17-20]*

OLD AGE HOMES — Great Britain
GREAT BRITAIN. Department of Health and Social Security
Residential accommodation for elderly people. — [London] : H.M.S.O., 1973. — 21p. — (Local authority building note ; 2)

NORMAN, A. J.
Severe dementia : the provision of longstay care / Alison Norman. — London : Centre for Policy on Ageing, 1987. — xxiv,275p. — (Policy Studies in Ageing ; No.7)

WILLCOCKS, Dianne M.
Private lives in public places : a research-based critique of residential life in local authority old people's homes / Dianne Willcocks, Sheila Peace, and Leonie Kellaher ; with a foreword by M. Powell Lawton. — London : Tavistock, 1987. — xii,212p. — *Bibliography: p193-201. — Includes index*

OLD AGE HOMES — Great Britain — Quality control
KANE, Eddie
Quality control in public and private homes for the elderly / Eddie Kane. — Norwich : University of East Anglia, 1985. — 40 leaves. — (Social work monographs ; 39). — *Bibliography: p40*

OLD AGE HOMES — Ireland
O'CONNOR, Joyce
"It's our home" : the quality of life in private and voluntary nursing homes / Joyce O'Connor, Marie Walsh. — Dublin : Stationery Office, 1986. — 167p. — (Report / National Council for the Aged ; no.14). — *Bibliography: p130-138*

O'CONNOR, Joyce
Nursing homes in the Republic of Ireland : a study of the private and voluntary sector / Joyce O'Connor, Kevin Thompstone. — Dublin : Stationery Office, 1986. — 154p. — (Report / National Council for the Aged ; no.13). — *Bibliography: p117-122*

OLD AGE PENSION ACT, 1969
The Old Age Pension Act, 1969. — [Copenhagen : Ministry of Social Affairs], 1970. — 17 leaves. — *Promulgated by the Ministry of Social Affairs on 15th April 1970*

OLD AGE PENSION (AMENDMENT) ACT, 1972
The Old Age Pension (Amendment) Act, 1972. — [Copenhagen : Ministry of Social Affairs?], 1972. — 15 leaves

OLD AGE PENSIONS — Law and legislation — Denmark
The Old Age Pension Act, 1969. — [Copenhagen : Ministry of Social Affairs], 1970. — 17 leaves. — *Promulgated by the Ministry of Social Affairs on 15th April 1970*

OLD AGE PENSIONS — Law and legislation — Great Britain
GREAT BRITAIN. Parliament. House of Commons. Library. Research Division
Social Security (Age of Retirement) Bill 1983/4 [Bill 16] / Julia Lourie. — [London] : the Division, 1983. — 20p. — (Reference sheet ; no.83/21). — *Bibliographical references: p15-18*

OLD AGE PENSIONS — Canada
BEATTIE, Earle
Canada's billion dollar pension scandal : how secure is your future? / Earle Beattie ; in consultation with Tom Delaney. — Toronto : Methuen, 1985. — 152p. — *References: p151-152*

OLD AGE PENSIONS — Denmark
Revalidering- og pensionsnaevnenes afgørelser i førtidspensionssager 1.april 1976 til 31 december 1978 : redegørelse fra sikringsstyrelsen. — [København] : Sikringsstyrelsen, 1980. — 106p. — (Sikringsstyrelsens undersøgelser ; nr.5). — *Includes bibliographical references*

OLD AGE PENSIONS — Denmark — Statistics
Afsluttende statistik fra invalideforsikringsretten og førtidspensionsudvalget. — [København] : Sikringsstyrelsen, 1978. — 60p. — (Sikringsstyrelsens undersøgelser ; nr3). — *Cover tittle. — Includes bibliographical references*

OLD-AGE PENSIONS — Finland
Old-age and invalidity pensions in Finland. — [Helsinki : National Pension Institute, 1957]. — 11,iiip

OLD AGE PENSIONS — France
CHADELAT, Jean-François
Les retraites des François : diversité et complexité des régimes / Jean-François Chadelat, Gérard Pellissier. — Paris : La Documentation française, 1986. — 142p. — (Notes et études documentaires ; no.4810). — *Bibliography: p141*

OLD AGE PENSIONS — Germany (West)
NOTTAGE, Raymond
Pensions : a plan for the future : based on a comparative study of the pensions systems of Great Britain and Germany / Raymond Nottage and Gerald Rhodes. — London : The Russell Press, 1986. — 53p

OLD AGE PENSIONS — Great Britain
GREAT BRITAIN. Parliament. House of Commons. Library. Research Division
Earnings rule for retirement pensioners. — [London] : the Division, 1976. — [12]p. — (Background paper ; no.53)

LYNES, Tony
Labour's pension plan / by Tony Lynes. — London : Fabian Society, 1969. — [2],33p. — (Fabian tract ; no. 396)

MIDWINTER, Eric
The wage of retirement : the case for a new pensions policy / Eric Midwinter. — London : Centre for Policy on Ageing, 1985. — 138p. — (Policy studies in ageing ; no.4)

NOTTAGE, Raymond
Pensions : a plan for the future : based on a comparative study of the pensions systems of Great Britain and Germany / Raymond Nottage and Gerald Rhodes. — London : The Russell Press, 1986. — 53p

PATERSON, Martin
Planning and implementing pensions : choices after 1988. — Cambridge : Woodhead-Faulkner, 1987. — [199]p. — *Includes bibliography and index*

SCHULLER, Tom
Pensions, bargaining and corporate policy / Tom Schuller. — Coventry : University of Warwick. School of Industrial and Business Studies. Industrial Relations Research Unit, 1986. — 17 leaves. — (Warwick papers in industrial relations ; no.12). — *Bibliography: p16*

OLD AGE PENSIONS — United States
KORCZYK, Sophie M.
Retirement income opportunities in an aging America : pensions and the economy / Sophie M. Korczyk. — Washington : Employee Benefit Research Institute, 1982. — 150p. — *Bibliography: p98-108*

SCHULZ, James H
The economics of aging / James H. Schulz. — 3rd ed. — New York : Van Nostrand Reinhold, [1985]. — p. cm. — *Includes index. — Bibliography: p*

Suggestions for research in the economics of pensions : report of an exploratory survey of the economic aspects of organized provision for the aged and surviving dependents. — New York : National Bureau of Economic Research, 1957. — 51p

OLD AGE PENSIONS — United States — History
Old age in a bureaucratic society : the elderly, the experts, and the state in American history / edited by David Van Tassel and Peter N. Stearns. — Westport, Conn. : Greenwood Press, c1986. — xx, 259 p.. — (Contributions to the study of aging ; no. 4). — *Includes bibliographies and index*

OLIGARCHY — Brazil — Paraíba (State) — History
LEWIN, Linda
Politic and Parentela in Paraíba : a case study of family-based oligarchy in Brazil / Linda Lewin. — Princeton, N.J. : Princeton University Press, c1987. — p. cm. — *Includes index. — Bibliography: p*

OLIGOPOLIES
WILLNER, Johan
Oligopolistic approaches to the measurement of the welfare losses of imperfect competition / Johan Willner. — °Abo : °Abo Akademi, 1987. — 83p. — (Meddelanden fr°an Ekonomisk-Statsvetens kapliga Fakulteten vid °Abo Akademi ; Ser.A:238). — *Bibliography: p54-56*

OLIGOPOLIES — Econometric models
SCHÄFER, Martin
Resource extraction and market structure / Martin Schäfer. — Berlin ; New York : Springer-Verlag, 1986. — 154p. — (Lecture notes in economics and mathematical systems ; 263). — *Bibliography: p[150]-151*

OLIVARES, GASPAR DE GUZMÁN, conde-duque de
ELLIOTT, J. H. (John Huxtable)
The Count-Duke of Olivares : the statesman in an age of decline / J.H. Elliott. — New Haven : Yale University Press, 1986. — p. cm. — *Includes index. — Bibliography: p*

O'MALLEY, DES
WALSH, Dick
Des O'Malley : a political profile / Dick Walsh. — Dingle : Brandon, 1986. — [160]p

OMAN — Economic conditions
Oman : economic, social and strategic developments / edited by B.R. Pridham. — London : Croom Helm, c1987. — xiv,254p. — *Includes index*

OMAN — History
BENNETT, Norman Robert
Arab versus European : diplomacy and war in nineteenth-century east central Africa / Norman Robert Bennett. — New York ; London : Africana Publishing, 1986. — 325p. — *Includes index. — Bibliography: p*

639

OMAN — History *continuation*
INNES, Neil McLeod
Minister in Oman / Neil McLeod Innes. — Cambridge : Oleander, c1987. — ix,292p. — *Bibliography: p286. — Includes index*

OMAN — National security
Oman : economic, social and strategic developments / edited by B.R. Pridham. — London : Croom Helm, c1987. — xiv,254p. — *Includes index*

OMAN — Social conditions
Oman : economic, social and strategic developments / edited by B.R. Pridham. — London : Croom Helm, c1987. — xiv,254p. — *Includes index*

OMBUDSMAN — Great Britain — Bibliography
GREAT BRITAIN. Civil Service Department. Central Management Library
Parliamentary commissioner for administration. — London : the Library, 1978. — 3p. — (Policy science documentation. Bibliography series ; B12)

OMBUDSMAN — Ireland
Ireland: annual report of the Ombudsman. — Dublin : Stationery Office, 1985-. — *Annual*

ON-LINE BIBLIOGRAPHIC SEARCHING
FOSTER, Allan
Online business sourcebook / by Allan Foster and Gerry Smith. — Hartlepool : Headland, 1985. — 1v.(looseleaf). — *Includes index*

GOLDSMITH, G.
Online searching made simple : a microcomputer interface for inexperienced users / G. Goldsmith and P.W. Williams. — London : British Library, c1986. — ix,113p. — (Library and information research report ; 41)

ONE-DIMENSIONAL MAN
ROTH, Roland
Rebellische Subjektivität : Herbert Marcuse und die neuen Protestbewegungen / Roland Roth. — Frankfurt : Campus, 1985. — 338p. — *Bibliography: p325-338*

ONE PARTY SYSTEMS — Africa, West
ZOLBERG, Aristide R.
Creating political order : the party-states of West Africa / Aristide R. Zolberg. — Chicago : Rand McNally, [1966]. — vi,168p

ONION INDUSTRY — Mexico
MEXICO. Dirección General de Economía Agrícola
Programa siembra-exportación de cebolla, temporada 1983-1984. — [México] : the Dirección, [ca.1984]. — 25p. — *Cover title: Cebolla, programa siembra exportación 1983-1984*

ONTARIO — Constitutional history
ROMNEY, Paul
Mr. Attorney : the Attorney General for Ontario in court, cabinet and legislature 1791-1899 / Paul Romney. — Toronto : Published for The Osgoode Society by University of Toronto Press, 1986. — xiii,396p. — *Notes: p[337]-381*

ONTARIO — Economic conditions
REA, K. J
The prosperous years : the economic history of Ontario, 1939-1975 / K.J. Rea. — Toronto ; Buffalo : University of Toronto Press, c1985. — xiv, 287 p.. — (Ontario historical studies series). — "A project of the Ontario historical studies series for the Government of Ontario.". — *Includes index. — Bibliography: p. [257]-277*

ONTARIO — Economic policy
REA, K. J
The prosperous years : the economic history of Ontario, 1939-1975 / K.J. Rea. — Toronto ; Buffalo : University of Toronto Press, c1985. — xiv, 287 p.. — (Ontario historical studies series). — "A project of the Ontario historical studies series for the Government of Ontario.". — *Includes index. — Bibliography: p. [257]-277*

ONTARIO — History
WHITE, Randall
Ontario : a political and economic history, 1610-1985 / by Randall White. — Toronto ; London : Dundurn, 1985. — [350]p. — *Includes bibliography and index*

ONTARIO — Politics and government
COPPS, Sheila
Nobody's baby : a survival guide to politics / Sheila Copps. — Toronto : Deneau, 1986. — 192p

HOY, Claire
Bill Davis : a biography / by Claire Hoy. — Toronto : New York : Methuen, c1985. — 413 p., [16] p. of plates. — *Includes index*

HUMPHRIES, Charles W
"Honest enough to be bold" : the life and times of Sir James Pliny Whitney / Charles W. Humphries. — Toronto ; Buffalo : Published by University of Toronto Press, c1985. — xii, 276 p., [14] p. of plates. — (The Ontario historical studies series). — *Includes index. — Bibliography: p. [269]-270*

JOHNSTON, Charles M.
E. C. Drury : agrarian idealist / Charles M. Johnston. — Toronto : University of Toronto Press, 1986. — xii,299p. — (Ontario Historical Studies Series). — *Includes references*

OLIVER, Peter
Unlikely Tory : the life and politics of Allan Grossman / Peter Oliver. — 1st ed. — Toronto, Ont. : L. & O. Dennys, c1985. — xi, 322 p., [8] p. of plates. — *Includes bibliographical references and index*

SPEIRS, Rosemary
Out of the blue : the fall of the Tory dynasty of Ontario / Rosemary Speirs. — Toronto : Macmillan of Canada, 1986. — xxii,246p

ONTARIO — Politics and government — 19th century
ROMNEY, Paul
Mr. Attorney : the Attorney General for Ontario in court, cabinet and legislature 1791-1899 / Paul Romney. — Toronto : Published for The Osgoode Society by University of Toronto Press, 1986. — xiii,396p. — *Notes: p[337]-381*

ONTARIO LIBERAL PARTY
COPPS, Sheila
Nobody's baby : a survival guide to politics / Sheila Copps. — Toronto : Deneau, 1986. — 192p

ONTOLOGY
DANIELS, Charles B.
Toward an ontology of number, mind and sign / Charles B. Daniels, James B. Freeman, Gerald W. Charlwood. — [Aberdeen] : Aberdeen University Press, 1986. — 156p. — (Scots philosophical monographs ; no.10). — *Bibliography: p153-155. — Includes index*

SELLARS, Wilfrid
Naturalism and ontology / Wilfrid Sellars. — Reseda, Calif. : Ridgeview, 1979. — viii, 182p. — *A revised and expanded version of the John Dewey lectures given at the University of Chicago in May 1974*

OPEC *See* Organization of the Petroleum Exporting Countries

OPEN AND CLOSED SHOP — Religious aspects — Catholic Church
MCLEAN, Edward B
Roman Catholicism and the right to work / Edward B. McLean. — Lanham : University Press of America, c1985. — ix, 175 p.. — *Bibliography: p. 167-175*

OPEN AND CLOSED SHOP — Great Britain
GREAT BRITAIN. Parliament. House of Commons. Library. Research Division
The closed shop / [Celia Nield]. — [London] : the Division, 1979. — 17p. — (Background paper ; no.74)

Practical guide to closed shop ballots. — London : Institute of Personnel Management, 1984. — vi,58p. — *Editor: Theon Wilkinson. — Bibliography: p57-58*

OPEN AND CLOSED SHOP — United States
MCLEAN, Edward B
Roman Catholicism and the right to work / Edward B. McLean. — Lanham : University Press of America, c1985. — ix, 175 p.. — *Bibliography: p. 167-175*

OPERATIONS RESEARCH
BAUMOL, William J.
Economic theory and operations analysis / William J. Baumol. — 4th ed. — Englewood Cliffs, N.J : Prentice-Hall, c1977. — xxi, 695 p. — (Prentice-Hall international series in management). — *Includes bibliographies and index*

Delivery of urban services : with a view towards applications in management science and operations research / edited by Arthur J. Swersey, Edward J. Ignall. — Amsterdam ; New York : North-Holland ; New York, NY, U.S.A. : Sole distributors for the U.S.A. and Canada, Elsevier Science Pub. Co., 1986. — vi, 274 p.. — (TIMS studies in the management science ; v. 22). — *Includes bibliographies*

MAKOWER, M. S.
Operational research / M.S. Makower and E. Williamson. — 4th ed. — Sevenoaks : Hodder and Stoughton, 1985. — 241p. — (Teach yourself books). — *Previous ed.: London : Teach Yourself Books, 1975. — Bibliography: p234-236. — Includes index*

Operational research techniques / S. French ... [et al.]. — London : Edward Arnold, 1986. — [256]p. — *Includes bibliography and index*

OPERATIONS RESEARCH — Data processing — Congresses
CONFERENCE "OR MODELS ON MICROCOMPUTERS" (1985 : Lisbon, Portugal)
OR models on microcomputers : proceedings of the Conference "OR Models on Microcomputers" held in Lisbon, Portugal, 25-27 September, 1985 / edited by J.D. Coelho and L.V. Tavares. — Amsterdam ; New York : North-Holland ; New York, N.Y. : Sole distributors for the U.S.A. and Canada, Elsevier Science Pub. Co., 1986. — p. cm

Impacts of microcomputers on operations research : proceedings of a symposium sponsored by the Computer Science Technical Section of the Operations Research Society of America, held on March 20-22, 1985, at the University of Colorado at Denver, Denver, Colorado, U.S.A. / editors, Saul I. Gass ... [et a.]. — New York : North-Holland, c1986. — viii, 255 p.. — (Publications in operations research series ; v. 5). — *Papers presented at the Symposium on Impacts of Microcomputers on Operations Research. — Includes bibliographies and index*

OPHIR
KEANE, A. H.
The gold of Ophir : whence brought and by whom? / by A.H.Keane. — New York : Negro Universities Press, 1969. — xviii,244p. — *Originally published in 1901*

OPPOSITION (POLITICAL SCIENCE)
ZIEGENHAGEN, Eduard A.
  The regulation of political conflict / Eduard A. Ziegenhagen. — New York : Praeger, 1986. — xix, 224 p.. — *Includes bibliographies and index*

OPPOSITION (POLITICAL SCIENCE) — Mexico — History — 20th century
Mexico's political stability : the next five years / edited by Roderic A. Camp. — Boulder : Westview Press, 1986. — ix, 279 p.. — (Westview special studies on Latin America and the Caribbean). — *Includes bibliographies and index.* — Contents: Overview / Roderic A. Camp -- The political consequences of changing socialization patterns / Daniel C. Levy -- How will economic recovery be managed? / William P. Glade -- Distributional and sectoral problems in the New Economic Policy / William P. Glade -- Leadership and change, Intellectuals and technocrats in Mexico / Peter H. Smith -- The impact of major groups on policy-making trends in government-business relations in Mexico / John Bailey -- The evolution of the Mexican military and its implications for civil-military relations / Edward J. Williams -- What explains the decline of the PRI and will it continue? / John Bailey -- Potential strengths of the political opposition and what it means to the PRI / Roderic A. Camp -- The implications of the border for Mexican-United States relations / Edward J. Williams -- The implications of Central American conflicts for Mexican politics / Daniel C. Levy

OPPOSITION (POLITICAL SCIENCE) — United States
FRESIA, Gerald John
  There comes a time : a challenge to the two party system / Gerald John Fresia. — New York : Praeger, 1986. — 255 p. — *Includes index.* — Bibliography: p. 217-249

OPPRESSION (PSYCHOLOGY)
BULHAN, Hussein Abdilahi
  Frantz Fanon and the psychology of oppression / Hussein Abdilahi Bulhan. — New York ; London : Plenum Press, c1985. — xiii, 299p. — (PATH in psychology). — *Includes index.* — *Includes bibliographical references*

OPTICAL DISKS — United States — Library applications
BARRETT, R.
  Further developments in optical disc technology and applications / R. Barrett. — Wetherby : British Library, c1984. — vii,35p. — (Library and Information research report ; 27)

OPTICAL STORAGE DEVICES
CENTRAL COMPUTER AND TELECOMMUNICATIONS AGENCY
  Data storage on optical disk : an experiment. — London : H.M.S.O., 1986. — 26p. — (Information technology in the civil service. IT series ; no.13)

GRAHAM, Margaret B. W.
  RCA and the VideoDisc : the business of research / Margaret B.W. Graham. — Cambridge : Cambridge University Press, 1986. — xiv,258p. — (Studies in economic history and policy : the United States in the twentieth century). — *Includes index*

HENDLEY, Tony
  CD-Rom and optical publishing systems : an assessment of the impact of optical read only memory systems on the information industry and a comparison between them and traditional paper, microfilm and on-line publishing systems / Tony Hendley. — Hatfield : Cimtech, 1987. — 151p. — (Cimtech publication ; 26) (British National Bibliography Research Fund report ; no.25)

OPUS DEI
ESCRIVA DE BALAGUER, Josemaría
  Conversations with Mgr Escriva de Balaguer : [recent interviews] / [by Pedro Rodriguez...[et al.]. — Dublin : Scepter Books, 1968. — 146p

ORAL COMMUNICATION
Language for hearers / edited by Graham McGregor. — Oxford : Pergamon, 1986. — [vii, 235]p. — (Language & communication library ; v.8). — *Includes index*

VENTOLA, Eija
  The structure of social interaction : a systemic approach to the semiotics of service encounters / Eija Ventola. — London : Pinter, 1987. — [270]p. — (Open linguistics series). — *Includes bibliography and index*

ORAL HISTORY
The Dissenters : voices from contemporary America / [compiled by] John Langston Gwaltney. — 1st ed. — New York : Random House, c1986. — xxviii, 321 p., [8] p. of plates

GERASSI, John
  The premature antifascists : North American volunteers in the Spanish Civil War, 1936-39 : an oral history / John Gerassi. — New York : Praeger, 1986. — xiii, 275 p.. — "Praeger special studies. Praeger scientific.". — *Includes index.* — Bibliography: p. 255-269

ROTHCHILD, Sylvia
  A special legacy : an oral history of Soviet Jewish emigrés in the United States / by Sylvia Rothchild. — New York : Simon and Schuster, c1985. — p. cm. — *Includes index*

ORDEAL — History
BARTLETT, Robert
  Trial by fire and water : the medieval judicial ordeal / Robert Bartlett. — Oxford : Clarendon, 1986. — [xiii,200]p. — *Includes bibliography and index*

ORDZHONIKIDZE, G. K.
KIRILLOV, V. S.
  Grigorii Konstantinovich Ordzhonikidze (Sergo) : biografiia / V. S. Kirillov, A. Ia. Sverdlov. — Izd. 2-e, dop. i isprav.. — Moskva : Politizdat, 1986. — 201p

ORGANIC WASTES AS FERTILIZER — United States
WINES, Richard A
  Fertilizer in America : from waste recycling to resource exploitation / Richard A. Wines. — Philadelphia : Temple University Press, 1985. — p. cm. — *Includes index.* — Bibliography: p

ORGANISATION COMMUNISTE INTERNATIONALISTE
ORGANISATION COMMUNISTE INTERNATIONALISTE
  Programme d'action de la classe ouvrière pour le socialisme, pour le gouvernement ouvrier. — Paris : Selio, 1968. — 22p. — (Documents de l'OCI ; no.1)

ORGANISATION DE L'ARMÉE SECRÈTE — History
KAUFFER, Rémi
  L' O. A. S. : histoire d'une organisation secrète / Rémi Kauffer. — Paris : Fayard, 1986. — 421p

ORGANISATION FOR ECONOMIC CO-OPERATION AND DEVELOPMENT — Economic assistance — Statistics
GREAT BRITAIN. overseas Development Administration. Statistics Division
  OECD and multilateral aid : geographical distribution 1977-1982. — [London] : the Administration, 1984. — 135p. — *Produced from an OECD computer tape*

ORGANISATION FOR ECONOMIC CO-OPERATION AND DEVELOPMENT. Development Centre
Development policies and the crisis of the 1980s / edited by Louis Emmerij. — Paris : OECD, 1987. — 178p. — (Development Centre seminars). — *Includes bibliographies.* — Contents: papers delivered at a seminar on "Alternative Development Strategies in the Light of Recent Experience", January,1987

ORGANISATION FOR ECONOMIC CO—OPERATION AND DEVELOPMENT. Development Centre — Research
ORGANISATION FOR ECONOMIC CO-OPERATION AND DEVELOPMENT. Development Centre
  Programme of research, 1987-1989. — Paris : OECD Development Centre, 1987. — 77p

ORGANISATION FOR ECONOMIC CO-OPERATION AND DEVELOPMENT. Water Management Research Group
ORGANISATION FOR ECONOMIC CO-OPERATION AND DEVELOPMENT. Water Management Research Group
  First report : 1969. — Paris : the Organisation, 1971. — 25p

ORGANISATION FOR ECONOMIC CO-OPERATION AND DEVELOPMENT COUNTRIES — Economic conditions — Mathematical models
JARRETT, Peter
  A revised supply block for the major seven countries in Interlink / by Peter Jarrett and Raymond Torres. — Paris : OECD, 1987. — 41p. — (Working papers / OECD Department of Economics and Statistics ; no.41). — *Bibliographical references: p23-24*

ORGANISATION FOR ECONOMIC CO-OPERATION AND DEVELOPMENT COUNTRIES — Economic policy
Structural adjustment and economic performance : synthesis report. — Paris : Organisation for Economic Co-operation and Development, 1987. — 39p

ORGANISATION OF THE PETROLEUM EXPORTING COUNTRIES — History
GHANEM, Shukri
  OPEC : the rise and fall of an exclusive club / Shukri Ghanem. — London : KPI, 1986. — x,233p. — *Includes bibliographies and index*

ORGANIZATION
BIDWELL, Charles E
  The organization and its ecosystem : a theory of structuring in organizations / by Charles E. Bidwell, John D. Kasarda. — Greenwich, Conn. : JAI Press, c1985. — xxiv, 248 p.. — (Monographs in organizational behavior and industrial relations ; v. 2). — *Includes indexes.* — Bibliography: p. 229-236

BURRELL, Gibson
  Sociological paradigms and organisational analysis : elements of the sociology of corporate life / Gibson Burrell, Gareth Morgan. — Aldershot : Gower, 1985, c1979. — [448]p. — *Originally published: London : Heinemann Educational, 1979.* — *Includes bibliography and index*

DAWSON, Sandra
  Analysing organisations / Sandra Dawson. — London : Macmillan, 1986. — xxiv,239p. — *Bibliography: p221-231*

DENHARDT, Robert B
  In the shadow of organization / Robert B. Denhardt. — Lawrence : Regents Press of Kansas, c1981. — viii, 157 p.. — *Includes index.* — Bibliography: p. 145-151

Organizing industrial development / editor, Rolf H. Wolff. — Berlin ; New York : W. de Gruyter, 1986. — p. cm. — (De Gruyter studies in organization ; 7). — *Includes index.* — Bibliography: p

ORGANIZATION — Addresses, essays, lectures
Human systems development / [edited by] Robert Tannenbaum, Newton Margulies, Fred Massarik, and associates. — 1st ed. — San Francisco : Jossey-Bass Publishers, 1985. — xxxi, 605 p.. — (The Jossey-Bass management series) (The Jossey-Bass social and behavioral science series). — *Includes bibliographies and indexes*

ORGANIZATION — Addresses, essays, lectures *continuation*
Organization--communication : emerging perspectives / Lee Thayer, editor. — Norwood, N.J. : Ablex Pub. Corp., c1986-. — v. <1, >. — (People, communication, organization). — *Includes bibliographies and indexes*

Power elites and organizations / edited by G. William Domhoff and Thomas R. Dye. — Beverly Hills : Sage Publications, c1986. — p. cm. — (Sage focus editions ; 82). — *Includes index*

ORGANIZATION — Case studies
LORSCH, Jay William, comp
Organization planning; cases and concepts / Edited by Jay W. Lorsch [and] Paul R. Lawrence. — Homewood, Ill. : R. D. Irwin, inc., 1972. — x, 341 p. — (The Irwin-Dorsey series in behavioral science). — *Bibliography: p. 73-74*

ORGANIZATION — Congresses
Organizational theory and inquiry : the paradigm revolution / edited by Yvonna S. Lincoln. — Beverly Hills : Sage Publications, c1985. — 231 p.. — (Sage focus editions ; v. 75). — *Based on papers presented at a conference held at the University of Kansas in November 1983. — Includes bibliographies*

ORGANIZATION — Dictionaries and encyclopedias
Encyclopedia of world problems and human potential / edited by Union of International Associations. — 2nd ed. — München ; London : K. F. Saur, 1986. — unpaged

ORGANIZATION — Mathematical models
Decision and organization : a volume in honor of Jacob Marschak / edited by C.B. McGuire and Roy Radner ; contributors, Kenneth J. Arrow ... [et al.]. — 2nd ed. — Minneapolis : University of Minnesota Press, c1986. — p. cm . — *Includes indexes. — "Publications of Jacob Marschak": p. — Bibliography: p*

ORGANIZATION — Research
ALDRICH, Howard
Population perspectives on organisations / Howard Aldrich in collaboration with Ellen R. Auster, Udo H. Staber and Catherine Zimmer. — Uppsala : [University of Uppsala], 1986. — 109p. — (Acta Universitatis Upsaliensis : Studia oeconomiae negotiorum ; 25) (Uppsala Lectures in Business ; 2). — *Bibliography: p95-104*

Survey item bank / [Bernard Stewart...et al.]. — [S.l.] : MCB/University Press. — *Sponsored by British Telecom*
Vol.2. — [1985]. — Various pagings

ORGANIZATION — Research — Congresses
Organizational theory and inquiry : the paradigm revolution / edited by Yvonna S. Lincoln. — Beverly Hills : Sage Publications, c1985. — 231 p.. — (Sage focus editions ; v. 75). — *Based on papers presented at a conference held at the University of Kansas in November 1983. — Includes bibliographies*

ORGANIZATION OF AFRICAN UNITY
ORGANIZATION OF AFRICAN UNITY
Resolutions adopted by the Council of Ministers of the Organization of African Unity : at its forty-fourth ordinary session, held at Addis Ababa from 21 to 26 July 1986 [and] Statements, declarations, decisions and resolutions adopted by the Assembly of Heads of State and Government of the Organization of African Unity : at its twenty-second ordinary session, held at Addis Ababa from 28 to 30 July 1986. — New York : United Nations, 1986. — *Resolutions, etc. transmitted to the Secretary General of the U.N. by the Permanent Representative of Algeria to the U.N. for distribution as an official U.N. document under cover of his letter dated 25 September 1986. — U.N. document A/41/654*

ORGANIZATION OF AFRICAN UNITY — History
AMATE, C. O. C.
Inside the OAU : Pan-Africanism in practice : C.O.C. Amate. — Basingstoke : Macmillan, 1986. — [608]p. — *Includes bibliography and index*

ORGANIZATION OF AMERICAN STATES
Anuario juridico interamericano = Inter-American juridical yearbook / Organizacion de los Estados Americanos. — Washington, D.C. : Organization of American States, 1949-1957. — Annual. — Text in English and Spanish. — *1949-1957 issuing body entitled Pan-American Union*

ORGANIZATION OF AMERICAN STATES — Bibliography
COLUMBUS MEMORIAL LIBRARY
Bibliography of books and articles in periodicals on the Organization of American States = : Bibliografía de libros y artículos de revistas sobre la Organización de los Estados Americanos. — Washington : Organization of American States, General Secretariat, Dept. of Publications, Columbus Memorial Library, 1977. — ii,22p. — (Documentation and information series ; no. 2). — *"OEA/SG/O.1/IV/III.2."*

ORGANIZATION OF ARAB PETROLEUM EXPORTING COUNTRIES — Bibliography
The annotated list of OAPEC publications / Organization of Arab Petroleum Exporting Countries. — Safat : Organization of Arab Petroleum Exporting Countries, 1984-

ORGANIZATION OF EASTERN CARIBBEAN STATES
DAVIDSON, Scott
Grenada : a study in politics and the limits of international law / Scott Davidson. — Aldershot : Avebury, c1987. — xii,196p. — *Bibliography: p184-190. — Includes index*

ORGANIZATION OF PETROLEUM EXPORTING COUNTRIES
AHRARI, Mohammed E
OPEC : the failing giant / Mohammed E. Ahrari. — Lexington, KY : University Press of Kentucky, 1986. — 256p. — *Includes index. — Bibliography: p.[232]-249*

ORGANIZATION OF REVOLUTIONARY WORKERS OF IRAN
ORGANIZATION OF REVOLUTIONARY WORKERS OF IRAN
Resolutions on Working Class Party, United Workers Front, United Democratic Anti-Imperialist Front. — Aliozadi : Organization of Revolutionary Workers of Iran, 1987. — 20p

ORGANIZATION OF THE PETROLEUM EXPORTING COUNTRIES
OPEC aid and the challenge of development / edited by Abdelkader Benamara and Sam Ifeagwu. — London : Croom Helm, c1987. — x,130p

OPEC and the world oil market : the genesis of the 1986 price crisis / edited by Robert Mabro. — Oxford : Oxford University Press for the Oxford Institute for Energy Studies, 1986. — [250]p

ORGANIZATION OF THE PETROLEUM EXPORTING COUNTRIES — History
EVANS, John, 19---
OPEC, its member states and the world energy market / compiled and written by John Evans. — Harlow : Longman, c1986. — xxiv,679p. — (A Keesing's reference publication). — *Includes index*

ORGANIZATIONAL BEHAVIOR
HARMON, Michael
Organization theory for public administration / Michael M. Harmon, Richard T. Mayer. — Boston : Little, Brown, 1986. — xiv, 443p. — *Includes index. — Bibliography: p.417-426*

HARRIMAN, Ann
Women/men/management / by Ann Harriman. — New York : Praeger Publishers, 1985. — p. cm. — *Includes index. — Bibliography: p*

HEARN, Jeff
'Sex' at 'work' : the power and paradox of organisation and sexuality / Jeff Hearn and Wendy Parkin. — Brighton : Wheatsheaf, 1987. — [224]p. — *Includes bibliography and index*

KAKABADSE, Andrew
Working in organisations / Andrew Kakabadse, Ron Ludlow and Susan Vinnicombe. — Aldershot : Gower, c1987. — x,453p. — *Includes bibliographies and index*

LAUFFER, Armand
Careers, colleagues, and conflicts : understanding gender, race and ethnicity in the workplace / Armand Lauffer. — Beverly Hills ; London : Sage, c1985. — 182 p. — (Sage human services guides ; v.43)

MCFARLAND, Dalton E
The managerial imperative : the age of macromanagement / Dalton E. McFarland. — Cambridge, Mass. : Ballinger, c1986. — xxiv, 369 p.. — *Includes bibliographies and index*

The Social psychology of education : current research and theory / edited by Robert S. Feldman. — Cambridge : Cambridge University Press, 1986. — 381p. — *Includes bibliography and index*

ORGANIZATIONAL BEHAVIOR — Addresses, essays, lectures
Human systems development / [edited by] Robert Tannenbaum, Newton Margulies, Fred Massarik, and associates. — 1st ed. — San Francisco : Jossey-Bass Publishers, 1985. — xxxi, 605 p.. — (The Jossey-Bass management series) (The Jossey-Bass social and behavioral science series). — *Includes bibliographies and indexes*

ORGANIZATIONAL BEHAVIOR — Research
Generalizing from laboratory to field settings : research findings from industrial-organizational psychology, organizational behavior, and human resource management / edited by Edwin A. Locke. — Lexington, Mass. : Lexington Books, c1986. — x, 291 p.. — (The Issues in organization and management series). — *Includes bibliography and index*

ORGANIZATIONAL CHANGE
DAVIES, Phillip L.
Are programme resources related to organizational change? / Dr. Phillip L. Davies and Professor Richard Rose. — Glasgow : University of Strathclyde. Centre for the Study of Public Policy, 1987. — 35p. — (Studies in public policy ; 159)

FÉDÉRATION CHRÉTIENNE DES OUVRIERS SUR MÉTAUX DE LA SUISSE.
Congrès (1979 : Montreux)
Les travailleurs face à la révolution technologique : FCOM congrès 1979. — [Genève] : the Fédération, [1979]. — 18p

GOLEMBIEWSKI, Robert T.
Humanizing public relations : perspectives on doing better-than-average when average ain't at all bad / Robert T. Golembiewski. — Mt. Airy, Md. : Lomond, 1985. — viii,377

HARMON, Michael
Organization theory for public administration / Michael M. Harmon, Richard T. Mayer. — Boston : Little, Brown, 1986. — xiv, 443p. — *Includes index. — Bibliography: p.417-426*

HUSE, Edgar F
Organization development and change / Edgar F. Huse, Thomas G. Cummings. — 3rd ed. — St. Paul, Minn. : West Pub. Co., c1985. — xv, 583 p.. — *Includes bibliographies and indexes*

ORGANIZATIONAL CHANGE
continuation

KAUFMAN, Herbert
Time, chance, and organizations : natural selection in a perilous environment / Herbert Kaufman. — Chatham, N.J. : Chatham House, c1985. — xii, 180 p.. — *Includes indexes.* — *Bibliography: p. 157-167*

LEVY, Amir
Organizational transformation : approaches, strategies, theories / Amir Levy, Uri Merry. — New York : Praeger, 1986. — xii, 335 p.. — *Includes index.* — *Bibliography: p. 309-331*

NORÉN, Anders E.
The Orrefors report : experimental activities with changed work organization and a new wage system : final report / Anders E. Norén [and] Jan-Peder Norstedt. — Stockholm : Swedish Employer's Confederation, 1975. — 54p

ORGANIZATIONAL CHANGE —
Addresses, essays, lectures

Human systems development / [edited by] Robert Tannenbaum, Newton Margulies, Fred Massarik, and associates. — 1st ed. — San Francisco : Jossey-Bass Publishers, 1985. — xxxi, 605 p.. — (The Jossey-Bass management series) (The Jossey-Bass social and behavioral science series). — *Includes bibliographies and indexes*

ORGANIZATIONAL CHANGE —
Dictionaries

HUCZYNSKI, Andrzej
Encyclopedia of organizational change methods / Andrzej Huczynski. — Aldershot : Gower, c1987. — xxvi,344p. — *Bibliography: p341-344.* — *Includes index*

ORGANIZATIONAL CHANGE —
Colombia — Case studies

SAVAGE, Charles H
Sons of the machine : case studies of social change in the workplace / Charles H. Savage and George F.F. Lombard. — Cambridge, Mass : MIT Press, c1986. — xvi, 313 p., [17] pages of plates. — (MIT Press series on organization studies ; 7). — *Includes index.* — *Bibliography: p. 283-291*

ORGANIZATIONAL CHANGE — Great Britain — Management — Case studies

CONFEDERATION OF BRITISH INDUSTRY
Managing change : the organisation of work / CBI. — London : Confederation of British Industry, 1985. — 99p

ORGANIZATIONAL CHANGE —
Scotland

STEWART, Valerie
Changing trains : messages for management from the ScotRail challenge / Valerie Stewart and Vivian Chadwick. — Newton Abbot : David & Charles, c1987. — 190p

ORGANIZATIONAL EFFECTIVENESS

AYUB, Mahmood Ali
Public industrial enterprises : determinants of performance / Mahmood Ali Ayub and Sven Olaf Hegstad. — Washington, D.C. : The World Bank, 1986. — xi,77p. — (Industry and finance series ; v.17). — *Includes bibliographical references*

DOWNS, George W
The search for government efficiency : from hubris to helplessness / George W. Downs, Patrick D. Larkey. — 1st ed. — Philadelphia : Temple University Press, c1986. — viii, 273 p.. — *Includes bibliographies*

GOLEMBIEWSKI, Robert T.
Humanizing public relations : perspectives on doing better-than-average when average ain't at all bad / Robert T. Golembiewski. — Mt. Airy, Md. : Lomond, 1985. — viii,377

KUHN, Arthur J
Organizational cybernetics and business policy : System design for performance control / Arthur J. Kuhn. — University Park : Pennsylvania State University Press, 1986. — p. cm. — *Includes index.* — *Bibliography: p*

ORGANIZATIONAL EFFECTIVENESS
— Case studies

PAUL, Ronald N
The 101 best performing companies in America / Ronald N. Paul, James W. Taylor. — Chicago, Ill. : Probus Pub. Co., c1986. — vii, 382 p.. — *Includes bibliographical references and index*

ORGANIZATIONAL EFFECTIVENESS
— Measurement

MUNDEL, Marvin Everett
Improving productivity and effectiveness / Marvin E. Mundel. — Englewood Cliffs, N.J. : Prentice-Hall, c1983. — x,467p. — (Prentice-Hall international series in industrial and systems engineering). — *Includes bibliographical references*

ORGANIZATIONS

MARCH, James G.
Ambiguity and choice in organizations / by James G. March and Johan P. Olsen; with contributions by Søren Christensen...[et al.]. — 2nd ed. — Bergen : Universitetsforlaget, 1979. — 408p. — *Bibliography: p397-402*

ORGANIZATSIIA VARSHAVSKOGO DOGOVORA

FARINGDON, Hugh
Confrontation : the strategic geography of NATO and the Warsaw Pact / Hugh Faringdon. — London : Routledge & Kegan Paul, 1986. — [352]p. — *Includes bibliography and index*

ORGANIZED CRIME — Australia

HALL, Richard
Disorganized crime / Richard Hall. — St. Lucia ; New York : University of Queensland Press, 1986. — 280 p., [7] p. of plates. — *Includes index.* — *Bibliography: p. [273]-276*

ORIENTATION (PSYCHOLOGY) —
Congresses

Attention and performance XI / edited by Michael I. Posner, Oscar S.M. Marin. — Hillsdale, N.J. : Lawrence Erlbaum Associates, 1985. — xxiii, 675p. — *"Proceedings of the Eleventh International Symposium on Attention and Performance, Eugene, Oregon, July 1-8, 1984"--P.* — *Includes bibliographies and indexes*

ORIGIN OF SPECIES

Darwin and modern science : essays in commemoration of the centenary of the birth of Charles Darwin and of the fiftieth anniversary of the publication of The Origin of Species / edited by A. C. Seward. — Cambridge : Cambridge University Press, 1910. — xvii,595p

ORIGINS OF MUHAMMADAN JURISPRUDENCE

A'ZAMĪ, Muḥammad Muṣṭafá
On Schacht's Origins of Muhammadan jurisprudence / M. Mustafa Al-Azami. — New York : Wiley, c1986. — p. cm. — *Includes index.* — *Bibliography: p*

ORISSA (INDIA) — Politics and government — Addresses, essays, lectures

Indian state politics : a case study of Orissa / edited by A.P. Padhi. — Delhi : B.R. Pub. Corp. ; New Delhi, India : Distributed by D.K. Publishers' Distributors, 1985. — xxx, 433 p.. — *Includes bibliographical references*

ORISSA (INDIA) — Statistics

Statistical outline of Orissa / Bureau of Statistics and Economics, Orissa. — Bhubaneswar : Bureau of Statistics and Economics, 1981-. — *Annual*

ORREFORS GLASSWORKS

NORÉN, Anders E.
The Orrefors report : experimental activities with changed work organization and a new wage system : final report / Anders E. Norén [and] Jan-Peder Norstedt. — Stockholm : Swedish Employer's Confederation, 1975. — 54p

ORTHODOX EASTERN CHURCH — Romania — History

PĂCURARIU, Mircea
Politica statului ungar faţă de Biserica românească din Transilvania în perioada dualismului (1867-1918) / Mircea Păcurariu. — Sibiu : Editura Institutului Biblic şi de Misiune al Bisericii Ortodoxe Române, 1986. — 301p

ORTHOPEDIC SHOES — England

BAINBRIDGE, Sheila
National Health surgical footwear : a survey carried out on behalf of the Department of Health and Social Security ... / Sheila Bainbridge ; [for the] Office of Population Censuses and Surveys, Social Survey Division. — London : H.M.S.O., 1979. — [10],77p

ORWELL, GEORGE. 1984

1984 und danach : Utopie, Realität, Perspektiren : Beiträge zum "Orwell-Jahr" / Horst Baier...[et al.] ; herausgegeben von Erhard R. Wiehn. — Konstanz : Universitätsverlag, 1984. — 148p. — *Includes bibliographic references*

ORWELL, GEORGE — Criticism and interpretation

WOODCOCK, George, 1912-
The crystal spirit : a study of George Orwell, George Woodcock. — 2nd ed. — London : Fourth Estate, 1984. — xiv,287p. — *Originally published: London : Cape, 1967*

OSAGE COUNTY (OKLA.) — Economic conditions

WILSON, Terry P.
The underground reservation : Osage oil / Terry P. Wilson. — Lincoln : University of Nebraska Press, c1985. — xiv, 263 p.. — *Includes index.* — *Bibliography: p. 237-249*

OSAGE INDIANS — Economic conditions

WILSON, Terry P.
The underground reservation : Osage oil / Terry P. Wilson. — Lincoln : University of Nebraska Press, c1985. — xiv, 263 p.. — *Includes index.* — *Bibliography: p. 237-249*

OSAGE INDIANS — History

WILSON, Terry P.
The underground reservation : Osage oil / Terry P. Wilson. — Lincoln : University of Nebraska Press, c1985. — xiv, 263 p.. — *Includes index.* — *Bibliography: p. 237-249*

OSTARA

DAIM, Wilfried
Der Mann, der Hitler die Ideen gab : die sektiererischen Grundlagen des Nationalsozialismus / Wilfried Daim. — 2e, erw. und verb. Aufl. — Wien : Hermann Böhlau, 1985. — 316p. — (Böhlaus zeitgeschichtliche Bibliothek ; Bd.4). — *First published 1958*

OSTEOMALACIA — Prevention

GREAT BRITAIN. Working Party on Fortification of Food with Vitamin D
Rickets and osteomalacia / report of the Working Party on Fortification of Food with Vitamin D. Committee on Medical Aspects of Food Policy. — London : H.M.S.O., 1980. — xii,66p. — (Report on health and social subjects ; 19). — *At head of title: Department of Health and Social Security.* — *Bibliography: p54-66*

OTECHESTVENNYE ZAPISKI

EMEL'IANOV, N. P.
"Otechestvennye zapiski" N. A. Nekrasova i M. E. Saltykova-Shchedrina (1868-1884) / N. P. Emel'ianov. — Leningrad : Khudozhestvennaia literatura, Leningradskoe otdelenie, 1986. — 333p

OUADDAI (CHAD) — Social conditions
HASSAN KHAYAR, Issa
Tchad : regards sur les élites ouaddaïennes / par Issa Hassan Khayar. — Paris : Centre National de la Recherche Scientifique, 1984. — 231p. — (Contributions à la connaissance des élites africaines ; 3). — *Bibliography: p215-231*

OUTER SPACE — Bibliography
DAG HAMMERSKJOLD LIBRARY
Outer space : a selective bibliography = L'espace extra-atmosph'erique : bibliographie s'elective / Dag Hammerskjold Library. — New York : United Nations, 1982. — x,123p. — (ST/LIB/SER.B/33). — *Prepared for the Second United Nations Conference on the Exploration and Peaceful Uses of Outer Space (UNISPACE 82), Vienna, 9-21 August 1982. — At head of title: Unispace 82*

OUTER SPACE — Exploration
MARSH, Peter, 1952-
The space business : a manual on the commercial uses of space / Peter Marsh. — Harmondsworth : Penguin, 1985. — 232p. — *Further reading: p[211]-217*

OVERIJSSEL (NETHERLANDS) — Economic policy
NETHERLANDS. Stuurgroep Integraal Structuurplan Noorden des Lands
Het Noorden : een versterkte bevolkingsgroei? Of juist niet! : een bewerking van het rapport Bevolkingsaspecten Noorden des Lands / Samensteller R. Idenburg. — 's-Gravenhage : Staatsuitgeverij, 1974. — 21p

NETHERLANDS. Werkgroep Beleidsdoelstellingen Analyse Noorden
ISP : integraal structuurplan Noorden des lands : rapport van de Werkgroep Beleidsdoelstellingen Analyse Noorden. — [s-Gravenhage] : the Werkgroep 2. — 1974. — 27p

OVERPRODUCTION — History
RAPOŠ, Pavel
Die kranke Wirtschaft : Kapitalismus und krise / Pavel Rapoš ; Übersetzung aus dem Slowakischen: Intertext. — Köln : Pahl-Rugenstein, 1984. — 321p. — *Originally published: Bratislava: Pravda, 1981*

OVERSEAS DEVELOPMENT INSTITUTE — History
CLARK, William, 1916-1985
From three worlds : memoirs / William Clark. — London : Sidgwick & Jackson, [1986]. — xi,292p

OWEN, ROBERT, 1771-1858
TAYLOR, Anne, 1932-
Visions of harmony : a study of nineteenth-century millenarianism / Anne Taylor. — Oxford : Clarendon, 1987. — 285p,[8]p of plates. — *Bibliography: p269-275. — Includes index*

PACEMAKER, ARTIFICIAL (HEART)
Les stimulateurs cardiaques. — [Paris] : La Documentation française, 1985. — 232p

PACIFIC AREA
Le Pacifique : nouveau centre du monde / [par] Georges Ordonnaud...[et al.]; [commissioné par l'] Institut du Pacifique. — Paris : Berger-Levrault, 1986. — 363p

Survey of major western Pacific economies. — 4th ed. — Canberra : Australian Government Publishing Service, 1986. — v,156p

PACIFIC AREA — Commerce
GOLDBERG, Michael A
The Chinese connection : getting plugged in to Pacific Rim real estate, trade, and capital markets / Michael A. Goldberg. — Vancouver : University of British Columbia Press, 1985. — xi, 158 p.. — *Includes indexes. — Bibliography: p. [121]-158*

Raw materials and Pacific economic integration / edited by Sir John Crawford and Saburo Okita assisted by ... [others]. — London : Croom Helm, 1978. — 343p. — *Bibliography: p.312-338. — Includes index*

PACIFIC AREA — Economic conditions
KRAUS, Willy
The economic development of the Pacific Basin : growth dynamics, trade relations and emerging cooperation / Willy Kraus, Wilfried Lütkenhorst. — New York : St. Martin's ; London : Hurst, c1986. — x,180p. — *Bibliography: p162-177. — Includes index*

PACIFIC AREA — Foreign economic relations
Economic relations in the Asian-Pacific region : report of a conference cosponsored by the Chinese Academy of Social Sciences and the Brookings Institution, June 1985 / edited by Bruce Dickson and Harry Harding. — Washington,D.C. : Brookings Institution, 1987. — ix,91p. — (Brookings dialogues on public policy)

PACIFIC AREA — Foreign relations
Security within the Pacific Rim / edited by Douglas T. Stuart. — Aldershot : Gower, c1987. — viii,166p. — *Includes index*

PACIFIC AREA — Strategic aspects
HAYES, Peter
American lake : nuclear peril in the Pacific / Peter Hayes, Lyuba Zarsky, Walden Bello. — Harmondsworth : Penguin, 1987. — xiv, 529p. — *First published by Penguin in Australia in 1986*

PACIFIC AREA — Yearbooks
Pacific Islands year book / editor: John Carter. — 15th ed. — Sydney ; New York : Pacific Publications, 1984. — 557p. — *Includes one folded map of the Pacific Islands in end-pocket*

PACIFIC AREA CO-OPERATION
NEW ZEALAND. Ministry of Foreign Affairs
The South Pacific Forum. — Wellington : the Ministry, 1986. — 12p. — (Information bulletin ; no.16)

PACIFIC OCEAN — Bibliography
FRY, Gerald W.
Pacific Basin and Oceania / Gerald W. Fry, Rufino Mauricio. — Oxford : Clio, c1987. — xxxvi,468p. — (World bibliographical series ; 70). — *Includes index*

PACIFIC OCEAN REGION — Relations — Canada — Congresses
Canada's strategies for the Pacific Rim / edited by Brian MacDonald. — Toronto, Ont., Canada : Canadian Institute of Strategic Studies, c1985. — 145 p.. — *Papers presented at a conference held in Victoria, B.C., Oct. 1984. — On cover: Proceedings, Fall 1984. — Includes bibliographies*

PACIFIC OCEAN REGION — Strategic aspects
The Anzac connection / edited by Desmond Ball. — Sydney ; London ; Boston : George Allen & Unwin, 1985. — xvi,169p

PACIFIC STATES — Commercial policy
The Pacific Rim era and the shipping. — Tokyo : Japan Maritime Research Institute, 1987. — 68p. — (Jamri report ; no.19)

PACIFICISM
The Sociology of war and peace / edited by Colin Creighton and Martin Shaw. — Basingstoke : Macmillan, 1987. — viii,245p. — (Explorations in sociology ; 24). — *Includes bibliographies and index*

PACIFISM
Articles of peace : celebrating fifty years of Peace News / edited by Gail Chester and Andrew Rigby. — Bridport : Prism Press, 1986. — [xiv],174p

Beyond survival : new directions for the disarmament movement / edited by Michael Albert and David Dellinger. — Boston : South End Press, 1983. — 365p

BONK, Heinz
Es gibt eine Kraft! : die revolutionäre Arbeiterbewegung im Kampf um Frieden und Abrüstung / Heinz Bonk. — Berlin : Dietz, 1981. — 229p

TEICHMAN, Jenny
Pacifism and the just war : a study in applied philosophy / Jenny Teichman. — Oxford : Basil Blackwell, 1986. — [128]p. — *Bibliography: p130. — Includes index*

PACIFISM — History
CALVOCORESSI, Peter
A time for peace : pacifism, internationalism and protest forces in the reduction of war / Peter Calvocoressi. — London : Hutchinson, 1987. — 195p. — *Includes index*

PACIFISM — Germany (West)
Neue Akzente der Friedenspädagogik / Peter Heitkämper (Hg.). — Münster : Lit, 1984. — 135p. — (Frieden - Ökologie - Entwicklung ; Bd.1)

PACIFISTS — Germany
KLEBERGER, Ilse
Die Vision vom Frieden : Bertha von Suttner / Ilse Kleburger. — Berlin : Klopp, 1985. — 210p

PACIFISTS — New Zealand
CRANE, Ernest
I can do no other : a biography of the Reverend Ormond Burton / Ernest Crane. — Auckland ; London : Hodder and Stoughton, 1986. — xii,338p. — *Bibliography: p328-9*

PAEA (TAHITI : REGION) — Population — Statistics
Tableaux normalisés du recensement général de la population : 15 octobre 1983. — [Papeete] : Institut territorial de la statistique Résultats de la commune de Paea. — [1985?]. — 4p,11 leaves

PAGANISM IN ART
WIND, Edgar
Pagan mysteries in the Renaissance / by Edgar Wind. — [2nd (enlarged) ed.]. — Oxford : Oxford University Press, 1980. — xiii,345p,[64]p of plates. — (Oxford paperbacks). — *This ed. originally published : Harmondsworth : Penguin, 1967. — Bibliography: p.305-315. — Includes index*

PAIN
SCARRY, Elaine
The body in pain : the making and unmaking of the world / Elaine Scarry. — New York : Oxford University Press, 1985. — p. cm. — *Includes index*

PAIN — Psychological aspects
KLEINMAN, Arthur
Social origins of distress and disease : depression, neurasthenia, and pain in modern China / Arthur Kleinman. — New Haven : Yale University Press, c1986. — xii, 264 p.. — *Includes index. — Bibliography: p. 241-254*

PAIN — psychology
KLEINMAN, Arthur
Social origins of distress and disease : depression, neurasthenia, and pain in modern China / Arthur Kleinman. — New Haven : Yale University Press, c1986. — xii, 264 p.. — *Includes index. — Bibliography: p. 241-254*

PAINE, THOMAS
PAINE, Thomas
The Thomas Paine reader / edited by Michael Foot and Isaac Kramnick. — Harmondsworth : Penguin, 1987. — 536p. — (Penguin classics)

PAINTING

BARRELL, John
The political theory of painting from Reynolds to Hazlitt : the body of the public / John Barrell. — New Haven ; London : Yale University Press, 1986. — [352]p. — *Includes index*

PAISLEY, IAN

BRUCE, Steve
God save Ulster : the religion and politics of Paisleyism / Steve Bruce. — Oxford : Clarendon, 1986. — xv,308p. — *Includes index*

MOLONEY, Ed
Paisley / Ed Moloney and Andy Pollak. — Dublin : Poolbeg, 1986. — 456p. — *Bibliography: p445-[448]*

PAKISTAN — Military policy

KAPUR, Ashok
Pakistan's nuclear development / Ashok Kapur. — London : Croom Helm, c1987. — [320]p. — *Includes index*

PAKISTAN

Pakistan: au official handbook / Pakistan. Directorate of Films and Publications.. — Islamabad : Directorate of Films and Publications, 1984-. — *Annual*

PAKISTAN — Appropriations and expenditures

The Federal Public Accounts Committee in Pakistan. — [Islamabad] : National Assembly Secretariat ; [1985]. — x,232p

PAKISTAN — Bibliography

Pakistan : a comprehensive bibliography of books and government publications with annotations, 1947-80 / compiled by Institute's research scholars under the direction of N.A. Baloch. — Islamabad : Institute of Islamic History, Culture, and Civilization, Islamic University, 1981. — xii,515p. — (Bibliographical series ; 4)

PAKISTAN — Census, 1981

1981 census report of Federally Administered Tribal Areas (FATA). — Islamabad : Population Census Organisation, 1984. — 116p. — (Census report ; no.62)

1981 census report of Pakistan. — Islamabad : Population Census Organisation, 1984. — iv,200p. — (Census report ; no.69)

Main findings of 1981 population census. — Islamabad : Population Census Organisation, [1983]. — 19p

PAKISTAN — Commercial policy

BHUTTO, Zulfikar Ali
Prime Minister Mr. Zulfikar Ali Bhutto : address at the Export Promotion Council Annual Meeting : Karachi, November 1, 1973. — [Islamabad : Department of Films and Publications, 1973]. — 15p

PAKISTAN — Constitution, 1985

Comparative statement of the constitution as it stood before the 20th March, 1985 and as it stands after that date. — Islamabad : Ministry of Justice and Parliamentary Affairs, 1985. — 73,73p. — *Opposite pages bear duplicate numbering*

The constitution of the Islamic Republic of Pakistan : as modified up to the 19th March, 1985. — Islamabad : Ministry of Justice and Parliamentary Affairs, 1985. — xviii,259p

PAKISTAN — Constitutional history

BARUA, B. P.
Politics and constitution-making in India and Pakistan / B. P. Barua ; foreword by Hugh Tinker. — New Delhi : Deep and Deep Publications, 1984. — 216p. — *Bibliography: p201-213*

PAKISTAN — Defenses

SAWHNEY, R. G.
Zia's Pakistan : implications for India's security / R. G. Sawhney. — New Delhi : ABC Publishing House, 1985. — xv,200p. — *Bibliography: p[181]-193*

PAKISTAN — Economic conditions

BHUTTO, Zulfikar Ali
Prime Minister Mr. Zulfikar Ali Bhutto : address at the Export Promotion Council Annual Meeting : Karachi, November 1, 1973. — [Islamabad : Department of Films and Publications, 1973]. — 15p

MADDISON, Angus
Class structure and economic growth : India and Pakistan since the Moghuls. — New York : Norton, [1972, c1971]. — 181 p. — *Bibliography: p. 173-176*

NASEEM, S. M
Underdevelopment, poverty, and inequality in Pakistan / S.M. Naseem. — Lahore : Vanguard Publications, 1981. — 323 p.. — *Includes index. — Bibliography: p. [305]-320*

Pakistan : reforms and development. — [Islamabad : Department of Films and Publications, Ministry of Information and Broadcasting, 1974?]. — 45p

PAKISTAN — Economic conditions — Statistics

Environment statistics of Pakistan / Federal Bureau of Statistics, Pakistan. — Karachi : Federal Bureau of Statistics, 1984-

PAKISTAN — Economic policy

NASEEM, S. M
Underdevelopment, poverty, and inequality in Pakistan / S.M. Naseem. — Lahore : Vanguard Publications, 1981. — 323 p.. — *Includes index. — Bibliography: p. [305]-320*

Pakistan, review of the sixth five-year plan. — Washington, D.C., U.S.A. : World Bank, c1984. — xci,167p. — (A World Bank country study). — *Summaries in English, French, and Spanish. — Includes bibliographical references*

PAKISTAN — Economic policy — Statistics

Federal government public sector development programme, 1985-86. — [Islamabad] : Planning Commission, Government of Pakistan, 1985. — xvi,223p

PAKISTAN — Emigration and immigration

SARMAD, Khwaja
Pakistani migration to the Middle East countries / Khwaja Sarmad. — Islamabad : Pakistan Institute of Development Economics, 1985. — 48p. — (Studies in population, labour force and migration project report ; no.9). — *Bibliography: p48-49*

PAKISTAN — Ethnic relations — Congresses

The State, religion, and ethnic politics : Afghanistan, Iran, and Pakistan / edited by Ali Banuazizi and Myron Weiner. — 1st ed. — [Syracuse, N.Y.] : Syracuse University Press, 1986. — xi, 390 p.. — (Contemporary issues in the Middle East). — *"Sponsored by the Joint Committee on the Near and Middle East and the Committee on South Asia of the American Council of Learned Societies and the Social Science Research Council.". — Includes bibliographies and index*

PAKISTAN — Foreign relations — Addresses, essays, lectures

ZIA-UL-HAQ, Mohammad
Pakistan's foreign relations : address to the nation / President General Mohammad Zia-ul-Haq. — Islamabad : Directorate of Films and Publications, Ministry of Information and Broadcasting, 1981. — 19p. — *English version of broadcast in Urdu given on radio and television from Rawalpindi on 24 June, 1981*

PAKISTAN — Foreign relations — Afghanistan

KULWANT KAUR
Pak-Afghanistan relations / Kulwant Kaur. — New Delhi : Deep & Deep Publications, c1985. — viii, 252 p.. — *Includes index. — Bibliography: p. [224]-250*

PAKISTAN — Foreign relations — India

SEMINAR ON INDO-PAK RELATIONS (1984 : New Delhi)
Studies in Indo-Pak relations : papers presented at the seminar on Indo-Pak relations by the Indian Centre for Regional Affairs, New Delhi, 24-25 April, 1984 / edited by V. D. Chopra ; with a sum-up by P. N. Haksar. — New Delhi : Patriot [for the Indian Centre for Regional Affairs], 1984. — xxxii,299p

PAKISTAN — Foreign relations — United States

The Red Army on Pakistan's border : policy implications for the United States / Theodore L. Eliot, Jr. ... [et al.]. — Washington : Pergamon-Brassey's, 1986. — p. cm. — (Special report). — *"May 1986.". — "A joint publication of the Institute for Foreign Policy Affairs, Inc. and the Center for Asian Pacific Affairs, the Asia Foundation."*

PAKISTAN — Foreign relations — United States — Addresses, essays, lectures

BHUTTO, Zulfikar Ali
Prime Minister Zulfikar Ali Bhutto : speeches and statements during visit to the United States of America in September 1973. — [Islamabad : Department of Films and Publications for the Ministry of Foreign Affairs, 1973. — 87p

PAKISTAN — Government publications — Bibliography

Pakistan : a comprehensive bibliography of books and government publications with annotations, 1947-80 / compiled by Institute's research scholars under the direction of N.A. Baloch. — Islamabad : Institute of Islamic History, Culture, and Civilization, Islamic University, 1981. — xii,515p. — (Bibliographical series ; 4)

PAKISTAN — History

BURKI, Shahid Javed
Pakistan : a nation in the making / Shahid Javed Burki. — Boulder, Colo. : Westview Press, 1986. — p. cm. — (Westview profiles. Nations of contemporary Asia). — *Includes index. — Bibliography: p*

PAKISTAN — Military policy

Pakistan's bomb : a documentary study / [compiled by] Sreedhar ; introduction by K. Subrahmanyam. — New Delhi : ABC Pub. House, 1986. — xviii, 331 p. — *Includes index. — Bibliography: p. [310]-316*

PAKISTAN — Military relations — Soviet Union

The Red Army on Pakistan's border : policy implications for the United States / Theodore L. Eliot, Jr. ... [et al.]. — Washington : Pergamon-Brassey's, 1986. — p. cm. — (Special report). — *"May 1986.". — "A joint publication of the Institute for Foreign Policy Affairs, Inc. and the Center for Asian Pacific Affairs, the Asia Foundation."*

PAKISTAN — Politics and government

AHMAD, Syed Nur
From martial law to martial law : politics in the Punjab, 1919-1958 / Syed Nur Ahmad ; edited by Craig Baxter ; from a translation from the Urdu by Mahmud Ali. — Boulder ; London : Westview, [1985]. — xiv,455p. — *Bibliography: p435*

GILBERT, Tony
Pakistan : regime of terror / Tony Gilbert. — London : Liberation, 1985. — 48p

KHAN, D. G. A
Disintegration of Pakistan / D.G.A. Khan. — Meerut : Meenakshi Prakashan, c1985. — vi, 252 p.. — *Includes index. — Bibliography: p. [242]-246*

PAKISTAN — Politics and government
continuation

KUKREJA, Veena
Military intervention in politics : a case study of Pakistan / Veena Kukreja ; foreword by Mahendra Prasad Singh. — New Delhi : Mrs. A. H. Marwah for NBO Publisher's Distributors, 1985. — 223p. — *Bibliography: p200-219*

PAKISTAN — Politics and government — 1971-

KAUSHIK, Surendra Nath
Pakistan under Bhutto's leadership / by Serundra Nath Kaushik. — New Dehli : Uppal, 1985. — xii,363p. — *Bibliography: p [335]-356*

KAUSHIK, Surendra Nath
Politics in Pakistan, with special reference to rise and fall of Bhutto / Surendra Nath Kaushik. — Jaipur, India : Aalekh, 1985. — iv, 152 p.. — (South Asian studies series). — *Summary: On the political scene of Pakistan under the leadership of Zulfikar Ali Bhutto. — Includes index. — Bibliography: p. [144]-146*

Pakistan : reforms and development. — [Islamabad : Department of Films and Publications, Ministry of Information and Broadcasting, 1974?]. — 45p

Pakistan and Asian peace / edited by V.D. Chopra ; with an introduction by Rasheeduddin Khan. — New Delhi : Patriot Publishers, 1985. — 288 p.. — *60-5. — Includes bibliographical references*

SAWHNEY, R. G.
Zia's Pakistan : implications for India's security / R. G. Sawhney. — New Delhi : ABC Publishing House, 1985. — xv,200p. — *Bibliography: p[181]-193*

ZIA-UL-HAQ, Mohammad
President of Pakistan, General Mohammad Zia-ul-Haq : interviews to foreign media. — Islamabad : Directorate of Films & Publications, Ministry of Information & Broadcasting, Government of Pakistan, <[1980?-1984? >. — 5v.. — *Includes indexes. — Contents: v. 1. March-December 1978 -- v. 2. January-December 1979 -- v. 3. January-December 1980 -- v. 4. January-December 1981 -- v. 5. January-December 1982*

PAKISTAN — Politics and government — 1971- — Congresses

The State, religion, and ethnic politics : Afghanistan, Iran, and Pakistan / edited by Ali Banuazizi and Myron Weiner. — 1st ed. — [Syracuse, N.Y.] : Syracuse University Press, 1986. — xi, 390 p.. — (Contemporary issues in the Middle East). — *"Sponsored by the Joint Committee on the Near and Middle East and the Committee on South Asia of the American Council of Learned Societies and the Social Science Research Council.". — Includes bibliographies and index*

PAKISTAN — Population

IRFAN, Mohammad
Poverty and household demographic behaviour in Pakistan : insights from PLM survey 1979 / Mohammad Irfan. — Islamabad : Pakistan Institute of Development Economics, 1986. — 57p. — (Studies in population, labour force and migration project report ; no.11). — *Bibliography: p[58-59]*

SATHAR, Zeba Ayesha
Socio-economic and demographic characteristics of the population in Pakistan : findings of the population, labour force and migration survey 1979-80 / Zeba A. Sathar, Syed Mubashir Ali [and] G. Mustafa Zahid. — Islamabad : Pakistan Institute of Development Ecomics, 1986. — 49p. — (Studies in population, labour force and migration project report ; no.8). — *Bibliography: p43-44*

PAKISTAN — Population — Statistics

1981 census report of Federally Administered Tribal Areas (FATA). — Islamabad : Population Census Organisation, 1984. — 116p. — (Census report ; no.62)

1981 census report of Pakistan. — Islamabad : Population Census Organisation, 1984. — iv,200p. — (Census report ; no.69)

Main findings of 1981 population census. — Islamabad : Population Census Organisation, [1983]. — 19p

PAKISTAN — Population, Rural

NABI, Ijaz
The agrarian economy of Pakistan : issues and policies / Ijaz Nabi, Navid Hamid, Shahid Zahid. — Karachi ; Oxford : Oxford University Press, 1986. — 337p. — *Bibliography: p319-324*

PAKISTAN — Social conditions

MADDISON, Angus
Class structure and economic growth : India and Pakistan since the Moghuls. — New York : Norton, [1972, c1971]. — 181 p. — *Bibliography: p. 173-176*

Pakistan : reforms and development. — [Islamabad : Department of Films and Publications, Ministry of Information and Broadcasting, 1974?]. — 45p

PAKISTAN — Social policy

Pakistan, review of the sixth five-year plan. — Washington, D.C., U.S.A. : World Bank, c1984. — xci,167p. — (A World Bank country study). — *Summaries in English, French, and Spanish. — Includes bibliographical references*

PAKISTAN. Agricultural Enquiry Committee

PAKISTAN. Agricultural Enquiry Committee
Report of the Agricultural Enquiry Committee. — [Islamabad] : Ministry of Food and Agriculture, 1975. — [iii],62p

PAKISTAN. National Assembly. Public Accounts Committee

The Federal Public Accounts Committee in Pakistan. — [Islamabad] : National Assembly Secretariat ; [1985]. — x,232p

PAKISTAN INSTITUTE OF DEVELOPMENT ECONOMICS — History

PAKISTAN INSTITUTE OF DEVELOPMENT ECONOMICS
Progress report, 1966/7-1968/9. — Karachi : Pakistan Institute of Development Economics, [1970?]. — 49p

PAKISTAN MOVEMENT

AHMAD, Syed Nur
From martial law to martial law : politics in the Punjab, 1919-1958 / Syed Nur Ahmad ; edited by Craig Baxter ; from a translation from the Urdu by Mahmud Ali. — Boulder ; London : Westview, [1985]. — xiv,455p. — *Bibliography: p435*

PALACIO, ALFREDO L.

GARCÍA COSTA, Victor O.
Alfredo L. Palacios : un socialismo argentino y para la Argentina / Victor O. García Costa. — Buenos Aires : Centro Editor de América Latina. — (Biblioteca Política Argentina ; 148) t.2. — Buenos Aires : Centro Editor de América Latina. — 143-289p. — (Biblioteca Política Argentina ; 148)

PALACIOS, ALFREDO L.

GARCÍA COSTA, Victor O.
Alfredo L. Palacios : un socialismo argentino y para la Argentina / Victor O. García Costa. — Buenos Aires : Centro Editor de América Latina. — (Biblioteca Política Argentina ; 147) t.1. — 1986. — 141p

PALENCIA (SPAIN) — Economic conditions

MARCOS MARTÍN, Alberto
Economía, sociedad, pobreza en Castilla : Palencia, 1500-1814 / Alberto Marcos Martín. — Palencia : Diputación Provincial 1. — 1985. — 358p

MARCOS MARTÍN, Alberto
Economía, sociedad, pobreza en Castilla : Palencia, 1500-1814 / Alberto Marcos Martín. — Palencia : Diputación Provincial. — *Bibliography: p[691]-715* 2. — 1985. — p369-742

PALESTINE — Emigration and immigration

SHAVIT, Yaacov
The new Hebrew nation : a study in Israeli heresy and fantasy / Yaacov Shavit. — London : Cass, 1987. — xv,192p. — *Bibliography: p164-174. — Includes index*

PALESTINE — Foreign opinion

Public opinion and the Palestine question / edited by Elia Zureik and Fouad Moughrabi. — London : Croom Helm, c1987. — 206p. — *Includes index*

PALESTINE — Foreign relations — Great Britain

ZWEIG, Ronald W.
Britain and Palestine during the Second World War / Ronald W. Zweig. — London : Royal Historical Society, 1986, c1985. — ix, 198p. — (Royal Historical Society studies in history series ; no.43). — *Bibliography: p.184-190*

PALESTINE — History — Addresses, essays, lectures

Palestine in the late Ottoman period : political, social and economic transformation / edited by David Kushner. — Jerusalem : Yad Izhak Ben-Zvi ; Leiden : Brill [distributor], 1986. — xi, 434p

PALESTINE — History — 1799-1917

BLUMBERG, Arnold
Zion before Zionism, 1838-1880 / Arnold Blumberg. — 1st ed. — Syracuse, N.Y. : Syracuse University Press, 1985. — xv, 235p. — *Includes index. — Bibliography: p.207-221*

PALESTINE — History — Arab riots, 1929

TAGGAR, Yehuda
The Mufti of Jerusalem and Palestine : Arab politics, 1930-1937 / Yehuda Taggar. — New York : Garland, 1986, c1987. — 472 p.. — (Outstanding theses from the London School of Economics and Political Science). — *Thesis (Ph. D.)--University of London, 1973. — Bibliography: p. 466-472*

PALESTINE — History — 1929-1948

ZWEIG, Ronald W.
Britain and Palestine during the Second World War / Ronald W. Zweig. — London : Royal Historical Society, 1986, c1985. — ix, 198p. — (Royal Historical Society studies in history series ; no.43). — *Bibliography: p.184-190*

PALESTINE — History — Arab rebellion, 1936-1939

BLACK, Ian
Zionism and the Arabs, 1936-1939 / Ian Black. — New York : Garland, 1986. — 435 p.. — (Outstanding theses from the London School of Economics and Political Science). — *Thesis (Ph. D.)--University of London, 1978. — Bibliography: p. 426-435*

TAGGAR, Yehuda
The Mufti of Jerusalem and Palestine : Arab politics, 1930-1937 / Yehuda Taggar. — New York : Garland, 1986, c1987. — 472 p.. — (Outstanding theses from the London School of Economics and Political Science). — *Thesis (Ph. D.)--University of London, 1973. — Bibliography: p. 466-472*

PALESTINE — History — Partition, 1947
HARON, Miriam Joyce
Palestine and the Anglo-American connection, 1945-1950 / Miriam Joyce Haron. — New York : P. Lang, c1986. — 209 p.. — (American university studies. Series IX. History ; vol. 17). — *Includes index.* — *Bibliography: p. [197]-201*

PALESTINE — International status
KIRISCI, Kemal
The PLO and world politics : a study of the mobilization of support for the Palestinian cause / Kemal Kirisci. — London : Pinter, 1986. — xi,198p. — *Bibliography: p188-192.* — *Includes index*

MALLISON, W. Thomas
The Palestine problem in international law and world order / W. Thomas Mallison and Sally V. Mallison. — London : Longman, 1986. — xvi,564p

PALESTINE — Politics and government
International documents on Palestine / Institute for Palestine Studies and the University of Kuwait. — Beirut : Institute for Palestine Studies, 1968-1981. — *Annual*

WHITFIELD, David
A land with people : a report from occupied Palestine / David Whitfield. — London : Morning Star, 1986. — 56p

PALESTINE — Politics and government — 1929-1948
NACHMANI, Amikam
Great power discord in Palestine : the Anglo-American Committee of Inquiry into the problems of European Jewry and Palestine, 1945-1946 / Amikam Nachmani. — London : Cass, 1987. — x,294p,18p of plates. — *Maps on lining papers.* — *Bibliography: p277-295.* — *Includes index*

PALESTINE — Politics and government — 1948-
EL-FARRA, Muhammad
Years of no decision / Muhammad El-Farra. — London : KP1, 1987. — xi,222p

PALESTINE ARABS — Legal status, laws, etc.
MALLISON, W. Thomas
The Palestine problem in international law and world order / W. Thomas Mallison and Sally V. Mallison. — London : Longman, 1986. — xvi,564p

PALESTINE LIBERATION ORGANISATION
KIRISCI, Kemal
The PLO and world politics : a study of the mobilization of support for the Palestinian cause / Kemal Kirisci. — London : Pinter, 1986. — xi,198p. — *Bibliography: p188-192.* — *Includes index*

PALESTINIAN ARABS
ATA, Ibrahim Wade
The West Bank Palestinian family / Ibrahim Wade Ata. — London : KPI, 1986. — xiii,166p. — *Bibliography: p152-160*

TURKI, Fawaz
The Disinherited : journal of a Palestinian exile. — 2nd Modern Reader pbk. ed. — New York ; london : [Modern Reader], 1974, c1972. — *Originally published in 1972.* — *Bibliographical references*

PALESTINIAN ARABS — Biography
TAGGAR, Yehuda
The Mufti of Jerusalem and Palestine : Arab politics, 1930-1937 / Yehuda Taggar. — New York : Garland, 1986, c1987. — 472 p.. — (Outstanding theses from the London School of Economics and Political Science). — *Thesis (Ph. D.)--University of London, 1973.* — *Bibliography: p. 466-472*

PALESTINIAN ARABS — Education (Higher)
ANABTAWI, Samir N.
Palestinian higher education in the West Bank and Gaza : a critical assessment / Samir N. Anabtawi. — London : KPI, 1986. — 94p

PALESTINIAN ARABS — History
GORNI, Yosef
Zionism and the Arabs 1882-1948 : a study of ideology / Yosef Gorny. — Oxford : Clarendon, 1987. — x,342p. — *Translation of: Ha-She' elah ha-'Arvit veha-be 'ayah ha-Yehundit.* — *Bibliography: p326-330.* — *Includes index*

PALESTINIAN ARABS — Legal status, laws, etc. — Israel
DAVIS, Uri
Israel : an apartheid state / Uri Davis. — London : Zed, 1987. — xiii,145p. — *Bibliography: p133-137.* — *Includes index*

PALESTINIAN ARABS — Politics and government
MILLER, Aaron David
The Arab states and the Palestine question : between ideology and self-interest / Aaron David Miller ; foreword by Alfred A. Atherton. — New York : Praeger Published with the Center for Strategic and International Studies, Georgetown University, Washington, D.C., c1986. — p. cm. — (The Washington papers ; 120). — *"Praeger special studies. Praeger scientific."*

PALESTINIAN ARABS — Gaza Strip — Social conditions
COSSALI, Paul
Stateless in Gaza / by Paul Cossali and Clive Robson ; translated from the Arabic by the authors. — London : Zed, 1986. — [192]p

PALESTINIAN ARABS — Israel
JURAYS, Ṣabrī
The Arabs in Israel / Sabri Jiryis ; translated from the Arabic by Inea Bushnaq. — New York : Monthly Review Press, c1976. — xviii, 314 p.. — *Updated translation of ha-'Aravim be-Yisrael.* — *Includes bibliographical references*

PALESTINIAN ARABS — Lebanon — Politics and government
KHALIDI, Rashid
Under siege : P.L.O. decisionmaking during the 1982 war / Rashid Khalidi. — New York : Columbia University Press, 1985. — p. cm. — *Includes index.* — *Bibliography: p*

PALESTINIAN ARABS — West Bank
TAGGART, Simon
Workers in struggle : Palestinian trade unions in the occupied West Bank / Simon Taggart. — London : Editpride, 1985. — 79p

PALMERSTON, HENRY JOHN TEMPLE, Viscount
WEBSTER, Sir Charles
The foreign policy of Palmerston, 1830-1841 : Britain, the Liberal movement and the Eastern question / by Sir Charles Webster. — London : Bell, 1951. — 2v

PAN-AFRICANISM
KRAFONA, Kwesi
The Pan-African movement : Ghana's contribution / Kwesi Krafona. — London : Afroworld, 1986. — 85p

LEGUM, Colin
Pan-Africanism : a short political guide / Colin Legum. — London : Pall Mall Press, 1962. — 296p

NYE, Joseph S.
Pan-Africanism and East African integration / Joseph S. Nye. — Cambridge, Mass. : Harvard University Press, 1965. — xvi,307p

PAN-AMERICANISM
GILDERHUS, Mark T
Pan American visions : Woodrow Wilson and regional integration in the western hemisphere, 1913-1921 / Mark T. Gilderhus. — Tucson : University of Arizona Press, c1986. — p. cm. — *Includes index.* — *Bibliography: p*

PAN-AMERICANISM — History
ALEN LASCANO, Luis C
Yrigoyen, Sandino y el panamericanismo / Luis C. Alen Lascano. — Buenos Aires : Centro Editor de América Latina, 1986. — 138p. — (Biblioteca Política Argentina ; 131). — *Bibliography: p138*

PANAMA — Census, 1980
Censos nacionales de 1980 : octavo censo de poblacion, cuarto censo de vivienda, 11 de mayo de 1980. — [Panama] : Dirección de Estadisticas y Censo
Volumen 4 : Caracteristicas economicas. — [1986]. — vii,333p

Censos nacionales de 1980 : octavo censo de poblacion, cuarto censo de vivienda, 11 de mayo de 1980. — [Panama] : Dirección de Estadística y Censo
Volumen 7: Sectores censales de los distritos de Panama, San Miguelito y Colon. — 1986. — vii,196p

PANAMA. Dirección de Estadística y Censo
Censos nacionales de 1980 : octavo censo de población, cuarto censo de vivienda, 11 de mayo de 1980. — [Panamá] : the Dirección, [1984-]

PANAMA — Economic conditions — 1979-
Panama : structural change and growth prospects. — Washington, D.C., U.S.A. : World Bank, 1985. — xxv,307p. — (A World Bank country study). — *"Report no. 5236-PAN.".* — *"February 28, 1985."*

PANAMA — Economic conditions — 1979- — Statistics
Censos nacionales de 1980 : octavo censo de poblacion, cuarto censo de vivienda, 11 de mayo de 1980. — [Panama] : Dirección de Estadisticas y Censo
Volumen 4 : Caracteristicas economicas. — [1986]. — vii,333p

PANAMA — Economic policy
Panama : structural change and growth prospects. — Washington, D.C., U.S.A. : World Bank, 1985. — xxv,307p. — (A World Bank country study). — *"Report no. 5236-PAN.".* — *"February 28, 1985."*

PANAMA — Population — Statistics
Censos nacionales de 1980 : octavo censo de poblacion, cuarto censo de vivienda, 11 de mayo de 1980. — [Panama] : Dirección de Estadística y Censo
Volumen 7: Sectores censales de los distritos de Panama, San Miguelito y Colon. — 1986. — vii,196p

PANAMA. Dirección de Estadística y Censo
Censos nacionales de 1980 : octavo censo de población, cuarto censo de vivienda, 11 de mayo de 1980. — [Panamá] : the Dirección, [1984-]

PANAMA — Race relations
CONNIFF, Michael L
Black labor on a white canal : Panama, 1904-1981 / Michael L. Conniff. — Pittsburgh : University of Pittsburgh Press, 1985. — p. cm. — *Includes index.* — *Bibliography: p*

PANAMA — Statistics, Vital
PANAMA. Dirección de Estadística y Censo
Censos nacionales de 1980 : octavo censo de población, cuarto censo de vivienda, 11 de mayo de 1980. — [Panamá] : the Dirección, [1984-]

PANARABISM
Pan-Arabism and Arab nationalism : the continuing debate / edited by Tawfic E. Farah ; foreword by James A. Bill. — Boulder : Westview Press, 1987. — xvi, 208 p.. — *Includes bibliographies and index*

PANKHURST, CHRISTABEL
CASTLE, Barbara
Sylvia and Christabel Pankhurst / Barbara Castle. — Harmondsworth : Penguin, 1987. — 159p. — *Bibliography: p157-159*

PANKHURST, E. SYLVIA
CASTLE, Barbara
Sylvia and Christabel Pankhurst / Barbara Castle. — Harmondsworth : Penguin, 1987. — 159p. — *Bibliography: p157-159*

CURTIN, Patricia R
E. Sylvia Pankhurst : portrait of a radical / by Patricia Romero Curtin. — New Haven : Yale University Press, c1986. — p. cm. — *Includes index. — Bibliography: p*

PANSLAVISM
GIZA, Antoni
Neoslawizm i polacy 1906-1910 / Antoni Giza. — Szczecin : Wyższa Szkoła Pedagogiczna, 1984. — 265p. — (Rozprawy i studia / Wyższa Szkola Pedagogiczna w Szczecinie ; t.61). — *Summary in German and Russian. — Bibliography: p237-251*

PAPACY — History
MOLLAT, Guillaume
The popes at Avignon, 1305-1378 / Guillaume Mollat ; translated from the 9th French edition. — London : Nelson, 1963. — xxii,361p . — *Bibliographies*

PAPARA (TAHITI) — Population — Statistics
Tableaux normalisés du recensement général de la population : 15 octobre 1983. — [Papeete] : Institut territorial de la statistique Résultats de la commune de Papara. — [1985?]. — 4p,11 leaves

PAPAU NEW GUINEA — Population — Statistics
1980 national population census : final figures : provincial summary : Enga Province. — Port Moresby : National Statistical Office, 1985. — iii,123p

PAPEETE (TAHITI) — Population — Statistics
Tableaux normalisés du recensement général de la population : 15 octobre 1983. — [Papeete] : Institut territorial de la statistique Résultats de la commune de Papeete. — [1985?]. — 16 leaves

PAPER INDUSTRY — Environmental aspects
Environmental considerations in the pulp and paper industry. — [Washington, D.C.] : World Bank, 1980. — [vi],101p. — *Prepared in co-operation with the World Bank by Beak Consultants Limited, Vancouver, B.C.. — Bibliography: p99-101*

PAPERMAKING — History
Papermaking : art and craft : an account derived from the exhibition presented in the Library of Congress, Washington, D.C. and opened on April 21, 1968. — Washington, D.C. : Library of Congress, 1968. — 96p. — *Bibliography: p[92]-93*

PAPERMAKING — Massachusetts — Berkshire County — History
MCGAW, Judith A.
Most wonderful machine : mechanization and social change in Berkshire paper making, 1801-1885 / Judith A. McGaw. — Princeton, N.J. : Princeton University Press, c1987. — xv, 439 p.. — *Includes index. — Bibliography: p. [413]-425*

PAPUA NEW GUINEA — Census, 1980
1980 national population census : final figures : provincial summary : Central Province. — Port Moresby : National Statistical Office, 1985. — iii,103p

1980 national population census : final figures : provincial summary : Chimbu Province. — Port Moresby : National Statistical Office, 1985. — iii,132p

1980 national population census : final figures : provincial summary : East Sepik Province. — Port Moresby : National Statistical Office, 1985. — iii,117p

1980 national population census : final figures : provincial summary : Western Highlands Province. — Port Moresby : National Statistical Office, 1985. — iii,134p

1980 national population census : final figures : provincial summary : Eastern Highlands Province. — Port Moresby : National Statistical Office, 1985. — 146p

1980 national population census : final figures : provincial summary : Enga Province. — Port Moresby : National Statistical Office, 1985. — iii,123p

1980 national population census : final figures : provincial summary : Morobe Province. — Port Moresby : National Statistical Office, 1985. — iii,172p

1980 national population census : final figures : provincial summary : National Capital District. — Port Moresby : National Statistical Office, 1985. — iii,87p

1980 national population census : final figures : provincial summary : Manus Province. — Port Moresby : National Statistical Office, 1985. — iii,96p

1980 national population census : final figures : provincial summary : New Ireland Province. — Port Moresby : National Statistical Office, 1986. — iii,118p

PAPUA NEW GUINEA — Economic conditions
BACCHUS, M. K.
Educational policy and development strategy in the Third World / M. Kazil Bacchus. — Aldershot : Avebury, c1987. — xi,233p

GOOD, Kenneth
Papua New Guinea : a false economy / Kenneth Good. — London : Anti-Slavery Society, 1986. — 107p. — (Indigenous peoples and development series ; rept. no.3)

PAPUA NEW GUINEA — Economic conditions — 1975-
GOODMAN, Raymond
The economy of Papua New Guinea : an independent review : a report to the Government of Papua New Guinea and the Government of Australia / Raymond Goodman, Charles Lepani, David Morawetz. — Canberra, Australia : Development Studies Centre, Australian National University, 1985. — xiii, 273 p.. — *Includes index. — Bibliography: p. 257-258*

PAPUA NEW GUINEA — Economic policy
GARNAUT, Ross
Exchange rate and macro-economic policy in independent Papua New Guinea / Ross Garnaut and Paul Baxter in consultation with Anne O. Krueger. — Canberra, Australia : Development Studies Centre, Australian National University, 1984. — xiv, 173 p.. — (Pacific research monograph ; no. 10). — *Includes bibliographical references*

GOODMAN, Raymond
The economy of Papua New Guinea : an independent review : a report to the Government of Papua New Guinea and the Government of Australia / Raymond Goodman, Charles Lepani, David Morawetz. — Canberra, Australia : Development Studies Centre, Australian National University, 1985. — xiii, 273 p.. — *Includes index. — Bibliography: p. 257-258*

PAPUA NEW GUINEA — Foreign relations — Indonesia
HARRIS, Stephen V.
Indonesia, Papua New Guinea and Australia : the Irian Jaya Problem of 1984 / Stephen V. Harris and Colin Brown. — Nathan : Centre for the Study of Australian-Asian Relations, Griffith University, 1980. — 83p. — (Australia-Asia papers ; no.29)

PAPUA NEW GUINEA — Industries — Statistics
labour productivity and industrial growth. — [Port Moresby?] : Department of Labour and Industry, 1982. — 12p,[142]leaves. — (Information paper / Department of Labour and Industry ; no.1-82)

PAPUA NEW GUINEA — Population — Statistics
1980 national population census : final figures : provincial summary : Central Province. — Port Moresby : National Statistical Office, 1985. — iii,103p

1980 national population census : final figures : provincial summary : Chimbu Province. — Port Moresby : National Statistical Office, 1985. — iii,132p

1980 national population census : final figures : provincial summary : East Sepik Province. — Port Moresby : National Statistical Office, 1985. — iii,117p

1980 national population census : final figures : provincial summary : Western Highlands Province. — Port Moresby : National Statistical Office, 1985. — iii,134p

1980 national population census : final figures : provincial summary : Eastern Highlands Province. — Port Moresby : National Statistical Office, 1985. — 146p

1980 national population census : final figures : provincial summary : Morobe Province. — Port Moresby : National Statistical Office, 1985. — iii,172p

1980 national population census : final figures : provincial summary : National Capital District. — Port Moresby : National Statistical Office, 1985. — iii,87p

1980 national population census : final figures : provincial summary : Manus Province. — Port Moresby : National Statistical Office, 1985. — iii,96p

1980 national population census : final figures : provincial summary : New Ireland Province. — Port Moresby : National Statistical Office, 1986. — iii,118p

PAPUA NEW GUINEA — Social conditions
READ, Kenneth E
Return to the high valley : coming full circle / Kenneth E. Read. — Berkeley : University of California Press, c1986. — xxi, 269 p., [8] p. of plates. — (Studies in Melanesian anthropology) . — *Includes bibliographical references and index*

PAPUA NEW GUINEA — Social life and customs
GELBER, Marilyn G
Gender and society in the New Guinea Highlands : an anthropological perspective on antagonism toward women / Marilyn G. Gelber. — Boulder : Westview Press, 1986. — xi, 180 p.. — (Women in cross-cultural perspective). — *Includes index. — Bibliography: p. [159]-175*

PAPUA NEW GUINEA — Social life and customs — Addresses, essays, lectures
Rituals of manhood : male initiation in Papua New Guinea / edited by Gilbert H. Herdt ; with an introduction by Roger M. Keesing. — Berkeley : University of California Press, c1982. — xxvi, 365 p.. — *Includes bibliographies and index*

PARADIGMS (SOCIAL SCIENCES) — Congresses
Organizational theory and inquiry : the paradigm revolution / edited by Yvonna S. Lincoln. — Beverly Hills : Sage Publications, c1985. — 231 p.. — (Sage focus editions ; v. 75). — *Based on papers presented at a conference held at the University of Kansas in November 1983. — Includes bibliographies*

PARAGUAY — Economic conditions — Statistics
HERKEN-KRAUER, Juan Carlos
Economic indicators for the Paraguayan economy, 1869-1932 : isolation and the world economy / by Juan Carlos Herken-Krauer. — 280 leaves. — *PhD (Econ) 1986 LSE*

PARAGUAY — History — To 1811
BENÍTEZ, Luis G.
Historia del Paraguay : época colonial / Luis G. Benítez. — Asunción : Comuneros S. A., [1985]. — 263p. — *Bibliography: p261-262*

PARAGUAY — History — 1870-1938
MACHUCA, Vicente
La Guerra del Chaco : desde la terminación del armisticio hasta el fin de la contienda / Vicente Machuca. — Asunción : NAPA, [1983]. — 562 p., [28] p. of plates. — (Colección Prisma). — *Includes bibliographical references*

WARREN, Harris Gaylord
Rebirth of the Paraguayan Republic : the first Colorado era, 1878-1904 / Harris Gaylord Warren with the assistance of Katherine F. Warren. — Pittsburgh, Pa. : University of Pittsburgh Press, 1985. — xvi, 379p. — (Pitt Latin American series). — *Includes index. — Bibliography: p 349-362*

PARAGUAY — Politics and government — 1938-1954
PRIETO YEGROS, Leandro
La infiltración comunista en los partidos politicos paraguayos : caso del "Bloque Liberación" del Partido Revolucionario Febrerista : (version documental / Leandro Prieto Yegros. — [Asunción] : Cuadernos Republicanos, [1985]. — 521p

PARAGUAY — Population — Statistics
The Paraguay Fertility Survey, 1979 : a summary of findings. — Voorburg : International Statistical Institute, 1983. — 16p. — (World Fertility Survey ; no.38)

PARAGUAY — Population — Statistics — Evaluation
SCHOEMAKER, Juan F.
Evaluación de la Encuesta Nacional de Fecundidad del Paraguay de 1979 / Juan F. Schoemaker. — Voorburg : International Statistical Institute, 1984. — 56p. — (Scientific reports / World Fertility Survey ; no.62)

PARAÍBA (BRAZIL : STATE) — Politics and government
LEWIN, Linda
Politic and Parentela in Paraíba : a case study of family-based oligarchy in Brazil / Linda Lewin. — Princeton, N.J. : Princeton University Press, c1987. — p. cm. — *Includes index. — Bibliography: p*

PARAPROFESSIONALS IN SOCIAL SERVICE
SCHINDLER, Ruben
Social care at the front line : a worldwide study of paraprofessionals / Ruben Schindler and Edward Allan Brawley. — New York ; London : Tavistock, 1987. — [240]p. — *Includes bibliography and index*

PARAPROFESSIONALS IN SOCIAL SERVICE — England
DIXON, Nora
A study of the role and function of social work assistants in four local authority social service departments / Nora Dixon, Rosemary Pugh-Thomas. — [London] : London Region North, Social Work Service, [1976]. — 76,[54]p . — *Bibliography: p76*

PARATRANSIT SERVICES — Europe — Congresses
ROUND TABLE ON TRANSPORT ECONOMICS (40th : 1978 : Paris)
Paratransit : report of the fortieth Round Table on Transport Economics : held in Paris on 26th-27th January, 1978. — Paris : European Conference of Ministers of Transport, 1979. — 165p. — *Includes bibliographical references*

PARENT AND CHILD
KNAPP, Ronald J
Beyond endurance : when a child dies / Ronald J. Knapp. — New York : Schocken Books, 1986. — xv, 271 p.. — *Includes index. — Bibliography: p. 263-265*

LABAND, David N
The roots of success : why children follow in their parents´ career footsteps / by David N. Laband, Bernard F. Lentz. — New York : Praeger, 1985. — p. cm. — *Includes index. — Bibliography: p*

NATIONAL COUNCIL FOR ONE PARENT FAMILIES
Time-off for child care : evidence to the House of Lords on the European Commission´s proposed directive on parental leave and leave for family reasons. — London : National Council for One Parent Families, 1984. — 24p

Parental behaviour / edited by Wladyslaw Sluckin and Martin Herbert. — Oxford : Basil Blackwell, 1986. — [288]p. — *Includes index*

PARENT AND CHILD — Longitudinal studies
GREEN, Richard
The "sissy boy syndrome" and the development of homosexuality / Richard Green. — New Haven : Yale University Press, c1987. — x, 416 p.. — *Includes index. — Bibliography: p. 399-409*

PARENT AND CHILD — Denmark
Parent-child relationship, post-divorce : a seminar report. — [Copenhagen : Socialforskningsinstituttet, 1984]. — 301p

PARENT AND CHILD — England
Lost in care : the problems of maintaining links between children in care and their families / Spencer Millham ... [et al.]. — Aldershot : Gower, c1986. — ix,258p. — *Includes index*

PARENT AND CHILD (LAW)
The father´s role : applied perspectives / edited by Michael E. Lamb. — New York : J. Wiley, c1986. — xiv, 461 p.. — (Wiley series on personality processes). — *"A Wiley-Interscience publication.". — Includes bibliographies and indexes*

PARENT AND CHILD (LAW) — Great Britain
HOGGETT, Brenda M.
Parents and children : the law of parental responsibility / Brenda M. Hoggett. — 3rd ed. — London : Sweet and Maxwell, 1987. — xxvi,213p. — *Previous ed.: 1981. — Bibliography: p193-204*

PARENTAL ACCEPTANCE — Cross-cultural studies
ROHNER, Ronald P
The warmth dimension : foundations of parental acceptance-rejection theory / Ronald P. Rohner. — Beverly Hills [Calif.] : Sage Publications, c1986. — 248 p.. — (New perspectives on family). — *Includes index. — Bibliography: p. 214-236*

PARENTAL BEHAVIOR IN ANIMALS
Parental behaviour / edited by Wladyslaw Sluckin and Martin Herbert. — Oxford : Basil Blackwell, 1986. — [288]p. — *Includes index*

PARENTAL REJECTION — Cross-cultural studies
ROHNER, Ronald P
The warmth dimension : foundations of parental acceptance-rejection theory / Ronald P. Rohner. — Beverly Hills [Calif.] : Sage Publications, c1986. — 248 p.. — (New perspectives on family). — *Includes index. — Bibliography: p. 214-236*

PARENTHOOD
LAROSSA, Ralph
Becoming a parent / by Ralph LaRossa. — Beverly Hills : Sage Publications, c1986. — p. cm. — (Family studies text series ; v. 3). — *Includes index. — Bibliography: p*

NEW, Caroline
For the children´s sake / Caroline New and Miriam David. — Harmondsworth : Penguin, 1985. — 379p. — (Pelican books). — *Bibliography: p355-366. — Includes index*

PARENTING
Parental behaviour / edited by Wladyslaw Sluckin and Martin Herbert. — Oxford : Basil Blackwell, 1986. — [288]p. — *Includes index*

PARENTING — United States
LAROSSA, Ralph
Becoming a parent / by Ralph LaRossa. — Beverly Hills : Sage Publications, c1986. — p. cm. — (Family studies text series ; v. 3). — *Includes index. — Bibliography: p*

PARENTS — Interviews
GREEN, Richard
The "sissy boy syndrome" and the development of homosexuality / Richard Green. — New Haven : Yale University Press, c1987. — x, 416 p.. — *Includes index. — Bibliography: p. 399-409*

PARENTS-IN-LAW
APTER, T. E.
Loose relations : your in-laws and you / Terri Apter. — London : Macmillan, 1986. — [250]p . — *Bibliography: p243-245. — Includes index*

PARETO, VILFREDO
POWERS, Charles H
Vilfredo Pareto / Charles H. Powers. — Newbury Park, Calif. : Sage Publications, c1987. — 167 p.. — (Masters of social theory ; v. 5). — *Includes indexes. — Bibliography: p. 159-160*

PARIS — History — Commune, 1871
SERMAN, William
La Commune de Paris (1871) / William Serman. — [Paris] : Fayard, 1986. — 621p. — *Bibliography: p[581]-600*

PARIS. Parlement — History — 18th century
BLUCHE, François
Les magistrats du Parlement de Paris au XVIIIe siècle / préface d´Emmanuel Le Roy Ladurie. — [nouv. ed.] — Paris : Economica, 1986. — xiii,481p. — *1er ed : 1961. — Bibliography: p399-426*

PARIS (FRANCE) — Ethnic relations
GREEN, Nancy L
The Pletzl of Paris : Jewish immigrant workers in the "belle epoque" / Nancy L. Green. — New York : Holmes & Meier, 1986. — ix, 270 p.. — *Includes index. — Bibliography: p. 249-263*

PARIS (FRANCE) — History — Revolution, 1789-1799
SLAVIN, Morris
The making of an insurrection : Parisian sections and the Gironde / Morris Slavin. — Cambridge, Mass. : Harvard University Press, 1986. — ix, 236 p.. — *Includes index. — Bibliography: p. [222]-228*

PARIS (FRANCE) — Politics and government
Paris: May 1986. — [London] : Rebel Press : Dark Star, 1986. — 55p

PARIS (FRANCE) — Popular culture — History — 19th century
SEIGEL, Jerrold E.
Bohemian Paris : culture, politics, and the boundaries of bourgeois life, 1830-1930 / Jerrold Seigel. — New York, N.Y., U.S.A. : Viking, 1986. — ix, 453 p.. — "Elisabeth Sifton books.". — Includes index. — Bibliography: p. 405-440

PARIS (FRANCE) — Population — Statistics
Recensement général de la population de 1982. — [Paris : Institut national de la statistique et des études économiques, 1985]
Résultats du sondage au 1/4 : population, emploi, ménages, familles, logements
Ville de Paris. — 540p

PARIS (FRANCE) — Social classes
PINÇON-CHARLOT, Monique
Ségrégation urbaine : classes sociales et équipements collectifs en région parisienne / Monique Pinçon-Charlot, Edmond Pretecielle, Paul Rendu. — Paris : Éditions Anthropos, 1986. — 291p. — Bibliography: p[230]-238

PARIS (FRANCE) — Social life and customs — 18th century
GARRIOCH, David
Neighbourhood and community in Paris, 1740-1790 / David Garrioch. — Cambridge : Cambridge University Press, 1986. — [xi,404]p. — (Cambridge studies in early modern history) . — Includes bibliography and index

ROCHE, Daniel
The people of Paris : an essay in popular culture in the 18th century / Daniel Roche ; translated by Marie Evans in association with Gwynne Lewis. — Leamington Spa : Berg, 1987. — 277p. — Translation of: Le peuple de Paris

PARIS PEACE CONFERENCE (1919-1920)
KARSKI, Jan
The Great Powers & Poland, 1919-1945 : from Versailles to Yalta / Jan Karski. — Lanham, MD : University Press of America, c1985. — xvi, 697 p.. — Includes index. — Bibliography: p. 627-671

WALWORTH, Arthur
Wilson and his peacemakers : American diplomacy at the Paris Peace Conference, 1919 / Arthur Walworth. — New York ; London : W.W. Norton, 1986. — xiii, 618p. — Includes index. — Bibliography: p.572-585

PARKS — United States — History — 19th century
SCHUYLER, David
The new urban landscape : the redefinition of city form in nineteenth-century America / David Schuyler. — Baltimore ; London : Johns Hopkins University Press, c1986. — xiv, 237p. — (New studies in American intellectual and cultural history). — Includes index. — Bibliography: p.227-232

PARLIAMENTARY PRACTICE — England
KNOWLES, Raymond S. B.
The law and practice of local authority meetings / Raymond S.B. Knowles. — [Rev. and substantially expanded ed.]. — Cambridge : ICSA Publishing, 1987. — [312]p. — Previous ed.: published as The law and practice relating to local authority meetings. Chichester : Rose, 1978. — Includes index

PARLIAMENTARY PRACTICE — European Economic Community countries — Comparative studies
KREMAIER, Franz
Das Europäische Parlament der EG und die Parlamentarische Versammlung des Europarates : eine vergleichende Strukturanalyse zur Begrifflichkeit... / Franz Kremaier. — München : Florentz, 1985. — (Europarecht - Völkerrecht ; Bd.9). — Bibliographical notes

PARLIAMENTARY PRACTICE — New Brunswick
NEW BRUNSWICK. Legislative Assembly
Speakers' rulings : 1784-1984 = Décisions des orateurs : 1784-1984. — Fredericton : Office of the Clerk, Legislative Assembly, 1985. — 321,358p

PARSONS, TALCOTT — Criticism and interpretation
HOLTON, R. J.
Talcott Parsons on economy and society / Robert J. Holton abd Bryan S. Turner. — London ; New York : Routledge & Kegan Paul, 1986. — vii, 276p

PART-TIME EMPLOYMENT — Great Britain
BLANCHFLOWER, David
Part-time employment in Great Britain : an analysis using establishment data / David Blanchflower, Bernard Corry. — [London] : Department of Employment, [1987]. — 77p. — (Research paper / Department of Employment ; no.57). — Bibliographical references: p73-77

HUMPHRIES, Judith
Part-time work / Judith Humphries. — 2nd ed. — London : Kogan Page, 1986. — 191p. — Previous ed.: 1983. — Bibliography: p184-185. — Includes index

PART-TIME EMPLOYMENT — United States
KAHNE, Hilda
Reconceiving part-time work : new perspectives for older workers and women / Hilda Kahne. — Totowa, N.J. : Rowman & Allanheld, 1985. — xv, 180 p.. — Includes index. — Bibliography: p. [160]-174

PART-TIME FARMING — Ireland
HIGGINS, J
A study of part-time farmers in the Republic of Ireland / J. Higgins. — Dublin : An Foras Taluntais, Economics and Rural Welfare Research Centre, [1983]. — 118 p.. — (Socio-economic research series ; no. 3). — Includes bibliographical references

PARTI COMMUNISTE FRANÇAIS
FALIGOT, Roger
Service B / Roger Faligot, Rémi Kauffer. — Paris : Fazard, [1985]. — 342p

NAUDY, Michel
P. C. F. : le suicide / Michel Naudy. — [Paris] : Albin Michel, 1986. — 209p

PARTI COMMUNISTE FRANÇAIS
Après le référendum et les élections legislatives...écarter tout ce qui divise ne retenir que ce qui unit. — Paris : Parti Communiste Français, 1962. — 47p

Le Parti Communiste Français des années sombres, 1938-1941 : actes du colloque organisé en Octobre 1983 par Centre de Recherches d'Histoire des Mauvements Sociaux et du Syndicalisme de l'Université de Paris-I...[et al.] / sous la direction de Jean-Pierre Azéma, Antoine Prost, Jean-Pierre Rioux. — Paris : Seuil, 1986. — 317p

Problèmes du mouvement communiste international / édité par le Comité Central de Parti Communiste Français. — [Paris] : Parti Communiste Français, 1963. — 95p

PARTI COMMUNISTE FRANÇAIS — History
SERRANO, Carlos
L'enjeu espagnol : PCF et guerre d'Espagne / Carlos Serrano. — Paris : Messidor/Éditions sociales, 1987. — 292p

PARTI LIBÉRAL SUISSE
Écologie et liberté : résumé des rapports présentés au Congrès du Parti Liberal Suisse à Crissier/VD le 4 février 1978. — [S.l.] : Parti liberal suisse, 1978. — 24p

PARTI LIBÉRAL SUISSE
Droits populaires et gouvernement : résumé des rapports presentés au Congrès du Parti libéral suisse à Cressier/NE le 26 mars 1977. — Berne : Parti Libéral Suisse, 1977. — 28p

PARTI LIBÉRAL SUISSE
Pour une politique libérale de la santé : rapport d'une commission d'étude du Parti libéral suisse. — Berne : Parti Libéral Suisse, 1977. — 15p

PARTI LIBÉRAL SUISSE
Pour une politique libérale de l'énergie : rapport d'une commission d'étude du Parti libéral suisse, 6 octobre 1978. — Berne : Parti Libéral Suisse, 1978. — 31p

PARTI LIBÉRAL SUISSE. Congrès (1977 : Troinex-Genève)
Enseignement : progrès ou impasse?: résumé des rapports présentés au Congrès du Parti Libéral Suisse. — [S.l.] : Parti Libéral Suisse, 1977. — 23p

PARTI QUÉBÉCOIS
Le Parti Québécois en bref. — Montreal : Éditions du Parti Québécois, 1973. — 32p. — (Le Citoyen ; 1)

Le militant du Parti Québécois. — Montreal : Les Éditions du Parti Québécois, 1972. — 48p

Qui finance le Parti Québécois?. — Montreal : Les Éditions du Parti Québécois, 1970. — 47p. — (Le Citoyen ; 4)

VAILLANCOURT, Yves
Le P.Q. et le social : éléments de bilan des politiques sociales du gouvernement du Parti québécois, 1976-1982 / Yves Vaillancourt ; avec la collaboration de Annie Autonès. — [Montréal] : Editions coopératives Albert Saint-Martin, c1983. — 165p. — (Collection "Actualité")

PARTI RADICAL-DÉMOCRATIQUE SUISSE
PARTI RADICAL-DÉMOCRATIQUE SUISSE
Objectifs 1975 : securité et liberté. — Lausanne : Parti Radical-Démocratique Suisse, 1975. — 68p

PARTI REPUBLICAIN
Liberté et progrès : manifeste du Parti Républicain. — [Paris] : Parti Républicain, 1982. — [16p]

PARTI ROYALISTE (France)
DESAUBLIAUX, Marc
La fin du Parti royaliste (1889-1890) / avec une preface du duc de Castries. — Paris : Editions Royaliste, [1986]. — 248p

PARTI SOCIALISTE BELGE
ABS, Robert
Histoire du Parti Socialiste Belge (1885-1960) : synthese historique / Robert Abs. — [s.l.] : Institut Emile Vandervelde : Fordation Louis de Brouckere, 1974. — 62p. — Bibliography: p47-62

Socialisme d'aujourd'hui : texte adopté par le congrès doctrinal du P.S.B. des 16 et 17 novembre 1974. — Bruxelles : Edition Rose au Poing, 1975. — 27p

PARTIDO AFRICANO DA INDEPENDENCIA DE LA GUINEE "PORTUGAISE" ET DES ILES DU CAP VERT
CABRAL, Amilcar
PAIGC : rapport general sur la lutte de liberation nationale / Amilcar Cabral. — Bissau : P.A.I.G.C., 1961. — 38p

CABRAL, Vasco
1956-1980 : PAIGC : 24 anos de luta / Vasco Cabral. — Bissau : PAIGC, 1980. — 29p

PARTIDO COMUNISTA DE ESPAÑA
PARTIDO COMUNISTA DE ESPAÑA
Asamblea para la Unidad de los Comunistas, 19-20 de Octubre de 1985 : texto íntegro. — Madrid : Ahora, 1985. — 177p

PARTIDO COMUNISTA DE ESPAÑA
continuation

PARTIDO COMUNISTA DE ESPAÑA. Comisión Económica
Una alternativa a la crisis : las propuestas del PCE / introducción de Nicolás Sartorius. — Barcelona : Partido Comunista de España : Planeta, 1985. — 224p. — (Colección textas ; 86)

SERRA Y MORET, Manuel
Introducción al "Manifiesto del Partido Comunista" y otros escritos / Manuel Serra y Moret ; estudio preliminar y notas aríticas a crgo de Antoni Jutglar. — [Barcelona] : Anthropos, Editorial del Hombre, 1984. — 279p. — (Historia, ideas y textos ; 9)

VILAR, Sergio
Porque se ha destruido el PCE / Sergio Vilar. — Barcelona : Plaza & Janes Editores, 1986. — 281p

PARTIDO COMUNISTA DE ESPAÑA — History

MORÁN, Gregorio
Miseria y grandeza del Partido Comunista de España, 1939-1985 / Gregorio Morán. — Barcelona : Planeta, 1986. — 648p. — (Espejo de España ; 122)

PARTIDO COMUNISTA PORTUGUÊS

Comment les communistes ont essayé de sêmparer du pouvoir au Portugal : supplément de Est et Ouest / edité par le Centre dÁrchives et de Documentation Politiques et Sociales. — Paris : Centre dÁrchives et de Documentation Politiques et Sociales, 1975. — 32p

PARTIDO OBRERO DE UNIFICACIÓN MARXISTA

ANDRADE, Juan
Notas sobre la guerra civil : (actuación del POUM) / Juan Andrade. — Madrid : Ediciones Libertarias, 1986. — 158p

PARTIDO REVOLUCIONARIO FEBRERISTA

PRIETO YEGROS, Leandro
La infiltración comunista en los partidos politicos paraguayos : caso del "Bloque Liberación" del Partido Revolucionario Febrerista : (version documental / Leandro Prieto Yegros. — [Asunción] : Cuadernos Republicanos, [1985]. — 521p

PARTIDO REVOLUCIONARIO INSTITUCIONAL

Mexico's political stability : the next five years / edited by Roderic A. Camp. — Boulder : Westview Press, 1986. — ix, 279 p.. — (Westview special studies on Latin America and the Caribbean). — *Includes bibliographies and index. — Contents: Overview / Roderic A. Camp -- The political consequences of changing socialization patterns / Daniel C. Levy -- How will economic recovery be managed? / William P. Glade -- Distributional and sectoral problems in the New Economic Policy / William P. Glade -- Leadership and change, Intellectuals and technocrats in Mexico / Peter H. Smith -- The impact of major groups on policy-making trends in government-business relations in Mexico / John Bailey -- The evolution of the Mexican military and its implications for civil-military relations / Edward J. Williams -- What explains the decline of the PRI and will it continue? / John Bailey -- Potential strengths of the political opposition and what it means to the PRI / Roderic A. Camp -- The implications of the border for Mexican-United States relations / Edward J. Williams -- The implications of Central American conflicts for Mexican politics / Daniel C. Levy*

PARTIDO SOCIALISTA DE CHILE — History

POLLACK, Benny
Revolutionary social democracy : the Chilean Socialist Party / Benny Pollack, Hernan Rosenkranz. — London : Pinter, 1986. — xiv,234p. — *Bibliography: p216-229 — Includes index*

PARTIDO SOCIALISTA OBERO ESPAÑOL — Congresses

PARTIDO SOCIALISTA OBRERO ESPAÑOL. Congreso (30 : 1984 : Madrid)
España, compromiso de solidaridad : resoluciones socialistas para los años 80. — [Madrid] : PSOE, 1985. — 181p

PARTIDO SOCIALISTA OBRERO ESPAÑOL

CARRASCAL, José María
La revolución del PSOE / José María Carrascal. — [Barcelona] : Plaza & Janes, [1985]. — 306p. — (Política española)

PARTIDO SOCIALISTA OBRERO ESPAÑOLA

DÍAZ, Elías
Socialismo en España : el Partido y el Estado / Elías Díaz. — 1a ed. — Madrid : Mezquita, 1982. — 253 p.. — (Serie política ; 4). — *Includes bibliographical references and index*

PARTIDUL COMUNIST ROMÂN — Congresses

PARTIDUL COMUNIST ROMÂN, Congresul (1984)
Congresul al XIII-lea al Partidul Comunist Român, 19-22 noiembrie 1984. — București : Editura Politica, 1985. — 766p

PARTIDUL COMUNIST ROMÂN — History — Sources

PARTIDUL COMUNIST ROMÂN
Epoca Nicolae Ceaușescu : Partidul Comunist Român centrul vital al întregii națiuni : documente ale plenarelor Comitetului Central și ale Comitetului Politic Executiv al Comitetului Central al Partidului Comunist Român, 1965-1985. — București : Editura Politică, 1986. — 4vols. — *Vol.1: 1965-1973; Vol.2: 1974-1977; Vol.3: 1978-1981; Vol.4: 1982-1985*

PARTIIA SOTSIALISTOV-REVOLIUTSIONEROV

GRIGOR'EV, V. K.
Razgrom melkoburzhuaznoi kontrrevoliutsii v Kazakhstane (1920-1922 gg.) / V. K. Grigor'ev. — Alma-Ata : Kazakhstan, 1984. — 174p

PARTIJ VAN DE ARBEID

PARTIJ VAN DE ARBEID
Verkiezingsprogramma van de Partij van de Arbeid voor de Tweede Kamerverkiezingen op 25 mei 1977. — [Amsterdam] : PvdA, 1977. — 94p. — *Cover-title : Voorwaarts...*

PARTISAN REVIEW (NEW YORK, N.Y. : 1934) — History

COONEY, Terry A
The rise of the New York Intellectuals : Partisan review and its circle / Terry A. Cooney. — Madison, Wis. : University of Wisconsin Press, 1986. — xi, 350p. — (History of American thought and culture). — *Includes index. — Bibliography: p.331-333*

PARTIT SOCIALISTA UNIFICAT DE CATALUNYA

Nuestra utopía : PSVC: cincuenta años de historia de Cataluña / colaboran: Andreu Mayayo...[et al.]. — Barcelona : Planeta, 1986. — 279p. — *At head of title: Nous Horitzons*

PARTNERSHIP — Taxation — Great Britain

GREAT BRITAIN. Board of Inland Revenue
Capital gains tax : partnerships. — London : the Board, 1975. — 8leaves

PARTNERSHIP — Canada — Cases

Cases and materials on partnerships and Canadian business corporations / by Stanley M. Beck ... [et al.]. — Toronto, Canada : Carswell, 1983. — xxix, 938 p.. — *"Table of cases": p. xxiii-xxix*

PARTY AFFILIATION — India

BRASS, Paul R.
Caste, faction and party in Indian politics / Paul R. Brass. — Delhi : Chanakya Publications
Vol.2: Election studies. — 1985. — 325p

PARTY AFFILIATION — West (U.S.)

Politics of realignment : party change in the mountain west / edited by Randy T. Simmons, Peter F. Galderisi, John G. Francis. — Boulder : Westview Press, 1986. — p. cm

PARTY OF LABOUR OF ALBANIA

LLESHI, Ismail
The PLA : on some aspects of contradictions in socialism / Ismail Lleshi. — Tirana : 8 Nentori Publishing House, 1985. — 74p

PASCAL (COMPUTER PROGRAM LANGUAGE)

KEMP, R.
Pascal for students / R. Kemp. — 2nd ed. — London : Edward Arnold, 1987. — ix,258p. — *Previous ed.: 1982. — Bibliography: p246-247. — Includes index*

KOFFMAN, Elliot B
Problem solving and structured programming in PASCAL / Elliot B. Koffman. — 2nd ed. — Reading, Mass. : Addison-Wesley Pub. Co., 1985. — p. cm. — *Includes index*

KOFFMAN, Elliot B
Turbo Pascal : a problem solving approach / Elliot B. Koffman. — Reading, Mass. : Addison-Wesley, c1986. — xvii, 532, [78] p.. — (Addison-Wesley series in computer science). — *Includes index*

MALLOZZI, John S.
Computability with Pascal / John S. Mallozzi, Nicholas J. De Lillo. — Englewood Cliffs : Prentice-Hall, 1984. — xii, 193p. — *Includes index. — Bibliography: p186-187*

REINGOLD, Edward M.
Data structures in Pascal / Edward M. Reingold, Wilfred J. Hansen. — Boston : Little, Brown, c1986. — xvi, 505 p.. — (Little, Brown computer systems series). — *Includes bibliographies and index*

PASSIVE RESISTANCE — Great Britain

Preparing for nonviolent direct action / Howard Clark...et al.. — [Nottingham] : Peace News ; [London] : CND, 1984. — 80p

PASSIVE RESISTANCE — United States

¡ Basta! : no mandate for war : a pledge of resistance handbook / by the Emergency Response Network ; edited by Ken Butigan, Terry Messman-Rucker, and Marie Pastrick. — Philadelphia : New Society, 1986. — 83,ivp. — *Bibliography: pi-iv*

PASSIVE RESISTANCE — India

OSTERGAARD, Geoffrey
Nonviolent revolution in India / Geoffrey Ostergaard. — Sevagram : J.P. Amrit Kosh ; New Delhi : Gandhi Peace Foundation, c1985. — xxiii, 419 p.. — *"Silver jubliee publication of the Gandhi Peace Foundation."--T.p. verso. — Includes index. — Bibliography: p. [370]-406*

PASTURE, RIGHT OF — Australia — New South Wales

COLLINS, C. M
The law of fences and pastures protection, New South Wales / Collins. — 2nd ed. / by H.K. Insall. — Sydney : Law Book Co., 1984. — xxi, 208 p.

PATAGONIA (ARGENTINA AND CHILE) — Description and travel

SOLARI YRIGOYEN, Hipólito
Testimonios australes / Hipólito Solari Yrigoyen. — Buenos Aires : Editorial Galerna, 1986. — 222p

PATAGONIA (ARGENTINA AND CHILE) — History, military — 20th century

MORENO, Carlos Alberto
Patagonia punto crítico : la Patagonia Central en los proyectos geopolíticos y en dos guerras mundiales / Carlos Alberto Moreno. — Chubut : Fondo Editorial de Canal 9 de Comodoro Rivadavia, 1985. — 177p. — *Bibliography: p175-176*

PATAGONIA (ARGENTINA AND CHILE) — Rural conditions

BAYER, Osvaldo
La Patagonia rebelde / Osvaldo Bayer. — [Buenos Aires] : Hyspamérica, c1986. — 429p. — (Biblioteca argentina de historia y política ; 1). — *Publicado originalmente en México por Nueva Imagen en 1980*

PATAGONIA (ARGENTINA AND CHILE) — Social life and customs

SOLARI YRIGOYEN, Hipólito
Testimonios australes / Hipólito Solari Yrigoyen. — Buenos Aires : Editorial Galerna, 1986. — 222p

PATAGONIA (ARGENTINA AND CHILE) — Strategic aspects

MORENO, Carlos Alberto
Patagonia punto crítico : la Patagonia Central en los proyectos geopolíticos y en dos guerras mundiales / Carlos Alberto Moreno. — Chubut : Fondo Editorial de Canal 9 de Comodoro Rivadavia, 1985. — 177p. — *Bibliography: p175-176*

PATEL, I. G

Essays on economic progress and welfare : in honour of I.G. Patel / edited by S. Guhan and Manu Shroff. — Delhi ; New York : Oxford University Press, 1986. — xvi, 330 p., [1] leaf of plates. — *Includes bibliographies and index*

PATENT LAWS AND LEGISLATION — European Economic Community Countries

Derecho de patentes : España y la Comunidad Económica Europea / Alberto Bercovitz...[et al.]. — Barcelona : Ariel, 1985. — 109p

PATENT LAWS AND LEGISLATION — Spain

Derecho de patentes : España y la Comunidad Económica Europea / Alberto Bercovitz...[et al.]. — Barcelona : Ariel, 1985. — 109p

PATENT LICENSES — European Economic Community countries

CAWTHRA, B. I.
Patent licensing in Europe / by B.I. Cawthra. — 2nd ed. — London : Butterworths, 1986. — xxi,249p. — *Previous ed.: 1978.* — *Bibliography: p236-240. — Includes index*

PATENT MEDICINES — Denmark

Engrosdistributionen af fabriksfremstillede laegemidler. — København : Monopoltilsynet, 1983. — 125p

PATENTS — European Economic Community countries

PATENTS (INTERNATIONAL LAW)

LADAS, Stephen Pericles
Patents, trademarks, and related rights : national and international protection / Stephen P. Ladas. — Cambridge (Mass.) : Harvard U.P., 1975. — 3v

PATERNAL DEPRIVATION

BILLER, Henry B
Child maltreatment and paternal deprivation / Henry Biller, Richard Solomon. — Lexington, Mass. : Lexington Books, c1986. — p. cm. — *Includes indexes. — Bibliography: p*

PATERNALISM — Moral and ethical aspects

VANDEVEER, Donald
Paternalistic intervention : the moral bounds of benevolence / Donald VanDeVeer. — Princeton, N.J. : Princeton University Press, c1986. — xii, 452 p.. — (Studies in moral, political, and legal philosophy). — *Includes bibliographical references and index*

PATERNALISM — Asia

PYE, Lucian W.
Asian power and politics : the cultural dimensions of authority / Lucian W. Pye with Mary W. Pye. — Cambridge, Mass. : Belknap Press, 1985. — p. cm. — *Includes index. — Bibliography: p*

PATRIARCHY

TRASK, Haunani-Kay
Eros and power : the promise of feminist theory / Haunani-Kay Trask. — Philadelphia : University of Pennsylvania Press, c1986. — xiv, 186 p.. — *Includes bibliographies and index*

PATRIARCHY — Europe, Northern — History

HOWELL, Martha C
Women, production, and patriarchy in late medieval cities / Martha C. Howell. — Chicago : University of Chicago Press, 1986. — xv, 285 p.. — (Women in culture and society). — *Includes index. — Bibliography: p. 261-277*

PATRIOTISM — France

BERGERON, Francis
Les droites dans la rue : nationaux et nationalistes sous la Troisiéme République / Francis Bergeron et Philippe Vilgier ; préface de Jean-François Chiappe. — [Bouére] : Dominique Martin Morin, 1985. — 175p

PATRIOTYCZNY RUCH ODRODZENIA NARODOWY

KUCIŃSKI, Jerzy
Geneza PRON / Jerzy Kuciński. — Warszawa : Książka i Weiedza, 1985. — 158p

PATRONAGE, POLITICAL — Scotland

SUNTER, Ronald M.
Patronage and politics in Scotland, 1707-1832 / Ronald M. Sunter. — Edinburgh : John Donald, c1986. — vii, 254p. — *Bibliography: p.238-242*

PATTERN PERCEPTION

HOFSTADTER, Douglas R.
Metamagical themas : questioning for the essence of mind and pattern : [an interlocked collection of literary, scientific and artistic studies] / Douglas R. Hofstadter. — Harmondsworth : Penguin, 1986, c1985. — xxviii,852p. — *Originally published: Basic Books, 1985. — Bibliography: p802-819*

PAUL, ALICE

LUNARDINI, Christine A.
From equal suffrage to equal rights : Alice Paul and the National Woman's Party, 1910-1928 / Christine A. Lunardini. — New York : New York University Press, 1986. — xx, 230 p.. — (The American social experience series ; 5). — *Includes index. — Bibliography: p. [206]-220*

PAVEMENTS — Organisation for Economic Co-operation and Development countries — Maintenance and repair

Pavement management systems : report / prepared by an OECD Scientific Expert Group. — Paris : Organisation for Economic Co-operation and Development, 1987. — 159p. — (Road transport research). — *Includes bibliographical references*

PAY EQUITY

HUTNER, Frances Cornwall
Equal pay for comparable worth : the working woman's issue of the eighties / Frances C. Hutner. — New York : Praeger, 1986. — xiii, 227 p.. — *Includes index. — Bibliography: p. 213-218*

PAY EQUITY — New York (State)

NEW YORK (State). Legislature. Assembly. Task Force on Women's Issues
Comparable worth, every woman's right / New York State Assembly, Task Force on Women's Issues. — [Albany] : The Task Force, [1983]. — ii,27p. — *"May 1983."*

PAY EQUITY — United States

CAMERAN, Lougy M.
The comparable worth controversy / Henry J. Aaron and Cameran Lougy. — Washington, D.C. : Brookings Institution, c1986. — p. cm. — *Includes index*

HUTNER, Frances Cornwall
Equal pay for comparable worth : the working woman's issue of the eighties / Frances C. Hutner. — New York : Praeger, 1986. — xiii, 227 p.. — *Includes index. — Bibliography: p. 213-218*

NEW YORK (State). Legislature. Assembly. Task Force on Women's Issues
Comparable worth, every woman's right / New York State Assembly, Task Force on Women's Issues. — [Albany] : The Task Force, [1983]. — ii,27p. — *"May 1983."*

PAY EQUITY — United States — Case studies

HUTNER, Frances Cornwall
Equal pay for comparable worth : the working woman's issue of the eighties / Frances C. Hutner. — New York : Praeger, 1986. — xiii, 227 p.. — *Includes index. — Bibliography: p. 213-218*

PAYMENT — Australia

AUSTRALIAN PAYMENTS SYSTEM COUNCIL
The Australian payments system. — [S.l.] : Australian Payments System Council, 1987. — vi,61p

PAYMENT — Developing countries

GHARTEY, J. B.
Crisis accountability and development in the Third World : the case of Africa / J.B. Ghartey. — Aldershot : Gower, c1987. — [259]p. — *Includes bibliography and index*

PAYMENT — Finland

HIRVENSALO, Inkeri
Suomen ja SNTL : n välinen clearing-maksujärjestelmë / Inkeri Hirvensalo. — Helsinki : Suomen Pankki, 1979. — 125p. — (Suomen Pankin julkaisuja ; Sarji A: 49). — *Bibliography: p[105]-107*

PAYMENT — Soviet Union

HIRVENSALO, Inkeri
Suomen ja SNTL : n välinen clearing-maksujärjestelmë / Inkeri Hirvensalo. — Helsinki : Suomen Pankki, 1979. — 125p. — (Suomen Pankin julkaisuja ; Sarji A: 49). — *Bibliography: p[105]-107*

PC-DOS (COMPUTER OPERATING SYSTEM)

EAGER, Bob
Introduction to PC-DOS / Bob Eager. — Wokingham : Addison Wesley, 1985

PC DOS (COMPUTER OPERATING SYSTEM) — Handbooks, manuals, etc.

MICROSOFT CORPORATION
Learning DOS : interactive guide to the PC Operating System : handbook / Microsoft Corporation. — [United States] : Microsoft Corporation, 1986. — ii,34p. — *"For IBM Personal Computers and compatibles"*

PEACE

Articles of peace : celebrating fifty years of Peace News / edited by Gail Chester and Andrew Rigby. — Bridport : Prism Press, 1986. — [xiv],174p

BEALE, Albert
Against all war : fifty years of Peace News 1936-1986 / Albert Beale. — Nottingham : Peace News, 1986. — 61p

PEACE *continuation*
Documents on the peace movement in Hungary / edited by Hugh Baldwin. — London : END. Hungary Working Group, 1986. — 53p

KIRANOVA, Evgenia
Black book on the militarist "democracy" in Turkey / Evgenia Kiranova. — Sofia : Sofia Press, 1980. — 16p

Konzepte zum Frieden : Vorschläge für eine neue Abrüstungs- und Entspannungspolitik der SPD / herausgegeben von Katrin Fuchs, Hajo Hoffmann und Horst Klaus. — Berlin : spw-Verlag, 1985. — 179p

LOEB, Paul Rogat
Hope in hard times : America's peace movement and the Reagan era / by Paul Rogat Loeb. — Lexington, Mass. : Lexington Books, [1986], c1987. — ix, 322 p.. — *Includes index. — Bibliography: p. [305]-306*

NATIONAL UNION OF MINEWORKERS
Miners United for peace. — London : National Union of Mineworkers, 1987. — [22p]. — (Campaign briefing ; 3)

Prospectus for a habitable planet / edited by Dan Smith and E. P. Thompson. — Harmondsworth : Penguin, 1987. — 240p

PURI, Rashmi-Sudha
Gandhi on war and peace / Rashmi-Sudha Puri. — New York : Praeger, 1987. — xiv, 244 p.. — *Includes index. — Bibliography: p. 229-238*

Roots of peace : the movement against militarism in Canada / edited by Eric Shragge, Ronald Babin, and Jean-Guy Vaillancourt. — Toronto : Between The Lines, 1986. — 203p. — *Bibliography: p181-194*

RUMMEL, R. J
In the minds of men : principles toward understanding and waging peace / R.J. Rummel. — Seoul, Korea : Sogang University Press, 1984. — xi, 297 p.. — *Includes bibliographies indexes*

The second superpower : the arms race and the Soviet Union / edited by Gerard Holden. — London : CND Publications, 1985. — 107p. — *Bibliography: p96-100*

STUDIE- EN DOCUMENTATIECENTRUM EMILE VANDERVELDE INSTITUUT
Socialisme, veiligheid en defensie : discussieweekend, Klemskerke, 15-18 november 1980 / algemeen concept : SEVI-werkgroep landsverdediging ; voorzitters discussiegroepen : Leo Peeters...[et al.]. — Brussel : Studie- en Documentatiecentrum Emile Vandervelde Instituut, 1981. — 58p. — (SEVI dossier ; nr.5)

SUTER, Keith D.
The Australian campaign for a Ministry for Peace / Keith D. Suter. — [Sydney] : United Nations Association of Australia, 1984. — iv,153p. — *Notes and references: p145-153*

TIUSHKEVICH, S. A.
Voina i sovremennost' / S. A. Tiushkevich ; otv. redaktor A. A. Babakov. — Moskva : Nauka, 1986. — 211p

Towards a just world peace : perspectives from social movements / editors Saul H. Mendlovitz, R.B.J. Walker. — London : Butterworths, 1987. — [424]p. — *Includes bibliographies*

The Uncertain course : new weapons, strategies and mind-sets / edited by Carl G. Jacobsen. — Oxford : Published for Stockholm International Peace Research Institute by Oxford University Press, 1987. — [408]p. — *Includes index*

World peace and the developing countries : annals of Pugwash 1985 / edited by Joseph Rotblat and Ubiratan D'Ambrosio. — Basingstoke : Macmillan, 1986. — xix,272p. — *Conference proceedings. — Includes index*

PEACE — Archival resources — United States — Directories
GREEN, Marguerite
Peace archives : a guide to library collections of the papers of American peace organizations and of leaders in the public effort for peace / compiled and edited by Marguerite Green. — Berkeley, CA : World Without War Council, 1986. — p. cm. — *Bibliography: p*

PEACE — Dictionaries
World encyclopedia of peace / honorary editor-in-chief Linus Pauling ; executive editors Ervin Laszlo, Jong Youl Yoo. — Oxford : Pergamon, 1986. — 4v.. — *In slip-case. — Includes bibliography and index*

PEACE — Library resources — United States — Directories
GREEN, Marguerite
Peace archives : a guide to library collections of the papers of American peace organizations and of leaders in the public effort for peace / compiled and edited by Marguerite Green. — Berkeley, CA : World Without War Council, 1986. — p. cm. — *Bibliography: p*

PEACE — Religious aspects — Catholic Church — Addresses, essays, lectures
Catholics and nuclear war : a commentary on The challenge of peace, the U.S. Catholic bishops' pastoral letter on war and peace / edited by Philip J. Murnion ; foreword by Theodore M. Hesburgh. — New York : Crossroad, 1983. — xxii, 346 p.. — *"A National Pastoral Life Center publication.". — Includes bibliographical references*

PEACE — Research
Essays in peace studies / edited by Vilho Harle. — Aldershot : Avebury, c1987. — xiii,209p. — *Originally published: Tampere : Tampere Peace Research Institute, 1986. — Bibliography: p193-207*

PEACE — Research — Directories
GREEN, Marguerite
Peace archives : a guide to library collections of the papers of American peace organizations and of leaders in the public effort for peace / compiled and edited by Marguerite Green. — Berkeley, CA : World Without War Council, 1986. — p. cm. — *Bibliography: p*

PEACE — Research — Africa
Africa : perspectives on peace and development / edited by Emmanuel Hansen. — London : Zed, 1987. — [256]p. — (The United Nations University studies in peace and regional security). — *Includes index*

PEACE — Societies, etc. — Directories
Peace movements of the world / edited by Alan J. Day. — Harlow : Longman, [1986]. — viii,398p. — (A Keesing's reference publication). — *Includes index*

PEACE — Study and teaching
Essays in peace studies / edited by Vilho Harle. — Aldershot : Avebury, c1987. — xiii,209p. — *Originally published: Tampere : Tampere Peace Research Institute, 1986. — Bibliography: p193-207*

Neue Akzente der Friedenspädagogik / Peter Heitkämper (Hg.). — Münster : Lit, 1984. — 135p. — (Frieden - Ökologie - Entwicklung ; Bd.1)

PEACE — Study and teaching — Africa
Africa : perspectives on peace and development / edited by Emmanuel Hansen. — London : Zed, 1987. — [256]p. — (The United Nations University studies in peace and regional security). — *Includes index*

PEACE — Study and teaching — Germany (West)
Neue Akzente der Friedenspädagogik / Peter Heitkämper (Hg.). — Münster : Lit, 1984. — 135p. — (Frieden - Ökologie - Entwicklung ; Bd.1)

PEACE — Study and teaching — United States
SMITH, Charles Duryea
The Hundred percent challenge : building a national institute of peace : a platform for planning, policy, and programming / edited by Charles Duryea Smith. — 1st ed. — Cabin John, MD : Seven Locks Press, 1985. — p. cm. — *Includes bibliographies and index*

PEACE CORPS (U.S.) — History
RICE, Gerard T
The bold experiment : JFK's Peace Corps / Gerard T. Rice. — Notre Dame, Ind. : University of Notre Dame Press, c1985. — xv, 349 p., [18] p. of plates. — *Includes index. — Bibliography: p. 304-343*

PEACE MOVEMENTS
REEVE, Gillian
Offence of the realm : how peace campaigners get bugged / Gillian Reeve [and] Joan Smith. — London : CND Publications, 1986. — 44p

PEACE NEWS
Articles of peace : celebrating fifty years of Peace News / edited by Gail Chester and Andrew Rigby. — Bridport : Prism Press, 1986. — [xiv],174p

BEALE, Albert
Against all war : fifty years of Peace News 1936-1986 / Albert Beale. — Nottingham : Peace News, 1986. — 61p

PEACE (PHILOSOPHY) — Study and teaching (Higher) — Israel
GORDON, Hayim
Dance, dialogue, and despair : existentialist philosophy and education for peace in Isreal / Haim Gordon. — University, Ala. : University of Alabama Press, c1986. — xvii, 250 p.. — (Judaic studies series). — *Includes index. — Bibliographical essay: p. 240-244*

PEARL HARBOR (HAWAII), ATTACK ON, 1941
PRANGE, Gordon William
Pearl Harbor : the verdict of history / by Gordon W. Prange, with Donald M. Goldstein, Katherine V. Dillon. — New York : McGraw-Hill Book Co., c1986. — p. cm. — *Includes index. — Bibliography: p*

PEARL HARBOR (HAWAII), ATTACK ON, 1941 — Historiography
MINTZ, Frank P
Revisionism and the origins of Pearl Harbor / Frank Paul Mintz. — Lanham, Md. ; London : University Press of America, c1985. — ix, 145p . — *Bibliography: p.127-145*

PEASANT UPRISINGS — India
Agrarian struggles in India after independence / edited by A. R. Desai. — Delhi : Oxford University Press, 1986. — xxvi,666p

PEASANT UPRISINGS — Japan
VLASTOS, Stephen
Peasant protests and uprisings in Tokugawa Japan / Stephen Vlastos. — Berkeley : University of California Press, c1986. — xii, 184 p.. — *Includes index. — Bibliography: p. [169]-179*

PEASANT UPRISINGS — Japan — History
BIX, Herbert P
Peasant protest in Japan, 1590-1884 / Herbert P. Bix. — New Haven [Conn.] : Yale University Press, c1986. — p. cm. — *Includes index. — Bibliography: p*

PEASANT UPRISINGS — Mexico — History
TUTINO, John
From insurrection to revolution in Mexico : social bases of agrarian violence, 1750-1940 / John Tutino. — Princeton, N.J. : Princeton University Press, c1986. — xx, 425 p.. — *Includes index. — Bibliography: p. [399]-417*

PEASANTRY
Peasants and peasant societies : selected readings / edited by Teodor Shanin. — 2nd ed. — Oxford : Basil Blackwell, 1987. — [510]p. — *Previous ed.: Harmondsworth : Penguin, 1971. — Includes bibliography and index*

PEASANTRY — Asia
SMIRENSKAĨĀ, Zhanna Dmitrievna
[Krest'ĩānstvo v stranakh Azii--obshchestvennoe soznanie i obshchestvennaĩā bor'ba. English]. Peasants in Asia--social consciousness and social struggle / by Zhanna D. Smirenskaia ; translated by Michael J. Buckley. — Athens, Ohio : Ohio University, Center for International Studies, Center for Southeast Asian Studies, 1986. — p. cm. — (Monographs in international studies. Southeast Asia series ; no. 73). — *Translation of: Krest'ĩānstvo v stranakh Azii-obshchestvennoe soznanie i obshchestvennaĩā bor'ba. — Bibliography: p*

PEASANTRY — Legal status, laws, etc. — Peru
PERU
[Laws, etc]. Estatuto de comunidades campesinas del Perú : Decreto supremo no.37-70-A. — Lima : [Empresa Editora del Diario Oficial "El Peruano"], 1970. — 27p

PEASANTRY — Africa
COLLOQUE DE LA SORBONNE "PARTICIPATION PAYSANNE ET DÉVELOPPEMENT AGRICOLE: L'EXEMPLE DES POLITIQUES DE L'EAU EN AFRIQUE" (1983 : Paris)
Les politiques de l'eau en Afrique : développement agricole et participation paysanne / actes du Colloque de la Sorbonne (organise par le) Centre d'Études Juridiques et Politiques du Monde Africai sous la direction de Gérard Conac, Claudette Savonnet-Guyot [et] Françoise Conac. — Paris : Economica, 1985. — 767p

PEASANTRY — Argentina — Political activity — History
LOZZA, Arturo Marcos
Tiempo de huelgas : los apasionados relatos del campesino y ferroviario Florindo Moretti sobre aquellas épocas de fundaciones, luchas y serenatas / Arturo Marcos Lozza. — Buenos Aires : Editorial Anteo, 1985. — 299p. — *Bibliography: p293-294*

PEASANTRY — Bangladesh
RAHMAN, Atiur
Peasants and classes : a study in differentiation in Bangladesh / Atiur Rahman ; preface by Terry Byres. — London : Zed, 1986. — [272]p. — *Includes bibliography and index*

PEASANTRY — Byelorussian S.S.R.
KOSTIUK, M. P.
Trudovoi vklad krest'ianstva v pobedu i uprochenie sotsializma : na materialakh BSSR / M. P. Kostiuk ; nauchnyi redaktor I. M. Ignatenko. — Minsk : Nauka i tekhnika, 1986. — 236p

PEASANTRY — China — History — 20th century
The Re-emergence of the Chinese peasantry : aspects of rural decollectivisation / edited by Ashwani Saith. — London : Croom Helm, c1987. — ix,277p. — *Includes bibliographies and index*

PEASANTRY — China — Hunan Province — History
PERDUE, Peter C.
Exhausting the earth : state and peasant in Hunan, 1500-1850 / Peter C. Perdue. — Cambridge, Mass. : Council on East Asian Studies, Harvard University ; Distributed by Harvard University Press, 1987. — p. cm. — (Harvard East Asian monographs ; 1987). — *Includes index. — Bibliography: p*

PEASANTRY — Colombia — History
LEGRAND, Catherine
Frontier expansion and peasant protest in Colombia, 1850-1936 / Catherine LeGrand. — 1st ed. — Albuquerque : University of New Mexico Press, c1986. — xviii, 302p. — *Includes index. — Bibliography: p.267-289*

PEASANTRY — Colombia — Political activity — History — 20th century
ZAMOSC, Leon
The agrarian question and the peasant movement in Colombia: struggles of the National Peasant Association 1967-1981 / Leon Zamosc. — Cambridge : Cambridge University Press, 1986. — [304]p. — (Cambridge Latin American studies ; 58). — *Bibliography: p416-438*

PEASANTRY — Developing countries
Third World peasantry : a continuing saga of deprivation / editors, R.P. Misra & Nguyen Tri Dung. — New Delhi : Sterling Publishers, c1986. — 2 v.. — *Includes bibliographies and indexes*

PEASANTRY — Egypt
ADAMS, Richard H
Development and social change in rural Egypt / Richard H. Adams, Jr. — 1st ed. — Syracuse, N.Y. : Syracuse University Press, 1986. — xii, 231 p.. — (Contemporary issues in the Middle East). — : *Revision of the author's thesis (Ph. D.)--University of California, Berkeley, 1981. — Includes index. — Bibliography: p. 213-224*

PEASANTRY — France
GROUPE POUR LA FONDATION DE L'UNION DES COMMUNISTES FRANÇAIS (marxiste-léniniste)
Le livre des paysans pauvres : 5 années de travail maoïste dans une campagne française / Groupe pour la fondation de l'Union des communistes de France marxiste-léniniste. — Paris : F. Maspero, 1976. — 302 p.. — (Collection Yenan) (Série Propositions et documents)

LAFONT, Jean
Paysannerie et capitalisme : analyse des principales tendances du développement récent de l'agriculture française / Jean Lafont. — Paris : Centre D'Études Prospectives D'Économie Mathématique Appliquées à la Planification, 1976. — 116p. — (Centre D'Études Prospectives D'Économie Mathématique Appliquées à la Planification ; 7701)

PEASANTRY — France — History — 16th century
LE ROY LADURIE, Emmanuel
The French peasantry 1450-1660 / Emmanuel Le Roy Ladurie ; translated by Alan Sheridan. — Aldershot : Scolar, 1987. — 447p. — *Translation of: Les masses profondes. — Bibliography: p431-436. — Includes index*

PEASANTRY — France — History — 17th century
LE ROY LADURIE, Emmanuel
The French peasantry 1450-1660 / Emmanuel Le Roy Ladurie ; translated by Alan Sheridan. — Aldershot : Scolar, 1987. — 447p. — *Translation of: Les masses profondes. — Bibliography: p431-436. — Includes index*

PEASANTRY — Germany — Political activity — History — 20th century
MOELLER, Robert G
German peasants and agrarian politics, 1914-1924 : the Rhineland and Westphalia / Robert G. Moeller. — Chapel Hill ; London : University of North Carolina Press, c1986. — xv, 286p. — *Includes index. — Bibliography: p 241-279*

PEASANTRY — Guatemala — History — 19th century
CAMBRANES, J. C
[Café y campesinos en Guatemala, 1853-1897. English]. Coffee and peasants : the origins of the modern plantation economy in Guatemala, 1853-1897 / J.C. Cambranes ; [English version revised by Carla Clason-Höök]. — Stockholm, Sweden : Institute of Latin American Studies, c1985. — 334 p.. — (Monografias / Institute of Latin American Studies ; no.10). — *Translation of: Café y campesinos en Guatemala, 1853-1897. — Bibliography: p. 327-332*

PEASANTRY — India
The Peasant movement today / Sunil Sahasrabudhey. — New Delhi : Ashish Pub. House, 1986. — xix, 224 p.. — *English and Hindi. — "Under the auspices of Gandhian Institute of Studies, Rajghat, Varanasi"--T.p. verso. — Includes bibliographies and index*

PEASANTRY — India — Hyderabad (State) — History
BHASKARA RAO, V.
Agrarian and industrial relations in Hyderabad State / V. Bhaskara Rao. — New Delhi : Associated Pub. House, c1985. — xi, 179 p.. — *Includes index. — Bibliography: p. [169]-173*

PEASANTRY — Japan — Political activity — History
BIX, Herbert P
Peasant protest in Japan, 1590-1884 / Herbert P. Bix. — New Haven [Conn.] : Yale University Press, c1986. — p. cm. — *Includes index. — Bibliography: p*

PEASANTRY — Karst (Yugoslavia and Italy)
DAVIS, James C
Rise from want : a peasant family in the machine age / James C. Davis. — Philadelphia : University of Pennsylvania Press, 1986. — xv, 165 p.. — *Includes index. — Bibliography: p. [153]-161*

PEASANTRY — Latin American
DEERE, Carmen Diana
The peasantry in political economy : trends of the 1980's / Carmen Diana Deere. — Amherst (Mass.) : University of Massachusetts at Amherst, International Area Studies Program, 1987. — 76p. — (Program in Latin American studies. Occasional papers series ; no.19)

PEASANTRY — Mexico
DE ROUFFIGNAC, Ann Elizabeth Lucas
The contemporary peasantry in Mexico : a class analysis / by Ann Elizabeth Lucas de Rouffignac. — New York : Praeger, 1985. — xix, 203p. — *Includes index. — Bibliography: p[186]-196*

YUNEZ-NAUDE, Antonio
Peasantry and agricultural exchange relations : an enquiry based on data for the Mexican economy / by Antonio Yunez-Naude. — 324 leaves. — *PhD (Econ) 1986 LSE. — Leaves 273-316 are appendices*

PEASANTRY — Peru
La cuestión rural en el Perú / Javier Iguiñiz. — 2a ed. — Lima : Pontifica Universidad Católica del Perú Fondo Editorial, 1986. — 332p. — *"Una recopilación de ensayos elaborados por profesores - investigadores de los Departamentos de Economía y Ciencias Sociales de la Pontifica Universidad Católica del Perú". — Includes bibliographies*

PEASANTRY — Peru — Cajamarca — History
TAYLOR, Lewis
Estates, freeholders and peasant communities in Cajamarca, 1876-1972 / by Lewis Taylor. — Cambridge : Centre of Latin American Studies, University of Cambridge, 1986. — 45p. — (Working papers / University of Cambridge, Centre of Latin American Studies ; no.42)

PEASANTRY — Philippines — Mindoro
LOPEZ-GONZAGA, Violeta
Peasants in the hills : a study of the dynamics of social change among the Buhid swidden cultivators in the Philippines / Violeta Lopez-Gonzaga. — Quezon City, Philippines : University of the Philippines Press, 1983. — xiv,226p. — *Bibliography: p[211]-219*

PEASANTRY — Poland — Political activity
STANKIEWICZ, Zbigniew
Kwestia chłopska w okresie narodzin polskiego ruchu robotniczego / Zbigniew Stankiewicz. — Warszawa : Ludowa Spółdzielnia Wydawnicza, 1985. — 329p. — *Bibliography: p305-[314]*

PEASANTRY — Romania — Political activity

DIMA, Romus
Organizarea politică a țărănimii : (sfîrșitul sec. XIX - începutul sec. XX) / Romus Dima. — București : Editura Științifică și Enciclopedică, 1985. — 405p. — *Bibliography: p384-393*

PEASANTRY — Russian S.F.S.R. — Siberia — History

GORIUSHKIN, L. M.
Krest'ianskoe dvizhenie v Sibiri 1907-1914 gg. : khronika i istoriografiia / L. M. Goriushkin, G. A. Nozdrin, A. N. Sagaidachnyi ; otv. redaktory L. M. Goriushkin, E. I. Solov'eva. — Novosibirsk : Nauka, Sibirskoe otdelenie, 1986. — 314p

Istoriia krest'ianstva Sibiri / Glavnaia redkollegiia: A. P. Derevianko...[et al.]. — Novosibirsk : Nauka, Sibirskoe otdelenie [4]: Krest'ianstvo Sibiri v period uprocheniia i razvitiia sotsializma / [otv. redaktor V. T. Aniskov]. — 1985. — 395

PEASANTRY — Soviet Union

STOLIAROV, Ivan
Zapiski russkogo krest'ianina = Récit d'un paysan russe / Ivan Stoliarov ; préface de Basile Kerblay; notes de Valérie Stoliaroff avec le concours d'Alexis Berelowitch. — Paris : Institut de'Études Slaves, 1986. — 202p. — (Cultures et sociétés de l'Est ; 6)

PEASANTRY — Soviet Union — History

Istoriia sovetskogo krest'ianstva / redkollegiia: V. P. Sherstobitov...[et al.]. — Moskva : Nauka. — (Istoriia krest'ianstva SSSR) 1: Krest'ianstvo v pervoe desiatiletie Sovetskoi vlasti 1917-1921 / redkollegiia: G. V. Sharapov...[et al.]. — 1986. — 455p

Istoriia sovetskogo krest'ianstva / redkollegiia: V. P. Sherstobitov...[et al.]. — Moskva : Nauka. — (Istoriia krest'ianstva SSSR) 2: Sovetskoe krest'ianstvo v period sotsialisticheskoi rekonstruktsii narodnogo khoziaistva. Konets 1927-1937 / redkollegiia: I. E. Zelenin...[et al.]. — 1986. — 448p

NEUPOKOEV, V. I.
Gosudarstvennye povinnosti krest'ian Evropeiskoi Rossii v kontse XVIII - nachale XIX veka / V. I. Neupokoev ; otv. redaktor P. G. Ryndziunskii. — Moskva : Nauka, 1987. — 286p

SHAPIRO, A. L.
Russkoe krest'ianstvo pered zakreposhcheniem (XIV-XVI vv.) / A. L. Shapiro. — Leningrad : Izd-vo Leningradskogo universiteta, 1987. — 254p

PEASANTRY — Soviet Union — Social life and customs

GROMYKO, M. M.
Traditsionnye normy povedeniia i formy obshcheniia russkikh krest'ian XIX v. / M. M. Gromyko ; otv. redaktory V. A. Aleksandrov, V. K. Sokolova. — Moskva : Nauka, 1986. — 274p

PEASANTRY — Transcaucasia — History

AVALIANI, S. L.
Krest'ianskii vopros v Zakavkaz'e / S. L. Avaliani ; podgotovka k izdaniiu G. N. Margiani ; vstupitel'nye stat'i G. N. Margiani i G. I. Megrelishrili. — Tbilisi : Metsniereba. — Vols.1-3 published in Odessa, 1912-1914; vol.4 published in Tbilisi, 1920
T.5 (dopolnitel'nyi). — 1986. — 120p

PEASANTRY — Yugoslavia — Slovenia — Case studies

DAVIS, James C
Rise from want : a peasant family in the machine age / James C. Davis. — Philadelphia : University of Pennsylvania Press, 1986. — xv, 165 p.. — *Includes index*. — *Bibliography: p. [153]-161*

PEASANTS' WAR, 1524-1525

BLICKLE, Peter
[Revolution von 1525. English]. The Revolution of 1525 : the German Peasants' War from a new perspective / Peter Blickle ; translated by Thomas A. Brady, Jr., and H.C. Erik Midelfort. — Baltimore : Johns Hopkins University Press, c1981. — p. cm. — *Translation of: Die Revolution von 1525.* — *Includes index.* — *Bibliography: p*

PEAT INDUSTRY — Developing countries

Fuel peat in developing countries / Bord na Móna (Irish Peat Development Authority). — Washington, D.C. : The World Bank, 1985. — xxi,146p. — (World Bank technical paper ; no.41). — *Bibliography: p129-146*

PEDDLERS AND PEDDLING — Peru — Lima

BUNSTER, Ximena
Sellers and servants : working women in Lima, Peru / Ximena Bunster, Elsa M. Chaney ; photos by Ellan Young. — New York : Praeger, 1985. — x, 258p. — *Includes index.* — *Bibliography: p.235-246*

PEDDLERS AND PEDDLING — United States — History

NAFF, Alixa
Becoming American : the early Arab immigrant experience / Alixa Naff. — Carbondale : Southern Illinois University Press, c1985. — p. cm. — (M.E.R.I. special studies). — *Includes index.* — *Bibliography: p*

PEDESTRIANS — Great Britain

NATIONAL CONSUMER COUNCIL
What's wrong with walking? : a consumer review of the pedestrian environment. — London : H.M.S.O., 1987. — 151p

PEDIATRICS — Great Britain

GREAT BRITAIN. Working Party on Fortification of Food with Vitamin D
Rickets and osteomalacia / report of the Working Party on Fortification of Food with Vitamin D. Committee on Medical Aspects of Food Policy. — London : H.M.S.O., 1980. — xii,66p. — (Report on health and social subjects ; 19). — *At head of title: Department of Health and Social Security.* — *Bibliography: p54-66*

PEDRO I, Emperor of Brazil

MACAULAY, Neill
Dom Pedro : the struggle for liberty in Brazil and Portugal, 1798-1834 / Neill Macaulay. — Durham, [N.C.] : Duke University Press, 1986. — xiv, 361 p.. — *Includes index.* — *Bibliography: p. [339]-344*

PEINADO PEINADO, RUFINO

PEINADO PEINADO, Rufino
Recuerdos de un carlista andaluz : un cruzado de la causa / [Rufino Peinado Peinado] ; Rafael Alvarez de Morales y Ruiz. — Córdoba : Instituto de H.a de Andalucía, [1982?]. — 245 p.. — (Publicaciones Instituto de Historia de Andalucía ; no. 13). — *Includes index*

PEKING (CHINA) — History

JOHNSTON, Reginald F.
Twilight in the forbidden city / Reginald F. Johnston ; with an introduction by Pamela Atwell. — Hong Kong : Oxford University Press, 1985. — xi,486p. — *Reprint of original published by Victor Gollancz in 1934*

PEMBROKE, WILLIAM MARSHAL, Earl of

DUBY, Georges
William Marshal : the flower of chivalry / Georges Duby ; translated from the French by Richard Howard. — London : Faber, 1986, c1985. — 155p. — *Translation of: Guillaume le Maréchal.* — *Bibliography: p154-155*

PENAL COLONIES — Australia

HUGHES, Robert, 1938-
The fatal shore : a history of the transportation of convicts to Australia, 1787-1868 / Robert Hughes. — London : Collins Harvill, 1987, c1986. — 680,[32]p of plates. — *Originally published: New York : Knopf, 1986.* — *Bibliography: p656-670.* — *Includes index*

PENAL COLONIES, BRITISH

HUGHES, Robert, 1938-
The fatal shore : a history of the transportation of convicts to Australia, 1787-1868 / Robert Hughes. — London : Collins Harvill, 1987, c1986. — 680,[32]p of plates. — *Originally published: New York : Knopf, 1986.* — *Bibliography: p656-670.* — *Includes index*

PENDLE (LANCASHIRE) — Industries — History

SWAIN, John T.
Industry before the Industrial Revolution : North-East Lancashire, c1500-1640 / John T. Swain. — Manchester : Printed for the Chetham Society by Manchester University Press, 1986. — 235p. — (Remains historical and literary connected with the palatine countries of Lancaster and Cheshire. 3rd series ; v.32) (Remains historical and literary connected with the palatine counties of Lancaster and Chester. 3rd series ; v.32). — *Bibliography: p210-224.* — *Includes index*

P'ENG TE-HUAI

P'ENG, Te-huai
[P'eng Te-huai tzu shu. English]. Memoirs of a Chinese marshal : the autobiographical notes of Peng Dehuai (1898-1974) / translated by Zheng Longpu ; English text edited by Sara Grimes. — 1st ed. — Beijing : Foreign Languages Press, 1984. — vi, 523 p., [15] p. of plates. — *Translation of: P'eng Te-huai tzu shu*

PENN, WILLIAM

PENN, William
The papers of William Penn / editors, Mary Maples Dunn, Richard S. Dunn...[et al.]. — Pennsylvania : University of Pennsylvania Press . — *Includes index*
V.5: William Penn's published writings 1660-1726 : an interpretive bibliography / [edited by] Edwin B. Bronner, David Fraser. — 1986. — xxvi,546p

PENNSYLVANIA — Economic policy

ALLEN, David N
Nurturing advanced technology enterprises : emerging issues in state and local economic development policy / David N. Allen and Victor Levine. — New York : Praeger, 1986. — xvi, 268 p.. — *Includes index.* — *Bibliography: p. 239-262*

PENNSYLVANIA — History — Insurrection of 1794

SLAUGHTER, Thomas P
The Whiskey Rebellion : frontier epilogue to the American Revolution / Thomas P. Slaughter. — New York : Oxford University Press, 1986. — p. cm. — *Includes index.* — *Bibliography: p*

PENNSYLVANIA — History — Colonial period, ca.1600-1775 — Sources

PENN, William
The papers of William Penn / editors, Mary Maples Dunn, Richard S. Dunn...[et al.]. — Pennsylvania : University of Pennsylvania Press . — *Includes index*
V.5: William Penn's published writings 1660-1726 : an interpretive bibliography / [edited by] Edwin B. Bronner, David Fraser. — 1986. — xxvi,546p

PENSION TRUSTS — Investments — Law and legislation — Great Britain

Pension fund investment / edited by A.G. Shepherd. — Cambridge [Cambridgeshire] ; Wolfeboro, NH, U.S.A. : Woodhead-Faulkner, 1987. — c. pm. — *Includes index*

PENSION TRUSTS — Social aspects — United States — Congresses
Should pension assets be managed for social/political purposes? : An EBRI Policy Forum, December 6, 1979 / edited by Dallas L. Salisbury. — Washington, D.C. : Employee Benefit Research Institute, c1980. — xii, 381 p.

PENSION TRUSTS — Great Britain — Accounting
MASCARENHAS, Amyas
Spicer and Pegler's accounts and audit of pension schemes / Amyas Mascarenhas. — London : Butterworths, 1987. — [150]p

PENSION TRUSTS — Great Britain — Investments
BLAKE, David Peter Courtney
The characteristics model of portfolio behaviour : with reference to United Kingdom private sector pension funds 1963-1978 / by David Peter Courtney Blake. — 322 leaves. — PhD (Econ) 1987 LSE

Pension fund investment / edited by A.G. Shepherd. — Cambridge [Cambridgeshire] ; Wolfeboro, NH, U.S.A. : Woodhead-Faulkner, 1987. — c. pm. — Includes index

PRODANO, Sylvio
Pension funds : investment and performance / Sylvio Prodano. — Aldershot : Gower, c1987. — xiii,166p. — (Gower studies in finance and investment ; 3). — Bibliography: 160-162. — Includes index

PENSION TRUSTS — Great Britain — Investments — Statistics
Insurance companies' and pension funds' investment. — London : HMSO, 1970-. — (Business monitor. MQ ; 5) (Business monitor. M ; 5). — Quarterly

PENSION TRUSTS — United States — Addresses, essays, lectures
Pensions, labor, and individual choice / edited by David A. Wise. — Chicago : University of Chicago Press, 1985. — p. cm. — (National Bureau of Economic Research project report). — Includes index. — Bibliography: p

PENSION TRUSTS — United States — Congresses
Issues in pension economics / edited by Zvi Bodie, John B. Shoven, and David A. Wise. — Chicago : University of Chicago Press, 1987. — ix, 376 p.. — (A National Bureau of Economic Research project report). — Includes bibliographies and indexes

PENSION TRUSTS — United States — Investments
KORCZYK, Sophie M.
Retirement income opportunities in an aging America : pensions and the economy / Sophie M. Korczyk. — Washington : Employee Benefit Research Institute, 1982. — 150p. — Bibliography: p98-108

PENSION TRUSTS — United States — Investments — Congresses
Should pension assets be managed for social/political purposes? : An EBRI Policy Forum, December 6, 1979 / edited by Dallas L. Salisbury. — Washington, D.C. : Employee Benefit Research Institute, c1980. — xii, 381 p.

PENSIONS — Law and legislation — Great Britain
GRAY, Kevin J.
Property, divorce and retirement pension rights / by K.J. Gray. British nationality and the right of abode 1948-1983 / by C.C. Turpin. — Deventer ; London : Kluwer, 1986. — vii,269p. — (Cambridge-Tilburg law lectures ; 5th ser., 1982). — Includes bibliographical references

GREAT BRITAIN. Department of Health and Social Security
Consultative document on equal status for men and women in occupational pension schemes. — [London] : the Department, [1976]. — [29]p

GREAT BRITAIN. Department of Health and Social Security
Second consultative document on equal treatment for men and women in occupational pension schemes. — [London] : the Department, [1977]. — 1v.(various pagings)

PENSIONS — Australia
Pensioner fringe benefits : their range, cost and value. — Canberra : Australian Government Publishing Service, 1984. — viii,162p. — Includes bibliographical references

PENSIONS — Canada
BEATTIE, Earle
Canada's billion dollar pension scandal : how secure is your future? / Earle Beattie ; in consultation with Tom Delaney. — Toronto : Methuen, 1985. — 152p. — References: p151-152

PENSIONS — Denmark
Samfundet og invalidepensionisterne. — 2 udg.. — [København] : Socialministeriet, 1971. — 30p

PENSIONS — Finland
Old-age and invalidity pensions in Finland. — [Helsinki : National Pension Institute, 1957]. — 11,iiip

PENSIONS — France
Évaluation et sauvegarde de l'assurance vieillesse : rapport au ministre des affaires sociales et de l'emploi / présenté par Raoul Briet, Alain Joubert. — [Paris : La Documentation française], 1987. — 187p. — (Collection des rapports officiéls)

PENSIONS — Great Britain
GREAT BRITAIN. Department of Health and Social Security
Consultative document on the termination of contracted-out employment and arrangements for paying state scheme premiums. — [London : the Department, 1975]. — 7p

GREAT BRITAIN. Department of Health and Social Security
Consultative document on tracing service for occupational pensions. — [London : the Department, 1976]. — [6]p

GREAT BRITAIN. Department of Health and Social Security
Note by the Department of Health and Social Security on the calculation of a guaranteed minimum pension. — [London : the Department, 1976?]. — [8]p

GREAT BRITAIN. Department of Health and Social Security
Second consultative document on the provision of information about G[uaranteed] M[inimum] P[ension]s. — [London : the Department, 1976]. — 12,7p

GREAT BRITAIN. Department of Health and Social Security
Social Security Pensions Act 1975 : commentary on the draft state scheme premiums (actuarial tables) regulations. — [London : the Department, 1976]. — 2,13p

GREAT BRITAIN. Government Actuary
Occupational pension schemes, 1983 : seventh survey. — London : H.M.S.O., 1986. — iv,111p

GREAT BRITAIN. Parliament. House of Commons. Library. Research Division
Earnings rule for retirement pensioners. — [London] : the Division, 1976. — [12]p. — (Background paper ; no.53)

GREAT BRITAIN. Parliament. House of Commons. Library. Research Division
State Earnings-Related Pension Scheme (SERPS) / Julia Lourie. — [London] : the Division, 1985. — 45p. — (Background paper ; no.168)

GREAT BRITAIN. Superannuation Funds Office
Occupational pension schemes : notes on approval under the Finance Act 1970 as amended by the Finance Act 1971. — New Malden : Joint Office of Inland Revenue Superannuation Funds Office and Occupational Pensions Board, [1979]. — 94p. — (I.R. ; 12 (1979)). — Includes index

PENSIONS — Great Britain — Taxation
FRY, V. C.
The taxation of occupational pension schemes in the UK / V. C. Fry, E. M. Hammond and J. A. Kay. — London : Institute for Fiscal Studies, 1985. — 66p. — (IFS report series ; No.14). — Cover title: Taxing pensions

PENSIONS — United States
IPPOLITO, Richard A
Pensions, economics, and public policy / Richard A. Ippolito. — Homewood, Ill. : Published for the Pension Research Council, Wharton School, University of Pennsylvania by Dow Jones-Irwin, 1986. — xxiii, 267 p.. — Includes index. — Bibliography: p. 253-256

PENSIONS — United States — Addresses, essays, lectures
Pensions, labor, and individual choice / edited by David A. Wise. — Chicago : University of Chicago Press, 1985. — p. cm. — (National Bureau of Economic Research project report). — Includes index. — Bibliography: p

PENSIONS — United States — Finance — Congresses
Issues in pension economics / edited by Zvi Bodie, John B. Shoven, and David A. Wise. — Chicago : University of Chicago Press, 1987. — ix, 376 p.. — (A National Bureau of Economic Research project report). — Includes bibliographies and indexes

PEOPLE'S ACTION PARTY (Singapore)
CHOO, Carolyn
Singapore, the PAP & the problem of political succession / Carolyn Choo. — Petaling Jaya, Selangor, Malaysia : Pelanduk Publications (M) ; Singapore : Sole distributor Asiapac Books & Educational Aids, [1985]. — x, 225 p.

PEOPLES TEMPLE
AHLBERG, Sture
Messianic movements : a comparative analysis of the Sabbatians, the People's Temple, and the Unification Church / by Sture Ahlberg. — Stockholm : Almqvist & Wiksell International, 1986. — 128 p.. — (Acta Universitatis Stockholmiensis. Stockholm studies in comparative religion ; 26). — Continuation of author's thesis (doctoral--Stockholm, 1977) originally presented as: Messianism in the State of Israel. — Includes indexes. — Bibliography: p. 118-122

PERAK (MALAYSIA) — Population — Statistics
Banci penduduk dan perumahan Malaysia 1980 = Population and housing census of Malaysia 1980. — Kuala Lumpur : Department of Statistics. — Text in Malay and English
Laporan penduduk negeri = State population report
Perak. — 1984. — 599p. — 1map

PERCEPTION
LINDSAY, Peter H.
Human information processing : An introduction to psychology / Peter H. Lindsay and Donald A. Norman. — 2d ed. — New York : Academic Press, c1977. — xxiii, 777 p. — Includes indexes. — Bibliography: p. [734]-762

PERELMAN, CHAIM
Practical reasoning in human affairs : studies in honor of Chaim Perelman / edited by James L. Golden and Joseph J. Pilotta. — Dordrecht ; Lancaster : Reidel, c1986. — x, 404p. — (Synthese library ; v. 183). — Includes bibliographies and indexes

PEREZ, ANTONIO — Correspondence
A Spaniard in Elizabethan England : the correspondence of Antonio Perez's exile / [compiled and annotated by] Gustav Ungerer. — London : Tamesis, 1974-1976. — 2v. — *Bibliographies*

PERFECTION (PHILOSOPHY) — History
MULLER, Virginia L.
The idea of perfectibility / Virginia L. Muller. — Lanham : University Press of America, c1985. — vii, 221 p.. — *Bibliography: p. 209-221*

PERFORMANCE — Congresses
Attention and performance XI / edited by Michael I. Posner, Oscar S.M. Marin. — Hillsdale, N.J. : Lawrence Erlbaum Associates, 1985. — xxiii, 675p. — *"Proceedings of the Eleventh International Symposium on Attention and Performance, Eugene, Oregon, July 1-8, 1984"--P. — Includes bibliographies and indexes*

PERFORMANCE — Evaluation
AUDIT COMMISSION FOR LOCAL AUTHORITIES IN ENGLAND AND WALES
Performance review in local government : a handbook for auditors and local authorities. — London : H.M.S.O., 1986. — 8booklets in ring binder. — *Includes bibliographies*

PERFORMING ARTS
VOGEL, Harold L.
Entertainment industry economics : a guide for financial analysis / Harold L. Vogel. — Cambridge : Cambridge University Press, 1986. — xx, 457p. — *Contains bibliographies*

PERFORMING ARTS — Psychological aspects
WILSON, Glenn, 1942-
The psychology of the performing arts / Glenn Wilson. — London : Croom Helm, c1985. — 180p. — *Bibliography: p165-172. — Includes index*

PERINATAL MORTALITY — Great Britain
GREAT BRITAIN. Working Party on Infant and Perinatal Mortality and Morbidity
Report. — [London] : Department of Health and Social Security, 1977. — 7,[12] leaves. — *Includes bibliographical references*

PERINATAL MORTALITY — Italy — Statistics
ITALY. Istituto Centrale di Statistica
Recenti livelli e caratteristiche della mortalità infantile in Italia : analisi delle informazioni e proposte di miglioramento. — [Roma] : Istituto Centrale di Statistica, 1983. — 102p. — (Collana di informazioni. Anno 7 ; 4)

PERINATAL MORTALITY — Syria — Statistics
VAIDYANATHAN, K. E.
Estimation of infant and child mortality in Syria from the 1970 Census data / K. E. Vaidyanathan. — Damascus : Central Bureau of Statistics, 1976. — 17p. — (Syrian Population Studies Series ; No.2)

PERIODICALS
Serials: proceedings of the UK Serials Group Conference. — [London] : UK Serials Group, 1985-. — (Serials monograph no.8). — *Annual*

PERIODICALS — Directories
Benn's media directory: incorporating Benn's press directory. — Tonbridge : Benn Business Information Services, 1986-. — *Annual*

PERIODICALS, PUBLISHING OF — Costs
PULLINGER, D. J.
BLEND-8 : cost appraisal / D.J. Pullinger. — London : British Library Research and Development Dept., c1987. — ix,41p. — (Library and information research report ; 53)

PERLIS (MALAYSIA) — Population — Statistics
Banci penduduk dan perumahan Malaysia 1980 = Population and housing census of Malaysia 1980. — Kuala Lumpur : Department of Statistics. — *Text in Malay and English*
Laporan penduduk negeri = State population report
Perlis. — 1984. — 555p

PERNAMBUCO (BRAZIL) — Economic conditions
HUGGINS, Martha Knisely
From slavery to vagrancy in Brazil : crime and social control in the Third World / Martha Knisely Huggins. — New Brunswick, N.J. : Rutgers University Press, c1984. — xix, 183p. — (Crime, law, and deviance series). — *Includes index. — Bibliography: p 159-167*

PERÓN, EVA DUARTE
La historia de Eva Perón : un ejemplo de amor entre una mujer y un pueblo. — Buenos Aires : Sánchez Teruelo
Tomo 1. — [1983]. — 320p

La historia de Eva Perón : un ejemplo de amor entre una mujer y un pueblo. — Buenos Aires : Sánchez Teruelo
Tomo 2. — 1985. — 321-560p

PERÓN, JUAN DOMINGO
CHÁVEZ, Fermín
Perón y el peronismo en la historia contemporánea / Fermín Chávez. — Buenos Aires : Editorial Oriente. — *Includes bibliographical references*
t.2. — 1984. — 298p

CRASSWELLER, Robert D.
Perón and the enigmas of Argentina / Robert D. Crassweller. — New York : W. W. Norton, 1987. — xi,432p. — *Bibliography: p406-[420]*

LUNA, Félix
Perón y su tiempo / Félix Luna. — Buenos Aires : Editorial Sudamericana
Vol.1: La Argentina era una fiesta 1946-1949. — 1984. — 607p. — *Includes 'Cronología - 4 de junio 1946 - 31 de diciembre 1949', p519-592*

LUNA, Félix
Perón y su tiempo / Félix Luna. — Buenos Aires : Editorial Sudamericana
Vol.2: La comunidad organizada, 1950-1952. — 1985. — 424p. — *Includes 'Cronología 1 de enero de 1950 - 31 de diciembre de 1952,' p [353]-393*

MACEYRA, Horacio
La segunda presidencia de Perón / Horacio Maceyra. — Buenos Aires : Centro Editor de América Latina, c1984. — 167 p.—. — (Biblioteca Política argentina ; 51) (Biblioteca Política argentina ; 51Las Presidencias peronistas). — *"Volumen especial (E)"--P. [4] of cover. — Includes bibliographies*

PAVÓN PEREYRA, Enrique
Perón tal como fue / Enrique Pavón Pereyra. — Buenos Aires : Centro Editor de América Latina. — (Biblioteca Política Argentina ; 137)
t.1. — 1986. — 139p

PERONISM
CHÁVEZ, Fermín
Perón y el peronismo en la historia contemporánea / Fermín Chávez. — Buenos Aires : Editorial Oriente. — *Includes bibliographical references*
t.2. — 1984. — 298p

GOLDAR, Ernesto
John William Cooke y el peronismo revolucionario / Ernesto Goldar. — Buenos Aires : Centro Editor de América Latina, 1985. — 140p. — (Biblioteca Política Argentina ; 99)

LATTUADA, Mario J.
La política agraria peronista (1943-1983) / Mario J. Lattuada. — Buenos Aires : Centro Editor de América Latina. — (Biblioteca Política Argentina ; 132)
t.1. — 1986. — 142p

MANGONE, Carlos
Universidad y peronismo (1946-1955) / Carlos Mongone y Jorge A. Warley. — Buenos Aires : Centro Editor de América Latina, 1986. — 161p. — (Biblioteca Política Argentina ; 83)

NARVAJA, Aurelio
Cuarenta años de Peronismo / Aurelio Narvaja, Angel Perelman, Jorge Abelardo Ramos. — Buenos Aires : Ediciones del Mar Dulce, 1985. — 158p

PAVÓN PEREYRA, Enrique
Perón tal como fue / Enrique Pavón Pereyra. — Buenos Aires : Centro Editor de América Latina. — (Biblioteca Política Argentina ; 137)
t.1. — 1986. — 139p

PERSECUTION — Europe — History
MOORE, R. I.
The formation of a persecuting society : power and deviance in Western Europe, 950-1250 / R.I. Moore. — Oxford : Basil Blackwell, 1987. — [192]p. — *Includes bibliography and index*

PERSECUTION — Europe — History — 16th century
LEVACK, Brian P.
The witch-hunt in early modern Europe / Brian P. Levack. — London : Longman, 1987. — [450]p. — *Bibliography: p435. — Includes index*

PERSECUTION — Europe — History — 17th century
LEVACK, Brian P.
The witch-hunt in early modern Europe / Brian P. Levack. — London : Longman, 1987. — [450]p. — *Bibliography: p435. — Includes index*

PERSECUTION — Soviet Union
Aufstehen! das Gericht kommt! : Gerichtsprozesse gegen Christen in der UdSSR / zusammengestellt und bearbeitet von H. Hartfeld. — Gummersbach : Friedensstimme, 1981. — 154p

PERSIAN GULF REGION — Armed Forces
MOTTALE, Morris Mehrdad
The arms buildup in the Persian Gulf / Morris Mehrdad Mottale. — Lanham, MD : University Press of America, c1986. — vii, 235 p.. — *Includes index. — Bibliography: p. 203-233*

PERSIAN GULF REGION — Defenses
EPSTEIN, Joshua M.
Strategy and force planning : the case of the Persian Gulf / Joshua M. Epstein. — Washington, D.C. : Brookings Institution, c1987. — xiii, 169 p.. — *Includes index. — Bibliography: p. 156-165*

SNYDER, Jed C
Defending the fringe : NATO, the Mediterranean, and the Gulf / Jed C. Snyder. — Boulder : Westview Press, 1986. — p. cm. — (SAIS papers in international affairs ; no. 11). — *Includes index*

PERSIAN GULF REGION — Foreign relations — Russia
YODFAT, Aryeh Y.
In the direction of the Persian Gulf : the Soviet Union and the Persian Gulf / A. Yodfat and M. Abir. — London : Cass, 1977. — xii,167p. — *Bibliography: p.154-158. — Includes index*

PERSIAN GULF REGION — Foreign relations — United States
KUNIHOLM, Bruce Robellet
The Persian Gulf and United States policy : a guide to issues and references / Bruce R. Kuniholm. — Claremont, Calif. : Regina Books, c1984. — vii, 220 p.. — (Guides to contemporary issues ; 3). — *Includes index. — Bibliography: p 145-211*

SIRRIYEH, Hussein
US policy in the Gulf, 1968-1977 : aftermath of British withdrawal / by Hussein Sirriyeh. — London : Ithaca, 1984. — 297p. — *Bibliography: p270-293. — Includes index*

PERSIAN GULF REGION — Foreign relations — United States — Bibliography

KUNIHOLM, Bruce Robellet
The Persian Gulf and United States policy : a guide to issues and references / Bruce R. Kuniholm. — Claremont, Calif. : Regina Books, c1984. — vii, 220 p.. — (Guides to contemporary issues ; 3). — Includes index. — Bibliography: p 145-211

PERSIAN GULF REGION — History

Arabia and the Gulf : from traditional society to modern states : essays in honour of M.A. Shaban's 60th birthday (16th November 1986) / edited by Ian Richard Netton. — London : Croom Helm, c1986. — [288]p. — Includes index

PERSIAN GULF REGION — Military relations — Soviet Union

EPSTEIN, Joshua M.
Strategy and force planning : the case of the Persian Gulf / Joshua M. Epstein. — Washington, D.C. : Brookings Institution, c1987. — xiii, 169 p.. — Includes index. — Bibliography: p. 156-165

PERSIAN GULF REGION — Military relations — United States

EPSTEIN, Joshua M.
Strategy and force planning : the case of the Persian Gulf / Joshua M. Epstein. — Washington, D.C. : Brookings Institution, c1987. — xiii, 169 p.. — Includes index. — Bibliography: p. 156-165

US strategic interests in the Gulf Region / edited by Wm.. — Boulder : Westview Press, 1987. — p. cm. — (Westview studies in regional security) (U.S. Army War College series on contemporary strategic issues). — Includes index

PERSIAN GULF REGION — Politics and government

HAMEED, Mazher A.
Saudi Arabia, the West and the security of the Gulf / Mazher A. Hameed ; foreword by James Schlesinger. — London : Croom Helm, 1986. — [xv,224]p. — Bibliography: p173-180. — Includes index

KUNIHOLM, Bruce Robellet
The Persian Gulf and United States policy : a guide to issues and references / Bruce R. Kuniholm. — Claremont, Calif. : Regina Books, c1984. — vii, 220 p.. — (Guides to contemporary issues ; 3). — Includes index. — Bibliography: p 145-211

MOTTALE, Morris Mehrdad
The arms buildup in the Persian Gulf / Morris Mehrdad Mottale. — Lanham, MD : University Press of America, c1986. — vii, 235 p.. — Includes index. — Bibliography: p. 203-233

NAKHLEH, Emile A.
The Gulf Cooperation Council : policies, problems, and prospects / Emile A. Nakhleh. — New York : Praeger, 1986. — xviii, 128 p.. — "Praeger special studies. Praeger scientific.". — Includes index. — Bibliography: p. 123-126

YODFAT, Aryeh Y.
In the direction of the Persian Gulf : the Soviet Union and the Persian Gulf / A. Yodfat and M. Abir. — London : Cass, 1977. — xii,167p. — Bibliography: p.154-158. — Includes index

PERSIAN GULF REGION — Politics and government — Bibliography

KUNIHOLM, Bruce Robellet
The Persian Gulf and United States policy : a guide to issues and references / Bruce R. Kuniholm. — Claremont, Calif. : Regina Books, c1984. — vii, 220 p.. — (Guides to contemporary issues ; 3). — Includes index. — Bibliography: p 145-211

PERSIAN GULF REGION — Strategic aspects

HAMEED, Mazher A.
Saudi Arabia, the West and the security of the Gulf / Mazher A. Hameed ; foreword by James Schlesinger. — London : Croom Helm, 1986. — [xv,224]p. — Bibliography: p173-180. — Includes index

US strategic interests in the Gulf Region / edited by Wm.. — Boulder : Westview Press, 1987. — p. cm. — (Westview studies in regional security) (U.S. Army War College series on contemporary strategic issues). — Includes index

PERSIAN GULF STATES — Foreign economic relations — Europe

YORKE, Valerie
European interests and Gulf oil / Valerie York and Louis Turner. — Aldershot : Gower, c1986. — x,125p. — (Energy papers ; no.17). — Includes index

PERSIAN LANGUAGE — Discourse analysis

BEEMAN, William O
Language, status, and power in Iran / William O. Beeman. — Bloomington : Indiana University Press, c1986. — xx, 255 p.. — (Advances in semiotics). — Includes indexes. — Bibliography: p. 213-235

PERSIAN LANGUAGE — Social aspects — Iran

BEEMAN, William O
Language, status, and power in Iran / William O. Beeman. — Bloomington : Indiana University Press, c1986. — xx, 255 p.. — (Advances in semiotics). — Includes indexes. — Bibliography: p. 213-235

PERSONAL INJURIES — England — Greater Manchester

GENN, Hazel
Meeting legal needs? : an evaluation of a scheme for personal injury victims / Hazel Genn. — Oxford : SSRC Centre for Socio-Legal Studies, 1982. — ix,69p. — A report commissioned by the Greater Manchester Legal Services Committee

PERSONALITY

COCHRAN, Larry
Position and the nature of personhood : an approach to the understanding of persons / Larry Cochran. — Westport, Conn. ; London : Greenwood Press, 1985. — xiv, 191p. — (Contributions in psychology ; no. 5). — Includes index. — Bibliography: p.[181]-187

DECI, Edward L
Intrinsic motivation and self-determination in human behavior / Edward L. Deci and Richard M. Ryan. — New York ; London : Plenum, c1985. — xv, 371 p.. — (Perspectives in social psychology). — Includes indexes. — Bibliography: p. 335-358

HAMPSON, Sarah E.
The construction of personality : an introduction / Sarah E. Hampson. — London ; Boston : Routledge & Kegan Paul, 1982. — 319p. — (Introductions to modern psychology). — Includes index. — Bibliography: p.[287]-310

JEHU, Derek
Learning theory and social work / Derek Jehu. — London : Routledge and Kegan Paul, 1967. — viii,139p. — Bibliography: p122-136. — Includes index

NEUMANN, Erich
The origins and history of consciousness / [by] Erich Neumann ; with a foreword by C. G. Jung ; translated from the German by R. F. C. Hull. — Princeton, N.J. : Princeton University Press, 1970. — xxiv,493p. — (Bollingen Series ; 42). — Originally published in German as 'Ursprungsgeschichte des Bewusstseins': Zurich: Rascher Verlag: 1949

Persons and personality : a contemporary enquiry / edited by Arthur Peacocke and Grant Gillett. — Oxford : Basil Blackwell, 1987. — viii,222p. — (Ian Ramsey Centre publication ; no.1). — Includes index

PERSONALITY — Research

HAMPSON, Sarah E.
The construction of personality : an introduction / Sarah E. Hampson. — London ; Boston : Routledge & Kegan Paul, 1982. — 319p. — (Introductions to modern psychology). — Includes index. — Bibliography: p.[287]-310

PERSONALITY AND CULTURE

LEE, Dorothy
Valuing the self : what we can learn from other cultures / Dorothy Lee. — Prospect Heights, I11 : Waveland Press, 1986. — xii,87p

WATSON, Lawrence Craig
Interpreting life histories : an anthropological inquiry / Lawrence C. Watson, Maria-Barbara Watson-Franke. — New Brunswick, N.J. : Rutgers University Press, c1985. — x, 228 p.. — Includes index. — Bibliography: p. [207]-222

PERSONALITY AND OCCUPATION — Michigan — Longitudinal studies

MORTIMER, Jeylan T.
Work, family, and personality : transition to adulthood / Jeylan T. Mortimer, Jon Lorence, Donald S. Kumka. — Norwood, N.J. : Ablex Pub. Corp., c1986. — viii, 267 p.. — (Modern sociology). — Includes index. — Bibliography: p. 231-255

PERSONALITY ASSESSMENT

Personality assessment in organizations / edited by H. John Bernardin and David A. Bownas. — New York : Praeger, 1985. — p. cm. — Includes index

PERSONALITY (LAW) — Australia

MURUMBA, Samuel K.
Commercial exploitation of personality / by Samuel K. Murumba. — North Ryde, N.S.W., 1986. — xvii,184p. — Bibliogrpahy: p.171-174. - Includes index. — Includes the text of a Draft Commonwealth Bill for an Unfair Publication Act

PERSONALITY TESTS

LAKE, Dale G
Measuring human behavior : tools for the assessment of social functioning / [by] Dale G. Lake, Matthew B. Miles [and] Ralph B. Earle, Jr. — New York : Teachers College Press, [1973]. — xviii, 422 p. — Includes bibliographies

PERSONALS — Great Britain — History

WINKWORTH, Stephen
Room two more guns : the intriguing history of the personal column of the Times / Stephen Winkworth. — London : Allen & Unwin, 1986. — [280]p. — Includes index

PERSONNEL MANAGEMENT

Flexibility and jobs : myths and realities : (a research report of the European Trade Union Institute) / (prepared by John Evans, Rafael Nedzynski and Gosta Karlsson). — Brussels : ETUI, [1985]. — 157p

Human resources management : a general manager's perspective : text and cases / Michael Beer ... [et al.]. — New York : Free Press, c1985. — p. cm. — Includes index

WATSON, Tony J.
Management, organisation and employment strategy : new directions in theory and practice / Tony J. Watson. — London : Routledge and Kegan Paul, 1986. — xiv,258p. — Bibliography: p241-253

PERSONNEL MANAGEMENT — Case studies

Human resources management : a general manager's perspective : text and cases / Michael Beer ... [et al.]. — New York : Free Press, c1985. — p. cm. — Includes index

PERSONNEL MANAGEMENT — Libraries
JOINT ANNUAL STUDY CONFERENCE OF THE COLLEGES OF FURTHER AND HIGHER EDUCATION GROUP AND THE EDUCATION LIBRARIANS GROUP OF THE LIBRARY ASSOCIATION (1985 : Chester)
Management issues in university libraries : proceedings of the Joint Annual Study Conference of the Colleges of Further and Higher Education Group and the Education Librarians Group of the Library Association, 1-4 April 1985 / edited by Tim Lomas. — London : Rossendale, c1986. — 84p

PERSONNEL MANAGEMENT — methods
MEISTER, David
Behavioral analysis and measurement methods / David Meister. — New York : Wiley, c1985. — xiii, 509 p.. — "A Wiley-Interscience publication.". — Includes bibliographies and index

PERSONNEL MANAGEMENT — Research
Generalizing from laboratory to field settings : research findings from industrial-organizational psychology, organizational behavior, and human resource management / edited by Edwin A. Locke. — Lexington, Mass. : Lexington Books, c1986. — x, 291 p.. — (The Issues in organization and management series). — Includes bibliographies and index

PERSONNEL MANAGEMENT — Canada
WELLS, Don
Soft sell : "quality of life" programs and the productivity race / by Don Wells. — Ottawa : Canadian Centre for Policy Alternatives, 1986. — xi,97p

PERSONNEL MANAGEMENT — Great Britain
ADVISORY, CONCILIATION AND ARBITRATION SERVICE
Developments in harmonisation. — [London : the Service], 1982. — 15p. — (Discussion paper ; no.1). — Includes Bibliographical references

PERSONNEL MANAGEMENT — Great Britain — Automation
NATIONAL CONFERENCE AND EXHIBITION ON COMPUTERS IN PERSONNEL (5th : 1986)
Computers in personnel : from potential to performance; published in association with CIP 86, the Fifth National Conference and Exhibition on Computers in Personnel, 8-10 July 1986 / edited by Terry Page. — Brighton : Institute of Manpower Studies, University of Sussex ; London : Institute of Personnel Management, 1986. — 105p. — (IMS Report ; No.120)

PERSONNEL MANAGEMENT — Great Britain — Case studies
CONFEDERATION OF BRITISH INDUSTRY
Managing change : the organisation of work / CBI. — London : Confederation of British Industry, 1985. — 99p

PERSONNEL MANAGEMENT — United States
GOLEMBIEWSKI, Robert T.
Humanizing public relations : perspectives on doing better-than-average when average ain't at all bad / Robert T. Golembiewski. — Mt. Airy, Md. : Lomond, 1985. — viii,377

PERSONNEL SERVICE IN SECONDARY EDUCATION — European Economic Community countries
MCMULLEN, I. R.
Guidance and orientation in secondary schools / I. R. McMullen. — Luxembourg : Office for Official Publications of the European Communities, 1977. — 60p. — (Education series / Commission of the European Communities ; no.2)

PERSONS (ISLAMIC LAW)
NASIR, Jamal J.
The Islamic law of personal status / Jamal J. Nasir. — London : Graham & Trotman, 1986. — xiv,328p. — Bibliography: p314-319. — Includes index

PEARL, David
A textbook on Muslim personal law / David Pearl. — 2nd ed. — London : Croom Helm, c1987. — 284p. — Previous ed.: published as a Textbook on Muslim Law. 1979. — Bibliography: p260-265. — Includes index

PERSUASION (PSYCHOLOGY)
Cognitive responses in persuasion / edited by Richard E. Petty, Thomas M. Ostrom, and Timothy C. Brock. — Hillsdale, N.J. : L. Erlbaum Associates, 1981. — xv,476p. — Includes index. — Bibliography: p

JOWETT, Garth
Propaganda and persuasion / by gGarth s. Jowett and Victoria O'Donnell. — Newbury Park, Calif. : Sage, c1986. — 236 p., [8] p. of plates. — (People and communication ; v. 18). — Includes index. — Bibliography: p. 219-225

PETTY, Richard E
Communication and persuasion : central and peripheral routes to attitude change / Richard E. Petty, John T. Cacioppo. — New York : Springer-Verlag, c1986. — xiv, 262 p.. — (Springer series in social psychology). — Includes indexes. — Bibliography: p. [225]-247

PERU — Economic conditions
Social and economic change in modern Peru / edited by Rory Miller, Clifford T. Smith and John Fisher. — [Liverpool] ([P.O. Box 147, Liverpool L69 3BX]) : Centre for Latin-American Studies, University of Liverpool, [1976]. — [5],197p. — (Monograph series / University of Liverpool. Centre for Latin-American Studies ; no.6). — 'The papers ... originated in a conference at the Centre for Latin-American Studies in Liverpool University in February 1974' - Introduction. — Bibliography: p.194-197

PERU — Economic conditions — 1968-
SALAVERRY LLOSA, José A.
Peru, desarrollo y política económica / José A. Salaverry Llosa. — [Lima] : Ministerio de Economía y Finanzas Dirección General de Asuntos Financieros, 1974. — 15leaves

PERU — Economic policy
BARUA CASTAÑEDA, Luis
Exposición televisada del Señor Ministro de Economía y Finanzas... con motivo de las medidas económicas complementarias que ha adoptado el Gobierno Revolucionario de la Fuerza Armada en la fecha / Luis Barua Castañeda. — [Lima] : Ministerio de Economía y Finanzas, Oficina de Relaciones Públicas, 1976. — 14leaves

JIMÉNEZ DE LUCIO, Alberto
Plan bienal 1975-76 del sector industria y turismo : exposición al pais por televisión y radio / Alberto Jiménez de Lucio. — [Lima : Ministerio de Industria y Turismo, Oficina de Relaciones Públicas e Información, ca.1975]. — [12]p. — Cover title: Perú en su mayor expansión industrial

SALAVERRY LLOSA, José A.
Peru, desarrollo y política económica / José A. Salaverry Llosa. — [Lima] : Ministerio de Economía y Finanzas Dirección General de Asuntos Financieros, 1974. — 15leaves

PERU — Executive departments — Legal status, laws, etc.
PERU
[Decreto ley no.17521]. Ley orgánica del Ministerio de Hacienda : Decreto ley no.17521. — [Lima : Presidencia?, 1969]. — [7]leaves

PERU
[Decreto ley no.17703]. El Ministerio de Hacienda sera denominado de Economía y Finanzas : Decreto ley no.17703. — [Lima : Presidencia?, 1969]. — 3leaves

PERU — History — Dictionaries
ALISKY, Marvin
Historical dictionary of Peru / Marvin Alisky. — Metuchen, N.J : Scarecrow Press, 1979. — (Latin American historical dictionaries ; no. 20). — Bibliography: p

PERU — Officials and employees
PERU. Dirección nacional de Personal. Programa Participación de los TAP
Nueva política de incentivos para los trabajadores de la administración pública. — [Lima] : the Dirección, [197-?]. — 35p. — Documento de trabajo. — Bibliography: p[35]

PERU — Politics and government — 1968-
RODRÍGUEZ RIVAS, Miguel
La participación en la administración pública a : programa; política y realidad / [Miguel Rodríguez Rivas]. — [Lima] : Instituto Nacional de Admnistración Pública, [197-?]. — 10leaves

TOVAR, Teresa
Velasquismo y movimiento popular : otra historia prohibida / Teresa Tovar. — Lima : Centro de Estudios y Promoción del Desarrollo, 1985. — 399p. — Bibliography: p395-399

VELASCO ALVARADO, Juan
Mansaje a la nación ... con motivo de los incidentes ocurridos en Lima los días 05 y 06 de febrero / Juan Velasco Alvarado. — Lima : [Secretaría de Prensa, Presidencia de la República], 1975. — 14p

PERU — Population — Statistics
O'MUIRCHEARTAIGH, C. A.
The magnitude and pattern of response variance in the Peru Fertility survey / C.A. O'Muircheartaigh. — Voorburg : International Statistical Institute, 1984. — 39p. — (Scientific reports / World Fertility Survey ; no.45)

PERU — Rural conditions
La cuestión rural en el Perú / Javier Iguíñiz. — 2a ed. — Lima : Pontifica Universidad Católica del Perú Fondo Editorial, 1986. — 332p. — "Una recopilación de ensayos elaborados por profesores - investigadores de los Departamentos de Economiá y Ciencias Sociales de la Pontífica Universidad Católica del Perú". — Includes bibliographies

PERU — Rural population
La cuestión rural en el Perú / Javier Iguíñiz. — 2a ed. — Lima : Pontifica Universidad Católica del Perú Fondo Editorial, 1986. — 332p. — "Una recopilación de ensayos elaborados por profesores - investigadores de los Departamentos de Economiá y Ciencias Sociales de la Pontífica Universidad Católica del Perú". — Includes bibliographies

PERU — Social conditions — Addresses, essays, lectures
Social and economic change in modern Peru / edited by Rory Miller, Clifford T. Smith and John Fisher. — [Liverpool] ([P.O. Box 147, Liverpool L69 3BX]) : Centre for Latin-American Studies, University of Liverpool, [1976]. — [5],197p. — (Monograph series / University of Liverpool. Centre for Latin-American Studies ; no.6). — 'The papers ... originated in a conference at the Centre for Latin-American Studies in Liverpool University in February 1974' - Introduction. — Bibliography: p.194-197

PERU — Statistics, Vital
MOSER, Kath
Levels and trends in child and adult mortality in Peru / Kath Moser. — Voorburg : International Statistical Institute, 1985. — 42p. — (Scientific reports / World Fertility Survey ; no.77)

PERU. Junta de Supervigilancia de Películas — Legal status, laws, etc.
PERU
[Laws, etc]. Junta de Supervigilancia de Películas y su reglamento. — Lima : Oficina Central de Información, 1974. — 25p

PERU. Junta Nacional de Mano de Obra
PERU. Servicio del Empleo y Recursos Humanos Junta Nacional de Mano de Obra. — [Lima : the Servicio, ca.1970]. — [12p]

PERU. Ministerio de Economía y Finanzas — Legal status, laws, etc.
PERU
[Decreto ley no.17703]. El Ministerio de Hacienda sera denominado de Economía y Finanzas : Decreto ley no.17703. — [Lima : Presidencia?, 1969]. — 3leaves

PERU. Ministerio de Hacienda — Legal status, laws, etc.
PERU
[Decreto ley no.17521]. Ley orgánica del Ministerio de Hacienda : Decreto ley no.17521. — [Lima : Presidencia?, 1969]. — [7]leaves

PERU
[Decreto ley no.17703]. El Ministerio de Hacienda sera denominado de Economía y Finanzas : Decreto ley no.17703. — [Lima : Presidencia?, 1969]. — 3leaves

PERU. Sistema Nacional de Información — Legal status, laws, etc.
PERU
[Laws, etc]. Ley orgánica del Sistema Nacional de Información. — Lima : [Oficina Central de Información, Oficina de Relaciones Públicas, ca.1975]. — 38p

PESSOA (Family)
LEWIN, Linda
Politic and Parentela in Paraíba : a case study of family-based oligarchy in Brazil / Linda Lewin. — Princeton, N.J. : Princeton University Press, c1987. — p. cm. — *Includes index. — Bibliography: p*

PESTICIDE RESIDUES IN FOOD
ERLICHMAN, James
Gluttons for punishment / James Erlichman. — Harmondsworth : Penguin Books, 1986. — 156p

PESTICIDES — Environmental aspects — Organisation for Economic Co-operation and Development countries
Water pollution by fertilizers and pesticides. — Paris : Organisation for Economic Co-operation and Development, 1986. — 144p. — *Includes bibliographical references*

PESTICIDES INDUSTRY — Developing countries
WEIR, David
The Bhopal syndrome : pesticide manufacturing and the Third World / by David Weir ; with an afterword by Claude Alvares. — Penang : International Organization of Consumers Union Regional Office for Asia and the Pacific, 1986. — vii,117p

PESTICIDES INDUSTRY — India — Accidents
MOREHOUSE, Ward
The Bhopal tragedy : what really happened and what it means for American workers and communities at risk / by Ward Morehouse and M. Arun Subramaniam. — [New York] : [Council on International and Public Affairs], [1986]. — xiii,190p. — *A report for the Citizens Commission on Bhopal. — Bibliography: p139-144*

PETRÓLEOS MEXICANOS
Energy efficiency and conservation in Mexico : perspectives on efficiency and conservation policies / edited by Oscar Guzmán, Antonio Yúnez-Naude, Miguel S. Wionczek. — Boulder, Colo. : Westview Press, 1986. — p. cm. — (Westview special studies on Latin America and the Caribbean). — *Bibliography: p*

PETROLEUM — Developing countries — Reserves
FEE, D. A.
Oil and gas databook for ACP countries : with special reference to the ACP countries / Derek Fee. — London : Graham & Trotman, 1985. — 215p

PETROLEUM — Taxation — Law and legislation — Great Britain
GREAT BRITAIN. Parliament. House of Commons. Library. Research Division
The Oil Taxation Bill / Timothy Edmonds. — [London] : the Division, 1983. — 6p. — (Reference sheet ; no.83/18)

PETROLEUM — South Africa — Transportation
SHIPPING RESEARCH BUREAU
Secret oil deliveries to South Africa 1981-1982 / published by The Shipping Research Bureau. — Amsterdam : the Bureau, 1984. — 104p

PETROLEUM CHEMICALS INDUSTRY
FAYAD, Marwan
The economics of the petrochemical industry / Marwan Fayad and Homa Motamen. — London : Pinter, 1986. — [xiii],241p. — *Bibliography: p144-151. — Includes index*

PETROLEUM CHEMICALS INDUSTRY — Management
BOWER, Joseph L
When markets quake : the management challenge of restructuring industry / Joseph L. Bower. — Boston, Mass. : Harvard Business School Press, c1986. — xi, 240 p.. — *Includes bibliographies and index*

PETROLEUM CHEMICALS INDUSTRY — China — Congresses
China's petroleum industry in the international context / edited by Fereidun Fesharaki and David Fridley. — Boulder [Colo.] : Westview Press, 1986. — xvii, 166 p.. — (Westview special studies in international economics and business). — *"Proceedings of the China Energy Workshop I: Petroleum Processing, conducted at the East-West Center, Honolulu, Hawaii, 25-26 April 1985, organized by the Resource Systems Institute of the East-West Center."*

PETROLEUM IN SUBMERGED LANDS — Asia, Southeastern
VALENCIA, Mark J.
South-East Asian seas : oil under troubled waters : hydrocarbon potential, jurisdictional issues, and international relations / Mark J. Valencia. — Oxford ; New York : Oxford University Press, 1985. — xiv,155p. — (Natural Resources of South-East Asia). — *Bibliography: p137-146*

PETROLEUM IN SUBMERGED LANDS — Georges Bank
MACLEISH, William H.
Oil and water : the struggle for Georges Bank / by William H. MacLeish. — 1st ed. — Boston : Atlantic Monthly Press, c1985. — 304 p.. — *Includes index*

PETROLEUM IN SUBMERGED LANDS — North Sea
DAM, Kenneth W
Oil resources : who gets what how? / Kenneth W. Dam. — Chicago : University of Chicago Press, 1976. — xi, 193 p.. — *Includes bibliographical references and index*

OKLAHOMA. University. Science and Public Policy Program. Technology Assessment Group
North Sea oil and gas : implications for future United States development / [by] Irvin L. White [and others] A study sponsored by the Council on Environmental Quality. — [1st ed.]. — Norman : University of Oklahoma Press, [c1973]. — xiii, 176 p. — *Includes bibliographical references*

PETROLEUM INDUSTRY AND TRADE
AHRARI, Mohammed E
OPEC : the failing giant / Mohammed E. Ahrari. — Lexington, KY : University Press of Kentucky, 1986. — 256p. — *Includes index. — Bibliography: p.[232]-249*

BROWN, Stewart L
Trading energy futures : a manual for energy industry professionals / Stewart L. Brown and Steven Errera. — New York : Quorum Books, c1986. — p. cm. — *Includes index. — Bibliography: p*

CLUBLEY, Sally
Trading in oil futures / Sally Clubley. — Cambridge : Woodhead-Faulkner, 1986. — [112]p. — *Includes index*

The International oil industry : an interdisciplinary perspective / edited by Judith Rees and Peter Odell. — Basingstoke : Macmillan, 1986. — xii,181p. — *Includes bibliographies and index*

MEIR, Shemuel
Strategic implications of the new oil reality / Shemuel Meir. — Boulder : Westview Press for Jaffee Center for Strategic Studies, Tel Aviv University, 1986. — 107p. — (JCSS study ; No.4)

ODELL, Peter R.
Oil and world power / Peter R. Odell. — 8th ed. — Harmondsworth : Penguin, 1986. — 314p

TÉTREAULT, Mary Ann
Revolution in the world petroleum market / Mary Ann Tetreault. — Westport, Conn. : Quorum Books, c1985. — p. cm. — *Includes bibliographies and index*

PETROLEUM INDUSTRY AND TRADE — Accounting
HEAZLEWOOD, C. T.
Financial accounting and reporting in the oil and gas industry : (a discussion of selected issues including a survey of United Kingdom company practices) / by C. T. Heazlewood. — [S.l.] : Institute of Chartered Accountants in England and Wales, [1987?]. — x,119p. — (Research paper / Institute of Chartered Accountants in England and Wales. Research Board). — *Bibliography: p107-119*

PETROLEUM INDUSTRY AND TRADE — Congresses
INTERNATIONAL ASSOCIATION OF ENERGY ECONOMISTS. North American Meeting (1985 : Philadelphia, Pa.)
World energy markets : stability or cyclical change? : proceedings, Seventh Annual North American Meeting, International Association of Energy Economists, Philadelphia, Pennsylvania, December 1985 / edited by William F. Thompson and David J. DeAngelo. — Boulder : Westview Press, 1985. — xiii, 690 p.. — (Westview special studies in natural resources and energy management). — *Includes bibliographies*

PETROLEUM INDUSTRY AND TRADE — Government ownership
DAM, Kenneth W
Oil resources : who gets what how? / Kenneth W. Dam. — Chicago : University of Chicago Press, 1976. — xi, 193 p.. — *Includes bibliographical references and index*

PETROLEUM INDUSTRY AND TRADE — Government ownership — Case studies
KLAPP, Merrie Gilbert
The sovereign entrepreneur : oil policies in advanced and less developed capitalist countries / Merrie Gilbert Klapp. — Itaca : Cornell University Press, 1987. — 244 p.. — (Cornell studies in political economy). — *Includes index. — Bibliography: p. 211-229*

PETROLEUM INDUSTRY AND TRADE — Government policy — Case studies
KLAPP, Merrie Gilbert
The sovereign entrepreneur : oil policies in advanced and less developed capitalist countries / Merrie Gilbert Klapp. — Itaca : Cornell University Press, 1987. — 244 p.. — (Cornell studies in political economy). — *Includes index. — Bibliography: p. 211-229*

PETROLEUM INDUSTRY AND TRADE — Government policy — Congresses

IAEE CONFERENCE ((7th : 1985 : Bonn, Germany)
Energy and economy, global interdependences : papers of the plenary sessions of the 1985 International Conference of the International Association of Energy Economists (IAEE) and its German Chapter, the Gesellschaft für Energiewissenschaft und Energiepolitik (GEE) / Mark Baier (Hrsg.). — Köln : Verlag TÜV Rheinland, c1986. — 183 p.. — *Includes bibliographies*

PETROLEUM INDUSTRY AND TRADE — Government policy — Great Britain

MCBETH, B. S.
British oil policy 1919-1939 / B.S. McBeth. — London : Cass, 1985. — xvii,171p,16p of plates . — *Bibliography: p150-164. — Includes index*

PETROLEUM INDUSTRY AND TRADE — Government policy — United States

BULL-BERG, Hans Jacob
American international oil policy : causal factors and effect / Hans Jacob Bull-Berg. — London : Pinter, 1987. — xvi,209p. — *Bibliography: p191-201. — Includes index*

PETROLEUM INDUSTRY AND TRADE — History

GREENE, William N
Strategies of the major oil companies / by William N. Greene. — Ann Arbor, Mich. : UMI Research Press, c1985. — p. cm. — (Research for business decisions ; no. 70). — : Revision of thesis (Ph.D.)--Harvard University, 1982. — *Includes index. — Bibliography: p*

PETROLEUM INDUSTRY AND TRADE — History — 20th century

GHANEM, Shukri
OPEC : the rise and fall of an exclusive club / Shukri Ghanem. — London : KPI, 1986. — x,233p. — *Includes bibliographies and index*

PETROLEUM INDUSTRY AND TRADE — International cooperation — Congresses

IAEE CONFERENCE ((7th : 1985 : Bonn, Germany)
Energy and economy, global interdependences : papers of the plenary sessions of the 1985 International Conference of the International Association of Energy Economists (IAEE) and its German Chapter, the Gesellschaft für Energiewissenschaft und Energiepolitik (GEE) / Mark Baier (Hrsg.). — Köln : Verlag TÜV Rheinland, c1986. — 183 p.. — *Includes bibliographies*

PETROLEUM INDUSTRY AND TRADE — Licenses — Great Britain

DAM, Kenneth W
Oil resources : who gets what how? / Kenneth W. Dam. — Chicago : University of Chicago Press, 1976. — xi, 193 p.. — *Includes bibliographical references and index*

PETROLEUM INDUSTRY AND TRADE — Licenses — Norway

DAM, Kenneth W
Oil resources : who gets what how? / Kenneth W. Dam. — Chicago : University of Chicago Press, 1976. — xi, 193 p.. — *Includes bibliographical references and index*

PETROLEUM INDUSTRY AND TRADE — Management — Case studies

GRAYSON, Leslie E
Who and how in planning for large companies / by Leslie E. Grayson. — New York : St. Martin's Press, 1986. — p. cm. — *Includes index*

PETROLEUM INDUSTRY AND TRADE — Political aspects — Near East

The politics of Middle Eastern Oil / [edited by] J. E. Peterson. — Washington : Middle East Institute, 1983. — xx,529p. — *Bibliography: p491-521*

PETROLEUM INDUSTRY AND TRADE — Political aspects — Soviet Union

STERN, Jonathan P.
Soviet oil and gas exports to the west : commercial transaction or security threat? / Jonathan P. Stern. — Aldershot : Gower, 1987. — xi,123p. — (Energy papers ; no.21). — *Bibliographical notes*

PETROLEUM INDUSTRY AND TRADE — Taxation

GOSS, Christopher
Petroleum and mining taxation : handbook on a method for equitable sharing of profits and risk / Christopher Goss. — Aldershot : Gower, c1986. — xiv,69p. — (Energy papers ; no.19)

PETROLEUM INDUSTRY AND TRADE — Argentina — History

GARCÍA MOLINA, Fernando
El general Uriburu y el petróleo / Fernando García Molina, Carlos A. Mayo. — Buenos Aires : Centro Editor de América Latina, 1985. — 156p. — (Biblioteca Política Argenta ; 96) . — *Bibliographical notes: p129-156*

PETROLEUM INDUSTRY AND TRADE — Canada

CANADA. Petroleum Incentives Administration
Annual report / Petroleum Incentives Administration. — Ottawa : Energy, Mines and Resources Canada, 1984-. — *Annual*

FOSTER, Peter
The blue-eyed sheiks : the Canadian oil establishment / Peter Foster. — Rev. and enl. ed. — Toronto : Totem, 1980. — 410p. — *First published 1979*

PETROLEUM INDUSTRY AND TRADE — China — Congresses

China's petroleum industry in the international context / edited by Fereidun Fesharaki and David Fridley. — Boulder [Colo.] : Westview Press, 1986. — xvii, 166 p.. — (Westview special studies in international economics and business). — *"Proceedings of the China Energy Workshop I: Petroleum Processing, conducted at the East-West Center, Honolulu, Hawaii, 25-26 April 1985, organized by the Resource Systems Institute of the East-West Center."*

PETROLEUM INDUSTRY AND TRADE — Ecuador

MARTZ, John D
Politics and petroleum in Ecuador / John D. Martz. — New Brunswick, N.J. : Transaction, c1986. — p. cm. — *Includes index. — Bibliography: p*

PETROLEUM INDUSTRY AND TRADE — Ecuador — Statistics

Estadistica mensual de hidrocarburos / Direccion Nacional de Hidrocarburos. — Quito : Dpto. de Estadistica e Informacion Hidrocarburifera, 1985-. — *Monthly*

PETROLEUM INDUSTRY AND TRADE — France

BONON, Jean-Pierre
La situation et l'avenir de l'industrie du pétrole / rapport présenté par Jean-Pierre Bonon, Gaston Richard. — Rouen : Comité économique et social de Haute-Normandie, 1986. — 2v. — *Cover title*

PETROLEUM INDUSTRY AND TRADE — Great Britain

BEAN, Charles R.
The macroeconomic consequences of North Sea Oil / C. Bean. — London : Centre for Labour Economics, London School of Economics, 1986. — 57p. — (Discussion paper / London School of Economics and Political Science. Centre for Labour Economics ; no.262). — *Bibliography: p53-57*

BEAN, Charles R.
Real wage rigidity and the effect of an oil discovery / C. Bean. — London : Centre for Labour Economics, London School of Economics, 1986. — 15p. — (Discussion paper / London School of Economics and Political Science. Centre for Labour Economics ; no.269). — *Bibliography: p13-15*

BRITISH NATIONAL OIL CORPORATION
The British National Oil Corporation. — [Glasgow] : the Corporation, 1978. — 12p

BRITISH NATIONAL OIL CORPORATION
Report and accounts / British National Oil Corporation. — London : the Corporation, 1976-1984. — *Annual. — Continued by Britoil annual report*

Britoil annual report. — Glasgow : Britoil, 1985-. — *Annual. — Continues: Report and accounts/British National Oil Corporation*

GREAT BRITAIN. Parliament. House of Commons. Library. Research Division
The economic background to the March 1986 budget : oil and the UK economy / Christopher Barclay. — [London] : the Division, 1986. — 13p. — (Background paper ; no.181)

KEMP, Alexander G.
Fiscal aspects of field abandonment in the UKCS / Alexander G. Kemp, David Rose, assisted by Barbara Creed. — Aberdeen : University of Aberdeen. Department of Economics, 1985. — iv,55p. — (North Sea study occasional paper ; no.22)

MACKAY, Donald Iain
The political economy of North Sea oil / D. I. MacKay & G. A. Mackay. — Boulder, Colo. : Westview Press, 1975. — ix, 193 p.. — *Includes bibliographical references and index*

PETROLEUM INDUSTRY AND TRADE — Italy

BAZZOLI, Luigi
Il miracolo Mattei / Luigi Bazzoli & Riccardo Renzi. — Milano : Rizzoli, 1984. — 258p. — *Bibliography: p251-2*

PETROLEUM INDUSTRY AND TRADE — Mexico — Energy consumption

Energy efficiency and conservation in Mexico : perspectives on efficiency and conservation policies / edited by Oscar Guzmán, Antonio Yúnez-Naude, Miguel S. Wionczek. — Boulder, Colo. : Westview Press, 1986. — p. cm. — (Westview special studies on Latin America and the Caribbean). — *Bibliography: p*

PETROLEUM INDUSTRY AND TRADE — Nigeria

State, oil, and agriculture in Nigeria / Michael Watts, editor. — Berkeley : Institute of International Studies, University of California, c1987. — xiv, 327 p.. — (Research series ; no. 66). — *Includes index. — Bibliography: p. 297-317*

PETROLEUM INDUSTRY AND TRADE — Norway

NORENG, Øjstein
Olje-Norge : det bevisstlose eksperiment / Øystein Noreng. — Oslo : Aschehoug, 1984. — 167p

PETROLEUM INDUSTRY AND TRADE — South Africa

SHIPPING RESEARCH BUREAU
Secret oil deliveries to South Africa 1981-1982 / published by The Shipping Research Bureau. — Amsterdam : the Bureau, 1984. — 104p

PETROLEUM INDUSTRY AND TRADE — United States

HULBERT, Mark
Interlock : the untold story of American banks, oil interests, the Shah's money, debts and the astounding connections between them / Mark Hulbert. — New York : Richardson and Snyder, 1982. — 272p

KARLSSON, Svante
Oil and the world order : American foreign oil policy / Svante Karlsson. — Leamington Spa : Berg, 1986. — 308p. — *Bibliography: p293-297. — Includes index*

PETROLEUM INDUSTRY AND TRADE — United States — Consolidation

GHOSH, Arabinda
Competition and diversification in the United States petroleum industry / Arabinda Ghosh. — Westport, Conn. : Quorum Books, c1985. — p. cm. — *Includes index. — Bibliography: p*

PETROLEUM INDUSTRY AND TRADE — United States — History

PAINTER, David S.
Private power and public policy : multinational oil corporations and United States foreign policy 1941-1954 / David S. Painter. — London : Tauris, 1986. — [300]p. — *Includes bibliography and index*

PETROLEUM INDUSTRY AND TRADE — Zimbabwe — Bibliography

GREAT BRITAIN. Parliament. House of Commons. Library. International Affairs Section
The Bingham Report : a background bibliography / [Carole B. Mann]. — [London] : the Library, 1978. — 6leaves. — (Reference sheet / House of Commons. Library. Research Division ; no.78/9)

GREAT BRITAIN. Parliament. House of Commons. Library. International Affairs Section
The Bingham Report : a background bibliography; addenda: November 1978-January 1979 / [Carole B. Mann]. — [London] : the Library, 1979. — 2leaves. — ([Reference sheet] / House of Commons. Library. [Research Division] ; no.78/9: Addenda)

PETROLEUM LAW AND LEGISLATION

BOLLECKER-STERN, Brigitte
Droit économique / Brigitte Bollecker-Stern, Maurice Dahan, Lazare Kopelmanas. — Paris : Pedone, 1978. — 166p. — (Cours et travaux / Institut des hautes études internationales de Paris)

HOOPER, Lisa
The regulation of lead levels in petrol / by Lisa Hooper. — Colchester : Department of Government University of Essex, 1987. — 27 p. — (Essex papers in politics and government ; no.36)

PETROLEUM LAW AND LEGISLATION — Great Britain

GREAT BRITAIN. Parliament. House of Commons. Library. Research Division
Oil and Gas (Enterprise) Bill / [B. L. Miller]. — [London] : the Division, 1982. — 17p. — (Reference sheet ; no.82/1). — *Bibliography: p15-17*

PETROLEUM LAW AND LEGISLATION — Nigeria

ETIKERENTSE, G.
Nigerian petroleum law / G. Etikerentse. — London : Macmillan, 1985. — x,356p. — *Includes index*

PETROLEUM PRODUCTS — Prices

STOURHARAS, Yannis
Are oil price movements perverse! : a critical explanation of oil price levels 1950-1985 / Yannis Stourharas. — Oxford : Oxford Institute for Energy Studies, 1985. — 61p. — *Bibliography: p59-61*

PETROLEUM PRODUCTS — Prices — Congresses

IAEE CONFERENCE ((7th : 1985 : Bonn, Germany)
Energy and economy, global interdependences : papers of the plenary sessions of the 1985 International Conference of the International Association of Energy Economists (IAEE) and its German Chapter, the Gesellschaft für Energiewissenschaft und Energiepolitik (GEE) / Mark Baier (Hrsg.). — Köln : Verlag TÜV Rheinland, c1986. — 183 p.. — *Includes bibliographies*

INTERNATIONAL ASSOCIATION OF ENERGY ECONOMISTS. North American Meeting (1985 : Philadelphia, Pa.)
World energy markets : stability or cyclical change? : proceedings, Seventh Annual North American Meeting, International Association of Energy Economists, Philadelphia, Pennsylvania, December 1985 / edited by William F. Thompson and David J. DeAngelo. — Boulder : Westview Press, 1985. — xiii, 690 p.. — (Westview special studies in natural resources and energy management). — *Includes bibliographies*

PETROLEUM PRODUCTS — Prices — Mathematical models

Macroeconomics [i.e. Macroeconimic] impacts of energy shocks / edited by Bert G. Hickman, Hillard G. Huntington, and James L. Sweeney. — Amsterdam ; New York : North-Holland ; New York, N.Y., U.S.A. : Sole distributors for the U.S.A. and Canada, Elsevier Science Pub. Co., 1987. — xvi, 331 p.. — (Contributions to economic analysis ; 163). — *Includes bibliographical references*

PETROLEUM PRODUCTS — Prices — Great Britain

ALOGOSKOUFIS, George S.
Competitiveness, oil prices and government expenditure in the United Kingdom business cycle / George Alogoskoufis. — London : Centre for Economic Policy Research, 1987. — 28p. — (Discussion paper series / Centre for Economic Policy Research ; no.184). — *Bibliography: p22-23*

PETROV, EVDOKIA

WHITLAM, Nicholas
Nest of traitors : the Petrov affair / Nicholas Whitlam, John Stubbs. — 2nd ed. — St. Lucia ; New York : University of Queensland Press, 1985. — xii, 259 p., [16] p. of plates. — *Includes index. — Bibliography: p. 251-253*

PETROV, VLADIMIR MIKHAĬLOVICH

WHITLAM, Nicholas
Nest of traitors : the Petrov affair / Nicholas Whitlam, John Stubbs. — 2nd ed. — St. Lucia ; New York : University of Queensland Press, 1985. — xii, 259 p., [16] p. of plates. — *Includes index. — Bibliography: p. 251-253*

PHARMACEUTICAL POLICY — Bangladesh

ROLT, Francis
Pills, policies and profits : reactions to the Bangladesh drug policy / by Francis Rolt. — London : War on Want, 1985. — 114p

PHILADELPHIA (PA.) — Commerce — History — 18th century

DOERFLINGER, Thomas M
A vigorous spirit of enterprise : merchants and economic development in Revolutionary Philadelphia / Thomas M. Doerflinger. — Chapel Hill : Published for the Institute of Early American History and Culture, Williamsburg, Va. by the University of North Carolina Press, c1986. — xvi, 413 p.. — *Includes index. — Bibliography: p. [383]-398*

PHILADELPHIA (PA.) — Economic conditions

DOERFLINGER, Thomas M
A vigorous spirit of enterprise : merchants and economic development in Revolutionary Philadelphia / Thomas M. Doerflinger. — Chapel Hill : Published for the Institute of Early American History and Culture, Williamsburg, Va. by the University of North Carolina Press, c1986. — xvi, 413 p.. — *Includes index. — Bibliography: p. [383]-398*

PHILANTHROPISTS — Moral and ethical aspects

Beneficence, philanthropy and the public good / edited by Ellen Frankel Paul...[et at]. — Oxford : Basil Blackwell for the Social Philosphy and Policy Center, Bowling Green State University, 1987. — 141p

PHILANTHROPISTS — Great Britain — Biography

BRADLEY, Ian, 1950-
Enlightened entrepreneurs / Ian Campbell Bradley. — London : Weidenfeld and Nicolson, 1987. — xii, 207p, 12p of plates. — *Bibliography: p202*

TYRRELL, Alex
Joseph Sturge and the "moral Radical party" in early Victorian Britain / Alex Tyrrell. — London : Helm, c1987. — [264]p. — *Bibliography: p249-250. — Includes index*

PHILANTHROPISTS — United States — Biography

NIELSEN, Waldemar A
The golden donors : a new anatomy of the great foundations / by Waldemar A. Nielsen. — 1st ed. — New York : E.P. Dutton, c1985. — xi, 468p. — "A Truman Talley book.". — *Includes bibliographical references and index*

PHILIP, JOHN

ROSS, Andrew, 19---
John Philip (1775-1851) : missions, race and politics in South Africa / Andrew Ross. — Aberdeen : Aberdeen University Press, 1986. — ix,249p. — *Bibliography: p240-242. — Includes index*

PHILIPPART, SIMON

KURGAN-VAN HENTENRYK, G
Rail, finance et politique : les entreprises Philippart, 1865-1890 / G. Kurgan-van Hentenryk. — Bruxelles, Belgique : Editions de l'Université de Bruxelles, 1982. — 392 p.. — (Université libre de Bruxelles, Faculté de philosophie et lettres ; 84). — *Includes index. — Bibliography: p. 366-370*

PHILIPPINES — Commercial policy

BAUTISTA, Romeo M.
Production incentives in Philippine agriculture : effects of trade and exchange rate policies / Romeo M. Bautista. — Washington, D.C. : International Food Policy Research Institute, 1987. — p. cm. — (Research report ; 59). — *Bibliography: p*

PHILIPPINES — Economic conditions — 1946-

CROUCH, Harold
Economic change, social structure and the political system in Southeast Asia : Philippine development compared with the other ASEAN countries / Harold Crouch. — Singapore : Institute of Southeast Asian Studies. Southeast Asian Studies Program, 1985. — 68p. — *Bibliography: p61-68*

Philippines : a framework for economic recovery. — Washington, D.C. : The World Bank, 1987. — xiv,156p. — (A World Bank country study). — *Includes bibliographical references*

PHILIPPINES — Economic policy

LEYCO-REYES, Soccoro
Social science education and national development in the Philippines / Soccoro Leyco-Reyes. — Singapore : Regional Institute of Higher Education and Development, 1985. — 167p. — (RIHED Research Series). — *Bibliography: p137-139*

Philippines : a framework for economic recovery. — Washington, D.C. : The World Bank, 1987. — xiv,156p. — (A World Bank country study). — *Includes bibliographical references*

PHILIPPINES — Foreign relations — United States

VAN DER KROEF, Justus Maria
Since Aquino : the Philippine tangle and the United States / Justus M. van der Kroef. — Baltimore (Md.) : University of Maryland School of Law, 1986. — 73p. — (Occasional papers/Reprints series in contemporary Asian studies ; no.6)

PHILIPPINES — History — 1946-

Crisis in the Philippines : the Marcos era and beyond / edited by John Bresnan. — Princeton, NJ : Princeton University Press, c1986. — xiv, 284p. — *Includes index.* — *Bibliography: p.[259]-267*

DAVIS, Leonard, 1931-
The Philippines : people, poverty and politics / Leonard Davis. — Basingstoke : Macmillan, 1987. — [256]p. — *Includes bibliography and index*

PHILIPPINES — Politics and government

VAN DER KROEF, Justus Maria
Since Aquino : the Philippine tangle and the United States / Justus M. van der Kroef. — Baltimore (Md.) : University of Maryland School of Law, 1986. — 73p. — (Occasional papers/Reprints series in contemporary Asian studies ; no.6)

PHILIPPINES — Politics and government — 1946-

DAVIS, Leonard, 1931-
The Philippines : people, poverty and politics / Leonard Davis. — Basingstoke : Macmillan, 1987. — [256]p. — *Includes bibliography and index*

PHILIPPINES — Politics and government — 1973-

CROUCH, Harold
Economic change, social structure and the political system in Southeast Asia : Philippine development compared with the other ASEAN countries / Harold Crouch. — Singapore : Institute of Southeast Asian Studies. Southeast Asian Studies Program, 1985. — 68p. — *Bibliography: p61-68*

DE LA TORRE, Edicio
Touching ground, taking root : theological and political reflections on the Philippine struggle / Edicio de la Torre. — London : Catholic Institute for International Relations in association with British Council of Churches, 1986. — ix,214p

LAWYERS COMMITTEE FOR INTERNATIONAL HUMAN RIGHTS
The Philippines : a country in crisis / a report by the Lawyers Committee for International Human Rights. — New York : the Committee, 1983. — iii,142p

PHILIPPINES — Relations — United States

Crisis in the Philippines : the Marcos era and beyond / edited by John Bresnan. — Princeton, NJ : Princeton University Press, c1986. — xiv, 284p. — *Includes index.* — *Bibliography: p.[259]-267*

PHILIPPINES — Social conditions

DAVIS, Leonard, 1931-
The Philippines : people, poverty and politics / Leonard Davis. — Basingstoke : Macmillan, 1987. — [256]p. — *Includes bibliography and index*

PHILIPPINES — Social policy

LEYCO-REYES, Soccoro
Social science education and national development in the Philippines / Soccoro Leyco-Reyes. — Singapore : Regional Institute of Higher Education and Development, 1985. — 167p. — (RIHED Research Series). — *Bibliography: p137-139*

PHILLIPS CURVE

ALOGOSKOUFIS, George S.
Monetary policy and the informational implications of the Phillips curve in an open economy / George Alogoskoufis. — London : Centre for Economic Policy Research, 1987. — v,30p. — (Discussion paper series / Centre for Economic Policy Research ; no.183). — *Bibliography: p29*

NEWELL, A.
The Phillips curve is a real wage equation / A. Newell and J. Symons. — London : Centre for Labour Economics, London School of Economics, 1986. — 32p. — (Discussion paper / London School of Economics and Political Science. Centre for Labour Economics ; no.246). — *Bibliography: p21-22*

PHILOSOPHERS — Directories

International directory of philosophy and philosophers, 1986-89 / editors: Ramona Cormier, Richard H. Lineback. — 6th ed. — Bowling Green, Ohio : Philosophy Documentation Center, c1986. — viii, 299p

PHILOSOPHERS — Austria — History and criticism — Congresses

POPPER-KOLLOQUIUM (1983 : Vienna)
Karl Popper : Philosophie und Wissenschaft : Beiträge zum Popper-Kolloquium / Friedrich Wallner (Hrsg). — Wien : Braumüller, 1985. — viii,148p. — (Philosophica ; 4). — *Bibliographies*

PHILOSOPHERS — Canada — Directories

Directory of American philosophers, 1986-87 / edited by Archie J. Bahm ; in cooperation with Richard H. Lineback. — 13th ed. — Bowling Green, Ohio : Philosophy Documentation Center, c1986. — x, 414p

PHILOSOPHERS — England — Biography

CRANSTON, Maurice
John Locke : a biography / Maurice Cranston. — Oxford : Oxford University Press, 1985, c1957. — [ix,512]p. — *Originally published: London : Longmans, Green, 1957.* — *Includes bibliography and index*

GLASSMAN, Peter J.
J.S. Mill : the evolution of a genius / by Peter Glassman. — Gainesville : University of Florida Press, c1985. — xvi, 188p. — *Includes index.* — *Bibliography: p.181-185*

POPPER, Karl R.
Unended quest : an intellectual autobiography / Karl Popper. — Rev. ed. — [London] : Flamingo, 1986. — 270p. — *Previous ed.: published as Autobiography of Karl Popper. La Salle, Ill. : Open Court, 1974.* — *Bibliography: p242-254.* — *Includes index*

PHILOSOPHERS — England — History and criticism — Congresses

POPPER-KOLLOQUIUM (1983 : Vienna)
Karl Popper : Philosophie und Wissenschaft : Beiträge zum Popper-Kolloquium / Friedrich Wallner (Hrsg). — Wien : Braumüller, 1985. — viii,148p. — (Philosophica ; 4). — *Bibliographies*

PHILOSOPHERS — France — Biography

HAYMAN, Ronald
Writing against : a biography of Sartre / Ronald Hayman. — London : Weidenfeld and Nicolson, c1986. — x,487p,[12]p of plates. — *Bibliography: p471-476.* — *Includes index*

PHILOSOPHERS — Germany — Biography

AITON, E. J.
Leibniz : a biography / E.J. Aiton. — Bristol : Hilger, c1985. — xiv,370p. — *Bibliography: p354-360.* — *Includes index*

BERGMANN, Peter
Nietzsche, "the last antipolitical German" / Peter Bergmann. — Bloomington : Indiana University Press, c1987. — 239 p.. — *Includes index.* — *Bibliography: p. [220]-231*

STUCKENBERG, J. H. W
The life of Immanuel Kant / by J.H.W. Stuckenberg ; with a new preface by Rolf George. — Lanham, MD : University Press of America, 1986. — xiv, 474 p.. — : *Reprint. Originally published: London : Macmillan, 1882.* — *Bibliography: p. [451]-474*

PHILOSOPHERS — Germany — Correspondence

ARENDT, Hannah
[Correspondence. Selections]. Hannah Arendt/Karl Jaspers : Briefwechsel 1926-1969 / herausgegeben von Lotte Köhler und Hans Saner. — Munich : Piper, c1985. — 859p, [8]p of plates. — *Includes indexes*

PHILOSOPHERS — Germany — History and criticism

HEIDEGGER, Martin
Nietzsche / Martin Heidegger. — San Francisco ; London : Harper and Row
Vol.3: The will to power as knowledge and as metaphysics / edited, with notes and an analysis, by David Farrell Krell ; translated from the German by Joan Stambaugh, David Farrell Krell and Frank A. Capuzzi. — 1987. — xiii,288p. — *Heidegger's German text originally published in 'Nietzsche', Erster Band, Zweiter Band, Verlag Günther Neske, Pfullingen, 1961.* — *Includes bibliographical references*

PHILOSOPHERS — Great Britain — Biography

ROGOW, Arnold A
Thomas Hobbes : radical in the service of reaction / Arnold A. Rogow. — New York ; London : W.W. Norton, c1986. — 287p. — *Includes index.* — *Bibliography: p.275-277*

PHILOSOPHERS — Hungary

SZIKLAI, László
Proletárforradalom után : Lukács György marxista fejlődése 1930-1945 / Sziklai László. — [Budapest] : Kossuth Könyvkiadó, 1986. — 361p. — *References: p331-[362]*

ZOLTAI, Dénes
Egy írástudó visszatér : Lukács György 1945 utáni munkásságáról / Zoltai Dénes. — [Budapest] : Kossuth Könyvkiadó, 1985. — 249p. — *Notes and references: p231-248*

PHILOSOPHERS — Italy — Biography

ROMANO, Sergio
Giovanni Gentile : la filosofia al potere / Sergio Romano. — Milano : Bompiani, 1984. — 352p, [32]p of plates

PHILOSOPHERS — Scotland

FERGUSON, Adam
The unpublished essays of Adam Ferguson / Adam Ferguson ; deciphered and commented upon by Winifred Philip. — Argyll : Winifred Philip. — *"Adam Ferguson's unpublished essays of which the manuscript is in the Archives of the Library of the University of Edinburgh"*
Vol.1. — 1986. — ii,128p

FERGUSON, Adam
The unpublished essays of Adam Ferguson / Adam Ferguson ; deciphered and commented upon by Winifred Philip. — Argyll : Winifred Philip. — *"Adam Ferguson's unpublished essays of which the manuscript is in the Archives of the Library of the University of Edinburgh"*
Vol.2. — 1986. — iii,141p

FERGUSON, Adam
The unpublished essays of Adam Ferguson / Adam Ferguson ; deciphered and commented upon by Winifred Philip. — Argyll : Winifred Philip. — *"Adam Ferguson's unpublished essays of which the manuscript is in the Archives of the Library of the University of Edinburgh"*
Vol.3. — 1986. — ii,207p

PHILOSOPHERS — United States — Biography

MARTINEAU, Alain
Herbert Marcuseś utopia / by Alain Martineau. — Montreal : Harvest House, 1986. — 156p

PHILOSOPHERS — United States — Biography *continuation*

The Philosophy of W.V. Quine / edited by Lewis Edwin Hahn and Paul Arthur Schilpp. — La Salle, Ill. : Open Court, 1986, c1985. — xvi, 705p. — (The Library of living philosophers ; v. 18). — Includes index. — "A bibliography of the publications of W.V. Quine": p

PHILOSOPHERS — United States — Directories

Directory of American philosophers, 1986-87 / edited by Archie J. Bahm ; in cooperation with Richard H. Lineback. — 13th ed. — Bowling Green, Ohio : Philosophy Documentation Center, c1986. — x, 414p

PHILOSOPHERS — Wales — Biography

JONES, Whitney R.D.
David Williams : the anvil and the hammer / Whitney R.D. Jones. — Cardiff : University of Wales Press, 1986. — xviii,266p. — *Bibliography: p.241-251. — Includes index*

PHILOSOPHERS, MODERN

BLACKHAM, H. J.
Six existentialist thinkers / H. J. Blackham. — London : Routledge & Kegan Paul, 1961. — vii,179p. — *First published 1952. — Bibliography: p169-173*

PHILOSOPHICAL ANTHROPOLOGY

MOULIN, Léo
La Gauche, la Droite et le péché originel et autres essais / Léo Moulin ; préface d'Alain Lancelot. — Paris : Librairie des Méridiens, 1984. — 234p. — *Includes bibliographic notes*

PHILOSOPHY

DESCARTES, René
Meditations on first philosophy : with selections from the Objections and replies / René Descartes ; translated by John Cottingham ; with an introduction by Bernard Williams. — Cambridge : Cambridge University Press, 1986. — [160]p. — *Translations from the Latin. — Includes index*

DESCARTES, René
[Selections. English]. The philosophical writings of Descartes / translated by John Cottingham, Robert Stoothoff, Dugald Murdoch. — Cambridge : Cambridge University Press
Vol.1. — 1985. — xii,418p. — *Translated from the Latin and French*

Ethics, science, and democracy : the philosophy of Abraham Edel / edited by Irving Louis Horowitz and H. Standish Thayer. — New Brunswick, N.J., U.S.A. : Transaction Books, c1986. — viii, 318p. — *"Festschrift honoring Abraham Edel"--Pref. — "Abraham Edel: philosophical bibliography, 1930-1985": p*

GARDNER, Martin, 1914-
The whys of a philosophical scrivener / Martin Gardner. — Oxford : Oxford University Press, 1985, c1983. — [464]p. — *Originally published: Brighton : Harvester, 1983. — Includes index*

MILL, John Stuart
Utilitarianism and other essays / J.S. Mill and Jeremy Bentham ; edited by Alan Ryan. — Harmondsworth : Penguin, 1987. — 344p. — (Penguin classics). — *Includes index*

WEIL, Simone
Formative writings, 1929-1941 / Simone Weil ; edited and translated by Dorothy Tuck McFarland and Wilhelmina van Ness. — London : Routledge & Kegan Paul, 1987. — [289]p. — *Translations from the French*

WIGGINS, David, 1933-
Needs, values, truth : essays in the philosophy of value / David Wiggins. — Oxford : Basil Blackwell, 1987. — ix,366p. — (Aristotelian Society series ; v.6)

PHILOSOPHY — Addresses, essays, lectures

JAMES, William, 1842-1910
Essays in philosophy / William James. — Cambridge, Mass ; London : Harvard University Press, 1978. — xxxv,410p. — (The works of William James ; [v.5]). — *Includes index*

LEWIS, David, 1941-
Philosophical papers / David Lewis. — New York : Oxford University Press
Vol.1. — 1983

LEWIS, David, 1941-
Philosophical papers / David Lewis. — New York : Oxford University Press
Vol. 2. — 1986. — xvii, 366p. — *Includes index and bibliographies. — Bibliography of the writings of David Lewis: p. 343-355*

Mind design : philosophy, psychology, artificial intelligence / edited by John Haugeland. — Cambridge, Mass. ; London : MIT Press, 1981. — xii,368p. — *A Bradford book*

Minds, machines and evolution : philosophical studies / edited by Christopher Hookway. — Cambridge : Cambridge University Press, 1984. — xi,177p. — *Includes bibliographies and index*

Rationality, relativism, and the human sciences / editors, J. Margolis, M. Krausz, and R.M. Burian. — Dordrecht ; Boston : M. Nijhoff, 1986. — p. cm. — (Studies of the Greater Philadelphia Philosophy Consortium). — *Includes bibliographical references and indexes*

SELLARS, Wilfrid
Pure pragmatics and possible worlds : the early essays of Wilfrid Sellars / edited and introduced by J. Sicha. — Reseda, Calif. : Ridgeview Pub. Co., c1980. — lxxx, 297 p.. — *Bibliography: p. lxxx*

PHILOSOPHY — Bibliography

BYNAGLE, Hans E
Philosophy : a guide to the reference literature / Hans E. Bynagle. — Littleton, Colo. : Libraries Unlimited, 1986. — x, 170 p.. — (Reference sources in the humanities series). — *Includes indexes*

PHILOSOPHY — Collected works

DESCARTES, René
[Selections. English]. The philosophical works of Descartes / rendered into English by Elizabeth S. Haldane and G.R.T. Ross. — Repr. with corr.. — Cambridge : Cambridge University Press
Vol.1. — 1931. — 452p. — *First edition published 1911*

PHILOSOPHY — Correspondence

SCHÜTZ, Alfred
Briefwechsel 1939-1959 / Alfred Schütz [und] Aron Gurwitsch ; herausgegeben von Richard Grathoff ; mit einer Einleitung von Ludwig Landgrebe. — München : Wilhelm Fink, 1985. — xxxviii,544p. — (Übergänge : Texte und Studien zu Handung, Sprache und Lebenswelt ; Bd.4). — *Bibliography: p531-534*

PHILOSOPHY — Dictionaries

COLLINSON, Diané
Fifty major philosophers : a reference guide / Diané Collinson. — London : Croom Helm, c1987. — 170p. — *Includes bibliographies*

PHILOSOPHY — Library resources

UNIVERSITY OF LONDON. Library Resources Coordinating Committee. Philosophy Subject Sub-committee
A guide to philosophy collections and reference literature in philosophy. — London : the Committee, 1987. — ii,[40]p

PHILOSOPHY — Political aspects — History

HOWARD, Dick
From Marx to Kant / Dick Howard. — Albany : State University of New York Press, 1985. — xiv, 300p. — (SUNY series in political thought)

PHILOSOPHY — United States — History

GABRIEL, Ralph Henry
The course of American democratic thought / Ralph Henry Gabriel. — 3rd ed. / with Robert H. Walker. — New York : Greenwood Press, 1986. — xix, 568 p.. — (Contributions in American studies ; no. 87). — *Includes index. — Bibliography: p. 541-547*

PHILOSOPHY, AMERICAN

GABRIEL, Ralph Henry
The course of American democratic thought / Ralph Henry Gabriel. — 3rd ed. / with Robert H. Walker. — New York : Greenwood Press, 1986. — xix, 568 p.. — (Contributions in American studies ; no. 87). — *Includes index. — Bibliography: p. 541-547*

PHILOSOPHY, ANCIENT

ARISTOTLE
A new Aristotle reader / edited by J.L. Ackrill. — Oxford : Clarendon, 1987. — [600]p. — *Translations from Classical Greek. — Includes bibliography*

PHILOSOPHY, BRITISH

Philosophy in Britain today / edited by S.G. Shanker. — London : Croom Helm, c1986. — 315p

PHILOSOPHY, CHINESE — 20th century

LOUIE, Kam
Inheriting tradition : interpretations of the classical philosophers in Communist China, 1949-1966 / Kam Louie. — Hong Kong ; New York : Oxford University Press, 1986. — xiv, 272 p.. — *Includes index. — Bibliography: p. [230]-260*

PHILOSOPHY, ENGLISH — 19th century

MILL, John Stuart
Newspaper writings / by John Stuart Mill ; edited by Ann P. Robson and John M. Robson. — Toronto : University of Toronto Press ; London : Routledge & Kegan Paul
1: December 1822 - July 1831. — 1986. — cxvii,333p. — (Collected works of John Stuart Mill ; v.22)

MILL, John Stuart
Newspaper writings / by John Stuart Mill ; edited by Ann P. Robson and John M. Robson. — Toronto : University of Toronto Press ; London : Routledge & Kegan Paul
2: August 1831 - October 1834. — 1986. — ix,335-751p. — (Collected works of John Stuart Mill ; v.23)

MILL, John Stuart
Newspaper writings / by John Stuart Mill ; edited by Ann P. Robson and John M. Robson. — Toronto : University of Toronto Press ; London : Routledge & Kegan Paul
3: January 1835 - June 1847. — 1986. — vii,753-1088p. — (Collected works of John Stuart Mill ; v.24)

MILL, John Stuart
Newspaper writings / by John Stuart Mill ; edited by Ann P. Robson and John M. Robson. — Toronto : University of Toronto Press ; London : Routledge & Kegan Paul
4: December 1847 - July 1873. — 1986. — vii,1089-1526p. — (Collected works of John Stuart Mill ; v.25)

PHILOSOPHY, ENGLISH — 18th century

WILLEY, Basil
The eighteenth century background studies on the idea of nature in the thought of the period / Basil Willey. — London : Chatto & Windus, 1940. — viii,302p

PHILOSOPHY, EUROPEAN

Philosophers ancient and modern / edited by Godfrey Vesey. — Cambridge : Cambridge University Press, c1986. — v,315p. — (Royal Institute of Philosophy lecture series ; 20). — *Supplement to Philosophy 1986. — Includes bibliographies and index*

PHILOSOPHY, EUROPEAN — History
The Figural and the literal : problems of language in the history of science and philosophy, 1630-1800 / edited by Andrew E. Benjamin, Geoffrey N. Cantor and John R.R. Christie. — Manchester : Manchester University Press, c1987. — 229p. — *Conference papers*

PHILOSOPHY, FRENCH
Philosophy in France today / edited by Alan Montefiore. — Cambridge : Cambridge University Press, 1983. — xxvi,201p

PLOURDE, Simonne
Vocabulaire philosophique de Gabriel Marcel / Simonne Plourde en collaboration avec Jeanne Parain-Vial, Abbé Marcel Belay, René Davignon ; avec une préface de Paul Ricoeur. — Montréal : Bellarmin, [1985]. — 583p. — (Collection Recherches. nouvelle série ; 6). — *Bibliography: p563-566*

PHILOSOPHY, FRENCH — Addresses, essays, lectures
POTTS, Denys Campion
French thought since 1600 / D. C. Potts and D. G. Charlton. — Rev. and reprinted from France : a companion to French studies / edited by D. G. Charlton. — London : Methuen ; [New York] : distributed by Harper & Row, 1974. — viii, 96 p. — (University paperbacks ; UP546). — *Includes bibliographies and index*

PHILOSOPHY, FRENCH — 18th century
CRANSTON, Maurice
Philosophers and pamphleteers : political theorists of the Enlightenment / Maurice Cranston. — Oxford : Oxford University Press, 1986. — [vii,168]p. — (OPUS). — *Includes bibliography and index*

PHILOSOPHY, FRENCH — 20th century
KAGRAMANOV, Iu. M.
Metamorfozy nigilizma : o "novykh filosofakh" i "novykh pravykh" / Iu. M. Kagramanov. — Moskva : Politizdat, 1986. — 158p. — (Sotsial'nyi progress i burzhuaznaia filosofiia)

PHILOSOPHY, GERMAN
Leitbilder des deutschen Konservatismus : Schopenhauer, Nietzsche, Spengler, Heidegger, Schelsky, Rohrmoser, Kaltenbrunner u.a. / Ludwig Elm (Hrsg.). — Cologne : Pahl-Rugenstein, 1984. — 285p. — *Includes bibliographic notes*

RUNDELL, John F.
Origins of modernity : the origins of modern social theory from Kant to Hegel to Marx / John F. Rundell. — Cambridge : Polity, 1987. — 249p. — *Bibliography: p234-241 Includes index*

PHILOSOPHY, KAGURU (AFRICAN PEOPLE)
BEIDELMAN, T. O
Moral imagination in Kaguru modes of thought / T.O. Beidelman. — Bloomington : Indiana University Press, c1986. — xiii, 231 p.. — (African systems of thought). — *Includes index. — Bibliography: p. [216]-224*

PHILOSOPHY, MARXIST
BHASKAR, Roy
Scientific realism and human emancipation / Roy Bhaskar. — London : Verso, 1986. — 308p

CATALANO, Joseph S
A commentary on Jean-Paul Sartre's Critique of dialectical reason, volume 1, Theory of practical ensembles / Joseph S. Catalano. — Chicago : University of Chicago Press, 1986. — x, 282 p.. — *Includes index. — Bibliography: p. [269]-273*

LORENZEN, Max-Otto
Der Geist der Dialektik oder die Erschöpfung der Kritik / Max-Otto Lorenzen. — Hannover : die Freie Gesellschaft, 1979. — 124p

Marxismus, Ideologie, Politik : Krise des Marxismus oder Krise des "Arguments"? / herausgegeben von Hans Heinz Holz, Thomas Metscher, Josef Schleifstein, Robert Steigerwald ; mit Beiträgen von Karl-Heinz Brown...[et al.]. — Frankfurt am Main : Verlag Marxistische Blätter, 1984. — 318p. — *Includes bibliographical notes*

PHILOSOPHY, MARXIST — Congresses
Rethinking Marx / edited by Sakari Hänninen and Leena Paldán ; contributors, Albers ... [et al.]. — Berlin : Argument-Verlag ; New York : International General/IMMRC, c1984. — 202 p.. — (Argument-Sonderband ; AS 109) (International Socialism-Discussion ; 5). — *Includes bibliographical references*

PHILOSOPHY, MARXIST — Hungary
SZIKLAI, László
Proletárforradalom után : Lukács György marxista fejlődése 1930-1945 / Sziklai László. — [Budapest] : Kossuth Könyvkiadó, 1986. — 361p. — *References: p331-[362]*

ZOLTAI, Dénes
Egy írástudó visszatér : Lukács György 1945 utáni munkásságáról / Zoltai Dénes. — [Budapest] : Kossuth Könyvkiadó, 1985. — 249p. — *Notes and references: p231-248*

PHILOSOPHY, MODERN — 19th century
GASCOIGNE, Robert
Religion, rationality, and community : sacred and secular in the thought of Hegel and his critics / by Robert Gascoigne. — The Hague ; Boston : M. Nijhoff, 1985. — xiv, 308p. — (International archives of the history of ideas ; 105). — *Bibliography: p.271-277*

PHILOSOPHY, MODERN — 20th century
After philosophy : end or transformation? / edited by Kenneth Baynes, James Bohman, and Thomas McCarthy. — Cambridge, Mass. : MIT Press, c1987. — xi, 488p. — *Includes bibliographies*

KAGRAMANOV, Iu. M.
Metamorfozy nigilizma : o "novykh filosofakh" i "novykh pravykh" / Iu. M. Kagramanov. — Moskva : Politizdat, 1986. — 158p. — (Sotsial'nyi progress i burzhuaznaia filosofiia)

PHILOSOPHY OF NATURE
SCHLESINGER, George N.
The intelligibility of nature / George N. Schlesinger. — Aberdeen : Aberdeen University Press, 1985. — [176]p. — (Scots philosophical monographs ; no.8). — *Includes bibliography*

PHILOSOPHY, PRIMITIVE
WALLACE, Edwin R
Freud and anthropology : a history and reappraisal / Edwin R. Wallace, IV. — New York : International Universities Press, c1983. — xi, 306p. — (Psychological issues ; monograph 55). — *Bibliography: p.281-294. — Includes index*

PHILOSOPHY, SPANISH — 20th century
DÍAZ, Elías
Pensamiento español en la ero de Franco (1939-1975) / Elías Díaz. — Madrid : Tecnos, 1983. — 219p. — *Bibliography: p[201]-206*

PHOSPHORUS INDUSTRY — Netherlands — Statistics
Fosfor in Nederland 1970-1983. — 's-Gravenhage : Staatsuitgeverij, 1985. — 71p. — *Title on back cover: Phosphorus in the Netherlands 1970-1983. — Bibliography: p66-71*

PHOTOGRAPHY, INDUSTRIAL — United States
NYE, David E.
Image worlds : corporate identities at General Electric, 1890-1930 / David E. Nye. — Cambridge, Mass. ; London : MIT Press, c1985. — xiv, 188p, [38]p of plates. — *Includes index. — Bibliography: p.[161]-182*

PHOTOGRAPHY OF WOMEN
ALLOULA, Malek
[Harem colonial. English]. The colonial harem / Malek Alloula ; translation by Myrna Godzich and Wlad Godzich ; introduction by Barbara Harlow. — Minneapolis : University of Minnesota Press, c1986. — xxii, 135 p.. — (Theory and history of literature ; v. 21). — *Translation of: Le harem colonial. — Bibliography: p. 135*

PHYSICAL GEOGRAPHY — Hong Kong
A Geography of Hong Kong / editors T.N. Chiu, C.L. So. — 2nd ed. / contributors P. Catt ... [et al.]. — Hong Kong ; Oxford : Oxford University Press, 1986. — [400]p. — *Previous ed.: 1983. — Includes bibliography and index*

PHYSICALLY HANDICAPPED — Employment — Great Britain
CONFEDERATION OF BRITISH INDUSTRY
Employing disabled people / CBI. — London : Confederation of British Industry, 1983. — 18p

PHYSICALLY HANDICAPPED — Home care — Great Britain
OWENS, Patricia
Community care and severe physical disability / Patricia Owens. — London : Bedford Square Press/NCVO, 1987. — iv,127p. — (Occasional papers on social administration ; no.82). — *Bibliography: p118-121*

PHYSICALLY HANDICAPPED — Institutional care — Great Britain
OWENS, Patricia
Community care and severe physical disability / Patricia Owens. — London : Bedford Square Press/NCVO, 1987. — iv,127p. — (Occasional papers on social administration ; no.82). — *Bibliography: p118-121*

PHYSICALLY HANDICAPPED — Transportation — Government policy — United States
KATZMANN, Robert A
Institutional disability : the saga of transportation policy for the disabled / Robert A. Katzmann. — Washington, D.C. : Brookings Institution, 1986. — p. cm. — *Includes index*

PHYSICALLY HANDICAPPED — Transportation — Law and legislation — United States
KATZMANN, Robert A
Institutional disability : the saga of transportation policy for the disabled / Robert A. Katzmann. — Washington, D.C. : Brookings Institution, 1986. — p. cm. — *Includes index*

PHYSICALLY HANDICAPPED — Great Britain — Bibliography
SHRIGLEY, Sheila
Selected official publications on the disabled 1948-1975 / compiled by Sheila M. Shrigley. — [London] : Department of Health and Social Security Library, 1975. — 6p. — (Bibliography series ; no.B28). — *Includes index*

PHYSICIAN AND PATIENT
Doctor-patient communication / edited by David Pendleton and John Hasler. — London : Academic Press, c1983. — x,293p. — *Includes bibliographies and index*

PHYSICIAN AND PATIENT — Wales
WELSH CONSUMER COUNCIL
Patient participation in general practice : a study of the Patients' Committee at Aberdare Health Centre, Mid Glamorgan. — Cardiff : the Council, 1978. — 71p. — *Bibliography: p69*

PHYSICIAN-PATIENT RELATIONS
FISHER, Sue
In the patient's best interest : women and the politics of medical decisions / Sue Fisher. — New Brunswick, N.J. : Rutgers University Press, c1986. — ix, 214 p.. — *Includes index. — Bibliography: p. 195-207*

PHYSICIANS
BENNET, Glin
The wound and the doctor : healing, technology and power in modern medicine / Glin Bennet. — London : Secker & Warburg, 1987. — [320]p. — *Includes index*

PHYSICIANS — economics — United States
FUCHS, Victor R
The health economy / Victor R. Fuchs. — Cambridge, Mass. ; London : Harvard University Press, 1986. — viii, 401p. — *Includes index*. — *Bibliography: p.385-386*

PHYSICIANS — Malpractice — Economic aspects — United States
DANZON, Patricia M.
Medical malpractice : theory, evidence and public policy / Patricia M. Danzon. — Cambridge, Mass. ; London : Harvard University Press, 1985. — vi,264p. — *Bibliography: p231-238. — Includes index*

PHYSICIANS — Malpractice — Germany — History — 20th century
LIFTON, Robert Jay
The Nazi doctors : medical killing and the psychology of genocide / Robert Jay Lifton. — London : Macmillan, 1986. — xiii,561p. — *Includes index*

PHYSICIANS — Malpractice — United States
WERTHMANN, Barbara
Medical malpractice law : how medicine is changing the law / Barbara Werthmann. — Lexington, Mass. : LexingtonBooks, c1984. — xii, 268 p.. — *Includes indexes*

PHYSICIANS — Supply and demand
Die Ärzteschwemme / Philipp Herder-Dorneich, Alexander Schuller (Hrsg.). — Baden-Baden : Nomos, 1985. — 232p. — (Ordnungspolitik im Gesundheitswesen ; Bd.4). — *Includes summaries in English*

PHYSICIANS — Australia — Social aspects
WILLIS, Evan
Medical dominance. — London : Allen and Unwin, Sept.1983. — 1v.

PHYSICIANS — Canada — History
HAMOWY, Ronald
Canadian medicine : a study in restricted entry / Ronald Hamowy. — Vancouver : Fraser Institute, 1984. — xxii,394p

PHYSICIANS — Germany (West)
Die Ärzteschwemme / Philipp Herder-Dorneich, Alexander Schuller (Hrsg.). — Baden-Baden : Nomos, 1985. — 232p. — (Ordnungspolitik im Gesundheitswesen ; Bd.4). — *Includes summaries in English*

PHYSICIANS — Great Britain — Supply and demand
GREAT BRITAIN. Working Party on Under-Doctored Areas
Draft report. — [London : Department of Health and Social Security], 1979. — [11]p

PHYSICIANS — United States — Biography
HAWKS, Esther Hill
A woman doctor's Civil War : Esther Hill Hawks' diary / edited with a foreword and afterword by Gerald Schwartz. — 1st ed. — Columbia, S.C. : University of South Carolina Press, c1984. — p. cm. — *Bibliography: p283-288. — Bibliography: p*

PHYSICIANS — United States — Supply and demand
BLUMBERG, Mark S
Trends and projections of physicians in the United States, 1967-2002 / By Mark S. Blumberg. — [Berkeley, Calif. : Carnegie Commission on Higher Education, 1971]. — vii, 83 p. — "A technical report sponsored by the Carnegie Commission on Higher Education.". — *Bibliography: p. 81-83*

PHYSICIANS (GENERAL PRACTICE) — Denmark
Laegeerhvervet : struktur, takster og indtjening. — København : Monopoltilsynet
1: Alment praktiserende laeger. — 1983. — 49p

PHYSICIANS (GENERAL PRACTICE) — Great Britain — History
LOUDON, Irvine
Medical care and the general practitioner 1750-1850 / Irvine Loudon. — Oxford : Clarendon, 1986. — xv,354p. — *Bibliography: p323-342. — Includes index*

PHYSICISTS — Great Britain — Biography
GJERTSEN, Derek
The Newton handbook / Derek Gjertsen. — London : Routledge & Kegan Paul, 1986. — xiv,665p

PHYSICS
JUNGNICKEL, Christa
Intellectual mastery of nature : theoretical physics from Ohum to Einstein / Christa Jungnickel and Russell McCormmach. — Chicago ; London : University of Chicago Press
Vol.2: The now mighty theoretical physics 1870-1925. — 1986. — xiv,435p. — *Bibliography: p373-414. — Includes index*

PHYSICS — Forecasting
ROYAL SOCIETY. Symposium (1986 : [London?])
Predictability in science and society : a joint symposium of the Royal Society and the British Academy held on 20 and 21 March 1986 / organized and edited by John Mason, P. Mathias, and J. H. Westcott. — London : Royal Society : British Academy, 1986. — viii,145p. — *Includes bibliographies*

PHYSICS — History
JUNGNICKEL, Christa
Intellectual mastery of nature / Christa Jungnickel and Russell McCormmach. — Chicago : University of Chicago Press, c1986-. — v. <1 >. — *Includes index*. — *Bibliography: v. 1, p. 311-338*. — Contents: v. 1. The torch of mathematics, 1800-1870

PHYSICS — History — 20th century
PAIS, Abraham
Inward bound : of matter and forces in the physical world / Abraham Pais. — Oxford : Clarendon, 1986. — [700]p. — *Includes bibliography and index*

PHYSICS — Philosophy
EARMAN, John
A primer on determinism / John Earman. — Dordrecht ; Lancaster : Reidel, c1986. — xiv, 273p. — (University of Western Ontario series in philosophy of science ; v. 32). — *Includes index*. — *Bibliography: p 257-269*

FINE, Arthur
The shaky game : Einstein, realism, and the quantum theory / Arthur Fine. — Chicago : University of Chicago Press, c1986. — xi, 186 p.. — (Science and its conceptual foundations). — *Includes index*. — *Bibliography: p. 173-179*

FREUDENTHAL, Gideon
[Atom und Individuum im Zeitalter Newtons. English]. Atom and individual in the age of Newton : on the genesis of the mechanistic world view / Gideon Freudenthal ; [translated by Peter McLaughlin from the German]. — New ed. — Dordrecht ; Boston : D. Reidel Pub. Co. ; Hingham, MA, U.S.A. : Sold and distributed in the U.S.A. and Canada by Kluwer Academic Publishers, c1985. — p. cm. — (Boston studies in the philosophy of science ; v. 88). — *Translation of: Atom und Individuum im Zeitalter Newtons. — Includes index*. — *Bibliography: p*

MACH, Ernst
[Principien der Wärmelehre. English]. Principles of the theory of heat : historically and critically elucidated / Ernst Mach ; with an introduction by Martin J. Klein ; edited by Brian McGuinness. — Dordrecht ; Lancaster : D. Reidel, c1986. — xxii, 456p. — (Vienna circle collection ; v. 17). — *Translation of: Die Principien der Wärmelehre. — Includes indexes*

PHYSIOCRATS
LLUCH, Ernest
Agronomía y fisiocracia en España (1750-1820) / Ernest Lluch y Lluís Argemí d 'Abadal ; prólogo y epílogo por Fabian Estapé. — Valencia : Institución Alfonso el Magnánimo : Institució Valenciana d'estudis i Investigació, [1985]. — lxi,215p. — (Estudios universitarios ; 11)

PI SUNYER, CARLES
PI SUNYER, Carles
La guerra. 1936-1939 : memòries / Cares Pi Sunyer ; recopilació revisió a cura de Núria Pi-Sunyer. — Barcelona : Editorial Pòrtic, 1986. — 251p

PIAGET, JEAN
CASE, Robbie
Intellectual development : birth to adulthood / Robbie Case. — Orlando : Academic Press, 1985. — xix, 460 p.. — (Developmental psychology series). — *Includes indexes*. — *Bibliography: p. 433-450*

The Future of Piagetian theory : the neo-Piagetians / edited by Valerie L. Shulman, Lillian C.R. Restaino-Baumann and Loretta Butler. — New York ; London : Plenum, c1985. — xxv,222p. — *Includes bibliographies and index*

GINSBURG, Herbert
Piaget's theory of intellectual development / Herbert Ginsburg, Sylvia Opper. — 2nd ed. — Englewood Cliffs ; London : Prentice-Hall, 1979. — xvi,253p. — *Previous ed.: 1969*. — *Bibliography: p.239-244. — Includes index*

PIAGET, JEAN — Congresses
Questions on social explanation : Piagetian themes reconsidered / edited by Luigia Camaioni and Cláudia de Lemos. — Amsterdam ; Philadelphia : J. Benjamins Pub. Co., 1985. — 141 p.. — (Pragmatics & beyond ; VI:4). — *Selection of the papers presented at the international conference in honour of Jean Piaget, held in Rome, 9-10 Oct. 1981, and sponsored by Rome University*. — *Bibliography: p. [131]-141*

PIAGET, JEAN — Contributions in theory of knowledge
KITCHENER, Richard F.
Piaget's theory of knowledge : genetic epistemology and scientific reason / Richard F. Kitchener. — New Haven [Conn.] ; London : Yale University Press, c1986. — [288]p. — *Includes bibliography and index*

PICKENS, F. W
EDMUNDS, John B
Francis W. Pickens and the politics of destruction / John B. Edmunds, Jr. — Chapel Hill : University of North Carolina Press, c1986. — xiii, 256 p.. — (The Fred W. Morrison series in Southern studies). — *Includes index*. — *Bibliography: p. [223]-239*

PICKERSGILL, J. W.
PICKERSGILL, J. W.
The road back : by a Liberal in opposition / J. W. Pickersgill. — Toronto : University of Toronto Press, 1986. — 320p

PICKETING — England — Orgreave (South Yorkshire)
JACKSON, Bernard
The battle for Orgreave / Bernard Jackson with Tony Wardle. — Brighton : Vanson Wardle Productions, [1986?]. — x,129p

PICTURE-WRITING — Australia — Northern Territory
MUNN, Nancy D.
Walbiri iconography : graphic representation and cultural symbolism in a central Australian society / Nancy D. Munn ; with a new afterword. — Chicago : University of Chicago Press, 1986. — xx, 244 p.. — : Reprint. *Originally published: Ithaca, N.Y. : Cornell University Press, 1973. — Includes index. — Bibliography: p. 235-239*

PIDGIN LANGUAGES
MÜHLHÄUSLER, Peter
Pidgin & creole linguistics / Peter Mühlhäusler. — Oxford : Blackwell, 1986. — 320p. — (Language in society ; 11). — *Bibliography: p297-317. — Includes index*

PINEAPPLE INDUSTRY — Hawaii — History
HAWKINS, Richard Adrian
Economic diversification in the American Pacific Territory of Hawai'i, 1893-1941 / Richard Adrian Hawkins. — 576 leaves. — *PhD (Econ) 1986 LSE. — Leaves 547-576 are appendices*

PINTUBI (AUSTRALIAN PEOPLE)
MYERS, Fred R.
Pintupi country, Pintupi self : sentiment, place and politics among Western Desert Aborigines / Fred R. Myers. — Washington, D.C. ; London : Smithsonian Institution Press, 1987. — [384]p. — (Smithsonian series in ethnographic inquiry ; 3)

PIONEER HEALTH CENTRE
PEARSE, Innes H.
The Peckham experiment : a study of the living structure of society / by Innes H. Pearse [and] Lucy H. Crocker. — Edinburgh : Scottish Academic Press, 1985. — xxx,333p. — *First published by Allen and Unwin in 1943*

PIONEERS — Pennsylvania — Correspondence
PENN, William
The papers of William Penn / editors, Mary Maples Dunn, Richard S. Dunn...[et al.]. — Pennsylvania : University of Pennsylvania Press . — *Includes index*
V.5: William Penn's published writings 1660-1726 : an interpretive bibliography / [edited by] Edwin B. Bronner, David Fraser. — 1986. — xxvi,546p

PIRAE (TAHITI) — Population — Statistics
Tableaux normalisés du recensement général de la population : 15 octobre 1983. — [Papeete] : Institut territorial de la statistique Résultats de la commune de Pirae. — [1985?]. — 4p,11 leaves

PIRATE RADIO BROADCASTING — Great Britain
Radio is my bomb : DIY manual for pirates. — London : Hooligan Press, 1987. — 72p

PIRATES — Persian Gulf — History — 18th century
AL-QĀSIMĪ, Muḥammad
The myth of Arab piracy in the Gulf / Muhammad Al-Qāsimi. — London : Croom Helm, c1986. — [xviii,450]p. — *Includes bibliography and index*

PIRATES — Persian Gulf — History — 19th century
AL-QĀSIMĪ, Muḥammad
The myth of Arab piracy in the Gulf / Muhammad Al-Qāsimi. — London : Croom Helm, c1986. — [xviii,450]p. — *Includes bibliography and index*

PITTERMANN, BRUNO
Bruno Pittermann : ein Leben für die Sozialdemokratie / Heinz Fischer, Leopold Gratz (Hrsg.). — Wien : Europaverlag, 1985. — 442p

PLAGUE — Italy — Florence — History
CARMICHAEL, Ann G.
Plague and the poor in Renaissance Florence / Ann G. Carmichael. — Cambridge : Cambridge University Press, 1986. — xv,180p. — (Cambridge history of medicine). — *Bibliography: p166-175. — Includes index*

PLAID CYMRU
PLAID CYMRU
General election programme: winning for Wales = Rhaglen etholiad cyffredinol: ennill dros Cymru. — Caerdydd : Plaid Cymru, 1987. — 31p

PLANNING
ABDULLAEVA, K. Sh.
Planirovanie i ekonomicheskoe stimulirovanie v sisteme upravleniia proizvodstvom : (opyt i rezul'taty eksperimental'nykh issledovanii) / K. Sh. Abdullaeva, E. G. Krushel', V. A. Galushkin. — Frunze : Ilim, 1983. — 162p. — *Bibliography: p154-[161]*

Strategic perspectives on planning practice / edited by Barry Checkoway. — Lexington, Mass. : Lexington Books, c1986. — x, 274 p.. — (Politics of planning series). — *Includes bibliographies and index*

PLANNING — Methodology
MOSER, Caroline O. N.
A theory and methodology of gender planning : meeting women's practical and strategic needs / Caroline O. N. Moser and Caren Levy. — London : Bartlett School of Architecture and Planning Development Planning Unit, 1986. — 33p. — (DPU gender and planning working paper ; no.11). — *Bibliography: p32-33*

PLANNING — Social aspects
MOSER, Caroline O. N.
A theory and methodology of gender planning : meeting women's practical and strategic needs / Caroline O. N. Moser and Caren Levy. — London : Bartlett School of Architecture and Planning Development Planning Unit, 1986. — 33p. — (DPU gender and planning working paper ; no.11). — *Bibliography: p32-33*

PLANNING — Barbados
Physical development plan for Barbados. — [Bridgetown?] : Town and Country Development Planning Office, 1970. — vii,134p

PLANNING — Bermuda
The Bermuda development plan 1983 : planning statement. — Hamilton : Department of Planning, 1983. — 77p

PLANNING — Great Britain
Chief planning inspector's report / Planning Inspectorate, Great Britain. — Bristol : Planning Inspectorate, 1985-. — *Annual*

Town and country planning / report of a Committee of Inquiry appointed by the Nuffield Foundation. — London : Nuffield Foundation, c1986. — xiv,204p

PLANNING — India
Studies in Indian planning and economic policy / edited by R. K. Sinha. — New Delhi : Deep & Deep, 1984. — 472p. — *Bibliography: p [466]-468*

PLANNING — Soviet Union — Mathematical models
Perspektivnoe otraslevoe planirovanie : ekonomiko-matematicheskie metody i modeli / otv. redaktor A. G. Aganbegian. — Novosibirsk : Nauka, Sibirskoe otdelenie, 1986. — 355p. — *Bibliography: p350-[356]*

Problemy narodno-khoziaistvennogo kriteriia optimal'nosti : materialy diskussii / [otv. redaktor N. P. Fedorenko]. — Moskva : Nauka, 1982. — 165p. — (Problemy sovetskoi ekonomiki)

Programmno-tselevoi metod v planirovanii / [otv. redaktor N. P. Fedorenko]. — Moskva : Nauka, 1982. — 150p. — (Problemy sovetskoi ekonomiki). — *Bibliography: p147-[149]*

PLANNING — Spain — Madrid
Madrid, Comunidad autónoma metropolitana / [equipo dirigido por] E. García de Enterría. — Madrid : Instituto de Estudios Económicos, 1983. — 482p. — (Colección Estudios / Instituto de Estudios Económicos)

PLANNING TECHNICS
SCHAEFER, Morris
Designing and using procedure in health and human services / by Morris Schaefer. — Beverly Hills : Sage Publications, c1985. — p. cm. — (Sage human services guides ; 39)

PLANT LAYOUT — Bibliography
DOMSCHKE, Wolfgang
Location and layout planning : an international bibliography / Wolfgang Domschke, Andreas Drexl. — Berlin ; New York : Springer-Verlag, 1985. — p. cm. — (Lecture notes in economics and mathematical systems ; 238)

PLANT PRODUCTS — Canada
PRESCOTT-ALLEN, Christine
The first resource : wild species in the North American economy / Christine Prescott-Allen and Robert Prescott-Allen. — New Haven : Yale University Press, c1986. — xv, 529 p.. — *"Published with support from the World Wildlife Fund and Philip Morris Incorporated.". — Includes index. — Bibliography: p. 463-507*

PLANT PRODUCTS — United States
PRESCOTT-ALLEN, Christine
The first resource : wild species in the North American economy / Christine Prescott-Allen and Robert Prescott-Allen. — New Haven : Yale University Press, c1986. — xv, 529 p.. — *"Published with support from the World Wildlife Fund and Philip Morris Incorporated.". — Includes index. — Bibliography: p. 463-507*

PLANT SHUTDOWNS
Deindustrialization and plant closure / [edited by] Paul D. Staudohar, Holly E. Brown. — Lexington, Mass. : D.C. Heath, c1987. — xxii, 348 p.. — *Includes index. — Bibliography: p. [335]-342*

PLANT SHUTDOWNS — Law and legislation — United States
Deindustrialization and plant closure / [edited by] Paul D. Staudohar, Holly E. Brown. — Lexington, Mass. : D.C. Heath, c1987. — xxii, 348 p.. — *Includes index. — Bibliography: p. [335]-342*

PLANT SHUTDOWNS — England — Corby (Northamptonshire)
MAUNDERS, A. R.
A process of struggle : the campaign for Corby steelmaking in 1979 / Allen Maunders. — Gower : Aldershot, c1987. — [295]p. — *Includes bibliography*

PLANT SHUTDOWNS — France
ROTHSTEIN, Lawrence E
Plant closings : the roles of myth, power, and politics / Lawrence E. Rothstein. — Dover, Mass. : Auburn House Pub. Co., c1986. — p. cm. — *Includes index*

PLANT SHUTDOWNS — United States
Deindustrialization and plant closure / [edited by] Paul D. Staudohar, Holly E. Brown. — Lexington, Mass. : D.C. Heath, c1987. — xxii, 348 p.. — *Includes index. — Bibliography: p. [335]-342*

ROTHSTEIN, Lawrence E
Plant closings : the roles of myth, power, and politics / Lawrence E. Rothstein. — Dover, Mass. : Auburn House Pub. Co., c1986. — p. cm. — *Includes index*

PLANTATION LIFE — Brazil — History
CONRAD, Robert Edgar
World of sorrow : the African slave trade to Brazil / Robert Edgar Conrad. — Baton Rouge : Louisiana State University Press, c1986. — 215 p.. — *Includes index. — Bibliography: p. 197-212*

PLANTATION LIFE — Caribbean Area — History
KLEIN, Herbert S
African slavery in Latin America and the Caribbean / Herbert S. Klein. — New York : Oxford University Press, 1986. — 311 p., [3] leaves of plates. — Includes index. — Bibliography: p. 273-294

PLANTATION LIFE — Georgia — History
SMITH, Julia Floyd
Slavery and rice culture in low country Georgia, 1750-1860 / Julia Floyd Smith. — Knoxville : University of Tennessee Press, c1985. — p. cm. — Includes index. — Bibliography: p

PLANTATION LIFE — Georgia — History — 19th century
MOHR, Clarence L
On the threshold of freedom : masters and slaves in Civil War Georgia / Clarence L. Mohr. — Athens, Ga. ; London : University of Georgia Press, c1986. — xxi, 397p, 18p of plates. — Includes index. — Bibliography: p.367-385

PLANTATION LIFE — Latin America — History
KLEIN, Herbert S
African slavery in Latin America and the Caribbean / Herbert S. Klein. — New York : Oxford University Press, 1986. — 311 p., [3] leaves of plates. — Includes index. — Bibliography: p. 273-294

PLANTATION LIFE — Southern States — History
WHITE, Deborah Gray
Ar'n't I a woman? : female slaves in the plantation South / Deborah Gray White. — 1st ed. — New York : Norton, c1985. — 216 p.. — Includes index. — Bibliography: p. [198]-208

PLANTATION LIFE — Virgin Islands of the United States — Saint John
OLWIG, Karen Fog
Cultural adaptation and resistance on St. John : three centuries of Afro-Caribbean life / Karen Fog Olwig. — Gainesville : University of Florida Press, c1985. — xii, 226 p.. — Cover title: Cultural adaptation & resistance on St. John. — Includes index. — Bibliography: p. [201]-216

PLANTATION LIFE — Virginia — History — 18th century
BREEN, T. H
Tobacco culture : the mentality of the great Tidewater planters on the eve of Revolution / T.H. Breen. — Princeton, N.J. : Princeton University Press, c1985. — xvi, 216p. — Includes index

PLANTATION OWNERS — Virginia — History — 18th century
BREEN, T. H
Tobacco culture : the mentality of the great Tidewater planters on the eve of Revolution / T.H. Breen. — Princeton, N.J. : Princeton University Press, c1985. — xvi, 216p. — Includes index

PLANTATIONS — Guatemala — History — 19th century
CAMBRANES, J. C
[Café y campesinos en Guatemala, 1853-1897. English]. Coffee and peasants : the origins of the modern plantation economy in Guatemala, 1853-1897 / J.C. Cambranes ; [English version revised by Carla Clason-Höök]. — Stockholm, Sweden : Institute of Latin American Studies, c1985. — 334 p.. — (Monografías / Institute of Latin American Studies ; no.10). — Translation of: Café y campesinos en Guatemala, 1853-1897. — Bibliography: p. 327-332

PLANTATIONS — Sri Lanka
ROTE, Ron
A taste of bitterness : the political economy of tea plantations in Sri Lanka / Ronald Rote. — Amsterdam : Free University Press, 1986. — xviii,282p. — Doctoral thesis for Free University of Amsterdam, 1986. — Bibliography: p231-245

PLANTS, PROTECTION OF — Bibliography
DAVID LUBIN MEMORIAL LIBRARY
FAO documentation : plant production and protection : 1979-1983 = Documentation de la FAO : production et protection des végétaux : 1979-1983 = Documentacion de la FAO : produccion y proteccion de plantas : 1979-1983. — Rome : Food and Agriculture Organization, 1985. — 112,13,34,12p. — In English with introductions also in French and Spanish

PLASTICS INDUSTRY AND TRADE — Great Britain
RUBBER AND PLASTICS PROCESSING INDUSTRY TRAINING BOARD
Towards a strategy for the plastics processing industry : a study based on a survey of plastics processing companies in South Wales during 1977, carried out by the Rubber and Plastics Processing Industry Training Board and commissioned by the Department of Industry. — London : Department of Industry, 1978. — 68p. — Bibliographical references: p42

PLASTICS INDUSTRY AND TRADE — Wales
RUBBER AND PLASTICS PROCESSING INDUSTRY TRAINING BOARD
Towards a strategy for the plastics processing industry : a study based on a survey of plastics processing companies in South Wales during 1977, carried out by the Rubber and Plastics Processing Industry Training Board and commissioned by the Department of Industry. — London : Department of Industry, 1978. — 68p. — Bibliographical references: p42

PLATO. Republic
CROSS, R. C. (Robert Craigie)
Plato's Republic : a philosophical commentary / R.C. Cross and A.D. Woozley. — London : Macmillan, 1964 (1980 [printing]). — xv,295p. — Originally published: London : Macmillan ; New York : St Martin's Press, 1964. — Bibliography: p289-291. — Includes index

PLATO. Republic. Book 1
LYCOS, Kimon
Plato on justice and power : reading Book 1 of Plato's Republic / Kimon Lycos. — Basingstoke : Macmillan, 1987. — ix,201p. — Bibliography: p194-197. — Includes index

PLATO
Plato, Popper and politics : some contributions to a modern controversy / edited by Renford Bambrough. — Cambridge : Heffer, 1967. — viii, 219p. — (Views and controversies about classical antiquity)

WHITE, Nicholas P.
A companion to Plato's 'Republic' / Nicholas P. White. — Oxford : Blackwell, 1979. — viii,275p. — Bibliography: p.267-272. — Includes index. — Includes a summary of the text

PLEA BARGAINING — England
BALDWIN, John, 1945—
Negotiated justice : pressures to plead guilty / John Baldwin & Michael McConville. — London : Martin Robertson, 1977. — xvi,128p. — (Law in society series). — Bibliography: p.121-126. — Includes index

PLEA BARGAINING — England — Birmingham
BALDWIN, John, 1945—
Negotiated justice : pressures to plead guilty / John Baldwin & Michael McConville. — London : Martin Robertson, 1977. — xvi,128p. — (Law in society series). — Bibliography: p.121-126. — Includes index

PLEBISCITE
FARLEY, Lawrence T.
Plebiscites and sovereignty : the crisis of political illegitimacy / Lawrence T. Farley. — Boulder, Colo. : Westview ; London : Mansell, 1986. — xiv,179p. — (Westview's special studies in international relations). — Bibliography: p149-165. — Includes index

PLEBISCITE — Puerto Rico
PUERTO RICO. Overseas Information Service
The plebiscite on the political status of Puerto Rico to be held on July 23, 1967. — San Juan : the Service, 1967. — vii,50p

PLUNKETT, HORACE
DIGBY, Margaret
Horace Plunkett : an Anglo-American Irishman / by Margaret Digby. — Oxford : Blackwell, 1949. — xv,314p, 9 plates

PLURALISM (SOCIAL SCIENCES)
Community power : directions for future research / edited by Robert J. Waste. — Beverly Hills : Sage Publications, 1986. — p. cm. — (Sage focus editions ; v. 79). — Includes bibliographies

CONFERENCE ON PLURALISM IN FEDERAL STATES (1983 : Kingston, Canada)
[Pluralism in Federal States]. — Kingston, Canada : International Political Science Association, 1983. — 13microfiches

WALZER, Michael
The politics of ethnicity / Michael Walzer...[et al.]. — Cambridge, Mass. ; London : Belknap Press of Harvard University Press, 1982. — vi,142p. — (Dimensions of ethnicity : Selections from the Harvard Encyclopedia of American ethnic groups). — Bibliography: p [139]-142

PLURALISM (SOCIAL SCIENCES) — History
MCNEILL, William H.
Polyethnicity and national unity in world history / William H. McNeill. — Toronto ; London : University of Toronto Press, 1986. — vii, 85p. — (The Donald G. Creighton lectures ; 1985)

PLURALISM (SOCIAL SCIENCES) — Canada
FRIESEN, John W.
When cultures clash : case studies in multiculturalism / John W. Friesen. — Calgary, Alberta : Detselig Enterprises, 1985. — 171p

PLURALISM (SOCIAL SCIENCES) — Poland
TOMASZEWSKI, Jerzy
Rzeczpospolita wielu narodów / Jerzy Tomaszewski. — Warszawa : Czytelnik, 1985. — 285

PLURALISM (SOCIAL SCIENCES) — Venezuela
ARROYO TALAVERA, Eduardo
Elections and negotiation : the limits of democracy in Venezuela / Eduardo Arroyo Talavera. — [New York, N.Y.] : Garland Pub., 1986. — 450 p.. — (Outstanding theses from the London School of Economics and Political Science). — Spine title: The limits of democracy in Venezuela, 1958-1981. — Thesis (Ph. D.)--University of London, 1983. — Bibliography: p. 421-450

PLYWOOD INDUSTRY — Northwest, Pacific — Management — Employee participation — Case studies
GREENBERG, Edward S.
Workplace democracy : the political effects of participation / Edward S. Greenberg. — Ithaca : Cornell University Press, 1986. — p. cm. — Includes index. — Bibliography: p

POETS, CUBAN — 20th century — Biography
VALLADARES, Armando
Against all hope : the prison memoirs of Armando Valladares / translated by Andrew Hurley. — London : Hamilton, 1986. — xiv,380p. — *Translation of: Contra toda esperanza*

POHER, ALAIN
BOISSONADE, Euloge
Jamais deux sans trois?... = ou, l'étonnant destin d'Alain Poher / Euloge Boissonade. — Paris : Editions France-Empire, 1986. — 238p

POLAND
TARAS, Ray
Poland, socialist state, rebellious nation / Ray Taras. — Boulder, Colo. : Westview Press, c1986. — p. cm. — (Westview profiles. Nations of contemporary Eastern Europe). — *Includes index. — Bibliography: p*

POLAND — Boundaries — Germany
MROCZKO, Marian
Polska myśl zachodnia 1918-1939 : (kształtowanie i upowszechnianie / Marian Mroczko. — Poznań : Instytut Zachodni, 1986. — 429p. — (Dzieje polskiej granicy zachodniej ; 6). — *Summary in English and German. — Bibliography: p352-393*

POLAND — Commerce
DĘBSKI, Jerzy
Integracja wielkich miast Polski w zakresie powiązań towarowych / Jerzy Dębski. — Wrocław : Ossolineum, 1980. — 125p. — (Prace geograficzne / Polska Akademia Nauk. Instytut Geografii i Przestrzennego Zagospodarowania ; Nr.135). — *Summary in Russian and English. — Bibliography: p115-119*

POLAND — Commerce — Great Britain
MIERZWA, Edward Alfred
Anglia a Polska w pierwszej połowie XVII w. / Edward Alfred Mierzwa. — Warszawa : Pa/nstwowe Wydawnictwo Naukowe, 1986. — 314p. — *Bibliography: p284-[300]*

POLAND — Economic conditions — 1918-1945
GOŁĘBIOWSKI, Jerzy
Sektor państwowy w gospodarce Polski międzywojennej / Jerzy GoŁębiowski. — Warszawa : Państwowe Wydawnictwo Naukowe, 1985. — 366p. — *Bibliography: p336-[355]*

POLAND — Economic conditions — 1945-
HIRSZOWICZ, Maria
The crisis : problems in Poland. — Munchen : Projekt 'Crises in Soviet-type systems'. — (Research project Crises in Soviet-type systems ; Study no.12)
Part 1 / M. Hirszowicz, P. Michel [and] G. Mink. — 1986. — 48p

Polska 1985 : spojrzenie na gospodarke / [opracowanie nieżaleznej grupy ekspertów z kraju]. — Paris : Spotkania, 1985. — 81p. — (Biblioteka Libertas ; 1)

POLAND — Economic Policy
CZEPURKO, Aleksander
Świat a gospodarka Polski. — Warszawa : Książka i Wiedza, 1986. — 191p

POLAND — Economic policy — 1945-
KARPIŃSKI, Andrzej
40 lat planowania w Polsce : problemy, ludzie, refleksje / Andrzej Karpiński. — Warszawa : Państwowe Wydawnictwo Ekonomiczne, 1986. — 421p. — *Bibliography: p413-[416]*

MAGIERSKA, Anna
Przywrócić Polsce : przemysł na Ziemiach Odzyskanych 1945-1946. — Warszawa : Państwowe Wydawnictwo Naukowe, 1986. — 467p. — *Bibliography: p439-[451]*

POLAND — Economic policy — 1966-1980
FLAKIERSKI, Henryk
Economic reform & income distribution : a case study of Hungary and Poland / by Henryk Flakierski. — Armonk, N.Y. : M.E. Sharpe, c1986. — xi, 194 p.. — *"Published simultaneously as vol. XXIV, no. 1-2, of Eastern European economics"--Verso t.p. — Bibliography: p. 165-194*

POLAND — Economic policy — 1981-
BAKA, Władysław
Czas reformy : wybór tekstów / WŁadysŁaw Baka. — Warszawa : Książka i Wiedza, 1986. — 382p. — (Refleksje & poglądy)

FLAKIERSKI, Henryk
Economic reform & income distribution : a case study of Hungary and Poland / by Henryk Flakierski. — Armonk, N.Y. : M.E. Sharpe, c1986. — xi, 194 p.. — *"Published simultaneously as vol. XXIV, no. 1-2, of Eastern European economics"--Verso t.p. — Bibliography: p. 165-194*

KOŹMIŃSKI, Andrzej K.
Gospodarka w punkcie zwrotnym / Andrzej K. Koźmiński. — Warszawa : Państwowe Wydawnictwo Ekonomiczne, 1985. — 91p

Polska 1985 : spojrzenie na gospodarke / [opracowanie nieżaleznej grupy ekspertów z kraju]. — Paris : Spotkania, 1985. — 81p. — (Biblioteka Libertas ; 1)

POLAND — Emigration and immigration
AVERY, D. H.
The Poles in Canada / D.H.Avery and J.K.Fedorowicz. — Ottawa : Canadian Historical Association, 1982. — 22p. — (Canada's ethnic groups. booklet ; no.4)

Pisarz na obczyźnie / praca zbiorowa pod redakcją Tadeusza Bujnickiego i Wojciecha Wyskiela. — Wrocław : Ossolineum, 1985. — 207p. — (Biblioteka polonijna ; 14). — *Summaries in English*

Writing home : immigrants in Brazil and the United States, 1890-1891 / Witold Kula...[et al.]; edited and translated by Josephine Wtulich. — Boulder, Colo. : East European Monographs ; New York : distributed by Columbia University Press, 1986. — xiii,698p. — (East European Monographs ; no.210). — *Translation of "Listy emigrantów z Brazylii i Stanów Zjednoczonych 1890-1891", Warsaw, 1972*

POLAND — Ethnic relations
CONFERENCE ON POLES AND JEWS: MYTH AND REALITY IN THE HISTORICAL CONTEXT (1983 : Columbia University)
Proceedings of the Conference on Poles and Jews--Myth and Reality in the Historical Context, held at Columbia University, March 6-10, 1983 / editorial staff, John Micgiel, Robert Scott, H.B. Segel. — New York : Institute on East Central Europe, Columbia University, 1986. — vi, 562 p.. — *Cover title: Poles and Jews. — "Sponsored by the Institute on East Central Europe, Columbia University, in collaboration with the Center for Israel and Jewish Studies, Columbia University"--Cover. — Includes bibliographies*

POLAND — Ethnic relations — Bibliography
LERSKI, Jerzy J
Jewish-Polish coexistence, 1772-1939 : a topical bibliography / compiled by George J. Lerski and Halina T. Lerski ; foreword by Lucjan Dobroszycki. — New York : Greenwood Press, 1986. — xiv, 230 p.. — (Bibliographies and indexes in world history ; no. 5). — *Includes index*

POLAND — Foreign economic relations
CZEPURKO, Aleksander
Świat a gospodarka Polski. — Warszawa : Książka i Wiedza, 1986. — 191p

GARLAND, John S
Industrial cooperation between Poland and the West / by John Garland. — Ann Arbor, Mich. : UMI Research Press, c1985. — p. cm. — (Research for business decisions ; no. 71). — : *Originally presented as the author's thesis (Indiana University, 1982). — Includes index. — Bibliography: p*

POLAND — Foreign economic relations — Great Britain
CIAMAGA, Lucjan
Polska-Wielka Brytania : gospodarka, stosunki ekonomiczne / Lucjan Ciamaga. — Warszawa : Państwowe Wydawnictwo Ekonomiczne, 1982. — 359p. — (Polska - RWPG - Świat)

POLAND — Foreign economic relations — Yugoslavia
RYŚ, Bronisław
Rozwój polsko-jugosłowiańskich stosunków gospodarczych / Bronisław Ryś. — Łódź : Wydawnictwo Łódskie, 1986. — 485p. — *Summary in Serbo Croat and German. — Bibliography: p467-[478]*

POLAND — Foreign relations — 1918-1945
KARSKI, Jan
The Great Powers & Poland, 1919-1945 : from Versailles to Yalta / Jan Karski. — Lanham, MD : University Press of America, c1985. — xvi, 697 p.. — *Includes index. — Bibliography: p. 627-671*

POLAND — Foreign relations — 1945-
PAŁYGA, Edward J.
Dypolomacja Polski Ludowej, 1944-1984 : (kierunki - tresci - mechanizmy) / Edward J. Pałyga. — Warszawa : Instytut Wydawniczy Zwigzków Zawodowych, 1986. — 370p. — *Bibliography: p354-[364]*

POLAND — Foreign relations — Germany
Studia z najnowszej historii niemiec i stosunków polsko-niemieckich / pod redakcją Stanisława Sierpowskiego. — Poznań : Uniwersytet im. Adama Mickiewicza, 1986. — 634p. — (Seria Historia / Uniwersytet im. Adama Mickiewicza w Poznaniu ; Nr.129). — *In Polish or German*

POLAND — Foreign relations — Germany (East)
Dokumenty i materiały do stosunków Polski z Niemiecką Republiką Demokratyczną / Komitet Redakcyjny: Kazimierz Wajda, Heinz Heitzer...[et al.]. — Wrocław : Ossolineum
T.1: Październik 1949-maj 1955 / opracowali Gerhard Keiderling...[et al.]. — 1986. — xxii,609p

POLAND — Foreign relations — Great Britain
MIERZWA, Edward Alfred
Anglia a Polska w pierwszej połowie XVII w. / Edward Alfred Mierzwa. — Warszawa : Pa/nstwowe Wydawnictwo Naukowe, 1986. — 314p. — *Bibliography: p284-[300]*

PRAŻMOWSKA, Anita
Britain, Poland and the Eastern Front, 1939 / Anita Prazmowska. — Cambridge : Cambridge University Press, 1987. — viii,231p. — (Soviet and East European studies). — *Bibliography: p220-224. — Includes index*

POLAND — Foreign relations — Italy
KIENIEWICZ, Stefan
L'Italie et l'insurrection polonaise de 1863 / Stefan Kieniewicz. — Wroclaw : Accademia Polacca Delle Scienze, 1975. — 20p

POLAND — Foreign relations — Soviet Union
GREAT BRITAIN. Parliament. House of Commons. Library. International Affairs Section
Poland, the USSR and the west / Richard Ware. — [London] : the Library, 1980. — 14p. — (Background paper / House of Commons. Library. [Research Division] ; no.87). — *Bibliographical references: p12*

POLAND — Foreign relations — Soviet Union *continuation*

GREAT BRITAIN. Parliament. House of Commons. Library. International Affairs Section
Poland, the USSR and the west / Richard Ware. — [London] : the Library, 1981. — 24p. — (Background paper / House of Commons. Library. [Research Division] ; no.87). — *Updated version of 1980 Background Paper no.87.* — *Bibliographical references: p12,24*

PLOSS, Sidney I
Moscow and the Polish crisis : an interpretation of Soviet policies and intentions / Sidney I. Ploss. — Boulder : Westview Press, 1986. — ix, 182 p.. — (Westview special studies on the Soviet Union and Eastern Europe). — *Includes bibliographical references and index*

Tajne rokowanie polsko-radzieckie w 1919 r. : materiały archiwalne i dokumenty / zebrała i opracowała Weronika Gosty'nska. — Warszawa : Pa'nstwowe Wydawnictwo Naukowe, 1986. — 412p. — *Documents in Polish, Russian, French or German.* — *Bibliography: p391-[396]*

POLAND — Foreign relations — United States

HOUGH, Jerry F.
The Polish crisis : American policy options : a staff paper / by Jerry F. Hough. — Washington : Brookings Institution, 1982. — viii,80p

KARSKI, Jan
The Great Powers & Poland, 1919-1945 : from Versailles to Yalta / Jan Karski. — Lanham, MD : University Press of America, c1985. — xvi, 697 p.. — *Includes index.* — *Bibliography: p. 627-671*

PEASE, Neal
Poland, the United States, and the stabilization of Europe, 1919-1933 / by Neal Pease. — New York ; Oxford : Oxford University Press, 1986. — vii, 238p. — *Includes index.* — *Bibliography: p.[222]-231*

POLAND — History

BROMKE, Adam
The meaning and uses of Polish history / Adam Bromke. — Boulder : East European Monographs ; New York : distributed by Columbia University Press, 1987. — viii,244p. — (East European Monographs ; 212)

POLAND — History — Study and teaching — Poland

BROMKE, Adam
The meaning and uses of Polish history / Adam Bromke. — Boulder : East European Monographs ; New York : distributed by Columbia University Press, 1987. — viii,244p. — (East European Monographs ; 212)

POLAND — History — Revolution, 1863-1864

KIENIEWICZ, Stefan
L'Italie et l'insurrection polonaise de 1863 / Stefan Kieniewicz. — Wroclaw : Accademia Polacca Delle Scienze, 1975. — 20p

POLAND — History — 20th century

ASCHERSON, Neal
The struggles for Poland / Neal Ascherson. — London : Joseph, 1987. — [288]p. — *Includes bibliography and index*

POLAND — History — 1918-1945

MACKIEWICZ, Stanisław
Historja Polski od 11 listopada 1918r. do 17 września 1939r. / Stanisław Mackiewicz (Cat). — 2-e wyd.. — London : Puls Publications, 1985. — 342p. — (Politicus ; 7). — *First published London, M. I. Kolin, 1941*

TOMASZEWSKI, Jerzy
Rzeczpospolita wielu narodów / Jerzy Tomaszewski. — Warszawa : Czytelnik, 1985. — 285

Wielkopolska a powstania śląskie 1919-1921 : praca zbiorowa / pod redakcją Krzysztofa Rzepy. — Poznań : Uniwersytet im. A. Mickiewicza, 1973. — 50p

POLAND — History — 1945-1980

GÓRA, Władysław
Trudny start : z dziejów Polski Ludowej 1944-1947 / Władysław Góra. — Warszawa : Instytut Wydawniczy Związków Zawodowych, 1985. — 221p. — (Historia - Współczesność - Ludzie)

POLAND — History — 1945-

GÓRA, Władysław
Polska Ludowa 1944-1984 : zarys dziejów politycznych / Władysław Góra. — Lublin : Wydawnictwo Lubelskie, 1986. — 718p. — *Bibliography: p[699]-704*

POLAND — History — 1980-

BARKER, Colin
Festival of the oppressed : Solidarity reform and revolution in Poland 1980-81 / Colin Barker. — London : Bookmarks, 1986. — 192p

HOUGH, Jerry F.
The Polish crisis : American policy options : a staff paper / by Jerry F. Hough. — Washington : Brookings Institution, 1982. — viii,80p

PLOSS, Sidney I
Moscow and the Polish crisis : an interpretation of Soviet policies and intentions / Sidney I. Ploss. — Boulder : Westview Press, 1986. — ix, 182 p.. — (Westview special studies on the Soviet Union and Eastern Europe). — *Includes bibliographical references and index*

POLAND — Industries

BARTOSIK, Zygmunt
Przemysł miedziowy / Zygmunt Bartosik. — Wrocław : Ossolineum, 1981. — 259p

BOSSAK, Jan W.
Structural adjustment policy and international competitiveness of Polish industry / Jan W. Bossak and Dariusz Zbytniewski. — Warsaw : Foreign Trade Research Institute, 1987. — 46p

MAGIERSKA, Anna
Przywrócić Polsce : przemysł na Ziemiach Odzyskanych 1945-1946. — Warszawa : Państwowe Wydawnictwo Naukowe, 1986. — 467p. — *Bibliography: p439-[451]*

POLAND — Poilitics and government — 1945-

TORAŃSKA, Teresa
Oni / Teresa Torańska. — Londyn : Aneks, 1985. — 365p

POLAND — Politics and government

KONARSKI, Marek
Stanowisko ministra w PRL : zagadnienia prawno-konstytucyjne / Marek Konarski. — Warszawa : Państwowe Wydawnictwo Naukowe, 1986. — 287p. — *Bibliography: p283-286*

POLAND — Politics and government — 1796-1918

JASZCZUK, Andrzej
Spór pozytywistów z konserwatystami o przyszŁość Polski 1870-1903 / Andrzej Jaszczuk. — Warszawa : Państwowe Wydawnictwo Naukowe, 1986. — 292p. — (Polska XIX i XX wieku : dzieje spoŁeczne)

POLAND — Politics and government — 1918-1945

COUTOUVIDIS, John
Poland 1939-1947 / John Coutouvidis & Jaime Reynolds. — [Leicester] : Leicester University Press, 1986. — xxi,393p,[8]p of plates. — (The Politics of liberation series). — *Bibliography: p372-382.* — *Includes index*

KOŁOMEJCZYK, Norbert
Polska Partia Robotnicza 1942-1948 / Norbert Kołomejczyk, Marian Malinowski. — Warszawa : Książka i Wiedza, 1986. — 540p. — *Bibliogpraphy: p526-[529]*

LATO, Stanisław
Ruch ludowy wobec sanacji : (z dziejów politycznych II Rzeczypospolitej) / Stanisław Lato. — Rzeszów : Krajowa Agencja Wydawnicza, 1985. — 217p

MAJCHROWSKI, Jacek
Silni, zwarci, gotowi : myśl polityczna Obozu Zjednoczenia Narodowego / Jacek Majchrowski. — Warszawa : Państwowe Wydawnictwo Naukowe, 1985. — 215,xvip. — *Bibliography: p202-[211]*

PAPIERZYŃSKA-TUREK, Mirosława
Sprawa ukraińska w Drugiej Rzeczypospolitej 1922-1926 / Mirosława Papierzyńska Turek. — Kraków : Wydawnictwo Literackie, 1979. — 389p. — *Bibliography: p359-379*

PEASE, Neal
Poland, the United States, and the stabilization of Europe, 1919-1933 / by Neal Pease. — New York ; Oxford : Oxford University Press, 1986. — vii, 238p. — *Includes index.* — *Bibliography: p.[222]-231*

TOMICKI, Jan
Lewica socjalistyczna w Polsce 1918-1939 / Jan Tomicki. — Warszawa : Książka i Wiedza, 1982. — 611p. — *Table of contents in Russian, German and English.* — *Bibliography: p577-[592]*

TORANSKA, Teresa
Oni : Stalin's Polish puppets / Teresa Toranska ; translated from the Polish by Agnieszka Kolakowska ; with an introduction by Harry Willetts. — London : Collins Harvill, 1987. — 384p. — *Translation of: Oni*

POLAND — Politics and government — 1945-1980

BŁAŻYŃSKI, Zbigniew
Mówi Józef Światło : za kulisami bezpieki i partii 1940-1955 / Zbigniew Błażyński ; słowo wstępne: Jan Nowak-Jezioranski. — Wyd. 3 (z erratami i uzupełnieniem). — Londyn : Polska Fundacja Kulturalna, 1986. — xv,319p. — *Part of the material contained in this book was published by Radio Free Europe as a pamphlet in 1955 and dropped over Poland from balloons, under the title "Za kulisami bezpieki i partii". Reprinted under title "Kulisy bezpieki i partii" in Warsaw 1979 by the clandestine Publishing House NOWA*

COUTOUVIDIS, John
Poland 1939-1947 / John Coutouvidis & Jaime Reynolds. — [Leicester] : Leicester University Press, 1986. — xxi,393p,[8]p of plates. — (The Politics of liberation series). — *Bibliography: p372-382.* — *Includes index*

POMIAN, Kryzsztof
Wymiary polskiego konfliktu 1956-1981 / Kryzsztof pomian. — Londyn : Aneks, 1985. — 174p

SYZDEK, Eleonora
Polityczne dylematy Władysława Gomułki / Eleonora Syzdek, Bronisław Syzdek. — Warszawa : Czytelnik, 1985. — 260p. — *Bibliography: p257-[261]*

TORANSKA, Teresa
Oni : Stalin's Polish puppets / Teresa Toranska ; translated from the Polish by Agnieszka Kolakowska ; with an introduction by Harry Willetts. — London : Collins Harvill, 1987. — 384p. — *Translation of: Oni*

POLAND — Politics and government — 1945-

GÓRA, Władysław
Polska Ludowa 1944-1984 : zarys dziejów politycznych / Władysław Góra. — Lublin : Wydawnictwo Lubelskie, 1986. — 718p. — *Bibliography: p[699]-704*

HIRSZOWICZ, Maria
The crisis : problems in Poland. — Munchen : Projekt 'Crises in Soviet-type systems'. — (Research project Crises in Soviet-type systems ; Study no.12)
Part 1 / M. Hirszowicz, P. Michel [and] G. Mink. — 1986. — 48p

POLAND — Politics and government — 1945- *continuation*

KAPLAN, Karel
The overcoming of the regime crisis after Stalin's death in Czechoslovakia, Poland and Hungary / Karel Kaplan. — Munchen : Projekt 'Crises in Soviet-type systems', 1986. — 119p. — (Research project Crises in Soviet-type systems ; Study no.11)

KARPIŃSKI, Jakub
Ustrój komunistyczny w Polsce / Jakub Karpiński. — Londyn : Aneks, 1985. — 228p

POLAND — Politics and government — 1980

MICHNIK, Adam
Z dziejów honoru w Polsce : wypisy więzienne / Adam Michnik. — Paryż : Instytut Literacki, 1985. — 285p. — (Biblioteka Kultury ; T.404)

POLAND — Politics and government — 1980-

GREAT BRITAIN. Parliament. House of Commons. Library. International Affairs Section
Poland - the continuing crisis / Richard Ware. — [London] : the Library, 1981. — 27p. — (Background paper / House of Commons. Library. [Research Division] ; no.97). — *Supplements Background Paper no.87*

GREAT BRITAIN. Parliament. House of Commons. Library. International Affairs Section
Poland, the USSR and the west / Richard Ware. — [London] : the Library, 1980. — 14p. — (Background paper / House of Commons. Library. [Research Division] ; no.87). — *Bibliographical references: p12*

GREAT BRITAIN. Parliament. House of Commons. Library. International Affairs Section
Poland, the USSR and the west / Richard Ware. — [London] : the Library, 1981. — 24p. — (Background paper / House of Commons. Library. [Research Division] ; no.87). — *Updated version of 1980 Background Paper no.87.* — *Bibliographical references: p12,24*

GREAT BRITAIN. Parliament. House of Commons. Library. International Affairs Section
Poland under martial law / Richard Ware. — [London] : the Library, 1982. — 38p. — (Background paper / House of Commons. Library. [Research Division] ; no.98)

JARUZELSKI, Wojciech
Przemówienia 1983 / Wojciech Jaruzelski. — Warszawa : Książka i Wiedza, 1984. — 341p

JARUZELSKI, Wojciech
Przemówienia 1984 / Wojciech Jaruzelski. — Warszawa : Książka i Wiedza, 1985. — 428p

JARUZELSKI, Wojciech
Przemówienia 1985 / Wojciech Jaruzelski. — Warszawa : Książka i Wiedza, 1986. — 500p

KĘPIŃSKI, Andrzej
Kto jest kim w Polsce-inaczej / Andrzej Kępiński, Zbigniew Kilar (współpraca). — Warszawa : Czytelnik
Cz.1. — 1985. — 420p

KĘPIŃSKI, Andrzej
Kto jest kim w Polsce - inaczej / Andrzej Kępiński, Zbigniew Kilar (współpraca). — Warszawa : Czytelnik
Cz.2. — 1986. — 454p

KUCIŃSKI, Jerzy
Geneza PRON / Jerzy Kuciński. — Warszawa : Książka i Weiedza, 1985. — 158p

MICHNIK, Adam
Takie czasy...rzecz o kompromisie / Adam Michnik. — Londyn : Aneks, 1985. — 140p

SANFORD, George
Military rule in Poland : the rebuilding of communist power, 1981-1983 / George Sanford. — London : Croom Helm, c1986. — 288p. — *Includes bibliography and index*

WEDEL, Janine
The private Poland / Janine Wedel. — New York, NY : Facts on File Inc., c1986. — xv, 230 p., [8] p. of plates. — *Includes index.* — *Bibliography: p. 223-226*

POLAND — Politics and government — 1980- — Addresses, essays, lectures

MICHNIK, Adam
Letters from prison and other essays / Adam Michnik ; translated by Maya Latynski ; foreword by Czeslaw Milosz ; introduction by Jonathan Schell. — Berkeley ; London : University of Calif. Press, c1985. — xlii, 354p. — *Translated from Polish*

POLAND — Population

LINK, Krzysztof
Społeczno-ekonomiczne czynniki tworzenia gospodarstw domowych / Krzysztof Link. — Warszawa : Szkoła Główna Planowania i Statystyki, 1986. — 155p. — (Kształtowanie procesów demograficznych a rozwój społeczno-gospodarczy Polski) (Monografie i opracowania / Szkoła Główna Planowania i Statystyki). — *Contents and summary in English and Russian*

OCHOCKI, Andrzej
Wpływ migracji na rozmieszczenie zasobów pracy w latach 1970-1983 / Andrzej Ochocki. — Warszawa : Szkoła Główna Planowania i Statystyki, 1986. — 155p. — (Kształtowanie procesów demograficznych a rozwój społeczno-gospodarczy Polski) (Monografie i opracowania / Szkoła Główna Planowania i Statystyki ; 221/8). — *Summary and contents in English and Russian*

POLSKA AKADEMIA NAUK. Komitet Nauk Demograficznych. Sekcja Demografii Historycznej
Przeszło's'c demograficzna Polski : materiały i studia / [komitet redakcyjny: Irena Gieysztorowa, Egon Vielrose (red. naczelny)...et al.]. — Warszawa : Państwowe Wydawnictwo Naukowe
12. — 1980. — 236p. — *Table of contents in English.* — *Contains "Bibliography of European historical demography 1971-1977", pt.1*

POLSKA AKADEMIA NAUK. Komitet Nauk Demograficznych. Sekcja Demografii Historycznej
Przeszło's'e demograficzna Polski : materiały i studia / [komitet redakcyjny: Stanisław Gierszewski, Egon Vielrose (red. naczelny)...et al.]. — Warszawa : Państwowe Wydawnictwo Naukowe
13. — 1981. — 185p. — *Table of contents in English.* — *Contains "Bibliography of European historical demography 1971-1977", pt.2*

Studia nad migracjami i przemianami systemu osadniczego w Polsce : opracowanie zbiorowe / pod redakcją Kazimierza Dziewo'nskiego i Piotra Korcellego. — Wrocław : Ossolineum, 1981. — 267p. — (Prace geograficzne / Polska Akademia Nauk. Instytut Geografii i Przestrzennego Zagospodarowania ; Nr.140). — *Summaries in Russian and English.* — *Bibliographies*

Wybrane uwarunkowania i konsekwencje procesu starzenia się ludności Polski / Ewa Frątczak...[et al.]. — Warszawa : Szkoła Główna Planowania i Statystyki, 1987. — 231p. — (Kształtowanie procesów demograficznych a rozwój społeczno-gospodarczy Polski) (Monografie i opracowania / Szkoła Główna Planowania i Statystyki ; 223/10). — *Contents and summary in English and Russian*

POLAND — Relations — Silesia

KOPEĆ, Eugeniusz
"My i oni" na polskim Śląsku (1918-1939) / Eugeniusz Kopeć. — Wyd. 2-e, popraw. i uzup. — Katowice : Wydawnictwo "Śląsk", 1986. — 238p

POLAND — Relations — Slavic countries

GIZA, Antoni
Neoslawizm i polacy 1906-1910 / Antoni Giza. — Szczecin : Wyższa Szkoła Pedagogiczna, 1984. — 265p. — (Rozprawy i studia / Wyższa Szkoła Pedagogiczna w Szczecinie ; t.61). — *Summary in German and Russian.* — *Bibliography: p237-251*

POLAND — Social conditions — 1945-

Social stratification in Poland : eight empirical studies / edited by Kazimierz M. Słomczyński and Tadeusz K. Krauze ; with a foreword by Gerhard Lenski. — Armonk, N.Y. : M.E. Sharpe, c1986. — p. cm. — *"Published simulanteously as International journal of sociology, vol. XVI, no. 1-2"--Verso of t.p.* — *Contents: Introduction : the context of recent Polish research on social stratification / Kazimierz M. Słomczyński and Tadeusz K. Krauze -- Social inequality and social mobility / Michael Pohoski -- Changes in social structure and its popular perception / Krystyna Janicka -- The attainment of occupation status / Kazimierz M. Słomczyński -- Dichotomous class images and worker' radicalism / Wojciech Zaborowski -- The subjective evaluation of social status / Kazimierz M. Słomvczyński -- The prestige of education / Zbigniew Sawinski -- Value systems among occupational groups / Maria Misztal -- Social mobility / Tadeusz K. Krauze and Kazimierz M. Słomczyński*

POLAND — Social life and customs — 1945-

WEDEL, Janine
The private Poland / Janine Wedel. — New York, NY : Facts on File Inc., c1986. — xv, 230 p., [8] p. of plates. — *Includes index.* — *Bibliography: p. 223-226*

POLAND — Social policy

OKRASA, W.
Social justice and the redistributive effect of social expenditure in Poland / W. Okrasa. — London : Suntory Toyota International Centre for Economics and Related Disciplines, 1987. — 18p. — (Welfare State Programme ; no.18). — *Bibliography: p18*

Polityka społeczna w okresie przemian : praca zbiorowa / pod redakcją naukowa Andrzeja Piekary i Jolanty Supińskiej. — Warszawa : Państwowe Wydawnictwo Ekonomiczne, 1985. — 473p. — (Polityka społeczna w PRL)

POLANYI, KARL

STANFIELD, J. Ron
The economic thought of Karl Polanyi : Lives and Livelihood / J.R. Stanfield. — Basingstoke : Macmillan, 1986. — x,162p. — *Includes index*

POLANYI, MICHAEL

PROSCH, Harry
Michael Polanyi : a critical exposition / by Harry Prosch. — Albany, NY : State University of New York Press, 1986. — x, 354p. — (A SUNY series in cultural perspectives). — *Includes index.* — *"Bibliography of Michael Polanyi's publications"- p 319-346*

POLAR REGIONS

SABIN, Francene
Arctic and Antarctic regions / by Francene Sabin ; illustrated by Allan Eitzen. — Mahwah, N.J. : Troll Associates, c1985. — p. cm. — *Summary: Briefly describes the frozen regions around the North Pole and the South Pole, which are alike in many ways and different in many others*

POLAR REGIONS — Juvenile literature

SABIN, Francene
Arctic and Antarctic regions / by Francene Sabin ; illustrated by Allan Eitzen. — Mahwah, N.J. : Troll Associates, c1985. — p. cm. — *Summary: Briefly describes the frozen regions around the North Pole and the South Pole, which are alike in many ways and different in many others*

POLES — Brazil

Writing home : immigrants in Brazil and the United States, 1890-1891 / Witold Kula...[et al.]; edited and translated by Josephine Wtulich. — Boulder, Colo. : East European Monographs ; New York : distributed by Columbia University Press, 1986. — xiii,698p. — (East European Monographs ; no.210). — *Translation of "Listy emigrantów z Brazylii i Stanów Zjednoczonych 1890-1891", Warsaw, 1972*

POLES — Germany — Berlin

PONIATOWSKA, Anna
Polacy w Berlinie 1918-1945 / Anna Poniatowska. — Poznań : Wydawnictwo Poznańskie, 1986. — 353p. — *Bibliography: p337-[342]*

POLES — United States

Writing home : immigrants in Brazil and the United States, 1890-1891 / Witold Kula...[et al.]; edited and translated by Josephine Wtulich. — Boulder, Colo. : East European Monographs ; New York : distributed by Columbia University Press, 1986. — xiii,698p. — (East European Monographs ; no.210). — *Translation of "Listy emigrantów z Brazylii i Stanów Zjednoczonych 1890-1891", Warsaw, 1972*

POLICE

KLOCKARS, Carl B
The idea of police / by Carl Klockars. — Beverly Hills, Calif. : Sage Publications, c1985. — p. cm. — (Law and criminal justice series ; v. 2). — *Includes index*

POLICE — Complaints against — England — Manchester (Greater Manchester)

WALKER, Martin, 1947-
With extreme prejudice : an investigation into police vigilantism in Manchester / Martin Walker. — London : Canary, 1986. — 203p

POLICE — Cross-cultural studies

BAYLEY, David H
Patterns of policing : a comparative international analysis / David H. Bayley. — New Brunswick, N.J. : Rutgers University Press, c1985. — xii, 263 p.. — (Crime, law, and deviance series). — *Includes index.* — *Bibliography: p. 245-258*

POLICE — Handbooks, manuals, etc

BECKER, Harold K
Handbook of the world's police / by Harold K. Becker, Donna Lee Becker ; maps by Ann Becker. — Metuchen, N.J. : Scarecrow Press, 1986. — ix, 340 p.. — *Bibliography: p. 8*

POLICE — Political aspects — India

MEHRA, Ajay K.
Police in changing India / Ajay K. Mehra. — New Delhi : Usha, 1985. — xiv,184p. — *Bibliography: p[172]-180*

POLICE — Recruiting — Congresses

NATO ADVANCED STUDY INSTITUTE ON "POLICE AND PSYCHOLOGY" (1985 : Skíathos, Greece)
Police selection and training : the role of psychology / editor, John C. Yuille ; [proceedings of the NATO Advanced Study Institute on "Police and Psychology," Skiathos, Greece, May 7-15, 1985]. — Dordrecht ; Boston : Martinus Nijhoff, 1986. — xvi, 376 p.. — (NATO ASI series. Series D. Behavioural and social sciences ; no. 30). — *"Published in cooperation with NATO Scientific Affairs Division.".* — *Includes bibliographies and index*

POLICE — Australia — Complaints against

Complaints against police : supplementary report. — Canberra : Australian Government Publishing Service, 1978. — xiii,131p. — (Report / Law Reform Commission ; no.9). — *Bibliography: p[126]-127*

POLICE — Canada — History

TALBOT, C. K.
Canada's constable's : the historical development of policing in Canada / by C. K. Talbot, C. H. S. Jayewardene, T. J. Juliani. — Ottawa : Crimcare Inc., 1985. — vii,331p. — *Based on: Talbot, C. K. 'The thin blue line' 1983; and Juliani, T. J. 'Urban centurions' 1984.* — *Bibliography: p294-320*

POLICE — England — Complaints against

BROWN, David C.
The police complaints procedure : a survey of complainants' views / by David Brown. — London : H.M.S.O., 1987. — v,91p. — (Home Office research study ; no.93). — *A Home Office Research and Planning Unit report*

POLICE — England — London

GREATER LONDON COUNCIL. Police Committee
Policing London : collected reports of the GLC Police Committee. — [London : the Council, 1986]. — 136p

LONDON STRATEGIC POLICY UNIT. Police Monitoring and Research Group
Policing Wapping : and account of the dispute 1986/7. — London : London Strategic Policy Unit, 1987-. — 47p. — (Briefing paper / London Strategic Policy Unit. Police Monitoring and Research Group ; no.3)

NATIONAL COUNCIL FOR CIVIL LIBERTIES
No way in Wapping : the effect of the policing of the News International dispute on Wapping residents. — London : National Council for Civil Liberties, 1986. — 40p

POLICE — England — London — Public opinion

LONDON STRATEGIC POLICY UNIT
Police complaints : a fresh approach. — London : London Strategic Policy Unit, 1987. — 67p. — (Briefing paper / Police Monitoring and Research Group ; no.4)

LONDON STRATEGIC POLICY UNIT. Police Monitoring and Research Group
Police accountability and a new strategic authority for London. — London : London Strategic Policy Unit. Police Monitoring and Research Group, 1986. — 64p. — (Briefing paper / London Strategic Policy Unit. Police Monitoring and Research Group ; no.2)

NATIONAL UNION OF TEACHERS
Police out of school. — London : National Union of Teachers : Hackney Teachers' Association, 1986. — 12p

POLICE — Europe

CRANFIELD-WOLFSON COLLOQUIUM ON MULTI-ETHNIC AREAS IN EUROPE (1983 : Cambridge)
Policing and social policy : [papers presented at the]...colloquium / edited by John Brown. — London : Police Review Publishing, [1984]. — 158p

POLICE — France — Finance

LINOTTE, Didier
La rationalisation des choix budgétaires de la police nationale / Didier Linotte. — Paris : Presses Universitaires de France, 1975. — 82p. — (Travaux et Recherches de l'Université de Droit, d'Economie et de Sciences Sociales de Paris / Série sciences administrative ; 8). — *Bibliography: p79-80*

POLICE — Great Britain

DOUGLASS, David
Come and wet this truncheon : the role of the police in the coal strike of 1984/85 / David John Douglass. — Doncaster : D. Douglass : Doncaster, Cambridge, South London, DAM-IWA : CaNary Press, 1986. — [40p]

GREGORY, Frank
Policing the democratic state : how much force? / Frank Gregory. — London : Centre for Security and Conflict Studies, 1986. — 25p. — (Conflict studies ; no.194)

GRIMSHAW, Roger
Interpreting policework : policy and practice in forms of beat policing / Roger Grimshaw and Tony Jefferson. — London : Allen & Unwin, 1987. — [288]p. — *Includes bibliography and index*

Police. — London : Conservative Study Group on Crime, 1986. — 14p. — (Occasional paper ; no.3)

The Police : powers, procedures and proprieties / edited by John Benyon and Colin Bourn ; with a foreword by Lord Scarman. — Oxford : Pergamon, 1986. — xxiv,334p. — *Bibliography: p299-312.* — *Includes index*

Policing and the community / edited by Peter Willmott. — London : Policy Studies Institute, 1987. — 67p. — (PSI discussion paper ; no.16)

SCARMAN, Leslie George Scarman, Baron
The Brixton disorders 10-12 April 1981 : report of an enquiry / by Lord Scarman. — London : H.M.S.O., 1981. — viii,168p. — (Cmnd. ; 8427). — *At head of title: Home Office Police Act 1964.* — *Map on folded sheet attached to inside cover.* — *Bibliography: p164-168*

POLICE — Great Britain — Attitudes

THOMAS, Terry, 1946-
The police and social workers / Terry Thomas. — Aldershot : Gower, c1986. — [120]p. — (Community care practice handbooks). — *Includes index*

POLICE — Great Britain — Complaints against

OLIVER, Ian Thomas
Police, government and accountability / Ian Oliver ; foreword by Sir Robert Mark. — Basingstoke : Macmillan, 1987. — x,280p. — *Bibliography: p266-271.* — *Includes index*

SCRATON, Phil
In the arms of the law : coroner's courts deaths in custody / Phil Scraton and Kathryn Chadwick. — London : Pluto, 1987. — [160]p

SPENCER, Sarah
Called to account : the case for police accountability in England and Wales / Sarah Spencer. — London : National Council for Civil Liberties, 1985. — 146p. — *Includes bibliography*

POLICE — Great Britain — Complaints aganist

HARRISON, John
Police misconduct : legal remedies / John Harrison. — London : Legal Action Group, 1987. — xxix,218p. — (Law and practice guide)

POLICE — Great Britain — Equipment and supplies

TechnoCop : new police technologies / by the BSSRS Technology of Political Control Group with RAMPET. — London : Free Association Books, 1985. — 112p. — *Bibliography: p109-110*

POLICE — Great Britain — History

Journal of the Police History Society. — Huntingdon : Police History Society, 1986-. — *Annual*

POLICE — Great Britain — Public opinion

DOWNES, David
Democratic policing : towards a Labour Party policy on police accountability / David Downes and Tony Ward. — London : Labour Campaign for Criminal Justice, 1986. — 70p. — *Bibliography: p64-70*

POLICE — India

INDIA. National Police Commission
Compendium of observations and recommendations of the National Police Commission. — [New Delhi : Controller of Publications, c1983]. — 138p

POLICE — India continuation

NATH, Trilok
The police problem / Trilok Nath. — New Delhi : Vision Books, 1983. — 164 p.. — *Includes index*

SHARMA, P. D.
Police and criminal justice administration in India / P. D. Sharma. — New Delhi : Upper Publishing House, 1985. — xv,247p. — *Bibliography: p227-236*

SHARMA, P. D.
Police and political order in India / P. D. Sharma. — New Delhi : Research Publications, 1984. — ix,292p

POLICE — India — Complaints against

MISRA, Shailendra
Police brutality : an analysis of police behaviour / Shailendra Misra. — New Delhi : Vikas Pub. House, c1986. — 139 p.. — *Includes index. — Bibliography: p. [133]-136*

POLICE — New Zealand

Policing at the crossroads / edited by Neil Cameron, Warren Young. — New Zealand : Allen and Unwin : Wellington : Port Nicholson Press, 1986. — 227p. — *Bibliography: p218-226*

POLICE — South Africa

SOUTHERN AFRICAN CATHOLIC BISHOPS' CONFERENCE
Report on police conduct during township protests, August-November 1984. — London : Southern African Catholic Bishops' Conference : Catholic Institute for International Relations, 1984. — 38p

POLICE — South Africa — Complaints against

LAWYERS COMMITTEE FOR HUMAN RIGHTS
The war against children : South Africa's youngest victims / Lawyers Committee for Human Rights ; with a foreword by Bishop Desmond Tutu. — New York : Lawyers Committee for Human Rights, [1986]. — vi,151p

POLICE — South Australia — Corrupt practices

BRIGHT, Charles
Reports commissioned by the Hon. K. T. Griffin, Attorney-General, South Australia into alleged corruption in the South Australian Police Force / [by Sir Charles Bright]. — Adelaide : Government Printer, 1982. — v,100p

POLICE — Spain — History

PUIG, Jaime J.
Historia de la Guardia Civil / Jaime J. Puig. — [Barcelona] : Mitre, 1984. — 419p. — *Bibliography: p417-419*

POLICE — United States

HAGEMAN, Mary J
Police-community relations / Mary Jeannette Hageman. — Beverly Hills, Calif. : Sage Publications, c1985. — 157p. — (Law and criminal justice series ; v. 6). — *Bibliography: p149-154*

POLICE — United States — Complaints against

HAGEMAN, Mary J
Police-community relations / Mary Jeannette Hageman. — Beverly Hills, Calif. : Sage Publications, c1985. — 157p. — (Law and criminal justice series ; v. 6). — *Bibliography: p149-154*

POLICE ADMINISTRATION — India

CHATURVEDI, S. K.
Metropolitan police administration in India / S. K. Chaturvedi. — Delhi : B. R. Publishing Corporation, 1985. — xxiii,188p. — *Bibliography: p.[169]-184*

SHARMA, P. D.
Police and political order in India / P. D. Sharma. — New Delhi : Research Publications, 1984. — ix,292p

POLICE AND CRIMINAL EVIDENCE ACT 1984

HARGREAVES, Fiona
A practitioner's guide to the Police and Criminal Evidence Act 1984 / Fiona Hargreaves [and] Howard Levenson. — [London] : Legal Action Group, 1985. — xxviii,429p. — *Contains the text of the act*

POLICE AND CRIMINAL EVIDENCE BILL 1982-83

GREAT BRITAIN. Parliament. House of Commons. Library. Research Division
Police and Criminal Evidence Bill (Bill 16, session 1982-83) / [Patrick Nealon]. — [London] : the Division, [1982]. — 25p. — (Reference sheet ; no.82/17). — *Includes bibliographical references*

POLICE AND CRIMINAL EVIDENCE BILL 1983-84

GREAT BRITAIN. Parliament. House of Commons. Library. Research Division
Police and Criminal Evidence Bill, 1983-84 [Bill 44] / [Patrick Nealon]. — [London] : the Division, 1983. — 11p. — (Reference sheet ; no.83/17). — *Bibliographical references: p10-11*

POLICE CHIEFS — Hungary — Biography

KOPÁCSI, Sándor
[Au nom de la classe ouvrière. English]. "In the name of the working class" : the inside story of the Hungarian Revolution / Sándor Kopácsi ; translated by Daniel and Judy Stoffman ; with a foreword by George Jonas. — 1st ed. — New York : Grove Press, 1987, c1986. — p. cm. — *Translation of: Au nom de la classe ouvrière. — Bibliography: p*

POLICE CORRUPTION — Bibliography

WALKER, Christine
Corruption in police forces, business & government. — [London] : Home Office Library, 1978. — 6leaves. — (Reading list / Home Office, Library)

POLICE CORRUPTION — Great Britain

HARRISON, John
Police misconduct : legal remedies / John Harrison. — London : Legal Action Group, 1987. — xxix,218p. — (Law and practice guide)

POLICE CORRUPTION — Hong Kong — History

LETHBRIDGE, H. J.
Hard graft in Hong Kong : scandal; corruption; the ICAC / H. J. Lethbridge. — Hong Kong ; Oxford : Oxford University Press, 1985. — viii,247p. — *Bibliography: p232-243*

POLICE MAGISTRATES — England

KING, Michael, 1942-
Black magistrates : a study of selection and appointment / by Michael King and Colin May. — London : Cobden Trust, 1985. — 198p. — *Includes bibliography*

POLICE PATROL

KLOCKARS, Carl B
The idea of police / by Carl Klockars. — Beverly Hills, Calif. : Sage Publications, c1985. — p. cm. — (Law and criminal justice series ; v. 2). — *Includes index*

POLICE PATROL — England

SOUTHGATE, Peter
Police-public encounters / by Peter Southgate with the assistance of Paul Ekblom. — London : H.M.S.O., 1986. — vi,143p. — (Home Office research study ; no.90). — *A Home Office Research and Planning Unit report*

POLICE PATROL — Great Britain

GRIMSHAW, Roger
Interpreting policework : policy and practice in forms of beat policing / Roger Grimshaw and Tony Jefferson. — London : Allen & Unwin, 1987. — [288]p. — *Includes bibliography and index*

POLICE POWER — England

ROBILLIARD, St. John A.
Police powers and the individual / St. John A. Robilliard and Jenny McEwan. — Oxford : Basil Blackwell, 1986. — [viii,260]p. — *Includes index*

POLICE POWER — Great Britain

GREAT BRITAIN. Parliament. House of Commons. Library. Research Division
Police and Criminal Evidence Bill, 1983-84 [Bill 44] / [Patrick Nealon]. — [London] : the Division, 1983. — 11p. — (Reference sheet ; no.83/17). — *Bibliographical references: p10-11*

GREAT BRITAIN. Parliament. House of Commons. Library. Research Division
Police and Criminal Evidence Bill (Bill 16, session 1982-83) / [Patrick Nealon]. — [London] : the Division, [1982]. — 25p. — (Reference sheet ; no.82/17). — *Includes bibliographical references*

GREATER LONDON COUNCIL
The control of protest : the new Public Order Bill : the Greater London Council's response, adopted 19 December 1985. — [London : the Council], 1986. — 51p. — (Policing London)

POLICE POWER — India — Tamil Nadu — History

ARNOLD, David
Police power and colonial rule, Madras, 1859-1947 / David Arnold. — Delhi ; New York : Oxford University Press, 1986. — x, 277 p.. — *Includes index. — Bibliography: p. [263]-270*

POLICE, PRIVATE

Private policing / [edited by Clifford D. Shearing and Philip C. Stenning. — Beverly Hills, Calif. : Sage Publications, 1986. — p. cm. — (Sage criminal justice systems annuals ; v. 23). — *Includes bibliographies and index*

POLICE QUESTIONING — Scotland

CURRAN, J. H.
Detention or voluntary attendance? : police use of detention under section 2, Criminal Justice (Scotland) Act 1980 / Joseph H. Curran, James K. Carnie. — Edinburgh : H.M.S.O., 1986. — xiv,94p. — (A Scottish Office social research study). — *Prepared under the auspices of the Scottish Office, Central Research Unit. — Bibliography: p93-94*

POLICE SERVICES FOR JUVENILES — Great Britain

ADVISORY COMMITTEE ON POLICE IN SCHOOLS
Policing schools. — London : Advisory Committee on Police in Schools, 1986. — 79p

POLICE SHOOTINGS — Northern Ireland — Investigation

TAYLOR, Peter, 1942-
Stalker : the search for the truth / Peter Taylor. — London : Faber, 1987. — xii,231p

POLICE SOCIAL WORK — Great Britain

THOMAS, Terry, 1946-
The police and social workers / Terry Thomas. — Aldershot : Gower, c1986. — [120]p. — (Community care practice handbooks). — *Includes index*

POLICE TRAINING — Congresses
NATO ADVANCED STUDY INSTITUTE ON "POLICE AND PSYCHOLOGY" (1985 : Skíathos, Greece)
Police selection and training : the role of psychology / editor, John C. Yuille ; [proceedings of the NATO Advanced Study Institute on "Police and Psychology," Skíathos, Greece, May 7-15, 1985]. — Dordrecht ; Boston : Martinus Nijhoff, 1986. — xvi, 376 p.. — (NATO ASI series. Series D. Behavioural and social sciences ; no. 30). — "Published in cooperation with NATO Scientific Affairs Division.". — Includes bibliographies and index

POLICE TRAINING — Great Britain
Police probationer training : the final report of the Stage II review, May 1986 / B. MacDonald (Director) ; Centre for Applied Research in Education, University of East Anglia. — London : H.M.S.O., 1987. — 243p. — Commissioned by the Home Office. — Bibliography: p241-243

POLICEWOMEN — Great Britain
JONES, Sandra
Policewomen and equality : formal policy v informal practice? / Sandra Jones. — Basingstoke : Macmillan, 1986. — xii,235p. — Bibliography: p225-229. — Includes index

POLICY SCIENCES
Advising the rulers / edited by William Plowden. — Oxford : Basil Blackwell, 1987. — [256]p. — Includes index

AHONEN, Pertti
Public policy evaluation as discourse / Perti Ahonen. — Helsinki : Finnish Political Science Association, 1983. — 191 p.. — Bibliography: p. 187-191

Doing cross-national research. — Aston : Aston Modern Languages Club
2: Research methods and problems in comparative public policy / edited by Steen Mangen [and] Linda Hantrais. — 1986. — 50p

HAMBLETON, Robin
Rethinking policy planning : a study of planning systems linking central and local government / Robin Hambleton. — [Bristol] : University of Bristol, School for Advanced Urban Studies, 1986. — v,189p. — (SAUS study ; no.2). — Bibliography: p175-189

HISKES, Anne L. Deckard
Science, technology, and policy decisions / Anne L. Hiskes and Richard P. Hiskes. — Boulder : Westview Press, 1986. — p. cm. — Includes index. — Bibliography: p

Improving policy analysis / edited by Stuart S. Nagel. — Beverly Hills ; London : Sage Publications, 1980. — 264p. — (Sage focus editions ; 16). — Includes bibliographies and index

LYNN, Laurence E.
Managing public policy / Laurence E. Lynn, Jr. — Boston : Little, Brown, c1987. — xiv, 282 p.. — (Little, Brown foundations of public management series). — Includes bibliographies and index

MERKHOFER, Miley W.
Decision science and social risk management : a comparative evaluation of cost-benefit analysis, decision analysis, and other formal decision-aiding approaches / Miley W. Merkhofer. — Dordrecht ; Boston : D. Reidel ; Norwell, MA : Sold and distributed in the U.S.A. and Canada by Kluwer Academic Publishers, 1986. — p. cm. — (Technology, risk, and society). — Includes index. — Bibliography: p

PETERS, B. Guy
American public policy : promise and performance / B. Guy Peters. — 2nd ed. — Basingstoke : Macmillan Education, 1986. — viii,344p. — 1st and 2nd U.S. eds have subtitle: Process and performance. — Previous ed.: New York : F. Watts, 1982. — Includes index

Policy analysis and deductive reasoning / edited by Gordon Tullock, Richard E. Wagner. — Lexington, Mass. : D.C. Heath ; Farnborough, Hants. ([1 Westmead, Farnborough, Hants. GU14 7RU]) : [Distributed by] Teakfield, 1978. — xii,207p. — (Policy Studies Organization series ; 15). — Based on symposia coordinated by the Policy Studies Organization. - 'Lexington Books'. — Includes index

POLICY SCIENCES — Addresses, essays, lectures
Bringing the state back in / edited by Peter B. Evans, Dietrich Rueschmeyer, Theda Skocpol. — Cambridge : Cambridge University Press, 1985. — x, 390p. — Contains bibliographies

The Collection and analysis of economic and consumer behavior data : in memory of Robert Ferber / edited by Seymour Sudman and Mary A. Spaeth. — Champaign, Ill. : Bureau of Economic and Business Research & Survey Research Laboratory, University of Illinois, c1984. — x, 406 p.. — Includes bibliographies

The Presidency and public policy making / George C. Edwards, III, Steven A. Shull, Norman C. Thomas, editors. — Pittsburgh, Pa. : University of Pittsburgh Press, c1985. — xix, 227 p.. — (Pitt series in policy and institutional studies). — Includes bibliographies and index

Public policy and social institutions / edited by Harrell R. Rodgers, Jr. — Greenwich, Conn. : JAI Press, c1984. — ix, 375 p.. — (Public policy studies ; v. 1). — Includes bibliographies and indexes

POLICY SCIENCES — Dictionaries
KRUSCHKE, Earl R.
The dictionary of public policy / Earl R. Kruschke, Byron M. Jackson. — Santa Barbara, Calif. : ABC-CLIO, 1987. — p. cm. — (CLIO dictionaries in political science ; 15). — Includes index. — Bibliography: p

POLICY SCIENCES — Methodology
Methodologies for analyzing public policies / [edited by] Frank P. Scioli, Jr., Thomas J. Cook. — Lexington, Mass. : Lexington Books, [1975]. — vii, 171 p.. — (Policy Studies Organization series ; 3). — Includes bibliographical references and indexes

POLICY SCIENCES — Moral and ethical aspects
TONG, Rosemarie
Ethics in policy analysis / Rosemarie Tong. — Englewood Cliffs, NJ : Prentice-Hall, c1986. — p. cm. — (Occupational ethics series). — Includes bibliographies and index

POLICY SCIENCES — Research
Comparative policy research : learning from experience / edited by Meinolf Dierkes, Hans N. Weiler, Ariane Berthoin Antal. — Aldershot : Gower, c1987. — vi,530p. — Includes index

POLICY SCIENCES — United States
On call : political essays / edited by June Jordan. — London : Pluto, 1986. — [224]p. — Includes bibliography

POLISARIO
KAMIL, Leo
Fueling the fire : U.S. policy and the Western Sahara conflict / Leo Kamil. — Trenton, New Jersey : Red Sea Press, 1987. — 104p. — Distributed in the UK by Spokesman, Nottingham. — Bibliography: p93-96. — Appendices give text of 1983 OAU peace plan: 1985 U.N. General Assembly resolution: and 1979 Algiers peace treaty between the Polisario Front and the Republic of Mauretania

POLISH LITERATURE — Foreign countries
Pisarz na obczyźnie / praca zbiorowa pod redakcją Tadeusza Bujnickiego i Wojciecha Wyskiela. — Wrocław : Ossolineum, 1985. — 207p. — (Biblioteka polonijna ; 14). — Summaries in English

POLITBURO See Kommunisticheskaia partiia Sovetskogo Soiuza. Tsentral'nyi komitet. Politbiuro

POLITICAL ANTHROPOLOGY — Africa, East
MAIR, Lucy Philip
Primitive government : a study of traditional political systems in eastern Africa / Lucy Mair. — Rev. ed. — Bloomington : Indiana University Press, c1977. — 244 p.. — Includes index. — Bibliography: p. 238-239

POLITICAL ANTHROPOLOGY — Australia
TESTART, Alain
Le communisme primitif / Alain Testart. — Paris : Editions de la Maison des sciences de l'homme
1: Economie et idéologie. — 1985. — 548p. — Bibliography: p523-[536]

POLITICAL ANTHROPOLOGY — Mexico
FRIEDRICH, Paul
The princes of Naranja : an essay in anthrohistorical method / by Paul Friedrich. — 1st ed. — Austin : University of Texas Press, 1986. — p. cm. — Bibliography: p

POLITICAL BALLADS AND SONGS — Netherlands
Het cirkus van vuile mong en zijn vieze gasten : teksten. — Waarschoot : Werkgroep voor Vormingstejater, 1975. — 45p

POLITICAL CLUBS — Yugoslavia
SEROKA, Jim
Political organizations in Yugoslavia / Jim Seroka and Rados Smiljkovic. — Durham, NC : Duke University Press, 1986. — p. cm. — (Duke Press policy studies). — Includes index

POLITICAL CONSULTANTS — Australia
WALTER, James
The ministers' minders : personal advisers in national government / James Walter. — Melbourne : Oxford University Press, 1986. — viii,237p. — Bibliography: p[218]-232

POLITICAL CONVENTIONS — United States — Addresses, essays, lectures
The Life of the parties : activists in presidential politics / edited by Ronald B. Rapoport, Alan I. Abramowitz, John McGlennon. — Lexington, Ky. : University Press of Kentucky, c1986. — x, 242 p.. — Includes bibliographies and index

POLITICAL CRIMES AND OFFENSES
CHRISTENSON, Ron
Political trials : Gordian knots in the law / Ron Christenson. — New Brunswick, N.J. : Transaction Books, c1986. — viii, 303 p.. — Includes index. — Bibliography: p. 285-294

POLITICAL CRIMES AND OFFENSES — United States
BARKAN, Steven E.
Protesters on trial : criminal justice in the Southern civil rights and Vietnam antiwar movements / Steven E. Barkan. — New Brunswick, N.J. : Rutgers University Press, c1985. — p. cm. — (Crime, law, and deviance series). — Includes index. — Bibliography: p

CHRISTENSON, Ron
Political trials : Gordian knots in the law / Ron Christenson. — New Brunswick, N.J. : Transaction Books, c1986. — viii, 303 p.. — Includes index. — Bibliography: p. 285-294

POLITICAL CRIMES AND OFFENSES — United States — Bibliography
Crime and punishment in America : a historical bibliography / [this bibliography was conceived and compiled from the periodicals database of the American Bibliographical Center by editors at ABC-Clio Information Services] ; [Lance Klass and Susan Kinnell, project coordinators ...]. — Santa Barbara, Calif. ; Oxford : The Information Service, c1984. — xii,346p. — (ABC-Clio research guides). — Includes index

POLITICAL ETHICS

BUDZISZEWSKI, J.
The resurrection of nature : political theory and the human character / J. Budziszewski. — Ithaca : Cornell University Press, 1986. — 218 p.. — *Includes index.* — *Bibliography: p. 205-212*

GODWIN, William
Enquiry concerning political justice, and its influence on modern morals and happiness / William Godwin. — [3rd ed. reprinted] / [edited with an introduction by Isaac Kramnick]. — Harmondsworth : Penguin, 1976. — 825p. — (Pelican classics). — *Third ed. originally published: in 2 vols. London : s.n., 1798.* — *Bibliography: p.801.* — *Includes index*

MÍGUEZ BONINO, José
Toward a Christian political ethics / José Míguez Bonino. — London : SCM Press, 1983. — 126p

REGAN, Richard J
The moral dimensions of politics / Richard J. Regan. — New York : Oxford University Press, c1986. — p. cm. — *Includes index.* — *Bibliography: p*

POLITICAL LEADERSHIP

BLONDEL, Jean
Political leadership : towards a general analysis / Jean Blondel. — London : Sage, 1987. — [256]p. — *Includes bibliography and index*

LITTLE, Graham
Political ensembles : a psychosocial approach to politics and leadership / Graham Little. — Melbourne ; New York : Oxford University Press, 1985. — viii, 223 p.. — *Includes index.* — *Bibliography: p. 202-216*

POLITICAL LEADERSHIP — India

PRASAD, Bimal
Gandhi, Nehru & J. P. : studies in leadership / Bimal Prasad. — Delhi : Chanakya Publications, 1985. — 294p. — *Bibliography: p283-287*

POLITICAL LEADERSHIP — Soviet Union

IATSKOV, V. Ia.
Kadrovaia politika KPSS : opyt i problemy / V. Ia. Iatskov. — Moskva : Mysl', 1986. — 315p

POLITICAL PARTICIPATION

CHEKKI, Dan A.
Participatory democracy in action : international profiles of community development / Dan A. Chekki. — Sahibabad : Vikas Publishing House PVT, [1979]. — xvi,306p. — *Bibliography: p293-300*

PICARD, Robert G
The press and the decline of democracy : the democratic socialist response in public policy / Robert G. Picard. — Westport, Conn. ; London : Greenwood Press, 1985. — 173p. — (Contributions to the study of mass media and communications ; no. 4). — *Includes index.* — *Bibliography: p [153]-168*

POLITICAL PARTICIPATION — Social aspects — Argentina

OLLIER, Maria Matilde
El fenómeno insurreccional y la cultura política (1969-1973) / Maria Matilde Ollier. — Buenos Aires : Centro Editor de América Latina, 1986. — 141p. — (Biblioteca Política Argentina ; 145). — *Bibliography: p139-141*

POLITICAL PARTICIPATION — Belgium

CAUWENBERGHE, Jean-Claude van
Rendre la ville aux citoyens : réflexions sur la participation des citoyens à la gestion de leur cité / Jean-Claude van Cauwenberghe ; préface de Emile Henry. — [Paris] : F. Nathan ; Bruxelles : Labor, cl1980. — 155 p.. — *Includes bibliographical references*

POLITICAL PARTICIPATION — India

BRASS, Paul R.
Caste, faction and party in Indian politics / Paul R. Brass. — Delhi : Chanakya Publications
Vol.2: Election studies. — 1985. — 325p

POLITICAL PARTICIPATION — Malawi

MTEWA, Mekki
Malawi democratic theory and public policy : a preface / by Mekki Mtewa. — Cambridge, Mass. : Schenkman Pub. Co., 1986. — p. cm. — *Includes index.* — *Bibliography: p*

POLITICAL PARTICIPATION — Michigan — Detroit — Case studies

HUCKFELDT, R. Robert
Politics in context : assimilation and conflict in urban neighborhoods / Robert Huckfeldt. — New York : Agathon Press, c1986. — viii, 191 p.. — *Includes index.* — *Bibliography: p. 177-185*

POLITICAL PARTICIPATION — Missouri — Kansas City

SHARP, Elaine B
Citizen demand-making in the urban context / Elaine B. Sharp. — University, AL : University of Alabama Press, c1986. — p. cm. — *Includes index.* — *Bibliography: p*

POLITICAL PARTICIPATION — New York (State) — Buffalo — Case studies

HUCKFELDT, R. Robert
Politics in context : assimilation and conflict in urban neighborhoods / Robert Huckfeldt. — New York : Agathon Press, c1986. — viii, 191 p.. — *Includes index.* — *Bibliography: p. 177-185*

POLITICAL PARTICIPATION — Ohio — Cincinnati

THOMAS, John Clayton
Between citizen and city : neighborhood organizations and urban politics in Cincinnati / John Clayton Thomas. — Lawrence : University Press of Kansas, c1986. — xii, 196 p.. — (Studies in government and public policy). — *Includes index.* — *Bibliography: p. 179-188*

POLITICAL PARTICIPATION — Papua New Guinea

Women and politics in Papua New Guinea / Maev O'Collins...[et al.]. — [Canberra, A.C.T.] : Department jof Political and Social Change, Australian National University, 1985. — 75p. — (Working paper / Department of Political and Social Change, Australian National University ; No.6). — *Cover title: Women in politics in Papua New Guinea.* — *Contains papers presented to the Australian National University Department of Political and Social Change fifth Annual Seminar on Papua New Guinea, May 1984*

POLITICAL PARTICIPATION — Peru

INSTITUTO NACIONAL DE ADMINISTRACIÓN PÚBLICA (Peru). Programa Apoyo a la Reforma de Gobiernos Locales
Participación popular y gobiernos locales. — Lima : the Programa, 1975. — 63p

RODRÍGUEZ RIVAS, Miguel
La participación en la administración pública a : programa; política y realidad / [Miguel Rodríguez Rivas]. — [Lima] : Instituto Nacional de Adminstración Pública, [197-?]. — 10leaves

POLITICAL PARTICIPATION — Spain

RAMIREZ, Manuel
La participatión politica / Manuel Ramirez. — Madrid : Tecnos, 1985. — 157p. — (Temas clave de la constitución española)

POLITICAL PARTICIPATION — Spain — Castellón de la Plana — History — 19th century

MARTÍ, Manuel
Cossieros i anticossieros : burgesia i política local, Castelló de la Plana, 1875-1891 / Manuel Martí. — [Castelló] : Diputació Provincial de Castelló, 1985. — 333 p.. — (Col·lecció universitària). — : *Originally presented as the author's thesis (llicenciatura--Universitat de València, 1984) under the title: Burgesia i política local, Castelló de la Plana, 1875-1891.* — *Bibliography: p. 323-333*

POLITICAL PARTICIPATION — Texas — San Antonio — Addresses, essays, lectures

The Politics of San Antonio : community, progress, & power / edited by David R. Johnson, John A. Booth, Richard J. Harris. — Lincoln : University of Nebraska Press, c1983. — xi, 248 p. — *Includes bibliographical references*

POLITICAL PARTICIPATION — United States

BENNETT, Stephen Earl
Apathy in America, 1960-1984 : causes and consequences of citizen political indifference / Stephen Earl Bennett. — Dobbs Ferry, N.Y. : Transnational Publishers, c1986. — x, 198 p.. — *Includes index.* — *Bibliography: p. 179-193*

Citizen participation in public decision making / edited by Jack DeSario and Stuart Langton. — New York : Greenwood Press, c1987. — xii, 237 p.. — (Contributions in political science ; no. 158). — *"Prepared under the auspices of the Policy Studies Organization.".* — *Includes bibliographies and index*

CONWAY, M. Margaret
Political participation in the United States / M. Margaret Conway. — Washington, D.C. : CQ Press, c1985. — p. cm. — *Includes index*

FRESIA, Gerald John
There comes a time : a challenge to the two party system / Gerald John Fresia. — New York : Praeger, 1986. — 255 p.. — *Includes index.* — *Bibliography: p. 217-249*

McCANN, Michael W.
Taking reform seriously : perspectives on public interest liberalism / Michael W. McCann. — Ithaca : Cornell University Press, 1986. — 345 p.. — *Includes index.* — *Bibliography: p. 321-335*

ZIMMERMAN, Joseph Francis
Participatory democracy : populism revived / Joseph F. Zimmerman. — New York : Praeger, 1986. — xi, 229 p.. — *Bibliography: p. 185-221*

POLITICAL PARTICIPATION — United States — Case studies

CLAVEL, Pierre
The progressive city : planning and participation, 1969-1984 / Pierre Clavel. — New Brunswick, N.J. : Rutgers University Press, c1986. — xviii, 262 p.. — *Includes index.* — *Bibliography: p. [241]-255*

POLITICAL PARTICIPATION — United States — History

CONWAY, M. Margaret
Political participation in the United States / M. Margaret Conway. — Washington, D.C. : CQ Press, c1985. — p. cm. — *Includes index*

POLITICAL PARTIES

DENIS, Serge
Syndicats, parti des travailleurs et parti ouvrier révolutionnaire / Serge Denis. — Montreal : Presses Socialistes Internationales, 1986. — 61p. — (Documents du Groupe socialiste des travailleurs du Québec ; 1)

Do elections matter? / Benjamin Ginsberg and Alan Stone, editors. — Armonk, N.Y. : M.E. Sharpe, c1986. — 240 p.. — *Includes bibliographies*

POLITICAL PARTIES
continuation

GARCÍA COTARELO, Ramón
Los partidos políticos / Ramón García Cotarelo. — Madrid : Editorial Sistema, [1985]. — 277p. — (Colección de Ciencas Sociales)

Political parties : electoral change and structural response / edited by Alan Ware. — Oxford : Basil Blackwell, 1987. — [240]p. — *Includes index*

POLITICAL PARTIES — Germany

Keine Stimme dem Radikalismus : Christliche, liberale und konservative Parteien in den Wahlen 1930-1933 / Günter Buchstab...[et al.] (Hrsg.). — Berlin : Colloquium, 1984. — 136p. — *Bibliography: p133-134*

POLITICAL PARTIES — Manifestos — History — 20th century

Ideology, strategy and party change : spatial analyses of post-war election programmes in 19 democracies / edited by Ian Budge, David Robertson, Derek Hearl. — Cambridge : Cambridge University Press, 1987. — xvii,494p. — *Bibliography: p472-483. — Includes index*

POLITICAL PARTIES — Membership — Great Britain

MANN, John
Labour and youth : the missing generation / John Mann [and] Phil Woolas. — London : Fabian Society, 1986. — 19 p. — (Fabian tract ; 515)

POLITICAL PARTIES — Religious aspects — Christianity

GUMMER, John Selwyn
Faith in politics : which way should Christians vote? / John Selwyn Gummer, Eric Heffer, Alan Beith. — London : SPCK, 1987. — 134p

POLITICAL PARTIES — Asia

Political parties of Asia and the Pacific / Haruhiro Fukui, editor-in-chief ; Colin A. Hughes ... [et al.], associate editors. — Westport, Conn. : Greenwood Press, 1985. — 2 v. (xviii, 1346 p.). — (The Greenwood historical encyclopedia of the world's political parties). — *Includes bibliographies and index. — Contents: [1] Afghanistan-Korea (ROK) -- [2] Laos-Western Samoa*

POLITICAL PARTIES — Brazil

LAMOUNIER, Bolivar
Political parties and democratic consolidation : the Brazilian case / Bolivar Lamounier [and] Rachel Meneguello. — Washington, D.C. : Latin American Program of the Woodrow Wilson International Center for Scholars, Smithsonian Institution and the World Peace Foundation, 1985. — 37p. — (Working papers / Woodrow Wilson International Center for Scholars. Latin American Program ; no.165). — *Bibliography: p32-37*

POLITICAL PARTIES — British Columbia

BLAKE, Donald E.
Two political worlds : parties and voting in British Columbia / Donald E. Blake, with the collaboration of David J. Elkins and Richard Johnston. — Vancouver : University of British Columbia Press, 1985. — x, 205 p. — *On spine: 2 political worlds. — Includes bibliographical references and index*

POLITICAL PARTIES — Canada

BASHEVKIN, Sylvia B.
Toeing the lines : women and party politics in English Canada / Sylvia B. Bashevkin. — Toronto : University of Toronto Press, 1985. — xvi,222p. — *References: p[177]-216*

BLAKE, Donald E.
Two political worlds : parties and voting in British Columbia / Donald E. Blake, with the collaboration of David J. Elkins and Richard Johnston. — Vancouver : University of British Columbia Press, 1985. — x, 205 p. — *On spine: 2 political worlds. — Includes bibliographical references and index*

National politics and community in Canada / edited by R. Kenneth Carty and W. Peter Ward. — Vancouver : University of British Columbia Press, 1986. — 200 p. — *Includes bibliographical references. — Contents: Canada as political community / R. Kenneth Carty & W. Peter Ward -- The Origins of Canadian politics and John A. Macdonald / Gordon Stewart -- Networks and associations and the nationalizing of sentiment in English Canada / Margaret Prang -- The Making of a Canadian political citizenship / R. Kenneth Carty & W. Peter Ward -- National political parties and the growth of the national political community / David E. Smith -- Leadership conventions and the development of the national political community in Canada / John C. Courtney -- Ceremonial politics / Christopher Armstrong -- Becoming Canadians / P.B. Waite -- Managing the periphery / Donald E. Blake -- The "French lieutenant" in Ottawa / John English*

UNDERHILL, F. H.
Canadian political parties / F. H. Underhill. — Ottawa : Canadian Historical Association, 1974. — 24p. — (Canadian Historical Association Booklets ; no.8). — *Bibliography: p21-22*

POLITICAL PARTIES — Chile

VALENZUELA, Arturo
Origins and characteristics of the Chilean party system : a proposal for a parliamentary form of government / Arturo Valenzuela. — Washington, D.C. : Latin American Program of the Woodrow Wilson International Center for Scholars, Smithsonian Institution and the World Peace Foundation, 1985. — 43p. — (Working papers / Woodrow Wilson International Center for Scholars. Latin American Program ; no.164)

POLITICAL PARTIES — China

SEYMOUR, James D
China's satellite parties / James D. Seymour. — Armonk, N.Y. : M.E. Sharpe, c1987. — xi, 149 p. — (Studies of the East Asian Institute). — *"An East-gate book.". — Includes index. — Bibliography: p. 135-144*

POLITICAL PARTIES — Denmark

KONSERVATIVE FOLKEPARTI (Denmark)
En fremtid i frihed : det konservative folkepartis program : ditto partiprogram er vedtaget på Det konservative folkepartis landsråd i Herning i September 1981 / Det konservative folkeparti. — København : Det konservative folkeparti, 1981. — 64p

POLITICAL PARTIES — Europe — Addresses, essays, lectures

The Future of party government. — Berlin ; New York : W. de Gruyter, 1986-. — p. cm. — (Series C--Political and social sciences =Sciences politiques et sociales ; 5). — *"A series under the general editorship of Rudolf Wildenmann.". — Includes index (v. 1). — Contents: v. 1. Visions and realities of party government / edited by Francis G. Castles and Rudolf Wildenmann*

POLITICAL PARTIES — Europe — History — 20th century

Party systems in Denmark, Austria, Switzerland, The Netherlands and Belgium / edited by Hans Daalder. — London : Pinter, 1987. — xiii,372p. — (European party systems) . — *Includes bibliographies and index*

POLITICAL PARTIES — France

WEISS, Dimitri
Centralité de l'entreprise et partis politiques / Dimitri Weiss. — [S.l.] : Revue française de Gestion, 1977. — 122p

POLITICAL PARTIES — Germany — History

Lexikon zur Parteiengeschichte : die bürgerlichen und kleinbürgerlichen Parteien und Verbände in Deutschland (1789-1945) : in vier Bänden / hrsg. von Dieter Fricke (Leiter des Herausgeberkollektivs)...[et al.]. — Köln : Pahl-Rugenstein. — (Geschichte der bürgerlichen und kleinbürgerlichen Parteien und Verbände)
Bd.4: Reichsverband der Deutschen Industrie - Zweckverband der freien Deutschturnsvereine. — 1986. — 743p. — *Includes bibliographies*

POLITICAL PARTIES — Germany (West)

MENG, Richard
Die sozialdemokratische Wende : Aussenbild und innerer Prozess der SPD 1981-1984 / Richard Meng. — Giessen : Focus, 1985. — 409p. — *Bibliography: p406-409*

OLZOG, Günter
Die politischen Parteien in der Bundesrepublik Deutschland : Geschichte, Programmatik, Organisation, Personen, Finanzierung / Günter Olzog, Hans-J. Liese. — Originalausg., 15.überarbeitete Aufl.. — München : Günter Olzog, 1985. — 205p. — (Geschichte und Staat ; Bd.104). — *Mit Text des Parteiengesetzes*

SIMON, Werner
Politische Bildung durch Parteien? : eine Untersuchung zur politischen Bildungsaufgabe der politischen Parteien in der Bundesrepublik Deutschland / Werner Simon. — Frankfurt am Main : Haag und Herchen, 1985. — 205p. — (Studien zur Politikdidaktik ; Bd.32). — *Bibliography: p187-205*

SMITH, Gordon, 1927-
Democracy in Western Germany : parties and politics in the Federal Republic / Gordon Smith. — 3rd ed. — Aldershot : Gower, c1986. — [240]p. — *Previous ed.: London : Heinemann, 1982. — Includes index*

POLITICAL PARTIES — Germany (West) — History

HUHN, Anne
"Einst kommt der Tag der Rache" : die rechtsextreme Herausforderung 1945 bis heute / Anne Huhn; Alwin Meyer. — Freiburg : Dreisam-Verlag, 1986. — 229p

PADGETT, Stephen
Political parties and elections in West Germany : the search for a new stability. — [2nd ed.] / Stephen Padgett, Tony Burkett. — London : Hurst, c1986. — xi,308p. — *Previous ed.: by Tony Burkett. Published as Parties and elections in West Germany. 1975. — Bibliography: p294-301. — Includes index*

POLITICAL PARTIES — Great Britain

BRADBURY CONTROLS LTD
Manifesto of manifestos U.K. general election 11th June, 1987 : a concise listing of the election policies extracted from the official party manifestos. — 4th ed.. — Ross-on-Wye : Hydatum, 1987. — iv,32p

FITZGERALD, Marian
Black people and party politics in Britain / Marian Fitzgerald. — London : Runnymede Trust, 1987. — 51p. — (Runnymede research report)

GUMMER, John Selwyn
Faith in politics : which way should Christians vote? / John Selwyn Gummer, Eric Heffer, Alan Beith. — London : SPCK, 1987. — 134p

INGLE, Stephen
The British party system / Stephen Ingle. — Oxford : Basil Blackwell, 1987. — [224]. — *Includes index*

LABOUR PARTY (Great Britain)
Britain will win : Labour manifesto, June 1987. — London : The Party, 1987. — 17 p

POLITICAL PARTIES — Great Britain
continuation

OSTROGORSKI, M.
Democracy and the organization of political parties / with a preface by...James Bryce ; edited...by Seymour Martin Lipset. — Chicago : Quadrangle
volume 1: England. — 1964. — lxxxii,350p. — *First published in English in 1902*

SDP-LIBERAL ALLIANCE
Britain united : the time has come : the SDP/Liberal Alliance programme for government. — London : The Alliance, [1987]. — [24] p.

POLITICAL PARTIES — Great Britain — Finance

EWING, K. D.
The funding of political parties in Britain / Keith Ewing. — Cambridge : Cambridge University Press, 1987. — 1v.. — *Includes bibliography and index*

POLITICAL PARTIES — Great Britain — History — 19th century

COX, Gary W.
The efficient secret : the Cabinet and the development of political parties in Victorian England / Gary W. Cox. — Cambridge : Cambridge University Press, 1987. — [208]p. — (Political economy of institutions and decisions). — *Includes bibliography and index*

POLITICAL PARTIES — India

GAUTAM, Om P.
The Indian National Congress : an analytical biography / Om P. Gautam. — Delhi : B. R. Publishing Corporation, 1985. — 400p. — *Bibliography: p368-389*

SADASIVAN, S. N
Party and democracy in India / S. N. Sadasivan. — New Delhi : Tata McGraw-Hill, c1977. — xv, 537 p.. — *A revision of the author's thesis, University of Poona.* — *Includes index.* — *Bibliography: p. [495]-512*

POLITICAL PARTIES — India — States

KOHLI, Atul
The state and poverty in India : the politics of reform / Atul Kohli. — Cambridge : Cambridge University Press, 1987. — x,262p. — (Cambridge South Asian studies ; no.37). — *Bibliography: p245-254.* — *Includes index*

POLITICAL PARTIES — Ireland

MAIR, Peter
The changing Irish party system : organisation, ideology and electoral competition / Peter Mair. — London : Pinter, 1987. — xii,245p. — (Recent changes in European party systems). — *Bibliography: p230-240.* — *Includes index*

POLITICAL PARTIES — Israel

ARIAN, Alan
Politics in Israel : the second generation / Asher Arian. — Chatham, N.J. : Chatham House, c1985. — p. cm. — *Includes index.* — *Bibliography: p*

POLITICAL PARTIES — Israel — Addresses, essays, lectures

Israel at the polls, 1981 : a study of the Knesset elections / edited by Howard R. Penniman and Daniel J. Elazar. — Washington : American Enterprise Institute for Public Policy Research ; Bloomington : Indiana University Press, c1986. — xiii, 280 p.. — (Jewish political and social studies). — *Includes bibliographies and index*

POLITICAL PARTIES — Japan

HVEBENAR, Ronald J.
The Japanese party system : from one-party rule to coalition government / Ronald J. Hrebenar with contributions by Peter Berton ... [et al.]. — Boulder, Colo. : Westview Press, 1986. — xviii, 330 p. — *Includes bibliographies and index*

POLITICAL PARTIES — Kenya — Bibliography

A guide to selected documents on political organisations in Kenya. — Nairobi : Kenya National Archives, 1984. — 42p

POLITICAL PARTIES — Mexico — History — 20th century

Mexico's political stability : the next five years / edited by Roderic A. Camp. — Boulder : Westview Press, 1986. — ix, 279 p.. — (Westview special studies on Latin America and the Caribbean). — *Includes bibliographies and index.* — Contents: Overview / Roderic A. Camp -- The political consequences of changing socialization patterns / Daniel C. Levy -- How will economic recovery be managed? / William P. Glade -- Distributional and sectoral problems in the New Economic Policy / William P. Glade -- Leadership and change, Intellectuals and technocrats in Mexico / Peter H. Smith -- The impact of major groups on policy-making trends in government-business relations in Mexico / John Bailey -- The evolution of the Mexican military and its implications for civil-military relations / Edward J. Williams -- What explains the decline of the PRI and will it continue? / John Bailey -- Potential strengths of the political opposition and what it means to the PRI / Roderic A. Camp -- The implications of the border for Mexican-United States relations / Edward J. Williams -- The implications of Central American conflicts for Mexican politics / Daniel C. Levy

POLITICAL PARTIES — Nigeria

ADAMU, Haroun
Nigeria : the meaning of the presidential system : 1979 General Elections / Haroun Adamu, Alaba Ogunsanwo. — Kano, Nigeria : Triumph Pub. Co., [1982?]. — x, 267 p.

POLITICAL PARTIES — Northern Ireland

NELSON, Sarah
Ulster's uncertain defenders : Protestant political, paramilitary and community groups and the Northern Ireland Conflict / Sarah Nelson. — Belfast : Appletree, 1984. — 219p. — (Modern Irish society). — *Bibliography: p210-215.* — *Includes index*

POLITICAL PARTIES — Norway — History

BJØRGUM, Jorunn
Venstre og kriseforliket : landbrukspolitikk og parlamentarisk spill 1934-1935 / Jorunn Bjørgum. — 2. utgave. — Oslo : Universitetsforlaget, 1978. — 191p. — *First published 1970.* — *Bibliography: p164*

LORENZ, Einhart
Det er ingen sak å få partiet lite : NKP 1923-1931 / Einhart Lorenz. — Olso : Pax, 1983. — 301p. — *Bibliography: p280-287*

Venstres hundre år / Ottar Grepstad, Jostein Nerbøvik (red.). — Oslo : Gyldendal Norsk Forlag, 1984. — 304p

POLITICAL PARTIES — Pacific Area

Political parties of Asia and the Pacific / Haruhiro Fukui, editor-in-chief ; Colin A. Hughes ... [et al.], associate editors. — Westport, Conn. : Greenwood Press, 1985. — 2 v. (xviii, 1346 p.). — (The Greenwood historical encyclopedia of the world's political parties). — *Includes bibliographies and index.* — Contents: [1] Afghanistan-Korea (ROK) -- [2] Laos-Western Samoa

POLITICAL PARTIES — Paraguay

PRIETO YEGROS, Leandro
La infiltración comunista en los partidos politicos paraguayos : caso del "Bloque Liberación" del Partido Revolucionario Febrerista : (version documental / Leandro Prieto Yegros. — [Asunción] : Cuadernos Republicanos, [1985]. — 521p

POLITICAL PARTIES — Quebec (Province)

VAILLANCOURT, Yves
Le P.Q. et la social : éléments de bilan des politiques sociales du gouvernement du Parti québécois, 1976-1982 / Yves Vaillancourt ; avec la collaboration de Annie Autonès. — [Montréal] : Editions coopératives Albert Saint-Martin, c1983. — 165p. — (Collection "Actualité")

POLITICAL PARTIES — Southern States — History — 20th century — Addresses, essays, lectures

The 1984 presidential election in the South : patterns of southern party politics / edited by Robert P. Steed, Laurence W. Moreland, and Tod A. Baker. — New York : Praeger, 1985. — p. cm. — *Includes index.* — *Bibliography: p*

POLITICAL PARTIES — Spain

CACIAGLI, Mario
Elecciones y partidos en la transición española / por Mario Caciagli. — Madrid : Centro de Investigaciones Sociologicas : Siglo Vientiuno, 1986. — x,292p

PASCUAL MARTÍNEZ, Pedro
Partidos politicos y constituciones de España / Pedro Pascual. — Madrid : Fragua, 1986. — x,521p. — *Bibliography: p515-521*

POLITICAL PARTIES — Spain — History

CARRASCAL, José María
La revolución del PSOE / José María Carrascal. — [Barcelona] : Plaza & Janes, [1985]. — 306p. — (Política española)

MONREAL, Antoni
El pensamiento político de Joaquín Maurín / Antoni Monreal. — [Barcelona] : Península, [1984]. — 204p. — (Historia, ciencia, sociedad ; 190)

POLITICAL PARTIES — United States

FRESIA, Gerald John
There comes a time : a challenge to the two party system / Gerald John Fresia. — New York : Praeger, 1986. — 255 p.. — *Includes index.* — *Bibliography: p. 217-249*

KOLBE, Richard L
American political parties : an uncertain future / Richard L. Kolbe. — New York, NY : Harper & Row, c1985. — xii, 353 p.. — *Includes bibliographies and index*

MAISEL, Louis Sandy
Parties and elections in America : the electoral process / Louis Sandy Maisel. — New York : Random House, 1986. — p. cm. — *Includes index.* — *Bibliography: p*

OSTROGORSKI, M.
Democracy and the organization of political parties / with a preface by...James Bryce ; edited...by Seymour Martin Lipset. — Chicago : Quadrangle
volume 2: United States. — 1964. — lxxvii,418p. — *First published in English in 1902*

WALZER, Michael
The politics of ethnicity / Michael Walzer...[et al.]. — Cambridge, Mass. ; London : Belknap Press of Harvard University Press, 1982. — vi,142p. — (Dimensions of ethnicity : Selections from the Harvard Encyclopedia of American ethnic groups). — *Bibliography: p [139]-142*

POLITICAL PARTIES — United States — Addresses, essays, lectures

The Life of the parties : activists in presidential politics / edited by Ronald B. Rapoport, Alan I. Abramowitz, John McGlennon. — Lexington, Ky. : University Press of Kentucky, c1986. — x, 242 p.. — *Includes bibliographies and index*

POLITICAL PARTIES — United States — History
EPSTEIN, Leon D
Political parties in the American mold / Leon D. Epstein. — Madison, Wis. : University of Wisconsin Press, 1986. — p. cm. — Includes index. — Bibliography: p

POLITICAL PARTIES — United States — History — Addresses, essays, lectures
MCCORMICK, Richard L
The party period and public policy : American politics from the Age of Jackson to the Progressive Era / Richard L. McCormick. — New York : Oxford University Press, 1986. — p. cm. — Includes index

POLITICAL PARTIES — Uruguay
GONZALEZ, Luis E.
Political parties and redemocratication in Uruguay / Luis E. Gonzalez. — Washington, D.C. : Latin American Program of the Woodrow Wilson International Center for Scholars and the World Peace Foundation, 1984. — 21p. — (Working papers / Woodrow Wilson International Center for Scholars. Latin American Program ; no.163)

POLITICAL PARTIES — West (U.S.)
Politics of realignment : party change in the mountain west / edited by Randy T. Simmons, Peter F. Galderisi, John G. Francis. — Boulder : Westview Press, 1986. — p. cm

POLITICAL PARTIES — Yugoslavia
SEROKA, Jim
Political organizations in Yugoslavia / Jim Seroka and Rados Smiljkovic. — Durham, NC : Duke University Press, 1986. — p. cm. — (Duke Press policy studies). — Includes index

POLITICAL PERSECUTION — Addresses, essays, lectures
Government violence and repression : an agenda for research / edited by Michael Stohl and George A. Lopez. — New York : Greenwood Press, 1986. — viii, 278 p.. — (Contributions in political science ; no. 148). — Includes index. — Bibliography: p. [269]-270

POLITICAL PERSECUTION — Germany — History — 20th century
BUCHSTAB, Günter
Verfolgung und Widerstand 1933-1945 : Christliche Demokraten gegen Hitler / Günter Buchstab, Brigitte Kaff, Hans-Otto Kleinmann. — Düsseldorf : Droste Verlag, 1986. — 288p. — Bibliography: p282-283

POLITICAL PERSECUTION — Philippines
LAWYERS COMMITTEE FOR INTERNATIONAL HUMAN RIGHTS
The Philippines : a country in crisis / a report by the Lawyers Committee for International Human Rights. — New York : the Committee, 1983. — iii, 142p

POLITICAL PLANNING
Strategic perspectives on planning practice / edited by Barry Checkoway. — Lexington, Mass. : Lexington Books, c1986. — x, 274 p.. — (Politics of planning series). — Includes bibliographies and index

POLITICAL PLANNING — Econometric models
Econometric contributions to public policy : proceedings of a conference held by the International Economic Association at Urbino, Italy / edited by Richard Stone and William Peterson. — London : Macmillan, 1978. — [416]p

POLITICAL PLANNING — Economic aspects
Econometric contributions to public policy : proceedings of a conference held by the International Economic Association at Urbino, Italy / edited by Richard Stone and William Peterson. — London : Macmillan, 1978. — [416]p

POLITICAL PLANNING — Evaluation
Evaluer les politiques publiques : méthodes, déontologie, organisation / Michel Deleau, président du group de travail. — [Paris : La Documentation française, 1986]. — 181p

POLITICAL PLANNING — Canada
LESLIE, Peter M.
Federal state, national economy / Peter M. Leslie. — Toronto : University of Toronto Press, [1987]. — xvi, 213p. — Notes: p[191]-205

POLITICAL PLANNING — France — Evaluation
Evaluer les politiques publiques : méthodes, déontologie, organisation / Michel Deleau, président du group de travail. — [Paris : La Documentation française, 1986]. — 181p

POLITICAL PLANNING — Great Britain
Policy change in government : three case studies / edited by Nicholas Deakin. — London : Royal Institute of Public Administration, 1986. — 91p

POLITICAL PLANNING — Japan — History
Democratizing Japan : the allied occupation / edited by Robert E. Ward and Sakamoto Yoshikazu. — Honolulu : University of Hawaii Press, c1987. — xv, 456 p., [1] folded leaf of plates. — One leaf of plates in pocket. — Based on papers presented at a conference sponsored by both the Japan Society for the Promotion of Science and the Joint Committee on Japanese Studies of the American Council of Learned Societies and the Social Science Research Council with support from the National Endowment for the Humanities. — Includes bibliographies and index

POLITICAL PLANNING — Latin America
SLOAN, John W
Public policy in Latin America : a comparative study / John W. Sloan. — Pittsburgh, Pa. : University of Pittsburgh Press, c1984. — xii, 276 p.. — (Pitt Latin American series) (Pitt series in policy and institutional studies). — Includes index. — Bibliography: p. 253-270

POLITICAL PLANNING — United States
BELL, Robert
The culture of policy deliberations / Robert Bell. — New Brunswick, N.J. : Rutgers University Press, c1985. — viii, 264 p.. — Includes index. — Bibliography: p. 227-253

PETERS, B. Guy
American public policy : promise and performance / B. Guy Peters. — 2nd ed. — Basingstoke : Macmillan Education, 1986. — viii, 344p. — 1st and 2nd U.S. eds have subtitle: Process and performance. — Previous ed.: New York : F. Watts, 1982. — Includes index

POLITICAL POSTERS, RUSSIAN
The Soviet political poster, 1917-1980 : from the USSR Lenin Library collection / [text and selection by Nina Baburina ; designed by Mikhail Anikst ; English translation by Boris Rubalsky]. — Harmmonsworth, Middx. : Penguin Books ; New York : Viking Penguin, 1985. — 9,183p. — Originally published in 3 vols. in English and Russian under the title: Sovetskii politicheskii plakat

POLITICAL PRISONERS
Disappeared! : technique of terror : a report / for the Independent Commission on International Humanitarian Issues ; preface by Simone Veil. — London : Zed, 1986. — [112]p

POLITICAL PRISONERS — Biography
Wall tappings : an anthology of writings by women prisoners / [compiled] by Judith A. Scheffler. — Boston : Northeastern University Press, c1986. — p. cm. — Bibliography: p

POLITICAL PRISONERS — Brazil
COMITÉ DE SOLIDARITÉ AVEC LE PEUPLE BRÉSILIEUN
[Manuel da Conceiçao]. — Geneve : Comité de Solidarité avec le Peuple Brésilieun, 1973. — 10p

CONCEICAO, Manuel da
Il était une fois dans le nord-est... / Manual da Conceiçao. — [S.l.] : Comité de Solidarité avec le Peuple brésilieu, 1976. — 18p

POLITICAL PRISONERS — China — Biography
CHENG, Nien
Life and death in Shanghai / Nien Cheng. — London : Grafton, 1986. — 496p. — Includes index

POLITICAL PRISONERS — Cuba
AMNESTY INTERNATIONAL
Political imprisonment in Cuba : a special report from Amnesty International. — London : Amnesty International, 1987. — 36p. — (Cuban-American National Foundation ; no.22)

POLITICAL PRISONERS — Greece
SIEGRIST, Roland
The protection of political detainees : the International Committee of the Red Cross in Greece 1967-1971 / Roland Siegrist. — Montreux : Editions Corbaz, 1985. — 171p. — Bibliography: p[157]-171

POLITICAL PRISONERS — Iran
LAFUE-VERON, Madeleine
Voyage au pays de la peur : Iran 1978 / Madeleine Lafue-Veron. — Genève : Comité Suisse de Défense des Prisonniers Politiques Iraniens, 1978. — [36p]

POLITICAL PRISONERS — Northern Ireland
BERESFORD, David
Ten men dead : the story of the 1981 Irish hunger strike / David Beresford. — London : Grafton, 1987. — 432p

POLITICAL PRISONERS — Poland
MICHNIK, Adam
Z dziejów honoru w Polsce : wypisy więzienne / Adam Michnik. — Paryż : Instytut Literacki, 1985. — 285p. — (Biblioteka Kultury ; T.404)

POLITICAL PRISONERS — Poland — Correspondence
MICHNIK, Adam
Letters from prison and other essays / Adam Michnik ; translated by Maya Latynski ; foreword by Czeslaw Milosz ; introduction by Jonathan Schell. — Berkeley ; London : University of Calif. Press, c1985. — xlii, 354p. — Translated from Polish

POLITICAL PRISONERS — Soviet Union
DELAUNAY, Vadim
Portrety v koliuchei rame = Portraits in a barbed wire frame / Vadim Delone ; predislovie Vladimira Bukovskogo. — London : Overseas Publications Interchange, 1984. — 217p

SOLZHENITSYN, Aleksandr
The Gulag Archipelago, 1918-1956 : an experiment in literary investigation / Alexander Solzhenitsyn. — London : Collins : Harvill Press. — Translation of: ´Arkhipelag Gulag, 1918-1956´. Paris : YMCA Press, 1973- [Vol.3]: [Parts] 5-7 / translated from the Russian by H.T. Willetts. — 1978. — x, 5-558p, [2]leaves of plates, [8]p of plates. — Includes index

POLITICAL PRISONERS — Soviet Union — Personal narratives
KUZNETSOV, Edward
Prison diaries / Edward Kuznetsov ; translated [from the Russian] by Howard Spier ; introduction by Leonard Schapiro. — London : Vallentine, Mitchell, 1975. — 256p, [4]p of plates. — Translation of: ´Dnevniki´. Paris : Les Editeurs Réunis, 1973

POLITICAL PRISONERS — Vietnam
FRONT SOLIDARITÉ INDOCHINE
Saigon : les prisonniers. — Paris : Front Solidarité Indochine, 1973. — 46p. — (Document / Front Solidarité Indochine ; no.6)

POLITICAL PSCYHOLOGY
ALMOND, Gabriel Abraham
The civic culture : political attitudes and democracy in five nations / by Gabriel A. Almond and Sidney Verba. — Princeton, N.J. : Princeton University Press, 1963. — xi, 562 p. — *Bibliographical footnotes*

POLITICAL PSYCHOLOGY
BARNER-BARRY, Carol
Psychological perspectives on politics / Carol Barner-Barry, Robert Rosenwein. — Englewood Cliffs, N.J. : Prentice-Hall, c1985. — ix, 342 p.. — *Includes index.* — *Bibliography: p. 309-336*

ELSHTAIN, Jean Bethke
Meditations on modern political thought : masculine/feminine themes from Luther to Arendt / Jean Bethke Elshtain. — New York : Praeger, 1986. — p. cm. — *Includes index.* — *Bibliography: p*

LITTLE, Graham
Political ensembles : a psychosocial approach to politics and leadership / Graham Little. — Melbourne ; New York : Oxford University Press, 1985. — viii, 223 p.. — *Includes index.* — *Bibliography: p. 202-216*

Political psychology : contemporary problems and issues / Margaret G. Hermann, general editor. — 1st ed. — San Francisco : Jossey-Bass Publishers, 1986. — p. cm. — (The Jossey-Bass social and behavioral science series) . — *Includes indexes.* — *Bibliography: p*

POLITICAL QUESTIONS AND JUDICIAL POWER — European Economic Community countries
VOLCANSEK, Mary L.
Judicial politics in Europe : an impact analysis / Mary L. Volcansek. — New York : P. Lang, c1986. — xi, 325 p.. — (American university studies. Series X, Political science ; vol. 7). — *Includes index.* — *Bibliography: p. [295]-313*

POLITICAL QUESTIONS AND JUDICIAL POWER — Great Britain
LEGOMSKY, Stephen H.
Immigration and the judiciary : law and politics in Britain and America / Stephen H. Legomsky. — Oxford : Clarendon, 1987. — xxxix,345p. — *Bibliography: p327-345*

POLITICAL QUESTIONS AND JUDICIAL POWER — Netherlands
JEUKENS, H. J. M.
Recht en politiek : enige aantekeningen bij een advies van de Hoge Raad / H. J. M. Jeukens. — Alphen aan den Rijn : Samsom, 1971. — 23p. — *Rede uitgesproken bij de drieënveertigste herdenking van de dies natalis van de Katholieke Hogeschool ite Tilburg op vrijdag 20 november 1970*

POLITICAL QUESTIONS AND JUDICIAL POWER — United States
DWORKIN, Ronald
A matter of principle / Ronald Dworkin. — Cambridge, Mass. ; London : Harvard University Press, 1985. — 425p

LEGOMSKY, Stephen H.
Immigration and the judiciary : law and politics in Britain and America / Stephen H. Legomsky. — Oxford : Clarendon, 1987. — xxxix,345p. — *Bibliography: p327-345*

POLITICAL QUESTIONS AND JUDICIAL POWER — United States — History
KACZOROWSKI, Robert J
The politics of judicial interpretation : the federal courts, Department of Justice and civil rights, 1866-1876 / by Robert J. Kaczorowski. — Dobbs Ferry, N.Y. : Oceana Publications, 1985. — xiv, 241 p. — (New York University School of Law series in legal history). — *"New York University School of Law, Linden studies in legal history.".* — *Includes bibliographies and index*

POLITICAL RIGHTS — New Zealand
ELKIND, Jerome B
A standard for justice : a critical commentary on the proposed Bill of Rights for New Zealand / Jerome B. Elkind and Antony Shaw ; with a foreword by P.T. Mahon. — Auckland ; New York : Oxford University Press, 1986. — xvi, 238 p.. — *Includes bibliographies and indexes*

POLITICAL RIGHTS — Legal status, laws, etc. — Indonesia
INTERNATIONAL COMMISSION OF JURISTS
Indonesia and the rule of law : twenty years of 'New Order' government : a study / prepared by the International Commission of Jurists and the Netherlands Institute of Human Rights ; edited by Hans Thoolen. — London : Pinter, 1987. — xii,208p. — *Includes index*

POLITICAL RIGHTS — Great Britain
GEISSELER, Andrea
Reformbestrebungen im Englischen Verfassungsrecht : Aussicht auf eine Grundrechtskodifizierung in Grossbritannien in naher Zukunft? / Andrea Geisseler. — Frankfurt am Main : Peter Lang, 1985. — xxxii,167p. — (Europäische Hochschulschriften. Reihe 2, Rechtswissenschaft ; Bd.465). — *Bibliography: pvii-xxix*

POLITICAL RIGHTS — India
HINGORANI, R. C.
Human rights in India / R.C. Hingorani. — New Delhi : Oxford & IBH, c1985. — vii, 181 p.. — *Includes bibliographical references and index*

POLITICAL SATIRE
LUKES, Steven
No laughing matter : a collection of political jokes / Steven Lukes, Itzhak Galnoor. — London ; Boston : Routledge & Kegan Paul, [1985]. — xiv,177p

POLITICAL SCIENCE
LEFORT, Claude
Essais sur le politique : XIXe-XXe siècles / Claude Lefort. — Paris : Seuil, [1986]. — 331p

AKZIN, Benjamin
On great powers and superpowers / Benjamin Akzin. — Den Haag : Martinus Nijhoff, [1972]. — p.610-626. — *Offprint of chapter from "Theory and politics/Theorie und Politik: Festschrift zum 70. Geburtstag für Carl Joachim Friedrich", ed. Klaus von Beyme, pub. Nijhoff,1972*

ANDERSEN, Alfred F.
Liberating the early American dream : a way to transcend the capitalist/communist dilemma nonviolently / by Alfred F. Andersen. — Ukiah, Calif. : Tom Paine Institute, c1985. — p. cm. — *Rev. ed. of: Updating the early American dream. c1984.* — *Includes index.* — *Bibliography: p*

Authority revisited / edited by J. Roland Pennock and John W. Chapman. — New York : New York University Press, 1987. — xii, 344 p.. — (Nomos ; 29). — *Includes bibliographies and index*

BAHRO, Rudolf
Building the Green movement / Rudolf Bahro ; translated by Mary Tyler. — London : GMP, c1986. — [224]p. — *Translated from the German*

BROWN, Alan
Modern political philosophy / Alan Brown. — Harmondsworth : Penguin Books, 1986. — 215p. — *Bibliography: p207-209*

Centre and periphery : spatial variation in politics / edited by Jean Gottmann. — Beverly Hills : Sage, 1980. — 226p. — (Sage focus editions ; 19). — *'The theme of Centre and Periphery was adopted for a symposium held by the Committee on Political Geography of the International Political Science Association in Paris in January 1978 ... based on papers offered at that meeting'*

CONNOLLY, William E
Politics and ambiguity / William E. Connolly. — Madison, Wis. : University of Wisconsin Press, 1987. — xiii, 168 p.. — (Rhetoric of the human sciences). — *Includes bibliographical references and index*

DI TELLA, Torcuato S.
Sociología de los procesos políticos : una perspectiva latinoamericana / Torcuato S. Di Tella. — [Buenos Aires] : Grupo Editor Latinoamericano, 1985. — 428p. — (Colección estudios políticos y sociales ; volumen 2). — *Bibliography: p[423-428]*

EULAU, Heinz
Politics, self, and society : a theme and variations / Heinz Eulau. — Cambridge, Mass. : Harvard University Press, 1986. — x, 567 p.. — *Includes index.* — *Bibliography: p. [534]-556*

Extremismus und streitbare Demokratie mit Beiträgen von Uwe Backes und Eckhard Jesse / herausgegeben von Wolfgang Michalka. — Stuttgart : Franz Steiner, 1987. — 128p. — (Neue politische Literatur. Beihefte Forschungsberichte zur internationalen Literatur ; 4)

FRIEDMANN, Friedrich Georg
Hannah Arendt : eine deutsche Jüdin im Zeitalter des Totalitarismus / Friedrich Georg Friedmann. — München : Piper, 1985. — 160p

Der Fürst dieser Welt : Carl Schmitt und die Folgen / herausgegeben von Jacob Taubes. — 2., verb. Auflage. — München : Fink, 1985. — 321p. — (Religionstheorie und politische Theologie ; Bd.1). — *First published 1983*

GODWIN, William
Enquiry concerning political justice, and its influence on modern morals and happiness / William Godwin. — [3rd ed. reprinted] / [edited with an introduction by Isaac Kramnick]. — Harmondsworth : Penguin, 1976. — 825p. — (Pelican classics). — *Third ed. originally published: in 2 vols. London : s.n., 1798.* — *Bibliography: p.801.* — *Includes index*

GRAHAM, David, 19---
The new enlightenment : the rebirth of liberalism / David Graham and Peter Clarke. — London : Macmillan in association with Channel Four Television Co., 1986. — xii,180p . — *Bibliography: p173-174.* — *Includes index*

GRAY, John, 1948 Nov.5-
Liberalism / John Gray. — Milton Keynes : Open University Press, 1986. — xi,106p. — (Concepts in the social sciences). — *Bibliography: p100-101.* — *Includes index*

HADDOCK, B. A. (Bruce Anthony)
Vico's political thought / B.A. Haddock. — Swansea : Mortlake Press, 1986. — vii,238p. — *Bibliography: p230-231*

HAGOPIAN, Mark N.
Ideals and ideologies of modern politics / Mark Hagopian. — New York ; Longman, c1985. — viii,263p. — *Includes bibliographies and index*

HAMPTON, Jean
Hobbes and the social contract tradition / Jean Hampton. — Cambridge : Cambridge University Press, 1986. — xii,299p. — *Bibliography: p285-291.* — *Includes index*

HARRIS, Peter B.
Foundations of political science / Peter Harris. — 2nd ed. — London : Hutchinson, 1986. — [352]p. — *Previous ed.: 1976.* — *Includes bibliographies and index*

LYBECK, Johan A.
The growth of government in developed economies / Johan A. Lybeck. — Aldershot : Gower, c1986. — xiv,257p. — *Includes bibliographies and index*

POLITICAL SCIENCE
continuation

LYCOS, Kimon
Plato on justice and power : reading Book 1 of Plato's Republic / Kimon Lycos. — Basingstoke : Macmillan, 1987. — ix,201p. — *Bibliography: p194-197. — Includes index*

MACCALLUM, Gerald C.
Political philosophy / Gerald C. MacCallum. — Englewood Cliffs, N.J. : Prentice-Hall, c1987. — x, 198 p.. — (Prentice-Hall foundations of philosophy series). — *Bibliography: p. 193-198*

MCLEAN, Iain
Public choice : an introduction / Iain McLean. — Oxford : Basil Blackwell, 1987. — [224]p. — *Includes bibliography and index*

MCLELLAN, David
Ideology / David McLellan. — Milton Keynes : Open University Press, 1986. — [112]p. — (Concepts in the social sciences). — *Includes bibliography and index*

MILNE, A. J. M.
The right to dissent : issues in political philosophy / by A.J.M. Milne. — Aldershot : Gower, 1986, c1983. — viii,197p. — (Avebury series in philosophy). — *Originally published: Amersham : Avebury, 1983*

Modern theories of exploitation / edited by Andrew Reeve. — London : Sage, 1987. — 209p. — (Sage modern politics series ; v.14). — *Includes bibliographies and index*

PAREKH, Bhikhu
The philosophy of political philosophy / Bhikhu Parekh. — [Hull] : Hull University Press, 1986. — 24p. — *Lecture delivered in the University of Hull 26 Feb. 1985*

PARRY, Geraint
Political elites / by Geraint Parry. — London : Allen & Unwin, 1969. — 3-169p. — *Pbk. Unpriced. sbn 04 320059 1. — bibl p159-164*

Political behavior annual. — Boulder, Colo. ; London : Westview Press, 1986-. — *Annual*

QUALTER, Terence H.
Conflicting political ideas in liberal democracies / Terence H. Qualter. — Toronto : Methuen, 1986. — ix,294p

Rational choice / edited by Jon Elster. — Oxford : Basil Blackwell, 1986. — [224]p. — (Readings in social and political theory). — *Includes index*

ROUSSEAU, Jean Jacques
[Du contrat social. English]. Of the social contract, or, Principles of political right & Discourse on political economy / by Jean-Jacques Rousseau ; translated with an introductory essay and annotations by Charles M. Sherover. — 1st ed. — New York : Harper & Row, c1984. — p. cm. — "Perennial Library.". — *Translation of: Du contrat social, and Discours sur l'oeconomie politique. — Includes bibliographical references and index*

SASSOON, Anne Showstack
Gramsci's politics / Anne Showstack Sassoon. — 2nd ed. — London : Hutchinson Education, 1987. — [261]p. — (Contemporary politics). — *Previous ed.: London : Croom Helm, 1980. — Includes bibliography and index*

SIMON, Herbert A.
Charles E. Merriam and the "Chicago School" of political science / Herbert A. Simon. — Urbana, Ill. : Department of Political Science. University of Illinois at Urbana-Champaign, 1987. — 11p. — *Edmund Jones James lecture. — Bibliography: p11*

POLITICAL SCIENCE — Anecdotes, facetiae, satire, etc.

The Oxford book of political anecdotes / edited by Paul Johnson. — Oxford : Oxford University Press, 1986. — [352]p. — *Includes index*

POLITICAL SCIENCE — Bibliography

GOOT, Murray
Henry Mayer's "Immortal works" : scholarly, semi-scholarly and nor very scholarly at all : a descriptive bibliography, with index, 1940-1985 / Murray Goot. — Canberra, A.C.T. : Australian National University for the Australasian Political Studies Association, 1986. — 245p

POLITICAL SCIENCE — Decision-making

HÖFFE, Otfried
Strategien der Humanität : zur Ethik öffentlicher Entscheidungsprozesse / Otfried Höffe. — Frankfurt am Main : Suhrkamp, 1985. — 372p. — *Published Freiburg: Karl Alber, 1975. — Bibliography: p341-362*

POLITICAL SCIENCE — Decision making — Mathematical models

BRAMS, Steven J
Rational politics : decisions, games, and strategy / Steven J. Brams. — Washington, D.C. : CQ Press, c1985. — xiv, 233 p.. — *Bibliography: p. 215-224. — Includes index*

POLITICAL SCIENCE — Dictionaries

The Blackwell encyclopaedia of political thought / edited by David Miller ... [et al.]. — Oxford : Blackwell Reference, 1987. — xii, 570p

DIETL, Clara-Erika
Wörterbuch für Rechts, Wirtschaft und Politik : mit erläuternden und rechtsvergleichenden Kommentaren. — 4., völlig neu bearbeitete und erw. Aufl.. — München : Beck ; New York : Bender
T.1: Englisch-Deutsch: einschliesslich der Besonderheiten des amerikanischen Sprachgebrauchs / von Clara-Erika Dietl, Anneliese A. Moss, Egon Lorenz ; unter Mitarbeit von Wiebke Buxbaum. — 1987. — lxxi,911p. — *English and German text. — Title on added title page : Dictionary of legal, commercial and political terms*

POLITICAL SCIENCE — Dictionaries and encyclopedias

Dictionnaire des oeuvres politiques / sous la direction de François Chatelet, Olivier Duhamel [et] Evelyne Pisier. — Paris : Presses Universitaires de France, 1986. — 904p

POLITICAL SCIENCE — Early works to 1700

HOBBES, Thomas
Leviathan / Thomas Hobbes ; edited with an introduction by C.B. Macpherson. — Harmondsworth : Penguin, 1968 (1981 [printing]). — 728p. — *Originally published: London : Andrew Crooke, 1651*

POLITICAL SCIENCE — History

Aspects of late medieval government and society : essays presented to J.R. Lander / edited by J. G. Rowe. — Toronto ; London : published in association with the University of Western Ontario by University of Toronto Press, 1986. — xx,276p

BOWIE, John
Western political thought : an historical introduction from the origins to Rousseau. — London : Cape, 1947. — 472p

D'ENTRÈVES, A. P.
The medieval contribution to political thought : Thomas Aquinas, Marsilius of Padua, Richard Hooker / by Alexander Passerin D'Entreves. — New York : Humanities, 1959. — viii,148p. — *On spine: Medieval contributions to political thought. — Originally published: Oxford University Press, 1939*

HELD, David
Models of democracy / David Held. — Cambridge : Polity in association with Blackwell, 1987. — xii,321p. — *Bibliography: p301-312. — Includes index*

History of political philosophy / edited by Leo Strauss [and] Joseph Cropsey. — 2nd ed. — Chicago : University of Chicago Press, 1973. — 849p

HOWARD, Dick
From Marx to Kant / Dick Howard. — Albany : State University of New York Press, 1985. — xiv, 300p. — (SUNY series in political thought)

JANOS, Andrew C
Politics and paradigms : changing theories of change in social science / Andrew C. Janos. — Stanford, Calif. : Stanford University Press, 1986. — p. cm. — *Includes index. — Bibliography: p*

MULLER, Virginia L.
The idea of perfectibility / Virginia L. Muller. — Lanham : University Press of America, c1985. — vii, 221 p.. — *Bibliography: p. 209-221*

Political thinkers / edited by David Muschamp. — Basingstoke : Macmillan, 1986. — ix,259p. — *Includes bibliographies and index*

SCHMID, J. J. von
Spinoza's staatkundige verhandeling in de ontwikkeling van de staatsleer / J. J. von Schmid. — Leiden : Brill, 1970. — 12p. — (Mededelingen vanwege het Spinozahuis ; 26)

Women in Western political philosophy : Kant to Nietzsche / edited by Ellen Kennedy and Susan Hendus. — Brighton : Wheatsheaf, 1987. — vi,215p. — *Bibliography: p202-210. — Includes index*

POLITICAL SCIENCE — Language — History

The Languages of political theory in early-modern Europe / edited by Anthony Pagden. — Cambridge : Cambridge University Press, 1987. — [viii,280]p. — (Ideas in context). — *Includes index*

POLITICAL SCIENCE — Mathematical models

ORDESHOOK, Peter C.
Game theory and political theory : an introduction / Peter C. Ordeshook. — Cambridge : Cambridge University Press, 1986. — viii,511p. — *Includes index*

POLITICAL SCIENCE — Philosophy

SAXONHOUSE, Arlene W
Women in the history of political thought : ancient Greece to Machiavelli / Arlene W. Saxonhouse. — New York ; Eastbourne : Praeger, 1985. — xii, 210p. — (Women and politics series). — *Includes index. — Bibliography: p.199-204*

POLITICAL SCIENCE — Research

EULAU, Heinz
Politics, self, and society : a theme and variations / Heinz Eulau. — Cambridge, Mass. : Harvard University Press, 1986. — x, 567 p.. — *Includes index. — Bibliography: p. [534]-556*

MANHEIM, Jarol B.
Empirical political analysis : research methods in political science / Jarol B. Manheim and Richard C. Rich, with contributions by Donna L. Bahry, Michael K. Brown, Philip A. Schrodt. — 2nd ed. — New York : Longman, c1986. — xii, 364 p.. — *Includes bibliographies and index*

POLITICAL SCIENCE — Study and teaching — Soviet Union

WILLIAMS, E. S.
The Soviet military : political education, training and morale / E.S. Williams ; with chapters by C.N. Donnelly and J.E. Moore ; foreword by Sir Curtis Keeble. — Basingstoke : Macmillan, 1987. — xv,203p,[16]p of plates. — (RUSI defence studies series). — *Bibliography: p196-198. — Includes index*

POLITICAL SCIENCE — Early works to 1700

BODIN, Jean
Les six livres de la République / Jean Bodin ; ouvrage publié avec le concours du Centre National des Lettres ; texte revu par Christiane Frémont, Marie-Dominique Couzinet, Henri Rochais. — [Paris] : Fayard, 1986. — . — (Corpus des oeuvres de philosophie en langue française / sous la direction de Michel Serres). — Also includes two other works by Jean Bodin: ´Apologie de René Herpin pour la République´ (1581), and ´Discours de Jean Bodin, sur le rehaussement et diminution tant d´or que d´argent, et le moyen d´y remedier, aux paradoxes du sieur de malestroit´ (1568,1578). Both appear in vol.6. — Reprint of 10th edition of work, published: Lyon: Gabriel Cartier, 1593. — Includes index at the end of vol.6

POLITICAL SCIENCE — England — History

Divine right and democracy : an anthology of political writing in Stuart England / edited by David Wootton. — Harmondsworth : Penguin, 1986. — 512p. — (Penguin classics)

POLITICAL SCIENCE — England — History — 17th century

SOMMERVILLE, J. P.
Politics and ideology in England, 1603-1640 / J.P. Sommerville. — London : Longman, 1986. — x,254p. — Includes index

POLITICAL SCIENCE — Europe

Contemporary political science in the USA and Western Europe / general editor G.Kh. Shakhnazarov ; [translated from the Russian by James Riordan]. — Moscow : Progress Publishers, c1985. — 431 p.. — (Criticism of bourgeois ideology and revisionism). — Title on verso of t.p.: Sovremenai͡a politicheskai͡a nauka v SShA i Zapadnoĭ Evrope. — Includes bibliographies and index

POLITICAL SCIENCE — Europe — History

KLOPPENBERG, James T
Uncertain victory : social democracy and progressivism in European and American thought, 1870-1920 / James T. Kloppenberg. — New York : Oxford University Press, 1986. — x, 546 p.. — Includes index. — Bibliography: p. [511]-528

The Languages of political theory in early-modern Europe / edited by Anthony Pagden. — Cambridge : Cambridge University Press, 1987. — [viii,280]p. — (Ideas in context) . — Includes index

POLITICAL SCIENCE — France — History

RILEY, Patrick
The general will before Rousseau : the transformation of the divine into the civic / Patrick Riley. — Princeton, N.J. : Princeton University Press, c1986. — xvii, 274p. — (Studies in moral, political, and legal philosophy). — Includes index

VERNON, Richard
Citizenship and order : studies in French political thought / Richard Vernon. — Toronto ; Buffalo : University of Toronto Press, c1986. — 264 p.. — Includes index. — Bibliography: p. [253]-260

POLITICAL SCIENCE — Germany

Leitbilder des deutschen Konservatismus : Schopenhauer, Nietzsche, Spengler, Heidegger, Schelsky, Rohrmoser, Kaltenbrunner u.a. / Ludwig Elm (Hrsg.). — Cologne : Pahl-Rugenstein, 1984. — 285p. — Includes bibliographic notes

POLITICAL SCIENCE — Great Britain — History — 17th century

POCOCK, J. G. A.
The ancient constitution and the feudal law : a study of English historical thought in the seventeenth century / J.G.A. Pocock. — Reissue with a retrospect [i.e. 2nd ed.]. — Cambridge : Cambridge University Press, 1987. — xv,402p. — Previous ed.: 1957. — Includes index

POLITICAL SCIENCE — Great Britain — History — 19th century

BRINTON, Crane
English political thought in the nineteenth century. — London : Benn, 1933. — 312p

POLITICAL SCIENCE — Hungary

GOMBÁR, Csaba
Egy állampolgár gondolatai : politikaelméleti írások / Gombár Csaba. — Budapest : Kossuth Könyvkiadó, 1984. — 244p. — Bibliographies

POLITICAL SCIENCE — India — Addresses, essays, lectures

Political thought in modern India / edited by Thomas Pantham, Kenneth L. Deutsch. — New Delhi : Beverly Hills, Calif. : Sage Publications, 1986. — p. cm. — Includes bibliographies

POLITICAL SCIENCE — Italy — History

ALBERTONI, Ettore A.
Mosca and the theory of elitism / Ettore A. Albertoni ; translated by Paul Goodrick. — Oxford : Basil Blackwell, 1987. — xvii,194p. — Translation of: Dottrina della classe politica e teoria delle elites. — Bibliography: p186-191. — Includes index

BELLAMY, Richard
Modern Italian social theory : ideology and politics from Pareto to the present / Richard Bellamy. — Cambridge : Polity in association with Blackwell, 1987. — 215p. — Bibliography: p204-210. — Includes index

POLITICAL SCIENCE — Poland

MAJCHROWSKI, Jacek
Silni, zwarci, gotowi : myśl polityczna Obozu Zjednoczenia Narodowego / Jacek Majchrowski. — Warszawa : Państwowe Wydawnictwo Naukowe, 1985. — 215,xvip. — Bibliography: p202-[211]

POLITICAL SCIENCE — Russia

WEBB, Sidney
Soviet communism : a new civilisation / by Sidney and Beatrice Webb. postscript added to the second edition. — [London] : Privately printed by the authors, 1937. — 72,33p

POLITICAL SCIENCE — Soviet Union — History

Obshchestvennaia mysl' v Rossii XIX v. / [redaktsionnaia kollegiia: A. N. Tsamutali...[et al.]. — Leningrad : Nauka, Leningradskoe otdelenie, 1986. — 244p. — (Trudy / Institut istorii SSSR, Leningradskoe otdelenie ; Vyp.16) . — Contains chart: "Skhema razvitiia dekabristskikh i sviazannykh s nimi organizatsii."

POLITICAL SCIENCE — United States

Contemporary political science in the USA and Western Europe / general editor G.Kh. Shakhnazarov ; [translated from the Russian by James Riordan]. — Moscow : Progress Publishers, c1985. — 431 p.. — (Criticism of bourgeois ideology and revisionism). — Title on verso of t.p.: Sovremenai͡a politicheskai͡a nauka v SShA i Zapadnoĭ Evrope. — Includes bibliographies and index

POLITICAL SCIENCE — United States — Addresses, essays, lectures

Left, right & babyboom : America´s new politics / edited by David Boaz. — Washington, D.C. : Cato Institute, c1986. — 122 p.

POLITICAL SCIENCE — United States — History

KAMMEN, Michael G
Spheres of liberty : changing perceptions of liberty in American culture / Michael Kammen. — Madison, Wis. : University of Wisconsin Press, 1986. — xiv, 191 p.. — (The Curti lectures ; 1985). — Includes bibliographical references and index. — Contents: Liberty, authority, and property in early America -- Ordered liberty and law in nineteenth-century America -- Liberty, justice, and equality in twentieth-century America -- Notes on liberty in American iconography

KLOPPENBERG, James T
Uncertain victory : social democracy and progressivism in European and American thought, 1870-1920 / James T. Kloppenberg. — New York : Oxford University Press, 1986. — x, 546 p.. — Includes index. — Bibliography: p. [511]-528

MADISON, James
The Federalist papers / James Madison, Alexander Hamilton and John Jay ; edited by Isaac Kramnick. — Harmondsworth : Penguin, 1987. — 515p

WHITE, Morton Gabriel
Philosophy, The Federalist, and the Constitution / Morton White. — New York ; Oxford : Oxford University Press, 1987. — xi, 273p. — Includes bibliographical references and index

POLITICAL SCIENCE — United States — History — 18th century

McDONALD, Forrest
Novus ordo seclorum : the intellectual origins of the Constitution / Forrest McDonald. — Lawrence, Kan. : University Press of Kansas, c1985. — xiii, 359 p.. — "The Constitution of the United States": p. [299]-311. — Includes index. — Bibliography: p. [313]-341

POLITICAL SOCIALIZATION

CARLSON, James M
Prime time law enforcement : crime show viewing and attitudes toward the criminal justice system / by James M. Carlson. — New York : Praeger, 1985. — p. cm. — Includes index. — Bibliography: p

POLITICAL SOCIALIZATION — Great Britain

BLUMLER, Jay G.
Political communication and the young voter : a panel study, 1970-1971, examining the role of election communication in the political socialisation of first time voters / Jay G. Blumler, Denis McQuail and T. J. Nossiter ; report to the Social Science Research Council, October 1975. — [London : Social Science Research Council, 1975]. — 1v. (various pagings). — Bibliographical references: end of vol.

BLUMLER, Jay G.
Political communication and the young voter in the general election of February 1974 : a panal study, 1970-1974, examining influences on the political socialisation of young voters between their first and second election campaigns / Jay G. Blumler, Denis McQuail and T. J. Nossiter ; report to the Social Science Research Council, July 1976. — [London : Social Science Research Council, 1976]. — 99 leaves. — Bibliographical references: p98-99

POLITICAL SOCIALIZATION — India — Case studies

SHARMA, Neena
Political socialization and its impact on attitudinal change towards social and political system : a case study of Harijan women of Delhi / Neena Sharma. — New Delhi : Inter-India Publications, 1985. — x, 157 p.. — Cover title: Political socialization & its impact on attitudinal change towards social & political system. — Includes index. — Bibliography: p. [146]-153

POLITICAL SOCIALIZATION — India — Delhi

SHARMA, Neena
Political socialization and its impact on attitudinal change towards social and political system : a case study of Harijan women of Delhi / Neena Sharma. — New Delhi : Inter-India Publications, 1985. — x, 157 p.. — *Cover title: Political socialization & its impact on attitudinal change towards social & political system. — Includes index. — Bibliography: p. [146]-153*

POLITICAL SOCIOLOGY

AGNEW, John A.
Place and politics : the geographical mediation of state and society / John A. Agnew. — Boston ; London : Allen & Unwin, 1987. — [288]p. — *Includes bibliography and index*

DOWSE, Robert E.
Political sociology / Robert E. Dowse and John A. Hughes. — 2nd ed. — Chichester : Wiley, c1986. — xi,398p,[416]p. — *Previous ed.: 1972. — Includes index*

EISENSTADT, S. N.
Centre formation, protest movements, and class structure in Europe and the United States / S.N. Eisenstadt, L. Roniger and A. Seligman. — London : Pinter, 1987. — 187p. — *Includes index*

GELLNER, Ernest
Culture, identity, and politics / Ernest Gellner. — Cambridge : Cambridge University Press, 1987. — [200]p. — *Includes bibliography and index*

KING, Roger, 1945-
The state in modern society : new directions in political sociology / Roger King with chapter 8 by Graham Gibbs. — Basingstoke : Macmillan, 1986. — [296]p. — *Includes bibliography and index*

LITTLE, Graham
Political ensembles : a psychosocial approach to politics and leadership / Graham Little. — Melbourne ; New York : Oxford University Press, 1985. — viii, 223 p.. — *Includes index. — Bibliography: p. 202-216*

MÉSZÁROS, István
Philosophy, ideology and social science : essays in negation and affirmation / István Mészáros. — Brighton : Harvester, 1986. — [272]p

The State in global perspective / edited by Ali Kazancigil. — Aldershot : Gower [with] UNESCO, 1986. — [350]p. — *Includes bibliography and index*

POLITICAL SOCIOLOGY — History

JANOS, Andrew C
Politics and paradigms : changing theories of change in social science / Andrew C. Janos. — Stanford, Calif. : Stanford University Press, 1986. — p. cm. — *Includes index. — Bibliography: p*

POLITICAL STABILITY

ZIEGENHAGEN, Eduard A.
The regulation of political conflict / Eduard A. Ziegenhagen. — New York : Praeger, 1986. — xix, 224 p.. — *Includes bibliographies and index*

POLITICAL STABILITY — Developing countries

The State and development in the Third World / edited by Atul Kohli. — Princeton, N.J. : Princeton University Press, 1986. — 288 p.. — (A World politics reader). — *"Essays collected...were published in World politics between 1976 and 1984"--Introd. — Includes bibliographical references*

POLITICAL STABILITY — Hong Kong

LIU, Siu-kai
Society and politics in Hong Kong / Lau Siu-kai. — Hong Kong : Chinese University Press ; New York : St. Martin's Press, 1983. — x, 205 p.. — *Includes index. — Bibliography: p. [191]-201*

POLITICIANS — Addresses, essays, lectures

Intellectuals in politics / edited by Nissan Oren. — Jerusalem : Magnes Press, Hebrew University, 1984. — 106 p.. — *Includes bibliographies*

POLITICIANS — Ireland — Biography

JENKINS, Brian
Sir William Gregory of Coole : the biography of an Anglo-Irishman / Brian Jenkins. — Gerrards Cross : Colin Smythe, 1986. — xi, 339p. — *Bibliography: p.323-332*

POLITICIANS — Argentina

GARCÍA COSTA, Victor O.
Alfredo L. Palacios : un socialismo argentino y para la Argentina / Victor O. García Costa. — Buenos Aires : Centro Editor de América Latina. — (Biblioteca Política Argentina ; 147) t.1. — 1986. — 141p

GARCÍA COSTA, Victor O.
Alfredo L. Palacios : un socialismo argentino y para la Argentina / Victor O. García Costa. — Buenos Aires : Centro Editor de América Latina. — (Biblioteca Política Argentina ; 148) t.2. — Buenos Aires : Centro Editor de América Latina. — 143-289p. — (Biblioteca Política Argentina ; 148)

POLITICIANS — Argentina — Biography

La historia de Eva Perón : un ejemplo de amor entre una mujer y un pueblo. — Buenos Aires : Sánchez Teruelo
Tomo 1. — [1983]. — 320p

La historia de Eva Perón : un ejemplo de amor entre una mujer y un pueblo. — Buenos Aires : Sánchez Teruelo
Tomo 2. — 1985. — 321-560p

QUIJADA, Mónica
Manuel Gálvez : 60 años de pensamiento nacionalista / Mónica Quijada. — Buenos Aires : Centro Editor de América Latina, 1985. — 139p. — *Bibliography: p133-139*

POLITICIANS — Australia

WALTER, James
The ministers' minders : personal advisers in national government / James Walter. — Melbourne : Oxford University Press, 1986. — viii,237p. — *Bibliography: p[218]-232*

POLITICIANS — Australia — Biography

RYDON, Joan
A federal legislature : the Australian Commonwealth Parliament 1901-1980 / Joan Rydon. — Melbourne : Oxford University Press, 1986. — 290p. — *Bibliography: p [281]-284*

POLITICIANS — Bangladesh

RAHMAN, Atiur
Rural power structure : a study of the local level leaders in Bangladesh / Atiur Rahman. — Dacca : Papri Publishers, 1981. — viii,63p. — *Bibliography: p59-63*

POLITICIANS — Canada — Biography

CAHILL, Jack
John Turner : the long run / by Jack Cahill. — Toronto, Ont. : McClelland and Stewart, c1984. — 234 p., [24] p. of plates. — *Includes index*

CHRÉTIEN, Jean
Straight from the heart / Jean Chrétien. — Toronto, Ont., Canada : Key Porter Books, c1985. — 231 p.. — *Includes index*

DAVEY, Keith
The rainmaker : a passion for politics / Keith Davey. — Toronto : Stoddart, 1986. — xii,383p

FLEMING, Donald M
So very near : the political memoirs of the Honourable Donald M. Fleming. — Toronto, Ont. : McClelland and Stewart, c1985. — 2 v.. — *Includes index. — Contents: v. 1. The rising years--v. 2. The summit years*

MACLAREN, Roy
Honourable mentions : the uncommon diary of an M.P. / Roy MacLaren. — Toronto : Deneau, 1986. — 226p

WHELAN, Eugene
Whelan : the man in the green stetson / by Eugene Whelan ; with Rick Archbold. — Toronto : Irwin Publishing, 1986. — 322p

POLITICIANS — China — Biography

LAMPTON, David M
Paths to power : elite mobility in contemporary China / by David M. Lampton with the assistance of Yeung Sai-cheung. — Ann Arbor : Center for Chinese Studies, Unversity of Michigan, 1985. — p. cm. — (Michigan monographs in Chinese studies ; no. 55). — *Includes index. — Bibliography: p*

POLITICIANS — Denmark — Biography

HOLCH, Mogens
K.Ø. Holch : landets sidste kgl. borgmester / Mogens Holch. — København : Dansk Historisk Håndbogsforlag, c1986. — 200p. — *Bibliography: p193*

POLITICIANS — England — London — Biography

CARVEL, John
Citizen Ken / John Carvel. — Rev. and enl. ed. — London : Hogarth, 1987. — 267p. — (Current affairs). — *Previous ed.: London : Chatto & Windus, 1984. — Includes index*

POLITICIANS — Georgia — Biography

CURRIE-MCDANIEL, Ruth
Carpetbagger of conscience : a biography of John Emory Bryant / Ruth Currie-McDaniel. — Athens : University of Georgia Press, c1987. — 238 p.. — *Includes index. — Bibliography: p. [221]-231*

POLITICIANS — Germany — Biography

BRAMWELL, Anna
Blood and soil : Richard Walther Darré and Hitler's 'Green Party' / [Anna Bramwell]. — Bourne End : Kensal, c1985. — viii,288p,[8]p of plates. — *Bibliography: p265-282. Includes index*

BUSSCHE, Albrecht von dem
Heinrich Alexander von Arnim : Liberalismus, Polenfrage und deutsche Einheit : das 19. Jahrhundert im Spiegel einer Biographie des preussischen Staatsmannes / von Albrecht von dem Bussche. — Osnabrück : Biblio Verlag, 1986. — x,426p. — *Bibliography: p339-344*

HAUPTS, Leo
Graf Brockdorff-Rantzou : Diplomat und Minister in Kaiser-reich und Republik / Leo Haupts. — Göttingen : Muster-Schmidt, c1984. — 106p. — (Persönlichkeit und Geschichte ; Bd.116/117). — *Bibliography: p103-106*

ZIMMERMANN, Mosche
[Vilhelm Mar, "ha-patri'arkh shel ha-Antishemiyut". English]. Wilhelm Marr, the patriarch of Antisemitism / by Moshe Zimmermann. — New York : Oxford University Press, 1986. — p. cm. — *Translation of: Vilhelm Mar, "ha-patri'arkh shel ha-Antishemiyut.". — Includes index*

POLITICIANS — Germany — History

ALFRED WEBER-KONGRESS (1st : 1984 : Heidelberg)
Alfred Weber als Politiker und Gelehrter : die Referate des Ersten Alfred Weber-Kongresses... / Eberhard Demm (Hrsg.). — Stuttgart : Steiner Verlag Wiesbaden, 1986. — 218p. — *Bibliography: p[205]-218*

POLITICIANS — Germany — Lower Saxony — Biography

RENZSCH, Wolfgang
Alfred Kubel : 30 Jahre Politik für Niedersachsen : eine politische Biographie / Wolfgang Renzsch. — Bonn : Neue Gesellschaft, 1985. — 232p. — *Bibliography: p222-229*

POLITICIANS — Germany — Prussia — Biography

BUSSCHE, Albrecht von dem
Heinrich Alexander von Arnim : Liberalismus, Polenfrage und deutsche Einheit : das 19. Jahrhundert im Spiegel einer Biographie des preussischen Staatsmannes / von Albrecht von dem Bussche. — Osnabrück : Biblio Verlag, 1986. — x,426p. — *Bibliography: p339-344*

DENNELER, Iris
Friedrich Karl von Savigny / von Iris Denneler. — Berlin : Stapp, 1985. — 140p. — (Preussische Köpfe ; 17). — *Cover title: Karl Friedrich von Savigny. — Bibliography: p125-129*

POLITICIANS — Germany (West) — Interviews

WEHNER, Herbert
Der Onkel : Herbert Wehner in Gesprächen und Interviews / herausgegeben von Knut Terjung. — Hamburg : Hoffman und Campe, 1986. — 287p

POLITICIANS — Great Britain

BROCKWAY, Fenner
98 not out / Fenner Brockway. — London : Quartet, 1986. — [140]p. — *Includes index*

POLITICIANS — Great Britain — Biography

BROWN, Gordon, 1951-
Maxton / by Gordon Brown. — Edinburgh : Mainstream, 1986. — 335p,[8]p of plates. — *Includes index*

HOWARD, Anthony
Rab : the life of R.A. Butler / Anthony Howard. — London : Cape, 1987. — xv,422p,[24]p of plates. — *Bibliography: p407-410. — Includes index*

JENKINS, Brian
Sir William Gregory of Coole : the biography of an Anglo-Irishman / Brian Jenkins. — Gerrards Cross : Colin Smythe, 1986. — xi, 339p. — *Bibliography: p.323-332*

LOFTHOUSE, Geoff
A very miner MP / by Geoff Lofthouse ; Foreword by Viscount Tonypandy. — Pontefract : Yorkshire Arts Circus, 1986. — 127p

TYRRELL, Alex
Joseph Sturge and the "moral Radical party" in early Victorian Britain / Alex Tyrrell. — London : Helm, c1987. — [264]p. — *Bibliography: p249-250. — Includes index*

WATKINSON, Harold Arthur
Turning points : a record of our times / Harold Watkinson. — Wilton : Michael Russell, 1986. — 228p

POLITICIANS — Great Britain — History — 19th century

JALLAND, Pat
Women, marriage and politics 1860-1914 / Pat Jalland. — Oxford : Clarendon, 1986. — [380]p,[8]p of plates. — *Includes bibliography and index*

POLITICIANS — Great Britain — History — 20th century

JALLAND, Pat
Women, marriage and politics 1860-1914 / Pat Jalland. — Oxford : Clarendon, 1986. — [380]p,[8]p of plates. — *Includes bibliography and index*

POLITICIANS — Hungary — Biography

NEMES, Dezső
Kun Béla politikai életútjáról / Nemes Dezső. — [Budapest] : Kossuth Könyvkiadó, 1985. — 186p

POLITICIANS — India

PRASAD, Bimal
Gandhi, Nehru & J. P. : studies in leadership / Bimal Prasad. — Delhi : Chanakya Publications, 1985. — 294p. — *Bibliography: p283-287*

POLITICIANS — India — Biography

ROSS, Alan
The emissary : G.D. Birla, Gandhi and independence / Alan Ross. — London : Collins Harvill, 1986. — [288]p. — *Includes bibliography and index*

POLITICIANS — Indiana — History

VANDERMEER, Philip R.
The Hoosier politician : officeholding and political culture in Indiana, 1896-1920 / Philip R. VanderMeer. — Urbana : University of Illinois Press, c1985. — p. cm. — *Includes index. — Bibliography: p*

POLITICIANS — Ireland — Biography

Daniel O'Connell : portrait of a radical / edited by Kevin B. Nowlan and Maurice R. O'Connell. — Belfast : Appletree Press, 1984. — 120p. — (The Thomas Davis lectures)

WALSH, Dick
Des O'Malley : a political profile / Dick Walsh. — Dingle : Brandon, 1986. — [160]p

POLITICIANS — Mexico

VALLARTA, Ignacio Luis
Vallarta en la reforma / prólogo y selección: Moisés González Navarro. — México, D.F. : Universidad Nacional Autónoma de México, 1956. — xxxv,232p. — (Biblioteca del estudiante Universitario ; 76)

POLITICIANS — Nevada — Biography

HOWARD, Anne Bail
The long campaign : a biography of Anne Martin / Anne Bail Howard. — Reno, Nevada : University of Nevada Press, c1985. — p. cm. — (Nevada studies in history and political science ; no. 20). — *Includes index. — Bibliography: p*

POLITICIANS — Northern Ireland — Biography

BRUCE, Steve
God save Ulster : the religion and politics of Paisleyism / Steve Bruce. — Oxford : Clarendon, 1986. — xv,308p. — *Includes index*

MOLONEY, Ed
Paisley / Ed Moloney and Andy Pollak. — Dublin : Poolbeg, 1986. — 456p. — *Bibliography: p445-[448]*

POLITICIANS — Ontario — Biography

MCDOUGALL, A. K.
John P. Robarts : his life and government / A.K. McDougall. — Toronto ; London : University of Toronto Press, c1986. — xiii,320,[17]p of plates. — (Ontario historical studies series). — *Bibliography: p299-305. — Includes index*

POLITICIANS — Palestine — Biography

TAGGAR, Yehuda
The Mufti of Jerusalem and Palestine : Arab politics, 1930-1937 / Yehuda Taggar. — New York : Garland, 1986, c1987. — 472 p. — (Outstanding theses from the London School of Economics and Political Science). — *Thesis (Ph. D.)--University of London, 1973. — Bibliography: p. 466-472*

POLITICIANS — Poland — Biography

KĘPIŃSKI, Andrzej
Kto jest kim w Polsce-inaczej / Andrzej Kępiński, Zbigniew Kilar (współpraca). — Warszawa : Czytelnik Cz.1. — 1985. — 420p

KĘPIŃSKI, Andrzej
Kto jest kim w Polsce - inaczej / Andrzej Kępiński, Zbigniew Kilar (współpraca). — Warszawa : Czytelnik Cz.2. — 1986. — 454p

POLITICIANS — Poland — Interviews

TORAŃSKA, Teresa
Oni / Teresa Torańska. — Londyn : Aneks, 1985. — 365p

POLITICIANS — Soviet Union

LAIRD, Roy D.
The Politburo : demographic trends, Gorbachev, and the future / Roy D. Laird. — Boulder, Colo. : Westview Press, 1986. — xv,198p. — (Westview special studies on the Soviet Union and Eastern Europe). — *Bibliography: p187-189*

POLITICIANS — Spain — Biography

AREILZA, José María de
Crónica de libertad, 1965-1975 / José María de Areilza. — Barcelona : Planeta, 1985. — 193p

POLITICIANS — Spain — Catalonia

BARCELÓ I SERRAMALERA, Mercè
El pensament polític de Serra i Moret : nació, democràcia i socialisme / Mercè Barceló i Serramalera ; pròleg d'Isidre Molas. — Barcelona : Edicions 62, 1986. — 205p. — *Bibliography: p191-205*

POLITICIANS — Sweden — Biography

WESTMAN, Karl Gustaf
Politiska anteckningar september 1939 - mars 1943 / K.G. Westman ; utgivna genom W.M. Carlgren. — Stockholm : Kungl. Samfundet för utgivande av handskrifter rörande Skandinaviens historia, 1981. — 237p.,[1] leaf of port. — (Handlingar / Kungl. Samfundet för utgivande av handskrifter rörande Skandinaviens historia ; del 6)

POLITICIANS — United States — Biography

OHL, John Kennedy
Hugh S. Johnson and the New Deal / John Kennedy Ohl. — Dekalb, Ill. : Northern Illinois University Press, 1985. — xi, 374p. — *Includes index. — Bibliography: p.[345]-359*

POLITICS — history — United States

HOLLINGSWORTH, J. Rogers
A political economy of medicine : Great Britain and the United States / J. Rogers Hollingsworth. — Baltimore : Johns Hopkins University Press, c1986. — xix, 312 p.. — *Includes index. — Bibliography: p. 275-303*

POLITICS AND CULTURE — Hungary

HERNÁDI, Miklós
Olyan amilyen? : körkép új kultúránkról / Hernádi Miklós. — Budapest : Kozmosz Könyvek, 1984. — 285p. — (Az én világom)

POLITICS AND EDUCATION

Critical pedagogy and cultural power / David W. Livingstone & contributors ; introduction by Paulo Freire and Henry Giroux. — Basingstoke : Macmillan, 1987. — xvi,342p. — *Bibliography: p293-335. — Includes index*

POLITICS AND EDUCATION — Chile — History — 20th century

FARRELL, Joseph P
The National Unified School in Allende's Chile : the role of education in the destruction of a revolution / Joseph P. Farrell. — Vancouver : University of British Columbia Press in association with the Centre for Research on Latin America and the Caribbean, York University, 1986. — viii, 268 p.. — (Latin American and Caribbean studies ; 1). — *Includes index. — Bibliography: p. [259]-263*

POLITICS AND EDUCATION — Soviet Union — Addresses, essays, lectures

SORRENTINO, Frank M.
Soviet politics and education / Frank M. Sorrentino and Frances R. Curcio. — Lanham, MD : University Press of America, c1985. — p. cm. — *Bibliography: p*

POLITICS AND EDUCATION — United States

Policy controversies in higher education / edited by Samuel K. Gove and Thomas M. Stauffer ; prepared under the auspices of the Policy Studies Organization. — New York : Greenwood Press, 1986. — xi, 274 p.. — (Contributions to the study of education ; no. 19). — *Includes index. — Bibliography: p. [261]-264*

POLITICS AND EDUCATION — United States — History
PETERSON, Paul E
The politics of school reform, 1870-1940 / Paul E. Peterson. — Chicago : University of Chicago Press, 1985. — x, 241 p.. — *Includes index. — Bibliography: p. [227]-234*

POLITICS AND GOVERNMENT — Classification
Classification of the functions of government. — New York : United Nations, 1980. — iii,52p. — (Statistical papers / United Nations, Statistical Office. Series M ; no.70) ([Document] (United Nations) ; ST/ESA/STAT/SER.M/70). — *Sales no.: E.80.XVII.17*

POLITICS AND LITERATURE
Literature, politics and theory : papers from the Essex Conference 1976-84 / edited by Francis Barker ... [et al.]. — London : Methuen, 1986. — [276]p. — (New accents)

POLITICS AND LITERATURE — Soviet Union — History
LITVINA, F. A.
Legal'nye formy propagandy raznochintsev-demokratov 60-70-kh gg. XIX v. : (literaturnye vechera, chteniia, sobraniia) / F. A. Litvina. — Kazan' : Izd-vo Kazanskogo universiteta, 1986. — 131p

POLITICS IN LITERATURE
PARKES, K. Stuart
Writers and politics in West Germany / K. Stuart Parkes. — London : Croom Helm, c1986. — 251p. — *Bibliography: p242-246. — Includes index*

POLITICS, PRACTICAL — Canada
SNIDER, Norman
The changing of the guard : how the Liberals fell from grace and the Tories rose to power / Norman Snider. — Toronto : Lester & Orpen Denys, 1985. — 206p

POLITICS, PRACTICAL — United States
ABNEY, Glenn
The politics of state and city administration / Glenn Abney and Thomas P. Lauth. — Albany, N.Y. : State University of New York Press, c1986. — p cm. — (SUNY series in public administration in the 1980's). — *Includes index*

POLL-TAX — Great Britain
SMITH, Stephen, 19---
Local taxes and local government / Stephen Smith and Duncan Squire. — London : Institute for Fiscal Studies : Distributed by Woodhead-Faulkner, c1987. — 80p. — (IFS report series ; no.25). — *Bibliography: p.77-79*

POLLUTANTS — Toxicology
BELLINI, James
High tech holocaust / James Bellini. — Newton Abbot : David & Charles, c1986. — 255p

POLLUTION — Economic aspects — England
BRITTAN, Yvonne
The impact of water pollution control on industry : a case study of fifty dischargers / Yvonne Brittan. — Oxford : Centre for Socio-Legal Studies, 1984. — vii,115p. — *Bibliography: p107*

POLLUTION — Environmental aspects — Bibliography
An Environmental bibliography : publications issued by UNEP or under its auspices, 1973-1980. — Nairobi : United Nations Environment Programme, 1981. — vi,67p. — (UNEP reference series ; 2). — *Includes indexes*

POLLUTION — Law and legislation — Great Britain
GREAT BRITAIN. Department of the Environment
A consultation paper on the review of the law of statutory nuisance and offensive trades. — London : the Department, [1979?]. — [30]p

POLLUTION — Law and legislation — United States
DURANT, Robert F.
When government regulates itself : EPA, TVA, and pollution control in the 1970s / Robert F. Durant. — Knoxville : University of Tennessee Press, c1985. — p. cm. — *Bibliography: p [169]-187. — Bibliography: p*

POLLUTION — Statistics — Bibliography
Directory of environment statistics. — New York : United Nations, 1983. — v,305p. — (Statistical papers / United Nations, Statistical Office. Series M ; no.75) ([Document] (United Nations) ; ST/ESA/STAT/SER.M/75). — *Sales no.: E.83.XVII.12*

POLLUTION — Europe
Acid rain. — London : Watt Committee on Energy, 1984. — 58 p.. — (Report / Watt Committee on Energy ; no. 14). — "*Papers presented at the fifteenth Consultative Council meeting of the Watt Committee on Energy, London, 1 December 1983*"

POLLUTION — Great Britain
GREAT BRITAIN. Department of the Environment
Inspecting industry: pollution and safety : action plan. — London : H.M.S.O., 1986. — 13p

Inspecting industry: pollution and safety : report and annexes / commissioned jointly by the Secretary of State for the Environment and for Employment. — London : H.M.S.O., 1986. — 110p. — (Efficiency scrutiny report)

NATIONAL SOCIETY FOR CLEAN AIR. Workshop (1984 : Oxford)
Regulating the impact of air pollution / [contributions by M. T. Westaway...et al.]. — Brighton : The Society, 1984. — Various pagings. — *Papers of a workshop held at Lincoln College, Oxford, 28 and 29 March 1984*

POLLUTION — Japan — Tokyo
TOKYO. Somukyoku. Shōgai Kankōbu. Gaijika
Tokyo fights pollution / [English text by Mitsuo Shono ; edited by the Liaison and Protocol Section, Bureau of General Affairs, Tokyo Metropolitan Government]. — Rev. ed. — [Tokyo : Tokyo Metropolitan Government], 1977. — ix, 222 p.. — (TMG municipal library ; no. 13). — *Revised translation of Tōkyō-to Kōgai Kenkyūjo Kōgai to Tōkyō-to*

POLLUTION — Organisation for Economic Co-operation and Development countries
YAKOWITZ, Harvey
Fate of small quantities of hazardous waste. — [Paris] : OECD, 1986. — 100p. — (OECD environment monographs ; no.6). — *Includes bibliographical references*

POLLUTION — Switzerland
GYSIN, Christoph H.
Externe Kosten der Energie in der Schweiz : methodische Grundlagen und Versuch einer Schätzung / Christoph H. Gysin. — Grüsch : Verlag Rüegger, 1985. — xi,220p. — *Bibliography: p205-220*

POLLUTION CONTROL INDUSTRY — Cost effectiveness
NICHOL, B. M.
The use of the EEC Council recommendation of 19 December 1978 regarding "Methods of evaluating the cost of pollution control to industry" / [B. M. Nichol]. — [London : Economies of Environmental Protection Division, Department of the Environment, 1979]. — 20leaves

POLSKA PARTIA ROBOTNICZA
KOWALSKI, Witold
Wkład PPR i PPS w rozwój spółdzielczości w Polsce w latach 1944-1948 / Witold Kowalski. — Warszawa : Książka i Wiedza, 1986. — 425p. — *Bibliography: p394-[413]*

POLSKA PARTIA ROBOTNICZA — History
KOŁOMEJCZYK, Norbert
Polska Partia Robotnicza 1942-1948 / Norbert Kołomejczyk, Marian Malinowski. — Warszawa : Książka i Wiedza, 1986. — 540p. — *Bibliogpraphy: p526-[529]*

POLSKA PARTIA SOCJALISTYCZNA
KOWALSKI, Witold
Wkład PPR i PPS w rozwój spółdzielczości w Polsce w latach 1944-1948 / Witold Kowalski. — Warszawa : Książka i Wiedza, 1986. — 425p. — *Bibliography: p394-[413]*

POLSKA PARTIA SOCJALNO-DEMOKRATYCZNA
NAJDUS, Walentyna
Polska Partia Socjalno-Demokratyczna Galicji i Śląska 1890-1919 / Walentyna Najdus. — Warszawa : Państwowe Wydawnictwo Naukowe, 1983. — 718p. — *Bibliography: p660-671*

POLYGAMY — Cross-cultural studies
BETZIG, L. L
Despotism and differential reproduction : a Darwinian view of history / L.L. Betzig. — New York : Aldine Pub., 1986. — p. cm. — *Bibliography: p*

POLYNESIANS IN EASTER ISLAND — History
BARTHEL, Thomas S.
[Achte Land. English]. The eighth land : the Polynesian discovery and settlement of Easter Island / Thomas S. Barthel ; translated for the German by Anneliese Martin. — Honolulu : University Press of Hawaii, c1978. — xi, 372 p.. — *Translation of Das achte Land. — Includes index. — Bibliography: p. [357]-362*

POLYTECHNICS AND COLLEGES FUNDING COUNCIL
GREAT BRITAIN. Department of Education and Science
Changes in structure and national planning for higher education. — [London] : the Department
Polytechnics and colleges sector : note. — 1987. — 49p

PONDICHERRY (INDIA) — Population — Statistics
Census of India 1981 / P. L. Samy, Director of Census Operations, Pondicherry. — [New Delhi : Controller of Publications] Series 32: Pondicherry. — [1985-]

PONDOS
SHOOTER, Joseph
The Kafirs of Natal and the Zulu country. — New York : Negro Universities Press, [1969]. — x, 403 p. — *Reprint of the 1857 ed*

POOR
LIPTON, Michael
Why poor people stay poor : urban bias in world development / Michael Lipton. — Cambridge : Harvard University Press, 1977, c1976. — 467 p.. — *Includes index. — Bibliography: p. 355-357*

NEAL, Marie Augusta
The just demands of the poor : essays in socio-theology / Marie Augusta Neal. — New York : Paulist Press, c1987. — v, 142 p.. — *Bibliography: p. 113-132*

POOR — Great Britain
PIACHAUD, David
Poor children : a tale of two decades / David Piachaud. — London : Child Poverty Action Group, 1986. — 16p. — *Bibliography: p15-16*

POOR — Health and hygiene — Great Britain
WHITEHEAD, Margaret
The health divide : inequalities in health in the 1980's / Margaret Whitehead. — London : Health Education Council, 1987. — iv,119p

POOR — History
MOLLAT, Michel
[Pauvres au Moyen Age. English]. The poor in the Middle Ages : an essay in social history / Michel Mollat ; translated by Arthur Goldhammer. — New Haven : Yale University Press, c1986. — p. cm. — *Translation of: Les Pauvres au Moyen Age.* — *Includes index.* — *Bibliography: p*

POOR — Hospital care — Scotland — Edinburgh (Lothian) — History — 18th century
RISSE, Guenter B.
Hospital life in Enlightenment Scotland : care and teaching at the Royal Infirmary of Edinburgh / Guenter B. Risse. — Cambridge : Cambridge University Press, 1986. — xiv,450p. — (Cambridge history of medicine). — *Includes index*

POOR — Housing — United States
Housing America's poor / edited by Peter D. Salins. — Chapel Hill : University of North Carolina Press, c1987. — p. cm. — (Urban and regional policy and development studies). — *Includes index*

POOR — Services for — England — History — 19th century
MARSHALL, J. D.
The Old Poor Law, 1795-1834 / prepared for the Economic History Society by J.D. Marshall. — 2nd ed. — Basingstoke : Macmillan, 1985. — 57p. — (Studies in economic and social history). — *Previous ed.: 1968.* — *Bibliography: p51-54.* — *Includes index*

POOR — Asia
Case studies on poverty programmes in Asia / edited by Swapna Mukhopadhyay. — Kuala Lumpur : Asian and Pacific Development Centre, 1985. — xv,271p. — *Bibliographies*

Fighting poverty : Asia's major challenge. — New Delhi : Asian Employment Programme, 1986. — 40p

The poor in Asia : productivity-raising programmes and strategies / edited by Swapna Mukhopadhyay. — Kuala Lumpur : Asian and Pacific Development Centre, 1985. — 772p. — *Bibliographies*

POOR — Canada
METTRICK, Alan
Last in line : on the road and out of work-- a desperate journey with Canada's unemployed / by Alan Mettrick. — Toronto, Ont., Canada : Key Porter Books, c1985. — x, 201 p.

POOR — Developing countries
CLAUSEN, A. W.
Poverty in developing countries, 1985 : address / by A. W. Clausen. — Washington, D.C. : World Bank, 1985. — 14p. — *Address given at the Martin Luther King, Jr., Center, Atlanta, Georgia on January 11, 1985*

POOR — England — Liverpool (Merseyside)
COONEY, Anthony
The sources of poverty : the causes of poverty in Liverpool in general and Toxteth in particular during the decade (1900-1910) of the Royal Commission on the Poor Law and Relief of Distress / Anthony Cooney. — Liverpool : Gild of St. George, 1984. — 77p. — *Bibliography: p77*

POOR — England — London — History — 19th century
DICKENS, Charles, 1812-1870
A December vision : his social journalism / Charles Dickens ; edited by Neil Philip and Victor Neuburg. — London : Collins, 1986. — 160p. — *Bibliography: p157-158.* — *Includes index*

POOR — England — Manchester (Greater Manchester)
MANCHESTER. City Council
Poverty in Manchester. — Manchester : [the Council], 1986. — 22p

POOR — France — Grenoble — History — 17th century
NORBERG, Kathryn
Rich and poor in Grenoble, 1600-1814 / Kathryn Norberg. — Berkeley ; London : University of California Press, c1985. — xii, 366p. — *Includes index.* — *Bibliography: p.345-352*

POOR — France — Grenoble — History — 18th century
NORBERG, Kathryn
Rich and poor in Grenoble, 1600-1814 / Kathryn Norberg. — Berkeley ; London : University of California Press, c1985. — xii, 366p. — *Includes index.* — *Bibliography: p.345-352*

POOR — Great Britain
BOOTH, Alan
Life on the margins : the politics of mass poverty / Alan Booth. — London : Communist Party, 1985. — 33p

CHILD POVERTY ACTION GROUP
Building one nation : memorandum to the Chancellor of the Exchequer. — London : Child Poverty Action Group, 1987. — 16p

CHILD POVERTY ACTION GROUP
Poverty: the facts. — London : Child Poverty Action Group, 1986. — 11p

LABOUR RESEARCH DEPARTMENT
The widening gap : rich and poor today. — London : Labour Research Department, 1987. — 44p

LISTER, Ruth
'A two-tier society' : response to the consultative document on Wages Councils from the Child Poverty Action Group / Ruth Lister, Fran Bennett and Jo Roll. — London : Child Poverty Action Group, 1985. — 18p

LOW PAY UNIT
The rising tide of poverty: joint briefing / Low Pay Unit [and] Child Poverty Action Group. — London : Low Pay : Child Poverty Action Group, 1986. — 7 leaves

NATIONAL COUNCIL FOR ONE PARENT FAMILIES
Fuel poverty : case-studies from one parent families. — London : National Council for One Parent Families, 1985. — 10p

POOR — Great Britain — Medical care
LIBERAL PARTY
Health care in the inner cities. — Hebden Bridge : Hebden Royd Publications, 1986. — 12p. — (Liberal Party Health panel papers ; no.15)

POOR — Great Britain — Nutrition
COLE-HAMILTON, Isobel
Tightening belts : a report on the impact of poverty on food / Isobel Cole-Hamilton and Tim Long. — 2nd ed. — London : London Food Commission, 1986. — viii,132p. — *Bibliography: p98-110*

POOR — Great Britain — Political aspects
FIELD, Frank, 1942-
Freedom and wealth in a socialist future / Frank Field. — Rev. and enl. ed. — London : Constable, 1987. — 288p. — *Previous ed.: London : Fontana, 1981.* — *Includes index*

POOR — Great Britain — Statistics
GREAT BRITAIN. Department of Health and Social Security
Low income families - 1983 : estimated numbers of families and persons with incomes at various levels relative to supplementary benefit level analysed by family type and economic status. — [London] : the Department, 1986. — [12]p

POOR — India
SOUZA, Alfred de
The social organisation of aging among the urban poor / Alfred de Souza. — New Delhi : Indian Social Institute, 1982. — 78p. — *Bibliography: p72-75*

POOR — India — Addresses, essays, lectures
The Indian city : poverty, ecology, and urban development / edited by Alfred de Souza. — New Delhi : Manohar, 1978. — xxix, 243 p.. — *Includes index.* — *Bibliography: p. [233]-238*

POOR — India — Karnataka
PRABHAKARA, N. R
Population growth and unemployment in India / N.R. Prabhakara, M.N. Usha. — New Delhi : Ashish Pub. House, 1986. — ix, 102 p.. — *Includes index.* — *Bibliography: p. 97-99*

POOR — Kenya
COLLIER, Paul
Labour and poverty in Kenya, 1900-1980 / Paul Collier and Deepak Lal. — Oxford : Clarendon, 1986. — xii,296p

GREER, Joel
Food poverty and consumption patterns in Kenya / Joel Greer and Erik Thorbecke. — Geneva : International Labour Office, 1986. — xii,170p

POOR — Latin America
ALTIMIR, Oscar
Measuring levels of living in Latin America : an overview of main problems / Oscar Altimir, Juan Sourrouille. — Washington, D.C., U.S.A. : World Bank, 1986 printing, c1980. — 75p. — (LSMS working papers ; no.3). — *Includes bibliographical references*

PFEFFERMANN, Guy P.
Public expenditure in Latin America : effects on poverty / Guy Pfeffermann. — Washington, D.C. : The World Bank, 1987. — 38p. — (World Bank discussion papers ; no.5). — *Includes bibliographical references*

Poverty in Latin America : the impact of depression. — Washington, D.C. : The World Bank, 1986. — 25p

POOR — Namibia
SMITH, Susanna
Namibia : a violation of trust : an Oxfam report on international responsibility for poverty in Namibia / Susanna Smith. — Oxford : Oxfam, 1986. — 99p. — *Bibliography: p99*

POOR — Pakistan
IRFAN, Mohammad
Poverty and household demographic behaviour in Pakistan : insights from PLM survey 1979 / Mohammad Irfan. — Islamabad : Pakistan Institute of Development Economics, 1986. — 57p. — (Studies in population, labour force and migration project report ; no.11). — *Bibliography: p[58-59]*

POOR — Pennsylvania — Philadelphia — History — 19th century
CLEMENT, Priscilla Ferguson
Welfare and the poor in the nineteenth-century city : Philadelphia, 1800-1854 / Priscilla Ferguson Clement. — Rutherford [N.J.] : Fairleigh Dickinson University Press, c1985. — p. cm. — *Includes index.* — *Bibliography: p*

POOR — Peru — Lima
BUNSTER, Ximena
Sellers and servants : working women in Lima, Peru / Ximena Bunster, Elsa M. Chaney ; photos by Ellan Young. — New York : Praeger, 1985. — x, 258p. — *Includes index.* — *Bibliography: p.235-246*

POOR — Scotland
Inequalities and childhood : the proceedings of a conference held on 26 April 1985 at the Queen's Hall, Edinburgh / edited by Eric Wilkinson and Rachel Jenkins. — Edinburgh : Scottish Child and Family Alliance, 1986. — 57p

SMAIL, Robin
Breadline Scotland : low pay and inequality north of the Border / Robin Smail. — London : Low Pay Unit, 1986. — 32p

POOR — Soviet Union — History — 20th century
MATTHEWS, Mervyn
Poverty in the Soviet Union : the life-styles of the underprivileged in recent years / by Mervyn Matthews. — Cambridge : Cambridge University Press, 1986. — [430]p. — *Includes bibliography and index*

POOR — Spain
La pobreza en España y sus causas / obra dirigida por Jesus Garcia Valcarcel. — 2a ed. — Madrid : Fundación AGAPE, 1985. — xx,759p

POOR — Spain — Castile
MARCOS MARTÍN, Alberto
Economía, sociedad, pobreza en Castilla : Palencia, 1500-1814 / Alberto Marcos Martín. — Palencia : Diputación Provincial
1. — 1985. — 358p

MARCOS MARTÍN, Alberto
Economia, sociedad, pobreza en Castilla : Palencia, 1500-1814 / Alberto Marcos Martín. — Palencia : Diputación Provincial. — *Bibliography: p[691]-715*
2. — 1985. — p369-742

POOR — Spain — Valladolid — History
MAZA ZORRILLA, Elena
Valladolid : sus pobres y la respuesta institucional (1750-1900) / Elena Maza Zorrila. — Valladolid : Universidad de Valladolid : Junta de Castille y León, 1985. — 405p. — *Bibliography: p381-392*

POOR — Swaziland
GUMA, X. P.
Some aspects of poverty among Swazi rural homesteads / X. P. Guma [and] M. Neocosmos. — Kwaluseni : Kwaluseni Campus, 1986. — ix,73p. — (Research paper / University of Swaziland. Social Science Research Unit ; no.23)

POOR — Switzerland
BEYELER-VON-BURG, Hélène
Des Suisses sans nom : les heimattoses d'anjourd'hui / Hélène Beyeler-von-Burg. — Pierrelaye : Éditions Science et Service, 1984. — 351p

POOR — United States
EDELMAN, Marian Wright
Families in peril : an agenda for social change / Marian Wright Edelman. — Cambridge, Mass. : Harvard University Press, 1987. — xii, 127 p.. — (The W.E.B. Du Bois lectures ; 1986). — *Includes index. — Bibliography: p. [115]-122*

POOR — United States — Case Studies
STACK, Carol B
All our kin: strategies for survival in a Black community / [by] Carol B. Stack. — [1st ed.]. — New York : Harper & Row, [1974]. — xxi, 175 p. — *Bibliography: p. [160]-167*

POOR AS CONSUMERS — Great Britain
Towards the sensitive bureaucracy : consumers, wlefare, and the new pluralism / editors, Drew Clode, Christopher Parker, Stuart Etherington. — [Brookfield, VT] : Gower Pub., 1986. — p. cm. — *Includes bibliographies and index*

Towards the sensitive bureaucracy : consumers, welfare and the new pluralism / edited by Drew Clode, Christopher Parker, Stuart Etherington. — Aldershot : Gower, c1987. — x,145p. — *Includes bibliographies and index*

POPIEŁUSZKO, JERZY
POPIEŁUSZKO, Jerzy
Zapiski 1980-1984 / Jersey Popiełuszko. — Paris : Editions Spotkania, 1985. — Various pagings

SIKORSKA, Grażyna
Prawda warta życie : Ks. Jerzy Popiełuszko / Grażyna Sikorska. — Londyn : Polska Fundacja Kulturalna, 1985. — xvi,148p

POPPER, KARL R.
Plato, Popper and politics : some contributions to a modern controversy / edited by Renford Bambrough. — Cambridge : Heffer, 1967. — viii, 219p. — (Views and controversies about classical antiquity)

POPPER, Karl R.
Unended quest : an intellectual autobiography / Karl Popper. — Rev. ed. — [London] : Flamingo, 1986. — 270p. — *Previous ed.: published as Autobiography of Karl Popper. La Salle, Ill. : Open Court, 1974. — Bibliography: p242-254. — Includes index*

POPPER, KARL R. — Congresses
POPPER-KOLLOQUIUM (1983 : Vienna)
Karl Popper : Philosophie und Wissenschaft : Beiträge zum Popper-Kolloquium / Friedrich Wallner (Hrsg). — Wien : Braumüller, 1985. — viii,148p. — (Philosophica ; 4). — *Bibliographies*

POPULAR CULTURE
BECKER, Howard S.
Art worlds / Howard S. Becker. — Berkeley ; London : University of California Press, 1984, c1982. — xiv,392p. — *Bibliography: p373-384*

BENNETT, Tony
Bond and beyond : the political career of a popular hero / Tony Bennett and Janet Woollacott. — Basingstoke : Macmillan Education, 1987. — xi,315p. — (Communications and culture). — *Includes index*

POPULAR FRONTS — History
The Popular Front in Europe / edited by Helen Graham, Paul Preston. — Basingstoke : Macmillan, 1987. — vii,171p. — *Includes index*

POPULAR FRONTS — Poland
KUCIŃSKI, Jerzy
Geneza PRON / Jerzy Kuciński. — Warszawa : Książka i Weiedza, 1985. — 158p

POPULAR LITERATURE — Soviet Union — History and criticism
BROOKS, Jeffrey
When Russia learned to read : literacy and popular literature, 1861-1917 / Jeffrey Brooks. — Princeton, N.J. : Princeton University Press, c1985. — xxii, 450 p.. — *Includes index. — Bibliography: p. 415-435*

POPULAR MOVEMENT FOR THE LIBERATION OF ANGOLA
HAMILL, James
The challenge to the M.P.L.A. : Angola's war: 1980-1986 / James Hamill. — Coventry : University of Warwick, 1986. — 74p. — (Working paper / University of Warwick. Department of Politics ; no.41)

POPULATION
ALDRICH, Howard
Population perspectives on organisations / Howard Aldrich in collaboration with Ellen R. Auster, Udo H. Staber and Catherine Zimmer. — Uppsala : [University of Uppsala], 1986. — 109p. — (Acta Universitatis Upsaliensis : Studia oeconomiae negotiorum ; 25) (Uppsala Lectures in Business ; 2). — *Bibliography: p95-104*

Concise report on the world population situation in 1983 : conditions, trends, prospects, policies. — New York : United Nations, 1984. — 108p. — (Population studies / Department of International Economic and Social Affairs ; no.85) ([Document] / United Nations ; ST/ESA/SER.A/85). — *Includes bibliographical references. — Sales no.: E.83.XIII.6*

LAROUCHE, Lyndon H.
There are no limits to growth / Lyndon H. LaRouche. — New York : New Benjamin Franklin House, 1983. — xix,225p

LOWRY, J. H.
World population and food supply / J.H. Lowry. — 3rd ed. — London : Edward Arnold, 1986. — [128]p. — *Previous ed.: 1976*

Population and development review. — New York : Population Council, 1975-. — *Quarterly*

La population mondiale : vers une stabilisation au XXIe siècle? / Olivier Belbeoch [et al.]. — Paris : La Documentation française, 1986. — 143p. — (Notes et études documentaires ; no.4806)

Population reports: Series L: Issues in world health / Population Information Program. — Baltimore, Md. : Population Information Program, John Hopkins University, 1980-. — *Irregular*

Population reports: Series M: Special topics / Population Information Program. — Baltimore, Md. : Population Information Program, John Hopkins University, 1985-. — *Every two months*

POPULATION — Dictionaries — English
Population terminology = Terminologie de la population = Terminología de población. — Washington, D.C. : The World Bank, 1986. — iii,27p. — (A World Bank glossary)

POPULATION — Dictionaries — Polyglot
PETERSEN, William
Dictionary of demography / William Petersen and Renee Petersen with the collaboration of an international panel of demographers. — Westport, Conn ; London : Greenwood Press, 1985
Multilingual glossary. — 1985. — 259p

POPULATION — Forecasting — Statistics
World population prospects : estimates and projections as assessed in 1984. — New York : United Nations, 1986. — x, 330p. — (Document ; ST/ESA/SER.A/98). — *UN Sales no.:E.86.XIII.3*

POPULATION — Genetic aspects
Genetic and population studies in Wales / edited by Peter S. Harper and Eric Sunderland. — Cardiff : University of Wales Press, 1986. — vii,432p. — *Includes index*

POPULATION — Government policy
HARF, James E.
The politics of global resources : population, food, energy and environment / James E. Harf and B. Thomas Trout. — Durham : Duke University Press, 1986. — xviii, 314p. — *Bibliography: p.[304]-309*

POPULATION — History
MCKEOWN, Thomas
The modern rise of population / Thomas McKeown. — London : Edward Arnold, 1976. — [5],168p. — *Includes index*

POPULATION — History — Congresses
Pre-industrial population change : the mortality decline and short-term population movements / edited by Tommy Bengtsson, Gunnar Fridlizius and Rolf Ohlsson. — Stockholm : Almqvist and Wiksell, 1984. — 419p. — *Conference papers*

POPULATION — History — 18th century
RILEY, James C
Population thought in the age of the demographic revolution / James C. Riley. — Durham, NC : Carolina Academic Press, c1985. — xvii, 225 p.. — *Includes index. — Bibliography: p. [179]-215*

POPULATION — Mathematical models
IMPAGLIAZZO, John
Deterministic aspects in mathematical demography / J. Impagliazzo ; with 53 illustrations. — Berlin ; New York : Springer-Verlag, 1985. — p. cm. — (Biomathematics ; v. 13). — *Includes index. — Bibliography: p. 179-182*

WEBB, Glenn F.
Theory of nonlinear age-dependent population dynamics / Glenn F. Webb. — New York : M. Dekker, c1985. — p. cm. — (Monographs and textbooks in pure and applied mathematics ; 89). — *Includes indexes. — Bibliography: p*

POPULATION — Political aspects

HARF, James E.
The politics of global resources : population, food, energy and environment / James E. Harf and B. Thomas Trout. — Durham : Duke University Press, 1986. — xviii, 314p. — *Bibliography: p.[304]-309*

POPULATION — Statistical methods

Indirect techniques for demographic estimation. — New York : United Nations, 1983. — xxv,304p. — (Population studies / Department of International Economic and Social Affairs ; no. 81). — *At head of title: Manual X.* — *"A collaboration of the Population Division of the Department of International Economic and Social Affairs of the United Nations Secretariat with the Committee on Population and Demography of the National Research Council, United States National Academy of Sciences.".* — *"ST/ESA/SER.A/81.".* — *"United Nations publication, sales no. E.83.XIII.2"--T.p. verso.* — *Includes bibliographical references*

POPULATION — Statistics

Age-sex composition of world population by major region and country, based on United Nations' population projections as assessed in 1978. — Tokyo : Institute of Population Problems, 1981. — iv,97p. — (Research series / Institute of Population Problems ; no.225). — *In Japanese with contents and forword also in English*

Economically active population : estimates and projections : 1950-2025 = Evaluations et projections de la population active : 1950-2025 = Estimaciones y proyecciones de la población económicamente activa : 1950-2025. — 3rd ed. — Geneva : International Labour Office V.4: Northern America, Europe, Oceania and USSR. — 1986. — xxvi,177p. — *Introduction and table headings in English, French and Spanish*

Economically active population : estimates and projections : 1950-2025 = Evaluations et projections de la population active : 1950-2025 = Estimaciones y proyecciones de la población económicamente activa : 1950-2025. — 3rd ed. — Geneva : International Labour Office V.5: World summary. — 1986. — xxvi,132p. — *Introductions and table headings in English, French and Spanish*

UNITED NATIONS. Department of International Economic and Social Affairs
World population prospects : estimates and projections as assessed in 1982 / Department of Economic and Social Affairs. — New York : United Nations, 1985. — (Population studies ; No.86)

VU, My T.
World population projections, 1985 : short- and long-term estimates by age and sex with related demographic statistics / My T. Vu. — Baltimore : Johns Hopkins University Press for the World Bank, 1985. — xxvi,451p

World population prospects : estimates and projections as assessed in 1984. — New York : United Nations, 1986. — x, 330p. — (Document ; ST/ESA/SER.A/98). — *UN Sales no.:E.86.XIII.3*

World population prospects as assessed in 1980 / Department of International Economic and Social Affairs. — New York : United Nations, 1981. — vi,101p. — (Population studies / Department of International Economic and Social Affairs ; no. 78). — *"ST/ESA/SER.A/78.".* — *Includes bibliographical references.* — *Sales no: E.81.XIII.8*

World population trends, population and development interrelations and population policies : 1983 monitoring report. — New York : United Nations. — (Population studies / Department of International Economic and Social Affairs ; no.93) ([Document] (United Nations) ; ST/ESA/SER.A/93)
V.1: Population trends. — 1985. — x,235p. — *Includes bibliographical references.* — *Sales no.: E.84.XIII.10*

POPULATION — Statistics — Data processing

PULLUM, Thomas W.
An assessment of the machine editing policies of the World Fertility Survey / Thomas W. Pullum, Nuri Ozsever, Trudy Harpham. — Voorburg : International Statistical Institute, 1984. — 39p. — (Scientific reports / World Fertility Survey ; no.54)

POPULATION — Statistics — Methodology

WUNSCH, Guillaume
Techniques d'analyse des données démographiques déficientes / Guillaume Wunsch. — Liège : Ordina, 1984. — v,221p

POPULATION — Italy — Statistics

Popolazione residente e presente dei comuni : censimenti dal 1861 al 1981 : circoscrizioni territoriali al 25 ottobre 1981. — Roma : Istituto Centrale di Statistica, 1985. — viii,383p

POPULATION — Netherlands — Statistics

Bevolkingsprognose voor Nederland 1984-2035. — 's-Gravenhage : Staatsuitgeverij, 1985. — 69p. — *Preface, contents list, summary and table headings in English.* — *Title on back cover: Population forecasts for the Netherlands, 1984-2035.* — *Bibliography: p46*

POPULATION ASSISTANCE, AMERICAN

World population and U.S. policy / Jane Menken, editor. — 1st ed. — New York : W.W. Norton, c1986. — p. cm. — *At head of title: The American Assembly, Columbia University.* — *Includes index*

POPULATION BIOLOGY — Mathematical models

WEBB, Glenn F.
Theory of nonlinear age-dependent population dynamics / Glenn F. Webb. — New York : M. Dekker, c1985. — p. cm. — (Monographs and textbooks in pure and applied mathematics ; 89). — *Includes indexes.* — *Bibliography: p*

POPULATION FORECASTING — Statistical methods

Indirect techniques for demographic estimation. — New York : United Nations, 1983. — xxv,304p. — (Population studies / Department of International Economic and Social Affairs ; no. 81). — *At head of title: Manual X.* — *"A collaboration of the Population Division of the Department of International Economic and Social Affairs of the United Nations Secretariat with the Committee on Population and Demography of the National Research Council, United States National Academy of Sciences.".* — *"ST/ESA/SER.A/81.".* — *"United Nations publication, sales no. E.83.XIII.2"--T.p. verso.* — *Includes bibliographical references*

POPULATION FORECASTING — Statistics

UNITED NATIONS. Department of International Economic and Social Affairs
World population prospects : estimates and projections as assessed in 1982 / Department of Economic and Social Affairs. — New York : United Nations, 1985. — (Population studies ; No.86)

VU, My T.
World population projections, 1985 : short- and long-term estimates by age and sex with related demographic statistics / My T. Vu. — Baltimore : Johns Hopkins University Press for the World Bank, 1985. — xxvi,451p

World population prospects as assessed in 1980 / Department of International Economic and Social Affairs. — New York : United Nations, 1981. — vi,101p. — (Population studies / Department of International Economic and Social Affairs ; no. 78). — *"ST/ESA/SER.A/78.".* — *Includes bibliographical references.* — *Sales no: E.81.XIII.8*

POPULATION FORECASTING — England — London

HOLLIS, John
The 1985 round of demographic projections for Greater London / prepared in the GLC Intelligence Unit by John Hollis, Carole Hills and Ian Longhurst. — [London] : Greater London Council, 1986. — 1v.(various pagings). — (Statistical series / Greater London Council ; no.52). — *Bibliographical references: p22*

POPULATION FORECASTING — Great Britain

GREAT BRITAIN. Department of the Environment
1983 based estimates of numbers of households in England, the regions, counties, metropolitan districts and London boroughs 1983-2001. — London : the Department, 1986. — vi,58,[11]p. — *Bibliography: Appendix E*

GREAT BRITAIN. Government Actuary
Variant population projections : variant population projections by sex and age for United Kingdom and selected constituent countries from mid 1983 : 1983-2023. — [London : H.M.S.O.], 1986. — vi,17p,. — (Series PP2 / Office of Population Censuses and Surveys ; no.14). — *Microfiches in end pocket*

Variant population projections: population projections by sex and age, with varying fertility assumptions, for Great Britain / Great Britain Office of Population, Censuses and Surveys. — London : Great Britain Office of Population, Censuses and Surveys, 1974-1983. — *Irregular.* — *Supersedes in part Registrar-General's statistical review of England and Wales*

POPULATION FORECASTING — Ireland

KEOGH, Gary
A statistical analysis of the Irish electoral register and its use for population estimation and sample surveys / Gary Keogh and Brendan J. Whelan. — Dublin, Ireland : Economic and Social Research Institute, 1986. — 126p. — (Papers / Economic and Social Research Institute ; 130). — *Bibliography: p99-100*

POPULATION POLICY

Concise report on the world population situation in 1983 : conditions, trends, prospects, policies. — New York : United Nations, 1984. — 108p. — (Population studies / Department of International Economic and Social Affairs ; no.85) ([Document] / United Nations ; ST/ESA/SER.A/85). — *Includes bibliographical references.* — *Sales no.: E.83.XIII.6*

CONSEIL INTERNATIONAL DES AGENCES BENEVOLES
Les questions de la population. — Genève : Conseil International des Agences Benevoles, 1974. — 96p. — (1CVA document ; no.19)

NERLOVE, Marc
Household and economy : welfare economics of endogenous fertility / Marc Nerlove, Assaf Razin, Efraim Sadka. — Boston : Academic Press, 1987. — xiii, 155 p.. — (Economic theory, econometrics, and mathematical economics). — *Includes bibliographies and indexes*

POPULATION POLICY — Addresses, essays, lectures

Population policy analysis : issues in American politics / edited by Michael E. Kraft, Mark Schneider. — Lexington, Mass. : Lexington Books, c1978. — xi, 204 p.. — (Policy Studies Organization series ; 17). — *"Collection of studies originated with a symposium on population policy which appeared in the winter, 1977 issue of the Policy studies journal.".* — *Includes bibliographical references and index*

POPULATION POLICY — Economic aspects
CLAUSEN, A. W.
Population growth and economic and social development : addresses / by A. W. Clausen. — Washington, D.C. : World Bank, 1984. — 36p. — Contents: Address to the National Leader's Seminar on Population and Development, Nairobi, Kenya, July 11, 1984 - Address to the International Population Conference, Mexico City, August 7, 1984

POPULATION POLICY — Mathematical models
NERLOVE, Marc
Population policy and individual choice : a theoretical investigation / Marc Nerlove, Assaf Razin, and Efraim Sadka. — Washington, D.C. : International Food Policy Research Institute, 1987. — p. cm. — (Research report / International Food Policy Research Institute ; 60). — "June 1987.". — Bibliography: p

POPULATION POLICY — Social aspects
CLAUSEN, A. W.
Population growth and economic and social development : addresses / by A. W. Clausen. — Washington, D.C. : World Bank, 1984. — 36p. — Contents: Address to the National Leader's Seminar on Population and Development, Nairobi, Kenya, July 11, 1984 - Address to the International Population Conference, Mexico City, August 7, 1984

POPULATION PROJECTIONS — Algeria
Projections provisoires de la population Algérienne de 1970 à 1985. — Algiers : Secretariat D'Etat Au Plan, Direction Des Statistiques, 1972. — 53p. — (Document de Travail)

POPULATION PROJECTIONS — Nigeria
Mid-year population projections by States 1963-2000. — Lagos : National Population Bureau, 1984. — 3 leaves

POPULATION PROJECTIONS — Seychelles
Population growth in the Sychelles. — 2nd ed.. — Mahe : Department of Finance, 1985. — 14p

POPULATION TRANSFERS — Serbs
PRVULOVICH, Žika Rad.
Serbia between the swastika and the red star / by Žika Rad. Prvulovich. — Birmingham : Ž. R. Prvulovich, 1986. — vi,240p. — Bibliography: p233-234

POPULISM — Soviet Union
KHEVROLINA, V. M.
Revoliutsionno-demokraticheskaia mysl' o vneshnei politike Rossii i mezhdunarodnykh otnosheniiakh (konets 60-kh - nachala 80-kh godov XIX v. / V. M. Khevrolina ; otv. redaktor A. L. Narochnitskii. — Moskva : Nauka, 1986. — 246p

POPULISM — United States
ZIMMERMAN, Joseph Francis
Participatory democracy : populism revived / Joseph F. Zimmerman. — New York : Praeger, 1986. — xi, 229 p.. — Bibliography: p. 185-221

POPULISM — United States — Addresses, essays, lectures
LONG, Huey Pierce
Kingfish to America, share our wealth : selected senatorial papers of Huey P. Long / edited and with an introduction by Henry M. Christman. — New York : Schocken Books, 1985. — xvi, 145 p.. — Includes index

POPULISM — United States — History — 20th century
The New populism : the politics of empowerment / edited by Harry C. Boyte and Frank Riessman. — Philadelphia : Temple University Press, 1986. — ix, 323 p.. — Includes index. — Bibliography: p. 319-323

PORNOGRAPHY — Social aspects
DWORKIN, Andrea
Pornography : men possessing women / Andrea Dworkin. — London : Women's Press, 1981. — 304p. — Originally published: New York : Perigee, 1981. — Bibliography: p239-285. — Includes index

Women against censorship / edited by Varda Burstyn ; essays by Varda Burstyn ... [et al.]. — Vancouver : Douglas & McIntyre, c1985. — 210 p.. — Bibliography: p. 201-205

PORT, Sir JOHN
PORT, Sir John
The notebook of Sir John Port / edited for the Selden Society by J. H. Baker. — London : Selden Society, 1986. — lvii,217p. — (Publications of the Selden Society ; 102)

PORT DISTRICTS — Alabama — Mobile — History — 19th century
AMOS, Harriet E.
Cotton City : urban development in antebellum Mobile / Harriet E. Amos. — University, Ala. : University of Alabama Press, c1985. — xvi, 311 p.. — Includes index. — Bibliography: p. 287-297

PORTFOLIO MANAGEMENT
HARRINGTON, Diana R.
Modern portfolio theory, the capital asset pricing model, and arbitrage pricing theory : a user's guide / Diana R. Harrington. — 2nd ed. — Englewood Cliffs, N.J. : Prentice-Hall, 1986, c1987. — p. cm. — : Previous ed. published as: Modern portfolio theory and the capital asset pricing model. 1983. — Includes bibliographies and index

KOBOLD, Klaus
Interest rate futures markets and capital market theory : theoretical concepts and empirical evidence / Klaus Kobold. — Berlin ; New York : W. de Gruyte, 1986. — p. cm. — (Series D--Economcis =Economique ; 1)

SENGUPTA, Jatikumar
Stochastic optimization and economic models / Jati K. Sengupta. — Dordrecht ; Boston : D. Reidel ; Norwell, MA, U.S.A. : Sold and distributed in the U.S.A. and Canada by Kluwer Academic, c1986. — x, 373 p.. — (Theory and decision library. Series B. Mathematical and statistical methods). — Includes bibliographies and indexes

PORTFOLIO MANAGEMENT — Great Britain
BLAKE, David Peter Courtney
The characteristics model of portfolio behaviour : with reference to United Kingdom private sector pension funds 1963-1978 / by David Peter Courtney Blake. — 322 leaves. — PhD (Econ) 1987 LSE

PORTLAND, WILLIAM CAVENDISH-BENTINCK, Duke of
HOWARTH, Patrick
Intelligence chief extraordinary : the life of the ninth Duke of Portland / Patrick Howarth. — London : Bodley Head, c1986. — 256p,[4]p of plates. — Bibliography: p244-245. — Includes index

PORTLAND (OR.) — Description and travel
Portland's changing landscape / edited by Larry W. Price. — Portland, Or. : Portland State University Department of Geography : Association of American Geographers, 1987. — xii,213p. — (Occasional papers / Portland State University Department of Geography ; no.4). — Bibliographies

PORTS (FINANCIAL ASSISTANCE) BILL 1980-81
GREAT BRITAIN. Parliament. House of Commons. Library. Research Division
Ports (Financial Assistance) Bill / Christopher Barclay, Robert Twigger, Celia Nield. — [London] : the Division, 1981. — 14p. — (Reference sheet ; no.81/12). — Bibliographical references: p14

PORTUGAL — Bibliography
UNWIN, P. T. H.
Portugal / P.T.H. Unwin, compiler. — Oxford : Clio, c1987. — xxxix,269p. — (World bibliographical series ; v.71). — Includes index

PORTUGAL — Colonies — History
CHANEY, Rick
Regional emigration and remittances in underdeveloped countries : the Portugese experience / by Rick Chaney. — New York : Praeger, 1986. — p. cm. — Includes index. — Bibliography: p

SOUZA, George Bryan
The survival of empire : Portuguese trade and society in China and the South China Sea, 1630-1754 / George Bryan Souza. — Cambridge : Cambridge University Press, 1986. — xx,282p. — Bibliography: p262-275. — Includes index

PORTUGAL — Commerce
EUROFI (U.K.) LIMITED
Portugal / compiled by Eurofi (U.K.) Limited. — Northill : Eurofi (U.K.), 1986. — 139p. — (European Business Reports / Eurofi (U.K.) Limited). — Bibliography: p137-139

PORTUGAL — Description and travel — 1981-
EUROFI (U.K.) LIMITED
Portugal / compiled by Eurofi (U.K.) Limited. — Northill : Eurofi (U.K.), 1986. — 139p. — (European Business Reports / Eurofi (U.K.) Limited). — Bibliography: p137-139

PORTUGAL — Economic conditions — 20th century
PORTUGAL. Instituto Nacional de Estatística
50 anos : Portugal 1935-1985 / [concepção e realização, Juvenal de Carvalho Machado]. — [Lisboa] : the Instituto, [1985]. — 73p

PORTUGAL — Economic conditions — 1974-
EUROFI (U.K.) LIMITED
Portugal / compiled by Eurofi (U.K.) Limited. — Northill : Eurofi (U.K.), 1986. — 139p. — (European Business Reports / Eurofi (U.K.) Limited). — Bibliography: p137-139

PORTUGAL — Economic conditions — 1974- — Addresses, essays, lectures
Portugal in the 1980's : dilemmas of democratic consolidation / edited by Kenneth Maxwell. — New York : Greenwood Press, 1986. — xiv, 254 p.. — (Contributions in political science ; no. 138Global perspectives in history and politics). — Includes index. — "Bibliography, sources for the study of contemporary portugal, Witney Schneidman": p. [233]-243

PORTUGAL — Economic conditions — 1974- — Econometric models
VILARES, Manuel José
Structural change in macroeconomic models : theory and estimation / by Manuel José Vilares. — Dordrecht ; Boston : Martinus Nijhoff, 1986. — p. cm. — (Advanced studies in theoretical and applied econometrics ; v. 6). — : Originally presented as author's thesis, University of Dijon. — Bibliography: p

PORTUGAL — Emigration and immigration
MARTINS, Vasco Manuel
Le Portugal et l'immigration Portugaise en France / Vasco Manuel Martins. — [Paris] : Agence de développement des relations interculturelles, 1984. — 51 leaves. — Bibliography: p45-47

PORTUGAL — Emigration and immigration — History — Case studies
BRETTELL, Caroline
Men who migrate, women who wait : population and history in a Portuguese parish / Caroline B. Brettell. — Princeton, N.J. : Princeton University Press, c1986. — xv, 329 p., [8] p. of plates. — Includes index. — Bibliography: p. [299]-319

PORTUGAL — Foreign relations — 1974- — Addresses, essays, lectures

Portugal in the 1980's : dilemmas of democratic consolidation / edited by Kenneth Maxwell. — New York : Greenwood Press, 1986. — xiv, 254 p.. — (Contributions in political science ; no. 138Global perspectives in history and politics). — Includes index. — "Bibliography, sources for the study of contemporary portugal, Witney Schneidman": p. [233]-243

PORTUGAL — Foreign relations — Guinea-Bissau

CABRAL, Amilcar
PAIGC : rapport general sur la lutte de liberation nationale / Amilcar Cabral. — Bissau : P.A.I.G.C., 1961. — 38p

PORTUGAL — Foreign relations — Spain

OLIVEIRA, Cesar de
Portugal y la Segunda República española, 1931-1936 / Cesar Oliveira. — Madrid : Ediciones Cultura Hispanica, Instituto de Cooperación Iberoamericana, 1986. — 291p. — Bibliography: p279-281

PORTUGAL — History — 1789-1900

MACAULAY, Neill
Dom Pedro : the struggle for liberty in Brazil and Portugal, 1798-1834 / Neill Macaulay. — Durham, [N.C.] : Duke University Press, 1986. — xiv, 361 p.. — Includes index. — Bibliography: p. [339]-344

PORTUGAL — History — 1974-

KAYMAN, Martin
Revolution and counter-revolution in Portugal / by Martin Kayman. — London : Merlin Press, 1986. — [275]p. — Includes index

PORTUGAL — Politics and government — 1974- — Addresses, essays, lectures

Portugal in the 1980's : dilemmas of democratic consolidation / edited by Kenneth Maxwell. — New York : Greenwood Press, 1986. — xiv, 254 p.. — (Contributions in political science ; no. 138Global perspectives in history and politics). — Includes index. — "Bibliography, sources for the study of contemporary portugal, Witney Schneidman": p. [233]-243

PORTUGAL — Population — Statistics

The Portugal Fertility Survey, 1979-80 : a summary of findings. — Voorburg : International Statistical Institute, 1983. — 23p. — (World Fertility Survey ; no.40)

PORTUGAL — Rural conditions

O'NEILL, Brian Juan
Social inequality in a Portuguese hamlet : land, late marriage and bastardy 1870-1978 / Brian Juan O'Neill. — Cambridge : Cambridge University Press, 1987. — xix,431p. — (Cambridge studies in social anthropology ; 63) . — Translation of: Proprietarios, lavradores e jornaleiras. — Bibliography: p401-418. — Includes index

PORTUGAL — Social conditions — 20th century

PORTUGAL. Instituto Nacional de Estatística
50 anos : Portugal 1935-1985 / [concepção e realização, Juvenal de Carvalho Machado]. — [Lisboa] : the Instituto, [1985]. — 73p

PORTUGAL — Social conditions — 20th century — Addresses, essays, lectures

Portugal in the 1980's : dilemmas of democratic consolidation / edited by Kenneth Maxwell. — New York : Greenwood Press, 1986. — xiv, 254 p.. — (Contributions in political science ; no. 138Global perspectives in history and politics). — Includes index. — "Bibliography, sources for the study of contemporary portugal, Witney Schneidman": p. [233]-243

PORTUGUESE — France

MARTINS, Vasco Manuel
Le Portugal et l'immigration Portugaise en France / Vasco Manuel Martins. — [Paris] : Agence de développement des relations interculturelles, 1984. — 51 leaves. — Bibliography: p45-47

PORTUGUESE IN CANADA

HIGGS, David
The Portuguese in Canada / David Higgs. — Ottawa : Canadian Historical Association, 1982. — 18p. — (Canada's ethnic groups. booklet ; n. 2)

PORTUGUESE LANGUAGE — Acquisition

CORRÊA, Letícia Maria Sicuro
On the comprehension of relative clauses : a developmental study with reference to Portuguese / Letícia Maria Sicuro Corrêa. — 291 leaves. — PhD (Arts) 1986 LSE

PORTUGUESE LANGUAGE — Relative clauses

CORRÊA, Letícia Maria Sicuro
On the comprehension of relative clauses : a developmental study with reference to Portuguese / Letícia Maria Sicuro Corrêa. — 291 leaves. — PhD (Arts) 1986 LSE

POSADA, ADOLFO

POSADA, Adolfo
Fragmentos de mis memorias / Adolfo Posada. — [Oviedo] : Universidad de Oviedo, Servicio de Publicaciones, Cátedra Aledo, c1983. — 363p. — Bibliography: p355-363

POSITIVISM

MÁRKUS, György
Language and production : a critique of the paradigms / by Gyorgy Markus. — Dordrecht ; Boston : D. Reidel Pub. Co. ; Hingham, MA, U.S.A. : Kluwer Academic Publishers [distributor], c1986. — p. cm. — (Boston studies in the philosophy of science ; v. 96). — Includes indexes. — Bibliography: p

POST OFFICE ENGINEERING UNION

POEU / Post Office Engineering Union. — London : POEU, 1969-1980. — Monthly. — Continues: POEU journal. Continued by POEU journal

POEU journal / Post Office Engineering Union. — London : POEU, 1958-1969. — Monthly. — Continued by: POEU

POEU journal / Post Office Engineering Union. — London : POEU, 1980-1985. — Monthly. — Continues: POEU. Continued by National Communications Union journal

POSTAL CARDS — Algeria

ALLOULA, Malek
[Harem colonial. English]. The colonial harem / Malek Alloula ; translation by Myrna Godzich and Wlad Godzich ; introduction by Barbara Harlow. — Minneapolis : University of Minnesota Press, c1986. — xxii, 135 p.. — (Theory and history of literature ; v. 21). — Translation of: Le harem colonial. — Bibliography: p. 135

POSTAL CARDS — Germany — History — 20th century

HOLT, Tonie
Germany awake! : the rise of National Socialism 1919-1939 / Tonie and Valmai Holt. — London : Longman, 1986. — vii,124p. — Includes index

POSTAL CARDS — Northern Ireland

KILLEN, John
John Bull's famous circus : Ulster history through the postcard, 1905-1985 / John Killen. — Dublin : O'Brien, 1985. — 160p

POSTAL SERVICE — Denmark — Employees

NORD-LARSEN, Mogens
Holdninger, normer og sygefravaer i P & T. — København : Socialforskningsenstituttet, 1986. — 59p. — (Meddelelse / Socialforskningsinstituttet ; 46)

POSTAL SERVICE — France — Statistics

FRANCE. Direction Générale des Postes
Statistiques / Direction Générale des Postes, France. — Paris : Imprimerie Nationale, 1983-. — Annual

POSTAL SERVICE — Great Britain

JOHNSON, Peter, 1949-
The British travelling post office / Peter Johnson. — London : Ian Allen, c1985. — 104p. — Bibliography: p.104

POSTAL SERVICE — Great Britain — History

AUSTEN, Brian
British mail-coach services, 1784-1850 / Brian Austen. — New York : Garland Pub., 1986. — p. cm. — (Outstanding theses from the London School of Economics and Political Science). — : Originally presented as the author's thesis (Ph. D.)--University of London, 1979. — Bibliography: p

POSTAL SERVICES — Spain — History

MADRAZO, Santos
El sistema de comunicaciones en España, 1750-1850 / Santos Madrazo. — [Madrid] : Colegio de Ingenieros de Caminos, Canales y Puertos : Ediciones Turner
2: [El tráfico y los sevicios]. — c1984. — 379-966p. — Bibliography: p883-924. — Number on spine: 20

POTOSÍ (BOLIVIA : DEPT.) — Economic conditions

COLE, Jeffrey A
The Potosí mita, 1573-1700 : compulsory Indian labor in the Andes / Jeffrey A. Cole. — Stanford, Calif. : Stanford University Press, 1985. — xi, 206p. — Includes index. — Bibliography: p.187-196

POTTERS — England — Longton (Staffordshire)

HART, Elizabeth Ann
Paintresses and potters : work, skill and social relations in a pottery in Stoke on Trent, 1981-1984 / Elizabeth Ann Hart. — 347 leaves, [12] leaves of plates. — PhD (Arts) 1987 LSE

POTTERY, ENGLISH — History

WEATHERILL, Lorna
The growth of the pottery industry in England, 1660-1815 / Lorna Weatherill. — New York : Garland Pub., 1986. — 498 p.. — (Outstanding theses from the London School of Economics and Political Science). — "Due to mis-pagination, there is no p. 149"--T.p. verso. — Thesis (Ph. D.)--London School of Economics and Political Science, 1981. — Bibliography: p. 470-498

POTTERY INDUSTRY — England — History

WEATHERILL, Lorna
The growth of the pottery industry in England, 1660-1815 / Lorna Weatherill. — New York : Garland Pub., 1986. — 498 p.. — (Outstanding theses from the London School of Economics and Political Science). — "Due to mis-pagination, there is no p. 149"--T.p. verso. — Thesis (Ph. D.)--London School of Economics and Political Science, 1981. — Bibliography: p. 470-498

POULTRY INDUSTRY — Trinidad and Tobago — Statitics

The broiler industry in Trinidad and Tobago : 1969-1971. — [Port of Spain] : Central Statistical Office, 1974. — iii,38p

POUND, BRITISH

BEAN, Charles R.
Sterling misalignment and British trade performance / C. Bean. — London : Centre for Labour Economics, London School of Economics, 1987. — 49p. — (Discussion paper / London School of Economics and Political Science. Centre for Labour Economics ; no.288). — Bibliography: p46-49

POUND, BRITISH
continuation
GREAT BRITAIN. Parliament. House of Commons. Library. Research Division
The exchange rate / Christopher Barclay. — [London] : the Division, 1981. — 25p. — (Background paper ; no.93). — *Bibliography: p24-25*

POVERTY
BOOTH, Alan
Life on the margins : the politics of mass poverty / Alan Booth. — London : Communist Party, 1985. — 33p

CHILD POVERTY ACTION GROUP
Poverty: the facts. — London : Child Poverty Action Group, 1986. — 11p

CONNOLLY, Kevin J.
The lost children : poverty and human development / Kevin Connolly. — [Exeter] : University of Exeter, 1985. — 20p. — (The Hugh Greenwood lecture ; 1985). — *Bibliography: p19-20*

DESAI, Meghnad
An econometric approach to the measurement of poverty / Meghnad Desai and Anup Shah. — London : Welfare State Programme Suntory-Toyota International Centre for Economics and Related Displines, 1985. — 20p. — (Discussion paper / Welfare State Programme. Suntory-Toyota International Centre For Economics and Related Disciplines ; no.2)

ELLIOTT, Charles, 1939-
Comfortable compassion? / Charles Elliott. — London : Hodder & Stoughton, 1987. — 194p

Employment and poverty in a troubled world : report of a meeting of high-level experts on employment. — Geneva : International Labour Office, 1985. — 55p

FLEW, Antony
The philosophy of poverty : Good Samaritans or Procrusteans / Antony Flew. — London : Social Affairs Unit, [1985]. — 21p. — (Taking thought for the poor). — *Cover title*

Focus / Institute for Research on Poverty, University of Wisconsin - Madison. — Madison : University of Wisconsin - Madison, Institute for Research on Poverty, 1985-. — *Quarterly*

LOW PAY UNIT
The rising tide of poverty: joint briefing / Low Pay Unit [and] Child Poverty Action Group. — London : Low Pay : Child Poverty Action Group, 1986. — 7 leaves

MCNAMARA, Robert S.
Economic interdependance and global poverty : the challenge of our time / Robert S. McNamara. — Durham, N.C. : Published by the Commission for International Justice and Peace of the Bishops' Conference of England and Wales, 1983. — 15p. — *First Barbara Ward Memorial Lecture*

PIACHAUD, David
Poor children : a tale of two decades / David Piachaud. — London : Child Poverty Action Group, 1986. — 16p. — *Bibliography: p15-16*

Poverty today / Peter Townsend, Charles Elliott, Zsusa Ferge and others. — Edinburgh (New College, The Mound, Edinburgh EH1 2LV) : Department of Christian Ethics and Practical Theology, 1986. — 18p. — (Occasional paper ; no.7). — *Proceedings of seminar. — At head of title: Edinburgh University Centre for Theology and Public Issues*

STEIDLMEIER, Paul
The paradox of poverty : a reappraisal of economic development policy / Paul Steidlmeier. — Cambridge, Mass. : Ballinger, 1987. — p. cm. — *Includes bibliographies and index*

POVERTY — Comparative studies
Dynamics of deprivation / edited by Zs. Ferge and S. M. Miller. — Aldershot : Gower, 1987. — [vii],329p. — (Studies in social policy and welfare ; 26). — *Bibliographies*

POVERTY — History
HAZLITT, Henry
The conquest of poverty / Henry Hazlitt. — Lanham : University Press of America, 1986, c1973. — p. cm. — : *Reprint. Originally published: New Rochelle, N.Y. : Arlington House, 1973. — Includes index*

POVERTY — Measurement — Mathematical models
COWELL, F. A.
Poverty measures, inequality and decomposability / F. A. Cowell. — [London : London School of Economics and Political Science], 1987. — 28p. — (Taxation, incentives and the distribution of income ; no.99). — *Economic and Social Research Council programme. — Bibliographical references: p27-28*

POVERTY — Prevention — Great Britain
WEBB, Sidney
The sphere of voluntary agencies in the prevention of destitution / by Sidney and Beatrice Webb. — London : National Committee for the Prevention of Destitution, 1911. — 46p

POVERTY — Psychological aspects
MOLLAT, Michel
[Pauvres au Moyen Age. English]. The poor in the Middle Ages : an essay in social history / Michel Mollat ; translated by Arthur Goldhammer. — New Haven : Yale University Press, c1986. — p. cm. — *Translation of: Les Pauvres au Moyen Age. — Includes index. — Bibliography: p*

POVERTY — India
Population, poverty, and hope. — New Delhi : Uppal, c1983. — xvii, 564 p. — *"Under the auspices of the Centre for Policy Research and Family Planning Foundation."*

POVERTY — Latin America
KANBUR, S. M. Ravi
Malnutrition and poverty in Latin America / S. M. Ravi Kanbur. — Coventry : University of Warwick. Department of Economics, 1987. — 62p. — (Warwick economic research papers ; no.278). — *Bibliography: p59-62*

POWER RESOURCES
CROWN AGENTS FOR OVERSEAS GOVERNMENTS AND ADMINISTRATIONS
Energy crisis in the eighties. — London : the Agents, 1980. — 48p. — *Crown Agents special review, July 1980*

Energie im Brennpunkt : Zwischenbilanz der Energiedebatte / Albrecht/Stegelmann [Herausgeber]. — München : High-Tech-Verlag Technik k sozialer Wandel, 1984. — 234p. — (Sozialverträglichkeit von Energieversorgungssystemen)

FRISCH, Jean-Romain
Future stresses for energy resources : energy abundance : myth or reality? / Jean-Romain Frisch. — London : Graham & Trotman, 1986. — xxxiv,226p. — *At head of title: World Energy Conference Conservation Commission. — Includes bibliography*

HALL, Charles A. S
Energy and resource quality : the ecology of the economic process / Charles A.S. Hall, Cutler J. Cleveland, Robert Kaufmann. — New York : Wiley, c1986. — xxi, 577 p.. — (Environmental science and technology). — *"A Wiley-Interscience publication.". — Includes index. — Bibliography: p. 535-568*

HAYES, Denis, 1944-
Rays of hope : the transition to a post-petroleum world / Denis Hayes. — 1st ed. — New York : Norton, c1977. — 240 p. — *"A Worldwatch Institute book.". — Includes bibliographical references and index*

POWER RESOURCES — Bibliography
STEENBLIK, Ronald P.
A guide to the periodic literature on energy and mineral resources available in London libraries / by Ronald P. Steenblik. — Rev. ed.. — [London?] : LSE International Resources Programme, 1986. — 27 leaves

POWER RESOURCES — Economic aspects — East Asia
Energy, security and economic development in East Asia / edited by Ronald C. Keith. — London : Croom Helm, c1986. — 303p. — *Bibliography: p287-293. — Includes index*

POWER RESOURCES — Forecasting — Social aspects — Case studies
The Politics of energy forecasting : a comparative study of energy forecasting in Western Europe and North America / edited by Thomas Baumgartner and Atle Midttun. — Oxford : Clarendon, 1987. — xiii,314p. — *Includes bibliographies and index*

POWER RESOURCES — Information services — England — London
STEENBLIK, Ronald P.
A guide to the periodic literature on energy and mineral resources available in London libraries / by Ronald P. Steenblik. — Rev. ed.. — [London?] : LSE International Resources Programme, 1986. — 27 leaves

POWER RESOURCES — Law and legislation — European Economic Community countries
DAINTITH, Terence
Energy strategy in Europe : the legal framework / by Terence Daintith and Leigh Hancher. — Berlin : W. de Gruyter, 1986. — ix,190p. — (Series A, Law / European University Institute ; 4). — *Includes bibliographical references and index*

POWER RESOURCES — Political aspects — East Asia
Energy, security and economic development in East Asia / edited by Ronald C. Keith. — London : Croom Helm, c1986. — 303p. — *Bibliography: p287-293. — Includes index*

POWER RESOURCES — Prices — Government policy — Developing countries
ENERGY PRICING POLICY WORKSHOP (1984 : Bangkok)
Criteria for energy pricing policy : a collection of papers commissioned for the Energy Pricing Policy Workshop organized under the Regional Energy Development Programme (RAS/84/001), Bangkok, 8-11 May 1984 / sponsored by the United Nations Development Programme (UNDP) ... (et al.) ; edited by Corazón Morales Siddayao. — London : Graham & Trotman, 1985. — 247p. — *Includes bibliographies and index*

POWER RESOURCES — Research — Great Britain
Energy technologies for the United Kingdom : 1986 appraisal of research, development and demonstration. — London : H.M.S.O., 1987. — vii,25p. — (Energy paper / Department of Energy ; 54). — *Prepared at the request of the Secretary of State for Energy's Advisory Council on Research and Development by the Chief Scientist's Group of the Energy Technology Support Unit*

POWER RESOURCES — Research — International Energy Agency countries
Collaborative projects in energy research, development and demonstration : a ten year review : 1976-1986. — Paris : International Energy Agency, 1987. — 243p

POWER RESOURCES — Research — Soviet Union
KELLY, William J
Energy research and development in the USSR : preparations for the twenty-first century / William J. Kelly, Hugh L. Shaffer, and J. Kenneth Thompson. — Durham, N.C. : Duke University Press, 1986. — p. cm. — (Duke Press policy studies). — *Includes bibliographies and index*

POWER RESOURCES — Research — Sweden
Energy ahead: Vattenfall annual R and D report. — Vallingby : Vattenfall, 1984-. — *Annual*

POWER RESOURCES — Research — United States — Addresses, essays, lectures
The Politics of energy research and development / edited by John Byrne and Daniel Rich. — New Brunswick, U.S.A. : Transaction Books, c1986. — 181 p.. — (Energy policy studies ; v. 3). — *Includes bibliographies*

POWER RESOURCES — Union lists
STEENBLIK, Ronald P.
A guide to the periodic literature on energy and mineral resources available in London libraries / by Ronald P. Steenblik. — Rev. ed.. — [London?] : LSE International Resources Programme, 1986. — 27 leaves

POWER RESOURCES — Asia — Congresses
PACIFIC TRADE AND DEVELOPMENT CONFERENCE (13th : 1983 : Manila, Philippines)
Energy and structural change in the Asia Pacific region : papers and proceedings of the Thirteenth Pacific Trade and Development Conference held in Manila, Philippines, January 24-28, 1983 / edited by Romeo M. Bautista and Seiji Naya. — [Manila, Philippines] : Philippine Institute for Development Studies : Asian Development Bank, 1984. — xxii,532p. — *Bibliography: p423-532*

POWER RESOURCES — Asia — Statistics
Asian energy problems : an Asian Development Bank survey. — New York : Praeger, 1982. — xxxviii,363p. — *Includes bibliographical references*

POWER RESOURCES — European Economic Community countries
Energy 2000 : a reference projection and alternative outlooks for the European Community and the world to the year 2000 / Jean-Francois Guilmot ... (et al.). — Cambridge : Published on behalf of the Commission of the European Communities by Cambridge University Press, 1986. — viii,261p

WEYMAN-JONES, Thomas G.
Energy in Europe issues and policies / Thomas G. Weyman-Jones. — London : Methuen, 1986. — xii,176p. — (The Methuen EEC series). — *Bibliography: p167-171. — Includes index*

POWER RESOURCES — European Economic Community Countries — Statistics
STATISTICAL OFFICE OF THE EUROPEAN COMMUNITIES
Energy: monthly statistics = énergie: statistiques mensuelles. — Luxembourg : [the Office], 1986-. — *Monthly. — In English and French*

POWER RESOURCES — France
Maîtrise de l'énergie et recherche : quel bilan? quel avenir? : journées organisées dans le cadre de la Fête de l'Industrie et de la Technologie (FIT) les 3,4,5,10 et 11 décembre 1985, à La Villette. — [Paris] : La Documentation française, [1987]. — 610p

POWER RESOURCES — France — Statistics
FRANCE. Observatoire de l'Energie
Bilans de l'énergie, 1970 à 1984. — Paris : Observatoire de l'Energie, 1985. — 45p. — (Collection chiffres et documents)

POWER RESOURCES — Great Britain — Forecasting
GREAT BRITAIN. Department of Energy
Energy projections 1979 : a paper. — [London] : the Department, [1979]. — 11,6p

POWER RESOURCES — Siberia, Western (R.S.F.S.R.) — Government policy
CHUNG, Han-Ku
Interest representation in Soviet policy-making : a case study of a Siberian energy coalition, 1969-1981 / Han-Ku Chung. — 176 leaves. — *PhD (Econ) 1986 LSE*

POWER RESOURCES — Spain — Congresses
SECTOR ENERGETICO ESPAÑOL ANTE LA ENTRADA EN LA CEE (Conferencia : 1985 : Madrid)
El sector energetico español ante la entrada en la CEE : conferencia, Madrid 20 y 21 de febrero de 1985 / organizada por: Instituto de Empresa. — Madrid : Instituto de Empresa, 1985. — 135p

POWER RESOURCES — Switzerland — Costs
GYSIN, Christoph H.
Externe Kosten der Energie in der Schweiz : methodische Grundlagen und Versuch einer Schätzung / Christoph H. Gysin. — Grüsch : Verlag Rüegger, 1985. — xi,220p. — *Bibliography: p205-220*

POWER RESOURCES — United States
CUFF, David J
The United States energy atlas / David J. Cuff, William J. Young. — 2nd ed. — New York : Macmillan Pub. Co. ; London : Collier Macmillan, c1985. — p. cm. — *Includes index. — Bibliography: p*

POWER RESOURCES — Zambia — Statistics
NATIONAL ENERGY COUNCIL (Zambia)
Energy production and consumption in Zambia 1978-1983. — [Lusaka] : National Energy Council, [1984?]. — 39p

POWER RESOURES — Pacific Area — Congresses
PACIFIC TRADE AND DEVELOPMENT CONFERENCE (13th : 1983 : Manila, Philippines)
Energy and structural change in the Asia Pacific region : papers and proceedings of the Thirteenth Pacific Trade and Development Conference held in Manila, Philippines, January 24-28, 1983 / edited by Romeo M. Bautista and Seiji Naya. — [Manila, Philippines] : Philippine Institute for Development Studies : Asian Development Bank, 1984. — xxii,532p. — *Bibliography: p423-532*

POWER (SOCIAL SCIENCES)
ALBERTONI, Ettore A.
Mosca and the theory of elitism / Ettore A. Albertoni ; translated by Paul Goodrick. — Oxford : Basil Blackwell, 1987. — xvii,194p. — *Translation of: Dottrina della classe politica e teoria delle elites. — Bibliography: p186-191. — Includes index*

BOCOCK, Robert
Hegemony / Robert Bocock. — Chichester : Ellis Horwood, 1986. — 136p. — *Bibliography: p.[130]-132*

COHEN, Abner
Two-dimensional man : an essay on the anthropology of power and symbolism in complex society / Abner Cohen. — London : Routledge and Kegan Paul, 1974. — xii,156p. — *Bibliography: p.139-148. — Includes index*

Community power : directions for future research / edited by Robert J. Waste. — Beverly Hills : Sage Publications, 1986. — p. cm. — (Sage focus editions ; v. 79). — *Includes bibliographies*

COUSINS, Norman
The pathology of power / by Norman Cousins ; introduction by George F. Kennan. — New York : Norton, 1987. — p. cm. — *Includes index*

DAM, Nikolaos van
The struggle for power in Syria : sectarianism, regionalism and tribalism in politics, 1961—1980 / Nikolaos van Dam. — 2nd ed. — London : Croom Helm, c1981. — 169 p

DAUDI, Philippe
Power in the organisation : the discourse of power in managerial praxis / Philippe Daudi. — Oxford : Blackwell, 1986. — [250]p. — *Translation of: Makt, diskurs ach handling. — Includes bibliography and index*

FRENCH, Marilyn
Beyond power : women, men and morals / Marilyn French. — London : Cape, 1985. — [640]p. — *Includes index*

GINSBERG, Benjamin
The captive public : how mass opinion promotes state power / Benjamin Ginsberg. — New York : Basic Books, c1986. — xi, 272 p.. — *Includes index. — Bibliography: p. [233]-249*

KIDRON, Michael
The book of business, money and power / Michael Kidron and Ronald Segal. — London : Pluto Projects, 1987. — 187p

Modern theories of exploitation / edited by Andrew Reeve. — London : Sage, 1987. — 209p. — (Sage modern politics series ; v.14). — *Includes bibliographies and index*

PFOHL, Stephen J
Images of deviance and social control : a sociological history / Stephen J. Pfohl. — New York : McGraw-Hill, c1985. — xiii, 402 p.. — *Cover title: Images of deviance & social control. — Includes bibliographies and index*

Pouvoirs et contre-pouvoirs dans la culture mexicaine / Louis Panabière, coordinateur. — Paris : CNRS, 1985. — 160p. — (Amérique latine-pays ibériques). — *Bibliography: p161*

Power / edited by Steven Lukes. — New York : New York University Press, 1986. — vi, 283 p.. — (Readings in social and political theory). — *Includes index. — Bibliography: p. [278]-280*

ROSENBAUM, Alan S
Coercion and autonomy : philosophical foundations, issues, and practices / Alan S. Rosenbaum. — New York : Greenwood Press, 1986. — xii, 196 p.. — (Contributions in philosophy ; no. 31). — *Includes index. — Bibliography: p. [187]-188*

POWER (SOCIAL SCIENCES) — Addresses, essays, lectures
Power elites and organizations / edited by G. William Domhoff and Thomas R. Dye. — Beverly Hills : Sage Publications, c1986. — p. cm. — (Sage focus editions ; 82). — *Includes index*

SRIVASTVA, Suresh
Executive power / Suresh Srivastva and associates. — San Francisco : Jossey-Bass Publishers, 1986. — xxii, 360 p.. — *Includes index. — Bibliography: p. 331-351*

POWER (SOCIAL SCIENCES) — Case studies
LAMPTON, David M
Paths to power : elite mobility in contemporary China / by David M. Lampton with the assistance of Yeung Sai-cheung. — Ann Arbor : Center for Chinese Studies, Unversity of Michigan, 1985. — p. cm. — (Michigan monographs in Chinese studies ; no. 55). — *Includes index. — Bibliography: p*

POWER (SOCIAL SCIENCES) — Congresses
Visibility and power : essays on women in society and development / edited by Leela Dube, Eleanor Leacock, Shirley Ardener. — Delhi ; New York : Oxford University Press, 1986. — L, 361 p.. — *Includes bibliographies and index*

POWER (SOCIAL SCIENCES) — History
MCDONOGH, Gary W
Good families of Barcelona : a social history of power in the industrial era / Gary Wray McDonogh. — Princeton, N.J. : Princeton University Press, c1986. — xiv, 262 p.. — *Includes index. — Bibliography: p. [227]-251*

PRAGMATICS — Addresses, essays, lectures
SELLARS, Wilfrid
Pure pragmatics and possible worlds : the early essays of Wilfrid Sellars / edited and introduced by J. Sicha. — Reseda, Calif. : Ridgeview Pub. Co., c1980. — lxxx, 297 p.. — *Bibliography: p. lxxx*

PRAIRIE PROVINCES — History — 19th century
ARTIBISE, Alan F. J
Prairie urban development, 1870-1930 / Alan F.J. Artibise. — Ottawa : Canadian Historical Association, 1981. — 42 p.. — (Historical booklet / Canadian Historical Association ; no.34). — *Bibliography: p. 24-25*

PRAIRIE PROVINCES — History — 20th century
ARTIBISE, Alan F. J
Prairie urban development, 1870-1930 / Alan F.J. Artibise. — Ottawa : Canadian Historical Association, 1981. — 42 p.. — (Historical booklet / Canadian Historical Association ; no.34). — *Bibliography: p. 24-25*

PRASAD, RAJENDRA
PRASAD, Rajendra
Dr. Rajendra Prasad : correspondence and select documents / edited by Valmiki Choudhary. — New Delhi : Allied Publishers Vol.2: (1938). — 1984. — 446p

PRASAD, Rajendra
Dr. Rajendra Prasad : correspondence and select documents / edited by Valmiki Choudhary. — New Delhi : Allied Publishers Vol.3: (January to July 1939). — 1984. — 444p

PRASAD, Rajendra
Dr. Rajendra Prasad : correspondence and select documents / edited by Valmiki Choudhary. — New Delhi : Allied Publishers Vol.4: (August to December 1939). — 1985. — 302p

PRASAD, Rajendra
Dr. Rajendra Prasad : correspondence and select documents / edited by Valmiki Choudhary. — New Delhi : Allied Publishers Vol.5: (1940 to 1942). — 1986. — 374p

PRASAD, Rajendra
Dr. Rajendra Prasad : correspondence and select documents / edited by Valmiki Choudhary. — New Delhi : Allied Publishers Vol.6: (1945 to 1946). — 1986. — 358p

PRASAD, Rajendra
Dr. Rajendra Prasad : correspondence and select documents / edited by Valmiki Choudhary. — New Delhi : Allied Publishers Vol.7: (1947). — 1987. — 534p

PRAVDA — History
ROXBURGH, Angus
Pravda : inside the Soviet news machine / by Angus Roxburgh. — London : Gollancz, 1987. — 285p,[4]p of plates. — *Includes index*

PRE-SENTENCE INVESTIGATION REPORTS
PERRY, Frederick George
Reports for criminal courts / F.G. Perry. — Ilkley (66 The Grove, Ilkley, W. Yorkshire LS29 9PA) : Owen Wells Publishing Company, 1979. — x,134p. — *Bibliography: p.127-132. — Includes index*

PRECIOUS METALS
CLARK, Grahame
Symbols of excellence : precious materials as expressions of status / Grahame Clark. — Cambridge : Cambridge University Press, 1986. — [144]p. — *Includes index*

PREFABRICATED BUILDINGS — Hungary — Budapest
25 [ie. huszonöt] éve az állami építöiparban a 100 éves Budapestért 1948-1973 / Kisvári János, and 43 sz. állami építöipari vállalat. — Budapest : Révai Nyomda, [1973?]. — 119p

PREFECTS (FRENCH GOVERNMENT)
CHAPMAN, Brian
The prefects and provincial France / Brian Chapman. — London : Allen and Unwin, 1955. — 246p. — *Bibliography: p239-242*

PREGNANCY
HALL, Marion, 1939-
Antenatal care assessed : a case study of an innovation in Aberdeen / Marion Hall, Sally Macintyre, Maureen Porter ; foreword by Ian MacGillivray. — Aberdeen : Aberdeen University Press, 1985. — xiii,139p. — *Bibliography: p125-131. — Includes index*

PREGNANCY — Psychological aspects
MERCER, Ramona Thieme
First-time motherhood : experiences from teens to forties / Ramona T. Mercer. — New York : Springer Pub. Co., c1986. — xv, 384 p.. — *Includes index. — Bibliography: p. 357-374*

PREGNANCY — Bangladesh — Matlab
BECKER, Stan
A validation study of backward and forward pregnancy histories in Matlab, Bangladesh / Stan Becker, Simeen Mahmud. — Voorburg : International Statistical Institute, 1984. — 37p. — (Scientific reports / World Fertility Survey ; no.52)

PREGNANCY, ADOLESCENT — Canada
Teenage pregnancy in industrialized countries : a study / conducted by the Alan Guttmacher Institute ; Elise F. Jones, study director ... [et al.]. — New Haven : Yale University Press, c1986. — p. cm. — *Includes index. — Bibliography: p*

PREGNANCY, ADOLESCENT — Europe
Teenage pregnancy in industrialized countries : a study / conducted by the Alan Guttmacher Institute ; Elise F. Jones, study director ... [et al.]. — New Haven : Yale University Press, c1986. — p. cm. — *Includes index. — Bibliography: p*

PREGNANCY, ADOLESCENT — United States
Teenage pregnancy in industrialized countries : a study / conducted by the Alan Guttmacher Institute ; Elise F. Jones, study director ... [et al.]. — New Haven : Yale University Press, c1986. — p. cm. — *Includes index. — Bibliography: p*

PREJUDICE
LYNCH, James
Prejudice reduction and the schools / James Lynch. — New York : Nichols Pub., 1987. — p. cm. — *Includes indexes. — Bibliography: p*

PREMIER-ALBANIAN COACHES — History
PREMIER-ALBANIAN COACHES
Premier Albanian Coaches : a history of independant [i.e. independent] bus and coach operation from 1923 / [written] by Ian F. Read ; based upon original research by J.E. Hewitt. — Watford : Premier Coaches (Watford), c1985. — [64]p. — *Ill on inside covers*

PRENATAL CARE — Great Britain
HALL, Marion, 1939-
Antenatal care assessed : a case study of an innovation in Aberdeen / Marion Hall, Sally Macintyre, Maureen Porter ; foreword by Ian MacGillivray. — Aberdeen : Aberdeen University Press, 1985. — xiii,139p. — *Bibliography: p125-131. — Includes index*

PRENATAL DIAGNOSIS — Denmark — Statistics
Fostervandsundersøgelser 1980-82. — [København] : Sundhedsstyrelsen, 1984. — 78p. — (Vitalstatistik / Sundhedsstyrelsen ; I:10:1984). — *Summary and table headings in English. — Bibliograpghy: p.46*

PRESBYTERIAN CHURCH — United States — Clergy — History — 18th century — Addresses, essays, lectures
Professions and professional ideologies in America / edited by Gerald L. Geison. — Chapel Hill : University of North Carolina Press, c1983. — x, 147 p.. — *Includes bibliographical references and index*

PRESBYTERIANS — Northern Ireland — Biography
BRUCE, Steve
God save Ulster : the religion and politics of Paisleyism / Steve Bruce. — Oxford : Clarendon, 1986. — xv,308p. — *Includes index*

PRESIDENTIAL CANDIDATES — United States — Biography
CEBULA, James E.
James M. Cox : journalist and politician / James E. Cebula. — New York : Garland, 1985. — 181 p.. — (Modern American history) . — *Includes index. — Bibliography: p. 171-173*

PRESIDENTS — Transition periods
Papers on presidential transitions and foreign policy. — Lanham, MD : University Press of America, <c1986- >. — v. <1-3 >. — *Includes bibliographies. — Contents: v. 1. History and current issues / edited by Kenneth W. Thompson -- v. 2. Problems and prospects / edited by Kenneth W. Thompson -- v. 3. Political transitions and foreign affairs in Britain and France / edited with a preface by Frederick C. Mosher*

PRESIDENTS — Pakistan — Interviews
ZIA-UL-HAQ, Mohammad
President of Pakistan, General Mohammad Zia-ul-Haq : interviews to foreign media. — Islamabad : Directorate of Films & Publications, Ministry of Information & Broadcasting, Government of Pakistan, < [1980?-1984? >. — 5v. — *Includes indexes. — Contents: v. 1. March-December 1978 -- v. 2. January-December 1979 -- v. 3. January-December 1980 -- v. 4. January-December 1981 -- v. 5. January-December 1982*

PRESIDENTS — Turkey — Biography
VOLKAN, Vamik D.
The immortal Atatürk : a psychobiography / Vamik D. Volkan and Norman Itzkowitz. — Chicago ; London : University of Chicago Press, 1984. — xxv,374p. — *Bibliography: p361-368. — Includes index*

PRESIDENTS — United States
The American presidency : perspectives from abroad / edited by Kenneth W. Thompson. — Lanham, MD : University Press of America, c1986. — xi, 127 p.. — *"A Miller Center tenth anniversary commemorative publication 1975-1985."*. — *"Co-published by arrangement with the White Burkett Miller Center of Public Affairs, University of Virginia"--Verso of t.p. — Includes bibliographies*

BERMAN, Larry
The new American presidency / Larry Berman. — Boston : Little Brown, c1987. — xi, 413 p.. — *Copyright date stamped on t.p. verso. — Includes index. — Bibliography: p. 383-391*

BOWLES, Nigel
The White House and Capitol Hill : the politics of presidential persuasion / Nigel Bowles. — Oxford : Clarendon, 1987. — [256]p. — *Includes index*

DENTON, Robert E., Jr
Presidential communication : description and analysis / Robert E. Denton, Jr. and Dan F. Hahn. — New York : Praeger, 1986. — xxiii, 332 p.. — *Includes bibliographies and index*

Five Virginia papers presented at the Miller Center Forums, 1984 / [by] Charles Bartlett...[et al.] ; [edited by Kenneth W. Thompson]. — Lanham ; London : University Press of America, 1984. — xi,114p. — (Virginia papers on the Presidency ; v.18)

PRESIDENTS — United States
continuation

Six Virginia papers presented at the Miller Center Forums, 1985 / by Arthur F. Burns...[et al.] ; [edited by Kenneth W. Thompson]. — Lanham ; London : University Press of America, 1986. — xi,88p. — (Virginia papers on the Presidency ; v.21)

Virginia papers on the Presidency / edited by Kenneth W. Thompson. — Lanham [Maryland] ; London : University Press of America
Vol.22
Part II: Five Virginia papers presented at Miller Center forums and conversations, 1985-86 / by Hedley W. Donovan...[et al.]. — 1986. — xi,96p

PRESIDENTS — United States — Addresses, essays, lectures

The Presidency and public policy making / George C. Edwards, III, Steven A. Shull, Norman C. Thomas, editors. — Pittsburgh, Pa. : University of Pittsburgh Press, c1985. — xix, 227 p.. — (Pitt series in policy and institutional studies). — *Includes bibliographies and index*

PRESIDENTS — United States — Archives — Catalogs

BURTON, Dennis A.
A guide to manuscripts in the Presidential Libraries / compiled and edited by Dennis A. Burton, James B. Rhoads, Raymond W. Smock. — College Park, Md. : Research Materials Corp., 1985. — p. cm. — *Includes index*

PRESIDENTS — United States — Biography

AMBROSE, Stephen E
Nixon : the education of a politician, 1913-1962 / Stephen E. Ambrose. — New York : Simon and Schuster, c1987. — 752 p., [16] p. of plates. — *Includes index.* — *Bibliography: p. 717-721*

The American presidents : the office and the men / edited by Frank N. Magill ; associate editor, John L. Loos. — Pasadena, Calif. : Salem Press, c1986. — 3 v.. — *Vol. 3 has index.* — *Includes bibliographies*

BAUER, K. Jack
Zachary Taylor : soldier, planter, statesman of the old Southwest / K. Jack Bauer. — Baton Rouge : Louisiana State University Press, c1985. — xxiv, 348 p.. — (Southern biography series). — *Includes index.* — *Bibliography: p. 329-338*

BORCH, Herbert von
John F. Kennedy : Amerikas unerfüllte Hoffnung / Herbert von Borch. — München : Piper, 1986. — 169p. — *Bibliography: p163-164*

BRENDON, Piers
Ike, his life and times / Piers Brendon. — 1st ed. — New York : Harper & Row, c1986. — xvi, 478 p., [16] p. of plates. — *Includes index.* — *Bibliography: p. [461]-462*

BURK, Robert Fredrick
Dwight D. Eisenhower, hero & politician / Robert F. Burk. — Boston : Twayne Publishers, c1986. — xii, 207 p., [14] p. of plates. — (Twayne's twentieth-century American biography series ; no. 2). — *Includes index.* — *Bibliography: p. 178-199*

FEHRENBACHER, Don Edward
Lincoln in text and context : collected essays / Don E. Fehrenbacher. — Stanford, Calif. : Stanford University Press, 1987. — p. cm. — *Includes index.* — *Bibliography: p*

The Johnson Presidency : twenty intimate perspectives of Lyndon B. Johnson / edited by Kenneth W. Thompson. — Lanham ; London : University Press of America, c1987. — [310]p. — (Portraits of American presidents ; 5)

MILLER, Richard Lawrence
Truman : the rise to power / Richard Lawrence Miller. — New York : McGraw-Hill, c1986. — viii, 536p, [8]p of plates. — *Includes index.* — *Bibliography: p [400]-401*

RICHARDS, Leonard L
The life and times of Congressman John Quincy Adams / Leonard L. Richards. — New York : Oxford University Press, 1986. — viii, 245 p.. — *Includes index.* — *Bibliography: p. 205-238*

PRESIDENTS — United States — Correspondence

JACKSON, Andrew
The papers of Andrew Jackson. — Knoxville, Tenn. : University of Tennessee Press
Vol.2: 1804-1813 / Harold D. Moser, Sharon Macpherson, editors. — 1984. — xxvii,634p

PRESIDENTS — United States — Election

MOSHER, Frederick C
Presidential transitions and foreign affairs / Frederick C. Mosher, W. David Clinton, Daniel G. Lang. — Baton Rouge : Louisiana State University Press, c1987. — xvii, 281 p.. — (Miller Center series on the American presidency). — *The recommendations of the Miller Center Commission on Presidential Transitions and Foreign Policy are included in the appendix.* — *Includes index.* — *Bibliography: p. [265]-273*

PRESIDENTS — United States — Election — History — Statistics

Presidential elections since 1789. — 3rd ed. — Washington, D.C. : Congressional Quarterly, c1983. — 211 p.. — *Includes index.* — *Bibliography: p. 199-201*

PRESIDENTS — United States — Election — 1920

CEBULA, James E.
James M. Cox : journalist and politician / James E. Cebula. — New York : Garland, 1985. — 181 p.. — (Modern American history). — *Includes index.* — *Bibliography: p. 171-173*

PRESIDENTS — United States — Election — 1952

GREENE, John Robert
The crusade : the presidential election of 1952 / John Robert Greene. — Lanham, Md. ; London : University Press of America, c1985. — vii, 343 p.. — *Includes index.* — *Bibliography: p.301-318*

PRESIDENTS — United States — Election — 1984

ABRAMSON, Paul R
Change and continuity in the 1984 elections / Paul R. Abramson, John H. Aldrich, David W. Rohde. — Rev. ed. — Washington, D.C. : CQ Press, c1987. — xvi, 378 p.. — *Includes index.* — *Bibliography: p. 359-367*

BROOKHISER, Richard
The outside story : how Democrats and Republicans re-elected Reagan / Richard Brookhiser. — 1st ed. — Garden City, N.Y. : Doubleday, 1986. — ix, 298 p.. — *Includes index*

COLLINS, Sheila D
From melting pot to rainbow coalition : the future of race in American politics / Sheila D. Collins. — New York : Monthly Review Press, 1986. — p. cm. — *Includes index.* — *Bibliography: p*

Elections '84. — London : United States Information Service, Embassy of the United States, [1984]. — 8leaflets in folder. — *Contents: Profiles of Reagan, Bush, Mondale and Ferraro with candidate lists for governorships, Senate and House of Representatives*

FERRARO, Geraldine
Ferraro, my story / Geraldine A. Ferraro, with Linda Bird Francke. — Toronto ; New York : Bantam Books, 1985. — 340 p., [24] p. of plates. — *Includes index*

PRESIDENTS — United States — Election — 1984 — Addresses, essays, lectures

The 1984 presidential election in the South : patterns of southern party politics / edited by Robert P. Steed, Laurence W. Moreland, and Tod A. Baker. — New York : Praeger, 1985. — p. cm. — *Includes index.* — *Bibliography: p*

The Election of 1984 : reports and interpretations / Gerald M. Pomper ... [et al.]. — Chatham, N.J. : Chatham House Publishers, c1985. — p. cm. — *Includes bibliographies and index*

PRESIDENTS — United States — Evaluation

BUCHANAN, Bruce
The citizen's presidency : standards of choice and judgment / Bruce Buchanan. — Washington, D.C. : CQ Press, c1987. — xii, 233 p.. — *Includes index.* — *Bibliography: p. 217-228*

PRESIDENTS — United States — History

The American presidents : the office and the men / edited by Frank N. Magill ; associate editor, John L. Loos. — Pasadena, Calif. : Salem Press, c1986. — 3 v.. — *Vol. 3 has index.* — *Includes bibliographies*

MARTIN, Lawrence
The presidents and the prime ministers : Washington and Ottawa face to face : the myth of bilateral bliss 1867-1982 / Lawrence Martin. — PaperJacks ed. — Toronto : PaperJacks, 1983,c1982. — 300p. — *Originally published: Toronto: Doubleday Canada, 1982*

PRESIDENTS — United States — History — 20th century

ARNOLD, Peri E.
Making the managerial presidency : comprehensive reorganization planning, 1905-1980 / Peri E. Arnold. — Princeton, N.J. : Princeton University Press, c1986. — p. cm. — *Includes index.* — *Bibliography: p*

CRABB, Cecil Van Meter
Presidents and foreign policy making : from FDR to Reagan / Cecil V. Crabb, Jr., Kevin V. Mulcahy. — Baton Rouge : Louisiana State University Press, c1986. — p. cm. — (Political traditions in foreign policy series). — *Includes bibliographical references and index*

SPEAR, Joseph C.
Presidents and the press : the Nixon legacy / Joseph C.Spear. — Cambridge, Massachusetts ; London : MIT Press, 1984

PRESIDENTS — United States — History — 20th century — Manuscripts — Catalogs

BURTON, Dennis A.
A guide to manuscripts in the Presidential Libraries / compiled and edited by Dennis A. Burton, James B. Rhoads, Raymond W. Smock. — College Park, Md. : Research Materials Corp., 1985. — p. cm. — *Includes index*

PRESIDENTS — United States — History — 20th century — Sources — Bibliography — Catalogs

BURTON, Dennis A.
A guide to manuscripts in the Presidential Libraries / compiled and edited by Dennis A. Burton, James B. Rhoads, Raymond W. Smock. — College Park, Md. : Research Materials Corp., 1985. — p. cm. — *Includes index*

PRESIDENTS — United States — Journeys

PLISCHKE, Elmer
Diplomat in chief : the President at the summit / Elmer Plischke. — New York ; Eastbourne : Praeger, 1986. — x,518p. — *Bibliography: p490-494*

PRESIDENTS — United States — Nomination — Addresses, essays, lectures

The Life of the parties : activists in presidential politics / edited by Ronald B. Rapoport, Alan I. Abramowitz, John McGlennon. — Lexington, Ky. : University Press of Kentucky, c1986. — x, 242 p.. — *Includes bibliographies and index*

PRESIDENTS — United States — Press conferences

Presidents, prime ministers, and the press / edited by Kenneth W. Thompson. — Lanham, MD : University Press of America, c1986. — xii, 85 p.. — (The White Burkett Miller Center series on the presidency and the press). — *"Tenth anniversary volume."*

PRESIDENTS — United States — Staff

KERNELL, Samuel
Chief of staff : twenty-five years of managing the presidency : contributions / by Samuel Kernell and Samuel L. Popkin ; foreword by Richard E. Neustadt. — Berkeley : University of California Press, c1986. — p. cm. — *Includes index*

PRESIDENTS — United States — Transition periods

BRAUER, Carl M.
Presidential transitions : Eisenhower through Reagan / Carl M. Brauer. — New York ; Oxford : Oxford University Press, 1986. — xvii, 310p. — *Includes bibliographical references*

MOSHER, Frederick C
Presidential transitions and foreign affairs / Frederick C. Mosher, W. David Clinton, Daniel G. Lang. — Baton Rouge : Louisiana State University Press, c1987. — xvii, 281 p.. — (Miller Center series on the American presidency). — *The recommendations of the Miller Center Commission on Presidential Transitions and Foreign Policy are included in the appendix. — Includes index. — Bibliography: p. [265]-273*

Papers on presidential transitions in foreign policy. — Lanham, Md. ; London : University Press of America
Vol.2: Problems and prospects / edited by Kenneth W. Thompson. — 1986. — [xi],144p

PRESIDENTS — Zaire

Les enseignements du discours présidentiel devant le Conseil Legislatif National 30 Novembre 1973. — Kinshasa : Université Nationale du Zaire, 1974. — 21p. — (Document du mois / Université Nationale du Zaire. Institut de Recherches Economiques ; vol.1, no.2)

PRESIDENT'S PRIVATE SECTOR SURVEY ON COST CONTROL (U.S.)

FITZGERALD, Randall
Porkbarrel : the unexpurgated Grace Commission story of congressional profligacy / Randall Fitzgerald and Gerald Lipson. — Washington, D.C. : Cato Institute, c1984. — xxxv, 114 p.. — *"This report was originally prepared under the title The cost of congressional encroachment"--T.p. verso*

PRESS

Pressa i obshchestvennoe mnenie / otv. redaktor V. S. Korobeinikov. — Moskva : Nauka, 1986. — 204p. — *Bibliography: p196-[203]*

PRESS — Africa

OCHS, Martin
The African press / Martin Ochs. — Cairo : American University, 1986. — [xi],138p. — *Bibliography: p[128]-130*

PRESS — England — History — 18th century

BLACK, Jeremy
The English press in the eighteenth century / Jeremy Black. — London : Croom Helm, c1987. — xv,321p. — *Bibliography: p310-316. — Includes index*

PRESS — France — Bibliography

PARBEL, Pierre
Bibliographie de la presse française : politique et d'information générale : des origines à 1944 / Pierre Parbel et Jean-Claude Poitelon. — Paris : Bibliothèque Nationale, 1986. — 44p

PRESS — France — History — 18th century

MURRAY, William James
The right-wing press in the French Revolution : 1789-92 / William James Murray. — London : Royal Historical Society, 1986, c1985. — viii, 349p. — (Royal Historical Society studies in history series ; no.44). — *Bibliography: p.314-326*

PRESS — Germany — History — 19th century

SAERBECK, Werner
Die Presse der deutschen Sozialdemokratie unter dem Sozialistengesetz / Werner Saerbeck. — Pfaffenweiler : Centaurus-Verlagsgesellschaft, 1986. — ix,271p. — *Bibliography: p259-271*

PRESS — India — History

SANKHDHER, Brijendra Mohan
Press, politics, and public opinion in India : dynamics of modernization and social transformation / B.M. Sankhdher ; foreword by Amba Prasad. — New Delhi : Deep & Deep Publications, c1984. — xxiv, 400 p.. — *Summary: On the role of the press in India, 1780-1835. — Includes index. — Bibliography: p. [353]-388*

PRESS — Scotland — History — 19th century

DONALDSON, William, 1944-
Popular literature in Victorian Scotland : language, fiction and the press / William Donaldson. — Aberdeen : Aberdeen University Press, 1986. — xii,186p. — *Includes index*

PRESS — Soviet Union

Pressa i obshchestvennoe mnenie / otv. redaktor V. S. Korobeinikov. — Moskva : Nauka, 1986. — 204p. — *Bibliography: p196-[203]*

PRESS AGENTS — Canada — Biography

GOSSAGE, Patrick
Close to the charisma : my years between the press and Pierre Elliott Trudeau / Patrick Gossage. — Toronto : McClelland and Stewart, c1986. — 271 p., [16] p. of plates

PRESS AND POLITICS

TATARYN, Lloyd
The pundits : power, politics & the press / Lloyd Tataryn. — Toronto, Canada : Deneau, 1985. — 198 p.. — *Includes index. — Bibliography: p. 181-191*

PRESS AND POLITICS — Bolivia — History — 20th century

KNUDSON, Jerry W
Bolivia, press and revolution, 1932-1964 / by Jerry W. Knudson. — Lanham, MD : University Press of America, c1986. — x, 488p. — *Includes bibliographical footnotes and index*

PRESS AND POLITICS — Germany — History — 19th century

SAERBECK, Werner
Die Presse der deutschen Sozialdemokratie unter dem Sozialistengesetz / Werner Saerbeck. — Pfaffenweiler : Centaurus-Verlagsgesellschaft, 1986. — ix,271p. — *Bibliography: p259-271*

PRESS AND POLITICS — Great Britain

HOLLINGSWORTH, Mark
The press and political dissent / Mark Hollingsworth. — London : Pluto, 1986. — viii,367p. — *Bibliography: p329-331. — Includes index*

PRESS AND POLITICS — Spain — History

SEMOLINOS ARRIBAS, Mercedes
Hitler y la prensa de la II República Española / Mercedes Semolinos Arribas. — Madrid : Centro de Investigaciones Sociológicas : Siglo Veintiuno de España, [1985]. — vi.,290p

PRESS, LABOR — Great Britain

McCARTHY, W. E. J.
The feasibility of establishing a new labour movement newspaper : a report by Lord McCarthy. — London : Trades Union Congress, 1983. — 40p

PRESS LAW — United States — Cases

SMOLLA, Rodney A
Suing the press / Rodney A. Smolla. — New York : Oxford University Press, 1986. — p. cm . — *Includes index. — Bibliography: p. — Contents: The thinning American skin -- The trials of Martin Luther King : the New York times case -- From chasing Communists to fighting Lillian Hellman : the libel suit as guerilla warfare -- Ariel Sharon v. Time magazine : the libel suit as politcal forum, international style -- "I read it in the Enquirer -- Carol Burnett and Henry Kissinger!" : the Carol Burnett case -- Jackie Onassis, Elizabeth Taylor, Clint Eastwood, and Mohammed Ali--of public personality and private property -- From "touching" to "missing" : libel arising from fiction and docudrama -- Of Vanessa Williams and Jerry Falwell : the contributions of Penthouse to the First Amendment -- Mobil Oil meets the Washington Post : can investigative journalism ever be objective? -- Westmoreland v. CBS : litigating the symbols and lessons of Vietnam -- "I'm okay but you're sued."*

PRESS, SOCIALIST — Germany — History — 19th century

SAERBECK, Werner
Die Presse der deutschen Sozialdemokratie unter dem Sozialistengesetz / Werner Saerbeck. — Pfaffenweiler : Centaurus-Verlagsgesellschaft, 1986. — ix,271p. — *Bibliography: p259-271*

PRESS, SOCIALIST — Sweden — Karlstad — History

ENGWALL, Lars
Från vag vision till komplex organisation : en studie av Värmlands Folkblads ekonomiska och organisatoriska utveckling / Lars Engwall. — Uppsala : Universitet ; Stockholm : distributed by Almqvist & Wiksell, 1985. — 448p. — *With English summary and abstract. — Bibliography: p415-432*

PRESSURE GROUPS — Canada

FORBES, James D.
Institutions and influence groups in Canadian farm and food policy / J. D. Forbes. — Toronto : Institute of Public Administration of Canada, 1985. — 131p. — (Monographs on Canadian public administration ; no.10). — *Includes bibliographical references*

MALVERN, Paul
Persuaders : influence peddling, lobbying and political corruption in Canada / Paul Malvern. — Toronto ; London : Methuen, 1985. — 350p . — *Includes bibliographical notes*

PROSS, A. Paul
Group politics and public policy / A. Paul Pross. — Toronto : Oxford University Press, 1986. — xi,343p. — *Bibliography: p321-333*

RIDDELL-DIXON, Elizabeth
The domestic mosaic : domestic groups and Canadian foreign policy / Elizabeth Riddell-Dixon. — Toronto, Canada : Canadian Institute of International Affairs, c1985. — xii, 120 p.. — *"Domestic sources of Canadian foreign policy ; 1"--Can. CIP. — Includes index. — Bibliography: p. 76-78*

PRESSURE GROUPS — Great Britain

HAMER, Mick
Wheels within wheels : a study of the road lobby / Mick Hamer. — London : Routledge & Kegan Paul, 1987. — [192]p. — (Geography, environment and planning). — *Includes index*

PRESSURE GROUPS — Great Britain — History

WOOTTON, Graham
Pressure groups in Britain, 1720-1970 : an essay in interpretation with original documents / Graham Wootton. — London : Allen Lane, 1975. — x,375p. — *Bibliography: p.112-119*

PRESSURE GROUPS — Kenya — Bibliography

A guide to selected documents on political organisations in Kenya. — Nairobi : Kenya National Archives, 1984. — 42p

PRESSURE GROUPS — Manitoba — Winnipeg

CHEKKI, Dan A.
Organised interest groups and the urban policy process / Dan A. Chekki and Roger T. Toews. — Winnipeg : Institute of Urban Studies, University of Winnipeg, 1985. — 87p. — (Report / University of Winnipeg, Institute of Urban Studies ; 9). — *Bibliography: p83-87*

PRESSURE GROUPS — Siberia, Western (R.S.F.S.R.)

CHUNG, Han-Ku
Interest representation in Soviet policy-making : a case study of a Siberian energy coalition, 1969-1981 / Han-Ku Chung. — 176 leaves. — *PhD (Econ) 1986 LSE*

PRESSURE GROUPS — United States

BAUER, Raymond A.
American business and public policy : the politics of foreign trade / Raymond A. Bauer, Ithiel de Sola Pool, Lewis Anthony Dexter. — New York : Atherton Press, 1963. — xxvii,499p

MCCANN, Michael W.
Taking reform seriously : perspectives on public interest liberalism / Michael W. McCann. — Ithaca : Cornell University Press, 1986. — 345 p. — *Includes index.* — *Bibliography: p. 321-335*

PRESSURE GROUPS — United States — Finance

BENNETT, James T
Destroying democracy : how government funds partisan politics / James T. Bennett, Thomas J. DiLorenzo. — Washington, D.C. : Cato Institute, c1985. — xiii, 561 p.. — *Includes index.* — *Bibliography: p. 505-543*

PRESSURE GROUPS — United States — History

WALLENFELDT, E. C
Roots of special interests in American higher education : a social psychological historical perspective / E.C. Wallenfeldt. — Lanham, MD : University Press of America, c1986. — p. cm. — *Includes index.* — *Bibliography: p*

PRESSURIZED WATER REACTORS

FRIENDS OF THE EARTH
Critical decision : should Britain buy the pressurised water reactor? : a report on the Sizewell Inquiry by Friends of the Earth / edited by Walt Patterson, Stewart Boyle, Juliette Majot. — London : Friends of the Earth Trust, 1986. — 135p. — *Bibliography: p103-109*

LAYFIELD, Sir Frank
Sizewell B public inquiry : report on applications by the Central Electricity Generating Board for consent for the construction of a pressurised water reactor and a direction that planning permission be deemed to be granted for that development : inquiry 11 January 1983-7 March 1985, presented to the Secretary of State for Energy on 5 December 1986 / Inspector: Sir Frank Layfield; Assessors: J. M. Alexander...[et al.]. — London : H.M.S.O., 1987. — 8v.. — *Summary of conclusions and recommendations issued separately.* — *Includes bibliographical references.* — *Includes index (in vol.8)*

LAYFIELD, Sir Frank
Sizewell B public inquiry : summary of conclusions and recommendations from the Inspector's report on the Central Electricity Generating Board's application for consent for the construction of a pressurised water reactor at Sizewell, Suffolk, together with chapters 2,47,90,104,108,109, of that report, being the concluding chapters referred to in that summary / Inspector: Sir Frank Layfield; Assessors: J. M. Alexander...[et al.]. — London : H.M.S.O., 1987. — 1v. (various pagings). — *Report presented to the Secretary of State for Energy on 5 December 1986*

Sizewell B public inquiry before Sir Frank Layfield (the Inspector) at The Maltings, Snape, Suffolk, 26 July 1982-7 March 1985 : transcript of proceedings. — [London : Department of Energy, 1985]. — 339microfiches. — *At head of title: Electric Lighting Act 1909 (as amended), Electricity Act 1957, Town and Country Planning Act 1971; Electricity Generating Stations and Overhead Lines (Inquiries Procedure) Rules 1981. — Transcripts prepared by J. L. Harpham Ltd., Official Shorthand Writers, Sheffield; filmed October 1985*

PRESTEL (VIDEOTEX SYSTEM)

REDFEARN, Judy
Libraries bring Prestel to the public : a summary of British Library-supported research 1979-1981 / Judy Redfearn. — [London] : British Library, c1983. — v,57p. — (Library and information research report ; 13)

YEATES, R.
Prestel in the public library. — Boston Spa : British Library Lending Division, July 1982. — [134]p. — (Library and information research reports ; 2)

PREVENTION OF TERRORISM BILL 1983-84

GREAT BRITAIN. Parliament. House of Commons. Library. Research Division
Prevention of Terrorism Bill 1983-4 [Bill 8] / [Patrick Nealon]. — [London] : the Division, [1983]. — 12p. — (Reference sheet ; no.83/13). — *Bibliographical references: p8-12*

PREVENTION OF TERRORISM (TEMPORARY PROVISIONS) ACT 1974

SCORER, Catherine
The new Prevention of Terrorism Act : the case for repeal. — Updated and expanded 3rd ed., covering the extension of the Act in 1984 to cover 'international terrorism' / Catherine Scorer, Sarah Spencer and Patricia Hewitt. — London : National Council for Civil Liberties, c1985. — 82p. — *Previous ed.: published as The Prevention of Terrorism Act. 1981*

PREVENTION OF TERRORISM (TEMPORARY PROVISIONS) ACT 1976

SCORER, Catherine
The new Prevention of Terrorism Act : the case for repeal. — Updated and expanded 3rd ed., covering the extension of the Act in 1984 to cover 'international terrorism' / Catherine Scorer, Sarah Spencer and Patricia Hewitt. — London : National Council for Civil Liberties, c1985. — 82p. — *Previous ed.: published as The Prevention of Terrorism Act. 1981*

PREVENTIVE DETENTION — North /America

Dangerousness : probability and prediction, psychiatry and public policy / edited by Christopher D. Webster, Mark H. Ben-Aron, Stephen J. Hucker. — Cambridge : Cambridge University Press, 1985. — xiii,236p. — *Includes bibliographies and index*

PRICE INDEXES

GREAT BRITAIN. Parliament. House of Commons. Library. Research Division
The measurement of inflation / R. Twigger. — [London] : the Division, 1982. — 12p. — (Background paper ; no.105). — *Bibliography: p12*

GREAT BRITAIN. Parliament. House of Commons. Library. Research Division
The measurement of inflation / Robert Twigger. — [London] : the Division, 1983. — 12p. — (Background paper ; no.120). — *June 1983 version*

GREAT BRITAIN. Parliament. House of Commons. Library. Research Division
The measurement of inflation / Robert Twigger. — [London] : the Division, 1983. — 12p. — (Background paper ; no.129). — *November 1983 version.* — *Bibliography: p12*

GREAT BRITAIN. Parliament. House of Commons. Library. Research Division
The measurement of inflation / Robert Twigger. — [London] : the Division, 1984. — 12p. — (Background paper ; no.142). — *June 1984 version.* — *Bibliography: p12*

GREAT BRITAIN. Parliament. House of Commons. Library. Research Division
The measurement of inflation / Robert Twigger. — [London] : the Division, 1985. — 12p. — (Background paper ; no.171). — *June 1985 version.* — *Bibliography: p12*

GREAT BRITAIN. Parliament. House of Commons. Library. Research Division
The measurement of inflation / Robert Twigger. — [London] : the Division, 1986. — 12p. — (Background paper ; no.182). — *May 1986 version.* — *Bibliography: p12*

Manual on producers' price indices for industrial goods. — New York : United Nations, 1979. — vi,79p. — (Statistical papers / United Nations, Statistical Office. Series M ; no.59 [i.e.66]) ([Document] / United Nations ; ST/ESA/STAT/SER.M/66). — *Cover and title page has Series M, no.59 instead of Series M, no.66.* — *Bibliography: p77-79.* — *Sales: E.79.XVII.11*

Price index numbers for current cost accounting : summary volume 1974-1982. — London : H.M.S.O., 1983. — 109p. — (Business monitor. MO ; 18). — *Continues: Price index numbers for current cost accounting*

Price index numbers for current cost accounting (monthly supplement). — London : HMSO, 1980-. — (Business monitor. MM ; 17) . — *Monthly*

PRICE INDEXES — Finland

HYRKKÖ, Jarmo
Tuottajahintaindeksit 1980=100 = Producer price indices 1980=100 / Jarmo Hyrkkö, Erkki Hakkarainen. — Helsinki : Tilastokeskus, 1984. — 104p. — (Tutkimuksai / Finland. Tilastokeskus ; no.105). — *In Finnish and English.* — *Bibliography: p29*

TUOMINEN, Pentti
Producer price indices : methods and practice : producer price index for manufactured products 1975=100 : basic price index for domestic supply 1975=100 : export price index 1975=100 : import price index 1975=100 / Pentti Tuominen. — Helsinki : Tilastokeskus, 1980. — 122p. — (Tutkimuksai / Finland. Tilastokeskus ; no.56)

PRICE INDEXES — Trinidad and Tobago
The index of retail prices, 1982. — [Port of Spain] : Central Statistical Office, 1984. — 20p. — (Statistical studies and papers ; no.10)

PRICE POLICY
ATTANASIO, O.
Staggered price decisions and aggregate nominal inertia : empirical evidence for the seven major OECD economies / O. P. Attanasio. — London : Centre for Labour Economics, London School of Economics, 1986. — 33p. — (Discussion paper / London School of Economics and Political Science. Centre for Labour Economics ; no.268). — *Bibliography: p31-33*

DORWARD, Neil
The pricing decision : economic theory and business practice / Neil Dorward. — London : Harper & Row, 1987. — [208]p. — *Includes index*

PRICE POLICY — Colombia — Addresses, essays, lectures
THOMAS, Vinod
Linking macroeconomic and agricultural policies for adjustment with growth : the Colombian experience / Vinod Thomas with contributions from Sebastian Edwards ... [et al.]. — Baltimore : Published for the World Bank [by] the Johns Hopkins University Press, c1985. — p. cm. — *"A World Bank publication."*. — *Includes index*

PRICE POLICY — Communist countries
RADNÓTI, Éva
Árpolitikai koncepciók és gazdaságunk fejlődése / Radnóti Éva. — Budapest : Közgazdasági és Jogi Könyvkiadó, 1984. — 233p. — (Időszerű közgazdasági kérdések). — *Bibliography: p229-[234]*

PRICE POLICY — Developing countries
JIMENEZ, Emmanuel
Pricing policy in the social sectors : cost recovery for education and health in developing countries / Emmanuel Jimenez. — Baltimore : Johns Hopkins University Press for the World Bank, 1987. — v,170p. — *Bibliographical references: p155-163*

PRICE POLICY — United States
LENT, Rebecca J.
Uncertainty, market disequilibrium and the firm's decision process : applications to the Pacific salmon market / Rebecca J. Lent. — Corvallis, Or. : Sea Grant College Program, Oregon State University, [1984]. — vii,109p. — *Bibliography: p94-97*

PRICE REGULATION
TIROLE, Jean
Concurrence imparfaite / Jean Tirole. — Paris : Economica, c1985. — 133p. — (Economie et statistiques avencées)

PRICE REGULATION — Great Britain
CAPIE, Forrest
Prices and price controls : are price controls a policy instrument? / Forrest Capie, Mahmoud Pradhan, Geoffrey E. Wood. — London : Centre for Banking and International Finance, City University, 1986. — 36p. — (Monetary history discussion paper series ; no.22). — *Bibliography: p36*

GREAT BRITAIN. Department of Prices and Consumer Protection
Consultative document on amendments to the price code : selective price restraint scheme : provisions to facilitate cross-subsidisation. — [London : the Department, 1976]. — 2,3p

GREAT BRITAIN. Department of Prices and Consumer Protection
Safeguards under clause 9 of the Price Commission Bill : a consultative document. — [London : the Department, 1977]. — [7]p

GREAT BRITAIN. Department of Prices and Consumer Protection
Selective Price Restraint Scheme : consultation document for organisations involved in negotiations. — [London : the Department, 1975]. — 5p

PRICE REGULATION — Poland
GRZYBOWSKI, Wacław
Stanowienie i kontrola cen / Wacław Grzybowski. — Warszawa : Instytut Wydawniczy Związków Zawodowych, 1986. — 239p. — *Bibliography: p236-[237]*

PRICES — Peru — Iquitos
PERU. Dirección General de Indicadores Económicos y Sociales. Area de Indices de Precios al Consumidor
Indices de precios al consumidor de la ciudad de Iquitos. — Lima : the Area, [1976]. — 16p. — *Base 1966 = 100.00*

PRICES
ATTANASIO, O.
Staggered price decisions and aggregate nominal inertia : empirical evidence for the seven major OECD economies / O. P. Attanasio. — London : Centre for Labour Economics, London School of Economics, 1986. — 33p. — (Discussion paper / London School of Economics and Political Science. Centre for Labour Economics ; no.268). — *Bibliography: p31-33*

IRELAND, Norman J.
Product differentiation and non-price competition / Norman Ireland. — Oxford : Basil Blackwell, 1987. — 1v.. — *Includes bibliography and index*

KROUSE, Clement G
Capital markets and prices : valuing uncertain income streams / Clement G. Krouse. — Amsterdam ; New York : North-Holland ; New York, N.Y. : Sole distributors for U.S.A. and Canada, Elsevier Science Pub. Co., 1986. — p. cm. — (Advanced textbooks in economics ; v. 25). — *Includes index*

PRICES — Government policy — India — Congresses
NATIONAL SEMINAR ON PRICE CONTROLS (1983 : Bombay, India)
Price controls in the Indian economy : papers and proceedings of a National Seminar on Price Controls / organised by the Times Research Foundation ; edited by G.B. Kulkarni. — 1st ed. — Pune : The Foundation, 1984. — 262 p.

PRICES — Mathematical models
HERD, Richard
Import and export price equations for manufactures / by Richard Herd. — [Paris] : OECD, 1987. — vi,37p. — (Working papers / OECD Department of Economics and Statistics ; no.43). — *Bibliography: p36-37*

Spatial pricing and differentiated markets / edited by G. Norman. — London : Pion, 1986. — 190p. — (London papers in regional science ; 16)

PRICES — Mathematical models — Congresses
Competition, instability, and nonlinear cycles : proceedings of an international conference, New School for Social Research, New York, USA, March 1985 / edited by Willi Semmler. — Berlin ; New York : Springer-Verlag, c1986. — p. cm. — (Lecture notes in economics and mathematical systems ; 275)

PRICES — Statistical methods
WOOD, G. Donald
The collection of price data for the measurement of living standards / G. Donald Wood, Jr., Jane A. Knight. — Washington, D.C., U.S.A. : The World Bank, c1985. — viii,61p. — (LSMS working papers ; no.21) (LSMS working papers ; no. 21). — *Summary in French and Spanish*. — *Bibliographical references: p61*

PRICES — Argentina — Statistics
Comercio interior / Instituto Nacional de Estadistica y Censos, Argentina. — Buenos Aires : Instituto Nacional de Estadistica, 1964-1972. — *Monthly*. — *Continued by: Precios al por mayor, capital federal*

Costa de vida / Instituto Nacional de Estadistica y Censos, Argentina. — Buenos Aires : Instituto Nacional de Estadistica y Censos, 1964-1972. — *Monthly*. — *Continued by: Indice de precios al consumidor*

Indice de precios al consumidor, capital federal / Instituto Nacional de Estadistica y Censos, Argentina. — Buenos Aires : Instituto Nacional de Estadistica y Censos, 1973-1984. — *Monthly*. — *Continues: Costa di vida-. Continued by Estadistica mensual*

Precios al por mayor, capital federal / Instituto Nacional de Estadistica y Censos, Argentina. — Buenos Aires : Instituto Nacional de Estadistica y Censos, 1956. — *Monthly*. — *1956-1972 entitled Indice de precios al por mayor*. — *Continues: Comercio interior- . Continued by Estadistica mensual*

PRICES — Australia — Tasmania
TASMANIA. Commonwealth Bureau of Census and Statistics. Tasmanian Office
Labour, wages and prices. — Hobart : [the Ofiice], 1970/71-1980/81. — *Annual*

PRICES — Egypt
AHMED, Sadiq
Reforming Egypt's pricing system / Sadiq Ahmed [and] Wafik Grais. — Safat : Industrial Bank of Kuwait, 1987. — 39p. — (IBK papers ; no.25)

PRICES — Great Britain
GREAT BRITAIN. Department of Employment
Retail prices indices 1914-1986. — London : H.M.S.O., 1987. — 45p

GREAT BRITAIN. Parliament. House of Commons. Library. Research Division
The measurement of inflation / R. Twigger. — [London] : the Division, 1982. — 12p. — (Background paper ; no.105). — *Bibliography: p12*

GREAT BRITAIN. Parliament. House of Commons. Library. Research Division
The measurement of inflation / Robert Twigger. — [London] : the Division, 1983. — 12p. — (Background paper ; no.120). — *June 1983 version*

GREAT BRITAIN. Parliament. House of Commons. Library. Research Division
The measurement of inflation / Robert Twigger. — [London] : the Division, 1983. — 12p. — (Background paper ; no.129). — *November 1983 version*. — *Bibliography: p12*

GREAT BRITAIN. Parliament. House of Commons. Library. Research Division
The measurement of inflation / Robert Twigger. — [London] : the Division, 1984. — 12p. — (Background paper ; no.142). — *June 1984 version*. — *Bibliography: p12*

GREAT BRITAIN. Parliament. House of Commons. Library. Research Division
The measurement of inflation / Robert Twigger. — [London] : the Division, 1985. — 12p. — (Background paper ; no.171). — *June 1985 version*. — *Bibliography: p12*

GREAT BRITAIN. Parliament. House of Commons. Library. Research Division
The measurement of inflation / Robert Twigger. — [London] : the Division, 1986. — 12p. — (Background paper ; no.182). — *May 1986 version*. — *Bibliography: p12*

Price index numbers for current cost accounting : summary volume 1974-1982. — London : H.M.S.O., 1983. — 109p. — (Business monitor. MO ; 18). — *Continues: Price index numbers for current cost accounting*

Price index numbers for current cost accounting (monthly supplement). — London : HMSO, 1980-. — (Business monitor. MM ; 17) . — *Monthly*

PRICES — Great Britain — History
DOWNS, André
General import restrictions and the behaviour of domestic prices and wages : the case of the British General Tariff of 1932 / by André Downs. — 245 leaves. — *PhD (Econ) 1986 LSE. — Leaves 210-245 are appendices*

PRICES — Hungary — Statistics
A fogyasztói árak valtozása a lakosság föbb rétegeinél. — Budapest : Központi Statisztikai Hivatal, 1980-. — *Annual*

PRICES — Japan
Price stabilizing effects of the Yen's appreciation and influence on enterprises and households. — Tokyo : Bank of Japan, 1987. — 28p. — (Special paper / Bank of Japan. Research and Statistics Department ; no.150)

PRICES — Netherlands — Econometric models
ZEELENBERG, C
Industrial price formation / C. Zeelenberg. — Amsterdam ; New York : North-Holland ; New York, N.Y., U.S.A. : Sole distributors for the U.S.A. and Canada, Elsevier Science Pub. Co., 1986. — p. cm. — (Contributions to economic analysis ; 158). — *Includes indexes. — Bibliography: p*

PRICES — Nigeria — Statistics
Consumer price index / Federal Office of Statistics, Lagos. — Lagos : Federal Office of Statistics, 1983-. — *3 per year*

PRICES — Organisation for Economic Co-operation and Development countries — Mathematical models
HERD, Richard
Import and export price equations for manufactures / by Richard Herd. — [Paris] : OECD, 1987. — vi,37p. — (Working papers / OECD Department of Economics and Statistics ; no.43). — *Bibliography: p36-37*

STIEHLER, Ulrich
Price determination in the major seven country models in INTERLINK / Ulrich Stiehler. — [Paris] : OECD, 1987. — iii,55p. — (Working papers / OECD Department of Economics and Statistics ; no.44). — *Bibliographical references: p54-55*

PRICES — Pakistan
AHMAD, Ehtisham
A complete set of shadow prices for Pakistan : illustrations for 1975-6 / Ehtisham Ahmad, David Coady and Nicholas Stern. — London : Suntory Toyota International Centre for Economics and Related Disciplines, 1987. — 42p. — (Development Research Programme London School of Economics and Political Science. / Suntory Toyota International Centre for Economics and Related Disciplines ; no.8)

PRICES — Peru — Arequipa (City)
PERU. Dirección General de Indicadores Económicos y Sociales
Indices de precios al consumidor de la ciudad de Arequipa, enero 1976. — Lima : the Dirección, [1976]. — 23p. — *Base 1966 = 100.00*

PRICES — Peru — Chiclayo
PERU. Dirección de Planificación Estadística. Division de Precios e Indices
Indices de precios al consumidor de la ciudad de Chiclayo, diciembre 1975. — Lima : the División, [1976]. — 15p. — *Base 1966 = 100.00*

PRICES — Peru — Cuzco (City)
PERU. Dirección General de Indicadores Económicos y Sociales. Area de Indices de Precios al Consumidor
Indices de precios al consumidor de la ciudad del Cuzco, enero 1976. — Lima : the Area, [1976]. — 17p. — *Base 1966 = 100.00*

PRICES — Peru — Huancayo
PERU. Dirección de Planificación Estadística. División de Precios e Indices
Indices de precios al consumidor de la ciudad de Huancayo, diciembre 1975. — Lima : the División, [1976]. — 14p. — *Base 1966 = 100.00*

PRICES — Peru — Piura (City)
PERU. Dirección General de Indicadores Económicos y Sociales. Area de Indices de Precios al Consumidor
Indices de precios al consumidor de la ciudad de Piura, enero 1976. — Lima : the Area, [1976]. — 19p. — *Base 1969 = 100.00*

PRICES — Peru — Trujillo
PERU. Dirección de Planificación Estadística. División de Precios e Indices
Indices de precios al consumidor de la ciudad de Trujillo, diciembre 1975. — Lima : the División, [1976]. — 15p. — *Base 1968 = 100.00*

PRICES — Poland
GRZYBOWSKI, Wacław
Stanowienie i kontrola cen / Wacław Grzybowski. — Warszawa : Instytut Wydawniczy Związków Zawodowych, 1986. — 239p. — *Bibliography: p236-[237]*

PRICES — Soviet Union
SKVORTSOV, L. I.
Tseny i tsenoobrazovanie v SSSR / L. I. Skvortsov. — Moskva : Vysshaia shkola, 1972. — 239p

PRICES — United States
FINANCIAL ACCOUNTING STANDARDS BOARD
Statement of financial accounting standards. — Stamford, Conn. : Financial Accounting Standards Board
No.89: Financial reporting and changing prices. — 1986. — 81p

PRICING POLICY
GEORGES, W
Analytical contribution accounting : the interface of cost accounting and pricing policy / Walter Georges and Robert W. McGee. — New York : Quorum Books, 1987. — xii, 254 p.. — *Includes index. — Bibliography: p. [225]-249*

PRIMARY HEALTH CARE — Nepal
JUSTICE, Judith
Policies, plans, and people : culture and health development in Nepal / Judith Justice. — Berkeley : University of California Press, c1986. — p. cm. — (Comparative studies of health systems and medical care). — *Includes index. — Bibliography: p*

PRIME MINISTERS — Alberta — Biography
WOOD, David G.
The Lougheed legacy / David G. Wood. — Toronto, Ont., Canada : Key Porter Books, c1985. — v, 250 p., [16] p. of plates. — *Includes index*

PRIME MINISTERS — British Columbia — Biography
GARR, Allen
Tough guy : Bill Bennett and the taking of British Columbia / by Allen Garr. — Toronto, Ont., Canada : Key Porter Books, c1985. — ix, 197 p., [16] p. of plates. — *Includes index. — Bibliography: p. 191-192*

PRIME MINISTERS — Canada — Biography
DONALDSON, Gordon
Eighteen men : the prime ministers of Canada / by Gordon Donaldson. — Toronto, Ont. : Doubleday Canada ; Garden City, N.Y. : Doubleday, 1985. — p. cm. — *Rev. ed. of: Sixteen men. — Includes index. — Bibliography: p*

PRIME MINISTERS — Canada — History
MARTIN, Lawrence
The presidents and the prime ministers : Washington and Ottawa face to face : the myth of bilateral bliss 1867-1982 / Lawrence Martin. — PaperJacks ed. — Toronto : PaperJacks, 1983,c1982. — 300p. — *Originally published: Toronto: Doubleday Canada, 1982*

PRIME MINISTERS — China — Biography
FANG, Percy Jucheng
Zhou Enlai : a profile / Percy Jucheng Fang, Lucy Guinong J. Fang. — 1st ed. — Beijing : Foreign Languages Press : Distributed by China International Book Trading Corporation, c1986. — iii, 238 p., [1] leaf of plates. — *Colophon title: Chou En-lai chuan lüeh. — Bibliography: p. 199-212*

PRIME MINISTERS — Great Britain — Biography
CALLAGHAN, James
Time and chance / James Callaghan. — London : Collins, 1987. — [420]p. — *Includes index*

DALYELL, Tam
Thatcher: patterns of deceit / by Tam Dalyell ; introduction by Paul Rogers. — London : Woolf, 1986. — [64]p. — (The Men and documents series). — *Includes index*

GILBERT, Bentley B.
David Lloyd George : a political life / Bentley Briakerhoff Gilbert. — London : Batsford
The architect of change, 1863-1912. — 1987. — 546p,[8]p of plates. — *Bibliography: p529-536. — Includes index*

HARRIMAN, Ed
Thatcher : a graphic guide / text: Ed Harriman ; illustrations: John Freeman. — London : Camden, 1986. — 169p. — (Graphic guide). — *Bibliography: p169*

JENKINS, Roy
Asquith / Roy Jenkins. — 3rd ed. — London : Collins, 1986. — [576]p. — *Previous ed.: 1978. — Includes index*

JENKINS, Roy
Baldwin / Roy Jenkins. — London : Collins, 1987. — 204p,[16]p of plates. — *Bibliography: p193-195. — Includes index*

MATTHEW, H. C. G.
Gladstone 1809-1874 / H.C.G. Matthew. — Oxford : Clarendon, 1986. — [230]p,[8]p of plates. — *Includes index*

MORGAN, Austen
J. Ramsay MacDonald / Austen Morgan. — Manchester : Manchester University Press, c1987. — 276p. — (Lives of the left). — *Includes index*

Salisbury : the man and his policies / edited by Lord Blake and Hugh Cecil. — Basingstoke : Macmillan, 1987. — ix,298p. — *Includes index*

WILSON, Harold, 1916-
Memoirs : the making of a Prime Minister 1916-64 / Harold Wilson. — London : Weidenfeld and Nicolson and Joseph, 1986. — 213p,[16]p of plates. — *Includes index*

ZALEWSKI, Marek J.
"Żelazna dama" z Downing Street / Marek J. Zalewski. — Warszawa : Krajowa Agencja Wydawnicza, 1985. — 272p

PRIME MINISTERS — India — Biography
NEHRU, Jawaharlal
Jawaharlal Nehru : an anthology / edited by Sarvepalli Gopal. — Delhi ; Oxford : Oxford University Press, 1983. — xxi,662p. — *Includes index*

PRIME MINISTERS — India — Correspondence
NEHRU, Jawaharlal
Letters to chief ministers, 1947-1964 / Jawaharlal Nehru ; general editor, G. Parthasarathi. — Delhi : Distributed by Oxford University Press, 1985-. — v. <1 >. — "A project of the Jawaharlal Nehru Memorial Fund"--T.p. verso. — Includes index. — Contents: v. 1. 1947-1949

PRIME MINISTERS — Ontario — Biography
HOY, Claire
Bill Davis : a biography / by Claire Hoy. — Toronto : New York : Methuen, c1985. — 413 p., [16] p. of plates. — Includes index

HUMPHRIES, Charles W
"Honest enough to be bold" : the life and times of Sir James Pliny Whitney / Charles W. Humphries. — Toronto ; Buffalo : Published by University of Toronto Press, c1985. — xii, 276 p., [14] p. of plates. — (The Ontario historical studies series). — Includes index. — Bibliography: p. [269]-270

JOHNSTON, Charles M.
E. C. Drury : agrarian idealist / Charles M. Johnston. — Toronto : University of Toronto Press, 1986. — xii,299p. — (Ontario Historical Studies Series). — Includes references

PRIME MINISTERS — Quebec (Province) — Biography
LÉVESQUE, René
Memoirs / René Levesque ; translated by Philip Stratford. — Toronto : McClelland and Stewart, 1986. — 368p. — Issued also in French under title: Mémoires

PRIME MINISTERS — Québec (Province) — Biography
THOMSON, Dale C
Jean Lesage & the quiet revolution / Dale C. Thomson. — Toronto, Canada : MacMillan of Canada, c1984. — x, 501 p., [16] p. of plates. — Includes bibliographical references and index

PRIME MINISTERS — Soviet Union — Biography
ABRAHAM, Richard
Alexander Kerensky : the first love of the revolution / Richard Abraham. — New York : Columbia University Press, 1987. — xiii, 503p, [32]p of plates. — Includes index. — Includes bibliographical references

PRIME MINISTERS — Trinidad and Tobago — Biography — Addresses, essays, lectures
Eric Williams, the man and the leader / edited by Ken I. Boodhoo. — Lanham, MD : University Press of America, c1986. — xviii, 143 p.. — Includes index. — "Bibliography of books, articles, and speeches by Eric Williams": p. 135-139

PRIME RATE — United States
BRADY, Thomas F.
The role of the prime rate in the pricing of business loans by commercial banks, 1977-84 / Thomas F. Brady. — Washington, D.C. : Board of Governors of the Federal Reserve System, 1985. — 25p. — (Staff study / Board of Governors of the Federal Reserve System (U.S.) ; 146)

PRIMO DE RIVERA, MIGUEL
RIAL, James H.
Revolution from above : the Primo de Rivera dictatorship in Spain, 1923-1930 / James H. Rial. — Cranbury, N.J. ; London : Associated University Presses, 1986. — 256 p.. — Includes index. — Bibliography: p. 235-251

PRIMROSE, ARCHIBALD PHILIP, Earl of Rosebery See Rosebery, Archibald Philip Primose, Earl of

PRINCESSES — Social conditions
STAFFORD, Pauline
Queens, concubines, and dowagers : the king's wife in the early Middle Ages / Pauline Stafford. — Athens, Ga. : University of Georgia Press, c1983. — xiii, 248 p.. — Includes index. — Bibliography: p. 211-226

PRINCIPAL COMPONENTS ANALYSIS
JOLLIFFE, I. T.
Principal component analysis / I.T. Jolliffe. — New York : Springer-Verlag, 1986. — (Springer series in statistics)

PRINTERS — Germany (West)
HEINE, Werner
Ein Tabu fällt : Kampf der Drucker um Arbeitszeitverkürzung und Lohnstruktur / Werner Heine ; mit ein Vorwort von Erwin Ferlemann. — Köln : Bund-Verlag, 1986. — 159p

PRINTING — France — History
DROZ, E.
Complément à la bibliographie de Pierre Haultin / E. Droz. — Genève : E. Droz, 1961. — p.375-394. — (Bibliothèque d'humanisme et renaissance. travaux et documents ; Tome 23). — Offprint

PRINTING — Sweden — History
LINDBERG, Sten G.
Svenska böcker 1483-1983 : bokhistoria i f'agelperspektiv / Sten G. Lindberg. — Stockholm : Bokbranschens marknadsinst, [1983]. — 61p

PRINTING, PUBLIC — Legal status, laws, etc. — Peru
PERU
[Laws, etc]. Ley orgánica de la Empresa Editora Perú : Decreto-ley no.21420. — Lima : [Empresa Editora Perú, ca.1976]. — 14p

PRISON ADMINISTRATION — India
CHADHA, Kumkum
The Indian jail : a contemporary document / Kumkum Chadha. — New Delhi : Vikas Pub. House, c1983. — viii, 251 p.. — Includes statistical tables

PRISON ADMINISTRATION — United States
POLLOCK, Joycelyn M.
Sex and supervision : guarding male and female inmates / Joycelyn M. Pollock ; foreword by Elaine A. Lord. — New York : Greenwood Press, 1986. — xiv, 160 p.. — (Contributions in criminology and penology ; no. 12). — Includes index. — Bibliography: p. [155]-157

PRISON ADMINISTRATION — United States — History
BAKER, J. E.
Prisoner participation in prison power / by J.E. Baker. — Metuchen, N.J. : Scarecrow Press, 1985. — xvi, 414 p.. — Includes bibliographies and index

PRISON DISCIPLINE — Addresses, essays, lectures
LYLE, William H., comp
Behavioral science and modern penology : a book of readings / edited by William H. Lyle, Jr., and Thetus W. Horner. — Springfield, Ill. : Thomas, [1973]. — xvi, 355 p. — Includes bibliographical references

PRISON DISCIPLINE — England
DITCHFIELD, John
Grievance procedures in prisons : a study of prisoners' applications and petitions / by John Ditchfield and Claire Austin. — London : H.M.S.O., 1986. — vi,71p. — (Home Office research study ; no.91). — A Home Office Research and Planning Unit report

PRISON PSYCHOLOGY
IRWIN, John
The jail : managing the underclass in American society / John Irwin. — Berkeley : University of California Press, c1985. — xvi, 148 p.. — Includes index. — Bibliography: p. 135-139

PRISON REFORM TRUST
Prisoners' information pack. — London : Prison Reform Trust, 1986. — 10 leaflets

PRISON REFORMERS — United States — History
BAKER, J. E.
Prisoner participation in prison power / by J.E. Baker. — Metuchen, N.J. : Scarecrow Press, 1985. — xvi, 414 p.. — Includes bibliographies and index

PRISON RIOTS — Mathematical models
A model for prison disturbances / E. C. Zeeman...[et al.]. — [London : Home Office, Prison Department, Directorate of Psychological Services], 1975. — 24p. — Bibliographical references: p24

PRISON SENTENCES — California
PETERSILIA, Joan
Prison versus probation in California : implications for crime and offender recidivism / Joan Petersilia, Susan Turner, with Joyce Peterson ; prepared for the National Institute of Justice, U.S. Department of Justice. — Santa Monica, CA. : Rand, [1986]. — xix, 63 p.. — "July 1986.". — "R-3323-NIJ.". — Bibliography: p. 59-63

PRISON WARDENS — Training of — Great Britain — Evaluation
BLANSHARD, A. J.
A systematic approach to the evaluation of training / A. J. Blanshard and P. Montgomery. — London : Home Office, Prison Department, Directorate of Psychological Services, 1978. — 15,[25]p. — (DPS report. Series 1 ; no.12). — Bibliography: second sequence, p[25]

PRISONERS — Addresses, essays, lectures
LYLE, William H., comp
Behavioral science and modern penology : a book of readings / edited by William H. Lyle, Jr., and Thetus W. Horner. — Springfield, Ill. : Thomas, [1973]. — xvi, 355 p. — Includes bibliographical references

PRISONERS — Legal status, laws, etc.
RODLEY, Nigel S.
The treatment of prisoners under international law / Nigel S. Rodley. — Paris : Unesco ; Oxford : Clarendon, 1987. — xxii,374. — Includes index

PRISONERS — Legal status, laws, etc — United States — History
BAKER, J. E.
Prisoner participation in prison power / by J.E. Baker. — Metuchen, N.J. : Scarecrow Press, 1985. — xvi, 414 p.. — Includes bibliographies and index

PRISONERS — Psychiatric care — Netherlands
EMMERICK, J. L. van
Recidivism among psychiatric offenders / Jos L. van Emmerik. — The Hague : Research and Documentation Centre, Ministry of Justice, 1985. — 20p. — ([Reports, papers, articles] ; 87). — Bibliographical references: p14. — "A summary of a survey of persons who were discharged between 1974 and 1979"

PRISONERS — California — Case studies
IRWIN, John
The jail : managing the underclass in American society / John Irwin. — Berkeley : University of California Press, c1985. — xvi, 148 p.. — Includes index. — Bibliography: p. 135-139

PRISONERS — England — London
LONDON STRATEGIC POLICY UNIT. Women's Equality Group
Women's prisoners : breaking the silence. — London : [the Group], 1987. — iii,184p

PRISONERS — Germany (West) — Suicidal behavior
CAMPAIGN AGAINST THE MODEL WEST GERMANY
[Reports]. — [Bochum] : Campaign against the Model West Germany
Nr.4: The Stammheim death. — [1977]. — 23p

PRISONERS — Great Britain
GREAT BRITAIN. Research and Advisory Group on the Long-Term Prison System
Special units for long-term prisoners: regimes, management and research : a report. — London : H.M.S.O., 1987. — 84p. — *Chairman: S. G. Norris*

GREAT BRITAIN. Working Group on the Review of the Role of the Probation Service in Adult Establishments
Report of the Working Group on the Review of the Role of the Probation Service in Adult Establishments. — [London : Home Office, Prison Department, 1985]. — 1v.(various pagings). — *Chairman: B.G. Chaplin*

PRISON REFORM TRUST
The remand explosion. — London : Prison Reform Trust, 1987. — 7p. — (Remand project paper ; no.10)

Prisoners' information pack. — London : Prison Reform Trust, 1986. — 10 leaflets

PRISONERS — Great Britain — Mortality
SCRATON, Phil
In the arms of the law : coroner's courts deaths in custody / Phil Scraton and Kathryn Chadwick. — London : Pluto, 1987. — [160]p

PRISONERS — India
CHADHA, Kumkum
The Indian jail : a contemporary document / Kumkum Chadha. — New Delhi : Vikas Pub. House, c1983. — viii, 251 p.. — *Includes statistical tables*

PRISONERS — India — Assam
Crime perspective in north-east India / edited by B. Datta Ray, D. N. Majumdar, D. Doley. — New Delhi : Omsons Publications, 1986. — vi,111p. — *Bibliography: p[105]-108*

PRISONERS — India — Meghalaya
Crime perspective in north-east India / edited by B. Datta Ray, D. N. Majumdar, D. Doley. — New Delhi : Omsons Publications, 1986. — vi,111p. — *Bibliography: p[105]-108*

PRISONERS — Scotland
MCKINLAY, Paul
Scottish prisons : lift the lid / Paul McKinlay. — Edinburgh : Fight Racism! Fight Imperialism!, 1986. — 39p

PRISONERS — United States — Psychology
POLLOCK, Joycelyn M.
Sex and supervision : guarding male and female inmates / Joycelyn M. Pollock ; foreword by Elaine A. Lord. — New York : Greenwood Press, 1986. — xiv, 160 p.. — (Contributions in criminology and penology ; no. 12). — *Includes index. — Bibliography: p. [155]-157*

PRISONERS, FOREIGN — Netherlands
BRAND-KOOLEN, M. J. M.
Migrants in detention / Maria Brand-Koolen. — The Hague : : Research and Documentation Centre, Ministry of Justice, 1985. — [32]p. — ([Reports, papers, articles] ; 81). — *Bibliography: p27-29*

PRISONERS OF WAR — Belgium
VLAEMYNCK, Carlos H.
Naar Engeland gedeporteerd : Vlaamse geïnterneerden of het eiland Man 1940-1945 / Carlos H. Vlaemynck. — Antwerpen : De Nederlandsche Boekhandel, 1984. — 80p. — *Bibliography: p75-76*

PRISONERS OF WAR — Isle of Man
VLAEMYNCK, Carlos H.
Naar Engeland gedeporteerd : Vlaamse geïnterneerden of het eiland Man 1940-1945 / Carlos H. Vlaemynck. — Antwerpen : De Nederlandsche Boekhandel, 1984. — 80p. — *Bibliography: p75-76*

PRISONERS OF WAR — United States
Der Ruf : Zeitung der deutschen Kriegsgefangenen in USA. — München ; London : K. G. Saur, 1945-1946. — *Monthly*

PRISONERS OF WAR, GERMAN
Der Ruf : Zeitung der deutschen Kriegsgefangenen in USA. — München ; London : K. G. Saur, 1945-1946. — *Monthly*

PRISONERS' WRITINGS
Wall tappings : an anthology of writings by women prisoners / [compiled] by Judith A. Scheffler. — Boston : Northeastern University Press, c1986. — p. cm. — *Bibliography: p*

PRISONS — Political aspects — Great Britain
Politics and prisons : Prison Reform Trust lectures 1985-86 / Robert Maclennan...[et al.]. — London : Prison Reform Trust, 1986. — 54p

PRISONS — California — Alcatraz — Rules and practice
UNITED STATES PENITENTIARY, ALCATRAZ, CALIFORNIA
Regulations for inmates : U.S.P., Alcatraz : revised 1956. — [San Francisco?] : Golden Gate National Parks Association, 1983. — 19 leaves. — *Cover title: Institution rules and regulations. — Reproduction of 1956 original*

PRISONS — Canada
GAMBERG, Herbert
The illusion of prison reform : corrections in Canada / Herbert Gamberg and Anthony Thomson. — New York : P. Lang, c1984. — 161 p.. — (American university studies. Series XI. Anthropology/sociology ; vol. 5). — *Bibliography: p. [145]-161*

PRISONS — Great Britain
CONSERVATIVE STUDY GROUP ON CRIME
Prison. — London : Conservative Study Group on Crime, 1986. — 16p

GREAT BRITAIN. Research and Advisory Group on the Long-Term Prison System
Special units for long-term prisoners: regimes, management and research : a report. — London : H.M.S.O., 1987. — 84p. — *Chairman: S. G. Norris*

Law and order prospects for the future / Malcolm Rifkind [et al.]. — Edinburgh : University of Edinburgh. Department of Christian Ethics and Practical Theology, 1986. — 82p. — (Occasional papers / University of Edinburgh. Department of Christian Ethics and Practical Theology ; no.10)

Politics and prisons : Prison Reform Trust lectures 1985-86 / Robert Maclennan...[et al.]. — London : Prison Reform Trust, 1986. — 54p

SHAW, Stephen
Conviction politics : a plan for penal policy / Stephen Shaw. — London : Fabian Society, 1987. — 25 p. — (Fabian tract ; 522)

STERN, Vivien
Bricks of shame : Britain's prisons / Vivien Stern. — Harmondsworth : Penguin, 1987. — 309p. — (Penguin special)

PRISONS — Great Britain — History — Bibliography
WALKER, Christine
Howard to Hull : 200 years of British prisons. — [London : Home Office Library], 1978. — 8leaves

PRISONS — India
CHADHA, Kumkum
The Indian jail : a contemporary document / Kumkum Chadha. — New Delhi : Vikas Pub. House, c1983. — viii, 251 p.. — *Includes statistical tables*

PRISONS — Netherlands
VINSON, T
Impressions of the Dutch prison system / Professor T. Vinson, Ms. M. Brouwers and Ms. M. Sampiemon. — The Hague : Research and Documentation Centre, Ministry of Justice, 1985. — 43p. — ([Reports, papers, articles] ; 84)

PRISONS — Scotland
MCKINLAY, Paul
Scottish prisons : lift the lid / Paul McKinlay. — Edinburgh : Fight Racism! Fight Imperialism!, 1986. — 39p

PRISONS — United States
GIALLOMBARDO, Rose
Society of women : a study of a women's prison / Rose Giallombardo. — New York ; London : Wiley, [1966]. — viii,248p

PRISONS — United States — Officials and employees
POLLOCK, Joycelyn M.
Sex and supervision : guarding male and female inmates / Joycelyn M. Pollock ; foreword by Elaine A. Lord. — New York : Greenwood Press, 1986. — xiv, 160 p.. — (Contributions in criminology and penology ; no. 12). — *Includes index. — Bibliography: p. [155]-157*

ZIMMER, Lynn Etta
Women guarding men / Lynn E. Zimmer ; foreword by James B. Jacobs. — Chicago : University of Chicago Press, 1986. — xiv, 264 p.. — (Studies in crime and justice). — *Includes index. — Bibliography: p. 239-259*

PRIVACY, RIGHT OF — Legal status, laws, etc. — Quebec (Province)
La protection de la vie privée des personnes bénéficiant de lois sociales au Québec. — [Québec : Yvon Blais, c1983]. — 142p. — *1982 prix Charles-Coderre pour l'avancement du droit social, décernés par le Fonds Charles-Coderre de Services Sociaux du Montréal métropolitain. — Contient le premier, le deuxième et le troisième prix*

PRIVACY, RIGHT OF — Canada
CANADA
Personal information index / Canada. — Ottawa : Canadian Government Publishing Centre, 1986-. — *Annual*

PRIVACY, RIGHT OF — Great Britain
CAMPBELL, Duncan, 1952-
On the record : surveillance, computers and privacy : the inside story / Duncan Campbell and Steve Connor. — London : Joseph, 1986. — 347p,[8]p of plates. — *Includes index*

GREAT BRITAIN. Parliament. House of Commons. Library. Research Division
Data protection and privacy / Barry K. Winetrobe. — [London] : the Division, 1982. — 23p. — (Background paper ; no.107)

PRIVACY, RIGHT OF — United States
EATON, Joseph W
Card-carrying Americans : privacy, security, and the national ID card debate / Joseph W. Eaton. — Totowa, NJ : Rowman &Allanheld, 1986. — p. cm. — *Includes index*

LAUDON, Kenneth C.
Dossier society : value choices in the design of national information systems / Kenneth C. Laudon. — New York : Columbia University Press, 1986. — xi, 421 p.. — (CORPS (computing, organizations, policy, and society) series). — *Includes index. — Bibliography: p. [403]-414*

RICHARDS, David A. J
Toleration and the Constitution / David A.J. Richards. — New York : Oxford University Press, 1986. — p. cm. — *Bibliography: p*

PRIVACY, RIGHT OF — United States — History
HIXSON, Richard F
Privacy in a public society : human rights in conflict / Richard F. Hixson. — New York : Oxford University Press, 1987. — xvi, 255 p.. — *Includes index. — Bibliography: p. 231-245*

PRIVATE COMPANIES — Registration and transfer — England
WINE, Humphrey
Buying and selling private companies and businesses / Humphrey Wine. — 3rd ed. — London : Butterworths, 1986. — [260]p. — *Previous ed.: 1983. — Includes index*

PRIVATE COMPANIES — Germany (West)
OLIVER, M. C
The private company in Germany : a translation and commentary / M.C. Oliver, M.A. Barrister. — 2nd ed. — Deventer, Netherlands ; New York : Kluwer Law and Taxation Publishers, c1986. — p. cm. — (Series on international corporate law ; 2). — Includes English and German text of Gesetz betreffend die Gesellschaften mit beschränkter Haftung

PRIVATE EYE
Malice in Wonderland : Robert Maxwell v. Private Eye / reported by John Jackson ; introduced and with an epilogue by Robert Maxwell ; edited by Joe Haines and Peter Donnelly ; cartoons by Charles Griffin and David Langdon. — London : Macdonald, 1986. — 191p

PRIVATE HEALTH CARE See Health facilities, Proprietary

PRIVATE PLOT AGRICULTURE — Soviet Union
SHMELEV, G.
Personal subsidiary farming under socialism / G. Shmelev ; translated from the Russian. — Moscow : Progress Publishers, 1986. — 110p

PRIVATE PRACTICE — United States
IMBER, Jonathan B.
Abortion and the private practice of medicine / Jonathan B. Imber. — New Haven : Yale University Press, c1986. — xviii, 164 p.. — Includes index. — Bibliography: p. 147-160

PRIVATE SCHOOLS — Great Britain
JOHNSON, Daphne, 1927-
Private schools and state schools : two systems or one? / Daphne Johnson. — Milton Keynes : Open University, 1987. — [192]p. — Includes bibliography and index

PRIVATIZATION
ALBREKTSEN, H. N.
Privatisering et alternativ / H. N. Albrektsen. — Oslo : Elingaard, 1975. — 85p. — (Nå debatt ; nr.3). — Bibliography: p81-85

BROCLAWSKI, Jean-Pierre
Les privatisations á l'étranger : Royaume-Uni, RFA, Italié, Espagne, Japon / Jean-Pierre Broclawski, Guy Longueville, Pierre Uhel ; études coordonnées par Jean-Jacques Santini. — [Paris : La Documentation française, 1986]. — 143p. — (Notes et études documentaires ; no.4821)

PRIVATIZATION — Congresses
Innovation and entrepreneurship in organizations : strategies for competitiveness, deregulation, and privatization / edited by Richard M. Burton and Børge Obel. — Amsterdam ; New York : Elsevier ; New York, NY, U.S.A. : Distributors for the U.S. and Canada, Elsevier Science Pub. Co., 1986. — vii, 207 p.. — Chiefly papers presented at a seminar held at the European Institute for Advanced Studies in Management, Brussels, in May 1985. — "Has been published in a special issue of Technovation, vol 5 (1986), issues 1-3.". — Includes bibliographies and index

PRIVATIZATION — Canada
GILLEN, David W
Canadian airline deregulation and privatization : assessing effects and prospects / by David W. Gillen, Tae H. Oum, Michael W. Tretheway. — Vancouver, Canada : Centre for Transportation Studies, University of British Columbia, c1985. — vi, 300 p.. — Bibliography: p. 297-300

PRIVATIZATION — Great Britain
ASCHER, Kate
The politics of privatisation : contracting out public services / Kate Ascher. — Basingstoke : Macmillan Education, 1987. — xiv,293p. — (Public policy and politics). — Bibliography: p271-273. — Includes index

GREAT BRITAIN. Department of the Environment
The National Rivers Authority : the government's proposals for a public regulatory body in a privatised water industry. — [London : the Department], 1987. — 42p

GREAT BRITAIN. Parliament. House of Commons. Library. Research Division
Airports Bill (Bill 60 of 1985/86) / Priscilla Baines. — [London] : the Division, 1986. — 31p. — (Reference sheet ; no.86/4). — Bibliographical references: p27-31

GREAT BRITAIN. Parliament. House of Commons. Library. Research Division
The financing of nationalised industries / C. R. Barclay. — [London] : the Division, 1980. — 26p. — (Background paper ; no.88). — Includes bibliographical references

GREAT BRITAIN. Parliament. House of Commons. Library. Research Division
The financing of nationalised industries / C. R. Barclay. — [New ed.]. — [London] : the Division, 1982. — 21p. — (Background paper ; no.103)

GREAT BRITAIN. Parliament. House of Commons. Library. Research Division
The Gas Bill (Bill 13 of 1985/6) / Christopher Barclay, Caroline Gilmour. — [London] : the Division, 1985. — 30p. — (Reference sheet ; no.85/10). — Bibliography: p28-30

GREAT BRITAIN. Parliament. House of Commons. Library. Research Division
Oil and Gas (Enterprise) Bill / [B. L. Miller]. — [London] : the Division, 1982. — 17p. — (Reference sheet ; no.82/1). — Bibliography: p15-17

GREAT BRITAIN. Parliament. House of Commons. Library. Research Division
Privatisation / Christopher Barclay. — [London] : the Division, 1983. — 14p. — (Background paper ; no.119). — Includes bibliographical references

GREAT BRITAIN. Parliament. House of Commons. Library. Research Division
Privatisation / Christopher Barclay. — [Rev.ed]. — [London] : the Division, 1984. — 21p. — (Background paper ; no.140). — Includes bibliographical references

GREAT BRITAIN. Parliament. House of Commons. Library. Research Division
Privatisation / Christopher Barclay, Neil Marsland. — [Rev. ed]. — [London] : the Division, 1985. — 29p. — (Background paper ; no.166). — Includes bibliographical references

GREAT BRITAIN. Parliament. House of Commons. Library. Research Division
Privatisation / Christopher Barclay. — Rev. ed. — [London] : the Division, 1986. — 26p. — (Background paper ; no.183)

GREAT BRITAIN. Parliament. House of Commons. Library. Research Division
Telecommunications Bill 1983/84 (Bill 5) / Christopher Barclay. — [London] : the Division, 1983. — 15p. — (Reference sheet ; no.83/11). — Bibliography: p11-13

GREAT BRITAIN. Parliament. House of Commons. Library. Research Division
Telecommunications Bill (Bill 15) / Christopher Barclay. — [London] : the Division, 1982. — 12p. — (Reference sheet ; no.82/15). — Bibliography: p11-12

HEUVERMANN, Arnulf
Die Liberalisierung des britischen Telekommunikationsmarktes / Arnulf Heuermann, Karl-Heinz Neumann. — Berlin : Springer-Verlag, 1985. — xii,401p. — (Schriftenreihe des Wissenschaftlichen Instituts für Kommunikationsdienste der Deutschen Bundespost ; Bd.3). — Bibliography: p [395]-401

LABOUR RESEARCH DEPARTMENT
Privatisation : paying the price. — London : LRD Publications, 1987. — 48p

Privatisation and regulation : the UK experience / edited by John Kay, Colin Mayer and David Thompson. — Oxford : Clarendon, 1986. — [288]p. — Includes bibliography

REDWOOD, John
Equity for everyman : new ways to widen ownership / John Redwood. — London : Centre for Policy Studies, 1986. — 39p. — (Policy study ; no.74)

PRIVATIZATION — Norway
ALBREKTSEN, H. N.
Privatisering et alternativ / H. N. Albrektsen. — Oslo : Elingaard, 1975. — 85p. — (Nå debatt ; nr.3). — Bibliography: p81-85

PRO-LIFE MOVEMENT — New York (State)
SPITZER, Robert J.
The Right to Life movement and third party politics / Robert J. Spitzer. — New York : Greenwood Press, c1987. — xii, 154 p.. — (Contributions in political science ; no. 160). — Includes index. — Bibliography: p. [141]-148

PROBABILITIES
BEAUMONT, G. P.
Probability and random variables / G.P. Beaumont. — Chichester : Ellis Horwood, 1986. — 345p. — (Ellis Horwood series in mathematics and its applications). — Text on lining papers. — Includes index

DACUNHA-CASTELLE, Didier
[Probabilités et statistiques. English]. Probability and statistics / Didier Dacunha-Castelle, Marie Duflo ; translated by David McHale. — New York : Springer-Verlag, c1986-. — p. cm. — 2 vols. — Translation of: Probabilités et statistiques. — Includes index. — Bibliography: v. 1, p

KOLMOGOROV, A. N.
Foundations of the theory of probability / by A.N. Kolmogorov ; translation edited by Nathan Morrison ; with an added bibliography by A.T. Bharucha-Reid. — 2nd ed. — New York : Chelsea Publishing, 1956. — viii, 84p

KYBURG, Henry E.
The logical foundations of statistical inference / by Henry E. Kyburg. — Dordrecht ; Boston : Reidel, 1974. — ix, 427 p.. — (Synthese library ; vol.65). — Includes bibliographical references and index

ROSENKRANTZ, Roger D.
Foundations and applications of inductive probability / R.D. Rosenkrantz. — Atascadero, Calif. : Ridgeview Publishing Co., 1981

SILVEY, S. D.
Statistical inference / S.D. Silvey. — [1st ed.], reprinted with corrections. — London : Chapman and Hall, 1975. — 3-192p. — (Monographs on applied probability and statistics). — Originally published: Harmondsworth : Penguin, 1970. — Bibliography: p.189-190. — Includes index

PROBATION — California
PETERSILIA, Joan
Prison versus probation in California : implications for crime and offender recidivism / Joan Petersilia, Susan Turner, with Joyce Peterson ; prepared for the National Institute of Justice, U.S. Department of Justice. — Santa Monica, CA. : Rand, [1986]. — xix, 63 p.. — "July 1986.". — "R-3323-NIJ.". — Bibliography: p. 59-63

PROBATION — England
JARVIS, F. V.
Jarvis's probation officers' manual. — 4th ed. / W.R. Weston. — London : Butterworths, 1987. — [350]p. — Previous ed.: 1980. — Includes index

PROBATION — England — Sheffield (South Yorkshire)

CELNICK, Anne
Hallam Project Evaluation Report. — [Sheffield] : Research Unit [of] South Yorkshire Probation Service, 1984. — ix,407p. — (Research Report / South Yorkshire Probation Service. Research Unit ; No.4). — Bibliography: p393-400

PROBATION — Great Britain

FEATHERSTONE, Bríd
"There is an alternative" : the promotional work of the probation service and social services departments : a review and guide to better practice / Bríd Featherstone. — London : Prison Reform Trust, 1987. — 67p. — Bibliography: p67-68

NATIONAL ASSOCIATION OF PROBATION OFFICERS
Probation; direction, innovation and change in the 1980's : proceedings of a professional conference held on 11-13 July 1984 at the University of York. — [London] : National Association of Probation Officers, 1984. — 39p

NATIONAL ASSOCIATION OF PROBATION OFFICERS
Probation - from court to community : proceedings of a professional conference held on 17-19 July 1985 at the University of Lancaster. — [London] : National Association of Probation Officers, 1985. — 41p. — Bibliographies

Probation and the community : a practice and policy reader / edited by John Harding. — London : Tavistock, 1987. — vii,248p. — Includes bibliographies and index

PROBATION — United States — Addresses, essays, lectures

Probation and justice : reconsideration of mission / edited by Patrick D. McAnany, Doug Thomson, David Fogel. — Cambridge, Mass. : Oelgeschlager, Gunn & Hain, c1984. — xi, 411 p.. — Includes bibliographies and index

PROBATION OFFICERS — Great Britain

GREAT BRITAIN. Working Group on the Review of the Role of the Probation Service in Adult Establishments
Report of the Working Group on the Review of the Role of the Probation Service in Adult Establishments. — [London : Home Office, Prison Department, 1985]. — 1v.(various pagings). — Chairman: B.G. Chaplin

PROBLEM CHILDREN

HERBERT, Martin
Behavioural treatment of children with problems : a practice manual / Martin Herbert. — 2nd ed. — London : Academic Press, 1987. — [250]p. — Previous ed.: published as Behavioural treatment of problem children. 1981. — Includes bibliography and index

PROBLEM FAMILIES — Counseling of — United States

Violence in the home : interdisciplinary perspectives / edited by Mary Lystad. — New York : Brunner/Mazel, c1986. — xxxv, 322 p.. — Includes bibliographies and indexes

PROBLEM FAMILIES — United States

EDELMAN, Marian Wright
Families in peril : an agenda for social change / Marian Wright Edelman. — Cambridge, Mass. : Harvard University Press, 1987. — xii, 127 p.. — (The W.E.B. Du Bois lectures ; 1986). — Includes index. — Bibliography: p. [115]-122

PROBLEM FAMILIES — United States — Addresses, essays, lectures

MOYNIHAN, Daniel P
Family and nation : the Godkin lectures, Harvard University / Daniel Patrick Moynihan. — 1st ed. — San Diego : Harcourt Brace Jovanovich, c1986. — xii, 207 p.. — Includes index. — Bibliography: p. 195-197

PROBLEM SOLVING

Applications of cognitive psychology : problem solving, education, and computing / edited by Dale E. Berger, Kathy Pezdek, William P. Banks. — Hillsdale, N.J. : L. Erlbaum Associates, 1987. — xii, 235 p.. — Includes bibliographies and indexes

GUNDERSON, Keith
Mentality and machines / Keith Gunderson. — 2nd ed. — London : Croom Helm, 1985. — xxii,260p. — Bibliography: p[249]-255

WETZEL, Gregory F.
The algorithmic process : an introduction to problem solving / Gregory F. Wetzel, William G. Bulgren. — Chicago : Science Research Associates, c1985. — p. cm. — Includes index. — Bibliography: p

PROCEDURE (JEWISH LAW)

QUINT, Emanuel B.
Jewish jurisprudence : its sources and modern applications / Emanuel B. Quint and Neil S. Hecht. — Chur : Harwood Academic Publishers
Vol.2. — 1986. — xvii,237p

PROCEDURE (LAW) — Great Britain

DEIGHAN, Maurice
County Court practice and procedure / by Maurice Deigham. — London : Fourmat, 1980. — xv, 125p. — (Lawyers' practice and procedure)

PRODUCE TRADE

BODY, Richard
Farming in the clouds / Richard Body. — London : Temple Smith, 1984. — 161p

PRODUCE TRADE — Government policy — Philippines

BAUTISTA, Romeo M.
Production incentives in Philippine agriculture : effects of trade and exchange rate policies / Romeo M. Bautista. — Washington, D.C. : International Food Policy Research Institute, 1987. — p. cm. — (Research report ; 59). — Bibliography: p

PRODUCE TRADE — Government policy — United States

JOHNSON, D. Gale
Agricultural policy and trade : adjusting domestic programs in an international framework : a task force report to the Trilateral Commission / authors, D. Gale Johnson, Kenzo Hemmi, Pierre Lardinois ; special consultants, T.K. Warley, P.A.J. Wijnmaalen. — New York : New York University Press, 1985. — xi, 132 p.. — (The Triangle papers ; 29). — Includes bibliographies

PRODUCE TRADE — Law and legislation — Great Britain

GREAT BRITAIN. Parliament. House of Commons. Library. Research Division
Agricultural Marketing Bill (Bill 7 of 1982-83) / [Priscilla Baines]. — [London] : the Division, [1982]. — 8p. — (Reference sheet ; no.82/12)

PRODUCE TRADE — Canada

NADEAU, Bertrand
Britain's entry into the European Economic Community and its effect on Canada's agricultural exports / Bertrand Nadeau. — Montreal : The Institute for Research on Public Policy/LInstitut de recherches politiques, 1985. — xx,111p. — (Essays in international economics). — Foreword and summary in English and French. — Bibliography: p95-100

PRODUCE TRADE — Europe, Eastern

DEUTSCH, Robert
The food revolution in the Soviet Union and Eastern Europe / Robert Deutsch. — Boulder, Colo. ; London : Westview Press, 1986. — xxi, 256p. — (Westview special studies on the Soviet Union and Eastern Europe). — Includes index. — Bibliography: p.149-241

PRODUCE TRADE — Hong Kong

Long-term economic and agricultural commodity projections for Hong Kong, 1970, 1975, and 1980. — Jerusalem : Publications Services Division of the Israel Program for Scientific Translations for the U.S. Department of Agriculture, 1969. — xiv,248p. — Contents: A contract study...for the United States Department of Agriculture under the principal research directorship of Anthony M. Tang

PRODUCE TRADE — Soviet Union

DEUTSCH, Robert
The food revolution in the Soviet Union and Eastern Europe / Robert Deutsch. — Boulder, Colo. ; London : Westview Press, 1986. — xxi, 256p. — (Westview special studies on the Soviet Union and Eastern Europe). — Includes index. — Bibliography: p.149-241

PRODUCE TRADE — Tanzania — Dar Es Salaam

SPORREK, Anders
Food marketing and urban growth in Dar Es Salaam / by Anders Sporrek. — Lund, Sweden : Royal University of Lund, Dept. of Geography ; Malmö, Sweden : CWK Gleerup, 1985. — 200 p.. — (Lund studies in geography. Ser. B. Human geography ; no. 51). — Bibliography: p. 193-200

PRODUCER COOPERATIVES

Labor-owned firms and workers' cooperatives / edited by Sune Jansson and Ann-Britt Hellmark. — Aldershot : Gower, c1986. — ix,162p

PRODUCER COOPERATIVES — European Economic Community countries

Prospects for workers' co-operatives. — Luxembourg : Office for Official Publications of the European Communities. — At head of title page: Commission of the European Communities
Vol. 1: Overview / by Mutual Aid Center, London. — 1984. — 1v.(various pagings)

Prospects for workers' co-operatives. — Luxembourg : Office for Official Publications of the European Communities. — At head of title page: Commission of the European Communities
Vol. 2: Country reports - first series : Denmark; Greece; Republic of Ireland; Netherlands; Spain: United Kingdom / by Mutual Aid Center, London. — 1984. — 1v.(various pagings)

Prospects for workers' co-operatives. — Luxembourg : Office for Official Publications of the European Communities. — At head of title page: Commission of the European Communities
Vol. 3: Country reports - second series : Belgium; France; Federal Republic of Germany; Italy / by Ten Cooperative de Conseils, Paris. — 1984. — 1v.(various pagings)

PRODUCER COOPERATIVES — France

Forms of organisation, type of employment, working conditions and industrial relations in co-operatives, any collectiveness or other self-managing structures of the EEC. — Luxembourg : Office for Official Publications of the European Communities, 1986. — i,119,C.102p. — (Programme of research and actions on the development of the labour market). — At head of title: Commission of the European Communities

PRODUCER COOPERATIVES — Great Britain

BERRY, John, 19---
Co-op management and employment / John Berry and Mark Roberts. — London : ICOM, 1984. — 83p. — (Running a workers co-op)

COCKERTON, Peter
The workers co-operative handbook : a comprehensive guide to setting up a workers co-operative / Peter Cockerton and Anna Whyatt. — New rev. ed. — London : ICOM, 1986. — 124p. — Previous ed.: 1984

PRODUCER COOPERATIVES — Great Britain *continuation*

Forms of organisation, type of employment, working conditions and industrial relations in co-operatives, any collectiveness or other self-managing structures of the EEC. — Luxembourg : Office for Official Publications of the European Communities, 1986. — i,119,C.102p. — (Programme of research and actions on the development of the labour market). — *At head of title: Commission of the European Communities*

PRODUCER COOPERATIVES — Great Britain — Employees

SIKKING, Maggi
Co-ops with a difference : worker co-ops for people with special needs / Maggi Sikking. — London : ICOM, 1986. — 65p. — *Bibliography: p61-62*

PRODUCER COOPERATIVES — Italy

Forms of organisation, type of employment, working conditions and industrial relations in co-operatives, any collectiveness or other self-managing structures of the EEC. — Luxembourg : Office for Official Publications of the European Communities, 1986. — i,119,C.102p. — (Programme of research and actions on the development of the labour market). — *At head of title: Commission of the European Communities*

PRODUCER COOPERATIVES — Northwest, Pacific — Management — Employee participation — Case studies

GREENBERG, Edward S.
Workplace democracy : the political effects of participation / Edward S. Greenberg. — Ithaca : Cornell University Press, 1986. — p. cm. — *Includes index.* — *Bibliography: p*

PRODUCER COOPERATIVES — Wales

RUBERY, Jill
Inflation, employment and income distribution in the recession / by Jill Rubery, Roger Tarling, Frank Wilkinson. — Luxembourg : Office for Official Publications of the European Communities, 1985. — iii,281p. — (Programme of research and action on the development of the labour market). — *At head of title: Commission of the European Communities*

PRODUCT COUNTERFEITING

FREEMANTLE, Brian
The steal : counterfeiting and industrial espionage / Brian Freemantle. — London : Joseph, 1986. — [256]p. — *Includes bibliography and index*

PRODUCT MANAGEMENT

IRELAND, Norman J.
Product differentiation and non-price competition / Norman Ireland. — Oxford : Basil Blackwell, 1987. — 1v.. — *Includes bibliography and index*

PRODUCT SAFETY

ABBOTT, Howard
Product liability : an exercise in corporate survival / by Howard Abbott. — London : Lloyd's of London, 1978

PRODUCT SAFETY — Organisation for Economic Co-operation and Development countries

ORGANISATION FOR ECONOMIC CO-OPERATION AND DEVELOPMENT. Committee on Consumer Policy
Product safety : developing and implementing measures / report by the OECD Committee on Consumer Policy. — Paris : Organisation for Economic Co-operation and Development, 1987. — 63p. — *Bibliographical references: p.8*

PRODUCTION (ECONOMIC THEORY)

BIASCA, Rodolfo Eduardo
Productividad : un enfoque integral del tema / Rodolfo Eduardo Biasca. — Buenos Aires : Ediciones Macchi, 1984. — 728p

DZIUBIK, S. D.
Rynok sredstv proizvodstva v sisteme planomerno organizovannoi ekonomiki / S. D. Dziubik. — L'vov : Vyshcha shkola, 1984. — 157p

OZHEREL'EV, O. I.
Sovershenstvovanie proizvodstvennykh otnoshenii / O. I. Ozherel'ev. — Moskva : Ekonomika, 1986. — 253p

POLIAKOV, R. I.
Obobshchestvlenie proizvodstva v usloviiakh razvitogo sotsializma / R. I. Poliakov. — Leningrad : Izd-vo Leningradskogo universiteta, 1984. — 222p

Production, circulation et monnaie / [par] R. Arena...[et al.] ; introduction: R. Arena, A. Graziani [et] post-face: J. Kregel. — Paris : Presses Universitaires de France, 1985. — 435p. — (Travaux et Recherches du Laboratoire Associé No.301. C.N.R.S.-Université de Nice). — *"Le présent ouvrage est né d'une rencontre...organisée par le L.A.T.A.P.S.E.S. (UA CNRS N°301), les 1 er et 2 février 1984 à l'Université de Nice".* — *Bibliograhie: p428-430*

PRODUCTION ENGINEERING

Manufacturing matters : the monthly newspaper of the Institution of Production Engineers. — No.1 (Nov.1983)-. — London (66 Little Ealing La., W5 4XX) : The Institution, 1983-. — v.. — *Description based on: No.2 (Dec. 1983)*

PRODUCTION ENGINEERING — Data processing

BESSANT, J. R.
Microprocessors in production processes / John Bessant. — London : Policy Studies Institute, 1982. — 134p. — (P.S.I. ; no.609)

PRODUCTION FUNCTIONS (ECONOMIC THEORY)

HEATHFIELD, David F.
An introduction to cost and production functions / David F. Heathfield and Sören Wibe. — Basingstoke : Macmillan, 1987. — 193p. — *Bibliography: p183-189.* — *Includes index*

RUBINOV, A. M.
Matematicheskie modeli rasshirennogo vosproizvodstva / A. M. Rubinov. — Leningrad : Nauka, Leningradskoe otdelenie, 1983. — 186p. — *Bibliography: p183-[185]*

PRODUCTION FUNCTIONS (ECONOMIC THEORY) — Case studies

Technology and employment in industry : a case study approach / edited by A.S. Bhalla ; preword by Amartya Sen. — 3rd, revised and enlarged ed. — Geneva : International Labour Office, 1985. — xviii,436p. — (A WEP Study)

PRODUCTION MANAGEMENT — Data processing

Information pack including bibliography on advanced manufacturing technology / compiled by Lucy Hamilton and John Devine ; foreword by Peter Willows. — London : Institution of Mechanical Engineers, 1986. — vi,98p. — (Information Pack ; 1). — *Annotated bibliography: p47-98*

PRODUCTION MANAGEMENT — Japan

SCHONBERGER, Richard J.
Japanese manufacturing techniques : nine hidden lessons in simplicity / Richard J. Schonberger. — New York : Free Press ; London : Collier Macmillan, c1982. — xii,260p . — *Bibliography: p247-251.* — *Includes index*

PRODUCTS LIABILITY

ABBOTT, Howard
Product liability : an exercise in corporate survival / by Howard Abbott. — London : Lloyd's of London, 1978

PRODUCTS LIABILITY — Agent Orange — United States

SCHUCK, Peter H
Agent Orange on trial : mass toxic disasters in the courts / Peter H. Schuck. — Cambridge, Mass. : Belknap Press of Harvard University Press, 1986. — ix, 347 p.. — *Includes index.* — *Bibliography: p. [301]-335*

PRODUCTS LIABILITY — Congresses

Comparative product liability / edited by C. J. Miller. — London : British Institute of International and Comparative Law, 1986. — xv,198p. — (United Kingdom comparative law series ; Vol.6). — *Based on revised papers and contributions originally submitted to a colloquium held by the United Kingdom National Committee for Comparative Law at the University of Edinburgh*

PRODUCTS LIABILITY — Great Britain

GRIFFITHS, William Hugh Griffiths, Baron
Developments in the law of product liability : being the presidential address of Lord Griffiths, president of the Holdsworth Club of the Faculty of Laws in the Univeristy of Birmingham, 1986-1987. — birmingham : The Holdsworth Club of the University of Birmingham, 1987. — 17p. — (The Holdsworth Club)

PROFESSIONAL EDUCATION — France — Champagne-Ardenne

Programme régional de formation professionnelle et d'apprentissage 1986-1987. — [Châlons-sur-Marne : Conseil régional], 1986. — 224p. — *Cover title*

PROFESSIONAL EDUCATION — Great Britain — Directories

A Dictionary of British qualifications : abbreviations and qualifying bodies. — London : Kogan Page, 1985. — [120]p

PROFESSIONAL ETHICS

Ethics in planning / edited by Martin Wachs. — New Brunswick, N.J. : Center for Urban Policy Research, c1985. — xxi, 372 p.. — *Includes index.* — *Bibliography: p. 356-365*

PROFESSIONS

MAY, William F.
The end of professionalism? / William F. May, Gilbert Smith [and] Alastair V. Campbell. — Edinburgh : Department of Christian Ethics and Practical Theology, 1985. — [42p]. — (Occasional paper / University of Edinburgh. Department of Christian Ethics and Practical Theology ; no.6). — *Contents: Adversarialism in America in the professions/William F. May - The challenge to professionalism/Gilbert Smith - Professionalism - a theological perspective/Alastair V. Campbell*

RAPOPORT, Rhona
Dual-career families re-examined : new integrations of work & family / Rhona & Robert N. Rapoport. — New York : Harper & Row, 1977, c1976. — 382 p. — (Harper colophon books ; CN 521). — *Sequel to the author's Dual-career families.* — *Bibliography: p. [373]-382*

PROFESSIONS — Law and legislation — European Economic Community countries

CRAYENCOUR, J.-P. de
The professions in the European Community : towards freedom of movement and mutual recognition of qualifications / J.-P. de Crayencour. — Luxembourg : Office for Official Publications of the European Communities, 1981. — 137p. — (The European perspectives series)

LASOK, Dominik
The professions and services in the European Economic Community / by D. Lasok. — Deventer, The Netherlands ; New York : Kluwer Law and Taxation Publishers, c1986. — p. cm

PROFESSIONS — Social aspects — England

The Professions in early modern England / edited by Wilfrid Prest. — London : Croom Helm, c1987. — [240]p. — *Includes index*

PROFESSIONS — Social aspects — United States — Addresses, essays, lectures

Professions and professional ideologies in America / edited by Gerald L. Geison. — Chapel Hill : University of North Carolina Press, c1983. — x, 147 p.. — *Includes bibliographical references and index*

PROFESSIONS — Sociological aspects

SAKS, Michael Paul
Professions and the public interest : the response of the medical profession to acupuncture in nineteenth and twentieth century Britain / Michael Paul Saks. — 676 leaves. — *PhD(Arts) 1986 LSE*

PROFESSIONS — Egypt — History

EGGER, Vernon
A Fabian in Egypt : Salāmah Mūsá and the rise of the professional classes in Egypt, 1909-1939 / Vernon Egger. — Lanham, MD : University Press of America, c1986. — xvi, 255 p.. — *Includes index.* — *Bibliography: p. 237-252*

PROFESSIONS — England — History

The Professions in early modern England / edited by Wilfrid Prest. — London : Croom Helm, c1987. — [240]p. — *Includes index*

PROFESSIONS — France — Statistical methods

SEYS, Baudouin
De l'ancien code à la nouvelle nomenclature des catégories socioprofessionnelles : étude méthodologique / Baudouin Seys. — Paris : I.N.S.E.E., 1986. — 203p. — (Archives et documents / Institut national de la statistique et des études économiques ; no.156). — *Bibliography: p.202-203*

PROFESSIONS — Soviet Union

ZIUZIN, D. I.
Kachestvo podgotovki spetsialistov kak sotsial'naia problema / D. I. Ziuzin. — Moskva : Nauka, 1978. — 164p

PROFESSIONS — Soviet Union — Sociological aspects

Sotsial'noe razvitie sovetskoi intelligentsii / otv. redaktor R. G. Ianovskii. — Moskva : Nauka, 1986. — 335p

PROFIT — Government policy — Great Britain

GREAT BRITAIN. Department of Prices and Consumer Protection
Safeguards under clause 9 of the Price Commission Bill : a consultative document. — [London : the Department, 1977]. — [7]p

PROFIT — Great Britain

HUGHES, John, 1927-
Nowt for nowt? or who got what, when? / John Hughes. — Nottingham : Institute for Workers Control, 1986. — 14p

PROFIT — Great Britain — Accounting

REVIEW BOARD FOR GOVERNMENT CONTRACTS
Report on the fifth general review of the profit formula for non-competitive government contracts. — London : H.M.S.O., 1987. — x,80p. — *Chairman: Sir Max Williams*

PROFIT — Norway

HALVORSEN, Ragnar
Lønnsomhetskrav : Strategi for lønnsom vekst sett fra Dyno Industrier A.S' side / Ragnar Halvorsen. — Bergen : Norges handelshøyskole, 1985. — 34p. — (Kristofer Lehmkuhl Forelesning ; 1985)

PROFIT — Organisation for Economic Co-operation and Development countries — Mathematical models

CHAN-LEE, James H.
Pure profit rates and Tobin's q in nine OECD countries / by James H. Chan-Lee. — [Paris] : OECD, 1986. — 41p. — (Working papers / OECD. Department of Economics and Statistics ; no.34). — *Bibliographical references: p.39-41*

PROFIT-SHARING

BLANCHFLOWER, D. G.
Profit related pay : prose discovered? / D. Blanchflower and A. Oswald. — London : Centre for Labour Economics, London School of Economics, 1987. — 15p. — (Discussion paper / London School of Economics and Political Science. Centre for Labour Economics ; no.287). — *Bibliography: p15*

BLANCHFLOWER, D. G.
Profit-sharing : can it work? / D. G. Blanchflower and A. J. Oswald. — London : Centre for Labour Economics, London School of Economics, 1986. — 28p. — (Discussion paper / London School of Economics and Political Science. Centre for Labour Economics ; no.255). — *Bibliography: p24-28*

BLANCHFLOWER, D. G.
Shares for employees : a test of their effects / D. G. Blanchflower and A. J. Oswald. — London : Centre for Labour Economics, London School of Economics, 1987. — 36p. — (Discussion paper / London School of Economics and Political Science. Centre for Labour Economics ; no.273). — *Bibliography: p34-36*

BRADLEY, Keith
Profit sharing in the retail trade sector : the relative performance of the John Lewis partnership / K. Bradley and S. Estrin. — London : Centre for Labour Economics, London School of Economics, 1987. — 30p. — (Discussion paper / London School of Economics and Political Science. Centre for Labour Economics ; no.279). — *Bibliography: p20-21*

PROFIT SHARING

ESTRIN, Saul
Will profit—sharing work / Saul Estrin and Sushil Wadhwani. — London : Employment Institute, 1986. — 36p. — *Bibliography: p34-35*

PROFIT-SHARING

WADHWANI, Sushil B.
Profit sharing as a cure for unemployment : some doubts / S. Wadhwani. — London : Centre for Labour Economics, London School of Economics, 1986. — 40p. — (Discussion paper / London School of Economics and Political Science. Centre for Labour Economics ; no.253). — *Bibliography: p38-40*

WEITZMAN, Martin L.
The case for profit—sharing / Martin L. Weitzman. — London : Employment Institute, 1986. — 32p

PROFIT SHARING — Taxation — Great Britain

GREAT BRITAIN. Board of Inland Revenue. Press Office
Profit sharing : tax relief. — London : the Board, 1978. — 13p. — (Press release / Inland Revenue Press Office)

PROFIT-SHARING — Great Britain

BRADLEY, Keith
The success story of the John Lewis Partnership : a study of comparative performance : a research report / prepared by Keith Bradley and Saul Estrin for Partnership Research Ltd.. — London : [Partnership Research Ltd.], 1986. — 29 leaves

ESTRIN, Saul
The micro-economic effects of profit-sharing : the British experience / S. Estrin and N. Wilson. — London : London School of Economics. Centre for Labour Economics, 1986. — 41p. — (Discussion paper / London School of Economics and Political Science. Centre for Labour Economics ; no.247)

WADHWANI, Sushil B.
Profit-sharing and Meade's discriminating labour-capital partnerships : a review article / S. Wadhwani. — London : Centre for Labour Economics, London School of Economics, 1987. — 42p. — (Discussion paper / London School of Economics and Political Science. Centre for Labour Economics ; no.276). — *Bibliography: p38-42*

PROFUMO, JOHN D.

KNIGHTLEY, Phillip
An affair of state : the Profumo case and the framing of Stephen Ward / by Phillip Knightley and Caroline Kennedy. — London : Cape, 1987. — [304]p. — *Includes bibliography and index*

PROGESSIVE CONSERVATIVE PARTY OF CANADA

CONRAD, Margaret
George Nowlan : Maritime Conservative in national politics / Margaret Conrad. — Toronto : University of Toronto Press, 1986. — xviii,357p. — *Notes: p[309]-343*

PROGRAM BUDGETING

WILDAVSKY, Aaron B
Budgeting : a comparative theory of budgetary processes / Aaron Wildavsky. — 2nd, rev. ed. — New Brunswick (U.S.A.) : Transaction Books, c1986. — xii, 403 p.. — *Includes bibliographies and index*

PROGRAMMING LANGUAGES (ELECTRONIC COMPUTERS)

MARCOTTY, Michael
Programming language landscape : syntax, semantics, and implementation / Michael Marcotty, Henry F. Ledgard. — 2nd ed. — Chicago : Science Research Associates, c1986. — xx, 569 p.. — *Rev. ed. of: The programming language landscape / Henry Ledgard. c1981.* — *Includes index.* — *Bibliography: p. 527-547*

STÜTTGEN, Heinrich J.
A hierarchical associative processing system / Heinrich J. Stüttgen. — Berlin ; New York : Springer-Verlag, c1985. — p. cm. — (Lecture notes in computer science ; 195). — *Bibliography: p*

PROGRAMMING LANGUAGES (ELECTRONIC COMPUTERS) — Semantics

IFIP WG 2.6 WORKING CONFERENCE ON DATA SEMANTICS (DS-1) (1985 : Hasselt)
Database semantics (DS-1) : proceedings of the IFIP WG 2.6 Working Conference on Data Semantics (DS-1) Hasselt, Belgium, 7-11 January, 1985 / edited by T.B. Steel, Jr., R. Meersman. — Amsterdam ; Oxford : North-Holland, 1986. — x,323p. — *Cover title: Database semantics.* — *Includes bibliographies*

PROGRAMMING (MATHEMATICS)

OKONJO-ADIGWE, Chiedu-Elue
Solution techniques for the multiple-vehicle travelling salesman problem / by Chiedu Elue Okonje-Adigwe. — 185 leaves. — *PhD (Econ) 1986 LSE*

PROGRESS

TODD, Emmanuel
The causes of progress : culture, authority and change / Emmanuel Todd ; translated by Richard Boulind. — Oxford : Basil Blackwell, 1987. — [iv,224]p. — (Family, sexuality and social relations in past times). — *Translation of: L'enfance du monde.* — *Includes bibliography and index*

PROGRESSIVE CONSERVATIVE PARTY OF CANADA
GRANATSTEIN, J. L
Sacred trust? : Brian Mulroney and the Conservative Party in power / by J.L. Granatstein, David Bercuson, William Young. — 1st ed. — Toronto, Canada : Doubleday Canada ; Garden City, N.Y. : Doubleday, 1986. — p. cm. — *Includes index*

PROGRESSIVE CONSERVATIVE PARTY OF ONTARIO
SPEIRS, Rosemary
Out of the blue : the fall of the Tory dynasty of Ontario / Rosemary Speirs. — Toronto : Macmillan of Canada, 1986. — xxii,246p

PROGRESSIVISM (UNITED STATES POLITICS)
TOBIN, Eugene M
Organize or perish : America's independent progressives, 1913-1933 / Eurgene M. Tobin. — Westport, Conn. ; London : Greenwood Press, c1986. — xiv, 279p. — (Contributions in American history ; no. 114). — *Includes index.* — *Bibliography: p [251]-260*

PROGRESSIVISM (UNITED STATES POLITICS) — Addresses, essays, lectures
MCCORMICK, Richard L
The party period and public policy : American politics from the Age of Jackson to the Progressive Era / Richard L. McCormick. — New York : Oxford University Press, 1986. — p. cm. — *Includes index*

PROHIBITED BOOKS — Bibliography
INDIA OFFICE LIBRARY AND RECORDS
Publications proscribed by the Government of India : a catalogue of the collections in the India Office Library and Records and the Department of Oriental Manuscripts and Printed Books, British Library Reference Division / edited by Graham Shaw and Mary Lloyd. — London : British Library, 1985. — [224]p. — *Includes index*

PROLETARIAT
Confrontation, class consciousness, and the labor process : studies in proletarian class formation / edited by Michael Hanagan and Charles Stephenson. — Westport, Conn. ; London : Greenwood Press, c1986. — viii, 261p. — (Contributions in labor studies ; no. 18). — *Includes index.* — *Bibliography: p.[241]-253*

PROLOG (COMPUTER PROGRAM LANGUAGE)
BRATKO, I.
Prolog programming for artificial intelligence / Ivan Bratko. — Wokingham : Addison-Wesley, 1986. — xvii,423p. — (International computer science series). — *Includes bibliographies and index*

PROPAGANDA
FOULKES, A. P.
Literature and propaganda / A.P. Foulkes. — London : Methuen, 1983. — viii,124p. — (New accents). — *Bibliography: p109-119.* — *Includes index*

GREAVES, Tony
[Leaflet delivery] / Tony Greaves. — Hebden Bridge : Association of Liberal Councillors, 1985. — [8p]. — (Activists' guide ; no.4)

JOWETT, Garth
Propaganda and persuasion / by gGarth s. Jowett and Victoria O'Donnell. — Newbury Park, Calif. : Sage, c1986. — 236 p., [8] p. of plates. — (People and communication ; v. 18). — *Includes index.* — *Bibliography: p. 219-225*

Propaganda, persuasion and polemic / editor Jeremy Hawthorn. — London : Edward Arnold, 1987. — 1v. — (Stratford-upon-Avon studies. second series). — *Includes index*

PROPAGANDA — Addresses, essays, lectures
Public communication campaigns / edited by Ronald E. Rice and William J. Paisley. — Beverly Hills : Sage Publications, c1981. — p. cm. — *Includes indexes. — Bibliography: p.* — Contents: Historical and theoretical foundations: Public communication campaigns / William Paisley. Theoretical foundations of campaigns / William McGuire. Mass communicating / Brenda Dervin -- Campaign experiences from the field: Anti-smoking campaigns / Alfred McAlister. Heart disease prevention / Nathan Maccoby and Douglas Solomon. Family planning communication campaigns / Shahnaz Taplin. Communication efforts to prevent wildfires / Troy Kurth, Eugene McNamara, and Donald Hansen. Campaigns to affect energy behavior / Barbara Farhar-Pilgrim and Floyd Shoemaker. Mass media in political campaigns / Steven Chaffee. Mass campaigns in the People's Republic of China / Alan Liu -- Putting theory into practice: Shaping persuasive messages with formative research / Edward Palmer. Evaluation of mass media prevention campaigns / Brian Flay and Thomas Cook. Mass media information campaign effectiveness / Charles Atkin. A social marketing perspective on campaigns / Douglas Solomon

PROPAGANDA, BRITISH
HAMILTON, W. Mark
The nation and the navy : methods and organization of British navalist propaganda, 1889-1914 / W. Mark Hamilton. — New York : Garland Pub., 1986. — p. cm. — (Outstanding theses from the London School of Economics and Political Science). — *Thesis (Ph.D.)--University of London, 1977.* — *Bibliography: p*

PROPAGANDA, COMMUNIST — Latin America — Congresses
The Red orchestra : instruments of Soviet policy in Latin America and the Caribbean / Dennis L. Bark, editor. — Stanford, Calif. : Hoover Institution Press, Stanford University, c1986. — ix, 139p. — *Includes bibliographies and index*

PROPAGANDA, COMMUNIST — Soviet Union
Voprosyteorii i praktiki ideologicheskoi raboty / Akademiia obshchestvennykh nauk pri TSK KPSS. — Moskva : Akademiia obschestvennykh nauk pri TSK KPSS, 1972-. — Annual. — Vyp.1-13 entitled Voprosyteorii i metodov idealogicheskoi raboty

PROPAGANDA, GERMAN — Soviet Union
ZETTERBERG, Seppo
Die Liga der Fremdvölker Russlands 1916-1918 : ein Beitrag zu Deutschlands antirussischem Propagandakreig unter den Fremdvölkern Russlands im ersten Weltkrieg / Seppo Zetterberg. — Helsinki : [Suomen Historiallinen Seura], 1978. — 279p. — (Studia historica veröffentlicht von der Finnischen Historischen Gesellschaft/Suomen Historiallinen Seura/Finska Historiska Samfundet ; vol.8). — *Bibliography: p263-271*

PROPAGANDA, RUSSIAN
STAAR, Richard Felix
USSR foreign policies after detente / Richard F. Staar. — Rev. ed. — Stanford, Calif. : Hoover Institution Press, Stanford University, c1987. — xxvii, 308 p.. — (Hoover Press publication ; 359). — *Includes index.* — *Bibliography: p. [275]-295*

PROPERTY
GRUNEBAUM, James O.
Private ownership / James O. Grunebaum. — London : Routledge & Kegan Paul, 1987. — ix, 213p. — (The problems of philosophy)

SUGDEN, Robert
The economics of rights, co-operation and welfare / Robert Sugden. — Oxford : Basil Blackwell, 1986. — [224]p. — *Includes index*

PROPERTY — Law and legislation — Great Britain
MURPHY, W. T.
Understanding property law / W. T. Murphy, Simon Roberts. — London : Fontana, 1987. — 215p. — (Understanding Law series) (Understanding law). — *Bibliography: p207-209*

PROPERTY — Moral and ethical aspects
GRUNEBAUM, James O.
Private ownership / James O. Grunebaum. — London : Routledge & Kegan Paul, 1987. — ix, 213p. — (The problems of philosophy)

PROPERTY — Germany (West) — Statistics
GERMANY (Federal Republic). Statistisches Bundesamt
Einkommens- und Verbrauchsstichprobe 1983. — Wiesbaden : the Bundesamt. — (Wirtschaftsrechnungen) Heft 2: Vermögenbestände und Schulden privater Haushalte. — 1986. — 540p

PROPERTY TAX — United States — States — Congresses
States under stress : a report on the finances of Massachusetts, Michigan, Texas, and California : California Policy Seminar conference report / Peggy B. Musgrave, editor. — Berkeley : Institute of Governmental Studies, University of California, [c1985]. — vii, 60 leaves. — "February 1985."

PROPORTIONAL REPRESENTATION — Great Britain
HAIN, Peter
Proportional misrepresentation : the case against PR in Britain / Peter Hain. — [S.l.] : Wildwood House, c1986. — 114 p

PROSECUTION — Europe — Decision-making — Congresses
EUROPEAN SEMINAR ON NON-PROSECUTION IN EUROPE (1986 : Helsinki)
Non-prosecution in Europe : report of the European seminar. — Helsinki : Helsinki Institute for Crime Prevention and Control, 1986. — 338p. — (Publication series / Helsinki Institute for Crime Prevention and Control ; no.9)

PROSECUTION — Scotland — Decision making
CHAMBERS, Gerry
Prosecuting sexual assault / G. Chambers, A. Millar. — Edinburgh : H.M.S.O., 1986. — ix,144p. — (A Scottish Office social research study). — *Prepared under the auspices of the Scottish Office Central Research Unit.* — *Bibliographical references: p142-143*

PROSELYTES AND PROSELYTING, JEWISH — Biography
FREY, Robert Seitz
The imperative of response : the holocaust in human context / Robert Seitz Frey, Nancy Thompson-Frey. — Lanham, MD : University Press of America, c1985. — xix, 165 p.. — *Bibliography: p. 144-164*

PROSPECTING — Environmental aspects — Georges Bank
MACLEISH, William H.
Oil and water : the struggle for Georges Bank / by William H. MacLeish. — 1st ed. — Boston : Atlantic Monthly Press, c1985. — 304 p.. — *Includes index*

PROSPECTING — British Columbia
Exploration in British Columbia / Ministry of Energy, Mines and Petroleum Resources. — Victoria : Ministry of Energy, Mines and Petroleum Resources, 1982

PROSTITUTES — India — Calcutta
JOARDAR, Biswanath
Prostitution in nineteenth and early twentieth century Calcutta / B. Joardar. — New Delhi : Inter-India Publications, 1985. — x, 87 p.. — 66-30. — *Includes index.* — *Bibliography: p. [76]-79*

PROSTITUTES — New South Wales — Sydney — Interviews
PERKINS, Roberta
  Being a prostitute : prostitute women and prostitute men / Roberta Perkins and Garry Bennett. — Sydney ; London : Allen & Unwin, 1985. — xx,318p. — *Bibliography: p313-315.* — *Includes index*

PROSTITUTION — Australia — History
  So much hard work : women and prostitution in Australian history / edited by Kay Daniels. — Sydney : Fontana : Collins, 1984. — 394 p.. — *Includes bibliographies*

PROSTITUTION — Canada
DAVIDSON, John
  The stroll : inner-city subcultures / John Davidson ; as told to Laird Stevens. — Toronto : NC Press Limited, 1986. — 165p

PROSTITUTION — Great Britain — Law and legislation
JOSEPHINE BUTLER SOCIETY
  Observations submitted to the Home Secretary on the Criminal Law Revision Committee's final reports on prostitution. — Hatfield : Josephine Butler Society, 1986. — 7p

PROSTITUTION — India — Calcutta
JOARDAR, Biswanath
  Prostitution in nineteenth and early twentieth century Calcutta / B. Joardar. — New Delhi : Inter-India Publications, 1985. — x, 87 p.. — 66-30. — *Includes index.* — *Bibliography: p. [76]-79*

PROSTITUTION — Ontario — Toronto
DAVIDSON, John
  The stroll : inner-city subcultures / John Davidson ; as told to Laird Stevens. — Toronto : NC Press Limited, 1986. — 165p

PROSTITUTION, MALE — New South Wales — Sydney
PERKINS, Roberta
  Being a prostitute : prostitute women and prostitute men / Roberta Perkins and Garry Bennett. — Sydney ; London : Allen & Unwin, 1985. — xx,318p. — *Bibliography: p313-315.* — *Includes index*

PROTEST SONGS — Netherlands
  Het cirkus van vuile mong en zijn vieze gasten : teksten. — Waarschoot : Werkgroep voor Vormingstejater, 1975. — 45p

PROTESTANT CHURCHES — Brazil — History
COOK, Guillermo
  The expectation of the poor : base ecclesial communities in Protestant perspective / Guillermo Cook. — Maryknoll, NY : Orbis Books, c1985. — p. cm. — *Includes index.* — *Bibliography: p*

PROTESTANT CHURCHES — Germany — Political aspects
NOORMANN, Harry
  Protestantismus und politisches Mandat 1945-1949 / Harry Noormaan. — Gütersloh : Gütersloher Verlagshaus. — *Bibliography: p295-317*
  Bd.1: Grundriss. — 1985. — 317p

NOORMANN, Harry
  Protestantismus und politisches Mandat 1945-1949 / Harry Noormann. — Gütersloh : Gütersloher Verlagshaus Mohn
  Bd.2: Dokumente und Kommentare. — 1985. — 287p

PROTESTANTISM
  The orange standard: monthly protestant magazine. — Birmingham : Cromwell, 1921

WEBER, Max
  The Protestant ethic and the spirit of capitalism / Max Weber ; translated by Talcott Parsons ; introduction by Anthony Giddens. — London : Unwin Paperbacks, 1985. — [320]p. — (Counterpoint). — *Translation of: Die protestantische Ethik und der 'Geist' des Kapitalismus.* — *Originally published: London : Allen & Unwin, 1930.* — *Includes index*

PROTESTANTISM — Doctrines — History
WELCH, Claude
  Protestant thought in the nineteenth century / Claude Welch. — New Haven [Conn.] ; London : Yale University Press
  Vol.2: 1870-1914. — c1985. — xii,315p. — *Includes index*

PROTESTANTS — Germany — Biography
SCHNÜBBE, Otto
  Paul Tillich und seine Bedeutung für den Protestantismus heute : das Prinzip der Rechtfertigung im theologischen, philosophischen und politischen Denken Paul Tillichs / Otto Schnübbe. — Hannover : Lutherhaus, 1985. — 288p

PROTESTANTS — Northern Ireland — Political activity
NELSON, Sarah
  Ulster's uncertain defenders : Protestant political, paramilitary and community groups and the Northern Ireland Conflict / Sarah Nelson. — Belfast : Appletree, 1984. — 219p. — (Modern Irish society). — *Bibliography: p210-215.* — *Includes index*

PROTESTANTS — Scotland — History
BRUCE, Steve
  No pope of Rome : anti-catholicism in modern Scotland / Steve Bruce. — Edinburgh : Mainstream, 1985. — 270p. — *Includes bibliographical notes*

PROTESTANTS — Ulster (Northern Ireland and Ireland) — History
CRAWFORD, Robert G
  Loyal to King Billy : a portrait of the Ulster Protestants / Robert G. Crawford. — New York : St. Martin's Press, 1987. — p. cm. — *Includes index.* — *Bibliography: p*

PROVIDENCE (R.I.) — History
GILKESON, John S.
  Middle-class Providence, 1820-1940 / John S. Gilkeson, Jr. — Princeton, N.J. : Princeton University Press, c1986. — ix, 380 p.. — *Includes index.* — *Bibliography: p. [357]-369*

PROVIDENCE (R.I.) — Social conditions
GILKESON, John S.
  Middle-class Providence, 1820-1940 / John S. Gilkeson, Jr. — Princeton, N.J. : Princeton University Press, c1986. — ix, 380 p.. — *Includes index.* — *Bibliography: p. [357]-369*

PROVIDER MOVEMENT
PROVIDER MOVEMENT
  [Manifesto]. — London : [the Providor Movement], 1984. — 48p

PROVINCIAL GOVERNMENTS — Canada
DYCK, Rand
  Provincial politics in Canada / Rand Dyck. — Scarborough : Prentice-Hall, 1986. — 626p. — *Bibliography: p587-616*

PROVISIONAL IRA
KEE, Robert
  Trial and error : the Maguires, the Guildford pub bombings and British justice / Robert Kee. — London : Hamish Hamilton, 1986. — 284p. — *Includes index*

PROVISIONAL IRA — History
MULLIN, Chris
  Error of judgment : the Birmingham bombings / by Chris Mullin. — London : Chatto & Windus, 1986. — [224]p

PRUSSIA — Politics and government — 1871-1888
GALL, Lothar
  Bismarck : the white revolutionary / Lothar Gall ; translated from the German by J.A. Underwood. — London : Allen & Unwin. — *Translation of: Bismarck.* — *Originally published under the title, Bismarck der weiss Revolutionaär, Frankfurt am Main : Ullstein, 1980*
  Vol.1: 1815-1871. — 1986. — [640]p. — *Includes bibliography and index*

PRUSSIA — Social conditions
BLASIUS, Dirk
  Bürgerliche Gesellschaft und Kriminalität : zur Sozialgeschichte Preussens im Vormärz / Dirk Blasius. — Göttingen : Vandenhoeck und Ruprecht, 1976. — 203 p. — (Kritische Studien zur Geschichtswissenschaft ; Bd. 22). — *Includes index.* — *Habilitationsschrift--Düsseldorf.* — *Bibliography: p. 186-198*

PRUSSIA (GERMANY) — Foreign relations — 1740-1786
DORAN, Patrick F
  Andrew Mitchell and Anglo-Prussian diplomatic relations during the Seven Years War / Patrick Francis Doran. — [Garland ed.]. — New York : Garland, 1986. — 408 p.. — (Outstanding theses from the London School of Economics and Political Science). — *Bibliography: p. [397]-408*

PRUSSIA (GERMANY) — Foreign relations — Great Britain
DORAN, Patrick F
  Andrew Mitchell and Anglo-Prussian diplomatic relations during the Seven Years War / Patrick Francis Doran. — [Garland ed.]. — New York : Garland, 1986. — 408 p.. — (Outstanding theses from the London School of Economics and Political Science). — *Bibliography: p. [397]-408*

PRUSSIA (GERMANY) — History
THADDEN, Rudolf von
  Prussia : the history of a lost state / Rudolf von Thadden ; translated by Angi Rutter. — Cambridge : Cambridge University Press, 1987. — xvii,161p. — *Translation of: Fragen an Preussen.* — *Includes index*

PRUSSIA (GERMANY) — History — 19th century
ENGELBERG, Ernst
  Bismarck : Urpreusse und Reichsgründer / Ernst Engelberg. — Berlin : Siedler, 1985. — xvi,839p

PRUSSIA (GERMANY) — History — 1918-1933
ORLOW, Dietrich
  Weimar Prussia, 1918-1925 : the unlikely rock of democracy / Dietrich Orlow. — Pittsburgh, Pa. : University of Pittsburgh Press, 1985. — xii, 363p. — *Includes index.* — *Bibliography: p.333-355*

PRUSSIA (GERMANY) — Industries
RICHTER, Friedrich
  Industriepolitik im agrarischen Osten : ein Beitrag zur Geschichte Ostpreussens zwischen den Weltkriegen : Bericht und Dokumentation / Friedrich Richter. — Wiesbaden : Franz Steiner, 1984. — 325p

PRUSSIA (GERMANY) — Politics and government — 1815-1870
BUSSCHE, Albrecht von dem
  Heinrich Alexander von Arnim : Liberalismus, Polenfrage und deutsche Einheit : das 19. Jahrhundert im Spiegel einer Biographie des preussischen Staatsmannes / von Albrecht von dem Bussche. — Osnabrück : Biblio Verlag, 1986. — x,426p. — *Bibliography: p339-344*

PSYCHIATRIC HOSPITAL CARE — Denmark — Statistics
  Befolkningens forbrug af psykiatriske sengepladser 1982. — [København] : Sundhedsstyrelsen, 1984. — 77p. — (Sygehusstatistik / Sundhedsstyrelsen ; II:21:1984). — *Some table headings in English.* — *Bibliography: p.36-37*

PSYCHIATRIC HOSPITAL CARE — Wales
GREAT BRITAIN. Working Party on Standards of Care for Mentally Ill and Mentally Handicapped Patients in Hospital
  Standards of care for mentally ill and mentally handicapped patients in hospital : report of the Working Party, presented to the Secretary of State for Wales. — [Cardiff : Welsh Office], 1978. — [38]p. — *Chairman: A. D. Lewis.* — *Bibliography: p[37]-[38]*

PSYCHIATRIC HOSPITALS — England — History
DIGBY, Anne
  Madness, morality and medicine : a study of the York Retreat, 1796-1914 / Anne Digby. — Cambridge : Cambridge University Press, 1985. — xvi,323p. — (Cambridge history of medicine)

PSYCHIATRIC HOSPITALS — England — Hampshire
Something to look forward to : an evaluation of a travelling day hospital for elderly mentally ill people / Neil Evans...[et al.]. — Portsmouth : Social Services Research and Intelligence Unit, 1986. — x,254p. — (SSRIU Report ; No.15). — *Bibliography: p[251]-254*

PSYCHIATRIC HOSPITALS — Great Britain
GOSTIN, Larry
  Institutions observed : towards a new concept of secure provision in mental health / Larry Gostin. — London : King Edward's Hospital Fund for London, 1986. — 179p. — *Bibliography: p165-172*

PSYCHIATRISTS — Algeria — Biography
BULHAN, Hussein Abdilahi
  Frantz Fanon and the psychology of oppression / Hussein Abdilahi Bulhan. — New York ; London : Plenum Press, c1985. — xiii, 299p. — (PATH in psychology). — *Includes index. — Includes bibliographical references*

PSYCHIATRY
HALLECK, Seymour L
  Psychiatry and the dilemmas of crime : a study of causes, punishment, and treatment / [by] Seymour L. Halleck. — [1st paperback ed.]. — Berkeley : University of California Press, 1971 [c1967]. — xiv, 382 p. — *Bibliography: p. 351-370*

The Power of psychiatry / edited by Peter Miller and Nikolas Rose. — Cambridge : Polity, 1986. — vii,326p. — *Includes index*

REES, Linford
  A short textbook of psychiatry / Linford Rees. — 3rd ed. — London : Hodder and Stoughton, 1982. — viii,371p. — (University medical texts) . — *Previous ed.: 1976. — Includes bibliographies and index*

Responding to mental illness / [editor, Gordon Horobin]. — London : Kogan Page, 1985. — 143p. — (Research highlights in social work ; 11)

PSYCHIATRY — England — History
SHOWALTER, Elaine
  The female malady : women, madness, and culture in England, 1830-1980 / Elaine Showalter. — New York : Pantheon Books, 1986. — p. cm. — *Includes index. — Bibliography: p*

PSYCHIATRY — Soviet Union
NIKOLAEV, E. B.
  Predavshie Gippokrata = The betrayal of Hippocrates / Evgenii Nikolaev. — London : Overseas Publications Interchange, 1984. — 324p

PSYCHICAL RESEARCH — Collected works
JAMES, William, 1842-1910
  Essays in psychical research / William James. — Cambridge, Mass. : Harvard Univ. Press, 1986. — xxxvi, 684p. — (The Works of William James ; [v.16]). — *Includes bibliographical references and index*

PSYCHOANALYSIS
FREUD, Sigmund
  Collected papers / Sigmund Freud ; edited by James Strachey ; translated by Joan Riviere. — London : Hogarth Press, 1950. — 5 vols. — *Bibliographies*

FREUD, Sigmund
  Introductory lectures on psycho-analysis : a course of twenty-eight lectures delivered at the University of Vienna; translated by Joan Rivière. — 2nd ed. — London : Allen and Unwin, 1952. — 395p

FREUD, Sigmund
  [Neue Folge der Vorlesungen zur Einführung in die Psychoanalyse. English]. New introductory lectures on psycho-analysis / Sigmund Freud ; translated by W. J. H. Sprott. — 3rd ed. — London : Hogarth Press, 1946. — 240p

FREUD, Sigmund
  [Übersicht der Übertragungsneurosen. English]. A phylogenetic fantasy : overview of the transference neuroses / Sigmund Freud ; edited and with an essay by Ilse Grubrich-Simitis ; translated by Axel Hoffer and Peter T. Hoffer. — Cambridge, Mass. : Belknap Press of Harvard University Press, 1987. — p. cm. — Translation of: Übersicht der Übertragungsneurosen. — *Bibliography: p*

KLEIN, Melanie
  The selected Melanie Klein / edited by Juliet Mitchell. — Harmondsworth : Penguin, 1986. — 256p. — *Bibliography: p.[242]-245*

KRISTEVA, Julia
  The Kristeva reader / Julia Kristeva ; edited by Toril Moi. — Oxford : Basil Blackwell, 1986. — vii,327p. — Translation of the French. — *Includes index*

STERN, Daniel N
  The interpersonal world of the infant : a view from psychoanalysis and developmental psychology / Daniel N. Stern. — New York : Basic Books, c1985. — x, 304p. — *Includes index. — Bibliography: p.278-294*

WALLACE, Edwin R
  Freud and anthropology : a history and reappraisal / Edwin R. Wallace, IV. — New York : International Universities Press, c1983. — xi, 306p. — (Psychological issues ; monograph 55). — *Bibliography: p.281-294. — Includes index*

WINNICOTT, D. W.
  Home is where we start from : essays by a psychoanalyst / D.W. Winnicott ; compiled and edited by Clare Winnicott, Ray Shepherd, Madeleine Davis. — Harmondsworth : Penguin, 1986. — 287p. — (Pelican books). — Originally published: New York : Norton, 1986. — *Includes index*

ZANUSO, Billa
  The young Freud : the origins of psychoanalysis in late nineteenth-century Viennese culture / Billa Zanuso. — Oxford : Basil Blackwell, 1986. — [v,192]p. — Translation of: La nascita della psicoanalisi. — *Includes bibliography and index*

PSYCHOANALYSIS — Case studies
MASSON, J. Moussaieff
  The assault on truth : Freud's suppression of the seduction theory / Jeffrey Moussaieff Masson. — New York, N.Y. : Penguin Books, 1985, c1984. — p. cm. — : Reprint. Originally published: New York : Farrar, Straus, and Giroux, 1984. — *Includes index. — Bibliography: p*

SACKS, Oliver
  The man who mistook his wife for a hat / Oliver Sacks. — London : Duckworth, 1985. — xii,233p. — *Includes bibliography and index*

PSYCHOANALYSIS — History
MASSON, J. Moussaieff
  The assault on truth : Freud's suppression of the seduction theory / Jeffrey Moussaieff Masson. — New York, N.Y. : Penguin Books, 1985, c1984. — p. cm. — : Reprint. Originally published: New York : Farrar, Straus, and Giroux, 1984. — *Includes index. — Bibliography: p*

PSYCHOANALYSIS — in infancy & childhood
STERN, Daniel N
  The interpersonal world of the infant : a view from psychoanalysis annd developmental psychology / Daniel N. Stern. — New York : Basic Books, c1985. — x, 304p. — *Includes index. — Bibliography: p.278-294*

PSYCHOANALYSIS — Political aspects
FROSH, Stephen
  The politics of psychoanalysis : an introduction to Freudian and post-Freudian theory / Stephen Frosh. — Basingstoke : Macmillan Education, 1987. — [272]p. — *Includes index*

PSYCHOHISTORY
POMPER, Philip
  The structure of mind in history : five major figures in psychohistory / Philip Pomper. — New York : Columbia University Press, 1985. — xvi, 192 p.. — *Includes index. — Bibliography: p. 177-182*

PSYCHOLINGUISTIC
Language for hearers / edited by Graham McGregor. — Oxford : Pergamon, 1986. — [vii, 235]p. — (Language & communication library ; v.8). — *Includes index*

PSYCHOLINGUISTICS
AITCHISON, Jean
  Words in the mind : an introduction to the mental lexicon / Jean Aitchison. — Oxford : Basil Blackwell, 1987. — [288]p. — *Includes bibliography and index*

Culture, communication and cognition : Vygotskian perspectives / edited by James V. Wertsch. — Cambridge : Cambridge University Press, 1985. — x,379p. — *Bibliographies*

GREENE, Judith
  Language understanding : a cognitive approach / Judith Greene. — Milton Keynes : Open University, 1986. — 158p. — (Open guides to psychology). — *Includes index. — Bibliography: p.153-155*

HÖRMANN, Hans
  [Einführung in die Psycholinguistik. English]. Meaning and context : an introduction to the psychology of language / Hans Hörmann ; edited and with an introduction by Robert E. Innis. — New York ; London : Plenum Press, c1986. — xiv, 294p. — (Cognition and language). — Rev. translation of: Einführung in die Psycholinguistik. — *Includes indexes. — Bibliography: p.271-286*

LINDSAY, Peter H.
  Human information processing : An introduction to psychology / Peter H. Lindsay and Donald A. Norman. — 2d ed. — New York : Academic Press, c1977. — xxiii, 777 p. — *Includes indexes. — Bibliography: p. [734]-762*

LOAR, Brian
  Mind and meaning / Brian Loar. — Cambridge : Cambridge University Press, 1981. — xi,268p. — (Cambridge studies in philosophy). — *Bibliography: p261-263. — Includes index*

PAIVIO, Allan
  Mental representations : a dual coding approach / Allan Paivio. — New York : Oxford University Press ; Oxford : Clarendon Press, 1986. — x, 322p. — (Oxford psychology series ; no. 9). — *Includes index. — Bibliography: p.277-305*

Social and functional approaches to language and thought / edited by Maya Hickmann ; with a foreword by Jerome Bruner. — Orlando : Academic Press, 1987. — p. cm. — *Includes index*

PSYCHOLINGUISTICS — Periodicals
Progress in the psychology of language. — Vol.1-. — London : Lawrence Erlbaum Associates, 1985-. — v.. — *Annual*

PSYCHOLINGUISTICS — Social aspects
WERTSCH, James V
Vygotsky and the social formation of mind / James V. Wertsch. — Cambridge, Mass. : Harvard University Press, 1985. — p. cm. — *Includes index. — Bibliography: p*

PSYCHOLOGICAL LITERATURE
REED, Jeffrey G.
Library use : a handbook for psychology / Jeffrey G. Reed and Pam M. Baxter. — Washington, DC : American Psychological Association, c1983. — 137 p.. — *Includes bibliographies and index*

PSYCHOLOGICAL RESEARCH
Frontiers of psychological research : readings from Scientific American / selected and introduced by Stanley Coopersmith. — San Francisco : Freeman, 1964. — xiii,322p. — *Bibliographies*

PSYCHOLOGICAL THEORY
HAMPSON, Sarah E.
The construction of personality : an introduction / Sarah E. Hampson. — London ; Boston : Routledge & Kegan Paul, 1982. — 319p. — (Introductions to modern psychology). — *Includes index. — Bibliography: p.[287]-310*

PSYCHOLOGISTS
The Power of psychology / edited by David Cohen. — London : Croom Helm, c1987. — 150p. — *Includes bibliographies and index*

PSYCHOLOGY
COHEN, David
Psychologists on psychology / David Cohen. — London : Ark, 1985. — 360p. — *Bibliography: p357-360*

FRANSELLA, Fay
Need to change? / Fay Fransella. — London : Methuen, 1975. — 144p

FREUD, Sigmund
Group psychology and the analysis of the ego / Sigmund Freud ; translated and edited by James Strachey. — London : Hogarth Press, 1959. — x,85p. — *Bibliographies*

Handbook of environmental psychology / edited by Daniel Stokols, Irwin Altman. — New York : Wiley, c1987. — 2 vols. — "A Wiley-Interscience publication.". — *Includes bibliographies and indexes*

HYLAND, Michael
Introduction to theoretical psychology / Michael Hyland. — London : Macmillan, 1981. — viii,147p. — *Bibliography: p140-147*

New directions in psychology. — New York : Holt
1 / Roger Brown [et al.]. — 1965. — ix,353p

The new psychologist: annual journal of the Open University Psychological Society. — Milton Keynes : Open University Psychological Department, 1982/3-. — *Annual*

The Power of psychology / edited by David Cohen. — London : Croom Helm, c1987. — 150p. — *Includes bibliographies and index*

PRICE-WILLIAMS, Douglass Richard
Introductory psychology : an approach for social workers / Douglass Richard Price-Williams. — London : Routledge and Kegan Paul, 1958. — viii,203p

Psychology for social workers / [edited by] Martin Herbert. — 2nd ed. — London : Macmillan, 1986. — [350]p. — (Psychology for professional groups). — *Previous ed.: 1981. — Includes bibliographies and index*

ROSE, Nikolas Simon
The psychological complex : psychology, politics and society in England, 1869-1939 / Nikolas Rose. — London : Routledge and Kegan Paul, 1985. — 293p. — *Bibliography: p255-285*

PSYCHOLOGY — Addresses, essays, lectures
Mind design : philosophy, psychology, artificial intelligence / edited by John Haugeland. — Cambridge, Mass. ; London : MIT Press, 1981. — xii,368p. — *A Bradford book*

PSYCHOLOGY — Cross-cultural studies
Field methods in cross-cultural research / edited by Walter J. Lonner, John W. Berry. — Beverly Hills : Sage Publications, c1986. — 368 p.. — (Cross-cultural research and methodology series ; v. 8). — *Includes indexes. — Bibliography: p. 325-349*

PSYCHOLOGY — Field work
Field methods in cross-cultural research / edited by Walter J. Lonner, John W. Berry. — Beverly Hills : Sage Publications, c1986. — 368 p.. — (Cross-cultural research and methodology series ; v. 8). — *Includes indexes. — Bibliography: p. 325-349*

PSYCHOLOGY — Handbooks
REED, Jeffrey G.
Library use : a handbook for psychology / Jeffrey G. Reed and Pam M. Baxter. — Washington, DC : American Psychological Association, c1983. — 137 p.. — *Includes bibliographies and index*

PSYCHOLOGY — History
HEARNSHAW, Leslie Spencer
The shaping of modern psychology / L.S. Hearnshaw. — London : Routledge & Kegan Paul, 1986. — [408]p. — *Includes bibliography and index*

Points of view in the modern history of psychology / edited by Claude E. Buxton. — New York : Academic Press, c1985. — xiv, 468 p.. — *Includes bibliographies and indexes*

PSYCHOLOGY — Library resources
REED, Jeffrey G.
Library use : a handbook for psychology / Jeffrey G. Reed and Pam M. Baxter. — Washington, DC : American Psychological Association, c1983. — 137 p.. — *Includes bibliographies and index*

PSYCHOLOGY — Philosophy
DECI, Edward L
Intrinsic motivation and self-determination in human behavior / Edward L. Deci and Richard M. Ryan. — New York ; London : Plenum, c1985. — xv, 371 p.. — (Perspectives in social psychology). — *Includes indexes. — Bibliography: p. 335-358*

Psychology : designing the discipline / Joseph Margolis ... [et al.]. — Oxford : Basil Blackwell, 1986. — [208]p. — *Includes index*

PSYCHOLOGY — Research
MISHLER, Elliot George
Research interviewing : context and narrative / Elliot G. Mishler. — Cambridge, Mass. : Harvard University Press, 1986. — xi, 189 p.. — *Includes index. — Bibliography: p. [171]-185*

SOMMER, Robert
A practical guide to behavioral research : tools and techniques / Robert Sommer and Barbara B. Sommer. — 2nd ed. — New York : Oxford University Press, 1986. — viii, 297 p.. — *Includes bibliographies and indexes*

PSYCHOLOGY — India
SINHA, Durganand
Psychology in a Third World country : the Indian experience / Durganand Sinha. — New Delhi ; London : Sage, 1986. — 160p. — *Bibliography: p.[131]-160*

PSYCHOLOGY — India — History
SINHA, Durganand
Psychology in a Third World country : the Indian experience / Durganand Sinha. — New Delhi ; London : Sage, 1986. — 160p. — *Bibliography: p.[131]-160*

PSYCHOLOGY — United States — History
FULLER, Robert C.
Americans and the unconscious / Robert C. Fuller. — New York : Oxford University Press, 1986. — p. cm. — *Includes index*

SCARBOROUGH, Elizabeth
Untold lives : the first generation of American women psychologists / Elizabeth Scarborough and Laurel Furumoto. — New York : Columbia University Press, 1987. — p. cm. — *Includes index. — Bibliography: p*

PSYCHOLOGY — United States — History — 19th century
O'DONNELL, John M.
The origins of behaviorism : American psychology, 1870-1920 / John M. O'Donnell. — New York ; London : New York University Press, 1985. — xii, 299p. — (The American social experience series ; 3). — *Includes bibliographical references and index*

SCARBOROUGH, Elizabeth
Untold lives : the first generation of American women psychologists / Elizabeth Scarborough and Laurel Furumoto. — New York : Columbia University Press, 1987. — p. cm. — *Includes index. — Bibliography: p*

PSYCHOLOGY — United States — History — 20th century
O'DONNELL, John M.
The origins of behaviorism : American psychology, 1870-1920 / John M. O'Donnell. — New York ; London : New York University Press, 1985. — xii, 299p. — (The American social experience series ; 3). — *Includes bibliographical references and index*

PSYCHOLOGY AND RELIGION — United States — History
FULLER, Robert C.
Americans and the unconscious / Robert C. Fuller. — New York : Oxford University Press, 1986. — p. cm. — *Includes index*

PSYCHOLOGY, CLINICAL
LEARY, Mark R
Social psychology and dysfunctional behavior : origins, diagnosis, and treatment / Mark R. Leary and Rowland S. Miller. — New York : Springer-Verlag, c1986. — xiii, 262 p.. — (Springer series in social psychology). — *Includes indexes. — Bibliography: p. [203]-244*

PSYCHOLOGY, COMPARATIVE
GRUBER, Howard E
Darwin on man : a psychological study of scientific creativity / Howard E. Gruber ; foreword to the 1st ed. by Jean Piaget. — 2d ed. — Chicago : University of Chicago Press, 1981. — xxvii, 310 p.. — *First ed., published in 1974, entered under title: Darwin on man. — Includes bibliographical references and index*

PSYCHOLOGY, FORENSIC — Congresses
Reconstructing the past : the role of psychologists in criminal trials / edited by Arne Trankell. — Deventer, The Netherlands : Kluwer, [1982]. — 398p. — *"This book contains papers and panels from the first international conference on Witness Psychology...Stockholm...September 1981"*

PSYCHOLOGY, INDUSTRIAL
International review of industrial and organizational psychology / edited by Cary L. Cooper and Ivan Robertson. — Chichester : Wiley, c1986. — xi,340p. — *Includes bibliographies and index*

International review of industrial and organizational psychology. — Chichester : John Wiley, 1986-. — *Annual*

LAUFFER, Armand
Careers, colleagues, and conflicts : understanding gender, race and ethnicity in the workplace / Armand Lauffer. — Beverly Hills ; London : Sage, c1985. — 182 p. — (Sage human services guides ; v.43)

PSYCHOLOGY, INDUSTRIAL
continuation

MEISTER, David
Behavioral analysis and measurement methods / David Meister. — New York : Wiley, c1985. — xiii, 509 p.. — "A Wiley-Interscience publication.". — Includes bibliographies and index

Motivation and work behavior / [compiled by] Richard M. Steers, Lyman W. Porter. — 4th ed. — New York : McGraw-Hill, c1987. — xii, 595 p.. — (McGraw-Hill series in management) . — Includes bibliographies and indexes

O'BRIEN, Gordon E.
Psychology of work and unemployment / Gordon E. O'Brien. — Chichester : Wiley, c1986. — xiii,315p. — (Wiley series in psychology and productivity at work). — Includes bibliographies and index

Personality assessment in organizations / edited by H. John Bernardin and David A. Bownas. — New York : Praeger, 1985. — p. cm. Includes index

PSYCHOLOGY, INDUSTRIAL — Addresses, essays, lectures

Psychology at work / edited by Peter B. Warr. — Harmondsworth : Penguin, 1971. — 460p. — (Penguin education). — bibl p403-444

PSYCHOLOGY, INDUSTRIAL — methods

MEISTER, David
Behavioral analysis and measurement methods / David Meister. — New York : Wiley, c1985. — xiii, 509 p.. — "A Wiley-Interscience publication.". — Includes bibliographies and index

PSYCHOLOGY, INDUSTRIAL — Research

Generalizing from laboratory to field settings : research findings from industrial-organizational psychology, organizational behavior, and human resource management / edited by Edwin A. Locke. — Lexington, Mass. : Lexington Books, c1986. — x, 291 p.. — (The Issues in organization and management series). — Includes bibliographies and index

PSYCHOLOGY, INDUSTRIAL — Europe

WEST EUROPEAN CONFERENCE ON THE PSYCHOLOGY OF WORK AND ORGANIZATION (1985 : Aachen, Germany)
The psychology of work and organization : current trends and issues : selected and edited proceedings of the West European Conference on the Psychology of Work and Organization, Aachen, F.R.G., 1-3 April, 1985 / edited by G. Debus and H.-W. Schroiff. — Amsterdam ; New York : North Holland ; New York, N.Y., U.S.A. : Sole distributors for the U.S.A. and Canada, Elsevier Science Pub. Co., 1986. — xi, 407 p.. — Includes bibliographies and indexes

PSYCHOLOGY, INDUSTRIAL — Soviet Union

VERSHININA, T. N.
Vzaimosviaz' tekuchesti i proizvodstvennoi adaptatsii rabochikh / T. N. Vershinina ; otv. redaktor Z. V. Kupriianova. — Novosibirsk : Nauka, Sibirskoe otdelenie, 1986. — 164p

PSYCHOLOGY, PATHOLOGICAL

EYSENCK, H. J.
Handbook of abnormal psychology / edited by H.J. Eysenck. — 2nd ed. — London : Pitman, 1973. — xvi,906p. — Previous ed. 1960. — Includes bibliographies and index

GOUDSMIT, W.
De mens in onvrijheid / W. Goudsmit. — Assen : Prakke, 1970. — 27p. — Rede uitgesproken bij de openbare canvaarding van het ambt van buitengewoon hoogleraar in de forensische psychiatrie aan de Rijksuniversiteit te Groningen op dinsdag 10 maart 1970. — Bibliography: p26-27

PSYCHOLOGY, PHYSIOLOGICAL

BARTLETT, Frederic C
Remembering : a study in experimental and social psychology / by Frederic C. Bartlett. — Cambridge : Cambridge University Press, 1967. — x,317p. — Previous ed: 1932

Human factors of information technology in the office / edited by Bruce Christie. — Chichester : Wiley, c1985. — ix,352p. — (Wiley series in information processing). — Bibliography: p326-340. — Includes index

Human motor behavior : an introduction / edited by J.A. Scott Kelso. — Hillsdale, N.J. ; London : L. Erlbaum, 1982. — xi,307p. — Includes bibliographies and indexes

PSYCHOLOGY, SOCIAL

LEARY, Mark R
Social psychology and dysfunctional behavior : origins, diagnosis, and treatment / Mark R. Leary and Rowland S. Miller. — New York : Springer-Verlag, c1986. — xiii, 262 p.. — (Springer series in social psychology). — Includes indexes. — Bibliography: p. [203]-244

PSYCHOMETRICS

BERDIE, Douglas R
Questionnaires : design and use / by Doug R. Berdie, John F. Anderson, Marsha A. Niebuhr. — 2nd ed. — Metuchen, N.J. : Scarecrow Press, 1986. — xii, 330 p.. — Includes indexes. — Bibliography: p. 67-204

DUNCAN, Otis Dudley
Notes on social measurement : historical and critical / Otis Dudley Duncan. — New York : Russell Sage Foundation, c1984. — xi, 256 p.. — Includes bibliographies and indexes

HOWELL, David C
Statistical methods for psychology / David C. Howell. — Boston, Mass. : Duxbury Press, c1982. — xvii, 583 p.. — Includes index. — Bibliography: p. 544-550

MARTIN, Paul, 1958-
Measuring behaviour : an introductory guide / Paul Martin, Patrick Bateson. — Cambridge : Cambridge University Press, 1986. — xii, 200p. — Includes index. — Bibliography: p.[163]-193

PSYCHOSEXUAL DEVELOPMENT

GREEN, Richard
The "sissy boy syndrome" and the development of homosexuality / Richard Green. — New Haven : Yale University Press, c1987. — x, 416 p.. — Includes index. — Bibliography: p. 399-409

PSYCHOTHERAPY

HALEY, Jay
Strategies of psychotherapy / by Jay Haley. — New York : Grune & Stratton, [1963]. — 204p . — Bibliography: p202-204

HOBSON, Robert F.
Forms of feeling : the heart of psychotherapy / Robert F. Hobson. — London : Tavistock, 1985. — xvi,318p. — Includes index

ROGERS, Carl R.
Client-centered therapy : its current practice, implications and theory / Carl R. Rogers ; with special chapters by Elaine Dorfman, Thomas Gordon, Nicholas Hobbs. — London : Constable, [1951]. — xii,560p. — Bibliography: p535-548

PSYCHOTHERAPY PATIENTS

KAY, Adah
Discharged to the community : a review of housing and support in London for people leaving psychiatric care / Adah Kay and Charlie Legg. — London : Good Practices in Mental Health, 1986. — vi,91p. — "Original research funded by the Greater London Council". — Bibliography: p89-91

PSYCHOTROPIC DRUGS — United States

STEPHENS, Richard C
Mind-altering drugs : use, abuse, and treatment / Richard C. Stephens. — Newbury Park, Calif. : SAGE Publications, c1987. — 133 p.. — (Law and critical justice series ; v. 9). — Includes index. — Bibliography: p. 125-128

PU YI, Emperor of China

POWER, Brian
The puppet Emperor : the life of Pu Yi, last Emperor of China / Brian Power. — London : Peter Owen, 1986. — 230p

PUBERTY RITES — Papua New Guinea — Addresses, essays, lectures

Rituals of manhood : male initiation in Papua New Guinea / edited by Gilbert H. Herdt ; with an introduction by Roger M. Keesing. — Berkeley : University of California Press, c1982. — xxvi, 365 p.. — Includes bibliographies and index

PUBIC HEALTH PERSONNEL — Education — Africa

LUTWAMA, J. S.
The place of public health education in programmes for the training of health team personnel / by Professor J. S. Lutwama. — Brazzaville : Regional Office for Africa, World Health Organization, 1971. — 44p. — (AFRO technical papers ; no.3). — Bibliographical references: p31. — Background paper for the technical discussions of the 21st session of the Regional Committee

PUBLIC ADMINISTRATION

BOOTH, Simon A. S.
Assessing capacity for innovation : the politics and management of change in public agencies / Simon Booth and Chris Moore. — Glasgow : Centre for the Study of Public Policy, University of Strathclyde, 1986. — 28p. — (Studies in public policy ; 155)

DENHARDT, Robert B
Theories of public organization / Robert B. Denhardt. — Monterey, Calif. : Brooks/Cole Pub. Co., c1984. — xiii, 208 p.. — Includes bibliographies and indexes

DOWNS, George W
The search for government efficiency : from hubris to helplessness / George W. Downs, Patrick D. Larkey. — 1st ed. — Philadelphia : Temple University Press, c1986. — viii, 273 p.. — Includes bibliographies

DUBHASHI, P. R.
Administrative reforms / P. R. Dubhashi. — Delhi : B. R. Publishing Corporation, 1986. — 207p

HARMON, Michael
Organization theory for public administration / Michael M. Harmon, Richard T. Mayer. — Boston : Little, Brown, 1986. — xiv, 443p. — Includes index. — Bibliography: p.417-426

PUBLIC ADMINISTRATION — Classification

Classification of the functions of government. — New York : United Nations, 1980. — iii,52p. — (Statistical papers / United Nations, Statistical Office. Series M ; no.70) ([Document] (United Nations) ; ST/ESA/STAT/SER.M/70). — Sales no.: E.80.XVII.17

PUBLIC ADMINISTRATION — Data processing

STEVENS, John M
Information systems and public management / by John M. Stevens. — New York : Praeger, 1985. — p. cm. — Includes index. — Bibliography: p

PUBLIC ADMINISTRATION — Data processing — Congresses

WORLD CONFERENCE ON INFORMATICS IN GOVERNMENT (1st : 1972 : Florence)
Papers of the first World Conference on Informatics in Government held October 16-20, 1972 in Florence, Italy / by the International Computation Centre, IBI-ICC. — Rome : IBI-ICC, [c1972]. — 3 v. (972 p.). — *Includes bibliographies*

PUBLIC ADMINISTRATION — Decision making

HOLCOMBE, Randall G
An economic analysis of democracy / Randall G. Holcombe. — Carbondale : Southern Illinois University Press, c1985. — xiii, 269 p.. — (Political and social economy). — *Includes index. — Bibliography: p. 257-266*

MAGAT, Wesley A
Rules in the making : a statistical analysis of regulatory agency behavior / Wesley A. Magat, Alan J. Krupnick, Winston Harrington. — Washington, D.C. : Resources for the Future, c1986. — xiii, 182 p.. — *Includes bibliographies and index*

PUBLIC ADMINISTRATION — Dictionaries

SHAFRITZ, Jay M
The Facts on File dictionary of public administration / Jay M. Shafritz. — New York, N.Y. : Facts on File, c1985. — 610 p.. — *Includes bibliographies*

PUBLIC ADMINISTRATION — Study and teaching

UNITED STATES CIVIL SERVICE COMMISSION. Bureau of Training
A study of the career education awards program of the National Institute of Public Affairs. — Washington, 1967. — v,173p. — *Bibliography: p170-173*

PUBLIC ADMINISTRATION — Study and teaching — Great Britain

Teaching public administration. — Manchester : Published by Department of Administrative Studies, University of Manchester in Association with the Joint University Council for Social and Public Administration, 1986-. — *Semi-annual*

PUBLIC ADMINISTRATION — Argentina

DROMI, José Roberto
Administración territorial y economía : (la provincia, la región y el municipio en Argentina / José Roberto Dromi. — Madrid : Instituto de Estudios de Administración Local, 1983. — 423p. — (Autores Hispanoamericanos de Derecho Público)

PUBLIC ADMINISTRATION — Europe

Bulletin des recherches. Research bulletin / European Group of Public Administration. — Roma : Formez Centro di Formazione e Studi per il Mezzogiorno, 1985-. — *Semi-annual. — Text in French and English*

PUBLIC ADMINISTRATION — Europe — Technological innovations

New technology in the public service : consolidated report. — Luxembourg : Office for Official Publications of the European Communities, 1986. — 75p

PUBLIC ADMINISTRATION — Great Britain

Policy management and policy assessment : developments in central government : proceedings of a one-day seminar organized by Peat Marwick in association with the Royal Institute of Public Adminstration. — London : Royal Institute of Public Administration, 1986. — 69p

PUBLIC ADMINISTRATION — Great Britain — Data processing

CENTRAL COMPUTER AND TELECOMMUNICATIONS AGENCY
Central Computer and Telecommunications Agency : progress report. — London : H.M.S.O., 1985. — vi,41p. — (Information technology in the civil service. IT series ; no.11)

Longer term review of administrative computing in central government : report / by the Steering Committee. — London : Civil Service Department, 1978. — 53p

PUBLIC ADMINISTRATION — Great Britain — Decision making

Policy change in government : three case studies / edited by Nicholas Deakin. — London : Royal Institute of Public Administration, 1986. — 91p

PUBLIC ADMINISTRATION — Great Britain — Effect of technological innovations on

New technology in the public service : United Kingdom. — Shankill, Co.Dublin : European Foundation for the Improvement of Living and Working Conditions, 1986. — 103p

PUBLIC ADMINISTRATION — Hungary

Politics and public administration in Hungary / edited by György Szoboszlai. — Budapest : Akadémiai Kiadó, 1985. — x,485p. — *Translated from the Hungarian. — Includes amended text of the Constitution of the Hungarian People's Republic: p427-484*

PUBLIC ADMINISTRATION — India

DUBHASHI, P. R.
Administrative reforms / P. R. Dubhashi. — Delhi : B. R. Publishing Corporation, 1986. — 207p

PUBLIC ADMINISTRATION — Ireland

INSTITUTE OF PUBLIC ADMINISTRATION (Dublin, Ireland)
Annual report / Institute of Public Administration, [Eire]. — Dublin : The Institute, 1984-. — *Annual. — In English and Irish*

PUBLIC ADMINISTRATION — New Zealand

The accountability of the executive / edited by T. M. Berthold. — Wellington : New Zealand Institute of Public Administration, 1981. — 110p. — *Includes bibliographical references*

PUBLIC ADMINISTRATION — New Zealand — Congresses

The path to reform / edited by C. Burns. — Wellington : New Zealand Institute of Public Administration, 1982. — 219p. — (Studies in public administration ; no.27). — *Includes bibliographical references. — Papers from the Institute's annual conference held in Wellington, Aug.1981*

PUBLIC ADMINISTRATION — Organisation for Economic Co-operation and Development countries — Public relations

Administration as service : the public as client. — Paris : Organisation for Economic Co-operation and Development, 1987. — 136p

PUBLIC ADMINISTRATION — Spain

España : un presente para el futuro. — [Madrid] : Instituto de Estudios Económicos. — (Colección tablero)
2: Las instituciones / E. García de Enterría...[et al.]. — c1984. — 445p

PUBLIC ADMINISTRATION — United States

LANE, Frederick S.
Current issues in public administration / Frederick S. Lane. — 2nd ed. — New York : St. Martin's Press, 1982

PUBLIC ADMINISTRATION — United States — History

ROHR, John A
To run a constitution : the legitimacy of the administrative state / John A. Rohr. — Lawrence, Kan. : University Press of Kansas, c1986. — xv, 272 p.. — (Studies in government and public policy). — *Includes index. — Bibliography: p. 215-264*

PUBLIC CONTRACTS — Price policy — Great Britain

REVIEW BOARD FOR GOVERNMENT CONTRACTS
Report on the fifth general review of the profit formula for non-competitive government contracts. — London : H.M.S.O., 1987. — x,80p. — *Chairman: Sir Max Williams*

PUBLIC CONTRACTS — European Economic Community countries

GREAT BRITAIN. Construction Industry Directorate
The EEC directives on the general right of establishment and freedom to provide services in the industrial field and the directives and decision on public works contracts : two summaries by the Construction Industry Directorate. — London : the Directorate, 1972. — 11 leaves

PUBLIC CONTRACTS — Great Britain

DINNAGE, Peter
Standard conditions of government contracts / Peter Dinnage and Owen D. Jolly. — London : Longman, c1986. — vii,263p. — (Crown Eagle government contracting series)

PUBLIC FINANCE — Finland — Statistics

FINLAND. Tilastokeskus
Julkisen sektorin talous ja toiminta = Public sector finances and activities. — Helsinki : Tilastokeskus, 1982. — 183p. — (Tilastollisia tiedonantoja = Statistical surveys ; no.68). — *Finnish and English*

PUBLIC GOODS — Cost effectiveness

CUMMINGS, Ronald G
Valuing environmental goods : an assessment of the contingent valuation method / R.G. Cummings, D.S. Brookshire, W.D. Schulze ; contributors, Richard Bishop ... [et al.] ; commentators, Kenneth Arrow ... [et al.]. — Totowa, N.J. : Rowman & Allanheld, 1986. — xiii, 270 p. — *Includes index. — Bibliography: p. [247]-258*

PUBLIC GOODS — Mathematical models

COWELL, F. A.
Unwillingness to pay : tax evasion and public good provision / Frank A. Cowell, James Gordon. — [London : London School of Economics and Political Science], 1986. — 26p. — (Taxation, incentives and the distribution of income ; no.103). — *Economic and Social Research Council programme. — Bibliographical references: p25-26*

PUBLIC GOODS — Valuation

CUMMINGS, Ronald G
Valuing environmental goods : an assessment of the contingent valuation method / R.G. Cummings, D.S. Brookshire, W.D. Schulze ; contributors, Richard Bishop ... [et al.] ; commentators, Kenneth Arrow ... [et al.]. — Totowa, N.J. : Rowman & Allanheld, 1986. — xiii, 270 p.. — *Includes index. — Bibliography: p. [247]-258*

PUBLIC HEALTH

HARPER, Andrew C
The health of populations : an introduction / Andrew C. Harper. — New York : Springer Pub. Co., c1986. — xvii, 222 p.. — *Includes index. — Bibliography: p. 199-216*

PUBLIC HEALTH — Congresses

Good health at low cost : proceedings of a conference held at the Bellagio Conference Center, Bellagio, Italy, April 29-May 3, 1985, sponsored by the Rockefeller Foundation / editors: Scott B. Halstead, Julia A. Walsh, Kenneth S. Warren. — New York : Rockefeller Foundation, 1985. — 248p

PUBLIC HEALTH — Economic aspects — Africa

WORLD HEALTH ORGANIZATION. Regional Committee for Africa
National health planning : its value and methods of preparation ; The place of public health in the economy of the African countries ; The principles and methods of evaluation of national health. — Brazzaville : Regional Office for Africa, World Health Organization, 1974. — 150p. — (AFRO technical papers ; no.7). — Includes bibliographies. — Background papers for the technical discussions of the 18th, 19th and the 20th sessions of the Regional Committee for Africa

PUBLIC HEALTH — Economic aspects — Denmark

LARSEN, Torben
Economic-statistical aspects of the development of national health services in Denmark 1966-1972 / by Torben Larsen and Sven Collatz Christensen. — Copenhagen : National Health Service, 1973. — 16, 3 leaves

PUBLIC HEALTH — Government policy

Epidemiology and health policy / edited by Sol Levine and Abraham M. Lilienfeld. — New York ; London : Tavistock, 1987. — xvi,301p. — (Contemporary issues in health, medicine, and social policy). — Includes bibliographies and index

PUBLIC HEALTH — History

MCKEOWN, Thomas
The modern rise of population / Thomas McKeown. — London : Edward Arnold, 1976. — [5],168p. — Includes index

PUBLIC HEALTH — History — 18th century

RILEY, James C., 1943-
The eighteenth-century campaign to avoid disease / James C. Riley. — Basingstoke : Macmillan, 1987. — xvii,213p. — Bibliography: p177-200. — Includes index

PUBLIC HEALTH — Information services — Great Britain

GREAT BRITAIN. Department of Health and Social Security
Information requirements of the health services : a consultative document. — [London : the Department, 1979]. — 4p

PUBLIC HEALTH — Moral and ethical aspects

Ethical dilemmas in health promotion / editor: Spyros Doxiadis ; editorial committee: Roger Blaney ... [et al.]. — Chichester : Wiley, c1987. — xiv,234p. — Includes index

PUBLIC HEALTH — Social aspects

Health and disease : a reader / edited by Nick Black ... [et al.]. — Milton Keynes : Open University Press, c1984. — xii,371p. — Includes bibliographies and index

PUBLIC HEALTH — Social aspects — Great Britain — Bibliography

BEST, K. W.
Selected references on social class and health / compiled by K. W. Best. — London : Department of Health and Social Security Library, 1977. — 4p. — (Bibliography series / Department of Health and Social Security Library ; no.B73)

PUBLIC HEALTH — Africa

Health by the people for the people : health for all by the year 2000. — Brazzaville : Regional Office for Africa, World Health Organization, 1978. — 147p. — (AFRO technical papers ; no.14). — At head of title; 30th anniversary of WHO. — Includes bibliographical references

Health progress in Africa : 1968-1973. — Brazzaville : Regional Office for Africa, World Health Organization, 1973. — 110p. — (AFRO technical papers ; no.6). — Includes bibliographical references

An integrated concept of the public health services in the African region / Contributors, B. Adjou-Moumouni...[et al.]. — Brazzaville : Regional Office for Africa, World Health Organization, 1970. — 108p. — (AFRO technical papers ; no.2). — Includes bibliographies

QUENUM, Comlan A. A.
The health development of African communities : ten years of reflexion / Comlan A. A. Quenum. — Brazzaville : Regional Office for Africa, World Health Organization, 1979. — 283p. — (AFRO technical papers ; no.15). — Includes bibliographical references

Towards a philosophy of health work in the African region. — Brazzaville : Regional Office for Africa, World Health Organization, 1970. — 38p. — (AFRO technical papers ; no.1). — Includes bibliographical references

PUBLIC HEALTH — Africa — Addresses, essays, lectures

Biomedical lectures / Contributors; A. Quenum...[et al.]. — Brazzaville : Regional Office for Africa, World Health Organization, 1972. — 83p. — (AFRO technical papers ; no.4). — Cover title: 1970-1971 series. — Includes bibliographies

Biomedical lectures / Contributors; P. Correa...[et al.]. — Brazzaville : Regional Office for Africa, World Health Organization, 1975. — 69p. — (AFRO technical papers ; no.11). — Cover title: 1970-1973 series. — Includes bibliographical references

Biomedical lectures / Contributors; A. M. Wright...[et al.]. — Brazzaville : Regional Office for Africa, World Health Organization, 1978. — 53p. — (AFRO technical papers ; no.13). — Cover title: 1976-1977 series. — Includes bibliographical references

PUBLIC HEALTH — Africa — Evaluation

WORLD HEALTH ORGANIZATION. Regional Committee for Africa
National health planning : its value and methods of preparation ; The place of public health in the economy of the African countries ; The principles and methods of evaluation of national health. — Brazzaville : Regional Office for Africa, World Health Organization, 1974. — 150p. — (AFRO technical papers ; no.7). — Includes bibliographies. — Background papers for the technical discussions of the 18th, 19th and the 20th sessions of the Regional Committee for Africa

PUBLIC HEALTH — Bangladesh

ZAMAN, Wasim Alimuz
Public participation in development and health programs : lessons from rural Bangladesh / Wasim Alimuz Zaman. — Lanham : University Press of America, c1984. — xix, 291 p.. — : Revision of thesis (Ph. D.)--Harvard University, 1982. — Includes bibliographical references

PUBLIC HEALTH — Canada

Health and Canadian society : sociological perspectives / [edited by David] Coburn...[et al.]. — 2nd ed. — [Markham, Ontario] : Fitzhenry & Whiteside, 1987. — vii,670p. — Includes references

PUBLIC HEALTH — China

China, the health sector / Dean T. Jamison ... [et al.]. — Washington, D.C., U.S.A. : World Bank, 1984. — xl,190p. — (A World Bank country study). — Six folded maps tipped in. — Includes bibliographical references

PIAZZA, Alan Lee
Food consumption and nutritional status in the P.R.C. / Alan Piazza. — Boulder : Westview Press, 1986. — p. cm. — (Westview special studies on China). — Bibliography: p

PUBLIC HEALTH — Colombia

COLOMBIA. Ministerio de Salud Pública
Niveles de atención médica para un sistema de regionalización en Colombia. — [Bogotá] : the Ministerio : Asociación Colombiana de Facultades de Medicina, INPES, [197-]. — 54p

PUBLIC HEALTH — Denmark

DENMARK. Sundhedsprioriteringsudvalget
Extract from the report on the Committee of Health Priorities. — Copenhagen : Ministry of the Interior, 1981. — 87p

PUBLIC HEALTH — Denmark — Statistics

LARSEN, Torben
Economic-statistical aspects of the development of national health services in Denmark 1966-1972 / by Torben Larsen and Sven Collatz Christensen. — Copenhagen : National Health Service, 1973. — 16, 3 leaves

Ti⁰ars-oversigt for sundhedsvaesenet 1973-82. — [København] : Sundhedsstyrelsen, 1985. — 107p. — (Statistiske oversigter / Sundhedsstyrelsen ; IV:1:1985). — Bibliography: p.107

PUBLIC HEALTH — Developing countries — Finance

AKIN, John S.
Financing health services in developing countries / [prepared by John Akin, Nancy Birdsall and David de Ferranti]. — Washington, D.C. : The World Bank, 1987. — vi,93p. — Bibliography: p85-93

PUBLIC HEALTH — Economic aspects — Developing countries

JIMENEZ, Emmanuel
Pricing policy in the social sectors : cost recovery for education and health in developing countries / Emmanuel Jimenez. — Baltimore : Johns Hopkins University Press for the World Bank, 1987. — v,170p. — Bibliographical references: p155-163

PUBLIC HEALTH — Europe — Forecasting

Health projections in Europe : Methods and applications. — Copenhagen : World Health Organization, Regional Office for Europe, 1986. — xxi,306p. — Includes bibliographical references

PUBLIC HEALTH — Finland

MATTILA, Antti
Features of public health in Finland / Antti Mattila. — Helsinki : WHO Committee for Finland, 1961. — 20p

PUBLIC HEALTH — Great Britain

LAING, William
Private health care, 1985 / William Laing. — London : Office of Health Economics, [1985]. — 55 p.

PUBLIC HEALTH — Great Britain — Bibliography

GRAYSON, Lesley
Unemployment and health : a review of the literature 1979-1986 / compiled by Lesley Grayson. — Letchworth : Technical Communications, 1986. — iv,27p

PUBLIC HEALTH — Great Britain — Finance

MAYS, Nicholas
Resource allocation in the Health Service : a review of the methods of the Resource Allocation Working Party / Nicholas Mays, Gwyn Bevan. — London : Bedford Square Press/NCVO, 1987. — 180p. — (Occasional papers on social administration ; 81). — Bibliography: p161-180

PUBLIC HEALTH — Great Britain — Statistics

STATISTICS USERS CONFERENCE (1980)
Health statistics in Britain : proceedings of the 1980 Statistics Users Conference; arranged by the Society for Social Medicine on behalf of the Standing Committee of Statistics Users. — Newcastle upon Tyne : University of Newcastle upon Tyne. Health Care Research Unit, 1980. — [96]p

PUBLIC HEALTH — Italy — Statistics
ITALY. Istituto Centrale di Statistica
I conti della protezione sociale : sanità, previdenza e assistenza anni 1960-1982. — Roma : Istituto Centrale di Statistica, 1983. — 195p. — (Bollettino mensile di statistica. Supplemento ; 1983 n.28)

PUBLIC HEALTH — Namibia
A nation in peril : health in apartheid Namibia. — London : International Defence and Aid Fund, 1985. — 40p. — (Fact paper on Southern Africa ; no.13)

PUBLIC HEALTH — Organisation for Economic Co-operation and Development countries
SCHIEBER, George J.
Financing and delivering health care : a comparative analysis of OECD countries / [George J. Schieber]. — Paris : Organisation for Economic Co-operation and Development, 1987. — 101p. — (Social policy studies / Organisation for Economic Co-operation and Development ; no.4). — *Includes bibliographical references*

PUBLIC HEALTH — South Africa
SOUTH AFRICA
White paper on the report of the Commission of Inquiry into Health Services (The Browne Report). — [Pretoria : Government Printer, 1986]. — 46p. — *In English and Afrikaans*

PUBLIC HEALTH — Tanzania — History
TURSHEN, Meredeth
The political ecology of disease in Tanzania / Meredeth Turshen. — New Brunswick, N.J. : Rutgers University Press, c1984. — xiv, 259 p., [2] leaves of plates. — *Includes index. — Bibliography: p. 211-239*

PUBLIC HEALTH — Wales — Citizen administration
Cynrychiolaeth fwy democrataidd ar awdurdodau iechyd Cymru = Making Welsh health authorities more democratic. — Cardiff : HMSO, 1974. — 24p. — *In English and Welsh*

PUBLIC HEALTH ACT 1936
GREAT BRITAIN. Department of the Environment
A consultation paper on the review of the law of statutory nuisance and offensive trades. — London : the Department, [1979?]. — [30]p

PUBLIC HEALTH ADMINISTRATION — Denmark
Public administration and health care in Denmark. — Copenhagen : National Board of Health of Denmark, 1984. — 32p

PUBLIC HEALTH ADMINISTRATION — Great Britain — Finance
MAYS, Nicholas
Resource allocation in the Health Service : a review of the methods of the Resource Allocation Working Party / Nicholas Mays, Gwyn Bevan. — London : Bedford Square Press/NCVO, 1987. — 180p. — (Occasional papers on social administration ; 81). — *Bibliography: p161-180*

PUBLIC HEALTH ADMINISTRATION — Nepal
JUSTICE, Judith
Policies, plans, and people : culture and health development in Nepal / Judith Justice. — Berkeley : University of California Press, c1986. — p. cm. — (Comparative studies of health systems and medical care). — *Includes index. — Bibliography: p*

PUBLIC HEALTH ADMINISTRATION — Wales
Cynrychiolaeth fwy democrataidd ar awdurdodau iechyd Cymru = Making Welsh health authorities more democratic. — Cardiff : HMSO, 1974. — 24p. — *In English and Welsh*

PUBLIC HEALTH LAWS
BASSETT, W. H.
Environmental health procedures / W.H. Bassett. — 2nd ed. — London : H.K. Lewis, 1987. — xxi, 405p

PUBLIC HEALTH LAWS — Peru
PERU
[Laws, etc]. Ley orgánica del sector salud. — [Lima] : Ministerio de Salud, Oficina de Relaciones Públicas e Informaciones, [ca.1975]. — [13]p

PUBLIC HEALTH PERSONNEL
WORLD HEALTH ORGANIZATION.
Regional Experts Meeting on Health Manpower Development (1977 : Brazzaville)
Health manpower development : the problems of the health team : report / of a WHO Regional Experts Meeting on Health Manpower Development. — Brazzaville : Regional Office for Africa, World Health Organization, 1977. — [viii]13p. — (AFRO technical report series ; no.4). — *Includes bibliographical references*

PUBLIC HEALTH PERSONNEL — Education — Europe
WORLD HEALTH ORGANIZATION. Meeting on Primary Health Care in Undergraduate Medical Education (1983 : Exeter)
Primary health care in undergraduate medical education : report on a WHO meeting : Exeter, 18-22 July 1983. — Copenhagen : World Health Organization, 1984. — 64p. — *Includes summaries in French, German and Russian. — Bibliography: p40*

PUBLIC HEALTH PERSONNEL — Africa
TEKSE, K.
Some estimates of vital rates for Sierra Leone / [K. Tekse]. Kenya National Tuberculosis Programme : evaluation of a test-run / [J. J. Rogowski...et al.]. Migration of health personnel of the African Region / [J. Vysohlid]. — Brazzaville : Regional Office for Africa, World Health Organization, 1975. — 124p. — (AFRO technical papers ; no.9). — *Includes bibliographical references*

PUBLIC HEALTH SECURITY ACT, 1971
The Public Health Security Act, 1971. — [Copenhagen : Sundhedsstyrelsen?], 1971. — 15 leaves

PUBLIC HOUSING — Law and legislation — England
HUGHES, D. J. (David John), 1945-
Public sector housing law / D.J. Hughes. — 2nd ed. — London : Butterworths, 1987. — xxxix,329p. — *Previous ed.: 1981. — Includes bibliographies and index*

WRIGHT, Christopher J.
Housing improvement and repair / Christopher J. Wright. — London : Sweet & Maxwell, 1986. — xiv,130p. — *Bibliography: p125. — Includes index*

PUBLIC HOUSING — Law and legislation — Great Britain
GREAT BRITAIN. Parliament. House of Commons. Library. Research Division
The Housing and Building Control Bill (Bill 3, session 1983/84) / [Christine Gillie, Barry Winetrobe]. — [London] : the Division, 1983. — 21p. — (Reference sheet ; no.83/10). — *Includes bibliographical references*

GREAT BRITAIN. Parliament. House of Commons. Library. Research Division
Housing and Planning Bill (Bill 63 of 1985/86) / Oonagh Gay, Barry Winetrobe, Betty Miller. — [London] : the Division, 1986. — 38p. — (Reference sheet ; no.86/5). — *Bibliographical references: p30-38*

PUBLIC HOUSING — Standards — England — London
GREATER LONDON COUNCIL. Industry and Employment Branch
Housing standards : a survey of new build local authority housing in London 1981-1984 / Industry and Employment Branch, Housing Department. — [London] : the Council, 1986. — 48p. — *Bibliographical references: p37*

PUBLIC HOUSING — England
HENDERSON, Jeff
Race, class and state housing : inequality and the allocation of public housing in Britain / Jeff Henderson and Valerie Karn. — Aldershot : Gower, c1987. — xxiii,331p. — (Studies in urban and regional policy ; 4). — *Bibliography: p313-320. — Includes index*

PUBLIC HOUSING — England — London
GREATER LONDON COUNCIL
Council house sales : the implications for local authority housing in London. — [London : the Council, 1984]. — [36]p

The tenant census / M. Wright. — Harrow : Department of Housing, 1986. — [8]p

PUBLIC HOUSING — England — London — Management
GREATER LONDON COUNCIL. Controller of Housing and Technical Services
Relationship breakdown : the implications for local authority tenancies and the impact of the 1980 Housing Act / report by Controller of Housing and Technical Services. — [London : the Council], 1985. — 12 leaves

TUCKLEY, Will
Relationship breakdown and local authority tenancies / survey designed and carried out by Jill Barelli and Lesley Roberts; survey analysed and report written by Will Tuckley, Policy Division, GLC Housing Department. — [London] : Greater London Council, [1985]. — ii,23p. — *Bibliographical references: p19. — A GLC survey of London housing authorities' policies toward relationship breakdown among tenants in local authority housing*

PUBLIC HOUSING — England — Manchester (Greater Manchester)
MANCHESTER. City Council
Housing defects in Manchester. — Manchester : [the Council], 1986. — [50p]

PUBLIC HOUSING — Great Britain
FORREST, Ray
Monitoring the right to buy, 1980-1982 / Ray Forrest, Alan Murie. — Bristol : University of Bristol, School for Advanced Urban Studies, 1984. — 85p. — (Working paper / University of Bristol, School for Advanced Urban Studies ; no.40)

GREAT BRITAIN. Department of the Environment
Shared ownership : a new choice for tenants : Minister's speech to Shelter conference, 27 July 1979 / John Stanley. — London : the Department, 1979. — 36p

MINFORD, Patrick
The housing morass : regulation, immobility and unemployment : an economic analysis of the consequences of government regulation, with proposals to restore the market in rented housing / Patrick Minford, Michael Peel and Paul Ashton. — London : Institute of Economic Affairs, 1987. — 162p. — (Hobart paperback ; 25). — *Bibliography: p157-162*

Public housing : current trends and future developments / edited by David Clapham and John English. — London : Croom Helm, 1987. — 174p. — *Bibliography: p165-170. — Includes index*

WILSON, Roger
Difficult housing estates / Roger Wilson. — London : Tavistock Publications, 1963. — 43p. — (Tavistock pamphlet ; no.5)

PUBLIC HOUSING — Great Britain — Finance
BAILEY, George
Newlife for old estates / Dr. George Bailey. — London : Conservative Political Centre, 1987. — 28p

SERVICES TO COMMUNITY ACTION AND TRADE UNIONS
"We are not for sale". — London : SCAT Publications
part 1: 10 point action plan to fight estate sales. — 1986. — 31p

PUBLIC HOUSING — Great Britain — Maintenance and repair
AUDIT COMMISSION FOR LOCAL AUTHORITIES IN ENGLAND AND WALES
Improving council house maintenance : a report by the Audit Commission. — London : H.M.S.O., 1986. — 89p

PUBLIC HOUSING — Great Britain — Management
MATTHEWS, Alison
Management cooperatives : the early stages / Alison Matthews. — London : H.M.S.O., 1981. — iv,34p. — *At head of cover title: Department of the Environment*

PUBLIC HOUSING — Great Britain — Management — History
POWER, Anne
Property before people : the management of twentieth-century council housing / Anne Power. — London : Allen & Unwin, 1987. — [272]p. — *Includes bibliography and index*

PUBLIC HOUSING — London metropolitan area — Tower Hamlets
PHILLIPS, Deborah
What price equality? : a report on the allocation of GLC housing in Tower Hamlets / by Deborah Phillips. — London : Greater London Council, 1986. — 83p. — (GLC housing research and policy report ; no.9). — *Title from cover*

PUBLIC HOUSING — Northern Ireland
BRETT, C. E. B.
Housing a divided community / C. E. B. Brett. — Dublin : Institute of Public Administration in association with Institute of Irish Studies, Queen's University of Belfast, 1986. — xi,171p. — *Bibliography: p152-3*

PUBLIC HOUSING — United States
Housing America's poor / edited by Peter D. Salins. — Chapel Hill : University of North Carolina Press, c1987. — p. cm. — (Urban and regional policy and development studies). — *Includes index*

Housing desegregation and federal policy / edited by John M. Goering. — Chapel Hill : University of North Carolina Press, c1986. — x, 343 p. — (Urban and regional policy and development studies). — *Includes bibliographies and index*

PUBLIC HOUSING — United States — Case studies
MERRY, Sally Engle
Urban danger : life in a neighborhood of strangers / Sally Engle Merry. — Philadelphia : Temple University Press, 1981. — x, 278 p.. — *Includes index. — Bibliography: p. [259]-272*

PUBLIC INTEREST — United States
MCCANN, Michael W.
Taking reform seriously : perspectives on public interest liberalism / Michael W. McCann. — Ithaca : Cornell University Press, 1986. — 345 p.. — *Includes index. — Bibliography: p. 321-335*

PERTSCHUK, Michael
Giantkillers / by Michael Pertschuk. — New York : Norton, c1986. — p. cm. — *Includes index*

PUBLIC INTEREST LAW
Public interest law / edited by Jeremy Cooper and Rajeev Dhavan. — Oxford : Basil Blackwell, 1986. — xviii,482p.. — *Includes index*

PUBLIC INTEREST LAW — Great Britain
Public interest law / edited by Jeremy Cooper and Rajeev Dhavan. — Oxford : Basil Blackwell, 1986. — xviii,482p.. — *Includes index*

PUBLIC INVESTMENTS — Evaluation — Mathematical models — Case studies
MENNES, L. B. M.
Multicoutry investment analysis / Loet B. M. Mennes, Ardy J. Stoutjesdijk. — Baltimore : Johns Hopkins University Press for the World Bank, 1985. — xii,228p. — (The planning of investment programs ; v.4) (A World Bank research publication). — *Includes bibliographical references*

PUBLIC INVESTMENTS — Dominica
Dominica, priorities and prospects for development. — Washington, D.C., U.S.A. : World Bank, c1985. — [xiv],105p. — (World Bank country study)

PUBLIC INVESTMENTS — Grenada
Grenada, economic report. — Washington, D.C., U.S.A. : World Bank, c1985. — [xii],90p. — (A World Bank country study)

PUBLIC INVESTMENTS — Haiti
Haiti : public expenditure review. — Washington, D.C. : The World Bank, 1987. — xix,254p. — (A World Bank country study). — *Includes bibliographical references*

PUBLIC INVESTMENTS — Kenya
Guidelines for the preparation, appraisal and approval of new public sector investment projects. — Nairobi : Ministry of Economic Planning and Development, 1983. — 49p

PUBLIC INVESTMENTS — Latin America
PFEFFERMANN, Guy P.
Public expenditure in Latin America : effects on poverty / Guy Pfeffermann. — Washington, D.C. : The World Bank, 1987. — 38p. — (World Bank discussion papers ; no.5). — *Includes bibliographical references*

PUBLIC INVESTMENTS — Saint Kitts-Nevis
St. Christopher and Nevis : economic report. — Washington, D.C., U.S.A. : World Bank, 1985. — xii,82p. — (World Bank country study)

PUBLIC INVESTMENTS — Saint Lucia
St. Lucia : economic performance and prospects. — Washington, D.C., U.S.A. : World Bank, 1985. — [xi],99p. — (World Bank country study). — *"Based on the findings of a World Bank mission to St. Lucia in February 1985"--Pref*

PUBLIC LAW — Great Britain
GANZ, Gabriele
Understanding public law / Gabriele Ganz. — London : Fontana, 1987. — 125p. — (Understanding law). — *Bibliography: p117*

Public law and politics / edited by Carol Harlow. — London : Sweet & Maxwell, 1986. — [250]p. — *Includes index*

PUBLIC LAW — Spain
MARTIN MATEO, Ramón
Derecho público de la economía / Ramón Martin Mateo. — Madrid : CEURA, 1985. — 416p. — *Bibliographies*

MUÑOZ MACHADO, Santiago
Derecho publico de las comunidades autonomas / Santiago Muñoz Machado. — Madrid : Editorial Civitas 1. — 1982. — 634p

MUÑOZ MACHADO, Santiago
Derecho publico de las comunidades autonomas / Santiago Muñoz Machado. — Madrid : Editorial Civitas 2. — 1982. — 471p

PUBLIC LIBRARIES — England
REDFEARN, Judy
Libraries bring Prestel to the public : a summary of British Library-supported research 1979-1981 / Judy Redfearn. — [London] : British Library, c1983. — v,57p. — (Library and information research report ; 13)

PUBLIC LIBRARIES — England — Services to the aged
DEE, Marianne
Library services to older people / Marianne Dee, Judith Bowen. — London : British Library, c1986. — viii,186p. — (Library and information research report ; 37)

PUBLIC LIBRARIES — England — Somerset
STOAKLEY, R. J.
Public library services points in Somerset : an appraisal report to the Libraries, Museums and Records Committee of Somerset County Council, 4th June, 1980 / Roger Stoakley. — Bridgwater (Mount St., Bridgwater, Somerset TA6 3ES) : Somerset County Library, 1980. — 28p,[4]fold.leaves of plates

STOAKLEY, Roger
The library service in Somerset : a report to the Libraries, Museums and Records Committee of the County Council, 19th June, 1985. — [Bridgwater] : Somerset County Council, 1985. — 15p

PUBLIC LIBRARIES — Great Britain
YEATES, R.
Prestel in the public library. — Boston Spa : British Library Lending Division, July 1982. — [134]p. — (Library and information research reports ; 2)

PUBLIC LIBRARIES — Great Britain — Acquisitions
SPILLER, David
Book selection : an introduction to principles and practice / David Spiller ; with an introduction by Brian Baumfield. — 4th ed. — London : Bingley, 1986. — ix,235p. — *Previous ed.: 1980. — Bibliography: p206-223. — Includes index*

PUBLIC LIBRARIES — Great Britain — Services to the blind
CRADDOCK, Peter
The public library and blind people : a survey and review of current practice / Peter Craddock. — London : British Library, c1985. — xv,106p. — (Library and information research report ; 36). — *Bibliography: p92-102*

PUBLIC OFFICERS — Political activity — Bibliography
GREAT BRITAIN. Civil Service Department. Central Management Library
The political activities of civil servants. — London : the Library, 1978. — 7p. — (Policy science documentation. Bibliography series ; B11)

PUBLIC OPINION
GINSBERG, Benjamin
The captive public : how mass opinion promotes state power / Benjamin Ginsberg. — New York : Basic Books, c1986. — xi, 272 p.. — *Includes index. — Bibliography: p. [233]-249*

Pressa i obshchestvennoe mnenie / otv. redaktor V. S. Korobeinikov. — Moskva : Nauka, 1986. — 204p. — *Bibliography: p196-[203]*

PUBLIC OPINION — Addresses, essays, lectures
WATKINS, Leslie
Private opinions public polls / Leslie Watkins, Robert M. Worcester. — [London] : Thames and Hudson, c1986. — 207p. — *Includes index*

PUBLIC OPINION — Africa
OLOKO, Olatunde
Dilemma of African modernisation : an inaugural lecture delivered at the University of Lagos, on Friday, 27th May, 1979 / by Olatunde Oloko. — [Lagos] : University of Lagos Press, 1981. — 54 p.. — (Inaugural lecture series / Lagos University Press)

PUBLIC OPINION — Canada
WEIMANN, Gabriel
Hate on trial : the Zundel Affair : thr media public opinion in Canada / Gabriel Weimann and Conrad Winn. — Oakville, Ontario : Mosaic Press, 1986. — 201p. — *Includes references*

PUBLIC OPINION — Canada — Congresses
Law in a cynical society? : Opinion and law in the 1980's : papers presented at a conference held in 1982 at the University of Manitoba / edited by Dale Gibson [and] Janet K. Baldwin. — Calgary : Carswell Legal Publications, 1985. — xviii,464p

PUBLIC OPINION — Europe
LLOYD, Michael Gordon
Legal databases in Europe : user attitudes and supplier strategies / Michael Lloyd. — Amsterdam ; New York : North-Holland ; New York, N.Y., U.S.A. : Sole distributors for the U.S.A. and Canada, Elsevier Science Pub. Co., c1986. — xiii, 218 p.. — *At head of title: Commission of the European Communities. — "Report no. EUR 10439 of the Commission of the European Communities"--T.p. verso. Bibliography: p.205*

PUBLIC OPINION — European Economic Community countries
HEWSTONE, Miles
Understanding attitudes to the European Community : a social-psychological study in four member states / Miles Hewstone. — Cambridge : Cambridge University Press, 1986. — 1v. — (European monographs in social psychology). — *Includes index*

PUBLIC OPINION — France
CARROLL, E. Malcolm
French public opinion and foreign affairs 1870-1914 / by E. Malcolm Carroll. — New York : the Century, 1931. — viii,348p

HERZLICH, Claudine
Health and illness : a social psychological analysis / Claudine Herzlich ; translated [from the French] by Douglas Graham. — London : Academic Press [for] the European Association of Experimental Social Psychology, 1973. — xvi,159p. — (European monographs in social psychology ; 5). — *Translation of: 'Santé et maladie'. Paris : Mouton, 1970. — Bibliography: p.151-154. — Includes index*

PUBLIC OPINION — Georgia — Augusta Region — History — 19th century
HARRIS, J. William
Plain folk and gentry in a slave society : white liberty and Black slavery in Augusta's hinterlands / J. William Harris. — 1st ed. — Middletown, Conn. : Wesleyan University Press ; Scranton, Pa. : Distributed by Harper & Row, 1985. — xv, 274 p.. — : *Originally presented as the author's thesis (Ph. D.--Johns Hopkins University, 1982.). — Includes index. — Bibliography: p. 253-261*

PUBLIC OPINION — Great Britain
BUNTING, Claire
Public attitudes to deafness : a survey carried out on behalf of the Department of Health and Social Security / Claire Bunting. — London : H.M.S.O., 1981. — vi,43p. — *At head of title: Office of Population Censuses and Surveys Social Survey Division*

PUBLIC OPINION — Great Britain — History — 19th century
YOKOYAMA, Toshio
Japan in the Victorian mind : a study of stereotyped images of a nation, 1850-80 / Toshio Yokoyama. — London : Macmillan, 1987. — xxiii,233p,[16]p of plates. — (St Antony's/Macmillan series). — *Bibliography: p208-219. — Includes index*

PUBLIC OPINION — Greece — Athens
CARTER, L. B.
The quiet Athenian / L.B. Carter. — Oxford : Clarendon, 1986. — [ix,224]p. — *Includes bibliography*

PUBLIC OPINION — India
INDRAYAN, N. K
Law and public opinion in India / N.K. Indrayan. — New Delhi : Deep & Deep Publications, c1985. — 311 p.. — *Includes index. — Bibliography: p. [302]-308*

PUBLIC OPINION — South Africa
NEUHAUS, Richard John
Dispensations : the future of South Africa as South Africans see it / by Richard John Neuhaus. — Grand Rapids, Mich. : W.B. Eerdmans Pub. Co., c1986. — p. cm. — *Includes bibliographical references*

ORKIN, Mark
Disinvestment, the struggle, and the future : what black South Africans really think / Mark Orkin. — Johannesburg : Ravan Press, 1986. — xii, 78 p.. — *A CASE/IBR study. — Includes bibliographies and index*

PUBLIC OPINION — Southern States
REED, John Shelton
The enduring South : subcultural persistence in mass society / John Shelton Reed ; with a new afterword by the author. — Chapel Hill : University of North Carolina Press, 1986, c1974. — p. cm. — *Includes index. — Bibliography: p*

PUBLIC OPINION — Soviet Union
The Other side : how Soviets and Americans perceive each other / edited by Jonathan J. Halperin. — New Brunswick, U.S.A. : Transaction Books, c1987. — p. cm. — *Includes index. — Bibliography: p*

Pressa i obshchestvennoe mnenie / otv. redaktor V. S. Korobeinikov. — Moskva : Nauka, 1986. — 204p. — *Bibliography: p196-[203]*

PUBLIC OPINION — United States
BENNETT, Stephen Earl
Apathy in America, 1960-1984 : causes and consequences of citizen political indifference / Stephen Earl Bennett. — Dobbs Ferry, N.Y. : Transnational Publishers, c1986. — x, 198 p.. — *Includes index. — Bibliography: p. 179-193*

GILBERT, James Burkhart
A cycle of outrage : juvenile delinquency and mass media in the 1950s / James Gilbert. — New York ; Oxford : Oxford University Press, 1986. — vi, 258p, [6]p of plates. — *Includes bibliographical references and index. — Bibliography: p*

GILBOA, Eytan
American public opinion toward Israel and the Arab-Israeli conflict / Eytan Gilboa. — Lexington, Mass. : Lexington Books, c1987. — xvi, 366 p.. — *Includes index. — Bibliography: p. [337]-347*

KLUEGEL, James R
Beliefs about inequality : Americans' views of what is and what ought to be / James R. Kluegel and Eliot R. Smith. — New York : A. de Gruyter, 1986. — p. cm. — *Includes index. — Bibliography: p*

LEVIN, Murray Burton
Talk radio and the American dream / by Murray B. Levin. — Lexington, Mass. : Lexington Books, c1987. — xv, 170 p.. — *Includes index*

LEWIS, Dan A
Fear of crime : incivility and the production of a social problem / Dan A. Lewis and Greta Salem. — New Brunswick, U.S.A. : Transaction Books, c1986. — p. cm. — *Includes index. — Bibliography: p*

NEUMAN, W. Russell
The paradox of mass politics : knowledge and opinion in the American electorate / W. Russell Neuman. — Cambridge, Mass. : Harvard University Press, 1986. — 241 p.. — *Includes index. — Bibliography: p. [222]-236*

The Other side : how Soviets and Americans perceive each other / edited by Jonathan J. Halperin. — New Brunswick, U.S.A. : Transaction Books, c1987. — p. cm. — *Includes index. — Bibliography: p*

PUBLIC OPINION — United States — History
Australia through American eyes, 1935-1945 : observations by American diplomats / selected, edited and with an introduction by P.G. Edwards. — St Lucia : University of Queensland Press ; Hemel Hempstead : Distributed by Prentice-Hall, 1979. — xi,104p. — *Bibliography: p.97-101. — Includes index*

HARTSFIELD, Larry K
The American response to professional crime, 1870-1917 / Larry K. Hartsfield. — Westport, Conn. ; London : Greenwood Press, c1985. — x, 226p. — (Contributions in criminology and penology ; no. 8). — *Includes index. — Bibliography: p.[209]-215p*

HOLMES, Jack E
The mood/interest theory of American foreign policy / Jack E. Holmes ; with a foreword by Frank L. Klingberg. — Lexington, Ky. : University Press of Kentucky, c1985. — xiii, 238 p.. — *Includes index. — Bibliography: p. [222]-225*

KAMMEN, Michael G
A machine that would go of itself : the Constitution in American culture / Michael Kammen. — 1st ed. — New York : Knopf, 1986. — xxii, 532 p., [16] p. of plates. — *Includes index. — Bibliography: p. 413-507*

PUBLIC OPINION — United States — History — 19th century
KNOBEL, Dale T
Paddy and the republic : ethnicity and nationality in antebellum America / by Dale T. Knobel. — 1st ed. — Middletown, Conn. : Wesleyan University Press ; Scranton, Pa. : Distributed by Harper & Row, c1986. — p. cm . — *Includes index. — Bibliography: p*

PUBLIC OPINION — Washington (State)
SUGAI, Wayne H
Nuclear power and ratepayer protest : the Washington Public Power Supply System / Wayne H. Sugai. — Boulder : Westview Press, 1987. — p. cm. — (Westview special studies in public policy and public systems management). — *Bibliography: p*

PUBLIC OPINION POLLS
MEGNAUD, Hélène Y.
Les sondages d'opinion / Hélène Y. Megnaud et Denis Duclos. — Paris : La Découverte, 1985. — 127p. — *Bibliography: p122-125*

PUBLIC ORDER ACT 1936
THORNTON, Peter, 1946-
We protest : the public order debate / Peter Thornton. — London : National Council for Civil Liberties, 1985. — [96]p

PUBLIC ORDER ACT 1986
THORNTON, Peter, 1946-
Public order law : including the Public Order Act 1986 / Peter Thornton. — London : Financial Training Publications, c1987. — xxi, 226p. — *Bibliography: p.[219]-220. — Includes the text of the Public Order Act 1986*

PUBLIC ORDER BILL 1985-86
GREAT BRITAIN. Parliament. House of Commons. Library. Research Division
Public Order Bill, Bill 40 of 1985-86 / Mary Baber, Jane Fiddick. — [London] : the Division, 1986. — 24p. — (Reference sheet ; no.86/1). — *Bibliographical references: p23-24*

GREATER LONDON COUNCIL
The control of protest : the new Public Order Bill : the Greater London Council's response, adopted 19 December 1985. — [London : the Council], 1986. — 51p. — (Policing London)

PUBLIC POLICY — United States

RUSHEFSKY, Mark R.
Making cancer policy / Mark R. Rushefsky. — Albany : State University of New York Press, c1986. — xiii, 257 p.. — (SUNY series in public administration in the 1980s). — *Includes index. — Bibliography: p. 225-245*

PUBLIC POLICY (INTERNATIONAL LAW)

MCDOUGAL, Myres Smith
Studies in world public order / by Myres S. McDougal and associates. — New Haven : New Haven Press ; Dordrecht : M. Nijhoff, 1986. — p. cm. — *Includes index*

PUBLIC POLICY (LAW)

Do elections matter? / Benjamin Ginsberg and Alan Stone, editors. — Armonk, N.Y. : M.E. Sharpe, c1986. — 240 p.. — *Includes bibliographies*

PUBLIC POLICY (LAW) — Great Britain

GREAT BRITAIN. Parliament. House of Commons. Library. Research Division
Public Order Bill, Bill 40 of 1985-86 / Mary Baber, Jane Fiddick. — [London] : the Division, 1986. — 24p. — (Reference sheet ; no.86/1). — *Bibliographical references: p23-24*

GREAT BRITAIN. Parliament. House of Commons. Library. Research Division
Review of public order legislation / [Patrick Nealon]. — [London] : the Division, 1980. — 21p. — (Background paper ; no.76)

GREATER LONDON COUNCIL
The control of protest : the new Public Order Bill : the Greater London Council's response, adopted 19 December 1985. — [London : the Council], 1986. — 51p. — (Policing London)

Law and order prospects for the future / Malcolm Rifkind [et al.]. — Edinburgh : University of Edinburgh. Department of Christian Ethics and Practical Theology, 1986. — 82p. — (Occasional papers / University of Edinburgh. Department of Christian Ethics and Practical Theology ; no.10)

THORNTON, Peter, 1946-
Public order law : including the Public Order Act 1986 / Peter Thornton. — London : Financial Training Publications, c1987. — xxi, 226p. — *Bibliography: p.[219]-220. — Includes the text of the Public Order Act 1986*

PUBLIC POLICY (LAW) — Great Britain — Bibliography

Urban riots and public order : a select bibliography, 1975-1985 / compiled by: E. Edwards, R. Golland & S. Leach [for the GLC Intelligence Unit]. — [S.l. : s.n. : Technical Communications [distributor], 1986]. — iii,159p

PUBLIC POLICY (LAW) — Great Britain — Information Services

Urban riots and public order : a select bibliography, 1975-1985 / compiled by: E. Edwards, R. Golland & S. Leach [for the GLC Intelligence Unit]. — [S.l. : s.n. : Technical Communications [distributor], 1986]. — iii,159p

PUBLIC POLICY (LAW) — United States

BELL, Robert
The culture of policy deliberations / Robert Bell. — New Brunswick, N.J. : Rutgers University Press, c1985. — viii, 264 p.. — *Includes index. — Bibliography: p. 227-253*

PUBLIC PROSECUTORS — Canada — History

STENNING, Philip C
Appearing for the Crown : a legal and historical review of criminal prosecutorial authority in Canada / a study conducted for the Law Reform Commission of Canada by Philip C. Stenning. — Cowansville, Qué. : Brown Legal Publications, c1986. — 426 p.. — *Includes indexes. — Bibliography: p. 385-396*

PUBLIC RECORDS — Great Britain

STOREY, Richard
Consolidated guide to the modern records centre / compiled by Richard Storey and Alistair Tough. — Coventry : University of Warwick Library, 1986. — 86p. — (Occasional publications / University of Warwick Library ; no.14)

PUBLIC RECORDS — Great Britain — Access control

CAMPBELL, Duncan, 1952-
On the record : surveillance, computers and privacy : the inside story / Duncan Campbell and Steve Connor. — London : Joseph, 1986. — 347p,[8]p of plates. — *Includes index*

PUBLIC RECORDS — Sri Lanka

SRI LANKA. Department of National Archives
Administration report of the Director of National Archives / Sri Lanka, Department of National Archives. — Colombo : [the Department], 1983-. — *Annual. — Added title in Sinhalese and Tamil*

PUBLIC RECORDS — United States — Access control

LAUDON, Kenneth C.
Dossier society : value choices in the design of national information systems / Kenneth C. Laudon. — New York : Columbia University Press, 1986. — xi, 421 p.. — (CORPS (computing, organizations, policy, and society) series). — *Includes index. — Bibliography: p. [403]-414*

PUBLIC RECORDS — United States — Data processing

LAUDON, Kenneth C.
Dossier society : value choices in the design of national information systems / Kenneth C. Laudon. — New York : Columbia University Press, 1986. — xi, 421 p.. — (CORPS (computing, organizations, policy, and society) series). — *Includes index. — Bibliography: p. [403]-414*

PUBLIC RELATIONS — England — Police

SOUTHGATE, Peter
Police-public encounters / by Peter Southgate with the assistance of Paul Ekblom. — London : H.M.S.O., 1986. — vi,143p. — (Home Office research study ; no.90). — *A Home Office Research and Planning Unit report*

PUBLIC RELATIONS — Great Britain — Police

Policing and the community / edited by Peter Willmott. — London : Policy Studies Institute, 1987. — 67p. — (PSI discussion paper ; no.16)

PUBLIC RELATIONS — United States

Views from the top : establishing the foundation for the future of business / edited by Jerome M. Rosow. — London : Sphere, 1987. — xv,[208]p. — *Originally published: Facts on File, 1985*

PUBLIC RELATIONS — United States — Police

HAGEMAN, Mary J
Police-community relations / Mary Jeannette Hageman. — Beverly Hills, Calif. : Sage Publications, c1985. — 157p. — (Law and criminal justice series ; v. 6). — *Bibliography: p149-154*

PUBLIC SCHOOLS — Brazil — Finance

Brazil : finance of primary education. — Washington, D.C. : The World Bank, 1986. — 78p. — (A World Bank country study). — *Bibliographical references: p55-56*

PUBLIC SCHOOLS — New York (N.Y.) — History

BRUMBERG, Stephan F
Going to America, going to school : the Jewish immigrant public school encounter in turn-of-the-century New York City / Stephan F. Brumberg. — New York : Praeger, 1986. — xiii, 282 p.. — *Includes bibliographies and indexes*

PUBLIC SCHOOLS — United States

ADELSON, Joseph
Inventing adolescence : the political psychology of everyday schooling / Joseph Adelson. — New Brunswick, N.J., U.S.A. : Transaction Books, c1986. — ix, 296 p.. — *Includes bibliographical references*

PUBLIC SCHOOLS — United States — Curricula — Censorship

ARONS, Stephen
Compelling belief : the culture of American schooling / Stephen Arons. — 1st paperback ed. — Amherst : University of Massachusetts Press, 1986, c1983. — xii, 228 p.. — : Reprint. *Originally published: New York : McGraw-Hill, c1983. — Includes index*

PUBLIC SERVICE EMPLOYMENT — Great Britain

Action on unemployment : 100 projects with unemployed people. — London : Church Action with the Unemployed, c1984. — 153p

PUBLIC SERVICE SUPERANNUATION ACT (CANADA)

NORWAY. Statistik Sentralbyrå
Kvartalsvis hasjonalregnskap = quarterly national accounts / Statistik Sentralbyrå, Norway. — Oslo : Statistik Sentralbyrå, 1978-. — *Annual*

CANADA. Treasury Board
Report on the administration of the Public Service Superannuation Act. — Ottawa : Canada. Treasury Board, 1984-. — *Annual. — Text in English and French*

PUBLIC SERVICES INTERNATIONAL

Info / Public Services International. — Ferney-Voltair : Public Services International, 1985-. — *Monthly*

PUBLIC TELEVISION — Government policy — United States

STONE, David M.
Nixon and the politics of public television / David M. Stone. — New York : Garland Pub., 1985. — xxi, 370p. — (Modern American history). — *Bibliography: p[342]-360*

PUBLIC UNIVERSITIES AND COLLEGES — United States — Directories

OHLES, John F
Public colleges and universities / John F. Ohles and Shirley M. Ohles. — Westport, Conn. ; London : Greenwood Press, 1986. — x, 1014p. — (Greenwood encyclopedia of American institutions). — *Includes index. — Includes bibliographical references*

PUBLIC UTILITIES — Employees — Great Britain

PARRY, Richard
Public employment in Britain and Germany / Richard Parry and Klaus-Dieter Schmidt. — Glasgow : University of Strathclyde. Centre for the Study of Public Policy, 1987. — 41p. — (Studies in public policy ; 157). — *Bibliography: p25-26*

PUBLIC UTILITIES — Law and legislation — United States

HJELMFELT, David C
Antitrust and regulated industries / David C. Hjelmfelt. — New York : Wiley Law Publications, c1985. — xxi, 465 p.. — (Federal practice library). — *Includes bibliographical references and index*

PUBLIC UTILITIES — Belize

DEVELOPMENT FINANCE CORPORATION (Belize). Investment Promotion Unit
Communication, transport and public utilities in Belize. — Belize City : the Corporation, 1980. — 11 leaves

PUBLIC UTILITIES — Canada — History

ARMSTRONG, Christopher
Monopoly's moment : the organization and regulation of Canadian utilities, 1830-1930 / Christopher Armstrong, H.V. Nelles. — Philadelphia : Temple University Press, 1986. — xvii, 393 p.. — (Technology and urban growth). — *Includes index.* — *Bibliography: p. 331-383*

PUBLIC UTILITIES — France

FRANCE. Haut Conseil du Secteur Public
Rapport. — Paris : Documentation Française, 1984-. — *Annual*

PUBLIC UTILITIES — Great Britain

LABOUR PARTY (Great Britain)
At your service! : Labour's charter for better local services. — London : Labour Party, 1986. — 15p

LABOUR RESEARCH DEPARTMENT
Privatisation : paying the price. — London : LRD Publications, 1987. — 48p

SERVICES TO COMMUNITY ACTION AND TRADE UNIONS
Hawley Group PLC Cleaning up? / researched by Services to Community Action and Trade Unions and Hillingdon Trade Union Support Unit. — London : SCAT Publications, 1986. — [8]p

SERVICES TO COMMUNITY ACTION AND TRADE UNIONS
The public cost of private contractors. — London : Services to Community Action and Trade Unions, 1985. — 64p

PUBLIC UTILITIES — Netherlands — Statistics

Vierde algemene bedrijfstelling, 1978. — 's-Gravenhage : Staatsuitgeverij. — *Rear cover title: Fourth general economic census, 1978: volume 2, part A: mining and quarrying, manufacturing, public utilities, construction and installation on construction projects d.2: Algemene sectorale gegevens A: Delfstoffenwinning, industrie, openbare nutsbedrijven, bouwnijverheid en bouwinstallatie.* — 1985. — 87p

PUBLIC UTILITIES — Scotland — Dumfries and Galloway

DUMFRIES AND GALLOWAY. Regional Council
Structure plan : report of survey : settlements and services (revised). — Dumfries : [the Regional Council], 1979. — 115p

PUBLIC UTILITIES — United States

CREW, Michael A.
The economics of public utility regulation / Michael A. Crew and Paul R. Kleindorfer. — London : Macmillan, 1986. — [256]p. — *Includes index*

Regulating utilities in an era of deregulation / edited by Michael A. Crew. — Basingstoke : Macmillan, 1987. — xii,201p. — *Conference proceedings.* — *Includes bibliographies and index*

PUBLIC UTILITIES STREET WORKS ACT 1950

GREAT BRITAIN
Public utilities street works : the government response to the Horne report on the review of the Public Utilities Street Works Act 1950. — London : H.M.S.O., 1986. — 32p. — *At head of title page: Department of Transport*

PUBLIC WELFARE

ALBEDA, W.
De crisis van de werkgelegenheid en de verzorgingsstaat : analyse en perspectief / W. Albeda. — Kampen : J. H. Kok, c1984. — 108p

BALLOCH, Susan
Caring for unemployed people : a study of the impact of unemployment on demand for personal social services / Susan Balloch...[et al.] for the Association of Metropolitan Authorities. — [London] : Bedford Square Press, NCVO for the Association of Metropolitan Authorities, [1985]. — xi,139p

JORDAN, Bill, 1941-
Rethinking welfare / Bill Jordan. — Oxford : Basil Blackwell, 1987. — [224]p. — *Includes index*

KEITH-LUCAS, Alan
Some casework concepts for the public welfare worker / Alan Keith-Lucas. — Chapel Hill : University of North Carolina Press, 1957. — 58p

Modern welfare states : a comparative view of trends and prospects / edited by Robert R. Friedmann, Neil Gilbert, Moshe Sherer. — Brighton : Wheatsheaf, 1987. — xiv,305p. — (Studies in international social policy and welfare). — *Conference proceedings.* — *Includes bibliographies and index*

PARTINGTON, Martin
Socio-legal studies and social welfare / Martin Partington ; a report for the Government and Law Committee of the Economic and Social Research Council. — London : Economic and Social Research Council, 1986. — 78p. — *Bibliography: p59-78*

PUBLIC WELFARE — Bibliography

STEWART, Gillian
The social services bibliography 1980-1985. — 3rd ed. / compiled by Gill Stewart and John Stewart in collaboration with Max McMurdo. — Lancaster : University of Lancaster, Department of Social Administration, 1985. — [205]p. — *Previous ed.: published as Personal social services bibliography. London : Library Association, 1980.* — *Includes index*

PUBLIC WELFARE — Cost effectiveness — Bibliography

SHRIGLEY, Sheila
Selected references on evaluation, cost-benefit analysis and cost-effectiveness in the social services / compiled by Sheila M. Shrigley. — London : Department of Health and Social Security Library, 1977-1978. — 6p. — (Bibliography series / Department of Health and Social Security Library ; no.B68). — *Includes supplement, compiled July 1978*

PUBLIC WELFARE — Data processing

SMITH, N. J.
Social welfare and computers : a general outline / N. J. Smith. — Melbourne : Longman Cheshire, 1985. — xiii,124p. — *Bibliography: p115-119*

PUBLIC WELFARE — Government policy — Great Britain

Challenges to social policy / edited by Richard Berthoud. — Aldershot : Gower, c1985. — x,220p. — *Includes bibliographies and index*

PUBLIC WELFARE — Law and legislation — Great Britain

Encyclopedia of social services law and practice. — [London] : Sweet & Maxwell : W. Green, 1981-. — 2v.(loose-leaf). — *Updated by loose-leaf supplements.* — *Includes indexes*

PUBLIC WELFARE — Political aspects — Australia

CASTLES, Francis G.
The working class and welfare : reflections on the political development of the welfare state in Australia and New Zealand, 1890-1980 / Francis G. Castles. — Sydney ; London : Allen & Unwin, 1985. — [xiv,140]p. — *Includes index*

PUBLIC WELFARE — Political aspects — New Zealand

CASTLES, Francis G.
The working class and welfare : reflections on the political development of the welfare state in Australia and New Zealand, 1890-1980 / Francis G. Castles. — Sydney ; London : Allen & Unwin, 1985. — [xiv,140]p. — *Includes index*

PUBLIC WELFARE — Religious aspects — Christianity

Not just for the poor : Christian perspectives on the welfare state / report of the Social Policy Committee of the Board for Social Responsibility. — London : Church House, c1986. — vii,146p. — *Bibliography: p145*

PUBLIC WELFARE — Australia — History

CASTLES, Francis G.
The working class and welfare : reflections on the political development of the welfare state in Australia and New Zealand, 1890-1980 / Francis G. Castles. — Sydney ; London : Allen & Unwin, 1985. — [xiv,140]p. — *Includes index*

PUBLIC WELFARE — Canada

The Canadian state : evolution and transition / edited by Jacqueline S. Ismael. — Edmonton, Alberta : University of Alberta Press, 1987. — xxv,390p

PUBLIC WELFARE — Canada — Congresses

Canadian social welfare policy : federal and provincial dimensions / edited by Jacqueline S. Ismael. — Kingston : McGill-Queen's University Press, 1985. — xviii, 187 p.. — (Canadian public administration series =Collection Administration publique canadienne). — *"The Institute of Public Administration of Canada.".* — *Proceedings of the First Conference on Provincial Social Welfare Policy, held at the University of Calgary, May 1982.* — *Includes bibliographies and index*

PUBLIC WELFARE — England — History

ROSE, Michael E.
The relief of poverty, 1834-1914 / prepared for the Economic History Society by Michael E. Rose. — 2nd ed. — Basingstoke : Macmillan, 1986. — [92p]. — (Studies in economic and social history). — *Previous ed.: 1972.* — *Includes bibliography and index*

PUBLIC WELFARE — England — History — 19th century

MARSHALL, J. D.
The Old Poor Law, 1795-1834 / prepared for the Economic History Society by J.D. Marshall. — 2nd ed. — Basingstoke : Macmillan, 1985. — 57p. — (Studies in economic and social history). — *Previous ed.: 1968.* — *Bibliography: p51-54.* — *Includes index*

PUBLIC WELFARE — Germany (West)

NAUJECK, Kurt
Die Anfänge des sozialen Netzes 1945-1952 / Kurt Naujeck. — Bielefeld : Kleine, c1984. — 276p. — (Wissenschaftliche Reihe ; Bd.19). — *Dissertation, Universität Düsseldorf, 1983.* — *Bibliography: p261-267*

PUBLIC WELFARE — Great Britain

BARR, N. A.
The economics of the welfare state / Nicholas Barr. — London : Weidenfeld and Nicholson, 1987. — xiv,475p. — *Bibliography: p432-459*

BERESFORD, Peter
Whose welfare : private care of public services? / Peter Beresford and Suzy Croft. — Brighton : Lewis Cohen Urban Studies Centre, 1986. — xvi,384p. — *Bibliography: p382-384*

PUBLIC WELFARE — Great Britain
continuation

Collaboration in community care : a discussion document. — London : H.M.S.O., 1978. — [6],64p. — *The Working Party on Collaboration between the health and social services in Community Care was the joint creation of the Standing Medical and the Standing Nursing and Midwifery Advisory Committees of the Central Health Services Council, and the Personal Social Services Council' - Introduction. — Chairman of the working party: Dame Albertine Winner. — Bibliography: p55-59*

CUTLER, Tony
Keynes, Beveridge and beyond / Tony Cutler, Karel Williams and John Williams. — London : Routledge and Kegan Paul, 1986. — [248]p. — *Includes bibliography and index*

DAVIES, Bleddyn
Matching resources to needs in community care : an evaluated demonstration of a long-term care model / Bleddyn Davies & David Challis. — Aldershot : Gower, c1986. — xxxii,658p. — *Bibliography: p571-642. — Includes index*

DAVIES, Stephen
Beveridge revisited : new foundations for tomorrow's welfare / Stephen Davies. — London : Centre for Policy Studies, 1986. — 48p. — (Policy study ; no.79)

GREAT BRITAIN. Department of Health and Social Security. Regional Directorate
Relations with social services : report of joint study...of the relationships between the Supplementary Benefits organisation and social services / by the Department's Regional Directorate and Social Work Service. — [London] : the Department, 1979. — viii,48p

GREAT BRITAIN. Department of Health and Social Security. Social Work Service. Development Group
Some brief notes on the Development Group. — [London] : the Group, 1978. — 3p

KNOX, Oliver
The wealthy wellfairs : how to care for the rich / Oliver Knox. — London : Centre for Policy Studies, 1986. — 38p. — (Pilot policy / Centre for Policy Studies)

LE GRAND, Julian
The middle classes and the welfare state / Julian Le Grand and David Winter. — London : Welfare State Programme. Suntory-Toyota International Centre for Economics and Related Disciplines, 1987. — 52p. — (Discussion paper / Welfare State Programme. Suntory-Toyota International Centre for Economics and Related Disciplines ; no.14). — *Bibliography: p51-52*

PERSONAL SOCIAL SERVICES COUNCIL
Personal social services : basic information. — [London] : the Council, 1977. — 27p

TOSSELL, David
Inside the caring services / David Tossell and Richard Webb. — London : Edward Arnold, 1986. — [272]p. — *Includes index*

Towards the sensitive bureaucracy : consumers, wlefare, and the new pluralism / editors, Drew Clode, Christopher Parker, Stuart Etherington. — [Brookfield, VT] : Gower Pub., 1986. — p. cm. — *Includes bibliographies and index*

Towards the sensitive bureaucracy : consumers, welfare and the new pluralism / edited by Drew Clode, Christopher Parker, Stuart Etherington. — Aldershot : Gower, c1987. — x,145p. — *Includes bibliographies and index*

PUBLIC WELFARE — Great Britain — Bibliography

ALLBROOKE, Jill C.
Selected references on joint planning and joint finance in the health and social services / compiled by Jill C. Allbrooke. — London : Department of Health and Social Security Library, 1979. — 4p. — (Bibliography series / Department of Health and Social Security Library ; no.B123)

SHRIGLEY, Sheila
Selected references on economies and resource allocation in the social services / compiled by Sheila M. Shrigley. — London : Department of Health and Social Security Library, 1977. — 8p. — (Bibliography series / Department of Health and Social Security Library ; no.B71)

PUBLIC WELFARE — Great Britain — History

CLARKE, John
Ideologies of welfare : from dreams to disillusion / John Clarke, Allan Cochrane and Carol Smart. — London : Hutchinson, 1987. — 206p. — (The state of welfare). — *Bibliography: p[197]-201*

PUBLIC WELFARE — Great Britain — History — 19th century

HENNOCK, E. P.
British social reform and German precedents : the case of social insurance 1880-1914 / E.P. Hennock. — Oxford : Clarendon, 1987. — vi,243p. — *Bibliography: p216-229. — Includes index*

PUBLIC WELFARE — Great Britain — History — 20th century

HENNOCK, E. P.
British social reform and German precedents : the case of social insurance 1880-1914 / E.P. Hennock. — Oxford : Clarendon, 1987. — vi,243p. — *Bibliography: p216-229. — Includes index*

WEBB, Adrian
Social work, social care and social planning : the personal social services since Seebohm / Adrian Webb and Gerald Wistow. — London : Longman, 1987. — [336]p. — (Social policy in modern Britain). — *Includes bibliography and index*

PUBLIC WELFARE — India

SHARMA, K. M.
Social assistance in India / K. M. Sharma. — Delhi : Macmillan Co. of India, 1976. — x,119p. — *Revision of author's thesis, University of Allahabad. — Bibliography: p [109]-114*

PUBLIC WELFARE — Ireland — Statistics

Statistical information on social welfare services / Department of Social Welfare, Ireland. — Dublin : Stationery Office, 1985-. — *Annual*

PUBLIC WELFARE — Mexico

INSTITUTO MEXICANO DEL SEGURO SOCIAL. Unidad de Promoción Voluntaria
Memoria de actividades 1977-1982 = Activities report 1977-1982. — [México] : the Unidad, 1982. — [34p]. — *Text in Spanish and English*

PUBLIC WELFARE — Middle East

Social welfare in the Middle East / edited by John Dixon. — London : Croom Helm, c1987. — xiii,218p. — (Croom Helm comparative social welfare series). — *Includes bibliographies and index*

PUBLIC WELFARE — New Zealand — History

CASTLES, Francis G.
The working class and welfare : reflections on the political development of the welfare state in Australia and New Zealand, 1890-1980 / Francis G. Castles. — Sydney ; London : Allen & Unwin, 1985. — [xiv,140]p. — *Includes index*

PUBLIC WELFARE — Northern Ireland

GREAT BRITAIN. Working Group on Revenue Resource Allocations to Health and Social Services Boards in Northern Ireland
Proposals for the allocation of revenue resources for health and personal social services (PARR) : report. — [Belfast] : the Department, 1978. — [76]p

PUBLIC WELFARE — Pennsylvania — Philadelphia — History — 19th century

CLEMENT, Priscilla Ferguson
Welfare and the poor in the nineteenth-century city : Philadelphia, 1800-1854 / Priscilla Ferguson Clement. — Rutherford [N.J.] : Fairleigh Dickinson University Press, c1985. — p. cm. — *Includes index. — Bibliography: p*

PUBLIC WELFARE — Scandinavia

ANDERSEN, Bent Rold
Two essays on the nordic welfare state / Bent Rold Andersen. — Copenhagen : Amtskommunernes og kommunernes forskningsinstitut, 1983. — 76p

PUBLIC WELFARE — Spain — Valladolid — History

MAZA ZORRILLA, Elena
Valladolid : sus pobres y la respuesta institucional (1750-1900) / Elena Maza Zorrila. — Valladolid : Universidad de Valladolid : Junta de Castille y León, 1985. — 405p. — *Bibliography: p381-392*

PUBLIC WELFARE — Switzerland

SEGALMAN, Ralph
The Swiss way of welfare : lessons for the Western world / Ralph Segalman. — New York : Praeger, 1985, c1986. — p. cm. — *Includes index. — Bibliography: p*

PUBLIC WELFARE — United States

MORONEY, Robert
Shared responsibility : families and social policy / Robert M. Moroney. — New York : Aldine Pub. Co., c1986. — xi, 218 p.. — *Includes index. — Bibliography: p. 177-211*

RODGERS, Harrell R
Poor women, poor families : the economic plight of America's female-headed households / Harrell R. Rodgers, Jr. — Armonk, N.Y. : M.E. Sharpe, c1986. — viii, 167 p.. — *Includes index. — Bibliography: p. 150-161*

WINEMAN, Steven
The politics of human services : radical alternatives to the welfare state / by Steven Wineman. — 1st ed. — Boston, MA : South End Press, c1984. — iv, 272 p.. — *Bibliography: p. 249-272*

PUBLIC WELFARE — Wales

GREAT BRITAIN. Welsh Office. Health and Social Work Department
Joint planning - health and local authorities : joint financing of personal social services projects. — Cardiff : the Office, 1977. — 4,4p. — (Health circular ; WHC (77)21)

PUBLIC WELFARE ADMINSTRATION — Australia

CARNEY, Terry
Australian social security law, policy and administration / Terry Carney & Peter Hanks. — Melbourne : Oxford University Press, 1986. — xxv,334p. — *Bibliography: p[311]-326*

PUBLISHERS AND PUBLISHING — Data processing — Handbooks, manuals, etc

Chicago guide to preparing electronic manuscripts for authors and publishers. — Chicago : University of Chicago Press, 1986. — xi, 143p. — (Chicago guides to writing, editing, and publishing). — *Includes index. — Bibliography: p 131*

PUBLISHERS AND PUBLISHING — Directories

5001 hard-to-find publishers and their addresses. — 1987 ed. — London : Alan Armstrong & Associates Ltd, 1987. — 114p

PUBLISHERS AND PUBLISHING — Management

BAILEY, Herbert Smith
The art and science of book publishing / Herbert S. Bailey. — New York : Harper and Row, [1970]. — xii,216p. — *Bibliography: p203-208*

PUBLISHERS AND PUBLISHING — Technological innovation

OAKESHOTT, Priscilla
The impact of new technology on the publication chain. — London : British Library, Research & Development Dept., May 1983. — [39]p. — (British National Bibliography research fund reports ; 11)

PUBLISHERS AND PUBLISHING — Technological innovations

HOROWITZ, Irving Louis
Communicating ideas : the crisis of publishing in a post-industrial society / Irving Louis Horowitz. — New York : Oxford University Press, 1986. — x, 240 p.. — *Includes index.* — *Bibliography: p. 217-230*

PUBLISHERS AND PUBLISHING — Canada — Statistics

Culture statistics: book publishing industry = Statistiques de la culture: l'industrie de l'édition du livre / Statistics Canada. — Ottawa : Statistics Canada, 1984-. — *Annual.* — *Title varies*

PUBLISHERS AND PUBLISHING — Commonwealth of Nations — Directories

Cassell and the Publishers Association directory of publishing. — 1987. — Eastbourne : Cassell, 1986. — [336]p. — *Includes index*

PUBLISHERS AND PUBLISHING — Denmark — History

Frimodts Forlag 100 °ar : 1884-1984. — Fredericia : Frimodt, 1984. — 26p

JØRGENSEN, Niels Chr.
BMFs historie 1883-1983 / Niels Chr. Jørgensen & Niels Erik Knudsen. — København : den Danske Boghandlermedhjælperforening, 1983. — 144p. — *Bibliography: p143*

PUBLISHERS AND PUBLISHING — European Economic Community Countries — Congresses

The impact of new technologies on publishing : proceedings of the symposium organized by the Commission of the European Communities, Directorate-General for Scientific and Technical Information and Information Management and held in Luxembourg, November 6-7, 1979 / symposium coordinator: J. Michel Gibb ; symposium editors: Marcel Maurice, Edward Phillips, Hans-Ludwig Scherff .... — London : Saur, c1980. — 195p

PUBLISHERS AND PUBLISHING — Germany — History

VERLAG ERNST WASMUTH
Einhundert Jahre Wasmuth-Bücher. — Tübingen : Ernst Wasmuth, [1975?]. — 16p

PUBLISHERS AND PUBLISHING — Great Britain — Biography

EDWARDS, Ruth Dudley
Victor Gollancz : a biography / by Ruth Dudley Edwards. — London : Gollancz, 1987. — 782p,[24]p of plates. — *Bibliography: p761-764.* — *Includes index*

JOSEPH, Richard, 1940-
Michael Joseph : master of words / Richard Joseph ; with a prologue by Monica Dickens. — Southampton : Ashford, 1986. — xviii,238p. — *Geneal. table on lining papers.* — *Bibliography: p217-229.* — *Includes index*

PUBLISHERS AND PUBLISHING — Wales

COUNCIL FOR THE WELSH LANGUAGE
Cyhoeddi yn yr iaith Gymraeg : asdroddiad i'r Gwir Anrhydeddus John Morris QC, AS, Ysgrifennydd Gwladol Cymru = Publishing in the Welsh Language : a report to the Rt. Hon. John Morris QC, MP, Secretary of State for Wales. — Cardiff : H.M.S.O., 1978. — vii,97p. — *Welsh and English text*

PUEBLA (MEXICO) — Industries

CASTAÑON R., Jesús
Los primeros 25 años de industrialización en Puebla / Jesús Castañon R.. — México : Ediciones del Boletín Bibliográfico de la Secretaría de Hacienda y Crédito Público, 1960. — 21p

PUERTO RICA — Foreign relations — Cuba

Castro's Puerto Rican obsession. — Washington, D.C. : Cuban-American National Foundation, 1987. — 53p

PUERTO RICANS — Illinois — Chicago — Ethnic identity

PADILLA, Felix M
Latino ethnic consciousness : the case of Mexican Americans and Puerto Ricans in Chicago / Felix M. Padilla. — Notre Dame, Ind. : University of Notre Dame Press, c1985. — ix, 187 p.. — *Includes index.* — *Bibliography: p. 173-183*

PUERTO RICO — Commerce — History

DIETZ, James L.
Economic history of Puerto Rico : institutional change and capitalist development / James L. Dietz. — Princeton, N.J. : Princeton University Press, c1986. — xxiii, 337p, [11]p of plates. — *Includes index.* — *Bibliography: p.[311]-326*

PUERTO RICO — Economic conditions

DIETZ, James L.
Economic history of Puerto Rico : institutional change and capitalist development / James L. Dietz. — Princeton, N.J. : Princeton University Press, c1986. — xxiii, 337p, [11]p of plates. — *Includes index.* — *Bibliography: p.[311]-326*

PUERTO RICO — Economic conditions — 1952-

MORALES, Julio
Puerto Rican poverty and migration : we just had to try elsewhere / Julio Morales. — New York : Praeger, 1986. — xvii, 253p. — *Includes index.* — *Bibliography: p.225-245*

PUERTO RICO — Emigration and immigration

MORALES, Julio
Puerto Rican poverty and migration : we just had to try elsewhere / Julio Morales. — New York : Praeger, 1986. — xvii, 253p. — *Includes index.* — *Bibliography: p.225-245*

PUERTO RICO — Executive departments

PUERTO RICO. Department of the Treasury
Organización y funcionamiento, Puerto Rico '83. — San Juan : the Department, [ca.1983]. — 23p

PUERTO RICO — Executive departments — Handbooks, manuals, etc.

PUERTO RICO. Office of the Governor
Manual de servicios de las agencias gubernamentales. — [San Juan] : the Office, [ca.1971]. — vi,346p

PUERTO RICO — Foreign relations — United States

CABRANES, José A.
Self-determination for Puerto Rico / José A. Cabranes. — [San Juan} : Office of the Commonwealth of Puerto Rico in Washington, D.C., [ca.1974]. — 14p

PUERTO RICO — History

DIETZ, James L.
Economic history of Puerto Rico : institutional change and capitalist development / James L. Dietz. — Princeton, N.J. : Princeton University Press, c1986. — xxiii, 337p, [11]p of plates. — *Includes index.* — *Bibliography: p.[311]-326*

PUERTO RICO — Politics and government

CABRANES, José A.
Self-determination for Puerto Rico / José A. Cabranes. — [San Juan} : Office of the Commonwealth of Puerto Rico in Washington, D.C., [ca.1974]. — 14p

GAUTIER, Carmen Eulalia
One aspect of the political dependence of Puerto Rico : the politics of the United States' financed poor relief in Puerto Rico / by Carmen E. Gautier. — 438 leaves. — *PhD (Econ) 1986 Ext*

PUERTO RICO — Politics and government — 1952-

PUERTO RICO. Overseas Information Service
The plebiscite on the political status of Puerto Rico to be held on July 23, 1967. — San Juan : the Service, 1967. — vii,50p

PUERTO RICO. Department of the Treasury

PUERTO RICO. Department of the Treasury
Organización y funcionamiento, Puerto Rico '83. — San Juan : the Department, [ca.1983]. — 23p

PUGLIA (ITALY) — Social conditions

SNOWDEN, Frank M.
Violence and great estates in the south of Italy : Apulia, 1900-1922 / Frank M. Snowden. — Cambridge : Cambridge University Press, 1986. — x,245p. — *Includes index*

PUKA PUKA (TUAMOTU ISLANDS) — Population — Statistics

Tableaux normalisés du recensement général de la population : 15 octobre 1983. — [Papeete] : Institut territorial de la statistique Résultats de la commune de Puka Puka. — [1985?]. — 4p,ll leaves

PULAU PINANG (MALAYSIA) — Population — Statistics

Banci penduduk dan perumahan Malaysia 1980 = Population and housing census of Malaysia 1980. — Kuala Lumpur : Department of Statistics. — *Text in Malay and English* Laporan penduduk negeri = State population report

PULITZER PRIZES

Outstanding international press reporting : Pulitzer Prize winning articles in foreign correspondence / editor Heinz-Dietrich Fischer. — Berlin ; New York : Walter de Gruyter
Vol.1: 1928-1945, from the consequences of World War I to the end of World War II. — 1984. — liii,368p

Outstanding international press reporting : Pulitzer Prize winning articles in foreign correspondence / editor Heinz-Dietrich Fischer. — Berlin ; New York : Walter de Gruyter
Vol.2: 1946-1962, from the end of World War II to the various stations of the Cold War. — 1985. — lxvii,304p

Outstanding international press reporting : Pulitzer Prize winning articles in foreign correspondence / editor Heinz-Dietrich Fischer. — Berlin ; New York : Walter de Gruyter
Vol.3: 1963-1977, from the escalation of the Vietnam war to the East Asian refugee problems. — 1986. — lxxii,309p

PUNAAUIA (TAHITI : REGION) — Population — Statistics

Tableaux normalisés du recensement général de la population : 15 octobre 1983. — [Papeete] : Institut territorial de la statistique Résultats de la commune de Punaauia. — [1985?]. — 11 leaves

PUNISHMENT — Congresseses
INTERNATIONAL CONFERENCE ON PRISON ABOLITION (2nd : 1985 : Amsterdam)
Abolitionism : towards a non-repressive approach to crime : proceedings of the Second International Conference on Prison Abolition, Amsterdam, 1985 / edited by Herman Bianchi, René van Swaaningen. — Amsterdam : Free University Press, 1986. — 247p

PUNISHMENT — Canada
GAMBERG, Herbert
The illusion of prison reform : corrections in Canada / Herbert Gamberg and Anthony Thomson. — New York : P. Lang, c1984. — 161 p.. — (American university studies. Series XI. Anthropology/sociology ; vol. 5). — *Bibliography: p. [145]-161*

PUNISHMENT — Great Britain — History — 19th century
FORSYTHE, W. J. (William James)
The reform of prisoners 1830-1900 / William James Forsythe. — London : Croom Helm, c1987. — 234p. — *Includes index*

PUNISHMENT — Nepal
VAIDYA, Tulasi Ram
Crime and punishment in Nepal : a historical perspective / Tulasi Ram Vaidya, Tri Ratna Manandhar. — Kathmandu : Bin Vaidya and Purna Devi Manandhar, 1985. — 302p. — *Bibliography: p295-300*

PUNISHMENT — United States
THOMAS, Charles Wellington
Corrections in America : problems of the past and the present / Charles W. Thomas. — Newbury Park, Ca. : Sage Publications, 1987. — 159p. (Law and criminal justice series ; v.7). — *Bibliography: p148-154*

PUNISHMENT — United States — Bibliography
Crime and punishment in America : a historical bibliography / [this bibliography was conceived and compiled from the periodicals database of the American Bibliographical Center by editors at ABC-Clio Information Services] ; [Lance Klass and Susan Kinnell, project coordinators ...]. — Santa Barbara, Calif. ; Oxford : The Information Service, c1984. — xii,346p. — (ABC-Clio research guides). — *Includes index*

PUNJAB (INDIA) — Politics and government
AHMAD, Syed Nur
From martial law to martial law : politics in the Punjab, 1919-1958 / Syed Nur Ahmad ; edited by Craig Baxter ; from a translation from the Urdu by Mahmud Ali. — Boulder ; London : Westview, [1985]. — xiv,455p. — *Bibliography: p435*

MADHOK, Balraj
Punjab problem, the Muslim connection / by Balraj Madhok. — New Delhi : Hindu World Publications : Distributors, Vision Books, c1985. — vii, 172 p.

MOHAN, Kamlesh
Militant nationalism in the Punjab 1919-1935 / by Kamlesh Mohan. — New Delhi : Manohar, 1985. — x,447p. — *Bibliography: p[398]-432*

NAYAR, Kuldip
Tragedy of Punjab : Operation Bluestar & after / Kuldip Nayar, Khushwant Singh. — New Delhi : Vision Books, 1984. — 192p

PURI, Nina
Political elite and society in the Punjab / Nina Puri. — New Delhi : Vikas, 1985. — vi,218p. — *Bibliography: p[194]-211*

RAI, Satya M
Punjab since partition / Satya M. Rai. — Delhi : Durga Publications, 1986. — xvii, 466 p.. — *Maps on lining papers. — Includes index. — Bibliography: p. [409]-435*

PUNK ROCK MUSIC — California — History and criticism
Hardcore California : a history of punk and new wave / Peter Belsito, Bob Davis. — Berkeley, CA : Last Gasp of San Francisco, c1983. — 128 p.. — *Contents: Los Angeles / text by Craig Lee and Shreader -- San Francisco / text by Peter Belsito*

PURCHASING POWER — Netherlands — Statistics
Koopkracht in kaart gebracht : een statistiek van de inkomensdynamiek. — 's-Gravenhage : Staatsuitgeverij, 1986. — 119p. — *Bibliography: p117-119*

PURITANS
HOLSTUN, James
A rational millennium : Puritan utopias of seventeenth-century England and America / James Holstun. — New York : Oxford University Press, 1987. — p. cm. — *Includes index. — Bibliography: p*

Puritanism and liberty : being the army debates (1647-9) from the Clarke manuscripts, with supplementary documents / selected and edited with an introduction by A.S.P. Woodhouse ; new preface by Ivan Roots. — 3rd ed. — London : Dent, 1986. — 506p. — (Everyman's library)

PURITANS — New England — Religious life
COHEN, Charles Lloyd
God's caress : the psychology of Puritan religious experience / Charles Lloyd Cohen. — New York : Oxford University Press, 1986. — p. cm. — *Includes index. — Bibliography: p*

PUSHKARNA BRAHMANS
ZEITLYN, Sushila Jane
Sacrifice and the sacred in a Hindu "tīrtha" : the case of Pushkar India / Sushila Jane Zeitlyn. — 377 leaves, [23] leaves of plates. — PhD (Econ) 1986 LSE

PUSHKIN, A. S.
NEVELEV, G. A.
"Istina sil'nee Tsaria..." : A. S. Pushkin v rabote nad istoriei dekabristov / G. A. Nevelev. — Moskva : Mysl', 1985. — 203p

PUT AND CALL TRANSACTIONS — United States
Financial futures and options in the U.S. economy : a study / by the staff of the Federal Reserve System ; edited by Myron L. Kwast. — [Washington : Board of Governors of the Federal Reserve System], 1986. — [ix],264p. — *Bibliography: p249-264*

PYGMIES — Addresses, essays, lectures
CAVALLI-SFORZA, Luigi Luca
African pygmies / edited by Luigi Luca Cavalli-Sforza. — Orlando : Academic Press, 1986. — p. cm. — *Bibliography: p427-453. — Bibliography: p*

QANTAS AIRWAYS — History
GUNN, John, 1925-
The defeat of distance : Qantas 1919-1939 / John Gunn. — St. Lucia ; London : University of Queensland, 1985. — xvi,400p. — *Map on lining papers. — Bibliography: p384-385. — Includes index*

QUADRATIC PROGRAMMING
MAGNUS, Jan R.
The exact moments of a ratio of quadratic forms / Jan R. Magnus. — London : London School of Economics and Political Science. Suntory Toyota International Centre for Economics and Related Disciplines, 1986. — 19p. — (Econometrics discussion paper ; 86/136). — *Bibliography: p18-19*

QUADRIPARTITE AGREEMENT ON BERLIN (1971)
KEITHLY, David M
Breakthrough in the Ostpolitik : the 1971 Quadripartite Agreement / David M. Keithly. — Boulder : Westview Press, 1986. — p. cm. — (Westview special studies in international relations). — *Includes index. — Bibliography: p*

QUADRUPLE ALLIANCE, 1718
MCKAY, Derek
Allies of convenience : diplomatic relations between Great Britain and Austria, 1714-1719 / Derek McKay. — New York : Garland Pub., 1986. — 378 p.. — (Outstanding theses from the London School of Economics and Political Science). — *Bibliography: p. 350-378*

QUALITY CIRCLES — Great Britain
Small group activities : quality circles : review of a conference held on 2 March 1983 at Millbank Tower, Millbank, London. — [London] : Work Research Unit, [1983]. — 15p

QUALITY CONTROL — Law and legislation — Addresses, essays, lectures
The regulation of quality : products, services, workplaces, and the environment / edited by Donald N. Dewees. — Toronto : Butterworths, 1983. — xvi,345p. — (Studies in law and economics)

QUALITY CONTROL — Great Britain
GREAT BRITAIN. Department of Trade and Industry
Register of quality assessed United Kingdom companies. — 3rd ed.. — London : HMSO, 1986

QUALITY OF LIFE
DEATON, Angus
The measurement of welfare : theory and practical guidelines / Angus Deaton. — Washington, D.C., U.S.A. : World Bank, 1985 printing, c1980. — 82p. — (LSMS working papers ; no.7) (LSMS working papers ; no. 7). — *Bibliographical references: p79-82*

The Quality of urban life : social, psychological, and physical conditions / edited by Dieter Frick in cooperation with Hans-Wolfgang Hoefert ... [et al.]. — Berlin ; New York : De Gruyter, 1986. — x, 262 p.. — *Includes bibliographies and index*

QUALITY OF LIFE — Handbooks, manuals, etc
MARLIN, John Tepper
Book of world city rankings / John Tepper Marlin, Immanuel Ness, and Stephen T. Collins. — New York : Free Press ; London : Collier Macmillan, c1986. — xiii, 604 p.. — *Includes bibliographies*

QUALITY OF LIFE — Moral and ethical aspects
GRIFFIN, James, 1933-
Well-being : its meaning, measurement and moral importance / James Griffin. — Oxford : Clarendon, 1986. — xii,412p. — *Bibliography: p391-402. — Includes index*

QUALITY OF LIFE — Asia
VISARIA, Pravin M
Poverty and living standards in Asia : an overview of the main results and lessons of selected household surveys / Pravin Visaria assisted by Shyamalendu Pal. — Washington, D.C., U.S.A. : World Bank, 1986 printing, c1980. — xii,224p. — (LSMS working papers ; no.2). — *Includes bibliographical references*

QUALITY OF LIFE — Communist countries
BROMLEI, N. Ia.
Obraz zhizni v usloviiakh sovershenstvovaniia sotsializma : opyt istoriko-sravnitel'nogo issledovaniia / N. Ia. Bromlei ; otv. redaktor E. I. Kapustin. — Moskva : Nauka, 1986. — 222p

QUALITY OF LIFE — Communist countries *continuation*
Obraz zhizni i planirovanie sotsial′nykh protsessov / pod redaktsiei G. Assmana, I. Ia. Pisarenko. — Minsk : Izd-vo ″Universitetskoe″, 1986. — 366p

QUALITY OF LIFE — Hungary — Statistical methods — Congresses
SCIENTIFIC CONFERENCE ON STATISTICAL PROBLEMS. Branch B (1961 : Budapest)
The standard of living : some problems of analysis and of international comparison / edited by M. Mód...[et al.]. — Budapest : Akadémiai Kiadó, 1962. — 294p

QUALITY OF LIFE — Norway — Statistics
Levekårsundersøkelsen 1983 = Survey of level of living 1983. — Oslo : Statistisk Sentralbyrå, 1985. — 223p. — (Norges offisielle statistikk ; B511). — *In Norwegian and English*

QUALITY OF LIFE — Scandinavia
Level of living and inequality in the Nordic countries : a comparative analysis of the Nordic comprehensive surveys. — Stockholm : Nordic Council and the Nordic Statistical Secretariat, 1984. — 226p. — *At head of title: Denmark, Finland, Norway, Sweden.* — *Includes bibliographical references*

QUALITY OF LIFE — Soviet Union
ISMAILOV, A. I.
Sotsialisticheskii byt Sovetskogo naroda : dostizheniia, retrospektiva, perspektivy / A. I. Ismailov, E. I. Ismailova, otv redaktor V. Ts. Naidakov. — Moskva : Nauka, 1986. — 157p

KAVALEROV, A. I.
Byt razvitogo sotsializma : sushchnost′ i osnovnye cherty / A. I. Kavalerov. — L′vov : Vyshcha shkola, 1985. — 144p

QUALITY OF LIFE — Soviet Union — Congresses
Quality of life in the Soviet Union / edited by Horst Herlemann. — Boulder, Colo. : Westview Press, 1987. — p. cm. — (A Westview special study)

QUALITY OF LIFE — Sri Lanka
DEATON, Angus
Three essays on a Sri Lanka household survey / Angus Deaton. — Washington, D.C., U.S.A. : World Bank, 1985 printing, c1981. — [iv],87p. — (LSMS working papers ; no.11). — *Bibliographical references: p85-87*

QUALITY OF LIFE — United States
Time, goods, and well-being / edited by F. Thomas Juster and Frank P. Stafford. — Ann Arbor, Mich. : Survey Research Center, Institute for Social Research, University of Michigan, 1985. — p. cm. — *Bibliography: p*

QUALITY OF LIFE — United States — Statistics
GOULD, Jay M
Quality of life in American neighborhoods : levels of affluence, toxic waste, and cancer mortality in residential Zip code areas / Jay M. Gould ; edited by Alice Tepper Marlin. — Boulder : Westview Press, 1986. — ix, 402 p.. — ″Published in cooperation with the Council on Economic Priorities.″

QUALITY OF PRODUCTS — United States — Case studies
Productivity and quality through people : practices of well-managed companies / edited by Y.K. Shetty and Vernon M. Buehler ; foreword by John A. Young. — Westport, Conn. : Quorum Books, 1985. — xvi, 351 p.. — *Includes index.* — *Bibliography: p. [329]-340*

QUALITY OF WORK LIFE
PARKER, Mike
Inside the circle : a union guide to quality of work life / by Mike Parker. — Boston, MA : South End Press, c1985. — p. cm. — *Includes index.* — *Bibliography: p*

QUALITY OF WORK LIFE — Societies, etc. — Directories
Conditions of work and quality of working life : a directory of institutions / edited by Linda Stoddart. — 2nd ed. — Geneva : International Labour Office, 1986. — xxi,306p

QUALITY OF WORK LIFE — Canada
WELLS, Don
Soft sell : ″quality of life″ programs and the productivity race / by Don Wells. — Ottawa : Canadian Centre for Policy Alternatives, 1986. — xi,97p

QUALITY OF WORK LIFE — Europe
MINE, Manabu
Humanisation of work and industrial relations : a study of Western Europe / Manabu Mine. — London : Work Research Unit, 1983. — 29p. — *At head of title page: Advisory, Conciliation and Arbitration Service*

QUALITY OF WORK LIFE — Japan
SELL, R. G.
Work organisation and attitudes in some Japanese factories : a report of a study tour / Reg Sell. — London : Work Research Unit, 1983. — 62p. — *At head of title page: Advisory, Conciliation and Arbitration Service.* — *Bibliographical references: p45*

QUALITY OF WORK LIFE — United States
HOWARD, Robert
Brave new workplace / Robert Howard. — New York : Penguin Books, 1986, c1985. — p. cm. — ″Elisabeth Sifton books.″. — *Includes index*

QUALITY OF WORK LIFE — United States — Case studies
JURAVICH, Tom
Chaos on the shop floor : a worker′s view of quality, productivity, and management / by Tom Juravich. — Philadelphia : Temple University Press, 1985. — ix, 160 p.. — (Labor and social change). — *Includes index.* — *Bibliography: p. 153-160*

Productivity and quality through people : practices of well-managed companies / edited by Y.K. Shetty and Vernon M. Buehler ; foreword by John A. Young. — Westport, Conn. : Quorum Books, 1985. — xvi; 351 p.. — *Includes index.* — *Bibliography: p. [329]-340*

QUALITY OF WORKLIFE
DELAMOTTE, Yves
Quality of working life in international perspective / Yves Delamotte and Shin-ichi Takezawa. — Geneva : International Labour Office, 1984. — ix,89p. — *Includes bibliographical references*

QUANTUM THEORY
FINE, Arthur
The shaky game : Einstein, realism, and the quantum theory / Arthur Fine. — Chicago : University of Chicago Press, c1986. — xi, 186 p.. — (Science and its conceptual foundations). — *Includes index.* — *Bibliography: p. 173-179*

QUARTZ FIBERS — Toxicology — West Virginia — Gauley Bridge
CHERNIACK, Martin
The Hawk′s Nest incident : America′s worst industrial disaster / Martin Cherniack ; foreword by Phillip Landrigan and Anthony Robbins. — New Haven : Yale University Press, c1986. — x, 194p, [16]p of plates. — *Includes index.* — *Bibliography: p.184-188*

QUEBEC (PROVINCE) — Autonomy and independence movements
Quebec since 1945 : selected readings / edited by Michael D. Behiels. — Toronto : Copp Clark Pitman, 1987. — 313p. — *Bibliography: p307-313*

QUÉBEC (PROVINCE) — Economic conditions
FÉDÉRATION DES TRAVAILLEURS DU QUÉBEC. Congrès (13th : 1973 : Montréal)
La politique de main dŏeuvre : le Québec dăbord. — Québec : Fédération des Travailleurs du Québec, 1973. — 23p. — (Document économique / Fédération des Travailleurs du Québec ; 1)

GREER, Allan
Peasant, lord and merchant : Rural society in three Quebec Parishes 1740-1840 / Allan Greer. — Toronto ; London : University of Toronto Press, 1985. — xvi,304p. — (Social history of Canada ; 39)

QUÉBEC (PROVINCE) — Economic conditions — Statistics
La situation économique au Québec : 1984 et 1 er semestre 1985. — Québec : Bureau de la statistique, 1985. — 208p

QUÉBEC (PROVINCE) — Ethnic relations
SEE, Katherine O′Sullivan
First world nationalisms : class and ethnic politics in Northern Ireland and Quebec / Katherine O′Sullivan See. — Chicago : University of Chicago Press, 1986. — p. cm. — *Includes index.* — *Bibliography: p*

QUEBEC (PROVINCE) — History
LOOMIS, D. G.
Not much glory : quelling the F.L.Q. / Dan G. Loomis. — Toronto : Deneau, 1984. — 199p

QUÉBEC (PROVINCE) — History — Autonomy and independence movements
SEE, Katherine O′Sullivan
First world nationalisms : class and ethnic politics in Northern Ireland and Quebec / Katherine O′Sullivan See. — Chicago : University of Chicago Press, 1986. — p. cm. — *Includes index.* — *Bibliography: p*

QUÉBEC (PROVINCE) — History — 1936-1960
Quebec since 1945 : selected readings / edited by Michael D. Behiels. — Toronto : Copp Clark Pitman, 1987. — 313p. — *Bibliography: p307-313*

QUEBEC (PROVINCE) — History — 1960-
Quebec since 1945 : selected readings / edited by Michael D. Behiels. — Toronto : Copp Clark Pitman, 1987. — 313p. — *Bibliography: p307-313*

QUEBEC (PROVINCE) — Politics and government
GROUPE SOCIALISTE DES TRAVAILLEURS DU QUÉBEC
La question nationale et la révolution prolétarienne au Canada : définition des mots dŏrdre du G.S.T.Q. au Québec dans la lutte pour la destruction de l′État fédéral. — Montreal : Presses Socialistes Internationales, 1978. — 61p. — (Documents du Groupe socialiste des travailleurs du Québec ; 3)

VAILLANCOURT, Yves
Le P.Q. et la social : éléments de bilan des politiques sociales du gouvernement du Parti québécois, 1976-1982 / Yves Vaillancourt ; avec la collaboration de Annie Autonès. — [Montréal] : Editions coopératives Albert Saint-Martin, c1983. — 165p. — (Collection ″Actualité″)

QUEBEC (PROVINCE) — Politics and government — 1960-
GAGNON, Lysiane
Chroniques politiques / Lysiane Gagnon. — Montréal : Boréal Express, 1985. — 461p

LÉVESQUE, René
Memoirs / René Levesque ; translated by Philip Stratford. — Toronto : McClelland and Stewart, 1986. — 368p. — *Issued also in French under title: Mémoires*

QUEBEC (PROVINCE) — Politics and government — 1960-

continuation

Old passions, new visions : social movements and political activisim in Quebec / edited by Marc Raboy ; translated by Robert Chodos. — Toronto, Ont. : Between the Lines, c1986. — 250 p.. — *Includes bibliographies*

QUÉBEC (PROVINCE) — Politics and government — 1960-

THOMSON, Dale C
Jean Lesage & the quiet revolution / Dale C. Thomson. — Toronto, Canada : MacMillan of Canada, c1984. — x, 501 p., [16] p. of plates. — *Includes bibliographical references and index*

QUÉBEC (PROVINCE) — Population — Statistics

Démographie québécoise : passé, présent, perspectives. — Québec : Bureau de la statistique du Québec, 1983. — xxxii,457p. — *Includes bibliographical references*

QUÉBEC (PROVINCE) — Population — Statistics — Forecasting

Perspectives démographiques infrarégionales, 1981-2001. — Québec : Bureau de la statistique, 1984. — 498p

QUÉBEC (PROVINCE) — Social conditions

GREER, Allan
Peasant, lord and merchant : Rural society in three Quebec Parishes 1740-1840 / Allan Greer. — Toronto ; London : University of Toronto Press, 1985. — xvi,304p. — (Social history of Canada ; 39)

QUEBEC (PROVINCE) — Social conditions

Old passions, new visions : social movements and political activisim in Quebec / edited by Marc Raboy ; translated by Robert Chodos. — Toronto, Ont. : Between the Lines, c1986. — 250 p.. — *Includes bibliographies*

QUEBEC (PROVINCE) — Social policy

VAILLANCOURT, Yves
Le P.Q. et la social : éléments de bilan des politiques sociales du gouvernement du Parti québécois, 1976-1982 / Yves Vaillancourt ; avec la collaboration de Annie Autonès. — [Montréal] : Editions coopératives Albert Saint-Martin, c1983. — 165p. — (Collection "Actualité")

QUEENS — Social conditions

STAFFORD, Pauline
Queens, concubines, and dowagers : the king's wife in the early Middle Ages / Pauline Stafford. — Athens, Ga. : University of Georgia Press, c1983. — xiii, 248 p.. — *Includes index.* — *Bibliography: p. 211-226*

QUEENSLAND — Emigration and immigration — History — 19th century

WOOLCOCK, Helen R.
Rights of passage : emigration to Australia in the nineteenth century / Helen R. Woolcock. — London : Tavistock, 1986. — [xv,304]p. — *Includes index*

QUESTIONNAIRES

BERDIE, Douglas R
Questionnaires : design and use / by Doug R. Berdie, John F. Anderson, Marsha A. Niebuhr. — 2nd ed. — Metuchen, N.J. : Scarecrow Press, 1986. — xii, 330 p.. — *Includes indexes.* — *Bibliography: p. 67-204*

OPPENHEIM, Abraham Naftali
Questionnaire design and attitude measurement / [by] A. N. Oppenheim. — New York : Basic Books, [1966]. — ix, 298 p. — (Basic topics in sociological method). — *Includes bibliographies*

Survey item bank / [Bernard Stewart...et al.]. — [S.l.] : MCB/University Press. — *Sponsored by British Telecom*
Vol.2. — [1985]. — Various pagings

QUETELET, ADOLPHE

Adolphe Quetelet : 1796-1874 : hommages et contributions. — Bruxelles : Palais des Académies, 1975. — 60p. — *Bibliography: p58-59*

QUINE, W. V.

KIRK, Robert, 19---
Translation determined / Robert Kirk. — Oxford : Clarendon, 1986. — [236]p. — *Includes bibliography and index*

QUINE, W. V

The Philosophy of W.V. Quine / edited by Lewis Edwin Hahn and Paul Arthur Schilpp. — La Salle, Ill. : Open Court, 1986, c1985. — xvi, 705p. — (The Library of living philosophers ; v. 18). — *Includes index.* — *"A bibliography of the publications of W.V. Quine": p*

QUINE, WILLARD VAN ORMAN

Can theories be refuted? : essays on the Duhem-Quine-thesis / [compiled by] S.G. Harding. — Dordrecht-Holland ; Boston : D. Reidel Pub. Co, [1975]. — (Synthese library ; 81). — *Includes bibliographies and index*

QUINET, EDGAR

FURET, François
La Gauche et la Révolution françoise au milieu du XIXe siècle : Edgar Quinet et la question du Jacobinisme (1865-1870) / François Furet ; textes présentés par Marina Valensise. — [Paris?] : Hachette, 1986. — 317p. — (Librarie du bicentenaire de la Revolution française). — *Includes bibliographic notes*

QUITMAN, JOHN ANTHONY

MAY, Robert E
John A. Quitman : Old South crusader / Robert E. May. — Baton Rouge : Louisiana State University Press, c1985. — p. cm. — (Southern biography series). — *Includes index.* — *Bibliography: p*

QUITO REGION (ECUADOR) — History

SALOMON, Frank
Native lords of Quito in the age of the Incas : the political economy of north Andean chiefdoms / Frank Salomon. — Cambridge : Cambridge University Press, 1986. — xviii,274p. — (Cambridge studies in social anthropology ; no.59)

RABBIS — United States — Biography

GOLDSTEIN, Israel
My world as a Jew : the memoirs of Israel Goldstein. — New York : Herzl Press ; London : Cornwall Books, c1984. — p. cm. — *Includes index*

RABKRIN See Soviet Union. Narodnyi kommissariat raboche-krest'iansko inspektsii

RACE AWARENESS

KATZ, Judy H.
White awareness : handbook for anti-racism training / by Judy H. Katz. — 1st ed. — Norman : University of Oklahoma Press, c1978. — x, 211 p.. — *Includes index.* — *Bibliography: p. 201-205*

RACE AWARENESS — Austria

Österreichbewusstsein - bewusst Österreicher sein? : Materialien zur Entwicklung des Österreichbewusstseins seit 1945 / herausgegeben von Dirk Lyon...[et al.]. — Wien : Österreichischer Bundesverlag, 1985. — 198p. — *Bibliography: p194-[199]*

RACE AWARENESS IN CHILDREN — Great Britain

WILSON, Anne, 19---
'Mixed race' children : a study of identity / Anne Wilson. — London : Allen & Unwin, 1987. — [172]p. — *Includes bibliography and index*

RACE DISCRIMINATION — Great Britain

The facts of racial disadvantage: a national survey : summary. — London : Commission for Racial Equality, 1980. — [2]p. — *Summary of report by David J. Smith.* — *Original report published by P.E.P., 1976*

RACE DISCRIMINATION

FRANKLIN, John Hope
Race and colour : an account of the conference held at Copenhagen, September 1965 [held under the joint sponsorship of the congress for Cultural Freedom and the American Academy of Arts and Sciences] / John Hope Franklin. — Paris : Congress for Cultural Freedom, 1966. — 24p

MULLARD, Chris
Race, class and idealogy : some formal notes / Chris Mullard. — London : Institute of Education.Race Relations Policy and Practise Research Unit, 1985. — 48p

RACE DISCRIMINATION — Government policy — Great Britain

GREAT BRITAIN. Home Office
Home Secretary's speech to the annual conference of the Race Relations Board in York on Friday, 13th September, 1974. — [London : Home Office, 1974]. — 7leaves

RACE DISCRIMINATION — Law and legislation — Great Britain

POULTER, Sebastian
English law and ethnic minority customs / Sebastian Poulter. — London : Butterworth, 1986. — xxviii,300p

RACE DISCRIMINATION — Psychological aspects

KATZ, Judy H.
White awareness : handbook for anti-racism training / by Judy H. Katz. — 1st ed. — Norman : University of Oklahoma Press, c1978. — x, 211 p.. — *Includes index.* — *Bibliography: p. 201-205*

RACE DISCRIMINATION — England — Liverpool (Merseyside)

LIVERPOOL BLACK CAUCUS
The racial politics of Militant in Liverpool : the black community's struggle for participation in local politics 1980-1986. — Liverpool : Merseyside Area Profile Group : Runnymede Trust, 1986. — 144p. — *Bibliography: p139-142*

RACE DISCRIMINATION — England — London

CAMDEN COMMITTEE FOR COMMUNITY RELATIONS
ILEA's anti-racist policy : what is it, what it will do, how it should work : a guide for Camden parents and community groups. — London : Camden Committee for Community Relations, 1984. — 29p

GREAT BRITAIN. Commission for Racial Equality
The Antwerp Arms Public House : report of a formal investigation. — London : the Commission, 1979. — 13p

RACE DISCRIMINATION — Great Britain

GORDON, Paul, 1954-
Different worlds : racism and discrimination in Britain / Paul Gordon and Anne Newnham. — London : Runnymede Trust, 1986. — 39p

GREAT BRITAIN. Commission for Racial Equality
Living in terror : a report on racial violence & harassment in housing. — London : the Commission, 1987. — 53p

LEECH, Kenneth
The fields of charity and sin / Kenneth Leech. — London : Race, Pluralism and Community Group Board for Social responsibility, 1986. — 14p. — (Theology and racism ; 3). — *Bibliography: p13*

RACE DISCRIMINATION — Great Britain *continuation*

NEWNHAM, Anne
Employment, unemployment and black people / Anne Newnham. — London : Runnymede Trust, 1986. — 30p. — (Runnymede research report). — *Bibliography:p.30*

PEARSON, Maggie
Equal opportunities in the NHS : a handbook / by Maggie Pearson. — Leeds : Training in Health and Race, 1985. — 39p

RACE DISCRIMINATION — Great Britain — Bibliography

GORDON, Paul
Anti-racist materials for adult and Community education / compiled by Paul Gordon. — London : Runnymeade Trust, 1986. — 22p

RACE DISCRIMINATION — Israel

DAVIS, Uri
Israel : an apartheid state / Uri Davis. — London : Zed, 1987. — xiii,145p. — *Bibliography: p133-137. — Includes index*

RACE DISCRIMINATION — South Africa

The Kairos document : a theological comment on the political crisis in South Africa. — London : Catholic Institute for International Relations : British Council of Churches, 1985. — 32p. — (Third World Theology)

RACE DISCRIMINATION — United States — History

Prejudice / Thomas F. Pettigrew ... [et al.]. — Cambridge, Mass. ; London : Belknap Press of Harvard University Press, 1982. — vi,127p. — (Dimensions of ethnicity). — *Bibliography: p124-127*

RACE DISCRIMINATION IN EMPLOYMENT — Great Britain

NATIONAL UNION OF PUBLIC EMPLOYEES
The report of the Race Equality Working Party. — London : NUPE, 1985. — 56p

RACE RELATIONS

BANTON, Michael
Racial theories / Michael Banton. — Cambridge : Cambridge University Press, 1987. — [192]p. — *Includes bibliography and index*

Ethnic conflict : international perspectives / edited by Jerry Boucher, Dan Landis, Karen Arnold Clark. — Newbury Park, Calif. : Sage Publications, c1987. — 331 p.. — (Sage focus editions ; 84). — *Includes bibliographies and index*

Race, class, and the world system : the sociology of Oliver C. Cox / Herbert M. Hunter and Sameer Y. Abraham, eds. — New York : Monthly Review Press, 1987. — p. cm. — *Bibliography: p*

REX, John
Race and ethnicity / John Rex. — Milton Keynes : Open University Press, 1986. — [160]p. — (Concepts in the social sciences). — *Includes bibliography and index*

Strategies for improving race relations : the Anglo-American experience / edited by John W. Shaw, Peter G. Nordlie, Richard M. Shapiro ; with a preface by Bhiku Parekh. — Manchester : Manchester University Press, c1987. — xiii,226p. — *Includes index*

Theories of race and ethnic relations / edited by John Rex and David Mason. — Cambridge : Cambridge University Press, 1986. — [x,526p] p. — (Comparative ethnic and race relations). — *Bibliography: p482-526*

RACE RELATIONS — Religious aspects — Christianity

HOLDEN, Tony
People, churches and multi-racial projects : an account of English Methodism's response to plural Britain / Tony Holden. — London : Division of Social Responsibility, Methodist Church, [1985]. — 151p. — *Bibliography: p142-151*

RACE RELATIONS — Religious aspects — Christianity — Public opinion

NEUHAUS, Richard John
Dispensations : the future of South Africa as South Africans see it / by Richard John Neuhaus. — Grand Rapids, Mich. : W.B. Eerdmans Pub. Co., c1986. — p. cm. — *Includes bibliographical references*

RACE RELATIONS — Great Britain

YOUNG, Ken, 1943-
The race relations adviser in local government / Ken Young and Pat Gay. — London : Local Authorities Race Relations Information Exchange, 1986. — 38p

RACE RELATIONS IN SCHOOL MANAGEMENT — Great Britain

Anti-racism : an assault on education and value / edited by Frank Palmer. — London : Sherwood Press, 1986. — xii,210p

RACISM

ALEXANDER, Peter
Racism, resistance and revolution / Peter Alexander. — London : Bookmarks, 1987. — 185p. — *Bibliography: p160*

CASHMORE, Ernest
The logic of racism / E. Ellis Cashmore. — London : Allen & Unwin, 1987. — vii,263p. — *Bibliography: p260-261. — Includes index*

DOWER, John W
War without mercy / John Dower. — New York : Pantheon Books, 1986. — p. cm. — *Includes index. — Bibliography: p*

KATZ, Judy H.
White awareness : handbook for anti-racism training / by Judy H. Katz. — 1st ed. — Norman : University of Oklahoma Press, c1978. — x, 211 p.. — *Includes index. — Bibliography: p. 201-205*

KIERNAN, V. G
The lords of human kind : black man, yellow man, and white man in an age of empire / V.G. Kiernan. — Columbia University Press morningside ed. — New York : Columbia University Press, 1987, c1969. — 336p, [16]p of plates. — : Reprint. Originally published: Boston : Little, Brown, 1969. — *Includes bibliographical references*

The Sociobiology of ethnocentrism : evolutionary dimensions of xenophobia, discrimination, racism and nationalism / edited by Vernon Reynolds, Vincent Falger and Ian Vine. — London : Croom Helm, c1987. — xx,327p. — *Bibliography: p274-314. — Includes index*

RACISM — History

ALEXANDER, Peter
Racism, resistance and revolution / Peter Alexander. — London : Bookmarks, 1987. — 185p. — *Bibliography: p160*

RACISM — Political aspects — New Zealand

SPOONLEY, P.
The politics of nostalgia : racism and the Extreme Right in New Zealand / Paul Spoonley. — Palmerston North : Dunmore Press, 1987. — 318p. — *Bibliography: p267-279*

RACISM — Study and teaching

LYNCH, James
Prejudice reduction and the schools / James Lynch. — New York : Nichols Pub., 1987. — p. cm. — *Includes indexes. — Bibliography: p*

RACISM — Australia — Broken Hill (N.S.W.)

KENNEDY, Brian Ernest
A tale of two mining cities : Johannesburg and Broken Hill 1885-1925 / Brian Kennedy. — Johannesburg : Ad. Donker, 1984. — xiii,146p. — *Bibliography: p136-142*

RACISM — Canada

BOLARIA, B. Singh
Racial oppression in Canada / B. Singh Bolaria, Peter S. Li. — Toronto, Canada : Garamond Press, c1985. — 232 p.. — *Bibliography: p. 199-221. — Includes index*

RACISM — England — West Midlands

CASHMORE, Ernest
The logic of racism / E. Ellis Cashmore. — London : Allen & Unwin, 1987. — vii,263p. — *Bibliography: p260-261. — Includes index*

RACISM — Europe

BELL, Andrew
Against racism and fascism in Europe / Andrew Bell. — Strasbourg : Socialist Group. European Parliament, 1986. — 47p

RACISM — France

GALLISSOT, René
Misère de l'antiracisme : racisme et identité nationale : le défi de l'immigration / René Gallissot. — Paris : Editions de l'Arcantère, 1985. — 154p

RACISM — Great Britain

GORDON, Paul
New right, new racism / Paul Gordon and Francesca Klug ; preface by David Edgar. — London : Searchlight, 1986. — 69p. — *Bibliography: p69*

GORDON, Paul, 1954-
Different worlds : racism and discrimination in Britain / Paul Gordon and Anne Newnham. — London : Runnymede Trust, 1986. — 39p

GORDON, Paul, 1954-
Racial violence and harassment / Paul Gordon. — London : Runnymede Trust, 1986. — vi,42p. — *Bibliography: p42*

THAKOORDIN, Jim
Eradicate racism : a murderous crime / Jim Thakoordin and Tony Gilbert. — London : Liberation, 1985. — 28p

WORKERS AGAINST RACISM
The roots of racism. — London : Junius Publications, 1985. — 85p

RACISM — Great Britain — History — 20th century

CARTER, Trevor
Shattering illusions : West Indians in British politics / Trevor Carter ; with Jean Coussins. — London : Lawrence and Wishart, 1986. — 158p

RACISM — South Africa

COONEY, Frank
Studies in race relations : South Africa and USA / Frank Cooney, Gordon Morton [and] Barry Wright. — Glasgow : Pulse Publications, 1986. — 84p

RACISM — South Africa — Johannesburg

KENNEDY, Brian Ernest
A tale of two mining cities : Johannesburg and Broken Hill 1885-1925 / Brian Kennedy. — Johannesburg : Ad. Donker, 1984. — xiii,146p. — *Bibliography: p136-142*

RACISM — United States

KATZ, Judy H.
White awareness : handbook for anti-racism training / by Judy H. Katz. — 1st ed. — Norman : University of Oklahoma Press, c1978. — x, 211 p.. — *Includes index. — Bibliography: p. 201-205*

Prejudice, discrimination, and racism / edited by John F. Dovidio and Samuel L. Gaertner. — Orlando : Academic Press, 1986. — xiii, 337 p.. — *Includes bibliographies and index*

RACISM — United States — Addresses, essays, lectures
DU BOIS, W. E. B
Against racism : unpublished essays, papers, addresses, 1887-1961 / by W.E.B. Du Bois ; edited by Herbert Aptheker. — Amherst : University of Massachusetts Press, 1985. — xx, 325 p.. — *Includes bibliographical references and index*

RACISM — United States — History
Prejudice / Thomas F. Pettigrew ... [et al.]. — Cambridge, Mass. ; London : Belknap Press of Harvard University Press, 1982. — vi,127p. — (Dimensions of ethnicity). — *Bibliography: p124-127*

RACISM — United States — History — 20th century
BLOOM, Jack M
Class, race, and the Civil Rights Movement / Jack M. Bloom. — Bloomington : Indiana University Press, c1987. — x, 267 p.. — (Blacks in the diaspora). — *Includes index. — Bibliography: p. [225]-237*

DRINNON, Richard
Keeper of concentration camps : Dillon S. Myer and American racism / Richard Drinnon. — Berkeley : University of California Press, c1987. — xxviii, 339 p.. — *Includes index. — Bibliography: p. 271-324*

RACISM IN TEXTBOOKS
Racialism and sexism in books - a checklist. — London : Commission for Racial Equality, 1977. — [1]p. — *First published in Interracial books for children, vol.5, no.3 (1974), and now reprinted from Education & community relations, September/October 1975*

RACISM IN TEXTBOOKS — Canada
Teaching prejudice - a view from Canada. — London : Commission for Racial Equality, [197-]. — [2]p. — *Summary of study by Garnet McDiarmid and David Pratt. — Reprint from Education & community relations, May 1972*

RADIALISM — United States — Periodicals — Biography
SKIDMORE, Gail
From radical left to extreme right : a bibliography of current periodicals of protest, controversy, advocacy, or dissent, with dispassionate content-summaries to guide librarians and other educators. — 3rd ed., completely rev. / by Gail Skidmore and Theodore Jurgen Spahn. — Metuchen, N.J. : Scarecrow Press, 1987. — p. cm. — *Rev. ed. of: From radical left to extreme right. 2nd ed. / by Robert H. Muller, Theodore Jurgen Spahn, and Janet M. Spahn. 1970-1976. — Includes indexes*

RADIATION
NATIONAL RADIOLOGICAL PROTECTION BOARD
Living with radiation. — 3rd ed. — Didcot : The Board, 1986. — *Previous ed: 1981*

RADICALISM
FRANSELLA, Fay
Need to change? / Fay Fransella. — London : Methuen, 1975. — 144p

The Radical papers / edited by Dimitrios I. Roussopoulos. — Montréal ; New York : Black Rose Books, 1987. — 160p

The revolution of everyday life : a new translation...of Traité de savoir-vivre à l'usage des jeunes générations / Raoul Vaneigem ; [translated by] Donald Nicholson-Smith. — [London?] : Left Bank Books : Rebel Press, 1983. — 216p

RADICALISM — Addresses, essays, lectures
Political violence and terror : motifs and motivations / edited by Peter H. Merkl. — Berkeley : University of California Press, c1986. — vi, 380 p.. — *Includes bibliographies and index*

RADICALISM — History
Cultural politics : radical movements in modern history / edited by Jerold M. Starr. — New York ; Eastbourne : Praeger, 1985. — xxiv,344p. — (Praeger special studies). — *Includes bibliographies and index*

RADICALISM — Islam
Radicalismes Islamiques / publié sous la direction de Olivier Carré et Paul Dumont. — Paris : Editions L'Harmattan. — *Includes bibliographic notes*
v.1: Iran, Liban,Turquie. — 1985. — 256p

Radicalismes Islamiques / publié sous la direction de Olivier Carré et Paul Dumont. — Paris : Editions L'Harmattan. — *Includes bibliographies*
v.2: Maroc, Pakistan, Inde, Yougoslavie, Mali. — 1986. — 181p

RADICALISM — Songs and music
Het cirkus van vuile mong en zijn vieze gasten : teksten. — Waarschoot : Werkgroep voor Vormingstejater, 1975. — 45p

RADICALISM — British Columbia — History
Fighting heritage : highlights of the 1930s struggle for jobs and militant unionism in British Columbia / edited by Sean Griffin. — Vancouver : Tribune Publishing Company, [1985]. — 159p

RADICALISM — California — Santa Monica — History
KANN, Mark E
Middle class radicalism in Santa Monica / Mark E. Kann. — Philadelphia : Temple University Press, 1986. — xiv, 322 p.. — *Includes index. — Bibliography: p. [289]-314*

RADICALISM — Europe
SHIPLEY, Peter
Patterns of protest in Western Europe / Peter Shipley. — London : Institute for the Study of Conflict, 1986. — 23p. — (Conflict studies ; no.189)

RADICALISM — Germany (West)
BACKES, Uwe
Totalitarismus, Extremismus, Terrorismus : ein Literaturführer und Wegweiser zur Extremismusforschung in der Bundesrepublik Deutschland / Uwe Backes, Eckhard Jesse. — 2. aktualisierte und erweiterte Auflage. — Opladen : Leske und Budrich, 1985. — 390p. — (Reihe Analysen ; 38)

RADICALISM — Great Britain — History — 17th century
GREAVES, Richard L
Deliver us from evil : the radical underground in Britain, 1660-1663 / Richard L. Greaves. — New York : Oxford University Press, 1986. — x, 291p. — *Includes index. — Includes bibliographical references*

RADICALISM — Ireland — History
IRISH CONFERENCE OF HISTORIANS (16th : 1983 : Maynooth)
Radicals, rebels & establishments : papers read before the Irish Confernce of Historians, Maynooth, 16-19 June 1983 / Ciaran Brady ... [et al.] ; edited by Patrick J. Corish. — Belfast : Appletree, 1985. — 237p. — (Historical studies ; 15)

RADICALISM — Moldavia
IOVVA, I. F.
Peredovaia Rossiia i obshchestvenno-politicheskoe dvizhenie v Moldavii : (pervaia polovina XIX v.) / I. F Iovva ; otv. redaktor S. S. Volk. — Kishinev : Shtiintsa, 1986. — 256p. — *Brief summary in English and French*

RADICALISM — Oklahoma — History
THOMPSON, John
Closing the frontier : radical response in Oklahoma, 1889-1923 / by John Thompson. — 1st ed. — Norman : University of Oklahoma Press, c1986. — xiii, 262 p. — *Includes index. — Bibliography: p. 249-258*

RADICALISM — Soviet Union — History
LITVINA, F. A.
Legal'nye formy propagandy raznochintsev-demokratov 60-70-kh gg. XIX v. : (literaturnye vechera, chteniia, sobraniia) / F. A. Litvina. — Kazan' : Izd-vo Kazanskogo universiteta, 1986. — 131p

Obshchestvennaia mysl' v Rossii XIX v. / [redaktsionnaia kollegiia: A. N. Tsamutali...[et al.]. — Leningrad : Nauka, Leningradskoe otdelenie, 1986. — 244p. — (Trudy / Institut istorii SSSR, Leningradskoe otdelenie ; Vyp.16) . — *Contains chart: "Skhema razvitiia dekabristskikh i sviazannykh s nimi organizatsii."*

PANTIN, I. K.
Revoliutsionnaia traditsiia v Rossii 1783-1883 gg. / I. K. Pantin, E. G. Plimak, V. G. Khoros. — Moskva : Mysl', 1986. — 341p

RADICALISM — Soviet Union — History — 19th century
Revoliutsionnoe demokraty i russkaia literatura XIX veka / otv. redaktory G. G. Elizavetina, A. S. Kurilov. — Moskva : Nauka, 1986. — 251p

RADICALISM — United States
FOSS, Daniel A.
Beyond revolution : a new theory of social movements / Daniel A. Foss, Ralph W. Larkin ; introduction by Stanley Aronowitz. — South Hadley, MA : Bergin & Garvey, c1985. — p. cm. — (Critical perspectives in social theory)

RADICALISM — United States — History — 20th century
HOMBERGER, Eric
American writers and radical politics, 1900-39 : equivocal commitments / Eric Homberger. — Basingstoke : Macmillan, 1986. — xiii,268p. — (Macmillan studies in American literature). — *Bibliography: p242-260. — Includes index*

RADICALISM — United States — History — 20th century — Addresses, essays, lectures
Race, politics, and culture : critical essays on the radicalism of the 1960's / edited by Adolph Reed, Jr. — Westport, Conn. : Greenwood Press, 1986. — xii, 287 p.. — (Contributions in Afro-American and African studies ; no. 95). — *Includes bibliographies and index*

RADICALISM — United States — Literary collections
LIPPARD, George
[Selections. 1986]. George Lippard, prophet of protest : writings of an American radical, 1822-1854 / edited with an introduction by David S. Reynolds. — New York : P. Lang, c1986. — xii, 335 p.. — *Cover title: George Lippard, an anthology. — Bibliography: p. 333-335*

RADICALS — Great Britain — Biography
CURTIN, Patricia R
E. Sylvia Pankhurst : portrait of a radical / by Patricia Romero Curtin. — New Haven : Yale University Press, c1986. — p. cm. — *Includes index. — Bibliography: p*

RADICALS — Great Britain — Directories
COMMON CAUSE PUBLICATIONS
The far left guide : directory of organisations and supporters. — Fleet, Hants : Common Cause Publications, 1985. — vi,33p

RADICALS — South Africa — Biography
KITSON, Norma
Where sixpence lives / Norma Kitson. — London : Hogarth, 1987, c1986. — 326p,[16]p of plates. — (Current affairs)

RADICALS — Soviet Union — Biography
LAZAREV, V. V.
Chaadaev. — Moskva : Iuridicheskaia literatura, 1986. — 110p. — (Iz istorii politicheskoi i pravovoi mysli). — *Bibliography: p107-[110]*

RADIO — Social aspects — Denmark
KÜHL, P. H.
Radio/TV undersøgelsen : nogle foreløbige resultater af / P. H. Kühl og Kaj Westergård. — [København : Socialforskningsinstituttet, 1965]. — 27 leaves. — (Studie (Socialforskningsinstituttet) ; nr.5)

RADIO BROADCASTING
CRISELL, Andrew
Understanding radio / Andrew Crisell. — London : Methuen, 1986. — 1v.. — (Studies in communication)

RADIO BROADCASTING — Legal status, laws, etc. — Peru
PERU
[Decreto supremo no.007-74-OCI]. Decreto supremo no.007-74-OCI. — [Lima : Presidencia?, 1974]. — 10leaves

RADIO BROADCASTING — Australia
AUSTRALIA. Department of Communications. Forward Development Unit
Future directions for commercial radio. — Canberra : Australian Government Publishing Service
V.1: Report. — 1986. — xxxv,173p. — *Includes bibliographical references*

AUSTRALIA. Department of Communications. Forward Development Unit
Future directions for commercial radio. — Canberra : Australian Government Publishing Service
V.2: Appendices. — 1986. — v,443p

RADIO BROADCASTING — Great Britain
CRISELL, Andrew
Understanding radio / Andrew Crisell. — London : Methuen, 1986. — 1v.. — (Studies in communication)

RADIO BROADCASTING POLICY — Australia
AUSTRALIA. Department of Communications. Forward Development Unit
Future directions for commercial radio : interim report : AM/FM conversion. — Canberra : Australian Government Publishing Service, 1986. — xxix,274p

AUSTRALIA. Department of Communications. Forward Development Unit
Future directions for commercial radio. — Canberra : Australian Government Publishing Service
V.1: Report. — 1986. — xxxv,173p. — *Includes bibliographical references*

AUSTRALIA. Department of Communications. Forward Development Unit
Future directions for commercial radio. — Canberra : Australian Government Publishing Service
V.2: Appendices. — 1986. — v,443p

RADIO BROADCASTING POLICY — Cuba
FREDERICK, Howard H
Cuban-American radio wars : ideology in international telecommunications / Howard H. Frederick. — Norwood, N.J. : Ablex Pub. Corporation, c1986. — viii, 200 p.. — (Communication and information science). — *Includes indexes. — Bibliography: p. 177-193*

RADIO BROADCASTING POLICY — Peru
PERU
[Decreto supremo no.007-74-OCI]. Decreto supremo no.007-74-OCI. — [Lima : Presidencia?, 1974]. — 10leaves

RADIO BROADCASTING POLICY — United States
FREDERICK, Howard H
Cuban-American radio wars : ideology in international telecommunications / Howard H. Frederick. — Norwood, N.J. : Ablex Pub. Corporation, c1986. — viii, 200 p.. — (Communication and information science). — *Includes indexes. — Bibliography: p. 177-193*

RADIO CORPORATION OF AMERICA
GRAHAM, Margaret B. W.
RCA and the VideoDisc : the business of research / Margaret B.W. Graham. — Cambridge : Cambridge University Press, 1986. — xiv,258p. — (Studies in economic history and policy : the United States in the twentieth century). — *Includes index*

RADIO FREE EUROPE
NOVOSTI PRESS AGENCY
Radio stations of the Cold War. — Moscow : Novosti Press, 1973. — 56p

NOWAK, Jan
Wojna w eterze : wspomnienia / Jan Nowak (Zdzisław Jeziorański). — 2-e wyd., popr.. — Londyn : Odnowa, 1986. — 302p

RADIO FREQUENCY ALLOCATION — Great Britain
Deregulation of the radio spectrum in the UK / by CSP International. — London : H.M.S.O., 1987. — [192]p. — *At head of title: Department of Trade and Industry. — Text on inside covers. — Bibliography: p185-192*

RADIO IN PROPAGANDA
NOWAK, Jan
Wojna w eterze : wspomnienia / Jan Nowak (Zdzisław Jeziorański). — 2-e wyd., popr.. — Londyn : Odnowa, 1986. — 302p

RADIO IN PROPAGANDA — Europe
NOVOSTI PRESS AGENCY
Radio stations of the Cold War. — Moscow : Novosti Press, 1973. — 56p

RADIO LIBERTY (Munich)
NOVOSTI PRESS AGENCY
Radio stations of the Cold War. — Moscow : Novosti Press, 1973. — 56p

RADIOACTIVE CONTAMINATION OF FOOD
GREAT BRITAIN. Ministry of Agriculture, Fisheries and Food
Radionuclide levels in food, animals and agricultural products : post Chernobyl monitoring in England and Wales / Ministry of Agriculture, Fisheries and Food, Welsh Office. — London : HMSO, c1987. — ii,203p

RADIOACTIVE POLLUTION — Mathematical models
International comparison study on reactor accident consequence modeling : summary report to CSNI / by an NEA group of experts. — Paris : Nuclear Energy Agency, 1984. — 110p. — *Bibliographical references: p73-76*

RADIOACTIVE POLLUTION — England — West Cumbria
Investigation of the possible increased incidence of cancer in West Cumbria : report of the independent advisory group / chairman Sir Douglas Black. — London : H.M.S.O., 1984. — 103p

RADIOACTIVE POLLUTION — Great Britain
Report on radioactive discharges, associated environmental monitoring and personal radiation doses resulting from operation of CEGB nuclear sites / Central Electricity Generating Board, Health and Safety Department. — London : CEGB, 1976-. — *Annual. — Title varies*

RADIOACTIVE POLLUTION OF THE SEA
CONNOLLY ASSOCIATION. Liverpool Branch. Conference (1985 : Liverpool)
The pollution and militarisation of the Irish Sea. — London : Four Provinces Book Shop, 1985. — 20p. — *Cover title: Irish sea, nuclear cesspool*

RADIOACTIVE WASTE DISPOSAL
Killingholme: development potential : the final report. — Newcastle upon Tyne : Coopers and Lybrand Associates, 1986. — [216p]

RADIOACTIVE WASTE DISPOSAL — England — Killingholme (Humberside)
Killingholme : the development potential. — [London] : Coopers and Lybrand Associates, 1986. — [11 leaves]

RADIOACTIVE WASTE DISPOSAL — Great Britain
GREAT BRITAIN. Radioactive Waste Management Advisory Committee
Annual report. — London : HMSO, 1980-. — *Annual*

RADIOACTIVE WASTES
IBRÜGGER, Lothar
General report on East-West scientific co-operation, the Chernobyl accident, and nuclear waste / Lothar Ibrügger. — Brussels : North Atlantic Assembly, 1986. — ii,33p

RADIOACTIVITY — Safety measures
HALVAS, J.
El programa de protección radiológica de la República Mexicana / J. Halvas, R. Díaz Perches, R. González Constandse. — México : Comisión Nacional de Energía Nuclear, 1964. — 8p. — ([Publicación] / Comisión Nacional de Energía Nuclear ; num.160). — *Text in Spanish and English. — Presentado al Décimo Congreso Internacional de Radiología en Montreal, el 26 de agosto al 1 de septiembre de 1962*

RADIOISOTOPES IN AGRICULTURE
GREAT BRITAIN. Ministry of Agriculture, Fisheries and Food
Radionuclide levels in food, animals and agricultural products : post Chernobyl monitoring in England and Wales / Ministry of Agriculture, Fisheries and Food, Welsh Office. — London : HMSO, c1987. — ii,203p

RAHMAN, SHEIKH MUJIBUR
ADDY, Premen
Bangladesh: distortions challenged : Sheikh Mujib's place in history and the truth about his opponents / Dr. Premen Addy, Dr. Gowher Rizvi [and] Abdul Matin. — London : Radical Asia Publications, 1986. — 30p. — (Bangladesh political scene ; no.4)

RAIATEA (SOCIETY ISLANDS) — Population — Statistics
Tableaux normalisés du recensement général de la population : 15 octobre 1983. — [Papeete] : Institut territorial de la statistique
Résultats de l'Ile de Raiatea. — [1985?]. — 4p,11 leaves

RAIFFEISEN, FRIEDRICH WILHELM — Biography
ARNOLD, Walter
Friedrich Wilhelm Raiffeisen : einer für alle - alle für einen / Walter Arnold, Fritz H. Lamparter. — Neuhausen-Stuttgart : Hänssler, 1985. — 209p. — *Bibliography: p192-193*

RAILRAODS — Statistics — European Economic Community countries
Carriage of goods by rail. — Luxembourg : Office des Publications Officielles des Communautés Européennes. — *On cover: Eurostat. — Text in Community languages*
1983. — 1985. — xxx, 145p

RAILROAD TERMINALS — England — London
LONDON STRATEGIC POLICY UNIT. Transport Group
The Channel Tunnel and London : an examination of British Rail's plans for London terminal facilities. — London : [the Group], 1987. — iv,84p. — *Bibliography: p77*

RAILROADS — Economic aspects
MAJUMDAR, J. (Jyotirmay)
The economics of railway traction / J. Majumdar. — Aldershot : Gower, c1985. — xxiii,497p. — *Bibliography: p489-497*

RAILROADS — Freight — Statistics

Carriage of goods: rail / Statistical Office of the European Communities. — Luxembourg : Office for Official Publications of the European Communities, 1983-. — *Annual. — Text in Community languages. — Title varies*

RAILROADS — History — 19th century

SCHIVELBUSCH, Wolfgang
The railway journey : the industrialization and perception of time and space in the 19th century / Wolfgang Schivelbusch. — New ed. — Leamington Spa : Berg, 1986. — xvi,203p,[16]p of plates. — *Translation of: Geschichte der Eisenbahnreise. — Previous ed.: New York : Urizen, 1979 : Oxford : Blackwell, 1980. — Bibliography: p198-200. — Includes index*

RAILROADS — Noise

BRITISH RAILWAYS BOARD. Process Technology Group. Physics Section
Railway noise and the environment : a summary. — Derby : the Board, 1974. — 22p. — (Technical note ; TNPHYS.4). — *Bibliographical references: p22*

RAILROADS — Passenger traffic

POTTER, Stephen, 1953-
On the right lines? : the limits of technological innovation / Stephen Potter. — London : Pinter, c1987. — viii,208p. — *Bibliography: p201-204. — Includes index*

RAILROADS — Africa, Southern

BUTTS, Kent Hughes
The geopolitics of southern Africa : South Africa as regional superpower / Kent Hughes Butts and Paul R. Thomas. — Boulder : Westview Press, 1986. — xiv, 193 p.. — (Westview special studies on Africa). — *Includes bibliographies and index*

RAILROADS — Australia

AUSTRALIA. Bureau of Transport Economics. Seminar on Australian Long Distance Surface Passenger Transport (1985 : Canberra)
Papers and proceedings. — Canberra : Australian Government Publishing Service, 1985. — viii,90p. — *Includes bibliographical references*

RAILROADS — Belgium — History — 19th century

KURGAN-VAN HENTENRYK, G
Rail, finance et politique : les entreprises Philippart, 1865-1890 / G. Kurgan-van Hentenryk. — Bruxelles, Belgique : Editions de l'Université de Bruxelles, 1982. — 392 p.. — (Université libre de Bruxelles, Faculté de philosophie et lettres ; 84). — *Includes index. — Bibliography: p. 366-370*

RAILROADS — Brazil — History

SILVA TELLES, Pedro C. da
A history of Brazilian railways / by Pedro C. da Silva Telles ; translated by Paul E. Waters. — Bromley : P.E. Waters
Part 1: The first railways. — [1984?]. — 69p. — (Brazilian railway history note ; no.3). — *"First published as Chapter 6 of 'Historia da Engenharia no Brasil (Séculos XVI a XIX)' by Pedro Carlos da Silva Telles. Rio de Janeiro: LTC -Livros Técnicos e Científicos Editora S.A.,1984."*

RAILROADS — England — Commuting traffic

RESEARCH PROJECTS LIMITED
The outer suburban commuter : the study at Berkhamsted and Harpenden / research undertaken by David Hollings...[et al.]. — London : Research Projects Limited, 1970. — 1v(various pagings). — *Prepared for the Passenger Departments, British Railways Board and London Midland Region, B. R.*

RAILROADS — England — Management — History

MASON, Nicholas Michael
Unprofitable railway companies in England and Wales, 1845-1923 : with special reference to the South Midlands / Nicholas Michael Mason. — New York : Garland Pub., 1986. — 510 p.. — (Outstanding theses from the London School of Economics and Political Science). — : *Originally presented as the author's thesis (Ph. D.)--University of London, 1982. — Bibliography: p. 493-510*

RAILROADS — England — Passenger traffic

RESEARCH PROJECTS LIMITED
Southern Region inner suburban services : management report. — London : Research Projects Limited, 1970. — 25leaves

RAILROADS — England — Kent — Passenger traffic

TAYLOR, NELSON AND ASSOCIATES
Study of off-peak travel in North Kent / prepared for British Railways Southern Region by Taylor, Nelson & Associates Limited. — Epsom : Taylor, Nelson & Associates Limited, 1969. — 22p,300/1leaves

RAILROADS — England — London

CAMPAIGN TO IMPROVE LONDON'S TRANSPORT
Railways for London : investment proposals for the LRT tube and BR network. — London : Campaign to Improve London's Transport, 1987. — 93p

LONDON REGIONAL PASSENGERS' COMMITTEE
The clandestine railway : a report / by the London Regional Passengers' Committee. — London : London Regional Passengers' Committee, [1986]. — 24p. — *Cover title*

RAILROADS — England — London Metropolitan Area — Commuting traffic — Evaluation

PEAT, MARWICK, MITCHELL & CO
An exploratory study into the evaluation of overcrowding on London commuter rail services. — London : Peat, Marwick, Mitchell & Co., 1973. — 60leaves. — *Report produced on behalf of the Department of the Environment. — Bibliographical references: leaves 59-60*

RAILROADS — England, Northern — History

HOLT, G. O.
The North West / G.O. Holt. — 2nd ed. / revised by Gordon Biddle. — [Newton Abbot] : David St. John Thomas, 1986. — 279p,17p of plates. — (A Regional history of the railways of Great Britain ; v.10). — *Previous ed.: Newton Abbot : David and Charles, 1978. — Bibliography: p273-275. — Includes index*

HOOLE, K.
The North East / by K. Hoole. — 3rd, rev. ed. — [Newton Abbot] : David St John Thomas ; Newton Abbot : David & Charles [distributor], c1986. — 245p,[21]p of plates. — (A Regional history of the railways of Great Britain ; v.4). — *Previous ed.: i.e. New ed. Newton Abbot : David and Charles, 1974. — Map on folded leaf tipped in. — Includes index*

RAILROADS — France — History — 19th century

KURGAN-VAN HENTENRYK, G
Rail, finance et politique : les entreprises Philippart, 1865-1890 / G. Kurgan-van Hentenryk. — Bruxelles, Belgique : Editions de l'Université de Bruxelles, 1982. — 392 p.. — (Université libre de Bruxelles, Faculté de philosophie et lettres ; 84). — *Includes index. — Bibliography: p. 366-370*

RAILROADS — Great Britain

BOOKER, Frank
The Great Western Railway : a new history / Frank Booker. — 2nd ed. — Newton Abbot : David St. John Thomas, 1985. — 208p,[8]p of plates. — *Previous ed.: 1977. — Previous ed.: Newton Abbot : David and Charles, 1977. — Bibliography: p201-203. — Includes index*

SEGLOW, Peter
Rail unions in Britain and W. Germany : a study of their structure and policies / Peter Seglow, Wolfgang Streeck, Pat Wallace. — London : Policy Studies Institute, 1982. — vii, 109p. — (Policy Studies Institute ; no. 604)

RAILROADS — Great Britain — Employees

WEISBERG, Jacob
Labour turnover : a case study of early quits in British Rail / by Jacob Weisberg. — 333 leaves . — *PhD (Econ) 1986 LSE. — Leaves 272-300 are appendices*

RAILROADS — Great Britain — History

HEAP, Christine
The pre-grouping railways : their development, and individual characters / Christine Heap, John van Riemsdijk. — London : H.M.S.O.. — (Science Museum books). — *At head of title: Science Museum*
Part 2. — 1980. — viii,89p

HEAP, Christine
The pre-grouping railways : their development, and individual characters / Christine Heap, John Van Riemsdijk. — London : H.M.S.O.. — *At head of title: Science Museum*
Part 3. — 1985. — viii, 83p

SIMMONS, Jack, 1915-
The railways of Britain / Jack Simmons. — 3rd ed. — London : Macmillan, 1986. — 256p. — *Previous ed.: 1968. — Bibliography: p246-249. — Includes index*

RAILROADS — Kazakh S.S.R. — History

AKHMEDZHANOVA, Z. K.
Zheleznodorozhnoe stroitel'stvo v Srednei Azii i Kazakhstane : (konets XIX-nachalo XX v.) / Z. K. Akhmedzhanova. — Tashkent : "Fan" Uzbekskoi SSR, 1984. — 126p

RAILROADS — Luxembourg — History — 19th century

KURGAN-VAN HENTENRYK, G
Rail, finance et politique : les entreprises Philippart, 1865-1890 / G. Kurgan-van Hentenryk. — Bruxelles, Belgique : Editions de l'Université de Bruxelles, 1982. — 392 p.. — (Université libre de Bruxelles, Faculté de philosophie et lettres ; 84). — *Includes index. — Bibliography: p. 366-370*

RAILROADS — Soviet Central Asia — History

AKHMEDZHANOVA, Z. K.
Zheleznodorozhnoe stroitel'stvo v Srednei Azii i Kazakhstane : (konets XIX-nachalo XX v.) / Z. K. Akhmedzhanova. — Tashkent : "Fan" Uzbekskoi SSR, 1984. — 126p

RAILROADS — United States — History

MERCER, Lloyd J
E.H. Harriman, master railroader / Lloyd J. Mercer. — Boston, Mass. : Twayne Publishers, c1985. — p. cm. — (The Evolution of American business). — *Includes index. — Bibliography: p*

RAILROADS — United States — History — 20th century

HEALY, Kent T
Performance of the U.S. railroads since World War II : a quarter century of private operation. — 1st ed. — New York : Vantage Press, c1985. — vii, 295 p.. — *Bibliography: p. 287-295*

RAILROADS — Wales — Management — History

MASON, Nicholas Michael
Unprofitable railway companies in England and Wales, 1845-1923 : with special reference to the South Midlands / Nicholas Michael Mason. — New York : Garland Pub., 1986. — 510 p.. — (Outstanding theses from the London School of Economics and Political Science). — : Originally presented as the author's thesis (Ph. D.)--University of London, 1982. — Bibliography: p. 493-510

RAILROADS, LOCAL AND LIGHT — England — London

LONDON TRANSPORT
Docklands rail study 1981. — London : London Transport
Appendices to main report. — 1981. — 1v (various pagings)

LONDON TRANSPORT
Docklands rail study 1981. — London : London Transport
Main report. — 1981. — 43p

RAILWAY MAIL SERVICE — Great Britain

JOHNSON, Peter, 1949-
The British travelling post office / Peter Johnson. — London : Ian Allen, c1985. — 104p. — Bibliography: p.104

RAILWAYS *See* Railroads

RAIN AND RAINFALL — Europe

Acid rain. — London : Watt Committee on Energy, 1984. — 58 p.. — (Report / Watt Committee on Energy ; no. 14). — "Papers presented at the fifteenth Consultative Council meeting of the Watt Committee on Energy, London, 1 December 1983"

RAIN FOREST — Asia, Southeastern

WHITMORE, T. C.
Tropical rain forests of the Far East / T.C. Whitmore ; with a chapter on soils by C.P. Burnham. — 2nd ed. — Oxford : Clarendon, 1984. — xvi,352p. — *Previous ed.: 1975.* — *Maps on lining papers.* — *Bibliography: p297-328.* — *Includes index*

RAIN FOREST ECOLOGY

INTERNATIONAL BOARD FOR SOIL RESEARCH AND MANAGEMENT
Report of the inaugural workshop and proposal for implementation of the tropical land clearing for sustainable agriculture network, August 27-September 2, 1985, Jakarta and Bulzittinggi, Indonesia. — Bangkok : International Board for Soil Research and Management, 1985. — 48p

RAIN FOREST ECOLOGY — Asia, Southeastern

WHITMORE, T. C.
Tropical rain forests of the Far East / T.C. Whitmore ; with a chapter on soils by C.P. Burnham. — 2nd ed. — Oxford : Clarendon, 1984. — xvi,352p. — *Previous ed.: 1975.* — *Maps on lining papers.* — *Bibliography: p297-328.* — *Includes index*

RAIVAVAE (AUSTRAL ISLANDS) — Population — Statistics

Tableaux normalisés du recensement général de la population : 15 octobre 1983. — [Papeete : Institut territorial de la statistique
Résultats de la commune de Raivavae. — [Papeete : Institut territorial de la statistique. — 4p,11 leaves

RAMMOHUN ROY, Raja

CRAWFORD, S. Cromwell
Ram Mohan Roy : social, political, and religious reform in 19th century India / S. Cromwell Crawford. — New York : Paragon House, c1987. — xvii, 263 p.. — *Includes index.* — *Bibliography: p. 253-255*

RAMMOHUN ROY, Raja — Ethics

CRAWFORD, S. Cromwell
Ram Mohan Roy : social, political, and religious reform in 19th century India / S. Cromwell Crawford. — New York : Paragon House, c1987. — xvii, 263 p.. — *Includes index.* — *Bibliography: p. 253-255*

RANGIROA (TUAMOTU ISLANDS) — Population — Statistics

Tableaux normalisés du recensement général de la population : 15 octobre 1983. — [Papeete] : Institut territorial de la statistique
Résultats de la commune de Rangiroa. — [1985?]. — 4p,ll leaves

RAPA (AUSTRAL ISLANDS) — Population — Statistics

Tableaux normalisés du recensement général de la population : 15 octobre 1983. — [Papeete] : Institut territorial de la statistique
Résultats de la commune de Rapa. — {1985?]. — 4p,11 leaves

RAPE

Rape / edited by Sylvana Tomaselli and Roy Porter. — Oxford : Basil Blackwell, 1986. — xii,292p,[16]p of plates. — *Bibliography: p280-281.* — *Includes index*

Violence against women : a critique of the sociobiology of rape / edited by Suzanne R. Sunday and Ethel Tobach. — New York : Gordian Press, 1985. — p. cm. — (A Genes and gender monograph). — *Includes index*

RAPE — Bibliography

WALKER, Christine
Rape. — [London] : Home Office Library, 1978. — 23leaves. — (Reading list / Home Office, Library)

RAPE — Law and legislation — England

ADLER, Zsuzsanna
Rape on trial / Zsuzsanna Adler. — London : Routledge & Kegan Paul, 1987. — viii,195p. — *Bibliography: p188-192.* — *Includes index*

RAPE — Legal status, laws, etc. — Bibliography

WALKER, Christine
Rape. — [London] : Home Office Library, 1978. — 23leaves. — (Reading list / Home Office, Library)

RAPE — Prevention

BART, Pauline B.
Stopping rape : successful survival strategies / Pauline B. Bart, Patricia H. O'Brien. — New York : Oxford : Pergamon, c1985. — xii,201p. — (The Athene series) (Pergamon international library). — *Bibliography: p187-191.* — *Includes index*

RAPE — England

BENN, Melissa
The rape controversy / Melissa Benn, Anna Coote, Tess Gill. — 3rd rev. and updated ed. — London : NCCL Rights for Women Unit, c1986. — 32p. — *Rev. ed.* — *Previous ed. i.e. 2nd ed.: 1983.* — *Bibliography: p32*

RAPE — England — History — 18th century

CLARK, Anna
Women's silence, men's violence : sexual assault in England 1770-1845 / Anna Clark. — London : Pandora Press, 1987. — viii,180p. — *Bibliography: p168-175*

RAPE — England — History — 19th century

CLARK, Anna
Women's silence, men's violence : sexual assault in England 1770-1845 / Anna Clark. — London : Pandora Press, 1987. — viii,180p. — *Bibliography: p168-175*

RAPE IN MARRIAGE — United States

FINKELHOR, David
License to rape : sexual abuse of wives / by David Finkelhor and Kersti Yllo. — New York : Holt, Rinehart and Winston, [1985]. — p. cm. — *Includes index.* — *Bibliography: p*

RAS TAFARI MOVEMENT

CAMPBELL, Horace
Rasta and resistance : from Marcus Garvey to Walter Rodney / Horace Campbell. — [London : Hansib, 1985]. — xiii,234p

RASKOLNIKS

RUMIANTSEVA, V. S.
Narodnoe antiserkovnoe dvizhenie v Rossii v XVII veke / V. S. Rumiantseva ; otv. redaktor I. A. Bulygin. — Moskva : Nauka, 1986. — 262p

RASSEMBLEMENT DU PEUPLE TOGOLAIS. Secretariat Administratif

EYADEMA, Etienne
Allocutions et discours : pronouces en 1969 / Le General Etienne Eyadema, President de la Republique Toglaise et President National du R.P.T.. — [S.l.] : Rassemblement du Peuple Togolais. Secretariat Administratif, 1973. — 42 leaves

RATE OF RETURN

DUVIGNEAU, J. Christian
Guidelines for calculating financial amd economic rates of return for DFC projects / J. Christian Duvigneau and Ranga N. Prasad. — Washington, D.C. : The World Bank, 1984. — xii,149p. — (World Bank technical paper ; no.33) (Industry and finance series ; v.9). — *Bibliography: p148-149*

RATE OF RETURN — Great Britain

STANNARD, R.
The required rate of return on investment : recent evidence from the private and public sectors / R. Stannard. — London : HM Treasury, 1985. — 12p. — (Government Economic Service working paper ; no.80) (Treasury working paper ; no.35). — *Bibliographical references: p12*

RATES BILL 1983-84

GREAT BRITAIN. Parliament. House of Commons. Library. Research Division
Rates Bill, Bill 79, 1983-84 / Barry K. Winetrobe. — [London] : the Division, 1984. — 18p. — (Reference sheet ; no.84/3). — *Includes bibliographical references*

RATING AND VALUATION (AMENDMENT) (SCOTLAND) BILL 1983-84

GREAT BRITAIN. Parliament. House of Commons. Library. Research Division
Rating & Valuation (Amendment) (Scotland) Bill, Bill 61 of 1983-84 / [Barry K. Winetrobe]. — [London] : the Division, 1983. — 9p. — (Reference sheet ; no.83/22). — *Includes bibliographical references*

RATIO ANALYSIS

WESTWICK, C. A.
How to use management ratios / C.A. Westwick. — 2nd ed. — Aldershot : Gower, 1987. — xviii,421p. — (A Gower workbook). — *Previous ed.: 1973.* — *Bibliography: p401-411.* — *Includes index*

RATIONAL EXPECTATIONS (ECONOMIC THEORY)

BHANDARI, Jagdeep S
Studies in international macroeconomics / Jagdeep S. Bhandari. — New York : Praeger, 1986. — p. cm. — *Includes index*

MACESICH, George
Monetary policy and rational expectations / George Macesich. — New York : Praeger, 1987. — x, 154 p.. — *Includes index.* — *Bibliography: p. [139]-147*

STRONG, Norman
Information and capital markets / Norman Strong and Martin Walker. — Oxford : Basil Blackwell, 1987. — [240]p. — *Includes bibliography and index*

RATIONAL EXPECTATIONS (ECONOMIC THEORY) — Mathematical models
CRIPPS, Martin William
Imperfect competition and strategic information transmission / Martin William Cripps. — 201 leaves. — *PhD (Econ) 1986 LSE*

RATIONALISM
INGRAM, David
Habermas and the dialectic of reason / David Ingram. — New Haven, CT : Yale University Press, c1987. — xvii, 263p. — *Includes index. — Bibliography: p.243-254*

MOSER, Paul K.
Empirical justification / Paul K. Moser. — Dordrecht ; Boston : D. Reidel Pub. Co. ; Hingham MA, U.S.A. : Sold and distributed in the U.S.A. and Canada by Kluwer Boston, c1985. — x, 263p. — (Philosophical studies series in philosophy ; v. 34). — *Includes indexes*

WATKINS, John W. N
Science and scepticism / John Watkins. — Princeton, N.J. : Princeton University Press, c1984. — xvii, 387 p.. — *Includes indexes. — Bibliography: p. 356-380*

RATIONALISM — Addresses, essays, lectures
Rationality : the critical view / Joseph Agassi, Ian Charles Jarvie, editors. — Dordrecht ; Boston : M. Nijhoff, 1986. — p. cm. — (Nijhoff international philosophy series ; 23). — *Includes indexes. — Bibliography: p*

RATIONALISM IN LITERATURE
HOLSTUN, James
A rational millennium : Puritan utopias of seventeenth-century England and America / James Holstun. — New York : Oxford University Press, 1987. — p. cm. — *Includes index. — Bibliography: p*

RATIONALIZATION (PSYCHOLOGY)
BILMES, Jack
Discourse and behavior / Jack Bilmes. — New York : Plenum Press, c1986. — p. cm. — *Includes index. — Bibliography: p*

RAW MATERIALS
Primary commodities : market developments and outlook / by the Commodities Division of the Research Department. — Washington, D.C. : International Monetary Fund, 1987. — vii,91p. — (World economic and financial surveys). — *Includes bibliographical references*

RAW MATERIALS — Economic aspects
Primary commodities : market developments and outlook / by the Commodities Division of the Research Department. — Washington, D.C. : International Monetary Fund, 1986. — vii,74p. — (World economic and financial surveys)

RAW MATERIALS — Government policy — Canada
CLARK-JONES, Melissa
A staple state : Canadian industrial resources in cold war / Melissa Clark-Jones. — Toronto : University of Toronto Press, 1987. — ix,260p. — (The State and economic life ; no.10). — *Bibliographical notes: p[225]-252*

RAW MATERIALS — Prices — Mathematical models
HOLTHAM, Gerald
OECD economic activity and non-oil commodity prices : reduced-form equations for INTERLINK / by Gerald Holtham, Martine Durand. — Paris : OECD, 1987. — 24p. — (Working papers / OECD Department 0f Economics and Statistics ; no.42). — *Bibliographical references: p24*

RAW MATERIALS — Pacific area
Raw materials and Pacific economic integration / edited by Sir John Crawford and Saburo Okita assisted by ... [others]. — London : Croom Helm, 1978. — 343p. — *Bibliography: p.312-338. — includes index*

RAWLS, JOHN. Theory of justice
Fondements d'une théorie de la justice : essais critiques sur la philosophie politique de John Rawls / publiés sous la direction de Jean Ladrière et Philippe Van Parijs. — Louvain-la-Neuve : Institut Supérieur de Philosophie, 1984. — x,275p. — (Essais philosophiques). — *Bibliography: p260-266*

REACTOR FUEL REPROCESSING — England — Cumbria
Public local inquiry into an application by British Nuclear Fuels Limited, referred to the Secretary of State under Section 35 of the Town and Country Planning Act 1971, for planning permission to establish a plant for reprocessing irradiated oxide nuclear fuels and support site services at Windscale and Calder Works, Sellafield, Cumbria; before the Hon. Mr Justice Parker (the Inspector), Sir Edward Pochin and Sir Frederick Warner (Assessors), at the Civic Hall, Whitehaven, Cumbria, on 14th June 1977 and succeeding days [to 4th November 1977] : transcript of proceedings. — [London : Department of the Environment, 1979]. — 144microfishes. — *At head of title: Town and Country Planning Act 1971. — Transcripts prepared by J. L. Harpham Ltd., Official Shorthand Writers, Sheffield; filmed August 1979*

SOUTHGATE, Mark
Windscale inquiry : index to the transcripts of the hearings held before Mr Justice Parker / compiled by Mark Southgate. — London : Department of Energy, 1978. — 4microfiches. — *At head of title: Departments of Industry, Trade and Prices and Consumer Protection Common Services: Libraries. — Comprises index of counsel, witnesses and representatives and subject index*

READ, KENNETH E
READ, Kenneth E
Return to the high valley : coming full circle / Kenneth E. Read. — Berkeley : University of California Press, c1986. — xxi, 269 p., [8] p. of plates. — (Studies in Melanesian anthropology) . — *Includes bibliographical references and index*

READING
Literacy, society, and schooling : a reader / edited by Suzanne de Castell, Allan Luke, Kieran Egan. — Cambridge : Cambridge University Press, 1986. — xiv,336p. — *Conference proceedings. — Includes bibliographies and indexes*

READING ABBEY
Reading Abbey cartularies : British Library manuscripts - Egerton 3031, Harley 1708 and Cotton Vespasian Exxv / edited by B.R. Kemp. — London : Royal Historical Society 2: Berkshire documents, Scottish charters and miscellaneous documents. — 1987. — [440]p. — (Camden fourth series ; v.33). — *Includes bibliography and index*

READING (ELEMENTARY)
Theory and practice of early reading / edited by Lauren B. Resnick, Phyllis A. Weaver. — Hillsdale, N.J. : Lawrence Erlbaun, 1979. — 3v . — *Based on papers presented at a series of 3 conferences, held at the Learning Research and Development Center, University of Pittsburgh, 1976. — Includes indexes. — Bibliography: p*

REAGAN, RONALD
KRIEGER, Joel
Reagan, Thatcher, and the politics of decline / Joel Krieger. — Cambridge : Polity, 1986. — [220]p. — (Europe and the international order) . — *Includes index*

Eagle resurgent? : the Reagan era in American foreign policy / edited by Kenneth A. Oye, Robert J. Lieber, Donald Rothchild. — Boston : Little, Brown, c1987. — viii, 472 p.. — *Includes bibliographical references and index*

HALLIDAY, Fred
Beyond Irangate : the Reagan doctrine and the Third World / Fred Halliday. — Amsterdam : Transnational Institute, 1987. — 38p. — (Transnational issues ; 1)

RAYACK, Elton
Not so free to choose : the political economy of Milton Friedman and Ronald Reagan / Elton Rayack. — New York : Praeger, 1987. — x, 215 p.. — *Includes index. — Bibliography: p. 203-208*

Reagan versus the Sandinistas : the undeclared war on Nicaragua / edited by Thomas W. Walker. — Boulder : Westview Press, 1986. — p. cm. — *Includes index*

REAGAN, RONALD — Addresses, essays, lectures
Evaluating U.S. foreign policy / edited by John A. Vasquez. — New York : Praeger, 1985. — p. cm. — *Includes index*

REAGAN, RONALD — Congresses
Reagan's leadership and the Atlantic Alliance : views from Europe and America / [edited by] Walter Goldstein. — Washington : Pergamon-Brassey, 1986. — p. cm. — *"Developed with the support of the Standing Conference of Atlantic Organizations.". — Papers presented at the 13th Annual Meeting of the Standing Conference of Atlantic Organizations, Wingspread House, Racine, Wisc., July 1985, sponsored by the Johnson Foundation and the Information Directorate of NATO*

REAGAN, RONALD — Journeys — Germany (West) — Addresses, essays, lectures
Bitburg in moral and political perspective / edited by Geoffrey H. Hartman. — Bloomington : Indiana University Press, c1986. — xvi, 284 p.. — *Bibliography: p. [281]-282*

REAL ANALYSIS
ROYDEN, H. L.
Real analysis / H.L.Royden. — 2nd ed.. — New York : Macmillan ; London : Collier Macmillan, 1968

REAL ESTATE DEVELOPMENT — Environmental aspects — Great Britain
GREAT BRITAIN INTERDEPARTMENTAL COMMITTEE ON THE REDEVELOPMENT OF CONTAMINATED LAND
Progress report of the Interdepartmental Committee on the Redevelopment of Contaminated Land, 1979. — [London : Department of the Environment, 1979]. — [12] . — *Bibliographical references: p[11]. — ICRCL 19/79*

REAL ESTATE DEVELOPMENT — Government policy — Great Britain
GREAT BRITAIN. Department of the Environment
The provision of land for private residential development. — London : H.M.S.O., 1977. — 8p. — (Development advice note ; 3)

GREAT BRITAIN. Department of the Environment
The United Kingdom's community land scheme. — [London] : the Department, 1976. — [4]. — (Planning in the United Kingdom). — *Prepared for the United Nations Conference on Human Settlements, 1976, Vancouver*

REAL ESTATE DEVELOPMENT — Argentina — History
MÍGUEZ, Eduardo José
Las tierras de los ingleses en la Argentina (1870-1914) / Eduardo José Míguez. — [Buenos Aires] : Editorial de Belgrano, 1985. — 348p. — *"El presente libro es una traducción y adaptación de mi tesis doctoral, titulada 'British interests in Argentine Land Development, 1870-1914. A study of British investment in Argentina', defendida en la Universidad de Óxford en abril de 1981.". — Bibliography: p[331]-342*

REAL ESTATE DEVELOPMENT — Australia — Melbourne (Vic.) — History — 20th century

LOGAN, William Stewart
The gentrification of inner Melbourne : a political geography of inner city housing / William Stewart Logan. — St Lucia ; London : University of Queensland Press, 1985. — xxxiii,328p. — (The University of Queensland Press scholars' library). — *Bibliography: p305-315. — Includes index*

REAL ESTATE DEVELOPMENT — England — Hertfordshire

MCNAMARA, Paul
Restraint policy and development interests : housing in Dacorum and North Hertfordshire / by Paul McNamara. — [Oxford : Oxford Polytechnic, Dept. of Town Planning], 1982. — iii,75p. — (Working paper / Oxford Polytechnic, Dept. of Town Planning ; no.76). — *Cover title: Housing in Dacorum & North Hertfordshire : restraint policy & development interests. — "... the eighth working paper forming part of an SSRC sponsored study entitled "Land release and development in areas of restraint" - p.i*

REAL ESTATE DEVELOPMENT — England — Reading (Berkshire) — History — 20th century

The National Health Service Central Register as an indicator of recent migration trends in Surrey. — [Kingston upon Thames] ([County Hall, Penrhyn Rd., Kingston upon Thames KT1 2DT]) : County Planning Department, Surrey County Council, 1985. — 14leaves. — (Technical report ; no.4/85). — *Cover title*

REAL ESTATE DEVELOPMENT — Great Britain

Planning control : philosophies, prospects and practice / edited by M.L. Harrison and R. Mordey. — London : Croom Helm, c1987. — 234p. — (Croom Helm series in geography and environment). — *Bibliography: p227-232. — Includes index*

REAL ESTATE DEVELOPMENT — Southern States

HEALY, Robert G
Competition for land in the American South : agriculture, human settlement, and the environment / Robert G. Healy. — Washington, D.C. : Conservation Foundation, c1985. — xxxii, 333 p.. — *Includes bibliographies and index*

REAL ESTATE INVESTMENT — Taxation — Law and legislation — United States — Congresses

Tax reform and real estate / edited by James R. Follain. — Washington, D.C. : Urban Institute Press, c1986. — xviii, 246 p.. — *Based on a conference held in Rosemont, Ill. on Oct. 4 and 5, 1985 which was organized and sponsored by the Office of Real Estate Research at the University of Illinois, Urbana-Champaign, in cooperation with Lambda Alpha International. — Includes bibliographies*

REAL ESTATE INVESTMENT — Taxation — United States — Congresses

Tax reform and real estate / edited by James R. Follain. — Washington, D.C. : Urban Institute Press, c1986. — xviii, 246 p.. — *Based on a conference held in Rosemont, Ill. on Oct. 4 and 5, 1985 which was organized and sponsored by the Office of Real Estate Research at the University of Illinois, Urbana-Champaign, in cooperation with Lambda Alpha International. — Includes bibliographies*

REAL ESTATE INVESTMENT — Argentina

MÍGUEZ, Eduardo José
Las tierras de los ingleses en la Argentina (1870-1914) / Eduardo José Míguez. — [Buenos Aires] : Editorial de Belgrano, 1985. — 348p. — *"El presente libro es una traducción y adaptación de mi tesis doctoral, titulada 'British interests in Argentine Land Development, 1870-1914. A study of British investment in Argentina', defendida en la Universidad de Oxford en abril de 1981.". — Bibliography: p[331]-342*

REAL ESTATE INVESTMENT — Pacific Area

GOLDBERG, Michael A
The Chinese connection : getting plugged in to Pacific Rim real estate, trade, and capital markets / Michael A. Goldberg. — Vancouver : University of British Columbia Press, 1985. — xi, 158 p. — *Includes indexes. — Bibliography: p. [121]-158*

REAL PROPERTY — Economic aspects — Great Britain

HARVEY, J
Urban land economics : the economics of real property / Jack Harvey. — Fully rev. 2nd ed. — Basingstoke : Macmillan Education, 1987. — xiv,408p. — *Previous ed: published as Economics of real property. 1981. — Bibliography: p387-391. — Includes index*

REAL PROPERTY — Law and legislation — Great Britain

GRAY, Kevin J.
Property, divorce and retirement pension rights / by K.J. Gray. British nationality and the right of abode 1948-1983 / by C.C. Turpin. — Deventer ; London : Kluwer, 1986. — vii,269p. — (Cambridge-Tilburg law lectures ; 5th ser., 1982). — *Includes bibliographical references*

REAL PROPERTY — Valuation — Hong Kong

CRUDEN, Gordon N.
Land compensation and valuation law in Hong Kong / Gordon N. Cruden. — Singapore : Butterworths, 1986. — xxxii,476p

REAL PROPERTY — England — Bibliography

BATES, David
A bibliography of Domesday book / David Bates. — Woodbridge : Boydell, 1986, c1985. — xi,166p

REAL PROPERTY — England — Cases

BURN, E. H.
Maudsley and Burn's land law : cases and materials. — 5th ed. / by E.H. Burn. — London : Butterworths, 1986. — [850]p. — *Previous ed.: published as Land law / by R.H. Maudsley and E.H. Burns. 1980. — Includes index*

REAL PROPERTY — England — London

GREEN, Shirley
Who owns London ? / Shirley Green. — London : Weidenfeld and Nicolson, c1986. — 224p

REAL PROPERTY — Spain — Barcelona

MASSANA, Carme
Indústria, ciutat i propietat : política econòmica i propietat urbana a l'àrea de Barcelona (1901-1939) / Carme Massana. — Barcelona : Curial, 1985. — 431p. — (Biblioteca de cultura catalana ; 57)

REAL PROPERTY AND TAXATION — United States — Congresses

Tax reform and real estate / edited by James R. Follain. — Washington, D.C. : Urban Institute Press, c1986. — xviii, 246 p.. — *Based on a conference held in Rosemont, Ill. on Oct. 4 and 5, 1985 which was organized and sponsored by the Office of Real Estate Research at the University of Illinois, Urbana-Champaign, in cooperation with Lambda Alpha International. — Includes bibliographies*

REAL PROPERTY, EXCHANGE OF — United States

LOGAN, John R.
Urban fortunes : the political economy of place / John R. Logan, Harvey L. Molotch. — Berkeley, CA : University of California Press, 1987. — p. cm. — *Includes index. — Bibliography: p*

REAL PROPERTY TAX — Law and legislation — Great Britain

GREAT BRITAIN. Parliament. House of Commons. Library. Research Division
Rates Bill, Bill 79, 1983-84 / Barry K. Winetrobe. — [London] : the Division, 1984. — 18p. — (Reference sheet ; no.84/3). — *Includes bibliographical references*

REAL PROPERTY TAX — Law and legislation — Peru

PERU
[Decreto supremo no.287-68-HC]. Income tax, real estate ownership value and stock assets : Supreme decree no.287-68-HC. — [Lima : Presidencia?, 1968]. — 106leaves. — *Translation from Spanish into English*

REAL PROPERTY TAX — Law and legislation — Scotland

GREAT BRITAIN. Parliament. House of Commons. Library. Research Division
Abolition of Domestic Rates etc. [Scotland] Bill, Bill 9 of 1986-87 / Barry Winetrobe, Rob Clements. — [London] : the Division, 1986. — 20p. — (Reference sheet ; no.86/16)

GREAT BRITAIN. Parliament. House of Commons. Library. Research Division
Rating & Valuation (Amendment) (Scotland) Bill, Bill 61 of 1983-84 / [Barry K. Winetrobe]. — [London] : the Division, 1983. — 9p. — (Reference sheet ; no.83/22). — *Includes bibliographical references*

REAL PROPERTY TAX — Appalachian Region

Who owns Appalachia? : landownership and its impact / the Appalachian Land Ownership Task Force ; with an introduction by Charles C. Geisler. — Lexington, Ky. : University Press of Kentucky, c1983. — xxxii, 235 p.. — *Map on lining papers. — Includes bibliographies and index*

REAL-TIME DATA PROCESSING

WARD, Paul T.
Structured development for real-time systems / by Paul T. Ward and Stephen J. Mellor. — New York : Yourden Press
Vol.1: Introduction and tools. — 1985. — 156p

REALISM

BHASKAR, Roy
Scientific realism and human emancipation / Roy Bhaskar. — London : Verso, 1986. — 308p

FINE, Arthur
The shaky game : Einstein, realism, and the quantum theory / Arthur Fine. — Chicago : University of Chicago Press, c1986. — xi, 186 p.. — (Science and its conceptual foundations). — *Includes index. — Bibliography: p. 173-179*

LARGEAULT, Jean
Principes de philosophie réaliste / Jean Largeault. — Paris : Klincksieck, 1985. — 271p

MARGOLIS, Joseph
Pragmatism without foundations : reconciling realism and relativism / Joseph Margolis. — Oxford : Basil Blackwell, 1986. — (The persistence of reality ; 1). — *Includes index*
1: Pragmatism without foundations : reconciling realism and relativism. — xix,320p

WRIGHT, Crispin
Realism, meaning and truth / Crispin Wright. — Oxford : Basil Blackwell, 1986 (1987 [printing]). — xii,386p. — *Bibliography: p363-375. — Includes index*

REALITY — Philosophy
RYN, Claes G.
Will, imagination, and reason : Irving Babbitt and the problem of reality / by Claes G. Ryn. — Chicago, IL : Regnery Gateway, [1986]. — p. cm. — *Bibliography: p*

REAO (TUAMOTU ISLANDS) — Population — Statistics
Tableaux normalisés du recensement général de la population : 15 octobre 1983. — [Papeete] : Institut territorial de la statistique Résultats de la commune de Reao. — [1985?]. — 4p,ll leaves

REASON OF STATE
ZIEGLER, Jean
Vive le pouvoir! : ou les délices de la raison d'état / Jean Ziegler. — Paris : Seuil, [1985]. — 281p

REASONING
GIERE, Ronald N.
Understanding scientific reasoning / Ronald N. Giere. — 2nd ed. — New York ; London : Holt, Rinehart and Winston, c1984. — xviii,391p. — *Previous ed.: 1979. — Bibliography: p371-373. — Includes index*

Practical reasoning in human affairs : studies in honor of Chaim Perelman / edited by James L. Golden and Joseph J. Pilotta. — Dordrecht ; Lancaster : Reidel, c1986. — x, 404p. — (Synthese library ; v. 183). — *Includes bibliographies and indexes*

REASONING (PSYCHOLOGY)
BARON, Jonathan
Rationality and intelligence / Jonathan Baron. — Cambridge : Cambridge University Press, 1985. — 299p

RECALL — United States
ZIMMERMAN, Joseph Francis
Participatory democracy : populism revived / Joseph F. Zimmerman. — New York : Praeger, 1986. — xi, 229 p.. — *Bibliography: p. 185-221*

RECEIVERS — Canada
BENNETT, Frank
Receiverships / by Frank Bennett. — Toronto, Canada : Carswell Co., 1985. — xlvii, 539 p.. — *Includes bibliographical references and indexes*

RECEIVERS — England
LIGHTMAN, Gavin
The law of receivers of companies / by Gavin Lightman and Gabriel Moss ; with a foreword by Sir John Vinelott. — London : Sweet & Maxwell, 1986. — xlix,358p. — *Includes index*

RECEIVERS — Ontario
BENNETT, Frank
Receiverships / by Frank Bennett. — Toronto, Canada : Carswell Co., 1985. — xlvii, 539 p.. — *Includes bibliographical references and indexes*

RECEIVERS — Scotland
GREENE, J. H.
The law and practice of receivership in Scotland / J.H. Greene, I.M. Fletcher. — London : Butterworths, 1987. — xxxviii,355p. — *Includes index*

RECIDIVISM — California
PETERSILIA, Joan
Prison versus probation in California : implications for crime and offender recidivism / Joan Petersilia, Susan Turner, with Joyce Peterson ; prepared for the National Institute of Justice, U.S. Department of Justice. — Santa Monica, CA. : Rand, [1986]. — xix, 63 p.. — *"July 1986.". — "R-3323-NIJ.". — Bibliography: p. 59-63*

RECIDIVISM — Netherlands
EMMERICK, J. L. van
Recidivism among psychiatric offenders / Jos L. van Emmerik. — The Hague : Research and Documentation Centre, Ministry of Justice, 1985. — 20p. — ([Reports, papers, articles] ; 87). — *Bibliographical references: p14. — "A summary of a survey of persons who were discharged between 1974 and 1979"*

RECIDIVISTS — United States — Case studies
SHOVER, Neal
Aging criminals / by Neal Shover. — Beverly Hills [Calif.] : Sage Publications, c1985. — p. cm. — (Sociological observations ; v. 17). — *Includes index. — Bibliography: p*

RECIFE HOUSE OF DETENTION — History — 19th century
HUGGINS, Martha Knisely
From slavery to vagrancy in Brazil : crime and social control in the Third World / Martha Knisely Huggins. — New Brunswick, N.J. : Rutgers University Press, c1984. — xix, 183p. — (Crime, law, and deviance series). — *Includes index. — Bibliography: p 159-167*

RECIPROCITY
BAUER, Raymond A.
American business and public policy : the politics of foreign trade / Raymond A. Bauer, Ithiel de Sola Pool, Lewis Anthony Dexter. — New York : Atherton Press, 1963. — xxvii,499p

WONNACOTT, Ronald J
Aggressive U.S. reciprocity evaluated with a new analytical approach to trade conflicts / R.J. Wonnacott. — Montreal, Quebec : Institute for Research on Public Policy, c1984. — xxi, 68 p.. — (Essays in international economics). — *Bibliography: p. 57-58*

RECLAMATION OF LAND — England
ROGER TYM AND PARTNERS
Evaluation of derelict land grant schemes / Roger Tym and Partners in association with Land Use Consultants ; [for the] Department of the Environment. — London : H.M.S.O., 1987. — v,122p. — *At head of cover title: Inner Cities Research Programme. — Commissioned by the Inner Cities Directorate of the Department of the Environment*

RECLAMATION OF LAND — Great Britain
BRADLEY, Christine
Community involvement in greening projects : a study on behalf of the Groundwork Foundation / by Christine Bradley. — Bolton : The Foundation, 1986. — 1v.. — *Includes index*

GREAT BRITAIN. Department of the Environment
"Waste of waste land" : the reclamation of derelict land and the prevention of dereliction in the United Kingdom. — [London] : the Department, 1976. — [21]p. — (Planning in the United Kingdom). — *Paper presented at the United Nations Conference on Human Settlements, 1976, Vancouver. — Bibliography: p[19-21]*

RECLAMATION OF LAND — Ukraine
UK-USSR Environmental Protection Agreement: area III (land reclamation) : report of a visit to the USSR (by a UK delegation) in 1976. — London : Planning, Regional and Minerals Directorate, Department of the Environment, [1977]. — 24p

RECLAMATION OF LAND — United States
NELSON, Robert Wayne
Wetland management strategies : balancing agriculture with conservation / by Robert Wayne Nelson. — 319 leaves. — *PhD (Econ) 1987 LSE. — Leaves 252-317 are appendices*

RECOGNITION(PSYCHOLOGY)
BARTLETT, Frederic C
Remembering : a study in experimental and social psychology / by Frederic C. Bartlett. — Cambridge : Cambridge University Press, 1967. — x,317p. — *Previous ed: 1932*

RECOLLECTION(PSYCHOLOGY)
BARTLETT, Frederic C
Remembering : a study in experimental and social psychology / by Frederic C. Bartlett. — Cambridge : Cambridge University Press, 1967. — x,317p. — *Previous ed: 1932*

RECOMBINANT DNA — Safety measures
Recombinant DNA safety considerations : safety considerations for industrial, agricultural and environmental applications of organisms derived by recombinant DNA techniques. — Paris : Organisation for Economic Co-operation and Development, 1986. — 69p. — *Includes bibliographical references*

RECONCILIATION
BEER, Jennifer E.
Peacemaking in your neighborhood : reflections on an experiment in community mediation / Jennifer E. Beer ; foreword by Elise Boulding. — Philadelphia, Pa. : New Society, 1986. — [viii],245p. — *Bibliography: p[235]-245*

RUSSELL, Joycelyne G.
Peacemaking in the Renaissance / Joycelyne G. Russell. — London : Duckworth, 1986. — x,278p,[8]p of plates. — *Bibliography: p257-267. — Includes index*

RECONSTRUCTION
BENEDICT, Michael Les
The fruits of victory : alternatives in restoring the Union, 1865-1877 / Michael Les Benedict. — Lanham ; London : University Press of America, 1987. — [174]p. — *Includes bibliography*

RABLE, George C
But there was no peace : the role of violence in the politics of Reconstruction / George C. Rable. — Athens : University of Georgia Press, c1984. — xiii, 257 p.. — *Includes index. — Bibliography: p. [247]-251*

RICHARDSON, Joe Martin
Christian reconstruction : the American Missionary Association and Southern Blacks, 1861-1890 / Joe M. Richardson. — Athens : University of Georgia Press, c1986. — ix, 348 p., [16] p. of plates. — *Includes index. — Bibliography: p. 323-335*

RECONSTRUCTION — Georgia
CURRIE-MCDANIEL, Ruth
Carpetbagger of conscience : a biography of John Emory Bryant / Ruth Currie-McDaniel. — Athens : University of Georgia Press, c1987. — 238 p. — *Includes index. — Bibliography: p. [221]-231*

DRAGO, Edmund L.
Black politicians and reconstruction in Georgia : a splendid failure / Edmund L. Drago. — Baton Rouge ; London : Louisiana State University Press, c1982. — xii,201p

DUNCAN, Russell
Freedom's shore : Tunis Campbell and the Georgia freedmen / by Russell Duncan. — Athens : University of Georgia Press, c1986. — p. cm. — *Includes index. — Bibliography: p*

WALLENSTEIN, Peter
From slave South to New South : public policy in nineteenth-century Georgia / Peter Wallenstein. — Chapel Hill : University of North Caroline Press, c1987. — xii, 284 p.. — (The Fred W. Morrison series in Southern studies). — *Includes index. — Bibliography: p. [257]-272*

RECONSTRUCTION (1939-1951) — Poland
MAGIERSKA, Anna
Przywrócić Polsce : przemysł na Ziemiach Odzyskanych 1945-1946. — Warszawa : Państwowe Wydawnictwo Naukowe, 1986. — 467p. — *Bibliography: p439-[451]*

RECREATION — Economic aspects — United States
WALSH, Richard G.
  Recreation economic decisions : comparing benefits and costs / Richard G. Walsh. — State College, Pa : Venture Publishing, 1986. — xiv,637p. — *Bibliographies*

RECREATION — Canada — Statistics
Tourism and recreation: a statistical digest = Tourisme et loisirs: résumé statistique / Statistics Canada. Travel, Tourism and Recreation Section. — Ottawa : Minister of Supply and Services, Canada, 1984-. — *Annual. — Text in English and French*

RECREATION — England — Devon
Leisure policies and programmes : a summary report on future possibilities. — Exeter : Devon County Council, 1985. — 28p. — *"This summary report shows the opportunities for future leisure provision by Devon's local authorities. The full report contains the survey material and analysis on which these possibilities are based."*

RECRUITING OF EMPLOYEES
SMITH, Mike, 1945-
  The theory and practice of systematic staff selection / Mike Smith and Ivan T. Robertson. — Basingstoke : Macmillan, 1986. — xii,321p. — *Bibliography: p291-313. — Includes index*

RECRUITING OF EMPLOYEES — Great Britain
GREAT BRITAIN. Equal Opportunities Commission
  Fair and efficient selection : guidance on equal opportunities policies in recruitment and selection procedures. — London : H.M.S.O., 1986. — 50p

RECRUITING OF EMPLOYEES — London
DAVIES, Tom
  Shutting out the inner city worker : recruitment and training practices of large employers in central London / Tom Davies, Charlie Mason. — Bristol : University of Bristol, School for Advanced Urban Studies, 1986. — 50p. — (Occasional paper / University of Bristol, School for Advanced Urban Studies ; 23)

RECURSIVE FUNCTIONS — Data processing
MALLOZZI, John S.
  Computability with Pascal / John S. Mallozzi, Nicholas J. De Lillo. — Englewood Cliffs : Prentice-Hall, 1984. — xii, 193p. — *Includes index. — Bibliography: p186-187*

RECYCLING (WASTE, ETC.)
EDWARDS, Peter
  Aquaculture : a component of low cost sanitation technology / Peter Edwards. — Washington, D.C. : The World Bank, 1985. — xi,45p. — (World Bank technical paper ; no.36) (UNDP project management report ; no.3) (Integrated resource recovery series ; no.3). — *At head of cover: "Integrated resource recovery". — Bibliographical references: p45*

Recycling from municipal refuse : a state-of-the-art review and annotated bibliography / Sanda Johnson Cointreau. — Washington, D.C. : The World Bank, 1984. — xiv,214p. — (World Bank technical paper ; no.30) (UNDP project management report ; no.1) (Integrated resource recovery series ; no.1). — *Bibliography: p25-189*

RECYCLING (WASTE, ETC.) — Bibliography
Recycling from municipal refuse : a state-of-the-art review and annotated bibliography / Sanda Johnson Cointreau. — Washington, D.C. : The World Bank, 1984. — xiv,214p. — (World Bank technical paper ; no.30) (UNDP project management report ; no.1) (Integrated resource recovery series ; no.1). — *Bibliography: p25-189*

RECYCLING (WASTE, ETC.) — Developing countries
OBENG, Letitia A.
  The co-composting of domestic solid and human wastes / Letitia A. Obeng and Frederick W. Wright. — Washington, D.C. : The World Bank, 1987. — xii,101p. — (World Bank technical paper ; no.57) (UNDP project management report ; no.7) (Intergrated resource recovery series ; no.7). — *At head of cover: "Integrated resource recovery"*

RED SEA — Relations — France
CAMPREDON, Jean-Pierre
  France, océan Indien, mer Rouge : études / menées sous la responsabilité de Jean-Pierre Campredon et Jean-Jacques Schweitzer. — Paris : Fondation pour les études de défense nationale, 1986. — 449p. — *Bibliography: p443-445*

REDDITCH (WORCESTERSHIRE) — City planning
ANSTIS, Gordon
  Redditch : success in the heart of England : the history of Redditch New Town, 1964-1985 / Gordon Anstis ; preface by Sir Edward Thompson ; foreword by Sir Michael Edwardes. — Stevenage, Herts. : Publications for Companies, 1985. — xvi,264p

REDUCING — Social aspects — United States — History
SCHWARTZ, Hillel
  Never satisfied : a cultural history of diets, fantasies, and fat / Hillel Schwartz. — New York : Free Press ; London : Collier Macmillan, c1986. — p. cm. — *Bibliography: p*

REFERENCE BOOKS — Bibliography
REED, Jeffrey G.
  Library use : a handbook for psychology / Jeffrey G. Reed and Pam M. Baxter. — Washington, DC : American Psychological Association, c1983. — 137 p. — *Includes bibliographies and index*

SHEEHY, Eugene Paul
  Guide to reference books / Eugene P. Sheehy. — 10th ed. — Chicago : American Library Association, 1986. — p. cm. — *Includes index*

Walford's guide to reference material. — 4th ed. — London : Library Association. — *Previous ed.: published as Guide to reference material. 1977*
Vol.3: Generalia, language & literature, the arts / edited by A.J. Walford and L.J. Taylor. — 1987. — x,872p. — *Includes index*

REFERENCE BOOKS — Criminal justice, Administration of
LUTZKER, Marilyn
  Criminal justice research in libraries : strategies and resources / Marilyn Lutzker and Eleanor Ferrall ; foreword by Edward Sagarin. — Westport, Conn. : Greenwood Press, c1986. — p. cm. — *Includes indexes*

REFERENCE BOOKS — Philosophy
UNIVERSITY OF LONDON. Library Resources Coordinating Committee. Philosophy Subject Sub-committee
  A guide to philosophy collections and reference literature in philosophy. — London : the Committee, 1987. — ii,[40]p

REFERENCE LIBRARIANS
Personnel issues in reference services / edited by Bill Katz and Ruth A. Fraley. — New York : Haworth Press, c1986. — xvi, 200 p.. — *Includes bibliographies*

REFERENCE LIBRARIES — Australia
Design for diversity : library services for higher education and research in Australia / edited by Harrison Bryan and Gordon Greenwood. — St. Lucia [Aus.] : University of Queensland Press, c1977. — xvi, 790 p., [11] p. of plates. — *Distributed by Prentice-Hall International, Hemel Hempstead, Eng. — Includes index. Bibliography: p. [713]-740*

REFERENCE SERVICES (LIBRARIES)
Personnel issues in reference services / edited by Bill Katz and Ruth A. Fraley. — New York : Haworth Press, c1986. — xvi, 200 p.. — *Includes bibliographies*

REFERENCE SERVICES (LIBRARIES) — England
REDFEARN, Judy
  Libraries bring Prestel to the public : a summary of British Library-supported research 1979-1981 / Judy Redfearn. — [London] : British Library, c1983. — v,57p. — (Library and information research report ; 13)

REFERENCE SERVICES (LIBRARIES) — Great Britain
YEATES, R.
  Prestel in the public library. — Boston Spa : British Library Lending Division, July 1982. — [134]p. — (Library and information research reports ; 2)

REFERENDUM — Bibliography
GREAT BRITAIN. Parliament. House of Commons. Library. Research Division
  The referendum. — [London] : the Division, 1975. — 10p. — [5]leaves. — (Reference sheet ; no.75/6)

REFERENDUM — Europe
Methods of consulting citizens on municipal affairs. — Strasbourg : Council of Europe, 1979. — iii,43p. — (Study series local and regional authorities in Europe ; study no. 18). — *"Prepared by the Secretariat of the Steering Committee for Regional and Municipal Matters with the assistance of two consultants, Mr. Bart (France) and Mr. Couchepin (Switzerland)"*

REFERENDUM — United States
ZIMMERMAN, Joseph Francis
  Participatory democracy : populism revived / Joseph F. Zimmerman. — New York : Praeger, 1986. — xi, 229 p.. — *Bibliography: p. 185-221*

REFORM JUDAISM — Great Britain — History
RAYNER, John Desmond
  Strengthen our hands. — [London?] : [Union of Liberal and Progressive Synagogues], 195-?]. — [12p]

REFORMATION — Great Britain — Sources
KNOX, John
  The political writings of John Knox : The first blast of the trumpet against the monstrous regiment of women and other selected works / edited and with an introduction by Marvin A. Breslow. — Washington : Folger Shakespeare Library ; London : Associated University Presses, c1985. — 160 p.. — *"Folger books.". — Includes bibliographies. — Contents: The first blast of the trumpet against the monstrous regiment of women (1558) -- Letter to the Regent of Scotland (1558) -- Appellation to the nobility (1558) -- Letter to the commonalty of Scotland (1558) -- The second blast (1558)*

REFORMATION — Wales
WILLIAMS, Glanmor
  Recovery, reorientation and reformation : Wales, c.1415-1642 / Glanmor Williams. — Oxford : Clarendon Press, 1987. — [500]p. — (The History of Wales ; 3). — *Includes bibliography and index*

REFORMATORIES FOR WOMEN — England — London
LONDON STRATEGIC POLICY UNIT. Women's Equality Group
  Women's prisoners : breaking the silence. — London : [the Group], 1987. — iii,184p

REFORMATORIES FOR WOMEN — United States
GIALLOMBARDO, Rose
  Society of women : a study of a women's prison / Rose Giallombardo. — New York ; London : Wiley, [1966]. — viii,248p

REFORMED CHURCH — Doctrines — Addresses, essays, lectures

KNOX, John
The political writings of John Knox : The first blast of the trumpet against the monstrous regiment of women and other selected works / edited and with an introduction by Marvin A. Breslow. — Washington : Folger Shakespeare Library ; London : Associated University Presses, c1985. — 160 p.. — "Folger books.". — Includes bibliographies. — Contents: The first blast of the trumpet against the monstrous regiment of women (1558) -- Letter to the Regent of Scotland (1558) -- Appellation to the nobility (1558) -- Letter to the commonalty of Scotland (1558) -- The second blast (1558)

REFORMERS — India — Biography

CRAWFORD, S. Cromwell
Ram Mohan Roy : social, political, and religious reform in 19th century India / S. Cromwell Crawford. — New York : Paragon House, c1987. — xvii, 263 p.. — Includes index. — Bibliography: p. 253-255

REFORMERS — Mexico — Jalisco

VALLARTA, Ignacio Luis
Vallarta en la reforma / prólogo y selección: Moisés González Navarro. — México, D.F. : Universidad Nacional Autónoma de México, 1956. — xxxv,232p. — (Biblioteca del estudiante Universitario ; 76)

REFORMERS — United States — Biography

American reformers : an H.W. Wilson biographical dictionary / editor, Alden Whitman. — New York : H.W. Wilson Co., 1985. — xx, 930 p.. — Includes bibliographies

REFUGEES

Refugees : the dynamics of displacement : a report / for the Independent Commission on International Humanitarian Issues ; preface by Sadruddin Aga Khan. — London : Zed, 1986. — [192]p

REFUGEES — Addresses, essays, lectures

Refugees and world politics ; edited by Elizabeth G. Ferris. — New York : Praeger, 1985. — p. cm. — Includes index. — Bibliography: p

REFUGEES — Education — Africa — Directories

Higher education in Africa : manual for refugees = Enseignement supérieur en Afrique : Manuel pour les réfugiés. — [Geneva?] : World University Service International, 1986. — xiii,784p

REFUGEES — Government policy — Great Britain — Handbooks, manuals, etc

BRITISH REFUGEE COUNCIL
Refugee adviser's handbook. — London : British Refugee Council, 1985. — 1v(loose-leaf)

REFUGEES — Government policy — United States — History — 20th century

LOESCHER, Gil
Calculated kindness : refugees and America's half-open door, 1945 to the present / Gil Loescher, John A. Scanlan. — New York : Free Press ; London : Collier Macmillan, c1986. — xviii, 346p. — Includes index. — Bibliography: p. 273-331

REFUGEES — Services for

GORDENKER, Leon
Refugees in international politics / Leon Gordenker. — London : Croom Helm, c1987. — 227p. — (The Croom Helm United Nations and its agencies series). — Bibliography: p215-220. — Includes index

REFUGEES — Afghanistan

Afghan resistance : the politics of survival / edited by Grant M. Farr, John G. Merriam. — Boulder, Colo. : Westview Press, 1987. — p. cm. — (Westview special studies in international relations). — Bibliography: p

REFUGEES — Africa

KIBREAB, Gaim
African refugees : reflections on the African refugee problem / Gaim Kibreab. — Trenton, N.J. : Africa World Press, 1985. — 125p. — Previously published as: Reflections on the African refugee problem, (1983)

WILLIAMS, Norman
Role of the Office of the United Nations High Commissioner for Refugees in Africa / prepared by Norman Williams, Joint Inspection Unit. — New York : United Nations, 1986. — 28p. — United Nations Joint Inspection Unit report (JIV/REP/86/2) circulated as annex to United Nations General Assembly document A/41/380.

REFUGEES — Africa — Education (Higher)

Higher education in Africa : manual for refugees = Enseignement supérieur en Afrique : Manuel pour les réfugiés. — [Geneva?] : World University Service International, 1986. — xiii,784p

REFUGEES — Central America

FERRIS, Elizabeth G
The Central American refugees / Elizabeth G. Ferris. — New York : Praeger, 1986. — p. cm

Out of the ashes : the lives and hopes of refugees from El Salvador and Guatemala / ... material was collated and texts translated. written and edited by the Refugee Team of ESCHR/GCHR. — London : Published jointly by El Salvador and Guatemala committees for Human Rights and WOW Campaigns Ltd, 1985. — 48p.. — Includes translations from the Spanish. — Ill on inside covers

REFUGEES — Central America — Congresses

Sanctuary : a resource guide for understanding and participating in the Central American refugees' struggle / Gary MacEoin, editor. — 1st ed. — San Francisco : Harper & Row, c1985. — 217 p. — Papers derived from the Inter-American Symposium on Sanctuary, held in Tucson, Ariz., Jan. 23-24, 1985, and sponsored by the Tucson Ecumenical Council's Task Force for Central America and others. — Bibliography: p. 207-211

REFUGEES — Denmark — Public opinion

KÖRMENDI, Eszter
Os og de andre : Danskernes holdinger til indvandrere og flygtninge = Danish attitudes towards immigrants and refugees / Eszter Körmendi. — København : Socialforskningsinstituttet, 1986. — 180p. — (Publikation / Socialforskningsinstituttet ; 153). — In Danish, with English summary. — Bibliography: p176-177

REFUGEES — Germany (West)

JACOBMEYER, Wolfgang
Vom Zwangsarbeiter zum heimatlosen Ausländer : die Displaced Persons in Westdeutschland 1945-1951 / Wolfgang Jacobmeyer. — Göttingen : Vandenhoeck & Ruprecht, 1985. — 323p. — (Kritische Studien zur Geschichtswissenschaft ; 65). — Bibliography: p311-319

REFUGEES — Pakistan

Afghan resistance : the politics of survival / edited by Grant M. Farr, John G. Merriam. — Boulder, Colo. : Westview Press, 1987. — p. cm. — (Westview special studies in international relations). — Bibliography: p

REFUGEES — United States

LOESCHER, Gil
Calculated kindness : refugees and America's half-open door, 1945 to the present / Gil Loescher, John A. Scanlan. — New York : Free Press ; London : Collier Macmillan, c1986. — xviii, 346p. — Includes index. — Bibliography: p. 273-331

REFUGEES, AFRICA

WILLIAMS, Norman
Role of the Office of the United Nations High Commissioner for Refugees in Africa / prepared by Norman Williams, Joint Inspection Unit. — New York : United Nations, 1986. — 28p. — United Nations Joint Inspection Unit report (JIV/REP/86/2) circulated as annex to United Nations General Assembly document A/41/380.

REFUGEES, ARAB

TURKI, Fawaz
The Disinherited : journal of a Palestinian exile. — 2nd Modern Reader pbk. ed. — New York ; london : [Modern Reader], 1974, c1972. — Originally published in 1972. — Bibliographical references

REFUGEES, ARAB — Social conditions

COSSALI, Paul
Stateless in Gaza / by Paul Cossali and Clive Robson ; translated from the Arabic by the authors. — London : Zed, 1986. — [192]p

REFUGEES, JEWISH — Netherlands

MOORE, Bob
Refugees from Nazi Germany in the Netherlands, 1933-1940 / by Bob Moore. — Dordrecht ; Boston : M. Nijhoff, 1986. — xiv, 241 p.. — (Studies in social history ; 9). — Includes index. — Bibliography: p. 221-233

REFUGEES, JEWISH — United States — History

CASTRO, Fidel
Fidel Castro habla a los trabajadores de América Latina sobre la deuda externa : diálogo sostenido con los delegados a la Conferencia Sindical de los Trabajadores de América Latina y el Caribe sobre la Deuda Externa, durante la sesión de clausura del evento, el jueves 18 de julio de 1985. — Buenos Aires : Editorial Anteo, 1985. — 102 p.

REFUGEES, POLITICAL — Biography

MONTSENY, Federica
El exodo : pasión y muerte de españoles en el exilio / Federica Montseny. — 1. ed. — Barcelona : Galba, 1977. — 305p. — (Memorias) (Galba ; 20)

REFUGEES, POLITICAL — Education — New York (N.Y.) — History

RUTKOFF, Peter M.
New School : a history of the New School for Social Research / Peter M. Rutkoff, William B. Scott. — New York : Free Press ; London : Collier Macmillan, c1986. — xiv, 314p, [16]p of plates. — Includes bibliographical references and index

REFUGEES, POLITICAL — Germany (West)

KLAUSMEIER, Simone
Vom Asylbewerber zum "Scheinasylanten" : Asylrecht und Asylpolitik in der Bundesrepublik Deutschland seit 1973 / Simone Klausmeier. — Berlin : Express Edition, 1984. — 127p. — Bibliography: p121-127

REFUGEES, POLITICAL — Great Britain

BRITISH REFUGEE COUNCIL
Settling for a future : proposals for a British policy on refugees. — London : British Refugee Council, 1987. — 26p

REFUGEES, POLITICAL — Netherlands

MOORE, Bob
Refugees from Nazi Germany in the Netherlands, 1933-1940 / by Bob Moore. — Dordrecht ; Boston : M. Nijhoff, 1986. — xiv, 241 p.. — (Studies in social history ; 9). — Includes index. — Bibliography: p. 221-233

REFUSE AND REFUSE DISPOSAL
GREAT BRITAIN. Central Directorate of Environmental Protection
Monitoring waste : the duty of care : the Government's response to the eleventh report of the Royal Commission on Environmental Pollution / Central Directorate of Environmental Protection, Department of the Environment. — London : H.M.S.O., 1986. — (Pollution paper ; no.24)

REFUSE AND REFUSE DISPOSAL — Economic aspects
WILCOX, Joan
Urban waste : economic aspects of technological alternatives / Joan Wilcox. — London : Department of the Environment, 1976. — 17,[9]leaves. — *Bibliography: second sequence, leaf [9]*

REFUSE AND REFUSE DISPOSAL — Belgium — East Flanders
ECONOMISCHE RAAD VOOR OOST-VLAANDEREN
Huisvuilverwijdering en -verwerking in Oost-Vlaanderen : huidige situatie en reorganisatievoorstellen / Economische Raad voor Oost-Vlaanderen. — Gent : Economische Raad voor Oost-Vlaanderen, 1972. — 28 leaves

REFUSE AND REFUSE DISPOSAL — England — Bedfordshire
BEDFORDSHIRE. County Planning Department
Waste disposal plan. — Bedford : [the Department], 1987. — 82p. — *Includes folded maps*

REFUSE AND REFUSE DISPOSAL — England — South East
SERPLAN. Waste Disposal Working Party
Waste disposal in the South East region / a report by the Waste Disposal Working Party. — London : London and South East Regional Planning Conference, 1986. — 27p

REFUSE AS FUEL — Europe
ABERT, James Goodear
Municipal waste processing in Europe : a status report on selected materials and energy recovery projects / James G. Abert. — Washington, D.C. : The World Bank, 1985. — xiv,157p. — (World Bank technical paper ; no.37) (UNDP project management report ; no.4) (Integrated resource recovery series ; no.4). — *At head of cover: "Integrated resource recovery". — Includes bibliographical references*

REGENTS — Great Britain — Biography
DUBY, Georges
William Marshal : the flower of chivalry / Georges Duby ; translated from the French by Richard Howard. — London : Faber, 1986, c1985. — 155p. — *Translation of: Guillaume le Maréchal. — Bibliography: p154-155*

REGIONAL DEVELOPMENT — Economic aspects — Case studies
The International Regional Policy Association yearbook 1984 : new spatial dynamics and economic crisis / edited by J. G. Lambooy. — Tampere : Finnpublishers Oy, 1984. — 93p

REGIONAL DEVELOPMENT — Switzerland
Le secteur tertiaire et le nouveau développement régional / par Jean Valarché...[et al.]. — Fribourg : Éditions Universitaires, [1985]. — 103p. — (Ökonomische kolloquien = Colloques économiques ; 17)

REGIONAL ECONOMIC DISPARITIES
BOOTH, Douglas E
Regional long waves, uneven growth, and the cooperative alternative / Douglas E. Booth. — New York : Praeger, 1987. — 121 p.. — *Includes index. — Bibliography: p. 109-115*

REGIONAL ECONOMIC DISPARITIES — Spain
PEREZ PEREZ, Luis
Approche méthodologique pour une délimitation des zones défavorisées : application au cas de la communauté autonome dÁragon / par Luis Perez Perez. — Montpellier : Institut Ayonomique Méditerranéen de Montpellier, 1985. — 148p. — (Collection "Thèses M. Sc." / Institut Agronomique Mèditerranéen de Montpellier). — *Bibliography:p65-68*

REGIONAL ECONOMICS
ARMSTRONG, Harvey
Regional policy : the way forward / Harvey Armstrong and Jim Taylor. — London : Employment Institute, [1987]. — 55 p. — *At head of title: Employment Institute*

BALCHIN, Paul N.
Regional and urban economics / Paul N. Balchin, Gregory H. Bull. — London : Harper & Row, 1987. — xiv,249p. — *Bibliography: p230-241. — Includes index*

BURDULI, V. Sh.
Sovershenstvovanic upravlenie ekonomikoi regiona : (na primere Gruzinskoi SSR) / V. Sh. Burduli. — Tbilisi : Metsniereba, 1985. — 200p

Le financement des petites et moyennes entreprises : analyse macroéconomique : adequation du système d'aides interventions économiques régionales / [realisée par Lucien Farhi, Jacques Pierre, Eric Taze]. — Paris : Société d'études pour le développement économique et social, 1983. — 199p

FOLMER, Hendrik
Regional economic policy : measurement of its effect / by Hendrik Folmer. — Dordrecht ; Lancaster : Nijhoff, 1986. — xiv, 272p. — (Studies in operational regional science). — *Bibliography: p.249-265*

Handbook of regional and urban economics / edited by Peter Nijkamp. — Amsterdam : North-Holland. — (Handbooks in economics ; 7)
Vol.1: Regional economics. — 1986. — xxii,702p. — *Bibliographies*

HEWINGS, Geoffrey J. D.
Regional input-output analysis / Geoffrey J.D. Hewings. — Beverly Hills, CA : Sage Publications, c1985. — 95p. — (Scientific geography series ; v. 6). — *Bibliography: p90-95*

HILHORST, J. G. M.
Regional planning : a systems approach / Jos G.M. Hilhorst. — Aldershot : Gower, 1985, c1971. — [166]p. — *Originally published: Rotterdam : Rotterdam University Press, 1971*

International economic restructuring and the regional community / edited by Herman Muegge and Walter B. Stöhr. — Aldershot : Avebury, c1987. — x,404p. — *Conference proceedings*

New technology and regional development / edited by Bert van der Knaap and Egbert Wever. — London : Croom Helm, c1987. — 188p. — *Conference papers. — Includes index*

Région et aménagement du territoire : mélanges offerts à Joseph Lajugie par ses collègues, ses élèves et ses amis. — Bordeaux : Editions Bière, 1985. — 898p. — *Bibliographies*

SCOTT, Allen John
High technology industry and regional development : a theoretical critique and reconstruction / A. J. Scott and M. Storper. — Reading : University of Reading. Department of Geography, 1986. — 25p. — (Geographical paper ; no.95). — *17th Norma Wilkinson memorial lecture. — Bibliography:p23-25*

REGIONAL ECONOMICS — Congresses
INTERNATIONAL SYMPOSIUM ON TECHNOLOGICAL CHANGE AND EMPLOYMENT: URBAN AND REGIONAL DIMENSIONS (1985 : Zandvoort, Netherlands)
Technological change, employment, and spatial dynamics : proceedings of an International Symposium on Technological Change and Employment: Urban and Regional Dimensions, held at Zandvoort, the Netherlands, April 1-3, 1985 / edited by Peter Nijkamp. — Berlin ; New York : Springer-Verlag, c1986. — vii, 466 p.. — (Lecture notes in economics and mathematical systems ; 270). — *Includes bibliographies*

REGIONAL ECONOMICS — Mathematical models
Spatial pricing and differentiated markets / edited by G. Norman. — London : Pion, 1986. — 190p. — (London papers in regional science ; 16)

REGIONAL MEDICAL PROGRAMS — Great Britain
HAYNES, Robin M.
The geography of health services in Britain / Robin Haynes. — London : Croom Helm, c1987. — [272]p. — *Includes bibliography and index*

REGIONAL PLANNING
DERBYSHIRE. County Council
Social policy indicators : an analysis of the 1981 census for Derbyshire / A. W. Johnson; editor. — [Matlock] : [the Council], 1986. — [vii,160p]. — *Annual*

ELSON, Martin J.
Green belts : conflict mediation in the urban fringe / Martin J. Elson. — London : Heinemann, 1986. — xxxi,304p. — *Includes index*

FALUDI, Andreas
A decision-centred view of environmental planning / by Andreas Faludi. — Oxford : Pergamon, 1987. — xiii,240p. — (Urban and regional planning series ; v.38). — *Includes bibliographies and index*

HELD, Daniel
Marché de l'emploi : entreprises et régions / Daniel Held et Denis Maillat. — [Lausanne] : Presses Polytechniques Romandes, 1984. — 205p. — (Collection "villes, régions et sociétés")

HILHORST, J. G. M.
Regional planning : a systems approach / Jos G.M. Hilhorst. — Aldershot : Gower, 1985, c1971. — [166]p. — *Originally published: Rotterdam : Rotterdam University Press, 1971*

International regional science review. — Philadelphia, P.A. : Regional Science Association, 1986-. — *Quarterly*

OWENS, Susan E.
Energy, planning and urban form / Susan Owens. — London : Pion, c1986. — 118p. — *Bibliography: p107-116. — Includes index*

Région et aménagement du territoire : mélanges offerts à Joseph Lajugie par ses collègues, ses élèves et ses amis. — Bordeaux : Editions Bière, 1985. — 898p. — *Bibliographies*

Regional dynamics of socioeconomic change / edited by Antoni Kuklinski, Olli Kultalahti & Briitta Koskiaho. — Tampere [Finland] : Finnpublishers, [1979]. — viii, 547 p.. — (Acta Universitatis Tamperensis : ser. A ; v. 100). — *Includes bibliographies*

Spatial cycles / edited by Leo van den Berg, Leland S. Burns and Leo H. Klaassen. — Aldershot : Gower, c1987. — xvii,277p. — *Includes bibliographies and index*

REGIONAL PLANNING *continuation*

WEINTRAUB, Dov
Basic social diagnosis for IRRD planning : conceptual framework, case studies and some generalisations / Dov Weintraub, Julia Margulies. — Aldershot : Gower, c1986. — 233p. — *Bibliography: p.219-227*

REGIONAL PLANNING — Case studies

The International Regional Policy Association yearbook 1984 : new spatial dynamics and economic crisis / edited by J. G. Lambooy. — Tampere : Finnpublishers Oy, 1984. — 93p

REGIONAL PLANNING — Congresses

SEMANA ECONÓMICA INTERNACIONAL (1st : 1970 : Barcelona)
La región y el desarrollo : (en España y a nivel internacional) / Selección y supervisión general de Ramón Roca-Sastre Moncunill. — [1. ed. — Barcelona] : DOPESA, [1972]. — 288p. — (Documento económico, 2). — *At head of title: Organizada por el semanario Mundo*

REGIONAL PLANNING — Dictionaries — Polyglot

LOGIE, Gordon
Glossary of land resources : English-French-Italian-Dutch-German-Swedish / Gordon Logie. — Amsterdam ; New York : Elsevier, 1984. — xxvii, 303 p.. — (International planning glossaries ; 4). — *Includes indexes. — Bibliography: p. 299-300*

REGIONAL PLANNING — Economic aspects

Le financement des petites et moyennes entreprises : analyse macroéconomique : adequation du système d'aides interventions économiques régionales / [realisée par Lucien Farhi, Jacques Pierre, Eric Taze]. — Paris : Société d'études pour le développement économique et social, 1983. — 199p

REGIONAL PLANNING — European Economic Community countries

COMMISSION OF THE EUROPEAN COMMUNITIES
The regional development programmes : Brussels / Commission of the European Communities. — [Washington, D.C. : sold by European Community Information Service], 1979. — (Regional policy series ; 17)

REGIONAL PLANNING — Government policy

Regional dynamics of socioeconomic change / edited by Antoni Kuklinski, Olli Kultalahti & Briitta Koskiaho. — Tampere [Finland] : Finnpublishers, [1979]. — viii, 547 p.. — (Acta Universitatis Tamperensis : ser. A ; v. 100). — *Includes bibliographies*

REGIONAL PLANNING — Law and legislation — England

GREAT BRITAIN. Department of the Environment
Speeding planning appeals : the handling of inquiries planning appeals : action plan [and review] / Department of the Environment. — London : H.M.S.O., 1986. — iv,182p

HEAP, Sir Desmond
An outline of planning law / Sir Desmond Heap. — 9th ed. — London : Sweet & Maxwell, 1987. — [350]p. — *Previous ed.: 1982. — Includes index*

REGIONAL PLANNING — Law and legislation — Europe

Planning law in Western Europe / edited by J.F. Garner and N.P. Gravells. — 2nd. rev. ed. — Amsterdam ; New York : North-Holland ; New York, N.Y., U.S.A. : Sole distributors for the U.S.A. and Canada, Elsevier Science Pub. Co., 1986. — p. cm. — *Bibliography: p*

REGIONAL PLANNING — Law and legislation — Great Britain

Challenging decision : papers from a conference held at Oxford, September 1985 / organised by the Bar Council, the Law Society and the Royal Institution of Chartered Surveyors. — London : Sweet & Maxwell, 1986. — vi,101p. — (Journal of planning and environmental law occasional papers ; no.12). — *Conference paper*

REGIONAL PLANNING — Law and legislation — Nigeria

OLA, C. S
Town and country planning and environmental laws in Nigeria / C.S. Ola. — 2nd ed. — Jericho, Ibadan, Nigeria : University Press, 1984. — xx, 275 p.. — *Rev. ed. of: Town and country planning law in Nigeria. 1977. — Based on a small part of author's thesis--University College, London. — Includes index. — Bibliography: p. 265-269*

REGIONAL PLANNING — Political aspects

SILLINCE, John
A theory of planning / John Sillince. — Aldershot : Gower, c1986. — [226]p. — *Includes index*

REGIONAL PLANNING — Bedfordshire — Citizen participation

BEDFORDSHIRE. County Council
County structure plan, public participation, phase 2 report / [Bedfordshire County Council]. — [Bedford ([County Hall, Bedford MK42 9AP]) : [The Council], 1976. — [225]p in various pagings

REGIONAL PLANNING — Botswana

NATIONAL DISTRICT DEVELOPMENT CONFERENCE (5th : 1978 : Gaborone)
A record of proceedings and actions. — Gaborone : Ministry of Local Government and Lands, 1978. — 88p

NATIONAL DISTRICT DEVELOPMENT CONFERENCE (7th : 1979 : Gaborone)
[Report]. — Gaborone : Ministry of Local Government and Lands, [1979]. — 279p

REGIONAL PLANNING — Canada

Canada : the state of the Federation 1985 / edited by Peter M. Leslie. — Kingston, Ontario : Queen's University (Kingston, Ont.), Institute of Intergovernmental Relations, 1985. — v,225p. — *Includes references*

The Canadian economy : a regional perspective / edited by Donald J. Savoie. — Toronto ; London : Methuen, 1986. — 291p

CULLINGWORTH, J. B
Urban and regional planning in Canada / J. Barry Cullingworth. — New Brunswick, U.S.A. : Transaction Books, c1987. — p. cm. — *Includes index. — Bibliography: p*

SAVOIE, Donald J.
Regional economic development : Canada's search for solutions / Donald J. Savoie. — Toronto ; London : University of Toronto Press, 1986. — 212p

REGIONAL PLANNING — Colombia

COLOMBIA. Unidad de Desarrollo Regional y Urbano
Estructura regional del desarrollo : modelo de regionalzación nodal, etapa 1; ordenamiento urbano y regional con base en el flujo de servicios. — Bogotá : la Unidad. — (Documento / Departamento Nacional de Planeación, Unidad de Desarrollo Regional y Urbano, División de Estudios Regionales ; 76/1)
Volumen 1. — 1976. — 44leaves

COLOMBIA. Unidad de Desarrollo Regional y Urbano
Estructura regional del desarrollo : modelo de regionalización [nodal], etapa 1; ordenamiento urbano y regional con base en el flujo de servicios. — Bogotá : la Unidad. — (Documento / Departamento Nacional de Planeación, Unidad de Desarrollo Regional y Urbano, División de Estudios Regionales ; 76/1)
Volumen 2: Anexo. — 1976. — 38leaves

REGIONAL PLANNING — Colombia — Bucaramanga

COLOMBIA. División de Estudios Regionales
Algunas consideraciones sobre el desarrollo de Bucaramanga y municipios asociados. — Bogotá : la División, 1976. — 10leaves. — (Documento / Departamento Nacional de Planeación, Unidad de Desarrollo Regional y Urbano, División de Estudios Regionales ; 76/4)

REGIONAL PLANNING — Developinmg countries — Mathematical models — Case studies — Congresses

Social accounting matrices : a basis for planning / edited by Graham Pyatt and Jeffery I. Round. — Washington, D.C., U.S.A. : World Bank, 1985. — p. cm. — *Bibliography: p*

REGIONAL PLANNING — Ecuador

ECUADOR. Junta Nacional de Planificación. División de Estudios Regionales
Regionalización del Ecuador : propuesta preliminar. — [Quito] : la División, 1976. — 26,[18]leaves

REGIONAL PLANNING — England

BRUTON, M. J.
Local planning in practice / Michael Bruton and David Nicholson. — London : Hutchinson, 1987. — 452p. — (The Built environment series). — *Bibliography: p421-440. — Includes index*

REGIONAL PLANNING — England — History — 20th century

MARTINS, Mario Rui
An organisational approach to regional planning / Mario Rui Martins. — Aldershot : Gower, c1986. — [246]p. — *Includes bibliography and index*

REGIONAL PLANNING — England — Avon

AVON. County Council
Structure plan, options in outline / Avon County Council Planning Department. — Bristol (Avon House North, St James Barton, Bristol BS99 7NB) : [The Department], [1977]. — [72]p

Avon county structure plan : written statement : as approved by the Secretary of State for the Environment. — Bristol : Avon County Planning Dept., 1985. — 40p

REGIONAL PLANNING — England — Berkshire

BERKSHIRE. Planning Department
Review of Berkshire's structure plans: submission document. — Reading : [the Department], 1986. — 145p. — *Includes folded map*

REGIONAL PLANNING — England — Buckinghamshire — Citizen participation

BUCKINGHAMSHIRE. County Council
Buckinghamshire county structure plan 1976, report on public participation / [Buckinghamshire County Council]. — [Aylesbury] ([County Hall, Aylesbury, Bucks.]) : [County Planning Department], [1976]. — [4],166p

REGIONAL PLANNING — England — Cornwall

CORNWALL (England : County). Planning Department
Cornwall county structure plan, the policy choices / [Cornwall County Council, Planning Department]. — [Truro] ([County Hall, Truro, Cornwall TR1 3AY]) : [The Department], 1976. — [4],34p

REGIONAL PLANNING — England — Devon

County structure plan : draft first alteration : explanatory memorandum. — Exeter : County Engineering and Planning Department, Devon County Council, 1984. — 85p. — *Folded map in back pocket. — Map in pocket attached to back cover*

DEVON. County Council
County structure plan : draft first alteration : written statement. — Exeter : [the Council], 1984. — 19p. — *Folded map in back pocket*

DEVON. County Council
County structure plan : first alteration : explanatory memorandum. — Exeter : [the Council], 1985. — 91p. — *Includes folded maps*

DEVON. County Council
County structure plan : second alteration : explanatory memorandum. — Exeter : [the Council], 1986. — 80p. — *Cover title: Devon county structure plan: second alteration: shopping: draft explanatory memorandum*

DEVON. County Council
Devon county structure plan. — Exeter : [the Council], 1981. — 212p

DEVON. County Council
Devon county structure plan : first alteration : written statement. — Exeter : [the Council], 1985. — 25p

DEVON. County Council
Devon county structure plan : first alteration : statement on publicity, public participation and consultation. — Exeter : [the Council], 1985. — 126p

DEVON. County Council
Devon county structure plan : second alteration : draft written statement. — Exeter : [County Council], 1986. — 12p. — *Cover title: Devon county structure plan: second alteration: shopping: draft written statement*

DEVON. County Council
Devon structure plan : second alteration : supplementary paper explaining the county council's consideration of alternative ways of meeting shopping needs in Exeter. — Exeter : [the Council], 1986. — 4p

REGIONAL PLANNING — England — Essex — History — 20th century

TOOGOOD, Norman Robert
History of county planning in Essex (1930-1974) / by Norman Robert Toogood. — 374 leaves (some folded). — *MPhil (Econ) 1986 LSE*

REGIONAL PLANNING — England — Hereford and Worcester

HEREFORD AND WORCESTER. County Council
Hereford and Worcester county structure plan : written statement. — Worcester : [the Council], 1985. — 37p. — *Includes folded map*

REGIONAL PLANNING — England — Hertfordshire

HERTFORDSHIRE. County Council
Hertfordshire county structure plan : explanatory memorandum. — Hertford : [the Council], 1987. — 115p

HERTFORDSHIRE. County Council
Hertfordshire county structure plan : 1986 review : technical notes. — [Hertford] : [the Council], 1986. — [98p in various pagings]

HERTFORDSHIRE. County Council
Hertfordshire county structure plan review ten years after : a monitoring study 1974-84. — 2nd ed. — [Hertford] : [the Council], 1986. — 136,[41]p. — *Bibliography: p[1-18]*

REGIONAL PLANNING — England — Hertfordshire — Citizen participation

HERTFORDSHIRE. County Council
Structure plan review : statement on publicity and consultation. — [Hertford] : [the Council], [1986]. — 8p. — *Cover title: Hertfordshire county structure plan: report of public participation*

REGIONAL PLANNING — England — Lancashire

LANCASHIRE. County Council
Lancashire structure plan : written statement. — Preston : [the Council], 1987. — v,51p. — *Includes folded map*

LANCASHIRE. County Council
Lancashire structure plan : explanatory memorandum. — Preston : [the Council], 1987. — 130p. — *Includes folded map*

REGIONAL PLANNING — England — London

LAMBETH
Revised Lambeth local plan : written statement and schedule of proposals (incorporating all changes proposed to the 1984 plan). — Lambeth : [the Council], 1986. — 184p. — *Includes folded map*

REGIONAL PLANNING — England — Somerset

SOMERSET. County Council
Somerset structure plan : alteration no.1 : explanatory memorandum. — Taunton : [the Council], 1986. — viii,143p. — *Includes folded map*

SOMERSET. County Council
Somerset structure plan : incorporating alteration no.1 : written statement. — Taunton : [the Council], 1986. — ii,65p. — *Folded map in back pocket*

REGIONAL PLANNING — England — Surrey

SURREY. County Council
Surrey structure plan : proposed first alteration : technical support information. — Kingston upon Thames : [the Council], 1985. — 86p

SURREY. County Council
Surrey structure plan : proposed first alteration : consultation draft. — Kingston upon Thames : [the Council], 1985. — iii,193p. — *Includes folded map*

SURREY. County Council
Surrey structure plan 1980 : proposed first alteration : report on publicity and public consultation. — Kingston upon Thames : [the Council], 1986. — 29p

SURREY. County Council
Surrey structure plan 1980 : proposed first alteration : the alterations. — Kingston upon Thames : [the Council], 1986. — 58p

SURREY. County Council
Surrey structure plan 1980 : proposed first alteration : explanatory memorandum. — Kingston upon Thames : [the Council], 1986. — iv,198p. — *Includes folded map*

SURREY. County Planning Department
Structure plan monitoring : employment and commercial data. — [Kingston upon Thames] : [the Department], 1985. — [25 leaves]. — (Technical report / Surrey. County Planning Department ; no.5/85). — *Bound with Employment and commuting in Surrey*

SURREY. County Planning Department
Surrey structure plan : monitoring technical report : ward population forecasts 1981-1991. — [Kingston upon Thames] : [the Department], 1987. — [16p]. — (Technical report / Surrey. County Planning Department ; no.5/87). — *Bound with Comparative statistics*

REGIONAL PLANNING — England — Sussex

EAST SUSSEX. Planning Department
County structure plan 1983 review : consultative draft. — Lewes : [the Department], 1983. — 13p

REGIONAL PLANNING — England — Warwickshire

WARWICKSHIRE. County Council
Warwickshire structure plan : progress and information report. — Warwick : [the Council], 1986. — 50p

WARWICKSHIRE. County Council
Warwickshire structure plan : information report, May 1987. — Warwick : [the Council], 1987. — 26,[14]p

REGIONAL PLANNING — England — West Midlands

WEST MIDLAND REGIONAL STUDY
A developing strategy for the West Midlands : report of the West Midland Regional Study : 1971, Technical appendix 2: housing study. — Birmingham : West Midland Regional Study, 1971. — 49,[78]p. — *Includes folded maps*

WEST MIDLANDS. County Council
West Midlands county structure plan, October 1980. — Birmingham : [the Council], 1980. — 171p. — *Includes folded map*

WEST MIDLANDS PLANNING AUTHORITIES' CONFERENCE
A developing strategy for the West Midlands. — Birmingham : West Midlands Planning Authorities' Conference, 1974. — 18,[24p]. — *Includes folded map*

REGIONAL PLANNING — Europe, Southern

HADJIMICHALIS, Costis
Uneven development and regionalism : state, territory and class in southern Europe / Costis Hadjimichalis. — London : Croom Helm, c1987. — 343p. — (Croom Helm series in geography and environment). — *Bibliography: p310-332. — Includes index*

REGIONAL PLANNING — European Economic Community countries

CLOUT, Hugh
Regional variations in the European Community / Hugh Clout. — Cambridge : Cambridge University Press, 1986. — 128p. — (Cambridge topics in geography) (Cambridge topics in geography. Second series). — *Bibliography: p124-126. — Includes index*

The contribution of infrastructure to regional development. — Luxembourg : Office for Official Publications of the European Communities. — *At head of title: Commission of the European Communities*
Annex: Companion volume to the Final report / by Infrastructure Study Group. — 1986. — 190p

The contribution of infrastructure to regional development. — Luxembourg : Office for Official Publications of the European Communities. — *At head of title: Commission of the European Communities*
Final report / by Dieter Biehl. — 1986. — 73p

INTERNATIONAL INSTITUTE OF MANAGEMENT
Regional incentives in the European Community : a comparative study : a report / by the International Institute of Management, Wissenschaftszentrum, Berlin to the Federal German Ministry for Economics, the Land of Hesse [Ministry for Economics and Technology], and the European Economic Community. — Brussels : Commission of the European Communities ; [Washington, D.C. : sold by European Community Information Service], 1979. — 268 p.. — (Regional policy series ; 15)

Regional accounts ESA : detailed tables by branches / Statistical Office of the European Communities. — Luxembourg : Statistical Office of the European Communities, 1979/80-. — *Irregular. — Text in Community languages*

REGIONAL PLANNING — European Economic Community countries
continuation

SWEENEY, G. P.
Innovation, entrepreneurs and regional development / G.P. Sweeney. — London : Pinter, 1987. — xvi,271p. — *Includes bibliographies and index*

VANHOVE, N.
Regional policy : a European approach / N. Vanhove, L.H. Klaassen. — 2nd ed. — Aldershot : Gower, c1987. — [xiv,450]p. — (Studies in spatial analysis). — *Previous ed.: Farnborough, Hampshire : Saxon House, 1980.* — *Bibliography: p433-448.* — *Includes index*

REGIONAL PLANNING — European Economic Community Countries — Statistics

Regions: statistical yearbook / Statistical Office of the European Communities. — Luxembourg : Statistical Office of the European Communities, 1986-. — *Annual.* — *Text in Community languages.* — *Continues: Yearbook of regional statistics/Statistical Office of the European Communities*

REGIONAL PLANNING — France

DATAR: rapport d'activité / Délégation à l'Aménagement du Territoire et à l'Action Régionale. — Paris : DATAR, 1984/85-. — *Annual*

FRANCE. Commission de réflexion sur l'Aménagement du territoire
Propositions pour l'aménagement du territoire / présenté par Olivier Guichard. — Paris : La Documentation française, 1986. — 61p. — (Collection des rapports officiels)

L'industrie et les régions / Ministère de l'Industrie et de la Recherche [et] Service d'Étude des Stratégies et des Statistiques Industrielles. — Paris : Documentation Française, 1981-. — (Traits fondamentaux du système industriel français). — *Annual*

TENZER, Nicolas
La région en quête d'avenir : compétences et moyens / Nicolas Tenzer. — Paris : La Documentation française, 1986. — 138p. — (Notes et études documentaires ; no.4816)

REGIONAL PLANNING — Great Britain

GREAT BRITAIN. Department of the Environment
United Kingdom memorandum on current trends and policies in the fields of housing, building and planning during the year 1975. — [London] : the Department, [1976]. — ii,28p. — *Prepared for the thirty-seventh session of the Committee on Housing, Building and Planning, United Nations Economic Commission for Europe*

GREAT BRITAIN. Parliament. House of Commons. Library. Research Division
Regional policy / Christopher Barclay. — [London] : the Division, 1983. — 17p. — (Background paper ; no.131)

JOHNSTONE, Derrick
Effective economic development : a discussion of local authority organization, management and training / by Derrick Johnstone. — Glasgow : The Planning Exchange, 1985. — 30leaves. — (Occasional paper ; no.19). — *Bibliography: leaves 28-30*

MORISON, Hugh
The regeneration of local economies / Hugh Morison. — Oxford : Clarendon, 1987. — viii,212p. — *Bibliography: p199-205.* — *Includes index*

Planning control : philosophies, prospects and practice / edited by M.L. Harrison and R. Mordey. — London : Croom Helm, c1987. — 234p. — (Croom Helm series in geography and environment). — *Bibliography: p227-232.* — *Includes index*

READE, Eric
British town and country planning / Eric Reade. — Milton Keynes : Open University Press, 1987. — xiii,270p. — *Bibliography: p243-266.* — *Includes index*

Regional problems, problem regions and public policy in the United Kingdom / edited by P.J. Damesick and P.A. Wood. — Oxford : Clarendon, 1987. — xii,275p. — *Includes bibliographies and index*

Rural planning : policy into action? / edited by Paul Cloke. — London : Harper & Row, 1987. — vi,229p. — *Includes bibliographies and index*

SYNNOTT, Michael Frederick
The relationship between the regional water authorities and local planning authorities / by Michael Frederick Synnott. — 350 leaves. — *PhD (Econ) 1986 LSE*

TRADES UNION CONGRESS
Urban and regional policy : a discussion document. — [London : National Economic Development Council, 1983]. — 4,32p. — *NEDC: (83)53*

REGIONAL PLANNING — Great Britain — Citizen participation

GREAT BRITAIN. Department of the Environment
Public participation in the statutory planning process : United Kingdom research programme. — [London] : the Department, 1976. — [11]p. — (Planning in the United Kingdom). — *Paper presented at the United Nations Conference on Human Settlements, 1976, Vancouver*

HUTTON, N. R.
Lay participation in a public local inquiry : a sociological case study / Neil Hutton. — Aldershot : Gower, c1986. — x,203p. — *Bibliography: p199-203*

ROYAL TOWN PLANNING INSTITUTE. Public Participation Working Party
The public and planning : means to better participation : final report of the Public Participation Working Party, Royal Town Planning Institute. — London : The Institute, 1982. — 96p

REGIONAL PLANNING — Great Britain — Evaluation

LANGLEY, P. E.
Evaluating the effectiveness of alternatives in structure planning / P. E. Langley. — London : Department of the Environment, 1974. — 13leaves. — (PDPS3 planning techniques paper ; 74/1). — *Bibliography: leaf 13*

REGIONAL PLANNING — Great Britain — History

HALL, Peter, 1932-
Urban and regional planning / Peter Hall. — 2nd ed. — London : Allen & Unwin, 1985, c1982. — [xv,336]p. — *Originally published: Harmondsworth : Penguin, 1982.* — *Includes index*

REGIONAL PLANNING — Great Britain — Law and legislation

MCAUSLAN, J. P. W. B.
Law, market and plan in the 1980's / J. P. W. B. McAuslan. — Cambridge : University of Cambridge. Department of Land Economy, 1982. — 20p. — *Denman Lecture 1982*

REGIONAL PLANNING — Guadeloupe

Rapport du schéma directeur d'aménagement et d'urbanisme. — [Basse-Terre?] : Atelier d'urbanisme et de d'aménagement de la Guadeloupe, [1976?]. — 144p. — *Three maps in end pocket*

REGIONAL PLANNING — India

BHATTACHARYA, Sib Nath
Strategy for economic development in agricultural, industrial and tertiary sectors in different Indian states / Sib Nath Bhattacharya. — New Delhi : Metropolitan, 1985. — xvi,244p. — *Bibliography: p[225]-244*

KUNDU, Amitabh
Location of public enterprises and regional development / Amitabh Kundu, Girish K. Misra, Rajkishor Meher. — New Delhi : Concept Pub. Co., 1986. — xv, 178 p.. — *Summary: Economic study of the impact of Bharat Heavy Electricals Limited on Bhopal City.* — *Includes index.* — *Bibliography: p. [170]-174*

REGIONAL PLANNING — India — Andhra Pradesh

Planning atlas of Andhra Pradesh / sponsors, Department of Finance & Planning, Government of Andhra Pradesh [and] Pilot Map Production Plant (C.S.T. & M.P.), Survey of India, Hyderabad [and] Department of Geography, Osmania University, Hyderabad. — Scales differ ; (E 77°--E 85°/N 20°--N 13°). — [S.l. : s.n.]. — *Editor: Afzal Mohammad.* — *"Andhra Pradesh Planning Atlas Project (Supplement) 1978-1980"--Page following verso t.p.* — *"Reg. no. 1200 PPE '79 (P.M.P. 34 -- 1: = 2,500,000) 520 '79-80"--Verso t.p.* — *"Based upon Survey of India maps, with the permission of the Surveyor general of India"--Verso t.p.* — *: "Revised maps ... mostly pertain to socio-economic characteristics"--Foreword.* — *Contents: Location & administrative divisions -- Land use -- Economic characteristics -- Socio-economic infrastructure*
Supplement. — c1980 (Hyderabad, A.P. : Print. Group of the Pilot Map Production Plant, Survey of India). — 1 atlas (xxi p., 40 leaves of plates)

REGIONAL PLANNING — Libya

Planning and development in modern Libya / edited by M. M. Burn, S. M. Ghanem and K. S. McLachlan. — London ; Wisbech : Society for Libyan Studies : Middle East and North African Studies Press, 1985. — x,234p. — *Includes bibliographic references*

REGIONAL PLANNING — Netherlands

NETHERLANDS. Stuurgroep Integraal Structuurplan Noorden des Lands
Het Noorden : een versterkte bevolkingsgroei? Of juist niet! : een bewerking van het rapport Bevolkingsaspecten Noorden des Lands / Samensteller R. Idenburg. — 's-Gravenhage : Staatsuitgeverij, 1974. — 21p

NETHERLANDS. Werkgroep Beleidsdoelstellingen Analyse Noorden
ISP : integraal structuurplan Noorden des lands : rapport van de Werkgroep Beleidsdoelstellingen Analyse Noorden. — [s-Gravenhage] : the Werkgroep 2. — 1974. — 27p

REGIONAL PLANNING — Nièvre, France (Dept.)

FRANCE. Comité départemental d'expansion économique et de productivité de la Nièvre
La Nièvre ... : pour un aménagement rural concerté / Comité départemental d'expansion économique et de productivité de la Nièvre, Direction departemental de l'agriculture de la Nièvre. — [Nevers?] : Le Comité, [1971?]. — 65p

REGIONAL PLANNING — Peru

10Peru. Programa de Adecuación del Sistema Financiero al Desarrollo Regional
Participación en el desarrollo regional. — Lima : the Programa, [ca.1974]. — 37leaves

REGIONAL PLANNING — Québec (Province)

FÉDÉRATION DES TRAVAILLEURS DU QUÉBEC. Congrès (13th : 1973 : Montréal)
Le développement régional : à la dérive. — Québec : Fédération des Travailleurs du Québec, 1973. — 51p. — (Document économique / Fédération des Travailleurs du Québec ; 2)

REGIONAL PLANNING — Scotland — Dumfries and Galloway

DUMFRIES AND GALLOWAY. Regional Council
  Structure plan : report of survey : population, employment and housing (revised). — Dumfries : [the Regional Council], 1979. — 105p

DUMFRIES AND GALLOWAY. Regional Council
  Structure plan : report of survey : finance (revised). — Dumfries : [the Regional Council], 1979. — 15p

DUMFRIES AND GALLOWAY. Regional Council
  Structure plan : report of survey : settlements and services (revised). — Dumfries : [the Regional Council], 1979. — 115p

DUNFRIES AND GALLOWAY. Regional Council
  Structure plan : report of survey : finance. — Dumfries : [the Regional Council], 1978. — 15p

REGIONAL PLANNING — Scotland — Lothian

LOTHIAN. Regional Council
  Lothian region structure plan : written statement. — Edinburgh : [the Regional Council], 1978. — 58p

LOTHIAN. Regional Council
  Lothian structure plan : report of survey. — Edinburgh : [the Regional Council], 1977. — 145p

REGIONAL PLANNING — Scotland — Lothian — Citizen participation

LOTHIAN. Regional Council
  Lothian structure plan : interim statement for public consultation. — Edinburgh : [the Regional Council], 1977. — 39p

LOTHIAN. Regional Council
  Lothian structure plan : public participation report. — Edinburgh : [the Regional Council], 1978. — 108,xvi p

REGIONAL PLANNING — Scotland — Strathclyde

STRATHCLYDE. Department of Physical Planning
  Strathclyde structure plan (update 1986) : written statement. — Glasgow : [the Department], 1986. — 50p

STRATHCLYDE. Regional Council
  The context of the regional report. — Glasgow : [the Council], 1975. — 144p. — Includes a folded map

STRATHCLYDE. Regional Council
  Development strategy. — Glasgow : [the Council], 1976. — 178p

STRATHCLYDE. Regional Council
  Strathclyde regional report, 1976. — Glasgow : [the Council], 1976. — 53p

STRATHCLYDE. Regional Council
  Strathclyde structure plan : the 'easy read'. — Glasgow : [the Council], [1982]. — 36p

STRATHCLYDE. Regional Council
  Strathclyde structure plan 1981 : the decision letter and approved policies. — Glasgow : [the Council], 1983. — 35p

STRATHCLYDE. Regional Council
  Strathclyde structure plan 1981 : update (1986) : consultative draft. — [Glasgow] : Strathclyde Regional Council, [1986]. — 73p. — Col. map (1 folded sheet) as insert

REGIONAL PLANNING — Scotland — Strathclyde — Citizen participation

STRATHCLYDE. Department of Physical Planning
  Strathclyde structure plan (update 1986) : consultation report. — Glasgow : [the Department], 1986. — 61p

REGIONAL PLANNING — Sunbelt States

ABBOTT, Carl
  The new urban America : growth and politics in Sunbelt cities / Carl Abbott. — Rev. ed. — Chapel Hill : University of North Carolina Press, c1987. — p. cm. — Includes index. — Bibliography: p

REGIONAL PLANNING — Wales — Anglesey

GWYNEDD. County Council
  Anglesey structure plan: written statement / Gwynedd County Council. — [Caernarvon] : Gwynedd County Council, 1974. — 69,66p. — English and Welsh texts back to back. — Welsh title: Sir Fôn: cynllun fframwaith

REGIONAL PLANNING — Wales — Caernarvonshire

GWYNEDD. County Council
  Caernarvonshire structure plan: written statement / Gwynedd County Council. — [Caernarvon] : Gwynedd County Council, 1974. — 91,81p. — English and Welsh texts back to back. — Welsh title: Sir Gaernarfon: cynllun fframwaith

REGIONAL PLANNING — Wales — Clwyd

CLWYD. County Council
  Clwyd county structure plan : public participation seminar : transportation : report of proceedings. — Mold : [the Council], 1975. — 28p

CLWYD. County Council
  Clwyd county structure plan : public partcipation and consultation : a summary of comments received on the policies contained in the draft written statement issued in March 1977. — Mold : [the Council], 1977. — 139p

CLWYD. County Council
  Clwyd county structure plan : report of survey (draft). — Mold : [the Council], 1977. — 235p. — Includes folded maps

CLWYD. County Council
  Clwyd county structure plan : written statement (draft). — Mold : [the Council], 1977. — v,187p

CLWYD. County Council
  Clwyd county structure plan : written statement (final draft). — Mold : [the Council], 1978. — ix,165p. — Folded map in back pocket

CLWYD. County Council
  Clwyd county structure plan : written statement. — Mold : [the Council], 1979. — x,197p. — Includes folded map

CLWYD. County Council
  Clwyd county structure plan : report of survey. — Mold [the Council]. — 1978. — Includes folded maps
  Technical appendix: population, housing and settlements. — 64p

REGIONAL PLANNING — Wales — Clwyd — Citizen participation

CLWYD. Council
  Clwyd county structure plan : public participatiuon seminar : minerals : report of proceedings. — Mold : [the Council], 1975. — 30p

CLWYD. County Council
  Clwyd county structure plan : public participation seminar : employment : report of proceedings. — Mold : [the Council], 1975. — 24p

CLWYD. County Council
  Clwyd county structure plan : public participation seminar : agriculture, woodlands and forestry : report of proceedings. — Mold : [the Council], 1975. — 41p

CLWYD. County Council
  Clwyd county structure plan : public participation seminar : rural communities : report of proceedings. — Mold : [the Council], 1975. — 25p

REGIONAL PLANNING — Wales — Clwyd — citizen participation

CLWYD. County Council
  Clwyd county structure plan : public participation seminar : urban communities : report of proceedings. — Mold : [the Council], 1975. — 23p

REGIONAL PLANNING — Wales — Clwyd — Citizen participation

CLWYD. County Council
  Clwyd county structure plan : public participation seminar : housing : report of proceedings. — Mold : [the Council], 1975. — 33p

CLWYD. County Council
  Clwyd county structure plan : public participation : local meetings, autumn 1974 and 1975 : summaries and reports. — Mold : [the Council], 1977. — 95p

CLWYD. County Council
  Clwyd county structure plan : draft written statement : public participation seminars July 1977, and report of local meetings, September 1977. — Mold : Clwyd County Council, 1977. — 35p

CLWYD. County Council
  Clwyd county structure plan : statement of public participation and consultation. — Mold : [the Council], 1979. — 108p

CLWYD. County Council
  Clwyd county structure plan : public participation : public meetings : public involvement in the preparation of the structure plan. — Mold : [the Council], 1979. — 31p. — Bibliography: p32-33

CLWYD. County Council
  Clwyd county structure plan : public participation : interpretive interviews : public involvement in the preparation of the structure plan. — Mold : [tThe Council], 1977. — 41p. — Bibliography: p(42-43)

CLWYD. County Council
  Clwyd county structure plan : public participation evaluation-seminars. — Mold : [the Council], 1976. — 28p

REGIONAL PLANNING — Wales — Dyfed

DYFED. County Council
  County of Dyfed structure plan : examination in public : report of panel. — Carmarthen : [the Council], 1981. — 63p

DYFED. County Council
  Dyfed county structure plan : project report. — Carmarthen : [the Council], 1975. — 40p

DYFED. County Council
  Dyfed county structure plan : written statement. — Carmarthen : [the council], 1980. — 142p. — Folded map in back pocket

DYFED. County Council
  Dyfed county structure plan : report of survey. — Carmarthen : [the Council], 1980. — [318p]

DYFED. County Council
  Dyfed county structure plan = Cymllun fframwaith sir Dyfed. — Carmarthen : [the Council], 1983. — 30,30p. — In English and Welsh. — Includes folded maps

DYFED. County Planning Department
  Dyfed county structure plan : draft written statement : consultation copy. — Carmarthen : [the Department], 1978. — [122p]

REGIONAL PLANNING — Wales — Dyfed — Citizen participation

DYFED. County Council
  Dyfed county structure plan : public participation and consultation. — Carmarthen : [the Council], 1980. — [322p]

REGIONAL PLANNING — Wales — Ghent

GOSS, Anthony
South Gwent : its development potential and relationship to the valleys and the Severn estuary / prepared by Professor Anthony Goss in association with Hubbard Ford and Partners for Gwent County Council. — Cwmbran : Gwent County Council, 1976. — vii,230p

REGIONAL PLANNING — Wales — Glamorgan

MID GLAMORGAN. County Council
Position and prospects 1975 : an analysis of the special problems of Mid Glamorgan and their solution / Mid Glamorgan County Council. — Cardiff : Mid Glamorgan County Council Vol.1. — 1975. — [xi],20p

MID GLAMORGAN. County Council
Position and prospects 1975 : an analysis of the special problems of Mid Glamorgan and their solution / Mid Glamorgan County Council. — Cardiff : Mid Glamorgan County Council Vol.2. — 1975. — [viii],138,vp

REGIONAL PLANNING — Wales — Gwent

GWENT. County Council
Gwent structure plan. — Cwmbran : [the Council], 1978. — 274,xviip

GWENT. County Council
Gwent structure plan : written statement of policies and proposals. — Cwmbran : [the Council], 1978. — 272,xxiip

REGIONAL PLANNING — Wales — Gwynedd

Structure plans for Gwynedd : report by the Panel conducting the examination in public. — [Cardiff? : Welsh Office?], 1976. — 95p

REGIONAL PLANNING — Wales — Powys

POWYS. County Council
Structure plan : written statement = Cynllun fframwaith : datganiad ysgrifenedig. — Llandrindod Wells : Powys Planning Department, 1979. — 91p. — *Cover title. — Maps inside covers*

POWYS. County Council
Structure plan : report of survey. — Llandrindod Wells : [the Council]. — 1979. — *Contents: Topic papers 7-11: - Health, education and welfare, Growth towns policy, Building conservation, Agriculture, forestry and nature conservation, minerals (brief discussion paper)*
Vol.2. — [238]p

POWYS. County Council
Structure play : report of survey. — Llandrindod Wells : [the Council]. — 1979. — *Contents: Topic papers 1-6: - Population, Employment, Industry, Settlement pattern, Tourism, Sport and Recreation [and] Transport*
vol.1. — [386]p

REGIONAL PLANNING — Wales — South Glamorgan

SOUTH GLAMORGAN
County of South Glamorgan : structure plan : proposed alterations : publicity and public participation statement. — [Cardiff] : [the Council], 1985. — 154p

SOUTH GLAMORGAN
County of South Glamorgan : structure plan : proposed alterations : written statement. — [Cardiff] : [the Council], 1985. — 44,xxxp

SOUTH GLAMORGAN
County of South Glamorgan structure plan proposed alterations : explanatory memorandum. — [Cardiff] : [the Council], 1986. — v,221,xxxxxp. — *Includes folded map*

SOUTH GLAMORGAN
South Glamorgan and its future : strategy for the 1990's : first review of the county structure plan : explanatory memorandum. — [Cardiff] : [the Council], 1984. — 49p. — *Includes folded map*

SOUTH GLAMORGAN
South Glamorgan and its future : strategy for the 1990's : first review of the county structure plan : draft policies. — [Cardiff] : [the Council], 1984. — 25p

REGIONAL PLANNING — Wales — West Glamorgan

WEST GLAMORGAN. County Council
The Celtic sea - oil and gas? : what are the issues?. — Swansea : [the Council], 1975. — v,26p

WEST GLAMORGAN. County Council
Community facilities : what are the issues?. — Swansea : [the Council], 1976. — 31p

WEST GLAMORGAN. County Council
Minerals : what are the issues?. — Swansea : [the Council], 1975. — iii,27p

WEST GLAMORGAN. County Council
Our countryside : what are the issues?. — Swansea : [the Council], 1975. — 31p

WEST GLAMORGAN. County Council
Our derelict land problem : what are the issues?. — Swansea : [the Council], 1975. — 27p

WEST GLAMORGAN. County Council
People and homes : what are the issues?. — Swansea : [the Council], 1975. — 37p

WEST GLAMORGAN. County Council
Transport : what are the issues?. — Swansea : [the Council], 1975. — iii,22p

WEST GLAMORGAN, County Council
Jobs today - and tomorrow? : what are the issues?. — Swansea : [the Council], 1976. — 43p

REGIONAL POWER UTILITY TARIFF SYMPOSIUM (1982 : Manila)

REGIONAL POWER UTILITY TARIFF SYMPOSIUM (1982 : Manila)
Costing and pricing electricity in developing countries : proceedings of the Asian Development Bank Regional Power Utility Tariff Symposium, August 1982 / edited by Mohan Munasinghe, Shyam Rungta. — Manila : Asian Development Bank, 1984. — xvii,648p. — *Includes bibliographical references*

REGIONALISM

Changing Britain, changing world : geographical perspectives. — Milton Keynes : Open University Press. — (Social sciences : a second level course) (D205; Units 26-29). — *At head of title: Open University*
Section 4: Geography matters
Block 7: The impact of geography on society / James Anderson...[et al.]. — 1985. — *Various pagings*

Geography and the urban environment : progress in research and applications. — Chichester : Wiley. — c1981
Vol.4 / edited by D.T. Herbert and R.J. Johnston. — xiii,354p. — *Includes bibliographies and index*

Région et aménagement du territoire : mélanges offerts à Joseph Lajugie par ses collègues, ses élèves et ses amis. — Bordeaux : Editions Bière, 1985. — 898p. — *Bibliographies*

Regional co-operation: recent developments / Commonwealth Secretariat. — London : Commonwealth Secretariat, 1984-. — *Irregular*

REGIONALISM — Australia

Uneven development and the geographical transfer of value / D.K. Forbes, P.J. Rimmer (eds.). — Canberra : Research School of Pacific Studies, The Australian National University, 1984. — 297p. — (Publication / Research School of Pacific Studies, Department of Human Geography, Australian National University ; HG/16). — *Original papers given at a Workshop on Geographical Transfer of Value held at ... the Australian National University in 1981*

REGIONALISM — Canada

Regionalism in Canada / edited by Robert J. Brym. — Toronto, Canada : Irwin Pub., c1986. — viii, 213 p.. — *Bibliography: p. 208-211*

REGIONALISM — Canary Islands

Contabilidad regional de Canarias / Consejería de Economía ye Comercio, Gobierno de Canarias. — Las Palmas : Gobierno de Canarias. Consejería de Economía y Comercio,, 1985-. — *Annual*

REGIONALISM — Colombia — History — 19th century

PARK, James William
Rafael Núñez and the politics of Colombian regionalism, 1863-1886 / James William Park. — ; Baton Rouge ; London : Louisiana State University Press, c1985. — xii, 304p. — *Includes index. — Bibliography: p.[279]-296*

REGIONALISM — Developing countries

Uneven development and the geographical transfer of value / D.K. Forbes, P.J. Rimmer (eds.). — Canberra : Research School of Pacific Studies, The Australian National University, 1984. — 297p. — (Publication / Research School of Pacific Studies, Department of Human Geography, Australian National University ; HG/16). — *Original papers given at a Workshop on Geographical Transfer of Value held at ... the Australian National University in 1981*

REGIONALISM — Europe

Regionalism in Europe / European Centre for Political Studies ; edited by Roger Morgan. — London : Policy Studies Institute, 1986. — [208]p. — *Includes bibliography*

REGIONALISM — France

Géopolitiques des régions françaises / sous la direction de Yves Lacoste ; Yves Lacoste ... [et al.]. — Paris : Fayard, 1986. — 3v. — *Contents: t.1. France septentrionale - t.2. La façade occidentale - t.3. La France du sud-est*

TENZER, Nicolas
La région en quête d'avenir : compétences et moyens / Nicolas Tenzer. — Paris : La Documentation française, 1986. — 138p. — (Notes et études documentaires ; no.4816)

REGIONALISM — South Asia — Congresses

South Asian regional cooperation : a socio-economic approach to peace and stability / edited by M. Abdul Hafiz, Iftekharuzzaman. — Dhaka : Bangladesh Institute of International and Strategic Studies, 1985. — xxxxiv, 290 p.. — *Summary: Papers presented at an International Conference on South Asian Regional Cooperation, held at Dhaka, January 14-16, 1985, under the aegis of the Bangladesh Institute of International and Strategic Studies. — Includes bibliographies and index*

REGIONALISM — Spain

Nacionalismo y regionalismo en España : (el horizonte político-institucional, económico, social, cultural e internacional de nuestro tiempo) : seminario en conmemoración del 28 de Febrero / presentación por Manuel Melero Muñoz. — Cordoba : Diputación Provincial de Cordoba, 1984. — 303p

REGIONALISM (INTERNATIONAL ORGANIZATION)

VYSOTSKII, A. F.
Morskoi regionalism : (mezhdunarodno-pravovye problemy regional'nogo sotrudnichestva gosudarstv) / A. F. Vysotskii. — Kiev : Naukova dumka, 1986. — 193p

REGISTERED HOMES ACT 1984

BIGGS, Simon
The Registered Homes Act 1984 : staff training issues / Simon Biggs. — London : Central Council for Education and Training in Social Work, 1986. — 47p. — (CCETSW paper ; 24). — *Bibliographical references: p46-47*

REGISTERS OF BIRTHS, ETC — Congresses
UNITED NATIONS/WORLD HEALTH ORGANIZATION WORKING GROUP ON DATA BASES FOR MEASUREMENT OF LEVELS, TRENDS, AND DIFFERENTIALS IN MORTALITY. Meeting (1981 : Bangkok, Thailand)
Data bases for mortality measurement : papers of the Meeting of the United Nations/World Health Organization Working Group on Data Bases for Measurement of Levels, Trends, and Differentials in Mortality, Bangkok, 20-23 October 1981. — New York : United Nations, 1984. — x,164p. — (Population studies / Department of International Economic and Social Affairs ; no. 84). — "ST/ESA/SER.A/84"--Verso t.p. — "United Nations publication, sales no. E.83.XIII.3"--Verso t.p. — Bibliography: p159-164

REGISTERS OF BIRTHS, ETC. — Great Britain — History
NISSEL, Muriel
People count : a history of the General Register Office / Muriel Nissel : [for the] Office of Population Censuses and Surveys. — London : H.M.S.O., 1987. — 157p. — Includes index

REGISTERS OF BIRTHS, ETC. — Portugal
AMORIM, Norberta
Método de exploração dos livros de registos paroquiais, e Cardanha e a sua população de 1573 a 1800 / por Norberta Amorim. — Lisboa : Instituto Nacional de Estatística, 1980. — 135p. — (Publicações do Centro de Estudos Demográficos). — Bibliogrpahy: p127

REHABILITATION
BROWN, Roy I.
Behavioural and social rehabilitation and training / Roy I. Brown and E. Anne Hughson. — Chichester : Wiley, c1987. — xi,192p. — Bibliography: p173-183. — Includes index

REHABILITATION — Law and legislation — Denmark
The Rehabilitation Act, 1970. — [Copenhagen : Ministry of Social Affairs?], 1970. — 11 leaves

REHABILITATION — Great Britain
STEIN, Mike
Leaving care / Mike Stein and Kate Carey. — Oxford : Blackwell, 1986. — [192]p. — (The Practice of social work ; 14). — Includes index

REHABILITATION ACT, 1970
The Rehabilitation Act, 1970. — [Copenhagen : Ministry of Social Affairs?], 1970. — 11 leaves

REHABILITATION CENTERS — Great Britain
CUMELLA, Stuart John
Patterns of resettlement of former clients of employment rehabilitation courses : a study of 307 persons within a year of leaving rehabilitation courses / by Stuart John Cumella. — 433 leaves. — PhD (Econ) 1986 Ext. — Leaves 401-433 are appendices

REHABILITATION OF CRIMINALS — Addresses, essays, lectures
Ecologic-biochemical approaches to treatment of delinquents and criminals / edited by Leonard J. Hippchen. — New York : Van Nostrand Reinhold Co., c1978. — xx,396p. — Bibliography: p389-392. — Bibliography: p. 389-392

REHABILITATION OF CRIMINALS — Canada
GAMBERG, Herbert
The illusion of prison reform : corrections in Canada / Herbert Gamberg and Anthony Thomson. — New York : P. Lang, c1984. — 161 p.. — (American university studies. Series XI. Anthropology/sociology ; vol. 5). — Bibliography: p. [145]-161

REHABILITATION OF CRIMINALS — Great Britain
BREED, Bryan
Off the record : an examination of the workings of the Rehabilitation of Offenders Act / Bryan Breed. — London : John Clare, [1987?]. — xvi,171p

Probation and the community : a practice and policy reader / edited by John Harding. — London : Tavistock, 1987. — vii,248p. — Includes bibliographies and index

REHABILITATION OF CRIMINALS — United States
CULLEN, Francis T
Reaffirming rehabilitation / Francis T. Cullen, Karen E. Gilbert ; foreword by Donald R. Cressey. — Cincinnati, Ohio : Anderson Pub. Co., c1982. — xxx, 315 p.. — (Criminal justice studies). — Includes bibliographical references and indexes

REHABILITATION OF JUVENILE DELINQUENTS
STUMPHAUZER, Jerome S
Helping delinquents change : a treatment manual of social learning approaches / Jerome S. Stumphauzer. — New York : Haworth Press, c1986. — p. cm. — "Published also as v. 8, no. 1/2 of the Child & youth services.". — Includes index. — Bibliography: p

REHABILITATION OF JUVENILE DELINQUENTS — England
GREAT BRITAIN. Department of Health and Social Security. Social Work Service. Development Group
Intermediate treatment, planning for action : reports of two study groups / Social Work Service, Development Group. — [London] ([Alexander Fleming House, Elephant and Castle, SE1 6BY]) : Department of Health and Social Security, 1977. — [3],79p

REHABILITATION OF JUVENILE DELINQUENTS — England — Derbyshire
Report of a seminar on community homes at Digby Hall, Leicester on June 30 - July 1 1975. — [London] : Department of Health and Social Security, [1975]. — 41p. — At head of title: Social Work Service Development Group and East Midlands Region in collaboration with the social services departments of Derbyshire and Lincolnshire

REHABILITATION OF JUVENILE DELINQUENTS — England — Durham (Durham)
Challenge alternative to care and custody project. — Durham : Durham Training and Enterprise, 1987. — 4p

The Challenge report : intensive I. T. in Durham. — Durham : Dragon Enterprises, 1985. — 16p

REHABILITATION OF JUVENILE DELINQUENTS — England — Isle of Wight
From approved school to community home : a Development Group exercise 15th - 17th October 1973 at Eastmore House, Isle of Wight County Council Social Services Department. — [London] : Department of Health and Social Security, [1973]. — [54]p. — At head of title: Social Work Service Development Group and London Region South

From approved school to community home : Eastmore House : report of a one day follow up exercise at Eastmore House, Isle of Wight County Council Social Services Department, on 7th January 1975. — [London : Department of Health and Social Security, 1975]. — 24p. — At head of title: Social Work Service Development Group and Southern Region

REHABILITATION OF JUVENILE DELINQUENTS — England — Lincolnshire
Report of a seminar on community homes at Digby Hall, Leicester on June 30 - July 1 1975. — [London] : Department of Health and Social Security, [1975]. — 41p. — At head of title: Social Work Service Development Group and East Midlands Region in collaboration with the social services departments of Derbyshire and Lincolnshire

REHABILITATION OF JUVENILE DELINQUENTS — England — London
"Approved school to community home" : St. Christopher's, Hillingdon : report of a Development Group Seminar October 4th-6th, 1973. — [London] : Department of Health and Social Security, [1973]. — 76p. — At head of title: Social Work Service, Development Group. — Includes bibliographical references

The Changing face of I.T. : intermediate treatment at Hambro House 1976-84 : articles from "Youth in society". — Leicester : National Youth Bureau, 1985. — 12p

REHABILITATION OF JUVENILE DELINQUENTS — France
Bilan d'activité du secteur associatif habilité / Ministère de la Justice, Direction de l'Education Surveillée. — Paris : Ministère de la Justice, 1981-. — Annual

REHABILITATION OF JUVENILE DELINQUENTS — Great Britain
ELY, Peter
Control without custody : non-custodial control of juvenile offenders / Peter Ely, Alan Swift, Alistair Sutherland ; with a section on costing by Martin Knapp. — Edinburgh : Scottish Academics, c1987. — viii,255p. — Bibliography: p242-249. — Includes index

GREAT BRITAIN. Department of Health and Social Security. Social Work Service. Development Group
Aspects of supervision and intermediate treatment : papers and discussion summaries from 3 seminars organised by the Development Group November 1976-January 1977. — London : the Department, [1977]. — 60p

SPEIRS, Sheila
Neighbourhood borstals : interim papers on their evaluation / by Sheila Speirs and David Grayson ; with preface and summary by Vernon Holloway. — London : Directorate of Psychological Services, Prison Department, 1977. — 1v. (various pagings). — (DPS report. Series 1 ; no.11). — Includes bibliographical references

REHABILITATION OF JUVENILE DELINQUENTS — Great Britain — Case studies
HAGARD, Michèle
Befriending : a sociological case-history / Michele Hagard & Vic Blickem. — Cambridge : Oleander, c1987. — 169p. — Bibliography: p168-169

REHABILITATION OF JUVENILE DELINQUENTS — United States
SHIREMAN, Charles H
Rehabilitating juvenile justice / Charles H. Shireman and Frederic G. Reamer. — New york : Columbia University Press, 1986. — ix, 188 p.. — Includes index. — Bibliography: p. [173]-184

REHABILITATION OF JUVENILE DELINQUENTS — Wales
The development of intermediate treatment : report of the residential workshops held at Carmarthen and Llandudno in March 1976 [organised by the] Welsh Office, Social Work Service. — [Cardiff] ([Pearl Assurance House, Greyfriars Rd, Cardiff CF1 3JL]) : [The Service], [1977]. — [1],131p

REHABILITATION OF JUVENILE DELINQUENTS — Wales
continuation

RESIDENTIAL WORKSHOP FOR INTERMEDIATE TREATMENT LIAISON OFFICERS (1977 : Abergavenny)
The development of a base for intermediate treatment : report of the Residential Workshop for Intermediate Treatment Liaison Officers held at The Hill Residential College, Abergavenny, 15 and 16 February 1977. — [Cardiff] ([Pearl Assurance House, Greyfriars Rd, Cardiff CF1 3JL]) : Welsh Office, Social Work Service, [1978]. — [1],i,179p

REHABILITATION OF JUVENILE DELINQUENTS — Wales — Congresses

RESIDENTIAL WORKSHOP FOR INTERMEDIATE TREATMENT LIAISON OFFICERS (1978 : Abergavenny)
The development of intermediate treatment in Wales : working paper no.2 : report of the Residential Workshop for Intermediate Treatment Liaison Officers held at The Hill Residential College, Abergavenny, 24 and 25 January 1978. — [Cardiff] : Welsh Office, Social Work Service, [1979]. — 47p

REIMS (FRANCE) — Politics and government

GORDON, David M.
Merchants and capitalists : industrialization and provincial politics in mid-nineteenth century France / by David M. Gordon. — University, Ala. : University of Alabama Press, c1985. — ix, 249p. — *Includes index. Bibliography: p.232-239*

RELATIVITY

MARGOLIS, Joseph
Pragmatism without foundations : reconciling realism and relativism / Joseph Margolis. — Oxford : Basil Blackwell, 1986. — (The persistence of reality ; 1). — *Includes index*
1: Pragmatism without foundations : reconciling realism and relativism. — xix,320p

RELIABILITY (ENGINEERING) — Mathematical models

BIROLINI, Alessandro
On the use of stochastic processes in modeling reliability problems / Alessandro Birolini. — Berlin ; New York : Springer-Verlag, c1985. — vi, 105 p.. — (Lecture notes in economics and mathematical systems ; 252). — *Includes index. — Bibliography: p. [89]-103*

RELIGION

MORRIS, Brian, 1930-
Anthropological studies of religion : an introductory text / Brian Morris. — Cambridge : Cambridge University Press, 1987. — [384]p. — *Includes bibliography and index*

Religion. — London : Academic Press, 1986. — *Quarterly*

RELIGION — Dictionaries

The Encyclopedia of religion / [editor in chief, Mircea Eliade ; editors, Charles J. Adams ... et al.]. — New York : Macmillan ; London : Collier Macmillan, c1987. — 16v. — *Includes bibliographies and index*

RELIGION — History — 20th century — Congresses

Religious movements : genesis, exodus, and numbers / edited by Rodney Stark. — New York : Paragon House Publishers, c1985. — v, 354 p.. — *"A New ERA book.". — "Essays ... were originally prepared for an international conference held in May 1982 on Orcas Island, Washington"--Editor's introd. — Includes bibliographies and index*

RELIGION — Philosophy

ARBIB, Michael A.
The construction of reality / Michael A. Arbib and Mary B. Hesse. — Cambridge : Cambridge University Press, 1986. — xii,286p. — *Bibliography: p268-275. — Includes index*

Religion and ideology : a reader / edited by Robert Bocock and Kenneth Thompson. — Manchester : Manchester University Press in association with the Open University, c1985. — [336]p. — *Includes bibliography and index*

SMART, Ninian
Religion and the western mind : Drummond lectures delivered at the University of Stirling, Scotland, March 1985, and other essays / Ninian Smart. — Basingstoke : Macmillan, 1987. — xi,142p. — (Library of philosophy and religion). — *Bibliography: p135-136. — Includes index*

RELIGION AND CIVILIZATION

VON DER MEHDEN, Fred R
Religion and modernization in Southeast Asia / Fred R. von der Mehden. — 1st ed. — Syracuse, N.Y. : Syracuse University Press, c1986. — viii, 240 p.. — *Includes index. — Bibliography: p. 225-233*

RELIGION AND CULTURE — Congresses

Religion and culture : essays in honor of Bernard Lonergan, S.J. / edited by Timothy P. Fallon and Philip Boo Riley. — Albany, NY : State University of New York Press, c1987. — x, 395 p.. — *Papers from the International Lonergan Symposium on Religion and Culture, held in March, 1984, at the University of Santa Clara. — Includes bibliographies and index*

RELIGION AND POLITICS — Congresses

Prophetic religions and politics / edited by Jeffrey K. Hadden and Anson D. Shupe. — New York : Paragon House, 1986, c1985. — p. cm. — (Religion and the political order ; v. 1) (Sociology of religion series). — *Papers presented at an international conference, held in Nov. 1984, in Martinique. — "A New ERA book.". — Includes bibliographies and index*

RELIGION AND POLITICS — India — History

WITZ, Cornelia
Religionspolitik in Britisch-Indien 1793-1813 : christliches Sendungsbewusstsein und Achtung hinduistischer Tradition im Widerstreit / von Cornelia Witz. — Stuttgart : Steiner Verlag Wiesbaden, 1985. — viii,137p. — (Beiträge zur Südasienforschung ; Bd.98). — *Summary and conclusion in English. — Bibliography: p117-127*

RELIGION AND RACE

The bible,racism and anti-semitism / John Austin Baker [et al.] ; edited by Kenneth Leech. — London : Race, Pluralism and Community Group, Board for Social Responsibility, 1985. — iv,54p. — (Theology and racism ; 1)

WILKINSON, John
Inheritors together : black people in the Church of England / John Wilkinson, Renate Wilkinson [and] James H. Evans. — London : Race, Pluralism and Community Group, Board for Social Responsibility, 1985. — iv,72p. — (Theology and racism ; 2)

RELIGION AND SOCIETY

MCLEOD, Hugh
Religion and the working class in nineteenth-century Britain / prepared for the Economic History Society by Hugh McLeod. — London : Macmillan, 1984. — 76p. — (Studies in economic and social history). — *Bibliography: p67-72. — Includes index*

RELIGION AND SOCIOLOGY

Disciplines of faith : studies in religion, politics and patriarchy / edited by Jim Obelkevich, Lyndal Roper, Raphael Samuel. — London : Routledge & Kegan Paul, 1987. — [572]p. — (History workshop series). — *Conference papers. — Includes index*

HOMAN, Roger
The sociology of religion : a bibliographical survey / compiled by Roger Homan ; G.E. Gorman, advisory editor. — New York : Greenwood Press, 1986. — x, 309 p.. — (Bibliographies and indexes in religious studies ; no. 9). — *Includes indexes*

MCGUIRE, Meredith B
Religion, the social context / Meredith B. McGuire. — 2nd ed. — Belmont, Calif. : Wadsworth Pub. Co., c1987. — xi, 301 p.. — *Includes indexes. — Bibliography: p. 263-289*

MADURO, Otto
[Religión y lucha de clases. English]. Religion and social conflicts / Otto Maduro ; translated from the Spanish by Robert R. Barr. — Maryknoll, NY : Orbis Books, c1982. — xxviii, 161 p.. — *Translation of: Religión y lucha de clases. — Bibliography: p. 158-161*

MOL, Hans
Faith and fragility : religion and identity in Canada / Hans Mol. — Burlington, Ont., Canada : Trinity Press, c1985. — viii, 354 p.. — *Includes index. — Bibliography: p. 301-338*

RELIGION AND SOCIOLOGY — Addresses, essays, lectures

Religion and the sociology of knowledge : modernization and pluralism in Christian thought and structure / edited by Barbara Hargrove. — New York : E. Mellen Press, c1984. — 402 p.. — (Studies in religion and society ; v. 8). — *Includes bibliographies*

RELIGION AND SOCIOLOGY — Bibliography

HOMAN, Roger
The sociology of religion : a bibliographical survey / compiled by Roger Homan ; G.E. Gorman, advisory editor. — New York : Greenwood Press, 1986. — x, 309 p.. — (Bibliographies and indexes in religious studies ; no. 9). — *Includes indexes*

RELIGION AND STATE — Bibliography

Religion and church and state : a bibliography selected from the ATLA religion database / edited by Albert E. Hurd. — rev. ed. — Chicago : American Theological Library Association, 1986. — 602p

RELIGION AND STATE — India — History

WITZ, Cornelia
Religionspolitik in Britisch-Indien 1793-1813 : christliches Sendungsbewusstsein und Achtung hinduistischer Tradition im Widerstreit / von Cornelia Witz. — Stuttgart : Steiner Verlag Wiesbaden, 1985. — viii,137p. — (Beiträge zur Südasienforschung ; Bd.98). — *Summary and conclusion in English. — Bibliography: p117-127*

RELIGION AND STATE — Near East

Nationalism and modernity : a Mediterranean perspective / edited by Joseph Alpher. — New York : Praeger, 1986. — vii, 143 p.. — *At head of title: Reuben Hecht Chair of Zionism and Jewish Political Thought. — "University of Haifa.". — Outgrowth of two seminars held at the University of Haifa in 1984 and 1985. — Includes bibliographies and index. — Contents: Introduction / Joseph Alpher -- State, nation, and religion / Hugh Seton-Watson -- State, nation, and religion in Islam / Bernard Lewis -- Will Israel ever become a nation? / Joseph Agassi -- Power or spirit : Jewish political thought in interbellum Europe / Paul Mendes-Flohr -- Zionism, marginalism, and cosmopolitan centralism / Dan V. Segre -- The international information revolution / Harlan Cleveland -- Language and nation : the Italian case / Sergio Romano -- Language and nation : the case of Arabic / Emmanuel Sivan -- Language conflict and national identity : a semiotic approach / Itamar Even-Zohar*

RELIGION AND STATE — Soviet Union

ANDERSON, John Philip
Soviet religious policy after Khrushchev / by John Philip Anderson. — 533 leaves. — *PhD (Econ) 1987 LSE*

RELIGION HISTORIANS — United States — Biography

AUSMUS, Harry J.
Will Herberg, from right to right / by Harry J. Ausmus ; with a foreword by Martin E. Marty. — Chapel Hill : University of North Carolina Press, c1987. — p. cm. — (Studies in religion). — *Includes index. — Bibliography: p*

RELIGIONS
New religious movements and rapid social change / edited by James A. Beckford on behalf of Research Committee 22 of the International Sociological Association. — London : Sage, 1986. — [288]p. — *Includes index*

SIEGEL, Paul N.
The meek and the militant : religion and power across the world / by Paul N. Siegel. — London : Zed, 1986. — [256]p. — *Includes bibliography and index*

RELIGIOUS BROADCASTING — Great Britain — History
WOLFE, Kenneth M.
The churches and the British Broadcasting Corporation, 1922-1956 : the politics of broadcast religion / Kenneth M. Wolfe. — London : SCM Press, 1984. — xxiv, 627p

RELIGIOUS EDUCATION — England — London
BRENT. Education Department
Brent religious education now and tomorrow. — Brent : [the Department], 1986. — 26p

RELIGIOUS LIBERTY — Great Britain
Puritanism and liberty : being the army debates (1647-9) from the Clarke manuscripts, with supplementary documents / selected and edited with an introduction by A.S.P. Woodhouse ; new preface by Ivan Roots. — 3rd ed. — London : Dent, 1986. — 506p. — (Everyman's library)

RELIGIOUS LIBERTY — Soviet Union
Aufstehen! das Gericht kommt! : Gerichtsprozesse gegen Christen in der UdSSR / zusammengestellt und bearbeitet von H. Hartfeld. — Gummersbach : Friedenstimme, 1981. — 154p

RELIGIOUS LIBERTY — Spain
ARBELOA, Víctor Manuel
Separación de Iglesia-Estado en España / Víctor Manuel Arbeloa. — Madrid : Mañana, 1977. — 76p. — (Colección Aperos del cristianismo ; 13). — *On cover: Separación de la Iglesia y el Estado en España. — Appendices (p. 46-[77]) contain legislation. — Includes bibliographical references*

RELIGIOUS LIBERTY — United States
The Assault on religion : commentaries on the decline of religious liberty / edited, with an introduction by Russell Kirk. — Lanham, MD : University Press of America ; Cumberland, Va. : Center for Judicial Studies, c1986. — ix, 115 p.

The First Amendment : the legacy of George Mason / edited by T. Daniel Shumate. — Fairfax : George Mason University Press ; London : Associated University Presses, c1985. — 201 p.. — (The George Mason lectures). — *Includes bibliographies and index*

RICHARDS, David A. J
Toleration and the Constitution / David A.J. Richards. — New York : Oxford University Press, 1986. — p. cm. — *Bibliography: p*

SHEPHERD, William C
To secure the blessings of liberty : American constitutional law and the new religious movements / William C. Shepherd. — New York : Crossroad Pub. Co. ; Chico, CA : Scholars Press, c1985. — x, 155 p.. — (Studies in religion / American Academy of Religion ; no. 35). — *Includes index. — Bibliography: p. [137]-144*

REMEDIAL TEACHING
MCGUINNESS, Diane
When children don't learn : understanding the biology and psychology of learning disabilities / Diane McGuinness. — New York : Basic Books, c1985. — x, 310p. — *Includes index. — Bibliography: p.277-295*

REMEDIES (LAW)
GRAY, Christine D.
Judicial remedies in international law / Christine D. Gray. — Oxford : Clarendon Press, 1987. — [300]p. — (Oxford monographs in international law). — *Includes bibliography and index*

REMINISCING
COLEMAN, Peter G.
Ageing and reminiscence processes : social and clinical implications / Peter G. Coleman. — Chichester : Wiley, c1986. — x,172p. — *Bibliography: p161-167. — Includes index*

RENAISSANCE
FERGUSON, Wallace Klippert
The renaissance in historical thought / Wallace Klippert Ferguson. — Boston, (Mass.) : Houghton Mifflin, 1948. — 429p

RENAISSANCE — Wales
WILLIAMS, Glanmor
Recovery, reorientation and reformation : Wales, c.1415-1642 / Glanmor Williams. — Oxford : Clarendon Press, 1987. — [500]p. — (The History of Wales ; 3). — *Includes bibliography and index*

RENEWABLE ENERGY SOURCES
BLACKBURN, John O.
The renewable energy alternative : how the United States and the world can prosper without nuclear energy or coal / John O. Blackburn. — Durham, N.C. : Duke University Press, 1987. — xi, 201 p.. — *Includes index. — Bibliography: p. [193]-196*

RENEWABLE ENERGY SOURCES — Economic aspects
The Economics of choice between energy sources : proceedings of a conference held by the International Economic Association in Tokyo, Japan / edited by Pierre Maillet, Douglas Hague and Chris Rowland. — Basingstoke : Macmillan, 1987. — xvi,493p. — *Includes index*

RENEWABLE ENERGY SOURCES — Environmental aspects — Great Britain
ATOMIC ENERGY RESEARCH ESTABLISHMENT. Energy Technology Support Unit
The environmental impact of the renewable energy sources : a review paper prepared for the Commission on Energy and the Environment. — Rev.ed. — [London] : Department of Energy, 1979. — 20p. — *First published 1978*

RENEWABLE ENERGY SOURCES — International Energy Agency countries
Renewable sources of energy. — Paris : International Energy Agency, 1987. — 334p. — *Includes bibliographies*

RENFREW (ONT. : COUNTY) — History
LEE-WHITING, Brenda
Harvest of stones : the German settlement in Renfrew County / Brenda Lee-Whiting. — Toronto ; Buffalo : University of Toronto Press, c1985. — xii, 323 p.. — *Includes index. — Bibliography: p. [301]-314*

RENT — Great Britain
MINFORD, Patrick
The housing morass : regulation, immobility and unemployment : an economic analysis of the consequences of government regulation, with proposals to restore the market in rented housing / Patrick Minford, Michael Peel and Paul Ashton. — London : Institute of Economic Affairs, 1987. — 162p. — (Hobart paperback ; 25). — *Bibliography: p157-162*

RENT CONTROL — Great Britain
GREAT BRITAIN. Parliament. House of Commons. Library. Research Division
The private rented sector and rent control / Oonagh Gay. — [London] : the Division, 1986. — 21p. — (Background paper ; no.189)

PROPHET, John
Fair rents : a practical guide to the law relating to the rents of residential tenancies including the work of rent officers, rent assessment committees and rent tribunals / by John Prophet. — 3rd ed. — London : Shaw and Sons, 1985. — xxxi,243p

RENT CONTROL — United States
BAIRD, Charles W
Rent control : the perennial folly / Charles W. Baird. — San Francisco, Calif. : Cato Institute, c1980. — p. cm. — (Cato public policy research monograph ; no. 2). — *Bibliography: p*

RENT (ECONOMIC THEORY)
DÄMPFLING, Björn
Die Marxsche Theorie der Grundrente : eine kritische Studie / Björn Dämpfling. — Hamburg : VSA-Verlag, 1985. — 161p. — *Bibliography: p154-161*

RENT STRIKES — England — London
MATHIESON, David
The St. Pancras rent strike 1960 : a study in consensus politics / David Mathieson. — London : Labour Heritage (the Labour Party), 1987. — 33p. — *Bibliography: p30-33*

RENTAL HOUSING — Law and legislation — England
YATES, David, 1946-
Landlord and tenant law / by David Yates and A.J. Hawkins. — 2nd ed. — London : Sweet & Maxwell, 1986. — cviii,839p. — *Previous ed.: 1981. — Includes index*

RENTAL HOUSING — Law and legislation — Great Britain
LUBA, Jan
Repairs : Tenant's rights / Jan Luba. — London : Legal Action Group, 1986. — xxxii,127p. — (Law and Practice Guide ; No.12)

PROPHET, John
Fair rents : a practical guide to the law relating to the rents of residential tenancies including the work of rent officers, rent assessment committees and rent tribunals / by John Prophet. — 3rd ed. — London : Shaw and Sons, 1985. — xxxi,243p

RENTAL HOUSING — Law and legislation — Northern Ireland
DOWLING, J.A.
Ejectment for non-payment of rent / by J. A. Dowling ; with a supplement for the Republic of Ireland by G. McCormack. — Belfast : Faculty of Law, the Queen's University of Belfast, 1986. — xvii,84p

RENTAL HOUSING — Maintenance and repair — Great Britain
LUBA, Jan
Repairs : Tenant's rights / Jan Luba. — London : Legal Action Group, 1986. — xxxii,127p. — (Law and Practice Guide ; No.12)

RENTAL HOUSING — England
WHITEHEAD, Christine M. E.
Private rented housing in the 1980s and 1990s / Christine M.E. Whitehead and Mark P. Kleinman. — Cambridge : Granta Editions, 1986. — x, 181p. — (Occasional paper / University of Cambridge, Department of Land Economy ; no.17). — *Bibliography: p.175-181*

RENTAL HOUSING — England — London
GREATER LONDON COUNCIL. Housing Department. Policy Division
The GLC and London's private rented sector. — [London] : the Council, 1984. — 1pamphlet (various pagings)

GREATER LONDON COUNCIL. Housing Department. Policy Division
Private tenants in London : the GLC survey 1983-84. — London : the Council, 1986. — 67p. — (GLC housing research and policy report ; no.5)

RENTAL HOUSING — Great Britain

GREAT BRITAIN. Parliament. House of Commons. Library. Research Division
The private rented sector and rent control / Oonagh Gay. — [London] : the Division, 1986. — 21p. — (Background paper ; no.189)

TODD, J. E.
Recent private lettings 1982-84 / Jean E. Todd ; [for the] Office of Population Censuses and Surveys, Social Survey Division. — London : H.M.S.O., 1986. — ii,46p

RENTAL HOUSING — London — Chelsea — Resident satisfaction

SMITH, Karen
'I'm not complaining' : the housing conditions of elderly private tenants / by Karen Smith. — [London] : Kensington and Chelsea Staying Put for the Elderly in association with SHAC, [1986]. — 84p

RENTAL HOUSING — London — Kensington — Resident satisfaction

SMITH, Karen
'I'm not complaining' : the housing conditions of elderly private tenants / by Karen Smith. — [London] : Kensington and Chelsea Staying Put for the Elderly in association with SHAC, [1986]. — 84p

REPARATION — Great Britain

BAILEY, Suzanne
Remedies for victims of crime / Suzanne Bailey, David Tucker. — London : Legal Action Group, 1984. — xxxi,133p. — (Law and Practice guide ; No.7)

GREAT BRITAIN. Home Office
Criminal injuries compensation : a statutory scheme / report of an interdepartmental working party. — London : H.M.S.O., 1986. — [90]p

REPARATION — Netherlands

DIJK, J. J. M. van
Compensation by the state or by the offender : the victim's perspective / Jan J. M. van Dijk. — The Hague : Research and Documentation Centre, Ministry of Justice, 1985. — 22p. — ([Reports, papers, articles] ; 78). — *Paper presented at the Conference on Victims, Restitution and Compensation in the Criminal Justice System, Cambridge, U.K. 13-16 August 1984. — Bibliography: p20-22*

REPORT ON THE SUPPLY OF PETROLEUM AND PETROLEUM PRODUCTS TO RHODESIA

GREAT BRITAIN. Parliament. House of Commons. Library. International Affairs Section
The Bingham Report : a background bibliography / [Carole B. Mann]. — [London] : the Library, 1978. — 6leaves. — (Reference sheet / House of Commons. Library. Research Division ; no.78/9)

GREAT BRITAIN. Parliament. House of Commons. Library. International Affairs Section
The Bingham Report : a background bibliography; addenda: November 1978-January 1979 / [Carole B. Mann]. — [London] : the Library, 1979. — 2leaves. — ([Reference sheet] / House of Commons. Library. [Research Division] ; no.78/9: Addenda)

REPORT WRITING

BERRY, Ralph
How to write a research paper / by Ralph Berry. — 2nd ed. — Oxford : Pergamon, 1986. — v,116p. — *Previous ed.: 1966*

WERNER, Oswald
Systematic fieldwork / Oswald Werner, G. Mark Schoepfle. — Newbury Park [Calif.] ; London : Sage
Vol.2: Ethnographic analysis and data management. — 1987. — 355p. — *Bibliography: p339-345*

REPORTERS AND REPORTING — Africa

HARRISON, Paul, 1945-
News out of Africa : Biafra to Band Aid / Paul Harrison, Robin Palmer. — London : Shipman, 1986. — x,147p. — *Bibliography: p141-142. — Includes index*

REPORTERS AND REPORTING — Canada

COMBER, Mary Anne
The newsmongers : how the media distort the political news / Mary Anne Comber and Robert S. Mayne. — Toronto : McClelland and Stewart, 1986. — 178p. — *Bibliography: p177-178*

REPRESENTATION OF THE PEOPLE BILL 1980-81

GREAT BRITAIN. Parliament. House of Commons. Library. Research Division
Representation of the People Bill [Bill 153 of 1980-81] / [Rosamund Coates]. — [London] : the Division, 1981. — 18p. — (Reference sheet ; no.81/16)

REPRESENTATIVE GOVERNMENT AND REPRESENTATION

BENJAMIN, Richard
Socialism and modern democratic techniques / Richard Benjamin. — Guildford : Labour Campaign for Electoral Reform, 1987. — 12p

GINSBERG, Benjamin
The captive public : how mass opinion promotes state power / Benjamin Ginsberg. — New York : Basic Books, c1986. — xi, 272 p.. — *Includes index. — Bibliography: p. [233]-249*

MONAHAN, Arthur P.
Consent, coercion, and limit : the medieval origins of parliamentary democracy / Arthur P. Monahan. — Kingston ; Montreal : McGill-Queen's University Press, 1987. — xx,345p. — (McGill-Queen's studies in the history of ideas ; 10). — *Bibliography: p [265]-325*

Die Unternehmung in der demokratischen Gesellschaft = : The business corporation in the democratic society / herausgegeben von Wolfgang Dorow. — Berlin ; New York : W. de Gruyter, 1987. — xiii, 390 p.. — *"Günter Dlugos zum 65. Geburtstagegewidmet.". — English and German. — Includes bibliographies*

REPRESENTATIVE GOVERNMENT AND REPRESENTATION — Case studies

Transitions from authoritarian rule : comparative perspectives / edited by Guillermo O'Donnell, Philippe C. Schmitter, and Laurence Whitehead. — Baltimore : Johns Hopkins University Press, c1986. — xii, 190 p.. — *Includes index. — Bibliography: p. 165-184. — Contents: Pt. 1, Southern Europe -- Pt. 2, Latin America -- Pt. 3, Comparative perspectives -- Pt. 4, Tentative conclusions and uncertain democracies*

REPRESENTATIVE GOVERNMENT AND REPRESENTATION — Congresses

Parlamento y democracia : problemas y perspectivas en los años 80 : textos del coloquio organizado por la Fundación Pablo Iglesias durante los días 23, 24 y 25 de septiembre de 1981 / Pierre Birnbaum ... [et al.] ; edición preparada por Mónica Threlfall. — Madrid : Editorial P. Iglesias, [1982?]. — 170 p.

REPRESENTATIVE GOVERNMENT AND REPRESENTATION — Europe, Southern — Case studies

Transitions from authoritarian rule / edited by Guillermo O'Donnell, Philippe C. Schmitter, and Laurence Whitehead ; [with a foreword by Abraham F. Lowenthal]. — Baltimore : Johns Hopkins University Press. — *Papers originally commissioned for conferences or meetings sponsored by the Latin American Program of the Woodrow Wilson International Center for Scholars between 1979 and 1981. — Includes index. — Bibliography: p. 187-212. — Contents: An introduction to southern European transitions from authoritarian rule : Italy, Greece, Portugal, Spain, and Turkey / Philippe C. Schmitter -- Political economy, legitimation, and the state in southern Europe / Salvador Giner -- The demise of the first Fascist regime and Italy's transition to democracy, 1943-1948 / Gianfranco Pasquino -- Political change in Spain and the prospects for democracy / José María Maravall and Julián Santamaría -- Regime overthrow and the prospects for democratic transition in Portugal / Kenneth Maxwell -- Regime change and the prospects for democracy in Greece, 1974-1983 / P. Nikiforos Diamandouros -- Democracy in Turkey : problems and prospects / Ilkay Sunar and Sabri Sayari*
Southern Europe. — c1986. — xii, 218 p.

REPRESENTATIVE GOVERNMENT AND REPRESENTATION — Finland

GRÖNHOLM, Christoffer
Kommunal självstyrelse och demokrati i Finland (inklusive en presentation av femkommunsundersökningen 1982) / Christoffer Grönholm. — Helsinki : Schildt, 1983. — 243p. — *Bibliography: p238-243*

REPRESENTATIVE GOVERNMENT AND REPRESENTATION — Germany

Deutscher und Britischer Parlamentarismus = British and German parliamentarism / herausgegeben von Adolf M. Birke und Kurt Kluxen. — München ; London : Saur, 1985. — 192p. — (Prinz-Albert-Studien = Prince Albert studies ; Bd.3). — *5 contibutions in German, 4 in English. — Proceedings of the yearly assembly of the Prinz-Albert-Gesellschaft, 1984. — Includes the statutes and list of members*

REPRESENTATIVE GOVERNMENT AND REPRESENTATION — Great Britain

CAIN, Bruce E
The personal vote : constituency service and electoral independence / Bruce Cain, John Ferejohn, Morris Fiorina. — Cambridge, Mass. : Harvard University Press, 1986. — p. cm. — *Includes index. — Bibliography: p*

Deutscher und Britischer Parlamentarismus = British and German parliamentarism / herausgegeben von Adolf M. Birke und Kurt Kluxen. — München ; London : Saur, 1985. — 192p. — (Prinz-Albert-Studien = Prince Albert studies ; Bd.3). — *5 contibutions in German, 4 in English. — Proceedings of the yearly assembly of the Prinz-Albert-Gesellschaft, 1984. — Includes the statutes and list of members*

REPRESENTATIVE GOVERNMENT AND REPRESENTATION — Latin America — Case studies

Transitions from authoritarian rule / edited by Guillermo O'Donnell, Philippe C. Schmitter, Laurence Whitehead. — Baltimore : Johns Hopkins University Press. — Papers originally commissioned for a conference sponsored by the Latin American Program of the Woodrow Wilson International Center for Scholars between 1979 and 1980. — Includes index. — Bibliography: p. — Contents: International aspects of democratization / Laurence Whitehead -- Some problems in the study of the transition to democracy / Adam Przeworski -- Paths toward redemocratization / Alfred Stepan -- Liberalization and democratization in South America ; perspectives from the 1970s / Robert R. Kaufman -- Demilitarization and the institutionalization of military-dominated polities in Latin America / Alain Rouquié -- Entrepreneurs and the transition process : the Brazilian case / Fernando H. Cardoso -- Economic policies and the prospects for successful transition from authoritarian rule in Latin America / John Sheahan
Comparative perspectives. — c1986. — p. cm

Transitions from authoritarian rule / edited by Guillermo O'Donnell, Philippe C. Schmitter, and Laurence Whitehead ; [with a foreword by Abraham F. Lowenthal]. — Baltimore : Johns Hopkins University Press. — Papers originally commissioned for a conference sponsored by the Latin American Program of the Woodrow Wilson International Center for Scholars between 1979 and 1981. — Includes index. — Bibliography: p. 221-236. — Contents: Introduction to the Latin American cases / Guillermo O'Donnell -- Political cycles in Argentina since 1955 / Marcelo Cavarozzi -- Bolivia's failed democratization, 1977-1980 / Laurence Whitehead -- The "liberalization" of authoritarian rule in Brazil / Luciano Martins -- The political evolution of the Chilean military regime and problems in the transition to democracy / Manuel Antonio Garretón -- Political liberalization in an authoritarian regime; the case of Mexico / Kevin J. Middlebrook -- Military interventions and "transfer of power to civilians" in Peru / Julio Cotler -- Uruguay's transition from collegial military-technocratic rule / Charles G. Gillespie -- Petroleum and political pacts : the transition to democracy in Venezuela / Terry Lynn Karl
Latin America. — c1986. — xii, 244 p.

REPRESENTATIVE GOVERNMENT AND REPRESENTATION — Spain — Congresses

Parlamento y democracia : problemas y perspectivas en los años 80 : textos del coloquio organizado por la Fundación Pablo Iglesias durante los días 23, 24 y 25 de septiembre de 1981 / Pierre Birnbaum ... [et al.] ; edición preparada por Mónica Threlfall. — Madrid : Editorial P. Iglesias, [1982?]. — 170 p.

REPRESENTATIVE GOVERNMENT AND REPRESENTATION — United States

CAIN, Bruce E
The personal vote : constituency service and electoral independence / Bruce Cain, John Ferejohn, Morris Fiorina. — Cambridge, Mass. : Harvard University Press, 1986. — p. cm. — Includes index. — Bibliography: p

REPRESENTATIVE GOVERNMENT AND REPRESENTATION — Venezuela

ARROYO TALAVERA, Eduardo
Elections and negotiation : the limits of democracy in Venezuela / Eduardo Arroyo Talavera. — [New York, N.Y.] : Garland Pub., 1986. — 450 p.. — (Outstanding theses from the London School of Economics and Political Science). — Spine title: The limites of democracy in Venezuela, 1958-1981. — Thesis (Ph. D.)--University of London, 1983. — Bibliography: p. 421-450

REPRESENTATIVE GOVERNMENT AND REPRESENTATION — Wales

JAMES, Arnold J.
Union to Reform : a history of the Parliamentary representation of Wales 1536 to 1832 / Arnold J. James, John E. Thomas. — Llandysul : Gomer Press, 1986. — xxiv,472p. — Bibliography: p469-[472]

REPRODUCTION

DALY, Martin
Sex, evolution, and behavior / Martin Daly and Margo Wilson. — 2nd ed. — Boston : Willard Grant Press, c1983. — xiv, 402 p.. — Includes index. — Bibliography: p. 345-389

REPUBLIC

CROSS, R. C. (Robert Craigie)
Plato's Republic : a philosophical commentary / R.C. Cross and A.D. Woozley. — London : Macmillan, 1964 (1980 [printing]). — xv,295p. — Originally published: London : Macmillan ; New York : St Martin's Press, 1964. — Bibliography: p289-291. — Includes index

REPUBLIC. BOOK 1

LYCOS, Kimon
Plato on justice and power : reading Book 1 of Plato's Republic / Kimon Lycos. — Basingstoke : Macmillan, 1987. — ix,201p. — Bibliography: p194-197. — Includes index

REPUBLICAN PARTY (U.S. : 1854-)

DIETZ, Terry
Republicans and Vietnam, 1961-1968 / Terry Dietz. — Westport, Conn. ; London : Greenwood Press, 1986. — xv, 184p. — (Contributions in political science ; no. 146). — Includes index. — Bibliography: p.[173]-177

REPUBLICANISM — Ireland

ADAMS, Gerry
The politics of Irish freedom / Gerry Adams. — Dingle : Brandon, 1986. — [192]p

REPUBLICANISM — Spain — History

GUTIÉRREZ LLORET, Rosa Ana
Republicanos y liberales : la revolución de 1868 y la I.a República en Alicante / Rosa Ana Gutiérrez Lloret. — Alicante : Instituto Juan Gil-Albert, 1985. — 188p. — Bibliography: p175-185

REPUBLICANISM — Spain — Catalonia

CULLA I CLARÀ, Joan B.
El republicanisme lerrouxista a Catalunya (1901-1923) / per Joan B. Culla i Clarà. — Barcelona : Curial, 1986. — 493p. — (Documents de cultura ; 19). — Bibliography: p[465]-478

REPUBLICANISM — Spain — Malaga

ARCAS CUBERO, Fernando
El republicanismo malagueño durante la Restauración (1875-1923) / Fernando Arcas Cubero. — Cordoba : Ayuntamiento Cordoba, 1985. — 600p. — Bibliography: p585-593

RESEARCH

FIEDLER, Judith
Field research : a manual for logistics and management of scientific studies in natural settings / Judith Fiedler. — 1st ed. — San Francisco : Jossey-Bass Publishers, 1978. — xviii, 188 p.. — (The Jossey-Bass social and behavioral science series). — Includes index. — Bibliography: p. 177-185

The university research system : the public policies of the home of scientists / edited by Bjorn Wittrock, Aant Elzinga. — Stockholm : Almqvist and Wiksell, 1985. — v,220p. — Bibliographies

RESEARCH — Government policy — Great Britain

COUNCIL FOR SCIENTIFIC POLICY. Working Group on the Reorientation of Scientific Research Activity
Report. — [London : the Council, 1970]. — 60p

RESEARCH — Methodology

MOORE, Nick
How to do research / Nick Moore. — 2nd ed. — London : Library Association, 1987. — viii,150p. — Previous ed.: 1983. — Bibliography: p147-148. — Includes index

STOCK, Molly
A practical guide to graduate research / Molly Stock. — New York : McGraw-Hill, c1985. — viii, 168 p.. — Includes index. — Bibliography: p. 162-164

RESEARCH — Methodology — Handbooks

REED, Jeffrey G.
Library use : a handbook for psychology / Jeffrey G. Reed and Pam M. Baxter. — Washington, DC : American Psychological Association, c1983. — 137 p.. — Includes bibliographies and index

RESEARCH — Methods — Handbooks

REED, Jeffrey G.
Library use : a handbook for psychology / Jeffrey G. Reed and Pam M. Baxter. — Washington, DC : American Psychological Association, c1983. — 137 p.. — Includes bibliographies and index

RESEARCH — Social aspects

JAGTENBERG, Tom
The social construction of science : a comparative study of goal direction, research evolution and legitimation / Tom Jagtenberg. — Dordrecht ; London : D. Reidel, c1983. — xviii, 237 p.. — (Sociology of the sciences monographs). — Includes indexes. — Bibliography: p. 223-231

RESEARCH — Australia

AUSTRALIAN SCIENCE AND TECHNOLOGY COUNCIL
Future directions for CSIRO : a report to the Prime Minister / by the Australian Science and Technology Council (ASTEC). — Canberra : Australian Government Publishing Service, 1985. — viii,94p. — Bibliographical references: p62-64

Technology and innovation. — Canberra : Economic Planning Advisory Council, 1986. — v,26p. — (Council paper / Economic Planning Advisory Council ; no.19). — Bibliographical references: p24

RESEARCH — European Economic Community countries

ECONOMIC AND SOCIAL COMMITTEE OF THE EUROPEAN COMMUNITIES
Organization and management of community research and development : study / Economic and Social Committee of the European Communities. — Brussels : General Secretariat of the Economic and Social Committee, 1980. — vi,159p

RESEARCH — Germany (West)

Frauen in Forschung und Lehre / Herausgeber: Der Bundesminister für Bildung und Wissenschaft. — Bad Honnef : Bock, 1985. — vi,147p. — (Studien zu Bildung und Wissenschaft ; 12). — Bibliography: p137-147

RESEARCH — Great Britain

Academic research in the United Kingdom : its organisation and effectiveness : proceedings of a symposium of the Association of Researchers in Medicine and Science / edited by Stephen A. Roberts. — London : Taylor Graham, c1984. — 112p

ADVISORY BOARD FOR THE RESEARCH COUNCILS
A strategy for the science base : a discussion document / prepared for the Secretary of State for Education and Science by the Advisory Board for the Research Councils. — London : H.M.S.O., 1987. — 50 p

COUNCIL FOR SCIENTIFIC POLICY. Working Group on the Reorientation of Scientific Research Activity
Report. — [London : the Council, 1970]. — 60p

RESEARCH — Great Britain
continuation
Current research in Britain: the humanities. — Boston Spa : British Library Lending Division, 1985-. — *Annual*

Exploitable areas of science. — London : HMSO, 1986. — *At head of title: Advisory Council for Applied Research and Development*

RESEARCH — Great Britain — Finance
MARTIN, Ben R.
An international comparison of government funding of academic and academically related research / Ben R. Martin and John Irvine ; with the assistance of Nigel Minchin. — London : Department of Education and Science, 1986. — (ABRC science policy study ; no. 2). — *Study carried out for the Advisory Board for the Research Councils by the Science Policy and Research Evaluation Group, Science Policy research Unit. — Spiral binding*

RESEARCH — Organisation for Economic Co-operation and Development countries — Evaluation
GIBBONS, Michael
Evaluation of research : a selection of current practices / [by Michael Gibbons and Luke Georghiou]. — Paris : OECD, 1987. — 77p. — *Bibliography: p73-75*

RESEARCH — Taiwan — Bibliography
Handbook of current research projects in the Republic of China. — Taipei : National Central Library, 1962. — 200p

RESEARCH — United States — Finance
Establishing cost allocation plans and indirect cost rates for research grants and contracts with the Department of Health, Education and Welfare. — [Washington, D.C. : Department of Health, Education, and Welfare, 1968]. — vii,36p. — *"OASC-4"*

RESEARCH AND DEVELOPMENT CONTRACTS — Developing countries
Démarches de recherche-développement appliquées au secteur de la production rurale des pays en voie de dévlopement / [Alain Lalau-Keraly...et al.]. — [Paris] : Bureau de liaison des agents de la coopération technique...[etc.], c1984. — 91p. — (Collection des ateliers technologique et développement ; no.2). — *Ce texte fait suite à un séminaire conçu par Alain Lalau-Keraly et Didier Pillot, avec rédaction finale par Jacques Bodichon. — Bibliography: p81-84*

RESEARCH AND DEVELOPMENT CONTRACTS — United States
Establishing cost allocation plans and indirect cost rates for research grants and contracts with the Department of Health, Education and Welfare. — [Washington, D.C. : Department of Health, Education, and Welfare, 1968]. — vii,36p. — *"OASC-4"*

RESEARCH GRANTS — Europe
A guide to European Community grants and loans 1986/87 : for commerce, industry, local authorities, academic and research institutions / compiled by Gay Scott. — 7th ed. — Newbury : Eurofi (UK), 1986. — 1v.(loose-leaf)

RESEARCH GRANTS — Europe — Handbooks, manuals, etc.
DAVISON, Ann
Grants from Europe : how to get money and influence policy / written for ERICA by Ann Davison. — 3rd ed.. — London : Bedford Square Press, 1986. — ix, 86p

RESEARCH, INDUSTRIAL — Government policy — Australia
AUSTRALIAN INDUSTRIAL RESEARCH AND DEVELOPMENT INCENTIVES BOARD
Future government support for innovation : the role and relevance of industrial R & D incentives / Australian Industrial Research and Development Incentives Board. — Canberra : Australian Government Publishing Service, 1985. — xv,[96]p

RESEARCH, INDUSTRIAL — Australia
AUSTRALIAN SCIENCE AND TECHNOLOGY COUNCIL
Future directions for CSIRO : a report to the Prime Minister / by the Australian Science and Technology Council (ASTEC). — Canberra : Australian Government Publishing Service, 1985. — viii,94p. — *Bibliographical references: p62-64*

RESEARCH, INDUSTRIAL — Australia — Public opinion
AUSTRALIA. Bureau of Industry Economics. Conference on Evaluation of Public Support for Industrial Research and Development (1986 : Canberra)
Evaluation of public support for industrial research and development : conference papers and proceedings Canberra 2 May 1986. — Canberra : Australian Government Publishing Service, 1986. — [vi,]113p. — *Bibliography: p31*

RESEARCH, INDUSTRIAL — European Economic Community countries — Finance — Directories
LOVASZ, J.
Incentives for industrial research, development and innovation : directory of direct and indirect public measures for promoting industrial research, development and innovation in the member states of the European Communities. — 2nd ed. / compiled for the Commission of the European Communities by J. Lovasz assisted by P. McCann. — London : Kogan Page, 1986. — [470]p. — *Previous ed.: 1985*

RESEARCH, INDUSTRIAL — Great Britain — Finance
UK science policy : a critical review of policies for publicly funded research / edited by Maurice Goldsmith. — London : Longman, 1984. — xxii,275p. — *Includes bibliographies and index*

RESEARCH, INDUSTRIAL — Soviet Union
GROSHEV, V. P.
Narodno-khoziaistvennyi nauchnyi kompleks / V. P. Groshev. — Moskva : Mysl', 1985. — 254p

RESEARCH, INDUSTRIES — United States
ZEGVELD, Walter
SDI and industrial technology policy : threat or opportunity? / Walter Zegveld and Christien Enzing. — London : Pinter, 1987. — 186p. — *Includes bibliographies and index*

RESEARCH INSTITUTES — United States — History
GEIGER, Roger L.
To advance knowledge : the growth of American research universities, 1900-1940 / Roger L. Geiger. — New York : Oxford University Press, 1986. — x, 325 p. — *Includes index. — Bibliography: p. 279-320*

RESEARCH LIBRARIES — Evaluation — Statistical methods
KANTOR, Paul B
Objective performance measures for academic and research libraries / by Paul B. Kantor. — Washington, D.C. : Association of Research Libraries, 1984. — viii, 76 p., [13] leaves. — *Bibliography: p. 75-76*

RESEARCH LIBRARIES — Finance
CUMMINGS, Martin M.
The economics of research libraries / Martin Marc Cummings. — Washington, D.C. : Council on Library Resources, 1986. — p. cm. — *"User fees and library economics : a selected, annotated bibliography / Jane A. Rosenberg": p. — Includes bibliographies and index*

RESEARCH PARKS
Science parks and technology complexes in relation to regional development. — [Paris] : Organisation for Economic Co-operation and Development, 1987. — i,38p

RESEARCHOFF. PUBNS. — European Economic Community countries 986
Aims and priorities of a common research and development policy : study. — Brussels : Economic and Social Committee, 1982. — 2,59p. — *At head of title: 'Economic and Social Committee of the European Communities'*

RESERVOIRS — Environmental aspects — England
LAND USE CONSULTANTS
Environmental appraisal of four alternative water resource schemes : Haweswater, Borrowbeck, Morecambe Bay, Hellifield; report of the Environmental Impact Study, November 1978 / prepared and published on behalf of the North West Water Authority by Land Use Consultants. — London : Land Use Consultants for the North West Water Authority, c1978. — xi,188p. — (Regional water resource studies). — *Bibliography: p187-188*

RESIDENTIAL MOBILITY — England — Bristol (Avon)
SHORT, John R.
Patterns of residential mobility in the private housing market : a case study of Bristol / John R. Short. — Bristol : University of Bristol. Department of Geography, 1977. — 15p. — (Bristol housing studies)

RESIDENTIAL MOBILITY — United States
NEWMAN, Sandra J
Federal policy and the mobility of older homeowners : the effects of the one-time capital gains exclusion / Sandra Newman, James Reschovsky ; project manager, Robert Marans. — Ann Arbor, Mich. : Survey Research Center, Institute for Social Research, University of Michigan, 1985. — p. cm. — (Research report series / Institute for social research). — *"ISR code no. 9020"--T.p. verso. — Bibliography: p*

RESOURCE ALLOCATION
CAMPBELL, Donald E.
Resource allocation mechanisms / Donald E. Campbell. — Cambridge : Cambridge University Press, 1987. — xiii,183p. — *Bibliography: p171-177. — Includes index*

RESOURCE RECOVERY FACILITIES — Europe
ABERT, James Goodear
Municipal waste processing in Europe : a status report on selected materials and energy recovery projects / James G. Abert. — Washington, D.C. : The World Bank, 1985. — xiv,157p. — (World Bank technical paper ; no.37) (UNDP project management report ; no.4) (Integrated resource recovery series ; no.4). — *At head of cover: "Integrated resource recovery". — Includes bibliographical references*

RESPECT FOR PERSONS
VANDEVEER, Donald
Paternalistic intervention : the moral bounds of benevolence / Donald VanDeVeer. — Princeton, N.J. : Princeton University Press, c1986. — xii, 452 p.. — (Studies in moral, political, and legal philosophy). — *Includes bibliographical references and index*

RESPIRATORY ORGANS — Diseases — Great Britain — Mortality
GREAT BRITAIN. Office of Population Censuses and Surveys
Trends in respiratory mortality 1951-1975. — London : H.M.S.O., 1981. — viii,55p. — (Series DH1 / Office of Population Censuses and Surveys ; no.7). — *Bibliographical references: p43-44*

RESPONSIBILITY
ROBINS, Michael H.
Promising, intending, and moral autonomy / Michael H. Robins. — Cambridge : Cambridge University Press, 1984. — xii,180p. — (Cambridge studies in philosophy). — *Bibliography: p171-177. — Includes index*

RESTAURANTS, LUNCH ROOMS, ETC. — Netherlands — Statistics
Vierde algemene bedrijfstelling, 1978. — 's-Gravenhage : Staatsuitgeverij
d.2: Algemene sectorale gegevens. — 1985
C: hotels, restaurants, cafés e.d.. — 61p

RESTAURANTS, LUNCH ROOMS, ETC. — Singapore — Statistics
Report on the censuses of wholesale trade, retail trade, restaurants and hotels, 1983. — Singapore : Department of Statistics, 1986. iv,231p

RESTITUTION — Great Britain
GOFF OF CHIEVELEY, Robert Goff, Baron
The law of restitution. — 3rd ed. / by Lord Goff of Chieveley and Gareth Jones. — London : Sweet & Maxwell, 1986. — xcix,770p . — Previous ed.: 1978. — Bibliography: p737-740. — Includes index

RESTRAINT OF TRADE
TREBILCOCK, Michael J.
The common law of restraint of trade : a legal and economic analysis / by Michael J. Trebilcock. — Toronto : Carswell, 1986. — xxvi,419p

RESTRAINT OF TRADE — Canada
Reaction : the new Combines Investigation Act / contributors include: Reuven Brenner....[et al.] ; edited by Walter Block. — [Vancouver] : The Fraser Institute, 1986. — xxix,208p. — Bibliography: p203-208

RESTRAINT OF TRADE — England
MEHIGAN, Simon
Restraint of trade and business secrets : law and practice / Simon Mehigan, David Griffiths. — London : Longman, c1986. — xxiv,247p. — (Longman commercial series). — Includes index

RESTRAINT OF TRADE — European Economic Community countries
KORAH, Valentine
An introductory guide to EEC Competition law and practice / Valentine Korah. — 3rd ed. — Oxford : ESC Publishing, 1986. — xxi,177p. — Cover title: EEC competition law and practice. — Includes bibliographies and index

RETAIL TRADE — Congresses
INTERNATIONAL CONFERENCE ON BUSINESS HISTORY (7th : 1981 : Fuji Education Center)
Development of mass marketing : the automobile and retailing industries : proceedings of the Fuji Conference / edited by Akio Okochi, Koichi Shimokawa. — Tokyo : University of Tokyo Press, 1981. — xiii,308p. — Includes references

RETAIL TRADE — Canada — Statistics
Retail chain and department stores = Magasins à détail à succursales et les grands magasins / Statistics Canada. — Ottawa : Statistics Canada, 1983-. — Annual. — Text in English and French

RETAIL TRADE — European Economic Community countries — Employees
BARTELS, Cornelis P. A.
Employment in retail trade in E.C. countries / by C. P. A. Bartels, F. G. M. Werkhoven, P. D. de Kruijk. — Luxembourg : Office for Official Publications of the European Communities, 1985. — vi, 101p. — At head of title: Commission of the European Communities

RETAIL TRADE — European Economic Community Countries — Statistics
Einzelhandel-Verkaufsindex = Retail sales - index numbers = Commerce de détail-indice des ventes / Statistical Office of the European Communities. — Luxembourg : Statistical Office of the European Communities, 1985-. — Monthly

RETAIL TRADE — Fiji — Statistics
Survey of distributive trade : 1983. — Suva : Bureau of Statistics, 1985. — 22,viip

RETAIL TRADE — France
CHAVANE, Laurence
Le phénomène Leclerc : de Landerneau à l'an 2000 / Laurence Chavane. — Paris : Plon, 1986. — 253p

RETAIL TRADE — Great Britain
BRADLEY, Keith
Profit sharing in the retail trade sector : the relative performance of the John Lewis partnership / K. Bradley and S. Estrin. — London : Centre for Labour Economics, London School of Economics, 1987. — 30p. — (Discussion paper / London School of Economics and Political Science. Centre for Labour Economics ; no.279). — Bibliography: p20-21

Business strategy and retailing / edited by Gerry Johnson. — Chichester : Wiley, c1987. — [300]p. — Includes index

Local shops : problems and prospects / Peter Jones and Rosemary Oliphant, editors. — Reading : Unit for Retail Planning Information, 1976. — 103p. — Includes bibliographies

RETAIL TRADE — Great Britain — Statistics
Census of distribution and other services. — London : HMSO, 1950-. — (Business monitor. SDO ; 10-23). — Occasional. — In thirteen parts plus supplement. — 1950-66 published by the Board of Trade; 1971- by the Business Statistics Office

Clothing and footwear shops. — London : HMSO, 1970-79. — (Business monitor. SD ; 2) (Business monitor. SDM ; 2). — Monthly. — Continued by: Retail sales

Consumer credit business of retailers. — London : HMSO, 1979-. — (Business monitor. SDM ; 8). — Monthly. — Continues: Instalment credit business of retailers

Durable goods shops. — London : HMSO, 1970-79. — (Business monitor. SD ; 3) (Business monitor. SDM ; 3). — Monthly. — Continued by: Retail sales

Food shops. — London : HMSO, 1970-79. — (Business monitor. SD ; 1) (Business monitor. SDM ; 1). — Monthly. — Continued by: Retail sales

Instalment credit business of retailers. — London : HMSO, 1974-1979. — (Business monitor. SD ; 8). — Monthly. — Continued by: Consumer credit business of retailers

Miscellaneous non-food shops. — London : HMSO, 1970-79. — (Business monitor. SD ; 4) (Business monitor. SDM ; 4). — Monthly. — Continued by: Retail sales

Retail sales. — London : HMSO, 1980-. — (Business monitor. SDM ; 28). — Monthly. — Continues: Food shops; Clothing and footwear shops; Durable goods shops; Miscellaneous non-food shops

Retailing. — London : HMSO, 1976-. — (Business monitor. SDA ; 25) (Business monitor. SDO ; 25). — Annual (1976-1980), occasional (1982)-

RETAIL TRADE — Italy — Statistics
ITALY. Istituto Centrale di Statistica
6 censimento generale dell'industria, del commercio, dei servizi e dell'artigianato 26 ottobre 1981. — Roma : the Istituto vol.3: Atti del censimento. — 1985. — 264p

RETAIL TRADE — Nigeria — Statistics
Distribution survey of Nigeria / Federal Office of Statistics, Nigeria. — Lagos : Federal Office of Statistics, 1978-. — Annual

RETAIL TRADE — Singapore — Statistics
Report on the censuses of wholesale trade, retail trade, restaurants and hotels, 1983. — Singapore : Department of Statistics, 1986. — iv,231p

RETAIL TRADE — Thailand — Statistics
Census of business trade and services 1966 : Southern region. — Bangkok : National Statistical Office, [1970?]. — 57p. — In English and Thai

Report : census of business trade and services 1977 : Bangkok Metropolitan, Nonthaburi, Pathum Thani and Samut Prakan. — Bangkok : National Statistical Office, [1980?]. — 96p. — In English and Thai

Report : census of business trade and services 1977 : whole kingdom. — Bangkok : National Statistical Office, [1980?]. — 75p

RETAIL TRADE — United States — Foreign ownership
KACKER, M. P
Transatlantic trends in retailing : takeovers and flow of know-how / Madhav P. Kacker. — Westport, Conn. : Quorum Books, c1985. — p. cm. — Includes index. — Bibliography: p

RETIREMENT
Retirement in industrialized societies : social, psychological and health factors / edited by Kyriakos S. Markides and Cary L. Cooper. — Chichester : Wiley, c1987. — ix,331p. — Includes bibliographies and index

SULLEROT, Evelyne
L'âge de travailler / Evelyne Sullerot. — [Paris] : Fayard, 1986. — 224p

RETIREMENT — Bibliography
MILETICH, John J
Retirement : an annotated bibliography / compiled by John J. Miletich. — New York : Greenwood Press, 1986. — xvii, 147 p.. — (Bibliographies and indexes in gerontology ; no. 2). — Includes indexes

RETIREMENT — Denmark
Revalidering- og pensionsnaevnenes afgørelser i førtidspensionssager 1.april 1976 til 31 december 1978 : redegørelse fra sikringsstyrelsen. — [København] : Sikringsstyrelsen, 1980. — 106p. — (Sikringsstyrelsens undersøgelser ; nr.5). — Includes bibliographical references

RETIREMENT — Great Britain
LYON, Phil
Nearing retirement : a study of late working lives / Phil Lyon. — Aldershot : Avebury, c1987. — xix,196p. — Bibliography: p186-196

MELLOR, Hugh W.
Work in later life : a plea for flexible retirement / Hugh Mellor. — London : Employment Institute, 1987. — 32p. — Bibliography: p29-30

RETIREMENT — Netherlands
De leefsituatie van de Nederlandse bevolking van 55 jaar en ouder 1982. — 's-Gravenhage : Staatsuitgeverij. — Summary and conclusions in English. — Title on back cover: Well-being of the elderly population in the Netherlands 1982 : a survey on people aged 55 years and over : Part 4. — Bibliography: p55
d.4: Gevolgen van uitreding uit het arbeidsproces : een panelanalyse 1976-1982. — 1985. — 55p

RETIREMENT AGE — Legal status, laws, etc. — Great Britain
GREAT BRITAIN. Parliament. House of Commons. Library. Research Division
Social Security (Age of Retirement) Bill 1983/4 [Bill 16] / Julia Lourie. — [London] : the Division, 1983. — 20p. — (Reference sheet ; no.83/21). — Bibliographical references: p15-18

RETIREMENT COMMUNITIES — California — Los Angeles — Case studies
SMITHERS, Janice A.
Determined survivors : community life among the urban elderly / by Janice A. Smithers. — New Brunswick, N.J. : Rutgers University Press, c1985. — p. cm. — Includes index. — Bibliography: p

RETIREMENT INCOME — Germany (West)
NOTTAGE, Raymond
Pensions : a plan for the future : based on a comparative study of the pensions systems of Great Britain and Germany / Raymond Nottage and Gerald Rhodes. — London : The Russell Press, 1986. — 53p

RETIREMENT INCOME — Great Britain
NOTTAGE, Raymond
Pensions : a plan for the future : based on a comparative study of the pensions systems of Great Britain and Germany / Raymond Nottage and Gerald Rhodes. — London : The Russell Press, 1986. — 53p

RETIREMENT INCOME — United States
KORCZYK, Sophie M.
Retirement income opportunities in an aging America : pensions and the economy / Sophie M. Korczyk. — Washington : Employee Benefit Research Institute, 1982. — 150p. — *Bibliography: p98-108*

SCHULZ, James H
The economics of aging / James H. Schulz. — 3rd ed. — New York : Van Nostrand Reinhold, [1985]. — p. cm. — *Includes index.* — *Bibliography: p*

RÉUNION
La Réunion dans l'océan Indien : colloque organisé par le Centre des Hautes Études sur l'Afrique et l'Asie Modernes : 24 et 25 octobre 1985 à la Sorbonne. — Paris : Le Centre des Hautes Études sur l'Afrique et l'Asie Modernes, 1986. — 239p. — (Publications du CHEAM ; 7). — *Includes bibliographical references*

REUTERS — History
LAWRENSON, John
The price of truth : the story of the Reuters £££ million / John Lawrenson & Lionel Barber. — Edinburgh : Mainstream, 1985. — 192p. — *Bibliography: p189. — Includes index*

REUTERSHAN, PAUL — Trials, litigation, etc
SCHUCK, Peter H
Agent Orange on trial : mass toxic disasters in the courts / Peter H. Schuck. — Cambridge, Mass. : Belknap Press of Harvard University Press, 1986. — ix, 347 p.. — *Includes index.* — *Bibliography: p. [301]-335*

REUTHER, WALTER
HANSEN, Beatrice
A political biography of Walter Reuther : the record of an opportunist / Beatrice Hausen. "Meany vs Reuther" / Farrell Dobbs. — New York : Pathfinder Press, 1987. — 27p

REVENUE — Belgium
Revenus et fiscalité des agriculteurs en Belgique : politique agricole commune / G. Bublot...[et al.] ; textes rassemblés par Max Frank. — [Bruxelles] : Université de Bruxelles, c1982. — 126p. — *At head of title: Politique agricole commune. — Bibliography: p126*

REVENUE — Canada
CARMICHAEL, Edward A
Tackling the federal deficit / Edward A. Carmichael. — Toronto : C.D. Howe Institute, [1984]. — 88 p.. — (Observation ; no. 26). — *Includes bibliographical references*

REVERSE DISCRIMINATION — Great Britain
EDWARDS, John, 1943-
Positive discrimination, social justice and social policy : moral scrutiny of a policy practice / John Edwards ; foreword by Lord Scarman. — London : Tavistock, 1987. — x,243p. — *Bibliography: p222-235. — Includes index*

REVIEW OF THE PUBLIC ORDER ACT 1936 AND RELATED LEGISLATION
THORNTON, Peter, 1946-
We protest : the public order debate / Peter Thornton. — London : National Council for Civil Liberties, 1985. — [96]p

REVIEW OF THE PUBLIC UTILITIES STREET WORKS ACT 1950
GREAT BRITAIN
Public utilities street works : the government response to the Horne report on the review of the Public Utilities Street Works Act 1950. — London : H.M.S.O., 1986. — 32p. — *At head of title page: Department of Transport*

REVOLUČNÍ ODBOROVÉ HNUTI
NEU, Rudolf
Výstavba a činnost' orgánov ROH / Rudolf Neu, Boris Vavro. — Bratislava : Práca, 1985. — 466p. — *Bibliography: p465-[467]*

REVOLUTIONISTS — Mexico
O'MALLEY, Ilene V
The myth of the revolution : hero cults and the institutionalization of the Mexican State, 1920-1940 / Ilene V. O'Malley. — New York : Greenwood Press, 1986. — xii, 199 p.. — (Contributions to the study of world history ; no. 1). — *Includes index. — Bibliography: p.[179]-194*

REVOLUTIONISTS — Algeria — Biography
BULHAN, Hussein Abdilahi
Frantz Fanon and the psychology of oppression / Hussein Abdilahi Bulhan. — New York ; London : Plenum Press, c1985. — xiii, 299p. — (PATH in psychology). — *Includes index. — Includes bibliographical references*

REVOLUTIONISTS — Angola — Biography
BRIDGLAND, Fred
Jonas Savimbi : a key to Africa / by Fred Bridgland. — Edinburgh : Mainstream, 1986. — [300]p. — *Includes bibliography and index*

REVOLUTIONISTS — Colombia — History — 20th century
ZAMOSC, Leon
The agrarian question and the peasant movement in Colombia : struggles of the National Peasant Association 1967-1981 / Leon Zamosc. — Cambridge : Cambridge University Press, 1986. — [304]p. — (Cambridge Latin American studies ; 58). — *Bibliography: p416-438*

REVOLUTIONISTS — Cuba — 19th Century — Biography
FRANCO, José Luciano
La vida heroica y ejemplar de Antonio Maceo (Cronología) / por José L. Franco. — La Habana : Comisión Nacional de la Academia de Ciencias, Instituto de Historia, 1963. — 117p

REVOLUTIONISTS — England — History — 17th century
HILL, Christopher, 1912-
The world turned upside down : radical ideas during the English Revolution / Christopher Hill. — Harmondsworth : Penguin, 1975. — 431p. — (Pelican books). — *Originally published: London : Temple Smith, 1972. — Includes index*

REVOLUTIONISTS — Germany — Biography
GEBHARDT, Manfred
Max Hoelz : Wege und Irrwege eines Revolutionärs : Biografie / von Manfred Gebhardt. — 2., durchgesehene Aufl.. — Berlin : Verlag Neves Leben, 1985, c1983. — [336]p. — *Bibliography: p333-[334]*

REVOLUTIONISTS — India — Biography
LEBRA-CHAPMAN, Joyce
The Rani of Jhansi : a study in female heroism in India / Joyce Lebra-Chapman. — Honolulu : University of Hawaii Press, c1986. — xii, 199 p., [2] leaves of plates. — *Includes index.* — *Bibliography: p. [185]-193*

REVOLUTIONISTS — Ireland — Biography
RYAN, Meda
Liam Lynch : the real chief / Meda Ryan. — Cork : Mercier, c1986. — 192p. — *Includes index*

ZAGLADINA, Kh. T
Dzheims Konnoli / Kh. T. Zagladina. — Moskva : Mysl', 1985. — 165p

REVOLUTIONISTS — Latin America — History
CABALLERO, Manuel
Latin America and the Comintern 1919-1943 / Manuel Caballero. — Cambridge : Cambridge University Press, 1986. — ix,213p. — (Cambridge Latin American studies ; 60). — *Bibliography: p196-205. — Includes index*

REVOLUTIONISTS — Nigeria, Northern — Biography
SULAIMAN, Ibraheem
A revolution in history : the jihad of Usman Dan Fodio / Ibraheem Sulaiman ; with a foreword by Shehu Usman M. Bugaje. — London : Mansell, 1986. — [208]p. — (East-West University Islamic studies)

REVOLUTIONISTS — Russian S.F.S.R. — Leningrad
Krushenie tsarizma : vospominaniia uchastnikov revoliutsionnogo dvizheniia v Petrograde (1907 g.- fevral' 1917 g.) / sostaviteli: R. Sh. Ganelin, V. A. Ulanov ; nauchnyi redaktor L. M. Spirin. — Leningrad : Lenizdat, 1986. — 429p. — (Biblioteka revoliutsionnykh memuarov "Iz iskry vozgoritsia plamia")

REVOLUTIONISTS — Russian S.F.S.R. — Siberia
Revoliutsionnoe i obshchestvennoe dvizhenie v Sibiri v kontse XIX - nachale XX v. / otv. redaktor L. M. Goriushkin. — Novosibirsk : Nauka, Sibirskoe otdelenie, 1986. — 220p

REVOLUTIONISTS — Soviet Union
BENNIGSEN, Alexandre
Sultan Galiev, le père de la révolution tiers-mondiste / Alexandre Bennigsen, Chantal Lemercier-Quelquejay. — Paris : Fayard, 1986. — 305p. — (Les inconnus de l'histoire)

REVOLUTIONISTS — Soviet Union — Bibliography
MERVAUD, Michel
Socialisme et liberté : la pensée et l'action de Nicolas Ogarev (1813-1877) / Michel Mervaud. — Rouen : Publications de l'Université de Rouen ; Paris : Institut d'études slaves, 1984. — 596p. — (Publications de l'Université de Rouen ; no.97) (Collection historique / Institut d'études slaves ; 31). — *Bibliography: p [545]-566*

REVOLUTIONISTS — Soviet Union — Biography
ANDREEV, A. A.
Vospominaniia, pis'ma / A. A. Andreev ; [sost.: N. A. Andreeva]. — Moskva : Politizdat, 1985. — 333p

Feliks Edmundovich Dzerzhinskii : biografiia / [redkollegiia: A. S. Velidov...et al.]. — Izd. 3-e, dop.. — Moskva : Politizdat, 1986. — 509p

KANATCHIKOV, S
[Iz istorii moego bytiĭa. English]. A radical worker in Tsarist Russia : the autobiography of Semën Ivanovich Kanatchikov / translated and edited by Reginald E. Zelnik. — Stanford, Calif. : Stanford University Press, 1986. — xxx, 472p, [3]p of plates. — *Translation of: Iz istorii moego bytiĭa*

KING, David, 1943-
Trotsky : a photographic biography / by David King ; commentary by James Ryan ; introduction by Tamara Deutscher. — Oxford : Basil Blackwell, 1986. — 334p

KIRILLOV, V. S.
Grigorii Konstantinovich Ordzhonikidze (Sergo) : biografiia / V. S. Kirillov, A. Ia. Sverdlov. — Izd. 2-e, dop. i isprav.. — Moskva : Politizdat, 1986. — 201p

Kirov i vremia / [sostaviteli: M. I. Bugaeva, D. L. Shumskii; redaktsionnaia kollegiia : V. I. Bokovnia...et al.]. — Leningrad : Lenizdat, 1986. — 316p

REVOLUTIONISTS — Soviet Union — Biography *continuation*
SERGE, Victor
Memoirs of a revolutionary / Victor Serge ; translated [with an introduction] by Peter Sedgwick. — London ; New York : Writers and Readers, 1984. — xxiv,403p. — *Translation of 'Mémoires d'un revolutionnaire', Paris: Editions du Seuil, 1951. — Bibliography: p[387]-391*

REVOLUTIONISTS — Soviet Union — History
DRUZHININ, N. M.
Izbrannye trudy / N. M. Druzhinin. — Moskva : Nauka
[1]: Revoliutsionnoe dvizhenie v Rossii v XIX v. / otv. redaktor S. S. Dmitriev. — 1985. — 484p

PANTIN, I. K.
Revoliutsionnaia traditsiia v Rossii 1783-1883 gg. / I. K. Pantin, E. G. Plimak, V. G. Khoros. — Moskva : Mysl', 1986. — 341p

REVOLUTIONISTS — Soviet Union — History — 19th century
OFFORD, Derek
The Russian revolutionary movement in the 1880s / Derek Offord. — Cambridge : Cambridge University Press, 1986. — 1v.. — *Bibliography: p277-294. — Includes index*

REVOLUTIONS
AVENAS, Denise
"Lutte ouvrière" et la révolution mondiale / Denise Avenas. — Paris : François Maspero, 1971. — 45p. — (Série "Marx ou crève" ; 3) (Cahiers rouges)

BAECHLER, Jean
Revolution / Jean Baechler ; translated [from the French] by Joan Vickers. — Oxford : Blackwell, 1975. — xxiv,208p. — (Key concepts in the social sciences). — *Translation of: 'Les Phénomènes révolutionnaires'. Paris : Presses universitaires de France, 1970. — Bibliography: p.207-208*

BERBEROGLU, Berch
The international of capital : imperialism and capitalist development on a world scale / Berch Berberoglu. — New York : Praeger, 1987. — p. cm. — *Bibliography: p*

CASTORIADIS, Cornelius
The imaginary institution of society / Cornelius Castoriadis ; translated by Kathleen Blamey. — Cambridge : Polity, 1987. — vii,418p. — *Translation of: L'institution imaginaire de la société. — Includes index*

JOES, Anthony James
From the barrel of a gun : armies and revolutions / Anthony J. Joes. — Washington, D.C. : Pergamon-Brassey's, 1986. — p. cm. — *Includes index. — Bibliography: p*

LENIN, V. I.
The state and revolution : the Marxist theory of the State and the tasks of the proletariat in the revolution / V. I. Lenin. — Moscow : Progress Publishers, 1949. — 139p

YACK, Bernard
The longing for total revolution : philosophic sources of social discontent from Rousseau to Marx and Nietzsche / Bernard Yack. — Princeton, N.J. : Princeton University Press, c1986. — xvii, 390 p.. — (Studies in moral, political, and legal philosophy). — *Includes index. — Bibliography: p. 370-385*

REVOLUTIONS — Cross-cultural studies — Congresses
Inequality and contemporary revolutions / Manus I. Midlarsky, editor. — Denver, Colo. : Graduate School of International Studies, University of Denver, c1986. — p. cm. — (Monograph series in world affairs ; v. 22, bk. 2). — *Includes bibliographies*

REVOLUTIONS — History
Revolution in history / edited by Roy Porter and Mikuláš Teich. — Cambridge : Cambridge University Press, 1986. — [vii,567]p. — *Includes index*

REVOLUTIONS — History — 20th century
Superpowers and revolution / edited by Jonathan R. Adelman. — New York : Praeger, 1986. — p. cm

REVOLUTIONS — Religious aspects — Christianity
ZWERLING, Philip
Nicaragua : a new kind of revolution / Philip Zwerling & Connie Martin. — Westport, Conn. : L. Hill, 1985. — xii, 251p

REVOLUTIONS — Europe — History
MULLETT, Michael A.
Popular culture and popular protest in late medieval and early modern Europe / Michael Mullett. — London : Croom Helm, c1987. — [9],176p. — *Bibliography: p170-171. — Includes index*

ZAGORIN, Perez
Revueltas y revoluciones en la Edad Moderna / Perez Zagorin. — Madrid : Catedra
1: Movimientos campesinos y urbanos. — 1985. — 325p

REVOLUTIONS — Latin America
BLAISIER, Cole
The hovering giant : U.S. responses to revolutionary change in Latin America / Cole Blasier. — Rev. ed. — Pittsburgh, Pa. : University of Pittsburgh Press, 1985. — xxi, 339 p.. — (Pitt Latin American series). — *Includes index. — Bibliography: p. 307-334*

DI TELLA, Torcuato S.
Sociología de los procesos políticos : una perspectiva latinoamericana / Torcuato S. Di Tella. — [Buenos Aires] : Grupo Editor Latinoamericano, 1985. — 428p. — (Colección estudios políticos y sociales ; volumen 2). — *Bibliography: p[423-428]*

New social movements and the state in Latin America / David Slater (ed.). — [Amsterdam] : CEDLA ; Cinnaminson, N.J., U.S.A. : Distributed by FORIS Publications USA, c1985. — 295 p.. — (Latin American studies ; 29). — *Papers from a CEDLA workshop held in Oct. 1983. — Includes bibliographies. — Contents: Social movements and a recasting of the political / D. Slater -- New social movements and the plurality of the social / E. Laclau -- Identity / T. Evers -- The pathways to encounter / L. Kowarick -- Base communities and urban social movements / N. Vink -- Urban social movements in Latin America / E. Henry -- The Peruvian state and regional crises / D. Slater -- The impact of sendero luminoso on regional and national politics in Peru / V. Gianotten ... [et al.] -- Social movements and revolution / J.L. Coraggio / Mobilisation without emancipation? / M. Molyneux -- Popular movement to "mass organization" / R. Reddock*

REVOLUTIONS — Mexico — History
TUTINO, John
From insurrection to revolution in Mexico : social bases of agrarian violence, 1750-1940 / John Tutino. — Princeton, N.J. : Princeton University Press, c1986. — xx, 425 p.. — *Includes index. — Bibliography: p. [399]-417*

REVOLUTIONS — Spain — History
BARCO TERUEL, Enrique
El "golpe" socialista del 6 de Octubre de 1934 / Enrique Barco Teruel. — Madrid : Dyrsa, 1984. — 361p

La revolución burguesa en España : actas del Coloquio hispano-alemán celebrado en Leipzig los dias 17 y 18 de noviembre de 1983 / edición e introducción de Alberto Gil Novales. — Madrid : Universidad Complutense, 1985. — 291p

ROSAL, Amaro del
1934 : Movimiento Revolucionario de Octubre / Amaro del Rosal. — [Madrid] : Akal, c1984. — xiii,313p. — (España sin espejo ; 1). — *Bibliography: p313*

REVOLUTIONS — Spain — Jaca
AZPÍROZ PASCUAL, José María
La sublevación de Jaca / José Maria Aspíroz Pascual, Fernando Elboj Broto. — Zaragoza : Guara, 1984. — 180p. — (Colección básica aragonesa ; 43). — *Bibliography: p[170]-174*

REYKJAVIK SUMMIT (1986)
GORBACHEV, M. S.
Speech given by the General Secretary of the Central Committee of the Communist Party of the Soviet Union (CPSU), M. S. Gorbachev, on Soviet television [following the Reykjavik Summit]. — New York : United Nations, 1986. — *Distributed by the Secretary General of the U.N. as an official document of the General Assembly and Security Council at the request of the Deputy Head of the U.S.S.R. delegation to the Forty First session of the General Assembly*

REYKJAVIK SUMMIT MEETING (1986 : Reykjavik)
GORBACHEV, M. S.
The results and lessons of Reykjavik : summit meeting in the Icelandic capital October 11-12, 1986 / Mikhail Gorbachev. — Moscow : Novosti Press Agency Publishing House, 1986. — 42p

RHETORIC
ANTCZAK, Frederick J.
Thought and character : the rhetoric of democratic education / Frederick J. Antczak. — 1st ed. — Ames : Iowa State University Press, 1985. — viii, 242 p.. — *Includes index. — Bibliography: p. 229-235*

WHITE, James Boyd
Heracles' bow : essays on the rhetoric and poetics of law / by James Boyd White. — Madison, Wis. : University of Wisconsin Press, 1985. — p. cm. — (Rhetoric of the human sciences). — *Includes index*

RHETORIC — Political aspects — United States
HAMMERBACK, John C
A war of words : Chicano protest in the 1960s and 1970s / John C. Hammerback, Richard J. Jensen, and Jose Angel Gutierrez. — Westport, Conn. ; London : Greenwood Press, 1985. — x, 187p. — (Contributions in ethnic studies ; no. 12). — *Includes index. — Bibliography: p.[173]-178*

RHINELAND (GERMANY) — History
KÖHLER, Henning
Adenauer und die rheinische Republik : der erste Anlauf 1918-1924 / Henning Köhler. — Opladen : Westdeutscher Verlag, 1986. — 287p . — *Bibliography: p281-284*

RHINELAND (GERMANY) — History — 20th century — Bibliography
IMPERIAL WAR MUSEUM. Library
The occupation of the Rhineland 1918-1930. — [London : the library, 1975]. — 4p. — (Booklist / Imperial War Museum ; no.1055)

RHINELAND (GERMANY) — Politics and government — History
KÖHLER, Henning
Adenauer und die rheinische Republik : der erste Anlauf 1918-1924 / Henning Köhler. — Opladen : Westdeutscher Verlag, 1986. — 287p . — *Bibliography: p281-284*

RHODESIA — Description and travel
KEANE, A. H.
The gold of Ophir : whence brought and by whom? / by A.H.Keane. — New York : Negro Universities Press, 1969. — xviii,244p. — *Originally published in 1901*

RHODESIA — Politics and government
HOWMAN, H. R. G.
H.R.G. Howman on provincialisation in Rhodesia, 1968-1969 : and rational and irrational elements / edited by G.C. Passmore. — Cambridge : African Studies Centre, [1986]. — xxvii,65p. — (Cambridge African occasional papers ; 4)

RHODESIA, SOUTHERN — History — 1965-
WINDRICH, Elaine
Britain and the politics of Rhodesian independence / Elaine Windrich. — London : Croom Helm, 1978. — 283p. — *Includes index*

RHODESIA, SOUTHERN — Politics and government — 1966-
WINDRICH, Elaine
Britain and the politics of Rhodesian independence / Elaine Windrich. — London : Croom Helm, 1978. — 283p. — *Includes index*

RHÔNE-ALPES (FRANCE) — Industries — Statistics
ROBERT, Jacqueline
1977 à 1982 : données sur l'industrie régionale / Jacqueline Robert. — Lyon : INSEE, 1985. — 143p. — (Les dossiers de l'INSEE Rhône-Alpes ; no.24)

RIBBON INDUSTRY — Switzerland — Basel — History
FINK, Paul
Vom Passementerhandwerk zur Bandindustrie : ein Beitrag zur Geschichte des alten Basel / Paul Fink ; herausgegeben von der Gesellschaft für das Gute und Gemeinnützige. — Basel : in Kommission bei Helbing & Lichtenhahn, 1979. — 101p. — *Bibliography: p100-101*

RICARDO, DAVID
David Ricardo : critical assessments / edited by John Cunningham Wood. — London : Croom Helm, c1985. — 4v. — (Croom Helm critical assessments of leading economists). — *In slipcase*

MARCUZZO, Maria Cristina
La teoria del gold standard : Ricardo e il suo tempo / Maria Cristina Marcuzzo, Annalisa Rosselli. — Bologna : Il Mulino, 1986. — 266p . — *Bibliography: p245-255*

RICE — Taiwan — Linear programming
HSIEH, S. C.
Application of linear programming to crop competition study in Taiwan (with special reference to rice and sugarcane competition in central Taiwan) / by S. C. Hsieh. — Taipei : Chinese-American Joint Commission on Rural Reconstruction, 1957. — [iv],95p. — (Economic digest series / Joint Commission on Rural Reconstruction ; no.10)

RICE — Taiwan — Marketing
YEH, S. M.
Rice marketing in Taiwan / by S. M. Yeh. — Taipei : Chinese-American Joint Commission on Rural Reconstruction, 1955. — [iv],18p. — (Economic digest series / Joint Commission on Rural Reconstruction ; no.7)

RICE TRADE — Asia, Southeastern
BRAY, Francesca
The rice economies : technology and development in Asian societies / Francesca Bray. — Oxford : Basil Blackwell, 1986. — 1v. . — *Includes bibliography and index*

RICE TRADE — East Asia
BRAY, Francesca
The rice economies : technology and development in Asian societies / Francesca Bray. — Oxford : Basil Blackwell, 1986. — 1v. . — *Includes bibliography and index*

RICE TRADE — Georgia — History
SMITH, Julia Floyd
Slavery and rice culture in low country Georgia, 1750-1860 / Julia Floyd Smith. — Knoxville : University of Tennessee Press, c1985. — p. cm. — *Includes index.* — *Bibliography: p*

RICE TRADE — Ghana
KONINGS, Piet
The State and rural class formation in Ghana : a comparative analysis / Piet Konings. — London : KPI, 1986. — xvi,391p. — *Bibliography: p356-377*

RICHMOND, Sir HERBERT
HUNT, Barry D.
Sailor-scholar : Admiral Sir Herbert Richmond 1871-1946 / Barry D. Hunt. — Waterloo, Ont. : Wilfred Laurier University Press ; Gerrards Cross : distributed by Smythe, c1982. — xii,259p. — *Bibliography: p238-248.* — *Includes index*

RICKETS — Prevention
GREAT BRITAIN. Working Party on Fortification of Food with Vitamin D
Rickets and osteomalacia / report of the Working Party on Fortification of Food with Vitamin D. Committee on Medical Aspects of Food Policy. — London : H.M.S.O., 1980. — xii,66p. — (Report on health and social subjects ; 19). — *At head of title: Department of Health and Social Security.* — *Bibliography: p54-66*

RIEBEN, HENRI
RIEBEN, Henri
Une lettre / Henri Rieben. — Lausanne : Fondation Jean Monnet pour l'Europe. Centre de Recherches Européennes, 1986. — 33p

RIEL, LOUIS
RIEL, Louis
[[Works]]. The collected writings of Louis Riel = Les ecrits complets de Louis Riel / Louis Riel ; general editor George F. G. Stanley. — Edmonton : University of Alberta Press. — *Text in English and French*
Vol.1: 29 December 1861 - 7 December 1875 / editor Raymond Huel. — 1985. — 546p. — *Bibliography and index in Vol.5*

RIEL, Louis
[[Works]]. The collected writings of Louis Riel = Les ecrits complets de Louis Riel / Louis Riel ; general editor George F. G. Stanley. — Edmonton : University of Alberta Press. — *Text in English and French*
Vol.2: 8 December 1875 - 4 June 1884 / editor Gilles Martel. — 1985. — 482p. — *Bibliography and index in Vol.5*

RIEL, Louis
[[Works]]. The collected writings of Louis Riel = Les ecrits complets de Louis Riel / Louis Riel ; general editor George F. G. Stanley. — Edmonton : University of Alberta Press. — *Text in English and French*
Vol.3: 5 June 1884 - 16November 1885 / editor Thomas Flanagan. — Edmonton : University of Alberta Press. — 637p. — *Text in English and French*

RIEL, Louis
[[Works]]. The collected writings of Louis Riel = Les ecrits complets de Louis Riel / Louis Riel ; general editor George F. G. Stanley. — Edmonton : University of Alberta Press. — *Text in English and French*
Vol.4: Poetry / editor Glen Campbell. — 1985. — 544p. — *Bibliography and index in Vol.5*

RIEL, Louis
[[Works]]. The collected writings of Louis Riel = Les ecrits complets de Louis Riel / Louis Riel ; general editor George F. G. Stanley. — Edmonton : University of Alberta Press. — *Text in English and French*
Vol.5: Reference / editors George F. G. Stanley, Thomas Flanagan, Claude Rocan. — 1985. — 360p. — *Contains bibliography, p131-205 and biographical index, p207-360*

SAINT-AUBIN, Bernard
Louis Riel : un destin tragique / Bernard Saint-Aubin. — Montréal : La Presse, 1985. — 313p

RIEL REBELLION — Collected works
RIEL, Louis
[[Works]]. The collected writings of Louis Riel = Les ecrits complets de Louis Riel / Louis Riel ; general editor George F. G. Stanley. — Edmonton : University of Alberta Press. — *Text in English and French*
Vol.2: 8 December 1875 - 4 June 1884 / editor Gilles Martel. — 1985. — 482p. — *Bibliography and index in Vol.5*

RIEL REBELLION, 1885
MCLEAN, Donald George
1885, Metis rebellion or government conspiracy? / Don McLean. — Winnipeg, Man., Canada : Pemmican Publications, c1985. — 137 p.. — *Bibliography: p. 125-127*

SAINT-AUBIN, Bernard
Louis Riel : un destin tragique / Bernard Saint-Aubin. — Montréal : La Presse, 1985. — 313p

RIEL REBELLION 1885 — Collected works
RIEL, Louis
[[Works]]. The collected writings of Louis Riel = Les ecrits complets de Louis Riel / Louis Riel ; general editor George F. G. Stanley. — Edmonton : University of Alberta Press. — *Text in English and French*
Vol.1: 29 December 1861 - 7 December 1875 / editor Raymond Huel. — 1985. — 546p. — *Bibliography and index in Vol.5*

RIEL, Louis
[[Works]]. The collected writings of Louis Riel = Les ecrits complets de Louis Riel / Louis Riel ; general editor George F. G. Stanley. — Edmonton : University of Alberta Press. — *Text in English and French*
Vol.3: 5 June 1884 - 16November 1885 / editor Thomas Flanagan. — Edmonton : University of Alberta Press. — 637p. — *Text in English and French*

RIEL, Louis
[[Works]]. The collected writings of Louis Riel = Les ecrits complets de Louis Riel / Louis Riel ; general editor George F. G. Stanley. — Edmonton : University of Alberta Press. — *Text in English and French*
Vol.4: Poetry / editor Glen Campbell. — 1985. — 544p. — *Bibliography and index in Vol.5*

RIEL, Louis
[[Works]]. The collected writings of Louis Riel = Les ecrits complets de Louis Riel / Louis Riel ; general editor George F. G. Stanley. — Edmonton : University of Alberta Press. — *Text in English and French*
Vol.5: Reference / editors George F. G. Stanley, Thomas Flanagan, Claude Rocan. — 1985. — 360p. — *Contains bibliography, p131-205 and biographical index, p207-360*

RIGHT AND LEFT (PHILOSOPHY)
MOULIN, Léo
La Gauche, la Droite et le péché originel et autres essais / Léo Moulin ; préface d'Alain Lancelot. — Paris : Librairie des Méridiens, 1984. — 234p. — *Includes bibliographic notes*

RIGHT AND LEFT (POLITICAL SCIENCE)
ANNE FRANK FOUNDATION
International seminar on the extreme right in Europe and the United States, 16,17 and 18 November, 1984 / Editor: Vera Ebels-Dolanová. — Amsterdam : Anne Frank Stichting, 1985. — vi,132p. — *Cover title: The extreme right in Europe and the United States*

BOURRICAUD, François
Le retour de la droite / François Bourricaud. — Paris : Calmann-Lévy, 1986. — 323p

DUDEK, Peter
Entstehung und Entwicklung des Rechtsextremismus in der Bundesrepublik : zur Tradition einer besonderen politischen Kultur / Peter Dudek, Hans-Gerd Jaschke. — Opladen : Westdeutscher Verlag. — *Bibliography: p [488]-496*
Bd.1. — 1984. — 507p

RIGHT AND LEFT (POLITICAL SCIENCE) *continuation*

DUDEK, Peter
Jugendliche Rechtsextremisten : zwischen Hakenkreuz und Odalsrune 1945 bis heute / Peter Dudek. — Köln : Bund-Verlag, 1985. — 243p. — *Bibliography: p237-240*

EDGAR, David
The new right and the church / David Edgar, Kenneth Leech and Paul Weller. — London : Jubilee Group, 1985-. — 58p. — *Bibliographies*

Extremismus und streitbare Demokratie mit Beiträgen von Uwe Backes und Eckhard Jesse / herausgegeben von Wolfgang Michalka. — Stuttgart : Franz Steiner, 1987. — 128p. — (Neue politische Literatur. Beihefte Forschungsberichte zur internationalen Literatur ; 4)

FÉHÉR, Ferenc
Eastern left, Western left : totalitarianism, freedom and democracy / Ferenc Féhér and Agnes Heller. — Cambridge : Polity, 1987, c1986. — 287p. — *Includes index*

GORDON, Paul
New right, new racism / Paul Gordon and Francesca Klug ; preface by David Edgar. — London : Searchlight, 1986. — 69p. — *Bibliography: p69*

GRAHAM, David, 19---
The new enlightenment : the rebirth of liberalism / David Graham and Peter Clarke. — London : Macmillan in association with Channel Four Television Co., 1986. — xii,180p . — *Bibliography: p173-174. — Includes index*

HARTMANN, Ulrich
Rechtsextremismus bei Jugendlichen : Anregungen, der wachsenden Gefahr entgegenzuwirken / Ulrich Hartmann, Hans-Peter und Sigrid Steffen. — München : Kösel-Verlag, c1985. — 160p. — *Bibliography: p154-[160]*

HUHN, Anne
"Einst kommt der Tag der Rache" : die rechtsextreme Herausforderung 1945 bis heute / Anne Huhn; Alwin Meyer. — Freiburg : Dreisam-Verlag, 1986. — 229p

KOELSCHTZKY, Martina
Die Stimme ihrer Herren : Ideologie und Strategie der 'Neuen Rechten' in der Bundesrepublik / Martina Koelschtzky. — Köln : Pahl-Rugenstein, 1986. — 124p. — *Bibliography: p121-124*

The new right : image and reality / Gerald Cohen...[et al.] ; with an introduction by Nicholas Deakin. — London : Runnymede Trust, 1986. — 55p

The new right and Christian values [a one day seminar, Wednesday, 13 February 1985, Martin Hall, New College, The Mound, Edinburgh]. — Edinburgh : University of Edinburgh. Department of Christian Ethics and Practical Theology, 1985. — [48]p. — (Occasional paper / Edinburgh University. Centre for Theology and Public Issues ; no.5)

OELEK, Sambal
Die Linke in den Wechseljahren : Gedankensplitter im Theorievakuum / Sambal Oelek. — Zürich : Rotpunktverlag, 1985. — 174p. — *Bibliography: p170-171, 174*

READER, Keith
Intellectuals and the Left in France since 1968 / Keith A. Reader. — Basingstoke : Macmillan, 1987. — xii,154p. — *Bibliography: p148-150. — Includes index*

WINEMAN, Steven
The politics of human services : radical alternatives to the welfare state / by Steven Wineman. — 1st ed. — Boston, MA : South End Press, c1984. — iv, 272 p.. — *Bibliography: p. 249-272*

RIGHT AND LEFT (POLITICAL SCIENCE) — Documentation — Germany (West)

DUDEK, Peter
Entstehung und Entwicklung des Rechtsextremismus in der Bundesrepublik : zur Tradition einer besonderen politischen Kultur / Peter Dudek, Hans-Gerd Jaschke. — Opladen : Westdeutscher Verlag
Bd.2: Dokumente und Materialien. — 1984. — 374p

RIGHT AND LEFT (POLITICAL SCIENCE) — Periodicals — Bibliography

SKIDMORE, Gail
From radical left to extreme right : a bibliography of current periodicals of protest, controversy, advocacy, or dissent, with dispassionate content-summaries to guide librarians and other educators. — 3rd ed., completely rev. / by Gail Skidmore and Theodore Jurgen Spahn. — Metuchen, N.J. : Scarecrow Press, 1987. — p. cm. — *Rev. ed. of: From radical left to extreme right. 2nd ed. / by Robert H. Muller, Theodore Jurgen Spahn, and Janet M. Spahn. 1970-1976. — Includes indexes*

RIGHT OF PROPERTY

PAUL, Ellen Frankel
Property rights and eminent domain / Ellen Frankel Paul. — New Brunswick, U.S.A. : Transaction Books, 1987. — 276 p.. — ([Social & moral thought series]). — *Series statement from jacket. — Includes bibliographies and indexes*

RIGHT OF PROPERTY — United States

PAUL, Ellen Frankel
Property rights and eminent domain / Ellen Frankel Paul. — New Brunswick, U.S.A. : Transaction Books, 1987. — 276 p.. — ([Social & moral thought series]). — *Series statement from jacket. — Includes bibliographies and indexes*

RIGHT TO COUNSEL — United States

CORTNER, Richard C
A "Scottsboro" case in Mississippi : the Supreme Court and Brown v. Mississippi / by Richard C. Cortner. — Jackson : University of Mississippi, c1986. — xiii, 174 p..— *Includes index. — Bibliography: p. 170*

RIGHT TO DIE

Voluntary euthanasia : experts debate the right to die / edited by A.B. Downing and Barbara Smoker. — Rev., enl. ed. — London : Peter Owen, c1986. — 303p. — *Originally published as: Euthanasia and the right to death:the case for voluntary euthanasia, 1969. — Bibliography:p302-303*

RIGHT TO DIE — Law and legislation — United States

CANTOR, Norman L
Legal frontiers of death and dying / by Norman L. Cantor. — Bloomington : Indiana University Press, c1987. — p. cm. — (Medical ethics series). — *Includes index*

RIGHT TO LABOR — France

LE GOFF, Jacques
Du silence à la parole : droit du travail, société, état, 1830-1985 / Jacques Le Goff ; préface de Marcel David ; postface d'Edmond Maire. — Quimperlé : Calligrammes, [1985]. — 374p

RIGHT TO LIFE PARTY

SPITZER, Robert J.
The Right to Life movement and third party politics / Robert J. Spitzer. — New York : Greenwood Press, c1987. — xii, 154 p.. — (Contributions in political science ; no. 160). — *Includes index. — Bibliography: p. [141]-148*

RIGHTS (PHILOSOPHY)

SHAPIRO, Ian
The evolution of rights in liberal theory / Ian Shapiro. — Cambridge : Cambridge University Press, 1986. — x,326p. — *Bibliography: p307-320. — Includes index*

RIMATARA (AUSTRAL ISLANDS) — Population — Statistics

Tableaux normalisés du recensement général de la population : 15 octobre 1983. — [Papeete] : Institut territorial de la statistique Résultats de la commune de Rimatara. — [1985?]. — 4p,11 leaves

RIO DE LA PLATA REGION (ARGENTINA AND URUGUAY — History

SABSAY, Fernando Leónidas
La sociedad argentina : España y el Rió de la Plata / Fernando L. Sabsay. — Buenos Aires : Ediciones Macchi, [1984]. — 288p. — (Colección Ciencas Economicas). — *Bibliography: p[287]-288*

RIO TINTO COMPANY — History — 19th century

FLORES CABALLERO, Manuel
Rio Tinto : la fiebre minera del XIX / Manuel Flores Caballero. — Huelva : Instituto de Estudios Onubenses "Padre Marchena" : Excma, Diputación Provincial, 1983. — 218p. — *Bibliography: p211-218*

RIOTS

RUDÉ, George
Paris and London in the eighteenth century : studies in popular protest / by George Rudé. — London : Collins, 1970. — 350p. — (Fontana history)

RIOTS — Colombia — Bogotá

BRAUN, Herbert
The assassination of Gaitán : public life and urban violence in Colombia / Herbert Braun. — Madison, Wis. : University of Wisconsin Press, 1985. — xiii, 282p. — *Includes index. — Bibliography: p.257-271*

RIOTS — England

BOWERY, Julian
The 1985 'riots' : 1981 revisited? / Julian Bowery. — [London] : Bartlett School of Architecture and Planning, 1986. — 42p. — (Town planning discussion paper ; no.47)

RIOTS — Great Britain

PRISON REFORM TRUST
The riots of '86 : evidence presented to H.M. Chief Inspector of Prisons. — London : Prison Reform Trust, 1986. — 22p

SCARMAN, Leslie George Scarman, Baron
The Brixton disorders 10-12 April 1981 : report of an enquiry / by Lord Scarman. — London : H.M.S.O., 1981. — viii,168p. — (Cmnd. ; 8427). — *At head of title: Home Office Police Act 1964. — Map on folded sheet attached to inside cover. — Bibliography: p164-168*

RIOTS — Great Britain — Bibliography

Urban riots and public order : a select bibliography, 1975-1985 / compiled by: E. Edwards, R. Golland & S. Leach [for the GLC Intelligence Unit]. — [S.l. : s.n. : Technical Communications [distributor], 1986. — iii,159p

RIOTS — Great Britain — Information Services

Urban riots and public order : a select bibliography, 1975-1985 / compiled by: E. Edwards, R. Golland & S. Leach [for the GLC Intelligence Unit]. — [S.l. : s.n. : Technical Communications [distributor], 1986. — iii,159p

RIOTS — Peru — History — 20th century

VELASCO ALVARADO, Juan
Mansaje a la nación ... con motivo de los incidentes ocurridos en Lima los días 05 y 06 de febrero / Juan Velasco Alvarado. — Lima : [Secretaría de Prensa, Presidencia de la República], 1975. — 14p

RISK

HANER, F. T
Country risk assessment : theory and worldwide practice / F.T. Haner and John S. Ewing. — New York : Praeger, 1985. — p. cm . — *Includes index. — Bibliography: p*

RISK *continuation*

HEFFERNAN, Shelagh A.
Sovereign risk analysis / Shelagh A. Heffernan. — London : Allen & Unwin, 1986. — [200]p. — Includes index

HEY, John D.
Uncertainty in microeconomics / John D. Hey. — Oxford : Martin Robertson, 1979. — ix,261p. — Bibliography: p.243-253. — Includes index

KRAYENBUEHL, Thomas E.
Country risk : assessment and monitoring / Thomas E. Krayenbuehl. — Cambridge : Woodhead-Faulkner, 1985. — x,180p. — Bibliography: p169. — Includes index

MARPLES, David R.
Chernobyl and nuclear power in the USSR / David R. Marples. — Basingstoke : Macmillan in association with Canadian Institute of Ukrainian Studies, University of Alberta, 1987, c1986. — xii,228p. — Originally published: New York : St. Martin's in association with Canadian Institute of Ukrainian Studies, University of Alberta, 1986. — Bibliography: p197-201. — Includes index

MORONE, Joseph G
Averting catastrophe : strategies for regulating risky technologies / Joseph G. Morone and Edward J. Woodhouse. — Berkeley : University of California Press, 1985, c1986. — p. cm. — Includes index. — Bibliography: p

RUBINSTEIN, Ariel
Similarity and decision-making under risk (is there a utility theory resolution to the Allais paradox?) / Ariel Rubinstein. — London : Suntory Toyota International Centre for Economics and Related Disciplines, 1987. — 15p. — (Theoretical economics ; 87/162). — Bibliography: p15

SHRADER-FRECHETTE, K. S.
Risk analysis and scientific method : methodological and ethical problems with evaluating societal hazards / K.S. Shrader-Frechette. — Dordrecht ; Boston : D. Reidel ; Hingham, MA, U.S.A. : Sold and distributed in the U.S.A. and Canada by Kluwer Academic Publishers, c1985. — x, 232 p.. — Includes indexes. — Bibliography: p. 217-226

RISK — Congresses

Hazards : technology and fairness / National Academy of Engineering. — Washington, D.C. : National Academy Press, 1986. — viii, 225 p.. — (Series on technology and social priorities). — Consists of papers based on the Symposium on Hazards: Technology and Fairness, held June 3-4, 1985. — Includes bibliographies and index

RISK — Mathematical models

LEAPE, Jonathan
Taxes and transaction costs in asset market equilibrium / Jonathan Leape. — Rev. ed. — [London : London School of Economics and Political Science], 1986. — 34p. — (Taxation, incentives and the distribution of income ; no.97). — Economic and Social Research Council programme. — Bibliographical references: p33-34

RISK (INSURANCE) — Congresses

GENEVA CONFERENCE ON THE VALUE OF LIFE AND SAFETY (1981)
The value of life and safety : proceedings of a conference held by the "Geneva Association" : collection of papers presented at the Geneva Conference on the Value of Life and Safety held at the University of Geneva, 30th, 31st March and 1st April 1981 / edited by M.W. Jones-Lee. — Amsterdam ; New York : North-Holland Pub. Co. ; New York, N.Y. : Sole distributors for the U.S.A. and Canada, Elsevier Science Pub. Co., 1982. — xvii, 309 p.. — Bibliography: p. xi

RISK (INSURANCE) — United States

ABRAHAM, Kenneth S.
Distributing risk : insurance, legal theory, and public policy / Kenneth S. Abraham. — New Haven : Yale University Press, c1986. — p. cm . — Includes index. — Bibliography: p

RISK MANAGEMENT

MACCRIMMON, Kenneth R
Taking risks : the management of uncertainty / Kenneth R. MacCrimmon and Donald A. Wehrung with William T. Stanbury. — New York : Free Press ; London : Collier Macmillan Publishers, c1985. — xv, 380p. — Includes index. — Bibliography: p.342-359

RISK PERCEPTION — Social aspects

DOUGLAS, Mary
Risk acceptability according to the social sciences / Mary Douglas. — London : Routledge & Kegan Paul, 1986, c 1985. — [115]p. — Originally published: New York : Russell Sage Foundation, 1985. — Includes bibliography

Risk and society : studies of risk generation and reactions to risk / edited by Lennart Sjöberg. — London : Allen & Unwin, 1987. — xvii,246p. — (The Risks & hazards series ; 3). — Includes bibliographies index

RITCHIE

RITCHIE, Charles
Diplomatic passport : more undiplomatic diaries, 1946-1962 / Charles Rtichie. — Toronto : Macmillan of Canada, 1986. — 200p. — (Macmillan paperbacks ; 12)

RITES AND CEREMONIES

FERNANDEZ, James W
Persuasions and performances : the play of tropes in culture / James W. Fernandez. — Bloomington : Indiana University Press, c1986. — xv, 304 p.. — Includes bibliographies and index

RITES AND CEREMONIES — Addresses, essays, lectures

RAPPAPORT, Roy A
Ecology, meaning, and religion / Roy A. Rappaport. — Richmond, Calif. : North Atlantic Books, c1979. — xi, 259 p.. — Includes bibliographical references and index

RITES AND CEREMONIES — Congresses

Women in ritual and symbolic roles / edited by Judith Hoch-Smith and Anita Spring. — New York ; London : Plenum Press, 1978. — xv,289p. — 'This volume of essays grew out of a symposium organized ... for the 1974 American Anthropological Association meetings in Mexico City' - Preface. — Includes bibliographies and index

RITES AND CEREMONIES — Hawaii

VALERI, Valerio
Kingship and sacrifice : ritual and society in ancient Hawaii / Valerio Valeri ; translated by Paula Wissing. — Chicago : University of Chicago Press, 1985. — p. cm. — Translated from the French. — Includes index. — Bibliography: p

RITES AND CEREMONIES — New Guinea

RUBEL, Paula G
Your own pigs you may not eat : a comparative study of New Guinea societies / Paula G. Rubel, Abraham Rosman. — Chicago : University of Chicago Press, 1978. — xiv, 368 p.. — Includes index. — Bibliography: p. 347-359

RIVAS, ANA MARÍA CASTILLO See Castillo Rivas, Ana María

RIVERS — Great Britain

GREAT BRITAIN. Department of the Environment
The National Rivers Authority : the government's proposals for a public regulatory body in a privatised water industry. — [London : the Department], 1987. — 42p

R.J. REYNOLDS INDUSTRIES — History

TILLEY, Nannie May
The R.J. Reynolds Tobacco Company / by Nannie May Tilley. — Chapel Hill : University of North Carolina Press, c1985. — p. cm. — Includes index

ROAD CONSTRUCTION — Government policy — Great Britain

GREAT BRITAIN. Department of Transport
Future organisation for road construction : a discussion paper. — [London] : the Department, 1978. — 6leaves

HAMER, Mick
Wheels within wheels : a study of the road lobby / Mick Hamer. — London : Routledge & Kegan Paul, 1987. — [192]p. — (Geography, environment and planning). — Includes index

ROAD CONSTRUCTION — Great Britain — Bibliography

WEBB, Sidney
Bibliography of road making and maintenance in Great Britain / by Sidney and Beatrice Webb. — London : Roads Improvement Association, 1906. — 35p

ROAD METERS — Calibration

SAYERS, Michael W.
Guidelines for conducting and calibrating road roughness measurements / Michael W. Sayers, Thomas D. Gillespie, and William D. O. Paterson. — Washington, D.C. : The World Bank, 1986. — vi,87p. — (World Bank technical paper ; no.46). — Bibliographical references: p87

ROADS — Riding qualities — Measurement

SAYERS, Michael W.
The international road roughness experiment : establishing correlation and a calibration standard for measurements / Michael W. Sayers, Thomas D. Gillespie, and Caesar A. V. Queiroz. — Washington, D.C. : The World Bank, 1986. — ix,453p. — (World Bank technical paper ; no.45). — Bibliographical references: p105-107

ROADS — Riding qualities — Testing

SAYERS, Michael W.
Guidelines for conducting and calibrating road roughness measurements / Michael W. Sayers, Thomas D. Gillespie, and William D. O. Paterson. — Washington, D.C. : The World Bank, 1986. — vi,87p. — (World Bank technical paper ; no.46). — Bibliographical references: p87

ROADS — England — Surrey

SURREY. County Council
Policy for the control of development associated with the national strategic road network in Surrey. — Kingston-upon-Thames : [the Council], 1983. — 13p. — Cover title: The control of development associated with the national strategic road network in Surrey

ROADS — Great Britain

ASSOCIATION OF COUNTY COUNCILS
The future of the trunk road system / Association of County Councils, Association of Metropolitan Authorities. — London : National Economic Development Office, [1984]. — [6]p. — (Discussion paper / Civil Engineering EDC ; 3)

GREAT BRITAIN
Public utilities street works : the government response to the Horne report on the review of the Public Utilities Street Works Act 1950. — London : H.M.S.O., 1986. — 32p. — At head of title page: Department of Transport

GREAT BRITAIN. Department of Transport
Roads in urban areas : supplement, a guide to revisions, 1979. — London : H.M.S.O., 1980. — [2]p

ROADS — Great Britain
continuation
GREAT BRITAIN. Standing Advisory Committee on Trunk Road Assessment
Urban road appraisal / Chairman: T. E. H. Williams. — London : H.M.S.O., 1986. — 200p. — *At head of title page: Department of Transport.* — *Bibliographical references: p181-183*

ROADS — Great Britain — Maintenance and Repair — Bibliography
WEBB, Sidney
Bibliography of road making and maintenance in Great Britain / by Sidney and Beatrice Webb. — London : Roads Improvement Association, 1906. — 35p

ROADS — Great Britain — Management
AUDIT COMMISSION FOR LOCAL AUTHORITIES IN ENGLAND AND WALES
Improving highways agency arrangements between counties and districts : an interim report. — London : H.M.S.O., 1987. — 80p

ROADS — Great Britain — Safety measures — Congresses
Roads to safety : a Conference on Road Safety, 13-14 June 1978, London, Department of Transport. — [London : Department of Transport, 1978]. — 48p

ROADS — Scotland — Fife — History
SILVER, Owen
The roads of Fife / Owen Silver. — Edinburgh : John Donald, 1987. — ix,197p. — (Scottish history and culture). — *Bibliography: p180-183*

ROADS — Spain — History
MADRAZO, Santos
El sistema de comunicaciones en España, 1750-1850 / Santos Madrazo. — [Madrid] : Colegio de Ingenieros de Caminos, Canales y Puertos : Ediciones Turner
7: [La red viaria]. — c1984. — 376p. — *Number on spine: 20*

ROBARTS, JOHN P.
MCDOUGALL, A. K.
John P. Robarts : his life and government / A.K. McDougall. — Toronto ; London : University of Toronto Press, c1986. — xiii,320,[17]p of plates. — (Ontario historical studies series). — *Bibliography: p299-305.* — *Includes index*

ROBBERY — England
BANTON, Michael
Investigating robbery / Michael Banton. — Aldershot : Gower, c1985. — [vii,126]p. — *Bibliography: p109-110.* — *Includes index*

ROBBERY — Great Britain
WALSH, Dermot
Heavy business : commercial burglary and robbery / Dermot Walsh. — London : Routledge & Kegan Paul, 1986. — xii,188p. — *Bibliography: p178-184.* — *Includes index*

ROBESPIERRE, MAXIMILIEN
JORDAN, David P.
The revolutionary career of Maximilien Robespierre / David P. Jordan. — New York : Free Press, c1985. — xii, 308p. — *Includes index.* — *Bibliography: p.299-304*

ROBOTICS — Great Britain — Industrial applications
NORTHCOTT, Jim
Robots in British industry : expectations and experience / Jim Northcott with Colin Brown...[et al.]. — London : Policy Studies Institute, 1986. — 215p. — (Research report / Policy Studies Institute ; no.660)

ROBOTS, INDUSTRIAL
ALEKSANDER, Igor
Decision and intelligence / Igor Aleksander, Henri Farreny and Malik Ghallab. — London : Kogan Page, c1987. — (Robot technology ; v.6). — *Bibliography: p193-200.* — *Includes index*
Vol.6: Decision autonomy and artificial intelligence. — 203p. — *Translation from the French*

Modelling and design of flexible manufacturing systems / edited by Andrew Kusiak. — Amsterdam : Elsevier, 1986. — ix,431p. — (Manufacturing research and technology ; 3)

NORTHCOTT, Jim
Robots in British industry : expectations and experience / Jim Northcott with Colin Brown...[et al.]. — London : Policy Studies Institute, 1986. — 215p. — (Research report / Policy Studies Institute ; no.660)

ROBSON, W. A., 1895-1980 — Bibliography
A bibliography of the writings of W. A. Robson / compiled by C. E. Hill ; preface by G. W. Jones. — London : London School of Economics and Political Science, 1986. — 81p. — (Greater London Papers ; no.17)

ROBUST STATISTICS
Robust statistics : the approach based on influence functions / Frank R. Hampel ... [et al.]. — New York : Wiley, 1985. — xxi, 502p. — (Wiley series in probability and mathematical statistics. Probability and mathematical statistics). — *Includes index.* — *Bibliography: p.439-464*

ROCKETS (ORDNANCE) — Government policy — Germany (West)
OBERMEYER, Ute
Das Nein der SPD - eine nene Ära? : SPD und Raketen 1977-1983 / Ute Obermeyer ; mit einem Vorwort von Karl Heinz Hansen. — Marburg : Verlag Arbeiterbewegung und Gesellschaftswissenschaft, 1985. — 170p. — (Schriftenreihe der Studiengesellschaft für sozialgeschichte und Arbeiterbewegung ; Bd.45)

ROCKINGHAM WHIG FACTION
O'GORMAN, Frank
The rise of party in England : the Rockingham Whigs, 1760-82 / Frank O'Gorman. — London : Allen and Unwin, 1975. — 3-662p. — *Bibliography: p.483-494.* — *Includes index*

ROCKWELL, NORMAN
The Saturday evening post Norman Rockwell book. — New York : Bonanza Books : Distributed by Crown Publishers, 1986, c1977. — vii, 152 p.

ROLE CONFLICT
BERG, Barbara J
The crisis of the working mother : resolving the conflict between family and work / by Barbara Berg. — New York : Summit Books, c1986. — p. cm. — *Includes bibliographical references*

ROLFE (Family)
BERRY, Veronica
The Rolfe papers : the chronicle of a Norfolk family, 1559-1908 / by Veronica Berry. — Norwich : V. Berry, 1979. — xvi, 280 p., [36] p. of plates. — *Includes index.* — *Bibliography: p. 225-227*

ROLPH, C. H.
ROLPH, C. H.
Further particulars / C.H. Rolph. — Oxford : Oxford University Press, 1987. — [288]p. — *Includes index*

ROMANIA — Church History
PĂCURARIU, Mircea
Politica statului ungar față de Biserica românească din Transilvania în perioada dualismului (1867-1918) / Mircea Păcurariu. — Sibiu : Editura Institutului Biblic și de Misiune al Bisericii Ortodoxe Române, 1986. — 301p

ROMANIA — Commerce — Great Britain
CERNOVODEANU, Paul
Relațiile comerciale româno-engleze în contextul politicii orientale a Marii Britanii (1803-1878) / Paul Cernovodeanu. — Cluj-Napoca : Editura Dacia, 1986. — 402p. — *English summary*

ROMANIA — Economic conditions
SCHAFARIK BRUNNER, Wladimir
Rom'ania szerepe h'aborus gazdálkodásunkban / 'irta Schafarik Brunner Wladimir. — Budapest : Sylvester irodalmi 'es nyomdai intézet R.T., 1935. — 137p. — (Közgazdas'agi Könyut'ar ; Köt.9)

TURNOCK, David
The Romanian economy in the twentieth century / David Turnock. — London : Croom Helm, c1986. — 296p[3]p of plates. — (Croom Helm series on the contemporary economic history of Europe). — *Bibliography: p281-285.* — *Includes index*

ROMANIA — Foreign economic relations — Hungary
SCHAFARIK BRUNNER, Wladimir
Rom'ania szerepe h'aborus gazdálkodásunkban / 'irta Schafarik Brunner Wladimir. — Budapest : Sylvester irodalmi 'es nyomdai intézet R.T., 1935. — 137p. — (Közgazdas'agi Könyut'ar ; Köt.9)

ROMANIA — History
A Concise history of Romania / edited by Andrei Oțetea ; English edition edited by Andrew Mackenzie. — London : Hale, 1985. — 591p,[24]p of plates. — *Based on: The history of the Romanian people. Bucharest : Scientific Publishing House. 1970. — Translation of: Istoria poporului român.* — *Bibliography: p559-566.* — *Includes index*

VENTOLIERE, Michel de la
...rien que la vérité / Michel de la Ventoliere. — London : Panopticum Press, [1970]. — 12p. — (Les documents politiques panopticum)

ROMANIA — History — To 1711
STOICESCU, Nicolae
Age-old factors of Romanian unity / Nicolae Stoicescu. — București : Editura Academiei Republicii Socialiste România, 1986. — 224p

ROMANIA — Politics and government
Culegere de decizii ale Plenului si Colegiilor Tribunalului Suprem al RPR. — Bucuresti : Plenului si Colegiilor Tribunalului Suprem, 1952-1954. — *Annual.* — *Continued by Culegere de decizii ale Tribunalului Suprem*

Culegere de decizii ale Tribunalului. — Bucuresti : Plenului si Colegiilor Tribunalului Suprem, 1958-1982. — *Annual.* — *Continues Culegere de decizii ale Plenului si Colegiilor Tribunalului Suprem al RPR*

ROMANIA — Politics and government — 1914-1944
IANCU, Gheorghe
Contribuția consiliului dirigent la consolidarea statului național unitar român (1918-1920) / Gheorghe Iancu. — Cluj-Napoca : Editura Dacia, 1985. — 315p

ROMANIA — Politics and government — 1944-
MĂNUCEANU, Vasile
Șapte vaci slabe : articole citite la microfonul postului de Radio "Europa Liberă" (1982-1983) / Vasile Mănuceanu. — Århus : Nord, 1984. — 237p

PARTIDUL COMUNIST ROMÂN
Epoca Nicolae Ceaușescu : Partidul Comunist Român centrul vital al întregii națiuni : documente ale plenarelor Comitetului Central și ale Comitetului Politic Executiv al Comitetului Central al Partidului Comunist Român, 1965-1985. — București : Editura Politică, 1986. — 4vols. — *Vol.1: 1965-1973; Vol.2: 1974-1977; Vol.3: 1978-1981; Vol.4: 1982-1985*

ROMANIA — Relations — Hungary — History
PĂCURARIU, Mircea
Politica statului ungar față de Biserica românească din Transilvania în perioada dualismului (1867-1918) / Mircea Păcurariu. — Sibiu : Editura Institutului Biblic și de Misiune al Bisericii Ortodoxe Române, 1986. — 301p

ROMANIA. Consiliul Dirigent
IANCU, Gheorghe
Contribuția consiliului dirigent la consolidarea statului național unitar român (1918-1920) / Gheorghe Iancu. — Cluj-Napoca : Editura Dacia, 1985. — 315p

ROME — History
WILKINSON, L. P.
The Roman experience / L. P. Wilkinson. — Lanham, Md. ; London : University Press of America, [1982?]. — [xii],220p. — *Originally published: Random House, 1974. — Bibliography: p[203]-207*

ROME — History — Republic, 265-30 B.C.
COWELL, F. R.
Cicero and the Roman Republic. — London : Pitman, 1948. — xiv,306p

COWELL, F. R.
Cicero and the Roman Republic. — 3rd ed. — Harmondsworth : Penguin, 1964. — xvii,398p

ROME — History — Empire, 284-476
FERRILL, Arther
The fall of the Roman Empire : the military explanation / Arther Ferrill. — London : Thames and Hudson, c1986. — 192p. — *Bibliography: p.182-187*

ROME — History, Military
FERRILL, Arther
The fall of the Roman Empire : the military explanation / Arther Ferrill. — London : Thames and Hudson, c1986. — 192p. — *Bibliography: p.182-187*

ROME — Social conditions
WILKINSON, L. P.
The Roman experience / L. P. Wilkinson. — Lanham, Md. ; London : University Press of America, [1982?]. — [xii],220p. — *Originally published: Random House, 1974. — Bibliography: p[203]-207*

ROME — Social life and customs
WILKINSON, L. P.
The Roman experience / L. P. Wilkinson. — Lanham, Md. ; London : University Press of America, [1982?]. — [xii],220p. — *Originally published: Random House, 1974. — Bibliography: p[203]-207*

ROME (ITALY) — Statistics
Notiziario statistico mensile del Comune di Roma / Ufficio di Statistica e Censimento. — Rome : Ufficio di Statistica e Censimento, 1984-. — *Monthly*

ROME&XHISTORY — Germanic Invasions, 3rd-6th centuries
FERRILL, Arther
The fall of the Roman Empire : the military explanation / Arther Ferrill. — London : Thames and Hudson, c1986. — 192p. — *Bibliography: p.182-187*

ROMULO, CARLOS PEÑA
ROMULO, Carlos Peña
Forty years : a Third World soldier at the UN / Carlos P. Romulo with Beth Day Romulo. — Westport, Conn. : Greenwood Press, c1986. — p. cm. — (Studies in freedom ; no. 3). — *Includes index. — Bibliography: p*

RONDA (SPAIN) — Social life and customs
CORBIN, J. R.
Urbane thought : culture and class in an Andalusian city / J.R. Corbin and M.P. Corbin. — Aldershot : Gower, c1987. — v,213p. — (Studies in Spanish anthropology ; 2). — *Bibliography: p193-199. — Includes index*

ROOSEVELT, FRANKLIN D
BENNETT, Edward Moore
Franklin D. Roosevelt and the search for security : American-Soviet relations, 1933-1939 / by Edward M. Bennett. — Wilmington, Del. : Scholarly Resources, 1985. — xix, 213p. — *Includes index. — Bibliography: p 197-203*

ROOSEVELT, FRANKLIN D.
DALLEK, Robert
Franklin D. Roosevelt and American foreign policy, 1932-1945 / Robert Dallek. — New York : Oxford University Press, 1979. — xii, 657 p. — *Includes index. — Bibliography: p. 619-628*

RÖSCH, AUGUSTIN
RÖSCH, Augustin
Kampf gegen den Nationalsozialismus / Augustin Rösch ; herausgegeben von Roman Bleistein. — Frankfurt am Main : Josef Knecht, 1985. — 492p. — *Bibliography: p481-484*

ROSEBERY, ARCHIBALD PHILIP PRIMROSE, Earl of
HAMILTON, Sir Edward, 1847-1908
The destruction of Lord Rosebery : from the diary of Sir Edward Hamilton, 1894-1895 / edited with an introductory essay by David Brooks. — London : Historians' Press, [1987?]. — x,290p. — (Sources for modern British history). — *Includes index*

ROSENBERG, HILARY
THOMSON, Alastair
A users guide to the Manpower Services Commission / Alastair Thomson and Hilary Rosenberg. — London : Kogan Page, 1986. — 332 p. — (10.1 Great Britain)

RÖSRATH (GERMANY) — Politics and government
GERNERT, Dörte
Demokratie auf dem Land : die Rösrather Sozialdemokratie und die Geschichte der Gemeinde bis 1933 / Dörte und Klaus-Dieter Gernert. — Remscheid : Verlag Ute Kierdorf, 1984. — 132p

RÖSRATH (GERMANY) — Social conditions
GERNERT, Dörte
Demokratie auf dem Land : die Rösrather Sozialdemokratie und die Geschichte der Gemeinde bis 1933 / Dörte und Klaus-Dieter Gernert. — Remscheid : Verlag Ute Kierdorf, 1984. — 132p

ROSSENDALE (LANCASHIRE : DISTRICT) — Economic history
TUPLING, G. H.
The economic history of Rossendale / by G. H. Tupling. — New York : Johnson Reprint Corporation, 1965. — xxiv,274p. — (Remains historical and literary connected with the Palatine Counties of Lancaster and Chester ; [2nd] Series volume 86). — *Originally published by the Chetham Society in 1927*

ROSSIISKAIA SOTSIAL-DEMOKRATICHESKAIA RABOCHAIA PARTIIA
Perepiska V. I. Lenina i rukovodimykh im uchrezhdenii RSDRP s partiinymi organizatsiiami 1905-1907 gg. : sbornik dokumentov. V piati tomakh. — Moskva : Mysl'
t.3: iiul'-avgust 1905 g.
Kn.1 / red. kollegiia D. I. Antoniuk...[et al.]. — 1986. — 368p

Perepiska V. I. Lenina i rukovodimykh im uchrezhdenii RSDRP s partiinymi organizatsiiami 1905-1907 gg. : sbornik dokumentov. V piati tomakh. — Moskva : Mysl'
t.3: iiul'-avgust 1905 g.
Kn.2 / red. kollegiia D. I. Antoniuk...[et al.]. — 1986. — 420p

ROSSIISKAIA SOTSIAL-DEMOKRATICHESKAIA RABOCHAIA PARTIIA. Peterburgskii komitet
Peterburgskii komitet RSDRP : protokoly i materialy zasedanii. Iiul' 1902-fevral' 1917 / [sbornik podgotovili: T. P. Bondarevskaia, T. A. Abrosimova, E. T. Leikina]. — Leningrad : Lenizdat, 1986. — 588p

SKRYPNIK, N. A.
Leninskaia partiia v bor'be za edinstvo rabochego klassa : (na materialakh Ukrainy) / N. A. Skrypnik. — Kiev : Vyshcha shkola, 1985. — 150p. — *Bibliography: p143-150*

ROSSIISKAIA SOTSIAL-DEMOKRATICHESKAIA RABOCHAIA PARTIIA — History
BROIDO, Vera
Lenin and the Mensheviks : the persecution of socialists under Bolshevism / by Vera Broido. — Aldershot : Gower, c1987. — viii,216p. — *Bibliography: p191-201. — Includes index*

ROTE ARMEE FRAKTION
CAMPAIGN AGAINST THE MODEL WEST GERMANY
[Reports]. — [Bochum] : Campaign against the Model West Germany
Nr.4: The Stammheim death. — [1977]. — 23p

ROTHFELS, HANS
Aspekte deutscher Aussenpolitik im 20. [i.e. zwanzigsten] Jahrhundert : Aufsätze Hans Rothfels z. Gedächtnis / hrsg. von Wolfgang Benz u. Hermann Graml. — Stuttgart : Deutsche Verlags-Anstalt, 1976. — 304 p.. — "Schriftenreihe der Vierteljahrshefte für Zeitgeschichte, Sondernummer.". — *Bibliography of H. Rothfels´ works: p.[287]-304. — Includes bibliographical references*

ROUSSEAU, JEAN-JACQUES — Contributions in philosophy of war
CARTER, Christine Jane
Rousseau and the problem of war / Christine Jane Carter. — New York : Garland Pub., 1987. — p. cm. — (Political theory and political philosophy). — *The author´s doctoral thesis, 1985. — Bibliography: p*

ROUSSEAU, JEAN-JACQUES — Contributions in political science
WOKLER, Robert
Social thought of J.J. Rousseau / Robert Wokler. — New York : Carland Pub., 1987. — p. cm. — (Political theory and political philosophy). — : *Originally presented as the author´s thesis under title: Rousseau on society, politics, music, and language. — Bibliography: p*

ROUSSEAU, JEAN-JACQUES — Contributions in sociology
WOKLER, Robert
Social thought of J.J. Rousseau / Robert Wokler. — New York : Carland Pub., 1987. — p. cm. — (Political theory and political philosophy). — : *Originally presented as the author´s thesis under title: Rousseau on society, politics, music, and language. — Bibliography: p*

ROUSSEAU, JEAN-JACQUES — Political and social views
BLUM, Carol
Rousseau and the republic of virtue : the language of politics in the French Revolution / Carol Blum. — Ithaca : Cornell University Press, 1986. — 302 p.. — *Includes index. — Bibliography: p. 283-294*

ROUSSEAU, JEAN-JACQUES, 1712-1778 — Criticism and interpretation
HOROWITZ, Asher
Rousseau, nature, and history / Asher Horowitz. — Toronto : University of Toronto Press, 1987. — xiii,273p. — *Bibliography: p [255]-263*

ROVERE, RICHARD HALWORTH
ROVERE, Richard Halworth
Final reports : personal reflections on politics and history in our time / Richard Rovere ; foreword by Arthur M. Schlesinger, Jr. — Middletown, Conn. : Wesleyan University Press ; Scranton, Pa. : Distributed by Harper & Row, 1986, c1984. — xviii, 244 p.. — (Wesleyan paperback). — *Includes index*

ROY, GABRIELLE
Kent / county editors: Winifred F. Bergess, Barbara R.M. Riddell, John Whyman. — London : British Library, c1982. — xviii,139p. — (Bibliography of British newspapers). — *Includes index*

ROYAL CANADIAN MOUNTED POLICE — History
MORRISON, William R
Showing the flag : the Mounted Police and Canadian sovereignty in the north, 1894-1925 / William R. Morrison. — Vancouver : University of British Columbia Press, 1985. — xix, 220 p., [16] p. of plates. — *Includes index.* — *Bibliography: p. [209]-216*

ROYAL COLLEGE OF NURSING
CLAY, Trevor
Nurses : power and politics / Trevor Clay in association with Alison Dunn and Neil Stewart. — London : Heinemann Medical, 1987. — 165p. — *Contains bibliographies*

ROYAL COMMISSION ON THE ECONOMIC UNION AND DEVELOPMENT PROSPECTS FOR CANADA
YUDELMAN, David
Mining and the MacDonald Commission : the state of the industry in the mid-1980s / David Yudelman. — [Kingston, Ont.] : Centre for Resource Studies, Queen's University, c1985. — x, 106 p.. — (Working paper / Centre for Resource Studies ; no. 34). — *Bibliography: p. 99-106*

ROYAL EXCHANGE ASSURANCE
JENKINS, D. T.
Indexes of the fire insurance policies of the Sun Fire Office and the Royal Exchange Assurance 1775-1787 : [an introduction]. — London : Economic and Social Research Council, 1986. — 35p. — *Bibliography: p32-35*

ROYAL EXCHANGE ASSURANCE
Fire policies 1775-1787. — London : Economic and Social Research Council, 1986. — 10microfiches

ROYAL INFIRMARY OF EDINBURGH — History
RISSE, Guenter B.
Hospital life in Enlightenment Scotland : care and teaching at the Royal Infirmary of Edinburgh / Guenter B. Risse. — Cambridge : Cambridge University Press, 1986. — xiv,450p. — (Cambridge history of medicine). — *Includes index*

ROYAL ULSTER CONSTABULARY
TAYLOR, Peter, 1942-
Stalker : the search for the truth / Peter Taylor. — London : Faber, 1987. — xii,231p

ROYALISTS — France
DESAUBLIAUX, Marc
La fin du Parti royaliste (1889-1890) / avec une preface du duc de Castries. — Paris : Editions Royaliste, [1986]. — 248p

RUBBER, ARTIFICIAL — History
HERBERT, Vernon
Synthetic rubber : a project that had to succeed / Vernon Herbert and Attilio Bisio. — Westport, Conn. ; London : Greenwood Press, 1985. — xi, 243p. — (Contributions in economic and economic history ; no. 63). — *Includes index.* — *Bibliography: p [233]-235*

RUBBER INDUSTRY AND TRADE — United States — History
HERBERT, Vernon
Synthetic rubber : a project that had to succeed / Vernon Herbert and Attilio Bisio. — Westport, Conn. ; London : Greenwood Press, 1985. — xi, 243p. — (Contributions in economic and economic history ; no. 63). — *Includes index.* — *Bibliography: p [233]-235*

RUDOLF II, Holy Roman Emperor
EVANS, R. J. W.
Rudolf II and his world : a study in intellectual history 1576-1612 / by R.J.W. Evans. — Oxford : Clarendon, 1984, c1973. — xv,323,[16]p. — *Originally published: 1973.* — *Bibliography: p299-310.* — *Includes index*

RUEFF, JACQUES
RUEFF, Jacques
Oeuvres complètes de Jacques Rueff. — Paris : Plon. — *Bibliography: p436-438*
Tome 1: De l'aube au crépuscule : autobiographie de l'auteur. — [1977]. — 443p

RUG AND CARPET INDUSTRY — Management — Case studies
JONES, Roger
The carpetmakers / Roger Jones, Chris Lakin. — London : McGraw-Hill, 1978

RUHR (GERMANY: REGION) — History — French occupation, 1923-1925
Die Ruhrkrise 1923 : Wendepunkt der internationalen Beziehungen nach dem Ersten Weltkrieg / Klaus Schwabe (Hrsg.). — Paderborn : Schöningh, 1984. — [vi], 111p

RUHR (GERMANY: REGION) — Politics and government
Die Ruhrkrise 1923 : Wendepunkt der internationalen Beziehungen nach dem Ersten Weltkrieg / Klaus Schwabe (Hrsg.). — Paderborn : Schöningh, 1984. — [vi], 111p

RULE OF LAW
DÍAZ, Elías
Estado de derecho y sociedad democrática / Elías Díaz. — Séptima edición. — Madrid : EDICUSA, 1979. — 204p. — (Divulgación universitaria. Temas políticos ; 5). — *Publicado originalmente en 1966.* — *Bibliography: p181-191*

RULE OF LAW — Gaza Strip
SHEHADEH, Raja
Occupier's law : a study of Israeli practices in the West Bank and Gaza / by Raja Shehadeh. — Washington, DC : Institute for Palestine Studies, 1985. — p. cm. — *Bibliography: p*

RULE OF LAW — South Africa
MATHEWS, Anthony S.
Freedom, state security and the rule of law : dilemmas of the apartheid society / Anthony S. Mathews. — Cape Town : Juta, 1986. — xxv,312p. — *Bibliography: p.xi-xiv.* - *Includes index*

RULE OF LAW — West Bank
SHEHADEH, Raja
Occupier's law : a study of Israeli practices in the West Bank and Gaza / by Raja Shehadeh. — Washington, DC : Institute for Palestine Studies, 1985. — p. cm. — *Bibliography: p*

RUPPIN, ARTHUR
RUPPIN, Arthur
Arthur Ruppin : memoirs, diaries, letters / edited with an introduction by Alex Bein ; translated from the German [MSS.] by Karen Gershon ; afterword by Moshe Dayan. — London : Weidenfeld and Nicolson, 1971. — xix,332,[16]p. — *Includes index*

RURAL CONDITIONS
KINSEY, B. H.
Creating rural employment / B.H. Kinsey. — London : Croom Helm, c1987. — [11],116p. — *Bibliography: p107-112.* — *Includes index*

RURAL DEVELOPMENT — Government policy — Australia
AUSTRALIA
Economic and rural policy : a Government policy statement. — Canberra : Australian Government Publishing Service, 1986. — 89p

RURAL DEVELOPMENT — Congo (Brazzaville)
NGUYEN, Gregory Tien Hung
Agriculture and rural development in the People's Republic of Congo / Gregory N.T. Hung. — Boulder : Westview Press, 1986. — p. cm. — (Westview special studies on Africa). — *Includes index.* — *Bibliography: p*

RURAL DEVELOPMENT
Anthropological contributions to planned change and development / edited by Harald O. Skar. — Göteborg, Sweden : Acta Universitatis Gothoburgensis, 1985. — iv, 191 p.. — (Gothenburg studies in social anthropology ; 8) . — *Includes bibliographies*

The assault on world poverty : problems of rural development, education and health / with a preface by Robert S. McNamara. — Baltimore ; London : Johns Hopkins University Press for the World Bank, 1975. — xiii,425p

KIM, Kyŏng-dong
Rethinking development : theories and experiences / by Kyong-Dong Kim. — Seoul : Seoul National University Press, c1985. — xiv, 292 p.. — (Korean studies series ; no. 7). — *Includes index.* — *Bibliography: p. [249]-273*

Local level planning and rural development : alternative strategies. — New Delhi : Concept, 1980. — 409 p.. — "United Nations Asian and Pacific Development Institute, Bangkok.". — "May 1980.". — *Includes index.* — *Bibliography: p. [372]-397*

WEINTRAUB, Dov
Basic social diagnosis for IRRD planning : conceptual framework, case studies and some generalisations / Dov Weintraub, Julia Margulies. — Aldershot : Gower, c1986. — 233p. — *Bibliography: p.219-227*

RURAL DEVELOPMENT — Addresses, essays, lectures
Indigenous knowledge systems and development / edited by David Brokensha, D. M. Warren, and Oswald Werner. — Washington, D.C. : University Press of America, c1980. — vii, 466 p.. — *Includes indexes.* — *Bibliography: p. 415-449*

RURAL DEVELOPMENT — Bibliography
DAVID LUBIN MEMORIAL LIBRARY
FAO documentation : rural development : 1980-1984 = Documentation de la FAO : developpement rural : 1980-1984 = Documentacion de la FAO : desarrollo rural : 1980-1984. — Rome : Food and Agriculture Organization, 1985. — [47]p. — *In English with introductions in French and Spanish*

RURAL DEVELOPMENT — Congresses
Integrated rural development - research results and programme implementation : Bonn Conference 1985 / Ernst Zurek (Editor). — Hamburg : Verlag Weltarchiv, 1985. — x,383p. — (Studien zur integrierten ländlichen Entwicklung ; 14). — *Papers presented at an international workshop on "Integrated rural development - concepts and experiences", Bonn, March 19 to 21, 1985*

RURAL DEVELOPMENT — Government policy — Great Britain
GREAT BRITAIN. Department of the Environment
Rural enterprise and development / Department of the Environment and Welsh Office. — London : H.M.S.O., 1987. — 40p

RURAL DEVELOPMENT — Social aspects — Great Britain
COUNTRYSIDE RECREATION RESEARCH ADVISORY GROUP CONFERENCE (1985 : Oxford)
Countryside leisure and jobs : proceedings of the...Conference, Oxford Polytechnic, September 18-19, 1985 / edited by Hilary Talbot-Ponsonby. — Bristol : Countryside Recreation Research Advisory Group, 1985. — 161p

RURAL DEVELOPMENT — Statistical methods
Guidelines for the computation of selected statistical indicators. — Rome : FAO, 1986. — vii,71p. — (FAO economic and social development paper ; 60)

RURAL DEVELOPMENT — Africa
Rural development and women in Africa. — Geneva : International Labour Office, c1984. — 157p. — (A WEP study)

RURAL DEVELOPMENT — Africa, Sub-Saharan
BOIRAL, P.
Paysans, experts et chercheurs en Afrique Noire : sciences sociales et développement rural / P. Boiral, J.- F. Lanteri, J.-P. Olivier de Sardan (sous la direction de). — Paris : Karthala, [1985]. — 224p

RURAL DEVELOPMENT — Alaska — Addresses, essays, lectures
Contemporary Alaskan native economies / edited by Steve J. Langdon. — Lanham, MD : University Press of America, c1986. — ix, 183 p.. — Includes bibliographies. — Contents: Economic growth and development strategies for rural Alaska / Bradford H. Tuck and Lee Huskey -- Subsistence as an economic system in Alaska / Thomas D. Lonner -- Contradictions in Alaskan native economy and society / Steve J. Langdon -- Limited entry policy and impacts on Bristol Bay fishermen / J. Anthony Koslow -- The Cape Romanzoff project / Dean F. Olson -- The Pribilof Island Aleuts / Michael K. Orbach and Beverly Holmes -- The economic efficiency of food production in a western Alaska Eskimo population / Robert J. Wolfe -- Subsistence and the North Slope Inupiat / John A. Kruse -- Subsistence beluga whale hunting in Alaska / Kerry D. Feldman -- Traditional subsistence activities and systems of exchange among the Nelson Island Yup'ik / Ann Fienup-Riordan

RURAL DEVELOPMENT — Asia
ETIENNE, Gilbert
[Développement rural en Asie. English]. Rural development in Asia : meetings with peasants / Gilbert Etienne ; translated by Arati Sharma. — Rev. ed. — New Delhi ; Beverly Hills, CA : Sage Publications, 1985. — 276 p.. — Translation of: Développement rural en Asie. — Bibliography: p. [272]-276

The poor in Asia : productivity-raising programmes and strategies / edited by Swapna Mukhopadhyay. — Kuala Lumpur : Asian and Pacific Development Centre, 1985. — 772p. — Bibliographies

The Rural non-farm sector in Asia / edited by Swapna Mukhopadhyay, Chee Peng Lim. — Kuala Lumpur, Malaysia : Asian and Pacific Development Centre, 1985. — xiv, 417 p.. — (The Human resource mobilization programme publications). — Includes bibliographies

RURAL DEVELOPMENT — Asia — Case studies
Rural development in Asia : case studies on programme implementation / edited by G. Shabbir Cheema. — New Delhi : Sterling, 1985. — vi,268p

RURAL DEVELOPMENT — Asia — Citizen participation
LOHANI, Prakash C
People's participation in development / Prakash Chandra Lohani. — 1st ed. — Kathmandu : Centre for Economic Development and Administration, Tribhuvan University, 1980. — 107 p.. — Includes bibliographical references

RURAL DEVELOPMENT — Bangladesh
ABDULLAH, Mohammad Mohiuddin
Rural development in Bangladesh : problems and prospects / Mohammud Mohiuddin Abdullah. — 2nd ed.. — Dacca : Jahan Publications, 1981. — iv,133p. — Bibliography: p134

RAHMAN, Atiur
Rural power structure : a study of the local level leaders in Bangladesh / Atiur Rahman. — Dacca : Papri Publishers, 1981. — viii,63p. — Bibliography: p59-63

ZAMAN, Wasim Alimuz
Public participation in development and health programs : lessons from rural Bangladesh / Wasim Alimuz Zaman. — Lanham : University Press of America, c1984. — xix, 291 p.. — : Revision of thesis (Ph. D.)--Harvard University, 1982. — Includes bibliographical references

RURAL DEVELOPMENT — Botswana
NATIONAL DISTRICT DEVELOPMENT CONFERENCE (5th : 1978 : Gaborone)
A record of proceedings and actions. — Gaborone : Ministry of Local Government and Lands, 1978. — 88p

NATIONAL DISTRICT DEVELOPMENT CONFERENCE (7th : 1979 : Gaborone)
[Report]. — Gaborone : Ministry of Local Government and Lands, [1979]. — 279p

RURAL DEVELOPMENT — Colombia
HELMSING, A. H. J.
Firms, farms, and the state in Colombia : a study of rural, urban, and regional dimensions of change / A.H.J. Helmsing. — Boston : Allen & Unwin, 1986. — xix, 297 p.. — Includes index. — Bibliography: p. 275-288

RURAL DEVELOPMENT — Developing countries
Macro policies for appropriate technology in developing countries / edited by Francis Stewart. — Boulder : Westview Press, 1986. — p. cm. — (Westview special studies in social, political, and economic development)

RURAL DEVELOPMENT — Egypt
ADAMS, Richard H
Development and social change in rural Egypt / Richard H. Adams, Jr. — 1st ed. — Syracuse, N.Y. : Syracuse University Press, 1986. — xii, 231 p.. — (Contemporary issues in the Middle East). — : Revision of the author's thesis (Ph. D.)--University of California, Berkeley, 1981. — Includes index. — Bibliography: p. 213-224

RURAL DEVELOPMENT — England
DEVELOPMENT COMMISSION FOR RURAL ENGLAND
Action for rural enterprise : a guide to the assistance available to business in rural areas of England from the government and other agencies. — [London : the Commission, 1987]. — 29p. — One of five publications in folder entitled Farming and rural enterprise

RURAL DEVELOPMENT — Ethiopia
MARIAM, Mesfin Wolde
Rural vulnerability to famine in Ethiopia, 1958-1977 / Mesfin Wolde Mariam. — London : Intermediate Technology Publications, 1986. — xii,191p

RURAL DEVELOPMENT — Ethiopia — Case studies
HAMER, John H.
Humane development : participation and change among the Sadáma of Ethiopia / John H. Hamer. — Tuscaloosa, Ala. : University of Alabama Press, c1987. — xi, 281 p.. — Includes index. — Bibliography: p. 267-276

RURAL DEVELOPMENT — Europe
NUTTALL, Trevor
Methods to stop rural depopulation and to involve citizens in the development of these regions / report prepared, under the guidance of the members of the Committee of Experts on Social and Economic Activities of the Steering Committee for Regional and Municipal Matters, by Trevor Nuttall. — Strasbourg : Council of Europe, 1980. — i,37p. — (Study series local and regional authorities in Europe ; study no. 22)

RURAL DEVELOPMENT — India
MAHESHWARI, Shriram
Rural development in India : a public policy approach / Shriram Maheshwari. — New Delhi ; London : Sage, 1985. — 231p. — Includes index

OOMMEN, T. K.
Social transformation in rural India : mobilization and state intervention / T.K. Oommen. — Delhi : Vikas, c1984. — xx, 326 p.. — Includes bibliographies and index

Population, poverty, and hope. — New Delhi : Uppal, c1983. — xvii, 564 p.. — "Under the auspices of the Centre for Policy Research and Family Planning Foundation."

RAO, Sudha V.
Education and rural development / Sudha V. Rao ; foreword by T. Scarlett Epstein. — New Delhi ; London : Sage, 1985. — 334p. — Bibliography: p321-328. — Includes index

RURAL DEVELOPMENT — India — Punjab
CHADHA, G. K
The state and rural transformation : the case of Punjab, 1950-85 / G.K. Chadha. — New Delhi ; Beverly Hills : Sage Publications, 1986. — p. cm. — Includes index. — Bibliography: p

RURAL DEVELOPMENT — Ireland
SCOTT, Ian, 19---
The periphery is the centre : a study of community development practice in the west of Ireland, 1983/84 / by Ian Scott. — Langholm (Langholm, Dumfriesshire, DG13 0HL) : Arkleton Trust, c1985. — x,93p,[4]p of plates. — Bibliography: p86-89

RURAL DEVELOPMENT — Kenya
LIVINGSTONE, Ian
Rural development, employment and incomes in Kenya / Ian Livingstone. — Aldershot : Gower, 1986. — xx,389p. — "A study prepared for the International Labour Office within the framework of the Jobs and Skills Programme for Africa (JASPA)" - t.p. verso

RURAL DEVELOPMENT — Korea (South)
KIM, Kyŏng-dong
Rethinking development : theories and experiences / by Kyong-Dong Kim. — Seoul : Seoul National University Press, c1985. — xiv, 292 p.. — (Korean studies series ; no. 7). — Includes index. — Bibliography: p. [249]-273

RURAL DEVELOPMENT — Nigeria — Congresses
Rural banking in Nigeria / edited by Adeniyi Osuntogun and Wole Adewunmi. — London ; New York : Longman, 1982. — p. cm. — Selected papers from a seminar held at the University of Ife, Mar. 29-Apr. 1, 1979, which was sponsored by the Nigerian Institute of Bankers. — Includes index

RURAL DEVELOPMENT — Organisation for Economic Co-operation and Development
Rural public management / Organisation for Economic Co—operation and Development. — Paris : Organisation for Economic Co—operation and Development, 1986. — 85p. — Bibliography: p83-85

RURAL DEVELOPMENT — Pakistan
NABI, Ijaz
The agrarian economy of Pakistan : issues and policies / Ijaz Nabi, Navid Hamid, Shahid Zahid. — Karachi ; Oxford : Oxford University Press, 1986. — 337p. — Bibliography: p319-324

RURAL DEVELOPMENT — Scotland
ALEXANDER, K. J. W.
Rural renewal : experience in the Highlands and Islands / Sir Kenneth Alexander. — Cambridge : University of Cambridge, Department of Land Economy, 1984. — 26p. — (The Denman lecture ; 1984)

RURAL DEVELOPMENT — Scotland
continuation
GREAT BRITAIN. Scottish Office
Rural Scotland. — [Edinburgh : the Office, 1987]. — 28p. — *One of five publications in folder entitled Farming and rural enterprise*

RURAL DEVELOPMENT — Singapore
Central government and local development in Indonesia / edited by Colin MacAndrews. — Singapore ; Oxford : Oxford University Press, 1986. — xv,253p. — (East Asian social science monographs)

RURAL DEVELOPMENT — Sudan
EL-ARIFI, Salih Abdalla
Local government and local participation in rural development in the Sudan / Salih Abdalla El-Arifi. — Khartoum : University of Khartoum. Faculty of Economic and Social Studies. Development Studies and Research Centre, 1978. — 34p. — (Monograph series / University of Khartoum. Faculty of Economic and Social Studies. Development Studies and Research Centre ; no.10). — *Bibliography: p29-34*

RURAL DEVELOPMENT — Tanzania
Towards rural development in Tanzania : some issues on policy implementation in the 1970s / edited by C. K. Omari. — Arusha : Eastern Africa Publications, 1984. — vii,178p

RURAL DEVELOPMENT — Wales
Action for rural enterprise in Wales / Manpower Services Commission, Mid Wales Development, Wales Tourist Board, Welsh Development Agency. — [Cardiff? : Welsh Development Agency?, 1987]. — 17,19p. — *In English and Welsh. — One of five publications in folder entitled Farming and rural enterprise*

RURAL DEVELOPMENT — Zimbabwe
ZIMBABWE CONFERENCE ON RECONSTRUCTION AND DEVELOPMENT (1981 : Salisbury)
Let's build Zimbabwe together : Conference documentation. — Causeway : Ministry of Economic Planning and Development, [1981]. — 111p. — *Cover title*

RURAL DEVELOPMENT PROJECTS — Congresses
Integrated rural development - research results and programme implementation : Bonn Conference 1985 / Ernst Zurek (Editor). — Hamburg : Verlag Weltarchiv, 1985. — x,383p. — (Studien zur integrierten ländlichen Entwicklung ; 14). — *Papers presented at an international workshop on "Integrated rural development - concepts and experiences", Bonn, March 19 to 21, 1985*

RURAL DEVELOPMENT PROJECTS — Evaluation — Statistical methods
SCOTT, Chris
Sampling for monitoring and evaluation / Chris Scott. — Washington, D.C. : The World Bank, 1985. — iii,44p. — *"A technical supplement to 'Monitoring and evaluation of agriculture and rural development projects' by Dennis J. Casley and Denis A. Lury". — Includes bibliographical references*

RURAL DEVELOPMENT PROJECTS — Management — Statistical methods
SCOTT, Chris
Sampling for monitoring and evaluation / Chris Scott. — Washington, D.C. : The World Bank, 1985. — iii,44p. — *"A technical supplement to 'Monitoring and evaluation of agriculture and rural development projects' by Dennis J. Casley and Denis A. Lury". — Includes bibliographical references*

RURAL DEVELOPMENT PROJECTS — Social aspects
Differential social impacts of rural resource development / editor Pamela D. Elkind-Savatsky ; associate editor Judith D. Kaufman. — Boulder, Colo. ; London : Westview Press, 1986. — xvii,293p. — (Social Impact Assessment Series ; no.13)

RURAL DEVELOPMENT PROJECTS — Bangladesh
ZAMAN, Wasim Alimuz
Public participation in development and health programs : lessons from rural Bangladesh / Wasim Alimuz Zaman. — Lanham : University Press of America, c1984. — xix, 291 p.. — : *Revision of thesis (Ph. D.)--Harvard University, 1982. — Includes bibliographical references*

RURAL DEVELOPMENT PROJECTS — Developing countries
Démarches de recherche-développement appliquées au secteur de la production rurale des pays en voie de dévloppement / [Alain Lalau-Keraly...et al.]. — [Paris] : Bureau de liaison des agents de la coopération technique...[etc.], c1984. — 91p. — (Collection des ateliers technologique et développement ; no.2). — *Ce texte fait suite à un séminaire conçu par Alain Lalau-Keraly et Didier Pillot, avec rédaction finale par Jacques Bodichon. — Bibliography: p81-84*

RURAL DEVELOPMENT PROJECTS — Developing countries — Management
HONADLE, George
Implementation for sustainability : lessons from integrated rural development / by George Honadle and Jerry VanSant. — West Hartford, Conn. : Kumarian Press, 1985. — xiv, 128 p.. — *Includes bibliographies and index*

KINSEY, B. H.
Agribusiness and rural enterprise / B.H. Kinsey. — London : Croom Helm, c1987. — [240]p. — *Includes bibliography and index*

RURAL DEVELOPMENT PROJECTS — Developing countries — Management — Case studies
HONADLE, George
Implementation for sustainability : lessons from integrated rural development / by George Honadle and Jerry VanSant. — West Hartford, Conn. : Kumarian Press, 1985. — xiv, 128 p.. — *Includes bibliographies and index*

RURAL DEVELOPMENT PROJECTS — Egypt
NIEUWENHUIJZE, C. A. O. van
The poor man's model of development : development potential at low levels of living in Egypt / by C. A. O. van Nieuwenhuijze, M. Fathalla al-Khatib, Adel Azer. — Leiden : E. J. Brill, 1985. — viii,206p. — (Social, economic and political studies of the Middle East ; 40)

RURAL DEVELOPMENT PROJECTS — India
SRIVASTAVA, A. K.
Integrated rural development programme in India : policy and administration / A. K. Srivastava. — New Delhi : Deep and Deep Publications, 1986. — 272p. — *Bibliography: p262-270*

RURAL ELECTRIFICATION — Economic aspects
MUNASINGHE, Mohan
Rural electrification for development : policy analysis and applications / Mohan Munasinghe. — Boulder, Colo. ; London : Westview, 1987. — xxiii,440p. — (Westview special studies in natural resources and energy management). — *Bibliography: p419-430*

RURAL ELECTRIFICATION — Government policy
MUNASINGHE, Mohan
Rural electrification for development : policy analysis and applications / Mohan Munasinghe. — Boulder, Colo. ; London : Westview, 1987. — xxiii,440p. — (Westview special studies in natural resources and energy management). — *Bibliography: p419-430*

RURAL FAMILIES — Africa, Sub-Saharan
Understanding Africa's rural households and farming systems / [edited by] Joyce Lewinger Moock. — Boulder : Westview Press, 1986. — p. cm. — (Westview special studies on Africa). — *Bibliography: p*

RURAL FAMILIES — Developing countries — Case studies
Agricultural household models : extensions, applications, and policy / Inderjit Singh. — Baltimore : Johns Hopkins University Press for the World Bank, 1986. — xi,335p. — *Includes bibliographical references*

RURAL FAMILIES — Great Britain — Bibliography
The farm as a family business : an annotated bibliography / edited by Andrew Errington ; contributions : Graham Crow ... [et al.]. — [Reading] : [Reading University], 1986. — 33p. — *Published as the result of a workshop organized by the Agricultural Manpower Society at Reading University, February 1985*

RURAL FAMILIES — India — Maps
DHURANDHER, K. P.
An atlas of assets and liabilities of Indian rural households / K. P. Dhurandher. — New Delhi : Vikas, 1985. — 180p. — *Contains 107 black and white maps*

RURAL GEOGRAPHY
GILG, Andrew W.
An introduction to rural geography / Andrew W. Gilg. — London : Edward Arnold, 1985. — [xvii,224]p. — *Includes bibliography and index*

PACIONE, Michael
Rural geography / Michael Pacione. — London : Harper & Row, 1984. — 384p. — *Includes bibliographies and index*

RURAL HEALTH — Nepal
ACHARD, Thomas
Primary health care in the hills of Nepal / Thomas Achard. — Kathmandu, Nepal : Integrated Hill Development Project, HMG/SATA, 1983. — 105p. — *Bibliography: p104-105*

JUSTICE, Judith
Policies, plans, and people : culture and health development in Nepal / Judith Justice. — Berkeley : University of California Press, c1986. — p. cm. — (Comparative studies of health systems and medical care). — *Includes index. — Bibliography: p*

RURAL HEALTH SERVICES — Planning — International cooperation
JUSTICE, Judith
Policies, plans, and people : culture and health development in Nepal / Judith Justice. — Berkeley : University of California Press, c1986. — p. cm. — (Comparative studies of health systems and medical care). — *Includes index. — Bibliography: p*

RURAL HEALTH SERVICES — Nepal
ACHARD, Thomas
Primary health care in the hills of Nepal / Thomas Achard. — Kathmandu, Nepal : Integrated Hill Development Project, HMG/SATA, 1983. — 105p. — *Bibliography: p104-105*

JUSTICE, Judith
Policies, plans, and people : culture and health development in Nepal / Judith Justice. — Berkeley : University of California Press, c1986. — p. cm. — (Comparative studies of health systems and medical care). — *Includes index. — Bibliography: p*

RURAL HEALTH SERVICES — Tanzania
Community health workers : the Tanzanian experience / Kris Heggenhougen ... [et al.] ; with special assistance from M.P. Mandara ; foreword by A.D. Chiduo. — Oxford : Oxford University Press, 1987. — xiv,205p. — (Oxford medical publications). — *Bibliography: p197-202. — Includes index*

RURAL HEALTH SERVICES — United States

Swing beds : assessing flexible health care in rural communities / edited by Joshua M. Wiener. — Washington, D.C. : Brookings Institution, 1987. — 140p. — (Brookings dialogues on public policy). — *Papers presented at a conference at the Brookings Institution. February 24, 1986*

RURAL POOR

LIPTON, Michael
Why poor people stay poor : urban bias in world development / Michael Lipton. — Cambridge : Harvard University Press, 1977, c1976. — 467 p. — *Includes index. — Bibliography: p. 355-357*

Local level planning and rural development : alternative strategies. — New Delhi : Concept, 1980. — 409 p.. — *"United Nations Asian and Pacific Development Institute, Bangkok.". — "May 1980.". — Includes index. — Bibliography: p. [372]-397*

RURAL POOR — Asia

Fighting poverty : Asia's major challenge. — New Delhi : Asian Employment Programme, 1986. — 40p

RURAL POOR — Great Britain

Deprivation and welfare in rural areas / edited by Philip Lowe, Tony Bradley and Susan Wright. — Norwich : Geo, [1986]. — viii,229p. — *Includes bibliographies*

RURAL POOR — India

BAJAJ, J. L
Rural poverty : issues and option / J.L. Bajaj, C. Shastri ; foreword, T.S. Papola. — Lucknow : Print House (India), c1985. — 252 p.. — *Includes bibliographies and index*

HIRWAY, Indira
Abolition of poverty in India : with special reference to target group approach in Gujarat / Indira Hirway. — New Delhi : Vikas Pub. House, c1986. — vi, 284 p. [i.e. 184]. — *Includes bibliographies and index*

OOMMEN, T. K.
Social transformation in rural India : mobilization and state intervention / T.K. Oommen. — Delhi : Vikas, c1984. — xx, 326 p.. — *Includes bibliographies and index*

RURAL POOR — India — Chakrabhavi

HADIMANI, R. N
The politics of poverty / R.N. Hadimani. — New Delhi : Ashish, 1984. — xxi, 194 p.. — *Summary: Study of the factors responsible for restricting the efficient implementation of the anti-poverty programs; based on empirical data from a village in Bangalore District, Karnataka. — Includes index. — Bibliography: p. 185-189*

RURAL POOR — India — Gujarat

HIRWAY, Indira
Abolition of poverty in India : with special reference to target group approach in Gujarat / Indira Hirway. — New Delhi : Vikas Pub. House, c1986. — vi, 284 p. [i.e. 184]. — *Includes bibliographies and index*

RURAL POOR — Kenya

GREER, Joel
Food poverty and consumption patterns in Kenya / Joel Greer and Erik Thorbecke. — Geneva : International Labour Office, 1986. — xii,170p

RURAL POPULATION

CAIN, Mead
Population growth and agrarian outcomes / Mead Cain [and] Geoffrey McNicoll. — New York : Population Council, 1986. — 25p. — (Working papers / Population Council. Center for Policy Studies ; no.128). — *Bibliography: p20-21*

RURAL POPULATION — Lesotho — Statistics

MOROJELE, C. M. H.
Basutoland village population lists / C. M. H. Morojele. — Maseni : Agricultural Department, 1960

RURAL PORT — India — Government policy

KOHLI, Atul
The state and poverty in India : the politics of reform / Atul Kohli. — Cambridge : Cambridge University Press, 1987. — x,262p. — (Cambridge South Asian studies ; no.37). — *Bibliography: p245-254. — Includes index*

RURAL SCHOOLS — Developing countries

LEWIS, Leonard John
The school and the rural environment / by L. J. Lewis. — London : Commonwealth Secretariat, 1970. — 10p. — *At head of title page: Commonwealth Conference on Education in Rural Areas. — CRE(70)LEAD/1*

RURAL SCHOOLS — Virginia — History — 19th century

LINK, William A
A hard country and a lonely place : schooling, society, and reform in rural Virginia, 1870-1920 / William A. Link. — Chapel Hill : University of North Carolina Press, c1986. — p. cm. — (The Fred W. Morrison series in Southern studies). — *Includes index. — Bibliography: p*

RURAL SCHOOLS — Virginia — History — 20th century

LINK, William A
A hard country and a lonely place : schooling, society, and reform in rural Virginia, 1870-1920 / William A. Link. — Chapel Hill : University of North Carolina Press, c1986. — p. cm. — (The Fred W. Morrison series in Southern studies). — *Includes index. — Bibliography: p*

RURAL TRANSIT — Europe

ROUND TABLE ON TRANSPORT ECONOMICS (65th : 1984 : Paris)
Public transport in rural areas : scheduled and non-scheduled services. — Paris : European Conference of Ministers of Transport, 1984. — 270p. — *Includes bibliographies*

RURAL-URBAN MIGRATION — Asia, Southeastern — Congresses

Urbanization and migration in ASEAN development / edited by Philip M. Hauser, Daniel B. Suits, Naohiro Ogawa. — Tokyo : National Institute for Research Advancement, 1985. — xiv,496p. — *Papers presented at Conference on Migration and Development in ASEAN in 1984. — Bibliographies*

RURAL-URBAN MIGRATION — Bolivia — Santa Cruz (Dept.) — Case studies

STEARMAN, Allyn MacLean
Camba and Kolla : migration and development in Santa Cruz, Bolivia / Allyn MacLean Stearman. — Orlando : University of Central Florida Press, c1985. — xi, 227p. — *Includes index. — Bibliography: p 211-217*

RURAL-URBAN MIGRATION — Caribbean Area

HOPE, Kempe R
Urbanization in the Commonwealth Caribbean / Kempe Ronald Hope. — Boulder, Colo. : Westview Press, 1986. — p. cm. — (Westview special studies on Latin America and the Caribbean). — *Includes index. — Bibliography: p*

RURAL-URBAN MIGRATION — Ethiopia — Bagēmder — Case studies

BAKER, Jonathan
The rural-urban dichotomy in the developing world : a case study from northern Ethiopia / Jonathan Baker. — Oslo : Norwegian University Press : Oxford ; New York : Distributed world-wide excluding Scandinavia by Oxford University Press, c1986. — 372 p.. — *Bibliography: p. [365]-372*

RURAL-URBAN MIGRATION — Europe

NUTTALL, Trevor
Methods to stop rural depopulation and to involve citizens in the development of these regions / report prepared, under the guidance of the members of the Committee of Experts on Social and Economic Activities of the Steering Committee for Regional and Municipal Matters, by Trevor Nuttall. — Strasbourg : Council of Europe, 1980. — i,37p. — (Study series local and regional authorities in Europe ; study no. 22)

RURAL-URBAN MIGRATION — Middle East — History — Congresses

The Middle East city : ancient traditions confront a modern world / edited by Abdulaziz Y. Saqqaf. — New York : Paragon House, c1987. — xx, 393 p.. — *Proceedings of a conference sponsored by the Middle East Chapter of the Professors World Peace Academy. — "A PWPA book.". — Includes bibliographies and index*

RURAL-URBAN MIGRATION — Russian S.F.S.R — Moscow — History

BRADLEY, Joseph
Muzhik and Muscovite : urbanization in late imperial Russia / Joseph Bradley. — Berkeley ; London : University of California Press, c1985. — xvi, 422p. — *Based on the author's doctoral thesis. — Includes index. — Bibliography: p.377-405*

RURAL-URBAN MIGRATION — Thailand

GOLDSTEIN, Sidney
Migration and fertility-related attitudes and behavior in urban Thailand / Sidney Goldstein, Alice Goldstein [and] Bhassorn Limanonda. — Bangkok : Chulalongkorn University. Institute of Population Studies, 1981. — 71p. — (Paper / Chulalongkorn University. Institute of Population Studies ; no.38)

RURAL WOMEN — Africa

Rural development and women in Africa. — Geneva : International Labour Office, c1984. — 157p. — (A WEP study)

RURAL WOMEN — Asia — Congresses

ILO TRIPARTITE ASIAN REGIONAL SEMINAR (1981 : Maharashtra, India)
Rural development and women in Asia : proceedings and conclusions of the ILO Tripartite Asian Regional Seminar, Mahabaleshwar, Maharashtra, India, 6-11 April 1981. — Geneva : ILO, 1982. — 88p. — (A WEP study)

RURAL WOMEN — Developing countries — Economic conditions

LOUTFI, Martha Fetherolf
Rural women : unequal partners in development / Martha Fetherolf Loutfi. — Geneva : International Labour Office, 1980. — (A WEP study)

RURAL WOMEN — Developing countries — Social conditions

LOUTFI, Martha Fetherolf
Rural women : unequal partners in development / Martha Fetherolf Loutfi. — Geneva : International Labour Office, 1980. — (A WEP study)

RURAL WOMEN — Iowa — Case studies

FINK, Deborah
Open country, Iowa : rural women, tradition and change / Deborah Fink. — Albany : State University of New York Press, c1986. — p. cm. — (SUNY series in the anthropology of work). — *Includes index*

RURAL WOMEN — Middle Atlantic States — History

JENSEN, Joan M
Loosening the bonds : Mid-Atlantic farm women, 1750-1850 / by Joan M. Jensen. — New Haven : Yale University Press, c1986. — p. cm. — *Includes index. — Bibliography: p*

RURAL WOMEN — United States — Case studies
FINK, Deborah
Open country, Iowa : rural women, tradition and change / Deborah Fink. — Albany : State University of New York Press, c1986. — p. cm. — (SUNY series in the anthropology of work). — Includes index

RURUTU (AUSTRAL ISLANDS) — Population — Statistics
Tableaux normalisés du recensement général de la population : 15 octobre 1983. — [Papeete] : Institut territorial de la statistique Résultats de la commune de Rurutu. — [Papeete] : Institut territorial de la statistique. — 4p,11 leaves

RUSKIN, JOHN — Influence
BORIS, Eileen
Art and labor : Ruskin, Morris, and the craftsman ideal in America / Eileen Boris. — Philadelphia : Temple University Press, 1986. — xviii, 261 p.. — (American civilization). — Includes index. — Bibliography: p. 195-247

RUSSELL, BERTRAND
KUNTZ, Paul Grimley
Bertrand Russell / by Paul Grimley Kuntz. — Boston : Twayne Publishers, c1986. — [16], 186p. — (Twayne's English authors series ; TEAS 421). — Includes index. — Bibliography: p 171-177

RUSSIA — Diplomatic and consular service
BESEDOVSKIĬ, Grigoriĭ Zinov'evich
[Na putīākh k termidoru. English]. Revelations of a Soviet diplomat / by Grigory Bessedovsky ; translated by Matthew Norgate. — Westport, Conn. : Hyperion Press, 1977. — 276 p.. — Abridged translation of Na putīākh k termidoru. — Reprint of the 1931 ed. published by Williams & Norgate, London. — Includes index

RUSSIA — Foreign relations — 1917-1945
BESEDOVSKIĬ, Grigoriĭ Zinov'evich
[Na putīākh k termidoru. English]. Revelations of a Soviet diplomat / by Grigory Bessedovsky ; translated by Matthew Norgate. — Westport, Conn. : Hyperion Press, 1977. — 276 p.. — Abridged translation of Na putīākh k termidoru. — Reprint of the 1931 ed. published by Williams & Norgate, London. — Includes index

RUSSIA — Foreign relations — Persian Gulf region
YODFAT, Aryeh Y.
In the direction of the Persian Gulf : the Soviet Union and the Persian Gulf / A. Yodfat and M. Abir. — London : Cass, 1977. — xii,167p. — Bibliography: p.154-158. — Includes index

RUSSIA — Politics and government
WEBB, Sidney
Soviet communism : a new civilisation / by Sidney and Beatrice Webb. postscript added to the second edition. — [London] : Privately printed by the authors, 1937. — 72,33p

RUSSIA — Politics and government — 19th century
MCAULEY, Mary
Politics and the Soviet Union / Mary McAuley. — Harmondsworth : Penguin, 1977. — 352p. — (Penguin education). — Bibliography: p.338-345. — Includes index

RUSSIA — Politics and government — 20th century
MCAULEY, Mary
Politics and the Soviet Union / Mary McAuley. — Harmondsworth : Penguin, 1977. — 352p. — (Penguin education). — Bibliography: p.338-345. — Includes index

RUSSIA — Politics and government — 1917-
MCNEAL, Robert Hatch
The Bolshevik tradition : Lenin, Stalin, Khrushchev, Brezhnev / Robert H. McNeal. — 2nd ed. — Englewood Cliffs ; London : Prentice-Hall, 1975. — xiii,210p. — Previous ed.: published as 'The Bolshevik tradition : Lenin, Stalin, Khrushchev'. Englewood Cliffs : Prentice-Hall, 1963. — Bibliography: p.196-204. — Includes index

RUSSIA. Gosudarstvennaia duma. 1st, 1906-1907
MARTIUKHOVA, M. A.
Na perelome revoliutsii : obshchestvenno-politicheskoe dvizhenie v Belorussii v sviazi s uchrezhdeniem Gosudarstvennoi dumy v Rossii (avgust 1905-iiul' 1906 g.) / M. A. Martiukhova ; pod redaktsiei T. E. Solodkova. — Minsk : Nauka i Tekhnika, 1986. — 140p

RUSSIA. Gosudarstvennaia duma. 4th, 1912-1917
BADAYEV, A. Y.
Bolsheviks in the Tsarist Duma / A. Y. Badayev ; [with an introduction by Tony Cliff]. — London : Bookmarks, 1987. — 248p. — Includes bibliographical notes

RUSSIA (1923- U.S.S.R.). Ob'edinennoe gosudarstvennoe politicheskoe upravlenie
BESEDOVSKIĬ, Grigoriĭ Zinov'evich
[Na putīākh k termidoru. English]. Revelations of a Soviet diplomat / by Grigory Bessedovsky ; translated by Matthew Norgate. — Westport, Conn. : Hyperion Press, 1977. — 276 p.. — Abridged translation of Na putīākh k termidoru. — Reprint of the 1931 ed. published by Williams & Norgate, London. — Includes index

RUSSIAN DIARIES — Bibliography
Vospominaniia i dnevniki XVIII-XX vv. : ukazatel' rukopisei / redaktsiia i predislovie S. V. Zhitomirskoi. — Moskva : Kniga, 1976. — 619p

RUSSIAN LITERATURE — History and criticism — 19th century
Revoliutsionnoe demokraty i russkaia literatura XIX veka / otv. redaktory G. G. Elizavetina, A. S. Kurilov. — Moskva : Nauka, 1986. — 251p

RUSSIAN LITERATURE — 20th century — History and criticism
TVARDOVSKII, Aleksandr
Pis'ma o literature, 1930-1970 / A. Tvardovskii. — Moskva : Sovetskii pisatel', 1985. — 510p

RUSSIAN PERIODICALS — Indexes
MOSKOVSKII GOSUDARSTVENNYI UNIVERSITET. Nauchnaia biblioteka im. A. M. Gor'kogo
Sistematicheskii ukazatel' k "Vestniku Moskovskogo universiteta" : (1946-1966) / sostavitel': M. K. Simon. — Moskva : Izd-vo Moskovskogo universiteta, 1969. — 493p

RUSSIAN S.F.S.R. — Officials and employees — Biography — Directories
HELF, Gavin
A biographical directory of Soviet regional party leaders / compiled by Gavin Helf. — Munich : Radio Liberty Research, RFE/RL Part 1: RSFSR oblasts, krais, and ASSRs. — 1987. — 90p

RUSSIANS — Foreign countries — Political activity
MILLER, Martin, A
The Russian revolutionary emigrés, 1825-1870 / Martin A. Miller. — Baltimore ; London : Johns Hopkins University Press, c1986. — xii, 292p. — (The Johns Hopkins University studies in historical and political science ; 104th ser., 2). — Includes index. — Bibliography: p.[271]-284

RUSSIANS — Alaska — History
Russia's American colony / edited by S. Frederick Starr. — Durham : Duke University Press, 1987. — p. cm. — (A Special study of the Kennan Institute for Advanced Russian Studies of the Woodrow Wilson International Center for Scholars). — Includes index. — Bibliography: p

RUSSIANS — Europe
TUDORIANU, N. L.
Ocherki rossiiskoi trudovoi emigratsii perioda imperializma : (v Germaniiu, Skandinavskie strany i SShA) / N. L. Tudorianu ; otv. redaktor E. M. Shchagin. — Kishinev : Shtiintsa, 1986. — 309p

RUSSIANS — Latvia
ZAVARINA, A. A.
Russkoe naselenie vostochnoi Latvii vo vtoroi polovine XIX - nachale XX veka : istoriko-etnograficheskii ocherk / A. A. Zavarina. — Riga : Zinatne, 1986. — 246p

RUSSIANS — United States
TUDORIANU, N. L.
Ocherki rossiiskoi trudovoi emigratsii perioda imperializma : (v Germaniiu, Skandinavskie strany i SShA) / N. L. Tudorianu ; otv. redaktor E. M. Shchagin. — Kishinev : Shtiintsa, 1986. — 309p

RUSSKAIA OSVOBODITEL'NAIA ARMIIA — History
ANDREYEV, Catherine
Vlasov and the Russian Liberation Movement : Soviet reality and émigré theories / Catherine Andreyev. — Cambridge : Cambridge University Press, 1987. — xiv,251p. — (Soviet and East European studies). — Bibliography: p224-239. — Includes index

RUSSO-JAPANESE WAR, 1904-1905 — Diplomatic history
WHITE, John Albert
The diplomacy of the Russo-Japanese War / John A. White. — Princeton : Princeton University Press, 1964. — xi,410p

RUSSO-POLISH WAR, 1919-1920 — Diplomatic history
Tajne rokowanie polsko-radzieckie w 1919 r. : materiały archiwalne i dokumenty / zebrała i opracowała Weronika Gosty'nska. — Warszawa : Pa'nstwowe Wydawnictwo Naukowe, 1986. — 412p. — Documents in Polish, Russian, French or German. — Bibliography: p391-[396]

RUTKOWSKI, JAN
TOPOLSKI, Jerzy
O nowy model historii : Jan Rutkowski (1886-1949) / Jerzy Topolski. — Warszawa : Państwowe Wydawnictwo Naukowe, 1986. — 310p

RYUKYU ISLANDS — Social life and customs
OUWEHAND, Cornelius
Hateruma : socio-religious aspects of a South Ryukyuan island culture / C. Ouwehand. — Leiden : Brill, 1985. — 324,(73)p

S. G. WARBURG & CO.
ATTALI, Jacques
A man of influence : Sir Siegmund Warburg 1902-82 / Jacques Attali ; translated by Barbara Ellis. — London : Weidenfeld and Nicholson, 1986. — vii,346p. — Translation of: Un homme d'influence

SAARLAND (GERMANY) — History — 20th century
LEMPERT, Peter
"Das Saarland den Saarländern!" : die frankophilen Bestrebungen im Saargebiet 1918-1935 / Peter Lempert. — Köln : dme-Verlag, 1985. — 542p. — (Kölner Schriften zur romanischen Kultur ; Bd.3). — Bibliography: p523-532

SAARLAND (GERMANY) — Politics and government

LEMPERT, Peter
"Das Saarland den Saarländern!" : die frankophilen Bestrebungen im Saargebiet 1918-1935 / Peter Lempert. — Köln : dme-Verlag, 1985. — 542p. — (Kölner Schriften zur romanischen Kultur ; Bd.3). — *Bibliography: p523-532*

SAARLAND (GERMANY) — Statistics

Statistisches Handbuch für das Saarland / Statistisches Amt, Saarland. — Saarbrücken : Statistisches Amt des Saarlandes, 1982-. — *Biennial*

SABBATHAIANS

AHLBERG, Sture
Messianic movements : a comparative analysis of the Sabbatians, the People's Temple, and the Unification Church / by Sture Ahlberg. — Stockholm : Almqvist & Wiksell International, 1986. — 128 p.. — (Acta Universitatis Stockholmiensis. Stockholm studies in comparative religion ; 26). — *Continuation of author's thesis (doctoral--Stockholm, 1977) originally presented as: Messianism in the State of Israel. — Includes indexes. — Bibliography: p. 118-122*

SACRIFICE

VALERI, Valerio
Kingship and sacrifice : ritual and society in ancient Hawaii / Valerio Valeri ; translated by Paula Wissing. — Chicago : University of Chicago Press, 1985. — p. cm. — *Translated from the French. — Includes index. — Bibliography: p*

SACRIFICE — Hinduism

ZEITLYN, Sushila Jane
Sacrifice and the sacred in a Hindu "tīrtha" : the case of Pushkar India / Sushila Jane Zeitlyn. — 377 leaves, [23] leaves of plates. — *PhD (Econ) 1986 LSE*

SAFETY EDUCATION, INDUSTRIAL

FOOD, DRINK AND TOBACCO INDUSTRY TRAINING BOARD
Training for health and safety at work : safety representatives and safety committees. — Gloucester : the Board, [1977]. — 12p

SAFETY REGULATIONS — Economic aspects — Congresses

GENEVA CONFERENCE ON THE VALUE OF LIFE AND SAFETY (1981)
The value of life and safety : proceedings of a conference held by the "Geneva Association" : collection of papers presented at the Geneva Conference on the Value of Life and Safety held at the University of Geneva, 30th, 31st March and 1st April 1981 / edited by M.W. Jones-Lee. — Amsterdam ; New York : North-Holland Pub. Co. ; New York, N.Y. : Sole distributors for the U.S.A. and Canada, Elsevier Science Pub. Co., 1982. — xvii, 309 p.. — *Bibliography: p. xi*

SAILORS' UNION OF THE PACIFIC — History

SCHWARTZ, Stephen
Brotherhood of the sea : a history of the Sailors' Union of the Pacific, 1885-1985 / by Stephen Schwartz ; foreword by Paul Dempster, preface by John F. Henning, introduction by Karl Kortum. — San Francisco, CA : Sailors' Union of the Pacific ; New Brunswick, USA : Distributed by Transaction Books, c1986. — p. cm. — *Includes index*

SAINT ÉTIENNE (LOIRE, FRANCE) — Politics and government

GORDON, David M.
Merchants and capitalists : industrialization and provincial politics in mid-nineteenth century France / by David M. Gordon. — University, Ala. : University of Alabama Press, c1985. — ix, 249p. — *Includes index. — Bibliography: p.232-239*

SAINT JOHN (NEW BRUNSWICK) — History

ACHESON, T. W.
Saint John : the making of a colonial urban community / T.W. Acheson. — Toronto ; London : University of Toronto Press, c1985. — 314p. — *Includes index*

SAINT JOHN (V.I.) — Race relations

OLWIG, Karen Fog
Cultural adaptation and resistance on St. John : three centuries of Afro-Caribbean life / Karen Fog Olwig. — Gainesville : University of Florida Press, c1985. — xii, 226 p.. — *Cover title: Cultural adaptation & resistance on St. John. — Includes index. — Bibliography: p. [201]-216*

SAINT KITTS-NEVIS — Economic conditions

St. Christopher and Nevis : economic report. — Washington, D.C., U.S.A. : World Bank, 1985. — xii,82p. — (World Bank country study)

SAINT LUCIA — Constitution

SAINT LUCIA
[Constitution (1967)]. Constitution of Saint Lucia : a summary. — Castries : Public Relations Office, 1967. — 13p

SAINT LUCIA — Economic conditions

St. Lucia : economic performance and prospects. — Washington, D.C., U.S.A. : World Bank, 1985. — [xi],99p. — (World Bank country study). — *"Based on the findings of a World Bank mission to St. Lucia in February 1985"--Pref*

SAINT VINCENT AND THE GRENADINES — Economic conditions

St. Vincent and the Grenadines : economic situations and selected development issues. — Washington, D.C., U.S.A. : World Bank, 1985. — xiii,108p. — (World Bank country study)

SAINT VINCENT AND THE GRENADINES — Economic policy

St. Vincent and the Grenadines : economic situations and selected development issues. — Washington, D.C., U.S.A. : World Bank, 1985. — xiii,108p. — (World Bank country study)

SAIONJI, KINMOCHI, Prince

CONNORS, Lesley
The Emperor's adviser : Saionji Kinmochi and pre-war Japanese politics / Lesley Connors. — London : Croom Helm, c1987. — 260p. — (The Nissan Institute / Croom Helm Japanese studies series). — *Includes index*

SAKATA, TOSHIBOMI

Satellites for arms control and crisis monitoring / edited by Bhupendra Jasani and Toshibomi Sakata. — Oxford : Oxford University Press, 1987. — xv,176p. — *Under the auspices of Sipri. — Includes index*

SALES — England

GOODE, R. M.
Proprietary rights and insolvency in sales transactions / by R.M. Goode. — London : Sweet & Maxwell, 1985. — xv,137p. — *Includes index*

SALES — Great Britain

Benjamin's sale of goods / [general editor, A.G. Guest]. — 3rd ed. — London : Sweet & Maxwell, 1987. — [xvi,1400]p. — (The Common law library ; no.11). — *Previous ed.: 1981. — Includes index*

SALES — Great Britain — Cases

IVAMY, E. R. Hardy
Casebook on sale of goods / E.R. Hardy Ivamy. — 5th ed. — London : Lloyd's of London, 1987. — [ix,200]p. — *Previous ed.: 1980. — Includes index*

SALES, CONDITIONAL — Canada

GEVA, Benjamin
Financing consumer sales and product defences in Canada and the United States / by Benjamin Geva. — [Agincourt, Ont.] : Carswell Legal Publications, 1984. — xlii, 340 p.. — *"Text on part V of the Bills of Exchange Act, FTC Trade Regulation Rule, provincial, federal, and uniform state legislation, legal doctrines and statutes pertaining to financing assignee, holder for value, holder in due course, direct lender, or credit card issuer, and related topics.". — Includes bibliographical references and index*

SALES TAX — Denmark

DENMARK. Udvalget om forbrugsbeskatning
Betaenkning om forbrugsbeskatning. — [København : Statens Trykningskontor], 1958. — 296p. — (Betaenkning ; nr.202)

SALINE WATER CONVERSION — Developing countries

The use of non-conventional water resources in developing countries. — New York : United Nations, 1985. — xviii,278p. — (Document / United Nations ; ST/ESA/149). — *Sales no.: E.84.II.A.14*

SALISBURY, ROBERT ARTHUR TALBOT GASCOYNE-CECIL, Marquess of

Salisbury : the man and his policies / edited by Lord Blake and Hugh Cecil. — Basingstoke : Macmillan, 1987. — ix,298p. — *Includes index*

SALMON-FISHERIES — Atlantic Ocean — Congresses

INTERNATIONAL ATLANTIC SALMON SYMPOSIUM (2nd : 1978 : Edinburgh)
Atlantic salmon, its future : proceedings of the second International Atlantic Salmon Symposium, Edinburgh 1978, sponsored by the International Atlantic Salmon Foundation and the Atlantic Salmon Research Trust / editor A.E.J. Went. — Farnham : Fishing News, 1980. — xi,253p. — *Includes bibliographies and index*

SALMON INDUSTRY — United States — Pacific States

LENT, Rebecca J.
Uncertainty, market disequilibrium and the firm's decision process : applications to the Pacific salmon market / Rebecca J. Lent. — Corvallis, Or. : Sea Grant College Program, Oregon State University, [1984]. — vii,109p. — *Bibliography: p94-97*

SALT INDUSTRY AND TRADE — Mexico — History

EWALD, Ursula
The Mexican salt industry, 1560-1980 : a study in change / Ursula Ewald. — Stuttgart ; New York : G. Fischer, 1985. — 480 p. — *Fourteen maps and one chart on folded leaves in pocket. — Includes index. — Bibliography: p. 375-413*

SALT INDUSTRY AND TRADE — Taiwan

Salt industry in Taiwan, Republic of China. — [Taipei : Ministry of Economic Affairs, 1958]. — 20p

SALTYKOV, M. E.

EMEL'IANOV, N. P.
"Otechestvennye zapiski" N. A. Nekrasova i M. E. Saltykova-Shchedrina (1868-1884) / N. P. Emel'ianov. — Leningrad : Khudozhestvennaia literatura, Leningradskoe otdelenie, 1986. — 333p

SALVAGE (WASTE, ETC.)

GREAT BRITAIN. Central Directorate of Environmental Protection
Monitoring waste : the duty of care : the Government's response to the eleventh report of the Royal Commission on Environmental Pollution / Central Directorate of Environmental Protection, Department of the Environment. — London : H.M.S.O., 1986. — (Pollution paper ; no.24)

SALVAGE (WASTE, ETC.)
continuation

LUND, Robert T.
Remanufacturing : the experience of the United States and implications for developing countries / Robert T. Lund. — Washington, D.C. : The World Bank, 1984. — xi,103p. — (World Bank technical paper ; no.31) (UNDP project management report ; no.2) (Integrated resource recovery series ; no.2). — *Includes bibliographical references*

SALVAGE (WASTE, ETC.) — Developing countries

LUND, Robert T.
Remanufacturing : the experience of the United States and implications for developing countries / Robert T. Lund. — Washington, D.C. : The World Bank, 1984. — xi,103p. — (World Bank technical paper ; no.31) (UNDP project management report ; no.2) (Integrated resource recovery series ; no.2). — *Includes bibliographical references*

SALVATION ARMY. Men's Social Service Department — History

MCKINLEY, Edward H
Somebody's brother : a history of the Salvation Army Men's Social Service Department, 1891-1985 / E.H. McKinley. — Lewiston [N.Y.] : Edwin Mellen Press, c1986. — xiii, 273 p., [40] p. of plates. — (Studies in American religion ; v. 21). — *Includes index. — Bibliography: p. 217-260*

SAMBIA (PAPUA NEW GUINEA PEOPLE)

HERDT, Gilbert H.
Sambia : ritual and gender in New Guinea / by Gilbert H. Herdt. — New York : Holt, Rinehart and Winston, 1986. — p. cm. — (Case studies in cultural anthropology). — *Includes index. — Bibliography: p*

SAMBO (FICTITIOUS CHARACTER)

BOSKIN, Joseph
Sambo : the rise & demise of an American jester / Joseph Boskin. — New York : Oxford University Press, 1986. — ix, 252 p. [8] p. of plates. — *Includes index. — Bibliography: p. 225-243*

SAMOANS — Anthropometry

The Changing Samoans : behavior and health in transition / edited by Paul T. Baker, Joel M. Hanna, and Thelma S. Baker. — New York : Oxford University Press, 1986. — p. cm. — *Includes index. — Bibliography: p*

SAMOANS — Health and hygiene

The Changing Samoans : behavior and health in transition / edited by Paul T. Baker, Joel M. Hanna, and Thelma S. Baker. — New York : Oxford University Press, 1986. — p. cm. — *Includes index. — Bibliography: p*

SAMPLING (STATISTICS)

Drawing inferences from self-selected samples / edited by Howard Wainer. — New York : Springer-Verlag, c1986. — xii, 163 p.. — *Papers from a conference sponsored by Educational Testing Service. — Includes indexes. — Bibliography: p. [153]-157*

MATÉRN, Bertil
Spatial variation / Bertil Matérn. — 2nd ed. — Berlin ; New York : Springer-Verlag, c1986. — 151 p.. — (Lecture notes in statistics ; v. 36). — *Includes indexes. — Bibliography: p. [140]-144*

YAMANE, Taro
Elementary sampling theory / Taro Yamane. — Englewood Cliffs : Prentice-Hall, [1967]. — x,405p

SAN ANTONIO (TEX.) — Politics and government — Addresses, essays, lectures

The Politics of San Antonio : community, progress, & power / edited by David R. Johnson, John A. Booth, Richard J. Harris. — Lincoln : University of Nebraska Press, c1983. — xi, 248 p.. — *Includes bibliographical references*

SAN FERNANDO (TRINIDAD AND TOBAGO) — Social conditions

CLARKE, Colin G.
East Indians in a West Indian town : San Fernando, Trinidad, 1930-1970 / Colin G. Clarke. — London : Allen & Unwin, 1986. — xi,193p,[4]p of plates. — (The London research series in geography ; 12). — *Bibliography: p176-187. — Includes index*

SAN FRANCISCO (CALIF.) — Economic conditions

ISSEL, William
San Francisco, 1865-1932 : politics, power, and urban development / William Issel and Robert W. Cherny. — Berkeley : University of California Press, c1986. — xiv, 294 p. [48] p. of plates. — *Includes index. — Bibliography: p. [261]-279*

MCDONALD, Terrence J
The parameters of urban fiscal policy : socio-economic change, political culture, and fiscal policy in San Francisco, 1860-1906. — Berkeley : University of California Press, c1986. — p. cm. — *Includes index. — Bibliography: p*

SAN FRANCISCO (CALIF.) — Politics and government

ISSEL, William
San Francisco, 1865-1932 : politics, power, and urban development / William Issel and Robert W. Cherny. — Berkeley : University of California Press, c1986. — xiv, 294 p. [48] p. of plates. — *Includes index. — Bibliography: p. [261]-279*

MCDONALD, Terrence J
The parameters of urban fiscal policy : socio-economic change, political culture, and fiscal policy in San Francisco, 1860-1906. — Berkeley : University of California Press, c1986. — p. cm. — *Includes index. — Bibliography: p*

SAN FRANCISCO (CALIF.) — Social conditions

MCDONALD, Terrence J
The parameters of urban fiscal policy : socio-economic change, political culture, and fiscal policy in San Francisco, 1860-1906. — Berkeley : University of California Press, c1986. — p. cm. — *Includes index. — Bibliography: p*

SAN MARINO — Census, 1976

5° censimento generale popolazione : 30 novembre 1976. — San Marino : Ufficio Statale di Statistica, 1979. — xiii,200 leaves

SAN MARINO — Industries — Statistics

1° censimento dell'industria e delle forze di lavoro : 10 luglio 1979. — San Marino : Ufficio Statale di Statistica, 1980. — xv,342 leaves

SAN MARINO — Population — Statistics

5° censimento generale popolazione : 30 novembre 1976. — San Marino : Ufficio Statale di Statistica, 1979. — xiii,200 leaves

Dinamica demografica ed evoluzione sociale nella Repubblica di San Marino. — San Marino : Ufficio Statale di Statistica, 1975. — ix,136 leaves

SAN MARINO — Social conditions — Statistics

Dinamica demografica ed evoluzione sociale nella Repubblica di San Marino. — San Marino : Ufficio Statale di Statistica, 1975. — ix,136 leaves

SAN MARINO — Statistics

Annuario statistico : 1972/1980. — San Marino : Ufficio Statale di Statistica, [1981?]. — f 4. — *Contents: Vol.1. Territorio, climatologia, popolazione - v.2. Sanitarie e sicurezza sociale - v.3. Istruzione, cultura e spettacolo, elezioni, giustizia, agricoltura, industrie, costruzioni e opere pubbliche - v.4. Trasporti e comunicazioni, commercio e turismo, prezzi, lavoro e retribuzioni, finanza pubblica, reddito nazionale*

SANATORIUMS — Soviet Union

POLTORANOV, V. V.
Zdravnitsy profsoiuzov SSSR : kurorty, sanatorii, pansionaty, doma otdykha / V. V. Poltoranov, S. Ia. Slutskii ; pod redaktsiei I. I. Kozlova. — Izd. 6-e, perer. i dop.. — Moskva : Profizdat, 1986. — 700p

SANCTIONS (INTERNATIONAL LAW)

MOORSOM, Richard
The scope for sanctions : economic measures against South Africa / Richard Moorsom. — London : Catholic Institute for International Relations, 1986. — [vi],102p

The Utility of international economic sanctions / edited by David Leyton-Brown. — London : Croom Helm, c1987. — 320p. — *Includes index*

SANCTIONS (INTERNATIONAL LAW) — Bibliography

Sanctions against South Africa : a selective bibliography = Les sanctions contre l'Afrique du Sud : bibliographie selective. — New York : United Nations, 1981. — vii,28p. — (Bibliographical series / Dag Hammarskjöld Library ; no.32 = Série bibliographique / Bibliothèque Dag Hammarskjöld ; no.32) ([Document] / United Nations ; ST/LIB/SER.B/32). — *In English, French, German, Italian and Russian. — Sales no: E/F/81.I.13*

SANCTIONS (LAW)

BAYLEY, David H
Social control and political change / by David H. Bayley. — [Princeton, N.J.] : Center of International Studies, Woodrow Wilson School of Public and International Affairs, Princeton University, c1985. — 135 p.. — (Research monograph / Center for International Studies, Woodrow Wilson School of Public and International Affairs ; no. 49). — *"December 1985.". — Includes bibliographical references*

SANCTUARY MOVEMENT

Sanctuary : a resource guide for understanding and participating in the Central American refugees' struggle / Gary MacEoin, editor. — 1st ed. — San Francisco : Harper & Row, c1985. — 217 p.. — *Papers derived from the Inter-American Symposium on Sanctuary, held in Tucson, Ariz., Jan. 23-24, 1985, and sponsored by the Tucson Ecumenical Council's Task Force for Central America and others. — Bibliography: p. 207-211*

SANDINO, AUGUSTO CÉSAR — Political and social views

HODGES, Donald Clark
Intellectual foundations of the Nicaraguan revolution / by Donald C. Hodges. — 1st ed. — Austin : University of Texas Press, 1986. — p. cm. — *Includes index. — Bibliography: p*

SANDINO, AUGUSTO CÉSAR — 1895-1934

ALEN LASCANO, Luis C
Yrigoyen, Sandino y el panamericanismo / Luis C. Alen Lascano. — Buenos Aires : Centro Editor de América Latina, 1986. — 138p. — (Biblioteca Política Argentina ; 131). — *Bibliography: p138*

SANDOZ, EDOUARD

RIEDL-EHRENBERG, Renate
Alfred Kern (1850-1893) : Edouard Sandoz (1853-1928) : Gründer der Sandoz AG, Basel / Renate Riedl-Ehrenberg. — Zürich : Verein für wirtschaftshistorische Studien, 1986. — 90p. — (Schweizer Pioniere der Wirtschaft und Technik ; 44). — *Bibliography: p84*

SANDOZ AG (Basel)

RIEDL-EHRENBERG, Renate
Alfred Kern (1850-1893) : Edouard Sandoz (1853-1928) : Gründer der Sandoz AG, Basel / Renate Riedl-Ehrenberg. — Zürich : Verein für wirtschaftshistorische Studien, 1986. — 90p. — (Schweizer Pioniere der Wirtschaft und Technik ; 44). — *Bibliography: p84*

SANE, INC — History
KATZ, Milton S.
Ban the bomb : a history of SANE, the Committee for a Sane Nuclear Policy, 1957-1985 / Milton S. Katz ; foreword by Benjamin Spock. — Westport, Conn. : Greenwood Press, c1986. — p. cm. — (Contributions in political science ; no. 147). — Includes index. — Bibliography: p

SANGER, MARGARET
MOORE, Gloria
Margaret Sanger and the birth control movement : a bibliography, 1911-1984 / by Gloria Moore and Ronald Moore. — Metuchen, N.J. : Scarecrow Press, 1986. — xvii, 211 p.. — Includes indexes. — Bibliography: xi-xii

SANGER, MARGARET — Bibliography
MOORE, Gloria
Margaret Sanger and the birth control movement : a bibliography, 1911-1984 / by Gloria Moore and Ronald Moore. — Metuchen, N.J. : Scarecrow Press, 1986. — xvii, 211 p.. — Includes indexes. — Bibliography: xi-xii

SANITARY ENGINEERING — Study and teaching (Higher) — Europe
Training of sanitary engineers in Europe / edited by Robert B. Dean. — Copenhagen : World Health Organization, 1985. — x,198p. — Includes bibliographical references

SANITARY ENGINEERS — Training of — Europe
Training of sanitary engineers in Europe / edited by Robert B. Dean. — Copenhagen : World Health Organization, 1985. — x,198p. — Includes bibliographical references

SANITATION — Statistics
The International Drinking Water Supply and Sanitation Decade : review of national baseline data (as at 31 December 1980). — Geneva : World Health Organization, 1984. — 169p. — (WHO offset publication ; no.85)

SANITATION ENGINEERING
EDWARDS, Peter
Aquaculture : a component of low cost sanitation technology / Peter Edwards. — Washington, D.C. : The World Bank, 1985. — xi,45p. — (World Bank technical paper ; no.36) (UNDP project management report ; no.3) (Integrated resource recovery series ; no.3). — At head of cover: "Integrated resource recovery". — Bibliographical references: p45

SANTA CATARINA (BRAZIL)
Santa Catarina ação da reconstrução: relatório / Conselho Extraordinário de Reconstruçao [and] Gabinete do Secretario Extraordinário para a Reconstrução. — FlorianópolisSanta Catarina : Conselho Extraordinario de Reconstrucao : Gabinete do Secretário Extraordinário para a Reconstrução, 1983-. — Annual

SÃO PAULO (BRAZIL : STATE) — Economic conditions
KUZNESOF, Elizabeth Anne
Household economy and urban development : São Paulo, 1765 to 1836 / Elizabeth Anne Kuznesof. — Boulder ; London : Westview Press, 1986. — xvii, 216p. — (Dellplain Latin American studies ; 18). — Includes index. — Bibliography: p199-211

SÃO PEDRO (RIO GRANDE DO SUL, BRAZIL) — History
PINHEIRO, José Feliciano Fernandes, Visconde de São Leopoldo
Anais da provincia de São Pedro : história da colonização alemã no Rio Grande do Sul / José Feliciano Fernandes Pinheiro, Visconde de São Leopoldo ; introdução de Viana Moog. — 4 edição. — Petrópolis : Vozes ; [Brasília] : Instituto Nacional do Livro, Ministério da Educação e Cultura, 1978. — 250p. — (Dimensões do Brasil ; 9). — Publicado originalmente em Rio de Janeiro, Regia, 1819-1822, com o título: "Annaes da capitania de S. Pedro

SAPINY (AFRICAN PEOPLE)
GOLDSCHMIDT, Walter Rochs
The Sebei / by Walter Goldschmidt. — New York : Holt, Rinehart, and Winston, c1986. — p. cm. — (Case studies in cultural anthropology). — Includes index. — Bibliography: p

SARAWAK (MALAYSIA) — Population — Statistics
Banci penduduk dan perumahan Malaysia 1980 = Population and housing census of Malaysia 1980. — Kuala Lumpur : Department of Statistics. — Text in Malay and English Laporan penduduk negeri = State population report
Sarawak. — 1980. — 2v. — 1map in v.2

SAROAKO (INDONESIA) — Economic conditions
ROBINSON, Kathryn May
Stepchildren of progress : the political economy of development in an Indonesian mining town / Kathryn May Robinson. — Albany, N.Y. : State University of New York Press, c1986. — xvi, 315 p.. — (SUNY series in the anthropology of work). — : Originally presented as the author's thesis (Ph.D.)--Australian National University, 1983. — Includes index. — Bibliography: p. 295-307

SAROAKO (INDONESIA) — Social conditions
ROBINSON, Kathryn May
Stepchildren of progress : the political economy of development in an Indonesian mining town / Kathryn May Robinson. — Albany, N.Y. : State University of New York Press, c1986. — xvi, 315 p.. — (SUNY series in the anthropology of work). — : Originally presented as the author's thesis (Ph.D.)--Australian National University, 1983. — Includes index. — Bibliography: p. 295-307

SARTRE, JEAN PAUL. Critique de la raison dialectique. 1, Théorie des ensembles pratiques
CATALANO, Joseph S
A commentary on Jean-Paul Sartre's Critique of dialectical reason, volume 1, Theory of practical ensembles / Joseph S. Catalano. — Chicago : University of Chicago Press, 1986. — x, 282 p.. — Includes index. — Bibliography: p. [269]-273

SARTRE, JEAN-PAUL
BOSCHETTI, Anna
Sartre et "les temps modernes" : une entreprise intellectuelle / Anna Boschetti. — Paris : Minuit, [1985]. — 324p

HAYMAN, Ronald
Writing against : a biography of Sartre / Ronald Hayman. — London : Weidenfeld and Nicolson, c1986. — x,487p,[12]p of plates. — Bibliography: p471-476. — Includes index

LÉVY, Benny
Le nom de l'homme : dialogue avec Sartre / Benny Lévy. — Lagrasse : Verdier, 1984. — 191p

SARTRE, JEAN PAUL — Contributions in political science
MERKEL, Bernard
The concept of freedom and the development of Sartre's early political thought / Bernard Merkel. — New York : Garland Pub., 1987. — p. cm. — (Political theory and political philosophy). — Thesis (Ph. D.)--University of Reading, 1984. — Bibliography: p

SARTRE, JEAN PAUL, 1905-1980
ABOULAFIA, Mitchell
The mediating self : Mead, Sartre, and self-determination / Mitchell Aboulafia. — New Haven : Yale University Press, c1986. — xvii, 139p. — Includes index. — Bibliography: p.127-131

SAS (COMPUTER SYSTEM) — Handbooks, manuals, etc
SAS INSTITUTE
SAS introductory guide for personal computers. — Version 6 ed. — Cary, N.C. : SAS Institute, 1985. — 111p

SAS INSTITUTE
SAS language guide for personal computers. — Version 6 ed. — Cary, N.C. : SAS Institute, 1985. — 429p

SAS INSTITUTE
SAS procedures guide for personal computers. — Version 6 ed. — Cary, N.C. : SAS Institute, 1985. — 373p

SAS INSTITUTE
SAS/STAT guide for personal computers. — Version 6 ed. — Cary, N.C. : SAS Institute, 1985. — 378p

SATURDAY EVENING POST — Illustrations
The Saturday evening post Norman Rockwell book. — New York : Bonanza Books : Distributed by Crown Publishers, 1986, c1977. — vii, 152 p.

SAUDI ARABIA — Economic conditions
AL-FARSY, Fouad
Saudi Arabia : a case study in development / Fouad Al-Farsy. — Completely revised and updated ed.. — London : KPI, 1986. — 264. — Bibliography: p[242]-255

SAUDI ARABIA — Economic policy
Fourth development plan 1985-1990. — [Riyadh] : Ministry of Planning, [1985]. — 435p

SAUDI ARABIA — Foreign relations
CORDESMAN, Anthony H.
Western strategic interests in Saudi Arabia / Anthony H. Cordesman. — London : Croom Helm, c1987. — 308p. — Bibliography: p267-290. — Includes index

GOLDBERG, Jacob
The foreign policy of Saudi Arabia : the formative years, 1902-1918 / Jacob Goldberg. — Cambridge, Mass. ; London : Harvard University Press, 1986. — viii,231p. — (Harvard Middle Eastern ; 19). — Includes index

SAUDI ARABIA — Foreign relations — Egypt
BADEEB, Saeed M
The Saudi-Egyptian conflict over North Yemen, 1962-1970 / Saeed M. Badeeb ; foreword by J.E. Peterson. — Boulder, Colo. : Westview Press ; Washington, D.C. : American-Arab Affairs Council, 1986. — xv, 148 p., [1] p. of plates. — Includes index. — Bibliography: p. 137-142

SAUDI ARABIA — Politics and government
AL-FARSY, Fouad
Saudi Arabia : a case study in development / Fouad Al-Farsy. — Completely revised and updated ed.. — London : KPI, 1986. — 264. — Bibliography: p[242]-255

SAUDI ARABIA — Social policy
Fourth development plan 1985-1990. — [Riyadh] : Ministry of Planning, [1985]. — 435p

SAUVÉ, JEANNE, 1922-
WOODS, Shirley E.
Her Excellency Jeanne Sauvé / Shirley E. Woods. — Toronto : Macmillan of Canada, 1986. — xii,242p

SAVEZ KOMUNISTA JUGOSLAVIJE
Savez komunista u borbi protiv antisocijalističkih delovanja i antikomunističkih ideologija / redakcioni odbor David Atlagić...[et al.]. — Beograd : Izdavački centar Komunist, 1986. — viii,555p

SAVEZ KOMUNISTA JUGOSLAVIJE — Congresses
SAVEZ KOMUNISTA JUGOSLAVIJE.
Centralni komitet. Sednica (3 : 1982)
Aktuelna idejno-politička pitanja društveno-ekonomske situacije i zadaci Saveza komunista u ostvarivanju stavova 12. kongresa SKJ : uvodno izlaganje Mitje Ribičiča, diskusija, zaključci. — Beograd : Izdavački Centae Komunist, 1982. — 212p

SAVEZ KOMUNISTA JUGOSLAVIJE — History
Istorija Saveza komunista Jugoslavije / autori: Janko Pleterski...[et al.] ; redaktsioni odbor: Takhir Abdulji...[et al.]. — Beograd : Izdavački centar komunist : Narodna knjiga : Rad, 1985. — xv,485p

SAVIGNY, FRIEDRICH KARL VON, 1779-1861
DENNELER, Iris
Friedrich Karl von Savigny / von Iris Denneler. — Berlin : Stapp, 1985. — 140p. — (Preussische Köpfe ; 17). — *Cover title: Karl Friedrich von Savigny.* — *Bibliography: p125-129*

SAVIMBI, JONAS
BRIDGLAND, Fred
Jonas Savimbi : a key to Africa / by Fred Bridgland. — Edinburgh : Mainstream, 1986. — [300]p. — *Includes bibliography and index*

SAVIMBI, JONAS MALHEIRO
DÖHNING, W
UNITA : União Nacional para a Independência Total de Angola / text by W. Döhning ; photographs by Cloete Breytenbach. — [Angola] : Kwacha Unita Press, 1984. — 93 p.

SAVING AND INVESTMENT — Addresses, essays, lectures
Public policy and capital formation : a study / by the Federal Reserve System, Board of Governors of the Federal Reserve System. — [Washington, D.C.] : the Board, 1981. — 326p. — *Includes bibliographical references*

SAVING AND INVESTMENT — Taxation — United States
NATIONAL BUREAU OF ECONOMIC RESEARCH
Taxes and capital formation : NBER summary report. — Cambridge (Mass.) : National Bureau of Economic Research, 1986. — 40p. — *This report summarizes the papers discussed at the NBER's conference on the effects of taxation on capital formation held on February 13-16 1986, in Palm Beach, Florida*

SAVING AND INVESTMENT — Bangladesh
RAHMAN, M. Akhlaqur
External assistance, saving and resource mobilization in Bangladesh / M. Akhlaqur Rahman, K. Mustahidur Rahman. — [Dacca] : External Resources Division, Ministry of Finance and Planning, [ca.1983]. — 95p. — *Bibliography: p94-95*

RANA, Pradumna B.
Improving domestic resource mobilization through financial development : Bangladesh / Pradumna B. Rana. — Manila : Asian Development Bank, 1986. — [v],52p. — *Includes bibliographical references*

SAVING AND INVESTMENT — China — History
LIPPIT, Victor D
The economic development of China / by Victor D. Lippit. — Armonk, N.Y. : M.E. Sharpe, c1987. — p. cm. — *Includes bibliographies and index*

SAVING AND INVESTMENT — Denmark
STETKAER, Karsten
Beregningen af erhvervsfordelte investeringer i nationalregnskabet 1966-81 / Karsten Stetkaer. — [København] : Danmarks Statistik, 1986. — 130p. — (Arbejdsnotat / Danmarks Statistik ; nr.14)

SAVING AND INVESTMENT — Europe
HALÁSZ, Sándor
A pénzintézeti betétek biztonsága : külöuös tekintettel a takarékpénztárakra / a kereskedelemügyi minister megbízásából ismerteti Halász Sándor. — Budapest : Kereskedelemügyi M. kir minster, 1904. — viii,348p

SAVING AND INVESTMENT — Great Britain
COLES, Adrian
Building Societies and the savings market / b Adrian Coles. — London : Building Societies Association, 1986. — 32p

SAVING AND INVESTMENT — Japan
BLUMENTHAL, Tuvia
Saving in postwar Japan. — Cambridge : East Asian Research Center, Harvard University; distributed by Harvard University Press, 1970. — xi, 117 p. — (Harvard East Asian monographs ; 35). — *Bibliography: p. 109-113*

SAVING AND INVESTMENT — Nigeria
State, oil, and agriculture in Nigeria / Michael Watts, editor. — Berkeley : Institute of International Studies, University of California, c1987. — xiv, 327 p.. — (Research series ; no. 66). — *Includes index.* — *Bibliography: p. 297-317*

SAVING AND INVESTMENT — Taiwan
HSING, Mo-huan
Capital formation in Taiwan 1951-1953 : a preliminary finding / by Mo-huan Hsing. — [Taipei] : Industrial Development Commission, 1955. — 22p

SAVING AND INVESTMENT — United States
Financial futures and options in the U.S. economy : a study / by the staff of the Federal Reserve System ; edited by Myron L. Kwast. — [Washington : Board of Governors of the Federal Reserve System], 1986. — [ix],264p. — *Bibliography: p249-264*

Responses to deregulation : retail deposit pricing from 1983 through 1985 / Patrick I. Mahoney...[et al.]. — Washington, D. C. : Board of Governors of the Federal Reserve System, 1987. — 29p. — (Staff study / Board of Governors of the Federal Reserve System ; 151). — *Includes bibliographical references*

SAVING AND INVESTMENT — United States — Addresses, essays, lectures
The Level and composition of household saving / edited by Patric H. Hendershott. — Cambridge, Mass. : Ballinger Pub. Co., [1985]. — p. cm. — *Includes bibliographies and index*

Public policy and capital formation : a study / by the Federal Reserve System, Board of Governors of the Federal Reserve System. — [Washington, D.C.] : the Board, 1981. — 326p. — *Includes bibliographical references*

SAVING AND INVESTMENT — United States — Congresses
Financing corporate capital formation / edited by Benjamin M. Friedman. — Chicago : University of Chicago Press, 1986. — 127 p.. — (A National Bureau of Economic Research project report). — *Papers presented at a conference held at Williamsburg, Va., Sept. 20-21, 1984, sponsored by the National Bureau of Economic Research.* — *Includes bibliographies and index*

SAVING AND INVESTMENT — Uruguay — History
ROCCA, José
La captación de excedentes financieros por el sistema bancario comercial. Uruguay, 1974-1982 / José Rocca, Jorge Simon. — Montevideo : Centro Interdisciplinario de Estudios sobre el Desarollo Uruguay, 1985. — 198p. — (Serie Investigaciones / Centro Interdisciplinario de Estudios sobre el Desarollo Uruguay ; no.19). — *Bibliography: p198*

SAVING AND THRIFT
Private saving and public debt / edited by Michael J. Boskin, John S. Flemming and Stefano Gorini. — Oxford : Basil Blackwell, 1987. — x,424p. — *Includes bibliographies and index*

SAVING AND THRIFT — Italy
LECALDANO SASSO LA TERZA, E.
Households' saving and the real rate of interest : the Italian experience, 1970-1983 / E. Lecaldano Sasso la Terza, G. Marotta, R. S. Masera. — [Roma] : Banca d'Italia, 1985. — 33p . addenda. — (Temi di discussione ; 47) (Servizio studi della Banca d'Italia). — *Bibliography: p32-33*

SAVING SNF THRIFT — Developing countries
VOGEL, Robert C.
Mobilizing small-scale savings : approaches, costs, and benefits / Robert C. Vogel and Paul Burkett. — Washington, D.C. : The World Bank, 1986. — vii,38p. — (Industry and finance series ; v.15). — *Bibliographical references: p30-38*

SAVINGS-BANKS — Europe
HALÁSZ, Sándor
A pénzintézeti betétek biztonsága : külöuös tekintettel a takarékpénztárakra / a kereskedelemügyi minister megbízásából ismerteti Halász Sándor. — Budapest : Kereskedelemügyi M. kir minster, 1904. — viii,348p

SCALES, JUNIUS IRVING
SCALES, Junius Irving
Cause at heart : a former Communist remembers / Junius Irving Scales and Richard Nickson ; foreword by Telford Taylor. — Athens : University of Georgia Press, c1987. — xxxv, 427 p.. — *Includes index*

SCANDINAVIA — Emigration and immigration — History — 19th century
LOWELL, Briant Lindsay
Scandinavian exodus : demography and social development of 19th-century rural communities / Briant Lindsay Lowell. — Boulder, Colo. ; London : Westview Press, 1987. — xxiii,262p. — (Brown University studies in population and development). — *Bibliography: p243-262*

SCANDINAVIA — Foreign economic relations — European Economic Community countries
MILJAN, Toivo
The reluctant Europeans : the attitudes of the Nordic countries towards European integration / Toivo Miljan. — London : C. Hurst, 1977. — viii,325p. — *Bibliography: p.301-318.* — *Includes index*

SCANDINAVIA — Foreign relations — Great Britain
OAKLEY, Stewart P
William III and the northern crowns during the Nine Years War, 1689-1697 / Stewart Philip Oakley. — New York : Garland Pub., 1987. — 504 p. (some folded). — (Outstanding theses from the London School of Economics and Political Science). — *Bibliography: p. 480-501*

SCANDINAVIA — Military relations — Soviet Union
BERNER, Örjan
[Sovjet & Norden. English]. Soviet policies toward the Nordic countries / Örjan Berner. — Lanham, MD : University Press of America ; [Cambridge, Mass.] : Center for International Affairs, Harvard University, c1986. — xii, 192 p., [1] leaf of plates. — *Shorter version published under title: Sovjet & Norden. c1985.* — *Bibliography: p. 187-192*

SCANDINAVIA — National security
Nordiske sikkerhedsproblemer / indledning af Bertel Heurlin. — [København] : Det Sikkerheds- og Nedrustningspolitiske Udvalg, 1984. — 178p. — (Det Sikkerheds- og Nedrustningspolitiske Udvalgs skriftserie). — *Includes bibliographical references*

SCANDINAVIA — Politics and government
ELIASSEN, Kjell A.
Skandinaviske politiske institutioner og politisk adfaerd 1970-1984 = Scandinavian political institutions and political behavior 1970-1984 / Kjell A. Eliassen [and] Mogens N. Pedersen. — Odense : Odense University Press, 1985. — vii,158p

SCANDINAVIA — Social conditions
Norden : the passion for equality / edited by Stephen R. Graubard. — Oslo : Norwegian University Press ; Oxford : Distributed by Oxford University Press, c1986. — 323p. — (Scandinavian library)

SCANDINAVIA — Social policy
ANDERSEN, Bent Rold
Two essays on the nordic welfare state / Bent Rold Andersen. — Copenhagen : Amtskommunernes og kommunernes forskningsinstitut, 1983. — 76p

PERSSON, Gunnar
The Scandinavian welfare state : anatomy, logic and some problems / Gunnar Persson. — London : Welfare State Programme. Suntory-Toyota International Centre for Economics and Related Disciplines, 1986. — 30p. — (Discussion paper / Welfare State Programme. Suntory-Toyota International Centre for Economics and Related Disciplines ; no.7). — *Bibliography: p29-30*

SCANDINAVIA — Strategic aspects
Nordiske sikkerhedsproblemer / indledning af Bertel Heurlin. — [København] : Det Sikkerheds- og Nedrustningspolitiske Udvalg, 1984. — 178p. — (Det Sikkerheds- og Nedrustningspolitiske Udvalgs skriftserie). — *Includes bibliographical references*

SCHACHT, JOSEPH. Origins of Muhammadan jurisprudence
A'ẒAMĪ, Muḥammad Muṣṭafá
On Schacht's Origins of Muhammadan jurisprudence / M. Mustafa Al-Azami. — New York : Wiley, c1986. — p. cm. — *Includes index. — Bibliography: p*

SCHEDULING (MANAGEMENT)
OKONJO-ADIGWE, Chiedu-Elue
Solution techniques for the multiple-vehicle travelling salesman problem / by Chiedu Elue Okonje-Adigwe. — 185 leaves. — *PhD (Econ) 1986 LSE*

SCHELLING, CEES
VERBEEK, Herman
Cees Schelling van de Voedingsbond / Herman Verbeek. — Groningen : Xeno, 1984. — 256p

SCHELSKY, HELMUT
Helmut Schelsky als Soziologe und politischer Denker : Grazer Gedächtnisschrift zum Andenken an den am 24. Februar 1984 verstorbenen Gelehrten / Ota Weinberger, Werner Krawietz (Hrsg.). — Stuttgart : Steiner-Verlag-Wiesbaden, 1985. — 172p

SCHILLER, HERBERT I.
Communication and domination : essays to honor Herbert I. Schiller / edited by Jörg Becker, Göran Hedebro, Leena Paldán. — Norwood, N.J. : Ablex, 1986. — p. cm. — *Includes index. — Bibliography: p*

SCHIZOPHRENIA — Treatment
WARNER, Richard
Recovery from schizophrenia : psychiatry and political economy / Richard Warner. — London : Routledge & Kegan Paul, 1985. — x, 380p. — *Bibliography: p.362-368*

SCHIZOPHRENIA — Treatment — Economic aspects
WARNER, Richard
Recovery from schizophrenia : psychiatry and political economy / Richard Warner. — London : Routledge & Kegan Paul, 1985. — x, 380p. — *Bibliography: p.362-368*

SCHIZOPHRENIA — Treatment — Political aspects
WARNER, Richard
Recovery from schizophrenia : psychiatry and political economy / Richard Warner. — London : Routledge & Kegan Paul, 1985. — x, 380p. — *Bibliography: p.362-368*

SCHLESWIG-HOLSTEIN (GERMANY) — History
RIEGLER, Claudius Helmut
Emigration und Arbeitswanderung aus Schweden nach Norddeutschland 1868-1914 / Claudius Helmut Riegler. — Neumunster : Wachholtz, 1985. — 293p. — (Studien zur Wirtschafts- und Sozialgeschichte Schleswig-Holsteins ; 8). — *Bibliography: p283-293*

STÜBER, Gabriele
Der Kampf gegen den Hunger 1945-1950 : der Ernährungslage in der britishchen Zone Deutschlands, insbesondere in Schleswig-Holstein und Hamburg / Gabriele Stüber. — Neumunster : Wachholtz, 1984. — 935p. — (Studien zur Wirtschafts- und Sozialgeschichte Schleswig-Holsteins ; Bd.6). — *Bibliography: p824-913*

SCHLESWIG-HOLSTEIN (GERMANY) — Social conditions
STÜBER, Gabriele
Der Kampf gegen den Hunger 1945-1950 : der Ernährungslage in der britishchen Zone Deutschlands, insbesondere in Schleswig-Holstein und Hamburg / Gabriele Stüber. — Neumunster : Wachholtz, 1984. — 935p. — (Studien zur Wirtschafts- und Sozialgeschichte Schleswig-Holsteins ; Bd.6). — *Bibliography: p824-913*

SCHMITT, CARL
Der Fürst dieser Welt : Carl Schmitt und die Folgen / herausgegeben von Jacob Taubes. — 2., verb. Auflage. — München : Fink, 1985. — 321p. — (Religionstheorie und politische Theologie ; Bd.1). — *First published 1983*

SCHOLARLY PUBLISHING — Technological innovations
HOROWITZ, Irving Louis
Communicating ideas : the crisis of publishing in a post-industrial society / Irving Louis Horowitz. — New York : Oxford University Press, 1986. — x, 240 p.. — *Includes index. — Bibliography: p. 217-230*

SCHOLARLY PUBLISHING — Asia, Southeastern — Congresses
SEMINAR ON ACADEMIC PUBLISHING IN THE ASEAN REGION (1985 : Singapore)
Academic publishing in ASEAN : problems and prospects : proceedings of the Seminar on Academic Publishing in the ASEAN Region held in Singapore from 9-11 September 1985 / edited by S. Gopinathan. — Singapore : Festival of Books Singapore, 1986. — 213 p.. — *Includes bibliographies*

SCHOLARS, JEWISH — United States — Biography
AUSMUS, Harry J.
Will Herberg, from right to right / by Harry J. Ausmus ; with a foreword by Martin E. Marty. — Chapel Hill : University of North Carolina Press, c1987. — p. cm. — (Studies in religion). — *Includes index. — Bibliography: p*

SCHOLARSHIPS — Directories
The Grants register 1987-89 / edited by Craig Alan Lerner, Roland Turner. — London : Macmillan, 1986. — [450]p. — *Includes index*

SCHOOL CHILDREN — Food — Great Britain
FAMILY POLICY STUDIES CENTRE
School meals and social security. — London : Family Policy Studies Centre, 1986. — 5p

HADJIPATERAS, Angela
The threat to free school meals : a survey of mothers' views / Angela Hadjipateras. — London : Child Poverty Action Group, 1986. — 8p

SCHOOL CHILDREN — Denmark — Recreation
JØRGENSEN, Per Schultz
Efter skoletid : en undersøgelse af de store skolebørns fritid / Per Schultz Jørgensen, Birthe Gamst, Bjarne Hjorth Andersen. — København : Socialforskningsinstituttet, 1986. — 220p. — (Publikation / Socialforskningsinstituttet ; 154). — *Bibliography: p215-217*

SCHOOL EMPLOYEES — Salaries, pensions, etc. — Norway — Statistics
Lønnsstatistikk for ansatte i skoleverket = Wage statistics for employees in publicly maintained schools / Norway. Statistiske Centralbyrå. — Oslo : Statistiske Centralbyrå, 1973-. — *Annual. — 1975-1983 entitled Lønns-og sysselsettingsstatistikk for ansatte i skoleverket: Wage and employment statistics for employees in publicly maintained schools*

SCHOOL FACILITIES — Extended use
WIDLAKE, Paul
Reducing educational disadvantage / Paul Widlake. — Milton Keynes : Open University Press, 1986. — vi,146p. — (Innovations in education). — *Includes index*

SCHOOL INTEGRATION — California — San Francisco
FINE, Doris R
When leadership fails : desegregation and demoralization in the San Francisco schools / Doris R. Fine. — New Brunswick, U.S.A. : Transaction Books, c1986. — ix, 222 p.. — (Observations in education). — *Includes bibliographical references and index*

SCHOOL INTEGRATION — Massachusetts — Boston
LUKAS, J. Anthony
Common ground : a turbulent decade in the lives of three American Families / J. Anthony Lukas. — New York : Vintage Books, 1986. — xiv,674p. — *Originally published: New York : Random House, 1985*

SCHOOL INTEGRATION — Tennessee — Nashville — History
PRIDE, Richard A
The burden of busing : the politics of desegregation in Nashville, Tennessee / Richard A. Pride, J. David Woodard. — Knoxville : University of Tennessee Press, [1985]. — xii, 302p. — *Includes index. — Bibliography: p 287-296*

SCHOOL INTEGRATION — United States — Case studies
MONTI, Daniel J
A semblance of justice : St. Louis school desegregation and order in urban America / Daniel J. Monti. — Columbia : University of Missouri Press, 1985. — xiv, 221 p.. — *Includes index. — Bibliography: p. 208-215*

SCHOOL LANDS — United States — History
HYMAN, Harold M
American singularity : the 1787 Northwest Ordinance, the 1862 Homestead and Morrill Acts, and the 1944 G.I. Bill / Harold M. Hyman. — Athens : University of Georgia Press, c1986. — x, 95 p.. — (The Richard B. Russell lectures ; no. 5). — *Includes index. — Bibliography: p. [77]-90*

SCHOOL MANAGEMENT AND ORGANISATION — England
Survey of organisation in multi-racial schools. — London : Commission for Racial Equality, 1977. — [3]p. — *Summary of Organisation in multi-racial schools, by H .E .R. Townsend and E .M .Britain. — Reprint from Education & community relations, November 1972*

SCHOOL MANAGEMENT AND ORGANIZATION — Decision making
MARCH, James G.
Ambiguity and choice in organizations / by James G. March and Johan P. Olsen; with contributions by Søren Christensen...[et al.]. — 2nd ed. — Bergen : Universitetsforlaget, 1979. — 408p. — *Bibliography: p397-402*

SCHOOL MANAGEMENT AND ORGANIZATION — California — San Francisco
FINE, Doris R
When leadership fails : desegregation and demoralization in the San Francisco schools / Doris R. Fine. — New Brunswick, U.S.A. : Transaction Books, c1986. — ix, 222 p.. — (Observations in education). — *Includes bibliographical references and index*

SCHOOL MANAGEMENT AND ORGANIZATION — Great Britain
BALL, Stephen, 1950-
The micro-politics of the school : towards a theory of school organization / Stephen J. Ball. — London : Methuen, 1987. — xi,307p. — *Bibliography: p284-298. — Includes index*

SCHOOL MANAGEMENT AND ORGANIZATION — Great Britain — History — 20th century
COOKE, George
Education committees / George Cooke and Peter Gosden. — Harlow : Councils and Education, 1986. — x,166p. — *Includes index*

SCHOOL MANAGEMENT AND ORGANIZATION — Japan
PASSIN, Herbert
Society and education in Japan / Herbert Passin. — 1st pbk. ed. — Tokyo ; New York : Kodansha International ; New York, N.Y. : distributed in the U.S. by Kodansha International/U.S.A. through Harper & Row, 1982. — 347 p.. — *Includes index. — Bibliography: p. 327-337*

SCHOOL MANAGEMENT AND ORGANIZATION — Quebec (Province)
MILNER, Henry
The long road to reform : restructuring public education in Quebec / Henry Milner. — Kingston ; Montreal : McGill-Queen's University Press, 1986. — xi,170p. — *Bibliographical notes: p[141]-165*

SCHOOL MANAGEMENT AND ORGANIZATION — United States
Political science and school politics : the princes and pundits / edited by Samuel K. Gove, Frederick M. Wirt. — Lexington, Mass. : Lexington Books, c1976. — x, 143 p.. — (Policy Studies Organization series ; 12). — *Includes bibliographical references and index*

Schooling in social context : qualitative studies / edited by George W. Noblit, William T. Pink. — Norwood, N.J. : Ablex Pub. Corp., c1987. — xviii, 332 p.. — *Includes bibliographies and indexes*

SCHOOL MANAGEMENT AND ORGANIZATION — Wales — Cardiff (South Glamorgan) — History — 20th century
GEEN, A. G.
Decision making and secondary education : a case study / by A.G. Geen. — Cardiff : University of Wales Press, 1986. — 160p

SCHOOLS — Great Britain — Social aspects
REID, Ivan
The sociology of school and education / Ivan Reid. — London : Fontana Press, 1986. — 320p. — *Bibliography: p294-314*

SCHOOLS — United States
MCNEIL, Linda M.
Contradictions of control : school structure and school knowledge / Linda M. McNeil. — New York ; London : Routledge and Kegan Paul, 1986. — xxiv,234p. — *Bibliography: p224-229*

SCHOOLS OF SOCIOLOGY
Structures of knowing / edited by Richard C. Monk. — Lanham ; London : University Press of America, 1987. — [522]p. — *Includes index*

SCHUMAN, ROBERT
BEYER, Henry
Robert Schuman : l'Europe par la réconciliation franco-allemande / Henry Beyer. — Lausanne : Centre de Recherches Européennes, 1986. — [174]p

LEJEUNE, René
Robert Schuman : une âme pour l'Europe / René Lejeune. — Paris : Saint-Paul, 1986. — 223p. — *Bibliography: p217-219*

SCHUMPETER, JOSEPH ALOIS — Congresses
Marx, Schumpeter, and Keynes : a centenary celebration of dissent / Suzanne W. Helburn and David F. Bramhall, editors. — Armonk, N.Y. : M.E. Sharpe, c1986. — xii, 343 p.. — *Papers presented at a symposium held Apr. 20-22, 1983 at the University of Colorado at Denver. — Includes bibliographies*

SCHURZ, CARL
Carl Schurz : Revolutionär und Staatsmann : sein Leben in selbstzeugnissen Bildern und Dokumenten = Revolutionary and statesman : his life in personal and official documents with illustrations / herausgegeben von/edited by Rüdiger Wersich. — 2.Aufl. — München : Moos, 1986. — *Parallel texts in German and English. — First published 1979*

SCHÜTZ, ALFRED — Correspondence
SCHÜTZ, Alfred
Briefwechsel 1939-1959 / Alfred Schütz [und] Aron Gurwitsch ; herausgegeben von Richard Grathoff ; mit einer Einleitung von Ludwig Landgrebe. — München : Wilhelm Fink, 1985. — xxxviii,544p. — (Übergänge : Texte und Studien zu Handung, Sprache und Lebenswelt ; Bd.4). — *Bibliography: p531-534*

SCHWARZHAUPT, ELISABETH
SALENTIN, Ursula
Elisabeth Schwarzhaupt : erste Ministerin der Bundesrepublik : ein demokratischer Lebensweg / Ursula Salentin. — Freiburg im Breisgan : Herder, 1986. — 126p

SCHWENKE, OLAF
SCHWENCKE, Olaf
Hoffen lernen : 12 Jahre Politik als Beruf : eine Zwischenbilanz / Olaf Schwencke. — Stuttgart : Radius, 1985. — 105p

SCIENCE
The Nature of scientific discovery : a symposium commemorating the 500th anniversary of the birth of Nicolaus Copernicus / Edited by Owen Gingerich. — [1st ed.]. — Washington : Smithsonian Institution Press ; [distributed by G. Braziller, New York, 1975]. — 616 p. — (Smithsonian international symposia series ; 5). — *"The fifth international symposium of the Smithsonian Institution organized jointly with the National Academy of Sciences in cooperation with the Copernicus Society of America.". — Bibliography: p. 23-26*

SCIENCE — Bibliography
COMMISSION OF THE EUROPEAN COMMUNITIES
Catalogue : EUR documents, 1968-1979 / Commission of the European Communities. — Luxembourg : Office for Official Publications of the European Communities, 1983. — xviii,301p. — (Information management / Commission of the European Communities)

SCIENCE — History
COHEN, I. Bernard
Revolution in science / I. Bernard Cohen. — Cambridge, Mass. ; London : Belknap Press, 1985. — xx, 711p. — *Bibliography: p.[623]-678*

GJERTSEN, Derek
The Newton handbook / Derek Gjertsen. — London : Routledge & Kegan Paul, 1986. — xiv,665p

SCIENCE — History — 19th century
KNIGHT, David, 1936 Nov. 30-
The age of science : the scientific world-view in the nineteenth century / David Knight. — Oxford : Basil Blackwell, 1986. — [230]p. — *Includes index*

SCIENCE — International cooperation
Nauchno-tekhnicheskii progress i sotrudnichestvo stran SEV / pod redaktsiei O. A. Chukanova, G. M. Kharakhash'iana, Iu. F. Kormnova. — Moskva : Mezhdunarodnye otnosheniia, 1973. — 205p

Nauchno-tekhnicheskoe sotrudnichestvo stran SEV : spravochnik / pod redaktsiei O. A. Chukanova. — Moskva : Ekonomika, 1986. — 287p

SCIENCE — Methodology
Can theories be refuted? : essays on the Duhem-Quine-thesis / [compiled by] S.G. Harding. — Dordrecht-Holland ; Boston : D. Reidel Pub. Co, [1975]. — (Synthese library ; 81). — *Includes bibliographies and index*

GIERE, Ronald N.
Understanding scientific reasoning / Ronald N. Giere. — 2nd ed. — New York ; London : Holt, Rinehart and Winston, c1984. — xviii,391p. — *Previous ed.: 1979. — Bibliography: p371-373. — Includes index*

Theories and observation in science / edited by Richard E. Grandy. — Atascadero, Calif. : Ridgeview Publishing Company, [c.1973]. — viii,184p. — *Bibliographies*

SCIENCE — Methodology — History
OLDROYD, D. R.
The arch of knowledge : an introductory study of the history of the philosophy and methodology of science / David Oldroyd. — London : Methuen, 1986. — 413p. — *Bibliography: p.[373]-383*

SCIENCE — Periodicals
Minerva : a review of science, learning and policy. — New York : International Council on the Future of the University, 1962-. — *Quarterly*

SCIENCE — Philosophy
BHASKAR, Roy
Scientific realism and human emancipation / Roy Bhaskar. — London : Verso, 1986. — 308p

Can theories be refuted? : essays on the Duhem-Quine-thesis / [compiled by] S.G. Harding. — Dordrecht-Holland ; Boston : D. Reidel Pub. Co, [1975]. — (Synthese library ; 81). — *Includes bibliographies and index*

EARMAN, John
A primer on determinism / John Earman. — Dordrecht ; Lancaster : Reidel, c1986. — xiv, 273p. — (University of Western Ontario series in philosophy of science ; v. 32). — *Includes index. — Bibliography: p 257-269*

HARRÉ, Rom
Varieties of realism : a rationale for the natural sciences / Rom Harré. — Oxford : Basil Blackwell, 1986. — vii,375p. — *Bibliography: p356-363. — Includes index*

JARDINE, N.
The fortunes of inquiry / Nicholas Jardine. — Oxford : Clarendon, 1986. — 240. — (Clarendon library of logic and philosphy). — *Includes index*

Kant's philosophy of physical science : Metaphysische Anfangsgründe der Naturwissenschaft, 1786-1986 / edited by Robert E. Butts. — Dordrecht ; Lancaster : Reidel, c1986. — xii, 363p. — (The University of Western Ontario series in philosophy of science ; v. 33). — *Includes index. — Includes bibliographies*

LOSEE, John
Philosophy of science and historical enquiry / John Losee. — Oxford : Clarendon, 1987. — [152]p. — *Includes index*

RICHARDS, Stewart
Philosophy and sociology of science : an introduction / Stewart Richards. — 2nd ed. — Oxford : Blackwell, 1987. — [240]p. — *Previous ed.: 1983. — Includes bibliography and index*

SCIENCE — Philosophy *continuation*

RICKERT, Heinrich
The limits of concept formation in natural science : a logical introduction to the historical sciences / Heinrich Rickert. — Abridged ed. / edited and translated by Guy Oakes. — Cambridge : Cambridge University Press, 1986. — xxxii,240p. — (Texts in German philosophy). — *Translation of: Die Grenzen der naturwissenschaftlichen Begriffsbildung. — Includes index*

VAN FRAASSEN, Bas C.
The scientific image / Bas C. Van Fraasen. — Oxford : Clarendon, 1980. — xi,235p. — (Clarendon library of logic and philosophy). — *Includes index*

WATKINS, John W. N
Science and scepticism / John Watkins. — Princeton, N.J. : Princeton University Press, c1984. — xvii, 387 p.. — *Includes indexes. — Bibliography: p. 356-380*

SCIENCE — Philosophy — History

GREENE, John C.
Science, ideology, and world view : esssays in the history of evolutionary ideas / John C. Greene. — Berkeley ; London : University of California Press, c1981. — x,202p. — *Includes index*

OLDROYD, D. R.
The arch of knowledge : an introductory study of the history of the philosophy and methodology of science / David Oldroyd. — London : Methuen, 1986. — 413p. — *Bibliography: p.[373]-383*

SCIENCE — Philosophy — History — 20th century

ALFORD, C. Fred
Science and the revenge of nature : Marcuse & Habermas / C. Fred Alford. — Gainesville, FL : University Presses of Florida, c1985. — x, 226 p.. — *Includes index. — Bibliography: p. 199-210*

SCIENCE — Social aspects

CLARKE, Robin
Science and technology in world development / Robin Clarke ; foreword by Amadou-Mahtar M'Bow. — Oxford : Oxford Univlrsity Press/Unesco, 1985. — vi,216p. — (OPUS)

HARDING, Sandra G
The science question in feminism / Sandra Harding. — Ithaca : Cornell University Press, 1986. — p. cm. — *Includes index. — Bibliography: p*

HISKES, Anne L. Deckard
Science, technology, and policy decisions / Anne L. Hiskes and Richard P. Hiskes. — Boulder : Westview Press, 1986. — p. cm. — *Includes index. — Bibliography: p*

Issues in radical science / edited by the Radical Science Collective. — London, Free Association Books, 1985. — [160]p. — (Radical science ; no.17)

JAGTENBERG, Tom
The social construction of science : a comparative study of goal direction, research evolution and legitimation / Tom Jagtenberg. — Dordrecht ; London : D. Reidel, c1983. — xviii, 237 p.. — (Sociology of the sciences monographs). — *Includes indexes. — Bibliography: p. 223-231*

PINCH, T. J
Confronting nature : the sociology of solar-neutrino detection / Trevor Pinch. — Dordrecht, Holland ; Boston : D. Reidel Pub. Co ; Higham, MA, U.S.A. : Sold and distributed in the U.S.A. and Canada by Kluwer Academic Publishers, c1986. — xi, 268 p.. — (Sociology of the sciences monographs). — *Includes index. — Bibliography: p. 249-258*

RICHARDS, Stewart
Philosophy and sociology of science : an introduction / Stewart Richards. — 2nd ed. — Oxford : Blackwell, 1987. — [240]p. — *Previous ed.: 1983. — Includes bibliography and index*

SALE, Kirkpatrick
Dwellers in the land : the bioregional vision / Kirkpatrick Sale. — San Francisco : Sierra Club Books, c1985. — x, 217 p.. — *Includes index. — Bibliography: p. 193-207*

Smothered by invention : technology in women's lives / edited by Wendy Faulkner and Erik Arnold. — London : Pluto, 1985. — [272]p

VANDERBURG, Willem H.
The growth of minds and cultures : a unified theory of the structure of human experience / Willem H. Vanderburg. — Toronto ; London : University of Toronto Press, c1985. — xxvi,334p. — *Includes index*

ZIMMERMAN, Jan
Once upon the future : a woman's guide to tomorrow's technology / Jan Zimmerman. — New York ; London : Pandora, 1986. — xviii,230p. — (Pandora Press focus). — *Includes index*

SCIENCE — Social aspects — Great Britain

ALTER, Peter
The reluctant patron : science and the state in Britain 1850-1920 / Peter Alter ; translated from the German by Angela Davis. — Oxford : Berg, 1987. — 292p. — *'This translation is based on Wissenschaft, Staat, Mäzene. Anfänge moderner Wissenschafts politik in Grossbritannien 1850-1920 (Stuttgart, 1982, but has been revised and updated by the author for this edition.'. — Translation based on a revised and updated edition of: Wissenschaft, Staat, Mäzene. — Bibliography: p261-282. — Includes index*

SCIENCE — Social aspects — United States

PEARSON, Willie
Black scientists, white society, and colorless science : a study of universalism in American science / Willie Pearson, Jr. — Millwood, N.Y. : Associated Faculty Press, c1985. — xi, 201 p. . — *Includes index. — Bibliography: p. 181-196*

SCIENCE — Social aspects — United States — Addresses, essays, lectures

The Rights of memory : essays on history, science, and American culture / edited by Taylor Littleton. — University, Ala. : University of Alabama Press, c1986. — viii, 227 p.. — (The Franklin lectures in the sciences & humanities). — *Includes bibliographies and index*

SCIENCE — Study and teaching (Higher)

The university research system : the public policies of the home of scientists / edited by Bjorn Wittrock, Aant Elzinga. — Stockholm : Almqvist and Wiksell, 1985. — v,220p. — *Bibliographies*

SCIENCE — Great Britain

Exploitable areas of science. — London : HMSO, 1986. — *At head of title: Advisory Council for Applied Research and Development*

SCIENCE — Great Britain — History — 19th century

ALTER, Peter
The reluctant patron : science and the state in Britain 1850-1920 / Peter Alter ; translated from the German by Angela Davis. — Oxford : Berg, 1987. — 292p. — *'This translation is based on Wissenschaft, Staat, Mäzene. Anfänge moderner Wissenschafts politik in Grossbritannien 1850-1920 (Stuttgart, 1982, but has been revised and updated by the author for this edition.'. — Translation based on a revised and updated edition of: Wissenschaft, Staat, Mäzene. — Bibliography: p261-282. — Includes index*

SCIENCE — Great Britain — History — 20th century

ALTER, Peter
The reluctant patron : science and the state in Britain 1850-1920 / Peter Alter ; translated from the German by Angela Davis. — Oxford : Berg, 1987. — 292p. — *'This translation is based on Wissenschaft, Staat, Mäzene. Anfänge moderner Wissenschafts politik in Grossbritannien 1850-1920 (Stuttgart, 1982, but has been revised and updated by the author for this edition.'. — Translation based on a revised and updated edition of: Wissenschaft, Staat, Mäzene. — Bibliography: p261-282. — Includes index*

SCIENCE — Soviet Union — History — 20th century

FORTESCUE, Stephen
The Communist Party and Soviet science / Stephen Fortescue. — Basingstoke : Macmillan in association with the Centre for Russian and East European Studies, University of Birmingham, 1986. — x,234p. — (Studies in Soviet history and society). — *Bibliography: p218-231. — Includes index*

SCIENCE — United States — History

GEIGER, Roger L.
To advance knowledge : the growth of American research universities, 1900-1940 / Roger L. Geiger. — New York : Oxford University Press, 1986. — x, 325 p.. — *Includes index. — Bibliography: p. 279-320*

SCIENCE AND CIVILIZATION

RAVETZ, Jerome R.
Scientific knowledge and its social problems / Jerome R. Ravetz. — New York : Oxford University Press, 1973. — x,449p

SCIENCE AND INDUSTRY — Soviet Union

GROSHEV, V. P.
Narodno-khoziaistvennyi nauchnyi kompleks / V. P. Groshev. — Moskva : Mysl', 1985. — 254p

SCIENCE AND STATE

HISKES, Anne L. Deckard
Science, technology, and policy decisions / Anne L. Hiskes and Richard P. Hiskes. — Boulder : Westview Press, 1986. — p. cm. — *Includes index. — Bibliography: p*

Science and technology policy in the 1980s and beyond / edited by Michael Gibbons, Philip Gummett, Bhalchandra Udgaonkar. — London : Longman, 1984. — xxvi,346p

SCIENCE AND STATE — Australia

Australia. — Paris : Organisation for Economic Co-operation and Development, 1986. — 119p. — (Reviews of national science and technology policy). — *Includes bibliographical references*

AUSTRALIAN SCIENCE AND TECHNOLOGY COUNCIL
Future directions for CSIRO : a report to the Prime Minister / by the Australian Science and Technology Council (ASTEC). — Canberra : Australian Government Publishing Service, 1985. — viii,94p. — *Bibliographical references: p62-64*

SCIENCE AND STATE — European Economic Community countries

ECONOMIC AND SOCIAL COMMITTEE OF THE EUROPEAN COMMUNITIES
Organization and management of community research and development : study / Economic and Social Committee of the European Communities. — Brussels : General Secretariat of the Economic and Social Committee, 1980. — vi,159p

SCIENCE AND STATE — Finland

Finland. — [Paris] : Organisation for Economic Co-operation and Development, [1987]. — 153p. — (Reviews of national science and technology policy). — *Includes bibliographical references*

SCIENCE AND STATE — Great Britain
INCE, Martin
　The politics of British science / Martin Ince. — Brighton : Wheatsheaf, 1986. — [256]p. — *Includes bibliography and index*

SCIENCE AND STATE — Netherlands
Netherlands. — Paris : OECD, 1987. — 141p. — (Reviews of national science and technology policy). — *Includes bibliographical references*

WETENSCHAPPELIJKE RAAD VOOR HET REGERINGSBELEID
　Externe adviesorganen van de centrale overheid : beschrijving, ontwikkelingen, aanbevelingen. — 's-Gravenhage : Staatsuitgeverij, 1977. — 227p. — (Rapporten aan de Regering / Wetenschappelijke Raad voor het Regeringsbeleid ; 12). — *Summary in English.* — *Bibliography: p111-121*

SCIENCE AND STATE — Portugal
Portugal. — [Paris] : Organisation for Economic Co-operation and Development, 1986. — 136p. — (Reviews of national science and technology policy). — *Bibliographical references: p82-85*

SCIENCE AND STATE — Sweden
Sweden. — Paris : Organisation for Economic Co-operation and Development, 1987. — 112p. — (Reviews of national science and technology policy). — *Bibliographical references: p88*

SCIENCE NEWS
GOLDSMITH, Maurice
　The science critic : a critical analysis of the popular presentation of science / Maurice Goldsmith. — London : Routledge, 1986. — xi, 217p. — *Bibliography: p.208-211*

SCIENTISTS, GERMAN
BOWER, Tom, 1946-
　The paperclip conspiracy : the battle for the spoils and secrets of Nazi Germany / Tom Bower. — London : Joseph, 1987. — xiv,336p,[12]p of plates. — *Bibliography: p326-327. — Includes index*

SCIENTISTS IN GOVERNMENT
Science for public policy / edited by Harvey Brooks and Chester L. Cooper. — Oxford : Pergamon, 1987. — viii,286p. — *Bibliography: p249-278. — Includes index*

SCIENTOLOGY
WHITEHEAD, Harriet
　Renunciation and reformulation : a study of conversion in an American sect / Harriet Whitehead. — Ithaca : Cornell University Press, 1987. — 299 p.. — (Anthropology of contemporary issues). — *Includes index.* — *Bibliography: p. 287-291*

SCOTLAND — Antiquities
WALKER, Bruce
　Exploring Scotland's heritage : Fife and Tayside / Bruce Walker and Graham Ritchie. — Edinburgh : H.M.S.O., 1987. — 202p. — (Exploring Scotland's heritage). — *At foot of t.p.: The Royal Commission on the Ancient and Historical Monuments of Scotland.* — *Bibliography: p.196-197*

SCOTLAND — Economic conditions
SALMOND, Alex
　The oil price collapse : some effects on the Scottish economy / Alex Salmond [and] Jim Walker. — Edinburgh : Royal Bank of Scotland, 1986. — [7p]

SCOTLAND — Economic conditions — 1973-
KEATING, Michael, 1950-
　Remaking urban Scotland : strategies for local economic development / Michael Keating and Robin Boyle. — Edinburgh : Edinburgh University Press, c1986. — x,174p. — (Scottish industrial policy series ; 3). — *Bibliography: p167-170. — Includes index*

SCOTLAND — Emigration and immigration
PRENTIS, Malcolm D
　The Scots in Australia : a study of New South Wales, Victoria and Queensland, 1788-1900 / Malcolm D. Prentis. — Sydney : Sydney University Press ; Beaverton, Or. : distributed by International Scholarly Book Services, 1983. — xv, 304 p.. — *Includes index.* — *Bibliography: p. 290-294*

SCOTLAND — History — 16th century
BROWN, Keith M.
　Bloodfeud in Scotland, 1573-1625 : violence, justice and politics in an early modern society / Keith M. Brown. — Edinburgh : John Donald, c1986. — x, 299p. — *Bibliography: p 285-293*

SCOTLAND — History — James VI, 1567-1625
GALLOWAY, Bruce
　The union of England and Scotland : 1603-1608 / Bruce Galloway. — Edinburgh : John Donald, c1986. — vii, 197p. — *Bibliography: p.179-192*

SCOTLAND — History — 17th century
BROWN, Keith M.
　Bloodfeud in Scotland, 1573-1625 : violence, justice and politics in an early modern society / Keith M. Brown. — Edinburgh : John Donald, c1986. — x, 299p. — *Bibliography: p 285-293*

HOPKINS, Paul
　Glencoe and the end of the Highland war / Paul Hopkins. — Edinburgh : John Donald, 1986. — 543p. — *Bibliography: p.500-509*

SCOTLAND — History — Charles I, 1625-1649
LEE, Maurice
　The road to revolution : Scotland under Charles I, 1625-37 / Maurice Lee, Jr. — Urbana : University of Illinois Press, c1985. — xvi, 258p, [11]p of plates. — *Includes bibliographical references and index*

SCOTLAND — History — 18th century
SMITH, Lawrence Bartlam
　Spain and Britain, 1715-1719 : the Jacobite issue / Lawrence Bartlam Smith. — New York : Garland Pub., 1987. — 361 p. — (Outstanding theses from the London School of Economics and Political Science). — *Thesis (Ph. D.)--University of London.* — *Bibliography: p. 344-361*

SCOTLAND — Industries
Dictionary of Scottish business biography 1860-1960 / editors, Anthony Slaven, Sydney Checkland ; associate editors, Sheila Hamilton ... [et al.]. — Aberdeen : Aberdeen University Press
Vol.1: The staple industries. — 1986. — xvi,496p. — *Includes indexes*

SCOTLAND — Learned institutions and societies
STEVENSON, David, 1942-
　Scottish texts and calendars : an analytical guide to serial publications / by David and Wendy B. Stevenson. — London : Royal Historical Society, 1987. — xii,233p. — (Royal Historical Society guides and handbooks ; no. 14) (Scottish History Society. 4 series ; v.23). — *Includes index*

SCOTLAND — Nobility
WORMALD, Jenny
　Lords and men in Scotland : bonds of manrent, 1442-1603 / Jenny Wormald. — Edinburgh : John Donald, 1985. — ix,475p

SCOTLAND — Politics and government
CAMPAIGN FOR A SCOTTISH ASSEMBLY
　[Discussion papers on the Scottish constitutional convention]. — Edinburgh : Campaign for a Scottish Assembly, 1985. — 8 leaflets

SCOTLAND — Politics and government — 18th century
SUNTER, Ronald M.
　Patronage and politics in Scotland, 1707-1832 / Ronald M. Sunter. — Edinburgh : John Donald, c1986. — vii, 254p. — *Bibliography: p.238-242*

SCOTLAND — Politics and government — 19th century
HUTCHISON, I. G. C.
　A political history of Scotland, 1832-1924 : parties, elections and issues / I.G.C. Hutchison. — Edinburgh : John Donald, 1986. — 371p. — *Bibliography: p.337-357*

SUNTER, Ronald M.
　Patronage and politics in Scotland, 1707-1832 / Ronald M. Sunter. — Edinburgh : John Donald, c1986. — vii, 254p. — *Bibliography: p.238-242*

SCOTLAND — Politics and government — 20th century
HUTCHISON, I. G. C.
　A political history of Scotland, 1832-1924 : parties, elections and issues / I.G.C. Hutchison. — Edinburgh : John Donald, 1986. — 371p. — *Bibliography: p.337-357*

SCOTLAND — Rural conditions
ALEXANDER, K. J. W.
　Rural renewal : experience in the Highlands and Islands / Sir Kenneth Alexander. — Cambridge : University of Cambridge, Department of Land Economy, 1984. — 26p. — (The Denman lecture ; 1984)

SHUCKSMITH, Mark
　Scotland's rural housing : a forgotten problem / Mark Shucksmith. — [Edinburgh] : Rural Forum, 1984. — 45p. — (Rural Forum discussion paper)

SCOTLAND — Social conditions
KELSALL, Helen M.
　Scottish lifestyle 300 years ago : new light on Edinburgh and Border families / Helen and Keith Kelsall. — Edinburgh : John Donald, 1986. — vii,224p. — *Bibliography: p201-202*

WORMALD, Jenny
　Lords and men in Scotland : bonds of manrent, 1442-1603 / Jenny Wormald. — Edinburgh : John Donald, 1985. — ix,475p

SCOTLAND — Social conditions — 20th century
MCKEAN, Charles
　The Scottish Thirties : an architectural introduction / Charles McKean. — Edinburgh : Scottish Academic Press, 1987. — 200p. — *Bibliography: p191*

SCOTLAND — Social life and customs
FENTON, Alexander
　The shape of the past 1 : essays in Scottish ethnology / Alexander Fenton. — Edinburgh : John Donald, 1985. — viii,186p. — *Bibliography: p176-186*

SCOTS — Australia — History — 19th century
PRENTIS, Malcolm D
　The Scots in Australia : a study of New South Wales, Victoria and Queensland, 1788-1900 / Malcolm D. Prentis. — Sydney : Sydney University Press ; Beaverton, Or. : distributed by International Scholarly Book Services, 1983. — xv, 304 p.. — *Includes index.* — *Bibliography: p. 290-294*

SCOTS IN CANADA
BUMSTED, J. M.
　The Scots in Canada / J.M. Bumsted. — Ottawa : Canadian Historical Association, 1982. — 19p. — (Canada's ethnic groups. booklet ; no. 1)

SCOTT, DUNCAN CAMPBELL, 1862-1947
TITLEY, E. Brian
　A narrow vision : Duncan Campbell Scott and the Administration of Indian affairs in Canada / E. Brian Titley. — Vancouver : University of British Columbia Press, 1986. — viii,245p

SCOTT, JEANNINE B
OBUDHO, Robert A
Afro-American demography and urban issues : a bibliography / compiled by R.A. Obudho and Jeannine B. Scott. — Westport, Conn. : Greenwood Press, 1985. — xxxix, 433 p.. — (Bibliographies and indexes in Afro-American and African studies ; no. 8). — *Includes index*

SCOTTISH EQUITABLE LIFE ASSURANCE SOCIETY
Scottish Equitable Life Assurance Society 1831-1981. — Edinburgh : Scottish Equitable Life Assurance Society, 1981. — 92p

SCOTTISH NATIONAL PARTY
SCOTTISH NATIONAL PARTY
Play the Scottish card : SNP general election manifesto 1987. — Edinburgh : Scottish National Party, 1987. — 27p

SCOTTISH TRADES UNION CONGRESS — History
TUCKETT, Angela
The Scottish Trades Union Congress : the first 80 years, 1897-1977 / Angela Tuckett. — Edinburgh : Mainstream Publishing in conjunction with the Scottish Trades Union Congress, 1986. — 444p

SDP/LIBERAL ALLIANCE
CARTER, Chris
The Alliance government : the first hundred days / Chris Carter. — Hebden Bridge : Hebden Royd Publications, 1986. — 45p. — (Hebden Royd paper ; no.4)

SDP LIBERAL ALLIANCE
OWEN, David, 1938-
The time has come : partnership for progress / David Owen and David Steel. — London : Weidenfeld and Nicholson, 1987. — 128p

SDP/LIBERAL ALLIANCE
SDP/LIBERAL ALLIANCE
The essential investment : Liberal/SDP Alliance Policies for Education. — Hebden Bridge : Hebden Royd Publications, [1987]. — [12 leaves]

SDP-LIBERAL ALLIANCE
SDP LIBERAL ALLIANCE
Freedom and choice for women : a Liberal-SDP Alliance policy proposal. — Hebden Bridge : Liberal Party Publications, 1986. — 35p

SDP-LIBERAL ALLIANCE
Government, law and justice : the case for a Ministry of Justice. — Hebden Bridge : Hebden Royd Publications, 1985. — 14p. — (Alliance paper ; no.1)

SDP/LIBERAL ALLIANCE
SDP/LIBERAL ALLIANCE
Jobs and competitiveness : SDP/Liberal Alliance budget priorities 1986. — London : [the Alliance], 1986. — [6p]

SDP LIBERAL ALLIANCE
WILSON, Des
Battle for power : [the inside story of the Alliance and the 1987 General Election] / Des Wilson. — London : Sphere, 1987. — xv,326p

SEA ISLANDS — History
HAWKS, Esther Hill
A woman doctor's Civil War : Esther Hill Hawks' diary / edited with a foreword and afterword by Gerald Schwartz. — 1st ed. — Columbia, S.C. : University of South Carolina Press, c1984. — p. cm. — *Bibliography: p283-288. — Bibliography: p*

SEA LEVEL
Sea surface studies : a global view / edited by R.J.N. Devoy. — London : Croom Helm, c1987. — [544]p

SEA-POWER — North Atlantic Ocean
Northern waters : security and resource issues / edited by Clive Archer and David Scrivener. — London : Croom Helm for the Royal Institute of International Affairs, c1986. — 240p. — *Includes index*

SEAFARERS' INTERNATIONAL UNION OF NORTH AMERICA
KAPLAN, William
Everything that floats : Pat Sullivan, Hal Banks, and the Seamen's Unions of Canada / William Kaplan. — Toronto : University of Toronto Press, 1987. — xii,241p — *Bibliography: p[227]-231*

SEASONAL VARIATIONS — Mathematical models
Seasonal adjustment of the monetary aggregates : report of the Committee of Experts on Seasonal Adjustment Techniques / Board of Governor of the Federal Reserve System. — Washington : The Board, 1981. — 55p

SECESSION
MAY, Robert E
John A. Quitman : Old South crusader / Robert E. May. — Baton Rouge : Louisiana State University Press, c1985. — p. cm. — (Southern biography series). — *Includes index. — Bibliography: p*

SECONDAT, CHARLES DE, baron de Montesquieu *See* Montesquieu, Charles de Secondat, baron de

SECRET SERVICE — Great Britain
HALL, Richard V.
A spy's revenge / Richard V. Hall. — Harmondsworth : Penguin, 1987. — 193p

SECRET SERVICE — Great Britain — History — 20th century
DOHERTY, Frank
The Stalker affair / Frank Doherty. — Cork : Mercier, c1986. — 90p

PINCHER, Chapman
Their trade is treachery / Chapman Pincher. — [New ed]. — London : Sidgwick & Jackson, 1982. — xi,317p. — *Previous ed.: 1981. — Includes index*

SECRET SERVICE — Soviet Union — History — 20th century
GLEES, Anthony
The secrets of the service : British intelligence and Communist subversion 1939-51 / Anthony Glees. — London : Cape, 1987. — 1v.. — *Includes bibliography and index*

SECRET SOCIETIES — Italy
DE LUTIIS, Giuseppe
Storia dei servizi segreti in Italia / Giuseppe de Lutiis. — Roma : Editori Riuniti, c1984. — 313p

SECTS
Cults, sects, and new religious movements : a bibliography of religions from the ATLA Religion Database / edited by Erica Treesh. — Chicago : American Theological Library Association, 1985. — 223p

ECCLESIASTICAL HISTORY SOCIETY. Summer Meeting (1985 : Lady Margaret Hall, Oxford)
Voluntary religion : papers read at the 1985 Summer Meeting and the 1986 Winter Meeting of the Ecclesiastical History Society / edited by W.J. Sheils and Diana Wood. — Oxford : Published for the Ecclesiastical History Society by Basil Blackwell, 1986. — xvi,521p. — (Studies in church history ; v.23). — *Includes index*

RODRÍGUEZ, Pepe
Esclavos de un mesías : sectas y lavado de cerebro / Pepe Rodríguez. — Barcelona : Elfos, 1984. — 277p. — (Temas de actualidad). — *Bibliography: p[276]-277*

Sickness and sectarianism : exploratory studies in medical and religious sectarianism / edited by R. Kenneth Jones. — Aldershot : Gower, c1985. — [176]p

SECTS — Congresses
Religious movements : genesis, exodus, and numbers / edited by Rodney Stark. — New York : Paragon House Publishers, c1985. — v, 354 p.. — *"A New ERA book.". — "Essays ... were originally prepared for an international conference held in May 1982 on Orcas Island, Washington"--Editor's introd. — Includes bibliographies and index*

SECTS — Law and legislation — United States
SHEPHERD, William C
To secure the blessings of liberty : American constitutional law and the new religious movements / William C. Shepherd. — New York : Crossroad Pub. Co. ; Chico, CA : Scholars Press, c1985. — x, 155 p.. — (Studies in religion / American Academy of Religion ; no. 35). — *Includes index. — Bibliography: p. [137]-144*

SECTS — Great Britain
WILSON, Bryan R.
Sects and society : a sociological study of three religious groups in Britain / Bryan Ronald Wilson. — London : Heinemann, 1961. — vi,397p

SECTS — United States
MELTON, J. Gordon
The encyclopedic handbook of cults in America / J. Gordon Melton. — New York : Garland Pub., 1986. — x, 272 p.. — (Garland reference library of social science ; v. 213). — *Includes bibliographies and index*

SECULARISM
FENN, Richard K
The spirit of revolt : anarchism and the cult of authority / Richard K. Fenn. — Totowa, NJ : Rowman & Littlefield, 1986. — p. cm. — *Includes index. — Bibliography: p*

SECURITIES
AGTMAEL, Antoine W. van
Emerging securities markets : investment banking opportunities in the developing world / by Antoine W. van Agtmael. — London : Euromoney, 1984. — xxvi,307p

International trade in services : securities. — Paris : Organisation for Economic Co-operation and Development, 1987. — 125p

The microstructure of securities markets / Kalman J. Cohen ... [et al.]. — Rev. — Englewood Cliffs, N.J. : Prentice-Hall, 1985. — p. cm. — *Includes index. — Bibliography: p*

SECURITIES — Canada
HUNTER, W. T.
Canadian financial markets / W. T. Hunter. — Peterborough, Canada : Broadview Press, 1986. — 193p. — *Includes references*

SECURITIES — United States
The microstructure of securities markets / Kalman J. Cohen ... [et al.]. — Rev. — Englewood Cliffs, N.J. : Prentice-Hall, 1985. — p. cm. — *Includes index. — Bibliography: p*

SECURITY CLASSIFICATION (GOVERNMENT DOCUMENTS) — United States
DEMAC, Donna A
Keeping America uninformed : government secrecy in the 1980's / Donna A. Demac ; preface by Ben H. Bagdikian. — New York : Pilgrim Press, c1984. — xii, 180 p.. — *Includes index. — Bibliography: p. 169-174*

SECURITY, INTERNATIONAL
BONK, Heinz
Es gibt eine Kraft! : die revolutionäre Arbeiterbewegung im Kampf um Frieden und Abrüstung / Heinz Bonk. — Berlin : Dietz, 1981. — 229p

The challenge of nuclear armaments : essays dedicated to Niels Bohr and his appeal for an open world / edited by A. Boserup, L. Christensen and O. Nathan. — Copenhagen : Rhodos International for the University of Copenhagen, 1986. — 346p

SECURITY, INTERNATIONAL
continuation

DAVID, Steven R
Third World coups d'état and international security / Steven R. David. — Baltimore : Johns Hopkins University Press, c1987. — p. cm. — *Includes index. — Bibliography: p*

DOROSHENKO, V. S.
Bor´ba KPSS za mezhdunarodnuiu razriadku i nesostoiatel´nost´ burzhuaznykh fal´sifikatsii / V. S. Doroshenko. — Kiev : Vyshcha shkola, 1985. — 204p. — *Bibliography: p202-[205]*

Escalation and intervention : multilateral security and its alternatives / edited by Arthur R. Day and Michael W. Doyle. — Boulder, Colo. : Westview ; London : Mansell, 1986. — x,181p. — (Westview special studies in international security). — *Published in cooperation with the United Nations Association of the United States of America. — Includes index*

Evropa XX veka : problemy mira i bezopasnosti / [red. kollegiia: A. O. Chubarian...et al.]. — Moskva : mezhdunarodnye otnosheniia, 1985. — 268p

FREEDMAN, Lawrence
Arms control : management or reform? / Lawrence Freedman. — London : Routledge & Kegan Paul, 1986. — 102p. — (Chatham House papers ; 31)

HAMEED, Mazher A.
Saudi Arabia, the West and the security of the Gulf / Mazher A. Hameed ; foreword by James Schlesinger. — London : Croom Helm, 1986. — [xv,224]p. — *Bibliography: p173-180. — Includes index*

Konzepte zum Frieden : Vorschläge für eine neue Abrüstungs- und Entspannungspolitik der SPD / herausgegeben von Katrin Fuchs, Hajo Hoffmann und Horst Klaus. — Berlin : spw-Verlag, 1985. — 179p

The Military buildup in the high North : American and Nordic perspectives / edited by Sverre Jervell and Kare Nyblom. — Lanham ; London : Center for International Affairs, Harvard University and University Press of America, c1986. — xiii,159p

Northern waters : security and resource issues / edited by Clive Archer and David Scrivener. — London : Croom Helm for the Royal Institute of International Affairs, c1986. — 240p. — *Includes index*

Nuclear non-proliferation and global security / edited by David B. Dewitt. — London : Croom Helm, c1987. — x,283p. — *Conference proceedings. — Includes index*

Overcoming threats to Europe : a new deal for confidence and security / edited by Sverre Lodgaard and Karl Birnbaum. — Oxford : Oxford University Press, 1987. — ix,235p. — *Under the auspices of Stockholm International Peace Research Institute. — Includes index*

PYM, Francis
Security and disarmament / Francis Pym. — London : Council for Arms Control, 1984. — 12p

SAVINOV, K. I.
Varshavskii dogovor - faktor mira, shchit sotsializma / K. I. Savinov. — Moskva : Mezhdunarodnye otnosheniia, 1986. — 267p

Security within the Pacific Rim / edited by Douglas T. Stuart. — Aldershot : Gower, c1987. — viii,166p. — *Includes index*

SEMENOV, V. A.
Politiki mira i kurs na konfrontatsiiu / V. A. Semenov. — Moskva : Mezhdunarodnye otnosheniia, 1986. — 146p

Sicherheit für Westeuropa : alternative Sicherheits- und Militärpolitik / "Generale für Frieden und Abrüstung". — Hamburg : Rasch und Röhring, 1985. — 223p

Space weapons and international security / edited by Bhupendra Jasani. — Oxford : Oxford University Press, 1986. — xvi,366p. — *Written for the Stockholm International Peace Research Institute. — Bibliography: p353-354 Includes index*

STUDIE- EN DOCUMENTATIECENTRUM EMILE VANDERVELDE INSTITUUT
Socialisme, veiligheid en defensie : discussieweekend, Klemskerke, 15-18 november 1980 / algemeen concept : SEVI-werkgroep landsverdediging ; voorzitters discussiegroepen : Leo Peeters...[et al.]. — Brussel : Studie- en Documentatiecentrum Emile Vandervelde Instituut, 1981. — 58p. — (SEVI dossier ; nr.5)

TIUSHKEVICH, S. A.
Voina i sovremennost´ / S. A. Tiushkevich ; otv. redaktor A. A. Babakov. — Moskva : Nauka, 1986. — 211p

SECURITY, INTERNATIONAL — Congresses

International security and arms control / edited by Ellen Propper Mickiewicz and Roman Kolkowicz. — New York : Praeger, 1986. — xii, 171 p.. — *Includes index*

SECURITY, INTERNATIONAL — History — 20th century

ALLSEBROOK, Mary
Prototypes of peacemaking : the first forty years of the United Nations / compiled and written by Mary Allsebrook ; introduction by Lord Caradon. — Harlow : Longman, c1986. — xvi,158p. — *Bibliography: p151-152. — Includes index*

SECURITY, INTERNATIONAL — Moral and ethical aspects

Ethics & European security / edited by Barrie Paskins. — London : Croom Helm, c1986. — 199p. — *Includes index*

SECURITY (PSYCHOLOGY)

WEIL, Simone
The need for roots : prelude to a declaration of duties towards mankind / Simone Weil ; [translated from the French by A. F. Wills] ; preface by T. S. Eliot. — Ark ed. — London : Routledge and Kegan Paul, 1987. — xv,288p. — *Translation of: L'Enracinement. — First French edition: 1949; this translation originally published: 1952*

SEED INDUSTRY AND TRADE — Argentina

JACOBS, Eduardo
La industría de semillas en la Argentina / Eduardo Jacobs, Marta Gutierrez. — [Buenos Aires] : CISEA, [1986]. — 242p. — (Documentos del CISEA ; 85). — *Bibliography: p239-242*

SEGREGATION — South Africa

SMITH, David M. (David Marshall)
Update : apartheid in South Africa / David M. Smith. — London : Dept. of Geography and Earth Science, Queen Mary College, 1983. — 76p. — (Special publication / Queen Mary College, Department of Geography and Earth Science ; 6). — *Bibliography: p. 74-76*

SEGREGATION — South Africa — History

CORNEVIN, Marianne
Apartheid : power and historical falsification / Marianne Cornevin. — Paris : Unesco, 1980. — 144 p.. — (Insights). — *Bibliography: p. [139]-144*

SEGREGATION IN EDUCATION — Law and legislation — Louisiana — History

LOFGREN, Charles A
The Plessy case : a legal-historical interpretation / Charles A. Lofgren. — New York : Oxford University Press, 1987. — p. cm . — *Includes index*

SEGREGATION IN EDUCATION — Law and legislation — United States — History

LOFGREN, Charles A
The Plessy case : a legal-historical interpretation / Charles A. Lofgren. — New York : Oxford University Press, 1987. — p. cm . — *Includes index*

TUSHNET, Mark V.
Segregated schools and legal strategy : the NAACP's capaign against segregated education, 1925-1950 / Mark Tushnet. — Chapel Hill : University of North Carolina Press, c1987. — p. cm. — *Includes index. — Bibliography: p*

SEGREGATION IN TRANSPORTATION — Law and legislation — Louisiana — History

LOFGREN, Charles A
The Plessy case : a legal-historical interpretation / Charles A. Lofgren. — New York : Oxford University Press, 1987. — p. cm . — *Includes index*

SEGREGATION IN TRANSPORTATION — Law and legislation — United States — History

LOFGREN, Charles A
The Plessy case : a legal-historical interpretation / Charles A. Lofgren. — New York : Oxford University Press, 1987. — p. cm . — *Includes index*

SEIGNIORIAL TENURE — Québec (Province) — Montréal (Region) — History

YOUNG, Brian J.
In its corporate capacity : the Seminary of Montreal as a business institution, 1816-1876 / Brian Young. — Kingston ; Montreal : McGill-Queen's University Press, 1986. — xix,295p. — *Bibliography: p[263]-285*

SEISMOLOGY — France

DESPEYROUX, J.
Nouveau zonage sismique de la France 1985 : en vue de l'application des règles parasismíques de construction et de la mise en oeuvre des plans d'exposition aux risques (PER) / J. Despeyroux, P. Godefroy. — [Paris : La Documentation française, 1986]. — 147p. — *Map in end pocket. — Bibliography: p95-97*

SELANGOR (MALAYSIA) — Population — Statistics

Banci penduduk dan perumahan Malaysia 1980 = Population and housing census of Malaysia 1980. — Kuala Lumpur : Department of Statistics. — *Text in Malay and English* Laporan penduduk negeri = State population report
Selangor. — 1983. — 599p. — 1map

SELECTIVITY (PSYCHOLOGY) — Congresses

Attention and performance XI / edited by Michael I. Posner, Oscar S.M. Marin. — Hillsdale, N.J. : Lawrence Erlbaum Associates, 1985. — xxiii, 675p. — *"Proceedings of the Eleventh International Symposium on Attention and Performance, Eugene, Oregon, July 1-8, 1984"--P. — Includes bibliographies and indexes*

SELF

Public self and private self / edited by Roy F. Baumeister. — New York : Springer-Verlag, c1986. — xiv, 257 p. — (Springer series in social psychology). — *Includes bibliographies and indexes*

Self and identity : psychosocial perspectives / edited by Krysia Yardley and Terry Honess. — Chichester : Wiley, c1987. — xvii,332p. — *Conference proceedings. — Includes bibliographies and index*

SELF — Addresses, essays, lectures

Reconstructing individualism : autonomy, individuality, and the self in Western thought / edited by Thomas C. Heller, Morton Sosna, and David E. Wellbery. — Stanford, Calif. : Stanford University Press, 1986. — xiv, 365p. — Includes index. — Includes bibliographical references

SELF-ACTUALIZATION (PSYCHOLOGY)

ABRAMSON, Jane B
Mothermania : a psychological study of mother-daughter conflict / Jane B. Abramson. — Lexington, Mass. : Lexington Books, c1987. — p. cm. — Includes index. — Bibliography: p

SELF-CONSCIOUSNESS — History — Addresses, essays, lectures

TUGENDHAT, Ernst
[Selbstbewusstsein und Selbstbestimmung. English]. Self-consciousness and self-determination / Ernst Tugendhat ; translated by Paul Stern. — Cambridge, Mass. : MIT Press, c1986. — xxxiv, 339 p.. — (Studies in contemporary German social thought). — Translation of: Selbstbewusstsein und Selbstbestimmung. — Includes index. — Bibliography: p. [333]-336

SELF-DEFENSE (INTERNATIONAL LAW)

KHARE, Subhas Chandra
Use of force under U.N. Charter / Subhas C. Khare ; foreword by Nagendra Singh. — 1st ed. — New Delhi, India : Metropolitan, 1985. — xii, 444 p.. — Spine title: Use of force under United Nations Charter. — : Originally presented as the author's thesis (LL. D.--Lucknow University). — Includes index. — Bibliography: p. [425]-439

TUCKER, Robert W
The inequality of nations / Robert W. Tucker. — New York : Basic Books, c1977. — x, 214 p.. — Includes bibliographical references and index

SELF-DETERMINATION, NATIONAL

CRISTESCU, Aureliu
The right to self-determination : historical and current development on the basis of United Nations instruments : study / prepared by Aureliu Cristescu [for] the Sub-Commission on Prevention of Discrimination and Protection of Minorities. — New York : United Nations, 1981. — v,125p

DELUPIS, Ingrid
International law and the independent state / Ingrid Detter De Lupis. — 2nd ed. — Aldershot : Gower, 1987. — xxvi,252p. — Previous ed.: 1974. — Includes index

GROS ESPIELL, Héctor
The right to self-determination : implimentation of United Nations resolutions / study prepared by Héctor Gros Espiell, special rapporteur of the Sub-Commission on Prevention of Discrimination and Protection of Minorities. — New York : United Nations, 1980. — vii,86p. — ([Document] / United Nations ; E/CN.4/Sub.2/405/Rev.1). — Bibliography: p.70-86

LOSONCZI, Pál
Erösödö népi-nemzeti egység, békés egymás mellett élés : válogatott beszédek, cikkek 1960-1984 / Losonczi. — Budapest : Kossuth Könyvkiadó, 1984. — 325p

Native power : the quest for autonomy and nationhood of indigenous peoples / edited by Jens Brøsted...[et al.]. — Bergen : Universitetsforlaget As, 1985. — 350p. — Includes bibliography of Helge Kleivan: p.342-348

SELF-DETERMINATION, NATIONAL — Addresses, essays, lectures

Native power : the quest for autonomy and nationhood of indigenous peoples / edited by Jens Brøsted ... [et al.]. — Bergen : Universitetsforlaget, c1985. — 350 p.. — Festschrift in memory of Helge Kleivan (1924-1983). — Includes bibliographies. — "Bibliography of Helge Kleivan": p. [341]-348

SELF-DETERMINATION, NATIONAL — Bibliography

Granting of independence to colonial countries and peoples : selective bibliography 1960-1980 = L'octroi de l'independance aux pays et aux peuples coloniaux : bibliographie sélective 1960-1980 / Dag Hammarskjöld Library. — New York : United Nations, 1981. — xiii,92p. — (Bibliographical series / Dag Hammarskjöld Library ; no. 31) ([Document] / United Nations ; ST/LIB/SER.B/31)

SELF-DETERMINATION, NATIONAL — Western Sahara

KAMIL, Leo
Fueling the fire : U.S. policy and the Western Sahara conflict / Leo Kamil. — Trenton, New Jersey : Red Sea Press, 1987. — 104p. — Distributed in the UK by Spokesman, Nottingham. — Bibliography: p93-96. — Appendices give text of 1983 OAU peace plan: 1985 U.N. General Assembly resolution: and 1979 Algiers peace treaty between the Polisario Front and the Republic of Mauretania

SELF-EMPLOYED — European Economic Community countries

GREAT BRITAIN. Construction Industry Directorate
The EEC directives on the general right of establishment and freedom to provide services in the industrial field and the directives and decision on public works contracts : two summaries by the Construction Industry Directorate. — London : the Directorate, 1972. — 11 leaves

SELF-EMPLOYED — Great Britain

GREAT BRITAIN. Parliament. House of Commons. Library. Research Division
Self-employed and national insurance. — [London] : the Division, [1975]. — 9 leaves. — (Background paper ; no.43). — Bibliographical references: leaves 8-9

SELF-GOVERNMENT IN EDUCATION — United States — History

ANTCZAK, Frederick J.
Thought and character : the rhetoric of democratic education / Frederick J. Antczak. — 1st ed. — Ames : Iowa State University Press, 1985. — viii, 242 p.. — Includes index. — Bibliography: p. 229-235

SELF HELP GROUPS — Ecuador — Guayaquil

MOSER, Caroline O. N.
Residential level struggle and consciousness : the experiences of poor women in Guayaquil, Ecuador / Caroline O. N. Moser. — London : Development Planning Unit, University College London, 1985. — 36p. — (DPU Gender and Planning Working Paper ; No.1). — Bibliography: p35-36

SELF-HELP GROUPS — Europe

Self-help and health in Europe : new approaches in health care / edited by Stephen Hatch and Ilona Kickbusch. — Copenhagen : WHO Regional Office for Europe, 1983

SELF-HELP GROUPS — United States

LIPNACK, Jessica
The networking book : people connecting with people / Jessica Lipnack and Jeffrey Stamps. — New York : Routledge & Kegan Paul, 1986. — xv, 192 p.. — Includes index. — Bibliography: p. 179-182

SELF-HELP HOUSING — Botswana

Administrative and operational procedures for programs for sites and services and area upgrading / J. Ronald Campbell, editor. — Washington, D.C. : The World Bank, 1985. — viii,230p. — (World Bank technical paper ; no.42)

SELF-PERCEPTION

KAUFMAN, Sharon R
The ageless self : sources of meaning in late life / Sharon R. Kaufman. — Madison, Wis. : University of Wisconsin Press, 1986. — xii, 208 p.. — (Life course studies). — Includes index. — Bibliography: p. 199-204

TURNER, John C
Rediscovering the social group : a self-categorization theory / John C. Turner with Michael A. Hogg ... (et al.). — Oxford : Basil Blackwell, 1987. — x,239p. — Bibliography: p209-232. — Includes index

SELF (PHILOSOPHY)

HANSON, Karen
The self imagined : philosophical reflection on the social character of psyche / Karen Hanson. — London : Routledge & Kegan Paul, 1986. — [160]p. — Includes index

SELF (PHILOSOPHY) — History — Addresses, essays, lectures

TUGENDHAT, Ernst
[Selbstbewusstsein und Selbstbestimmung. English]. Self-consciousness and self-determination / Ernst Tugendhat ; translated by Paul Stern. — Cambridge, Mass. : MIT Press, c1986. — xxxiv, 339 p.. — (Studies in contemporary German social thought). — Translation of: Selbstbewusstsein und Selbstbestimmung. — Includes index. — Bibliography: p. [333]-336

SELF (PHILOSOPHY) — History — 20th century

ABOULAFIA, Mitchell
The mediating self : Mead, Sartre, and self-determination / Mitchell Aboulafia. — New Haven : Yale University Press, c1986. — xvii, 139p. — Includes index. — Bibliography: p.127-131

SELF-PRESENTATION

Public self and private self / edited by Roy F. Baumeister. — New York : Springer-Verlag, c1986. — xiv, 257 p. — (Springer series in social psychology). — Includes bibliographies and indexes

SELF-REALIZATION

LEE, Dorothy
Valuing the self : what we can learn from other cultures / Dorothy Lee. — Prospect Heights, Ill : Waveland Press, 1986. — xii,87p

SELLING — Automobiles — Congresses

INTERNATIONAL CONFERENCE ON BUSINESS HISTORY (7th : 1981 : Fuji Education Center)
Development of mass marketing : the automobile and retailing industries : proceedings of the Fuji Conference / edited by Akio Okochi, Koichi Shimokawa. — Tokyo : University of Tokyo Press, 1981. — xiii,308p. — Includes references

SEMANTICS

ALLAN, Keith
Linguistic meaning / Keith Allan. — London ; New York : Routledge & Kegan Paul, 1986. — 2v.

GRONINGEN ROUND TABLE (3rd : 1976)
Syntax and semantics. — New York ; London : Academic Press. — Bibliographies
Vol.10: Selections from the third Groningen Round Table / edited by Frank Henry, Helmut S. Schnelle. — 1960. — xii,378p

NELSON, Katherine
Making sense : the acquisition of shared meaning / Katherine Nelson. — Orlando [Fla.] : Academic Press, 1985. — p. cm. — Includes index

SEMANTICS (LAW)
GOODRICH, Peter
Legal discourse : studies in linguistics, rhetoric and legal analysis / Peter Goodrich. — London : Macmillan, 1987. — x,266p. — (Language, discourse, society series). — Bibliography: p247-258. — Includes index

SEMANTICS (PHILOSOPHY)
APPIAH, Anthony
For truth in semantics / Anthony Appiah. — Oxford : Basil Blackwell, 1986. — xix,186p. — (Philosophical theory). — Bibliography: p174-177. — Includes index

QUINE, W. V
Word and object / W. V. Quine. — [Cambridge] : Technology Press of the Massachusetts Institute of Technology, [1960]. — 294 p. — (Studies in communication). — Includes bibliographies

SEMICONDUCTOR INDUSTRY — Europe
MALERBA, Franco
The semiconductor business : the economics of rapid growth and decline / Franco Malerba. — Madison, Wis. : University of Wisconsin Press, 1985, c1984. — p. cm. — Based on the author's thesis (Ph. D.)--Yale University. — Includes index. — Bibliography: p

SEMICONDUCTOR INDUSTRY — Japan
MALERBA, Franco
The semiconductor business : the economics of rapid growth and decline / Franco Malerba. — Madison, Wis. : University of Wisconsin Press, 1985, c1984. — p. cm. — Based on the author's thesis (Ph. D.)--Yale University. — Includes index. — Bibliography: p

SEMICONDUCTOR INDUSTRY — United States
MALERBA, Franco
The semiconductor business : the economics of rapid growth and decline / Franco Malerba. — Madison, Wis. : University of Wisconsin Press, 1985, c1984. — p. cm. — Based on the author's thesis (Ph. D.)--Yale University. — Includes index. — Bibliography: p

SEMINAR ON ECONOMIC MODELLING IN NEW ZEALAND (1984 : Wellington)
SEMINAR ON ECONOMIC MODELLING IN NEW ZEALAND (1984 : Wellington)
Economic modelling in New Zealand : proceedings of a seminar sponsored by the New Zealand Planning Council, Wellington, December 1984 / edited by Brian Silverstone and Graeme Wells. — Wellington : New Zealand Planning Council, 1986. — viii,131p. — Includes bibliographical references

SEMINAR ON INDUSTRIAL DEMOCRACY AND EMPLOYEE PARTICIPATION (1984 : Melbourne)
SEMINAR ON INDUSTRIAL DEMOCRACY AND EMPLOYEE PARTICIPATION (1984 : Melbourne)
Industrial Democracy and employee participation. — Canberra : Australian Government Publishing Service, 1985. — ix,272p. — Proceedings of a seminar held by the Federal Government in conjunction with the National Labour Consultative Council's Committee on Employee Participation

SEMIOTICS
KRISTEVA, Julia
The Kristeva reader / Julia Kristeva ; edited by Toril Moi. — Oxford : Basil Blackwell, 1986. — vii,327p. — Translation of the French. — Includes index

Television mythologies : stars, shows & signs / edited by Len Masterman. — London : Comedia/MK Media in association with Boyars, c1984. — iv,143p. — (Comedia series ; no. 24)

SEMIOTICS — Social aspects
WERTSCH, James V
Vygotsky and the social formation of mind / James V. Wertsch. — Cambridge, Mass. : Harvard University Press, 1985. — p. cm. — Includes index. — Bibliography: p

SENEGAL — History — Dictionaries
COLVIN, Lucie Gallistel
Historical dictionary of Senegal / by Lucie Gallistel Colvin. — Metuchen, N.J. : Scarecrow Press, 1981. — xiv, 339 p.. — (African historical dictionaries ; no. 23). — Bibliography: p. 297-339

SENEGAL — Population — Statistics — Evaluation
GUEYE, Lamine
Enquête Sénégalaise sur la fécondité : rapport d'évaluation / Lamine Gueye. — Voorburg : International Statistical Institute, 1984. — 57p. — (Scientific reports / World Fertility Service ; no.49)

SENEGAL — Relations — United States
Senegalese opinion on selected African and international issues : (World Survey III series). — [Washington, D.C.] : United States Information Agency, 1966. — xiv, 23p. — R-68-66

SENEGALESE — Attitudes
Senegalese opinion on selected African and international issues : (World Survey III series). — [Washington, D.C.] : United States Information Agency, 1966. — xiv, 23p. — R-68-66

SENILE DEMENTIA — Australia
HENDERSON, A. S.
The problem of dementia in Australia / by A. S. Henderson and A. F. Jorm. — Canberra : Australian Government Publishing Service, 1986. — v,56p. — Bibliographical references: p53-56

SENILE DEMENTIA — Great Britain
NORMAN, A. J.
Severe dementia : the provision of longstay care / Alison Norman. — London : Centre for Policy on Ageing, 1987. — xxiv,275p. — (Policy Studies in Ageing ; No.7)

SENTENCES (CRIMINAL PROCEDURE) — Legal status, laws, etc — Great Britain
GREAT BRITAIN. Parliament. House of Commons. Library. Research Division
Criminal Justice Bill 1981-82 [Bill 32] / [Patrick Nealon]. — [London] : the Division, 1982. — 25p. — (Reference sheet ; no.82/3). — Bibliography: p18-25

SENTENCES (CRIMINAL PROCEDURE) — England
The Psychology of sentencing : approaches to consistency and disparity / edited by Donald C. Pennington and Sally Lloyd-Bostock. — Oxford : Centre for Social-Legal Studies, 1987. — [xvi,240]p. — Includes bibliographies and index

SENTENCES (CRIMINAL PROCEDURE) — Great Britain
BURNEY, Elizabeth
Sentencing young people : what went wrong with the Criminal Justice Act 1982 / Elizabeth Burney. — Aldershot : Gower, c1985. — 120p

FUCHS, Claus
Der Community Service als Alternative zur Freiheitsstrafe / Claus Fuchs. — Pfaffenweiler : Centaurus-Verlagsgesellschaft, 1985. — lvi,369p. — (Beiträge zur rechtssoziologischen Forschung ; Bd.2). — Bibliography: pxvi-lvi

Sentencing reform : guidance or guidelines? / edited by Martin Wasik and Ken Pease. — Manchester : Manchester University Press, c1987. — viii,208p. — Includes bibliographies and index

SENTENCES (CRIMINAL PROCEDURE) — United States
Reform and punishment : essays on criminal sentencing / Michael Tonry and Franklin E. Zimring, editors. — Chicago ; London : University of Chicago Press, 1983. — viii,210p. — (Studies in crime and justice). — Includes bibliographies and index

Sentencing reform : guidance or guidelines? / edited by Martin Wasik and Ken Pease. — Manchester : Manchester University Press, c1987. — viii,208p. — Includes bibliographies and index

SENUFO (AFRICAN PEOPLE)
GLAZE, Anita J.
Art and death in a Senufo village / Anita J. Glaze. — Bloomington : Indiana University Press, c1981. — xvi, 267 p., [2] leaves of plates. — (Traditional arts of Africa). — Includes index. — Bibliography: p. [246]-254

SEPARATE PROPERTY — United States — History
SALMON, Marylynn
Women and the law of property in early America / Marylynn Salmon. — Chapel Hill ; London : University of North Carolina Press, c1986. — xvii, 267 p.. — (Studies in legal history). — Based on the author's thesis (Ph. D.). — Includes indexes. — Bibliography: p. 239-251

SEPARATION OF POWERS — India
KRISHNAPURAM, R. Mohan
Sovereignty of Parliament in India / R. Mohan Krishnapuram ; foreword by J. M. L. Sinha. — New Delhi : Deep & Deep, 1985. — 214p. — Bibliography: p[211]-212

SEPARATION OF POWERS — United States
FISHER, Louis
The politics of shared power : Congress and the executive / Louis Fisher. — 2nd ed. — Washington, D.C. : CQ Press, c1987. — xi, 241 p.. — Includes indexes. — Includes bibliographies

MERRY, Henry J
The constitutional system : the group character of the elected institutions / Henry J. Merry. — New York : Praeger, 1986. — x, 215 p.. — Includes bibliographies and index

SEPARATION (PSYCHOLOGY)
GROSSMAN, Tracy Barr
Mothers and children facing divorce / by Tracy Barr Grossman. — Ann Arbor, Mich. : UMI Research Press, c1986. — 208 p. — (Research in clinical psychology ; no. 15). — : Revision of thesis (Ph.D.)--University of Michigan, 1984. — Includes index. — Bibliography: p. [203]-205

SERBIA — History — 1945-
PRVULOVICH, Žika Rad.
Serbia between the swastika and the red star / by Žika Rad. Prvulovich. — Birmingham : Ž. R. Prvulovich, 1986. — vi,240p. — Bibliography: p233-234

SERFDOM — Soviet Union
DRUZHININ, N. M.
Izbrannye trudy / N. M. Druzhinin. — Moskva : Nauka
[2]: Sotsial'no-ekonomicheskaia istoriia Rossii / otv. redaktor S. S. Dmitriev. — 1987. — 421p

SERFDOM — Soviet Union — History
NEUPOKOEV, V. I.
Gosudarstvennye povinnosti krest'ian Evropeiskoi Rossii v kontse XVIII - nachale XIX veka / V. I. Neupokoev ; otv. redaktor P. G. Ryndziunskii. — Moskva : Nauka, 1987. — 286p

SHAPIRO, A. L.
Russkoe krest'ianstvo pered zakreposhcheniem (XIV-XVI vv.) / A. L. Shapiro. — Leningrad : Izd-vo Leningradskogo universiteta, 1987. — 254p

SERIAL PUBLICATIONS — Scotland — Bibliography

STEVENSON, David, 1942-
Scottish texts and calendars : an analytical guide to serial publications / by David and Wendy B. Stevenson. — London : Royal Historical Society, 1987. — xii,233p. — (Royal Historical Society guides and handbooks ; no. 14) (Scottish History Society. 4th series ; v.23). — *Includes index*

SERRA I MORET, MANUEL

BARCELÓ I SERRAMALERA, Mercè
El pensament polític de Serra i Moret : nació, democràcia i socialisme / Mercè Barceló i Serramalera ; pròleg d'Isidre Molas. — Barcelona : Edicions 62, 1986. — 205p. — *Bibliography: p191-205*

SERRA Y MORET, MANUEL

SERRA Y MORET, Manuel
Introducción al "Manifiesto del Partido Comunista" y otros escritos / Manuel Serra y Moret ; estudio preliminar y notas aríticas a crgo de Antoni Jutglar. — [Barcelona] : Anthropos, Editorial del Hombre, 1984. — 279p. — (Historia, ideas y textos ; 9)

SERRANO SUÑER, RAMÓN

GARRIGA, Ramón
Franco-Serrano Suñer : un drama político / Ramón Garriga Alemany. — Barcelona : Planeta, 1986. — 209p

SERVANTS — England — Liverpool (Merseyside)

Born to serve : domestic service in Liverpool 1850-1950. — Liverpool : Second Chance to Learn Project, 1987. — 53p

SERVICE B

FALIGOT, Roger
Service B / Roger Faligot, Rémi Kauffer. — Paris : Fazard, [1985]. — 342p

SERVICE INDUSTRIES

The emerging service economy / edited by Orio Giarini for the Services World Forum. — Oxford : Pergamon, 1987. — xii,298p. — *Bibliography: p283-293. — Includes index*

KAKABADSE, Mario A.
International trade in services : prospects for liberalisation in the 1990s / Mario A. Kakabadse. — London : Croom Helm for the Atlantic Institute for International Affairs, c1987. — [80]p. — (Atlantic paper ; no.64)

RIDDLE, Dorothy I
Service-led growth : the role of the service sector in world development / Dorothy I. Riddle. — New York : Praeger, 1985. — p. cm . — *Includes index. — Bibliography: p*

SERVICE INDUSTRIES — Government policy — Congresses

Production and trade in services : policies and their underlying factors bearing upon international service transactions : report / by the UNCTAD secretariat. — New York : United Nations, 1985. — vii,64p. — *At head of title: United Nations Conference on Trade and Development, Geneva. — "TD/B/941/Rev.1"--T.p. verso. — "United Nations publication sales no. E.84.II.D.2"--T.p. verso. — Includes bibliographical references*

SERVICE INDUSTRIES — International cooperation — Congresses

Production and trade in services : policies and their underlying factors bearing upon international service transactions : report / by the UNCTAD secretariat. — New York : United Nations, 1985. — vii,64p. — *At head of title: United Nations Conference on Trade and Development, Geneva. — "TD/B/941/Rev.1"--T.p. verso. — "United Nations publication sales no. E.84.II.D.2"--T.p. verso. — Includes bibliographical references*

SERVICE INDUSTRIES — Law and legislation — European Economic Community countries

LASOK, Dominik
The professions and services in the European Economic Community / by D. Lasok. — Deventer, The Netherlands ; New York : Kluwer Law and Taxation Publishers, c1986. — p. cm

SERVICE INDUSTRIES — Asia, Southeastern

The Pacific challenge in international business / edited by W. Chan Kim and Philip K.Y. Young ; with a foreword by Vern Terpstra. — Ann Arbor, Mich. : UMI Research Press, 1987. — viii, 342 p.. — (Research for business decisions ; no. 72). — *Includes bibliographies and index*

SERVICE INDUSTRIES — Denmark

Servicesektorens rolle i dansk økonomi. — København : Industriministeriet, 1984. — 96p

SERVICE INDUSTRIES — East Asia

The Pacific challenge in international business / edited by W. Chan Kim and Philip K.Y. Young ; with a foreword by Vern Terpstra. — Ann Arbor, Mich. : UMI Research Press, 1987. — viii, 342 p.. — (Research for business decisions ; no. 72). — *Includes bibliographies and index*

SERVICE INDUSTRIES — Europe — Technological innovations — Bibliography

New technology and the quality of life : the service sector in Europe : an annotated bibliography (with supplement in French) / edited by W. O'Conghaile and V. Di Martino. — Dublin : European Foundation for the Improvement of Living and Working Conditions, 1986. — 272p

SERVICE INDUSTRIES — France — Statistics

DEMAILLY, Dominique
Rétropolation 1959-1969 de comptes détaillés des biens et des services / Dominique Demailly, Alain Tranap. — Paris : I.N.S.E.E., 1986. — 71p. — (Archives et documents / Institut national de la statistique et des études économiques ; no.164)

DEPOUTOT, Raoul
Indices de chiffres d'affaires dans le commerce et les services : 1976-1984 / Raoul Depoutot, Marie-Line Honnibal. — Paris : I.N.S.E.E., 1986. — 113p. — (Archives et documents / Institut national de la statistique et des études économiques ; no.163)

Enquête annuelle d'entreprise dans les services. — Paris : INSEE, 1984-. — (Les collections de l'Insée. série E). — *Annual*

SERVICE INDUSTRIES — Great Britain — Forecasting

RAJAN, Amin
Services — the second industrial revolution? : business and jobs outlook for UK growth industries : an employer-based study by the Institute of Manpower Studies for the Occupations Study Group / by Amin Rajan. — London : Butterworths, 1987. — xviii,257p. — *An employer-based study by the Institute of Manpower Studies for the Occupations Study Group. — Bibliography: p240-244*

SERVICE INDUSTRIES — Italy — Statistics

ITALY. Istituto Centrale di Statistica
6 censimento generale dell'industria, del commercio, dei servizi e dell'artigianato 26 ottobre 1981. — Roma : the Istituto vol.3: Atti del censimento. — 1985. — 264p

SERVICE INDUSTRIES — London

Services and employment growth in London, 1971-91 / James Simmie ... [et al.]. — London : Bartlett School of Architecture and Planning, 1985. — 32p. — (Town planning discussion paper ; no.45)

SERVICE INDUSTRIES — Organisation for Economic Co-operation and Development countries — Statistics — Measurement

Measurement of value added at constant prices in service activities : national accounts : sources and methods (1) = Mesure de la valeur ajoutée aux prix constants dans les activités de service : comptes nationaux : sources et méthodes (1). — Paris : Organisation for Economic Co-operation and Development, 1987. — 105p

SERVICE INDUSTRIES — Singapore — Statistics

Report on the census of services / Department of Statistics, Singapore. — Singapore : Department of Statistics, 1984-. — *Biennial. — Continues: Report on the survey of services*

Report on the survey of services / Department of Statistics, Singapore. — Singapore : Department of Statistics, 1976-1982. — *Biennial. — Continued by: Report on the census of services*

SERVICE INDUSTRIES — Thailand — Statistics

Census of business trade and services 1966 : Southern region. — Bangkok : National Statistical Office, [1970?]. — 57p. — *In English and Thai*

Report : census of business trade and services 1977 : Bangkok Metropolitan, Nonthaburi, Pathum Thani and Samut Prakan. — Bangkok : National Statistical Office, [1980?]. — 96p. — *In English and Thai*

Report : census of business trade and services 1977 : whole kingdom. — Bangkok : National Statistical Office, [1980?]. — 75p

SERVICE INDUSTRIES — Togo — Statistics

Enquête sur les entreprises industrielles commerciales et de services du Togo : exercice 1976. — Lomé : Direction de la Statistique, 1976. — 116p

Enquête sur les entreprises industrielles commerciales et des services du Togo : exercices 1981 et 1982. — Lomé : Direction de la Statistique, 1986. — 300p

SERVICE INDUSTRIES — United States

ECALLE, François
La révolution tertiaire aux Etats-Unis / François Ecalle. — Paris : La Documentation française, 1986. — 113p. — (Notes et études documentaires ; no.4814). — *Bibliography: p111-112*

SERVICE INDUSTRIES — United States — Communication systems — Congresses

Services in transition : the impact of information technology on the service sector / edited by Gerald Faulhaber, Eli Noam, Roberta Tasley. — Cambridge, Mass. : Ballinger Pub. Co., c1986. — xix, 218 p.. — *Papers presented at the Conference on the Impact of Information Technology on the Service Sector, held at the Wharton School, University of Pennsylvania, Feb. 7-8, 1985. — Includes bibliographies and index*

SERVICE INDUSTRIES WORKERS — Europe — Effect of technological innovations on — Bibliography

New technology and the quality of life : the service sector in Europe : an annotated bibliography (with supplement in French) / edited by W. O'Conghaile and V. Di Martino. — Dublin : European Foundation for the Improvement of Living and Working Conditions, 1986. — 272p

SERVICE INDUSTRIES WORKERS — Great Britain — Supply and demand — Forecasting
RAJAN, Amin
  Services — the second industrial revolution? : business and jobs outlook for UK growth industries : an employer-based study by the Institute of Manpower Studies for the Occupations Study Group / by Amin Rajan. — London : Butterworths, 1987. — xviii,257p. — *An employer-based study by the Institute of Manpower Studies for the Occupations Study Group.* — Bibliography: p240-244

SETTLEMENTS (LAW) — England
JACKSON, Joseph
  Jackson's matrimonial finance and taxation. 4th ed. / by Joseph Jackson and D.T.A. Davies. — London : Butterworths, 1986. — 1v. . — *Previous ed.: 1980.* — *Includes index*

SEVEN YEARS' WAR, 1756-1763
KENNETT, Lee
  The French armies in the Seven Years' War : a study in military organization and administration / Lee Kennett. — Durham, N.C. : Duke University Press, 1967. — xvi,165p

SEVEN YEARS' WAR, 1756-1763 — Diplomatic history
DORAN, Patrick F
  Andrew Mitchell and Anglo-Prussian diplomatic relations during the Seven Years War / Patrick Francis Doran. — [Garland ed.]. — New York : Garland, 1986. — 408 p.. — (Outstanding theses from the London School of Economics and Political Science). — Bibliography: p. [397]-408

SEVEN YEARS' WAR, 1756-1763 — Economic aspects — France
RILEY, James C
  The Seven Years War and the old regime in France : the economic and financial toll / James C. Riley. — Princeton, N.J. : Princeton University Press, 1986. — xxii, 256p. — *Includes index*

SEVERN, RIVER, ESTUARY (ENGLAND AND WALES) — Bridges
SECOND SEVERN CROSSING GROUP
  Study of second Severn crossing. : final report, July 1986 : summary / Second Severn Crossing Group. — London : Her Majesty's Stationery Office, 1986. — 48p. — *At head of title: Department of Transport*

SEVERN TUNNEL (ENGLAND) AND WALES
SECOND SEVERN CROSSING GROUP
  Study of second Severn crossing. : final report, July 1986 : summary / Second Severn Crossing Group. — London : Her Majesty's Stationery Office, 1986. — 48p. — *At head of title: Department of Transport*

SEVILLE (SPAIN) — History — 20th century
MACARRO VERA, José Manuel
  La utopia revolucionaria : Sevilla en la Segunda Republica / José Manuel Macarro Vera. — Sevilla : Monte de Piedad y Caja de Ahorros de Sevilla, 1985. — 518p

SEWAGE DISPOSAL — England — South East
SERPLAN. Waste Disposal Working Party
  Waste disposal in the South East region / a report by the Waste Disposal Working Party. — London : London and South East Regional Planning Conference, 1986. — 27p

SEWAGE IRRIGATION — Hygienic aspects — Developing countries
  Wastewater irrigation in developing countries : health effects and technical solutions / Hillel I. Shuval ...[et al.]. — Washington, D.C. : The World Bank, 1986. — xxxi,324p. — (World Bank technical paper ; no51) (UNDP project management report ; no.6) (Integrated resource recovery series ; no.6). — *Bibliographical references: p307-324*

SEX
CARPENTER, Edward, 1844-1929
  Selected writings / Edward Carpenter. — London : GMP. — (Gay modern classics) Vol.1: Sex / with an introduction by Nöel Grieg. — 1984. — 318p. — *Includes index*

DALY, Martin
  Sex, evolution, and behavior / Martin Daly and Margo Wilson. — 2nd ed. — Boston : Willard Grant Press, c1983. — xiv, 402 p.. — *Includes index.* — Bibliography: p. 345-389

SEX — Addresses, essays, lectures
  Sexuality, new perspectives / edited by Zira DeFries, Richard C. Friedman, and Ruth Corn. — Westport, Conn. : Greenwood Press, 1985. — xii, 362 p.. — (Contributions in psychology ; no. 6). — *Includes bibliographies and index*

SEX — Religious aspects — Unification Church
GRACE, James H
  Sex and marriage in the Unification movement : a sociological study / James H. Grace ; with a preface by Mac Linscott Ricketts. — New York : E. Mellen Press, c1985. — 284 p.. — (Studies in religion and society ; v. 13). — Bibliography: p. [275]-284

SEX — Statistics
  Age-sex composition of world population by major region and country, based on United Nations' population projections as assessed in 1978. — Tokyo : Institute of Population Problems, 1981. — iv,97p. — (Research series / Institute of Population Problems ; no.225). — *In Japanese with contents and forword also in English*

ZOUGHLAMI, Younès
  The demographic characteristics of household populations / Younès Zoughlami, Diana Allsopp. — Voorburg : International Statistical Institute, 1985. — 82p. — (Comparative studies / World Fertility Survey ; no.45). — *Bibliographical references: p31*

SEX AND LAW — Europe — Congresses
CRIMINOLOGICAL RESEARCH CONFERENCE (15th : 1982)
  Sexual behaviour and attitudes and their implications for criminal law : reports presented to the Fifteenth Criminological Research Conference 1982. — Strasbourg : Council of Europe, 1984. — 207p. — (Collected studies in criminological research ; v.21). — *On cover: European Committee on Crime Problems*

SEX (BIOLOGY)
FRAYSER, Suzanne G
  Varieties of sexual experience : an anthropological perspective on human sexuality / Suzanne G. Frayser. — New Haven, Conn. : HRAF Press, 1985. — xii, 546 p.. — "Ethnographic bibliography": p. 495-510. — *Includes index.* — Bibliography: p. 511-527

SEX CRIMES — United States
GOLDSTEIN, Seth L
  The sexual exploitation of children : a practical guide to assessment, investigation, and intervention / Seth L. Goldstein. — New York : Elsevier, c1987. — xix, 433 p.. — (Elsevier series in practical aspects of criminal and forensic investigations). — *Includes bibliographies and index*

SEX CUSTOMS
  The Cultural construction of sexuality / edited by Pat Caplan. — London : Tavistock, 1987. — xi,304p. — *Includes bibliographies and index*

SEX CUSTOMS — Cross-cultural studies
FRAYSER, Suzanne G
  Varieties of sexual experience : an anthropological perspective on human sexuality / Suzanne G. Frayser. — New Haven, Conn. : HRAF Press, 1985. — xii, 546 p.. — "Ethnographic bibliography": p. 495-510. — *Includes index.* — Bibliography: p. 511-527

SEX CUSTOMS — Barbados
DANN, Graham
  The Barbadian male : sexual attitudes and practice / Graham Dann. — London : Macmillan Caribbean, 1987. — [224]p. — *Includes bibliography and index*

SEX CUSTOMS — Canada
KINSMAN, Gary
  The regulation of desire : sexuality in Canada / Gary Kinsman. — Montréal ; New York : Black Rose Books, 1987. — 233p. — *Includes references*

SEX CUSTOMS — Europe — History
MOSSE, George L
  Nationalism and sexuality : respectability and abnormal sexuality in modern Europe / George L. Mosse. — 1st ed. — New York : H. Fertig, 1985. — viii, 232 p., [10] p. of plates. — *Includes index.* — Bibliography: p. 195-223

SEX CUSTOMS — Germany — Case studies
MOSSE, George L
  Nationalism and sexuality : respectability and abnormal sexuality in modern Europe / George L. Mosse. — 1st ed. — New York : H. Fertig, 1985. — viii, 232 p., [10] p. of plates. — *Includes index.* — Bibliography: p. 195-223

SEX CUSTOMS — Great Britain — Case studies
MOSSE, George L
  Nationalism and sexuality : respectability and abnormal sexuality in modern Europe / George L. Mosse. — 1st ed. — New York : H. Fertig, 1985. — viii, 232 p., [10] p. of plates. — *Includes index.* — Bibliography: p. 195-223

SEX CUSTOMS — Great Britain — History — Sources
  The Sexuality debates / edited by Sheila Jeffreys. — London : Routledge & Kegan Paul, 1987. — [630]p. — (Women's source library). — *Includes index*

SEX CUSTOMS — Papua New Guinea
HERDT, Gilbert H.
  Sambia : ritual and gender in New Guinea / by Gilbert H. Herdt. — New York : Holt, Rinehart and Winston, 1986. — p. cm. — (Case studies in cultural anthropology). — *Includes index.* — Bibliography: p

SEX CUSTOMS — Rome
KIEFER, Otto
  Sexual life in ancient Rome / by Otto Kiefer. — London : Abbey Library, 1934. — viii,380p

SEX CUSTOMS — United States
BERTELSON, David
  Snowflakes and snowdrifts : individualism and sexuality in America / David Bertelson. — Lanham, MD : University Press of America, c1986. — ix, 282 p.. — *Includes index.* — Bibliography: p. 255-275

SEX DIFFERENCES
ARCHER, John, 1944-
  Sex and gender / John Archer, Barbara Lloyd. — Cambridge : Cambridge University Press, 1985. — ix, 355p — *"First published in 1982 by Penguin" - t.p. verso.* — Bibliography: p.300-330

CARPENTER, Edward, 1844-1929
  Selected writings / Edward Carpenter. — London : GMP. — (Gay modern classics) Vol.1: Sex / with an introduction by Nöel Grieg. — 1984. — 318p. — *Includes index*

NICHOLSON, John, 1945-
  Men and women: how different are they? / John Nicholson. — Rev. and expanded ed. — Oxford : Oxford University Press, 1984. — 193p. — *Previous ed.: published as A question of sex. London : Fontana, 1979.* — Bibliography: p180-188. — *Includes index*

SEX DIFFERENCES — Addresses, essays, lectures
HALL, Roberta L
Male-female differences : a bio-cultural perspective / Roberta L. Hall, with Patricia Draper ... [et al.]. — New York ; Eastbourne : Praeger, 1985. — vii, 309p. — *Includes index*

SEX DIFFERENCES IN EDUCATION
MCGUINNESS, Diane
When children don't learn : understanding the biology and psychology of learning disabilities / Diane McGuinness. — New York : Basic Books, c1985. — x, 310p. — *Includes index. — Bibliography: p.277-295*

SEX DIFFERENCES IN EDUCATION — Great Britain
SMITH, Stuart
Separate tables? : an investigation into single-sex setting in mathematics / Stuart Smith. — London : H.M.S.O., 1986. — (Research series / Equal Opportunities Commission)

WHYTE, Judith
Girls into science and technology : the story of a project / Judith Whyte. — London : Routledge & Kegan Paul, 1986

SEX DIFFERENCES (PSYCHOLOGY)
ARCHER, John, 1944-
Sex and gender / John Archer, Barbara Lloyd. — Cambridge : Cambridge University Press, 1985. — ix, 355p. — *"First published in 1982 by Penguin" - t.p. verso. — Bibliography: p.300-330*

DENMARK. Kommissionen vedrørende kvindernes stilling i samfundet
Bilag til betaenkning og ligestilling : afgivet af et udvalg under kommissionen vedrørende kvindernes stilling i samfundet. — København : the Kommissionen, 1968. — 88p. — *Includes bibliographies. — Contents: Psykologiske kønsforskelle/Carl Weltzer - Sociologiske kønsforskelle/Benedicte Madsen*

MACKIE, Marlene
Constructing women and men : gender socialization / Marlene Mackie. — Toronto : Holt, Rinehart and Winston of Canada, 1987. — v,314p. — *Bibliography: p[276]-308*

RANCOUR-LAFERRIERE, Daniel
Signs of the flesh : an essay on the evolution of hominid sexuality / Daniel Rancour-Laferriere. — Berlin ; New York : Mouton, c1985. — x, 473 p.. — (Approaches to semiotics ; 71). — *Includes index. — Bibliography: p. [389]-452*

SEX DISCRIMINATION — Law and legislation — South Australia
SOUTH AUSTRALIA. Equal Opportunities Branch
Australian equal opportunity legislation. — [Adelaide] : the Branch, 1986. — 3 leaves. — (Equal employment opportunity management planning information sheet)

SEX DISCRIMINATION — Law and legislation — United States
Women's work, men's work : sex segregation on the job / Barbara F. Reskin and Heidi I. Hartmann, editors ; Committee on Women's Employment and Related Social Issues, Commission on Behavioral and Social Sciences and Education, National Research Council. — Washington, D.C. : National Academy Press, 1986. — xii, 173 p.. — *Includes index. — Bibliography: p. 141-161*

SEX DISCRIMINATION AGAINST WOMEN
ALDRICH, Mark
The economics of comparable worth / Mark Aldrich, Robert Buchele. — Cambridge, Mass. : Ballinger Pub. Co., 1986. — p. cm. — *Includes bibliographies and index*

SEX DISCRIMINATION AGAINST WOMEN — Cross-cultural studies
Women in the world, 1975-1985 : the women's decade / Lynne B. Iglitzin and Ruth Ross, editors. — 2nd rev. ed. — Santa Barbara, Calif. : ABC-Clio Information Services, c1985. — p. cm. — (Studies in international and comparative politics ; 16). — *Includes bibliographies and index*

SEX DISCRIMINATION AGAINST WOMEN — Law and legislation — Great Britain
LEONARD, Alice M.
Judging inequality : the effectiveness of the tribunal system in sex discrimination and equal pay cases / Alice M. Leonard. — London : Cobden Trust, c1987. — [160]p. — *Includes bibliography*

SEX DISCRIMINATION AGAINST WOMEN — Law and legislation — United States
RUBIN, Eva R
The Supreme Court and the American Family : ideology and issues / Eva R. Rubin. — New York : Greenwood Press, 1986. — 251 p.. — (Contributions in American studies ; [no. 85]). — *Series no. from jacket. — Includes indexes. — Bibliography: p. [225]-236*

SEX DISCRIMINATION AGAINST WOMEN — European Economic Community countries
European women in paid employment 1984 : Do they feel discriminated against and vulnerable at work? Are they equipped to take up the challenge of technology. — Luxembourg : Office for Official Publications of the European Communities, 1984. — 118p. — *At head of title page: Commission of the European Communities*

SEX DISCRIMINATION AGAINST WOMEN — Great Britain
GREAT BRITAIN. Equal Opportunities Commission
Men's jobs? women's jobs? : practical guidance on why many jobs are done only by men or only by women, and how this pattern 'job segregation' can and should be changed. — London : HMSO, 1986. — vii,34p. — *At head of title: Equal Opportunities Commission*

SEX DISCRIMINATION AGAINST WOMEN — Great Britain — Statistics
Women and men in Britain: a statistical profile / Equal Opportunities Commission. — London : HMSO, 1985-. — *Annual*

SEX DISCRIMINATION BILL 1985-86
GREAT BRITAIN. Parliament. House of Commons. Library. Research Division
Sex Discrimination Bill [HL] (Bill 151 of 1985-86) / Celia Nield. — [London] : the Division, 1986. — 32p. — (Reference sheet ; no.86/12). — *Bibliographical references: p32*

SEX DISCRIMINATION IN CRIMINAL JUSTICE ADMINISTRATION — United States
ROSS, Robert R.
Female offender : correctional afterthoughts / by Robert R. Ross, Elizabeth A. Fabiano. — Jefferson, N.C. : McFarlane, 1986. — p. cm. — *Includes index. — Bibliography: p*

SEX DISCRIMINATION IN EDUCATION — Great Britain
Untying the apron strings : anti-sexist provision for the under-fives / edited by Naima Browne and Pauline France. — Milton Keynes : Open University Press, 1986. — xii,175p. — (Gender and education). — *Bibliography: p162-168. — Includes index*

VAN DYKE, Ruth Marie
Secondary school careers advice, examination choices and adult aspirations : the maintenance of gender stratification / Ruth Marie Van Dyke. — 472 leaves. — *PhD (Econ) 1986 LSE. — Leaves 373-447 are appendices*

SEX DISCRIMINATION IN EMPLOYMENT
COCKBURN, Cynthia
Machinery of dominance : women, men and technical know-how / Cynthia Cockburn. — London : Pluto, 1985. — 282p. — *Includes index*

Gender in the workplace / Clair Brown and Joseph A. Pechman, editors. — Washington, D.C. : Brookings Institution, c1987. — xiv, 316 p.. — *Includes bibliographical references and index*

RESSNER, Ulla
The hidden hierarchy : democracy and equal opportunities / Ulla Ressner. — Aldershot : Avebury, c1987. — 120p

WILLNER, Johan
Who will be assigned to the well-paid occupations? : a study of sex discrimination in the allocation of the work force under imperfect competition / Johan Willner. — Åbo : Åbo Akademi, 1986. — 47p. — (Meddelanden från Ekonomisk-Statsvetenskapliga Fakulteten Vid Åbo Akademi. Serie A ; 235). — *Bibliography: p45-47*

SEX DISCRIMINATION IN EMPLOYMENT — Law and legislation — Great Britain
GREAT BRITAIN. Department of Health and Social Security
Consultative document on equal status for men and women in occupational pension schemes. — [London} : the Department, [1976]. — [29]p

GREAT BRITAIN. Department of Health and Social Security
Second consultative document on equal treatment for men and women in occupational pension schemes. — [London] : the Department, [1977]. — 1v.(various pagings)

GREAT BRITAIN. Parliament. House of Commons. Library. Research Division
Sex Discrimination Bill [HL] (Bill 151 of 1985-86) / Celia Nield. — [London] : the Division, 1986. — 32p. — (Reference sheet ; no.86/12). — *Bibliographical references: p32*

LEONARD, Alice M.
Judging inequality : the effectiveness of the tribunal system in sex discrimination and equal pay cases / Alice M. Leonard. — London : Cobden Trust, c1987. — [160]p. — *Includes bibliography*

SEX DISCRIMINATION IN EMPLOYMENT — Canada
GANNAGÉ, Charlene
Double day, double bind : women garment workers / by Charlene Gannagé. — Toronto, Ont. : Women's Press, 1986. — 235 p., [1] leaf of plates. — (Women's press issues). — *Bibliography: p. 227-235*

SEX DISCRIMINATION IN EMPLOYMENT — Cyprus
HOUSE, William J.
Labour market segmentation and sex discrimination in Cyprus : some empirical evidence / by William J. House. — [Nicosia] : Department of Statistics and Research, [1985]. — v,39p

SEX DISCRIMINATION IN EMPLOYMENT — Developing countries
Sex inequalities in urban employment in the Third World : a study prepared for the International Labour Office within the framework of the World Employment Programme with the financial support of the United Nations Fund for Population Activities (UNFPA) / edited by Richard Anker and Catherine Hein. — Basingstoke : Macmillan, 1986. — [304]p. — (Macmillan series of ILO studies). — *Includes index*

SEX DISCRIMINATION IN EMPLOYMENT — Great Britain

COCKBURN, Cynthia
Two track training : sex inequalities and the YTS / Cynthia Cockburn. — Basingstoke : Macmillan Education, 1987. — [256]p. — (Youth questions)

GRAHAM, Cosmo
The role of ACAS conciliation in equal pay and sex discrimination cases / Cosmo Graham, Norman Lewis ; [for the] Equal Opportunities in Commission. — Manchester : Equal Opportunities Commission, 1985. — 70p. — *Bibliographical references: p69-70*

GREAT BRITAIN. Equal Opportunities Commission
Fair and efficient selection : guidance on equal opportunities policies in recruitment and selection procedures. — London : H.M.S.O., 1986. — 50p

In a man's world : essays on women in male-dominated professions / edited by Anne Spencer & David Podmore. — London : Tavistock, 1987. — 240p. — (Social science paperbacks ; 342). — *Includes bibliographies and index*

JONES, Sandra
Policewomen and equality : formal policy v informal practice? / Sandra Jones. — Basingstoke : Macmillan, 1986. — xii,235p. — *Bibliography: p225-229. — Includes index*

LEEVERS, Kate
Women at work in housing / Kate Leevers ; with illustrations by Candy Walker. — London : HERA, 1986. — 32p

LEONARD, Alice M.
Pyrrhic victories : winning sex discrimination and equal pay cases in the industrial tribunals, 1980-84 / Alice M. Leonard. — London : H.M.S.O., 1987. — 55p. — (Research series / Equal Opportunities Commission)

MALLIER, A. T.
Women and the economy : a comparative study of Britain and the USA / A.T. Mallier and M.J. Rosser. — Basingstoke : Macmill, 1987. — xiii,221p. — *Bibliography: p200-211. — Includes index*

NATIONAL AND LOCAL GOVERNMENT OFFICERS ASSOCIATION
How equal are your opportunities? : comparisons of local improvements won by NALGO branches. — London : NALGO, 1986. — 44p

ROBARTS, Sadie
Positive action for women : changing the workplace. — [2nd ed.] / Paddy Stamp & Sadie Robarts. — London : National Council for Civil Liberties, c1986. — vi,135p. — *Previous ed.: 1981. — Bibliography: p135-135*

TZANNATOS, Z.
A general equilibrium model of discrimination and its effect on incomes / Z. Tzannatos. — London : Centre for Labour Economics, London School of Economics, 1986. — 28p. — (Discussion paper / London School of Economics and Political Science. Centre for Labour Economics ; no.244). — *Bibliography: p26-28*

VAN DYKE, Ruth Marie
Secondary school careers advice, examination choices and adult aspirations : the maintenance of gender stratification / Ruth Marie Van Dyke. — 472 leaves. — *PhD (Econ) 1986 LSE. — Leaves 373-447 are appendices*

SEX DISCRIMINATION IN EMPLOYMENT — Great Britain — History

WALBY, Sylvia
Patriarchy at work : patriarchal and capitalist relations in employment / Sylvia Walby. — Cambridge : Polity, 1986. — vii,292p. — (Feminist perspectives from Polity Press). — *Bibliography: p260-281. — Includes index*

SEX DISCRIMINATION IN EMPLOYMENT — Palestine

BERNSTEIN, Deborah
The struggle for equality : urban women workers in pre-state Israeli society / by Deborah Bernstein. — New York : Praeger, 1986. — p. cm. — *"Praeger special studies. Praeger scientific.". — Includes index. — Bibliography: p*

SEX DISCRIMINATION IN EMPLOYMENT — United States

Gender in the workplace / Clair Brown and Joseph A. Pechman, editors. — Washington, D.C. : Brookings Institution, c1987. — xiv, 316 p.. — *Includes bibliographical references and index*

HARRIMAN, Ann
Women/men/management / by Ann Harriman. — New York : Praeger Publishers, 1985. — p. cm. — *Includes index. — Bibliography: p*

MALLIER, A. T.
Women and the economy : a comparative study of Britain and the USA / A.T. Mallier and M.J. Rosser. — Basingstoke : Macmill, 1987. — xiii,221p. — *Bibliography: p200-211. — Includes index*

Women's work, men's work : sex segregation on the job / Barbara F. Reskin and Heidi I. Hartmann, editors ; Committee on Women's Employment and Related Social Issues, Commission on Behavioral and Social Sciences and Education, National Research Council. — Washington, D.C. : National Academy Press, 1986. — xii, 173 p.. — *Includes index. — Bibliography: p. 141-161*

SEX DISCRIMINATION IN EMPOYMENT — United States — History

Working women : past, present, future / edited by Karen Shallcross Koziara, Michael H. Moskow, Lucretia Dewey Tanner. — Washington, D.C. : Bureau of National Affairs, 1987. — p. cm. — (Industrial Relations Research Association series). — *Includes index*

SEX IN TELEVISION

GUNTER, Barrie
Television and sex role stereotyping / Barrie Gunter. — London : Libbey, c1986. — 89p. — (Television research monograph). — *Bibliography: p83-89*

SEX INSTRUCTION FOR CHILDREN — Great Britain

ALLEN, Isobel
Education in sex and personal relationships / Isobel Allen. — London : Policy Studies Institute, 1987. — 238p

SEX OF CHILDREN, PARENTAL PREFERENCES FOR

WARREN, Mary Anne
Gendercide : the implications of sex selection / Mary Anne Warren. — Totowa, N.J. : Rowman & Allanheld, 1985. — viii, 209 p.. — (New feminist perspectives). — *Includes bibliographies and index*

SEX OFFENSES

FINKELHOR, David
A sourcebook on child sexual abuse / David Finkelhor and associates. — Beverly Hills : Sage Publications, c1986. — p. cm. — *Includes index. — Bibliography: p*

SEX ORIENTED BUSINESSES — Law and legislation — England

MANCHESTER, Colin
Sex shops and the law / Colin Manchester. — Aldershot : Gower, c1986. — xx,264p. — *Includes index*

SEX PRESELECTION

WARREN, Mary Anne
Gendercide : the implications of sex selection / Mary Anne Warren. — Totowa, N.J. : Rowman & Allanheld, 1985. — viii, 209 p.. — (New feminist perspectives). — *Includes bibliographies and index*

SEX (PSYCHOLOGY)

RANCOUR-LAFERRIERE, Daniel
Signs of the flesh : an essay on the evolution of hominid sexuality / Daniel Rancour-Laferriere. — Berlin ; New York : Mouton, c1985. — x, 473 p.. — (Approaches to semiotics ; 71). — *Includes index. — Bibliography: p. [389]-452*

SEX ROLE

ARCHER, John, 1944-
Sex and gender / John Archer, Barbara Lloyd. — Cambridge : Cambridge University Press, 1985. — ix, 355p. — *"First published in 1982 by Penguin" - t.p. verso. — Bibliography: p.300-330*

ASSOCIATION OF SOCIAL ANTHROPOLOGISTS OF THE COMMONWEALTH. Conference (1977 : Swansea)
Sex and age as principles of social differentiation / edited by J.S. La Fontaine. — London : Academic Press, 1978. — vii,188p. — (Monographs / Association of Social Anthropologists of the Commonwealth ; 17). — *'The papers presented here represent six out of eight papers delivered at the Conference of the Association of Social Anthropologists at Swansea in April 1977' - Preface. — Includes bibliographies and index*

CONNELL, R. W.
Gender and power : society, the person and sexual politics / R.W. Connell. — Cambridge : Polity in association with Blackwell, 1987. — [290]p. — *Includes bibliography and index*

MACKIE, Marlene
Constructing women and men : gender socialization / Marlene Mackie. — Toronto : Holt, Rinehart and Winston of Canada, 1987. — v,314p. — *Bibliography: p[276]-308*

RANCOUR-LAFERRIERE, Daniel
Signs of the flesh : an essay on the evolution of hominid sexuality / Daniel Rancour-Laferriere. — Berlin ; New York : Mouton, c1985. — x, 473 p.. — (Approaches to semiotics ; 71). — *Includes index. — Bibliography: p. [389]-452*

ROWAN, John
The horned god : feminism and men as wounding and healing / John Rowan. — London : Routledge & Kegan Paul, 1987. — xi,155p. — *Bibliography: Includes p143-150. — index*

TRASK, Haunani-Kay
Eros and power : the promise of feminist theory / Haunani-Kay Trask. — Philadelphia : University of Pennsylvania Press, c1986. — xiv, 186 p.. — *Includes bibliographies and index*

SEX ROLE — Addresses, essays, lectures

HALL, Roberta L
Male-female differences : a bio-cultural perspective / Roberta L. Hall, with Patricia Draper ... [et al.]. — New York ; Eastbourne : Praeger, 1985. — vii, 309p. — *Includes index*

Men in families / edited by Robert A. Lewis and Robert E. Salt. — Beverly Hills : Sage Publications, c1985. — p. cm. — (Sage focus editions ; v. 76). — *Includes bibliographical references*

Sexuality, new perspectives / edited by Zira DeFries, Richard C. Friedman, and Ruth Corn. — Westport, Conn. : Greenwood Press, 1985. — xii, 362 p.. — (Contributions in psychology ; no. 6). — *Includes bibliographies and index*

SEX ROLE — Case studies

KAHN, Miriam
Always hungry, never greedy : food and the expression of gender in a Melanesian society / Miriam Kahn. — Cambridge : Cambridge University Press, 1986. — xx,187p. — *Bibliography: p174-181. — Includes index*

SEX ROLE — Brazil
GREGOR, Thomas
Anxious pleasures : the sexual lives of an Amazonian people / Thomas Gregor. — Chicago : University of Chicago Press, 1985. — xii, 223 p.. — *Includes index. Bibliography: p. [211]-216*

SEX ROLE — Denmark
DENMARK. Kommissionen vedrørende kvindernes stilling i samfundet
Bilag til betaenkning og ligestilling : afgivet af et udvalg under kommissionen vedrørende kvindernes stilling i samfundet. — København : the Kommissionen, 1968. — 88p. — *Includes bibliographies.* — Contents: Psykologiske kønsforskelle/Carl Weltzer - Sociologiske kønsforskelle/Benedicte Madsen

SEX ROLE — Developing countries — Case studies
Gender roles in development projects : a case book / editors, Catherine Overholt ... [et al.]. — West Hartford, Conn. : Kumarian Press, 1985. — p. cm. — *Bibliography: p*

SEX ROLE — Great Britain — Case studies
HILL, Malcolm
Sharing child care in early parenthood / Malcolm Hill. — London : Routledge & Kegan Paul, 1987. — [360]p. — *Includes bibliography and index*

SEX ROLE — Greece
Gender & power in rural Greece / edited by Jill Dubisch. — Princeton, N.J. : Princeton University Press, c1986. — p. cm. — *Includes index.* — *Bibliography: p*

SEX ROLE — Papua New Guinea
GELBER, Marilyn G
Gender and society in the New Guinea Highlands : an anthropological perspective on antagonism toward women / Marilyn G. Gelber. — Boulder : Westview Press, 1986. — xi, 180 p.. — (Women in cross-cultural perspective). — *Includes index.* — *Bibliography: p. [159]-175*

SEX ROLE — United States
BERTELSON, David
Snowflakes and snowdrifts : individualism and sexuality in America / David Bertelson. — Lanham, MD : University Press of America, c1986. — ix, 282 p.. — *Includes index.* — *Bibliography: p. 255-275*

MCBROOM, Patricia
The third sex : the new professional woman / Patricia A. McBroom. — New York : W. Morrow, [1986]. — p. cm. — *Includes index*

PLECK, Joseph H
Working wives, working husbands / Joseph H. Pleck. — Beverly Hills, Calif. : Published in cooperation with the National Council on Family Relations [by] Sage Publications, c1985. — 167 p.. — (New perspectives on family). — *Bibliography: p. 160-167*

SEX ROLE IN CHILDREN — Longitudinal studies
GREEN, Richard
The "sissy boy syndrome" and the development of homosexuality / Richard Green. — New Haven : Yale University Press, c1987. — x, 416 p.. — *Includes index.* — *Bibliography: p. 399-409*

SEX ROLE IN THE WORK ENVIRONMENT
Gender in the workplace / Clair Brown and Joseph A. Pechman, editors. — Washington, D.C. : Brookings Institution, c1987. — xiv, 316 p.. — *Includes bibliographical references and index*

HEARN, Jeff
'Sex' at 'work' : the power and paradox of organisation and sexuality / Jeff Hearn and Wendy Parkin. — Brighton : Wheatsheaf, 1987. — [224]p. — *Includes bibliography and index*

SEX ROLE IN THE WORK ENVIRONMENT — United States
Gender in the workplace / Clair Brown and Joseph A. Pechman, editors. — Washington, D.C. : Brookings Institution, c1987. — xiv, 316 p.. — *Includes bibliographical references and index*

SEX ROLES
SYDIE, R. A
Natural women, cultured men : a feminist perspective on sociological theory / R.A. Sydie. — Milton Keynes : Open University Press, 1987. — x,268p. — *Bibliography: p247-258.* — *Includes index*

SEX ROLES — Public opinion
GUNTER, Barrie
Television and sex role stereotyping / Barrie Gunter. — London : Libbey, c1986. — 89p. — (Television research monograph). — *Bibliography: p83-89*

SEX ROLEWOMEN — Developing countries 976/3 — Developing countries — Social conditions
Geography of gender in the Third World / edited by Janet Henshall Momsen and Janet Townsend. — London : Hutchinson Education, 1987. — [304]p. — *Written by the Women & Geography Study Group of the Institute of British Geographers.* — *Includes bibliography and index*

SEXISM
BENOKRAITIS, Nijole V.
Modern sexism : blatant, subtle and covert discrimination / Nijole V. Benokraitis, Joe R. Feagin. — Englewood Cliffs, N.J. ; London : Prentice-Hall, c1986. — xiii,187p. — *Includes index*

HARDING, Sandra G
The science question in feminism / Sandra Harding. — Ithaca : Cornell University Press, 1986. — p. cm. — *Includes index.* — *Bibliography: p*

Human rights for humankind : sexism. — Canberra : Australian Government Publishing Service, 1984. — 29p

SEXISM — Australia
Human rights for humankind : sexism. — Canberra : Australian Government Publishing Service, 1984. — 29p

SEXISM — Mexico
O'MALLEY, Ilene V
The myth of the revolution : hero cults and the institutionalization of the Mexican State, 1920-1940 / Ilene V. O'Malley. — New York : Greenwood Press, 1986. — xii, 199 p.. — (Contributions to the study of world history ; no. 1). — *Includes index.* — *Bibliography: p.[179]-194*

SEXISM — U.S
HARRIMAN, Ann
Women/men/management / by Ann Harriman. — New York : Praeger Publishers, 1985. — p. cm. — *Includes index.* — *Bibliography: p*

SEXISM IN LANGUAGE
BARON, Dennis E
Grammar and gender / Dennis Baron. — New Haven : Yale University Press, c1986. — p. cm . — *Includes index.* — *Bibliography: p*

SEXISM IN TEXTBOOKS
MICHEL, Andrée
Down with stereotypes! : eliminating sexism from children's literature and school textbooks / Andrée Michel. — Paris : Unesco, 1986. — 105p. — *Bibliography: p103-105*

Racialism and sexism in books - a checklist. — London : Commission for Racial Equality, 1977. — [1]p. — *First published in Interracial books for children, vol.5, no.3 (1974), and now reprinted from Education & community relations, September/October 1975*

SEXUAL BEHAVIOR IN ANIMALS
DALY, Martin
Sex, evolution, and behavior / Martin Daly and Margo Wilson. — 2nd ed. — Boston : Willard Grant Press, c1983. — xiv, 402 p.. — *Includes index.* — *Bibliography: p. 345-389*

SEXUAL BEHAVIOR SURVEYS — Caribbean Area
HAREWOOD, Jack
Mating and fertility : results from three WFS surveys in Guyana, Jamaica and Trinidad and Tobago / Jack Harewood. — Voorburg : International Statistical Institute, 1984. — 65p. — (Scientific reports / World Fertility Survey ; no.67)

SEXUAL CUSTOMS — Caribbean Area
HAREWOOD, Jack
Mating and fertility : results from three WFS surveys in Guyana, Jamaica and Trinidad and Tobago / Jack Harewood. — Voorburg : International Statistical Institute, 1984. — 65p. — (Scientific reports / World Fertility Survey ; no.67)

SEXUAL DEVIATION
Variant sexuality : research and theory / edited by Glenn D. Wilson. — London : Croom Helm, c1987. — 268p. — *Includes bibliographies and index*

SEXUAL DISORDERS — Addresses, essays, lectures
Sexuality, new perspectives / edited by Zira DeFries, Richard C. Friedman, and Ruth Corn. — Westport, Conn. : Greenwood Press, 1985. — xii, 362 p.. — (Contributions in psychology ; no. 6). — *Includes bibliographies and index*

SEXUAL DIVISION OF LABOR
Gender and the labour process / edited by David Knights, Hugh Willmott. — Aldershot : Gower, c1986. — vii,186p. — *Includes bibliographies and index*

TESTART, Alain
Essai sur les fondements de la division sexuelle du travail chez les chasseurs-cueilleurs / Alain Testart. — Paris : École des Hautes Études en Sciences Sociales, 1986. — 102p. — (Cahiers de l'homme : ethnologie, géographie, linguistique. nouvelle série ; 25). — *Bibliography: p91-99*

SEXUAL DIVISION OF LABOR — Developing countries
Geography of gender in the Third World / edited by Janet Henshall Momsen and Janet Townsend. — London : Hutchinson Education, 1987. — [304]p. — *Written by the Women & Geography Study Group of the Institute of British Geographers.* — *Includes bibliography and index*

SEXUAL DIVISION OF LABOR — England
BREAKWELL, Glynis M.
Young women in 'gender-atypical' jobs : the case of trainee technicians in the engineering industry / Glynis M. Breakwell, Barbara Weinberger. — [London] : Department of Employment, [1987]. — 39p. — (Research paper / Department of Employment ; no.49). — *Bibliographical references: p22*

SEXUAL DIVISION OF LABOR — France — Auffay — History
GULLICKSON, Gay L.
Spinners and weavers of Auffay : rural industry and the sexual division of labor in a French village, 1750-1850 / Gay L. Gullickson. — Cambridge : Cambridge University Press, 1986. — [xi,400]p. — *Bibliography: p395-400*

SEXUAL DIVISION OF LABOR — Great Britain — History
COHN, Samuel
The process of occupational sex-typing : the feminization of clerical labor in Great Britain / Samuel Cohn. — Philadelphia : Temple University Press, 1985. — p. cm. — (Women in the political economy). — *Includes index.* — *Bibliography: p*

SEXUAL DIVISION OF LABOR — United States
PLECK, Joseph H
Working wives, working husbands / Joseph H. Pleck. — Beverly Hills, Calif. : Published in cooperation with the National Council on Family Relations [by] Sage Publications, c1985. — 167 p.. — (New perspectives on family). — *Bibliography: p. 160-167*

SEXUAL ETHICS — Addresses, essays, lectures
Sexuality, new perspectives / edited by Zira DeFries, Richard C. Friedman, and Ruth Corn. — Westport, Conn. : Greenwood Press, 1985. — xii, 362 p.. — (Contributions in psychology ; no. 6). — *Includes bibliographies and index*

SEXUAL ETHICS — Canada
KINSMAN, Gary
The regulation of desire : sexuality in Canada / Gary Kinsman. — Montréal ; New York : Black Rose Books, 1987. — 233p. — *Includes references*

SEXUAL ETHICS — Europe — History
MOSSE, George L
Nationalism and sexuality : respectability and abnormal sexuality in modern Europe / George L. Mosse. — 1st ed. — New York : H. Fertig, 1985. — viii, 232 p., [10] p. of plates. — *Includes index.* — *Bibliography: p. 195-223*

SEXUAL INTERCOURSE
DWORKIN, Andrea
Intercourse / Andrea Dworkin. — London : Secker & Warburg, 1987. — [288]p. — *Includes bibliography and index*

SEXUALLY ABUSED CHILDREN
FINKELHOR, David
Child sexual abuse : new theory and research / David Finkelhor. — New York : Free Press, c1984. — xii, 260 p.. — *Includes index.* — *Bibliography: p. 240-255*

FINKELHOR, David
A sourcebook on child sexual abuse / David Finkelhor and associates. — Beverly Hills : Sage Publications, c1986. — p. cm. — *Includes index.* — *Bibliography: p*

SEXUALLY ABUSED CHILDREN — Case studies
MASSON, J. Moussaieff
The assault on truth : Freud's suppression of the seduction theory / Jeffrey Moussaieff Masson. — New York, N.Y. : Penguin Books, 1985, c1984. — p. cm. — : Reprint. Originally published: New York : Farrar, Straus, and Giroux, 1984. — *Includes index.* — *Bibliography: p*

SEXUALLY TRANSMITTED DISEASES — Study and teaching — Great Britain
GREAT BRITAIN. Department of Health and Social Security
AIDS : monitoring response to the public education campaign February 1986-February 1987 : report on four surveys during the first year of advertising. — London : H.M.S.O., 1987. — 141p. — *Research programme designed and executed by British Market Research Bureau Ltd.. — Four microfiches in end pocket*

SEYCHELLES — Appropriations and expenditures — Statistics
Sources and methods of estimating national accounts for Seychelles at current and constant prices. — Victoria : Statistics Division, 1984. — xii,305p. — *Bibliography: p305*

SEYCHELLES — Economic policy
Seychelles structure plan 1975. — [Victoria : Government Printer, ca. 1975]. — 14p. — 3maps

SEYCHELLES — Population
PEDERSEN, Jon
The social construction of fertility : population processes on a plantation in the Seychelles / Jon Pedersen. — Oslo : Department of Social Anthropology, Oslo University, 1985. — 230p. — (Oslo occasional papers in social anthropology ; no.10). — *Thesis submitted for the "Magistergrad" at the Institute of Social Anthropology, University of Oslo, April 1982.* — *Bibliography: p218-230*

SEYCHELLES — Population — Statistics
Population growth in the Sychelles. — 2nd ed.. — Mahe : Department of Finance, 1985. — 14p

SEYCHELLES — Social conditions (— 1976)
PEDERSEN, Jon
The social construction of fertility : population processes on a plantation in the Seychelles / Jon Pedersen. — Oslo : Department of Social Anthropology, Oslo University, 1985. — 230p. — (Oslo occasional papers in social anthropology ; no.10). — *Thesis submitted for the "Magistergrad" at the Institute of Social Anthropology, University of Oslo, April 1982.* — *Bibliography: p218-230*

SEYCHELLES — Social policy
Seychelles structure plan 1975. — [Victoria : Government Printer, ca. 1975]. — 14p. — 3maps

SEYN, F. A.
LUNTINEN, Pertti
F.A. Seyn : a political biography of a Tsarist imperialist as administrator of Finland / Pertti Luntinen. — Helsinki : SHS, 1985. — 343p. — (Studia historica ; 19)

SH·I·AH — History — 20th century
Shi'ism, resistance and revolution / edited by Martin Kramer. — London : Mansell, 1987. — [352]p. — *Conference proceedings.* — *Includes index*

SH·I·AH — Near East — History
Shi'ism, resistance and revolution / edited by Martin Kramer. — London : Mansell, 1987. — [352]p. — *Conference proceedings.* — *Includes index*

SHAKERS — United States
BREWER, Priscilla J
Shaker communities, Shaker lives / Priscilla J. Brewer. — Hanover : University Press of New England, 1986. — xviii, 273 p.. — *Includes index.* — *Bibliography: p. 259-268*

SHAKESPEARE, WILLIAM. Hamlet
KNIGHTS, L. C.
An approach to 'Hamlet' / L. C. Knights. — London : Chatto & Windus, 1960. — 91 p

SHAMANISM — Korea (South)
KENDALL, Laurel
Shamans, housewives, and other restless spirits : women in Korean ritual life / Laurel Kendall. — Honolulu : University of Hawaii Press, c1985. — xiii, 234 p.. — (Studies of the East Asian Institute). — *Includes index.* — *Bibliography: p. [213]-222*

SHAMANS — Korea (South)
KENDALL, Laurel
Shamans, housewives, and other restless spirits : women in Korean ritual life / Laurel Kendall. — Honolulu : University of Hawaii Press, c1985. — xiii, 234 p.. — (Studies of the East Asian Institute). — *Includes index.* — *Bibliography: p. [213]-222*

SHAME — Social aspects — Melanesia
EPSTEIN, A. L.
The experience of shame in Melanesia : an essay on the anthropology of affect / by A.L. Epstein. — London : Royal Anthropological Institute, 1984. — iv,58p. — (Occasional paper / Royal Anthropological Institute of Great Britain and Ireland ; no.40)

SHANGHAI (CHINA) — Economic conditions
HONIG, Emily
Sisters and strangers : women in the Shanghai cotton mills, 1919-1949 = [Shang-hai sha ch'ang nü kung] / Emily Honig. — Stanford, Calif. : Stanford University Press, 1986. — ix, 299 p.. — *Parallel title in Chinese characters.* — *Includes index.* — *Bibliography: p. [279]-289*

SHARED HOUSING — Great Britain
THOMAS, Andrew, 1950-
The 1985 physical and social survey of houses in multiple occupation in England and Wales / Andrew D. Thomas with Alan Hedges. — London : H.M.S.O., 1986. — vi,163p. — *Carried out for the Dept. of the Environment*

SHATT AL'-ARAB RIVER (IRAQ AND IRAN)
SCHOFIELD, Richard N.
Evolution of the Shatt al-'Arab boundary dispute / by Richard N. Schofield. — Wisbech : Middle East and North African Studies Press, 1986. — viii,111p. — *Bibliography: p87-94*

SHAW, BERNARD
SHAW, Bernard
Bernard Shaw : the diaries, 1885-1897 with early autobiographical notebooks and diaries, and an abortive 1917 diary / edited & annotated by Stanley Weintraub ; transliterated by Stanley Rypins, with additional transliterations & transcriptions by Blanche Patch ... [et al.]. — University Park, Pa. : Pennsylvania State University Press, 1986. — p. cm. — *Includes index*

SHAYKH AL-ISLÁM — Turkey
REPP, R. C.
The Müfti of Istanbul : a study in the development of the Ottoman learned hierarchy / by R.C. Repp. — London : Published by Ithaca Press for the Board of the Faculty of Oriental Studies, Oxford University, c1986. — xxi,325p. — (Oxford Oriental Institute monographs ; no.8). — *Includes index*

SHEEP BREEDING — Australia — History
GARRAN, J. C.
Merinos, myths and Macarthurs : Australian graziers and their sheep, 1788-1900 / J. C. Garran and L. White. — Rushcutters Bay, N.S.W. : Australian National University Press, 1985. — xv,288p. — *Bibliography: p[261]-270*

SHEFFIELD (SOUTH YORKSHIRE) — Economic conditions
HOMES AND JOBS CONFERENCE (1986 : Sheffield)
Building for our future needs : homes and jobs. — Sheffield : Sheffield City Council, 1986. — 64p. — *Includes information pack in seven sections*

SHEFFIELD. Department of Employment and Economic Development
Sheffield : working it out : an outline employment plan for Sheffield. — Sheffield : [the Department] and Central Policy Unit, 1987. — 28p

SHEFFIELD (SOUTH YORKSHIRE) — Economic policy
SHEFFIELD. City Council
Sheffield : putting you in the picture : Sheffield City Council 1980-1986. — Sheffield : Central Policy Unit, Sheffield City Council, 1986. — 43p

SHEFFIELD (SOUTH YORKSHIRE) — Social conditions
BEATTIE, Geoffrey
Survivors of steel city : a portrait of Sheffield / Geoffrey Beattie. — London : Chatto & Windus, 1986. — 204p. — *Bibliography: p203-204*

SHEFFIELD (SOUTH YORKSHIRE) — Social policy

BARNES, Marian
Social work in general practice : the situation in Sheffield / Marian Barnes. — Sheffield : Research and Information Section, City of Sheffield Family and Community Services Department. — *Bibliography: p32* report no.12. — 1982. — 31p

SHEFFIELD. City Council
Sheffield : putting you in the picture : Sheffield City Council 1980-1986. — Sheffield : Central Policy Unit, Sheffield City Council, 1986. — 43p

SHELTER

SHELTER campaign news. — London : SHELTER, 1987-. — *Quarterly*

SHENZHEN (CHINA) — Economic policy

Modernization in China : the case of the Shenzhen special economic zone / editors Kwan-yiu Wong, David K.Y. Chu. — Oxford : Oxford University Press, 1986. — xi,229p. — *Bibliography: p[218]-224*

SHERPAS — Social life and customs

FÜRER-HAIMENDORF, Christoph von
The Sherpas transformed : social change in a Buddhist society of Nepal / Christoph von Fürer-Haimendorf. — New Delhi : Sterling, 1984. — xiii,197p. — *Bibliography: [189]-192*

SHETLAND ISLANDS — Historical geography

KNOX, Susan A.
The making of the Shetland landscape / Susan A. Knox. — Edinburgh : John Donald, c1985. — x, 255p. — *Bibliography: p.242-251*

SHIFT SYSTEMS

LABOUR RESEARCH DEPARTMENT
Shift work and unsocial hours : a negotiators' guide. — London : Labour Research Department, 1987. — 48p

SHIFT SYSTEMS — Bibliography

Annotated bibliography on working time. — Geneva : International Labour Office, 1986. — v,100p

SHIFT SYSTEMS — Effect of technological innovations on

GHOBADIAN, Abby
The effects of new technological change on shift work in the brewing industry / Abby Ghobadian. — Aldershot : Gower, c1986. — xiv,192p. — *Includes bibliography*

SHIFTING CULTIVATION — Philippines — Mindoro

LOPEZ-GONZAGA, Violeta
Peasants in the hills : a study of the dynamics of social change among the Buhid swidden cultivators in the Philippines / Violeta Lopez-Gonzaga. — Quezon City, Philippines : University of the Philippines Press, 1983. — xiv,226p. — *Bibliography: p[211]-219*

SHIMAMURA, HŌGETSU

NOLTE, Sharon H
Liberalism in modern Japan : Ishibashi Tanzan and his teachers, 1905-1960 / Sharon H. Nolte. — Berkeley : University of California Press, c1987. — xii, 378 p.. — *Includes index. — Bibliography: p. 343-370*

SHIPBUILDING — Employees

STRÅTH, Bo
Varvsarbetare i två varvsstäder : en historisk studie av verkstadsklubbarna vid varven i Göteborg och Malmö / Bo Stråth. — Göteborg : Svenska Varv AB, [1982]. — ii,372p. — *English summary, p329-354. — Bibliography: p363-370*

SHIPBUILDING INDUSTRY — Safety regulations — Great Britain

GREAT BRITAIN. Factory Inspectorate.
Shipbuilding National Industry Group
Shipbuilding and ship-repairing : health and safety 1971-78. — London : H.M.S.O., 1980. — 28p

SHIPBUILDING INDUSTRY — Europe

STRÅTH, Bo
The politics of de-industrialisation : the contraction of the West European shipbuilding industry / Bo Stråth. — London : Croom Helm, c1987. — xi,295p. — *Bibliography: 271-288. — Includes index*

SHIPBUILDING INDUSTRY — Great Britain

GREAT BRITAIN. Parliament. House of Commons. Library. Research Division
Shipbuilding in crisis : Christopher Barclay. — [London] : the Division, 1983. — 12p. — (Background paper ; no.133)

GREAT BRITAIN. Parliament. House of Commons. Library. Research Division
The shipbuilding industry / Christopher Barclay, Samantha Bennett. — [London] : the Division, 1985. — 14p. — (Background paper ; no.173)

SHIPBUILDING INDUSTRY — Sweden

STRÅTH, Bo
Varvsarbetare i två varvsstäder : en historisk studie av verkstadsklubbarna vid varven i Göteborg och Malmö / Bo Stråth. — Göteborg : Svenska Varv AB, [1982]. — ii,372p. — *English summary, p329-354. — Bibliography: p363-370*

SHIPBUILDING INDUSTRY — United States

WHITEHURST, Clinton H.
The U.S. shipbuilding industry : past, present, and future / by Clinton H. Whitehurst, Jr. — Annapolis, MD : Naval Institute Press, c1986. — xvi, 282 p.. — *Includes index. — Bibliography: p. 270-278*

SHIPHAM (SOMERSET) — Social conditions

GREAT BRITAIN. Shipham Survey Committee
Interim report on metal contamination at Shipham : a report for Sedgemoor District Council prepared by the Department of the Environment and the Ministry of Agriculture, Fisheries and Food with the advice of the Department of Health and Social Security. — [London : Department of the Environment, 1979]. — [6]p. — *Alternative title: Soil contamination at Shipham: interim report on survey*

SHIPMENT OF GOODS — Australia — Costs

CONLON, R. M
Distance and duties : determinants of manufacturing in Australia and Canada / by R.M. Conlon. — Ottawa, Canada : Carleton University Press, c1985. — ix, 217 p.. — (Carleton library series ; 135). — *Bibliography: p. 210-217*

SHIPMENT OF GOODS — Canada — Costs

CONLON, R. M
Distance and duties : determinants of manufacturing in Australia and Canada / by R.M. Conlon. — Ottawa, Canada : Carleton University Press, c1985. — ix, 217 p.. — (Carleton library series ; 135). — *Bibliography: p. 210-217*

SHIPPING

JANSSON, Jan Owen
Liner shipping economics / J.O. Jansson and D. Shneerson. — London : Chapman and Hall, 1987. — x,299p. — *Bibliography: p289-292. — Includes index*

JAPAN MARITIME RESEARCH INSTITUTE
Medium to long term analysis of the shipping market (1986-2000). — Tokyo : Japan Maritime Research Institute, 1987. — 86p

SHIPPING — Argentina — Statistics

INSTITUTO NACIONAL DE ESTADÍSTICA Y CENSOS (Argentina)
Navegación comercial argentina, 1976. — [Buenos Aires] : the Instituto, [ca.1977]. — 154p

SHIPPING — Asia, Southeastern

NAIDU, G
The thrust towards shipping co-operation / G. Naidu. — Kuala Lumpur : Institute of Strategic and International Studies, 1986. — 16p. — (ISIS ASEAN studies). — *Bibliography: p13*

SHIPPING — Cameroon — Statistics

Les cahiers statistiques du C.N.C.C. / Conseil National des Chargeurs du Cameroun. — [Douala] : Conseil National des Chargeurs du Cameroun, 1982-. — *Irregular*

SHIPPING — Canada — Statistics

Coastwise shipping statistics = Statistiques du cabotage / Statistics Canada. — Ottawa : Statistics Canada, 1983-. — *Annual. — Text in English and French*

SHIPPING — France

Enquête annuelle d'entreprise: auxiliaires des transports maritimes / Ministère de l'Urbanisme, du Logement et des Transports, Département des Statistiques des Transports. — Paris : Ministère de l'Urbanisme, du Logement et des Transports, 1982-. — *Annual*

SHIPPING — Pacific States

The Pacific Rim era and the shipping. — Tokyo : Japan Maritime Research Institute, 1987. — 68p. — (Jamri report ; no.19)

SHIPPING — Soviet Union

BERGSTRAND, Simon
The impact of Soviet shipping / Simon Bergstrand & Rigas Doganis. — London : Allen & Unwin, 1987. — xvi,184p. — *Bibliography: p177-179. — Includes index*

SHIPPING — Wales — Cardiff

JENKINS, David, 1957-
Jenkins Brothers of Cardiff : a Ceredigion family's shipping ventures / David Jenkins. — Cardiff : National Museum of Wales, 1985. — 112p. — *Includes references p109-112*

SHIPPING CONFERENCE — History

BERRIDGE, G. R.
The politics of the South Africa run : European Shipping and Pretoria / G.R. Berridge. — Oxford : Clarendon, 1987. — [298]p. — *Includes bibliography and index*

SHIPPING CONFERENCES — Law and legislation

Carriage of goods by sea / edited by Peter Koh Soon Kwang. — Singapore : Butterworths, 1986. — xviii,198p

JUDA, Lawrence
The UNCTAD Liner Code : United States maritime policy at the crossroads / Lawrence Juda. — Boulder, Colo. : Westview Press, 1983. — xiv, 234 p.. — (A Westview replica edition). — *"Appendix 1: The Convention on a Code of Conduct for Liner Conferences, and the Resolutions adopted by the United Nations Conference of Plenipotentiaries": p. 169-207. — Includes index. — Bibliography: p. 215-229*

STURMEY, S. G.
Workbook on the application of the Unctad Code / by S.G. Sturmey. — 2nd ed. — London : Seatrade Academy, 1985. — ix,159p, [40]p. — *Includes index*

SHIPPING CONFERENCES — Law and legislation — United States

JUDA, Lawrence
The UNCTAD Liner Code : United States maritime policy at the crossroads / Lawrence Juda. — Boulder, Colo. : Westview Press, 1983. — xiv, 234 p.. — (A Westview replica edition). — *"Appendix 1: The Convention on a Code of Conduct for Liner Conferences, and the Resolutions adopted by the United Nations Conference of Plenipotentiaries": p. 169-207. — Includes index. — Bibliography: p. 215-229*

SHIPS — Cargo

Prospects of demand for containerships in the second half of the 1980s. — Tokyo : Japan Maritime Research Institute, 1986. — 58p. — (Jamri report ; no.18)

SHIPS — Maintenance and repair — Safety regulations — Great Britain
GREAT BRITAIN. Factory Inspectorate. Shipbuilding National Industry Group
Shipbuilding and ship-repairing : health and safety 1971-78. — London : H.M.S.O., 1980. — 28p

SHIPS — Safety regulations
[International Convention for the Safety of Life at Sea (1974). Protocols, amendments, etc.].
Consolidated text of the 1974 SOLAS Convention, the 1978 SOLAS Protocol, the 1981 and 1983 SOLAS amendments. — London : International Maritime Organization, 1986. — vii,439p

SHIPS — Safety regulations — Congresses
INTERNATIONAL CONFERENCE ON SHIP SAFETY AND MARINE SURVEYING (1986 : Malmo, Sweden)
International Conference on Ship Safety and Marine Surveying : [proceedings] / [organized by] the Nautical Institute and the World Maritime University, Malmo, Sweden, 8-9 May 1986. — London : Nautical Institute, 1986. — 158p

SHIPS — Great Britain — Nationality — Statistics
Nationality of vessels in United Kingdom seaborne trade. — London : HMSO, 1973-. — (Business monitor. MA ; 8) (Business monitor. M ; 8). — Annual

SHIPS — Greece — Scrapping
APOSTOLOPOULOS, Yannis N.
Maritime industrial area : a new investment concept for shipping and industry / Yannis N. Apostolopoulos. — Athens : Development Division, Hellenic Industrial Development Bank, 1984. — 135p. — *Bibliography: p133-135*

SHIPYARDS — British Columbia — History
TAYLOR, G. W.
Shipyards of British Columbia : the principal companies / G. W. Taylor. — Victoria, B.C. : Morriss Publishing, 1986. — 216p. — *Bibliography: p210-212*

SHIPYARDS — Northern Ireland — Belfast — History
MOSS, Michael S.
Shipbuilders to the world : 125 years of Harland and Wolff, Belfast, 1861-1986 / Michael Moss and John R. Hume. — Belfast : Blackstaff, 1986. — xvii,601p,[10]p of plates. — *Bibliography: p502-505. — Includes index*

SHOPLIFTING — England
MURPHY, Daniel J. I.
Customers and thieves : an ethnography of shoplifting / Daniel J.I. Murphy. — Aldershot : Gower, 1986. — xi,266. — *Bibliography: p246-256. — Includes index*

SHOPPING — England — Devon
DEVON. County Council
County structure plan : second alteration : explanatory memorandum. — Exeter : [the Council], 1986. — 80p. — *Cover title: Devon county structure plan: second alteration: shopping: draft explanatory memorandum*

DEVON. County Council
Devon county structure plan : second alteration : draft written statement. — Exeter : [County Council], 1986. — 12p. — *Cover title: Devon county structure plan: second alteration: shopping: draft written statement*

SHOPPING — England — East Sussex
EAST SUSSEX (County). Planning Department
County structure plan, 1976 review : County Council approved / East Sussex [County Planning Department]. — Lewes (Southover House, Southover Rd, Lewes, E. Sussex BN7 1YA) : The Department, 1976. — [3],10p

SHOPPING — England — Exeter (Devon)
DEVON. County Council
Devon structure plan : second alteration : supplementary paper explaining the county council's consideration of alternative ways of meeting shopping needs in Exeter. — Exeter : [the Council], 1986. — 4p

SHOPPING — Great Britain
FAMILY POLICY STUDIES CENTRE
The Shops Bill: the family dimension. — London : Family Policy Studies Centre, 1986. — 16p

SHOPPING CENTERS — England — Chelmsford (Essex)
CHELMSFORD (District). Council
Rural areas study, subject report, shopping and services / Chelmsford District Council. — Chelmsford (Planning Department, Burgess Well Rd, Coval La., Chelmsford, [Essex]) : [The Council], 1976. — [2] leaves,7[i.e.9]p

SHOPPING CENTERS — Singapore
SIM, Loo Lee
A study of planned shopping centres in Singapore / Sim Loo Lee. — Singapore : Published by Singapore University Press for the Centre for Advanced Studies, c1984. — xiv, 124 p., [5] p. of plates. — *: Originally presented as the author's thesis (Ph.D.--National University of Singapore). — Includes index. — Bibliography: p. 115-121*

SHOPS BILL 1980-81
GREAT BRITAIN. Parliament. House of Commons. Library. Research Division
Shops Bill, Bill 26 (Revised) 80-81 / [Joanna Roll]. — [London] : the Division, [1981]. — 13p. — (Reference sheet ; no.81/7)

SHOPS BILL 1985-86
GREAT BRITAIN. Parliament. House of Commons. Library. Research Division
Shops Bill (Bill 94 of 1985-86) / Fiona Poole. — [London] : the Division, 1986. — 23p. — (Reference sheet ; no.86/7). — *Bibliographical references: p22-23*

SHORE PROTECTION — United States — Congresses
Cities on the beach : management issues of developed coastal barriers / edited by Rutherford H. Platt, Sheila G. Pelczarski, Barbara K.R. Burbank. — Chicago, Ill. : Department of Geography, University of Chicago, 1987. — p. cm. — (Research paper / University of Chicago. Dept. of Geography ; no. 224). — *Bibliography: p*

SHORT-TERM COUNSELING
MAPLE, Frank F
Dynamic interviewing : an introduction to counseling / by Frank F. Maple. — Beverly Hills ; London : Sage Publications, c1985. — 174p. — (Sage Human services guides ; 41). — *Bibliography: p 173-174*

SHORT-TERM MEMORY
BADDELEY, Alan D.
Working memory / Alan Baddeley. — Oxford : Clarendon, 1986. — xi,289p. — (Oxford psychology series ; no.11) (Oxford science publications). — *Bibliography: p260-278. — Includes index*

SHORTIS, VALENTINE FRANCIS CUTHBERT
FRIEDLAND, Martin L.
The case of Valentine Shortis : a true story of crime and politics in Canada / Martin L. Friedland. — Toronto : University of Toronto Press, 1986. — xi,324p

SHOTTON (CLWYD) — Industries — History
REDHEAD, Brian
The Summers of Shotton / Brian Redhead & Sheila Gooddie. — London : Hodder and Stoughton, 1987. — 160p. — *Map on lining papers. — Bibliography: p156. — Includes index*

SHROPSHIRE — Rural conditions
SHROPSHIRE. Planning Department. Policy and Information Group
Report of the 1984 rural facilities survey. — [Shrewsbury] : [the Department], 1985. — iii,34 leaves. — (Working paper / Shropshire Planning Department ; 85/7)

SHROPSHIRE. Planning Department. Policy and Information Group
Rural facilities survey : methodology report. — [Shrewsbury] : [the Group], 1986. — 51 leaves. — (Working paper / Shropshire. Planning Department ; 86/2)

SIBERIA (R.S.F.S.R.) — Economic conditions
Siberia : problems and prospects for regional development / edited by Alan Wood. — London : Croom Helm, c1987. — 233p. — *Includes index*

SIBERIA (R.S.F.S.R.) — Historiography
VOLCHENKO, A. V.
Ocherki istoriografii rabochego klassa Sibiri 1917-1937 gg. / A. V. Volchenko, A. S. Moskovskii ; otv. redaktor I. M. Savitskii. — Novosibirsk : Nauka, Sibirskoe otdelenie, 1986. — 159p

SIBERIA (R.S.F.S.R.) — History — 1904-1914
Revoliutsionnoe i obshchestvennoe dvizhenie v Sibiri v kontse XIX - nachale XX v. / otv. redaktor L. M. Goriushkin. — Novosibirsk : Nauka, Sibirskoe otdelenie, 1986. — 220p

SIBERIA (R.S.F.S.R.) — Rural conditions
Istoriia krest'ianstva Sibiri / Glavnaia redkollegiia: A. P. Dereviankо...[et al.]. — Novosibirsk : Nauka, Sibirskoe otdelenie [4]: Krest'ianstvo Sibiri v period uprocheniia i razvitiia sotsializma / [otv. redaktor V. T. Aniskov]. — 1985. — 395

SIBSAGAR DISTRICT (INDIA) — Rural conditions — Case studies
BORAH, K. C
Income, expenditure, and saving in rural India : a micro-level study / K.C. Borah. — Delhi, India : Mittal Publications : Distributed by Mittal Publishers' Distributors, 1985. — xviii, 221 p.. — *: Revision of the author's thesis (Ph.D.--Dibrugarh University, 1977). — Summary: Based on survey conducted in Sibsagar District, Assam. — Includes index. — Bibliography: p. [209]-217*

SICILY — History
FINLEY, M. I.
A history of Sicily / M.I. Finley, Denis Mack Smith and Christopher Duggan. — London : Chatto & Windus, 1986. — x,246p,[16]p of plates. — *Bibliography: p234-238. — Includes index*

SICK — Psychology
CALNAN, Michael
Health and illness : the lay perspective / Michael Calnan. — London : Tavistock, 1987. — [192]p. — *Includes index*

SICK LEAVE — Great Britain
TRADES UNION CONGRESS
TUC guide to employers' statutory sick pay. — London : Trades Union Congress, 1982. — 60p

SICKLE CELL ANEMIA — Great Britain
PRASHAR, Usha
Sickle cell anaemia : who cares? / Usha Prashar, Elizabeth Anionwu, Milica Brozovic. — London : Runnymede Trust, 1985. — 62p. — *Bibliography: p62*

SIDAMO (AFRICAN PEOPLE)
HAMER, John H.
Humane development : participation and change among the Sadáma of Ethiopia / John H. Hamer. — Tuscaloosa, Ala. : University of Alabama Press, c1987. — xi, 281 p.. — *Includes index. — Bibliography: p. 267-276*

SIEFF, MARCUS JOSEPH SIEFF, Baron
SIEFF, Marcus Joseph, Baron Sieff of Brimpton
Don't ask the price : memoirs of the president of Marks & Spencer / Marcus Sieff. — London : Weidenfeld and Nicolson, c1986. — 260p, 8p of plates

SIEMENS, CARL FRIEDRICH VON
GOETZELER, Herbert
Wilhelm und Carl Friedrich von Siemens : die zweite Unternehmergeneration / Herbert Goetzeler, Lothar Schoen. — Stuttgart : Franz Steiner Verlag Wiesbaden, 1986. — 131p. — *Includes bibliographies*

SIEMENS, WILHELM VON
GOETZELER, Herbert
Wilhelm und Carl Friedrich von Siemens : die zweite Unternehmergeneration / Herbert Goetzeler, Lothar Schoen. — Stuttgart : Franz Steiner Verlag Wiesbaden, 1986. — 131p. — *Includes bibliographies*

SIEMENS AG — History
GOETZELER, Herbert
Wilhelm und Carl Friedrich von Siemens : die zweite Unternehmergeneration / Herbert Goetzeler, Lothar Schoen. — Stuttgart : Franz Steiner Verlag Wiesbaden, 1986. — 131p. — *Includes bibliographies*

SIENKIEWICZ, HENRYK
PŁYGAWKO, Danuta
Sienkiewicz w Szwajcarii : z dziejów akcji ratunkowej dla Polski w czasie pierwszej wojny światowej / Danuta Płygawko. — Poznań : Uniwersytet im. Adama Mickiewicza, 1986. — 171p. — (Seria Historia / Uniwersytet im. Adama Mickiewicza w Poznaniu ; Nr.122). — *Summary in French and English.* — *Bibliography: p[154]-159*

SIERRA LEONE — Description and travel
MIGEOD, Frederick William Hugh
A view of Sierra Leone / by Frederick William Hugh Migeod. — New York : Negro Universities Press, 1970. — x,351p. — *Originally published in 1926 by Kegan Paul, Trench, Trubner & Co. Ltd., London*

SIERRA LEONE — History — Dictionaries
FORAY, Cyril P.
Historical dictionary of Sierra Leone / by Cyril P. Foray. — Metuchen, N.J. : Scarecrow Press, 1977. — lvii, 279 p.. — (African historical dictionaries ; no. 12). — *Bibliography: p. 237-279*

SIERRA LEONE — Rural conditions
JOHNNY, Michael
Informal credit for integrated rural development in Sierra Leone / Michael Johnny. — Hamburg : Weltarchiv, 1985. — xviii,212p. — (Studien zur integrierten ländlichen Entwicklung ; 6). — *Bibliography: p199-212*

SIERRA LEONE — Statistics, Vital — Estimates
TEKSE, K.
Some estimates of vital rates for Sierra Leone / K. Tekse]. Kenya National Tuberculosis Programme : evaluation of a test-run / [J. J. Rogowski...et al.]. Migration of health personnel of the African Region / [J. Vysohlid]. — Brazzaville : Regional Office for Africa, World Health Organization, 1975. — 124p. — (AFRO technical papers ; no.9). — *Includes bibliographical references*

SIGN LANGUAGE — Case studies
WASHABAUGH, William
Five fingers for survival / William Washabaugh. — Ann Arbor, Mich. : Karoma, 1986. — xiv,198p. — *Bibliography: p193-198*

SIKHS — Education — Great Britain
Sikh children in Britain. — London : Commission for Racial Equality, 1977. — [1]p. — *Summary of work with same title by Alan G. James.* — *Reprint from Education & community relations, October 1974*

SIKHS — British Columbia — Vancouver — Economic conditions
CHADNEY, James G
The Sikhs of Vancouver / by James G. Chadney. — New York : AMS Press, c1984. — p. cm. — (Immigrant communities & ethnic minorities in the United States & Canada ; 1). — *Includes index.* — *Bibliography: p*

SIKHS — British Columbia — Vancouver — Social conditions
CHADNEY, James G
The Sikhs of Vancouver / by James G. Chadney. — New York : AMS Press, c1984. — p. cm. — (Immigrant communities & ethnic minorities in the United States & Canada ; 1). — *Includes index.* — *Bibliography: p*

SIKHS — India — Punjab
NAYAR, Kuldip
Tragedy of Punjab : Operation Bluestar & after / Kuldip Nayar, Khushwant Singh. — New Delhi : Vision Books, 1984. — 192p

SIKKIM (INDIA) — Economic policy
Sikkim state development programme / Planning and Development Department, Sikkim. — Gangtok : Plannning and Development Department, 1980/81-. — Annual

SIKKIM (INDIA) — Politics and government
SENGUPTA, Nirmalananda
State government and politics, Sikkim / Nirmalananda Sengupta. — New Delhi : Sterling, c1985. — xii, 308 p.. — *Includes index.* — *Bibliography: p. [289]-301*

SIKKIM (INDIA) — Social policy
Sikkim state development programme / Planning and Development Department, Sikkim. — Gangtok : Plannning and Development Department, 1980/81-. — Annual

SILESIA — Relations — Poland
KOPEĆ, Eugeniusz
"My i oni" na polskim Śląsku (1918-1939) / Eugeniusz Kopeć. — Wyd. 2-e, popraw. i uzup. — Katowice : Wydawnictwo "Śląsk", 1986. — 238p

SILESIA — Social conditions
KOPEĆ, Eugeniusz
"My i oni" na polskim Śląsku (1918-1939) / Eugeniusz Kopeć. — Wyd. 2-e, popraw. i uzup. — Katowice : Wydawnictwo "Śląsk", 1986. — 238p

SILESIA, UPPER (POLAND AND CZECHOSLOVAKIA) — Foreign relations — Germany
OPITZ, Michael
Schlesien bleibt unser : Deutschlands Kampf um Oberschlesien 1919-1921 / Michael Opitz. — Kiel : Arndt, 1985. — 252p. — *Bibliography: p248-251*

SILESIA, UPPER (POLAND AND CZECHOSLOVAKIA) — History — Partition, 1919-1922
OPITZ, Michael
Schlesien bleibt unser : Deutschlands Kampf um Oberschlesien 1919-1921 / Michael Opitz. — Kiel : Arndt, 1985. — 252p. — *Bibliography: p248-251*

Wielkopolska a powstania śląskie 1919-1921 : praca zbiorowa / pod redakcją Krzysztofa Rzepy. — Poznań : Uniwersytet im. A. Mickiewicza, 1973. — 50p

SILICOSIS — West Virginia — Gauley Bridge
CHERNIACK, Martin
The Hawk's Nest incident : America's worst industrial disaster / Martin Cherniack ; foreword by Phillip Landrigan and Anthony Robbins. — New Haven : Yale University Press, c1986. — x, 194p, [16]p of plates. — *Includes index.* — *Bibliography: p.184-188*

SILK INDUSTRY — Connecticut — South Manchester — Employees — History — 19th century
MARGRAVE, Richard Dobson
The emigration of silk workers from England to the United States in the nineteenth century : with special reference to Coventry, Macclesfield, Paterson, New Jersey, and South Manchester, Connecticut / Richard Dobson Margrave. — New York : Garland, 1986. — 421 p.. — (Outstanding theses from the London School of Economics and Political Science). — *Thesis (Ph. D.)--London School of Economics and Political Science, 1981.* — *Bibliography: p. [384]-421*

SILK INDUSTRY — England — Employees — History — 19th century
MARGRAVE, Richard Dobson
The emigration of silk workers from England to the United States in the nineteenth century : with special reference to Coventry, Macclesfield, Paterson, New Jersey, and South Manchester, Connecticut / Richard Dobson Margrave. — New York : Garland, 1986. — 421 p.. — (Outstanding theses from the London School of Economics and Political Science). — *Thesis (Ph. D.)--London School of Economics and Political Science, 1981.* — *Bibliography: p. [384]-421*

SILK INDUSTRY — New Jersey — Paterson — Employees — History — 19th century
MARGRAVE, Richard Dobson
The emigration of silk workers from England to the United States in the nineteenth century : with special reference to Coventry, Macclesfield, Paterson, New Jersey, and South Manchester, Connecticut / Richard Dobson Margrave. — New York : Garland, 1986. — 421 p.. — (Outstanding theses from the London School of Economics and Political Science). — *Thesis (Ph. D.)--London School of Economics and Political Science, 1981.* — *Bibliography: p. [384]-421*

SILK MANUFACTURE AND TRADE — China
ENG, Robert Y.
Economic imperialism in China : silk production and exports, 1861-1932 / Robert Y. Eng. — Berkeley, (Calif.) : University of California. Institute of East Asian Studies, 1986. — (China research monograph ; 31). — *Bibliography: p205-243*

SILVER MINES AND MINING — Bolivia — Potosí (Dept.) — History
COLE, Jeffrey A
The Potosí mita, 1573-1700 : compulsory Indian labor in the Andes / Jeffrey A. Cole. — Stanford, Calif. : Stanford University Press, 1985. — xi, 206p. — *Includes index.* — *Bibliography: p.187-196*

SILVER MINES AND MINING — Wales — Cardiganshire — Statistics
BURT, Roger, 1942-
The mines of Cardiganshire : metalliferous and associated minerals 1845-1913 / Roger Burt, Peter Waite, Ray Burnley. — Exeter : Department of Economic History, University of Exeter, in association with the Northern Mine Research Society, [1985]. — xxviii, 92p

SIMON, SHENA
SIMON, Joan
Shena Simon : feminist and educationalist / Joan Simon. — [Manchester] : [J. Simon], 1986. — [250 leaves]. — *Bibliography: p[4]*

SIMPLEXES (MATHEMATICS)
CHUANG, Min Hwei
A sparse matrix implementation of the simplex method : its application to a class of combinatorial optimization problems / by Chuang Min Hwei. — 210 leaves. — PhD (Econ) 1986 LSE

SIN, ORIGINAL

MOULIN, Léo
La Gauche, la Droite et le péché originel et autres essais / Léo Moulin ; préface d'Alain Lancelot. — Paris : Libriarie des Méridiens, 1984. — 234p. — *Includes bibliographic notes*

SINCLAIR, Sir CLIVE, 1940-

ADAMSON, Ian
Sinclair and the sunrise technology : the deconstruction of a myth / Ian Adamson and Richard Kennedy. — Harmondsworth : Penguin, 1986. — 262p

SINGAPORE

People's Action Party, 1954-1984 : Petir, 30th anniversary issue. — [Singapore] : Central Executive Committee, People's Action Party, [1984]. — 216 p.. — *Chinese, English, Malay, and Tamil. — Cover title: Partai Tindakan Rakyat, 1954-1984*

SINGAPORE — Civilization

CLAMMER, John
Singapore : ideology, society, culture / by John Clammer. — Singapore : Chopmen Publishers, 1985. — 169p. — *Includes bibliographic notes*

SINGAPORE — Commerce

LIM, Linda
Trade, employment and industrialisation in Singapore / Linda Lim and Pang Eng Fong. — Geneva : International Labour Office, 1986. — xi,110p. — *Includes bibliographical references*

SINGAPORE — Economic conditions

LIM, Chong-Yah
Economic restructuring in Singapore / Lim Chong-Yah. — Singapore : Federal Publications, 1984. — v,117p. — *Bibliography: p109*

SINGAPORE. Economic Committee
The Singapore economy : new directions : report / of the Economic Committee. — Singapore : Ministry of Trade and Industry, 1986. — 234p

Singapore : resources and growth / edited by Lim Chong-Yah and Peter J. Lloyd. — Singapore ; Oxford : Oxford University Press, 1986. — xiii,279p. — *Bibliographies*

SINGAPORE — Economic conditions — Statistics

Economic and social statistics Singapore 1960-1982. — Singapore : Department of Statistics, 1983. — x,270p

SINGAPORE — Economic policy

The Political economy of the new Asian industrialism / edited by Frederic C. Deyo. — Ithaca, N.Y. : Cornell University Press, 1987. — 252 p.. — (Cornell studies in political economy). — *Includes bibliographies and index. — Contents: Export-oriented industrializing states in the capitalist world system / Richard E. Barrett and Soomi Chin -- The origins and development of the Northeast Asian political economy / Bruce Cumings -- State and foreign capital in the East Asian NICs / Stephan Haggard and Tun-jen Cheng -- Political institutions and economic performance / Chalmers Johnson -- The interplay of state, social class, and world system in East Asian development / Hagen Koo -- State and labor / Frederic C. Deyo -- Class, state, and dependence in East Asia / Peter Evans -- Coalitions, institutions, and linkage sequencing toward a strategic capacity model of East Asian development / Frederic C. Deyo*

SINGAPORE. Economic Committee
The Singapore economy : new directions : report / of the Economic Committee. — Singapore : Ministry of Trade and Industry, 1986. — 234p

SINGAPORE — Ethnic relations

CHEW, Sock Foon
Ethnicity and nationality in Singapore / by Chew Sock Foon. — Athens, Ohio : Ohio University Center for International Studies, Center for Southeast Asian Studies, 1987. — xv, 229 p.. — (Monographs in international studies. Southeast Asia series ; no. 78). — *Bibliography: p. 213-229*

SINGAPORE — History

SONG, Ong Siang
One hundred years' history of the Chinese in Singapore / Song Ong Siang ; introduction by Edwin Lee. — Singapore ; Oxford : Oxford University Press, 1984. — xxii,602p,[113]leaves of plates. — *Facsim of: 1st ed. London : John Murray, 1923. — Includes index*

SINGAPORE — Industries

LIM, Linda
Trade, employment and industrialisation in Singapore / Linda Lim and Pang Eng Fong. — Geneva : International Labour Office, 1986. — xi,110p. — *Includes bibliographical references*

SINGAPORE — Politics and government

Central government and local development in Indonesia / edited by Colin MacAndrews. — Singapore ; Oxford : Oxford University Press, 1986. — xv,253p. — (East Asian social science monographs)

CHOO, Carolyn
Singapore, the PAP & the problem of political succession / Carolyn Choo. — Petaling Jaya, Selangor, Malaysia : Pelanduk Publications (M) ; Singapore : Sole distributor Asiapac Books & Educational Aids, [1985]. — x, 225 p.

The Straits Times: weekly overseas edition. — Singapore : Straits Times, 1987-. — *Weekly*

SINGAPORE — Social conditions

CLAMMER, John
Singapore : ideology, society, culture / by John Clammer. — Singapore : Chopmen Publishers, 1985. — 169p. — *Includes bibliographic notes*

Singapore : resources and growth / edited by Lim Chong-Yah and Peter J. Lloyd. — Singapore ; Oxford : Oxford University Press, 1986. — xiii,279p. — *Bibliographies*

SINGAPORE — Social conditions — Statitics

Economic and social statistics Singapore 1960-1982. — Singapore : Department of Statistics, 1983. — x,270p

SINGLE MEN — United States

RUBINSTEIN, Robert L
Singular paths : old men living alone / Robert L. Rubinstein. — New York : Columbia University Press, 1986. — viii, 265 p.. — (Columbia studies of social gerontology and aging). — *Includes index. — Bibliography: p. [257]-261*

SINGLE-PARENT FAMILY

Social security and family law : with special reference to the one-parent family : a comparative survey / edited by Alec Samuels. — [s.l.] : United Kingdom National Committee of Comparative Law, 1979. — 327p. — (United Kingdom comparative law series ; v. 4) . — *Includes bibliographies. — Based on revised papers and contributions originally submitted to a colloquium held by the United Kingdom National Committee for Comparative Law at the University of Nottingham*

SINGLE-PARENT FAMILY — Canada

SCHLESINGER, Benjamin
The one-parent family in the 1980s : perpectives and annotated bibliography 1978-1984 / Benjamin Schlesinger. — [5th ed.]. — Toronto ; London : University of Toronto, 1985. — 284p. — *Four previous editions covered period 1930-1978*

SINGLE-PARENT FAMILY — Canada — Bibliography

SCHLESINGER, Benjamin
The one-parent family in the 1980s : perpectives and annotated bibliography 1978-1984 / Benjamin Schlesinger. — [5th ed.]. — Toronto ; London : University of Toronto, 1985. — 284p. — *Four previous editions covered period 1930-1978*

SINGLE PARENT FAMILY — Great Britain

NATIONAL COUNCIL FOR ONE PARENT FAMILIES
Fuel poverty : case-studies from one parent families. — London : National Council for One Parent Families, 1985. — 10p

SINGLE PARENT FAMILY — Great Britain — Medical care

Caring for health : health issues for one-parent families : report of a conference organised by the National Council for One Parent Families in collaboration with the King's Fund, held at the King's Fund Centre on 12th October 1984. — London : King's Fund Centre : One Parent Families, 1985. — 25p

SINGLE-PARENT FAMILY — United States

SCHLESINGER, Benjamin
The one-parent family in the 1980s : perpectives and annotated bibliography 1978-1984 / Benjamin Schlesinger. — [5th ed.]. — Toronto ; London : University of Toronto, 1985. — 284p. — *Four previous editions covered period 1930-1978*

SINGLE-PARENT FAMILY — United States — Bibliography

SCHLESINGER, Benjamin
The one-parent family in the 1980s : perpectives and annotated bibliography 1978-1984 / Benjamin Schlesinger. — [5th ed.]. — Toronto ; London : University of Toronto, 1985. — 284p. — *Four previous editions covered period 1930-1978*

SINGLE PARENTS — Employment — Australia

FREY, Dianne
Survey of sole parent pensioners' workforce barriers / Dianne Frey. — Woden, ACT : Department of Social Security, 1986. — 40p. — (Background/discussion paper / Social Security Review ; no.12). — *Includes bibliographical references*

SINGLE PARENTS — Government policy — Australia

RAYMOND, Judy
Bringing up children alone : policies for sole parents / Judy Raymond. — Canberra : Australian Government Publishing Service, 1987. — xi,145p. — (Issues paper / Social Security Review ; no.3). — *Bibliography: p139-145*

SINGLE PARENTS — Legal status, laws, etc. — England

Legal rights of single mothers / One Parent Families. — [London] : National Council for One Parent Families, 1986, c1984. — 41p. — *Cover title*

SINGLE PARENTS — Australia

Labour force status and other characteristics of sole parents : 1974-1985. — Woden, ACT : Department of Social Security, 1986. — 33p. — (Background paper / Social Security Review ; no.8)

Overseas countries' assistance to sole parents / [Robyn Bradley...[et al.]. — Woden, ACT : Department of Social Security, 1986. — [115]p. — (Background/discussion paper / Social Security Review ; no.14). — *Bibliography: p111*

SINGLE PARENTS — Australia — Finance

Overseas countries' assistance to sole parents / [Robyn Bradley...[et al.]]. — Woden, ACT : Department of Social Security, 1986. — [115]p. — (Background/discussion paper / Social Security Review ; no.14). — *Bibliography: p111*

SINGLE PARENTS — Great Britain — Medical care

Caring for health : health issues for one-parent families : report of a conference organised by the National Council for One Parent Families in collaboration with the King's Fund, held at the King's Fund Centre on 12th October 1984. — London : King's Fund Centre : One Parent Families, 1985. — 25p

SINGLE PEOPLE — Housing — England — Gloucester (Gloucestershire)

COWEN, Harry
The hidden homeless : a report of a survey on homelessness and housing amongst single young Blacks in Gloucester / Harry Cowen with Richard Lording. — Gloucester (15 Brunswick Rd, Gloucester GL1 1HG) : Gloucester Community Relations Council, 1982. — 54p

SINGLE PEOPLE — Housing — England — London

SINGLE HOMELESSNESS IN LONDON WORKING PARTY
Single homelessness in London 1986 : a report. — London : Greater London Council, 1986. — 54p. — *A joint GLC and London Boroughs Working Party. — Bibliography: p54*

SINGLE PEOPLE — California — Los Angeles — Case studies

SMITHERS, Janice A.
Determined survivors : community life among the urban elderly / by Janice A. Smithers. — New Brunswick, N.J. : Rutgers University Press, c1985. — p. cm. — *Includes index. — Bibliography: p*

SINGLE TAX

GASTON, Paul M
Women of Fair Hope / Paul M. Gaston. — Athens : University of Georgia Press, c1984. — xiv, 143 p.. — (Mercer University Lamar memorial lectures ; no. 25). — *Includes index. — Bibliography: p. [119]-133*

SINGLE WOMEN — United States — Psychology

RICHARDSON, Laurel Walum
The new other woman : contemporary single women in affairs with married men / Laurel Richardson. — New York : Free Press ; London : Collier Macmillan, c1985. — p. cm. — *Includes index. — Bibliography: p*

SINKIANG PROVINCE (CHINA) — Foreign relations — Soviet Union

WHITING, Allen S.
Sinkiang : pawn or pivot? / Allen S. Whiting and Sheng Shih-ts'ai. — East Lansing, Mich. : Michigan State University Press, 1958. — xxii,314p. — *Bibliography: p303-307*

SINKIANG PROVINCE (CHINA) — History

WHITING, Allen S.
Sinkiang : pawn or pivot? / Allen S. Whiting and Sheng Shih-ts'ai. — East Lansing, Mich. : Michigan State University Press, 1958. — xxii,314p. — *Bibliography: p303-307*

SINKIANG PROVINCE (CHINA) — Politics and government

WHITING, Allen S.
Sinkiang : pawn or pivot? / Allen S. Whiting and Sheng Shih-ts'ai. — East Lansing, Mich. : Michigan State University Press, 1958. — xxii,314p. — *Bibliography: p303-307*

SINKIANG UIGHUR AUTONOMOUS REGION (CHINA) — Politics and government

FORBES, Andrew D. W.
Warlords and Muslims in Chinese Central Asia : a political history of republican Sinkiang, 1911-1949 / Andrew D.W. Forbes. — Cambridge : Cambridge University Press, 1986. — xvi,376p. — *Bibliography: p345-364. — Includes index*

SINN FEIN

SINN FEIN
For freedom, justice, peace. — Derry : Sinn Fein Director of Elections, [1987]. — [16 leaves]

SINO-INDIAN BORDER DISPUTE — 1957-

BANERJEE, D. K.
Sino-Indian border dispute / D. K. Banerjee. — New Delhi : Intellectual Publishing House, 1985. — xii,116p. — *Bibliography: p[110]-112*

SINO-JAPANESE CONFLICT, 1937-1945

CHIANG, May-ling Soong, 1897-
Selected speeches / by Madame Chiang Kai-shek. — Taipei : Government Information Office, 1957. — 73p

SIRÁCKY, ANDREJ

ŠIŠKA, Miroslav
Publicista Andrej Sirácky : Miroslav Šiška. — Praha : Vydavatelství Novinař, 1986. — 248,19p

SIT-DOWN STRIKES — Netherlands

Bedrijfsbezetting : een nieuwe aktievorm in Nederland / [Projektgroep "Arbeid en Vorming"] ; [Lucy van Houwelingen...et al.]. — [Utrecht : "Arbeid en Vorming", 1974]. — 59p. — *Bibliography: p59*

SKEPTICISM

DOOB, Leonard William
Slightly beyond skepticism : social science and the search for morality / Leonard W. Doob. — New Haven : Yale University Press, c1987. — ix, 319 p.. — *Includes index. — Bibliography: p. 281-306*

FERREIRA, M. Jamie
Scepticism and reasonable doubt : the British naturalist tradition in Wilkins, Hume, Reid and Newman / M. Jamie Ferreira. — Oxford : Clarendon, 1986. — [264]p. — *Includes bibliography and index*

WATKINS, John W. N
Science and scepticism / John Watkins. — Princeton, N.J. : Princeton University Press, c1984. — xvii, 387 p.. — *Includes indexes. — Bibliography: p. 356-380*

SKILLED LABOR — Europe — History

LINDER, Marc
European labor aristocracies : trade unionism, the hierarchy of skill, and the stratification of the manual working class before the First World War / Marc Linder. — Frankfurt : Campus, 1985. — 343 p.. — *Includes bibliographical references*

SKILLED LABOR — Great Britain — History

LINDER, Marc
European labor aristocracies : trade unionism, the hierarchy of skill, and the stratification of the manual working class before the First World War / Marc Linder. — Frankfurt : Campus, 1985. — 343 p.. — *Includes bibliographical references*

SKILLS DEVELOPMENT FUND (Singapore)

LIM, Chong-Yah
Economic restructuring in Singapore / Lim Chong-Yah. — Singapore : Federal Publications, 1984. — v,117p. — *Bibliography: p109*

SLAVE TRADE — Bibliography

MILLER, Joseph Calder
Slavery : a worldwide bibliography, 1900-1982 / Joseph C. Miller. — White Plains, N.Y. : Kraus International, 1985. — xxvii, 451 p.. — *Includes bibliographical references and indexes*

SLAVE-TRADE — Africa

Africans in bondage : studies in slavery and the slave trade : essays in honor of Philip D. Curtin on the occasion of the twenty-fifth anniversary of African Studies at the University of Wisconsin / edited by Paul E. Lovejoy. — Madison : African Studies Program, University of Wisconsin-Madison : Distributed by the University of Wisconsin Press, c1986. — 378p. — *Includes index. — Includes bibliographies*

ELTIS, David
Economic growth and the ending of the transatlantic slave trade / David Eltis. — New York : Oxford University Press, 1987. — xiii, 418 p.. — *Includes index. — Bibliography: p. 399-404*

SLAVE-TRADE — America

ELTIS, David
Economic growth and the ending of the transatlantic slave trade / David Eltis. — New York : Oxford University Press, 1987. — xiii, 418 p.. — *Includes index. — Bibliography: p. 399-404*

SLAVE-TRADE — American

Africans in bondage : studies in slavery and the slave trade : essays in honor of Philip D. Curtin on the occasion of the twenty-fifth anniversary of African Studies at the University of Wisconsin / edited by Paul E. Lovejoy. — Madison : African Studies Program, University of Wisconsin-Madison : Distributed by the University of Wisconsin Press, c1986. — 378p. — *Includes index. — Includes bibliographies*

SLAVE TRADE — Brazil — History

CONRAD, Robert Edgar
World of sorrow : the African slave trade to Brazil / Robert Edgar Conrad. — Baton Rouge : Louisiana State University Press, c1986. — 215 p.. — *Includes index. — Bibliography: p. 197-212*

SLAVE TRADE — Caribbean Area — History

KLEIN, Herbert S
African slavery in Latin America and the Caribbean / Herbert S. Klein. — New York : Oxford University Press, 1986. — 311 p., [3] leaves of plates. — *Includes index. — Bibliography: p. 273-294*

SLAVE-TRADE — England — Bristol (Avon) — History — 18th century

Bristol, Africa and the eighteenth-century slave trade to America. — [Bristol] : Bristol Record Society. — (Bristol Record Society's publications ; v.38)
Vol.1: The years of expansion 1698-1729 / edited by David Richardson. — 1986. — xxix,203p

SLAVE-TRADE — Great Britain

ELTIS, David
Economic growth and the ending of the transatlantic slave trade / David Eltis. — New York : Oxford University Press, 1987. — xiii, 418 p.. — *Includes index. — Bibliography: p. 399-404*

SLAVE TRADE — Latin America — History

KLEIN, Herbert S
African slavery in Latin America and the Caribbean / Herbert S. Klein. — New York : Oxford University Press, 1986. — 311 p., [3] leaves of plates. — *Includes index. — Bibliography: p. 273-294*

SLAVE-TRADE — United States — History — 18th century

Bristol, Africa and the eighteenth-century slave trade to America. — [Bristol] : Bristol Record Society. — (Bristol Record Society's publications ; v.38)
Vol.1: The years of expansion 1698-1729 / edited by David Richardson. — 1986. — xxix,203p

SLAVE TRADE — Virginia — Danville — History

SIEGEL, Frederick F
The roots of southern distinctiveness : tobacco and society in Danville, Virginia, 1780-1865 / by Frederick F. Siegel. — Chapel Hill, N.C. : University of North Carolina Press, c1987. — p. cm. — *Includes index.* — *Bibliography: p*

SLAVEHOLDERS — Georgia — Augusta Region — Attitudes

HARRIS, J. William
Plain folk and gentry in a slave society : white liberty and Black slavery in Augusta's hinterlands / J. William Harris. — 1st ed. — Middletown, Conn. : Wesleyan University Press ; Scranton, Pa. : Distributed by Harper & Row, 1985. — xv, 274 p.. — *: Originally presented as the author's thesis (Ph. D.--Johns Hopkins University, 1982.).* — *Includes index.* — *Bibliography: p. 253-261*

SLAVERY

SAWYER, Roger
Slavery in the twentieth century / Roger Sawyer. — London : Routledge & Kegan Paul, 1986. — [261]p. — *Includes bibliography and index*

SLAVERY — Bibliography

MILLER, Joseph Calder
Slavery : a worldwide bibliography, 1900-1982 / Joseph C. Miller. — White Plains, N.Y. : Kraus International, 1985. — xxvii, 451 p.. — *Includes bibliographical references and indexes*

SLAVERY — Law and legislation — United States — History

CURTIS, Michael Kent
No state shall abridge : the 14th amendment and the Bill of Rights / Michael Kent Curtis. — Durham, N.C. : Duke University Press, 1986. — xii, 275 p.. — *Includes index.* — *Bibliography: p. [221]-266*

SLAVERY — Political aspects — Africa — History

In resistance : studies in African, Caribbean and Afro-American history / edited by Gary Y. Okihiro. — London : University of Massachusetts Press/Eurospan, 1987. — [272]p

SLAVERY — Political aspects — Caribbean Area — History

In resistance : studies in African, Caribbean and Afro-American history / edited by Gary Y. Okihiro. — London : University of Massachusetts Press/Eurospan, 1987. — [272]p

SLAVERY — Political aspects — United States — History

In resistance : studies in African, Caribbean and Afro-American history / edited by Gary Y. Okihiro. — London : University of Massachusetts Press/Eurospan, 1987. — [272]p

SLAVERY — Africa

Africans in bondage : studies in slavery and the slave trade : essays in honor of Philip D. Curtin on the occasion of the twenty-fifth anniversary of African Studies at the University of Wisconsin / edited by Paul E. Lovejoy. — Madison : African Studies Program, University of Wisconsin-Madison : Distributed by the University of Wisconsin Press, c1986. — 378p. — *Includes index.* — *Includes bibliographies*

Slaves and slavery in Muslim Africa / edited with an introduction by John Ralph Willis. — London ; Totowa, N.J. : Frank Cass
Vol.1: Islam and the ideology of enslavement. — 1985. — xiv,267p. — *Contains glossary and index of Arabic words and terms*

Slaves and slavery in Muslim Africa / edited with an introduction by John Ralph Willis. — London ; Totowa, N. J. : Frank Cass
Vol.2: The servile estate. — 1985. — xiv,198p. — *Contains glossary and index of arabic words and terms*

SLAVERY — America

Africans in bondage : studies in slavery and the slave trade : essays in honor of Philip D. Curtin on the occasion of the twenty-fifth anniversary of African Studies at the University of Wisconsin / edited by Paul E. Lovejoy. — Madison : African Studies Program, University of Wisconsin-Madison : Distributed by the University of Wisconsin Press, c1986. — 378p. — *Includes index.* — *Includes bibliographies*

SLAVERY — Brazil — History

CONRAD, Robert Edgar
World of sorrow : the African slave trade to Brazil / Robert Edgar Conrad. — Baton Rouge : Louisiana State University Press, c1986. — 215 p. — *Includes index.* — *Bibliography: p. 197-212*

SLAVERY — Caribbean Area — History

KLEIN, Herbert S
African slavery in Latin America and the Caribbean / Herbert S. Klein. — New York : Oxford University Press, 1986. — 311 p., [3] leaves of plates. — *Includes index.* — *Bibliography: p. 273-294*

SLAVERY — Georgia — Condition of slaves

SMITH, Julia Floyd
Slavery and rice culture in low country Georgia, 1750-1860 / Julia Floyd Smith. — Knoxville : University of Tennessee Press, c1985. — p. cm. — *Includes index.* — *Bibliography: p*

SLAVERY — Georgia — History

MOHR, Clarence L
On the threshold of freedom : masters and slaves in Civil War Georgia / Clarence L. Mohr. — Athens, Ga. ; London : University of Georgia Press, c1986. — xxi, 397p, 18p of plates. — *Includes index.* — *Bibliography: p.367-385*

SLAVERY — Georgia — Augusta Region — Public opinion

HARRIS, J. William
Plain folk and gentry in a slave society : white liberty and Black slavery in Augusta's hinterlands / J. William Harris. — 1st ed. — Middletown, Conn. : Wesleyan University Press ; Scranton, Pa. : Distributed by Harper & Row, 1985. — xv, 274 p.. — *: Originally presented as the author's thesis (Ph. D.--Johns Hopkins University, 1982.).* — *Includes index.* — *Bibliography: p. 253-261*

SLAVERY — Great Britain — Anti-slavery movements

DRESCHER, Seymour
Capitalism and antislavery : British mobilization in comparative perspective / Seymour Drescher ; foreword by Christine Bolt. — London : Macmillan, 1986. — [368]p. — (The second Anstey memorial lecture in the University of Kent at Canterbury ; 1984). — *Includes bibliography and index*

ELTIS, David
Economic growth and the ending of the transatlantic slave trade / David Eltis. — New York : Oxford University Press, 1987. — xiii, 418 p.. — *Includes index.* — *Bibliography: p. 399-404*

FLADELAND, Betty
Abolitionists and working-class problems in the age of industrialization / Betty Fladeland. — London : Macmillan, 1984. — xiv,232p. — *Includes index*

WALVIN, James
England, slaves and freedom, 1776-1838 / James Walvin. — Basingstoke : Macmillan, 1986. — [176]p. — *Includes index*

SLAVERY — Latin America — History

KLEIN, Herbert S
African slavery in Latin America and the Caribbean / Herbert S. Klein. — New York : Oxford University Press, 1986. — 311 p., [3] leaves of plates. — *Includes index.* — *Bibliography: p. 273-294*

SLAVERY — Southern States

SHORE, Laurence
Southern capitalists : the ideological leadership of an elite, 1832-1885 / by Laurence Shore. — Chapel Hill : University of North Carolina Press, c1986. — p. cm. — (The Fred W. Morrison series in southern studies). — *Includes index.* — *Bibliography: p*

SLAVERY — Southern States — Addresses, essays, lectures

HUGHES, Henry
[Selections. 1985]. Selected writings of Henry Hughes, antebellum Southerner, slavocrat, sociologist / edited, with a critical essay, by Stanford M. Lyman. — Jackson : University Press of Mississippi, c1985. — xxi, 235 p.. — *Includes bibliographical references*

SLAVERY — Southern States — Condition of slaves

WHITE, Deborah Gray
Ar'n't I a woman? : female slaves in the plantation South / Deborah Gray White. — 1st ed. — New York : Norton, c1985. — 216 p.. — *Includes index.* — *Bibliography: p. [198]-208*

SLAVERY — Tennessee — Emancipation

CIMPRICH, John
Slavery's end in Tennessee, 1861-1865 / John Cimprich. — University, Ala. : University of Alabama Press, c1985. — 191 p.. — *Includes index.* — *Bibliography: p. 181-185*

SLAVERY — United States

NEWMAN, Francis Wilson
Anglo-Saxon abolition of Negro slavery / by F. W. Newman. — New York : Negro Universities Press, 1969. — 135p. — *Originally published in 1889*

SLAVERY — United States — Anti-slavery movements

The Black abolitionist papers / C. Peter Ripley, editor ; Jeffrey S. Rossbach, associate editor ... [et al.]. — Chapel Hill : University of North Carolina Press, c1985-. — p. cm. — *Includes index.* — *Contents: v. 1. The British Isles, 1830-1865*

JONES, Howard
Mutiny on the Amistad : the saga of a slave revolt and its impact on American abolition, law, and diplomacy / Howard Jones. — New York : Oxford University Press, 1987. — ix, 271 p., [12] p. of plates. — *Includes index.* — *Bibliography: p. 221-259*

WYATT-BROWN, Bertram
Yankee saints and Southern sinners / Bertram Wyatt-Brown. — Baten Rouge ; London : Louisiana State University Press, c1985. — xi, 227p. — *Includes index*

SLAVERY — United States — Anti-slavery movements — Sources

The black abolitionist papers / C. Peter Ripley, Editor. — Chapel Hill ; London : University of North Carolina Press
Vol.2: Canada, 1830-1865. — 1986. — xxviii,560p

SLAVERY — United States — Emancipation

Freedom : a documentary history of emancipation 1861-1867 : selected from the holdings of the National Archives of the United States. — Cambridge : Cambridge University Press
Series 1
Vol.1: The destruction of slavery / Ira Berlin ... [et al.]. — 1985. — xxxviii,852p. — *Includes index*

SLAVERY — United States — Historiography

SMITH, John David
An old creed for the new South : proslavery ideology and historiography, 1865-1918 / John David Smith. — Westport, Conn. : Greenwood Press, 1985. — ix, 314 p. — (Contributions in Afro-American and African studies ; no. 89). — *Includes index.* — *Bibliography: p. [295]-299*

SLAVERY — United States — Insurrections, etc
JONES, Howard
Mutiny on the Amistad : the saga of a slave revolt and its impact on American abolition, law, and diplomacy / Howard Jones. — New York : Oxford University Press, 1987. — ix, 271 p., [12] p. of plates. — *Includes index.* — *Bibliography: p. 221-259*

SLAVERY — Virgin Islands of the United States — Saint John — History
OLWIG, Karen Fog
Cultural adaptation and resistance on St. John : three centuries of Afro-Caribbean life / Karen Fog Olwig. — Gainesville : University of Florida Press, c1985. — xii, 226 p.. — *Cover title: Cultural adaptation & resistance on St. John.* — *Includes index.* — *Bibliography: p. [201]-216*

SLAVERY — West Indies, British
NEWMAN, Francis Wilson
Anglo-Saxon abolition of Negro slavery / by F. W. Newman. — New York : Negro Universities Press, 1969. — 135p. — *Originally published in 1889*

SLAVERY AND ISLAM — Africa
Slaves and slavery in Muslim Africa / edited with an introduction by John Ralph Willis. — London ; Totowa, N.J. : Frank Cass Vol.1: Islam and the ideology of enslavement. — 1985. — xiv,267p. — *Contains glossary and index of Arabic words and terms*

Slaves and slavery in Muslim Africa / edited with an introduction by John Ralph Willis. — London ; Totowa, N. J. : Frank Cass Vol.2: The servile estate. — 1985. — xiv,198p. — *Contains glossary and index of arabic words and terms*

SLAVERY IN THE UNITED STATES — History
FRANKLIN, John Hope
From slavery to freedom : a history of Negro Americans / John Hope Franklin. — 5th ed. — New York : Knopf, 1980. — xxvii, 554, xxxix, p.. — *Includes index.* — *Bibliography: p. 507-546*

SLAVIC COUNTRIES — Library resources
AMERICAN COUNCIL OF LEARNED SOCIETIES. Joint Committee on Soviet Studies. Subcommittee on Bibliography, Information Retrieval and Documentation
International directory of librarians and library specialists in the Slavic and East European field / prepared under the auspices of the Subcommittee on Bibliography,Information Retrieval and Documentation of the Joint Committee on Soviet Studies of the American Council of Learned Societies and the Social Science Research Council. — New York : American Council of Learned Societies, 1985. — 58p

SLAVIC COUNTRIES — Relations — Poland
GIZA, Antoni
Neoslawizm i polacy 1906-1910 / Antoni Giza. — Szczecin : Wyższa Szkoła Pedagogiczna, 1984. — 265p. — (Rozprawy i studia / Wyższa Szkola Pedagogiczna w Szczecinie ; t.61). — *Summary in German and Russian.* — *Bibliography: p237-251*

SLAVIC LANGUAGES — Library resources
AMERICAN COUNCIL OF LEARNED SOCIETIES. Joint Committee on Soviet Studies. Subcommittee on Bibliography, Information Retrieval and Documentation
International directory of librarians and library specialists in the Slavic and East European field / prepared under the auspices of the Subcommittee on Bibliography,Information Retrieval and Documentation of the Joint Committee on Soviet Studies of the American Council of Learned Societies and the Social Science Research Council. — New York : American Council of Learned Societies, 1985. — 58p

SLAVS, SOUTHERN — Hungary
LÁSZLÓ, Lajos
Jégszikrák : (A hazai nemzetiségek életéb"ol) / László Lajos. — [Budapest] : Népszava, 1984. — 177p

SLOVAK AMERICANS — Minnesota — Minneapolis — Social life and customs
The Bohemian Flats / compiled by the workers of the Writers' Program of the Work Projects Administration in the State of Minnesota ; with an introduction by Thaddeus Radzilowsky. — St. Paul : Minnesota Historical Society Press, 1986. — p. cm. — (Borealis books). — : Reprint. Originally published: Minneapolis : University of Minnesota Press, 1941. With new introd. and index. — *Bibliography: p[189]-203*

SLOVAK SOCIALIST REPUBLIC (CZECHOSLOVAKIA) — History
KLIMKO, Jozef
Tretia riša a ľudácky režim na Slovensku / Jozef Klimko. — Bratislava : Obzor, 1986. — 249p. — *Bibliography: p233-[243]*

SLOVAK SOCIALIST REPUBLIC (CZECHOSLOVAKIA) — History — Uprising, 1944
CHŇOUPEK, Bohuš
Les résistants de la dernière chance : combattants français dans les maquis slovaques, 1944-45 / Bohuš Chňoupek. — Paris : Jacques Grancher, 1986. — 189p

SLOVENES — Austria — Carinthia
Carinthischer Herbst = Koroška jesen. — Klagenfurt : Karel Smolle, [1978?]. — 31p. — *Text in German and Slovene*

ZWITTER, Fran
To destroy Nazism or to reward it? : an aspect of the question of Slovene Carinthia / Fran Zwitter. — Beograd : Yugoslav Institute for International Affairs, 1947. — 30p

SLUMS
Perspectives in urban geography. — New Delhi : Concept Publishing Vol.7: Slums, urban decline and revitalization / edited by C. S. Yadav. — 1987. — 288p. — *Includes bibliographies and index*

SLUMS — Denmark
JØRGENSEN, Jørgen
Betonbørn / Jørgen Jørgensen. — Aarhus : Modtryk, 1978. — 94p

SLUMS — England — London — History
WOHL, Anthony S
The eternal slum : housing and social policy in Victorian London / Anthony S. Wohl. — Montreal : McGill-Queen's University Press, 1977. — xxiv, 386 p., [8] leaves of plates. — (Studies in urban history ; 5). — *"A note on sources": p. 341-355.* — *Includes index*

SLUMS — India — Bombay
JHA, S. S.
Structure of urban poverty : the case of Bombay slums / S. S. Jha. — London : Sangam Books, 1986. — xvii,184p

SLUMS — Pakistan — Layāri
HAFEEZ, Sabeeha
Poverty, voluntary organizations, and social change : a study of an urban slum in Pakistan / Sabeeha Hafeez. — 1st ed. — Karachi : Royal Book Co., c1985. — 248 p.. — *Includes index*

SMALL BUSINESS
GREAT BRITAIN. Parliament. House of Commons. Library. Research Division
Small firms : the international scene / Timothy Edmonds. — [London] : the Division, 1984. — 20p. — (Background paper ; no.134)

HAMERTON, A. S.
Valuation of small business goodwill / A. S. Hamerton. — Huddersfield : Polytechnic. Department of Accountancy and Finance, 1986. — [84p]

The Performance of small firms : profits, jobs and failures / David Storey ... (et al.). — London : Croom Helm, c1987. — 342p. — *Bibliography: p327-334.* — *Includes index*

The Survival of the small firm / edited by James Curran, John Stanworth, David Watkins. — Aldershot : Gower, c1986. — 2v.

UNION DES INDUSTRIES DE LA COMMUNAUTÉ EUROPEENNE
Rôle et avenir des petites et moyennes entreprises industrielles. — Bruxelles : U.N.I.C.E., [1970]. — 32p

SMALL BUSINESS — Information services — Great Britain
Information and the small manufacturing firm : report of a study of information use and needs in small manufacturing firms in the UK and the current pattern of information provision : funded by the British Library Research and Development Department. — Edinburgh : Capital Planning Information, 1982. — v,133p. — *Bibliography: p71-75.* — *Includes index*

Information and the small manufacturing firm : seminar report : summary report of the proceedings of a two-day seminar held at Dunchurch College of Management, 18-19 November 1982 / compiled by Capital Planning Information. — Edinburgh : Capital Planning Information, [1983?]. — 25 leaves. — (British Library Research and Development Department report ; no.5734)

TROTT, Fiona
Information for industry : a study of the information needs of small firms and the relevance of public information services / Fiona Trott with an external assessment by John Martyn. — [London] : British Library, c1986. — xi,94p. — (Library and information research report ; 51). — *Bibliography: p89-91*

SMALL BUSINESS — Management
Growing concerns : building and managing the smaller business / David E. Gumpert, editor. — New York : Wiley, c1984. — ix, 418 p.. — (Harvard business review executive book series) . — *"Harvard business review"--Cover.* — *Includes bibliographical references and indexes*

SMALL BUSINESS — Asia
The Rural non-farm sector in Asia / edited by Swapna Mukhopadhyay, Chee Peng Lim. — Kuala Lumpur, Malaysia : Asian and Pacific Development Centre, 1985. — xiv, 417 p. — (The Human resource mobilization programme publications). — *Includes bibliographies*

SMALL BUSINESS — Australia
Small business review 1985. — Canberra : Australian Government Publishing Service, 1986. — vii,121p. — *Bibliographical references: p117-119*

SMALL BUSINESS — Developing countries
GREAT BRITAIN. Overseas Development Administration. Economic Planning Staff
Project handbook : small-scale enterprises. — [London] : the Adminstration, [1979]. — 10leaves. — *Bibliography: leaf[10]*

HULL, Galen
A small business agenda : trends in a global economy / Galen Spencer Hull. — Lanham, MD : University Press of America, c1986. — x, 128 p.. — *Bibliography: p. 125-127*

SMALL BUSINESS — Developing countries — Finance
LEVITSKY, Jacob
World Bank lending to small enterprises : a review / Jacob Levitsky. — Washington, D.C. : The World Bank, 1986. — viii,53p. — (Industry and finance series ; v.16). — *Includes bibliographical references*

SMALL BUSINESS — Europe
Entrepreneurship in Europe : the social processes / edited by Robert Goffee and Richard Scase. — London : Croom Helm, c1987. — 197p. — (Social analysis). — *Includes bibliographies and index*

SMALL BUSINESS — Europe
continuation

Small business in Europe / edited by Paul Burns and Jim Dewhurst. — Basingstoke : Macmillan, 1986. — xx,211p. — (Macmillan small business series). — *Includes index*

SMALL BUSINESS — European Economic Community countries

The promotion of the small and medium—sized enterprises : opinion. — Brussels : Economic and Social Committee of the European Communities, 1982. — iii, 70p

STOREY, David J.
Job creation in small and medium sized enterprises / by David J. Storey. — Luxembourg : Office for Official Publications of the European Communities. — *At head of title: Commission of the European Communities*
Vol.1: Summary report; Issues for research and policy; United Kingdom; Italy : main report. — 1987. — 215p. — (Programme of research and actions on the development of the labour market)

STOREY, David J.
Job creation in small and medium sized enterprises / by David J. Storey, Steven G. Johnson. — Luxembourg : Office for Official Publications of the European Communities. — *At head of title: Commission of the European Communities*
Vol.2: Federal Republic of Germany; France; Netherlands; Belgium; Luxembourg : main report. — 1987. — 216—486p. — (Programme of research and actions on the development of the labour market)

STOREY, David J.
Job creation in small and medium sized enterprises / by David J.Storey, StevenG. Johnson. — Luxembourg : Office for Official Publications of the European Communities. — *At head of title: Commission of the European Communities*
Vol.3: Spain, Ireland, Denmark, Greece, Portugal : main report. — 1987. — 488-663p. — (Programme of research and actions on the development of the labour market)

SMALL BUSINESS — France — Finance

Le financement des petites et moyennes entreprises : analyse macroéconomique : adequation du système d'aides interventions économiques régionales / [realisée par Lucien Farhi, Jacques Pierre, Eric Taze]. — Paris : Société d'études pour le développement économique et social, 1983. — 199p

SMALL BUSINESS — Great Britain

BINKS, Martin
The birth of enterprise : an analytical and empirical study of the growth of small firms / Martin Binks and John Coyne. — London : Institute of Economic Affairs, 1983. — (Hobart paper ; 98)

CRAIG, Christine, 1921—
Payment structures and smaller firms : women's employment in segmented labour markets / by Christine Craig, Elizabeth Garnsey, Jill Rubery. — London : Department of Employment, [1985?]. — 109p. — (Research paper / Department of Employment ; no.48)

GREAT BRITAIN. Parliament. House of Commons. Library. Research Division
Small firms / Timothy Edmonds, Christopher Barclay. — [London] : the Division, 1983. — 27p. — (Background paper ; no.117)

GREAT BRITAIN. Parliament. House of Commons. Library. Research Division
Small firms / Timothy Edmonds, Christopher Barclay. — [London] : the Divsion, 1984. — 30p. — (Baackground paper ; no.144)

GREAT BRITAIN. Parliament. House of Commons. Library. Research Division
Small firms / Timothy Edmonds, Christopher Barclay. — [Rev. ed] — [London] : the Division, 1985. — 36p. — (Background paper ; no.174)

GREAT BRITAIN. Parliament. House of Commons. Library. Research Division
Small firms / Timothy Edmonds. — Rev. ed. — [London] : the Division, 1986. — 25p. — (Background paper ; no.184)

GREEN, Howard
Redundant space : a productive asset : converting property for small business use / Howard Green and Paul Foley. — London : Harper & Rowe on behalf of the Small Business Research Trust, 1986. — 140p. — *Bibliography: p136. — Includes index*

HART, P. E.
Job generation and size of firm / P. E. Hart. — London : National Institute of Economic and Social Research, 1987. — 24p. — (Discussion paper / National Institute of Economic and Social Research ; no.125). — *Bibliography: p22*

JACKSON, Annabel
Managing workspaces : prepared for the Department of the Environment / by Annabel Jackson, Daphne Mair and Rupert Nabarro, Land and Urban Analysis Ltd.. — London : H.M.S.O., 1987. — 133p. — (Case studies of good practice in urban regeneration). — *Commissioned by the Inner Cities Directorate of the Department of the Environment. — Bibliography: p132*

Local employment initiatives : local enterprise agencies in Great Britain : a study of their impact, operational lessons and policy implications / by Community Initiatives Research Trust (CIRT) Liverpool. — Luxembourg : Office for Official Publications of the European Communities, 1985. — iv, 61p. — (Programme of research and action on the development of the labour market). — *At head of title: Commission of the European Communities*

PERRY, Martin
Small factories and economic development / Martin Perry. — Aldershot : Gower, c1986. — [245]p. — *Includes bibliography*

Readings in small business / edited by Graham Beaver ... [et al.]. — Aldershot : Gower, c1986. — [400]p. — *Conference proceedings*

Small firms growth and development / edited by Michael Scott ... [et al.]. — Aldershot : Gower, c1986. — xix,325p. — *Includes bibliographies*

STOREY, D. J. (David John), 1947-
Are small firms the answer to unemployment? / D.J.Storey and S.Johnson. — London : Employment Institute, 1987. — 47p. — *At head of title: Employment Institute*

SMALL BUSINESS — Great Britain — Societies, etc

Information and the small manufacturing firm : report of a study of information use and needs in small manufacturing firms in the UK and the current pattern of information provision : funded by the British Library Research and Development Department. — Edinburgh : Capital Planning Information, 1982. — v,133p. — *Bibliography: p71-75. — Includes index*

Information and the small manufacturing firm : seminar report : summary report of the proceedings of a two-day seminar held at Dunchurch College of Management, 18-19 November 1982 / compiled by Capital Planning Information. — Edinburgh : Capital Planning Information, [1983?]. — 25 leaves. — (British Library Research and Development Department report ; no.5734)

SMALL BUSINESS — Great Britain — Technological innovations

NORTHCOTT, Jim
Promoting innovation 2 : microelectronics consultancy support / Jim Northcott...[et al.]. — London : Policy Studies Institute, 1986. — 181p. — (PSI Research Report ; 662)

SMALL BUSINESS — Netherlands

RAAD VOOR HET MIDDEN- EN KLEINBEDRIJF
Beroepskenmerken en bedrijfsbeëindiging : raaport inzake de beroepspositie, de beroepsgeschiedenis en de beëindigingsmotieven van ondernemers die bedrijfsbeëindigingshulp bij de Stichting Ontwikkeling en Sanering voor het Midden- en Kleinbedrijf hebben anngevraagd. — 's-Gravenhage : Raad voor het Midden- en Kleinbedrijf, 1969. — 60p. — *Summaries in French, German and English*

Voorjaarsnota / Raad voor het Midden-en Kleinbedrijf. — 's-Gravenhage : Raad voor het Midden-en Keinbedrijf, 1984-. — *Annual*

SMALL BUSINESS — United States

HULL, Galen
A small business agenda : trends in a global economy / Galen Spencer Hull. — Lanham, MD : University Press of America, c1986. — x, 128 p.. — *Bibliography: p. 125-127*

SMART (COMPUTER PROGRAM)

INNOVATIVE SOFTWARE
[Smart software demonstration pack]. — [s.l.] : Innovative Software, c1986. — 22p,80p,+ 11 disks. — *Contents: 2 leaflets entitled - The Smart demo-pack and Introducing Smart; also eleven disks*

ŠMERAL, BOHUMÍR

WHEATON, Bernard
Radical socialism in Czechoslovakia : Bohumír Šmeral, the Czech road to socialism and the origins of the Czechoslovak Communist Party (1917-1921) / Bernard Wheaton. — Boulder, Colo. : East European Monographs ; New York : distributed by Columbia University Press, 1986. — xxvii,204p. — (East European Monographs ; no.213). — *Bibliography: p191-199*

SMITH, ADAM

SMITH, Adam, 1723-1790
The correspondence of Adam Smith / edited by Ernest Campbell Mossner and Ian Simpson Ross. — [2nd ed.]. — Oxford : Clarendon, 1987. — xxxi,464p. — (The Glasgow edition of the works and correspondence of Adam Smith ; 6). — *Previous ed.: 1977. — Includes index*

SMOKING

WILKINSON, James, 1941-
Tobacco : the truth behind the smokescreen / James Wilkinson. — Harmondsworth : Penguin, 1986. — 158p. — *Cover title: Tobacco: the facts.... — Bibliography: p.[142]-143*

SMOKING — Government policy — Addresses, essays, lectures

Smoking and society : toward a more balanced assessment / edited by Robert D. Tollison. — Lexington, Mass. : Lexington Books, c1986. — ix, 368 p.. — *Includes bibliographies and indexes*

SMOKING — Social aspects — Addresses, essays, lectures

Smoking and society : toward a more balanced assessment / edited by Robert D. Tollison. — Lexington, Mass. : Lexington Books, c1986. — ix, 368 p.. — *Includes bibliographies and indexes*

SMOKING — Australia — History

WALKER, R. B
Under fire : a history of tobacco smoking in Australia / Robin Walker. — Carlton, Vic. : Melbourne University Press ; Beaverton, OR : International Scholarly Book Services, 1984. — ix, 155 p., [12] p. of plates. — *Includes bibliographical references and index*

SMOKING — Great Britain

RAW, Martin
Helping people to stop smoking : the development, role and potential of support services in the UK / Martin Raw and Julie Heller. — [London?] : Health Education Council, 1984. — 134p. — *Bibliography: p125-128*

SNOWDEN, PHILIP
Philip Snowden : the first Labour Chancellor of the Exchequer / edited by Keith Laybourn and David James. — Bradford : Bradford Libraries and Information Service, 1987. — 111p. — *Includes index*

SOAP OPERAS — United States
CASSATA, Mary
life on daytime television : tuning-in American serial drama / by Mary Cassata and Thomas Skill. — Norwood, N.J. : Ablex Publishing Corporation, 1983. — xxxv,214p. — *Bibliography: p187-202*

SOAP OPERAS — United States — Addresses, essays, lectures
CASSATA, Mary B.
Life on daytime television : tuning-in American serial drama / by Mary Cassata and Thomas Skill. — Norwood, N.J. : Ablex Pub. Corp., c1983. — xxxv, 214 p.. — (Communication and information science). — *Includes indexes.* — "The daytime serial : a bibliography of scholarly writings, 1943-1981" / Patricia Tegler: p. 187-196. — *Bibliography: p. 197-202*

SOCCER — Great Britain
REDHEAD, Steve
Sing when you're winning : the last football book / Steve Redhead. — London : Pluto, 1987, c1986. — 144p. — *Bibliography: p144*

SOCCER — Great Britain — Fans — Bibliography
SHRIGLEY, Sheila
Selected references on soccer hooliganism / compiled by Sheila M. Shrigley. — London : Department of Health and Social Security Library, 1979. — 4p. — (Bibliography series / Department of Health and Social Security Library ; no.B122)

SOCIAL ACCOUNTING — Statistical methods
GROOTAERT, Christiaan
The labor market and social accounting : a framework of data presentation / Christiaan Grootaert. — Washington, D.C. : World Bank, c1982 ((1985 printing)). — 36p. — (LSMS working papers ; no.17) (LSMS working papers ; no. 17). — *Bibliographical references: p36*

SOCIAL ACCOUNTING — Developinmg countries — Case studies — Congresses
Social accounting matrices : a basis for planning / edited by Graham Pyatt and Jeffery I. Round. — Washington, D.C., U.S.A. : World Bank, 1985. — p. cm. — *Bibliography: p*

SOCIAL ACCOUNTING — Developinmg countries — Methodology — Congresses
Social accounting matrices : a basis for planning / edited by Graham Pyatt and Jeffery I. Round. — Washington, D.C., U.S.A. : World Bank, 1985. — p. cm. — *Bibliography: p*

SOCIAL ACCOUNTING — Indonesia — Statistics
Sistem neraca sosial ekonomi Indonesia, 1975 = Social accounting matrix Indonesia, 1975. — Jakarta : Biro Pusat Statistik. — *Tables in Indonesian with list of tables in English* Vol.2. — [1983]. — xx,311 leaves

Social accounting matrix Indonesia, 1975. — Jakarta : Biro Pusat Statistik. — *Bibliography: p101-105*
Vol.1. — [1982]. — v,105p

SOCIAL ACTION
BILMES, Jack
Discourse and behavior / Jack Bilmes. — New York : Plenum Press, c1986. — p. cm. — *Includes index. — Bibliography: p*

INGRAM, David
Habermas and the dialectic of reason / David Ingram. — New Haven, CT : Yale University Press, c1987. — xvii, 263p. — *Includes index. — Bibliography: p.243-254*

SOCIAL ADJUSTMENT — Congresses
Development of antisocial and prosocial behavior : research, theories, and issues / edited by Dan Olweus, Jack Block, Marian Radke-Yarrow. — Orlando : Academic Press, 1986. — xiii, 432 p.. — (Developmental psychology series). — *Based on a conference on the development of antisocial and prosocial behavior, held at Voss, Norway, 7/4-10/82.* — *Includes bibliographies and indexes*

SOCIAL CASE WORK
Ego-oriented casework : problems and perspectives : papers from the Smith College School for Social Work / edited by Howard J. Parad anbd Roger R. Miller. — New York : Family Service Association of America, 1963. — 312p

JEHU, Derek
Learning theory and social work / Derek Jehu. — London : Routledge and Kegan Paul, 1967. — viii,139p. — *Bibliography: p122-136. — Includes index*

MAPLE, Frank F
Dynamic interviewing : an introduction to counseling / by Frank F. Maple. — Beverly Hills ; London : Sage Publications, c1985. — 174p. — (Sage Human services guides ; 41). — *Bibliography: p 173-174*

Perspectives on patch / edited by Ian Sinclair [and] David N. Thomas. — London : National Institute for Social Work, 1983. — 77p. — (National Institute for Social Work paper ; no.14). — *Bibliography: p[79-81]*

WILLIAMSON, Howard
Strategies for intervention : an approach to youth and community work in an area of social deprivation / Howard Williamson [and] Kaye Weatherspoon. — Cardiff : University College, Social Research Unit, 1985. — 99p. — *Bibliography: p99*

SOCIAL CASE WORK — Great Britain
DAVIES, Bleddyn
Matching resources to needs in community care : an evaluated demonstration of a long-term care model / Bleddyn Davies & David Challis. — Aldershot : Gower, c1986. — xxxii,658p. — *Bibliography: p571-642. — Includes index*

SOCIAL CASEWORK
BARNES, Marian
Social work in general practice : the situation in Sheffield / Marian Barnes. — Sheffield : Research and Information Section, City of Sheffield Family and Community Services Department. — *Bibliography: p32*
report no.12. — 1982. — 31p

SOCIAL CHANGE
Beyond progress and development : macro-political and macro-societal change / edited by Jan Berting and Wim Blockmans. — Aldershot : Avebury, 1987. — vii,93p. — (Issues in interdisciplinary studies ; no.4). — *Conference proceedings*

BOUDON, Raymond
Theories of social change : a critical appraisal / Raymond Boudon ; translated by J.C. Whitehouse. — Cambridge : Polity, 1986. — vi,253p. — (Social and political theory). — *Translation of: La place du désordre. — Includes index*

CAMPBELL, Angus
The human meaning of social change / Edited by Angus Campbell and Philip E. Converse. — New York : Russell Sage Foundation, [1972]. — x, 547 p. — (Publications of Russell Sage Foundation). — *Includes bibliographical references*

Collaborative research and social change : applied anthropology in action / edited by Donald D. Stull, Jean J. Schensul. — Boulder, CO : Westview Press, 1986. — p. cm. — (Westview special studies in applied anthropology). — *Includes index*

DAVIS, Nanette J
From crime to choice : the transformation of abortion in America / Nanette J. Davis. — Westport, Conn. : Greenwood Press, c1985. — p. cm. — (Contributions in women's studies ; no. 60). — *Includes index. — Bibliography: p*

EISENSTADT, S. N.
Centre formation, protest movements, and class structure in Europe and the United States / S.N. Eisenstadt, L. Roniger and A. Seligman. — London : Pinter, 1987. — 187p. — *Includes index*

MADURO, Otto
[Religión y lucha de clases. English]. Religion and social conflicts / Otto Maduro ; translated from the Spanish by Robert R. Barr. — Maryknoll, NY : Orbis Books, c1982. — xxviii, 161 p.. — *Translation of: Religión y lucha de clases. — Bibliography: p. 158-161*

MARRIS, Peter
Loss and change / Peter Marris. — rev. ed. — London : Routledge and Kegan Paul, 1986. — xiv,178p. — (Reports / Institute of Community Studies). — *Bibliography:p172-174*

Speaking of faith : cross-cultural perspectives on women, religion and social change / Diana L. Eck and Devaki Jain editors. — London : Women's Press, 1986. — 288p. — *Conference papers*

SOCIAL CHANGE — Case studies
SIDER, Gerald M.
Culture and class in anthropology and history : a Newfoundland illustration / Gerald M. Sider. — Cambridge : Cambridge University Press, 1986. — xi, 205p, [8] p of plates. — (Cambridge studies in social anthropology ; 60) . — *Bibliography: p.195-200*

SOCIAL CHANGE — Congresses
Behavioral and social science : fifty years of discovery : in commemoration of the fiftieth anniversary of the "Ogburn report," Recent social trends in the United States / Neil J. Smelser and Dean R. Gerstein, editors ; Committee on Basic Research in the Behavioral and Social Sciences, Commission on Behavioral and Social Sciences and Education, National Research Council. — Washington, D.C. : National Academy Press, 1986. — x, 298 p.. — *Symposium held Nov. 29-30, 1983. — Includes bibliographies*

Communications for national development : lessons from experience / [edited by] Robert D. Graff. — Cambridge, Mass. : Oelgeschlager, Gunn & Hain, c1983. — ix, 395 p.. — *Based on papers and discussions of three successive Salzburg Seminars, held Sept. 1979, Sept. 1980, and Mar. 1981 in Salzburg, Austria. — Bibliography: p. 373-380*

SOCIAL CHANGE — Cross-cultural studies
The cultural transition : human experience and social transformation in the Third World and Japan / edited by Merry I. White and Susan Pollack. — London : Routledge and Kegan Paul, 1986. — xiii,302p

Women living change / edited by Susan C. Bourque and Donna Robinson Divine. — Philadelphia : Temple University Press, 1985. — p. cm. — (Women in the political economy) . — *Includes index*

SOCIAL CHANGE — History
JANOS, Andrew C
Politics and paradigms : changing theories of change in social science / Andrew C. Janos. — Stanford, Calif. : Stanford University Press, 1986. — p. cm. — *Includes index. — Bibliography: p*

SOCIAL CHANGE — Mathematical models
PLEWIS, Ian
Analysing change : measurement and explanation using longitudinal data / Ian Plewis. — Chichester : Wiley, c1985. — xii,182p. — *Bibliography: p169-175. — Includes index*

SOCIAL CHOICE

ATKINSON, A. B.
James Buchanan's contribution to economics / A. B. Atkinson. — [London : London School of Economics and Political Science], 1986. — 13p. — (Taxation, incentives and the distribution of income ; no.100). — *Economic and Social Research Council programme.* — *Bibliographical references: p11-13*

MCLEAN, Iain
Public choice : an introduction / Iain McLean. — Oxford : Basil Blackwell, 1987. — [224]p. — *Includes bibliography and index*

MERKHOFER, Miley W.
Decision science and social risk management : a comparative evaluation of cost-benefit analysis, decision analysis, and other formal decision-aiding approaches / Miley W. Merkhofer. — Dordrecht ; Boston : D. Reidel ; Norwell, MA : Sold and distributed in the U.S.A. and Canada by Kluwer Academic Publishers, 1986. — p. cm. — (Technology, risk, and society). — *Includes index.* — *Bibliography: p*

Rational choice / edited by Jon Elster. — Oxford : Basil Blackwell, 1986. — [224]p. — (Readings in social and political theory). — *Includes index*

RINGEN, Stein
The possibility of politics : a study in the political economy of the welfare state / Stein Ringen. — Oxford : Clarendon, 1987. — x,303p. — *Bibliography: p267-295.* — *Includes index*

SOCIAL CHOICE — Congresses

Experimental social dilemmas / Henk A.M. Wilke, Dave M. Messick, Christel G. Rutte, eds. — Frankfurt am Main ; New York : P. Lang, c1986. — vi, 234 p.. — (Psychologie des Entscheidungsverhaltens und des Konfliktes = Psychology of decisions and conflict ; Bd. 3). — *Papers were presented at a conference held at the University of Groningen in the spring of 1984.* — *Includes bibliographies*

SOCIAL CHOICE — Mathematical models

ARROW, Kenneth Joseph
Social choice and multicriterion decision-making / Kenneth J. Arrow and Hervé Raynaud. — Cambridge, Mass. : MIT Press, c1986. — p. cm. — *Includes index.* — *Bibliography: p*

SOCIAL CLASSES — India

KAMBLE, J. R.
Pursuit of equality in Indian history / J. R. Kamble. — New Delhi : National Publishing House, 1985. — xi,414p. — *Bibliography: p386-394*

SOCIAL CLASSES

BERKI, R. N.
State, class, nation / R. N. Berki. — Hull : Hull University Press, 1986. — 20p

BOCOCK, Robert
Hegemony / Robert Bocock. — Chichester : Ellis Horwood, 1986. — 136p. — *Bibliography: p.[130]-132*

CAPLOW, Theodore
The sociology of work / by Theodore Caplow. — Westport, Conn. : Greenwood Press, 1978, c1954. — viii, 330 p.. — *Reprint of the ed. published by University of Minnesota Press, Minneapolis.* — *Includes index.* — *Bibliography: p. 303-322*

LANE, David
The end of inequality? : stratification under state socialism / David Lane. — Harmondsworth : Penguin, 1971. — 156p. — (Penguin modern sociology monographs) (Penguin education). — *Bibliographyp.141-147.* — *Includes index*

PHILLIPS, Anne, 1950-
Divided loyalties : dilemmas of sex and class / Anne Phillips. — London : Virago, 1987. — 192p. — *Bibliography: p177-185.* — *Includes index*

Poverty today / Peter Townsend, Charles Elliott, Zsusa Ferge and others. — Edinburgh (New College, The Mound, Edinburgh EH1 2LV) : Department of Christian Ethics and Practical Theology, 1986. — 18p. — (Occasional paper ; no.7). — *Proceedings of seminar.* — *At head of title: Edinburgh University Centre for Theology and Public Issues*

Social inequality : selected readings / edited by André Béteille. — Harmondsworth : Penguin, 1969. — 397p. — (Penguin education) (Penguin modern sociology). — *bibl p381-384*

STINCHCOMBE, Arthur L.
Stratification and organization : selected papers / Arthur L. Stinchcombe. — Cambridge : Cambridge University Press in collaboration with Maison des Sciences del' Homme, Paris, 1986. — viii,381p. — (Studies in rationality and social change). — *Includes bibliography: p364-372.* — *Includes index*

SOCIAL CLASSES — Case studies

SIDER, Gerald M.
Culture and class in anthropology and history : a Newfoundland illustration / Gerald M. Sider. — Cambridge : Cambridge University Press, 1986. — xi, 205p, [8] p of plates. — (Cambridge studies in social anthropology ; 60) . — *Bibliography: p.195-200*

SOCIAL CLASSES — Health and hygiene — Great Britain — Bibliography

BEST, K. W.
Selected references on social class and health / compiled by K. W. Best. — London : Department of Health and Social Security Library, 1977. — 4p. — (Bibliography series / Department of Health and Social Security Library ; no.B73)

SOCIAL CLASSES — History — Addresses, essays, lectures

Proletarians and protest : the roots of class formation in an industrializing world / edited by Michael Hanagan and Charles Stephenson. — New York : Greenwood Press, 1986. — viii, 250 p.. — (Contributions in labor studies ; no. 17). — *Includes index.* — *Bibliography: p. [231]-241*

SOCIAL CLASSES — Australia — History

MACINTYRE, Stuart
Winners and losers : the pursuit of social justice in Australian history / Stuart Macintyre. — Sydney ; London : Allen & Unwin, 1985. — xxii,174p. — *Includes index*

SOCIAL CLASSES — Bangladesh

JAHANGIR, B. K.
Rural society, power structure and class practice / B. K. Jahangir. — Dacca : Centre for Social Studies, 1982. — 165p. — *Bibliography: p158-165*

SOCIAL CLASSES — Canada

FORCESE, Dennis
The Canadian class structure / Dennis Forcese. — 3rd ed. — Toronto : McGraw-Hill Ryerson, [1986]. — xi,202p. — (McGraw-Hill Ryerson Series in Canadian Sociology). — *Bibliography: p185-194*

SOCIAL CLASSES — China — History

LIPPIT, Victor D
The economic development of China / by Victor D. Lippit. — Armonk, N.Y. : M.E. Sharpe, c1987. — p. cm. — *Includes bibliographies and index*

SOCIAL CLASSES — Egypt

ANSARI, Hamied
Egypt, the stalled society / Hamied Ansari. — Albany : State University of New York Press, c1986. — xiv, 308 p.. — (SUNY series in Near Eastern studies). — *Includes indexes.* — *Bibliography: p. 291-295*

SOCIAL CLASSES — England — Oldham, Lancs. — History

FOSTER, John, 1940-
Class struggle and the Industrial Revolution : early industrial capitalism in three English towns / John Foster ; with a foreword by E.J. Hobsbawm. — London : Weidenfeld and Nicolson, 1974. — xiii,346p. — *Bibliography: p.337-338.* — *Includes index*

SOCIAL CLASSES — England — West Midlands

CASHMORE, Ernest
The logic of racism / E. Ellis Cashmore. — London : Allen & Unwin, 1987. — vii,263p. — *Bibliography: p260-261.* — *Includes index*

SOCIAL CLASSES — Europe

The Social basis of European fascist movements / edited by Detlef Mühlberger. — London : Croom Helm, c1987. — [384]p. — *Includes index*

SOCIAL CLASSES — Europe, Eastern

MATEJKO, Alexander J
Comparative work systems : ideologies and reality in Eastern Europe / Alexander J. Matejko. — New York : Praeger, 1985. — p. cm. — *Includes index.* — *Bibliography: p*

SOCIAL CLASSES — Fiji

TOREN, Christina Camden
Symbolic space and the construction of hierarchy : an anthropological and cognitive development study in a Fijian village / by Christina Toren. — 523 leaves. — *PhD (Arts) 1986 LSE.* — *Leaves 432-512 are appendices*

SOCIAL CLASSES — France — Nomenclature

SEYS, Baudouin
De l'ancien code à la nouvelle nomenclature des catégories socioprofessionnelles : étude méthodologique / Baudouin Seys. — Paris : I.N.S.E.E., 1986. — 203p. — (Archives et documents / Institut national de la statistique et des études économiques ; no.156). — *Bibliography: p.202-203*

SOCIAL CLASSES — France — Statistics

DESPLANQUES, Guy
Cycle de vie et milieu social / Guy Desplanques. — Paris : INSEE, 1987. — 272p. — (Les collections de l'INSEE. Série D. Démographie et emploi ; no.117)

SOCIAL CLASSES — France — Paris region

PINÇON-CHARLOT, Monique
Ségrégation urbaine : classes sociales et équipements collectifs en région parisienne / Monique Pinçon-Charlot, Edmond Preteceille, Paul Rendu. — Paris : Editions Anthropos, 1986. — 291p. — *Bibliography: p[230]-238*

SOCIAL CLASSES — Germany — History

SPEIER, Hans
[Angestellten vor dem Nationalsozialismus. English]. German white-collar workers and the rise of Hitler / Hans Speier. — New Haven : Yale University Press, c1986. — xxv, 208 p.. — *Translation of: Die Angestellten vor dem Nationalsozialismus.* — *Includes index.* — *Bibliography: p. 191-203*

SOCIAL CLASSES — Ghana

KONINGS, Piet
The State and rural class formation in Ghana : a comparative analysis / Piet Konings. — London : KPI, 1986. — xvi,391p. — *Bibliography: p356-377*

SOCIAL CLASSES — Great Britain

LABOUR RESEARCH DEPARTMENT
The widening gap : rich and poor today. — London : Labour Research Department, 1987. — 44p

SOCIAL CLASSES — Great Britain
continuation

LE GRAND, Julian
The middle classes and the welfare state / Julian Le Grand and David Winter. — London : Welfare State Programme. Suntory-Toyota International Centre for Economics and Related Disciplines, 1987. — 52p. — (Discussion paper / Welfare State Programme. Suntory-Toyota International Centre for Economics and Related Disciplines ; no.14). — *Bibliography: p51-52*

WORKERS POWER
The class struggle and the elections : a workers' manifesto. — London : Workers Power, 1987. — 58p

SOCIAL CLASSES — Great Britain — Case studies

HILL, Malcolm
Sharing child care in early parenthood / Malcolm Hill. — London : Routledge & Kegan Paul, 1987. — [360]p. — *Includes bibliography and index*

SOCIAL CLASSES — Guyana

JEFFREY, Henry B.
Guyana : politics, economics and society : beyond the Burnham era / Henry B. Jeffrey and Colin Baber. — Boulder, Colo. : L. Rienner Publishers, 1986. — viii, 203p. — (Marxist regimes series). — *Includes index. — Bibliography: p [187]-191*

SOCIAL CLASSES — India

SHARMA, A. K.
Social inequality and demographic processes / A.K. Sharma. — Delhi, India : Mittal Publications : Distributed by Mittal Publishers' Distributors, 1985. — x, 170 p.. — *Includes bibliographies and index*

SOCIAL CLASSES — India — Congresses

Social stratification in India / edited by K.L. Sharma. — New Delhi : Manohar, 1986. — xxvi, 343 p.. — *Summary: Papers presented at a workshop, organized by the Northern Regional Centre of the Indian Council of Social Science Research and Jawaharlal Nehru University, 1983. — Includes bibliographies and index*

SOCIAL CLASSES — India — West Bengal

BOSE, P. K.
Classes and class relations among tribals of Bengal / Pradip Kumar Bose. — 1st ed. — Delhi : Ajanta Publications : Distributors, Ajanta Books International, 1985. — viii, 132 p.. — *Includes index. — Bibliography: p. [126]-128*

SOCIAL CLASSES — Iraq

BATATU, Hanna
The old social classes and the revolutionary movements of Iraq : a study of Iraq's old landed and commercial classes and of its Communists, Ba'thists, and Free Officers / Hanna Batatu. — Princeton, N.J. : Princeton University Press, c1978. — xxiv, 1283 p., [8] leaves of plates. — (Princeton studies on the Near East). — *Includes indexes. — Bibliography: p. [1231]-1252*

SOCIAL CLASSES — Malaya

SUNDARAM, Jomo Kwame
A question of class : capital, the state and uneven development in Malaya / Jomo Kwame Sundaram. — Singapore : Oxford University Press, 1986. — xxiii,360p. — (East Asian Social Science Monographs). — *Bibliography: p331-354*

SOCIAL CLASSES — Nicaragua

COLBURN, Forrest D
Post-revolutionary Nicaragua : state, class, and the dilemmas of agrarian policy / Forrest D. Colburn. — Berkeley : University of California Press, c1986. — xi, 145p. — *Includes index. — Bibliography: p.133-138*

SOCIAL CLASSES — Nigeria, Northern

LUBECK, Paul M.
Islam and urban labor in Northern Nigeria : the making of a Muslim working class / Paul M. Lubeck. — Cambridge : Cambridge Univesity Press, 1986. — [368]p. — (African studies series ; 52). — *Includes bibliography and index*

SOCIAL CLASSES — Poland

Social stratification in Poland : eight empirical studies / edited by Kazimierz M. Słomczyński and Tadeusz K. Krauze ; with a foreword by Gerhard Lenski. — Armonk, N.Y. : M.E. Sharpe, c1986. — p. cm. — "Published simulanteously as International journal of sociology, vol. XVI, no. 1-2"--Verso of t.p. — Contents: Introduction : the context of recent Polish research on social stratification / Kazimierz M. Słomczyński and Tadeusz K. Krauze -- Social inequality and social mobility / Michael Pohoski -- Changes in social structure and its popular perception / Krystyna Janicka -- The attainment of occupation status / Kazimierz M. Słomczyński -- Dichotomous class images and worker' radicalism / Wojciech Zaborowski -- The subjective evaluation of social status / Kazimierz M. Słomvczyńki -- The prestige of education / Zbigniew Sawinski -- Value systems among occupational groups/ Maria Misztal -- Social mobility / Tadeusz K. Krauze and Kazimierz M. Słomczyński

SOCIAL CLASSES — Russian S.F.S.R — Moscow — History

BRADLEY, Joseph
Muzhik and Muscovite : urbanization in late imperial Russia / Joseph Bradley. — Berkeley ; London : University of California Press, c1985. — xvi, 422p. — *Based on the author's doctoral thesis. — Includes index. — Bibliography: p.377-405*

SOCIAL CLASSES — Scotland

WORMALD, Jenny
Lords and men in Scotland : bonds of manrent, 1442-1603 / Jenny Wormald. — Edinburgh : John Donald, 1985. — ix,475p

SOCIAL CLASSES — Southern States

BLOOM, Jack M
Class, race, and the Civil Rights Movement / Jack M. Bloom. — Bloomington : Indiana University Press, c1987. — x, 267 p.. — (Blacks in the diaspora). — *Includes index. — Bibliography: p. [225]-237*

SOCIAL CLASSES — Soviet Union

SELUNSKAIA, V. M.
Sotsial'naia struktura Sovetskogo obshchestva : istoriia i sovremennost' / V. M. Selunskaia. — Moskva : Politizdat, 1987. — 286p

SOCIAL CLASSES — Spain — Barcelona — History

AMELANG, James S.
Honored citizens of Barcelona : patrician culture and class relations, 1490-1714 / James S. Amelang. — Princeton, N.J. : Princeton University Press, c1986. — xxvi, 259p. — *Includes index. — Bibliography: p.223-252*

SOCIAL CLASSES — Spain — Catalonia

Conflict in Catalonia : images of an urban society / edited by Gary W. McDonogh. — Gainesville : University Presses of Florida, University of Florida Press, c1986. — 102 p.. — (University of Florida monographs. Social sciences ; no. 71). — *Includes bibliographies and index*

SOCIAL CLASSES — United States

BENSMAN, Joseph
American society : the welfare state & beyond / Joseph Bensman & Arthur J. Vidich. — Rev. — South Hadley, Mass. : Bergin & Garvey Publishers, 1986. — p. cm. — : *Previous ed. published as: The new American society. 1971. — Includes index. — Bibliography: p*

SOCIAL CLASSES — United States — History

FORM, William Humbert
Divided we stand : working-class stratification in America / William Form. — Urbana : University of Illinois Press, c1985. — p. cm. — *Includes index. — Bibliography: p*

SOCIAL CLASSES — Uzbek S.S.R. — History

MUKMINOVA, R. G.
Sotsial'naia differentsiatsiia naseleniia gorodov Uzbekistana, konets XV-XVI v. / R. G. Mukminova. — Tashkent : "Fan" Uzbekskoi SSR, 1985. — 135p

SOCIAL CONDITIONS — Burkina Faso — Statistics

Statistiques Sociales. — Ouagadougou : Institut National de la Statistique et de la Démographie, 1984. — 108p

SOCIAL CONFLICT

FOLEY, Duncan K
Money, accumulation, and crisis / Duncan K. Foley. — Chur, Switzerland ; New York : Harwood Academic Publishers, c1986. — 60 p.. — (Fundamentals of pure and applied economics ; vol. 2Marxian economics section). — *Includes index. — Bibliography: p. 55-58*

ROEMER, John E
Value, exploitation, and class / John E. Roemer. — Chur, Switzerland ; New York : Horwood Academic Publishers, c1986. — p. cm. — (Fundamentals of pure and applied economics ; vol. 4. Marxian economics section). — *Includes index. — Bibliography: p*

SHIPLEY, Peter
Patterns of protest in Western Europe / Peter Shipley. — London : Institute for the Study of Conflict, 1986. — 23p. — (Conflict studies ; no.189)

SOCIAL CONFLICT — Economic aspects

DICKHUT, Willi
Krisen und Klassenkampf / Willi Dickhut. — Stuttgart : Verlag Neuer Weg, 1985. — 292p

SOCIAL CONFLICT — Religious aspects — Christianity

KEE, Alistair
Domination or liberation : the place of religion in social conflict / Alistair Kee. — London : SCM, 1986. — [144]p

SOCIAL CONFLICT — Arab countries

Forbidden agendas : intolerance and defiance in the Middle East / selected and introduced by Jon Rothschild. — London : Al Saqi Books ; London : Zed Press [distributor], 1984. — 400p . — " *The articles in this anthology were first published in the journal 'Khamsin' 1976-83"*

SOCIAL CONFLICT — Denmark

MØLLER, Iver Hornemann
Klassekamp og sociallovgivning 1850-1970 / Iver Hornemann Møller. — København : Socialistiske Økonomers Forlag, 1981. — 296p

PETERSEN, Jens Peter Østerby
Arbeijderne og krisen : forholdet mellem AOF's arbejderuddannelse, reformismen og arbejderbevidstheden i 30 'erne / Jens Peter Østerby Petersen & Jens Skovholm. — København : Litteratur & Samfund, 1978. — 240p. — *Bibliography: p237-239*

SOCIAL CONFLICT — Mexico — Morelos — Case studies

ROMANUCCI-ROSS, Lola
Conflict, violence, and morality in a Mexican village / Lola Romanucci-Ross ; with a new afterword. — University of Chicago Press ed. — Chicago : University of Chicago Press, 1986. — ix, 222 p.. — : *Reprint. Originally published: Palo Alto, Calif. : National Press Books, 1973. — Bibliography: p. 218-222*

SOCIAL CONFLICT — Near East
Forbidden agendas : intolerance and defiance in the Middle East / selected and introduced by Jon Rothschild. — London : Al Saqi Books ; London : Zed Press [distributor], 1984. — 400p . — " The articles in this anthology were first published in the journal 'Khamsin' 1976-83"

SOCIAL CONFLICT — Norway
Styrk fagbevegelsens kampkraft : faglig studiebok fra AKP (m-l). — Oslo : Forlaget Oktober, 1975. — 205p

SOCIAL CONFLICT — Spain — Basque Provinces
Conflicto en Euskadi / Juan J. Linz con la colaboración de Manuel Gómez-Reino, Francisco Andrés Orizo y Darío Vila. — Madrid : Espasa Calpe, 1986. — 699p

SOCIAL CONFLICT — Spain — Cantabria
ORTIZ REAL, Javier
Cantabria en el siglo XV : aproximación al estudio de los conflictos sociales / Javier Ortiz Real. — Santander : Tantín, 1985. — 212p. — *Bibliography: p207-212*

SOCIAL CONFLICT — Spain — Catalonia
Conflict in Catalonia : images of an urban society / edited by Gary W. McDonogh. — Gainesville : University Presses of Florida, University of Florida Press, c1986. — 102 p.. — (University of Florida monographs. Social sciences ; no. 71). — *Includes bibliographies and index*

SOCIAL CONFLICT — Spain — Madrid — History — 20th century
JULIÁ DÍAZ, Santos
Madrid, 1931-1934 : de la fiesta popular a la lucha de clases / por Santos Juliá Díaz. — Madrid : Siglo Veintiuno, 1984. — 509p

SOCIAL CONFLICT — Spain — Zaragoza
PINILLA NAVARRO, Vicente
Conflictividad social y revuelta politica en Zaragoza (1854-1856) / Vicente Pinilla Navarro. — Zaragoza : Diputación General de Aragon, 1985. — 244p. — *Bibliography: p234-244*

SOCIAL CONTRACT
BRENNAN, Geoffrey
The reason of rules : constitutional political economy / Geoffrey Brennan [and] James M. Buchanan. — Cambridge : Cambridge University Press, 1985. — xiv,153p

LESSNOFF, Michael H.
Social contract / Michael Lessnoff. — London : Macmillan, 1986. — x,178p. — (Issues in political theory). — *Bibliography: p169-173. — Includes index*

ROUSSEAU, Jean Jacques
[Du contrat social. English]. Of the social contract, or, Principles of political right & Discourse on political economy / by Jean-Jacques Rousseau ; translated with an introductory essay and annotations by Charles M. Sherover. — 1st ed. — New York : Harper & Row, c1984. — p. cm. — "Perennial Library.". — Translation of: Du contrat social, and Discours sur l'oeconomie politique. — *Includes bibliographical references and index*

SOCIAL CONTROL
BAYLEY, David H
Social control and political change / by David H. Bayley. — [Princeton, N.J.] : Center of International Studies, Woodrow Wilson School of Public and International Affairs, Princeton University, c1985. — 135 p.. — (Research monograph / Center for International Studies, Woodrow Wilson School of Public and International Affairs ; no. 49). — "December 1985.". — *Includes bibliographical references*

DUSSICH, John P. J.
New perspectives in control theory : social coping of youth under supervision / John P. J. Dussich. — Köln : Carl Heymanns Verlag, c1985. — 306,liip. — (Interdisziplinäre Beiträge zur kriminologischen Forschung.; Band 11). — Text in English, with German summary. — *Bibliography: p281-306*

LEWIS, Dan A
Fear of crime : incivility and the production of a social problem / Dan A. Lewis and Greta Salem. — New Brunswick, U.S.A. : Transaction Books, c1986. — p. cm. — *Includes index. — Bibliography: p*

PFOHL, Stephen J
Images of deviance and social control : a sociological history / Stephen J. Pfohl. — New York : McGraw-Hill, c1985. — xiii, 402 p.. — Cover title: Images of deviance & social control. — *Includes bibliographies and index*

ROSENBAUM, Alan S
Coercion and autonomy : philosophical foundations, issues, and practices / Alan S. Rosenbaum. — New York : Greenwood Press, 1986. — xii, 196 p.. — (Contributions in philosophy ; no. 31). — *Includes index. — Bibliography: p. [187]-188*

SAXONHOUSE, Arlene W
Women in the history of political thought : ancient Greece to Machiavelli / Arlene W. Saxonhouse. — New York ; Eastbourne : Praeger, 1985. — xii, 210p. — (Women and politics series). — *Includes index. — Bibliography: p.199-204*

Women, violence and social control / edited by Jalna Hanmer and Mary Maynard. — Basingstoke : Macmillan, 1987. — xi,213p. — (Explorations in sociology ; 23). — Conference proceedings. — *Bibliography: p193-209. — Includes index*

SOCIAL CREDIT
COONEY, Anthony
Social credit politics / Anthony Cooney. — Liverpool : Gild of St. George, 1985. — 64p. — *Bibliography: p62-64*

SOCIAL DARWINISM
HOLBROOK, David
Evolution and the humanities / David Holbrook. — Aldershot : Gower, c1987. — [230]p. — (Avebury series in philosophy). — *Includes bibliography and index*

SOCIAL DEMOCRATIC PARTY
EVANS, Roy
Racial justice : an SDP approach to equal opportunities / Roy Evans and Dr Francis Bridger. — London : SDP Open Forum Committee, 1985. — 38p. — (SDP Open Forum ; no.12)

HOWE, Geoffrey Sir
Partnership for paralysis : Liberal and SDP policies examined / Sir Geoffrey Howe. — London : Conservative Political Centre, 1987. — 14p

SDP/LIBERAL ALLIANCE
The essential investment : Liberal/SDP Alliance Policies for Education. — Hebden Bridge : Hebden Royd Publications, [1987]. — [12 leaves]

SDP-LIBERAL ALLIANCE
People in power : why constitutional reform matters to everyone in Britain. — Hebden Bridge : Liberal Party ; London : Social Democratic Party, 1986. — 16p

SOCIAL DEMOCRATIC PARTY
How to get the money in!. — London : Peter Luff, 1983. — 51p

SOCIAL DEMOCRATIC PARTY
The only way to a fairer Britain. — London : SDP, 1985. — [86p]

SUTHERLAND, H.
Modelling the SDP tax/benefit scheme / Holly Sutherland. — [London : London School of Economics and Political Science], 1986. — 25p. — (Taxation, incentives and the distribution of income ; no.101). — Economic and Social Research Council programme. — *Bibliographical references: p25*

SOCIAL DEMOCRATIC PARTY. SDP Liberal Alliance See SDP Liberal Alliance

SOCIAL ENVIRONMENT — United States
The elderly : victims and deviants / edited by Carl D. Chambers ... [et al.]. — Athens, Ohio : Ohio University Press, 1987. — p. cm. — *Includes bibliographies*

SOCIAL ETHICS
ALMOND, Brenda
Moral concerns / Brenda Almond. — Atlantic Highlands, NJ : Humanities Press International, 1987. — xiii, 152p

BOOKCHIN, Murray
The modern crisis / Murray Bookchin. — Philadelphia : New Society Publishers, 1986. — xi,167p. — Published in cooperation with Institute for Social Ecology, Rochester, Vermont

OLDENQUIST, Andrew
The non-suicidal society / Andrew Oldenquist. — Bloomington : Indiana University Press, c1986. — p. cm. — *Includes index. — Bibliography: p*

WEIL, Simone
The need for roots : prelude to a declaration of duties towards mankind / Simone Weil ; [translated from the French by A. F. Wills] ; preface by T. S. Eliot. — Ark ed. — London : Routledge and Kegan Paul, 1987. — xv,288p. — Translation of: L'Enracinement. — First French edition: 1949; this translation originally published: 1952

SOCIAL ETHICS — Addresses, essays, lectures
New directions in ethics : the challenge of applied ethics / edited by Joseph P. MeMarco, Richard M. Fox. — New York ; London : Routledge & Kegan Paul, 1986. — xi, 335p. — *Includes bibliographical references*

NIEBUHR, Reinhold
The essential Reinhold Niebuhr : selected essays and addresses / edited and introduced by Robert McAfee Brown. — New Haven : Yale University Press, c1986. — p. cm. — *Includes index*

SOCIAL EVOLUTION
HALLPIKE, C. R.
The principles of social evolution / C.R. Hallpike. — Oxford : Clarendon, 1986. — xi,412p. — *Bibliography: p379-402. — Includes index*

RITCHEY, Thomas P.
Towards a theory of non-linear social evolution / Thomas P. Ritchey. — Malmö : Liber, 1983. — 164p. — *Bibliography: p156-164*

SOCIAL EVOLUTION — Congresses
The Burden of being civilized : an anthropological perspective on the discontents of civilization / Miles Richardson and Malcolm C. Webb, editors. — Athens : University of Georgia Press, c1986. — x, 156 p.. — (Southern Anthropological Society proceedings ; no. 18). — Includes papers presented at a symposium, held in Baton Rouge, Feb. 12-14, 1983, as part of the annual meeting of the Southern Anthropological Society. — *Includes index. — Bibliography: p. [127]-145*

SOCIAL EXCHANGE
HOLLANDER, Edwin Paul
Leadership dynamics : a practical guide to effective relationships / Edwin P. Hollander. — New York : Free Press, c1978. — xii, 212 p.. — *Includes indexes. — Bibliography: p. 185-201*

SOCIAL GROUP WORK
BROWN, Allan
Groupwork / Allan Brown. — 2nd ed. — Aldershot : Gower, c1986. — [110]p. — (Community care practice handbooks ; 2). — Previous ed.: London : Heinemann Education, 1979. — *Includes bibliography and index*

SOCIAL GROUP WORK *continuation*

HEAP, Ken
The practice of social work with groups : a systematic approach / Ken Heap. — London : Allen & Unwin, 1985. — xiii,208p. — (National Institute social services library ; no.49). — *Bibliography: p193-204. — Includes index*

SOCIAL GROUP WORK — Great Britain

A Community social worker's handbook / Roger Hadley ... [et al.]. — London : Tavistock, 1987. — [224]p. — *Includes bibliography and index*

ELY, Peter
Social work in a multi-racial society / Peter Ely and David Denney. — Aldershot : Gower, c1987. — vi,231p. — (Issues in social work). — *Bibliography: p201-218. — Includes index*

HENDERSON, Paul, 1942-
Skills in neighbourhood work / Paul Henderson, David N. Thomas. — 2nd ed. — London : Allen & Unwin, 1987. — xviii,358p. — *Previous ed.: 1980. — Bibliography : p334-346. — Includes index*

What a way to run a railroad : an analysis of radical failure / by Charles Landry ... [et al.]. — London : Comedia, 1985. — vi,101p

SOCIAL GROUP WORK — Great Britain — Abstracts

TAYLOR, Marilyn
Community work in the U.K. 1982-6 : a review and digest of abstracts / by Marilyn Taylor and Frances Presley ; edited by Gabriel Chanan. — London : Library Association in association with Caboste Gulbenkian Foundation, c1987. — 148p. — *Co-published with Community Projects Foundation*

SOCIAL GROUPS

ANDORKA, Rudolf
A társadalmi mobilitás változásai Magyarországon / Andorka Rudolf. — Budapest : Gondslat, 1982. — 326p. — *References: p303-326*

COHEN, Abner
Two-dimensional man : an essay on the anthropology of power and symbolism in complex society / Abner Cohen. — London : Routledge and Kegan Paul, 1974. — xii,156p. — *Bibliography: p.139-148. — Includes index*

Contact and conflict in intergroup encounters / edited by Miles Hewstone and Rupert Brown. — Oxford : Basil Blackwell, 1986. — xiii,231p. — (Social psychology and society). — *Bibliography: p196-221 Includes index*

Theories of group behavior / edited by Brian Mullen and George R. Goethals. — New York : Springer-Verlag, c1987. — xiii, 243 p.. — (Springer series in social psychology). — *Includes bibliographies and index*

THIBAUT, John W
The social psychology of groups / John W. Thibaut and Harold H. Kelley ; with a new introduction by the authors. — New Brunswick, U.S.A. : Transaction Books, 1985. — p. cm. — : *Reprint. Originally published: New York : Wiley, 1959. — Includes index. — Bibliography: p*

TURNER, John C.
Rediscovering the social group : a self-categorization theory / John C. Turner with Michael A. Hogg ... (et al.). — Oxford : Basil Blackwell, 1987. — x,239p. — *Bibliography: p209-232. — Includes index*

SOCIAL HISTORY

Affari sociali internazionali. — Milan : Franco Angeli Editore, 1973-. — *Quarterly.*

HOMANS, George Caspar
Certainties and doubts : collected papers, 1962-1985 / George Caspar Homans. — New Brunswick, N.J. : Transaction Books, c1987. — p. cm. — *Bibliography: p*

Sistema : revista de ciencias sociales. — Madrid : Agisa, 1982-. — *Irregular*

Social movements in an organization society : collected essays / edited by Mayer N. Zald and John D. McCarthy. — New Brunswick, N.J., U.S.A. : Transaction Books, c1986. — p. cm. — *Includes index. — Bibliography: p*

Women, religion, and social change / edited by Yvonne Yazbeck Haddad and Ellison Banks Findly. — Albany : State University of New York Press, c1985. — xxi, 508 p.. — *Proceedings of the Hartford Symposium on Women, Religion, and Social Change. — Includes bibliographies and index*

SOCIAL HISTORY — Medieval, 500-1500

GIVEN-WILSON, Chris
The English nobility in the late Middle Ages : the fourteenth-century political community / Chris Given-Wilson. — London : Routledge and Kegan Paul, 1987. — xxii,222p

MOLLAT, Michel
[Pauvres au Moyen Age. English]. The poor in the Middle Ages : an essay in social history / Michel Mollat ; translated by Arthur Goldhammer. — New Haven : Yale University Press, c1986. — p. cm. — *Translation of: Les Pauvres au Moyen Age. — Includes index. — Bibliography: p*

SOCIAL HISTORY — Modern, 1500-

AMELANG, James S.
Honored citizens of Barcelona : patrician culture and class relations, 1490-1714 / James S. Amelang. — Princeton, N.J. : Princeton University Press, c1986. — xxvi, 259p. — *Includes index. — Bibliography: p.223-252*

POLANYI, Karl
The great transformation / Karl Polanyi ; foreword by Robert M. MacIver. — Boston : Beacon Press, 1957. — xii,315p

SOCIAL HISTORY — 16th century

Handbuch der Europäischen Wirtschafts- und Sozialgeschichte / herausgegeben von Wolfram Fischer...[et al.]. — Stuttgart : Klett-Cotta Bd.3: Europäische Wirtschafts- und Sozialgeschichte vom ausgehenden Mittelalter bis zur Mitte des 17. Jahrhunderts / unter Mitarbeit von Norbert Angermann...[et al.] ; herausgegeben von Hermann Kellenbenz. — 1986. — xxvi,1326p

SOCIAL HISTORY — 1945-

ALMOND, Gabriel Abraham
The civic culture : political attitudes and democracy in five nations / by Gabriel A. Almond and Sidney Verba. — Princeton, N.J. : Princeton University Press, 1963. — xi, 562 p. — *Bibliographical footnotes*

SOCIAL HISTORY — 1960-1970

LEE, Martin A
Acid dreams : the CIA, LSD, and the sixties rebellion / by Martin A. Lee and Bruce Shlain. — 1st Grove Press ed. — New York : Grove Press, 1986. — xxi, 343p, [12] p of plates. — *Includes index. — Bibliography: p.320-329*

SOCIAL INDICATORS — Colombia

COLOMBIA. Unidad de Desarrollo Regional y Urbano
Estudio sobre algunos indicadores socioeconómicos para centros urbanos con población superior a 20.000 habitantes. — Bogotá : the Unidad, 1973. — 54leaves. — (Documento / Departamento Nacional de Planeación, Unidad de Desarrollo Regional y Urbano, División de Estudios Regionales ; 73/3)

SOCIAL INDICATORS — Indonesia

Indikator kesejahteraan rakyat = Welfare indicators / Biro Pusat Statistik, Indonesia. — Jakarta : Biro Pusat Statistik, Indonesia, 1983-

SOCIAL INDICATORS — Japan

JAPAN. Statistics Bureau
Statistical indicators on social life. — [Tokyo] : the Bureau, 1984. — xiii,621p. — *Text in Japanese and English*

SOCIAL INDICATORS — Scandinavia

Level of living and inequality in the Nordic countries : a comparative analysis of the Nordic comprehensive surveys. — Stockholm : Nordic Council and the Nordic Statistical Secretariat, 1984. — 226p. — *At head of title: Denmark, Finland, Norway, Sweden. — Includes bibliographical references*

SOCIAL INSTITUTIONS — Addresses, essays, lectures

Macroeconomic conflict and social institutions / edited by Shlomo Maital, Irwin Lipnowski. — Cambridge, Mass. : Ballinger Pub. Co., 1985. — p. cm. — *Chiefly papers originating from a session on "Income policy as a social institution," at the American Economic Association's 95th Annual Meeting in New York, Dec. 28-30, 1982. — Includes bibliographies and index*

SOCIAL INSTITUTIONS — Congresses

The Social fabric : dimensions and issues / [edited] by James F. Short, Jr. — Beverly Hills, Calif. : Sage Publications, c1986. — p. cm. — (American Sociological Association presidential series). — *Based on papers presented at the 79th Annual Meeting of the American Sociological Association, held in San Antonio, Tex., Aug. 27-31, 1984. — Includes bibliographies and index*

SOCIAL INSTITUTIONS — Pennsylvania — Hazleton

AURAND, Harold W
Population change and social continuity : ten years in a coal town / Harold W. Aurand. — Selinsgrove [Pa.] : Susquehanna University Press ; London : Associated University Presses, c1986. — 139 p. — *Includes index. — Bibliography: p. 131-134*

SOCIAL INTEGRATION — Russian S.F.S.R — Moscow — History

BRADLEY, Joseph
Muzhik and Muscovite : urbanization in late imperial Russia / Joseph Bradley. — Berkeley ; London : University of California Press, c1985. — xvi, 422p. — *Based on the author's doctoral thesis. — Includes index. — Bibliography: p.377-405*

SOCIAL INTERACTION

Contact and conflict in intergroup encounters / edited by Miles Hewstone and Rupert Brown. — Oxford : Basil Blackwell, 1986. — xiii,231p. — (Social psychology and society). — *Bibliography: p196-221 Includes index*

The dilemma of difference : a multidisciplinary view of stigma / edited by Stephen C. Ainlay, Gaylene Becker, and Lerita M. Coleman. — New York ; London : Plenum, c1986. — xxiii, 262p. — (Perspectives in social psychology). — *Includes bibliographical references and index*

Friendship and social interaction / edited by Valerian J. Derlega and Barbara A. Winstead. — New York : Springer-Verlag, c1986. — p. cm. — (Springer series in social psychology). — *Includes index. — Bibliography: p*

MCGRATH, Joseph Edward
Time and human interaction : toward a social psychology of time / by Joseph E. McGrath and Janice R. Kelly. — New York : Guilford Press, 1986. — p. cm. — (The Guilford social psychology series). — *Includes index. — Bibliography: p*

PIN, Emile Jean
The pleasure of your company : a socio-psychological analysis of modern sociability / Emile Jean Pin ; in collaboration with Jamie Turndorf. — New York : Praeger, 1985. — p. cm. — *Includes indexes. — Bibliography: p*

Theories of group behavior / edited by Brian Mullen and George R. Goethals. — New York : Springer-Verlag, c1987. — xiii, 243 p.. — (Springer series in social psychology). — *Includes bibliographies and index*

SOCIAL INTERACTION
continuation

TURNER, John C.
  Rediscovering the social group : a self-categorization theory / John C. Turner with Michael A. Hogg ... (et al.). — Oxford : Basil Blackwell, 1987. — x,239p.
  Bibliography: p209-232. — Includes index

VENTOLA, Eija
  The structure of social interaction : a systemic approach to the semiotics of service encounters / Eija Ventola. — London : Pinter, 1987. — [270]p. — (Open linguistics series). — *Includes bibliography and index*

SOCIAL INTERACTION — Congresses

Justice in social relations / edited by Hans Werner Bierhoff, Ronald L. Cohen, and Jerald Greenberg. — New York : Plenum Press, c1986. — xvi, 364 p.. — (Critical issues in social justice). — *Includes bibliographies and indexes*

SOCIAL INTERACTION — Great Britain

HEWITT, Roger
  White talk black talk : inter-racial friendship and communication amongst adolescents / Roger Hewitt. — Cambridge : Cambridge University Press, 1986. — [264]p. — (Comparative ethnic and race relations). — *Includes bibliography and index*

SOCIAL INTERACTION — Michigan — Detroit — Case studies

HUCKFELDT, R. Robert
  Politics in context : assimilation and conflict in urban neighborhoods / Robert Huckfeldt. — New York : Agathon Press, c1986. — viii, 191 p.. — *Includes index. — Bibliography: p. 177-185*

SOCIAL INTERACTION — New York (State) — Buffalo — Case studies

HUCKFELDT, R. Robert
  Politics in context : assimilation and conflict in urban neighborhoods / Robert Huckfeldt. — New York : Agathon Press, c1986. — viii, 191 p.. — *Includes index. — Bibliography: p. 177-185*

SOCIAL INTERACTION — Papua New Guinea

LEDERMAN, Rena
  What gifts engender : social relations and politics in Mendi, Highland Papua New Guinea / Rena Lederman. — Cambridge : Cambridge University Press, 1986. — [297]p. — *Includes bibliography and index*

SOCIAL INTERACTION — West Bank

SHINAR, Dov
  Palestinian voices : communication and nation building in the West Bank / Dov Shinar. — Boulder, Colo. : L. Rienner, 1987. — xi, 211 p. . — *Includes index. — Bibliography: p. 201-202*

SOCIAL JUSTICE

ARKES, Hadley
  First things : an inquiry into the first principles of morals and justice / Hadley Arkes. — Princeton, N.J. : Princeton University Press, c1986. — xii, 432p. — *Includes index*

Justice : views from the social sciences / edited by Ronald L. Cohen. — New York : Plenum Press, c1986. — p. cm. — (Critical issues in social justice). — *Includes bibliographies and index*

MOWER, A. Glenn
  International cooperation for social justice : global and regional protection of economic/social rights / A. Glenn Mower, Jr. — Westport, Conn. : Greenwood Press, c1985. — p. cm. — (Studies in human rights ; no. 6). — *Includes index. — Bibliography: p*

PRAKASH, Om
  Guided incomes policy / Om Prakash. — New Delhi : Sterling, c1983. — vi, 214 p.. — *Includes bibliographical references and index*

SOCIAL JUSTICE — Congresses

Justice in social relations / edited by Hans Werner Bierhoff, Ronald L. Cohen, and Jerald Greenberg. — New York : Plenum Press, c1986. — xvi, 364 p.. — (Critical issues in social justice). — *Includes bibliographies and indexes*

SOCIAL LEARNING

The dilemma of difference : a multidisciplinary view of stigma / edited by Stephen C. Ainlay, Gaylene Becker, and Lerita M. Coleman. — New York ; London : Plenum, c1986. — xxiii, 262p. — (Perspectives in social psychology). — *Includes bibliographical references and index*

SOCIAL LEARNING — Congresses

Questions on social explanation : Piagetian themes reconsidered / edited by Luigia Camaioni and Cláudia de Lemos. — Amsterdam ; Philadelphia : J. Benjamins Pub. Co., 1985. — 141 p.. — (Pragmatics & beyond ; VI:4). — *Selection of the papers presented at the international conference in honour of Jean Piaget, held in Rome, 9-10 Oct. 1981, and sponsored by Rome University. — Bibliography: p. [131]-141*

SOCIAL LEGISLATION

Dilemmas of law in the welfare state / edited by Gunther Teubner. — Berlin : W. de Gruyter, 1986. — viii,341p. — (Series A, Law / European University Institute ; 3). — *Includes bibliographies and index*

SOCIAL LEGISLATION — Canada — Addresses, essays, lectures

The regulation of quality : products, services, workplaces, and the environment / edited by Donald N. Dewees. — Toronto : Butterworths, 1983. — xvi,345p. — (Studies in law and economics)

SOCIAL LEGISLATION — European Economic Community countries

PHILIP, Christian
  Droit social européen / par Christian Philip. — Paris : Masson, 1985. — 218p

SOCIAL LEGISLATION — France — History

STONE, Judith F.
  The search for social peace : reform legislation in France, 1890-1914 / Judith F. Stone. — Albany : State University of New York Press, c1985. — p. cm

SOCIAL LEGISLATION — Near East

Social legislation in the contemporary Middle East / edited by Laurence O. Michalak, Jeswald W. Salacuse. — Berkeley : Institute of International Studies, University of California, Berkeley, 1986. — p. cm. — (Research series ; no. 64). — *Includes index*

SOCIAL MEDICINE

Applications of social science to clinical medicine and health policy / edited by Linda H. Aiken and David Mechanic. — New Brunswick, N.J. : Rutgers University Press, c1986. — p. cm. — *Sponsored by the Medical Sociology Section of the American Sociological Association*

CALNAN, Michael
  Health and illness : the lay perspective / Michael Calnan. — London : Tavistock, 1987. — [192]p. — *Includes index*

Concepts of health, illness and disease : a comparative perspective / edited by Caroline Currer and Meg Stacey. — Leamington Spa : Berg, 1986. — 1v.. — *Includes bibliography and index*

EASTHOPE, Gary
  Healers and alternative medicine : a sociological examination / Gary Easthope. — Aldershot : Gower, c1986. — [viii,151]p. — *Bibliography: p142-149. — Includes index*

HART, Nicky
  The sociology of health and medicine / by Nicky Hart. — Ormskirk : Causeway, 1985. — [80]p. — (Themes & perspectives in sociology). — *Includes bibliography and index*

ILLICH, Ivan
  Limits to medicine : medical nemesis, the expropriation of health / Ivan Illich. — [New ed.]. — London : Boyars, 1976. — viii,294p. — (Open forum). — *Previous ed.: published as 'Medical nemesis, the expropriation of health'. London : Calder and Boyars, 1975. — Includes index*

ILLICH, Ivan
  Limits to medicine : medical nemesis : the expropriation of health / Ivan Illich. — [New ed.]. — Harmondsworth : Penguin, 1977. — 296p. — (Pelican books). — *This ed. originally published: London : Boyars, 1976. — Includes index*

Sociology as applied to medicine / edited by Donald L. Patrick and Graham Scambler ; with a foreword by Margot Jefferys. — 2nd ed. — London : Bailliére Tindall, 1986. — xii,259p. — (Concise medical textbooks). — *Previous ed.: 1982. — Bibliography: p252-253. — Includes index*

TURNER, Bryan S.
  Medical power and social knowledge / Bryan S. Turner. — London : Sage, 1987. — [288]p. — *Includes bibliography and index*

SOCIAL MEDICINE — Addresses, essays, lectures

Medical science and the advancement of world health / edited by Robert Lanza. — New York : Praeger, 1985. — p. cm. — *Includes index*

SOCIAL MEDICINE — Bibliography

BIEGEL, David E
  Social networks and mental health : an annotated bibliography / David E. Biegel, Ellen McCardle, Susan Mendelson ; foreword by Stephen E. Goldston. — Beverly Hills, Calif. : Sage Publications, [1985]. — 391 p.. — *Includes indexes*

SOCIAL MEDICINE — China

KLEINMAN, Arthur
  Social origins of distress and disease : depression, neurasthenia, and pain in modern China / Arthur Kleinman. — New Haven : Yale University Press, c1986. — xii, 264 p.. — *Includes index. — Bibliography: p. 241-254*

SOCIAL MEDICINE — France

HERZLICH, Claudine
  Health and illness : a social psychological analysis / Claudine Herzlich ; translated [from the French] by Douglas Graham. — London : Academic Press [for] the European Association of Experimental Social Psychology, 1973. — xvi,159p. — (European monographs in social psychology ; 5). — *Translation of: 'Santé et maladie'. Paris : Mouton, 1970. — Bibliography: p.151-154. — Includes index*

SOCIAL MEDICINE — Great Britain

WHITEHEAD, Margaret
  The health divide : inequalities in health in the 1980's / Margaret Whitehead. — London : Health Education Council, 1987. — iv,119p

SOCIAL MEDICINE — Tanzania — History

TURSHEN, Meredeth
  The political ecology of disease in Tanzania / Meredeth Turshen. — New Brunswick, N.J. : Rutgers University Press, c1984. — xiv, 259 p., [2] leaves of plates. — *Includes index. — Bibliography: p. 211-239*

SOCIAL MEDICINE — United States

Applications of social science to clinical medicine and health policy / edited by Linda H. Aiken and David Mechanic. — New Brunswick, N.J. : Rutgers University Press, c1986. — p. cm. — *Sponsored by the Medical Sociology Section of the American Sociological Association*

SOCIAL MOBILITY
MACH, Bogdan W.
Social mobility and social structure / Bogdan W. Mach and Włodzimierz Wesołowski. — London : Routledge & Kegan Paul, 1986. — vi,118p. — (International library of sociology). — Translation of Ruchliwość a teoria struktury społecznej (Warsaw, 1982)

SOCIAL MOBILITY — Cross-cultural studies
KASARDA, John D
Status enhancement and fertility : reproductive responses to social mobility and educational opportunity / John D. Kasarda, John O.G. Billy, Kirsten West. — Orlando, Fla. : Academic Press, 1986. — xii, 266 p.. — (Studies in population). — Includes indexes. — Bibliography: p.216-250

SOCIAL MOBILITY — Canada
Ascription and achievement : studies in mobility and status attainment in Canada / by Monica Boyd ... [et al.]. — Ottawa, Canada : Carleton University Press ; Don Mills, Ont., Canada : Distributed by Oxford University Press Canada, c1985. — 539 p.. — (Carleton library series ; 133). — Includes bibliographies

SOCIAL MOBILITY — China — Case studies
LAMPTON, David M
Paths to power : elite mobility in contemporary China / by David M. Lampton with the assistance of Yeung Sai-cheung. — Ann Arbor : Center for Chinese Studies, Unversity of Michigan, 1985. — p. cm. — (Michigan monographs in Chinese studies ; no. 55). — Includes index. — Bibliography: p

SOCIAL MOBILITY — Great Britain
PAYNE, Geoff
Mobility and change in modern society / Geoff Payne. — Basingstoke : Macmillan, 1987. — xiii,174p. — Bibliography: p155-165. — Includes index

SOCIAL MOBILITY — Hungary
ANDORKA, Rudolf
A társadalmi mobilitás változásai Magyarországon / Andorka Rudolf. — Budapest : Gondslat, 1982. — 326p. — References: p303-326

SOCIAL MOBILITY — India
SURESH KUMAR
Social mobility in industrializing society / Suresh Kumar. — Jaipur : Rawat Publications, 1986. — x, 188 p.. — Includes bibliographies and index

SOCIAL MOBILITY — Poland
Social stratification in Poland : eight empirical studies / edited by Kazimierz M. Słomczyński and Tadeusz K. Krauze ; with a foreword by Gerhard Lenski. — Armonk, N.Y. : M.E. Sharpe, c1986. — p. cm. — "Published simulanteously as International journal of sociology, vol. XVI, no. 1-2"-Verso of t.p. — Contents: Introduction : the context of recent Polish research on social stratification / Kazimierz M. Słomczyński and Tadeusz K. Krauze -- Social inequality and social mobility / Michael Pohoski -- Changes in social structure and its popular perception / Krystyna Janicka -- The attainment of occupation status / Kazimierz M. Słomczyński -- Dichotomous class images and worker' radicalism / Wojciech Zaborowski -- The subjective evaluation of social status / Kazimierz M. Słomvczyński -- The prestige of education / Zbigniew Sawinski -- Value systems among occupational groups/ Maria Misztal -- Social mobility / Tadeusz K. Krauze and Kazimierz M. Słomczyński

SOCIAL MOBILITY — United States — Case studies
MACLEOD, Jay
Ain't no makin' it : leveled aspirations in a low-income neighbourhood / Jay MacLeod. — London : Tavistock, 1987. — [208]p. — Includes bibliography and index

SOCIAL MOVEMENTS
FOSS, Daniel A.
Beyond revolution : a new theory of social movements / Daniel A. Foss, Ralph W. Larkin ; introduction by Stanley Aronowitz. — South Hadley, MA : Bergin & Garvey, c1985. — p. cm. — (Critical perspectives in social theory)

LOO, Hans van der
Een wenkend perspectief? : nieuwe sociale bewegingen en culturele veranderingen / Hans van der Loo, Erik Snel en Bart van Steenbergen. — Amersfoort : De Horstink, 1984. — 247p. — (Strategieën). — Bibliography: p234-247

Mouvements populaires et conscience sociale XVIe-XIXe siècles : actes du Colloque de Paris, 24-26 mai 1984 / vecueillis et presentés par Jean Nicolas. — Paris : C.N.R.S. Université Paris VII, 1985. — 773p

Social movements in an organization society : collected essays / edited by Mayer N. Zald and John D. McCarthy. — New Brunswick, N.J., U.S.A. : Transaction Books, c1986. — p. cm. — Includes index. — Bibliography: p

SOCIAL MOVEMENTS — England — History — 19th century
DINWIDDY, J. R.
From Luddism to the First Reform Bill : reform in England 1810-1832 / J.R. Dinwiddy. — Oxford : Basil Blackwell, 1986. — [96]p. — (Historical Association studies). — Includes bibliography and index

SOCIAL MOVEMENTS — England — History — 20th century
LANSBURY, Coral
The old brown dog : women, workers, and vivisection in Edwardian England / Coral Lansbury. — Madison, Wis. : University of Wisconsin Press, 1985. — p. cm. — Includes index

SOCIAL MOVEMENTS — India — History
OSTERGAARD, Geoffrey
Nonviolent revolution in India / Geoffrey Ostergaard. — Sevagram : J.P. Amrit Kosh ; New Delhi : Gandhi Peace Foundation, c1985. — xxiii, 419 p.. — "Silver jubliee publication of the Gandhi Peace Foundation."--T.p. verso. — Includes index. — Bibliography: p. [370]-406

SOCIAL MOVEMENTS — Latin America
New social movements and the state in Latin America / David Slater (ed.). — [Amsterdam] : CEDLA ; Cinnaminson, N.J., U.S.A. : Distributed by FORIS Publications USA, c1985. — 295 p.. — (Latin American studies ; 29). — Papers from a CEDLA workshop held in Oct. 1983. — Includes bibliographies. — Contents: Social movements and a recasting of the political / D. Slater -- New social movements and the plurality of the social / E. Laclau -- Identity / T. Evers -- The pathways to encounter / L. Kowarick -- Base communities and urban social movements / N. Vink -- Urban social movements in Latin America / E. Henry -- The Peruvian state and regional crises / D. Slater -- The impact of sendero luminoso on regional and national politics in Peru / V. Gianotten ... [et al.] -- Social movements and revolution / J.L. Coraggio / Mobilisation without emancipation? / M. Molyneux -- Popular movement to "mass organization" / R. Reddock

SOCIAL MOVEMENTS — Netherlands
LOO, Hans van der
Een wenkend perspectief? : nieuwe sociale bewegingen en culturele veranderingen / Hans van der Loo, Erik Snel en Bart van Steenbergen. — Amersfoort : De Horstink, 1984. — 247p. — (Strategieën). — Bibliography: p234-247

SOCIAL MOVEMENTS — Peru
TOVAR, Teresa
Velasquismo y movimiento popular : otra historia prohibida / Teresa Tovar. — Lima : Centro de Estudios y Promoción del Desarrollo, 1985. — 399p. — Bibliography: p395-399

SOCIAL MOVEMENTS — Quebec (Province)
Old passions, new visions : social movements and political activisim in Quebec / edited by Marc Raboy ; translated by Robert Chodos. — Toronto, Ont. : Between the Lines, c1986. — 250 p.. — Includes bibliographies

SOCIAL MOVEMENTS — United States — History
EVANS, Sara M
Free spaces : the sources of democratic change in America / Sara M. Evans and Harry C. Boyte. — 1st ed. — New York : Harper & Row, c1986. — xi, 228 p.. — Includes index. — Bibliography: p. [203]-219

SOCIAL NORMS
BILMES, Jack
Discourse and behavior / Jack Bilmes. — New York : Plenum Press, c1986. — p. cm. — Includes index. — Bibliography: p

SOCIAL PARTICIPATION
ALMOND, Gabriel Abraham
The civic culture : political attitudes and democracy in five nations / by Gabriel A. Almond and Sidney Verba. — Princeton, N.J. : Princeton University Press, 1963. — xi, 562 p. — Bibliographical footnotes

CHEKKI, Dan A.
Participatory democracy in action : international profiles of community development / Dan A. Chekki. — Sahibabad : Vikas Publishing House PVT, [1979]. — xvi,306p. — Bibliography: p293-300

FLORO, George K.
Sociology for life : expanding circles of social participation through scholarship, community service, and teaching / George K. Floro. — Lanham : University Press of America, c1986. — xvii, 135 p.. — Includes index. — Bibliography: p. 125-128

SOCIAL PERCEPTION
BANDURA, Albert
Social foundations of thought and action : a social cognitive theory / Albert Bandura. — Englewood Cliffs, N.J. : Prentice-Hall, c1986. — p. cm. — (Prentice-Hall series in social learning theory). — Includes index. — Bibliography: p

Communication by children and adults : social, cognitive and strategic processes / edited by Howard E. Sypher, James L. Applegate. — Beverley Hills ; London : Sage, c1984. — 328p. — (Sage series In interpersonal communication ; v.5). — Includes index

The Development of social cognition / edited by John B. Pryor, Jeanne D. Day. — New York : Springer-Verlag, c1985. — xiv, 239p. — Includes bibliographies and indexes

LEWICKI, Paweł
Nonconscious social information processing / Pawel Lewicki. — Orlando : Academic Press, 1986. — p. cm. — Includes bibliographical references and index

SOCIAL PERCEPTION — Addresses, essays, lectures
Handbook of social cognition / edited by Robert S. Wyer, Jr., Thomas K. Srull. — Hillsdale, N.J. ; London : L. Erlbaum Associates, 1984. — 3v. — Includes bibliographies and indexes

SOCIAL PERCEPTION — Congresses
Experimental social dilemmas / Henk A.M. Wilke, Dave M. Messick, Christel G. Rutte, eds. — Frankfurt am Main ; New York : P. Lang, c1986. — vi, 234 p.. — (Psychologie des Entscheidungsverhaltens und des Konfliktes =Psychology of decisions and conflict ; Bd. 3). — Papers were presented at a conference held at the University of Groningen in the spring of 1984. — Includes bibliographies

SOCIAL PERCEPTION — Handbooks
Handbook of social cognition / edited by Robert S. Wyer, Jr., Thomas K. Srull. — Hillsdale, N.J. ; London : L. Erlbaum Associates, 1984. — 3v. — *Includes bibliographies and indexes*

SOCIAL PERCEPTION IN CHILDREN
Communication by children and adults : social, cognitive and strategic processes / edited by Howard E. Sypher, James L. Applegate. — Beverley Hills ; London : Sage, c1984. — 328p. — (Sage series In interpersonal communication ; v.5). — *Includes index*

SOCIAL POLICY
ABEL-SMITH, Brian
Future directions for social protection : a report on a European Symposium held in Athens, June 1986 / Brian Abel-Smith [and] Marios Raphael. — Athens : M.K. Publishers, 1986. — 68p

CHARLES, Susan
The economic approach to social policy / S.T. Charles, A.L. Webb. — Brighton : Wheatsheaf, 1986. — xii,247p. — *Includes index*

Critics of capitalism : Victorian reactions to 'political economy' / edited by Elisabeth Jay and Richard Jay. — Cambridge : Cambridge University Press, 1986. — vii,268p. — (Cambridge English prose texts). — *Bibliography: p262-268*

Econometric contributions to public policy : proceedings of a conference held by the International Economic Association at Urbino, Italy / edited by Richard Stone and William Peterson. — London : Macmillan, 1978. — [416]p

HELLER, Peter S.
Ageing and social expenditure in the major industrial countries, 1980-2025 / by Peter S. Heller, Richard Hemming and Peter W. Kohnert. — Washington, D.C. : The World Bank, 1986. — viii,76p. — (Occasional paper / International Monetary Fund ; no.47). — *Bibliographical references: p74-76*

HILL, Michael, 1937-
Analysing social policy / Michael Hill and Glen Bramley. — Oxford : Basil Blackwell, 1986. — [vii,256]p. — *Includes bibliography and index*

HINDESS, Barry
Freedom, equality and the market : arguments on social policy / Barry Hindess. — London : Tavistock, 1987. — 183p. — *Bibliography: p168-172.* — *Includes index*

MOSER, Caroline O. N.
A theory and methodology of gender planning : meeting women's practical and strategic needs / Caroline O. N. Moser and Caren Levy. — London : Bartlett School of Architecture and Planning Development Planning Unit, 1986. — 33p. — (DPU gender and planning working paper ; no.11). — *Bibliography: p32-33*

Public/private interplay in social protection : a comparative study / edited by Martin Rein and Lee Rainwater ; with Ellen Immergut, Michael O'Higgins, and Harald Russig. — Armonk, N.Y. : M.E. Sharpe, c1986. — viii, 215 p.. — (Comparative public policy analysis). — *Includes bibliographies*

SOCIAL POLICY — Congresses
Behavioral and social science : fifty years of discovery : in commemoration of the fiftieth anniversary of the "Ogburn report," Recent social trends in the United States / Neil J. Smelser and Dean R. Gerstein, editors ; Committee on Basic Research in the Behavioral and Social Sciences, Commission on Behavioral and Social Sciences and Education, National Research Council. — Washington, D.C. : National Academy Press, 1986. — x, 298 p.. — *Symposium held Nov. 29-30, 1983.* — *Includes bibliographies*

SOCIAL POLICY — Decision making
BULMER, Martin
Social science and social policy / Martin Bulmer with Keith G. Banting ... [et al.]. — London : Allen & Unwin, 1986. — [272]p. — (Contemporary social research series ; 12). — *Includes bibliography and index*

The Research relationship : practice and politics in social policy research / edited by G. Clare Wenger. — London : Allen & Unwin, 1987. — xix,228p. — (Contemporary social research series ; 15). — *Includes bibliographies and index*

SOCIAL POLICY — United States — Addresses, essays, lectures
Women, biology, and public policy / edited by Virginia Sapiro. — Beverly Hills, Calif. : Sage Publications, c1985. — p. cm. — (Sage yearbooks in women's policy studies ; v. 10). — *Contents: Biology and women's policy, a view from the biological sciences / Ruth Bleier -- Biology and women's policy, a view from the social sciences / Virginia Sapiro -- Male and female hormones / Marianne H. Whatley -- Fetal personhood and women's policy / Janet Gallagher -- Childbirth management and medical monopoly / Barbara Katz Rothman -- Occupational safety and health as a women's policy issue / Graham K. Wilson and Virginia Sapiro -- Older women / Laura Katz Olson -- The politics of a biosocial approach to crime / Susette M. Talarico -- Women's biology and the U.S. military / Judith Hicks Stiehm -- Women as "at risk" reproducers / Jane S. Jaquette and Kathleen A. Staudt*

SOCIAL PREDICTION — Mathematical models
Catastrophe or new society? : a Latin American world model / Amílcar O. Herrera ... [et al.]. — Ottawa : International Development Research Centre, c1976. — 108 p.. — "IDRC-064e.". — *Includes bibliographical references*

SOCIAL PROBLEMS
Options for youth / John Fethney (ed.) ; with a foreword by Philip Morgan. — [Chichester] : Angel, [c1985]. — 144p. — *Cover title*

SOCIAL PROBLEMS — Congresses
Redefining social problems / edited by Edward Seidman and Julian Rappaport. — New York : Plenum Press, c1986. — xxii, 311p. — (Perspectives in social psychology). — *Includes bibliographies and index*

SOCIAL PROBLEMS — Literary collections
LIPPARD, George
[Selections. 1986]. George Lippard, prophet of protest : writings of an American radical, 1822-1854 / edited with an introduction by David S. Reynolds. — New York : P. Lang, c1986. — xii, 335 p.. — *Cover title: George Lippard, an anthology.* — *Bibliography: p. 333-335*

SOCIAL PSYCHIATRY
LEARY, Mark R
Social psychology and dysfunctional behavior : origins, diagnosis, and treatment / Mark R. Leary and Rowland S. Miller. — New York : Springer-Verlag, c1986. — xiii, 262 p.. — (Springer series in social psychology). — *Includes indexes.* — *Bibliography: p. [203]-244*

SOCIAL PSYCHOLOGY
BANDURA, Albert
Social foundations of thought and action : a social cognitive theory / Albert Bandura. — Englewood Cliffs, N.J. : Prentice-Hall, c1986. — p. cm. — (Prentice-Hall series in social learning theory). — *Includes index.* — *Bibliography: p*

BARTLETT, Frederic C
Remembering : a study in experimental and social psychology / by Frederic C. Bartlett. — Cambridge : Cambridge University Press, 1967. — x,317p. — *Previous ed: 1932*

BERKOWITZ, Leonard
A survey of social psychology / Leonard Berkowitz. — 3rd ed. — New York : Holt, Rinehart and Winston, c1986. — xiv, 536 p.. — *Includes indexes.* — *Bibliography: p. 477-519*

BILLIG, Michael
Arguing and thinking : a rhetorical approach to social psychology / Michael Billig. — Cambridge : Cambridge University Press, 1987. — vi,290p. — (European monographs in social psychology). — *Bibliography: p265-282.* — *Includes index*

BULHAN, Hussein Abdilahi
Frantz Fanon and the psychology of oppression / Hussein Abdilahi Bulhan. — New York ; London : Plenum Press, c1985. — xiii, 299p. — (PATH in psychology). — *Includes index.* — *Includes bibliographical references*

DOISE, Willem
Levels of explanation in social psychology / Willem Doise ; translated from the French by Elizabeth Mapstone. — Cambridge : Cambridge University Press, 1986. — 1v. — (European monographs in social psychology). — *Translation of: L'explication en psychologie sociale.* — *Includes bibliography and index*

EISER, J. Richard
Social psychology : attitudes, cognition and social behaviour / J. Richard Eiser. — Rev. and updated ed. — Cambridge : Cambridge University Press, 1986. — [x,605]p. — *Previous ed.: published as Cognitive social psychology, London : McGraw-Hill, 1980.* — *Includes index*

FENN, Richard K
The spirit of revolt : anarchism and the cult of authority / Richard K. Fenn. — Totowa, NJ : Rowman & Littlefield, 1986. — p. cm. — *Includes index.* — *Bibliography: p*

HOMANS, George Caspar
Certainties and doubts : collected papers, 1962-1985 / George Caspar Homans. — New Brunswick, N.J. : Transaction Books, c1987. — p. cm. — *Bibliography: p*

Issues in contemporary German social psychology : history, theories and application / edited by Gün R. Semin and Barbara Krahé. — London : Sage, 1987. — xii,281p. — *Translated from German.* — *Includes bibliographies and index*

KERSHAW, Ian
The 'Hitler myth' : image and reality in the Third Reich / Ian Kershaw. — Oxford : Clarendon, 1987. — xii,297p. — *Rev. ed. of: Der Hitler-Mythos. 1980.* — *Bibliography: p277-287.* — *Includes index*

LEARY, Mark R
Social psychology and dysfunctional behavior : origins, diagnosis, and treatment / Mark R. Leary and Rowland S. Miller. — New York : Springer-Verlag, c1986. — xiii, 262 p.. — (Springer series in social psychology). — *Includes indexes.* — *Bibliography: p. [203]-244*

MANGHAM, Iain
Organizations as theatre : a social psychology of dramatic appearances / Iain L. Mangham, Michael A. Overington. — Chichester : Wiley, c1987. — [450]p. — *Includes index*

MEAD, George Herbert
George Herbert Mead on social psychology : selected papers / edited and with an introduction by Anselm Strauss. — Chicago ; London : University of Chicago Press, [1964]. — xxv,358p. — *Bibliography: p355-358*

PIN, Emile Jean
The pleasure of your company : a socio-psychological analysis of modern sociability / Emile Jean Pin ; in collaboration with Jamie Turndorf. — New York : Praeger, 1985. — p. cm. — *Includes indexes.* — *Bibliography: p*

SOCIAL PSYCHOLOGY
continuation

RAVEN, Bertram H.
Social psychology / Bertram H. Raven, Jeffrey Z. Rubin. — 2nd ed.. — New York ; Chichester : Wiley, 1983. — *Previous ed.: 1976*

ROSE, Nikolas Simon
The psychological complex : psychology, politics and society in England, 1869-1939 / Nikolas Rose. — London : Routledge and Kegan Paul, 1985. — 293p. — *Bibliography: p255-285*

Self and identity : psychosocial perspectives / edited by Krysia Yardley and Terry Honess. — Chichester : Wiley, c1987. — xvii,332p. — *Conference proceedings. — Includes bibliographies and index*

The Social dimension : European developments in social psychology / edited by Henri Tajfel ; preparation for publication completed by Colin Fraser and Joseph M.F. Jaspars. — Cambridge : Cambridge University Press, 1984. — 2v.(xxii,715,xiip). — (European studies in social psychology). — *Includes bibliographies and index*

Social psychology : a practical manual / edited by Glynis M. Breakwell, Hugh Foot and Robin Gilmour. — London : British Psychological Society and Macmillan, 1982. — xi,256p. — *Includes bibliographies*

The Social psychology of education : current research and theory / edited by Robert S. Feldman. — Cambridge : Cambridge University Press, 1986. — 381p. — *Includes bibliographies and index*

Theories of group behavior / edited by Brian Mullen and George R. Goethals. — New York : Springer-Verlag, c1987. — xiii, 243 p.. — (Springer series in social psychology). — *Includes bibliographies and index*

ULLMANN-MARGALIT, Edna
The emergence of norms / Edna Ullmann-Margalit. — Oxford : Clarendon Press, 1977. — xiii,206p. — (Clarendon library of logic and philosophy). — *Bibliography: p.198-201. — Includes index*

WEIL, Simone
The need for roots : prelude to a declaration of duties towards mankind / Simone Weil ; [translated from the French by A. F. Wills] ; preface by T. S. Eliot. — Ark ed. — London : Routledge and Kegan Paul, 1987. — xv,288p. — *Translation of: L'Enracinement. — First French edition: 1949; this translation originally published: 1952*

WEYANT, James M
Applied social psychology / James M. Weyant. — New York : Oxford University Press, 1986. — viii, 241 p.. — *Includes indexes. — Bibliography: p. 205-228*

SOCIAL PSYCHOLOGY — Addresses, essays, lectures

Gedrag en struktuur : de relevantie van microtheorieën voor de verklaring van macroverschijnselen / onder redaktie van W. Arts, S. Lindenberg en R. Wippler. — [Rotterdam] : Universitaire Pers Rotterdam, 1976. — xv, 237 p. — (Mens en maatschappij. Boekaflevering ; 1976). — *Includes index. — Bibliography: p. 217-231*

SOCIAL PSYCHOLOGY — Congresses

Redefining social problems / edited by Edward Seidman and Julian Rappaport. — New York : Plenum Press, c1986. — xxii, 311p. — (Perspectives in social psychology). — *Includes bibliographies and index*

SOCIAL PSYCHOLOGY — Dictionaries

The Dictionary of personality and social psychology / edited by Rom Harré and Roger Lamb. — Oxford : Blackwell, 1986. — xi,402p. — (Blackwell reference). — *Includes bibliographies and index*

SOCIAL PSYCHOLOGY — History — 20th century

ABOULAFIA, Mitchell
The mediating self : Mead, Sartre, and self-determination / Mitchell Aboulafia. — New Haven : Yale University Press, c1986. — xvii, 139p. — *Includes index. — Bibliography: p.127-131*

SOCIAL PSYCHOLOGY — Russian S.F.S.R — Leningrad — Addresses, essays, lectures

Research in Soviet social psychology / edited by L.H. Strickland, V.P. Trusov, and E. Lockwood ; translated by E. Lockwood. — Berlin ; New York : Springer-Verlag, c1986. — vii, 99 p.. — (Recent research in psychology). — *Translation of original essays by social psychologists working at the Institute of Psychology in Leningrad. — Includes bibliographies*

SOCIAL PSYCHOLOGY — Soviet Union — Addresses, essays, lectures

Research in Soviet social psychology / edited by L.H. Strickland, V.P. Trusov, and E. Lockwood ; translated by E. Lockwood. — Berlin ; New York : Springer-Verlag, c1986. — vii, 99 p.. — (Recent research in psychology). — *Translation of original essays by social psychologists working at the Institute of Psychology in Leningrad. — Includes bibliographies*

SOCIAL REFORMERS — Alabama — Fairhope — History — Addresses, essays, lectures

GASTON, Paul M
Women of Fair Hope / Paul M. Gaston. — Athens : University of Georgia Press, c1984. — xiv, 143 p.. — (Mercer University Lamar memorial lectures ; no. 25). — *Includes index. — Bibliography: p. [119]-133*

SOCIAL REFORMERS — Great Britain — Biography

DINNAGE, Rosemary
Annie Besant / Rosemary Dinnage. — Harmondsworth : Penguin, 1986. — 127p,[8]p of plates. — (Lives of modern women). — *Bibliography: p124. — Includes index*

HINDE, Wendy
Richard Cobden : a Victorian outsider : a biography / by Wendy Hinde. — New Haven : Yale University Press, 1987. — p. cm. — *Includes index. — Bibliography: p*

SOCIAL REFORMERS — Great Britian — Biography

EDSALL, Nicholas C
Richard Cobden, independent radical / Nicholas C. Edsall. — Cambridge, Mass. ; London : Harvard University Press, 1986. — xiv, 465p. — *Includes index. — Bibliography: p.[429]-433*

SOCIAL REFORMERS — United States — Biography

American reformers : an H.W. Wilson biographical dictionary / editor, Alden Whitman. — New York : H.W. Wilson Co., 1985. — xx, 930 p.. — *Includes bibliographies*

BORDIN, Ruth Birgitta Anderson
Frances Willard : a biography / by Ruth Bordin. — Chapel Hill ; London : University of North Carolina Press, c1986. — xv, 294p. — *Includes index. — Bibliography: p.277-287*

SOCIAL ROLE — Cross-cultural studies

The cultural transition : human experience and social transformation in the Third World and Japan / edited by Merry I. White and Susan Pollack. — London : Routledge and Kegan Paul, 1986. — xiii,302p

SOCIAL ROLE — Denmark

DENMARK. Kommissionen vedrørende kvindernes stilling i samfundet
Bilag til betaenkning og ligestilling : afgivet af et udvalg under kommissionen vedrørende kvindernes stilling i samfundet. — København : the Kommissionen, 1968. — 88p. — *Includes bibliographies. — Contents: Psykologiske kønsforskelle/Carl Weltzer - Sociologiske kønsforskelle/Benedicte Madsen*

SOCIAL SCIENCE — Data processing

NORUŠIS, M. J
SPSS/PC⁺ / SPSS Inc. ; Marija J. Norušis. — Chicago, Ill. : SPSS, c1986. — p. cm. — *On t.p. the registered trademark symbol "TM" is subscript following "SPSS/PC⁺" in the title. — Includes index. — Bibliography: p*

SOCIAL SCIENCE LITERATURE — Publishing

HOROWITZ, Irving Louis
Communicating ideas : the crisis of publishing in a post-industrial society / Irving Louis Horowitz. — New York : Oxford University Press, 1986. — x, 240 p.. — *Includes index. — Bibliography: p. 217-230*

SOCIAL SCIENCE RESEARCH

Evaluation review: a journal of applied social research. — Beverly Hills : Sage, 1986-. — *Semi-annual*

SOCIAL SCIENCE RESEARCH — Great Britain

Current research in Britain: social sciences / British Library. — Boston Spa : British Library Lending Division, 1985-. — *Annual. — Continues Research in British universities, polytechnics and colleges*

SOCIAL SCIENCES

Économies et sociétés: philosophie et sciences de l'homme. — Paris : Presses Universitaires de France, 1967-. — *Monthly*

FRISBY, David
Society / David Frisby and Derek Sayer. — Chichester : Ellis Horwood, 1986. — 129p. — (Key ideas). — *Includes index*

HUGHES, H. Stuart
Consciousness and society : the reorientation of European social thought 1890-1930 / H. Stuart Hughes. — London : Paladin, 1974. — xi,433,xv p. — *Originally published: New York : Knopf, 1958 ; London : MacGibbon and Kee, 1959. — Includes index*

The philosophy of social explanation / edited by Alan Ryan. — London : Oxford University Press, 1973. — [5],228p. — (Oxford readings in philosophy). — *Bibliographyp.223-226. — Includes index*

SOCIAL SCIENCES — Abstracting and indexing

ASSIA (Applied social sciences index and abstracts / the Library Association). — London : Library Association, 1987-. — *Bimonthly*

SOCIAL SCIENCES — Addresses, essays, lectures

The Goodman lectures 1973-1982, at the Royal Society. — [London] : Aitchison Fund, c1985. — 261p

SOCIAL SCIENCES — Bibliography

ESRC DATA ARCHIVE
ESRC Data Archive catalogue. — Cambridge : Chadwyck-Healey, 1986. — 2v.. — *Includes index*

Sources of information in the social sciences. — 3rd ed. / William H. Webb, editor ; Alan R. Beals ... [et al.]. — Chicago : American Library Association, 1986. — p. cm. — *Rev. ed. of: Sources of information in the social sciences / Carl M. White and associates. 2nd ed. 1973. — Includes index*

SOCIAL SCIENCES — Computer programs
DE JONG, Lucy
Statistical package for social sciences : a summary or facilities available and a guide to their use / Lucy de Jong. — [London?] : Civil Service Department, Behavioural Sciences Research Division, 1974. — 15p. — (BSRD statistical and computer paper ; no.13)

SOCIAL SCIENCES — Data processing
GARSON, G. David
Academic microcomputing : a resource guide / G. David Garson. — Beverly Hills : Sage Publications, c1987. — 175 p.. — *Includes bibliographies*

Information and communication technologies : social science research and training. — London : Economic and Social Research Council. — *At head of title: A report by the ESRC Programme on Information and Communication Technologies* Vol 2: National directory / edited by Robin E. Mansell ; assisted by Barbara J. Richards. — 1986

MELODY, William H.
Information and communication technologies : social science research and training. — London : Economic and Social Research Council. — *At head of title: A report by the ESRC Programme on Information and Communication Technologies* Vol 1: An over-view of research / William H. Melody, Robin E. Mansell. — 1986

SOCIAL SCIENCES — Dictionaries and encyclopedias
Encyclopedia of world problems and human potential / edited by Union of International Associations. — 2nd ed. — München ; London : K. F. Saur, 1986. — unpaged

SOCIAL SCIENCES — Forecasting
ROYAL SOCIETY. Symposium (1986 : [London?])
Predictability in science and society : a joint symposium of the Royal Society and the British Academy held on 20 and 21 March 1986 / organized and edited by John Mason, P. Mathias, and J. H. Westcott. — London : Royal Society : British Academy, 1986. — viii,145p. — *Includes bibliographies*

SOCIAL SCIENCES — History
MANICAS, Peter T.
A history and philosophy of the social sciences / Peter T. Manicas. — Oxford : Basil Blackwell, 1987. — vii,345p. — *Bibliography: p319-335. — Includes index*

SOCIAL SCIENCES — History — 20th century
Advances in the social sciences 1900-1980 : what, who, where, how? : written under the auspices of the Wissenschaftszentrum, Berlin, June 1982 / editors Karl W. Deutsch, Andrei S. Markovits, John Platt. — London : University Press of America, 1987. — [478]p. — *Conference papers. — Includes index*

SOCIAL SCIENCES — Information services
International journal of information management. — Guildford : Butterworth Scientific, 1986-. — *Quarterly. — Continues: Social science information studies*

SOCIAL SCIENCES — International cooperation — Case studies
LENGYEL, Peter
International social science, the UNESCO experience / Peter Lengyel. — New Brunswick, U.S.A. : Transaction Books, c1986. — xii, 133 p.. — *Includes index. — Bibliography: p. 123-129*

SOCIAL SCIENCES — Mathematical models
MOULIN, Hervé
89 exercises with solutions from Game theory for the social sciences, 2nd and revised edition / Hervé Moulin. — New York : New York University Press, 1986, c1985. — p. cm. — (Studies in game theory and mathematical economics). — *Includes index*

MOULIN, Hervé
[Théorie des jeux pour l'économie et la politique. English]. Game theory for the social sciences / Hervé Moulin. — 2nd, rev. ed. — New York : New York University Press, 1986, c1985. — p. cm. — (Studies in game theory and mathematical economics). — *Translation of: Théorie des jeux pour l'économie et la politique. — Includes index. — Bibliography: p*

SOCIAL SCIENCES — Mathematics
BRADLEY, Ian
Matrices and society / Ian Bradley and Ronald L. Meek. — Princeton, N.J. : Princeton University Press, 1986. — p. cm. — *Bibliography: p*

SOCIAL SCIENCES — Methodology
ABELL, Peter
The syntax of social life : the theory and method of comparative narratives / Peter Abell. — Oxford : Clarendon, 1987. — [192]p. — *Includes bibliography and index*

ARGYRIS, Chris
Action science / Chris Argyris, Robert Putnam, Diana McLain Smith. — 1st ed. — San Francisco : Jossey-Bass, 1985. — xx, 480 p.. — (The Jossey-Bass social and behavioral science series) (The Jossey-Bass management series). — *Includes index. — Bibliography: p. 451-465*

CRANO, William D.
Principles and methods of social research / William D. Crano, Marilynn B. Brewer. — Newton, MA : Allyn and Bacon, c1986. — p. cm. — *Includes index*

DIXON, Beverly R.
A handbook of social science research. — [British ed.], Beverly R. Dixon, Gary D. Bouma, G.B.J. Atkinson. — Oxford : Oxford University Press, 1987. — xiii,225p. — *Previous ed.: published as The research process. 1984. — Includes index*

HAKIM, C.
Research design : strategies and choices in the design of social research / Catherine Hakim. — London : Allen & Unwin, 1987. — [xii,216] p. — (Contemporary social research series ; no.13). — *Bibliography: p263-308. — Includes index*

JARVIE, I. C.
Thinking about society : theory and practice / I. C. Jarvie. — Dordrecht : Reidel, 1986. — xviii,519p. — (Boston studies in the philosophy of science ; v.93)

KIDDER, Louise H
Research mathods in social relations / Louise H. Kidder, Charles Judd, with Eliot R. Smith. — 5th ed. — New York ; London : Holt, Rinehart and Winston, c1986. — xii, 563p. — *"Published for the Society for the Psychological Study of Social Issues.". — Includes indexes. — Bibliography: p.521-548*

KIRK, Jerome
Reliability and validity in qualitative research / Jerome Kirk [and] Marc L. Miller. — Beverly Hills ; London : Sage, c1986. — 87 p. — (Qualitative research methods ; v.1)

Liberating theory / by Michael Albert ... [et al.]. — 1st ed. — Boston, MA : South End Press, c1986. — 197 p.. — *Bibliography: p. 195-197*

MYRDAL, Gunnar
Value in social theory : a selection of essays on methodology / by Gunnar Myrdal ; edited by Paul Streeten. — London : Routledge and Kegan Paul, 1958. — (International library of sociology and social reconstruction)

PHILLIPS, D. C. (Denis Charles)
Philosophy, science, and social inquiry : contemporary methodological controversies in social science and related applied fields of research / D.C. Phillips. — Oxford : Pergamon, 1987. — [245]p

PRZEWORSKI, Adam
The logic of comparative social inquiry / Adam Przeworski and Henry Teune. — New York : Wiley, 1970. — (Comparative studies in behavioral science)

SOMMER, Robert
A practical guide to behavioral research : tools and techniques / Robert Sommer and Barbara B. Sommer. — 2nd ed. — New York : Oxford University Press, 1986. — viii, 297 p.. — *Includes bibliographies and indexes*

SOCIAL SCIENCES — Methodology — Congresses
Metatheory in social science : pluralisms and subjectivities / edited by Donald W. Fiske and Richard A. Shweder. — Chicago : University of Chicago Press, 1986. — x, 390 p.. — (Chicago original paperbacks). — *Proceedings of a conference on "Potentialities for Knowledge in Social Science," held at the University of Chicago, Sept. 11-14, 1983. — Includes indexes. — Bibliography: p. 371-377*

SOCIAL SCIENCES — Methodology — History
TURNER, Stephen P.
The search for a methodology of social science / Stephen P. Turner. — Dordrecht, Holland ; Boston : D. Reidel Pub. Co. ; Hingham, MA : Sold and distributed in the U.S.A. and Canada by Kluwer Academic Publishers, c1985. — p. cm. — (Boston studies in the philosophy of science ; vol. 92). — *Includes index. — Bibliography: p*

SOCIAL SCIENCES — Methodology — Moral and ethical aspects
PUNCH, Maurice
The politics and ethics of fieldwork / Maurice Punch. — Beverly Hills : Sage Publications, c1986. — 93 p.. — (Qualitative research methods ; v. 3). — *"A Sage university paper"--Cover. — Bibliography: p. 85-91*

SOCIAL SCIENCES — Philosophy
BHASKAR, Roy
Scientific realism and human emancipation / Roy Bhaskar. — London : Verso, 1986. — 308p

CASTORIADIS, Cornelius
The imaginary institution of society / Cornelius Castoriadis ; translated by Kathleen Blamey. — Cambridge : Polity, 1987. — vii,418p. — *Translation of: L'institution imaginaire de la société. — Includes index*

DOYAL, Len
Empiricism, explanation and rationality : an introduction to the philosophy of the social sciences / Len Doyal and Roger Harris. — London : Routledge & Kegan Paul, 1986. — [218]p. — *Includes bibliography and index*

European philosophy and the human and social sciences / edited by Simon Glynn. — Aldershot : Gower, c1986. — xi,229p. — (Avebury series in philosophy)

FAY, Brian
Critical social science : liberation and its limits / Brian Fay. — Ithaca, N.Y. : Cornell University Press, [1987]. — p. cm. — *Includes index. — Bibliography: p*

JARVIE, I. C.
Thinking about society : theory and practice / I. C. Jarvie. — Dordrecht : Reidel, 1986. — xviii,519p. — (Boston studies in the philosophy of science ; v.93)

MANICAS, Peter T.
A history and philosophy of the social sciences / Peter T. Manicas. — Oxford : Basil Blackwell, 1987. — vii,345p. — *Bibliography: p319-335. — Includes index*

SOCIAL SCIENCES — Philosophy
continuation

Philosophy and practice / edited by A. Phillips Griffiths. — Cambridge : Cambridge University Press, 1985. — vii,290p. — (Royal Institute of Philosophy lecture series ; 18). — "Supplement to Philosophy, 1985". — Includes bibliographies and index

WALZER, Michael
Interpretation and social criticism / Michael Walzer. — Cambridge, Mass. : Harvard University Press, 1987. — viii, 96 p.. — (The Tanner lectures on human values). — Includes bibliographical references and index

SOCIAL SCIENCES — Philosophy — Congresses

Metatheory in social science : pluralisms and subjectivities / edited by Donald W. Fiske and Richard A. Shweder. — Chicago : University of Chicago Press, 1986. — x, 390 p.. — (Chicago original paperbacks). — *Proceedings of a conference on "Potentialities for Knowledge in Social Science," held at the University of Chicago, Sept. 11-14, 1983.* — Includes indexes. — Bibliography: p. 371-377

SOCIAL SCIENCES — Philosophy — History

RUNDELL, John F.
Origins of modernity : the origins of modern social theory from Kant to Hegel to Marx / John F. Rundell. — Cambridge : Polity, 1987. — 249p. — *Bibliography: p234-241 Includes index*

SOCIAL SCIENCES — Philosophy — History — 19th century

POPE, Whitney
Alexis de Tocqueville : his social and political theory / by Whitney Pope. — Beverly Hills, Calif. : Sage, c1985. — p. cm. — (Masters of social theory ; v. 4). — Includes index. — Bibliography: p

SOCIAL SCIENCES — Research

ADAMS, Gerald R.
Understanding research methods / Gerald R. Adams & Jay D. Schvaneveldt. — New York : Longman, 1984, c1985. — p. cm. — *Includes index.* — Bibliography: p

Advances in the social sciences 1900-1980 : what, who, where, how? : written under the auspices of the Wissenschaftszentrum, Berlin, June 1982 / editors Karl W. Deutsch, Andrei S. Markovits, John Platt. — London : University Press of America, 1987. — [478]p. — *Conference papers. — Includes index*

ARGYRIS, Chris
Action science / Chris Argyris, Robert Putnam, Diana McLain Smith. — 1st ed. — San Francisco : Jossey-Bass, 1985. — xx, 480 p.. — (The Jossey-Bass social and behavioral science series) (The Jossey-Bass management series). — Includes index. — Bibliography: p. 451-465

BULMER, Martin
Social science and social policy / Martin Bulmer with Keith G. Banting ... [et al.]. — London : Allen & Unwin, 1986. — [272]p. — (Contemporary social research series ; 12). — *Includes bibliography and index*

CRANO, William D.
Principles and methods of social research / William D. Crano, Marilyn B. Brewer. — Newton, MA : Allyn and Bacon, c1986. — p. cm. — *Includes index*

FIEDLER, Judith
Field research : a manual for logistics and management of scientific studies in natural settings / Judith Fiedler. — 1st ed. — San Francisco : Jossey-Bass Publishers, 1978. — xviii, 188 p.. — (The Jossey-Bass social and behavioral science series). — Includes index. — *Bibliography: p. 177-185*

HUNT, Morton M.
Profiles of social research : the scientific study of human interactions / Morton Hunt. — New York : Russell Sage Foundation, c1985. — p. cm. — Includes index. — Bibliography: p

KIDDER, Louise H
Research mathods in social relations / Louise H. Kidder, Charles Judd, with Eliot R. Smith. — 5th ed. — New York ; London : Holt, Rinehart and Winston, c1986. — xii, 563p. — "Published for the Society for the Psychological Study of Social Issues.". — Includes indexes. — Bibliography: p.521-548

PRZEWORSKI, Adam
The logic of comparative social inquiry / Adam Przeworski, Henry Teune. — Malabar, Fla. : R.E. Krieger Pub. Co., 1982, c1970. — xii, 153 p.. — : Reprint. Originally published: New York : Wiley Interscience, 1970. — Includes index. — Bibliography: p. 135-150

The Research relationship : practice and politics in social policy research / edited by G. Clare Wenger. — London : Allen & Unwin, 1987. — xix,228p. — (Contemporary social research series ; 15). — *Includes bibliographies and index*

RIGGS, Fred W.
Help for social scientists : a new kind of reference process / by Fred W. Riggs. — Paris : Unesco, 1986. — vi,48p. — (Reports and papers in the social sciences ; no.57). — *Bibliographical references: p48*

Social sciences and farming systems research : methodological perspectives on agricultural development / edited by Jeffrey R. Jones, Ben J. Wallace. — Boulder : Westview Press, 1986. — p. cm

SOMMER, Robert
A practical guide to behavioral research : tools and techniques / Robert Sommer and Barbara B. Sommer. — 2nd ed. — New York : Oxford University Press, 1986. — viii, 297 p.. — *Includes bibliographies and indexes*

The Use and abuse of social science / edited by Frank Heller. — London : Sage, 1986. — x,294p. — *Includes bibliographies and index*

SOCIAL SCIENCES — Research — Case studies

LENGYEL, Peter
International social science, the UNESCO experience / Peter Lengyel. — New Brunswick, U.S.A. : Transaction Books, c1986. — xii, 133 p.. — Includes index. — Bibliography: p. 123-129

SOCIAL SCIENCES — Research — Congresses

Metatheory in social science : pluralisms and subjectivities / edited by Donald W. Fiske and Richard A. Shweder. — Chicago : University of Chicago Press, 1986. — x, 390 p.. — (Chicago original paperbacks). — *Proceedings of a conference on "Potentialities for Knowledge in Social Science," held at the University of Chicago, Sept. 11-14, 1983.* — Includes indexes. — Bibliography: p. 371-377

SOCIAL SCIENCES — Research — Data processing

CORNFORD, Tony
Designing a computer workstation for researchers in the quantitative social sciences / Tony Cornford, Brian Hayes. — [London : London School of Economics and Political Science], 1986. — 19p. — (Taxation, incentives and the distribution of income ; no.93). — *Economic and Social Research Council programme.* — Bibliographical references: p19

SOMMER, Robert
A practical guide to behavioral research : tools and techniques / Robert Sommer and Barbara B. Sommer. — 2nd ed. — New York : Oxford University Press, 1986. — viii, 297 p.. — *Includes bibliographies and indexes*

SOCIAL SCIENCES — Research — Methodology

New tools for social scientists : advances and applications in research methods / edited by William D. Berry, Michael S. Lewis-Beck. — Beverly Hills : Sage Publications, c1986. — 288 p.. — *Includes bibliographies*

SOCIAL SCIENCES — Research — Moral and ethical aspects

PUNCH, Maurice
The politics and ethics of fieldwork / Maurice Punch. — Beverly Hills : Sage Publications, c1986. — 93 p.. — (Qualitative research methods ; v. 3). — "A Sage university paper"--Cover. — Bibliography: p. 85-91

SOCIAL SCIENCES — Research — Great Britain

The social science PhD : the ESRC inquiry on submission rates / chairman: Graham Winfield. — London : Economic and Social Research Council
Background papers. — 1987. — 232p

SOCIAL SCIENCES — Research — Great Britain — Directories

Information and communication technologies : social science research and training. — London : Economic and Social Research Council. — *At head of title: A report by the ESRC Programme on Information and Communication Technologies*
Vol 2: National directory / edited by Robin E. Mansell ; assisted by Barbara J. Richards. — 1986

MELODY, William H.
Information and communication technologies : social science research and training. — London : Economic and Social Research Council. — *At head of title: A report by the ESRC Programme on Information and Communication Technologies*
Vol 1: An over-view of research / William H. Melody, Robin E. Mansell. — 1986

SOCIAL SCIENCES — Research — Great Britain — Government policy — History — 20th century

Social science research and government : comparative essays on Britain and the United States / edited by Martin Bulmer. — Cambridge : Cambridge University Press, 1987. — [424]p

SOCIAL SCIENCES — Research — United States — Case studies

HUNT, Morton M.
Profiles of social research : the scientific study of human interactions / Morton Hunt. — New York : Russell Sage Foundation, c1985. — p. cm. — Includes index. — Bibliography: p

SOCIAL SCIENCES — Research — United States — Congresses

Behavioral and social science : fifty years of discovery : in commemoration of the fiftieth anniversary of the "Ogburn report," Recent social trends in the United States / Neil J. Smelser and Dean R. Gerstein, editors ; Committee on Basic Research in the Behavioral and Social Sciences, Commission on Behavioral and Social Sciences and Education, National Research Council. — Washington, D.C. : National Academy Press, 1986. — x, 298 p.. — *Symposium held Nov. 29-30, 1983. — Includes bibliographies*

SOCIAL SCIENCES — Research — United States — Finance

The Nationalization of the social sciences / Samuel Z. Klausner and Victor M. Lidz, editors. — Philadelphia : University of Pennsylvania Press, 1986. — xiv, 296 p.. — *Includes bibliographical references and index*

SOCIAL SCIENCES — Research — United States — Government policy — History — 20th century

Social science research and government : comparative essays on Britain and the United States / edited by Martin Bulmer. — Cambridge : Cambridge University Press, 1987. — [424]p

SOCIAL SCIENCES — Scholarships, fellowships, etc. — Great Britain

BRITISH ACADEMY
Guide to awards in the humanities and social sciences, 1986-87. — London : British Academy, 1986. — 27p

SOCIAL SCIENCES — Statistical methods

ALDENDERFER, Mark S.
Cluster analysis / by Mark S. Aldenderfer and Roger K. Blashfield. — Beverly Hills : Sage, 1984. — (Quantitative applications in the social sciences ; 44)

DAVIS, James A.
The logic of causal order / James A. Davis. — Beverly Hills ; London : Sage, c1985. — 72 p. — (Quantitative applications in the social sciences ; 55)

Drawing inferences from self-selected samples / edited by Howard Wainer. — New York : Springer-Verlag, c1986. — xii, 163 p.. — *Papers from a conference sponsored by Educational Testing Service. — Includes indexes. — Bibliography: p. [153]-157*

SOCIAL SCIENCES — statistical methods

FOX, James Alan
Randomized response : a method for sensitive surveys / James Alan Fox, Paul E.Tracy. — Beverly Hills : Sage, 1986. — (Quantitative applications in the social sciences ; 58) (Sage University Paper)

SOCIAL SCIENCES — Statistical methods

KIECOLT, K. Jill
Secondary analysis of survey data / K. Jill Kiecolt [and] Laura E. Nathan. — Beverly Hills ; London : Sage, c1985. — 88 p. — (Quantitative applications in the social sciences ; 53)

KISH, Leslie
Statistical design for research / Leslie Kish. — New York : Wiley, 1987. — p. cm. — (Wiley series in probability and mathematical statistics. Applied probability and statistics section). — *Includes index. — Bibliography: p*

REID, Stuart
Working with statistics : an introduction to quantitative methods for social scientists / Stuart Reid. — Cambridge : Polity, 1987. — xviii,183p. — *Bibliography: p176-177. — Includes index*

SOCIAL SCIENCES — Statistical methods — Congresses

Small area statistics : an international symposium / edited by R. Platek ... [et al.]. — New York : Wiley, 1986. — p. cm. — (Wiley series in probability and mathematical statistics. Applied probability and statistics). — *Includes index*

SOCIAL SCIENCES — Statistical methods — Mathematical models

LONG, J. Scott
Covariance structure models : an introduction to LISREL / J. Scott Long. — Beverly Hills : Sage Publications, c1983. — 95 p.. — (Sage university papers series. Quantitative applications in the social sciences ; no. 07-034). — *Bibliography: p. 91-93*

SOCIAL SCIENCES — Study and teaching

Changing the curriculum / edited by John F. Kerr. — London : University of London Press, c1968. — 112p. — *Bibliographies*

L.S.E. quarterly. — Oxford : Blackwell, 1987-. — *Quarterly*

SOCIAL SCIENCES — Study and teaching — Philippines

LEYCO-REYES, Soccoro
Social science education and national development in the Philippines / Soccoro Leyco-Reyes. — Singapore : Regional Institute of Higher Education and Development, 1985. — 167p. — (RIHED Research Series). — *Bibliography: p137-139*

SOCIAL SCIENCES — Study and teaching (Secondary) — England — London

INNER LONDON EDUCATION AUTHORITY. Inspectorate
History and social sciences at secondary level. — [London : the Authority]
Part 3: Social sciences. — [1983]. — 108p. — *Bibliography: p104-106*

SOCIAL SCIENCES — Terminology

RIGGS, Fred W.
Help for social scientists : a new kind of reference process / by Fred W. Riggs. — Paris : Unesco, 1986. — vi,48p. — (Reports and papers in the social sciences ; no.57). — *Bibliographical references: p48*

SOCIAL SCIENCES — Africa, Sub-Saharan

BOIRAL, P.
Paysans, experts et chercheurs en Afrique Noire : sciences sociales et développement rural / P. Boiral, J.- F. Lanteri, J.-P. Olivier de Sardan (sous la direction de). — Paris : Karthala, [1985]. — 224p

SOCIAL SCIENCES — China

New directions in the social sciences and humanities in China / edited by Michael B. Yahuda. — Basingstoke : Macmillan, 1987. — xxi,169p. — *Includes index*

SOCIAL SCIENCES — Europe — History

HUGHES, H. Stuart
Consciousness and society / H. Stuart Hughes. — Brighton : Harvester Press, 1979. — xi,433,xv p. — (Set books / Open University). — *Originally published: New York : Knopf, 1958 ; London : MacGibbon and Kee, 1959. — Bibliography: p.432-433. — Includes index*

SOCIAL SCIENCES — Great Britain — Research

The social science PhD : the ESRC inquiry on submission rates / chairman: Graham Winfield. — London : Economic and Social Research Council
The report. — 1987. — 133p

SOCIAL SCIENCES — Great Britain — Research grants

BRITISH ACADEMY
Guide to awards in the humanities and social sciences, 1986-87. — London : British Academy, 1986. — 27p

SOCIAL SCIENCES — Spain

DÍAZ, Elías
Pensamiento español en la ero de Franco (1939-1975) / Elías Díaz. — Madrid : Tecnos, 1983. — 219p. — *Bibliography: p[201]-206*

SOCIAL SCIENCES AND ETHICS

TONG, Rosemarie
Ethics in policy analysis / Rosemarie Tong. — Englewood Cliffs, NJ : Prentice-Hall, c1986. — p. cm. — (Occupational ethics series). — *Includes bibliographies and index*

SOCIAL SCIENTISTS — Japan — Biography

HIRSI, Atsuko
Individualism and socialism : Kawai Eijirō's life and thought (1891-1944) / Atsuko Hirai. — Cambridge, Mass. : Council on East Asian Studies, Harvard University : Distributed by Harvard University Press, 1986. — p. cm. — (Harvard East Asian monographs ; 127). — *Includes index. — Bibliography: p*

SOCIAL SECURITY

ABEL-SMITH, Brian
Future directions for social protection : a report on a European Symposium held in Athens, June 1986 / Brian Abel-Smith [and] Marios Raphael. — Athens : M.K. Publishers, 1986. — 68p

ATKINSON, A. B.
Income maintenance and social insurance : a survey / A. B. Atkinson. — London : Suntory-Toyota International Centre for Economics and Related Disciplines, London School of Economics, 1985. — 234p. — (Welfare State Programme ; no.5). — *Bibliography: p205-234*

Caring costs : the social security implications. — [London] : Family Policy Studies Centre, 1986. — 16 leaves. — *Bibliography: p16*

Incomes from work : between equity and efficiency. — Geneva : International Labour Office, 1987. — viii,169p. — (World labour report ; 3). — *Bibliography: p165-169*

INTERNATIONAL SOCIAL SECURITY ASSOCIATION
Volume and cost of sickness benefits in kind and cash (1967-1970). — Geneva : International Social Security Association
Part 1: National analyses: report of the Permanent Committee on Medical Care and Sickness Insurance. — 1973. — iv,209p

National welfare benefits handbook / Child Poverty Action Group. — London : Child Poverty Action Group, 1982/3-. — *Annual*

PARTINGTON, Martin
Socio-legal studies and social welfare / Martin Partington ; a report for the Government and Law Committee of the Economic and Social Research Council. — London : Economic and Social Research Council, 1986. — 78p. — *Bibliography: p59-78*

Public/private interplay in social protection : a comparative study / edited by Martin Rein and Lee Rainwater ; with Ellen Immergut, Michael O'Higgins, and Harald Russig. — Armonk, N.Y. : M.E. Sharpe, c1986. — viii, 215 p.. — (Comparative public policy analysis). — *Includes bibliographies*

SOCIAL SECURITY — Congresses

Essays in social security economics : selected papers of a conference of the International Institute of Management, Wissenschaftszentrum Berlin / edited by J.-Matthias Graf von der Schulenburg. — Berlin ; New York : Springer-Verlag, 1986. — p. cm. — (Microeconomic studies). — *: "Contributions to this book were presented at the Workshop on the Origin and Future of Social Security Schemes held at the International Institute of Management of the Science Centre, Berlin, December 13-14, 1984"---Acknowledgement. — Includes indexes*

SOCIAL SECURITY — Finance

Financing social security : the options : an international analysis. — Geneva : International Labour Office, 1984. — x,145p. — *Includes bibliographical references*

SOCIAL SECURITY — Government policy — Australia

CARNEY, Terry
Australian social security law, policy and administration / Terry Carney & Peter Hanks. — Melbourne : Oxford University Press, 1986. — xxv,334p. — *Bibliography: p[311]-326*

SOCIAL SECURITY — Law and legislation — Addresses, essays, lectures

Fifty years of labour law and social security : studies at the occasion of the fiftieth [sic] anniversary of the chair in sociaal recht at the Rijksuniversiteit Leiden, the Netherlands. — Deventer ; London : Kluwer, 1986. — viii,166p . — *Authors listed on cover as: M.G. Rood ... [et al.]*

SOCIAL SECURITY — Law and legislation — Australia

CARNEY, Terry
Australian social security law, policy and administration / Terry Carney & Peter Hanks. — Melbourne : Oxford University Press, 1986. — xxv,334p. — *Bibliography: p[311]-326*

SOCIAL SECURITY — Law and legislation — European Economic Community countries

Compendium of Community Provisions on social security / Commission of the European Communities. — Luxembourg : Office for Official Publications of the European Communities, 1981. — 389p

Compendium of Community provisions on Social Security / Commission of the European Communities. — 1st updating (30 June) 1981. — Luxembourg : Office for Official Publications of the European Communities, 1981. — 99p

Compendium of Community provisions on social security. — 2nd updating (31 December 1981). — Luxembourg : Office for Official Publications of the European Communities. — 131p

Compendium of Community provisions on social security. — 2nd ed. (31 December 1982). — Luxembourg : Office for Official Publications of the European Communities, 1982. — 410p

Compendium of Community provisions on social security. — 2nd ed. (updating supplement — 30 June 1985). — Luxembourg : Office for Official Publications of the European Communities, 1986. — 223p

SOCIAL SECURITY — Law and legislation — Great Britain

GREAT BRITAIN
C.P.A.G.'s supplementary benefit and family income supplement : the legislation / commentary by John Mesher. — 4th ed. — London : Sweet & Maxwell, 1987. — [500]p. — *Previous ed.: 1985*

GREAT BRITAIN. Parliament. House of Commons. Library. Research Division
Health and Social Security Bill 1983 / Keith Cuninghame, Julia Lourie, Christine Gillie. — [London] : the Division, 1983. — 50p. — (Reference sheet ; no.83/24). — *Includes bibliographical references*

GREAT BRITAIN. Parliament. House of Commons. Library. Research Division
Social Security and Housing Benefits Bill 1982/83 (Bill 109) / Julia Lourie. — [London] : the Division, 1983. — 23p. — (Reference sheet ; no.83/7). — *Bibliographical references: p14-15*

GREAT BRITAIN. Parliament. House of Commons. Library. Research Division
Social Security Bill 1980/81 (Bill 68) / [Julia Lourie]. — [London] : the Division, 1981. — 10p. — (Reference sheet ; no.81/8). — *Bibliography: p8-10*

GREAT BRITAIN. Parliament. House of Commons. Library. Research Division
Social Security Bill 1984/5 [Bill 10] / Julia Lourie. — [London] : the Division, 1984. — 23p. — (Reference sheet ; no.84/11). — *Bibliographical references: p18-23*

GREAT BRITAIN. Parliament. House of Commons. Library. Research Division
Social Security Bill 1985/6 [Bill 59] / Julia Lourie, Christine Gillie. — [London] : the Division, 1986. — 52p. — (Reference sheet ; no.86/3). — *Bibliographical references: p46-52*

GREAT BRITAIN. Parliament. House of Commons. Library. Research Division
Social Security (Contributions) Bill 1980-81 [Bill 4] / [Julia Lourie]. — [London] : the Division, 1980. — 19p. — (Reference sheet ; no.80/16). — *Bibliographical references: p17-19*

GREAT BRITAIN. Parliament. House of Commons. Library. Research Division
The Social Security (No.2) Bill 1979/80 (Bill 180) / Julia Lourie, Christine Fretten. — [London] : the Division, 1980. — 13p. — (Reference sheet ; no.80/11). — *Bibliography: p10-13*

JOYCE, Josephine
Tolley's guide to Statutory Sick Pay : implementing and operating SSP in practice / Josephine Joyce with assistance from Veronica Cowan ; consultant: Erich Suter. — 2nd ed. — Croydon : Tolley, 1986. — x,93p

SOCIAL SECURITY — Law and legislation — Great Britain — Bibliography

GREAT BRITAIN. Parliament. House of Commons. Library. Research Division
Social Security Bill (No.86 of 1979/80) / [Julia Lourie]. — [London] : the Division, 1979. — 5p. — (Reference sheet ; no.79/16)

SOCIAL SECURITY — Law and legislation — Spain

SPAIN
[Laws, etc]. Legislación de seguridad social / edición preparada por Antonio Ojeda Aviles, María Fernanda Fernández López y Félix Salvador Pérez. — [Madrid] : Tecnos, c1984. — 615p. — (Biblioteca de textos legales)

SOCIAL SECURITY — Law and legislation — United States

LIGHT, Paul Charles
Artful work : the politics of social security reform / Paul Light. — 1st ed. — New York : Random House, c1985. — xiv, 255 p.. — *Includes index*

SOCIAL SECURITY — Argentina — History

ISUANI, Ernesto A.
Los orígenes conflictivos de la seguridad social argentina / Ernesto A. Isuani. — Buenos Aires : Centro Editor de América Latina, 1985. — 140p. — (Biblioteca Política Argentina ; 129). — *Bibliography: p137-140*

SOCIAL SECURITY — Australia

CASS, Bettina
The case for review of aspects of the Australian social security system / Bettina Cass. — Woden ACT : Department of Social Security, 1986. — 19 leaves. — (Background/discussion paper / Social Security Review ; no.1). — *Bibliographical references: p[18-19]*

CASS
Income support for families with children / Bettina Cass. — Canberra : Australian Government Publishing Service, 1986. — xiii,126p. — (Issues paper / Social Security Review ; no.1). — *Bibliography: p115-120*

CROMPTON, Cathy
Too old for a job, too young for a pension? : income support for older people out of work / Cathy Crompton. — Canberra : Australian Government Publishing Service, 1986. — x,69p. — (Issues paper / Social Security Review ; no.2). — *Bibliogaphy: p67-69*

DONALD, Owen
Social security reform / Owen Donald. — Woden, ACT : Department of Social Security, 1986. — 21 leaves. — (Background/discussion paper / Social Security Review ; no.2)

FREY, Dianne
Survey of sole parent pensioners' workforce barriers / Dianne Frey. — Woden, ACT : Department of Social Security, 1986. — 40p. — (Background/discussion paper / Social Security Review ; no.12). — *Includes bibliographical references*

GRIFFITHS, Bob
Overseas countries' maintenance provisions / Bob Griffiths, Shelley Cooper and Neil McVicar. — Woden, ACT : Department of Social Security, 1986. — [45]p. — (Background/discussion paper / Social Security Review ; no.13). — *Bibliography: p[40-41]*

HARDING, Ann
Assistance for families with children and the Social Security Review / Ann Harding. — Woden, ACT : Department of Social Security, 1986. — [18] leaves. — (Background/discussion paper / Social Security Review ; no.4). — *Bibliographical references: p[18-19]*

JOHNSTONE, Helen
Older unemployed people in the Illawarra Region, New South Wales / Helen Johnstone. — Woden, ACT : Department of Social Security, 1986. — 14 leaves. — (Background/discussion paper / Social Security Review ; no.7). — *Bibliographical references: p14*

Labour force status and other characteristics of sole parents : 1974-1985. — Woden, ACT : Department of Social Security, 1986. — 33p. — (Background paper / Social Security Review ; no.8)

OGBORN, Keith
Social security and the labour force-looking ahead / Keith Ogborn. — Woden, ACT : Department of Social Security, 1986. — 20 leaves. — (Background/discussion paper / Social Security Review ; no.3)

OGBORN
Workfare in America : an initial guide to the debate / Keith Ogborn. — Woden, ACT : Department of Social Security, 1986. — 27p. — (Background/discussion paper / Social Security Review ; no.6). — *Bibliography: p24-27*

Overseas countries' assistance to sole parents / [Robyn Bradley...[et al.]]. — Woden, ACT : Department of Social Security, 1986. — [115]p. — (Background/discussion paper / Social Security Review ; no.14). — *Bibliography: p111*

Pensioner fringe benefits : their range, cost and value. — Canberra : Australian Government Publishing Service, 1984. — viii,162p. — *Includes bibliographical references*

RAYMOND, Judy
Bringing up children alone : policies for sole parents / Judy Raymond. — Canberra : Australian Government Publishing Service, 1987. — xi,145p. — (Issues paper / Social Security Review ; no.3). — *Bibliography: p139-145*

ROBINSON, Judi
Australian families : current situation and trends; 1969-1985 / Judi Robinson and Bob Griffiths. — Woden, ACT : Department of Social Security, 1986. — 27leaves. — (Background paper / Social Security Review ; no.10) (Research paper / Development Division, Department of Social Security ; no.30). — *Includes bibliographical references*

The treatment of disabled persons in social security and taxation law. — Canberra : Australian Government Publishing Service, 1986. — viii,149p. — (Occasional paper / Human Rights Commission ; no.11). — *Bibliography: p134-149*

WHITEFORD, Peter
Issues in assistance for families - horizontal and vertical equity considerations / Peter Whiteford. — Woden, ACT : Department of Social Security, 1986. — iii,56p. — (Background/discussion paper / Social Security Review ; no.5) (Research paper / Department of Social Security ; no.29). — *Bibliography: p52-56*

SOCIAL SECURITY — Austria

TOMANDL, Theodor
Social partnership : the Austrian system of industrial relations and social insurance / Theodor Tomandl, Karl Fuerboeck. — Ithaca, NY : ILR Press, New York State School of Industrial and Labor Relations, Cornell University, c1986. — viii, 165 p.. — (Cornell international industrial and labor relations report ; no. 12). — *Includes index. — Bibliography: p. 157-159*

SOCIAL SECURITY — Brazil

PASSARINHO, Jarbas G.
Resposta às dez principais objeções à integração do seguro de acidentes do trabalho na previdência social / Jarbas G. Passarinho. — [Brazília] : Ministério do Trabalho e Previdência Social, Serviço de Documentação, Seção de Publicação, 1967. — 9p

SOCIAL SECURITY — Canada
BEATTIE, Earle
Canada's billion dollar pension scandal : how secure is your future? / Earle Beattie ; in consultation with Tom Delaney. — Toronto : Methuen, 1985. — 152p. — *References: p151-152*

SOCIAL SECURITY — Denmark
Børnetilskud og andre familieydelser i årene 1970-1981. — [København] : Sikringsstyrelsen, 1983. — 64p. — (Sikringsstyrelsens undersøgelser ; nr.8)

National Health Security Act, 1975. — Copenhagen : Ministry of Social Affairs, [1975]. — 14 leaves

The Public Health Security Act, 1971. — [Copenhagen : Sundhedsstyrelsen?], 1971. — 15 leaves

SOCIAL SECURITY — Denmark — Copenhagen — Statistics
Kontanthjaelp i København 1983. — [København : Kobenhavns Statistiske Kontor, 1983?]. — 79p. — (Undersøgelser fra Københavns Statistiske Kontor ; nr.21). — *Includes English summary*

SOCIAL SECURITY — Egypt
TADROS, Helmi R
Social security and the family in Egypt / by Helmi R. Tadros. — New York, NY (866 United Nations Plaza, New York 10017) : American University in Cairo, c1984. — ix, 87 p.. — (The Cairo papers in social science ; v. 7, monograph 1). — *Summary in Arabic. Title on added t.p.: al-Ta'mīnāt al-ijtimā'īyah fī Miṣr. — "March 1984.". — Bibliography: p. 49-50*

SOCIAL SECURITY — European Economic Community countries
Comparative tables of the social security schemes in the member states of the European Communities. — 13th ed. / (situation at 1 July 1984). — Luxembourg : Office for Official Publications of the European Communities General scheme : (employees in industry and commerce). — 1985. — 119p

SOCIAL SECURITY — Finland
Social insurance in Finland. — Helsinki : Ministry of Social Affairs and Health, 1981. — 47p

SOCIAL SECURITY — Germany — History
RITTER, Gerhard A.
Social welfare in Germany and Britain : origins and development / Gerhard A. Ritter ; translated from the German by Kim Traynor. — Leamington Spa : Berg, c1986. — xi,211p. — *Translation of: Sozialversicherung in Deutschland und England. — Bibliography: p199-206. — Includes index*

SOCIAL SECURITY — Germany. West — Statistics
GERMANY (FEDERAL REPUBLIC). Statistisches Bundesamt
Sozialleistungen: Reihe S.7: Einmalige Leistungen der Hilfe zum Lebensunterhalt. — Wiesbaden : Statistisches Bundesamt, 1981/81-. — *Annual*

SOCIAL SECURITY — Great Britain
ATKINSON, A. B.
Taxation of husband and wife in the UK and changes in the tax-benefit system / A. B. Atkinson and H. Sutherland. — [London : London School of Economics and Political Science], 1987. — 42p. — (Taxation, incentives and the distribution of income ; no.104). — *Economic and Social Research Council programme. — Bibliographical references: p42*

BEENSTOCK, Michael
Work, welfare and taxation : a study of labour supply incentives in the UK / Michael Beenstock and associates. — London : Allen & Unwin, 1987. — xi,275p. — *Bibliography : p268-271. — Includes index*

BERTHOUD, Richard
Standing up for claimants : welfare rights work in local authorities / Richard Berthoud, Sheila Benson and Sandra Williams. — London : Policy Studies Institute, 1986. — 82p. — (Research report / Policy Studies Institute ; no.663)

CHILD POVERTY ACTION GROUP
Burying Beveridge : a detailed response to the Green Paper: Reform of Social Security / [Ruth Lister...et al.]. — London : Child Poverty Action Group, 1985. — 187p

CHURCH OF ENGLAND. Board for Social Responsibility
Reform of social security : response of the Board for Social Responsibility General Synod of the Church of England to the DHSS green paper. — London (Church House, Dean's Yard, SW1P 3NZ) : The Board, 1985. — 5p

Desperate measures : the DHSS supplementary benefit regulations for board and lodging. — [Rev. and updated]. — London : CHAR, 1985. — 49p

Family impact: 1986 Social Security Bill. — London : Family Policy Studies Centre, 1986. — 16p. — (Family policy briefing papers). — *Bibliography: p16*

FAMILY POLICY STUDIES CENTRE
School meals and social security. — London : Family Policy Studies Centre, 1986. — 5p

FAMILY POLICY STUDIES CENTRE
The social fund: a briefing. — London : Family Policy Studies Centre, 1986. — 8p. — *Bibliography: p8*

Fringe benefits, labour costs and social security / edited by Graham L Reid and Donald J. Robertson. — London : Allen and Unwin, 1965. — 336p

GREAT BRITAIN. Parliament. House of Commons. Library. Research Division
Child benefit. — [London] : the Division, [1977]. — 13p. — (Background paper ; no.59)

GREAT BRITAIN. Parliament. House of Commons. Library. Research Division
Self-employed and national insurance. — [London] : the Division, [1975]. — 9 leaves. — (Background paper ; no.43). — *Bibliographical references: leaves 8-9*

GREAT BRITAIN. Parliament. House of Commons. Library. Research Division
Social security reform : reponses to the green paper / Julia Lourie. — [London] : the Division, 1985. — 38p. — (Reference sheet ; no.85/6). — *Includes bibliographical references*

KNOX, Oliver
The wealthy wellfairs : how to care for the rich / Oliver Knox. — London : Centre for Policy Studies, 1986. — 38p. — (Pilot policy / Centre for Policy Studies)

LAND, Hilary
Women and economic dependency / Hilary Land. — Manchester : Equal Opportunities Commission, 1986. — 81p

LAND, Hilary
Women won't benefit : the impact of the Social Security Bill on women's rights / Hilary Land and Sue Ward. — London : National Council for Civil Liberties. Rights for Women Unit, 1986. — 48p

LEWIS, Paul
Reform of social security : the effects of the Social Security Bill on young people / Paul Lewis. — London : Youthaid, 1986. — 38p

LISTER, Ruth
What future for social security : a preliminary commentary on the Green Paper on the reform of social security / Ruth Lister, Jo Roll and Roger Smith. — London : Child Poverty Action Group, 1985. — 24p

RAYNES, Harold Ernest
Social security in Britain : a history / Harold E. Raynes. — 2nd ed. — London : Pitman, 1960. — viii,264p

Rights to non-means-tested social security benefits. — London : Child Poverty Action Group, 1981-. — *Annual*

Statutory sick pay / Department of Health and Social Security. — London : HMSO, 1986-

SUTHERLAND, H.
Modelling the SDP tax/benefit scheme / Holly Sutherland. — [London : London School of Economics and Political Science], 1986. — 25p. — (Taxation, incentives and the distribution of income ; no.101). — *Economic and Social Research Council programme. — Bibliographical references: p25*

SOCIAL SECURITY — Great Britain — History
RITTER, Gerhard A.
Social welfare in Germany and Britain : origins and development / Gerhard A. Ritter ; translated from the German by Kim Traynor. — Leamington Spa : Berg, c1986. — xi,211p. — *Translation of: Sozialversicherung in Deutschland und England. — Bibliography: p199-206. — Includes index*

SOCIAL SECURITY — Great Britain — Law and legislation
SOCIAL SECURITY CONSORTIUM
Of little benefit : a critical guide to the Social Security Act 1986. — London : Social Security Consortium, 1986. — 24p

SOCIAL SECURITY — Great Britain — Statistics
GREAT BRITAIN. Department of Health and Social Security
Supplementary benefit statistics. — Newcastle upon Tyne : [the Department], 1983-. — *Annual*

SOCIAL SECURITY — India
SHARMA, K. M.
Social assistance in India / K. M. Sharma. — Delhi : Macmillan Co. of India, 1976. — x,119p. — *Revision of author's thesis, University of Allahabad. — Bibliography: p [109]-114*

SOCIAL SECURITY — Law and legislation
Social security and family law : with special reference to the one-parent family : a comparative survey / edited by Alec Samuels. — [s.l.] : United Kingdom National Committee of Comparative Law, 1979. — 327p. — (United Kingdom comparative law series ; v. 4) . — *Includes bibliographies. — Based on revised papers and contributions originally submitted to a colloquium held by the United Kingdom National Committee for Comparative Law at the University of Nottingham*

SOCIAL SECURITY — Netherlands — Statistics
Ontvangers van periodieke bijstand / Centraal Bureau voor de Statistiek, Netherlands. — 's-gravenhage : Staatsuitgeverij, 1982-. — *Annual*

SOCIAL SECURITY — New Zealand — Finance
HOWELL, T. A.
Changing a winning scheme : a Nuffield Fellowship study of New Zealand's social security cash benefits / T. A. Howell. — London : Department of Health and Social Security, 1975. — 110p

SOCIAL SECURITY — Peru
CONSEJO NACIONAL PARA LA SEGURIDAD SOCIAL (Peru)
Consejo Nacional para la Seguridad Social. — [Lima] : the Consejo, [197-?]. — 9p

SOCIAL SECURITY — Québec (Province)
PERREAULT, Géraldine
La situation des jeunes à l'aide sociale. — Québec : [Ministère de la main-d'oeuvre et de la sécurité du revenu], 1984. — iv,103p. — (Études monographiques en sécurité du revenu ; no.1)

SOCIAL SECURITY — Scandinavia — Statistics
Social security in the Nordic countries : scope, expenditure and financing 1981. — Helsinki : Nordic Statistical Secretariat. — 187p. — (Nordisk statistisk skriftserie = Statistical reports of the Nordic countries ; 44)

SOCIAL SECURITY — Spain
ORDEIG FOS, José María
El sistema español de seguridad social / José María Ordeig Fos. — 2-a ed. — Madrid : Edersa, 1986. — xxi,558p

SOCIAL SECURITY — United States
LIGHT, Paul Charles
Artful work : the politics of social security reform / Paul Light. — 1st ed. — New York : Random House, c1985. — xiv, 255 p.. — Includes index

Work, health, and income among the elderly / Gary Burtless, editor. — Washington, D.C. : Brookings Institution, c1987. — xiii, 276 p.. — (Studies in social economics). — Includes bibliographical references and index

SOCIAL SECURITY — United States — Congresses
Checks and balances in social security : symposium in honor of Robert J. Myers / symposium convened and directed by Yung-Ping Chen ; edited by Yung-Ping Chen and George F. Rohrlich. — Lanham, MD : University Press of America, c1986. — xxiv, 357 p.. — Spine title: Checks & balances in social security. — Includes bibliographies

SOCIAL SECURITY — United States — Finance
LIGHT, Paul Charles
Artful work : the politics of social security reform / Paul Light. — 1st ed. — New York : Random House, c1985. — xiv, 255 p.. — Includes index

SOCIAL SECURITY — United States — History
ACHENBAUM, W. Andrew
Social security : visions and revisions / W. Andrew Achenbaum. — Cambridge : Cambridge University Press, 1986. — [304]p. — (A Twentieth Century Fund study). — Includes index

SOCIAL SECURITY — United States — Law and Legislation
Proposals to deal with the social security notch problem. — Washington, D.C. : American Enterprise Institute for Public Policy Research, 1985. — 34p. — (AEI legislative analyses)

SOCIAL SECURITY (AGE OF RETIREMENT) BILL 1983-84
GREAT BRITAIN. Parliament. House of Commons. Library. Research Division
Social Security (Age of Retirement) Bill 1983/4 [Bill 16] / Julia Lourie. — [London] : the Division, 1983. — 20p. — (Reference sheet ; no.83/21). — Bibliographical references: p15-18

SOCIAL SECURITY AND HOUSING BENEFITS BILL 1982-83
GREAT BRITAIN. Parliament. House of Commons. Library. Research Division
Social Security and Housing Benefits Bill 1982/83 (Bill 109) / Julia Lourie. — [London] : the Division, 1983. — 23p. — (Reference sheet ; no.83/7). — Bibliographical references: p14-15

SOCIAL SECURITY BENEFICIARIES — Legal status, laws, etc. — Quebec (Province)
La protection de la vie privée des personnes bénéficiant de lois sociales au Québec. — [Québec : Yvon Blais, c1983]. — 142p. — 1982 prix Charles-Coderre pour l'avancement du droit social, décernés par le Fonds Charles-Coderre du Centre de Services Sociaux du Montréal métropolitain. — Contient le premier, le deuxième et le troisième prix

SOCIAL SECURITY BILL 1979-80
GREAT BRITAIN. Parliament. House of Commons. Library. Research Division
Social Security Bill (No.86 of 1979/80) / [Julia Lourie]. — [London] : the Division, 1979. — 5p. — (Reference sheet ; no.79/16)

SOCIAL SECURITY BILL 1980-81
GREAT BRITAIN. Parliament. House of Commons. Library. Research Division
Social Security Bill 1980/81 (Bill 68) / [Julia Lourie]. — [London] : the Division, 1981. — 10p. — (Reference sheet ; no.81/8). — Bibliography: p8-10

SOCIAL SECURITY BILL 1984-85
GREAT BRITAIN. Parliament. House of Commons. Library. Research Division
Social Security Bill 1984/5 [Bill 10] / Julia Lourie. — [London] : the Division, 1984. — 23p. — (Reference sheet ; no.84/11). — Bibliographical references: p18-23

SOCIAL SECURITY BILL 1985-86
GREAT BRITAIN. Parliament. House of Commons. Library. Research Division
Social Security Bill 1985/6 [Bill 59] / Julia Lourie, Christine Gillie. — [London] : the Division, 1986. — 52p. — (Reference sheet ; no.86/3). — Bibliographical references: p46-52

SOCIAL SECURITY (CONTRIBUTIONS) BILL 1980-81
GREAT BRITAIN. Parliament. House of Commons. Library. Research Division
Social Security (Contributions) Bill 1980-81 [Bill 4] / [Julia Lourie]. — [London] : the Division, 1980. — 19p. — (Reference sheet ; no.80/16). — Bibliographical references: p17-19

SOCIAL SECURITY COURTS — Great Britain — Bibliography
WHITEHEAD, D. W.
Selected references on social security adjudication and appeals procedure / compiled by D. W. Whitehead. — London : Department of Health and Social Security Library, 1978. — 5p. — (Bibliography series / Department of Health and Social Security Library ; no.J13)

SOCIAL SECURITY COURTS — United States
COFER, M. Donna Price
Judges, bureaucrats, and the question of independence : a study of the Social Security Administration hearing process / Donna Price Cofer. — Westport, Conn. : Greenwood Press, 1985. — xvii, 245 p.. — (Contributions in political science ; no. 130). — Includes index. — Bibliography: p. [231]-235

SOCIAL SECURITY (NO.2) BILL 1979-80
GREAT BRITAIN. Parliament. House of Commons. Library. Research Division
The Social Security (No.2) Bill 1979/80 (Bill 180) / Julia Lourie, Christine Fretten. — [London] : the Division, 1980. — 13p. — (Reference sheet ; no.80/11). — Bibliography: p10-13

SOCIAL SERVICE
BARTLETT, Harriet M.
Analyzing social work practice by fields / Harriet M. Bartlett. — New York : National Association of Social Workers, [1961]. — 69p

FLORO, George K.
Sociology for life : expanding circles of social participation through scholarship, community service, and teaching / George K. Floro. — Lanham : University Press of America, c1986. — xvii, 135 p.. — Includes index. — Bibliography: p. 125-128

JORDAN, Bill, 1941-
Rethinking welfare / Bill Jordan. — Oxford : Basil Blackwell, 1987. — [224]p. — Includes index

KADUSHIN, Alfred
The social work interview / Alfred Kadushin. — 2nd ed. — New York : Columbia University Press, 1983. — 423 p.. — Includes index. — Bibliography: p. [403]-416

MEYER, Carol H.
Social work practice : a response to the urban crisis / Carol H. Meyer. — London : Collier-Macmillan, 1970. — 227p

Psychology for social workers / [edited by] Martin Herbert. — 2nd ed. — London : Macmillan, 1986. — [350]p. — (Psychology for professional groups). — Previous ed.: 1981. — Includes bibliographies and index

Social work departments as organisations / [Joyce Lishman: editor]. — Aberdeen : University of Aberdeen, Department of Social Work, 1982. — 111p. — (Research highlights in Social work ; no.4)

SOCIAL SERVICE — Addresses, essays, lectures
The Field of social work / [edited by] Arthur E. Fink, Jane H. Pfouts, Andrew W. Dobelstein. — 8th ed. — Beverly Hills, Calif. : Sage Publications, c1985. — 400 p.. — Includes bibliographies and index

SOCIAL SERVICE — Data processing
SMITH, N. J.
Social welfare and computers : a general outline / N. J. Smith. — Melbourne : Longman Cheshire, 1985. — xiii,124p. — Bibliography: p115-119

SOCIAL SERVICE — Psychological aspects
NICOLSON, Paula
Applied psychology for social workers / Paula Nicolson and Rowan Bayne. — London : Macmillan, 1984. — x,166p. — (Practical social work). — Bibliography: p[159]-164

SOCIAL SERVICE — Team-work
ATHERTON, James S.
Professional supervision in group care : a contract-based approach / James S. Atherton. — London : Tavistock Publications, 1986. — [192]p. — (Residential social work). — Includes index

SOCIAL SERVICE — Vocational guidance — Great Britain
JORDAN, Bill, 1941-
Invitation to social work / Bill Jordan. — Oxford : Robertson, 1984. — 198p. — (Invitation series). — Bibliography: p190-193. — Includes index

SOCIAL SERVICE — Africa
Health by the people for the people : health for all by the year 2000. — Brazzaville : Regional Office for Africa, World Health Organization, 1978. — 147p. — (AFRO technical papers ; no.14). — At head of title; 30th anniversary of WHO. — Includes bibliographical references

SOCIAL SERVICE — Denmark
JEPPESEN, Kirsten Just
Private hjaelpeorganisationer : på det sociale område / Kirsten Just Jeppesen, Dorte Høeg. — København : Socialforskningsinstituttet, 1987. — 182p. — (Publikation / Socialforskningsinstituttet ; 160). — Bibliography: p179-180

SOCIAL SERVICE — Denmark — Bibliography
Bibliography of foreign-language literature on industrial relations and social services in Denmark. — København : Arbejds- og socialministeriernes bibliotek, 1975. — 28 leaves

SOCIAL SERVICE — Developing countries — Finance
JIMENEZ, Emmanuel
Pricing policy in the social sectors : cost recovery for education and health in developing countries / Emmanuel Jimenez. — Baltimore : Johns Hopkins University Press for the World Bank, 1987. — v,170p. — *Bibliographical references: p155-163*

SOCIAL SERVICE — France
[Institutions sociales de la France. English]. The Social institutions of France : translations from the first French edition = [Les institutions sociales de la France] / coordinated by Roy Evans with the assistance of Patricia G. Evans. — New York : Gordon and Breach, c1983. — xxii, 802 p.. — : *"Original French work was produced under the direction of Pierre Laroque"--P. v. — Includes bibliographical references*

SOCIAL SERVICE — France — Nomenclature
FRANCE. Ministerè des Affaires Sociales et de la Solidarité Nationale. Service des Statistiques, des Etudes et des Systèmes d'Information
Nomenclatures applicables aux unités de production des établissements sanitaires, sociaux et médico-sociaux et aux prestations qui y sont servies : période de validité: exercice 1986. — [Paris] : Ministère des Affaires Sociales et de la Solidarité Nationale, SESI, 1986. — 194p. — (Solidarité santé. Cahiers statistiques ; no.7 bis)

SOCIAL SERVICE — Great Britain
BERESFORD, Peter
Whose welfare : private care of public services? / Peter Beresford and Suzy Croft. — Brighton : Lewis Cohen Urban Studies Centre, 1986. — xvi,384p. — *Bibliography: p382-384*

BROWN, Muriel
Introduction to social administration in Britain / Muriel Brown. — 6th ed. — London : Hutchinson, 1985. — 304p. — (Hutchinson university library). — *Previous ed.: 1982. — Includes bibliographies and index*

CURRIE, Robin
A unitary approach to social work : application in practice : an analysis of a patch system and team approach within a unitary framework in a social services department / Robin Currie and Brian Parrott. — new ed. — Birmingham : British Association of Social Workers, 1986. — 64p. — (BASW publications)

DAVIES, Bleddyn
Matching resources to needs in community care : an evaluated demonstration of a long-term care model / Bleddyn Davies & David Challis. — Aldershot : Gower, c1986. — xxxii,658p. — *Bibliography: p571-642. — Includes index*

DAVIES, Martin, 1936-
The essential social worker : a guide to positive practice / Martin Davies. — 2nd ed / with an appendix on 'Law and the social worker' by Caroline Ball. — Aldershot : Gower, c1985. — 278p. — (Community care practice handbooks ; 5). — *Previous ed.: London : Heinemann Educational, 1981. — Bibliography: p258-270. — Includes index*

DAY, Peter R.
Sociology in social work practice / Peter R. Day. — Basingstoke : Macmillan Education, 1987. — vii,157p. — (Practical social work). — *Bibliography: p141-149. — Includes index*

FEATHERSTONE, Bríd
"There is an alternative" : the promotional work of the probation service and social services departments : a review and guide to better practice / Bríd Featherstone. — London : Prison Reform Trust, 1987. — 67p. — *Bibliography: p67-68*

The future role of social services departments / John Rea Price [et al.]. — London : Policy Studies Institute, 1987. — 40p

LEAT, Diana
Paying for care : a study of policy and practice in paid care schemes / Diana Leat [and] Pat Gay. — London : Policy Studies Institute, 1987. — 81p. — (Research report / Policy Studies Institute ; no.661). — *Bibliography: p79-81*

SULLIVAN, Michael, 19---
Sociology and social welfare / Michael Sullivan. — London : Allen & Unwin, 1987. — [172]p. — (Studies in sociology ; 14). — *Includes bibliography and index*

SOCIAL SERVICE — Great Britain — Bibliography
Studies on community health and personal social services / Department of Health and Social Security Library, Great Britain. — London : DHSS, 1972. — *Annual*

SOCIAL SERVICE — Great Britain — Finance
DAVIES, Bleddyn
Matching resources to needs in community care : an evaluated demonstration of a long-term care model / Bleddyn Davies & David Challis. — Aldershot : Gower, c1986. — xxxii,658p. — *Bibliography: p571-642. Includes index*

SOCIAL SERVICE — Hong Kong
The Common welfare : Hong Kong's social services / edited by John F. Jones. — Hong Kong : Chinese University Press ; Manila, Philippines : United Nations Social Welfare and Development Centre for Asia and the Pacific, c1981. — xix, 148 p.. — *Includes index. — Bibliography: p. [131]-146*

SOCIAL SERVICE — India
Essays on economic progress and welfare : in honour of I.G. Patel / edited by S. Guhan and Manu Shroff. — Delhi ; New York : Oxford University Press, 1986. — xvi, 330 p., [1] leaf of plates. — *Includes bibliographies and index*

Social development : essays in honour of SMT Durgabai Deshmukh / edited by B. N. Ganguli. — New Delhi : Sterling Publishers : Council for Social Development, 1977. — viii,303p. — *Bibliography: p287-290*

SOCIAL SERVICE — Ireland — Tallaght (Dublin) — Case studies
LAVAN, Ann
Social need and community social services : voluntary-statutory co-operation in Tallaght : a social policy research report / by Ann Lavan. — Tallaght, Co. Dublin : Tallaght Welfare Society, c1981. — x, 261 p.. — *Includes bibliographical references*

SOCIAL SERVICE — South Africa
SOUTH AFRICA. Department of Co-operation and Development. Division of Social Work
Social work practice. — Pretoria : [the Department], 1984-. — *3 per year*

SOCIAL SERVICE — South Australia
SOUTH AUSTRALIA. Department for Community Welfare
Regional community welfare services : a plan of development. — [Adelaide] : the Department, 1983. — [40]p. — *Cover title. — Submission to the National Commission on Social Welfare*

SOCIAL SERVICE — Taiwan
A brief report on social welfare service of the Republic of China. — [Taipei] : Ministry of Interior, 1962. — iii,42p

Social welfare services in the Republic of China. — [Taipei] : Ministry of Interior, 1958. — 38p

SOCIAL SERVICE — United States
Social planning and human service delivery in the voluntary sector / edited by Gary A. Tobin. — Westport, Conn. : Greenwood Press, 1985. — xxx, 290 p.. — (Studies in social welfare policies and programs ; no. 1). — *Includes index. — Bibliography: p. [261]-276*

SOSIN, Michael
Private benefits : material assistance in the private sector / Michael Sosin. — Orlando : Academic Press, 1986. — xvii, 195 p.. — (Institute for Research on Poverty monograph series). — *Includes index. — Bibliography: p. 179-184*

SOCIAL SERVICE — United States — Addresses, essays, lectures
The Field of social work / [edited by] Arthur E. Fink, Jane H. Pfouts, Andrew W. Dobelstein. — 8th ed. — Beverly Hills, Calif. : Sage Publications, c1985. — 400 p.. — *Includes bibliographies and index*

SOCIAL SERVICE AND RACE RELATIONS — Great Britain
Race and social work : a guide to training / edited by Vivienne Coombe and Alan Little. — London : Tavistock, 1986. — xiii,233p. — (Social science paperbacks ; 330). — *Includes bibliographies and index*

SOCIAL SERVICE, RURAL — Great Britain
Deprivation and welfare in rural areas / edited by Philip Lowe, Tony Bradley and Susan Wright. — Norwich : Geo, [1986]. — viii,229p. — *Includes bibliographies*

SOCIAL SERVICE, RURAL — Northern Ireland
CECIL, Rosanne
Informal welfare : a sociological study of care in Northern Ireland / Rosanne Cecil, John Offer and Fred St. Leger. — Aldershot : Gower, c1987. — vii,166p. — *Bibliography: p154-162. — Includes index*

SOCIAL SETTLEMENTS — Scotland — Dumfries and Galloway
DUMFRIES AND GALLOWAY. Regional Council
Structure plan : report of survey : settlements and services (revised). — Dumfries : [the Regional Council], 1979. — 115p

SOCIAL SKILLS
BINSTED, Don
Developments in interpersonal skills training / Don Binsted. — Aldershot : Gower, c1986. — vi,208p. — *Bibliography: p206-208*

SOCIAL SKILLS IN CHILDREN
Children's social behavior : development, assessment, and modification / edited by Phillip S. Strain, Michael J. Guralnick, Hill M. Walker. — Orlando [Fla.] : Academic Press, 1986. — xiii, 460 p.. — *Includes bibliographies and index*

SOCIAL SKILLS IN CHILDREN — Therapeutic use
Children's social behavior : development, assessment, and modification / edited by Phillip S. Strain, Michael J. Guralnick, Hill M. Walker. — Orlando [Fla.] : Academic Press, 1986. — xiii, 460 p.. — *Includes bibliographies and index*

SOCIAL STATUS — Cross-cultural studies
KASARDA, John D
Status enhancement and fertility : reproductive responses to social mobility and educational opportunity / John D. Kasarda, John O.G. Billy, Kirsten West. — Orlando, Fla. : Academic Press, 1986. — xii, 266 p.. — (Studies in population). — *Includes indexes. — Bibliography: p.216-250*

SOCIAL STATUS — Canada
Ascription and achievement : studies in mobility and status attainment in Canada / by Monica Boyd ... [et al.]. — Ottawa, Canada : Carleton University Press ; Don Mills, Ont., Canada : Distributed by Oxford University Press Canada, c1985. — 539 p.. — (Carleton library series ; 133). — *Includes bibliographies*

SOCIAL STATUS — United States
The Egalitarian city : issues of rights, distribution, access, and power / edited by Janet K. Boles. — New York : Praeger, 1986. — xiv, 223 p.. — *Includes bibliographies*

SOCIAL STRUCTURE

ASSOCIATION OF SOCIAL ANTHROPOLOGISTS OF THE COMMONWEALTH. Conference (1977 : Swansea)
Sex and age as principles of social differentiation / edited by J.S. La Fontaine. — London : Academic Press, 1978. — vii,188p. — (Monographs / Association of Social Anthropologists of the Commonwealth ; 17). — *The papers presented here represent six out of eight papers delivered at the Conference of the Association of Social Anthropologists at Swansea in April 1977´ - Preface. — Includes bibliographies and index*

Charisma, history, and social structure / edited by Ronald M. Glassman and William H. Swatos, Jr. — New York : Greenwood Press, 1986. — viii, 240 p.. — (Contributions in sociology ; no. 58). — *Includes index. — Bibliography: p. [223]-232. — Contents: Introduction / Ronald M. Glassman and William H. Swatos, Jr. -- On the interpretation and misinterpretation of the concept of charismatic leadership. Bureaucracy and charisma : a philosophy of history / H.H. Gerth and C. Wright Mills. Reflections on charismatic leadership / Reinhard Bendix. Charisma and modernity : the use and abuse of a concept / Joseph Bensman and Michael Givant. Charisma and illegitimate authority / Richard S. Bell -- Charisma and religion. Charismatic Calvinism : forging a missing link / William H. Swatos, Jr. Hasidism and Moonism : charisma in the counterculture / Alan L. Berger. Against Satan : charisma and tradition in Iran / Michael S. Kimmel and Rahmat Tavakol -- The fate of charisma in the modern world. Manufactured charisma and legitimacy / Ronald M. Glassman. The disenchantment of charisma : on revolution in a rationalized world / William H. Swatos, Jr. Hitler's dictatorial charisma / Arthur Schweitzer. The historic fate of the charisma of r*

FAIA, Michael A.
Dynamic functionalism : strategy and tactics / Michael A. Faia. — Cambridge : Cambridge University Press, 1986. — xiv,187p. — (The Arnold and Caroline Rose monograph series of the American Sociological Association) (ASA rose monograph series). — *Bibliography: p174-184. — Includes index*

LEY, David
A social geography of the city / David Ley. — New York : Harper & Row, c1983. — xii,449p. — (Harper & Row series in geography). — *Bibliography: p.401-441*

MACH, Bogdan W.
Social mobility and social structure / Bogdan W. Mach and Włodzimierz Wesołowski. — London : Routledge & Kegan Paul, 1986. — vi,118p. — (International library of sociology). — *Translation of Ruchliwość a teoria struktury społecznej (Warsaw, 1982)*

Social movements in an organization society : collected essays / edited by Mayer N. Zald and John D. McCarthy. — New Brunswick, N.J., U.S.A. : Transaction Books, c1986. — p. cm. — *Includes index. — Bibliography: p*

TESTART, Alain
Les chasseurs-cueilleurs, ou l´origine des inégalités / Alain Testart. — Paris : Société d´ethnographie, 1982. — 254p. — (Mémoires de la Société d´ethnographie ; 26). — *Bibliography: p227-247*

SOCIAL STRUCTURE — Comparative studies

Comparative studies of social structure : recent research on France, the United States, and the Federal Republic of Germany / edited by Wolfgang Teckenberg. — Armonk, NY : M.E. Sharpe, c1987. — p. cm. — *"Published simultaneously as vol. XVII, no. 1-2 of International journal of sociology"--Verso of t.p. — Bibliography: p. — Contents: Intergenerational and career mobility in the Federal Republic of Germany and the United States / Peter Kappelhoff and Wolfgang Teckenberg -- Employment and career mobility of women in France and the Federal Republic of Germany / Wolfgang König -- Entry into the labor market and occupation career in the Federal Republic of Germany / Hans-Peter Blossfeld -- Class position and income inequality / Michael Terwey -- Positional and sectoral differences in income / Max Haller*

SOCIAL STRUCTURE — Psychological aspects — Bibliography

BIEGEL, David E
Social networks and mental health : an annotated bibliography / David E. Biegel, Ellen McCardle, Susan Mendelson ; foreword by Stephen E. Goldston. — Beverly Hills, Calif. : Sage Publications, [1985]. — 391 p.. — *Includes indexes*

SOCIAL STRUCTURE — Africa, Sub-Saharan — History

DIOP, Cheikh Anta
[Afrique noire pré-coloniale. English]. Precolonial Black Africa : a comparative study of the political and social systems of Europe and Black Africa, from antiquity to the formation of modern states / Cheikh Anta Diop ; translated by Harold J. Salemson. — Westport, Conn. : L. Hill, 1986. — p. cm. — *Translation of: L´Afrique noire pré-coloniale*

SOCIAL STRUCTURE — Denmark

Sociale netvaerk og socialpolitik : en undersøgelse i to lokalområder / Mogens Kjaer Jensen...[et al.]. — København : Socialforskningsinstituttet, 1987. — 202p. — (Publikation / Socialforskningsinstituttet ; 163). — *Bibliography: p199-200*

SOCIAL STRUCTURE — Europe — History

DIOP, Cheikh Anta
[Afrique noire pré-coloniale. English]. Precolonial Black Africa : a comparative study of the political and social systems of Europe and Black Africa, from antiquity to the formation of modern states / Cheikh Anta Diop ; translated by Harold J. Salemson. — Westport, Conn. : L. Hill, 1986. — p. cm. — *Translation of: L´Afrique noire pré-coloniale*

SOCIAL STRUCTURE — Europe, Eastern

Sotsial'naia struktura i politicheskie dvizheniia v stranakh Tsentral'noi i Iugo-Vostochnoi Evropy : mezhvoennyi period / otv. redaktor A. Kh. Klevanskii. — Moskva : Nauka, 1986. — 244p

SOCIAL STRUCTURE — France

Comparative studies of social structure : recent research on France, the United States, and the Federal Republic of Germany / edited by Wolfgang Teckenberg. — Armonk, NY : M.E. Sharpe, c1987. — p. cm. — *"Published simultaneously as vol. XVII, no. 1-2 of International journal of sociology"--Verso of t.p. — Bibliography: p. — Contents: Intergenerational and career mobility in the Federal Republic of Germany and the United States / Peter Kappelhoff and Wolfgang Teckenberg -- Employment and career mobility of women in France and the Federal Republic of Germany / Wolfgang König -- Entry into the labor market and occupation career in the Federal Republic of Germany / Hans-Peter Blossfeld -- Class position and income inequality / Michael Terwey -- Positional and sectoral differences in income / Max Haller*

SOCIAL STRUCTURE — Germany (West)

Comparative studies of social structure : recent research on France, the United States, and the Federal Republic of Germany / edited by Wolfgang Teckenberg. — Armonk, NY : M.E. Sharpe, c1987. — p. cm. — *"Published simultaneously as vol. XVII, no. 1-2 of International journal of sociology"--Verso of t.p. — Bibliography: p. — Contents: Intergenerational and career mobility in the Federal Republic of Germany and the United States / Peter Kappelhoff and Wolfgang Teckenberg -- Employment and career mobility of women in France and the Federal Republic of Germany / Wolfgang König -- Entry into the labor market and occupation career in the Federal Republic of Germany / Hans-Peter Blossfeld -- Class position and income inequality / Michael Terwey -- Positional and sectoral differences in income / Max Haller*

SOCIAL STRUCTURE — Iran — Case studies

GOODELL, Grace E
The elementary structures of political life : rural development in Pahlavi Iran / Grace E. Goodell. — New York : Oxford University Press, 1986. — vii, 362 p.. — *Includes index. — Bibliography: p. 345-350*

SOCIAL STRUCTURE — Japan

IGA, Mamoru
The thorn in the chrysanthemum : suicide and economic success in modern Japan / Mamoru Iga ; forewords by Edwin S. Shneidman and David K. Reynolds. — Berkeley : University of California Press, c1986. — xiv, 231 p.. — *Includes index. — Bibliography: p. 205-217*

SOCIAL STRUCTURE — Libya

ANDERSON, Lisa
The state and social transformation in Tunisia and Libya, 1830-1980 / Lisa Anderson. — Princeton, N.J. : Princeton University Press, c1986. — xxiv, 325 p.. — (Princeton studies on the Near East). — *Includes index. — Bibliography: p. 295-311*

SOCIAL STRUCTURE — Pennsylvania — Hazleton

AURAND, Harold W
Population change and social continuity : ten years in a coal town / Harold W. Aurand. — Selinsgrove [Pa.] : Susquehanna University Press ; London : Associated University Presses, c1986. — 139 p.. — *Includes index. — Bibliography: p. 131-134*

SOCIAL STRUCTURE — Portugal — History

O´NEILL, Brian Juan
Social inequality in a Portuguese hamlet : land, late marriage and bastardy 1870-1978 / Brian Juan O´Neill. — Cambridge : Cambridge University Press, 1987. — xix,431p. — (Cambridge studies in social anthropology ; 63) . — *Translation of: Proprietarios, lavradores e jornaleiras. — Bibliography: p401-418. — Includes index*

SOCIAL STRUCTURE — Russian S.F.S.R. — Buriat A.S.S.R.

MITUPOV, K. B-M.
Stanovlenie sotsialisticheskoi sotsial'noi struktury Buriatii 1938-1960 gg. / K. B-M. Mitupov ; otv.redaktor V. B. Tel'pukhovskii. — Novosibirsk : Nauka, Sibirskoe otdelenie, 1986. — 133p

SOCIAL STRUCTURE — Soviet Union

SELUNSKAIA, V. M.
Sotsial'naia struktura Sovetskogo obshchestva : istoriia i sovremennost' / V. M. Selunskaia. — Moskva : Politizdat, 1987. — 286p

SOCIAL STRUCTURE — Spain

Estructuras sociales y cuestión nacional en España / Francesc Hernández y Francesc Mercadé, compiladores ; prologo de Salvador Giner. — Barcelona : Ariel, 1986. — 512p

SOCIAL STRUCTURE — Tunisia

ANDERSON, Lisa
The state and social transformation in Tunisia and Libya, 1830-1980 / Lisa Anderson. — Princeton, N.J. : Princeton University Press, c1986. — xxiv, 325 p.. — (Princeton studies on the Near East). — Includes index. — Bibliography: p. 295-311

SOCIAL STRUCTURE — United States

CLARK, Gordon L
Judges and the cities : interpreting local autonomy / Gordon L. Clark. — Chicago : University of Chicago Press, c1985. — xv, 247 p.. — Includes index. — Bibliography: p. 231-242

Comparative studies of social structure : recent research on France, the United States, and the Federal Republic of Germany / edited by Wolfgang Teckenberg. — Armonk, NY : M.E. Sharpe, c1987. — p. cm. — "Published simultaneously as vol. XVII, no. 1-2 of International journal of sociology"--Verso of t.p. — Bibliography: p. — Contents: Intergenerational and career mobility in the Federal Republic of Germany and the United States / Peter Kappelhoff and Wolfgang Teckenberg -- Employment and career mobility of women in France and the Federal Republic of Germany / Wolfgang König -- Entry into the labor market and occupation career in the Federal Republic of Germany / Hans-Peter Blossfeld -- Class position and income inequality / Michael Terwey -- Positional and sectoral differences in income / Max Haller

SOCIAL SURVEYS

BELSON, William A.
Validity in survey research : with special reference to the techniques of intensive interviewing and progressive modification for testing and constructing difficult or sensitive measures for use in survey research : a report / by William A. Belsen. — Aldershot : Gower, c1986. — xviii,565p. — Fiche in pocket. — Includes index

CONVERSE, Jean M.
Survey questions : Handcrafting the standardized questionnaire / Jean M. Converse [and] Stanley Presser. — Beverly Hills : Sage Publications, 1986. — 80p. — (Quantitative applications in the social sciences ; 63). — Bibliography: p76-79

JOLLIFFE, F. R.
Survey design and analysis / F.R. Jolliffe. — Chichester : Ellis Horwood, 1986. — 178p. — (Statistics and operational research)

MISHLER, Elliot George
Research interviewing : context and narrative / Elliot G. Mishler. — Cambridge, Mass. : Harvard University Press, 1986. — xi, 189 p.. — Includes index. — Bibliography: p. [171]-185

SHESKIN, Ira M.
Survey research for geographers / Ira M. Sheskin. — Washington, DC : Association of American Geographers, 1985. — 112p. — (Resource Publications in geography). — Bibliography: p.105-112

WORLD FERTILITY SURVEY. Seminar on Collection and Analyis of Data on Community and Institutional Factors (1983 : London)
The Collection and analysis of community data / edited by John B. Casterline. — Voorburg : International Statistical Institute : World Fertility Survey, 1985. — xvi, 286p. — Includes bibliographical references

SOCIAL SURVEYS — Response rate

MARCKWARDT, Albert M.
Response rates, callbacks and coverage : the WFS experience / Albert M. Marckwardt. — Voorburg : International Statistical Institute, 1984. — 32p. — (Scientific reports / World Fertility Survey ; no.55)

SOCIAL SURVEYS — Australia — Sydney (N.S.W.)

DAY, Alice Taylor
We can manage : expectations about care and varieties of family support among people 75 years and over / Alice T. Day. — Melbourne : Institute of Family Studies, c1985. — xii, 168 p.. — (Institute of Family Studies monograph ; no. 5). — "February 1985.". — Bibliography: p. 162-168

SOCIAL SURVEYS — Great Britain

GREAT BRITAIN. Office of Population Censuses and Surveys. Social Survey Division
Annual report / Social Survey Division, Office of Population Censuses and Surveys. — London : OPCS, 1984/85-. — Annual

SOCIAL SURVEYS — India

PRAKASH, Om
Caste Hindu and scheduled caste children in rural India / Om Prakash and Arun K. Sen. — New Delhi : Ess Ess Publications, 1985. — xiv, 184 p.. — Spine title: Hindu caste and scheduled caste children in rural India. — Includes index. — Bibliography: p. [155]-182

SOCIAL SURVEYS — India — Nagpur

SHAMKUNWAR, M. R.
Scheduled castes : socio-economic survey / by M. R. Shamkunwar. — Allahabad [India] : Kitab Mahal, 1985. — vii,151p. — Bibliography: p[141]-143

SOCIAL SURVEYS — Southern States

REED, John Shelton
The enduring South : subcultural persistence in mass society / John Shelton Reed ; with a new afterword by the author. — Chapel Hill : University of North Carolina Press, 1986, c1974. — p. cm. — Includes index. — Bibliography: p

SOCIAL SYSTEMS

BURNS, Tom R.
The shaping of social organization : social rule system theory with applications / by Tom R. Burns and Helena Flam ; with Reinier de Man ... [et al]. — London : Sage, 1987. — [432]p. — Includes bibliography and index

JESSOP, Bob
Economy, state and the law in autopoietic theory / by Bob Jessop. — Colchester : Department of Government University of Essex, 1987. — 48 p. — (Essex papers in politics and government ; no.42)

SOCIAL SYSTEMS — Congresses

The Social fabric : dimensions and issues / [edited] by James F. Short, Jr. — Beverly Hills, Calif. : Sage Publications, c1986. — p. cm. — (American Sociological Association presidential series) — Based on papers presented at the 79th Annual Meeting of the American Sociological Association, held in San Antonio, Tex., Aug. 27-31, 1984. — Includes bibliographies and index

SOCIAL VALUES

IGA, Mamoru
The thorn in the chrysanthemum : suicide and economic success in modern Japan / Mamoru Iga ; forewords by Edwin S. Shneidman and David K. Reynolds. — Berkeley : University of California Press, c1986. — xiv, 231 p.. — Includes index. — Bibliography: p. 205-217

SOCIAL VALUES — Congresses

Values in conflict : Blacks and the American ambivalence toward violence / edited by Charles A. Frye. — Washington, D.C. : University Press of America, c1980. — iii, 169 p.. — Includes bibliographies and index

SOCIAL WORK ADMINISTRATION

SCHAEFER, Morris
Designing and using procedure in health and human services / by Morris Schaefer. — Beverly Hills : Sage Publications, c1985. — p. cm. — (Sage human services guides ; 39)

Social work departments as organisations / [Joyce Lishman: editor]. — Aberdeen : University of Aberdeen, Department of Social Work, 1982. — 111p. — (Research highlights in Social work ; no.4)

SOCIAL WORK EDUCATION — Great Britain

CCETSW reporting / Central Council for Education and Training in Social Work. — London : CCETSW, 1985-. — Irregular

CENTRAL COUNCIL FOR EDUCATION AND TRAINING IN SOCIAL WORK
Council policy on training for community work within the personal social services. — [London] : the Council, 1979. — 14p

SOCIAL WORK WITH BLACKS — Great Britain

Social work with black children and their families / edited by Shama Ahmed, Juliet Cheetham and John Small. — London : Batsford in association with British Agencies for Adoption and Fostering, 1986. — 207p. — (Child care policy and practice). — Includes bibliographies and index

SOCIAL WORK WITH CHILDREN — Great Britain

FAMILY RIGHTS GROUP
The link between prevention and care : papers from a seminar organised by FRG in 1984 for social work managers and practitioners. — London : Family Rights Group, 1985. — 44p

SOCIAL WORK WITH DELINQUENTS AND CRIMINALS — Great Britain

Probation and the community : a practice and policy reader / edited by John Harding. — London : Tavistock, 1987. — vii,248p. — Includes bibliographies and index

SOCIAL WORK WITH DELINQUENTS AND CRIMINALS — Great Britain — Congresses

Supervision and intermediate treatment : the report of a seminar at Scarborough, February 1976. — [London] : Department of Health and Social Security, Social Work Service, [1978]. — v,107p

SOCIAL WORK WITH DELINQUENTS AND CRIMINALS — Massachusets

MILLER, Alden D
Delinquency and community : creating opportunities and controls / Alden D. Miller, Lloyd E. Ohlin. — Beverly Hills : Sage Publications, c1985. — 208 p.. — Includes bibliographies

SOCIAL WORK WITH DELINQUENTS AND CRIMINALS — Scotland — Strathclyde

STRATHCLYDE. Social Work Department
Services to the offender : who cares? : report of a special officer/member group of the council's social work committee on social work with offenders in Strathclyde. — Glasgow : [the Department], 1978. — 47 leaves

SOCIAL WORK WITH IMMIGRANTS — Denmark

HENRIKSEN, Ingrid
Mødet mellem indvandrerfamilier og social- og sundhedssystemet. — København : Socialforskningsinstituttet, 1987. — 208p. — (Publikation / Socialforskningsinstituttet ; 158). — Bibliography: p203-206

SOCIAL WORK WITH IMMIGRANTS — Great Britain

Race and social work : a guide to training / edited by Vivienne Coombe and Alan Little. — London : Tavistock, 1986. — xiii,233p. — (Social science paperbacks ; 330). — Includes bibliographies and index

SOCIAL WORK WITH MINORITIES — Great Britain
ELY, Peter
Social work in a multi-racial society / Peter Ely and David Denney. — Aldershot : Gower, c1987. — vi,231p. — (Issues in social work). — Bibliography: p201-218. — Includes index

NATIONAL ASSOCIATION FOR MATERNAL AND CHILD WELFARE. Conference (72nd : 1985 : Westminster)
"Ethnic minorities" : 'between two cultures' : a study of issues affecting ethnic minority families : seventy second Annual Conference report, 1985 Wednesday 26th June, Westminster London SW1 / [National Association for Maternal and Child Welfare]. — [London] : [National Association for Maternal and Child Welfare], [1985]. — 52p

Social work with black children and their families / edited by Shama Ahmed, Juliet Cheetham and John Small. — London : Batsford in association with British Agencies for Adoption and Fostering, 1986. — 207p. — (Child care policy and practice). — Includes bibliographies and index

SOCIAL WORK WITH MINORITY YOUTH — Great Britain — Case studies
PANEL TO PROMOTE THE CONTINUING DEVELOPMENT OF TRAINING FOR PART-TIME AND VOLUNTARY YOUTH AND COMMUNITY WORKERS
Working with black youth : complementary or competing perspectives? / the report of the Panel to Promote the Continuing Development of Training for Part-time and Voluntary Youth and Community Workers ; written by Gus John and Nigel Parkes. — Leicester : National Youth Bureau, 1984. — 11p. — (Extension report ; no.2). — Bibliography: p11

SOCIAL WORK WITH THE AGED
GREENE, Roberta
Social work with the aged and their families / Roberta Greene. — New York : Aldine de Gruyter, c1986. — p. cm. — Includes index. — Bibliography: p

SOCIAL WORK WITH THE AGED — Great Britain
CENTRAL COUNCIL FOR EDUCATION AND TRAINING IN SOCIAL WORK
A happier old age : a discussion document on elderly people in our society (DHSS/Welsh office). — [London] : the Council, 1979. — 3leaves

GREAT BRITAIN. Department of Health and Social Security. Social Services Inspectorate. Development Group
Assessment procedures for elderly people referred for local authority residential care : a Development Group project 1984-1985. — [London : the Department], 1985. — 23,vi,17p. — Bibliography: end pages 1-17

PERSONAL SOCIAL SERVICES COUNCIL. Policy Group on the Elderly
Comments on "A happier old age". — London : the Council, [ca.1978]. — 25p. — Bibliographical references: p24-25

SOCIAL WORK WITH THE MENTALLY HANDICAPPED — Great Britain
GILBERT, Peter
Mental handicap : a practical guide for social workers / Peter Gilbert. — Sutton : Business Press International, 1985. — 128p. — Includes bibliographies

SOCIAL WORK WITH YOUTH
DUSSICH, John P. J.
New perspectives in control theory : social coping of youth under supervision / John P. J. Dussich. — Köln : Carl Heymanns Verlag, c1985. — 306,liip. — (Interdisziplinäre Beiträge zur kriminologischen Forschung ; Band 11). — Text in English, with German summary. — Bibliography: p281-306

GROSS, Fanny A.
Youth in crisis / Fanny A. Gross. — Cape Town : Juta, 1985. — xv,134p

SOCIAL WORK WITH YOUTH — Great Britain
PALEY, John
Rethinking youth social work / John Paley, Jim Thomas and Jerry Norman. — Leicester : National Youth Bureau, 1986. — iv,42p

Youth work / edited by Tony Jeffs and Mark Smith. — Basingstoke : Macmillan Education, 1987. — x,158p. — (Practical social work). — Bibliography: p153-155. — Includes index

SOCIAL WORK WITH YOUTH — Scotland
PETRIE, Cairine
The nowhere girls / Cairine Petrie. — Aldershot : Gower, c1986. — [364]p. — Bibliography: p325-343. — Includes index

SOCIAL WORK WITH YOUTH — South Africa
GROSS, Fanny A.
Youth in crisis / Fanny A. Gross. — Cape Town : Juta, 1985. — xv,134p

SOCIAL WORK WITH YOUTH — Wales — Cardiff
WILLIAMSON, Howard
Strategies for intervention : an approach to youth and community work in an area of social deprivation / Howard Williamson [and] Kaye Weatherspoon. — Cardiff : University College, Social Research Unit, 1985. — 99p. — Bibliography: p99

SOCIAL WORKERS
MATTINSON, Janet
The reflection process in casework supervision / Janet Mattinson. — [London] : Institute of Marital Studies, The Tavistock Institute of Human Relations : Distributed by Research Publications Services, 1975. — 149p

SOCIAL WORKERS — In-service training — Great Britain
BIGGS, Simon
The Registered Homes Act 1984 : staff training issues / Simon Biggs. — London : Central Council for Education and Training in Social Work, 1986. — 47p. — (CCETSW paper ; 24). — Bibliographical references: p46-47

SOCIAL WORKERS — Great Britain
BROWN, Roberts, 1949-
Social workers at risk : the prevention and management of violence / Robert Brown, Stanley Bute, Peter Ford. — Basingstoke : Macmillan, 1986. — xii,145p. — (Practical social work). — Bibliography: p135-139. — Includes index

COUSINS, Christine
Controlling social welfare : a sociology of state welfare work and organization / Christine Cousins. — Brighton : Wheatsheaf, 1987. — viii,219p. — Bibliography: p189-208. — Includes index

FORD, Kathy
Student supervision / Kathy Ford and Alan Jones. — Basingstoke : Macmillan Education, 1987. — x,162p. — (Practical social work). — Bibliography: p154-157. — Includes index

JONES, Ray, 1949-
Like distant relatives : adolescents' perceptions of social work and social workers / Ray Jones. — Aldershot : Gower, c1987. — [200]p. — Includes bibliography and index

SOCIAL WORKERS — Great Britain — Attitudes
THOMAS, Terry, 1946-
The police and social workers / Terry Thomas. — Aldershot : Gower, c1986. — [120]p. — (Community care practice handbooks). — Includes index

SOCIAL WORKERS — Great Britain — Job stress
FINEMAN, Stephen
Social work stress and intervention / Stephen Fineman. — Aldershot : Gower, 1986, c1985. — ix,174p. — Originally published: 1985. — Bibliography: p167-171. — Includes index

SOCIAL WORKERS — United States
CHERNISS, Cary
Staff burnout : job stress in the human services / Cary Cherniss. — Beverly Hills ; London : Sage, 1980. — 199p. — (Sage studies in community mental health ; 2). — Bibliography: p193-197

COUSINS, Christine
Controlling social welfare : a sociology of state welfare work and organization / Christine Cousins. — Brighton : Wheatsheaf, 1987. — viii,219p. — Bibliography: p189-208. — Includes index

SOCIAL WORKERS — United States — Biography — Dictionaries
Biographical dictionary of social welfare in America / Walter I. Trattner, editor. — New York : Greenwood Press, 1986. — xiv, 897 p.. — Includes index

SOCIALDEMOKRATISCHE PARTEI DEUTSCHLANDS
Konzepte zum Frieden : Vorschläge für eine neue Abrüstungs- und Entspannungspolitik der SPD / herausgegeben von Katrin Fuchs, Hajo Hoffmann und Horst Klaus. — Berlin : spw-Verlag, 1985. — 179p

SOCIALE SERURITY — Italy — Statistics
ITALY. Istituto Centrale di Statistica
I conti della protezione sociale : sanità, previdenza e assistenza anni 1960-1982. — Roma : Istituto Centrale di Statistica, 1983. — 195p. — (Bollettino mensile di statistica. Supplemento ; 1983 n.28)

SOCIALE SERVICE — Italy — Statistics
ITALY. Istituto Centrale di Statistica
I conti della protezione sociale : sanità, previdenza e assistenza anni 1960-1982. — Roma : Istituto Centrale di Statistica, 1983. — 195p. — (Bollettino mensile di statistica. Supplemento ; 1983 n.28)

SOCIALISM — Spain
FRAGA IRIBARNE, Manuel
Cambio que fracasó / Manuel Fraga Iribarne. — Barcelona : Planeta, 1986. — 230p

SOCIALISM
ALTHUSSER, Louis
For Marx / Louis Althusser ; translated by Ben Brewster. — London : Verso, 1979

Analytical Marxism / edited by John Roemer. — Cambridge : Cambridge University Press, 1986. — [324]p. — (Studies in Marxism and social theory). — Includes bibliography

BOBBIO, Norberto
Which socialism? : Marxism, socialism and democracy / Norberto Bobbio ; translated by Roger Griffin ; edited and introduced by Richard Bellamy. — Cambridge : Polity, c1987. — 242p. — Translation of: Quale socialismo. — Includes index

BRÉLAZ, Michel
Henri de Man : une autre idée du socialisme / Michel Brélaz. — Genève : Antipodes, 1985. — 814p. — Bibliography: p739-790

CROZIER, Brian
Socialism : dream and reality / Brian Crozier. — London : Sherwood Press, 1987. — xv, 145p

ENGELS, Friedrich
Socialism, Utopian and scientific : with the essay on "the mark" / by Frederick Engels ; translated by Edward Aveling. — Westport, Conn. : Greenwood Press, 1977. — 93p. — Reprint of edition originally published in 1935 by International Publishers, New York

GRLIČKOV, Aleksandar
Raskršća socijalizma / Aleksandar Grličkov. — Beograd : Izdavački centar Komunist, 1984. — 358p

HATTERSLEY, Roy
Choose freedom : the future for democratic socialism / Roy Hattersley. — London : Joseph, 1987. — [352]p. — Includes index

SOCIALISM — continuation

HIRST, Paul Q.
Law, socialism and democracy / Paul Q. Hirst. — London : Allen & Unwin, 1986. — [200]p. — *Includes bibliography and index*

Karl Marx, the Materialist Messiah / edited by Kevin B. Nowlan. — Dublin : Published in collaboration with Radio Telefís Éireann, 1984. — 99p. — (The Thomas Davis lecture series). — *Bibliography: p98-99*

KOMMUNISTISCHE ORGANISATIE ROTTERDAM EN OMSTREKEN (MARXISTISCH-LENINISTISCH)
Politieke stellingname beginselverklaring doel en taken / von de Kommunistische Organisatie Rotterdam en Omstreken (marxistisch-leninistisch). — Rotterdam : Koro (ml), 1974. — 16p

LANE, David
The end of inequality? : stratification under state socialism / David Lane. — Harmondsworth : Penguin, 1971. — 156p. — (Penguin modern sociology monographs) (Penguin education). — *Bibliographyp.141-147. — Includes index*

LICHTHEIM, George
[Selections. 1986]. Thoughts among the ruins : collected essays on Europe and beyond / George Lichtheim ; new introduction by Walter Laqueur. — New Brunswick (U.S.A.) : Transaction Books, [1986], c1973. — xxix, 492 p.. — *"First paperback edition"--T.p. verso. — "Introduction ... first appeared in Commentary magazine, August 1973"--T.p. verso. — : Reprint. Originally published: Collected essays. New York : Viking Press, 1973*

MARX, Karl, 1818-1883
Capital : a critique of political economy. — London : Lawrence and Wishart. — *Based on the 1893 German edition*
Vol.2: The process of circulation of capital / edited by Friedrich Engels. — 1956. — xii,551p

MOORE, Barrington
Authority and inequality under capitalism and socialism / Barrington Moore Jr. — Oxford : Clarendon, 1987. — x,142p. — *Includes index*

POPOV, Iu. N.
Essays in political economy / Yuri Popov ; [translated from the Russian by Yuri Sdobnikov]. — Moscow : Progress Publishers. — (Progress guides to the social sciences)
[2]: Socialism and the socialist orientation. — 1985. — 262p

POPOV, M.V.
Planomernoe razreshenie protivorechii razvitiia sotsializma kak pervoi fazy kommunizma / M.V. Popov. — Leningrad : Izd-vo Leningradskogo universiteta, 1986. — 156p

Rethinking socialist economics : a new agenda for Britain / edited by Peter Nolan and Suzanne Paine. — Cambridge : Polity, 1986. — [300]p

Socialism on the threshold of the twenty-first century / edited by Miloš Nicolić. — London : Verso, 1985. — ix,311p

SOCIALISM — Addresses, essays, lectures

Ein Gespräch mit Jürgen Kuczynski über Arbeiterklasse, Alltag, Geschichte, Kultur und vor allem über Krieg und Frieden [/ Frank Deppe...et al.]. — Marburg : Verlag Arbeiterbewegung und Gesellschaftswissenschaft, 1984. — 141p. — (Schriftenreihe der Studiengesellschaft für Sozialgeschichte und Arbeiterbewegung ; Bd.48)

LUXEMBURG, Rosa
[Selections. English]. Rosa Luxemburg speaks / Edited with an introd. by Mary-Alice Waters. — New York : Pathfinder Press, 1970. — 473 p. — *"A Merit book."*

MEYLAN, René
Sentinelle toujours vivante : [recueil d'articles], 1964-1970 / René Meylan. — Neuchâtel, case postale 859 : Parti socialiste neuchâtelois, [1975]. — 226 p.. — *Collection of articles originally published in La Sentinelle. — Includes index*

NOVE, Alec
Socialist economics : selected readings / edited by Alec Nove and D.M. Nuti. — Harmondsworth : Penguin, 1972. — 526p. — (Penguin education) (Penguin modern economics readings). — *Bibliographyp.511-515. — Includes index*

SOCIALISM — Bibliography

Petite bibliographie sociale en 4 langues, Chinois, François, Anglais, Allemand. — London : Carl Slienger, 1975. — [10p]. — (Bibliography of socialism ; vol.3). — *Originally published by Bureau des "Temps Nouveaux", Paris, 1907*

SOCIALISM — Collected works

LUXEMBURG, Rosa
[Selections. English]. Rosa Luxemburg speaks / Edited with an introd. by Mary-Alice Waters. — New York : Pathfinder Press, 1970. — 473 p. — *"A Merit book."*

SOCIALISM — Economic aspects — Great Britain

Socialist enterprise : reclaiming the economy / by Diana Gilhespy...[et al.]. — Nottingham : New Socialist / Spokesman, 1986. — 230p. — *Bibliography: p.226-229*

SOCIALISM — History

Istoriia sotsialisticheskikh uchenii 1986 : sbornik statei / otv. redaktor L. S. Chikolini. — Moskva : Nauka, 1986. — 283p

Non-market socialism in the nineteenth and twentieth centuries / edited by Maximilien Rubel and John Crump. — Basingstoke : Macmillan, 1987. — [176]p. — *Includes bibliography and index*

ZIEGLER, Jean
Vive le pouvoir! : ou les délices de la raison d'état / Jean Ziegler. — Paris : Seuil, [1985]. — 281p

SOCIALISM — History — Sources

MARX, Karl, 1818-1883
[Collected works]. Werke, Artikel, Entwurfe : Juli 1851 bis Dezember 1852 / Karl Marx, Friedrich Engels ; [Bearbeitung des Bandes: Martin Hundt...et al.]. — Berlin : Dietz, 1985. — 2v. — (Karl Marx Friedrich Engels Gesamtausgabe (MEGA). 1 Abt. ; Bd.11)

SOCIALISM — History — 20th century

The international working-class movement : problems of history and theory / General editorial committee: B. N. Ponomarev...[et al.]. — Moscow : Progress
Vol.5: The builder of socialism and fighter against fascism / Editorial board: S. S. Salychev...[et al.]. — 1985. — 757p

SOCIALISM — Spain — Catalonia

Nuestra utopía : PSVC: cincuenta años de historia de Cataluña / colaboran: Andreu Mayayo...[et al.]. — Barcelona : Planeta, 1986. — 279p. — *At head of title: Nous Horitzons*

SOCIALISM — Uruguay

BOTTARO, José R.
25 años de movimiento Sindical Uruguayo / suplemento especial de Avanzada / José R. Bottaro. — Montevideo : Acción Sindical Uruguaya, [1985]. — 288p

SOCIALISM — Africa

Africa : problems in the transition to socialism / edited by Barry Munslow. — London : Zed, 1986. — [240]p. — *Includes index*

SOCIALISM — Albania

LLESHI, Ismail
The PLA : on some aspects of contradictions in socialism / Ismail Lleshi. — Tirana : 8 Nentori Publishing House, 1985. — 74p

SOCIALISM — Argentina — History

MUNCK, Ronnie
Argentina : from anarchism to Peronism / Ronaldo Munck, Ricardo Falcon, Bernardo Galitelli ; edited and translated by Ronaldo Munck. — London : Zed, 1987. — [272]p. — *Includes bibliography and index*

SOCIALISM — Australia

PERCY, Jim
Socialist election strategy today / Jim Percy. — Chippendale, NSW : Pathfinder Press, 1984. — 22p

SOCIALISM — Australia — History

BURGMANN, Verity
'In our time' : socialism and the rise of Labor, 1885-1905 / Verity Burgmann. — Sydney ; London : Allen & Unwin, 1985. — [ix,240]p. — *Bibliography: p213-226. — Includes index*

SOCIALISM — Austria

MAGAZINER, Alfred
Die Bahnbrecher : aus der Geschichte der Arbeiterbewegung / Alfred Magaziner. — Wien : Europaverlag, c1985. — 189p

SCHÖLER, Uli
"Otto Bauer - nein danke"? : Austromarxismusdiskussion und historische Bezüge für eine Strandortbestimmung marxistischer Sozialdemokraten / Uli Schöler. — Berlin : Demokratische Verlagskooperative, 1984. — 89p. — *Bibliography: p87-89*

SOCIALISM — Belgium

Socialisme d'aujourd'hui : texte adopté par le congrès doctrinal du P.S.B. des 16 et 17 novembre 1974. — Bruxelles : Edition Rose au Poing, 1975. — 27p

SOCIALISM — Canada

SCOTT, Frank R.
A new endeavour : selected political essays, letters, and addresses / edited and introduced by Michiel Horn. — Toronto : University of Toronto Press, 1986. — xlix,144p

SOCIALISM — Canada — History — Congresses

"Building the Co-operative Commonwealth" : essays on the Democratic Socialist tradition in Canada / edited by J. William Brennan. — Regina : University of Regina, Canadian Plains Research Center, 1985. — xiii,255p. — (Canadian Plains proceedings ; 13). — *"Based on papers delivered at the Regina Conference, June 23-25, 1983, commemorating the 50th anniversary of the Regina Manifesto". — Includes references*

SOCIALISM — Chile

WINN, Peter
Weavers of revolution : the Yarur workers and Chile's road to socialism / Peter Winn. — New York : Oxford University Press, 1986. — xiv, 328 p.. — *Includes index. — Bibliography: p. 300-315*

SOCIALISM — Czechoslovakia — History

WHEATON, Bernard
Radical socialism in Czechoslovakia : Bohumír Šmeral, the Czech road to socialism and the origins of the Czechoslovak Communist Party (1917-1921) / Bernard Wheaton. — Boulder, Colo. : East European Monographs ; New York : distributed by Columbia University Press, 1986. — xxvii,204p. — (East European Monographs ; no.213). — *Bibliography: p191-199*

SOCIALISM — Denmark

PETERSEN, Jens Peter Østerby
Arbejderne og krisen : forholdet mellem AOF's arbejderuddannelse, reformismen og arbejderbevidstheden i 30´erne / Jens Peter Østerby Petersen & Jens Skovholm. — København : Litteratur & Samfund, 1978. — 240p. — *Bibliography: p237-239*

SOCIALISM — Developing countries

MARTON, Imre
Contribution to a critique of an interpretation of specific Third World traits / Imre Marton. — Budapest : Institute for World Economics of the Hungarian Academy of Sciences : sold by Kultúra, 1978. — 120 p.. — (Studies on developing countries ; no. 97). — *Includes bibliographical references*

The Socialist Third World : urban development and territorial planning / edited by Dean Forbes and Nigel Thrift. — Oxford : Basil Blackwell, 1987. — [288]p. — *Includes bibliography and index*

SOCIALISM — Europe

Les états-unis socialistes d'Europe / brochure diffusée par la Ligue Révolutionnaire des Travailleurs (Belgique), la Ligue Communiste (France) et la Ligue Marxiste Révolutionnaire (Suisse). — Paris : François Maspero, 1972. — 48p. — (Classique rouge ; no.10)

KʹEDROS, André
Les socialistes au pouvoir en Europe (1981-1985) / André Kʹedros. — Paris : Plon, 1986. — 403p

RADICE, Giles
Socialists in the recession : the search for solidarity / Giles Radice and Lisanne Radice. — Basingstoke : Macmillan, 1986. — ix,172p. — *Bibliography: p166-167. — Includes index*

SOCIALISM — Europe — History

BIRCHALL, Ian
Bailing out the system : reformist socialism in Western Europe : 1944-1985 / Ian Birchall. — London : Bookmarks, 1986. — 287p. — *Bibliography: p.[267]-278*

EVANS, Richard J.
Comrades and sisters : feminism, socialism and pacifism in Europe 1870-1945 / Richard J. Evans. — Brighton : Wheatsheaf, 1987. — [240]p. — *Includes index*

KLOPPENBERG, James T
Uncertain victory : social democracy and progressivism in European and American thought, 1870-1920 / James T. Kloppenberg. — New York : Oxford University Press, 1986. — x, 546 p.. — *Includes index. — Bibliography: p. [511]-528*

SOCIALISM — Europe — History — 20th century

KIRBY, D. G. (David Gordon)
War, peace and revolution : international socialism at the crossroads 1914-1918 / David Kirby. — Aldershot : Gower, 1986. — ix,310p. — *Bibliography: p284-301. — Includes index*

SOCIALISM — Europe, Eastern

Socialist economy and economic policy / edited by G. Fink. — Wien : Springer-Verlag, 1985. — 279p. — (Studien über Wirtschafts- und Systemvergleiche ; Bd.13). — *"Essays in honour of Friedrich Levcik". — Includes bibliographies*

SOCIALISM — France

DROIT, Michel
Lettre ouverte à ceux qui en ont plus qu'assez du socialisme / Michel Droit. — Paris : Albin Michel, [1985]. — 183p

FONTENEAU, Alain
La gauche face à la crise / Alain Fonteneau, Pierre Alain Muet. — [Paris] : Presses de la Fondation nationale des sciences politiques, 1985. — 389p. — *Bibliography: p[377]-381*

GAUDIN, Jean-Claude
La gauche à l'imparfait / Jean-Claude Gaudin. — Paris : France-Empire, 1985. — 299p

SOCIALISM — France — History

FESSARD DE FOUCAULT, Bertrand
Charles Maurras et le socialisme / Bertrand Fessard de Foucault. — [Paris : Royaliste, ca.1984]. — 296p. — (Collection lys rouge). — *Bibliography: p290*

LE BRAS-CHOPARD, Armelle
De l'égalité dans la différence : le socialisme de Pierre Leroux / Armelle Le Bras-Chopard. — [Paris] : Presses de la Fondation nationale des sciences politiques, 1986. — 460p. — *Bibliography: p[435]-455*

SOCIALISM — France — History — 20th century

READER, Keith
Intellectuals and the Left in France since 1968 / Keith A. Reader. — Basingstoke : Macmillan, 1987. — xii,154p. — *Bibliography: p148-150. — Includes index*

SOCIALISM — Germany

PARK, Ho-Leong
Sozialismus und Nationalismus : Grundsatzdiskussionen über Nationalismus, Imperialismus, Militarismus und Krieg in der deutschen Sozialdemokratie vor 1914 / von Ho-Leong Park ; mit einem Vorwort von Wolf-Dieter Narr. — Berlin : Schelzky und Jeep, 1986. — 349p. — *Bibliography: p323-349*

SOCIALISM — Germany — History

BREUILLY, John
Joachim Friedrich Martens (1806-1877) und die deutsche Arbeiterbewegung / John Breuilly, Wieland Sachse. — Göttingen : Otto Schwartz, 1984. — (xviii),489p. — (Göttinger Beiträge zur Wirtschafts- und Sozialgeschichte ; Bd.8). — *Bibliography: p469-485*

MAEHL, William Harvey
The German Socialist Party : champion of the First Republic, 1918-1933 / William Harvey Maehl. — Philadelphia : American Philosophical Society, 1986. — xvii, 270p, [12]p of plates. — (Memoirs of the American Philosophical Society ; v.169). — *Bibliography: p.239-253*

SOCIALISM — Germany (West)

Sozialisten und Demokratie / herausgegeben vom Koordinationsrat der Projektgruppe Anti-Repression. — Offenbach : Sozialistisches Büro, 1980. — 95p. — (Links-reprint ; Heft 2)

SOCIALISM — Great Britain

MILITANT
Marxism on trial : defend the Liverpool socialists. — London : Militant Publications, 1986. — 32p

SELBOURNE, David
Left behind : journeys into British politics / David Selbourne. — London : Cape, 1987. — xvii,174p

SMITH, Martin, 1951-
The consumer case for socialism / Martin Smith. — London : Fabian Society, 1986. — 32p. — (Fabian tract ; 513)

Socialist organiser / Socialist Campaign for a Labour Victory. — London : Socialist Campaign for a Labour Victory, 1979-. — *Weekly. — September 1985 entitled: Workers' Liberty*

The radical challenge : the response of social democracy / edited by Alastair Kilmarnock. — London : Andre Deutsch, 1987. — 168p. — *Includes index*

WATKINS, Steve
Medicine and labour : the politics of a profession / Steve Watkins. — London : Lawrence and Wishart, 1987. — 272p

WEBB, Sidney
Socialism in England / Sidney Webb. — Aldershot : Gower, c1987. — lvi,136p. — *Facsim of ed. published London : Sonnenschein, 1890. — Includes index*

SOCIALISM — Great Britain — History

GORNY, Joseph
The British Labour movement and Zionism 1917-1948 / Joseph Gorny. — London : Cass, 1983. — xvi,251p. — *Bibliography: p239-242. — Includes index*

LUNDH, Christer
Gillesocialismen i England 1912-1923 : inspirationskälla för svensk arbetarrörelse / Christer Lundh. — Lund : Ekonomisk-historiska föreningen, 1982. — 130p. — (Skrifter utgivna av ekonomisk-historiska föreningen ; vol.37). — *Bibliography: p127-130*

NORMAN, E. R.
The Victorian Christian Socialists / Edward Norman. — Cambridge : Cambridge University Press, 1987. — [v,315]p. — *Includes index*

SOCIALISM — Great Britain — History — 19th century

CLAEYS, Gregory
Machinery, money and the millenium : from moral economy to socialism, 1815-60 / Gregory Claeys. — Cambridge : Polity, c1987. — xxx,245p. — *Bibliography: p223-239. — Includes index*

SOCIALISM — Great Britain — History — 20th century

BORNSTEIN, Sam
Against the stream : a history of the Trotskyist movement in Britain, 1924-38 / Sam Bornstein and Al Richardson. — London : Socialist Platform, 1986. — xii,302p

MACINTYRE, Stuart
A proletarian science : Marxism in Britain 1917-1933 / Stuart Macintyre. — Paperback ed, with corrections. — London : Lawrence and Wishart, 1986. — [xiii],286p. — *Originally published: Cambridge: Cambridge University Press, 1980. — Bibliography: p[271]-280*

SOCIALISM — Grenada — History

PRYOR, Frederic L
Revolutionary Grenada : a study in political economy / Frederic L. Pryor. — New York : Praeger, 1986. — xx, 395 p.. — *Includes index. — Bibliography: p. 375-382*

SOCIALISM — Hungary

KÁDÁR, János
Béke, f"uggetlenség, honvédelem : beszédek és cikkek 1957-1985 / Kádár János. — Budapest : Zrínyi Katonai Kiadó, 1985. — 342p

KASPER, Egon F.
Ungarn : Lebenskünstler auf der Suche nach der kleinen Freiheit / Egon F. Kasper. — München : printul, 1986. — xiip,p9-213

LOSONCZI, Pál
Erösödö népi-nemzeti egység, békés egymás mellett élés : válogatott beszédek, cikkek 1960-1984 / Losonczi. — Budapest : Kossuth Könyvkiadó, 1984. — 325p

SOCIALISM — India

JOSHI, P. C.
Marxism and social revolution in India and other essays / P. C. Joshi. — New Delhi : Patriot Publishers, 1986. — xiv,227p

SOCIALISM — Latin America

CHILCOTE, Ronald H
Latin America : capitalist and socialist perspectives of development and underdevelopment / Ronald H. Chilcote and Joel C. Edelstein. — Boulder ; London : Westview Press, 1986. — xv, 175p. — (Latin American perspectives series ; no. 3). — *"This is a complete revision and expansion of our introduction to Latin America : the struggle with dependency and beyond, published in 1974"--Pref. — Includes index. — Bibliography: p.153-164*

SOCIALISM — Latin America — History

GARCÍA PONCE, Antonio
¿ Adecos, tucanes o marxistas? : una historia de la izquierda: 1959-1984 / Antonio García Ponce. — Caracas : Domingo-Fuentes, 1985. — 204p

SOCIALISM — Netherlands

KOMMUNISTISCHE ORGANISATIE ROTTERDAM EN OMSTREKEN (MARXISTISCH-LENINISTISCH)
Politieke stellingname beginselverklaring doel en taken / von de Kommunistische Organisatie Rotterdam en Omstreken (marxistisch-leninistisch). — Rotterdam : Koro (ml), 1974. — 16p

PARTIJ VAN DE ARBEID
Verkiezingsprogramma van de Partij van de Arbeid voor de Tweede Kamerverkiezingen op 25 mei 1977. — [Amsterdam] : PvdA, 1977. — 94p. — *Cover-title : Voorwaarts...*

SOCIALISM — Poland — History

KOZŁOWSKI, Czesław
Tradycje polskiego ruchu robotniczego / Czesław Kozłowski. — Warszawa : Książka i Wiedza, 1986. — 119p. — *Bibliography: p119*

NAJDUS, Walentyna
Polska Partia Socjalno-Demokratyczna Galicji i Śląska 1890-1919 / Walentyna Najdus. — Warszawa : Państwowe Wydawnictwo Naukowe, 1983. — 718p. — *Bibliography: p660-671*

TOMICKI, Jan
Lewica socjalistyczna w Polsce 1918-1939 / Jan Tomicki. — Warszawa : Książka i Wiedza, 1982. — 611p. — *Table of contents in Russian, German and English. — Bibliography: p577-[592]*

SOCIALISM — Poland — Łódz

SAMUŚ, Paweł
Dzieje SDKPiL w Łódzi 1893-1918 / Paweł Samuś. — Łódz : Wydawnictwo Łódzkie, 1984. — 288p. — *Bibliography: p281-[289]*

SOCIALISM — South Africa

Contending ideologies in South Africa / edited by James Leatt, Theo Kneifel, and Klaus Nürnberger. — Grand Rapids : W.B. Eerdmans, 1986. — x, 318 p.. — *Includes index. — Bibliography: p. [303]-309*

SOCIALISM — Soviet Union

KELLEY, Donald R
The politics of developed socialism : the Soviet Union as a post-industrial state / Donald R. Kelley. — New York : Greenwood Press, 1986. — viii, 215 p.. — (Contributions in political science ; no. 149). — *Includes index. — Bibliography: p. [205]-209*

SOCIALISM — Soviet Union — History

MERVAUD, Michel
Socialisme et liberté : la pensée et l'action de Nicolas Ogarev (1813-1877) / Michel Mervaud. — Rouen : Publications de l'Université de Rouen ; Paris : Institut d'études slaves, 1984. — 596p. — (Publications de l'Université de Rouen ; no.97) (Collection historique / Institut d'études slaves ; 31). — *Bibliography: p [545]-566*

SOCIALISM — Spain

BIGLINO CAMPOS, Paloma
El socialismo español y la cuestion agraria (1890-1936) / Paloma Biglino Campos. — Madrid : Centro de Publicaciones, Ministerio de Trabajo y Seguridad Social, 1986. — 564p. — *Bibliography: p543-564*

DÍAZ, Elías
Socialismo en España : el Partido y el Estado / Elías Díaz. — 1a ed. — Madrid : Mezquita, 1982. — 253 p. — (Serie política ; 4). — *Includes bibliographical references and index*

Leviatan : revista de hechos e ideas. — Madrid : Leviatan, 1984-. — *Quarterly*

PARIS EGUILAZ, Higinio
España en el socialismo actual / por Higinio Paris Eguilaz. — Madrid : [s.n.], 1984. — 235p

PARTIDO SOCIALISTA OBRERO ESPANOL
Un año para la esperanza : [365 días de gobierno socialista]. — Madrid : Equipo de Documentación Política, 1983. — 175p

PARTIDO SOCIALISTA OBRERO ESPAÑOL. Congreso (30 : 1984 : Madrid)
España, compromiso de solidaridad : resoluciones socialistas para los años 80. — [Madrid] : PSOE, 1985. — 181p

SOTELO, Ignacio
Los socialistas en el poder / Ignacio Sotelo. — Madrid : El País, 1986. — 315p

SOCIALISM — Spain — Bibliography

LAMBERET, Renée
Movimientos obreros y socialistas : (cronologia y bibliografia) : España 1700-1939 : libros y folletos / Renée Lamberet, Luis Moreno Herrero. — [2a ed]. — Madrid : Júcar. — (Crónica general de España ; 37). — *First ed. published Paris, 1953*
T.1
Vol.1: 1700-1788. — 1985. — xlvii,467p

SOCIALISM — Spain — Chronology

LAMBERET, Renée
Movimientos obreros y socialistas : (cronologia y bibliografia) : España 1700-1939 : libros y folletos / Renée Lamberet, Luis Moreno Herrero. — [2a ed]. — Madrid : Júcar. — (Crónica general de España ; 37). — *First ed. published Paris, 1953*
T.1
Vol.1: 1700-1788. — 1985. — xlvii,467p

SOCIALISM — Spain — History

BARCO TERUEL, Enrique
El "golpe" socialista del 6 de Octubre de 1934 / Enrique Barco Teruel. — Madrid : Dyrsa, 1984. — 361p

CARRASCAL, José María
La revolución del PSOE / José María Carrascal. — [Barcelona] : Plaza & Janes, [1985]. — 306p. — (Política española)

Pablo Iglesias : el socialismo en España. — Barcelona : Anthropos, 1985. — 192p. — *Numero extraordinario 6 de "Anthropos: boletín de información y documentación", No.45-46-47, 1985*

ROSAL, Amaro del
1934 : Movimiento Revolucionario de Octubre / Amaro del Rosal. — [Madrid] : Akal, c1984. — xiii,313p. — (España sin espejo ; 1). — *Bibliography: p313*

El socialismo en España : desde la fundación del PSOE hasta 1975 / S. Castillo...[et al.]; coordinado por Santos Juliá. — Madrid : Editorial Pablo Iglesias, 1986. — 466p. — (Anales de historia de la Fundación Pablo Iglesias ; Vol.1). — *Bibliography: p[435]-466*

SOCIALISM — Spain — History — 20th Century

AVILÉS FARRÉ, Juan
La izquierda burguesa en la II Republica / Juan Avilés Farré. — Madrid : Espasa—Calpe, 1985. — 397p

SOCIALISM — Spain — History — 20th century

SERRA Y MORET, Manuel
Introducción al "Manifiesto del Partido Comunista" y otros escritos / Manuel Serra y Moret ; estudio preliminar y notas arίticas a crgo de Antoni Jutglar. — [Barcelona] : Anthropos, Editorial del Hombre, 1984. — 279p. — (Historia, ideas y textos ; 9)

SOCIALISM — Spain — Andalusia — History

Seis estudios sobre el proletariado andaluz (1868-1939) / R. Rodriguez Aguilera...[et al.]. — Córdoba : Excmo. Ayuntamiento de Córdoba, Delegación de Cultura, 1984. — 247p

SOCIALISM — Spain — Asturias — History

Octubre 1934 : cincuenta años para la reflexión / [por] G. Jackson ... [et al.]. — Madrid : Siglo Veintiuno, 1985. — viii,344p. — *'En la edición de la presente obra ha colaborado la Fundación José Barreiro, de Oviedo' — half-title. — Bibliography: p.[320]-344*

SOCIALISM — Spain — Catalonia

BARCELÓ I SERRAMALERA, Mercè
El pensament polític de Serra i Moret : nació, democràcia i socialisme / Mercè Barceló i Serramalera ; pròleg d'Isidre Molas. — Barcelona : Edicions 62, 1986. — 205p. — *Bibliography: p191-205*

CAMPALANS, Rafael
Catalanisme i socialisme : el debat de 1923 / R. Campalans i A. Fabri i Ribas ; edició a cura de Jesús M. Rodés. — [Barcelona] : La Magrana, [1985]. — xliv,114p. — (Biblioteca dels clàssics del nacionalisme català ; 10). — *Iniciativa conjunta d'Edicions de la Magrana i de la Diputació de Barcelona*

LORÉS, Jaume
El 1984 de Catalunya : una crònica apassionada / Jaume Lorés. — Barcelona : Edicions 62, [1985]. — 203p. — (Llibres a l'abast ; 206)

NIN, Andres
Socialisme i nacionalisme (1912-1934) : escrits republicans, socialistes i comunistes / Andreu Nin ; edició a cura de Pelai Pagès. — Barcelona : Edicions de la Magrana, 1985. — li,191p. — (Biblioteca dels Clàssics del Nacionalisme Català ; 11). — *Bibliography: p [xlv] - xlvii*

SOCIALISM — Spain — Catalonia — History — 20th century

CAMINAL I BADIA, Miquel
Joan Comorera / Miquel Caminal i Badia. — Barcelona : Empúries. — (Biblioteca universal Empúries)
Volum 2: Guerra i revolució (1936-1939). — [1984]. — 294p

CAMINAL I BADIA, Miquel
Joan Comorera / Miquel Caminal i Badia. — Barcelona : Empúries. — (Biblioteca universal Empúries)
Volum 3: Comunisme i nacionalisme (1939-1958). — [1985]. — 393p

SOCIALISM — Spain — Seville — History

MACARRO VERA, José Manuel
La utopia revolucionaria : Sevilla en la Segunda Republica / José Manuel Macarro Vera. — Sevilla : Monte de Piedad y Caja de Ahorros de Sevilla, 1985. — 518p

SOCIALISM — Spain — Vitoria

RIVERA BLANCO, Antonio
Situación y comportamiento de la clase obrera en Vitoria (1900-1915) / Antonio Rivera Blanco. — [Bibao] : Servicio Editorial, Universidad del Vasco, [1985]. — 195p

SOCIALISM — Sweden — History

Marx i Sverige : 100 år med Marx i svensk historia, vetenskap och politik / redigerad ar Lars Vikström. — Stockholm : Arbetarkultur, 1983. — 258p. — (Teori & praxis ; 6)

SOCIALISM — Switzerland

PLATTEN, Fritz
Die Reise Lenins durch Deutschland im plombierten Wagen / Fritz Platten. — Frankfurt am Main : isp, 1985. — 152p. — *First published in 1924*

SOCIALISM — Ukraine — History

SKRYPNIK, N. A.
Leninskaia partiia v bor'be za edinstvo rabochego klassa : (na materialakh Ukrainy) / N. A. Skrypnik. — Kiev : Vyshcha shkola, 1985. — 150p. — *Bibliography: p143-150*

SOCIALISM — United States — History

KLOPPENBERG, James T
Uncertain victory : social democracy and progressivism in European and American thought, 1870-1920 / James T. Kloppenberg. — New York : Oxford University Press, 1986. — x, 546 p.. — *Includes index. Bibliography: p. [511]-528*

SOCIALISM AND CHRISTIANITY
CHARLTON, William
 The Christian response to industrial capitalism / William Charlton, Tatiana Mallinson, Robert Oakeshott. — London : Sheed & Ward, 1986. — 263p

GOLLWITZER, Helmut
 Christentum/Demokratie/Sozialismus / Helmut Gollwitzer. — Berlin : Argument-Verlag. — 1980
 1: Aufsätze zu Christentum und Sozialismus. — 94p. — (Argument-Studienhefte ; 39). — *Bibliography: p95*

WEHNER, Herbert
 Christentum und demokratischer Sozialismus : Beiträge zu einer unbequemen Partnerschaft / Herbert Wehner ; hrsg. von Rüdiger Reitz. — Freibury : Br : Dreisam, 1985. — 243p

SOCIALISM AND RELIGION
CLUB DE L'HORLOGE
 Socialisme et religion sont-ils compatibles?. — Paris : Editions Albatros, 1986. — 268p

 Labour prophet. — Manchester ; London : Labour Prophet, 1892-1898. — *Monthly.* — *Continued by: Labour Church Record*

MOULIN, Léo
 La Gauche, la Droite et le péché originel et autres essais / Léo Moulin ; préface d'Alain Lancelot. — Paris : Libriarie des Méridiens, 1984. — 234p. — *Includes bibliographic notes*

SOCIALISM AND YOUTH — Great Britain
YETTRAM, Pamela June
 Contrary imaginations : causes and consequences of left wing ideology among student activists in the mid-seventies / by Pamela J. Yettram. — 511 leaves. — *PhD (Econ) 1986 LSE. — Leaves 457-486 are appendices*

SOCIALISM, CHRISTIAN — Great Britain
FLETCHER, Eric George Molyneux, Baron
 Random reminiscences / of Lord Fletcher of Islington. — London : Bishopsgate Press, 1986. — xii,269p

NORMAN, E. R.
 The Victorian Christian Socialists / Edward Norman. — Cambridge : Cambridge University Press, 1987. — [v,315]p. — *Includes index*

SOCIALISM IN ZAMBIA
KANDEKE, Timothy K.
 Fundamentals of Zambian humanism / Timothy K. Kandeke. — Lusaka : NECZAM, c1977. — xxvii, 249 p.. — *Includes bibliographical references and index*

SOCIALIST PARTIES — Directories
HOBDAY, Charles
 Communist and Marxist parties of the world / compiled and written by Charles Hobday. — Harlow : Longman, 1986. — 529p. — (A Keesing's reference publication). — *Bibliography: p508-513. — Includes index*

SOCIALIST PARTIES — History
PRZEWORSKI, Adam
 Paper stones : a history of electoral socialism / Adam Przeworski and John Sprague. — Chicago : University of Chicago Press, 1986. — vi, 224 p.. — *Includes indexes.* — *Bibliography: p. [203]-216*

SOCIALIST PARTIES — Poland — History
KOZŁOWSKI, Czesław
 Tradycje polskiego ruchu robotniczego / Czesław Kozłowski. — Warszawa : Książka i Wiedza, 1986. — 119p. — *Bibliography: p119*

SOCIALISTS — Argentina
GARCÍA COSTA, Victor O.
 Alfredo L. Palacios : un socialismo argentino y para la Argentina / Victor O. García Costa. — Buenos Aires : Centro Editor de América Latina. — (Biblioteca Política Argentina ; 147)
 t.1. — 1986. — 141p

GARCÍA COSTA, Victor O.
 Alfredo L. Palacios : un socialismo argentino y para la Argentina / Victor O. García Costa. — Buenos Aires : Centro Editor de América Latina. — (Biblioteca Política Argentina ; 148)
 t.2. — Buenos Aires : Centro Editor de América Latina. — 143-289p. — (Biblioteca Política Argentina ; 148)

SOCIALISTS — Austria — Biography
 Bruno Pittermann : ein Leben für die Sozialdemokratie / Heinz Fischer, Leopold Gratz (Hrsg.). — Wien : Europaverlag, 1985. — 442p

MAGAZINER, Alfred
 Die Bahnbrecher : aus der Geschichte der Arbeiterbewegung / Alfred Magaziner. — Wien : Europaverlag, c1985. — 189p

SOCIALISTS — Canada — Biography
FRANCIS, R. Douglas
 Frank H. Underhill : intellectual provocateur / R. Douglas Francis. — Toronto : University of Toronto Press, 1986. — x,219p. — *Notes: p [183]-206*

SOCIALISTS — France — Biography
BEECHER, Jonathan
 Charles Fourier : the visionary and his world / Jonathan Beecher. — Berkeley : University of California Press, 1987. — p. cm. — *Includes index.* — *Bibliography: p*

BRUGAS, Jacques
 Edouard Herriot / Jacques Brugas. — Roanne : Horvath, 1985. — 143p. — *Bibliography: p141-142*

FESSARD DE FOUCAULT, Bertrand
 Charles Maurras et le socialisme / Bertrand Fessard de Foucault. — [Paris : Royaliste, ca.1984]. — 296p. — (Collection lys rouge). — *Bibliography: p290*

 Die geteilte Utopie : Sozialisten in Frankreich und Deutschland : Biografische Vergleiche zur politischen Kultur / herausgegeben von Marieluise Christadler ; mit einem Vorwort von Alfred Grosser. — Opladen : Leske und Budrich, 1985. — 379p. — *Bibliographies*

SOCIALISTS — Germany — Biography
FRANKENTHAL, Käte
 Jüdin, Intellektuelle, Sozialistin : Lebenserinnerungen einer Ärztin in Deutschland und im Exil / Käte Frankenthal ; herausgegeben von Kathleen M. Pearle und Stephan Leibfried. — Frankfurt/Main : Campus, 1985. — 250p

FRIEDERICI, Hans Jürgen
 Ferinand Lassalle : eine politische Biographie / Hans Jürgen Friederici. — Berlin : Dietz, 1985. — 240p

 Die geteilte Utopie : Sozialisten in Frankreich und Deutschland : Biografische Vergleiche zur politischen Kultur / herausgegeben von Marieluise Christadler ; mit einem Vorwort von Alfred Grosser. — Opladen : Leske und Budrich, 1985. — 379p. — *Bibliographies*

JUNG, Werner
 August Bebel : deutscher Patriot und internationaler Sozialist : seine Stellung zu Patriotismus und Internationalismus / Werner Jung. — Pfaffenweiler : Centaurus-Verlagsgesellschaft, 1986. — 539p. — (Reihe Geschichtswissenschaft ; Bd.6). — *Bibliography: p521-538*

SOCIALISTS — Great Britain — Biography
BROWN, Gordon, 1951-
 Maxton / by Gordon Brown. — Edinburgh : Mainstream, 1986. — 335p,[8]p of plates. — *Includes index*

SOCIALISTS — Great Britain — Directories
COMMON CAUSE PUBLICATIONS
 The far left guide : directory of organisations and supporters. — Fleet, Hants : Common Cause Publications, 1985. — vi,33p

SOCIALISTS — Ireland — Biography
ZAGLADINA, Kh. T
 Dzheims Konnoli / Kh. T. Zagladina. — Moskva : Mysl', 1985. — 165p

SOCIALISTS — New York (N.Y.) — History — 20th century
WALD, Alan M.
 The New York intellectuals : the rise and decline of the anti-Stalinist left from the 1930s to the 1980s / by Alan M. Wald. — Chapel Hill : University of North Carolina Press, c1987. — p. cm. — *Includes index.* — *Bibliography: p*

SOCIALISTS — Poland — Biography
ETTINGER, Elżbieta
 Rosa Luxemburg : a life / Elżbieta Ettinger. — London : Harrap, 1987. — xv, 286p, [24]p of plates

MICHTA, Norbert
 Julian Marchlewski / Norbert Michta. — Warszawa : Iskry, 1979. — 113p. — (Współczesne zyciorysy Polaków)

PATERCZYK, Zygmunt
 Marcin Kasprzak i jego "sprawa" : anatomia funkcjonowania niesłusznego oskarżenia / Zygmunt Paterczyk. — Warszawa : Państwowe Wydawnictwo Naukowe, 1985. — 351p. — (Biblioteka kroniki Wielkopolski). — *Bibliography: p335-[340]*

SOCIALISTS — Spain — Catalonia — Biography
BALCELLS, Albert
 Rafael Campalans, socialisme català : biografia i textos / Albert Balcells. — [Barcelona?] : L'Abadia de Montserrat, 1985. — 444p

CAMINAL I BADIA, Miquel
 Joan Comorera / Miquel Caminal i Badia. — Barcelona : Empúries. — (Biblioteca universal Empúries)
 Volum 2: Guerra i revolució (1936-1939). — [1984]. — 294p

CAMINAL I BADIA, Miquel
 Joan Comorera / Miquel Caminal i Badia. — Barcelona : Empúries. — (Biblioteca universal Empúries)
 Volum 3: Comunisme i nacionalisme (1939-1958). — [1985]. — 393p

SOCIALISTS — United States — Biography — Dictionaries
 Biographical dictionary of the American Left / edited by Bernard K. Johnpoll and Harvey Klehr. — Westport, Conn. : Greenwood Press, 1986. — xiii, 493 p.. — *Includes index*

SOCIALIZATION
 Between two worlds : children from the Soviet Union in Israel / edited by Tamar Ruth Horowitz. — Lanham [Md.] : University Press of America, c1986. — vi, 233 p.. — *Includes bibliographies*

 Language socialization across cultures / edited by Bambi B. Schieffelin and Elinor Ochs. — Cambridge : Cambridge University Press, 1986. — 1v.. — (Studies in the social and cultural foundations of language ; 3). — *Includes index*

LARSON, Karen A.
 Learning without lessons : socialization and language change in Norway / Karen A. Larson. — Lanham, Md. ; London : University Press of America, c1985. — x,133p. — *Bibliography: p121-130. — Includes index*

LEE, Dorothy
 Valuing the self : what we can learn from other cultures / Dorothy Lee. — Prospect Heights, Ill : Waveland Press, 1986. — xii,87p

MACKIE, Marlene
 Constructing women and men : gender socialization / Marlene Mackie. — Toronto : Holt, Rinehart and Winston of Canada, 1987. — v,314p. — *Bibliography: p[276]-308*

SOCIALIZATION — Addresses, essays, lectures

The Child's construction of social inequality / edited by Robert L. Leahy. — New York ; London : Academic Press, 1983. — xv, 349p. — (Developmental psychology series). — *Includes bibliographies and indexes*

SOCIALIZATION — Cross-cultural studies

ROHNER, Ronald P
The warmth dimension : foundations of parental acceptance-rejection theory / Ronald P. Rohner. — Beverly Hills [Calif.] : Sage Publications, c1986. — 248 p.. — (New perspectives on family). — *Includes index. — Bibliography: p. 214-236*

SOCIALLY HANDICAPPED — Health and hygiene — Great Britain

LYONS, N. J.
A summary of investigations into the relationships between standardised mortality ratio and measures of social deprivation, and a consideration of the effect of social deprivation on hospital use / N. J. Lyons. — [London : Department of Health and Social Security, 1977]. — 6leaves

SOCIALLY HANDICAPPED — India — Government policy — Congresses

Seventh Plan and development of weaker sections : questions, challenges, and alternatives / edited by Jose Kananaikil. — New Delhi : Indian Social Institute, c1985. — xv, 188 p.. — *Includes index. — Bibliography: p. [171]-186*

SOCIALLY HANDICAPPED YOUTH — United States — Case studies

MACLEOD, Jay
Ain't no makin' it : leveled aspirations in a low-income neighbourhood / Jay MacLeod. — London : Tavistock, 1987. — [208]p. — *Includes bibliography and index*

SOCIALOGISTS — Germany — Bibliography

KAESTNER, Jürgen
Personalbibliographie Heinz Maus (1911-1978) : ein Beitrag zur Geschichte der deutschen Soziologie / Jürgen Kaestner. — Berlin : Wissenschaftlicher Autoren-Verlag (WAV), 1984. — 80p

SOCIETY ISLANDS — Population — Statistics

Tableaux normalisés du recensement général de la population : 15 octobre 1983. — [Papeete] : Institut territorial de la statistique

Tableaux normalisés du recensement général de la population : 15 octobre 1983. — [Papeete] : Institut territorial de la statistique
Résultats de la commune de Huahine. — [1985?]. — 4p,11 leaves

Tableaux normalisés du recensement général de la population : 15 octobre 1983. — [Papeete] : Institut territorial de la statistique
Résultats de la commune de Maupiti. — [1985?]. — 4p,11 leaves

Tableaux normalisés du recensement général de la population : 15 octobre 1983. — [Papeete] : Institut territorial de la statistique
Résultats de la commune de Tahaa. — [1985?]. — 11 leaves

Tableaux normalisés du recensement général de la population : 15 octobre 1983. — [Papeete] : Institut territorial de la statistique
Résultats de la Commune de Taputapuatea. — [1985?]. — 4p,11 leaves

Tableaux normalisés du recensement général de la population : 15 octobre 1983. — [Papeete] : Institut territorial de la statistique
Résultats de la commune de Tumaraa. — [1985?]. — 4p,11 leaves

Tableaux normalisés du recensement général de la population : 15 octobre 1983. — [Papeeta] : Institut territorial de la statistique
Résultats de la commune de Uturoa. — [1985?]. — 4p,11 leaves

Tableaux normalisés du recensement général de la population : 15 octobre 1983. — [Papeete] : Institut territorial de la statistique
Résultats de la subdivision administrative des Iles Sous le Vent. — [1985?]. — 4p,12 leaves

Tableaux normalisés du recensement général de la population : 15 octobre 1983. — [Papeete] : Institut territorial de la statistique
Résultats de la subdivision adminstrative des Iles du Vent. — [1985?]. — 4p,12 leaves

Tableaux normalisés du recensement général de la population : 15 octobre 1983. — [Papeete] : Institut territorial de la statistique
Résultats de l'Ile de Raiatea. — [1985?]. — 4p,11 leaves

SOCIETY OF FRIENDS — Biography

PENN, William
The papers of William Penn / editors, Mary Maples Dunn, Richard S. Dunn...[et al.]. — Pennsylvania : University of Pennsylvania Press . — *Includes index*
V.5: William Penn's published writings 1660-1726 : an interpretive bibliography / [edited by] Edwin B. Bronner, David Fraser. — 1986. — xxvi,546p

SOCIETY OF FRIENDS — History — 17th century — Sources

PENN, William
The papers of William Penn / editors, Mary Maples Dunn, Richard S. Dunn...[et al.]. — Pennsylvania : University of Pennsylvania Press . — *Includes index*
V.5: William Penn's published writings 1660-1726 : an interpretive bibliography / [edited by] Edwin B. Bronner, David Fraser. — 1986. — xxvi,546p

SOCIETY OF FRIENDS — History — 18th century — Sources

PENN, William
The papers of William Penn / editors, Mary Maples Dunn, Richard S. Dunn...[et al.]. — Pennsylvania : University of Pennsylvania Press . — *Includes index*
V.5: William Penn's published writings 1660-1726 : an interpretive bibliography / [edited by] Edwin B. Bronner, David Fraser. — 1986. — xxvi,546p

SOCIETY, PRIMITIVE

BIEBUYCK, Daniel Prosper
Tradition and creativity in tribal art / edited and with an introduction by Daniel P. Biebuyck. — Berkeley ; London (2 Brook St., W1Y 1AA) : University of California Press, 1969. — xx,236p,64plates. — *bibl p215-224*

DURKHEIM, Émile
Primitive classification / by Émile Durkheim and Marcel Mauss ; translated from the French and edited with an introduction by Rodney Needham. — 2nd ed. — London : Cohen and West, 1970. — xlviii,96p. — *Second ed. originally published 1969. Previous ed. of this translation 1963. Originally published as 'De quelques formes primitives de classification' in 'Année Sociologique', 1903. — bibl p89-93*

TESTART, Alain
Le communisme primitif / Alain Testart. — Paris : Editions de la Maison des sciences de l'homme
1: Economie et idéologie. — 1985. — 548p. — *Bibliography: p523-[536]*

SOCIOBIOLOGY

BADCOCK, C. R.
The problem of altruism : Freudian-Darwinian solutions / C.R. Badcock. — Oxford : Basil Blackwell, 1986. — [270]p. — *Includes bibliography and index*

BETZIG, L. L
Despotism and differential reproduction : a Darwinian view of history / L.L. Betzig. — New York : Aldine Pub., 1986. — p. cm. — *Bibliography: p*

Essays in human sociobiology / edited by Jan Wind. — London : Academic Press. — *"This volume is a slightly adapted reprint of the Journal of Human Evolution 13/1 (1984)"*
Vol.1 / contributions by R. Cliquet...[et al.]. — 1985. — 164p

Essays in human sociobiology. — Brussels : Vrije Universiteit, Pleinlaan 2. — (V. U. B. Study series ; 26). — *Includes references*
Vol.2 / edited by Jan Wind and Vernon Reynolds. — 1986. — xv,253p

PERPER, Timothy
Sex signals : the biology of love / Timothy Perper. — Philadelphia : ISI Press, c1985. — xvi, 323 p.. — *Includes index. — Bibliography: p. 296-314*

Violence against women : a critique of the sociobiology of rape / edited by Suzanne R. Sunday and Ethel Tobach. — New York : Gordian Press, 1985. — p. cm. — (A Genes and gender monograph). — *Includes index*

SOCIOBIOLOGY — Addresses, essays, lectures

Women, biology, and public policy / edited by Virginia Sapiro. — Beverly Hills, Calif. : Sage Publications, c1985. — p. cm. — (Sage yearbooks in women's policy studies ; v. 10). — *Contents: Biology and women's policy, a view from the biological sciences / Ruth Bleier -- Biology and women's policy, a view from the social sciences / Virginia Sapiro -- Male and female hormones / Marianne H. Whatley -- Fetal personhood and women's policy / Janet Gallagher -- Childbirth management and medical monopoly / Barbara Katz Rothman -- Occupational safety and health as a women's policy issue / Graham K. Wilson and Virginia Sapiro -- Older women / Laura Katz Olson -- The politics of a biosocial approach to crime / Susette M. Talarico -- Women's biology and the U.S. military / Judith Hicks Stiehm -- Women as "at risk" reproducers / Jane S. Jaquette and Kathleen A. Staudt*

SOCIOECONOMIC FACTORS

HO, Teresa J.
Measuring health as a component of living standards / Teresa J. Ho. — Washington, D.C., U.S.A. : World Bank, c1982 ((1985 printing)). — 58p. — (LSMS working papers ; no.15) (LSMS working papers ; no. 15). — *Bibliography: p56-58*

SOCIOLINGUISTICS

HAARMANN, Harald
Language in ethnicity : a view of basic ecological relations / by Harald Haarmann. — Berlin ; New York : Mouton de Gruyter, c1986. — p. cm. — (Contributions to the sociology of language ; 44). — *Includes indexes. — Bibliography: p*

HORVATH, Barbara M.
Variation in Australian English : the sociolects of Sydney / Barbara M. Horvath. — Cambridge : Cambridge University Press, 1985. — xi,200p. — (Cambridge studies in linguistics ; 45). — *Bibliography: p190-196. — Includes index*

Language socialization across cultures / edited by Bambi B. Schieffelin and Elinor Ochs. — Cambridge : Cambridge University Press, 1986. — 1v.. — (Studies in the social and cultural foundations of language ; 3). — *Includes index*

The Languages of political theory in early-modern Europe / edited by Anthony Pagden. — Cambridge : Cambridge University Press, 1987. — [viii,280]p. — (Ideas in context) . — *Includes index*

MILROY, Lesley
Language and social networks / Lesley Milroy. — 2nd ed. — Oxford : Basil Blackwell, 1987. — xi,232p. — (Language in society ; 2). — *Previous ed.: 1980. — Bibliography: p219-228. — Includes index*

SOCIOLINGUISTICS
continuation

MÜHLHÄUSLER, Peter
Pidgin & creole linguistics / Peter Mühlhäusler. — Oxford : Blackwell, 1986. 320p. — (Language in society ; 11). — *Bibliography: p297-317. — Includes index*

Social and functional approaches to language and thought / edited by Maya Hickmann ; with a foreword by Jerome Bruner. — Orlando : Academic Press, 1987. — p. cm. — *Includes index*

VENTOLA, Eija
The structure of social interaction : a systemic approach to the semiotics of service encounters / Eija Ventola. — London : Pinter, 1987. [270]p. — (Open linguistics series). — *Includes bibliography and index*

SOCIOLINGUISTICS — Cross-cultural studies

WODAK, Ruth
The language of love and guilt : mother-daughter relationships from a cross-cultural perspective / Ruth Wodak, Muriel Schulz. — Amsterdam ; Philadelphia : J. Benjamins, 1986. — xiv, 253 p.. — *Includes indexes. — Bibliography: p. [220]-247*

SOCIOLINGUISTICS — Methodology

MILROY, Lesley
Observing and analysing natural language : a critical account of sociolinguistic method / Lesley Milroy. — Oxford : Basil Blackwell, 1987. — [240]p. — (Language in society). — *Includes bibliography and index*

SOCIOLINGUISTICS — Belgium

MCRAE, Kenneth D.
Conflict and compromise in multilingual societies : Belgium / Kenneth D.McRae. — Waterloo, Ont. : Wilfrid Laurier University Press, 1986. — xiv, 387p

SOCIOLINGUISTICS — Fiji

SIEGEL, Jeff
Language contact in a plantation environment : a sociolinguistic history of Fiji / Jeff Siegel. — Cambridge : Cambridge University Press, 1987. — [324]p. — (Studies in the social and cultural foundations of language ; 5). — *Includes bibliography and index*

SOCIOLINGUISTICS — Hong Kong

GIBBONS, John, 1946-
Code-mixing and code choice : a Hong Kong case study / John Gibbons. — Clevedon : Multilingual Matters, c1987. — [184]p. — (Multilingual matters ; 27). — *Includes bibliography and index*

SOCIOLOGICAL JURISPRUDENCE

ADLER, Zsuzsanna
Rape on trial / Zsuzsanna Adler. — London : Routledge & Kegan Paul, 1987. — viii,195p. — *Bibliography: p188-192. — Includes index*

Dilemmas of law in the welfare state / edited by Gunther Teubner. — Berlin : W. de Gruyter, 1986. — viii,341p. — (Series A, Law / European University Institute ; 3). — *Includes bibliographies and index*

FRIEDMAN, Lawrence M.
Total justice / Lawrence M. Friedman. — New York : Russell Sage Foundation, c1985. — ix, 166 p.. — "75th anniversary series"--Jacket. — *Includes bibliography and index*

HONORÉ, Tony
Making law bind : essays legal and philosophical / Tony Honoré. — Oxford : Clarendon, 1987. — [288]p. — *Includes index*

HUND, John
Legal ideology and politics in South Africa : a social science approach / by John Hund and Hendrik W. van der Merwe. — 1st ed. — Lanham, MD : University Press of America ; Rondebosch, South Africa : Centre for Intergroup Studies, c1986. — 132 p.. — *Includes index. — Bibliography: p. 122-126*

MCDOUGAL, Myres Smith
Studies in world public order / by Myres S. McDougal and associates. — New Haven : New Haven Press ; Dordrecht : M. Nijhoff, 1986. — p. cm. — *Includes index*

Marriage and property / edited by Elizabeth M. Craik ; foreword by J. Steven Watson. — Aberdeen : Aberdeen University Press, 1984. — vi,192p. — *Includes bibliographies and index*

PARTINGTON, Martin
Socio-legal studies and social welfare / Martin Partington ; a report for the Government and Law Committee of the Economic and Social Research Council. — London : Economic and Social Research Council, 1986. — 78p. — *Bibliography: p59-78*

The social dimensions of law / Neil Boyd...[et al.]. — Scarborough, Ontario : Prentice-Hall Canada Inc., [1986]. — xii,259p. — *Includes references*

UNGER, Roberto Mangabeira
The critical legal studies movement / Roberto Mangabeira Unger. — Cambridge, Mass. : Harvard University Press, 1986. — 128 p.. — *Includes index. — Bibliography: p. [121]-122*

SOCIOLOGICAL JURISPRUDENCE — Addresses, essays, lectures

Sociology of law and legal anthropology in the Dutch speaking countries / J. van Houtte, editor. — Dordrecht ; Boston : M. Nijhoff Publishers, 1985. — p. cm. — (Nijhoff law specials). — *Bibliography of 'The sociology of law in Dutch-speaking countries': p67-102. — Bibliography of 'Current legal anthropology in the Netherlands': p149-162*

SOCIOLOGISTS — Germany — Biography

Helmut Schelsky als Soziologe und politischer Denker : Grazer Gedächtnisschrift zum Andenken an den am 24. Februar 1984 verstorbenen Gelehrten / Ota Weinberger, Werner Krawietz (Hrsg.). — Stuttgart : Steiner-Verlag-Wiesbaden, 1985. — 172p

SOCIOLOGISTS — Germany (West)

ADORNO-SYMPOSIUM (1984 : Hamburg)
Hamburger Adorno-Symposium / herausgegeben von Michael Löbig und Gerhard Schweppenhäuser. — Lüneberg : Dietrich zu Klampen Verlag, 1984. — 169p. — *Includes bibliographic notes*

SOCIOLOGISTS — Soviet Union — Directories

VORONITSYN, Sergei
A directory of prominent Soviet economists, sociologists, and demographers by institutional affiliation / compiled by Sergei Voronitsyn ; edited by: Robert Farrell. — Munich : Radio Liberty, 1987. — 118p

SOCIOLOGY

BEETHAM, David
Bureacracy / David Beetham. — Milton Keynes : Open University Press, 1987. — [112] p. — (Concepts in the social sciences). — *Includes bibliography and index*

Berkeley journal of sociology. — Berkeley, Calif. : University of California at Berkeley, 1967-. — *Annual*

BOTTOMORE, Tom
Sociology : a guide to problems and literature / Tom Bottomore. — 3rd ed. — London : Allen & Unwin, 1987. — [368]p. — *Previous ed.: 1971. — Includes bibliography and index*

CAPLOW, Theodore
The sociology of work / by Theodore Caplow. — Westport, Conn. : Greenwood Press, 1978, c1954. — viii, 330 p.. — *Reprint of the ed. published by University of Minnesota Press, Minneapolis. — Includes index. — Bibliography: p. 303-322*

Classic disputes in sociology / edited by R. J. Anderson, J. A. Hughes, W. W. Sharrock. — London : Allen and Unwin, 1987. — x,245p. — *Bibliographies*

ELIAS, Norbert
Involvement and detachment / Norbert Elias ; German editor, Michael Schröter ; translated by Edmund Jephcott. — Oxford : Basil Blackwell, 1987. — [150]p. — *Translation of: Engagement und Distanzierung. — Includes index*

Ethnomethodological studies of work / edited by Harold Garfinkel. — London ; New York : Routledge and Kegan Paul, 1986. — viii,196p

European sociological review. — Oxford : Oxford University Press, 1985-. — *3 per year*

Family portraits / edited by Digby Anderson and Graham Dawson. — London : Social Affairs Unit, c1986. — 127p

FLORO, George K.
Sociology for life : expanding circles of social participation through scholarship, community service, and teaching / George K. Floro. — Lanham : University Press of America, c1986. — xvii, 135 p.. — *Includes index. — Bibliography: p. 125-128*

FRANKEL, Boris
The post-industrial Utopians / Boris Frankel. — Cambridge : Polity, 1987. — xi,303p. — *Includes index*

GIDDENS, Anthony
Social theory and modern sociology / Anthony Giddens. — Stanford : Stanford University Press, 1987. — ix,310p

HARALAMBOS, Michael
Sociology : themes and perspectives / Michael Haralambos ; with Robin Heald. — London : Bell & Hyman, 1985. — xiv,594. — *Bibliography: p560-584*

HOMANS, George Caspar
Certainties and doubts : collected papers, 1962-1985 / George Caspar Homans. — New Brunswick, N.J. : Transaction Books, c1987. — p. cm. — *Bibliography: p*

International sociology / International Sociological Association. — Cardiff : University College, Cardiff, 1986-. — *Quarterly*

LIAZOS, Alexander
Sociology : a liberating perspective / Alezander Liazos. — London : Allyn and Bacon, 1985. — xviii,461p. — *Bibliography: p[415]-444*

MERLE, Marcel
The sociology of international relations / Marcel Merle ; translated from the French by Dorothy Parkin. — Leamington Spa : Berg, c1987. — 430p. — *Translation of: Sociologie des relations internationales. — Bibliography: p421-424. — Includes index*

MIRANDA, Michel
La société incertaine : pour un imaginaire social contemporain / Michel Miranda. — Paris : Librairie des Meridiens, 1986. — iii,208p

MULLAN, Bob
Sociologists on sociology / Bob Mullan. — London : Croom Helm, c1987. — 322p. — *Bibliography: p298-318. — Includes index*

Network: newsletter of the British Sociological Association. — London : British Sociological Association, 1975-. — *3 per year*

The new introducing sociology / [editor] Peter Worsley ; [contributors] Frank Bechhofer ... [et al.]. — Harmondsworth : Penguin, 1987. — 559 p

PARRY, Geraint
Political elites / by Geraint Parry. — London : Allen & Unwin, 1969. — 3-169p. — *Pbk. Unpriced. sbn 04 320059 1. — bibl p159-164*

Social theory today / edited by Anthony Giddens and Jonathan H. Turner. — Cambridge : Polity, 1987. — [400]p. — *Includes bibliography and index*

SOCIOLOGY *continuation*

The Sociobiology of ethnocentrism : evolutionary dimensions of xenophobia, discrimination, racism and nationalism / edited by Vernon Reynolds, Vincent Falger and Ian Vine. — London : Croom Helm, c1987. — xx,327p. — *Bibliography: p274-314. Includes index*

Sociology from crisis to science / edited by Ulf Himmelstrand. — London : Sage, 1986. — 2v.. — *Includes bibliography and index*

SYDIE, R. A
Natural women, cultured men : a feminist perspective on sociological theory / R.A. Sydie. — Milton Keynes : Open University Press, 1987. — x,268p. — *Bibliography: p247-258. Includes index*

TURGOT, Anne Robert Jacques, baron de l'Aulne
Turgot on progress, sociology and economics / translated [from the French], edited and with an introduction by Ronald L. Meek. — London : Cambridge University Press, 1973. — [6],185p. — (Cambridge studies in the history and theory of politics). — *Includes index. Contents:- A philosophical review of the successive advances of the human mind - On universal history - Reflections on the formation and the distribution of wealth. Translation of 'Réflexions sur la formation et la distribution des richesses'.* [s.l.]: [s.n.], 1788

TURNER, Jonathan H
The structure of sociological theory / Jonathan H. Turner. — 4th ed. — Chicago, Ill. : Dorsey Press, 1986. — xvii, 478, xviii p.. — *Includes bibliographical references and indexes*

SOCIOLOGY — Addresses, essays, lectures

DEMERATH, Nicholas Jay, comp
System, change, and conflict : a reader on contemporary sociological theory and the debate over functionalism / edited by N. J. Demerath and Richard A. Peterson. — New York : Free Press, [1967]. — viii, 533 p. — *Bibliographical footnotes*

Gedrag en struktuur : de relevantie van microtheorieën voor de verklaring van macroverschijnselen / onder redaktie van W. Arts, S. Lindenberg en R. Wippler. — [Rotterdam] : Universitaire Pers Rotterdam, 1976. — xv, 237 p. — (Mens en maatschappij. Boekaflevering ; 1976). — *Includes index. Bibliography: p. 217-231*

Sociology on trial / edited by Maurice Stein and Arthur Vidich. — Englewood Cliffs, N.J. : Prentice-Hall, c1963. — 182p. — (Spectrum books in sociology)

SOCIOLOGY — Bibliography

BARDIS, Panos Demetrios
Dictionary of quotations in sociology / Panos Bardis. — Westport, Conn. : Greenwood Press, 1985. — xiv, 356 p.. — *Includes indexes. Bibliography: p. [315]-325*

SOCIOLOGY — Biographical method

MATTHEWS, Sarah H
Friendships through the life-course : oral biographies in old age / by Sarah H. Matthews. — Beverly Hills : Sage Publications, c1986. — p. cm. — (Sage library of social research ; v. 161). — *Includes index. Bibliography: p*

SOCIOLOGY — Congresses

Economy and society in the transformation of the world / edited by Mike Gonzalez, Salustiano del Campo Urbano, Roberto Mesa. — London : United Nations University in association with Macmillan, 1984. — viii,206p. — ('The Transformation of the world' series ; v.2). — *Conference proceedings. — Includes index*

The Social fabric : dimensions and issues / [edited] by James F. Short, Jr. — Beverly Hills, Calif. : Sage Publications, c1986. — p. cm. — (American Sociological Association presidential series). — *Based on papers presented at the 79th Annual Meeting of the American Sociological Association, held in San Antonio, Tex., Aug. 27-31, 1984. — Includes bibliographies and index*

SOCIOLOGY — Correspondence

SCHÜTZ, Alfred
Briefwechsel 1939-1959 / Alfred Schütz [und] Aron Gurwitsch ; herausgegeben von Richard Grathoff ; mit einer Einleitung von Ludwig Landgrebe. — München : Wilhelm Fink, 1985. — xxxviii,544p. — (Übergänge : Texte und Studien zu Handung, Sprache und Lebenswelt ; Bd.4). — *Bibliography: p531-534*

SOCIOLOGY — Dictionaries

BARDIS, Panos Demetrios
Dictionary of quotations in sociology / Panos Bardis. — Westport, Conn. : Greenwood Press, 1985. — xiv, 356 p.. — *Includes indexes. Bibliography: p. [315]-325*

BOUDON, Raymond
Dictionnaire critique de la sociologie / Raymond Boudon [et] François Bourricaud. — 2nd ed. — Paris : Presses Universitaires de France, 1986. — xix,714p. — *Bibliographies*

SOCIOLOGY — History

Classic disputes in sociology / edited by R. J. Anderson, J. A. Hughes, W. W. Sharrock. — London : Allen and Unwin, 1987. — x,245p. — *Bibliographies*

HAWTHORN, Geoffrey
Enlightenment and despair : a history of social theory / Geoffrey Hawthorn. — 2nd ed. — Cambridge : Cambridge University Press, 1987. — xii,312p. — *Previous ed. : 1976. — Bibliography: p276-303. — Includes index*

NISBET, Robert, 1913-
The making of modern society / Robert Nisbet. — Brighton : Wheatsheaf, 1986. — [240]p. — *Includes index*

RUNDELL, John F.
Origins of modernity : the origins of modern social theory from Kant to Hegel to Marx / John F. Rundell. — Cambridge : Polity, 1987. — 249p. — *Bibliography: p234-241 Includes index*

Structures of knowing / edited by Richard C. Monk. — Lanham ; London : University Press of America, 1987. — [522]p. — *Includes index*

SOCIOLOGY — History — 20th century

ALEXANDER, Jeffrey C.
Sociological theory since 1945 / Jeffrey C. Alexander. — London : Hutchinson Education, 1987. — [432]p. — *Includes index*

Burzhuaznaia sotsiologiia na iskhode XX veka : kritika noveishikh tendentsii / otv. redaktor V. N. Ivanov. — Moskva : Nauka, 1986. — 278p. — *Summary and table of contents in English*

SOCIOLOGY — Methodology

ALEXANDER, Jeffrey C
Twenty lectures : sociological theory since World War II / Jeffrey C. Alexander. — New York : Columbia University Press, 1987. — x, 393 p.. — *Includes bibliographical references and index*

KRAUSZ, Ernest
Sociological research : a philosophy of science perspective / Ernest Krausz. — Assen, The Netherlands ; Wolfeboro, N.H., U.S.A. : Van Gorcum, 1986. — p. cm. — *At head of title: Sponsored by the Sociological Institute for Community Studies, Bar-Ilan University, Israel. — Includes indexes. Bibliography: p*

Sociological research methods : an introduction / edited by Martin Bulmer. — 2nd ed. — Basingstoke : Macmillan, 1984 (1986 [printing]). — xv,351p. — *Previous ed.: 1977. — Bibliography: p321-351*

TANCHER, V. V.
Metodologicheskii krizis sovremennoi burzhuaznoi sotsiologii / V. V. Tancher. — Kiev : Naukova dumka, 1985. — 183p. — (Voprosy ideologicheskoi bor'by i kontrpropagandy)

SOCIOLOGY — Philosophy

FREUDENTHAL, Gideon
[Atom und Individuum im Zeitalter Newtons. English]. Atom and individual in the age of Newton : on the genesis of the mechanistic world view / Gideon Freudenthal ; [translated by Peter McLaughlin from the German]. — New ed. — Dordrecht ; Boston : D. Reidel Pub. Co. ; Hingham, MA, U.S.A. : Sold and distributed in the U.S.A. and Canada by Kluwer Academic Publishers, c1985. — p. cm. — (Boston studies in the philosophy of science ; v. 88). — *Translation of: Atom und Individuum im Zeitalter Newtons. — Includes index. — Bibliography: p*

INGRAM, David
Habermas and the dialectic of reason / David Ingram. — New Haven, CT : Yale University Press, c1987. — xvii, 263p. — *Includes index. — Bibliography: p.243-254*

JARVIE, I. C.
Thinking about society : theory and practice / I. C. Jarvie. — Dordrecht : Reidel, 1986. — xviii,519p. — (Boston studies in the philosophy of science ; v.93)

MCKEGANEY, Neil P.
Enter the sociologist : reflections on the practice of sociology / edited by Neil P. McKeganey and Sarah Cunningham-Burley. — Aldershot : Avebury, 1987. — xi,203p. — *Bibliography p: 196-203*

SOCIOLOGY — Political aspects — Soviet Union

SHLAPENTOKH, Vladimir
The politics of sociology in the Soviet Union / by Vladimir E. Shlapentokh. — Boulder : Westview Press, 1987, c1986. — p. cm. — (Delphic monograph series). — *Includes index. — Bibliography: p*

SOCIOLOGY — Quotations, maxims, etc — History — Sources

BARDIS, Panos Demetrios
Dictionary of quotations in sociology / Panos Bardis. — Westport, Conn. : Greenwood Press, 1985. — xiv, 356 p.. — *Includes indexes. Bibliography: p. [315]-325*

SOCIOLOGY — Research

KRAUSZ, Ernest
Sociological research : a philosophy of science perspective / Ernest Krausz. — Assen, The Netherlands ; Wolfeboro, N.H., U.S.A. : Van Gorcum, 1986. — p. cm. — *At head of title: Sponsored by the Sociological Institute for Community Studies, Bar-Ilan University, Israel. — Includes indexes. — Bibliography: p*

SOCIOLOGY — Study and teaching

Sociological theory 1984 / editor: Randall Collins. — San Francisco : Jossey-Bass, 1984. — xxi,428p. — (The Jossey-Bass social and behavioral science series). — *Includes bibliographic references*

SOCIOLOGY — Canada — History

SHORE, Marlene
The science of social redemption : McGill, the Chicago School, and the origins of social research in Canada. — Toronto : University of Toronto Press, 1987. — xviii,340p. — *Bibliographical notes: p[275]-324*

SOCIOLOGY — German — History

COLLINS, Randall
Max Weber : a skeleton key / by Randall Collins. — Beverly Hills : Sage Publications, c1985. — p. cm. — (Masters of social theory ; v. 3). — *Includes index*

SOCIOLOGY — Germany

COLLINS, Randall
Weberian sociological theory / Randall Collins. — Cambridge : Cambridge University Press, 1986

SOCIOLOGY — Germany
continuation

RAMMSTEDT, Otthein
Deutsche Soziologie 1933-1945 : die Normalität einer Anpassung / Otthein Rammstedt. — Frankfurt am Main : Suhrkamp, 1986. — 412p. — *Bibliography: p169-[190]*

WIEHN, Erhard R.
Gesammelte Schriften zur Soziologie / Erhard R. Wiehn. — Konstanz : Hartung-Gorre. — *Bibliographies*
1. — 1986. — 762p

SOCIOLOGY — Germany — Bibliography

RAMMSTEDT, Otthein
Deutsche Soziologie 1933-1945 : die Normalität einer Anpassung / Otthein Rammstedt. — Frankfurt am Main : Suhrkamp, 1986. — 412p. — *Bibliography: p169-[190]*

SOCIOLOGY — Germany — History

Max Weber and his contemporaries / edited by Wolfgang J. Mommsen and Jürgen Osterhammel ; the German Historical Institute. — London : Allen & Unwin, 1987. — xiv,591p. — *Conference proceedings. — Includes index*

SOCIOLOGY — Great Britain

DAY, Peter R.
Sociology in social work practice / Peter R. Day. — Basingstoke : Macmillan Education, 1987. — vii,157p. — (Practical social work). — *Bibliography: p141-149. — Includes index*

SOCIOLOGY — Great Britain — History

SCHNEIDER, Louis
Paradox and society : the work of Bernard Mandeville / Louis Schneider ; editorial foreword by Jay Weinstein. — New Brunswick, N.J. : Transaction Books, c1986. — p. cm. — *Includes index. — Bibliography: p*

SOCIOLOGY — Hungary — History

NÉMEDI, Dénes
A népi szociográfia 1930-1938 / Némedi Dénes. — Budapest : Gondolat, 1985. — 293p. — *Bibliography: p251-252*

SOCIOLOGY — India — Research — India

Survey of research in sociology and social anthropology, 1969-1979. — 1st ed. — New Delhi : Satvahan, 1985-1986. — 3 v.. — *"A project sponsored by the Indian Council of Social Science Research.". — Includes bibliographies and indexes*

SOCIOLOGY — Italy

POWERS, Charles H
Vilfredo Pareto / Charles H. Powers. — Newbury Park, Calif. : Sage Publications, c1987. — 167 p.. — (Masters of social theory ; v. 5). — *Includes indexes. — Bibliography: p. 159-160*

SOCIOLOGY — Korea — Addresses, essays, lectures

LEE, Man-Gap
Sociology and social change in Korea / by Man-Gap Lee. — [Seoul] : Seoul National University Press, c1982. — v, 336 p.. — *Includes bibliographical references and index*

SOCIOLOGY — Quebec (Province)

WEINSTEIN, Michael A.
Culture critique : Fernand Dumont and New Quebec sociology / Michael A. Weinstein. — Montréal : New World Perspectives, 1985. — 123p. — *Bibliography p[124]*

SOCIOLOGY — Southern States — Addresses, essays, lectures

HUGHES, Henry
[Selections. 1985]. Selected writings of Henry Hughes, antebellum Southerner, slavocrat, sociologist / edited, with a critical essay, by Stanford M. Lyman. — Jackson : University Press of Mississippi, c1985. — xxi, 235 p.. — *Includes bibliographical references*

SOCIOLOGY — Soviet Union

CHAGIN, B. A.
Istoricheskii materializm v SSSR v perekhodnyi period 1917-1936 gg. : istoriko-sotsiologicheskii ocherk / B. A. Chagin, V. I. Klushin ; otv. redaktor A. A. Fedoseev. — Moskva : Nauka, 1986. — 439p

SHLAPENTOKH, Vladimir
The politics of sociology in the Soviet Union / by Vladimir E. Shlapentokh. — Boulder : Westview Press, 1987, c1986. — p. cm. — (Delphic monograph series). — *Includes index. — Bibliography: p*

SOCIOLOGY — United Satates

HOLTON, R. J.
Talcott Parsons on economny and society / Robert J. Holton abd Bryan S. Turner. — London ; New York : Routledge & Kegan Paul, 1986. — vii, 276p

SOCIOLOGY — United States

BALDWIN, John D.
George Herbert Mead : a unifying theory for sociology / by John D. Baldwin. — Beverly Hills, Calif. : Sage Publications, c1986. — 168p. — (Masters of social theory ; v. 6). — *Includes index. — Bibliography: p.165-168*

Race, class, and the world system : the sociology of Oliver C. Cox / Herbert M. Hunter and Sameer Y. Abraham, eds. — New York : Monthly Review Press, 1987. — p. cm. — *Bibliography: p*

SOCIOLOGY AND RELIGION — Congresses

Religious movements : genesis, exodus, and numbers / edited by Rodney Stark. — New York : Paragon House Publishers, c1985. — v, 354 p.. — *"A New ERA book.". — "Essays ... were originally prepared for an international conference held in May 1982 on Orcas Island, Washington"--Editor's introd. — Includes bibliographies and index*

SOCIOLOGY, CHRISTIAN

MADURO, Otto
[Religión y lucha de clases. English]. Religion and social conflicts / Otto Maduro ; translated from the Spanish by Robert R. Barr. — Maryknoll, NY : Orbis Books, c1982. — xxviii, 161 p.. — *Translation of: Religión y lucha de clases. — Bibliography: p. 158-161*

WALKER, J. A.
Sociology and Christianity : some conflicts and their resolutions / J.A. Walker. — Leicester : UCCF Associates, [1985?]. — 10p. — *Originally published: in Christian graduate, June 1977. — Bibliography: p10*

SOCIOLOGY, CHRISTIAN — Addresses, essays, lectures

Religion and the sociology of knowledge : modernization and pluralism in Christian thought and structure / edited by Barbara Hargrove. — New York : E. Mellen Press, c1984. — 402 p.. — (Studies in religion and society ; v. 8). — *Includes bibliographies*

SOCIOLOGY, CHRISTIAN — Canada — 19th century

COOK, Ramsay
The regenerators : social criticism in late Victorian English Canada / Ramsay Cook. — Toronto : University of Toronto Press, 1985. — x,291p. — *Includes bibliographical references*

SOCIOLOGY, CHRISTIAN — Latin America

MADURO, Otto
[Religión y lucha de clases. English]. Religion and social conflicts / Otto Maduro ; translated from the Spanish by Robert R. Barr. — Maryknoll, NY : Orbis Books, c1982. — xxviii, 161 p.. — *Translation of: Religión y lucha de clases. — Bibliography: p. 158-161*

SOCIOLOGY, CHRISTIAN (BAPTIST)

GREENHOUSE, Carol J.
Praying for justice : faith, order, and community in an American town / Carol J. Greenhouse. — Ithaca : Cornell University Press, 1986. — p. cm. — (Anthropology of contemporary issues). — *Includes index. — Bibliography: p*

SOCIOLOGY, MEDICAL — China

KLEINMAN, Arthur
Social origins of distress and disease : depression, neurasthenia, and pain in modern China / Arthur Kleinman. — New Haven : Yale University Press, c1986. — xii, 264 p.. — *Includes index. — Bibliography: p. 241-254*

SOCIOLOGY, MILITARY — History — 18th century — Congresses

Adapting to conditions : war and society in the eighteenth century / edited by Maarten Ultee. — University, AL : University of Alabama Press, c1986. — viii, 197p. — *Includes index*

SOCIOLOGY, MILITARY — Latin America — Addresses, essays, lectures

The Latin American military institution / edited by Robert Wesson. — New York : Praeger, 1986. — xiii, 234p. — *"Published with the support of the Hoover Institution, Stamford University, Stamford, California" - t.p.. — Includes bibliographical notes and index*

SOCIOLOGY, RURAL

Rural landscapes and communities : essays presented to Desmond McCourt / edited by Colin Thomas. — Blackrock : Irish Academic Press, c1986. — 256p. — *Includes index*

SOCIOLOGY, RURAL — Sweden — Locknevi (Småland)

MILLER, Roger
Social change in 19th-century Swedish agrarian society / by Roger Miller, Torvald Gerger. — Stockholm : Almqvist & Wiksell International, 1985. — 130p. — (Acta universitatis Stockholmiensis. Stockholm studies in human geography ; 5) (Stockholm studies in human geography ; 5)

SOCIOLOGY, URBAN

GURR, Ted Robert
The state and the city / Ted Robert Gurr, Desmond S. King. — Basingstoke : Macmillan, 1987. — [272]p. — (Sociology, politics and cities)

MCGAHAN, Peter
Urban sociology in Canada / Peter McGahan. — 2nd ed. — Toronto : Butterworths, 1986. — vi,334p. — *Bibliography: p[271]-323*

MCKEOWN, Kieran
Marxist political economy and Marxist urban sociology : a review and elaboration of recent developments / Kieran McKeown. — Basingstoke : Macmillan, 1987. — [256]p. — *Includes bibliography and index*

SANDERCOCK, Leonie
Urban political economy : the Australian case / Leonie Sandercock, Michael Berry. — Sydney ; Boston : G. Allen & Unwin, 1983. — xi, 193 p.. — *Includes index. — Bibliography: p. 179-187*

SAUNDERS, Peter, 1950-
Social theory and the urban question / Peter Saunders. — 2nd ed. — London : Hutchinson Education, 1986. — [348]p. — *Previous ed.: 1981. — Includes bibliography and index*

Social process and the city / edited by Peter Williams. — London : Allen & Unwin, 1983. — 233p. — (Urban studies yearbook ; 1)

SOCIOLOGY, URBAN — Australia — Jabiru (Northern Territory)

LEA, John P.
Yellowcake and crocodiles : town planning, government and society in Northern Australia / John P. Lea, Robert B. Zehner. — London : Allen & Unwin, 1986. — xxiv,200p. — (Studies in society ; 34). — *Bibliography: p179-192. — Includes index*

SOCIOLOGY, URBAN — France — Paris region

PINÇON-CHARLOT, Monique
Ségrégation urbaine : classes sociales et équipements collectifs en région parisienne / Monique Pinçon-Charlot, Edmond Preteceille, Paul Rendu. — Paris : Editions Anthropos, 1986. — 291p. — *Bibliography: p[230]-238*

SOCIOLOGY, URBAN — India

Indian cities : ecological perspectives / edited by Vinod K. Tewari, Jay A. Weinstein, V. L. S. Prakasa Rao. — New Delhi : Concept Publishing Company, 1986. — 289p. — *Bibliography: p273-284*

SOCIOLOGY, URBAN — United States

LOGAN, John R.
Urban fortunes : the political economy of place / John R. Logan, Harvey L. Molotch. — Berkeley, CA : University of California Press, 1987. — p. cm. — *Includes index. — Bibliography: p*

SOCIOMETRY

DUNCAN, Otis Dudley
Notes on social measurement : historical and critical / Otis Dudley Duncan. — New York : Russell Sage Foundation, c1984. — xi, 256 p.. — *Includes bibliographies and indexes*

SOCJALDEMOCRACJA KROLESTWA POLSKIEGO I LITWY — History

SAMUŚ, Paweł
Dzieje SDKPiL w Łódzi 1893-1918 / Paweł Samuś. — Łódz : Wydawnictwo Łódzkie, 1984. — 288p. — *Bibliography: p281-[289]*

SODOMY

ROSSMAN, Parker
Sexual experience between men and boys / Parker Rossman. — Hounslow : Temple Smith, 1985, c1976. — 247p. — *Originally published: New York : Association Press, c1976. — Bibliography: p236-244. — Includes index*

SOETOMO, RADEN

Toward a glorius Indonesia : reminiscences and observations of Dr. Soetomo / edited, annotated, and introduced by Paul W. van der Veur ; translated by Suharni Soemarmo and Paul W. van der Veur. — Athens, Ohio : Ohio University, Center for International Studies, 1987. — p. cm. — (Monographs in international studies. Southeast Asia series ; no. 81). — *Translation of Dr. Soetomo's Kenang-kenangan; Poespita mantja nagara; and, Poespa-rinontjé*

SOFTWARE, COMPUTER — Accounting

Accounting treatment of software. — Paris : OECD, 1986. — 33p. — (Working document / OECD Working Group on Accounting Standards ; no.1). — *Bibliographical references: p33*

SOIL CONSERVATION — Southern States

HEALY, Robert G
Competition for land in the American South : agriculture, human settlement, and the environment / Robert G. Healy. — Washington, D.C. : Conservation Foundation, c1985. — xxxii, 333 p.. — *Includes bibliographies and index*

SOIL DEGRADATION

BLAIKIE, Piers M.
Land degradation and society / Piers Blaikie and Harold Brookfield ; with contributions by Bryant Allen ... [et al.]. — London : Methuen, 1987. — xxiv,296p. — *Bibliography: p251-284. — Includes index*

SOIL EROSION — Tanzania

ÖSTBERG, Wilhelm
The Kondoa transformation : coming to grips with soil erosion in Central Tanzania / Wilhelm Östberg. — Uppsala : Scandinavian Institute of African Studies, 1986. — 99p. — (Research reports / Scandinavian Institute of African Studies ; no.76). — *Bibliography: p97-99*

SOIL MANAGEMENT — Congresses

EXPERT CONSULTATION ON BETTER EXPLOITATION OF PLANT NUTRIENTS (1977 : Rome City)
Improved use of plant nutrients : report of the expert consultation on better exploitation of plant nutrients held in Rome 18-22 April 1977. — Rome : Food and Agriculture Organization of the United Nations, 1978. — vii, 152 p.. — (FAO soils bulletin ; 37). — *On t.p.: Soil Resources, Management and Conservation Service, Land and Water Development Division. — Includes bibliographies*

SOIL POLLUTION — England — Shipham (Somerset)

GREAT BRITAIN. Shipham Survey Committee
Interim report on metal contamination at Shipham : a report for Sedgemoor District Council prepared by the Department of the Environment and the Ministry of Agriculture, Fisheries and Food with the advice of the Department of Health and Social Security. — [London : Department of the Environment, 1979]. — [6]p. — *Alternative title: Soil contamination at Shipham: interim report on survey*

SOIL RESEARCH

INTERNATIONAL BOARD FOR SOIL RESEARCH AND MANAGEMENT
Report of the inaugural workshop and proposal for implementation of the tropical land clearing for sustainable agriculture network, August 27-September 2, 1985, Jakarta and Bulzittinggi, Indonesia. — Bangkok : International Board for Soil Research and Management, 1985. — 48p

SOILS

BRIDGES, E. M.
World soils / by E. M. Bridges. — London : Cambridge U.P, 1970. — [1],89p,8plates. — *bibl p85-86*

SOLAR ACCESS RIGHTS — Australia

BRADBROOK, Adrian J
Solar energy and the law / by Adrian J. Bradbrook. — Sydney : Law Book Co., 1984. — xxxiii, 324 p.. — *Includes bibliographical references and indexes*

SOLAR ENERGY

HAYES, Denis, 1944-
Rays of hope : the transition to a post-petroleum world / Denis Hayes. — 1st ed. — New York : Norton, c1977. — 240 p. — *"A Worldwatch Institute book.". — Includes bibliographical references and index*

SOLAR ENERGY — Law and legislation — Australia

BRADBROOK, Adrian J
Solar energy and the law / by Adrian J. Bradbrook. — Sydney : Law Book Co., 1984. — xxxiii, 324 p.. — *Includes bibliographical references and indexes*

SOLAR NEUTRINOS — Measurement

PINCH, T. J
Confronting nature : the sociology of solar-neutrino detection / Trevor Pinch. — Dordrecht, Holland ; Boston : D. Reidel Pub. Co ; Higham, MA, U.S.A. : Sold and distributed in the U.S.A. and Canada by Kluwer Academic Publishers, c1986. — xi, 268 p.. — (Sociology of the sciences monographs). — *Includes index. — Bibliography: p. 249-258*

SOLAR RADIATION — Great Britain

Climate in the United Kingdom : a handbook of solar radiation, temperature and other data for thirteen principal cities and towns / edited by John Page and Ralph Lebens for David Bartholomew. — London : H.M.S.O., 1986. — x, 391p. — *Produced for the Energy Technology Support Unit of the Department of Energy. — Bibliography: p.389-391*

SOLDIERS — Education, Non-military — Soviet Union

WILLIAMS, E. S.
The Soviet military : political education, training and morale / E.S. Williams ; with chapters by C.N. Donnelly and J.E. Moore ; foreword by Sir Curtis Keeble. — Basingstoke : Macmillan, 1987. — xv,203p,[16]p of plates. — (RUSI defence studies series). — *Bibliography: p196-198. — Includes index*

SOLDIERS — United States — Biography

ANSCHEL, Eugene
Homer Lea, Sun Yat-sen, and the Chinese revolution / by Eugene Anschel. — New York : Praeger, 1984. — xvi, 269 p.. — *Includes index. — Bibliography: p. 253-262*

SOLIDARNOŚĆ

BARKER, Colin
Festival of the oppressed : Solidarity reform and revolution in Poland 1980-81 / Colin Barker. — London : Bookmarks, 1986. — 192p

GREAT BRITAIN. Parliament. House of Commons. Library. International Affairs Section
Poland - the continuing crisis / Richard Ware. — [London] : the Library, 1981. — 27p. — (Background paper / House of Commons. Library. [Research Division] ; no.97). — *Supplements Background Paper no.87*

GREAT BRITAIN. Parliament. House of Commons. Library. International Affairs Section
Poland under martial law / Richard Ware. — [London] : the Library, 1982. — 38p. — (Background paper / House of Commons. Library. [Research Division] ; no.98)

LEWANDOWSKI, Janusz
Samorząd w dobie "Solidarności" : współpraca samorządów pracowniczych Pomorza Gdańskiego na tle sytuacji w kraju w latach 1980/81 / opracował Janusz Lewandowski przy współpracy Jana Szomburga. — Londyn : Odnowa, 1985. — 109p

POMIAN, Krzysztof
Wymiary polskiego konfliktu 1956-1981 / Krzysztof pomian. — Londyn : Aneks, 1985. — 174p

SOLIDARNOŚĆ — Biography

CRAIG, Mary, 1928-
The crystal spirit : Lech Walesa and his Poland / Mary Craig. — London : Hodder and Stoughton, 1986. — [384p]

SOLO (INDONESIA) — Social conditions

SIEGEL, James T.
Solo in the new order : language and hierarchy in an Indonesian city / James T. Siegel. — Princeton, N.J. : Princeton University Press, c1986. — p. cm. — *Includes index. — Bibliography: p*

SOLOMON ISLANDS — Religion

KEESING, Roger M.
Kwaio religion : the living and the dead in a Solomon Island society / Roger M. Keesing. — New York : Columbia University Press, 1982. — xi, 257p. — *Includes index. — Bibliography: p.[249]-253*

SOLVENT ABUSE

WATSON, Joyce
Solvent abuse : the adolescent epidemic? / Joyce M. Watson. — London : Croom Helm, c1986. — 234p. — *Includes index*

SOMALIA — Foreign relations — Ethiopia
SPENCER, John Hathaway
Ethiopia, the Horn of Africa, and U.S. policy / John H. Spencer. — Cambridge, Mass : Institute for Foreign Policy Analysis, 1977. — 69 p. — (Foreign policy report). — *Includes bibliographical references*

SOMALIA — History
LAITIN, David D.
Somalia : nation in search of a state / David D. Laitin and Said S. Samatar. — Boulder, Co. ; London : Westview, 1987. — 198p. — (Profiles : nations of contemporary Africa). — *Bibliography: p182-183. — Includes index*

SOMALIA — History — Dictionaries
CASTAGNO, Margaret
Historical dictionary of Somalia / by Margaret Castagno. — Metuchen, N.J. : Scarecrow Press, 1975. — xxviii, 213 p.. — (African historical dictionaries ; no. 6). — *Bibliography: p. 165-213*

SOMALIA — Politics and government
LEWIS, I. M.
A pastoral democracy : a study of pastoralism and politics among the Northern Somali of the Horn of Africa / I. M. Lewis. — London : Oxford University Press, 1961. — xiii,320p

SOMALIA — Social life and customs
LEWIS, I. M.
A pastoral democracy : a study of pastoralism and politics among the Northern Somali of the Horn of Africa / I. M. Lewis. — London : Oxford University Press, 1961. — xiii,320p

SOMARY, FELIX
SOMARY, Felix
The raven of Zürich : the memoirs of Felix Somary / translated from the German by A.J. Sherman ; with a foreword by Otto Von Habsburg. — London : Hurst, c1986. — xii,310p,[1]p of plates. — *Translation of: Erinnerungen aus meinem Leben. — Includes index*

SOMATOFORM DISORDERS — China
KLEINMAN, Arthur
Social origins of distress and disease : depression, neurasthenia, and pain in modern China / Arthur Kleinman. — New Haven : Yale University Press, c1986. — xii, 264 p.. — *Includes index. — Bibliography: p. 241-254*

SOMERSET. Library Service
STOAKLEY, Roger
The library service in Somerset : a report to the Libraries, Museums and Records Committee of the County Council, 19th June, 1985. — [Bridgwater] : Somerset County Council, 1985. — 15p

SOREL, GEORGES
Cahiers Georges Sorel. — Paris : Societé d'Etudes Soréliennes, 1983-. — *Annual*

SOTHEBY'S (Firm)
HOGREFE, Jeffrey
"Wholly unacceptable" : the bitter battle for Sotheby's / Jeffrey Hogrefe. — 1st ed. — New York : W. Morrow, c1986. — 238 p.. — *Includes index*

SOTHO (AFRICAN PEOPLE)
LYE, William F.
Transformations on the highveld : the Tswana and Southern Sotho / William F. Lye and Colin Murray. — Cape Town ; London : David Philip, 1985. — 160p. — (The people of Southern Africa ; no.2). — *Bibliographies*

SOUQ AL-MANAKH
DARWICHE, Fida
The Gulf stock exchange crash : the rise and fall of the Souq Al-Manakh / Fida Darwiche. — London : Croom Helm, c1986. — xii,162p. — *Bibliography: p145-153. — Includes index*

SOUTH AFRICA — Bibliography
Who's who of Southern Africa. — Parkhurst : Who's Who of Southern Africa C.C., 1985-. — *Annual. — 1945 edition entitled South Africa Who's Who*

SOUTH AFRICA — Census, 1985
Bevolkingsensus 1985 : geografiese verspreiding van die bevolking met 'n oorsig vir 1960-1985 = Population census 1985 : geographical distribution of the population with a review for 1960-1985. — Pretoria : Central Statistical Services, 1986. — 493p. — (Report no.02-85-01). — *Text in Afrikaans and English*

Bevolkingsensus 1985 : nywerheid volgens ontwikkelingstreek, statistiese streek en distrik = Population census 1985 : industry by development region, statistical region and district. — Pretoria : Central Statistical Services, 1986. — 545p. — (Report no.02-85-03). — *Text in Afrikaans and English*

Bevolkingsensus 1985 : maatskaplike eienskappe : statistieke oor ouderdom, huwelikstaat, land van geboorte, land van burgerskap en onderwyspeil = Population census 1985 : social characteristics : statistics according to age, marital status, country of birth, country of citizenship and level of education. — Pretoria : Central Statistical Services, 1986. — 203p. — (Report no.02-85-06). — *Text in Afrikaans and English*

Bevolkingsensus 1985 : ekonomiese eienskappe : statistieke oor beroep, nywerheid en identiteit van werkgewer = Population census 1985 : economic characteristics : statistics according to occupation, industry and identity of employer. — Pretoria : Central Statistical Services, 1986. — 276p. — (Report no.02-85-07). — *Text in Afrikaans and English*

Bevolkingsensus 1985 : statistieke oor ouderdom, onderwyspeil en beroep volgens voorstad, nywerheid en identitian van werkgewer vir die uitgesoekte statistiese streek = Population census 1985 : statistics according to age, level of education and occupation by suburb, industry and identity of employer for the selected statistical region (s). — Pretoria : Central Statistical Services, 1986. — 9v. — (Report nos.02-85-08 to 02-85-16). — *Text in Afrikaans and English*

SOUTH AFRICA — Commerce
ANDOR, Lydia Eve
South Africa's chrome, manganese, platinum and vanadium : foreign views on the mineral dependency issue 1970-1984 : a select and annotated bibliography / L. E. Andor. — Braamfontein, [R.S.A.] : South African Institute of International Affairs, 1985. — 222p. — (South African Institute of International Affairs Bibliographical Series ; No.13)

MOORSOM, Richard
The scope for sanctions : economic measures against South Africa / Richard Moorsom. — London : Catholic Institute for International Relations, 1986. — [vi],102p

SOUTH AFRICA — Commercial policy — History — 20th century
BERRIDGE, G. R.
The politics of the South Africa run : European Shipping and Pretoria / G.R. Berridge. — Oxford : Clarendon, 1987. — [298]p. — *Includes bibliography and index*

SOUTH AFRICA — Constitutional history
MARAIS, D.
Constitutional development of South Africa / D. Marais. — 2nd ed. — Braamfontein : Macmillan, 1985. — 100p. — *"Statutes": p100. — Bibliography: p98-99*

South Africa : a plural society in transition / editors, D.J. van Vuuren ... [et al.]. — Durban ; Stoneham, MA : Butterworths, c1985. — 510 p.. — *Includes bibliographies and index*

SOUTH AFRICA — Economic conditions
Black advancement in the South African economy / edited by Roy Smollan. — Basingstoke : Macmillam, 1986. — 256p. — *Bibliography: p243-250*

SOUTH AFRICA — Economic conditions — Statistics
SOUTH AFRICA. Department of Finance
Inland revenue statistical bulletin = Binnelandse inkomste statistiese bulletin / Department of Finance, South Africa. — Pretoria : Government Printer, 1983-. — *Annual. — Text in English and Afrikaans*

SOUTH AFRICA — Economic conditions — 1918-
STADLER, Alf
The political economy of modern South Africa. — London : Croom Helm, 1987. — 197p. — *Bibliography: p190-193. — Includes index*

SOUTH AFRICA — Economic conditions — 1961-
LOMBARD, J. A.
Die ekonomiese stelsel van Suid-Afrika / J. A. Lombard, J. J. Stadler, P. J. Haasbroek. — Pretoria : HAVM Opvoedkundige Uitgewers, 1985. — (x),369p

MOORSOM, Richard
The scope for sanctions : economic measures against South Africa / Richard Moorsom. — London : Catholic Institute for International Relations, 1986. — [vi],102p

South African review 3 / edited and compiled by SARS (South African Research Service). — Johannesburg : Ravan Press, 1986. — xiv,397p

SOUTH AFRICA — Economic policy
LOUW, Leon
South Africa, the solution / Leon Louw and Frances Kendall. — Bisho, Ciskei : Amagi, [1986]. — xvi,237p. — *Bibliography: p235-237*

SOUTH AFRICA — Ethnic relations
The Politics of race, class and nationalism in twentieth century South Africa / edited by Shula Marks and Stanley Trapido. — Harlow : Longman, 1987. — 1v.. — *Includes index*

The South African society : realities and future prospects / Human Sciences Research Council. — New York : Greenwood Press, c1987. — p. cm. — (Contributions in ethnic studies ; no. 21). — *"Final report of the Main Committee of the HSRC Investigation into Intergroup Relations"--Pref. — Includes index. — Bibliography: p*

SOUTH AFRICA — Ethnic relations — Addresses, essays, lectures
VAN DER ROSS, R. E
Coloured viewpoint : a series of articles in the Cape times, 1958-1965 / by R.E. van der Ross ; compiled by J.L. Hattingh, H.C. Bredekamp. — Bellville : Western Cape Institute for Historical Research (IHR), University of the Western Cape, 1984. — xii, 279 p.. — (Publication series / Western Cape Institute for Historical Research (IHR) ; B2)

SOUTH AFRICA — Foreign economic relations
BARCLAYS SHADOW BOARD
Barclays Shadow report 1986. — London : End loans to South Africa, 1986. — 18p

HANLON, Joseph
The sanctions handbook : for or against? / Joseph Hanlon and Roger Omond. — Harmondsworth : Penguin Books, 1987. — 399p

SOUTH AFRICA — Foreign economic relations — Africa, Southern
BUTTS, Kent Hughes
The geopolitics of southern Africa : South Africa as regional superpower / Kent Hughes Butts and Paul R. Thomas. — Boulder : Westview Press, 1986. — xiv, 193 p.. — (Westview special studies on Africa). — *Includes bibliographies and index*

SOUTH AFRICA — Foreign economic relations — Africa, Southern
continuation

Confrontation and liberation in southern Africa : regional directions after the Nkomati Accord / edited by Ibrahim S. R. Msabaha and Timothy M. Shaw. — Boulder, Colo : Westview Press, 1987. — xii, 315 p., [1] leaf of plates. — (Westview special studies on Africa). — *Bibliography: p. [307]-315*

SOUTH AFRICA — Foreign enonomic relations — Great Britain

LABOUR RESEARCH DEPARTMENT
Profiting from apartheid : Britain's links with South Africa. — London : Labour Research Department, 1986. — 54p

SOUTH AFRICA — Foreign relations

Confidential U.S. State Department Central Files : South Africa : internal and foreign affairs, 1945-1949 / edited by Paul Kesaris. — Frederick, MD : University Publications of America, 1986. — 14microfilms. — *Contents: Documents from the records of the Department of State, Central Files: South Africa*

EVANS, M.
The front-line states, South Africa and southern African security : military prospects and perspectives / M. Evans. — Harare : University of Zimbabwe, 1986. — 19p. — *Reprinted from Zambezia. — Bibliography: p18-19*

JASTER, Robert S.
South Africa and its neighbours : the dynamics of regional conflict / Robert S. Jaster. — London : International Institute for Strategic Studies, 1986. — 78p. — (Adelphi papers ; 209)

SOUTH AFRICA — Foreign relations — Bibliography

LESTER, Robert
internal affairs, decimal number 848A and foreign affairs, decimal numbers 748A and 711.48A / edited by Paul Kesaris ; guide compiled by Robert Lester. — Frederick, MD : University Publications of America, 1986. — x,38p. — *Contents: Index to U.S. State Department documents filed at the National Archives and available on 14 microfilms*

SOUTH AFRICA — Foreign relations — 1948-1961

Confidential U.S. State Department Central Files : South Africa : internal and foreign affairs, 1950-1954 / edited by Paul Kesaris. — Frederick, MD : University Publications of America, 1986. — 23microfilms. — *Contents: Documents from the records of the Department of State, Central Files: South Africa*

Confidential U.S. State Department Central Files : South Africa : internal and foreign affairs, 1945-1949 / edited by Paul Kesaris. — Frederick, MD : University Publications of America, 1986. — 14microfilms. — *Contents: Documents from the records of the Department of State, Central Files: South Africa*

SOUTH AFRICA — Foreign relations — 1948-1961 — Bibliography

LESTER, Robert
internal affairs, decimal number 848A and foreign affairs, decimal numbers 748A and 711.48A / edited by Paul Kesaris ; guide compiled by Robert Lester. — Frederick, MD : University Publications of America, 1986. — x,38p. — *Contents: Index to U.S. State Department documents filed at the National Archives and available on 14 microfilms*

LESTER, Robert
A guide to confidential U.S. State Department central files : South Africa : 1950-1954 : internal affairs, decimal numbers 745A, 845A, and 945A and foreign affairs, decimal numbers 645A and 611.45A : edited by Paul Kesaris / guide compiled by Robert Lester. — Frederick, MD : University Publications of America, 1986. — x,70p. — *Contents: Index to U.S. State Department documents filed at the National Archives and available on 23 microfilms*

SOUTH AFRICA — Foreign relations — Africa, Southern

BUTTS, Kent Hughes
The geopolitics of southern Africa : South Africa as regional superpower / Kent Hughes Butts and Paul R. Thomas. — Boulder : Westview Press, 1986. — xiv, 193 p.. — (Westview special studies on Africa). — *Includes bibliographies and index*

Confrontation and liberation in southern Africa : regional directions after the Nkomati Accord / edited by Ibrahim S. R. Msabaha and Timothy M. Shaw. — Boulder, Colo : Westview Press, 1987. — xii, 315 p., [1] leaf of plates. — (Westview special studies on Africa). — *Bibliography: p. [307]-315*

South African review 3 / edited and compiled by SARS (South African Research Service). — Johannesburg : Ravan Press, 1986. — xiv,397p

SOUTH AFRICA — Foreign relations — Botswana

NYELELE, Libero
The raid on Gaborone : June 14, 1985, a memorial / Libero Nyelele and Ellen Drake. — Gaborone : Nyelele and Drake, 1985. — 39p

SOUTH AFRICA — Foreign relations — Canada

BABB, Glenn
South Africa: where we stand / Glenn Babb. Clark's South Africa policy: a Canadian disgrace / Kenneth H. W. Hilborn. — Toronto : Citizens for Foreign Aid Reform, 1987. — [20p]. — (C. FAR Canadian Issues Series ; 15)

Canada and South Africa : challenge and response / editor: Douglas G. Anglin. — Ottawa : The Norman Paterson School of International Affairs, Carleton University, 1986. — vii,64p. — (Carleton International Proceedings). — *Proceedings of a Forum held in Ottawa, Ontario, March 1986*

SOUTH AFRICA — Foreign relations — Lesotho

Massacre at Maseru : South African aggression against Lesotho. — London : International Defence and Aid Fund, 1985. — 36p. — (Fact paper on Southern Africa ; no.12)

SOUTH AFRICA — Foreign relations — Soviet Union

CAMPBELL, Kurt M.
Soviet policy towards South Africa / Kurt M. Campbell. — Basingstoke : Macmillan, 1986. — xii,223p. — *Bibliography: p201-217. — Includes index*

SOUTH AFRICA — Foreign relations — United States

COKER, Christopher
The United States and South Africa, 1968-1985 : constructive engagement and its critics / Christopher Coker. — Durham, N.C. : Duke University Press, 1986. — xi, 327p. — *Includes index. — Bibliography: p.286-296*

DANAHER, Kevin
In whose interest? : a guide to U.S.-South Africa relations / Kevin Danaher. — 1st ed. — Washington, D.C. : Institute for Policy Studies, c1985. — p. cm. — *Includes index. — Bibliography: p*

SOUTH AFRICA — Foreign relations — United States — Bibliography

KETO, C. Tsehloane
American-South African relations, 1784-1980 : review and select bibliography / by C. Tsehloane Keto. — Athens, Ohio : Ohio University Center for International Studies, Africa Studies Program, 1985. — x, 159 p.. — (Monographs in international studies. African series ; no. 45). — *Includes index*

SOUTH AFRICA — History

ATTWELL, Michael
South Africa : background to the crisis / Michael Attwell. — London : Sidgwick and Jackson, 1986. — xxx,224p. — (A Weekend World Analysis)

DAVENPORT, T. R. H.
South Africa : a modern history / T.R.H. Davenport. — 3rd ed., updated and extensively rev. — Basingstoke : Macmillan, 1987. — xxiv,692p. — (Cambridge Commonwealth series). — *Previous ed.: 1978. — Bibliography: p590-655. — Includes index*

LEACH, Graham
South Africa : no easy path to peace / Graham Leach. — London : Routledge and Kegan Paul, 1986. — xxi,266p. — *Bibliography: p251-252*

LOUW, Leon
South Africa, the solution / Leon Louw and Frances Kendall. — Bisho, Ciskei : Amagi, [1986]. — xvi,237p. — *Bibliography: p235-237*

OMER-COOPER, J. D.
History of Southern Africa / J.D. Omer-Cooper. — London : James Currey, 1987. — [320]p. — *Includes bibliography and index*

TROUP, Freda
South Africa : an historical introduction / Freda Troup. — [New ed.]. — Harmondsworth : Penguin, 1975. — xviii,454p,[8]p of plates. — (Penguin African library). — *Previous ed.: London : Eyre Methuen, 1972. — Bibliography: p.427-431. — Includes index*

VAN JAARSVELD, F. A.
Omstrede Suid-Afrikaanse verlede : geskiedenisideologie en die historiese skuldvraagstuk / F. A. van Jaarsveld. — Johannesburg : Lex Patria, 1984. — 221p

SOUTH AFRICA — History — Great Trek, 1836-1840

GORIS, J. M.
België en de Boerenrepublieken : Belgisch-Zuidafrikaanse betrekkingen (ca.1835-1895) / J. M. Goris. — Retie : Kempische Boekhandel, 1983. — 620p. — (Belgie Zuid-Afrika ; Deel 1)

SOUTH AFRICA — History — 1836-1909

GORIS, J. M.
België en de Boerenrepublieken : Belgisch-Zuidafrikaanse betrekkingen (ca.1835-1895) / J. M. Goris. — Retie : Kempische Boekhandel, 1983. — 620p. — (Belgie Zuid-Afrika ; Deel 1)

SOUTH AFRICA — History — 1836-1909 — Sources

HOBHOUSE, Emily
Boer war letters / edited by Rykie Van Reenen. — Cape Town : Human and Rousseau, 1984. — 557p. — *Bibliography: p543-546*

SOUTH AFRICA — History — 1909-1961

MANDELA, Nelson
No easy walk to freedom : articles, speeches and trial addresses of Nelson Mandela / with a foreword by Ruth First. — Harare : Zimbabwe Publishing House, 1983. — 189p. — *First published 1965*

SOUTH AFRICA — History — 1961-
MANDELA, Nelson
No easy walk to freedom : articles, speeches and trial addresses of Nelson Mandela / with a foreword by Ruth First. — Harare : Zimbabwe Publishing House, 1983. — 189p. — *First published 1965*

SOUTH AFRICA — Industries — Statistics
Bevolkingsensus 1985 : nywerheid volgens ontwikkelingstreek, statistiese streek en distrik = Population census 1985 : industry by development region, statistical region and district. — Pretoria : Central Statistical Services, 1986. — 545p. — (Report no.02-85-03). — *Text in Afrikaans and English*

SOUTH AFRICA — Military relations — Africa, Southern
Destructive engagement : Southern Africa at war / editors Phyllis Johnson and David Martin ; foreword by Julius K. Nyerere. — Harare : Zimbabwe Publishing House for the Southern African Research and Documentation Centre, 1986. — xxi,378p

SOUTH AFRICA — National security
MATHEWS, Anthony S.
Freedom, state security and the rule of law : dilemmas of the apartheid society / Anthony S. Mathews. — Cape Town : Juta, 1986. — xxv,312p. — *Bibliography: p.xi-xiv. - Includes index*

SOUTH AFRICA — Occupations
Working in South Africa / editors Ken Dovey, Lorraine Laughton, Jo-Anne Durandt. — Johannesburg : Ravan Press, 1985. — ix,397p

SOUTH AFRICA — Occupations — Statistics
Bevolkingsensus 1985 : ekonomiese eienskappe : statistieke oor beroep, nywerheid en identiteit van werkgewer = Population census 1985 : economic characteristics : statistics according to occupation, industry and identity of employer. — Pretoria : Central Statistical Services, 1986. — 276p. — (Report no.02-85-07). — *Text in Afrikaans and English*

SOUTH AFRICA — Politics and government
ATKINSON, David
"Bloody confrontation or constructive compromise?" / David Atkinson, Paul Howell and Sir Fergus Montgomery. — Strasbourg : European Parliament, 1986. — i,13p

The Kairos document : a theological comment on the political crisis in South Africa. — 2nd rev.ed. — London : Catholic Institute for International Relations. — viii,35p. — (Third World Theology)

LEMON, Anthony
Apartheid in transition / Anthony Lemon. — Aldershot : Gower, 1987. — [410]p. — *Includes bibliography and index*

LOUW, Leon
South Africa, the solution / Leon Louw and Frances Kendall. — Bisho, Ciskei : Amagi, [1986]. — xvi,237p. — *Bibliography: p235-237*

MARAIS, D.
Constitutional development of South Africa / D. Marais. — 2nd ed. — Braamfontein : Macmillan, 1985. — 100p. — *"Statutes": p100. — Bibliography: p98-99*

Transformation: critical perspectives on Southern Africa. — Durban : University of Natal. Economic History Department, 1986-. — *Irregular*

Umkhanyiseli. — Goodwood : Western Cape Development Board, 1986-. — *Monthly*

SOUTH AFRICA — Politics and government — 1948-1961 — Bibliography
LESTER, Robert
internal affairs, decimal number 848A and foreign affairs, decimal numbers 748A and 711.48A / edited by Paul Kesaris ; guide compiled by Robert Lester. — Frederick, MD : University Publications of America, 1986. — x,38p. — *Contents: Index to U.S. State Department documents filed at the National Archives and available on 14 microfilms*

SOUTH AFRICA — Politics and government — 20th century
MANDELA, Winnie
Part of my soul / Winnie Mandela ; edited by Anne Benjamin and adapted by Mary Benson. — Harmondsworth : Penguin, 1985. — 164p

The Politics of race, class and nationalism in twentieth century South Africa / edited by Shula Marks and Stanley Trapido. — Harlow : Longman, 1987. — 1v.. — *Includes index*

South Africa : a plural society in transition / editors, D.J. van Vuuren ... [et al.]. — Durban ; Stoneham, MA : Butterworths, c1985. — 510 p.. — *Includes bibliographies and index*

SOUTH AFRICA — Politics and government — 1909-1948
Confidential U.S. State Department Central Files : South Africa : internal and foreign affairs, 1945-1949 / edited by Paul Kesaris. — Frederick, MD : University Publications of America, 1986. — 14microfilms. — *Contents: Documents from the records of the Department of State, Central Files: South Africa*

SOUTH AFRICA — Politics and government — 1909-1948 — Bibliography
LESTER, Robert
internal affairs, decimal number 848A and foreign affairs, decimal numbers 748A and 711.48A / edited by Paul Kesaris ; guide compiled by Robert Lester. — Frederick, MD : University Publications of America, 1986. — x,38p. — *Contents: Index to U.S. State Department documents filed at the National Archives and available on 14 microfilms*

SOUTH AFRICA — Politics and government — 1948-1961
Confidential U.S. State Department Central Files : South Africa : internal and foreign affairs, 1950-1954 / edited by Paul Kesaris. — Frederick, MD : University Publications of America, 1986. — 23microfilms. — *Contents: Documents from the records of the Department of State, Central Files: South Africa*

Confidential U.S. State Department Central Files : South Africa : internal and foreign affairs, 1945-1949 / edited by Paul Kesaris. — Frederick, MD : University Publications of America, 1986. — 14microfilms. — *Contents: Documents from the records of the Department of State, Central Files: South Africa*

SOUTH AFRICA — Politics and government — 1948-1961 — Bibliography
LESTER, Robert
A guide to confidential U.S. State Department central files : South Africa : 1950-1954 : internal affairs, decimal numbers 745A, 845A, and 945A and foreign affairs, decimal numbers 645A and 611.45A / edited by Paul Kesaris / guide compiled by Robert Lester. — Frederick, MD : University Publications of America, 1986. — x,70p. — *Contents: Index to U.S. State Department documents filed at the National Archives and available on 23 microfilms*

SOUTH AFRICA — Politics and government — 1961-1978
FATTON, Robert
Black consciousness in South Africa : the dialectics of ideological resistance to white supremacy / Robert Fatton, Jr. — Albany : State University of New York Press, c1986. — ix, 189 p.. — (SUNY series in African politics and society). — *: Revision of the author's thesis (Ph.D.)--University of Notre Dame. — Includes index. — Bibliography: p. 171-185*

SOUTH AFRICA — Politics and government — 1969-
DE VILLIERS, Dirk
PW / Dirk en Johanna de Villiers. — Kaapstad : Tafelberg, 1984. — 376p

SOUTH AFRICA — Politics and government — 1978-
ATTWELL, Michael
South Africa : background to the crisis / Michael Attwell. — London : Sidgwick and Jackson, 1986. — xxx,224p. — (A Weekend World Analysis)

BERRIDGE, G. R.
The politics of the South Africa run : European Shipping and Pretoria / G.R. Berridge. — Oxford : Clarendon, 1987. — [298]p. — *Includes bibliography and index*

BREWER, John D.
After Soweto : an unfinished journey / John D. Brewer. — Oxford : Clarendon, 1986. — [416]p. — *Includes bibliography and index*

BREYTENBACH, Breyten
End papers : essays, letters, articles of faith, workbook notes / Breyten Breytenbach. — London : Faber, 1986. — 270p

Canada and South Africa : challenge and response / editor: Douglas G. Anglin. — Ottawa : The Norman Paterson School of International Affairs, Carleton University, 1986. — vii,64p. — (Carleton International Proceedings). — *Proceedings of a Forum held in Ottawa, Ontario, March 1986*

CARTER, Gwendolen M.
Continuity and change in Southern Africa / Gwendolen M. Carter. — [S.l.] : African Studies Association ; [Gainesville, Fla.] : Center for African Studies, University of Florida, 1985. — x,117p. — (Carter lectures on Africa). — *Includes bibliographies*

CATHOLIC INSTITUTE FOR INTERNATIONAL RELATIONS
South Africa in the 1980s : state of emergency. — 3rd ed.. — London : CIIR, 1986. — 94p

Contending ideologies in South Africa / edited by James Leatt, Theo Kneifel, and Klaus Nürnberger. — Grand Rapids : W.B. Eerdmans, 1986. — x, 318 p.. — *Includes index. — Bibliography: p. [303]-309*

FATTON, Robert
Black consciousness in South Africa : the dialectics of ideological resistance to white supremacy / Robert Fatton, Jr. — Albany : State University of New York Press, c1986. — ix, 189 p.. — (SUNY series in African politics and society). — *: Revision of the author's thesis (Ph.D.)--University of Notre Dame. — Includes index. — Bibliography: p. 171-185*

GREAT BRITAIN. Parliament. House of Commons. Library. International Affairs Section
The situation in South Africa / Chris Bowlby, Jennifer Tanfield. — [London] : the Library, 1985. — 33p. — (Background paper / House of Commons. Library. [Research Division] ; no.176). — *Bibliography: p33*

GREAT BRITAIN. Parliament. House of Commons. Library. International Affairs Section
The South African crisis / Chris Bowlby. — [London] : the Library, 1987. — 49p. — (Background paper / House of Commons. Library. [Research Division] ; no.192). — *Bibliography: p49*

SOUTH AFRICA — Politics and government — 1978- *continuation*

LEACH, Graham
South Africa : no easy path to peace / Graham Leach. — London : Routledge and Kegan Paul, 1986. — xxi,266p. — *Bibliography: p251-252*

MURRAY, Martin
South Africa : time of agony, time of destiny : the upsurge of popular protest / Martin Murray. — London : Verso, 1987. — [500]p. — *Includes index*

South African review 3 / edited and compiled by SARS (South African Research Service). — Johannesburg : Ravan Press, 1986. — xiv,397p

SOUTH AFRICA — Politics and government — 1978- — Government

South Africa, a chance for liberalism? : papers presented during a seminar of the Friedrich Naumann Foundation in December 1983. — 1. Aufl. — Sankt Augustin [Germany] : Liberal Verlag, 1985. — vi, 407 p.. — (Schriften der Friedrich-Naumann-Stiftung. Liberale Texte). — *Includes bibliographies*

SOUTH AFRICA — Politics and government — 1978- — Public opinion

NEUHAUS, Richard John
Dispensations : the future of South Africa as South Africans see it / by Richard John Neuhaus. — Grand Rapids, Mich. : W.B. Eerdmans Pub. Co., c1986. — p. cm. — *Includes bibliographical references*

SOUTH AFRICA — Population — Statistics

Bevolkingsensus 1985 : geografiese verspreiding van die bevolking met 'n oorsig vir 1960-1985 = Population census 1985 : geographical distribution of the population with a review for 1960-1985. — Pretoria : Central Statistical Services, 1986. — 493p. — (Report no.02-85-01). — *Text in Afrikaans and English*

Bevolkingsensus 1985 : maatskaplike eienskappe : statistieke oor ouderdom, huwelikstaat, land van geboorte, land van burgerskap en onderwyspeil = Population census 1985 : social characteristics : statistics according to age, marital status, country of birth, country of citizenship and level of education. — Pretoria : Central Statistical Services, 1986. — 203p. — (Report no.02-85-06). — *Text in Afrikaans and English*

Bevolkingsensus 1985 : ekonomiese eienskappe : statistieke oor beroep, nywerheid en identiteit van werkgewer = Population census 1985 : economic characteristics : statistics according to occupation, industry and identity of employer. — Pretoria : Central Statistical Services, 1986. — 276p. — (Report no.02-85-07). — *Text in Afrikaans and English*

Bevolkingsensus 1985 : statistieke oor ouderdom, onderwyspeil en beroep volgens voorstad, nywerheid en identiteit van werkgewer vir die uitgesoekte statistiese streek = Population census 1985 : statistics according to age, level of education and occupation by suburb, industry and identity of employer for the selected statistical region (s). — Pretoria : Central Statistical Services, 1986. — 9v. — (Report nos.02-85-08 to 02-85-16). — *Text in Afrikaans and English*

SOUTH AFRICA — Population density — Statistics

Bevolkingsensus 1985 : geografiese verspreiding van die bevolking met 'n oorsig vir 1960-1985 = Population census 1985 : geographical distribution of the population with a review for 1960-1985. — Pretoria : Central Statistical Services, 1986. — 493p. — (Report no.02-85-01). — *Text in Afrikaans and English*

SOUTH AFRICA — Race relations

ALEXANDER, Neville
Sow the wind : contemporary speeches / Neville Alexander. — Johannesburg : Skotaville, 1985. — xi,180p

Apartheid in crises / edited by Mark A. Uhlig. — Harmondsworth : Penguin Books, 1986. — viii,334p

CATHOLIC INSTITUTE FOR INTERNATIONAL RELATIONS
South Africa in the 1980s : state of emergency. — 3rd ed.. — London : CIIR, 1986. — 94p

COONEY, Frank
Studies in race relations : South Africa and USA / Frank Cooney, Gordon Morton [and] Barry Wright. — Glasgow : Pulse Publications, 1986. — 84p

CORNEVIN, Marianne
Apartheid : power and historical falsification / Marianne Cornevin. — Paris : Unesco, 1980. — 144 p.. — (Insights). — *Bibliography: p. [139]-144*

DANAHER, Kevin
In whose interest? : a guide to U.S.-South Africa relations / Kevin Danaher. — 1st ed. — Washington, D.C. : Institute for Policy Studies, c1985. — p. cm. — *Includes index.* — *Bibliography: p*

DENMAN, Earl
The fiercest fight : a documented account of the struggle against apartheid in South Africa / by Earl Denman ; foreword by Gonville ffrench-Beytagh. — Worthing : Churchman, 1985. — xxii,190p

FATTON, Robert
Black consciousness in South Africa : the dialectics of ideological resistance to white supremacy / Robert Fatton, Jr. — Albany : State University of New York Press, c1986. — ix, 189 p.. — (SUNY series in African politics and society). — : *Revision of the author's thesis (Ph.D.)--University of Notre Dame.* — *Includes index.* — *Bibliography: p. 171-185*

GREAT BRITAIN. Parliament. House of Commons. Library. International Affairs Section
The situation in South Africa / Chris Bowlby, Jennifer Tanfield. — [London] : the Library, 1985. — 33p. — (Background paper / House of Commons. Library. [Research Division] ; no.176). — *Bibliography: p33*

GREAT BRITAIN. Parliament. House of Commons. Library. International Affairs Section
The South African crisis / Chris Bowlby. — [London] : the Library, 1987. — 49p. — (Background paper / House of Commons. Library. [Research Division] ; no.192). — *Bibliography: p49*

The Kairos document : a theological comment on the political crisis in South Africa. — London : Catholic Institute for International Relations : British Council of Churches, 1985. — 32p. — (Third World Theology)

LAPPING, Brian
Apartheid : a history / Brian Lapping in association with Granada Television. — London : Grafton, 1986. — xxi,200p,[32]p of plates. — *Bibliography : p185-190* — *Includes index*

LEMON, Anthony
Apartheid in transition / Anthony Lemon. — Aldershot : Gower, 1987. — [410]p. — *Includes bibliography and index*

LOUW, Leon
South Africa, the solution / Leon Louw and Frances Kendall. — Bisho, Ciskei : Amagi, [1986]. — xvi,237p. — *Bibliography: p235-237*

LOVE, Janice
The U.S. anti-apartheid movement : local activism in global politics / Janice Love. — New York : Praeger, 1985. — p. cm. — *Includes index.* — *Bibliography: p*

MANDELA, Winnie
Part of my soul / Winnie Mandela ; edited by Anne Benjamin and adapted by Mary Benson. — Harmondsworth : Penguin, 1985. — 164p

REDDY, E. S.
Apartheid, the United Nations and the international community : a collection of speeches and papers / E. S. Reddy. — New Delhi : Vikas, 1986. — x,157p

SMITH, David M. (David Marshall)
Update : apartheid in South Africa / David M. Smith. — London : Dept. of Geography and Earth Science, Queen Mary College, 1983. — 76p. — (Special publication / Queen Mary College, Department of Geography and Earth Science ; 6). — *Bibliography: p. 74-76*

SUTTNER, Raymond
30 years of the Freedom Charter / Raymond Suttner, Jeremy Cronin. — Johannesburg : Ravan Press, 1985. — xi,266p

TUTU, Desmond
Crying in the wilderness : the struggle for justice in South Africa / Desmond Tutu ; introduced and edited by John Webster ; foreword by Trevor Huddleston. — Rev. and updated. — London : Mowbray, 1986. — xix,124p,[8]p of plates. — (Mowbrays popular Christian paperbacks). — *Previous ed.: published as Bishop Desmond Tutu : the voice of one crying in the wilderness. 1982.* — *Bibliography: p124*

SOUTH AFRICA — Race relations — Addresses, essays, lectures

VAN DER ROSS, R. E
Coloured viewpoint : a series of articles in the Cape times, 1958-1965 / by R.E. van der Ross ; compiled by J.L. Hattingh, H.C. Bredekamp. — Bellville : Western Cape Institute for Historical Research (IHR), University of the Western Cape, 1984. — xii, 279 p.. — (Publication series / Western Cape Institute for Historical Research (IHR) ; B2)

SOUTH AFRICA — Race relations — Bibliography

Apartheid : a selective bibliography on the racial policies of the government of the Republic of South Africa. — New York : United Nations, 1970. — 57p. — ([Document] / United Nations ; ST/LIB/22/Rev.1). — *In various languages.* — *Prepared by the Dag Hammarskjöld Library*

SOUTH AFRICA — Race relations — Public opinion

NEUHAUS, Richard John
Dispensations : the future of South Africa as South Africans see it / by Richard John Neuhaus. — Grand Rapids, Mich. : W.B. Eerdmans Pub. Co., c1986. — p. cm. — *Includes bibliographical references*

SOUTH AFRICA — Relations — Foreign countries

GREAT BRITAIN. Parliament. House of Commons. Library. International Affairs Section
The situation in South Africa / Chris Bowlby, Jennifer Tanfield. — [London] : the Library, 1985. — 33p. — (Background paper / House of Commons. Library. [Research Division] ; no.176). — *Bibliography: p33*

GREAT BRITAIN. Parliament. House of Commons. Library. International Affairs Section
The South African crisis / Chris Bowlby. — [London] : the Library, 1987. — 49p. — (Background paper / House of Commons. Library. [Research Division] ; no.192). — *Bibliography: p49*

SOUTH AFRICA — Relations — United States

LOVE, Janice
The U.S. anti-apartheid movement : local activism in global politics / Janice Love. — New York : Praeger, 1985. — p. cm. — *Includes index.* — *Bibliography: p*

SOUTH AFRICA — Religion

The Kairos document : a theological comment on the political crisis in South Africa. — 2nd rev.ed. — London : Catholic Institute for International Relations, 1986. — viii,35p. — (Third World Theology)

SOUTH AFRICA — Religion
continuation

The Kairos document : a theological comment on the political crisis in South Africa. — London : Catholic Institute for International Relations : British Council of Churches, 1985. — 32p. — (Third World Theology)

SOUTH AFRICA — Social conditions

ALEXANDER, Neville
Sow the wind : contemporary speeches / Neville Alexander. — Johannesburg : Skotaville, 1985. — xi,180p

LEMON, Anthony
Apartheid in transition / Anthony Lemon. — Aldershot : Gower, 1987. — [410]p. — *Includes bibliography and index*

SOUTH AFRICA — Social conditions — 1961-

BREYTENBACH, Breyten
End papers : essays, letters, articles of faith, workbook notes / Breyten Breytenbach. — London : Faber, 1986. — 270p

FATTON, Robert
Black consciousness in South Africa : the dialectics of ideological resistance to white supremacy / Robert Fatton, Jr. — Albany : State University of New York Press, c1986. — ix, 189 p.. — (SUNY series in African politics and society). — : *Revision of the author's thesis (Ph.D.)--University of Notre Dame. — Includes index. — Bibliography: p. 171-185*

NAIDOO, Beverley
Censoring reality : an examination of books on South Africa / by Beverley Naidoo. — [London] (Mawbey School, Coopers Rd. SE1) : [ILEA Centre for Anti-Racist Education and the British Defence and Aid Fund for Southern Africa], c1984. — 44p. — *Text on inside covers. — Bibliography: p44*

The South African society : realities and future prospects / Human Sciences Research Council. — New York : Greenwood Press, c1987. — p. cm. — (Contributions in ethnic studies ; no. 21). — *"Final report of the Main Committee of the HSRC Investigation into Intergroup Relations"--Pref. — Includes index. — Bibliography: p*

SOUTH AFRICA — Social life and customs

MOYA, Lily
Not either an experimental doll : the separate worlds of three South African women / Shula Marks (editor). — London : Women's Press, 1987. — 217p,[16]p of plates. — *Letters written between Lily Moya and Mabel Palmer*

SOUTH AFRICA — Social policy

SOUTH AFRICA. Department of Co-operation and Development. Division of Social Work
Social work practice. — Pretoria : [the Department], 1984-. — *3 per year*

SOUTH AFRICA — Statistics

SOUTH AFRICA. Directorate Agricultural Economic Trends
Kortbegrip van Landboustatistiek = abstract of agricultural statistics. — Pretoria : the Department, 1985-. — *Annual*

SOUTH AFRICA — Statistics, Vital

South African life tables = Suid-Afrikaanse lewenstabelle / Central Statistical Services, South Africa. — Pretoria : Government Printer, 1969/71-. — *Irregular. — Text in English and Afrikaans. — 1969/71 issuing body entitled: South Africa. Department of Statistics*

SOUTH AFRICA — Relations — United States

SEIDMAN, Ann
The roots of crisis in Southern Africa / Ann Seidman. — Trenton, N.J. : Africa World Press, 1985. — xvii,209p. — (Impact audit ; No.4). — *Bibliography: p175-180*

SOUTH AFRICA. Department of Home Affairs

SOUTH AFRICA. Department of Home Affairs
Annual report = Jaarverslag / Department of Home Affairs, South Africa. — Pretoria : Government Printer, 1984/85-. — *Annual. — Text in English and Afrikaans*

SOUTH AFRICA. Department of Mineral and Energy Affairs

SOUTH AFRICA. Department of Mineral and Energy Affairs. Minerals Bureau
Directory / Minerals Bureau, Department of Mineral and Energy Affairs, South Africa. — Braamfontein : Minerals Bureau, 1984-. — *Annual*

SOUTH AFRICA. Department of Trade and Industry

SOUTH AFRICA (Department of Trade and Industry)
Annual report = Jaarverslag / Department of Trade and Industry, South Africa. — [Pretoria] : Department of Trade and Industry, 1984-. — *Annual. — Text in English and Afrikaans*

SOUTH AFRICA. Directorate Agricultural Economic Trends

SOUTH AFRICA. Directorate Agricultural Economic Trends
Kortbegrip van Landboustatistiek = abstract of agricultural statistics. — Pretoria : the Department, 1985-. — *Annual*

SOUTH AFRICA WAR, 1899-1902 — Correspondence

HOBHOUSE, Emily
Boer war letters / edited by Rykie Van Reenen. — Cape Town : Human and Rousseau, 1984. — 557p. — *Bibliography: p543-546*

SOUTH AFRICAN ESSAYS (ENGLISH)

BREYTENBACH, Breyten
End papers : essays, letters, articles of faith, workbook notes / Breyten Breytenbach. — London : Faber, 1986. — 270p

SOUTH AFRICAN WAR, 1899-1902 — History

LEE, Emanoel C. G.
To the bitter end : a photographic history of the Boer War 1899-1902 / Emanoel Lee. — London : Viking, 1985. — 1v.. — *Includes index*

SOUTH AMERICA — Politics and government — 20th century — Case studies

O'DONNELL, Guillermo A
Modernization and bureaucratic-authoritarianism : studies in South American politics / [by] Guillermo A. O'Donnell. — Berkeley : Institute of International Studies, University of California, [1973]. — xv, 219 p. — (Politics of modernization series ; no. 9). — *Bibliography: p. 201-219*

SOUTH ASIA — Atlases

DUTT, Ashok K.
Fully annotated atlas of South Asia / Ashok K. Dutt [and] M. Margaret Geib. — Boulder, Colo. : Westview Press, 1987. — xxiii,231p. — *Bibliography: p225-231*

SOUTH ASIA — Bibliography

South Asian studies : papers presented at a colloquium 24-26 April 1985 / edited by Albertine Gaur. — London : British Library, 1986. — xvi,327p. — (British library occasional papers ; 7)

SOUTH ASIA — Economic policy — Congresses

South Asian regional cooperation : a socio-economic approach to peace and stability / edited by M. Abdul Hafiz, Iftekharuzzaman. — Dhaka : Bangladesh Institute of International and Strategic Studies, 1985. — xxxxiv, 290 p.. — *Summary: Papers presented at an International Conference on South Asian Regional Cooperation, held at Dhaka, January 14-16, 1985, under the aegis of the Bangladesh Institute of International and Strategic Studies. — Includes bibliographies and index*

SOUTH ASIA — Foreign economic relations — Asia, Southeastern

ASEAN-South Asia economic relations / edited by Charan D. Wadhva and Mukul G. Asher. — Singapore : Institute of Southeast Asian Studies, c1985. — 384 p

SOUTH ASIA — Foreign relations — Great Britain

MOORE, R. J. (Robin James)
Making the new Commonwealth / R.J. Moore. — Oxford : Clarendon, 1987. — [224]p. — *Includes bibliography and index*

SOUTH ASIA — Foreign relations — Soviet Union

RAM, Raghunath
Super powers and Indo-Pakistani sub-continent : perceptions and policies / Raghunath Ram. — New Delhi : Raaj Prakashan, 1985. — 427p. — *Bibliography: p[402]-411*

Soviet-American relations with Pakistan, Iran and Afghanistan / edited by Hafeez Malik. — Basingstoke : Macmillan, 1986. — [480]p. — *Includes index*

SOUTH ASIA — Foreign relations — United States

RAM, Raghunath
Super powers and Indo-Pakistani sub-continent : perceptions and policies / Raghunath Ram. — New Delhi : Raaj Prakashan, 1985. — 427p. — *Bibliography: p[402]-411*

Soviet-American relations with Pakistan, Iran and Afghanistan / edited by Hafeez Malik. — Basingstoke : Macmillan, 1986. — [480]p. — *Includes index*

SOUTH ASIA — History — Addresses, essays, lectures

Subaltern studies. — Delhi ; Oxford : Oxford University Press
4: Writings on South Asian history and society / edited by Ranajit Guha. — 1985. — 383 p

SOUTH ASIA — Library resources — Great Britain — Directories

Directory of South Asian library resources in the UK and the Republic of Ireland / edited by S. Gunasingam. — London : South Asia Library Group, 1987. — 177p

SOUTH ASIA — Politics and government

MISHRA, Pramod Kumar
India, Pakistan, Nepal, and Bangladesh : India as a factor in the intra-regional interaction in South Asia / P. K. Mishra. — Delhi : Sundeep Prakashan, 1979. — viii, 286 p.. — *Based on the author's thesis (M. Phil.) School of International Studies, Jawaharlal Nehru University, 1972, with title: Pakistan Nepal relations. — Includes index. — Bibliography: p. [271]-279*

Pakistan and Asian peace / edited by V.D. Chopra ; with an introduction by Rasheeduddin Khan. — New Delhi : Patriot Publishers, 1985. — 288 p.. — *60-5. — Includes bibliographical references*

RAM, Raghunath
Super powers and Indo-Pakistani sub-continent : perceptions and policies / Raghunath Ram. — New Delhi : Raaj Prakashan, 1985. — 427p. — *Bibliography: p[402]-411*

SOUTH ASIA — Politics and government — Congresses

South Asian regional cooperation : a socio-economic approach to peace and stability / edited by M. Abdul Hafiz, Iftekharuzzaman. — Dhaka : Bangladesh Institute of International and Strategic Studies, 1985. — xxxxiv, 290 p.. — *Summary: Papers presented at an International Conference on South Asian Regional Cooperation, held at Dhaka, January 14-16, 1985, under the aegis of the Bangladesh Institute of International and Strategic Studies. — Includes bibliographies and index*

SOUTH ASIA — Relations — India

BINDRA, S. S
India and her neighbours : a study of political, economic, and cultural relations, and interactions / S.S. Bindra. — New Delhi : Deep & Deep, c1984. — 404 p.. — *Includes index. — Bibliography: p. [364]-398*

SOUTH ASIA — Rural conditions

Rice societies : Asian problems and prospects / edited by Irene Nørlund, Sven Cederroth, Ingela Gerdin. — London : Curzon, 1986. — x,321p. — (Studies on Asian topics ; 10). — *Includes bibliographies*

SOUTH ASIA — Social conditions — Addresses, essays, lectures

Subaltern studies. — Delhi ; Oxford : Oxford University Press
4: Writings on South Asian history and society / edited by Ranajit Guha. — 1985. — 383 p

SOUTH ASIA — Social policy — Congresses

South Asian regional cooperation : a socio-economic approach to peace and stability / edited by M. Abdul Hafiz, Iftekharuzzaman. — Dhaka : Bangladesh Institute of International and Strategic Studies, 1985. — xxxxiv, 290 p.. — *Summary: Papers presented at an International Conference on South Asian Regional Cooperation, held at Dhaka, January 14-16, 1985, under the aegis of the Bangladesh Institute of International and Strategic Studies. — Includes bibliographies and index*

SOUTH ATLANTIC REGION — Defenses

MILIA, Juan Guillermo
El valor estrategico y económico del Atlantico sur y la guerra de las Malvinas / Juan Guillermo Milia. — [Buenos Aires] : OIKOS, [1985]. — 34p. — *Bibliography: p[35-36]*

SOUTH ATLANTIC REGION — Economic aspects

MILIA, Juan Guillermo
El valor estrategico y económico del Atlantico sur y la guerra de las Malvinas / Juan Guillermo Milia. — [Buenos Aires] : OIKOS, [1985]. — 34p. — *Bibliography: p[35-36]*

SOUTH AUSTRALIA. Justices Act

NAFFIN, Ngaire
Domestic violence and the law : a study of S.99 of the Justices Act (S. A.) / by Naffin. — [Adelaide] : Women's Adviser's Office, Department of the Premier and Cabinet, 1985. — iv,iii,170p. — *Includes bibliographical references*

SOUTH AUSTRALIA — Officials and employees

SOUTH AUSTRALIA. Public Service Board
The ethnic composition of the South Australian public service. — [Adelaide] : the Board, 1982. — iii,102,4p

SOUTH AUSTRALIA. Committee on Aboriginal Employment

SOUTH AUSTRALIA. Committee on Aboriginal Employment
Report of the Committee on Aboriginal Employment. — Adelaide : Equal Opportunities Branch, Public Service Board, [1983]. — 34 leaves. — *Includes bibliographical references*

SOUTH AUSTRALIA. Department for Community Welfare

SOUTH AUSTRALIA. Department for Community Welfare
The services of the Department for the care of the young offender, the support of the family, the protection of the community. — [Adelaide] : the Department, 1975. — 36 leaves

SOUTH AUSTRALIA. Department of Agriculture. Economics Division — Research

SOUTH AUSTRALIA. Department of Agriculture. Research Policy Advisory Committee
Research priorities in the Economics Division. — Adelaide : the Department, 1982. — ii,60 leaves. — (Technical report / Department of Agriculture ; no.11). — *Includes bibliographical references*

SOUTH AUSTRALIA. Enquiry into Hospital Services in South Australia

SOUTH AUSTRALIA. Enquiry into Hospital Services in South Australia
Report of the Enquiry into Hospital Services in South Australia. — Adelaide : [South Australian Health Commission], 1983. — xix,456p. — *Bibliography: p451-454. — Chairman: Sidney Sax*

SOUTH AUSTRALIA. Police Department — Corrupt practices

BRIGHT, Charles
Reports commissioned by the Hon. K. T. Griffin, Attorney-General, South Australia into alleged corruption in the South Australian Police Force / [by Sir Charles Bright]. — Adelaide : Government Printer, 1982. — v,100p

SOUTH AUSTRALIA. Task Force on Child Sexual Abuse

SOUTH AUSTRALIA. Task Force on Child Sexual Abuse
Community disscussion paper. — Adelaide : South Australian Health Commission, 1985. — 89p. — *Includes bibliography references*

SOUTH AUSTRALIA. Task Force on Child Sexual Abuse
Final report of the Task Force on Child Sexual Abuse. — Adelaide : South Australian Health Commission, 1986. — viii,358p. — *Bibliography: p347-358*

SOUTH CAROLINA — Governors — Biography

EDMUNDS, John B
Francis W. Pickens and the politics of destruction / John B. Edmunds, Jr. — Chapel Hill : University of North Carolina Press, c1986. — xiii, 256 p.. — (The Fred W. Morrison series in Southern studies). — *Includes index. — Bibliography: p. [223]-239*

SOUTH CAROLINA — Politics and government — 1775-1865

EDMUNDS, John B
Francis W. Pickens and the politics of destruction / John B. Edmunds, Jr. — Chapel Hill : University of North Carolina Press, c1986. — xiii, 256 p.. — (The Fred W. Morrison series in Southern studies). — *Includes index. — Bibliography: p. [223]-239*

SOUTH-EAST ASIA LIBRARY GROUP

SOUTH-EAST ASIA LIBRARY GROUP
Newsletter / South-East Asia Library Group. — Hull : South-East Asia Library Group, 1982-. — *Biennial*

SOUTH EAST (ENGLAND) — Economic conditions — Statistics

Regional trends in the south east: the south east regional monitor / London and South East Regional Planning Conference. — London : London and South East Regional Planning Conference, 1983/4-. — *Annual*

SOUTH EAST (ENGLAND) — Social conditions — Statistics

Regional trends in the south east: the south east regional monitor / London and South East Regional Planning Conference. — London : London and South East Regional Planning Conference, 1983/4-. — *Annual*

SOUTH GLAMORGAN — Economic conditions

SOUTH GLAMORGAN
1986 social survey employment and economic activity results: county electoral divisions. — [Cardiff] : [the Council], 1986. — ii,55p

SOUTH GLAMORGAN — Economic conditions — Statistics

SOUTH GLAMORGAN
[1981 census of population] : statistical atlas : summary tables : employment and travel : new communities. — [Cardiff] : [the Council], 1981. — 14p

SOUTH GLAMORGAN — Population

SOUTH GLAMORGAN
1981 census area profiles : South Glamorgan electoral divisions. — [Cardiff] : [the Council], 1981. — 39p

SOUTH GLAMORGAN
1981 census community profiles : county of South Glamorgan. — [Cardiff] : [the Council], 1981. — 67 leaves

SOUTH GLAMORGAN
1986 social survey : selected characteristics of pensionable age population : county electoral divisions. — [Cardiff] : [the Council], 1987. — ii,35p

SOUTH GLAMORGAN — Population — Statistics

SOUTH GLAMORGAN
[1981 census of population] : statistical atlas : summary tables : employment and travel : new communities. — [Cardiff] : [the Council], 1981. — 14p

SOUTH GLAMORGAN
[1981 census of population] : statistical atlas summary tables : new communities. — [Cardiff] : [the Council], 1981. — 7 leaves

SOUTH GLAMORGAN — Social conditions

SOUTH GLAMORGAN
1986 social survey : selected characteristics of pensionable age population : county electoral divisions. — [Cardiff] : [the Council], 1987. — ii,35p

SOUTH GLAMORGAN
South Glamorgan social survey : 1986 profiles : county electoral divisions. — [Cardiff] : [the Council], 1987. — vi,140p

SOUTH PACIFIC FORUM

NEW ZEALAND. Ministry of Foreign Affairs
The South Pacific Forum. — Wellington : the Ministry, 1986. — 12p. — (Information bulletin ; no.16)

SOUTHALL (MIDDLESEX) — Race relations

Southall : the birth of a black community / Campaign Against Racism and Fascism/Southall Rights. — London : Institute of Race Relations, c1981. — 70p,[4]p of plates. — *Ill on inside covers. — Bibliography: p65-66*

SOUTHAMPTON INSURRECTION, 1831 — Fiction

STYRON, William
The confessions of Nat Turner / William Styron. — New York : Bantam, 1983. — xv,347p

SOUTHERN CONE OF SOUTH AMERICA — Economic policy

RAMOS, Joseph R
Neoconservative economics in the southern cone of Latin America, 1973-1983 / Joseph Ramos. — Baltimore : Johns Hopkins University Press, c1986. — xviii, 200p. — (The Johns Hopkins studies in development). — *Includes index. — Bibliography: p.185-191*

SOUTHERN STATES — Civilization

KIRBY, Jack Temple
Media-made Dixie : the South in the American imagination / Jack Temple Kirby. — Rev. ed. — Athens : University of Georgia Press, c1986. — p. cm. — *Includes index. — Bibliography: p*

SOUTHERN STATES — Civilization — 1775-1865

WYATT-BROWN, Bertram
Yankee saints and Southern sinners / Bertram Wyatt-Brown. — Baten Rouge ; London : Louisiana State University Press, c1985. — xi, 227p. — *Includes index*

SOUTHERN STATES — Economic conditions

SHORE, Laurence
Southern capitalists : the ideological leadership of an elite, 1832-1885 / by Laurence Shore. — Chapel Hill : University of North Carolina Press, c1986. — p. cm. — (The Fred W. Morrison series in southern studies). — *Includes index. — Bibliography: p*

WRIGHT, Gavin
Old South, New South : revolutions in the southern economy since the Civil War / Gavin Wright. — New York : Basic Books, c1986. — x, 321 p.. — *Includes index. — Bibliography: p. 304-309*

SOUTHERN STATES — Economic conditions — Addresses, essays, lectures

Essays on the postbellum southern economy / by Thavolia Glymph ... [et al.] ; introduction by Thavolia Glymph ; edited by Thavolia Glymph and John J. Kushma. — 1st ed. — College Station [Tex.] : Published for the University of Texas at Arlington by Texas A&M University Press, c1985. — p. cm. — (The Walter Prescott Webb memorial lectures ; 18). — *Includes bibliographies*

SOUTHERN STATES — Economic conditions — 1945-

Agricultural change : consequences for southern farms and rural communities / edited by Joseph J. Molnar. — Boulder : Westview Press, c1986. — xxii, 440 p. — (Westview special studies in agricultural science and policy). — *Includes bibliographies and indexes*

SOUTHERN STATES — Historiography

KIRBY, Jack Temple
Media-made Dixie : the South in the American imagination / Jack Temple Kirby. — Rev. ed. — Athens : University of Georgia Press, c1986. — p. cm. — *Includes index. — Bibliography: p*

WOODWARD, C. Vann
Thinking back : the perils of writing history / C. Vann Woodward. — Baton Rouge ; London : Louisiana State University Press, c1986. — x, 158p. — *Includes index. — Bibliography: p 147-151*

SOUTHERN STATES — History — 1775-1865

SHORE, Laurence
Southern capitalists : the ideological leadership of an elite, 1832-1885 / by Laurence Shore. — Chapel Hill : University of North Carolina Press, c1986. — p. cm. — (The Fred W. Morrison series in southern studies). — *Includes index. — Bibliography: p*

SOUTHERN STATES — History — 1865-1877

RABLE, George C
But there was no peace : the role of violence in the politics of Reconstruction / George C. Rable. — Athens : University of Georgia Press, c1984. — xiii, 257 p.. — *Includes index. — Bibliography: p. [247]-251*

SOUTHERN STATES — History

SHORE, Laurence
Southern capitalists : the ideological leadership of an elite, 1832-1885 / by Laurence Shore. — Chapel Hill : University of North Carolina Press, c1986. — p. cm. — (The Fred W. Morrison series in southern studies). — *Includes index. — Bibliography: p*

SOUTHERN STATES — History — 20th century

DANIEL, Pete
Standing at the crossroads : Southern life since 1900 / Pete Daniel ; consulting editor, Eric Foner. — 1st ed. — New York : Hill and Wang, 1986. — viii, 259 p.. — (American century series). — *Includes index. — Bibliography: p.233-251*

SOUTHERN STATES — Industries — History

WRIGHT, Gavin
Old South, New South : revolutions in the southern economy since the Civil War / Gavin Wright. — New York : Basic Books, c1986. — x, 321 p.. — *Includes index. — Bibliography: p. 304-309*

SOUTHERN STATES — Politics and government — 1865-1950

LISIO, Donald J
Hoover, Blacks, and lily-whites : a study of Southern strategies / Donald J. Lisio. — Chapel Hill ; London : University of North Carolina Press, c1985. — xxii, 373p. — (The Fred W. Morrison series in Southern studies). — *Includes index. — Bibliography: p.357-364*

SOUTHERN STATES — Politics and government — 1951- — Addresses, essays, lectures

The 1984 presidential election in the South : patterns of southern party politics / edited by Robert P. Steed, Laurence W. Moreland, and Tod A. Baker. — New York : Praeger, 1985. — p. cm. — *Includes index. — Bibliography: p*

SOUTHERN STATES — Popular culture

REED, John Shelton
Southern folk, plain & fancy : native white social types / John Shelton Reed. — Athens : University of Georgia Press, c1986. — xii, 119 p., [1] leaf of plates. — (Lamar memorial lectures / Mercer University ; no. 29). — *Lectures delivered Oct. 1985. — Includes index. — Bibliography: p. 105-113*

SOUTHERN STATES — Race relations

BLOOM, Jack M
Class, race, and the Civil Rights Movement / Jack M. Bloom. — Bloomington : Indiana University Press, c1987. — x, 267 p.. — (Blacks in the diaspora). — *Includes index. — Bibliography: p. [225]-237*

LISIO, Donald J
Hoover, Blacks, and lily-whites : a study of Southern strategies / Donald J. Lisio. — Chapel Hill ; London : University of North Carolina Press, c1985. — xxii, 373p. — (The Fred W. Morrison series in Southern studies). — *Includes index. — Bibliography: p.357-364*

SOUTHERN STATES — Race relations — Addresses, essays, lectures

HUGHES, Henry
[Selections. 1985]. Selected writings of Henry Hughes, antebellum Southerner, slavocrat, sociologist / edited, with a critical essay, by Stanford M. Lyman. — Jackson : University Press of Mississippi, c1985. — xxi, 235 p.. — *Includes bibliographical references*

SOUTHERN STATES — Rural conditions

Agricultural change : consequences for southern farms and rural communities / edited by Joseph J. Molnar. — Boulder : Westview Press, c1986. — xxii, 440 p. — (Westview special studies in agricultural science and policy). — *Includes bibliographies and indexes*

SOUTHERN STATES — Social conditions

DANIEL, Pete
Standing at the crossroads : Southern life since 1900 / Pete Daniel ; consulting editor, Eric Foner. — 1st ed. — New York : Hill and Wang, 1986. — viii, 259 p.. — (American century series). — *Includes index. — Bibliography: p.233-251*

REED, John Shelton
The enduring South : subcultural persistence in mass society / John Shelton Reed ; with a new afterword by the author. — Chapel Hill : University of North Carolina Press, 1986, c1974. — p. cm. — *Includes index. — Bibliography: p*

SOUTHERN STATES — Social conditions — Congresses

The Web of southern social relations : women, family, & education / edited by Walter J. Fraser, Jr., R. Frank Saunders, Jr., and Jon L. Wakelyn. — Athens : University of Georgia Press, c1985. — xvii, 257 p.. — *Includes bibliographies and index*

SOUTHERN STATES — Social life and customs

REED, John Shelton
The enduring South : subcultural persistence in mass society / John Shelton Reed ; with a new afterword by the author. — Chapel Hill : University of North Carolina Press, 1986, c1974. — p. cm. — *Includes index. — Bibliography: p*

REED, John Shelton
Southern folk, plain & fancy : native white social types / John Shelton Reed. — Athens : University of Georgia Press, c1986. — xii, 119 p., [1] leaf of plates. — (Lamar memorial lectures / Mercer University ; no. 29). — *Lectures delivered Oct. 1985. — Includes index. — Bibliography: p. 105-113*

SOUTHPORT LIBERAL ASSOCIATION — History

BRAHAM, Michael
Southport Liberal Association : the first 100 years / by Michael Braham. — [Southport] : The author, 1985. — 82p. — *Bibliography: p82*

SOUTHWARK (LONDON, ENGLAND) — Economic conditions

SOUTHWARK
A working community. — Southwark : [the Council], 1986. — iv,93p

SOUTHWARK (LONDON, ENGLAND) — Social conditions

SOUTHWARK
A working community. — Southwark : [the Council], 1986. — iv,93p

SOUTHWARK (LONDON, ENGLAND) — Social policy

LOWE, Clare
Outside the Act : a study of young single homeless people in the London borough of Southwark / Clare Lowe. — Southwark : Southwark Housing Departmnt. Research and Development Group, 1986. — 54p. — *At head of title: Southwark housing*

SOVEREIGNTY

DELUPIS, Ingrid
International law and the independent state / Ingrid Detter De Lupis. — 2nd ed. — Aldershot : Gower, 1987. — xxvi,252p. — *Previous ed.: 1974. — Includes index*

GILSON, Bernard
The conceptual system of sovereign equality / by Bernard Gilson. — Leuven : Peeters, 1984. — vi,602p. — (Philosophie du droit international). — *Includes bibliography*

HINSLEY, F. H.
Sovereignty / F.H. Hinsley. — 2nd ed. — Cambridge : Cambridge University Press, 1986. — [272]p. — *Previous ed.: London : Watts, 1966. — Includes bibliography and index*

SOVEREIGNTY *continuation*

SCHMITT, Carl
[Politische Theologie. English]. Political theology : four chapters on the concept of sovereignty / Carl Schmitt ; translated by George Schwab. — Cambridge, Mass. ; London : MIT, 1985. — xxvi, 70p. — (Studies in contemporary German social thought). — *Translation of: Politische Theologie. — Includes index*

SOVET EKONOMICHESKOI VZAIMOPOMOSHCHI

Nauchno-tekhnicheskii progress i sotrudnichestvo stran SEV / pod redaktsiei O. A. Chukanova, G. M. Kharakhash'iana, Iu. F. Kormnova. — Moskva : Mezhdunarodnye otnosheniia, 1973. — 205p

Nauchno-tekhnicheskoe sotrudnichestvo stran SEV : spravochnik / pod redaktsiei O. A. Chukanova. — Moskva : Ekonomika, 1986. — 287p

PIREC, Dušan
Kriza realnog socijalizma? : društveno-ekonomske karakteristike i protivurečnosti istočnoevropskih socijalističkih zemalja / Dušan Pirec. — Beograd : Ekonomika, 1985. — 412p. — *Bibliography: p369-392*

Soglasovanie ekonomicheskoi politiki stran SEV / otv. redaktor O. T. Bogomolov. — Moskva : Nauka, 1986. — 287p

SOVET EKONOMICHESKOI VZAIMOPOMOSHCHI — Commerce — Statistics

Comecon foreign trade data / edited by the Vienna Institute for Comparative Economic Studies. — London : Macmillan, 1980-

SOVET EKONOMICHESKOI VZAIMOPOMOSHCHI — Foreign economic relations — Statistics

Comecon foreign trade data / edited by the Vienna Institute for Comparative Economic Studies. — London : Macmillan, 1980-

SOVET EKONOMICHESKOÏ VZAIMOPOMOSHCHI — History

WALLACE, William V.
Comecon, trade and the West / William V. Wallace and Roger A. Clarke. — London : Pinter, 1986. — xi,176p. — *Bibliography: p170-172. — Includes index*

SOVIET CENTRAL ASIA — History — Revolution of 1905

Revoliustiia 1905-1907 gg. v Srednem Azii i Kazakhstane / [B. V. Lunin...et al.; otv. redaktor Kh. Z. Ziiaev]. — Tashkent : "Fan" Uzbekskoi SSR, 1985. — 206p

Revoliutsiia 1905-1907 gg. v Srednei Azii i Kazakhstane / [B. V. Lunin...et al.; otv. red. Kh. Z. Ziiaev]. — Tashkent : "Fan" Uzbekskoi SSR, 1985. — 206p

SOVIET FAR EAST (R.S.F.S.R.) — History — Revolution, 1917-1921

SAMOILOV, A. D.
Na strazhe zavoevanii Oktiabria : (krakh kontrrevoliutsii na Dal'nem Vostoke) / A. D. Samoilov. — Moskva : Mysl', 1986. — 301p

SOVIET UNION

JENSEN, Bent
Sovjetunionen : historie, ideologi, økonomi og politik / Bent Jensen. — København : Forsvarets Oplysnings- og Velfaerdstjeneste, 1985. — [119p]. — (Forsvaret i samfundet). — *Bibliography: p112-[114]. — FKO PUB 493-60*

The USSR today and tomorrow : problems and challenges / edited by Uri Ra'anan and Charles M. Perry. — Lexington, Mass. : Lexington Books, c1987. — p. cm

SOVIET UNION — Administrative and political divisions

POLIAKOV, Iu. A.
Sovetskaia strana posle okonchaniia Grazhdanskoi voiny : territoriia i naselenie / Iu. A. Poliakov. — Moskva : Nauka, 1986. — 270p

SOVIET UNION — Appropriations and expenditures

The Costs and benefits of the Soviet empire, 1981-1983 / Charles Wolf, Jr. ... [et al.]. — Santa Monica, CA : Rand, [1986]. — xv, 46 p.. — *"Prepared for the Director of Net Assessment, Office of the Secretary of Defense."*. — *"August 1986."*. — *"R-3419-NA."*. — *Includes bibliographical references*

SOVIET UNION — Armed forces

LEE, William Thomas
Soviet military policy since World War II / William T. Lee, Richard F. Staar ; foreword by William R. van Cleave. — Stanford, Calif. : Hoover Institution Press, Stanford University, c1986. — xxii, 263 p.. — (Hoover Press publication). — *Includes index. — Bibliography: p. [249]-258*

SOVIET UNION — Armed Forces — Appropriations and expenditures

A dollar cost comparison of Soviet and US defense activities, 1966-1976. — [Washington] : Central Intelligence Agency, 1977. — 15p. — SR 77-1000IU

SOVIET UNION — Armed forces — History

BESKROVNYI, L. G.
Armiia i flot Rossii v nachale XX v. : ocherki voenno-ekonomicheskogo potentsiala / L. G. Beskrovnyi ; otv. redaktor A. L. Narochnitskii. — Moskva : Nauka, 1986. — 237p

SOVIET UNION — Armed forces — Political activity

Voennye organizatsii partii bol'shevikov v 1917 godu / otv. redaktor Iu. I. Korablev. — Moskva : Nauka, 1986. — 253p

SOVIET UNION — Armed Forces — Political activity

WILLIAMS, E. S.
The Soviet military : political education, training and morale / E.S. Williams ; with chapters by C.N. Donnelly and J.E. Moore ; foreword by Sir Curtis Keeble. — Basingstoke : Macmillan, 1987. — xv,203p,[16]p of plates. — (RUSI defence studies series). — *Bibliography: p196-198. — Includes index*

SOVIET UNION — Bibliography

HORAK, Stephan M.
Russia, the USSR, and Eastern Europe : a bibliographic guide to English language publications, 1975-1980 / Stephan M. Horak. — Littleton, Colo. : Libraries Unlimited, 1982. — 279 p.. — *Supplements: Russia, the USSR, and Eastern Europe : a bibliographic guide to English language publications, 1964-1974 / Stephan M. Horak. 1978. — Includes index*

SOVIET UNION — Biography — Bibliography

Vospominaniia i dnevniki XVIII-XX vv. : ukazatel' rukopisei / redaktsiia i predislovie S. V. Zhitomirskoi. — Moskva : Kniga, 1976. — 619p

SOVIET UNION — Boundaries

POLIAKOV, Iu. A.
Sovetskaia strana posle okonchaniia Grazhdanskoi voiny : territoriia i naselenie / Iu. A. Poliakov. — Moskva : Nauka, 1986. — 270p

Zakon Soiuza Sovetskikh Sotsialisticheskikh Respublik o gosudarstvennoi granitse SSSR : politiko-pravovoi kommentarii / [avtorskii kollektiv : N. M. Atasian...et al; nauchno-redaktsionnaia kollegiia : V. N. Kudriavtsev...et al.]. — Moskva : Voennoe izd-vo, 1986. — 150p

SOVIET UNION — Census — History — Study and teaching

Research guide to the Russian and Soviet censuses / edited by Ralph S. Clem. — Ithaca : Cornell University Press, 1986. — p. cm. — *Includes index*

SOVIET UNION — Church history — 17th century

RUMIANTSEVA, V. S.
Narodnoe antitserkovnoe dvizhenie v Rossii v XVII veke / V. S. Rumiantseva ; otv. redaktor I. A. Bulygin. — Moskva : Nauka, 1986. — 262p

SOVIET UNION — Civilization

SCHAPIRO, Leonard
Russian studies / Leonard Schapiro ; edited by Ellen Dahrendorf ; with and introduction by Harry Willetts. — London : Collins Harvill, 1986. — 400p. — *Includes index*

SOVIET UNION — Civilization — 18th century — Ukrainian influences

SAUNDERS, David
The Ukrainian impact on Russian culture 1750-1850 / by David Saunders. — Edmonton : Canadian Institute of Ukrainian Studies, University of Alberta, 1985. — x, 415p. — (The Canadian library in Ukrainian studies). — *Thesis (Ph.D.) - St. Antony's College, Oxford, [1983?]. — Bibliography: p.330-406*

SOVIET UNION — Civilization — 18th century — Ukranian influences

SAUNDERS, David
The Ukrainian impact on Russian culture 1750-1850 / by David Saunders. — Edmonton : Canadian Institute of Ukrainian Studies, University of Alberta, 1985. — x, 415p. — (The Canadian library in Ukrainian studies). — *Thesis (Ph.D.) - St. Antony's College, Oxford, [1983?]. — Bibliography: p.330-406*

SOVIET UNION — Civilization — 19th century — Ukrainian influences

SAUNDERS, David
The Ukrainian impact on Russian culture 1750-1850 / by David Saunders. — Edmonton : Canadian Institute of Ukrainian Studies, University of Alberta, 1985. — x, 415p. — (The Canadian library in Ukrainian studies). — *Thesis (Ph.D.) - St. Antony's College, Oxford, [1983?]. — Bibliography: p.330-406*

SOVIET UNION — Civilization — 1917-

TUCKER, Robert C.
Political culture and leadership in Soviet Russia : from Lenin to Gorbachev / Robert C. Tucker. — Brighton : Wheatsheaf, 1987. — x,214p. — *Includes index*

SOVIET UNION — Commerce

Effektivnost' sotsialisticheskoi vnutrennei torgovli / R. A. Maksimento...[et al.] ; pod redaktsiei V. I. Ivanitskogo i L. Rendosha. — Kiev : Vyshcha shkola, 1985. — 174p

SOKOLOFF, Georges
The economy of détente : the Soviet Union and western capital / Georges Sokoloff ; translated from the French by Jean Kirby. — Leamington Spa : Berg, c1987. — [236]p. — *Translation of: L'économie de la détente. — Includes bibliography and index*

SOVIET UNION — Commerce — United States

LUNDBORG, Per
The economics of export embargo : the case of the US-Soviet grain suspension / Per Lundborg. — London : Croom Helm, c1987. — xi,127p. — *Bibliography: p119-122. — Includes index*

SOVIET UNION — Commercial policy

SOKOLOFF, Georges
The economy of détente : the Soviet Union and western capital / Georges Sokoloff ; translated from the French by Jean Kirby. — Leamington Spa : Berg, c1987. — [236]p. — *Translation of: L'économie de la détente. — Includes bibliography and index*

SOVIET UNION — Constitution

UNION OF SOVIET SOCIALIST REPUBLICS
[Constitution (1977)]. Constitution (fundamental law) of the Union of Soviet Socialist Republics : adopted at the Seventh (Special) Session of the Supreme Soviet of the USSR, Ninth Convocation, on October 7, 1977. — Moscow : Novosti Press Agency, 1985. — 86p

SOVIET UNION — Constitution — Dictionaries

The Soviet constitution : a dictionary / [edited by V. N. Kudriavtsev...et al.]. — Moscow : Progress, 1986. — 300p

SOVIET UNION — Constitutional law

KABALKIN, A. Iu.
Sotsial'no-ekonomicheskie prava sovetskikh grazhdan : (v otrasliakh prava tsivilisticheskogo profilia) / A. Iu. Kabalkin ; otv. red. V. M. Chkhikvadze. — Moskva : Nauka, 1986. — 207p

Zakon Soiuza Sovetskikh Sotsialisticheskikh Respublik o gosudarstvennoi granitse SSSR : politiko-pravovoi kommentarii / [avtorskii kollektiv : N. M. Atasian...et al; nauchno-redaktsionnaia kollegiia : V. N. Kudriavtsev...et al.]. — Moskva : Voennoe izd-vo, 1986. — 150p

SOVIET UNION — Defences — History

BESKROVNYI, L. G.
Armiia i flot Rossii v nachale XX v. : ocherki voenno-ekonomicheskogo potentsiala / L. G. Beskrovnyi ; otv. redaktor A. L. Narochnitskii. — Moskva : Nauka, 1986. — 237p

SOVIET UNION — Defenses

The second superpower : the arms race and the Soviet Union / edited by Gerard Holden. — London : CND Publications, 1985. — 107p. — Bibliography: p96-100

SOVIET UNION — Economic conditions

BLACK, Cyril Edwin
Understanding Soviet politics : the perspective of Russian history / Cyril E. Black. — Boulder, Colo. : Westview Press, 1986. — p. cm. — A collection of previously published essays. — Includes index

LAFONT, Jean
L'accumulation du capital et les crises dans l'URSS contemporaine : une première approche / Jean Lafont et Danièle Leborgne. — Paris : Centre D'Études Prospectives d'Économie Mathématique Appliquées à la Planification, 1979. — 98p. — (Centre d'Études Prospectives d'Économie Mathématique Appliquées à la Planification ; 7910). — Bibliography: p93-98

Sotsial'no-ekonomicheskii potentsial sela : problemy razvitiia i ispol'zovaniia / otv. redaktor L. V. Nikiforov. — Moskva : Nauka, 1986. — 205p. — (Problemy sovetskoi ekonomiki)

Sotsial'no-ekonomicheskoe razvitie Rossii : sbornik statei k 100-letiiu so dnia rozhdeniia Nikolaia Mikhailovicha Druzhinina / otv. redaktor S. L. Tikhvinskii. — Moskva : Nauka, 1986. — 267p

Soviet economy. — Silver Spring : V. H. Winston (Published in association with the Joint Committee on Soviet Studies of the American Council of Learned Societies and the Social Science Research Council), 1985-. — Quarterly

SOVIET UNION — Economic conditions — To 1861

DRUZHININ, N. M.
Izbrannye trudy / N. M. Druzhinin. — Moskva : Nauka
[2]: Sotsial'no-ekonomicheskaia istoriia Rossii / otv. redaktor S. S. Dmitriev. — 1987. — 421p

POSOSHKÓV, Iván
The book of poverty and wealth / Iván Pososhkóv ; edited and translated by A.P. Vlasto and L.R. Lewitter ; introduction and commentaries by L.R. Lewitter. — London : Athlone, 1987. — 440p. — Translation of: Kniga o skúdosti i bogátstve. — Bibliography: p401-430. — Includes index

SOVIET UNION — Economic conditions — 1861-1917 — Addresses, essays, lectures

The City in late imperial Russia / edited by Michael F. Hamm. — Bloomington : Indiana University Press, c1986. — viii, 372p. — (Indiana-Michigan series in Russian and East European studies). — Papers from a meeting of the American Association for the Advancement of Slavic Studies, held in Kansas City, Mo., Oct. 1983. — Includes index. — Bibliography: p.[355]-359

SOVIET UNION — Economic conditions — 1917-

The Soviet Union : contributors: M. S. Pletushkov...[et al.]. — Moscow : Progress Publishers, 1986. — 248p

SOVIET UNION — Economic conditions — 1918-1945

Istoriia sovetskogo krest'ianstva / redkollegiia: V. P. Sherstobitov...[et al.]. — Moskva : Nauka. — (Istoriia krest'ianstva SSSR)
2: Sovetskoe krest'ianstvo v period sotsialisticheskoi rekonstruktsii narodnogo khoziaistva. Konets 1927-1937 / redkollegiia: I. E. Zelenin...[et al.]. — 1986. — 448p

Kalendar'-ezhegodnik kommunista na 1931 god. — Moskva : Moskovskii rabochii, 1931

REIMAN, Michal
[Geburt des Stalinismus. English]. The birth of Stalinism : the USSR on the eve of the "second revolution" / by Michal Reiman ; translated by George Saunders. — Bloomington : Indiana University Press, c1987. — xii, 188 p.. — (Indiana-Michigan series in Russian and East European studies). — Translation of: Die Geburt des Stalinismus. — Includes index. — Bibliography: p. 155-181

SOVIET UNION — Economic conditions — 1918-

Economically active population : estimates and projections : 1950-2025 = Evaluations et projections de la population active : 1950-2025 = Estimaciones y proyecciones de la población económicamente activa : 1950-2025. — 3rd ed. — Geneva : International Labour Office
V.4: Northern America, Europe, Oceania and USSR. — 1986. — xxvi,177p. — Introduction and table headings in English, French and Spanish

MATTHEWS, Mervyn
Poverty in the Soviet Union : the life-styles of the underprivileged in recent years / by Mervyn Matthews. — Cambridge : Cambridge University Press, 1986. — [430]p. — Includes bibliography and index

SOVIET UNION — Economic conditions — 1965-1975

NOVE, Alec
The Soviet economic system / Alec Nove. — 3rd ed. — Boston ; London : Allen & Unwin, 1986. — [420]p. — Previous ed.: 1980. — Includes bibliography and index

SOVIET UNION — Economic conditions — 1976-

BIALER, Seweryn
The Soviet paradox : external expansion, internal decline / Seweryn Bialer. — 1st ed. — New York : Knopf, 1986. — ix, 391p. — Includes index. — Bibliography: p.379-386

BUCK, Trevor
Modern Soviet economic performance / Trevor Buck and John Cole. — Oxford : Basil Blackwell, 1987. — viii,192p. — Bibliography: p180-187. — Includes index

DESAI, Padma
The Soviet economy in decline? / Padma Desai. — Oxford : Basil Blackwell, 1987. — [280]p. — Includes bibliography and index

Ekonomicheskie problemy razvitogo sotsializma / red. kollegiia I. I. Lukinov...[et al.]. — Kiev : Naukova dumka
T.4: Ekonomicheskaia struktura obshchestva i razitie sotsialisticheskogo obraza zhizni / red. kollegiia V. E. Kozak...[et al.]. — 1985. — 270p

From Brezhnev to Gorbachev : domestic affairs and Soviet foreign policy / edited by Hans-Joachim Veen. — Leamington Spa : Berg, 1987. — xii,378p. — Revised ed. of Wohin entwickelt sich die Sowjetunion?

KERBLAY, Basile
Les soviétiques des années 80 / Basile Kerblay, Marie Lavigne. — Paris : Armand Colin, 1985. — 214p. — Bibliography: p211-[212]

LUDWIKOWSKI, Rett R
The crisis of communism : its meaning, origins, and phases / Rett R. Ludwikowski. — Washington : Pergamon-Brassey's International Defense Publishers, 1986. — xii, 84 p.. — (Foreign policy report). — "A Publication of the Institute for Foreign Policy Analysis, Inc.". — Includes bibliographical references

NOVE, Alec
The Soviet economic system / Alec Nove. — 3rd ed. — Boston ; London : Allen & Unwin, 1986. — [420]p. — Previous ed.: 1980. — Includes bibliography and index

SCHROEDER, Gertrude
The system versus progress : Soviet economic problems / Gertrude Schroeder ; introduced by Phil Hanson. — London : Centre for Research into Communist Economies, 1986. — 100p. — (The State of communist economies ; 2). — Bibliography: p99-100

SCRIVENER, Ronald Stratford
U.S.S.R. economic handbook / Ronald Stratford Scrivener. — London : Euromonitor, 1986. — [250]p

SOVIET UNION — Economic conditions — 1981-

KRICKUS, Richard J
The superpowers in crisis : implications of domestic discord / Richard J. Krickus. — Washington ; London : Pergamon-Brassey's International Defence Publishers, 1987. — xiii, 236p. — Includes bibliographies

MAKOVETSKAIA, M. I.
Effektivnost' sotsialisticheskogo vosproizvodstva : (sushchnost', kriterii, izmerenie) / M. I. Makovetskaia ; otv. redaktor I. P. Suslov. — Novosibirsk : Nauka, Sibirskoe otdelenie, 1982. — 112p. — Bibliography: p109-112

SOVIET UNION — Economic integration

KISS, Károly
Domestic integration of the Soviet economy : the case of the Central Asian Republics. — Budapest : Hungarian Scientific Council for World Economy, 1987. — 127p. — (Trends in world economy ; no.56). — Bibliography: p119-127

SOVIET UNION — Economic policy

DZIUBIK, S. D.
Rynok sredstv proizvodstva v sisteme planomerno organizovannoi ekonomiki / S. D. Dziubik. — L'vov : Vyshcha shkola, 1984. — 157p

Khoziaistvennyi mekhanizm obshchestvennykh formatsii / pod obshchei redaktsiei L. I. Abalkina. — Moskva : Mysl', 1986. — 268p

ORESHIN, V. P.
Planirovanie proizvodstvennoi infrastruktury : kompleksnyi podkhod / V. P. Oreshin. — Moskva : Ekonomika, 1986. — 143p. — Bibliography: p140-142

SOVIET UNION — Economic policy
continuation

Planovoe upravlenie ekonomikoi razvitogo sotsializma / redaktsionnaia kollegiia: A. S. Emel'ianov...[et al.]. — Kiev : Naukova dumka. — *V piati tomakh*. — *Bibliography: p303-[307]*
T.2: Resursy narodnogo khoziaistva: planirovanie i effektivnost' ispol'zovaniia / redaktsionnaia kollegiia: I. K. Bondar'...[et al.]. — 1985. — 308p

SOVIET UNION — Economic policy — Data processing

URINSON, Ia. M.
Sovershenstvovanie tekhnologii narodnokhoziaistvennogo planirovaniia / Ia. M. Urinson. — Moskva : Ekonomika, 1986. — 197p

SOVIET UNION — Economic policy — Dictionaries

Upravlenie ekonomiki: [slovar'-spravochnik] : osnovnye poniatiia i kategorii / pod redaktsiei R. A. Belousova i A. Z. Selezneva. — Moskva : Ekonomika, 1986. — 302p

SOVIET UNION — Economic policy — Mathematical models

Programmno-tselevoi metod v planirovanii / [otv. redaktor N. P. Fedorenko]. — Moskva : Nauka, 1982. — 150p. — (Problemy sovetskoi ekonomiki). — *Bibliography: p147-[149]*

SOVIET UNION — Economic policy — 1917-1928

DMITRENKO, V. P.
Sovetskaia ekonomicheskaia politika v pervye gody proletarskoi diktatury : problemy regulirovaniia rynochnykh otnoshenii / V. P. Dmitrenko ; otv. redaktor Iu. A. Poliakov. — Moskva : Nauka, 1986. — 252p

Ekonomicheskaia politika Sovetskogo gosudarstva v perekhodnyi period ot kapitalizma k sotsializmu / otv. redaktor M. P. Kim. — Moskva : Nauka, 1986. — 254p

SOVIET UNION — Economic policy — 1917-

Soviet industrialisation and Soviet maturity / edited by Keith Smith. — London : Routledge & Kegan Paul, 1986. — [228]p. — (Economy and society paperbacks). — *Articles originally published: in Economy and society. Includes bibliography*

SOVIET UNION — Economic policy — 1928-1932

VIOLA, Lynne
The best sons of the fatherland : workers in the vanguard of soviet collectivization / Lynne Viola. — New York : Oxford University Press, 1987. — p. cm. — *Includes index.* — *Bibliography: p*

SOVIET UNION — Economic policy — 1946-1950

POLIAK, G. B.
Poslevoennoe vosstanovlenie narodnogo khoziaistva / G. B. Poliak. — Moskva : Finansy i statistika, 1986. — 166p. — (SSSR-bratstvo narodov)

SOVIET UNION — Economic policy — 1981-

ABALKIN, L. I.
Novyi tip ekonomicheskogo myshleniia / L. I. Abalkin. — Moskva : Ekonomika, 1987. — 189p

ALYMOV, A. N.
Sbalansirovannost' narodno-khoziaistvennogo razvitiia : (regional'nye i otraslevye problemy) / A. N. Alymov, F. D. Zastavnyi, D. K. Preiger. — Kiev : Naukova dumka, 1986. — 221p. — (Ekonomika razvitogo sotsializma). — *Bibliography: p218-[222]*

BECKER, Abraham Samuel
Soviet central decisionmaking and economic growth : a summing up / Abraham S. Becker. — Santa Monica, CA : Rand, [1986]. — xi, 53 p.. — *"A Project Air Force report prepared for the United States Air Force."*. — *"January 1986."*. — *"R-3349-AF."*. — *Includes bibliographical references*

The Costs and benefits of the Soviet empire, 1981-1983 / Charles Wolf, Jr. ... [et al.]. — Santa Monica, CA : Rand, [1986]. — xv, 46 p.. — *"Prepared for the Director of Net Assessment, Office of the Secretary of Defense."*. — *"August 1986."*. — *"R-3419-NA."*. — *Includes bibliographical references*

DESAI, Padma
The Soviet economy in decline? / Padma Desai. — Oxford : Basil Blackwell, 1987. — [280]p. — *Includes bibliography and index*

Ekonomicheskie problemy razvitogo sotsializma / red. kollegiia I. I. Lukinov...[et al.]. — Kiev : Naukova dumka
T.3: Povyshenie effektivnosti sotsialisticheskogo vosproizvodstva / red. kollegiia V. I. Kononenko...[et al.]. — 1985. — 270p

GORBACHEV, M. S.
Selected speeches and articles / Mikhail Gorbachev. — 2nd updated ed. — Moscow : Progress, 1987. — 605p

OZHEREL'EV, O. I.
Sovershenstvovanie proizvodstvennykh otnoshenii / O. I. Ozherel'ev. — Moskva : Ekonomika, 1986. — 253p

PALKIN, Iu. I.
Ekonomicheskie zakony i ekonomicheskaia politika KPSS / Iu. I. Palkin, P. S. Eshchenko. — Kiev : Vishcha shkola, 1985. — 245p

Planovoe upravlenie ekonomikoi razvitogo sotsializma / redaktsionnaia kollegiia: A. S. Emel'ianov...[et al.]. — Kiev : Naukova dumka. — *V piati tomakh*
T.1: Narodno-khoziaistvennye proportsii, ikh planirovanie i prognozirovanie / otv. redaktor A. S. Emel'ianov. — 1985. — 316p.
Bibliography: p311-[314]

Planovoe upravlenie ekonomikoi razvitogo sotsializma / redaktsionnaia kollegiia: A. S. Emel'ianov...[et al.]. — Kiev : Naukova dumka. — *V piati tomath*
T.3: Nauchno-tekhnicheskii progress i planovoe investirovanie v narodnoe khoziaistvo / otv. redaktor S. M. Iampol'skii. — 1986. — 307p.
— *Bibliography: p305-[308]*

Planovoe upravlenie ekonomikoi razvitogo sotsializma / redaktsionnaia kollegiia: A. S. Emel'ianov...[et al.]. — Kiev : Naukova dumka. — *V piati tomakh*
T.4: Nauchno-metodicheskie osnovy planirovaniia i prognozirovaniia razvitiia ekonomiki / otv. redaktor V. F. Besedin. — 1986. — 322p. — *Bibliography: p318-[323]*

Planovoe upravlenie ekonomikoi razvitogo sotsializma / redaktsionnaia kollegiia: A. S. Emel'ianov...[et al.]. — Kiev : Naukova dumka. — *V piati tomakh*
T.5: Otraslevye problemy planovogo razvitiia ekonomiki respubliki / otv. redaktor A. S. Emel'ianov. — 1986. — 403p. — *Bibliography: p299-[302]*

Rezervy povysheniia effektivnosti narodno-khoziaistvennogo kompleksa / [avtorskii kollektiv: V. G. Lebedev...et al.]. — Moskva : Mysl', 1985. — 222p

Rol' finansov v sotsial'no-ekonomicheskom razvitii strany / pod redaktsiei G. V. Bazarovoi. — Moskva : Finansy i statistika, 1986. — 230p

The Soviet Union 1984/85 : events, problems, perspectives / edited by the Federal Institute for East European and International Studies. — Boulder, Colo. : Westview Press, 1986. — xix,349p. — (Westview Special Studies on the Soviet Union and Eastern Europe)

The Soviet Union under Gorbachev / edited by Martin McCauley. — Basingstoke : Macmillan in association with School of Slavonic and East European Studies, University of London, 1987. — [272]p. — (Studies in Russia and East Europe). — *Includes index*

The Soviet Union under Gorbachev : prospects for reform / edited by David A. Dyker. — London : Croom Helm, c1987. — [224]p. — *Includes index*

Struktura narodnogo khoziaistva v usloviiakh intensifikatsii ekonomiki / otv. redaktor V. P. Loginov. — Moskva : Nauka, 1986. — 267p

SOVIET UNION — Economic policy — 1985-

Soviet law and economy / edited by Olimpiad S. Ioffe and Mark W. Janis. — Dordrecht : Martinus Nijhoff, 1987. — xii,335p. — (Law in Eastern Europe ; no.32)

SOVIET UNION — Economic policy 1981-

Razvitoi sotsializm : voprosy teorii i istorii / otv. redaktor S. S. Khromov. — Moskva : Nauka, 1986. — 245p

SOVIET UNION — Emigration and immigration — Case studies

ROSNER, Lydia S
The Soviet way of crime : beating the system in the Soviet Union and the U.S.A. / Lydia S. Rosner. — South Hadley, Mass. : Bergin & Garvey Publishers, 1986. — xvii, 140 p.. — *Includes bibliographies and index*

SOVIET UNION — Emigration and immigration — History

TUDORIANU, N. L.
Ocherki rossiiskoi trudovoi emigratsii perioda imperializma : (v Germaniiu, Skandinavskie strany i SShA) / N. L. Tudorianu ; otv. redaktor E. M. Shchagin. — Kishinev : Shtiintsa, 1986. — 309p

SOVIET UNION — Ethnic relations

KLIER, John
Russia gathers her Jews : the origins of the "Jewish question" in Russia, 1772-1825 / John Doyle Klier. — DeKalb, Ill. : Northern Illinois University Press, 1986. — xxiv, 236p. — *Map on lining papers. — Includes index. — Bibliography: p. [213]-223*

KPSS - organizator bratskoi druzhby narodov SSSR / [redaktsionnaia kollegiia: V. A. Smyshliaev...et al.]. — Leningrad : Izd-vo Leningradskogo universiteta, 1973. — 153p. — (Uchenie zapiski kafedr obshchestvennykh nauk vuzov Leningrada. Istoriia KPSS ; vyp.13)

MOTYL, Alexander J
Will the non-Russians rebel? : theoretical perspectives on state, ethnicity, and stability in the USSR / Alexander J. Motyl. — Ithaca, N.Y. : Cornell University Press, 1987. — p. cm. — (Studies in Soviet history and society). — *Includes index. — Bibliography: p*

ROTHCHILD, Sylvia
A special legacy : an oral history of Soviet Jewish emigrés in the United States / by Sylvia Rothchild. — New York : Simon and Schuster, c1985. — p. cm. *Includes index*

TSAMERIAN, I. P.
Natsional'nye otnosheniia v SSSR / I. P. Tsamerian. — Moskva : Mysl', 1987. — 181p

SOVIET UNION — Ethnic relations — Addresses, essays, lectures

KAHAN, Arcadius
Essays in Jewish social and economic history / Arcadius Kahan ; edited by Roger Weiss ; with an introduction by Jonathan Frankel. — Chicago : University of Chicago Press, 1986. — xx, 208 p.. — *Includes bibliographical references and index*

SOVIET UNION — Ethnic relations — Historiography

Natsional'nye otnosheniia v SSSR v trudakh uchenykh soiuznykh respublik / otv. redaktor V. P. Sherstobitov. — Moskva : Nauka, 1986. — 348p. — (Natsional'nye otnosheniia v sovremennuiu epokhu)

SOVIET UNION — Foreign economic relations

Soviet law and economy / edited by Olimpiad S. Ioffe and Mark W. Janis. — Dordrecht : Martinus Nijhoff, 1987. — xii,335p. — (Law in Eastern Europe ; no.32)

STAAR, Richard Felix
USSR foreign policies after detente / Richard F. Staar. — Rev. ed. — Stanford, Calif. : Hoover Institution Press, Stanford University, c1987. — xxvii, 308 p.. — (Hoover Press publication ; 359). — Includes index. — Bibliography: p. [275]-295

SOVIET UNION — Foreign economic relations — Europe, Eastern

CRANE, Keith
The Soviet economic dilemma of eastern Europe / Keith Crane. — Santa Monica, CA : Rand, [1986]. — xiii, 70 p.. — "A Project Air Force report prepared for the United States Air Force.". — "R-3368-AF.". — "May 1986.". — Bibliography: p. 65-70

SELUCKY, Radoslav
The present dilemma of Soviet-East European integration / Radoslav Selucky. — Munchen : Projekt ´Crises in Soviet-type systems´, 1985. — 24p. — (Research project Crises in Soviet-type systems ; Study no.7)

SOVIET UNION — Foreign economic relations — Sweden

ATTMAN, Artur
Swedish aspirations and the Russian market during the 17th century / Artur Attman. — Göteborg : Kung 1. Vetenskaps-och Vitterhets-Samhället, 1985. — 41p. — (Acta Regiae Societatis Scientiarum et Litterarum Gothoburgensis. Humaniora ; 24). — Bibliography: p38-40

SOVIET UNION — Foreign opinion — 1917-

BUBIS, Mordecai Donald
The Soviet Union and Stalinism in the ideological debates of American Trotskyism (1937-51) / by Mordecai Donald Bubis. — 330 leaves. — PhD (Econ) 1986 LSE

SOVIET UNION — Foreign opinion, American

The Other side : how Soviets and Americans perceive each other / edited by Jonathan J. Halperin. — New Brunswick, U.S.A. : Transaction Books, c1987. — p. cm. — Includes index. — Bibliography: p

SOVIET UNION — Foreign relatins — 1975-

SAVIGEAR, Peter
Cold war or detente in the 1980s : the international politics of American-Soviet relations / Peter Savigear. — Brighton : Wheatsheaf, 1987. — [192]p. — Includes bibliography and index

SOVIET UNION — Foreign relations

CARRÈRE D'ENCAUSSE, Hélène
Ni paix ni guerre : le nouvel Empire soviétique ou du bon usage de la détente / Hélène Carrère d'Encausse. — [S.l.] : Flammarion, c1986. — 417 p

The Costs and benefits of the Soviet empire, 1981-1983 / Charles Wolf, Jr. ... [et al.]. — Santa Monica, CA : Rand, [1986]. — xv, 46 p.. — "Prepared for the Director of Net Assessment, Office of the Secretary of Defense.". — "August 1986.". — "R-3419-NA.". — Includes bibliographical references

MAY, Brian, 1914-
Is Russia really a threat? / Brian May. — Hebden Bridge : Hebden Royd Publications, 1986. — 32p. — (Liberal challenge booklet ; no.7). — Bibliography: p31-32

SOVIET UNION — Foreign relations — 19th century

GEYER, Dietrich
Russian imperialism : the interaction of domestic and foreign policy, 1860-1914 / Dietrich Geyer ; translated from the German by Bruce Little. — Leamington Spa : Berg, 1987. — [368]p. — Translation of: Der russische Imperialismus. — Includes bibliography and index

SOVIET UNION — Foreign relations — Historiography

Problemy metodologii i istochnikovedeniia istorii vneshnei politiki Rossii : sbornik statei / otv. redaktor A. L. Narochnitskii. — Moskva : Nauka, 1986. — 286p. — Bibliography: p280-[287]

SOVIET UNION — Foreign relations — 1689-1725

BARANY, George
The Anglo-Russian entente cordiale of 1697-1698 : Peter I and William III at Utrecht / George Barany. — Boulder : East European Monographs ; New York : Columbia University Press [distributor], 1986. — 101p, plates. — (East European monographs ; no.207)

SOVIET UNION — Foreign relations — 19th century

KHEVROLINA, V. M.
Revoliutsionno-demokraticheskaia mysl' o vneshnei politike Rossii i mezhdunarodnykh otnosheniiakh (konets 60-kh - nachala 80-kh godov XIX v. / V. M. Khevrolina ; otv. redaktor A. L. Narochnitskii. — Moskva : Nauka, 1986. — 246p

SOVIET UNION — Foreign relations — 1894-1917

IGNAT'EV, A. V.
Vneshniaia politika Rossii v 1905-1907 gg. / A. V. Ignat'ev ; otv. redaktor A. L. Narochnitskii. — Moskva : Nauka, 1986. — 300p

SOLOV'EV, O. F.
Obrechennyi al'ians : zagovor imperialistov protiv narodov Rossii. 1914-1917 gg. / O. F. Solov'ev. — Moskva : Mysl', 1986. — 254p

SOVIET UNION — Foreign relations — 1917-1945

The Cold war past and present / edited by Richard Crockatt and Steve Smith. — London : Allen & Unwin, 1987. — [248]p. — Includes bibliography and index

DORSEY, Gray L
Beyond the United Nations : changing discourse in international politics and law / Gray L. Dorsey. — Lanham ; London : University Press of America, c1986. — xi, 111p. — (Exxon Education Foundation series on rhetoric and political discourse ; v. 5). — Bibliography: p. 103-111. — Bibliography: p.103-111

Istoriia mezhdunarodnykh otnoshenii i vneshnei politiki SSSR, 1917-1987 : v trekh tomakh. — Moskva : Mezhdunarodnye otnosheniia
T.1: 1917-1945 / redaktor toma I. A. Kirilin. — 1986. — 412p

Istoriia vneshnei politiki SSSR, 1917-1985 / pod redaktsiei A. A. Gromyko, B. N. Ponomareva. — Izd. 5-e, perer. i dop.. — Moskva : Nauka
T.1: 1917-1945 gg.. — 1986. — 534p

SOVIET UNION — Foreign relations — 1945-

The Cold war past and present / edited by Richard Crockatt and Steve Smith. — London : Allen & Unwin, 1987. — [248]p. — Includes bibliography and index

DUNCAN, W. Raymond
The Soviet Union and Cuba : interests and influence / by W. Raymond Duncan. — New York : Praeger, 1985. — xv, 220p. — (Studies of influence in international relations). — Includes index. — Bibliography: p.205-209

GATI, Charles
Hungary and the Soviet bloc / by Charles Gati. — Durham [N.C.] : Duke University Press, 1986. — 244 p.. — Includes index. — Bibliography: p. [233]-237

HART, Thomas G.
Sino-Soviet relations : re-examining the prospects for normalization / Thomas G. Hart. — Aldershot : Gower, 1987. — [170]p. — (Swedish studies in international relations). — Bibliography: p121-126. — Includes index

Istoriia vneshnei politiki SSSR, 1917-1985 / pod redaktsiei A. A. Gromyko, B. N. Ponomareva. — Izd. 5-e, perer. i dop.. — Moskva : Nauka. — Bibliographoy: p654-[682]
T.2: 1945-1985 gg.. — 1986. — 691p

MCCGWIRE, Michael K.
Military objectives in Soviet foreign policy / Michael K. McCGwire. — Washington, D.C. : Brookings Institution, c1987. — xiv, 530p. — Includes bibliographies and index

MAKINDA, Samuel M.
Superpower diplomacy in the Horn of Africa / Samuel M. Makinda. — London : Croom Helm, c1987. — 241p. — Bibliography: p225-234. — Includes index

PAGE, Stephen
The Soviet Union and the Yemens : influence on asymmetrical relationships / Stephen Page. — New York : Praeger, 1985. — p. cm. — (Studies of influence in international relations). — Includes index. — Bibliography: p

PHILLIPS, Ann L
Soviet policy toward East Germany reconsidered : the postwar decade / Ann L. Phillips. — Westport, Conn. : Greenwood Press, 1986. — xii, 262 p.. — (Contributions in political science ; no. 142). — Includes index. — Bibliography: p. [233]-256

The Soviet Union and the Third World : the last three decades / edited by Andrzej Korbonski and Francis Fukuyama. — Ithaca, N.Y. : Cornell University Press, c1987. — p. cm. — "A book from the Rand/UCLA Center for the Study of Soviet International Behavior.". — Includes index

Superpowers and revolution / edited by Jonathan R. Adelman. — New York : Praeger, 1986. — p. cm

SOVIET UNION — Foreign relations — 1945- — Bibliography

LESTER, Robert
A guide to confidential U.S. State Department central files : the Soviet Union internal affairs 1945-1949 / compiled by Robert Lester. — Frederick, MD : University Publications of America, Inc., 1985. — ix,85p. — Contents: A guide to the microfilm set of documents from the State Department central files deposited in the National Archives

LESTER, Robert
A guide to U.S. State Department central files : the Soviet Union internal affairs 1950-1954 and foreign affairs 1950-1954 / compiled by Robert Lester. — Frederick, MD : University Publications of America, Inc., 1985. — ix,120p. — Contents: A guide to the microfilm set of documents from State Department central files deposited in the National Archives

SOVIET UNION — Foreign relations — 1953-1975

HERRMANN, Richard K.
Perceptions and behavior in Soviet foreign policy / Richard K. Herrmann. — Pittsburgh, Pa. : University of Pittsburgh Press, c1985. — xxi, 266 p.. — (Pitt series in policy and institutional studies) (Series in Russian and East European studies ; no. 7). — Includes index. — Bibliography: p. 249-261

SOVIET UNION — Foreign relations — 1953-1975 *continuation*

KHRUSHCHEV, N.
For victory in peaceful competition with capitalism : with a special preface written for the English edition / Nikita S. Khrushchev. — London : Hutchinson, 1960. — 784p

UNION OF SOVIET SOCIALIST REPUBLICS. Ministerstvo inostrannykh del
SSSR v bor'be protiv kolonializma i neokolonializma, 1960-mart 1986 gg. : dokumenty i materialy / red. kollegiia: A. A. Gromyko...[et al.]. — Moskva : Politizdat. —
V dvukh tomakh
T.1: (1960-1981 gg.). — 1986. — 542p

UNION OF SOVIET SOCIALIST REPUBLICS. Ministerstvo inostrannykh del
Za mir i bezopasnost' narodov : dokumenty vneshnei politiki SSSR 1968 god / [redaktsionnaia kollegiia: G. K. Deev...et al.]. — Moskva : Politizdat
Kn.1: [ianvar'-iiun']. — 1985. — 428p

UNION OF SOVIET SOCIALIST REPUBLICS. Ministerstvo inostrannykh del
Za mir i bezopasnost' narodov : dokumenty vneshnei politiki SSSR 1968 god / [redaktsionnaia kollegiia: G. K. Deev...et al.]. — Moskva : Politizdat
Kn.2: [iiul'-dekabr']. — 1985. — 428p

SOVIET UNION — Foreign relations — 1953-1975 — Congresses

The Red orchestra : instruments of Soviet policy in Latin America and the Caribbean / Dennis L. Bark, editor. — Stanford, Calif. : Hoover Institution Press, Stanford University, c1986. — ix, 139p. — *Includes bibliographies and index*

SOVIET UNION — Foreign relations — 1975-

BECKER, Jillian
The Soviet connection : state sponsorship of terrorism / Jillian Becker. — London : Alliance Publishers for the Institute for European Defence and Strategic Studies, 1985. — 55p. — (Occasional paper / Institute for European Defence Strategic Studies ; no.13)

BEYME, Klaus von
The Soviet Union in world politics / Klaus von Beyme. — Aldershot : Gower, c1987. — xi,219p. — *Bibliography: p203-211. — Includes index*

BIALER, Seweryn
The Soviet paradox : external expansion, internal decline / Seweryn Bialer. — 1st ed. — New York : Knopf, 1986. — ix, 391p. — *Includes index. — Bibliography: p.379-386*

DALLY, Peter
The Sino-Soviet split : a trap for the West / by Peter Dally. — Cheltenham (31 Seneca Way, Cheltenham, Glos. GL50 45F) : British Anti-Communist Council, c1984. — 67p

DOROSHENKO, V. S.
Bor'ba KPSS za mezhdunarodnuiu razriadku i nesostoiatel'nost' burzhuaznykh fal'sifikatsii / V. S. Doroshenko. — Kiev : Vyshcha shkola, 1985. — 204p. — *Bibliography: p202-[205]*

GOLITSYN, Anatoliy
New lies for old : the communist strategy of deception and disinformation / Anatoliy Golitsyn. — London : Bodley Head, 1984. — 412p. — *Originally published: New York : Dodd, Mead, 1983. — Includes index*

HERRMANN, Richard K.
Perceptions and behavior in Soviet foreign policy / Richard K. Herrmann. — Pittsburgh, Pa. : University of Pittsburgh Press, c1985. — xxi, 266 p.. — (Pitt series in policy and institutional studies) (Series in Russian and East European studies ; no. 7). — *Includes index. — Bibliography: p. 249-261*

LEONHARD, Wolfgang
The Kremlin and the West : a realistic approach / Wolfgang Leonhard ; translated by Houchang E. Chehabi. — New York : W. W. Norton, 1986. — xii,228p

LISKA, George
Rethinking US-Soviet relations / George Liska. — Oxford : Basil Blackwell, 1987. — [256]p. — *Includes index*

PARCHOMENKO, Walter
Soviet images of dissidents and nonconformists / Walter Parchomenko. — New York ; London : Praeger, 1986. — xv, 251 p.. — *"Praeger special studies. Praeger scientific.". — Includes index. — Bibliography: p. 213-243*

SEMENOV, V. A.
Politiki mira i kurs na konfrontatsiiu / V. A. Semenov. — Moskva : Mezhdunarodnye otnosheniia, 1986. — 146p

Soviet-East European relations as a problem for the West / edited by Richard D. Vine. — London : Croom Helm, c1987. — 262p. — (An Atlantic Institute for International Affairs research volume). — *Includes index*

Soviet-Latin American relations in the 1980s / edited by Augusto Varas. — Boulder : Westview Press, 1987. — p. cm. — (Westview special studies on Latin America and the Caribbean)

The Soviet Union 1984/85 : events, problems, perspectives / edited by the Federal Institute for East European and International Studies. — Boulder, Colo. : Westview Press, 1986. — xix,349p. — (Westview Special Studies on the Soviet Union and Eastern Europe)

STAAR, Richard Felix
USSR foreign policies after detente / Richard F. Staar. — Rev. ed. — Stanford, Calif. : Hoover Institution Press, Stanford University, c1987. — xxvii, 308 p.. — (Hoover Press publication ; 359). — *Includes index. — Bibliography: p. [275]-295*

UNION OF SOVIET SOCIALIST REPUBLICS. Ministerstvo inostrannykh del
SSSR v bor'be protiv kolonializma i neokolonializma, 1960-mart 1986 gg. : dokumenty i materialy / red. kollegiia: A. A. Gromyko...[et al.]. — Moskva : Politizdat. —
V dvukh tomakh
T.1: (1960-1981 gg.). — 1986. — 542p

UNION OF SOVIET SOCIALIST REPUBLICS. Ministerstvo inostrannykh del
SSSR v bor'be protiv kolonializma i neokolonializma, 1960-mart 1986 gg. : dokumenty i materialy / red. kollegiia: A. A. Gromyko...[et al.]. — Moskva : Politizdat. —
V dvukh tomakh
T.2: (1981-mart 1986 gg.). — 1986. — 431p

VAN OUDENAREN, John
Interviews by Soviet officials in the Western media : two case studies / John Van Oudenaren. — Santa Monica : Rand, 1985. — 63p. — *Bibliography: p57-63*

SOVIET UNION — Foreign relations — 1975- — Congresses

The Red orchestra : instruments of Soviet policy in Latin America and the Caribbean / Dennis L. Bark, editor. — Stanford, Calif. : Hoover Institution Press, Stanford University, c1986. — ix, 139p. — *Includes bibliographies and index*

SOVIET UNION — Foreign relations — 1975- — Sources

Soviet foreign policy documents 1984 / [edited by] Darshan Singh. — New Delhi : Sterling Publishers Private, 1986. — xxiv,231p

SOVIET UNION — Foreign relations — Afghanistan

RASHIDOV, R. T.
Sovetsko-afganskie otnosheniia i ikh burzhuaznye fal'sifikatovy (1978-1983) / R. T. Rashidov. — Tashkent : "Fan" Uzbekskoi SSR, 1986. — 114p

SHAMS-UD-DIN
Soviet Afghan relations / Shams Ud Din. — Calcutta ; New Delhi : K. P. Bagchi, 1985,1984. — vii,168p. — *Bibliography: p [155]-160*

TRASK, Roger
Afghanistan : grasping of the nettle of peace / Roger Trask. — London : Morning Star, 1987. — 24p

VOLODARSKII, M. I.
Sovety i ikh iuzhnye sosedi Iran i Afganistan (1917-1933) / M. I. Volodarskii ; predislovie S. Mogilevskogo. — London : Overseas Publications Interchange, 1985. — 241p. — *Bibliography: p235*

SOVIET UNION — Foreign relations — Africa

LAÏDI, Zaki
Les contraintes Dûne rivalité : les superpuissances et lÁfríque (1960-1985) / Zaki Laïdi. — Paris : La Découverte, 1986. — 299p. — *Bibliography: p284-292*

SOVIET UNION — Foreign relations — Algeria

SHVEDOV, A. A.
Sovetsko-alzhirskie otnosheniia / A. A. Shvedov, A. B. Podtserob. — Moskva : Progress, 1986. — 260p. — *Bibliography: p247-[261]*

SOVIET UNION — Foreign relations — Arab countries — History — 20th century

BEHBEHANI, Hashim S. H.
The Soviet Union and Arab nationalism, 1917-1966 / Hashim S. H. Behbehani. — London : KPI, 1986. — 252p. — *Bibliography: p237-247*

SOVIET UNION — Foreign relations — Asia, Southeastern

MCLANE, Charles B.
Soviet strategies in southeast Asia : an exploration of eastern policy under Lenin and Stalin / Charles B. McLane. — Princeton : Princeton University Press, 1966. — 563p

SOVIET UNION — foreign relations — Caribbean Area

MANFARLANE, S. Neil
Superpower rivalry and Soviet policy in the Caribbean Basin / S. N. MacFarlane. — Ottawa : Canadian Institue for International Peace and Security, 1986. — 70p. — (Occasional papers / Canadian Institute for International Peace and Security ; no.1)

SOVIET UNION — Foreign relations — China

DALLY, Peter
The Sino-Soviet split : a trap for the West / by Peter Dally. — Cheltenham (31 Seneca Way, Cheltenham, Glos. GL50 45F) : British Anti-Communist Council, c1984. — 67p

HART, Thomas G.
Sino-Soviet relations : re-examining the prospects for normalization / Thomas G. Hart. — Aldershot : Gower, 1987. — [170]p. — (Swedish studies in international relations). — *Bibliography: p121-126. — Includes index*

LEDOVSKII, A. M.
Kitaiskaia politika SShA i sovetskaia diplomatiia 1942-1954 / A. M. Ledovskii. — Moskva : Nauka (IVL), 1985. — 286p. — *English summary*

SOVIET UNION — Foreign relations — China — Sinkiang Province

WHITING, Allen S.
Sinkiang : pawn or pivot? / Allen S. Whiting and Sheng Shih-ts'ai. — East Lansing, Mich. : Michigan State University Press, 1958. — xxii,314p. — *Bibliography: p303-307*

SOVIET UNION — Foreign relations — Czechoslovakia

FLORIA, B. N.
Rossiia i cheshskoe vosstanie protiv Gabsburgov / B. N. Floria ; otv. redaktor A. S. Myl'nikov. — Moskva : Nauka, 1986. — 206p

SOVIET UNION — Foreign relations — Developing countries

FUKUYAMA, Francis
Moscow's post-Brezhnev reassessment of the Third World / Francis Fukuyama. — Santa Monica (Calif.) : Rand, 1986. — xi,91p. — *Bibliography: p87-91*

The Soviet Union and the Third World : the last three decades / edited by Andrzej Korbonski and Francis Fukuyama. — Ithaca, N.Y. : Cornell University Press, c1987. — p. cm. — *"A book from the Rand/UCLA Center for the Study of Soviet International Behavior.". — Includes index*

SOVIET UNION — Foreign relations — Developing countries — Congresses

East-West tensions in the Third World / Marshall D. Shulman, editor. — 1st ed. — New York : W.W. Norton, c1986. — 243 p.. — *Background papers prepared for the 70th American Assembly at Arden House, Harriman, N.Y., Nov. 21, 1985. — At head of title: American Assembly. — Includes index*

SOVIET UNION — Foreign relations — Europe

JENTLESON, Bruce W.
Pipeline politics : the complex political economy of East-West energy trade / Bruce W. Jentleson. — Ithaca, N.Y. : Cornell University Press, 1986. — 263 p.. — (Cornell studies in political economy). — *Includes index. — Bibliography: p. 247-256*

MINC, Alain
Le syndrone finlandais / Alain Minc. — Paris : Seuil, [1986]. — 232p

PLATT, Alan
Soviet-West European relations : recent trends and near-term prospects / Alan Platt. — Santa Monica (Calif.) : Rand, 1986. — xiii,50p

VAN OUDENAREN, John
Soviet policy toward western Europe : objectives, instruments, results / John Van Oudenaren. — Santa Monica, CA : Rand, [1986]. — xi, 118 p.. — *"A Project Air Force report, prepared for the United States Air Force.". — "February 1986.". — "R-3310-AF.". — Bibliography: p. 117-118*

SOVIET UNION — Foreign relations — Europe, Eastern

Dominant powers and subordinate states : the United States in Latin America and the Soviet Union in Eastern Europe / edited by Jan F. Triska. — Durham, [N.C.] : Duke University Press, 1986. — xi, 504 p.. — (Duke Press policy studies). — *Includes index. — Bibliography: p. [471]-498*

FEHÉR, Ferenc
Eastern Europe under the shadow of a new Rapallo / Ferenc Fehér [and] Agnes Heller. — Munchen : Projekt 'Crises in Soviet-type systems', 1984. — 38p. — (Research project Crises in Soviet-type systems ; Study no.6)

GATI, Charles
Hungary and the Soviet bloc / by Charles Gati. — Durham [N.C.] : Duke University Press, 1986. — 244 p.. — *Includes index. — Bibliography: p. [233]-237*

SSSR v bor'be protiv fashistskoi agressii 1933-1945 / otv. redaktor A. L. Norochnitskii. — 2-e izd., perer. i dop.. — Moskva : Nauka, 1986. — 349p. — *1st ed. 1976*

SOVIET UNION — Foreign relations — Finland

LUNTINEN, Pertti
F.A. Seyn : a political biography of a Tsarist imperialist as administrator of Finland / Pertti Luntinen. — Helsinki : SHS, 1985. — 343p. — (Studia historica ; 19)

SOVIET UNION — Foreign relations — Germany

LEONHARD, Wolfgang
Der Schock des Hitler-Stalin-Paktes : Grinnerungen aus der Sowjetunion, Westeuropa und USA / Wolfgang Leonhard. — Freiburg im Breisgau : Herder, 1986. — 220p. — *Bibliographical notes*

ZETTERBERG, Seppo
Die Liga der Fremdvölker Russlands 1916-1918 : ein Beitrag zu Deutschlands antirussischem Propagandakreig unter den Fremdvölkern Russlands im ersten Weltkrieg / Seppo Zetterberg. — Helsinki : [Suomen Historiallinen Seura], 1978. — 279p. — (Studia historica veröffentlicht von der Finnischen Historischen Gesellschaft/Suomen Historiallinen Seura/Finska Historiska Samfundet ; vol.8). — *Bibliography: p263-271*

SOVIET UNION — Foreign relations — Germany (East)

PHILLIPS, Ann L
Soviet policy toward East Germany reconsidered : the postwar decade / Ann L. Phillips. — Westport, Conn. : Greenwood Press, 1986. — xii, 262 p. — (Contributions in political science ; no. 142). — *Includes index. — Bibliography: p. [233]-256*

SOVIET UNION — Foreign relations — Great Britain

BARANY, George
The Anglo-Russian entente cordiale of 1697-1698 : Peter I and William III at Utrecht / George Barany. — Boulder : East European Monographs ; New York : Columbia University Press [distributor], 1986. — 101p, plates. — (East European monographs ; no.207)

KITCHEN, Martin
British policy towards the Soviet Union during the Second World War / Martin Kitchen. — Basingstoke : Macmillan, 1986. — viii,309p. — *Bibliography: p297-309. — Includes index*

RYZHIKOV, V. A.
Sovetsko-angliiskie otnosheniia : osnovnye etapy istorii / V. A. Ryzhikov. — Moskva : Mezhdunarodnye otnosheniia, 1987. — 276p

VOLKOV, F. D.
Secrets from Whitehall and Downing Street / Fyodor Volkov. — Moscow : Progress, 1986. — 334p

SOVIET UNION — Foreign relations — Hungary

GATI, Charles
Hungary and the Soviet bloc / by Charles Gati. — Durham [N.C.] : Duke University Press, 1986. — 244 p.. — *Includes index. — Bibliography: p. [233]-237*

SOVIET UNION — Foreign relations — India

KIDWAI, M. Saleem
Indo-Soviet relations / M. Saleem Kidwai. — New Delhi, India : Rima Pub. House, 1985. — vi, 144 p.. — *: Revision of the author's thesis (Ph. D.--Aligarh Muslim University). — Includes index. — Bibliography: p. [127]-141*

SINGH, S. Nihal
The yogi and the bear : story of Indo-Soviet relations / S. Nihal Singh. — London : Mansell, 1986. — [328]p

SOVIET UNION — Foreign relations — Iran

VOLODARSKII, M. I.
Sovety i ikh iuzhnye sosedi Iran i Afganistan (1917-1933) / M. I. Volodarskii ; predislovie S. Mogilevskogo. — London : Overseas Publications Interchange, 1985. — 241p. — *Bibliography: p235*

SOVIET UNION — Foreign relations — Latin America — Congresses

The Red orchestra : instruments of Soviet policy in Latin America and the Caribbean / Dennis L. Bark, editor. — Stanford, Calif. : Hoover Institution Press, Stanford University, c1986. — ix, 139p. — *Includes bibliographies and index*

SOVIET UNION — Foreign relations — Libya

SHVEDOV, A. A.
Sovetsko-liviiskie otnosheniia / A. Shvedov, V. Rumiantsev. — Moskva : Progress, 1986. — 186p

SOVIET UNION — Foreign relations — Near East

Soviet-American relations with Pakistan, Iran and Afghanistan / edited by Hafeez Malik. — Basingstoke : Macmillan, 1986. — [480]p. — *Includes index*

SOVIET UNION — Foreign relations — Poland

GREAT BRITAIN. Parliament. House of Commons. Library. International Affairs Section
Poland, the USSR and the west / Richard Ware. — [London] : the Library, 1980. — 14p. — (Background paper / House of Commons. Library. [Research Division] ; no.87). — *Bibliographical references: p12*

GREAT BRITAIN. Parliament. House of Commons. Library. International Affairs Section
Poland, the USSR and the west / Richard Ware. — [London] : the Library, 1981. — 24p. — (Background paper / House of Commons. Library. [Research Division] ; no.87). — *Updated version of 1980 Background Paper no.87. — Bibliographical references: p12,24*

PLOSS, Sidney I
Moscow and the Polish crisis : an interpretation of Soviet policies and intentions / Sidney I. Ploss. — Boulder : Westview Press, 1986. — ix, 182 p.. — (Westview special studies on the Soviet Union and Eastern Europe). — *Includes bibliographical references and index*

Tajne rokowanie polsko-radzieckie w 1919 r. : materiały archiwalne i dokumenty / zebrała i opracowała Weronika Gosty'nska. — Warszawa : Pa'nstwowe Wydawnictwo Naukowe, 1986. — 412p. — *Documents in Polish, Russian, French or German. — Bibliography: p391-[396]*

SOVIET UNION — Foreign relations — South Africa

CAMPBELL, Kurt M.
Soviet policy towards South Africa / Kurt M. Campbell. — Basingstoke : Macmillan, 1986. — xii,223p. — *Bibliography: p201-217. — Includes index*

SOVIET UNION — Foreign relations — South Asia

RAM, Raghunath
Super powers and Indo-Pakistani sub-continent : perceptions and policies / Raghunath Ram. — New Delhi : Raaj Prakashan, 1985. — 427p . — *Bibliography: p[402]-411*

Soviet-American relations with Pakistan, Iran and Afghanistan / edited by Hafeez Malik. — Basingstoke : Macmillan, 1986. — [480]p. — *Includes index*

SOVIET UNION — Foreign relations — United States

BENNETT, Edward Moore
Franklin D. Roosevelt and the search for security : American-Soviet relations, 1933-1939 / by Edward M. Bennett. — Wilmington, Del. : Scholarly Resources, 1985. — xix, 213p. — *Includes index. — Bibliography: p 197-203*

BIALER, Seweryn
The Soviet paradox : external expansion, internal decline / Seweryn Bialer. — 1st ed. — New York : Knopf, 1986. — ix, 391p. — *Includes index. — Bibliography: p.379-386*

DURCH, William J.
The future of the ABM treaty / William J. Durch. — London : International Institute for Strategic Studies, 1987. — 80p. — (Adelphi papers ; 223)

ELLEINSTEIN, Jean
Goliath contre Goliath : histoire des relations américano-soviétiques / Jean Elleinstein. — Paris : Fayard
1: L'enfance des grands (1941-1949). — 1986. — 550p. — *Bibliography: p[493]-500*

GORBACHEV, M. S.
The results and lessons of Reykjavik : summit meeting in the Icelandic capital October 11-12, 1986 / Mikhail Gorbachev. — Moscow : Novosti Press Agency Publishing House, 1986. — 42p

GORBACHEV, M. S.
Speech given by the General Secretary of the Central Committee of the Communist Party of the Soviet Union (CPSU), M. S. Gorbachev, on Soviet television [following the Reykjavik Summit]. — New York : United Nations, 1986. — *Distributed by the Secretary General of the U.N. as an official document of the General Assembly and Security Council at the request of the Deputy Head of the U.S.S.R. delegation to the Forty First session of the General Assembly*

GRIFFITHS, John, 1942 Apr. 5-
The Cuban missile crisis / John Griffiths. — Hove : Wayland, 1986. — [80]p. — (Flashpoints). — *Includes bibliography and index*

HALLENBERG, Jan
Foreign policy change : United States foreign policy toward the Soviet Union and the People's Republic of China, 1961-1980 / Jan Hallenberg. — [Stockholm] : Dept. of Political Science, University of Stockholm, 1984. — 347 p.. — (Stockholm studies in politics ; 25). — *Errata slip inserted. — : Originally presented as the author's thesis (doctoral--University of Stockholm, 1984). — Bibliography: p. 333-347*

KRICKUS, Richard J
The superpowers in crisis : implications of domestic discord / Richard J. Krickus. — Washington ; London : Pergamon-Brassey's International Defence Publishers, 1987. — xiii, 236p. — *Includes bibliographies*

LISKA, George
Rethinking US-Soviet relations / George Liska. — Oxford : Basil Blackwell, 1987. — [256]p. — *Includes index*

SAVIGEAR, Peter
Cold war or detente in the 1980s : the international politics of American-Soviet relations / Peter Savigear. — Brighton : Wheatsheaf, 1987. — [192]p. — *Includes bibliography and index*

WEIHMILLER, Gordon R.
U.S. - Soviet summits : an account of East-West diplomacy at the top, 1955-1985 / Gordon R. Weihmiller ; epilogue by Dusko Doder, foreword by David D. Newsom. — Lanham, Md. : University Press of America ; Washington, D.C. : Institute for the Study of Diplomacy, 1986. — xv,211p. — *Bibliography: p209-211*

SOVIET UNION — Foreign relations — United States — Addresses, essays, lectures

Shared destiny : fifty years of Soviet-American relations / edited by Mark Garrison and Abbott Gleason. — Boston : Beacon Press, c1985. — xxxii, 167 p.. — *Includes bibliographies and index*

SOVIET UNION — Foreign relations — United States — Case studies

STOESSINGER, John George
Nations in darkness--China, Russia, and America / John G. Stoessinger. — 4th ed. — New York : Random House, 1986. — x, 301 p. . — *Includes index. — Bibliography: p. 281-286*

SOVIET UNION — Foreign relations — United States — Congresses

Public diplomacy : USA versus USSR / Richard F. Staar, editor ; foreword by W. Glenn Campbell. — Stanford, Calif. : Hoover Institution Press, Stanford University, c1986. — xvii, 305 p.. — (Hoover Press publication ; 345). — *Papers originally presented at a workshop, held in October 1984, sponsored by the Hoover Institution at Stanford University. — Includes bibliographies and index*

SOVIET UNION — Foreign relations — Yemen

PAGE, Stephen
The Soviet Union and the Yemens : influence on asymmetrical relationships / Stephen Page. — New York : Praeger, 1985. — p. cm. — (Studies of influence in international relations). — *Includes index. — Bibliography: p*

SOVIET UNION — Foreign relations — Yemen (People's Democratic Republic)

PAGE, Stephen
The Soviet Union and the Yemens : influence on asymmetrical relationships / Stephen Page. — New York : Praeger, 1985. — p. cm. — (Studies of influence in international relations). — *Includes index. — Bibliography: p*

SOVIET UNION — Foreign relations — Yugoslavia

GIBIANSKII, L. Ia.
Sovetskii Soiuz i novaia Iugoslaviia 1941-1947 gg. / L. Ia. Gibianskii ; otv. redaktor V. K. Volkov. — Moskva : Nauka, 1987. — 201p

SOVIET UNION — Historiography

IGNATENKO, T. A.
Kritika men'shevistskoi kontseptsii istorii Oktiabria v sovetskoi istoriografii (1917 g.- seredina 30-kh godov) / T. A. Ignatenko ; otv. redaktor V. P. Naumov. — Moskva : Nauka, 1986. — 146p

SOVIET UNION — History

ACTON, Edward
Russia / Edward Acton. — London : Longman, 1986. — [xiv,288]p. — (The Present and the past). — *Includes bibliography and index*

BESANÇON, Alain
Présent soviétique et passé russe / Alain Besançon. — Nouvelle éd., rev. et augm. — Paris : Hachette, 1986. — 448p. — *New ed. of texts published 1967-1981. — Includes: "Court traité de soviétologie" and "Anatomie d'un spectre"*

BLACK, Cyril Edwin
Understanding Soviet politics : the perspective of Russian history / Cyril E. Black. — Boulder, Colo. : Westview Press, 1986. — p. cm. — *A collection of previously published essays. — Includes index*

SOVIET UNION — History — Bibliography

HARTLEY, Janet M.
Guide to documents and manuscripts in the United Kingdom relating to Russia and the Soviet Union / Janet M. Hartley. — London : Mansell, 1987. — xxiii,526p. — *Includes index*

SOVIET UNION — History — Philosophy

CHAGIN, B. A.
Istoricheskii materializm v SSSR v perekhodnyi period 1917-1936 gg. : istoriko-sotsiologicheskii ocherk / B. A. Chagin, V. I. Klushin ; otv. redaktor A. A. Fedoseev. — Moskva : Nauka, 1986. — 439p

SOVIET UNION — History — Sources

Vospominaniia i dnevniki XVIII-XX vv. : ukazatel' rukopisei / redaktsiia i predislovie S. V. Zhitomirskoi. — Moskva : Kniga, 1976. — 619p

SOVIET UNION — History — Peter I, 1689-1725

POSOSHKÓV, Iván
The book of poverty and wealth / Iván Pososhkóv ; edited and translated by A.P. Vlasto and L.R. Lewitter ; introduction and commentaries by L.R. Lewitter. — London : Athlone, 1987. — 440p. — *Translation of: Kniga o skúdosti i bogátstve. — Bibliography: p401-430. — Includes index*

SOVIET UNION — History — 19th century

DRUZHININ, N. M.
Izbrannye trudy / N. M. Druzhinin. — Moskva : Nauka
[1]: Revoliutsionnoe dvizhenie v Rossii v XIX v. / otv. redaktor S. S. Dmitriev. — 1985. — 484p

WESTWOOD, J. N.
Endurance and endeavour : Russian history, 1812-1986 / J.N. Westwood. — 3rd ed. — Oxford : Oxford University Press, 1987. — [560]p. — (The Short Oxford history of the modern world). — *Previous ed.: 1981. — Includes bibliography and index*

SOVIET UNION — History — Conspiracy of December, 1825 — Historiography

NEVELEV, G. A.
"Istina sil'nee Tsaria..." : A. S. Pushkin v rabote nad istoriei dekabristov / G. A. Nevelev. — Moskva : Mysl', 1985. — 203p

SOVIET UNION — History — Nicholas II, 1894-1917

FITZLYON, Kyril
Rossiia nakanune revoliutsii / Kirill Zinov'ev (Fittslaion). — London : Overseas Publications Interchange, 1983. — 123p. — (Vchera. Segodnia. Zavtra ; 1)

GEYER, Dietrich
The Russian Revolution / Dietrich Geyer ; translated from the German by Bruce Little. — Leamington Spa : Berg, 1987. — viii,163p. — *Translation of: Die Russische Revolution. — Bibliography: p155-159. — Includes index*

LINCOLN, W. Bruce
Passage through Armageddon : the Russians in war and revolution, 1914-1918 / W. Bruce Lincoln. — New York : Simon and Schuster, c1986. — 637 p., [16] p. of plates. — *Includes index. — Bibliography: p. 581-613*

SOVIET UNION — History — 1894-1917

SOLOV'EV, O. F.
Obrechennyi al'ians : zagovor imperialistov protiv narodov Rossii. 1914-1917 gg. / O. F. Solov'ev. — Moskva : Mysl', 1986. — 254p

SOVIET UNION — History — Nicholas II, 1894-1917

WOOD, Anthony, 1923-
The Russian Revolution / Anthony Wood. — 2nd ed. — London : Longman, 1986. — [ix,112]p. — (Seminar studies in history). — *Previous ed.: 1979. — Includes bibliography and index*

SOVIET UNION — History — 20th century

SERGE, Victor
Memoirs of a revolutionary / Victor Serge ; translated [with an introduction] by Peter Sedgwick. — London ; New York : Writers and Readers, 1984. — xxiv,403p. — *Translation of 'Mémoires d'un revolutionnaire', Paris: Editions du Seuil, 1951. — Bibliography: p[387]-391*

TREADGOLD, Donald W.
Twentieth century Russia / Donald W. Treadgold. — 5th ed. — Boston : Houghton Mifflin, c1981. — xiii, 555 p.. — *Includes index. — Bibliography: p. 495-521*

WESTWOOD, J. N.
Endurance and endeavour : Russian history, 1812-1986 / J.N. Westwood. — 3rd ed. — Oxford : Oxford University Press, 1987. — [560]p. — (The Short Oxford history of the modern world). — *Previous ed.: 1981. Includes bibliography and index*

SOVIET UNION — History — Revolution of 1905

IGNAT'EV, A. V.
Vneshniaia politika Rossii v 1905-1907 gg. / A. V. Ignat'ev ; otv. redaktor A. L. Narochnitskii. — Moskva : Nauka, 1986. — 300p

Revoliustiia 1905-1907 gg. v Srednem Azii i Kazakhstane / [B. V. Lunin...et al.; otv. redaktor Kh. Z. Ziiaev]. — Tashkent : "Fan" Uzbekskoi SSR, 1985. — 206p

Revoliutsiia 1905-1907 gg. v Srednei Azii i Kazakhstane / [B. V. Lunin...et al.; otv. red. Kh. Z. Ziiaev]. — Tashkent : "Fan" Uzbekskoi SSR, 1985. — 206p

SOVIET UNION — History — Revolution of 1905 — Congresses

1905 : la première révolution russe / édité par François-Xavier Coquin, Céline Gervais-Francelle. — Paris : Publications de la Sorbonne : Institut d'études slaves, 1986. — 568p. — (Publications de la Sorbonne. Série internationale ; 26) (Collection historique de l'Institut d'études slaves ; 32). — *Actes du colloque international, organisé en juin 1981 à l'Université de Paris I. — Contributions in French or English*

SOVIET UNION — History — February Revolution, 1917

ABRAHAM, Richard
Alexander Kerensky : the first love of the revolution / Richard Abraham. — New York : Columbia University Press, 1987. — xiii, 503p, [32]p of plates. — *Includes index. — Includes bibliographical references*

SOVIET UNION — History — Revolution, 1917-1921

ANDREEV, Leonid
Pered zadachami vremeni : politicheskie stat'i 1917-1919 godov / Leonid Andreev ; sostavlenie i podgotovka teksta Richard Devisa. — Benson, Vt. : Chalidze Publications, 1985. — 204p

BURBANK, Jane
Intelligentsia and revolution : Russian views of Bolshevism, 1917-1922 / Jane Burbank. — New York : Oxford University Press, 1986. — viii, 340 p.. — *Includes index. — Bibliography: p. 315-326*

GEYER, Dietrich
The Russian Revolution / Dietrich Geyer ; translated from the German by Bruce Little. — Leamington Spa : Berg, 1987. — viii,163p. — *Translation of: Die Russische Revolution. — Bibliography: p155-159. — Includes index*

Istoricheskii opyt Velikogo Oktiabria : k 90-letiiu akademika I. I. Mintsa / otv. redaktor S. L. Tikhvinskii. — Moskva : Nauka, 1986. — 399p. — *Bibliografiia trudov akademika I. I. Mintsa, 1975-1984 gg. : p23-[34]*

KOCHAN, Lionel
Russia in revolution 1890-1918 / by Lionel Kochan. — London : Paladin, 1970. — 334p. — *Originally published (B66-21946), London: Weidenfeld & Nicolson, 1967. — bibl p315-326*

LINCOLN, W. Bruce
Passage through Armageddon : the Russians in war and revolution, 1914-1918 / W. Bruce Lincoln. — New York : Simon and Schuster, c1986. — 637 p., [16] p. of plates. — *Includes index. — Bibliography: p. 581-613*

POLIAKOV, Iu. A.
Sovetskaia strana posle okonchaniia Grazhdanskoi voiny : territoriia i naselenie / Iu. A. Poliakov. — Moskva : Nauka, 1986. — 270p

SOVIET UNION — History — Revolution 1917-1921

POPOV, A. L.
Oktiabr'skii perevorot : fakty i dokumenty / sostavil A. L. Popo ; pod redaktsiei i so vstupitel'noi stat'eiu "Khod revoliutsii" N. A. Rozhkova. — Petrograd : Novaia Epokha, 1918. — 415p. — (Arkhiv revoliutsii 1917 goda)

SOVIET UNION — History — Revolution, 1917-1921

Velikii Oktiabr' : problemy istorii / otv. redaktor Iu. A. Poliakov. — Moskva : Nauka, 1987. — 286p

VOLIN
La révolution inconnue : Russie 1917-1921 / Voline. — [Nouvelle ed.]. — Paris : Pierre Belfond, 1986. — 734p. — *New ed. with previously unpublished "Conclusions"*

WOOD, Anthony, 1923-
The Russian Revolution / Anthony Wood. — 2nd ed. — London : Longman, 1986. — [ix,112]p. — (Seminar studies in history). — *Previous ed.: 1979. — Includes bibliography and index*

SOVIET UNION — History — Revolution, 1917-1921 — Causes

LINCOLN, W. Bruce
Passage through Armageddon : the Russians in war and revolution, 1914-1918 / W. Bruce Lincoln. — New York : Simon and Schuster, c1986. — 637 p., [16] p. of plates. — *Includes index. — Bibliography: p. 581-613*

SOVIET UNION — History — Revolution, 1917-1921 — Chronology

Bor'ba za ustanovlenie i uprochenie Sovetskoi vlasti : khronika sobytii, 26 oktiabria 1917 g. - 10 ianvaria 1918 g. / [sostaviteli: L. M. Gavrilov, V. V. Farsobin, R. G. Tsypkina; red. kollegiia: I. G. Dykov...[et al.]. — Moskva : Izd-vo AN SSSR, 1962. — 696p. — *Vol.5 of "Velikaia Oktiabr'skaia sotsialisticheskaia revoliutsiia: khronika sobytii"*

Velikaia Oktiabr'skaia sotsialisticheskaia revoliutsiia : khronika sobytii. — Moskva : Nauka. — Vols. 1-4 published 1957-1961; Vol.5, 1962
[6]: 11 ianvariia - 5 marta 1918 g. / otv. redaktor V. D. Polikarpov. — 1986. — 510p

SOVIET UNION — History — Revolution, 1917-1921 — Foreign public opinion, German — Sources

The German revolution and the debate on Soviet power : documents, 1918-1919 : preparing the founding conference / edited by John Riddell. — New York : Anchor : Distributed by Pathfinder Press, 1986. — xx,540p. — (The Communist International in Lenin's time). — *Bibliography: p528*

SOVIET UNION — History — Revolution, 1917-1921 — Historiography

IGNATENKO, T. A.
Kritika men'shevistskoi kontseptsii istorii Oktiabria v sovetskoi istoriografii (1917 g.- seredina 30-kh godov) / T. A. Ignatenko ; otv. redaktor V. P. Naumov. — Moskva : Nauka, 1986. — 146p

Velikii Oktiabr' i ukreplenie edinstva Sovetskogo obshchestva / [otv. redaktor: A. I. Vdovin]. — Moskva : Izd-vo Moskovskogo universiteta, 1987. — 384p. — (Voprosy metodologii i istorii istoricheskoi nauki ; vyp.5)

SOVIET UNION — History — Revolution, 1917-1921 — Influence

Pervyi kongress Kominterna : Velikii Oktiabr' i rozhdenie mezhdunarodnogo kommunisticheskogo dvizheniia / [otv. redaktor K. K. Shirinia]. — Moskva : Politizdat, 1986. — (Osnovnye etapy istorii mezhdunarodnogo kommunisticheskogo dvizheniia)

SOVIET UNION — History — 1917-1936

CARR, Edward Hallett
The Bolshevik revolution, 1917-1923 / by Edward Hallett Carr. — New York ; London : Norton. — (A history of Soviet Russia) volume 2. — 1985. — 400p

CARR, Edward Hallett
The Bolshevik revolution, 1917-1923 / by Edward Hallett Carr. — New York ; London : Norton. — (A history of Soviet Russia) volume 3. — 1985. — 614p

DURANTY, Walter
USSR : the story of Soviet Russia / Walter Duranty. — London : Hamish Hamilton, 1944. — 293p

GELLER, Mikhail
Utopiia u vlasti : istoriia Sovetskogo Soiuza s 1917 goda do nashikh dnei / Mikhail Geller, Aleksandr Nekrich. — London : Overseas Publications Interchange
1: [1917-1938]. — 1982. — 380p

SOVIET UNION — History — 1917-

GELLER, Mikhail
Utopia in power : the history of the Soviet Union from 1917 to the presents / by Mikhail Heller and Aleksandr Nekrich ; translated from the Russian by Phyllis B. Carlos. — London : Hutchinson, 1986, c1985. — 877p. — *On t.p. the letter 'o' in "power" is represented by a hammer and sickle. — Translated from the Russian. — Originally published as L'utopie au pouvoir: Paris : Calam-Levy, 1982. — Bibliography: p820-845. — Includes index*

RAȚIU, Ion
Moscow challenges the world / Ion Rațiu ; with an introduction by Brian Crozier. — London : Sherwood Press, 1986. — [vi],410p. — *Bibliography: p381-388*

The Soviet Union : contributors: M. S. Pletushkov...[et al.]. — Moscow : Progress Publishers, 1986. — 248p

SOVIET UNION — History — 1917- — Historiography

Velikii Oktiabr' i ukreplenie edinstva Sovetskogo obshchestva / [otv. redaktor: A. I. Vdovin]. — Moskva : Izd-vo Moskovskogo universiteta, 1987. — 384p. — (Voprosy metodologii i istorii istoricheskoi nauki ; vyp.5)

SOVIET UNION — History — 1917- — Sources

Sovetskoe obshchestvo v vospominaniiakh i dnevnikakh : annotirovannyi bibliograficheskii ukazatel 'knig, publikatsii v sbornikakh i zhurnalakh / [sostaviteli: K. I. Butina...et al.] ; nauchnaia redaktsiia; V. Z. Drobizheva. — Moskva : Kniga
T.1: 1917-1941. — 1987. — 477p

SOVIET UNION — History — 1925-1953

GELLER, Mikhail
Utopiia u vlasti : istoiia Sovetskogo Soiuza s 1917 goda do nashikh dnei / Mikhail Geller, Aleksandr Nekrich. — London : Overseas Publications Interchange
2: [1939-1980]. — 1982. — 551p

SOVIET UNION — History — 1925-1953 — Bibliography

LESTER, Robert
A guide to confidential U.S. State Department central files : the Soviet Union internal affairs 1945-1949 / compiled by Robert Lester. — Frederick, MD : University Publications of America, Inc., 1985. — ix,85p. — *Contents: A guide to the microfilm set of documents from the State Department central files deposited in the National Archives*

LESTER, Robert
A guide to U.S. State Department central files : the Soviet Union internal affairs 1950-1954 and foreign affairs 1950-1954 / compiled by Robert Lester. — Frederick, MD : University Publications of America, Inc., 1985. — ix,120p. — *Contents: A guide to the microfilm set of documents from State Department central files deposited in the National Archives*

SOVIET UNION — History — 1939-1945

KAROL, K. S.
Solik : inside the USSR, 1939-46 / by K.S. Karol ; translated from the French by Eamonn McArdle. — London : Pluto, 1986. — [448]p. — *Translation of: Solik*

SOVIET UNION — History — 1953-1980

GELLER, Mikhail
Utopiia u vlasti : istoiia Sovetskogo Soiuza s 1917 goda do nashikh dnei / Mikhail Geller, Aleksandr Nekrich. — London : Overseas Publications Interchange
2: [1939-1980]. — 1982. — 551p

SOVIET UNION — History — 1953-

Khrushchev and Khrushchevism / edited by Martin McCauley. — Basingstoke : Macmillan in association with the school of Slavonic and East European Studies University of London, 1987. — [240]p. — (Studies in Russia and East Europe). — *Includes index*

SOVIET UNION — History — 1953- — Bibliography

LESTER, Robert
A guide to U.S. State Department central files : the Soviet Union internal affairs 1950-1954 and foreign affairs 1950-1954 / compiled by Robert Lester. — Frederick, MD : University Publications of America, Inc., 1985. — ix,120p. — *Contents: A guide to the microfilm set of documents from State Department central files deposited in the National Archives*

SOVIET UNION — History, Military — 1917-

SEATON, Albert
The Soviet army, 1918 to the present / by Albert and Joan Seaton. — London : Bodley Head, 1986. — [288]p. — *Includes bibliography and index*

SOVIET UNION — Industries — Location

KHRUSHCHEV, A. T.
Geografiia promyshlennosti SSSR / A. T. Khrushchev. — 3-e izd., perer. i dop.. — Moskva : Mysl, 1986. — 415p

Planirovanie razmeshcheniia proizvoditel'nykh sil SSSR : osushchestvlenie politiki KPSS na etapakh sotsialisticheskogo stroitel'stva / [red. kollegiia: V. P. Mozhin...et al.]. — Moskva : Ekonomika
Ch.2: Planirovanie razmeshcheniia proizvoditel'nykh sil na etape razvitogo sotsializma. — 1986. — 382p

ZASTAVNYI, F. D.
Sovershenstvovanie territorial'noi organizatsii proizvoditel'nykh sil : teoriia, metody, praktika / F. D. Zastavnyi ; otv. redaktor N. T. Agafonov. — Leningrad : Nauka, Leningradskoe otdelenie, 1986. — 139p

SOVIET UNION — Military policy

DONNELLY, C. N.
Heirs of Clausewitz : change and continuity in the Soviet war machine / C. N. Donnelly. — London : Alliance Publishers for the Institute for European Defence and Strategic Studies, 1985. — 40p. — (Occasional paper / Institute for European Defence and Strategic Studies ; no.16)

GREEN, William
Soviet nuclear weapons policy : a research guide / William Green. — Boulder, Colo. : Westview Press, 1987, c1983. — p. cm. — (A Westview replica edition). — *Includes bibliographies and indexes*

JOHNSON, Nicholas L.
Soviet military strategy in space / Nicholas L. Johnson. — London : Jane's, 1987. — 287p

LEE, William Thomas
Soviet military policy since World War II / William T. Lee, Richard F. Staar ; foreword by William R. van Cleave. — Stanford, Calif. : Hoover Institution Press, Stanford University, c1986. — xxii, 263 p.. — (Hoover Press publication). — *Includes index. — Bibliography: p. [249]-258*

MCCGWIRE, Michael K.
Military objectives in Soviet foreign policy / Michael K. MccGwire. — Washington, D.C. : Brookings Institution, c1987. — xiv, 530p. — *Includes bibliographies and index*

MANFARLANE, S. Neil
Superpower rivalry and Soviet policy in the Caribbean Basin / S. N. MacFarlane. — Ottawa : Canadian Institue for International Peace and Security, 1986. — 70p. — (Occasional papers / Canadian Institute for International Peace and Security ; no.1)

SEATON, Albert
The Soviet army, 1918 to the present / by Albert and Joan Seaton. — London : Bodley Head, 1986. — [288]p. — *Includes bibliography and index*

SHENFIELD, Stephen
The nuclear predicament : explorations in Soviet ideology / Stephen Shenfield. — London : [for] The Royal Institute of International Affairs [by] Routledge & Kegan Paul, 1987. — [96]p. — (Chatham House papers ; 37)

STAAR, Richard Felix
USSR foreign policies after detente / Richard F. Staar. — Rev. ed. — Stanford, Calif. : Hoover Institution Press, Stanford University, c1987. — xxvii, 308 p.. — (Hoover Press publication ; 359). — *Includes index. — Bibliography: p. [275]-295*

THOMAS, Hugh, 1931-
Mr Gorbachev's own star wars / Hugh Thomas. — London : Centre for Policy Studies, 1986. — 15p. — (C.P.S. policy challenge)

TRITTEN, James John
Soviet naval forces and nuclear warfare : weapons, employment, and policy / James J. Tritten. — Boulder, Colo. : Westview Press, 1986. — xiii, 282 p.. — (Westview special studies in military affairs). — : *Revision of the author's thesis (University of Southern California, 1984) under the title: The strategic employment of the Soviet Navy in a nuclear war. — Includes bibliographies and index*

VAN OUDENAREN, John
Soviet policy toward western Europe : objectives, instruments, results / John Van Oudenaren. — Santa Monica, CA : Rand, [1986]. — xi, 118 p.. — *"A Project Air Force report, prepared for the United States Air Force.". — "February 1986.". — "R-3310-AF.". — Bibliography: p. 117-118*

SOVIET UNION — Military relations — Finland

BERNER, Örjan
[Sovjet & Norden. English]. Soviet policies toward the Nordic countries / Örjan Berner. — Lanham, MD : University Press of America ; [Cambridge, Mass.] : Center for International Affairs, Harvard University, c1986. — xii, 192 p., [1] leaf of plates. — *Shorter version published under title: Sovjet & Norden. c1985. — Bibliography: p. 187-192*

SOVIET UNION — Military relations — Near East

KARSH, Efraim
The cautious bear : Soviet military engagement in Middle East wars in the post-1967 era / Ephraim [i.e. Efraim] Karsh. — Jerusalem, Israel : Published for the Jaffee Center for Strategic Studies by the Jerusalem Post ; Boulder, Colo. : Westview Press, c1985. — 97 p.. — (JCSS study ; no. 3). — *Bibliography: p. 91-97*

SOVIET UNION — Military relations — Pakistan

The Red Army on Pakistan's border : policy implications for the United States / Theodore L. Eliot, Jr. ... [et al.]. — Washington : Pergamon-Brassey's, 1986. — p. cm. — (Special report). — *"May 1986.". — "A joint publication of the Institute for Foreign Policy Affairs, Inc. and the Center for Asian Pacific Affairs, the Asia Foundation."*

SOVIET UNION — Military relations — Persian Gulf Region

EPSTEIN, Joshua M.
Strategy and force planning : the case of the Persian Gulf / Joshua M. Epstein. — Washington, D.C. : Brookings Institution, c1987. — xiii, 169 p.. — *Includes index. — Bibliography: p. 156-165*

SOVIET UNION — Military relations — Scandinavia

BERNER, Örjan
[Sovjet & Norden. English]. Soviet policies toward the Nordic countries / Örjan Berner. — Lanham, MD : University Press of America ; [Cambridge, Mass.] : Center for International Affairs, Harvard University, c1986. — xii, 192 p., [1] leaf of plates. — *Shorter version published under title: Sovjet & Norden. c1985. — Bibliography: p. 187-192*

SOVIET UNION — Military relations — United States

LEONARD, Ellis P
[Orthopedic surgery of the dog and cat]. Leonard's Orthopedic surgery of the dog and cat. — 3rd ed. / J.W. Alexander. — Philadelphia : Saunders, 1985. — ix, 242 p.. — *Includes bibliographies and index*

SOVIET UNION — National security

The Race for security : arms and arms control in the Reagan years / edited by Robert Travis Scott. — Lexington, Mass. : Lexington Books, c1987. — p. cm. — *Includes index*

SOVIET UNION — Politics and government

BESANÇON, Alain
Présent soviétique et passé russe / Alain Besançon. — Nouvelle éd., rev. et augm. — Paris : Hachette, 1986. — 448p. — *New ed. of texts published 1967-1981. — Includes: "Court traité de soviétologie" and "Anatomie d'un spectre"*

BLACK, Cyril Edwin
Understanding Soviet politics : the perspective of Russian history / Cyril E. Black. — Boulder, Colo. : Westview Press, 1986. — p. cm. — *A collection of previously published essays. — Includes index*

FÉHÉR, Ferenc
Eastern left, Western left : totalitarianism, freedom and democracy / Ferenc Féhér and Agnes Heller. — Cambridge : Polity, 1987, c1986. — 287p. — *Includes index*

PUSHKAREV, Sergei
Samoupravlenie i svoboda v Rossii / Sergei Pushkarev. — Frankfurt am Main : Posev, 1985. — 171p

SOVIET UNION — Politics and Government

USSR facts and figures annual. — Gulf Breeze : Academic International Press, 1986-. — *Annual*

SOVIET UNION — Politics and government

ZEMTSOV, I. G.
Policy dilemmas and the struggle for power in the Kremlin : the Andropov period / by Ilya Zemtsov. — Fairfax, Va : Hero Books, [1985]. — x,213p. — *Bibliography: p209-212*

SOVIET UNION — Politics and government — To 1533

KOLLMANN, Nancy Shields
Kinship and politics : the making of the Muscovite political system, 1345-1547 / Nancy Shields Kollmann. — Stanford, Calif. : Stanford University Press, 1987. — x, 324 p.. — *Includes index. — Bibliography: p. [289]-308*

SOVIET UNION — Politics and government — 1533-1613

KOLLMANN, Nancy Shields
Kinship and politics : the making of the Muscovite political system, 1345-1547 / Nancy Shields Kollmann. — Stanford, Calif. : Stanford University Press, 1987. — x, 324 p.. — *Includes index. — Bibliography: p. [289]-308*

SOVIET UNION — Politics and government — 19th century

MILLER, Martin, A
The Russian revolutionary emigrés, 1825-1870 / Martin A. Miller. — Baltimore ; London : Johns Hopkins University Press, c1986. — xii, 292p. — (The Johns Hopkins University studies in historical and political science ; 104th ser., 2). — *Includes index. — Bibliography: p.[271]-284*

PANTIN, I. K.
Revoliutsionnaia traditsiia v Rossii 1783-1883 gg. / I. K. Pantin, E. G. Plimak, V. G. Khoros. — Moskva : Mysl', 1986. — 341p

SOVIET UNION — Politics and government — 1881-1894

OFFORD, Derek
The Russian revolutionary movement in the 1880s / Derek Offord. — Cambridge : Cambridge University Press, 1986. — 1v.. — *Bibliography: p277-294. — Includes index*

SOVIET UNION — Politics and government — 1894-1917

GALAI, Shmuel
The liberation movement in Russia, 1900-1905 / Shmuel Galai. — Cambridge : Cambridge University Press, 1973. — x,325p. — (Soviet and East European Studies). — *Bibliography: p277-315*

GEYER, Dietrich
The Russian Revolution / Dietrich Geyer ; translated from the German by Bruce Little. — Leamington Spa : Berg, 1987. — viii,163p. — *Translation of: Die Russische Revolution. — Bibliography: p155-159. — Includes index*

KOCHAN, Lionel
Russia in revolution 1890-1918 / by Lionel Kochan. — London : Paladin, 1970. — 334p. — *Originally published (B66-21946), London: Weidenfeld & Nicolson, 1967. — bibl p315-326*

WOOD, Anthony, 1923-
The Russian Revolution / Anthony Wood. — 2nd ed. — London : Longman, 1986. — [ix,112]p. — (Seminar studies in history). — *Previous ed.: 1979. — Includes bibliography and index*

SOVIET UNION — Politics and government — 20th century — Addresses, essays, lectures

SORRENTINO, Frank M.
Soviet politics and education / Frank M. Sorrentino and Frances R. Curcio. — Lanham, MD : University Press of America, c1985. — p. cm. — *Bibliography: p*

SOVIET UNION — Politics and government — 1904-1914

BADAYEV, A. Y.
Bolsheviks in the Tsarist Duma / A. Y. Badayev ; [with an introduction by Tony Cliff]. — London : Bookmarks, 1987. — 248p. — *Includes bibliographical notes*

WILLIAMS, Robert Chadwell
The other Bolsheviks : Lenin and his critics, 1904-1914 / Robert C. Williams. — Bloomington : Indiana University Press, c1986. — 233 p.. — *Includes index. — Bibliography: p. 222-228*

SOVIET UNION — Politics and government — 1917 — Posters

The Soviet political poster, 1917-1980 : from the USSR Lenin Library collection / [text and selection by Nina Baburina ; designed by Mikhail Anikst ; English translation by Boris Rubalsky]. — Harmmonsworth, Middx. : Penguin Books ; New York : Viking Penguin, 1985. — 9,183p. — *Originally published in 3 vols. in English and Russian under the title: Sovetskii politicheskii plakat*

SOVIET UNION — Politics and government — 1917-1936

ANDREEV, Leonid
Pered zadachami vremeni : politicheskie stat'i 1917-1919 godov / Leonid Andreev ; sostavlenie i podgotovka teksta Richard Devisa. — Benson, Vt. : Chalidze Publications, 1985. — 204p

BROIDO, Vera
Lenin and the Mensheviks : the persecution of socialists under Bolshevism / by Vera Broido. — Aldershot : Gower, c1987. — viii,216p. — *Bibliography: p191-201. — Includes index*

ČAVOŠKI, Kosta
The enemies of the people / Kosta Čavoški. — London : Centre for Research into Communist Economies, 1986. — 76p. — (Economics and society ; 1). — *Text on inside covers. — Bibliography: p75-76*

GEYER, Dietrich
The Russian Revolution / Dietrich Geyer ; translated from the German by Bruce Little. — Leamington Spa : Berg, 1987. — viii,163p. — *Translation of: Die Russische Revolution. — Bibliography: p155-159. — Includes index*

Kalendar'-ezhegodnik kommunista na 1931 god. — Moskva : Moskovskii rabochii, 1931

REIMAN, Michal
[Geburt des Stalinismus. English]. The birth of Stalinism : the USSR on the eve of the "second revolution" / by Michal Reiman ; translated by George Saunders. — Bloomington : Indiana University Press, c1987. — xii, 188 p.. — (Indiana-Michigan series in Russian and East European studies). — *Translation of: Die Geburt des Stalinismus. — Includes index. — Bibliography: p. 155-181*

WOOD, Anthony, 1923-
The Russian Revolution / Anthony Wood. — 2nd ed. — London : Longman, 1986. — [ix,112]p. — (Seminar studies in history). — *Previous ed.: 1979. — Includes bibliography and index*

SOVIET UNION — Politics and government — 1917-

AGURSKY, Mikhail
The third Rome : national Bolshevism in the USSR / Mikhail Agursky ; foreword by Leonard Shapiro. — Boulder : Westview Press, 1987. — p. cm. — *Includes index. — Bibliography: p*

BARGHOORN, Frederick Charles
Politics in the USSR / Frederick C. Barghoorn, Thomas F. Remington. — 3rd ed. — Boston : Little, Brown, 1986. — xiii, 530p. — (Little, Brown series in comparative politics. A Country study). — *Includes index*

KELLEY, Donald R
The politics of developed socialism : the Soviet Union as a post-industrial state / Donald R. Kelley. — New York : Greenwood Press, 1986. — viii, 215 p.. — (Contributions in political science ; no. 149). — *Includes index. — Bibliography: p. [205]-209*

LAIRD, Roy D.
The Politburo : demographic trends, Gorbachev, and the future / Roy D. Laird. — Boulder, Colo. : Westview Press, 1986. — xv,198p. — (Westview special studies on the Soviet Union and Eastern Europe). — *Bibliography: p187-189*

SHLAPENTOKH, Vladimir
The politics of sociology in the Soviet Union / by Vladimir E. Shlapentokh. — Boulder : Westview Press, 1987, c1986. — p. cm. — (Delphic monograph series). — *Includes index. — Bibliography: p*

The Soviet Union : contributors: M. S. Pletushkov...[et al.]. — Moscow : Progress Publishers, 1986. — 248p

TUCKER, Robert C.
Political culture and leadership in Soviet Russia : from Lenin to Gorbachev / Robert C. Tucker. — Brighton : Wheatsheaf, 1987. — x,214p. — *Includes index*

SOVIET UNION — Politics and government — 1936-1953

DUNMORE, Timothy
Soviet politics, 1945-53 / Timothy Dunmore. — London : Macmillan, 1984. — vi,167p. — *Includes index*

SOVIET UNION — Politics and government — 1953-1982

COLTON, Timothy J.
The dilemma of reform in the Soviet Union / Timothy J. Colton. — Rev. and expanded ed. — New York : Council of Foreign relations, 1986. — p. cm. — *Includes index*

KHRUSHCHEV, N.
For victory in peaceful competition with capitalism : with a special preface written for the English edition / Nikita S. Khrushchev. — London : Hutchinson, 1960. — 784p

PARCHOMENKO, Walter
Soviet images of dissidents and nonconformists / Walter Parchomenko. — New York ; London : Praeger, 1986. — xv, 251 p.. — *"Praeger special studies. Praeger scientific.". — Includes index. — Bibliography: p. 213-243*

SOVIET UNION — Politics and government — 1953-

AVIDAR, Yosef
[Yehasim ben ha-miflagah le-ven ha-tsava bi-Verit ha-Mo'atsot, 1953 'ad 1964. English]. The party and the army in the Soviet Union / Yosef Avidar. — University Park : Pennsylvania State University Press, 1985. — p. cm. — *Translation of: ha-Yehasim ben ha-miflagah le-ven ha-tsava bi-Verit ha-Mo'atsot, 1953 'ad 1964. — Includes index. — Bibliography: p*

BIALER, Seweryn
The Soviet paradox : external expansion, internal decline / Seweryn Bialer. — 1st ed. — New York : Knopf, 1986. — ix, 391p. — *Includes index. — Bibliography: p.379-386*

From Brezhnev to Gorbachev : domestic affairs and Soviet foreign policy / edited by Hans-Joachim Veen. — Leamington Spa : Berg, 1987. — xii,378p. — *Revised ed. of Wohin entwickelt sich die Sowjetunion?*

LEONHARD, Wolfgang
The Kremlin and the West : a realistic approach / Wolfgang Leonhard ; translated by Houchang E. Chehabi. — New York : W. W. Norton, 1986. — xii,228p

WALKER, Martin, 1947-
The waking giant : the Soviet Union under Gorbachev / Martin Walker. — London : Joseph, 1986. — xxviii,282p. — *Includes index*

SOVIET UNION — Politics and government — 1953-
continuation

YANOV, Alexander
The Russian challenge and the year 2000 / Alexander Yanov ; translated by Iden J. Rosenthal. — Oxford : Basil Blackwell, 1987. — xvi,302p. — *Translation from the Russian.* — *Includes index*

SOVIET UNION — Politics and government — 1982-

COLTON, Timothy J.
The dilemma of reform in the Soviet Union / Timothy J. Colton. — Rev. and expanded ed. — New York : Council of Foreign relations, 1986. — p. cm. — *Includes index*

GORBACHEV, M. S.
Selected speeches and articles / Mikhail Gorbachev. — 2nd updated ed. — Moscow : Progress, 1987. — 605p

KERBLAY, Basile
Les soviétiques des années 80 / Basile Kerblay, Marie Lavigne. — Paris : Armand Colin, 1985. — 214p. — *Bibliography: p211-[212]*

LUDWIKOWSKI, Rett R
The crisis of communism : its meaning, origins, and phases / Rett R. Ludwikowski. — Washington : Pergamon-Brassey's International Defense Publishers, 1986. — xii, 84 p.. — (Foreign policy report). — *"A Publication of the Institute for Foreign Policy Analysis, Inc.".* — *Includes bibliographical references*

PARCHOMENKO, Walter
Soviet images of dissidents and nonconformists / Walter Parchomenko. — New York ; London : Praeger, 1986. — xv, 251 p.. — *"Praeger special studies. Praeger scientific.".* — *Includes index.* — *Bibliography: p. 213-243*

Problemy partiinogo i gosudarstvennogo stroitel'stva / Akademiia obschestvennykh nauk pri TSK KPSS. — Moskva : Akademiia obschestvennykh nauk pri TSK KPSS, 1982-. — *Annual*

The Soviet Union 1984/85 : events, problems, perspectives / edited by the Federal Institute for East European and International Studies. — Boulder, Colo. : Westview Press, 1986. — xix,349p. — (Westview Special Studies on the Soviet Union and Eastern Europe)

The Soviet Union under Gorbachev / edited by Martin McCauley. — Basingstoke : Macmillan in association with School of Slavonic and East European Studies, University of London, 1987. — [272]p. — (Studies in Russia and East Europe). — *Includes index*

The Soviet Union under Gorbachev : prospects for reform / edited by David A. Dyker. — London : Croom Helm, c1987. — [224]p. — *Includes index*

SOVIET UNION — Popular culture

BROOKS, Jeffrey
When Russia learned to read : literacy and popular literature, 1861-1917 / Jeffrey Brooks. — Princeton, N.J. : Princeton University Press, c1985. — xxii, 450 p.. — *Includes index.* — *Bibliography: p. 415-435*

SOVIET UNION — Population

Dinamika naseleniia SSSR 1960-1980gg. / [E. K. Vasil'eva...et al.]. — Moskva : Finansy i statistika, 1985. — 174p. — *Bibliography: p [172-173]*

DROBIZHEV, V. Z.
U istokov sovetskoi demografii. — Moskva : Mysl', 1987. — 221p. — *Bibliography: p192-[199]*

POLIAKOV, Iu. A.
Sovetskaia strana posle okonchaniia Grazhdanskoi voiny : territoriia i naselenie / Iu. A. Poliakov. — Moskva : Nauka, 1986. — 270p

Razmeshchenie naseleniia v SSSR : regional'nyi aspekt dinamiki i politiki narodonaseleniia / [B. S. Khorev...et al.]. — Moskva : Mysl', 1986. — 220p. — *Bibliography: p212-[219]*

ZHURAVLEVA, N. I.
Antisovetizm burzhuaznoi demografii / N. I. Zhuravleva. — Moskva : Mysl', 1987. — 189p. — (Kritika burzhuaznoi ideologii i revizionizma). — *Bibliography: p177-[190]*

SOVIET UNION — Population — Study and teaching

Research guide to the Russian and Soviet censuses / edited by Ralph S. Clem. — Ithaca : Cornell University Press, 1986. — p. cm. — *Includes index*

SOVIET UNION — Population policy

Demograficheskaia politika sotsialisticheskogo obshchestva / otv. redaktor T. V. Riabushkin. — Moskva : Nauka, 1986. — 190p

HEITLINGER, Alena
Reproduction, medicine and the socialist state / Alena Heitlinger. — Basingstoke : Macmillan, 1987. — xv,318p. — *Bibliography: p280-303.* — *Includes index*

Rasselenie : voprosy teorii i razvitie : (na primere Ukrainskoi SSR) / [G. S. Ftomov...et al., otv. redaktor F. D. Zastavnyi]. — Kiev : Naukova dumka, 1985. — 261p

Razmeshchenie naseleniia v SSSR : regional'nyi aspekt dinamiki i politiki narodonaseleniia / [B. S. Khorev...et al.]. — Moskva : Mysl', 1986. — 220p. — *Bibliography: p212-[219]*

Vosproizvodstvo naseleniia i trudovykh resursov v usloviiakh razvitogo sotsializma / redaktsionnaia kollegiia: V. S. Steshenko...[et al.]. — Kiev : Naukova dumka. — *V 4-kh tomkh*
T.1: Razvitie naseleniia i ego trudovogo potentsiala / otv. redaktor V. S. Steshenko. — 1985. — 318p

SOVIET UNION — Public opinion

FEHÉR, Ferenc
Eastern left : western left : a contribution to the morphology of a problematic relationship / Ferenc Fehér [and] Agnes Heller. — Munchen : Projekt 'Crises in Soviet-type systems', 1986. — 40p. — (Research project Crises in Soviet-type systems ; Study no.10)

SOVIET UNION — Relations — Argentina

ECHAGÜE, Carlos
El socialimperialismo Ruso en la Argentina / Carlos Echagüe. — Buenos Aires : Agora, 1984. — 367p

VACS, Aldo César
Los socios discretos : el nuevo carácter de las relaciones internacionales entre la Argentina y la Unión Soviética / Aldo César Vacs. — Buenos Aires : Sudoamericana, 1984. — 183p. — *Bibliography: p[187-193]*

SOVIET UNION — Relations — Bulgaria

Internatsional'noe sotrudnichestvo KPSS i BKP : istorii i sovremennost' / pod obshchei redaktsiei A. G. Egorova (SSSR) i D. Elazara (NRB). — Moskva : Politizdat, 1985. — 415p

SOVIET UNION — Relations — Cuba

DUNCAN, W. Raymond
The Soviet Union and Cuba : interests and influence / by W. Raymond Duncan. — New York : Praeger, 1985. — xv, 220p. — (Studies of influence in international relations). — *Includes index.* — *Bibliography: p.205-209*

Letopis' vazhneishikh sobytii sovetskokubinskoi druzhby i sotrudnichestva 1959-1985 / [sostavitel': M. V. Grishchenko; otv. redaktor I. N. Mel'nikova]. — Kiev : Naukova dumka, 1987. — 136p

SOVIET UNION — Relations — Europe, Eastern

JOHNSON, A. Ross
The impact of eastern Europe on Soviet policy toward western Europe / A. Ross Johnson. — Santa Monica, CA. : Rand, [1986]. — xv, 79 p. . — *"A project Air Force report prepared for the United States Air Force.".* — *"March 1986.".* — *"R-3332-AF.".* — *Includes bibliographical references*

SOVIET UNION — Relations — Germany

AGURSKY, Mikhail
The third Rome : national Bolshevism in the USSR / Mikhail Agursky ; foreword by Leonard Shapiro. — Boulder : Westview Press, 1987. — p. cm. — *Includes index.* — *Bibliography: p*

SOVIET UNION — Relations — Great Britain

RYLE, Claire
Citizens' diplomacy : a handbook on Anglo-Soviet initiatives / Claire Ryle and Jim Garrison. — London : Merlin, 1986. — 90p

SOVIET UNION — Relations — India

Studies in Indo-Soviet relations / P.N. Haksar ... [et al.] ; V.D. Chopra, editor. — New Delhi : Published by Patriot Publishers on behalf of Indian Centre for Regional Affairs, 1986. — 288 p.. — *Includes bibliographical references and index*

SOVIET UNION — Relations — Iran — Azerbaijan

NISSMAN, David B.
The Soviet Union and Iranian Azerbaijan : the use of nationalism for political penetration / David B. Nissman. — Boulder, Colo. : Westview Press, 1987. — ix,123p. — (Westview special studies on the Soviet Union and Eastern Europe). — *Bibliography: p109-113*

SOVIET UNION — Relations — Latin America

Soviet-Latin American relations in the 1980s / edited by Augusto Varas. — Boulder : Westview Press, 1987. — p. cm. — (Westview special studies on Latin America and the Caribbean)

SOVIET UNION — Relations — Moldavia

IOVVA, I. F.
Peredovaia Rossiia i obshchestvenno-politicheskoe dvizhenie v Moldavii : (pervaia polovina XIX v.) / I. F Iovva ; otv. redaktor S. S. Volk. — Kishinev : Shtiintsa, 1986. — 256p. — *Brief summary in English and French*

SOVIET UNION — Relations — United States

AILES, Catherine P.
Cooperation in science and technology : an evaluation of the U.S.-Soviet agreement / Catherine P. Ailes and Arthur E. Pardee. — Boulder : Westview, 1986. — xxiii,334p

HAMMER, Armand
Witness to history / by Armand Hammer with Neil Lyndon. — New York ; London : Simon & Schuster, 1987. — [512]p. — *Includes index*

RICHMOND, Yale
U.S.-Soviet cultural exchanges, 1958-1986 : who wins? / Yale Richmond ; foreword by Marshall D. Shulmam. — Boulder : Westview Press, 1987. — xvi, 170 p.. — (Westview special studies on the Soviet Union and Eastern Europe). — *Includes index.* — *Bibliography: p. 161-163*

SOVIET UNION — Relations (Military) with the United States

FREEDMAN, Lawrence
US intelligence and the Soviet strategic threat / Lawrence Freedman. — 2nd ed. — London : Macmillan, 1986. — [288]p. — *Previous ed.: 1977.* — *Includes bibliography and index*

SOVIET UNION — Religion
KAHLE, Wilhelm
Die lutherischen Kirchen und Gemeinden in der Sowjetunion : seit 1938/1940 / Wilhelm Kahle. — Gütersloh : Gütersloher Verlagshaus Mohn, 1985. — 279p. — (Die lutherische Kirche, Geschichte und Gestalten ; Bd.8). — *Bibliography: p264-269*

SOVIET UNION — Revolution, 1917-1921 — Personal narratives
PATIN, Louise
Journal d'une institutrice française en Russie pendant la révolution, 1917-1919 / Louise Pation ; préface de Geneviève Legras. — Paris : La Table Ronde ; Pontoise : Edijac, 1987. — 249p

SOVIET UNION — Rural conditions
Sotsial'no-ekonomicheskii potentsial sela : problemy razvitiia i ispol'zovaniia / otv. redaktor L. V. Nikiforov. — Moskva : Nauka, 1986. — 205p. — (Problemy sovetskoi ekonomiki)

Sovremennye etnosotsial'nye protsessy na sele / otv. redaktor Iu. V. Arutiunian. — Moskva : Nauka, 1986. — 247p. — *Table of contents in English*

STOLIAROV, Ivan
Zapiski russkogo krest'ianina = Récit d'un paysan russe / Ivan Stoliarov ; préface de Basile Kerblay; notes de Valérie Stoliaroff avec le concours d'Alexis Berelowitch. — Paris : Institut d'Études Slaves, 1986. — 202p. — (Cultures et sociétés de l'Est ; 6)

SOVIET UNION — Social conditions
BLACK, Cyril Edwin
Understanding Soviet politics : the perspective of Russian history / Cyril E. Black. — Boulder, Colo. : Westview Press, 1986. — p. cm. — *A collection of previously published essays. — Includes index*

ISMAILOV, A. I.
Sotsialisticheskii byt Sovetskogo naroda : dostizheniia, retrospektiva, perspektivy / A. I. Ismailov, E. I. Ismailova, otv redaktor V. Ts. Naidakov. — Moskva : Nauka, 1986. — 157p

JONES, Ellen
Modernization, value change and fertility in the Soviet Union / Ellen Jones, Fred W. Grupp. — Cambridge : Cambridge University Press, 1987. — xiv,420p. — (Soviet and East European studies). — *Includes index*

KAVALEROV, A. I.
Byt razvitogo sotsializma : sushchnost' i osnovnye cherty / A. I. Kavalerov. — L'vov : Vyshcha shkola, 1985. — 144p

KOCHAN, Lionel
Russia in revolution 1890-1918 / by Lionel Kochan. — London : Paladin, 1970. — 334p. — *Originally published (B66-21946), London: Weidenfeld & Nicolson, 1967. — bibl p315-326*

SELUNSKAIA, V. M.
Sotsial'naia struktura Sovetskogo obshchestva : istoriia i sovremennost' / V. M. Selunskaia. — Moskva : Politizdat, 1987. — 286p

Sotsial'no-ekonomicheskii potentsial sela : problemy razvitiia i ispol'zovaniia / otv. redaktor L. V. Nikiforov. — Moskva : Nauka, 1986. — 205p. — (Problemy sovetskoi ekonomiki)

Sotsial'no-ekonomicheskoe razvitie Rossii : sbornik statei k 100-letiiu so dnia rozhdeniia Nikolaia Mikhailovicha Druzhinina / otv. redaktor S. L. Tikhvinskii. — Moskva : Nauka, 1986. — 267p

Working papers / University of Illinois at Urbana-Champaign, Soviet Interview Project. — [S.l.] : University of Illinois at Urbana-Champaign, 1980-

SOVIET UNION — Social conditions — 1801-1917
KANATCHIKOV, S
[Iz istorii moego bytiia. English]. A radical worker in Tsarist Russia : the autobiography of Semën Ivanovich Kanatchikov / translated and edited by Reginald E. Zelnik. — Stanford, Calif. : Stanford University Press, 1986. — xxx, 472p, [3]p of plates. — *Translation of: Iz istorii moego bytiia*

SOVIET UNION — Social conditions — 1917-
The Soviet Union : contributors: M. S. Pletushkov...[et al.]. — Moscow : Progress Publishers, 1986. — 248p

SOVIET UNION — Social conditions — 1970-
BIALER, Seweryn
The Soviet paradox : external expansion, internal decline / Seweryn Bialer. — 1st ed. — New York : Knopf, 1986. — ix, 391p. — *Includes index. — Bibliography: p.379-386*

From Brezhnev to Gorbachev : domestic affairs and Soviet foreign policy / edited by Hans-Joachim Veen. — Leamington Spa : Berg, 1987. — xii,378p. — *Revised ed. of Wohin entwickelt sich die Sowjetunion?*

KERBLAY, Basile
Les soviétiques des années 80 / Basile Kerblay, Marie Lavigne. — Paris : Armand Colin, 1985. — 214p. — *Bibliography: p211-[212]*

LUDWIKOWSKI, Rett R
The crisis of communism : its meaning, origins, and phases / Rett R. Ludwikowski. — Washington : Pergamon-Brassey's International Defense Publishers, 1986. — xii, 84 p.. — (Foreign policy report). — *"A Publication of the Institute for Foreign Policy Analysis, Inc."*. — *Includes bibliographical references*

Razvitoi sotsializm : voprosy teorii i istorii / otv. redaktor S. S. Khromov. — Moskva : Nauka, 1986. — 245p

SOVIET UNION — Social conditions — 1970- — Congresses
Quality of life in the Soviet Union / edited by Horst Herlemann. — Boulder, Colo. : Westview Press, 1987. — p. cm. — (A Westview special study)

SOVIET UNION — Social life and customs — 19th century
GROMYKO, M. M.
Traditsionnye normy povedeniia i formy obshcheniia russkikh krest'ian XIX v. / M. M. Gromyko ; otv. redaktory V. A. Aleksandrov, V. K. Sokolova. — Moskva : Nauka, 1986. — 274p

SOVIET UNION — Social life and customs — 1970-
Sotsial'no kul'turnyi oblik sovetskikh natsii : po rezul'tatam etnosotsiologicheskogo issledovaniia / otv. redaktory: Iu. V. Arutiunian, Iu. V. Bromlei. — Moskva : Nauka, 1986. — 453p. — *Table of contents in English*

SOVIET UNION — Social policy
KELLEY, Donald R
The politics of developed socialism : the Soviet Union as a post-industrial state / Donald R. Kelley. — New York : Greenwood Press, 1986. — viii, 215 p.. — (Contributions in political science ; no. 149). — *Includes index. — Bibliography: p. [205]-209*

SOVIET UNION — Statistics
USSR facts and figures annual. — Gulf Breeze : Academic International Press, 1986-. — *Annual*

SOVIET UNION — Statistics — Handbooks, manuals, etc — Bibliography
GILLULA, James W.
Bibliography of regional statistical handbooks in the U.S.S.R. / by James W. Gillula. — 2nd ed. — Washington, D.C. : Foreign Demographic Analysis Division, Bureau of the Census, 1980. — v,99p

SOVIET UNION — Relations — Europe
JOHNSON, A. Ross
The impact of eastern Europe on Soviet policy toward western Europe / A. Ross Johnson. — Santa Monica, CA. : Rand, [1986]. — xv, 79 p. . — *"A project Air Force report prepared for the United States Air Force."*. — *"March 1986."*. — *"R-3332-AF."*. — *Includes bibliographical references*

SOVIET UNION. Armiia — History
AVIDAR, Yosef
[Yeḥasim ben ha-miflagah le-ven ha-tsava bi-Verit ha-Mo'atsot, 1953 'ad 1964. English]. The party and the army in the Soviet Union / Yosef Avidar. — University Park : Pennsylvania State University Press, 1985. — p. cm. — *Translation of: ha-Yeḥasim ben ha-miflagah le-ven ha-tsava bi-Verit ha-Mo'atsot, 1953 'ad 1964. — Includes index. — Bibliography: p*

SOVIET UNION. Armiia — History
SEATON, Albert
The Soviet army, 1918 to the present / by Albert and Joan Seaton. — London : Bodley Head, 1986. — [288]p. — *Includes bibliography and index*

SOVIET UNION. Armiia — Political activity
AVIDAR, Yosef
[Yeḥasim ben ha-miflagah le-ven ha-tsava bi-Verit ha-Mo'atsot, 1953 'ad 1964. English]. The party and the army in the Soviet Union / Yosef Avidar. — University Park : Pennsylvania State University Press, 1985. — p. cm. — *Translation of: ha-Yeḥasim ben ha-miflagah le-ven ha-tsava bi-Verit ha-Mo'atsot, 1953 'ad 1964. — Includes index. — Bibliography: p*

SOVIET UNION. Ministerstvo inostrannykh del
STAAR, Richard Felix
USSR foreign policies after detente / Richard F. Staar. — Rev. ed. — Stanford, Calif. : Hoover Institution Press, Stanford University, c1987. — xxvii, 308 p.. — (Hoover Press publication ; 359). — *Includes index. — Bibliography: p. [275]-295*

SOVIET UNION. Voenno-morskoĭ flot
TRITTEN, James John
Soviet naval forces and nuclear warfare : weapons, employment, and policy / James J. Tritten. — Boulder, Colo. : Westview Press, 1986. — xiii, 282 p.. — (Westview special studies in military affairs). — *: Revision of the author's thesis (University of Southern California, 1984) under the title: The strategic employment of the Soviet Navy in a nuclear war. — Includes bibliographies and index*

SOVIET UNION — Foreign relations — 1975-
VAN OUDENAREN, John
Soviet policy toward western Europe : objectives, instruments, results / John Van Oudenaren. — Santa Monica, CA : Rand, [1986]. — xi, 118 p.. — *"A Project Air Force report, prepared for the United States Air Force."*. — *"February 1986."*. — *"R-3310-AF."*. — *Bibliography: p. 117-118*

SOVIET UNION — Foreign relations — Germany
CARR, Edward Hallett
German-Soviet relations between the two world wars, 1919-1939 / Edward H. Carr. — Baltimore : Johns Hopkins Press, 1951. — 146p

SOVIET UNION, NORTHERN — Ethnic relations
KUOLJOK, Kerstin Eidlitz
The revolution in the north : Soviet ethnography and nationality policy / Kerstin Eidlitz Kuoljok ; translated by T. J. M. Gray and N. Tomkinson. — Uppsala : [Universitet] ; Stockholm : Almquist and Wiksell, 1985. — x,185p. — (Acta Universitatis Upsaliensis / Studia Multiethnica Upsaliensia ; no.I) (Uppsala Research Reports in Cultural Anthropology ; 1). — *Bibliography: p173-182*

SOVIET UNION, NORTHERN — Native races

Problemy sovremennogo sotsial'nogo razvitiia narodnostei Severa / otv. redaktory V. I. Boiko, Iu. P. Nikitin, A. I. Solomakha. — Novosibirsk : Nauka, Sibirskoe otdelenie, 1987. — 254p. — (Sotsial'noe i ekonomicheskoe razvitie narodnostei Severa)

Sotsial'nye problemy truda u narodnostei Severa / otv. redaktor V. I Boiko. — Novosibirsk : Nauka, Sibirskoe otdelenie, 1986. — 213p. — (Sotsial'noe i ekonomicheskoe razvitie narodnostei Severa)

SOVIET UNION, NORTHERN — Social conditions

Problemy sovremennogo sotsial'nogo razvitiia narodnostei Severa / otv. redaktory V. I. Boiko, Iu. P. Nikitin, A. I. Solomakha. — Novosibirsk : Nauka, Sibirskoe otdelenie, 1987. — 254p. — (Sotsial'noe i ekonomicheskoe razvitie narodnostei Severa)

Sotsial'nye problemy truda u narodnostei Severa / otv. redaktor V. I Boiko. — Novosibirsk : Nauka, Sibirskoe otdelenie, 1986. — 213p. — (Sotsial'noe i ekonomicheskoe razvitie narodnostei Severa)

SOVIET UNION X HISTORY — February Revolution, 1917

IGNATENKO, I. M.
Fevral'skaia burzhuazno-demokraticheskaia revoliutsiia v Belorussii / I. M. Ignatenko. — Minsk : Nauka i tekhnika, 1986. — 341p

SOVIETS — Russian S.F.S.R. — Leningrad

Leningradskii Sovet v gody Grazhdanskoi voiny i sotsialisticheskogo stroitel'stva 1917-1937 gg. : sbornik statei / [redaktsionnaia kollegiia: M. P. Iroshnikov...et al.]. — Leningrad : Nauka, Leningradskoe otdelenie, 1986. — 258p

SOVIETS — Russian S.F.S.R. — Moscow

BRITISH LIBRARY OF POLITICAL AND ECONOMIC SCIENCE
Rare printed material relating to Moscow, 1887-1923 : contents of the microfilm. — Hebdon Bridge, W. Yorks. : Altair Publishing, [1987]. — 35p

MOSCOW (R.S.F.S.R.). Sovet deputatov trudiashchikhsia
Sobranie postanovlenii i rasporiazhenii Moskovskogo Soveta Rabochikh i Krasnoarmeiskikh Deputatov, Nos.1-46 : (1 May 1918-30 September 1919). — Moskva : Izd. Iuridicheskogo Otdela, 1918-1919. — (Rare printed material relating to Moscow, 1887-1923)

MOSCOW (R.S.F.S.R.). Sovet deputatov trudiashchikhsia. Ispolnitel'nyi komitet
Otchet Ispolnitel'nogo Komiteta Moskovskogo Soveta R.K. i K.D. 2-mu Ob"edinennomu Gubernskomu S"ezdu Sovetov za iiun'-noiabr' 1920g.. — Moscow : [s.n.], 1920. — 624p. — (Rare printed material relating to Moscow 1887-1923)

MOSCOW (R.S.F.S.R.: Guberniia). Ispolnitel'nyi komitet
Otchet o deiatel'nosti Moskovskogo Gubernskogo Ispolnitel'nogo Komiteta i Gubernskogo Ekonomicheskogo Soveshchaniia s 1/X 1922g..-po 1/X1923g.. — Moskva : Tip. Administrativnago Otdela M.S. im M. I. Rogova. — (Rare printed material relating to Moscow, 1887-1923)
Vyp.1: Otchet Gubispolkoma / (sostavlen pod redaktsiei Organiz. - Instr. otd. M.S.R.,K. i K.D.). — 1924. — 649p

SOVIETS — Ukraine

PETLIAK, F. A.
Partiinoe rukovodstvo Sovetami na Ukraine v gody Velikoi Otechestvennoi voiny (1941-1945) / F. A. Petliak. — Kiev : Vyshcha shkola, 1986. — 181p

SOZIALDEMOKRATISCHE PARTEI DEUTSCHLANDS

MENG, Richard
Die sozialdemokratische Wende : Aussenbild und innerer Prozess der SPD 1981-1984 / Richard Meng. — Giessen : Focus, 1985. — 409p. — *Bibliography: p406-409*

OBERMEYER, Ute
Das Nein der SPD - eine nene Ära? : SPD und Raketen 1977-1983 / Ute Obermeyer ; mit einem Vorwort von Karl Heinz Hansen. — Marburg : Verlag Arbeiterbewegung und Gesellschaftswissenschaft, 1985. — 170p. — (Schriftenreihe der Studiengesellschaft für sozialgeschichte und Arbeiterbewegung ; Bd.45)

SPD und Grüne : das neue Bündnis? / Wolfram Bickerich (Hg.). — Reinbek bei Hamburg : Rowohlt Taschenbuch Verlag, 1985. — 282p

SOZIALDEMOKRATISCHE PARTEI DEUTSCHLANDS — History

MAEHL, William Harvey
The German Socialist Party : champion of the First Republic, 1918-1933 / William Harvey Maehl. — Philadelphia : American Philosophical Society, 1986. — xvii, 270p, [12]p of plates. — (Memoirs of the American Philosophical Society ; v.169). — *Bibliography: p.239-253*

MILLER, Susanne
A history of German Social Democracy from 1848 to the present / Susanne Miller, Heinrich Potthoff ; translated from the German by J.A. Underwood. — Leamington Spa : Berg, c1986. — xii,330p. — *Translation of: Kleine Geschichte der SPD. — Bibliography: p320-325. — Includes index*

SOZIALDEMOKRATISCHE PARTIE DEUTSCHLANDS — History

AUERNHEIMER, Gustav
Genosse Herr Doktor : zur Rolle von Akademikern in der deutschen Sozialdemokratie 1890 bid 1933 / Gustav Auernheimer. — Giessen : Focus-verlag, 1985. — 240p. — *Bibliography: p223-240*

SOZIALISTISCHE EINHEITSPARTEI DEUTSCHLANDS — History

Dokumente zur Geschichte der SED. — Berlin : Dietz. — (Schriftenreihe Geschichte)
Bd.2: 1945 bis 1971 / [Redaktion: Günter Benser...et al.]. — 1986. — 340p

SOZIALISTISCHE EINHEITSPARTEI DEUTSCHLANDS — History — Sources

Dokumente zur Geschichte der SED. — Berlin : Dietz. — (Schriftenreihe Geschichte)
Bd.2: 1945 bis 1971 / [Redaktion: Günter Benser...et al.]. — 1986. — 340p

SOZIALISTISCHE FRONT

RABE, Bernd
Die "Sozialistische Front" : Sozialdemokraten gegen den Faschismus 1933-1936 / Bernd Rabe ; [Vortwort: Peter von Oertzen]. — Hanover : Fackelträger-Verlag, 1984. — 120p. — *Includes bibliographic notes*

SPACE COLONIES

LAROUCHE, Lyndon H.
There are no limits to growth / Lyndon H. LaRouche. — New York : New Benjamin Franklin House, 1983. — xix,225p

SPACE FLIGHT

MARSH, Peter, 1952-
The space business : a manual on the commercial uses of space / Peter Marsh. — Harmondsworth : Penguin, 1985. — 232p. — *Further reading: p[211]-217*

SPACE IN ECONOMICS

Location theory / Jean Jaskold Gabszewicz ... [et. al.]. — Chur, Switzerland ; New York : Harwood Academic Publishers, c1986. — vii, 190 p.. — (Fundamentals of pure and applied economics ; v. 5Regional and urban economics section). — *Includes bibliographies and index*

Région et aménagement du territoire : mélanges offerts à Joseph Lajugie par ses collègues, ses élèves et ses amis. — Bordeaux : Editions Bière, 1985. — 898p. — *Bibliographies*

SPACE IN ECONOMICS — Mathematical models

Spatial pricing and differentiated markets / edited by G. Norman. — London : Pion, 1986. — 190p. — (London papers in regional science ; 16)

SPACE LAW

BOGAERT, E. R. C. van
Aspects of space law / E.R.C. van Bogaert. — Deventer ; London : Kluwer, c1986. — ix, 307p. — *Includes index. — Bibliography: p.287-303*

Pravovye problemy poletov cheloveka v kosmos / otv. redaktor V. S. Vereshchetin. — Moskva : Nauka, 1986. — 222p

SPACE PERCEPTION

OSTROWETSKY, Sylvia
L'imaginaire bâtisseur : les villes nouvelles françaises / préface de Louis Marin. — Paris : Librairie des Méridiens, 1983. — viii,345p. — *Bibliography: p331-342*

TOREN, Christina Camden
Symbolic space and the construction of hierarchy : an anthropological and cognitive development study in a Fijian village / by Christina Toren. — 523 leaves. — *PhD (Arts) 1986 LSE. — Leaves 432-512 are appendices*

SPACE SCIENCES — France

CHABBERT, Bernard
Les fils d'Ariane / Bernard Chabbert. — Paris : Plon, 1986. — 248p

SPACE STATIONS — Legal status, laws, etc

UNIVERSITY OF COLOGNE. Institute of Air and Space Law. International Colloquium (1984 : Hamburg)
Space stations : legal aspects of scientific and commercial use in a framework of transatlantic cooperation : proceedings... / organized by the Institute...and the German Society of Aeronautics and Astronautics in cooperation with the Federal Ministry for Research and Technology ; edited by Karl-Heinz Böckstiegel. — Cologne : Carl Heymanns, 1985. — vii,253p. — (Studies in Air and Space Law ; Vol.5)

SPACE WARFARE

BANKS, Robert
Special report on the exploitation of space / Robert Banks. — Brussels : North Atlantic Assembly, 1986. — ii,31p

BARNABY, Frank
What on earth is Star Wars? : a guide to the Strategic Defence Initiative / Frank Barnaby. — London : Fourth Estate, 1986. — [184]p. — *Includes bibliography and index*

BULKELEY, Rip
Space weapons : deterrence or delusion? / Rip Bulkeley and Graham Spinardi ; edited by Christopher Meredith ; foreword by Brian Aldiss. — Cambridge : Polity, 1986. — xv,378p. — *Bibliography: p347-358. — Includes index*

JOHNSON, Nicholas L.
Soviet military strategy in space / Nicholas L. Johnson. — London : Jane's, 1987. — 287p

Krieg der Sterne : ein amerikanischer Traum für Europa / herausgegeben von Andreas Orth. — Frankfurt am Main : Robinson, 1985. — 183p

MARSH, Peter, 1952-
The space business : a manual on the commercial uses of space / Peter Marsh. — Harmondsworth : Penguin, 1985. — 232p. — *Further reading: p[211]-217*

SPACE WARFARE
continuation

SCHROEER, Dietrich
Directed-energy weapons and strategic defence : a primer / Dietrich Schroeer. — London : International Institute for Strategic Studies, 1987. — 69p. — (Adelphi papers ; 221)

THOMAS, Hugh, 1931-
Mr Gorbachev's own star wars / Hugh Thomas. — London : Centre for Policy Studies, 1986. — 15p. — (C.P.S. policy challenge)

SPACE WEAPONS
Space weapons and international security / edited by Bhupendra Jasani. — Oxford : Oxford University Press, 1986. — xvi,366p. — *Written for the Stockholm International Peace Research Institute.* — Bibliography: p353-354 Includes index

"Zvezdnye voiny" : illiuzii i opasnosti / [redaktor L. I. Dvinina]. — Moskva : Voennoe izd-vo, 1985. — 55p

SPAIN — Armed Forces
PEREDA, Antonio
La tropa atropellada : el servicio militar hoy / Antonio Pereda. — [Madrid] : Revolución, [1984]. — 192p. — (Colección nuestra lucha)

SPAIN — Armed forces — Civil rights — Congresses
Libertades publicas y fuerzas armadas : actas de las jornadas de estudio celebradas en el Instituto de Derechos Humanos de la Universidad Complutense, Madrid, 4-24 Febrero, 1984 / presentación y edición a cargo de Luis Prieto y Carlos Bruquetas. — Madrid : Centro de Publicaciones del Ministerio de Educación y Ciencia, 1985. — 926p. — *Bibliography: p915-917*

SPAIN — Armed forces — Political activity
CAPARRÓS, Francisco
La UMD : militares rebeldes / Francisco Caparrós. — Barcelona : Argos Vergara, 1983. — 170p

FERNÁNDEZ, Carlos
Tensiones militares durante el franquismo / Carlos Fernández. — Barcelona : Plaza & Janes Editores, 1985. — 223p. — *Bibliography: p[219]-223*

LLEIXÀ, Joaquim
Cien años de militarismo en España : funciones estatales confiadas al Ejército en la Restauración y el franquismo / Joaquim Lleixà. — Barcelona : Editorial Anagrama, 1986. — 217p

SPAIN — Boundaries — France
FERNANDEZ DE CASADEVANTE ROMANI, Carlos
La frontera hispano-francesca y las relaciones de vecindad : (especial referncia al sector fronterizo del País Vasco) / Carlos Fernandez de Casadevante Romani. — [Bilbao] : Universidad del País Vasco, 1985. — xx,547p. — *Bibliography: p[507]-539*

SPAIN — Census, 1981
Censo de población de 1981. — Madrid : Instituto Nacional de Estadistica
t.2: Resultados por Comunidades Autónomas
1a parte: Características de la población. — 1985. — 17v

SPAIN — Civilization
CROW, John Armstrong
Spain : the root and the flower : an interpretation of Spain and the Spanish people / John A. Crow. — 3rd ed., expanded and updated. — Berkeley : University of California Press, c1985. — x, 455 p.. — *Includes index.* — Bibliography: p. 435-439

SPAIN — Colonies — America
CASAS, Bartolomé de las
Brevísima relación de la destrucción de las Indias / Bartolomé de las Casas. — [Madrid] : Anjana, [ca.1983]. — 104p. — *Publicado originalmente en 1552*

SPAIN — Colonies — America — Administration
COLE, Jeffrey A
The Potosí mita, 1573-1700 : compulsory Indian labor in the Andes / Jeffrey A. Cole. — Stanford, Calif. : Stanford University Press, 1985. — xi, 206p. — *Includes index.* — Bibliography: p.187-196

SPAIN — Colonies — America — Economic policy
ANDRIEN, Kenneth J.
Crisis and decline : the Viceroyalty of Peru in the seventeenth century / Kenneth J. Andrien. — 1st ed. — Albuquerque : University of New Mexico Press, c1985. — x, 287 p.. — *Includes index.* — Bibliography: p. 263-275

SPAIN — Commerce
EUROFI (U.K.) LIMITED
Spain / compiled by Eurofi (U.K.) Limited. — Northill : Eurofi (U.K.), 1986. — 173p. — (European Business Reports / Eurofi (U.K.) Limited). — *Bibliography: p171-173*

GUIMERÁ RAVINA, Agustín
Burgesía extranjera y comercio atlántico : la empresa comercial irlandesa en Canarias : 1703-1771 / Agustín Guimerá Ravina. — Tenerife : Consejería de Cultura y Deportes, 1985. — 478p

SPAIN — Commerce — European Economic Community countries
ALONSO, Jose Antonio
La empresa exportadora español frente a Iberoamerica y la CEE / Jose Antonio Alonso, Vicente Donoso. — Madrid : Ediciones Cultura Hispanica del Instituto de Cooperación Iberoamericana, 1985. — xiii,263p. — *Bibliography: p193-199*

SPAIN — Commerce — Latin America
ALONSO, Jose A.
Efectos de la adhesión de España a la CEE sobre las exportaciones de Iberoamerica / Jose A. Alonso, Vicente Donoso. — Madrid : Ediciones Cultura Hispanica, 1983. — 316p. — *Bibliography: p305-310*

ALONSO, Jose Antonio
La empresa exportadora español frente a Iberoamerica y la CEE / Jose Antonio Alonso, Vicente Donoso. — Madrid : Ediciones Cultura Hispanica del Instituto de Cooperación Iberoamericana, 1985. — xiii,263p. — *Bibliography: p193-199*

SPAIN — Commercial policy
ESCUELA SUPERIOR DE GESTIÓN COMERCIAL Y MARKETING (ESIC). Gabinete de Estudios
Consecuencias para la economia española de la integracion de España en la C.E.E.. — Madrid : Ediciones ESIC, 1986. — 227p. — (Estudios ESIC ; 11)

SPAIN — Constitution
Comentarios a la Constitución / Fernando Garrido Falla...[et al.]. — 2a ed.. — Madrid : Editorial Civitas, 1985. — 2503p

ESTEBAN, Jorge de
El régimen constitucional español / Jorge de Esteban y Luis López Guerra con la colaboración de Joaquín García Morillo y Pablo Pérez Tremps. — Barcelona : Labor
1. — 1984. — 352p

ESTEBAN, Jorge de
El régimen constitucional español / Jorge de Esteban y Luis López Guerra con la colaboración de Eduardo Espín y Joaquín Garcia Morillo. — Barcelona : Labor
2. — 1984. — 425p

JUAN ASENJO, Oscar de
La Constitución economica española : iniciativa económica pública "versus" iniciativa económica privada en la Constitución española de 1978 / Oscar de Juan Asenjo. — Madrid : Centor de Estudios Constitucionales, 1984. — 371p. — (Estudios constitucionales). — *Bibliography: p345-371*

SANCHEZ AGESTA, Luis
Sistema politico de la Constitución española de 1978 : ensayo de un sistema : (diez lecciones sobre la Constitución de 1978) / Luis Sanchez Agesta. — 4a ed. — Madrid : Editorial Revista de Derecho Privado, 1985. — 559p

SPAIN — Constitutional history
ATTARD, Emilio
El cambio, antes y después : dos años de felipismo / Emilio Attard. — Barcelona : Argos Vergara, 1984. — 295,xp

BALLBÉ, Manuel
Orden público y militarismo en la España constitucional (1812-1983) / Manuel Ballbé ; prólogo de Eduardo García de Entrería. — 2a ed. — Madrid : Alianza, 1985. — iv,488p

BONIME-BLANC, Andrea R
Spain's transition to democracy : the politics of constitution-making / Andrea R. Bonime-Blanc. — Boulder : Westview Press, 1986. — p. cm. — (Studies of the Research Institute on International Change, Columbia University). — *Includes index.* — Bibliography: p

PASCUAL MARTÍNEZ, Pedro
Partidos politicos y constituciones de España / Pedro Pascual. — Madrid : Fragua, 1986. — x,521p. — *Bibliography: p515-521*

SPAIN — Constitutional law
Comentarios a la Constitución / Fernando Garrido Falla...[et al.]. — 2a ed.. — Madrid : Editorial Civitas, 1985. — 2503p

ESTEBAN, Jorge de
El régimen constitucional español / Jorge de Esteban y Luis López Guerra con la colaboración de Joaquín García Morillo y Pablo Pérez Tremps. — Barcelona : Labor
1. — 1984. — 352p

ESTEBAN, Jorge de
El régimen constitucional español / Jorge de Esteban y Luis López Guerra con la colaboración de Eduardo Espín y Joaquín Garcia Morillo. — Barcelona : Labor
2. — 1984. — 425p

GARCÍA-ESCUDERO MARQUEZ, Piedad
El nuevo régimen local español : estudio sistemático de la Ley 7/1985 de 2 de abril, reguladora de las bases del régimen local / Piedad García-Escudero Marquez, Benigno Pendás García ; prólogo de Fernando Sainz Moreno. — Barcelona : Praxis, 1985. — xii,564p. — *Bibliographies*

MUÑOZ MACHADO, Santiago
El Estado, el derecho interno y la Comunidad Europea / Santiago Muñoz Machado. — Madrid : Editorial Civitas, 1986. — 300p. — *Bibliography: p[291]-300*

RAMIREZ, Manuel
La participatión politica / Manuel Ramirez. — Madrid : Tecnos, 1985. — 157p. — (Temas clave de la constitución española)

SANCHEZ AGESTA, Luis
Sistema politico de la Constitución española de 1978 : ensayo de un sistema : (diez lecciones sobre la Constitución de 1978) / Luis Sanchez Agesta. — 4a ed. — Madrid : Editiorial Revista de Derecho Privado, 1985. — 559p

El sistema juridico de las comunidades autonomas / Eliseo Aja...[et al.]. — Madrid : Tecnos, 1985. — 476p. — *Bibliograhies*

SOLÉ TURA, Jordi
Nacionalidades y nacionalismos en España : autonomías, federalismo, autodeterminación / Jordi Solé Tura. — Madrid : Alianza Editorial, 1985. — 233p. — *Bibliography: p227-233*

TORRES DEL MORAL, Antonio
Principios de derecho constitucional español / Antonio Torres del Moral. — Madrid : Atomo ediciones
1. — 1985. — xv,351p

SPAIN — Constitutional law
continuation

TORRES DEL MORAL, Antonio
Principios de derecho constitucional español / Antonio Torres del Moral. — Madrid : Atomo ediciones 2. — 1986. — xi,446p

VANDELLI, Luciano
El ordenamiento español de las comunidades autónomas / Luciano Vandelli ; prologo de Eduardo García de Enterria ; traducción española: Fernando Lopez Ramón, Pablo Lucas Murillo de la Cueva. — Madrid : Instituto de Estudios de Administración Local, 1982. — 431p. — *Bibliography: p415-431*

SPAIN — Defenses

FISAS, Vicenç
Una alternativa a la politica de defensa en España / Vicenç Fisas Armengol. — Barcelona : Fontamara, 1985. — 293p. — (Paz y conflictos). — *Bibliography: p111-126*

SPAIN — Description and travel — 1981

EUROFI (U.K.) LIMITED
Spain / compiled by Eurofi (U.K.) Limited. — Northill : Eurofi (U.K.), 1986. — 173p. — (European Business Reports / Eurofi (U.K.) Limited). — *Bibliography: p171-173*

SPAIN — Economic conditions

Acracia. — Barcelona : Acracia, 1886-1888. — *Irregular*

La modernización económica de España 1830-1930 / compilación de Nicolás Sánchez-Albornoz. — Madrid : Alianza Editorial, 1985. — 343p

La pobreza en España y sus causas / obra dirigida por Jesus Garcia Valcarcel. — 2a ed. — Madrid : Fundación AGAPE, 1985. — xx,759p

UNIVERSIDAD COMPLUTENSE DE MADRID. Coloquio sobre la España Contemporánea (1 : Madrid : 1983)
España, 1898-1936, estructuras y cambio : Coloquio de la Universidad Complutense sobre la España Contemporánea / edición de José Luis García Delgado ; M. Tuñón de Lara. — Madrid : the Universidad, 1984. — 452p

VOLTES, Pedro
Cuestiones vivas de la historia economica de España / Pedro Voltes. — Madrid : Tecnos, 1985. — 141p. — *Bibliography: p141*

SPAIN — Economic conditions — 19th century

OJEDA, Germán
Asturias en la industrialización española, 1833-1907 / por Germán Ojeda. — Madrid : Siglo veintiuno ; Oviedo : Universidad de Oviedo, Servicio de publicaciones, 1985. — xi,472p. — *Bibliography: p[437]-459*

SPAIN — Economic conditions — 20th century

NIETO DE ALBA, Ubaldo
De la dictadura al socialismo democrático : análisis sobre el cambio de modelo socioeconómico en España / Ubaldo Nieto de Alba. — Madrid : Unión Editorial, 1984. — 269p

SPAIN — Economic conditions — 1918-1975

HERNÁNDEZ ANDREU, Juan
España y la crisis de 1929 / Juan Hernández Andreu. — Madrid : Espasa-Calpe, 1986. — 260p. — *Bibliography: p[167]-172*

SERRA Y MORET, Manuel
Introducción al "Manifiesto del Partido Comunista" y otros escritos / Manuel Serra y Moret ; estudio preliminar y notas aríticas a crgo de Antoni Jutglar. — [Barcelona] : Anthropos, Editorial del Hombre, 1984. — 279p. — (Historia, ideas y textos ; 9)

TAMAMES, Ramón
Estructura económica de España / Ramón Tamames. — [Madrid] : Alianza Editorial, c1985. — xxx,772p. — (Alianza universidad textos ; [97])

SPAIN — Economic conditions — 1975-

ARGANDOÑA, Antonio
Para entender la crisis económica española / Antonio Argandoña. — 2a ed. — Madrid : Tecnos, 1984. — 221p

BELTRÁN, Lucas
La nueva economía liberal : un horizonte para la economía española / Lucas Bettrán. — [Madrid] : Instituto de Economía de Mercado : Fundación Canovas del Castillo, c1982. — 188p. — (Biblioteca del pensamiento conservador. Moderna). — *Bibliography: p183-185*

BRAÑA, Javier
El Estadio y el cambio tecnológico en la industrialización tardía : un analisis del caso español / Javier Braña, Mikel Buesa, Jose Molero. — México ; Madrid : Fondo de Cultura Económica, 1984. — 380p. — *Bibliography: p345-375*

España : un presente para el futuro. — [Madrid] : Instituto de Estudios Económicos. — (Colección tablero)
1: La sociedad / J. Linz...[et al.]. — c1984. — 448p

España : un presente para el futuro. — [Madrid] : Instituto de Estudios Económicos. — (Colección tablero)
2: Las instituciones / E. García de Enterría...[et al.]. — c1984. — 445p

EUROFI (U.K.) LIMITED
Spain / compiled by Eurofi (U.K.) Limited. — Northill : Eurofi (U.K.), 1986. — 173p. — (European Business Reports / Eurofi (U.K.) Limited). — *Bibliography: p171-173*

Nuevas tecnologías, economía y sociedad en España / Manuel Castells...[et al.] ; prólogo de Felipe González. — Madrid : Alianza Editorial Vol.1. — 1986. — xvi,493p

Nuevas tecnologías, economía y sociedad en España / Manuel Castells...[et al.] ; prólogo Felipe González. — Madrid : Alianza Editorial . — *Bibliography: p[1047]-1056* Vol.2. — 1986. — x,503-1056p

SÁNCHEZ CREUS, Fernando
Estudio socio-laboral de la empresa española : segundo análisis / estudio dirigido por Fernando Sánchez Creus y Emilio Arevalo Eizaguirre. — [Madrid] : Asociación para el Progreso de la Dirección, 1983. — 259p

TAMAMES, Ramón
Estructura económica de España / Ramón Tamames. — [Madrid] : Alianza Editorial, c1985. — xxx,772p. — (Alianza universidad textos ; [97])

SPAIN — Economic policy

BELTRÁN, Lucas
La nueva economía liberal : un horizonte para la economía española / Lucas Bettrán. — [Madrid] : Instituto de Economía de Mercado : Fundación Canovas del Castillo, c1982. — 188p. — (Biblioteca del pensamiento conservador. Moderna). — *Bibliography: p183-185*

LLUCH, Ernest
Agronomía y fisiocracia en España (1750-1820) / Ernest Lluch y Lluís Argemí d´Abadal ; prólogo y epílogo por Fabian Estapé. — Valencia : Institución Alfonso el Magnánimo : Institució Valenciana d'estudis i Investigació, [1985]. — lxi,215p. — (Estudios universitarios ; 11)

MARAVALL, Fernando
Economía y política industrial en España / Fernando Maravall. — Madrid : Ediciones Pirámide, 1987. — 231p. — *Bibliographies*

La modernización económica de España 1830-1930 / compilación de Nicolás Sánchez-Albornoz. — Madrid : Alianza Editorial, 1985. — 343p

RIAL, James H.
Revolution from above : the Primo de Rivera dictatorship in Spain, 1923-1930 / James H. Rial. — Cranbury, N.J. ; London : Associated University Press, 1986. — 256 p.. — *Includes index.* — *Bibliography: p. 235-251*

SPAIN. Ministerio de Economía y Hacienda. Secretaría General de Economía y Planificación
Programa económico a medio plazo. — [Madrid] : the Ministerio, [1985]. — 6v. in case

SPAIN — Economic policy — 1975-

ARGANDOÑA, Antonio
Para entender la crisis económica española / Antonio Argandoña. — 2a ed. — Madrid : Tecnos, 1984. — 221p

ESCUELA SUPERIOR DE GESTIÓN COMERCIAL Y MARKETING (ESIC). Gabinete de Estudios
Consecuencias para la economia española de la integracion de España en la C.E.E.. — Madrid : Ediciones ESIC, 1986. — 227p. — (Estudios ESIC ; 11)

GÁMIR, Luis
Contra el paro y la crisis en España / Luis Gamir. — Barcelona : Planeta, 1985. — 330p

JUAN ASENJO, Oscar de
La Constitución económica española : iniciativa económica pública "versus" iniciativa económica privada en la Constitución española de 1978 / Oscar de Juan Asenjo. — Madrid : Centor de Estudios Constitucionales, 1984. — 371p. — (Estudios constitucionales). — *Bibliography: p345-371*

MARTIN MATEO, Ramón
Derecho público de la economía / Ramón Martin Mateo. — Madrid : CEURA, 1985. — 416p. — *Bibliographies*

PARIS EGUILAZ, Higinio
España en el socialismo actual / por Higinio Paris Eguilaz. — Madrid : [s.n.], 1984. — 235p

PARTIDO COMUNISTA DE ESPAÑA. Comisión Económica
Una alternativa a la crisis : las propuestas del PCE / introducción de Nicolás Sartorius. — Barcelona : Partido Comunista de España : Planeta, 1985. — 224p. — (Colección textas ; 86)

PARTIDO SOCIALISTA OBRERO ESPANOL
Un año para la esperanza : [365 días de gobierno socialista]. — Madrid : Equipo de Documentación Política, 1983. — 175p

SPAIN — Foreign economic relations

ALONSO, Antonio
España en el Mercado Común : del Acuerdo del 70 a la Comunidad de Doce / Antonio Alonso ; prólogo de José María de Areilza. — Madrid : Espasa-Calpe, 1985. — 331p. — (Nueva Europa ; 1)

SPAIN — Foreign opinion, British

MALTBY, William S.
The black legend in England, 1558-1660 / by William Saunders Maltby. — Ann Arbor : University Microfilms, [1986]. — 203p. — *Dissertation (PhD)-Duke University, 1966.* — *Bibliography: p191-202*

SPAIN — Foreign relations — Treaties

Tratado de adhesión de España a las Comunidades Europeas. — Madrid : Tecnos, 1986. — xv,583p. — (Practica juridica)

SPAIN — Foreign relations — 18th century

SMITH, Lawrence Bartlam
Spain and Britain, 1715-1719 : the Jacobite issue / Lawrence Bartlam Smith. — New York : Garland Pub., 1987. — 361 p.. — (Outstanding theses from the London School of Economics and Political Science). — *Thesis (Ph. D.)--University of London.* — *Bibliography: p. 344-361*

SPAIN — Foreign relations — 20th century
RUBIO GARCÍA, Leandro
España y la O.T.A.N. / Leandro Rubio García. — [Zaragoza] : Caja de Ahorros de Zaragoza, Aragón y Rioja, [ca.1982]. — 78p. — (Serie papeles diversos / Caja de Ahorros de Zaragoza, Aragón y Rioja)

SPAIN — Foreign relations — 1939-1975
LLEONART Y AMSELEM, A. J.
España y ONU / A. J. Lleonart y Amselem, F. M. Castiella y Maiz. — Madrid : Consejo Superior de Investigaciones Cientificas. — (España y la Organización de las Naciones Unidas ; 1). — Bibliography: p[433]-443
1 (1945-46): La "Cuestion Española" : documentación basica, sistematizada y anotada. — 1978. — lxxv,451p

LLEONART Y AMSELEM, A. J.
España y ONU / por A. J. Lleonart y Amselem. — Madrid : Consejo Superior de Investigaciones Cientificas. — (España y la Organización de las Naciones Unidas ; 2). — Summary in English. — p[327]-332
2 (1947): La "Cuestion Española" : estudio introductivo y corpus documental. — 1983. — xxxi,340p

LLEONART Y AMSELEM, A. J.
España y ONU / A. J. Lleonart y Amselem. — Madrid : Consejo Superior de Investigaciones Cientificas. — (España y la Organización de las Naciones Unidas ; 3). — Summary in English
3(1948-49): La "Cuestion Española" : estudios introductivos y corpus documental. — 1985. — xxv,400p

SPAIN — Foreign relations — France
ACUÑA, Ramón Luis
Como los dientes de una sierra : (Francia-España de 1975 a 1985, una década) / Ramón Luis Acuña. — Barcelona : Plaza & Janes, 1986. — 300p. — Bibliography: p [285]-288

FERNANDEZ DE CASADEVANTE ROMANI, Carlos
La frontera hispano-francesca y las relaciones de vecindad : (especial referncia al sector fronterizo del País Vasco) / Carlos Fernandez de Casadevante Romani. — [Bilbao] : Universidad del País Vasco, 1985. — xx,547p. — Bibliography: p[507]-539

JENSEN, De Lamar
Diplomacy and dogmatism : Bernardino de Mendoza and the French Catholic League / De Lamar Jensen. — Cambridge, Mass. : Harvard University Press, 1964. — xii,322p. — Bibliography: p241-263

SPAIN — Foreign relations — Germany
RUIZ HOLST, Matthias
Neutralität oder Kriegsbeteiligung? : die deutsch-spanischen Verhandlungen im Jahre 1940 / Matthias Ruiz Holst. — Pfaffenweiler : Centaurus-Verlagsgesellschaft, 1986. — vi,231p. — Bibliography: p225-231

SPAIN — Foreign relations — Great Britain
MALTBY, William S.
The black legend in England, 1558-1660 / by William Saunders Maltby. — Ann Arbor : University Microfilms, [1986]. — 203p. — Dissertation (PhD)-Duke University, 1966. — Bibliography: p191-202

SMITH, Lawrence Bartlam
Spain and Britain, 1715-1719 : the Jacobite issue / Lawrence Bartlam Smith. — New York : Garland Pub., 1987. — 361 p.. — (Outstanding theses from the London School of Economics and Political Science). — Thesis (Ph. D.)--University of London. — Bibliography: p. 344-361

SPAIN — Foreign relations — Italy
SAZ CAMPOS, Ismael
Mussolini contra la II República : hostilidad, conspiraciones, intervención (1931-1936) / Ismael Saz. — Valencia : Edicions Alfons el Magnànim, Institució Valenciana d'Estudis i Investigació, 1986. — 265p. — Bibliography: p[255]-265

TUSELL GÓMEZ, Javier
Franco y Mussolini : la política española durante la segunda guerra mundial / Xavier Tusell, Genoveva García Queipo de Llano. — Barcelona : Planeta, 1985. — 299p. — (Espejo de España ; 109). — Bibliography: p293-296

SPAIN — Foreign relations — Portugal
OLIVEIRA, Cesar de
Portugal y la Segunda República española, 1931-1936 / Cesar Oliveira. — Madrid : Ediciones Cultura Hispanica, Instituto de Cooperación Iberoamericana, 1986. — 291p. — Bibliography: p279-281

SPAIN — History — Civil War, 1936-1939
AMETLLA, Claudi
Catalunya paradís perdut : (la guerra civil i revolució anarco-comunista) / Claudi Ametlla ; pròleg del Molt Honorable President de la Generalitat Jordi Pujol. — Barcelona : Editorial Selecta, 1984. — 228p

El final de la guerra civil / [Redactor José Manuel Martínez Bande]. — Madrid : San Martin, 1985. — 396p. — (Monografias de la guerra de España ; no.17). — At head of title: 'Servizio Histórico Militar'. — Contains 10 folding maps. — Bibliography: p[393]-396

SPAIN — History — Civil War, 1936-1939 — Personal narratives
SOMMERFIELD, John
Volunteer in Spain / John Sommerfield. — London : Lawrence & Wishart Ltd., 1937. — 159p

SPAIN — History — Republic, 1931-1939
DÍAZ FERNÁNDEZ, José
Octubre rojo en Asturias / prólogo de J. Díaz Fernández ; introducción de José Manuel López de Abiada. — Gijon : Silverio Cañada, 1984. — 1,205p. — (Colección Reconquista : Libros de Asturias recuperados ; 4). — Reprint of original edition published by Agencia General de Libreria y Artes Gráficas, with a foreword by J. Díaz Fernández - Madrid, 1935

SPAIN — History — Ferdinand and Isabella, 1479-1516
KAMEN, Henry
Spain 1469-1714 : a society of conflict / Henry Kamen. — London : Longman, 1983. — xiv,305p. — Bibliography: p284-293. — Includes index

SPAIN — History — Charles I, 1516-1556
LOVETT, A. W.
Early Habsburg Spain 1517-1598 / A.W. Lovett. — Oxford : Oxford University Press, 1986. — [viii,300]p. — Includes bibliography and index

SPAIN — History — House of Austria, 1516-1700
KAMEN, Henry
Spain 1469-1714 : a society of conflict / Henry Kamen. — London : Longman, 1983. — xiv,305p. — Bibliography: p284-293. — Includes index

SPAIN — History — Philip II, 1556-1598
LOVETT, A. W.
Early Habsburg Spain 1517-1598 / A.W. Lovett. — Oxford : Oxford University Press, 1986. — [viii,300]p. — Includes bibliography and index

SPAIN — History — Philip V, 1700-1746
KAMEN, Henry
Spain 1469-1714 : a society of conflict / Henry Kamen. — London : Longman, 1983. — xiv,305p. — Bibliography: p284-293. — Includes index

SPAIN — History — 19th century
INIGO GÍAS, María Pilar
Zaragoza esparterista (1840-1843) / Maria Pilar Inigo Gias. — Zaragoza : Ayuntamiento de Zaragoza, 1983. — 111p. — Bibliography: p77-81

SPAIN — History — Napoleonic Conquest, 1808-1813
MONTÓN, Juan Carlos
La revolución armada del Dos de Mayo en Madrid / Juan Carlos Montón. — Madrid : Istmo, 1983. — 332p,[4]leaves of plates. — Bibliography: p.323-329

SPAIN — History — Revolution, 1854
URQUIJO Y GOITIA, José Ramón de
La revolución de 1854 en Madrid / José Ramón de Urquijo y Goitia. — Madrid : Consejo Superior de Investigaciones Científicas, Instituto de Historia "Jerónimo Zurita", 1984. — xxi,594p. — Bibliography: p578-584

SPAIN — History — 1868-1931
ARCAS CUBERO, Fernando
El republicanismo malagueño durante la Restauración (1875-1923) / Fernando Arcas Cubero. — Cordoba : Ayuntamiento Cordoba, 1985. — 600p. — Bibliography: p585-593

SPAIN — History — Carlist War, 1873-1876
PEINADO PEINADO, Rufino
Recuerdos de un carlista andaluz : un cruzado de la causa / [Rufino Peinado Peinado] ; Rafael Alvarez de Morales y Ruiz. — Córdoba : Instituto de H.a de Andalucía, [1982?]. — 245 p.. — (Publicaciones Instituto de Historia de Andalucía ; no. 13). — Includes index

SPAIN — History — 20th century
GARRIGA, Ramón
El general Juan Yagüe : figura clave para conocer nuestra historia / Ramón Garriga. — Barcelona : Planeta, 1985. — 282p

GÓMEZ MOLLEDA, María Dolores
La masonería en la crisis española del siglo XX / María Dolores Gómez Molleda. — Madrid : Taurus, 1986. — 537p

HERMET, Guy
L'Espagne au XXe siècle / Guy Hermet. — Paris : Presses Universitaires de France, 1986. — 315p. — Bibliography: p[311]-315

INIESTA CANO, Carlos
Memorias y recuerdos : los años que le vivido en le proceso histórico de España / Carlos Iniesta Cano ; prólogo de Emilio Romero. — Barcelona : Planeta, 1984. — 270p

SPAIN — History — Dictatorship, 1923-1930
AZPÍROZ PASCUAL, José María
La sublevación de Jaca / José Maria Aspíroz Pascual, Fernando Elboj Broto. — Zaragoza : Guara, 1984. — 180p. — (Colección básica aragonesa ; 43). — Bibliography: p[170]-174

MERINO, Julio
Todos contra la monarquia (1930-1931) / Julio Merino. — Barcelona : Plaza & Janes, 1985. — 391p. — (Episodios estelares de la España del siglo XX)

SPAIN — History — 1923-1930 — Congresses
La crisis de la Restauración : España, entre la primera guerra mundial y la Segunda Republica / [contributions by] J. Aróstegui...[et al.] ; edición al cuidado de Jose Luis Garcia Delgado. — Madrid : Siglo Vientiuno, 1986. — ix,429p. — II Coloquio de Segovia sobre Historia Contemporánea de España, dirigido por M. Tuñón de Lara

SPAIN — History — Revolution, 1931
MERINO, Julio
Todos contra la monarquia (1930-1931) / Julio Merino. — Barcelona : Plaza & Janes, 1985. — 391p. — (Episodios estelares de la España del siglo XX)

SPAIN — History — Republic, 1931-1939
BARCO TERUEL, Enrique
El "golpe" socialista del 6 de Octubre de 1934 / Enrique Barco Teruel. — Madrid : Dyrsa, 1984. — 361p

SPAIN — History — Republic, 1931-1939
continuation

GRANT, Ted
 The Spanish revolution 1931-37 / Ted Grant and Peter Taaffe. — London : Militant Publications, 1985. — 64p. — (Marxist studies pamphlets ; 2). — *Bibliography: p63*

MUNIESA, Bernat
 La burguesía catalana ante la II República española / Bernat Muniesa ; prólogo de Antoni Jutglar. — Barcelona : Anthropos. — (Historia, ideas y textos ; 10)
 1: "Il trovatore" frente a Wotan. — 1985. — 321p

MUNIESA, Bernat
 La burguesía catalana ante la II República española (1931-1936) / Bernat Muniesa. — Barcelona : Anthropos. — (Historia, ideas y textos ; 12)
 2: El triunfo de Wagner sobre Verdi. — 1986. — 262p

OLIVEIRA, Cesar de
 Portugal y la Segunda República española, 1931-1936 / Cesar Oliveira. — Madrid : Ediciones Cultura Hispanica, Instituto de Cooperación Iberoamericana, 1986. — 291p. — *Bibliography: p279-281*

Spain in conflict 1931-1939 : democracy and its enemies / edited by Martin Blinkhorn. — London : Sage, 1986. — [304]p. — *Includes bibliography and index*

SPAIN — History — Civil War, 1936-1939

ANDRADE, Juan
 Notas sobre la guerra civil : (actuación del POUM) / Juan Andrade. — Madrid : Ediciones Libertarias, 1986. — 158p

CARR, Raymond
 The civil war in Spain 1936-39 / Raymond Carr. — London : Weidenfeld and Nicolson, 1986. — xvii,328p. — *Originally published under the title The Spanish tragedy, the Civil War in perspective. — Bibliography: p304-313*

A day mournful and overcast : an "uncontrollable" from the Iron Column. — [s.l] : [s.n], 1987. — 27p. — *Originally published, by Nosotros, the daily newspaper in Valencia of the Iron Column in 1937*

SPAIN — History — Civil war, 1936-1939

FERNÁNDEZ SORIA, Juan Manuel
 Educación y cultura en la Guerra Civil : (España 1936-39) / Juan Manual Fernández Soria. — Valencia : NAU Llibres, 1984. — 311p

SPAIN — History — Civil War, 1936-1939

GIRONA I ALBUIXEC, Albert
 Guerra i revolució al País Valenciá (1936-1939) / Albert Girona i Albuixec ; pròleg de Joan Brines. — Valencia : Eliseu Climent, 1986. — 554p. — (Tres i quatre : biblioteca d'estudis i investigacions ; 8)

GRANT, Ted
 The Spanish revolution 1931-37 / Ted Grant and Peter Taaffe. — London : Militant Publications, 1985. — 64p. — (Marxist studies pamphlets ; 2). — *Bibliography: p63*

La guerra civil española : 50 años después / Manuel Tuñón de Lara...[et al.]. — 2a. ed. — Barcelona : Labor, 1985. — 476p. — *Includes Bibliographies*

La guerra civil española : una reflexión moral, 50 años después / José Luis L. Aranguren...[et al.] ; bajo la dirección de Ramón Tamames. — Barcelona : Planeta, 1986. — 219p. — (Espejo de España ; 119)

HERNÁNDEZ GARCÍA, Antonio
 La represión en La Rioja durante la Guerra Civil / Antonio Hernández García. — Logroño : A. Hernández García, 1984. — 3v

HORE, Charlie
 Spain 1936 : popular front on worker's power / Charlie Hore. — London : Socialist Workers Party, 1986. — 36p

SPAIN — History — Civil War, 1936-1939

KELSEY, Graham
 Civil war and civil peace : libertarian Aragon 1936-37 / Graham Kelsey. — Cambridge : Cambridge Free Press, 1985. — 78p. — (Anarchist encyclopaedia ; monograph 1). — *Bibliography: p73-78*

SPAIN — History — Civil War, 1936-1939

NADAL SANCHEZ, Antonio
 Guerra civil en Málaga / Antonio Nadal. — Málaga : Arguval, 1984. — 474p

SPAIN — History — Civil War, 1936-1939

PAECHTER, Henri
 Espagne 1936-1937 : la guerre dévore le révolution / Henri Paechter. — Ed. rev. et augm. par l'auteur. — Paris : Spartacus, 1986. — 235p. — *First ed. "Espagne: creuset politique" published under pseudonyme Henri Rabasseire (Paris: Fustier, 1939)*

SPAIN — History — Civil War, 1936-1939

PALACIO, Léo
 1936: la maldonne espagnole : ou la guerre d'Espagne comme répétition générale du deuxième conflit mondial / Léo Palacio ; préface d'André Fontaine. — Toulouse : Privat, 1986. — iii,490p. — *Bibliography: p[445]-447*

ROCKER, Rudolf
 The tradedy of Spain / Rudolf Rocker. — London ; Doncaster : ASP, 1986. — 48p

SPAIN — History — Civil War, 1936-1939 — Bibliography

GARCÍA DURÁN, Juan
 La guerra civil española, fuentes : archivos, bibliografía y filmografía / Juan García Durán. — Barcelona : Crítica, c1985. — 443p. — (Crítica/historia)

SPAIN — History — Civil War, 1936-1939 — Foreign participation

In defence of liberty : Spain 1936-9 : International Brigade Memorial. — London : International Brigade Association, 1986. — 24p

SPAIN — History — Civil War, 1936-1939 — Foreign participation — French

SERRANO, Carlos
 L'enjeu espagnol : PCF et guerre d'Espagne / Carlos Serrano. — Paris : Messidor/Éditions sociales, 1987. — 292p

SPAIN — History — Civil War, 1936-1939 — Foreign public opinion

FYRTH, Jim
 The signal was Spain : the Spanish aid Movement in Britain, 1936-39 / Jim Fyrth. — London : Lawrence and Wishart ; New York : St. Martin's Press, 1986. — 344p. — *Cover and spine title: The signal was Spain: the Aid Spain movement in Britain, 1936-39*

SPAIN — History — Civil War, 1936-1939 — Participation, American

GERASSI, John
 The premature antifascists : North American volunteers in the Spanish Civil War, 1936-39 : an oral history / John Gerassi. — New York : Praeger, 1986. — xiii, 275 p.. — *"Praeger special studies. Praeger scientific.". — Includes index. — Bibliography: p. 255-269*

SPAIN — History — Civil War, 1936-1939 — Participation, British

CLARK, Bob, 1909-
 No boots to my feet : experiences of a Britisher in Spain 1937-38 / by Bob Clark ; with a foreword by Jack Jones. — Stoke-on-Trent : Student Bookshops Ltd, c1984. — 120p

SPAIN — History — Civil War, 1936-1939 — Participation, Canadian

GERASSI, John
 The premature antifascists : North American volunteers in the Spanish Civil War, 1936-39 : an oral history / John Gerassi. — New York : Praeger, 1986. — xiii, 275 p.. — *"Praeger special studies. Praeger scientific.". — Includes index. — Bibliography: p. 255-269*

SPAIN — History — Civil War, 1936-1939 — Participation, Foreign

Für Spaniens Freiheit : Österreicher an der Seite der Spanischen Republik 1936-1939 : eine Dokumentation / Herausgeber: Dokumentationsarchiv des österreichischen Widerstandes ; Auswahl und Bearbeitung: Mag. Brigitte Galanda...[et al.]. — Wien : Österreichischer Bundesverlag : Jugend und Volk Verlagsges, 1986. — 462p,[32p] of ill. — (Österreicher im Exil 1934-1945)

SPAIN — History — Civil War, 1936-1939 — Personal narratives

BORKENAU, Franz
 The Spanish cockpit : an eyewitness account of the political and social conflicts of the Spanish Civil War / Franz Borkenau. — London : Pluto, 1986, c1937. — [320]p. — (Liberation classics). — *Originally published: London : Faber, 1937*

EDMONDS, Lloyd
 Letters from Spain / Lloyd Edmonds ; edited by Amirah Inglis. — Sydney ; London : Allen & Unwin, 1985. — xiv,200p

GREGORY, Walter
 The shallow grave : a memoir of the Spanish Civil War / Walter Gregory ; edited by David Morris and Anthony Peters ; foreword by Jack Jones. — London : Gollancz, 1986. — [192]p. — *Includes index*

INIESTA CANO, Carlos
 Memorias y recuerdos : los años que le vivido en le proceso histórico de España / Carlos Iniesta Cano ; prólogo de Emilio Romero. — Barcelona : Planeta, 1984. — 270p

MONTSENY, Federica
 El exodo : pasión y muerte de españoles en el exilio / Federica Montseny. — 1. ed. — Barcelona : Galba, 1977. — 305p. — (Memorias) (Galba ; 20)

ORWELL, George
 Homage to Catalonia. — Complete ed. — London : Secker & Warburg, 1986. — [272]p. — (The Complete works of George Orwell ; v.6). — *Author: George Orwell. — Previous ed.: i.e. 2nd ed. 1951*

SPAIN — History — Civil war, 1936-1939 — Personal narratives

PI SUNYER, Carles
 La guerra. 1936-1939 : memòries / Cares Pi Sunyer ; recopilació revisió a cura de Núria Pi-Sunyer. — Barcelona : Editorial Pòrtic, 1986. — 251p

SPAIN — History — Civil War, 1936-1939 — Personal narratives

TARÍN-IGLESIAS, Manuel
 Los años rojos / Manuel Tarín-Iglesias. — Barcelona : Planeta, 1985. — 251p

SPAIN — History — Civil War, 1936-1939 — Personal narratives, American

GERASSI, John
 The premature antifascists : North American volunteers in the Spanish Civil War, 1936-39 : an oral history / John Gerassi. — New York : Praeger, 1986. — xiii, 275 p.. — *"Praeger special studies. Praeger scientific.". — Includes index. — Bibliography: p. 255-269*

SPAIN — History — Civil War, 1936-1939 — Personal narratives, British

CLARK, Bob, 1909-
 No boots to my feet : experiences of a Britisher in Spain 1937-38 / by Bob Clark ; with a foreword by Jack Jones. — Stoke-on-Trent : Student Bookshops Ltd, c1984. — 120p

SPAIN — History — Civil War, 1936-1939 — Personal narratives, Canadian

GERASSI, John
 The premature antifascists : North American volunteers in the Spanish Civil War, 1936-39 : an oral history / John Gerassi. — New York : Praeger, 1986. — xiii, 275 p.. — *"Praeger special studies. Praeger scientific.". — Includes index. — Bibliography: p. 255-269*

SPAIN — History — Civil War. 1936-1939 — Photography
Images of the Spanish Civil War / introduction by Raymond Carr. — London : Allen & Unwin, 1986. — 192p. — *Bibliography: p.191*

SPAIN — History — Civil War, 1936-1939 — Refugees
MONTSENY, Federica
El exodo : pasión y muerte de españoles en el exilio / Federica Montseny. — 1. ed. — Barcelona : Galba, 1977. — 305p. — (Memorias) (Galba ; 20)

SPAIN — History — Civil War, 1936-1939 — Sources
Cockburn in Spain : despatches from the Spanish Civil War / edited by James Pettifer. — London : Lawrence and Wishart, 1986. — 208p

GARCÍA DURÁN, Juan
La guerra civil española, fuentes : archivos, bibliografía y filmografía / Juan García Durán. — Barcelona : Crítica, c1985. — 443p. — (Crítica/historia)

The Guardian book of the Spanish Civil War / edited by R. H . Haigh, D. S. Morris, A. R. Peters. — Aldershot : Wildwood House, 1987. — xx,382p

SPAIN — History — 1939-1975
CIERVA, Ricardo de la
Pro y contra Franco : franquismo y antifranquismo / Ricardo de la Cierva [y] Sergio Vilar. — Barcelona : Planeta, 1985. — 279p. — (Espejo de España ; 114)

EL PAÍS. Equipo de Investigación
Golpe mortal : asesinato de Carrero y agonía del franquismo / El País, Equipo de Investigación ; Ismael Fuente, Javier García y Joaquín Prieto. — [Madrid : Promotora de Informaciones], 1983. — 374p

FERNÁNDEZ, Carlos
Tensiones militares durante el franquismo / Carlos Fernández. — Barcelona : Plaza & Janes Editores, 1985. — 223p. — *Bibliography: p[219]-223*

SUÁREZ FERNÁNDEZ, Luis
Francisco Franco y su tiempo / Luis Suárez Fernández. — Madrid : Fundación Nacional Francisco Franco, 1984. — 8 v.. — (Azor ; núm. 2). — *Includes indexes. — Bibliography: v. 1, p. 37-51*

TUSELL GOMEZ, Javier
Franco y los católicos : la política interior española entre 1945 y 1957 / Javier Tusell. — [Madrid] : Alianza, 1984. — 461p. — (Alianza universidad ; 413)

SPAIN — History — 1975-
España diez años después de Franco (1975-1985) / [articulos por] Rafael Abella ... [et al.] ; introducción de Manuel Fraga Iribarne. — Barcelona : Planeta, 1986. — xiii,243p. — (Espejo de España ; 120)

SPAIN — Industries
CAPDEVILA BATLLES, José
Agricultura e industria española frente a la CEE : aspectos jurídicos, económicos y políticos / José Capdevila Batlles ; prólogo de Edgard Pisani. — Barcelona : Editorial Aedos, 1985. — 252p. — *Bibliography: p245-252*

La empresa española ante la CEE / selección de textos y coordinación Eduardo Bueno Campos. — Madrid : Instituto de Estudios Económicos, 1984. — xxvii,184p. — *Revista del Instituto de Estudios Económicos, 1984, No.2*

La empresa española en las Comunidades Europeas : temas clave de gestión / por Lluís Riera i Figueras...[et al.] ; prólogo por Manuel Marín. — Barcelona : Editorial Hispano Europea, 1986. — 423p. — (Colección ESADE " Estudios de la Empresa). — *Bibliographies*

Informe anual sobre la industria española. — Madrid : Ministerio de Industria y Energia, 1984-. — *Annual*

MARAVALL, Fernando
Economía y política industrial en España / Fernando Maravall. — Madrid : Ediciones Pirámide, 1987. — 231p. — *Bibliographies*

SPAIN — Industries — Finance
GUTIÉRREZ, Fernando
La empresa española y su financiación (1963-1982) : (análisis elaborado a partir de una muestra de 21 empresas cotizadas en Bolsa) / Fernando Guti'errez, Eduardo Fernández. — [Madrid] : Banco de España, 1985. — 128p. — (Estudios económicos / Banco de España, servicio de Estudios ; no.38). — *Bibliography: p128*

SPAIN — Industries — History
OJEDA, Germán
Asturias en la industrialización española, 1833-1907 / por Germán Ojeda. — Madrid : Siglo veintiuno ; Oviedo : Universidad de Oviedo, Servicio de publicaciones, 1985. — xi,472p. — *Bibliography: p[437]-459*

SPAIN — Intellectual life — 20th century
DÍAZ, Elías
Pensamiento español en la ero de Franco (1939-1975) / Elías Díaz. — Madrid : Tecnos, 1983. — 219p. — *Bibliography: p[201]-206*

FERNÁNDEZ SORIA, Juan Manuel
Educación y cultura en la Guerra Civil : (España 1936-39) / Juan Manual Fernández Soria. — Valencia : NAU Llibres, 1984. — 311p

SPAIN — Kings and rulers — Biography
NOURRY, Philippe
Juan Carlos : un roi pour les républicains / Philippe Nourry. — 2e éd.. — Paris : Le Centurion, 1986. — 430p

SPAIN — Military policy
ARROJO, Pedro
OTAN : debate directo / Pedro Arrojo. — Zaragoza : Centro de Documentación por la Paz yel Desarme, [1984]. — 32p

España, Europa, occidente : una política integrada de seguridad / textos de: José María de Areilza...[et al.] ; editado por: Bernhard Hagemeyer...[et al.]. — Madrid : Distribución y Comunicación, 1984. — 177p. — *Papers presented at an international colloquium organized by the Konrad Adenauer Stiftung in Madrid, 26-28 October, 1983*

España y la OTAN : textos y documentos / edición preparada por Celestino del Arenal y Francisco Aldecoa. — Madrid : Tecnos, 1986. — 492p. — (Colección Relaciones exteriores de España)

FISAS, Vicenç
Una alternativa a la politica de defensa en España / Vicenç Fisas Armengol. — Barcelona : Fontamara, 1985. — 293p. — (Paz y conflictos). — *Bibliography: p111-126*

SPAIN — Nobility — Biography
MALTBY, William S.
Alba : a biography of Fernando Alvarez de Toledo, third Duke of Alba, 1507-1582 / William S. Maltby. — Berkeley, Calif. ; London : University of California Press, c1983. — xvii, 377p, [8]p of plates. — *Bibliographical notes: p.321-361. — Includes index*

SPAIN — Politics and government
Acracia. — Barcelona : Acracia, 1886-1888. — *Irregular*

Leviatan : revista de hechos e ideas. — Madrid : Leviatan, 1984-. — *Quarterly*

SECO SERRANO, Carlos
Militarismo y civilismo en la España contemporánea / Carlos Seco Serrano. — Madrid : Instituto de Estudios Económicos, 1984. — 458p

YUSTE, José Luis
Las cuentas pendientes de la política en España / José Luis Yuste. — Madrid : Espasa Calpe, 1986. — 382p

SPAIN — Politics and government — 1621-1665
ELLIOTT, J. H. (John Huxtable)
The Count-Duke of Olivares : the statesman in an age of decline / J.H. Elliott. — New Haven : Yale University Press, 1986. — p. cm. — *Includes index. — Bibliography: p*

SPAIN — Politics and government — 19th century
La revolución burguesa en España : actas del Coloquio hispano-alemán celebrado en Leipzig los dias 17 y 18 de noviembre de 1983 / edición e introducción de Alberto Gil Novales. — Madrid : Universidad Complutense, 1985. — 291p

SANCHIS DE LOS SANTOS, Ramón de
Los golpes de Estado en España : de Espoz y Mina a Miláns del Bosch, pasando por Espartero, Prim y otros / Ramón de Sanchis de los Santos ; prologo de: Ramón Serrano Suñer. — Madrid : Vassallo de Mumbert, 1985. — 431p

SPAIN — Politics and government — 1808-1814
MERCADER RIBA, Juan
Jose Bonaparte Rey de España (1808-1813) / Juan Mercader Riba. — Madrid : Consejo Superior de Investigaciones Científicas, Instituto de Historia "Jerónimo Zurita". — *Part 1, "Historia externa del reinado", published 1971*
[2]: Estructura de estado español bonapartista. — 1983. — 634p

SPAIN — Politics and government — 1868-1875
GUTIÉRREZ LLORET, Rosa Ana
Republicanos y liberales : la revolución de 1868 y la I.a República en Alicante / Rosa Ana Gutiérrez Lloret. — Alicante : Instituto Juan Gil-Albert, 1985. — 188p. — *Bibliography: p175-185*

SPAIN — Politics and government — 1886-1931
COMALADA, Angel
España: el ocaso de un parlamento. 1921-1923 / Angel Comalada. — Barcelona : Ediciones Península, 1985. — 172p. — (Temas de historia y política contemporánea ; 18). — *Bibliography: p167-172*

TUSELL GOMEZ, Javier
La derecha española contemporánea : sus orígenes: el maurismo / Javier Tusell, Juan Avilés. — Madrid : Espasa Calpe, 1986. — 376p. — *Bibliography: p371-376*

UNIVERSIDAD COMPLUTENSE DE MADRID. Coloquio sobre la España Contemporánea (1 : Madrid : 1983)
España, 1898-1936, estructuras y cambio : Coloquio de la Universidad Complutense sobre la España Contemporánea / edición de José Luis García Delgado ; M. Tuñón de Lara. — Madrid : the Universidad, 1984. — 452p

SPAIN — Politics and government — 20th century
CARRASCAL, José María
La revolución del PSOE / José María Carrascal. — [Barcelona] : Plaza & Janes, [1985]. — 306p. — (Política española)

MONREAL, Antoni
El pensamiento político de Joaquín Maurín / Antoni Monreal. — [Barcelona] : Península, [1984]. — 204p. — (Historia, ciencia, sociedad ; 190)

SANCHIS DE LOS SANTOS, Ramón de
Los golpes de Estado en España : de Espoz y Mina a Miláns del Bosch, pasando por Espartero, Prim y otros / Ramón de Sanchis de los Santos ; prologo de: Ramón Serrano Suñer. — Madrid : Vassallo de Mumbert, 1985. — 431p

SPAIN — Politics and government — 1923-1930

RIAL, James H.
Revolution from above : the Primo de Rivera dictatorship in Spain, 1923-1930 / James H. Rial. — Cranbury, N.J. ; London : Associated University Press, 1986. — 256 p.. — *Includes index. -- Bibliography: p. 235-251*

SPAIN — Politics and government — 1923-1930 — Congresses

La crisis de la Restauración : España, entre la primera guerra mundial y la Segunda Republica / [contributions by] J. Aróstegui...[et al.] ; edición al cuidado de Jose Luis Garcia Delgado. — Madrid : Siglo Vientiuno, 1986. — ix,429p. — *II Coloquio de Segovia sobre Historia Contemporánea de España, dirigido por M. Tuñón de Lara*

SPAIN — Politics and government — 1931-1939

AVILÉS FARRÉ, Juan
La izquierda burguesa en la II Republica / Juan Avilés Farré. — Madrid : Espasa—Calpe, 1985. — 397p

MORODO, Raúl
Los orígines ideologicos del franquismo : Acción Española / Raúl Morodo. — Madrid : Alianza, 1985. — 227p. — (Alianza universidad ; 429)

ROSAL, Amaro del
1934 : Movimiento Revolucionario de Octubre / Amaro del Rosal. — [Madrid] : Akal, c1984. — xiii,313p. — (España sin espejo ; 1). — *Bibliography: p313*

TUÑON DE LARA, Manuel
Tres claves de la Segunda República : la cuestión agraria, los aparatos del Estado, Frente Popular / Manuel Tuñon de Lara. — Madrid : Alianza Editorial, 1985. — 367p. — *Bibliographies*

TUSELL GÓMEZ, Javier
Las constituyentes de 1931 : unas elecciones de transición / Javier Tusell ; [con la colaboración de Octavio Ruiz Manjón y Genoveva García Queipo de Llano]. — Madrid : Centro de Investigaciones Sociológicas, 1982. — 206p. — (Colección monografías / Centro de Investigaciones sociológicas ; núm.59). — *Publicado originalmente en Madrid por Universidad Nacional de Educación a Distancia, 1981-1982*

SPAIN — Politics and government — 1939-1945

GARRIGA, Ramón
Franco-Serrano Suñer : un drama político / Ramón Garriga Alemany. — Barcelona : Planeta, 1986. — 209p

JÁUREGUI, Fernando
Crónica del antifranquismo / Fernando Jáuregui, Pedro Vega. — Barcelona : Argos Vergara
2. — 1984. — 428p

SPAIN — Politics and government — 1939-1975

ALVÁREZ ALVÁREZ, Julian
Burocracia y poder político en el regimen franquista : el papel de los Cuerpos de funcionarios en 1938 y 1975 / Julian Alvárez Alvárez. — [Madrid : Instituto Nacional de Administración Pública, c1984. — 130p. — (Publicaciones del Instituto Nacional de Administración Pública) (Biblioteca básica de administración pública. Serie general). — *Bibliography: p127-128*

AREILZA, José María de
Crónica de libertad, 1965-1975 / José María de Areilza. — Barcelona : Planeta, 1985. — 193p

BASTIDA, Francisco J.
Jueces y franquismo : el pensamiento político del Tribunal Supremo en la dictadura / prólogo de J. A. González Casanova. — Barcelona : Editorial Ariel, 1986. — 205p

BERNÁLDEZ, José María
El patrón de la derecha : biografía de Fraga / José María Bernáldez. — [Barcelona] : Plaza & Janes, [1985]. — 281p. — (Biografías y memorias)

CIERVA, Ricardo de la
Pro y contra Franco : franquismo y antifranquismo / Ricardo de la Cierva [y] Sergio Vilar. — Barcelona : Planeta, 1985. — 279p. — (Espejo de España ; 114)

DOMINGUEZ, Javier
Organizaciones obreras cristianas en la oposición al franquismo (1951-1975) : (con 65 documentos clandestinos e inéditos) / Javier Dominquez. — Bilbao : Mensajero, 1985. — 479p

FERNÁNDEZ, Carlos
Franquismo y transición politica en Galicia : (apuntes para una historia de nuestro pasado reciente) 1939-1979 / Carlos Fernández ; con la colaboración de Carlos Luis Rodríguez. — La Coruña : Ediciós do Castro, 1985. — 476p. — (Documentos para a historia contemporánea de Galicia). — *Bibliography: p469-476*

FERRANDO BADÍA, Juan
El regimen de Franco : un enfoque politico-juridico / Juan Ferrando Badía. — Madrid : Tecnos, 1984. — 302p

GILMOUR, David
The transformation of Spain : from Franco to the constitutional monarchy / David Gilmour. — London : Quartet, 1985. — xi,322p. — *Ill on lining papers. — Bibliography: p299-306. — Includes index*

MOYA, Carlos
Señas de Leviatán : estado nacional y sociedad industrial : España 1936-1980 / Carlos Moya. — Madrid : Alianza, 1984. — 356p. — *Bibliographies*

TUSELL GOMEZ, Javier
Franco y los católicos : la política interior española entre 1945 y 1957 / Javier Tusell. — [Madrid] : Alianza, 1984. — 461p. — (Alianza universidad ; 413)

SPAIN — Politics and government — 1975-

ATTARD, Emilio
El cambio, antes y después : dos años de felipismo / Emilio Attard. — Barcelona : Argos Vergara, 1984. — 295,xp

BERNÁLDEZ, José María
El patrón de la derecha : biografía de Fraga / José María Bernáldez. — [Barcelona] : Plaza & Janes, [1985]. — 281p. — (Biografías y memorias)

CACIAGLI, Mario
Elecciones y partidos en la transición española / por Mario Caciagli. — Madrid : Centro de Investigaciones Sociologicas : Siglo Vientiuno, 1986. — x,292p

CAPARRÓS, Francisco
La UMD : militares rebeldes / Francisco Caparrós. — Barcelona : Argos Vergara, 1983. — 170p

DÍAZ, Elías
Socialismo en España : el Partido y el Estado / Elías Díaz. — 1a ed. — Madrid : Mezquita, 1982. — 253 p.. — (Serie política ; 4). — *Includes bibliographical references and index*

España : un presente para el futuro. — [Madrid] : Instituto de Estudios Económicos. — (Colección tablero)
2: Las instituciones / E. García de Enterría...[et al.]. — c1984. — 445p

España diez años después de Franco (1975-1985) / [articulos por] Rafael Abella ... [et al.] ; introducción de Manuel Fraga Iribarne. — Barcelona : Planeta, 1986. — xiii,243p. — (Espejo de España ; 120)

FRAGA IRIBARNE, Manuel
Razón de Estado y pasión de Estado / Manuel Fraga Iribarne. — [Barcelona] : Planeta. — *"Discursos parlamentarios pronunciados entre 1978 y 1984"*
1. — 1985. — 332p

FRAGA IRIBARNE, Manuel
Razón de Estado y pasión de Estado / Manuel Fraga Iribarne. — [Barcelona] : Planeta. — *"Discursos parlamentarios pronunciados entre 1978 y 1984"*
2. — 1985. — xi,333-632p

GILMOUR, David
The transformation of Spain : from Franco to the constitutional monarchy / David Gilmour. — London : Quartet, 1985. — xi,322p. — *Ill on lining papers. — Bibliography: p299-306. — Includes index*

MARAVALL, José María
La política de la transición / José María Maravall. — 2a ed. — Madrid : Taurus, 1985. — 301p

PARTIDO SOCIALISTA OBRERO ESPANOL
Un año para la esperanza : [365 días de gobierno socialista]. — Madrid : Equipo de Documentación Política, 1983. — 175p

SANCHEZ AGESTA, Luis
Sistema politico de la Constitución española de 1978 : ensayo de un sistema : (diez lecciones sobre la Constitución de 1978) / Luis Sanchez Agesta. — 4a ed. — Madrid : Editorial Revista de Derecho Privado, 1985. — 559p

SARASQUETA, Antxon
De Franco a Felipe : (España 1975-1985) / Antxon Sarasqueta. — [Barcelona] : Plaza & Janes, [1984]. — 271p. — (Politica Española)

SOLÉ TURA, Jordi
Nacionalidades y nacionalismos en España : autonomías, federalismo, autodeterminación / Jordi Solé Tura. — Madrid : Alianza Editorial, 1985. — 233p. — *Bibliography: p227-233*

SOTELO, Ignacio
Los socialistas en el poder / Ignacio Sotelo. — Madrid : El País, 1986. — 315p

SPAIN — Politics and government — 1976-

MARTÍN VILLA, Rodolfo
Al servicio del Estado / Rodolfo Martín Villa. — Barcelona : Editorial Planeta, 1984. — 229p

SPAIN — Population

RODRÍGUEZ OSUNA, Jacinto
Población y territorio en España : siglos XIX y XX / Jacinto Rodríguez Osuna. — Madrid : Espasa-Calpe, 1985. — 219p. — *Bibliography: p[215]-219*

SPAIN — Population — Statistics

ALCOBENDAS TIRADO, María Pilar
Datos sobre el trabajo de la mujer en España / María Pilar Alcobendas Tirado. — Madrid : Centro de Investigaciones Sociológicas, 1983. — 217 p. ;c19 cm. — (Colección Monografías ; no. 68). — *Bibliography: p. 209-213*

Censo de población de 1981. — Madrid : Instituto Nacional de Estadistica
t.2: Resultados por Comunidades Autónomas 1a parte: *Características de la población.* — 1985. — 17v

SPAIN — Relations — Argentina

SABSAY, Fernando Leónidas
La sociedad argentina : España y el Rió de la Plata / Fernando L. Sabsay. — Buenos Aires : Ediciones Macchi, [1984]. — 288p. — (Colección Ciencas Economicas). — *Bibliography: p[287]-288*

SPAIN — Relations — Europe

HERRERO DE MIÑON, Miguel
España y la Comunidad Económica Europea : Un sí para... / Miguel Herrero de Miñon. — Barcelona : Planeta, 1986. — 225p

SPAIN — Relations — France
SERRANO, Carlos
L'enjeu espagnol : PCF et guerre d'Espagne / Carlos Serrano. — Paris : Messidor/Éditions sociales, 1987. — 292p

SPAIN — Relations — Germany
SEMOLINOS ARRIBAS, Mercedes
Hitler y la prensa de la II República Española / Mercedes Semolinos Arribas. — Madrid : Centro de Investigaciones Sociológicas : Siglo Veintiuno de España, [1985]. — vi.,290p

SPAIN — Relations — Latin America
The Iberian-Latin American connection : implications for U.S. foreign policy / edited by Howard J. Wiarda. — Boulder, Colo. ; London : Westview Press ; Washington, D.C. : American Enterprise Institute, 1986. — xiii,482p. — (Westview special studies on Latin America and the Caribbean). — *Bibliographical notes*

SABSAY, Fernando Leónidas
La sociedad argentina : España y el Rió de la Plata / Fernando L. Sabsay. — Buenos Aires : Ediciones Macchi, [1984]. — 288p. — (Colección Ciencas Economicas). — *Bibliography: p[287]-288*

SPAIN — Relations — Morocco
COMALADA, Angel
España: el ocaso de un parlamento. 1921-1923 / Angel Comalada. — Barcelona : Ediciones Península, 1985. — 172p. — (Temas de historia y política contemporánea ; 18). — *Bibliography: p167-172*

SPAIN — Rural conditions
Historia agraria de la España contemporánea. — Barcelona : Crítica. — (Crítica/historia ; 33)
2: Expansión y crisis (1850-1900) / editores Ramón Garrabou y Jesús Sanz Fernández. — c1985. — 542p

SPAIN — Rural conditions — History
LLUCH, Ernest
Agronomía y fisiocracia en España (1750-1820) / Ernest Lluch y Lluís Argemí d'Abadal ; prólogo y epílogo por Fabian Estapé. — Valencia : Institución Alfonso el Magnánimo : Institució Valenciana d'estudis i Investigació, [1985]. — lxi,215p. — (Estudios universitarios ; 11)

SPAIN — Social conditions
La pobreza en España y sus causas / obra dirigida por Jesus Garcia Valcarcel. — 2a ed. — Madrid : Fundación AGAPE, 1985. — xx,759p

SPAIN — Social conditions — 19th century
MONLAU, Pere Felip
Condiciones de vida y trabajo obrero en España a mediados del siglo XIX / Pere Felip Monlau y Joaquim Salarich ; estudio preliminar y notas críticas a cargo de Antoni Jutglar. — Barcelona : Anthropos, 1984. — 290p. — (Historia, ideas y textos ; 6). — *Reprint of "Higiene industrial" by P. F. Monlau (Madrid, 1856) and "Higiene del tejedor" by J. Salarich (Vich, 1858)*

SPAIN — Social conditions — 1886-1939
UNIVERSIDAD COMPLUTENSE DE MADRID. Coloquio sobre la España Contemporánea (1 : Madrid : 1983)
España, 1898-1936, estructuras y cambio : Coloquio de la Universidad Complutense sobre la España Contemporánea / edición de José Luis García Delgado ; M. Tuñón de Lara. — Madrid : the Universidad, 1984. — 452p

SPAIN — Social conditions — 20th century
NIETO DE ALBA, Ubaldo
De la dictadura al socialismo democrático : análisis sobre el cambio de modelo socioeconómico en España / Ubaldo Nieto de Alba. — Madrid : Unión Editorial, 1984. — 269p

SPAIN — Social conditions — 1939-1975
MOYA, Carlos
Señas de Leviatán : estado nacional y sociedad industrial : España 1936-1980 / Carlos Moya. — Madrid : Alianza, 1984. — 356p. — *Bibliographies*

SPAIN — Social conditions — 1975-
España : un presente para el futuro. — [Madrid] : Instituto de Estudios Económicos. — (Colección tablero)
1: La sociedad / J. Linz...[et al.]. — c1984. — 448p

Nuevas tecnologías, economía y sociedad en España / Manuel Castells...[et al.] ; prólogo de Felipe González. — Madrid : Alianza Editorial Vol.1. — 1986. — xvi,493p

Nuevas tecnologías, economía y sociedad en España / Manuel Castells...[et al.] ; prólogo Felipe González. — Madrid : Alianza Editorial . — *Bibliography: p[1047]-1056*
Vol.2. — 1986. — x,503-1056p

SPAIN — Social life and customs
FERNANDEZ, James W
Persuasions and performances : the play of tropes in culture / James W. Fernandez. — Bloomington : Indiana University Press, c1986. — xv, 304 p.. — *Includes bibliographies and index*

SPAIN — Social policy
PARTIDO SOCIALISTA OBRERO ESPANOL
Un año para la esperanza : [365 días de gobierno socialista]. — Madrid : Equipo de Documentación Política, 1983. — 175p

RIAL, James H.
Revolution from above : the Primo de Rivera dictatorship in Spain, 1923-1930 / James H. Rial. — Cranbury, N.J. ; London : Associated University Press, 1986. — 256 p.. — *Includes index.* — *Bibliography: p. 235-251*

SAMANIEGO BONEU, Mercedes
La elite dirigente del Instituto Nacional de Previsión : un equipo pluriideológico durante la II República / Mercedes Samaniego Boneu. — Salamanca : Departamento de Historia Contemporánea, Universidad de Salamanca, 1984. — 57p. — (Temas científicos, literarios e históricos ; 50) (Estudios y documentos / Departamento de Historia Contemporánea, Universidad de Salamanca ; 2)

SPAIN. Comisión de Reformas Sociales — History
PALOMARES IBÁÑEZ, Jesús María
La Comisión de Reformas Sociales y la cuestión social en Ferrol (1884-1903) / Jesús Ma. Palomares Ibáñes, Ma. del Carmen Fernández Casanova. — [Santiago de Compostela] : Universidad de Santiago de Compostela, 1984. — 202p. — (Monografías de la Universidad de Santiago de Compostela ; no.93)

SPAIN. Guardia Civil — History
PUIG, Jaime J.
Historia de la Guardia Civil / Jaime J. Puig. — [Barcelona] : Mitre, 1984. — 419p. — *Bibliography: p417-419*

SPAIN. Ministerio de Industria y Energía
Informe anual sobre la industria española. — Madrid : Ministerio de Industria y Energia, 1984-. — *Annual*

SPAIN. Ministerio de Trabajo y Seguridad Social
Estadistica de regulacion de empleo / Ministerio de Trabajo y Seguridad Social, Spain. — Madrid : Ministerio de Trabajo y Seguridad Social. Servicio de Publicaciones, 1984-. — *Quarterly*

SPAIN. Tribunal Supremo
BASTIDA, Francisco J.
Jueces y franquismo : el pensamiento político del Tribunal Supremo en la dictadura / prólogo de J. A. González Casanova. — Barcelona : Editorial Ariel, 1986. — 205p

SPANISH LANGUAGE — Dictionaries — English
Population terminology = Terminologie de la population = Terminología de población. — Washington, D.C. : The World Bank, 1986. — iii,27p. — (A World Bank glossary)

SPANISH LANGUAGE — Social aspects — United States — Addresses, essays, lectures
Spanish language use and public life in the United States / edited by Lucía Elías-Olivares ... [et al.]. — Berlin ; New York : Mouton, c1985. — 238 p.. — (Contributions to sociology of language ; 35). — *Includes bibliographies*

SPANISH LANGUAGE — United States — Addresses, essays, lectures
Spanish language use and public life in the United States / edited by Lucía Elías-Olivares ... [et al.]. — Berlin ; New York : Mouton, c1985. — 238 p.. — (Contributions to sociology of language ; 35). — *Includes bibliographies*

SPARE SURVEILLANCE
Satellites for arms control and crisis monitoring / edited by Bhupendra Jasani and Toshibomi Sakata. — Oxford : Oxford University Press, 1987. — xv,176p. — *Under the auspices of Sipri.* — *Includes index*

SPASOWSKI, ROMUALD
SPASOWSKI, Romuald
The liberation of one / Romuald Spasowski. — 1st ed. — San Diego : Harcourt Brace Jovanovich, c1986. — 687 p., [16] p. of plates. — *Includes index*

SPATIAL ANALYSIS (STATISTICS)
NATO ADVANCED RESEARCH WORKSHOP ON ANALYSIS OF QUALITATIVE DATA (1983 : Amsterdam, Netherlands)
Measuring the unmeasurable / editor-in-chief, Peter Nijkamp, co-editors, Helga Leitner, Neil Wrigley. — Dordrecht ; Boston : M. Nijhoff ; Hingham, MA : Distributors for the U.S. and Canada, 1985. — ix, 713 p.. — (NATO ASI series. Series D. Behavioural and social sciences ; no. 22). — *"Proceedings of the NATO Advanced Research Workshop on Analysis of Qualitative Data, Amsterdam, The Netherlands, March 28-April 1, 1983"--T.p. verso.* — *Includes bibliographies*

UNWIN, David J.
Introductory spatial analysis / David Unwin. — London : Methuen, 1981. — xii,212p. — *Includes bibliographies and index*

SPATIAL SYSTEMS
Urban systems : contemporary approaches to modelling / edited by C.S. Bertuglia ... [et al.]. — London : Croom Helm, c1987. — 677p. — *Bibliography: p597-650.* — *Includes index*

SPECIAL DISTRICTS — Illinois
CHICOINE, David L
Governmental structure and local public finance / David L. Chicoine, Norman Walzer. — Boston, Mass. : Oelgeschlager, Gunn & Hain, c1985. — xi, 235 p.. — *Includes bibliographies and index*

SPECIAL DRAWING RIGHTS
The role of the SDR in the international monetary system : studies by the Research and Treasurer's Departments of the International Monetary Fund. — Washington, D. C. : International Monetary Fund, 1987. — vii,62p. — (Occasional paper / International Monetary Fund ; no.51). — *Bibliography: p60-62*

SPECULATION
The GT guide to world equity markets / edited by Charles G. Hildeburn ; editorial advisor David Galloway ; assistant editors Bryan de Caires, Quek Peck Lim, Andrew Luglis-Taylor. — London : Euromoney Publications, 1986. — xi,290p

SPECULATION
continuation

STEIN, Jerome L.
The economics of futures markets / Jerome L. Stein. — Oxford : Basil Blackwell, 1986. — [250]p. — *Includes bibliography and index*

SPECULATION — Mathematical models

GHOSH, S.
Stabilizing speculative commodity markets / S. Ghosh, C.L. Gilbert and A.J. Hughes Hallett. — Oxford : Clarendon, 1987. — [448]p. — *Includes bibliography and index*

SPEECH ACTS (LINGUISHES)

ALLAN, Keith
Linguistic meaning / Keith Allan. — London ; New York : Routledge & Kegan Paul, 1986. — 2v.

SPEECH ACTS (LINGUISTICS)

BILMES, Jack
Discourse and behavior / Jack Bilmes. — New York : Plenum Press, c1986. — p. cm. — *Includes index. — Bibliography: p*

PREISLER, Bent
Linguistic sex roles in conversation : social variation in the expression of tentativeness in English / Bent Preisler. — Berlin ; New York : Mouton de Gruyter, c1986. — p. cm. — (Contributions to the sociology of language ; 45). — *Includes indexes. — Bibliography: p*

SPEECH AND SOCIAL STATUS — Indonesia — Solo

SIEGEL, James T.
Solo in the new order : language and hierarchy in an Indonesian city / James T. Siegel. — Princeton, N.J. : Princeton University Press, c1986. — p. cm. — *Includes index. — Bibliography: p*

SPEECH PERCEPTION

VOSS, Bernd
Slips of the ear : investigations into the speech perception behaviour of German speakers of English / Bernd Voss. — Tübingen : G. Narr, c1984. — 184 p.. — (Tübinger Beiträge zur Linguistik ; 254). — *Bibliography: p. 126-134*

SPEECH SYNTHESIS

WITTEN, I. H
Making computers talk : an introduction to speech synthesis / Ian H. Witten. — Englewood Cliffs, N.J. : Prentice-Hall, c1986. — ix, 150 p.. — *Includes bibliographies and index*

SPENCER, JOHN POYNTZ SPENCER, Earl — Correspondence

SPENCER, John Poyntz Spencer, Earl
The red earl : the papers of the fifth Earl Spencer 1835-1910 / edited by Peter Gordon. — Nothampton : Northamptonshire Record Society
Vol.2: 1885-1910. — 1986. — xii, 387p, [9]p of plates. — (The Publications of the Northamptonshire Record Society ; v.34)

SPENDINGS TAX — United States

TEPLITZ, Paul V
Alternative tax proposals : how the numbers add up / Paul V. Teplitz, Stephen H. Brooks. — Lexington, Mass. : Lexington Books, c1986. — xii, 131 p.. — *Includes bibliographies and index*

SPIES — Canada

STAFFORD, David
Camp X / David Stafford. — New York : Dodd, Mead, 1987. — p. cm. — *Includes index. — Bibliography: p*

SPIES — Great Britain

WEST, Nigel
Molehunt : the full story of the Soviet spy in MI5 / Nigel West. — London : Weidenfeld and Nicholson, 1987. — 208p. — *Bibliography: p.197-199*

SPIES — Great Britain — Biography

PENROSE, Barrie
Conspiracy of silence : the secret life of Anthony Blunt / Barrie Penrose and Simon Freeman. — London : Grafton, 1986. — xix,588p,[20]p of plates. — *Bibliography: p565-567. — Includes index*

SPINOZA, BENEDICTUS DE

SCHMID, J. J. von
Spinoza's staatkundige verhandeling in de ontwikkeling van de staatsleer / J. J. von Schmid. — Leiden : Brill, 1970. — 12p. — (Mededelingen vanwege het Spinozahuis ; 26)

SPIRITUALITY — History of doctrines — 16th century

COHEN, Charles Lloyd
God's caress : the psychology of Puritan religious experience / Charles Lloyd Cohen. — New York : Oxford University Press, 1986. — p. cm. — *Includes index. — Bibliography: p*

SPIRITUALITY — History of doctrines — 17th century

COHEN, Charles Lloyd
God's caress : the psychology of Puritan religious experience / Charles Lloyd Cohen. — New York : Oxford University Press, 1986. — p. cm. — *Includes index. — Bibliography: p*

SPOKANE (WASH.) — Economic conditions

FAHEY, John
The inland empire, unfolding years, 1879-1929 / John Fahey. — Seattle : University of Washington Press, c1986. — p. cm. — *Includes index. — Bibliography: p*

SPOKANE (WASH.) — Social conditions

FAHEY, John
The inland empire, unfolding years, 1879-1929 / John Fahey. — Seattle : University of Washington Press, c1986. — p. cm. — *Includes index. — Bibliography: p*

SPONSORS — Europe — History

LYNCH, Joseph H.
Godparents and kinship in early medieval Europe / Joseph H. Lynch. — Princeton, N.J. : Princeton University Press, 1986. — xiv, 378 p.. — *Includes index. — Bibliography: p [340]-369*

SPORTS — History

BELL, J. Bowyer
To play the game : an analysis of sports / J. Bowyer Bell. — New Brunswick, U.S.A. : Transaction Books, c1986. — p. cm. — *Includes index*

SPORTS — Political aspects — Argentina

ROMERO, Amílcar G.
Deporte, violencia y política : (crónica negra 1958-1983) / Amílcar G. Romero. — Buenos Aires : Editor Centro de América Latina, 1985. — 136p. — (Biblioteca Política Argentina ; 118). — *Bibliography: p[137]*

SPORTS — Political aspects — Ireland

MANDLE, W. F.
The Gaelic Athletic Association & Irish nationalist politics, 1884-1924 / W.F. Mandle. — London : Christopher Helm, 1987. — xi,240p. — *Bibliography: p225-229. — Includes index*

SPORTS — Social aspects

ELIAS, Norbert
The quest for excitement : sport and leisure in the civilizing process / Norbert Elias and Eric Dunning. — Oxford : Basil Blackwell, 1986. — x,313p. — *Ill on lining papers. — Includes index*

SPORTS — Social aspects — History

COMMONWEALTH AND INTERNATIONAL CONFERENCE ON SPORT, PHYSICAL EDUCATION, DANCE, RECREATION AND HEALTH (8th : 1986 : Glasgow)
Sport, Culture, Society : international, historical and sociological perspectives : proceedings of the VIII Commonwealth and International Conference on Sport, Physical Education, Dance, Recreation and Health, Conference '86 Glasgow, 18-23 July / edited by J.A. Mangan and R.B. Small. — London : Spon, 1986. — xi,348p. — *Includes bibliographies and index*

SPORTS — Social aspects — Great Britain

HARGREAVES, John, 19---
Sport, power and culture : a social and historical analysis of popular sports in Britain / John Hargreaves. — Cambridge : Polity in association with Basil Blackwell, 1986. — [275]p. — *Includes bibliography and index*

Sport, leisure and social relations / edited by John Horne, David Jary and Alan Tomlinson. — London : Routledge and Kegan Paul, 1987. — (Sociological review monograph ; 33)

SPORTS — Finland — Statistics

FINLAND. Tilastokeskus
Kulttuuritilasto : Tilastotietoja taiteesta, tiedonvälityksestä, vapaa-ajasta, urheilusta ja nuorisotoiminnasta vuosilta 1930-1977 = Cutlural statistics : Statistical information on arts, communication, leisure, sports and youth activities in 1930-1977. — Helsinki : Tilastokeskus, 1978. — 256p. — (Tilastollisia tiedonantoja = Statistical surveys ; no.60). — *In Finnish, Swedish and English*

FINLAND. Tilastokeskus
Kulttuuritilasto 1981 : Tilastotietoja taiteesta, tiedonvälityksestä, vapaa-ajasta, urheilusta ja nuorisotojmminnasta = Cultural statistics 1981 : Statistical information on arts, communication, leisure, sports and youth activities. — Helsinki : Tilastokeskus, 1984. — 683p. — (Tilastollisia tiedonantoja = Statistical surveys ; no.73). — *In Finnish, Swedish and English*

SPORTS — Great Britain — History

HARGREAVES, John, 19---
Sport, power and culture : a social and historical analysis of popular sports in Britain / John Hargreaves. — Cambridge : Polity in association with Basil Blackwell, 1986. — [275]p. — *Includes bibliography and index*

SPORTS AND STATE

The Politics of sport / edited by Lincoln Allison. — Manchester : Manchester University Press, c1986. — [240]p. — *Includes index*

SPORTS AND STATE — South Africa

JARVIE, Grant
Class, race and sport in South Africa's political economy / Grant Jarvie. — London : Routledge & Kegan Paul, 1985. — ix,107p. — *Bibliography: p97-103. — Includes index*

SPORTS SPECTATORS — History

GUTTMANN, Allen
Sports spectators / Allen Guttmann. — New York : Columbia University Press, 1986. — viii, 236 p.. — *Includes index. — Bibliography: p. [187]-217*

SPRY, IRENE M — Addresses, essays, lectures

Explorations in Canadian economic history : essays in honour of Irene M. Spry / edited by Duncan Cameron. — Ottawa, Canada : University of Ottawa Press, 1985. — 330 p. — *Bibliography: p. 327-330*

SPSS/PC+ (COMPUTER SYSTEM)

NORUŠIS, M. J
SPSS/PC+ / SPSS Inc. ; Marija J. Norušis. — Chicago, Ill. : SPSS, c1986. — p. cm. — *On t.p. the registered trademark symbol "TM" is subscript following "SPSS/PC+" in the title. — Includes index. — Bibliography: p*

SPY STORIES
RUFF, Ivan
Dead reckoning / Ivan Ruff. — London : Heinemann, 1987. — 229p. — *Spy novel written by former LSE student, with some of the plot taking place in and around the LSE*

SQUATTER SETTLEMENTS — Great Britain — Handbooks, manuals, etc.
Ideal home / Jon Preston...[et al.]. — Survival edition. — [London? : Suspect : Hooligan, 1986]. — [127p]

SQUATTER SETTLEMENTS — Pakistan — Lahore
SHAH, Nasra M
Basic needs, woman, and development : a survey of squatters in Lahore, Pakistan / by Nasra M. Shah and Muhammad Anwar. — Honolulu : East-West Population Institute, East-West Center ; Ottawa : International Development Research Centre, c1986. — xii, 163 p.. — *Bibliography: p. [159]-163*

SQUATTERS — England
Squatters' handbook. — 8th ed. — London : Advisory Service for Squatters, 1986. — [50]p. — *Previous ed.: 1980. — Includes bibliography and index*

SQUATTERS — Kenya — History — 20th century
KANOGO, Tabitha
Squatters and the roots of Mau Mau / Tabitha Kanogo. — London : Currey, 1987. — [224]p. — (East African studies). — *Includes bibliography and index*

SRI LANKA — Census, 1981
Sri Lanka census of population and housing 1981 : district report. — [Colombo] : Department of Census and Statistics, [1984-85]. — 1v (in 24 parts)

SRI LANKA — Commerce
ATHUKORALA, Premachandra
Export instability and growth : problems and prospects for the developing economies / Premachandra Athukorala and Frank Cong Hiep Huynh. — London : Croom Helm, c1987. — 244p. — *Bibliography: p221-237. — Includes index*

SRI LANKA — Economic conditions
Review of the economy / Central Bank of Ceylon. — Colombo : Central Bank of Ceylon, 1975-1984. — Annual. — *Continued by: Review of the economy/Central Bank of Sri Lanka*

Review of the economy / Central Bank of Sri Lanka. — Colombo : Central Bank of Sri Lanka, 1985-. — *Annual*

SRI LANKA — Ethnic relations
DE SILVA, K. M
Managing ethnic tensions in multi-ethnic societies : Sri Lanka, 1880-1985 / K.M. de Silva. — Lanham, MD : University Press of America, c1986. — xix, 429 p.. — *Includes index. — Bibliography: p. 379-391*

VAIDIKA, Vedapratāpa
Ethnic crisis in Sri Lanka : India's options / V.P. Vaidik. — 1st ed. — New Delhi, India : National, 1986. — viii, 239 p.. — *Includes index. — Bibliography: p. [221]-231*

SRI LANKA — Foreign relations
KODIKARA, Shelton U
Foreign policy of Sri Lanka : a Third World perspective / Shelton U. Kodikara. — Delhi : Chanakya Publications, 1982. — 224 p., [1] leaf of plates. — *Includes bibliographical references and index*

SRI LANKA — Foreign relations — China
KUMAR, Vijay
India and Sri Lanka-China Relations (1948-84) / Vijay Kumar. — New Delhi : Uppal Publishing House, 1986. — 196p. — *Bibliography: p181-187*

SRI LANKA — Foreign relations — India
KUMAR, Vijay
India and Sri Lanka-China Relations (1948-84) / Vijay Kumar. — New Delhi : Uppal Publishing House, 1986. — 196p. — *Bibliography: p181-187*

SRI LANKA — Governors — Biography
JENKINS, Brian
Sir William Gregory of Coole : the biography of an Anglo-Irishman / Brian Jenkins. — Gerrards Cross : Colin Smythe, 1986. — xi, 339p. — *Bibliography: p.323-332*

SRI LANKA — History
GOONERATNE, Yasmine
Relative merits : a personal memoir of the Bandaranaike family of Sri Lanka / Yasmine Gooneratne. — London : Hurst, 1986. — 269p. — *Bibliography: p251-253*

SRI LANKA — Languages
COORAY, L. J. M.
Changing the language of the law : the Sri Lanka experience / L. J. Mark Cooray. — Québec : Presses de l'Université Laval, 1985. — 183p. — (Travaux du Centre international de recherche sur le bilinguisme ; A-20)

SRI LANKA — Neutrality
SENGUPTA, Jyoti
Non-alignment : search for a destination / Jyoti Sengupta. — Calcutta : Naya Prokash, 1979. — xxii,208p

SRI LANKA — politics and govenment
KUMAR, Vijay
India and Sri Lanka-China Relations (1948-84) / Vijay Kumar. — New Delhi : Uppal Publishing House, 1986. — 196p. — *Bibliography: p181-187*

SRI LANKA — Politics and government
DE SILVA, K. M
Managing ethnic tensions in multi-ethnic societies : Sri Lanka, 1880-1985 / K.M. de Silva. — Lanham, MD : University Press of America, c1986. — xix, 429 p.. — *Includes index. — Bibliography: p. 379-391*

VAIDIKA, Vedapratāpa
Ethnic crisis in Sri Lanka : India's options / V.P. Vaidik. — 1st ed. — New Delhi, India : National, 1986. — viii, 239 p.. — *Includes index. — Bibliography: p. [221]-231*

SRI LANKA — Population — Statistics
Sri Lanka census of population and housing 1981 : district report. — [Colombo] : Department of Census and Statistics, [1984-85]. — 1v (in 24 parts)

SRI LANKA — Relations — India
VAIDIKA, Vedapratāpa
Ethnic crisis in Sri Lanka : India's options / V.P. Vaidik. — 1st ed. — New Delhi, India : National, 1986. — viii, 239 p.. — *Includes index. — Bibliography: p. [221]-231*

SRI LANKA — Bibliography
SAMARAWEERA, Vijaya
Sri Lanka / Vijaya Samaraweera, compiler. — Oxford : Clio, c1987. — xliii,195p. — (World bibliographical series ; 20). — *Includes index*

SRI LANKA. Department of National Archives
SRI LANKA. Department of National Archives
Administration report of the Director of National Archives / Sri Lanka, Department of National Archives. — Colombo : [the Department], 1983-. — Annual. — *Added title in Sinhalese and Tamil*

SRI LANKA. Ministry of Industries and Scientific Affairs
Administration report of the Ministry of Industries and Scientific Affairs / Sri Lanka. — [Colombo] : Ministry of Industries and Scientific Affairs, 1982/83-. — *Annual*

ST. HUGH'S COLLEGE — History
St. Hugh's : one hundred years of women's education in Oxford / edited by Penny Griffin. — Basingstoke : Macmillan, 1986. — [336]p. — *Includes bibliography and index*

ST. VINCENT'S COMMUNITY HOME
St. Vincent's Community Home, Formby, Lancashire / report of the working party. — [London : Department of Health and Social Security], 1975. — 12p

STABLE POPULATION MODEL
IMPAGLIAZZO, John
Deterministic aspects in mathematical demography / J. Impagliazzo ; with 53 illustrations. — Berlin ; New York : Springer-Verlag, 1985. — p. cm. — (Biomathematics ; v. 13). — *Includes index. — Bibliography: p. 179-182*

STADIA — Great Britain — Safety measures
GREAT BRITAIN, Home Office
Guide to safety at sports grounds. — London : H.M.S.O., 1986. — 75p. — *First published 1973*

STALIN, JOSEPH
JACOBY, Russell
Stalin, marxism-Leninism and the left : Russell Jacoby. — Somerville, Mass. : New England Free Press, 1976. — 63p

SOUVARINE, Boris
[Staline. English]. Stalin : a critical survey of Bolshevism. — New York : Arno Press, 1972 [c1939]. — xiv, 690 p. — (World affairs: national and international viewpoints)

STALIN, JOSEPH, 1879-1953
CAMERON, Kenneth Neill
Stalin : Man of contradiction / Kenneth Neill Cameron. — Toronto : NC Press Limited, 1987. — 190p. — *Bibliography: p181-184*

STALKER, JOHN
TAYLOR, Peter, 1942-
Stalker : the search for the truth / Peter Taylor. — London : Faber, 1987. — xii,231p

STAMP-DUTIES — Legal aspects, laws, etc. — Great Britain
MONROE, J. G
Monroe and Nock The law of stamp duties. — 6th ed. / by R.S. Nock. — London : Sweet & Maxwell, 1986. — xli,371p. — *Previous ed.: published as The law of stamp duties. 1976. — Includes index*

STANDARD CHARTERED PLC
STANDARD CHARTERED PLC
Annual report / Standard Chartered PLC. — London : Standard Chartered PLC, 1986-. — *Annual*

STANFORD UNIVERSITY — Students — Attitudes — Case studies
KATCHADOURIAN, Herant A
Careerism and intellectualism among college students / Herant A. Katchadourian, John Boli ; with the assistance of Nancy Olsen, Raymond F. Bacchetti, Sally Mahoney. — 1st ed. — San Francisco : Jossey-Bass Publishers, 1985. — xxvi, 324 p.. — (The Jossey-Bass higher education series). — *Includes indexes. — Bibliography: p. 311-316*

STARVATION
LAPPÉ, Frances Moore
World hunger : twelve myths / by Frances Moore Lappé and Joseph Collins. — New York : Grove Press, 1986. — [x],208p

STATE AID TO HIGHER EDUCATION — Great Britain
GREAT BRITAIN. Parliament. House of Commons. Library. Research Division
The future of higher education / Kay Andrews. — [London] : the Division, 1984. — 25p. — (Reference sheet ; no.84/9). — *Bibliography: p21-24*

STATE BONDS — Law and legislation — United States — History

ORTH, John V
The judicial power of the United States : the eleventh amendment in American history / John V. Orth. — New York : Oxford University Press, 1986. — p. cm. — *Includes index. — Bibliography: p*

STATE FARMS — Russsian S.F.S.R. — Ural Mountains region

Sovkhozy Urala v period sotsializma (1938-1985 gg.) : sbornik nauchnykh trudov / [otv. redaktor R. P. Tolmacheva]. — Sverdlovsk : AN SSR, Ural'skii nauchnyi tsentr, 1986. — 77p

STATE GOVERNMENTS

ABNEY, Glenn
The politics of state and city administration / Glenn Abney and Thomas P. Lauth. — Albany, N.Y. : State University of New York Press, c1986. — p cm. — (SUNY series in public administration in the 1980's). — *Includes index*

NOTHDURFT, William E
Renewing America : natural resource assets and state economic development / William E. Nothdurft. — Washington, D.C. : Council of State Planning Agencies, c1984. — xii, 198 p.. — (Studies in renewable resource policy). — *Includes index. — Bibliography: p. 181-189*

State politics and the new federalism : readings and commentary / edited by Marilyn Gittell. — New York : Longman, c1986. — xv, 544 p.. — *Includes index. — Bibliography: p. 533-535*

STATE GOVERNMENTS — India

GEHLOT, N. S.
State governors in India : trends and issues / N. S. Ghelot [i.e. Gehlot]. — New Delhi : Gitanjali, 1985. — x,388p. — *Bibliography: p367-382*

STATE-LOCAL RELATIONS — England — Bristol

GARRISH, Stephen
Centralisation and decentralisation in England and France / Stephen Garrish. — Bristol : University of Bristol, School for Advanced Urban Studies, 1986. — xvi,160p. — (Occasional paper / University of Bristol, School for Advanced Urban Studies ; 27)

STATE-LOCAL RELATIONS — France — Bordeaux

GARRISH, Stephen
Centralisation and decentralisation in England and France / Stephen Garrish. — Bristol : University of Bristol, School for Advanced Urban Studies, 1986. — xvi,160p. — (Occasional paper / University of Bristol, School for Advanced Urban Studies ; 27)

STATE-LOCAL RELATIONS — United States

Intergovernmental relations and public policy / edited by J. Edwin Benton and David R. Morgan ; prepared under the auspices of the Policy Studies Organization. — New York : Greenwood Press, 1986. — viii, 224 p.. — (Contributions in political science ; no. 156). — *Includes index. — Bibliography: p. [213]-216*

STATE SUCCESSION

YILMA MAKONNEN
The Nyerere doctrine of state succession : Dar es Salaam to Vienna / Yilma Makonnen. — Arusha ; New York : Eastern Africa Publications, 1985. — p. cm. — *Includes bibliographies and index*

STATE, THE

Aspects of late medieval government and society : essays presented to J.R. Lander / edited by J. G. Rowe. — Toronto ; London : published in association with the University of Western Ontario by University of Toronto Press, 1986. — xx,276p

BERKI, R. N.
State, class, nation / R. N. Berki. — Hull : Hull University Press, 1986. — 20p

BODIN, Jean
Les six livres de la République / Jean Bodin ; ouvrage publié avec le concours du Centre National des Lettres ; texte revu par Christiane Frémont, Marie-Dominique Couzinet, Henri Rochais. — [Paris] : Fayard, 1986. — . — (Corpus des oeuvres de philosophie en langue française / sous la direction de Michel Serres). — *Also includes two other works by Jean Bodin: 'Apologie de René Herpin pour la République' (1581), and 'Discours de Jean Bodin, sur le rehaussement et diminution tant d'or que d'argent, et le moyen d'y remedier, aux paradoxes du sieur de malestroit' (1568,1578). Both appear in vol.6. — Reprint of 10th edition of work, published: Lyon: Gabriel Cartier, 1593. — Includes index at the end of vol.6*

DUNLEAVY, Patrick
Theories of the state : the politics of liberal democracy / Patrick Dunleavy and Brendan O'Leary. — Basingstoke : Macmillan Education, 1987. — [400]p

GELLNER, Ernest
Culture, identity, and politics / Ernest Gellner. — Cambridge : Cambridge University Press, 1987. — [200]p. — *Includes bibliography and index*

KING, Roger, 1945-
The state in modern society : new directions in political sociology / Roger King with chapter 8 by Graham Gibbs. — Basingstoke : Macmillan, 1986. — [296]p. — *Includes bibliography and index*

LESSNOFF, Michael H.
Social contract / Michael Lessnoff. — London : Macmillan, 1986. — x,178p. — (Issues in political theory). — *Bibliography: p169-173. — Includes index*

LEVINE, Andrew
The end of the state / Andrew Levine. — London : Verso, 1987. — [200]p

SCHLESINGER, Arthur M. (Arthur Meier), 1917-
Creativity in statecraft / by Arthur Schlesinger, Jr. — Washington : Library of Congress, 1983. — iii,34p. — (Occasional papers of the Council of Scholars ; no. 1). — *Includes bibliographical references*

SMITH, Anthony D. (Anthony David)
The ethnic origins of nations / Anthony D. Smith. — Oxford : Basil Blackwell, 1986. — 1v.. — *Includes bibliography and index*

The State in global perspective / edited by Ali Kazancigil. — Aldershot : Gower [with] UNESCO, 1986. — [350]p. — *Includes bibliography and index*

VINCENT, Andrew
Theories of the state / Andrew Vincent. — Oxford : Basil Blackwell, 1987. — [224]p. — *Includes bibliography and index*

WEISS, Paul
Toward a perfected state / Paul Weiss. — Albany, N.Y. : State University of New York Press, c1986. — xii, 459 p.. — (SUNY series in systematic philosophy). — *Includes indexes. — Bibliography: p. 387-435*

STATE, THE — Addresses, essays, lectures

Bringing the state back in / edited by Peter B. Evans, Dietrich Rueschmeyer, Theda Skocpol. — Cambridge : Cambridge University Press, 1985. — x, 390p. — *Contains bibliographies*

STATE, THE — History

States in history / edited by John A. Hall. — Oxford : Basil Blackwell, 1986. — [256]p. — *Includes index*

STATE UNIVERSITIES AND COLLEGES — United States — Directories

OHLES, John F
Public colleges and universities / John F. Ohles and Shirley M. Ohles. — Westport, Conn. ; London : Greenwood Press, 1986. — x, 1014p. — (Greenwood encyclopedia of American institutions). — *Includes index. — Includes bibliographical references*

STATES, SIZE OF

KOHR, Leopold
The breakdown of nations / Leopold Kohr ; foreword by Ivan Illich. — London : Routledge & Kegan Paul, 1986. — xxvi,244p. — *First published 1957. — Bibliography: p235-237*

STATES, SMALL

KOHR, Leopold
The breakdown of nations / Leopold Kohr ; foreword by Ivan Illich. — London : Routledge & Kegan Paul, 1986. — xxvi,244p. — *First published 1957. — Bibliography: p235-237*

STATESMAN — Canada — Biography

BISSELL, Claude
The imperial Canadian : Vincent Massey in office / Claude Bissell. — Toronto ; London : University of Toronto Press, c1986. — xii, 361p, [23]p of plates. — *Sequel to: Young Vincent Massey*

STATESMAN — Soviet Union — Biography

SCHMIDT-HÄUER, Christian
Gorbachev : the path to power / Christian Schmidt-Häuer ; with an appendix on the Soviet economy by Maria Huber ; edited by John Man ; translated by Ewald Osers and Chris Romberg. — London : I. B. Tauris, 1986. — v,218p

STATESMAN — United States — Biography

Carl Schurz : Revolutionär und Staatsmann : sein Leben in selbstzeugnissen Bildern und Dokumenten = Revolutionary and statesman : his life in personal and official documents with illustrations / herausgegeben von/edited by Rüdiger Wersich. — 2.Aufl. — München : Moos, 1986. — *Parallel texts in German and English. — First published 1979*

STATESMEN

SCHLESINGER, Arthur M. (Arthur Meier), 1917-
Creativity in statecraft / by Arthur Schlesinger, Jr. — Washington : Library of Congress, 1983. — iii,34p. — (Occasional papers of the Council of Scholars ; no. 1). — *Includes bibliographical references*

STATESMEN — Addresses, essays, lectures

Intellectuals in politics / edited by Nissan Oren. — Jerusalem : Magnes Press, Hebrew University, 1984. — 106 p.. — *Includes bibliographies*

STATESMEN — Italy — Biography

DE GASPERI, Maria Romana
Mio caro padre : con otto testimonianze / Maria Romana de Gasperi. — 3 ed. — Brescia : Morcelliana, 1981. — 223p. — *First published 1979*

STATESMEN — Australia — Biography

HUDSON, W. J.
Casey / W. J. Hudson. — Melbourne : Oxford University Press, 1986. — xii,361p

STATESMEN — Brazil — Biography

LACOMBE, Américo Jacobina
A sombra de Rui Barbosa / Américo Jacobina Lacombe. — [São Paulo] : Companhia Editora Nacional ; [Brasília : Instituto Nacional do Livro, MEC, 1978]. — x,226p. — (Brasiliana ; volume 365)

STATESMEN — Bulgaria — Addresses, essays, lectures
ZHIVKOV, Todor
Velik sin na Bŭlgariia : dokladi, statii, rechi, razmisli za Georgi Dimitrov / Todor Zhivkov. — Sofiia : Partizdat, 1982. — 454p

STATESMEN — Bulgaria — Biography
Georgi Dimitrov : biografiia / [Dobrin Michev...et al.]. — []2. dop. izd.]. — Sofiia : Partizdat, 1982. — 663p

STATESMEN — Canada — Biography
GRUENDING, Dennis
Emmett Hall : establishment radical / Dennis Gruending. — Toronto, Canada : Macmillan of Canada, c1985. — ix, 246 p., [16] p. of plates. — Includes index. — Bibliography: p. 231-243

STATESMEN — Finland — Biography
JÄGERSKIÖLD, Stig
Mannerheim : Marshal of Finland / Stig Jägerskiöld. — London : Hurst, c1986. — x,210p,[8]p of plates. — Translation of: Gustaf Mannerheim 1867-1951. — Bibliography: p200-202. — Includes index

WARNER, Oliver
Marshal Mannerheim and the Finns / Oliver Warner. — London : Weidenfeld and Nicholson, 1967. — 232p

STATESMEN — Germany — Biography
GALL, Lothar
Bismarck : the white revolutionary / Lothar Gall ; translated from the German by J.A. Underwood. — London : Allen & Unwin. — Translation of: Bismarck. — Originally published under the title, Bismarck der weiss Revolutionaär, Frankfurt am Main : Ullstein, 1980
Vol.1: 1815-1871. — 1986. — [640]p. — Includes bibliography and index

GALL, Lothar
Bismarck : the white revolutionary / Lothar Gall ; translated from the German by J.A. Underwood. — London : Allen & Unwin
Vol.2: 1871-1898. — 1987. — [384]p. — Translation of: Bismarck. — Includes bibliography and index

STATESMEN — Great Britain — Biography
DALTON, Hugh
The political diary of Hugh Dalton, 1918-40, 1945-60 / edited by Ben Pimlott. — London : Cape in association with the London School of Economics and Political Science, 1986. — 737p,[16]p of plates. — Includes index

JAMES, Robert Rhodes
Anthony Eden / Robert Rhodes James. — London : Weidenfeld and Nicolson, c1986. — xiv,665,[16]p of plates. — Includes index

Philip Snowden : the first Labour Chancellor of the Exchequer / edited by Keith Laybourn and David James. — Bradford : Bradford Libraries and Information Service, 1987. — 111p. — Includes index

SPENCER, John Poyntz Spencer, Earl
The red earl : the papers of the fifth Earl Spencer 1835-1910 / edited by Peter Gordon. — Nothampton : Northamptonshire Record Society
Vol.2: 1885-1910. — 1986. — xii, 387p, [9]p of plates. — (The Publications of the Northamptonshire Record Society ; v.34)

STATESMEN — Great Britain — Correspondence
WELLINGTON, Arthur Wellesley, Duke of Wellington / ed. by R. J. Olney and Julia Melvin. — London : H.M.S.O.
2: Political correspondence, November 1834 — April 1835. — 1986. — v, 664p. — (Prime Ministers' papers series)

STATESMEN — India — Biography
COPLEY, Antony
Gandhi : against the tide / Antony Copley. — Oxford : Basil Blackwell, 1987. — v,118p. — (Historical Association studies). — Bibliography: p107-110. — Includes index

EDWARDES, Michael, 1923-
The myth of the Mahatma : Gandhi, the British and the Raj / Michael Edwardes. — London : Constable, 1986. — 270p,[24]p of plates. — Bibliography: p261-262. — Includes index

GANDHI, M. K.
The moral and political writings of Mahatma Gandhi / edited by Raghavan Iyer. — Oxford : Clarendon
Vol.3: Non-violent resistance and social transformation. — 1987. — xx,641p. — Bibliography: p625-630. — Includes index

STATESMEN — Japan — Biography
CONNORS, Lesley
The Emperor's adviser : Saionji Kinmochi and pre-war Japanese politics / Lesley Connors. — London : Croom Helm, c1987. — 260p. — (The Nissan Institute / Croom Helm Japanese studies series). — Includes index

STATESMEN — Nigeria — Biography
PADEN, John N.
Ahmadu Bello, Sardauna of Sokoto : values and leadership in Nigeria / John N. Paden. — London : Hodder and Stoughton, 1986. — xi,799p,[24]p of plates. — Includes bibliographies and index

STATESMEN — Soviet Union — Biography
KING, David, 1943-
Trotsky : a photographic biography / by David King ; commentary by James Ryan ; introduction by Tamara Deutscher. — Oxford : Basil Blackwell, 1986. — 334p

STATESMEN — Spain — Biography
BERNÁLDEZ, José María
El patrón de la derecha : biografía de Fraga / José María Bernáldez. — [Barcelona] : Plaza & Janés, [1985]. — 281p. — (Biografías y memorias)

ELLIOTT, J. H. (John Huxtable)
The Count-Duke of Olivares : the statesman in an age of decline / J.H. Elliott. — New Haven : Yale University Press, 1986. — p. cm. — Includes index. — Bibliography: p

MALTBY, William S.
Alba : a biography of Fernando Alvarez de Toledo, third Duke of Alba, 1507-1582 / William S. Maltby. — Berkeley, Calif. ; London : University of California Press, c1983. — xvii, 377p, [8]p of plates. — Bibliographical notes: p.321-361. — Includes index

STATESMEN — United States — Biography
GALBRAITH, John Kenneth
A view from the stands : of people, politics, military power, and the arts / John Kenneth Galbraith ; with notes by the author ; arranged and edited by Andrea D. Williams. — Boston : Houghton Mifflin, 1986. — p. cm. — Includes index

TOULOUSE, Mark G.
The transformation of John Foster Dulles : from prophet of realism to priest of nationalism / Mark G. Toulouse. — [Macon, GA) : Mercer University Press, c1985. — xlii, 277 p.. — Includes index. — Bibliography: p. [255]-269

WRIGHT, Esmond
Franklin of Philadelphia / Esmond Wright. — Cambridge, Mass. : Belknap Press of Harvard University Press, 1986. — p. cm. — Includes index. — Bibliography: p

STATESMEN — United States — Interviews
CHARLTON, Michael
From deterrence to defence : the inside story of strategic policy / Michael Charlton. — Cambridge, Mass. : Harvard University Press, 1987, c1986. — p. cm. — Based on the author's BBC radio series, The Star wars history. — Includes index

STATICS AND DYNAMICS (SOCIAL SCIENCES)
HARRIS, Milton
Dynamic economic analysis / Milton Harris. — New York : Oxford University Press, 1987. — p. cm. — Includes index. — Bibliography: p

STATISICAL SERVICES
NIITAMO, Olavi E.
Tilastollinen tietohuolto 1980-luvulla = Statistical information service in the 1980's / Olavi E. Niitamo. — Helsinki : Tilastokeskus, 1981. — 37p. — (Tutkimuksia / Finland. Tilastokeskus ; no.68). — In Finnish and English

STATISTICAL DICISION
BROSS, Irwin D. J
Design for decision. — New York : Macmillan, [1953]. — 276 p

STATISTICAL HYPOTHESIS TESTING
JUDGE, George G
Improved methods of inference in econometrics / George G. Judge and Thomas A. Yancey. — Amsterdam ; New York : North-Holland ; New York, N.Y., U.S.A. : Elsevier Science Pub. Co. [distributor], 1986. — xvi, 291 p.. — (Studies in mathematical and managerial economics ; v. 34). — Includes bibliographies and indexes

STATISTICAL OFFICE OF THE EUROPEAN COMMUNITIES
Eurostat news / Statistical Office of the European Communities. — Luxembourg : Statistical Office of the European Communities, 1976-. — Quarterly

STATISTICAL OFFICE OF THE EUROPEAN COMMUNITIES — Catalogs
STATISTICAL OFFICE OF THE EUROPEAN COMMUNITIES
Catalogue of Eurostat publications. — Luxembourg : Office for Official Publications of the European Communities, 1986. — 48p

STATISTICAL SERVICES
SLATTERY, Martin
Official statistics / Martin Slattery. — London : Tavistock, 1986. — 154p. — (Society now) (Social science paperbacks ; 337). — Bibliography: p143-148. — Includes index

Statistics sources : a subject guide to data on industrial, business, educational, financial, and other topics for the United States and internationally / Jacqueline Wasserman O'Brien and Steven R. Wasserman, editors; Kenneth Clansky, assistant editor. — 10th ed. — Detroit : Gale Research Company
Vol.1: A-J. — 1986. — xxix,1001p

Statistics sources : a subject guide to data on industrial, business, educational, financial, and other topics for the United States and internationally / Jacqueline Wasserman O'Brien and Steven R. Wasserman, editors; Kenneth Clansky, assistant editor. — 10th ed. — Detroit : Gale Research Company
Vol.2: K-Z. — 1986. — viii,1003-2014p

STATISTICAL SERVICES — Finland
NIITAMO, O. E.
Long-term planning in the Central Statistical Office of Finland / Niitamo, O. E., Laihonen, A., Tiihonen, P.. — Helsinki : Tilastokeskus, 1981. — 53p,[13]p. — (Tutkimuksia / Finland. Tilastokeskus ; no.71)

STATISTICS
Annales de l'INSEE / Institut National de la Statistique et des Études Économiques. — Paris : Institut National de la Statistique et des Etudes Économiques, 1969-1985. — 3 per year. — Continued by Annales d'Economie et de Statistique/Institut National de la Statistique et des Etudes Economiques

Annales d'économie et de statistique / Institut National de la Statistique et des Études Économiques. — Paris : Institut National de la Statistique et des Etudes Économiques, 1986-. — Quarterly. — Continues Annales de l'INSEE and Cahiers du Séminaire d'Econométrie

STATISTICS
continuation

EHRENBERG, A. S. C
A primer in data reduction : an introductory statistics textbook / A.S.C. Ehrenberg. — Chichester [West Sussex] ; New York : Wiley, c1982. — p. cm. — *Includes index*

Journal of economic and social measurement (formerly Review of public data use). — Amsterdam ; New York : North-Holland, 1986-. — *Quarterly*

KMENTA, Jan
Elements of econometrics / Jan Kmenta. — 2nd ed. — New York : Macmillan ; London : Collier Macmillan, c1986. — xii, 786p. — *Includes index*

MOSES, Lincoln E
Think and explain with statistics / by Lincoln Moses. — Reading, Mass. : Addison-Wesley Pub. Co., c1986. — xii, 483 p.. — *Includes index*

STATISTICS — Charts, diagrams, etc.
CHAPMAN, Myra
Plain figures / Myra Chapman ; in collaboration with Basil Mahon. — London : Her Majesty's Stationery Office, 1986. — 111p. — At head of title: Cabinet Office (Management and Personnel Office) [and] Civil Service College

STATISTICS — Data processing — Handbooks, manuals, etc
SAS INSTITUTE
SAS/STAT guide for personal computers. — Version 6 ed. — Cary, N.C. : SAS Institute, 1985. — 378p

STATISTICS — Dictionaries
Encyclopedia of statistical sciences. — New York ; Chichester : Wiley
Vol.7: Plackett family of distributions to Regression, Wrong. — c1986. — ix,714p. — *Includes bibliographies*

STATISTICS — Graphic methods
DU TOIT, S. H. C
Graphical exploratory data analysis / S.H.C. du Toit, A.G.W. Steyn, R.H. Stumpf. — New York : Springer-Verlag, c1986. — p. cm. — (Springer texts in statistics). — *Includes index. — Bibliography: p*

STATISTICS — History
PETERS, William Stanley
Counting for something : statistical principles and personalities / William S. Peters. — New York : Springer-Verlag, c1987. — xviii, 275 p.. — (Springer texts in statistics). — *Includes index. — Bibliography: p. [261]-268*

STATISTICS — History — 19th century — Bibliography
WESTFALL, Gloria
Bibliography of official statistical yearbooks and bulletins / Gloria Westfall. — Alexandria, Va. : Chadwyck-Healey ; Cambridge : Distributed by Chadwyck-Healey, 1986. — [260]p. — (Government documents bibliographies)

STATISTICS — History — 20th century — Bibliography
WESTFALL, Gloria
Bibliography of official statistical yearbooks and bulletins / Gloria Westfall. — Alexandria, Va. : Chadwyck-Healey ; Cambridge : Distributed by Chadwyck-Healey, 1986. — [260]p. — (Government documents bibliographies)

STATISTICS — Programmed instruction
KAZMIER, Leonard J.
Statistical analysis for business and economics : programmed for effective learning / Leonard J. Kazmier. — 3rd ed. — New York ; London : McGraw-Hill, 1978. — xv,646p. — *With answers. — Previous ed.: 1973. — Includes index*

STATISTICS — Finland
Suomen taloushistoria. — Helsinki : Kustannusosakeyhtiö Tammi. — *Text in English and Finnish*
vol.3: Historiallinen tilasto / toimittanut Kaarina Vattula ; English translation by Sinikka Lampivuo. — 1983. — 470p

STATISTICS CANADA. Travel, Tourism and Recreation Section
Tourism and recreation: a statistical digest = Tourisme et loisirs: résumé statistique / Statistics Canada. Travel, Tourism and Recreation Section. — Ottawa : Minister of Supply and Services, Canada, 1984-. — *Annual. — Text in English and French*

STATUS OFFENDERS — Government policy — United States
Neither angels nor thieves : studies in deinstitutionalization of status offenders / Joel F. Handler and Julie Zatz, editors. — Washington, D.C. : National Academy Press, 1982. — xiii, 949 p.. — "Panel on the Deinstitutionalization of Children and Youth; Committee on Child Development Research and Public Policy; Assembly of Behavioral and Social Sciences, National Research Council.". — *Includes bibliographies and index*

STATUS OFFENDERS — United States — Case studies
Neither angels nor thieves : studies in deinstitutionalization of status offenders / Joel F. Handler and Julie Zatz, editors. — Washington, D.C. : National Academy Press, 1982. — xiii, 949 p.. — "Panel on the Deinstitutionalization of Children and Youth; Committee on Child Development Research and Public Policy; Assembly of Behavioral and Social Sciences, National Research Council.". — *Includes bibliographies and index*

STATUTES — England
CROSS, Sir Rupert
Statutory interpretation / by the late Sir Rupert Cross. — 2nd ed. / by John Bell and Sir George Engle. — London : Butterworths, 1987. — [200]p. — *Previous ed.: 1976. — Includes index*

STATUTES — United States
BARDACH, Eugene
The implementation game : what happens after a bill becomes a law / Eugene Bardach. — Cambridge, Mass. ; London : M.I.T. Press, 1977. — xi,323p. — (MIT studies in American politics and public policy / Massachusetts Institute of Technology ; 1). — *Includes index*

STEAMBOATS — History — 19th century
WOOLCOCK, Helen R.
Rights of passage : emigration to Australia in the nineteenth century / Helen R. Woolcock. — London : Tavistock, 1986. — [xv,304]p. — *Includes index*

STEDELIJK HOGER INSTITUUT VOOR SOCIALE STUDIE
STEDELIJK HOGER INSTITUUT VOOR SOCIALE STUDIE. Werkgroep Inspraak Zwartboek / Werkgroep Inspraak SHISS. — Gent : the Werkgroep, [1975]. — 72p. — *Cover title*

STEEL INDUSTRY AND TRADE
Ailing steel : the transoceanic quarrel / [edited by] Walter H. Goldberg. — Aldershot : Gower, c1986. — xxiv,535p

Crisis in the international steel industry : conference sponsored by the International Law Institute, August 5-8, 1984, Lake Como, Italy. — Washington, D.C. : International Law Institute, 1986. — 143p. — (ILI program proceedings ; 3)

The steel market / Organisation for Economic Co-operation and Development. — Paris : OECD, 1981-. — *Annual*

STEEL INDUSTRY AND TRADE — Government policy — Europe
MÉNY, Yves
La crise de la sidérurgie européenne 1974-1984 / Yves Mény et Vincent Wright ; avec la collaboration de Patrick A. Messerlin... [et al.]. — [Paris] : Presses universitaires de France, [1985]. — 306p

STEEL INDUSTRY AND TRADE — Government policy — European Economic Community countries
LEVINE, Michael K
Inside international trade policy formulation : a history of the 1982 US-EC steel arrangements / by Michael K. Levine. — New York : Praeger, 1985. — p. cm. — *Includes index*

STEEL INDUSTRY AND TRADE — Government policy — United States
LEVINE, Michael K
Inside international trade policy formulation : a history of the 1982 US-EC steel arrangements / by Michael K. Levine. — New York : Praeger, 1985. — p. cm. — *Includes index*

STEEL INDUSTRY AND TRADE — Planning — Mathematical models
KENDRICK, David A.
The planning of investment programs in the steel industry / David A. Kendrick, Alexander Meeraus, Jaime Alatorre. — Baltimore : Johns Hopkins University Press for the World Bank, 1984. — xv,310p. — (The planning of investment programs ; v.3) (A World Bank research publication). — *Bibliographical references: p303-304*

STEEL INDUSTRY AND TRADE — Belgium — Management — Case studies
GANDOIS, Jean
Mission acier : mon aventure belge / Jean Gandois. — Gembloux : Duculot Perspectives, 1986. — 141p

STEEL INDUSTRY AND TRADE — Canada
Metallurgical works in Canada : primary iron and steel = L'activité métallurgique au Canada : fer et acier de première fusion / Energy, Mines and Resources Canada. — Ottawa : Energy, Mines and Resources Canada, 1986-. — *Annual. — Text in English and French*

STEEL INDUSTRY AND TRADE — England — Sheffield Region (South Yorkshire) — History
TWEEDALE, Geoffrey
Sheffield steel and America : a century of commercial and technological interdependence, 1830-1930 / Geoffrey Tweedale. — Cambridge : Cambridge University Press, 1987. — xv,296p . — *Bibliography: p263-287. — Includes index*

STEEL INDUSTRY AND TRADE — Europe
MÉNY, Yves
La crise de la sidérurgie européenne 1974-1984 / Yves Mény et Vincent Wright ; avec la collaboration de Patrick A. Messerlin... [et al.]. — [Paris] : Presses universitaires de France, [1985]. — 306p

The Politics of steel : Western Europe and the steel industry in the crisis years (1974-1984) / edited by Yves Mény and Vincent Wright. — Berlin ; New York : W. de Gruyter, 1986. — p. cm. — (Series C, Political and social sciences =Sciences politiques et sociales ; 7). — *Includes index*

STEEL INDUSTRY AND TRADE — European Economic Community countries
FORUTAN SABZAVARI, Faezeh
The EEC steel industry and the mid 1970s crisis : some aspects of trade policy / by Faezeh Forutan Sabzavari. — 348 leaves. — *PhD (Econ) 1986 LSE*

STEEL INDUSTRY AND TRADE — France — Lorraine
GENDARME, René
Les coulées du futur : sidérurgie lorraine / René Gendarme. — Nancy : Presses Universitaires de Nancy ; Metz : Editions Serpenoise, 1985. — 314p

STEEL INDUSTRY AND TRADE — Germany — Rhineland
Stahl '85 : der letzte Tango am Rhein, Ruhr, Saar? / [Verfasser: Winfried Wolf]. — Frankfurt/M. : isp-Verlag, c1984. — 110p

STEEL INDUSTRY AND TRADE — Germany — Ruhr River Valley
Stahl '85 : der letzte Tango am Rhein, Ruhr, Saar? / [Verfasser: Winfried Wolf]. — Frankfurt/M. : isp-Verlag, c1984. — 110p

STEEL INDUSTRY AND TRADE — Germany — Saarland
Stahl '85 : der letzte Tango am Rhein, Ruhr, Saar? / [Verfasser: Winfried Wolf]. — Frankfurt/M. : isp-Verlag, c1984. — 110p

STEEL INDUSTRY AND TRADE — Germany (West)
Stahl '85 : der letzte Tango am Rhein, Ruhr, Saar? / [Verfasser: Winfried Wolf]. — Frankfurt/M. : isp-Verlag, c1984. — 110p

STEEL INDUSTRY AND TRADE — Great Britain
GREAT BRITAIN. Parliament. House of Commons. Library. Research Division
The British Steel Corporation and the steel industry / [Christopher Barclay]. — [London] : the Division, 1980. — 18p. — *Bibliography: p16-18*

STEEL INDUSTRY AND TRADE — Great Britain — History — 19th century
ERICKSON, Charlotte
British industrialists : steel and hosiery 1850-1950 / Charlotte Erickson. — Aldershot : Gower in association with he London School of Economics and Political Science, c1986. — xxi,276p. — *Originally published: Cambridge : Cambridge University Press, 1959. — Bibliography: p248-257. — Includes index*

STEEL INDUSTRY AND TRADE — Great Britain — History — 20th century
ERICKSON, Charlotte
British industrialists : steel and hosiery 1850-1950 / Charlotte Erickson. — Aldershot : Gower in association with he London School of Economics and Political Science, c1986. — xxi,276p. — *Originally published: Cambridge : Cambridge University Press, 1959. — Bibliography: p248-257. — Includes index*

STEEL INDUSTRY AND TRADE — India
KRISHNA MOORTHY, K.
Engineering change : India's iron and steel / K. Krishna Moorthy. — Indiranagar : Technology Books, 1984. — 434p. — *Includes bibliographic notes*

STEEL INDUSTRY AND TRADE — Mexico — Planning — Mathematical models
KENDRICK, David A.
The planning of investment programs in the steel industry / David A. Kendrick, Alexander Meeraus, Jaime Alatorre. — Baltimore : Johns Hopkins University Press for the World Bank, 1984. — xv,310p. — (The planning of investment programs ; v.3) (A World Bank research publication). — *Bibliographical references: p303-304*

STEEL INDUSTRY AND TRADE — Spain — Basque provinces — History
GONZÁLEZ PORTILLA, Manuel
La siderurgia vasca (1880-1901) : nuevas tecnologías, empresarios y Política económica / Manuel González Portilla. — Bilbao : Servicio Editorial Universidad del País Vasco, 1985. — 345p

STEEL INDUSTRY AND TRADE — Sweden — History
AXELSSON, Björn
Wikmanshyttans uppgång och fall : en kommentar till angreppssättet i en företagshistorisk studie / Björn Axelsson. — Uppsala : Uppsala Universitet, 1982. — 152p. — (Acta Universitatis Upsaliensis. Studien Oeconomiae Negotiorum ; 15). — *Doctoral thesis, Uppsala University 1981. — Bibliography: p147-152*

STEEL INDUSTRY AND TRADE — United States
BARNETT, Donald F
Up from the ashes : steel minimill in the U.S. / Donald F. Barnett and Robert W. Crandall. — Washington, D.C. : Brookings Institution, c1986. — p. cm. — *Includes bibliographical references and indexes*

STEEL INDUSTRY AND TRADE — United States — History
TWEEDALE, Geoffrey
Sheffield steel and America : a century of commercial and technological interdependence, 1830-1930 / Geoffrey Tweedale. — Cambridge : Cambridge University Press, 1987. — xv,296p. — *Bibliography: p263-287. — Includes index*

STEEL INDUSTRY AND TRADE — Wales — Shotton (Clwyd) — History
REDHEAD, Brian
The Summers of Shotton / Brian Redhead & Sheila Gooddie. — London : Hodder and Stoughton, 1987. — 160p. — *Map on lining papers. — Bibliography: p156. — Includes index*

STEEL INDUSTRY MANAGEMENT ASSOCIATION
BAMBER, Greg J.
Militant managers? : managerial unionism and industrial relations / Greg Bamber. — Aldershot : Gower, c1986. — [176]p. — *Includes bibliography and index*

STEEL MINIMILLS — United States
BARNETT, Donald F
Up from the ashes : steel minimill in the U.S. / Donald F. Barnett and Robert W. Crandall. — Washington, D.C. : Brookings Institution, c1986. — p. cm. — *Includes bibliographical references and indexes*

STEREOTYPE (PSYCHOLOGY)
BOSKIN, Joseph
Sambo : the rise & demise of an American jester / Joseph Boskin. — New York : Oxford University Press, 1986. — ix, 252 p. [8] p. of plates. — *Includes index. — Bibliography: p. 225-243*

STEREOTYPE (PSYCHOLOGY) — Case studies
JOB, Eena
Eighty plus : outgrowing the myths of old age / Eena Job. — St Lucia, Queensland : University of Queensland Press ; Lawrence, Mass. : Distributed in the USA and Canada by Technical Impex, 1984. — viii, 235 p.. — *Includes index. — Bibliography: p. [219]-227*

STERILIZATION, EUGENIC — Germany
BOCK, Gisela
Zwangssterilisation im Nationalsozialismus : Studien zur Rassenpolitik und Frauenpolitik / Gisela Bock. — Opladen : Westdeutscher Verlag, 1986. — 494p. — *Bibliography: p469-492*

STERILIZATION OF WOMEN — Germany
BOCK, Gisela
Zwangssterilisation im Nationalsozialismus : Studien zur Rassenpolitik und Frauenpolitik / Gisela Bock. — Opladen : Westdeutscher Verlag, 1986. — 494p. — *Bibliography: p469-492*

STERN
BAHNSEN, Uwe
Der "Stern" - Prozess : Heidemann und Kujau vor Gericht / Uwe Bahnsen. — Mainz : v. Hase und Kochler, 1986. — 192p

BISSINGER, Manfred
Hitlers Sternstunde : Kujau, Heidemann und die Millionen / Manfred Bissinger. — Hamburg : Rasch und Röhring, 1984. — 238p

STEVENS, ISAAC INGALLS
Indians, superintendents, and councils : northwestern Indian policy, 1850-1855 / edited by Clifford E. Trafzer. — Lanham, MD : University Press of America, c1986. — xi, 173 p.. — *Includes index. — Bibliography: p. 137-161*

STIGMA (SOCIAL PSYCHOLOGY)
The dilemma of difference : a multidisciplinary view of stigma / edited by Stephen C. Ainlay, Gaylene Becker, and Lerita M. Coleman. — New York ; London : Plenum, c1986. — xxiii, 262p. — (Perspectives in social psychology). — *Includes bibliographical references and index*

Stress and stigma : explanation and evidence in the sociology of crime and illness / edited by Uta E. Gerhardt and Michael E.J. Wadsworth. — Frankfurth : Campus ; London : Macmillan, 1985. — 206p. — *Includes bibliographies*

STOCHASTIC ANALYSIS
BURRIDGE, Peter
Forecasting and signal extraction in autoregressive-moving average models / Peter Burridge and Kenneth F. Wallis. — Coventry : University of Warwick. Department of Economics, 1986. — 60p. — (Warwick economic research papers ; no.274). — *Bibliography: p58-59*

STOCHASTIC PROCESSES
BIROLINI, Alessandro
On the use of stochastic processes in modeling reliability problems / Alessandro Birolini. — Berlin ; New York : Springer-Verlag, c1985. — vi, 105 p.. — (Lecture notes in economics and mathematical systems ; 252). — *Includes index. — Bibliography: p. [89]-103*

FARMER, Roger E. A.
Closed-form solutions to dynamic stochastic choice problems / Roger E. A. Farmer. — Coventry : University of Warwick. Department of Economics, 1987. — 20p. — (Warwick economic research papers ; no.282). — *Bibliography: p19-20*

SENGUPTA, Jatikumar
Stochastic optimization and economic models / Jati K. Sengupta. — Dordrecht ; Boston : D. Reidel ; Norwell, MA, U.S.A. : Sold and distributed in the U.S.A. and Canada by Kluwer Academic, c1986. — x, 373 p.. — (Theory and decision library. Series B. Mathematical and statistical methods). — *Includes bibliographies and indexes*

STOCHASTIC PROGRAMMING
KLEIN HANEVELD, Willem K.
Duality in stochastic linear and dynamic programming / Willem K. Klein Haneveld. — Berlin ; New York : Springer-Verlag, c1986. — p. cm. — (Lecture notes in economics and mathematical systems ; 274). — *Includes bibliographies and index*

STOCK EXCHANGE (London)
THOMAS, W. A.
The big bang / W.A. Thomas. — Oxford : Philip Allan, 1986. — [160]p. — *Includes bibliography and index*

STOCK-EXCHANGE
The GT guide to world equity markets / edited by Charles G. Hildeburn ; editorial advisor David Galloway ; assistant editors Bryan de Caires, Quek Peck Lim, Andrew Luglis-Taylor. — London : Euromoney Publications, 1986. — xi,290p

KROUSE, Clement G
Capital markets and prices : valuing uncertain income streams / Clement G. Krouse. — Amsterdam ; New York : North-Holland ; New York, N.Y. : Sole distributors for U.S.A. and Canada, Elsevier Science Pub. Co., 1986. — p. cm. — (Advanced textbooks in economics ; v. 25). — *Includes index*

STOCK EXCHANGE
The microstructure of securities markets / Kalman J. Cohen ... [et al.]. — Rev. — Englewood Cliffs, N.J. : Prentice-Hall, 1985. — p. cm. — *Includes index*. — *Bibliography: p*

STOCK-EXCHANGE
NICKELL, Stephen
Myopia, the 'dividend puzzle', and share prices / S. Nickell and S. Wadhwani. — London : Centre for Labour Economics, London School of Economics, 1987. — 41p. — (Discussion paper / London School of Economics and Political Science. Centre for Labour Economics ; no.272). — *Bibliography: p37-41*

STOCK-EXCHANGE — Periodicals
The City Press : the City of London newspaper. — London : The City Press, 1945-1975. — *Weekly*

STOCK-EXCHANGE — Great Britain
Conflicts of interest in the changing financial world / edited by R.M. Goode. — London : Institute of Bankers, 1986. — 1v.. — *Conference proceedings.* — *Includes index*

WEBBER, Alan
The activities of the regional units of the Stock exchange, 1973-86 / Alan Webber. — London : City University, 1987. — 40p. — (Discussion paper series / City University. Centre for Banking and International Finance ; no.57). — *Bibliography: p38-40*

STOCK-EXCHANGE — Ireland — History
THOMAS, W. A.
The stock exchanges of Ireland / W.A. Thomas. — Liverpool : Cairns, 1986. — 273p,8p of plates. — (Studies in financial and economic history ; v.1). — *Includes index*

STOCK-EXCHANGE — Queensland — Brisbane — History
LOUGHEED, A. L
The Brisbane Stock Exchange, 1884-1984 / A.L. Lougheed. — Brisbane, Qld. : Boolarong Publications, 1984. — xiii, 182 p.. — *Includes bibliographical references*

STOCK EXCHANGE — United States
The microstructure of securities markets / Kalman J. Cohen ... [et al.]. — Rev. — Englewood Cliffs, N.J. : Prentice-Hall, 1985. — p. cm. — *Includes index*. — *Bibliography: p*

STOCK OWNERSHIP
SPEISER, Stuart M
The USOP handbook : a guide to designing universal share ownership plans for the United States and Great Britain / by Stuart M. Speiser. — New York, N.Y. : Council on International and Public Affairs, c1986. — 168 p.. — *"Published on cooperation with the Center for Study of Expanded Capital Ownership.".* — *Bibliography: p. 165-168*

STOCK OWNERSHIP — Great Britain
HELLER, Robert
Shares for employees / by Robert Heller. — London : Poland Street Publications, 1984. — 131p

SCOTT, John, 1949-
The controlling constellations directory of 100 large companies / John Scott. — [Leicester] ([c/o Dept. of Sociology, University of Leicester, University Rd, Leicester LE1 7RH]) : J. Scott, [1984]. — [108]p. — *'Working paper for the Company Analysis Project 1984'*

SPEISER, Stuart M
The USOP handbook : a guide to designing universal share ownership plans for the United States and Great Britain / by Stuart M. Speiser. — New York, N.Y. : Council on International and Public Affairs, c1986. — 168 p.. — *"Published on cooperation with the Center for Study of Expanded Capital Ownership.".* — *Bibliography: p. 165-168*

STOCK OWNERSHIP — United States
SPEISER, Stuart M
The USOP handbook : a guide to designing universal share ownership plans for the United States and Great Britain / by Stuart M. Speiser. — New York, N.Y. : Council on International and Public Affairs, c1986. — 168 p.. — *"Published on cooperation with the Center for Study of Expanded Capital Ownership.".* — *Bibliography: p. 165-168*

STOCKHOLDERS
BLANCHFLOWER, D. G.
Shares for employees : a test of their effects / D. G. Blanchflower and A. J. Oswald. — London : Centre for Labour Economics, London School of Economics, 1987. — 36p. — (Discussion paper / London School of Economics and Political Science. Centre for Labour Economics ; no.273). — *Bibliography: p34-36*

RYDQVIST, Kristian
The pricing of shares with different voting power and the theory of oceanic games / Kristian Rydqvist. — Stockholm : Stockholm School of Economics, The Economic Research Institute, 1987. — 177p. — *"A dissertation for the Doctor's Degree in Business Administration, Stockholm School of Economics, 1987".* — *Bibliography: p166-173*

STOCKHOLDERS — Great Britain
GOODISON, Nicholas
Shares for all : steps towards a share-owning society / Sir Nicholas Goodison. — London : Centre for Policy Studies, 1986. — 16p

LETWIN, Shirley Robin
Every adult a share-owner : the case for universal share ownership / Shirley Robin Letwin [and] William Letwin. — London : Centre for Policy Studies, 1986. — 31p. — (Policy study ; no.80)

REDWOOD, John
Equity for everyman : new ways to widen ownership / John Redwood. — London : Centre for Policy Studies, 1986. — 39p. — (Policy study ; no.74)

STOCKHOLDERS — United States
Patterns of power : an introductory study of corporate control for the members of the Securities and Exchange Commission. — [Hampton, Va.] (532 Settlers Landing Rd., P.O. Box 302, Hampton 23669) : Foundation for the Study of Philanthropy, c1982. — 3, ii-v, 151 leaves. — *Includes index*. — *Bibliography: leaves 135-140*

STOCKMAN, DAVID ALAN
GREENYA, John
The real David Stockman / by John Greenya and Anne Urban ; introduction by Ralph Nader. — New York : St. Martin's Press, 1986. — p. cm. — *On t.p. "real" is italicized*

STOCKMANN, DAVID ALAN
ULLMANN, Owen
Stockmann : the man, the myth, the future / by Owen Ullmann. — New York : Fine, 1986. — 343p

STOCKS — Law and legislation — Great Britain
WYATT, Michael, 1952-
Company acquisition of own shares / Michael Wyatt. — London : Longman, c1986. — [180]p. — *New ed.: Previous ed.: 1983.* — *Includes index*

STOCKS — Prices
RAPPAPORT, Alfred
Creating shareholder value : the new standard for business performance / Alfred Rappaport. — New York : Free Press ; London : Collier Macmillan, c1986. — xv, 270 p.. — *Includes index*. — *Bibliography: p. 241-257*

RYDQVIST, Kristian
The pricing of shares with different voting power and the theory of oceanic games / Kristian Rydqvist. — Stockholm : Stockholm School of Economics, The Economic Research Institute, 1987. — 177p. — *"A dissertation for the Doctor's Degree in Business Administration, Stockholm School of Economics, 1987".* — *Bibliography: p166-173*

STOCKS — Great Britain
BANNOCK, Graham
Going public : the markets in unlisted securities / Graham Bannock with Alan Doran. — London : Harper & Row, 1987. — xvi,105p. — (Harper & Row series in accounting and finance). — *Originally published: London : Economist Publications, 1985.* — *Includes index*

STOCKS — India
MUKHERJEE, Amitava
The proximate determinants of money stock in a developing economy (1951-52 to 1979-80) / Amitava Mukherjee. — Calcutta : Firma KLM, 1981. — 128p. — *Bibliography: p122-128*

STOCZNIA GDAŃSKA IM. LENINA STRIKE, GDAŃSK, POLAND, 1980
Zapis rokowań gdańskich, sierpień 1980 / [zebrali i opracowali: Andrzej Drzycimski i Tadeusz Skutnik]. — Paris : Spotkania, [1986]. — 435p

STOKES, CHARLES
HARMAN, Nicholas
Bwana Stokesi and his African conquests / Nicholas Harman. — London : Cape, 1986. — xv,272p,[16]p of plates. — *Includes index*

STOLIAROV, IVAN
STOLIAROV, Ivan
Zapiski russkogo krest'ianina = Récit d'un paysan russe / Ivan Stoliarov ; préface de Basile Kerblay; notes de Valérie Stoliaroff avec le concours d'Alexis Berelowitch. — Paris : Institut de'Études Slaves, 1986. — 202p. — (Cultures et sociétés de l'Est ; 6)

STOLYPIN, P. A.
ZENKOVSKY, Alexander V.
Stolypin : Russia's last great reformer / Alexander V. Zenkovsky ; translated by Margaret Patoski. — Princeton, N.J. : Kingston Press, 1986. — x,146p

STONEHENGE (WILTSHIRE, ENGLAND)
NATIONAL COUNCIL FOR CIVIL LIBERTIES
Stonehenge : a report into the civil liberties implications of the events relating to the convoys of summer 1985 and 1986. — London : National Council for Civil Liberties, 1986. — 43p

STORAGE AND MOVING TRADE — Netherlands — Statistics
Vierde algemene bedrijfstelling, 1978. — 's-Gravenhage : Staatsuitgeverij. — *Rear cover title: Fourth general economic census, 1978: volume 2, part D: transport and storage*
d.2: Algemene sectorale gegevens D: transport en opslag. — 1985. — 71p

STORE HOURS — Law and legislation — Great Britain
GREAT BRITAIN. Parliament. House of Commons. Library. Research Division
Shops Bill, Bill 26 (Revised) 80-81 / [Joanna Roll]. — [London] : the Division, [1981]. — 13p. — (Reference sheet ; no.81/7)

GREAT BRITAIN. Parliament. House of Commons. Library. Research Division
Shops Bill (Bill 94 of 1985-86) / Fiona Poole. — [London] : the Division, 1986. — 23p. — (Reference sheet ; no.86/7). — *Bibliographical references: p22-23*

STORE HOURS — Great Britain
Effects of Sunday trading : the regulation of retail trading hours / J. A. Kay...[et al.]. — London : Institute for Fiscal Studies, 1984. — 110p. — (IFS report series ; no.13). — *Bibliography: p98-100*

STORE LOCATION — Great Britain
Local shops : problems and prospects / Peter Jones and Rosemary Oliphant, editors. — Reading : Unit for Retail Planning Information, 1976. — 103p. — *Includes bibliographies*

STORES, RETAIL
FAMILY POLICY STUDIES CENTRE
The Shops Bill: the family dimension. — London : Family Policy Studies Centre, 1986. — 16p

Local shops : problems and prospects / Peter Jones and Rosemary Oliphant, editors. — Reading : Unit for Retail Planning Information, 1976. — 103p. — *Includes bibliographies*

STORES, RETAIL — England — London
SMITH, Gordon, 1959-
Retail warehouses in London / Gordon Smith. — [London] : London Research Centre, 1986. — iii,[44]p. — (Reviews and studies series ; no.30). — *Bibliographical references: p16-17*

STORY, JOSEPH
NEWMYER, R. Kent
Supreme Court Justice Joseph Story : statesman of the Old Republic / R. Kent Newmyer. — Chapel Hill : University of North Carolina Press, c1985. — p. cm. — (Studies in legal history). — *Includes index.* — *Bibliography: p*

STORYTELLERS — Italy
MATHIAS, Elizabeth
Italian folktales in America : the verbal art of an immigrant woman / Elizabeth Mathias and Richard Raspa ; foreword by Roger D. Abrahams. — Detroit : Wayne State University Press, 1985. — p. cm. — (Wayne State University Folklore Archive study series). — *Includes 22 tales as told by Clementina Todesco.* — *Includes indexes.* — *Bibliography: p*

STORYTELLERS — United States
MATHIAS, Elizabeth
Italian folktales in America : the verbal art of an immigrant woman / Elizabeth Mathias and Richard Raspa ; foreword by Roger D. Abrahams. — Detroit : Wayne State University Press, 1985. — p. cm. — (Wayne State University Folklore Archive study series). — *Includes 22 tales as told by Clementina Todesco.* — *Includes indexes.* — *Bibliography: p*

STRATEGIC DEFENCE INITIATIVE
CANADIAN CENTRE FOR ARMS CONTROL AND DISARMAMENT
The economics of the strategic defence initiative : critical questions for Canada. — Ottawa, Ont. : Canadian Centre for Arms Control and Disarmament, 1985. — vi,16p. — (Issue brief / Canadian Centre for Arms Control and Disarmament ; no.4)

STRATEGIC DEFENSE INITIATIVE
Arms control and the strategic defense initiative : three perspectives. — Muscatine, Iowa : Stanley Foundation, 1985. — 32p. — (Occasional paper / Stanley Foundation ; 36). — *Contents: Soviet interpretation and response/Jerry F. Hough - A new dilemma for NATO/Stanley R. Sloan - Breaking the deadlock/Paul C. Warnke and David Linebaugh*

BYERS, R. B
Aerospace defence : Canada's future role? / R.B. Byers, John Hamre, G.R. Lindsey. — Toronto, Canada : Canadian Institute of International Affairs, 1985. — 56 p.. — (Wellesley papers ; 9/1985). — *Includes bibliographies.* — *Contents: Defending North America / G.R. Lindsey -- Continental air defence, United States security policy, and Canada-United States defence relations / John Hamre -- NORAD, Star Wars, and strategic doctrine / R.B. Byers*

CHARLTON, Michael
From deterrence to defence : the inside story of strategic policy / Michael Charlton. — Cambridge, Mass. : Harvard University Press, 1987, c1986. — p. cm. — *Based on the author's BBC radio series, The Star wars history.* — *Includes index*

DESCHAMPS, Louis
The SDI and European security interests / Louis Deschamps. — London : Croom Helm for the Atlantic Institute for International Affairs, c1987. — 64p. — (Atlantic paper ; no.62)

ENNALS, J. R.
Star Wars : a question of initiative / Richard Ennals. — Chichester : Wiley, c1986. — xiv,236p. — *Includes index*

JASTROW, Robert
How to make nuclear weapons obsolete / Robert Jastrow. — 1st ed. — Boston : Little, Brown, c1985. — 175 p.. — *Includes index.* — *Bibliography: p. 143-150*

Konzepte zum Frieden : Vorschläge für eine neue Abrüstungs- und Entspannungspolitik der SPD / herausgegeben von Katrin Fuchs, Hajo Hoffmann und Horst Klaus. — Berlin : spw-Verlag, 1985. — 179p

PAYNE, Keith B
Strategic defense : "star wars" in perspective / [by Keith B. Payne ; foreword by Zbigniew Brzezinski]. — Lanham, MD : Hamilton Press, c1986. — xviii, 250 p.. — *Includes bibliographies and index*

Strategic defense : folly or future? / [edited by] P. Edward Haley, Jack Merritt. — Boulder : Westview Press, 1986. — p. cm. — *Includes index.* — *Bibliography: p*

The Strategic Defense Initiative : new perspectives on deterrence / edited by Dorinda G. Dallmeyer ; in association with Daniel S. Papp. — Boulder : Westview Press, 1986. — xi, 112 p.. — (A Dean Rusk Center monograph). — *Includes index*

VAN CLEAVE, William R
Fortress U.S.S.R. : the Soviet strategic defense initiative and the U.S. strategic defense reponse / William R. Van Cleave. — Stanford, Calif. : Hoover Institution Press, Stanford University, c1986. — 60 p.. — *Bibliography: p. [57]-60*

ZEGVELD, Walter
SDI and industrial technology policy : threat or opportunity? / Walter Zegveld and Christien Enzing. — London : Pinter, 1987. — 186p. — *Includes bibliographies and index*

"Zvezdnye voiny" : illiuzii i opasnosti / [redaktor L. I. Dvinina]. — Moskva : Voennoe izd-vo, 1985. — 55p

STRATEGIC DEFENSE INITIATIVE — Bibliography
LAWRENCE, Robert M.
Strategic Defense Initiative : bibliography and research guide / Robert M. Lawrence. — Boulder, Colo. : Westview ; London : Mansell in cooperation with the Center for Space Law and Policy, University of Colorado at Boulder, 1987. — xiii,352p. — *Bibliography: p211-293*

STRATEGIC DEFENSE INITIATIVE — Congresses
The Strategic defense debate : can "Star Wars" make us safe? / edited by Craig Snyder. — Philadelphia : University of Pennsylvania Press, 1986. — xx, 247 p.. — *At head of title: The World Affairs Council of Philadelphia.* — *Based on a conference sponsored by the World Affairs Council of Philadelphia, held Oct. 3-4, 1985.* — *Includes index*

STRATEGIC DEFENSE INITIATIVE — Study and teaching
LAWRENCE, Robert M.
Strategic Defense Initiative : bibliography and research guide / Robert M. Lawrence. — Boulder, Colo. : Westview ; London : Mansell in cooperation with the Center for Space Law and Policy, University of Colorado at Boulder, 1987. — xiii,352p. — *Bibliography: p211-293*

STRATEGIC FORCES — Soviet Union
GREEN, William
Soviet nuclear weapons policy : a research guide / William Green. — Boulder, Colo. : Westview Press, 1987, c1983. — p. cm. — (A Westview replica edition). — *Includes bibliographies and indexes*

STRATEGIC MATERIALS — Commerce — South Africa
ANDOR, Lydia Eve
South Africa's chrome, manganese, platinum and vanadium : foreign views on the mineral dependency issue 1970-1984 : a select and annotated bibliography / L. E. Andor. — Braamfontein, [R.S.A.] : South African Institute of International Affairs, 1985. — 222p. — (South African Institute of International Affairs Bibliographical Series ; No.13)

STRATEGIC PLANNING
GODET, Michel
Scenarios and strategic management / by Michel Godet ; translated from the French by David Green and Alan Rodney. — London : Butterworths, 1987. — xviii,210p. — *Translation of: Prospective and planification stratégique.* — *Bibliography: p207-210.* — *Includes index*

ITAMI, Hiroyuki
Mobilizing invisible assets / Hiroyuki Itami with Thomas W. Roehl. — Cambridge, Mass. : Harvard University Press, 1987. — p. cm. — *Includes index.* — *Bibliography: p*

NAYLOR, Thomas H.
The corporate strategy matrix / Thomas H. Naylor. — New York : Basic Books, c1986. — xii, 290 p.. — *Includes index.* — *Bibliography: p. 276-280*

Strategic perspectives on planning practice / edited by Barry Checkoway. — Lexington, Mass. : Lexington Books, c1986. — x, 274 p.. — (Politics of planning series). — *Includes bibliographies and index*

STRATEGIC PLANNING — Case studies
GRAYSON, Leslie E
Who and how in planning for large companies / by Leslie E. Grayson. — New York : St. Martin's Press, 1986. — p. cm. — *Includes index*

STRATEGIC PLANNING — Great Britain
PETRELLI, Robert
Structure planning and the coordination of policies within British local authorities. — 316 leaves. — *PhD (Econ) 1986 LSE*

STRATEGIC PLANNING — Japan
[Nichi-Bei kigyō no keiei hikaku. English]. Strategic vs. evolutionary management : a U.S.-Japan comparison of strategy and organization / Tadao Kagono ... [et al.] ; in collaboration with Shiori Sakamoto, Johhny K. Johansson. — Amsterdam ; New York : North-Holland ; New York : Sole distributors for the U.S.A. and Canada, Elsevier Science Pub. Co., 1985. — p. cm. — (Advanced series in management ; v. 10). — *Translation of: Nichi-Bei kigyō no keiei hikaku*

STRATEGIC PLANNING — United States
[Nichi-Bei kigyō no keiei hikaku. English].
Strategic vs. evolutionary management : a U.S.-Japan comparison of strategy and organization / Tadao Kagono ... [et al.] ; in collaboration with Shiori Sakamoto, Johhny K. Johansson. — Amsterdam ; New York : North-Holland ; New York : Sole distributors for the U.S.A. and Canada, Elsevier Science Pub. Co., 1985. — p. cm. — (Advanced series in management ; v. 10). — *Translation of: Nichi-Bei kigyō no keiei hikaku*

STRATEGY
L'année strategique. — [Paris] : Editions Maritimes, 1985-. — *Annual*

BARNABY, Frank
What on earth is Star Wars? : a guide to the Strategic Defence Initiative / Frank Barnaby. — London : Fourth Estate, 1986. — [184]p. — *Includes bibliography and index*

Contemporary strategy / John Baylis...[et al.]. — 2nd ed, rev. and enl.. — London : Croom Helm. — *Previous ed: 1975*
1: Theories and concepts. — 1987. — x,326p

Contemporary strategy / John Baylis...[et al.]. — 2nd ed, rev. and enl.. — London : Croom Helm. — *Previous ed.: 1975*
2: The nuclear powers. — 1987. — ix,209p

Doctrine, the Alliance and arms control / edited by Robert O'Neill. — Basingstoke : Macmillan in association with International Institute for Strategic Studies, 1986. — 232p. — (International Institute for Strategic Studies conference papers). — *Includes index*

HENDRICKSON, David C
The future of American strategy / David C. Hendrickson. — New York : Holmes & Meier, 1986. — p. cm. — *Includes index.* — *Bibliography: p*

The Logic of nuclear terror Roman Kolkowicz, editor. — Boston, Mass. ; London : Published under the auspices of the University of California Project on Politics and War [by] Allen & Unwin, c1987. — xi,289p. — *Includes index*

STRATEGY — History
LIDER, Julian
Origins and development of West German military thought. — Aldershot : Gower. — (Swedish studies in international relations ; 16)
Vol.1: 1949-1966 / Julian Lider. — c1986. — ix,433p

STRATEGY — History — 20th century
ROBERTS, Adam
Nations in arms : the theory and practice of territorial defence / Adam Roberts. — 2nd (rev. and enl.) ed. / foreword by McGeorge Bundy. — Basingstoke : Macmillan, 1986. — [290]p. — (Studies in international security). — *Previous ed.: London : Chatto and Windus for The International Institute for Strategic Studies, 1976. — Includes index*

STRATEGY — Political aspects — Soviet Union — History — 20th century
TOPITSCH, Ernst
Stalin's war : the Soviet long-term strategy against the West considered as rational power politics / Ernst Topitsch ; translated by Arthur Taylor. — London : Fourth Estate, 1987. — [192]p. — *Translation from the German.* — *Includes index*

STRATHCLYDE — Emigration and immigration — History
GALLAGHER, Tom, 1954-
Glasgow : the uneasy peace : religious tension in modern Scotland, 1819-1914 / Tom Gallagher. — Manchester : Manchester University Press, c1987. — ix,382p. — *Bibliography: p357-366.* — *Includes index*

STRATHCLYDE — Religious life and customs
GALLAGHER, Tom, 1954-
Glasgow : the uneasy peace : religious tension in modern Scotland, 1819-1914 / Tom Gallagher. — Manchester : Manchester University Press, c1987. — ix,382p. — *Bibliography: p357-366.* — *Includes index*

STRATHCLYDE (SCOTLAND) — Economic conditions
STRATHCLYDE. Regional Council
Economic policy. — Glasgow : [the Council], 1976. — iv,158p

STRATHCLYDE (SCOTLAND) — Economic policy
STRATHCLYDE. Regional Council
Economic policy. — Glasgow : [the Council], 1976. — iv,158p

STREET-RAILROADS — Hongkong — Employees
Hongkong Tramways Ltd : analysis of individual workers reactions to management policies and techniques. — [S.l.] : [S.n.], 1960. — 33 leaves

STRESS IN CHILDREN — Bibliography
SHRIGLEY, Sheila
Selected references on children in war time and other social disturbances / compiled by Sheila M. Shrigley. — [London] : Department of Health and Social Security Library, 1975. — 3p. — (Bibliography series ; no.B25)

STRESS (PHYSIOLOGY)
Environmental stress / edited by Gary W. Evans. — Cambridge [Cambridgeshire] ; New York : Cambridge University Press, 1982. — xiv, 386 p.. — *Includes bibliographies and indexes*

STRESS (PSYCHOLOGY)
Environmental stress / edited by Gary W. Evans. — Cambridge [Cambridgeshire] ; New York : Cambridge University Press, 1982. — xiv, 386 p.. — *Includes bibliographies and indexes*

In support of families / edited by Michael W. Yogman and T. Berry Brazelton. — Cambridge, Mass. : Harvard University Press, 1986. — 293 p.. — *Includes index.* — *Bibliography: p. [257]-283*

LEFCOURT, Herbert M
Humor and life stress : antidote to adversity / Herbert M. Lefcourt, Rod A. Martin. — New York : Springer-Verlag, c1986. — p. cm. — *Includes index.* — *Bibliography: p*

STRESS (PSYCHOLOGY) — Social aspects
Social support, life events, and depression / edited by Nan Lin, Alfred Dean, and Walter M. Ensel. — New York : Academic Press, 1986. — p. cm. — *Includes index*

STRESS (PSYCHOLOGY) — Social aspects — Research
Social support, life events, and depression / edited by Nan Lin, Alfred Dean, and Walter M. Ensel. — New York : Academic Press, 1986. — p. cm. — *Includes index*

STRIKERS AND LOCK-OUTS — Coal mining — England — Barnsley (South Yorkshire)
BARNSLEY WOMEN AGAINST PIT CLOSURES
Barnsley Women Against Pit Closures. — Barnsley (Barnsley Women Against Pit Closures). — (Women Against Pit Closures ; vol.2) (People's History of Yorkshire ; no.12) vol.2. — 1985. — 109p

STRIKES AND LOCK-OUTS
Streik-Widerstand gegen Kapital und Kabinett / Frank Deppe [...et al.]. — Frankfurt am Main : Nachrichten Verlagsgesellschaft, 1985. — 331p

Strike action. — London : Dark Star ; Manchester : Direct Action Movement, 1984. — [8p]

STRIKES AND LOCK-OUTS — Coal-miners — Great Britain
DOUGLASS, David
Come and wet this truncheon : the role of the police in the coal strike of 1984/85 / David John Douglass. — Doncaster : D. Douglass : Doncaster, Cambridge, South London, DAM-IWA : CaNary Press, 1986. — [40p]

STRIKES AND LOCK-OUTS — Coal mining — Great Britain
Digging deeper : issues in the miners strike / edited by Huw Beynon. — London : Verso, 1985. — [280]p

STRIKES AND LOCK-OUTS — Newspapers — England — London
LONDON STRATEGIC POLICY UNIT. Police Monitoring and Research Group
Policing Wapping : and account of the dispute 1986/7. — London : London Strategic Policy Unit, 1987-. — 47p. — (Briefing paper / London Strategic Policy Unit. Police Monitoring and Research Group ; no.3)

STRIKES AND LOCK-OUTS — Social aspects
NAYLOR, Robin
Strikes, free riders and social customs / Robin Naylor. — Coventry : University of Warwick, 1987. — 34p. — (Warwick Economic Research Papers ; no.275). — *Bibliography: p30-32*

STRIKES AND LOCK-OUTS — Transport workers — Ireland — Dublin
MCCAMLEY, Bill
The role of the rank and file in the 1935 Dublin tram and bus strike / Bill McCamley. — Dublin : Labour History Workshop, 1981. — [35p]

STRIKES AND LOCK-OUTS — England — London — Printers
NATIONAL COUNCIL FOR CIVIL LIBERTIES
No way in Wapping : the effect of the policing of the News International dispute on Wapping residents. — London : National Council for Civil Liberties, 1986. — 40p

STRIKES AND LOCKOUTS — Agricultural laborers — Patagonia (Argentina and Chile)
BAYER, Osvaldo
La Patagonia rebelde / Osvaldo Bayer. — [Buenos Aires] : Hyspamérica, c1986. — 429p. — (Biblioteca argentina de historia y política ; 1). — *Publicado originalmente en México por Nueva Imagen en 1980*

STRIKES AND LOCKOUTS — Coal mining — England — Doncaster (South Yorkshire)
A year of our lives : a colliery community in the great coal strike of 1984/85 / compiled and narrated by David John Douglass. — [S.l.] : Hooligan Press, [1986]. — [100]p

STRIKES AND LOCKOUTS — Coal mining — Scotland — Mauchline (Ayrshire)
LEVY, Catriona
A very hard year : the 1984-85 miners' strike in Mauchline / compiled by Catriona Levy and Mauchline miners' wives. — Glasgow : Workers' Educational Association, [1985]. — 34p

STRIKES AND LOCKOUTS — Law and legislation
The strike / [Angarita Barón Ciro...et al.]. — Milano : Giuffrè, 1987. — xvi,554p. — (Inchieste di diritto comparato / M. Rotondi ; 9). — *Contributions by various authors in English, Italian, French, Spanish, German or Portuguese*

STRIKES AND LOCKOUTS — Law and legislation — United States
GOULD, William B
Strikes, dispute procedures, and arbitration : essays on labor law / William B. Gould IV. — Westport, Conn. : Greenwood Press, c1985. — p. cm. — (Contributions in American studies ; no. 82). — Includes index. — Bibliography: p

STRIKES AND LOCKOUTS — Meat industry — Minnesota — Austin
HALSTEAD, Fred
The 1985-86 Hormel meat-packers strike in Austin, Minnesota / Fred Halstead. — New York : Pathfinder Press, 1986. — 44p

STRIKES AND LOCKOUTS — Metal workers — Germany (West)
BAHNMÜLLER, Reinhard
Der Streik : Tarifkonflikt um Arbeitszeitverkürzung in der Metallindustrie 1984 / Reinhard Bahnmüller. — Hamburg : VSA-Verlag, 1985. — 204p. — Bibliography: p202-204

STRIKES AND LOCKOUTS — Printers — Germany (West)
HEINE, Werner
Ein Tabu fällt : Kampf der Drucker um Arbeitszeitverkürzung und Lohnstruktur / Werner Heine ; mit ein Vorwort von Erwin Ferlemann. — Köln : Bund-Verlag, 1986. — 159p

STRIKES AND LOCKOUTS — Public utilities — Law and legislation — Great Britain
MORRIS, Gillian, 1953-
Strikes in essential services / Gillian S. Morris. — London : Mansell, 1986. — x,221p. — (Studies in labour and social law). — Bibliography: p209-215. — Includes index

STRIKES AND LOCKOUTS — Railroads — Argentina — History
LOZZA, Arturo Marcos
Tiempo de huelgas : los apasionados relatos del campesino y ferroviario Florindo Moretti sobre aquellas épocas de fundaciones, luchas y serenatas / Arturo Marcos Lozza. — Buenos Aires : Editorial Anteo, 1985. — 299p. — Bibliography: p293-294

STRIKES AND LOCKOUTS — Argentina — History
LOZZA, Arturo Marcos
Tiempo de huelgas : los apasionados relatos del campesino y ferroviario Florindo Moretti sobre aquellas épocas de fundaciones, luchas y serenatas / Arturo Marcos Lozza. — Buenos Aires : Editorial Anteo, 1985. — 299p. — Bibliography: p293-294

STRIKES AND LOCKOUTS — Europe
HIBBS, Douglas A.
The political economy of industrial democracies / Douglas A. Hibbs, Jr. — Cambridge, Mass. ; London : Harvard University Press, 1987. — viii, 327 p.. — Includes bibliographical references and index

STRIKES AND LOCKOUTS — France — History — 19th century
PERROT, Michelle
Workers on strike : France 1871-1890 / Michelle Perrot ; translated from the French by Chris Turner with the assistance of Erica Carter and Claire Laudet. — Leamington Spa : Berg, c1987. — 321p. — Translation of: Jeunesse de la grève, France 1871-1890. — Bibliography: p320-321

STRIKES AND LOCKOUTS — France — Paris
Paris: May 1986. — [London] : Rebel Press : Dark Star, 1986. — 55p

STRIKES AND LOCKOUTS — Germany (West)
BAHNMÜLLER, Reinhard
Der Streik : Tarifkonflikt um Arbeitszeitverkürzung in der Metallindustrie 1984 / Reinhard Bahnmüller. — Hamburg : VSA-Verlag, 1985. — 204p. — Bibliography: p202-204

STRIKES AND LOCKOUTS — Netherlands
Bedrijfsbezetting : een nieuwe aktievorm in Nederland / [Projektgroep "Arbeid en Vorming"] ; [Lucy van Houwelingen...et al.]. — [Utrecht : "Arbeid en Vorming", 1974]. — 59p. — Bibliography: p59

STRIKES AND LOCKOUTS — Poland
Zapis rokowań gdańskich, sierpień 1980 / [zebrali i opracowali: Andrzej Drzycimski i Tadeusz Skutnik]. — Paris : Spotkania, [1986]. — 435p

STRIKES AND LOCKOUTS — Spain
GÁMIR, Luis
Contra el paro y la crisis en España / Luis Gamir. — Barcelona : Planeta, 1985. — 330p

STRIKES AND LOCKOUTS — Spain — Cantabria — History — 20th century
ARGOS VILLAR, José Carlos
El movimiento obrero en Cantabria (1955-1977) / José Carlos Argos Villar, José Emilio Gómez Díaz ; prólogo de J.R. Saiz Viadero. — [Santander?] : J.E. Gómez Díaz, [1982?]. — 227 p.. — (Puntal libros)

STRIKES AND LOCKOUTS — Spain — Madrid — History — 20th century
JULIÁ DÍAZ, Santos
Madrid, 1931-1934 : de la fiesta popular a la lucha de clases / por Santos Juliá Díaz. — Madrid : Siglo Veintiuno, 1984. — 509p

STRIKES AND LOCKOUTS — United States
HIBBS, Douglas A.
The political economy of industrial democracies / Douglas A. Hibbs, Jr. — Cambridge, Mass. ; London : Harvard University Press, 1987. — viii, 327 p.. — Includes bibliographical references and index

STRIP MINING — Environmental aspects — Ukraine
UK-USSR Environmental Protection Agreement: area III (land reclamation) : report of a visit to the USSR (by a UK delegation) in 1976. — London : Planning, Regional and Minerals Directorate, Department of the Environment, [1977]. — 24p

STRIP MINING — Law and legislation — United States
SHOVER, Neal
Enforcement or negotiation : constructing a regulatory bureaucracy / Neal Shover, Donald Clelland, John Lynxwiler. — Albany, NY : State University of New York Press, c1986. — p. cm. — (SUNY series in critical issues in criminal justice). — Includes index. — Bibliography: p

STRUCTURAL ANTHROPOLOGY
ROSSI, Ino
The logic of culture : advances in structural theory and methods / Ino Rossi and contributors. — London : Tavistock Publications, 1982. — viii,296p

STRUCTURALISM
WEEDON, Chris
Feminist practice and poststructuralist theory / Chris Weedon. — Oxford : Basil Blackwell, 1987. — 1v. — Includes bibliography and index

STRUCTURALISM — Addresses, essays, lectures
Structuralism and since : from Lévi-Strauss to Derrida / edited, with an introduction, by John Sturrock. — Oxford ; New York : Oxford University Press, [1981] c1979. — 190 p.. — Includes bibliographies and index

STRUCTURALISM — History
MERQUIOR, J. G.
From Prague to Paris : a critique of structuralist and post-structuralist thought / J.G. Merquior. — London : Verso, 1986. — xi,286p. — Bibliography: p261-276. — Includes index

STRUCTURALISM (LITERARY ANALYSIS)
Post-structuralism and the question of history / edited by Derek Attridge, Geoff Bennington and Robert Young. — Cambridge : Cambridge University Press, 1987. — [304]p. — Includes index

STRUCTURED PROGRAMMING
KOFFMAN, Elliot B
Problem solving and structured programming in PASCAL / Elliot B. Koffman. — 2nd ed. — Reading, Mass. : Addison-Wesley Pub. Co., 1985. — p. cm. — Includes index

STUART, HOUSE OF
GREGG, Edward
The Protestant succession in international politics, 1710-1716 / Edward Gregg. — New York : Garland, 1986. — 456 p. — (Outstanding theses from the London School of Economics and Political Science). — Bibliography: p. 417-456

STUDENT ADJUSTMENT
KAAYK, Jan
Education, estrangement and adjustment : a study among pupils and school leavers in Bukumbi, a rural community in Tanzania / Jan Kaayk ; [translation, V. A. February]. — The Hague : Mouton, [1976]. — xv, 267 p.. — (Change and continuity in Africa). — Includes index. — Bibliography: p. 265-267

STUDENT ASPIRATION — United States
LEVINE, David O.
The American college and the culture of aspiration, 1915-1940 / David O. Levine. — Ithaca : Cornell University Press, 1986. — 281 p.. — Includes index. — Bibliography: p. 255-275

STUDENT ASPIRATIONS — California — Stanford — Case studies
KATCHADOURIAN, Herant A
Careerism and intellectualism among college students / Herant A. Katchadourian, John Boli ; with the assistance of Nancy Olsen, Raymond F. Bacchetti, Sally Mahoney. — 1st ed. — San Francisco : Jossey-Bass Publishers, 1985. — xxvi, 324 p.. — (The Jossey-Bass higher education series). — Includes indexes. — Bibliography: p. 311-316

STUDENT MOBILITY — Egypt — Statistics
1976 Population and housing census : total Republic. — Cairo : Central Agency for Public Mobilisation and Statistics
Vol. 2: Fertility and internal migration and movement of workers and students. — 1980. — 440p

STUDENT MOVEMENTS — Great Britain
YETTRAM, Pamela June
Contrary imaginations : causes and consequences of left wing ideology among student activists in the mid-seventies / by Pamela J. Yettram. — 511 leaves. — PhD (Econ) 1986 LSE. — Leaves 457-486 are appendices

STUDENT NONVIOLENT COORDINATING COMMITTEE (U.S.) — Biography
FORMAN, James
The making of Black revolutionaries / James Forman. — 2d ed. — Washington, DC : Open Hand Pub., c1985. — xxiii, 568 p.. — Includes index

STUDENTS — Belgium
STEDELIJK HOGER INSTITUUT VOOR SOCIALE STUDIE. Werkgroep Inspraak
Zwartboek / Werkgroep Inspraak SHISS. — Gent : the Werkgroep, [1975]. — 72p. — Cover title

STUDENTS — Crimes against — England — Manchester (Greater Manchester)
WALKER, Martin, 1947-
With extreme prejudice : an investigation into police vigilantism in Manchester / Martin Walker. — London : Canary, 1986. — 203p

STUDENTS — Political activity
STEDELIJK HOGER INSTITUUT VOOR SOCIALE STUDIE. Werkgroep Inspraak
Zwartboek / Werkgroep Inspraak SHISS. — Gent : the Werkgroep, [1975]. — 72p. — *Cover title*

STUDENTS — Belgium — Statistics
Recensement de la population et des logements au 1er mars 81. — Bruxelles : Institut national de statistique
Résultats généraux
Population scolaire et niveau d'instruction. — 1986. — 307p

STUDENTS — Finland — Socioeconomic status
HERMUNEN, Hannele
Oppilaiden sosiaalinen tauste 1980 / Hannele Hermunen. — Helsinki : Tilastokeskus, 1984. — 86p. — (Tutkimuksia / Finland. Tilastokeskus ; no.111)

STUDENTS — France
De la misère en milieu étudiant considérée sous ses aspects économique, politique, psychologique, sexuel et notamment intellectuel, et de quelques moyens pour y remédier / par des membres de l'Internationale situationniste et des étudiants de Strasbourg. — Strasbourg : l'Internationale situationniste, 1967. — [28p]

STUDENTS — Great Britain — Political activity
YETTRAM, Pamela June
Contrary imaginations : causes and consequences of left wing ideology among student activists in the mid-seventies / by Pamela J. Yettram. — 511 leaves. — *PhD (Econ) 1986 LSE. — Leaves 457-486 are appendices*

STUDENTS — United States — Psychology
ADELSON, Joseph
Inventing adolescence : the political psychology of everyday schooling / Joseph Adelson. — New Brunswick, N.J., U.S.A. : Transaction Books, c1986. — ix, 296 p.. — *Includes bibliographical references*

STUDENTS, BLACK — France
TRAORE, Sekou
La Fédération des Étudiants d'Afrique Noire en France (F.E.A.N.F.) / Sekou Traore. — Paris : L'Harmattan, 1985. — 102p. — *Bibliography: p97-100*

STUDENTS, FOREIGN
International comparisons in overseas student affairs / edited by Stephen Shotnes. — London : UK Council for Overseas Student Affairs, 1986. — 91p

STUDENTS, FOREIGN — Bibliography
ALTBACH, Philip G
Bibliography of foreign students and international study / by Philip G. Altbach, David H. Kelly, and Y. G-M. Lulat. — New York : Praeger, 1985. — p. cm. — (The Praeger special studies series in comparative education). — *"Published in cooperation with the Comparative Education Center, State University of New York, Buffalo."*

STUDENTS, FOREIGN — Legal status, laws, etc. — Great Britain
GREAT BRITAIN. Parliament. House of Commons. Library. Research Division
Education (Fees and Awards) Bill (Bill 135 of 1982/83) / Kay Andrews. — [London] : the Division, 1983. — 16p. — (Reference sheet ; no.83/9). — *Bibliographical references: p14-16*

STUDENTS, INTERCHANGE OF — European Economic Community countries
Pupil exchange in the European Community : Venice Colloquium, 24—28 October 1977. — Luxembourg : Office for Official Publications of the European Communities, 1978. — 68p. — (Education series / Commission of the European Communities ; no.5)

STUDENTS, RATING OF — Germany (West)
GREAT BRITAIN. Department of Education and Science. Inspectorate of Schools
Education in the Federal Republic of Germany : aspects of curriculum and assessment : a paper by HMI. — London : H.M.S.O., 1986. — 49p

STUDY, METHOD OF
DUNLEAVY, Patrick
Studying for a degree in the humanities and social sciences / Patrick Dunleavy. — Basingstoke : Macmillan Education, 1986. — [224]p. — *Includes bibliography and index*

SALIMBENE, Suzanne
Strengthening your study skills : a guide for overseas students / Suzanne Salimbene. — [London] : University of London, Institute of Education, c1982. — 96p. — *Bibliography: p96*

STURGE, JOSEPH
TYRRELL, Alex
Joseph Sturge and the "moral Radical party" in early Victorian Britain / Alex Tyrrell. — London : Helm, c1987. — [264]p. — *Bibliography: p249-250. — Includes index*

SUBCONSCIOUSNESS
FULLER, Robert C.
Americans and the unconscious / Robert C. Fuller. — New York : Oxford University Press, 1986. — p. cm. — *Includes index*

SUBCONSIOUSNESS
LEWICKI, Paweł
Nonconscious social information processing / Pawel Lewicki. — Orlando : Academic Press, 1986. — p. cm. — *Includes bibliographical references and index*

SUBJECT HEADINGS — Bibliography
Thesaurus guide : analytical directory of selected vocabularies for information retrievel, 1985 / prepared by Gesellschaft für Information und Dokumentation for the Commission of the European Communities. — Amsterdam ; Luxembourg : Elsevier : Office for Official Publications of the European Communities, 1985. — xxxvi,749p

SUBSIDIARY CORPORATIONS — Management
PRATTEN, Cliff, 1936-
The management of operating businesses by large companies / Cliff Pratten. — Aldershot : Gower, c1986. — [vii,122]p

SUBSIDIARY CORPORATIONS — Taxation
Cross-border transactions between related companies : a summary of tax rules / edited by William R. Lawlor. — Deventer, The Netherlands ; Boston : Kluwer Law and Taxation Publishers, c1985. — p. cm. — *Derived from an international tax planning symposium in New York sponsored by Ernst & Whinney. — "Current to January 1985"--Foreword*

SUBSIDIES — England
DEVELOPMENT COMMISSION FOR RURAL ENGLAND
Action for rural enterprise : a guide to the assistance available to business in rural areas of England from the government and other agencies. — [London : the Commission, 1987]. — 29p. — *One of five publications in folder entitled Farming and rural enterprise*

GREAT BRITAIN. Department of the Environment
Consultation document on proposals to increase local authority powers with serious inner area problems to assist industry. — [London : the Department, 1977]. — 9 leaves

SUBSIDIES — Europe — Handbooks, manuals, etc.
DAVISON, Ann
Grants from Europe : how to get money and influence policy / written for ERICA by Ann Davison. — 3rd ed.. — London : Bedford Square Press, 1986. — ix, 86p

SUBSIDIES — European Economic Community countries — Directories
SCOTT, Gay
A guide to European Community grants and loans, 1985/86 for commerce, industry, local authorities, academic and research institutions / compiled by Gay Scott. — 6th ed : Northill, Beds. : Eurofi, 1985. — 1v(loose-leaf)

SUBSIDIES — Great Britain
GREAT BRITAIN. Department of Industry
Incentives for industry in the areas for expansion : special development areas, development areas, intermediate areas, Northern Ireland / [prepared for the Department of Industry by the Central Office of Information]. — [London : the Department], 1976. — 44p

GREAT BRITAIN. Department of Industry
Industry Act 1972 : criteria for assistance to industry. — [London : the Department, 1975]. — 16,3p

GREAT BRITAIN. Department of Industry
Wool textile industry scheme : an assessment of the effects of selective assistance under the Industry Act 1972 / analysis and consultations...carried out by Dilys Gane. — London : the Department, 1978. — ii,41,[35]p

SUBSIDIES — Scotland
GREAT BRITAIN. Scottish Office
Rural Scotland. — [Edinburgh : the Office, 1987]. — 28p. — *One of five publications in folder entitled Farming and rural enterprise*

SUBSIDIES — Wales
Action for rural enterprise in Wales / Manpower Services Commission, Mid Wales Development, Wales Tourist Board, Welsh Development Agency. — [Cardiff? : Welsh Development Agency?, 1987]. — 17,19p. — *In English and Welsh. — One of five publications in folder entitled Farming and rural enterprise*

SUBSISTENCE ECONOMY — Alaska — Addresses, essays, lectures
Contemporary Alaskan native economies / edited by Steve J. Langdon. — Lanham, MD : University Press of America, c1986. — ix, 183 p.. — *Includes bibliographies. — Contents: Economic growth and development strategies for rural Alaska / Bradford H. Tuck and Lee Huskey -- Subsistence as an economic system in Alaska / Thomas D. Lonner -- Contradictions in Alaskan native economy and society / Steve J. Langdon -- Limited entry policy and impacts on Bristol Bay fishermen / J. Anthony Koslow -- The Cape Romanzoff project / Dean F. Olson -- The Pribilof Island Aleuts / Michael K. Orbach and Beverly Holmes -- The economic efficiency of food production in a western Alaska Eskimo population / Robert J. Wolfe -- Subsistence and the North Slope Inupiat / John A. Kruse -- Subsistence beluga whale hunting in Alaska / Kerry D. Feldman -- Traditional subsistence activities and systems of exchange among the Nelson Island Yup'ik / Ann Fienup-Riordan*

SUBSTANCE ABUSE
The Steel drug : cocaine in perspective / Patricia G. Erickson ... [et al.]. — Lexington, Mass. : Lexington Books, c1987. — xviii, 169 p.. — *Includes index. — Bibliography: p. [151]-159*

SUBSTANCE ABUSE — Dictionaries

SPEARS, Richard A
The slang and jaron of drugs and drink / by Ricard A. Spears. — Metuchen, N.J. : Scarecrow Press, 1986. — xv, 585 p.. — *Bibliography: p. [562]-575*

SUBSTANCE ABUSE — dictionaries

SPEARS, Richard A
The slang and jaron of drugs and drink / by Ricard A. Spears. — Metuchen, N.J. : Scarecrow Press, 1986. — xv, 585 p.. — *Bibliography: p. [562]-575*

SUBSTANCE ABUSE — Slang — Dictionaries

SPEARS, Richard A
The slang and jaron of drugs and drink / by Ricard A. Spears. — Metuchen, N.J. : Scarecrow Press, 1986. — xv, 585 p.. — *Bibliography: p. [562]-575*

SUBSTANCE ABUSE — Terminology

SPEARS, Richard A
The slang and jaron of drugs and drink / by Ricard A. Spears. — Metuchen, N.J. : Scarecrow Press, 1986. — xv, 585 p.. — *Bibliography: p. [562]-575*

SUBSTANCE ABUSE — United States

Chemical dependencies : patterns, costs, and consequences / edited by Carl D. Chambers ... [et al.]. — Athens, Ohio : Ohio University Press, 1987. — p. cm. — *Includes bibliographies*

SUBURBAN LIFE — California — Orange County — Case studies

BALDASSARE, Mark
Trouble in paradise : the suburban transformation in America / Mark Baldassare. — New York : Columbia University Press, 1986. — xi, 251 p. — *Includes index. — Bibliography: p. [231]-240*

SUBURBAN LIFE — United States

BALDASSARE, Mark
Trouble in paradise : the suburban transformation in America / Mark Baldassare. — New York : Columbia University Press, 1986. — xi, 251 p.. — *Includes index. — Bibliography: p. [231]-240*

SUBURBS — Congresses

INTERNATIONAL SYMPOSIUM ON THE CRISIS OF THE CENTRAL CITY AND THE TAKE-OFF OF SUBURBIA (1984 : Munich & Vienna)
The take-off of suburbia and the crisis of the central city : proceedings of the International Symposium in Munich and Vienna 1984 / edited by Günter Heinritz and Elisabeth Lichtenberger. — Stuttgart : Steiner, 1986. — [viii],301p. — (Erdkundliches Wissen ; Heft 76)

SUBURBS — California — Orange County — Case studies

BALDASSARE, Mark
Trouble in paradise : the suburban transformation in America / Mark Baldassare. — New York : Columbia University Press, 1986. — xi, 251 p.. — *Includes index. — Bibliography: p. [231]-240*

SUBURBS — United States

BALDASSARE, Mark
Trouble in paradise : the suburban transformation in America / Mark Baldassare. — New York : Columbia University Press, 1986. — xi, 251 p.. — *Includes index. — Bibliography: p. [231]-240*

SUBVERSIVE ACTIVITIES — France

GAUCHER, Roland
Le réseau Curiel : ou, La subversion humanitaire / Roland Gaucher. — Paris : Editions Jean Picollec, 1981. — 433p

SUBVERSIVE ACTIVITIES — Great Britain — History — 17th century

GREAVES, Richard L
Deliver us from evil : the radical underground in Britain, 1660-1663 / Richard L. Greaves. — New York : Oxford University Press, 1986. — x, 291p. — *Includes index. — Includes bibliographical references*

SUBVERSIVE ACTIVITIES — United States

HOFFMAN, Bruce
Terrorism in the United States and the potential threat to nuclear facilities / Bruce Hoffman ; prepared for the U.S. Department of Energy. — Santa Monica, CA : Rand, [1986]. — ix, 56 p.. — "R-3351-DOE.". — "January 1986.". — *Bibliography: p. 55-56*

SUBVERSIVE ACTIVITIES — United States — History — 20th century

EWALD, William Bragg
McCarthyism and consensus / William Bragg Ewald, Jr. — Lanham [Md.] : University Press of America, c1986. — viii, 68 p.. — (The Credibility of institution, policies and leadership ; v. 13). — "Co-published by arrangement with the White Burkett Miller Center of Public Affairs, University of Virginia"--T.p. verso. — Contents: Rotunda lecture: "McCarthyism revisited" / William Bragg Ewald, Jr. -- Miller Center discussion: "McCarthyism and consensus."

SCHRECKER, Ellen
No ivory tower : McCarthyism and the universities / Ellen Schrecker. — New York : Oxford University Press, 1986. — p. cm. — *Includes index. — Bibliography: p*

SUBWAYS — England — London

GREAT BRITAIN. Department of Transport
Crime on the London Underground / report of a study by the Department of Transport in conjunction with London Underground ... [et al.]. — London : H.M.S.O., 1986. — 118p

SUCCESS

ROSS, Percy
Ask for the moon--and get it! : the secret to getting what you want by knowing how to ask / Percy Ross with Dick Samson. — New York : Putnam, c1987. — 219 p.

SUCCESS IN BUSINESS — Great Britain

GOLDSMITH, Walter
The new elite : Britain's top chief executives / Walter Goldsmith and Berry Ritchie. — London : Weidenfeld and Nicolson, 1987. — ix,179p

LESSEM, Ronnie
The roots of excellence / Ronnie Lessem. — London : Fontana/Collins, 1985. — 313p

SUCCESS IN BUSINESS — Japan

IGA, Mamoru
The thorn in the chrysanthemum : suicide and economic success in modern Japan / Mamoru Iga ; forewords by Edwin S. Shneidman and David K. Reynolds. — Berkeley : University of California Press, c1986. — xiv, 231 p.. — *Includes index. — Bibliography: p. 205-217*

SUCCESS IN BUSINESS — United States — Addresses, essays, lectures

Making it in America : the role of ethnicity in business enterprise, education, and work choices / edited by M. Mark Stolarik and Murray Friedman. — Lewisburg [Pa.] : Bucknell University Press ; London : Associated University Presses, c1986. — 143 p.. — *Includes bibliographies and index. — Contents: Ethnicity and business enterprise / Ivan Light, Randall M. Miller ; comments, Kenneth L. Kusmer -- Ethnicity and education / David Hogan, Mark Hutter ; comments, Henry P. Drewry -- Ethnicity and the world of work / Milton Cantor, Dennis Clark ; comments, Arthur B. Shostak -- Making it in America--and in the world / Michael Novak -- Conclusion / M. Mark Stolarik*

SUCCESS IN BUSINESS — United States — Case studies

PAUL, Ronald N
The 101 best performing companies in America / Ronald N. Paul, James W. Taylor. — Chicago, Ill. : Probus Pub. Co., c1986. — vii, 382 p.. — *Includes bibliographical references and index*

SUDAN — Biography

DENG, Francis Mading
The man called Deng Majok : a biography of power, polygyny, and change / Francis Mading Deng. — New Haven : Yale University Press, c1986. — p. cm. — *Includes index*

SUDAN — Economic conditions

ALI, Ali Abdel Gadir
Some aspects of the Sudan economy / Ali Abdel Gadir Ali. — Khartoum : University of Khartoum. Faculty of Economic and Social Studies. Development Studies and Research Centre, 1984. — 30p. — (Postgraduate teaching material series / University of Khartoum. Faculty of Economic and Social Studies. Development Studies and Research Centre ; no.1). — *Bibliography: p29-30*

NIBLOCK, Timothy
Class and power in Sudan : the dynamics of Sudanese politics, 1898-1985 / Tim Niblock. — Basingstoke : Macmillan, 1987. — [310]p. — *Includes index*

NIMERI, Sayed
The five year plan (1970-1975) : some aspects of the plan and its performance / Sayed Nimeri. — Khartoum : University of Khartoum. Faculty of Economic and Social Studies. Development Studies and Research Centre, 1977. — 55p. — (Monograph series / University of Khartoum. Faculty of Economic and Social Studies. Development Studies and Research Centre ; no.1). — *Bibliography: p[56]*

SÖRBÖ, Gunnar M.
How to survive development : the story of New Halfa / Gunnar M. Sörbö. — Khartoum : University of Khartoum. Faculty of Economic and Social Studies. Development Studies and Research Centre, 1977. — 52p. — (Monograph series / University of Khartoum. Faculty of Economic and Social Studies. Development Studies and Research Centre ; no.6). — *Bibliography: p[2]*

SØRBØ, Gunnar M.
Tenants and nomads in Eastern Sudan : a study of economic adaptations in the New Halfa Scheme / Gunnar M. Sørbø. — Uppsala : Scandinavian Institute of African Studies, 1985. — 159p

SUDAN — Economic policy

INTERNATIONAL LABOUR ORGANIZATION. Identification and Programming Mission to the Republic of the Sudan (1985)
After the famine : a programme of action to strengthen the survival strategies of affected populations / report of the ILO Identification and Programming Mission to the Republic of the Sudan, September 1985. — Geneva : ILO, c1986. — xi,309p

NIMERI, Sayed
An evaluation of the six year development plan of the Sudan (1977/78-1982/83) / Sayed Nimeri. — Khartoum : University of Khartoum. Faculty of Economic and Social Studies. Development Studies. Development Studies and Research Centre, 1978. — 55p. — (Monograph series / University of Khartoum. Faculty of Economic and Social Studies. Development Studies and Research Centre ; no.7). — *Bibliography: p54-55*

SUDAN — Foreign economic relations — Great Britain

BADAL, Raphael Koba
Origins of the underdevelopment of the Southern Sudan : British administrative neglect / Raphael Koba Badal. — Khartoum : University of Khartoum. Faculty of Economic and Social Studies. Development Studies and Research Centre, 1983. — 51p. — (Monograph series / University of Khartoum. Faculty of Economic and Social Studies. Development and Research Centre ; no.16)

SUDAN — History

GARANG, John
John Garang speaks / by John Garang ; edited and introduced by Mansour Khalid. — London : KPI Limited, 1987. — xiii,147p

SUDAN — History — 1899-1956

DALY, M. W.
Empire on the Nile : the Anglo-Eqyptian Sudan, 1898-1934 / M.W. Daly. — Cambridge : Cambridge University Press, 1986. — [xi,810]p. — *Includes bibliography and index*

HASABU, Afaf Abdel Majid Abu
Factional conflict in the Sudanese nationalist movement 1918-1948 / Araf [sic.] Abdel Majid Abu Hasabu. — Khartoum : Graduate College, University of Khartoum, 1985. — 179p. — (Graduate College publications / University of Khartoum ; no.12). — *Bibliography: p174-179*

SUDAN — History — Civil War, 1955-1972

ASSEFA, Hizkias
Mediation of civil wars / Hizkias Assefa. — Boulder, Colo. : Westview Press, 1986. — p. cm. — (Westview special studies in peace, conflict, and conflict resolution). — *Includes index.* — *Bibliography: p*

SUDAN — History — 1956-

Sudan since independence : studies of the political development since 1956 / edited by Muddathir Abd al-Rahim ... [et al.]. — Aldershot : Gower, c1986. — xi,181p. — *Includes bibliographies and index*

SUDAN — Industries

AFFAN, Bodour O. Abu
Industrial policies and industrialization in the Sudan / Bodour Osman Abu Affan. — Khartoum : University of Khartoum, 1985. — 180p. — (Graduate college publications / University of Khartoum ; no.16). — *Bibliography: p174-180*

SUDAN — Politics and government

The British in the Sudan, 1898-1956 : the sweetness and the sorrow / edited by Robert O. Collins and Francis M. Deng. — London : Macmillan in association with St. Antony's College, Oxford, 1984. — xxii,258p,[12]p of plates. — (St. Antony's/Macmillan series). — *Bibliography: p251. — Includes index*

DALY, M. W.
Empire on the Nile : the Anglo-Eqyptian Sudan, 1898-1934 / M.W. Daly. — Cambridge : Cambridge University Press, 1986. — [xi,810]p. — *Includes bibliography and index*

NIBLOCK, Timothy
Class and power in Sudan : the dynamics of Sudanese politics, 1898-1985 / Tim Niblock. — Basingstoke : Macmillan, 1987. — [310]p. — *Includes index*

SUDAN PEOPLES LIBERATION MOVEMENT

Sudan today : a collection of talks given at the Africa Centre, London, March 1985. — London : Sudan Peoples Liberation Movement, 1985. — 56p

SUDAN — Social conditions

AL-SHAHI, Ahmed
Themes for northern Sudan / Ahmed Al-Shahi. — London : Ithaca for the British Society for Middle Eastern Studies, 1986. — 152p. — (BRISMES Series ; no.1). — *Bibliography: p146-148. — Includes index*

NIBLOCK, Timothy
Class and power in Sudan : the dynamics of Sudanese politics, 1898-1985 / Tim Niblock. — Basingstoke : Macmillan, 1987. — [310]p. — *Includes index*

SØRBØ, Gunnar M.
Tenants and nomads in Eastern Sudan : a study of economic adaptations in the New Halfa Scheme / Gunnar M. Sørbø. — Uppsala : Scandinavian Institute of African Studies, 1985. — 159p

SUDDEN DEATH IN INFANTS — Government policy — United States

BERGMAN, Abraham B.
The "discovery" of sudden infant death syndrome : lessons in the practice of political medicine / Abraham B. Bergman. — New York : Praeger, 1986. — xii, 237 p.. — *Bibliography: p. 191-195*

SUDDEN DEATH IN INFANTS — United States — Political aspects

BERGMAN, Abraham B.
The "discovery" of sudden infant death syndrome : lessons in the practice of political medicine / Abraham B. Bergman. — New York : Praeger, 1986. — xii, 237 p.. — *Bibliography: p. 191-195*

SUDDEN INFANT DEATH — prevention & control — United States

BERGMAN, Abraham B.
The "discovery" of sudden infant death syndrome : lessons in the practice of political medicine / Abraham B. Bergman. — New York : Praeger, 1986. — xii, 237 p.. — *Bibliography: p. 191-195*

SUDETENLAND (CZECHOSLOVAKIA) — History — 20th century — Sources

Kampf - Widerstand - Verfolgung der sudetendeutschen Sozialdemokraten : Dokumentation der deutschen Sozialdemokraten aus der Tschechoslowakei im Kampf gegen Henlein und Hitler / erarbeitet von Adolf Hasenöhrl. — Stuttgart : Seliger-Gemeinde, 1983. — 649p

SUEZ CANAL — History

THOMAS, Hugh
The Suez affair. — Weidenfeld & Nicolson, 1967. — 259p.,ill.,24cm

SUEZ CANAL (EGYPT)

REID, Escott
Hungary and Suez 1956 : a view from New Delhi / Escott Reid. — Oakville [Ontario] : Mosaic Press, 1986. — 163p

SUEZ CANAL (EGYPT) — History

FAWZI, Mahmoud
Suez 1956 : an Egyptian perspective / by Mahmoud Fawzi. — London : Shorouk International, [1986]. — 149p

SUFFOLK — History

MACCULLOCH, Diarmaid
Suffolk and the Tudors : politics and religion in an English county 1500-1600 / Diarmaid MacCulloch. — Oxford : Clarendon, 1986. — [360]p. — *Includes index*

SUFFRAGE — Germany (West)

JESSE, Eckhard
Wahlrecht zwischen Kontinuität und Reform : eine Analyse der Wahlsystemdiskussion und der Wahlrechtsänderungen in der Bundesrepublik Deutschland 1949-1983 / Eckhard Jesse ; [herausgegeben von der Kommission für Geschichte des Parlamentarismus und der politischen Parteien]. — Düsseldorf : Droste, 1985. — 440p. — (Beiträge zur Geschichte des Parlamentarismus und der politischen Parteien ; Bd.78)

SUFFRAGE — South Africa

TATZ, Colin Martin
Shadow and substance in South Africa : a study in land and franchise policies affecting Africans, 1910-1960 / Colin Tatz. — Pietermaritzburg : University of Natal Press, 1962. — vi,238p

SUFFRAGETTES — Spain — History

FAGOAGA, Concha
La voz y el voto de las mujeres 1877-1931 / Concha Fagoaga. — Barcelona : Icaria Antrazyt, 1985. — 214p. — *Bibliography: p199-203*

SUFFRAGETTES — United States

FOWLER, Robert Booth
Carrie Catt : feminist politician / Robert Booth Fowler. — Boston : Northeastern University Press, c1986. — xx, 226 p.. — *Includes index.* — *Bibliography: p. 201-218*

SUFFRAGETTES — United States — Biography

LUNARDINI, Christine A.
From equal suffrage to equal rights : Alice Paul and the National Woman's Party, 1910-1928 / Christine A. Lunardini. — New York : New York University Press, 1986. — xx, 230 p.. — (The American social experience series ; 5). — *Includes index.* — *Bibliography: p. [206]-220*

SUFISM — Soviet Union — History

BENNIGSEN, Alexandre
Mystics and commissars : Sufism in the Soviet Union / Alexandre Bennigsen, S. Enders Wimbush. — London : Hurst, 1985. — [200]p. — *Includes bibliography and index*

SUGAO (INDIA) — Economic conditions

DANDEKAR, Hemalata C.
Men to Bombay, women at home : urban influence on Sugao village, Deccan Maharashtra, India 1942-1982 / Hemalata C. Dandekar. — Michigan : Ann Arbor : University of Michigan Center for South and Southeast Asian Studies, 1986. — xix,325p. — (Michigan papers on South and Southeast Asia). — *Bibliography: p311-317*

SUGAO (INDIA) — Social conditions

DANDEKAR, Hemalata C.
Men to Bombay, women at home : urban influence on Sugao village, Deccan Maharashtra, India 1942-1982 / Hemalata C. Dandekar. — Michigan : Ann Arbor : University of Michigan Center for South and Southeast Asian Studies, 1986. — xix,325p. — (Michigan papers on South and Southeast Asia). — *Bibliography: p311-317*

SUGAR — Manufacture and refining — Taiwan

The sugar industry in Taiwan, Republic of China. — [Taipei : Ministry of Economic Affairs, 1958]. — 16,[24]p

SUGAR CANE INDUSTRY — Dominican Republic

PLANT, Roger
Sugar and modern slavery : a tale of two countries / Roger Plant. — London : Zed, 1987. — [208]p. — *Includes bibliography and index*

SUGAR GROWING — Taiwan

The sugar industry in Taiwan, Republic of China. — [Taipei : Ministry of Economic Affairs, 1958]. — 16,[24]p

SUGAR GROWING — Taiwan — Linear programming

HSIEH, S. C.
Application of linear programming to crop competition study in Taiwan (with special reference to rice and sugarcane competition in central Taiwan) / by S. C. Hsieh. — Taipei : Chinese-American Joint Commission on Rural Reconstruction, 1957. — [iv],95p. — (Economic digest series / Joint Commission on Rural Reconstruction ; no.10)

SUGAR TRADE

BROWN, James G.
The international sugar industry : developments and prospects / James G. Brown. — Washington, D. C. : The World Bank, 1987. — xii,69p. — (World Bank staff commodity working papers ; no.18). — *Includes bibliographical references*

SUGAR TRADE — Government policy

BROWN, James G.
The international sugar industry : developments and prospects / James G. Brown. — Washington, D. C. : The World Bank, 1987. — xii,69p. — (World Bank staff commodity working papers ; no.18). — *Includes bibliographical references*

SUGAR WORKERS — Dominican Republic

PLANT, Roger
Sugar and modern slavery : a tale of two countries / Roger Plant. — London : Zed, 1987. — [208]p. — *Includes bibliography and index*

SUGARCANE — Fiji

BROOKFIELD, Harold Chillingworth
Land, cane and coconuts : papers on the rural economy of Fiji / H. C. Brookfield, F. Ellis, R. G. Ward. — Canberra [A.C.T.] : Australian National University, 1985. — 251p. — (Australian National University Department of Human Geography Publication ; HG/17). — *Includes bibliographies*

SUGARCANE — Taiwan

HSIEH, S. C.
Application of linear programming to crop competition study in Taiwan (with special reference to rice and sugarcane competition in central Taiwan) / by S. C. Hsieh. — Taipei : Chinese-American Joint Commission on Rural Reconstruction, 1957. — [iv],95p. — (Economic digest series / Joint Commission on Rural Reconstruction ; no.10)

SUICIDE

BARRACLOUGH, Brian
Suicide : clinical and epidemiological studies. Brian Barraclough with Jennifer Hughes. — London : Croom Helm, c1987. — 188p. — *Bibliography: p181-185. — Includes index*

BAUDELOT, Christian
Durkheim et le suicide / Christian Baudelot et Roger Establet. — [Paris] : Presses universitaires de France, [1984]. — 125p. — (Philosophies ; 3)

SHNEIDMAN, Edwin S
Definition of suicide / Edwin S. Shneidman. — New York : Wiley, c1985. — p. cm. — "A Wiley-Interscience publication.". — *Bibliography: p239-247. — Bibliography: p*

SUICIDE — Bibliography

MCINTOSH, John L
Research on suicide : a bibliography / compiled by John L. McIntosh. — Westport, Conn. ; London : Greenwood Press, 1985. — xiii, 323p. — (Bibliographies and indexes in psychology ; no. 2). — *Includes index. — Bibliography: p*

SUICIDE — in adolescence

HAWTON, Keith
Suicide and attempted suicide among children and adolescents / by Keith Hawton. — Beverly Hills ; London : Sage, c1986. — 159 p. — (Developmental clinical psychology and psychiatry series ; v. 5). — *Includes index. — Bibliography: p. 145-153*

Suicide in adolescence : suicidal behaviour among adolescents / edited by René F.W. Diekstra and Keith Hawton. — Dordrecht ; Boston : Nijhoff, 1986. — p. cm. — *Includes indexes*

SUICIDE — in infancy & childhood

HAWTON, Keith
Suicide and attempted suicide among children and adolescents / by Keith Hawton. — Beverly Hills ; London : Sage, c1986. — 159 p. — (Developmental clinical psychology and psychiatry series ; v. 5). — *Includes index. — Bibliography: p. 145-153*

SUICIDE — Prevention

HAWTON, Keith
Suicide and attempted suicide among children and adolescents / by Keith Hawton. — Beverly Hills ; London : Sage, c1986. — 159 p. — (Developmental clinical psychology and psychiatry series ; v. 5). — *Includes index. — Bibliography: p. 145-153*

SUICIDE — Prevention — Addresses, essays, lectures

Suicide in adolescence : suicidal behaviour among adolescents / edited by René F.W. Diekstra and Keith Hawton. — Dordrecht ; Boston : Nijhoff, 1986. — p. cm. — *Includes indexes*

SUICIDE — prevention & control

Suicide in adolescence : suicidal behaviour among adolescents / edited by René F.W. Diekstra and Keith Hawton. — Dordrecht ; Boston : Nijhoff, 1986. — p. cm. — *Includes indexes*

SUICIDE — Japan

IGA, Mamoru
The thorn in the chrysanthemum : suicide and economic success in modern Japan / Mamoru Iga ; forewords by Edwin S. Shneidman and David K. Reynolds. — Berkeley : University of California Press, c1986. — xiv, 231 p.. — *Includes index. — Bibliography: p. 205-217*

SUICIDE — United States — Bibliography

MCINTOSH, John L
Research on suicide : a bibliography / compiled by John L. McIntosh. — Westport, Conn. ; London : Greenwood Press, 1985. — xiii, 323p. — (Bibliographies and indexes in psychology ; no. 2). — *Includes index. — Bibliography: p*

SUICIDE

POPE, Whitney
Durkheim's Suicide : a classic analyzed / Whitney Pope. — Chicago ; London : University of Chicago Press, 1982. — 229 p. — (Midway reprint). — *Originally published: University of Chicago Press, 1976*

SUKARNO, President of Indonesia

LEGGE, J. D.
Sukarno : a political biography / J.D. Legge. — Rev. ed. — London : Allen & Unwin, [1985]. — x,431p,[8]p of plates. — *Previous ed.: London : Allen Lane, 1972. — Includes index*

SUKYO MAHIKARI

DAVIS, Winston Bradley
Dojo : magic and exorcism in modern Japan / Winston Davis. — Stanford, Calif. : Stanford University Press, 1980. — xvi, 332 p.. — *Includes bibliographical references and index*

SULPHUR — Environmental aspects

Air-borne sulphur pollution : effects and control : report prepared within the framework of the Convention on Long-range Transboundary Air Pollution. — New York : United Nations, 1984. — xiii,265p. — (Air pollution studies ; no.1). — *Sales no: E.84.II.E.8*

SULTAN GALIEV, MIRSAID

BENNIGSEN, Alexandre
Sultan Galiev, le père de la révolution tiers-mondiste / Alexandre Bennigsen, Chantal Lemercier-Quelquejay. — Paris : Fayard, 1986. — 305p. — (Les inconnus de l'histoire)

SUN, YAT-SEN

ANSCHEL, Eugene
Homer Lea, Sun Yat-sen, and the Chinese revolution / by Eugene Anschel. — New York : Praeger, 1984. — xvi, 269 p.. — *Includes index. — Bibliography: p. 253-262*

SUN, YAT-SEN — Exile, 1896-1897 — England — London

WONG, J. Y
The origins of an heroic image : Sun Yatsen in London, 1896-1897 / J.Y. Wong. — Hong Kong ; Oxford : Oxford University Press, 1986. — xviii, 330p, [8]p of plates. — (East Asian historical monographs). — *Includes index. — Bibliography: p.299-319*

SUN FIRE OFFICE

JENKINS, D. T.
Indexes of the fire insurance policies of the Sun Fire Office and the Royal Exchange Assurance 1775-1787 : [an introduction]. — London : Economic and Social Research Council, 1986. — 35p. — *Bibliography: p32-35*

SUN FIRE OFFICE

Fire policies 1775-1787. — London : Economic and Social Research Council, [1986]. — 24microfiches

SUNDAY LEGISLATION — Great Britain

Effects of Sunday trading : the regulation of retail trading hours / J. A. Kay...[et al.]. — London : Institute for Fiscal Studies, 1984. — 110p. — (IFS report series ; no.13). — *Bibliography: p98-100*

GREAT BRITAIN. Parliament. House of Commons. Library. Research Division
Shops Bill, Bill 26 (Revised) 80-81 / [Joanna Roll]. — [London] : the Division, [1981]. — 13p. — (Reference sheet ; no.81/7)

GREAT BRITAIN. Parliament. House of Commons. Library. Research Division
Shops Bill (Bill 94 of 1985-86) / Fiona Poole. — [London] : the Division, 1986. — 23p. — (Reference sheet ; no.86/7). — *Bibliographical references: p22-23*

TOWNSEND, Christopher
Why keep Sunday special? / Christopher Townsend and Michael Schluter ; foreword by Sir Norman Anderson. — Cambridge : Jubilee Centre Publications, 1985. — 87p. — (Jubilee Centre Paper ; no.5). — *Bibliography: p84-87*

SUNDAY-SCHOOLS — England — History

CLIFF, Philip B.
The rise and development of the Sunday school movement in England, 1780-1980 / Philip B. Cliff. — Redhill : National Christian Education Council, c1986. — [416]p. — *Includes bibliography and index*

SUNDERLAND (TYNE AND WEAR) — Religion

MILBURN, G. E.
Religion in Sunderland in the mid-nineteenth century / G. E. Milburn. — Sunderland : Sunderland Polytechnic. Department of Geography and History, 1983. — 73p. — (Occasional paper / Sunderland Polytechnic. Department of Geography and History ; no.3)

SUNTORY-TOYOTA INTERNATIONAL CENTRE FOR ECONOMICS AND RELATED DISCIPLINES

Bulletin / Suntory-Toyota International Centre for Economics and Related Disciplines. — London : Suntory-Toyota International Centre for Economics and Related Disciplines, 1986-. — 3 per year

SUOMEN KOMUNISTINEN PUOLUE

HYVÄRINEN, Matti
The Finnish Communist Party : the failure of attempts to modernize a C.P. / Matti Hyvärinen, Jukka Paastela. — Tampere : Tampereen yliopisto, Politiikan tutkimuksen laitos, 1985. — 42 leaves. — (Tutkielmia / Tampereen yliopisto, Politiikan tutkimuksen laitosOccasional papers / University of Tampere, Department of Political Science ; 39). — *Bibliography: leaves 35-42*

SUPERCALC (COMPUTER PROGRAM)
THOMAS, Tom E.
Financial decision making with VisiCalc and SuperCalc / Tom E. Thomas. — Englewood Cliffs, N.J. : Prentice-Hall, 1985. — p. cm. — Includes index

SUPERCOMPUTERS
LAZOU, Christopher
Supercomputers and their use / Christopher Lazou. — Oxford : Clarendon, 1986. — xi,227p. — (Oxford science publications). — Bibliography: p215-218. — Includes index

SUPERMARKETS — Denmark
Engroshandelen med dagligvarer : markedsstruktur, konkurrenceforhold, prisdannelse, indtjening. — København : Monopoltilsynet, 1982. — 372p. — Bibliography: p217

SUPERVISION OF SOCIAL WORKERS
ATHERTON, James S.
Professional supervision in group care : a contract-based approach / James S. Atherton. — London : Tavistock Publications, 1986. — [192]p. — (Residential social work). — Includes index

FORD, Kathy
Student supervision / Kathy Ford and Alan Jones. — Basingstoke : Macmillan Education, 1987. — x,162p. — (Practical social work). — Bibliography: p154-157. — Includes index

SUPERVISORS, INDUSTRIAL
WHITE, G. C.
Redesign of work organisations - its impact on supervisors / Geoff White. — London : Work Research Unit, 1983. — 10p. — (WRU occasional paper ; 26). — At head of title page: Advisory, Conciliation and Arbitration Service. — Bibliographical references: p9-10

SUPERVISORS, INDUSTRIAL — Great Britain
INDUSTRIAL TRAINING SERVICE
Supervision - now and then : a report of a research study into the role and training of supervisors in the iron and steel industry carried out by Industrial Training Service on behalf of the Iron and Steel Industry Training Board. — [London] ([190 Fleet St., EC4A 2AH]) : [Iron and Steel Industry Training Board], [1980]. — 19p

SUPPLEMENTAL SECURITY INCOME PROGRAM — Australia
CROMPTON, Cathy
Too old for a job, too young for a pension? : income support for older people out of work / Cathy Crompton. — Canberra : Australian Government Publishing Service, 1986. — x,69p. — (Issues paper / Social Security Review ; no.2). — Bibliogaphy: p67-69

SUPPLEMENTAL SECURITY INCOME PROGRAM — Great Britain
GREAT BRITAIN. Department of Health and Social Security. Regional Directorate
Relations with social services : report of joint study...of the relationships between the Supplementary Benefits organisation and social services / by the Department's Regional Directorate and Social Work Service. — [London] : the Department, 1979. — viii,48p

SUPPLEMENTAL SECURITY INCOME PROGRAM — Great Britain — Statistics
GREAT BRITAIN. Department of Health and Social Security
Supplementary benefit statistics. — Newcastle upon Tyne : [the Department], 1983-. — Annual

SUPPLEMENTARY EMPLOYMENT — European Economic Community countries — Statistics
ALDEN, Jeremy
Multiple job holders : an analysis of second jobs in the European Community / by Jeremy Alden and Richard Spooner. — Luxembourg : Office for Official Publications of the European Communities, 1982. — xii,161p

SUPPLEMENTARY EMPLOYMENT — Germany (West)
SMITH, Stephen
The shadow economy in Britain and Germany : based on a comparative research project undertaken by the Institute for Fiscal Studies, London, and the Institut für Angewandte Wirtschaftforschung Tübingen / Stephen Smith and Susanne Wied-Nebbeling. — London : Anglo-German Foundation for the Study of Industrial Society, c1986. — 102 p

SUPPLEMENTARY EMPLOYMENT — Great Britain
SMITH, Stephen
The shadow economy in Britain and Germany : based on a comparative research project undertaken by the Institute for Fiscal Studies, London, and the Institut für Angewandte Wirtschaftforschung Tübingen / Stephen Smith and Susanne Wied-Nebbeling. — London : Anglo-German Foundation for the Study of Industrial Society, c1986. — 102 p

SUPPLY AND DEMAND
AHMAD, E.
Demand response in Pakistan : a modification of the linear expenditure system for 1976 / E. Ahmad, H. M. Leung and N. H. Stern. — London : Suntory Toyota International Centre for Economics and Related Disciplines, 1987. — 18p. — (Development research programme / London School of Economics and Political Science. Suntory Toyota International Centre for Economics and Related Disciplines ; no.6). — Bibliography: p17

SUPPLY AND DEMAND — Transportation — Mathematical models
MOSLER, Karl C.
Continuous location of transportation networks / K. C. Mosler. — Berlin ; London : Sringer-Verlag, 1987. — 158p. — Bibliography: p143-153

SUPPLY-SIDE ECONOMICS
ATTANASIO, O.
Real effects of demand- and supply -side policies in interdependent economies / O. Attanasio and F. van der Ploeg. — London : Centre for Labour Economics, London School of Economics, 1987. — 42p. — (Discussion paper / London School of Economics and Political Science. Centre for Labour Economics ; no.282). — Bibliography: p29-31

International monetary problems and supply-side economics : essays in honour of Lorie Tarshis / edited by Jon S. Cohen and G.C. Harcourt. — Basingstoke : Macmillan, 1986. — viii,162p. — Includes bibliographies and index

SUPPLY-SIDE ECONOMICS — Organisation for Economic Co-operation and Development countries — Mathematical models
JARRETT, Peter
A revised supply block for the major seven countries in Interlink / by Peter Jarrett and Raymond Torres. — Paris : OECD, 1987. — 41p. — (Working papers / OECD Department of Economics and Statistics ; no.41). — Bibliographical references: p23-24

SUPPLY-SIDE ECONOMICS — United States
Economic report of the people / Center for Popular Economics. — 1st ed. — Boston : South End Press, c1986. — xvii, 260 p.. — The crossed out word "President" appears in the title before the word "people.". — Includes bibliographies and index

SUPPLY-SIDE ECONOMICS — United States — Congresses
The Legacy of Reaganomics : prospects for long-term growth / edited by Charles R. Hulten and Isabel V. Sawhill. — Washington, D.C. : Urban Institute Press, 1984. — p. cm. — (The Changing domestic priorities series). — Papers presented at a conference held Sept. 22, 1983, under the auspices of the Urban Institute Changing Domestic Priorities project. — Includes bibliographical references

SUPPORT (DOMESTIC RELATIONS) — Great Britain
GREAT BRITAIN. Parliament. House of Commons. Library. Research Division
Matrimonial and Family Proceedings Bill (H.L.) 1983-4 [Bill 96] / [Patrick Nealon]. — [London] : the Division, 1984. — 11p. — (Research note ; no.141)

SURETY OF THE PEACE — England
GREAT BRITAIN. Law Commission
Criminal law : binding over - the issues / The Law Commission. — London : H.M.S.O., 1987. — vi,113p. — (Working paper / The Law Commission ; no.103)

SURETYSHIP AND GUARANTY — South Africa
CANEY, L. R.
The law of suretyship in South Africa / by L.R. Caney. — 2nd ed. / with a chapter on the Roman law by R.O. Donnellan. — Cape Town : Juta, 1970. — xxiii,249p. — Bibliography: p.xi. - Includes index

SURFACE ROUGHNESS — Measurement
SAYERS, Michael W.
The international road roughness experiment : establishing correlation and a calibration standard for measurements / Michael W. Sayers, Thomas D. Gillespie, and Caesar A. V. Queiroz. — Washington, D.C. : The World Bank, 1986. — ix,453p. — (World Bank technical paper ; no.45). — Bibliographical references: p105-107

SURINAM — Social conditions
CHIN, Henk E.
Surinam : politics, economics and society / Henk E. Chin and Hans Buddingh'. — London : Pinter, 1987. — [220]p. — (Marxist regimes series). — Includes bibliography and index

SURREY — Economic conditions
SURREY. County Planning Department
Structure plan monitoring : employment and commercial data. — [Kingston upon Thames] : [the Department], 1985. — [25 leaves]. — (Technical report / Surrey. County Planning Department ; no.5/85). — Bound with Employment and commuting in Surrey

SURREY — Population — Statistics
SURREY. County Planning Department
Comparative statistics : census of population 1971 and 1981. — [Kingston upon Thames] : [the Department], 1985. — [100 leaves]. — (Technical report / Surrey. County Planning Department ; no.8/85). — Bound with other publications on population in Surrey

SURREY. County Planning Department
Surrey structure plan : monitoring technical report : ward population forecasts 1981-1991. — [Kingston upon Thames] : [the Department], 1987. — [16p]. — (Technical report / Surrey. County Planning Department ; no.5/87). — Bound with Comparative statistics

SURREY. County Planning Department
Surrey structure plan : monitoring technical report : population forecasts, 1981-1991 and 1991-2001. — [Kingston upon Thames] : [the Department], 1987. — [19 leaves]. — (Technical report / Surrey. County Planning Department ; no.4/87). — Bound with Comparative statistics

SURREY — Statistics, Vital
SURREY. County Planning Department
Births and deaths in Surrey - vital statistics. — [Kingston upon Thames] : [the Department], 1985. — 31 leaves. — (Technical report / Surrey. County Planning Department ; no.2/85). — Bound with Comparative statistics

SURVEYS
BELSON, William A.
Validity in survey research : with special reference to the techniques of intensive interviewing and progressive modification for testing and constructing difficult or sensitive measures for use in survey research : a report / by William A. Belsen. — Aldershot : Gower, c1986. — xviii,565p. — Fiche in pocket. — Includes index

SURVEYS *continuation*
Survey item bank / [Bernard Stewart...et al.]. — [S.l.] : MCB/University Press. — *Sponsored by British Telecom* Vol.2. — [1985]. — Various pagings

SURVIVORS' BENEFITS — France
BORREL, Catherine
Le veuvage avant soixante ans : ses conséquences financières. — Paris : La Documentation française. — (Documents du centre d'étude des revenus et des coûts ; no.81) 1: Les premiers mois du veuvage / ...réalisée par Catherine Borrel et Philippe Madinier. — 1986. — 146p

SUTCLIFFE, PETER, 1946-
WARD JOUVE, Nicole
"The streetcleaner : the Yorkshire Ripper case on trial / Nicole Ward Jouve. — London : Boyars, 1986. — 231p

SUTTNER, BERTHA VON
KLEBERGER, Ilse
Die Vision vom Frieden : Bertha von Suttner / Ilse Kleburger. — Berlin : Klopp, 1985. — 210p

SVARĀJYA PĀRṬĪ (India)
BAKSHI, S. R
Swaraj Party and the Indian National Congress / S.R. Bakshi. — New Delhi : Vikas Pub. House, c1985. — vi, 200 p.. — *Bibliography: p [191]-195.* — *Bibliography: p. [191]-195*

SVENSKA KYRKAN
Aktiva i Svenska kyrkan : en livsstilstudie / [Hans L. Zetterberg...et al.]. — [s.l.] : Verbum, 1983. — 236p

SVENSKA TÄNDSTICKS AKTIEBOLAGET — History
HILDEBRAND, Karl-Gustav
Expansion, crisis, reconstruction 1917-1939 / Karl-Gustav Hildebrand ; translation by Michael Callow. — Stockholm : Liber Forlag, 1985. — 496p. — (The Swedish Match Company, 1917-1939. studies in business internationalisation). — *Bibliography: p473-484*

SVERIGES KOMMUNISTISKA PARTI
HERMANSSON, Jörgen
Kommunism på svenska? : SKP/VPK:s idéutveckling efter Komintern / Jörgen Hermansson. — Uppsala : Uppsala universitet ; Stockholm : Distributed by Almqvist & Wiksell, 1984. — 388p. — (Acta Universitatis Upsaliensis). — *With English summary.* — *Doktorsavhandling framlagd vid Uppsala universitet 1984*

SW-AT KOHISTAN (PAKISTAN) — History
JAHANZEB, Miangul, Wali of Swat
The last Wali of Swat : an autobiography / as told to Fredrik Barth. — Oslo : Universitetsforlaget : Distributed world-wide excluding Scandinavia by Oxford University Press, c1985. — 199p, 8p of plates. — *Bibliography:p.191-192*

SWAHILI LANGUAGE — Zaire — History
FABIAN, Johannes
Language and colonial power : the appropriation of Swahili in the former Belgian Congo 1880-1938 / Johannes Fabian. — Cambridge : Cambridge University Press, 1986. — viii,206p. — (African studies series ; 48). — *Bibliography: p188-199.* — *Includes index*

SWALCAP
GOSLING, Jane
SWALCAP : a guide for librarians and systems managers / Jane Gosling. — Aldershot : Gower, c1987. — 129 p

SWAZILAND — Population
TESTERINK-MAAS, E. M. W. M.
Demographic response on commercialization in agriculture : a case study of Swaziland / E. M. W. M. Testerink-Maas. — Kwaluseni : Kwaluseni Campus, 1985. — iii,76p. — (Research paper / University of Swaziland. Social Science Research Unit ; no.16). — *Bibliography: p76*

SWAZILAND — Rural conditions
GUMA, X. P.
Some aspects of poverty among Swazi rural homesteads / X. P. Guma [and] M. Neocosmos. — Kwaluseni : Kwaluseni Campus, 1986. — ix,73p. — (Research paper / University of Swaziland. Social Science Research Unit ; no.23)

RUSSELL, Margo
Rural homestead income in central Swaziland / Margo Russell and Makhosazana Ntshingila. — Kwaluseni : Kwaluseni Campus, 1984. — 61p. — (Research paper / University of Swaziland. Social Science Research Unit ; no.13)

SWEDEN — Commerce
ERIKSSON, Gösta A.
Finnish and Swedish iron export to England in the 18th and 19th centuries with an excursus / Gösta A. Eriksson. — ˚Abo : ˚Abo Akademis, 1987. — 43p. — (Meddelanden fr˚an Ekonomisk-Statsveten skapliga Fakulteten vid ˚Abo Akademi ; Ser.A.:239). — *Bibliography: p42-43*

SWEDEN — Economic conditions — 1945-
MEYERSON, Per-Martin
Eurosclerosis : the case of Sweden : a critical examination of some central problems in the Swedish economy and in Swedish politics / by Per-Martin Meyerson ; [translated by Victor J. Kayfetz]. — Stockholm : Federation of Swedish Industries, c1985. — 118 p.. — *Bibliography: p. 114-118*

The Swedish economy / Barry P. Bosworth ... [et al.] ; Barry P. Bosworth and Alice M. Rivlin, editors. — Washington, D.C. : Brookings Institution, c1987. — p. cm. — *Includes bibliographical references and index*

SWEDEN — Economic policy
The Swedish economy / Barry P. Bosworth ... [et al.] ; Barry P. Bosworth and Alice M. Rivlin, editors. — Washington, D.C. : Brookings Institution, c1987. — p. cm. — *Includes bibliographical references and index*

SWEDEN — Foreign economic relations — Soviet Union
ATTMAN, Artur
Swedish aspirations and the Russian market during the 17th century / Artur Attman. — Göteborg : Kung 1. Vetenskaps-och Vitterhets-Samhället, 1985. — 41p. — (Acta Regiae Societatis Scientiarum et Litterarum Gothoburgensis. Humaniora ; 24). — *Bibliography: p38-40*

SWEDEN — Foreign relations
Utrikesfragor : Utrikesdepartementet. — Stockholm : Utrikesdepartementet, 1950/51-1981. — *Annual*

SWEDEN — Foreign relations — 1950-
GOLDMANN, Kjell
Democracy and foreign policy : the case of Sweden / Kjell Goldmann, Sten Berglund, Gunnar Sjöstedt. — Aldershot : Gower, c1986. — xiv,206p. — (Swedish studies in international relations). — *Bibliography: p190-196.* — *Includes index*

SWEDEN — History — Christina, 1632-1654
ROBERTS, Michael
Sweden's age of greatness, 1632-1718 / Edited by Michael Roberts. — New York : St. Martin's Press, [1973]. — x, 314 p. — (Problems in focus series). — *Bibliography: p. [288]-295*

SWEDEN — History — House of Pfalz-Zweibrücken, 1654-1718
ROBERTS, Michael
Sweden's age of greatness, 1632-1718 / Edited by Michael Roberts. — New York : St. Martin's Press, [1973]. — x, 314 p. — (Problems in focus series). — *Bibliography: p. [288]-295*

SWEDEN — Industries
BENGTSSON, Tommy
Industri under avspärrning : studier i svensk textilproduktion 1935-1950 / Tommy Bengtsson. — Lund : Ekonomisk-Historiska Föreningen, 1980. — 215p. — *Bibliography: p211-215*

PANAS, Epaminondas E.
Almost homogeneous functions : a theoretical and empirical analysis with special emphasis on labour input : the case of Swedish manufacturing industries / Epaminondas E. Panas. — Uppsala : Uppsala University, 1985. — 130p. — (Acta universitatis Upsaliensis. Studia oeconomica Upsaliensia ; 11). — *Bibliographies*

SWEDEN — Industries — History — 18th century
ISACSON, Maths
Proto-industrialisation in Scandinavia : craft skills in the industrial revolution / Maths Isacson and Lars Magnusson. — Leamington Spa : Berg, c1987. — 151p,[12]p of plates. — *Bibliography: p138-146.* — *Includes index*

SWEDEN — Industries — History — 19th century
ISACSON, Maths
Proto-industrialisation in Scandinavia : craft skills in the industrial revolution / Maths Isacson and Lars Magnusson. — Leamington Spa : Berg, c1987. — 151p,[12]p of plates. — *Bibliography: p138-146.* — *Includes index*

SWEDEN — Manufactures
PANAS, Epaminondas E.
Almost homogeneous functions : a theoretical and empirical analysis with special emphasis on labour input : the case of Swedish manufacturing industries / Epaminondas E. Panas. — Uppsala : Uppsala University, 1985. — 130p. — (Acta universitatis Upsaliensis. Studia oeconomica Upsaliensia ; 11). — *Bibliographies*

SWEDEN — Politics and government — 1905-
HADENIUS, Stig
[Svensk politik under 1900-talent. English]. Swedish politics during the 20th century / Stig Hadenius. — [Stockholm] : Swedish Institute, c1985. — 173 p.. — (Sweden books). — *Translation of: Svensk politik under 1900-talet.* — *Bibliography: p. 172-173*

HERMANSSON, Jörgen
Kommunism på svenska? : SKP/VPK:s idéutveckling efter Komintern / Jörgen Hermansson. — Uppsala : Uppsala universitet ; Stockholm : Distributed by Almqvist & Wiksell, 1984. — 388p. — (Acta Universitatis Upsaliensis). — *With English summary.* — *Doktorsavhandling framlagd vid Uppsala universitet 1984*

SWEDEN — Politics and government — 1950-1973
BIRGERSSON, Bengt Owe
Den svenska folkestyrelsen / Bengt Owe Birgersson, Jörgen Westerståhl. — 2nd ed.. — Stockholm : Liber Förlag : Jurist- och Samhällsvetareförbundets, c1982. — 216p

SWEDEN — Politics and government — 1973-
BIRGERSSON, Bengt Owe
Den svenska folkestyrelsen / Bengt Owe Birgersson, Jörgen Westerståhl. — 2nd ed.. — Stockholm : Liber Förlag : Jurist- och Samhällsvetareförbundets, c1982. — 216p

SWEDEN — Politics and government — 1973- *continuation*
MEYERSON, Per-Martin
Eurosclerosis : the case of Sweden : a critical examination of some central problems in the Swedish economy and in Swedish politics / by Per-Martin Meyerson ; [translated by Victor J. Kayfetz]. — Stockholm : Federation of Swedish Industries, c1985. — 118 p.. — *Bibliography: p. 114-118*

SWEDEN — Population — Statistics
Fertility survey in Sweden, 1981 : a summary of findings. — Voorburg : International Statistical Institute, 1984. — 18p. — (World Fertility Survey ; no.43)

SWEDEN — Religious life and customs
Aktiva i Svenska kyrkan : en livsstilstudie / [Hans L. Zetterberg...et al.]. — [s.l.] : Verbum, 1983. — 236p

SWEDEN — Social conditions — 1945-
Welfare in transition : a survey of living conditions in Sweden 1968-1981 / edited by Robert Erikson and Rune Åberg. — Oxford : Clarendon, 1987. — xv,297p. — *Bibliography: p291-297*

SWEDES — Germany — History
RIEGLER, Claudius Helmut
Emigration und Arbeitswanderung aus Schweden nach Norddeutschland 1868-1914 / Claudius Helmut Riegler. — Neumunster : Wachholtz, 1985. — 293p. — (Studien zur Wirtschafts- und Sozialgeschichte Schleswig-Holsteins ; 8). — *Bibliography: p283-293*

SWEDES — Germany — Schleswig-Holstein — History
RIEGLER, Claudius Helmut
Emigration und Arbeitswanderung aus Schweden nach Norddeutschland 1868-1914 / Claudius Helmut Riegler. — Neumunster : Wachholtz, 1985. — 293p. — (Studien zur Wirtschafts- und Sozialgeschichte Schleswig-Holsteins ; 8). — *Bibliography: p283-293*

SWEDES — Soviet Union
JONSSON, Karl
Sågverksarbetare i österled : liv och leverne kring det svenska sågverket i Kovda / berättet av Karl Jonsson och nedtecknat av Linnéa Jonsson. — 2:a upplagan. — [s.l. : s.n.], 1981. — 136p. — *Bibliography: p135-136*

SWEDISH LANGUAGE — Dictionaries — English
EDSTRÖM, N. F.
Ekonomi ordbok : svensk-engelsk fackordbok för ekonomifunktionen med begreppsförklaringar / N.F. Edström, L.A. Samuelson, O.K. Böök. — 2. uppl. — Stockholm : Norstedt & Söners, 1984. — 145p

SWEDISH MATCH COMPANY *See* Svenska Tändsticks Aktiebologet

ŚWIATŁO, JÓZEF
BŁAŻYŃSKI, Zbigniew
Mówi Józef Światło : za kulisami bezpieki i partii 1940-1955 / Zbigniew Błażyński ; słowo wstępne: Jan Nowak-Jezioranski. — Wyd. 3 (z erratami i uzupełnieniem). — Londyn : Polska Fundacja Kulturalna, 1986. — xv,319p. — *Part of the material contained in this book was published by Radio Free Europe as a pamphlet in 1955 and dropped over Poland from balloons, under the title "Za kulisami bezpieki i partii". Reprinted under title "Kulisy bezpieki i partii" in Warsaw 1979 by the clandestine Publishing House NOWA*

SWINE — Ecomomic aspects — Denmark
Investering i svinestalde. — København : I kommission hos Landhusholdningsselskabets Forlag, 1975. — 24p. — (Meddelelse / Det landøkonomiske Driftsbureau ; nr.18)

SWISS — Argentina — History — 19th century
CARRON, Alexandre
Nos cousins d'Amérique : histoire de l'émigration valaisanne au XIXe siècle / Alexandre Carron [et] Christophe Carron. — Sierre : Monographic SA, 1986. — 300p

SWITZERLAND — Biography
Who's who in Switzerland including the Principality of Liechtenstein 1986-1987. — Geneva : Nagel, 1986. — 564p

SWITZERLAND — Boundaries
RÉGIONS FRONTALIÈRES (1980 : Berne)
Régions frontalières = Grenzregionen = Regioni di frontiera / éditeurs/Herausgeber/editori, Basilio Biucchi, Gaston Gaudard. — Saint-Saphorin : Georgi, c1981. — 276p. — (Thema-Hefte / Schweizerischer Nationalfonds zur Förderung der wissenschaftlichen Forschung, Programmleitung). — *Travaux éxécutés dans le cadre du programme national "Problèmes régionaux en Suisse, notamment dans les zones de montagne et les zones frontalières" du Fonds national suisse de la recherche scientifique. — Avec contributions en français, allemand et italien*

SWITZERLAND — Constitution
FLEINER, Thomas
The concept of the constitution of Switzerland : the Swiss Constitution explained to a foreign audience / Thomas Fleiner. — Riehen : Joint Center for Federal and Regional Studies, 1983. — 25 leaves. — (Kleine Institutsreihe ; no.7)

SWITZERLAND — Economic conditions — 1918-
RÉGIONS FRONTALIÈRES (1980 : Berne)
Régions frontalières = Grenzregionen = Regioni di frontiera / éditeurs/Herausgeber/editori, Basilio Biucchi, Gaston Gaudard. — Saint-Saphorin : Georgi, c1981. — 276p. — (Thema-Hefte / Schweizerischer Nationalfonds zur Förderung der wissenschaftlichen Forschung, Programmleitung). — *Travaux éxécutés dans le cadre du programme national "Problèmes régionaux en Suisse, notamment dans les zones de montagne et les zones frontalières" du Fonds national suisse de la recherche scientifique. — Avec contributions en français, allemand et italien*

Le secteur tertiaire et le nouveau développement régional / par Jean Valarché...[et al.]. — Fribourg : Éditions Universitaires, [1985]. — 103p. — (Ökonomische kolloquien = Colloques économiques ; 17)

SWITZERLAND — Economic conditions — 1945-
GENBERG, Hans
External influences on the Swiss economy under fixed and flexible exchange rates / Hans Genberg and Alexander K. Swoboda. — Grüsch : Rüegger, c1985. — ii, 182 p.. — (Schweizerisches Institut für Aussenwirtschafts-, Struktur- und Regionalforschung an der Hochschule St. Gallen ; Bd. 10). — *Bibliography: p. 178-182*

SWITZERLAND — Emigration and immigration
FEDERAZIONE COLONIE LIBERE ITALIANE IN SVIZZERA
"Passaporti, prego!" : ricordi e testimonianze di emigrati italiani / Federazione colonie libere italiane in Svizzera ; [Tullio Agelli...et al.]. — Zurigo : Federazione colonie libere italiane in Svizzera, 1985. — 210p

SWITZERLAND — Emigration and immigration — History — 19th century
CARRON, Alexandre
Nos cousins d'Amérique : histoire de l'émigration valaisanne au XIXe siècle / Alexandre Carron [et] Christophe Carron. — Sierre : Monographic SA, 1986. — 300p

SWITZERLAND — Foreign economic relations
BORNER, Silvio
Internationalization of industry : an assessment in the light of a small open economy (Switzerland) / Silvio Borner. — Berlin ; New York : Springer-Verlag, c1986. — p. cm. — *Bibliography: p*

JOLLES, Paul R.
Von der Handelspolitik zur Aussenwirtschaftspolitik : ausgewählte Reden und Aufsätze / Paul R. Jolles ; herausgegeben von den Direktionsmitgliedern des Bundesamtes für Aussenwirtschaft aus Anlass des vierzigjährigen Dienstjubiläums von Staatssekretär...Paul R. Jolles. — Bern : Verlag Stämpfli, 1983. — 403p. — *Bibliography: p399-403*

SWITZERLAND — Foreign economic relations — France
WACKERMANN, Gabriel
Belfort, Colmar, Mulhouse, Bâle, Fribourg-en-Brisgau : un espace économique transfrontalier / Gabriel Wackermann. — [Paris : La Documentation française, 1986]. — 143p. — (Notes et études documentaires ; no.4824). — *Bibliography: p139-142*

SWITZERLAND — Foreign economic relations — Germany (West)
WACKERMANN, Gabriel
Belfort, Colmar, Mulhouse, Bâle, Fribourg-en-Brisgau : un espace économique transfrontalier / Gabriel Wackermann. — [Paris : La Documentation française, 1986]. — 143p. — (Notes et études documentaires ; no.4824). — *Bibliography: p139-142*

SWITZERLAND — Foreign relations — Sources
COMMISSION NATIONALE POUR LA PUBLICATION DE DOCUMENTS DIPLOMATIQUES SUISSES
Documents diplomatiques suisses = Diplomatische Dokumente der Schweiz = Documenti diplomatici svizzeri : 1848-1945. — Bern : Benteli
Band 3: 1873-1889 / unter der Leitung von Erwin Bucher und Peter Stadler, bearbeitet von Heinz Krummenacher und Martin Lüdi. — [1986]. — cviii,995p

SWITZERLAND — History
BONJOUR, Edgar
A short history of Switzerland / by E. Bonjour, H.S. Offler, and G.R. Potter. — Westport, Conn. : Greenwood Press, 1985, c1952. — p. cm. — *Reprint. Originally published: Oxford : Oxford University Press, 1952. — Includes index. — Bibliography: p*

SWITZERLAND — Industries
BORNER, Silvio
Internationalization of industry : an assessment in the light of a small open economy (Switzerland) / Silvio Borner. — Berlin ; New York : Springer-Verlag, c1986. — p. cm. — *Bibliography: p*

SCHWAMM, Henri
La pénétration industrielle suisse dans le marché commun / Henri Schwamm. — Lausanne : Feuille dÁvis de Lausanne, 1971. — 19p

SWITZERLAND — Intellectual life — 20th century
GREEN, Martin Burgess
Mountain of truth : the counterculture begins, Ascona, 1900-1920 / Martin Green. — Hanover, N.H. : Published for Tufts University by University Press of New England, 1986. — 287 p., [12] p. of plates. — *Includes index. — Bibliography: p. [275]-281*

SWITZERLAND — Politics and government
NÜSSLI, Kurt
Föderalismus in der Schweiz : Konzepte, Indikatoren, Daten / Kurt Nüssli. — Zürich : Rüegger, 1985. — 383p. — (Zürcher Beiträge zur politischen Wissenschaft ; Bd.12). — *Bibliography: p367-381*

SWITZERLAND — Politics and government — 1945- — Addresses, essays, lectures
MEYLAN, René
Sentinelle toujours vivante : [recueil d'articles], 1964-1970 / René Meylan. — Neuchâtel, case postale 859 : Parti socialiste neuchâtelois, [1975]. — 226 p.. — *Collection of articles originally published in La Sentinelle. — Includes index*

SWITZERLAND — Population
Les Suisses vont-ils disparaître? : la population de la Suisse: problèmes, perspectives, politiques. — [Berne] : Commission "Politiques de la population" (Société Suisse de Statistique et d'Économie Politique-Groupe d'Étude "Demographie"), 1985. — x,245p

SWITZERLAND — Social conditions
RÉGIONS FRONTALIÈRES (1980 : Berne)
Régions frontalières = Grenzregionen = Regioni di frontiera / éditeurs/Herausgeber/editori, Basilio Biucchi, Gaston Gaudard. — Saint-Saphorin : Georgi, c1981. — 276p. — (Thema-Hefte / Schweizerischer Nationalfonds zur Förderung der wissenschaftlichen Forschung, Programmleitung). — *Travaux éxécutés dans le cadre du programme national "Problèmes régionaux en Suisse, notamment dans les zones de montagne et les zones frontalières" du Fonds national suisse de la recherche scientifique. — Avec contributions en français, allemand et italien*

SWITZERLAND — Social policy
SEGALMAN, Ralph
The Swiss way of welfare : lessons for the Western world / Ralph Segalman. — New York : Praeger, 1985, c1986. — p. cm. — *Includes index. — Bibliography: p*

SWITZERLAND. Commission d'experts chargée d'examiner la revision de l'assurance-accidents
SWITZERLAND. Commission d'experts chargée d'examiner la revision de l'assurance-accidents
Rapport de la commission d'experts chargée d'examiner la revision de l'assurance-accidents : du 14 septembre 1973. — Berne : the Commission, 1973. — ix,223p

SWITZERLAND. Office fédéral de la protection de l'environnement
Office fédéral de la protection de l'environnement 1971-1981 : textes rédigés à l'occasion de son dixième anniversaire. — Berne : the Office, 1981. — 160p

SYMBOLIC INTERACTIONISM
Women and symbolic interaction / edited by Mary Jo Deegan, Michael R. Hill. — Boston, Mass. ; London : Allen & Unwin, 1987. — xii,458p. — *Includes index*

SYMBOLISM
CLARK, Grahame
Symbols of excellence : precious materials as expressions of status / Grahame Clark. — Cambridge : Cambridge University Press, 1986. — [144]p. — *Includes index*

FERNANDEZ, James W
Persuasions and performances : the play of tropes in culture / James W. Fernandez. — Bloomington : Indiana University Press, c1986. — xv, 304 p.. — *Includes bibliographies and index*

WAGNER, Roy
Symbols that stand for themselves / Roy Wagner. — Chicago : University of Chicago Press, 1986. — p. cm. — *Sequel to: The invention of culture. — Includes index. — Bibliography: p*

SYMBOLISM IN ART
WIND, Edgar
Pagan mysteries in the Renaissance / by Edgar Wind. — [2nd (enlarged) ed.]. — Oxford : Oxford University Press, 1980. — xiii,345p,[64]p of plates. — (Oxford paperbacks). — *This ed. originally published : Harmondsworth : Penguin, 1967. — Bibliography: p.305-315. — Includes index*

SYMPOSIUM ON ARTIFICIAL AUDITORY STIMULATION (1982 : Erlangen)
SYMPOSIUM ON ARTIFICIAL AUDITORY STIMULATION (1982 : Erlangen)
Discussions on artificial auditory stimulation : symposium 29 September - 2 October 1982, Erlangen, Federal Republic of Germany / edited by W. D. Keidel, P. Finkenzeller. — Luxembourg : Office for Official Publications of the European Communities, 1984. — ix,182p. — (EUR ; 8980). — *Series title: Medicine. — Bibliography: p155-179*

SYNDICALISM — France — History
PAPAYANIS, Nicholas
Alphonse Merrheim : the emergence of reformism in revolutionary syndicalism, 1871-1925 / by Nicholas Papayanis. — Dordrecht ; Lancaster : Nijhoff, 1985. — xx,184p. — (Studies in social history ; 8). — *Bibliography: p169. — Includes index*

SYNDICALISM — France — History — 19th century
SCHÖTTLER, Peter
Naissance des Bourses du travail : un appareil idéologique d'État à la fin du XIXe siècle / Peter Schöttler ; traduction française de Jean-Pierre Lefebvre et de l'auteur. — Paris : Presses Universitaires de France, 1982. — 294p

SYNDICALISM — Great Britain — History
LUNDH, Christer
Gillesocialismen i England 1912-1923 : inspirationskälla för svensk arbetarrörelse / Christer Lundh. — Lund : Ekonomisk-historiska föreningen, 1982. — 130p. — (Skrifter utgivna av ekonomisk-historiska föreningen ; vol.37). — *Bibliography: p127-130*

SYNDICATES (FINANCE) — Great Britain
MACVE, Richard
A survey of Lloyd's syndicate accounts : financial reporting at Lloyd's in 1985 / Richard Macve. — Englewood Cliffs ; London : Prentice Hall International in association with The Institute of Chartered Accountants in England and Wales, 1986. — xxv,263p. — (Research studies in accounting). — *Bibliography: p261-262. — Includes index*

SYRIA — Boundaries
BAYLSON, Joshua C.
Territorial allocation by imperial rivalry : the human legacy in the Near East / by Joshua C. Baylson. — Chicago, Ill. : University of Chicago, Dept. of Geography, 1987. — p. cm. — (Research paper / The University of Chicago, Department of Geography ; no. 221). — *Includes index. — Bibliography: p*

SYRIA — Census, 1970
Population census in Syrian Arab Republic : 1970. — [Damascus] : Central Bureau of Statistics, 1970. — 2v. — *In English and Arabic*

VAIDYANATHAN, K. E.
Estimation of fertility in Syria from the 1970 Census data on past live births. — Damascus : Central Bureau of Statistics, 1976. — 22p. — (Syrian Population Studies Series ; no. 1)

SYRIA — Foreign relations — Lebanon
WEINBERGER, Naomi Joy
Syrian intervention in Lebanon : the 1975-76 civil war / Naomi Joy Weinberger. — New York : Oxford University Press, 1986. — ix, 367 p.. — *Includes index. — Bibliography: p. [339]-348*

SYRIA — History — 20th century
SEALE, Patrick
The struggle for Syria : a study of post-war Arab politics 1945-1958 / by Patrick Seale. — 2nd ed. — with a foreword by Albert Hourani. — London : Tauris, 1986. — [370]p. — *Previous ed.: London : Oxford University Press, 1965. — Includes bibliography and index*

SYRIA — Politics and government
DAM, Nikolaos van
The struggle for power in Syria : sectarianism, regionalism and tribalism in politics, 1961—1980 / Nikolaos van Dam. — 2nd ed. — London : Croom Helm, c1981. — 169 p

KHOURY, Philip S.
Syria and the French mandate : the politics of Arab nationalism, 1920-1945 / by Philip S. Khoury. — London : Tauris, 1987. — [650]p. — *Includes bibliography and index*

ROBERTS, David, 19---
The Ba'th and the creation of modern Syria / David Roberts. — London : Croom Helm, c1987. — 182p. — *Bibliography: p167-169. — Includes index*

SYRIA — Population — Statistics
Follow-up demographic survey : final report 1976-1979. — [Damascus] : Central Bureau of Statistics, 1981. — 115p

Population census in Syrian Arab Republic : 1970. — [Damascus] : Central Bureau of Statistics, 1970. — 2v. — *In English and Arabic*

SYRIA — Social conditions
LEWIS, Norman N.
Nomads and settlers in Syria and Jordan, 1800-1980 / Norman N. Lewis. — Cambridge : Cambridge University Press, 1987. — xvii,249p. — (Cambridge Middle East library). — *Bibliography: p238-244. — Includes index*

SYRIA — Statistics, vital
Pregnancy follow-up study in Syria : 1976-1979. — [Damascus] : Central Bureau of Statistics, 1984. — 90p

SYRIAN AMERICANS — History
NAFF, Alixa
Becoming American : the early Arab immigrant experience / Alixa Naff. — Carbondale : Southern Illinois University Press, c1985. — p. cm. — (M.E.R.I. special studies). — *Includes index. — Bibliography: p*

SYSTEM ANALYSIS
DONALD, Archibald Gordon
Management, information and systems / by Archie Donald. — 2nd ed. — Oxford : Pergamon, 1979. — xiii,253p. — (Pergamon international library). — *Previous ed.: 1967. — Bibliography: p.246-249. — Includes index*

HAWRYSZKIEWYCZ, I. T
Database analysis and design / I.T. Hawryszkiewycz. — Chicago : Science Research Associates, c1984. — xx, 578 p.. — *Includes index. — Bibliography: p. 561-571*

LESLIE, Robert E.
Systems analysis and design : method and invention / Robert E. Leslie. — Englewood Cliffs, N.J. : Prentice-Hall, c1986. — vi, 490 p.. — *Includes index. — Bibliography: p. 463-464*

PERKINSON, Richard C
Data analysis : the key to data base design / Richard C. Perkinson. — Wellesley, Mass. : QED Information Sciences, c1984. — xvii, 285 p.. — *Bibliography: p. 283-285*

SYSTEM ANALYSIS — Collected works
MAGIROS, Demetrios G
[Selections. 1985]. Selected papers of Demetrios C. Magiros : applied mathematics, nonlinear mechanics, and dynamical systems analysis / edited by S.G. Tzafestas. — Dordrecht, Holland : D. Reidel Pub. Co. ; Hingham, MA, U.S.A. : Sold and distributed in the U.S.A. and Canada by Kluwer Academic Publishers, c1985. — xv, 518 p.. — *"Published on behalf of the Greek Mathematical Society.". — Bibliography: p. 511-518*

SYSTEM ANALYSIS — Congresses

IFAC/IFORS CONFERENCE ON SYSTEMS APPROACHES TO DEVELOPING COUNTRIES (1973 : Algiers)
Systems approaches to developing countries : proceedings / Edited by M. A. Cuenod [and] S. Kahne. — Pittsburgh : Distributed by Instrument Society of America, [1973]. — ix, 515 p. — "A publication of the International Federation of Automatic Control.". — English or French. — Includes bibliographical references

SYSTEM DESIGN

ADDIS, T. R.
Designing knowledge-based systems / T.R. Addis. — London : Kogan Page, 1985. — 322p. — Bibliography: p303-310. — Includes index

BRITISH COMPUTER SOCIETY. Human Computer Interaction Specialist Group. Conference (2nd : 1986 : University of York)
People and computers : designing for usability : proceedings of the Second Conference of the British Computer Society, Human Computer Interaction Specialist Group, University of York, 23-26 September 1986 / edited by M.D. Harrison, A.F. Monk. — Cambridge : Cambridge University Press on behalf of the British Computer Society, 1986. — xiii,650p. — (The British Computer Society Workshop series). — Bibliography: p615-644. — Includes index

GILBERT, Philip
Software design and development / Philip Gilbert. — Chicago : Science Research Associates, c1983. — xvi, 681 p.. — (SRA computer science series). — Includes bibliographies and index

HAWRYSZKIEWYCZ, I. T
Database analysis and design / I.T. Hawryszkiewycz. — Chicago : Science Research Associates, c1984. — xx, 578 p.. — Includes index. — Bibliography: p. 561-571

LESLIE, Robert E.
Systems analysis and design : method and invention / Robert E. Leslie. — Englewood Cliffs, N.J. : Prentice-Hall, c1986. — vi, 490 p.. — Includes index. — Bibliography: p. 463-464

MACRO, Allen
The craft of software engineering / Allen Marco, John Buxton. — Wokingham : Addison-Wesley, c1987. — [376]p. — (International computer science series). — Includes index

PERKINSON, Richard C
Data analysis : the key to data base design / Richard C. Perkinson. — Wellesley, Mass. : QED Information Sciences, c1984. — xvii, 285 p.. — Bibliography: p. 283-285

SHNEIDERMAN, Ben
Designing interactive computer systems / Ben Shneiderman. — Reading, Mass. : Addison-Wesley, 1986. — p. cm. — Includes indexes. — Bibliography: p

User centered system design : new perspectives on human-computer interaction / edited by Donald A. Norman, Stephen W. Draper. — Hillsdale, N.J. ; London : Lawrence Erlbaum Associates, 1986. — xiii, 526p. — Includes index. — Bibliography: p.[499]-512

WARD, Paul T.
Structured development for real-time systems / by Paul T. Ward and Stephen J. Mellor. — New York : Yourden Press
Vol.1: Introduction and tools. — 1985. — 156p

SYSTEM THEORY

JESSOP, Bob
Economy, state and the law in autopoietic theory / by Bob Jessop. — Colchester : Department of Government University of Essex, 1987. — 48 p. — (Essex papers in politics and government ; no.42)

KUHN, Arthur J
Organizational cybernetics and business policy : System design for performance control / Arthur J. Kuhn. — University Park : Pennsylvania State University Press, 1986. — p. cm. — Includes index. — Bibliography: p

TABLE RONDE DES AIDES EXTÉRIEURES AU RWANDA (3ièm : 1982 : Kigali)

TABLE RONDE DES AIDES EXTÉRIEURES AU RWANDA (3ème : 1982 : Kigali)
[Report]. — Kigali : Ministère du Plan, [1983?]. — 326p

TABOO

WALLACE, Edwin R
Freud and anthropology : a history and reappraisal / Edwin R. Wallace, IV. — New York : International Universities Press, c1983. — xi, 306p. — (Psychological issues ; monograph 55). — Bibliography: p.281-294. — Includes index

TACITUS, COMELIUS

VOLPILHAC-AUGER, Catherine
Tacite et Montesquieu / Catherine Volpilhac-Auger. — Oxford : Voltaire Foundation, 1985. — vii,202p. — (Studies on Voltaire and the eighteenth century ; 232). — Bibliography: p.193-198

TAHAA (SOCIETY ISLANDS) — Population — Statistics

Tableaux normalisés du recensement général de la population : 15 octobre 1983. — [Papeete] : Institut territorial de la statistique
Résultats de la commune de Tahaa. — [1985?]. — 11 leaves

TAHITI (SOCIETY ISLANDS) — Economic conditions — Statistics

Tableaux normalisés du recensement général de la population : 15 octobre 1983. — [Papeete] : Institut territorial de la statistique
Résultats de la zone rurale de Tahiti. — [1985?]. — 4p,11 leaves

Tableaux normalisés du recensement général de la population : 15 octobre 1983. — [Papeete] : Institut territorial de la statistique
Résultats de la zone urbaine de Tahiti. — [1985?]. — 11 leaves

TAHITI (SOCIETY ISLANDS) — Population — Statistics

Tableaux normalisés du recensement général de la population : 15 octobre 1983. — [Papeete] : Institut territorial de la statistique
Résultats de la commune de Arue. — [1985?]. — 4p,11 leaves

Tableaux normalisés du recensement général de la population : 15 octobre 1983. — [Papeete] : Institut territorial de la statistique
Résultats de la commune de Faaa. — [1985?]. — 12 leaves

Tableaux normalisés du recensement général de la population : 15 octobre 1983. — [Papeete] : Institut territorial de la statistique
Résultats de la commune de Hitiaa o te ra. — [1985?]. — 4p,11 leaves

Tableaux normalisés du recensement général de la population : 15 octobre 1983. — [Papeete] : Institut territorial de la statistique
Résultats de la commune de Mahina. — [1985?]. — 15 leaves

Tableaux normalisés du recensement général de la population : 15 octobre 1983. — [Papeete] : Institut territorial de la statistique
Résultats de la commune de Paea. — [1985?]. — 4p,11 leaves

Tableaux normalisés du recensement général de la population : 15 octobre 1983. — [Papeete] : Institut territorial de la statistique
Résultats de la commune de Papara. — [1985?]. — 4p,11 leaves

Tableaux normalisés du recensement général de la population : 15 octobre 1983. — [Papeete] : Institut territorial de la statistique
Résultats de la commune de Papeete. — [1985?]. — 16 leaves

Tableaux normalisés du recensement général de la population : 15 octobre 1983. — [Papeete] : Institut territorial de la statistique
Résultats de la commune de Pirae. — [1985?]. — 4p,11 leaves

Tableaux normalisés du recensement général de la population : 15 octobre 1983. — [Papeete] : Institut territorial de la statistique
Résultats de la commune de Punaauia. — [1985?]. — 11 leaves

Tableaux normalisés du recensement général de la population : 15 octobre 1983. — [Papeete] : Institut territorial de la statistique
Résultats de la commune de Taiarapu-Est. — [1985?]. — 4p,11 leaves

Tableaux normalisés du recensement général de la population : 15 octobre 1983. — [Papeete] : Institut territorial de la statistique
Résultats de la commune de Taiarapu-Ouest. — [1985?]. — 4p,11 leaves

Tableaux normalisés du recensement général de la population : 15 octobre 1983. — [Papeete] : Institut territorial de la statistique
Résultats de la commune de Teva i Uta. — [1985?]. — 4p,11 leaves

Tableaux normalisés du recensement général de la population : 15 octobre 1983. — [Papeete] : Institut territorial de la statistique
Résultats de la zone rurale de Tahiti. — [1985?]. — 4p,11 leaves

Tableaux normalisés du recensement général de la population : 15 octobre 1983. — [Papeete] : Institut territorial de la statistique
Résultats de la zone urbaine de Tahiti. — [1985?]. — 11 leaves

Tableaux normalisés du recensement général de la population : 15 octobre 1983. — [Papeete] : Institut territorial de la statistique
Résultats de l'Ile de Tahiti. — [1985?]. — 12 leaves

TAHUATA (MARQUESAS ISLANDS) — Population — Statistics

Tableaux normalisés du recensement général de la population : 15 octobre 1983. — [Papeete] : Institut territorial de la statistique
Résultats de la commune de Tahuata. — [1985?]. — 4p,11 leaves

TAIARAPU-EST (TAHITI : REGION) — Population — Statistics

Tableaux normalisés du recensement général de la population : 15 octobre 1983. — [Papeete] : Institut territorial de la statistique
Résultats de la commune de Taiarapu-Est. — [1985?]. — 4p,11 leaves

TAIARAPU-OUEST (TAHITI : REGION) — Population — Statistics

Tableaux normalisés du recensement général de la population : 15 octobre 1983. — [Papeete] : Institut territorial de la statistique
Résultats de la commune de Taiarapu-Ouest. — [1985?]. — 4p,11 leaves

TAIWAN

101 questions about Taiwan. — 6th ed. — [Taipei : Free China Review, 1962]. — 60p

TAIWAN — Economic conditions

The economy of Taiwan, Republic of China. — [Taipei : Ministry of Economic Affairs, 1958]. — 12p

TAIWAN — Economic conditions — 1945

YIN, K. Y.
Economic development in Taiwan, 1950-1960 : record and prospects / by K. Y. Yin. — Taipei : Council for United States Aid, 1962. — 57p

TAIWAN — Economic conditions — 1945-

Basic information about Taiwan's economy. — Taipei : Industrial Development and Investment Center, 1961. — 21p

CHEN, Cheng
Premier Chen Cheng's report to the Legislative Yuan : verbal report, September 20, 1960. — [Taipei] : Government Information Office, 1960. — 15,11p. — *In English and Chinese*

CHEN, Cheng
Premier Chen Cheng's reports to 25th session of Legislative Yuan and 3rd session of National Assembly, February and March, 1960. — [Taipei] : Government Information Office, 1960. — 26,26p. — *In English and Chinese*

Economic miracle in free China. — [Taipei : China Publishing Company, 1962]. — 48p

Facts for investors in Taiwan. — [Taipei] : Industrial Development Commission, 1958. — ii,60p

A general review of the economy of Taiwan in 1960. — [Taipei : Bank of Taiwan], 1961. — 32p. — *Reprint from the Bank of Taiwan's Annual Report, 1960*

GOLD, Thomas B
State and society in the Taiwan miracle / Thomas B. Gold. — Armonk, N.Y. : M.E. Sharpe, c1986. — xiv, 162 p.. — "An East gate book"--Half t.p. verso. — Includes index. — *Bibliography: p. 147-155*

LI, K. T.
A review of the economic situation in Taiwan in 1958 : by K. T. Li. — [Taipei : Industrial Development Commission?], 1959. — 20p

Models of development : a comparative study of economic growth in South Korea and Taiwan / edited by Lawrence J. Lau. — San Francisco, Calif. : ICS Press, Institute for Contemporary Studies, c1986. — xv, 217 p.. — *Includes index. — Bibliography: p. 203-208*

Taiwan today. — [Taipei] : Council for United States Aid, 1959. — [26]p

TAIWAN — Economic policy

CHENG, Chen
Report on free China / by Chen Cheng. — Taipei : Government Information Bureau, 1954. — 60p. — *Submitted to the second session of the First National Assembly on March 4, 1954*

Highlights of the second four-year plan for the economic development in Taiwan. — [Taipei] : Economic Stabilization Board, 1957. — [iv],51p

HSIEH, S. C.
An analytical review of agricultural development in Taiwan : an input-output and productivity approach / by S. C. Hsieh and T. H. Lee. — Taipei : Chinese-American Joint Commission on Rural Reconstruction, 1958. — [vi],84p. — (Economic digest series / Joint Commission on Rural Reconstruction ; no.12)

The Political economy of the new Asian industrialism / edited by Frederic C. Deyo. — Ithaca, N.Y. : Cornell University Press, 1987. — 252 p.. — (Cornell studies in political economy). — *Includes bibliographies and index. — Contents: Export-oriented industrializing states in the capitalist world system / Richard E. Barrett and Soomi Chin -- The origins and development of the Northeast Asian political economy / Bruce Cumings -- State and foreign capital in the East Asian NICs / Stephan Haggard and Tun-jen Cheng -- Political institutions and economic performance / Chalmers Johnson -- The interplay of state, social class, and world system in East Asian development / Hagen Koo -- State and labor / Frederic C. Deyo -- Class, state, and dependence in East Asia / Peter Evans -- Coalitions, institutions, and linkage sequencing toward a strategic capacity model of East Asian development / Frederic C. Deyo*

SHEN, T. H.
Economic significance of agricultural development in Taiwan / by T. H. Shen. — Taipei : Committee D, Economic Stabilization Board, 1955. — 41p

TAIWAN — Economic policy — 1945-

Models of development : a comparative study of economic growth in South Korea and Taiwan / edited by Lawrence J. Lau. — San Francisco, Calif. : ICS Press, Institute for Contemporary Studies, c1986. — xv, 217 p.. — *Includes index. — Bibliography: p. 203-208*

TAIWAN — Foreign relations — 1945-

CHEN, Cheng
Vice President and Premier Chen Cheng's oral report to the 30th session of the Legislative Yuan, September 18, 1962. — [Taipei] : Government Information Office, 1962. — 10,6p . — *In English and Chinese*

CHEN, Cheng
Vice President and Premier Chen Cheng's oral report to the 31st session of the Legislative Yuan, February 19, 1963. — [Taipei] : Government Information Office, 1963. — 7,5p. — *In English and Chinese*

TAIWAN — Foreign relations — United States

Congress, the Presidency, and the Taiwan Relations Act / edited by Louis W. Koenig, James C. Hsiung, and King-Yuh Chang. — New York : Praeger, 1985. — p. cm. — *Includes index. — Bibliography: p*

TAIWAN — History — 1945- — Addresses, essays, lectures

China, seventy years after the 1911 Hsin-Hai Revolution / edited by Hungdah Chiu with Shao-Chuan Leng. — Charlottesville : University Press of Virginia, 1984. — x, 601 p.. — *Papers from the Tenth Annual Meeting of the Mid-Atlantic Regional Conference of the Association for Asian Studies, held at the University of Maryland, Oct. 17-18, 1981 and the Twenty-third Annual Meeting of the American Association for Chinese Studies, held at Ohio State University, Nov. 7-8, 1981. — Includes bibliographical references and index*

TAIWAN — Industries

Industry in China. — 2nd ed.. — [Taipei : Industrial Development and Investment Center], 1962. — 14p

Industry in Taiwan. — [Taipei : Industrial Development and Investment Center, 1961]. — 14p

LI, K. T.
The growth of private industry in free China / K. T. Li. — Taipei : [Ministry of Economic Affairs?], 1959. — 40p

LI, K. T.
A review of industrial development in Taiwan, 1957 / by K. T. Li. — [Taipei] : Industrial Development Commission, 1958. — 13p

TAIWAN — Politics and government — 1945-1975

CHENG, Chen
An oral report on Free China by Premier Chen Cheng to the second session of the first National Assembly on March 4, 1954. — [Taipei] : Government Information Bureau, 1954. — 23,17p. — *In English and Chinese*

CHENG, Chen
Report on free China / by Chen Cheng. — Taipei : Government Information Bureau, 1954. — 60p. — *Submitted to the second session of the First National Assembly on March 4, 1954*

CHIANG, Kai-shek, 1887-1975
President Chiang Kai-shek's address at the opening of the second session of the first National Assembly on February 19, 1954. — [Taipei] : Government Information Bureau, [1954]. — 16,15p. — *In English and Chinese*

CHIANG, Kai-shek, 1887-1975
Selected speeches and messages in 1955. — [Taipei] : Government Information Office, [1955]. — 65p

CHIANG, May-ling Soong, 1897-
Selected speeches / by Madame Chiang Kai-shek. — Taipei : Government Information Office, 1957. — 73p

TAIWAN — Politics and government — 1945-

CHEN, Cheng
Premier Chen Cheng's report to the Legislative Yuan : verbal report, September 20, 1960. — [Taipei] : Government Information Office, 1960. — 15,11p. — *In English and Chinese*

CHEN, Cheng
Premier Chen Cheng's reports to 25th session of Legislative Yuan and 3rd session of National Assembly, February and March, 1960. — [Taipei] : Government Information Office, 1960. — 26,26p. — *In English and Chinese*

CHEN, Cheng
Vice President and Premier Chen Cheng's oral report to the 30th session of the Legislative Yuan, September 18, 1962. — [Taipei] : Government Information Office, 1962. — 10,6p . — *In English and Chinese*

CHEN, Cheng
Vice President and Premier Chen Cheng's oral report to the 31st session of the Legislative Yuan, February 19, 1963. — [Taipei] : Government Information Office, 1963. — 7,5p. — *In English and Chinese*

CHIANG, Kai-shek, 1887-1975
President Chiang Kai-shek's selected speeches and messages in 1962. — [Taipei] : Government Information Office, 1963. — 59p

GOLD, Thomas B
State and society in the Taiwan miracle / Thomas B. Gold. — Armonk, N.Y. : M.E. Sharpe, c1986. — xiv, 162 p.. — "An East gate book"--Half t.p. verso. — Includes index. — *Bibliography: p. 147-155*

TAIWAN — Rural conditions

KIRBY, E. Stuart
Rural progress in Taiwan / by E. Stuart Kirby. — Taipei : Chinese-American Joint Commission on Rural Reconstruction, 1960. — [vii],160p

TAIWAN — Social conditions

GOLD, Thomas B
State and society in the Taiwan miracle / Thomas B. Gold. — Armonk, N.Y. : M.E. Sharpe, c1986. — xiv, 162 p.. — "An East gate book"--Half t.p. verso. — Includes index. — *Bibliography: p. 147-155*

TSAI, Wen-hui
From tradition to modernity : a socio-historical interpretation on China's struggle toward modernization since the mid-19th century / Wen-hui Tsai. — Baltimore : University of Maryland School of Law, 1986. — 76p. — (Occasional papers/reprint series in contemporary Asian studies. 1986 ; no.1 (72))

TAIWAN — Social policy

Social welfare services in the Republic of China. — [Taipei] : Ministry of Interior, 1958. — 38p

TAIWAN FERTILIZER CO., LTD.

Taiwan Fertilizer Co., Ltd.. — Taipei : [Government Information Office], 1957. — [20]p

TAIWAN RELATIONS ACT

Congress, the Presidency, and the Taiwan Relations Act / edited by Louis W. Koenig, James C. Hsiung, and King-Yuh Chang. — New York : Praeger, 1985. — p. cm. — *Includes index. — Bibliography: p*

TAKAROA (TUAMOTU ISLANDS) — Population — Statistics
Tableaux normalisés du recensement général de la population : 15 octobre 1983. — [Papeete] : Institut territorial de la statistique Résultats de la commune de Takaroa. — [1985?]. — 2p,ll leaves

TALES — Italy
MATHIAS, Elizabeth
Italian folktales in America : the verbal art of an immigrant woman / Elizabeth Mathias and Richard Raspa ; foreword by Roger D. Abrahams. — Detroit : Wayne State University Press, 1985. — p. cm. — (Wayne State University Folklore Archive study series). — *Includes 22 tales as told by Clementina Todesco.* — *Includes indexes.* — *Bibliography: p*

TALES — Papua New Guinea — History and criticism
LEROY, John D.
Fabricated world : an interpretation of Kewa tales / John LeRoy. — Vancouver : University of British Columbia Press, 1985. — xii, 319 p.. — *Includes index.* — *Bibliography: p. [304]-311*

TALES — United States
MATHIAS, Elizabeth
Italian folktales in America : the verbal art of an immigrant woman / Elizabeth Mathias and Richard Raspa ; foreword by Roger D. Abrahams. — Detroit : Wayne State University Press, 1985. — p. cm. — (Wayne State University Folklore Archive study series). — *Includes 22 tales as told by Clementina Todesco.* — *Includes indexes.* — *Bibliography: p*

TALK SHOWS — United States
LEVIN, Murray Burton
Talk radio and the American dream / by Murray B. Levin. — Lexington, Mass. : Lexington Books, c1987. — xv, 170 p.. — *Includes index*

TALLENSI (AFRICAN PEOPLE)
FORTES, Meyer
The web of kinship among the Tallensi : the second part of an analysis of the social structure of a Trans-Volta tribe / Meyer Fortes. — London : Oxford University Press, 1949. — xiv,358p

TAMIL NADU (INDIA) — Economic conditions — Statistics
Statistical handbook of Tamil Nadu / Department of Statistics, Madras. — Madras : Department of Statistics, 1982-. — *Annual*

TAMILS — India
FRIES, Yvonne
The undesirables : the expatriation of the Tamil people "of recent Indian origin" from the plantations in Sri Lanka to India / Yvonne Fries, Thomas Bibin. — Calcutta : K P Bagchi, 1984. — 253 p.. — *Bibliography: p [248]-253*

TAMILS — Sri Lanka
FRIES, Yvonne
The undesirables : the expatriation of the Tamil people "of recent Indian origin" from the plantations in Sri Lanka to India / Yvonne Fries, Thomas Bibin. — Calcutta : K P Bagchi, 1984. — 253 p.. — *Bibliography: p [248]-253*

LAMBALLE, Alain
Le problème tamoul à Sri Lanka / Alain Lamballe. — Paris : Éditions L'Harmattan, 1985. — xiv, 515p. — *Bibliography: p491-515*

TANAKA, ŌDŌ
NOLTE, Sharon H
Liberalism in modern Japan : Ishibashi Tanzan and his teachers, 1905-1960 / Sharon H. Nolte. — Berkeley : University of California Press, c1987. — xii, 378 p.. — *Includes index.* — *Bibliography: p. 343-370*

TANKERS — Law and legislation — Great Britain
VENTRIS, F. M.
Tanker voyage charter parties / by F. M. Ventris. — [S.l.] : Kluwer Law Publishers ; [chichester] : Barry Rose, 1986. — xvi,411p

TANKS (MILITARY SCIENCE) — History
WILSON, A. Gordon
Walter Wilson : portrait of an inventor / A Grodon Wilson ; edited by Rodney Dale. — London : Duckworth, 1986. — 173p

TANZANIA — Economic policy
LUTTRELL, William L
Post-capitalist industrialization : planning economic independence in Tanzania / William L. Luttrell. — New York : Praeger, 1986. — xv, 189 p.. — *Includes index.* — *Bibliography: p. 181-184*

TURSHEN, Meredeth
The political ecology of disease in Tanzania / Meredeth Turshen. — New Brunswick, N.J. : Rutgers University Press, c1984. — xiv, 259 p., [2] leaves of plates. — *Includes index.* — *Bibliography: p. 211-239*

TANZANIA — Industries
African industrialisation : technology and change in Tanzania / C.E. Barker ... [et al.]. — Aldershot : Gower, c1986. — xiv,227p. — *Bibliography: p215-221.* — *Includes index*

LUTTRELL, William L
Post-capitalist industrialization : planning economic independence in Tanzania / William L. Luttrell. — New York : Praeger, 1986. — xv, 189 p.. — *Includes index.* — *Bibliography: p. 181-184*

SKARSTEIN, Rune
Industrial development in Tanzania : some critical issues / Rune Skarstein, Sammuel M. Wangwe. — Uppsala : Scandinavian Institute of African Studies ; Dar es Salaam : Tanzania Publishing House, 1986. — [xii],291p. — *Bibliography: p275-291*

TANZANIA — Politics and government — 1964-
Villagers, villages, and the state in modern Tanzania / edited by R.G. Abrahams. — Cambridge : African Studies Centre, 1985. — ii,167p. — (Cambridge African monograph ; 4) . — *Includes bibliographies*

TANZANIA — Rural conditions
ÖSTBERG, Wilhelm
The Kondoa transformation : coming to grips with soil erosion in Central Tanzania / Wilhelm Östberg. — Uppsala : Scandinavian Institute of African Studies, 1986. — 99p. — (Research reports / Scandinavian Institute of African Studies ; no.76). — *Bibliography: p97-99*

TAPESTRY, FLEMISH
YATES, Frances A.
The Valois tapestries / Frances A. Yates. — 2nd ed. — London : Routledge and Kegan Paul, 1975. — xxvii,151p,[40]p of plates,[8] leaves of plates. — *Previous ed.: London : Warburg Institute, 1959.* — *Includes index*

TAPUTAPUATEA (RAIATEA : REGION) — Population — Statistics
Tableaux normalisés du recensement général de la population : 15 octobre 1983. — [Papeete] : Institut territorial de la statistique Résultats de la Commune de Taputapuatea. — [1985?]. — 4p,11 leaves

TARIFF — Law and legislation
GENERAL AGREEMENT ON TARIFFS AND TRADE (Organization)
Text of the General Agreement. — Geneva : the Organization, 1986. — vi,96p

The texts of the Tokyo Round Agreements. — Geneva : General Agreement on Tariffs and Trade, 1986. — vii,208p

TARIFF — Law and legislation — Canada — Congresses
The legal framework for Canada-United States trade / edited by Maureen Irish and Emily F. Carasco. — Toronto : Carswell, 1987. — xxxviii,275p

TARIFF — Law and legislation — European Economic Community countries
The European Community and GATT / edited by Meinhard Hilf, Francis G. Jacobs, and Ernst-Ulrich Petersmann. — Deventer, the Netherlands ; Boston : Kluwer, c1986. — xvii, 398 p.. — (Studies in transnational economic law ; v. 4). — *Includes bibliographical references and index*

TARIFF — Law and legislation — Mexico
KATE, Adriaan ten
Measuring nominal & effective protection : the case of Mexico / Adriaan Ten Kate. — Aldershot : Avebury, 1987. — 1v.. — *Includes index*

TARIFF — Law and legislation — United States — Congresses
The legal framework for Canada-United States trade / edited by Maureen Irish and Emily F. Carasco. — Toronto : Carswell, 1987. — xxxviii,275p

TARIFF — Canada
C. D. HOWE INSTITUTE
Policy harmonization : the effects of a Canadian-American free trade area / C. D. Howe Institute. — Toronto : the Institute, 1986. — xv,164p. — *Includes bibliographical references*

The Free trade papers / edited by Duncan Cameron. — Toronto : James Lorimer & Company, 1986. — xlix,227p

WONNACOTT, R. J.
Selected new developments in international trade theory / R. J. Wonnacott. — Montreal : The Institute for Research on Public Policy/LInstitut de recherches politiques, 1984. — xxi,40p. — (Essays in international economics). — *Prefatory material in English and French.* — *Bibliography: p27-29*

TARIFF — Canada — History — 19th century
FORSTER, Jakob Johann Benjamin
A conjunction of interests : business, politics, and tariffs, 1825-1879 / Ben Forster. — Toronto ; Buffalo : University of Toronto Press, c1986. — vi, 288 p.. — (The State and economic life ; 8). — *Includes index.* — *Bibliography: p. [259]-276*

TARIFF — Great Britain
SELF, Robert C.
Tories and tariffs : the Conservative Party and the politics of tariff reform, 1922-1932 / Robert C. Self. — New York : Garland Pub., 1986. — xxv, 817 p.. — (Outstanding theses from the London School of Economics and political Science). — *Bibliography: p. [784]-817*

TARIFF — Great Britain — History
DOWNS, André
General import restrictions and the behaviour of domestic prices and wages : the case of the British General Tariff of 1932 / by André Downs. — 245 leaves. — *PhD (Econ) 1986 LSE.* — *Leaves 210-245 are appendices*

TARIFF — United States
C. D. HOWE INSTITUTE
Policy harmonization : the effects of a Canadian-American free trade area / C. D. Howe Institute. — Toronto : the Institute, 1986. — xv,164p. — *Includes bibliographical references*

The Free trade papers / edited by Duncan Cameron. — Toronto : James Lorimer & Company, 1986. — xlix,227p

TARIFF PREFERENCES — Congresses

UNITED NATIONS. Conference on Trade and Development. Secretariat
Operation and effects of the generalized system of preferences : fifth review : selected studies submitted to the Special Committee on Preferences at its ninth session : Geneva 27 May-4 June 1980. — New York : United Nations, 1981. — vi,81p. — ([Document] / United Nations ; TD/B/C.5/71). — *Includes bibliographical references.* — *Sales no.: E.81.II.D.6*

UNITED NATIONS. Conference on Trade and Development. Secretariat
Operation and effects of the generalized system of preferences : sixth review : selected studies submitted to the Special Committee on Preferences at its tenth session Geneva, 11-27 May 1981. — New York : United Nations, 1982. — vi,82p. — ([Document] / United Nations ; TD/B/C.5/79). — *Includes bibliographical references.* — *Sales no.: E.82.II.D.10*

UNITED NATIONS. Conference on Trade and Development. Secretariat
Operation and effects of the generalized system of preferences : seventh and eighth reviews : selected studies submitted to the Special Committee on Preferences at its eleventh session Geneva, 3-11 May 1982 and at its twelfth session Geneva, 24 April-4 May 1984. — New York : United Nations, 1985. — vi,99p. — ([Document] / United Nations ; TD/B/C.5/100). — *Includes bibliographical references.* — *Sales no.: E.85.II.D.15*

TARIFF PREFERENCES — European Economic Community countries

The Significance of the EEC's generalised system of preferences : trade effects and links with other community aid policies / Axel Borrmann ... [et al.]. — Hamburg : Verlag Weltarchiv, 1985. — 420 p.. — (Publication of HWWA-Institut für Wirtschaftsforschung-Hamburg). — *Bibliography: p. 405-420*

TARPENBEK (Ship)

GREAT BRITAIN. Department of Trade
The Tarpenbek incident. — London : the Department, 1979. — 31p

TASCA, ANGELO

DE GRAND, Alexander J.
In Stalin's shadow : Angelo Tasca and the crisis of the left in Italy and France, 1910-1945 / Alexander J. De Grand. — Dekalb, Ill. : Northern Illinois University Press, 1986. — viii, 231p. — *Includes index.* — *Contains bibliographical references*

TASMANIA — History — 1803-1851

The diaries and letters of G. T. W. B. Boyes. — Melbourne ; Auckland : Oxford University Press. — *Bibliography: p647-657*
vol.1: 1820-1832 / edited by Peter Chapman. — 1985. — xxvi,692p

TASMANIA — Population

TASMANIA. Commonwealth Bureau of Census and Statistics. Tasmanian Office
Demography. — Hobart : [the office], 1970-1981. — *Annual*

TASMANIAN DEVELOPMENT AUTHORITY

TASMANIAN DEVELOPMENT AUTHORITY
Review of operations / Tasmanian Development Authority. — Hobart : the Authority, 1984/5-. — *Annual*

TATAKOTO (TUAMOTU ISLANDS) — Population — Statistics

Tableaux normalisés du recensement général de la population : 15 octobre 1983. — [Papeete] : Institut territorial de la statistique
Résultats de la commune de Tatakoto. — [1985?]. — 4p,ll leaves

TATAR A.S.S.R. — Politics and government

BENNIGSEN, Alexandre
Sultan Galiev, le père de la révolution tiers-mondiste / Alexandre Bennigsen, Chantal Lemercier-Quelquejay. — Paris : Fayard, 1986. — 305p. — (Les inconnus de l'histoire)

TATARS — Russian S.F.S.R — Tatarskaīa A.S.S.R — History

RORLICH, Azade-Ayse
The Volga Tatars : a profile in national resilience / Azade-Ayse Rorlich. — Stanford, Calif. : Hoover Institution Press, Stanford University, 1986. — xvi, 288 p.. — (Studies of nationalities in the USSR). — *Includes index.* — *Bibliography: p. [253]-275*

TATARSKAĪA A.S.S.R. (R.S.F.S.R.) — History

RORLICH, Azade-Ayse
The Volga Tatars : a profile in national resilience / Azade-Ayse Rorlich. — Stanford, Calif. : Hoover Institution Press, Stanford University, 1986. — xvi, 288 p.. — (Studies of nationalities in the USSR). — *Includes index.* — *Bibliography: p. [253]-275*

TAX ADMINISTRATION AND PROCEDURE

RAAD, C. van
Nondiscrimination in international tax law / Kees van Raad. — Deventer ; Boston : Kluwer Law and Taxation, c1986. — xix, 284 p.. — (Series on international taxation ; no. 6). — *Bibliography: p. 271-284*

TAX ADMINISTRATION AND PROCEDURE — Great Britain

GREAT BRITAIN. Board of Inland Revenue
PAYE - possible future developments : a review by the Inland Revenue of the Pay As You Earn system and of possible alternative methods of collecting tax from wages and salaries. — [London] : the Board, 1979. — 50p

GREAT BRITAIN. Treasury
The reform of personal taxation : presented to Parliament by the Chancellor of the Exchequer by Command of her Majesty March 1986. — London : H.M.S.O., 1986. — 82p. — (Cmnd ; 9756). — *Green Paper on the reform of personal taxation*

TAX COLLECTION — China — History

MANN, Susan
Local merchants and the Chinese bureaucracy, 1750-1950 / Susan Mann. — Stanford, Calif. : Stanford University Press, 1987. — viii, 278 p.. — *Includes index.* — *Bibliography: p. [255]-267*

TAX EVASION — Mathematical models

COWELL, F. A.
Unwillingness to pay : tax evasion and public good provision / Frank A. Cowell, James Gordon. — [London : London School of Economics and Political Science], 1986. — 26p. — (Taxation, incentives and the distribution of income ; no.103). — *Economic and Social Research Council programme.* — *Bibliographical references: p25-26*

GORDON, James
Modelling tax evasion where honesty may be the best policy / James Gordon. — [London : London School of Economics and Political Science], 1987. — 38p. — (Taxation, incentives and the distribution of income ; no.102). — *Economic and Social Research Council programme.* — *Bibliographical references: p37-38*

TAX EVASION — Germany (West)

SMITH, Stephen
The shadow economy in Britain and Germany : based on a comparative research project undertaken by the Institute for Fiscal Studies, London, and the Institut für Angewandte Wirtschaftforschung Tübingen / Stephen Smith and Susanne Wied-Nebbeling. — London : Anglo-German Foundation for the Study of Industrial Society, c1986. — 102 p

TAX EVASION — Great Britain

GILLARD, Michael
In the name of charity : the Rossminster affair / Michael Gillard. — London : Chatto & Windus, 1987. — xi,316p,[8]p of plates. — *Includes index*

GREAT BRITAIN. Parliament. House of Commons. Library. Research Division
The black economy / Jennifer Tanfield. — [London] : the Division, 1984. — 10p. — (Background paper ; no.151). — *Bibliographical references: p9-10*

SMITH, Stephen
The shadow economy in Britain and Germany : based on a comparative research project undertaken by the Institute for Fiscal Studies, London, and the Institut für Angewandte Wirtschaftforschung Tübingen / Stephen Smith and Susanne Wied-Nebbeling. — London : Anglo-German Foundation for the Study of Industrial Society, c1986. — 102 p

SMITH, Stephen, 19---
Britain's shadow economy / Stephen Smith. — Oxford : Clarendon, 1986. — [192]p. — *Includes bibliography and index*

TAX HAVENS

ARNOLD, Brian J
The taxation of controlled foreign corporations : an international comparison / Brian J. Arnold. — Toronto, Ont. : Canadian Tax Foundation, c1986. — xxiii, 816. — (Canadian tax paper ; no. 78). — *Includes index.* — *Bibliography: p. 797-811*

GRUNDY, Milton
Grundy's tax havens : a world survey. — 4th ed. / edited by John Walters ; with an introduction by Milton Grundy. — London : Sweet & Maxwell, 1983. — vii,219p. — *Previous ed.: London : Bodley Head, 1974*

Grundy's tax havens : a world survey / edited by Milton Grundy. — 3rd ed.. — London : Bodley Head, 1974. — viii,160p

TAX INCIDENCE — Québec (Province)

White paper on the personal tax and transfer systems / [prepared by the Ministère des finances ; edited by the Direction générale de publications gouvernementales]. — Québec : Le Ministere, 1984. — 380p. — *Cover title.* — *Inclues index.* — *Includes index*

TAX PLANNING — Great Britain

BALLARDIE
Tolley's tax efficient personal investments : [a detailed explanatory guide to tax efficient investments for the individual] / [Patricia Ballardie] ; [edited by David Marks]. — Croydon, Surrey : Tolley, 1986. — ix,103p

GAMMIE, Malcolm
Tax strategy for companies. — 4th ed / by Malcolm Gammie. — London : Longman Professional, 1986. — xxviii,511p. — *Previous ed.: 1983.* — *Includes index*

TAXATION

AGNELL, Jonas
Tax reforms and asset markets / Jonas Agnell. — Stockholm : Industrial Institute for Economic and Social Research : Distributed by Almqvist & Wiksell, 1985. — 181p. — *Bibliography: p170-181*

Inflation, trade and taxes : essays in honor of Alice Bourneuf / edited by David A. Belsley...[et al.]. — Columbus : Ohio State University Press, 1976. — 252p

MYLES, G. D.
Optimal commodity taxation with imperfect competition / G. D. Myles. — Coventry : University of Warwick, 1987. — 46p. — (Warwick economic research papers ; no.280). — *Bibliography: p46*

TAXATION *continuation*

Staat und Politische Ökonomie heute : Horst Claus Recktenwald zum 65. Geburtstag = Public sector and political economy today: essays in honour of Horst Claus Recktenwald / herausgegeben von Horst Hanusch, Karl W. Roskamp, Jack Wiseman. — Stuttgart : Gustav Fischer, 1985. — xii,393p. — *Includes bibliographies*

Taxation : an international perspective : proceedings of an international conference / contributors include: James M. Buchanan...[et al.] ; Walter Block and Michael Walker, editors. — Vancouver : The Fraser Institute, 1984. — 447p. — *Proceedings of a symposium held in Vancouver, British Columbia, on August 27-29, 1980*

TAXATION — Environmental aspects — Australia

Fiscal measures and the environment impacts and potential. — Canberra : Australian Government Publishing Service, 1985. — x,25p. — (Environment papers / Department of Arts, Heritage and Environment). — *Bibliographical references: p23*

TAXATION — Law and legislation — France

FRANCE
[Code général des impôts]. Code général des impôts. — [7e éd]. — Paris : Dalloz, 1985. — lvi,1685p. — (Petits codes Dalloz). — *Previous ed.: 1983. Includes index*

TAXATION — Law and legislation — Great Britain

BOOTH, Neil D.
Residence, domicile and UK taxation / Neil D. Booth. — London : Butterworths, 1986. — [250]p. — *Includes index*

COOKE, R. M.
Establishing a business in the United Kingdom / R. M. Cooke and D. C. Borer. — 3rd ed. — London : Institute of Chartered Accountants, 1986. — viii,226p

GREAT BRITAIN. Board of Inland Revenue
The Inland Revenue and the taxpayer : proposals in response to the recommendations of the Keith Committee on income tax, capital gains tax and corporation tax : a consultative document / Board of Inland Revenue. — London : H.M.S.O., 1986. — 170p

LAW SOCIETY. Revenue Law Committee
Tax law in the melting pot / a study by the Revenue Law Committee of the Law Society of the 'Ramsay' doctrine after 'Furniss v. Dawson', with proposals. — [London] : Law Society, c1985. — iii,119p. — *Bibliography: p.119*

PINSON, Barry
Pinson on revenue law : comprising income tax; capital gains tax; development land tax; corporation tax; inheritance tax; value added tax; stamp duties; tax planning. — 17th ed. / by Barry Pinson with Roger Thomas. — London : Sweet & Maxwell, 1986. — lxxx,780p . — *Previous ed.: 1985. — Includes index*

WHITEHOUSE, Chris, 1948-
Revenue law : principles and practice / Chris Whitehouse, Elizabeth Stuart-Buttle. — 5th ed. — London : Butterworths, 1987. — xxxi,671p. — *Previous ed.: 1986. — Includes index*

TAXATION — Law and legislation — Hong Kong

FLUX, David
Hong Kong taxation : law and practice / David Flux. — 1986-87 ed. — Hong Kong : Chinese University Press, 1986. — xxxiv,492p

TAXATION — Law and legislation — Korea (South)

Business laws in Korea : investment, taxation, and industrial property / Chan-jin Kim, editor. — Seoul, Korea : Panmun Book Co., 1982. — xii, 799 p.. — *Includes bibliographical references*

TAXATION — Law and legislation — Peru

PERU
[Decreto supremo no.287-68-HC]. Income tax, real estate ownership value and stock assets : Supreme decree no.287-68-HC. — [Lima : Presidencia?, 1968]. — 106leaves. — *Translation from Spanish into English*

TAXATION — Law and legislation — Scotland

JONES, Martyn H.
Revenue law in Scotland / Martyn H. Jones, Simon A. Mackintosh. — London : Butterworths, 1986. — 181p. — *Includes index*

TAXATION — Law and legislation — Soviet Union

NEWCITY, Michael A
Taxation in the Soviet Union / Michael A. Newcity. — New York : Praeger, c1986. — xiii, 392 p. — *"Praeger special studies. Praeger scientific.". — Includes index. — Bibliography: p. 368-377*

TAXATION — Law and legislation — United States

BRAYTON, Flint
The macroeconomic and sectoral effects of the Economic Recovery Tax Act : some simulation results / Flint Brayton, Peter B. Clark. — Washington, D.C. : Board of Governors of the Federal Reserve System, 1985. — 17p. — (Staff study / Board of Governors of the Federal Reserve System (U.S.) ; 148)

TAXATION — Asia, Southeastern

Fiscal issues in south-east Asia : comparative studies of selected economies / edited by Parthasarathi Shome. — Singapore ; Oxford : Oxford University Press, 1986. — x,237p. — *Bibliography: p[220]-233*

TAXATION — Australia

AUSTRALIA. National Taxation Summit (1985 : Canberra)
Record of proceedings, Monday 1-Thursday 4 July 1985. — Canberra : Australian Government Publishing Service, 1985. — xvi,240p

KEATING, Paul
Reform of the Australian taxation system : statement / by the Treasurer the Hon. Paul Keating, M.P.. — Canberra : Australian Government Publishing Service, 1985. — iv,81p

TAXATION — Developing countries

AHMAD, Ehtisham
The analysis of tax reform for developing countries : lessons from research on Pakistan and India / Ehtisham Ahmad and Nicholas Stern. — London : Suntory Toyota International Centre for Economics and Related Disciplines, 1986. — 31p. — (Development research programme / London School of Economics and Political Science. Suntory Toyota International Centre for Economics and Related Disciplines ; no.2). — *Bibliography: p30-31*

AHMAD, Ehtisham
Taxation for developing countries / Ehtisham Ahmad and Nicholas Stern. — London : Suntory Toyota International Centre for Economics and Related Disciplines, 1985. — 125p. — (Development research programme / London School of Economics and Political Science. Suntory Toyota International Centre for Economics and Related Disciplines ; no.1). — *This is a revised version of Public economics for developing countries, 1985. — Bibliography: p117-125*

LEECHOR, Chad
Tax policy and tax reform in semi-industrial countries / Chad Leechor. — Washington, D.C. : The World Bank, 1986. — viii,63p. — (Industry and finance series ; v.13). — *Bibliographical references: p62-63*

TAXATION — France — Dauphiné — History

HICKEY, Daniel
The coming of French absolutism : the struggle for tax reform in the Province of Dauphiné, 1540-1650 / Daniel Hickey. — Toronto ; London : University of Toronto Press, c1986. — 273 p.

TAXATION — Great Britain

BEENSTOCK, Michael
Work, welfare and taxation : a study of labour supply incentives in the UK / Michael Beenstock and associates. — London : Allen & Unwin, 1987. — xi,275p. — *Bibliography : p268-271. — Includes index*

CHILD POVERTY ACTION GROUP
Building one nation : memorandum to the Chancellor of the Exchequer. — London : Child Poverty Action Group, 1987. — 16p

CONFEDERATION OF BRITISH INDUSTRY
Tax : time for change. — London : Confederation of British Industry, 1985. — 126p

GREAT BRITAIN. Treasury
The reform of personal taxation : presented to Parliament by the Chancellor of the Exchequer by Command of her Majesty March 1986. — London : H.M.S.O., 1986. — 82p. — (Cmnd ; 9756). — *Green Paper on the reform of personal taxation*

KAY, J. A., 1948-
The British tax system / J.A. Kay, M.A. King. — 4th ed. — Oxford : Oxford University Press, 1986. — viii,261p. — *Previous ed.: 1983. — Bibliography: p241-250. — Includes index*

Leaving Britain? : a tax and legal guide for intending emigrants / edited by Tax Haven Review, Technical Services Group. — London : Tax Haven Review, 1976. — 63p

LISTER, Ruth
Opportunity lost : a response to the Green Paper on the Reform of Personal Taxation from the Child Poverty Action Group / Ruth Lister and Fran Bennett. — London : Child Poverty Action Group, 1986. — 34p

TAXATION — Great Britain — Forms

JAMES, Simon, 1952-
The comprehensibility of taxation : a study of taxation and communications / Simon James, Alan Lewis and Frances Allison. — Aldershot : Avebury, c1987. — xiii,314p. — *Includes bibliographies and index*

TAXATION — Great Britain — Statistics

GREAT BRITAIN. Parliament. House of Commons. Library. Research Division
The burden of taxation 1978-1982 / Jennifer Tanfield. — [London] : the Division, 1982. — 20p. — (Research note ; no.70)

TAXATION — India

AHMAD, Ehtisham
The analysis of tax reform for developing countries : lessons from research on Pakistan and India / Ehtisham Ahmad and Nicholas Stern. — London : Suntory Toyota International Centre for Economics and Related Disciplines, 1986. — 31p. — (Development research programme / London School of Economics and Political Science. Suntory Toyota International Centre for Economics and Related Disciplines ; no.2). — *Bibliography: p30-31*

TAXATION — Pakistan

AHMAD, Ehtisham
The analysis of tax reform for developing countries : lessons from research on Pakistan and India / Ehtisham Ahmad and Nicholas Stern. — London : Suntory Toyota International Centre for Economics and Related Disciplines, 1986. — 31p. — (Development research programme / London School of Economics and Political Science. Suntory Toyota International Centre for Economics and Related Disciplines ; no.2). — *Bibliography: p30-31*

TAXATION — Puerto Rico

PUERTO RICO. Department of the Treasury. Office of Economic and Financial Research
Aspectos mas importantes del sistema tributario de Puerto Rico. — San Juan : the Office, 1974. — viii,126p

PUERTO RICO. Department of the Treasury. Office of Public Relations
Contribuciones en Puerto Rico. — [Rev. ed]. — San Juan : the Office, 1962. — vi,113p

PUERTO RICO. Department of the Treasury. Office of Public Relations
Contribuciones en Puerto Rico. — [Rev. ed] — San Juan : the Office, 1964. — vii,116p

TAXATION — South Africa

SOUTH AFRICA. Department of Finance
Inland revenue statistical bulletin = Binnelandse inkomste statistiese bulletin / Department of Finance, South Africa. — Pretoria : Government Printer, 1983-. — *Annual. — Text in English and Afrikaans*

TAXATION — Soviet Union — History

NEUPOKOEV, V. I.
Gosudarstvennye povinnosti krest'ian Evropeiskoi Rossii v kontse XVIII - nachale XIX veka / V. I. Neupokoev ; otv. redaktor P. G. Ryndziunskii. — Moskva : Nauka, 1987. — 286p

TAXATION — Taiwan

Taxes in Taiwan currently in effect, with illustrations. — Taipei : Industrial Development and Investment Center, 1961. — ii,31p

TAXATION — United States

HERSHEY, Barry J.
The American tax system : a call for reform / by Barry J. Hershey. — New York : Philosophical Library, 1984. — xiii, 158 p.. — *Includes index. — Bibliography: p. 147-149*

Tax reform and U.S. economy / papers by Henry J. Aaron...[et al.] ; edited by Joseph A. Pechman. — Washington, D.C. : Brookings Institution, 1987. — 107p. — (Brookings dialogues on public policy). — *Papers presented at a conference at the Brookings institution, December 2, 1986*

TAXATION — United States — Mathematical models

A General equilibrium model for tax policy evaluation / Charles L. Ballard ... [et al.]. — Chicago : University of Chicago Press, 1985. — p. cm. — (A National Bureau of Economic Research monograph). — *Includes index. — Bibliography: p*

TAXATION — United States — States — Congresses

States under stress : a report on the finances of Massachusetts, Michigan, Texas, and California : California Policy Seminar conference report / Peggy B. Musgrave, editor. — Berkeley : Institute of Governmental Studies, University of California, [c1985]. — vii, 60 leaves. — *"February 1985."*

TAXATION, DOUBLE

Cross-border transactions between related companies : a summary of tax rules / edited by William R. Lawlor. — Deventer, The Netherlands ; Boston : Kluwer Law and Taxation Publishers, c1985. — p. cm. — *Derived from an international tax planning symposium in New York sponsored by Ernst & Whinney. — "Current to January 1985"--Foreword*

RAAD, C. van
Nondiscrimination in international tax law / Kees van Raad. — Deventer ; Boston : Kluwer Law and Taxation, c1986. — xix, 284 p.. — (Series on international taxation ; no. 6). — *Bibliography: p. 271-284*

TAXATION, DOUBLE — Treaties

United Nations model double taxation convention between developed and developing countries. — New York : United Nations, 1980. — iv,265p. — ([Document] / United Nations ; ST/ESA/102). — *At head of title: Department of International Economic and Social Affairs*

TAXATION, DOUBLE — Soviet Union

NEWCITY, Michael A
Taxation in the Soviet Union / Michael A. Newcity. — New York : Praeger, c1986. — xiii, 392 p.. — "Praeger special studies. Praeger scientific.". — *Includes index. — Bibliography: p. 368-377*

TAXATION OF ALIENS

RAAD, C. van
Nondiscrimination in international tax law / Kees van Raad. — Deventer ; Boston : Kluwer Law and Taxation, c1986. — xix, 284 p.. — (Series on international taxation ; no. 6). — *Bibliography: p. 271-284*

TAXATION OF ALIENS — Soviet Union

NEWCITY, Michael A
Taxation in the Soviet Union / Michael A. Newcity. — New York : Praeger, c1986. — xiii, 392 p.. — "Praeger special studies. Praeger scientific.". — *Includes index. — Bibliography: p. 368-377*

TAXATION OF ARTICLES OF CONSUMPTION — Mathematical models

GORDON, Jim
The grouping of commodities for tax purposes / Jim Gordon. — [London : London School of Economics and Political Science], 1986. — 15p. — (Taxation, incentives and the distribution of income ; no.94). — *Economic and Social Research Council programme. — Bibliographical references: p15*

TAXATION OF ARTICLES OF CONSUMPTION — United States

A Citizen's guide to the new tax reforms : fair tax, simple tax, flat tax / Joseph A. Pechman, editor. — Totowa, N.J. : Rowman & Allanheld, 1985. — p. cm. — *Includes index*

TAXATION OF BONDS, SECURITIES, ETC. — Peru

PERU
[Decreto supremo no.287-68-HC]. Income tax, real estate ownership value and stock assets : Supreme decree no.287-68-HC. — [Lima : Presidencia?, 1968]. — 106leaves. — *Translation from Spanish into English*

TAXATION OF PERSONAL PROPERTY — Great Britain

WALKER, Andrew
Housing taxation : owner-occupation and the reform of housing finance / Andrew Walker. — London : Catholic Housing Aid Society, c1986. — 99 p. — (CHAS occasional paper ; 9). — *Bibliography: p96-99*

TAYLOR, ZACHARY

BAUER, K. Jack
Zachary Taylor : soldier, planter, statesman of the old Southwest / K. Jack Bauer. — Baton Rouge : Louisiana State University Press, c1985. — xxiv, 348 p.. — (Southern biography series). — *Includes index. — Bibliography: p. 329-338*

TAYSIDE (SCOTLAND) — Antiquities

WALKER, Bruce
Exploring Scotland's heritage : Fife and Tayside / Bruce Walker and Graham Ritchie. — Edinburgh : H.M.S.O., 1987. — 202p. — (Exploring Scotland's heritage). — *At foot of t.p.: The Royal Commission on the Ancient and Historical Monuments of Scotland. — Bibliography: p.196-197*

TEA — Sri Lanka

ROTE, Ron
A taste of bitterness : the political economy of tea plantations in Sri Lanka / Ronald Rote. — Amsterdam : Free University Press, 1986. — xviii,282p. — *Doctoral thesis for Free University of Amsterdam, 1986. — Bibliography: p231-245*

TEA PLANTATION WORKERS — Sri Lanka

ROTE, Ron
A taste of bitterness : the political economy of tea plantations in Sri Lanka / Ronald Rote. — Amsterdam : Free University Press, 1986. — xviii,282p. — *Doctoral thesis for Free University of Amsterdam, 1986. — Bibliography: p231-245*

TEA TRADE

FORREST, Denys
The world tea trade : a survey of the production, distribution and consumption of tea / Denys Forrest. — Cambridge : Woodhead-Faulkner, 1985. — [256]p. — *Included bibliography and indes*

TEA TRADE — Mathematical models

AKIYAMA, Takamasa
A new global tea model : specification, estimation, and simulation / Takamasa Akiyama and Pravin K. Trivedi. — Washington, D.C. : The World Bank, 1987. — vi,130p. — (World Bank staff commodity working papers ; no.17). — *Bibliographical references: p129-130*

TEACHERS — In-service training — European Economic Community countries

BELBENOIT, G.
In—service education and training of teachers in the European Community / by G. Belbenoit. — Luxembourg : Office for Official Publications of the European Communities, 1979. — 204p. — (Education series / Commission of the European Communities ; no.8)

TEACHERS — Salaries, pensions, etc. — Law and legislation — Great Britain

GREAT BRITAIN. Parliament. House of Commons. Library. Research Division
Education (Amendment) Bill, [Bill 12 of 1985/86] / Kay Andrews. — [London] : the Division, 1985. — 18p. — (Reference sheet ; no.85/8). — *Bibliographical references: p17-18*

GREAT BRITAIN. Parliament. House of Commons. Library. Research Division
The Teachers' Pay and Conditions Bill [Bill 10], session 1986/87 / Christine Gillie, Gillian Allen. — [London] : the Division, 1986. — 24p. — (Reference sheet ; no.86/15). — *Bibliographical references: p20-24*

TEACHERS — Salaries, pensions, etc — United States — Congresses

Public sector payrolls / edited by David A. Wise. — Chicago : University of Chicago Press, 1987. — ix, 327 p. — (A National Bureau of Economic Research project report). — *Papers presented at a conference held in Williamsburg, Va., Nov. 15-17, 1984. — Includes bibliographies and indexes*

TEACHERS — England — London — Political activity

MARKS, John, 1934-
London's schools : when even the Communist Party gives up! / John Marks. — London : Aims of Industry, 1985. — 6p

TEACHERS' PAY AND CONDITIONS BILL 1986-87

GREAT BRITAIN. Parliament. House of Commons. Library. Research Division
The Teachers' Pay and Conditions Bill [Bill 10], session 1986/87 / Christine Gillie, Gillian Allen. — [London] : the Division, 1986. — 24p. — (Reference sheet ; no.86/15). — *Bibliographical references: p20-24*

TEACHERS, TRAINING OF — Great Britain

GREAT BRITAIN. Department of Education and Science. Inspectorate of Schools
Quality in schools: the initial training of teachers : a survey of initial teacher training in the public sector in England, Northern Ireland and Wales / carried out by HMI and the Inspectorate in Northern Ireland January 1983 to January 1985. — London : H.M.S.O., 1987. — 158p

TEACHING

SCRUTON, Roger
Education and indoctrination : an attempt at definition and a review of social and political implications / Roger Scruton, Angela Ellis-Jones and Dennis O'Keeffe. — Harrow : Education Research Centre, 1985. — 64p

TEACHING TEAMS — England — Suffolk

REDMONDS, Jo
A study of co-operative teaching in primary schools / Jo Redmonds. — [Ipswich] : Education Department, 1987. — 53,iip. — (Research paper / Suffolk. Education Department ; no.6). — Bibliography: pi-ii

TECHNICAL ASSISTANCE

HÖLL, Otmar
Österreichische Entwicklungshilfe 1970-1983 : kritische Analyse und internationale Vergleich / Otmar Höll. — Wien : Braumuller, 1986. — 187p. — (Informationen zur Weltpolitik ; 7). — Bibliography: p183-187

TECHNICAL ASSISTANCE — Anthropological aspects

Anthropological contributions to planned change and development / edited by Harald O. Skar. — Göteborg, Sweden : Acta Universitatis Gothoburgensis, 1985. — iv, 191 p.. — (Gothenburg studies in social anthropology ; 8) . — Includes bibliographies

TECHNICAL ASSISTANCE — Anthropological aspects — Case studies

Practicing development anthropology / edited by Edward C. Green. — Boulder, Colo. : Westview Press, 1986. — xi, 283 p.. — (Westview special studies in applied anthropology). — Includes bibliographies and index

TECHNICAL ASSISTANCE — Dictionaries

The World Bank glossary = Glossaire de la Banque mondiale. — Washington, D.C. : The World Bank
V.1: English-French, French-English. — 1986. — 429p. — In English and French

The World Bank glossary = Glosario del Banco Mundial. — Washington, D.C. : The World Bank
V.2: English-Spanish, Spanish-English. — 1986. — v,360p. — In English and Spanish

TECHNICAL ASSISTANCE — Evaluation

CRUISE O'BRIEN, Rita
Third country training : an evaluation / Rita Cruise O'Brien, Jake Jacobs. — London : Ministry of Overseas Development, 1977. — [75]p

TECHNICAL ASSISTANCE, AMERICAN — Nepal

20 years of Nepalese-American cooperation : a summary of American aid to Nepal, 1951-1971. — [Kathmandu? : s.n., 1971?]. — 42p. — Cover title

TECHNICAL ASSISTANCE, BRITISH

GREAT BRITAIN. Overseas Development Administration
United Kingdom memorandum to the Development Assistance Committee of the Organisation for Economic Cooperation and Development. — [London] : the Administration, 1979. — 13p

TECHNICAL ASSISTANCE, BRITISH — Administration

GREAT BRITAIN. Overseas Development Administration
Minister's seminar on aid procedures : Deputy Secretaries' working group. — [London : the Administration, ca.1979]. — 14p

TECHNICAL ASSISTANCE, BRITISH — Directories

GREAT BRITAIN. Department of the Environment
British services overseas. — [London] : the Department, 1976. — 15p. — A contribution by the United Kingdom to the United Nations Conference on Human Settlements, 1976, Vancouver

TECHNICAL ASSISTANCE, BRITISH — Evaluation

GREAT BRITAIN. Overseas Development Administration. Evaluation Unit
Guidelines for the preparation of evaluation studies. — London : the Unit, 1979. — 9,2p

TECHNICAL ASSISTANCE, BRITISH — Bangladesh

CRACKNELL, Basil E.
A review of the ODM's training cooperation with Bangladesh / B. E. Cracknell, R. Stoneman, R. B. W. Haines. — London : Manpower Planning Unit, Ministry of Overseas Development with the cooperation of the British Council, London and Dacca, 1977. — 14p

TECHNICAL ASSISTANCE, BRITISH — Bangladesh — Evaluation

CRACKNELL, Basil E.
An evaluation of the training received by Bangladesh study fellows in the UK / B. E. Cracknell, R. Stoneman, R. B. W. Haines. — London : Manpower Planning Unit, Ministry of Overseas Development with the co-operation of the British Council, London & Dacca, 1977. — 31p

TECHNICAL ASSISTANCE, BRITISH — Sri Lanka

ODM's training cooperation with Sri Lanka : report of a mission to Sri Lanka, 12-23 October 1977 / B.E. Cracknell...[et al.]. — London : Manpower Planning Unit, Ministry of Overseas Development ; Colombo : British Council, 1977. — 48p

TECHNICAL ASSISTANCE, BRITISH — Thailand

CRACKNELL, Basil E.
ODM's training co-operation with Thailand : report of a visit to Thailand, 4-12 October 1977 / B.E. Cracknell and R. Stoneman. — London : Manpower Planning Unit, Ministry of Overseas Development, 1977. — 13,[6]p

TECHNICAL ASSISTANCE, CANADIAN — Bibliography

VANDERWAL, Andrew
Canadian development assistance : a selected bibliography 1978-1984 / Andrew Vanderwal ; edited by Rede Widstrand and Vivian Cummins. — Ottawa : Norman Paterson School of International Affairs, [1985]. — 39p. — (Bibliography series / Norman Paterson School of International Affairs ; 7)

TECHNICAL EDUCATION — Evaluation

HUNTING, Gordon
Evaluating vocational training programs : a practical guide / Gordon Hunting, Manuel Zymelman, Martin Godfrey. — Washington, D.C. : The World Bank, 1986. — vii,96p

TECHNICAL EDUCATION — Europe — Directories

Training of sanitary engineers in Europe / edited by Robert B. Dean. — Copenhagen : World Health Organization, 1985. — x,198p. — Includes bibliographical references

TECHNICAL EDUCATION — United States

BINKIN, Martin
Military technology and defense manpower / Martin Binkin. — Washington, D.C. : Brookings Institution, 1986. — p. cm. — (Studies in defense policy). — Includes index

TECHNICAL INNOVATIONS — Developing countries

Technical cooperation among developing countries news : TCDC news / United Nations. Development Programme. — New York : UNDP, 1979-1984. — Quarterly. — Continued by: Cooperation south: the magazine of technical co-operation among developing countries

TECHNOCRACY

Citizen participation in public decision making / edited by Jack DeSario and Stuart Langton. — New York : Greenwood Press, c1987. — xii, 237 p.. — (Contributions in political science ; no. 158). — "Prepared under the auspices of the Policy Studies Organization.". — Includes bibliographies and index

TECHNOLOGICAL FORECASTING

NATIONAL ECONOMIC DEVELOPMENT COUNCIL. Economic Development Committee for the Information Technology Industry. Long-Term Perspectives Group
IT futures : what current forecasting literature says about the social impact of information technology : a report / prepared by John Bessant ... [et al.] for the Long-Term Perspectives Group [of the Information Technology Economic Development Committee]. — London : National Economic Development Office, 1985. — vi,118p. — Chairman: Alan Benjamin

TECHNOLOGICAL INNOVATION — Economic aspects

GRAVES, John, 19---
Liberating technology : steps towards a benevolent society / John Graves ; with a foreword by Jo Campling. — London : Owen, 1986. — 175p. — Bibliography: p171. — Includes index

TECHNOLOGICAL INNOVATION — Social aspects

GRAVES, John, 19---
Liberating technology : steps towards a benevolent society / John Graves ; with a foreword by Jo Campling. — London : Owen, 1986. — 175p. — Bibliography: p171. — Includes index

TECHNOLOGICAL INNOVATIONS

ARNOLD, Erik
Parallel convergence : national strategies in information technology / Erik Arnold and Ken Guy. — London : Pinter, 1986. — [230]p. — Includes bibliography and index

BODDY, David
Managing new technology / David Boddy and David A. Buchanan. — Oxford : Blackwell, 1986. — vii,253p. — Includes index

COOLEY, Mike
Interview : Mike Cooley on new technology. — London : Hackney Job Share Project, 1985. — 6 leaves

DESAI, Meghnad
Financial innovations : measuring the opportunity for product innovation / M. Desai and W. Low. — London : Economic and Social Research Council : London School of Economics, 1986. — [41]p. — (ESRC/LSE econometrics project discussion paper ; A.58). — Bibliography: p36

Industrial technological development : a network approach / edited by Håkan Håkansson. — London : Croom Helm, c1987. — 234p. — (UWIST/Croom Helm series on management and new information technology)

TECHNOLOGICAL INNOVATIONS
continuation

KANTER, Rosabeth Moss
The change masters / Rosabeth Moss Kanter. — London : Allen & Unwin, 1984, c1983. — 432p. — *Originally published: New York : Simon and Schuster, 1983. — Includes index*

MEGARRY, Jacquetta
Inside information : computers, communications and people / Jacquetta Megarry. — London : British Broadcasting Corporation, 1985. — 224p. — *Includes index*

The Myth of the information revolution : social and ethical implications of communication technology / edited by Michael Traber. — London : Sage, 1986. — viii,146p. — (Sage communications in society series). — *Includes index*

POLLACK, Jonathan D.
The R and D process and technological innovation in the Chinese industrial system / Jonathan D. Pollack. — Santa Monica (Calif:) : Rand, 1985. — iii,12p

POTTER, Stephen, 1953-
On the right lines? : the limits of technological innovation / Stephen Potter. — London : Pinter, c1987. — viii,208p. — *Bibliography: p201-204. — Includes index*

RAY, George
The diffusion of mature technologies / George F. Ray. — Cambridge : Cambridge University Press, 1984. — ix,96p. — (Occasional papers / National Institute of Economic and Social Research ; 36)

Science, technology and the labour process : Marxist studies / edited by Les Levidow and Bob Young. — London : Free Association Books
Vol.2. — 1985. — v,232p. — *Includes bibliographies*

The Spatial impact of technological change / edited by John F. Brotchie, Peter Hall & Peter W. Newton. — London : Croom Helm, c1987. — xxv,460p

STRUICK VAN BEMMELEN, Ton
Interim report of the Sub-Committee on Advanced Technology and Technology Transfer / Ton Struick van Bemmelen. — Brussels : North Atlantic Assembly, 1986. — ii,33p

Technical change and industrial policy / edited by Keith Chapman and Graham Humphrys. — Oxford : Basil Blackwell, 1987. — 264p. — (Institute of British Geographers special publications ; 19). — *Conference papers. — Includes bibliographies and index*

Technical working papers / National Bureau of Economic Research. — Cambridge (Mass.) : National Bureau of Economic Research, 1985-

Technology, innovation and change / edited by Brian Elliott. — Edinburgh : University of Edinburgh, Centre of Canadian Studies, 1986. — x,94p. — *Bibliographies*

TECHNOLOGICAL INNOVATIONS — Congresses

INTERNATIONAL SYMPOSIUM ON TECHNOLOGICAL CHANGE AND EMPLOYMENT: URBAN AND REGIONAL DIMENSIONS (1985 : Zandvoort, Netherlands)
Technological change, employment, and spatial dynamics : proceedings of an International Symposium on Technological Change and Employment: Urban and Regional Dimensions, held at Zandvoort, the Netherlands, April 1-3, 1985 / edited by Peter Nijkamp. — Berlin ; New York : Springer-Verlag, c1986. — vii, 466 p.. — (Lecture notes in economics and mathematical systems ; 270). — *Includes bibliographies*

TECHNOLOGICAL INNOVATIONS — Economic aspects

COOMBS, Rod
Economics and technological change / Rod Coombs, Paolo Saviotti and Vivien Walsh. — Basingstoke : Macmillan Education, 1987. — xv,296p. — *Bibliography: p279-292. — Includes index*

Entrepreneurship & technology : world experiences and policies / editors, Wayne S. Brown & Roy Rothwell. — Harlow : Longman, 1986. — 222p. — *Includes bibliographies*

FOSTER, Richard N.
Innovation : the attacker's advantage / Richard N. Foster. — London : Macmillan, 1986. — [320]p. — *Includes bibliography and index*

New technology and regional development / edited by Bert van der Knaap and Egbert Wever. — London : Croom Helm, c1987. — 188p. — *Conference papers. — Includes index*

ROSEGGER, Gerhard
The economics of production and innovation : an industrial perspective / by Gerhard Rosegger. — 2nd ed. / with a foreword by Bela Gold. — Oxford : Pergamon, 1986. — xvii,281p. — (Omega management science series). — *Previous ed.: 1980. — Bibliography: p271-272. — Includes index*

SCOTT, Allen John
High technology industry and regional development : a theoretical critique and reconstruction / A. J. Scott and M. Storper. — Reading : University of Reading. Department of Geography, 1986. — 25p. — (Geographical paper ; no.95). — *17th Norma Wilkinson memorial lecture. — Bibliography: p23-25*

TECHNOLOGICAL INNOVATIONS — Economic aspects — Developing countries

Macro policies for appropriate technology in developing countries / edited by Francis Stewart. — Boulder : Westview Press, 1986. — p. cm. — (Westview special studies in social, political, and economic development)

TECHNOLOGICAL INNOVATIONS — Economic aspects — Europe

A High technology gap? : Europe, America, and Japan / Andrew J. Pierre, editor ; Frank Press ... [et al.] ; introduction by Robert D. Hormats. — New York, N.Y. : Council on Foreign Relations, c1987. — xii, 114 p.. — (Europe/America ; 6). — *Includes bibliographical references*

TECHNOLOGICAL INNOVATIONS — Economic aspects — Great Britain

Industrial change in the United Kingdom / edited by William F. Lever. — Harlow : Longman Scientific & Technical, 1987. — 272p . — *Includes bibliographies and index*

TECHNOLOGICAL INNOVATIONS — Economic aspects — Japan

A High technology gap? : Europe, America, and Japan / Andrew J. Pierre, editor ; Frank Press ... [et al.] ; introduction by Robert D. Hormats. — New York, N.Y. : Council on Foreign Relations, c1987. — xii, 114 p.. — (Europe/America ; 6). — *Includes bibliographical references*

TECHNOLOGICAL INNOVATIONS — Economic aspects — Latin America

Technology generation in Latin American manufacturing industries : theory and case-studies concerning its nature, magnitude and consequences / edited by Jorge M. Katz. — Basingstoke : Macmillan, 1987. — x,549p. — *Includes index*

TECHNOLOGICAL INNOVATIONS — Economic aspects — United States

A High technology gap? : Europe, America, and Japan / Andrew J. Pierre, editor ; Frank Press ... [et al.] ; introduction by Robert D. Hormats. — New York, N.Y. : Council on Foreign Relations, c1987. — xii, 114 p.. — (Europe/America ; 6). — *Includes bibliographical references*

TECHNOLOGICAL INNOVATIONS — Government policy

Entrepreneurship & technology : world experiences and policies / editors, Wayne S. Brown & Roy Rothwell. — Harlow : Longman, 1986. — 222p. — *Includes bibliographies*

TECHNOLOGICAL INNOVATIONS — Government policy — France

Innovation policy : France. — Paris : OECD, 1986. — 296p. — *Bibliographical references: p237-242, 296*

TECHNOLOGICAL INNOVATIONS — Government policy — Ireland

Innovation policy : Ireland. — Paris : Organisation for Economic Co-operation and Development, 1987. — 75p. — *Bibliographical references: p55*

TECHNOLOGICAL INNOVATIONS — History — Addresses, essays, lectures

Technological change and workers' movements / edited by Melvyn Dubofsky. — Beverly Hills : Sage Publications, c1985. — p. cm. — (Explorations in the world-economy ; v. 4). — : "Originally presented at the Third U.S.-U.S.S.R. Colloquium on World Labor and Social Change held at the State University of New York at Binghamton in January 1983"--Introd

TECHNOLOGICAL INNOVATIONS — Law and legislation

DESJARDINS, André
Les changements technologiques : recueil de clauses-types / par André Desjardins. — Québec : Centre de recherche et de statistiques sur le marché du travail, 1985. — 121p

TECHNOLOGICAL INNOVATIONS — Law and legislation — Québec (Province)

DESJARDINS, André
Les changements technologiques : recueil de clauses-types / par André Desjardins. — Québec : Centre de recherche et de statistiques sur le marché du travail, 1985. — 121p

TECHNOLOGICAL INNOVATIONS — Management — Congresses

Innovation and entrepreneurship in organizations : strategies for competitiveness, deregulation, and privatization / edited by Richard M. Burton and Børge Obel. — Amsterdam ; New York : Elsevier ; New York, NY, U.S.A. : Distributors for the U.S. and Canada, Elsevier Science Pub. Co., 1986. — vii, 207 p.. — *Chiefly papers presented at a seminar held at the European Institute for Advanced Studies in Management, Brussels, in May 1985. — "Has been published in a special issue of Technovation, vol 5 (1986), issues 1-3.". — Includes bibliographies and index*

INTERNATIONAL CONFERENCE ON PRODUCT INNOVATION MANAGEMENT ((4th : 1985 : Innsburg, Austria and lgls, Austria)
The art and science of innovation management : an international perspective : proceedings of the Fourth International Conference on Product Innovation Management, Innsbruck/Igls, Austria, August 26-28, 1985 / edited by Heinz Hübner. — Amsterdam ; New York : Elsevier, 1986. — p. cm

TECHNOLOGICAL INNOVATIONS — Social aspects

FÉDÉRATION CHRÉTIENNE DES OUVRIERS SUR MÉTAUX DE LA SUISSE. Congrès (1979 : Montreux)
Les travailleurs face à la révolution technologique : FCOM congrès 1979. — [Genève] : la Fédération, [1979]. — 18p

TECHNOLOGICAL INNOVATIONS — Social aspects
continuation

MAITRA, Priyatosh
Population, technology and development : a critical analysis / Priyatosh Maitra. — Aldershot : Gower, c1986. — [216]p. — *Includes bibliography and index*

MOLE, Veronica
Enterprising innovation : an alternative approach / Veronica Mole and Dave Elliott. — London : Pinter, 1987. — x,180p. — *Bibliography: p164-169. — Includes index*

Public acceptance of new technologies : an international review / edited by Roger Williams and Stephen Mills. — London : Croom Helm, c1986. — 443p. — *Conference proceedings. — Includes index*

SIMPSON, David, 1936-
The challenge of new technology / David Simpson, Jim Love, Jim Walker. — Brighton : Wheatsheaf, 1987. — ix,159p. — *Bibliography: p148-151. — Includes index*

Smothered by invention : technology in women's lives / edited by Wendy Faulkner and Erik Arnold. — London : Pluto, 1985. — [272]p

Social responses to technological change / edited by Augustine Brannigan and Sheldon Goldenberg. — Westport, Conn. : Greenwood Press, c1985. — p. cm. — (Contributions in sociology ; no. 56). — *Includes index. — Bibliography: p*

WILLMAN, Paul
Technological change, collective bargaining, and industrial efficiency / Paul Willman. — Oxford : Clarendon, 1986. — [xvii.264]p. — *Includes index*

ZIMMERMAN, Jan
Once upon the future : a woman's guide to tomorrow's technology / Jan Zimmerman. — New York ; London : Pandora, 1986. — xviii,230p. — (Pandora Press focus). — *Includes index*

TECHNOLOGICAL INNOVATIONS — Social aspects — Argentina

SALEÑO, Nicanor
La Argentina : productividad tecnológica y cambio social; escenario prospectivo para el tercer milenio / Nicanor Saleño. — [Buenos Aires?] : Pleamar, c1984. — 199p. — (Economía y sociedad)

TECHNOLOGICAL INNOVATIONS — Social aspects — Switzerland

FÉDÉRATION CHRÉTIENNE DES OUVRIERS SUR MÉTAUX DE LA SUISSE. Congrès (1979 : Montreux)
Les travailleurs face à la révolution technologique : FCOM congrès 1979. — [Genève] : the Fédération, [1979]. — 18p

TECHNOLOGICAL INNOVATIONS — Argentina

SALEÑO, Nicanor
La Argentina : productividad tecnológica y cambio social; escenario prospectivo para el tercer milenio / Nicanor Saleño. — [Buenos Aires?] : Pleamar, c1984. — 199p. — (Economía y sociedad)

TECHNOLOGICAL INNOVATIONS — Australia

Technology and innovation. — Canberra : Economic Planning Advisory Council, 1986. — v,26p. — (Council paper / Economic Planning Advisory Council ; no.19). — *Bibliographical references: p24*

TECHNOLOGICAL INNOVATIONS — Canada

MARTIN, Fernand
The regional factor in the diffusion of innovations / Fernand Martin. — Montreal : Université de Montréal. Departement des Sciences Economiques, 1976. — 25p. — (Cahier / Université de Montréal. Departement des Sciences Economiques ; no.7601). — *Bibliography: p23-25*

TECHNOLOGICAL INNOVATIONS — Developing countries

Cooperation south: the magazine of technical co-operation among developing countries / United Nations. Development Programme. — New York : UNDP, 1985-. — *Quarterly. — Continues:*

TECHNOLOGICAL INNOVATIONS — Developing countries — Case studies

Technology and employment in industry : a case study approach / edited by A.S. Bhalla ; preword by Amartya Sen. — 3rd, revised and enlarged ed. — Geneva : International Labour Office, 1985. — xviii,436p. — (A WEP Study)

TECHNOLOGICAL INNOVATIONS — Europe

WOODS, Stan
Western Europe : technology and the future / Stanley Woods. — London : Croom Helm for the Atlantic Institute for International Affairs, c1987. — [180]p. — (Atlantic paper ; no.63)

TECHNOLOGICAL INNOVATIONS — European Economic Community countries

CLAYTON, M.
Study into EC-wide criteria for the identification of new technology based enterprises / M. Clayton, T. Mitchell. — Luxembourg : Office for Official Publications of the European Communities, 1984. — iv,174p. — (EUR ; 8926). — *Includes bibliographical references*

TECHNOLOGICAL INNOVATIONS — European Economic community countries — Bibliography — Catalogs

COMMISSION OF THE EUROPEAN COMMUNITIES. Library
Recent publications on the European Communities received by the Library : supplement. — [Luxembourg : Office for Official Publications of the European Communities]
1985/2: Bibliography on technological innovation. — 1985. — 584,40 columns. — *In Community languages*

TECHNOLOGICAL INNOVATIONS — France

Innovation policy : France. — Paris : OECD, 1986. — 296p. — *Bibliographical references: p237-242, 296*

TECHNOLOGICAL INNOVATIONS — Great Britain

NORTHCOTT, Jim
Promoting innovation 2 : microelectronics consultancy support / Jim Northcott...[et al.]. — London : Policy Studies Institute, 1986. — 181p. — (PSI Research Report ; 662)

PRIDE, Emrys
Pride in Britain's high-tech process / Emrys Pride. — Brigend : D. Brown
Part 1: From distressed areas to development agency. — 1985. — 72p

WINTERTON, Jonathan
New technology : the bargaining issues / Jonathan and Ruth Winterton. — Leeds ; Nottingham : Published by the Universities of Leeds and Nottingham in association with the Institute of Personnel Management, 1985. — v,37p. — (Leeds-Nottingham occasional papers in industrial relations ; 7)

TECHNOLOGICAL INNOVATIONS — India

BIRLA INSTITUTE OF SCIENTIFIC RESEARCH. Economic Research Division
Capital and technological progress in the Indian economy, 1950/51 - 1980/81. — New Delhi : Radiant Publishers, 1985. — xvi,198p. — *Bibliography: p192-198*

LALL, Sanjaya
Learning to industrialize : the acquisition of technological capability by India / Sanjaya Lall. — Basingstoke : Macmillan, 1987. — [280]p. — *Includes index*

TECHNOLOGICAL INNOVATIONS — Ireland

Innovation policy : Ireland. — Paris : Organisation for Economic Co-operation and Development, 1987. — 75p. — *Bibliographical references: p55*

TECHNOLOGICAL INNOVATIONS — Nigeria

FADAHUNSI, Akin
The development process and technology : a case for a resources based development strategy in Nigeria / Akin Fadahunsi. — Uppsala : Scandinavian Institute of African Studies, 1986. — 41p. — (Research report / Scandinavian Institute of African Studies ; no.77). — *Bibliographies*

ONU, C. Ogbonnaya
Technology and national development : the Nigerian state / by C. Ogbonnaya Onu. — Aba : Aduco Nigeria, [1985?]. — x,189p

TECHNOLOGICAL INNOVATIONS — Québec (Province)

BENOIT, Carmelle
L'incidence de la machine a traitement de textes sur l'emploi et le travail / Carmelle Benoit, Alfred Cossette, Prisco Cardillo ; en collaboration avec Réal Morrissette, Emmanuel Nyahoho. — Québec : Ministère du travail : Ministère de la main-d'oeuvre et de la sécurité du revenu, 1984. — xxi,249p. — *Bibliographical references: p243-249*

TECHNOLOGICAL INNOVATIONS — Soviet Union

BUGAVEI, V. Iu.
Ekonomicheskie problemy tekhnicheskogo progressa / V. Iu. Bugavei, M I. Panova. — Moskva : Mysl', 1974. — 285p

HOFFMANN, Erik P.
Technocratic socialism : the Soviet Union in the advanced industrial era / Erik P. Hoffmann and Robbin F. Laird. — Durham : Duke University Press, 1985. — 228p. — (Duke Press policy studies). — *Includes index. — Bibliography: p.[201]-225*

Rabochii klass i nauchno-tekhnicheskii progress / otv. redaktor G. V. Osipov. — Moskva : Nauka, 1986. — 187p

TECHNOLOGICAL INNOVATIONS — Soviet Union — Finance

Planovoe upravlenie ekonomikoi razvitogo sotsializma / redaktsionnaia kollegiia: A. S. Emel'ianov...[et al.]. — Kiev : Naukova dumka . — *V piati tomath*
T.3: Nauchno-tekhnicheskii progress i planovoe investirovanie v narodnoe khoziaistvo / otv. redaktor S. M. Iampol'skii. — 1986. — 307p. — *Bibliography: p305-[308]*

TECHNOLOGICAL INNOVATIONS — Spain

BRAÑA, Javier
El Estadio y el cambio tecnológico en la industrialización tardía : un analisis del caso español / Javier Braña, Mikel Buesa, Jose Molero. — México ; Madrid : Fondo de Cultura Económica, 1984. — 380p. — *Bibliography: p345-375*

Nuevas tecnologías, economía y sociedad en España / Manuel Castells...[et al.] ; prólogo de Felipe González. — Madrid : Alianza Editorial
Vol.1. — 1986. — xvi,493p

TECHNOLOGICAL INNOVATIONS — Spain *continuation*
Nuevas tecnologías, economía y sociedad en España / Manuel Castells...[et al.] ; prólogo Felipe González. — Madrid : Alianza Editorial. — *Bibliography: p[1047]-1056* Vol.2. — 1986. — x,503-1056p

TECHNOLOGICAL INNOVATIONS — United States
ZEGVELD, Walter
SDI and industrial technology policy : threat or opportunity? / Walter Zegveld and Christien Enzing. — London : Pinter, 1987. — 186p. — *Includes bibliographies and index*

TECHNOLOGICAL INNOVATIONS — United States — Congresses
Technology venturing : American innovation and risk-taking / edited by Eugene B. Konecci and Robert Lawrence Kuhn. — New York : Praeger, c1985. — p. cm. — *Derived from a conference held at the University of Texas at Dallas, Feb. 5-7, 1984. — Includes index*

TECHNOLOGY
MARTIN, James
Technology's crucible / James Martin. — Englewood Cliffs, N.J. : Prentice-Hall, c1987. — p. cm

TECHNOLOGY — Bibliography
COMMISSION OF THE EUROPEAN COMMUNITIES
Catalogue : EUR documents, 1968-1979 / Commission of the European Communities. — Luxembourg : Office for Official Publications of the European Communities, 1983. — xviii,301p. — (Information management / Commission of the European Communities)

TECHNOLOGY — Congresses
Technology and human productivity : challenges for the future / edited by John W. Murphy and John T. Pardeck. — New York : Quorum Books, 1986. — xx, 236 p.. — *"Result of the proceedings of the conference titled 'Technology and human productivity: myth or reality,' held at Arkansas State University, April 12-13, 1985"--Foreword. — Includes index. — Bibliography: p. [225]-228*

TECHNOLOGY — Economic aspects — Soviet Union
BUGAVEI, V. Iu.
Ekonomicheskie problemy tekhnicheskogo progressa / V. Iu. Bugavei, M I. Panova. — Moskva : Mysl', 1974. — 285p

TECHNOLOGY — History
[Histoire des techniques. English]. History of techniques / edited by Bertrand Gille ; translated from the French by J. Brainch ... [et al.] ; translation revised by A. Keller ; additional bibliography provided by E.F. Kranakis. — New York : Gordon and Breach Science Publishers, c1986. — p. cm. — *Translation of: Histoire des techniques. — Includes index. — Bibliography: p. — Contents: v. 1. Techniques and civilizations -- v. 2. Techniques and sciences*

TECHNOLOGY — International cooperation
Nauchno-tekhnicheskii progress i sotrudnichestvo stran SEV / pod redaktsiei O. A. Chukanova, G. M. Kharakhash'iana, Iu. F. Kormnova. — Moskva : Mezhdunarodnye otnosheniia, 1973. — 205p

SHARP, Margaret, 1938-
European technological collaboration / Margaret Sharp and Claire Shearman. — London : Routledge & Kegan Paul, 1987. — xii, 122p. — (Chatham House papers ; 36)

Strany SEV v mezhdunarodnom obmene tekhnologiei / pod redaktsiei O. T. Bogomolova, A. N. Bykova. — Moskva : Mezhdunarodnye otnosheniia, 1986. — 319p

TECHNOLOGY — Moral and ethical aspects
Contemporary moral controversies in technology / edited by A. Pablo Iannone. — New York : Oxford University Press, 1987. — xv, 336 p.. — *Bibliography: p. 334-336*

GRANT, George
Technology and justice / George Grant. — Toronto : Anansi, 1986. — 133p

TECHNOLOGY — Philosophy
AGASSI, Joseph
Technology, philosophical and social aspects / Joseph Agassi. — Dordrecht, Holland : D. Reidel ; Hingham, MA, U.S.A. : Sold and distributed in the U.S.A. and Canada by Kluwer Academic Publishers, c1985. — xix, 272 p.. — (Episteme ; v. 11). — *Includes indexes. — Bibliography: p. 260-261*

DEGREGORI, Thomas R
A theory of technology : continuity and change in human development / Thomas R. DeGregori. — Ames, Iowa : Iowa State University Press, c1985. — xiii, 263 p.. — *Includes indexes. — Bibliography: p. 221-251*

TECHNOLOGY — Religious aspects
VON DER MEHDEN, Fred R
Religion and modernization in Southeast Asia / Fred R. von der Mehden. — 1st ed. — Syracuse, N.Y. : Syracuse University Press, c1986. — viii, 240 p.. — *Includes index. — Bibliography: p. 225-233*

TECHNOLOGY — Social aspects
AGASSI, Joseph
Technology, philosophical and social aspects / Joseph Agassi. — Dordrecht, Holland : D. Reidel ; Hingham, MA, U.S.A. : Sold and distributed in the U.S.A. and Canada by Kluwer Academic Publishers, c1985. — xix, 272 p.. — (Episteme ; v. 11). — *Includes indexes. — Bibliography: p. 260-261*

CLARKE, Robin
Science and technology in world development / Robin Clarke ; foreword by Amadou-Mahtar M'Bow. — Oxford : Oxford Univlrsity Press/Unesco, 1985. — vi,216p. — (OPUS)

COOLEY, Mike
Interview : Mike Cooley on new technology. — London : Hackney Job Share Project, 1985. — 6 leaves

DEGREGORI, Thomas R
A theory of technology : continuity and change in human development / Thomas R. DeGregori. — Ames, Iowa : Iowa State University Press, c1985. — xiii, 263 p.. — *Includes indexes. — Bibliography: p. 221-251*

FORESTER, Tom
High-tech society : the story of the information technology revolution / Tom Forester. — Oxford : Basil Blackwell, 1987. — viii,311p. — *Bibliography: p290-296. — Includes index*

FRANCIS, Arthur
New technology at work / Arthur Francis. — Oxford : Clarendon, 1986. — [224]p

HISKES, Anne L. Deckard
Science, technology, and policy decisions / Anne L. Hiskes and Richard P. Hiskes. — Boulder : Westview Press, 1986. — p. cm. — *Includes index. — Bibliography: p*

NATIONAL ECONOMIC DEVELOPMENT COUNCIL. Economic Development Committee for the Information Technology Industry. Long-Term Perspectives Group
IT futures : what current forecasting literature says about the social impact of information technology : a report / prepared by John Bessant ... [et al.] for the Long-Term Perspectives Group [of the Information Technology Economic Development Committee]. — London : National Economic Development Office, 1985. — vi,118p. — *Chairman: Alan Benjamin*

Technology and international relations / edited by Otto Hieronymi ; with contributions by Michel Barjon ... [et al.]. — Basingstoke : Macmillan, 1987. — 194p

Technology and the human prospect : essays in honour of Christopher Freeman / edited by Roy M. MacLeod. — London : Pinter, 1986. — [300]p. — *Includes bibliography and index*

VANDERBURG, Willem H.
The growth of minds and cultures : a unified theory of the structure of human experience / Willem H. Vanderburg. — Toronto ; London : University of Toronto Press, c1985. — xxvi,334p. — *Includes index*

WENK, E
Tradeoffs : imperatives of choice in a high-tech world / Edward Wenk, Jr. — Baltimore : Johns Hopkins University Press, c1986. — p. cm. — *Includes index. — Bibliography: p*

WINTERTON, Jonathan
New technology : the bargaining issues / Jonathan and Ruth Winterton. — Leeds ; Nottingham : Published by the Universities of Leeds and Nottingham in association with the Institute of Personnel Management, 1985. — v,37p. — (Leeds-Nottingham occasional papers in industrial relations ; 7)

TECHNOLOGY — Social aspects — Bibliography
GRAYSON, Lesley
The social and economic impact of new technology 1984-1986 : a select bibliography / compiled by Leslie Grayson. — Letchworth : Technical Communications, 1986. — vi,116p

TECHNOLOGY — Social aspects — Germany (West)
SCHMIDT, Karlheinz
Der Traum vom deutschen Silicon Valley / Karlheinz Schmidt. — Landsberg am Lech : Verlag Moderne Industrie, 1985. — 225p. — *Bibliography: p211*

TECHNOLOGY — Social aspects — Soviet Union
HOFFMANN, Erik P.
Technocratic socialism : the Soviet Union in the advanced industrial era / Erik P. Hoffmann and Robbin F. Laird. — Durham : Duke University Press, 1985. — 228p. — (Duke Press policy studies). — *Includes index. — Bibliography: p.[201]-225*

TECHNOLOGY — Social aspects — Yugoslavia
ILIĆ, Zdravko
Balkanski atomski soko : bezbednosne, ekonomske, moralne i ekološke posledice gradnje atomskih elektrana / Zdravko Ilić. — Beograd : "Četvrti Jul", 1986. — 184p

TECHNOLOGY — China — Government policy
KANG, Chong-Sook
Technologie-Transfer nach China 1949-1982 / Chong-Sook Kang. — Frankfurt am Main : Campus Verlag, 1985. — 306p. — *Bibliography: p269-306*

TECHNOLOGY — Developing countries — Case studies
Technology and employment in industry : a case study approach / edited by A.S. Bhalla ; preword by Amartya Sen. — 3rd, revised and enlarged ed. — Geneva : International Labour Office, 1985. — xviii,436p. — (A WEP Study)

TECHNOLOGY — Europe
BONIFACE, Pascal
La puce, les hommes et la bombe : lÈurope face aux nouveau défis technologiques et militaires / Pascal Boniface, François Heisbourg ; Préface dAndré Fontaine. — Paris : Hachette, [1986]. — 321p. — *Bibliography: p310-314*

TECHNOLOGY — Europe
continuation

SHARP, Margaret, 1938-
European technological collaboration / Margaret Sharp and Claire Shearman. — London : Routledge & Kegan Paul, 1987. — xii, 122p. — (Chatham House papers ; 36)

TECHNOLOGY — Great Britain
Exploitable areas of science. — London : HMSO, 1986. — *At head of title: Advisory Council for Applied Research and Development*

TECHNOLOGY — Netherlands
Netherlands. — Paris : OECD, 1987. — 141p. — (Reviews of national science and technology policy). — *Includes bibliographical references*

TECHNOLOGY — United States
BINKIN, Martin
Military technology and defense manpower / Martin Binkin. — Washington, D.C. : Brookings Institution, 1986. — p. cm. — (Studies in defense policy). — *Includes index*

TECHNOLOGY — United States — History — 19th century — Addresses, essays, lectures
Military enterprise and technological change : perspectives on the American experience / edited by Merritt Roe Smith. — Cambridge, Mass. : MIT Press, c1985. — 391 p.. — *Includes bibliographical references and index*

TECHNOLOGY — United States — History — 20th century — Addresses, essays, lectures
Military enterprise and technological change : perspectives on the American experience / edited by Merritt Roe Smith. — Cambridge, Mass. : MIT Press, c1985. — 391 p.. — *Includes bibliographical references and index*

TECHNOLOGY AND CIVILIZATION
MCLUHAN, Marshall
Understanding media : the extensions of man / Marshall McLuhan ; Marshall McLuhan. — London : ARK, 1987. — 359 p

SALE, Kirkpatrick
Dwellers in the land : the bioregional vision / Kirkpatrick Sale. — San Francisco : Sierra Club Books, c1985. — x, 217 p.. — *Includes index. — Bibliography: p. 193-207*

TECHNOLOGY AND CIVILIZATION — Congresses
Irrigation civilizations : a comparative study : a symposium on method and result in cross-cultural regularities / [by] Julian H. Steward ... [et al.]. — Westport, Conn. : Greenwood Press, [1981]. — v, 78 p. — : *Reprint. Originally published: Washington, D.C. : Social Science Section, Dept. of Cultural Affairs, Pan American Union, 1955. (Social science monographs ; 1). — Includes bibliographies. — Contents: Introduction / by Julian H. Steward -- Developmental stages in ancient Mesopotamia / by Robert M. Adams -- Development of civilization on the coast of Peru / by Donald Collier -- The agricultural bases of urban civilization in Mesoamerica / by Angel Palerm -- Developmental aspects of hydraulic societies / by Karl A. Wittfogel -- Discussion: symposium on irrigation civilizations / by Ralph L. Beals -- Some implications of the symposium / by Julian H. Steward*

TECHNOLOGY AND CIVILIZATION — Forecasting
MUMFORD, Lewis
The future of technics and civilization / Lewis Mumford ; with an introduction by Colin Ward. — London : Freedom Press, 1986. — 184p. — *First published 1934*

TECHNOLOGY AND STATE
HISKES, Anne L. Deckard
Science, technology, and policy decisions / Anne L. Hiskes and Richard P. Hiskes. — Boulder : Westview Press, 1986. — p. cm. — *Includes index. — Bibliography: p*

Science and technology policy in the 1980s and beyond / edited by Michael Gibbons, Philip Gummett, Bhalchandra Udgaonkar. — London : Longman, 1984. — xxvi,346p.

Science parks and technology complexes in relation to regional development. — [Paris] : Organisation for Economic Co-operation and Development, 1987. — i,38p

Technology and international relations / edited by Otto Hieronymi ; with contributions by Michel Barjon ... [et al.]. — Basingstoke : Macmillan, 1987. — 194p

WENK, E
Tradeoffs : imperatives of choice in a high-tech world / Edward Wenk, Jr. — Baltimore : Johns Hopkins University Press, c1986. — p. cm. — *Includes index. — Bibliography: p*

TECHNOLOGY AND STATE — Case studies
National policies for developing high technology industries : international comparisons / edited by Francis W. Rushing and Carole Ganz Brown. — Boulder, Colo. : Westview Press, c1986. — xiv, 247 p.. — (Westview special studies in science, technology, and public policy). — *Includes bibliographies*

TECHNOLOGY AND STATE — Australia
Australia. — Paris : Organisation for Economic Co-operation and Development, 1986. — 119p. — (Reviews of national science and technology policy). — *Includes bibliographical references*

TECHNOLOGY AND STATE — Finland
Finland. — [Paris] : Organisation for Economic Co-operation and Development, [1987]. — 153p. — (Reviews of national science and technology policy). — *Includes bibliographical references*

TECHNOLOGY AND STATE — Great Britain
UK science policy : a critical review of policies for publicly funded research / edited by Maurice Goldsmith. — London : Longman, 1984. — xxii,275p. — *Includes bibliographies and index*

TECHNOLOGY AND STATE — Nigeria
ONU, C. Ogbonnaya
Technology and national development : the Nigerian state / by C. Ogbonnaya Onu. — Aba : Aduco Nigeria, [1985?]. — x,189p

TECHNOLOGY AND STATE — Portugal
Portugal. — [Paris] : Organisation for Economic Co-operation and Development, 1986. — 136p. — (Reviews of national science and technology policy). — *Bibliographical references: p82-85*

TECHNOLOGY AND STATE — Soviet Union
HOFFMANN, Erik P.
Technocratic socialism : the Soviet Union in the advanced industrial era / Erik P. Hoffmann and Robbin F. Laird. — Durham : Duke University Press, 1985. — 228p. — (Duke Press policy studies). — *Includes index. — Bibliography: p.[201]-225*

TECHNOLOGY AND STATE — Sweden
Sweden. — Paris : Organisation for Economic Co-operation and Development, 1987. — 112p. — (Reviews of national science and technology policy). — *Bibliographical references: p88*

TECHNOLOGY ASSESSMENT
MORONE, Joseph G
Averting catastrophe : strategies for regulating risky technologies / Joseph G. Morone and Edward J. Woodhouse. — Berkeley : University of California Press, 1985, c1986. — p. cm. — *Includes index. — Bibliography: p*

SHRADER-FRECHETTE, K. S.
Risk analysis and scientific method : methodological and ethical problems with evaluating societal hazards / K.S. Shrader-Frechette. — Dordrecht ; Boston : D. Reidel ; Hingham, MA, U.S.A. : Sold and distributed in the U.S.A. and Canada by Kluwer Academic Publishers, c1985. — x, 232 p.. — *Includes indexes. — Bibliography: p. 217-226*

TECHNOLOGY ASSESSMENT — Congresses
Hazards : technology and fairness / National Academy of Engineering. — Washington, D.C. : National Academy Press, 1986. — viii, 225 p.. — (Series on technology and social priorities). — *Consists of papers based on the Symposium on Hazards: Technology and Fairness, held June 3-4, 1985. — Includes bibliographies and index*

TECHNOLOGY TRANSFER
BOLLECKER-STERN, Brigitte
Droit économique / Brigitte Bollecker-Stern, Maurice Dahan, Lazare Kopelmanas. — Paris : Pedone, 1978. — 166p. — (Cours et travaux / Institut des hautes études internationales de Paris)

DELAPIERRE, Michel
L'informatique du Nord au Sud : un complexe industriel transnationalisé / Michel Delapierre, Jean-Benoît Zimmermann. — Paris : La Documentation française, 1986. — 143p. — (Notes et études documentaires ; no.4809)

Multinationals, governments and international technology transfer / edited by A.E. Safarian and Gilles Y. Bertin. — London : Croom Helm, c1987. — [240]p. — (Croom Helm series in international business). — *Includes bibliography and index*

PANEL ON THE IMPACT OF NATIONAL SECURITY CONTROLS ON INTERNATIONAL TECHNOLOGY TRANSFER
Balancing the national interest : U.S. national security export controls and global economic competition. — Washington : National Academy Press, 1987. — xiii,321p. — *Bibliography: p297-309*

STRUICK VAN BEMMELEN, Ton
Interim report of the Sub-Committee on Advanced Technology and Technology Transfer / Ton Struick van Bemmelen. — Brussels : North Atlantic Assembly, 1986. — ii,33p

Technology transfer : geographic, economic, cultural, and technical dimensions / edited by A. Coskun Samli. — Westport, Conn. : Quorum Books, c1985. — p. cm. — *Includes index. — Bibliography: p*

TECHNOLOGY TRANSFER — Addresses, essays, lectures
The Political economy of international technology transfer / edited by John R. McIntyre and Daniel S. Papp. — Westport, Conn. : Quorum Books, c1986. — p. cm. — *Includes index. — Bibliography: p*

TECHNOLOGY TRANSFER — Bibliography
UNITED NATIONS. Conference on Trade and Development. Committee on Transfer of Technology
Bibliography of documents on transfer and development of technology that have been prepared by or for the UNCTAD Secretariat. — [New York] : the Conference, 1986. — iii,34p. — ([Document] / United Nations ; TD/B/C.6/INF.2/Rev.5)

TECHNOLOGY TRANSFER — Congresses
International technology transfer : concepts, measures, and comparisons / edited by Nathan Rosenberg and Claudio Frischtak. — New York : Praeger, 1985. — p. cm. — *Includes bibliographies and index*

TECHNOLOGY TRANSFER — Economic aspects — Europe

A High technology gap? : Europe, America, and Japan / Andrew J. Pierre, editor ; Frank Press ... [et al.] ; introduction by Robert D. Hormats. — New York, N.Y. : Council on Foreign Relations, c1987. — xii, 114 p.. — (Europe/America ; 6). — *Includes bibliographical references*

TECHNOLOGY TRANSFER — Economic aspects — Japan

A High technology gap? : Europe, America, and Japan / Andrew J. Pierre, editor ; Frank Press ... [et al.] ; introduction by Robert D. Hormats. — New York, N.Y. : Council on Foreign Relations, c1987. — xii, 114 p.. — (Europe/America ; 6). — *Includes bibliographical references*

TECHNOLOGY TRANSFER — Economic aspects — United States

A High technology gap? : Europe, America, and Japan / Andrew J. Pierre, editor ; Frank Press ... [et al.] ; introduction by Robert D. Hormats. — New York, N.Y. : Council on Foreign Relations, c1987. — xii, 114 p.. — (Europe/America ; 6). — *Includes bibliographical references*

TECHNOLOGY TRANSFER — Government policy — United States

MORSE, Ronald A.
Getting America ready for Japanese science and technology / Ronald A. Morse, Richard J. Samuels. — Lanham ; London : University Press of America, 1986. — [196]p

TECHNOLOGY TRANSFER — China

KANG, Chong-Sook
Technologie-Transfer nach China 1949-1982 / Chong-Sook Kang. — Frankfurt am Main : Campus Verlag, 1985. — 306p. — *Bibliography: p269-306*

TECHNOLOGY TRANSFER — Communist countries

Strany SEV v mezhdunarodnom obmene tekhnologiei / pod redaktsiei O. T. Bogomolova, A. N. Bykova. — Moskva : Mezhdunarodnye otnosheniia, 1986. — 319p

TECHNOLOGY TRANSFER — Developing countries

BURCH, David, 1942 Jan. 16-
Overseas aid and the transfer of technology : the political economy of agricultural mechanisation in the Third World / David Burch. — Aldershot : Avebury, c1987. — xiv,370p. — *Bibliography: p354-370*

Guidelines for the acquisition of foreign technology in developing countries : with special reference to technology licence agreements. — New York : United Nations, 1973. — xi,55p. — ([Documents] / United Nations ; ID/98). — *"Prepared by Rana K.D.N. Singh...in co-operation with the secretariat of UNIDO"*. — Sales no.: E.73.II.B.1

STEWART, Charles T.
Technology transfer and human factors / Charles T. Stewart, Jr., Yasumitsu Nihei. — Lexington, Mass. : Lexington Books, c1987. — xiii, 200 p.. — *Includes bibliographies and index*

TECHNOLOGY TRANSFER — Europe, Eastern

Strany SEV v mezhdunarodnom obmene tekhnologiei / pod redaktsiei O. T. Bogomolova, A. N. Bykova. — Moskva : Mezhdunarodnye otnosheniia, 1986. — 319p

TECHNOLOGY TRANSFER — Japan

MORSE, Ronald A.
Getting America ready for Japanese science and technology / Ronald A. Morse, Richard J. Samuels. — Lanham ; London : University Press of America, 1986. — [196]p

STEWART, Charles T.
Technology transfer and human factors / Charles T. Stewart, Jr., Yasumitsu Nihei. — Lexington, Mass. : Lexington Books, c1987. — xiii, 200 p.. — *Includes bibliographies and index*

TECHNOLOGY TRANSFER — Soviet Union

SOKOLOFF, Georges
The economy of détente : the Soviet Union and western capital / Georges Sokoloff ; translated from the French by Jean Kirby. — Leamington Spa : Berg, c1987. — [236]p. — *Translation of: L'économie de la détente*. — *Includes bibliography and index*

TECHNOLOGY TRANSFER — United States

SOKOLOFF, Georges
The economy of détente : the Soviet Union and western capital / Georges Sokoloff ; translated from the French by Jean Kirby. — Leamington Spa : Berg, c1987. — [236]p. — *Translation of: L'économie de la détente*. — *Includes bibliography and index*

STEWART, Charles T.
Technology transfer and human factors / Charles T. Stewart, Jr., Yasumitsu Nihei. — Lexington, Mass. : Lexington Books, c1987. — xiii, 200 p.. — *Includes bibliographies and index*

TEESSIDE (YORKSHIRE) — Social conditions

NICHOLAS, Katharine
The social effects of unemployment in Teesside / Katharine Nicholas. — Manchester : Manchester University Press, c1986. — ix,236p . — *Bibliography: p227-231*. — *Includes index*

TEHERAN CONFERENCE (1943)

EUBANK, Keith
Summit at Teheran / by Keith Eubank. — New York : W. Morrow, 1985. — 528p, 16p of plates. — *Bibliography: p 509-517*

MAYLE, Paul D.
Eureka summit : agreement in principle and the Big Three at Tehran, 1943 / Paul D. Mayle. — Newark : University of Delaware Press ; London : Associated University Presses, c1987. — 210 p.. — *Includes index*. — *Bibliography: p. 193-203*

TELECOMMUNICATION

HILTZ, Starr Roxanne
The network nation : human communication via computer / Starr Roxanne Hiltz, Murray Turoff ; with forewords by Suzanne Keller and Herbert R.J. Grosch. — Reading, Mass. ; London : Addison-Wesley, 1978. — xxxv,528 [i.e.536]p. — *Text on lining paper*. — *Bibliography(21p.)*. — *Includes index*

ROGERS, Everett M
Communication technology / Everett M. Rogers. — New York : Free Press, c1986. — p. cm. — (Series in communication technology and society). — *Includes index*. — *Bibliography: p*

TELECOMMUNICATION — Bibliography

SNOW, Marcellus S
Telecommunication economics and international regulatory policy : an annotated bibliography / compiled by Marcellus S. Snow and Meheroo Jussawalla. — New York : Greenwood Press, 1986. — xiv, 216 p.. — (Bibliographies and indexes in economics and economic history ; no. 4). — *Includes indexes*

TELECOMMUNICATION — Economic aspects — Australia

ERGAS, H.
Telecommunications and the Australian economy : report to the Department of Communications / H. Ergas. — Canberra : Australian Government Publishing Service, 1986. — ix,112p. — *Includes bibliographical references*

TELECOMMUNICATION — Law and legislation — Economic aspects — United States

Telecommunications in the post-divestiture era : essays in honor of Jasper N. Dorsey and Ben T. Wiggins / edited by Albert L. Danielsen, David R. Kamerschen. — [Lexington, Mass.] : Lexington Books, c1986. — xiv, 252 p.. — *Includes bibliographies and index*

TELECOMMUNICATION — Law and legislation — Australia

Freedom of expression and section 116 of the Broadcasting and Television Act 1942. — Canberra : Australian Government Publishing Service, 1985. — vii,22p. — (Report / Human Rights Commission ; no.16)

TELECOMMUNICATION — Law and legislation — Great Britain

GREAT BRITAIN. Parliament. House of Commons. Library. Research Division
Telecommunications Bill (Bill 15) / Christopher Barclay. — [London] : the Division, 1982. — 12p. — (Reference sheet ; no.82/15). — *Bibliography: p11-12*

TELECOMMUNICATION — Law and legislation — United States

KELLEY, David
Laissez parler : freedom in the electronic media / David Kelley, Roger Donway. — Bowling Green, Ohio : Social Philosophy & Policy Center, Bowling Green State University, c1983. — 49 p. — (Studies in social philosophy & policy ; no. 1). — *Includes bibliographical references*

TELECOMMUNICATION — Management

SHERMAN, Barry L.
Telecommunications management : the broadcast & cable industries / Barry L. Sherman. — New York ; London : McGraw–Hill, 1987. — (McGraw-Hill series in mass communication)

TELECOMMUNICATION — Political aspects — Europe

The Politics of the communications revolution in Western Europe / edited by Kenneth Dyson and Peter Humphreys. — London : Cass, 1986. — 233p. — *Includes index*

TELECOMMUNICATION — Research — Australia

AUSTRALIAN SCIENCE AND TECHNOLOGY COUNCIL
Telecommunications research and development in Australia : a report to the Prime Minister / by the Australian Science and Technology Council (ASTEC). — Canberra : Australian Government Publishing Service, 1985. — vii,47p. — *Bibliographical references: p47*

TELECOMMUNICATION — Denmark — Employees

NORD-LARSEN, Mogens
Holdninger, normer og sygefravaer i P & T. — København : Socialforskningsinstituttet, 1986. — 59p. — (Meddelelse / Socialforskningsinstituttet ; 46)

TELECOMMUNICATION — Developing countries

HUDSON, Heather E
When telephones reach the village : the role of telecommunications in rural development / Heather E. Hudson. — Norwood, N.J. : Ablex Pub. Corp., 1984, c1983. — p. cm. — (Communication and information science). — *Includes indexes*. — *Bibliography: p*

TELECOMMUNICATION — European Economic Community countries

The effects of new information technology on the less-favoured regions of the Community / by Andrew Gillespie ... [et al.]. — Luxembourg : Office for Official Publications of the European Communities, 1985. — ix,192p. — (Regional policy series ; no.23). — *At head of title page: Commission of the European Communities*

TELECOMMUNICATION — France — Statistics
MOLINA, Valérie
Images économiques des entreprises. — Paris : I.N.S.E.E.
Dossier sectoriel no.7: Transports et télécommunications au 1-1-1983 / Valérie Molina. — 1986. — 55p

TELECOMMUNICATION — Great Britain
HARPER, J. M.
Telecommunications and computing : the uncompleted revolution : a survey in plain English of the state of the common ground of telecommunications, computing, office machinery and cable television in the UK / J. M. Harper. — London : Communications Educational Services, 1986. — xix,200p

New management: the Journal of the Communication Managers' Association. — Reading : Communication Managers' Association, 1986-. — *Monthly March issue is the annual report of the Communication Managers' Association*

TELECOMMUNICATION — United States
Telecommunications in the post-divestiture era : essays in honor of Jasper N. Dorsey and Ben T. Wiggins / edited by Albert L. Danielsen, David R. Kamerschen. — [Lexington, Mass.] : Lexington Books, c1986. — xiv, 252 p.. — *Includes bibliographies and index*

TELECOMMUNICATION CABLES — Great Britain
INFORMATION TECHNOLOGY ADVISORY PANEL
Report on cable systems. — London : H.M.S.O., 1982. — 54p. — *At head of title: Cabinet Office. Information Technology Advisory Panel*

TELECOMMUNICATION EQUIPMENT INDUSTRY
SCIBERRAS, E.
Telecommunications industry / by E. Sciberras and B.D. Payne. — Harlow : Longman, 1986. — xi,179p. — (Technical change and international competitiveness ; 2)

TELECOMMUNICATION EQUIPMENT INDUSTRY — Technological innovations
SCIBERRAS, E.
Telecommunications industry / by E. Sciberras and B.D. Payne. — Harlow : Longman, 1986. — xi,179p. — (Technical change and international competitiveness ; 2)

TELECOMMUNICATION POLICY
HILLS, Jill
Deregulating telecoms : competition and control in the United States, Japan and Britain / by Jill Hills. — London : Pinter, 1986. — [200]p. — *Includes bibliography and index*

SAUVANT, Karl P
International transactions in services : the politics of transborder data flows / Karl P. Sauvant. — Boulder : Westview Press, 1986. — p. cm. — (The Atwater series on the world information economy) (Westview special studies in international economics and business)

TELECOMMUNICATION POLICY — Bibliography
SNOW, Marcellus S
Telecommunication economics and international regulatory policy : an annotated bibliography / compiled by Marcellus S. Snow and Meheroo Jussawalla. — New York : Greenwood Press, 1986. — xiv, 216 p.. — (Bibliographies and indexes in economics and economic history ; no. 4). — *Includes indexes*

TELECOMMUNICATION POLICY — Australia
ERGAS, H.
Telecommunications and the Australian economy : report to the Department of Communications / H. Ergas. — Canberra : Australian Government Publishing Service, 1986. — ix,112p. — *Includes bibliographical references*

TELECOMMUNICATION POLICY — Canada
Telecommunications policy and regulation : the impact of competition and technological change / edited by W. T. Stanbury. — Montreal : The Institute for Research on Public Policy/L'Institut de recherches poliques, 1986. — xii,529p

TELECOMMUNICATION POLICY — Great Britain
HEUVERMANN, Arnulf
Die Liberalisierung des britischen Telekommunikationsmarktes / Arnulf Heuermann, Karl-Heinz Neumann. — Berlin : Springer-Verlag, 1985. — xii,401p. — (Schriftenreihe des Wissenschaftlichen Instituts für Kommunikationsdienste der Deutschen Bundespost ; Bd.3). — *Bibliography: p [395]-401*

TELECOMMUNICATION POLICY — Organisation for Economic Co-operation and Development countries
Trends of change in telecommunications policy. — Paris : OECD, 1987. — 353p. — (Information, computer and communications policy ; no.13). — *Contents: Documents from the discussions of the Second Special Session of the OECD Committee for Information, Computer and Communications Policy*

TELECOMMUNICATIONS
WEDELL, George
Media in competition : the future of print and electronic media in 22 countries / George Wedell and Georg-Michael Luyken ; with contributions by Alberto Cavallari...[et al.]. — Manchester : European Institute for the Media, 1986. — 173p. — (Euromedia Indicator ; No.1). — *Includes summaries in French and German*

TELECOMMUNICATIONS — Law and legislation — Great Britain
GREAT BRITAIN. Parliament. House of Commons. Library. Research Division
Telecommunications Bill 1983/84 (Bill 5) / Christopher Barclay. — [London] : the Division, 1983. — 15p. — (Reference sheet ; no.83/11). — *Bibliography: p11-13*

TELECOMMUNICATIONS — Denmark
Aarsberetning / Fyns Kommunale Telefonselskab, Denmark. — [Copenhagen] : Fyns Kommunale Telefonselskab, 1955-1976. — Annual. — *Title varies.* — *Continued by: Beretning og regnskab*

Beretning og arsregnskab / Fyns Kommunale Telefonselskab, Denmark. — [Copenhagen] : Fyns Kommunale Telefonselskab, 1984-. — Annual. — *Continues: Beretning og regnskab*

Beretning og regnskab / Fyns Kommunale Telefonselskab, Denmark. — [Copenhagen] : Fyns Kommunale Telefonselskab, 1977-1980. — Annual. — *Continues: Aarsberetning. Continued by: Beretning og arsregnskab*

TELECOMMUNICATIONS — France — Statistics
FRANCE. Direction Générale des Télécommunications
Statistique annuelle / Direction Générale des Telecommunications, France. — Paris : Ministere des Postes et Telecommunications, 1984-. — Annual

TELECOMMUNICATIONS BILL 1982-83
GREAT BRITAIN. Parliament. House of Commons. Library. Research Division
Telecommunications Bill (Bill 15) / Christopher Barclay. — [London] : the Division, 1982. — 12p. — (Reference sheet ; no.82/15). — *Bibliography: p11-12*

TELECOMMUNICATIONS BILL 1983-84
GREAT BRITAIN. Parliament. House of Commons. Library. Research Division
Telecommunications Bill 1983/84 (Bill 5) / Christopher Barclay. — [London] : the Division, 1983. — 15p. — (Reference sheet ; no.83/11). — *Bibliography: p11-13*

TELECOMMUTING — United States
RAMSOWER, Reagan Mays
Telecommuting : the organizational and behavioral effects of working at home / by Reagan Mays Ramsower. — Ann Arbor, Mich. : UMI Research Press, c1985. — p. cm. — (Research for business decisions ; no. 75). — : *Revision of thesis (Ph. D.)--University of Minnesota, 1983.* — *Includes index.* — *Bibliography: p*

TELECONFERENCING
ROGERS, Everett M
Communication technology / Everett M. Rogers. — New York : Free Press, c1986. — p. cm. — (Series in communication technology and society). — *Includes index.* — *Bibliography: p*

TELEPHONE — United States — Rates — Peak-load pricing — Mathematical models
PARK, Rolla Edward
Optimal peak-load pricing for local telephone calls : technical appendixes / Rolla Edward Park, Bridger M. Mitchell. — Santa Monica, CA : Rand, c1986. — x, 72 p.. — *"R-3404/1-RC.". — "June 1986.".* — *Bibliography: p. 70-72*

TELEVISION — Censorship — United States
SPITZER, Matthew Laurence
Seven dirty words and six other stories : controlling the content of print and broadcast / Matthew Laurence Spitzer. — New Haven : Yale University Press, 1986. — p. cm. — *Includes index*

TELEVISION — Law and legislation
TAISHOFF, Marika Natasha
State responsibility and the direct broadcast satellite / Marika Natasha Taishoff. — London : Pinter, 1987. — xii,203p. — *"A publication of the Graduate Institute of International Studies".* — *Half t.p. verso.* — *Bibliography: p183-197.* — *Includes index*

TELEVISION — Social aspects
GUNTER, Barrie
Television and sex role stereotyping / Barrie Gunter. — London : Libbey, c1986. — 89p. — (Television research monograph). — *Bibliography: p83-89*

TELEVISION — Social aspects — Denmark
KÜHL, P. H.
Radio/TV undersøgelsen : nogle foreløbige resultater af / P. H. Kühl og Kaj Westergård. — [København : Socialforskningsinstituttet, 1965]. — 27 leaves. — (Studie (Socialforskningsinstituttet) ; nr.5)

TELEVISION ADVERTISING AND CHILDREN
MCNEAL, James U
Children as consumers : insights and implications / James U. McNeal. — Lexington, Mass. : Lexington Books, c1987. — xvi, 211 p.. — *Includes index.* — *Bibliography: p. [191]-205*

TELEVISION AND CHILDREN
HODGE, Robert
Children and television : a semiotic approach / Robert Hodge and David Tripp. — Cambridge : Polity, 1986. — vi,233p. — *Bibliography: p219-225.* — *Includes index*

PALMER, Patricia
The lively audience : a study of children around the TV set / Patricia Palmer. — London : Allen & Unwin, 1986. — x,166p. — *Bibliography: p154-164.* — *Includes index*

TELEVISION AND CHILDREN — Cross-cultural studies
Television and the aggressive child : a cross-national comparison / edited by L. Rowell Huesmann, Leonard D. Eron. — Hillsdale, N.J. : L. Erlbaum Associates, 1986. — p. cm. — *Includes bibliographies and index*

TELEVISION AND CHILDREN — United States

VOORT, T. H. A. van der
Television violence : a child's-eye view / T.H.A. van der Voort. — Amsterdam ; Oxford : North-Holland, 1986. — xiii, 440p. — (Advances in psychology ; 32). — Includes indexes. — Bibliography: p 403-423

TELEVISION AND POLITICS — Great Britain

BLUMLER, Jay G.
Political communication and the young voter : a panel study, 1970-1971, examining the role of election communication in the political socialisation of first time voters / Jay G. Blumler, Denis McQuail and T. J. Nossiter ; report to the Social Science Research Council, October 1975. — [London : Social Science Research Council, 1975]. — 1v. (various pagings). — Bibliographical references: end of vol.

BLUMLER, Jay G.
Political communication and the young voter in the general election of February 1974 : a panal study, 1970-1974, examining influences on the political socialisation of young voters between their first and second election campaigns / Jay G. Blumler, Denis McQuail and T. J. Nossiter ; report to the Social Science Research Council, July 1976. — [London : Social Science Research Council, 1976]. — 99 leaves. — Bibliographical references: p98-99

GUNTER, Barrie
Television coverage of the 1983 general election : audiences, appreciation and public opinion / Barrie Gunter, Michael Svennevig and Mallory Wober. — Aldershot : Gower, c1986. — v,138p. — Bibliography: p134-136

Media monitoring report : July 1985-June 1986 / edited by: Simon Clark ; foreword by: Lord Chalfont. — London : Media Monitoring Unit, 1986. — xxiii,314p

TELEVISION AUDIENCES — Great Britain

MORLEY, Dave
Family television : cultural power and domestic leisure / by David Morley. — London : Comedia, 1986. — 178p. — Includes bibliography

The Television audience : patterns of viewing : an update. — 2nd ed. / G.J. Goodhardt ... [et al.]. — Aldershot : Gower, c1987. — xv,134p. — Previous ed.: / G.J. Goodhardt, A.S.C. Ehrenberg, M.A. Collins - Farnborough : Saxon House, 1975. — Bibliography: p128-129. — Includes index

TELEVISION BROADCASTING

Research on the range and quality of broadcasting services : a report for the Committee on Financing the BBC / West Yorkshire Media in Politics Group, Centre for Television Research, The University of Leeds. — London : H.M.S.O., 1986. — 180p. — At head of t.p.: Home Office. — Includes bibliographical references

TELEVISION BROADCASTING — Research — Addresses, essays, lectures

Broadcasting research methods / [edited] by Joseph R. Dominick and James E. Fletcher. — Newton, Mass. : Allyn and Bacon, 1984. — p. cm. — Includes bibliographies and indexes

TELEVISION BROADCASTING — Social aspects

LODZIAK, Conrad
The power of television : a critical appraisal / Conrad Lodziak. — London : Pinter, 1987. — 217p. — Includes index

Television in society / edited by Arthur Asa Berger ; with an introduction by the author. — New Brunswick, U.S.A. : Transaction Books, c1987. — 282 p.. — "Collection of articles from Society magazine"--Introd. — Bibliography: p. 269-277

TELEVISION BROADCASTING — Social aspects — Canada

UNGERLIEDER, Charles S.
Television and society : an investigative approach / Charles S. Ungerlieder, Ernest Krieger. — Toronto : Irwin, 1985. — 243p

TELEVISION BROADCASTING — Australia

AUSTRALIA. Department of Communications
Equalisation of regional commercial television : draft indicative plan. — Canberra : Australian Government Publishing Service
Pts.1 and 2: General considerations, consultants' methodologies and general reports. — 1986. — ix,246p

AUSTRALIA. Department of Communications
Equalisation of regional commercial television : draft indicative plan. — Canberra : Australian Government Publishing Service
Pt.3: Discussion of individual approved markets. — 1986. — vii,400p

AUSTRALIA. Department of Communications. Forward Development Unit
Ownership and control of commercial television : future policy directions. — Canberra : Australian Government Publishing Service
V.1: Report. — 1986. — xxxi,268p. — Includes bibliographical references

AUSTRALIA. Department of Communications. Forward Development Unit
Ownership and control of commercial television : future policy directions. — Canberra : Australian Government Publishing Service
V.2: Appendices. — 1986. — v,535p

TELEVISION BROADCASTING — Canada — History

UNGERLIEDER, Charles S.
Television and society : an investigative approach / Charles S. Ungerlieder, Ernest Krieger. — Toronto : Irwin, 1985. — 243p

TELEVISION BROADCASTING — European Economic Community countries — Congresses

EUROPEAN INSTITUTE FOR THE MEDIA. Colloquia (1985)
Television in Europe. — [Manchester] : the Institute
Vol.1: Broadcasting policies in the E.E.C. : proceedings of the colloquia, Manchester, 24-25 January 1985. — 1985. — 145p

TELEVISION BROADCASTING — European Economic Community Countries — Congresses

EUROPEAN INSTITUTE FOR THE MEDIA. Colloquia (1985 : Paris)
Television in Europe. — [Manchester] : the Institute
Vol. 2: Politiques de radiodiffusion dans la C.E.E. : actes des colloques, Paris, 13 et 14 Juin 1985. — 1985. — 227p

TELEVISION BROADCASTING — Great Britain

Research on the range and quality of broadcasting services : a report for the Committee on Financing the BBC / West Yorkshire Media in Politics Group, Centre for Television Research, The University of Leeds. — London : H.M.S.O., 1986. — 180p. — At head of t.p.: Home Office. — Includes bibliographical references

TELEVISION BROADCASTING — Ireland — History — Congresses

Television and Irish society : 21 years of Irish television / edited by Martin McLoone and John MacMahon. — Dublin, Ireland : Radio Telefís Eireann, 1984. — 151 p.. — Includes bibliographies. — Contents: The future of public service broadcasting / T.V. Finn -- From kitchen sink to soap / Luke Gibbons -- Strumpet city / Martin McLoone -- Twenty years of current affairs on RTE / Mary Kelly -- The Late late show / Maurice Earls -- The presentation of women in Irish television drama / Barbara O'Connor -- Form, content, and Irish television / Kevin Rockett

TELEVISION BROADCASTING OF NEWS

ROBINSON, John P
The main source : learning from television news / John P. Robinson, Mark R. Levy in association with Dennis K. Davis, W. Gill Woodall, Michael Gurevitch. — Beverly Hills : Sage Publications, c1986. — p. cm. — (People and communication ; v. 17). — Includes index. — Bibliography: p

TELEVISION BROADCASTING OF NEWS — Great Britain

GUNTER, Barrie
Television coverage of the 1983 general election : audiences, appreciation and public opinion / Barrie Gunter, Michael Svennevig and Mallory Wober. — Aldershot : Gower, c1986. — v,138p. — Bibliography: p134-136

TELEVISION BROADCASTING POLICY — Australia

AUSTRALIA. Department of Communications
Equalisation of regional commercial television : draft indicative plan. — Canberra : Australian Government Publishing Service
Pts.1 and 2: General considerations, consultants' methodologies and general reports. — 1986. — ix,246p

AUSTRALIA. Department of Communications
Equalisation of regional commercial television : draft indicative plan. — Canberra : Australian Government Publishing Service
Pt.3: Discussion of individual approved markets. — 1986. — vii,400p

AUSTRALIA. Department of Communications. Forward Development Unit
Ownership and control of commercial television : future policy directions. — Canberra : Australian Government Publishing Service
V.1: Report. — 1986. — xxxi,268p. — Includes bibliographical references

AUSTRALIA. Department of Communications. Forward Development Unit
Ownership and control of commercial television : future policy directions. — Canberra : Australian Government Publishing Service
V.2: Appendices. — 1986. — v,535p

TELEVISION BROADCASTING POLICY — Great Britain

GREAT BRITAIN. Parliament. House of Commons. Library. Research Division
Broadcasting 1980 / [Fiona Poole]. — [London] : the Division, 1980. — 15p. — (Reference sheet ; no.80/8). — Includes bibliographical references

TELEVISION IN POLITICS — Great Britain

FERGUSON, Bob
Television on history : representations of Ireland / Bob Ferguson. — 2nd ed. — London : Department of English and Media Studies, University of London Institute of Education in association with Comedia, 1985. — iv,27p. — (Media analysis paper ; 5). — Previous ed.: 198-?

TELEVISION PLAYS — Ireland — History and criticism — Congresses

Television and Irish society : 21 years of Irish television / edited by Martin McLoone and John MacMahon. — Dublin, Ireland : Radio Telefís Eireann, 1984. — 151 p.. — Includes bibliographies. — Contents: The future of public service broadcasting / T.V. Finn -- From kitchen sink to soap / Luke Gibbons -- Strumpet city / Martin McLoone -- Twenty years of current affairs on RTE / Mary Kelly -- The Late late show / Maurice Earls -- The presentation of women in Irish television drama / Barbara O'Connor -- Form, content, and Irish television / Kevin Rockett

TELEVISION PROGRAMS

Television mythologies : stars, shows & signs / edited by Len Masterman. — London : Comedia/MK Media in association with Boyars, c1984. — iv,143p. — (Comedia series ; no. 24)

TELEVISION SERIALS — United States
CASSATA, Mary
life on daytime television : tuning-in American serial drama / by Mary Cassata and Thomas Skill. — Norwood, N.J. : Ablex Publishing Corporation, 1983. — xxxv,214p. — *Bibliography: p187-202*

TELEVISION SERIALS — United States — Addresses, essays, lectures
CASSATA, Mary B.
Life on daytime television : tuning-in American serial drama / by Mary Cassata and Thomas Skill. — Norwood, N.J. : Ablex Pub. Corp., c1983. — xxxv, 214 p. — (Communication and information science). — *Includes indexes.* — "The daytime serial : a bibliography of scholarly writings, 1943-1981" / Patricia Tegler: p. 187-196. — *Bibliography: p. 197-202*

TELLICO DAM (TENN.)
WHEELER, William Bruce
TVA and the Tellico Dam, 1936-1979 : a bureaucratic crisis in post-industrial America / by William Bruce Wheeler and Michael J. McDonald. — 1st ed. — Knoxville : University of Tennessee Press, c1986. — xii, 290 p.. — *Includes index.* — *Bibliography: p. [226]-275*

TEMPERANCE SOCIETIES — Norway — History
KAASALIA, T. H.
Med skjold og fakkel : det Norske Totalavholdsselskaps barnearbeid i 100 år : 1874/1974 / T. H. Kaasalia. — [s.l.] : Magne, 1974. — 48p

TEMPORARY EMPLOYMENT — France — Statistics
Le travail temporaire en 1983 : enquête annuelle d'entreprise dans les services résultats détaillés. — [Paris] : INSEE, 1985. — 63p. — (Archives et documents / Institut National de la Statistique et des Études Économiques ; no.135)

TEMPORARY EMPLOYMENT — Great Britain
LABOUR RESEARCH DEPARTMENT
Temporary workers : a negotiator's guide. — London : Labour Research Department, 1987. — 49p

TENNESEE — Rural conditions
MONTELL, William Lynwood
Killings : folk justice in the Upper South / William Lynwood Montell. — Lexington, KY : University Press of Kentucky, 1986. — p. cm. — *Includes index.* — *Bibliography: p*

TENNESSEE — History — Civil War, 1861-1865
CIMPRICH, John
Slavery's end in Tennessee, 1861-1865 / John Cimprich. — University, Ala. : University of Alabama Press, c1985. — 191 p.. — *Includes index.* — *Bibliography: p. 181-185*

TENNESSEE — History — Civil War, 1861-1865 — Social aspects
BAILEY, Fred Arthur
Class and Tennessee's Confederate generation / by Fred Arthur Bailey. — Chapel Hill : University of North Carolina Press, c1987. — x, 205 p.. — (The Fred W. Morrison series in Southern studies). — *Includes index.* — *Bibliography: p. [191]-196*

TENNESSEE — Race relations
CIMPRICH, John
Slavery's end in Tennessee, 1861-1865 / John Cimprich. — University, Ala. : University of Alabama Press, c1985. — 191 p.. — *Includes index.* — *Bibliography: p. 181-185*

TENNESSEE VALLEY AUTHORITY
DURANT, Robert F.
When government regulates itself : EPA, TVA, and pollution control in the 1970s / Robert F. Durant. — Knoxville : University of Tennessee Press, c1985. — p. cm. — *Bibliography: p [169]-187.* — *Bibliography: p*

WHEELER, William Bruce
TVA and the Tellico Dam, 1936-1979 : a bureaucratic crisis in post-industrial America / by William Bruce Wheeler and Michael J. McDonald. — 1st ed. — Knoxville : University of Tennessee Press, c1986. — xii, 290 p.. — *Includes index.* — *Bibliography: p. [226]-275*

TENSE (LOGIC)
NEEDHAM, Paul
Temporal perspective : a logical analysis of temporal reference in English / Paul Needham. — Uppsala : [Philosophical Society : Dept. of Philosophy, University of Uppsala], 1975. — 112 p.. — (Philosophical studies ; no. 25). — Thesis--Uppsala. — *Includes index.* — *Bibliography: p. 108-109*

TERMINAL CARE — Law and legislation — United States
CANTOR, Norman L
Legal frontiers of death and dying / by Norman L. Cantor. — Bloomington : Indiana University Press, c1987. — p. cm. — (Medical ethics series). — *Includes index*

TERMINAL CARE — Great Britain
CONFERENCE ON CARE FOR THE DYING (1985 : London)
Proceedings of the Conference on Care for the Dying, 3 December 1985, Central Hall, Westminster / [organised by] Department of Health and Social Security, National Association of Health Authorities in England and Wales. — London : H.M.S.O., 1986. — 78p

TERMINALS (TRANSPORTATION)
Bulk shipping and terminal logistics / Ernst G. Frankel...[et al.]. — Washington, D.C. : The World Bank, 1985. — xvi,288p. — (World Bank technical paper ; no.38)

TERRITORIAL WATERS — Political aspects
Maritime boundaries and ocean resources / edited by Gerald Blake ; International Geographical Union Study Group on the World Political Map. — London : Croom Helm, c1987. — 284p. — *Bibliography: p257-271.* — *Includes index*

TERRITORIAL WATERS — Asia, Southeastern
VALENCIA, Mark J.
South-East Asian seas : oil under troubled waters : hydrocarbon potential, jurisdictional issues, and international relations / Mark J. Valencia. — Oxford ; New York : Oxford University Press, 1985. — xiv,155p. — (Natural Resources of South-East Asia). — *Bibliography: p137-146*

TERRORISM
ALEXANDER, Yonah
State sponsored terrorism : low intensity warfare / Yonah Alexander. — London : Centre for Contemporary Studies, 1986. — 16p. — (Occasional paper / Centre for Contemporary Studies ; no.3)

BECKER, Jillian
The Soviet connection : state sponsorship of terrorism / Jillian Becker. — London : Alliance Publishers for the Institute for European Defence and Strategic Studies, 1985. — 55p. — (Occasional paper / Institute for European Defence Strategic Studies ; no.13)

BEQUAI, August
Technocrimes / by August Bequai. — Lexington, Mass. : Lexington Books, c1987. — p. cm. — *Includes index.* — *Bibliography: p*

CHALIAND, Gérard
Terrorism : from popular struggle to media spectacle / Gerard Chaliand. — London : Sagi, 1987. — [144]p. — Translation of: Terrorismes et guérillas. — *Includes index*

Contemporary research on terrorism / edited by Paul Wilkinson and Alasdair M. Stewart in association with George D. Smith, Andre Ya Dean and Thomas Schiller. — Aberdeen : Aberdeen University Press, 1987. — xx,634p. — *Bibliography: p599-623.* — *Includes index*

DOBSON, Christopher
War without end : the terrorists : an intelligence dossier / Christopher Dobson and Ronald Payne. — London : Harrap, 1986. — 279p

GREAT BRITAIN. Parliament. House of Commons. Library. International Affairs Section
International responses to terrorism / Chris Bowlby. — [London] : the Library, 1987. — 27p. — (Background paper / House of Commons. Library. [Research Division] ; no.200). — *Bibliography: p27*

HERMAN, Edward S.
The real terror network : terrorism in fact and propaganda / Edward S. Herman. — Montréal : Black Rose, 1985. — ix,252p. — *Includes bibliographical notes*

Inter 85 : a review of international terrorism in 1985 / [edited by] Ariel Merari...[et al.]. — Boulder, Colo. : Westview Press, [1986?]. — 130p. — Originally published: Jerusalem: The Jerusalem Post for the Jaffee Center for Strategic Studies, 1986

LAQUEUR, Walter
The age of terrorism / Walter Laqueur. — London : Weidenfeld & Nicolson, 1987. — 385p. — *Bibliography: p.323-333*

Legislative responses to terrorism / edited by Yonah Alexander, Allan S. Nanes. — Dordrecht [Holland] ; Boston : M. Nijhoff, 1986. — p. cm. — (International studies on terrorism ; v. 1)

MCFORAN, Desmond
The world held hostage : the war waged by international terrorism / Desmond McForan. — London : Oak-Tree Books, 1986. — xv, 262p, [5]p of plates. — *Bibliography: p.247-256*

MILBANK, David L
International and transnational terrorism : diagnosis and prognosis. — [Washington : Central Intelligence Agency], 1976. — iii,45p. — (Research study - Central Intelligence Agency). — Cover title. — "PR 76 10030.". — *Includes bibliographical references*

RUBENSTEIN, Richard E.
Alchemists of revolution : terrorism in the modern world / Richard E. Rubenstein. — London : Tauris, 1987. — [250]p

Terrorism : how the west can win / edited by Benjamin Netanyahu. — London : Weidenfeld and Nicolson, 1986. — xv,254p

Terrorism and international order / Lawrence Freedman...[et al.]. — London : Routledge and Kegan Paul, 1986. — [vii], [112]p. — (Chatham House special paper). — *Bibliographical notes*

WILKINSON, Paul
Terrorism and the liberal state / Paul Wilkinson. — 2nd ed. rev., extended and updated. — Basingstoke : Macmillan, 1986. — xiv,322p. — Previous ed.: 1977. — *Bibliography: p303.* — *Includes index*

TERRORISM — Addresses, essays, lectures
Government violence and repression : an agenda for research / edited by Michael Stohl and George A. Lopez. — New York : Greenwood Press, 1986. — viii, 278 p.. — (Contributions in political science ; no. 148). — *Includes index.* — *Bibliography: p. [269]-270*

Political violence and terror : motifs and motivations / edited by Peter H. Merkl. — Berkeley : University of California Press, c1986. — vi, 380 p.. — *Includes bibliographies and index*

TERRORISM — Bibliography
LAKOS, Amos
International terrorism : a bibliography / Amos Lakos. — Boulder, Colo. : Westview ; London : Mansell, 1986. — xii,481p. — *Includes index*

TERRORISM — Finance
ADAMS, James, 1951-
The financing of terror / James Adams. — Sevenoaks : New English Library, 1986. — x,293p. — *Bibliography: p280-284.* — *Includes index*

TERRORISM — History — Dictionaries
ROSIE, George
The directory of international terrorism / George Rosie ; additional research by Paul Rosie. — Edinburgh : Mainstream, 1986. — 310p. — *Bibliography: p307-310*

TERRORISM — Legal status, laws, etc — Great Britain
GREAT BRITAIN. Parliament. House of Commons. Library. Research Division
Prevention of Terrorism Bill 1983-4 [Bill 8] / [Patrick Nealon]. — [London] : the Division, [1983]. — 12p. — (Reference sheet ; no.83/13). — *Bibliographical references: p8-12*

TERRORISM — Prevention
Terrorism and international order / Lawrence Freedman...[et al.]. — London : Routledge and Kegan Paul, 1986. — [vii], [112]p. — (Chatham House special paper). — *Bibliographical notes*

TERRORISM — Statistics
Inter 85 : a review of international terrorism in 1985 / [edited by Ariel Merari...[et al.]. — Boulder, Colo. : Westview Press, [1986?]. — 130p. — *Originally published: Jerusalem: The Jerusalem Post for the Jaffee Center for Strategic Studies, 1986*

TERRORISM — Armenia
GUNTER, Michael M
"Pursuing the just cause of their people" : a study of contemporary Armenian terrorism / Michael M. Gunter. — New York : Greenwood Press, 1986. — viii, 182 p.. — (Contributions in political science ; no. 152). — *Includes index.* — *Bibliography: p. [159]-169*

TERRORISM — Europe
HAMON, Alain
Action directe : du terrorisme français a l'euroterrorisme / Alain Hamon, Jean Charles Marchand. — Paris : Le Seuil, 1986. — 251p

TERRORISM — France
HAMON, Alain
Action directe : du terrorisme français a l'euroterrorisme / Alain Hamon, Jean Charles Marchand. — Paris : Le Seuil, 1986. — 251p

TERRORISM — Germany (West)
BACKES, Uwe
Totalitarismus, Extremismus, Terrorismus : ein Literaturführer und Wegweiser zur Extremismusforschung in der Bundesrepublik Deutschland / Uwe Backes, Eckhard Jesse. — 2. aktualisierte und erweiterte Auflage. — Opladen : Leske und Budrich, 1985. — 390p. — (Reihe Analysen ; 38)

TERRORISM — Great Britain
The Angry Brigade, 1967-1984 : documents and chronology / introduction by Jean Weir. — London : Elephant Editions, 1985. — 73p. — (Anarchist pocketbooks ; 3). — *First published in 1978 by Bratach Dubh Anarchist Pamphlets*

TERRORISM — Great Britain — Prevention
SCORER, Catherine
The new Prevention of Terrorism Act : the case for repeal. — Updated and expanded 3rd ed., covering the extension of the Act in 1984 to cover 'international terrorism' / Catherine Scorer, Sarah Spencer and Patricia Hewitt. — London : National Council for Civil Liberties, c1985. — 82p. — *Previous ed.: published as The Prevention of Terrorism Act. 1981*

TERRORISM — Ireland
Lest we forget : an Irish record of one year, July 1920-July 1921. — London : Vacher, 1921. — 48p

TERRORISM — Italy
Armed struggle in Italy : a chronology. — London : Bratach Dubh, 1979. — 94p. — (Anarchist pamphlets ; no.4)

WAGNER-PACIFICI, Robin Erica
The Moro morality play : terrorism as social drama / Robin Erica Wagner-Pacifici. — Chicago : The University of Chicago Press, c1986. — p. cm. — *Includes index.* — *Bibliography: p*

TERRORISM — Near East
TAHERI, Amir
Holy terror : The inside story of Islamic terrorism / Amir Taheri. — London : Hutchinson, 1987. — 313p. — *Spine title: Holy terror: Islamic terrorism and the West.* — *Bibliography: p[295]-301*

TERRORISM — Northern Ireland — History — Addresses, essays, lectures
Ireland's terrorist dilemma / [edited by Yonah Alexander and Alan O'Day. — Dordrecht [Netherlands] ; Lancaster : M. Nijhoff, 1986. — 279p. — (International studies on terrorism ; v. 2). — *Bibliography: p.261-277*

TERRORISM — Pakistan
GILBERT, Tony
Pakistan : regime of terror / Tony Gilbert. — London : Liberation, 1985. — 48p

TERRORISM — Spain — History — 20th century
EL PAÍS. Equipo de Investigación
Golpe mortal : asesinato de Carrero y agonía del franquismo / El País, Equipo de Investigación ; Ismael Fuente, Javier García y Joaquín Prieto. — [Madrid : Promotora de Informaciones], 1983. — 374p

TERRORISM — Turkey
GUNTER, Michael M
"Pursuing the just cause of their people" : a study of contemporary Armenian terrorism / Michael M. Gunter. — New York : Greenwood Press, 1986. — viii, 182 p.. — (Contributions in political science ; no. 152). — *Includes index.* — *Bibliography: p. [159]-169*

TERRORISM — United States
HOFFMAN, Bruce
Terrorism in the United States and the potential threat to nuclear facilities / Bruce Hoffman ; prepared for the U.S. Department of Energy. — Santa Monica, CA : Rand, [1986]. — ix, 56 p.. — "R-3351-DOE.". — "January 1986.". — *Bibliography: p. 55-56*

TERRORISM — United States — Congresses
Values in conflict : Blacks and the American ambivalence toward violence / edited by Charles A. Frye. — Washington, D.C. : University Press of America, c1980. — iii, 169 p.. — *Includes bibliographies and index*

TERRORISM — Yugoslavia
PLANTAGENET, Edouard E.
Les crimes de l'O.R.I.M. : organisation terroriste / Edouard E. Plantagenet. — Paris : La Paix, 1920. — 38p

TERRORISM IN MASS MEDIA — Italy
WAGNER-PACIFICI, Robin Erica
The Moro morality play : terrorism as social drama / Robin Erica Wagner-Pacifici. — Chicago : The University of Chicago Press, c1986. — p. cm. — *Includes index.* — *Bibliography: p*

TERRORISM IN MASS MEDIA — United States
HERMAN, Edward S.
The real terror network : terrorism in fact and propaganda / Edward S. Herman. — Montréal : Black Rose, 1985. — ix,252p. — *Includes bibliographical notes*

TERRORISTS — Germany (West)
CAMPAIGN AGAINST THE MODEL WEST GERMANY
[Reports]. — [Bochum] : Campaign against the Model West Germany
Nr.4: The Stammheim death. — [1977]. — 23p

TEVA I UTA (TAHITI : REGION) — Population — Statistics
Tableaux normalisés du recensement général de la population : 15 octobre 1983. — [Papeete] : Institut territorial de la statistique
Résultats de la commune de Teva i Uta. — [1985?]. — 4p,11 leaves

TEXAS — History — Republic, 1836-1846
MONTEJANO, David
Anglos and Mexicans in the making of Texas, 1836-1986 / by David Montejano. — 1st ed. — Austin : University of Texas Press, 1987. — p. cm. — *Includes index.* — *Bibliography: p*

TEXAS — History — 1846-1950
MONTEJANO, David
Anglos and Mexicans in the making of Texas, 1836-1986 / by David Montejano. — 1st ed. — Austin : University of Texas Press, 1987. — p. cm. — *Includes index.* — *Bibliography: p*

TEXAS — Race relations
MONTEJANO, David
Anglos and Mexicans in the making of Texas, 1836-1986 / by David Montejano. — 1st ed. — Austin : University of Texas Press, 1987. — p. cm. — *Includes index.* — *Bibliography: p*

TEXT PROCESSING (COMPUTER SCIENCE)
Text processing and document manipulation : proceedings of the international conference, University of Nottingham, 14-16 April 1986 / edited by J.C. van Vliet. — Cambridge : Published by Cambridge University Press on behalf of British Computer Society, 1986. — viii,277p. — (The British Computer Society Workshop series). — *Bibliography: p261-275*

TEXT RETRIEVAL '85 CONFERENCE
Integrating text with non-text : a picture is worth 1K words / edited by Robert Kimberley : proceedings of the Institute of Information Scientists Text Retrieval '85 Conference. — London : Taylor Graham, 1986. — 120p

TEXTILE INDUSTRY — Automation
BENGTSSON, Tommy
Industri under avspärrning : studier i svensk textilproduktion 1935-1950 / Tommy Bengtsson. — Lund : Ekonomisk-Historiska Föreningen, 1980. — 215p. — *Bibliography: p211-215*

TEXTILE INDUSTRY — Economic aspects
INTERNATIONAL CONFERENCE ON BUSINESS HISTORY ((8th : 1981 : Fuji Education Center)
The Textile industry and its business climate : proceedings of the Fuji Conference / International Conference on Business History 8 ; edited by Akio Okochi, Shin-ichi Yonekawa. — Tokyo : University of Tokyō Press, c1982. — xii, 299 p.. — *Includes bibliographical references and index*

TEXTILE INDUSTRY — Colombia — Location
HELMSING, A. H. J.
Firms, farms, and the state in Colombia : a study of rural, urban, and regional dimensions of change / A.H.J. Helmsing. — Boston : Allen & Unwin, 1986. — xix, 297 p.. — *Includes index.* — *Bibliography: p. 275-288*

TEXTILE INDUSTRY — France — Auffay — Employees
GULLICKSON, Gay L.
Spinners and weavers of Auffay : rural industry and the sexual division of labor in a French village, 1750-1850 / Gay L. Gullickson. — Cambridge : Cambridge University Press, 1986. — [xi,400]p. — *Bibliography: p395-400*

TEXTILE INDUSTRY — Mexico — Puebla — History
CASTAÑON R., Jesús
 Los primeros 25 años de industrialización en Puebla / Jesús Castañon R.. — México : Ediciones del Boletín Bibliográfico de la Secretaría de Hacienda y Crédito Público, 1960. — 21p

TEXTILE INDUSTRY — Pennsylvania — Philadelphia — History
SHELTON, Cynthia J.
 The mills of Manayunk : industrialization and social conflict in the Philadelphia region, 1787-1837 / Cynthia J. Shelton. — Baltimore : Johns Hopkins University Press, c1986. — xii, 227 p.. — (Studies in industry and society ; 5). — : Revision of thesis (Ph. D.)--UCLA, 1982. — Includes index. — Bibliography: p. 211-215

TEXTILE INDUSTRY — Peru
PERU. Servicio del Empleo y Recursos Humanos
 Estructura salarial y ocupacional de la industria textil de Lima y Callao. — Lima : the Servicio, 1965. — 58p

TEXTILE INDUSTRY — Sweden
BENGTSSON, Tommy
 Industri under avspärrning : studier i svensk textilproduktion 1935-1950 / Tommy Bengtsson. — Lund : Ekonomisk-Historiska Föreningen, 1980. — 215p. — Bibliography: p211-215

TEXTILE INDUSTRY — Taiwan
The textile industry in Taiwan, Republic of China. — [Taipei : Ministry of Economic Affairs, 1958]. — [20]p

TEXTILE INDUSTRY AND TRADE — England — Oldham (Lancashire)
PHILANDER
 A manufacturer's business a hundred years ago : notes on the account books of Joseph Wrigley of Stonebreaks (1711-1781) / compiled by 'Philander' (Samuel Andrew). — Oldham : Saddleworth Historical Society, 1879. — 46p. — Reprinted from the Oldham Chronicle

TEXTILE MACHINERY INDUSTRY — European Economic Community countries
FISHWICK, Frank
 The textile machinery industry in the EEC / F. Fishwick. — Luxembourg : Office for Official Publications of the European Communities, 1984. — ix, 96p. — At head of title page: Commission of the European Communities

TEXTILE WORKERS
Social and labour practices of multinational enterprises in the textiles, clothing, and footwear industries. — Geneva : International Labour Office, 1984. — xii,184p. — Includes bibliographies

TEXTILE WORKERS — Chile
WINN, Peter
 Weavers of revolution : the Yarur workers and Chile's road to socialism / Peter Winn. — New York : Oxford University Press, 1986. — xiv, 328 p.. — Includes index. — Bibliography: p. 300-315

TEXTILE WORKERS — Egypt — Political activity
GOLDBERG, Ellis
 Tinker, tailor, and textile worker : class and politics in Egypt, 1930-1952 / Ellis Goldberg. — Berkeley : University of California Press, 1986. — p. cm. — Includes index. — Bibliography: p

THAILAND — Civilization
KEYES, Charles F
 Thailand, Buddhist kingdom as modern nation-state / Charles F. Keyes. — Boulder : Westview Press, 1986. — p. cm. — (Westview profiles. Nations of contemporary Asia). — Includes index. — Bibliography: p

THAILAND — Economic conditions
INTERNATIONAL BANK FOR RECONSTRUCTION AND DEVELOPMENT
 Thailand : managing public resources for structural adjustment. — Washington, D.C., U.S.A. : World Bank, c1984. — Lxviii,275p. — (A World Bank country study). — Summaries in English, French, and Spanish. — Includes bibliographical references

KEYES, Charles F
 Thailand, Buddhist kingdom as modern nation-state / Charles F. Keyes. — Boulder : Westview Press, 1986. — p. cm. — (Westview profiles. Nations of contemporary Asia). — Includes index. — Bibliography: p

Thailand: economic conditions in... and outlook for... / Bank of Thailand, Department of Economic Research. — Bangkok : Bank of Thailand. Department of Economic Research, 1979/80-. — Annual. — Text in Thai and English. — Year dates included in title

THAILAND — Economic policy
INTERNATIONAL BANK FOR RECONSTRUCTION AND DEVELOPMENT
 Thailand : managing public resources for structural adjustment. — Washington, D.C., U.S.A. : World Bank, c1984. — Lxviii,275p. — (A World Bank country study). — Summaries in English, French, and Spanish. — Includes bibliographical references

NITSMER, Samart
 Economics curricula and their relevance to policy-making in Thailand / Samart Nitsmer. — Singapore : Regional Institute of Higher Education and Development, 1984. — 197p. — (RIHED Research Series). — Bibliography: p [147]-152

Summary of the Fourth Five-Year Plan, 1977-1981. — Bangkok : National Economic and Social Development Board, [1976?]. — ii,33p

THAILAND — Foreign relations
BRAILEY, Nigel J
 Thailand and the fall of Singapore : a frustrated Asian revolution / Nigel J. Brailey. — Boulder, Colo. : Westview Press, c1986. — p. cm. — (Westview special studies on South and Southeast Asia). — Includes index. — Bibliography: p

THAILAND — Industries — Statistics
Census of business trade and services 1966 : Southern region. — Bangkok : National Statistical Office, [1970?]. — 57p. — In English and Thai

Population by detailed classification of industry : 1980 population and housing census : whole kingdom and Bangkok metropolis. — [Bangkok] : National Statistical Office, [1985?]. — 144p. — In English and Thai. — Cover title

Report : census of business trade and services 1977 : Bangkok Metropolitan, Nonthaburi, Pathum Thani and Samut Prakan. — Bangkok : National Statistical Office, [1980?]. — 96p. — In English and Thai

Report : census of business trade and services 1977 : whole kingdom. — Bangkok : National Statistical Office, [1980?]. — 75p

THAILAND — Native races
TAPP, Nicholas
 The Hmong of Thailand : opium people of the Golden Triangle / Nicholas Tapp. — London : Anti-Slavery Society, 1986. — 72p. — (Indigenous peoples and development series. report no.4). — Bibliography: p69-70

THAILAND — Occupations — Statistics
Population by detailed classification of industry : 1980 population and housing census : whole kingdom and Bangkok metropolis. — [Bangkok] : National Statistical Office, [1985?]. — 144p. — In English and Thai. — Cover title

Population by detailed clssification [i.e. classification] of occupation : 1980 population and housing census : whole kingdom and Bangkok metropolis. — [Bangkok] : National Statistical Office, [1985?]. — 120p. — In English and Thai

THAILAND — Politics and government
BRAILEY, Nigel J
 Thailand and the fall of Singapore : a frustrated Asian revolution / Nigel J. Brailey. — Boulder, Colo. : Westview Press, c1986. — p. cm. — (Westview special studies on South and Southeast Asia). — Includes index. — Bibliography: p

Government and politics of Thailand / edited by Somsakdi Xuto. — Singapore ; Oxford : University Press, 1987. — xii,243p. — Bibliography: p[217]-229

KEYES, Charles F
 Thailand, Buddhist kingdom as modern nation-state / Charles F. Keyes. — Boulder : Westview Press, 1986. — p. cm. — (Westview profiles. Nations of contemporary Asia). — Includes index. — Bibliography: p

THAILAND — Population
GOLDSTEIN, Sidney
 Migration in Thailand : a twenty-five-year review / Sidney Goldstein and Alice Goldstein. — Honululu, Hawaii : East-West Center, [1986]. — vii, 54 p.. — (Papers of the East-West Population Institute ; no. 100). — Expanded version of a paper presented at the annual meeting of thePopulation Association of America, Boston, March 1985. — "July 1986.". — Bibliography: p. 51-54

THAILAND — Population — Statistics
PEJARANONDA, Chintana
 Household structure and factor affecting size of household. — [Bangkok] : National Statistical Office, 1985. — 32p. — (1980 population and housing census. Subject report ; no.6). — In English and Thai. — Cover title

Report : the survey of population change : 1974-1976. — Bangkok : National Statistical Office, [1978?]. — 89p. — In Thai and English

Report on population characteristics : the 1984 survey of population change. — [Bangkok] : National Statistical Office, [1985?]. — 152p. — In English and Thai. — Cover title

THAILAND — Social conditions
KEYES, Charles F
 Thailand, Buddhist kingdom as modern nation-state / Charles F. Keyes. — Boulder : Westview Press, 1986. — p. cm. — (Westview profiles. Nations of contemporary Asia). — Includes index. — Bibliography: p

THAILAND — Social policy
Summary of the Fourth Five-Year Plan, 1977-1981. — Bangkok : National Economic and Social Development Board, [1976?]. — ii,33p

THAMES RIVER (ENGLAND) — Bridges — Drawings
PENTON, Howard
 County of London sketches of bridges over the Thames / sketches by Howard Penton ; letterpress by Charles Palmer. — [London : Walter Emden, 1903]. — [24] leaves of plates. — Spine title: Sketches of bridges over the Thames. — Printed protectives include notes on each bridge

THATCHER, MARGARET
KRIEGER, Joel
 Reagan, Thatcher, and the politics of decline / Joel Krieger. — Cambridge : Polity, 1986. — [220]p. — (Europe and the international order) . — Includes index

COLE, John, 1927-
 The Thatcher years : a decade of revolution in British politics / John Cole. — London : BBC Books, 1987. — viii,216p. — Bibliography: p [210]

THATCHER, MARGARET
continuation

CREWE, Ivor
Thatcherism : its origins, electoral impact and implications for Down's theory of party strategy / Ivor Crewe and Donald D. Searing. — Colchester : University of Essex. Department of Government, 1986. — [48p]. — (Essex papers in politics and government ; no.37)

DALYELL, Tam
Thatcher: patterns of deceit / by Tam Dalyell ; introduction by Paul Rogers. — London : Woolf, 1986. — [64]p. — (The Men and documents series). — *Includes index*

HARRIMAN, Ed
Thatcher : a graphic guide / text: Ed Harriman ; illustrations: John Freeman. — London : Camden, 1986. — 169p. — (Graphic guide). — *Bibliography: p169*

LUNDBERG, Lars-Olof
Thatcher och facket : brittisk fackföreningsrörelse under den konservativa regeringen / Lars-Olof Lundberg. — Stockholm : Tiden, 1984. — 224p. — *Bibliography: p216-218*

ZALEWSKI, Marek J.
"Żelazna dama" z Downing Street / Marek J. Zalewski. — Warszawa : Krajowa Agencja Wydawnicza, 1985. — 272p

THEATER — History — 20th century
STOURÁC, Richard
Theatre as a weapon : workers' theatre in the Soviet Union, Germany and Britain, 1917-1934 / Richard Stourac and Kathleen McCreery. — London : Routledge & Kegan Paul, 1986. — xvi,336p. — *Bibliography: p324-326.* — *Includes index*

THEATER — Political aspects
STOURÁC, Richard
Theatre as a weapon : workers' theatre in the Soviet Union, Germany and Britain, 1917-1934 / Richard Stourac and Kathleen McCreery. — London : Routledge & Kegan Paul, 1986. — xvi,336p. — *Bibliography: p324-326.* — *Includes index*

THEATER — Political aspects — Québec (Province)
NARDOCCHIO, Elaine F
Theatre and politics in modern Québec / Elaine F. Nardocchio. — Edmonton, Alta., Canada : University of Alberta Press, 1986. — xii, 157 p.. — *Includes index.* — *Bibliography: p. 133-148*

THEATER — Québec (Province) — History — 20th century
NARDOCCHIO, Elaine F
Theatre and politics in modern Québec / Elaine F. Nardocchio. — Edmonton, Alta., Canada : University of Alberta Press, 1986. — xii, 157 p.. — *Includes index.* — *Bibliography: p. 133-148*

THEATER AND SOCIETY — Québec (Province)
NARDOCCHIO, Elaine F
Theatre and politics in modern Québec / Elaine F. Nardocchio. — Edmonton, Alta., Canada : University of Alberta Press, 1986. — xii, 157 p.. — *Includes index.* — *Bibliography: p. 133-148*

THEOLOGY — Addresses, essays, lectures
NIEBUHR, Reinhold
The essential Reinhold Niebuhr : selected essays and addresses / edited and introduced by Robert McAfee Brown. — New Haven : Yale University Press, c1986. — p. cm. — *Includes index*

THEOLOGY, DOCTRINAL — History
WELCH, Claude
Protestant thought in the nineteenth century / Claude Welch. — New Haven [Conn.] ; London : Yale University Press Vol.2: 1870-1914. — c1985. — xii,315p. — *Includes index*

THEORIE DES KOMMUNIKATIVEN HANDELNS
INGRAM, David
Habermas and the dialectic of reason / David Ingram. — New Haven, CT : Yale University Press, c1987. — xvii, 263p. — *Includes index.* — *Bibliography: p.243-254*

THEORY OF JUSTICE
Fondements d'une théorie de la justice : essais critiques sur la philosophie politique de John Rawls / publiés sous la direction de Jean Ladrière et Philippe Van Parijs. — Louvain-la-Neuve : Institut Supérieur de Philosophie, 1984. — x,275p. — (Essais philosophiques). — *Bibliography: p260-266*

THEOSOPHISTS — Great Britain — Biography
DINNAGE, Rosemary
Annie Besant / Rosemary Dinnage. — Harmondsworth : Penguin, 1986. — 127p,[8]p of plates. — (Lives of modern women). — *Bibliography: p124.* — *Includes index*

THERAPEUTIC SYSTEMS
Alternative therapy / [report of the Board of Science and Education]. — London : British Medical Association, 1986. — 164p. — *Bibliography: p163-164*

Sickness and sectarianism : exploratory studies in medical and religious sectarianism / edited by R. Kenneth Jones. — Aldershot : Gower, c1985. — [176]p

THERAPEUTIC SYSTEMS — Religious aspects
Sickness and sectarianism : exploratory studies in medical and religious sectarianism / edited by R. Kenneth Jones. — Aldershot : Gower, c1985. — [176]p

THERAPEUTIC SYSTEMS — Social aspects
EASTHOPE, Gary
Healers and alternative medicine : a sociological examination / Gary Easthope. — Aldershot : Gower, c1986. — [viii,151]p. — *Bibliography: p142-149.* — *Includes index*

THESAURI — Bibliography
Thesaurus guide : analytical directory of selected vocabularies for information retrieval, 1985 / prepared by Gesellschaft für Information und Dokumentation for the Commission of the European Communities. — Amsterdam ; Luxembourg : Elsevier : Office for Official Publications of the European Communities, 1985. — xxxvi,749p

THIEVES — United States — Case studies
SHOVER, Neal
Aging criminals / by Neal Shover. — Beverly Hills [Calif.] : Sage Publications, c1985. — p. cm. — (Sociological observations ; v. 17). — *Includes index.* — *Bibliography: p*

THIRD INTERNATIONAL
GRANT, Ted, 19---
The rise and fall of the Communist International / by Ted Grant ; introduction by Alan Woods. — London : Militant Publications, 1985. — 47p. — (Marxist studies ; 3). — *Contents: The rise and fall of the Communist International. Originally published: s.l. : s.n., 1975. - The evolution of the Comintern / Anon. Originally published: s.l. : s.n., 1936*

THIRD INTERNATIONAL — History
CABALLERO, Manuel
Latin America and the Comintern 1919-1943 / Manuel Caballero. — Cambridge : Cambridge University Press, 1986. — ix,213p. — (Cambridge Latin American studies ; 60). — *Bibliography: p196-205.* — *Includes index*

THIRD INTERNATIONAL — History — Sources
The German revolution and the debate on Soviet power : documents, 1918-1919 : preparing the founding congress / edited by John Riddell. — New York : Anchor Foundation, 1986. — xx,540p. — (Communist International in Lenin's time)

THIRD PARTIES (UNITED STATES POLITICS)
FRESIA, Gerald John
There comes a time : a challenge to the two party system / Gerald John Fresia. — New York : Praeger, 1986. — 255 p.. — *Includes index.* — *Bibliography: p. 217-249*

SPITZER, Robert J.
The Right to Life movement and third party politics / Robert J. Spitzer. — New York : Greenwood Press, c1987. — xii, 154 p.. — (Contributions in political science ; no. 160). — *Includes index.* — *Bibliography: p. [141]-148*

THIRTY YEARS WAR, 1618-1648
PAGÈS, Georges
La guerre de trente ans, 1618-1648 / G. Pagès. — Paris : Payot, 1949. — 270p. — *Bibliography: p[269]-270*

THIRTY YEAR'S WAR, 1618-1648
SCHORMANN, Gerhard
Der dreissigjährige Krieg / Gerhard Schormann. — Göttingen : Vandenhoeck & Ruprecht, 1985. — 151p. — *Bibliography: p145-147*

THISTED (DENMARK) — Economic conditions
Analyse af Hjørring og Thisted amter. — København : Boligministeriets kommitterede i byplansager, 1960. — 60p. — *Cover title: Hjørring og Thisted amter*

THOMAS, Aquinas, Saint
D'ENTRÈVES, A. P.
The medieval contribution to political thought : Thomas Aquinas, Marsilius of Padua, Richard Hooker / by Alexander Passerin D'Entreves. — New York : Humanities, 1959. — viii,148p. — *On spine: Medieval contributions to political thought.* — *Originally published: Oxford University Press, 1939*

THOMPSON-FREY, NANCY
FREY, Robert Seitz
The imperative of response : the holocaust in human context / Robert Seitz Frey, Nancy Thompson-Frey. — Lanham, MD : University Press of America, c1985. — xix, 165 p.. — *Bibliography: p. 144-164*

THOUGHT AND THINKING
BARON, Jonathan
Rationality and intelligence / Jonathan Baron. — Cambridge : Cambridge University Press, 1985. — 299p

BODEN, Margaret A
Artificial intelligence and natural man / Margaret A. Boden. — 2nd ed., expanded. — New York : Basic Books, c1987. — xii, 576 p.. — *Includes index.* — *Bibliography: p. [501]-528*

Social and functional approaches to language and thought / edited by Maya Hickmann ; with a foreword by Jerome Bruner. — Orlando : Academic Press, 1987. — p. cm. — *Includes index*

TIBET — Foreign relations — India
LAMB, Alastair
British India and Tibet, 1766-1910 / Alastair Lamb. — 2nd ed. — London : Routledge and Kegan Paul, 1986. — xiv,353p. — *Bibliography: p323-338*

TIBET — Politics and government
GOODMAN, Michael Harris
The last Dalai Lama : a biography / Michael Harris Goodman. — London : Sidgwick and Jackson, 1986. — xiii,364p. — *Bibliography: p353-357*

TIBET — Religion
GOODMAN, Michael Harris
The last Dalai Lama : a biography / Michael Harris Goodman. — London : Sidgwick and Jackson, 1986. — xiii,364p. — *Bibliography: p353-357*

TIBET (CHINA) — Foreign relations — China
WALT VAN PRAAG, M. C. van
The status of Tibet : history, rights, and prospects in international law / by Michael C. Van Walt, van Praag ; with a foreword by Franz Michael and an introduction by Rikhi Jaipal. — Boulder, Colo. : Westview Press, 1987. — xxiv, 381 p., [1] p. of plates. — *Includes index. — Bibliography: p. 343-359*

TIBET (CHINA) — History
GRUNFELD, A. Tom
The making of modern Tibet / A. Tom Grunfeld. — London : Zed Books, 1987. — x,277p. — *Includes index*

TIBET (CHINA) — International status
WALT VAN PRAAG, M. C. van
The status of Tibet : history, rights, and prospects in international law / by Michael C. Van Walt, van Praag ; with a foreword by Franz Michael and an introduction by Rikhi Jaipal. — Boulder, Colo. : Westview Press, 1987. — xxiv, 381 p., [1] p. of plates. — *Includes index. — Bibliography: p. 343-359*

TIBET (CHINA) — Politics and government — 1951-
WALT VAN PRAAG, M. C. van
The status of Tibet : history, rights, and prospects in international law / by Michael C. Van Walt, van Praag ; with a foreword by Franz Michael and an introduction by Rikhi Jaipal. — Boulder, Colo. : Westview Press, 1987. — xxiv, 381 p., [1] p. of plates. — *Includes index. — Bibliography: p. 343-359*

TIBUAI (AUSTRAL ISLANDS) — Population — Statistics
Tableaux normalisés du recensement général de la popultion : 15 octobre 1983. — [Papeete] : Institut territorial de la statistique Résultats de la commune de Tubuai. — [1985?]. — 4p,11 leaves

TIENTSIN (CHINA) — Industries — History
HERSHATTER, Gail
The workers of Tianjin, 1900-1949 / Gail Hershatter. — Stanford, Calif. : Stanford University Press, 1986. — viii, 313p. — *Includes index. — Bibliography: p.[285]-301*

TIKHOMIROV, M. N.
CHISTIAKOVA, E. V.
Mikhail Nikolaevich Tikhomirov (1893-1965) / E. V. Chistiakova ; otv. redaktor V. I. Buganov. — Moskva : Nauka, 1987. — 157p. — (Nauchnye biografii)

TILLAGE — Economic aspects — Denmark
IVERSEN, Kjeld Kryhlmand
Reduceret jordbehandling : driftsøkonomi og energieffektivitet / Kjeld Kryhlmand Iversen, Arne Serup Møller. — København : Statens Jordbrugsøkonomiske Institut i kommission hos Landhusholdningsselskabets Forlag, 1987. — 75p. — (Rapport / Statens Jordbrugsøkonomiske Institut ; nr.29). — *Includes English summary. — Bibliography: p64-66*

TILLAGE — Denmark — Energy conservation
IVERSEN, Kjeld Kryhlmand
Reduceret jordbehandling : driftsøkonomi og energieffektivitet / Kjeld Kryhlmand Iversen, Arne Serup Møller. — København : Statens Jordbrugsøkonomiske Institut i kommission hos Landhusholdningsselskabets Forlag, 1987. — 75p. — (Rapport / Statens Jordbrugsøkonomiske Institut ; nr.29). — *Includes English summary. — Bibliography: p64-66*

TILLICH, PAUL
SCHNÜBBE, Otto
Paul Tillich und seine Bedeutung für den Protestantismus heute : das Prinzip der Rechtfertigung im theologischen, philosophischen und politischen Denken Paul Tillichs / Otto Schnübbe. — Hannover : Lutherhaus, 1985. — 288p

TIME
The Nature of time / edited by Raymond Flood and Michael Lockwood. — Oxford : Basil Blackwell, 1986. — [240]p. — *Includes bibliography and index*

TARSKI, Ignacy
[Czynnik czasu w procesie transportowym. English]. The time factor in transportation processes / Ignacy Tarski ; [translated by Olgierd Wojtasiewicz]. — Amsterdam ; New York : Elsevier ; Warszawa : Wydawnictwa Komunikacji i Łączności, 1987. — viii, 259 p.. — (Developments in civil engineering ; 15). — *Translation of: Czynnik czasu w procesie transportowym. — Includes index. — Includes bibliographies*

TIME — Psychological aspects
MCGRATH, Joseph Edward
Time and human interaction : toward a social psychology of time / by Joseph E. McGrath and Janice R. Kelly. — New York : Guilford Press, 1986. — p. cm. — (The Guilford social psychology series). — *Includes index. — Bibliography: p*

TIME — Social aspects
MCGRATH, Joseph Edward
Time and human interaction : toward a social psychology of time / by Joseph E. McGrath and Janice R. Kelly. — New York : Guilford Press, 1986. — p. cm. — (The Guilford social psychology series). — *Includes index. — Bibliography: p*

TIME AND ECONOMIC REACTIONS
Ekonomiia vremeni i effektivnost' sotsialisticheskogo proizvodstva / pod redaktsiei M. S. Atlas, A. G. Griaznovoi. — Moskva : Ekonomika, 1986. — 237p

TIME MANAGEMENT
Management of work and personal life : problems and opportunities / edited by Mary Dean Lee and Rabindra N. Kanungo. — New York, N.Y. : Praeger, 1984. — p. cm. — *Includes index. — Bibliography: p*

Time use studies : dimensions and applications / edited by Dagfinn °As [and others]. — Helsinki : Tilastokeskus, 1986. — 190p. — (Tutkimuksia / Finland. Tilastokeskus ; no.128)

TIME MANAGEMENT — United States
PLECK, Joseph H
Working wives, working husbands / Joseph H. Pleck. — Beverly Hills, Calif. : Published in cooperation with the National Council on Family Relations [by] Sage Publications, c1985. — 167 p.. — (New perspectives on family). — *Bibliography: p. 160-167*

TIME MANAGEMENT — United States — Social aspects
Time, goods, and well-being / edited by F. Thomas Juster and Frank P. Stafford. — Ann Arbor, Mich. : Survey Research Center, Institute for Social Research, University of Michigan, 1985. — p. cm. — *Bibliography: p*

TIME MANAGEMENT SURVEYS — Developing countries
ACHARYA, Meena
Time use data and the living standards measurement study / Meena Acharya. — Washington, D.C., U.S.A. : World Bank, c1982 ((1985 printing)). — 72p. — (LSMS working papers ; no.18) (LSMS working papers ; no. 18). — *Bibliographical references: p69-72*

TIME MANAGEMENT SURVEYS — United States
Time, goods, and well-being / edited by F. Thomas Juster and Frank P. Stafford. — Ann Arbor, Mich. : Survey Research Center, Institute for Social Research, University of Michigan, 1985. — p. cm. — *Bibliography: p*

TIME-SERIES ANALYSIS
ANDERSON, T. W.
The statistical analysis of time series / T.W. Anderson. — New York ; Chichester : Wiley, 1971. — xiv,704p. — (Wiley series in probability and mathematical statistics). — *bibl p680-688*

BROCKWELL, P. J
Time series : theory and methods / P.J. Brockwell, R.A. Davis. — New York : Springer-Verlag, c1987. — p. cm. — (Springer series in statistics). — *Includes index. — Bibliography: p*

DROBNY, A.
Some long-run features of dynamic time series models : the implications of cointegration / A. Drobny and S. G. Hall. — London : National Institute of Economic and Social Research, 1987. — 12p. — (Discussion paper / National Institute of Economic and Social Research ; no.129). — *Bibliography: p13-14*

Essays in time series and allied processes : papers in honour of E. J. Hannan / edited by J. Gani and M. B. Priestley. — Sheffield : Allied Probability Trust, 1986. — viii,438p. — (Journal of Allied Probability special volume ; 23A (1986))

HARVEY, A. C.
Estimation, smoothing, interpolation and distribution for structural time series models in discrete and continuous time / A. C. Harvey and J. H. Stock. — London : Economic and Social Research Council : London School of Economics, 1986. — [39p]. — (ESRC/LSE econometrics project discussion paper ; A.62). — *Bibliography: p[32-33]*

TAYLOR, Stephen, 1954-
Modelling financial time series / Stephen Taylor. — Chichester : Wiley, c1986. — xvi,268p. — *Bibliography: p256-261. — Includes index*

TIME-SERIES ANALYSIS — Congresses
Time series and econometric modelling / Ian B. MacNeill & Gary J. Umphrey, editors ; associate editors, Richard A.L. Carter, A. Ian McLeod, Aman Ullah. — Dordrecht ; Boston : D. Reidel ; Norwell, MA, U.S.A. : Sold and distributed in the U.S.A. and Canada by Kluwer Academic Publishers, c1987. — p. cm. — (Advances in the statistical sciences ; v. 3) (The University of Western Ontario series in philosophy of science ; v. 36)

TIMES
WINKWORTH, Stephen
Room two more guns : the intriguing history of the personal column of the Times / Stephen Winkworth. — London : Allen & Unwin, 1986. — [280]p. — *Includes index*

TIMOR ISLAND (INDONESIA) — History
RAMOS-HORTA, Jose
Funu : the unfinished saga of East Timor / Jose Ramos-Horta ; preface by Noam Chomsky. — Trenton, New Jersey : Red Sea Press, 1987. — xvi,207p

TIMOR ISLAND (INDONESIA) — Politics and government
RAMOS-HORTA, Jose
Funu : the unfinished saga of East Timor / Jose Ramos-Horta ; preface by Noam Chomsky. — Trenton, New Jersey : Red Sea Press, 1987. — xvi,207p

TIN INDUSTRY — Bolivia
AYUB, Mahmood Ali
The economics of tin mining in Bolivia / Mahmood Ali Ayub, Hideo Hashimoto. — Washington, D.C. : World Bank, 1985. — v, 106p. — *Bibliography: p.105-106*

TIN INDUSTRY — Bolivia
continuation

CRABTREE, John
The great tin crash : Bolivia and the world tin market / [John Crabtree, Gavan Duffy and Jenny Pearce]. — London : Latin American Bureau, 1987. — 104p. — *Bibliography: p103*

TIN MINES AND MINING — Bolivia

AYUB, Mahmood Ali
The economics of tin mining in Bolivia / Mahmood Ali Ayub, Hideo Hashimoto. — Washington, D.C. : World Bank, 1985. — v, 106p. — *Bibliography: p.105-106*

CRABTREE, John
The great tin crash : Bolivia and the world tin market / [John Crabtree, Gavan Duffy and Jenny Pearce]. — London : Latin American Bureau, 1987. — 104p. — *Bibliography: p103*

TIN MINES AND MINING — England — Dartmoor — History — Pictorial works

GREEVES, Tom
Tin mines and miners of Dartmoor : a photographic record / Tom Greeves. — Exeter : Devon Books, 1986. — [96]p. — *Includes bibliography and index*

TINIDAD AND TOBAGO — Statistics, Vital

Marriages and divorces report, 1979-1983. — [Port of Spain] : Central Statistical Office, 1985. — v,19p

TIRUNELVELI DISTRICT (INDIA) — Social conditions

FANSELOW, Frank Sylvester
Trade, kinship and Islamisation : a comparative study of the social and economic organisation of Muslim and Hindu traders in Tirunelveli district, South India / by Frank Sylvester Fanselow. — 306 leaves. — *PhD (Econ) 1986 LSE*

TITHES — Wales — Clwyd

The tithe war. — Hawarden : Clwyd Record Office, 1978. — 12p. — *Bibliography: p12*

TOBACCO — Economic aspects — Addresses, essays, lectures

Smoking and society : toward a more balanced assessment / edited by Robert D. Tollison. — Lexington, Mass. : Lexington Books, c1986. — ix, 368 p.. — *Includes bibliographies and indexes*

TOBACCO — Physiological effect — Addresses, essays, lectures

Smoking and society : toward a more balanced assessment / edited by Robert D. Tollison. — Lexington, Mass. : Lexington Books, c1986. — ix, 368 p.. — *Includes bibliographies and indexes*

TOBACCO HABIT

WILKINSON, James, 1941-
Tobacco : the truth behind the smokescreen / James Wilkinson. — Harmondsworth : Penguin, 1986. — 158p. — *Cover title: Tobacco: the facts.... — Bibliography: p.[142]-143*

TOBACCO HABIT — Treatment — Great Britain

RAW, Martin
Helping people to stop smoking : the development, role and potential of support services in the UK / Martin Raw and Julie Heller. — [London?] : Health Education Council, 1984. — 134p. — *Bibliography: p125-128*

TOBACCO HABIT — Australia — History

WALKER, R. B
Under fire : a history of tobacco smoking in Australia / Robin Walker. — Carlton, Vic. : Melbourne University Press ; Beaverton, OR : International Scholarly Book Services, 1984. — ix, 155 p., [12] p. of plates. — *Includes bibliographical references and index*

TOBACCO INDUSTRY

WILKINSON, James, 1941-
Tobacco : the truth behind the smokescreen / James Wilkinson. — Harmondsworth : Penguin, 1986. — 158p. — *Cover title: Tobacco: the facts.... — Bibliography: p.[142]-143*

TOBACCO INDUSTRY — Social aspects — Developing countries

NATH, Uma Ram
Smoking : Third World alert / Uma Ram Nath. — Oxford : Oxford University Press, 1986. — [270]p. — *Includes bibliography and index*

TOBACCO INDUSTRY — Developing countries

NATH, Uma Ram
Smoking : Third World alert / Uma Ram Nath. — Oxford : Oxford University Press, 1986. — [270]p. — *Includes bibliography and index*

TOBACCO INDUSTRY — Germany — History

BUSCHAK, Willy
Von Menschen, die wie Menschen leben wollten : die Geschichte der Gewerkschaft Nahrung-Genuss-Gaststätten und ihrer Vorläufer / Willy Buschak ; Vorwork: Günter Döding. — Köln : Bund, 1985. — 645p. — *Bibliography: p634-639*

TOBACCO INDUSTRY — United States — History

TILLEY, Nannie May
The R.J. Reynolds Tobacco Company / by Nannie May Tilley. — Chapel Hill : University of North Carolina Press, c1985. — p. cm. — *Includes index*

TOBACCO INDUSTRY — Virginia — History — 18th century

BREEN, T. H
Tobacco culture : the mentality of the great Tidewater planters on the eve of Revolution / T.H. Breen. — Princeton, N.J. : Princeton University Press, c1985. — xvi, 216p. — *Includes index*

TOBACCO INDUSTRY — Virginia — Danville — History

SIEGEL, Frederick F
The roots of southern distinctiveness : tobacco and society in Danville, Virginia, 1780-1865 / by Frederick F. Siegel. — Chapel Hill, N.C. : University of North Carolina Press, c1987. — p. cm. — *Includes index. — Bibliography: p*

TOCQUEVILLE, ALEXIS DE

BOESCHE, Roger
The strange liberalism of Alexis de Tocqueville / Roger Boesche. — Ithaca, N.Y. ; London : Cornell University Press, 1987. — 288p. — *Includes index. — Bibliography: p.267-281*

POPE, Whitney
Alexis de Tocqueville : his social and political theory / by Whitney Pope. — Beverly Hills, Calif. : Sage, c1985. — p. cm. — (Masters of social theory ; v. 4). — *Includes index. — Bibliography: p*

TOCQUEVILLE, ALEXIS DE — Correspondence

TOCQUEVILLE, Alexis de
[Works]. Oeuvres complètes / Alexis de Tocqueville. — Paris : Gallimard
Tom.7: Correspondance étrangère d'Alexis de Tocqueville : Amérique, Europe continentale / .... établi par Françoise Mélonio, Lise Queffélec et Anthony Pleasance ; .... soumis pour contrôle et approbation à Jean-Claude Lamberti et à David Lee. — 1986. — 398p

TODESCO, CLEMENTINA

MATHIAS, Elizabeth
Italian folktales in America : the verbal art of an immigrant woman / Elizabeth Mathias and Richard Raspa ; foreword by Roger D. Abrahams. — Detroit : Wayne State University Press, 1985. — p. cm. — (Wayne State University Folklore Archive study series). — *Includes 22 tales as told by Clementina Todesco. — Includes indexes. — Bibliography: p*

TOGO — Census, 1981

Aperçu des resultats d'ensemble du recensement général de la population et de l'habitat au Togo de novembre 1981 : caractéristiques de la population. — [Lomé] : Bureau Central du Recensement, 1986. — 70p

Recensement général de la population et de l'habitat 9-22 novembre 1981. — [Lomé] : Bureau Central du Recensement
vol.2: Caractéristiques socio-culturelles : résultats définitifs. — 1985. — 327p

Recensement général de la population et de l'habitat 9-22 novembre 1981. — [Lomé] : Bureau Central du Recensement
vol.3: Activités economiques
tome 1: Résultats globaux: ensemble du pays: urbain et rural et ville de Lomé : résultats définitifs. — 1985. — 246p

Recensement général de la population et de l'habitat 9-22 novembre 1981. — [Lomé] : Bureau Central du Recensement
vol.4: Mouvements naturels: migrations : résultats définitifs. — 1985. — 252p

TOGO — Commerce — Statistics

Annuaire des statistiques du commerce exterieur / Direction de la Statistique, Togo. — Lome : Direction de la Statistique, 1978/79-. — *Annual*

Commerce exterieur du Togo, 1937-1956. — Lomé : Service de la Statistique Générale du Togo, [1957]. — 42 leaves

Enquête sur les entreprises industrielles commerciales et des services du Togo : exercices 1981 et 1982. — Lomé : Direction de la Statistique, 1986. — 300p

TOGO — Economic conditions — Statistics

Indicateurs de l'economie togolaise / Direction de la Statistique, Togo. — Lomé : Direction de la Statistique, 1972-. — *Annual*

TOGO — Industries — Statistics

Enquête sur les entreprises industrielles commerciales et de services du Togo : exercice 1976. — Lomé : Direction de la Statistique, 1976. — 116p

Enquête sur les entreprises industrielles commerciales et des services du Togo : exercices 1981 et 1982. — Lomé : Direction de la Statistique, 1986. — 300p

TOGO — Politics and government

EYADEMA, Etienne
Allocutions et discours : pronouces en 1969 / Le General Etienne Eyadema, President de la Republique Toglaise et President National du R.P.T.. — [S.l.] : Rassemblement du Peuple Togolais. Secretariat Administratif, 1973. — 42 leaves

RASSEMBLEMENT DU PEUPLE TOGOLAIS. Secretariat Administratif
Statuts du Rassemblement du Peuple Togolais. — [s.l.] : Rassemblement du Peuple Togolais, 1972. — 15 leaves

TOGO — Population — Statistics

Aperçu des resultats d'ensemble du recensement général de la population et de l'habitat au Togo de novembre 1981 : caractéristiques de la population. — [Lomé] : Bureau Central du Recensement, 1986. — 70p

TOGO — Population — Statistics
continuation

Recensement général de la population et de l'habitat 9-22 novembre 1981. — [Lomé] : Bureau Central du Recensement
vol.2: Caractéristiques socio-culturelles : résultats définitifs. — 1985. — 327p

Recensement général de la population et de l'habitat 9-22 novembre 1981. — [Lomé] : Bureau Central du Recensement
vol.3: Activités economiques
tome 1: Résultats globaux: ensemble du pays: urbain et rural et ville de Lomé : résultats définitifs. — 1985. — 246p

Recensement général de la population et de l'habitat 9-22 novembre 1981. — [Lomé] : Bureau Central du Recensement
vol.4: Mouvements naturels: migrations : résultats définitifs. — 1985. — 252p

TOGO — Statistics, Vital
Recensement général de la population et de l'habitat 9-22 novembre 1981. — [Lomé] : Bureau Central du Recensement
vol.4: Mouvements naturels: migrations : résultats définitifs. — 1985. — 252p

TOKYO (JAPAN) — Economic conditions
ORII, S.
The changing face of Tokyo : urban redevelopment / S. Orii. — London : Yamaichi Research Institute of Securities and Economics, Inc., 1987. — 29p. — (Yamaichi investment report ; 87-03)

TOKYO (JAPAN) — Politics and government
The fiscal outlook for the metropolis of Tokyo. — Tokyo : Tokyo Metropolitan Government, 1986. — viii,143p. — (TMG municipal library ; no.21)

TOKYO (JAPAN) — Social conditions
ORII, S.
The changing face of Tokyo : urban redevelopment / S. Orii. — London : Yamaichi Research Institute of Securities and Economics, Inc., 1987. — 29p. — (Yamaichi investment report ; 87-03)

TOKYO ROUND (1973-1979)
WINHAM, Gilbert R
International trade and the Tokyo Round negotiation / Gilbert R. Winham. — Princeton, N.J. : Princeton University Press, c1986. — xiv, 449 p.. — Includes index. — Bibliography: p. 425-437

TOKYO ROUND (1973-1979)
WINHAM, Gilbert R
International trade and the Tokyo Round negotiation / Gilbert R. Winham. — Princeton, N.J. : Princeton University Press, c1986. — xiv, 449 p.. — Includes index. — Bibliography: p. 425-437

TOKYO ROUND AGREEMENTS
The texts of the Tokyo Round Agreements. — Geneva : General Agreement on Tariffs and Trade, 1986. — vii,208p

TŌKYŌ SHIBAURA DENKI KABUSHIKI KAISHA
HONGO, Takanobu
[Mokuhyō kanri no shinkō. English].
Management by objectives : a Japanese experience / by Takanobu Hongo. — Tokyo : Asian Productivity Organization, 1980. — viii,86p. — Translation of: Mokuhyō kanri no shinkō

TOKYO TRIAL, 1946-1948 — Congresses
The Tokyo war crimes trial : an international symposium / edited by C. Hosoya ... [et al.]. — 1st ed. — Tokyo : Kodansha ; New York, N.Y. : Distributed in the U.S. by Kodansha International through Harper & Row, 1986. — 226 p.. — "Record of ... International Symposium on the Tokyo War Crimes Trial was held in Tokyo on 28-29 May 1983"--p. 11. — Colophon inserted. — Includes index. — Bibliography: p. 209-212

TOLL ROADS — Developing countries
BANISTER, David
Toll road pricing on inter urban highways in developing countries / David Banister. — London : Bartlett School of Architecture and Planning, 1986. — [31]p. — (Town planning discussion paper ; no.46)

TOLL ROADS — Great Britain
TANNER, J. C.
A theoretical study of the possible use of tolls to relieve traffic congestion in urban areas / by J. C. Tanner. — London : Road Research Laboratory, Department of Scientific and Industrial Research, 1960. — 4,iip. — (Research note ; No.RN/3819/JCT). — Bibliographical references: p4

TOM, PETRUS
TOM, Petrus
My life struggle : the story of Petrus Tom. — Braamfontein, South Africa : Ravan Press, 1985. — 68 p., [1] leaf of plates. — (Ravan worker series)

TOMATO INDUSTRY — Mexico
MEXICO. Dirección General de Economía Agrícola
Programa siembra-exportación de tomate, temporada 1983-1984. — [México] : the Dirección, [ca.1985]. — 27p. — Cover title: Tomate, programa siembra exportación 1983-1984

TONGA — Industries — Statistics
Industrial employment and output survey, January 1980. — [Nukuʹalofa : Statistics Department], 1980. — 12p

Survey of employment and output in the manufacturing sector, 1979. — [Nukuʹalofa : Statistics Department], 1979. — 14p

TORADJAS — Rites and ceremonies
VOLKMAN, Toby Alice
Feasts of honor : ritual and change in the Toraja highlands / Toby Alice Volkman. — Urbana : University of Illinois Press, c1985. — xi, 216 p.. — (Illinois studies in anthropology ; no. 16). — : Originally presented as the author's thesis (Ph. D.--Cornell University, 1980) under title: The pig has eaten the vegetables. — Includes index. — Bibliography: p. [201]-207

TORADJAS — Social conditions
VOLKMAN, Toby Alice
Feasts of honor : ritual and change in the Toraja highlands / Toby Alice Volkman. — Urbana : University of Illinois Press, c1985. — xi, 216 p.. — (Illinois studies in anthropology ; no. 16). — : Originally presented as the author's thesis (Ph. D.--Cornell University, 1980) under title: The pig has eaten the vegetables. — Includes index. — Bibliography: p. [201]-207

TORFAEN (GWENT) — Social policy
HUNT, John
Housing and care for elderly people / John Hunt. — Cwmbran : Cwmbran Development Corporation ; Torfaen : Torfaen Borough Council, 1985. — xv,109p

TORONTO GENERAL HOSPITAL
O'MALLEY, Martin
Hospital : life and death in a major medical centre / Martin O'Halley. — Toronto : Macmillan of Canada, 1986. — xv,239p

TORRES STRAIT ISLANDERS — Employment
AUSTRALIA. Committee of Review of Aboriginal Employment and Training Programs
Aboriginal employment and training programs : report of the Committee of Review. — Canberra : Australian Government Publishing Service, 1985. — ix,453p

TORRES STRAIT ISLANDERS — Training of
AUSTRALIA. Committee of Review of Aboriginal Employment and Training Programs
Aboriginal employment and training programs : report of the Committee of Review. — Canberra : Australian Government Publishing Service, 1985. — ix,453p

TORT LIABILITY OF HOSPITALS — United States
WERTHMANN, Barbara
Medical malpractice law : how medicine is changing the law / Barbara Werthmann. — Lexington, Mass. : LexingtonBooks, c1984. — xii, 268 p.. — Includes indexes

TORTS
The Law of tort : policies and trends in liability for damage to property and economic loss / edited by Michael Furmston. — London : Duckworth, 1986. — vi,231p. — (Colston papers ; no.36). — Conference proceedings. — Includes index

TORTS — Australia
TRINDADE, Francis A
The law of torts in Australia / F.A. Trindade, Peter Cane. — Melbourne ; New York : Oxford University Press, 1985. — lxv, 763 p.. — Includes indexes

TORTS — England
BURROWS, A. S.
Remedies for torts and breach of contract / A.S. Burrows. — London : Butterworths, 1987. — lviii,435p. — Includes index

HARLOW, Carol
Understanding tort law : Carol Harlow. — London : Fontana, 1987. — 160p. — (Understanding law) (Understanding law). — Bibliography: p147-151

SALMOND, Sir John
Salmond and Heuston on the law of torts. — 19th ed. / by R.F.V. Heuston and R.A. Buckley. — London : Sweet & Maxwell, 1987. — [700]p. — Previous ed.: 1981. — Includes index

WINFIELD, Sir Percy Harry
Winfield and Jolowicz on tort. — 12th ed / by W.V.H. Rogers. — London : Sweet & Maxwell, 1984. — lxiii,767p. — Previous ed.: 1979. — Includes index

TORTS — Germany (West)
MARKESINIS, B. S.
A comparative introduction to the German law of tort / B.S. Markesinis. — Oxford : Clarendon, 1986. — xxix,610p. — Spine title: The German law of torts. — Includes bibliographies and index

TORTS — Great Britain
STANTON, K. M.
Breach of statutory duty in tort / by K.M. Stanton. — London : Sweet & Maxwell, 1986. — xvii,155p. — (Modern legal studies). — Includes index

TORTURE
HERMAN, Edward S.
The real terror network : terrorism in fact and propaganda / Edward S. Herman. — Montréal : Black Rose, 1985. — ix,252p. — Includes bibliographical notes

SCARRY, Elaine
The body in pain : the making and unmaking of the world / Elaine Scarry. — New York : Oxford University Press, 1985. — p. cm. — Includes index

TORTURE — Congresses
La torture : le corps et la parole : les actes du IIIe Colloque Interuniversitaire, Fribourg 1985 / Guy Aurenche...[et al.]. — Fribourg : Éditions Universitaires, 1985. — 193p

TOTALITARIANISM
BARRETT, Jeffrey W
 Impulse to revolution in Latin America / by Jeffrey W. Barrett. — New York : Praeger, 1985. — ix, 357p. — (Praeger special studies)

FÉHÉR, Ferenc
 Eastern left, Western left : totalitarianism, freedom and democracy / Ferenc Féhér and Agnes Heller. — Cambridge : Polity, 1987, c1986. — 287p. — *Includes index*

MERLO, Arturo
 Argentina totalitaria / Arturo Merlo. — Buenos Aires : Editorial Occidente, 1984. — 253p. — *Bibliography: p251-253*

TOTALITARIANISM — Addresses, essays, lectures
FRIEDRICH, Carl J.
 Totalitarianism in perspective : three views / Carl J. Friedrich, Michael Curtis, Benjamin R. Barber. — London : Pall Mall Press, 1969. — xii,164p. — *Originally published, New York: Praeger, 1969*

FRIEDRICH, Carl J
 Totalitarianism in perspective: three views / [by] Carl J. Friedrich, Michael Curtis [and] Benjamin R. Barber. — New York : Praeger, [1969]. — xii, 164 p. — *Includes bibliographical references. — Contents: Conceptual foundations of totalitarianism, by B. B. Barber.--Retreat from totalitarianism, by M. Curtis.--The evolving theory and practice of totalitarian regimes, by C. J. Friedrich*

TOTEM UND TABU
WALLACE, Edwin R
 Freud and anthropology : a history and reappraisal / Edwin R. Wallace, IV. — New York : International Universities Press, c1983. — xi, 306p. — (Psychological issues ; monograph 55). — *Bibliography: p.281-294. — Includes index*

TOTEMISM
DURKHEIM, Emile
 The elementary forms of the religious life / Emile Durkheim ; translated [from the French] by Joseph Ward Swain. — 2nd ed. / introduction by Robert Nisbet. — London : Allen and Unwin, 1976. — xix,456p. — *This translation originally published as 1st ed.: 1915. - Translation of: 'Les Formes élémentaires de la vie religieuse, le système totémique en Australiè. Paris : F. Alcan, 1912. — Includes index*

WALLACE, Edwin R
 Freud and anthropology : a history and reappraisal / Edwin R. Wallace, IV. — New York : International Universities Press, c1983. — xi, 306p. — (Psychological issues ; monograph 55). — *Bibliography: p.281-294. — Includes index*

TOURISM — Pakistan
 Visitors to museums, historical places and archaeological sites : annual report / Ministry of Culture and Tourism, Pakistan. — Islamabad : Ministry of Culture and Tourism, 1983-. — *Annual*

TOURIST CAMPS, HOSTELS, ETC. — Great Britain — History
WARD, Colin
 Goodnight campers! : the history of the British holiday camp / Colin Ward and Dennis Hardy. — London : Mansell, 1986. — [256]p. — (Studies in history, planning and the environment) (An Alexandrine Press book). — *Includes index*

TOURIST TRADE
KRIPPENDORF, Jost
 The holiday people : towards a new understanding of leisure and travel / Jost Krippendorf ; translated by Vera Andrassy. — London : Heinemann, 1987. — 1v.. — *Translation of: Die Ferienmenschen. — Includes bibliography and index*

PEARCE, Douglas G.
 Tourism today : a geographical analysis / Douglas Pearce. — London : Longman, 1987. — [288]p. — *Includes bibliography and index*

WANHILL, Stephen Robert Charles
 Making tourism work / S. R. C. Wanhill. — [Guildford] : University of Surrey, 1987. — 16p

TOURIST TRADE — Environmental aspects
EDINGTON, John M.
 Ecology, recreation and tourism / John M. Edington and M. Ann Edington. — Cambridge : Cambridge University Press, 1986. — [220]p. — *Includes index*

TOURIST TRADE — Political aspects
 Who from their labours rest? : conflict and practice in rural tourism / edited by Mary Bouquet and Michael Winter. — Aldershot : Avebury, c1987. — viii,158p. — *Bibliography: p157-158*

TOURIST TRADE — Social aspects
 Who from their labours rest? : conflict and practice in rural tourism / edited by Mary Bouquet and Michael Winter. — Aldershot : Avebury, c1987. — viii,158p. — *Bibliography: p157-158*

TOURIST TRADE — Statistics — Standards
 Provisional guidelines on statistics of international tourism. — New York : United Nations, 1978. — vi,52p. — (Statistical papers / United Nations, Statistical Office. Series M ; no.62) ([Document] / United Nations ; ST/ESA/STAT/SER.M/62). — *Bibliography: p25. — Sales no.: E.78.XVII.6*

TOURIST TRADE — Canada — Statistics
 Tourism and recreation: a statistical digest = Tourisme et loisirs: résumé statistique / Statistics Canada. Travel, Tourism and Recreation Section. — Ottawa : Minister of Supply and Services, Canada, 1984-. — *Annual. — Text in English and French*

TOURIST TRADE — Caribbean area
BRYDEN, John
 Tourism and development : a case study of the Commonwealth Caribbean / John M. Bryden. — London : Cambridge University Press, 1973. — xii,236p. — *Bibliographyp.222-227. — Includes index*

TOURIST TRADE — Developing countries
ENGLISH, E. Philip
 The great escape? : an examination of North-South tourism / E. Philip English. — Ottawa : North-South Institute, 1986. — ix,89p . — *Bibliography: p83-87*

HONG, Evelyne
 See the Third World while it lasts : the social and environmental impact of tourism with special reference to Malaysia / Evelyne Hong. — Penang : Consumers' Associaton of Penang, 1986. — 98p

TOURIST TRADE — England
ENGLISH TOURIST BOARD
 A study of tourism in the North West. — London : the Board, 1975. — 6,7,32 leaves. — *Report "Tourism in the North West" commissioned by the English Tourist Board on behalf of the North West Tourist Board. — Contents: The future of tourism in the North West / North West Tourist Board - The work of the North West Tourist Board / the Board - Tourism in the North West / PA Management Consultants*

TOURIST TRADE — England — Planning
INBUCON/AIC MANAGEMENT CONSULTANTS. Marketing and Business Planning Division
 Strategy for tourism : conclusions and recommendations : a report commissioned by the English Tourist Board for the South East England Tourist Board. — [London : English Tourist Board, 1974]. — iii,34p

TOURIST TRADE — England — Yorkshire
PA MANAGEMENT CONSULTANTS. Economic Studies and Market Research Division
 Tourism in Yorkshire. — London : English Tourist Board, [1973]. — 39 leaves. — *Cover title: A study of tourism in Yorkshire. — Commissioned by the English Tourist Board on behalf of the Yorkshire, Cleveland and Humberside Tourist Board*

TOURIST TRADE — European Economic Community countries
 Tourism : opinion. — Brussels : Economic and Social Committee of the European Communities, 1984. — i,59p. — *At head of title page: Economic and Social Committee of the European Communities*

TOURIST TRADE — Fiji
BRITTON, Stephen G
 Tourism and underdevelopment in Fiji / Stephen G. Britton. — Canberra, Australia ; New York, N.Y., U.S.A. : Australian National University ; Canberra : Distributed by ANU Press, 1983. — xiv, 232 p.. — (Monograph / Development Studies Centre ; no. 31). — *Bibliography: p. 219-226*

TOURIST TRADE — France
PY, Pierre
 Le tourisme : Un phénomène économique / Pierre Py. — Paris : La Documentation française, 1986. — 144p. — (Notes et études documentaires ; no.4811). — *Bibliography: p141-144*

TOURIST TRADE — Gambia — Statistics
 Tourist statistics / Central Statistics Department, Ministry of Economic Planning and Industrial Development, Gambia. — Banjul : Ministry of Economic Planning and Industrial Development, 1977/78-. — *Annual. — Title varies*

TOURIST TRADE — Great Britain
MEDLIK, S.
 Paying guests : a report on the challenge and opportunity of travel and tourism / Professor S. Medlik. — London : Confederation of British Industry, 1985. — 54p

TOURIST TRADE — Great Britain — Statistics
BRITISH TOURIST AUTHORITY. Research Department
 The British on holiday : a summary of regular surveys on holidaytaking by British adults 1951-1974. — London : the Authority, 1974. — 11p

 Overseas travel and tourism. — London : HMSO, 1973-. — (Business monitor. MQ ; 6) (Business monitor. M ; 6). — *Quarterly*

 Overseas travel and tourism. — London : HMSO, 1973-. — (Business monitor. MA ; 6) (Business monitor. M ; 6)

TOURIST TRADE — Jamaica — Statistics
 A survey on visitor expenditure in Jamaica / Ministry of Tourism, Jamaica. — Kingston : Ministry of Tourism, 1981-. — *Annual*

TOURIST TRADE — Louisiana — Henderson
ESMAN, Marjorie R
 Henderson, Louisiana : cultural adaptation in a Cajun community / by Marjorie R. Esman. — New York : Holt, Rinehart, and Winston, c1985. — xv, 137 p.. — (Case studies in cultural anthropology). — *Includes index. — Bibliography: p. 133-134*

TOURIST TRADE — Malaysia
HONG, Evelyne
 See the Third World while it lasts : the social and environmental impact of tourism with special reference to Malaysia / Evelyne Hong. — Penang : Consumers' Associaton of Penang, 1986. — 98p

TOURIST TRADE — Manitoba
MANITOBA. Business Development and Tourism Department
Annual report / Business Development and Tourism Department, Manitoba. — Winnipeg : [the Department], 1983/84-. — *Annual*

TOURIST TRADE — Pakistan
International tourism in Pakistan : a survey report. — Islamabad : Ministry of Culture and Tourism (Tourism Division), Planning, Development and Research Wing, 1985. — iii,60p

TOURIST TRADE — Pakistan — Galliat
Tourism in Murree and Galliat : a survey report. — Islamabad : Ministry of Culture and Tourism (Tourism Division), Planning, Development and Research Wing, 1985. — ix,106 leaves

TOURIST TRADE — Pakistan — Murree
Tourism in Murree and Galliat : a survey report. — Islamabad : Ministry of Culture and Tourism (Tourism Division), Planning, Development and Research Wing, 1985. — ix,106 leaves

TOURIST TRADE — Scotland
RURAL FORUM SCOTLANDRURAL FORUM
Tourism in the rural economy : a Rural Forum report. — Edinburgh ([The Gateway, North Methven St., Perth PH1 5PP]) : Rural Forum, 1984. — i,59leaves

TOURIST TRADEOFF. PUBNS. — European Economic Community countries 986
The tourism sector in the community : a study of concentration, competition and competitiveness / C. Casini ... [et al.]. — Luxembourg : Office for Official Publications of the European Communities, 1985. — 182p. — *At head of title page: Commission of the European Communities*

TOWER HAMLETS (LONDON) — Race relations
PHILLIPS, Deborah
What price equality? : a report on the allocation of GLC housing in Tower Hamlets / by Deborah Phillips. — London : Greater London Council, 1986. — 83p. — (GLC housing research and policy report ; no.9). — *Title from cover*

TOWER HAMLETS (LONDON, ENGLAND) — City planning
TOWER HAMLETS. Planning Department
Tower Hamlets borough plan, adopted 12th March, 1986. — Tower Hamlets : [the Department], 1986. — v,190,A35p. — *Cover title: Adopted borough plan*

TOWER HAMLETS (LONDON, ENGLAND) — Economic conditions
TOWER HAMLETS. Planning Department. Directorate of Development
Workers in Tower Hamlets. — Tower Hamlets : [the Directorate], 1986. — 42 leaves. — *At head of title: Planning research and information*

TOWER HAMLETS (LONDON, ENGLAND) — Population
MOKONE, Moji
A count of the Bangladeshi population in Tower Hamlets / Moji Mokone and David Wickens. — Tower Hamlets : Planning Department, 1987. — [24]p. — (Planning research and information / Tower Hamlets. Planning Department)

TOWERS, GRAHAM F.
FULLERTON, Douglas H.
Graham Towers and his times : a biography / by Douglas H. Fullerton. — Toronto : McClelland and Stewart, 1986. — 348p

TRADE ADJUSTMENT ASSISTANCE
BANKS, Gary
Economic policy and the adjustment problem / by Gary Banks and Jan Tumlir. — Aldershot : Gower for the Trade Policy Research Centre, 1986. — x,101p. — (Thames essay ; no.45). — *Bibliography: p92-97*

MCCLAM, Warren D.
Adjustment performance of open economies : some international comparisons / by W. D. McClam and P. S. Andersen. — Basle : Bank for International Settlements, 1983. — 100p. — (BIS economic papers ; no.10)

TRADE ADJUSTMENT ASSISTANCE — United States
LAWRENCE, Robert Z.
Saving free trade : a pragmatic approach / Robert Z. Lawrence and Robert E. Litan. — Washington, D.C. : Brookings Institution, 1986. — p. cm. — *Includes bibliographical references and index*

TRADE AND PROFESSIONAL ASSOCIATIONS — Europe — Directories
Directory of European industrial & trade associations = Répertoire des associations européennes dans l'industrie et le commerce = Handbuch der europäischen Verbände im Bereich der gewerblichen Wirtschaft / editor: Richard Leigh. — Edition 4. — Beckenham : CBD Research Ltd, 1986. — lvi,406p. — *A CBD Research publication. — Previous editions published with title: Directory of European Associations. Part 1*

TRADE AND PROFESSIONAL ASSOCIATIONS — Great Britain — Directories
Trade associations and professional bodies of the United Kingdom / edited by Patricia Millard. — 8th ed. (rev. and enl.). — Oxford : Pergamon, 1987. — vii,513p. — *Previous ed.: 1985*

TRADE-MARKS (INTERNATIONAL LAW)
LADAS, Stephen Pericles
Patents, trademarks, and related rights : national and international protection / Stephen P. Ladas. — Cambridge (Mass.) : Harvard U.P., 1975. — 3v

TRADE REGULATION
LOWENFELD, Andreas F.
International economic law. — New York : Matthew Bender
Vol.1: International private trade / Andreas F. Lowenfeld. — 2nd ed. — 1981. — xi,183,177,7,8p. — *Includes Documents Supplement*

LOWENFELD, Andreas F.
International economic law. — New York : Matthew Bender
Vol.2: International private investment / Andreas F. Lowenfeld. — 2nd ed. — 1982. — xi,207,355,2,12p. — *Includes Documents Supplement*

LOWENFELD, Andreas F.
International economic law. — New York : Matthew Bender
Vol.3: Trade controls for political ends / Andreas F. Lowenfeld. — 2nd ed. — 1983. — x,621,910,5,21p. — *Includes Documents Supplement*

LOWENFELD, Andreas F.
International economic law. — New York : Matthew Bender
Vol.4: The international monetary system / Andreas F. Lowenfeld. — 2nd ed. — 1984. — xvi,404,473,4,17p. — *Includes Documents Supplement*

LOWENFELD, Andreas F.
International economic law. — New York : Matthew Bender
Vol.6: Public controls on international trade / Andreas F. Lowenfeld. — 2nd ed. — 1983. — xvii,457,775,4,22p. — *Includes Documents Supplement*

TILLINGHAST, David R.
International economic law. — New York : Matthew Bender
Vol.5: Tax aspects of international transactions / David R. Tillinghast. — 2nd ed. — 1984. — xv,473,177,12,10p. — *Bibliography*

TRADE REGULATION — Congresses
Innovation and entrepreneurship in organizations : strategies for competitiveness, deregulation, and privatization / edited by Richard M. Burton and Børge Obel. — Amsterdam ; New York : Elsevier ; New York, NY, U.S.A. : Distributors for the U.S. and Canada, Elsevier Science Pub. Co., 1986. — vii, 207 p.. — *Chiefly papers presented at a seminar held at the European Institute for Advanced Studies in Management, Brussels, in May 1985. "Has been published in a special issue of Technovation, vol 5 (1986), issues 1-3.". — Includes bibliographies and index*

Mainstreams in industrial organization / edited by H.W. de Jong, W.G. Shepherd. — Dordrecht ; Boston : Kluwer Academic Publishers, 1986. — 2 v. (x, 465 p.). — (Studies in industrial organization ; 6). — *Essays and part of the discussions presented at a conference held Aug. 21-23, 1985 at the University of Amsterdam. — Bibliography: p. 463-465. — Contents: bk. 1. Theory and international aspects -- bk. 2. Policies, antitrust, deregulation, and industrial*

TRADE REGULATION — History
EKELUND, Robert B
Mercantilism as a rent-seeking society : economic regulation in historical perspective / by Robert B. Ekelund and Robert D. Tollison. — 1st ed. — College Station, Tex. : Texas A&M University Press, 1981. — xiii, 169 p.. — (Texas A & M University economics series ; no. 5). — *Includes index. — Bibliography: p. [157]-164*

TRADE REGULATION — Canada — Addresses, essays, lectures
The regulation of quality : products, services, workplaces, and the environment / edited by Donald N. Dewees. — Toronto : Butterworths, 1983. — xvi,345p. — (Studies in law and economics)

TRADE REGULATION — Great Britain
MACKIE, P. J.
The British transport industry and the European Community : a study of regulation and modal split in the long distance and international freight market / Peter J. Mackie, David Simon and Anthony E. Whiteing. — Aldershot : Gower, c1987. — xvi,184p. — (Institute for Transport Studies ; 3). — *Bibliography: p154-159. — Includes index*

UTTON, M. A.
The economics of regulating industry / M.A. Utton. — Oxford : Basil Blackwell, 1986. — [288]p. — *Includes bibliography and index*

TRADE REGULATION — India — History
MARATHE, Shared S.
Regulation and development : India's experience of controls over industry / Shared S. Marathe ; under the auspices of the Centre for Policy Research. — New Delhi ; Beverly Hills : Sage Publications, 1986. — p. cm. — *Includes index. — Bibliography: p*

TRADE REGULATION — Soviet Union
Soviet law and economy / edited by Olimpiad S. Ioffe and Mark W. Janis. — Dordrecht : Martinus Nijhoff, 1987. — xii,335p. — (Law in Eastern Europe ; no.32)

TRADE REGULATION — United States
ADAMS, Walter
The bigness complex : industry, labor, and government in the American economy / Walter Adams and James W. Brock. — 1st ed. — New York : Pantheon Books, 1986. — xiii, 426 p.. — *Includes indexes. — Bibliography: p. 381-413*

TRADE REGULATION — United States
continuation

BAIN, Joe Staten
Industrial organization : a treatise / by Joe S. Bain, P. David Qualls. — Greenwich, Conn. : JAI Press, c1987. — 2 v.. — (Monographs in organizational behavior and industrial relations ; v. 6). — *Includes bibliographies and index*

Breaking up Bell : essays on industrial organisation and regulation / [a CERA research study] ; edited by David S. Evans ; with contributions by Robert Bornholz ... [et al.]. — New York ; Oxford : North-Holland, c1983. — xiv,298p. — *Bibliography: p283-291.* — *Includes index*

Economic regulatory policies / edited by James E. Anderson. — Lexington, Mass. ; London : Lexington Books, 1976. — xiv, 215p. — (Policy studies organization series ; 10)

LEONE, Robert A
Who profits : winners, losers, and government regulation / Robert A. Leone. — New York : Basic Books, 1986. — xiii, 248 p.. — *Includes index.* — *Bibliography: p. 231-237*

POSNER, Richard A.
Economic analysis of law. — 3rd ed. — Boston : Little, Brown and Company, c1986. — xxi,666p

TRADE UNION BILL 1983-84

GREAT BRITAIN. Parliament. House of Commons. Library. Research Division
Trade Union Bill (Bill 43, 1983-84) / Celia Neald. — [London] : the Division, 1983. — 27p. — (Reference sheet ; no.83/16). — *Bibliographical references: p26-27*

TRADE-UNIONS

DENIS, Serge
Syndicats, parti des travailleurs et parti ouvrier révolutionnaire / Serge Denis. — Montreal : Presses Socialistes Internationales, 1976. — 61p. — (Documents du Groupe socialiste des travailleurs du Québec ; 1)

A framework for international trade union cooperation : main document adopted by the 11th World Trade Union Congress, Berlin, GDR, 16-22 September 1986. — Prague : World Federation of Trade Unions, 1986. — 34p

HAZLITT, Henry
The conquest of poverty / Henry Hazlitt. — Lanham : University Press of America, 1986, c1973. — p. cm. — : *Reprint. Originally published: New Rochelle, N.Y. : Arlington House, 1973.* — *Includes index*

TRADE UNIONS

Journal of labor research. — Fairfax, VA : Department of Economics, George Mason University, 1986-. — Quarterly

TRADE-UNIONS

PARKER, Mike
Inside the circle : a union guide to quality of work life / by Mike Parker. — Boston, MA : South End Press, c1985. — p. cm. — *Includes index.* — *Bibliography: p*

PLOEG, Frederick van der
Monopoly unions, investment and employment : benefits of contingent wage strategies / F. van der Ploeg. — London : Centre for Labour Economics, London School of Economics, 1987. — 18p. — (Discussion paper / London School of Economics and Political Science. Centre for Labour Economics ; no.280). — *Bibliography: p17-18*

Trade unions and the economic crisis of the 1980s / edited by William Brierley. — Aldershot : Gower, c1987. — [220]p

Union farm : a story for children and adults; illustrations by Diana John. — London : Labour Research Department, 1985. — 24p

WILLMAN, Paul
Technological change, collective bargaining, and industrial efficiency / Paul Willman. — Oxford : Clarendon, 1986. — [xvii.264]p. — *Includes index*

TRADE-UNIONS — Agricultural laborers — Patagonia (Argentina and Chile)

BAYER, Osvaldo
La Patagonia rebelde / Osvaldo Bayer. — [Buenos Aires] : Hyspamérica, c1986. — 429p. — (Biblioteca argentina de historia y política ; 1). — *Publicado originalmente en México por Nueva Imagen en 1980*

TRADE-UNIONS — Automobile industry workers — Great Britain

THORNETT, Alan
From militancy to marxism : a personal and political account of organising car workers / Alan Thornett. — London : Left View Books, 1987. — 280p

TRADE-UNIONS — Automobile industry workers — United States

ANDERSON, John
Fifty years of the U.A.W. : from sit-downs to concessions / John Anderson. — 2nd ed. — Chicago, (Ill.) : Bookmarks, 1986. — 44p

TRADE-UNIONS — Bank employees — Australia

GRIFFIN, Gerard
White collar militancy : the Australian banking and insurance unions / Gerard Griffin. — Sydney ; London : Croom Helm, 1985. — xvi,234p. — *Bibliography: p217-230*

TRADE-UNIONS — Building trades — United States

SILVER, Marc L.
Under construction : work and alienation in the building trades / Marc L. Silver. — Albany : State University of New York Press, c1986. — xi, 251 p.. — (SUNY series in the sociology of work). — *Includes indexes.* — *Bibliography: p. 229-242*

TRADE-UNIONS — Carpenters — Nova Scotia — Halifax — History

MCKAY, Ian
The craft transformed : an essay on the carpenters of Halifax, 1885-1985 / Ian McKay. — Halifax : Holdfast Press : Distributed by Formac Pub., Co., 1985. — ix, 148 p.. — "Written to mark the centenary of Local 83 of the United Brotherhood of Carpenters and Joiners of America"--P. [vii]. — *Bibliography: p. [145]-148*

TRADE-UNIONS — Communication and traffic — United States — History

SCHACHT, John N.
The making of telephone unionism, 1920-1947 / John N. Schacht. — New Brunswick, N.J. : Rutgers University Press, c1985. — p. cm. — *Includes index.* — *Bibliography: p*

TRADE-UNIONS — Directories

Trade unions of the world / edited and compiled by F. John Harper. — Harlow : Longman, c1987. — viii,503p. — (A Keesing's reference publication)

TRADE-UNIONS — Electric industry workers — France

ELECTRICITY COUNCIL. Overseas Activities Section
The trade unions in France, with particular reference to the electricity supply industry. — London : the Council, 1972. — 12leaves. — *Bibliography: leaf [12]*

TRADE-UNIONS — Fishers — Canada — History

CLEMENT, Wallace
The struggle to organize : resistance in Canada's fishery / by Wallace Clement. — Toronto, Ont. : McClelland and Stewart, c1986. — 219 p.. — *Includes index.* — *Bibliography: p. 197-209*

TRADE-UNIONS — Fishers — Newfoundland — History

INGLIS, Gordon
More than just a union : the story of the NFFAWU / Gordon Inglis. — St. John's, Nfld. : Jesperson Press, 1985. — 331 p., [8] p. of plates. — *Includes index.* — *Bibliography: p. [317]-323*

TRADE-UNIONS — Foundrymen — South Africa — History

WEBSTER, Eddie
Cast in a racial mould : labour process and trade unionism in the foundries / Eddie Webster. — Johannesburg : Ravan Press, 1985. — xv, 299 p., [6] p. of plates. — *Includes index.* — *Bibliography: p. [281]-293*

TRADE-UNIONS — Health facilities — Soviet Union

POLTORANOV, V. V.
Zdravnitsy profsoiuzov SSSR : kurorty, sanatorii, pansionaty, doma otdykha / V. V. Poltoranov, S. Ia. Slutskii ; pod redaktsiei I. I. Kozlova. — Izd. 6-e, perer. i dop.. — Moskva : Profizdat, 1986. — 700p

TRADE-UNIONS — Industrial technicians — Great Britain

SMITH, Chris
Technical workers : class, labour and trade unionism / Chris Smith. — Basingstoke : Macmillan Education, 1987. — xiv,322p. — *Bibliography: p304-313.* — *Includes index*

TRADE-UNIONS — Information services — Great Britain

O'NEILL, Patti
Information and trade unions : a report to the Commonwealth Relations Trust / by Patti O'Neill. — Ilford : Trade Union Information Group, c1986. — 13,[8]p. — *Cover title.* — *Text on inside covers*

TRADE-UNIONS — Insurance companies — Australia

GRIFFIN, Gerard
White collar militancy : the Australian banking and insurance unions / Gerard Griffin. — Sydney ; London : Croom Helm, 1985. — xvi,234p. — *Bibliography: p217-230*

TRADE UNIONS — International cooperation

MAHLEIN, Leonhard
Gewerkschaften international : im Spannungsfeld zwischen Ost und West : aus eigener Sicht / Leonhard Mahlein. — Frankfurt am Main : Nachrichten-Verlags-Gesellschaft, 1984. — 205p. — *Bibliography: p9*

TRADE-UNIONS — Law and legislation — Digests

INTERNATIONAL LABOUR OFFICE. Freedom of Association Committee
Freedom of association : digest of decisions and principles of the Freedom of Association Committee of the governing body of the ILO. — 3rd ed. — Geneva : International Labour Office, 1985. — xii, 140 [i.e. 262] p.

TRADE-UNIONS — Law and legislation — Australia

SMITH, Douglas W.
Trade union law in Australia : the legal status of Australian trade unions / Douglas W. Smith and Donald W. Rawson ; with a foreward by J. E. Isaac. — 2nd ed. — Sydney : Butterworths, 1985. — xvii,204p

TRADE-UNIONS — Law and legislation — Great Britain

Freedom and fairness : empowering people at work / edited by Ken Coates ; with contributions from Stephen Bodington...[et al.] ; foreword by John Prescott. — Nottingham : Spokesman for the Institute for Workers' Control, 1986. — 157p

TRADE UNIONS — Law and legislation — Great Britain
GREAT BRITAIN. Department of Employment
Trade union immunities. — London :
H.M.S.O., 1981. — (Cmnd. ; 8128)

TRADE-UNIONS — Law and legislation — Great Britain
GREAT BRITAIN. Department of Employment
Trade unions and their members / presented to
Parliament by the Secretary of State for
Employment and the Paymaster General ... —
London : H.M.S.O., 1987. — iii,33p. — (Cm. ; 95)

GREAT BRITAIN. Parliament. House of
Commons. Library. Research Division
Employment Bill (Bill 56 1981-82) / Celia
Nield. — [London] : the Division, 1982. —
30p. — (Reference sheet ; no.82/5). —
Bibliography: p28-30

GREAT BRITAIN. Parliament. House of
Commons. Library. Research Division
Employment Bill (Bill 97, 1979-80) / Celia
Nield. — Rev. ed. — [London] : the Division,
1980. — 53p. — (Reference sheet ; no.79/17).
— *First Published in 1979. — Includes bibliographical references*

GREAT BRITAIN. Parliament. House of
Commons. Library. Research Division
Trade Union Bill (Bill 43, 1983-84) / Celia
Neald. — [London] : the Division, 1983. —
27p. — (Reference sheet ; no.83/16). —
Bibliographical references: p26-27

Trade unions and the law in the 1980's. —
Oxford (23 Worcester Place, Oxford OX1 2JW)
: Trade Union Research Unit, 1985. — 18p. —
(Discussion paper ; no.33). — *Cover title*

TRADE-UNIONS — Law and legislation — Nigeria
UVIEGHARA, E. E
Trade union law in Nigeria / by E. E.
Uvieghara. — Benin City, Nigeria : Ethiope
Pub. Co., 1976. — xxxiii, 248 p.. — (Ethiope
law series ; no. 4). — *Includes index*

TRADE-UNIONS — Law and legislation — United States
GOULD, William B
Strikes, dispute procedures, and arbitration :
essays on labor law / William B. Gould IV. —
Westport, Conn. : Greenwood Press, c1985. —
p. cm. — (Contributions in American studies ;
no. 82). — *Includes index. — Bibliography: p*

TRADE-UNIONS — Law and legislation — United States — Congresses
The Changing law of fair representation / Jean
T. McKelvey, editor. — Ithaca, NY : ILR
Press, New York State School of Industrial and
Labor Relations, Cornell University, 1985. —
iv, 298 p.. — *Papers presented at a national conference sponsored by the Extension Division of the New York State School of Industrial and Labor Relations, Cornell University, October 20 and 21, 1983. — Includes bibliographical references and indexes*

TRADE-UNIONS — Merchant seamen — Canada — History
GREEN, Jim
Against the tide : the story of the Canadian
Seamen's Union / Jim Green. — Toronto :
Progress Books, 1986. — 324p. —
Bibliography: p297-316

TRADE-UNIONS — Merchant seamen — Pacific States — History
SCHWARTZ, Stephen
Brotherhood of the sea : a history of the
Sailors' Union of the Pacific, 1885-1985 / by
Stephen Schwartz ; foreword by Paul
Dempster, preface by John F. Henning,
introduction by Karl Kortum. — San
Francisco, CA : Sailors' Union of the Pacific ;
New Brunswick, USA : Distributed by
Transaction Books, c1986. — p. cm. —
Includes index

TRADE-UNIONS — Metal workers — Germany (West)
BAHNMÜLLER, Reinhard
Der Streik : Tarifkonflikt um
Arbeitszeitverkürzung in der Metallindustrie
1984 / Reinhard Bahnmüller. — Hamburg :
VSA-Verlag, 1985. — 204p. — *Bibliography: p202-204*

TRADE-UNIONS — Periodicals — Bibliography
TRADES UNION CONGRESS. Library
List of current trade union periodicals / Trades
Union Congress Library. — London : Trades
Union Congress Library, 1986. — 17p

TRADES UNION CONGRESS. Library
Periodicals list / Trades Union Congress
Library. — London : Trades Union Congress
Library, 1986. — 27p

TRADE-UNIONS — Postal Service — Great Britain
TERRY, Michael
Political change and union democracy : the
negotiation of internal order in the Union of
Communication Workers / Michael Terry and
Anthony Ferner. — Coventry : University of
Warwick. School of Industrial and Business
Studies. Industrial Relations Research Unit,
1986. — 23 leaves. — (Warwick papers in
industrial relations ; no.10). — *Bibliography: p23*

TRADE UNIONS — Railway workers — Germany — History
SEGLOW, Peter
Rail unions in Britain and W. Germany : a
study of their structure and policies / Peter
Seglow, Wolfgang Streeck, Pat Wallace. —
London : Policy Studies Institute, 1982. — vii,
109p. — (Policy Studies Institute ; no. 604)

TRADE UNIONS — Railway workers — Great Britain — History
SEGLOW, Peter
Rail unions in Britain and W. Germany : a
study of their structure and policies / Peter
Seglow, Wolfgang Streeck, Pat Wallace. —
London : Policy Studies Institute, 1982. — vii,
109p. — (Policy Studies Institute ; no. 604)

TRADE-UNIONS — Recognition — Elections — Law and legislation — United States
WILLIAMS, Robert E.
NLRB regulation of election conduct / by
Robert E. Williams ; with acknowledgement to
Peter A. Janus and Kenneth C. Huhn. — Rev
ed. — Philadelphia, Pa. : Industrial Research
Unit, Wharton School, University of
Pennsylvania, c1985. — xv, 539 p.. — (Labor
relations and public policy series ; no. 8). —
Includes bibliographical references and index

TRADE-UNIONS — Shipbuilding industry employees — Sweden
STRÅTH, Bo
Varvsarbetare i två varvsstäder : en historisk
studie av verkstadsklubbarna vid varven i
Göteborg och Malmö / Bo Stråth. — Göteborg
: Svenska Varv AB, [1982]. — ii,372p. —
English summary, p329-354. — Bibliography: p363-370

TRADE-UNIONS — Sugar workers — Indonesia — Java — History
INGLESON, John
In search of justice : workers and unions in
colonial Java, 1908-1926 / John Ingleson. —
Singapore ; New York : Oxford University
Press, 1986. — xiii, 342 p., [1] p. of plates. —
(Southeast Asia publications series / Asian
Studies Association of Australia ; no. 12). —
Includes index. — Bibliography: p. [327]-337

TRADE-UNIONS — Telephone workers — United States — History
SCHACHT, John N.
The making of telephone unionism, 1920-1947
/ John N. Schacht. — New Brunswick, N.J. :
Rutgers University Press, c1985. — p. cm. —
Includes index. — Bibliography: p

TRADE UNIONS — Tobacco workers — Germany — History
BUSCHAK, Willy
Von Menschen, die wie Menschen leben
wollten : die Geschichte der Gewerkschaft
Nahrung-Genuss-Gaststätten und ihrer
Vorläufer / Willy Buschak ; Vorwork: Günter
Döding. — Köln : Bund, 1985. — 645p. —
Bibliography: p634-639

TRADE-UNIONS — Transport workers — United States
CRONIN, Sean
The Transport Workers Union of America :
the Irish connection / Sean Cronin. — Dublin
: Labour History Workshop, 1984. — 22 leaves

TRADE UNIONS — Uruguay
BOTTARO, José R.
25 años de movimiento Sindical Uruguayo :
suplemento especial de Avanzada / José R.
Bottaro. — Montevideo : Acción Sindical
Uruguaya, [1985]. — 288p

TRADE-UNIONS — Africa
SÉMINAIRE PANAFRICAIN SUR LA
POLITIQUE EN MATIÈRE DE FORMATION
SYNDICALE (1972 : Lagos, Nigeria)
La formation syndicale au cours des années 70.
— Bruxelles : Confederation Internationale des
Syndicats Libres, 1972. — 69p

TRADE-UNIONS — Africa — Political activity
SIBIRI, Sieba
Syndicalisme et politique : vrais et faux
problemes / Sieba Sibiri. — [S.l.] : [s.n.],
[1970]. — 14 leaves

TRADE-UNIONS — Argentina — History
BILSKY, Edgardo J.
La F.O.R.A. y el movimiento obrero
(1900-1910) / Edgardo J. Bilsky. — Buenos
Aires : Centro Editor de América Latina. —
(Biblioteca Política Argentina ; 97). —
Bibliographic notes: p97-108
t.1. — 1985. — 108p

BILSKY, Edgardo J.
La F.O.R.A. y el movimiento obrero
(1900-1910) / Edgardo J. Bilsky. — Buenos
Aires : Centro Editor de América Latina. —
(Biblioteca Política Argentina ; 98)
t.2. — 1985. — 109-243p

TRADE-UNIONS — Argentina — History
FALCÓN, Ricardo
Los orígenes del movimiento obrero
(1857-1899) / Ricardo Falcón. — Buenos Aires
: Centro Editor de América Latina, c1984. —
129p. — (Biblioteca política argentina ; 53). —
Includes bibliographical references

TRADE-UNIONS — Argentina — History
FERNÁNDEZ, Arturo
Ideologías de los grupos dirigentes sindicales /
Arturo Fernández. — Buenos Aires : Centro
Editor de América Latina. — (Biblioteca
Política Argentina ;· 144). — *Bibliography: p141-143*
t.2: (1966-1973). — 1986. — 143p

FERNÁNDEZ, Arturo
Las prácticas sociales del sindicalismo
(1976-1982) / Arturo Fernández. — Buenos
Aires : Centro Editor de América Latina, 1985.
— 145p. — (Biblioteca Política Argentina ;
113). — *Bibliography: p143-144*

TRADE-UNIONS — Australia — History
Common cause : essays in Australian and New
Zealand labour history / edited by Eric Fry. —
Wellington ; London : Allen & Unwin, 1986.
— [xvi,210]p. — *Includes bibliography and index*

TRADE-UNIONS — Austria
The trade union situation and industrial
relations in Austria : report of an ILO mission.
— Geneva : International Labour Office, 1986.
— xiii,107p. — *Includes bibliographical references*

TRADE-UNIONS — Belgium
EUROPEAN TRADE UNION INSTITUTE
The trade union movement in Belgium. — Brussels : European Trade Union Institute, 1987. — 75p. — (Info ; 18)

TRADE UNIONS — British Columbia — History
Fighting heritage : highlights of the 1930s struggle for jobs and militant unionism in British Columbia / edited by Sean Griffin. — Vancouver : Tribune Publishing Company, [1985]. — 159p

TRADE UNIONS — Canada — History
KAPLAN, William
Everything that floats : Pat Sullivan, Hal Banks, and the Seamen's Unions of Canada / William Kaplan. — Toronto : University of Toronto Press, 1987. — xii,241p. — *Bibliography: p[227]-231*

Lectures in Canadian labour and working-class history / edited by W. J. C. Cherwinski and Gregory S. Kealey. — St. John's Newfoundland : Committee on Canadian Labour History, Department of History, Memorial University of Newfoundland, 1985. — 198p

TRADE-UNIONS — Canada — Atlantic Provinces
FORSEY, Eugene Albert
Perspectives on the Atlantic Canadian Labour Movement and the working-class experience / Eugene A. Forsey, J. Albert Richardson, Gregory S. Kealey. — New Brunswick : Centre for Canadian Studies, Mount Allison University, 1985. — 62p. — (Winthrop Pickard Bell Lectures in Maritime Studies ; 4)

TRADE UNIONS — Chile
CHILE SOLIDARITY CAMPAIGN
Chile : trade unions and the coup. — London : Chile Solidarity Campaign, 1974. — 12p

TRADE-UNIONS — China
LEE, Lai To
Trade unions in China, 1949 to the present : the organization and leadership of the All-China Federation of Trade Unions / Lee Lai To. — Singapore : Singapore University Press, National University of Singapore, c1986. — xii, 206 p.. — *Includes index. — Bibliography: p. [192]-201*

TRADE-UNIONS — China — Shanghai — Political activity — History — 20th century
HONIG, Emily
Sisters and strangers : women in the Shanghai cotton mills, 1919-1949 = [Shang-hai sha ch'ang nü kung] / Emily Honig. — Stanford, Calif. : Stanford University Press, 1986. — ix, 299 p.. — *Parallel title in Chinese characters. — Includes index. — Bibliography: p. [279]-289*

TRADE-UNIONS — Communist countries
Trade unions in communist states / edited by Alex Pravda and Blair A. Ruble. — Boston ; London : Allen & Unwin, 1986. — [250]p. — *Includes index*

TRADE-UNIONS — Czechoslovakia
NEU, Rudolf
Výstavba a činnosť orgánov ROH / Rudolf Neu, Boris Vavro. — Bratislava : Práca, 1985. — 466p. — *Bibliography: p465-[467]*

TRADE-UNIONS — Europe — History
LIEBERMAN, Sima
Labor movements and labor thought : Spain, France, Germany, and the United States / Sima Lieberman. — New York ; Eastbourne : Praeger, 1986. — ix, 288p. — *Includes bibliographies and index*

LINDER, Marc
European labor aristocracies : trade unionism, the hierarchy of skill, and the stratification of the manual working class before the First World War / Marc Linder. — Frankfurt : Campus, 1985. — 343 p.. — *Includes bibliographical references*

TRADE-UNIONS — France
ELECTRICITY COUNCIL. Overseas Activities Section
The trade unions in France, with particular reference to the electricity supply industry. — London : the Council, 1972. — 12leaves. — *Bibliography: leaf [12]*

ERBÈS-SEGUIN, Sabine
Syndicats et relations de travail dans la vie économique française / Sabine Erbès-Seguin. — Lille : Presses Universitaires de Lille, 1985. — 137p. — *Bibliography: p135-137*

TRADE-UNIONS — France — Officials and employees — Biography
PAPAYANIS, Nicholas
Alphonse Merrheim : the emergence of reformism in revolutionary syndicalism, 1871-1925 / by Nicholas Papayanis. — Dordrecht ; Lancaster : Nijhoff, 1985. — xx,184p. — (Studies in social history ; 8). — *Bibliography: p169. — Includes index*

TRADE-UNIONS — Germany — History
ABENDROTH, Wolfgang
Die Aktualität der Arbeiterbewegung : Beiträge zu ihrer Theorie und Geschichte / Wolfgang Abendroth ; herausgegeben von Joachim Perels. — Frankfurt am Main : Suhrkamp, 1985. — 225p. — *Bibliography: p225-[226]*

TRADE-UNIONS — Germany — History
DEUTSCHE GEWERKSCHAFTSKONGRESS (10 : 1919 : Nürnberg)
Zur Sozialisierungsfrage : die Arbeitgemeinschaft der industriellen und gewerklichen Arbeitgeber und Arbeitnehmer Deutschlands : Vier Referate / erstattet auf dem Zehnten Deutschen Gewerkschaftskongress zu Nürnberg. — Berlin : Verlag des "Allgemeinen Deutschen Gewerkschaftsbundes", 1919. — 68p. — *Sonderabdruck aus dem Protokoll der Verhandlungen des Zehnten Deutschen Gewerkschaftskongresses, abgehalten in der Zeit vom 30. Juni bis 5. Juli zu Nürnberg*

TRADE-UNIONS — Germany (East)
WILKE, Alfred
Die gewerkschaftlichen Revisionskommissionen : Arbeitsmaterial für die Tätigkeit der Revisionskommissionen des FDGB sowie der Industriegewerkschaften und Gewerkschaften / Alfred Wilke. — Berlin : Tribüne, [1981]. — 47p

TRADE-UNIONS — Germany (West)
ELECTRICITY COUNCIL. Overseas Activities Section
The trade unions in the Federal Republic of Germany. — London : the Council, 1972. — 10leaves. — *Bibliography: leaf [9]*

TRADE-UNIONS — Great Britain
BAIN, George Sayers
The growth of white-collar unionism / by George Sayers Bain. — Oxford : Clarendon P, 1970. — xvi,233p,fold plate. — *bibl p219-220*

BATSTONE, Eric
Unions, unemployment and innovation / Eric Batstone and Stephen Gourlay with Hugo Levie and Roy Moore. — Oxford : Blackwell, 1986. — [300]p. — *Includes bibliography and index*

FOGARTY, Michael P.
Trade Unions and British industrial development / Michael Fogarty with Douglas Brooks. — London : Policy Studies Institute, 1986. — 184p. — (Research report / Policy Studies Institute ; [no.658]). — *Bibliographical references*

HAYEK, F. A.
1980's unemployment and the unions : essays on the impotent price structure of Britain and monopoly in the labour market / F.A. Hayek. — 2nd ed / With a postscript on British trade unions and the law, From Toff Vale to Tebbit, by Charles G. Hanson. — London : Institute of Economic Affairs, 1984. — 80p. — (Hobart paper ; 87)

LABOUR RESEARCH DEPARTMENT
Bashing the unions : LRD's guide to the Green Paper. — London : LRD Publications, 1987. — 20p

LABOUR RESEARCH DEPARTMENT
Unions at work : a handbook for shop stewards and staff reps. — London : LRD Publications, 1986. — 48p

TRADE UNIONS — Great Britain
LUNDBERG, Lars-Olof
Thatcher och facket : brittisk fackföreningsrörelse under den konservativa regeringen / Lars-Olof Lundberg. — Stockholm : Tiden, 1984. — 224p. — *Bibliography: p216-218*

TRADE-UNIONS — Great Britain
ROOTS, Paul
Do companies get the trade unions they deserve? / Paul Roots. — Nottingham : Trent Polytechnic, 1984. — 57p. — *Trent Business School. Open lectures on industrial relations: the changing contours of collective bargaining*

STEPHENS, Mark
Roots of power : 150 years of British trade unions: a personal view / Mark Stephens. — Stevenage : SPA Books, 1986. — xiii,239p

TRADE-UNIONS — Great Britain
VORNEHM, Norbert
Organisation und Basis : zur Anatomie britischer Gewerkschaften / Norbert Vornehm. — Köln : Bund, 1985. — 160p. — (Schriftenreihe der Otto Brenner Stiftung ; 36). — *Dissertation, Universität Konstanz, 1984, under title "Norm und Funktion gewerkschaftlicher Basisstrukturen in Wales". — Bibliography: p153-160*

TRADE-UNIONS — Great Britain — Dictionaries
JONES, Jack, 1913-
A-Z of trade unionism and industrial relations / Jack Jones and Max Morris. — London : Sphere Books, 1986. — xii,355p

TRADE-UNIONS — Great Britain — Directories
Directory of employers' associations, trade unions, joint organisations, &c / Department of Employment. — London : H.M.S.O., 1986-. — 1v.(loose-leaf). — *Includes index*

TRADE-UNIONS — Great Britain — Elections
A Guide on workplace balloting / compiled by Theon Wilkinson. — London : Institute of Personnel Management, 1987. — [84]p. — *Prepared by the IPM National Committee on Employee Relations. — Includes bibliography*

TRADE-UNIONS — Great Britain — History
LINDER, Marc
European labor aristocracies : trade unionism, the hierarchy of skill, and the stratification of the manual working class before the First World War / Marc Linder. — Frankfurt : Campus, 1985. — 343 p.. — *Includes bibliographical references*

MARSH, Arthur
Historical directory of trade unions / Arthur Marsh and Victoria Ryan ; foreword by Lord Briggs. — Aldershot : Gower
Vol.3: Including unions in building and allied trades, transport, woodworkers and allied trades, leather workers, enginemen and tobacco workers. — c1987. — xxiii,525p. — *Bibliography: pxiii-xxiii. — Includes index*

PELLING, Henry
A history of British trade unionism / by Henry Pelling. — 3rd ed. — London : Macmillan, 1976. — xiii,326p,8leaves of plates. — *Also published: Harmondsworth : Penguin, 1976. - Previous ed.: 1972. — Bibliography: p.306-316. — Includes index*

TRADE-UNIONS — Great Britain — History *continuation*
PELLING, Henry
A history of British trade unionism / by Henry Pelling. — 4th ed. — London : Macmillan, 1987. — [336]p. — *Previous ed.: 1976.* — *Includes bibliography and index*

TRADE UNIONS — Great Britain — History — 20th century
BEAUMONT, P. B.
The decline of trade union organisation / P.B. Beaumont. — London : Croom Helm, c1987. — 206p. — *Includes index*

TRADE-UNIONS — Great Britain — Political activity
FATCHETT, Derek
Trade unions and politics in the 1980s : the 1984 act and political funds / Derek Fatchett. — London : Croom Helm, c1987. — 135p. — *Bibliography: p:131-132.* — *Includes index*

TAYLOR, Andrew, 1954-
The trade unions and the Labour Party / Andrew Taylor. — London : Croom Helm, c1987. — 320p. — *Bibliography: p298-306.* — *Includes index*

TRADE-UNIONS — Hungary
The trade union situation and industrial relations in Hungary : report of an ILO mission. — Geneva : International Labour Office, 1984. — x,100p. — *Includes bibliographical references*

TRADE-UNIONS — Iceland
MAGNÚSSON, Magnús S.
Iceland in transition : labour and socio-economic change before 1940 / Magnús S. Magnússon. — Lund : Ekonomisk-Historiska Föreningen i Lund, 1985. — 306p. — (Skrifter Utgivna av Ekonomisk-Historiska Föreningen i Lund ; Vol.45). — *Bibliography: p289-303*

TRADE-UNIONS — India
FERNANDES, Walter
Trade-unions and industrial relations in India / Walter Fernandes. — New Delhi : Indian Social Institute, 1984. — 43p. — (Monograph series / Indian Social Institute ; 20)

TRADE-UNIONS — India — History
RAMANUJAM, G.
Indian labour movement / G. Ramanujam. — New Delhi : Sterling Publishers, c1986. — xvi, 423 p.. — *Includes bibliographical references and index*

TRADE-UNIONS — India — Officials and employees
MASIHI, Edwin J
Trade union leadership in India : a sociological perspective / Edwin J. Masihi. — Delhi : Ajanta Publications : Distributors, Ajanta Books International, 1985. — xvi, 240 p.. — *Includes index.* — *Bibliography: p. [223]-233*

TRADE-UNIONS — India — Punjab — Officials and employees — Case studies
SOOD, Santosh
Trade union leadership in India : a case study / Santoosh Sood. — New Delhi : Deep & Deep, 1984. — 262p. — *Bibliography: p [249]-258*

TRADE-UNIONS — Indonesia — Java — History
INGLESON, John
In search of justice : workers and unions in colonial Java, 1908-1926 / John Ingleson. — Singapore ; New York : Oxford University Press, 1986. — xiii, 342 p., [1] p. of plates. — (Southeast Asia publications series / Asian Studies Association of Australia ; no. 12). — *Includes index.* — *Bibliography: p. [327]-337*

TRADE-UNIONS — Iran — History — 20th century
FLOOR, Willem
Labour unions, law and conditions in Iran (1900-1941) / by Willem Floor. — Durham City (South End House, South Road, Durham City, DH1 3TG) : Centre for Middle Eastern and Islamic Studies, University of Durham, c1985. — 124p. — (Occasional paper series ; no.26 (1985)). — *Bibliography: p119-124*

TRADE-UNIONS — Ireland — History
BOYD, Andrew
The rise of the Irish trade unions / Andrew Boyd. — [2nd ed]. — [S.l.] : Anvil, 1985. — 160p. — *Bibliography: p[151]-153*

TRADE-UNIONS — Louisiana — History
COOK, Bernard A
Louisiana labor from slavery to "right-to-work" / Bernard A. Cook, James R. Watson. — Lanham : University Press of America, c1985. — p. cm

TRADE UNIONS — Netherlands
VERBEEK, Herman
Cees Schelling van de Voedingsbond / Herman Verbeek. — Groningen : Xeno, 1984. — 256p

TRADE-UNIONS — New Zealand — Directories
Trade union directory / New Zealand Federation of Labour. — Wellington : Zew Zealand Federation of Labour, 1986-. — *Annual*

TRADE-UNIONS — New Zealand — History
Common cause : essays in Australian and New Zealand labour history / edited by Eric Fry. — Wellington ; London : Allen & Unwin, 1986. — [xvi,210]p. — *Includes bibliography and index*

TRADE-UNIONS — Newfoundland — History
GILLESPIE, Bill
A class act : an illustrated history of the labour movement in Newfoundland and Labrador / Bill Gillespie. — St. John's, Newfoundland : The Newfoundland Federation and Labrador Federation of Labour, 1986. — 148p. — *Bibliography: p141-148*

TRADE-UNIONS — Norway
EUROPEAN TRADE UNION INSTITUTE
The trade union movement in Norway. — Brussels : European Trade Union Institute, 1987. — 57p. — (Info ; 19)

The trade union situation and industrial relations in Norway : report of an ILO mission. — Geneva : International Labour Office, 1984. — x,90p. — *Includes bibliographical references*

TRADE-UNIONS — Poland — Biography
CRAIG, Mary, 1928-
The crystal spirit : Lech Walesa and his Poland / Mary Craig. — London : Hodder and Stoughton, 1986. — [384p]

TRADE-UNIONS — Poland — History
Ruch zawodowy w Polsce : zarys dziejów / pod redakcją Stanisława Kalabińskiego. — Warszawa : Instytut Wydawniczy CRZZ
T.2: 1918-1944
Cz.1: Do 1929 / opracowali Lucjan Kieszczyński, Maria Korniluk. — 1980. — 502p. — *Bibliography: p445-[455]*

TRADE-UNIONS — Russian S.F.S.R. — Moscow
IONOV, I. N.
Profsoiuzy rabochikh Moskvy v revoliutsii 1905-1907 gg. / I. N. Ionov; otv. redaktor A. M. Sinitsyn. — Moskva : Nauka, 1986. — 166p

TRADE-UNIONS — Scotland
TUCKETT, Angela
The Scottish Trades Union Congress : the first 80 years, 1897-1977 / Angela Tuckett. — Edinburgh : Mainstream Publishing in conjunction with the Scottish Trades Union Congress, 1986. — 444p

TRADE-UNIONS — Scotland — History
MACDOUGALL, Ian
Labour in Scotland : a pictorial history from the eighteenth century to the present / Ian MacDougall. — Edinburgh : Mainstream, 1985. — 270p. — *Bibliography: p[271]*

TRADE-UNIONS — Senegal — Political activity
UNION PROGRESSISTE SÉNÉGALAISE
Syndicalisme et politique. — [S.l.] : Union Progressiste Sénégalaise, 1973. — 20p

TRADE-UNIONS — South Africa — Biography
BAARD, Frances
My spirit is not banned : as told by Frances Baard to Barbie Schreiner. — Harare : Zimbabwe Publishing House, 1986. — 92p

TRADE-UNIONS — South Africa — History
WEBSTER, Eddie
Cast in a racial mould : labour process and trade unionism in the foundries / Eddie Webster. — Johannesburg : Ravan Press, 1985. — xv, 299 p., [6] p. of plates. — *Includes index.* — *Bibliography: p. [281]-293*

TRADE-UNIONS — South America — History
BERGQUIST, Charles W
Labor in Latin America : comparative essays on Chile, Argentina, Venezuela, and Colombia / Charles Bergquist. — Stanford, Calif. : Stanford University Press, 1986. — xiv, 397p. — *Includes index.* — *Includes bibliographical references*

TRADE-UNIONS — Soviet Union
Soviet policies on labour productivity and trade unions : a report based on Russian publications. — London : Labour Information Office, United States Information Service, [1958?]. — 5p

TRADE UNIONS — Spain
EUROPEAN TRADE UNION INSTITUTE
The trade union movement in Spain. — Brussels : European Trade Union Institute, 1986. — 68p. — (Info ; 17)

TRADE-UNIONS — Spain
Que es la C.N.T.?. — Barcelona : Federacion Local de Barcelona, 1977. — 9p

The trade union situation and industrial relations in Spain : report of an ILO mission. — Geneva : International Labour Office, 1985. — xiii,138p. — *Includes bibliographical references*

TRADE-UNIONS — Spain — History
ROSAL, Amaro del
1934 : Movimiento Revolucionario de Octubre / Amaro del Rosal. — [Madrid] : Akal, c1984. — xiii,313p. — (España sin espejo ; 1). — *Bibliography: p313*

TRADE-UNIONS — Spain — History — Sources
UNION GENERAL DE TRABAJADORES DE ESPAÑA
Actas de la Unión General de Trabajadores de España / [notas de introducción por Amaro del Rosal Días]. — Madrid : Fundación Pablo Iglesias
Vol.2: 1899-1904. — 1985. — 687p

UNION GENERAL DE TRABAJADORES DE ESPAÑA
Actas de la Unión General de Trabajadores de España / [brevas notas de introducción por Amaro del Rosal Días]. — Madrid : Fundación Pablo Iglesias
Vol.4: 1910-1913. — 1985. — 492p

TRADE-UNIONS — Spain — Political activity
MARTÍN VILLA, Rodolfo
Al servicio del Estado / Rodolfo Martín Villa. — Barcelona : Editorial Planeta, 1984. — 229p

TRADE-UNIONS — Spain — Asturias — History
Octubre 1934 : cincuenta años para la reflexión / [por] G. Jackson ... [et al.]. — Madrid : Siglo Veintiuno, 1985. — viii,344p. — 'En la edición de la presente obra ha colaborado la Fundación José Barreiro, de Oviedo' — half-title. — Bibliography: p.[320]-344

TRADE-UNIONS — Spain — Asturias — Political activity — History
Octubre 1934 : cincuenta años para la reflexión / [por] G. Jackson ... [et al.]. — Madrid : Siglo Veintiuno, 1985. — viii,344p. — 'En la edición de la presente obra ha colaborado la Fundación José Barreiro, de Oviedo' — half-title. — Bibliography: p.[320]-344

TRADE-UNIONS — Spain — Cantabria — History
ARGOS VILLAR, José Carlos
El movimiento obrero en Cantabria (1955-1977) / José Carlos Argos Villar, José Emilio Gómez Díaz ; prólogo de J. R. Saiz Viadero. — Santander : Puntal Libros, [1982]. — 227p

TRADE-UNIONS — Spain — Cantabria — History — 20th century
ARGOS VILLAR, José Carlos
El movimiento obrero en Cantabria (1955-1977) / José Carlos Argos Villar, José Emilio Gómez Díaz ; prólogo de J.R. Saiz Viadero. — [Santander?] : J.E. Gómez Díaz, [1982?]. — 227 p.. — (Puntal libros)

TRADE-UNIONS — Spain — Madrid — History — 20th century
JULIÁ DÍAZ, Santos
Madrid, 1931-1934 : de la fiesta popular a la lucha de clases / por Santos Juliá Díaz. — Madrid : Siglo Veintiuno, 1984. — 509p

TRADE-UNIONS — Sweden
NORDIN, Rune
Den svenska arbetarrörelsen : idé, organisation och historia i sammandrag / Rune Nordin. — 3e. rev. uppl.. — Stockholm : Tiden, 1983. — 167p

TRADE-UNIONS — Sweden — History
NORDIN, Rune
Den svenska arbetarrörelsen : idé, organisation och historia i sammandrag / Rune Nordin. — 3e. rev. uppl.. — Stockholm : Tiden, 1983. — 167p

TRADE-UNIONS — Turkey
Defence of Abdullah Bastürk : trade unionism on trial in Turkey. — [s.l.] : Public Services International, 1981. — 199p

TRADE-UNIONS — United States — Bibliography
MILES, Dione
Something in common : an IWW bibliography / compiled by Dione Miles. — Detroit : Wayne State University Press, 1986. — 560 p.. — On cover: Archives of Labor and Urban Affairs, Walter P. Reuther Library, Wayne State University. — Includes index

TRADE-UNIONS — United States — Biography
HANSEN, Beatrice
A political biography of Walter Reuther : the record of an opportunist / Beatrice Hausen. "Meany vs Reuther" / Farrell Dobbs. — New York : Pathfinder Press, 1987. — 27p

TRADE-UNIONS — United States — History
LIEBERMAN, Sima
Labor movements and labor thought : Spain, France, Germany, and the United States / Sima Lieberman. — New York ; Eastbourne : Praeger, 1986. — ix, 288p. — Includes bibliographies and index

STEPHENSON, Charles
Life and labor : dimensions of American working-class history / by Charles Stephenson and Robert Asher. — Albany : State University of New York Press, c1986. — p. cm. — (American labor history series). — Includes index

TRADE-UNIONS — United States — History — Sources
The Samuel Gompers papers / editor, Stuart B. Kaufman. — Urbana, Ill. : University of Illinois Press
volume 1: The making of a union leader, 1850-86. — 1986. — xxxvi,529p

TRADE-UNIONS — United States — History — 20th century
ZIEGER, Robert H
American workers, American unions, 1920-1985 / Robert H. Zieger. — Baltimore : Johns Hopkins University Press, c1986. — xii, 233 p.. — (The American moment). — Includes index. — Bibliography: p. [201]-220

TRADE-UNIONS — United States — Organizing — History
SUGGS, George G.
Union busting in the Tri-State : the Oklahoma, Kansas, and Missouri metal workers' strike of 1935 / by George G. Suggs, Jr. — Norman : University of Oklahoma Press, c1986. — xiv, 282 p.. — Includes index. — Bibliography: p. [231]-260

TRADE-UNIONS — United States — Political activity
MINK, Gwendolyn
Old labor and new immigrants in American political development : union, party, and state, 1875-1920 / Gwendolyn Mink. — Ithaca, N.Y. : Cornell University Press, 1986. — p. cm. — Includes index. — Bibliography: p

VALE, Vivian
Labour in American politics / Vivian Vale. — London : Routledge and K. Paul, 1971. — [6],172p. — Originally published, New York: Barnes & Noble, 1971. — bibl p161-166

TRADE-UNIONS — West Bank
TAGGART, Simon
Workers in struggle : Palestinian trade unions in the occupied West Bank / Simon Taggart. — London : Editpride, 1985. — 79p

TRADE-UNIONS — Yugoslavia
The trade union situation and industrial relations in Yugoslavia. — Geneva : International Labour Office, 1985. — xii,104p. — Includes bibliographical references

TRADE-UNIONS AND COMMUNISM
Trade unions in communist states / edited by Alex Pravda and Blair A. Ruble. — Boston ; London : Allen & Unwin, 1986. — [250]p. — Includes index

TRADE-UNIONS AND MASS MEDIA — United States — History
DOUGLAS, Sara U
Labor's new voice : unions and the mass media / by Sara U. Douglas. — Norwood, N.J. : Ablex, 1986. — p. cm. — (Communication and information science). — Includes index. — Bibliography: p

TRADE-UNIONS AND YOUTH — Germany — History
BRÜLLS, Klaus
Neubeginn oder Wiederaufbau? : Gewerkschaftsjugend in der britischen Zone 1945-1950 / Klaus Brülls. — Marburg : Verlag Arbeiterbewegung und Gesellschaftswissenschaft, 1985. — 384p. — (Schriftenreihe der Studiengesellschaft für Sozialgeschichte und Arbeiterbewegung ; Bd.52). — Bibliography: p349-384

TRADE-UNIONS, BLACK — South Africa
MCSHANE, Denis
Power! : black workers, their unions and the struggle for freedom in South Africa / Denis MacShane, Martin Plant, David Ward. — Nottingham : Spokesman, 1984. — 195p

TRADE-UNIONS, BLACK — South Africa — Biography
TOM, Petrus
My life struggle : the story of Petrus Tom. — Braamfontein, South Africa : Ravan Press, 1985. — 68 p., [1] leaf of plates. — (Ravan worker series)

TRADE-UNIONS, BLACK — South Africa — History
WEBSTER, Eddie
Cast in a racial mould : labour process and trade unionism in the foundries / Eddie Webster. — Johannesburg : Ravan Press, 1985. — xv, 299 p., [6] p. of plates. — Includes index. — Bibliography: p. [281]-293

TRADE-UNIONS, CATHOLIC — Spain
DOMINGUEZ, Javier
Organizaciones obreras cristianas en la oposición al franquismo (1951-1975) : (con 65 documentos clandestinos e inéditos) / Javier Dominquez. — Bilbao : Mensajero, 1985. — 479p

TRADEMARKS — Great Britain
KERLY, Sir Duncan M.
Kerly's law of trade marks and trade names. — 12th ed / by T.A. Blanco White and Robin Jacob. — London : Sweet & Maxwell, 1986. — [830]p. — Previous ed.: 1983. — Includes index

TRADES UNION CONGRESS
TUC-LABOUR PARTY LIAISON COMMITTEE
Low pay : policies and priorities. — London : TUC : Labour Party, 1986. — 26p. — (Jobs and industry)

TUC-LABOUR PARTY LIAISON COMMITTEE
People at work : new rights, new responsibilities. — London : TUC : Labour Party, 1986. — 22p. — (Jobs and industry)

TRADES UNION CONGRESS — Decision making
WOLFE, Joel D
Workers, participation, and democracy : internal politics in the British union movement / Joel D. Wolfe. — Westport, Conn. ; London : Greenwood Press, c1985. — xii, 258p. — (Contributions in political science ; no. 136). — Includes index. — Bibliography: p.[219]-243

TRADES-UNIONS — Economic aspects
CARRUTH, Alan
On union preferences and labour market models : insiders and outsiders / A. A. Carruth [and] A. J. Oswald. — London : Centre for Labour Economics, London School of Economics, 1986. — 30p. — (Discussion paper / London School of Economics and Political Science. Centre for Labour Economics ; no.256)

KIDD, D. P.
A dynamic model of trade union behaviour / D. P. Kidd and A. J. Oswald. — London : Centre for Labour Economics, London School of Economics, 1986. — 25p. — (Discussion paper / London School of Economics and Political Science. Centre for Labour Economics ; no.259). — Bibliography: p24-25

OSWALD, A. J.
New research on the economics of trade unions and labour contracts / A. Oswald. — London : Centre for Labour Economics, London School of Economics, 1986. — 34p. — (Discussion paper / London School of Economics and Political Science. Centre for Labour Economics ; no.261). — Bibliography: p20-34

TRADES-UNIONS — Public utilities
Info / Public Services International. — Ferney-Voltair : Public Services International, 1985-. — Monthly

TRADING COMPANIES
CHO, Tong-sŏng
The general trading company : concept and strategy / Dong-Sung Cho. — Lexington, Mass. : Lexington Books, c1987. — xv, 159 p.. — *Includes index. — Bibliography: p. [149]-155*

TRADING COMPANIES — Developing countries
State trading and development : a perspective view of state trading organizations in developing countries as instruments of national development and channels of international cooperation / edited by Praxy Fernandes. — Ljubljana, Yugoslavia : International Center for Public Enterprises in Developing Countries, 1982. — 277p. — *Includes bibliographical references*

TRAFFIC ACCIDENTS — Great Britain — Congresses
Roads to safety : a Conference on Road Safety, 13-14 June 1978, London, Department of Transport. — [London : Department of Transport, 1978]. — 48p

TRAFFIC CONGESTION — Great Britain
TANNER, J. C.
A theoretical study of the possible use of tolls to relieve traffic congestion in urban areas / by J. C. Tanner. — London : Road Research Laboratory, Department of Scientific and Industrial Research, 1960. — 4,iip. — (Research note ; No.RN/3819/JCT). — *Bibliographical references: p4*

TRAFFIC ENGINEERING — England — Reading (Berkshire)
GREAT BRITAIN. Traffic Advisory Unit
Comprehensive traffic management in Reading. — London : the Unit, 1972. — [32]leaves. — (Report ; no.11)

TRAFFIC ENGINEERING — Great Britain — Congresses
BEESLEY, M. E
Influence of measures designed to restrict the use of certain transport modes / [M.E. Beesley]. — Paris : European Conference of Ministers of Transport, 1979. — 59p. — *At head of title: Economic Research Centre. — Subtitle: Report of the forty-second Round Table on Transport Economics, held in Paris on 9th-10th November 1978. — Includes bibliographical references*

TRAFFIC ESTIMATION — Great Britain — Mathematical models
HASKEY, J. C.
A general investigation into the efficacy of trip distribution models / J. C. Haskey. — [London] : Mathematical Advisory Unit, Department of the Environment, 1973. — [76] leaves. — *MAU-N-244*

TRAFFIC FLOW — Sweden — Stockholm
STOCKHOLMS LÄNS LANDSTING. Trafiknämnden
Trafikundersökningar i Stockholmsregionen hösten 1971. — [Stockholm : the Landsting]. — *Cover part-title: Vardagsresandet i Stockholmsregionen*
Resultatrapport nr. 1: Befolkningen, arbetsplatserna större centra, transportapparaten : vardagsresandet. — [1983?]. — 140p

STOCKHOLMS LÄNS LANDSTING. Trafiknämnden
Trafikundersökningar i Stockholmsregionen hösten 1971. — [Stockholm : the Landsting] Resultatrapport nr. 2: Hushållens tid, sysslor, förflyttningar: vardag, lördag, söndag. — [1974?]. — 125p

STOCKHOLMS LÄNS LANDSTING. Trafiknämnden
Trafikundersökningar i Stockholmsregionen hösten 1971. — [Stockholm : the Landsting] Rapport nr.3: TU 71:s uppläggning, redovisning, användning en bruksanvisning. — [1974?]. — Various pagination

TRAFFIC REGULATIONS
ADAMS, John, 1938 Aug.13-
Risk and freedom : the record of road safety regulation / John G. U. Adams. — cardiff : Transport Publishing Projects, 1985. — ix, 202p

TRAFFIC REGULATIONS — Great Britain
GREAT BRITAIN. Department of the Environment
Control of Heavy commercial vehicles : legal powers. — [London] : the Department, [1975]. — 5p. — (Lorry plans advice note)

TRAFFIC SAFETY
ADAMS, John, 1938 Aug.13-
Risk and freedom : the record of road safety regulation / John G. U. Adams. — cardiff : Transport Publishing Projects, 1985. — ix, 202p

TRAFFIC SAFETY — Canada
Road safety annual report = rapport annuel sécurité routière / Road Safety and Motor Vehicle Regulation Directorate. — Ottawa : Transport Canada, 1984-. — Annual. — *Text in English and French*

TRAFFIC SAFETY — Europe — Congresses
ROUND TABLE ON TRANSPORT ECONOMICS ((53rd : 1980 : Paris, France)
The working conditions of professional drivers : effects on productivity and road safety : report of the fifty-third Round Table on Transport Economics held in Paris on 11th-12th December 1980 ... / M.G. Gutmann. — Paris : Economic Research Centre, European Conference of Ministers of Transport, 1981. — 59p. — *Bibliography: p37*

TRAFFIC SAFETY — Great Britain
GREAT BRITAIN. Department of the Environment
Control of heavy commercial vehicles : the environmental and road safety effects of lorry plans. — [London] : the Department, [1975]. — [8]p. — (Lorry plans advice note). — *Bibliographical references: p[8]*

TRAFFIC SIGNS AND SIGNALS — Great Britain
GREAT BRITAIN. Department of the Environment
Control of heavy commercial vehicles : signs. — [London] : the Department, [1975]. — 5p. — (Lorry plans advice note)

TRAFFIC SURVEYS — England
GREAT BRITAIN. Traffic Advisory Unit
Urban congestion study 1976 : interim report (thirteen towns and cities in England, excluding London). — London : the Unit, 1978. — 15,[14]leaves

TRAFFIC SURVEYS — England — London
GREATER LONDON COUNCIL. Transportation and Development Department
Company assisted motoring in London. — [London] : the Council, 1985. — 1v. (various pagings). — (Reviews and studies series / Greater London Council ; no.27)

Traffic monitoring review (1981) / data collected and processed by members of the Survey Services Group of the Greater London Council Intelligence Unit and report written by Peter Munt. — [London] : Greater London Council, 1981. — 61p. — (Statistical series / Greater London Council ; no.4)

Traffic monitoring review (1985) / data collected and processed by members of the Traffic Survey and Traffic Monitoring Sections of the Greater London Council Intelligence Unit and report written by Peter Munt. — [London] : Greater London Council, 1985. — 109p. — (Statistical series / Greater London Council ; no.41)

Traffic monitoring review (1986) / data collected and processed by members of the Traffic Survey and Traffic Monitoring Sections of the Greater London Council Intelligence Unit and report written by Peter Munt. — [London] : Greater London Council, 1986. — 100p. — (Statistical series / Greater London Council ; no.53)

TRAFFIC SURVEYS — Great Britain — Methodology
GREAT BRITAIN. Department of the Environment
Control of heavy commercial vehicles : survey techniques for lorry plans. — [London] : the Department, [1975]. — 8p. — (Lorry plans advice note)

TRAFFIC SURVEYS — Sweden — Stockholm
STOCKHOLMS LÄNS LANDSTING. Trafiknämnden
Trafikundersökningar i Stockholmsregionen hösten 1971. — [Stockholm : the Landsting]. — *Cover part-title: Vardagsresandet i Stockholmsregionen*
Resultatrapport nr. 1: Befolkningen, arbetsplatserna större centra, transportapparaten : vardagsresandet. — [1983?]. — 140p

STOCKHOLMS LÄNS LANDSTING. Trafiknämnden
Trafikundersökningar i Stockholmsregionen hösten 1971. — [Stockholm : the Landsting] Resultatrapport nr. 2: Hushållens tid, sysslor, förflyttningar: vardag, lördag, söndag. — [1974?]. — 125p

STOCKHOLMS LÄNS LANDSTING. Trafiknämnden
Trafikundersökningar i Stockholmsregionen hösten 1971. — [Stockholm : the Landsting] Rapport nr.3: TU 71:s uppläggning, redovisning, användning en bruksanvisning. — [1974?]. — Various pagination

TRANQUILIZING DRUGS
Tranquillisers : social, psychological, and clinical perspectives / edited by Jonathan Gabe and Paul Williams ; forewords by Michael Shepherd and Margot Jefferys. — London : Tavistock, 1986. — xv,311p. — *Includes bibliographies and index*

TRANSACTION COSTS — Mathematical models
LEAPE, Jonathan
Taxes and transaction costs in asset market equilibrium / Jonathan Leape. — Rev. ed. — [London : London School of Economics and Political Science], 1986. — 34p. — (Taxation, incentives and the distribution of income ; no.97). — *Economic and Social Research Council programme. — Bibliographical references: p33-34*

TRANSFER OF TRAINING
ANNETT, John
Transfer of learning and training : basic issues, policy implications, how to promote transfer / John Annett, John Sparrow. — [Sheffield] : Manpower Services Commission, [1985]. — 13p. — (Research & development ; no.23). — *Bibliography: p13*

TRANSFER PAYMENTS — Organisation for Economic Co-operation and Development countries — Data processing
VARLEY, Rita
The government household transfer data base : 1960-1984 / by Rita Varley. — Paris : OECD, 1986. — ii,48p. — (Working papers / OECD Department of Economics and Statistics ; no.36). — *Bibliographical references: p7*

TRANSFER PAYMENTS — Organisation for Economic Co-operation and Development countries — Statistics
VARLEY, Rita
The government household transfer data base : 1960-1984 / by Rita Varley. — Paris : OECD, 1986. — ii,48p. — (Working papers / OECD Department of Economics and Statistics ; no.36). — *Bibliographical references: p7*

TRANSFER PAYMENTS — Québec (Province)
White paper on the personal tax and transfer systems / [prepared by the Ministère des finances ; edited by the Direction générale de publications gouvernementales]. — Québec : Le Ministere, 1984. — 380p. — *Cover title.* — *Inclues index.* — *Includes index*

TRANSFER PRICING
ECCLES, Robert G.
The transfer pricing problem : a theory for practice / Robert G. Eccles. — Lexington, Mass. : Lexington Books ; [Aldershot] : Gower [distributor], c1985. — xviii,342p. — *Bibliography: p325-332.* — *Includes index*

TRANSFERENCE (PSYCHOLOGY)
FREUD, Sigmund
[Übersicht der Übertragungsneurosen. English]. A phylogenetic fantasy : overview of the transference neuroses / Sigmund Freud ; edited and with an essay by Ilse Grubrich-Simitis ; translated by Axel Hoffer and Peter T. Hoffer. — Cambridge, Mass. : Belknap Press of Harvard University Press, 1987. — p. cm. — *Translation of: Übersicht der Übertragungsneurosen.* — *Bibliography: p*

TRANSIENTS, RELIEF OF — Government policy — United States
CROUSE, Joan M.
The homeless transient in the Great Depression : New York State, 1929-1941 / Joan M. Crouse. — Albany, N.Y. : State University of New York Press, c1986. — xii, 319 p., [8] p. of plates. — : *Revision of thesis (doctoral)--State University of New York at Buffalo.* — *Includes index.* — *Bibliography: p. 296-306*

TRANSIENTS, RELIEF OF — New York (State) — History — 20th century
CROUSE, Joan M.
The homeless transient in the Great Depression : New York State, 1929-1941 / Joan M. Crouse. — Albany, N.Y. : State University of New York Press, c1986. — xii, 319 p., [8] p. of plates. — : *Revision of thesis (doctoral)--State University of New York at Buffalo.* — *Includes index.* — *Bibliography: p. 296-306*

TRANSIT, INTERNATIONAL — Europe — Congresses
ROUND TABLE ON TRANSPORT ECONOMICS (45th : 1979 : Paris)
Infrastructural capacity problems raised by international transit : report of the Forty-fifth Round Table on Transport Economics held in Paris on 8th and 9th February. 1979. — Paris : European Conference of Ministers of Transport, 1979. — 135p. — *At head of title: Economic Research Centre.* — *Includes bibliographical references*

TRANSIT, INTERNATIONAL — Great Britain
MACKIE, P. J.
The British transport industry and the European Community : a study of regulation and modal split in the long distance and international freight market / Peter J. Mackie, David Simon and Anthony E. Whiteing. — Aldershot : Gower, c1987. — xvi,184p. — (Institute for Transport Studies ; 3). — *Bibliography: p154-159.* — *Includes index*

TRANSKEI — History
BLONDEL, Alain
The parrot's egg / Alain Blondel and Shena Lamb ; photographs by Ali Hashemian. — Johannesburg : Ravan Press, 1985. — 159p. — *Bibliography: p158-159*

TRANSKEI — Politics and government
BEINART, William
Hidden struggles in rural South Africa : politics & popular movements in the Transkei & Eastern Cape 1890-1930 / William Beinart, Colin Bundy. — London : Currey, 1987. — xxvi,326p. — *Includes index*

TRANSKEI — Social conditions
BLONDEL, Alain
The parrot's egg / Alain Blondel and Shena Lamb ; photographs by Ali Hashemian. — Johannesburg : Ravan Press, 1985. — 159p. — *Bibliography: p158-159*

TRANSLATING AND INTERPRETING
KIRK, Robert, 19---
Translation determined / Robert Kirk. — Oxford : Clarendon, 1986. — [236]p. — *Includes bibliography and index*

TRANSLATION OF: DEL BUEN SALVAJE AL BUEN REVOLUCIONARIO
RANGEL, Carlos
[Del buen salvaje al buen revolucionario. English]. The Latin Americans : their love-hate relationship with the United States / Carlos Rangel. — Rev. ed. with a new introduction by the author. — New Brunswick, N.J. (U.S.A.) : Transaction Books, c1987. — p. cm. — *Includes bibliographical references and index*

TRANSPLANTATION OF ORGANS, TISSUES, ETC — Law and legislation
COWEN, Zelman
Reflections on medicine, biotechnology, and the law / Sir Zelman Cowen. — [Lincoln, NE] : University of Nebraska College of Law : Distributed by the University of Nebraska Press, 1986, c1985. — p. cm. — *"Eleventh in the series of Roscoe Pound lectures at the University of Nebraska College of Law"--Foreword*

TRANSPORT ACT 1978
GREAT BRITAIN. Welsh Office
Transport Act 1978 : public transport planning in non-metropolitan counties. — Cardiff : the Office, 1978. — 10p. — (Circular ; no.78/115)

TRANSPORT, AUTOMOTIVE — Law and legislation — Great Britain
OPEN TECH TRANSPORT PROJECT
Your guide to the 1985 Transport Act / Open Tech Transport Project. — London : Transport Publishing Projects, 1986. — xviii,130p

TRANSPORT BILL 1980-81
GREAT BRITAIN. Parliament. House of Commons. Library. Research Division
The Transport Bill 1980-81 / C. R. Barclay. — [London] : the Division, 1981. — 21p. — (Reference sheet ; no.81/1). — *Bibliography: p20-21*

TRANSPORT BILL 1981-82
GREAT BRITAIN. Parliament. House of Commons. Library. Research Division
Transport Bill (Bill 57 of 1981-82) / [Priscilla Baines]. — [London] : the Division, 1982. — 11p. — (Reference sheet ; no.82/6)

TRANSPORT BILL 1982-83
GREAT BRITAIN. Parliament. House of Commons. Library. Research Division
Transport Bill (Bill 5 of 1982-83) / Priscilla Baines. — [London] : the Division, 1982. — 14p. — (Reference sheet ; no.82/11). — *Includes bibliographical references*

TRANSPORT BILL 1984-85
GREAT BRITAIN. Parliament. House of Commons. Library. Research Division
Transport Bill, Bill 68 of 1984-85 / Priscilla Baines. — [London] : the Division, 1985. — 34p. — (Reference sheet ; no.85/4). — *Includes bibliographical references*

TRANSPORTATION — Statistics — European Economic Community countries
Carriage of goods by inland waterways. — Luxembourg : Office for Official Publications of the European Communities, 1985. — *Text in Community languages* 1983. — xxx,170p

TRANSPORTATION
Analytical studies in transport economics / edited by Andrew F. Daughety. — Cambridge : Cambridge University Press, 1985. — viii,253p. — *Includes bibliographies and index*

ROUND TABLE ON TRANSPORT ECONOMICS (43rd : 1978 : Paris)
Indicators for evaluating transport output : report of the forty-third Round Table on Transport Economics : held in Paris on 23rd and 24th November 1978. — Paris : European Conference of Ministers of Transport, 1979. — 78p. — *Includes bibliographical references*

TARSKI, Ignacy
[Czynnik czasu w procesie transportowym. English]. The time factor in transportation processes / Ignacy Tarski ; [translated by Olgierd Wojtasiewicz]. — Amsterdam ; New York : Elsevier ; Warszawa : Wydawnictwa Komunikacji i Łączności, 1987. — viii, 259 p.. — (Developments in civil engineering ; 15). — *Translation of: Czynnik czasu w procesie transportowym.* — *Includes index.* — *Includes bibliographies*

TRANSPORTATION — Bibliography
Catalogue of studies in the field of transport, 1985 / Department of International Economic and Social Affairs. — New York : United Nations, 1985. — 125p. — *"United Nations publication no. E.85.II.10"--T.p. verso.* — *Includes indexes*

TRANSPORTATION — Congresses
Transportation and mobility in an era of transition / editors, Gijsbertus R.M. Jansen, Peter Nijkamp, Cees J. Ruijgrok. — Amsterdam ; New York : North-Holland ; New York, N.Y., U.S.A. : Sole distributors for the U.S.A. and Canada, Elsevier Science Pub. Co., 1985. — p. cm. — (Studies in regional science and urban economics ; v. 13)

TRANSPORTATION — Cost effectiveness
ADLER, Hans A.
Economic appraisal of transport projects : a manual with case studies. — Rev. ed. — Baltimore : Johns Hopkins University Press for the World Bank, 1987. — xii,235p. — (EDI series in economic development). — *Bibliography: p208-230*

TRANSPORTATION — Cost effectiveness — Case studies
ADLER, Hans A.
Economic appraisal of transport projects : a manual with case studies. — Rev. ed. — Baltimore : Johns Hopkins University Press for the World Bank, 1987. — xii,235p. — (EDI series in economic development). — *Bibliography: p208-230*

TRANSPORTATION — Dictionaries — Polyglot
LOGIE, Gordon
Glossary of transport : English, French, Italian, Dutch, German, Swedish / Gordon Logie. — Amsterdam ; New York : Elsevier Scientific Pub. Co. ; New York : distributors for the U.S. and Canada, Elsevier/North-Holland, 1980. — xxvii, 296 p.. — (International planning glossaries ; 2)

TRANSPORTATION — History
VANCE, James E
Capturing the horizon : the historical geography of transportation since the transportation revolution of the sixteenth century / James E. Vance, Jr. — New York : Harper & Row, c1986. — xv, 656 p.. — *Includes bibliographies and index*

TRANSPORTATION — Law and legislation — Great Britain
GREAT BRITAIN. Parliament. House of Commons. Library. Research Division
The Transport Bill 1980-81 / C. R. Barclay. — [London] : the Division, 1981. — 21p. — (Reference sheet ; no.81/1). — *Bibliography: p20-21*

TRANSPORTATION — Management
Managing transport systems : a cybernetic perspective / edited by Paul Keys and Michael C. Jackson. — Aldershop : Gower, c1985 (1987 [printing]). — xi,191p. — *Conference proceedings.* — *Includes index*

TRANSPORTATION — Mathematical models

MOSLER, Karl C.
Continuous location of transportation networks / K. C. Mosler. — Berlin ; London : Sringer-Verlag, 1987. — 158p. — *Bibliography: p143-153*

TRANSPORTATION — Passenger traffic

INTERNATIONAL UNION OF PUBLIC TRANSPORT INTERNATIONAL CONGRESS. International Commission for Regional Transport (Railways, Motorbuses, Waterways) (40th : 1973 : The Hague)
The social function of regional transport : the possibilty of reconciling economic and social considerations in the operation of regional public transport undertakings / H. J. van Zuylen. — Brussels : International Union of Public Transport, 1973. — 27p

INTERNATIONAL UNION OF PUBLIC TRANSPORT INTERNATIONAL CONGRESS. International Regional Light Railways and Motor Transport Commission (37th : 1967 : Barcelona)
Man and public transport : sociological remarks on the relations between man and public transport / H. J.van Zuylen. — Brussels : International Union of Public Transport, 1967. — 23p

TRANSPORTATION — Passenger traffic — Finance

ROUND TABLE ON TRANSPORT ECONOMICS (67th : 1984 : Paris)
Aims and effects of public financial support for passenger transport. — Paris : European Conference of Ministers of Transport, 1984. — 77p. — *Bibliography: p58-61*

TRANSPORTATION — Planning

Transportation planning in a changing world / edited by P. Nijkamp and S. Reichman. — Aldershot : Gower in association with the European Science Foundation, c1987. — xii,340p. — *Includes bibliographies and index*

TRANSPORTATION — Planning — Congresses

Transportation and mobility in an era of transition / editors, Gijsbertus R.M. Jansen, Peter Nijkamp, Cees J. Ruijgrok. — Amsterdam ; New York : North-Holland ; New York, N.Y., U.S.A. : Sole distributors for the U.S.A. and Canada, Elsevier Science Pub. Co., 1985. — p. cm. — (Studies in regional science and urban economics ; v. 13)

TRANSPORTATION — Planning — Social aspects

Transport sociology : social aspects of transport planning / edited by Enne de Boer. — Oxford : Pergamon, 1986. — xi,235p. — ([Urban and regional planning series] ; [v.35]). — *Includes bibliographies and index*

TRANSPORTATION — Australia — Passenger traffic

AUSTRALIA. Bureau of Transport Economics. Seminar on Australian Long Distance Surface Passenger Transport (1985 : Canberra)
Papers and proceedings. — Canberra : Australian Government Publishing Service, 1985. — viii,90p. — *Includes bibliographical references*

TRANSPORTATION — Belize

DEVELOPMENT FINANCE CORPORATION (Belize). Investment Promotion Unit
Communication, transport and public utilities in Belize. — Belize City : the Corporation, 1980. — 11 leaves

TRANSPORTATION — Brazil — Statistics

Séries estatísticas retrospectivas. — Rio de Janeiro : IBGE
V.2: O Brasil, suas riquezas naturais, suas indústrias
T.3: *Indústria de transportes, indústria fabril.* — 1986. — 273,148p. — Facsimile of 1909 edition

TRANSPORTATION — Denmark — Copenhagen

DENMARK. Kommission vedrørende samfaerdselsforholdene i hovedstadsområdet
Betaenkning vedrørende forslag til et trafikråd for storkøbenhavn / af givet den 28. juni 1955 af den af boligministeriet den 4. december 1950 nedsatte kommission vedrørende samfaerdselsforholdene i hovedstadsområdet. — [København : Statens Trykningskontor], 1955. — 227p. — (Betaenkning ; nr.132)

TRANSPORTATION — England — London — Passenger traffic

CAMPAIGN TO IMPROVE LONDON'S TRANSPORT
Railways for London : investment proposals for the LRT tube and BR network. — London : Campaign to Improve London's Transport, 1987. — 93p

FULLER, Ken
All change please : the alternative plan for London's transport / Ken Fuller. — London : Campaign to Improve London's Transport, 1986. — 49p

LONDON STRATEGIC POLICY UNIT. Transport Group
London corridor assessment studies : joint strategic response to the first stage reports. — London : London Strategic Policy Unit, 1987. — 39p

TRANSPORTATION — England — London — Passenger Traffic

LONDON STRATEGIC POLICY UNIT. Transport Group
London corridor assessment studies : joint strategic response to the Draft Terms of Reference for Stage 2. — London : London Strategic Policy Unit, 1987. — 10p

TRANSPORTATION — England — London — Passenger traffic

LONDON STRATEGIC POLICY UNIT. Transport Policy Group
Transport policies for London 1987-88. — London : [the Group], 1986. — 56p

Popular planning transport guide. — London : Industry and Employment Branch. Popular Planning Unit
no.3 s/h Notes from the Underground. — 1986. — 131p

TRANSPORTATION — England — South Yorkshire

Transport policies and programme / South Yorkshire County Council. — Barnsley : South Yorkshire County Council, 1986-87

TRANSPORTATION — England — West Yorkshire — Passenger traffic

WEST YORKSHIRE PASSENGER TRANSPORT AUTHORITY
Keeping it all together : a statement of intended policies. — Leeds : [the Authority], 1986. — [8p]

TRANSPORTATION — Europe — Congresses

ROUND TABLE ON TRANSPORT ECONOMICS (41st : 1978 : Paris)
The role of transport in counter-cyclical policy : report of the forty-first Round Table on Transport Economics, held in Paris on 2nd-3rd March, 1978 ... — Paris : Organisation for Economic Co-operation and Development. — 61p. — *At head of title: Economic Research Centre.* — *Bibliography: p47-48*

TRANSPORTATION — Europe — Passenger traffic

ROUND TABLE ON TRANSPORT ECONOMICS (68th : 1984 : Paris)
Changes in transport users' motivations for modal choice : passenger transport. — Paris : European Conference of Ministers of Transport, 1985. — 102p. — *Includes bibliographies*

TRANSPORTATION — Europe — Planning

SIMPSON, Barry J.
Planning and public transport in Great Britain, France and West Germany / Barry J. Simpson. — Harlow : Longman Scientific & Technical, 1987. — [208]p. — *Includes bibliography and index*

TRANSPORTATION — Finland — Accounting

HAMUNEN, Eeva
Kansantalouden tilinpito : liikenne kansantalouden tilinpidossa = National accounts : transport and communication in national accounts / Eeva Hamunen. — Helsinki : Tilastokeskus, 1982. — 77p. — (Tutkimuksia / Finland. Tilastokeskus ; no.85). — *In Finnish and English*

TRANSPORTATION — France — Statistics

MOLINA, Valérie
Images économiques des entreprises. — Paris : I.N.S.E.E.
Dossier sectoriel no.7: Transports et télécommunications au 1-1-1983 / Valérie Molina. — 1986. — 55p

TRANSPORTATION — Great Britain — History

BAGWELL, Philip S.
The transport revolution from 1770 / Philip S. Bagwell. — London : Batsford, 1974. — 460p. — *Bibliography: p.419-446.* — *Includes index*

TRANSPORTATION — Great Britain — Passenger traffic

Go public / Transport 2000. — London : Transport 2000, 1984

Passenger transport : planning for radical change / edited by J.D. Carr. — Aldershot : Gower, c1986. — xii,209p. — *Conference proceedings.* — *Includes index*

TRANSPORTATION — Great Britain — Planning

Passenger transport : planning for radical change / edited by J.D. Carr. — Aldershot : Gower, c1986. — xii,209p. — *Conference proceedings.* — *Includes index*

WHITE, Peter R.
Public transport : its planning, management and operation / Peter White. — 2nd ed. — London : Hutchinson, 1986. — 222p. — (The Built environment series). — *Previous ed.: published as Planning for public transport. 1976.* — *Includes bibliographies and index*

TRANSPORTATION — Great Britain — Statistics

STATISTICS USERS' CONFERENCE ON TRANSPORT STATISTICS (1983 : London)
The annual conference of the Standing Committee of Statistics Users. — London : Standing Committee of Statistics Users, 1983. — 248p. — *Cover title: Transport statistics conference, November 16th, 1983*

TRANSPORTATION — Malaysia — History

KAUR, Amarjit
Bridge and barrier : transport and communications in colonial Malaya 1870-1957 / Amarjit Kaur. — Oxford : Oxford University Press, 1985. — 235p

TRANSPORTATION — Netherlands — Statistics

Vierde algemene bedrijfstelling, 1978. — 's-Gravenhage : Staatsuitgeverij. — *Rear cover title: Fourth general economic census, 1978: volume 2, part D: transport and storage*
d.2: Algemene sectorale gegevens
D: transport en opslag. — 1985. — 71p

Zakboek verkeers-en vervoersstatistieken. — š-Gravenhage : Staatsuitgeverij, 1985. — 89p. — *Contents list in English.* — *Title on back cover: Pocket yearbook: traffic and transport statistics 1984*

TRANSPORTATION — New Zealand

Industrial relations in transport : proceedings of a seminar / edited by Kevin Hince. — Wellington : Victoria University of Wellington. Industrial Relations Centre : Chartered Institute of Transport in New Zealand, 1985. — 55p

TRANSPORTATION — Northeastern States — Finance — Mathematical models

GOLDMAN, A. J.
A transport improvement problem transformable to a best-path problem / by A. J. Goldman and G. L. Nemhauser. — [Washington, D.C.] : U.S. Department of Transportation, 1967. — [27p]. — (Northeast Corridor Transportation Project technical paper ; no.9). — *Bibliographical references: p[26]*

TRANSPORTATION — Northeastern States — Mathematical models

Approaches to the modal split : intercity transportation : papers / by J. A. Josephs...[et al.]. — [Washington, D.C.] : U.S. Department of Commerce, 1967. — 7,12,[35],[33],18p. — (Northeast Corridor Transportation Project technical paper ; no.7). — *Includes bibliographical references*

TRANSPORTATION — Northeastern States — Passenger traffic — Statistical methods

QUANDT, Richard E.
The abstract mode model : theory and measurement / by Richard E. Quandt and William J. Baumol. — [Washington, D.C.] : U.S. Department of Commerce, 1966. — 28p. — (Northeast Corridor Transportation Project technical paper ; no.4). — *Bibliography: p28*

TRANSPORTATION — Northeastern States — Planning

GLANCY, David M.
Description of the area system for the Northeast Corridor Transportation Project / by David M. Glancy. — [Washington, D.C.] : U.S. Department of Commerce, 1965. — [16],7 leaves. — (Northeast Corridor Transportation Project technical paper ; no.2)

SHULDINER, Paul W.
A strategy for the generation of transportation alternatives / by Paul W. Shuldiner. — [Washington, D.C.] : U.S. Department of Transportation, 1968. — 27p. — (Northeast Corridor Transportation Project technical paper ; no.10)

Study design. — [Washington, D.C.] : U.S. Department of Commerce, 1966. — 40p. — (Northeast Corridor Transportation Project technical paper ; no.5)

TRANSPORTATION — Northeastern States — Planning — Mathematical models

Analysis of a market-split model / by A. J. Goldman...[et al.]. — [Washington, D.C.] : U.S. Department of Transportation, 1967. — 38p. — (Northeast Corridor Transportation Project technical paper ; no.8)

TRANSPORTATION — Portugal — Statistics

PORTUGAL. Instituto Nacional de Estatística
Recenseamento das empresas do sector dos transportes, 1982. — Lisboa : the Instituto, [1986]. — xvii,371p

TRANSPORTATION — Spain — History

MADRAZO, Santos
El sistema de comunicaciones en España, 1750-1850 / Santos Madrazo. — [Madrid] : Colegio de Ingenieros de Caminos, Canales y Puertos : Ediciones Turner
2: [El tráfico y los sevicios]. — c1984. — 379-966p. — *Bibliography: p883-924.* — *Number on spine: 20*

MADRAZO, Santos
El sistema de comunicaciones en España, 1750-1850 / Santos Madrazo. — [Madrid] : Colegio de Ingenieros de Caminos, Canales y Puertos : Ediciones Turner
7: [La red viaria]. — c1984. — 376p. — *Number on spine: 20*

TRANSPORTATION — Spain — Passenger traffic — Statistics

DIEZ NICOLAS, Juan
Movimientos de población en áreas urbanas españolas / Juan Díez Nicolás, Francisco Alvira Martín. — Madrid : Centro de Estudios de Ordenación del Territorio y Medio Ambiente, 1985. — 666p. — (Monografías / Centro de Estudios de Ordenación del Territorio y Media Ambiente ; 18)

TRANSPORTATION — Sri Lanka — Statistics

Transport statistics in Sri Lanka. — 3rd. — Colombo : Ministry of Finance and Planning, 1982. — viii,34p

TRANSPORTATION — Taiwan

FEI, W. H.
Transportation development in Taiwan / by W. H. Fei. — [Taipei] : Industrial Development Commission, 1958. — 27p

TRANSPORTATION — Wales — Planning

GREAT BRITAIN. Welsh Office
Transport Act 1978 : public transport planning in non-metropolitan counties. — Cardiff : the Office, 1978. — 10p. — (Circular ; no.78/115)

TRANSPORTATION — Wales — Statistics

Welsh transport statistics = Ystadegau trafnidiaeth Cymru / Welsh Office. — Cardiff : Economic and Statistical Services, Welsh Office, 1985-. — *Annual*

TRANSPORTATION — Wales — Clwyd — Citizens participation

CLWYD. County Council
Clwyd county structure plan : public participation seminar : transportation : report of proceedings. — Mold : [the Council], 1975. — 28p

TRANSPORTATION — Wales — West Glamorgan

WEST GLAMORGAN. County Council
Transport : what are the issues?. — Swansea : [the Council], 1975. — iii,22p

TRANSPORTATION AND STATE

INTERNATIONAL CONFERENCE ON TRAVEL BEHAVIOUR (1985 : Noordwijk)
Behavioural research for transport policy. — Utrecht : VNU Science Press, 1986. — xv,490p . — *Bibliographies*

TRANSPORTATION AND STATE — Europe

ROUND TABLE ON TRANSPORT ECONOMICS (65th : 1984 : Paris)
Public transport in rural areas : scheduled and non-scheduled services. — Paris : European Conference of Ministers of Transport, 1984. — 270p. — *Includes bibliographies*

ROUND TABLE ON TRANSPORT ECONOMICS (67th : 1984 : Paris)
Aims and effects of public financial support for passenger transport. — Paris : European Conference of Ministers of Transport, 1984. — 77p. — *Bibliography: p58-61*

TRANSPORTATION AND STATE — France

MERLIN, Pierre
Les politiques de transport urbain / Pierre Merlin. — Paris : La Documentation française, 1985. — 143p. — (Notes et études documentaires ; 4797)

TRANSPORTATION, AUTOMOTIVE

The Economic and social effects of the spread of motor vehicles : an international centenary tribute / edited by Theo Barker. — Basingstoke : Macmillan, 1987. — xiii,324p. — *Includes index*

TRANSPORTATION, AUTOMOTIVE — Environmental aspects — Organisation for Economic Co-operation and Development countries

Environmdntal effects of automotive transport : the OECD compass project. — Paris : Organisation for Economic Co-operation and Development, 1986. — 172p. — *Includes bibliographies*

TRANSPORTATION, AUTOMOTIVE — Forecasting — Congresses

ROUND TABLE ON TRANSPORT ECONOMICS
The future of the use of the car : 55th, 56th and 57th Round Tables on Transport Economics / Economic Research Centre. — Paris : European Conference of Ministers of Transport, 1982. — 233p. — *Bibliography: p165-168.* — *Contents: Round Table 55, Forecasts for the ownership and use of a car -- Round Table 56, Cost of using a car (perception and fiscal policy) -- Round Table 57, Interrelationships between car use and changing space-time patterns*

TRANSPORTATION, AUTOMOTIVE — Law and legislation — Great Britain

GREAT BRITAIN. Parliament. House of Commons. Library. Research Division
Transport Bill (Bill 57 of 1981-82) / [Priscilla Baines]. — [London] : the Division, 1982. — 11p. — (Reference sheet ; no.82/6)

GREAT BRITAIN. Parliament. House of Commons. Library. Research Division
Transport Bill, Bill 68 of 1984-85 / Priscilla Baines. — [London] : the Division, 1985. — 34p. — (Reference sheet ; no.85/4). — *Includes bibliographical references*

TRANSPORTATION, AUTOMOTIVE — Social aspects

The Economic and social effects of the spread of motor vehicles : an international centenary tribute / edited by Theo Barker. — Basingstoke : Macmillan, 1987. — xiii,324p. — *Includes index*

TRANSPORTATION, AUTOMOTIVE — Statistics

Carriage of goods: road / Statistical Office of the European Communities. — Luxembourg : Office for Official Publications of the European Communities, 1983-. — *Annual.* — *Text in Community languages.* — *Title varies*

TRANSPORTATION, AUTOMOTIVE — Great Britain — Congresses

BEESLEY, M. E
Influence of measures designed to restrict the use of certain transport modes / [M.E. Beesley]. — Paris : European Conference of Ministers of Transport, 1979. — 59p. — *At head of title: Economic Research Centre.* — *Subtitle: Report of the forty-second Round Table on Transport Economics, held in Paris on 9th-10th November 1978.* — *Includes bibliographical references*

TRANSPORTATION, AUTOMOTIVE — Ireland — Freight

Road freight transport survey / Central Statistics Office, Ireland. — Dublin : Stationary Office, 1984-. — *Annual*

TRANSPORTATION, AUTOMOTIVE — South Australia — Statistics

Motor vehicle census : 30th September, 1976 / South Australia. — Adelaide : Australian Bureau of Statistics, 1976. — 23p

TRANSPORTATION PLANNING — Methodology

ROYAL INSTITUTE OF PUBLIC ADMINISTRATION. Local Government Operational Research Unit
Interaction analysis in structure planning - a transport case study : report / K. S. Barnes and J. A. Green. — London : Department of the Environment : Department of Transport, 1979. — x,72p. — (Research report / Departments of the Environment and Transport ; 28). — *Bibliography: p65-72*

TRANSPORTATION PLANNING — England — West Midlands

WEST MIDLANDS. County Council
Rapid transit for the West Midlands : a study carried out by the West Midlands County Council and West Midlands Passenger Transport Executive Joint Transportation Planning Unit, with advice from Halcrow, Fox and Associates, and Roger Tym and Partners. — Birmingham : West Midlands County Council : West Midlands Passenger Transport Executive, 1984. — 82p

WEST MIDLANDS. County Council
Rapid transit for the West Midlands : fact sheets. — Birmingham : West Midlands County Council : West Midlands Passenger Transport Executive, 1985. — 6 sheets

TRANSPORTATION POLICY

GILLINGWATER, David
The regulation and control of transport / D. Gillingwater. — Loughborough : University of Technology, 1985. — 61p. — *Bibliography: p60-61*

TRANSVAAL (SOUTH AFRICA) — Finance

SOUTH AFRICA, Department of the Auditor General
Report of the Auditor General on the accounts of the Central Transvaal Area Bantu Affairs Administration Board. — Pretoria : [the Department], 1973-1982/83. — Annual. — text in English and Afrikaans. — *continued by: Report of the Auditor-General on the accounts of the Central Transvaal Area Development Board*

SOUTH AFRICA. Department of the Auditor General
Report of the Auditor-General on the accounts of the Central Transvaal Area Development Board. — Pretoria : [the Department], 1983/84-. — Annual. — Text in Afrikaans and English. — *Continues: Report of the Auditor General on the accounts of the Central Transvaal Area Bantu Affairs Administration Board*

TRANSVESTISM — Cross-cultural studies

WHITAM, Frederick L
Male homosexuality in four societies : Brazil, Guatemala, the Philippines, and the United States / Frederick L. Whitam and Robin M. Mathy ; foreword by Milton Diamond. — New York : Praeger, 1985. — p. cm. — *Includes indexes. — Bibliography: p*

TRANSYLVANIA (ROMANIA) — History

MEDGYESI, Pál
Erdély romlásának okairól / Medgyesi Pál. — Budapest : Magvető Kiadó, 1984. — 60p. — (Gondolkodó Magyarok)

PĂCURARIU, Mircea
Politica statului ungar față de Biserica românească din Transilvania în perioada dualismului (1867-1918) / Mircea Păcurariu. — Sibiu : Editura Institutului Biblic și de Misiune al Bisericii Ortodoxe Române, 1986. — 301p

TRANSYLVANIA (ROMANIA) — History — 1919-

IANCU, Gheorghe
Contribuția consiliului dirigent la consolidarea statului national unitar român (1918-1920) / Gheorghe Iancu. — Cluj-Napoca : Editura Dacia, 1985. — 315p

TRAVELERS — German

ESSNER, Cornelia
Deutsche Afrikareisende im neunzehnten Jahrhundert : zur Sozialgeschichte des Reisens / Cornelia Essner. — Stuttgart : Steiner-Verlag-Wiesbaden, 1985. — 235p. — (Beiträge zur Kolonial- und Überseegeschichte ; Bd.32). — *Bibliography: p210-235*

TRAVELERS — Africa

ESSNER, Cornelia
Deutsche Afrikareisende im neunzehnten Jahrhundert : zur Sozialgeschichte des Reisens / Cornelia Essner. — Stuttgart : Steiner-Verlag-Wiesbaden, 1985. — 235p. — (Beiträge zur Kolonial- und Überseegeschichte ; Bd.32). — *Bibliography: p210-235*

TRAVELLING-SALESMAN PROBLEM

OKONJO-ADIGWE, Chiedu-Elue
Solution techniques for the multiple-vehicle travelling salesman problem / by Chiedu Elue Okonje-Adigwe. — 185 leaves. — *PhD (Econ) 1986 LSE*

TREASON — Bibliography

IMPERIAL WAR MUSEUM. Library
Bibliography of espionage and treason. — [London] : the Library, [1955]. — 21p. — (Booklist / Imperial War Museum Library ; no.1244)

IMPERIAL WAR MUSEUM. Library
Espionage and treason : a list of selected references. — [London] : the Library, [1963]. — 8p. — (Booklist / Imperial War Museum Llibrary ; no.1244). — *Supplement to booklist published in 1955*

TREASON — England — History — 16th century

SMITH, Lacey Baldwin
Treason in Tudor England : politics and paranoia / Lacey Baldwin Smith. — London : Cape, 1986. — [320]p. — *Includes bibliography and index*

TREATIES

BLIX, Hans
The treaty maker's handbook / Edited by Hans Blix and Jirina H. Emerson. — [Uppsala] : Dag Hammarskjöld Foundation ; Dobbs Ferry, N.Y. : Oceana Publications, 1973. — 355 p. — *An expanded and rev. ed. of a compilation of passages from treaties which exemplify several types of constitutional rules relating to formal treaty provisions. The material was originally prepared for use at 2 seminars on the law of treaties which were arr. by the Dag Hammarskjöld Foundation and held in Uppsala in 1966 and 1967*

TREATIES — Bibliography

A select bibliography on the law of treaties between states and international organizations or between international organizations. — New York : United Nations, 1985. — iii,33p. — ([Document] / United Nations ; ST/LIB/SER.B/36). — *In various languages. — Prepared by the Dag Hammerskjöld Library*

TREATIES — Collections

International organization and integration : annotated basic doucments of international organizations and arrangements / selected by Louis B. Sohn. — Student ed. — Dordrecht [Netherlands] ; Boston : Nijhoff ; Norwell, MA, USA : Distributors for the U.S. and Canada, Kluwer Academic Publishers, 1986. — xxviii, 1082 p.. — *Based on the five-volume set International organization and integration. — Includes index*

Multilateral treaties between ASEAN countries / editor-in-chief Visu Sinnadurai. — Singapore : Butterworth, 1986. — 235p. — (ASEAN law series)

TREATIES — History — 19th century

DEGENHARDT, Henry W.
Treaties and alliances of the world / compiled and written by Henry W. Degenhardt general editor, Alan J. Day. — 4th ed. — Harlow : Longman, 1986. — x,495p. — (A Keesing's reference publication). — *Previous ed.: 1981. — Bibliography: p473-474. — Includes index*

TREATIES — History — 20th century

DEGENHARDT, Henry W.
Treaties and alliances of the world / compiled and written by Henry W. Degenhardt general editor, Alan J. Day. — 4th ed. — Harlow : Longman, 1986. — x,495p. — (A Keesing's reference publication). — *Previous ed.: 1981. — Bibliography: p473-474. — Includes index*

TREATIES, ETC. SOUTH AFRICA

Confrontation and liberation in southern Africa : regional directions after the Nkomati Accord / edited by Ibrahim S. R. Msabaha and Timothy M. Shaw. — Boulder, Colo : Westview Press, 1987. — xii, 315 p., [1] leaf of plates. — (Westview special studies on Africa). — *Bibliography: p. [307]-315*

TREATIES, ETC. UNITED STATES

PÉREZ, Louis A.
Cuba under the Platt Amendment, 1902-1934 / Louis A. Pérez, Jr. — Pittsburg, Pa. : University of Pittsburgh Press, c1986. — xiii, 410p. — (Pitt Latin American series). — *Includes index. — Bibliography: p.[387]-402*

TREATY-MAKING POWER — United States

Congress, the Presidency, and the Taiwan Relations Act / edited by Louis W. Koenig, James C. Hsiung, and King-Yuh Chang. — New York : Praeger, 1985. — p. cm. — *Includes index. — Bibliography: p*

TREATY OF PARIS (1783) — Addresses, essays, lectures

Peace and the peacemakers : the treaty of 1783 / edited by Ronald Hoffman and Peter J. Albert. — Charlottesville : Published for the United States Capitol Historical Society by the University Press of Virginia, 1985. — p. cm. — (Perspectives on the American Revolution). — *Includes index*

TREATY OF VERSAILLES (1919)

SCHWABE, Klaus
[Deutsche Revolution und Wilson-Frieden. English]. Woodrow Wilson, Revolutionary Germany, and peacemaking, 1918-1919 : missionary diplomacy and the realities of power / by Klaus Schwabe ; translated from German by Rita and Robert Kimber. — Chapel Hill : University of North Carolina Press, c1985. — ix, 565p. — *"Supplementary volumes to The papers of Woodrow Wilson, Arthur S. Link, editor"--Half t.p. — Translation of: Deutsche Revolution und Wilson-Frieden. — Includes index. — Bibliography: p [533]-547*

TREE CROPS — Great Britain

NATIONAL FARMERS' UNION
Farming trees : the case for government support for woodland on farms / National Farmers' Union. — London : The Union, 1986

TREES — Great Britain — Statistics

LOCKE, G. M. L.
Census of woodlands and trees 1979-82 / G. M. L. Locke. — London : H.M.S.O., 1987. — v,123p. — (Forestry Commission bulletin ; 63)

TRENTINO-ALTO ADIGE (ITALY) — History

STUHLPFARRER, Karl
Umsiedlung Südtirol 1939-1940 / Karl Stuhlpfarrer. — Wien : Löcker, 1985. — 2v.

VOLGGER, Friedl
Mit Südtirol am Scheideweg : erlebte Geschichte / Friedl Volgger. — Innsbruck : Haymon, 1984. — 319p

TRENTINO-ALTO ADIGE (ITALY) — Politics and government

VOLGGER, Friedl
Mit Südtirol am Scheideweg : erlebte Geschichte / Friedl Volgger. — Innsbruck : Haymon, 1984. — 319p

TRESPASS — England

BIRTS, Peter W.
Trespass : summary procedure for possession of land / Peter W. Birts, Alan Willis. — London : Butterworths, 1987. — xi,143p. — *Includes index*

TRESPASS — Great Britain

NATIONAL COUNCIL FOR CIVIL LIBERTIES
Stonehenge : a report into the civil liberties implications of the events relating to the convoys of summer 1985 and 1986. — London : National Council for Civil Liberties, 1986. — 43p

TRIAGE (MEDICINE) — Moral and ethical aspects — Congresses
Ethics and critical care medicine / edited by John C. Moskop and Loretta Kopelman. — Dordrecht ; Lancaster : D. Reidel, c1985. — xx, 236p. — (Philosophy and medicine ; v. 19). — *Based on papers presented at a symposium held at East Carolina University School of Medicine in Greenville, N.C. on Mar. 17-19, 1983; sponsored by the East Carolina University School of Medicine and others. — Includes bibliographies and index*

TRIALS — France — Statistics
FRANCE. Ministerè de la justice
Les procès civils 1982-1983. — Paris : the Ministerè, [1985]. — 476p. — *(Statistique annuelle / France. Ministerè de la justice ; 2)*

TRIALS (COMMERCIAL CRIMES) — Soviet Union
EVEL'SON, Evgeniia
Sudebnye protsessy po ekonomicheskim delam v SSSR (shestidesiatye gody) / Evgeniia Evel'son. — London : Overseas Publications Interchange, 1986. — 370p. — *Published in conjunction with the Soviet and East European Research Centre of the Hebrew University, Jerusalem. — Bibliography: p365-370*

TRIALS (FORGERY) — Germany (West)
BAHNSEN, Uwe
Der "Stern" - Prozess : Heidemann und Kujau vor Gericht / Uwe Bahnsen. — Mainz : v. Hase und Kochler, 1986. — 192p

BISSINGER, Manfred
Hitlers Sternstunde : Kujau, Heidemann und die Millionen / Manfred Bissinger. — Hamburg : Rasch und Röhring, 1984. — 238p

TRIALS (FRAUD) — England
GREAT BRITAIN. Fraud Trials Committee
Fraud Trials Committee report / chairman, Lord Roskill. — London : H.M.S.O., 1986. — xi,245p

TRIALS (HATE PROPAGANDA) — Canada — Public opinion
WEIMANN, Gabriel
Hate on trial : the Zundel Affair : thr media public opinion in Canada / Gabriel Weimann and Conrad Winn. — Oakville, Ontario : Mosaic Press, 1986. — 201p. — *Includes references*

TRIALS (LIBEL) — England
Malice in Wonderland : Robert Maxwell v. Private Eye / reported by John Jackson ; introduced and with an epilogue by Robert Maxwell ; edited by Joe Haines and Peter Donnelly ; cartoons by Charles Griffin and David Langdon. — London : Macdonald, 1986. — 191p

TRIALS (MURDER) — Canada — History
FRIEDLAND, Martin L.
The case of Valentine Shortis : a true story of crime and politics in Canada / Martin L. Friedland. — Toronto : University of Toronto Press, 1986. — xi,324p

TRIALS (MURDER) — England — London
DEVLIN, Patrick Devlin, Baron
Easing the passing : the trial of Dr John Bodkin Adams / Patrick Devlin. — London : Bodley Head, 1985. — [256]p

TRIALS (MURDER) — Mississippi — DeKalb
CORTNER, Richard C
A "Scottsboro" case in Mississippi : the Supreme Court and Brown v. Mississippi / by Richard C. Cortner. — Jackson : University of Mississippi, c1986. — xiii, 174 p.. — *Includes index. — Bibliography: p. 170*

TRIALS (POLITICAL CRIMES AND OFFENSES)
CHRISTENSON, Ron
Political trials : Gordian knots in the law / Ron Christenson. — New Brunswick, N.J. : Transaction Books, c1986. — viii, 303 p.. — *Includes index. — Bibliography: p. 285-294*

TRIALS (POLITICAL CRIMES AND OFFENSES) — United States
CHRISTENSON, Ron
Political trials : Gordian knots in the law / Ron Christenson. — New Brunswick, N.J. : Transaction Books, c1986. — viii, 303 p.. — *Includes index. — Bibliography: p. 285-294*

TRIALS (RIOTS) — England — Sheffield (South Yorkshire)
JACKSON, Bernard
The battle for Orgreave / Bernard Jackson with Tony Wardle. — Brighton : Vanson Wardle Productions, [1986?]. — x,129p

TRIALS (SEX CRIMES) — Scotland
CHAMBERS, Gerry
Prosecuting sexual assault / G. Chambers, A. Millar. — Edinburgh : H.M.S.O., 1986. — ix,144p. — (A Scottish Office social research study). — *Prepared under the auspices of the Scottish Office Central Research Unit. — Bibliographical references: p142-143*

TRIBES — Congresses
INTERNATIONAL CONGRESS OF ANTHROPOLOGICAL AND ETHNOLOGICAL SCIENCES ((10th : 1978 : New Delhi, India)
The tribal world and its transformation / edited by Bhupinder Singh, J.S. Bhandari. — New Delhi : Concept, 1980, c1978. — xx, 276 p.. — (Xth ICAES series ; no. 1). — *Includes bibliographical references and index*

TRIBES — Iran — Luristan
BLACK-MICHAUD, Jacob
Sheep and land : the economics of power in a tribal society / Jacob Black-Michaud. — Cambridge : Cambridge University Press, 1986. — xiv,231p. — (Collection production pastorale et société ; 4). — *English text with foreword in French. — Bibliography: p218-225. — Includes index*

TRIBES AND TRIBAL SYSTEM — India
KURUP, Ayyappan Madhava
Continuity and change in a little community : a study of the Bharias of Patalkot in Madhya Pradesh / A. M. Kurup. — New Delhi : Concept Publishing, 1985. — 140p. — *Includes references*

VIDYARTHI, Lalita Prasad
The tribal culture of India / L. P. Vidyarthi, B. K. Rai. — 2nd ed. — New Delhi : Concept Publishing, 1985. — 488p. — *Previous ed: 1976. — Includes bibliographical references*

TRIDENT (WEAPONS SYSTEMS) — Bibliography
GREAT BRITAIN. Parliament. House of Commons. Library. Research Division
The future of Britain's strategic nuclear force : the Trident II decision / [J. B. Poole]. — [London] : the Division, 1982. — 5leaves. — (Reference sheet ; no.82/8)

TRIDENT (WEAPONS SYSTEMS) — Government policy — Great Britain
MCINNES, Colin
Trident : the only option? / by Colin McInnes. — London : Brassey's Defence, 1986. — xv,235p. — *Bibliography: p228-231. — Includes index*

TRINIDAD AND TOBAGO — Description and travel
DAUXION LAVAYSSE, Jean François
A statistical, commercial and political description of Venezuela, Trinidad, Margarita, and Tobago : containing various anecdotes and observations, illustrative of the past and present state of these interesting countries; from the French of M. Lavaysse : with an introduction and explanatory notes, by the editor [E. B. i.e. Edward Blaquiere]. — Westport, Conn. : Negro Universities Press, 1969. — xxxix,479p. — *Translation of: Voyages aux îles de Trinidad, de Tabago, de la Marguerite, and dans diverses parties de Venezuela. — Reprint of the 1820 edition*

TRINIDAD AND TOBAGO — Economic conditions
HOPE, Kempe R
Economic development in the Caribbean / Kempe Ronald Hope. — New York : Praeger, 1986. — xv, 215p. — *Includes bibliographical references and index*

MACDONALD, Scott B
Trinidad and Tobago : democracy and development in the Caribbean / Scott B. MacDonald. — New York : Praeger, 1986. — ix, 231p. — *Bibliography: p.221-228*

TRINIDAD AND TOBAGO — Economic conditions — Statistics
Business surveys 1978. — Port of Spain : Central Statistical Office, Ministry of Finance, 1983. — xvi,60p

TRINIDAD AND TOBAGO — Officials and employees — Statistics
The growth of the public service 1973-1978 and projected growth 1979-1983. — [Port of Spain?] : Personnel Department, [1980]. — 27p

TRINIDAD AND TOBAGO — Politics and government
MACDONALD, Scott B
Trinidad and Tobago : democracy and development in the Caribbean / Scott B. MacDonald. — New York : Praeger, 1986. — ix, 231p. — *Bibliography: p.221-228*

TRINIDAD AND TOBAGO — Politics and government — Addresses, essays, lectures
Eric Williams, the man and the leader / edited by Ken I. Boodhoo. — Lanham, MD : University Press of America, c1986. — xviii, 143 p.. — *Includes index. — "Bibliography of books, articles, and speeches by Eric Williams": p. 135-139*

TRINIDAD AND TOBAGO — Population
SINGH, Susheela
Guyana, Jamaica and Trinidad and Tobago : socio—economic differentials in cumulative fertility / Susheela Singh. — Voorburg : International Statistical Institute, 1984. — 89p. — (Scientific reports / World Fertility Survey ; no.57)

TRINIDAD AND TOBAGO — Population — Statistics
ABDULAH, Norma
Contraceptive use and fertility in the Commonwealth Caribbean / Norma Abdulah, Jack Harewood. — Voorburg : International Statistical Institute, 1984. — 55p. — (Scientific reports / World Fertility Survey ; no.60)

HUNTE, Desmond
Evaluation of the Trinidad and Tobago Fertility Survey 1977 / Desmond Hunte. — Voorburg : International Statistical Institute, 1983. — 55p. — (Scientific reports / World Fertility Survey ; no.44)

LIGHTBOURNE, Robert E.
Fertility preferences in Guyana, Jamaica and Trinidad and Tobago, from World Fertility Survey, 1975-77 : a multiple indicator approach / R.E. Lightbourne. — Voorburg : International Statistical Institute, 1984. — 128p. — (Scientific reports / World Fertility Survey ; no.68)

Population abstract : 1970-1981. — Port of Spain : Central Statistical Office, 1986. — ix,48p

TRINIDAD AND TOBAGO — Social conditions
MACDONALD, Scott B
Trinidad and Tobago : democracy and development in the Caribbean / Scott B. MacDonald. — New York : Praeger, 1986. — ix, 231p. — *Bibliography: p.221-228*

TRINIDAD AND TOBAGO — Statistics, Vital

EBANKS, G. Edward
Infant and child mortality and fertility : Trinidad and Tobago, Guyana and Jamaica / G. Edward Ebanks. — Voorburg : International Statistical Institute, 1985. — 68p. — (Scientific reports / World Fertility Survey ; no.75)

TRINIDAD AND TOBAGO — Bibliography

CHAMBERS, Frances
Trinidad and Tobago / Frances Chambers, compiler ; edited by Sheila Herstein. — Oxford : Clio, c1986. — xv,213p. — (World bibliographical series ; 74). — *Includes index*

TRIP GENERATION — Spain — Statistics

DIEZ NICOLAS, Juan
Movimientos de población en áreas urbanas españolas / Juan Díez Nicolás, Francisco Alvira Martín. — Madrid : Centro de Estudios de Ordenación del Territorio y Medio Ambiente, 1985. — 666p. — (Monografías / Centro de Estudios de Ordenación del Territorio y Media Ambiente ; 18)

TRIPARTITE DECLARATION OF PRINCIPLES CONCERNING MULTINATIONAL ENTERPRISES AND SOCIAL POLICY

INTERNATIONAL LABOUR OFFICE
Safety and health practices of multinational enterprises. — Geneva : I.L.O., 1984. — viii,90p

TRIPLE ALLIANCE, 1717

MCKAY, Derek
Allies of convenience : diplomatic relations between Great Britain and Austria, 1714-1719 / Derek McKay. — New York : Garland Pub., 1986. — 378 p.. — (Outstanding theses from the London School of Economics and Political Science). — *Bibliography: p. 350-378*

TRIPURA (INDIA) — Population — Statistics

Census of India 1981. — [Delhi : Controller of Publications]
Series 21: Tripura. — [1985]

TROTSKII, L.

BEILHARZ, Peter
Trotsky, Trotskyism and the transition to socialism / Peter Beilharz. — London : Croom Helm, c1987. — 197p. — *Includes index*

BORNSTEIN, Sam
Against the stream : a history of the Trotskyist movement in Britain, 1924-38 / Sam Bornstein and Al Richardson. — London : Socialist Platform, 1986. — xii,302p

TROTŜKIĬ, L.

KING, David, 1943-
Trotsky : a photographic biography / by David King ; commentary by James Ryan ; introduction by Tamara Deutscher. — Oxford : Basil Blackwell, 1986. — 334p

TROTSKII, LEV

BUBIS, Mordecai Donald
The Soviet Union and Stalinism in the ideological debates of American Trotskyism (1937-51) / by Mordecai Donald Bubis. — 330 leaves. — *PhD (Econ) 1986 LSE*

TRUCK DRIVERS — Europe — Congresses

ROUND TABLE ON TRANSPORT ECONOMICS ((53rd : 1980 : Paris, France)
The working conditions of professional drivers : effects on productivity and road safety : report of the fifty-third Round Table on Transport Economics held in Paris on 11th-12th December 1980 ... / M.G. Gutmann. — Paris : Economic Research Centre, European Conference of Ministers of Transport, 1981. — 59p. — *Bibliography: p37*

TRUCKING — Government policy — United States — History

CHILDS, William R.
Trucking and the public interest : the emergence of federal regulation, 1914-1940 / William R. Childs. — Knoxville : University of Tennessee Press, c1985. — xiv, 243 p.. — *Includes index*. — *Bibliography: p. [222]-233*

TRUCKING — Law and legislation — Great Britain

GREAT BRITAIN. Parliament. House of Commons. Library. Research Division
Lorry weights / [Priscilla Baines]. — [London] : the Division, [1982]. — 13p. — (Reference sheet ; no.82/16). — *Bibliographical references: p12-13*

TRUCKING — Law and legislation — United States — History

CHILDS, William R.
Trucking and the public interest : the emergence of federal regulation, 1914-1940 / William R. Childs. — Knoxville : University of Tennessee Press, c1985. — xiv, 243 p.. — *Includes index*. — *Bibliography: p. [222]-233*

TRUCKING — Canada — Statistics

Trucking in Canada = le camionnage au Canada / Statistics Canada, Surface and Marine Transport Section. — Ottawa : Statistics Canada, 1984-. — Annual. — *In English and French*. — 1984-

TRUCKING — Europe — Labor productivity — Congresses

ROUND TABLE ON TRANSPORT ECONOMICS ((53rd : 1980 : Paris, France)
The working conditions of professional drivers : effects on productivity and road safety : report of the fifty-third Round Table on Transport Economics held in Paris on 11th-12th December 1980 ... / M.G. Gutmann. — Paris : Economic Research Centre, European Conference of Ministers of Transport, 1981. — 59p. — *Bibliography: p37*

TRUCKING — United States — History

CHILDS, William R.
Trucking and the public interest : the emergence of federal regulation, 1914-1940 / William R. Childs. — Knoxville : University of Tennessee Press, c1985. — xiv, 243 p.. — *Includes index*. — *Bibliography: p. [222]-233*

TRUCKS — Environmental aspects — Great Britain

GREAT BRITAIN. Department of the Environment
Control of heavy commercial vehicles : the environmental and road safety effects of lorry plans. — [London] : the Department, [1975]. — [8]p. — (Lorry plans advice note). — *Bibliographical references: p[8]*

TRUCKS — Legal status, laws, etc. — Great Britain

GREAT BRITAIN. Department of the Environment
Control of Heavy commercial vehicles : legal powers. — [London] : the Department, [1975]. — 5p. — (Lorry plans advice note)

TRUCKS — Routes — Great Britain

GREAT BRITAIN. Department of the Environment
Control of heavy commercial vehicles : survey techniques for lorry plans. — [London] : the Department, [1975]. — 8p. — (Lorry plans advice note)

GREAT BRITAIN. Department of the Environment
Control of heavy commercial vehicles : signs. — [London] : the Department, [1975]. — 5p. — (Lorry plans advice note)

TRUCKS — Great Britain

GREAT BRITAIN. Department of the Environment
Control of heavy commercial vehicles : vehicle operating costs for the evaluation of lorry plans. — [London] : the Department, [1975]. — 4p. — (Lorry plans advice note)

TRUDEAU, PIERRE ELLIOTT — Friends and associates

GOSSAGE, Patrick
Close to the charisma : my years between the press and Pierre Elliott Trudeau / Patrick Gossage. — Toronto : McClelland and Stewart, c1986. — 271 p., [16] p. of plates

TRUMAN, HARRY S.

DUNAR, Andrew J.
The Truman scandals and the politics of morality / Andrew J. Dunar. — Columbia : University of Missouri Press, 1984. — viii, 213p. — *Bibliography: p.199-205*

MILLER, Richard Lawrence
Truman : the rise to power / Richard Lawrence Miller. — New York : McGraw-Hill, c1986. — viii, 536p, [8]p of plates. — *Includes index*. — *Bibliography: p [400]-401*

TRUMAN, HARRY S. — Congresses

Harry S. Truman, the man from Independence / edited by William F. Levantrosser ; prepared under the auspices of Hofstra University. — New York : Greenwood Press, c1986. — x, 427 p.. — (Contributions in political science ; no. 145). — *Papers presented at the Hofstra University International Conference on Harry S. Truman, held Apr. 14-16, 1983*. — *Includes bibliographies and index*

TRUST (PSYCHOLOGY)

LEVIN, Murray Burton
Talk radio and the American dream / by Murray B. Levin. — Lexington, Mass. : Lexington Books, c1987. — xv, 170 p.. — *Includes index*

TRUSTS AND TRUSTEES — England

HACKNEY, Jeffrey
Understanding equity and trusts / Jeffrey Hackney. — London : Fontana, 1987. — 182p. — (Understanding law) (Understanding law). — *Bibliography: p169-175*

HAYTON, David J.
Cases and commentary on the law of trusts / Hayton and Marshall. — 8th ed. / by David J. Hayton. — London : Stevens, 1986. — [796]p. — *Previous ed.: / Nathan and Marshall. 1980*. — *Includes index*

OAKLEY, A. J.
Constructive trusts / by A.J. Oakley. — 2nd ed. — London : Sweet & Maxwell, 1987. — [200]p. — (Modern legal studies). — *Previous ed.: 1978*. — *Includes index*

RIDDALL, J. G.
The law of trusts / J.G. Riddall. — 3rd ed. — London : Butterworths, 1987. — [420]p. — *Previous ed.: 1982*. — *Includes index*

UNDERHILL, Sir Arthur
Law relating to trusts and trustees / Underhill and Hayton. — 14th ed. / by David J. Hayton. — London : Butterworths, 1987. — cxxxv,858p. — *Previous ed.: published as Underhill's law relating to trusts and trustees. 1979*. — *Includes index*

TRUSTS, INDUSTRIAL — History — Congresses

INTERNATIONAL CONFERENCE ON BUSINESS HISTORY ((10th : 1983 : Fuji Education Center)
Family business in the era of industrial growth : its ownership and management : proceedings of the Fuji Conference / the International Conference on Business History, 10 ; edited by Akio Okochi, Shigeaki Yasuoka. — [Tokyo] : University of Tokyo Press, c1984. — xiii, 318 p.. — *Includes bibliographical references and index*

TRUTH

GANDHI, M. K.
The moral and political writings of Mahatma Gandhi. — Oxford : Clarendon
volume 2: Truth and non-violence / edited by Raghavan Iyer. — 1986. — xxii,678p. — *Bibliography:p659-664*

TRUTH *continuation*
ODDIE, Graham
Likeness to truth / Graham Oddie. — Dordrecht ; Lancaster : Reidel, c1986. — xv, 218p. — (The University of Western Ontario series in philosophy of science ; v. 30). Includes index. — Bibliography: p.212-215

TSK KPSS. Politbi͡uro
STAAR, Richard Felix
USSR foreign policies after detente / Richard F. Staar. — Rev. ed. — Stanford, Calif. : Hoover Institution Press, Stanford University, c1987. — xxvii, 308 p.. — (Hoover Press publication ; 359). — Includes index. — Bibliography: p. [275]-295

TSWANA (AFRICAN PEOPLE)
LYE, William F.
Transformations on the highveld : the Tswana and Southern Sotho / William F. Lye and Colin Murray. — Cape Town ; London : David Philip, 1985. — 160p. — (The people of Southern Africa ; no.2). — Bibliographies

TUAMOTU ISLANDS — Population — Statistics
Tableaux normalisés du recensement général de la population : 15 octobre 1983. — [Papeete] : Institut territorial de la statistique
Résultats de la subdivision administrative des Iles Tuamotu-Gambier. — [1985?]. — 4p,12 leaves

Tableaux normalisés du recensement général de la population : 15 octobre 1983. — [Papeete] : Institut territorial de la statistique
Résultats des Tuamotu de l'Ouest. — [1985?]. — 4p,11 leaves

Tableaux normalisés du recensement général de la population : 15 octobre 1983. — [Papeete] : Institut territorial de la statistique
Résultats des Tuamotu Nord-Est. — [1985?]. — 4p,12 leaves

TUBERCULOSIS — Kenya — Prevention
TEKSE, K.
Some estimates of vital rates for Sierra Leone / [K. Tekse]. Kenya National Tuberculosis Programme : evaluation of a test-run / [J. J. Rogowski...et al.]. Migration of health personnel of the African Region / [J. Vysohlid]. — Brazzaville : Regional Office for Africa, World Health Organization, 1975. — 124p. — (AFRO technical papers ; no.9). — Includes bibliographical references

TUCHOLSKY, KURT — Biography
AUSTERMANN, Anton
Kurt Tucholsky : der Journalist und sein Publikum / Anton Austermann. — München : Piper, 1985. — 202p. — (Serie Piper ; Bd.5214)

TUCHOLSKY, KURT — History and criticism
AUSTERMANN, Anton
Kurt Tucholsky : der Journalist und sein Publikum / Anton Austermann. — München : Piper, 1985. — 202p. — (Serie Piper ; Bd.5214)

TUCSON (ARIZ.) — History
SHERIDAN, Thomas E
Los Tucsonenses : the Mexican community in Tucson, 1854-1941 / Thomas E. Sheridan. — Tucson : University of Arizona Press, c1986. — xiv, 327 p., [28] p. of plates. — Includes index. — Bibliography: p. 303-314

TUMARAA (RAIATEA : REGION) — Population — Statistics
Tableaux normalisés du recensement général de la population : 15 octobre 1983. — [Papeete] : Institut territorial de la statistique
Résultats de la commune de Tumaraa. — [1985?]. — 4p,11 leaves

TUMORS IN CHILDREN — Statistics
Childhood cancer in Britain : incidence, survival and mortality / G. J. Draper...[et al.] ; [for the] Office of Population Censuses and Surveys. — London : H.M.S.O., 1982. — vii,87p. — (Studies on medical and population subjects ; no.37). — Bibliographical references: p87

TUNISIA — Emigration and immigration
MAZOUZ, Mohamed
La Tunisie et l'immigration Tunisienne en France / Mohamed Mazouz. — [Paris] : Agence de développement des relations interculturelles, 1984. — 48 leaves. — Includes bibliographical references

TUNISIA — Politics and government
ANDERSON, Lisa
The state and social transformation in Tunisia and Libya, 1830-1980 / Lisa Anderson. — Princeton, N.J. : Princeton University Press, c1986. — xxiv, 325 p.. — (Princeton studies on the Near East). — Includes index. — Bibliography: p. 295-311

TUNISIA — Rural conditions
ANDERSON, Lisa
The state and social transformation in Tunisia and Libya, 1830-1980 / Lisa Anderson. — Princeton, N.J. : Princeton University Press, c1986. — xxiv, 325 p.. — (Princeton studies on the Near East). — Includes index. — Bibliography: p. 295-311

TUNISIANS — France
MAZOUZ, Mohamed
La Tunisie et l'immigration Tunisienne en France / Mohamed Mazouz. — [Paris] : Agence de développement des relations interculturelles, 1984. — 48 leaves. — Includes bibliographical references

TUNNELS — English Channel
The Tunnel : the Channel and beyond / editor, Bronwen Jones ; contributing authors, John Ardill ... [et al.]. — Chichester : Ellis Horwood, 1987. — xxxi,334p. — Includes bibliography and index

TUPAMAROS
MERCADER, Antonio
Los Tupamaros : estrategia y acción / Antonio Mercader y Jorge de Vera. — Barcelona : Editorial Anagrama, [1986]. — 161p. — (Colección documentos ; 9). — New edition of 'Tupamaros: estrategia y acción', Montevideo, Editoria Alfa, 1969.

TURBO PASCAL (COMPUTER PROGRAM)
EDWARDS, Charles C.
Advanced techniques in Turbo Pascal / Charles C. Edwards. — San Francisco : Sybex, 1987. — xxiii,311p

KOFFMAN, Elliot B
Turbo Pascal : a problem solving approach / Elliot B. Koffman. — Reading, Mass. : Addison-Wesley, c1986. — xvii, 532, [78] p.. — (Addison-Wesley series in computer science) . — Includes index

TUREIA (TUAMOTU ISLANDS) — Population — Statistics
Tableaux normalisés du recensement général de la population : 15 octobre 1983. — [Papeete] : Institut territorial de la statistique
Résultats de la commune de Tureia. — [1985?]. — 4p,11 leaves

TURIN (ITALY) — Politics and government — 1860-1954
PASSERINI, Luisa
Fascism in popular memory : the cultural experience of the Turin working class / Luisa Passerini ; translated by Bob Lumley and Jude Bloomfield. — Cambridge : Cambridge University Press, 1987. — x,244p. — (Studies in modern capitalism = Etudes sur le capitalisme moderne). — Translation of: Torino operaia e Fascismo. — Includes index

TURIN (ITALY) — Social conditions
PASSERINI, Luisa
Fascism in popular memory : the cultural experience of the Turin working class / Luisa Passerini ; translated by Bob Lumley and Jude Bloomfield. — Cambridge : Cambridge University Press, 1987. — x,244p. — (Studies in modern capitalism = Etudes sur le capitalisme moderne). — Translation of: Torino operaia e Fascismo. — Includes index

TURKEY — Armed Forces — Political activity
BIRAND, Mehmet Ali, 1941-
The generals' coup in Turkey : an inside story of 12 September 1980 / Mehmet Ali Birand ; translated by M.A. Dikerdem. — London : Brassey's Defence, c1987. — xiii,220p. — Translated from the Turkish

TURKEY — Economic conditions — 1918-1960
Turkey in transition : new perspectives / edited by İrvin C. Schick and Ertuğrul Ahmet Tonak ; with translations by Rezan Benatar, İrvin Cemil Schick, Ronnie Margulies. — New York : Oxford University Press, 1987. — xii, 405 p.. — Includes bibliographies and index

TURKEY — Economic conditions — 1960-
KOPITS, George
Structural reform, stabilization, and growth in Turkey / by George Kopits. — Washington, D.C. : International Monetary Fund : External Relations Dept., Publication Services, IMF [distributor], c1987. — v,46p. — (Occasional paper ; no. 52). — "May 1987.". — Bibliographical references: p46

SHABON, Anwar
The political, economic, and labor climate in Turkey / by Anwar M. Shabon and Isik U. Zeytinoglu. — Philadelphia, Pa., U.S.A. : Industrial Research Unit, Wharton School, University of Pennsylvania, c1985. — xiii, 277 p.. — (Multinational industrial relations series. No. 10. European studies ; 10b). — Includes index

Turkey in transition : new perspectives / edited by İrvin C. Schick and Ertuğrul Ahmet Tonak ; with translations by Rezan Benatar, İrvin Cemil Schick, Ronnie Margulies. — New York : Oxford University Press, 1987. — xii, 405 p.. — Includes bibliographies and index

TURKEY — Economic policy
KOPITS, George
Structural reform, stabilization, and growth in Turkey / by George Kopits. — Washington, D.C. : International Monetary Fund : External Relations Dept., Publication Services, IMF [distributor], c1987. — v,46p. — (Occasional paper ; no. 52). — "May 1987.". — Bibliographical references: p46

TURKEY — Emigration and immigration
GOKALP, Altan
La Turquie et l'émigration Turque / Altan Gokalp. — [Paris] : Agence de développement des relations interculturelles, 1984. — 47 leaves . — Includes bibliographical references

TURKEY — Foreign relations
Turkish review: quarterly digest. — Ankara : Directorate General of Press and Information, 1985-. — Quarterly

TURKEY — Foreign relations — France
SAAKIAN, R. G.
Franko-turetskie otnosheniia i Kilikiia v 1918-1923 gg. / R. G. Saakian. — Erevan : Izd-vo AN Armianskoi SSR, 1986. — 281p. — Summary in French. — Bibliography: p245-272

TURKEY — Foreign relations — Great Britain
HELLER, Joseph, 1937-
British policy towards the Ottoman Empire 1908-1914 / Joseph Heller. — London : Cass, 1983. — xi,228p. — Bibliography: p214-218. — Includes index

TURKEY — Foreign relations — Great Britain *continuation*

ROBERTSON, John
Turkey and Allied strategy, 1941-1945 / John Robertson. — New York : Garland Pub., 1986. — xvi, 309 p.. — (Outstanding theses from the London School of Economics and Political Science). — : *Originally presented as the author's thesis (Ph.D.--University of London, 1982) under title: Anglo-Turkish relations 1941-1945.* — *Includes index.* — *Bibliography: p. 272-295*

TURKEY — Foreign relations — Greece

PHOTIADES, Kostas
The annihilation of the Greeks in Pontus by the Turks / Kostas Photiades. — [S.l.] : Union of the Fighters for the Liberation of the Greek lands seized by Turkey, 1987. — 38p

TURKEY — History

SHAW, Stanford J.
History of the Ottoman Empire and modern Turkey / Stanford Shaw [and Ezel Kural Shaw]. — Cambridge : Cambridge University Press. — *In 2 vols*
Vol.1: Empire of the Gazis : the rise and decline of the Ottoman Empire, 1280-1808 / [by Stanford Shaw]. — 1976 [i.e. 1977]. — xv,351p. — *Published in the United States: 1976.* — *Bibliography: p.ix-xii.* — *Includes index*

TURKEY — History — Ottoman Empire, 1288-1918

DAVIS, Fanny
The Ottoman lady : a social history from 1718 to 1918 / Fanny Davis. — Westport, Conn. : Greenwood Press, c1986. — xv, 321 p.. — (Contributions in women's studies ; no. 70). — *Includes bibliographies and index*

REPP, R. C.
The Müfti of Istanbul : a study in the development of the Ottoman learned hierarchy / by R.C. Repp. — London : Published by Ithaca Press for the Board of the Faculty of Oriental Studies, Oxford University, c1986. — xxi,325p. — (Oxford Oriental Institute monographs ; no.8). — *Includes index*

SHAW, Stanford J.
History of the Ottoman Empire and modern Turkey / Stanford Shaw [and Ezel Kural Shaw]. — Cambridge : Cambridge University Press. — *In 2 vols*
Vol.1: Empire of the Gazis : the rise and decline of the Ottoman Empire, 1280-1808 / [by Stanford Shaw]. — 1976 [i.e. 1977]. — xv,351p. — *Published in the United States: 1976.* — *Bibliography: p.ix-xii.* — *Includes index*

TURKEY — History — Ottoman Empire, 1288-1918 — Addresses, essays, lectures

Palestine in the late Ottoman period : political, social and economic transformation / edited by David Kushner. — Jerusalem : Yad Izhak Ben-Zvi ; Leiden : Brill [distributor], 1986. — xi, 434p

TURKEY — History — 1918-1960

Turkey in transition : new perspectives / edited by İrvin C. Schick and Ertuğrul Ahmet Tonak ; with translations by Rezan Benatar, İrvin Cemil Schick, Ronnie Margulies. — New York : Oxford University Press, 1987. — xii, 405 p.. — *Includes bibliographies and index*

TURKEY — History — 1960-

INFO-TÜRK AGENCY
Black book on the militarist "democracy" in Turkey / Info-Türk. — Brussels : Info-Türk Agency, 1986. — 405p. — *Contains historical summary (1923-1980). p398-405*

Turkey in transition : new perspectives / edited by İrvin C. Schick and Ertuğrul Ahmet Tonak ; with translations by Rezan Benatar, İrvin Cemil Schick, Ronnie Margulies. — New York : Oxford University Press, 1987. — xii, 405 p.. — *Includes bibliographies and index*

TURKEY — Military policy

Militarist "democracy" in Turkey. — Bruxelles : Info-Türk, 1983. — 51p

TURKEY — Military relations — United States

CAMPANY, Richard C
Turkey and the United States : the arms embargo period / Richard C. Campany, Jr. — New York : Praeger, 1986. — p. cm. — *Includes index.* — *Bibliography: p*

HALLEY, Laurence
Ancient affections : ethnic groups and foreign policy / Laurence Halley. — New York : Praeger, 1985. — viii, 180 p.. — *Includes index.* — *Bibliography: p. 172-174*

TURKEY — Neutrality

ROBERTSON, John
Turkey and Allied strategy, 1941-1945 / John Robertson. — New York : Garland Pub., 1986. — xvi, 309 p.. — (Outstanding theses from the London School of Economics and Political Science). — : *Originally presented as the author's thesis (Ph.D.--University of London, 1982) under title: Anglo-Turkish relations 1941-1945.* — *Includes index.* — *Bibliography: p. 272-295*

TURKEY — Politics and government

KIRANOVA, Evgenia
Black book on the militarist "democracy" in Turkey / Evgenia Kiranova. — Sofia : Sofia Press, 1980. — 16p

Militarist "democracy" in Turkey. — Bruxelles : Info-Türk, 1983. — 51p

Turkish review: quarterly digest. — Ankara : Directorate General of Press and Information, 1985-. — *Quarterly*

TURKEY — Politics and government — 1909—

TOPRAK, Binnaz
Islam and political development in Turkey / by Binnaz Toprak. — Leiden : Brill, 1981. — 164 p. — (Social, economic and political studies of the Middle East ; v. 32)

TURKEY — Politics and government — 1918-1960

ROBERTSON, John
Turkey and Allied strategy, 1941-1945 / John Robertson. — New York : Garland Pub., 1986. — xvi, 309 p.. — (Outstanding theses from the London School of Economics and Political Science). — : *Originally presented as the author's thesis (Ph.D.--University of London, 1982) under title: Anglo-Turkish relations 1941-1945.* — *Includes index.* — *Bibliography: p. 272-295*

TURKEY — Politics and government — 1960-

BIRAND, Mehmet Ali, 1941-
The generals' coup in Turkey : an inside story of 12 September 1980 / Mehmet Ali Birand ; translated by M.A. Dikerdem. — London : Brassey's Defence, c1987. — xiii,220p. — *Translated from the Turkish*

INFO-TÜRK AGENCY
Black book on the militarist "democracy" in Turkey / Info-Türk. — Brussels : Info-Türk Agency, 1986. — 405p. — *Contains historical summary (1923-1980). p398-405*

SHABON, Anwar
The political, economic, and labor climate in Turkey / by Anwar M. Shabon and Isik U. Zeytinoglu. — Philadelphia, Pa., U.S.A. : Industrial Research Unit, Wharton School, University of Pennsylvania, c1985. — xiii, 277 p.. — (Multinational industrial relations series. No. 10. European studies ; 10b). — *Includes index*

Turkey in transition : new perspectives / edited by İrvin C. Schick and Ertuğrul Ahmet Tonak ; with translations by Rezan Benatar, İrvin Cemil Schick, Ronnie Margulies. — New York : Oxford University Press, 1987. — xii, 405 p.. — *Includes bibliographies and index*

TURKEY — Politics and government — 1918-1960

Turkey in transition : new perspectives / edited by İrvin C. Schick and Ertuğrul Ahmet Tonak ; with translations by Rezan Benatar, İrvin Cemil Schick, Ronnie Margulies. — New York : Oxford University Press, 1987. — xii, 405 p.. — *Includes bibliographies and index*

TURKEY — Population — Statistics — Evaluation

ÜNER, Sunday
Evaluation of the Turkish Fertility Survey 1978 / Sunday Üner. — Voorburg : International Statistical Institute, 1983. — 37p. — (Scientific reports / World Fertility Survey ; no. 43)

TURKEY — Relations — Armenia

SONYEL, Salahi Ramsdan
The Ottoman Armenians : victims of great power diplomacy / by Salahi Ramsdan Sonyel. — London : K. Rustem, 1987. — xv,426p. — *Bibliography: p[365]-386*

TURKEY — Strategic aspects

CAMPANY, Richard C
Turkey and the United States : the arms embargo period / Richard C. Campany, Jr. — New York : Praeger, 1986. — p. cm. — *Includes index.* — *Bibliography: p*

TURKEY. Ba͞g-Kur — Statistics

TURKEY. Ba͞g-Kur
Istatistik yilli͞gi / Ba͞g-Kur, Turkey. — Ankara : Ba͞g-Kur, 1980-. — *Annual.* — *Text in Turkish and English*

TURKS — France

GOKALP, Altan
La Turquie et l'émigration Turque / Altan Gokalp. — [Paris] : Agence de développement des relations interculturelles, 1984. — 47 leaves. — *Includes bibliographical references*

TURKS — Germany (West)

WALLRAFF, Günter
Ganz unten / Günter Wallraff. — Köln : Kiepenheuer & Witsch, c1985. — 254 p

TURNER, JOHN N

CAHILL, Jack
John Turner : the long run / by Jack Cahill. — Toronto, Ont. : McClelland and Stewart, c1984. — 234 p., [24] p. of plates. — *Includes index*

TURNER, NAT — Fiction

STYRON, William
The confessions of Nat Turner / William Styron. — New York : Bantam, 1983. — xv,347p

TUSKEGEE (ALA.) — Race relations

NORRELL, Robert J
Reaping the whirlwind : the civil rights movement in Tuskegee / Robert J. Norrell. — 1st ed. — New York : Knopf : Distributed by Random House, 1985. — x, 254 p., [8] p. of plates. — : *Revision of author's thesis (Ph. D.)--University of Virginia.* — *Includes index.* — *Bibliography: p. 237-242*

TUSKEGEE INSTITUTE

NORRELL, Robert J
Reaping the whirlwind : the civil rights movement in Tuskegee / Robert J. Norrell. — 1st ed. — New York : Knopf : Distributed by Random House, 1985. — x, 254 p., [8] p. of plates. — : *Revision of author's thesis (Ph. D.)--University of Virginia.* — *Includes index.* — *Bibliography: p. 237-242*

TUVALU — Economic policy

Development plan : 1973-1976 : first annual review. — Tarawa : Government Printing Works, [1973?]. — iii,132p

TUVALU — Social policy

Development plan : 1973-1976 : first annual review. — Tarawa : Government Printing Works, [1973?]. — iii,132p

TVARDOVSKII, ALEKSANDR — Correspondence
TVARDOVSKII, Aleksandr
Pis'ma o literature, 1930-1970 / A. Tvardovskii. — Moskva : Sovetskii pisatel', 1985. — 510p

TWENTIETH CENTURY
KOHN, Hans
The twentieth century / Hans Kohn. — London : Gollancz, 1950. — xi,242p

TWENTIETH CENTURY — Forecasts
JAY, Peter, 1937-
Apocalypse 2000 : economic breakdown and the suicide of democracy, 1989-2000 / Peter Jay and Michael Stewart. — London : Sidgwick and Jackson, 1987. — ix,254p

MARTIN, James
Technology's crucible / James Martin. — Englewood Cliffs, N.J. : Prentice-Hall, c1987. — p. cm

Shaping the future : thoughts on the world to come / by the...Bishop of Birmingham...[et al.]. — Wellington, N.Z. : Progressive Publishing Society, 1943. — 55p

TWENTIETH CENTURY — Forecasts — Congresses
ROUND TABLE ON TRANSPORT ECONOMICS
The future of the use of the car : 55th, 56th and 57th Round Tables on Transport Economics / Economic Research Centre. — Paris : European Conference of Ministers of Transport, 1982. — 233p. — *Bibliography: p165-168. — Contents: Round Table 55, Forecasts for the ownership and use of a car -- Round Table 56, Cost of using a car (perception and fiscal policy) -- Round Table 57, Interrelationships between car use and changing space-time patterns*

TWENTY-FIRST CENTURY — Forecasts
MCHALE, John
The ecological context. — New York : G. Braziller, [1970]. — 188 p. — *Bibliography: p. 175-188*

MARTIN, James
Technology's crucible / James Martin. — Englewood Cliffs, N.J. : Prentice-Hall, c1987. — p. cm

TWYMAN (Family)
LUKAS, J. Anthony
Common ground : a turbulent decade in the lives of three American Families / J. Anthony Lukas. — New York : Vintage Books, 1986. — xiv,674p. — *Originally published: New York : Random House, 1985*

TYPEWRITING — Psychological aspects
Cognitive aspects of skilled typewriting / edited by William E. Cooper. — New York : Springer-Verlag, c1983. — xii, 417 p. — *Includes bibliographies and indexes*

TYROL (AUSTRIA) — History — Uprising of 1809
EYCK, F. Gunther
Loyal rebels : Andreas Hofer and the Tyrolean uprising of 1809 / F. Gunther Eyck. — Lanham, MD : University Press of America, c1986. — xvii, 278 p., [1] p. of plates. — *Includes index. — Bibliography: p. 255-266*

UA HUKA (MARQUESAS ISLANDS) — Population — Statistics
Tableaux normalisés du recensement général de la population : 15 octobre 1983. — [Papeete] : Institut territorial de la statistique Résultats de la commune de Ua Huka. — [1985?]. — 4p,11 leaves

UA POU (MARQUESAS ISLANDS) — Population — Statistics
Tableaux normalisés du recensement général de la population : 15 octobre 1983. — [Papeete] : Institut territorial de la statistique Résultats de la commune de Ua Pou. — [1985?]. — 4p,11 leaves

UBALDI, BALDO DEGLI — Contributions in political science
CANNING, Joseph
The political thought of Baldus de Ubaldis / Joseph Canning. — Cambridge : Cambridge University Press, 1987. — xi,300p. — (Cambridge studies in medieval life and thought. Fourth series ; 6). — *Bibliography: p278-290. — Includes index*

UGANDA — Armed Forces — Political activity
OMARA-OTUNNU, Amii
Politics and the military in Uganda, 1890-1985 / Amii Omara-Otunnu. — Basingstoke : Macmillan in association with St. Antony's College, Oxford, 1987. — xx,218p. — (St Antony's / Macmillan series). — *Bibliography: p204-209. — Includes index*

UGANDA — History — 1979-
BWENGYE
The agony of Uganda : from Idi Amin to Obote : repressive rule and bloodshed : causes, effects and the cure / Francis Aloysius Wazarwalu Bwengye ; foreword by Grove Stuart Ibingira. — London : Regency Press, 1985. — xx,379p. — *Bibliography: p374-379*

UGANDA — Politics and government
BWENGYE
The agony of Uganda : from Idi Amin to Obote : repressive rule and bloodshed : causes, effects and the cure / Francis Aloysius Wazarwalu Bwengye ; foreword by Grove Stuart Ibingira. — London : Regency Press, 1985. — xx,379p. — *Bibliography: p374-379*

FURLEY, Oliver
Uganda's retreat from turmoil? / Oliver Furley. — London : Centre for Security and Conflict Studies, 1986. — 32p. — (Conflict studies ; 196)

OMARA-OTUNNU, Amii
Politics and the military in Uganda, 1890-1985 / Amii Omara-Otunnu. — Basingstoke : Macmillan in association with St. Antony's College, Oxford, 1987. — xx,218p. — (St Antony's / Macmillan series). — *Bibliography: p204-209. — Includes index*

SATHYAMURTHY, T. V.
The political development of Uganda : 1900-1986 / T.V. Sathyamurthy. — Aldershot : Gower, c1986. — xviii,781p. — *Bibliography: p747-763. — Includes index*

UKRAINE — Dictionaries and encyclopedias
Ukrainskaia Sovetskaia Sotsialisticheskaia Respublika : entsiklopedicheskii spravochnik / [glavnyi redatfor F. S. Babichev]. — Kiev : Glavnaia redaktsiia USE, 1987. — 513p

UKRAINE — Economic policy
ALYMOV, A. N.
Sbalansirovannost' narodno-khoziaistvennogo razvitiia : (regional'nye i otraslevye problemy) / A. N. Alymov, F. D. Zastavnyi, D. K. Preiger. — Kiev : Naukova dumka, 1986. — 221p. — (Ekonomika razvitogo sotsializma). — *Bibliography: p218-[222]*

Planovoe upravlenie ekonomikoi razvitogo sotsializma / redaktsionnaia kollegiia: A. S. Emel'ianov...[et al.]. — Kiev : Naukova dumka . — *V piati tomakh*
T.1: Narodno-khoziaistvennye proportsii, ikh planirovanie i prognozirovanie / otv. redaktor A. S. Emel'ianov. — 1985. — 316p. — *Bibliography: p311-[314]*

Planovoe upravlenie ekonomikoi razvitogo sotsializma / redaktsionnaia kollegiia: A. S. Emel'ianov...[et al.]. — Kiev : Naukova dumka . — *V piati tomath*
T.3: Nauchno-tekhnicheskii progress i planovoe investirovanie v narodnoe khoziaistvo / otv. redaktor S. M. Iampol'skii. — 1986. — 307p. — *Bibliography: p305-[308]*

Planovoe upravlenie ekonomikoi razvitogo sotsializma / redaktsionnaia kollegiia: A. S. Emel'ianov...[et al.]. — Kiev : Naukova dumka . — *V piati tomakh*
T.4: Nauchno-metodicheskie osnovy planirovaniia i prognozirovaniia razvitiia ekonomiki / otv. redaktor V. F. Besedin. — 1986. — 322p. *Bibliography: p318-[323]*

Planovoe upravlenie ekonomikoi razvitogo sotsializma / redaktsionnaia kollegiia: A. S. Emel'ianov...[et al.]. — Kiev : Naukova dumka . — *V piati tomakh*
T.5: Otraslevye problemy planovogo razvitiia ekonomiki respubliki / otv. redaktor A. S. Emel'ianov. — 1986. — 403p. — *Bibliography: p299-[302]*

UKRAINE — History — 1921-1944
CONQUEST, Robert
The harvest of sorrow : Soviet collectivisation and the terror-famine / by Robert Conquest. — London : Hutchinson, 1986. — viii,412,[8]p of plates. — *Bibliography: p394-396. — Includes index*

UKRAINE — History — 1921-1944 — Congresses
Famine in Ukraine, 1932-1933 / edited by Roman Serbyn and Bohdan Krawchenko. — Edmonton : Canadian Institute of Ukrainian Studies, 1986. — 192p. — (Canadian library in Ukrainian Studies). — *Selected papers from a conference held in 1983 at the Université du Québec à Montréal*

UKRAINE — History — German occupation, 1941-1944
Sovetskaia Ukraina v gody Velikoi Otechestvennoi voiny 1941-1945 / [glav. red. kollegiia: V. I. Iurchuk...et al.]. — Izd. 2-e, dop.. — Kiev : Naukova dumka. — *In 3 vols.*
2: Ukrainskaia SSR v period korennogo pereloma v khode Velikoi Otechestvennoi voiny (19 noiabria 1942g.-konets 1943g.) / red. kollegiia: V. N. Nemiatyi...et al.]. — 1985. — 509p

Sovetskaia Ukraina v gody Velikoi Otechestvennoi voiny 1941-1945 : dokumenty i materialy / [glav. red. kollegiia: V. I. Iurchuk...et al.]. — Izd. 2-e, dop.. — Kiev : Naukova dumka
3: Ukrainskaia SSR v zavershaiushchii period Velikoi Otechestvennoi voiny (1944-1945 gg.) / [red. kollegiia: P. I. Denisenko...et al.]. — 1985. — 508p

Ukraine during World War II : history and its aftermath : a symposium / edited by Yury Boshyk with the assistance of Roman Waschuk and Andriy Wynnyckyj. — Edmonton : Canadian Institute of Ukrainian Studies, University of Alberta ; Downsview, Ont., Canada : Distributed by University of Toronto Press, 1986. — xviii, 291 p., [8] p. of plates. — (The Canadian library in Ukrainian studies). — *Includes index. — Bibliography: p. [267]-285*

UKRAINE — History — German occupation, 1941-1945
Sovetskaia Ukraina v gody Velikoi Otechestvennoi voiny 1941-1945 : dokumenty i materialy / [glav. red. kollegiia: V. I. Iurchuk...et al.]. — Izd. 2-e, dop.. — Kiev : Naukova dumka. — *In 3 vols.*
1: Ukrainskaia SSR v pervyi period Velikoi Otechestvennoi voiny (22 iiunia 1941 g.-18 noiabria 1942) / [red. kollegiia: D. F. Grigorovich...et al.]. — 1985. — 516p

UKRAINE — Politics and government
PETLIAK, F. A.
Partiinoe rukovodstvo Sovetami na Ukraine v gody Velikoi Otechestvennoi voiny (1941-1945) / F. A. Petliak. — Kiev : Vyshcha shkola, 1986. — 181p

UKRAINE — Population policy
Rasselenie : voprosy teorii i razvitie : (na primere Ukrainskoi SSR) / [G. S. Ftomov...et al., otv. redaktor F. D. Zastavnyi]. — Kiev : Naukova dumka, 1985. — 261p

UKRAINE, WESTERN — History
PAPIERZYŃSKA-TUREK, Mirosława
Sprawa ukraińska w Drugiej Rzeczypospolitej 1922-1926 / Mirosława Papierzyńska Turek. — Kraków : Wydawnictwo Literackie, 1979. — 389p. — *Bibliography: p359-379*

UKRAINIANS — Government policy — History
PETRYSHYN, Jaroslav
Peasants in the promised land : Canada and the Ukrainians, 1891-1914 / Jaroslav Petryshyn with L. Dzubak. — Toronto : James Lorimer, 1985. — xi,265p. — *Bibliography: p[240]-255*

UKRAINIANS — Canada — History
PETRYSHYN, Jaroslav
Peasants in the promised land : Canada and the Ukrainians, 1891-1914 / Jaroslav Petryshyn with L. Dzubak. — Toronto : James Lorimer, 1985. — xi,265p. — *Bibliography: p[240]-255*

UKRAINIANS — Canada — History — Sources
A delicate and difficult question : documents in the history of Ukrainians in Canada, 1899-1962 / [compiled by] Bohdan S. Kordan, Lubomyr Y. Luciuk. — Kingston, Ontario : Limestone Press, 1986. — [11],174p. — (Builders of Canada Series ; No.3). — *Bibliography: p174*

UKRAINIANS — Galicia (Poland and Ukraine) — History
KOZIK, Jan
The Ukrainian national movement in Galicia : 1815-1849 / Jan Kozik ; edited with an introduction by Lawrence D. Orton ; translated from the Polish by Andrew Gorski and Lawrence D. Orton. — Edmonton : University of Alberta, Canadian Institute of Ukrainian Studies, 1986. — xx,498p. — (Canadian library in Ukrainian studies). — *Abridged translation of "Ukraiński ruch narodowy w Galicji w latach 1830-1848" (Cracow, 1973) and "Miedzy reakcją a rewolucją" (Warsaw, 1975). — Bibliography: p[451]-471*

UKRAINIANS — Poland
PAPIERZYŃSKA-TUREK, Mirosława
Sprawa ukraińska w Drugiej Rzeczypospolitej 1922-1926 / Mirosława Papierzyńska Turek. — Kraków : Wydawnictwo Literackie, 1979. — 389p. — *Bibliography: p359-379*

UKRAINIANS — Prairie Provinces — History
KEYWAN, Zonia
Greater than kings / text by Zonia Keywan ; photographs by Martin Coles. — Montreal : Clio Editions, 1986. — 165p. — *Originally published: Montreal : Harvest House, 1977*

ULSTER (NORTHERN IRELAND AND IRELAND) — History
CRAWFORD, Robert G
Loyal to King Billy : a portrait of the Ulster Protestants / Robert G. Crawford. — New York : St. Martin's Press, 1987. — p. cm. — *Includes index. — Bibliography: p*

CURL, James Stevens
The Londonderry Plantation 1609-1914 : the history, architecture, and planning of the estates of the City of London and its Livery Companies in Ulster / James Stevens Curl. — Chichester : Phillimore, 1986. — xxiii,503p. — *Bibliography: p484-492*

ULSTER (NORTHERN IRELAND AND IRELAND) — Politics and government
CRAWFORD, Robert G
Loyal to King Billy : a portrait of the Ulster Protestants / Robert G. Crawford. — New York : St. Martin's Press, 1987. — p. cm. — *Includes index. — Bibliography: p*

ULSTER UNIONIST PARTY — History
BIGGS-DAVISON, John
The cross of St Patrick : the Catholic Unionist tradition in Ireland / John Biggs-Davison and George Chowdharay-Best. — Bourne End : Kensal, c1984. — 487p,[8] of plates. — *Bibliography: p453-471. — Includes index*

GAILEY, Andrew
Ireland and the death of kindness : the experience of constructive unionism 1890-1905 / Andrew Gailey. — Cork : Cork University Press, 1987. — xiv,345p. — (Studies in Irish history). — *Bibliography: p323-336. — Includes index*

ULTRA VIRES — Great Britain
Reform of the ultra vires rule / D. D. Prentice [for the] Department of Trade and Industry. — [London] : Department of Trade and Industry, 1986]. — 4,81p

UNCERTAINTY
DRÈZE, Jacques H.
Essays on economic decisions under uncertainty / Jacques H. Drèze. — Cambridge : Cambridge University Press, c1987. — xxvii,424p. — *Includes bibliographies and index*

HEY, John D.
Uncertainty in microeconomics / John D. Hey. — Oxford : Martin Robertson, 1979. — ix,261p. — *Bibliography: p.243-253. — Includes index*

MARCH, James G.
Ambiguity and choice in organizations / by James G. March and Johan P. Olsen ; with contributions by Søren Christensen...[et al.]. — 2nd ed. — Bergen : Universitetsforlaget, 1979. — 408p. — *Bibliography: p397-402*

SENGUPTA, Jatikumar
Stochastic optimization and economic models / Jati K. Sengupta. — Dordrecht ; Boston : D. Reidel ; Norwell, MA, U.S.A. : Sold and distributed in the U.S.A. and Canada by Kluwer Academic, c1986. — x, 373 p. — (Theory and decision library. Series B. Mathematical and statistical methods). — *Includes bibliographies and indexes*

Surveys in the economics of uncertainty / edited by John D. Hey and Peter J. Lambert. — Oxford : Basil Blackwell, 1987. — 232p. — *Includes bibliographies and index*

UNDERDEVELOPED AREAS — Economic policy
The assault on world poverty : problems of rural development, education and health / with a preface by Robert S. McNamara. — Baltimore ; London : Johns Hopkins University Press for the World Bank, 1975. — xiii,425p

DASGUPTA, Ajit Kumar
Economic theory and the developing countries / Ajit K. Dasgupta. — London : Macmillan, 1974. — ix,132p. — *Bibliography: p.120-128. — Includes index*

UNDERDEVELOPED AREAS — Peasantry
MIGDAL, Joel Samuel
Peasants, politics and revolution : pressures towards political and social change in the Third World / Joel S. Migdal. — Princeton ; London : Princeton University Press, 1974 [i.e. 1975]. — x,300p. — *Published in the United States: 1974. — Bibliography: p.275-296. — Includes index*

UNDERDEVELOPED AREAS — Social conditions
MIGDAL, Joel Samuel
Peasants, politics and revolution : pressures towards political and social change in the Third World / Joel S. Migdal. — Princeton ; London : Princeton University Press, 1974 [i.e. 1975]. — x,300p. — *Published in the United States: 1974. — Bibliography: p.275-296. — Includes index*

UNDERDEVELOPED AREAS — Unemployed
HOFFMANN, Helga
Desemprego e subemprego no Brasil / Helga Hoffmann. — São Paulo : Editora Ática, 1977. — 183 p.. — (Ensaios ; 24). — *: Originally presented as the author's thesis, Universidade de São Paulo. — Bibliography: p. [175]-183*

UNDERDEVELOPED ARES — Taxation
United Nations model double taxation convention between developed and developing countries. — New York : United Nations, 1980. — iv,265p. — ([Document] / United Nations ; ST/ESA/102). — *At head of title: Department of International Economic and Social Affairs*

UNDEREMPLOYMENT — Brazil
HOFFMANN, Helga
Desemprego e subemprego no Brasil / Helga Hoffmann. — São Paulo : Editora Ática, 1977. — 183 p.. — (Ensaios ; 24). — *: Originally presented as the author's thesis, Universidade de São Paulo. — Bibliography: p. [175]-183*

UNDERGROUND LITERATURE — China — Bibliography — Catalogs
HOOVER INSTITUTION ON WAR, REVOLUTION, AND PEACE
Unofficial documents of the Democracy Movement in Communist China, 1978-1981 = : Chung-kuo min chu yun tung tzu liao : a checklist of Chinese materials in the Hoover Institution on War, Revolution and Peace / compiled by I-mu. — Stanford, Calif. : East Asian Collection, Hoover Institution, 1986. — viii, 100 p. — (Hoover Press bibliographical series ; 67). — *English and Chinese*

UNDERGROUND PRESS — United States
PECK, Abe
Uncovering the sixties : the life and times of the underground press / by Abe Peck. — 1st ed. — New York : Pantheon Books, 1985. — p. cm. — *Includes index. — Bibliography: p*

UNDERGROUND RAILROAD
Popular planning transport guide. — London : Industry and Employment Branch. Popular Planning Unit
no.3 s/h Notes from the Underground. — 1986. — 131p

UNDERHILL, FRANK H.
FRANCIS, R. Douglas
Frank H. Underhill : intellectual provocateur / R. Douglas Francis. — Toronto : University of Toronto Press, 1986. — x,219p. — *Notes: p [183]-206*

UNEMPLOYED
Youth, unemployment and training : a collection of national perspectives / edited by Rob Fiddy. — London : Falmer, 1985. — 247 p. — (Politics and education series)

UNEMPLOYED — Diseases and hygiene
SMITH, Richard, 1952-
Unemployment and health : a disaster and a challenge / Richard Smith. — Oxford : Oxford University Press, 1987. — [160]p. — (Oxford medical publications). — *Includes bibliographies and index*

UNEMPLOYED — Education — England
MCDONALD, Joan
Education for unemployed adults : problems and good practice : a paper / by Joan McDonald. — [London] : Department of Education and Science, [1985?]. — 36p

UNEMPLOYED — Education — Great Britain
SENIOR, Barbara
Educational responses to adult unemployment / Barbara Senior and John Naylor. — London : Croom Helm, c1987. — 174p. — (Radical forum on adult education series). — *Includes index*

UNEMPLOYED — Government policy — Great Britain
TODD, Graham
Job creation in the UK : a national survey of local models / by Graham Todd. — London : Economist Publications ; Paris : OECD, 1986. — 98p. — (Sepcial report / Economist Intelligence Unit ; no.1075)

UNEMPLOYED — Health and hygiene
Health policy implications of unemployment / edited by G. Westcott, P. -G Svensson, H. F. K. Zöllner. — Copenhagen : World Health Organization, 1985. — vii,409p. — *Includes summaries in French, German and Russian. Includes bibliographical references*

UNEMPLOYED — Training of — Denmark
ROSDAHL, Anders
Uddannelses- og ivaerksaetterydelsen til langtidsledige / Anders Rosdahl og Inge Maerkedahl. — København : Socialforskningsinstituttet, 1987. — 12,161,78p. — (Publikation / Socialforskningsinstituttet ; 161). — *Contents: d.1: Konklusion og perspektiver - d.2: Spørgeskemaundersøgelsen/Anders Rosdahl - d.3: Den intensive undersøgelse/Inge Maerkedahl*

UNEMPLOYED — Training of — Great Britain
FINN, Dan
Training without jobs : new deals and broken promises : from raising the school leaving age to the Youth Training Scheme / Dan Finn. — London : Macmillan, 1987. — xxi,242p. — (Youth questions). — *Bibliography: p217-231. — Includes index*

UNEMPLOYED — Australia
Relocation assistance scheme : review of operational statistics, October 1976 to September 1980. — Canberra : Australian Government Publishing Service, 1983. — vii,38p. — (Research report / Bureau of Labour Market Research ; no.1). — *Bibliographical references: p38*

UNEMPLOYED — Australia — Interviews
TURNER, Michele
Stuck! : unemployed people talk to Michele Turner. — Ringwood, Vic., Australia ; New York, N.Y., U.S.A. : Penguin Books, 1983. — 263 p.. — (An Australian original)

UNEMPLOYED — Australia — Illawarra (N.S.W. : Region)
JOHNSTONE, Helen
Older unemployed people in the Illawarra Region, New South Wales / Helen Johnstone. — Woden, ACT : Department of Social Security, 1986. — 14 leaves. — (Background/discussion paper / Social Security Review ; no.7). — *Bibliographical references: p14*

UNEMPLOYED — Austria
BIFFL, G.
The causes of low unemployment in Austria / G. Biffl, A. Guger [and] W. Pollan. — Buckingham : University of Buckingham. Employment Research Centre, 1987. — 30p. — (Occasional papers in employment studies / University of Buckingham. Employment Research Centre ; no.7). — *Bibliography: p27-29*

UNEMPLOYED — Brazil
HOFFMANN, Helga
Desemprego e subemprego no Brasil / Helga Hoffmann. — São Paulo : Editora Ática, 1977. — 183 p.. — (Ensaios ; 24). — : *Originally presented as the author's thesis, Universidade de São Paulo. — Bibliography: p. [175]-183*

UNEMPLOYED — Canada
METTRICK, Alan
Last in line : on the road and out of work-- a desperate journey with Canada's unemployed / by Alan Mettrick. — Toronto, Ont., Canada : Key Porter Books, c1985. — x, 201 p.

UNEMPLOYED — Canada — History
BROWN, Lorne
When freedom was lost : the unemployed, the agitator, and the state / Lorne Brown. — Montréal : Black Rose Books, 1987. — 208p. — *Includes bibliographic references*

UNEMPLOYED — England — Attitudes
BANKS, Michael H.
Youth unemployment : social and psychological perspectives / Michael H. Banks, Philip Ullah. — [London] : Department of Employment, [1987]. — 91p. — (Research paper / Department of Employment ; no.61). — *Bibliographical references: p86-88*

UNEMPLOYED — England — Bolton (Greater Manchester)
THURNHAM, Peter
Operation long-stop : a time limit to unemployment : a redirection of the Community Programme based on the Bolton Pilot Scheme / Peter Thurnham. — London : Conservative Political Centre, 1987. — 55p. — *Bibliography: p52-53*

UNEMPLOYED — England — London
HAMMERSMITH AND FULHAM. Directorate of Development Planning
The long-term unemployed : a study of their characteristics and problems. — Hammersmith : [the Directorate], 1985. — 120p. — (Research report / Hammersmith and Fulham. Directorate of Development Planning ; 71)

HAMMERSMITH AND FULHAM. Unemployment and Economic Development Group
The long-term unemployed : a joint strategy for the support, training and provision of employment opportunities for long-term unemployed adults. — Hammersmith : [the Group], 1985. — 124p

UNEMPLOYED — England — Skelmersdale (Lancashire)
RILEY, Frank
People in need of a future : a survey of the long-term unemployed in Skelmersdale / Frank Riley. — Skelmersdale : Workbase, 1986. — iv,33 leaves

UNEMPLOYED — France
FRANCE. Agence nationale pour l'emploi. Division des Etudes
Les demandeurs d'emploi de longue durée : analyse d'une population. — [Paris : Agence nationale pour l'emploi, 1983. — 2v. — *Vol.2 contains annexes*

UNEMPLOYED — Great Britain
Adult education with the unemployed / edited by Bruce Spencer. — Leeds : University of Leeds. Department of Adult and Continuing Education, 1986. — 90p

BALLOCH, Susan
Caring for unemployed people : a study of the impact of unemployment on demand for personal social services / Susan Balloch...[et al.] for the Association of Metropolitan Authorities. — [London] : Bedford Square Press, NCVO for the Association of Metropolitan Authorities, [1985]. — xi,139p

BURTON, John, 1945-
Would workfare work? : a feasibility study of a workfare system to replace long-term unemployment in the U.K. / John Burton. — Buckingham : University of Buckingham. Employment Research Centre, 1987. — 64p. — (Occasional papers in employment studies / University of Buckingham. Employment Research Centre ; no.9)

FEDERATION OF CLAIMANTS UNIONS
On the dole : a claimants union guide for the unemployed. — London : Federation of Claimants Unions, 1985. — 37p

HORTON, Claire
Nothing like a job / Claire Horton. — London : Lasso Co-operative, 1985. — 70p. — *Bibliography: p70*

JACKMAN, Richard
A job guarantee for long-term unemployed people / Richard Jackman. — London : Employment Institute, 1986. — 67p

UNELL, Judith
Opportunity costs : government funding and volunteering by unemployed young people / Judith Unell. — Leicester : National Youth Bureau, 1984. — 24p. — *Bibliography: p24*

UNEMPLOYED — Great Britain — Rehabilitation
CUMELLA, Stuart John
Patterns of resettlement of former clients of employment rehabilitation courses : a study of 307 persons within a year of leaving rehabilitation courses / by Stuart John Cumella. — 433 leaves. — *PhD (Econ) 1986 Ext. — Leaves 401-433 are appendices*

UNEMPLOYED — Great Britain — Services for
CUMELLA, Stuart John
Patterns of resettlement of former clients of employment rehabilitation courses : a study of 307 persons within a year of leaving rehabilitation courses / by Stuart John Cumella. — 433 leaves. — *PhD (Econ) 1986 Ext. — Leaves 401-433 are appendices*

UNEMPLOYED — India
CHAUDHARY, Shobha Kant
Planning and employment trends in Indai / S. K. Chaudhary. — New Delhi : Deep and Deep Publications, 1987. — 300p. — *Bibliography: p290-298*

UNEMPLOYED — Netherlands
AKTIECOMITÉ WERKLOZE VROUWEN
Eisenaktieboek / Aktiecomité Werkloze Vrouwen. — Amsterdam : the Aktiecomité, [1971?]. — 22p

UNEMPLOYED — O.E.C.D. countries
ORGANISATION FOR ECONOMIC CO-OPERATION AND DEVELOPMENT
Entry of young people into working life : general report / [Organisation for Economic Co-operation and Development]. — Paris : O.E.C.D. ; [London] : [H.M.S.O.], 1977. — 106p. — *Bibliography: p.103-106*

UNEMPLOYED — Puerto Rico
GUZMAN SOTO, Vicente
El problema del desempleo en Puerto Rico / Vicente Guzman Soto y Vernon R. Esteves. — San Juan : Banco Gubernamental de Fomento para Puerto Rico, [ca.1963]. — v,25p

UNEMPLOYED — United States
BURTON, John, 1945-
Would workfare work? : a feasibility study of a workfare system to replace long-term unemployment in the U.K. / John Burton. — Buckingham : University of Buckingham. Employment Research Centre, 1987. — 64p. — (Occasional papers in employment studies / University of Buckingham. Employment Research Centre ; no.9)

MAHARIDGE, Dale
Journey to nowhere : the saga of the new underclass / by Dale Maharidge ; photographs by Michael Williamson. — Garden City, N.Y. : Doubleday, 1984. — p. cm. — *"Dolphin book."*

UNEMPLOYMENT
ALBEDA, W.
De crisis van de werkgelegenheid en de verzorgingsstaat : analyse en perspectief / W. Albeda. — Kampen : J. H. Kok, c1984. — 108p

Die Arbeitsgesellschaft zwischen Sachgesetzlichkeit und Ethik / Anton Rauscher (Hrsg.). — Köln : J. P. Bachem, 1985. — 174p. — (Mönchengladbacher Gespräche ; Bd.6) (Veröffentlichungen der Kathelischen Sozialwissenschaftlichen Zentralstelle Mönchengladbach)

BERG SØRENSEN, Torben
Fyret! : arbejdsløse mœnds erfaringer / Torben Berg Sørensen. — [s.l.] : Tiderne Skifter, 1984. — 235p. — *Bibliography: p228-235*

UNEMPLOYMENT *continuation*

DESAI, Meghnad
Money, inflation and unemployment : an econometric model of the Keynes effect / M. Desai and G. Weber. — London : Economic and Social Research Council : London School of Economics, 1986. — [77p]. — (ESRC/LSE econometrics project discussion paper ; A.59). — *Bibliography: p[69.71]*

Employment and poverty in a troubled world : report of a meeting of high-level experts on employment. — Geneva : International Labour Office, 1985. — 55p

FOLMER, Hendrik
Differences in characteristics between unemployed with different spells of unemployment / Hendrik Folmer and Jouke van Dijk. — Groningen : University of Groningen. Faculty of Economics. Institute of Economic Research. — 24p. — (Research memorandum / University of Groningen. Faculty of Economics. Institute of Economic Research ; nr.181). — *Bibliography: p18-19*

HASLUCK, Chris
Urban unemployment : local labour markets and employment initiatives / Chris Hasluck. — London : Longman, 1987. — 248p. — *Bibliography : p228-243. — Includes index*

JACKMAN, Richard
Innovative supply-side policies to reduce unemployment / R. Jackman and R. Layard. — London : Centre for Labour Economics, London School of Economics, 1987. — 34p. — (Discussion paper / London School of Economics and Political Science. Centre for Labour Economics ; no.281). — *Bibliography: p33-34*

LEADBEATER, Charles
In search of work / Charles Leadbeater and John Lloyd. — Harmondsworth : Penguin, 1987. — 232p. — *'Based on a special report "Work - the way ahead", published by the Financial Times in 1986'. — Bibliography: p[214]-218*

METCALF, David
Cutting work time as a cure for unemployment / David Metcalf. — Buckingham : University of Buckingham. Employment Research Centre, 1987. — 32p. — (Occasional papers in employment studies (University of Buckingham. Employment Research Centre) ; no.6)

NEWELL, A.
Corporatism, the laissez-faire and the rise in unemployment / A. Newell and J. S. V. Symons. — London : Centre for Labour Economics, London School of Economics, 1986. — 62p. — (Discussion paper / London School of Economics and Political Science. Centre for Labour Economics ; no.260). — *Bibliography: p60-62*

NEWELL, A.
Mid 1980s unemployment / A. Newell and J. S. V. Symons. — London : Centre for Labour Economics, London School of Economics, 1987. — 96p. — (Discussion paper / London School of Economics and Political Science. Centre for Labour Economics ; no.283). — *Bibliography: p94-96*

NEWELL, A.
Wages and employment between the wars / A. Newell and J. S. V. Symons. — London : Centre for Labour Economics, London School of Economics, 1986. — 36p. — (Discussion paper / London School of Economics and Political Science. Centre for Labour Economics ; no.257)

SHACKLETON, J. R.
Wages and unemployment / J. R. Shackleton. — Buckingham : University of Buckingham. Employment Research Centre, 1987. — 44p. — (Occasional papers in employment studies / University of Buckingham. Employment Research Centre ; no.8). — *Bibliography: p40-43*

SINCLAIR, P. J. N.
Unemployment : economic theory and evidence / Peter Sinclair. — Oxford : Basil Blackwell, 1987. — viii,312p. — *Bibliography: p297-305. — Includes index*

Unemployed people : social and psychological perspectives / edited by David Fryer and Philip Ullah. — Milton Keynes : Open University Press, 1987. — [320]p. — *Includes index*

Unemployment and the structure of labor markets / edited by Kevin Lang and Jonathan S. Leonard. — Oxford : Blackwell, 1987. — vi,253p. — *Bibliography: p234-243. — Includes index*

WADHWANI, Sushil B.
Profit sharing as a cure for unemployment : some doubts / S. Wadhwani. — London : Centre for Labour Economics, London School of Economics, 1986. — 40p. — (Discussion paper / London School of Economics and Political Science. Centre for Labour Economics ; no.253). — *Bibliography: p38-40*

WHITING, Edwin
A guide to unemployment reduction measures / Edwin Whiting. — Basingstoke : Macmillan, 1986. — [280]p. — *Includes index*

UNEMPLOYMENT — Bibliography

GRAYSON, Lesley
Unemployment and health : a review of the literature 1979-1986 / compiled by Lesley Grayson. — Letchworth : Technical Communications, 1986. — iv,27p

UNEMPLOYMENT — Effect of inflation on

BRUNO, Michael
Economics of worldwide stagflation / Michael Bruno and Jeffrey D. Sachs. — Cambridge, Mass. : Harvard University Press, 1985. — 315p. — *Includes index. — Bibliography: p.[297]-310*

PETERSEN, Uwe
Arbeitslosigkeit unser Schicksal? : Wirtschaftspolitik in der Stagflation / Uwe Petersen. — Frankfurt am Main : Peter Lang, 1985. — 133p. — (Europöische Hochschulschriften. Reihe 5, Volks- und Betriebswirtschaft ; Bd.661). — *Bibliography: p130-133*

UNEMPLOYMENT — Effect of inflation on — History — 20th century

MCLEOD, Alex N.
The fearsome dilemma : simultaneous inflation and unemployment / by Alex N. McLeod. — Lanham, MD : University Press of America, c1984. — xi, 197 p.. — *Includes index. — Bibliography: p. 185-188*

UNEMPLOYMENT — Government policy — Great Britain

GREAT BRITAIN. Parliament. House of Commons. Library. Research Division
The economics of special employment measures / Christopher Barclay. — [London] : the Division, 1985. — 24p. — (Background paper ; no.160). — *Bibliographical references: p24*

GREAT BRITAIN. Parliament. House of Commons. Library. Research Division
Special measures to alleviate unemployment in Great Britain. — [London] : the Division, 1977. — 12, [4]p. — (Background paper ; no.61). — *Includes Department of Employment press notice: 'New help for 230,000 unemployed youngsters'*

GREAT BRITAIN. Parliament. House of Commons. Library. Research Division
Unemployment / [Christopher Barclay, Paul Hutt, Celia Nield]. — [London] : the Division, 1980. — 43p. — (Background paper)

GREAT BRITAIN. Parliament. House of Commons. Library. Research Division
Unemployment / Christopher Barclay...[et al.]. — [London] : the Division, 1981. — 67p. — (Background paper ; no.92). — *Revised version of Background Paper no.77*

Unemployment and labour market policies / edited by P.E. Hart. — Aldershot : Gower, c1986. — 198p. — (Joint studies in public policy ; 12). — *Conference proceedings. — At head of title: National Institute of Economic and Social Research, Policy Studies Institute, Royal Institute of International Affairs. — Includes index*

UNEMPLOYMENT — History

BELLAN, R. C.
The unnecessary evil : an answer to Canada's high unemployment / Ruben Bellan. — Toronto : McLelland and Stewart, 1986. — 173p

UNEMPLOYMENT — Mathematical models

LINDBECK, Assar
Cooperation, harassment and involuntary unemployment / by Assar Lindbeck and Dennis D. Snower. — Stockholm : Institute for International Economic Studies, University of Stockholm, 1985. — 52p. — (Seminar Paper / Stockholms Universitet. Institutet för internationell ekonomi ; No.321). — *Bibliography: p52*

UNEMPLOYMENT — Psychological aspects

Health policy implications of unemployment / edited by G. Westcott, P. -G Svensson, H. F. K. Zöllner. — Copenhagen : World Health Organization, 1985. — vii,409p. — *Includes summaries in French, German and Russian. — Includes bibliographical references*

UNEMPLOYMENT — Religious aspects — Christianity

STORKEY, Alan
Transforming economics : a Christian way to employment / Alan Storkey. — London : SPCK, 1986. — xi,212p. — (Third way books). — *Bibliography: p205-206. — Includes index*

UNEMPLOYMENT — Research — Bibliography

World Employment Programme : research in retrospect and prospect. — Geneva : International Labour Office, 1976. — 278p. — *Bibliography: p245-273*

UNEMPLOYMENT — Social aspects

Die Arbeitsgesellschaft zwischen Sachgesetzlichkeit und Ethik / Anton Rauscher (Hrsg.). — Köln : J. P. Bachem, 1985. — 174p. — (Mönchengladbacher Gespräche ; Bd.6) (Veröffentlichungen der Kathelischen Sozialwissenschaftlichen Zentralstelle Mönchengladbach)

BERG SØRENSEN, Torben
Fyret! : arbejdsløse mænds erfaringer / Torben Berg Sørensen. — [s.l.] : Tiderne Skifter, 1984. — 235p. — *Bibliography: p228-235*

UNEMPLOYMENT — Social aspects — Denmark

BERG SØRENSEN, Torben
Fyret! : arbejdsløse mænds erfaringer / Torben Berg Sørensen. — [s.l.] : Tiderne Skifter, 1984. — 235p. — *Bibliography: p228-235*

UNEMPLOYMENT — Social aspects — England — Teesside (Yorkshire) — History — 20th century

NICHOLAS, Katharine
The social effects of unemployment in Teesside / Katharine Nicholas. — Manchester : Manchester University Press, c1986. — ix,236p. — *Bibliography: p227-231. — Includes index*

UNEMPLOYMENT — Social aspects — Great Britain

BALLOCH, Susan
Caring for unemployed people : a study of the impact of unemployment on demand for personal social services / Susan Balloch...[et al.] for the Association of Metropolitan Authorities. — [London] : Bedford Square Press, NCVO for the Association of Metropolitan Authorities, [1985]. — xi,139p

UNEMPLOYMENT — Australia

PISSARIDES, Christopher A.
Real wages and unemployment in Australia / C. Pissarides. — London : Centre for Labour Economics, London School of Economics, 1987. — 39p. — (Discussion paper / London School of Economics and Political Science. Centre for Labour Economics ; no.286). — *Bibliography: p38-39*

Trends in the labour market. — Canberra : Economic Planning Advisory Council, 1986. — v,31p. — (Council paper / Economic Planning Advisory Council ; no.21). — *Bibliographical references: p29*

Unemployment and the labour market : anatomy of the problem. — Canberra : Australian Government Publishing Service, 1986. — xv,243p. — (Research report / Bureau of Labour Market Research ; no.9). — *Bibliographical references: p225-243*

UNEMPLOYMENT — Australia — Congresses

Unemployment in the eighties / edited by Robert Castle and John Mangan. — Melbourne, Australia : Longman Cheshire, 1984. — 249 p.. — (Australian studies). — *"... arises out of a conference held at the University of Wollongong on the 9 and 10 July 1982 ..."--Foreword. — Includes bibliographies and index*

UNEMPLOYMENT — Australia — Longitudinal studies

The first wave of the Australian longitudinal survey : facts and figures about young CES registrants / Jan Muir...[et al.]. — Canberra : Australian Government Publishing Service, 1986. — xxi,220p. — (Monograph series / Bureau of Labour Market Research ; no.12). — *Bibliographical references: p219-220*

UNEMPLOYMENT — Canada

BELLAN, R. C.
The unnecessary evil : an answer to Canada's high unemployment / Ruben Bellan. — Toronto : McLelland and Stewart, 1986. — 173p

UNEMPLOYMENT — Denmark

BERG SØRENSEN, Torben
Fyret! : arbejdsløse mœnds erfaringer / Torben Berg Sørensen. — [s.l.] : Tiderne Skifter, 1984. — 235p. — *Bibliography: p228-235*

PLOUG, Niels
10 år med arbejdsløshed / Niels Ploug. — København : Socialforskningsinstituttet, 1986. — 48p. — (Pjece / Socialforskningsinstituttet ; 18). — *Bibliography: p47-48*

UNEMPLOYMENT — Egypt

ABDEL-FADIL, Mahmoud
Informal sector employment in Egypt / Mahmoud Abdel-Fadil. — Geneva : International Labour Office, 1983. — viii,39p. — (Employment opportunities and equity in Egypt ; no.1). — *Bibliographical references: p35-39. — A technical paper of the ILO/UNDP comprehensive employment strategy mission to Egypt, 1980*

EL-ISSAWY, Ibrahim H.
Employment inadequacy in Egypt / Ibrahim H. El-Issawy. — Geneva : International Labour Office, 1983. — 32p. — (Employment opportunities and equity in Egypt ; no.3). — *Bibliographical references: p29-32. — A technical paper of the ILO/UNDP comprehensive employment strategy mission to Egypt, 1980*

EL-ISSAWY, Ibrahim H.
Labour force, employment and unemployment / Ibrahim H. El-Issawy. — Geneva : International Labour Office, 1983. — ix,80p. — (Employment opportunities and equity in Egypt ; no.4). — *Bibliographical references: p52-56. — A technical paper of the ILO/UNDP comprehensive employment strategy mission to Egypt, 1980*

UNEMPLOYMENT — England — Bristol (Avon)

BODDY, Martin
Sunbelt city? : a study of economic change in Britain's M4 growth corridor / Martin Boddy, John Lovering and Keith Bassett. — Oxford : Clarendon Press, 1986. — vii,235p. — (Inner Cities Research Programme series ; 3). — *Bibliography: p221-226. — Includes index*

UNEMPLOYMENT — England — London

BUCK, N. H.
The London employment problem / Nick Buck, Ian Gordon and Ken Young, with John Ermisch and Liz Mills. — Oxford : Clarendon Press, 1986. — xvi,213p. — (Inner Cities Research Programme series ; 5). — *Bibliography: p199-205. — Includes index*

UNEMPLOYMENT — European Economic Community countries

Definitions of registered unemployed / Statistical Office of the European Communities. — Luxembourg : Office for Official Publications of the European Communities, 1982. — 172p. — *Title and text in Community languages*

Definitions of registered unemployed. — Luxembourg : Office for Official Publications of the European Communities, 1984. — 376p. — *Text in Community languages*

GREAT BRITAIN. Parliament. House of Commons. Library. Research Division
Why the USA creates new jobs and why Europe does not / Christopher Barclay. — [London] : the Division, 1985. — 25p. — (Background paper ; no.170)

Local employment initiatives : report on a series of local consultations held in European Countries 1982—1983 : main report / by the Centre for Employment Initiatives, London. — Luxembourg : Office for Official Publications of the European Communities, 1985. — 159p. — (Programme of research and actions on the development of the labour market). — *At head of title: Commission of the European Communities*

Local employment initiatives : an evaluation of support agencies / by Centre for Research on European Women - CREW, Brussels. — Luxembourg : Office for Official Publications of the European Communities, 1985. — 356p. — (Programme of Research and Actions on the Development of the Labour Market). — *At head of title: Commission of the European Communities*

Local employment initiatives : a manual on intermediary and support organisations : main report / by The Centre for Employment Initiatives, London. — Luxembourg : Office for Official Publications of the European Communities, 1985. — 90p. — (Programme of research and actions on the development of the labour market). — *At head of title: Commission of the European Communities*

UNEMPLOYMENT — Finland — Mathematical models

ERIKSSON, Tor
Some investigations into Finnish unemployment dynamics / Tor Eriksson. — Åbo : Åbo Akademi, 1985. — 309p. — (Meddelanden från Stiftelsens för Åbo Akademi Forskningsinstitutt ; Nr.107). — *Bibliographies*

UNEMPLOYMENT — France — Costs

JUNANKAR, P. N.
Costs of unemployment / by P.N.Junankar. — Luxembourg : Office for Official Publications of the European Communities. — (Programme of research and actions on the development of the labour market). — *At head of title:Commission of the European Communities* Main report. — 1986. — vi,35p

UNEMPLOYMENT — France — Statistics

Données statistiques sur les zones d'emploi. — Paris : I.N.S.E.E., 1986. — 92p. — (Archives et documents / Institut national de la statistique et des études économiques ; no.162)

Les zones d'emploi : indicateurs socio-économiques. — Paris : Délégation a l'aménagement du territoire et a l'action régionale, 1986. — 59p

UNEMPLOYMENT — Germany — History — 20th century

The German unemployed : experiences and consequences of mass unemployment from the Weimar Republic to the Third Reich / edited by Richard J. Evans and Dick Geary. — London : Croom Helm, c1987. — xviii,314p. — *Includes index*

Unemployment and the Great Depression in Weimar Germany / edited by Peter D. Stachura. — Basingstoke : Macmillan, 1986. — [350]p. — *Includes index*

UNEMPLOYMENT — Germany (West) — Costs

JUNANKAR, P. N.
Costs of unemployment / by P.N.Junankar. — Luxembourg : Office for Official Publications of the European Communities. — (Programme of research and actions on the development of the labour market). — *At head of title:Commission of the European Communities* Main report. — 1986. — vi,35p

UNEMPLOYMENT — Great Britain

CARRUTH, Alan
Testing for multiple natural rates of unemployment in the British economy : a preliminary investigation / A. A. Carruth [and] A. J. Oswald. — London : Centre for Labour Economics, London School of Economics, 1986. — 43p. — (Discussion paper / London School of Economics and Political Science. Centre for Labour Economics ; no.265). — *Bibliography: p39-43*

CONFEDERATION OF BRITISH INDUSTRY
Company responses to unemployment. — London : Confederation of British Industry, 1985. — 64p

EICHENGREEN, Barry
Juvenile unemployment in interwar Britain : the emergence of a problem / Barry Eichengreen. — London : Centre for Economic Policy Research, 1987. — 27p. — (Discussion paper series / Centre for Economic Policy Research ; no.194)

The Experience of unemployment / edited by Sheila Allen ... [et al.]. — Basingstoke : Macmillan, 1986. — xi,204p. — (Explorations in sociology). — *Bibliography: p185-198. — Includes index*

GREAT BRITAIN. Parliament. House of Commons. Library. Research Division
Unemployment / [Christopher Barclay, Paul Hutt, Celia Nield]. — [London] : the Division, 1980. — 43p. — (Background paper)

GREAT BRITAIN. Parliament. House of Commons. Library. Research Division
Unemployment / Christopher Barclay...[et al.]. — [London] : the Division, 1981. — 67p. — (Background paper ; no.92). — *Revised version of Background Paper no.77*

HARRIS, Ralph
Myths on unemployment : the count, some courses and cures / Ralph Harris. — London : Aims of Industry, 1987. — 17p

HAYEK, F. A.
1980's unemployment and the unions : essays on the impotent price structure of Britain and monopoly in the labour market / F.A. Hayek. — 2nd ed / With a postscript on British trade unions and the law, From Toff Vale to Tebbit, by Charles G. Hanson. — London : Institute of Economic Affairs, 1984. — 80p. — (Hobart paper ; 87)

KNIGHT, K. G.
Unemployment : an economic analysis / K.G. Knight. — London : Croom Helm, c1987. — 411p. — *Bibliography: p386-408. — Includes index*

UNEMPLOYMENT — Great Britain
continuation

LAYARD, Richard
How to beat unemployment / Richard Layard with assistance from Andrew Sentance. — Oxford : Oxford University Press, 1986. — 201p. — Bibliography: p192-197. — Includes index

METCALF, David
Alternatives to unemployment : special employment measures in Britain / David Metcalf. — London : Policy Studies Institute, 1982. — 66p. — (Policy Studies Institute ; no. 610)

MICHAEL, I. M.
Employment creation in the US and UK : an econometric comparison / I. M. Michael. — London : Bank of England, 1986. — 74p. — (Discussion paper / Bank of England ; no.27). — Bibliography: p71-74

MINFORD, Patrick
The housing morass : regulation, immobility and unemployment : an economic analysis of the consequences of government regulation, with proposals to restore the market in rented housing / Patrick Minford, Michael Peel and Paul Ashton. — London : Institute of Economic Affairs, 1987. — 162p. — (Hobart paperback ; 25). — Bibliography: p157-162

NATIONAL ECONOMIC DEVELOPMENT OFFICE
Job generation in areas of high unemployment : memorandum / by the Director General. — [London] : National Economic Development Council, 1985. — 1v (various pagings). — Bibliography: Annex D. — NEDC: (85) 74

NEWNHAM, Anne
Employment, unemployment and black people / Anne Newnham. — London : Runnymede Trust, 1986. — 30p. — (Runnymede research report). — Bibliography:p.30

STANDING, Guy
Unemployment and labour market flexibilty : the United Kingdom / Guy Standing. — Geneva : International Labour Office, 1986. — xi,147p. — Including bibliographical references

STOREY, D. J. (David John), 1947-
Are small firms the answer to unemployment? / D.J.Storey and S.Johnson. — London : Employment Institute, 1987. — 47p. — At head of title: Employment Institute

TRINDER, C.
Unemployment and labour supply in National Institute Model 8 / C. Trinder [and] R. Biswas. — London : National Institute of Economic and Social Research, 1986. — 36p. — (Discussion paper / National Institute of Economic and Social Research ; no.112). — Bibliography: p36

Unemployment : personal and social consequences / edited by Stephen Fineman ; foreword by Adrian Sinfield. — London : Tavistock, 1987. — xii,260p. — (Social science paperbacks ; 348). — Includes bibliographies and index

WILSON, Thomas, 1916-
Unemployment and the labour market / Tom Wilson ; with a commentary by Geoffrey E. Wood. — London : Institute of Economic Affairs, 1987. — 70p. — (Occasional paper / Institute of Economic Affairs ; 75)

UNEMPLOYMENT — Great Britain — History — 20th century

The Road to full employment / edited by Sean Glynn, Alan Booth. — London : Allen & Unwin, 1987. — ix,214p. — Bibliography: p198-210. — Includes index

UNEMPLOYMENT — Great Britain — Statistics

[UK occupation and employment trends to 1990]. UK occupation and employment trends to 1990 : an employer-based study of the trends and their underlying causes / edited by Amin Rajan and Richard Pearson. — London : Butterworths, 1986. — xxiv, 249p. — 'By the Institute of Manpower Studies for the Occupations Study Group' — cover. — Bibliography: p.201

UNEMPLOYMENT — India — Karnataka

PRABHAKARA, N. R
Population growth and unemployment in India / N.R. Prabhakara, M.N. Usha. — New Delhi : Ashish Pub. House, 1986. — ix, 102 p.. — Includes index. — Bibliography: p. 97-99

UNEMPLOYMENT — Ireland

MALONEY, Oliver
Unemployment: what can be done? / Oliver Maloney and Fr. John Sweeney. — Dublin : Irish Messenger Publications, 1985. — 30p

UNEMPLOYMENT — Italy — Costs

JUNANKAR, P. N.
Costs of unemployment / by P.N.Junankar. — Luxembourg : Office for Official Publications of the European Communities. — (Programme of research and actions on the development of the labour market). — At head of title:Commission of the European Communities Main report. — 1986. — vi,35p

UNEMPLOYMENT — London

ALLAN, Malcolm
Creating a local economic development network : a case study of Hammersmith and Fulham / Malcolm Allan, Mike Fenton, Andy Flockhart. — Glasgow : The Planning Exchange, 1985. — iii,82p

UNEMPLOYMENT — London Metropolitan Area

Monitoring manufacturing employment change in London, 1976-1978 / Roger Leigh ... [et al.]. — [London] : Middlesex Polytechnic, London Industry and Employment Research Group Vol.1: The implications for local economic policy. — [1983?]. — xv,216p

Monitoring manufacturing employment change in London, 1976-1981 / Roger Leigh ... [et al.]. — [London] : Middlesex Polytechnic, London Industry and Employment Research Group Vol.2: Industrial Sector Studies. — [1983]. — 150p

UNEMPLOYMENT — Netherlands

AKTIECOMITÉ WERKLOZE VROUWEN
Eisenaktieboek / Aktiecomité Werkloze Vrouwen. — Amsterdam : the Aktiecomité, [1971?]. — 22p

UNEMPLOYMENT — Organisation for Economic Co-operation and Development countries

Employment and unemployment : some issues and facts. — [Paris] : OECD, 1986. — 20p. — Includes bibliographical references. — Contents: Background paper for OECD meeting of the Manpower and Social Affairs Committee at ministerial level

UNEMPLOYMENT — Scotland — Clydeside (Strathclyde)

The city in transition : policies and agencies for the economic regeneration of Clydeside / edited by William Lever and Chris Moore. — Oxford : Clarendon Press, 1986. — xvi,173p. — (Inner Cities Research Programme series ; 4). — Bibliography: p163-167. — Includes index

UNEMPLOYMENT — Scotland — Strathclyde

STRATHCLYDE. Chief Executive's Department
Unemployment in Strathclyde. — Glasgow : [the Department], 1985. — 13 leaves

STRATHCLYDE. Regional Council. Economic and Industrial Development Committee
Unemployment in Strathclyde in April 1987. — Glasgow : [the Committee], 1987. — [10p]

STRATHCLYDE. Regional Council. Economic and Industrial Development Committee
Unemployment in Strathclyde in February 1987. — Glasgow : [the Committee], 1987. — [10p]

UNEMPLOYMENT — United States

GREAT BRITAIN. Parliament. House of Commons. Library. Research Division
Why the USA creates new jobs and why Europe does not / Christopher Barclay. — [London] : the Division, 1985. — 25p. — (Background paper ; no.170)

MICHAEL, I. M.
Employment creation in the US and UK : an econometric comparison / I. M. Michael. — London : Bank of England, 1986. — 74p. — (Discussion paper / Bank of England ; no.27). — Bibliography: p71-74

UNEMPLOYMENT — United States — Congresses

FREEMAN, Richard B
The Black youth employment crisis / Richard B. Freeman and Harry J. Holzer. — Chicago : University of Chicago Press, 1986. — p. cm. — (A National Bureau of Economic Research project report). — Includes bibliographies and indexes

UNEMPLOYMENT — United States — History

BERNSTEIN, Irving
A caring society : the New Deal, the worker, and the Great Depression : a history of the American worker, 1933-1941 / Irving Bernstein. — Boston : Houghton Mifflin, 1985. — 338 p., [24] p. of plates. — Includes index. — Bibliography: p. 309-326

UNEMPLOYMENT — Wales — South Glamorgan

SOUTH GLAMORGAN
1986 social survey employment and economic activity results: county electoral divisions. — [Cardiff] : [the Council], 1986. — ii,55p

UNEMPLOYMENT, STRUCTURAL — Great Britain

Global restructuring local response / edited by Philip Cooke. — London : Economic and Social Research Council, 1986. — 308p. — A report commissioned by the Environment and Planning Committee of the ESRC. — Includes bibliographies

UNEMPLOYMENTOFF. PUBNS. — Great Britain — Costs 986

JUNANKAR, P. N.
Costs of unemployment / by P.N.Junankar. — Luxembourg : Office for Official Publications of the European Communities. — (Programme of research and actions on the development of the labour market). — At head of title:Commission of the European Communities Main report. — 1986. — vi,35p

UNESCO

HOLLY, Daniel
L'Unesco : le tiers-monde et l'économie mondiale / Daniel A. Holly. — Montréal : Presses de l'Université de Montréal ; Genève : Institute Universitaire de Hautes Études Internationales, 1981. — 176p. — Bibliography: p161-172

LENGYEL, Peter
International social science, the UNESCO experience / Peter Lengyel. — New Brunswick, U.S.A. : Transaction Books, c1986. — xii, 133 p.. — Includes index. — Bibliography: p. 123-129

PACE-UK report on 'the crisis facing UNESCO'. — London : PACE-UK, 1985. — 57,3p

UNESCO — History

A chronology of Unesco, 1945-1985 : facts and events in Unesco's history arranged by dates with references to documentary sources in the Unesco Archives and supplementary information in the annexes 1-15. — Paris : Unesco, 1985. — 69p

UNESCO — History
continuation

WELLS, Clare
The UN, UNESCO and the politics of knowledge / Clare Wells. — London : : Macmillan, 1987. — [272]p. — *Includes index*

UNESCO — United States

BEHRSTOCK, Julian
The eighth case : troubled times at the United Nations / Julian Behrstock. — Lanham : University Press of America, c1987. — p. cm. — *Includes bibliographical references and index*

UNIÃO NACIONAL PARA A INDEPENDÊNCIA TOTAL DE ANGOLA

DÖHNING, W
UNITA : União Nacional para a Independência Total de Angola / text by W. Döhning ; photographs by Cloete Breytenbach. — [Angola] : Kwacha Unita Press, 1984. — 93 p.

UNICEF

UNICEF
Annual report / United Nations. Children's Fund. — New York : UNICEF, 1982-. — *Annual*

UNICEF — Bibliography

UNICEF
Geographical index to UNICEF documents 1946 to 1972. — New York : UNICEF, 1974. — 324p. — (Documents / United Nations ; E/ICEF/INDEX/2) ([Document] - United Nations ; E/ICEF/Index/2). — *Cover title*

UNICEF — History

BLACK, Maggie
The children and the nations : the story of UNICEF / by Maggie Black. — New York : UNICEF, 1986. — x,502p. — *Includes bibliographical references*

UNIFICATION CHURCH

AHLBERG, Sture
Messianic movements : a comparative analysis of the Sabbatians, the People's Temple, and the Unification Church / by Sture Ahlberg. — Stockholm : Almqvist & Wiksell International, 1986. — 128 p.. — (Acta Universitatis Stockholmiensis. Stockholm studies in comparative religion ; 26). — *Continuation of author's thesis (doctoral--Stockholm, 1977) originally presented as: Messianism in the State of Israel. — Includes indexes. — Bibliography: p. 118-122*

UNIFICATION CHURCH — Doctrines

GRACE, James H
Sex and marriage in the Unification movement : a sociological study / James H. Grace ; with a preface by Mac Linscott Ricketts. — New York : E. Mellen Press, c1985. — 284 p.. — (Studies in religion and society ; v. 13). — *Bibliography: p. [275]-284*

UNIFORMS — Social aspects

JOSEPH, Nathan
Uniforms and nonuniforms : communication through clothing / Nathan Joseph. — New York : Greenwood Press, 1986. — vi, 248 p.. — (Contributions in sociology ; no. 61). — *Includes index. — Bibliography: p. [221]-238*

UNILEVER LIMITED — Management

Geoffrey Heyworth : Baron Heyworth of Oxton : a memoir. — [London] ([PO Box 68, Unilever Hse., Blackfriars, EC4P 4BQ]) : [Unilever], c1985. — 71p

UNIMAR GROUP

BOYD, Stewart C.
Minet Holdings plc, W. M. D. Underwriting Agencies Limited : investigation under Section 165 (1) (b) of the Companies Act 1948 : interim report / S. C. Boyd, P. W. G. DuBuisson, inspectors appointed by the Secretary of State for Trade and Industry. — London : H.M.S.O., 1986. — 88p

UNION CARBIDE CORPORATION

CHERNIACK, Martin
The Hawk's Nest incident : America's worst industrial disaster / Martin Cherniack ; foreword by Phillip Landrigan and Anthony Robbins. — New Haven : Yale University Press, c1986. — x, 194p, [16]p of plates. — *Includes index. — Bibliography: p.184-188*

SUFRIN, Sidney C.
Bhopal, its setting, responsibility, and challenge / Sidney C. Surfin. — Delhi : Ajanta Publications : Distributors, Ajanta Books International, 1985. — 98 p.. — 60-9

UNION CARBIDE LTD. (India)

SUFRIN, Sidney C.
Bhopal, its setting, responsibility, and challenge / Sidney C. Surfin. — Delhi : Ajanta Publications : Distributors, Ajanta Books International, 1985. — 98 p.. — 60-9

UNION CASTLE MAIL STEAMSHIP COMPANY — History

BERRIDGE, G. R.
The politics of the South Africa run : European Shipping and Pretoria / G.R. Berridge. — Oxford : Clarendon, 1987. — [298]p. — *Includes bibliography and index*

UNION DE CENTRO DEMOCRATICO

MARTÍN VILLA, Rodolfo
Al servicio del Estado / Rodolfo Martín Villa. — Barcelona : Editorial Planeta, 1984. — 229p

UNIÓN GENERAL DE TRABAJADORES DE ESPAÑA — History

ROSAL, Amaro del
1934 : Movimiento Revolucionario de Octubre / Amaro del Rosal. — [Madrid] : Akal, c1984. — xiii,313p. — (España sin espejo ; 1). — *Bibliography: p313*

UNION GENERAL DE TRABAJADORES DE ESPAÑA — History — Sources

UNION GENERAL DE TRABAJADORES DE ESPAÑA
Actas de la Unión General de Trabajadores de España / [notas de introducción por Amaro del Rosal Días]. — Madrid : Fundación Pablo Iglesias
Vol.2: 1899-1904. — 1985. — 687p

UNION GENERAL DE TRABAJADORES DE ESPAÑA
Actas de la Unión General de Trabajadores de España / [brevas notas de introducción por Amaro del Rosal Días]. — Madrid : Fundación Pablo Iglesias
Vol.4: 1910-1913. — 1985. — 492p

UNION GÉNÉRALE DES ISRAÉLITES DE FRANCE

COHEN, Richard I
The burden of conscience : French Jewish leadership during the holocaust / Richard I. Cohen. — Bloomington : Indiana University Press, c1987. — p. cm. — (The Modern Jewish experience). — *Includes index. — Bibliography: p*

UNION LIBÉRALE-DEMOCRATIQUE SUISSE

Relations cantons-confédération : résumé des rapports presentés au Congrès de l'Union libérale-democratique suisse à Neuchâtel le 5 avril 1975. — [S.l.] : Union libérale-démocratique suisse, 1975. — 27p

UNIÓN MILITAR DEMOCRÁTICA

CAPARRÓS, Francisco
La UMD : militares rebeldes / Francisco Caparrós. — Barcelona : Argos Vergara, 1983. — 170p

UNION OF COMMUNICATION WORKERS

Annual conference report / Union of Communication Workers. — London : Union of Communication Workers, 1986-. — *Annual*

TERRY, Michael
Political change and union democracy : the negotiation of internal order in the Union of Communication Workers / Michael Terry and Anthony Ferner. — Coventry : University of Warwick. School of Industrial and Business Studies. Industrial Relations Research Unit, 1986. — 23 leaves. — (Warwick papers in industrial relations ; no.10). — *Bibliography: p23*

UNION OF CONSTRUCTION, ALLIED TRADES AND TECHNICIANS

UCATT viewpoint : journal of the Union of Construction, Allied Trades and Technicians. — London : UCATT, 1985-. — *Monthly*

UNION OF LIBERAL AND PROGRESSIVE SYNAGOGUES — History

RAYNER, John Desmond
Strengthen our hands. — [London?] : [Union of Liberal and Progressive Synagogues], 195-?]. — [12p]

UNION PACIFIC CORPORATION

UNION PACIFIC CORPORATION
Annual report / Union Pacific Corporation. — New York : Union Pacific Corporation, 1982-. — *Annual. — Continues: Missouri Pacific Corporation. Annual report*

UNION PROGRESSISTE SÉNÉGALAISE

UNION PROGRESSISTE SÉNÉGALAISE
Syndicalisme et politique. — [S.l.] : Union Progressiste Sénégalaise, 1973. — 20p

UNITED ARAB EMIRATES

United Arab Emirates / Middle East Research Institute, University of Pennsylvania. — London : Croom Helm, c1985. — 198p. — (MERI report)

UNITED ARAB EMIRATES — History

TARYAM, Abdullah Omran
The establishment of the United Arab Emirates 1950-85 / Abdullah Omran Taryam. — London : Croom Helm, c1987. — 290p. — *Includes index*

UNITED ARAB REPUBLIC — Statistics

Basic statistics = Statistiques de base / Central Agency for Public Mobilisation and Statistics, United Arab Republic. — Cairo : Central Agency for Public Mobilisation and Statistics, 1964. — *Text in English and French*

UNITED AUTOMOBILE WORKERS UNION

ANDERSON, John
Fifty years of the U.A.W. : from sit-downs to concessions / John Anderson. — 2nd ed. — Chicago, (Ill.) : Bookmarks, 1986. — 44p

UNITED BISCUITS

MCTIERNAN, M. P.
Workers' alternative plans : a case study at United Biscuits Liverpool plant / M. P. McTiernan. — Coventry : University of Warwick. School of Industrial and Business Studies. Industrial Relations Research Unit, 1986. — 13p. — (Warwick papers in industrial relations ; no.7). — *Bibliography: p13*

UNITED BROTHERHOOD OF CARPENTERS AND JOINERS OF AMERICA. Local 83 (Halifax, N.S.) — History

MCKAY, Ian
The craft transformed : an essay on the carpenters of Halifax, 1885-1985 / Ian McKay. — Halifax : Holdfast Press : Distributed by Formac Pub., Co., 1985. — ix, 148 p.. — *"Written to mark the centenary of Local 83 of the United Brotherhood of Carpenters and Joiners of America"--P. [vii]. — Bibliography: p. [145]-148*

UNITED COUNTIES OMNIBUS COMPANY

WARWICK, Roger M.
An illustrated history of United Counties Omnibus Company Limited / Roger M. Warwick. — Northampton : R. M. Warwick, 1985
Part 7: 1952-1961. — 108p

UNITED FRUIT COMPANY

SCHLESINGER, Stephen C
Bitter fruit : the untold story of the American coup in Guatemala / Stephen Schlesinger and Stephen Kinzer. — 1st ed. — Garden City, N.Y. : Doubleday, 1982. — xv, 320 p., [16] p. of plates. — *Includes index. — Bibliography: p. [293]-305*

UNITED KINGDOM IMMIGRANTS ADVISORY SERVICE

UNITED KINGDOM IMMIGRANTS ADVISORY SERVICE
Annual report / United Kingdom Immigrants Advisory Service. — London : United Kingdom Immigrants Advisory Service, 1983/84-. — *Annual*

UNITED NATIONS

Diplomacy at the UN / edited and introduced by G.R. Berridge and A. Jennings. — London : Macmillan, 1985. — xvii,227p. — *Includes index*

DORSEY, Gray L
Beyond the United Nations : changing discourse in international politics and law / Gray L. Dorsey. — Lanham ; London : University Press of America, c1986. — xi, 111p. — (Exxon Education Foundation series on rhetoric and political discourse ; v. 5). — *Bibliography: p. 103-111. — Bibliography: p.103-111*

International organization and integration : annotated basic doucments of international organizations and arrangements / selected by Louis B. Sohn. — Student ed. — Dordrecht [Netherlands] ; Boston : Nijhoff ; Norwell, MA, USA : Distributors for the U.S. and Canada, Kluwer Academic Publishers, 1986. — xxviii, 1082 p.. — *Based on the five-volume set International organization and integration. — Includes index*

JAKOBSON, Max
Trettioåttonde våningen : håkomster och anteckningar 1965-1971 / Max Jakobson ; översättning av Henrik von Bonsdorff. — Helsinki : Holger Schildts, 1983. — 351p. — *Translated into Swedish from Finnish. — Originally published Helsinki Keuruu, 1983*

KHARE, Subhas Chandra
Use of force under U.N. Charter / Subhas C. Khare ; foreword by Nagendra Singh. — 1st ed. — New Delhi, India : Metropolitan, 1985. — xii, 444 p.. — *Spine title: Use of force under United Nations Charter. — : Originally presented as the author's thesis (LL. D.--Lucknow University). — Includes index. — Bibliography: p. [425]-439*

ROCHE, Douglas
United Nations : divided world / Douglas Roche. — Toronto : NC Press, 1984. — 152p. — *Bibliography: p[151]-152p*

SHORE, William I
Fact-finding in the maintenance of international peace / by William I. Shore. Pref. by A. J. P. Tammes. — Dobbs Ferry, N.Y. : Oceana Publications, 1970. — ii, 183 p. — *Bibliography: p. 154-167*

SOCIÉTE FRANÇAISE POUR LE DROIT INTERNATIONAL. Colloque (19e : 1985 : Nice)
Les nations unies et le droit international économique : [actes du colloque]. — Paris : A. Pedone, 1986. — vii,383p

STEELE, David, 19---
The reform of the United Nations / David Steele. — London : Croom Helm, c1987. — 191p. — (The Croom Helm United Nations and its agencies series). — *Bibliography: p181-186. — Includes index*

SUTER, Keith D.
Peace working : the United Nations and disarmament / Keith D. Suter. — Sydney : United Nations Association of Australia, 1985. — 189p

The United Nations at forty : a foundation to build on. — New York : United Nations, 1985. — vi,[202]p. — *Sales no. : E.85.I.24*

URQUHART, Brian
The United Nations and international law: : the Rede Lecture / Brian Urquhart. — Cambridge : Cambridge University Press, 1985. — 20p

UNITED NATIONS — Armed Forces — History

ALLSEBROOK, Mary
Prototypes of peacemaking : the first forty years of the United Nations / compiled and written by Mary Allsebrook ; introduction by Lord Caradon. — Harlow : Longman, c1986. — xvi,158p. — *Bibliography: p151-152. — Includes index*

UNITED NATIONS — Documentation

UNITED NATIONS. Dag Hammarskjold Library
United Nations document series symbols 1946-1977 : cumulative list with indexes. — New York : United Nations, 1978. — 312p. — (Dag Hammarskjold Library Bibliographical Series ; no.5/Rev.3). — *U.N. document no.ST/LIB/Ser.B/5/Rev.3 U.N. sales no.E.79.I.3*

UNITED NATIONS — Government publications

UNITED NATIONS
United Nations documentation : a brief guide. — New York : United Nations, 1981. — 51p. — (Document / United Nations ; ST/LIB/34/Rev.1). — *UN doc. no.: ST/LIB/34/Rev. 1. — Bibliography: p46-47. — Bibliography: p. 46-47*

UNITED NATIONS — History

ROMULO, Carlos Peña
Forty years : a Third World soldier at the UN / Carlos P. Romulo with Beth Day Romulo. — Westport, Conn. : Greenwood Press, c1986. — p. cm. — (Studies in freedom ; no. 3). — *Includes index. — Bibliography: p*

The United Nations and disarmament, 1945-1985 / United Nations Department for Disarmament Affairs. — New York : United Nations, 1985. — x, 166 p.. — *"United Nations publication sales no. E.85.IX.6"--T.p. verso*

UNITED NATIONS — Management

BEIGBEDER, Yves
Management problems in United Nations organizations : reform or decline? / Yves Beigbeder. — London : Pinter, 1987. — x,174p. — (Studies in international political economy). — *Bibliography: p170-172. — Includes index*

UNITED NATIONS — Officials and employees, American

BEHRSTOCK, Julian
The eighth case : troubled times at the United Nations / Julian Behrstock. — Lanham : University Press of America, c1987. — p. cm. — *Includes bibliographical references and index*

UNITED NATIONS — Developing countries

The international law of development : basic documents / compiled and edited by A. Peter Mutharika. — Dobbs Ferry, N.Y. : Oceana
Vol.2. — 1978. — vii,647-1303p

UNITED NATIONS — Nepal — Economic assistance

Policy approaches to development issues : a review of Nepal's relation with ESCAP along with policy statements of Nepalese delegations since its thirteenth session / edited by Rabindra K. Shakya. — Kathmandu : National Planning Commission Secretariat, 1983. — [iv],68p

UNITED NATIONS — Palestine

MALLISON, W. Thomas
The Palestine problem in international law and world order / W. Thomas Mallison and Sally V. Mallison. — London : Longman, 1986. — xvi,564p

UNITED NATIONS — Philippines — History

ROMULO, Carlos Peña
Forty years : a Third World soldier at the UN / Carlos P. Romulo with Beth Day Romulo. — Westport, Conn. : Greenwood Press, c1986. — p. cm. — (Studies in freedom ; no. 3). — *Includes index. — Bibliography: p*

UNITED NATIONS — South Africa

REDDY, E. S.
Apartheid, the United Nations and the international community : a collection of speeches and papers / E. S. Reddy. — New Delhi : Vikas, 1986. — x,157p

UNITED NATIONS — Spain

LLEONART Y AMSELEM, A. J.
España y ONU / A. J. Lleonart y Amselem, F. M. Castiella y Maiz. — Madrid : Consejo Superior de Investigaciones Cientificas. — (España y la Organización de las Naciones Unidas ; 1). — *Bibliography: p[433]-443*
1 (1945-46): La "Cuestion Española" : documentación basica, sistematizada y anotada. — 1978. — lxxv,451p

LLEONART Y AMSELEM, A. J.
España y ONU / por A. J. Lleonart y Amselem. — Madrid : Consejo Superior de Investigaciones Cientificas. — (España y la Organización de las Naciones Unidas ; 2). — *Summary in English. — p[327]-332*
2 (1947): La "Cuestion Española" : estudio introductivo y corpus documental. — 1983. — xxxi,340p

LLEONART Y AMSELEM, A. J.
España y ONU / A. J. Lleonart y Amselem. — Madrid : Consejo Superior de Investigaciones Cientificas. — (España y la Organización de las Naciones Unidas ; 3). — *Summary in English*
3(1948-49): La "Cuestion Española" : estudios introductivos y corpus documental. — 1985. — xxv,400p

UNITED NATIONS — United States

BEHRSTOCK, Julian
The eighth case : troubled times at the United Nations / Julian Behrstock. — Lanham : University Press of America, c1987. — p. cm. — *Includes bibliographical references and index*

BLOOMFIELD, Lincoln P.
The United Nations and U.S. foreign policy : a new look at the national interest / Lincoln P. Bloomfield. — Rev. ed. — London : University of London Press, 1969. — xviii,268p

UNITED NATIONS. Conference on the Law of the Sea (3rd : 1973-1982 : New York, etc.) — Documentation

The law of the sea : master file containing references to official documents of the Third United Nations Conference on the Law of the Sea. — New York : United Nations, 1985. — xiii,176p. — *Sales no.: E.85.V.9*

UNITED NATIONS. Conference on Trade and Development

UNITED NATIONS. Conference on Trade and Development. Committee on Transfer of Technology
Bibliography of documents on transfer and development of technology that have been prepared by or for the UNCTAD Secretariat. — [New York] : the Conference, 1986. — iii,34p. — ([Document] / United Nations ; TD/B/C.6/INF.2/Rev.5)

UNITED NATIONS. Conference on Trade and Development — Bibliography

UNCTAD 1963-1983 : bibliography = CNUCED 1963-1983 : bibliographie. — Geneva : United Nations Library, 1983. — ii,81p. — (Publications / United Nations Library. Series C. special bibliographies, repertoires and indexes ; no.4 = Publications / Nations Unie, Bibliothèque. Serie C. Bibliographies speciales, repertoires et index ; no.4)

UNITED NATIONS. Development Programme

Cooperation south: the magazine of technical co-operation among developing countries / United Nations. Development Programme. — New York : UNDP, 1985-. — Quarterly. — Continues:

Technical cooperation among developing countries news : TCDC news / United Nations. Development Programme. — New York : UNDP, 1979-1984. — Quarterly. — Continued by: Cooperation south: the magazine of technical co-operation among developing countries

UNITED NATIONS. Economic and Social Commission for Asia and the Pacific

Industry and technology development news: Asia and the Pacific / United Nations. Economic and Social Commission for Asia and the Pacific. — Bangkok : United Nations. Economic and Social Commission for Asia and the Pacific, 1984-. — Annual. — Continues: Industrial development news: Asia and the Pacific

Quarterly bulletin of statistics for Asia and the Pacific / Economic and Social Commission for Asia and the Pacific, United Nations. — Bangkok : Economic and Social Commission for Asia and the Pacific, 1971-. — Quarterly

UNITED NATIONS. Economic and Social Commission for Asia and the Pacific — Relations — Nepal

Policy approaches to development issues : a review of Nepal's relation with ESCAP along with policy statements of Nepalese delegations since its thirteenth session / edited by Rabindra K. Shakya. — Kathmandu : National Planning Commission Secretariat, 1983. — [iv],68p

UNITED NATIONS. Economic and Social Commission for Western Asia — Statistics

External trade bulletin of the ESCWA region / United Nations. Economic and Social Commission for Western Asia. — Baghdad : ESCWA, 1985-. — Annual

UNITED NATIONS. Economic Commission for Africa

ECA index: bibliography of selected ECA documents / United Nations. Economic Commission for Africa. — Addis Ababa : United Nations. Economic Commission for Africa, 1975-. — Annual. — Text in English and French

UNITED NATIONS. Environment Programme

AHMAD, Yusuf J.
Desertification : financial support for the biosphere / Yusuf J. Ahmad, Mohammed Kassas ; sponsored by the United Nations Environment Programme. — London : Hodder and Stoughton, 1987. — xviii,187p. — Includes index

UNITED NATIONS. Environment Programme
Evaluation report. — Nairobi : United Nations. Environment Programme, 1985-. — Annual

UNITED NATIONS. Environment Programme
Report on new projects. — New York : United Nations, 1984-. — Annual

UNITED NATIONS. General Assembly

PETERSON, M. J.
The General Assembly in world politics / M.J. Peterson. — Boston [Mass.] ; London : Allen & Unwin, 1986. — [240]p. — Includes index

SCHWEBEL, Stephen M.
The legal effect of resolutions and codes of conduct of the United Nations. — Deventer : Kluwer, 1986. — 16p. — (Forum internationale ; no. 7). — Includes bibliographical references

UNITED NATIONS. General Assembly. Charter of Economic Rights and Duties of States

BULAJIĆ, Milan
Principles of international development law : progressive development of the principles of international law relating to the new international economic order / Milan Bulajić. — Dordrecht, Netherlands ; Boston : Martinus Nijhoff Publishers, 1986. — 403p. — Bibliography: p.359-366

UNITED NATIONS. Industrial Development Organization — Documentation — Bibliography

UNITED NATIONS. Industrial Development Organization
Index to documents issued by the Committee for Industrial Development, Centre for Industrial Development and Division for Industrial Development from inception to end of 1966. — New York : United Nations Industrial Development Organization, 1967. — v,114p. — (Document / United Nations ; ID/SER.G/1). — United Nations document no.ID/SER.G/1

UNITED NATIONS

Everyone's United Nations. — 10th ed. — New York : United Nations, 1986. — 484p. — Sales no: E.85.I.24

UNITED NATIONS — Membership

TSIANG, Tingfu F.
The Charter of the United Nations and the package deal / by Tingfu F. Tsiang. — New York : Chinese Delegation to the United Nations, 1955. — 37p

UNITED NATIONS — Resolutions

SCHWEBEL, Stephen M.
The legal effect of resolutions and codes of conduct of the United Nations. — Deventer : Kluwer, 1986. — 16p. — (Forum internationale ; no. 7). — Includes bibliographical references

UNITED NATIONS — Taiwan

TSIANG, Tingfu F.
The Charter of the United Nations and the package deal / by Tingfu F. Tsiang. — New York : Chinese Delegation to the United Nations, 1955. — 37p

UNITED NATIONS CHILDREN'S FUND

The state of the world's children / United Nations Children's Fund. — London : Published for UNICEF by the Oxford University Press 1981-. — Annual

UNITED NATIONS COMMISSION ON INTERNATIONAL TRADE LAW

DORE, Isaak I.
Arbitration and conciliation under the UNCITRAL rules : a textual analysis / Issaak I. Dore. — Dordrecht ; Boston : Nijhoff, 1986. — p. cm

UNITED NATIONS CONFERENCE ON THE LAW OF THE SEA

Malaysia and the United Nations Conference on the Law of the Sea : selected documents / edited by Hamzah Ahmad. — [Kuala Lumpur : s.n.], 1983. — v,319p. — Cover title: Malaysia and the law of the sea

UNITED NATIONS CONVENTION ON THE LAW OF THE SEA (1982 : Montego Bay)

The law of the sea : multilateral treaties relevant to the United Nations Convention on the Law of the Sea. — New York : United Nations, 1985. — ix,108p. — Sales no.: E.85.V.11

The law of the sea : pollution by dumping : legislative history of Articles 1, paragraph 1 (5), 210 and 216 of the United Nations Convention on the Law of the Sea. — New York : United Nations, 1985. — V,77p. — Sales no.: E.85.V.12

UNITED NATIONS. ECONOMIC COMMISSION FOR AFRICA

Africa index: selected articles on socio-economic development / United Nations. Economic Commission for Africa. — Addis Ababa : United Nations. Economic Commission for Africa, 1971-. — 3 times a year. — Text in English and French

UNITED NATIONS ENVIRONMENT PROGRAMME — Catalogs

An Environmental bibliography : publications issued by UNEP or under its auspices, 1973-1980. — Nairobi : United Nations Environment Programme, 1981. — vi,67p. — (UNEP reference series ; 2). — Includes indexes

UNITED NATIONS HIGH COMMISSIONER FOR REFUGEES IN AFRICA

WILLIAMS, Norman
Role of the Office of the United Nations High Commissioner for Refugees in Africa / prepared by Norman Williams, Joint Inspection Unit. — New York : United Nations, 1986. — 28p. — United Nations Joint Inspection Unit report (JIV/REP/86/2) circulated as annex to United Nations General Assembly document A/41/380.

UNITED STATED — History — 1815-1861 — Collected works

WEBSTER, Daniel
The papers of Daniel Webster / Charles M. Wiltse, editor-in-chief. — Hanover, N.H. ; London : published for Dartmouth College by the University Press of New England
Series 4: Speeches and formal writings
Vol.1: 1800-1833 / Charles M. Wiltse editor ; Alan R. Berolzheimer, assistant editor. — 1986. — xx,641p

UNITED STATES. Constitution

Beyond confederation : origins of the constitution and American national identity / edited by Richard Beeman, Stephen Botein, and Edward C. Carter II. — Chapel Hill : University of North Carolina Press, c1987. — p. cm. — "Published for the Institute of Early American History and Culture, Williamsburg, Virginia.". — Includes index

UNITED STATES. Economic Recovery Tax Act

BRAYTON, Flint
The macroeconomic and sectoral effects of the Economic Recovery Tax Act : some simulation results / Flint Brayton, Peter B. Clark. — Washington, D.C. : Board of Governors of the Federal Reserve System, 1985. — 17p. — (Staff study / Board of Governors of the Federal Reserve System (U.S.) ; 148)

UNITED STATES. Migrant Health Act 1962

JOHNSTON, Helen L.
Health for the nation's harvesters : a history of the Migrant Health Program in its economic and social setting / Helen L. Johnston. — Farmington Hills, Mich. : National Migrant Worker Council, 1985. — 252p. — *Bibliography: p[193]-206*

UNITED STATES. Taiwan Relations Act

Congress, the Presidency, and the Taiwan Relations Act / edited by Louis W. Koenig, James C. Hsiung, and King-Yuh Chang. — New York : Praeger, 1985. — p. cm. — *Includes index. — Bibliography: p*

UNITED STATES

Facts about the United States. — [Washington, D.C.?] : United States Information Service, 1951. — 68p

UNITED STATES — Air defenses, Military

BYERS, R. B
Aerospace defence : Canada's future role? / R.B. Byers, John Hamre, G.R. Lindsey. — Toronto, Canada : Canadian Institute of International Affairs, 1985. — 56 p.. — (Wellesley papers ; 9/1985). — *Includes bibliographies.* — Contents: Defending North America / G.R. Lindsey -- Continental air defence, United States security policy, and Canada-United States defence relations / John Hamre -- NORAD, Star Wars, and strategic doctrine / R.B. Byers

UNITED STATES — Appropriations and expenditures

LEONARD, Herman B
Checks unbalanced : the quiet side of public spending / Herman B. Leonard. — New York : Basic Books, c1986. — xii, 289 p.. — *Includes index. — Bibliography: p. 265-279*

LEVITT, M. S.
Measuring changes in central government productivity in the United States / M. S. Levitt. — London : National Institute of Economic and Social Research, 1986. — 24p. — (Discussion paper / National Institute of Economic and Social Research ; no.119)

UNITED STATES — Armed Forces

GABRIEL, Richard A
Military incompetence : why the American military doesn't win / Richard A. Gabriel. — 1st ed. — New York : Hill and Wang, 1985. — p. cm. — *Bibliography: p*

UNITED STATES — Armed Forces — Addresses, essays, lectures

Toward a more effective defense : report of the Defense Organization Project / edited by Barry M. Blechman and William J. Lynn. — Cambridge, Mass. : Ballinger Pub. Co., 1985. — xiii, 247 p.. — *Includes bibliographies and index*

UNITED STATES — Armed Forces — Afro-American troops

MCGUIRE, Phillip
Taps for a Jim Crow army : letters from black soldiers in World War II / Phillip McGuire ; with a foreword by Benjamin Quarles. — Santa Barbara, Calif. : ABC-Clio, c1983. — li, 278 p. . — *Includes index. — Bibliography: p. 263*

UNITED STATES — Armed Forces — Appropriations and expenditures

A dollar cost comparison of Soviet and US defense activities, 1966-1976. — [Washington] : Central Intelligence Agency, 1977. — 15p. — *SR 77-10001U*

EPSTEIN, Joshua M.
The 1988 defense budget / Joshua M. Epstein. — Washington, D.C. : Brookings Institution, 1987. — viii,57p. — (Studies in defense policy)

UNITED STATES — Armed Forces — History — 19th century — Addresses, essays, lectures

Military enterprise and technological change : perspectives on the American experience / edited by Merritt Roe Smith. — Cambridge, Mass. : MIT Press, c1985. — 391 p.. — *Includes bibliographical references and index*

UNITED STATES — Armed Forces — History — 20th century — Addresses, essays, lectures

Military enterprise and technological change : perspectives on the American experience / edited by Merritt Roe Smith. — Cambridge, Mass. : MIT Press, c1985. — 391 p.. — *Includes bibliographical references and index*

UNITED STATES — Armed Forces — Military life

MCGUIRE, Phillip
Taps for a Jim Crow army : letters from black soldiers in World War II / Phillip McGuire ; with a foreword by Benjamin Quarles. — Santa Barbara, Calif. : ABC-Clio, c1983. — li, 278 p. . — *Includes index. — Bibliography: p. 263*

UNITED STATES — Armed Forces — Pay, allowances, etc — Congresses

Public sector payrolls / edited by David A. Wise. — Chicago : University of Chicago Press, 1987. — ix, 327 p.. — (A National Bureau of Economic Research project report). — *Papers presented at a conference held in Williamsburg, Va., Nov. 15-17, 1984. — Includes bibliographies and indexes*

UNITED STATES — Armed Forces — Recruiting, enlistment, etc

BINKIN, Martin
Military technology and defense manpower / Martin Binkin. — Washington, D.C. : Brookings Institution, 1986. — p. cm. — (Studies in defense policy). — *Includes index*

HOSEK, James R
Educational expectations and enlistment decisions / James R. Hosek, Christine E. Peterson, Rick A. Eden. — Santa Monica, CA. : Rand, [1986]. — xiii, 41 p.. — "Prepared for the Office of the Assistant Secretary of Defense/Force Management and Personnel.". — "March 1986.". — R-3350-FMP.". — *Bibliography: p. 41*

UNITED STATES — Armed forces — Recruiting, enlistment, etc. — Forecasting

COTTERMAN, Robert F.
Forecasting enlistment supply : a time series of cross sections model / Robert F. Cotterman. — Santa Monica, Calif. : Rand, 1986. — xvi,74p. — *Bibliography: p73-74*

UNITED STATES — Armed Forces — Search and rescue operations — History — 20th century

RYAN, Paul B
The Iranian rescue mission : why it failed / by Paul B. Ryan. — Annapolis, Md. : Naval Institute Press, c1985. — xiii, 185p. — *Includes index. — Bibliography: p [177]-180*

UNITED STATES — Biography

American reformers : an H.W. Wilson biographical dictionary / edited by Alden Whitman. — New York : H.W. Wilson Co., 1985. — xx, 930 p.. — *Includes bibliographies*

BUEL, Joy Day
The way of duty : a woman and her family in revolutionary America / Joy Day Buel and Richard Buel, Jr. — New York ; London : Norton, c1984. — xviii,309p. — *Bibliography: p299-301. — Includes index*

HUGHES, Jonathan R. T
The vital few : the entrepreneur and American economic progress / Jonathan Hughes. — Expanded ed. — New York : Oxford University Press, 1986. — p. cm. — *Includes index. — Bibliography: p*

Indian lives : essays on nineteenth- and twentieth-century Native American leaders / edited by L.G. Moses and Raymond Wilson. — 1st ed. — Albuquerque : University of New Mexico Press, c1985. — 227p. — *Includes index. — Bibliography: p.[215]-216*

Who's who in American politics 1985-1986 / edited by Jaques Cattell Press. — 10th ed.. — New York ; London : R. R. Bowker, 1985. — xxii,1761p

UNITED STATES — Census — Indexes

SCHULZE, Suzanne
Population information in nineteenth century census volumes / by Suzanne Schulze. — Phoenix, AZ : Oryx Press, 1983. — ix, 446 p.. — *Continued by: Population information in twentieth century census volumes, 1900-1940. — Bibliography: p. 437-438*

UNITED STATES — Civilization

GABRIEL, Ralph Henry
The course of American democratic thought / Ralph Henry Gabriel. — 3rd ed. / with Robert H. Walker. — New York : Greenwood Press, 1986. — xix, 568 p.. — (Contributions in American studies ; no. 87). — *Includes index. — Bibliography: p. 541-547*

KAMMEN, Michael G
A machine that would go of itself : the Constitution in American culture / Michael Kammen. — 1st ed. — New York : Knopf, 1986. — xxii, 532 p., [16] p. of plates. — *Includes index. — Bibliography: p. 413-507*

UNITED STATES — Civilization — Addresses, essays, lectures

The Rights of memory : essays on history, science, and American culture / edited by Taylor Littleton. — University, Ala. : University of Alabama Press, c1986. — viii, 227 p.. — (The Franklin lectures in the sciences & humanities). — *Includes bibliographies and index*

UNITED STATES — Civilization — 20th century

BROOKEMAN, Christopher
American culture and society since the 1930s / Christopher Brookeman. — 1st American ed. — New York : Schocken Books, 1984. — xv, 241 p., [8] p. of plates. — *Includes index. — Bibliography: p. 227-233*

UNITED STATES — Civilization — 1945-

BOYER, Paul S
By the bomb's early light : American thought and culture at the dawn of the atomic age / Paul Boyer. — New York : Pantheon, 1985. — xx, 440p. — *Includes bibliographical references and index*

UNITED STATES — Commerce

BANK OF JAPAN. Research and Statistics Department
On the U.S. trade imbalances. — Tokyo : Bank of Japan. Research and Statistics Department, 1986. — 28p. — (Special paper / Bank of Japan. Research and Statistics Department ; no.144)

HEFFER, Jean
Le port de New York et le commerce extérieur américain 1860-1900 / Jean Heffer. — Paris : Université de Paris 1, Panthéon-Sorbonne, 1986. — ii,568p. — (Publications de la Sorbonne. Série internationale ; 25)

UNITED STATES — Commerce — Case studies

Revitalizing American industry : lessons from our competitors / Milton S. Hochmuth and William H. Davidson, editors. — Cambridge, Mass. : Ballinger Pub. Co., 1985. — p. cm. — *Includes bibliographies and index*

UNITED STATES — Commerce — History — 19th century

SCHROEDER, John H.
Shaping a maritime empire : the commercial and diplomatic role of the American Navy, 1829-1861 / John H. Schroeder. — Westport, Conn. ; London : Greenwood Press, 1985. — 229p. — (Contributions in military studies ; no. 48). — "Notes on sources": p. [215]-219. — *Includes bibliographical references and index*

UNITED STATES — Commerce — Canada

Building a Canadian-American free trade area : papers / by Donald S. MacDonald...[et al.] ; edited by Edward R. Fried, Frank Stone, Philip H. Trezise. — Washington, D.C. : Brookings Institution, 1987. — xii,217p. — (Brookings dialogues on public policy)

LIPSEY, Richard G.
Taking the initative : Canada's trade options in a turbulent world / Richard G. Lipsey and Murray G. Smith. — Toronto : C.D. Howe Institute, 1985. — xi.183p. — (Observation / C.D. Howe Institute ; no.27). — *Includes references*

WINHAM, Gilbert R.
Canada - U.S. sectoral trade study : the impact of free trade : a background paper prepared for Royal Commission on the Economic Union and Development Prospects for Canada, Ottawa, Ontario - April 1985 / Gilbert R. Winham ; with the assistance of David Black...[et al.]. — Halifax, N.S. : Dalhousie University, Centre for Foreign Policy Studies, 1986. — viii,323p

WONNACOTT, Ronald J
Aggressive U.S. reciprocity evaluated with a new analytical approach to trade conflicts / R.J. Wonnacott. — Montreal, Quebec : Institute for Research on Public Policy, c1984. — xxi, 68 p.. — (Essays in international economics). — *Bibliography: p. 57-58*

UNITED STATES — Commerce — China — History — 19th century

CHINA AND THE RED BARBARIANS: AMERICAN AND BRITISH RELATIONS WITH CHINA IN THE 19TH CENTURY (Symposium : 1972 : London)
China and the red barbarians : [papers read at the Symposium]. — London : National Maritime Museum, 1973. — 26p. — (Maritime monographs and reports ; no.8)

UNITED STATES — Commerce — Japan

MCCREARY, Don R
Japanese-U.S. business negotiations : a cross-cultural study / Don R. McCreary. — New York : Praeger, 1986. — viii, 121 p.. — "Praeger special studies. Praeger scientific.". — *Includes index. — Bibliography: p. 109-115*

WONNACOTT, Ronald J
Aggressive U.S. reciprocity evaluated with a new analytical approach to trade conflicts / R.J. Wonnacott. — Montreal, Quebec : Institute for Research on Public Policy, c1984. — xxi, 68 p.. — (Essays in international economics). — *Bibliography: p. 57-58*

UNITED STATES — Commerce — Soviet Union

LUNDBORG, Per
The economics of export embargo : the case of the US-Soviet grain suspension / Per Lundborg. — London : Croom Helm, c1987. — xi,127p. — *Bibliography: p119-122. — Includes index*

UNITED STATES — Commercial policy

BAUER, Raymond A.
American business and public policy : the politics of foreign trade / Raymond A. Bauer, Ithiel de Sola Pool, Lewis Anthony Dexter. — New York : Atherton Press, 1963. — xxvii,499p

DESTLER, I. M
American trade politics : system under stress / I.M. Destler. — Washington, DC : Institute for International Economics ; New York, NY : Twentieth Century Fund, 1986. — xiii, 366 p.. — *Includes bibliographical references and index*

HART, Michael
Some thoughts on Canada-United States sectoral free trade / Michael Hart. — Montreal, Quebec : Institute for Research on Public Policy, c1985. — xiii, 54 p.. — (Essays in international economics). — *Bibliography: p. 43-44*

JOHNSON, D. Gale
Agricultural policy and trade : adjusting domestic programs in an international framework : a task force report to the Trilateral Commission / authors, D. Gale Johnson, Kenzo Hemmi, Pierre Lardinois ; special consultants, T.K. Warley, P.A.J. Wijnmaalen. — New York : New York University Press, 1985. — xi, 132 p.. — (The Triangle papers ; 29). — *Includes bibliographies*

LAWRENCE, Robert Z.
Saving free trade : a pragmatic approach / Robert Z. Lawrence and Robert E. Litan. — Washington, D.C. : Brookings Institution, 1986. — p. cm. — *Includes bibliographical references and index*

LOVETT, William Anthony
World trade rivalry : trade equity and competing industrial policies / William A. Lovett. — Lexington, Mass. : Lexington Books, c1987. — p. cm. — *Includes index. — Bibliography: p*

U.S. trade policies in a changing world economy / edited by Robert M. Stern. — Cambridge, Mass. : MIT Press, c1987. — 437 p.. — *Includes bibliographies and indexes*

WONNACOTT, Paul
The United States and Canada : the quest for freer trade : an examination of selected issues / Paul Wonnacott ; with an appendix by John Williamson. — Washington, DC : Institute for International Economics, 1987. — p. cm. — (Policy analyses in international economics ; 16). — *Bibliography: p*

UNITED STATES — Commercial policy — Case studies

HUFBAUER, Gary Clyde
Trade protection in the United States : thirty-one case studies / Gary Clyde Hufbauer, assisted by Diane T. Berliner, Kimberly Ann Elliott. — Washington, DC : Institute for International Economics, 1985. — p. cm. — *Bibliography: p*

UNITED STATES — Congress

MERVIN, David
"Congressional government" revisited / David Mervin. — Coventry : University of Warwick, 1987. — 19p. — (Politics Working papers (University of Warwick) ; no.44)

UNITED STATES — Constitution

MADISON, James
The Federalist papers / James Madison, Alexander Hamilton and John Jay ; edited by Isaac Kramnick. — Harmondsworth : Penguin, 1987. — 515p

The United States of America : a government by the people. — [Washington, D.C.] : United States Information, 1966. — 106p

UNITED STATES — Constitutional history

Beyond confederation : origins of the constitution and American national identity / edited by Richard Beeman, Stephen Botein, and Edward C. Carter II. — Chapel Hill : University of North Carolina Press, c1987. — p. cm. — "Published for the Institute of Early American History and Culture, Williamsburg, Virginia.". — *Includes index*

CURRIE, David P
The constitution in the Supreme Court : the first hundred years, 1789-1888 / David P. Currie. — Chicago ; London : University of Chicago Press, c1985. — xiii, 504 p.. — "Tables of cases": p. 477-486. — *Includes bibliographical references and indexes*

Essays on the making of the Constitution / edited by Leonard W. Levy. — 2nd ed. — New York : Oxford University Press, 1987. — p. cm. — *Bibliography: p*

KAMMEN, Michael G
A machine that would go of itself : the Constitution in American culture / Michael Kammen. — 1st ed. — New York : Knopf, 1986. — xxii, 532 p., [16] p. of plates. — *Includes index. — Bibliography: p. 413-507*

MERRY, Henry J
The constitutional system : the group character of the elected institutions / Henry J. Merry. — New York : Praeger, 1986. — x, 215 p.. — *Includes bibliographies and index*

ROHR, John A
To run a constitution : the legitimacy of the administrative state / John A. Rohr. — Lawrence, Kan. : University Press of Kansas, c1986. — xv, 272 p.. — (Studies in government and public policy). — *Includes index. — Bibliography: p. 215-264*

WHITE, Morton Gabriel
Philosophy, The Federalist, and the Constitution / Morton White. — New York ; Oxford : Oxford University Press, 1987. — xi, 273p. — *Includes bibliographical references and index*

UNITED STATES — Constitutional history — Bibliography

The Dynamic Constitution : a historical bibliography / Suzanne Robitaille Ontiveros, editor ; foreword by Ralph C. Chandler. — Santa Barbara, Calif. : ABC-CLIO, c1986. — xvii, 343 p.. — (ABC-Clio research guides ; 19) . — *Includes indexes*

UNITED STATES — Constitutional history — Sources

The Founders' Constitution / edited by Philip B. Kurland and Ralph Lerner. — Chicago ; London : University of Chicago Press, 1987. — 5v. — *Includes bibliographical references and index. — Contents: v. 1. Major themes*

Free government in the making : readings in American political thought / [edited by] Alpheus Thomas Mason and Gordon E. Baker. — 4th ed. — New York : Oxford University Press, 1985. — xviii, 793p. — *Includes bibliographical references*

UNITED STATES — Constitutional law

LOFGREN, Charles A
"Government from reflection and choice" : constitutional essays on war, foreign relations, and federalism / Charles A. Lofgren. — New York : Oxford University Press, c1986. — xviii, 235p. — *Includes index*

MENDELSON, Wallace
Supreme Court statecraft : the rule of law and men / by Wallace Mendelson. — 1st ed. — Ames : Iowa State University Press, 1985. — p. cm. — *Includes index*

SHEPHERD, William C
To secure the blessings of liberty : American constitutional law and the new religious movements / William C. Shepherd. — New York : Crossroad Pub. Co. ; Chico, CA : Scholars Press, c1985. — x, 155 p.. — (Studies in religion / American Academy of Religion ; no. 35). — *Includes index. — Bibliography: p. [137]-144*

UNITED STATES — Constitutional law — Amendments — 11th

ORTH, John V
The judicial power of the United States : the eleventh amendment in American history / John V. Orth. — New York : Oxford University Press, 1986. — p. cm. — *Includes index. — Bibliography: p*

UNITED STATES — Constitutional law — Amendments — 14th — History

CURTIS, Michael Kent
No state shall abridge : the 14th amendment and the Bill of Rights / Michael Kent Curtis. — Durham, N.C. : Duke University Press, 1986. — xii, 275 p.. — *Includes index. — Bibliography: p. [221]-266*

UNITED STATES — Constitutional law — Interpretation and construction

CURRIE, David P
The constitution in the Supreme Court : the first hundred years, 1789-1888 / David P. Currie. — Chicago ; London : University of Chicago Press, c1985. — xiii, 504 p.. — *"Tables of cases": p. 477-486. — Includes bibliographical references and indexes*

MACEDO, Stephen
The New Right v. the Constitution / Stephen Macedo. — Washington, D.C. : Cato Institute, c1986. — xiv, 60 p. — *Includes bibliographical references*

RICHARDS, David A. J
Toleration and the Constitution / David A.J. Richards. — New York : Oxford University Press, 1986. — p. cm. — *Bibliography: p*

UNITED STATES — Constitutional law — Interpretation and construction — History

WOLFE, Christopher
The rise of modern judicial review : from constitutional interpretation to judge-made law / Christopher Wolfe. — New York : Basic Books, c1986. — ix, 392 p.. — ([Basic series in American government]). — *Series statement from jacket. — Includes indexes. — Bibliography: p. 357-380*

UNITED STATES — Defenses

American defense annual. — Lexington (Mass.) : Lexington Books, 1985/86-. — *Annual*

UNITED STATES. Department of Defense
Report to the Congress of the strategic defense initiative. — Washington D.C. : [the Department], 1985-. — *Annual*

UNITED STATES — Defenses — Addresses, essays, lectures

Toward a more effective defense : report of the Defense Organization Project / edited by Barry M. Blechman and William J. Lynn. — Cambridge, Mass. : Ballinger Pub. Co., 1985. — xiii, 247 p.. — *Includes bibliographies and index*

UNITED STATES — Diplomatic and consular service

HEINRICHS, Waldo H
American ambassador : Joseph C. Grew and the development of the United States diplomatic tradition / Waldo H. Heinrichs, Jr. — New York : Oxford University Press, 1986, c1966. — p. cm. — : Reprint. Originally published: Boston : Little, Brown, 1966. — *Includes index. — Bibliography: p*

UNITED STATES — Diplomatic and consular service — Australia — History

Australia through American eyes, 1935-1945 : observations by American diplomats / selected, edited and with an introduction by P.G. Edwards. — St Lucia : University of Queensland Press ; Hemel Hempstead : Distributed by Prentice-Hall, 1979. — xi,104p. — *Bibliography: p.97-101. — Includes index*

UNITED STATES — Directories — Bibliography

LARSON, Donna Rae
Guide to U.S. government directories / Donna Rae Larson. — [Phoenix] : Oryx Press Volume 2: 1980-1984. — 1985. — xviii,214p

UNITED STATES — Economic conditions

BOWLES, Samuel
Understanding capitalism : competition, command, and change in the U.S. economy / by Samuel Bowles and Richard Edwards. — New York, NY : Harper & Row, c1985. — p. cm. — *Includes index*

Essays in American economic history / edited by A. W. Coats and Ross M. Robertson. — London : Edward Arnold, 1969. — x,307p. — *bibl*

HUGHES, Jonathan R. T
The vital few : the entrepreneur and American economic progress / Jonathan Hughes. — Expanded ed. — New York : Oxford University Press, 1986. — p. cm. — *Includes index. — Bibliography: p*

Long-term factors in American economic growth / edited by Stanley L. Engerman and Robert E. Gallman. — Chicago : University of Chicago Press, 1986. — p. cm. — (Studies in income and wealth ; v. 51). — *Includes indexes*

UNITED STATES — Economic conditions — Maps

Atlas of the United States : a thematic and comparative approach / [edited by] Jilly Glassborow, Gillian Freeman. — New York : Macmillan : Nomad : Michael W. Dempsey, 1985. — 127p

UNITED STATES — Economic conditions — Regional disparities

BOOTH, Douglas E
Regional long waves, uneven growth, and the cooperative alternative / Douglas E. Booth. — New York : Praeger, 1987. — 121 p.. — *Includes index. — Bibliography: p. 109-115*

UNITED STATES — Economic conditions — To 1865 — Congresses

Quantity & quiddity : essays in U.S. economic history / Peter Kilby, editor ; Jeremy Atack ... [et al.]. — 1st ed. — Middletown, Conn. : Wesleyan University Press ; Scranton, Pa. : Distributed by Harper & Row, c1987. — xxiii, 423 p.. — *Papers presented at a symposium in honor of Stanley Lebergott, Mar. 28th and 29th, 1985. — "Selected publications of Stanley Lebergott": p. 399-405. — Includes bibliographical references and index*

UNITED STATES — Economic conditions — 1865-1918 — Congresses

Quantity & quiddity : essays in U.S. economic history / Peter Kilby, editor ; Jeremy Atack ... [et al.]. — 1st ed. — Middletown, Conn. : Wesleyan University Press ; Scranton, Pa. : Distributed by Harper & Row, c1987. — xxiii, 423 p.. — *Papers presented at a symposium in honor of Stanley Lebergott, Mar. 28th and 29th, 1985. — "Selected publications of Stanley Lebergott": p. 399-405. — Includes bibliographical references and index*

UNITED STATES — Economic conditions — 1918-1945

POTTER, Jim
The American economy between the World Wars / Jim Potter. — Rev. ed. — London : Macmillan, 1985. — 183p — *Previous ed.: 1974. — Bibliography: p174-176. — Includes index*

UNITED STATES. Congress. Joint Economic Committee. Fortieth Anniversary Symposium (1986 : Washington, D.C.)
The changing American economy : papers from the Fortieth Anniversary Symposium of the Joint Economic Committee of the United States Congress / edited by David R. Obey and Paul Sarbanes. — Oxford : Basil Blackwell, 1986. — viii,242p. — *Includes index*

UNITED STATES — Economic conditions — 1918-1945 — Bibliography

The Great Depression : a historical bibliography. — Santa Barbara, Calif. ; Oxford : ABC-Clio Information Services, c1984. — xii, 260p. — (ABC-Clio research guides ; 4). — *Includes index*

UNITED STATES — Economic conditions — 1945-

Economically active population : estimates and projections : 1950-2025 = Evaluations et projections de la population active : 1950-2025 = Estimaciones y proyecciones de la población económicamente activa : 1950-2025. — 3rd ed. — Geneva : International Labour Office V.4: Northern America, Europe, Oceania and USSR. — 1986. — xxvi,177p. — *Introduction and table headings in English, French and Spanish*

HEALY, Kent T
Performance of the U.S. railroads since World War II : a quarter century of private operation. — lst ed. — New York : Vantage Press, c1985. — vii, 295 p.. — *Bibliography: p. 287-295*

Liberating theory / by Michael Albert ... [et al.]. — 1st ed. — Boston, MA. : South End Press, c1986. — 197 p.. — *Bibliography: p. 195-197*

SCHULTZE, Charles L
Other times, other places : macroeconomic lessons from U.S. and European history / Charles L. Schultze. — Washington, D.C. : Brookings Institution, c1986. — p. cm. — *Includes index*

UNITED STATES. Congress. Joint Economic Committee. Fortieth Anniversary Symposium (1986 : Washington, D.C.)
The changing American economy : papers from the Fortieth Anniversary Symposium of the Joint Economic Committee of the United States Congress / edited by David R. Obey and Paul Sarbanes. — Oxford : Basil Blackwell, 1986. — viii,242p. — *Includes index*

WOLFF, Edward N.
Growth, accumulation, and unproductive activity : an analysis of the postwar U.S. economy / Edward N. Wolff. — Cambridge : Cambridge University Press, 1987. — xi,201p. — *Bibliography: p193-195. — Includes index*

UNITED STATES — Economic conditions — 1971-1981

BOWLES, Samuel
Beyond the wasteland : a democratic alternative to economic decline / Samuel Bowles, David M. Gordon & Thomas E. Weisskopf. — London : Verso, 1984. — xxi,328p. — *Originally published: Garden City, N.Y. : Anchor Press/Doubleday, 1983. — Includes index*

UNITED STATES — Economic conditions — 1971-1981 — Congresses

How open is the U.S. economy? / edited by R.W. Hafer. — Lexington, Mass. : Lexington Books, c1986. — xviii, 248 p. — *Papers presented at the Federal Reserve Bank of St. Louis's Tenth Annual Economic Conference, Oct. 12-13, 1985. — Includes bibliographies and index*

UNITED STATES — Economic conditions — 1981-

BOWLES, Samuel
Beyond the wasteland : a democratic alternative to economic decline / Samuel Bowles, David M. Gordon & Thomas E. Weisskopf. — London : Verso, 1984. — xxi,328p. — *Originally published: Garden City, N.Y. : Anchor Press/Doubleday, 1983. — Includes index*

Economic report of the people / Center for Popular Economics. — 1st ed. — Boston : South End Press, c1986. — xvii, 260 p.. — *The crossed out word "President" appears in the title before the word "people.". — Includes bibliographies and index*

GENETSKI, Robert J.
Taking the voodoo out of economics / by Robert J. Genetski. — Chicago : Regnery Books, 1986. — 189p. — *Bibliographical notes: p187-189*

UNITED STATES — Economic conditions — 1981- *continuation*

KRICKUS, Richard J
The superpowers in crisis : implications of domestic discord / Richard J. Krickus. — Washington ; London : Pergamon-Brassey's International Defence Publishers, 1987. — xiii, 236p. — *Includes bibliographies*

MAHARIDGE, Dale
Journey to nowhere : the saga of the new underclass / by Dale Maharidge ; photographs by Michael Williamson. — Garden City, N.Y. : Doubleday, 1984. — p. cm. — *"Dolphin book."*

MALKIN, Lawrence
The national debt / Lawrence Malkin. — 1st ed. — New York : Holt, c1987. — ix, 309 p.. — *Includes index.* — *Bibliography: p. 277-298*

STERNLIEB, George
Patterns of development / by George Sternlieb. — New Brunswick, N.J. : Center for Urban Policy Research, c1986. — p. cm. — *Includes index.* — *Bibliography: p*

Tax reform and U.S. economy / papers by Henry J. Aaron...[et al.] ; edited by Joseph A. Pechman. — Washington, D.C. : Brookings Institution, 1987. — 107p. — (Brookings dialogues on public policy). — *Papers presented at a conference at the Brookings institution, December 2, 1986*

WATKINS, Alfred J.
Till debt do us part : who wins, who loses, and who pays for the international debt crisis / Alfred J. Watkins. — London : University Press of America, 1987. — [108]p

WINIECKI, Jan
Economic prospects - East and West : a view from the East / Jan Winiecki ; comment: Roger Clarke. — London : Centre for Research into Communist Economies, 1987. — 136p. — (Understanding economic systems ; 3) . — *Bibliography: 123-127*

UNITED STATES — Economic conditions — 1981- — Congresses

American futures : political and economic trends and prospects : papers / presented to a conference at the Swedish Institute of International Affairs on June 16-18, 1983 ; edited by Leon N. Lindberg, Atis Lejins, and Katarina Engberg. — Stockholm : The Institute, [1984]. — x, 130 p.. — (Conference papers / the Swedish Institute of International Affairs ; 4, 1984). — *Includes bibliographies.* — *Contents: The American economy in the 1980's / Leon N. Lindberg -- Long-term trends in American economy and possible future / Michel Aglietta -- The US hegemony in the postwar world economy / Lars Mjøset -- Fragmentation and continuity / Reinhard Rode -- Gulliver's digestion / Harald Müller -- Party decline and party reform / Alan Ware -- The changing political role of business in the USA / Graham K. Wilson -- Social movements and the left opposition in the USA / Ib Jørgensen -- American futures and public policy / Virginia Sapiro*

The Legacy of Reaganomics : prospects for long-term growth / edited by Charles R. Hulten and Isabel V. Sawhill. — Washington, D.C. : Urban Institute Press, 1984. — p. cm. — (The Changing domestic priorities series). — *Papers presented at a conference held Sept. 22, 1983, under the auspices of the Urban Institute Changing Domestic Priorities project.* — *Includes bibliographical references*

UNITED STATES — Economic policy

GRAY, H. Peter
International trade, employment and structural adjustment : the United States / H. Peter Gray, Thomas Pugel and Ingo Walter. — Geneva : International Labour Office, 1986. — x,108p. — (Employment, adjustment and industrialisation ; 3). — *Includes bibliographical references*

The Great society and its legacy : twenty years of U.S. social policy / Marshall Kaplan and Peggy Cuciti, editors. — Durham, N.C. : Duke University Press, 1986. — p. cm. — *Includes index*

GREENBERG, Edward S.
Capitalism and the American political ideal / by Edward S. Greenberg. — Armonk, N.Y. : M.E. Sharpe, 1985. — p. cm

UNITED STATES — Economic policy — Congresses

The Integration question : political economy and public policy in Canada and North America / edited by Jon H. Pammett and Brian W. Tomlin. — Don Mills, Ont. ; Reading, Mass. : Addison-Wesley Publishers, c1984. — 262 p.. — : *Revised papers of the Conference on Integration and Fragmentation in Canada and North America held March, 1982 at Carleton University, and sponsored by the Carleton Dept. of Political Science in cooperation with Norman Paterson School of International Affairs.* — *Includes bibliographies and index*

UNITED STATES — Economic policy — Mathematical models

The U.S. economy in an interdependent world : a multicountry model / Guy V.G. Stevens ... [et al.]. — Washington, D.C. : Board of Governors of the Federal Reserve System : Copies obtained from Publications Services, Board of Governors of the Federal Reserve System, 1984. — x,590p. — *Includes bibliographical references and indexes*

UNITED STATES — Economic policy — To 1933

NELSON, John R.
Liberty and property : political economy and policymaking in the new nation, 1789-1812 / John R. Nelson, Jr. — Baltimore : Johns Hopkins University Press, c1987. — p. cm. — (The Johns Hopkins University studies in historical and political science ; 105th ser., 2). — *Bibliography: p*

TICKNER, J. Ann
Self-reliance versus power politics : the American and Indian experience in building nation states / J. Ann Tickner. — New York : Columbia University Press, 1987. — xi, 282 p.. — (The Political economy of international change). — *Includes index.* — *Bibliography: p. [231]-267*

UNITED STATES — Economic policy — 1933-1945 — Addresses, essays, lectures

LONG, Huey Pierce
Kingfish to America, share our wealth : selected senatorial papers of Huey P. Long / edited and with an introduction by Henry M. Christman. — New York : Schocken Books, 1985. — xvi, 145 p.. — *Includes index*

UNITED STATES — Economic policy — 1933-1945 — Bibliography

The Great Depression : a historical bibliography. — Santa Barbara, Calif. ; Oxford : ABC-Clio Information Services, c1984. — xii, 260p. — (ABC-Clio research guides ; 4). — *Includes index*

UNITED STATES — Economic policy — 1971-1981

HILL, Robert Bernard
Economic policies and black progress : myths and realities / Robert B. Hill. — Washington, D.C. (733 15th St., N.W., Suite 1020, Washington 20005) : National Urban League, Research Dept., c1981. — vi, 144 p.. — *Bibliography: p. 90-99*

UNITED STATES — Economic policy — 1971-1981 — Congresses

How open is the U.S. economy? / edited by R.W. Hafer. — Lexington, Mass. : Lexington Books, c1986. — xviii, 248 p.. — *Papers presented at the Federal Reserve Bank of St. Louis's Tenth Annual Economic Conference, Oct. 12-13, 1985.* — *Includes bibliographies and index*

UNITED STATES — Economic policy — 1971-

Economic regulatory policies / edited by James E. Anderson. — Lexington, Mass. ; London : Lexington Books, 1976. — xiv, 215p. — (Policy studies organization series ; 10)

GROSS, Bertram
Friendly fascism : the new face of power in America / Bertram Gross. — Montréal : Black Rose Books, 1985. — xxvii,409p

UNITED STATES — Economic policy — 1981-

Economic report of the people / Center for Popular Economics. — 1st ed. — Boston : South End Press, c1986. — xvii, 260 p.. — *The crossed out word "President" appears in the title before the word "people.".* — *Includes bibliographies and index*

LEE, Dwight R
Regulating government : a preface to constitutional economics / Dwight R. Lee, Richard B. McKenzie. — Lexington, Mass. : Lexington Books, c1987. — xiv, 192 p.. — *Includes bibliographical references and index*

MALKIN, Lawrence
The national debt / Lawrence Malkin. — 1st ed. — New York : Holt, c1987. — ix, 309 p.. — *Includes index.* — *Bibliography: p. 277-298*

MORSE, Ronald A.
Getting America ready for Japanese science and technology / Ronald A. Morse, Richard J. Samuels. — Lanham ; London : University Press of America, 1986. — [196]p

PETERSON, Paul E
When federalism works / Paul E. Peterson, Barry G. Rabe, Kenneth K. Wong. — Washington, D.C. : Brookings Institution, c1986. — xvi, 245 p.. — *Includes bibliographical references and index*

RAYACK, Elton
Not so free to choose : the political economy of Milton Friedman and Ronald Reagan / Elton Rayack. — New York : Praeger, 1987. — x, 215 p.. — *Includes index.* — *Bibliography: p. 203-208*

State politics and the new federalism : readings and commentary / edited by Marilyn Gittell. — New York : Longman, c1986. — xv, 544 p.. — *Includes index.* — *Bibliography: p. 533-535*

UNITED STATES — Economic policy — 1981- — Congresses

Japan and the United States today : exchange rates, macroeconomic policies, and financial market innovations / Hugh T. Patrick, Ryuichiro Tachi, editors. — New York : Center on Japanese Economy and Business, Columbia University, 1986, c1987. — vii, 234 p.. — *Papers presented at a conference held in New York, June 4-5, 1986, sponsored by the Center on Japanese Economy and Business at the Graduate School of Business, Columbia University, and the Institute of Fiscal and Monetary Policy of the Japanese Ministry of Finance, together with the Foundation for Advanced Information and Research, Japan.* — *Includes bibliographies*

The Legacy of Reaganomics : prospects for long-term growth / edited by Charles R. Hulten and Isabel V. Sawhill. — Washington, D.C. : Urban Institute Press, 1984. — p. cm. — (The Changing domestic priorities series). — *Papers presented at a conference held Sept. 22, 1983, under the auspices of the Urban Institute Changing Domestic Priorities project.* — *Includes bibliographical references*

UNITED STATES — Economic polity — 1981-

BLOCK, Walter
The U.S. bishops and their critics : an economic and ethical perspective / Walter Block. — Vancouver : Fraser Institute, 1986. — 127p

UNITED STATES — Emigration and immigration

CARLSON, Robert A.
The Americanization syndrome : a quest for conformity / Robert A. Carlson. — [Rev. and updated ed.]. — London : Croom Helm, c1987. — 197p. — (Croom Helm series on theory and practice of adult education in North America). — Previous ed.: published as the quest for conformity. New York : London : Wiley, 1975. — Includes index

FRANCIS, Samuel T.
Illegal immigration : a threat to US security / Samuel T. Francis. — London : Centre for Security and Conflict Studies, 1986. — 27p. — (Conflict studies ; no.192)

GREGORY, Peter
The myth of market failure : employment and the labor market in Mexico / Peter Gregory. — Baltimore : Johns Hopkins University Press for the World Bank, 1986. — viii,299p. — Bibliography: p281-291

LOESCHER, Gil
Calculated kindness : refugees and America's half-open door, 1945 to the present / Gil Loescher, John A. Scanlan. — New York : Free Press ; London : Collier Macmillan, c1986. — xviii, 346p. — Includes index. — Bibliography: p. 273-331

SARAN, Parmatma
The Asian Indian experience in the United States / Parmatma Saran. — New Delhi : Vikas, 1985. — x,131p. — Bibliography: p [123]-126

Urban ethnicity in the United States : new immigrants and old minorities / edited by Lionel Maldonado and Joan Moore. — Beverly Hills ; London : Sage Publications, c1985. — 304p. — (Urban affairs annual reviews ; v. 29). — "Published in cooperation with the Urban Research Center, University of Wisconsin--Milwaukee.". — Bibliography: p 277-301

UNITED STATES — Emigration and Immigration

VAN VUGT, William
British emigration during the early 1850's : with special reference to emigration to the USA / by William E. Van Vugt. — 351 leaves. — PhD (Econ) 1986 LSE. — Leaves 287-322 are appendices

UNITED STATES — Emigration and immigration — Bibliography

CORDASCO, Francesco
The new American immigration : evolving patterns of legal and illegal emigration : a bibliography of selected references / Francesco Cordasco. — New York : Garland, 1987. — xxviii, 418 p.. — (Garland reference library of social science ; vol. 376). — Includes index

UNITED STATES — Emigration and immigration — History

MINK, Gwendolyn
Old labor and new immigrants in American political development : union, party, and state, 1875-1920 / Gwendolyn Mink. — Ithaca, N.Y. : Cornell University Press, 1986. — p. cm. — Includes index. — Bibliography: p

UNITED STATES — Emigration and immigration — History — Addresses, essays, lectures

Immigration / Richard A. Easterlin ... [et al.]. — Cambridge, Mass. : Belknap Press of Harvard University Press, 1982, c1980. — vi, 159 p.. — (Dimensions of ethnicity). — Selections from the Harvard encyclopedia of American ethnic groups. — Bibliography: p. [155]-159. — Contents: Economic and social characteristics of the immigrants / Richard A. Easterlin -- Settlement patterns and spatial distribution / David Ward -- A history of U.S. immigration policy / William S. Bernard -- Naturalization and citizenship / Reed Ueda

UNITED STATES — Emigration and immigration — History — 18th century

BAILYN, Bernard
Voyagers to the west : a passage in the peopling of America on the eve of the Revolution / Bernard Bailyn with the assistance of Barbara DeWolfe. — London : Tauris, 1987, c1986. — [550]p. — Originally published: New York : Knopf, 1986. — Includes bibliography and index

UNITED STATES — Emigration and immigration — History — 19th century

MARGRAVE, Richard Dobson
The emigration of silk workers from England to the United States in the nineteenth century : with special reference to Coventry, Macclesfield, Paterson, New Jersey, and South Manchester, Connecticut / Richard Dobson Margrave. — New York : Garland, 1986. — 421 p.. — (Outstanding theses from the London School of Economics and Political Science). — Thesis (Ph. D.)--London School of Economics and Political Science, 1981. — Bibliography: p. [384]-421

UNITED STATES — Emigration and immigration — History — 20th century

REIMERS, David M
Still the golden door : the third world comes to America / David M. Reimers. — New York : Columbia University Press, c1985. — xviii, 319p. — Includes index. — Bibliography: p.[219]-312

UNITED STATES — Emigration and Immigration — Australia

AITCHISON, Raymond
The Americans in Australia / Ray Aitchison. — Melbourne (Vic.) : Australasian Educa Press, 1986. — 165p. — (Australian ethnic heritage series). — Bibliography: p162-163

UNITED STATES — Ethnic relations

HAMMERBACK, John C
A war of words : Chicano protest in the 1960s and 1970s / John C. Hammerback, Richard J. Jensen, and Jose Angel Gutierrez. — Westport, Conn. ; London : Greenwood Press, 1985. — x, 187p. — (Contributions in ethnic studies ; no. 12). — Includes index. — Bibliography: p.[173]-178

KNOBEL, Dale T.
Paddy and the republic : ethnicity and nationality in antebellum America / by Dale T. Knobel. — 1st ed. — Middletown, Conn. : Wesleyan University Press ; Scranton, Pa. : Distributed by Harper & Row, c1986. — p. cm . — Includes index. — Bibliography: p

ROSENWAIKE, Ira
On the edge of greatness : a portrait of American Jewry in the early national period / Ira Rosenwaike. — [Cincinnati] : American Jewish Archives, c1985. — xvi, 189 p.. — (Publications of the American Jewish Archives ; no. 14). — Bibliography: p. 171-189

UNITED STATES — Ethnic relations — Abstracts

The Jewish experience in America : a historical bibliography. — Santa Barbara, Calif. ; Oxford : ABC-Clio, 1983. — vi,190p. — "Compiled from the periodicals database of the American Bibliographical Center by editors at ABC-Clio Information Services"

UNITED STATES — Ethnic relations — Addresses, essays, lectures

Anti-Semitism in American history / edited by David A. Gerber. — Urbana : University of Illinois Press, c1986. — p. cm. — Includes index. — Bibliography: p

KAHAN, Arcadius
Essays in Jewish social and economic history / Arcadius Kahan ; edited by Roger Weiss ; with an introduction by Jonathan Frankel. — Chicago : University of Chicago Press, 1986. — xx, 208 p.. — Includes bibliographical references and index

UNITED STATES — Executive departments

FITZGERALD, Randall
Porkbarrel : the unexpurgated Grace Commission story of congressional profligacy / Randall Fitzgerald and Gerald Lipson. — Washington, D.C. : Cato Institute, c1984. — xxxv, 114 p.. — "This report was originally prepared under the title The cost of congressional encroachment"--T.p. verso

Making government work : from White House to Congress / edited by Robert E. Hunter, Wayne L. Berman, John F. Kennedy ; foreword by Amos A. Jordan. — Boulder : Westview Press, 1986. — xi, 292 p.. — Rev. ed. of: Making the government work / edited by Robert E. Hunter, Wayne L. Berman. 1985. — Published in cooperation with the Center for Strategic and International Studies, Georgetown University. — Bibliography: p. 274-279

UNITED STATES — Executive departments — Reorganization — History — 20th century

ARNOLD, Peri E.
Making the managerial presidency : comprehensive reorganization planning, 1905-1980 / Peri E. Arnold. — Princeton, N.J. : Princeton University Press, c1986. — p. cm. — Includes index. — Bibliography: p

UNITED STATES — Foreign economic relations

JONES, Joseph Marion
The fifteen weeks : (February 21-June 5, 1947) / Joseph Marion Jones. — San Diego ; London : Harcourt Brace Jovanovich, c1955. — viii,296p

PHAUP, E. Dwight
The World Bank : how it can serve U.S. interests / E. Dwight Phaup. — Washington, D.C. : Heritage Foundation, 1984. — vi,57p

ROOSA, Robert V.
The United States and Japan in the international monetary system 1946-1985 / Robert V. Roosa. — New York : Group of Thirty, 1986. — ii,75p. — (Occasional papers / Group of Thirty ; no.21)

UNITED STATES — Foreign economic relations — Mathematical models

The U.S. economy in an interdependent world : a multicountry model / Guy V.G. Stevens ... [et al.]. — Washington, D.C. : Board of Governors of the Federal Reserve System : Copies obtained from Publications Services, Board of Governors of the Federal Reserve System, 1984. — x,590p. — Includes bibliographical references and indexes

UNITED STATES — Foreign economic relations — Africa

MOSS, Joanna
Emerging Japanese economic influence in Africa : implications for the United States / Joanna Moss & John Ravenhill. — Berkeley : Institute of International Studies, University of California, c1985. — xi, 150 p.. — (Policy papers in international affairs ; no. 21). — Includes index. — Bibliography: p. 139-143

UNITED STATES — Foreign economic relations — Arab countries — Addresses, essays, lectures

U.S.-Arab economic relations : a time of transition / edited by Michael R. Czinkota and Scot Marciel. — New York : Praeger, 1985. — p. cm. — Includes index

UNITED STATES — Foreign economic relations — Canada

CLARKSON, Stephen
Canada and the Reagan challenge : crisis and adjustment, 1981-85 / Stephen Clarkson. — New updated ed. — Toronto : J. Lorimer, 1985. — xv, 431 p.. — Includes index. — Bibliography: p. 378-409

UNITED STATES — Foreign economic relations — Canada
continuation

GWYN, Richard J.
The 49th paradox : Canada in North America / Richard Gwyn. — Toronto, Ont. : McClelland and Stewart, c1985. — 362 p.. — *Includes index. — Bibliography: p. 341-348*

The legal framework for Canada-United States trade / edited by Maureen Irish and Emily F. Carasco. — Toronto : Carswell, 1987. — xxxviii,275p

WONNACOTT, Paul
The United States and Canada : the quest for freer trade : an examination of selected issues / Paul Wonnacott ; with an appendix by John Williamson. — Washington, DC : Institute for International Economics, 1987. — p. cm. — (Policy analyses in international economics ; 16). — *Bibliography: p*

UNITED STATES — Foreign economic relations — Canada — Congresses

The Integration question : political economy and public policy in Canada and North America / edited by Jon H. Pammett and Brian W. Tomlin. — Don Mills, Ont. ; Reading, Mass. : Addison-Wesley Publishers, c1984. — 262 p.. — : *Revised papers of the Conference on Integration and Fragmentation in Canada and North America held March, 1982 at Carleton University, and sponsored by the Carleton Dept. of Political Science in cooperation with Norman Paterson School of International Affairs. — Includes bibliographies and index*

UNITED STATES — Foreign economic relations — China

Economic relations in the Asian-Pacific region : report of a conference cosponsored by the Chinese Academy of Social Sciences and the Brookings Institution, June 1985 / edited by Bruce Dickson and Harry Harding. — Washington,D.C. : Brookings Institution, 1987. — ix,91p. — (Brookings dialogues on public policy)

UNITED STATES — Foreign economic relations — Europe — Addresses, essays, lectures

New directions in economic and security policy : U.S.-West European relations in a period of crisis and indecision / edited by Werner J. Feld. — Boulder : Westview Press, 1985. — xiii, 93 p.. — *"Sixth biannual symposium published in cooperation with the Institute for the Comparative Study of Public Policy, the University of New Orleans/the University of Innsbruck.". — Includes bibliographies*

UNITED STATES — Foreign economic relations — European Economic Community countries

LEVINE, Michael K
Inside international trade policy formulation : a history of the 1982 US-EC steel arrangements / by Michael K. Levine. — New York : Praeger, 1985. — p. cm. — *Includes index*

UNITED STATES — Foreign economic relations — Japan — Congresses

Japan and the United States today : exchange rates, macroeconomic policies, and financial market innovations / Hugh T. Patrick, Ryuichiro Tachi, editors. — New York : Center on Japanese Economy and Business, Columbia University, 1986, c1987. — vii, 234 p.. — *Papers presented at a conference held in New York, June 4-5, 1986, sponsored by the Center on Japanese Economy and Business at the Graduate School of Business, Columbia University, and the Institute of Fiscal and Monetary Policy of the Japanese Ministry of Finance, together with the Foundation for Advanced Information and Research, Japan. — Includes bibliographies*

Law and trade issues of the Japanese economy : American and Japanese perspectives / edited by Gary R. Saxonhouse and Kozo Yamamura. — Seattle : University of Washington Press ; [Tokyo] : University of Tokyo Press, c1986. — xx, 290 p.. — *Based on a workshop held in Sept. 1983, sponsored by the Committee on Japanese Economic Studies. — Includes bibliographies and index*

UNITED STATES — Foreign economic relations — Latin America

CLAYTON, Lawrence A
Grace : W.R. Grace & Co., the formative years, 1850-1930 / Lawrence A. Clayton. — Ottawa, Ill. : Jameson Books, c1985. — xiii, 403 p., [35] p. of plates. — *Includes index. — Bibliography: p. 387-394*

The United States and Latin America in the 1980s : contending perspectives on a decade of crisis / Kevin J. Middlebrook and Carlos Rico, editors. — Pittsburgh, PA : University of Pittsburgh Press, 1985. — xii, 648p. — (Pitt Latin American series). — *Includes index*

UNITED STATES — Foreign opinion

The American presidency : perspectives from abroad / edited by Kenneth W. Thompson. — Lanham, MD : University Press of America, c1986. — xi, 127 p.. — *"A Miller Center tenth anniversary commemorative publication 1975-1985.". — "Co-published by arrangement with the White Burkett Miller Center of Public Affairs, University of Virginia"--Verso of t.p. — Includes bibliographies*

UNITED STATES — Foreign opinion, African

African student outlook : a comparison of findings at English and French-speaking universities. — [Washington, D.C.] : United States Information Agency, 1965. — vi,29p. — R-115-65

East African university student views on international and continental issues. — [Washington, D.C.] : United States Information Agency, 1965. — vii,25p. — R-39-65

UNITED STATES — Foreign opinion, European

The standing of the U.S. in West European opinion-1965 : (World Survey III series). — [Washington, D.C.] : United States Information Agency, 1965. — xii,59p. — R-145-65

UNITED STATES — Foreign opinion, Nigerian

Nigerian opinion on selected national and international issues : (World Survey III series). — [Washington, D.C.] : United States Information Agency, 1966. — xi,42p. — R-32-66

UNITED STATES — Foreign opinion, Russian

The Other side : how Soviets and Americans perceive each other / edited by Jonathan J. Halperin. — New Brunswick, U.S.A. : Transaction Books, c1987. — p. cm. — *Includes index. — Bibliography: p*

UNITED STATES — Foreign population

LYMAN, Stanford M
Chinatown and Little Tokyo : power, conflict, and community among Chinese and Japanese immigrants to America / Stanford Morris Lyman. — Millwood, N.Y. : Associated Faculty Press, c1986. — xiv, 282 p.. — (Minority structures and race and ethnic relations series). — *Bibliography: p. 255-272*

UNITED STATES — Foreign public opinion

HASELER, Stephen
Anti-Americanism : steps on a dangerous path / Stephen Haseler. — London : Alliance Publishers for the Institute for European Defence and Strategic Studies, 1986. — 64p. — (Occasional paper / Institute for European Defence and Strategic Studies ; no.18)

UNITED STATES — Foreign relations

The American character and the formation of United States foreign policy / edited by Michael P. Hamilton. — Grand Rapids, Mich. : W.B. Eerdmans Pub. Co., c1986. — p. cm. — *Contents: Formative events from Columbus to World War I / Marcus Cunliffe, Robert L. Beisner -- The modern age / John L. Gaddis, Charles M. Lichenstein -- Religious influences on United States foreign policy / Robert N. Bellah, Earl H. Brill -- Profits at what costs? / Richard J. Barnet, Dale R. Weigel -- Ethnicity and race as factors in the formation of United States foreign policy / Elliot P. Skinner -- The American character and the formation of United States foreign policy / McGeorge Bundy, Alton Frye*

Cultural change in the United States since World War II / edited by Maurice Gonnand, Sergio Perosa, Christopher W.E. Bigsby ; with contributions from Zoltan Abadi-Nagy...[et al.]. — Amsterdam : Free University Press, 1986. — 102p. — (European contributions to American studies ; 9). — *Includes bibliographies*

FOX, William T R
A continent apart : the United States and Canada in world politics / William T.R. Fox. — Toronto ; Buffalo : University of Toronto Press, c1985. — xv, 188 p.. — (The Bissell lectures ; 1982-3). — *Includes bibliographical references and index*

HOLMES, Jack E
The mood/interest theory of American foreign policy / Jack E. Holmes ; with a foreword by Frank L. Klingberg. — Lexington, Ky. : University Press of Kentucky, c1985. — xiii, 238 p.. — *Includes index. — Bibliography: p. [222]-225*

HUNT, Michael H
Ideology and U.S. foreign policy / Michael H. Hunt. — New Haven : Yale University Press, 1987. — p. cm. — *Includes index. — Bibliography: p*

The national interest. — Washington, D. C. : National Affairs, Inc., 1985-. — *Quarterly*

SARAVANAMUTTU, Paikiasothy
The influence of an idea on foreign policy : the case of domino theory in American foreign policy in Indochina, 1945-56 / P. Saravanamuttu. — 348 leaves. — *PhD (Econ) 1986 LSE*

UNITED STATES — Foreign relations — Bibliography

GOEHLERT, Robert
The Department of State and American diplomacy : a bibliography / Robert U. Goehlert, Elizabeth R. Hoffmeister. — New York : Garland Pub., 1986. — xxviii, 349 p.. — (Garland reference library of social science ; vol. 333). — *Includes indexes*

UNITED STATES — Foreign relations — Chronology

BRUNE, Lester H
Chronological history of United States foreign relations, 1776 to January 20, 1981 / Lester H. Brune. — New York ; London : Garland, 1985. — 2 v. (xviii, 1289 p.). — (Garland reference library of social science ; v. 196). — *Includes index. — Bibliography: p.1198-1209*

UNITED STATES — Foreign relations — Dictionaries

Encyclopedia of American foreign policy : studies of the principal movements and ideas / Alexander DeConde, editor. — New York : Scribner, c1978. — 3 v. (xii, 1201 p.). — *Includes bibliographies and index*

FINDLING, John E
Dictionary of American diplomatic history / John E. Findling. — Westport, Conn. : Greenwood Press, 1980. — xviii, 622 p.. — *Includes bibliographies and index*

UNITED STATES — Foreign relations — Law and legislation

LOFGREN, Charles A
"Government from reflection and choice" : constitutional essays on war, foreign relations, and federalism / Charles A. Lofgren. — New York : Oxford University Press, c1986. — xviii, 235p. — Includes index

UNITED STATES — Foreign relations — Philosophy

HUNT, Michael H
Ideology and U.S. foreign policy / Michael H. Hunt. — New Haven : Yale University Press, 1987. — p. cm. — Includes index. — Bibliography: p

UNITED STATES — Foreign relations — Public opinion — History

HOLMES, Jack E
The mood/interest theory of American foreign policy / Jack E. Holmes ; with a foreword by Frank L. Klingberg. — Lexington, Ky. : University Press of Kentucky, c1985. — xiii, 238 p.. — Includes index. — Bibliography: p. [222]-225

UNITED STATES — Foreign relations — Sources — Germany

Dokumente zur Deutschlandpolitik. — Frankfurt : Metzner (for) Bundesministerium für innerdeutsche Beziechungen Reihe 1: Vom 3. September 1939 bis 8. Mai 1945 / bearbeitet von Rainer A. Blasius [and others]. — 1984-

UNITED STATES — Foreign relations — 1783-1815

LANG, Daniel George
Foreign policy in the early republic : the law of nations and the balance of power / Daniel George Lang. — Baton Rouge : Louisiana State University Press, c1985. — 175 p.. — (Political traditions in foreign policy series). — Includes index. — Bibliography: p. 165-170

UNITED STATES — Foreign relations — 1829-1837

BELOHLAVEK, John M
Let the eagle soar! : The foreign policy of Andrew Jackson / John M. Belohlavek. — Lincoln : University of Nebraska Press, c1985. — x, 328 p.. — Includes index. — Bibliography: p. [309]-318

UNITED STATES — Foreign relations — 20th century

Amerikanskii ekspansionizm : noveishee vremia / otv. redaktor G. N. Sevost'ianov. — Moskva : Nauka, 1986. — 610p

CRABB, Cecil Van Meter
Presidents and foreign policy making : from FDR to Reagan / Cecil V. Crabb, Jr., Kevin V. Mulcahy. — Baton Rouge : Louisiana State University Press, c1986. — p. cm. — (Political traditions in foreign policy series). — Includes bibliographical references and index

HEINRICHS, Waldo H
American ambassador : Joseph C. Grew and the development of the United States diplomatic tradition / Waldo H. Heinrichs, Jr. — New York : Oxford University Press, 1986, c1966. — p. cm. — : Reprint. Originally published: Boston : Little, Brown, 1966. — Includes index. — Bibliography: p

LEFFLER, Melvyn P.
The elusive quest : the America's pursuit of European stability and French security, 1919-1933 / by Melvyn P. Leffler. — Chapel Hill : University of North Carolina Press, c1979. — xvi, 409 p.. — Includes index. — Bibliography: p. 369-393

Modern American diplomacy / edited by John M. Carroll and George C. Herring. — Wilmington, Del. : Scholarly Resources Inc., 1986. — p. cm. — Includes index. — Bibliography: p

RYAN, Henry Butterfield
The vision of Anglo-America : the US-UK alliance and the emerging Cold War, 1943-1946 / Henry Butterfield Ryan. — Cambridge : Cambridge University Press, 1987. — [vi,240]p. — Bibliography: p281-301. — Includes index

UNITED STATES — Foreign relations — 20th century — Philosophy

HALLE, Louis Joseph
History, philosophy, and foreign relations : background for the making of foreign policy / Louis J. Halle ; with a preface by Kenneth W. Thompson. — Lanham : University Press of America ; [s.l.] : The White Burkett Miller Center of Public Affairs, University of Virginia, c1987. — xii, 404 p.. — (Papers on presidential transitions and foreign policy ; v. 7). — Includes bibliographies

UNITED STATES — Foreign relations — 1913-1921

FERRELL, Robert H
Woodrow Wilson and World War I, 1917-1921 / by Robert H. Ferrell. — 1st ed. — New York ; London : Harper & Row, c1985. — xii, 346p, [26]p of plates. — (New American nationl series). — Includes index. — Bibliography: p.303-333

GILDERHUS, Mark T
Pan American visions : Woodrow Wilson and regional integration in the western hemisphere, 1913-1921 / Mark T. Gilderhus. — Tucson : University of Arizona Press, c1986. — p. cm. — Includes index. — Bibliography: p

WALWORTH, Arthur
Wilson and his peacemakers : American diplomacy at the Paris Peace Conference, 1919 / Arthur Walworth. — New York ; London : W.W. Norton, 1986. — xiii, 618p. — Includes index. — Bibliography: p.572-585

UNITED STATES — Foreign relations — 1921-1923

PEASE, Neal
Poland, the United States, and the stabilization of Europe, 1919-1933 / by Neal Pease. — New York ; Oxford : Oxford University Press, 1986. — vii, 238p. — Includes index. — Bibliography: p.[222]-231

UNITED STATES — Foreign relations — 1923-1929

PEASE, Neal
Poland, the United States, and the stabilization of Europe, 1919-1933 / by Neal Pease. — New York ; Oxford : Oxford University Press, 1986. — vii, 238p. — Includes index. — Bibliography: p.[222]-231

UNITED STATES — foreign relations — 1929-1933

PEASE, Neal
Poland, the United States, and the stabilization of Europe, 1919-1933 / by Neal Pease. — New York ; Oxford : Oxford University Press, 1986. — vii, 238p. — Includes index. — Bibliography: p.[222]-231

UNITED STATES — Foreign relations — 1933-1945

BENNETT, Edward Moore
Franklin D. Roosevelt and the search for security : American-Soviet relations, 1933-1939 / by Edward M. Bennett. — Wilmington, Del. : Scholarly Resources, 1985. — xix, 213p. — Includes index. — Bibliography: p 197-203

DALLEK, Robert
Franklin D. Roosevelt and American foreign policy, 1932-1945 / Robert Dallek. — New York : Oxford University Press, 1979. — xii, 657 p. — Includes index. — Bibliography: p. 619-628

MATRAY, James Irving
The reluctant crusade : American foreign policy in Korea, 1941-1950 / James Irving Matray. — Honolulu : University of Hawaii Press, c1985. — xii, 351 p.. — Includes index. — Bibliography: p.[319]-330

TOULOUSE, Mark G.
The transformation of John Foster Dulles : from prophet of realism to priest of nationalism / Mark G. Toulouse. — [Macon, GA] : Mercer University Press, c1985. — xlii, 277 p.. — Includes index. — Bibliography: p. [255]-269

UNITED STATES — Foreign relations — 1945-1953

BEST, Richard A
Co-operation with like-minded peoples : British influences on American security policy, 1945-1949 / Richard A. Best, Jr. — Westport, Conn. : Greenwood Press, 1986. — x, 226 p.. — (Contributions in American history ; no. 116). — Includes index. — Bibliography: p. [197]-212

EDMONDS, Robin
Setting the mould : the United States and Britain 1945-1950 / Robin Edmonds. — Oxford : Clarendon, 1986. — [450]p. — Includes bibliography and index

HARBUTT, Fraser J
The iron curtain : Churchill, America, and the origins of the Cold War / Fraser J. Harbutt. — New York ; Oxford : Oxford University Press, 1986. — xiv, 370p. — Includes index. — Bibliography: p.341-353

MATRAY, James Irving
The reluctant crusade : American foreign policy in Korea, 1941-1950 / James Irving Matray. — Honolulu : University of Hawaii Press, c1985. — xii, 351 p.. — Includes index. — Bibliography: p.[319]-330

TOULOUSE, Mark G.
The transformation of John Foster Dulles : from prophet of realism to priest of nationalism / Mark G. Toulouse. — [Macon, GA] : Mercer University Press, c1985. — xlii, 277 p.. — Includes index. — Bibliography: p. [255]-269

UNITED STATES — Foreign relations — 1945-1953 — Congresses

Harry S. Truman, the man from Independence / edited by William F. Levantrosser ; prepared under the auspices of Hofstra University. — New York : Greenwood Press, c1986. — x, 427 p.. — (Contributions in political science ; no. 145). — Papers presented at the Hofstra University International Conference on Harry S. Truman, held Apr. 14-16, 1983. — Includes bibliographies and index

UNITED STATES — Foreign relations — 1945-

BLOOMFIELD, Lincoln P.
The United Nations and U.S. foreign policy : a new look at the national interest / Lincoln P. Bloomfield. — Rev. ed. — London : University of London Press, 1969. — xviii,268p

BLUM, William
The CIA : a forgotten history : US global interventions since World War 2 / William Blum. — London : Zed, 1986. — [432]p. — Includes index

BROWN, Eugene
J. William Fulbright : advice and dissent / Eugene Brown. — Iowa City : University of Iowa Press, c1985. — x, 171p. — Includes index. — Bibliography: p.153-167

CHADDA, Maya
Paradox of power : the United States in Southwest Asia, 1973-1984 / Maya Chadda ; foreword by Afaf Mansot. — Santa Barbara, Calif. : ABC-CLIO, c1986. — xvi, 278 p.. — Includes index. — Bibliography: p. 259-265

CONFERENCE ON FOREIGN ASPECTS OF UNITED STATES NATIONAL SECURITY (1958 : Washington, D.C.)
Foreign aspects of U.S. national security : conference report and proceedings. — Washington, D.C. : Committee for International Economic Growth, 1958. — 120p

UNITED STATES — Foreign relations — 1945- *continuation*

DARBY, Phillip
Three faces of imperialism : British and American approaches to Asia and Africa, 1870-1970 / Phillip Darby. — New Haven : Yale University Press, 1987. — 267p. — *Includes index. — Bibliography: p.[256]-262*

The deadly connection : nuclear war and U.S. intervention / [articles and speeches on behalf of the] New England Regional Office of the American Friends Service Committee edited by Joseph Gerson ; forward by Thomas J. Gumbleton. — Philadelphia : New Society Publishers, 1986. — xi,253p

The Diplomacy of human rights / edited by David D. Newsom. — Lanham, MD. : University Press of America ; [Washington, D.C.] : Institute for the Study of Diplomacy, c1986. — p. cm. — *Includes bibliographies*

GARRETT, Stephen A.
From Potsdam to Poland : American policy toward Eastern Europe / Stepehn A. Garrett. — New York : Praeger, 1986. — ix, 237 p.. — *Includes index. — Bibliography: p. 221-232*

HERMAN, Edward S.
The real terror network : terrorism in fact and propaganda / Edward S. Herman. — Montréal : Black Rose, 1985. — ix,252p. — *Includes bibliographical notes*

HORNE, Gerald
Black and red : W.E.B. Du Bois and the Afro-American response to the Cold War, 1944-1963 / Gerald Horne. — Albany, N.Y. : State University of New York Press, c1985. — xii, 457p. — (SUNY series in Afro-American society). — *Includes index. — Bibliography: p.437-440*

ISAACSON, Walter
The wise men : six friends and the world they made : Acheson, Bohlen, Harriman, Kennan, Lovett, McCloy / by Walter Isaacson and Evan Thomas. — London : Faber, 1986. — 853p,[16]p of plates. — *Bibliography: p814-830. — Includes index*

KEGLEY, Charles W.
American foreign policy : pattern and process / Charles W. Kegley, Jr. and Eugene R. Wittkopf. — 3rd ed. — Basingstoke : Macmillan Education, 1987. — xiii,681p. — *Previous ed.: New York : St. Martin's Press, 1982. — Bibliography: p627-662. — Includes index*

LOWENTHAL, Abraham F
Partners in conflict, the United States and Latin America / Abraham F. Lowenthal. — Baltimore, Md. : Johns Hopkins University Press, c1987. — xi, 240 p.. — *Includes index. — Bibliography: p. 201-235*

MAKINDA, Samuel M.
Superpower diplomacy in the Horn of Africa / Samuel M. Makinda. — London : Croom Helm, c1987. — 241p. — *Bibliography: p225-234. — Includes index*

MORTIMER, Edward
Roosevelt's children : tomorrow's world leaders and their world / by Edward Mortimer. — London : Hamilton, 1987. — xxiii,422p. — *Includes index*

The 'Special relationship' : Anglo-American relations since 1945 / edited by Wm. Roger Louis and Hedley Bull. — Oxford : Clarendon, 1986. — [xviii,450]p. — *Includes index*

Staying the course : Henry M. Jackson and national security / edited by Dorothy Fosdick. — Seattle : University of Washington Press, c1987. — p. cm

STIVERS, William
America's confrontation with revolutionary change in the Middle East 1948-83 / William Stivers. — London : Macmillan, 1986. — [208]p. — *Includes index*

Superpowers and revolution / edited by Jonathan R. Adelman. — New York : Praeger, 1986. — p. cm

UNITED STATES — Foreign relations — 1945- — Decision making

CHANG, Jaw-ling Joanne
United States-China normalization : an evaluation of foreign policy decision making / Jaw-ling Joanne Chang. — [Baltimore] : School of Law, University of Maryland, 1986. — 246p. — (Occasional papers?reprints series in contemporary Asian studies ; 1986; no.4(75)). — *Bibliography: p205-225*

UNITED STATES — Foreign relations — 1945- — Decision making — Case studies

NEUSTADT, Richard E
Thinking in time : the uses of history for decision-makers / Richard E. Neustade, Ernest R. May. — New York : Free Press ; London : Collier Macmillan, c1986. — p. cm. — *Includes index. — Bibliography: p*

UNITED STATES — Foreign relations — 1963-1969 — Sources — Bibliography

The Johnson years / edited by Robert A. Divine. — Lawrence, Kan. : University Press of Kansas, 1987-. — v. <1 >. — *Includes index. — Contents: v. 1. Foreign policy, the Great Society, and the White House*

UNITED STATES — Foreign relations — 1969-1974

SCHURMANN, Franz
The foreign politics of Richard Nixon : the grand design / Franz Schurmann. — Berkeley, CA : Institute of International Studies, University of California, Berkeley, 1986. — p. cm. — (Research series ; no. 65). — *Includes index. — Bibliography: p*

STRONG, Robert J.
Bureaucracy and statesmanship : Henry Kissinger and the making of American foreign policy / Robert J. Strong. — Lanham ; London : University Press of America, c1987. — [124]p. — *Includes bibliography*

UNITED STATES — Foreign relations — 1974-1977

STRONG, Robert J.
Bureaucracy and statesmanship : Henry Kissinger and the making of American foreign policy / Robert J. Strong. — Lanham ; London : University Press of America, c1987. — [124]p. — *Includes bibliography*

UNITED STATES — Foreign relations — 1977-1981

MURAVCHIK, Joshua
The uncertain crusade : Jimmy Carter and the dilemmas of human rights policy / Joshua Muravchik ; foreword by Jeane Kirkpatrick. — Lanham, Md. ; London : Hamilton Press, c1986. — xxii, 247p. *Includes bibliographies and index*

UNITED STATES — Foreign relations — 1981-

BERRYMAN, Phillip
Inside Central America : the essential facts past and present on El Salvador, Nicaragua, Honduras, Guatemala and Costa Rica / Phillip Berryman. — London : Pluto, 1985. — [176]p. — *Includes bibliography and index*

BEST, Edward
US policy and regional security in Central America / Edward Best. — [London] : IISS, c1987. — 182p. — *Includes index*

COHEN, Benjamin J
In whose interest? : international banking and American foreign policy / Benjamin J. Cohen. — New Haven ; London : Yale University Press, c1986. — xi, 347p. — *"A Council on Foreign Relations book.". — Includes index*

DICKEY, Christopher
With the Contras : a reporter in the wilds of Nicaragua / Christopher Dickey. — New York : Simon and Schuster, c1985. — 327 p., [9] p. of plates. — *Includes index. — Bibliography: p. 273-315*

Eagle resurgent? : the Reagan era in American foreign policy / edited by Kenneth A. Oye, Robert J. Lieber, Donald Rothchild. — Boston : Little, Brown, c1987. — viii, 472 p.. — *Includes bibliographical references and index*

INTERNATIONAL TRIBUNAL ON THE REAGAN ADMINISTRATION'S FOREIGN POLICY - FACTS AND JUDGEMENT (1984 : Brussels)
The Reagan administration's foreign policy : facts and judgement of the International Tribunal / [papers of the International Conference and proceedings of the International Tribunal on the Reagan Administration's Foreign Policy - Facts and Judgement, organized in Brussels, Belgium, by the International Progress Organization (28-30 September 1984)] ; edited by Hans Köchler. — London : Third World Centre, (1985?). — 470p. — (Studies in international relations ; 11) . — *Includes two papers in French*

LEFEVER, Ernest W.
Ethics and United States foreign policy / Ernest W. Lefever. — Lanham : University Press of America ; London : Distributed by Eurospan, c1986. — [236]p. — *Includes bibliography and index*

LISKA, George
Rethinking US-Soviet relations / George Liska. — Oxford : Basil Blackwell, 1987. — [256]p. — *Includes index*

NEWSUM, H. E.
United States foreign policy towards Southern Africa : Andrew Young and beyond / H.E. Newsum and Olayiwola Abegunrin. — Basingstoke : Macmillan, 1987. — ix,164p. — *Bibliography: p156-157. - Includes index*

NOVIK, Nimrod
Encounter with reality : Reagan and the Middle East during the first term / Nimrod Novik. — Jerusalem, Israel : Jerusalem Post ; Boulder, Colo. : Westview Press, c1985. — 106 p.. — (JCSS study ; no. 1). — *Bibliography: p. 99-106*

Reagan versus the Sandinistas : the undeclared war on Nicaragua / edited by Thomas W. Walker. — Boulder : Westview Press, 1986. — p. cm. *Includes index*

SAVIGEAR, Peter
Cold war or detente in the 1980s : the international politics of American-Soviet relations / Peter Savigear. — Brighton : Wheatsheaf, 1987. — [192]p. — *Includes bibliography and index*

UNITED STATES — Foreign relations — 1981- — Addresses, essays, lectures

Evaluating U.S. foreign policy / edited by John A. Vasquez. — New York : Praeger, 1985. — p. cm. — *Includes index*

UNITED STATES — Foreign relations — 1981- — Congresses

Reagan's leadership and the Atlantic Alliance : views from Europe and America / [edited by] Walter Goldstein. — Washington : Pergamon-Brassey, 1986. — p. cm. — *"Developed with the support of the Standing Conference of Atlantic Organizations.". — Papers presented at the 13th Annual Meeting of the Standing Conference of Atlantic Organizations, Wingspread House, Racine, Wisc., July 1985, sponsored by the Johnson Foundation and the Information Directorate of NATO*

UNITED STATES — Foreign relations — Africa

African crisis areas and U.S. foreign policy / edited by Gerald J. Bender, James S. Coleman, Richard L. Sklar. — Berkeley : University of California Press, 1986, c1985. — p. cm. — *Includes index. — Bibliography: p*

LAÏDI, Zaki
Les contraintes Dŭne rivalité : les superpuissances et lÁfrique (1960-1985) / Zaki Laïdi. — Paris : La Découverte, 1986. — 299p. — *Bibliography: p284-292*

UNITED STATES — Foreign relations — Africa, Southern

NEWSUM, H. E.
United States foreign policy towards Southern Africa : Andrew Young and beyond / H.E. Newsum and Olayiwola Abegunrin. — Basingstoke : Macmillan, 1987. — ix,164p. — *Bibliography: p156-157. - Includes index*

UNITED STATES — Foreign relations — Asia, Southeastern

HESS, Gary R
The United States' emergence as a Southeast Asian power, 1940-1950 / Gary R. Hess. — New York : Columbia University, 1987. — p. cm. — *Includes index. — Bibliography: p*

UNITED STATES — Foreign relations — Canada

CLARKSON, Stephen
Canada and the Reagan challenge : crisis and adjustment, 1981-85 / Stephen Clarkson. — New updated ed. — Toronto : J. Lorimer, 1985. — xv, 431 p. — *Includes index. — Bibliography: p. 378-409*

DORAN, Charles F
Canada and Congress : lobbying in Washington / by Charles F. Doran, Joel J. Sokolsky. — Halifax, N.S., Canada : Centre for Foreign Policy Studies, Dalhousie University, 1985. — vi, 257 p.. — *Includes bibliographies*

FOX, William T. R
A continent apart : the United States and Canada in world politics / William T.R. Fox. — Toronto ; Buffalo : University of Toronto Press, c1985. — xv, 188 p.. — (The Bissell lectures ; 1982-3). — *Includes bibliographical references and index*

MARTIN, Lawrence
The presidents and the prime ministers : Washington and Ottawa face to face : the myth of bilateral bliss 1867-1982 / Lawrence Martin. — PaperJacks ed. — Toronto : PaperJacks, 1983,c1982. — 300p. — *Originally published: Toronto: Doubleday Canada, 1982*

UNITED STATES — Foreign relations — Caribbean area

POLICY ALTERNATIVES FOR THE CARIBBEAN AND CENTRAL AMERICA
Changing course : blueprint for peace in Central America and the Caribbean / PACCA. — Washington D.C. : Institute for Policy Studies, 1984. — 116p

UNITED STATES — Foreign relations — Central America

BERRYMAN, Phillip
Inside Central America : the essential facts past and present on El Salvador, Nicaragua, Honduras, Guatemala and Costa Rica / Phillip Berryman. — London : Pluto, 1985. — [176]p. — *Includes bibliography and index*

BEST, Edward
US policy and regional security in Central America / Edward Best. — [London] : IISS, c1987. — 182p. — *Includes index*

COHEN, Joshua
Inequity and intervention : the federal budget and Central America / Joshua Cohen and Joel Rogers. — 1st ed. — Boston, MA : South End Press, c1986. — xi, 66 p. — (PACCA series on the domestic roots of United States foreign policy). — *Bibliographical notes: p.57-62*

Confronting revolution : security through diplomacy in Central America / Morris Blachman, William LeoGrande, and Kenneth Sharpe, editors. — New York : Pantheon Books, [1986]. — ix, 438p. — *Includes bibliographies and index*

FAGEN, Richard R
Forging peace : the challenge of Central America / Richard R. Fagen ; foreword by George McGovern. — Oxford : Basil Blackwell, 1987. — [160]p. — (A PACCA book). — *Includes index*

POLICY ALTERNATIVES FOR THE CARIBBEAN AND CENTRAL AMERICA
Changing course : blueprint for peace in Central America and the Caribbean / PACCA. — Washington D.C. : Institute for Policy Studies, 1984. — 116p

SAUVAGE, Léo
Les États-Unis face à l'Amerique centrale / Léo Sauvage. — Paris : Balland, [1985]. — 285p

WILLIAMS, Robert G
Export agriculture and the crisis in Central America / by Robert G. Williams. — Chapel Hill : University of North Carolina Press, c1986. — xvi, 257p. — *Includes index. — Bibliography: p.[239]-248*

UNITED STATES — Foreign relations — China

ANSCHEL, Eugene
Homer Lea, Sun Yat-sen, and the Chinese revolution / by Eugene Anschel. — New York : Praeger, 1984. — xvi, 269 p.. — *Includes index. — Bibliography: p. 253-262*

CHANG, Jaw-ling Joanne
United States-China normalization : an evaluation of foreign policy decision making / Jaw-ling Joanne Chang. — [Baltimore] : School of Law, University of Maryland, 1986. — 246p. — (Occasional papers?reprints series in contemporary Asian studies ; 1986; no.4(75)). — *Bibliography: p205-225*

The China Hands' legacy : ethics and diplomacy / edited by Paul Gordon Lauren. — Boulder : Westview Press, 1987. — xi, 196 p.. — *Includes bibliographies and index*

GREGOR, A. James
The China connection : U.S. policy and the People's Republic of China / A. James Gregory. — Stanford, Calif. : Hoover Institution Press, Stanford University, 1986. — x, 263 p.. — *Map on lining papers. — Includes index. — Bibliography: p. [241]-254*

HALLENBERG, Jan
Foreign policy change : United States foreign policy toward the Soviet Union and the People's Republic of China, 1961-1980 / Jan Hallenberg. — [Stockholm] : Dept. of Political Science, University of Stockholm, 1984. — 347 p.. — (Stockholm studies in politics ; 25). — *Errata slip inserted. — : Originally presented as the author's thesis (doctoral--University of Stockholm, 1984). — Bibliography: p. 333-347*

KUSANO, Atsushi
Two Nixon shocks and Japan-U.S. relations / Atsushi Kusano. — Princeton, N.J. : Princeton University. Woodrow Wilson School of Public and International Affairs, 1987. — 46p. — (Research monograph / Princeton University. Woodrow Wilson School of Public and International Affairs ; no.50)

LEDOVSKII, A. M.
Kitaiskaia politika SShA i sovetskaia diplomatiia 1942-1954 / A. M. Ledovskii. — Moskva : Nauka (IVL), 1985. — 286p. — *English summary*

UNITED STATES — Foreign relations — China — Case studies

STOESSINGER, John George
Nations in darkness--China, Russia, and America / John G. Stoessinger. — 4th ed. — New York : Random House, 1986. — x, 301 p. . — *Includes index. — Bibliography: p. 281-286*

UNITED STATES — Foreign relations — Cuba

PÉREZ, Louis A.
Cuba under the Platt Amendment, 1902-1934 / Louis A. Pérez, Jr. — Pittsburg, Pa. : University of Pittsburgh Press, c1986. — xiii, 410p. — (Pitt Latin American series). — *Includes index. — Bibliography: p.[387]-402*

UNITED STATES — Foreign relations — Developing countries

HALLIDAY, Fred
Beyond Irangate : the Reagan doctrine and the Third World / Fred Halliday. — Amsterdam : Transnational Institute, 1987. — 38p. — (Transnational issues ; 1)

THORNTON, Thomas Perry
The challenge to U.S. policy in the Third World : global responsibilities and regional devolution / Thomas Perry Thornton. — Boulder : Westview Press with the Foreign Policy Institute, School of Advanced International Studies, Johns Hopkins University, 1986. — p. cm. — (SAIS papers in international affairs ; no. 9). — *Includes index*

UNITED STATES — Foreign relations — Developing countries — Congresses

East-West tensions in the Third World / Marshall D. Shulman, editor. — 1st ed. — New York : W.W. Norton, c1986. — 243 p.. — *Background papers prepared for the 70th American Assembly at Arden House, Harriman, N.Y., Nov. 21, 1985. — At head of title: American Assembly. — Includes index*

UNITED STATES — Foreign relations — East Asia

BISSON, Thomas Arthur
America's far eastern policy / T. A. Bisson. — New York : Institute of Pacific Relations, 1945. — xiii,235p

GRISWOLD, Alfred Whitney
The far eastern policy of the United States / Alfred W. Griswold. — New Haven : Yale University Press, 1962. — 530p

UNITED STATES — Foreign relations — Egypt

WEINBAUM, Marvin G.
Egypt and the politics of U.S. economic aid / Marvin G. Weinbaum. — Boulder ; London : Westview, 1986. — xii,192p. — *Bibliography: p183-187*

UNITED STATES — Foreign relations — El Salvador

REED, Roger
El Salvador and the crisis in Central America / Roger Reed. — Washington, D.C. : Council for Inter-American Security, c1984. — 59 p.. — *Includes bibliographical references*

UNITED STATES — Foreign relations — Ethiopia

SPENCER, John Hathaway
Ethiopia, the Horn of Africa, and U.S. policy / John H. Spencer. — Cambridge, Mass : Institute for Foreign Policy Analysis, 1977. — 69 p. — (Foreign policy report). — *Includes bibliographical references*

UNITED STATES — Foreign relations — Europe

BEUGEL, Ernst Hans van der
From Marshall Aid to Atlantic partnership : European integration as a concern of American foreign policy / Ernst Hans van der Beugel. — Amsterdam : Elsevier, 1966. — 480p

JENTLESON, Bruce W.
Pipeline politics : the complex political economy of East-West energy trade / Bruce W. Jentleson. — Ithaca, N.Y. : Cornell University Press, 1986. — 263 p.. — (Cornell studies in political economy). — *Includes index. — Bibliography: p. 247-256*

LANGER, Peter H.
Transatlantic discord and NATO's crisis of cohesion / Peter H. Langer. — Washington, D.C. : Pergamon-Brassey's, 1986. — p. cm. — (Foreign policy report). — "A publication of the Institute for Foreign Policy Analysis, Inc.". — *Bibliography: p*

UNITED STATES — Foreign relations — Europe *continuation*

LEFFLER, Melvyn P.
The elusive quest : the America's pursuit of European stability and French security, 1919-1933 / by Melvyn P. Leffler. — Chapel Hill : University of North Carolina Press, c1979. — xvi, 409 p.. — *Includes index. — Bibliography: p. 369-393*

OLDAG, Andreas
Allianzpolitische Konflikte in der NATO : die sicherheitspolitischen Interessen der USA und Westeuropas zu Beginn der 80er Jahre / Andreas Oldag. — Baden-Baden : Nomos Verlagsgesellschaft, 1985. — vi,185p. — (Darstellungen zur internationalen Politik und Entwicklungspolitik ; 15). — *Bibliography: p169-185*

WALWORTH, Arthur
Wilson and his peacemakers : American diplomacy at the Paris Peace Conference, 1919 / Arthur Walworth. — New York ; London : W.W. Norton, 1986. — xiii, 618p. — *Includes index. — Bibliography: p.572-585*

UNITED STATES — Foreign relations — Europe — Congresses

Reagan's leadership and the Atlantic Alliance : views from Europe and America / [edited by] Walter Goldstein. — Washington : Pergamon-Brassey, 1986. — p. cm. — *"Developed with the support of the Standing Conference of Atlantic Organizations.". — Papers presented at the 13th Annual Meeting of the Standing Conference of Atlantic Organizations, Wingspread House, Racine, Wisc., July 1985, sponsored by the Johnson Foundation and the Information Directorate of NATO*

UNITED STATES — Foreign relations — Europe, Eastern

GARRETT, Stephen A.
From Potsdam to Poland : American policy toward Eastern Europe / Stepehn A. Garrett. — New York : Praeger, 1986. — ix, 237 p.. — *Includes index. — Bibliography: p. 221-232*

GORDON, Lincoln
Eroding empire : Western relations with Eastern Europe / Lincoln Gordon, with J.F. Brown ... [et al.]. — Washington, D.C. : Brookings Institution, c1987. — xv, 359 p.. — *Includes bibliographical references and index*

UNITED STATES — Foreign relations — France

LEFFLER, Melvyn P.
The elusive quest : the America's pursuit of European stability and French security, 1919-1933 / by Melvyn P. Leffler. — Chapel Hill : University of North Carolina Press, c1979. — xvi, 409 p.. — *Includes index. — Bibliography: p. 369-393*

UNITED STATES — Foreign relations — Germany

FROHN, Axel
Neutralisierung als Alternative zur Westintegration : die Deutschlandpolitik der Vereinigten Staaten von Amerika 1945-1949 / von Axel Frohn. — Frankfurt : Metzner, 1985. — 170p. — (Dokumente zur Deutschlandpolitik. Beihefte ; Bd.7). — *Bibliography: p145-162*

UNITED STATES — Foreign relations — Germany — Addresses, essays, lectures

FLETCHER, Willard Allen
United States-German relations, past and present / Willard Allen Fletcher, Stephen F. Szabo, Stanley R. Sloan. — Washington : Library of Congress, 1984. — iii,25p. — *Bibliography: p23-25*

UNITED STATES — Foreign relations — Germany — Congresses

America and the Germans : an assessment of a three hundred year history / Frank Trommler and Joseph McVeigh, editors. — Philadelphia, Pa. : University of Pennsylvania Press. — *Rev. versions of papers presented at the Tricentennial Conference of German-American History, Politics and Culture, held at the University of Pennsylvania, Philadelphia, Oct.3-6, 1983*
Vol.1: Immigration, language, ethnicity. — 1985. — xxxii,376p

America and the Germans : an assessment of a three hundred year history / Frank Trommler and Joseph McVeigh, editors. — Philadelphia, Pa. : University of Pennsylvania Press. — *Rev. versions of papers presented at the Tricentennial Conference of German-American History, Politics and Culture, held at the University of Pennsylvania, Philadelphia, Oct. 3-6, 1983*
Vol.2: The relationship in the twentieth century. — 1985. — xvii,369p

UNITED STATES — Foreign relations — Germany (West) — Addresses, essays, lectures

FLETCHER, Willard Allen
United States-German relations, past and present / Willard Allen Fletcher, Stephen F. Szabo, Stanley R. Sloan. — Washington : Library of Congress, 1984. — iii,25p. — *Bibliography: p23-25*

UNITED STATES — Foreign relations — Great Britain

British documents on foreign affairs - reports and papers from the Foreign Office confidential print / general editors: Kenneth Bourne and D. Cameron Watt. — [Frederick, Md.] : University Publications of America
Part I: From the mid-nineteenth century to the first world war
Series C: North America, 1837-1914 / editor: Kenneth Bourne. — 1986. —

DANCHEV, Alex
Very special relationship : Field-Marshall Sir John Dill and the Anglo-American alliance 1941-44 / Alex Danchev. — London : Brassey's Defence, 1986. — xv,201p. — *Bibliography: p183-197. — Includes index*

EDMONDS, Robin
Setting the mould : the United States and Britain 1945-1950 / Robin Edmonds. — Oxford : Clarendon, 1986. — [450]p. — *Includes bibliography and index*

HALL, Christopher, 1956-
Britain, America and arms control,1921-37 / Christopher Hall. — Basingstoke : Macmillan, 1987. — vii,295p. — *Bibliography: p276-285. — Includes index*

HARON, Miriam Joyce
Palestine and the Anglo-American connection, 1945-1950 / Miriam Joyce Haron. — New York : P. Lang, c1986. — 209 p.. — (American university studies. Series IX. History ; vol. 17). — *Includes index. — Bibliography: p. [197]-201*

HELMREICH, Jonathan E
Gathering rare ores : the diplomacy of uranium acquisition, 1943-1954 / Jonathan E. Helmreich. — Princeton, N.J. : Princeton University Press, c1986. — xiv, 303 p.. — *Includes index. — Bibliography: p. 287-291*

MASTERSON, William H
Tories and Democrats : British diplomats in the pre-Jacksonian America / by William H. Masterson ; foreword by Frank E. Vandiver. — 1st ed. — College Station : Texas A&M University Press, c1985. — xvi, 280p, [8]p of plates. — *Includes index. — Bibliography: p.[259]- 274*

RYAN, Henry Butterfield
The vision of Anglo-America : the US-UK alliance and the emerging Cold War, 1943-1946 / Henry Butterfield Ryan. — Cambridge : Cambridge University Press, 1987. — [vi,240]p. — *Bibliography: p281-301. — Includes index*

The 'Special relationship' : Anglo-American relations since 1945 / edited by Wm. Roger Louis and Hedley Bull. — Oxford : Clarendon, 1986. — [xviii,450]p. — *Includes index*

THORNE, Christopher
Allies of a kind : the United States, Britain, and the war against Japan, 1941-1945 / Christopher Thorne. — Oxford : Oxford University Press, 1979. — xxii, 772 p. — *Includes index. — Bibliography: p. [732]-746*

WRIGHT, Oliver
Anglo-American relations : the Atlantic grows wider / Sir Oliver Wright. — London : David Davies Memorial Institute of International Studies, 1986. — 16p. — *Annual memorial lecture, 1986*

UNITED STATES — Foreign relations — Great Britain — History

SOSIN, Jack M
English America and imperial inconstancy : the rise of provincial autonomy, 1696-1716 / J.M. Sosin. — Lincoln, Neb. ; London : University of Nebraska Press, 1985. — xii, 287p. — *Includes index*

UNITED STATES — Foreign relations — Grenada

DAVIDSON, Scott
Grenada : a study in politics and the limits of international law / Scott Davidson. — Aldershot : Avebury, c1987. — xii,196p. — *Bibliography: p184-190. — Includes index*

UNITED STATES — Foreign relations — Guatemala

SCHLESINGER, Stephen C
Bitter fruit : the untold story of the American coup in Guatemala / Stephen Schlesinger and Stephen Kinzer. — 1st ed. — Garden City, N.Y. : Doubleday, 1982. — xv, 320 p., [16] p. of plates. — *Includes index. — Bibliography: p. [293]-305*

UNITED STATES — Foreign relations — India — History

CHOPRA, V. D.
Pentagon shadow over India / V. D. Chopra ; with an introduction by T. N. Kaul. — New Delhi : Patriot Publishers, 1985. — xvi,223p

UNITED STATES — Foreign relations — Indochina

SARAVANAMUTTU, Paikiasothy
The influence of an idea on foreign policy : the case of domino theory in American foreign policy in Indochina, 1945-56 / P. Saravanamuttu. — 348 leaves. — *PhD (Econ) 1986 LSE*

UNITED STATES — Foreign relations — Iran

HULBERT, Mark
Interlock : the untold story of American banks, oil interests, the Shah's money, debts and the astounding connections between them / Mark Hulbert. — New York : Richardson and Snyder, 1982. — 272p

HUYSER, Robert E.
Mission to Tehran / by Robert E. Huyser ; introduction by Alexander M. Haig. — London : Deutsch, 1986. — [320]p. — *Includes index*

RYAN, Paul B
The Iranian rescue mission : why it failed / by Paul B. Ryan. — Annapolis, Md. : Naval Institute Press, c1985. — xiii, 185p. — *Includes index. — Bibliography: p [177]-180*

UNITED STATES — Foreign relations — Israel

Dynamics of dependence : U.S.-Israeli relations / edited by Gabriel Sheffer. — Boulder, Colo. : Westview Press, 1987. — x, 210 p.. — (Studies in international politics). — *Includes bibliographies and index*

HARON, Miriam Joyce
Palestine and the Anglo-American connection, 1945-1950 / Miriam Joyce Haron. — New York : P. Lang, c1986. — 209 p.. — (American university studies. Series IX. History ; vol. 17). — *Includes index. — Bibliography: p. [197]-201*

ROSE, John
Israel : the hijack state : America's watchdog in the Middle East / John Rose. — London : Bookmarks, 1986. — 78p

UNITED STATES — Foreign relations — Italy

AGA ROSSI, Elena
L'Italia nella sconfitta : politica interna e situazione internazionale durante la seconda guerra mondiale / Elena Aga-Rossi ; introduzione di Renzo De Felice. — Napoli : Edizioni scientifiche italiane, c1985. — 485 p.. — (Biblioteca storica ; 4). — *Includes bibliographical references and index*

UNITED STATES — Foreign relations — Japan

HEINRICHS, Waldo H
American ambassador : Joseph C. Grew and the development of the United States diplomatic tradition / Waldo H. Heinrichs, Jr. — New York : Oxford University Press, 1986, c1966. — p. cm. — : Reprint. Originally published: Boston : Little, Brown, 1966. — *Includes index. — Bibliography: p*

KUSANO, Atsushi
Two Nixon shocks and Japan-U.S. relations / Atsushi Kusano. — Princeton, N.J. : Princeton University. Woodrow Wilson School of Public and International Affairs, 1987. — 46p. — (Research monograph / Princeton University. Woodrow Wilson School of Public and International Affairs ; no.50)

LIBAL, Michael
Japans Weg in den Krieg : die Aussenpolitik der Kabinette Konoye 1940/1941 : Michael Libal. — Düsseldorf : Droste, [1971]. — 261p

TOKINOYA, Atsushi
The Japan—US alliance : a Japanese perspective / Atsushi Tokinoya. — London : International Institute for Strategic Studies, 1986. — 47p. — (Adelphi papers ; 212)

UNITED STATES — Foreign relations — Korea

MATRAY, James Irving
The reluctant crusade : American foreign policy in Korea, 1941-1950 / James Irving Matray. — Honolulu : University of Hawaii Press, c1985. — xii, 351 p.. — *Includes index. — Bibliography: p.[319]-330*

UNITED STATES — Foreign relations — Korea — Congresses

One hundred years of Korean-American relations, 1882-1982 / edited by Yur-Bok Lee and Wayne Patterson. — University, Ala. : University of Alabama Press, c1986. — x, 188p . — *Based on papers presented at the annual meeting of the American Historical Association or that of the Association for Asian Studies in 1982. — Includes index. — Bibliography: p.163-181*

UNITED STATES — Foreign relations — Korea (South)

MOON, Changjoo
The balance of power in Asia and U.S.-Korea relations = : [Asia ŭi seryŏk kyunhyŏng kwa Han-Mi kwan'gye] / Changjoo Moon. — Seoul, Korea : Gimm-Young Press ; Maple Shade, N.J. : Distributive Office for the U.S.A., Gimm-Young Co., c1983. — 386 p.. — *English and Korean. — Includes bibliographical references*

UNITED STATES — Foreign relations — Latin America

BLACK, Jan Knippers
Sentinels of empire : United States and Latin American militarism / Jan Knippers Black. — Westport, Conn. : Greenwood Press, 1986. — xix, 240p. — (Contributions in political science ; no. 144). — *Includes index. — Bibliography: p.[221]-236*

BLAISIER, Cole
The hovering giant : U.S. responses to revolutionary change in Latin America / Cole Blasier. — Rev. ed. — Pittsburgh, Pa. : University of Pittsburgh Press, 1985. — xxi, 339 p.. — (Pitt Latin American series). — *Includes index. — Bibliography: p. 307-334*

Cono sur / Facultad Latinoamericana de Ciencias Sociales. — Santiago : Facultad Latinoamericana de Ciencias Sociales, 1987-. — 6 per year

Dominant powers and subordinate states : the United States in Latin America and the Soviet Union in Eastern Europe / edited by Jan F. Triska. — Durham, [N.C.] : Duke University Press, 1986. — xi, 504 p.. — (Duke Press policy studies). — *Includes index. — Bibliography: p. [471]-498*

GILDERHUS, Mark T
Pan American visions : Woodrow Wilson and regional integration in the western hemisphere, 1913-1921 / Mark T. Gilderhus. — Tucson : University of Arizona Press, c1986. — p. cm. — *Includes index. — Bibliography: p*

KRYZANEK, Michael J
U.S.-Latin American relations / Michael J. Kryzanek. — New York : Praeger, 1985. — xxx, 242p. — *Bibliography: p.227-234*

Latin American views of U.S. policy / edited by Robert G. Wesson, Heraldo Munoz. — New York : Praeger, 1986. — vii, 153p. — (Praeger special studies)

LOWENTHAL, Abraham F
Partners in conflict, the United States and Latin America / Abraham F. Lowenthal. — Baltimore, Md. : Johns Hopkins University Press, c1987. — xi, 240 p.. — *Includes index. — Bibliography: p. 201-235*

The United States and Latin America in the 1980s : contending perspectives on a decade of crisis / Kevin J. Middlebrook and Carlos Rico, editors. — Pittsburgh, PA : University of Pittsburgh Press, 1985. — xii, 648p. — (Pitt Latin American series). — *Includes index*

WIARDA, Howard J.
Population, internal unrest, and U.S. security in Latin America / Howard J. Wiarda and Iêda Siqueira Wiarda. — Amherst : University of Massachusetts at Amherst, 1986. — 50p. — (Program in Latin American studies. Occasional papers series ; no.18)

UNITED STATES — Foreign relations — Libya

MCCORMICK, Bob
Libya : the truth behind the bombings / Bob McCormick. — London : Straight Left, 1987. — 12p

Mad dogs : the US raids on Libya / edited by Mary Kaldor and Paul Anderson ; introduction by Mary Kaldor. — London : Pluto in association with European Nuclear Disarmament, 1986. — 172p

WORLD ISLAMIC CALL SOCIETY
God is great. — Rome : World Islamic Call Society, 1986. — [36p]

UNITED STATES — Foreign relations — Mexico

VÁZQUEZ, Josefina Zoraida
The United States and Mexico / Josefina Zoraida Vázquez and Lorenzo Meyer. — Chicago : University of Chicago Press, 1985. — xiii, 220p. — (The United States and the world. foreign perspectives). — *Includes index. — Bibliography: p.199-207*

UNITED STATES — Foreign relations — Middle East

NOVIK, Nimrod
Encounter with reality : Reagan and the Middle East during the first term / Nimrod Novik. — Jerusalem, Israel : Jerusalem Post ; Boulder, Colo. : Westview Press, c1985. — 106 p.. — (JCSS study ; no. 1). — *Bibliography: p. 99-106*

UNITED STATES — Foreign Relations — Morocco

KAMIL, Leo
Fueling the fire : U.S. policy and the Western Sahara conflict / Leo Kamil. — Trenton, New Jersey : Red Sea Press, 1987. — 104p. — *Distributed in the UK by Spokesman, Nottingham. — Bibliography: p93-96. — Appendices give text of 1983 OAU peace plan: 1985 U.N. General Assembly resolution: and 1979 Algiers peace treaty between the Polisario Front and the Republic of Mauretania*

UNITED STATES — Foreign relations — Near East

CHADDA, Maya
Paradox of power : the United States in Southwest Asia, 1973-1984 / Maya Chadda ; foreword by Afaf Mansot. — Santa Barbara, Calif. : ABC-CLIO, c1986. — xvi, 278 p.. — *Includes index. — Bibliography: p. 259-265*

LATTER, Richard
The making of American foreign policy in the Middle East, 1945-1948 / Richard Latter. — New York : Garland, 1986. — 463 p.. — (Outstanding theses from the London School of Economics and Political Science). — *Thesis (Ph. D.)--University of London, 1976. — Bibliography: p. 457-463*

Soviet-American relations with Pakistan, Iran and Afghanistan / edited by Hafeez Malik. — Basingstoke : Macmillan, 1986. — [480]p. — *Includes index*

STIVERS, William
America's confrontation with revolutionary change in the Middle East 1948-83 / William Stivers. — London : Macmillan, 1986. — [208]p. — *Includes index*

UNITED STATES — Foreign relations — Nicaragua

BERMANN, Karl
Under the big stick : Nicaragua and the United States since 1848 / by Karl Bermann. — Boston : South End Press, c1986. — ix, 339 p., [2] p. of plates. — *Includes index. — Bibliography: p. [303]-329*

GROSSMAN, Karl
Nicaragua, America's new Vietnam? / text and photos by Karl Grossman. — Sag Harbor, N.Y. : Permanent Press, c1984. — 228 p.. — *Bibliography: p. 227-228*

Reagan versus the Sandinistas : the undeclared war on Nicaragua / edited by Thomas W. Walker. — Boulder : Westview Press, 1986. — p. cm. — *Includes index*

ROBINSON, William I.
David and Goliath : Washington's war against Nicaragua / William I. Robinson and Kent W. Norsworthy. — London : Zed, 1987. — [272]p. — *Includes bibliography and index*

UNITED STATES — Foreign relations — Nigeria

ATE, Bassey E
Decolonization and dependence : the development of Nigerian-U.S. relations / Bassey E. Ate. — Boulder, Colo. : Westview Press, 1985. — p. cm. — (Westview special studies on Africa). — *Includes index. — Bibliography: p*

UNITED STATES — Foreign relations — Pakistan

The Red Army on Pakistan's border : policy implications for the United States / Theodore L. Eliot, Jr. ... [et al.]. — Washington : Pergamon-Brassey's, 1986. — p. cm. — (Special report). — "May 1986.". — "A joint publication of the Institute for Foreign Policy Affairs, Inc. and the Center for Asian Pacific Affairs, the Asia Foundation."

UNITED STATES — Foreign relations — Pakistan — Addresses, essays, lectures

BHUTTO, Zulfikar Ali
Prime Minister Zulfikar Ali Bhutto : speeches and statements during visit to the United States of America in September 1973. — [Islamabad : Department of Films and Publications for the Ministry of Foreign Affairs, 1973. — 87p

UNITED STATES — Foreign relations — Persian Gulf Region

KUNIHOLM, Bruce Robellet
The Persian Gulf and United States policy : a guide to issues and references / Bruce R. Kuniholm. — Claremont, Calif. : Regina Books, c1984. — vii, 220 p.. — (Guides to contemporary issues ; 3). — Includes index. — Bibliography: p 145-211

UNITED STATES — Foreign relations — Persian Gulf region

SIRRIYEH, Hussein
US policy in the Gulf, 1968-1977 : aftermath of British withdrawal / by Hussein Sirriyeh. — London : Ithaca, 1984. — 297p. — Bibliography: p270-293. — Includes index

UNITED STATES — Foreign relations — Persian Gulf Region — Bibliography

KUNIHOLM, Bruce Robellet
The Persian Gulf and United States policy : a guide to issues and references / Bruce R. Kuniholm. — Claremont, Calif. : Regina Books, c1984. — vii, 220 p. — (Guides to contemporary issues ; 3). — Includes index. — Bibliography: p 145-211

UNITED STATES — Foreign relations — Philippines

VAN DER KROEF, Justus Maria
Since Aquino : the Philippine tangle and the United States / Justus M. van der Kroef. — Baltimore (Md.) : University of Maryland School of Law, 1986. — 73p. — (Occasional papers/Reprints series in contemporary Asian studies ; no.6)

UNITED STATES — Foreign relations — Poland

HOUGH, Jerry F.
The Polish crisis : American policy options : a staff paper / by Jerry F. Hough. — Washington : Brookings Institution, 1982. — viii,80p

KARSKI, Jan
The Great Powers & Poland, 1919-1945 : from Versailles to Yalta / Jan Karski. — Lanham, MD : University Press of America, c1985. — xvi, 697 p.. — Includes index. — Bibliography: p. 627-671

PEASE, Neal
Poland, the United States, and the stabilization of Europe, 1919-1933 / by Neal Pease. — New York ; Oxford : Oxford University Press, 1986. — vii, 238p. — Includes index. — Bibliography: p.[222]-231

UNITED STATES — Foreign relations — Puerto Rico

CABRANES, José A.
Self-determination for Puerto Rico / José A. Cabranes. — [San Juan] : Office of the Commonwealth of Puerto Rico in Washington, D.C., [ca.1974]. — 14p

UNITED STATES — Foreign relations — South Africa

COKER, Christopher
The United States and South Africa, 1968-1985 : constructive engagement and its critics / Christopher Coker. — Durham, N.C. : Duke University Press, 1986. — xi, 327p. — Includes index. — Bibliography: p.286-296

DANAHER, Kevin
In whose interest? : a guide to U.S.-South Africa relations / Kevin Danaher. — 1st ed. — Washington, D.C. : Institute for Policy Studies, c1985. — p. cm. — Includes index. — Bibliography: p

UNITED STATES — Foreign relations — South Africa — Bibliography

KETO, C. Tsehloane
American-South African relations, 1784-1980 : review and select bibliography / by C. Tsehloane Keto. — Athens, Ohio : Ohio University Center for International Studies, Africa Studies Program, 1985. — x, 159 p.. — (Monographs in international studies. African series ; no. 45). — Includes index

UNITED STATES — Foreign relations — South Asia

RAM, Raghunath
Super powers and Indo-Pakistani sub-continent : perceptions and policies / Raghunath Ram. — New Delhi : Raaj Prakashan, 1985. — 427p . — Bibliography: p[402]-411

Soviet-American relations with Pakistan, Iran and Afghanistan / edited by Hafeez Malik. — Basingstoke : Macmillan, 1986. — [480]p. — Includes index

UNITED STATES — Foreign relations — Soviet Union

BENNETT, Edward Moore
Franklin D. Roosevelt and the search for security : American-Soviet relations, 1933-1939 / by Edward M. Bennett. — Wilmington, Del. : Scholarly Resources, 1985. — xix, 213p. — Includes index. — Bibliography: p 197-203

BIALER, Seweryn
The Soviet paradox : external expansion, internal decline / Seweryn Bialer. — 1st ed. — New York : Knopf, 1986. — ix, 391p. — Includes index. — Bibliography: p.379-386

DURCH, William J.
The future of the ABM treaty / William J. Durch. — London : International Institute for Strategic Studies, 1987. — 80p. — (Adelphi papers ; 223)

ELLEINSTEIN, Jean
Goliath contre Goliath : histoire des relations américano-soviétiques / Jean Elleinstein. — Paris : Fayard
1: L'enfance des grands (1941-1949). — 1986. — 550p. — Bibliography: p[493]-500

GORBACHEV, M. S.
The results and lessons of Reykjavik : summit meeting in the Icelandic capital October 11-12, 1986 / Mikhail Gorbachev. — Moscow : Novosti Press Agency Publishing House, 1986. — 42p

GORBACHEV, M. S.
Speech given by the General Secretary of the Central Committee of the Communist Party of the Soviet Union (CPSU), M. S. Gorbachev, on Soviet television [following the Reykjavik Summit]. — New York : United Nations, 1986. — Distributed by the Secretary General of the U.N. as an official document of the General Assembly and Security Council at the request of the Deputy Head of the U.S.S.R. delegation to the Forty First session of the General Assembly

GRIFFITHS, John, 1942 Apr. 5-
The Cuban missile crisis / John Griffiths. — Hove : Wayland, 1986. — [80]p. — (Flashpoints). — Includes bibliography and index

HALLENBERG, Jan
Foreign policy change : United States foreign policy toward the Soviet Union and the People's Republic of China, 1961-1980 / Jan Hallenberg. — [Stockholm] : Dept. of Political Science, University of Stockholm, 1984. — 347 p.. — (Stockholm studies in politics ; 25). — Errata slip inserted. — : Originally presented as the author's thesis (doctoral--University of Stockholm, 1984). — Bibliography: p. 333-347

KRICKUS, Richard J
The superpowers in crisis : implications of domestic discord / Richard J. Krickus. — Washington ; London : Pergamon-Brassey's International Defence Publishers, 1987. — xiii, 236p. — Includes bibliographies

LISKA, George
Rethinking US-Soviet relations / George Liska. — Oxford : Basil Blackwell, 1987. — [256]p. — Includes index

SAVIGEAR, Peter
Cold war or detente in the 1980s : the international politics of American-Soviet relations / Peter Savigear. — Brighton : Wheatsheaf, 1987. — [192]p. — Includes bibliography and index

WEIHMILLER, Gordon R.
U.S. - Soviet summits : an account of East-West diplomacy at the top, 1955-1985 / Gordon R. Weihmiller ; epilogue by Dusko Doder, foreword by David D. Newsom. — Lanham, Md. : University Press of America ; Washington, D.C. : Institute for the Study of Diplomacy, 1986. — xv,211p. — Bibliography: p209-211

UNITED STATES — Foreign relations — Soviet Union — Addresses, essays, lectures

Shared destiny : fifty years of Soviet-American relations / edited by Mark Garrison and Abbott Gleason. — Boston : Beacon Press, c1985. — xxxii, 167 p.. — Includes bibliographies and index

UNITED STATES — Foreign relations — Soviet Union — Case studies

STOESSINGER, John George
Nations in darkness--China, Russia, and America / John G. Stoessinger. — 4th ed. — New York : Random House, 1986. — x, 301 p. . — Includes index. — Bibliography: p. 281-286

UNITED STATES — Foreign relations — Soviet Union — Congresses

Public diplomacy : USA versus USSR / Richard F. Staar, editor ; foreword by W. Glenn Campbell. — Stanford, Calif. : Hoover Institution Press, Stanford University, c1986. — xvii, 305 p.. — (Hoover Press publication ; 345). — Papers originally presented at a workshop, held in October 1984, sponsored by the Hoover Institution at Stanford University. — Includes bibliographies and index

UNITED STATES — Foreign relations — Taiwan

Congress, the Presidency, and the Taiwan Relations Act / edited by Louis W. Koenig, James C. Hsiung, and King-Yuh Chang. — New York : Praeger, 1985. — p. cm. — Includes index. — Bibliography: p

UNITED STATES — Foreign relations — Vietnam

KAHIN, George McTurnan
Intervention : how America became involved in Vietnam / by George McT. Kahin. — 1st ed. — New York : Knopf, c1986. — xii, 550 p.. — "A portion of this work was originally published in Pacific affairs, winter 1979-1980"--T.p. verso. — Includes index. — Bibliography: p. [433]-538

UNITED STATES — Foreign Relations — Western Sahara
KAMIL, Leo
Fueling the fire : U.S. policy and the Western Sahara conflict / Leo Kamil. — Trenton, New Jersey : Red Sea Press, 1987. — 104p. — *Distributed in the UK by Spokesman, Nottingham. — Bibliography: p93-96. — Appendices give text of 1983 OAU peace plan: 1985 U.N. General Assembly resolution: and 1979 Algiers peace treaty between the Polisario Front and the Republic of Mauretania*

UNITED STATES — Foreign relations administration
MOSHER, Frederick C
Presidential transitions and foreign affairs / Frederick C. Mosher, W. David Clinton, Daniel G. Lang. — Baton Rouge : Louisiana State University Press, c1987. — xvii, 281 p.. — (Miller Center series on the American presidency). — *The recommendations of the Miller Center Commission on Presidential Transitions and Foreign Policy are included in the appendix. — Includes index. — Bibliography: p. [265]-273*

Papers on presidential transitions in foreign policy. — Lanham, Md. ; London : University Press of America
Vol.2: Problems and prospects / edited by Kenneth W. Thompson. — 1986. — [xi],144p

The President, the Congress, and foreign policy / [foreword by] Edmund S. Muskie, Kenneth Rush ; Kenneth W. Thompson [rapporteur]. — Lanham : University Press of America, c1986. — xv, 311 p.. — *"A joint policy project of the Association of Former Members of Congress and the Atlantic Council of the United States. — Includes bibliographies*

UNITED STATES — Government policy — Developing countries
THORNTON, Thomas Perry
The challenge to U.S. policy in the Third World : global responsibilities and regional devolution / Thomas Perry Thornton. — Boulder : Westview Press with the Foreign Policy Institute, School of Advanced International Studies, Johns Hopkins University, 1986. — p. cm. — (SAIS papers in international affairs ; no. 9). — *Includes index*

UNITED STATES — Government publications
HERNON, Peter
GPO's depository library program : a descriptive analysis / by Peter Hernon, Charles R. McClure, Gary R. Purcell. — Norwood, N.J. : Ablex Pub. Corp., 1985. — p. cm. — *Includes index. — Bibliography: p*

UNITED STATES — Government publications — Bibliography
LARSON, Donna Rae
Guide to U.S. government directories / Donna Rae Larson. — [Phoenix] : Oryx Press
Volume 2: 1980-1984. — 1985. — xviii,214p

SCHWARZHOPF, LeRoy C.
Government reference books 82/83 : a biennial guide to U.S. government publications : eighth biennial volume / compiled by LeRoy C. Schwarzkopf. — Littleton, Col. : Libraries Unlimited, 1984. — xxiii,370p

SCHWARZKOPF, LeRoy C
Guide to popular U.S. government publications / compiled by LeRoy C. Schwarzkopf. — Littleton, Colo. : Libraries Unlimited, 1986. — xxxii, 432 p.. — *Includes indexes*

Using government publications. — Phoenix : Oryx Press
volume 2: Finding statistics and using special techniques / by Jean L. Sears and Marilyn K. Moody. — 1986. — viii,231p

UNITED STATES — Government publications — Handbooks, manuals, etc.
Using government publications. — Phoenix : Oryx Press
volume 2: Finding statistics and using special techniques / by Jean L. Sears and Marilyn K. Moody. — 1986. — viii,231p

UNITED STATES — Government publications — Indexes
SCHWARTZ, Julia
Easy access to information in United States government documents / Julia Schwartz. — Chicago : American Library Association, 1986. — xi, 49 p.

UNITED STATES — Historical geography
MEINIG, D. W.
The shaping of America : a geographical perspective on 500 years of history / D.W. Meinig. — New Haven ; London : Yale University Press
Vol.1: Atlantic America, 1492-1800. — c1986. — xxii,500p. — *Map on lining papers. — Bibliography: p461-479. — Includes index*

UNITED STATES — Historiography
BAKER, Susan Stout
Radical beginnings : Richard Hofstadter and the 1930s / Susan Stout Baker. — Westport, Conn. ; London : Greenwood Press, 1985. — xxi, 268p. — (Contributions in American history ; no. 112). — *Includes index. — Bibliography: p.[253]-259*

UNITED STATES — Historiography — Addresses, essays, lectures
The Rights of memory : essays on history, science, and American culture / edited by Taylor Littleton. — University, Ala. : University of Alabama Press, c1986. — viii, 227 p.. — (The Franklin lectures in the sciences & humanities). — *Includes bibliographies and index*

UNITED STATES — History
A Master's due : essays in honor of David Herbert Donald / edited by William J. Cooper, Jr., Michael F. Holt, and John McCardell. — Baton Rouge : Louisiana State University Press, c1985. — p. cm. — *"The principal writings of David Herbert Donald": p. — Includes index. — Contents: Introduction: David Herbert Donald / Ari Hoogenboom -- The election of 1840, voter mobilization, and the emergence of the second American party system / Michael F. Holt -- "The only door" / William J. Cooper, Jr. -- [etc.] The ceremonies of politics / Jean H. Baker -- American historians and Antebellum southern slavery, 1959-1984 / Peter Kolchin -- Ethnic roots of southern violence / Grady McWhiney -- Family, kinship, and neighborhood in an Antebellum southern community / Robert C. Kenzer -- Trent's Simms / John McCardell -- "Gotta mind to move, a mind to settle down" / Sydney Nathans -- Jazz, segregation, and desegregation / Stanley P. Hirshson -- The "Long march through the institutions" / Irwin Unger*

MORISON, Samuel Eliot
The Oxford history of the United States 1783-1917 / S. E. Morison. — Oxford : Oxford University Press
Vol. 2. — 1927. — x,531p

SCHLESINGER, Arthur M. (Arthur Meier), 1917-
The cycles of American history / Arthur M. Schlesinger. — London : Deutsch, 1987. — xiii,498p

UNITED STATES — History — Philosophy
HOLMES, Jack E
The mood/interest theory of American foreign policy / Jack E. Holmes ; with a foreword by Frank L. Klingberg. — Lexington, Ky. : University Press of Kentucky, c1985. — xiii, 238 p.. — *Includes index. — Bibliography: p. [222]-225*

UNITED STATES — History — Colonial period, ca. 1600-1775 — Addresses, essays, lectures
NASH, Gary B
Race, class, and politics : essays on American colonial and revolutionary society / Gary B. Nash ; with a foreword by Richard S. Dunn. — Urbana : University of Illinois Press, c1986. — p. cm. — *Includes index*

UNITED STATES — History — Revolution, 1775-1783
COUNTRYMAN, Edward
The American Revolution / Edward Countryman ; consulting editor Eric Foner. — London : Tauris, 1986. — [280]p. — *Includes bibliography and index*

UNITED STATES — History — Revolution, 1775-1783 — Causes
TYLER, John W.
Smugglers & patriots : Boston merchants and the advent of the American Revolution / John W. Tyler. — Boston : Northeastern University Press, c1986. — xiv, 349p. — *Includes index. — Bibliography: p 319-335*

UNITED STATES — History — Revolution, 1775-1783 — Causes — Case studies
BREEN, T H
Tobacco culture : the mentality of the great Tidewater planters on the eve of Revolution / T.H. Breen. — Princeton, N.J. : Princeton University Press, c1985. — xvi, 216p. — *Includes index*

UNITED STATES — History — Revolution, 1775-1783 — Economic aspects
TYLER, John W.
Smugglers & patriots : Boston merchants and the advent of the American Revolution / John W. Tyler. — Boston : Northeastern University Press, c1986. — xiv, 349p. — *Includes index. — Bibliography: p 319-335*

UNITED STATES — History — Revolution, 1775-1783 — Foreign public opinion
SAINSBURY, John
Disaffected patriots : London supporters of revolutionary America / John Sainsbury. — Kingston, Ont. : McGill — Queen's University Press, 1987. — xi, 305p. — *Bibliography: p.[281]-296*

UNITED STATES — History — Revolution, 1775-1783 — Peace — Addresses, essays, lectures
Peace and the peacemakers : the treaty of 1783 / edited by Ronald Hoffman and Peter J. Albert. — Charlottesville : Published for the United States Capitol Historical Society by the University Press of Virginia, 1985. — p. cm. — (Perspectives on the American Revolution). — *Includes index*

UNITED STATES — History — Revolution, 1775-1783 — Religious aspects
BONOMI, Patricia U
Under the cope of heaven : religion, society, and politics in Colonial America / Patricia U. Bonomi. — New York : Oxford University Press, 1986. — p. cm. — *Includes index. — Bibliography: p*

UNITED STATES — History — Revolution, 1775-1783 — Social aspects — Addresses, essays, lectures
NASH, Gary B
Race, class, and politics : essays on American colonial and revolutionary society / Gary B. Nash ; with a foreword by Richard S. Dunn. — Urbana : University of Illinois Press, c1986. — p. cm. — *Includes index*

UNITED STATES — History — 1801-1809 — Collected works
WEBSTER, Daniel
The papers of Daniel Webster / Charles M. Wiltse and Michael J. Birkner, editors. — Hanover, N.H. ; London : published for Dartmouth College by the University Press of New England
Series 1: Correspondence
Vol.7: 1850-1852. — 1986. — xxxiii,695p

UNITED STATES — History — 1801-1809 — Collected works
continuation

WEBSTER, Daniel
The papers of Daniel Webster / Charles M. Wiltse, editor- in-chief. — Hanover, N.J. : published for Dartmouth College by the University Press of New England
Series 3: Diplomatic papers
Vol.1: 1841-1843 / Kenneth E. Shewmaker, editor. — 1983. — xliv,960p

WEBSTER, Daniel
The papers of Daniel Webster / Charles M. Wiltse, editor-in-chief. — Hanover, N.H. ; London : published for Dartmouth College by the University Press of New England
Series 4: Speeches and formal writings
Vol.1: 1800-1833 / Charles M. Wiltse editor ; Alan R. Berolzheimer, assistant editor. — 1986. — xx,641p

UNITED STATES — History — 1809-1817 — Collected works

WEBSTER, Daniel
The papers of Daniel Webster / Charles M. Wiltse and Michael J. Birkner, editors. — Hanover, N.H. ; London : published for Dartmouth College by the University Press of New England
Series 1: Correspondence
Vol.7: 1850-1852. — 1986. — xxxiii,695p

WEBSTER, Daniel
The papers of Daniel Webster / Charles M. Wiltse, editor- in-chief. — Hanover, N.J. : published for Dartmouth College by the University Press of New England
Series 3: Diplomatic papers
Vol.1: 1841-1843 / Kenneth E. Shewmaker, editor. — 1983. — xliv,960p

WEBSTER, Daniel
The papers of Daniel Webster / Charles M. Wiltse, editor-in-chief. — Hanover, N.H. ; London : published for Dartmouth College by the University Press of New England
Series 4: Speeches and formal writings
Vol.1: 1800-1833 / Charles M. Wiltse editor ; Alan R. Berolzheimer, assistant editor. — 1986. — xx,641p

UNITED STATES — History — 1815-1861 — Collected works

WEBSTER, Daniel
The papers of Daniel Webster / Charles M. Wiltse and Michael J. Birkner, editors. — Hanover, N.H. ; London : published for Dartmouth College by the University Press of New England
Series 1: Correspondence
Vol.7: 1850-1852. — 1986. — xxxiii,695p

WEBSTER, Daniel
The papers of Daniel Webster / Charles M. Wiltse, editor- in-chief. — Hanover, N.J. : published for Dartmouth College by the University Press of New England
Series 3: Diplomatic papers
Vol.1: 1841-1843 / Kenneth E. Shewmaker, editor. — 1983. — xliv,960p

UNITED STATES — History — War with Mexico, 1845-1848 — Campaigns

BAUER, K. Jack
Zachary Taylor : soldier, planter, statesman of the old Southwest / K. Jack Bauer. — Baton Rouge : Louisiana State University Press, c1985. — xxiv, 348 p.. — (Southern biography series). — *Includes index.* — *Bibliography: p. 329-338*

UNITED STATES — History — Civil War, 1861-1865 — Causes

WYATT-BROWN, Bertram
Yankee saints and Southern sinners / Bertram Wyatt-Brown. — Baten Rouge ; London : Louisiana State University Press, c1985. — xi, 227p. — *Includes index*

UNITED STATES — History — Civil War, 1861-1865 — Civilian relief

RICHARDSON, Joe Martin
Christian reconstruction : the American Missionary Association and Southern Blacks, 1861-1890 / Joe M. Richardson. — Athens : University of Georgia Press, c1986. — ix, 348 p., [16] p. of plates. — *Includes index.* — *Bibliography: p. 323-335*

UNITED STATES — History — Civil War, 1861-1865 — Historiography — Addresses, essays, lectures

Why the South lost the Civil War / Richard E. Beringer ... [et al.]. — Athens : University of Georgia Press, c1986. — xi, 582 p., [24] p. of plates. — *Includes index.* — *Bibliography: p. [537]-555*

UNITED STATES — History — Civil War, 1861-1865 — Medical care

HAWKS, Esther Hill
A woman doctor's Civil War : Esther Hill Hawks' diary / edited with a foreword and afterword by Gerald Schwartz. — 1st ed. — Columbia, S.C. : University of South Carolina Press, c1984. — p. cm. — *Bibliography: p283-288.* — *Bibliography: p*

UNITED STATES — History — Civil War, 1861-1865 — Personal narratives

HAWKS, Esther Hill
A woman doctor's Civil War : Esther Hill Hawks' diary / edited with a foreword and afterword by Gerald Schwartz. — 1st ed. — Columbia, S.C. : University of South Carolina Press, c1984. — p. cm. — *Bibliography: p283-288.* — *Bibliography: p*

UNITED STATES — History — Civil War, 1861-1865 — Religious aspects

RICHARDSON, Joe Martin
Christian reconstruction : the American Missionary Association and Southern Blacks, 1861-1890 / Joe M. Richardson. — Athens : University of Georgia Press, c1986. — ix, 348 p., [16] p. of plates. — *Includes index.* — *Bibliography: p. 323-335*

UNITED STATES — History — Civil War, 1861-1865 — Social aspects

BAILEY, Fred Arthur
Class and Tennessee's Confederate generation / by Fred Arthur Bailey. — Chapel Hill : University of North Carolina Press, c1987. — x, 205 p.. — (The Fred W. Morrison series in Southern studies). — *Includes index.* — *Bibliography: p. [191]-196*

UNITED STATES — History — Civil War, 1861-1865 — Women

HAWKS, Esther Hill
A woman doctor's Civil War : Esther Hill Hawks' diary / edited with a foreword and afterword by Gerald Schwartz. — 1st ed. — Columbia, S.C. : University of South Carolina Press, c1984. — p. cm. — *Bibliography: p283-288.* — *Bibliography: p*

UNITED STATES — History — 1933-1945

LEUCHTENBURG, William Edward
Franklin D. Roosevelt and the New Deal, 1932-1940. — [1st ed.]. — New York : Harper & Row, [1963]. — 393 p. — (The New American Nation series). — *Includes bibliography*

OHL, John Kennedy
Hugh S. Johnson and the New Deal / John Kennedy Ohl. — Dekalb, Ill. : Northern Illinois University Press, 1985. — xi, 374p. — *Includes index.* — *Bibliography: p.[345]-359*

UNITED STATES — History — 1933-1945 — Dictionaries

Historical dictionary of the new deal : from inauguration to preparation for war / edited by James S. Olson. — Westport, Conn. ; London : Greenwood Press, c1985. — viii, 611p. — *Includes index.* — *Bibliography: p.563-575*

UNITED STATES — History, Military — 20th century

GABRIEL, Richard A
Military incompetence : why the American military doesn't win / Richard A. Gabriel. — 1st ed. — New York : Hill and Wang, 1985. — p. cm. — *Bibliography: p*

WHITNAH, Donald Robert
The American occupation of Austria : planning and early years / Donald R. Whitnah and Edgar L. Erickson. — Westport, Conn. ; London : Greenwood Press, c1985. — xiv, 352p, [12]p of plates. — (Contributions in military history ; no. 46). — *Includes index.* — *Bibliography: p.[329]-333*

UNITED STATES — History, Military — 20th century — Bibliography

BEEDE, Benjamin R
Intervention and counterinsurgency : an annotated bibliography of the small wars of the United States, 1898-1984 / Benjamin R. Beede. — New York : Garland Pub., 1985. — xxxviii, 321 p.. — (Wars of the United States ; vol. 5) (Garland reference library of social science ; vol. 251). — *Includes indexes*

UNITED STATES — History, Naval — Bibliography

KINNELL, Susan K
American maritime history : a bibliography / Susan K. Kinnell, Susanne R. Ontiveros, editors. — Santa Barbara, Calif. : ABC-Clio, c1986. — x, 260 p.. — (ABC-Clio research guides ; 17). — *Includes indexes*

UNITED STATES — History, Naval — To 1900

SCHROEDER, John H.
Shaping a maritime empire : the commercial and diplomatic role of the American Navy, 1829-1861 / John H. Schroeder. — Westport, Conn. ; London : Greenwood Press, 1985. — 229p. — (Contributions in military studies ; no. 48). — *"Notes on sources": p. [215]-219.* — *Includes bibliographical references and index*

UNITED STATES — Industries

GREAT BRITAIN. Parliament. House of Commons. Library. Research Division
Why the USA creates new jobs and why Europe does not / Christopher Barclay. — [London] : the Division, 1985. — 25p. — (Background paper ; no.170)

HICKS, Donald A
Advanced industrial development : restructuring, relocation, and renewal / Donald A. Hicks. — Boston, MA : Published by Oelgeschlager, Gunn & Hain in association with Lincoln Institute of Land Policy, c1985. — xx, 321 p.. — *"A Lincoln Institute of Land Policy book.".* — *Includes index.* — *Bibliography: p. [279]-310*

UNITED STATES — Industries — Case studies

Industrial strategy and planning in Mexico and the United States / edited by Sidney Weintraub. — Boulder, Colo. : Westview Press, 1986. — xiv, 279 p.. — (Westview special studies in international economics and business) . — *Includes bibliographies and index.* — *Contents: Industrial policy in the United States / William Diebold -- The new industrialization strategy in Mexico for the eighties / René Villarreal Arrambide -- Industrial strategy in the United States and the impact on Mexico / Sidney Weintraub -- The petrochemical industry in Mexico / Francisco Barnés de Castro, Lars Christianson -- The Mexican iron and steel industry / Gerardo M. Bueno, Gustavo S. Cortés, Rafael R. Rubio -- Steel in transition / Robert Crandall -- The U.S. motor vehicle industry / Neil D. Schuster -- Industry on the northern border of Mexico / José Luis Fernández, Jesús Tamayo -- Industry on the southern border of the United States / Jerry R. Ladman -- A United States view / Clark Reynolds -- A Mexican view / Francisco Javier Alejo*

UNITED STATES — Industries — Case studies *continuation*

RAMSEY, Douglas K.
The corporate warriors / Douglas K. Ramsey. — London : Grafton, 1987. — xxi,261p. — *Bibliography: p261*

Revitalizing American industry : lessons from our competitors ; Milton S. Hochmuth and William H. Davidson, editors. — Cambridge, Mass. : Ballinger Pub. Co., 1985. — p. cm. — *Includes bibliographies and index*

UNITED STATES — Industries — History

HUNTER, Louis C.
A history of industrial power in the United States 1780-1930 / Louis C. Hunter. — Charlottesville, Va : Published for the Hagley Museum and Library by the University Press of Virginia. — *Includes bibliographical references and indexes*
Vol.2: Steam power. — 1985. — xxii,732p

UNITED STATES — Industries — History — Congresses

Quantity & quiddity : essays in U.S. economic history / Peter Kilby, editor ; Jeremy Atack ... [et al.]. — 1st ed. — Middletown, Conn. : Wesleyan University Press ; Scranton, Pa. : Distributed by Harper & Row, c1987. — xxiii, 423 p.. — *Papers presented at a symposium in honor of Stanley Lebergott, Mar. 28th and 29th, 1985. "Selected publications of Stanley Lebergott": p. 399-405. — Includes bibliographical references and index*

UNITED STATES — Industries — Location

HICKS, Donald A
Advanced industrial development : restructuring, relocation, and renewal / Donald A. Hicks. — Boston, MA : Published by Oelgeschlager, Gunn & Hain in association with Lincoln Institute of Land Policy, c1985. — xx, 321 p.. — "A Lincoln Institute of Land Policy book.". — *Includes index. — Bibliography: p. [279]-310*

UNITED STATES — Industries — Reorganization

GRAY, H. Peter
International trade, employment and structural adjustment : the United States / H. Peter Gray, Thomas Pugel and Ingo Walter. — Geneva : International Labour Office, 1986. — x,108p. — (Employment, adjustment and industrialisation ; 3). — *Includes bibliographical references*

UNITED STATES — Industries — Statistics

Industrial production. — 1986 ed. — Washington, D.C. : Board of Governors of the Federal Reserve System, 1986. — viii,440p. — *"With a description of the methodology"*

UNITED STATES — Intellectual life

GABRIEL, Ralph Henry
The course of American democratic thought / Ralph Henry Gabriel. — 3rd ed. / with Robert H. Walker. — New York : Greenwood Press, 1986. — xix, 568 p.. — (Contributions in American studies ; no. 87). — *Includes index. — Bibliography: p. 541-547*

UNITED STATES — Intellectual life — Addresses, essays, lectures

The Rights of memory : essays on history, science, and American culture / edited by Taylor Littleton. — University, Ala. : University of Alabama Press, c1986. — viii, 227 p.. — (The Franklin lectures in the sciences & humanities). — *Includes bibliographies and index*

UNITED STATES — Intellectual life — 1865-1918

SMITH, John David
An old creed for the new South : proslavery ideology and historiography, 1865-1918 / John David Smith. — Westport, Conn. : Greenwood Press, 1985. — ix, 314 p.. — (Contributions in Afro-American and African studies ; no. 89). — *Includes index. — Bibliography: p. [295]-299*

UNITED STATES — Intellectual life — 20th century

BLOOM, Allan David
The closing of the American mind / Allan Bloom. — New York : Simon and Schuster, c1987. — 392p. — *Includes index*

GOTTFRIED, Paul
The search for historical meaning : Hegel and the postwar American right / Paul Edward Gottfried. — DeKalb, Ill. : Northern Illinois University Press, 1986. — xv, 178 p.. — *Includes index. — Bibliography: p. [163]-170*

UNITED STATES — Manufactures

SOMKID JATUSRIPITAK
The exporting behavior of manufacturing firms / by Somkid Jatusripitak. — Ann Arbor, Mich. : UMI Research Press, c1986. — xii, 115 p.. — (Research for business decisions ; no. 87) . — : A revision of author's thesis (Ph. D.)--Northwestern University, 1984. — *Includes index. — Bibliography: p. [107]-112*

UNITED STATES — Military policy

Amerikanskii ekspansionizm : noveishee vremia / otv. redaktor G. N. Sevost'ianov. — Moskva : Nauka, 1986. — 610p

BEST, Richard A
Co-operation with like-minded peoples : British influences on American security policy, 1945-1949 / Richard A. Best, Jr. — Westport, Conn. : Greenwood Press, 1986. — x, 226 p.. — (Contributions in American history ; no. 116). — *Includes index. — Bibliography: p. [197]-212*

CABLE, Larry E.
Conflict of myths : the development of American counterinsurgency doctrine and the Vietnam War / Larry E. Cable. — New York : New York University Press, 1986. — p. cm. — *Includes index. — Bibliography: p*

CHARLES, Daniel
Nuclear planning in NATO : pitfalls of first use / Daniel Charles. — Cambridge, Mass. : Ballinger Pub. Co., c1987. — xv, 177 p.. — "A Federation of American Scientists book.". — *Includes bibliographies and index*

CHARLTON, Michael
From deterrence to defence : the inside story of strategic policy / Michael Charlton. — Cambridge, Mass. : Harvard University Press, 1987, c1986. — p. cm. — Based on the author's BBC radio series, The Star wars history. — *Includes index*

CHARLTON, Michael, 1927-
The Star Wars history : from deterrence to defence : the American strategic debate / Michael Charlton. — London : BBC Publications, 1986. — 154p. — *Includes index*

COX, Andrew
Congress, Parliament and defence : the impact of legislative reform on defence accountability in Britain and America / Andrew Cox and Stephen Kirby. — Basingstoke : Macmillan, 1986. — 1v.. — *Includes index*

The deadly connection : nuclear war and U.S. intervention / [articles and speeches on behalf of the] New England Regional Office of the American Friends Service Committee edited by Joseph Gerson ; forward by Thomas J. Gumbleton. — Philadelphia : New Society Publishers, 1986. — xi,253p

HAYES, Peter
American lake : nuclear peril in the Pacific / Peter Hayes, Lyuba Zarsky, Walden Bello. — Harmondsworth : Penguin, 1987. — xiv, 529p. — *First published by Penguin in Australia in 1986*

HENDRICKSON, David C
The future of American strategy / David C. Hendrickson. — New York : Holmes & Meier, 1986. — p. cm. — *Includes index. — Bibliography: p*

KATU, Michio
To win a nuclear war : the Pentagon's secret strategy / Michio Katu and Daniel Axelrod ; with an introduction by Daniel Ellsberg. — Boston : Southend ; London : Zed, 1986. — [350]p

KAUFMANN, William W
A thoroughly efficient Navy / William W. Kaufmann. — Washington, D.C. : Brookings Institution, c1987. — p. cm. — (Studies in defense policy). — *Includes index*

KNELMAN, Fred H
Reagan, God, and the bomb : from myth to policy in the nuclear arms race / F.H. Knelman. — Toronto, Ont. : McClelland and Stewart, c1985. — vii, 343 p.. — *Bibliography: p. 313-330*

STARES, Paul B
Space and national security / Paul B. Stares. — Washington, D.C. : Brookings Institution, c1987. — p. cm. — *Includes bibliographical references and index*

UNITED STATES — Military policy — Addresses, essays, lectures

The national strategy : its theory and practice in the United States, 1945-1960 / edited by Norman A. Graebner. — New York : Oxford University Press, 1986. — p. cm. — *Includes index*

Toward a more effective defense : report of the Defense Organization Project / edited by Barry M. Blechman and William J. Lynn. — Cambridge, Mass. : Ballinger Pub. Co., 1985. — xiii, 247 p.. — *Includes bibliographies and index*

UNITED STATES — Military relations — Canada

BYERS, R. B
Aerospace defence : Canada's future role? / R.B. Byers, John Hamre, G.R. Lindsey. — Toronto, Canada : Canadian Institute of International Affairs, 1985. — 56 p.. — (Wellesley papers ; 9/1985). — *Includes bibliographies. — Contents: Defending North America / G.R. Lindsey -- Continental air defence, United States security policy, and Canada-United States defence relations / John Hamre -- NORAD, Star Wars, and strategic doctrine / R.B. Byers*

LITTLETON, James
Target nation : Canada and the western intelligence network / James Littleton. — 1st ed. — Toronto, Canada : L. & O. Dennys : CBC Enterprises, c1986. — viii, 228 p.. — *Includes index. — Bibliography: p. 209-220*

UNITED STATES — Military relations — Developing countries

LEONARD, Ellis P
[Orthopedic surgery of the dog and cat]. Leonard's Orthopedic surgery of the dog and cat. — 3rd ed. / J.W. Alexander. — Philadelphia : Saunders, 1985. — ix, 242 p.. — *Includes bibliographies and index*

UNITED STATES — Military relations — Great Britain

BEST, Richard A
Co-operation with like-minded peoples : British influences on American security policy, 1945-1949 / Richard A. Best, Jr. — Westport, Conn. : Greenwood Press, 1986. — x, 226 p.. — (Contributions in American history ; no. 116). — *Includes index. — Bibliography: p. [197]-212*

UNITED STATES — Military relations — Israel

HALSELL, Grace
Prophecy and politics : militant evangelists on the road to nuclear war / Grace Halsell. — Westport, Conn. : Lawrence Hill & Co., c1986. — 210 p.. — *Includes index*

UNITED STATES — Military relations — Latin America

BLACK, Jan Knippers
Sentinels of empire : United States and Latin American militarism / Jan Knippers Black. — Westport, Conn. : Greenwood Press, 1986. — xix, 240p. — (Contributions in political science ; no. 144). — Includes index. — Bibliography: p.[221]-236

SCHOULTZ, Lars
National security and United States policy toward Latin America / Lars Schoultz. — Princeton, N.J. : Princeton University Press, c1987. — xx, 377 p.. — Includes index. — Bibliography: p. 331-365

UNITED STATES — Military relations — Nicaragua

DICKEY, Christopher
With the Contras : a reporter in the wilds of Nicaragua / Christopher Dickey. — New York : Simon and Schuster, c1985. — 327 p., [9] p. of plates. — Includes index. — Bibliography: p. 273-315

INTERNATIONAL COURT OF JUSTICE
[Judgements]. Military and paramilitary activities in and against Nicaragua : (Nicaragua v. United States of America). Merits. 27 June 1986 = Activités militaires et paramilitaires au Nicaragua c. Etats-Unis d'America. Fond. 27 June 1986. — New York : United Nations, 1986. — 142 bis. — U.N. Security Council document S/18221 conveying the judgment of the Court at the request of the Permanent Representative of Nicaragua to the United Nations

UNITED STATES — Military relations — Persian Gulf Region

EPSTEIN, Joshua M.
Strategy and force planning : the case of the Persian Gulf / Joshua M. Epstein. — Washington, D.C. : Brookings Institution, c1987. — xiii, 169 p.. — Includes index. — Bibliography: p. 156-165

US strategic interests in the Gulf Region / edited by Wm.. — Boulder : Westview Press, 1987. — p. cm. — (Westview studies in regional security) (U.S. Army War College series on contemporary strategic issues). — Includes index

UNITED STATES — Military relations — Turkey

CAMPANY, Richard C
Turkey and the United States : the arms embargo period / Richard C. Campany, Jr. — New York : Praeger, 1986. — p. cm. — Includes index. — Bibliography: p

HALLEY, Laurence
Ancient affections : ethnic groups and foreign policy / Laurence Halley. — New York : Praeger, 1985. — viii, 180 p.. — Includes index. — Bibliography: p. 172-174

UNITED STATES — Moral conditions

OLDENQUIST, Andrew
The non-suicidal society / Andrew Oldenquist. — Bloomington : Indiana University Press, c1986. — p. cm. — Includes index. — Bibliography: p

UNITED STATES — National security

BERKOWITZ, Bruce D.
American security : dilemmas for a modern democracy / Bruce D. Berkowitz. — New Haven ; London : Yale University Press, c1986. — xvi, 282p. — Includes index

BEST, Richard A
Co-operation with like-minded peoples : British influences on American security policy, 1945-1949 / Richard A. Best, Jr. — Westport, Conn. : Greenwood Press, 1986. — x, 226 p.. — (Contributions in American history ; no. 116). — Includes index. — Bibliography: p. [197]-212

COMMITTEE FOR ECONOMIC DEVELOPMENT
Nuclear energy and national security : a statement on national policy / by the Research and Policy Committee of the Committee for Economic Development. — Washington : Committee for Economic Development, 1976. — 80 p.

COX, Andrew
Congress, Parliament and defence : the impact of legislative reform on defence accountability in Britain and America / Andrew Cox and Stephen Kirby. — Basingstoke : Macmillan, 1986. — 1v.. — Includes index

DIXON, James H.
National security policy formulation : institutions, processes and issues / James H. Dixon and associates. — Lanham ; London : University Press of America, c1984. — vi,237p. — Bibliography: p226-230. — Includes index

MÜLLER, Kurt E
Language competence : implications for national security / Kurt E. Müller. — New York : Published with the Center for Strategic and International Studies, Georgetown University, Washington, D.C. by Praeger, 1986. — p. cm. — (The Washington papers ; 119). — Bibliography: p

PANEL ON THE IMPACT OF NATIONAL SECURITY CONTROLS ON INTERNATIONAL TECHNOLOGY TRANSFER
Balancing the national interest : U.S. national security export controls and global economic competition. — Washington : National Academy Press, 1987. — xiii,321p. — Bibliography: p297-309

Population growth in Latin America and U.S. national security / edited by John Saunders. — Boston ; London : Allen & Unwin, 1986. — xxvii,305p. — Includes bibliographies and index

The Race for security : arms and arms control in the Reagan years / edited by Robert Travis Scott. — Lexington, Mass. : Lexington Books, c1987. — p. cm. — Includes index

SCHOULTZ, Lars
National security and United States policy toward Latin America / Lars Schoultz. — Princeton, N.J. : Princeton University Press, c1987. — xx, 377 p.. — Includes index. — Bibliography: p. 331-365

Staying the course : Henry M. Jackson and national security / edited by Dorothy Fosdick. — Seattle : University of Washington Press, c1987. — p. cm

UNITED STATES — National security — Addresses, essays, lectures

The national strategy : its theory and practice in the United States, 1945-1960 / edited by Norman A. Graebner. — New York : Oxford University Press, 1986. — p. cm. — Includes index

UNITED STATES — National security — Law and legislation — History

BIGEL, Alan I.
The Supreme Court on emergency powers, foreign affairs, and protection of civil liberties, 1935-1975 / Alan I. Bigel. — Lanham, MD : University Press of America, c1986. — xv, 211 p.. — : Originally presented as the author's thesis (doctoral--New School for Social Research). — Includes indexes. — Bibliography: p. 194-203

UNITED STATES — Officials and employees

LEVITT, M. S.
Measuring changes in central government productivity in the United States / M. S. Levitt. — London : National Institute of Economic and Social Research, 1986. — 24p. — (Discussion paper / National Institute of Economic and Social Research ; no.119)

UNITED STATES — Officials and employees — Biography

DRINNON, Richard
Keeper of concentration camps : Dillon S. Myer and American racism / Richard Drinnon. — Berkeley : University of California Press, c1987. — xxviii, 339 p.. — Includes index. — Bibliography: p. 271-324

UNITED STATES — Officials and employees — Salaries, allowances, etc — Congresses

Public sector payrolls / edited by David A. Wise. — Chicago : University of Chicago Press, 1987. — ix, 327 p.. — (A National Bureau of Economic Research project report). — Papers presented at a conference held in Williamsburg, Va., Nov. 15-17, 1984. — Includes bibliographies and indexes

UNITED STATES — Politics and government

The American presidents : the office and the men / edited by Frank N. Magill ; associate editor, John L. Loos. — Pasadena, Calif. : Salem Press, c1986. — 3 v.. — Vol. 3 has index. — Includes bibliographies

American studies / Mid America American Studies Association and University of Kansas. — Kansas : Mid-America American Studies Association, 1985-

DENTON, Robert E., Jr
Political communication in America / Robert E. Denton, Gary C. Woodward. — New York : Praeger, 1985. — p. cm. — Includes index

HARRIS, Fred R
America's democracy : the ideal and the reality / Fred R. Harris. — 3rd ed. — Glenview, Ill. ; London : Scott, Foresman, c1986. — 702, xxxp . — Includes bibliographical references and index

Politicheskoe razvitie Velikobritanii i SShA v XVII-XIX vv. : mezhvuzovskii sbornik nauchnykh trudov / [red. kollegiia: G. R. Levin...et al.]. — Leningrad : LGPI im. A. I. Gertsena, 1985. — 104p

The United States of America : a government by the people. — [Washington, D.C.] : United States Information, 1966. — 106p

UNITED STATES — Politics and government — Addresses, essays, lectures

Politics in Britain and the United States : comparative perspectives / edited by Richard Hodder-Williams and James Ceaser. — Durham : Duke University Press, 1986. — xvi, 232p. — Includes index. — Contains bibliographies

UNITED STATES — Politics and government — Miscellanea

AUSTIN, Erik W
Political facts of the United States since 1789 / Erik W. Austin ; with the assistance of Jerome M. Clubb. — New York : Columbia University Press, 1986. — p. cm. — Bibliography: p

ROGIN, Michael Paul
"Ronald Reagan," the movie : and other episodes in political demonology / Michael Rogin. — Berkeley : University of California Press, 1987. — p. cm. — Includes index

UNITED STATES — Politics and government — Periodicals — Bibliography

SKIDMORE, Gail
From radical left to extreme right : a bibliography of current periodicals of protest, controversy, advocacy, or dissent, with dispassionate content-summaries to guide librarians and other educators. — 3rd ed., completely rev. / by Gail Skidmore and Theodore Jurgen Spahn. — Metuchen, N.J. : Scarecrow Press, 1987. — p. cm. — Rev. ed. of: From radical left to extreme right. 2nd ed. / by Robert H. Muller, Theodore Jurgen Spahn, and Janet M. Spahn. 1970-1976. — Includes indexes

UNITED STATES — Politics and government — Statistics

AUSTIN, Erik W
Political facts of the United States since 1789 / Erik W. Austin ; with the assistance of Jerome M. Clubb. — New York : Columbia University Press, 1986. — p. cm. — *Bibliography: p*

UNITED STATES — Politics and government — Colonial period, ca. 1600-1775

GREENE, Jack P.
Peripheries and center : constitutional development in the extended polities of the British Empire and the United States, 1607-1788 / Jack P. Greene. — London : University of Georgia Press, 1987. — [288]p

SOSIN, Jack M
English America and imperial inconstancy : the rise of provincial autonomy, 1696-1716 / J.M. Sosin. — Lincoln, Neb. ; London : University of Nebraska Press, 1985. — xii, 287p. — *Includes index*

UNITED STATES — Politics and government — Colonial period, ca. 1600-1775 — Addresses, essays, lectures

NASH, Gary B
Race, class, and politics : essays on American colonial and revolutionary society / Gary B. Nash ; with a foreword by Richard S. Dunn. — Urbana : University of Illinois Press, c1986. — p. cm. — *Includes index*

UNITED STATES — Politics and government — Revolution, 1775-1783

GREENE, Jack P.
Peripheries and center : constitutional development in the extended polities of the British Empire and the United States, 1607-1788 / Jack P. Greene. — London : University of Georgia Press, 1987. — [288]p

TICKNER, J. Ann
Self-reliance versus power politics : the American and Indian experience in building nation states / J. Ann Tickner. — New York : Columbia University Press, 1987. — xi, 282 p.. — (The Political economy of international change). — *Includes index.* — *Bibliography: p. [231]-267*

UNITED STATES — Politics and government — 1783-1789

Beyond confederation : origins of the constitution and American national identity / edited by Richard Beeman, Stephen Botein, and Edward C. Carter II. — Chapel Hill : University of North Carolina Press, c1987. — p. cm. — *"Published for the Institute of Early American History and Culture, Williamsburg, Virginia.".* — *Includes index*

GREENE, Jack P.
Peripheries and center : constitutional development in the extended polities of the British Empire and the United States, 1607-1788 / Jack P. Greene. — London : University of Georgia Press, 1987. — [288]p

MADISON, James
The Federalist papers / James Madison, Alexander Hamilton and John Jay ; edited by Isaac Kramnick. — Harmondsworth : Penguin, 1987. — 515p

UNITED STATES — Politics and government — 1783-1865

TICKNER, J. Ann
Self-reliance versus power politics : the American and Indian experience in building nation states / J. Ann Tickner. — New York : Columbia University Press, 1987. — xi, 282 p.. — (The Political economy of international change). — *Includes index.* — *Bibliography: p. [231]-267*

UNITED STATES — Politics and government — 1789-1815

NELSON, John R.
Liberty and property : political economy and policymaking in the new nation, 1789-1812 / John R. Nelson, Jr. — Baltimore : Johns Hopkins University Press, c1987. — p. cm. — (The Johns Hopkins University studies in historical and political science ; 105th ser., 2). — *Bibliography: p*

UNITED STATES — Politics and government — 19th century

OSTROGORSKI, M.
Democracy and the organization of political parties / with a preface by...James Bryce ; edited...by Seymour Martin Lipset. — Chicago : Quadrangle
volume 2: United States. — 1964. — lxxvii,418p. — *First published in English in 1902*

UNITED STATES — Politics and government — 1815-1861

SHIELDS, Johanna Nicol
The line of duty : maverick congressmen and the development of American political culture, 1836-1860 / Johanna Nicol Shields. — Westport, Conn. : Greenwood Press, c1985. — p. cm. — (Contributions in American studies ; no. 80). — *Includes index.* — *Bibliography: p*

UNITED STATES — Politics and government — 1815-1861 — Literary collections

LIPPARD, George
[Selections. 1986]. George Lippard, prophet of protest : writings of an American radical, 1822-1854 / edited with an introduction by David S. Reynolds. — New York : P. Lang, c1986. — xii, 335 p.. — *Cover title: George Lippard, an anthology.* — *Bibliography: p. 333-335*

UNITED STATES — Politics and government — 1825-1829

HARGREAVES, Mary W. M.
The presidency of John Quincy Adams / Mary W.M. Hargreaves. — Lawrence, Kan. : University Press of Kansas, c1985. — xv, 398 p.. — (American presidency series). — *Includes index.* — *Bibliography: p. 325-380*

UNITED STATES — Politics and government — 1829-1837

ELLIS, Richard E
The Union at risk : Jacksonian democracy, states' rights, and the nullification crisis / Richard E. Ellis. — New York : Oxford University Press, 1987. — p. cm. — *Includes index*

JACKSON, Andrew
The papers of Andrew Jackson. — Knoxville, Tenn. : University of Tennessee Press
Vol.2: 1804-1813 / Harold D. Moser, Sharon Macpherson, editors. — 1984. — xxvii,634p

Jacksonian democracy / [edited by] James L. Bugg, Jr., Peter C. Stewart. — 2nd ed. — Lanham, Md. ; London : University Press of America, 1986. — 166p. — : Reprint. Originally published: 2nd ed. Hinsdale, Ill. : Dryden Press, c1976. — *Bibliography: p.[160]-166*

UNITED STATES — Politics and government — 1849-1877

CLAY, Cassius Marcellus
The life of Cassius Marcellus Clay : memoirs, writings, and speeches showing his conduct in the overthrow of American slavery, the salvation of the Union, and the restoration of the autonomy of the states / [by Cassius Marcellus Clay]. — New York : Negro Universities Press. — *Reprint of 1886 edition*
[Vol.1]. — 1969. — xiii,600p

UNITED STATES — Politics and government — 1849-1877 — Addresses, essays, lectures

Abraham Lincoln and the American political tradition / edited by John L. Thomas. — Amherst : University of Massachusetts Press, 1986. — 162 p.. — *"The essays in this volume were presented in briefer form as papers at a conference on "Lincoln and the American Political Tradition" held at Brown University, June 7-9, 1984, and sponsored by the university's John Hay Library and the Lincoln Group of Boston."--Acknowledgements.* — *Includes bibliographies*

UNITED STATES — Politics and government — 1865-1900

Carl Schurz : Revolutionär und Staatsmann : sein Leben in selbstzeugnissen Bildern und Dokumenten = Revolutionary and statesman : his life in personal and official documents with illustrations / herausgegeben von/edited by Rüdiger Wersich. — 2.Aufl. — München : Moos, 1986. — *Parallel texts in German and English.* — *First published 1979*

UNITED STATES — Politics and government — 1865-1933

TOBIN, Eugene M
Organize or perish : America's independent progressives, 1913-1933 / Eugene M. Tobin. — Westport, Conn. ; London : Greenwood Press, c1986. — xiv, 279p. — (Contributions in American history ; no. 114). — *Includes index.* — *Bibliography: p [251]-260*

UNITED STATES — Politics and government — 1865-1933 — Addresses, essays, lectures

MCCORMICK, Richard L
The party period and public policy : American politics from the Age of Jackson to the Progressive Era / Richard L. McCormick. — New York : Oxford University Press, 1986. — p. cm. — *Includes index*

UNITED STATES — Politics and government — 20th century

ARNOLD, Peri E.
Making the managerial presidency : comprehensive reorganization planning, 1905-1980 / Peri E. Arnold. — Princeton, N.J. : Princeton University Press, c1986. — p. cm. — *Includes index.* — *Bibliography: p*

GREENBERG, Edward S.
Capitalism and the American political ideal / by Edward S. Greenberg. — Armonk, N.Y. : M.E. Sharpe, 1985. — p. cm

WALZER, Michael
The politics of ethnicity / Michael Walzer...[et al.]. — Cambridge, Mass. ; London : Belknap Press of Harvard University Press, 1982. — vi,142p. — (Dimensions of ethnicity : Selections from the Harvard Encyclopedia of American ethnic groups). — *Bibliography: p [139]-142*

UNITED STATES — Politics and government — 20th century — Manuscripts — Catalogs

BURTON, Dennis A.
A guide to manuscripts in the Presidential Libraries / compiled and edited by Dennis A. Burton, James B. Rhoads, Raymond W. Smock. — College Park, Md. : Research Materials Corp., 1985. — p. cm. — *Includes index*

UNITED STATES — Politics and government — 20th century — Sources — Bibliography — Catalogs

BURTON, Dennis A.
A guide to manuscripts in the Presidential Libraries / compiled and edited by Dennis A. Burton, James B. Rhoads, Raymond W. Smock. — College Park, Md. : Research Materials Corp., 1985. — p. cm. — *Includes index*

UNITED STATES — Politics and government — 1901-1953

CEBULA, James E.
James M. Cox : journalist and politician / James E. Cebula. — New York : Garland, 1985. — 181 p.. — (Modern American history) . — Includes index. — Bibliography: p. 171-173

UNITED STATES — Politics and government — 1913-1921

FERRELL, Robert H
Woodrow Wilson and World War I, 1917-1921 / by Robert H. Ferrell. — 1st ed. — New York ; London : Harper & Row, c1985. — xii, 346p, [26]p of plates. — (New American nationl series). — Includes index. — Bibliography: p.303-333

UNITED STATES — Politics and government — 1933-1945

BERMAN, Larry
The new American presidency / Larry Berman. — Boston : Little Brown, c1987. — xi, 413 p.. — Copyright date stamped on t.p. verso. — Includes index. — Bibliography: p. 383-391

MORGAN, Chester M
Redneck liberal : Theodore G. Bilbo and the New Deal / Chester M. Morgan. — Baton Rouge : Louisiana State University Press, c1985. — p. cm. — Includes index. — Bibliography: p

STEELE, Richard W
Propaganda in an open society : the Roosevelt administration and the media, 1933-1941 / Richard W. Steele. — Westport, Conn. ; London : Greenwood Press, c1985. — x, 231p. — (Contributions in American history ; no. 111). — Includes index. — Bibliography: p.[213]-224

UNITED STATES — Politics and government — 1933-1945 — Addresses, essays, lectures

LONG, Huey Pierce
Kingfish to America, share our wealth : selected senatorial papers of Huey P. Long / edited and with an introduction by Henry M. Christman. — New York : Schocken Books, 1985. — xvi, 145 p.. — Includes index

UNITED STATES — Politics and government — 1945-1953

DUNAR, Andrew J.
The Truman scandals and the politics of morality / Andrew J. Dunar. — Columbia : University of Missouri Press, 1984. — viii, 213p. — Bibliography: p.199-205

GREENE, John Robert
The crusade : the presidential election of 1952 / John Robert Greene. — Lanham, Md. ; London : University Press of America, c1985. — vii, 343 p.. — Includes index. — Bibliography: p.301-318

UNITED STATES — Politics and government — 1945-1953 — Congresses

Harry S. Truman, the man from Independence / edited by William F. Levantrosser ; prepared under the auspices of Hofstra University. — New York : Greenwood Press, c1986. — x, 427 p.. — (Contributions in political science ; no. 145). — Papers presented at the Hofstra University International Conference on Harry S. Truman, held Apr. 14-16, 1983. — Includes bibliographies and index

UNITED STATES — Politics and government — 1945-

BERMAN, Larry
The new American presidency / Larry Berman. — Boston : Little Brown, c1987. — xi, 413 p.. — Copyright date stamped on t.p. verso. — Includes index. — Bibliography: p. 383-391

BRAUER, Carl M.
Presidential transitions : Eisenhower through Reagan / Carl M. Brauer. — New York ; Oxford : Oxford University Press, 1986. — xvii, 310p. — Includes bibliographical references

CHARLTON, Michael, 1927-
The Star Wars history : from deterrence to defence : the American strategic debate / Michael Charlton. — London : BBC Publications, 1986. — 154p. — Includes index

GIBBONS, William Conrad
The U.S. government and the Vietnam war : executive and legislative roles and relationships / William Conrad Gibbons ; with a new preface by the author. — Princeton, N.J. : Princeton University Press, [1986-. — p. cm. — "Prepared for the Committee on Foreign Relations, United States Senate, by the Congressional Research Service, Library of Congress.". — : "Originally published by the U.S. Government Printing Office in April 1984"--T.p. verso. — Includes bibliographical references and indexes. — Contents: pt. 1. 1945-1960 -- pt. 2. 1961-1964

GOTTFRIED, Paul
The search for historical meaning : Hegel and the postwar American right / Paul Edward Gottfried. — DeKalb, Ill. : Northern Illinois University Press, 1986. — xv, 178 p.. — Includes index. — Bibliography: p. [163]-170

GRANT, Alan R.
The American political process / Alan R. Grant. — 3rd ed. — Aldershot : Gower, c1986. — ix,302p. — Previous ed.: London : Heinemann, 1982. — Includes index

GROSS, Bertram
Friendly fascism : the new face of power in America / Bertram Gross. — Montréal : Black Rose Books, 1985. — xxvii,409p

Liberating theory / by Michael Albert ... [et al.]. — 1st ed. — Boston, MA. : South End Press, c1986. — 197 p.. — Bibliography: p. 195-197

NEUMAN, W. Russell
The paradox of mass politics : knowledge and opinion in the American electorate / W. Russell Neuman. — Cambridge, Mass. : Harvard University Press, 1986. — 241 p.. — Includes index. — Bibliography: p. [222]-236

SPEAR, Joseph C.
Presidents and the press : the Nixon legacy / Joseph C.Spear. — Cambridge, Massachusetts ; London : MIT Press, 1984

ULLMANN, Owen
Stockmann : the man, the myth, the future / by Owen Ullmann. — New York : Fine, 1986. — 343p

UNITED STATES — Politics and government — 1945- — Congresses

The Role of government in the United States : practice and theory / edited by Robert E. Cleary. — Lanham, Md. : University Press of America, c1985. — 245 p.. — "A report of a conference at the College of Public and International Affairs of the American University, Washington, D.C., March 2-3, 1984.". — Includes bibliographical references

UNITED STATES — Politics and government — 1945- — Decision making — Case studies

NEUSTADT, Richard E
Thinking in time : the uses of history for decision-makers / Richard E. Neustade, Ernest R. May. — New York : Free Press ; London : Collier Macmillan, c1986. — p. cm. — Includes index. — Bibliography: p

UNITED STATES — Politics and government — 1945- — Public opinion

BENNETT, Stephen Earl
Apathy in America, 1960-1984 : causes and consequences of citizen political indifference / Stephen Earl Bennett. — Dobbs Ferry, N.Y. : Transnational Publishers, c1986. — x, 198 p.. — Includes index. — Bibliography: p. 179-193

LEVIN, Murray Burton
Talk radio and the American dream / by Murray B. Levin. — Lexington, Mass. : Lexington Books, c1987. — xv, 170 p.. — Includes index

UNITED STATES — Politics and government — 1961-1963

DIETZ, Terry
Republicans and Vietnam, 1961-1968 / Terry Dietz. — Westport, Conn. ; London : Greenwood Press, 1986. — xv, 184p. — (Contributions in political science ; no. 146). — Includes index. — Bibliography: p.[173]-177

UNITED STATES — Politics and government — 1961-1963 — Addresses, essays, lectures

Race, politics, and culture : critical essays on the radicalism of the 1960's / edited by Adolph Reed, Jr. — Westport, Conn. : Greenwood Press, 1986. — xii, 287 p.. — (Contributions in Afro-American and African studies ; no. 95). — Includes bibliographies and index

UNITED STATES — Politics and government — 1963-1969

The Johnson Presidency : twenty intimate perspectives of Lyndon B. Johnson / edited by Kenneth W. Thompson. — Lanham ; London : University Press of America, c1987. — [310]p. — (Portraits of American presidents ; 5)

ZAREFSKY, David
President Johnson's war on poverty : rhetoric and history / David Zarefsky. — University, Ala. : University of Alabama Press, c1986. — xxiii, 275p. — Includes index. — Bibliography: p 256-266

UNITED STATES — Politics and government — 1963-1969 — Addresses, essays, lectures

Race, politics, and culture : critical essays on the radicalism of the 1960's / edited by Adolph Reed, Jr. — Westport, Conn. : Greenwood Press, 1986. — xii, 287 p.. — (Contributions in Afro-American and African studies ; no. 95). — Includes bibliographies and index

UNITED STATES — Politics and government — 1963-1969 — Sources — Bibliography

The Johnson years / edited by Robert A. Divine. — Lawrence, Kan. : University Press of Kansas, 1987-. — v. <1 >. — Includes index. — Contents: v. 1. Foreign policy, the Great Society, and the White House

UNITED STATES — Politics and government — 1965-1969

DIETZ, Terry
Republicans and Vietnam, 1961-1968 / Terry Dietz. — Westport, Conn. ; London : Greenwood Press, 1986. — xv, 184p. — (Contributions in political science ; no. 146). — Includes index. — Bibliography: p.[173]-177

UNITED STATES — Politics and government — 1974-

BARDACH, Eugene
The implementation game : what happens after a bill becomes a law / Eugene Bardach. — Cambridge, Mass. ; London : M.I.T. Press, 1977. — xi,323p. — (MIT studies in American politics and public policy / Massachusetts Institute of Technology ; 1). — Includes index

UNITED STATES — Politics and government — 1977-

SHAFER, Byron E.
The changing structure of American politics / Byron E. Shafer. — Oxford : Clarendon Press, 1986. — 20p. — *An inaugural lecture delivered before the University of Oxford on 27 January 1986*

UNITED STATES — Politics and government — 1981

BROOKHISER, Richard
The outside story : how Democrats and Republicans re-elected Reagan / Richard Brookhiser. — 1st ed. — Garden City, N.Y. : Doubleday, 1986. — ix, 298 p.. — *Includes index*

UNITED STATES — Politics and government — 1981-

BURT, Martha R
Testing the social safety net : the impact of changes in support programs during the Reagan administration / Martha R. Burt, Karen J. Pittman. — Washington, D.C. : Urban Institute Press, c1985. — xix, 183 p.. — (The Changing domestic priorities series). — *Includes bibliographical references*

COLLINS, Sheila D
From melting pot to rainbow coalition : the future of race in American politics / Sheila D. Collins. — New York : Monthly Review Press, 1986. — p. cm. — *Includes index. — Bibliography: p*

DEMAC, Donna A
Keeping America uninformed : government secrecy in the 1980's / Donna A. Demac ; preface by Ben H. Bagdikian. — New York : Pilgrim Press, c1984. — xii, 180 p.. — *Includes index. — Bibliography: p. 169-174*

FERRARO, Geraldine
Ferraro, my story / Geraldine A. Ferraro, with Linda Bird Francke. — Toronto ; New York : Bantam Books, 1985. — 340 p., [24] p. of plates. — *Includes index*

FERRIS, Elizabeth G
The Central American refugees / Elizabeth G. Ferris. — New York : Praeger, 1986. — p. cm

FURGURSON, Ernest B.
Hard right : the rise of Jesse Helms / by Ernest B. Furgurson. — 1st ed. — New York : Norton, c1986. — p. cm

GREEN, David G
The new conservatism : the counter-revolution in political, economic, and social thought / David G. Green. — New York : St. Martin's Press, 1987. — xi, 238 p.. — *Includes index. — Bibliography: p. 221-232*

GREENYA, John
The real David Stockman / by John Greenya and Anne Urban ; introduction by Ralph Nader. — New York : St. Martin's Press, 1986. — p. cm. — *On t.p. "real" is italicized*

HALSELL, Grace
Prophecy and politics : militant evangelists on the road to nuclear war / Grace Halsell. — Westport, Conn. : Lawrence Hill & Co., c1986. — 210 p.. — *Includes index*

IDE, Arthur Frederick
Tomorrow's tyrants : the radical right & the politics of hate / by Arthur Frederick Ide. — Dallas : Monument Press, 1985. — p. cm. — *Includes bibliographical references and index*

KNELMAN, Fred H
Reagan, God, and the bomb : from myth to policy in the nuclear arms race / F.H. Knelman. — Toronto, Ont. : McClelland and Stewart, c1985. — vii, 343 p.. — *Bibliography: p. 313-330*

KRICKUS, Richard J
The superpowers in crisis : implications of domestic discord / Richard J. Krickus. — Washington ; London : Pergamon-Brassey's International Defence Publishers, 1987. — xiii, 236p. — *Includes bibliographies*

KRIEGER, Joel
Reagan, Thatcher, and the politics of decline / Joel Krieger. — Cambridge : Polity, 1986. — [220]p. — (Europe and the international order) . — *Includes index*

MCKAY, David H.
Politics and power in the U.S.A. : [a guide to the basic institutions of the American Federal Government] / David McKay. — Harmondsworth : Penguin, 1987. — 240p. — *Bibliography: p[229]-231*

The New populism : the politics of empowerment / edited by Harry C. Boyte and Frank Riessman. — Philadelphia : Temple University Press, 1986. — ix, 323 p.. — *Includes index. — Bibliography: p. 319-323*

On call : political essays / edited by June Jordan. — London : Pluto, 1986. — [224]p. — *Includes bibliography*

PETERS, B. Guy
American public policy : promise and performance / B. Guy Peters. — 2nd ed. — Basingstoke : Macmillan Education, 1986. — viii,344p. — *1st and 2nd U.S. eds have subtitle: Process and performance. — Previous ed.: New York : F. Watts, 1982. — Includes index*

Six Virginia papers presented at the Miller Center Forums, 1985 / by Arthur F. Burns...[et al.] ; [edited by Kenneth W. Thompson]. — Lanham ; London : University Press of America, 1986. — xi,88p. — (Virginia papers on the Presidency ; v.21)

State politics and the new federalism : readings and commentary / edited by Marilyn Gittell. — New York : Longman, c1986. — xv, 544 p.. — *Includes index. — Bibliography: p. 533-535*

STOCKMAN, David A.
The triumph of politics / David A. Stockman. — London : Bodley Head, c1986. — 440p,[16]p of plates

UNITED STATES — Politics and government — 1981- — Addresses. essays, lectures

Left, right & babyboom : America's new politics / edited by David Boaz. — Washington, D.C. : Cato Institute, c1986. — 122 p.

UNITED STATES — Politics and government — 1981- — Congresses

American futures : political and economic trends and prospects : papers / presented to a conference at the Swedish Institute of International Affairs on June 16-18, 1983 ; edited by Leon N. Lindberg, Atis Lejins, and Katarina Engberg. — Stockholm : The Institute, [1984]. — x, 130 p.. — (Conference papers / the Swedish Institute of International Affairs ; 4, 1984). — *Includes bibliographies. — Contents: The American economy in the 1980's / Leon N. Lindberg -- Long-term trends in American economy and possible future / Michel Aglietta -- The US hegemony in the postwar world economy / Lars Mjøset -- Fragmentation and continuity / Reinhard Rode -- Gulliver's digestion / Harald Müller -- Party decline and party reform / Alan Ware -- The changing political role of business in the USA / Graham K. Wilson -- Social movements and the left opposition in the USA / Ib Jørgensen -- American futures and public policy / Virginia Sapiro*

UNITED STATES — Popular culture

BOSKIN, Joseph
Sambo : the rise & demise of an American jester / Joseph Boskin. — New York : Oxford University Press, 1986. — ix, 252 p. [8] p. of plates. — *Includes index. — Bibliography: p. 225-243*

UNITED STATES — Population

KITAGAWA, Evelyn Mae
Differential mortality in the United States : a study in socioeconomic epidemiology / [by] Evelyn M. Kitagawa and Philip M. Hauser. — Cambridge, Mass. : Harvard University Press, 1973. — xx, 255 p. — (Vital and health statistics monographs). — *Bibliography: p. 248-251*

UNITED STATES — Population — History — 19th century — Sources — Indexes

SCHULZE, Suzanne
Population information in nineteenth century census volumes / by Suzanne Schulze. — Phoenix, AZ : Oryx Press, 1983. — ix, 446 p.. — *Continued by: Population information in twentieth century census volumes, 1900-1940. — Bibliography: p. 437-438*

UNITED STATES — Population policy

World population and U.S. policy / Jane Menken, editor. — 1st ed. — New York : W.W. Norton, c1986. — p. cm. — *At head of title: The American Assembly, Columbia University. — Includes index*

UNITED STATES — Population policy — Addresses, essays, lectures

Population policy analysis : issues in American politics / edited by Michael E. Kraft, Mark Schneider. — Lexington, Mass. : Lexington Books, c1978. — xi, 204 p.. — (Policy Studies Organization series ; 17). — *"Collection of studies originated with a symposium on population policy which appeared in the winter, 1977 issue of the Policy studies journal.". — Includes bibliographical references and index*

UNITED STATES — Public lands — History

HYMAN, Harold M
American singularity : the 1787 Northwest Ordinance, the 1862 Homestead and Morrill Acts, and the 1944 G.I. Bill / Harold M. Hyman. — Athens : University of Georgia Press, c1986. — x, 95 p.. — (The Richard B. Russell lectures ; no. 5). — *Includes index. — Bibliography: p. [77]-90*

UNITED STATES — Race question — Addresses, essays, lectures

BLAUNER, Robert
Racial oppression in America / Robert Blauner. — New York ; London : Harper and Row, 1972. — x,309p. — *Includes index*

UNITED STATES — Race relations

BLOOM, Jack M
Class, race, and the Civil Rights Movement / Jack M. Bloom. — Bloomington : Indiana University Press, c1987. — x, 267 p.. — (Blacks in the diaspora). — *Includes index. — Bibliography: p. [225]-237*

BOGGS, James
Racism and the class struggle : further pages from a black worker's notebook. — New York : [Monthly Review Press, 1970]. — 190 p

BOSKIN, Joseph
Sambo : the rise & demise of an American jester / Joseph Boskin. — New York : Oxford University Press, 1986. — ix, 252 p. [8] p. of plates. — *Includes index. — Bibliography: p. 225-243*

COONEY, Frank
Studies in race relations : South Africa and USA / Frank Cooney, Gordon Morton [and] Barry Wright. — Glasgow : Pulse Publications, 1986. — 84p

Housing desegregation and federal policy / edited by John M. Goering. — Chapel Hill : University of North Carolina Press, c1986. — x, 343 p.. — (Urban and regional policy and development studies). — *Includes bibliographies and index*

Prejudice, discrimination, and racism / edited by John F. Dovidio and Samuel L. Gaertner. — Orlando : Academic Press, 1986. — xiii, 337 p.. — *Includes bibliographies and index*

UNITED STATES — Race relations
continuation

Strategies for improving race relations : the Anglo-American experience / edited by John W. Shaw, Peter G. Nordlie, Richard M. Shapiro ; with a preface by Bhiku Parekh. — Manchester : Manchester University Press, c1987. — xiii,226p. — *Includes index*

UNITED STATES — Race relations — Addresses, essays, lectures

DU BOIS, W. E. B
Against racism : unpublished essays, papers, addresses, 1887-1961 / by W.E.B. Du Bois ; edited by Herbert Aptheker. — Amherst : University of Massachusetts Press, 1985. — xx, 325 p.. — *Includes bibliographical references and index*

KING, Martin Luther
A testament of hope : the essential writings of Martin Luther King, Jr. / edited by James Melvin Washington. — 1st ed. — San Francisco : Harper & Row, c1986. — xxvi, 676 p.. — *Includes index. — Bibliography: p. 654-661*

NASH, Gary B
Race, class, and politics : essays on American colonial and revolutionary society / Gary B. Nash ; with a foreword by Richard S. Dunn. — Urbana : University of Illinois Press, c1986. — p. cm. — *Includes index*

UNITED STATES — Relations Europeans

The standing of the U.S. in West European opinion-1965 : (World Survey III series). — [Washington, D.C.] : United States Information Agency, 1965. — xii,59p. — *R-145-65*

UNITED STATES — Relations — Nigerians

Nigerian university student views on national and international issues. — [Washington, D. C.] : United States Information Agency, 1966. — viii,35p. — *R-44-66*

UNITED STATES — Relations — Africa

East African university student views on international and continental issues. — [Washington, D.C.] : United States Information Agency, 1965. — vii,25p. — *R-39-65*

UNITED STATES — Relations — African

African student outlook : a comparison of findings at English and French-speaking universities. — [Washington, D.C.] : United States Information Agency, 1965. — vi,29p. — *R-115-65*

UNITED STATES — Relations — Canada

GWYN, Richard J.
The 49th paradox : Canada in North America / Richard Gwyn. — Toronto, Ont. : McClelland and Stewart, c1985. — 362 p.. — *Includes index. — Bibliography: p. 341-348*

LEYTON-BROWN, David
Weathering the storm : Canadian-U.S. relations, 1980-83 / by David Leyton-Brown. — Toronto, Ont. : Canadian-American Committee, [1985]. — xi, 86 p.. — *Includes bibliographical references*

Southern exposure : Canadian perspectives on the United States / edited with an introduction by David H. Flaherty, William R. McKercher. — Toronto : McGraw-Hill Ryerson, 1986. — x,246p. — *Bibliography: p233-237*

UNITED STATES — Relations — China

Confidential U.S. State Department Central Files : United States-China relations, 1940-1949 / edited by Paul Kesaris. — Frederick, MD : University Publications of America, 1985. — 7microfilms. — *Contents: Documents from the records of the Department of State, Central Files: China*

UNITED STATES — Relations — China — Bibliography

Confidential U.S. State Department Central Files : United States - China relations, 1940-1949 / edited by Robert Lester. — Frederick, Md. : University Publications of America, 1985. — 7p. — *Contents: Index to documents from Department of State Central Files*

UNITED STATES — Relations — Cuba

FREDERICK, Howard H
Cuban-American radio wars : ideology in international telecommunications / Howard H. Frederick. — Norwood, N.J. : Ablex Pub. Corporation, c1986. — viii, 200 p.. — (Communication and information science). — *Includes indexes. — Bibliography: p. 177-193*

UNITED STATES — Relations — Europe

SERVAN-SCHREIBER, J. J.
The American challenge / J. J. Servan-Schreiber ; translated from the French by Ronald Steel ; with a foreword by Arthur Schlesinger, Jr.. — New York : Atheneum, 1979. — 254p. — *Originally published as Le défi américain, by Denöel, 1967*

UNITED STATES — Relations — Latin America

The Iberian-Latin American connection : implications for U.S. foreign policy / edited by Howard J. Wiarda. — Boulder, Colo. ; London : Westview Press ; Washington, D.C. : American Enterprise Institute, 1986. — xiii,482p. — (Westview special studies on Latin America and the Caribbean). — *Bibliographical notes*

RANGEL, Carlos
[Del buen salvaje al buen revolucionario. English]. The Latin Americans : their love-hate relationship with the United States / Carlos Rangel. — Rev. ed. with a new introduction by the author. — New Brunswick, N.J. (U.S.A.) : Transaction Books, c1987. — p. cm. — *Includes bibliographical references and index*

UNITED STATES — Relations — Mexico — Congresses

Missions in conflict : essays on U.S.-Mexican relations and Chicano culture / Renate von Bardeleben (managing editor). — Tübingen : Narr, 1986. — xxi,304p. — *Collection of essays first presented at First International Symposium on Chicano Culture, 1984, Mainz*

UNITED STATES — Relations — Nigeria

Nigerian opinion on selected national and international issues : (World Survey III series). — [Washington, D.C.] : United States Information Agency, 1966. — xi,42p. — *R-32-66*

UNITED STATES — Relations — Philippines

Crisis in the Philippines : the Marcos era and beyond / edited by John Bresnan. — Princeton, NJ : Princeton University Press, c1986. — xiv, 284p. — *Includes index. — Bibliography: p.[259]-267*

UNITED STATES — Relations — Senegal

Senegalese opinion on selected African and international issues : (World Survey III series). — [Washington, D.C.] : United States Information Agency, 1966. — xiv, 23p. — *R-68-66*

UNITED STATES — Relations — South Africa

LOVE, Janice
The U.S. anti-apartheid movement : local activism in global politics / Janice Love. — New York : Praeger, 1985. — p. cm. — *Includes index. — Bibliography: p*

UNITED STATES — Relations — Soviet Union

AILES, Catherine P.
Cooperation in science and technology : an evaluation of the U.S.-Soviet agreement / Catherine P. Ailes and Arthur E. Pardee. — Boulder : Westview, 1986. — xxiii,334p

HAMMER, Armand
Witness to history / by Armand Hammer with Neil Lyndon. — New York ; London : Simon & Schuster, 1987. — [512]p. — *Includes index*

RICHMOND, Yale
U.S.-Soviet cultural exchanges, 1958-1986 : who wins? / Yale Richmond ; foreword by Marshall D. Shulman. — Boulder : Westview Press, 1987. — xvi, 170 p.. — (Westview special studies on the Soviet Union and Eastern Europe). — *Includes index. — Bibliography: p. 161-163*

UNITED STATES — Relations (Military) — Central America — Moral and ethical aspects

¡ Basta! : no mandate for war : a pledge of resistance handbook / by the Emergency Response Network ; edited by Ken Butigan, Terry Messman-Rucker, and Marie Pastrick. — Philadelphia : New Society, 1986. — 83,ivp. — *Bibliography: pi-iv*

UNITED STATES — Relations (Military) with the Soviet Union

FREEDMAN, Lawrence
US intelligence and the Soviet strategic threat / Lawrence Freedman. — 2nd ed. — London : Macmillan, 1986. — [288]p. — *Previous ed.: 1977. — Includes bibliography and index*

UNITED STATES — Religion

American studies / Mid America American Studies Association and University of Kansas. — Kansas : Mid-America American Studies Association, 1985-

Cultural change in the United States since World War II / edited by Maurice Gonnand, Sergio Perosa, Christopher W.E. Bigsby ; with contributions from Zoltan Abadi-Nagy...[et al.]. — Amsterdam : Free University Press, 1986. — 102p. — (European contributions to American studies ; 9). — *Includes bibliographies*

MELTON, J. Gordon
The encyclopedic handbook of cults in America / J. Gordon Melton. — New York : Garland Pub., 1986. — x, 272 p.. — (Garland reference library of social science ; v. 213). — *Includes bibliographies and index*

UNITED STATES — Religion — Biography — Dictionaries

MELTON, J. Gordon
Biographical dictionary of American cult and sect leaders / J. Gordon Melton. — New York ; London : Garland Publishing, 1986. — xii, 354 p.. — (Garland reference library of social science ; v.212). — *Includes index*

UNITED STATES — Religion — To 1800

BONOMI, Patricia U
Under the cope of heaven : religion, society, and politics in Colonial America / Patricia U. Bonomi. — New York : Oxford University Press, 1986. — p. cm. — *Includes index. — Bibliography: p*

UNITED STATES — Religion — 19th century

MCDANNELL, Colleen
The Christian home in Victorian America, 1840-1900 / Colleen McDannell. — Bloomington : Indiana University Press, c1986. — xvii, 193p. — (Religion in North America). — *Includes index. — Bibliography: p. 178-186*

UNITED STATES — Religion — 1960-

FLOWERS, Ronald B
Religion in strange times : the 1960s and 1970s / by Ronald B. Flowers. — Macon, GA : Mercer University Press, c1984. — xiv, 242 p.. — *Includes index. — Bibliography: p. 229-230*

UNITED STATES — Rural conditions

ATACK, Jeremy
To their own soil : agriculture in the Antebellum North / Jeremy Atack, Fred Bateman. — 1st ed. — Ames : Iowa State University Press, 1987. — xi, 322 p.. — (The Henry A. Wallace series on agricultural history and rural studies). — Includes index. — Bibliography: p. 299-312

UNITED STATES — Social conditions

KIRSCHNER, D. S.
The paradox of professionalism : reform and public service in urban America, 1900-1940 / by D.S. Kirschner. — Westport, Conn. ; London : Greenwood, 1987. — [224]p. — (Contributions in American history ; no.119). — Includes bibliography and index

UNITED STATES — Social conditions — Congresses

Redefining social problems / edited by Edward Seidman and Julian Rappaport. — New York : Plenum Press, c1986. — xxii, 311p. — (Perspectives in social psychology). — Includes bibliographies and index

UNITED STATES — Social conditions — To 1865

ROSENWAIKE, Ira
On the edge of greatness : a portrait of American Jewry in the early national period / Ira Rosenwaike. — [Cincinnati] : American Jewish Archives, c1985. — xvi, 189 p.. — (Publications of the American Jewish Archives ; no. 14). — Bibliography: p. 171-189

WYATT-BROWN, Bertram
Yankee saints and Southern sinners / Bertram Wyatt-Brown. — Baten Rouge ; London : Louisiana State University Press, c1985. — xi, 227p. — Includes index

UNITED STATES — Social conditions — To 1865 — Addresses, essays, lectures

NASH, Gary B
Race, class, and politics : essays on American colonial and revolutionary society / Gary B. Nash ; with a foreword by Richard S. Dunn. — Urbana : University of Illinois Press, c1986. — p. cm. — Includes index

UNITED STATES — Social conditions — To 1865 — Literary collections

LIPPARD, George
[Selections. 1986]. George Lippard, prophet of protest : writings of an American radical, 1822-1854 / edited with an introduction by David S. Reynolds. — New York : P. Lang, c1986. — xii, 335 p.. — Cover title: George Lippard, an anthology. — Bibliography: p. 333-335

UNITED STATES — Social conditions — 1865-1918 — Addresses, essays, lectures

From Paddy to Studs : Irish-American communities in the turn of the century era, 1880 to 1920 / edited by Timothy J. Meagher. — Westport, Conn. ; London : Greenwood Press, 1986. — xiv, 202 p.. — (Contributions in ethnic studies ; no. 13). — Includes index. — Bibliography: p. [189]-194

UNITED STATES — Social conditions — 1918-1932

Social change and new modes of expression : the United States, 1910-1930 / edited by Rob Kroes [and] Alessandro Portelli. — Amsterdam : Free University Press, 1986. — 222p. — (European contributions to American studies ; 10). — Bibliographies

UNITED STATES — Social conditions — 1933-1945

BROOKEMAN, Christopher
American culture and society since the 1930s / Christopher Brookeman. — 1st American ed. — New York : Schocken Books, 1984. — xv, 241 p., [8] p. of plates. — Includes index. — Bibliography: p. 227-233

UNITED STATES — Social conditions — 1933-1945 — Bibliography

The Great Depression : a historical bibliography. — Santa Barbara, Calif. ; Oxford : ABC-Clio Information Services, c1984. — xii, 260p. — (ABC-Clio research guides ; 4). — Includes index

UNITED STATES — Social conditions — 1945-

BROOKEMAN, Christopher
American culture and society since the 1930s / Christopher Brookeman. — 1st American ed. — New York : Schocken Books, 1984. — xv, 241 p., [8] p. of plates. — Includes index. — Bibliography: p. 227-233

CAMPBELL, Angus
The human meaning of social change / Edited by Angus Campbell and Philip E. Converse. — New York : Russell Sage Foundation, [1972]. — x, 547 p. — (Publications of Russell Sage Foundation). — Includes bibliographical references

Cultural change in the United States since World War II / edited by Maurice Gonnand, Sergio Perosa, Christopher W.E. Bigsby ; with contributions from Zoltan Abadi-Nagy...[et al.]. — Amsterdam : Free University Press, 1986. — 102p. — (European contributions to American studies ; 9). — Includes bibliographies

The Dissenters : voices from contemporary America / [compiled by] John Langston Gwaltney. — 1st ed. — New York : Random House, c1986. — xxviii, 321 p., [8] p. of plates

GILBERT, James Burkhart
A cycle of outrage : juvenile delinquency and mass media in the 1950s / James Gilbert. — New York ; Oxford : Oxford University Press, 1986. — vi, 258p, [6]p of plates. — Includes bibliographical references and index. — Bibliography: p

ISSEL, William
Social change in the United States, 1945-1983 / William Issel. — Basingstoke : Macmillan, 1985. — xi,228p. — (The Contemporary United States). — Bibliography: p218-223. — Includes index

Liberating theory / by Michael Albert ... [et al.]. — 1st ed. — Boston, MA. : South End Press, c1986. — 197 p.. — Bibliography: p. 195-197

UNITED STATES — Social conditions — 1960-1980

The Great society and its legacy : twenty years of U.S. social policy / Marshall Kaplan and Peggy Cuciti, editors. — Durham, N.C. : Duke University Press, 1986. — p. cm. — Includes index

OLDENQUIST, Andrew
The non-suicidal society / Andrew Oldenquist. — Bloomington : Indiana University Press, c1986. — p. cm. — Includes index. — Bibliography: p

UNITED STATES — Social conditions — 1960-1980 — Public opinion

LEVIN, Murray Burton
Talk radio and the American dream / by Murray B. Levin. — Lexington, Mass. : Lexington Books, c1987. — xv, 170 p.. — Includes index

UNITED STATES — Social conditions — 1960-

HAMMERBACK, John C
A war of words : Chicano protest in the 1960s and 1970s / John C. Hammerback, Richard J. Jensen, and Jose Angel Gutierrez. — Westport, Conn. ; London : Greenwood Press, 1985. — x, 187p. — (Contributions in ethnic studies ; no. 12). — Includes index. — Bibliography: p.[173]-178

UNITED STATES — Social conditions — 1980-

LITTWIN, Susan
The postponed generation : why America's kids are growing up later / Susan Littwin. — New York : Morrow, c1986. — p. cm

MAHARIDGE, Dale
Journey to nowhere : the saga of the new underclass / by Dale Maharidge ; photographs by Michael Williamson. — Garden City, N.Y. : Doubleday, 1984. — p. cm. — "Dolphin book."

OLDENQUIST, Andrew
The non-suicidal society / Andrew Oldenquist. — Bloomington : Indiana University Press, c1986. — p. cm. — Includes index. — Bibliography: p

UNITED STATES — Social life and customs — 1783-1865

RORABAUGH, W J
The craft apprentice : from Franklin to the machine age in America / W.J. Rorabaugh. — New York : Oxford University Press, 1986. — p. cm. — Includes index

UNITED STATES — Social life and customs — 1971-

FISHLOCK, Trevor
The state of America / Trevor Fishlock. — London : Faber, 1987, c1986. — 194p. — Originally published: London : Murray, 1986. — Includes index

UNITED STATES — Social policy

BURT, Martha R
Testing the social safety net : the impact of changes in support programs during the Reagan administration / Martha R. Burt, Karen J. Pittman. — Washington, D.C. : Urban Institute Press, c1985. — xix, 183 p.. — (The Changing domestic priorities series). — Includes bibliographical references

GELB, Joyce
Women and public policies / Joyce Gelb and Marian Lief Palley. — rev. ed. — Princeton : Princeton University Press, 1987. — xvi,241p

The Great society and its legacy : twenty years of U.S. social policy / Marshall Kaplan and Peggy Cuciti, editors. — Durham, N.C. : Duke University Press, 1986. — p. cm. — Includes index

GREENBERG, Edward S.
Capitalism and the American political ideal / by Edward S. Greenberg. — Armonk, N.Y. : M.E. Sharpe, 1985. — p. cm

SCHORR, Alvin Louis
Common decency : domestic policies after Reagan / Alvin L. Schorr ; with a contribution by James P. Comer. — New Haven ; London : Yale University Press, c1986. — ix, 246p. — Includes bibliographies and index

Social planning and human service delivery in the voluntary sector / edited by Gary A. Tobin. — Westport, Conn. : Greenwood Press, 1985. — xxx, 290 p.. — (Studies in social welfare policies and programs ; no. 1). — Includes index. — Bibliography: p. [261]-276

UNITED STATES — Social policy — Addresses, essays, lectures

The Media, social science, and social policy for children / Eli A. Rubinstein and Jane D. Brown, editors. — Norwood, N.J. : Ablex Pub. Corp., 1985. — xv, 240 p.. — (Child and family policy ; v. 5). — Includes bibliographies and indexes

Public policy and social institutions / edited by Harrell R. Rodgers, Jr. — Greenwich, Conn. : JAI Press, c1984. — ix, 375 p.. — (Public policy studies ; v. 1). — Includes bibliographies and indexes

UNITED STATES — Social policy — Case studies

BOLT, Christine
American Indian policy and American reform : case studies of the campaign to assimilate the American Indians / Christine Bolt. — London : Allen & Unwin, 1987. — [xii,288]p. — *Includes bibliography and index*

UNITED STATES — Social policy — Congresses

Behavioral and social science : fifty years of discovery : in commemoration of the fiftieth anniversary of the "Ogburn report," Recent social trends in the United States / Neil J. Smelser and Dean R. Gerstein, editors ; Committee on Basic Research in the Behavioral and Social Sciences, Commission on Behavioral and Social Sciences and Education, National Research Council. — Washington, D.C. : National Academy Press, 1986. — x, 298 p.. — *Symposium held Nov. 29-30, 1983.* — *Includes bibliographies*

UNITED STATES — Social policy — 1980-

BENNETT, James T
Destroying democracy : how government funds partisan politics / James T. Bennett, Thomas J. DiLorenzo. — Washington, D.C. : Cato Institute, c1985. — xiii, 561 p.. — *Includes index.* — *Bibliography: p. 505-543*

PETERSON, Paul E
When federalism works / Paul E. Peterson, Barry G. Rabe, Kenneth K. Wong. — Washington, D.C. : Brookings Institution, c1986. — xvi, 245 p.. — *Includes bibliographical references and index*

State politics and the new federalism : readings and commentary / edited by Marilyn Gittell. — New York : Longman, c1986. — xv, 544 p.. — *Includes index.* — *Bibliography: p. 533-535*

UNITED STATES — Statistical services

Statistics sources : a subject guide to data on industrial, business, educational, financial, and other topics for the United States and internationally / Jacqueline Wasserman O'Brien and Steven R. Wasserman, editors; Kenneth Clansky, assistant editor. — 10th ed. — Detroit : Gale Research Company
Vol.1: A-J. — 1986. — xxix,1001p

Statistics sources : a subject guide to data on industrial, business, educational, financial, and other topics for the United States and internationally / Jacqueline Wasserman O'Brien and Steven R. Wasserman, editors; Kenneth Clansky, assistant editor. — 10th ed. — Detroit : Gale Research Company
Vol.2: K-Z. — 1986. — viii,1003-2014p

UNITED STATES — Statistical services — Bibliography

STRATFORD, Juri
Guide to statistical materials produced by governments and associations in the United States / Juri Stratford and Jean Slemmons Stratford. — Alexandria, Va. : Chadwyck-Healey Inc. ; Cambridge : Chadwyck-Healey Ltd. [distributor], 1987. — 279p. — (Government documents bibliographies). — *Includes index*

UNITED STATES — Statistics

Using government publications. — Phoenix : Oryx Press
volume 2: Finding statistics and using special techniques / by Jean L. Sears and Marilyn K. Moody. — 1986. — viii,231p

UNITED STATES — Statistics, Vital

KITAGAWA, Evelyn Mae
Differential mortality in the United States : a study in socioeconomic epidemiology / [by] Evelyn M. Kitagawa and Philip M. Hauser. — Cambridge, Mass. : Harvard University Press, 1973. — xx, 255 p. — (Vital and health statistics monographs). — *Bibliography: p. 248-251*

UNITED STATES — Foreign relations — 1945-1953

HARON, Miriam Joyce
Palestine and the Anglo-American connection, 1945-1950 / Miriam Joyce Haron. — New York : P. Lang, c1986. — 209 p.. — (American university studies. Series IX. History ; vol. 17). — *Includes index.* — *Bibliography: p. [197]-201*

UNITED STATES — Relations — South Africa

SEIDMAN, Ann
The roots of crisis in Southern Africa / Ann Seidman. — Trenton, N.J. : Africa World Press, 1985. — xvii,209p. — (Impact audit ; No.4). — *Bibliography: p175-180*

UNITED STATES. Army — Biography

BAUER, K. Jack
Zachary Taylor : soldier, planter, statesman of the old Southwest / K. Jack Bauer. — Baton Rouge : Louisiana State University Press, c1985. — xxiv, 348 p.. — (Southern biography series). — *Includes index.* — *Bibliography: p. 329-338*

BRENDON, Piers
Ike, his life and times / Piers Brendon. — 1st ed. — New York : Harper & Row, c1986. — xvi, 478 p., [16] p. of plates. — *Includes index.* — *Bibliography: p. [461]-462*

BURK, Robert Fredrick
Dwight D. Eisenhower, hero & politician / Robert F. Burk. — Boston : Twayne Publishers, c1986. — xii, 207 p., [14] p. of plates. — (Twayne's twentieth-century American biography series ; no. 2). — *Includes index.* — *Bibliography: p. 178-199*

HERSHEY, Lewis Blaine
Lewis B. Hershey, Mr. Selective Service / George Q. Flynn. — Chapel Hill : University of North Carolina Press, c1985. — p. cm. — *Includes index.* — *Bibliography: p*

UNITED STATES. Central Intelligence Agency — History

BESCHLOSS, Michael R.
Mayday : Eisenhower, Khrushchev and the U-2 affair / Michael R. Beschloss. — London : Faber, 1986. — xvi,494p,[24]p of plates. — *Bibliography: p416-422.* — *Includes index*

BLUM, William
The CIA : a forgotten history : US global interventions since World War 2 / William Blum. — London : Zed, 1986. — [432]p. — *Includes index*

UNITED STATES. Congress

BOWLES, Nigel
The White House and Capitol Hill : the politics of presidential persuasion / Nigel Bowles. — Oxford : Clarendon, 1987. — [256]p. — *Includes index*

CAIN, Bruce E
The personal vote : constituency service and electoral independence / Bruce Cain, John Ferejohn, Morris Fiorina. — Cambridge, Mass. : Harvard University Press, 1986. — p. cm. — *Includes index.* — *Bibliography: p*

COX, Andrew
Congress, Parliament and defence : the impact of legislative reform on defence accountability in Britain and America / Andrew Cox and Stephen Kirby. — Basingstoke : Macmillan, 1986. — 1v.. — *Includes index*

FITZGERALD, Randall
Porkbarrel : the unexpurgated Grace Commission story of congressional profligacy / Randall Fitzgerald and Gerald Lipson. — Washington, D.C. : Cato Institute, c1984. — xxxv, 114 p.. — *"This report was originally prepared under the title The cost of congressional encroachment"--T.p. verso*

Making government work : from White House to Congress / edited by Robert E. Hunter, Wayne L. Berman, John F. Kennedy ; foreword by Amos A. Jordan. — Boulder : Westview Press, 1986. — xi, 292 p.. — *Rev. ed. of: Making the government work / edited by Robert E. Hunter, Wayne L. Berman. 1985.* — *Published in cooperation with the Center for Strategic and International Studies, Georgetown University.* — *Bibliography: p. 274-279*

UNITED STATES. Congress — Biography

BROWN, Eugene
J. William Fulbright : advice and dissent / Eugene Brown. — Iowa City : University of Iowa Press, c1985. — x, 171p. — *Includes index.* — *Bibliography: p.153-167*

UNITED STATES. Congress — Committees — History — Handbooks, manuals, etc

STUBBS, Walter
Congressional committees, 1789-1982 : a checklist / compiled by Walter Stubbs. — Westport, Conn. : Greenwood Press, c1985. — p. cm. — (Bibliographies and indexes in law and political science ; no. 6). — *Includes index.* — *Bibliography: p*

UNITED STATES. Congress — Committees — Seniority system

TOBIN, Maurice B
Hidden power : the seniority system and other customs of Congress / Maurice B. Tobin ; edited by Joan Shaffer. — New York : Greenwood Press, 1986. — xiii, 134 p.. — (Contributions in political science ; no. 155). — *Includes index.* — *Bibliography: p. [115]-121*

UNITED STATES. Congress — Elections, 1984

ABRAMSON, Paul R
Change and continuity in the 1984 elections / Paul R. Abramson, John H. Aldrich, David W. Rohde. — Rev. ed. — Washington, D.C. : CQ Press, c1987. — xvi, 378 p.. — *Includes index.* — *Bibliography: p. 359-367*

Elections '84. — London : United States Information Service, Embassy of the United States, [1984]. — 8leaflets in folder. — *Contents: Profiles of Reagan, Bush, Mondale and Ferraro with candidate lists for governorships, Senate and House of Representatives*

UNITED STATES. Congress — Elections, 1984 — Addresses, essays, lectures

The Election of 1984 : reports and interpretations / Gerald M. Pomper ... [et al.]. — Chatham, N.J. : Chatham House Publishers, c1985. — p. cm. — *Includes bibliographies and index*

UNITED STATES. Congress — Ethics — Addresses, essays, lectures

Representation and responsibility : exploring legislative ethics / edited by Bruce Jennings and Daniel Callahan. — New York : Plenum Press, 1985. — p. cm. — (Hastings Center series in ethics). — *Includes index.* — *Bibliography: p*

UNITED STATES. Congress — History — 19th century

SHIELDS, Johanna Nicol
The line of duty : maverick congressmen and the development of American political culture, 1836-1860 / Johanna Nicol Shields. — Westport, Conn. : Greenwood Press, c1985. — p. cm. — (Contributions in American studies ; no. 80). — *Includes index.* — *Bibliography: p*

UNITED STATES. Congress — Powers and duties

FISHER, Louis
The politics of shared power : Congress and the executive / Louis Fisher. — 2nd ed. — Washington, D.C. : CQ Press, c1987. — xi, 241 p.. — *Includes indexes.* — *Includes bibliographies*

UNITED STATES. Congress. House — Biography

FERRARO, Geraldine
  Ferraro, my story / Geraldine A. Ferraro, with Linda Bird Francke. — Toronto ; New York : Bantam Books, 1985. — 340 p., [24] p. of plates. — *Includes index*

MAY, Robert E
  John A. Quitman : Old South crusader / Robert E. May. — Baton Rouge : Louisiana State University Press, c1985. — p. cm. — (Southern biography series). — *Includes index. — Bibliography: p*

UNITED STATES. Congress. House — Committees

PARKER, Glenn R
  Factions in House committees / Glenn R. Parker and Suzanne L. Parker. — Knoxville : University of Tennessee Press, c1985. — xx, 312 p.. — *Includes index. — Bibliography: p. 299-308*

UNITED STATES. Congress. House — Election districts

Congressional districts in the 1980s. — Washington, D.C. : Congressional Quarterly, c1983. — p. cm

UNITED STATES. Congress. House — Election districts — History

PARSONS, Stanley B
  United States congressional districts and data, 1843-1883 / Stanley B. Parsons, William W. Beach, Michael J. Dubin. — Scale not given. — New York : Greenwood Press, 1986. — 1 atlas (xxviii, 225 p.)

UNITED STATES. Congress. House — Election districts — Maps

PARSONS, Stanley B
  United States congressional districts and data, 1843-1883 / Stanley B. Parsons, William W. Beach, Michael J. Dubin. — Scale not given. — New York : Greenwood Press, 1986. — 1 atlas (xxviii, 225 p.)

UNITED STATES. Congress. House — Election districts — Statistics

PARSONS, Stanley B
  United States congressional districts and data, 1843-1883 / Stanley B. Parsons, William W. Beach, Michael J. Dubin. — Scale not given. — New York : Greenwood Press, 1986. — 1 atlas (xxviii, 225 p.)

UNITED STATES. Congress. House — Voting

PARKER, Glenn R
  Factions in House committees / Glenn R. Parker and Suzanne L. Parker. — Knoxville : University of Tennessee Press, c1985. — xx, 312 p.. — *Includes index. — Bibliography: p. 299-308*

UNITED STATES. Congress. Senate — Biography

FURGURSON, Ernest B.
  Hard right : the rise of Jesse Helms / by Ernest B. Furgurson. — 1st ed. — New York : Norton, c1986. — p. cm

MORGAN, Chester M
  Redneck liberal : Theodore G. Bilbo and the New Deal / Chester M. Morgan. — Baton Rouge : Louisiana State University Press, c1985. — p. cm. — *Includes index. — Bibliography: p*

UNITED STATES. Congress. Senate — Elections, 1984

SNIDER, William D
  Hunt and Helms : North Carolina chooses a Senator / by William D. Snider. — Chapel Hill : University of North Carolina Press, c1985. — p. cm. — *Includes index*

UNITED STATES. Constitutional Convention (1787)

MCDONALD, Forrest
  Novus ordo seclorum : the intellectual origins of the Constitution / Forrest McDonald. — Lawrence, Kan. : University Press of Kansas, c1985. — xiii, 359 p.. — *"The Constitution of the United States": p. [299]-311. — Includes index. — Bibliography: p. [313]-341*

UNITED STATES. Department of Defense

UNITED STATES. Department of Defense
  Report to the Congress of the strategic defense initiative. — Washington D.C. : [the Department], 1985-. — *Annual*

UNITED STATES. Department of Defense — Appropriations and expenditures

EPSTEIN, Joshua M.
  The 1988 defense budget / Joshua M. Epstein. — Washington, D.C. : Brookings Institution, 1987. — viii,57p. — (Studies in defense policy)

UNITED STATES. Department of State — Bibliography

GOEHLERT, Robert
  The Department of State and American diplomacy : a bibliography / Robert U. Goehlert, Elizabeth R. Hoffmeister. — New York : Garland Pub., 1986. — xxviii, 349 p.. — (Garland reference library of social science ; vol. 333). — *Includes indexes*

UNITED STATES. Environmental Protection Agency

DURANT, Robert F.
  When government regulates itself : EPA, TVA, and pollution control in the 1970s / Robert F. Durant. — Knoxville : University of Tennessee Press, c1985. — p. cm. — *Bibliography: p [169]-187. — Bibliography: p*

UNITED STATES. Environmental Protection Agency — Management — Decision making

MAGAT, Wesley A
  Rules in the making : a statistical analysis of regulatory agency behavior / Wesley A. Magat, Alan J. Krupnick, Winston Harrington. — Washington, D.C. : Resources for the Future, c1986. — xiii, 182 p.. — *Includes bibliographies and index*

UNITED STATES. Federal Trade Commission

HASIN, Bernice Rothman
  Consumers, commissions, and Congress : law, theory, and the Federal Trade Commission, 1968-1985 / Bernice Rothman Hasin. — New Brunswick (U.S.A.) : Transaction Books, c1987. — ix, 236 p.. — *Based on the author's doctoral dissertation, University of California. — Includes bibliographies and index*

UNITED STATES. Forest Service — History

ROBBINS, William G.
  American forestry : a history of national, state, and private cooperation / by William G. Robbins. — Lincoln : University of Nebraska Press, c1985. — xv, 344 p. — *Includes index. — Bibliography: p. 271-326*

UNITED STATES. Government Printing Office

HERNON, Peter
  GPO's depository library program : a descriptive analysis / by Peter Hernon, Charles R. McClure, Gary R. Purcell. — Norwood, N.J. : Ablex Pub. Corp., 1985. — p. cm. — *Includes index. — Bibliography: p*

UNITED STATES. Immigration and Naturalization Service

HARWOOD, Edwin
  In liberty's shadow : illegal aliens and immigration law enforcement / Edwin Harwood. — Stanford, Calif. : Hoover Institution Press, Stanford University, c1986. — xvi, 224 p.. — (Hoover Press publication ; 331). — *Includes index. — Bibliography: p. [193]-220*

UNITED STATES. Joint Chiefs of Staff — Reorganization

The Reorganization of the Joint Chiefs of Staff : a critical analysis / Allan R. Millett ... [et al.]. — Washington : Pergamon-Brassey's International Defense Publishers, 1986. — xi, 80 p. — (Foreign policy report). — *"A publication of the Institute for Foreign Policy Analysis, Inc.". — Includes bibliographical references*

UNITED STATES. National Labor Relations Board

WILLIAMS, Robert E.
  NLRB regulation of election conduct / by Robert E. Williams ; with acknowledgement to Peter A. Janus and Kenneth C. Huhn. — Rev ed. — Philadelphia, Pa. : Industrial Research Unit, Wharton School, University of Pennsylvania, c1985. — xv, 539 p.. — (Labor relations and public policy series ; no. 8). — *Includes bibliographical references and index*

UNITED STATES. National Recovery Administration — Officials and employees — Biography

OHL, John Kennedy
  Hugh S. Johnson and the New Deal / John Kennedy Ohl. — Dekalb, Ill. : Northern Illinois University Press, 1985. — xi, 374p. *Includes index. — Bibliography: p.[345]-359*

UNITED STATES. National Technical Information Service — Catalogs

THOMAS SLATNER AND CO.
  Citations from the NTIS database : computer network protocols (1973-1984). — Springfield, VA : National Technical Information Service, [1984]. — v,16,166,39p. — *A bibliography containing "citations concerning the design, network analysis, and formulation of computer network protocols"*

UNITED STATES. Navy

KAUFMANN, William W
  A thoroughly efficient Navy / William W. Kaufmann. — Washington, D.C. : Brookings Institution, c1987. — p. cm. — (Studies in defense policy). — *Includes index*

UNITED STATES. Navy — History

DINGMAN, Roger
  Power in the Pacific : the origins of naval arms limitation, 1914-1922 / Roger Dingman. — Chicago : University of Chicago Press, 1976. — xiii, 318 p.. — *Includes index. — Bibliography: p. 287-310*

UNITED STATES. Navy — History — 19th century

SCHROEDER, John H.
  Shaping a maritime empire : the commercial and diplomatic role of the American Navy, 1829-1861 / John H. Schroeder. — Westport, Conn. ; London : Greenwood Press, 1985. — 229p. — (Contributions in military studies ; no. 48). — *"Notes on sources": p. [215]-219. — Includes bibliographical references and index*

UNITED STATES. Office of Surface Mining Reclamation and Enforcement

SHOVER, Neal
  Enforcement or negotiation : constructing a regulatory bureaucracy / Neal Shover, Donald Clelland, John Lynxwiler. — Albany, NY : State University of New York Press, c1986. — p. cm. — (SUNY series in critical issues in criminal justice). — *Includes index. — Bibliography: p*

UNITED STATES. Office of the Comptroller of the Currency

ROBERTSON, Ross M
  The Comptroller and bank supervision: a historical appraisal / [by] Ross M. Robertson. — Washington : Office of the Comptroller of the Currency, [1968]. — x,262p. *Bibliography: p247-253*

UNITED STATES. Social Security Administration
COFER, M. Donna Price
Judges, bureaucrats, and the question of independence : a study of the Social Security Administration hearing process / Donna Price Cofer. — Westport, Conn. : Greenwood Press, 1985. — xvii, 245 p.. — (Contributions in political science ; no. 130). — Includes index. — Bibliography: p. [231]-235

UNITED STATES. Supreme Court
BICKEL, Alexander M.
The least dangerous branch : the Supreme Court at the bar of politics / Alexander M. Bickel. — 2nd ed. / with a new foreword by Harry H. Wellington. — New Haven ; London : Yale University Press, c1986. — xii,303p. — Previous ed.: Indianapolis : Bobbs-Merrill, 1962. — Includes index

CURRIE, David P
The constitution in the Supreme Court : the first hundred years, 1789-1888 / David P. Currie. — Chicago ; London : University of Chicago Press, c1985. — xiii, 504 p.. — "Tables of cases": p. 477-486. — Includes bibliographical references and indexes

ESTREICHER, Samuel
Redefining the Supreme Court's role : a theory of managing the federal judicial process / Samuel Estreicher and John Sexton. — New Haven : Yale University Press, c1986. — p. cm . — Includes index. — Bibliography: p

MENDELSON, Wallace
Supreme Court statecraft : the rule of law and men / by Wallace Mendelson. — 1st ed. — Ames : Iowa State University Press, 1985. — p. cm. — Includes index

RUBIN, Eva R
The Supreme Court and the American Family : ideology and issues / Eva R. Rubin. — New York : Greenwood Press, 1986. — 251 p.. — (Contributions in American studies ; [no. 85]). — Series no. from jacket. — Includes indexes. — Bibliography: p. [225]-236

SCHWARTZ, Bernard
The unpublished opinions of the Warren court / Bernard Schwartz. — New York : Oxford University Press, 1985. — p. cm

TRIBE, Laurence H
God save this honorable court : how the choice of justices can change our lives / Laurence H. Tribe. — 1st ed. — New York : Random House, c1985. — p. cm. — Includes index

VINING, Joseph
The authoritative and the authoritarian / Joseph Vining. — Chicago : University of Chicago Press, 1986. — xiii, 261 p.. — Includes indexes. — Bibliography: p. 239-242

UNITED STATES. Supreme Court — History
BIGEL, Alan I.
The Supreme Court on emergency powers, foreign affairs, and protection of civil liberties, 1935-1975 / Alan I. Bigel. — Lanham, MD : University Press of America, c1986. — xv, 211 p.. — ; Originally presented as the author's thesis (doctoral--New School for Social Research). — Includes indexes. — Bibliography: p. 194-203

BINDLER, Norman
The conservative court, 1910-1930 / by Norman Bindler. — Port Washington, N.Y. : Associated Faculty Press, 1986. — p. cm. — (The Supreme Court in American life series). — Includes index. — Bibliography: p

WILKINSON, Charles F.
American Indians, time, and the law : native societies in a modern constitutional democracy / Charles F. Wilkinson. — New Haven ; London : Yale University Press, c1987. — xi, 225 p.. — "Supreme Court cases in Indian law during the modern era": p. 123-132. — Includes index. — Bibliography: p. 133-219

UNITED STATES PENITENTIARY, ALCATRAZ, CALIFORNIA — Rules and practice
UNITED STATES PENITENTIARY, ALCATRAZ, CALIFORNIA
Regulations for inmates : U.S.P., Alcatraz : revised 1956. — [San Francisco?] : Golden Gate National Parks Association, 1983. — 19 leaves. — Cover title: Institution rules and regulations. — Reproduction of 1956 original

UNITES STATES — Armed forces — Germany
SEILER, Signe
Die GIs : amerikanische Soldaten in Deutschland / Signe Seiler. — Hamburg : Rowohlt, 1985. — 281p. — Bibliography: p278-281

UNIVERSAL NEGRO IMPROVEMENT ASSOCIATION — History
STEIN, Judith
The world of Marcus Garvey : race and class in modern society / Judith Stein. — Baton Rouge ; London : Louisiana State University Press, c1986. — xii, 294p. — Includes index. — Bibliography: p.281-284

UNIVERSITÄT MÜNCHEN — Riot, 1943
DUMBACH, Annette E
Shattering the German night : the story of the White Rose / by Annette E. Dumbach and Jud Newborn. — 1st ed. — Boston : Little, Brown, c1986. — xi, 259 p.. — Includes index. — Bibliography: p. 243-247

UNIVERSITIES AND COLLEGES
ANDERSEN, Alfred F.
Liberating the early American dream : a way to transcend the capitalist/communist dilemma nonviolently / by Alfred F. Andersen. — Ukiah, Calif. : Tom Paine Institute, c1985. — p. cm. — Rev. ed. of: Updating the early American dream. c1984. — Includes index. — Bibliography: p

The university research system : the public policies of the home of scientists / edited by Bjorn Wittrock, Aant Elzinga. — Stockholm : Almqvist and Wiksell, 1985. — v,220p. — Bibliographies

UNIVERSITIES AND COLLEGES — Directories
International handbook of universities : and other institutions of higher education. — 10th ed. — London : Macmillan for the International Association of Universities, 1986. — [630]p. — Previous ed.: 1983. — Includes index

UNIVERSITIES AND COLLEGES — Government policy — Great Britain
GREAT BRITAIN. Parliament. House of Commons. Library. Research Division
The future of higher education / Kay Andrews. — [London] : the Division, 1984. — 25p. — (Reference sheet ; no.84/9). — Bibliography: p21-24

UNIVERSITIES AND COLLEGES — Graduate work
STOCK, Molly
A practical guide to graduate research / Molly Stock. — New York : McGraw-Hill, c1985. — viii, 168 p.. — Includes index. — Bibliography: p. 162-164

UNIVERSITIES AND COLLEGES — Political aspects — Argentina — History
MANGONE, Carlos
Universidad y peronismo (1946-1955) / Carlos Mongone y Jorge A. Warley. — Buenos Aires : Centro Editor de América Latina, 1986. — 161p. — (Biblioteca Política Argentina ; 83)

UNIVERSITIES AND COLLEGES — Africa — Directories
Higher education in Africa : manual for refugees = Enseignement supérieur en Afrique : Manuel pour les réfugiés. — [Geneva?] : World University Service International, 1986. — xiii,784p

UNIVERSITIES AND COLLEGES — Australia — Finance — History
GALLAGHER, A. P.
Coordinating Australian university development : a study of the Australian Universities Commission, 1959-1970 / A.P. Gallagher. — St. Lucia ; New York : University of Queensland Press, c1982. — xii, 244 p.. — (The University of Queensland Press scholars' library). — Includes index. — Bibliography: p. [230]-238

UNIVERSITIES AND COLLEGES — Australia — Statistics
AUSTRALIA. Commonwealth Bureau of Census and Statistics
University statistics. — Canberra : [the Bureau], 1978-1980. — Annual

UNIVERSITIES AND COLLEGES — Canada — Finance
BIRD, Richard M.
Private support for universities / Richard M. Bird and Meyer W. Bucovetsky. — Ontario : Commission on the Future Development of the Universities of Ontario, 1984. — 88p

UNIVERSITIES AND COLLEGES — Canada — Finance — Statistics
Canadian universities, income and expenditure = Universités canadiennes, recettes et dépenses / Dominion Bureau of Statistics, Canada. — Ottawa : Dominion Bureau of Statistics, 1961/62-1968/69. — Annual. — Text in English and French. — Continued by : University financial statistics

University financial statistics = Universités statistiques financières / Statistics Canada. — Ottawa : Statistics Canada, 1971/72-1976/77. — Irregular. — Text in English and French. — Continues: Canadian universities, income and expenditure. Continued by: University finance: trend analysis

UNIVERSITIES AND COLLEGES — China — Administration
China : management and finance of higher education. — Washington, D.C. : The World Bank, 1986. — [xxiii],126p. — (A World Bank country study). — Bibliographical references: p124-126

UNIVERSITIES AND COLLEGES — China — Finance
China : management and finance of higher education. — Washington, D.C. : The World Bank, 1986. — [xxiii],126p. — (A World Bank country study). — Bibliographical references: p124-126

UNIVERSITIES AND COLLEGES — Denmark
Higher education in Denmark : a short survey of the organization and activities of the universities and other institutions of higher education in Denmark. — Copenhagen : Danish Ministry of Education, 1954. — 55p

UNIVERSITIES AND COLLEGES — Developing countries — Admission
KLITGAARD, Robert E
Elitism and meritocracy in developing countries : selection policies for higher education / Robert Klitgaard. — Baltimore : Johns Hopkins University Press, c1986. — xi, 191 p.. — (The Johns Hopkins studies in development) . — Includes index. — Bibliography: p. 161-183

UNIVERSITIES AND COLLEGES — Europe — Entrance requirements
COX, Edwin H.
Academic recognition of diplomas in the European Community : present state and prospects / by Edwin Cox. — Brussels : Commission of the European Communities, 1977c1979. — 75p. — (Education series / Commission of the European Communities ; no. 10)

UNIVERSITIES AND COLLEGES — Germany — Faculty — Attitudes — History — 20th century

GALLIN, Alice
Midwives to Nazism : university professors in Weimar Germany, 1925-1933 / Alice Gallin. — Macon, Ga. : Mercer, c1986. — viii, 134 p.. — Includes index. — Bibliography: p. [115]-128

UNIVERSITIES AND COLLEGES — Great Britain — Administration

GREAT BRITAIN. Department of Education and Science
Changes in structure and national planning for higher education. — [London] : the Department
Polytechnics and colleges sector : note. — 1987. — 49p

GREAT BRITAIN. Department of Education and Science
Changes in structure and national planning for higher education. — [London] : the Department
Universities Funding Council : note. — 1987. — 18p

UNIVERSITIES AND COLLEGES — Great Britain — Data processing

HOLLIGAN, Patrick J.
Access to academic networks / Patrick J. Holligan. — London : Taylor Graham on behalf of the Primary Communications Research Centre, c1986. — 91p. — Bibliography: p87-91

UNIVERSITIES AND COLLEGES — Great Britain — Directories

A Dictionary of British qualifications : abbreviations and qualifying bodies. — London : Kogan Page, 1985. — [120]p

UNIVERSITIES AND COLLEGES — Great Britain — Finance

GREAT BRITAIN. Department of Education and Science
Changes in structure and national planning for higher education. — [London] : the Department
Contracts between the funding bodies and higher education institutions : note. — 1987. — 16p

UNIVERSITIES AND COLLEGES — Great Britain — Graduate work

Academic research in the United Kingdom : its organisation and effectiveness : proceedings of a symposium of the Association of Researchers in Medicine and Science / edited by Stephen A. Roberts. — London : Taylor Graham, c1984. — 112p

Current research in Britain: social sciences / British Library. — Boston Spa : British Library Lending Division, 1985-. — Annual. — Continues Research in British universities, polytechnics and colleges

UNIVERSITIES AND COLLEGES — Nigeria

OJO, Folayan
Nigerian universities and high level manpower development / by Folayan Ojo. — Lagos : Lagos University Press, 1985. — 135p. — Bibliography: p126-135

UNIVERSITIES AND COLLEGES — Organisation for Economic Co-operation and Development countries

TAYLOR, William
Universities under scrutiny / [Professor William Taylor]. — Paris : Organisation for Economic Co-operation and Development, 1987. — 113p. — Bibliography: p107-113

UNIVERSITIES AND COLLEGES — Organisation for Economic Co-operation and Development countries — Graduate work

BLUME, S.
Post-graduate education in the 1980's / [Prof. S. Blume and Mrs. O. Amsterdamska]. — Paris : Organisation for Economic Co-operation and Development, 1987. — 81p. — Bibliographical references: p81

UNIVERSITIES AND COLLEGES — South Africa

COOVADIA, H. M.
From ivory tower to a people's university / H. M. Coovadia. — [Cape Town] : University of Cape Town, 1986. — 25 p. — "The twenty-seventh T. B. Davie Memorial Lecture delivered in the Jameson Hall, University of Cape Town on 25 September 1986"

NOLAN, Albert
Academic freedom : a service to the people / Albert Nolan. — Cape Town : University of Cape Town, 1986. — 12p. — 28th T. B. Davie Memorial lecture

UNIVERSITIES AND COLLEGES — United States

GEIGER, Roger L.
To advance knowledge : the growth of American research universities, 1900-1940 / Roger L. Geiger. — New York : Oxford University Press, 1986. — x, 325 p.. — Includes index. — Bibliography: p. 279-320

LEVINE, David O.
The American college and the culture of aspiration, 1915-1940 / David O. Levine. — Ithaca : Cornell University Press, 1986. — 281 p.. — Includes index. — Bibliography: p. 255-275

UNIVERSITIES AND COLLEGES — Finance — Statistics

University finance: trend analysis = Finance des universités: analysis des tendances / Statistics Canada. — Ottawa : Statistics Canada, 1974/75-. — Irregular. — Text in English and French. — Continues: University financial statistics

UNIVERSITIES AND COLLEGES, BLACK — South Africa — History

NKOMO, Mokubung O
Student culture and activism in black South African universities : the roots of resistance / Mokubung O. Nkomo ; foreword by Johnnetta B. Cole. — Westport, Conn. : Greenwood Press, 1984. — xxiii, 209 p.. — (Contributions in Afro-American and African studies ; no. 78) . — Includes index. — Bibliography: p. [179]-200

UNIVERSITIES FUNDING COUNCIL

GREAT BRITAIN. Department of Education and Science
Changes in structure and national planning for higher education. — [London] : the Department
Universities Funding Council : note. — 1987. — 18p

UNIVERSITY COLLEGE OF NORTH WALES

WILLIAMS, J. Gwynn
The founding of the University College of North Wales, Bangor / J. Gwynn Williams. — [Bangor] : University College of North Wales, 1985. — 31p

UNIVERSITY COLLEGE OF NORTH WALES — History

WILLIAM, J. Gwynn
The University College of North Wales : foundations 1884-1927 / J. Gwynn Williams. — Cardiff : University of Wales Press, 1985. — xvii,499p,[73]p of plates. — Bibliography: p472-481. — Includes index

UNIVERSITY COOPERATION — Commonwealth of Nations

COMMONWEALTH INFORMATION PROGRAMME
Cooperation in education. — London : Commonwealth Secretariat, 1974. — 13p. — (Notes on the Commonwealth)

UNIVERSITY COOPERATION — European Economic Community countries

SMITH, Alan
Joint programmes of study : an instrument of European Co—operation in higher education / by Alan Smith. — Luxembourg : Office for Official Publications of the European Communities, 1979. — vii, 188p. — (Education series / Commission of the European Communities ; no.7)

UNIVERSITY OF ASTON IN BIRMINGHAM

WALFORD, Geoffrey
Restructuring universities : politics and power in the management of change / Geoffrey Walford. — London : Croom Helm, c1987. — 197p. — Bibliography: p183-192p. — Includes index

UNIVERSITY OF ESSEX — Students

YETTRAM, Pamela June
Contrary imaginations : causes and consequences of left wing ideology among student activists in the mid-seventies / by Pamela J. Yettram. — 511 leaves. — PhD (Econ) 1986 LSE. — Leaves 457-486 are appendices

UNIVERSITY OF KANSAS. School of Medicine

BECKER, Howard Saul
Boys in white : student culture in medical school / Howard S. Becker ... [et al.]. — New Brunswick, N.J. : Transaction Books, 1977, c1961. — xiv, 456 p.. — Reprint of the ed. published by University of Chicago Press, Chicago

UNIVERSITY OF KUWAIT

International documents on Palestine / Institute for Palestine Studies and the University of Kuwait. — Beirut : Institute for Palestine Studies, 1968-1981. — Annual

UNIVERSITY OF LONDON — Dissertations — Bibliography

Theses and dissertations accepted for higher degrees / University of London. — London : University of London, 1959-1977. — Continues: Theses and dissertations and published work accepted for higher degrees/University of London.- Continued by: Theses and dissertations accepted for the degrees of M. Phil. and Ph. D in the University of London/University of London

Theses and dissertations accepted for the degrees of M.Phil and Ph.D in the University of London / University of London. — London : University of London Library, 1977-. — Continues: Theses and dissertations accepted for higher degrees/University of London

UNIVERSITY OF LONDON — History

HARTE, Negley
The University of London 1836-1986 : an illustrated history / Negley Harte ; with a foreword by HRH Princess Anne. — London : Athlone, 1986. — 303p. — Ill on lining papers. — Bibliography: p292-295. — Includes index

UNIVERSITY OF LONDON — Libraries — Directories

UNIVERSITY OF LONDON
Guide to the library resources of the University of London / compiled by Kenneth Garside. — [London] : University of London, Library Resources Co-ordinating Committee, 1983. — vii,179p. — Includes index

UNIVERSITY OF LONDON. Institute of Education — History
UNIVERSITY OF LONDON. Institute of Education
The Institute : a personal account of the history of the University of London Institute of Education, 1932-1972 / C. Willis Dixon. — London : The Institute, 1986. — x,286p

UNIVERSITY OF WARWICK. Library. Modern Records Centre
STOREY, Richard
Consolidated guide to the modern records centre / compiled by Richard Storey and Alistair Tough. — Coventry : University of Warwick Library, 1986. — 86p. — (Occasional publications / University of Warwick Library ; no.14)

UNIVERSITY PRESSES — Asia, Southeastern — Congresses
SEMINAR ON ACADEMIC PUBLISHING IN THE ASEAN REGION (1985 : Singapore)
Academic publishing in ASEAN : problems and prospects : proceedings of the Seminar on Academic Publishing in the ASEAN Region held in Singapore from 9-11 September 1985 / edited by S. Gopinathan. — Singapore : Festival of Books Singapore, 1986. — 213 p.. — *Includes bibliographies*

UNMARRIED COUPLES — Legal status, laws, etc — United States
WEITZMAN, Lenore J
The marriage contract : spouses, lovers and the law / Lenore J. Weitzman. — New York : Free Press, c1981. — p. cm. — *Includes index*

UNMARRIED MOTHERS — Legal status, laws, etc. — England
Legal rights of single mothers / One Parent Families. — [London] : National Council for One Parent Families, 1986, c1984. — 41p. — *Cover title*

UNTOUCHABLES
Census of India 1981. — [Delhi : Controller of Publications]
Series 23: West Bengal / S. N. Ghosh, Director of Census Operations, West Bengal. — [1984]

SHAMKUNWAR, M. R.
Scheduled castes : socio-economic survey / by M. R. Shamkunwar. — Allahabad [India] : Kitab Mahal, 1985. — vii,151p. — *Bibliography: p[141]-143*

Struggle for status / edited by Prakash N. Pimpley, Satish K. Sharma. — Delhi : B.R. Pub. Corp. ; New Delhi : D.K. Publishers' Distributors, 1985. — xii, 232 p.. — *Includes bibliographies and index*

UNTOUCHABLES — Case studies
SHARMA, Neena
Political socialization and its impact on attitudinal change towards social and political system : a case study of Harijan women of Delhi / Neena Sharma. — New Delhi : Inter-India Publications, 1985. — x, 157 p.. — *Cover title: Political socialization & its impact on attitudinal change towards social & political system. — Includes index. — Bibliography: p. [146]-153*

UNTOUCHABLES — Politics and suffrage — History
GUPTA, S. K.
The scheduled castes in modern Indian politics : their emergence as a political power / S. K. Gupta. — New Delhi : Munshiram Manoharlal, 1985. — xi,355p. — *Bibliography: p[333]-342*

UPPER CLASSES — Great Britain — Attitudes
PARKER, Peter, 1954-
The old lie : the Great War and the public school ethos / Peter Parker. — London : Constable, 1987. — 319p,[16]p of plates. — *Bibliography: p297-306. — Includes index*

UPPER CLASSES — Great Britain — History
DAVIDOFF, Leonore
The best circles : society, etiquette and the Season / Leonore Davidoff ; new introduction by Victoria Glendinning. — London : Cresset Library, 1986, c1973. — xii,127p. — *Originally published: London : Croom Helm, 1974. — Bibliography: p118-120. — Includes index*

UPPER CLASSES — United States — Case studies
OSTRANDER, Susan A
Women of the upper class / Susan A. Ostrander. — Philadelphia : Temple University Press, 1984. — x, 183 p.. — (Women in the political economy). — *Bibliography: p. 175-183*

UPPER VOLTA — Bibliography
MCFARLAND, Daniel Miles
Historical dictionary of Upper Volta (Haute Volta) / by Daniel Miles McFarland. — Metuchen, N.J. : Scarecrow Press, 1978. — xxi, 217 p.. — (African historical dictionaries ; no. 14). — *Bibliography: p. 163-217*

UPPER VOLTA — History — Chronology
MCFARLAND, Daniel Miles
Historical dictionary of Upper Volta (Haute Volta) / by Daniel Miles McFarland. — Metuchen, N.J. : Scarecrow Press, 1978. — xxi, 217 p.. — (African historical dictionaries ; no. 14). — *Bibliography: p. 163-217*

UPPER VOLTA — History — Dictionaries
MCFARLAND, Daniel Miles
Historical dictionary of Upper Volta (Haute Volta) / by Daniel Miles McFarland. — Metuchen, N.J. : Scarecrow Press, 1978. — xxi, 217 p.. — (African historical dictionaries ; no. 14). — *Bibliography: p. 163-217*

URAL MOUNTAINS REGION (R.S.F.S.R.) — Population
Osobennosti vosproizvodstva i migratsii naseleniia na Urale : sbornik nauchnykh trudov / [otv. redaktor I. P. Mokerov]. — Sverdlovsk : AN SSSR, Ural'skii nauchnyi tsentr, 1986. — 101p

URANIUM INDUSTRY
OWEN, Anthony David
The economics of uranium / Anthony David Owen. — New York : Praeger, 1985. — p. cm. — *Includes index. — Bibliography: p*

Uranium : resources, production and demand : a joint report / by the OECD Nuclear Energy Agency and the International Atomic Energy Agency. — Paris : Organisation for Economic Co-operation and Development, 1983. — 348p. — *On front cover: "December 1983"*

Uranium : resources, production and demand : a joint report / by the OECD Nuclear Energy Agency and the International Atomic Energy Agency. — Paris : Organisation for Economic Co-operation and Development, 1986. — 413p. — *Includes supplement: Overview*

URANIUM INDUSTRY — Political aspects — History
HELMREICH, Jonathan E
Gathering rare ores : the diplomacy of uranium acquisition, 1943-1954 / Jonathan E. Helmreich. — Princeton, N.J. : Princeton University Press, c1986. — xiv, 303 p.. — *Includes index. — Bibliography: p. 287-291*

URANIUM INDUSTRY — United States
OWEN, Anthony David
The economics of uranium / Anthony David Owen. — New York : Praeger, 1985. — p. cm. — *Includes index. — Bibliography: p*

URANIUM MINES AND MINING — Social aspects — Australia — Jabiru (Northern Territory)
LEA, John P.
Yellowcake and crocodiles : town planning, government and society in Northern Australia / John P. Lea, Robert B. Zehner. — London : Allen & Unwin, 1986. — xxiv,200p. — (Studies in society ; 34). — *Bibliography: p179-192. — Includes index*

URANIUM MINES AND MINING — Mexico — Hygienic aspects
HALVAS, J.
Condiciones de trabajo y niveles de radiación existentes en las minas que actualmente explota la Comisión Nacional de Energía Nuclear y la planta pilota de la misma / J. Halvas, J. Télich, R. González C.. — México : Comisión Nacional de Energía Nuclear, 1964. — 117-136p. — ([Publicación] / Comisión Nacional de Energía Nuclear ; num.157). — *Text in Spanish and English. — Esto artículo forma parte del Simposio sobre Higiene y Seguridad Radiológicas en la Extracción y Elaboración de los Materiales Nucleares, en Viena, el 26-31 de agosto de 1963*

URBAN ANTHROPOLOGY — Case studies
MERRY, Sally Engle
Urban danger : life in a neighborhood of strangers / Sally Engle Merry. — Philadelphia : Temple University Press, 1981. — x, 278 p.. — *Includes index. — Bibliography: p. [259]-272*

URBAN BEAUTIFICATION — England
JURUE
Greening city sites : prepared for the Department of the Environment / by JURUE. — London : H.M.S.O., 1987. — 127p. — (Case studies of good practice in urban regeneration). — *Commissioned by the Inner Cities Directorate of the Department of the Environment*

URBAN ECONOMICS
The Capitalist city : global restructuring and community politics / edited by Michael Peter Smith & Joe R. Feagin. — Oxford : Basil Blackwell, 1987. — vi,393p. — *Includes bibliographies and index*

Critical issues in urban economic development / edited by Victor A. Hausner. — Oxford : Clarendon. — (Publications in the inner cities research programme series ; 8)
Vol.1. — 1986. — [240]p. — *Includes index*

DRENNAN, Matthew P.
Modeling metropolitan economies for forecasting and policy analysis / Matthew P. Drennan. — New York : New York University Press, 1985. — p. cm. — *Includes index. — Bibliography: p*

Handbook of regional and urban economics / edited by Peter Nijkamp. — Amsterdam : North-Holland. — (Handbooks in economics ; 7)
Vol.1: Regional economics. — 1986. — xxii,702p. — *Bibliographies*

HARVEY, J.
Urban land economics : the economics of real property / Jack Harvey. — Fully rev. 2nd ed. — Basingstoke : Macmillan Education, 1987. — xiv,408p. — *Previous ed: published as Economics of real property. 1981. — Bibliography: p387-391. — Includes index*

HASLUCK, Chris
Urban unemployment : local labour markets and employment initiatives / Chris Hasluck. — London : Longman, 1987. — 248p. — *Bibliography : p228-243. — Includes index*

LOGAN, John R.
Urban fortunes : the political economy of place / John R. Logan, Harvey L. Molotch. — Berkeley, CA : University of California Press, 1987. — p. cm. — *Includes index. — Bibliography: p*

SANDERCOCK, Leonie
Urban political economy : the Australian case / Leonie Sandercock, Michael Berry. — Sydney ; Boston : G. Allen & Unwin, 1983. — xi, 193 p.. — *Includes index. — Bibliography: p. 179-187*

Spatial cycles / edited by Leo van den Berg, Leland S. Burns and Leo H. Klaassen. — Aldershot : Gower, c1987. — xvii,277p. — *Includes bibliographies and index*

URBAN ECONOMICS
continuation

Urban systems : contemporary approaches to modelling / edited by C.S. Bertuglia ... [et al.]. — London : Croom Helm, c1987. — 677p. — *Bibliography: p597-650. — Includes index*

URBAN ECONOMICS — Congresses

Advances in urban systems modelling / editors, Bruce Hutchinson and Michael Batty. — Amsterdam ; New York : North-Holland ; New York, N.Y., U.S.A. : Sole distributors for the U.S.A. and Canada, Elsevier Science Pub. Co., 1986. — xi, 432 p.. — (Studies in regional science and urban economics ; v. 15). — *Based on the papers originally presented at the International Symposium on New Directions in Urban Systems Modelling held at the University of Waterloo in July, 1983. — Includes bibliographies*

The economics of urbanization and urban policies in developing countries / edited by George S. Tolley, Vinod Thomas. — Washington, D.C. : The World Bank, 1987. — xii,184p. — (A World Bank symposium). — *Includes bibliographies*

The Future of the metropolis : Berlin, London, Paris, New York : economic aspects / editors, Hans-Jürgen Ewers, John B. Goddard, and Horst Matzerath. — Berlin ; New York : W. de Gruyter, 1986. — xi, 484 p.. — *"Presents the papers of an international conference ... held at the Technical University Berlin in October 1984"--Pref. — Includes bibliographies*

URBAN ECONOMICS — History

WRIGLEY, E. A.
People, cities and wealth : the transformation of traditional society / E.A. Wrigley. — Oxford : Basil Blackwell, 1987. — [400]p. — *Includes bibliography and index*

URBAN HEALTH — United States

GINZBERG, Eli
Local health policy in action : the Municipal Health Services Program / Eli Ginzberg, Edith Davis, Miriam Ostow. — Totowa, N.J. : Rowman & Allanheld, c1985. — xiv, 136 p.. — (LandMark studies). — *Includes bibliographies and index*

URBAN HOMESTEADING — United States

VARADY, David P
Neighborhood upgrading : a realistic assessment / David P. Varady. — Albany : State University of New York Press, c1986. — p. cm. — (SUNY series on urban public policy). — *Includes index. — Bibliography: p*

URBAN POLICY

STEINBERGER, Peter J.
Ideology and the urban crisis / Peter J. Steinberger. — Albany : State University of New York Press, c1985. — ix, 175 p.. — (SUNY series in urban public policy). — *Includes index. — Bibliography: p. 163-170*

URBAN POLICY — Congresses

The Future of the metropolis : Berlin, London, Paris, New York : economic aspects / editors, Hans-Jürgen Ewers, John B. Goddard, and Horst Matzerath. — Berlin ; New York : W. de Gruyter, 1986. — xi, 484 p.. — *"Presents the papers of an international conference ... held at the Technical University Berlin in October 1984"--Pref. — Includes bibliographies*

URBAN POLICY — Moral and ethical aspects

Ethics in planning / edited by Martin Wachs. — New Brunswick, N.J. : Center for Urban Policy Research, c1985. — xxi, 372 p.. — *Includes index. — Bibliography: p. 356-365*

URBAN POLICY — Research — Great Britain

GREAT BRITAIN. Department of the Environment
Brief for external research on inner city areas. — [London : the Department, 1977]. — 8 leaves

GREAT BRITAIN. Department of the Environment
Invitation to submit proposals for research on inner city areas. — London : the Department, 1977. — 4 leaves

URBAN POLICY — Asia

Basic needs and the urban poor : the provision of communal services / edited by P. J. Richards and A. M. Thomson. — London : Croom Helm, 1984. — 276p. — *Includes bibliographical references. — A study prepared for the International Labour Office within the framework of the World Employment Programme*

SIVARAMAKRISHNAN, K. C.
Metropolitan management : the Asian experience / K. C. Sivaramakrishnan and Leslie Green. — New York : Oxford University Press for the Economic Development Institute of the World Bank, 1986. — xiv,290p. — (EDI series in economic development). — *Includes bibliographical references*

URBAN POLICY — Asia — Congresses

Cities in conflict : studies in the planning and management of Asian cities / edited by John P. Lea and John M. Courtney. — Washington, D.C., U.S.A. : World Bank, 1985. — p. cm. — (A World Bank symposium). — *Outgrowth of a symposium held in Sydney, Australia, June 13-17, 1983, sponsored by the World Bank in association with the Commonwealth Association of Architects and the Royal Australian Institute of Architects. — Bibliography: p*

URBAN POLICY — Australia

SANDERCOCK, Leonie
Urban political economy : the Australian case / Leonie Sandercock, Michael Berry. — Sydney ; Boston : G. Allen & Unwin, 1983. — xi, 193 p.. — *Includes index. — Bibliography: p. 179-187*

URBAN POLICY — Australia — Addresses, essays, lectures

Australian urban politics : critical perspectives / edited by John Halligan and Chris Paris, with the assistance of Jan Wells. — Melbourne, Australia : Longman Cheshire, 1984. — xi, 247 p.. — (Australian studies). — *Includes index. — Bibliography: p. [222]-249*

URBAN POLICY — Caribbean Area

HOPE, Kempe R
Urbanization in the Commonwealth Caribbean / Kempe Ronald Hope. — Boulder, Colo. : Westview Press, 1986. — p. cm. — (Westview special studies on Latin America and the Caribbean). — *Includes index. — Bibliography: p*

URBAN POLICY — China

Chinese cities : the growth of the metropolis since 1949 / editor, Victor F. S. Sit ; contributors, Dong Liming ... [et al.]. — Oxford : Oxford University Press, 1985. — xvi,239p

URBAN POLICY — Developing countries — Congresses

The economics of urbanization and urban policies in developing countries / edited by George S. Tolley, Vinod Thomas. — Washington, D.C. : The World Bank, 1987. — xii,184p. — (A World Bank symposium). — *Includes bibliographies*

URBAN POLICY — England

GREAT BRITAIN. Department of the Environment
Consultation document on proposals to increase local authority powers with serious inner area problems to assist industry. — [London : the Department, 1977]. — 9 leaves

URBAN POLICY — England — Birmingham (West Midlands)

BIRMINGHAM. Environmental Health Department
HMO's : a new initiative : tackling the problems of houses in multiple occupation in Birmingham's inner city. — Birmingham : [the Department], 1986. — 8p. — (Urban renewal)

THOMAS, Andrew D.
Managing houses in multiple occupation : a preliminary report on Birmingham's Housing Action Team / Andrew D. Thomas. — Birmingham : Environmental Health Department, 1986. — 64p. — (Urban renewal)

URBAN POLICY — England — Hertfordshire

MCNAMARA, Paul
Restraint policy and development interests : housing in Dacorum and North Hertfordshire / by Paul McNamara. — [Oxford : Oxford Polytechnic, Dept. of Town Planning], 1982. — iii,75p. — (Working paper / Oxford Polytechnic, Dept. of Town Planning ; no.76). — *Cover title: Housing in Dacorum & North Hertfordshire : restraint policy & development interests. — "... the eighth working paper forming part of an SSRC sponsored study entitled "Land release and development in areas of restraint" - p.i*

URBAN POLICY — Great Britain

Managing the city : the aims and impacts of urban policy / edited by Brian Robson. — London : Croom Helm, c1987. — [240]p. — (Croom Helm series in geography and environment). — *Includes index*

Regional problems, problem regions and public policy in the United Kingdom / edited by P.J. Damesick and P.A. Wood. — Oxford : Clarendon, 1987. — xii,275p. — *Includes bibliographies and index*

TRADES UNION CONGRESS
Urban and regional policy : a discussion document. — [London : National Economic Development Council, 1983]. — 4,32p. — *NEDC: (83)53*

URBAN POLICY — India — Punjab — Congresses

Urbanisation & urban development in Punjab / editor, S.N. Misra. — 1st ed. — Amritsar : Guru Ram Dass P.G. School of Planning, Guru Nanak Dev University, 1985. — ii, 224 p., [14] leaves of plates. — 84-24. — *Summary: Papers presented at the ICSSR North Western Regional Centre Seminar on Urbanisation & Urban Development in Punjab, 1983, GRPG School of Planning, Guru Nanak Dev University. — Includes bibliographies*

URBAN POLICY — Japan

Urban policies in Japan : a review / by the OECD Group on Urban Affairs undertaken in 1984/5 at the request of the Government of Japan. — Paris : Organisation for Economic Co-operation and Development, 1986. — 107p. — *Includes bibliographical references*

URBAN POLICY — Manitoba — Winnipeg — Citizen participation

CHEKKI, Dan A.
Organised interest groups and the urban policy process / Dan A. Chekki and Roger T. Toews. — Winnipeg : Institute of Urban Studies, University of Winnipeg, 1985. — 87p. — (Report / University of Winnipeg, Institute of Urban Studies ; 9). — *Bibliography: p83-87*

URBAN POLICY — Middle West

The Metropolitan Midwest : policy problems and prospects for change / edited by Barry Checkoway and Carl V. Patton. — Urbana : University of Illinois Press, c1985. — 309 p.. — *Includes bibliographies*

URBAN POLICY — Nigeria

UYANGA, Joseph T
Towards a Nigerian national urban policy / Joseph Uyanga. — Ibadan, Nigeria : Ibadan University Press, 1982. — ix, 211 p.. — *Includes bibliographies*

URBAN POLICY — Organisation for Economic Co-operation and Development countries
Managing and financing urban services. — Paris : Organisation for Economic Co-operation and Development, 1987. — 94p. — *Bibliography: p77*

URBAN POLICY — Pakistan — Layāri
HAFEEZ, Sabeeha
Poverty, voluntary organizations, and social change : a study of an urban slum in Pakistan / Sabeeha Hafeez. — 1st ed. — Karachi : Royal Book Co., c1985. — 248 p.. — *Includes index*

URBAN POLICY — Sweden — Malmö
General plan för Malmö / verkställd på stadsingenjörskontoret av Martin Weibull. — Malmö : Stadsingenjörskontoret
Del 2: Inventering av näringsliv och allmänna institutioner. — 1952. — 353,41p

URBAN POLICY — Turkey
DANIELSON, Michael N
The politics of rapid urbanization : government and growth in modern Turkey / Michael N. Danielson, Ruşen Keleş. — New York : Holmes & Meier, 1984. — p. cm. — *Includes index. — Bibliography: p*

URBAN POLICY — United States
DRENNAN, Matthew P.
Modeling metropolitan economies for forecasting and policy analysis / Matthew P. Drennan. — New York : New York University Press, 1985. — p. cm. — *Includes index. — Bibliography: p*

Ethics in planning / edited by Martin Wachs. — New Brunswick, N.J. : Center for Urban Policy Research, c1985. — xxi, 372 p.. — *Includes index. — Bibliography: p. 356-365*

VARADY, David P
Neighborhood upgrading : a realistic assessment / David P. Varady. — Albany : State University of New York Press, c1986. — p. cm. — (SUNY series on urban public policy). — *Includes index. — Bibliography: p*

URBAN POLICY — United States — Addresses, essays, lectures
Urban policy problems : federal policy and institutional change / Mark S. Rosentraub, ed. — New York : Praeger, 1986. — p. cm. — *Published in cooperation with the Policy Studies Organization. — Includes index. — Bibliography: p*

The Urban predicament / edited by William Gorham, Nathan Glazer. — Washington : Urban Institute, c1976. — xix, 363 p.. — *Includes bibliographical references and index*

URBAN POLICY — United States — History
FOGLESONG, Richard E.
Planning the capitalist city : the colonial era to thhe 1920s / by Richard E. Foglesong. — Princeton, N.J. : Princeton University Press, c1986. — x, 286 p. — *Includes index. — Bibliography: p. 258-279*

URBAN POOR — Services for
Basic needs and the urban poor : the provision of communal services / edited by P. J. Richards and A. M. Thomson. — London : Croom Helm, 1984. — 276p. — *Includes bibliographical references. — A study prepared for the International Labour Office within the framework of the World Employment Programme*

URBAN POOR — United States — Case studies
MACLEOD, Jay
Ain't no makin' it : leveled aspirations in a low-income neighbourhood / Jay MacLeod. — London : Tavistock, 1987. — [208]p. — *Includes bibliography and index*

URBAN PROGRAMME
GREAT BRITAIN. Parliament. House of Commons. Library. Research Division
The urban programme / Christine Gillie. — [London] : the Division, 1982. — 20p. — (Reference sheet ; no.82/9). — *Bibliography: p17-20*

GREAT BRITAIN. Parliament. House of Commons. Library. Research Division
The urban programme / Oonagh Gay. — [London] : the Division, 1986. — 30p. — (Reference sheet ; no.86/13). — *Updates Reference sheets 82/9 and 84/7. — Bibliographical references: p24-30*

URBAN PROGRAMMME
GREAT BRITAIN. Parliament. House of Commons. Library. Research Division
The urban programme / Oonagh Gay. — [London] : the Division, 1984. — 27p. — (Reference sheet ; no.84/7). — *Bibliographical references: p23-27*

URBAN RENEWAL
Perspectives in urban geography. — New Delhi : Concept Publishing
Vol.7: Slums, urban decline and revitalization / edited by C. S. Yadav. — 1987. — 288p. — *Includes bibliographies and index*

URBAN RENEWAL — Case studies
UNIVERSITY COLLEGE LONDON. Development Planning Unit
Evaluating community participation in urban development projects : proceedings of a workshop held at the DPU 14th January 1983 / edited by Caroline O. N. Moser. — London : Development Planning Unit, Bartlett School of Architecture and Planning, University College London, 1983. — 67p. — (Working paper / University College London, Development Planning Unit ; No.14)

URBAN RENEWAL — Citizen participation — Case studies
UNIVERSITY COLLEGE LONDON. Development Planning Unit
Evaluating community participation in urban development projects : proceedings of a workshop held at the DPU 14th January 1983 / edited by Caroline O. N. Moser. — London : Development Planning Unit, Bartlett School of Architecture and Planning, University College London, 1983. — 67p. — (Working paper / University College London, Development Planning Unit ; No.14)

URBAN RENEWAL — England
GREAT BRITAIN. Department of the Environment. Yorkshire and Humberside Regional Office
General improvement areas. — [Leeds] : the Office, 1971. — 33,[7]p

JURUE
Evaluation of industrial and commercial improvement areas / JURUE ; [for the] Department of the Environment. — London : H.M.S.O., 1986. — vi,51p. — *At head of cover title: Inner Cities Research Programme. — Commissioned by the Inner Cities Directorate of the Department of the Environment. — Bibliographical references: p51*

URBAN RENEWAL — England — Finance
GREAT BRITAIN. Department of the Environment
Consultation document on proposals to increase local authority powers with serious inner area problems to assist industry. — [London : the Department, 1977]. — 9 leaves

URBAN RENEWAL — Great Britain
BRADLEY, Christine
Community involvement in greening projects : a study on hehalf of the Groundwork Foundation / by Christine Bradley. — Bolton : The Foundation, 1986. — 1v.. — *Includes index*

Environmental economy / editors, Richard Brooker and Matthew Corder. — London : Spon, 1986. — [200]p. — *Includes bibliography and index*

GREAT BRITAIN. Department of the Environment
Demonstration sites in the United Kingdom. — [London] : the Department, 1976. — 19p. — *(Planning in the United Kingdom). — Paper presented at the United Nations Conference on Human Settlements, 1976, Vancouver*

TOWN AND COUNTRY PLANNING ASSOCIATION
Whose responsibility? : reclaiming the inner cities. — London : TCPA, 1986. — 40p

URBED (URBAN AND ECONOMIC DEVELOPMENT) LTD.
Re-using redundant buildings : prepared for the Department of the Environment / by URBED (Urban and Economic Development) Ltd.. — London : H.M.S.O., 1987. — 115p. — (Case studies of good practice in urban regeneration). — *Commissioned by the Inner Cities Directorate of the Department of the Environment*

URBAN RENEWAL — India — Addresses, essays, lectures
The Indian city : poverty, ecology, and urban development / edited by Alfred de Souza. — New Delhi : Manohar, 1978. — xxix, 243 p.. — *Includes index. — Bibliography: p. [233]-238*

URBAN RENEWAL — London — Fulham
WHITTING, Gill
Implementing an inner city policy : a case study of the London Borough of Hammersmith & Fulham inner area programme / Gill Whitting. — Bristol : University of Bristol, School for Advanced Urban Studies, 1985. — 85p. — (Occasional paper / School for Advanced Urban Studies ; 22)

URBAN RENEWAL — London — Hammersmith
WHITTING, Gill
Implementing an inner city policy : a case study of the London Borough of Hammersmith & Fulham inner area programme / Gill Whitting. — Bristol : University of Bristol, School for Advanced Urban Studies, 1985. — 85p. — (Occasional paper / School for Advanced Urban Studies ; 22)

URBAN RENEWAL — Middle West
The Metropolitan Midwest : policy problems and prospects for change / edited by Barry Checkoway and Carl V. Patton. — Urbana : University of Illinois Press, c1985. — 309 p.. — *Includes bibliographies*

URBAN RENEWAL — Northern Ireland — Belfast
DAWSON, Gerry
Planning in the shadow of urban civil conflict : a case study from Belfast / by Gerry Dawson. — Liverpool : University of Liverpool, Dept. of Civic Design, 1984. — 48 leaves. — (Working paper / Dept. of Civic Design, University of Liverpool ; WP24)

URBAN RENEWAL — Organisation for Economic Co-operation and Development countries
Maintenance and modernisation of urban housing. — Paris : Organisation for Economic Co-operation and Development, 1986. — 88p. — *At head of cover: OECD urban affairs programme*

URBAN RENEWAL — Scotland — Glasgow (Strathclyde)
Regenerating the inner city : Glasgow's experience / edited by David Donnison and Alan Middleton. — London : Routledge & Kegan Paul, 1987. — [304]p. — (Geography, environment and planning). — *Includes bibliography and index*

URBAN RENEWAL — United States
VARADY, David P
Neighborhood upgrading : a realistic assessment / David P. Varady. — Albany : State University of New York Press, c1986. — p. cm. — (SUNY series on urban public policy). — *Includes index. — Bibliography: p*

URBAN RENEWAL — United States — Case studies
MERRY, Sally Engle
Urban danger : life in a neighborhood of strangers / Sally Engle Merry. — Philadelphia : Temple University Press, 1981. — x, 278 p.. — Includes index. — Bibliography: p. [259]-272

URBAN RENEWAL — United States — Citizen participation
DELGADO, Gary
Organizing the movement : the roots and growth of ACORN / Gary Delgado ; with a foreword by Richard A. Cloward and Frances Fox Piven. — Philadelphia : Temple University Press, 1986. — xx, 269 p.. — (Labor and social change). — Includes index. — Bibliography: p. 253-261

WILLIAMS, Michael R.
Neighborhood organizations : seeds of a new urban life / Michael R. Williams. — Westport, Conn. : Greenwood Press, 1985. — xiii, 278 p.. — (Contributions in political science ; no. 131). — Includes index. — Bibliography: p. [261]-269

URBAN-RURAL MIGRATION
PERRY, Ronald
Counterurbanisation : international case studies of socio-economic change in the rural areas / Ronald Perry, Ken Dean and Bryan Brown with the assistance of David Shaw. — Norwich : Geo, c1986. — xiii,246p. — Bibliography: p224-242. — Includes index

URBAN-RURAL MIGRATION — History — Addresses, essays, lectures
Proletarians and protest : the roots of class formation in an industrializing world / edited by Michael Hanagan and Charles Stephenson. — New York : Greenwood Press, 1986. — viii, 250 p.. — (Contributions in labor studies ; no. 17). — Includes index. — Bibliography: p. [231]-241

URBAN-RURAL MIGRATION — Korea (South)
LEE, On-Jook
Urban-to-rural return migration in Korea / Lee On-Jook. — [Seoul] : Seoul National University Press, c1980. — xii, 182 p.. — ″A publication of the Population and Development Studies Center.″. — Includes indexes. — Bibliography: p. 169-174

URBAN TRANSPORTATION
The Geography of urban transportation / edited by Susan Hanson. — New York : Guilford Press, c1986. — viii, 424 p.. — Includes bibliographies and index

Urban transport. — Washington, D.C. : The World Bank, 1986. — xi,61p. — (A World Bank policy study). — Bibliography: p59-61

URBAN TRANSPORTATION — Mathematical models
HOLZAPFEL, Helmut
Trip relationships in urban areas / Helmut Holzapfel. — Aldershot : Gower, c1986. — [137]p. — Bibliography: p127-137

VAUGHAN, Rodney
Urban spatial traffic patterns / Rodney Vaughan. — London : Pion, 1987. — 334p. — Bibliography: p[315]-330

URBAN TRANSPORTATION — Statistics
International statistical handbook of public transport = Recueil international de statistiques des transports publics = Internationales Statistik-Handbuch für den öffentlichen Verkehr / by Lee H. Rogers, compiler/editor in collaboration with UITP Documentation Centre. — Bruxelles, Belgique : International Union of Public Transport, c1985. — 3 v. (1645 p.). — Cover title: UITP handbook of public transport = Recueil UITP des transports publics = UITP-Handbuch für öffentlichen Verkehr

URBAN TRANSPORTATION — Asia, Southeastern
RIMMER, Peter J.
Rikisha to rapid transport : urban public transport systems and policy in southeast Asia / Peter J. Rimmer. — Sydney ; Oxford : Pergamon, 1986. — xxvi,387p. Bibliography: p333-371

URBAN TRANSPORTATION — Great Britain
WELSBY, J. K.
Conurbation transport : ten years on; synopsis of forum contribution / by J. K. Welsby. — [London] : Department of the Environment : Department of Transport, [1976]. — 12leaves. — At head of title: Tenth Symposium on the Future of Conurbation Transport

URBAN TRANSPORTATION — Great Britain — Planning
DUPREE, Harry
Urban transportation : the new town solution / Harry Dupree. — Aldershot : Gower, c1987. — xxii,267p,[18]p of plates. — Bibliography: p253-256. — Includes index

URBAN TRANSPORTATION — India
DARBÉRA, Richard
Le planificateur et le cyclopousse : les avatars de la politique des transports urbains en Inde / Richard Darbéra, Bernard Henri Nicot ; préface de Ralph Gakenheimer. — Caen : Paradigme, 1986. — xiii, 190p. — Bibliography:p135-142

URBAN TRANSPORTATION — Japan
MCDONALD, Graeme
The development of medium capacity transport systems in Japan / Graeme McDonald. — Reading : University of Reading. Department of Geography, 1986. — 61p. — (Geographical papers ; no94). — Bibliography: p61

URBAN TRANSPORTATION POLICY — France
MERLIN, Pierre
Les politiques de transport urbain / Pierre Merlin. — Paris : La Documentation française, 1985. — 143p. — (Notes et études documentaires ; 4797)

URBAN WOMEN — Employment — United States
LOPATA, Helena Znaniecka
City women : work, jobs, occupations, careers / Helena Znaniecka Lopata, with Cheryl Allyn Miller and Debra Barnewolt. — New York : Praeger, 1984-. — v. <1 >. — Includes bibliographies and index. — Contents: v. 1. America

URBANIZATION
Perspectives in urban geography. — New Delhi : Concept Publishing
Vol.1: New directions in urban geography / edited by C. S. Yadav. — 1986. — 347p. — Includes bibliographies and index

Perspectives in urban geography. — New Delhi : Concept Publishing
Vol.3: Comparative urbanization : city growth and change / edited by C. S. Yadav. — 1986. — 420p. — Includes bibliographies and index

Perspectives in urban geography. — New Delhi : Concept Publishing
Vol. 5: Urban research methods : central place, hierarchical and city size models / edited by C. S. Yadav. — 1986. — 320p. — Includes bibliographies and index

Urbanization and counter-urbanization / edited by Brian J.L. Berry. — Beverly Hills ; London : Sage Publications, [1977]. — 334p. — (Urban affairs annual reviews ; vol.11). — Published in the United States: 1976. — Includes bibliographies

URBANIZATION — Addresses, essays, lectures
World patterns of modern urban change : essays in honor of Chauncy D. Harris / edited by Michael P. Conzen. — Chicago : University of Chicago, Dept. of Geography, 1985. — p. cm. — (Research paper / the University of Chicago, Department of Geography ; no. 217-218). — Includes index

URBANIZATION — History
KONVITZ, Josef W
The urban millennium : the city-building process from the early Middle Ages to the present / Josef W. Konvitz. — Carbondale : Southern Illinois University Press, c1985. — p. cm. — Includes index. — Bibliography: p

URBANIZATION — Research
Pathologies of urban processes / edited by Kingsley E. Haynes, Antoni Kuklinski and Olli Kultalahti. — Tampere : Finn publishers, 1985. — xxv,448p. — Bibliograhies

Perspectives in urban geography. — New Delhi : Concept Publishing
Vol.2: Comparative urban research / edited by C. S. Yadav. — 1986. — 219p. — Includes bibliographies and index

URBANIZATION — Social aspects — India
KOPARDEKAR, H. D.
Social aspects of urban development : a case study of the pattern of urban development in the developing countries / H. D. Kopardekar. — New Delhi : Sangam Books, 1986. — viii,392p. — Bibliography: p377-387

URBANIZATION — Africa — Bibliography
AJAEGBU, Hyacinth I.
African urbanization : a bibliography / compiled by Hyacinth I. Ajaegbu. — London : International African Institute, 1972. — vi,78p

URBANIZATION — Africa, Sub-Saharan
MITCHELL, J. Clyde
Cities, society and social perception : a Central African perspective / J. Clyde Mitchell. — Oxford : Clarendon, 1987. — xxii,336p. — Bibliography: p317-331. — Includes index

URBANIZATION — Ahmedabad
DOSHI, Harish
Traditional neighbourhood in a modern city / Harish Doshi. — New Delhi : Abhinav Publications, 1974. — x,154p. — Bibliographic references: p[147]-150

URBANIZATION — Asia, Southeastern — Congresses
Urbanization and migration in ASEAN development / edited by Philip M. Hauser, Daniel B. Suits, Naohiro Ogawa. — Tokyo : National Institute for Research Advancement, 1985. — xiv,496p. — Papers presented at Conference on Migration and Development in ASEAN in 1984. — Bibliographies

URBANIZATION — Canada
MCGAHAN, Peter
Urban sociology in Canada / Peter McGahan. — 2nd ed. — Toronto : Butterworths, 1986. — vi,334p. — Bibliography: p[271]-323

URBANIZATION — Colombia
HELMSING, A. H. J.
Firms, farms, and the state in Colombia : a study of rural, urban, and regional dimensions of change / A.H.J. Helmsing. — Boston : Allen & Unwin, 1986. — xix, 297 p.. — Includes index. — Bibliography: p. 275-288

URBANIZATION — Developing countries
TODARO, Michael P.
International migration, domestic unemployment, and urbanization : a three-sector model / Michael P. Todaro. — New York : Population Council, 1986. — 29p. — (Working papers / Population Council, New York. Center for Policy Studies ; no.124). — Bibliography: p24-25

URBANIZATION — Developing countries — Congresses
The economics of urbanization and urban policies in developing countries / edited by George S. Tolley, Vinod Thomas. — Washington, D.C. : The World Bank, 1987. — xii,184p. — (A World Bank symposium). — Includes bibliographies

URBANIZATION — Ethiopia — Bagēmder — Case studies
BAKER, Jonathan
The rural-urban dichotomy in the developing world : a case study from northern Ethiopia / Jonathan Baker. — Oslo : Norwegian University Press : Oxford ; New York : Distributed world-wide excluding Scandinavia by Oxford University Press, c1986. — 372 p.. — Bibliography: p. [365]-372

URBANIZATION — India
Perspectives in urban geography. — New Delhi : Concept Publishing
Vol.3: Comparative urbanization : city growth and change / edited by C. S. Yadav. — 1986. — 420p. — Includes bibliographies and index

RAJ BALA
Trends in urbanisation in India, 1901-1981 / Raj Bala. — Jaipur : Rawat Publication, 1986. — xxvi, 231 p.. — Based on the author's thesis (Ph. D.--Panjab University, Chandigarh). — Includes index. — Bibliography: p. [202]-226

Urban growth and urban planning : political context and people's priorities / edited by Alfred de Souza. — New Delhi : Indian Social Institute, c1983. — xi, 163 p.. — Includes index. — Bibliography: p. [155]-160. — Contents: The challenge of urbanisation and the response / C.S. Chandrasekhara -- Patterns of urban growth, 1971-81 / Ashish Bose -- An approach to urban land policy / Louis Menezes -- Planning for the urban poor: basic needs and priorities / E.F.N. Ribeiro -- Ahmedabad slums: redefining strategies for action / Kirtee Shah -- Rural-urban migration of women: some implications for urban planning / Andrea Menefee Singh -- Urban growth and urban planning / Alfred de Souza

URBANIZATION — India — Addresses, essays, lectures
The Indian city : poverty, ecology, and urban development / edited by Alfred de Souza. — New Delhi : Manohar, 1978. — xxix, 243 p.. — Includes index. — Bibliography: p. [233]-238

URBANIZATION — India — History
NAQVI, Hameeda Khatoon
Urbanisation and urban centres under the Great Mughals 1556-1707 : an essay in interpretation / Hameeda Khatoon Naqvi. — Simla : Indian Institute of Advanced Study
Vol.1. — 1971. — 210p. — Bibliography: p [187]-192

RAJ BALA
Trends in urbanisation in India, 1901-1981 / Raj Bala. — Jaipur : Rawat Publication, 1986. — xxvi, 231 p.. — Based on the author's thesis (Ph. D.--Panjab University, Chandigarh). — Includes index. — Bibliography: p. [202]-226

URBANIZATION — India — Maharashtra
KOPARDEKAR, H. D.
Social aspects of urban development : a case study of the pattern of urban development in the developing countries / H. D. Kopardekar. — New Delhi : Sangam Books, 1986. — viii,392p. — Bibliography: p377-387

URBANIZATION — India — Punjab — Congresses
Urbanisation & urban development in Punjab / editor, S.N. Misra. — 1st ed. — Amritsar : Guru Ram Dass P.G. School of Planning, Guru Nanak Dev University, 1985. — ii, 224 p., [14] leaves of plates. — 84-24. — Summary: Papers presented at the ICSSR North Western Regional Centre Seminar on Urbanisation & Urban Development in Punjab, 1983, GRPG School of Planning, Guru Nanak Dev University. — Includes bibliographies

URBANIZATION — Kenya
Approaches to rural-urban development : proceedings of a workshop organised by the Institute for Development Studies, University of Nairobi, 22 May 1985 / edited by Hugh E. Evans [and] George M. Ruigu. — Nairobi : University of Nairobi. Institute for Development, 1985. — 40p. — (Occasional paper / University of Nairobi. Institute for Development Studies ; no.46)

URBANIZATION — Latin America
ROBERTS, Bryan
Cities of peasants : the political economy of urbanization in the Third World / Bryan Roberts. — Beverly Hills ; London : Sage Publications, 1979. — vi, 207 p. — (Explorations in urban analysis ; v. 1). — Includes indexes. — Bibliography: p. [178]-199

URBANIZATION — Mexico
RAMOS G., Sergio
Urbanización y servicios públicos en México / Sergio Ramos G.. — México D.F. : Universidad Nacional Autónoma de México, Instituto de Investigaciones Sociales, 1972. — 192p

URBANIZATION — Middle East — History — Congresses
The Middle East city : ancient traditions confront a modern world / edited by Abdulaziz Y. Saqqaf. — New York : Paragon House, c1987. — xx, 393 p. — Proceedings of a conference sponsored by the Middle East Chapter of the Professors World Peace Academy. — "A PWPA book.". — Includes bibliographies and index

URBANIZATION — Nigeria
UYANGA, Joseph T
Towards a Nigerian national urban policy / Joseph Uyanga. — Ibadan, Nigeria : Ibadan University Press, 1982. — ix, 211 p.. — Includes bibliographies

URBANIZATION — Nigeria — Congresses
Urbanization processes and problems in Nigeria / edited by P. O. Sada and J. S. Oguntoyinbo. — Ibadan : Ibadan University Press, 1981. — xi,202p. — Papers from the 17th annual Conference of the Nigerian Geographical Association with the theme 'Urban systems and the process of development'. — First published 1978

URBANIZATION — Nigeria — Lagos — History
BARNES, Sandra T.
Patrons and power : creating a political community in metropolitan Lagos / Sandra T. Barnes. — Manchester : Manchester University Press, c1986. — [336]p. — (International African library ; v.1). — Includes bibliography and index

URBANIZATION — Norway
TORSTENSON, Joel S.
Urbanization and community building in modern Norway / by Joel S. Torstenson, Michael F. Metcalf, Tor Fr. Rasmussen. — Oslo : Urbana, 1985. — xviii,313p. — Bibliographies

URBANIZATION — Russian S.F.S.R — Moscow — History
BRADLEY, Joseph
Muzhik and Muscovite : urbanization in late imperial Russia / Joseph Bradley. — Berkeley ; London : University of California Press, c1985. — xvi, 422p. — Based on the author's doctoral thesis. — Includes index. — Bibliography: p.377-405

URBANIZATION — Russian S.F.S.R. — Siberia
Urbanizatsiia sovetskoi Sibiri / otv. redaktor V. V. Alekseev. — Novosibirsk : Nauka, Sibirskoe otdelenie, 1987. — 222p

URBANIZATION — Southern States — History — 19th century
LARSEN, Lawrence Harold
The rise of the urban South / Lawrence H. Larsen. — Lexington, Ky. : University Press of Kentucky, c1985. — xi, 220 p.. — Includes index. — Bibliography: p. [192]-213

URBANIZATION — Soviet Union — History — Addresses, essays, lectures
The City in late imperial Russia / edited by Michael F. Hamm. — Bloomington : Indiana University Press, c1986. — viii, 372p. — (Indiana-Michigan series in Russian and East European studies). — Papers from a meeting of the American Association for the Advancement of Slavic Studies, held in Kansas City, Mo., Oct. 1983. — Includes index. — Bibliography: p.[355]-359

URBANIZATION — Sudan
AHMED, Abdel Ghaffar M.
Urbanisation and exploration : the role small centres / Abdel Ghaffar M. Ahmed and Mustafa Abdel Rahman. — Khartoum : University of Khartoum. Faculty of Economic and Social Studies. Development Studies and Research Centre, 1979. — 45p. — (Monograph series / University of Khartoum. Faculty of Economic and Social Studies. Development Studies and Research Centre ; no.11)

URBANIZATION — Tanzania — Dar Es Salaam
SPORREK, Anders
Food marketing and urban growth in Dar Es Salaam / by Anders Sporrek. — Lund, Sweden : Royal University of Lund, Dept. of Geography ; Malmö, Sweden : CWK Gleerup, 1985. — 200 p.. — (Lund studies in geography. Ser. B. Human geography ; no. 51). — Bibliography: p. 193-200

URBANIZATION — Turkey
DANIELSON, Michael N
The politics of rapid urbanization : government and growth in modern Turkey / Michael N. Danielson, Ruşen Keleş. — New York : Holmes & Meier, 1984. — p. cm. — Includes index. — Bibliography: p

URBANIZATION — United States — History — 20th century
TEAFORD, Jon C
The twentieth-century American city : problem, promise, and reality / Jon C. Teaford. — Baltimore ; London : Johns Hopkins University Press, c1986. — x, 177p. — (The American moment). — Includes index. — Bibliography: p.[157]-169

URIBURU, JOSÉ FÉLIX
GARCÍA MOLINA, Fernando
El general Uriburu y el petróleo / Fernando García Molina, Carlos A. Mayo. — Buenos Aires : Centro Editor de América Latina, 1985. — 156p. — (Biblioteca Política Argentina ; 96) . — Bibliographical notes: p129-156

URQUHART, LESLIE
KENNEDY, K. H.
Mining tsar : the life and times of Leslie Urquhart / K.H. Kennedy. — Sydney ; London : Allen & Unwin, 1986. — [276]p. — Bibliography: p346-351. — Includes index

URUGUAY — Dictionaries and encyclopedias
WILLIS, Jean L
Historical dictionary of Uruguay / by Jean L. Willis. — Metuchen, N.J. : Scarecrow Press, 1974. — vii, 275 p. — (Latin American historical dictionaries, no. 11). — Bibliography: p. 261-275

URUGUAY — Economic conditions — 1973-

GONZÁLEZ GARCÍA, José I.
La segmentación del mercado del credito y sus impactos sobre la distribución del ingreso / José I. González. — Montevideo : Centro Interdisciplinario de Estudios sobre el Desarollo Uruguay, 1984. — 123p. — (Serie Investigaciones / Centro Interdisciplinario de Estudios sobre el Desarollo Uruguay ; no.18). — *Bibliography: p89-92*

URUGUAY — Economic policy

GONZÁLEZ GARCÍA, José I.
La segmentación del mercado del credito y sus impactos sobre la distribución del ingreso / José I. González. — Montevideo : Centro Interdisciplinario de Estudios sobre el Desarollo Uruguay, 1984. — 123p. — (Serie Investigaciones / Centro Interdisciplinario de Estudios sobre el Desarollo Uruguay ; no.18). — *Bibliography: p89-92*

URUGUAY — History — 1904-1973

MERCADER, Antonio
Los Tupamaros : estrategia y acción / Antonio Mercader y Jorge de Vera. — Barcelona : Editorial Anagrama, [1986]. — 161p. — (Colección documentos ; 9). — *New edition of 'Tupamaros: estrategia y acción', Montevideo, Editoria Alfa, 1969.*

URUGUAY — Politics and government

GONZALEZ, Luis E.
Political parties and redemocratication in Uruguay / Luis E. Gonzalez. — Washington, D.C. : Latin American Program of the Woodrow Wilson International Center for Scholars and the World Peace Foundation, 1984. — 21p. — (Working papers / Woodrow Wilson International Center for Scholars. Latin American Program ; no.163)

U.S. NUCLEAR REGULATORY COMMISSION

ADATO, Michelle
Safety second : the NRC and America's nuclear power plants / The Union of Concerned Scientists ; contributors, Michelle Adato, principal author, James MacKenzie, Robert Pollard, Ellyn Weiss. — Bloomington : Indiana University Press, c1987. — 194 p.. — *Includes index.* — *Bibliography: p. [164]-187*

USURY

LANGHOLM, Odd
The Aristotelian analysis of usury / Odd Langholm. — Bergen : Universitetsforlaget ; London : [Distributed by] Global Book Resources, c1984. — 153p. — *Bibliography: p.[152]-153*

UTILITARIANISM

MILL, John Stuart
Newspaper writings / by John Stuart Mill ; edited by Ann P. Robson and John M. Robson. — Toronto : University of Toronto Press ; London : Routledge & Kegan Paul
1: December 1822 - July 1831. — 1986. — cxvii,333p. — (Collected works of John Stuart Mill ; v.22)

MILL, John Stuart
Newspaper writings / by John Stuart Mill ; edited by Ann P. Robson and John M. Robson. — Toronto : University of Toronto Press ; London : Routledge & Kegan Paul
2: August 1831 - October 1834. — 1986. — ix,335-751p. — (Collected works of John Stuart Mill ; v.23)

MILL, John Stuart
Newspaper writings / by John Stuart Mill ; edited by Ann P. Robson and John M. Robson. — Toronto : University of Toronto Press ; London : Routledge & Kegan Paul
3: January 1835 - June 1847. — 1986. — vii,753-1088p. — (Collected works of John Stuart Mill ; v.24)

MILL, John Stuart
Newspaper writings / by John Stuart Mill ; edited by Ann P. Robson and John M. Robson. — Toronto : University of Toronto Press ; London : Routledge & Kegan Paul
4: December 1847 - July 1873. — 1986. — vii,1089-1526p. — (Collected works of John Stuart Mill ; v.25)

UTILITARIANISM — England

STEPHEN, Sir Leslie
The English utilitarians / by Sir Leslie Stephen. — New York : Kelley
Vol.1: Jeremy Bentham. — 1968. — 326p

STEPHEN, Sir Leslie
The English utilitarians / by Sir Leslie Stephen. — London : Duckworth
Vol.3: John Stuart Mill. — 1900

UTOPIAN SOCIALISM

INGRISCH, Doris
Das Rollenbild der Frau bei den Frühsozialisten / Doris Ingrisch. — Linz : Tranner, 1985. — 119p. — (Linzer Schriften zur Sozial- und Wirtschaftsgeschicte ; Bd.13). — *Bibliography : p114-119*

UTOPIAN SOCIALISM — History

BEECHER, Jonathan
Charles Fourier : the visionary and his world / Jonathan Beecher. — Berkeley : University of California Press, 1987. — p. cm. — *Includes index.* — *Bibliography: p*

UTOPIAN SOCIALISM — France

DUMONT, René
Les raisons de la colère, ou L'utopie et les Verts / René Dumont ; avec Charlotte Paquet. — Paris : Éditions Entente, 1986. — 137p. — *Bibliography: p135-137*

UTOPIAS

GASTON, Paul M
Women of Fair Hope / Paul M. Gaston. — Athens : University of Georgia Press, c1984. — xiv, 143 p.. — (Mercer University Lamar memorial lectures ; no. 25). — *Includes index.* — *Bibliography: p. [119]-133*

HOLSTUN, James
A rational millennium : Puritan utopias of seventeenth-century England and America / James Holstun. — New York : Oxford University Press, 1987. — p. cm. — *Includes index.* — *Bibliography: p*

MARTINEAU, Alain
Herbert Marcuses utopia / by Alain Martineau. — Montreal : Harvest House, 1986. — 156p

UTOPIAS — History

Istoriia sotsialisticheskikh uchenii 1986 : sbornik statei / otv. redaktor L. S. Chikolini. — Moskva : Nauka, 1986. — 283p

RICŒUR, Paul
Lectures on ideology and utopia / Paul Ricoeur ; edited by George H. Taylor. — New York : Columbia University Press, 1986. — xxxvi, 353 p.. — *Includes index.* — *Bibliography: p. [329]-337*

UTOPIAS IN LITERATURE

KUMAR, Krishan, 1942-
Utopia and anti-Utopia in modern times / Krishan Kumar. — Oxford : Basil Blackwell, 1986. — [352]p. — *Includes bibliography and index*

UTTAR PRADESH (INDIA) — Politics and government

BRASS, Paul R.
Caste, faction and party in Indian politics / Paul R. Brass. — Delhi : Chanakya Publications
Vol.2: Election studies. — 1985. — 325p

UTUROA (RAIATEA) — Population — Statistics

Tableaux normalisés du recensement général de la population : 15 octobre 1983. — [Papeeta] : Institut territorial de la statistique Résultats de la commune de Uturoa. — [1985?]. — 4p,11 leaves

UZBEK S.S.R. — Economic conditions

ZIIADULLAEV, S. K.
Industriia Sovetskogo Uzbekistana / S. K. Ziiadullaev. — Tashkent : Uzbekistan, 1984. — 229p

UZBEK S.S.R. — Economic policy

ABDUSALIAMOV, M.
Proizvoditel'nye sily i sovershenstvovanie ekonomicheskikh sviazei Uzbekistana / M. Abdusaliamov, A. Alimov, I. Musienko ; otv. redaktor K. N. Bedrintsev. — Tashkent : "Fan" Uzbekskoi SSR, 1986. — 141p

UZBEK S.S.R. — Industries

ABDUSALIAMOV, M.
Proizvoditel'nye sily i sovershenstvovanie ekonomicheskikh sviazei Uzbekistana / M. Abdusaliamov, A. Alimov, I. Musienko ; otv. redaktor K. N. Bedrintsev. — Tashkent : "Fan" Uzbekskoi SSR, 1986. — 141p

ZIIADULLAEV, S. K.
Industriia Sovetskogo Uzbekistana / S. K. Ziiadullaev. — Tashkent : Uzbekistan, 1984. — 229p

UZBEK S.S.R. — Social conditions

MUKMINOVA, R. G.
Sotsial'naia differentsiatsii naseleniia gorodov Uzbekistana, konets XV-XVI v. / R. G. Mukminova. — Tashkent : "Fan" Uzbekskoi SSR, 1985. — 135p

VACATIONS — Great Britain — Statistics

BRITISH TOURIST AUTHORITY. Research Department
The British on holiday : a summary of regular surveys on holidaytaking by British adults 1951-1974. — London : the Authority, 1974. — 11p

VACATIONS, EMPLOYEE — Law and legislation — Denmark

The Holidays with Pay Act, 1971. — [Copenhagen : Ministry of Labour?], 1971. — 8 leaves

VAGRANCY — Brazil — Pernambuco — History — 19th century

HUGGINS, Martha Knisely
From slavery to vagrancy in Brazil : crime and social control in the Third World / Martha Knisely Huggins. — New Brunswick, N.J. : Rutgers University Press, c1984. — xix, 183p. — (Crime, law, and deviance series). — *Includes index.* — *Bibliography: p 159-167*

VAIZEY, JOHN

VAIZEY, John
Scenes from institutional life and other writings / John Vaizey. — London : Weidenfeld and Nicolson, 1986. — vi,164p. — *Bibliography: p163-164*

VALCO *See* Volta Aluminium Company

VALE OF BELVOIR (LEICESTERSHIRE DISTRICT) — Industries

Belvoir prospect / National Coal Board, South Nottinghamshire and South Midlands areas. — [London? : National Coal Board?]
Vol.1: Surface and underground works, joint conclusion / Leonard and Partners with Owen Luder Partnership, Thyssen (G.B.) Ltd.. — 1977. — [2] leaves, 1 map

VALE OF BELVOIR (LEICESTERSHIRE: DISTRICT) — Industries

Belvoir prospect / National Coal Board, South Nottinghamshire and South Midlands areas. — [London? : National Coal Board?]
Vol.2: Surface works report / Leonard and Partners in association with Owen Luder Partnership. — 1977. — 96p

VALE OF BELVOIR (LEICESTERSHIRE: DISTRICT) — Industries
continuation

Belvoir prospect / National Coal Board, South Nottinghamshire and South Midlands areas. — [London? : National Coal Board?]
Vol.2: Surface works report / Leonard and Partners in association with Owen Luder Partnership
Appendices
Plans. — 1977. — *1v. of plans*

Belvoir prospect / National Coal Board, South Nottinghamshire and South Midlands areas. — [London? : National Coal Board?]
Vol.2: Surface works report / Leonard and Partners in association with Owen Luder Partnership
Plans. — 1977. — *50plans*

Belvoir prospect / National Coal Board, South Nottinghamshire and South Midlands areas. — [London? : National Coal Board?]
Surface works report / Leonard and Parners in association with Owen Luder Partnership
Appendices. — 1977. — 352p

VALENCIA (SPAIN) — Foreign economic relations — America — History — 18th century
RIBES, Vicent
Los valencianos y América : el comercio valenciano con Indias en el siglo XVIII / Vicent Ribes. — Valencia : Diputació Provincial de València, [1985]. — 193p. — (História i societat ; 2)

VALENCIA (SPAIN) — History — Auntonomy and independence movements
ALCARAZ RAMOS, Manuel
Cuestión nacional y autonomía Valenciana / Manuel Alcaraz Ramos. — Alicante : Instituto Juan Gil-Albert, 1985. — 221p. — *Bibliography: p15-221*

VALENCIA (SPAIN: REGION) — History
GIRONA I ALBUIXEC, Albert
Guerra i revolució al País Valenciá (1936-1939) / Albert Girona i Albuixec ; pròleg de Joan Brines. — Valencia : Eliseu Climent, 1986. — 554p. — (Tres i quatre : biblioteca d'estudis i investigacions ; 8)

VALLADARES, ARMANDO — Biography — Imprisonment
VALLADARES, Armando
Against all hope : the prison memoirs of Armando Valladares / translated by Andrew Hurley. — London : Hamilton, 1986. — xiv,380p. — *Translation of: Contra toda esperanza*

VALLADOLID (SPAIN) — Economic conditions — History
MAZA ZORRILLA, Elena
Valladolid : sus pobres y la respuesta institucional (1750-1900) / Elena Maza Zorrila. — Valladolid : Universidad de Valladolid : Junta de Castille y León, 1985. — 405p. — *Bibliography: p381-392*

VALLADOLID (SPAIN) — Social conditions
PRADO MOURA, Angel de
El movimiento obrero en Valladolid durante la II República (1931-1936) / Angel de Prado Moura. — Valladolid : Junta de Castilla y Leon, 1985. — 234p. — *Bibliography: p231-232*

VALLADOLID (SPAIN) — Social conditions — History
MAZA ZORRILLA, Elena
Valladolid : sus pobres y la respuesta institucional (1750-1900) / Elena Maza Zorrila. — Valladolid : Universidad de Valladolid : Junta de Castille y León, 1985. — 405p. — *Bibliography: p381-392*

VALLARTA, IGNACIO LUIS
VALLARTA, Ignacio Luis
Vallarta en la reforma / prólogo y selección: Moisés González Navarro. — México, D.F. : Universidad Nacional Autónoma de México, 1956. — xxxv,232p. — (Biblioteca del estudiante Universitario ; 76)

VALOIS TAPESTRIES
YATES, Frances A.
The Valois tapestries / Frances A. Yates. — 2nd ed. — London : Routledge and Kegan Paul, 1975. — xxvii,151p,[40]p of plates,[8] leaves of plates. — *Previous ed.: London : Warburg Institute, 1959. — Includes index*

VALUE
KROTOV, M. I.
Potrebitel'naia stoimost' pri sotsializme / M. I. Krotov. — Moskva : Ekonomika, 1983. — 151p

NELL, Edward J.
On monetary circulation and the rate of exploitation / Edward Nell. — London : Thames Polytechnic, 1986. — 36p. — (Thames papers in political economy)

PACK, Spencer J
Reconstructing Marxian economics : Marx based upon a Sraffian commodity theory of value / by Spencer J. Pack. — New York : Praeger, 1985. — p. cm. — *Includes index. Bibliography: p*

ROLAND, Gérard
La valeur d'usage chez Karl Marx / Gérard Roland. — Bruxelles : Université de Bruxelles, [1985]. — 200p. — *Bibliography: p191-196*

The Value dimension : Marx versus Ricardo and Sraffa / edited by Ben Fine. — London : Routledge & Kegan Paul, 1986. — 239p. — (Economy and society). — *Includes bibliographies*

VALUE — Addresses, essays, lectures
SHAW, George Bernard
Bernard Shaw & Karl Marx : a symposium, 1884-1889. — Folcroft, Pa. : Folcroft Library Editions, 1977. — ix, 200 p., [1] fold. leaf of plates. — *Reprint of the 1930 ed. printed for Random House by R. W. Ellis, The Georgian Press, New York*

VALUE ADDED
WOOD, E. G
The nature and uses of added value / by E. G. Wood. — [London : s.n., 1978?]. — 28 leaves. — *Includes various reprinted articles on added value*

VALUE ADDED — Great Britain
GREAT BRITAIN. Central Statistical Office
Value added and the national accounts. — [London : the Office, 1977]. — 6p. — *"Paper to be presented at seminar on value added: 6 December 1977"*

VALUE ADDED — Great Britain — Industries — Statistics
MITCHELL, B.
Measuring value added from the census of production / by Dr. B. Mitchell. — [Newport, Gwent?] : Business Statistics Office, 1977. — 9 leaves. — *At haed of title page: "Seminar on value added"*

VALUE ADDED — Organisation for Economic Co-operation and Development countries — Statistical methods
Measurement of value added at constant prices in service activities : national accounts : sources and methods (1) = Mesure de la valeur ajoutée aux prix constants dans les activités de service : comptes nationaux : sources et méthodes (1). — Paris : Organisation for Economic Co-operation and Development, 1987. — 105p

VALUE-ADDED TAX — Great Britain
GREAT BRITAIN. Parliament. House of Commons. Library. Research Division
Vat : the EEC and the UK tax system / Timothy Edmonds. — [London] : the Division, 1984. — 27p. — (Background paper ; no.154)

VALUE-ADDED TAX — Spain
LAMPREAVE PEREZ, Jose Luis
La empresa española ante el impuesto sobre el valor añadido : medidas de adaptación y ajuste / Jose Luis Lampreave Perez, Juan Antonio Gimeno Ullastres y Alberto Terol Esteban ; prologo: César Albiñana García-Quintana. — Madrid : Instituto de Estudios Fiscales, 1985. — 493p

VALUES
KANE, R
Free will and values / R. Kane. — Albany : State University of New York Press, c1985. — vii, 229 p.. — (SUNY series in philosophy). — *Includes indexes. Bibliography: p. 206-218*

LEE, Dorothy
Valuing the self : what we can learn from other cultures / Dorothy Lee. — Prospect Heights, I11 : Waveland Press, 1986. — xii,87p

VALVERDE (SPAIN) — Emigration and immigration
RAMÍREZ COPEIRO DEL VILLAR, Jesús
Ingleses en Valverde : aspecto humano de la minería inglesa en la provincia de Huelva / por Jesús Ramírez Copeiro del Villar. — Huelva : Jesús Ramírez Copeiro del Villar, Granada no.13, Valverde de Camino (Huelva), 1985. — 281p. — *Bibliography: p279-281*

VANCOUVER (B.C.) — Economic conditions
CHADNEY, James G
The Sikhs of Vancouver / by James G. Chadney. — New York : AMS Press, c1984. — p. cm. — (Immigrant communities & ethnic minorities in the United States & Canada ; 1). — *Includes index. — Bibliography: p*

VANCOUVER (B.C.) — History
Vancouver past : essays in social history : Vancouver centennial issue of BC Studies / edited by Robert A. J. McDonald and Jean Barman. — Vancouver : University of Columbia Press, 1986. — 327p. — *Includes bibliographic references*

VANCOUVER (B.C.) — Social conditions
CHADNEY, James G
The Sikhs of Vancouver / by James G. Chadney. — New York : AMS Press, c1984. — p. cm. — (Immigrant communities & ethnic minorities in the United States & Canada ; 1). — *Includes index. — Bibliography: p*

Vancouver past : essays in social history : Vancouver centennial issue of BC Studies / edited by Robert A. J. McDonald and Jean Barman. — Vancouver : University of Columbia Press, 1986. — 327p. — *Includes bibliographic references*

VANCOUVER (B.C.) — Social conditions — History
Working lives : Vancouver 1886-1986 / The Working Lives Collective. — Vancouver : New Star Books, 1985. — 211p. — *References: p202-208*

VANDALISM — Great Britain
WILSON, John
Violence and vandalism / John Wilson. — Oxford : Education Data Surveys, 1986. — 56p

VÄNSTERPARTIET KOMMUNISTERNA
HERMANSSON, Jörgen
Kommunism på svenska? : SKP/VPK:s idéutveckling efter Komintern / Jörgen Hermansson. — Uppsala : Uppsala universitet ; Stockholm : Distributed by Almqvist & Wiksell, 1984. — 388p. — (Acta Universitatis Upsaliensis). — *With English summary. — Doktorsavhandling framlagd vid Uppsala universitet 1984*

VANUATU — Census, 1946
NEW HEBRIDES. Bureau of Statistics
Detailed census of part of native population in sexes and estimated figures of other areas in which census has not yet been taken. — Vila : British Residence, 1946. — 2 leaves

VANUATU — Population — Statistics
NEW HEBRIDES. Bureau of Statistics
Detailed census of part of native population in sexes and estimated figures of other areas in which census has not yet been taken. — Vila : British Residence, 1946. — 2 leaves

Report of the Vanuatu urban census 1986. — [Port Vila?] : National Planning and Statistics Office, 1986. — 157p

VANUATU — Statistics
NEW HEBRIDES. Bureau of Statistics
Facts and figures about the New Hebrides Condominium. — Vila : the Bureau, 1976. — [4]p

NEW HEBRIDES. Bureau of Statistics
Facts and figures about the New Hebrides Condominium. — Vila : the Bureau, 1977. — [4]p

VÄRMLANDS FOLKBLAD
ENGWALL, Lars
Från vag vision till komplex organisation : en studie av Värmlands Folkblads ekonomiska och organisatoriska utveckling / Lars Engwall. — Uppsala : Universitet ; Stockholm : distributed by Almqvist & Wiksell, 1985. — 448p. — *With English summary and abstract. — Bibliography: p415-432*

VATICAN CITY — Foreign relations — Great Britain
CHADWICK, Owen
Britain and the Vatican during the Second World War / Owen Chadwick. — Cambridge : Cambridge University Press, 1986. — [ix,644]p. — (The Ford lectures). — *Includes bibliography and index*

VATICAN COUNCIL (2nd : 1962-1965)
ZABŁOCKI, Janusz
Kościół i świat współczesny : wprowadzenie do soborowej konstytucji pastoralnej "Gaudium et spes" / Janusz Zabłocki. — 2nd ed. — Warszawa : Ośrodek Dokumentacji i Studiów Społecznych, 1986. — 457p

VATICAN COUNCIL (2ND: 1962-1965)
CASANOVA, Antoine
Le concile vingt ans après : essai d'approche marxiste / Antoine Casanova. — Paris : Messidor, [1985]. — 263p

VATTENFALL
VATTENFALL
Annual report / Vattenfall, Sweden. — Vällingby : Vattenfall, 1984-. — *Annual*

VEGETABLES — England — London — Marketing
DAVIS, Keith
London's wholesale fruit and vegetable markets : a survey of the four east London markets / Keith Davis, Tim Catchpole. — [London] : London Research Centre, 1986. — 65p. — (Reviews and studies series ; no.31). — *Re-issue of the Greater London Council's study report of February 1986 with an appendix added giving a detailed analysis of the survey data including comparisons between the markets*

A new site for Covent Garden Market : report on a feasibility study for the Nine Elms area. — [London] : Covent Garden Market Authority, 1964. — 34leaves. — [21]folded leaves

VENDETTA — Scotland — History
BROWN, Keith M.
Bloodfeud in Scotland, 1573-1625 : violence, justice and politics in an early modern society / Keith M. Brown. — Edinburgh : John Donald, c1986. — x, 299p. — *Bibliography: p 285-293*

VENEZUELA — Armed Forces — Appropriations and expenditures
LOONEY, Robert E
The political economy of Latin American defense expenditures : case studies of Venezuela and Argentina / Robert E. Looney. — Lexington, Mass. : Lexington Books, c1986. — xxii, 325 p.. — *Includes index. — Bibliography: p. [309]-314*

VENEZUELA — Defenses
LOONEY, Robert E
The political economy of Latin American defense expenditures : case studies of Venezuela and Argentina / Robert E. Looney. — Lexington, Mass. : Lexington Books, c1986. — xxii, 325 p.. — *Includes index. — Bibliography: p. [309]-314*

VENEZUELA — Description and travel
DAUXION LAVAYSSE, Jean François
A statistical, commercial and political description of Venezuela, Trinidad, Margarita, and Tobago : containing various anecdotes and observations, illustrative of the past and present state of these interesting countries; from the French of M. Lavaysse : with an introduction and explanatory notes, by the editor [E. B. i.e. Edward Blaquiere]. — Westport, Conn. : Negro Universities Press, 1969. — xxxix,479p. — *Translation of: Voyages aux îles de Trinidad, de Tabago, de la Marguerite, and dans diverses parties de Venezuela. — Reprint of the 1820 edition*

VENEZUELA — Foreign relations — Germany
HERWIG, Holger H
Germany's vision of empire in Venezuela, 1871-1914 / Holger H. Herwig. — Princeton, N.J. : Princeton University Press, c1986. — xii, 285 p.. — *Includes index. — Bibliography: p. [247]-272*

VENEZUELA — History — Anglo-German Blockade, 1902
HERWIG, Holger H
Germany's vision of empire in Venezuela, 1871-1914 / Holger H. Herwig. — Princeton, N.J. : Princeton University Press, c1986. — xii, 285 p.. — *Includes index. — Bibliography: p. [247]-272*

VENEZUELA — Politics and government — 1958-
ARROYO TALAVERA, Eduardo
Elections and negotiation : the limits of democracy in Venezuela / Eduardo Arroyo Talavera. — [New York, N.Y.] : Garland Pub., 1986. — 450 p.. — (Outstanding theses from the London School of Economics and Political Science). — *Spine title: The limites of democracy in Venezuela, 1958-1981. — Thesis (Ph. D.)--University of London, 1983. — Bibliography: p. 421-450*

VENSTRE (Norway)
BJØRGUM, Jorunn
Venstre og kriseforliket : landbrukspolitikk og parlamentarisk spill 1934-1935 / Jorunn Bjørgum. — 2. utgave. — Oslo : Universitetsforlaget, 1978. — 191p. — *First published 1970. — Bibliography: p164*

Venstres hundre år / Ottar Grepstad, Jostein Nerbøvik (red.). — Oslo : Gyldendal Norsk Forlag, 1984. — 304p

VENTURE CAPITAL
PENCE, Christine Cope
How venture capitalists make investment decisions / by Christine Cope Pence. — Ann Arbor, Mich. : UMI Research Press, c1982. — x, 138 p.. — (Research for business decisions ; no. 53). — *: A revision of the author's thesis, University of California, Irvine, 1981. — Includes index. — Bibliography: p. [133]-135*

VENTURE CAPITAL — European Economic Community countries
ADAM INTERNATIONAL BV
European venture capital pilot scheme : final report. — Luxembourg : Office for Official Publications of the European Communities, 1984. — iii,87p. — (EUR ; 9082). — *Series title: Innovation. — Bibliography: p69-70*

VENTURE CAPITAL — Great Britain
CLARK, Rodney
Venture capital in Britain, America and Japan / Rodney Clark. — London : Croom Helm, c1987. — [144]p

VENTURE CAPITAL — Japan
CLARK, Rodney
Venture capital in Britain, America and Japan / Rodney Clark. — London : Croom Helm, c1987. — [144]p

VENTURE CAPITAL — United States
CLARK, Rodney
Venture capital in Britain, America and Japan / Rodney Clark. — London : Croom Helm, c1987. — [144]p

VENTURE CAPITAL — United States — Addresses, essays, lectures
Entrepreneurship, intrapreneurship, and venture capital : the foundation of economic renaissance / edited by Robert D. Hisrich. — Lexington, Mass. : Lexington Books, c1986. — xiv, 144 p.. — *Includes bibliographies. — Contents: Importance of entrepreneurship in economic development / Howard H. Stevenson and William A. Sahlman -- Role of entrepreneurship in economic development / Donald L. Sexton -- Building indigenous companies / Raymond W. Smilor -- Entrepreneurship and intrapreneurship / Robert D. Hisrich -- The role of venture capital in the economic renaissance of an area / Barry M. Davis -- Entrepreneurs, angels, and economic renaissance / William E. Wetzel, Jr*

VENTURE CAPITAL — United States — Congresses
Technology venturing : American innovation and risk-taking / edited by Eugene B. Konecci and Robert Lawrence Kuhn. — New York : Praeger, c1985. — p. cm. — *Derived from a conference held at the University of Texas at Dallas, Feb. 5-7, 1984. — Includes index*

VERBAL ABILITY
ROSS, Percy
Ask for the moon--and get it! : the secret to getting what you want by knowing how to ask / Percy Ross with Dick Samson. — New York : Putnam, c1987. — 219 p.

VERBAL BEHAVIOR
PAIVIO, Allan
Mental representations : a dual coding approach / Allan Paivio. — New York : Oxford University Press ; Oxford : Clarendon Press, 1986. — x, 322p. — (Oxford psychology series ; no. 9). — *Includes index. — Bibliography: p.277-305*

VERENIGDE OOST-INDISCHE COMPAGNIE
KORTE, J. P. de
De jaarlijkse financiele verantwoording in de VOC : Verenigde Oostindische Compagnie / door J. P. de Korte. — Leiden : Martinus Nijhoff, 1984. — xiv,95p,76 leaves. — (Werken uitgegeven door de Vereeniging het Nederlandsch Economisch-Historisch Archief ; 17)

VERLAG ERNST WASMUTH — History
VERLAG ERNST WASMUTH
Einhundert Jahre Wasmuth-Bücher. — Tübingen : Ernst Wasmuth, [1975?]. — 16p

VESTNIK MOSKOVSKOGO UNIVERSITETA — Indexes
MOSKOVSKII GOSUDARSTVENNYI UNIVERSITET. Nauchnaia biblioteka im. A. M. Gor'kogo
Sistematicheskii ukazatel' k "Vestniku Moskovskogo universiteta" : (1946-1966) / sostavitel': M. K. Simon. — Moskva : Izd-vo Moskovskogo universiteta, 1969. — 493p

VETERANS — Education — Law and legislation — United States — History
HYMAN, Harold M
American singularity : the 1787 Northwest Ordinance, the 1862 Homestead and Morrill Acts, and the 1944 G.I. Bill / Harold M. Hyman. — Athens : University of Georgia Press, c1986. — x, 95 p.. — (The Richard B. Russell lectures ; no. 5). — Includes index. — Bibliography: p. [77]-90

VETERANS — Tennessee
BAILEY, Fred Arthur
Class and Tennessee's Confederate generation / by Fred Arthur Bailey. — Chapel Hill : University of North Carolina Press, c1987. — x, 205 p. — (The Fred W. Morrison series in Southern studies). — Includes index. — Bibliography: p. [191]-196

VICE-PRESIDENTIAL CANDIDATES — United States — Biography
FERRARO, Geraldine
Ferraro, my story / Geraldine A. Ferraro, with Linda Bird Francke. — Toronto ; New York : Bantam Books, 1985. — 340 p., [24] p. of plates. — Includes index

VICEROYS — India — Biography
ZIEGLER, Philip
Mountbatten : the official biography / Philip Ziegler. — London : Collins, 1985. — 786p,[48]p of plates. — Geneal.table on lining papers. — Bibliography: p751-756. — Includes index

VICO, GIAMBATTISTA — Contributions in political science
HADDOCK, B. A. (Bruce Anthony)
Vico's political thought / B.A. Haddock. — Swansea : Mortlake Press, 1986. — vii,238p. — Bibliography: p230-231

VICTIMS OF CRIME — Great Britain
SMITH, Susan J.
Crime, space and society / Susan J. Smith. — Cambridge : Cambridge University Press, 1986. — xii,228p. — (Cambridge human geography). — Bibliography: p197-221. — Includes index

VICTIMS OF CRIMES
CRIMINOLOGICAL RESEARCH CONFERENCE (16th : 1984 : Strasbourg)
Research on victimisation : Strasbourg 26-29 November 1984 : Secretariat report / prepared by the Directorate of Legal Affairs. — Strasbourg : Council of Europe, 1986. — 165p. — Bibliography: p123-157

VICTIMS OF CRIMES — Congresses
CRIMINOLOGICAL RESEARCH CONFERENCE (16th : 1984)
Regaining a sense of community and order : general report of the 16th Criminological Research Conference of the European Committee on Crime Problems : research on victimization / Jan J. M. Dijk. — The Hague : Research and Documentation Centre, Ministry of Justice, 1985. — [21]p. — ([Reports, papers, articles] ; 80). — Bibliography: p[21]

CRIMINOLOGICAL RESEARCH CONFERENCE (16th : 1984)
Research on victimisation : reports presented to the sixteenth Criminological Research Conference (1984). — Strasbourg : Council of Europe, 1985. — 168p. — (Collected studies in criminological research ; v.23). — On cover: European Committee on Crime Problems

VICTIMS OF CRIMES — Government policy — Canada
ROCK, Paul
A view from the shadows : the Ministry of the Solicitor General of Canada and the making of the justice for victims of crime initiative / Paul Rock. — Oxford : Clarendon, 1986. — xix,396p. — (Oxford socio-legal studies)

VICTIMS OF CRIMES — Services for — Great Britain
MAGUIRE, Mike
The effects of crime and the work of victims support schemes / Mike Maguire and Claire Corbett. — Aldershot : Gower, c1987. — xiii,276p. — (Cambridge studies in criminology ; 56). — Bibliography: p263-276

VICTIMS OF CRIMES — Council of Europe countries
CRIMINOLOGICAL RESEARCH CONFERENCE (16th : 1984 : Strasbourg)
Research on victimisation : Strasbourg 26-29 November 1984 : Secretariat report / prepared by the Directorate of Legal Affairs. — Strasbourg : Council of Europe, 1986. — 165p. — Bibliography: p123-157

VICTIMS OF CRIMES — England — Liverpool (Merseyside)
JONKER, Joan
Victims of violence / Joan Jonker. — London : Fontana, 1986. — 223p

VICTIMS OF CRIMES — Netherlands
DIJK, J. J. M. van
Compensation by the state or by the offender : the victim's perspective / Jan J. M. van Dijk. — The Hague : Research and Documentation Centre, Ministry of Justice, 1985. — 22p. — ([Reports, papers, articles] ; 78). — Paper presented at the Conference on Victims, Restitution and Compensation in the Criminal Justice System, Cambridge, U.K. 13-16 August 1984. — Bibliography: p20-22

VICTIMS OF CRIMES — United States
YIN, Peter
Victimization and the aged / Peter Yin. — Springfield, Ill. : Thomas, c1985. — ix, 211 p.. — Includes indexes. — Bibliography: p. 175-188

VICTORIA, Queen of Great Britain
WEINTRAUB, Stanley
Victoria : biography of a queen / Stanley Weintraub. — London : Allen & Unwin, 1987. — [704]p. — Includes index

VICTORIA — Governors — Biography
ROBERTS, Shirley
Charles Hotham : a biography / Shirley Roberts. — Carlton : Melbourne University Press ; Ashford : HB Sales [distributor], 1985. — xi,201p. — Bibliography: p193-195. — Includes index

VIDEO DISC PLAYERS — Design and construction
GRAHAM, Margaret B. W.
RCA and the VideoDisc : the business of research / Margaret B.W. Graham. — Cambridge : Cambridge University Press, 1986. — xiv,258p. — (Studies in economic history and policy : the United States in the twentieth century). — Includes index

VIDEO DISCS
GRAHAM, Margaret B. W.
RCA and the VideoDisc : the business of research / Margaret B.W. Graham. — Cambridge : Cambridge University Press, 1986. — xiv,258p. — (Studies in economic history and policy : the United States in the twentieth century). — Includes index

HENDLEY, Tony
Videodiscs,compact discs and digital optical disk systems : an introduction to the technologies and the systems and their potential for information storage,retrieval and dissemination / by Tony Hendley. — Hatfield : Cimtech, 1985

VIDEO DISPLAY TERMINALS — Hygienic aspects
GRANDJEAN, E.
Ergonomics in computerized offices / Etienne Grandjean. — London : Taylor & Francis, 1987. — [225]p. — Includes bibliography and index

VIDEO RECORDINGS
GREAT BRITAIN. Parliament. House of Commons. Library. Research Division
"Video nasties" : a background to the Video Recordings Bill, 1983-84 / [Jane Fiddick]. — [London] : the Division, 1983. — 29p. — (Background paper ; no.130)

VIDEOTEX SYSTEMS
ROGERS, Everett M
Communication technology / Everett M. Rogers. — New York : Free Press, c1986. — p. cm. — (Series in communication technology and society). — Includes index. — Bibliography: p

VIENNA (AUSTRIA) — History — Siege, 1683 — Bibliography
HOSKINS, Janina W
Victory at Vienna : the Ottoman siege of 1683 : a historical essay and a selective list of reading materials / Janina W. Hoskins. — Washington : European Division, Library of Congress, 1983. — 44p

VIET CONG
The Viet Cong infrastructure : a background paper. — Saigon : U.S. Mission in Vietnam, 1970. — 48p. — Cover title. — Includes bibliographical references

VIETNAM — Economic conditions
DACY, Douglas C.
Foreign aid, war, and economic development : South Vietnam, 1955-1975 / Dougxlas C. Dacy. — Cambridge : Cambridge University Press, 1986. — xix,300p. — Bibliography: p283-293. — Includes index

FFORDE, Adam
The limits of national liberation : problems of economic management in the Democratic Republic of Vietnam, with a statistical appendix / Adam Fforde and Suzanne H. Paine. — London : Croom Helm, c1987. — 245p. — Bibliography: p237-246

NGUYEN, Anh Tuan
South Vietnam, trail and experience : a challenge for development / by Nguyen Anh Tuan. — Athens, Ohio : Ohio University Center for International Studies, Center for Southeast Asian Studies, 1986. — p. cm. — (Monographs in international studies. Southeast Asia series ; no. 80). — Bibliography: p

POPKIN, Samuel L.
The rational peasant : the political economy of rural society in Vietnam / Samuel L. Popkin. — Berkeley ; London : University of California Press, 1979. — xxi,307p. — Bibliography: p.269-287. — Includes index

TAN, Teng Lang
Economic debates in Vietnam : issues and problems in reconstruction and development (1975-84) / by Tan Teng Lang. — Singapore : Institute of Southeast Asian Studies, 1985. — vi, 60 p.. — (Research notes and discussions paper / Institute of Southeast Asian Studies ; no. 55). — Bibliography: p. 57-60

VIETNAM — Economic policy
FFORDE, Adam
The limits of national liberation : problems of economic management in the Democratic Republic of Vietnam, with a statistical appendix / Adam Fforde and Suzanne H. Paine. — London : Croom Helm, c1987. — 245p. — Bibliography: p237-246

NGUYEN, Anh Tuan
South Vietnam, trail and experience : a challenge for development / by Nguyen Anh Tuan. — Athens, Ohio : Ohio University Center for International Studies, Center for Southeast Asian Studies, 1986. — p. cm. — (Monographs in international studies. Southeast Asia series ; no. 80). — Bibliography: p

VIETNAM — Economic policy
continuation

TAN, Teng Lang
Economic debates in Vietnam : issues and problems in reconstruction and development (1975-84) / by Tan Teng Lang. — Singapore : Institute of Southeast Asian Studies, 1985. — vi, 60 p.. — (Research notes and discussions paper / Institute of Southeast Asian Studies ; no. 55). — *Bibliography: p. 57-60*

VIETNAM — Foreign relations — Canada

LEVANT, Victor
Quiet complicity : Canadian involvement in the Vietnamese War / Victor Levant. — Toronto : Between The Lines, 1986. — 322p. — *Bibliography: p297-313*

VIETNAM — Foreign relations — United States

KAHIN, George McTurnan
Intervention : how America became involved in Vietnam / by George McT. Kahin. — 1st ed. — New York : Knopf, c1986. — xii, 550 p.. — *"A portion of this work was originally published in Pacific affairs, winter 1979-1980"--T.p. verso. — Includes index. — Bibliography: p. [433]-538*

VIETNAM — Government publications — Bibliography

Thu-tich vê ân-phâm-công Viêt-Nam : 1960-1969 = Bibliography on Vietnamese official publications : 1960-1969. — Saigon : Directorate of National Archives and Libraries, [1970]. — [134]p. — *In Vietnamese, French and English*

VIETNAM — History — 1945-1975

DELLINGER, David
Vietnam revisited : from covert action to invasion to reconstruction / David Dellinger. — Boston, MA : South End Press, c1986. — vi, 232 p.. — *Bibliography: p. 221-232*

LEVANT, Victor
Quiet complicity : Canadian involvement in the Vietnamese War / Victor Levant. — Toronto : Between The Lines, 1986. — 322p. — *Bibliography: p297-313*

VIETNAM — History — 1975-

DELLINGER, David
Vietnam revisited : from covert action to invasion to reconstruction / David Dellinger. — Boston, MA : South End Press, c1986. — vi, 232 p.. — *Bibliography: p. 221-232*

VIETNAM — Politics and government

POPKIN, Samuel L.
The rational peasant : the political economy of rural society in Vietnam / Samuel L. Popkin. — Berkeley ; London : University of California Press, 1979. — xxi,307p. — *Bibliography: p.269-287. — Includes index*

VIETNAM — Politics and government — 20th century

THAI, Quang Trung
Collective leadership and factionalism : an essay on Ho Chi Minh's legacy / Thai Quang Trung. — Singapore : Institute of Southeast Asian Studies, c1985. — viii, 136 p.. — *Bibliography: p. [113]-136*

VIETNAM — Politics and government — 1945-1975

DACY, Douglas C.
Foreign aid, war, and economic development : South Vietnam, 1955-1975 / Dougxlas C. Dacy. — Cambridge : Cambridge University Press, 1986. — xix,300p. — *Bibliography: p283-293. — Includes index*

KAHIN, George McTurnan
Intervention : how America became involved in Vietnam / by George McT. Kahin. — 1st ed. — New York : Knopf, c1986. — xii, 550 p.. — *"A portion of this work was originally published in Pacific affairs, winter 1979-1980"--T.p. verso. — Includes index. — Bibliography: p. [433]-538*

NGUYEN, Anh Tuan
South Vietnam, trail and experience : a challenge for development / by Nguyen Anh Tuan. — Athens, Ohio : Ohio University Center for International Studies, Center for Southeast Asian Studies, 1986. — p. cm. — (Monographs in international studies. Southeast Asia series ; no. 80). — *Bibliography: p*

VIETNAM — Rural conditions

POPKIN, Samuel L.
The rational peasant : the political economy of rural society in Vietnam / Samuel L. Popkin. — Berkeley ; London : University of California Press, 1979. — xxi,307p. — *Bibliography: p.269-287. — Includes index*

SCOTT, James Cameron
The moral economy of the peasant : rebellion and subsistence in Southeast Asia / James C. Scott. — New Haven ; London : Yale University Press, 1976 [i.e. 1977]. — ix,246p. — *Published in the United States: 1976. — Includes index*

VIETNAMESE CONFLICT, 1961-1975

NIXON, Richard
No more Vietnams / Richard Nixon. — London : W.H. Allen, 1986, c1985. — [240]p. — *Originally published: New York : Arbor House, 1985*

SUMMERS, Harry G
Vietnam war almanac / Harry G. Summers, Jr. — New York, N.Y. : Facts on File, c1985. — x, 414 p. — *Includes index. — Bibliography: p. 369-382*

THOMPSON, Sir Robert Grainger Ker
No exit from Vietnam / Sir Robert G. K. Thompson. — London : Chatto & Windus, 1969. — 208p

VIETNAMESE CONFLICT, 1961-1975 — Influence

HELLMANN, John
American myth and the legacy of Vietnam / John Hellmann. — New York : Columbia University Press, 1986. — xiv, 241p. — *Includes bibliographical references and index. — Bibliography: p. [225]-233*

VIETNAMESE CONFLICT, 1961-1975 — Literature and the war

HELLMANN, John
American myth and the legacy of Vietnam / John Hellmann. — New York : Columbia University Press, 1986. — xiv, 241p. — *Includes bibliographical references and index. — Bibliography: p. [225]-233*

VIETNAMESE CONFLICT, 1961-1975 — Motion pictures and the war

HELLMANN, John
American myth and the legacy of Vietnam / John Hellmann. — New York : Columbia University Press, 1986. — xiv, 241p. — *Includes bibliographical references and index. — Bibliography: p. [225]-233*

VIETNAMESE CONFLICT, 1961-1975 — personal narratives

To bear any burden : the Vietnam war and its aftermath in the words of Americans and southeast Asians / Al Santoli. — London : Abacus, 1986,c1985. — xxii,367p. — *Includes chronology of events, p[337]-352*

VIETNAMESE CONFLICT, 1961-1975 — Personal narratives, American

LEWIS, Lloyd B
The tainted war : culture and identity in Vietnam War narratives / Lloyd B. Lewis. — Westport, Conn. : Greenwood Press, 1985. — xvi, 193 p. — (Contributions in military studies ; no. 44). — *Includes index. — Bibliography: p. [177]-186*

VIETNAMESE CONFLICT, 1961-1975 — Protest movements

HAASKEN, Georg
Protest in der Klemme : soziale Bewegungen in der Bundesrepublik / Georg Haasken, Michael Wigbers. — Frankfurt am Main : Verlag Neue Kritik, 1986. — 212p. — *Bibliography: p203-[212]*

VIETNAMESE CONFLICT, 1961-1975 — Protest movements — United States

BARKAN, Steven E.
Protesters on trial : criminal justice in the Southern civil rights and Vietnam antiwar movements / Steven E. Barkan. — New Brunswick, N.J. : Rutgers University Press, c1985. — p. cm. — (Crime, law, and deviance series). — *Includes index. — Bibliography: p*

VIETNAMESE CONFLICT, 1961-1975 — Psychological aspects

LEWIS, Lloyd B
The tainted war : culture and identity in Vietnam War narratives / Lloyd B. Lewis. — Westport, Conn. : Greenwood Press, 1985. — xvi, 193 p.. — (Contributions in military studies ; no. 44). — *Includes index. — Bibliography: p. [177]-186*

VIETNAMESE CONFLICT, 1961-1975 — Social aspects — United States

LEWIS, Lloyd B
The tainted war : culture and identity in Vietnam War narratives / Lloyd B. Lewis. — Westport, Conn. : Greenwood Press, 1985. — xvi, 193 p.. — (Contributions in military studies ; no. 44). — *Includes index. — Bibliography: p. [177]-186*

VIETNAMESE CONFLICT, 1961-1975 — United States

CABLE, Larry E.
Conflict of myths : the development of American counterinsurgency doctrine and the Vietnam War / Larry E. Cable. — New York : New York University Press, 1986. — p. cm. — *Includes index. — Bibliography: p*

DIETZ, Terry
Republicans and Vietnam, 1961-1968 / Terry Dietz. — Westport, Conn. ; London : Greenwood Press, 1986. — xv, 184p. — (Contributions in political science ; no. 146). — *Includes index. — Bibliography: p.[173]-177*

GIBBONS, William Conrad
The U.S. government and the Vietnam war : executive and legislative roles and relationships / William Conrad Gibbons ; with a new preface by the author. — Princeton, N.J. : Princeton University Press, [1986-. — p. cm. — *"Prepared for the Committee on Foreign Relations, United States Senate, by the Congressional Research Service, Library of Congress.". — : "Originally published by the U.S. Government Printing Office in April 1984"--T.p. verso. — Includes bibliographical references and indexes. — Contents: pt. 1. 1945-1960 -- pt. 2. 1961-1964*

HELLMANN, John
American myth and the legacy of Vietnam / John Hellmann. — New York : Columbia University Press, 1986. — xiv, 241p. — *Includes bibliographical references and index. — Bibliography: p. [225]-233*

KAHIN, George McTurnan
Intervention : how America became involved in Vietnam / by George McT. Kahin. — 1st ed. — New York : Knopf, c1986. — xii, 550 p.. — *"A portion of this work was originally published in Pacific affairs, winter 1979-1980"--T.p. verso. — Includes index. — Bibliography: p. [433]-538*

VILLAGES — Botswana — Statistics

1981 population and housing census : guide to the villages and towns of Botswana. — Gaborone : Central Statistics Office, [1983]. — 1 vol.(various pagings)

VILLAGES — England — Planning
PARSONS, D. J.
Rural gentrification : the influence of rural settlement planning policies / D. J. Parsons. — [Brighton : University of Sussex, 1980]. — 36p. — (University of Sussex Research Papers in Geography)

VILLAGES — Great Britain
WILLETT, Rodney
Village ventures : rural communities in action / written for Rural Voice by Rodney Willett. — London : Published in association with Rural Voice by Bedford Square Press/NCVO, 1985. — 44p

VILLAGES — Japan
FUKUTAKE, Tadashi
[Nihon no nōson. English]. Rural society in Japan / Tadashi Fukutake ; translated by the staff of the Japan Interpreter. — Tokyo : University of Tokyo Press, c1980. — xii, 218 p. — Translation of: Nihon no nōson. 2nd ed., 1978. — Includes index

VILLAGES — Mexico
FRIEDRICH, Paul
The princes of Naranja : an essay in anthrohistorical method / by Paul Friedrich. — 1st ed. — Austin : University of Texas Press, 1986. — p. cm. — Bibliography: p

VILLAGES — Portugal — History
O'NEILL, Brian Juan
Social inequality in a Portuguese hamlet : land, late marriage and bastardy 1870-1978 / Brian Juan O'Neill. — Cambridge : Cambridge University Press, 1987. — xix,431p. — (Cambridge studies in social anthropology ; 63) . — Translation of: Proprietarios, lavradores e jornaleiras. — Bibliography: p401-418. — Includes index

VILLAGES — Soviet Union
Sotsial'no-ekonomicheskii potentsial sela : problemy razvitiia i ispol'zovaniia / otv. redaktor L. V. Nikiforov. — Moskva : Nauka, 1986. — 205p. — (Problemy sovetskoi ekonomiki)

VILLAGES — Tanzania
Villagers, villages, and the state in modern Tanzania / edited by R.G. Abrahams. — Cambridge : African Studies Centre, 1985. — ii,167p. — (Cambridge African monograph ; 4) . — Includes bibliographies

VILNIUS (LITHUANIA) — Ethnic relations — Addresses, essays, lectures
KAHAN, Arcadius
Essays in Jewish social and economic history / Arcadius Kahan ; edited by Roger Weiss ; with an introduction by Jonathan Frankel. — Chicago : University of Chicago Press, 1986. — xx, 208 p.. — Includes bibliographical references and index

VIOLENCE
AHN, Chung-si
Social development and political violence : a cross-national causal analysis / by Chung-si Ahn. — [Seoul?] : Seoul National University Press, c1981. — xviii, 191 p.. — (International studies series ; no. 3). — Includes indexes. — Bibliography: p. [175]-182

The Anthropology of violence / edited by David Riches. — Oxford : Basil Blackwell, 1986. — [224]p. — Includes index

BROWN, Seyom
The causes and prevention of war / by Seyom Brown. — New York : St. Martin's Press, c1987. — xiv, 274 p.. — Includes bibliographies and index

POYNER, Barry
Violence to staff : a basis for assessment and prevention / Barry Poyner, Caroline Warne ; [for the] Health and Safety Executive. — [London : H.M.S.O., 1986]. — 16p

Unhappy families : clinical and research perspectives on family violence / [edited by] Eli H. Newberger, Richard Bourne. — Littleton, Mass. : PSG, c1985. — p. cm. — Includes index

The Violent society / edited by Eric Moonman ; foreword by Lord Scarman. — London : Cass, 1987. — 167p

VIOLENCE — Prediction — North America
Dangerousness : probability and prediction, psychiatry and public policy / edited by Christopher D. Webster, Mark H. Ben-Aron, Stephen J. Hucker. — Cambridge : Cambridge University Press, 1985. — xiii,236p. — Includes bibliographies and index

VIOLENCE — Research
Violence against women : a critique of the sociobiology of rape / edited by Suzanne R. Sunday and Ethel Tobach. — New York : Gordian Press, 1985. — p. cm. — (A Genes and gender monograph). — Includes index

VIOLENCE — Canada — History
TORRANCE, Judy Margaret Curtis
Public violence in Canada, 1867-1982 / Judy M. Torrance. — Kingston : McGill-Queen's University Press, c1986. — xii, 270 p.. — Includes index. — Bibliography: p. [245]-260

VIOLENCE — Great Britain
WILSON, John
Violence and vandalism / John Wilson. — Oxford : Education Data Surveys, 1986. — 56p

Women, violence and social control / edited by Jalna Hanmer and Mary Maynard. — Basingstoke : Macmillan, 1987. — xi,213p. — (Explorations in sociology ; 23). — Conference proceedings. — Bibliography: p193-209. — Includes index

VIOLENCE — India
PANDEY, Sachchidanand
Naxal violence : a socio-political study / Sachchidanand Pandey. — Delhi : Chanakya Publications, 1985. — vi,156p. — Bibliography: p144-153

VIOLENCE — Kentucky — History
MONTELL, William Lynwood
Killings : folk justice in the Upper South / William Lynwood Montell. — Lexington, KY : University Press of Kentucky, 1986. — p. cm. — Includes index. — Bibliography: p

VIOLENCE — Mexico — Morelos — Case studies
ROMANUCCI-ROSS, Lola
Conflict, violence, and morality in a Mexican village / Lola Romanucci-Ross ; with a new afterword. — University of Chicago Press ed. — Chicago : University of Chicago Press, 1986. — ix, 222 p.. — : Reprint. Originally published: Palo Alto, Calif. : National Press Books, 1973. — Bibliography: p. 218-222

VIOLENCE — Netherlands
Democratie en geweld : probleemanalyse naar aanleiding van de gebeurtenissen in Amsterdam op 30 april 1980. — 's-Gravenhage : Staatsuitgeverij, 1980. — 32 p.. — (Rapporten aan de regering ; 20). — Prepared by the Wetenschappelijke Raad voor het Regeringsbeleid. — Includes bibliographical references

VIOLENCE — Northern Ireland — History
MACDONALD, Michael, 19---
Children of wrath : political violence in Northern Ireland / Michael MacDonald. — Cambridge : Pality, 1986. — [220]p. — Includes index

VIOLENCE — Southern States — History — 19th century
RABLE, George C
But there was no peace : the role of violence in the politics of Reconstruction / George C. Rable. — Athens : University of Georgia Press, c1984. — xiii, 257 p. — Includes index. — Bibliography: p. [247]-251

VIOLENCE — Spain — Basque provinces
REINARES, Fernando
Violencia y politica en Euskadi / Fernando Reinares. — Bilbao : Désclee de Brouwer, 1984. — 254p. — Bibliography: p251-252

VIOLENCE — Tennessee — History
MONTELL, William Lynwood
Killings : folk justice in the Upper South / William Lynwood Montell. — Lexington, KY : University Press of Kentucky, 1986. — p. cm. — Includes index. — Bibliography: p

VIOLENCE — United States
GOLDSTEIN, Jeffrey H
Aggression and crimes of violence / Jeffrey H. Goldstein. — 2nd ed. — New York : Oxford University Press, 1986. — ix, 230p. — Includes index. — Bibliography: p.[189]-215

VIOLENCE — United States — Congresses
Values in conflict : Blacks and the American ambivalence toward violence / edited by Charles A. Frye. — Washington, D.C. : University Press of America, c1980. — iii, 169 p.. — Includes bibliographies and index

VIOLENCE IN HOSPITALS — Great Britain
GREAT BRITAIN. Health Services Advisory Committee
Violence to staff in the health services. — [London : H.M.S.O., 1987]. — 12p

VIOLENCE IN MOTION PICTURES
BJÖRKQVIST, Kaj
Violent films, anxiety and aggression : experimental studies of the effect of violent films on the level of anxiety and aggressiveness in children / Kaj Björkqvist. — Helsinki : Societas Scientiarum Fennica, 1985. — 75p. — (Commentationes Scientarum Socialium ; 30). — Bibliography: p71-75

VIOLENCE IN SPORTS — History
GUTTMANN, Allen
Sports spectators / Allen Guttmann. — New York : Columbia University Press, 1986. — viii, 236 p.. — Includes index. — Bibliography: p. [187]-217

VIOLENCE IN SPORTS — Argentina
ROMERO, Amílcar G.
Deporte, violencia y politica : (crónica negra 1958-1983) / Amílcar G. Romero. — Buenos Aires : Editor Centro de América Latina, 1985. — 136p. — (Biblioteca Política Argentina ; 118). — Bibliography: p[137]

VIOLENCE IN TELEVISION
Violence on television : report of the Wyatt Committee. — London : British Broadcasting Corporation, 1987. — 23p

VIOLENCE IN TELEVISION — Cross-cultural studies
Television and the aggressive child : a cross-national comparison / edited by L. Rowell Huesmann, Leonard D. Eron. — Hillsdale, N.J. : L. Erlbaum Associates, 1986. — p. cm. — Includes bibliographies and index

VIOLENCE IN TELEVISION — United States
VOORT, T. H. A. van der
Television violence : a child's-eye view / T.H.A. van der Voort. — Amsterdam ; Oxford : North-Holland, 1986. — xiii, 440p. — (Advances in psychology ; 32). — Includes indexes. — Bibliography: p 403-423

VIOLENT CRIMES — Denmark
Gadevold / af Flemming Balvig...[et al.]. — [København] : Det Kriminalpraeventive Råd, [1985]. — 173p

VIOLENT CRIMES — England — Liverpool (Merseyside)
JONKER, Joan
Victims of violence / Joan Jonker. — London : Fontana, 1986. — 223p

VIOLENT CRIMES — Great Britain
BROWN, Roberts, 1949-
Social workers at risk : the prevention and management of violence / Robert Brown, Stanley Bute, Peter Ford. — Basingstoke : Macmillan, 1986. — xii,145p. — (Practical social work). — *Bibliography: p135-139.* — *Includes index*

VIOLENT CRIMES — United States — Prevention
CURRIE, Elliott
Confronting crime : an American challenge / Elliott Currie. — 1st ed. — New York : Pantheon Books, c1985. — viii, 326 p.. — *Includes index.* — *Bibliography: p. 279-316*

VIRGINIA — History — Colonial period, ca. 1600-1775
BREEN, T. H
Tobacco culture : the mentality of the great Tidewater planters on the eve of Revolution / T.H. Breen. — Princeton, N.J. : Princeton University Press, c1985. — xvi, 216p. — *Includes index*

VIRGINIA — History — Revolution, 1775-1783 — Causes — Case studies
BREEN, T. H
Tobacco culture : the mentality of the great Tidewater planters on the eve of Revolution / T.H. Breen. — Princeton, N.J. : Princeton University Press, c1985. — xvi, 216p. — *Includes index*

VIRGINIA — Rural conditions
LINK, William A
A hard country and a lonely place : schooling, society, and reform in rural Virginia, 1870-1920 / William A. Link. — Chapel Hill : University of North Carolina Press, c1986. — p. cm. — (The Fred W. Morrison series in Southern studies). — *Includes index.* — *Bibliography: p*

VISICALC (COMPUTER PROGRAM)
THOMAS, Tom E.
Financial decision making with VisiCalc and SuperCalc / Tom E. Thomas. — Englewood Cliffs, N.J. : Prentice-Hall, 1985. — p. cm. — *Includes index*

VISITS OF STATE — Germany (West) — Addresses, essays, lectures
Bitburg in moral and political perspective / edited by Geoffrey H. Hartman. — Bloomington : Indiana University Press, c1986. — xvi, 284 p.. — *Bibliography: p. [281]-282*

VISITS OF STATE — United States
BHUTTO, Zulfikar Ali
Prime Minister Zulfikar Ali Bhutto : speeches and statements during visit to the United States of America in September 1973. — [Islamabad : Department of Films and Publications for the Ministry of Foreign Affairs, 1973. — 87p

PLISCHKE, Elmer
Diplomat in chief : the President at the summit / Elmer Plischke. — New York ; Eastbourne : Praeger, 1986. — x,518p. — *Bibliography: p490-494*

VISUAL PERCEPTION
ARNHEIM, Rudolf
Art and visual perception : a psychology of the creative eye / Rudolf Arnheim. — New version, expanded and rev. ed. — Berkeley : University of California Press, [1974]. — x, 508 p., [2] leaves of plates. — *Includes index.* — *Bibliography: p. [487]-501*

VISUALIZATION
KOSSLYN, Stephen Michael
Image and mind / Stephen Michael Kosslyn. — Cambridge, Mass. : Harvard University Press, 1980. — p. cm. — *Includes index.* — *Bibliography: p*

VITAMIN D
GREAT BRITAIN. Working Party on Fortification of Food with Vitamin D
Rickets and osteomalacia / report of the Working Party on Fortification of Food with Vitamin D. Committee on Medical Aspects of Food Policy. — London : H.M.S.O., 1980. — xii,66p. — (Report on health and social subjects ; 19). — At head of title: Department of Health and Social Security. — *Bibliography: p54-66*

VITORIA (SPAIN) — History
RIVERA BLANCO, Antonio
Situación y comportamiento de la clase obrera en Vitoria (1900-1915) / Antonio Rivera Blanco. — [Bibao] : Servicio Editorial, Universidad del Vasco, [1985]. — 195p

VIVISECTION — England — History
LANSBURY, Coral
The old brown dog : women, workers, and vivisection in Edwardian England / Coral Lansbury. — Madison, Wis. : University of Wisconsin Press, 1985. — p. cm. — *Includes index*

VIZCAYA (SPAIN) — Economic conditions
Los grandes problemas infraestructurales de Bizkaia / [realizado por] Jon Imanol Azua Mendía...[et al.]. — Bilbao : Diputación Foral de Vizcaya, 1983-. — v. <1>

VLACHS *See* Aromanians

VLASOV, A. A.
ANDREYEV, Catherine
Vlasov and the Russian Liberation Movement : Soviet reality and émigré theories / Catherine Andreyev. — Cambridge : Cambridge University Press, 1987. — xiv,251p. — (Soviet and East European studies). — *Bibliography: p224-239. Includes index*

VOCATIONAL EDUCATION
HAYES, Chris
Research and development to improve education and training effectiveness : report prepared at the request of the Manpower Services Commission / Chris Hayes, Alan Anderson, Nickie Fonda, Institute of Manpower Studies. — [Sheffield : Manpower Services Commission, 1985]. — vi,95p

VOCATIONAL EDUCATION — Evaluation
HUNTING, Gordon
Evaluating vocational training programs : a practical guide / Gordon Hunting, Manuel Zymelman, Martin Godfrey. — Washington, D.C. : The World Bank, 1986. — vii,96p

VOCATIONAL EDUCATION — Colombia — Case studies
PSACHAROPOULOS, George
Diversified secondary education and development : evidence from Colombia and Tanzania / George Psacharopoulos and William Loxley. — Baltimore : Johns Hopkins University Press for the World Bank, 1985. — x,243p. — *Bibliographical references: p229-238*

VOCATIONAL EDUCATION — Great Britain
HAYES, Chris
Research and development to improve education and training effectiveness : report prepared at the request of the Manpower Services Commission / Chris Hayes, Alan Anderson, Nickie Fonda, Institute of Manpower Studies. — [Sheffield : Manpower Services Commission, 1985]. — vi,95p

KEEP, Ewart
Britain's attempts to create a national vocational educational and training system : a review of progress / Ewart Keep. — Coventry : University of Warwick, 1987. — 37p. — (Warwick papers in industrial relations ; no.16) . — *Bibliography: p32-37*

LAW, Bill
The pre-vocational franchise : organising community-linked education for adult and working life / Bill Law. — London : Harper & Row, 1986. — ix,199p. — (Harper education series). — *Bibliography: p193-196.* — *Includes index*

PRAIS, S. J.
Educating for productivity : comparisons of Japanese and English schooling and vocational preparation / S. J. Prais. — London : National Institute of Economic and Social Research, 1986. — 33,[10]p. — (Discussion paper / National Institute of Economic and Social Research ; no.121)

VOCATIONAL EDUCATION — Ireland
MCCARTHY, J. R.
Study while you work : vocational courses in further education for 16-19 year old employees / J. R. McMarthy, R. H. McDowell and C. J. McIlheney. — Belfast : Northern Ireland Council for Educational Research, 1985. — vi,59p. — (Publications of the Northern Ireland Council for Educational Research ; 31). — *Bibliography: p.59*

VOCATIONAL EDUCATION — Japan
PRAIS, S. J.
Educating for productivity : comparisons of Japanese and English schooling and vocational preparation / S. J. Prais. — London : National Institute of Economic and Social Research, 1986. — 33,[10]p. — (Discussion paper / National Institute of Economic and Social Research ; no.121)

VOCATIONAL EDUCATION — Tanzania — Case studies
PSACHAROPOULOS, George
Diversified secondary education and development : evidence from Colombia and Tanzania / George Psacharopoulos and William Loxley. — Baltimore : Johns Hopkins University Press for the World Bank, 1985. — x,243p. — *Bibliographical references: p229-238*

VOCATIONAL GUIDANCE — European Economic Community countries
MCMULLEN, I. R.
Guidance and orientation in secondary schools / I. R. McMullen. — Luxembourg : Office for Official Publications of the European Communities, 1977. — 60p. — (Education series / Commission of the European Communities ; no.2)

VOCATIONAL GUIDANCE — Great Britain — Management
RANSON, Stewart
The management of change in the careers service / by Stewart Ranson and Peter Ribbins ; with Lesley Chesterfield and Tony Smith. — Birmingham : INLOGOV, 1986. — 200p

VOCATIONAL INTERESTS
LABAND, David N
The roots of success : why children follow in their parents' career footsteps / by David N. Laband, Bernard F. Lentz. — New York : Praeger, 1985. — p. cm. — *Includes index.* — *Bibliography: p*

VOCATIONAL INTERESTS — California — Stanford — Case studies
KATCHADOURIAN, Herant A
Careerism and intellectualism among college students / Herant A. Katchadourian, John Boli ; with the assistance of Nancy Olsen, Raymond F. Bacchetti, Sally Mahoney. — 1st ed. — San Francisco : Jossey-Bass Publishers, 1985. — xxvi, 324 p.. — (The Jossey-Bass higher education series). — *Includes indexes.* — *Bibliography: p. 311-316*

VOCATIONAL QUALIFICATIONS — Great Britain
Review of vocational qualifications in England and Wales : a report by the working group, April 1986 / [for the] Manpower Services Commission. — London : H.M.S.O., 1986. — 61p. — *Chairman: H. G. De Ville*

VOCATIONAL REHABILITATION
STACE, Sheila
Vocational rehabilitation for women with disabilities / Sheila Stace. — Geneva : International Labour Office, 1986. — viii,38p. — *Bibliography: p33-36*

VOCATIONAL REHABILITATION — European Economic Community countries
CROXEN, Mary
Overview : disability and employment / report by Dr. Mary Croxen. — Luxembourg : Office for Official Publications of the European Communities, 1984. — 1v.(various pagings). — *At head of title page: Commission of the European Communities*

Journal of the community network of rehabilitation centres. — Brussels : Commission of the European Communities, 1986-. — *6 per year*

VOGEL, JULIUS
DALZIEL, Raewyn
Julius Vogel : business politician / by Raewyn Dalziel. — Auckland : Auckland University Press, 1986. — 368p

VOLCANISM
Disaster prevention and mitigation : a compendium of current knowledge. — Geneva : New York
V.1: Volcanological aspects. — 1976. — iv,38p. — *Bibliographical references: p33-38.* "UNDRO/28/75"

VOLGGER, FRIEDL
VOLGGER, Friedl
Mit Südtirol am Scheideweg : erlebte Geschichte / Friedl Volgger. — Innsbruck : Haymon, 1984. — 319p

VOLTA ALUMINIUM COMPANY
Essays from the Ghana-Valco renegotiations, 1982-85 / edited by Fui S. Tsikata. — [Accra] : Ghana Publishing Corporation, 1986. — viii,163p. — *Bibliographies*

VOLTAIRE — Biography
MASON, Haydn Trevor
Voltaire : a biography / Haydn Mason. — Baltimore, Md. : Johns Hopkins University Press, 1981. — xiii, 194 p., [8] p. of plates. — *Includes index. — Bibliography: p. 186-187*

VOLUNTARISM
ROBICHAUD, Jean-Bernard
Voluntary action : provincial policies and practices / Jean-Bernard Robichaud. — Ottawa : Canadian Council on Social Development, 1985. — iv,100p. — *Bibliography: p66-67*

VOLUNTARISM — England — Liverpool (Merseyside)
CLAY, Dave
Voluntary issues: a conference review / compiled by Dave Clay, Mike Walsh [and] Hilary Jones. — Liverpool : Liverpool Community Organisations Committee, 1985. — 8p

VOLUNTARISM — England — London
Introducing community and voluntary services. — Croydon : Community and Voluntary Services, Croydon Social Services Dept., 1986. — 18p

VOLUNTARISM — Great Britain
UNELL, Judith
Opportunity costs : government funding and volunteering by unemployed young people / Judith Unell. — Leicester : National Youth Bureau, 1984. — 24p. — *Bibliography: p24*

VOLUNTARISM — Great Britain — Bibliography
HARRIS, Margaret
Organising voluntary agencies : a guide through the literature / Margaret Harris and David Billis. — [London] : Bedford Square Press : NCVO, [1986]. — 125p

VOLUNTARISM — Ireland — Directories
Directory of national voluntary organisations, social service agencies and other useful public bodies. — 5th ed. (1985)-. — Dublin (71 Lower Leeson St., Dublin 2) : NSSB, 1985-. — v.. — *Full name of the body: National Social Service Board. — Continues: Directory of social service organisations*

VOLUNTARISM — Mexico
INSTITUTO MEXICANO DEL SEGURO SOCIAL. Unidad de Promoción Voluntaria
Memoria de actividades 1977-1982 = Activities report 1977-1982. — [México] : the Unidad, 1982. — [34p]. — *Text in Spanish and English*

VOLUNTARISM — United States
KAMINER, Wendy
Women volunteering : the pleasure, pain, and politics of unpaid work from 1830 to the present / Wendy Kaminer. — 1st ed. — Garden City, N.Y. : Anchor Press, 1984. — xix, 237 p.. — *Includes index. — Bibliography: p. [227]-228*

Social planning and human service delivery in the voluntary sector / edited by Gary A. Tobin. — Westport, Conn. : Greenwood Press, 1985. — xxx, 290 p.. — (Studies in social welfare policies and programs ; no. 1). — *Includes index. — Bibliography: p. [261]-276*

VOLUNTARISM — United States — Congresses
COMMITTEE ON AN AGING SOCIETY (U.S.)
Productive roles in an older society / Committee on an Aging Society, Institute of Medicine and National Research Council. — Washington, D.C. : National Academic Press, 1986. — vii, 154 p.. — (America's aging). — *"This report ... presents the papers commissioned for the May 1983 Symposium on Unpaid Productive Roles in an Aging Society"--Pref. — Includes bibliographies and index*

VOLUNTARY EUTHANASIA SOCIETY
Voluntary euthanasia : experts debate the right to die / edited by A.B. Downing and Barbara Smoker. — Rev., enl. ed. — London : Peter Owen, c1986. — 303p. — *Originally published as: Euthanasia and the right to death:the case for voluntary euthanasia, 1969. — Bibliography:p302-303*

VOLUNTEER WORKERS IN EDUCATION
ADVISORY COUNCIL FOR ADULT AND CONTINUING EDUCATION
Volunteers in adult education : a research report for the Advisory Council / by Dorothea Hall ; assisted by Ieuan Hughes and Colette Laplace under the direction of Barry Elsey. — Leicester : ACACE, c1983. — viii,132p. — *Bibliography: p109-110*

VOLUNTEER WORKERS IN SOCIAL SERVICE — Northern Ireland
CECIL, Rosanne
Informal welfare : a sociological study of care in Northern Ireland / Rosanne Cecil, John Offer and Fred St. Leger. — Aldershot : Gower, c1987. — vii,166p. — *Bibliography: p154-162. — Includes index*

VOLUNTEER WORKERS IN SOCIAL SERVICE — Pakistan — Layari
HAFEEZ, Sabeeha
Poverty, voluntary organizations, and social change : a study of an urban slum in Pakistan / Sabeeha Hafeez. — 1st ed. — Karachi : Royal Book Co., c1985. — 248 p.. — *Includes index*

VOLUNTEERS — Nicaragua
Brigadista : harvest and war in Nicaragua / edited by Jeffrey Jones. — New York : Praeger, 1986. — xxviii, 227p. — *Includes index*

VOLUNTEERS — United States
Brigadista : harvest and war in Nicaragua / edited by Jeffrey Jones. — New York : Praeger, 1986. — xxviii, 227p. — *Includes index*

VOLVO KALMAR
Volvo Kalmar revisited : ten years of experience / Stefan Agurén [et al.]. — Stockholm : Efficiency and Participation Development Council, 1984. — 107p

VOTERS, REGISTRATION OF — United States
The Voting Rights Act : consequences and implications / edited by Lorn S. Foster. — New York : Praeger, 1985. — p. cm. — *Includes index*

VOTING
Do elections matter? / Benjamin Ginsberg and Alan Stone, editors. — Armonk, N.Y. : M.E. Sharpe, c1986. — 240 p.. — *Includes bibliographies*

GINSBERG, Benjamin
The captive public : how mass opinion promotes state power / Benjamin Ginsberg. — New York : Basic Books, c1986. — xi, 272 p.. — *Includes index. — Bibliography: p. [233]-249*

HOLCOMBE, Randall G
An economic analysis of democracy / Randall G. Holcombe. — Carbondale : Southern Illinois University Press, c1985. — xiii, 269 p.. — (Political and social economy). — *Includes index. — Bibliography: p. 257-266*

VOTING — History
PRZEWORSKI, Adam
Paper stones : a history of electoral socialism / Adam Przeworski and John Sprague. — Chicago : University of Chicago Press, 1986. — vi, 224 p.. — *Includes indexes. — Bibliography: p. [203]-216*

VOTING — British Columbia
BLAKE, Donald E.
Two political worlds : parties and voting in British Columbia / Donald E. Blake, with the collaboration of David J. Elkins and Richard Johnston. — Vancouver : University of British Columbia Press, 1985. — x, 205 p.. — *On spine: 2 political worlds. — Includes bibliographical references and index*

VOTING — Canada
BLAKE, Donald E.
Two political worlds : parties and voting in British Columbia / Donald E. Blake, with the collaboration of David J. Elkins and Richard Johnston. — Vancouver : University of British Columbia Press, 1985. — x, 205 p.. — *On spine: 2 political worlds. — Includes bibliographical references and index*

VOTING — Great Britain
ASSOCIATION OF LIBERAL COUNCILLORS
Knocking on doors : why do we do it?. — Hebden Bridge : Association of Liberal Councillors, [1983]. — 11p. — (ALC activists' guide ; no.3)

BBC newsnight constituency survey : Greenwich survey 21 February 1987. — London : BBC, 1987. — 11p

BLUMLER, Jay G.
Political communication and the young voter : a panel study, 1970-1971, examining the role of election communication in the political socialisation of first time voters / Jay G. Blumler, Denis McQuail and T. J. Nossiter ; report to the Social Science Research Council, October 1975. — [London : Social Science Research Council, 1975]. — 1v. (various pagings). — *Bibliographical references: end of vol.*

VOTING — Great Britain
continuation

BLUMLER, Jay G.
Political communication and the young voter in the general election of February 1974 : a panal study, 1970-1974, examining influences on the political socialisation of young voters between their first and second election campaigns / Jay G. Blumler, Denis McQuail and T. J. Nossiter ; report to the Social Science Research Council, July 1976. — [London : Social Science Research Council, 1976]. — 99 leaves. — *Bibliographical references: p98-99*

MCLEAN, Iain
Consumer's guide to tactical voting / Iain McLean. — London : Centre for Electoral Choice, 1987. — 21p

SCARBROUGH, Elinor
The British electorate twenty years on : reviewing electoral change and election surveys / by Elinor Scarbrough. — Colchester : Department of Government University of Essex, 1986. — 34 p. — (Essex papers in politics and government ; no.35)

VOTING — Great Britain — History — 20th century

MCALLISTER, Ian
The nationwide competition for votes : the 1983 British election / Ian McAllister & Richard Rose. — London : Pinter in association with the Centre for the Study of Public Policy, c1984. — viii,257p. — *Bibliography: p248-254. — Includes index*

VOTING — United States

NEUMAN, W. Russell
The paradox of mass politics : knowledge and opinion in the American electorate / W. Russell Neuman. — Cambridge, Mass. : Harvard University Press, 1986. — 241 p.. — *Includes index. — Bibliography: p. [222]-236*

WALZER, Michael
The politics of ethnicity / Michael Walzer...[et al.]. — Cambridge, Mass. ; London : Belknap Press of Harvard University Press, 1982. — vi,142p. — (Dimensions of ethnicity : Selections from the Harvard Encyclopedia of American ethnic groups). — *Bibliography: p [139]-142*

VOTING — United States — History — Bibliography

The American electorate : a historical bibliography. — Santa Barbara, Calif. : ABC-Clio Information Services, 1983. — xii, 388 p. — (ABC-Clio research guides ; 8). — *Includes indexes. — "This bibliography was conceived and compiled from the periodicals database of the American Bibliographical Center by editors at ABC-Clio Information Services."*

VOYAGES AND TRAVELS

WOOLCOCK, Helen R.
Rights of passage : emigration to Australia in the nineteenth century / Helen R. Woolcock. — London : Tavistock, 1986. — [xv,304]p. — *Includes index*

VUYLSTEKE, JULIUS

VERSCHAEREN, J.
Julius Vuylsteke (1836-1903) : Klavwaard & Geus / J. Verschaeren. — Kortrijk : Van Ghemmert, 1984. — 486p. — *Bibliography: p12-21*

VYGOTSKIĬ, L. S.

WERTSCH, James V
Vygotsky and the social formation of mind / James V. Wertsch. — Cambridge, Mass. : Harvard University Press, 1985. — p. cm. — *Includes index. — Bibliography: p*

VYGOTSKIĬ, LEV SEMENOVICH

Culture, communication and cognition : Vygotskian perspectives / edited by James V. Wertsch. — Cambridge : Cambridge University Press, 1985. — x,379p. — *Bibliographies*

WAGE — Cost-of-living adjustments — United States

HENDRICKS, Wallace E
Wage indexation in the United States : Cola or Uncola? / Wallace E. Hendricks, Lawrence M. Kahn. — Cambridge, MA : Ballinger Pub. Co., [1985]. — p. cm. — *Includes index. — Bibliography: p*

WAGE PAYMENT SYSTEMS — Legal status, laws, etc. — Great Britain

GREAT BRITAIN. Parliament. House of Commons. Library. Research Division
Wages Bill (Bill 70 of 1985-86) / Fiona Poole, Celia Nield. — [London] : the Division, 1986. — 35p. — (Reference sheet ; no.86/6). — *Bibliographical references: p33-35*

WAGE PAYMENT SYSTEMS — Belgium

Wage payment systems : surveys : Belgium. — Dublin : European Foundation for the Improvement of Living and Working Conditions, 1982. — 1v (various pagings)

WAGE PAYMENT SYSTEMS — European Economic Community countries

Wage payment systems : survey : consolidated report. — Dublin : European Foundation for the Improvement of Living and Working Conditions, 1982. — 1v (various pagings)

WAGE PAYMENT SYSTEMS — France

Wage payment systems : surveys : France. — Dublin : European Foundation for the Improvement of Living and Working Conditions, 1982. — 1v (various pagings)

WAGE PAYMENT SYSTEMS — Germany (West)

Wage payment systems : surveys : Federal Republic of Germany. — Dublin : European Foundation for the Improvement of Living and Working Conditions, 1982. — 1v (various pagings). — *Bibliography: p55-56*

WAGE PAYMENT SYSTEMS — Great Britain

GRAYSON, David
Progressive payment systems / David Grayson. — London : Work Research Unit, 1984. — 37p. — (WRU occasional paper ; 28). — *Bibliography: p36-37*

Wage payment systems : surveys : United Kingdom. — Dublin : European Foundation for the Improvement of Living and Working Conditions, 1982. — 1v (various pagings). — *Bibliography: p95-96*

WAGE PAYMENT SYSTEMS — Italy

Wage payment systems : surveys : Italy. — Dublin : European Foundation for the Improvement of Living and Working Conditions, 1982. — 1v (various pagings)

WAGE PAYMENT SYSTEMS — Luxembourg

Wage payment systems : surveys : Luxembourg. — Dublin : European Foundation for the Improvement of Living and Working Conditions, 1982. — 1v (various pagings)

WAGE-PRICE POLICY

HOLDEN, K.
The economics of wage controls / K. Holden, D.A. Peel and J.L. Thompson. — London : Macmillan, 1987. — [200]p. — *Includes index*

WAGE-PRICE POLICY — Congresses

Economic and social partnership and incomes policy = : Pacto social e política de rendimentos / edited by Aníbal A. Cavaco Silva. — Lisboa : Faculdade de Ciências Humanas da Universidade Católica Portuguesa, c1984. — 304 p.. — *English, French, and Portuguese. — Papers and comemntary presented at the Conference on "Economic and Social Partnership and Incomes Policy" organized by the Austrian Embassy in Portugal and the Faculty of Social Sciences of the Portuguese Catholic University, held Mar. 15-16, 1983, in Lisbon. — Includes bibliographical references*

WAGE-PRICE POLICY — History

Wage restraint and the control of inflation : an international survey / edited by Beth Bilson. — London : Croom Helm, c1987. — 190p

WAGE-PRICE POLICY — Pennsylvania

PERRIN, Suzanne M.
Comparable worth and public policy : the case of Pennsylvania / by Suzanne M. Perrin. — Philadelphia, Pa : Industrial Research Unit, University of Pennsylvania, 1985. — viii,123p. — (Labor Relations and Public Policy Series ; No.29)

WAGES — Netherlands — Statistics

NETHERLANDS. Centraal Bureau voor de Statistiek
Loonstructuuronderzoek : verdiende lonen van werknemers in de nijverheid en dienstensector. — s-Gravenhage : Staatsuitgeverij, 1983. — 52p. — *Title on back cover: Survey into the structure of earnings 1979: earnings of employees (manual and non-manual) in industry and services*

NETHERLANDS. Centraal Bureau voor de Statistiek
Loonstructuuronderzoek 1976 : verdiende lonen van werknemers in transport-, opslag-, communicatiebedrijven en overige dienstverlening. — s-Gravenhage : Staatsuitgeverij, 1981. — 56p. — *Title on back cover: Survey into the structure of earnings 1976: earnings of employees (manual and non-manual) in transport, storage, communication and other services*

WAGES

CARTTER, Allan Murray
Theory of wages nd employment / by Allan M. Cartter. — Homewood, Ill. : Irwin, 1959. — xii,193p

FOSTER, N.
Public and private sector pay : some further results / N. Foster, S. G. B. Henry and C. Trinder. — London : National Institute of Economic and Social Research, 1986. — 19p. — (Discussion paper / National Institute of Economic and Social Research ; no.120). — *Bibliography: p19*

GAUSDEN, Robert
Real wages and employment : a survey of studies based on the Granger-Causality testing approach / Robert Gausden. — London : National Institute of Economic and Social Research, 1986. — 40p. — (Discussion paper / National Institute of Economic and Social Research ; no.123). — *Bibliography: p39-40*

NEWELL, A.
The Phillips curve is a real wage equation / A. Newell and J. Symons. — London : Centre for Labour Economics, London School of Economics, 1986. — 32p. — (Discussion paper / London School of Economics and Political Science. Centre for Labour Economics ; no.246). — *Bibliography: p21-22*

NEWELL, A.
Wages and employment between the wars / A. Newell and J. S. V. Symons. — London : Centre for Labour Economics, London School of Economics, 1986. — 36p. — (Discussion paper / London School of Economics and Political Science. Centre for Labour Economics ; no.257)

OSWALD, A. J.
A theory of non-contingent wage contracts / A. Oswald. — London : Centre for Labour Economics, London School of Economics, 1986. — 36p. — (Discussion paper / London School of Economics and Political Science. Centre for Labour Economics ; no.266). — *Bibliography: p34-36*

PLOEG, Frederick van der
Monopoly unions, investment and employment : benefits of contingent wage strategies / F. van der Ploeg. — London : Centre for Labour Economics, London School of Economics, 1987. — 18p. — (Discussion paper / London School of Economics and Political Science. Centre for Labour Economics ; no.280). — *Bibliography: p17-18*

WAGES continuation

PUBLIC ADMINISTRATION SERVICE
Introduction and administration of position classification and pay plans / [prepared for the United Nations Secretariat by the Public Administration Service]. — New York : United Nations, 1976. — xxxiii, 159 p. — ([Document - United Nations] ; ST/ESA/ser.E/5). — "United Nations publication. Sales no. E.77.II.H.1.". — Bibliography: p. 155-159

SHACKLETON, J. R.
Wages and unemployment / J. R. Shackleton. — Buckingham : University of Buckingham. Employment Research Centre, 1987. — 44p. — (Occasional papers in employment studies / University of Buckingham. Employment Research Centre ; no.8). — Bibliography: p40-43

WORSWICK, G. D. N.
Real wages and employment / G. D. N. Worswick [and] R. Gansden. — London : National Institute of Economic and Social Research, 1986. — 53p. — (Discussion paper / National Institute of Economic and Social Research ; no.122). — Bibliography: p[52-53]

WAGES — Clothing workers — Great Britain — History — 20th century

CANNING, David
A report on the Department of Employment's study 'Wages floors in the clothing industry 1950-81' / by David Canning and Roger Tarling ; commissioned by the National Union of Tailors and Garment Workers. — London (16 Charles Square W1 6HP) : [The Union?], [1985?]. — 21p. — Cover title

WAGES — Cost-of-living adjustments

SACHS, Jeffrey
Wage indexation, flexible exchange rates, and macro-economic policy / by Jeffrey Sachs. — [Washington, D.C. : Board of Governors of the Federal Reserve System], 1979. — 36p. — (International finance discussion papers ; no.137). — Bibliographical references: p34-36

WAGES — Econometric models
Efficiency wage models of the labor market / edited by George A. Akerlof and Janet L. Yellen. — Cambridge : Cambridge University Press, 1986. — ix,178p. — Includes bibliographies

WAGES — Effect of business cycles on

MICHIE, Jonathan
Wages in the business cycle : an empirical and methodological analysis / Jonathan Michie. — London : Pinter, 1987. — [256]p. — Includes bibliogrphy and index

WAGES — Government policy — Mexico
MEXICO. Secretaría del Trabajo y Previsión Social
1973, salarios...un movimiento de justicia. — [México : the Secretaría, 1973]. — 96p

WAGES — Hairdressing — Great Britain
A cut below the rest : pay and conditions in hairdressing / Dominic Byrne...[et al.]. — London : Low Pay Unit, 1987. — 38p

WAGES — Hispanic Americans — Addresses, essays, lectures
Hispanics in the U.S. economy / edited by George J. Borjas, Marta Tienda. — Orlando : Academic Press, 1985. — p. cm. — Includes index. — Bibliography: p

WAGES — Law and legislation — Belgium
FÉDERATION DES ENTREPRISES DE BELGIQUE
Protection de la rémunération des travailleurs : saisie et cession. — Bruxelles : the Fédération, [ca.1979]. — 94p

WAGES — Law and legislation — Great Britain

DAVIDSON, Fraser
A guide to the Wages Act 1986 / Fraser P. Davidson. — London : Financial Training, 1986. — [vi],136p. — Includes the text of the Wages Act 1986

GREAT BRITAIN. Parliament. House of Commons. Library. Research Division
Wages Bill (Bill 70 of 1985-86) / Fiona Poole, Celia Nield. — [London] : the Division, 1986. — 35p. — (Reference sheet ; no.86/6). — Bibliographical references: p33-35

SUTER, Erich
Cashless pay and deductions : implications of the Wages Act 1986 / by Erich Suter and Phil Long. — London : Institute of Personnel Management, 1987. — vii,95p. — Bibliography: p95

WAGES — Mathematical models

LINDBECK, Assar
Cooperation, harassment and involuntary unemployment / by Assar Lindbeck and Dennis D. Snower. — Stockholm : Institute for International Economic Studies, University of Stockholm, 1985. — 52p. — (Seminar Paper / Stockholms Universitet. Institutet för internationell ekonomi ; No.321). — Bibliography: p52

WAGES — Medical personnel — England

ROGERS, D. A.
Labour cost differentials / [D. A. Rogers]. — [Croydon : South East Thames Regional Health Authority, ca.1977]. — [3]leaves

WAGES — Metal workers — Germany (West)

BAHNMÜLLER, Reinhard
Der Streik : Tarifkonflikt um Arbeitszeitverkürzung in der Metallindustrie 1984 / Reinhard Bahnmüller. — Hamburg : VSA-Verlag, 1985. — 204p. — Bibliography: p202-204

WAGES — Minimum wage

STARR, Gerald Frank
Minimum wage fixing : an international review of practices and problems / Gerald Starr. — Geneva : International Labour Office, 1981. — xi,203p. — Includes bibliographical references

WAGES — Minimum wage — Great Britain
Wages councils : a submission to government. — London (Room 463, Church House, Dean's Yard, Westminster, SW1P 3N2) : Industrial and Economic Affairs Committee, 1985. — 14p. — (Working papers ; 19)

WAGES — Printers — Germany (West)

HEINE, Werner
Ein Tabu fällt : Kampf der Drucker um Arbeitszeitverkürzung und Lohnstruktur / Werner Heine ; mit ein Vorwort von Erwin Ferlemann. — Köln : Bund-Verlag, 1986. — 159p

WAGES — Public utilities

FOSTER, N.
Public and private sector pay : some further results / N. Foster, S. G. B. Henry and C. Trinder. — London : National Institute of Economic and Social Research, 1986. — 19p. — (Discussion paper / National Institute of Economic and Social Research ; no.120). — Bibliography: p19

WAGES — Public utilities — Great Britain
Public sector pay trends : a review. — London : Incomes Data Services, 1986. — 51 leaves

RAHMAN, Nasreen
Council non-manual workers and low pay / Nasreen Rahman. — London : Low Pay Unit, 1986. — 32p. — (Low pay pamphlet ; no.41)

WAGES — Statistical methods

GROOTAERT, Christiaan
The role of employment and earnings in analyzing levels of living / Christiaan Grootaert. — Washington D.C. : The World Bank, 1986. — xiv,278p. — (LSMS working papers ; no.27). — Bibliographical references: p269-278

WAGES — Statistics
Incomes from work : between equity and efficiency. — Geneva : International Labour Office, 1987. — viii,169p. — (World labour report ; 3). — Bibliography: p165-169

WAGES — Statistics — Sources
Statistical sources and methods. — Geneva : International Labour Office
V.2: Employment, wages and hours of work (establishment surveys). — 1987. — vii,241p. — Includes bibliographical references. — A technical guide to series published in the Bulletin of Labour Statistics and the Year Book of Labour Statistics

WAGES — Women — England — London

PITCHER, Jane
Women and low pay : initiatives / Jane Pitcher. — Hackney : Research and Intelligence Section, Chief Executive's Office, London Borough of Hackney, 1985. — [26p]. — (Research note / Hackney. Chief Executive's Office. Research and Intelligence Section ; 11). — At Head of cover title: Research in Hackney. — Formerly Working note 20

WAGES — Women — France

EUVRARD, Françoise
Mères de famille : coûts et revenus de lâctivité professionnelle / [étude...réalisée par Françoise Euvrard...Marie-Gabrielle David et Kristof Starzek. — [Paris] : Centre dÉtude des Revenus et des Coûts, 1985. — 163p. — (Documents du Centre dÉtude des Revenus et des Coûts ; no.75)

WAGES — Women — Great Britain

CRAIG, Christine, 1921—
Payment structures and smaller firms : women's employment in segmented labour markets / by Christine Craig, Elizabeth Garnsey, Jill Rubery. — London : Department of Employment, [1985?]. — 109p. — (Research paper / Department of Employment ; no.48)

WAGES — Women — Great Britain — History

MORRIS, Jenny
Women workers and the sweated trades : the origins of minimum wage legislation / Jenny Morris. — Aldershot : Gower, 1986. — [256]p. — Includes bibliography

WAGES — Youth — European Economic Community countries

MARSDEN, David, 19——
Wage differential between young and adults and its relation with youth unemployment / by David Marsden. — Luxembourg : Office for Official Publications of the European Communities, 1985. — 96p. — (Programme of research and actions on the development of the labour market). — At head of title: Commission of the European Communities

WAGES — Youth — Great Britain

MARSDEN, David, 19——
Wage differential between young and adults and its relation with youth unemployment / by David Marsden. — Luxembourg : Office for Official Publications of the European Communities, 1985. — 96p. — (Programme of research and actions on the development of the labour market). — At head of title: Commission of the European Communities

WILLMORE, Ian
The future of the Wages Councils : arguments against abolition or the exclusion of young people / Ian Willmore. — London : Youthaid, 1985. — 7 leaves. — (MP's briefing paper ; no.5)

WAGES — Asia — Congresses
Wage determination in Asia and the Pacific : the views of employers' organisations : reports and documents submitted to an ILO/DANIDA regional seminar, (Singapore, 8-12 October 1979). — Geneva : International Labour Office, 1980. — ii,169p. — (Labour-management relations series ; 58)

WAGES — Australia

PISSARIDES, Christopher A.
Real wages and unemployment in Australia / C. Pissarides. — London : Centre for Labour Economics, London School of Economics, 1987. — 39p. — (Discussion paper / London School of Economics and Political Science. Centre for Labour Economics ; no.286). — *Bibliography: p38-39*

Wage fixation in Australia / edited by John Niland. — Sydney ; London : Allen & Unwin, 1986. — [270]p. — *Includes bibliography and index*

WAGES — Australia — Tasmania

TASMANIA. Commonwealth Bureau of Census and Statistics. Tasmanian Office
Labour, wages and prices. — Hobart : [the Office], 1970/71-1980/81. — *Annual*

WAGES — Caribbean Area — Congresses

REGIONAL SEMINAR ON WAGE DETERMINATION FOR CARIBBEAN COUNTRIES (1978 : Kingston, Jamaica)
Wage determination in English-speaking Caribbean countries : record of proceedings of, and documents submitted to, ILO/DANIDA regional seminar, (Kingston, Jamaica, 1-7 March 1978). — Geneva : International Labour Office, 1979. — 121p. — (Labour-management relations series ; 57). — *Includes bibliographical references*

WAGES — Cyprus — Statistics

HOUSE, William J.
Wage structure, manpower analysis and the market in Cyprus / by William J. House. — [Nicosia] : Department of Statistics and Research, [1984]. — 78p. — *Bibliography: p77-78*

Statistics of wages, salaries and hours of work / Department of Statistics and Research, Ministry of Finance. — Nicosia : Department of Statistics and Research, 1984-. — *Annual*

WAGES — Denmark — Statistics

Structure of earnings : principal results : 1978/79. — Luxembourg : Office des publications officielles des Communautés européennes. — *Introduction in Community languages, table headings in English and French. Includes complete set of tables on microfiche*
V.5: Danmark. — 1984. — xcix,603p

WAGES — Developing countries

NEWELL, A.
Wages and employment in the O.E.C.D. countries / A. Newell and J. S. V. Symons. — London : Centre of Labour Economics, London School of Economics, 1985. — 60p. — (Discussion paper / London School of Economics and Political Science. Centre for Labour Economics ; no.219). — *Bibliography: p59-60*

Wage policy issues in economic development : the proceedings of a symposium held by the International Institute for Labour Studies at Egelund, Denmark, 23-27 October 1967 / edited by Anthony D. Smith, with a preface by R. W. Cox. — London : Macmillan, 1969. — xv,408p

WAGES — Egypt

HANSEN, Bent
Employment opportunities and equity in a changing economy : Egypt in the 1980s : a labour market approach : report of an inter-agency team financed by the United Nations Development Programme and organised by the International Labour Office / Bent Hansen, Samir Radwan. — Geneva : International Labour Office, 1982. — xviii,292p. — (A WEP study). — *Includes bibliographical references*

STARR, Gerald Frank
Wages in the Egyptian formal sector / Gerald Starr ; with the collaboration of M. A. F. Mongi. — Geneva : International Labour Office, 1983. — 46p. — (Employment opportunities and equity in Egypt ; no.5). — *Bibliographical references: p45-46. — A technical paper of the ILO/UNDP comprehensive employment strategy mission to Egypt, 1980*

WAGES — European Economic Community countries

La flexibilité du travail en Europe : une étude comparative des transformations du rapport salarial dans sept pays de 1973 à 1985 / sous la direction de Robert Boyer. — Paris : Editions La Découverte, 1986. — 330p. — (Economie critique)

WAGES — European Economic Community countries — Statistics — Sources

MARSDEN, David
A guide to current sources of wage statistics in the European Community / by David Marsden ; with the assistance of Lydia Redlbacher. — Luxembourg : Office for Official Publications of the European Communities, 1984. — 169p

WAGES — France

Constat de L'évolution récente des revenus en France (1981-1984) / [étude...réalisée sous la direction de Jean-Etienne Chapron]. — [Paris] : La Documentation française, 1985. — 197p. — (Documents du Centre dÉtude des Revenus et des Coûts ; no.76)

Constat de l'évolution récente des revenus en France 1982-1985 / ...réalisée sous la direction de Jean-Etienne Chapron et Jean-Jacques Malpot. — Paris : La Documentation française, 1986. — 183p. — (Documents du Centre d'étude des revenus et des coûts ; no.82)

MAURICE, Marc
The social foundations of industrial power : a comparison of France and Germany / Marc Maurice, François Sellier, and Jean-Jacques Silvestre ; translated by Arthur Goldhammer. — Cambridge, Mass ; London : MIT Press, c1986. — xi, 292p. — *Translation of: Politique d'éducation et organisation industrielle en France et en Allemagne. — Includes index*

Les revenus des Français : la croissance et la crise (1960-1983) : Quatrième rapport de synthèse / ...établi sous la direction de Alain Foulon. — Paris : Centre dÉtude des Revenus et des Coûts : La Documentation française, [1985]. — 282p. — (Documents du Centre dÉtude des Revenus et des Coûts ; no.77)

Revenus et consommation des Français : le grand tournant / sous la direction de Michel Gaspard. — Paris : La Documentation française, 1985. — 187p. — (Notes et études documentaires ; no.4800)

WAGES — France — Statistics

Structure of earnings 1978/79 : principal results. — Luxembourg : Office des publications officielles des Communautés européennes. — *Introduction in Community languages, table headings in English and French. — Includes complete set of tables on microfiche*
V.2: France. — 1983. — xcix,603p

WAGES — Germany (West)

MAURICE, Marc
The social foundations of industrial power : a comparison of France and Germany / Marc Maurice, François Sellier, and Jean-Jacques Silvestre ; translated by Arthur Goldhammer. — Cambridge, Mass ; London : MIT Press, c1986. — xi, 292p. — *Translation of: Politique d'éducation et organisation industrielle en France et en Allemagne. — Includes index*

WAGES — Germany (West) — Statistics

GERMANY (Federal Republic). Statistisches Bundesamt
Gewerbliche Wirtschaft und Dienstleistungsbereich : Arbeiterverdienste 1972. — Stuttgart : W. Kohlhammer, 1976. — 210p. — (Preise, Löhne, Wirtschaftsrechnungen ; Reihe 17. Gehalts- und Lohnstrukturerhebungen ; 1)

Struture of earnings : principal results : 1978/79. — Luxembourg : Office des publications officielles des Communautés européennes. — *Introduction in community laguages, table headings in English and French*
V.7: BR Deutschland. — 1985. — xcix,603p

WAGES — Great Britain

BEAN, Charles R.
Real wage rigidity and the effect of an oil discovery / C. Bean. — London : Centre for Labour Economics, London School of Economics, 1986. — 15p. — (Discussion paper / London School of Economics and Political Science. Centre for Labour Economics ; no.269). — *Bibliography: p13-15*

BICKERSTAFFE, Rodney
Privatisation and low pay : the impact of government policies / Rodney Bickerstaffe. — Nottingham : Trent Polytechnic, 1984. — 46p. — *Trent Business School. Open lectures on industrial relations: the changing contours of collective bargaining*

BLANCHFLOWER, D. G.
Internal and external influences upon pay settlements : new survey evidence / D. G. Blanchflower and A. J. Oswald. — London : Centre for Labour Economics, London School of Economics, 1987. — 16p. — (Discussion paper / London School of Economics and Political Science. Centre for Labour Economics ; no.275). — *Bibliography: p15-16*

BROSNAN, Peter
Cheap labour : Britain's false economy : the costs of a low wage economy versus a national minimum wage / Peter Brosnan and Frank Wilkinson. — London : Low Pay Unit, 1987. — 44p

CARRUTH, Alan
Wage inflexibility in Britain / A. A. Carruth and A. J. Oswald. — London : Centre for Labour Economics, London School of Economics, 1986. — 51p. — (Discussion paper / London School of Economics and Political Science. Centre for Labour Economics ; no.258). — *Bibliography: p49-51*

FOSTER, N.
Public and private sector pay : some further results / N. Foster, S. G. B. Henry and C. Trinder. — London : Centre for Labour Economics, London School of Economics, 1986. — 21p. — (Discussion paper / London School of Economics and Political Science. Centre for Labour Economics ; no.267). — *Bibliography: p21*

HUGHES, John, 1927-
Nowt for nowt? or who got what, when? / John Hughes. — Nottingham : Institute for Workers Control, 1986. — 14p

LEE, Kevin
An empirical investigation of the frequency of industrial wage change in the U.K. / Kevin Lee. — London : Centre for Labour Economics, London School of Economics, 1987. — 46p. — (Discussion paper / London School of Economics and Political Science ; no.271). — *Bibliography: p44-46*

LISTER, Ruth
'A two-tier society' : response to the consultative document on Wages Councils from the Child Poverty Action Group / Ruth Lister, Fran Bennett and Jo Roll. — London : Child Poverty Action Group, 1985. — 18p

TUC-LABOUR PARTY LIAISON COMMITTEE
Low pay : policies and priorities. — London : TUC : Labour Party, 1986. — 26p. — (Jobs and industry)

WAGES — Great Britain — History
DOWNS, André
General import restrictions and the behaviour of domestic prices and wages : the case of the British General Tariff of 1932 / by André Downs. — 245 leaves. — *PhD (Econ) 1986 LSE. — Leaves 210-245 are appendices*

WAGES — Great Britain — Statistics
Structure of earnings : principal results : 1978/79. — Luxembourg : Office des publications officielles des Communautés européennes. — *Table headings in English and French, introductions in Community languages* Vol.10: United Kingdom. — 1986. — c,603p

WAGES — Hungary
FALUS-SZIKRA, Katalin
The system of incomes and incentives in Hungary / Katalin Falus-Szikra. — Budapest : Akadémiai Kiadó, 1985. — xiii,317p. — *Translated from Hungarian*

WAGES — India — Manufactures — Statistics
INDIA. Labour Bureau
Third occupational wage survey. — Delhi : Controller of Publications, 1984
Report on selected manufacturing industries, 1977-79. — 5v.

WAGES — India — Statistics
INDIA. Labour Bureau
Labour Bureau's labour : master reference book on labour statistics 1984. — Shinla : Labour Bureau, Ministry of Labour and Rehabilitation, 1984. — 471p

WAGES — Japan
NIHON RÔDÔ KYÔKAI
Wages and hours of work. — [Rev. ed]. — Tokyo : Japan Institute of Labour, 1984. — 36p. — (Japanese industrial relations series ; 3)

WAGES — Luxembourg — Statistics
Structure of earnings : principal results : 1978/79. — Luxembourg : Office des publications officielles des Communautés européennes. — *Introduction in Community languages, table headings in English and French. — Includes complete set of tables on microfiche*
V.3 : Luxembourg. — 1984. — xcix,603p

WAGES — Mexico
GREGORY, Peter
The myth of market failure : employment and the labor market in Mexico / Peter Gregory. — Baltimore : Johns Hopkins University Press for the World Bank, 1986. — viii,299p. — *Bibliography: p281-291*

MEXICO. Secretaría del Trabajo y Previsión Social
1973, salarios...un movimiento de justicia. — [México : the Secretaría, 1973]. — 96p

WAGES — Netherlands — Statistics
NETHERLANDS. Centraal Bureau voor de Statistiek
Loonstructuuronderzoek 1974 : verdiende lonen van werknemers in de groot- en kleinhandel, het bank- en verzekeringsbedrijf : algemene resultaten. — s-Gravenhage : Staatsuitgeverij, 1979. — 63p. — *Summary in English. — Title on back cover: Survey into the structure of earnings 1974: earnings of employees (manual and non-manual) in wholesale and retail trade, banking and insurance: general results*

Structure of earnings : principal results : 1978/79. — Luxembourg : Office des publications officielles des Communautés européennes. — *Introduction in Community languages, table headings in English and French*
V.6: Nederland. — 1985. — xcix,603p

Verdiende lonen van werknemers in nijverheid en dienstensector ontleend aan het halfjaarlijks loononderzoek : methodebeschrijving en reeksen 1947-1983. — 's-Gravenhage : Staatsuitgeverij, 1985. — 176p. — *Title on back cover: Earnings of employees (manual and non-manual) in industry and services derived from the half yearly survey on earnings: methodology, series 1947-1983*

WAGES — Norway — Statistics
Lønninger og inntekter 1982 = Wages, salaries and income 1982. — Oslo : Statistisk Sentralbyrå, 1985. — 96p. — (Norges offisielle statistikk ; B536). — *In Norwegian and English*

WAGES — Pacific Area — Congresses
Wage determination in Asia and the Pacific : the views of employers' organisations : reports and documents submitted to an ILO/DANIDA regional seminar, (Singapore, 8-12 October 1979). — Geneva : International Labour Office, 1980. — ii,169p. — (Labour-management relations series ; 58)

WAGES — Scotland
SMAIL, Robin
Breadline Scotland : low pay and inequality north of the Border / Robin Smail. — London : Low Pay Unit, 1986. — 32p

WAGES — Sri Lanka — Statistics
Sample survey of earnings, hours of work : June, 1980. — 8th ed. — Colombo : Department of Labour, 1983. — xi,41p

WAGES — United States
NICKELL, Stephen
The real wage-employment relationship in the United States / S. J. Nickell and J. S. V. Symons. — London : Centre for Labour Economics, London School of Economics, 1986. — 22p. — (Discussion paper / London School of Economics and Political Science. Centre for Labour Economics ; no.264). — *Bibliography: p18-19*

WAGES — Statistics
Structure of earnings : principal results : 1978/79. — Luxembourg : Office des publications officielles des Communautés européennes. — *Introduction in Community languages, table headings in English and French. — Includes complete set of tables on microfiche*
V.4: Belgique/België. — 1984. — xcix,603p

WAGES AND LABOR PRODUCTIVITY
Payment by results. — Geneva : International Labour Office, 1984. — xii,164p. — *Includes bibliographical references*

WAGES BILL 1985-86
GREAT BRITAIN. Parliament. House of Commons. Library. Research Division
Wages Bill (Bill 70 of 1985-86) / Fiona Poole, Celia Nield. — [London] : the Division, 1986. — 35p. — (Reference sheet ; no.86/6). — *Bibliographical references: p33-35*

WALBIRI (AUSTRALIAN PEOPLE)
MUNN, Nancy D.
Walbiri iconography : graphic representation and cultural symbolism in a central Australian society / Nancy D. Munn ; with a new afterword. — Chicago : University of Chicago Press, 1986. — xx, 244 p.. — : Reprint. *Originally published: Ithaca, N.Y. : Cornell University Press, 1973. — Includes index. — Bibliography: p. 235-239*

WALDEGRAVE, WILLIAM
BYNG, Julian
Distant views of William Waldegrave's Oxford speech / Julian Byng, Tony Paterson [and] Graham Pye. — London : Centre for Policy Studies, 1986. — 63p

WALES — Administrative and political divisions
GREAT BRITAIN. Welsh Office
The Local Government Area Changes Regulations 1976 (S.I.no.246). — Cardiff : the Office, 1976. — 5p. — (Circular ; no.76/43)

WALES — History
WILLIAMS, Glanmor
Recovery, reorientation and reformation : Wales, c.1415-1642 / Glanmor Williams. — Oxford : Clarendon Press, 1987. — [500]p. — (The History of Wales ; 3). — *Includes bibliography and index*

WALES — History — To 1536
DAVIES, R. R.
Conquest, coexistence and change : Wales 1063-1415 / by R.R. Davies. — Oxford : Oxford University Press, 1987. — [520]p. — (The History of Wales ; v.2). — *Includes bibliography and index*

WILLIAMS, Glanmor
Recovery, reorientation and reformation : Wales, c.1415-1642 / Glanmor Williams. — Oxford : Clarendon Press, 1987. — [500]p. — (The History of Wales ; 3). — *Includes bibliography and index*

WALES — Industries
SADLER, Peter G.
The Welsh social accounts 1968 : a labour dimension / Peter Sadler, Richard Jarvis. — [Cardiff] ([Crown Building, Cathays Park, Cardiff CF1 3NQ]) : Welsh Council, 1979. — ix,38,7m[15]p. — *Bibliography: p.36-37*

WALES — Industries — Statistics
GREAT BRITAIN. Welsh Office. Economic Services Division
The index of industrial production for Wales, 1975 based : sources and methods. — Cardiff : the Office, [ca.1978]. — 16,[9]p

WALES — Politics and government
JAMES, Arnold J.
Union to Reform : a history of the Parliamentary representation of Wales 1536 to 1832 / Arnold J. James, John E. Thomas. — Llandysul : Gomer Press, 1986. — xxiv,472p. — *Bibliography: p469-[472]*

WALES — Politics and government — 20th century
The National question again : Welsh political identity in the 1980s / edited by John Osmond. — Llandysul : Gomer, 1985. — xlvi,323p

WALES — Population
Genetic and population studies in Wales / edited by Peter S. Harper and Eric Sunderland. — Cardiff : University of Wales Press, 1986. — vii,432p. — *Includes index*

WALES — Rural conditions
WELSH AGRICULTURAL ORGANISATION SOCIETY
Annual report / Welsh Agricultural Organisation Society. — Aberystwyth : [the Society], 1934-1947. — *Annual. — Continued by: Rural Wales: a yearbook of Welsh agricultural cooperation/Welsh Agricultural Organisation Society*

WELSH AGRICULTURAL ORGANISATION SOCIETY
Annual report: rural Wales / Welsh Agricultural Organisation Society. — Aberystwyth : [the Society], 1981-. — *Annual. — Title varies. — Continues: Rural Wales: a yearbook of Welsh agricultural cooperation/Welsh Agricultural Organisation Society*

WELSH AGRICULTURAL ORGANISATION SOCIETY
Rural Wales: a yearbook of Welsh agricultural cooperation / Welsh Agricultural Organisation Society. — Aberystwyth : [the Society], 1949/50-1980. — *Annual. — Continues: Welsh Agricultural Organisation Society. Annual report. — Continued by: Welsh Agricultural Organisation Society. Annual report: rural Wales*

WALES, SOUTH — Gentry — History
HOWELL, David W.
Patriarchs and parasites : the gentry of south-west Wales in the eighteenth century / David W. Howell. — Cardiff : University of Wales Press, 1986. — ix,310p. — *Bibliography: p247-257. — Includes index*

WAŁĘSA, LECH
CRAIG, Mary, 1928-
The crystal spirit : Lech Walesa and his Poland / Mary Craig. — London : Hodder and Stoughton, 1986. — [384p]

WALKER, PETER, 1932-
WALKER, Peter, 1932-
Trust the people : the selected essays and speeches of Peter Walker / edited by Neale Stevenson ; with an introduction by Robert Rhodes James. — London : Collins, 1987. — 206p

WALL STREET
AULETTA, Ken
Greed and glory on Wall Street : the fall of the house of Lehman / Ken Auletta. — Harmondsworth : Penguin Books, 1986. — xi,253p

WALLINGFORD COMMUNITY HOSPITAL
Wallingford Community Hospital research project : report of an ad-hoc Working Party formed to consider detailed proposals for the pattern of medical working appropriate to this new concept. — [Oxford] : Oxford Regional Hospital Board, 1973. — 30, [11]leaves. — *Chairman: A. E. Bennett*

WALLIS AND FUTUNA — Census, 1983
Territoire des îles Wallis et Futuna : résultats du recensement de la population, 15 Février 1983. — Paris : Institut National de la Statistique et des Études Économiques, 1983. — 35,26p

WALLIS AND FUTUNA — Population — Statistics
Territoire des îles Wallis et Futuna : résultats du recensement de la population, 15 Février 1983. — Paris : Institut National de la Statistique et des Études Économiques, 1983. — 35,26p

WALLO (ETHIOPIA) — Politics and government
MCCANN, James
From poverty to famine in northeast Ethiopia : a rural history, 1900-1935 / James McCann. — Philadelphia : University of Pennsylvania Press, 1986. — p. cm. — (University of Pennsylvania Press publications in ethnohistory). — *Includes index. — Bibliography: p*

WALLO (ETHIOPIA) — Rural conditions
MCCANN, James
From poverty to famine in northeast Ethiopia : a rural history, 1900-1935 / James McCann. — Philadelphia : University of Pennsylvania Press, 1986. — p. cm. — (University of Pennsylvania Press publications in ethnohistory). — *Includes index. — Bibliography: p*

WALPOLE, ROBERT
PLUMB, J. H.
Sir Robert Walpole / by J. H. Plumb. — London : Cresset
vol.2: The King's minister. — 1960. — xi,363p

WAMIRA (PAPUA NEW GUINEA PEOPLE)
KAHN, Miriam
Always hungry, never greedy : food and the expression of gender in a Melanesian society / Miriam Kahn. — Cambridge : Cambridge University Press, 1986. — xx,187p. — *Bibliography: p174-181. — Includes index*

WANDSWORTH (LONDON, ENGLAND)
The Changing face of I.T. : intermediate treatment at Hambro House 1976-84 : articles from "Youth in society". — Leicester : National Youth Bureau, 1985. — 12p

WANG, AN
WANG, An
Lessons, an autobiography / An Wang ; with Eugene Linden. — Reading, Mass. : Addison-Wesley, 1986. — p. cm. — *Includes index*

WANG LABORATORIES, INC — History
WANG, An
Lessons, an autobiography / An Wang ; with Eugene Linden. — Reading, Mass. : Addison-Wesley, 1986. — p. cm. — *Includes index*

WAPPING POST
Wapping post. — London : Wapping Post, 1986-1987. — *Irregular*

WAR
BROWN, Seyom
The causes and prevention of war / by Seyom Brown. — New York : St. Martin's Press, c1987. — xiv, 274 p.. — *Includes bibliographies and index*

DYER, Gwynne
War / Gwynne Dyer. — London : Bodley Head, 1986, c1985. — [352]p. — *Includes index*

GOŁĄB, Zdzisław
Wojna a system obronny państwa / Zdzisław Gołąb. — Warszawa : Wydawnictwo Ministerstwa Obrony Narodowej, 1984. — 312p. — *Bibliography: p[311]-312*

MERCER, Derrik
The fog of war : the media on the battlefield / by Derrik Mercer, Geoff Mungham, Kevin Williams ; foreword by Sir Tom Hopkinson. — London : Heinemann, 1987. — xvi,413p

PURI, Rashmi-Sudha
Gandhi on war and peace / Rashmi-Sudha Puri. — New York : Praeger, 1987. — xiv, 244 p.. — *Includes index. — Bibliography: p. 229-238*

SCARRY, Elaine
The body in pain : the making and unmaking of the world / Elaine Scarry. — New York : Oxford University Press, 1985. — p. cm. — *Includes index*

STOESSINGER, John G.
Why nations go to war / John G. Stoessinger. — 4th ed. — Basingstoke : Macmillan Education, 1987, c1985. — xiii,221p. — *Previous ed.: New York : St. Martin's, 1982. — Includes bibliographies*

TIUSHKEVICH, S. A.
Voina i sovremennost' / S. A. Tiushkevich ; otv. redaktor A. A. Babakov. — Moskva : Nauka, 1986. — 211p

The Uncertain course : new weapons, strategies and mind-sets / edited by Carl G. Jacobsen. — Oxford : Published for Stockholm International Peace Research Institute by Oxford University Press, 1987. — [408]p. — *Includes index*

Voenno-teoreticheskoe nasledie V. I. Lenina i problemy sovremennoi voiny / pod redaksiei A. S. Milovidova. — Moskva : Voennoe izd-vo, 1987. — 359p

WAR — History
LUARD, Evan
War in international society / Evan Luard. — London : Tauris, 1986. — [480]p. — *Includes bibliography and index*

WAR — Moral and ethical aspects
BAILEY, Sydney D. (Sydney Dewson)
War and conscience in the nuclear age / Sydney D. Bailey. — Basingstoke : Macmillan, 1987. — xviii,210p. — *Bibliography: p200-202. — Includes index*

WAR — Religious aspects — Islam
CHARNAY, Jean Paul
L'Islam et la guerre : de la guerre juste à la révolution sainte / Jean Paul Charnay. — Paris : Fayard, 1986. — 354p. — *Bibliography: p [341]-342*

WAR AND EMERGENCY LEGISLATION
SINGHVI, Abhishek Manu
The state of emergency and permissible measures of derogation / A. M. Singhvi. — [Bombay] : [Lawasia-Bar Association of India], 1986. — 45p. — *Working paper of the Joint Regional Conference (Asia) of the International Bar Association, Law Asia and Bar Association of India (Bombay, Feb.22-23, 1986) on Topic 2 "International support for protection of human rights". — Includes references, p30-41*

WAR AND EMERGENCY LEGISLATION — Ireland — History
FARRELL, Michael, 1944-
The apparatus of repression : emergency legislation / by Michael Farrell. — Derry, Field Day Theatre, 1986. — 31p. — (A Field Day pamphlet ; no.11). — *Text on inside back cover. — Bibliography: p28-29*

MULLOY, Eanna
Dynasties of coercion : emergency legislation / by Eanna Mulloy. — Derry : Field Day Theatre, 1986. — 26p. — (A Field Day pamphlet ; no.10). — *Text on inside back cover. — Bibliography: p24*

WAR AND EMERGENCY LEGISLATION — Northern Ireland — History
MCGRORY, Patrick J.
Law and the constitution : present discontents : emergency legislation / by Patrick J. McGrory. — Derry : Field Day Theatre, 1986. — 28p. — (A Field Day pamphlet ; no.12). — *Text on inside back cover. — Bibliography: p26*

WAR AND EMERGENCY POWERS
SINGHVI, Abhishek Manu
The state of emergency and permissible measures of derogation / A. M. Singhvi. — [Bombay] : [Lawasia-Bar Association of India], 1986. — 45p. — *Working paper of the Joint Regional Conference (Asia) of the International Bar Association, Law Asia and Bar Association of India (Bombay, Feb.22-23, 1986) on Topic 2 "International support for protection of human rights". — Includes references, p30-41*

WAR AND EMERGENCY POWERS — Great Britain
GREAT BRITAIN. Parliament. House of Commons. Library. Research Division
Emergency powers / [J. B. Poole]. — [London] : the Division, [1979]. — 7p. — (Background paper ; no.66)

WAR AND EMERGENCY POWERS — United States
LOFGREN, Charles A
"Government from reflection and choice" : constitutional essays on war, foreign relations, and federalism / Charles A. Lofgren. — New York : Oxford University Press, c1986. — xviii, 235p. — *Includes index*

WAR AND EMERGENCY POWERS — United States — History
BIGEL, Alan I.
The Supreme Court on emergency powers, foreign affairs, and protection of civil liberties, 1935-1975 / Alan I. Bigel. — Lanham, MD : University Press of America, c1986. — xv, 211 p.. — : *Originally presented as the author's thesis (doctoral--New School for Social Research). — Includes indexes. — Bibliography: p. 194-203*

WAR AND SOCIALISM
STUDIE- EN DOCUMENTATIECENTRUM EMILE VANDERVELDE INSTITUUT
Socialisme, veiligheid en defensie : discussieweekend, Klemskerke, 15-18 november 1980 / algemeen concept : SEVI-werkgroep landsverdediging ; voorzitters discussiegroepen : Leo Peeters...[et al.]. — Brussel : Studie- en Documentatiecentrum Emile Vandervelde Instituut, 1981. — 58p. — (SEVI dossier ; nr.5)

WAR AND SOCIETY
The origins of war in early modern Europe / edited by Jeremy Black. — Edinburgh : John Donald Publishers, 1987. — xiii,271p. — *Bibliography: p261-271*

WAR AND SOCIETY
continuation

The Sociology of war and peace / edited by Colin Creighton and Martin Shaw. — Basingstoke : Macmillan, 1987. — viii,245p. — (Explorations in sociology ; 24). — *Includes bibliographies and index*

WAR CRIME TRIALS — Bibliography
TUTOROW, Norman E
War crimes, war criminals, and war crimes trials : an annotated bibliography and source book / compiled and edited by Norman E. Tutorow with the special assistance of Karen Winnovich. — New York : Greenwood Press, 1986. — xx, 548 p.. — (Bibliographies and indexes in world history ; no. 4). — *Includes index*

WAR CRIME TRIALS — Canada
ZUMBAKIS, S. Paul
Soviet evidence in North American courts : an analysis of problems and concerns with reliance on communist source evidence in alleged war criminal trials / S. Paul Zumbakis. — Toronto : Canadians for Justice, 1986. — 168p

WAR CRIME TRIALS — France
Procès da'près-guerre : "Je suis partout", René Hardy, Orodour-sur-Glane, Oberg et Knochen / présenté et étobli par Jean-Marc Théolleyre. — Paris : Éditions la Découverte, 1985. — 221p

WAR CRIME TRIALS — United States
ZUMBAKIS, S. Paul
Soviet evidence in North American courts : an analysis of problems and concerns with reliance on communist source evidence in alleged war criminal trials / S. Paul Zumbakis. — Toronto : Canadians for Justice, 1986. — 168p

WAR CRIMES — Bibliography
TUTOROW, Norman E
War crimes, war criminals, and war crimes trials : an annotated bibliography and source book / compiled and edited by Norman E. Tutorow with the special assistance of Karen Winnovich. — New York : Greenwood Press, 1986. — xx, 548 p.. — (Bibliographies and indexes in world history ; no. 4). — *Includes index*

WAR CRIMES — Germany
LIFTON, Robert Jay
The Nazi doctors : medical killing and the psychology of genocide / Robert Jay Lifton. — London : Macmillan, 1986. — xiii,561p. — *Includes index*

WAR CRIMINALS — Bibliography
TUTOROW, Norman E
War crimes, war criminals, and war crimes trials : an annotated bibliography and source book / compiled and edited by Norman E. Tutorow with the special assistance of Karen Winnovich. — New York : Greenwood Press, 1986. — xx, 548 p.. — (Bibliographies and indexes in world history ; no. 4). — *Includes index*

WAR CRIMINALS — Canada
TOLSTOY, Nikolai
Trial and error : Canada's Commission of Inquiry on War Criminals and the Soviets / Nikolai Tolstoy. — Toronto : Justinian Press, 1986. — 28p

WAR CRIMINALS — Germany — Biography
LINKLATER, Magnus
The Fourth Reich : Klaus Barbie and the neo-Fascist connection / Magnus Linklater, Isabel Hilton and Neal Ascherson with Mark Hosenball in Washington, Jon Swain in Paris and Tana de Zulueta in Rome. — London : Hodder and Stoughton, 1984 (1985 [printing]). — [iv,448]p. — (Coronet books)

WAR CRIMINALS — Germany (West)
FRIEDRICH, Jörg
Die Kalte Amnestie : NS-Täter in der Bundesrepublik / Jörg Friedrich. — Frankfurt am Main : Fischer Taschenbuch Verlag, 1984. — 431p. — *Bibliographical notes*

WAR CRIMINALS — Ukraine
Ukraine during World War II : history and its aftermath : a symposium / edited by Yury Boshyk with the assistance of Roman Waschuk and Andriy Wynnyckyj. — Edmonton : Canadian Institute of Ukrainian Studies, University of Alberta ; Downsview, Ont., Canada : Distributed by University of Toronto Press, 1986. — xviii, 291 p., [8] p. of plates. — (The Canadian library in Ukrainian studies). — *Includes index*. — *Bibliography: p. [267]-285*

WAR (INTERNATIONAL LAW)
BAILEY, Sydney D. (Sydney Dewson)
War and conscience in the nuclear age / Sydney D. Bailey. — Basingstoke : Macmillan, 1987. — xviii,210p. — *Bibliography: p200-202*. — *Includes index*

The current legal regulation of the use of force / edited by A. Cassese. — Dordrecht ; Lancaster : Martinus Nijhoff, 1986. — xiv,536p. — (Developments in international law). — *Includes bibliographical references*

The current legal regulation of the use of force / edited by A. Cassese. — Dordrecht ; Lancaster : Martinus Nijhoff, 1986. — xiv,536p. — (Developments in international law). — *Includes bibliographical notes*

GAINSBOROUGH, J. R.
The Arab-Israeli conflict : a politico-legal analysis / J.R. Gainsborough. — Aldershot : Gower, c1986 (1987 [printing]). — xxxv,345p. — *Bibliography: p319-334*. — *Includes index*

WAR OF THE PACIFIC, 1879-1884 — Chile
SATER, William F.
Chile and the War of the Pacific / William F. Sater. — Lincoln ; London : University of Nebraska Press, 1986. — 343p — *Includes index*. — *Bibliography: p.[323]-335*

WAR (PHILOSOPHY) — History — 18th century
CARTER, Christine Jane
Rousseau and the problem of war / Christine Jane Carter. — New York : Garland Pub., 1987. — p. cm. — (Political theory and political philosophy). — *The author's doctoral thesis, 1985. — Bibliography: p*

WAR VICTIMS — Legal status, laws, etc
SINGH, Nagendra
Enforcement of human rights in peace and war and the future of humanity / Nagendra Singh. — Dordrecht ; Boston : Nijhoff ; Calcutta : Eastern Law House Private Ltd., 1986. — p. cm

WAR WIDOWS — Services for — Israel
SHAMGAR-HANDELMAN, Lea
Israeli war widows : beyond the glory of heroism / Lea Shamgar-Handelman. — South Hadley, Mass. : Bergin & Garvey, 1986. — xiii, 219 p.. — *Includes index*. — *Bibliography: p. 211-216*

WAR WIDOWS — Israel — Psychology
SHAMGAR-HANDELMAN, Lea
Israeli war widows : beyond the glory of heroism / Lea Shamgar-Handelman. — South Hadley, Mass. : Bergin & Garvey, 1986. — xiii, 219 p.. — *Includes index*. — *Bibliography: p. 211-216*

WAR WIDOWS — Israel — Social conditions
SHAMGAR-HANDELMAN, Lea
Israeli war widows : beyond the glory of heroism / Lea Shamgar-Handelman. — South Hadley, Mass. : Bergin & Garvey, 1986. — xiii, 219 p.. — *Includes index*. — *Bibliography: p. 211-216*

WARBURG, Sir SIEGMUND
ATTALI, Jacques
A man of influence : Sir Siegmund Warburg 1902-82 / Jacques Attali ; translated by Barbara Ellis. — London : Weidenfeld and Nicholson, 1986. — vii,346p. — *Translation of: Un homme d'influence*

WARD, STEPHEN
KNIGHTLEY, Phillip
An affair of state : the Profumo case and the framing of Stephen Ward / by Phillip Knightley and Caroline Kennedy. — London : Cape, 1987. — [304]p. — *Includes bibliography and index*

WARSAW TREATY ORGANIZATION
DEAN, Jonathan
Watershed in Europe : dismantling the East-West military confrontation / Jonathan Dean. — Lexington, Mass. : Lexington Books, 1986, c1987. — p. cm. — *Includes index*

NELSON, Daniel N.
Alliance behavior in the Warsaw Pact / Daniel N. Nelson. — Boulder : Westview Press, 1986. — xvii, 134 p.. — (Westview special studies on the Soviet Union and Eastern Europe). — *Includes index*. — *Bibliography: p. [123]-127*

SAVINOV, K. I.
Varshavskii dogovor - faktor mira, shchit sotsializma / K. I. Savinov. — Moskva : Mezhdunarodnye otnosheniia, 1986. — 267p

Vneshniaia politika stran Varshavskogo Dogovora : (pervaia polovina 80-kh godov) / otv. redaktor I. I. Orlik. — Moskva : Nauka, 1986. — 319p

WARSAW TREATY ORGANIZATION — Congresses
Security in the North : Nordic and superpower perceptions : papers / presented to a seminar on "The North and the superpowers : mutual security policy perceptions" on March 16, 1983 ; edited by Bo Huldt and Atis Lejins. — Stockholm : Swedish Institute of International Affairs, [1984]. — vii, 78 p.. — (Conference papers / the Swedish Institute of International Affairs ; 5, 1984). — *Includes bibliographies*. — *Contents: Perceptions in international politics and national security / Christer Jönsson -- Nordic perceptions of the great powers and Nordic security / Kari Möttölä -- The USA and security in the Nordic countries / Svein Melby -- Soviet perceptions of Nordic security problems / Bjarne Nörretranders -- The big powers and Nordic security / Sverre Lodgaard*

WARSAW TREATY ORGANIZATION — History — Sources
UNION OF SOVIET SOCIALIST REPUBLICS. Ministerstvo inostrannykh del
Organizatsiia Varshavskogo Dogovora 1955-1985 : dokumenty i materialy / [otv. redaktor V. F. Mal'tsev. — Moskva : Politizdat, 1986. — 421p

WARSHIPS — Europe
FALTAS, Sami
Arms markets and armament policy : the changing structure of naval industries in Western Europe / by S. Faltas. — Dordrecht, Netherlands ; Boston : M. Nijhoff ; Norwell, MA, USA : Distributors for the U.S. and Canada, Kluwer Academic Publishers, 1986. — 417 p.. — (Studies in industrial organization ; v. 7). — : *Originally presented as the author's thesis (doctoral)--Free University, Amsterdam*. — *Bibliography: p. [358]-370*

WASHINGTON, GEORGE — Influence
HIGGINBOTHAM, Don
George Washington and the American military tradition / Don Higginbotham. — Athens : University of Georgia Press, c1985. — xii, 170 p.. — (Mercer University Lamar memorial lectures ; no. 27). — *Includes index*. — *Bibliography: p. [139]-161*

WASHINGTON, GEORGE — Military leadership
HIGGINBOTHAM, Don
George Washington and the American military tradition / Don Higginbotham. — Athens : University of Georgia Press, c1985. — xii, 170 p.. — (Mercer University Lamar memorial lectures ; no. 27). — *Includes index*. — *Bibliography: p. [139]-161*

WASHINGTON, D.C — Social conditions — Addresses, essays, lectures
The Urban predicament / edited by William Gorham, Nathan Glazer. — Washington : Urban Institute, c1976. — xix, 363 p.. — *Includes bibliographical references and index*

WASHINGTON PUBLIC POWER SUPPLY SYSTEM — Finance
SUGAI, Wayne H
Nuclear power and ratepayer protest : the Washington Public Power Supply System / Wayne H. Sugai. — Boulder : Westview Press, 1987. — p. cm. — (Westview special studies in public policy and public systems management). — *Bibliography: p*

WASHINGTON (STATE) — Economic conditions
FAHEY, John
The inland empire, unfolding years, 1879-1929 / John Fahey. — Seattle : University of Washington Press, c1986. — p. cm. — *Includes index. — Bibliography: p*

WASHINGTON (STATE) — Social conditions
FAHEY, John
The inland empire, unfolding years, 1879-1929 / John Fahey. — Seattle : University of Washington Press, c1986. — p. cm. — *Includes index. — Bibliography: p*

WASTE DISPOSAL IN THE OCEAN — Government policy — European Economic Community countries
The Oslo and Paris Commissions : the first decade. — London : Oslo and Paris Commissions, c1984. — x,377p. — *Contains summaries of the presentations prepared by all contracting parties of the Olso and Paris Conventions*

WASTE IN GOVERNMENT SPENDING — United States
FITZGERALD, Randall
Porkbarrel : the unexpurgated Grace Commission story of congressional profligacy / Randall Fitzgerald and Gerald Lipson. — Washington, D.C. : Cato Institute, c1984. — xxxv, 114 p.. — *"This report was originally prepared under the title The cost of congressional encroachment"--T.p. verso*

Fraud, waste, and abuse in government : causes, consequences, and cures / edited by Jerome B. McKinney and Michael Johnston. — Philadelphia : Institute for the Study of Human Issues, 1986. — p. cm. — *Includes index*

WASTE LANDS — Great Britain
GREAT BRITAIN. Department of the Environment
"Waste of waste land" : the reclamation of derelict land and the prevention of dereliction in the United Kingdom. — [London] : the Department, 1976. — [21]p. — (Planning in the United Kingdom). — *Paper presented at the United Nations Conference on Human Settlements, 1976, Vancouver. — Bibliography: p[19-21]*

WASTE LANDS — Ukraine
UK-USSR Environmental Protection Agreement: area III (land reclamation) : report of a visit to the USSR (by a UK delegation) in 1976. — London : Planning, Regional and Minerals Directorate, Department of the Environment, [1977]. — 24p

WASTE PRODUCTS AS FUEL — Europe
ABERT, James Goodear
Municipal waste processing in Europe : a status report on selected materials and energy recovery projects / James G. Abert. — Washington, D.C. : The World Bank, 1985. — xiv,157p. — (World Bank technical paper ; no.37) (UNDP project management report ; no.4) (Integrated resource recovery series ; no.4). — *At head of cover: "Integrated resource recovery". — Includes bibliographical references*

WATER — Economic aspects — Bibliography
Water resources, planning and management : a select bibliography = Les ressources en eau, leur planification et leur gestion : bibliographie sélective. — New York : United Nations, 1977. — vi,117p. — (Bibliographical series / Dag Hammarskjöld Library ; no.23 = Série bibliographique / Bibliotheque Dag Hammarskjöld ; no.23) ([Document] / United Nations ; ST/LIB/SER.B/23). — *In various languages. — Sales no: E/F.77.I.4*

WATER — Law and legislation — Ghana
Ghana : water supply and control : a record and analysis of legislation / A. J. Adamson...[et al.]. — London : Commonwealth Secretariat, [1985]. — xv,133p. — (Law and human ecology in the Commonwealth ; vol.1). — *Bibliography: p113-122. — Includes index*

WATER — Nitrogen content
GREAT BRITAIN. Central Directorate of Environmental Protection
Nitrate in water : a report of the Nitrate Coordination Group / Central Directorate of Environmental Protection, Department of the Environment. — London : H.M.S.O., 1986. — (Pollution paper ; no.26)

WATER — Pollution
GREAT BRITAIN. Central Directorate of Environmental Protection
Nitrate in water : a report of the Nitrate Coordination Group / Central Directorate of Environmental Protection, Department of the Environment. — London : H.M.S.O., 1986. — (Pollution paper ; no.26)

ORGANISATION FOR ECONOMIC CO-OPERATION AND DEVELOPMENT. Water Management Sector Group
Report of the Water Management Sector Group on eutrophication control. — Paris : the Organisation, 1974. — 19p. — *Includes bibliographical references*

WATER — Pollution — Law and legislation — Great Lakes Region
MULDOON, Paul R.
Cross-border litigation : environmental rights in the Great Lakes ecosystem / by Paul R. Muldoon, with David A. Scriven and James B. Olson. — Toronto : Carswell, 1986. — xxxv,410p

WATER — Pollution — Law and legislation — United States
MAGAT, Wesley A
Rules in the making : a statistical analysis of regulatory agency behavior / Wesley A. Magat, Alan J. Krupnick, Winston Harrington. — Washington, D.C. : Resources for the Future, c1986. — xiii, 182 p.. — *Includes bibliographies and index*

WATER — Pollution — England
BRITTAN, Yvonne
The impact of water pollution control on industry : a case study of fifty dischargers / Yvonne Brittan. — Oxford : Centre for Socio-Legal Studies, 1984. — vii,115p. — *Bibliography: p107*

WATER — Pollution — Organisation for Economic Co-operation and Development countries
Water pollution by fertilizers and pesticides. — Paris : Organisation for Economic Co-operation and Development, 1986. — 144p. — *Includes bibliographical references*

WATER — Purification
Wastewater irrigation in developing countries : health effects and technical solutions / Hillel I. Shuval ...[et al.]. — Washington, D.C. : The World Bank, 1986. — xxxi,324p. — (World Bank technical paper ; no51) (UNDP project management report ; no.6) (Integrated resource recovery series ; no.6). — *Bibliographical references: p307-324*

WATER-MELON INDUSTRY — Mexico
MEXICO. Dirección General de Economía Agrícola
Programa siembra-exportación de sandia, temporada 1983-1984. — [México] : the Dirección, [ca.1985]. — 25p. — *Cover title: Sandia, programa siembra exportación 1983-1984*

WATER-POWER — Economic aspects — United States — History
HUNTER, Louis C.
A history of industrial power in the United States 1780-1930 / Louis C. Hunter. — Charlottesville, Va : Published for the Hagley Museum and Library by the University Press of Virginia. — *Includes bibliographical references and indexes*
Vol.2: Steam power. — 1985. — xxii,732p

WATER-POWER — Finland
CHRISTIERNIN, Georg
Finland's water-power and electrification / Georg Christiernin. — Helsingfors : Government Printing Office, 1924. — 11p

WATER QUALITY MANAGEMENT — United States — Cost effectiveness
SMITH, V. Kerry
Measuring water quality benefits / V. Kerry Smith, William H. Desvousges. — Boston : Kluwer-Nijhoff Pub. ; Norwell, MA : Distributors for the U.S. and Canada, Kluwer Academic Publishers, c1986. — xiv, 327 p.. — (International series in economic modeling). — *Includes bibliographies and index*

WATER RESOURCES BOARD
GREAT BRITAIN. Countryside Commission
Memorandum to Secretaries of State for Environment and for Wales on the future organisation of water and sewage services. — [Cheltenham] : the Commission, 1972. — 9p

WATER RESOURCES DEVELOPMENT
BURTON, Ian
Water management and the environment / [Professor Ian Burton]. — Paris : Organisation for Economic Co-operation and Development, 1973. — iii,64p. — *Bibliographical references: p60-64*

WATER RESOURCES DEVELOPMENT — Bibliography
Water resources, planning and management : a select bibliography = Les ressources en eau, leur planification et leur gestion : bibliographie sélective. — New York : United Nations, 1977. — vi,117p. — (Bibliographical series / Dag Hammarskjöld Library ; no.23 = Série bibliographique / Bibliotheque Dag Hammarskjöld ; no.23) ([Document] / United Nations ; ST/LIB/SER.B/23). — *In various languages. — Sales no: E/F.77.I.4*

WATER RESOURCES DEVELOPMENT — Eanvironmental aspects — Netherlands
ORGANISATION FOR ECONOMIC CO-OPERATION AND DEVELOPMENT. Environment Directorate
Water management in the Netherlands. — Paris : the Organisation, 1976. — 50p. — (Study on economic and policy instruments for water management)

WATER RESOURCES DEVELOPMENT — Economic aspects
WRIGHT, William A.
Economic and social purposes related to water management : by William A. Wright. — Paris : OECD, 1972. — ii,50p. — *Bibliography: p41-50. — A paper prepared for the Panel on Integrated Water Resources Management Water Management Sector Group*

WATER RESOURCES DEVELOPMENT — Environmental aspects — Great Britain
ORGANISATION FOR ECONOMIC CO-OPERATION AND DEVELOPMENT. Environment Directorate
Water management in the United Kingdom. — Paris : the Organisation, 1976. — ii,41p. — (Study on economic and policy instruments for water management). — *Bibliography: p41*

WATER RESOURCES DEVELOPMENT — Environmental aspects — Canada

ORGANISATION FOR ECONOMIC CO-OPERATION AND DEVELOPMENT. Environment Directorate
Water management in Canada. — Paris : the Organisation, 1976. — i,61p. — (Study on economic and policy instruments for water management). — *Includes bibliographical references*

WATER RESOURCES DEVELOPMENT — Environmental aspects — England

LAND USE CONSULTANTS
Environmental appraisal of four alternative water resource schemes : Haweswater, Borrowbeck, Morecambe Bay, Hellifield; report of the Environmental Impact Study, November 1978 / prepared and published on behalf of the North West Water Authority by Land Use Consultants. — London : Land Use Consultants for the North West Water Authority, c1978. — xi,188p. — (Regional water resource studies). — *Bibliography: p187-188*

WATER RESOURCES DEVELOPMENT — Environmental aspects — Finland

ORGANISATION FOR ECONOMIC CO-OPERATION AND DEVELOPMENT. Environment Directorate
Water management in Finland. — Paris : the Organisation, 1976. — 34p. — (Study on economic and policy instruments for water management)

WATER RESOURCES DEVELOPMENT — Environmental aspects — France

ORGANISATION FOR ECONOMIC CO-OPERATION AND DEVELOPMENT. Environment Directorate
Water management in France. — Paris : the Organisation, 1976. — 65p. — (Study on economic and policy instruments for water management). — *Includes bibliographical references*

WATER RESOURCES DEVELOPMENT — Environmental aspects — Germany (West)

ORGANISATION FOR ECONOMIC CO-OPERATION AND DEVELOPMENT. Environment Directorate
Water management in the Federal Republic of Germany. — Paris : the Organisation, 1976. — v,55p. — (Study on economic and policy instruments for water management)

WATER RESOURCES DEVELOPMENT — Environmental aspects — Japan

ORGANISATION FOR ECONOMIC CO-OPERATION AND DEVELOPMENT. Environment Directorate
Water management in Japan. — Paris : the Organisation, 1976. — 49p. — (Study on economic and policy instruments for water management)

WATER RESOURCES DEVELOPMENT — Government policy — Brazil

BRAZIL. Divisão de Controle de Recursos Hídricos
Plano nacional de recursos hídricos : documento preliminar, consolidando informações já disponíveis. — [Brasília] : the Divisão, 1985. — 321p

WATER RESOURCES DEVELOPMENT — Planning — Bibliography

Water resources, planning and management : a select bibliography = Les ressources en eau, leur planification et leur gestion : bibliographie sélective. — New York : United Nations, 1977. — vi,117p. — (Bibliographical series / Dag Hammarskjöld Library ; no.23 = Série bibliographique / Bibliotheque Dag Hammarskjöld ; no.23) ([Document] / United Nations ; ST/LIB/SER.B/23). — *In various languages.* — Sales no: E/F.77.I.4

WATER RESOURCES DEVELOPMENT — Research

ORGANISATION FOR ECONOMIC CO-OPERATION AND DEVELOPMENT. Water Management Research Group
First report : 1969. — Paris : the Organisation, 1971. — 25p

WATER RESOURCES DEVELOPMENT — Social aspects

WRIGHT, William A.
Economic and social purposes related to water management : by William A. Wright. — Paris : OECD, 1972. — ii,50p. — *Bibliography: p41-50.* — *A paper prepared for the Panel on Integrated Water Resources Management Water Management Sector Group*

WATER RESOURCES DEVELOPMENT — Developing countries

The use of non-conventional water resources in developing countries. — New York : United Nations, 1985. — xviii,278p. — (Document / United Nations ; ST/ESA/149). — *Sales no.: E.84.II.A.14*

WATER RESOURCES DEVELOPMENT — Great Britain

GREAT BRITAIN. Countryside Commission
Memorandum to Secretaries of State for Environment and for Wales on the future organisation of water and sewage services. — [Cheltenham] : the Commission, 1972. — 9p

WATER RESOURCES DEVELOPMENT — Mexico — Mexico (State)

MEXICO (Mexico: State). Dirección de Comunicaciones y Obras Públicas
Uso del agua en el Estado de México / [Alberto J. Flores, Alberto Barrios A.]. — [México] : the Dirección, [1975]. — 16p

WATER RESOURCES DEVELOPMENT — Québec (Province)

BOURASSA, Robert
Power from the north / Robert Bourassa ; with a foreword by James Schlesinger. — Scarborough, Ontario : Prentice-Hall, 1985. — x,181p

WATER RESOURCES DEVELOPMENT — Scotland

SEWELL, W. R. Derrick
Institutional innovation in water management : the Scottish experience / by W.R.D. Sewell, J.T. Coppock, Alan Pitkethly. — Norwich : Geo, c1985. — xi,160p. — *Bibliography: p151-158.* — *Includes index*

WATER RESOURCES DEVELOPMENT — Sudan

SHEPHERD, Andrew
Water planning in arid Sudan / Andrew Shepherd, Malcolm Norris, John Watson. — London : Published for the Development Administration Group, Institute of Local Government Studies, University of Birmingham by Ithaca, 1986. — [288]p. — (Middle East science policy studies ; no.10)

WATER RESOURCES DEVELOPMENT — United States

ORGANISATION FOR ECONOMIC CO-OPERATION AND DEVELOPMENT. Environment Directorate
Water management in the United States. — Paris : the Organisation, 1976. — v,127p. — (Study on economic and policy instruments for water management). — *Bibliographical references: p126-127*

WATER REUSE — Hygienic aspects — Developing countries

Wastewater irrigation in developing countries : health effects and technical solutions / Hillel I. Shuval ...[et al.]. — Washington, D.C. : The World Bank, 1986. — xxxi,324p. — (World Bank technical paper ; no51) (UNDP project management report ; no.6) (Integrated resource recovery series ; no.6). — *Bibliographical references: p307-324*

WATER RIGHTS — United States — History

HUNTER, Louis C.
A history of industrial power in the United States 1780-1930 / Louis C. Hunter. — Charlottesville, Va : Published for the Hagley Museum and Library by the University Press of Virginia. — *Includes bibliographical references and indexes*
Vol.2: Steam power. — 1985. — xxii,732p

WATER-SUPPLY — Canada — Management

ORGANISATION FOR ECONOMIC CO-OPERATION AND DEVELOPMENT. Environment Directorate
Water management in Canada. — Paris : the Organisation, 1976. — i,61p. — (Study on economic and policy instruments for water management). — *Includes bibliographical references*

WATER-SUPPLY — Colorado River Watershed (Colo.-Mexico) — Collected works

E. BOLLAY ASSOCIATES
Park range atmospheric water resources program. — [Washington] : U.S. Dept. of the Interior, Bureau of Reclamation; [for sale by the Supt. of Docs., U.S. Govt. Print. Off., 1967-. — x,iiip. — (A water resources technical publication) (Research report no. 5). — *Bibliography: v. 1, p. v.* — *Contents: [1] Phase 1*

WATER-SUPPLY — Finland — Management

ORGANISATION FOR ECONOMIC CO-OPERATION AND DEVELOPMENT. Environment Directorate
Water management in Finland. — Paris : the Organisation, 1976. — 34p. — (Study on economic and policy instruments for water management)

WATER-SUPPLY — France

ORGANISATION FOR ECONOMIC CO-OPERATION AND DEVELOPMENT. Environment Directorate
Water management in France. — Paris : the Organisation, 1976. — 65p. — (Study on economic and policy instruments for water management). — *Includes bibliographical references*

WATER-SUPPLY — Germany (West) — Management

ORGANISATION FOR ECONOMIC CO-OPERATION AND DEVELOPMENT. Environment Directorate
Water management in the Federal Republic of Germany. — Paris : the Organisation, 1976. — v,55p. — (Study on economic and policy instruments for water management)

WATER-SUPPLY — Great Britain

GREAT BRITAIN. Department of the Environment
The National Rivers Authority : the government's proposals for a public regulatory body in a privatised water industry. — [London : the Department], 1987. — 42p

WATER-SUPPLY — Great Britain — Bibliography

ELLENDER, Pat
Water industry in England and Wales / [compiled by Pat Ellender]. — [London] : Water Information Centre, National Water Council, [1976]. — [21]p. — (Water Information Centre bibliography ; no.1)

WATER-SUPPLY — Great Britain — Congresses

NATIONAL WATER CONFERENCE (1975 : Bournemouth)
Proceedings, report. — [London?] : National Water Council, [ca.1975]. — 77p

WATER-SUPPLY — Great Britain — Management

ORGANISATION FOR ECONOMIC CO-OPERATION AND DEVELOPMENT. Environment Directorate
Water management in the United Kingdom. — Paris : the Organisation, 1976. — ii,41p. — (Study on economic and policy instruments for water management) — *Bibliography: p41*

SYNNOTT, Michael Frederick
The relationship between the regional water authorities and local planning authorities / by Michael Frederick Synnott. — 350 leaves. — *PhD (Econ) 1986 LSE*

WATER-SUPPLY — Japan

ORGANISATION FOR ECONOMIC CO-OPERATION AND DEVELOPMENT. Environment Directorate
Water management in Japan. — Paris : the Organisation, 1976. — 49p. — (Study on economic and policy instruments for water management)

WATER-SUPPLY — Netherlands

ORGANISATION FOR ECONOMIC CO-OPERATION AND DEVELOPMENT. Environment Directorate
Water management in the Netherlands. — Paris : the Organisation, 1976. — 50p. — (Study on economic and policy instruments for water management)

WATER-SUPPLY — Organisation for Economic Co-operation and Development Countries — Price policy

Pricing of water services. — Paris : Organisation for Economic Co-operation and Development, 1987. — 145p. — *Bibliographical references: p138-145*

WATER-SUPPLY — Statistics

The International Drinking Water Supply and Sanitation Decade : review of national baseline data (as at 31 December 1980). — Geneva : World Health Organization, 1984. — 169p. — (WHO offset publication ; no.85)

WATER-SUPPLY — United States

ORGANISATION FOR ECONOMIC CO-OPERATION AND DEVELOPMENT. Environment Directorate
Water management in the United States. — Paris : the Organisation, 1976. — v,127p. — (Study on economic and policy instruments for water management). — *Bibliographical references: p126-127*

WATER-SUPPLY ENGINEERING — Developing countries

Community piped water supply systems in developing countries : a planning manual / Daniel A. Okun and Walter R. Ernst. — Washington, D.C. : The World Bank, 1987. — x,249p. — (World Bank technical paper ; no.60). — *Bibliography: p212-222*

WATER USE — Great Britain — Congresses

NATIONAL WATER CONFERENCE (1975 : Bournemouth)
Proceedings, report. — [London?] : National Water Council, [ca.1975]. — 77p

WATERWORKS — Developing countries — Planning

Community piped water supply systems in developing countries : a planning manual / Daniel A. Okun and Walter R. Ernst. — Washington, D.C. : The World Bank, 1987. — x,249p. — (World Bank technical paper ; no.60). — *Bibliography: p212-222*

WATKINSON, HAROLD

WATKINSON, Harold Arthur
Turning points : a record of our times / Harold Watkinson. — Wilton : Michael Russell, 1986. — 228p

WAYFARING LIFE — Law and legislation — England

FORRESTER, Bill
The travellers' handbook : a guide to the law affecting gypsies / by Bill Forrester. — London : InterChange, 1985. — ix,124p. — *Bibliography: p104-105. — Includes index*

WEALTH

BENARD, Jean
Economie publique / Jean Benard. — Paris : Economica, c1985. — 430p. — (Collection "Economie"). — *Bibliography: p[401]-414*

HOLTHAM, G. H.
Wealth and inflation effects in the aggregate consumption function / by G. H. Holtham, H. Kato. — [Paris] : OECD, 1986. — 37p. — (Working papers / OECD Department of Economics and Statistics ; no.35). — *Bibliographical references: p19*

Introduction to economics. — Milton Keynes : Open University Press. — (Social Sciences : a second level course)
Block 5: Income and wealth. — 1985. — [26],29p. — (D210 ; 18-19). — *At head of title: The Open University. — Contents: Unit 18: Redistribution and the fiscal system/prepared for the course team by Julian Le Grand - Unit 19: income and wealth in the USSR/prepared for the course team by Alastair McAuley*

KIDRON, Michael
The book of business, money and power / Michael Kidron and Ronald Segal. — London : Pluto Projects, 1987. — 187p

KOTLIKOFF, Laurence J.
The contribution of intergenerational transfers to total wealth : a reply / Laurence J. Kotkikoff, Lawrence H. Summers. — Cambridge, Mass. : NBER, 1986. — 24p. — (NBER working paper series ; no.1827). — *Bibliography: p22-24*

TURGOT, Anne Robert Jacques, baron de l'Aulne
Turgot on progress, sociology and economics / translated [from the French], edited and with an introduction by Ronald L. Meek. — London : Cambridge University Press, 1973. — [6],185p. — (Cambridge studies in the history and theory of politics). — *Includes index. — Contents:- A philosophical review of the successive advances of the human mind - On universal history - Reflections on the formation and the distribution of wealth. Translation of 'Réflexions sur la formation et la distribution des richesses'. [s.l.]: [s.n.], 1788*

WEALTH — Addresses, essays, lectures

The Collection and analysis of economic and consumer behavior data : in memory of Robert Ferber / edited by Seymour Sudman and Mary A. Spaeth. — Champaign, Ill. : Bureau of Economic and Business Research & Survey Research Laboratory, University of Illinois, c1984. — x, 406 p.. — *Includes bibliographies*

WEALTH — Congresses

International comparisons of the distribution of household wealth / edited by Edward N. Wolff. — Oxford : Clarendon, 1987. — xii,283p. — *Includes bibliographies and index*

WEALTH — Denmark

Udviklingen i formuefordelingen 1960-1977. — [København] : Lavindkomstkommissionen, 1979. — 167p. — (Delrapport / Lavindkomstkommissionen ; 2)

WEALTH — Germany (West) — Statistics

GERMANY (Federal Republic). Statistisches Bundesamt
Einkommens- und Verbrauchsstichprobe 1983. — Wiesbaden : the Bundesamt. — (Wirtschaftsrechnungen)
Heft 2: Vermögensbestände und Schulden privater Haushalte. — 1986. — 540p

WEALTH — Great Britain

ATKINSON, A. B.
Trends in the distribution of wealth in Britain 1923-1981 / A. B. Atkinson, J. Gordon, A. J. Harrison. — [London : London School of Economics and Political Science], 1986. — 41p. — (Taxation, incentives and the distribution of income ; no.70). — *Economic and Social Research Council programme. — Bibliographical references: p33*

WEALTH — Hungary

FELLNER, Frigyes
Csonka-Magyarország nemzeti vagyona / írta Fellner Frigyes. — Budapest : Magyar Tudományos Akadémia, 1929. — 94p

WEALTH, ETHICS OF

MCKENZIE, Richard B
The fairness of markets : a search for justice in a free society / Richard B. McKenzie. — Lexington, Mass. : Lexington Books, c1987. — xiv, 235 p.. — *Includes bibliographies and index*

WEAPONS SYSTEMS

BARNABY, Frank
What on earth is Star Wars? : a guide to the Strategic Defence Initiative / Frank Barnaby. — London : Fourth Estate, 1986. — [184]p. — *Includes bibliography and index*

Emerging technologies and military doctrines : a political assessment / edited by Frank Barnaby and Marlies ter Borg. — Basingstoke : Macmillan, 1986. — xxi,328p. — *Includes index*

WEATHER CONTROL — Steamboat Springs region — Collected works

E. BOLLAY ASSOCIATES
Park range atmospheric water resources program. — [Washington] : U.S. Dept. of the Interior, Bureau of Reclamation; [for sale by the Supt. of Docs., U.S. Govt. Print. Off., 1967-. — x,iiip. — (A water resources technical publication) (Research report no. 5). — *Bibliography: v. 1, p. v. — Contents: [1] Phase 1*

WEATHER FORECASTING — Economic aspects

MAUNDER, W. J., 1932-
The uncertainty business : risks and opportunities in weather and climate / W.J. Maunder ; with a foreword by John R. Mather. — London : Methuen, 1986. — xxviii,420p. — *Bibliography: p361-403. — Includes indexes*

WEBB, BEATRICE

CAINE, Barbara
Destined to be wives : the sisters of Beatrice Webb / Barbara Caine. — Oxford : Clarendon, 1986. — [xii,280]p,[16]p of plates. — *Includes bibliography and index*

WEBER, ALFRED — History and criticism

ALFRED WEBER-KONGRESS (1st : 1984 : Heidelberg)
Alfred Weber als Politiker und Gelehrter : die Referate des Ersten Alfred Weber-Kongresses... / Eberhard Demm (Hrsg.). — Stuttgart : Steiner Verlag Wiesbaden, 1986. — 218p. — *Bibliography: p[205]-218*

WEBER, MAX

BUSS, Andreas E.
Max Weber and Asia : contributions to the sociology of development / Andreas E. Buss. — München ; London : Weltforum Verlag, 1985. — 115p. — (Materialien zu Entwicklung und Politik ; 27). — *Bibliography: p107-115*

Max Weber and his contemporaries / edited by Wolfgang J. Mommsen and Jürgen Osterhammel ; the German Historical Institute. — London : Allen & Unwin, 1987. — xiv,591p. — *Conference proceedings. — Includes index*

Max Weber in Asian studies / edited by Andreas E. Buss. — Leiden : Brill, 1985. — 252p. — (International Studies in Sociology and Social Anthropology ; 42). — *Bibliographies*

WEBER, MAX
continuation

Max Weber, rationality and modernity / edited by Scott Lash, Sam Whimster. — London : Allen & Unwin, 1987. — xvii,394p. — *Bibliography: p378-389. — Includes index*

SAHAY, Arun
Max Weber and modern sociology / edited by Arun Sahay ; contributors John Rex [and others]. — London : Routledge and K. Paul, 1971. — [6],111p

WRONG, Dennis Hume, comp
Max Weber / Edited by Dennis Wrong. — Englewood Cliffs, N.J. : Prentice-Hall, [1970]. — viii, 214 p. — (Makers of modern social science) (A Spectrum book). — *Bibliography: p. 211-212*

WEBER, MAX — criticism and interpretation

COLLINS, Randall
Weberian sociological theory / Randall Collins. — Cambridge : Cambridge University Press, 1986

WEBER, MAX — Criticism and interpretation

SCHÖLLGEN, Gregor
Max Webers Anliegen : Rationalisierung als Forderung und Hypothek / Gregor Schöllgen. — Darmstadt : Wissenschaftliche Buchgessellschaft, 1985. — [xi],150p. — *Bibliography: p[143]-148*

WEBER, MAX — History and criticism

COLLINS, Randall
Max Weber : a skeleton key / by Randall Collins. — Beverly Hills : Sage Publications, c1985. — p. cm. — (Masters of social theory ; v. 3). — *Includes index*

WEBSTER, DANIEL, 1782-1852

WEBSTER, Daniel
The papers of Daniel Webster / Charles M. Wiltse, editor- in—chief. — Hanover, N.J. : published for Dartmouth College by the University Press of New England
Series 3: Diplomatic papers
Vol.1: 1841-1843 / Kenneth E. Shewmaker, editor. — 1983. — xliv,960p

WEBSTER, Daniel
The papers of Daniel Webster / Charles M. Wiltse, editor-in-chief. — Hanover, N.H. ; London : published for Dartmouth College by the University Press of New England
Series 4: Speeches and formal writings
Vol.1: 1800-1833 / Charles M. Wiltse editor ; Alan R. Berolzheimer, assistant editor. — 1986. — xx,641p

WEBSTER, DANIEL, 1782-1852 — Correspondence

WEBSTER, Daniel
The papers of Daniel Webster / Charles M. Wiltse and Michael J. Birkner, editors. — Hanover, N.H. ; London : published for Dartmouth College by the University Press of New England
Series 1: Correspondence
Vol.7: 1850-1852. — 1986. — xxxiii,695p

WEEKLY REST-DAY

TOWNSEND, Christopher
Why keep Sunday special? / Christopher Townsend and Michael Schluter ; foreword by Sir Norman Anderson. — Cambridge : Jubilee Centre Publications, 1985. — 87p. — (Jubilee Centre Paper ; no.5). — *Bibliography: p84-87*

WEHNER, HERBERT — Interviews

WEHNER, Herbert
Der Onkel : Herbert Wehner in Gesprächen und Interviews / herausgegeben von Knut Terjung. — Hamburg : Hoffman und Campe, 1986. — 287p

WEIHAIWEI (CHINA) — Politics and government

ATWELL, Pamela
British mandarins and Chinese reformers : the British administration of Weihaiwei (1898-1930) and the territory's return to Chinese rule / Pamela Atwell ; with a foreword by N. J. Miners. — Hong Kong : Oxford University Press, 1985. — xviii,302p. — (East Asian historical monographs). — *Bibliography: p[284]-294*

WEISSE ROSE (Resistance group)

DUMBACH, Annette E
Shattering the German night : the story of the White Rose / by Annette E. Dumbach and Jud Newborn. — 1st ed. — Boston : Little, Brown, c1986. — xi, 259 p.. — *Includes index. — Bibliography: p. 243-247*

WEIZMANN, CHAIM

ROSE, Norman
Chaim Weizmann : a biography / Norman Rose. — London : Weidenfeld and Nicolson, 1986. — xiv,520p. — *Bibliography: p.463-470*

WELFARE ECONOMICS

BARR, N. A.
The economics of the welfare state / Nicholas Barr. — London : Weidenfeld and Nicholson, 1987. — xiv,475p. — *Bibliography: p432-459*

BOOKCHIN, Murray
The modern crisis / Murray Bookchin. — Philadelphia : New Society Publishers, 1986. — xi,167p. — *Published in cooperation with Institute for Social Ecology, Rochester, Vermont*

CAMPBELL, Donald E.
Resource allocation mechanisms / Donald E. Campbell. — Cambridge : Cambridge University Press, 1987. — xiii,183p. — *Bibliography: p171-177. — Includes index*

DEATON, Angus
The measurement of welfare : theory and practical guidelines / Angus Deaton. — Washington, D.C., U.S.A. : World Bank, 1985 printing, c1980. — 82p. — (LSMS working papers ; no.7) (LSMS working papers ; no. 7). — *Bibliographical references: p79-82*

HAZLITT, Henry
The conquest of poverty / Henry Hazlitt. — Lanham : University Press of America, 1986, c1973. — p. cm. — : Reprint. Originally published: New Rochelle, N.Y. : Arlington House, 1973. — *Includes index*

PFEIFFER, Lucien
Libre entreprise et socialismes. — Paris : Nouvelle Société des Éditions Encre, 1986. — 192p

STIGLITZ, Joseph E.
Economics of the public sector / Joseph E. Stiglitz. — New York ; London : Norton, 1986. — xxiii,509p. — *Bibliography: p577-586*

WELFARE ECONOMICS — Addresses, essays, lectures

Economic justice : selected readings / [edited by] Edmund S. Phelps. — Harmondsworth : Penguin Education, 1973. — 479p. — (Penguin modern economics readings) (Penguin education). — *Includes bibliographies and index*

WELFARE ECONOMICS — Econometric models

BOHM, Peter
Social efficiency : a concise introduction to welfare economics / Peter Bohm. — 2nd ed. — London : Macmillan Education, 1987. — [160]p. — *Previous ed.: New York : Wiley, 1973. — Includes bibliography and index*

WELFARE ECONOMICS — Mathematical models

KING, Mervyn A.
The empirical analysis of tax reforms / Mervyn A. King. — [London : London School of Economics and Political Science], 1986. — 51p. — (Taxation, incentives and the distribution of income ; no.96). — *Economic and Social Research Council programme. — Paper presented to the Symposium on Empirical Public Finance at the Fifth World Congress of the Econometric Society, MIT, 1985. — Bibliographical references: p44-47*

WELFARE FRAUD — Great Britain

GREAT BRITAIN. Department of Health and Social Security
Evidence by the Department of Health and Social Security to the Royal Commission on Criminal Procedure. — [London : the Department, 1978]. — 13,4p

GREAT BRITAIN. Department of Health and Social Security. Co-ordinating Committee on Abuse
Second report : action taken against social security fraud and abuse from September 1977-December 1978, and work still in hand / by the Coordinating Committee on Abuse. — [London : the Department, 1979]. — 14,3p

WELFARE RECIPIENTS — Employment — Australia

OGBORN
Workfare in America : an initial guide to the debate / Keith Ogborn. — Woden, ACT : Department of Social Security, 1986. — 27p. — (Background/discussion paper / Social Security Review ; no.6). — *Bibliography: p24-27*

WELFARE RECIPIENTS — Employment — United States

OGBORN
Workfare in America : an initial guide to the debate / Keith Ogborn. — Woden, ACT : Department of Social Security, 1986. — 27p. — (Background/discussion paper / Social Security Review ; no.6). — *Bibliography: p24-27*

WELFARE RECIPIENTS — United States

KIMMICH, Madeleine H
America's children, who cares? : growing needs and declining assistance in the Reagan era / Madeleine H. Kimmich. — Washington, D.C. : Urban Institute Press, c1985. — xvii 112 p.. — (The Changing domestic priorities series). — *Includes bibliographical references*

WELFARE STATE

ANDERSEN, Bent Rold
Two essays on the nordic welfare state / Bent Rold Andersen. — Copenhagen : Amtskommunernes og kommunernes forskningsinstitut, 1983. — 76p

ATKINSON, A. B.
The welfare state in Britain 1970-1985 : extent and effectiveness / A.B. Atkinson, J. Hills and J. Le Grand. — London : Suntory-Toyota International Centre for Economics and Related Disciplines, 1986. — 64p. — (Discussion paper / Welfare State Programme. Suntory-Toyota International Centre for Economics and Related Disciplines ; no.9). — *Bibliography: p61-64*

CAHN, Edgar S.
Service credits : a new currency for the welfare state / Edgar S. Cahn [and] Nicholas Barr. — London : Welfare State Programme Suntory-Toyota International Centre for Economics and Related Disciplines, 1986. — 48p. — (Discussion paper / Welfare State Programme. Suntory-Toyota International Centre for Economics and Related Disciplines ; no.8)

The Changing face of welfare / edited by Adalbert Evers, Helga Nowotny and Helmut Wintersberger. — Aldershot : Gower, c1987. — xv,246p. — (Studies in social policy and welfare ; 27). — *Includes bibliographies and index*

WELFARE STATE
continuation

COUSINS, Christine
Controlling social welfare : a sociology of state welfare work and organization / Christine Cousins. — Brighton : Wheatsheaf, 1987. — viii,219p. — *Bibliography: p189-208. — Includes index*

CUTLER, Tony
Keynes, Beveridge and beyond / Tony Cutler, Karel Williams and John Williams. — London : Routledge and Kegan Paul, 1986. — [248]p. — *Includes bibliography and index*

DAVIES, Stephen
Beveridge revisited : new foundations for tomorrow's welfare / Stephen Davies. — London : Centre for Policy Studies, 1986. — 48p. — (Policy study ; no.79)

GLENNERTER, Howard
Research directions on the future of the welfare state : a view from social administration / Howard Glennerter. — London : Welfare State Programme. Suntory-Toyota International Centre for Economics and Related Disciplines, 1985. — 39p. — (Discussion paper / Welfare State Programme. Suntory-Toyota International Centre for Economics and Related Disciplines ; no.4). — *Bibliography: p34-39*

GOODIN, Robert E.
The middle class infiltration of the welfare state : some evidence from Australia / Robert E. Goodin and Julian Le Grand. — London : Welfare State Programme. Suntory-Toyota International Centre for Economics and Related Disciplines, 1986. — 29p. — (Discussion paper / Welfare State Programme. Suntory-Toyota International Centre for Economics and Related Disciplines ; no.10). — *Bibliography: p27-29*

GREENBERG, Edward S.
Capitalism and the American political ideal / by Edward S. Greenberg. — Armonk, N.Y. : M.E. Sharpe, 1985. — p. cm

Growth to limits : the western European welfare states since World War II / edited by Peter Flora. — Berlin ; New York : W. de Gruyter, 1986-. — v. <1-2, >. — (Series C–Political and social sciences =Sciences politiques et sociales ; 6). — *Includes bibliographies. — Contents: v. 1. Sweden, Norway, Finland, Denmark -- v. 2. Germany, United Kingdom, Ireland, Italy*

JOHNSON, Norman
The welfare state in transition : the theory and practice of welfare pluralism / Norman Johnson. — Brighton : Wheatsheaf, 1987. — [224]p. — *Includes bibliography and index*

JOHNSON, Paul
The historical dimensions of the welfare state 'crisis' / Paul Johnson. — London : Welfare State Programme. Suntory-Toyota International Centre for Economics and Related Disciplines, 1985. — 41p. — (Discussion paper / Welfare State Programme. Suntory-Toyota International Centre for Economics and Related Disciplines ; no.3)

Law, rights and the welfare state / edited by C.J.G. Sampford and D.J. Galligan. — London : Croom Helm, c1986. — xv,215p. — *Bibliography: p200-207. — Includes index*

MEYERSON, Per-Martin
Eurosclerosis : the case of Sweden : a critical examination of some central problems in the Swedish economy and in Swedish politics / by Per-Martin Meyerson ; [translated by Victor J. Kayfetz]. — Stockholm : Federation of Swedish Industries, c1985. — 118 p.. — *Bibliography: p. 114-118*

Not just for the poor : Christian perspectives on the welfare state / report of the Social Policy Committee of the Board for Social Responsibility. — London : Church House, c1986. — vii,146p. — *Bibliography: p145*

PASCALL, Gillian
Social policy : a feminist analysis / Gillian Pascall. — London : Tavistock, 1986. — [v,220]p. — *Includes bibliography and index*

PERSSON, Gunnar
The Scandinavian welfare state : anatomy, logic and some problems / Gunnar Persson. — London : Welfare State Programme. Suntory-Toyota International Centre for Economics and Related Disciplines, 1986. — 30p. — (Discussion paper / Welfare State Programme. Suntory-Toyota International Centre for Economics and Related Disciplines ; no.7). — *Bibliography: p29-30*

Public/private interplay in social protection : a comparative study / edited by Martin Rein and Lee Rainwater ; with Ellen Immergut, Michael O'Higgins, and Harald Russig. — Armonk, N.Y. : M.E. Sharpe, c1986. — viii, 215 p.. — (Comparative public policy analysis). — *Includes bibliographies*

RAINWATER, Lee
Income packaging in the welfare state : a comparative study of family income / Lee Rainwater, Martin Rein, and Joseph Schwartz. — New York : Oxford University Press, 1986. — p. cm. — *Includes index. — Bibliography: p*

RINGEN, Stein
The possibility of politics : a study in the political economy of the welfare state / Stein Ringen. — Oxford : Clarendon, 1987. — x,303p. — *Bibliography: p267-295. — Includes index*

TITMUSS, Richard M.
The philosophy of welfare : selected writings of Richard M. Titmuss / edited by Brian Abel-Smith and Kay Titmuss ; with an introduction by S.M. Miller. — London : Allen & Unwin, 1987. — xvi,282p. *Includes index*

WICKS, Malcolm
A future for all : do we need the Welfare State? / Malcolm Wicks. — Harmondsworth : Penguin, 1987. — 301p. — *Bibliography: p.[258]-280*

WINEMAN, Steven
The politics of human services : radical alternatives to the welfare state / by Steven Wineman. — 1st ed. — Boston, MA : South End Press, c1984. — iv, 272 p.. — *Bibliography: p. 249-272*

WELFARE STATE — Addresses, essays, lectures

HARTMANN, Jürgen
Youth in the welfare society : a reader on theoretical concepts and empirical studies in youth research / Jürgen Hartmann. — Uppsala, Sweden : Distribution, Dept. of Sociology, Uppsala University, [1984]. — 103 p.. — *Includes bibliographies*

WELFARE STATE — Congresses

Futures for the welfare state / edited by Norman Furniss. — Bloomington : Indiana University Press, c1986. — vi, 444 p.. — *Bibliography: p. 404-431*

The Welfare state East and West / edited by Richard Rose and Rei Shiratori. — New York : Oxford University Press, 1986. — p. cm. — *Papers derived from meetings held at the University of Strathclyde, Scotland and at Nikko, Japan, and from a seminar held in Tokyo, and produced under the auspices of the Institute for Political Studies in Japan*

WELFARE STATE — History

ASHFORD, Douglas E.
The emergence of the welfare states / Douglas E. Ashford. — Oxford : Basil Blackwell, 1986. — x,352p. — *Bibliography: p319-342. — Includes index*

GOODIN, Robert E.
Not only the poor : the middle classes and the welfare state / Robert E. Goodin, Julian Le Grand with John Dryzek ... [et al.]. — London : Allen & Unwin, 1987. — [288]p. — *Includes bibliography and index*

WELFARE STATE — Political aspects

HARRIS, David, 19---
Justifying state welfare : the new right versus the old left / David Harris ; with a foreword by David Miller. — Oxford : Basil Blackwell, 1987. — viii,181p. — *Bibliography: p175-178. — Includes index*

WELFARE WORK IN INDUSTRY — Germany — History

SACHSE, Carola
Industrial housewives : social work for women in the factories in Nazi Germany / Carola Sachse. — New York, N.Y. : The Institute for Research in History and the Haworth Press, c1987. — p. cm. — *"Has also been published as Women & history, number 11, 1986"--T.p. verso. — Bibliography: p*

WELLCOME, Sir HENRY SOLOMON

HALL, A. Rupert
Physic and philanthropy : a history of the Wellcome Trust 1936-1986 / A.R. Hall and B.A. Bembridge ; with a foreword by Sir David Steel. — Cambridge : Cambridge University Press, 1986. — xii,479p. — *Includes index*

WELLCOME FOUNDATION — History

One hundred years : Wellcome 1880-1980 : in pursuit of excellence / [written by Gilbert Macdonald]. — London : Wellcome Foundation, 1980. — 120p

WELLCOME TRUST

HALL, A. Rupert
Physic and philanthropy : a history of the Wellcome Trust 1936-1986 / A.R. Hall and B.A. Bembridge ; with a foreword by Sir David Steel. — Cambridge : Cambridge University Press, 1986. — xii,479p. — *Includes index*

WELLINGTON, ARTHUR WELLESLEY, Duke of

MATHER, F. C.
Achilles or Nestor? : the Duke of Wellington in British politics after the great Reform Act / F. C. Mather. — Southampton : University of Southampton, 1986. — 21p. — *A public lecture delivered on 6 February 1986. — Bibliography: p17-21*

THOMPSON, Neville
Wellington after Waterloo / Neville Thompson. — London : Routledge & Kegan Paul, 1986. — [320]p. — *Includes index*

WELLINGTON, Arthur Wellesley, Duke of
Wellington / ed. by R. J. Olney and Julia Melvin. — London : H.M.S.O. 2: Political correspondence, November 1834 — April 1835. — 1986. — v, 664p. — (Prime Ministers' papers series)

WELLINGTON

WELLINGTON, Arthur Wellesley, Duke of
Wellington / ed. by R. J. Olney and Julia Melvin. — London : H.M.S.O. 2: Political correspondence, November 1834 — April 1835. — 1986. — v, 664p. — (Prime Ministers' papers series)

WELSH — Canada

GREENSLADE, David
. — Cowbridge : D. Brown and Sons, 1986. — xv,303p

WELSH — United States

GREENSLADE, David
. — Cowbridge : D. Brown and Sons, 1986. — xv,303p

WELSH AGRICULTURAL ORGANISATION SOCIETY

WELSH AGRICULTURAL ORGANISATION SOCIETY
Annual report / Welsh Agricultural Organisation Society. — Aberystwyth : [the Society], 1934-1947. — Annual. — *Continued by: Rural Wales: a yearbook of Welsh agricultural cooperation/Welsh Agricultural Organisation Society*

WELSH AGRICULTURAL ORGANISATION SOCIETY
continuation

WELSH AGRICULTURAL ORGANISATION SOCIETY
Annual report: rural Wales / Welsh Agricultural Organisation Society. — Aberystwyth : [the Society], 1981-. — Annual. — Title varies. — Continues: Rural Wales: a yearbook of Welsh agricultural cooperation/Welsh Agricultural Organisation Society

WELSH AGRICULTURAL ORGANISATION SOCIETY
Rural Wales: a yearbook of Welsh agricultural cooperation / Welsh Agricultural Organisation Society. — Aberystwyth : [the Society], 1949/50-1980. — Annual. — Continues: Welsh Agricultural Organisation Society. Annual report. — Continued by: Welsh Agricultural Organisation Society. Annual report: rural Wales

WELSH LANGUAGE

COUNCIL FOR THE WELSH LANGUAGE
Cyhoeddi yn yr iaith Gymraeg : asdroddiad i'r Gwir Anrhydeddus John Morris QC, AS, Ysgrifennydd Gwladol Cymru = Publishing in the Welsh Language : a report to the Rt. Hon. John Morris QC, MP, Secretary of State for Wales. — Cardiff : H.M.S.O., 1978. — vii,97p. — Welsh and English text

COUNCIL FOR THE WELSH LANGUAGE
Dyfodol i'r iaith Gymraeg = A future for the Welsh language : adroddiad i'r Gwir Anrhydeddus John Morris Q.C., A.S., Ysgrifennydd Gwladol Cymru = a report to the Right Hon. John Morris Q.C., M.P., Secretary of State for Wales / Cyngor yr Iaith Gymraeg = Council for the Welsh Language. — Caerdydd [i.e. Cardiff] : H.M.S.O., 1978. — vii,78p. — Parallel Welsh and English text

WELSH LANGUAGE — Study and teaching (Preschool) — Wales
Y gymraeg mewn addysg feithrin = The Welsh language in nursery education. — Cardiff : HMSO, 1975. — [34]p. — In English and Welsh

WELWYN GARDEN CITY (HERTFORDSHIRE) — City planning
Welwyn Garden City : town centre study : a report for public discussion / David Overton with the assistance of the County Surveyor. — Hertford : Hertfordshire County Council, 1973. — 22p. — Includes folded map

WEST BANK — Defenses
SHALEV, Ariyeh
[Kav haganah bi-Yehudah uva-Shomron. English]. The West Bank : line of defense / by Aryeh Shalev ; with a historical supplement by Mordechai Gichon. — New York : Praeger, 1985. — p. cm. — "A JCSS book.". — Translation of: Kav haganah bi-Yehudah uva-Shomron. — Includes index. — Bibliography: p

WEST BANK — Family relationships
ATA, Ibrahim Wade
The West Bank Palestinian family / Ibrahim Wade Ata. — London : KPI, 1986. — xiii,166p. — Bibliography: p152-160

WEST BANK — History
PERETZ, Don
The West Bank : history, politics, society, and economy / Don Peretz. — Boulder, Colo. : Westview Press, 1986. — xi,173p. — (Westview special studies on the Middle East)

WEST BANK — International status
MISHAL, Shaul
The PLO under 'Arafat : between gun and olive branch / Shaul Mishal. — New Haven ; London : Yale University Press, c1986. — xiv, 190p. — Includes index

WEST BANK — Politics and government
BENVENISTI, Meron
Conflicts and contradictions / Meron Benvenisti. — 1st ed. — New York : Villard Books, 1986. — xii, 210 p.. — Includes index

PERETZ, Don
The West Bank : history, politics, society, and economy / Don Peretz. — Boulder, Colo. : Westview Press, 1986. — xi,173p. — (Westview special studies on the Middle East)

WEST BENGAL (INDIA) — Economic conditions
BOSE, P. K.
Classes and class relations among tribals of Bengal / Pradip Kumar Bose. — 1st ed. — Delhi : Ajanta Publications : Distributors, Ajanta Books International, 1985. — viii, 132 p.. — Includes index. — Bibliography: p. [126]-128

WEST BENGAL (INDIA) — Ethnic relations
BOSE, P. K.
Classes and class relations among tribals of Bengal / Pradip Kumar Bose. — 1st ed. — Delhi : Ajanta Publications : Distributors, Ajanta Books International, 1985. — viii, 132 p.. — Includes index. — Bibliography: p. [126]-128

WEST BENGAL (INDIA) — Politics and government
ROYCHOUDHURY, Profulla
Left experiment in West Bengal / Profulla Roy Choudhury. — New Delhi : Patriot Publishers, 1985, c1984. — 201, [3] p.. — Bibliography: p. [202]-[204]

SAMANTA, Amiya K.
Left extremist movement in West Bengal : an experiment in armed agrarian struggle / Amiya K. Samanta. — Calcutta : Firma KLM, 1984. — x,361p. — Bibliography: 329-348

WEST BENGAL (INDIA) — Population — Statistics
Census of India 1981. — [Delhi : Controller of Publications]
Series 23: West Bengal / S. N. Ghosh, Director of Census Operations, West Bengal. — [1984]

WEST BENGAL (INDIA) — Scheduled tribes
BOSE, P. K.
Classes and class relations among tribals of Bengal / Pradip Kumar Bose. — 1st ed. — Delhi : Ajanta Publications : Distributors, Ajanta Books International, 1985. — viii, 132 p.. — Includes index. — Bibliography: p. [126]-128

WEST BURRA (SCOTLAND) — Social conditions
BYRON, Reginald
Sea change : a Shetland society, 1970-79 / Reginald Byron. — St John's : Institute of Social and Economic Research Memorial University of Newfoundland, 1986. — vii,164p

WEST GLAMORGAN (WALES) — Economic conditions
WEST GLAMORGAN, County Council
Jobs today - and tomorrow? : what are the issues?. — Swansea : [the Council], 1976. — 43p

WEST INDIANS — Canada
WALKER, James W. St. G.
The West Indians in Canada / James W. St. G. Walker. — Ottawa : Canadian Historical Association, 1984. — 27p. — (Canadian Historical Association booklet ; no.6). — Bibliography: p25-26

WEST INDIANS — Europe — History — 20th century
The Caribbean in Europe : aspects of the West Indian experience in Britain, France and the Netherlands / edited by Colin Brock. — London : Cass, 1986. — viii,243p. — (Legacies of West Indian slavery). — Conference proceedings. — Includes index

WEST INDIANS — Great Britain — History — 20th century
The Caribbean in Europe : aspects of the West Indian experience in Britain, France and the Netherlands / edited by Colin Brock. — London : Cass, 1986. — viii,243p. — (Legacies of West Indian slavery). — Conference proceedings. — Includes index

CARTER, Trevor
Shattering illusions : West Indians in British politics / Trevor Carter ; with Jean Coussins. — London : Lawrence and Wishart, 1986. — 158p

WEST INDIANS — Great Britain — Languages
EDWARDS, Viv
Language in a black community / Viv Edwards. — Clevedon : Multilingual Matters, c1986. — 169p. — (Multilingual matters ; 24). — Bibliography: p153-164. — Includes index

WEST INDIANS — Panama Canal (Panama)
CONNIFF, Michael L
Black labor on a white canal : Panama, 1904-1981 / Michael L. Conniff. — Pittsburgh : University of Pittsburgh Press, 1985. — p. cm . — Includes index. — Bibliography: p

WEST INDIES — Emigration and immigration
CONNIFF, Michael L
Black labor on a white canal : Panama, 1904-1981 / Michael L. Conniff. — Pittsburgh : University of Pittsburgh Press, 1985. — p. cm . — Includes index. — Bibliography: p

WEST INDIES, BRITISH — Dictionaries and encyclopedias
LUX, William
Historical dictionary of the British Caribbean / by William Lux. — Metuchen, N.J. : Scarecrow Press, 1975. — 266 p.. — (Latin American historical dictionaries ; no. 12). — Bibliography: p. 251-266

WEST INDIES, FRENCH — Dictionaries and encyclopedias
GASTMANN, Albert L
Historical dictionary of the French and Netherlands Antilles / by Albert Gastmann. — Metuchen, N.J. : Scarecrow Press, 1978. — viii, 162 p.. — (Latin American historical dictionaries ; no. 18). — Includes bibliographies

WEST INDIES, FRENCH — History
GARRETT, Mitchell Bennett
The French colonial question 1789-1791 : dealings of the constituent assembly with problems arising from the revolution in the West Indies / by Mitchell Bennett Garrett. — New York : Negro Universities Press, 1970. — iv,167p. — Reprint of 1916 edition. — Bibliography: p[135]-160

WEST INDIES, FRENCH — History — Archival resources
Guide des sources de l'histoire de l'Amérique latine et des Antilles dans les archives françaises. — Paris : Archives nationales, 1984. — 711p

WEST MIDLANDS — Economic conditions
WEST MIDLANDS. County Council
A time for action : economic and social trends in the West Midlands : a discussion document prepared by the West Midlands County Council. — Birmingham : [the Council], 1974. — 29p

WEST MIDLANDS. County Council
Visit to EEC and EIB, September 1975, European Economic Community : Economic trends in the West Midlands. — Birmingham : [the Council], 1975. — 36p

WEST MIDLANDS — Social conditions

WEST MIDLANDS. County Council
A time for action : economic and social trends in the West Midlands : a discussion document prepared by the West Midlands County Council. — Birmingham : [the Council], 1974. — 29p

WEST MIDLANDS (ENGLAND) — Economic conditions

Crisis in the industrial heartland : a study of the West Midlands / Ken Spencer...[et al.]. — Oxford : Clarendon Press, 1986. — xviii,219p. — (Inner Cities Research Programme series ; 6). — *Bibliography: p200-210. — Includes index*

WEST MIDLANDS. County Council
Economic and social trends in the West Midlands : policy proposals. — Birmingham : [the Council], 1975. — 49p. — *Cover title: A time for action*

WEST MIDLANDS. County Council. Economic Development Committee
Action in the local economy : progress report of the Economic Development Committee, West Midlands County Council. — Birmingham : [the Council], 1984. — 36p

WEST MIDLANDS (ENGLAND) — Economic policy

Crisis in the industrial heartland : a study of the West Midlands / Ken Spencer...[et al.]. — Oxford : Clarendon Press, 1986. — xviii,219p. — (Inner Cities Research Programme series ; 6). — *Bibliography: p200-210. — Includes index*

WEST MIDLANDS (ENGLAND) — Race relations

CASHMORE, Ernest
The logic of racism / E. Ellis Cashmore. — London : Allen & Unwin, 1987. — vii,263p. — *Bibliography: p260-261. — Includes index*

WEST MIDLANDS (ENGLAND) — Social conditions

WEST MIDLANDS. County Council
Economic and social trends in the West Midlands : policy proposals. — Birmingham : [the Council], 1975. — 49p. — *Cover title: A time for action*

WEST (U.S.) — Politics and government

Politics of realignment : party change in the mountain west / edited by Randy T. Simmons, Peter F. Galderisi, John G. Francis. — Boulder : Westview Press, 1986. — p. cm

WESTERN AND NORTHERN TERRITORIES (POLAND) — History

MROCZKO, Marian
Polska myśl zachodnia 1918-1939 : (kształtowanie i upowszechnianie / Marian Mroczko. — Poznań : Instytut Zachodni, 1986. — 429p. — (Dzieje polskiej granicy zachodniej ; 6). — *Summary in English and German. — Bibliography: p352-393*

WESTERN AUSTRALIA. Commonwealth Bureau of Census and Statistics. Western Australian Office

WESTERN AUSTRALIA. Commonwealth Bureau of Census and Statistics. Western Australian Office
Building and housing. — Perth : [Office], 1968/9-. — *Annual. — Supercedes in part its Statistical register of Western Australia: part 12. Retail prices, wages, employment and miscellaneous*

WESTERN AUSTRALIA. Commonwealth Bureau of Census and Statistics. Western Australian Office
Divorce / Western Australian Office, Commonwealth Bureau of Census and Statistics. — Perth : [the Office], 1947-1980. — *Annual*

WESTERN HIGHLANDS PROVINCE (PAPUA NEW GUINEA) — Population — Statistics

1980 national population census : final figures : provincial summary : Western Highlands Province. — Port Moresby : National Statistical Office, 1985. — iii,134p

WESTERN SAHARA — Dictionaries and encyclopedias

HODGES, Tony
Historical dictionary of Western Sahara / by Tony Hodges. — Metuchen, N.J. : Scarecrow Press, 1982. — xxxix, 431 p.. — (African historical dictionaries ; no. 35). — *Bibliography: p. 371-431*

WESTERN SAHARA — Foreign Relations — United States

KAMIL, Leo
Fueling the fire : U.S. policy and the Western Sahara conflict / Leo Kamil. — Trenton, New Jersey : Red Sea Press, 1987. — 104p. — *Distributed in the UK by Spokesman, Nottingham. — Bibliography: p93-96. — Appendices give text of 1983 OAU peace plan: 1985 U.N. General Assembly resolution: and 1979 Algiers peace treaty between the Polisario Front and the Republic of Mauretania*

WESTERN SAHARA — History — 1975-

KAMIL, Leo
Fueling the fire : U.S. policy and the Western Sahara conflict / Leo Kamil. — Trenton, New Jersey : Red Sea Press, 1987. — 104p. — *Distributed in the UK by Spokesman, Nottingham. — Bibliography: p93-96. — Appendices give text of 1983 OAU peace plan: 1985 U.N. General Assembly resolution: and 1979 Algiers peace treaty between the Polisario Front and the Republic of Mauretania*

WESTMAN, KARL GUSTAF

WESTMAN, Karl Gustaf
Politiska anteckningar september 1939 - mars 1943 / K.G. Westman ; utgivna genom W.M. Carlgren. — Stockholm : Kungl. Samfundet för utgivande av handskrifter rörande Skandinaviens historia, 1981. — 237p.,[1] leaf of port. — (Handlingar / Kungl. Samfundet för utgivande av handskrifter rörande Skandinaviens historia ; del 6)

WESTMINSTER, HUGH RICHARD ARTHUR GROSVENOR, Duke of, F45, 11843468

FIELD, Leslie
Bendor : the golden Duke of Westminster / Leslie Field. — London : Weidenfeld and Nicolson, 1983. — ix,292p,[16]p of plates. — *Ill on lining papers. — Bibliography: p273-281. — Includes index*

WESTMINSTER (LONDON) — City planning

PIMLICO NEIGHBOURHOOD AID CENTRE HOUSING GROUP
Planning, policy and eviction in Pimlico : a report / by the Pimlico Neighbourhood Aid Centre Housing Group. — London : Pimlico Neighbourhood Aid Centre, 1974. — 13p

WESTMINSTER (LONDON, ENGLAND) — Economic conditions

WESTMINSTER. Finance Department. Policy Unit
Financial effects of GLC abolition : a Westminster briefing paper for industry and commerce. — Westminster : [the Department], 1985. — 8p

WESTMINSTER (LONDON, ENGLAND) — Industries

WESTMINSTER. Finance Department. Policy Unit
Financial effects of GLC abolition : a Westminster briefing paper for industry and commerce. — Westminster : [the Department], 1985. — 8p

WETLAND CONSERVATION — Government policy — Great Britain

PENNING-ROWSELL, Edmund C.
Floods and drainage : British policies for hazard reduction, agricultural improvement and wetland conservation / E.C. Penning-Rowsell, D.J. Parker, D.M. Harding. — London : Allen & Unwin, 1986. — xx,199p. — (The Risks & hazards series ; v.2). — *Bibliography: p178-192. — Includes index*

WETLAND CONSERVATION — United States

NELSON, Robert Wayne
Wetland management strategies : balancing agriculture with conservation / by Robert Wayne Nelson. — 319 leaves. — *PhD (Econ) 1987 LSE. — Leaves 252-317 are appendices*

WETLAND ECOLOGY — England — Somerset

NATURE CONSERVANCY COUNCIL. South West Region
The Somerset wetlands project : report by a working party. — [S.l.] : the Council, 1977. — 22leaves. — *Cover title: The Somerset wetlands project; a consultation paper*

NATURE CONSERVANCY COUNCIL. South West Region
The Somerset wetlands project : summary of responses to the consultation paper. — [s.l.] : the Council, 1978. — 16p

WETLANDS — United States

NELSON, Robert Wayne
Wetland management strategies : balancing agriculture with conservation / by Robert Wayne Nelson. — 319 leaves. — *PhD (Econ) 1987 LSE. — Leaves 252-317 are appendices*

WEY AND ARUN CANAL (ENGLAND) — History

VINE, P. A. L.
London's lost route to the sea : an historical account of the inland navigations which linked the Thames to the English Channel / P.A.L. Vine. — 4th ed. — Newton Abbot : David & Charles, 1986. — xvii,278p,[32]p of plates. — *Previous ed.: 1973. — Bibliography: p242-246. — Includes index*

WHALES

DAY, David, 1947-
The whale war / David Day. — London : Routledge & Kegan Paul, 1987. — 168p,[8]p of plates. — *Includes index*

WHALING — Arctic Ocean — History

BOCKSTOCE, John R
Whales, ice, and men : the history of whaling in the western Arctic / John R. Bockstoce. — 1st ed. — Seattle : University of Washington Press in association with the New Bedford Whaling Museum, Massachusetts, 1986. — 400 p.. — *Cover title: Whales, ice & men. — Includes index. — Bibliography: p. 383-393*

WHEAT — Economic aspects — Hungary — Congresses

A magyar buza minösége, ára és értékesítése : a Magyar Közgazdasági Társaság ankétja / contributions by Éber Antal...[et al.]. — Budapest : Gergely R., 1930. — 202p. — (Közgazdasági Könyvtár ; köt.9). — *Proceedings of a conference "A magyar buza minösége, ára és értékesítése", [Budapest?], 1929-1930 ????????*

WHEAT — Prices — Pakistan

AHMAD, E.
The demand for wheat under non-linear pricing in Pakistan / E. Ahmad, H. M. Leung and N. H. Stern. — London : Suntory Toyota International Centre for Economics and Related Disciplines, 1987. — 17p. — (Development research programme / London School of Economics and Political Science. Suntory Toyota International Centre for Economics and Related Disciplines ; no.5). — *Bibliography: p17*

WHEAT — Taiwan

TSUI, Young-chi
A study of wheat in Taiwan / by Young-chi Tsui. — Taipei : Chinese-American Joint Commission on Rural Reconstruction, 1957. — iii,109p. — (Economic digest series / Joint Commission on Rural Reconstruction ; no.9)

WHEAT TRADE — Australia

AUSTRALIA. Bureau of Agricultural Economics
Wheat: situation and outlook. — Canberra : [the Bureau], 1951-1980. — *Annual*

WHEATLEY, JOHN WHEATLEY, Lord

WHEATLEY, John Wheatley, Lord
One man's judgement : an autobiography / Lord Wheatley. — London : Butterworths, 1987. — [220]p. — *Includes index*

WHELAN, EUGENE F.

WHELAN, Eugene
Whelan : the man in the green stetson / by Eugene Whelan ; with Rick Archbold. — Toronto : Irwin Publishing, 1986. — 322p

WHEN THE WIND BLOWS

KILBORN, Richard W.
The multi-media melting pot : marketing When the wind blows / by Richard Kilborn. — London : Comedia, 1986. — 117p. — *Bibliography: p114-117*

WHIG PARTY (GREAT BRITAIN)

MURRAY, John Joseph
George I, the Baltic and the Whig split of 1717 : a study in diplomacy and propaganda / John J. Murray. — London : Routledge and Kegan Paul, 1969. — xv,366p

WHISKEY INSURRECTION, 1794

SLAUGHTER, Thomas P
The Whiskey Rebellion : frontier epilogue to the American Revolution / Thomas P. Slaughter. — New York : Oxford University Press, 1986. — p. cm. — *Includes index.* — *Bibliography: p*

WHITE COLLAR CRIMES

LEVI, Michael
Regulating fraud : white-collar crime and the criminal process / Michael Levi. — London : Tavistock, 1987. — [416]p. — *Includes bibliography and index*

WHITE COLLAR CRIMES — United States

COLEMAN, James William
The criminal elite : the sociology of white collar crime / James W. Coleman. — New York : St. Martin's Press, c1985. — xi, 260 p.. — *Includes bibliographies and index*

WHITE COLLAR WORKERS — Germany — History

SPEIER, Hans
[Angestellten vor dem Nationalsozialismus. English]. German white-collar workers and the rise of Hitler / Hans Speier. — New Haven : Yale University Press, c1986. — xxv, 208 p.. — *Translation of: Die Angestellten vor dem Nationalsozialismus.* — *Includes index.* — *Bibliography: p. 191-203*

WHITE COLLAR WORKERS — Germany — Political activity — History

SPEIER, Hans
[Angestellten vor dem Nationalsozialismus. English]. German white-collar workers and the rise of Hitler / Hans Speier. — New Haven : Yale University Press, c1986. — xxv, 208 p.. — *Translation of: Die Angestellten vor dem Nationalsozialismus.* — *Includes index.* — *Bibliography: p. 191-203*

WHITE COLLAR WORKERS — Great Britain

CRUM, R. E.
Non—productive activities in U.K. manufacturing industry : a report by the School of Social Studies of the University of East Anglia (Norwich) to the U.K. Department of Industry and the European Economic Community / R. E. Crum [and] G. Gudgin. — Luxembourg : Office for Official Publications of the European Communities, 1977. — ix, 176p. — (Regional policy series ; no.3)

WHITE COLLAR WORKERS — Switzerland — History

KÖNIG, Mario
Warten und Aufrücken : die Angestellten in der Schweiz 1870-1950 / Mario König, Hannes Siegrist, Rudolf Vetterli. — Zürich : Chronos, 1985. — 644p. — *Bibliography: p628-638*

WHITE COLLAR WORKERS — United States — Effect of technological innovations on — Congresses

Technology and the transformation of white-collar work / edited by Robert E. Kraut. — Hillsdale, N.J. : L. Erlbaum Associates, c1987. — x,281p. — *Presented at a conference sponsored by Bell Communications Research, June 1984.* — *Includes bibliography and indexes*

WHITEHEAD, ALFRED NORTH

LECLERC, Ivor
Whitehead's philosophy between rationalism and empiricism / Ivor Leclerc. — Leuven : Center for Metaphysics and Philosophy of God, Institute of Philosophy, 1984. — iv,69p

WHITNEY, Sir JAMES PLINY

HUMPHRIES, Charles W
"Honest enough to be bold" : the life and times of Sir James Pliny Whitney / Charles W. Humphries. — Toronto ; Buffalo : Published by University of Toronto Press, c1985. — xii, 276 p., [14] p. of plates. — (The Ontario historical studies series). — *Includes index.* — *Bibliography: p. [269]-270*

WHOLESALE TRADE — Denmark

Engrosdistributionen af fabriksfremstillede laegemidler. — København : Monopoltilsynet, 1983. — 125p

Engroshandelen med dagligvarer : markedsstruktur, konkurrenceforhold, prisdannelse, indtjening. — København : Monopoltilsynet, 1982. — 372p. — *Bibliography: p217*

WHOLESALE TRADE — Fiji — Statistics

Survey of distributive trade : 1983. — Suva : Bureau of Statistics, 1985. — 22,viip

WHOLESALE TRADE — Great Britain — Statistics

Wholesaling and dealing. — London : HMSO, 1974. — vi,[142]p. — (Business monitor. SDO ; 26)

WHOLESALE TRADE — Singapore — Statistics

Report on the censuses of wholesale trade, retail trade, restaurants and hotels, 1983. — Singapore : Department of Statistics, 1986. — iv,231p

WHOLESALE TRADE — Thailand — Statistics

Census of business trade and services 1966 : Southern region. — Bangkok : National Statistical Office, [1970?]. — 57p. — *In English and Thai*

Report : census of business trade and services 1977 : Bangkok Metropolitan, Nonthaburi, Pathum Thani and Samut Prakan. — Bangkok : National Statistical Office, [1980?]. — 96p. — *In English and Thai*

Report : census of business trade and services 1977 : whole kingdom. — Bangkok : National Statistical Office, [1980?]. — 75p

WIDOWERS — United States — Life skills guides

RUBINSTEIN, Robert L
Singular paths : old men living alone / Robert L. Rubinstein. — New York : Columbia University Press, 1986. — viii, 265 p.. — (Columbia studies of social gerontology and aging). — *Includes index.* — *Bibliography: p. [257]-261*

WIDOWS — Economic aspects — France

BORREL, Catherine
Le veuvage avant soixante ans : ses conséquences financières. — Paris : La Documentation française. — (Documents du centre d'étude des revenus et des coûts ; no.81) 1: Les premiers mois du veuvage / ...réalisée par Catherine Borrel et Philippe Madinier. — 1986. — 146p

WIEHN, ERHARD R. — Collected works

WIEHN, Erhard R.
Gesammelte Schriften zur Soziologie / Erhard R. Wiehn. — Konstanz : Hartung-Gorre. — *Bibliographies*
1. — 1986. — 762p

WIFE ABUSE — Bibliography

ALLBROOKE, Jill C.
Selected references on battered women, 1975-1978 / compiled by Jill C. Allbrooke. — London : Department of Health and Social Security Library, 1978. — 7p. — (Bibliography series / Department of Health and Social Security Library ; no.B111)

ENGELDINGER, Eugene A
Spouse abuse : an annotated bibliography of violence between mates / by Eugene A. Engeldinger. — Metuchen, N.J. : Scarecrow Press, 1986. — xiv, 317 p.. — *Includes indexes*

WIGGINS, BEN T

Telecommunications in the post-divestiture era : essays in honor of Jasper N. Dorsey and Ben T. Wiggins / edited by Albert L. Danielsen, David R. Kamerschen. — [Lexington, Mass.] : Lexington Books, c1986. — xiv, 252 p.. — *Includes bibliographies and index*

WIKMANSHYTTAN (Firm) — History

AXELSSON, Björn
Wikmanshyttans uppgång och fall : en kommentar till angreppssättet i en företaghistorisk studie / Björn Axelsson. — Uppsala : Uppsala Universitet, 1982. — 152p. — (Acta Universitatis Upsaliensis. Studien Oeconomiae Negotiorum ; 15). — *Doctoral thesis, Uppsala University 1981.* — *Bibliography: p147-152*

WILAYAH PERSEKUTUAN (MALAYSIA) — Population — Statistics

Banci penduduk dan perumahan Malaysia 1980 = Population and housing census of Malaysia 1980. — Kuala Lumpur : Department of Statistics. — *Text in Malay and English*
Laporan penduduk negeri = State population report
Wilayah Persekutuan. — 1983. — 297p. — 1map

WILDLIFE CONSERVATION

DAY, David, 1947-
The whale war / David Day. — London : Routledge & Kegan Paul, 1987. — 168p,[8]p of plates. — *Includes index*

WILDLIFE CONSERVATION — Great Britain

ADAMS, W. M.
Nature's place : conservation sites and countryside change / W.M. Adams. — London : Allen & Unwin, 1986. — [160p]. — *Includes bibliography and index*

WILDLIFE CONSERVATION — Kenya

YEAGER, Rodger
Wildlife, wild death : land use and survival in eastern Africa / Rodger Yeager, Norman N. Miller. — Albany, NY : State University of New York Press in association with the African-Caribbean Institute, 1986. — p. cm. — *Includes index.* — *Bibliography: p*

WILDLIFE CONSERVATION — Tanzania

YEAGER, Rodger
Wildlife, wild death : land use and survival in eastern Africa / Rodger Yeager, Norman N. Miller. — Albany, NY : State University of New York Press in association with the African-Caribbean Institute, 1986. — p. cm. — *Includes index.* — *Bibliography: p*

WILDLIFE CONSERVATION — Yukon Territory — History

MCCANDLESS, Robert G
Yukon wildlife : a social history / Robert G. McCandless. — Edmonton, Alta., Canada : University of Alberta Press, c1985. — xvii, 200 p.. — *Includes index.* — *Bibliography: p. 189-[193]*

WILDLIFE MANAGEMENT — Law and legislation — Yukon Territory — History

MCCANDLESS, Robert G
Yukon wildlife : a social history / Robert G. McCandless. — Edmonton, Alta., Canada : University of Alberta Press, c1985. — xvii, 200 p.. — *Includes index.* — *Bibliography: p. 189-[193]*

WILDLIFE MANAGEMENT — Yukon Territory — History

MCCANDLESS, Robert G
Yukon wildlife : a social history / Robert G. McCandless. — Edmonton, Alta., Canada : University of Alberta Press, c1985. — xvii, 200 p.. — *Includes index.* — *Bibliography: p. 189-[193]*

WILKES, JOHN, 1727-1797

RUDÉ, George
Wilkes and liberty : a social study / George Rudé. — London : Lawrence and Wishart, 1983. — xiv, 240p. — *Originally published: Oxford: Clarendon Press, 1962.* — *Bibliography: p.224-228*

WILLARD, FRANCES ELIZABETH

BORDIN, Ruth Birgitta Anderson
Frances Willard : a biography / by Ruth Bordin. — Chapel Hill ; London : University of North Carolina Press, c1986. — xv, 294p. — *Includes index.* — *Bibliography: p.277-287*

WILLIAM III, King of England

OAKLEY, Stewart P
William III and the northern crowns during the Nine Years War, 1689-1697 / Stewart Philip Oakley. — New York : Garland Pub., 1987. — 504 p. (some folded). — (Outstanding theses from the London School of Economics and Political Science). — *Bibliography: p. 480-501*

WILLIAMS, DAVID, 1738-1816

JONES, Whitney R.D.
David Williams : the anvil and the hammer / Whitney R.D. Jones. — Cardiff : University of Wales Press, 1986. — xviii,266p. — *Bibliography: p.241-251.* — *Includes index*

WILLIAMS, ERIC EUSTACE — Addresses, essays, lectures

Eric Williams, the man and the leader / edited by Ken I. Boodhoo. — Lanham, MD : University Press of America, c1986. — xviii, 143 p.. — *Includes index.* — *"Bibliography of books, articles, and speeches by Eric Williams": p. 135-139*

WILSON, HAROLD, 1916-

WILSON, Harold, 1916-
Memoirs : the making of a Prime Minister 1916-64 / Harold Wilson. — London : Weidenfeld and Nicolson and Joseph, 1986. — 213p,[16]p of plates. — *Includes index*

WILSON, WALTER

WILSON, A. Gordon
Walter Wilson : portrait of an inventor / A Grodon Wilson ; edited by Rodney Dale. — London : Duckworth, 1986. — 173p

WILSON, WOODROW

FERRELL, Robert H
Woodrow Wilson and World War I, 1917-1921 / by Robert H. Ferrell. — 1st ed. — New York ; London : Harper & Row, c1985. — xii, 346p, [26]p of plates. — (New American nationl series). — *Includes index.* — *Bibliography: p.303-333*

SCHWABE, Klaus
[Deutsche Revolution und Wilson-Frieden. English]. Woodrow Wilson, Revolutionary Germany, and peacemaking, 1918-1919 : missionary diplomacy and the realities of power / by Klaus Schwabe ; translated from German by Rita and Robert Kimber. — Chapel Hill : University of North Carolina Press, c1985. — ix, 565p. "Supplementary volumes to The papers of Woodrow Wilson, Arthur S. Link, editor"--Half t.p. — *Translation of: Deutsche Revolution und Wilson-Frieden.* — *Includes index.* — *Bibliography: p [533]-547*

WALWORTH, Arthur
Wilson and his peacemakers : American diplomacy at the Paris Peace Conference, 1919 / Arthur Walworth. — New York ; London : W.W. Norton, 1986. — xiii, 618p. *Includes index.* — *Bibliography: p.572-585*

WILTSHIRE — Bibliography — Union lists

Wiltshire / county editor: R.K. Bluhm. — London : Library Association Special, Reference and Information Section, 1975. — 28p. — (Bibliography of British newspapers)

WINCHESTER (HAMPSHIRE) — Social conditions — History

KEENE, Derek
Survey of medieval Winchester / Derek Keene with a contribution by Alexander R. Rumble. — Oxford : Clarendon, 1985. — 2v.(xxxviii,1490p,[10]p of plates). — (Winchester studies ; 2). — *Maps (6 folded sheets) and table (1 folded sheet) in pocket in first volume.* — *Includes index*

WIND POWER — European Economic Community countries

MUSGROVE, P.
Wind energy evaluation for the European Communities / P. Musgrove. — Luxembourg : Office for the Official Publications of the European Communities, 1984. — vii,136p. — (EUR ; 8996). — *Bibliographical references: p102-107.* — *Contract no.: XVII/AR/82/255*

WINDWARD ISLANDS (SOCIETY ISLANDS) — Population — Statistics

Tableaux normalisés du recensement général de la population : 15 octobre 1983. — [Papeete] : Institut territorial de la statistique Résultats de la subdivision adminstrative des Iles du Vent. — [1985?]. — 4p,12 leaves

WINNIPEG (MAN.) — Politics and government

CHEKKI, Dan A.
Organised interest groups and the urban policy process / Dan A. Chekki and Roger T. Toews. — Winnipeg : Institute of Urban Studies, University of Winnipeg, 1985. — 87p. — (Report / University of Winnipeg, Institute of Urban Studies ; 9). — *Bibliography: p83-87*

WIRE-TAPPING — Government policy — Great Britain

GREAT BRITAIN. Parliament. House of Commons. Library. Research Division
Telephone tapping and electronic surveillance devices / [Margaret M. Camsell]. — [London] : the Division, 1980. — 14p. — (Reference sheet ; no.80/12)

WIT AND HUMOR — Therapeutic use

LEFCOURT, Herbert M
Humor and life stress : antidote to adversity / Herbert M. Lefcourt, Rod A. Martin. — New York : Springer-Verlag, c1986. — p. cm. — *Includes index.* — *Bibliography: p*

WITCHCRAFT — History

KLAITS, Joseph
Servants of Satan : the age of the witch hunts / Joseph Klaits. — Bloomington, IN : Indiana University Press, c1985. — p. cm. — *Bibliography: p[196]-206.* — *Bibliography: p*

WITCHCRAFT — Africa, Central

EVANS-PRITCHARD, Sir Edward Evan
Witchcraft, oracles and magic among the Azande / Sir Edward Evans-Pritchard ; with a foreword by C. G. Seligman. — Oxford : Clarendon Press, 1937. — 558p

WITCHCRAFT — Europe

QUAIFE, G. R
Godly zeal and furious rage : the witch in early modern Europe / G.R. Quaife. — New York : St. Martin's Press, 1987. — p. cm. — *Includes index.* — *Bibliography: p*

WITCHCRAFT — Europe — History — 16th century

LEVACK, Brian P.
The witch-hunt in early modern Europe / Brian P. Levack. — London : Longman, 1987. — [450]p. — *Bibliography: p435.* — *Includes index*

WITCHCRAFT — Europe — History — 17th century

LEVACK, Brian P.
The witch-hunt in early modern Europe / Brian P. Levack. — London : Longman, 1987. — [450]p. — *Bibliography: p435.* — *Includes index*

WITCHCRAFT — France, Southern — History

LE ROY LADURIE, Emmanuel
Jasmin's witch / Emmanuel Le Roy Ladurie ; translated by Brian Pearce. — London : Scholar, 1987. — 222p. — *Translation of: La sorcière de Jasmin.* — *Bibliography: p183-202.* — *Includes index*

WITCHCRAFT — Papua New Guinea

KNAUFT, Bruce M
Good company and violence : sorcery in a lowland New Guinea society / Bruce M. Knauft. — Berkeley : University of California Press, c1985. — p. cm. — *Includes index.* — *Bibliography: p*

WITNESSES — Great Britain

JUSTICE
Witnesses in the criminal courts : a report / by Justice ; chairman of committee Peter Crawford. — London : Justice, 1986. — 25p

WITTGENSTEIN, LUDWIG

SHANKER, S. G
Wittgenstein and the turning point in the philosophy of mathematics / S. G. Shanker. — London : Croom Helm, c1986. — [320]p. — *Includes bibliography and index*

WINCH, Peter
Trying to make sense / Peter Winch. — Oxford : Basil Blackwell, 1987. — [224]p. — *Includes index*

WITTGENSTEIN, LUDWIG — History and Criticism

KAMPITS, Peter
Ludwig Wittgenstein : Wege und Unwege zu seinen Denken / Peter Kampits. — Graz : Verlog Styria, 1985. — 223p. — *With bibliographical notes*

WIVES — Employment — Canada

HARPELL, Cindy
An analysis of dual-earner families in Canada / Cindy Harpell. — Kingston, Ont., Canada : Industrial Relations Centre, Queen's University at Kingston, 1985. — 48 p.. — (School of Industrial Relations research essay series ; no. 2). — *Bibliography: p. 47-48*

WIVES — Employment — Germany (East)
KOCH, Petra
Familienpolitik der DDR im Spannungsfeld zwischen Familie und Berufstätigkeit von Frauen / Petra Koch [und] Hans Günther Knöbel. — Pfaffenweiler : Centaurus-Verlagsgesellschaft, 1986. — vii,171p. — *Bibliography: p124-143*

WIVES — Employment — Great Britain — Mathematical models
GOMULKA, J.
The employment of married women in the UK: 1970-1983 / Joanna Gomulka, Nicholas Stern. — [London : London School of Economics and Political Science], 1986. — 58p. — (Taxation, incentives and the distribution of income ; no.98). — *Economic and Social Research Council programme. — Bibliographical references: p57-58*

WOLA (PAPUA NEW GUINEA PEOPLE)
SILLITOE, Paul
Give and take : exchange in Wola society / Paul Sillitoe. — New York : St. Martin's Press, 1979. — xiv, 316 p., [4] leaves of plates. — *Includes index. — Bibliography: p. [303]-308*

WOLFF
LANG, Jochen von
Der Adjutant : der Mann zwischen Hitler und Himmler / Jochen v. Lang ; unter Mitarbeit von Claus Sibyll. — München : Herbig, 1985. — 428p

WOLFF, JOSEPH
DAVY, Yvonne
Trail of peril : the story of Joseph Wolff / Yvonne Davy. — Washington, D.C. : Review and Herald Pub. Association, c1984. — 94 p.

WOMAN (CHRISTIAN THEOLOGY) — Addresses, essays, lectures
KNOX, John
The political writings of John Knox : The first blast of the trumpet against the monstrous regiment of women and other selected works / edited and with an introduction by Marvin A. Breslow. — Washington : Folger Shakespeare Library ; London : Associated University Presses, c1985. — 160 p.. — *"Folger books.". — Includes bibliographies. — Contents: The first blast of the trumpet against the monstrous regiment of women (1558) -- Letter to the Regent of Scotland (1558) -- Appellation to the nobility (1558) -- Letter to the commonalty of Scotland (1558) -- The second blast (1558)*

WOMAN (PHILOSOPHY)
SAXONHOUSE, Arlene W
Women in the history of political thought : ancient Greece to Machiavelli / Arlene W. Saxonhouse. — New York ; Eastbourne : Praeger, 1985. — xii, 210p. — (Women and politics series). — *Includes index. — Bibliography: p.199-204*

WOMAN'S CHRISTIAN TEMPERANCE UNION
BORDIN, Ruth Birgitta Anderson
Frances Willard : a biography / by Ruth Bordin. — Chapel Hill ; London : University of North Carolina Press, c1986. — xv, 294p. — *Includes index. — Bibliography: p.277-287*

WOMEN — Finland — Social conditions — Statistics
TASA-ARVOASIAIN NEUVOTTELUKUNTA
Tilastotietoja naisten asemasta = : Statistics about the position of women in Finland / Tasa-arvoasiain neuvottelukunta. — Helsinki : [Valtioneuvoston kanslia], 1975. — xi, 107 p. — (Valtioneuvoston kanslian julkaisuja ; 1975:5). — *English and Finnish*

WOMEN
INGRISCH, Doris
Das Rollenbild der Frau bei den Frühsozialisten / Doris Ingrisch. — Linz : Tranner, 1985. — 119p. — (Linzer Schriften zur Sozial- und Wirtschaftsgeschicte ; Bd.13). — *Bibliography : p114-119*

SAXONHOUSE, Arlene W
Women in the history of political thought : ancient Greece to Machiavelli / Arlene W. Saxonhouse. — New York ; Eastbourne : Praeger, 1985. — xii, 210p. — (Women and politics series). — *Includes index. — Bibliography: p.199-204*

WOMEN — Bibliography
PRESLEY, Frances
Women and community 1983-4 : a review and bibliography / Frances Presley. — London : Community Projects Foundation, 1985. — 28p

WOMEN — Congresses
Women's worlds : from the new scholarship / edited by Marilyn Safir ... [et al] ; in cooperation with the Society for the Psychological Study of Social Issues. — New York : Praeger, 1985. — p. cm. — *Papers presented at the First International Interdisciplinary Congress on Women held at the University of Haifa, Haifa, Israel, Dec. 28, 1981-Jan. 1, 1982. — Includes index*

WOMEN — Drug use
Adverse effects : women and the pharmaceutical industry / edited by Kathleen McDonnell. — Penang : International Organization of Consumers Unions Regional Office for Asia and the Pacific, 1986. — 217p

WOMEN — Education — Australia — South Australia — History — Case studies
MACKINNON, Alison
One foot on the ladder : origins and outcomes of girls' secondary schooling in South Australia / Alison Mackinnon. — St. Lucia ; New York : University of Queensland Press, 1984. — xii, 209 p.. — (The University of Queensland Press scholars' library). — *Includes index. — Bibliography: p. [197]-205*

WOMEN — Education — European Economic Community countries
BYRNE, Eileen Maire
Equality of education and training for girls (10—18 years) / by Eileen M. Byrne. — Luxembourg : Office for Official Publications of the European Communities, 1979. — iv, 80p. — (Education series / Commission of the European Communities ; no.9)

WOMEN — Education — Great Britain — History
The Education papers : women's quest for equality in Britain, 1850-1912 / edited by Dale Spender. — London : Routledge & Kegan Paul, 1987. — [365]p. — (Women's source library). — *Includes index*

WOMEN — Education — India
VOHRA, Roopa
Status education and problems of Indian women / Roopa Vohra, Arun K. Sen. — 2nd ed. — Delhi : Akshat Publications, 1986. — xx,148p. — *Bibliography: 141-148*

WOMEN — Education — Spain — Statistics
ALCOBENDAS TIRADO, María Pilar
Datos sobre el trabajo de la mujer en España / María Pilar Alcobendas Tirado. — Madrid : Centro de Investigaciones Sociológicas, 1983. — 217 p. ;c19 cm. — (Colección Monografías ; no. 68). — *Bibliography: p. 209-213*

WOMEN — Employment
BEECHEY, Veronica
Unequal work / Veronica Beechey. — London : Verse, 1987. — [240]p. — (Questions for feminism). — *Includes index*

CHABAUD-RYCHTER, Danielle
Espace et temps du travail domestique / Danielle Chabaud-Rychter, Dominique Fongeyrollas-Schwebel [et] Françoise Southounax. — Paris : Libraries des Méridiens, 1985. — 156p

Equal pay for women : progress and problems in seven countries / edited by Barrie O. Pettman with the assistance of John Fyfe. — Bradford (200 Keighley Rd, Bradford, W. Yorkshire BD9 4JZ) : MCB Books [for] the International Institute of Social Economics, 1975. — ix,173p

Feminism and political economy : women's work, women's struggles / edited by Heather Jon Maroney and Meg Luxton. — Toronto ; New York ; London : Methuen, 1987. — xii,333p. — *Bibliography: p.285-318*

Gender and the labour process / edited by David Knights, Hugh Willmott. — Aldershot : Gower, c1986. — vii,186p. — *Includes bibliographies and index*

MARSHALL, Kate
Real freedom : women's liberation and socialism / Kate Marshall. — London : Junius, 1982. — ii,139p

METCALFE, Beverly Alban
The effects of socialisation on women's management careers : a review / Beverly Alban Metcalfe. — Bradford : MCB University Press, 1985. — 50p. — (Management bibliographies and reviews ; ol.2,no.3). — *Bibliography: p42-50*

MITTER, Swasti
Common fate, common bond : women in the global economy / Swasti Mitter. — London : Pluto, 1986. — [224]p. — *Includes index*

NATIONAL RESEARCH COUNCIL (U.S.). Committee on Women's Employment and Related Social Issues. Panel on Technology and Women's Employment
Computer chips and paper clips : technology and women's employment / Heidi I. Hartmann, Robert E. Kraut, and Louise A. Tilly, editors ; Panel on Technology and Women's Employment, Committee on Women's Employment and Related Social Issues, Commission on Behavioral and Social Sciences and Education, National Research Council. — Washington, D.C. : National Academy Press, 1986-1987. — 2 v.. — *Includes bibliographies and index. — Contents: v. 1. [without special title] -- v. 2. Case studies and policy perspectives / Heidi I. Hartmann, editor*

STACE, Sheila
Vocational rehabilitation for women with disabilities / Sheila Stace. — Geneva : International Labour Office, 1986. — viii,38p. — *Bibliography: p33-36*

Women and work : an annual review. — Beverly Hills : Sage Publications, 1985. — *Annual*

WOMEN — Employment — Government policy — United States
NATIONAL RESEARCH COUNCIL (U.S.). Committee on Women's Employment and Related Social Issues. Panel on Technology and Women's Employment
Computer chips and paper clips : technology and women's employment / Heidi I. Hartmann, Robert E. Kraut, and Louise A. Tilly, editors ; Panel on Technology and Women's Employment, Committee on Women's Employment and Related Social Issues, Commission on Behavioral and Social Sciences and Education, National Research Council. — Washington, D.C. : National Academy Press, 1986-1987. — 2 v.. — *Includes bibliographies and index. — Contents: v. 1. [without special title] -- v. 2. Case studies and policy perspectives / Heidi I. Hartmann, editor*

WOMEN — Employment — Law and legislation — Canada — Congresses
Women, the law, and the economy / the editorial board, E. Diane Pask, Kathleen E. Mahoney, Catherine A. Brown. — Toronto ; Boston : Butterworths, c1985. — xix, 393 p.. — *Proceedings of the Women, Law and the Economy Conference held at the Banff Springs Hotel in 1983. Bibliography: p. 377-393*

WOMEN — Employment — Social aspects — United States
KAMINER, Wendy
Women volunteering : the pleasure, pain, and politics of unpaid work from 1830 to the present / Wendy Kaminer. — 1st ed. — Garden City, N.Y. : Anchor Press, 1984. — xix, 237 p.. — *Includes index. — Bibliography: p. [227]-228*

WOMEN — Employment — Australia — South Australia — History — Case studies
MACKINNON, Alison
One foot on the ladder : origins and outcomes of girls' secondary schooling in South Australia / Alison Mackinnon. — St. Lucia ; New York : University of Queensland Press, 1984. — xii, 209 p.. — (The University of Queensland Press scholars' library). — *Includes index. — Bibliography: p. [197]-205*

WOMEN — Employment — Canada
NORTH-SOUTH INSTITUTE
Women in industry : north-south connections / a study by the North-South Institute. — Ottawa : The Institute, 1985. — vii,75p. — *Bibliography: p70-75*

WOMEN — Employment — Canada — Congresses
Women, the law, and the economy / the editorial board, E. Diane Pask, Kathleen E. Mahoney, Catherine A. Brown. — Toronto ; Boston : Butterworths, c1985. — xix, 393 p.. — *Proceedings of the Women, Law and the Economy Conference held at the Banff Springs Hotel in 1983. — Bibliography: p. 377-393*

WOMEN — Employment — Canada — History — 20th century
PIERSON, Ruth Roach
They're still women after all : the Second World War and Canadian womanhood / Ruth Roach Pierson. — Toronto, Ont. : McClelland and Stewart, c1986. — 301 p.. — (The Canadian social history series). — *Includes index. — Bibliography: p. 221-236*

WOMEN — Employment — China
PECK, Stacey
Halls of jade, walls of stone : women in China today / Stacey Peck. — London : Grafton, 1986, c1985. — 288p. — *Bibliography: p [284]-285*

WOMEN — Employment — China — Tientsin — History
HERSHATTER, Gail
The workers of Tianjin, 1900-1949 / Gail Hershatter. — Stanford, Calif. : Stanford University Press, 1986. — viii, 313p. — *Includes index. — Bibliography: p.[285]-301*

WOMEN — Employment — Cyprus — Statistics
HOUSE, William J.
Discrimination and segregation of women workers in Cyprus / by William J. House. — [Nicosia] : Department of Statistics and Research, [1983?]. — 82p. — *Bibliography: p80-82*

Survey on the employment status of women in Cyprus. — [Nicosia] : Department of Statistics and Research, [1983]. — 121p. — *Bibliography: p54*

WOMEN — Employment — Developing countries
BOSERUP, Ester
Woman's role in economic development / Ester Boserup. — Brookfield, VT : Gower Pub. Co., 1986. — p. cm. — : Reprint. Originally published: New York : St. Martin's Press, 1970. — *Includes index. — Bibliography: p*

NORTH-SOUTH INSTITUTE
Women in industry : north-south connections / a study by the North-South Institute. — Ottawa : The Institute, 1985. — vii,75p. — *Bibliography: p70-75*

Sex inequalities in urban employment in the Third World : a study prepared for the International Labour Office within the framework of the World Employment Programme with the financial support of the United Nations Fund for Population Activities (UNFPA) / edited by Richard Anker and Catherine Hein. — Basingstoke : Macmillan, 1986. — [304]p. — (Macmillan series of ILO studies). — *Includes index*

WOMEN — Employment — Developing countries — Case studies
Gender roles in development projects : a case book / editors, Catherine Overholt ... [et al.]. — West Hartford, Conn. : Kumarian Press, 1985. — p. cm. — *Bibliography: p*

WOMEN — Employment — England — London
PITCHER, Jane
Women and low pay : initiatives / Jane Pitcher. — Hackney : Research and Intelligence Section, Chief Executive's Office, London Borough of Hackney, 1985. — [26p]. — (Research note / Hackney. Chief Executive's Office. Research and Intelligence Section ; 11). — *At Head of cover title: Research in Hackney. — Formerly Working note 20*

WOMEN — Employment — England — London — Bermondsey
HAW, Catherine Elise
Employment and well-being : a social-psychological study of Bermondsey housewives and women workers / Catherine Elise Haw. — 2v(708 leaves). — *PhD (Econ) 1986 LSE. — Leaves 581-686 are appendices*

WOMEN — Employment — Europe — Congresses
REGIONAL TRADE UNION SEMINAR (1968 : Paris)
Employment of womwn : regional trade union seminar, Paris, 26th-29th November, 1968 : final report. — Paris : OECD, 1970. — 385p. — (International seminars / Organisation for Economic Co-operation and Development ; 1968-2). — *Includes bibliographical references*

WOMEN — Employment — Europe — History — Addresses, essays, lectures
Women and work in preindustrial Europe / edited by Barbara A. Hanawalt. — Bloomington : Indiana University Press, c1986. — xviii, 233 p.. — *Includes bibliographies and index*

WOMEN — Employment — Europe, Northern — History
HOWELL, Martha C
Women, production, and patriarchy in late medieval cities / Martha C. Howell. — Chicago : University of Chicago Press, 1986. — xv, 285 p.. — (Women in culture and society). — *Includes index. — Bibliography: p. 261-277*

WOMEN — Employment — European Economic Community countries
European women in paid employment 1984 : Do they feel discriminated against and vulnerable at work? Are they equipped to take up the challenge of technology. — Luxembourg : Office for Official Publications of the European Communities, 1984. — 118p. — *At head of title page: Commission of the European Communities*

WOMEN — Employment — Germany — History
FRANZOI, Barbara
At the very least she pays the rent : women and German industrialization 1871-1914 / Barbara Franzoi. — Westport, Conn. ; London : Greenwood Press, 1985. — xii, 206p, 10p of plates. — (Contributions in women's studies ; no.57). — *Bibliography: p.[187]-199*

SACHSE, Carola
Industrial housewives : social work for women in the factories in Nazi Germany / Carola Sachse. — New York, N.Y. : The Institute for Research in History and the Haworth Press, c1987. — p. cm. — *"Has also been published as Women & history, number 11, 1986"--T.p. verso. — Bibliography: p*

WOMEN — Employment — Great Britain
CRAIG, Christine, 1921—
Payment structures and smaller firms : women's employment in segmented labour markets / by Christine Craig, Elizabeth Garnsey, Jill Rubery. — London : Department of Employment, [1985?]. — 109p. — (Research paper / Department of Employment ; no.48)

DEX, Shirley
Women's occupational mobility : a lifetime perspective / Shirley Dex. — London : Macmillan, 1987. — xii,157p. — *Bibliography: p148-154. — Includes index*

GREAT BRITAIN. Equal Opportunities Commission
Men's jobs? women's jobs? : practical guidance on why many jobs are done only by men or only by women, and how this pattern 'job segregation' can and should be changed. — London : HMSO, 1986. — vii,34p. — *At head of title: Equal Opportunities Commission*

In a man's world : essays on women in male-dominated professions / edited by Anne Spencer & David Podmore. — London : Tavistock, 1987. — 240p. — (Social science paperbacks ; 342). — *Includes bibliographies and index*

MALLIER, A. T.
Women and the economy : a comparative study of Britain and the USA / A.T. Mallier and M.J. Rosser. — Basingstoke : Macmill, 1987. — xiii,221p. — *Bibliography: p200-211. — Includes index*

NEWELL, Marie-Louise
The next job after the first baby : occupational transition among women born in 1946 / Marie-Louise and Heather Joshi. — London : London School of Hygiene and Tropical Medicine, 1986. — 68p. — (CPS research paper ; 86-3). — *Bibliography: p37-38*

ROBARTS, Sadie
Positive action for women : changing the workplace. — [2nd ed.] / Paddy Stamp & Sadie Robarts. — London : National Council for Civil Liberties, c1986. — vi,135p. — *Previous ed.: 1981. — Bibliography: p135-135*

WEBSTER, Barbara
Bearing the burden : women's work and local government / Barbara Webster. — London : Local Government Campaign Unit, 1987. — 27p. — *Bibliographies*

WOMEN — Employment — Great Britain — History
COHN, Samuel
The process of occupational sex-typing : the feminization of clerical labor in Great Britain / Samuel Cohn. — Philadelphia : Temple University Press, 1985. — p. cm. — (Women in the political economy). — *Includes index. — Bibliography: p*

Our work, our lives, our words : women's history and women's work / edited by Leonore Davidoff and Belinda Westover. — Basingstoke : Macmillan Education, 1986. — xiii,189p. — (Women in society)

WALBY, Sylvia
Patriarchy at work : patriarchal and capitalist relations in employment / Sylvia Walby. — Cambridge : Polity, 1986. — vii,292p. — (Feminist perspectives from Polity Press). — *Bibliography: p260-281. — Includes index*

WOMEN — Employment — Great Britain — History — 20th century
BRAYBON, Gail
Out of the cage : women's experiences in two world wars / Gail Braybon and Penny Summerfield. — London : Pandora, 1987. — [280]p. — *Includes bibliography and index*

WOMEN — Employment — Great Britain — Religious aspects — Christianity
DAWSON, Rosemary
And all that is unseen : a new look at women's work / by Rosemary Dawson ; the report of the Industrial and Economic Affairs Committee of the General Synod Board for Social Responsibility. — London : Church House, 1986. — vi,62p. — *Bibliography: p60*

WOMEN — Employment — India
VOHRA, Roopa
Status education and problems of Indian women / Roopa Vohra, Arun K. Sen. — 2nd ed. — Delhi : Akshat Publications, 1986. — xx,148p. — *Bibliography: 141-148*

WOMEN — Employment — India — Bibliography
Women at work in India : a bibliography / compiled by Suchitra Anant, S. V. Ramani Rao, Kabita Kapoor. — New Delhi ; London : Sage, 1986. — 238p

WOMEN — Employment — India — Delhi
KARLEKAR, Malavika
Poverty and women's work : a study of sweeper women in Delhi / Malavika Karlekar. — New Delhi : Vikas Pub. House, c1982. — vi, 158 p.. — *Includes index. — Bibliography: p. [149]-152*

WOMEN — Employment — Ireland — Statistics
BLACKWELL, John, 1941-
Women in the labour force : (a statistical digest) / John Blackwell. — Dublin : Employment Equality Agency, 1986. — 134p. — *Bibliographical references: p133-134*

WOMEN — Employment — Netherlands
AKTIECOMITÉ WERKLOZE VROUWEN
Eisenaktieboek / Aktiecomité Werkloze Vrouwen. — Amsterdam : the Aktiecomité, [1971?]. — 22p

WOMEN — Employment — Norway
LEIRA, Arnlaug
Kvinner på en oljearbeidsplass : rapport fra en undersøkelse ved Condeep - anlegget i Stavanger / Arnlaug Leira. — Stavanger : Rogalandsforskning, 1978. — 88p. — (Rogalandsforskning rapport ; nr.6). — *Bibliography: p85-88*

WOMEN — Employment — Pakistan
IRFAN, Mohammad
The determinants of female labour force participation in Pakistan / Mohammad Irfan. — Islamabad : Pakistan Institute of Development Economics, 1986. — [54p]. — (Studies in population, labour force and migration project report ; no.5). — *Bibliography: p[49]*

WOMEN — Employment — Peru — Lima
BUNSTER, Ximena
Sellers and servants : working women in Lima, Peru / Ximena Bunster, Elsa M. Chaney ; photos by Ellan Young. — New York : Praeger, 1985. — x, 258p. — *Includes index. — Bibliography: p.235-246*

WOMEN — Employment — Portugal
SILVA, Manuela
The employment of women in Portugal / report by Manuela Silva. — Luxembourg : Office for Official Publications of the European Communities, 1984. — xv,218p. — *At head of title page: Commission of the European Communities*

WOMEN — Employment — Puerto Rico
PUERTO RICO. Bureau of Labor Statistics
La participación de la mujer en la fuerza laboral : promedio años naturales 1960, 1970 y 1980. — [San Juan] : the Bureau, 1981. — 17leaves

WOMEN — Employment — Puerto Rico — Statistics
PUERTO RICO. Bureau of Labor Statistics
La participación de la mujer en la fuerza laboral : promedio años naturales 1960, 1970 y 1980. — [San Juan] : the Bureau, 1981. — 17leaves

WOMEN — Employment — Spain — Statistics
ALCOBENDAS TIRADO, María Pilar
Datos sobre el trabajo de la mujer en España / María Pilar Alcobendas Tirado. — Madrid : Centro de Investigaciones Sociológicas, 1983. — 217 p. ;c19 cm. — (Colección Monografías ; no. 68). — *Bibliography: p. 209-213*

WOMEN — Employment — Swaziland
ARMSTRONG, A.
A sample survey of women in wage employment in Swaziland / A. Armstrong. — Kwaluseni : Kwaluseni Campus, 1985. — 45p. — (Research paper / University of Swaziland. Social Science Research Unit ; no.15). — *Bibliography: p45*

WOMEN — Employment — United States
BOSE, Christine E
Jobs and gender : a study of occupational prestige / by Christine E. Bose. — New York : Praeger, 1985. — p. cm. — *Includes index. — Bibliography: p*

HARRIMAN, Ann
Women/men/management / by Ann Harriman. — New York : Praeger Publishers, 1985. — p. cm. — *Includes index. — Bibliography: p*

KAHNE, Hilda
Reconceiving part-time work : new perspectives for older workers and women / Hilda Kahne. — Totowa, N.J. : Rowman & Allanheld, 1985. — xv, 180 p.. — *Includes index. — Bibliography: p. [160]-174*

MALLIER, A. T.
Women and the economy : a comparative study of Britain and the USA / A.T. Mallier and M.J. Rosser. — Basingstoke : Macmill, 1987. — xiii,221p. — *Bibliography: p200-211. — Includes index*

RODGERS, Harrell R
Poor women, poor families : the economic plight of America's female-headed households / Harrell R. Rodgers, Jr. — Armonk, N.Y. : M.E. Sharpe, c1986. — viii, 167 p.. — *Includes index. — Bibliography: p. 150-161*

Women's career development / editors, Barbara A. Gutek and Laurie Larwood. — Newbury Park, Calif. : Sage Publications, c1987. — 191 p.. — *Includes bibliographies and index*

Women's work, men's work : sex segregation on the job / Barbara F. Reskin and Heidi I. Hartmann, editors ; Committee on Women's Employment and Related Social Issues, Commission on Behavioral and Social Sciences and Education, National Research Council. — Washington, D.C. : National Academy Press, 1986. — xii, 173 p.. — *Includes index. — Bibliography: p. 141-161*

WOMEN — Employment — United States — History
WEINER, Lynn Y.
From working girl to working mother : the female labor force in the United States, 1820-1980 / by Lynn Y. Weiner. — Chapel Hill ; London : University of North Carolina, c1985. — xii, 187p. — *Includes index. — Bibliography: p [165]-180*

Working women : past, present, future / edited by Karen Shallcross Koziara, Michael H. Moskow, Lucretia Dewey Tanner. — Washington, D.C. : Bureau of National Affairs, 1987. — p. cm. — (Industrial Relations Research Association series). — *Includes index*

WOMEN — Employment — United States — History — 19th century — Congresses
"To toil livelong day" : America's women at work, 1780-1980 / Carol Groneman and Mary Beth Norton, editors. — Ithaca, N.Y. : Cornell University Press, 1987. — p. cm. — *Papers presented at the Sixth Berkshire Conference on the History of Women held at Smith College June 1-3, 1984. — Includes index*

WOMEN — Employment — United States — History — 20th century — Congresses
"To toil livelong day" : America's women at work, 1780-1980 / Carol Groneman and Mary Beth Norton, editors. — Ithaca, N.Y. : Cornell University Press, 1987. — p. cm. — *Papers presented at the Sixth Berkshire Conference on the History of Women held at Smith College June 1-3, 1984. — Includes index*

WOMEN — Employment — United States — Longitudinal studies
Midlife women at work : a fifteen-year perspective / edited by Lois Banfill Shaw. — Lexington, Mass. : Lexington Books, c1986. — xi, 142 p.. — *Based on data from the National Longitudinal Surveys of Labor Market Experience of Mature Women begun in 1967 by the Ohio State University Center for Human Resource Research. — Includes bibliographies and index*

WOMEN — Employment — United States — Psychological aspects
Women's career development / editors, Barbara A. Gutek and Laurie Larwood. — Newbury Park, Calif. : Sage Publications, c1987. — 191 p.. — *Includes bibliographies and index*

WOMEN — Employment — Wales — South Glamorgan
SOUTH GLAMORGAN
1986 social survey : selected female variables : county electoral divisions. — [Cardiff] : [the Council], 1987. — ii,33p

WOMEN — Food — Psychological aspects
Fed up and hungry : women, oppression and food / Marilyn Lawrence (editor) ; with a foreword by Susie Orbach. — London : Women's Press, 1987. — 236p

WOMEN — Food — Social aspects
Fed up and hungry : women, oppression and food / Marilyn Lawrence (editor) ; with a foreword by Susie Orbach. — London : Women's Press, 1987. — 236p

WOMEN — Government policy — United States — Addresses, essays, lectures
Women, biology, and public policy / edited by Virginia Sapiro. — Beverly Hills, Calif. : Sage Publications, c1985. — p. cm. — (Sage yearbooks in women's policy studies ; v. 10). — *Contents: Biology and women's policy, a view from the biological sciences / Ruth Bleier -- Biology and women's policy, a view from the social sciences / Virginia Sapiro -- Male and female hormones / Marianne H. Whatley -- Fetal personhood and women's policy / Janet Gallagher -- Childbirth management and medical monopoly / Barbara Katz Rothman -- Occupational safety and health as a women's policy issue / Graham K. Wilson and Virginia Sapiro -- Older women / Laura Katz Olson -- The politics of a biosocial approach to crime / Susette M. Talarico -- Women's biology and the U.S. military / Judith Hicks Stiehm -- Women as "at risk" reproducers / Jane S. Jaquette and Kathleen A. Staudt*

WOMEN — Health and hygiene
Adverse effects : women and the pharmaceutical industry / edited by Kathleen McDonnell. — Penang : International Organization of Consumers Unions Regional Office for Asia and the Pacific, 1986. — 217p

WOMEN — Health and hygiene
continuation

DEKONINCK, Maria
Essai sur la santé des femmes / Maria DeKoninck, Francine Saillant, Lise Dunnigan. — [Québec] : Gouvernement du Québec, Conseil du statut de la femme, [1983]. — xviii,294p. — *Bibliography: p275-294.* — *Contents: Pouvoir, dépendance et santé des femmes / Maria DeKoninck, Francine Saillant -- Réflexion sur la sexualité / Lise Dunnigan*

WOMEN — Health and hygiene — Addresses, essays, lectures

Women, biology, and public policy / edited by Virginia Sapiro. — Beverly Hills, Calif. : Sage Publications, c1985. — p. cm. — (Sage yearbooks in women's policy studies ; v. 10). — *Contents: Biology and women's policy, a view from the biological sciences / Ruth Bleier -- Biology and women's policy, a view from the social sciences / Virginia Sapiro -- Male and female hormones / Marianne H. Whatley -- Fetal personhood and women's policy / Janet Gallagher -- Childbirth management and medical monopoly / Barbara Katz Rothman -- Occupational safety and health as a women's policy issue / Graham K. Wilson and Virginia Sapiro -- Older women / Laura Katz Olson -- The politics of a biosocial approach to crime / Susette M. Talarico -- Women's biology and the U.S. military / Judith Hicks Stiehm -- Women as "at risk" reproducers / Jane S. Jaquette and Kathleen A. Staudt*

WOMEN — Health and hygiene — Cross-cultural studies

Women's medicine : a cross-cultural study of indigenous fertility regulation / Lucile F. Newman, editor, with the assistance of James M. Nyce. — New Brunswick, N.J. : Rutgers University Press, c1985. — x, 203 p.. — (The Douglass series on women's lives and the meaning of gender). — *Includes bibliographies*

WOMEN — Health and hygiene — England — London

DOYAL, Lesley
Unhaealthy lives : being a woman in London / Lesley Doyal, Women's Studies Unit, the Polytechnic of North London : a report commissioned by the Greater London Council Industry and Employment Branch. — [London : Greater London Council, 1986]. — 26p. — *Includes bibliographical references*

WOMEN — Health and hygiene — Québec (Province)

DEKONINCK, Maria
Essai sur la santé des femmes / Maria DeKoninck, Francine Saillant, Lise Dunnigan. — [Québec] : Gouvernement du Québec, Conseil du statut de la femme, [1983]. — xviii,294p. — *Bibliography: p275-294.* — *Contents: Pouvoir, dépendance et santé des femmes / Maria DeKoninck, Francine Saillant -- Réflexion sur la sexualité / Lise Dunnigan*

WOMEN — History

LERNER, Gerda
Women and history / Gerda Lerner. — New York : Oxford University Press, c1986-. — v. <1 >. — *Includes index.* — *Bibliography: v. 1, p. 283-303.* — *Contents: v. 1. The creation of patriarchy*

WOMEN — History — Middle Ages, 500-1500

HOWELL, Martha C
Women, production, and patriarchy in late medieval cities / Martha C. Howell. — Chicago : University of Chicago Press, 1986. — xv, 285 p.. — (Women in culture and society). — *Includes index.* — *Bibliography: p. 261-277*

WOMEN — Housing — England — London

Women and housing policy : reports submitted to the GLC Housing and Women's Committees. — London : Greater London Council, 1986. — 100p. — (GLC housing research and policy report ; no.3). — *Research commissioned and coordinated by GLC Housing Department Policy and Resources Branch, Policy Division*

WOMEN — Language

BARON, Dennis E
Grammar and gender / Dennis Baron. — New Haven : Yale University Press, c1986. — p. cm . — *Includes index.* — *Bibliography: p*

WOMEN — Legal status, law, etc — Cross-cultural studies

Women in the world, 1975-1985 : the women's decade / Lynne B. Iglitzin and Ruth Ross, editors. — 2nd rev. ed. — Santa Barbara, Calif. : ABC-Clio Information Services, c1985. — p. cm. — (Studies in international and comparative politics ; 16). — *Includes bibliographies and index*

WOMEN — Legal status, laws, etc — Canada — Congresses

Women, the law, and the economy / the editorial board, E. Diane Pask, Kathleen E. Mahoney, Catherine A. Brown. — Toronto ; Boston : Butterworths, c1985. — xix, 393 p.. — *Proceedings of the Women, Law and the Economy Conference held at the Banff Springs Hotel in 1983.* — *Bibliography: p. 377-393*

WOMEN — Legal status, laws, etc. — Great Britain

LAND, Hilary
Women and economic dependency / Hilary Land. — Manchester : Equal Opportunities Commission, 1986. — 81p

WOMEN — Legal status, laws, etc — Spain

ALCOBENDAS TIRADO, María Pilar
Datos sobre el trabajo de la mujer en España / María Pilar Alcobendas Tirado. — Madrid : Centro de Investigaciones Sociológicas, 1983. — 217 p. ;c19 cm. — (Colección Monografías ; no. 68). — *Bibliography: p. 209-213*

WOMEN — Legal status, laws, etc. — Spain — History

FAGOAGA, Concha
La voz y el voto de las mujeres 1877-1931 / Concha Fagoaga. — Barcelona : Icaria Antrazyt, 1985. — 214p. — *Bibliography: p199-203*

WOMEN — Legal status, laws. etc — Swaziland

ARMSTRONG, Alice Kavanaugh
Law and the other sex : the legal position of women in Swaziland / by Alice Kavanagh Armstrong [and] Ronald Thandabantu Nhlapo. — Mbabane : Webster, [1985?]. — 150p. — *Bibliography: p148-150*

WOMEN — Legal status, laws, etc — United States

MACKINNON, Catharine A
Feminism unmodified : discourses on life and law / Catharine A. MacKinnon. — Cambridge, Mass. : Harvard University Press, 1987. — p. cm. — *Includes index.* — *Bibliography: p*

WOMEN — Legal status, laws, etc — United States — Bibliography

ARIEL, Joan
Women's legal rights in the United States : a selective bibliography / compiled by Joan Ariel, Ellen Broidy, and Susan Searing with assistance from Kay Cassell. — Chicago, Ill. : American Library Association, 1985. — vii, 55 p.. — *"Sponsored by the Discussion Goup on Women's Materials and Women Library Users of the Reference and Adult Services Division of the American Library Association."--T.p. verso*

WOMEN — Legal status, laws, etc — United States — History

SALMON, Marylynn
Women and the law of property in early America / Marylynn Salmon. — Chapel Hill ; London : University of North Carolina Press, c1986. — xvii, 267 p.. — (Studies in legal history). — *Based on the author's thesis (Ph. D.).* — *Includes indexes.* — *Bibliography: p. 239-251*

WOMEN — Medical care

DEKONINCK, Maria
Essai sur la santé des femmes / Maria DeKoninck, Francine Saillant, Lise Dunnigan. — [Québec] : Gouvernement du Québec, Conseil du statut de la femme, [1983]. — xviii,294p. — *Bibliography: p275-294.* — *Contents: Pouvoir, dépendance et santé des femmes / Maria DeKoninck, Francine Saillant -- Réflexion sur la sexualité / Lise Dunnigan*

For alma mater : theory and practice in feminist scholarship / edited by Paula A. Treichler, Cheris Kramarae, Beth Stafford. — Urbana : University of Illinois Press, c1985. — xv, 450 p., [10] p. of plates. — *Includes bibliographies and index*

WOMEN — Medical care — Québec (Province)

DEKONINCK, Maria
Essai sur la santé des femmes / Maria DeKoninck, Francine Saillant, Lise Dunnigan. — [Québec] : Gouvernement du Québec, Conseil du statut de la femme, [1983]. — xviii,294p. — *Bibliography: p275-294.* — *Contents: Pouvoir, dépendance et santé des femmes / Maria DeKoninck, Francine Saillant -- Réflexion sur la sexualité / Lise Dunnigan*

WOMEN — Mental health — England — London — Bermondsey

HAW, Catherine Elise
Employment and well-being : a social-psychological study of Bermondsey housewives and women workers / Catherine Elise Haw. — 2v(708 leaves). — *PhD (Econ) 1986 LSE.* — *Leaves 581-686 are appendices*

WOMEN — Miscellanea — Addresses, essays, lectures

The Female body in western culture : contemporary perspectives / Susan Rubin Suleiman, editor. — Cambridge, Mass. : Harvard University Press, 1986. — p. cm. — *Includes bibliographies*

WOMEN — Psychology

CHERNIN, Kim
The hungry self : women, eating, and identity / Kim Chernin. — London : Virago, 1986, c1985. — xv,213p. — *Originally published: New York : Times Books, 1985*

WOMEN — psychology

FISHER, Sue
In the patient's best interest : women and the politics of medical decisions / Sue Fisher. — New Brunswick, N.J. : Rutgers University Press, c1986. — ix, 214 p.. — *Includes index.* — *Bibliography: p. 195-207*

RUSSELL, Diana E H
The secret trauma : incest in the lives of girls and women / Diana E.H. Russell. — New York : Basic Books, c1986. — xviii, 426 p.. — *Includes index.* — *Bibliography: p. [413]-417*

WOMEN — Psychology

WESTCOTT, Marcia
The feminist legacy of Karen Horney / Marcia Westkott. — New Haven : Yale University Press, c1986. — p. cm. — *Includes index.* — *Bibliography: p*

WOMEN — Psychology — Cross-cultural studies

Women living change / edited by Susan C. Bourque and Donna Robinson Divine. — Philadelphia : Temple University Press, 1985. — p. cm. — (Women in the political economy) . — *Includes index*

WOMEN — Services for — South Australia

Women and welfare : South Australia. — [Adelaide] : Adviser on Women and Welfare : Women's Advisory Unit, [1980?]. — 23p

WOMEN — Services for — United States

The Woman client : providing human services in a changing world / edited by Dianne S. Burden and Naomi Gottlieb. — New York ; London : Tavistock, 1987. — x,299p. — *Includes bibliographies and index*

WOMEN — Sexual behavior — Addresses, essays, lectures

Sexuality, new perspectives / edited by Zira DeFries, Richard C. Friedman, and Ruth Corn. — Westport, Conn. : Greenwood Press, 1985. — xii, 362 p.. — (Contributions in psychology ; no. 6). — *Includes bibliographies and index*

WOMEN — Social conditions

BERNARD, Jessie Shirley
The female world from a global perspective / by Jessie Bernard. — Bloomington : Indiana University Press, c1987. — p. cm. — *Includes index. — Bibliography: p*

Caught up in conflict : women's responses to political strife / edited by Rosemary Ridd and Helen Callaway. — Basingstoke : Macmillan Education in association with the Oxford University Women's Studies Committee, 1986. — xii,246p. — (Women in society). — *Includes bibliographies and index*

CHERNIN, Kim
The hungry self : women, eating, and identity / Kim Chernin. — London : Virago, 1986, c1985. — xv,213p. — *Originally published: New York : Times Books, 1985*

DEKONINCK, Maria
Essai sur la santé des femmes / Maria DeKoninck, Francine Saillant, Lise Dunnigan. — [Québec] : Gouvernement du Québec, Conseil du statut de la femme, [1983]. — xviii,294p. — *Bibliography: p275-294. — Contents: Pouvoir, dépendance et santé des femmes / Maria DeKoninck, Francine Saillant -- Réflexion sur la sexualité / Lise Dunnigan*

Feminism and political economy : women's work, women's struggles / edited by Heather Jon Maroney and Meg Luxton. — Toronto ; New York ; London : Methuen, 1987. — xii,333p. — *Bibliography: p285-318*

Feminism as critique : essays on the politics of gender in late-capitalist societies / edited by Seyla Benhabib and Drucilla Cornell. — Cambridge : Polity, 1987. — 193p. — (Feminist perspectives). — *Includes index*

FIGES, Eva
Patriarchal attitudes : women in society / by Eva Figes ; with a new introduction by the author. — Basingstoke : Macmillan, 1986. — 191p. — *Originally published: London : Faber, 1970. — Bibliography: p188. — Includes index*

HAUG, Frigga
Female sexualization : a collective work of memory / Frigga Haug and others ; translated from the German by Erica Carter. — London : Verso, 1987. — 301p. — (Questions for feminism). — *Translation of: Frauenformen. 2. Sexualisierung. — Bibliography: p295-301*

MARSHALL, Kate
Real freedom : women's liberation and socialism / Kate Marshall. — London : Junius, 1982. — ii,139p

MATTELART, Michèle
Women, media and crisis : femininity and disorder / Michèle Mattelart. — London : Comedia, 1986. — 123p. — (Comedia series ; 33). — *Includes bibliography*

MOSER, Caroline O. N.
Housing policy and women : towards a gender aware approach : draft document commissioned by United Nations Centre for Human Settlements. — London : Development Planning Unit, Bartlett School of Architecture and Planning, University College, 1985. — 37p. — (DPU gender and planning working paper ; no.7). — *Bibliography: p35-37*

NORRIS, Pippa
Politics and sexual equality : the comparative position of women in Western democracies / Pippa Norris. — Brighton : Wheatsheaf, 1987. — [160]p. — *Includes bibliography and index*

OAKLEY, Ann
Telling the truth about Jerusalem : a collection of essays and poems / Ann Oakley. — Oxford : Basil Blackwell, 1986. — [288]p. — *Includes index*

PHILLIPS, Anne, 1950-
Divided loyalties : dilemmas of sex and class / Anne Phillips. — London : Virago, 1987. — 192p. — *Bibliography: p177-185. — Includes index*

ROWBOTHAM, Sheila
Woman's consciousness, man's world / Sheila Rowbotham. — Harmondsworth : Penguin, 1973. — xvi,136p. — (A pelican original). — *Bibliography: p.127-131. — Includes index*

Smothered by invention : technology in women's lives / edited by Wendy Faulkner and Erik Arnold. — London : Pluto, 1985. — [272]p

Speaking of faith : cross-cultural perspectives on women, religion and social change / Diana L. Eck and Devaki Jain editors. — London : Women's Press, 1986. — 288p. — *Conference papers*

Women and the state : the shifting boundaries of public and private / edited by Anne Showstack Sassoon. — London : Hutchinson Education, 1987. — [304]p. — (Contemporary politics). — *Includes index*

Women in Western political philosophy : Kant to Nietzsche / edited by Ellen Kennedy and Susan Hendus. — Brighton : Wheatsheaf, 1987. — vi,215p. — *Bibliography: p202-210. — Includes index*

Women, social science and public policy / edited by Jacqueline Goodnow & Carole Pateman for the Academy of Social Sciences in Australia. — Sydney ; London : Allen & Unwin, 1985. — xvi,162p

ZIMMERMAN, Jan
Once upon the future : a woman's guide to tomorrow's technology / Jan Zimmerman. — New York ; London : Pandora, 1986. — xviii,230p. — (Pandora Press focus). — *Includes index*

WOMEN — Social conditions — Atlases

SEAGER, Joni
Women in the world : an international atlas / Joni Seager and Ann Olson. — London : Pan, 1986. — 128p. — *Bibliography: p121-126*

WOMEN — Social conditions — Cross-cultural studies

Women in the world, 1975-1985 : the women's decade / Lynne B. Iglitzin and Ruth Ross, editors. — 2nd rev. ed. — Santa Barbara, Calif. : ABC-Clio Information Services, c1985. — p. cm. — (Studies in international and comparative politics ; 16). — *Includes bibliographies and index*

Women living change / edited by Susan C. Bourque and Donna Robinson Divine. — Philadelphia : Temple University Press, 1985. — p. cm. — (Women in the political economy). — *Includes index*

WOMEN — Social conditions — New Zealand

CONEY, Sandra
Every girl : a social history of women and the YWCA in Auckland, 1885-1985 / Sandra Coney. — Auckland, N.Z. : Auckland YWCA, 1986. — 292p

WOMEN — Societies and clubs — New Zealand

CONEY, Sandra
Every girl : a social history of women and the YWCA in Auckland, 1885-1985 / Sandra Coney. — Auckland, N.Z. : Auckland YWCA, 1986. — 292p

WOMEN — Socioeconomic status

PHILLIPS, Anne, 1950-
Divided loyalties : dilemmas of sex and class / Anne Phillips. — London : Virago, 1987. — 192p. — *Bibliography: p177-185. — Includes index*

WOMEN — Suffrage — Great Britain

LANSBURY, Coral
The old brown dog : women, workers, and vivisection in Edwardian England / Coral Lansbury. — Madison, Wis. : University of Wisconsin Press, 1985. — p. cm. — *Includes index*

WOMEN — Suffrage — Great Britain — History

HOLTON, Sandra Stanley
Feminism and democracy : women's suffrage and reform politics in Britain, 1900-1918 / Sandra Stanley Holton. — Cambridge : Cambridge University Press, 1986. — xip,201p,[4]p of plates. — *Bibliography: p187-195. — Includes index*

WOMEN — Suffrage — Great Britain — History — Bibliography

GREAT BRITAIN. Home Office. Library
Women's suffrage. — [London : the Library, ca.1978]. — [2]leaves

WOMEN — Suffrage — New Jersey — History — 20th century

GORDON, Felice D.
After winning : the legacy of the New Jersey suffragists, 1920-1947 / Felice D. Gordon. — New Brunswick, N.J. : Rutgers University Press, c1986. — x, 262 p.. — *Includes index. — Bibliography: p. [245]-251*

WOMEN — Suffrage — Spain — History

FAGOAGA, Concha
La voz y el voto de las mujeres 1877-1931 / Concha Fagoaga. — Barcelona : Icaria Antrazyt, 1985. — 214p. — *Bibliography: p199-203*

WOMEN — Tobacco use

JACOBSON, Bobbie
Beating the ladykillers : women and smoking / Bobbie Jacobson. — London : Pluto, 1986. — [192]p. — *Includes index*

WOMEN — Africa, Southern — Economic conditions — Bibliography

Women in Southern Africa : a bibliography / Durban Women's Bibliography Group. — Durban, South Africa : The Group, [1985]. — 107 p.. — *"February 1985."*

WOMEN — Africa, Southern — Social conditions — Bibliography

Women in Southern Africa : a bibliography / Durban Women's Bibliography Group. — Durban, South Africa : The Group, [1985]. — 107 p.. — *"February 1985."*

WOMEN — Alabama — Fairhope — Biography — Addresses, essays, lectures

GASTON, Paul M
Women of Fair Hope / Paul M. Gaston. — Athens : University of Georgia Press, c1984. — xiv, 143 p.. — (Mercer University Lamar memorial lectures ; no. 25). — *Includes index. — Bibliography: p. [119]-133*

WOMEN — Albania — Social conditions

On the road of the emancipation of the Albanian women : papers read in the session held on the occasion of the 40th anniversary of the 1st Congress of the Anti-fascist Women's Union of Albania (Berat, 4 November 1984). — Tirana : 8 Nentori Publishing House, 1985. — 63p

WOMEN — Algeria — Social conditions

ALLOULA, Malek
[Harem colonial. English]. The colonial harem / Malek Alloula ; translation by Myrna Godzich and Wlad Godzich ; introduction by Barbara Harlow. — Minneapolis : University of Minnesota Press, c1986. — xxii, 135 p.. — (Theory and history of literature ; v. 21). — *Translation of: Le harem colonial. — Bibliography: p. 135*

WOMEN — Australia — History — Modern period, 1600-

HUNT, Susan Jane
Spinifex and hessian : women's lives in North-Western Australia 1860-1900 / Susan Jane Hunt. — Nedlands : University of Western Australia Press, 1986. — x,168p. — (Western Australian experience series). — *Cover title: Spinifex and hessian: women in North-West Australia, 1860-1900. — Bibliography: p152-159*

WOMEN — Australia — Social conditions

Australian women : new feminist perspectives / edited by Norma Grieve and Ailsa Burns. — Melbourne ; New York : Oxford University Press, 1986. — xii, 412 p.. — *Bibliography: p. [358]-395*

Australian women and the political system / edited by Marian Simms. — Melbourne, Australia : Longman Cheshire, 1984. — xviii, 222 p. — (Australian studies). — *Includes index. — Bibliography: p. [204]-217*

Women, social science and public policy / edited by Jacqueline Goodnow & Carole Pateman for the Academy of Social Sciences in Australia. — Sydney ; London : Allen & Unwin, 1985. — xvi,162p

WOMEN — Australia — South Australia — Social conditions — Case studies

MACKINNON, Alison
One foot on the ladder : origins and outcomes of girls' secondary schooling in South Australia / Alison Mackinnon. — St. Lucia ; New York : University of Queensland Press, 1984. — xii, 209 p.. — (The University of Queensland Press scholars' library). — *Includes index. — Bibliography: p. [197]-205*

WOMEN — Canada — Bibliography

NEW BRUNSWICK. Women's Employment Policy Coordinator
Bibliography : women's issues. — Fredericton : Department of Labour and Human Resources, 1984. — [7] leaves,iii,153p. — *An updated version of a bibliography prepared by Catherine Bowlen*

WOMEN — Canada — Crimes against

No safe place : violence against women and children / edited by Connie Guberman & Margie Wolfe. — Toronto, Ont. : Women's Press, c1985. — 165 p.. — *Includes bibliographical references*

WOMEN — Canada — Economic conditions

NORTH-SOUTH INSTITUTE
Women in industry : north-south connections / a study by the North-South Institute. — Ottawa : The Institute, 1985. — vii,75p. — *Bibliography: p70-75*

WOMEN — Canada — Economic conditions — Congresses

Women, the law, and the economy / the editorial board, E. Diane Pask, Kathleen E. Mahoney, Catherine A. Brown. — Toronto ; Boston : Butterworths, c1985. — xix, 393 p.. — *Proceedings of the Women, Law and the Economy Conference held at the Banff Springs Hotel in 1983. — Bibliography: p. 377-393*

WOMEN — Canada — History — 20th century

PIERSON, Ruth Roach
Canadian women and the Second World War / Ruth Roach Pierson. — Ottawa : Canadian Historical Association, 1983. — 31p. — (Historical booklet / Canadian Historical Association ; no.37). — *Bibliography: p.28-29*

WOMEN — Canada — Social conditions

The politics of diversity : feminism, Marxism and nationalism / edited by Roberta Hamilton and Michèle Barrett. — [London] : Verso, 1986

WOMEN — Caribbean Area

Integrating women into development programs : a guide for implementation for Latin America and the Caribbean / by Karen White...[et al.] ; tables prepared by Roxana Moayedi. — Washington, D.C. : International Centre for Research on Women, 1986. — iv,87p. — *Prepared for the Bureau for Latin America and the Caribbean, U.S. Agency for International Development*

WOMEN — Caribbean Area — Social conditions

Women of the Caribbean / edited by Pat Ellis. — London : Zed, 1986. — [176]p. — *Includes bibliography and index*

WOMEN — Chile

CHILE SOLIDARITY CAMPAIGN
Women in Chile : information pack. — London : Chile Solidarity Campaign, 1985. — 14 leaves

WOMEN — China — Bibliography

CHENG, Lucie
Women in China : bibliography of available English Language materials / compiled by Lucie Cheng, Charlotte Furth, and Hon-ming Yip. — Berkeley : Institute of East Asian Studies. Center for Chinese Studies, 1984. — xiv,109p

WOMEN — China — Case studies

PECK, Stacey
Halls of jade, walls of stone : women in China today / Stacey Peck. — London : Grafton, 1986, c1985. — 288p. — *Bibliography: p [284]-285*

WOMEN — China — Social conditions

CUSACK, Dymphna
Chinese women speak / Dymphna Cusack. — London : Century Hutchinson, 1985, c1958. — 262p. — (Century travellers series). — *Originally published: London : Angus & Robertson, 1959*

PECK, Stacey
Halls of jade, walls of stone : women in China today / Stacey Peck. — London : Grafton, 1986, c1985. — 288p. — *Bibliography: p [284]-285*

WOMEN — Developing countries

BOSERUP, Ester
Woman's role in economic development / Ester Boserup. — Brookfield, VT : Gower Pub. Co., 1986. — p. cm. — : Reprint. Originally published: New York : St. Martin's Press, 1970. — *Includes index. — Bibliography: p*

WOMEN — Developing countries — Economic conditions

BUVINIĆ, Maria
Woman-headed households : the ignored factor in development planning / Maria Buvinić, Nadia H. Youssef with Barbara Von Elm. — Washington, D.C. : International Center for Research on Women, 1978. — iii,iii,119p. — *Report submitted to AID/WID. — Bibliography: p[115-119]*

NORTH-SOUTH INSTITUTE
Women in industry : north-south connections / a study by the North-South Institute. — Ottawa : The Institute, 1985. — vii,75p. — *Bibliography: p70-75*

WOMEN — Developing countries — Economic conditions — Case studies

Gender roles in development projects : a case book / editors, Catherine Overholt ... [et al.]. — West Hartford, Conn. : Kumarian Press, 1985. — p. cm. — *Bibliography: p*

WOMEN — Developing countries — Social conditions

BUVINIĆ, Maria
Woman-headed households : the ignored factor in development planning / Maria Buvinić, Nadia H. Youssef with Barbara Von Elm. — Washington, D.C. : International Center for Research on Women, 1978. — iii,iii,119p. — *Report submitted to AID/WID. — Bibliography: p[115-119]*

SAFILIOS-ROTHSCHILD, Constantina
The status of women and fertility in the Third World in the 1970-80 decade / Constantina Safilios-Rothschild. — New York : Population Council, 1985. — 49p. — (Working papers / Population Council. Center for Policy Studies ; no.118). — *Bibliography: p25-28*

Women, state and ideology : studies from Africa and Asia / edited by Haleh Afshar. — London : Macmillan, 1987. — [250]p. — *Includes index*

WOMEN — Developing countries — Social conditions — Congresses

Visibility and power : essays on women in society and development / edited by Leela Dube, Eleanor Leacock, Shirley Ardener. — Delhi ; New York : Oxford University Press, 1986. — L, 361 p.. — *Includes bibliographies and index*

WOMEN — Ecuador — Guayaquil

MOSER, Caroline O. N.
Residential level struggle and consciousness : the experiences of poor women in Guayaquil, Ecuador / Caroline O. N. Moser. — London : Development Planning Unit, University College London, 1985. — 36p. — (DPU Gender and Planning Working Paper ; No.1). — *Bibliography: p35-36*

WOMEN — Egypt — Social conditions

TUCKER, Judith E.
Women in nineteenth-century Egypt / Judith E. Tucker. — Cambridge : Cambridge University Press, 1985. — xii,251p. — (Cambridge Middle East library). — *Bibliography: p239-247. — Includes index*

WOMEN — England — History — 16th century

HENDERSON, Katherine U
Half humankind : contexts and texts of the controversy about women in England, 1540-1640 / Katherine Usher Henderson, Barbara F. McManus. — Urbana : University of Illinois Press, c1985. — p. cm. — *Includes index. — Bibliography: p*

WOMEN — England — History — 16th century — Sources

HENDERSON, Katherine U
Half humankind : contexts and texts of the controversy about women in England, 1540-1640 / Katherine Usher Henderson, Barbara F. McManus. — Urbana : University of Illinois Press, c1985. — p. cm. — *Includes index. — Bibliography: p*

WOMEN — England — History — 17th century

HENDERSON, Katherine U
Half humankind : contexts and texts of the controversy about women in England, 1540-1640 / Katherine Usher Henderson, Barbara F. McManus. — Urbana : University of Illinois Press, c1985. — p. cm. — *Includes index. — Bibliography: p*

WOMEN — England — History — 17th century — Sources

HENDERSON, Katherine U
Half humankind : contexts and texts of the controversy about women in England, 1540-1640 / Katherine Usher Henderson, Barbara F. McManus. — Urbana : University of Illinois Press, c1985. — p. cm. — *Includes index. — Bibliography: p*

WOMEN — England — London — Social conditions

HAMILTON, Jane
Women in Camden 1981 / Jane Hamilton [and] Peter Land. — Camden : Department of Planning and Communications, 1982. — 11p. — (Planning and Communication notes)

WOMEN — England — Nottinghamshire

WITHAM, Joan
Hearts and minds : the story of the women of Nottinghamshire in the miners' strike, 1984-1985 / Joan Witham. — London : Canary, 1986. — 217p. — *Includes index*

WOMEN — England, Northern — Crimes against
WARD JOUVE, Nicole
"The streetcleaner : the Yorkshire Ripper case on trial / Nicole Ward Jouve. — London : Boyars, 1986. — 231p

WOMEN — Europe — Economic conditions — Addresses, essays, lectures
Women and work in preindustrial Europe / edited by Barbara A. Hanawalt. — Bloomington : Indiana University Press, c1986. — xviii, 233 p.. — *Includes bibliographies and index*

WOMEN — Finland — Statistics
TASA-ARVOASIAIN NEUVOTTELUKUNTA
Tilastotietoja naisten asemasta = : Statistics about the position of women in Finland / Tasa-arvoasiain neuvottelukunta. — Helsinki : [Valtioneuvoston kanslia], 1975. — xi, 107 p. — (Valtioneuvoston kanslian julkaisuja ; 1975:5). — *English and Finnish*

WOMEN — France — Institutional care
RIPA, Yannick
La ronde des folles : femme, folie et enfermement au XIXe siècle, (1838-1870) / Yannick Ripa. — Paris : Aubier, 1986. — 216p

WOMEN — France — Statistics
Femmes en chiffres. — [Paris] : CNIDF-INSEE, [1986]. — 94p. — *Bibliography: p94*

WOMEN — Germany — Economic conditions
FRANZOI, Barbara
At the very least she pays the rent : women and German industrialization 1871-1914 / Barbara Franzoi. — Westport, Conn. ; London : Greenwood Press, 1985. — xii, 206p, 10p of plates. — (Contributions in women's studies ; no.57). — *Bibliography: p.[187]-199*

WOMEN — Germany — History
LEHKER, Marianne
Frauen im Nationalsozialismus : wie aus Opfern Handlanger der Täter wurden : eine nötige Trauerarbeit / Marianne Lehker. — Frankfurt : Materialis, 1984. — 132p. — *Bibliography: p123-132*

WOMEN — Germany — History — 20th century
KOONZ, Claudia
Mothers in the fatherland : women, the family and Nazi politics / Claudia Koonz. — London : Jonathan Cape, 1987, c1986. — [700]p. — *Originally published: New York : St. Martin's Press, 1986. — Includes bibliography and index*

WOMEN — Germany — Social conditions
LEHKER, Marianne
Frauen im Nationalsozialismus : wie aus Opfern Handlanger der Täter wurden : eine nötige Trauerarbeit / Marianne Lehker. — Frankfurt : Materialis, 1984. — 132p. — *Bibliography: p123-132*

WOMEN — Germany — Social conditions — History
BUSSEMER, Herrad-Ulrike
Frauenemanzipation und Bildungsbürgertum : Sozialgeschichte der Frauenbewegung in der Reichsgründungszeit / Herrad-Ulrike Bussemer. — Weinheim : Beltz Verlag, 1985. — 360p. — (Ergebnisse der Frauenforschung ; Bd.7). — *Bibliography: p[350]-360*

WOMEN — Germany (West)
HÜBNER, Irene
"-wie eine zweite Haut" : Ausländerinnen in Deutschland / Irene Hübner. — Weinheim : Beltz, 1985. — 211p. — *Bibliography: p209-210*

WOMEN — Great Britain — Crimes against
Women, violence and social control / edited by Jalna Hanmer and Mary Maynard. — Basingstoke : Macmillan, 1987. — xi,213p. — (Explorations in sociology ; 23). — *Conference proceedings. — Bibliography: p193-209. — Includes index*

WOMEN — Great Britain — Economic conditions
LAND, Hilary
Women and economic dependency / Hilary Land. — Manchester : Equal Opportunities Commission, 1986. — 81p

Women in Britain today / edited by Veronica Beechey and Elizabeth Whitelegg. — Milton Keynes : Open University Press, 1986. — 216p. — *Includes bibliographies and index*

WOMEN — Great Britain — Health and hygiene
FOLEY, Roni
Women and health care : self-help health groups in Britain / Roni Foley. — Southampton : University of Southampton. Department of Sociology and Social Administration, 1985. — 37p. — *A research project funded by the Equal Opportunities Commission*

WOMEN — Great Britain — History
TURNBULL, Annmarie
Women with a past : a brief account of some aspects of women's history in Britain in the 19th and 20th centuries / Annmarie Turnbull, Anna Davin and Patricia de Wolfe. — London : Feminist Library and Information Centre, 1980. — 31p

WOMEN — Great Britain — History — 17th century
The Women's sharp revenge : five women's pamphlets from the Renaissance / edited by Simon Shepherd. — London : Fourth Estate, c1985. — 207p. — *Bibliography: p199-200. — Includes index*

WOMEN — Great Britain — Social conditions
BRAYBON, Gail
Out of the cage : women's experiences in two world wars / Gail Braybon and Penny Summerfield. — London : Pandora, 1987. — [280]p. — *Includes bibliography and index*

CAINE, Barbara
Destined to be wives : the sisters of Beatrice Webb / Barbara Caine. — Oxford : Clarendon, 1986. — [xii,280]p,[16]p of plates. — *Includes bibliography and index*

COOTE, Anna
Sweet freedom : the struggle for women's liberation / Anna Coote and Beatrix Campbell. — 2nd ed. — Oxford : Basil Blackwell, 1987. — [224]p. — *Previous ed.: 1982. — Includes index*

Eighteenth-century women : an anthology / [compiled by] Bridget Hill. — London : Allen & Unwin, 1984. — ix,271p. — *Bibliography: p258-264. — Includes index*

JALLAND, Pat
Women, marriage and politics 1860-1914 / Pat Jalland. — Oxford : Clarendon, 1986. — [380]p,[8]p of plates. — *Includes bibliography and index*

LAND, Hilary
Women won't benefit : the impact of the Social Security Bill on women's rights / Hilary Land and Sue Ward. — London : National Council for Civil Liberties. Rights for Women Unit, 1986. — 48p

MARSHALL, Kate
Moral panics and Victorian values / Kate Marshall. — 2nd ed. — London : Junius Publications, 1986. — 62p

PASCALL, Gillian
Social policy : a feminist analysis / Gillian Pascall. — London : Tavistock, 1986. — [v,220]p. — *Includes bibliography and index*

SDP LIBERAL ALLIANCE
Freedom and choice for women : a Liberal-SDP Alliance policy proposal. — Hebden Bridge : Liberal Party Publications, 1986. — 35p

SOUHAMI, Diane
A woman's place : the changing picture of women in Britain / Diane Souhami. — Harmondsworth : Penguin, 1986. — 160p. — *Bibliography: p158*

Women : neglected majority or monstrous regiment?. — London : Papermac, 1987. — 115p. — (Days of decision)

Women and social policy : a reader / edited by Clare Ungerson. — Basingstoke : Macmillan Education, 1985. — x,278p. — (Women in society). — *Bibliography: p261-274. — Includes index*

Women in Britain today / edited by Veronica Beechey and Elizabeth Whitelegg. — Milton Keynes : Open University Press, 1986. — 216p. — *Includes bibliographies and index*

Women, violence and social control / edited by Jalna Hanmer and Mary Maynard. — Basingstoke : Macmillan, 1987. — xi,213p. — (Explorations in sociology ; 23). — *Conference proceedings. — Bibliography: p193-209. — Includes index*

The Women's sharp revenge : five women's pamphlets from the Renaissance / edited by Simon Shepherd. — London : Fourth Estate, c1985. — 207p. — *Bibliography: p199-200. — Includes index*

WOMEN — Great Britain — Social conditions — History
KELLY, Jane Catherine
The creation of "moral woman" : a sociological history with reference to Britain in the nineteenth and twentieth centuries / by Jane Catherine Kelly. — 210 leaves. — *PhD (Econ) 1986 LSE*

WOMEN — Great Britain — Social conditions — Sources
Barbara Leigh Smith Bodichon and the Langham Place Group / edited by Candida Ann Lacey. — New York ; London : Routledge & Kegan Paul, 1987. — vii,485p.. — (Women's source library). — *Includes index*

WOMEN — Great Britain — Social conditions — Statistics
Women and men in Britain: a statistical profile / Equal Opportunities Commission. — London : HMSO, 1985-. — *Annual*

WOMEN — Greece — Social conditions
Gender & power in rural Greece / edited by Jill Dubisch. — Princeton, N.J. : Princeton University Press, c1986. — p. cm. — *Includes index. — Bibliography: p*

WOMEN — India — Bibliography
PANDIT, Harshida
Women of India : an annotated bibliography / Harshida Pandit. — New York : Garland Pub., 1985. — p. cm. — (Garland reference library of social science ; vol. 152). — *Includes index*

WOMEN — India — Economic conditions
Women's oppression : patterns and perspectives / edited by Susheela Kaushik. — New Delhi : Shakti Books, c1985. — vi, 134 p.. — (Women in society). — *Includes index. — Bibliography: p. [111]-131. — Contents: Equality / Sarah Joseph -- Patriarchal ideology and women's oppression / Bikram Nanda and Anjana Mangalagiri -- Patriarchy and women's oppression / Manoshi Mitra -- The economics of women's oppression / Suguna Paul -- Rural women, class formations, and development / K. Murali Manohar -- Cultural roots of oppression / Usha Nayar -- Muslim women, a political profile / Archana Chaturvedi -- Development process / Neera Chandhoke*

WOMEN — India — Social conditions
DEVENDRA, Kiran
Status and position of women in India : with special reference to women in contemporary India / Kiran Devendra. — New Delhi : Shakti Books, 1985. — xxi,186p. — *Bibliography: p[173]-181*

WOMEN — India — Social conditions
continuation

POITEVIN, Guy
Inde : village au féminin : la peine d'exister / Guy Poitevin. — Paris : L'Harmattan, 1985. — 246p. — *Bibliography: p249*

Social development : essays in honour of SMT Durgabai Deshmukh / edited by B. N. Ganguli. — New Delhi : Sterling Publishers : Council for Social Development, 1977. — viii,303p. — *Bibliography: p287-290*

VOHRA, Roopa
Status education and problems of Indian women / Roopa Vohra, Arun K. Sen. — 2nd ed. — Delhi : Akshat Publications, 1986. — xx,148p. — *Bibliography: 141-148*

Women's oppression : patterns and perspectives / edited by Susheela Kaushik. — New Delhi : Shakti Books, c1985. — vi, 134 p.. — (Women in society). — *Includes index. — Bibliography: p. [111]-131. — Contents: Equality / Sarah Joseph -- Patriarchal ideology and women's oppression / Bikram Nanda and Anjana Mangalagiri -- Patriarchy and women's oppression / Manoshi Mitra -- The economics of women's oppression / Suguna Paul -- Rural women, class formations, and development / K. Murali Manohar -- Cultural roots of oppression / Usha Nayar -- Muslim women, a political profile / Archana Chaturvedi -- Development process / Neera Chandhoke*

WOMEN — India — Social conditions — Bibliography

PANDIT, Harshida
Women of India : an annotated bibliography / Harshida Pandit. — New York : Garland Pub., 1985. — p. cm. — (Garland reference library of social science ; vol. 152). — *Includes index*

WOMEN — Iowa — Case studies

FINK, Deborah
Open country, Iowa : rural women, tradition and change / Deborah Fink. — Albany : State University of New York Press, c1986. — p. cm. — (SUNY series in the anthropology of work). — *Includes index*

WOMEN — Iran

Women and the family in Iran / edited by Asghar Fathi. — Leiden : E. J. Brill, 1985. — 239p. — (Social, economic and political studies of the Middle East ; v.38)

WOMEN — Ireland — Social conditions

BEALE, Jenny
Women in Ireland : voices of change / Jenny Beale. — Basingstoke : Macmillan Education, 1986. — xii,219p. — (Women in society). — *Bibliography: p209-212. — Includes index*

WOMEN — Japan

EKKEN, Kaibara Atsunobu
The way of contentment ; and Women and wisdom of Japan [Greater learning for women] / Kaibara Ekken ; translated from the Japanese by Ken Hoshino. — Washington, D.C. : University Publications of America, 1979. — 124,64p. — (Studies in Japanese history and civilization). — *At head of title: Wisdom of the East. — Reprint the way of contentment (London: John Murray, 1913) and Women and wisdom of Japan [Greater learning for women] (London: John Murray, 1905)*

WOMEN — Korea (South) — Religious life

KENDALL, Laurel
Shamans, housewives, and other restless spirits : women in Korean ritual life / Laurel Kendall. — Honolulu : University of Hawaii Press, c1985. — xiii, 234 p.. — (Studies of the East Asian Institute). — *Includes index. — Bibliography: p. [213]-222*

WOMEN — Latin America

Integrating women into development programs : a guide for implementation for Latin America and the Caribbean / by Karen White...[et al.] ; tables prepared by Roxana Moayedi. — Washington, D.C. : International Centre for Research on Women, 1986. — iv,87p. — *Prepared for the Bureau for Latin America and the Caribbean, U.S. Agency for International Development*

WOMEN — Mediterranean Region — Social conditions

Women of the Mediterranean / edited by Monique Gadant ; translated by A.M. Berrett. — London : Zed, 1986. — [240]p. — *Translated from the French. — Includes bibliography and index*

WOMEN — Mexican-American Border Region — Social conditions

Women on the U.S.-Mexico border : responses to change / edited by Vicki L. Ruiz and Susan Tiano. — Boston ; London : Allen & Unwin, c1987. — xi,247p. — (Thematic studies in Latin America). — *Includes bibliography and index*

WOMEN — New Brunswick — Bibliography

NEW BRUNSWICK. Women's Employment Policy Coordinator
Bibliography : women's issues. — Fredericton : Department of Labour and Human Resources, 1984. — [7] leaves,iii,153p. — *An updated version of a bibliography prepared by Catherine Bowlen*

WOMEN — New Brunswick — Congresses

"NEW DIRECTIONS FOR NEW BRUNSWICK": A CONFERENCE FOR WOMEN (Memramcook : 1974)
A report on new directions for New Brunswick : a conference for women. — [Memramcook? : the Conference, [1974?]. — 3,3 leaves. — *Headings for workshops also given in French*

WOMEN — New Zealand — Social conditions

WARING, Marilyn
Women, politics and power / essays by Marilyn Waring. — Wellington : Allen and Unwin New Zealand, [1985]. — 121p

WOMEN — New Zealand — North Island — History

BINNEY, Judith
Ngā Mōrehu : the survivors / Judith Binney and Gillian Chaplin. — Auckland ; Oxford : Oxford University Press, 1986. — 218p. — *Bibliography: p212-215*

WOMEN — New Zealand — North Island — Social conditions

BINNEY, Judith
Ngā Mōrehu : the survivors / Judith Binney and Gillian Chaplin. — Auckland ; Oxford : Oxford University Press, 1986. — 218p. — *Bibliography: p212-215*

WOMEN — Nicaragua — Social conditions

ANGEL, Adriana
The tiger's milk : women of Nicaragua / Adriana Angel, Fiona Macintosh. — London : Virago, 1987. — 142p

WOMEN — Norway — Social conditions

Patriarchy in a welfare society / edited by Harriet Holter. — Oslo : Universitetsforlaget ; London : Global [distributor], c1984. — 235p. — *Bibliography: p223-234*

WOMEN — Papua New Guinea

GELBER, Marilyn G
Gender and society in the New Guinea Highlands : an anthropological perspective on antagonism toward women / Marilyn G. Gelber. — Boulder : Westview Press, 1986. — xi, 180 p.. — (Women in cross-cultural perspective). — *Includes index. — Bibliography: p. [159]-175*

WOMEN — Papua New Guinea — Goroka District

SEXTON, Lorraine
Mothers of money, daughters of coffee : the Wok Meri movement / by Lorraine Sexton. — Ann Arbor, Mich. : UMI Research Press, c1986. — p. cm. — (Studies in cultural anthropology ; no. 10). — *: Revision of thesis (Ph. D.)--Temple University, 1980. — Includes index. — Bibliography: p*

WOMEN — Poland — Statistics

POLAND. Główny Urząd Statystyczny
Kobieta w Polsce. — Warszawa : Główny Urząd Statystyczny, 1985. — 116p

WOMEN — Puerto Rico

The Puerto Rican woman : perspectives on culture, history, and society / edited by Edna Acosta-Belén. — 2nd ed. — New York : Praeger, 1986. — xii, 212 p.. — *Includes index. — Bibliography: p. 189-208*

WOMEN — Puerto Rico — Social conditions

The Puerto Rican woman : perspectives on culture, history, and society / edited by Edna Acosta-Belén. — 2nd ed. — New York : Praeger, 1986. — xii, 212 p.. — *Includes index. — Bibliography: p. 189-208*

WOMEN — Québec (Province) — Social conditions

DEKONINCK, Maria
Essai sur la santé des femmes / Maria DeKoninck, Francine Saillant, Lise Dunnigan. — [Québec] : Gouvernement du Québec, Conseil du statut de la femme, [1983]. — xviii,294p. — *Bibliography: p275-294. — Contents: Pouvoir, dépendance et santé des femmes / Maria DeKoninck, Francine Saillant -- Réflexion sur la sexualité / Lise Dunnigan*

WOMEN — Russia — History — Congresses

Women in Russia / edited by Dorothy Atkinson, Alexander Dallin, and Gail Warshofsky Lapidus. — Stanford, Calif. : Stanford University Press, 1977. — xiii, 410 p.. — *Based on a conference held at Stanford University, May 29-June 1, 1975. — Includes bibliographical references and index*

WOMEN — Russia — Social conditions — Congresses

Women in Russia / edited by Dorothy Atkinson, Alexander Dallin, and Gail Warshofsky Lapidus. — Stanford, Calif. : Stanford University Press, 1977. — xiii, 410 p.. — *Based on a conference held at Stanford University, May 29-June 1, 1975. — Includes bibliographical references and index*

WOMEN — South Africa — Biography

BAARD, Frances
My spirit is not banned : as told by Frances Baard to Barbie Schreiner. — Harare : Zimbabwe Publishing House, 1986. — 92p

WOMEN — South Australia

Women and welfare : South Australia. — [Adelaide] : Adviser on Women and Welfare : Women's Advisory Unit, [1980?]. — 23p

WOMEN — Southern States — Social conditions — Congresses

The Web of southern social relations : women, family, & education / edited by Walter J. Fraser, Jr., R. Frank Saunders, Jr., and Jon L. Wakelyn. — Athens : University of Georgia Press, c1985. — xvii, 257 p.. — *Includes bibliographies and index*

WOMEN — Soviet Union — Social conditions

Soviet social scientists talking : an official debate about women / edited by Mary Buckley. — London : Macmillan, 1986. — xii,107p. — *Bibliography: p107*

WOMEN — Spain — Statistics
ALCOBENDAS TIRADO, María Pilar
Datos sobre el trabajo de la mujer en España / María Pilar Alcobendas Tirado. — Madrid : Centro de Investigaciones Sociológicas, 1983. — 217 p. ;c19 cm. — (Colección Monografías ; no. 68). — Bibliography: p. 209-213

WOMEN — Sudan — Social conditions
GRUENBAUM, Ellen
Patterns of family living : a case study of two villages on the Rahad River / Ellen Gruenbaum. — Khartoum : University of Khartoum. Faculty of Economic and Social Studies. Development Studies and Research Centre, 1979. — 55p. — (Monograph series / University of Khartoum. Faculty of Economic and Social Studies. Development Studies and Research Centre ; no.12). — *Bibliography: p54-55*

WOMEN — Tanzania — History
TURSHEN, Meredeth
The political ecology of disease in Tanzania / Meredeth Turshen. — New Brunswick, N.J. : Rutgers University Press, c1984. — xiv, 259 p., [2] leaves of plates. — *Includes index. Bibliography: p. 211-239*

WOMEN — Thailand — Bangkok — Social conditions
THORBEK, Susanne
Voices from the city : women of Bangkok / Susanne Thorbek. — London : Zed, 1987. — [224]p. — *Includes bibliography and index*

WOMEN — Turkey — History
DAVIS, Fanny
The Ottoman lady : a social history from 1718 to 1918 / Fanny Davis. — Westport, Conn. : Greenwood Press, c1986. — xv, 321 p.. — (Contributions in women's studies ; no. 70). — *Includes bibliographies and index*

WOMEN — United States
KAMINER, Wendy
Women volunteering : the pleasure, pain, and politics of unpaid work from 1830 to the present / Wendy Kaminer. — 1st ed. — Garden City, N.Y. : Anchor Press, 1984. — xix, 237 p.. — *Includes index. Bibliography: p. [227]-228*

WOMEN — United States — Crimes against
No safe place : violence against women and children / edited by Connie Guberman & Margie Wolfe. — Toronto, Ont. : Women's Press, c1985. — 165 p.. — *Includes bibliographical references*

WOMEN — United States — Economic conditions
HEWLETT, Sylvia Ann
A lesser life : the myth of women's liberation in America / Sylvia A. Hewlett. — New York, N.Y. : W. Morrow, 1986. — p. cm

WOMEN — United States — Economic conditions — Congresses
"To toil livelong day" : America's women at work, 1780-1980 / Carol Groneman and Mary Beth Norton, editors. — Ithaca, N.Y. : Cornell University Press, 1987. — p. cm. — *Papers presented at the Sixth Berkshire Conference on the History of Women held at Smith College June 1-3, 1984. — Includes index*

WOMEN — United States — Economic conditions — Maps
GIBSON, Anne
The women's atlas of the United States / Anne Gibson and Timothy Fast. — New York : Facts on File Publications, 1986. — p. cm. — *Includes index. — Bibliography: p. — Contents: Demographics -- Education -- Employment -- Family -- Health -- Crime -- Politics*

WOMEN — United States — History
OGDEN, Annegret S
The great American housewife : from helpmate to wage earner, 1776-1986 / Annegret S. Ogden. — Westport, Conn. : Greenwood Press, 1986. — xxiii, 256 p.. — (Contributions in women's studies ; no. 61). — *Includes index. — Bibliography: p. [241]-247*

WOMEN — United States — History — Sources
CONWAY, Jill K.
The female experience in eighteenth- and nineteenth-century America : a guide to the history of American women / Jill K. Conway, with the assistance of Linda Kealey, Janet E. Schulte. — New York : Garland Pub., 1982. — xxiv, 290 p.. — (Garland reference library of social science ; v. 35). — *Includes bibliographies and index*

COTT, Nancy F
Root of bitterness : documents of the social history of American women / edited, with an introduction, and a new foreword by Nancy F. Cott. — Boston : Northeastern University Press, 1986, c1972. — p. cm. — : *Originally published: New York : Dutton, c1972. — Bibliography: p*

WOMEN — United States — History — 18th century
BUEL, Joy Day
The way of duty : a woman and her family in revolutionary America / Joy Day Buel and Richard Buel, Jr. — New York ; London : Norton, c1984. — xviii,309p. — *Bibliography: p299-301. — Includes index*

WOMEN — United States — History — 18th century — Bibliography
CONWAY, Jill K.
The female experience in eighteenth- and nineteenth-century America : a guide to the history of American women / Jill K. Conway, with the assistance of Linda Kealey, Janet E. Schulte. — New York : Garland Pub., 1982. — xxiv, 290 p.. — (Garland reference library of social science ; v. 35). — *Includes bibliographies and index*

WOMEN — United States — History — 19th century — Bibliography
CONWAY, Jill K.
The female experience in eighteenth- and nineteenth-century America : a guide to the history of American women / Jill K. Conway, with the assistance of Linda Kealey, Janet E. Schulte. — New York : Garland Pub., 1982. — xxiv, 290 p.. — (Garland reference library of social science ; v. 35). — *Includes bibliographies and index*

WOMEN — United States — Maps
GIBSON, Anne
The women's atlas of the United States / Anne Gibson and Timothy Fast. — New York : Facts on File Publications, 1986. — p. cm. — *Includes index. — Bibliography: p. — Contents: Demographics -- Education -- Employment -- Family -- Health -- Crime -- Politics*

WOMEN — United States — Psychology
ABRAMSON, Jane B
Mothermania : a psychological study of mother-daughter conflict / Jane B. Abramson. — Lexington, Mass. : Lexington Books, c1987. — p. cm. — *Includes index. — Bibliography: p*

WOMEN — United States — Social conditions
HEWLETT, Sylvia Ann
A lesser life : the myth of women's liberation in America / Sylvia A. Hewlett. — New York, N.Y. : W. Morrow, 1986. — p. cm

IDE, Arthur Frederick
Tomorrow's tyrants : the radical right & the politics of hate / by Arthur Frederick Ide. — Dallas : Monument Press, 1985. — p. cm. — *Includes bibliographical references and index*

WOMEN — United States — Social conditions — Maps
GIBSON, Anne
The women's atlas of the United States / Anne Gibson and Timothy Fast. — New York : Facts on File Publications, 1986. — p. cm. — *Includes index. — Bibliography: p. — Contents: Demographics -- Education -- Employment -- Family -- Health -- Crime -- Politics*

WOMEN — United States — Social conditions — Sources
COTT, Nancy F
Root of bitterness : documents of the social history of American women / edited, with an introduction, and a new foreword by Nancy F. Cott. — Boston : Northeastern University Press, 1986, c1972. — p. cm. — : *Originally published: New York : Dutton, c1972. — Bibliography: p*

WOMEN AND LAND USE PLANNING
MOSER, Caroline O. N.
A theory and methodology of gender planning : meeting women's practical and strategic needs / Caroline O. N. Moser and Caren Levy. — London : Bartlett School of Architecture and Planning Development Planning Unit, 1986. — 33p. — (DPU gender and planning working paper ; no.11). — *Bibliography: p32-33*

WOMEN AND MILITARISM
MARSHALL, Catherine, b. 1880
Militarism versus feminism : writings on women and war / Catherine Marshall, C.K. Ogden and Mary Sargant Florence ; edited by Margaret Kamester and Jo Vellacott. — London : Virago, 1987. — x,178p. — *Originally published: London : Allen & Unwin, 1915. — Includes bibliography and index*

WOMEN AND PEACE
DEMING, Barbara
Prisons that could not hold / Barbara Deming ; introduction by Grace Paley ; photo essay edited by Joan E. Biren. — San Francisco : Spinsters Ink, 1985. — 230p

Women and peace : theoretical, historical and practical perspectives / edited by Ruth Roach Pierson with the assistance of Joanne Thompson, Somer Brodribb, Paula Bourne. — London : Croom Helm, c1987. — xvi,249p. — *Conference papers. — Includes index*

WOMEN AND PEACE — Addresses, essays, lectures
We are ordinary women : a chronicle of the Puget Sound Women's Peace Camp / by Peace Camp participants. — 1st ed. — Seattle : Seal Press, 1985. — p. cm

WOMEN AND POLITICS
NORRIS, Pippa
Politics and sexual equality : the comparative position of women in Western democracies / Pippa Norris. — Brighton : Wheatsheaf, 1987. — [160]p. — *Includes bibliography and index*

WOMEN AND RELIGION
Speaking of faith : cross-cultural perspectives on women, religion and social change / Diana L. Eck and Devaki Jain editors. — London : Women's Press, 1986. — 288p. — *Conference papers*

Women, religion, and social change / edited by Yvonne Yazbeck Haddad and Ellison Banks Findly. — Albany : State University of New York Press, c1985. — xxi, 508 p.. — *Proceedings of the Hartford Symposium on Women, Religion, and Social Change. — Includes bibliographies and index*

WOMEN AND RELIGION — Congresses
Women in ritual and symbolic roles / edited by Judith Hoch-Smith and Anita Spring. — New York ; London : Plenum Press, 1978. — xv,289p. — *'This volume of essays grew out of a symposium organized ... for the 1974 American Anthropological Association meetings in Mexico City' - Preface. — Includes bibliographies and index*

WOMEN AND RELIGION — Social aspects

Women, religion, and social change / edited by Yvonne Yazbeck Haddad and Ellison Banks Findly. — Albany : State University of New York Press, c1985. — xxi, 508 p.. — *Proceedings of the Hartford Symposium on Women, Religion, and Social Change.* — *Includes bibliographies and index*

WOMEN AND RELIGION — England — History

Religion in the lives of English women, 1760-1930 / edited by Gail Malmgreen. — London : Croom Helm, c1986. — [224]p. — *Includes index*

WOMEN AND SOCIALISM

ELDERGILL, Anselm
Woman's lot : political purdah and the Labour Party / Anselm Eldergill. — Nottingham : Institute of Workers' Control, 1987. — 38p. — (IWC pamphlet ; no.89)

EVANS, Richard J.
Comrades and sisters : feminism, socialism and pacifism in Europe 1870-1945 / Richard J. Evans. — Brighton : Wheatsheaf, 1987. — [240]p. — *Includes index*

GUTIÉRREZ ALVAREZ, José
Mujeres socialistas / José Gutiérrez Alvarez. — Barcelona : Editorial Hacer, [1986]. — 157p

INGRISCH, Doris
Das Rollenbild der Frau bei den Frühsozialisten / Doris Ingrisch. — Linz : Tranner, 1985. — 119p. — (Linzer Schriften zur Sozial- und Wirtschaftsgeschichte ; Bd.13). — *Bibliography : p114-119*

MARSHALL, Kate
Real freedom : women's liberation and socialism / Kate Marshall. — London : Junius, 1982. — ii,139p

WOMEN AND SOCIALISM — Great Britain — History

BRULEY, Sue
Leninism, Stalinism, and the women's movement in Britain, 1920-1939 / Susan Bruley. — New York : Garland Pub., 1986. — p. cm. — (Outstanding theses from the London School of Economics and Political Science). — *Thesis (Ph.D.)--University of London, 1980.* — *Bibliography: p*

WOMEN AND WAR

Caught up in conflict : women's responses to political strife / edited by Rosemary Ridd and Helen Callaway. — Basingstoke : Macmillan Education in association with the Oxford University Women's Studies Committee, 1986. — xii,246p. — (Women in society). — *Includes bibliographies and index*

WOMEN AS COLLEGE TEACHERS

AUT woman / Association of University Teachers. — London : Association of University Teachers, 1984-. — *Quarterly*

WOMEN, AUSTRALIAN (ABORIGINAL)

AUSTRALIA. Office of the Status of Women. Aboriginal Women's Task Force
Women's business : report of the Aboriginal Women's Task Force / by Phyllis Daylight and Mary Johnstone. — Canberra : Australian Government Publishing Service, 1986. — xiii,139p. — *Includes bibliographical references*

WOMEN, AUSTRALIAN (ABORIGINAL) — Congresses

We are bosses ourselves : the status and role of Aboriginal women today / edited by Fay Gale. — Canberra : Australian Institute of Aboriginal Studies ; Atlantic Highlands, NJ : Sold and distributed in North and South America by Humanities Press, 1983. — x, 175 p.. — (AIAS new series ; no. 41). — *Collection from first Australia-wide meeting of Aboriginal women at 1980 ANZAAS Conference in Adelaide*

WOMEN, BLACK — Education

Slipping through the cracks : the status of black women / edited by Margaret C. Simms and Julianne Molveaux. — New Brunswick ; Oxford : Transaction Books, 1986. — 302p

WOMEN, BLACK — Employment

Slipping through the cracks : the status of black women / edited by Margaret C. Simms and Julianne Molveaux. — New Brunswick ; Oxford : Transaction Books, 1986. — 302p

WOMEN, BLACK — Africa, Southern — Social conditions

Women in Southern Africa / edited by Christine N. Qunta. — London : Allison & Busby, 1987. — [192]p. — *Includes index*

WOMEN, BLACK — South Africa

BLONDEL, Alain
The parrot's egg / Alain Blondel and Shena Lamb ; photographs by Ali Hashemian. — Johannesburg : Ravan Press, 1985. — 159p. — *Bibliography : p158-159*

LAWSON, Lesley
Working women in South Africa / Lesley Lawson for the Sached Trust. — London : Pluto, 1986. — [144]p. — *Includes bibliography*

WOMEN, BLACK — South Africa — Social conditions

LAWSON, Lesley
Working women in South Africa / Lesley Lawson for the Sached Trust. — London : Pluto, 1986. — [144]p. — *Includes bibliography*

WOMEN CLERKS — Great Britain — History

COHN, Samuel
The process of occupational sex-typing : the feminization of clerical labor in Great Britain / Samuel Cohn. — Philadelphia : Temple University Press, 1985. — p. cm. — (Women in the political economy). — *Includes index.* — *Bibliography: p*

WOMEN CLOTHING WORKERS — Canada

GANNAGÉ, Charlene
Double day, double bind : women garment workers / by Charlene Gannagé. — Toronto, Ont. : Women's Press, 1986. — 235 p., [1] leaf of plates. — (Women's press issues). — *Bibliography: p. 227-235*

WOMEN CLOTHING WORKERS — Canada — Interviews

GANNAGÉ, Charlene
Double day, double bind : women garment workers / by Charlene Gannagé. — Toronto, Ont. : Women's Press, 1986. — 235 p., [1] leaf of plates. — (Women's press issues). — *Bibliography: p. 227-235*

WOMEN CLOTHING WORKERS — Great Britain — Attitudes

CLOTHING AND ALLIED PRODUCTS INDUSTRY TRAINING BOARD
The aspirations of female shop-floor workers : a report of the survey undertaken by Board staff. — [Leeds] : the Board, c1979. — 109p

WOMEN COLONIAL ADMINISTRATORS — Nigeria — History

CALLAWAY, Helen
Gender, culture and empire : European women in colonial Nigeria / Helen Callaway. — Basingstoke : Macmillan in association with St. Antony's College, Oxford, 1987. — xiv,278p. — (St. Antony's/Macmillan series). — *Bibliography: p252-266.* — *Includes index*

WOMEN CORRECTIONAL PERSONNEL — United States

POLLOCK, Joycelyn M.
Sex and supervision : guarding male and female inmates / Joycelyn M. Pollock ; foreword by Elaine A. Lord. — New York : Greenwood Press, 1986. — xiv, 160 p. — (Contributions in criminology and penology ; no. 12). — *Includes index.* — *Bibliography: p. [155]-157*

ZIMMER, Lynn Etta
Women guarding men / Lynn E. Zimmer ; foreword by James B. Jacobs. — Chicago : University of Chicago Press, 1986. — xiv, 264 p.. — (Studies in crime and justice). — *Includes index.* — *Bibliography: p. 239-259*

WOMEN DOMESTICS — Peru — Lima

BUNSTER, Ximena
Sellers and servants : working women in Lima, Peru / Ximena Bunster, Elsa M. Chaney ; photos by Ellan Young. — New York : Praeger, 1985. — x, 258p. — *Includes index.* — *Bibliography : p.235-246*

WOMEN DOMESTICS — South Africa

GORDON, Suzanne
A talent for tomorrow : life stories of South African servants / Suzanne Gordon ; photographs by Ingrid Hudson. — Johannesburg : Ravan Press, 1985. — xxvii,294p. — *Bibliography : p288-289*

WOMEN DOMESTICS — United States — History

ROLLINS, Judith
Between women : domestics and their employers / Judith Rollins. — Philadelphia : Temple University Press, 1985. — p. cm. — *Includes index.* — *Bibliography: p*

WOMEN DOMESTICS — United States — Interviews

ROLLINS, Judith
Between women : domestics and their employers / Judith Rollins. — Philadelphia : Temple University Press, 1985. — p. cm. — *Includes index.* — *Bibliography: p*

WOMEN ENGINEERS

BYRNE, Eileen. M.
Women and engineering : a comparative overview of new initiatives / Eileen M. Byrne. — Canberra : Australian Government Publishing Service, 1985. — xiii,181p. — (Monograph series / Bureau of Labour Market Research ; no.11). — *Bibliography: p162-181*

WOMEN ENGINEERS — Australia

BYRNE, Eileen. M.
Women and engineering : a comparative overview of new initiatives / Eileen M. Byrne. — Canberra : Australian Government Publishing Service, 1985. — xiii,181p. — (Monograph series / Bureau of Labour Market Research ; no.11). — *Bibliography: p162-181*

WOMEN EXECUTIVES

Businesswoman : present and future / edited by David Clutterbuck and Marion Devine. — London : Macmillan, 1987. — xi,176p. — *Includes bibliographies and index*

JACOBSON, Aileen
Women in charge : dilemmas of women in authority / Aileen Jacobson. — New York : Van Nostrand Reinhold, 1985. — p. cm. — *Includes index.* — *Bibliography: p*

WOMEN EXECUTIVES — Training of — Great Britain

HENNESSEY, Jan
Self-development for women managers : a report by the Anne Shaw Organisation / Jan Hennessey, Martin Hughes. — [Sheffield] : Manpower Services Commission, [1984]. — 35p. — (Research & development ; no.19). — *Bibliographical references: p29*

WOMEN HEADS OF HOUSEHOLDS — Developing countries

BUVINIĆ, Maria
Woman-headed households : the ignored factor in development planning / Maria Buvinić, Nadia H. Youssef with Barbara Von Elm. — Washington, D.C. : International Center for Research on Women, 1978. — iii,iii,119p. — *Report submitted to AID/WID.* — *Bibliography: p[115-119]*

WOMEN HEADS OF HOUSEHOLDS — United States
RODGERS, Harrell R
Poor women, poor families : the economic plight of America's female-headed households / Harrell R. Rodgers, Jr. — Armonk, N.Y. : M.E. Sharpe, c1986. — viii, 167 p.. — *Includes index. — Bibliography: p. 150-161*

WOMEN HEADS OF STATE — Addresses, essays, lectures
KNOX, John
The political writings of John Knox : The first blast of the trumpet against the monstrous regiment of women and other selected works / edited and with an introduction by Marvin A. Breslow. — Washington : Folger Shakespeare Library ; London : Associated University Presses, c1985. — 160 p.. — "Folger books.". — *Includes bibliographies. — Contents: The first blast of the trumpet against the monstrous regiment of women (1558) -- Letter to the Regent of Scotland (1558) -- Appellation to the nobility (1558) -- Letter to the commonalty of Scotland (1558) -- The second blast (1558)*

WOMEN IMMIGRANTS — Canada — History — Congresses
Looking into my sister's eyes : an exploration in women's history / edited by Jean Burnet. — Toronto : Multicultural History Society of Ontario, 1986. — x,245. — *Papers presented at a conference 'Immigration and ethnicity in Ontario: an exploration in women's history' held at the University of Toronto in May 1985. — Includes bibliographical references*

WOMEN IMMIGRANTS — Great Britain — History
Worlds apart : women under immigration and nationality law / edited by Jacqueline Bhabha, Francesca Klug and Sue Shutter. — London : Pluto, 1985. — [vi,176]p. — *At head of title: The Women, Immigration and Nationality Group. — Includes bibliography*

WOMEN IMMIGRANTS — Ontario — History — Congresses
Looking into my sister's eyes : an exploration in women's history / edited by Jean Burnet. — Toronto : Multicultural History Society of Ontario, 1986. — x,245. — *Papers presented at a conference 'Immigration and ethnicity in Ontario: an exploration in women's history' held at the University of Toronto in May 1985. — Includes bibliographical references*

WOMEN IN AGRICULTURE — Great Britain
GASSON, Ruth
Opportunities for women in agriculture / Ruth Gasson. — Ashford : School of Rural Economics, Wye College, 1981. — iii,22p. — (Occasional papers / Wye College. Department of Environmental Studies and Countryside Planning ; no.5). — *Bibliography: p21-22*

WOMEN IN AGRICULTURE — Middle Atlantic States — History
JENSEN, Joan M
Loosening the bonds : Mid-Atlantic farm women, 1750-1850 / by Joan M. Jensen. — New Haven : Yale University Press, c1986. — p. cm. — *Includes index. — Bibliography: p*

WOMEN IN ART
Looking on : images of feminity in the visual arts and media / edited by Rosemary Betterton. — London : Pandora, 1987. — 293p. — (Pandora Press popular culture critical readers). — *Bibliography: p280-284. — Includes index*

WOMEN IN ART — Addresses, essays, lectures
The Female body in western culture : contemporary perspectives / Susan Rubin Suleiman, editor. — Cambridge, Mass. : Harvard University Press, 1986. — p. cm. — *Includes bibliographies*

WOMEN IN BUSINESS — Developing countries — Case studies
Gender roles in development projects : a case book / editors, Catherine Overholt ... [et al.]. — West Hartford, Conn. : Kumarian Press, 1985. — p. cm. — *Bibliography: p*

WOMEN IN BUSINESS — Egypt
SULLIVAN, Earl L
Women in Egyptian public life / Earl L. Sullivan. — 1st ed. — Syracuse, N.Y. : Syracuse University Press, 1986. — xiii, 223 p.. — (Contemporary issues in the Middle East). — *Includes index. — Bibliography: p. 207-215*

WOMEN IN CHRISTIANITY — History
Religion in the lives of English women, 1760-1930 / edited by Gail Malmgreen. — London : Croom Helm, c1986. — [224]p. — *Includes index*

WOMEN IN CIVIL SERVICE — United States — History — 19th century
ARON, Cindy Sondik
Ladies and gentlemen of the civil service : middle-class workers in Victorian America / Cindy Sondik Aron. — New York : Oxford University Press, 1987. — viii, 234 p. — *Includes index. — Bibliography: p. 195-227*

WOMEN IN COOPERATIVE SOCIETIES — Great Britain — Case studies
CENTRE FOR RESEARCH ON EUROPEAN WOMEN
New types of employment initiatives especially as relating to women / by the Centre for Research on European Women. — Luxembourg : Office for Official Publications of the European Communities, 1984. — 1v.(various pagings). — *At head of title page: Commission of the European Communities*

WOMEN IN COOPERATIVE SOCIETIES — Italy — Case studies
CENTRE FOR RESEARCH ON EUROPEAN WOMEN
New types of employment initiatives especially as relating to women / by the Centre for Research on European Women. — Luxembourg : Office for Official Publications of the European Communities, 1984. — 1v.(various pagings). — *At head of title page: Commission of the European Communities*

WOMEN IN DEVELOPMENT
Geography of gender in the Third World / edited by Janet Henshall Momsen and Janet Townsend. — London : Hutchinson Education, 1987. — [304]p. — *Written by the Women & Geography Study Group of the Institute of British Geographers. — Includes bibliography and index*

WOMEN IN DEVELOPMENT — Asia
Missing women : development planning in Asia and the Pacific / edited by Noeleen Heyzer. — Kuala Lumpur : Asian and Pacific Development Centre, 1985. — xxxii,419p. — *Bibliography: p406-419*

WOMEN IN DEVELOPMENT — Developing countries — Congresses
Visibility and power : essays on women in society and development / edited by Leela Dube, Eleanor Leacock, Shirley Ardener. — Delhi ; New York : Oxford University Press, 1986. — L, 361 p.. — *Includes bibliographies and index*

WOMEN IN DEVELOPMENT — Pacific Area
Missing women : development planning in Asia and the Pacific / edited by Noeleen Heyzer. — Kuala Lumpur : Asian and Pacific Development Centre, 1985. — xxxii,419p. — *Bibliography: p406-419*

WOMEN IN DEVELOPMENT — Turkey
ABADAN-UNAT, Nermin
Women in the developing world : evidence from Turkey / Nermin Abadan-Unat. — Denver, Colo. : Graduate School of International Studies, University of Denver, 1986. — p. cm. — (Monograph series in world affairs ; v. 22, bk. 1). — *Bibliography: p*

WOMEN IN EDUCATION
For alma mater : theory and practice in feminist scholarship / edited by Paula A. Treichler, Cheris Kramarae, Beth Stafford. — Urbana : University of Illinois Press, c1985. — xv, 450 p., [10] p. of plates. — *Includes bibliographies and index*

WOMEN IN ENGINEERING
BYRNE, Eileen. M.
Women and engineering : a comparative overview of new initiatives / Eileen M. Byrne. — Canberra : Australian Government Publishing Service, 1985. — xiii,181p. — (Monograph series / Bureau of Labour Market Research ; no.11). — *Bibliography: p162-181*

WOMEN IN ENGINEERING — Australia
BYRNE, Eileen. M.
Women and engineering : a comparative overview of new initiatives / Eileen M. Byrne. — Canberra : Australian Government Publishing Service, 1985. — xiii,181p. — (Monograph series / Bureau of Labour Market Research ; no.11). — *Bibliography: p162-181*

WOMEN IN ENGINEERING — England
BREAKWELL, Glynis M.
Young women in 'gender-atypical' jobs : the case of trainee technicians in the engineering industry / Glynis M. Breakwell, Barbara Weinberger. — [London] : Department of Employment, [1987]. — 39p. — (Research paper / Department of Employment ; no.49). — *Bibliographical references: p22*

WOMEN IN FINANCE — California — San Francisco
MCBROOM, Patricia
The third sex : the new professional woman / Patricia A. McBroom. — New York : W. Morrow, [1986]. — p. cm. — *Includes index*

WOMEN IN FINANCE — New York (N.Y.)
MCBROOM, Patricia
The third sex : the new professional woman / Patricia A. McBroom. — New York : W. Morrow, [1986]. — p. cm. — *Includes index*

WOMEN IN LITERATURE
SWINDELLS, Julia
Victorian writing and working women : the other side of silence / Julia Swindells. — Cambridge : Polity, 1985. — [240]p. — *Includes index*

WOMEN IN MASS MEDIA
Out of focus : writings on women and the media / Kath Davies, Julienne Dickey and Teresa Stratford, editors. — London : Women's Press, 1987. — ix,230p. — *Bibliography: p227-230*

WOMEN IN MASS MEDIA — Great Britain
DICKEY, Julienne
Women in focus : guidelines for eliminating media sexism / Julienne Dickey and CPBF London Women's Group. — London : Campaign for Press and Broadcasting Freedom, 1985. — 44p

WOMEN IN POLITICS
Caught up in conflict : women's responses to political strife / edited by Rosemary Ridd and Helen Callaway. — Basingstoke : Macmillan Education in association with the Oxford University Women's Studies Committee, 1986. — xii,246p. — (Women in society). — *Includes bibliographies and index*

COCKBURN, Cynthia
Women, trade unions and political parties / Cynthia Cockburn. — London : Fabian Society, 1987. — 27 p. — (Fabian research series ; no.349)

WOMEN IN POLITICS — Australia
Australian women and the political system / edited by Marian Simms. — Melbourne, Australia : Longman Cheshire, 1984. — xviii, 222 p.. — (Australian studies). — *Includes index. — Bibliography: p. [204]-217*

WOMEN IN POLITICS — Canada
BASHEVKIN, Sylvia B.
Toeing the lines : women and party politics in English Canada / Sylvia B. Bashevkin. — Toronto : University of Toronto Press, 1985. — xvi,222p. — *References: p[177]-216*

COPPS, Sheila
Nobody's baby : a survival guide to politics / Sheila Copps. — Toronto : Deneau, 1986. — 192p

The politics of diversity : feminism, Marxism and nationalism / edited by Roberta Hamilton and Michèle Barrett. — [London] : Verso, 1986

WOMEN IN POLITICS — Canada — History — 20th century
KOME, Penney
Women of influence : Canadian women and politics / Penney Kome. — 1st ed. — Toronto, Canada : Doubleday Canada Ltd. ; Garden City, N.Y. : Doubleday, 1985. — p. cm. — *Includes index*

WOMEN IN POLITICS — Egypt
SULLIVAN, Earl L
Women in Egyptian public life / Earl L. Sullivan. — 1st ed. — Syracuse, N.Y. : Syracuse University Press, 1986. — xiii, 223 p.. — (Contemporary issues in the Middle East). — *Includes index. — Bibliography: p. 207-215*

WOMEN IN POLITICS — Germany (West)
Die quotierte Hälfte : Frauenpolitik in den grün-alternativen Parteien / herausgegeben von Regina Michalik und Elke A. Richardsen. — Berlin : LitPol, 1985. — 151p

WOMEN IN POLITICS — Great Britain
CAMPBELL, Beatrix
The iron ladies : why do women vote Tory? / Beatrix Campbell. — London : Virago, 1987. — 314p.

ELDERGILL, Anselm
Woman's lot : political purdah and the Labour Party / Anselm Eldergill. — Nottingham : Institute of Workers' Control, 1987. — 38p. — (IWC pamphlet ; no.89)

LABOUR PARTY (Great Britain). National Executive Committee
Labour's ministry for women : N.E.C. discussion document. — London : Labour Party, 1986. — 35p

WOMEN IN POLITICS — Great Britain — History — 19th century
Equal or different : women's politics 1800-1914 / edited by Jane Rendall. — Oxford : Basil Blackwell, 1987. — [288]p. — *Includes index*

WOMEN IN POLITICS — India — Case studies
SHARMA, Neena
Political socialization and its impact on attitudinal change towards social and political system : a case study of Harijan women of Delhi / Neena Sharma. — New Delhi : Inter-India Publications, 1985. — x, 157 p.. — *Cover title: Political socialization & its impact on attitudinal change towards social & political system. — Includes index. — Bibliography: p. [146]-153*

WOMEN IN POLITICS — India — History
KAUR, Manmohan
Manmohan Kaur. — New Delhi : Sterling, 1985. — 282p. — *Bibliography: p[253]-263*

WOMEN IN POLITICS — India — Delhi
SHARMA, Neena
Political socialization and its impact on attitudinal change towards social and political system : a case study of Harijan women of Delhi / Neena Sharma. — New Delhi : Inter-India Publications, 1985. — x, 157 p.. — *Cover title: Political socialization & its impact on attitudinal change towards social & political system. — Includes index. — Bibliography: p. [146]-153*

WOMEN IN POLITICS — New Jersey — History — 20th century
GORDON, Felice D.
After winning : the legacy of the New Jersey suffragists, 1920-1947 / Felice D. Gordon. — New Brunswick, N.J. : Rutgers University Press, c1986. — x, 262 p.. — *Includes index. — Bibliography: p. [245]-251*

WOMEN IN POLITICS — New Zealand
WARING, Marilyn
Women, politics and power / essays by Marilyn Waring. — Wellington : Allen and Unwin New Zealand, [1985]. — 121p

WOMEN IN POLITICS — Papua New Guinea
Women and politics in Papua New Guinea / Maev O'Collins...[et al.]. — [Canberra, A.C.T.] : Department jof Political and Social Change, Australian National University, 1985. — 75p. — (Working paper / Department of Political and Social Change, Australian National University ; No.6). — *Cover title: Women in politics in Papua New Guinea. — Contains papers presented to the Australian National University Department of Political and Social Change fifth Annual Seminar on Papua New Guinea, May 1984*

Women in politics in Papua New Guinea / [by] Maev o'Collins...[et al.]. — [Canberra) : Dept. of Political and Social Change, Australian National University, 1985. — 75p. — (Working Paper / Department of Political and Social Change, Australian National University ; No.6). — *Bibliography: p72-74*

WOMEN IN POLITICS — Spain — History
DI FEBO, Giuliana
Resistencia y movimiento de mujeres en España 1936-1976 / Giuliana Di Febo. — [Barcelona] : Icaria, 1979. — 239p

WOMEN IN POLITICS — United States
BECKWITH, Karen
American women and political participation : the impacts of work, generation and feminism / Karen Beckwith. — New York ; London : Greenwood, 1986. — xiv,185p. — (Contributions in women's studies ; no.68). — *Bibliography: p169-177. — Includes index*

GELB, Joyce
Women and public policies / Joyce Gelb and Marian Lief Palley. — rev. ed. — Princeton : Princeton University Press, 1987. — xvi,241p

Women leaders in contemporary U.S. politics / edited by Frank P. Le Veness & Jane P. Sweeney. — Boulder, Colo. : L. Rienner, 1987. — ix, 164 p.. — *Bibliography: p. 151-161. — Contents: Women in the political arena / Frank P. Le Veness and Jane P. Sweeney -- Shirley Chisholm / Reba Carruth and Vivian Jenkins Nelsen -- Diane Feinstein / Kirsten Amunsden -- Congresswoman Geraldine A. Ferraro / Arthur J. Hughes and Frank P. LeVeness -- Margaret M. Heckler / Arthur A. Belonzi -- Elizabeth Holtzman / Joseph C. Bertolini -- Nancy Landon Kassebaum / Linda K. Richter -- Jeane Kirkpatrick / Naomi B. Lynn -- Barbara Mikulski / Jane P. Sweeney -- Sandra Day O'Connor / Orma Linford -- The unnamed political woman / Irene J. Dabrowski*

WOMEN IN POLITICS — United States — Biography
FOWLER, Robert Booth
Carrie Catt : feminist politician / Robert Booth Fowler. — Boston : Northeastern University Press, c1986. — xx, 226 p.. — *Includes index. — Bibliography: p. 201-218*

Women leaders in contemporary U.S. politics / edited by Frank P. Le Veness & Jane P. Sweeney. — Boulder, Colo. : L. Rienner, 1987. — ix, 164 p.. — *Bibliography: p. 151-161. — Contents: Women in the political arena / Frank P. Le Veness and Jane P. Sweeney -- Shirley Chisholm / Reba Carruth and Vivian Jenkins Nelsen -- Diane Feinstein / Kirsten Amunsden -- Congresswoman Geraldine A. Ferraro / Arthur J. Hughes and Frank P. LeVeness -- Margaret M. Heckler / Arthur A. Belonzi -- Elizabeth Holtzman / Joseph C. Bertolini -- Nancy Landon Kassebaum / Linda K. Richter -- Jeane Kirkpatrick / Naomi B. Lynn -- Barbara Mikulski / Jane P. Sweeney -- Sandra Day O'Connor / Orma Linford -- The unnamed political woman / Irene J. Dabrowski*

WOMEN IN POLITICS — United States — History — Addresses, essays, lectures
Freedom, feminism, and the state : an overview of individualist feminism / edited by Wendy McElroy ; foreword by Lewis Perry. — Washington, D.C. : Cato Institute, c1982. — xi, 357 p.. — *Includes index. — Bibliography: p. 349-352*

WOMEN IN PUBLIC LIFE — Egypt
SULLIVAN, Earl L
Women in Egyptian public life / Earl L. Sullivan. — 1st ed. — Syracuse, N.Y. : Syracuse University Press, 1986. — xiii, 223 p.. — (Contemporary issues in the Middle East). — *Includes index. — Bibliography: p. 207-215*

WOMEN IN PUBLIC LIFE — Middle Atlantic States — History
JENSEN, Joan M
Loosening the bonds : Mid-Atlantic farm women, 1750-1850 / by Joan M. Jensen. — New Haven : Yale University Press, c1986. — p. cm. — *Includes index. — Bibliography: p*

WOMEN IN RURAL DEVELOPMENT — Asia — Congresses
ILO TRIPARTITE ASIAN REGIONAL SEMINAR (1981 : Maharashtra, India)
Rural development and women in Asia : proceedings and conclusions of the ILO Tripartite Asian Regional Seminar, Mahabaleshwar, Maharashtra, India, 6-11 April 1981. — Geneva : ILO, 1982. — 88p. — (A WEP study)

WOMEN IN RURAL DEVELOPMENT — Developing countries
LOUTFI, Martha Fetherolf
Rural women : unequal partners in development / Martha Fetherolf Loutfi. — Geneva : International Labour Office, 1980. — (A WEP study)

WOMEN IN SCIENCE
HARDING, Sandra G
The science question in feminism / Sandra Harding. — Ithaca : Cornell University Press, 1986. — p. cm. — *Includes index. — Bibliography: p*

WOMEN IN TECHNOLOGY — Great Britain
KELLY, Alison, 1947-
Girls into science and technology : final report / Alison Kelly, Judith Whyte and Barbara Smail. — Manchester : GIST, 1984. — 45p. — *Final report from the Girls into Science and Technology project to the Joint Panel on Women and Under Achievement of the Equal Opportunities Commission and the Social Science Research Council. — Bibliography: p43-45*

WOMEN IN THE CIVIL SERVICE
RESSNER, Ulla
The hidden hierarchy : democracy and equal opportunities / Ulla Ressner. — Aldershot : Avebury, c1987. — 120p

WOMEN IN THE CIVIL SERVICE — Great Britain
Equal opportunities for men and women in the Civil Service. — London (St Andrews House, 40 Broadway, SW1H OBT) : Council of Civil Service Unions, [1985]. — 38p

WOMEN IN THE COMPUTER SERVICE INDUSTRY

DEAKIN, Rose
Women and computing : the golden opportunity / Rose Deakin. — London : Macmillan, 1984. — 149p. — (Papermac computer library). — *Includes index*

WOMEN IN THE PROFESSIONS — United States

MCBROOM, Patricia
The third sex : the new professional woman / Patricia A. McBroom. — New York : W. Morrow, [1986]. — p. cm. — *Includes index*

WOMEN IN TRADE UNIONS

COCKBURN, Cynthia
Women, trade unions and political parties / Cynthia Cockburn. — London : Fabian Society, 1987. — 27 p. — (Fabian research series ; no.349)

WOMEN IN TRADE UNIONS — Canada

GANNAGÉ, Charlene
Double day, double bind : women garment workers / by Charlene Gannagé. — Toronto, Ont. : Women's Press, 1986. — 235 p., [1] leaf of plates. — (Women's press issues). — *Bibliography: p. 227-235*

WOMEN IN TRADE-UNIONS — Germany (West)

Träumen verboten : gewerkschaftliche Frauenpolitik für die 90er Jahre / Karin Roth u.a.. — Hamburg : VSA-Verlag, 1984. — 240p

WOMEN IN TRADE-UNIONS — Great Britain

BOSTON, Sarah
Women workers and the trade unions / Sarah Boston. — Updated ed. — London : Lawrence and Wishart, 1987. — 371p. — *Previous ed. published as 'Women workers and the trade union movement', London: Davis-Poynter, 1980. — Bibliography: p[352]-357*

WOMEN, JEWISH — New York (N.Y.) — History

EWEN, Elizabeth
Immigrant women in the land of dollars : life and culture on the Lower East Side, 1890-1925 / Elizabeth Ewen. — New York : Monthly Review Press, 1985. — p. cm. — (New feminist library)

WOMEN, JEWISH — Palestine — Employment

BERNSTEIN, Deborah
The struggle for equality : urban women workers in pre-state Israeli society / by Deborah Bernstein. — New York : Praeger, 1986. — p. cm. — "Praeger special studies. Praeger scientific.". — *Includes index. — Bibliography: p*

WOMEN LEGISLATORS — Canada — Biography

COPPS, Sheila
Nobody's baby : a survival guide to politics / Sheila Copps. — Toronto : Deneau, 1986. — 192p

WOMEN, MUSLIM — Turkey

ABADAN-UNAT, Nermin
Women in the developing world : evidence from Turkey / Nermin Abadan-Unat. — Denver, Colo. : Graduate School of International Studies, University of Denver, 1986. — p. cm. — (Monograph series in world affairs ; v. 22, bk. 1). — *Bibliography: p*

WOMEN PETROLEUM INDUSTRY WORKERS — Norway

LEIRA, Arnlaug
Kvinner på en oljearbeidsplass : rapport fra en undersøkelse ved Condeep - anlegget i Stavanger / Arnlaug Leira. — Stavanger : Rogalandsforskning, 1978. — 88p. — (Rogalandsforskning rapport ; nr.6). — *Bibliography: p85-88*

WOMEN PHYSICIANS — Great Britain — Congresses

Women in medicine : proceedings of a conference organised by the Department of Health and Social Security on 4-5 July 1975. — [London] : Department of Health and Social Security, [1976]. — [76]p. — (Report on health and social subjects)

WOMEN, POOR — Pakistan — Lahore

SHAH, Nasra M
Basic needs, woman, and development : a survey of squatters in Lahore, Pakistan / by Nasra M. Shah and Muhammad Anwar. — Honolulu : East-West Population Institute, East-West Center ; Ottawa : International Development Research Centre, c1986. — xii, 163 p.. — *Bibliography: p. [159]-163*

WOMEN, POOR — United States

RODGERS, Harrell R
Poor women, poor families : the economic plight of America's female-headed households / Harrell R. Rodgers, Jr. — Armonk, N.Y. : M.E. Sharpe, c1986. — viii, 167 p.. — *Includes index. — Bibliography: p. 150-161*

WOMEN PRISONERS — Biography

Wall tappings : an anthology of writings by women prisoners / [compiled] by Judith A. Scheffler. — Boston : Northeastern University Press, 1986. — p. cm. — *Bibliography: p*

WOMEN PRISONERS — Northern Ireland — Armagh — Searching

Strip searching : an inquiry into the strip searching of women remand prisoners at Armagh Prison between 1982 and 1985. — London : National Council for Civil Liberties, c1986. — 36p

WOMEN PRISONERS — Poland

KOLARCZYK, Tadeusz
Przestępczość kobiet : aspekty kryminologiczne i penitencjarne / Tadeusz Kolarczyk, Jacek Roman Kubiak, Piotr Wierzbicki. — Warszawa : Wydawnictwo Prawnicze, 1984. — 312p. — *Summary in English*

WOMEN PRISONERS — United States

DEMING, Barbara
Prisons that could not hold / Barbara Deming ; introduction by Grace Paley ; photo essay edited by Joan E. Biren. — San Francisco : Spinsters Ink, 1985. — 230p

WOMEN PSYCHOLOGISTS — United States — Biography

SCARBOROUGH, Elizabeth
Untold lives : the first generation of American women psychologists / Elizabeth Scarborough and Laurel Furumoto. — New York : Columbia University Press, 1987. — p. cm. — *Includes index. — Bibliography: p*

WOMEN REFUGEES — Bibliography

A selected and annotated bibliography on refugee women. — [Geneva : UNHCR Refugee Documentation Centre], 1985. — viii,69p. — *"A joint project of the Office of the United Nations High Commissioner for Refugees and the Refugee Policy Group for the United Nations Decade for Women*

WOMEN SCHOLARS

For alma mater : theory and practice in feminist scholarship / edited by Paula A. Treichler, Cheris Kramarae, Beth Stafford. — Urbana : University of Illinois Press, c1985. — xv, 450 p., [10] p. of plates. — *Includes bibliographies and index*

WOMEN SCIENTISTS — Great Britain

KELLY, Alison, 1947-
Girls into science and technology : final report / Alison Kelly, Judith Whyte and Barbara Smail. — Manchester : GIST, 1984. — 45p. — *Final report from the Girls into Science and Technology project to the Joint Panel on Women and Under Achievement of the Equal Opportunities Commission and the Social Science Research Council. — Bibliography: p43-45*

WOMEN SLAVES — Southern States

WHITE, Deborah Gray
Ar'n't I a woman? : female slaves in the plantation South / Deborah Gray White. — 1st ed. — New York : Norton, c1985. — 216 p.. — *Includes index. — Bibliography: p. [198]-208*

WOMEN SOCIAL REFORMERS — Great Britain — Biography

CURTIN, Patricia R
E. Sylvia Pankhurst : portrait of a radical / by Patricia Romero Curtin. — New Haven : Yale University Press, c1986. — p. cm. — *Includes index. — Bibliography: p*

WOMEN SOCIAL REFORMERS — New Jersey — History — 20th century

GORDON, Felice D.
After winning : the legacy of the New Jersey suffragists, 1920-1947 / Felice D. Gordon. — New Brunswick, N.J. : Rutgers University Press, c1986. — x, 262 p.. — *Includes index. — Bibliography: p. [245]-251*

WOMEN SOLDIERS

Loaded questions : women in the military / edited by W. Chapkis. — Amsterdam ; Washington : Transnational Institute, 1981. — 97p

WOMEN TEACHERS — Germany (West)

Frauen in Forschung und Lehre / Herausgeber: Der Bundesminister für Bildung und Wissenschaft. — Bad Honnef : Bock, 1985. — vi,147p. — (Studien zu Bildung und Wissenschaft ; 12). — *Bibliography: p137-147*

WOMEN TECHNICIANS

COCKBURN, Cynthia
Machinery of dominance : women, men and technical know-how / Cynthia Cockburn. — London : Pluto, 1985. — 282p. — *Includes index*

WOMEN TEXTILE WORKERS — China — Shanghai — History — 20th century

HONIG, Emily
Sisters and strangers : women in the Shanghai cotton mills, 1919-1949 = [Shang-hai sha ch'ang nü kung] / Emily Honig. — Stanford, Calif. : Stanford University Press, 1986. — ix, 299 p.. — *Parallel title in Chinese characters. — Includes index. — Bibliography: p. [279]-289*

WOMEN VOLUNTEERS IN SOCIAL SERVICE — United States

KAMINER, Wendy
Women volunteering : the pleasure, pain, and politics of unpaid work from 1830 to the present / Wendy Kaminer. — 1st ed. — Garden City, N.Y. : Anchor Press, 1984. — xix, 237 p.. — *Includes index. — Bibliography: p. [227]-228*

WOMEN WHITE COLLAR WORKERS — Effect of automation on

CHALUDE, Monique
Office automation and work for women / Monique Chalude ; scientific direction: Marcel Bolle de Bal. — Luxembourg : Office for Official Publications of the European Communities, 1984. — ii, F, 135p. — *At head of title page: Commission of the European Communities*

WOMEN WHITE COLLAR WORKERS — Effect of technological innovations on
NATIONAL RESEARCH COUNCIL (U.S.). Committee on Women's Employment and Related Social Issues. Panel on Technology and Women's Employment
 Computer chips and paper clips : technology and women's employment / Heidi I. Hartmann, Robert E. Kraut, and Louise A. Tilly, editors ; Panel on Technology and Women's Employment, Committee on Women's Employment and Related Social Issues, Commission on Behavioral and Social Sciences and Education, National Research Council. — Washington, D.C. : National Academy Press, 1986-1987. — 2 v.. — Includes bibliographies and index. — Contents: v. 1. [without special title] -- v. 2. Case studies and policy perspectives / Heidi I. Hartmann, editor

WOMEN WHITE COLLAR WORKERS — United States — Effect of technological innovations on
GINZBERG, Eli
 Technology and employment : concepts and clarifications / Eli Ginzberg, Thierry J. Noyelle, and Thomas M. Stanback, Jr. — Boulder : Westview Press, 1986. — xi, 111 p.. — (Conservation of Human Resources studies in the new economy). — Includes bibliographies and index

WOMEN'S CLOTHING INDUSTRY — Canada
GANNAGÉ, Charlene
 Double day, double bind : women garment workers / by Charlene Gannagé. — Toronto, Ont. : Women's Press, 1986. — 235 p., [1] leaf of plates. — (Women's press issues). — Bibliography: p. 227-235

WOMEN'S RIGHTS
COREA, Gena
 The mother machine : reproductive technologies from artificial insemination to artificial wombs / Gena Corea. — 1st ed. — New York : Harper & Row, c1985. — p. cm. — Includes index. — Bibliography: p

 Feminism and equality / edited by Anne Phillips. — Oxford : Basil Blackwell, 1987. — 202p. — (Readings in social and political theory). — Includes index

 Feminism and political economy : women's work, women's struggles / edited by Heather Jon Maroney and Meg Luxton. — Toronto ; New York ; London : Methuen, 1987. — xii,333p. — Bibliography: p285-318

FRASER, Arvonne S
 The U.N. Decade for Women : documents and dialogue / Arvonne S. Fraser. — Boulder : Westview Press, 1987. — p. cm. — (Westview special studies on women in contemporary society)

NORRIS, Pippa
 Politics and sexual equality : the comparative position of women in Western democracies / Pippa Norris. — Brighton : Wheatsheaf, 1987. — [160]p. — Includes bibliography and index

WOMEN'S RIGHTS — History — Addresses, essays, lectures
SCHNEIR, Miriam, comp
 Feminism : the essential historical writings / Edited, and with an introd. and commentaries, by Miriam Schneir. — [1st ed.]. — New York : Random House, [1972]. — xxi, 360 p. — Bibliography: p. 356-360

WOMEN'S RIGHTS — Austria
PAULI, Ruth
 Emanzipation in Österreich : der lange Marsch in die Sackgasse / Ruth Pauli. — Graz : Böhlau, 1986. — 163p. — Bibliography: p163

WOMEN'S RIGHTS — Canada
GANNAGÉ, Charlene
 Double day, double bind : women garment workers / by Charlene Gannagé. — Toronto, Ont. : Women's Press, 1986. — 235 p., [1] leaf of plates. — (Women's press issues). — Bibliography: p. 227-235

WOMEN'S RIGHTS — Germany — History — 19th century
BUSSEMER, Herrad-Ulrike
 Frauenemanzipation und Bildungsbürgertum : Sozialgeschichte der Frauenbewegung in der Reichsgründungszeit / Herrad-Ulrike Bussemer. — Weinheim : Beltz Verlag, 1985. — 360p. — (Ergebnisse der Frauenforschung ; Bd.7). — Bibliography: p[350]-360

WOMEN'S RIGHTS — India
DEVENDRA, Kiran
 Status and position of women in India : with special reference to women in contemporary India / Kiran Devendra. — New Delhi : Shakti Books, 1985. — xxi,186p. — Bibliography: p[173]-181

KAUR, Manmohan
 Manmohan Kaur. — New Delhi : Sterling, 1985. — 282p. — Bibliography: p[253]-263

WOMEN'S RIGHTS — New Brunswick
NEW BRUNSWICK ADVISORY COUNCIL ON THE STATUS OF WOMEN
 Being there : everywomen's guide to political action. — Moncton : the Council, 1983. — 31p

WOMEN'S RIGHTS — New Brunswick — History
TULLOCH, Elspeth
 We, the undersigned : a historical overview of New Brunswick women's political and legal status, 1784-1984 / Elspeth Tulloch for the New Brunswick Advisory Council on the Status of Women. — Moncton : New Brunswick Advisory Council on the Status of Women, 1985. — xx,147p. — Bibliography: p143-147

WOMEN'S RIGHTS — Spain
FAGOAGA, Concha
 La voz y el voto de las mujeres 1877-1931 / Concha Fagoaga. — Barcelona : Icaria Antrazyt, 1985. — 214p. — Bibliography: p199-203

WOMEN'S RIGHTS — Swaziland
ARMSTRONG, Alice Kavanaugh
 Law and the other sex : the legal position of women in Swaziland / by Alice Kavanagh Armstrong [and] Ronald Thandabantu Nhlapo. — Mbabane : Webster, [1985?]. — 150p. — Bibliography: p148-150

WOMEN'S RIGHTS — Turkey
ABADAN-UNAT, Nermin
 Women in the developing world : evidence from Turkey / Nermin Abadan-Unat. — Denver, Colo. : Graduate School of International Studies, University of Denver, 1986. — p. cm. — (Monograph series in world affairs ; v. 22, bk. 1). — Bibliography: p

WOMEN'S RIGHTS — United States
MANSBRIDGE, Jane J
 Why we lost the ERA / Jane J. Mansbridge. — Chicago : University of Chicago Press, 1986. — p. cm. — Includes index. — Bibliography: p

WOMEN'S RIGHTS — United States — History
LUNARDINI, Christine A.
 From equal suffrage to equal rights : Alice Paul and the National Woman's Party, 1910-1928 / Christine A. Lunardini. — New York : New York University Press, 1986. — xx, 230 p. — (The American social experience series ; 5). — Includes index. — Bibliography: p. [206]-220

WOMEN'S STUDIES
For alma mater : theory and practice in feminist scholarship / edited by Paula A. Treichler, Cheris Kramarae, Beth Stafford. — Urbana : University of Illinois Press, c1985. — xv, 450 p., [10] p. of plates. — Includes bibliographies and index

WOMEN'S STUDIES — Congresses
Women's worlds : from the new scholarship / edited by Marilyn Safir ... [et al] ; in cooperation with the Society for the Psychological Study of Social Issues. — New York : Praeger, 1985. — p. cm. — Papers presented at the First International Interdisciplinary Congress on Women held at the University of Haifa, Haifa, Israel, Dec. 28, 1981-Jan. 1, 1982. — Includes index

WOMEN'S STUDIES — United States
Feminist scholarship : challenge, discovery, and impact / Ellen Carol DuBois ... [et al.]. — Urbana : University of Illinois Press, c1985. — p. cm. — Includes index. — Bibliography: p

WOOD-CARVING, PRIMITIVE — New Guinea
GERBRANDS, Adrian A.
 Wow-ipits : eight Asmat woodcarvers of New Guinea / Adrian A. Gerbrands ; [translated from the dutch by Inez Wolf Seeger]. — The Hague : Mouton, c1967. — 191p. — (Art in its context : studies in ethno-aesthetics. field reports ; v.3). — Bibliography: p[173]-174

WOOD-PULP INDUSTRY — Environmental aspects
Environmental considerations in the pulp and paper industry. — [Washington, D.C.] : World Bank, 1980. — [vi],101p. — Prepared in co-operation with the World Bank by Beak Consultants Limited, Vancouver, B.C.. — Bibliography: p99-101

WOODCRAFT FOLK
Woodcraft focus: a journal for youth leaders and parents. — London : Woodcraft Folk, 1987-. — Quarterly

WOODWARD, C. VANN
WOODWARD, C. Vann
 Thinking back : the perils of writing history / C. Vann Woodward. — Baton Rouge ; London : Louisiana State University Press, c1986. — x, 158p. — Includes index. — Bibliography: p 147-151

WOODWORKERS — Great Britain — Recruiting
FURNITURE AND TIMBER INDUSTRY TRAINING BOARD
 Education for our industries : a report / by the Furniture and Timber Industry Training Board. — [High Wycombe] : the Board, 1978. — 35p

WOOL — Australia — Marketing — Mathematical models
CASSIDY, Peter
 The Australian wool supply pipeline, technology and marketing logistics : low cost alternatives / by Peter Cassidy, Ian Toft, Owen McCarthy. — Kelvin Grove, Qld. : Brisbane College of Advanced Education, 1986. — 104p. — (Monographs / Brisbane College of Advanced Education Business Research Centre ; no.2)

WOOL-COMBING — History — 19th century
HONEYMAN, Katrina
 Technology and enterprise : Isaac Holden and the mechanisation of woolcombing in France, 1848-1914 / Katrina Honeyman and Jordan Goodman. — Aldershot : Scolar [for] the Pasold Research Fund, 1986. — ix,121p,[4]p of plates. — (Pasold studies in textile history ; 6)

WOOL TRADE AND INDUSTRY — Australia
CASSIDY, Peter
 The Australian wool supply pipeline, technology and marketing logistics : low cost alternatives / by Peter Cassidy, Ian Toft, Owen McCarthy. — Kelvin Grove, Qld. : Brisbane College of Advanced Education, 1986. — 104p. — (Monographs / Brisbane College of Advanced Education Business Research Centre ; no.2)

WOOL TRADE AND INDUSTRY — Australia — History
GARRAN, J. C.
Merinos, myths and Macarthurs : Australian graziers and their sheep, 1788-1900 / J. C. Garran and L. White. — Rushcutters Bay, N.S.W. : Australian National University Press, 1985. — xv,288p. — *Bibliography: p[261]-270*

WOOL TRADE AND INDUSTRY — Australia — Statistics
AUSTRALIAN BUREAU OF STATISTICS
Wool statistics, Australia. — Canberra : [the Bureau], 1969/70-1980/81. — Annual. — *Continues Statistical bulletin: Wool production and utilization, Australia*

WOOL TRADE AND INDUSTRY — Great Britain
GREAT BRITAIN. Department of Industry
Wool textile industry scheme : an assessment of the effects of selective assistance under the Industry Act 1972 / analysis and consultations...carried out by Dilys Gane. — London : the Department, 1978. — ii,41,[35]p

WOOL TRADE AND INDUSTRY — Great Britain — History — 20th century
HARDILL, Irene
The regional implications of restructuring in the wool textile industry / Irene Hardill. — Aldershot : Gower, c1987. — xvi,256p

WOOLEN AND WORSTED MANUFACTURE — France — History — 19th century
HONEYMAN, Katrina
Technology and enterprise : Isaac Holden and the mechanisation of woolcombing in France, 1848-1914 / Katrina Honeyman and Jordan Goodman. — Aldershot : Scolar [for] the Pasold Research Fund, 1986. — ix,121p,[4]p of plates. — (Pasold studies in textile history ; 6)

WORD PROCESSING
PFAFFENBERGER, Bryan
The scholar's personal computing handbook : a practical guide / Bryan Pfaffenberger. — Boston : Little, Brown, c1986. — xiii, 359 p.. — (The Little, Brown microcomputer bookshelf). — *Includes bibliographies and index*

WORDSTAR (COMPUTER PROGRAM) — Handbooks, manuals, etc.
AMSTRAD CONSUMER ELECTRONICS
WordStar 1512 : [documentation] / Amstrad Consumer Electronics. — Brentwood : Amstrad Consumer Electronics, c1986. — 1v.(loose-leaf)

WORK
ABENDROTH, Wolfgang
Die Aktualität der Arbeiterbewegung : Beiträge zu ihrer Theorie und Geschichte / Wolfgang Abendroth ; herausgegeben von Joachim Perels. — Frankfurt am Main : Suhrkamp, 1985. — 225p. — *Bibliography: p225-[226]*

ATKINSON, John
New forms of work organisation / by John Atkinson and Nigel Meager. — Brighton : Institute of Manpower Studies, 1986. — iv,181p. — (IMS report ; No.121)

Ethnomethodological studies of work / edited by Harold Garfinkel. — London ; New York : Routledge and Kegan Paul, 1986. — viii,196p

HOWARD, Robert
Brave new workplace / Robert Howard. — New York : Penguin Books, 1986, c1985. — p. cm. — "Elisabeth Sifton books.". — *Includes index*

LEADBEATER, Charles
In search of work / Charles Leadbeater and John Lloyd. — Harmondsworth : Penguin, 1987. — 232p. — 'Based on a special report "Work - the way ahead", published by the Financial Times in 1986'. — *Bibliography: p [214]-218*

RINEHART, James W.
The tyranny of work : alienation and the labour process / James W. Rinehart ; with the assistance of Seymour Faber. — 2nd ed. — Toronto : Harcourt Brace Jovanovich, 1987. — x,226p. — *Bibliography: p[211]-222*

SMITH, Stephen
The shadow economy in Britain and Germany : based on a comparative research project undertaken by the Institute for Fiscal Studies, London, and the Institut für Angewandte Wirtschaftsforschung Tübingen / Stephen Smith and Susanne Wied-Nebbeling. — London : Anglo-German Foundation for the Study of Industrial Society, c1986. — 102 p

Work, employment and society / British Sociological Association. — London : British Sociological Association, 1987-. — Quarterly

WORK — Psychological aspects
ALVESSON, Mats
[Organisationsteori och teknokratiskt medvetande. English]. Organization theory and technocratic consciousness : rationality, ideology, and quality of work / Mats Alvesson. — Berlin ; New York : W. De Gruyter, 1987. — p. cm. — (De Gruyter studies in organization ; 8). — *Translation of: Organisationsteori och teknokratiskt medvetande. — Includes index. — Bibliography: p*

Management of work and personal life : problems and opportunities / edited by Mary Dean Lee and Rabindra N. Kanungo. — New York, N.Y. : Praeger, 1984. — p. cm. — *Includes index. — Bibliography: p*

SCHWALBE, Michael L.
The psychosocial consequences of natural and alienated labor / Michael L. Schwalbe. — Albany, N.Y. : State University of New York Press, c1986. — ix, 233 p.. — (SUNY series in the sociology of work). — *Includes index. — Bibliography: p. 215-227*

WORK — Social aspects
OPEN UNIVERSITY
Work and society. — Milton Keynes : Open University Press. — (DE325. Block 1, Units 1-4)
Block 1: Analysing work : problems and issues / Ruth Finnegan...[et al.]. — 1985. — 113p

OPEN UNIVERSITY
Work and society. — Milton Keynes : Open University Press. — (DE325. Block 4, Units 13-16)
Block 4: Work, culture and society / Rosemary Deem...[et al.]. — 1985. — 93p

WORK — Social aspects — South Africa
Working in South Africa / editors Ken Dovey, Lorraine Laughton, Jo-Anne Durandt. — Johannesburg : Ravan Press, 1985. — ix,397p

WORK AND FAMILY — Michigan — Longitudinal studies
MORTIMER, Jeylan T.
Work, family, and personality : transition to adulthood / Jeylan T. Mortimer, Jon Lorence, Donald S. Kumka. — Norwood, N.J. : Ablex Pub. Corp., c1986. — viii, 267 p.. — (Modern sociology). — *Includes index. — Bibliography: p. 231-255*

WORK AND FAMILY — United States
BERG, Barbara J
The crisis of the working mother : resolving the conflict between family and work / by Barbara Berg. — New York : Summit Books, c1986. — p. cm. — *Includes bibliographical references*

GROLLMAN, Earl A
The working parent dilemma : how to balance the responsibilities of children and careers / Earl A. Grollman and Gerri L. Sweder. — 1st ed. — Boston : Beacon Press, 1986. — xv, 190 p.. — *Includes index. — Bibliography: p. 181-185*

WORK DESIGN — Social aspects
ALVESSON, Mats
Consensus, control and critique : three paradigms of work organization research / Mats Alvesson. — Aldershot : Avebury, c1987. — viii,162p. — *Translation from the Swedish. — Bibliography: p151-162*

WORK DESIGN — Great Britain
ASSOCIATION OF PROFESSIONAL, EXECUTIVE, CLERICAL AND COMPUTER STAFF
Job design & new technology : guidelines / APEX. — London : The Association, 1985

WORK ENVIRONMENT
MITTER, Swasti
Common fate, common bond : women in the global economy / Swasti Mitter. — London : Pluto, 1986. — [224]p. — *Includes index*

Working conditions and environment : a worker's education manual. — Geneva : International Labour Office, 1983. — vi, 81 p., [6] p. of plates. — "A selection of recommended ILO publications and documents": p. 75. — "ILO films and film strips": p. 76

WORK ENVIRONMENT — Societies, etc. — Directories
Conditions of work and quality of working life : a directory of institutions / edited by Linda Stoddart. — 2nd ed. — Geneva : International Labour Office, 1986. — xxi,306

WORK ENVIRONMENT — Europe — Congresses
Work and health in the 1980s : experiences of direct workers' participation in occupational health / Sebastiano Bagnara, Raffaello Misiti, Helmut Wintersberger, eds. — Berlin : Edition Sigma, c1985. — 384 p.. — "Wissenschaftszentrum Berlin, International Institute for Comparative Social Research/Labor Policy"--Cover. — *Includes bibliographies*

WORK GROUPS
WOODCOCK, Mike
Team development manual / Mike Woodcock. — Aldershot : Gower, 1984, c1979. — [200]p. — *Bibliography: p210-213*

WORK GROUPS — Sweden
RESSNER, Ulla
Group organised work in the automated office / Ulla Ressner and Evy Gunnarsson. — Aldershot : Gower, c1986. — 122p. — *Bibliography: p111-122*

WORK IN LITERATURE
SWINDELLS, Julia
Victorian writing and working women : the other side of silence / Julia Swindells. — Cambridge : Polity, 1985. — [240]p. — *Includes index*

WORK MEASUREMENT
MEISTER, David
Behavioral analysis and measurement methods / David Meister. — New York : Wiley, c1985. — xiii, 509 p.. — "A Wiley-Interscience publication.". — *Includes bibliographies and index*

WORK SHARING
HUMPHREYS, Peter C.
Worksharing and the public sector / Peter C. Humphreys. — Dublin : Institute of Public Administration, 1986. — xii,239p. — *Bibliography: p195-210*

WORK SHARING — Germany (West)
CASEY, Bernard
Worksharing and young persons : recent experiences in Great Britain, the Federal Republic of Germany and The Netherlands : main report / by Bernard Casey. — Luxembourg : Office for Official Publications of the European Communities, 1984. — 62p. — *At head of title page: Commission of the European Communities*

WORK SHARING — Great Britain
CASEY, Bernard
Worksharing and young persons : recent experiences in Great Britain, the Federal Republic of Germany and The Netherlands : main report / by Bernard Casey. — Luxembourg : Office for Official Publications of the European Communities, 1984. — 62p. — *At head of title page: Commission of the European Communities*

WORK SHARING — Ireland
HUMPHREYS, Peter C.
Worksharing and the public sector / Peter C. Humphreys. — Dublin : Institute of Public Administration, 1986. — xii,239p. — *Bibliography: p195-210*

WORK SHARING — Netherlands
CASEY, Bernard
Worksharing and young persons : recent experiences in Great Britain, the Federal Republic of Germany and The Netherlands : main report / by Bernard Casey. — Luxembourg : Office for Official Publications of the European Communities, 1984. — 62p. — *At head of title page: Commission of the European Communities*

WORKERS' COMPENSATION — Law and legislation — Great Britain
LEWIS, Richard, 19---
Compensation for industrial injury : a guide to the revised scheme of benefits for work accidents and diseases / by Richard Lewis. — Abingdon : Professional Books, 1987. — 359p

WORKERS' COMPENSATION — Brazil
PASSARINHO, Jarbas G.
Resposta às dez principais objeções à integração do seguro de acidentes do trabalho na previdência social / Jarbas G. Passarinho. — [Brazília] : Ministério do Trabalho e Previdência Social, Serviço de Documentação, Seção de Publicação, 1967. — 9p

WORKERS' COMPENSATION — Denmark
Arbejdsskadeforsikringen beretning for årene 1980 og 1981. — [København] : Sikringsstyrelsen, 1982. — 53p. — (Sikringsstyrelsens undersøgelser ; nr.7)

WORKER'S COMPENSATION — Denmark
Beretning fra Sikringsstyrelsen : arbejdsskadeforsikringen for årene 1977,1978 og 1979. — København : [Sikringsstyrelsen], 1980. — 150p

WORKERS' COMPENSATION — United States — Addresses, essays, lectures
Workers' compensation benefits : adequacy, equity, and efficiency / John D. Worrall and David Appel, editors. — Ithaca, NY : ILR Press, New York State School of Industrial and Labor Relations, Cornell University, c1985. — p. cm. — *Includes index. — Bibliography: p*

WORKERS POWER
WORKERS POWER
The class struggle and the elections : a workers' manifesto. — London : Workers Power, 1987. — 58p

WORKING CAPITAL
VICKERS, Douglas
Money capital in the theory of the firm : a preliminary analysis / Douglas Vickers. — Cambridge : Cambridge University Press, 1987. — x,244p. — *Bibliography: p232-238. — Includes index*

WORKING CLASS WOMEN
MARSHALL, Kate
Real freedom : women's liberation and socialism / Kate Marshall. — London : Junius, 1982. — ii,139p

WORKING CLASS WOMEN — Biography — History and criticism
SWINDELLS, Julia
Victorian writing and working women : the other side of silence / Julia Swindells. — Cambridge : Polity, 1985. — [240]p. — *Includes index*

WORKING CLASS WOMEN — England — Barnsley (South Yorkshire)
BARNSLEY WOMEN AGAINST PIT CLOSURES
Barnsley Women Against Pit Closures. — Barnsley (Barnsley Women Against Pit Closures). — (Women Against Pit Closures ; vol.2) (People's History of Yorkshire ; no.12) vol.2. — 1985. — 109p

WORKING CLASS WOMEN — India — Bibliography
Women at work in India : a bibliography / compiled by Suchitra Anant, S. V. Ramani Rao, Kabita Kapoor. — New Delhi ; London : Sage, 1986. — 238p

WORKING MOTHERS
SCARR, Sandra
Mother care/ other care : [the child-care dilemma for women and children] / Sandra Scarr and Judy Dunn. — 2nd ed. — Harmondsworth : Penguin, 1987. — 239p. — *Originally published: New York: Basic Books, 1984. — Bibliography: [p221]-229*

WORKING MOTHERS — United States — Biography
LUBIN, Aasta S
Managing success : high-echelon careers and motherhood / Aasta S. Lubin. — New York : Columbia University Press, 1987. — p. cm. — *Includes index. — Bibliography: p*

WORKING MOTHERS — United States — Psychology
BERG, Barbara J
The crisis of the working mother : resolving the conflict between family and work / by Barbara Berg. — New York : Summit Books, c1986. — p. cm. — *Includes bibliographical references*

WORKS COUNCILS — Great Britain — Directories
Directory of employers' associations, trade unions, joint organisations, &c / Department of Employment. — London : H.M.S.O., 1986-. — 1v.(loose-leaf). — *Includes index*

WORKS COUNCILS — Hungary — History
RÁCZ, János
Az üzemi bizottságok a magyar demokratikus átalakulásban (1944-1948) / Rácz János. — Budapest : Akadémiai Kiadó, 1971. — 159p

WORKS COUNCILS — Iran
BAYAT, Assef
Workers and revolution in Iran : a Third World experience of workers' control / Assef Bayat. — London : Zed, 1987. — 227p. — *Bibliography: p208-222. — Includes index*

WORKSHOPS — Great Britain
JACKSON, Annabel
Managing workspaces : prepared for the Department of the Environment / by Annabel Jackson, Daphne Mair and Rupert Nabarro, Land and Urban Analysis Ltd.. — London : H.M.S.O., 1987. — 133p. — (Case studies of good practice in urban regeneration). — *Commissioned by the Inner Cities Directorate of the Department of the Environment. — Bibliography: p132*

WORLD BANK
Between two worlds : the World Bank's next decade / Richard E. Feinberg, editor ; Gerald K. Helleiner ... [et al., contributors]. — New Brunswick (USA) : Transaction Books, c1985. — p. cm. — (U.S.-Third World policy perspectives ; no. 7)

CLAUSEN, A. W
The development challenge of the eighties : A.W. Clausen at the World Bank : major policy addresses, 1981-1986. — Washington, D.C., U.S.A. : The Bank, 1986. — p. cm

MILLER, Morris
Coping is not enough! : the international debt crisis and the roles of the World Bank and International Monetary Fund / Morris Miller. — Homewood, Ill. : Dow Jones-Irwin, c1986. — xiii, 268 p.. — *Includes bibliographical references and index*

PHAUP, E. Dwight
The World Bank : how it can serve U.S. interests / E. Dwight Phaup. — Washington, D.C. : Heritage Foundation, 1984. — vi,57p

La réunion du Groupe consultatif de la Banque Mondiale pour le Zaire, Novembre 1973. — Kinshasa : Université Nationale du Zaire, Institut de Recherches Economiques, 1974. — 16p. — (Document du mois / Université Nationale du Zaire. Institute de Recherches Economiques ; vol.1, no.1)

RODEN, Hanne
The World Bank : introduction to its involvement in urbanisation in the 3rd World : the care of Botswana / Hanne Roden. — Copenhagen : [s.n.], 1984. — 186p

VENUGOPAL REDDY, Y
World Bank, borrowers' perspectives / Y. Venugopal Reddy. — New Delhi : Sterling Publishers, c1985. — x, 143 p.. — *Includes index*

WORLD BANK
Catalog: World Bank publications. — Washington, D.C. : World Bank, 1973-1984. — Annual. — *Continued by: World Bank: new publications*

WORLD BANK
General conditions applicable to loan and guarantee agreements. — [Washington, D.C.] : the Bank, 1974. — iii,18p. — *At head of title page: International Bank for Reconstruction and Development*

WORLD BANK
New publications / World Bank. — Washington, D.C. : World Bank Publications, 1985-. — *Quarterly*

WORLD BANK — Bibliography
WORLD BANK
Index of publications / World Bank. — Alton : Microinfo for World Bank, 1987-. — *Irregular*

WORLD BANK — Case studies
PAUL, Samuel
Community participation in development projects : the World Bank experience / Samuel Paul. — Washington, D.C. : The World Bank, 1987. — 37p. — (World Bank discussion papers ; no.6). — *Includes bibliographical references*

WORLD BANK — Finance
Disbursement handbook. — Washington D. C. : The World Bank, 1986. — iv,58p

WORLD BANK — History
CLARK, William, 1916-1985
From three worlds : memoirs / William Clark. — London : Sidgwick & Jackson, [1986]. — xi,292p

WORLD BANK — Language — Glossaries, etc.
Borrowing and lending terminology : English-French-Spanish = Terminologie des emprunts et des prêts : Français-anglais-espagnol = Terminología de empréstitos y prśetamos : Español-inglés-francés. — Washington, D.C. : The World Bank, 1984. — vii,56p. — (A World Bank glossary). — *In English, French and Spanish*

WORLD BANK — Language — Glossaries, etc. *continuation*

The World Bank glossary = Glossaire de la Banque mondiale. — Washington, D.C. : The World Bank
V.1: English-French, French-English. — 1986. — 429p. — *In English and French*

The World Bank glossary = Glosario del Banco Mundial. — Washington, D.C. : The World Bank
V.2: English-Spanish, Spanish-English. — 1986. — v,360p. — *In English and Spanish*

WORLD BANK — Legal status, laws, etc.

WORLD BANK
Articles of agreement of the International Bank for Reconstruction and Development : as amended effective December 17, 1965. — Washington, D.C. : the Bank, 1980. — 24p

WORLD BANK
By-laws of the International Bank for Reconstruction and Development : as amended through September 26, 1980. — Washington, D.C. : the Bank, 1980. — 6p

WORLD BANK
Loan regulations no.3 : applicable to loans made by the Bank to member governments : dated February 15, 1961 as amended February 9, 1967. — [Washington, D.C.?] : the Bank, 1967. — iv,35p

WORLD BANK
Loan regulations no.4 : applicable to loans made by the Bank to borrowers other than member governments : dated Februrary 15, 1961 as amended February 9, 1967. — [Washington, D.C.?] : the Bank, 1967. — iv,40p

WORLD BANK — Membership

WORLD BANK
Telephone directory. — Washington, D.C. : The World Bank, 1987. — 174p

WORLD BANK — Asia

PAL, Mahendra
World Bank and the Third World countries of Asia : (with special reference to India) / Mahendra Pal. — New Delhi : National, 1985. — x,407p. — *Bibliography: p[379]-389*

WORLD BANK — Developing countries

BAUM, Warren C
Investing in development : lessons of World Bank experience / Warren C. Baum and Stokes M. Tolbert. — New York : Published for the World Bank [by] Oxford University Press, c1985. — p. cm. — *Includes index*

WORLD BANK — Switzerland

VÖLK, Karl
The World Bank group and Switzerland / Dr. Karl Völk. — [Basle] : Union Bank of Switzerland, 1987. — 76p

WORLD BANK. Operations Evaluation Department

Annual review of project performance audit results. — Washington, DC : World Bank, 1982-1983

WORLD BANK

CLAUSEN, A. W.
The development challenge of the eighties : A. W. Clausen at the World Bank : major policy addresses, 1981-1986 / A. W. Clausen. — Washington, D.C. : The World Bank, 1986. — xxvii,496p. — *Contents: Addresses to various bodies by A. W. Clausen, ex-President of the World Bank*

LEVITSKY, Jacob
World Bank lending to small enterprises : a review / Jacob Levitsky. — Washington, D.C. : The World Bank, 1986. — viii,53p. — (Industry and finance series ; v.16). — *Includes bibliographical references*

WORLD BANK — Congresses

LONDON SYMPOSIUM ON THE WORLD BANK'S ROLE (1985)
Recovery in the developing world. — Washington, D.C. : The World Bank, 1986. — vi,122p. — *Bibliography: p121-122*

WORLD DISARMAMENT CAMPAIGN (UK) — History

BROCKWAY, Fenner
98 not out / Fenner Brockway. — London : Quartet, 1986. — [140]p. — *Includes index*

WORLD EMPLOYMENT PROGRAMME — Research — Bibliography

Bibliography of published research of the World Employment Programme. — 5th ed. — Geneva : International Labour Office, 1984. — vi,151p

Bibliography of published research of the World Employment Programme. — 6th ed. — Geneva : International Labour Office, 1986. — vii,177p. — *Includes supplement*

World Employment Programme : research in retrospect and prospect. — Geneva : International Labour Office, 1976. — 278p. — *Bibliography: p245-273*

WORLD FEDERATION OF TRADE UNIONS

A framework for international trade union cooperation : main document adopted by the 11th World Trade Union Congress, Berlin, GDR, 16-22 September 1986. — Prague : World Federation of Trade Unions, 1986. — 34p

WORLD FERTILITY SURVEY — Data processing

PULLUM, Thomas W.
An assessment of the machine editing policies of the World Fertility Survey / Thomas W. Pullum, Nuri Ozsever, Trudy Harpham. — Voorburg : International Statistical Institute, 1984. — 39p. — (Scientific reports / World Fertility Survey ; no.54)

Software user's manual. — Voorburg : International Statistical Institute, 1984. — 269p. — (Basic documentation / World Fertility Survey ; no.12)

WORLD FERTILITY SURVEY — Statistical methods

MARCKWARDT, Albert M.
Response rates, callbacks and coverage : the WFS experience / Albert M. Marckwardt. — Voorburg : International Statistical Institute, 1984. — 32p. — (Scientific reports / World Fertility Survey ; no.55)

WORLD HEALTH

Medical science and the advancement of world health / edited by Robert Lanza. — New York : Praeger, 1985. — p. cm. — *Includes index*

WORLD HEALTH — Addresses, essays, lectures

Medical science and the advancement of world health / edited by Robert Lanza. — New York : Praeger, 1985. — p. cm. — *Includes index*

WORLD HEALTH ORGANIZATION

Medical specialization in relation to health needs : report on a WHO meeting : Abano Terme, Italy, 22-25 October 1984. — Copenhagen : World Health Organization, 1986. — 67p. — *Summary in French, German, and Russian*. — *Bibliography: p42*

WORLD HEALTH ORGANIZATION. Regional Experts Meeting on Health Manpower Development (1977 : Brazzaville)

WORLD HEALTH ORGANIZATION. Regional Experts Meeting on Health Manpower Development (1977 : Brazzaville)
Health manpower development : the problems of the health team : report / of a WHO Regional Experts Meeting on Health Manpower Development. — Brazzaville : Regional Office for Africa, World Health Organization, 1977. — [viii]13p. — (AFRO technical report series ; no.4). — *Includes bibliographical references*

WORLD HISTORY

MONTBRIAL, Thierry de
La revanche de lhistoire / Thierry de Montbrial. — Paris : Julliard, c1985. — 197p. — (Commentaire Julliard)

WORLD MAPS

The Times concise atlas of the world / maps prepared and printed by John Bartholomew and Son Ltd.. — 5th ed. — London : Times Books, 1986. — 44p,148 maps,96p

WORLD POLITICS

Buffer states in world politics / edited by John Chay, Thomas E. Ross. — Boulder : Westview Press, 1986. — p. cm. — (Westview special studies in international relations). — *Includes index*

The Christian science monitor. — Boston (Mass) : Christian Science Publishing Society, 1987-. — *Weekly*

Deutschland und der Westen : Vorträge und Diskussionsbeiträge des Symposions zu Ehren von Gordon A. Craig veranstaltet von der Freien Universität Berlin vom 1.-3. Dezember 1983 / herausgegeben von Henning Köhler. — Berlin : Colloquium Verlag, 1984. — 218p. — (Studien zur europäischen Geschichte ; Bd.15). — *Includes three chapters in English*

FALK, Richard A.
A world order perspective on authoritarian tendencies / Richard A. Falk. — New York : Institute for World Order, 1980. — 67p. — (World Order Models Project working paper ; no.10)

Israel, the Middle East and the great powers : studies in the contemporary history and politics of the Middle East and the Arab-Israel conflict / edited by Israel Stockman-Shomron. — [Jerusalem] : Shikmona Publishing Co., 1984. — 389p

KOTHARI, Rajni
Towards a just world / Rajni Kothari. — New York : Institute for World Order, 1980. — 42p. — (World Order Models Project working paper ; no.11)

MCNEILL, William Hardy
The pursuit of power : technology, armed force, and society since A.D. 1000 / William H. McNeill. — Chicago : University of Chicago Press, 1982. — x, 405 p.. — *Includes bibliographical references and index*

Le monde diplomatique. — Paris : Le Monde, 1984

Politique internationale. — Paris : Politique Internationale, 1985-. — *Quarterly*

Prognosen für Europa : die siebziger Tahre zwischen Ost und West. — Opladen : Leske Verlag, 1968. — 140p

The Straits Times: weekly overseas edition. — Singapore : Straits Times, 1987-. — *Weekly*

Times of India. — Bombay : Times of India, 1986-. — *Monthly*

WORLD POLITICS — Addresses, essays, lectures

Ein Gespräch mit Jurgen Kuczynski über Arbeiterklasse, Alltag, Geschichte, Kultur und vor allem über Krieg und Frieden [/ Frank Deppe...et al.]. — Marburg : Verlag Arbeiterbewegung und Gesellschaftswissenschaft, 1984. — 141p. — (Schriftenreihe der Studiengesellschaft für Sozialgeschichte und Arbeiterbewegung ; Bd.48)

Refugees and world politics ; edited by Elizabeth G. Ferris. — New York : Praeger, 1985. — p. cm. — Includes index. — Bibliography: p

WORLD POLITICS — Chronology

[Nihon Kyosanto no rokujunen. English]. Sixty-year history of Japanese Communist Party / Central Committee, Japanese Communist Party. — Tokyo : Japan Press Service, 1984. — 714 p. — Translation of: Nihon Kyōsantō no rokujūnen. 1982

WORLD POLITICS — 1900-1945

CHOUDHURY, Veena
Indian nationalism and external forces, 1920-47 / Veena Choudhury. — Delhi : Capital Pub. House, 1985. — xii, 234 p.. — Includes index. — Bibliography: p. [210]-228

WORLD POLITICS — 20th century

DUROSELLE, Jean-Baptiste
Histoire diplomatique de 1919 à nos jours / Jean-Baptiste Duroselle. — 9e edition. — Paris : Dalloz, 1985. — 962p. — Bibliographie: p881-908

KROMBACH, Hayo Benedikt Ernst Désiré
Scientific and philosophical thought about the discourse of international relations in the 20th century : a hermeneutic inquiry into the implications of the idea of nuclear war / Hayo Benedikt Ernst Désiré Krombach. — 606 leaves. — PhD (Econ) 1986 LSE

Outstanding international press reporting : Pulitzer Prize winning articles in foreign correspondence / editor Heinz-Dietrich Fischer. — Berlin ; New York : Walter de Gruyter
Vol.1: 1928-1945, from the consequences of World War I to the end of World War II. — 1984. — liii,368p

Outstanding international press reporting : Pulitzer Prize winning articles in foreign correspondence / editor Heinz-Dietrich Fischer. — Berlin ; New York : Walter de Gruyter
Vol.2: 1946-1962, from the end of World War II to the various stations of the Cold War. — 1985. — lxvii,304p

Outstanding international press reporting : Pulitzer Prize winning articles in foreign correspondence / editor Heinz-Dietrich Fischer. — Berlin ; New York : Walter de Gruyter
Vol.3: 1963-1977, from the escalation of the Vietnam war to the East Asian refugee problems. — 1986. — lxxii,309p

WORLD POLITICS — 20th century — Library resources — California — Stanford

The Library of the Hoover Institution on War, Revolution, and Peace / edited by Peter Duignan. — Stanford, Calif. : Hoover Institution, Stanford University, 1985. — p. cm . — Bibliography: p

WORLD POLITICS — 20th century — Philosophy

HALLE, Louis Joseph
History, philosophy, and foreign relations : background for the making of foreign policy / Louis J. Halle ; with a preface by Kenneth W. Thompson. — Lanham : University Press of America ; [s.l.] : The White Burkett Miller Center of Public Affairs, University of Virginia, c1987. — xii, 404 p. — (Papers on presidential transitions and foreign policy ; v. 7). — Includes bibliographies

WORLD POLITICS — 1919-1932

Die Ruhrkrise 1923 : Wendepunkt der internationalen Beziehungen nach dem Ersten Weltkrieg / Klaus Schwabe (Hrsg.). — Paderborn : Schöningh, 1984. — [vi], 111p

WORLD POLITICS — 1933-1945

The Cold war past and present / edited by Richard Crockatt and Steve Smith. — London : Allen & Unwin, 1987. — [248]p. — Includes bibliography and index

WORLD POLITICS — 1945-1955

CHOUDHURY, Veena
Indian nationalism and external forces, 1920-47 / Veena Choudhury. — Delhi : Capital Pub. House, 1985. — xii, 234 p.. — Includes index. — Bibliography: p. [210]-228

HARBUTT, Fraser J
The iron curtain : Churchill, America, and the origins of the Cold War / Fraser J. Harbutt. — New York ; Oxford : Oxford University Press, 1986. — xiv, 370p. — Includes index. — Bibliography: p.341-353

Kalter Krieg und Deutsche Frage : Deutschland im Widerstreit der Mächte 1945-1952 / herausgegeben von Josef Foschepoth. — Göttingen : Vandenhoeck und Ruprecht, 1985. — 388p. — (Veröffentlichungen des Deutschen Historischen Instituts London = Publications of the German Historical Insitute London ; Bd.16). — Bibliograhical notes

NACHMANI, Amikam
Great power discord in Palestine : the Anglo-American Committee of Inquiry into the problems of European Jewry and Palestine, 1945-1946 / Amikam Nachmani. — London : Cass, 1987. — x,294p,18p of plates. — Maps on lining papers. — Bibliography: p277-295. — Includes index

THOMAS, Hugh, 1931-
Armed truce : the beginnings of the Cold War 1945-46 / Hugh Thomas. — London : Hamilton, 1986. — xviii,667p. — Includes index

WORLD POLITICS — 1945-

Berlin between two worlds / edited by Ronald A. Francisco and Richard L. Merritt. — Boulder, Colo. ; London : Westview Press, 1986. — xiii,184p

BERRIDGE, G. R.
International politics : states, power and conflict since 1945 / G.R. Berridge. — Brighton : Wheatsheaf, 1987. — xii,228p. — Includes index

BETTS, Richard K.
Nuclear blackmail and nuclear balance / Richard K. Betts. — Washington, D.C. : Brookings Institution, c1987. — p. cm. — Includes bibliographical references and index

CALVOCORESSI, Peter
World politics since 1945 / Peter Calvocoressi. — 5th ed. — London : Longman, 1987. — [564]p. — Previous ed.: 1982. — Includes index

CASTRO, Fidel
Fidel Castro : nothing can stop the course of history / interview by Jeffrey M. Elliot and Mervyn M. Dymally. — New York ; London : Pathfinder Press, 1986. — 258p

The challenge of nuclear armaments : essays dedicated to Niels Bohr and his appeal for an open world / edited by A. Boserup, L. Christensen and O. Nathan. — Copenhagen : Rhodos International for the University of Copenhagen, 1986. — 346p

The Cold war past and present / edited by Richard Crockatt and Steve Smith. — London : Allen & Unwin, 1987. — [248]p. — Includes bibliography and index

Documents in communist affairs. — Brighton : Wheatsheaf
1985 / edited by Bogdan Szajkowski. — 1986. — [352]p

GRADER, Sheila Lillian
The problem of ideology and international relations / by Sheila Grader. — 271 leaves. — PhD (Econ) 1986 LSE

HANSON, Eric O
The Catholic Church in world politics / Eric O. Hanson. — Princeton, N.J. : Princeton University Press, c1987. — p. cm. — Includes index. — Bibliography: p

HELMREICH, Jonathan E
Gathering rare ores : the diplomacy of uranium acquisition, 1943-1954 / Jonathan E. Helmreich. — Princeton, N.J. : Princeton University Press, c1986. — xiv, 303 p.. — Includes index. — Bibliography: p. 287-291

HOFFMANN, Stanley
Janus and Minerva : essays in the theory and practice of international politics / Stanley Hoffmann. — Boulder : Westview Press, 1987. — xiv, 457 p.. — Includes bibliographies

HOXHA, Enver
The superpowers, 1959-1984 : extracts from the political diary / Enver Hoxha. — Tirana : Nentori Publishing House for the Institute of Marxist-Leninist Studies at the Central Committee of Party of Labour of Albania, 1986. — 678p

KEITHLY, David M
Breakthrough in the Ostpolitik : the 1971 Quadripartite Agreement / David M. Keithly. — Boulder : Westview Press, 1986. — p. cm. — (Westview special studies in international relations). — Includes index. — Bibliography: p

KHRUSHCHEV, N.
For victory in peaceful competition with capitalism : with a special preface written for the English edition / Nikita S. Khrushchev. — London : Hutchinson, 1960. — 784p

LUNDESTAD, Geir
East, west, north, south : major developments in international politics 1945-1986 / Geir Lundestad ; translated from the Norwegian by Gail Adams Kvam. — Oslo : Norwegian University Press ; Oxford : Distributed world-wide excluding Scandinavia by Oxford University Press, c1986. — 308p. — Translation of: Øst, vest, nord, sør. hovedlinjer i internasjonal politikk 1945-1985. — Bibliography: p290-295. — Includes index

MCNAMARA, Robert S.
Blundering into disaster : surviving the first century of the nuclear age / by Robert McNamara. — London : Bloomsbury, 1987. — [194]p. — Originally published: New York : Pantheon Books, 1986

MAKINDA, Samuel M.
Superpower diplomacy in the Horn of Africa / Samuel M. Makinda. — London : Croom Helm, c1987. — 241p. — Bibliography: p225-234. — Includes index

MALCOLMSON, Robert W
Nuclear fallacies : how we have been misguided since Hiroshima / Robert W. Malcolmson. — Kingston : McGill-Queen's University Press, c1985. — xi, 152 p.. — Includes index. — Bibliography: p. [117]-127

NOLTE, Ernst
Deutschland und der kalte Krieg / Ernst Nolte. — München : Piper, 1974. — 755p

SCRUTON, Roger
World studies : education or indoctrination / Roger Scruton. — London : Institute for European Defence and Strategic Studies, 1985. — 69p. — (Occasional paper / Institute for European Defence and Strategic Studies ; no.15)

WORLD POLITICS — 1945- *continuation*
SENGUPTA, Jyoti
Non-alignment : search for a destination / Jyoti Sengupta. — Calcutta : Naya Prokash, 1979. — xxii,208p

The Yalta agreements : documents prior to, during and after the Crimea Conference 1945. — London : Polish Government in Exile, 1986. — xv,183p. — Bibliography: p148

WORLD POLITICS — 1945- — Addresses, essays, lectures
Neorealism and its critics / Robert O. Keohane, editor. — New York : Columbia University Press, c1986. — p. cm. — (The Political economy of international change). — Includes index. — Bibliography: p. — Contents: Realism, neorealism, and the study of world politics / Robert O. Keohane -- Laws and theories / Kenneth N. Waltz -- Reductionist and systemic theories / Kenneth N. Waltz -- Political structures / Kenneth N. Waltz -- Anarchic orders and balances of power / Kenneth N. Waltz -- Continuity and transformation in the world polity / John Gerard Ruggie -- Theory of world politics / Robert O. Keohane -- Social forces, states, and world orders / Robert W. Cox -- The poverty of neorealism / Richard K. Ashley -- The richness of the tradition of political realism / Robert G. Gilpin -- Reflections on theory of international politics / Kenneth N. Waltz

The Origins of the cold war and contemporary Europe / edited with an introd. by Charles S. Maier. — New York : New Viewpoints, 1978. — xvi, 255 p.. — (Modern scholarship on European history). — Includes index. — Bibliography: p. 245-248

WORLD POLITICS — 1965-1975
HALLIDAY, Fred
The making of the second cold war / Fred Halliday. — 2nd ed. — London : Verso, 1986. — [256]p. — Previous ed.: 1983. — Includes bibliography and index

WORLD POLITICS — 1965-
World outlook: a journal of international affairs. — Hanover (NH) : World outlook, 1986

WORLD POLITICS — 1975-1985
HALLIDAY, Fred
The making of the second cold war / Fred Halliday. — 2nd ed. — London : Verso, 1986. — [256]p. — Previous ed.: 1983. — Includes bibliography and index

KNELMAN, Fred H
Reagan, God, and the bomb : from myth to policy in the nuclear arms race / F.H. Knelman. — Toronto, Ont. : McClelland and Stewart, c1985. — vii, 343 p.. — Bibliography: p. 313-330

LEONARD, Ellis P
[Orthopedic surgery of the dog and cat]. Leonard's Orthopedic surgery of the dog and cat. — 3rd ed. / J.W. Alexander. — Philadelphia : Saunders, 1985. — ix, 242 p.. — Includes bibliographies and index

SEMENOV, V. A.
Politiki mira i kurs na konfrontatsiiu / V. A. Semenov. — Moskva : Mezhdunarodnye otnosheniia, 1986. — 146p

Soviet-East European relations as a problem for the West / edited by Richard D. Vine. — London : Croom Helm, c1987. — 262p. — (An Atlantic Institute for International Affairs research volume). — Includes index

WORLD POLITICS — 1985-1995
CORDESMAN, Anthony H.
Western strategic interests in Saudi Arabia / Anthony H. Cordesman. — London : Croom Helm, c1987. — 308p. — Bibliography: p267-290. — Includes index

DALLY, Peter
The Sino-Soviet split : a trap for the West / by Peter Dally. — Cheltenham (31 Seneca Way, Cheltenham, Glos. GL50 45F) : British Anti-Communist Council, c1984. — 67p

Dealignment : a new foreign policy perspective / edited by Mary Kaldor and Richard Falk with the assistance of Gerard Holden. — Oxford : Basil Blackwell, 1987. — viii,265p. — Includes index

Prospectus for a habitable planet / edited by Dan Smith and E. P. Thompson. — Harmondsworth : Penguin, 1987. — 240p

WINDASS, Stan
The rite of war / by Stan Windass. — London : Brassey's, 1986. — viii,132p

WORLD POLITICS — 1986-
The Neutral democracies and the new Cold War / edited by Bengt Sundelius. — Boulder, Colo. : Westview Press, 1987. — xi, 245 p.. — (Westview special studies in international relations). — "Published in cooperation with the Swedish Institute of International Affairs, Stockholm.". — Includes index. — Bibliography: p. 218-220

WORLD WAR — Economic aspects — Moldavian S.S.R.
SHORNIKOV, P. M.
Promyshlennost' i rabochii klass Moldavskoi SSR v gody Velikoi Otechestvennoi voiny / P. M. Shornikov ; otv. redaktor I. E. Levit. — Kishinev : Shtiintsa, 1986. — 148p. — Brief summary in English and French

WORLD WAR, 1914-1918 — Causes
HAMILTON, W. Mark
The nation and the navy : methods and organization of British navalist propaganda, 1889-1914 / W. Mark Hamilton. — New York : Garland Pub., 1986. — p. cm. — (Outstanding theses from the London School of Economics and Political Science). — Thesis (Ph.D.)--University of London, 1977. — Bibliography: p

Military strategy and the origins of the First World War / edited by Steven E. Miller. — Princeton, N.J. : Princeton University Press, 1985. — 186p. — (An International security reader). — "The contents of this book were first published in International security" - verso t.p.

The Origins of the First World War : great power rivalry and German war aims / edited by H.W. Koch. — 2nd ed. — Basingstoke : Macmillan, 1984 (1985 [printing]). — viii,402p. — Previous ed.: 1972. — Bibliography: p387-395. — Includes index

WORLD WAR, 1914-1918 — Civilian relief — Poland
PŁYGAWKO, Danuta
Sienkiewicz w Szwajcarii : z dziejów akcji ratunkowej dla Polski w czasie pierwszej wojny światowej / Danuta Płygawko. — Poznań : Uniwersytet im. Adama Mickiewicza, 1986. — 171p. — (Seria Historia / Uniwersytet im. Adama Mickiewicza w Poznaniu ; Nr.122). — Summary in French and English. — Bibliography: p[154]-159

WORLD WAR, 1914-1918 — Diplomatic history
HARDARSON, S. B. Jensdottír
Anglo-Icelandic relations during the First World War / S.B. Jensdottir Hardarson. — New York : Garland Pub., 1986. — 220 p.. — (Outstanding theses from the London School of Economics and Political Science). — Thesis (M.A.)--London School of Economics and Political Science, 1980. — Includes index. — Bibliography: p. 217-220

HARTLEY, Stephen
The Irish question as a problem in British foreign policy, 1914-18 / Stephen Hartley. — Basingstoke : Macmillan in association with King's College, London, 1987. — xi,243p. — (Studies in military and strategic history). — Bibliography:p228-236. — Includes index

JONES, A. Phillip
Britain's search for Chinese cooperation in the First World War / A. Phillip Jones. — New York : Garland, 1986. — p. cm. — (Outstanding theses from the London School of Economics and Political Science). — Thesis (Ph.D.)--University of London, 1976. — Bibliography: p

JONES, Simon Mark
Domestic factors in Italian intervention in the First World War / Simon Mark Jones. — New York : Garland, 1986. — 292 p.. — (Outstanding theses from the London School of Economics and Political Science). — Thesis (Ph.D.)--London School of Economics and Political Science. — Bibliography: p. 275-292

WALWORTH, Arthur
Wilson and his peacemakers : American diplomacy at the Paris Peace Conference, 1919 / Arthur Walworth. — New York ; London : W.W. Norton, 1986. — xiii, 618p. — Includes index. — Bibliography: p.572-585

WORLD WAR, 1914-1918 — Economic aspects — Brazil
FRITSCH, Winston
Brazil and the Great War, 1914-1918 / Winston Fritsch. — Rio de Janeiro, RJ : Departamento de Economia, Pontifícia Universidade Católica do Rio de Janeiro, [1984]. — 54 leaves. — (Texto para discussão / Departamento de Economia, PUC/RJ ; no. 62) . — "January 1984.". — Includes bibliographical references

WORLD WAR, 1914-1918 — Economic aspects — Europe
KIRBY, D. G. (David Gordon)
War, peace and revolution : international socialism at the crossroads 1914-1918 / David Kirby. — Aldershot : Gower, c1986. — ix,310p. — Bibliography: p284-301. — Includes index

WORLD WAR, 1914-1918 — Economic aspects — France
GODFREY, John F.
Capitalism at war : industrial policy and bureaucracy in France, 1914-1918 / John F. Godfrey ; with a foreword by Jay Winter. — Leamington Spa : Berg, 1987. — xiv,313p. — Bibliography: p301-309. — Includes index

WORLD WAR, 1914-1918 — Finance
DOMÁNY, Gyula
A háborus valuta / írta Domány Gyula. — Budapest : Benkö Gyula cs. és kir. udvari könyvkereskedése, 1917. — 141p

WORLD WAR, 1914-1918 — Moral and ethical aspects
FRIEDRICH, Ernst
War against war! / Ernst Friedrich ; introduction by Douglas Kellner. — London : Journeyman Press, 1987. — 263p. — Parallel English, French, German and Dutch text. — Originally published: Frankfurt am Main: Zweitausendeins, 1924

WORLD WAR, 1914-1918 — Peace
SCHWABE, Klaus
[Deutsche Revolution und Wilson-Frieden. English]. Woodrow Wilson, Revolutionary Germany, and peacemaking, 1918-1919 : missionary diplomacy and the realities of power / by Klaus Schwabe ; translated from German by Rita and Robert Kimber. — Chapel Hill : University of North Carolina Press, c1985. — ix, 565p. — "Supplementary volumes to The papers of Woodrow Wilson, Arthur S. Link, editor"--Half t.p. — Translation of: Deutsche Revolution und Wilson-Frieden. — Includes index. — Bibliography: p [533]-547

WALWORTH, Arthur
Wilson and his peacemakers : American diplomacy at the Paris Peace Conference, 1919 / Arthur Walworth. — New York ; London : W.W. Norton, 1986. — xiii, 618p. — Includes index. — Bibliography: p.572-585

WORLD WAR, 1914-1918 — Pictorial works
FRIEDRICH, Ernst
War against war! / Ernst Friedrich ; introduction by Douglas Kellner. — London : Journeyman Press, 1987. — 263p. — *Parallel English, French, German and Dutch text. — Originally published: Frankfurt am Main: Zweitausendeins, 1924*

WORLD WAR, 1914-1918 — Reparations
FRAGA, Arminio
German reparations and Brazilian debt : a comparative study / Arminio Fraga. — Princeton, N.J. : Princeton University. Department of Economics. International Finance Section, 1986. — 34p. — (Essays in international finance ; no.163). — *Bibliography: p28-29*

WORLD WAR, 1914-1918 — Social aspects — Great Britain
WINTER, J. M.
The Great War and the British people / J.M. Winter. — London : Macmillan, 1986, c1985. — xiv,360p. — *Bibliography: p334-349. — Includes index*

WORLD WAR, 1914-1918 — Territorial questions — Near East
BAYLSON, Joshua C.
Territorial allocation by imperial rivalry : the human legacy in the Near East / by Joshua C. Baylson. — Chicago, Ill. : University of Chicago, Dept. of Geography, 1987. — p. cm. — (Research paper / The University of Chicago, Department of Geography ; no. 221). — *Includes index. — Bibliography: p*

WORLD WAR, 1914-1918 — Africa
Africa and the First World War / edited by Melvin E. Page. — London : Macmillan, 1987. — [270]p. — *Includes bibliography and index*

WORLD WAR, 1914-1918 — Argentina and Chile — Patagonia
MORENO, Carlos Alberto
Patagonia punto crítico : la Patagonia Central en los proyectos geopolíticos y en dos guerras mundiales / Carlos Alberto Moreno. — Chubut : Fondo Editorial de Canal 9 de Comodoro Rivadavia, 1985. — 177p. — *Bibliography: p175-176*

WORLD WAR, 1914-1918 — China
JONES, A. Phillip
Britain's search for Chinese cooperation in the First World War / A. Phillip Jones. — New York : Garland, 1986. — p. cm. — (Outstanding theses from the London School of Economics and Political Science). — *Thesis (Ph.D.)--University of London, 1976. — Bibliography: p*

WORLD WAR, 1914-1918 — Europe, Eastern
War and society in East Central Europe. — Boulder, Colo. : Social Science Monographs, 1985. — (East European monographs ; no.196) vol.19: East Central European society in World War 1 / Béla K. Király Nándor F. Dreisziger, and Albert A. Nofi; editors. — xi,623p

WORLD WAR, 1914-1918 — Germany
KUNZ, Andreas
Civil servants and the politics of inflation in Germany, 1914-1924 / Andreas Kunz. — Berlin ; New York : De Gruyter, 1986. — xix, 427 p.. — (Veröffentlichungen der Historischen Kommission zu Berlin ; Bd. 66) (Beiträge zu Inflation und Wiederaufbau in Deutschland und Europa 1914-1924 ; Bd. 7). — *Includes indexes. — Bibliography: p. [393]-413*

WORLD WAR, 1914-1918 — Great Britain
BABINGTON, Anthony
For the sake of example : capital courts martial, 1914-1920 / Anthony Babington ; with a postscript by...Frank Richardson. — London : Paladin Grafton Books, 1985. — x,309p. — *Bibliography: p301-304*

BIRD, J. C
Control of enemy alien civilians in Great Britain, 1914-1918 / J.C. Bird. — New York : Garland Pub., 1986. — 355 p.. — (Outstanding theses from the London School of Economics and Political Science). — *Bibliography: p. 346-355*

FRENCH, David, 1954-
British strategy & war aims, 1914-16 / David French. — London : Allen & Unwin, 1986. — xiv,274p. — *Bibliography: p250-274. — Includes index*

PARKER, Peter, 1954-
The old lie : the Great War and the public school ethos / Peter Parker. — London : Constable, 1987. — 319p,[16]p of plates. — *Bibliography: p297-306. — Includes index*

WILSON, Trevor, 1928-
The myriad faces of war : Britain and the Great War, 1914-1918 / Trevor Wilson. — Cambridge : Polity, 1986. — xvi,864p. — *Includes index*

WORLD WAR, 1914-1918 — Great Britain — Propaganda
REEVES, Nicholas
Official British film propaganda during the First World War / published in association with the Imperial War Museum ; Nicholas Reeves. — London : Croom Helm, c1986. — xiii,288p,[8]p of plates. — *List of films: p261-271. — Bibliography: p271-278. — Includes index*

WORLD WAR, 1914-1918 — Ireland
Ireland and the First World War / [a collection of essays compiled by Trinity History Workshop] edited by David Fitzpatrick. — Dublin : Trinity History Workshop, 1986. — x,108p

WORLD WAR, 1914-1918 — Italy
JONES, Simon Mark
Domestic factors in Italian intervention in the First World War / Simon Mark Jones. — New York : Garland, 1986. — 292 p.. — (Outstanding theses from the London School of Economics and Political Science). — *Thesis (Ph.D.)--London School of Economics and Political Science. — Bibliography: p. 275-292*

WORLD WAR, 1914-1918 — Poland
PŁYGAWKO, Danuta
Sienkiewicz w Szwajcarii : z dziejów akcji ratunkowej dla Polski w czasie pierwszej wojny światowej / Danuta Pływawko. — Poznań : Uniwersytet im. Adama Mickiewicza, 1986. — 171p. — (Seria Historia / Uniwersytet im. Adama Mickiewicza w Poznaniu ; Nr.122). — *Summary in French and English. — Bibliography: p[154]-159*

WORLD WAR, 1914-1918 — Soviet Union
LINCOLN, W. Bruce
Passage through Armageddon : the Russians in war and revolution, 1914-1918 / W. Bruce Lincoln. — New York : Simon and Schuster, c1986. — 637 p., [16] p. of plates. — *Includes index. — Bibliography: p. 581-613*

ZETTERBERG, Seppo
Die Liga der Fremdvölker Russlands 1916-1918 : ein Beitrag zu Deutschlands antirussischem Propagandakrieg unter den Fremdvölkern Russlands im ersten Weltkrieg / Seppo Zetterberg. — Helsinki : [Suomen Historiallinen Seura], 1978. — 279p. — (Studia historica publicata von der Finnischen Historischen Gesellschaft/Suomen Historiallinen Seura/Finska Historiska Samfundet ; vol.8). — *Bibliography: p263-271*

WORLD WAR, 1914-1918 — United States
FERRELL, Robert H
Woodrow Wilson and World War I, 1917-1921 / by Robert H. Ferrell. — 1st ed. — New York ; London : Harper & Row, c1985. — xii, 346p, [26]p of plates. — (New American nationl series). — *Includes index. — Bibliography: p.303-333*

WORLD WAR, 1939-1945
MANDEL, Ernest
The meaning of the Second World War / by Ernest Mandel. — London : Verso, 1986. — [208]p. — *Includes index*

Vtoraia mirovaia voina : itogi i uroki / [redaktsiia: S. A. Tiushkevich...et al.]. — Moskva : Voennoe izd-vo, 1985. — 440p

WORLD WAR, 1939-1945 — Atrocities
KOLB, Eberhard
Bergen-Belsen : vom "Aufenthaltslager" zum Konzentrationslager 1943-1945 / Eberhard Kolb. — Göttingen : Vandenhoek und Ruprecht, 1985. — 105 (12)p

LIFTON, Robert Jay
The Nazi doctors : medical killing and the psychology of genocide / Robert Jay Lifton. — London : Macmillan, 1986. — xiii,561p. — *Includes index*

MORLOK, Karl
Wo bringt ihr uns hin? : "Geheime Reichssache" Grafeneck / Karl Morlok. — Stuttgart : Quell, 1985. — 96p. — *Bibliography: p96*

WORLD WAR, 1939-1945 — Atrocities — Bibliography
TUTOROW, Norman E
War crimes, war criminals, and war crimes trials : an annotated bibliography and source book / compiled and edited by Norman E. Tutorow with the special assistance of Karen Winnovich. — New York : Greenwood Press, 1986. — xx, 548 p.. — (Bibliographies and indexes in world history ; no. 4). — *Includes index*

WORLD WAR, 1939-1945 — Campaigns — Western
SHULMAN, Milton
Defeat in the West / Milton Shulman. — Rev. ed. / with an introduction by Max Hastings. — London : Secker & Warburg, 1986. — [365]p. — *Previous ed.: 1947. — Includes bibliography and index*

WORLD WAR, 1939-1945 — Campaigns — Europe
EISENHOWER, David
Eisenhower : at war 1943-1945 / David Eisenhower. — London : Collins, 1986. — xxvii,977p,[32]p of plates. — *Bibliography: p847-857. — Includes index*

WORLD WAR, 1939-1945 — Campaigns — Near East
GAUNSON, A. B.
The Anglo-French clash in Lebanon and Syria, 1940-45 / A.B. Gaunson. — London : Macmillan, 1986. — xi,233p,[8]p of plates. — *Bibliography: p219-225. — Includes index*

WORLD WAR, 1939-1945 — Casualties (Statistics, etc.)
SORGE, Martin K
The other price of Hitler's war : German military and civilian losses resulting from World War II / Martin K. Sorge. — New York : Greenwood Press, 1986. — xx, 175 p., [15] p. of plates. — (Contributions in military studies ; no. 55). — *Includes index. — Bibliography: p. [153]-164*

WORLD WAR, 1939-1945 — Catholic Church — Germany
RÖSCH, Augustin
Kampf gegen den Nationalsozialismus / Augustin Rösch ; herausgegeben von Roman Bleistein. — Frankfurt am Main : Josef Knecht, 1985. — 492p. — *Bibliography: p481-484*

WORLD WAR, 1939-1945 — Causes
IRIYE, Akira
The origins of the Second World War in Asia and the Pacific / Akira Iriye. — London : Longman, 1987. — 1v.. — (Origins of modern wars). — *Includes bibliography and index*

WORLD WAR, 1939-1945 — Causes
continuation

LEONHARD, Wolfgang
Der Schock des Hitler-Stalin-Paktes : Grinnerungen aus der Sowjetunion, Westeuropa und USA / Wolfgang Leonhard. — Freiburg im Breisgau : Herder, 1986. — 220p.
Bibliographical notes

LIBAL, Michael
Japans Weg in den Krieg : die Aussenpolitik der Kabinette Konoye 1940/1941 : Michael Libal. — Düsseldorf : Droste, [1971]. — 261p

WORLD WAR, 1939—1945 — Causes

TAYLOR, A. J. P.
The origins of the Second World War / by A. J. P. Taylor. — London : Hamish Hamilton, 1961. — 296p

WORLD WAR, 1939-1945 — Collaborationists — Czechoslovakia — Slovak Socialist Republic

KLIMKO, Jozef
Tretia ríša a ľudácky režim na Slovensku / Jozef Klimko. — Bratislava : Obzor, 1986. — 249p. — *Bibliography: p233-[243]*

WORLD WAR, 1939-1945 — Collaborationists — France

BÉDARIDA, François
Résistants et collaborateurs : les français dans les années noires / présenté par François Bédarida. — Paris : Seuil, [1985]. — 129p

LOTTMAN, Herbert R.
The people's anger : justice and revenge in post-liberation France / Herbert R. Lottman. — London : Hutchinson, 1986. — 332p,[8]p of plates. — *Includes index*

WORLD WAR, 1939-1945 — Collaborationists — Ukraine

Ukraine during World War II : history and its aftermath : a symposium / edited by Yury Boshyk with the assistance of Roman Waschuk and Andriy Wynnyckyj. — Edmonton : Canadian Institute of Ukrainian Studies, University of Alberta ; Downsview, Ont., Canada : Distributed by University of Toronto Press, 1986. — xviii, 291 p., [8] p. of plates. — (The Canadian library in Ukrainian studies). — *Includes index. — Bibliography: p. [267]-285*

WORLD WAR, 1939-1945 — Concentration camps — Germany (West)

KOLB, Eberhard
Bergen-Belsen : vom "Aufenthaltslager" zum Konzentrationslager 1943-1945 / Eberhard Kolb. — Göttingen : Vandenhoek und Rupredit, 1985. — 105 (12)p

WORLD WAR, 1939-1945 — Deportations from France

KLARSFELD, Serge
Vichy-Auschwitz : le rôle de Vichy dans la solution finale de la question juive en France / Serge Klarsfeld. — Paris : Fayard [2]: 1943-1944. — 1985. — 408p

WORLD WAR, 1939-1945 — Destruction and pillage — Germany

SORGE, Martin K
The other price of Hitler's war : German military and civilian losses resulting from World War II / Martin K. Sorge. — New York : Greenwood Press, 1986. — xx, 175 p., [15] p. of plates. — (Contributions in military studies ; no. 55). — *Includes index. — Bibliography: p. [153]-164*

WORLD WAR, 1939-1945 — Diplomatic history

AGA ROSSI, Elena
L'Italia nella sconfitta : politica interna e situazione internazionale durante la seconda guerra mondiale / Elena Aga-Rossi ; introduzione di Renzo De Felice. — Napoli : Edizioni scientifiche italiane, c1985. — 485 p.. — (Biblioteca storica ; 4). — *Includes bibliographical references and index*

DANCHEV, Alex
Very special relationship : Field-Marshall Sir John Dill and the Anglo-American alliance 1941-44 / Alex Danchev. — London : Brassey's Defence, 1986. — xv,201p.
Bibliography: p183-197. — Includes index

DAY, David
Menzies & Churchill at war : a controversial new account of the 1941 struggle for power / David Day. — North Ryde : Angus & Robertson, 1986. — xii,271p

EUBANK, Keith
Summit at Teheran / by Keith Eubank. — New York : W. Morrow, 1985. — 528p, 16p of plates. — *Bibliography: p 509-517*

KHARLAMOV, N. M.
Difficult mission : war memoirs / N. Kharlamov. — Moscow : Progress, 1986. — 228p

KITCHEN, Martin
British policy towards the Soviet Union during the Second World War / Martin Kitchen. — Basingstoke : Macmillan, 1986. — viii,309p.
Bibliography: p297-309. — Includes index

LIBAL, Michael
Japans Weg in den Krieg : die Aussenpolitik der Kabinette Konoye 1940/1941 : Michael Libal. — Düsseldorf : Droste, [1971]. — 261p

MAYLE, Paul D.
Eureka summit : agreement in principle and the Big Three at Tehran, 1943 / Paul D. Mayle. — Newark : University of Delaware Press ; London : Associated University Presses, c1987. — 210 p.. — *Includes index. — Bibliography: p. 193-203*

RUIZ HOLST, Matthias
Neutralität oder Kriegsbeteiligung? : die deutsch-spanischen Verhandlungen im Jahre 1940 / Matthias Ruiz Holst. — Pfaffenweiler : Centaurus-Verlagsgesellschaft, 1986. — vi,231p. — *Bibliography: p225-231*

THORNE, Christopher
Allies of a kind : the United States, Britain, and the war against Japan, 1941-1945 / Christopher Thorne. — Oxford : Oxford University Press, 1979. — xxii, 772 p. — *Includes index. — Bibliography: p. [732]-746*

WORLD WAR, 1939-1945 — Economic aspects — Germany

BOELCKE, Willi A.
Die Kosten von Hitlers Krieg : Kriegsfinanzierung und finanzielles Kriegserbe in Deutschland 1933-1948 / Willi A. Boelcke. — Paderborn : Schöningh, 1985. — 220p. — *Includes bibliograhical references*

WORLD WAR, 1939-1945 — Economic aspects — Italy

RASPIN, Angela
The Italian war economy, 1940-1943 : with particular reference to Italian relations with Germany / Angela Raspin. — New York : Garland Pub., 1986. — p. cm. — (Outstanding theses from the London School of Economics and Political Science). — Thesis (Ph. D.)--London University, 1980. — *Bibliography: p*

WORLD WAR, 1939-1945 — Economic aspects — Soviet Union

POLIAK, G. B.
Poslevoennoe vosstanovlenie narodnogo khoziaistva / G. B. Poliak. — Moskva : Finansy i statistika, 1986. — 166p. — (SSSR-bratstvo narodov)

WORLD WAR, 1939-1945 — Finance — Germany

BOELCKE, Willi A.
Die Kosten von Hitlers Krieg : Kriegsfinanzierung und finanzielles Kriegserbe in Deutschland 1933-1948 / Willi A. Boelcke. — Paderborn : Schöningh, 1985. — 220p. — *Includes bibliograhical references*

ERHARD, Ludwig
Kriegsfinanzierung und Schuldenkonsolidierung / Ludwig Erhard ; mit Vorbemerkungen von Ludwig Erhard, Theodor Eschenburg, Günter Schmölders. — Faks.-Dr. d. Denkschr. von 1943-44. — Frankfurt/M ; Berlin ; Wien : Propyläen, 1977. — xxxiv, 268 p. — *On spine: Denkschrift 1943/44. — "Eine Veröffentlichung der Ludwig-Erhard-Stiftung e.V. Bonn. Materialien zur Zeitgeschichte."*

WORLD WAR, 1939-1945 — Forced repatriation

PRVULOVICH, Žika Rad.
Serbia between the swastika and the red star / by Žika Rad. Prvulovich. — Birmingham : Ž. R. Prvulovich, 1986. — vi,240p. — *Bibliography: p233-234*

WORLD WAR, 1939-1945 — Jews

BISS, Andreas
Wir hielten die Vernichtung an : der Kampf gegen die "Endlösung" 1944 / Andreas Biss ; mit einer Nachbemerkung von Hans Dieter Heilmann. — Herbstein : März Verlag, 1985. — 403p

Der Mord an den Juden im Zweiten Weltkrieg : Entschlussbildung und Verwicklichung / herausgegeben von Eberhard Jäckel und Jürgen Rohwer. — Stuttgart : Deutsche Verlags-Anstalt, 1985. — 252p

WORLD WAR, 1939-1945 — Military intelligence — Great Britain

RENIER, Olive
Assigned to listen : the Evesham experience 1939-43 / by Olive Renier, Vladimir Rubinstein. — [S.l.] : B.B.C. External Services, 1986. — 154p

WORLD WAR, 1939-1945 — Participation, Afro-American

MCGUIRE, Phillip
Taps for a Jim Crow army : letters from black soldiers in World War II / Phillip McGuire ; with a foreword by Benjamin Quarles. — Santa Barbara, Calif. : ABC-Clio, c1983. — li, 278 p. . — *Includes index. — Bibliography: p. 263*

WORLD WAR, 1939-1945 — Participation, Female — Bibliography

IMPERIAL WAR MUSEUM. Library
The women's part in the Second World War : a selection of references. — [London] : the Library, [1958]. — 28p. — (Booklist / Imperial War Museum Library ; no.1234)

WORLD WAR, 1939-1945 — Peace

LAMB, Richard
The ghosts of peace, 1935-1945 / Richard Lamb. — Salisbury : Michael Russell, 1987. — 353 p.

WORLD WAR, 1939-1945 — Personal narratives, American

MCGUIRE, Phillip
Taps for a Jim Crow army : letters from black soldiers in World War II / Phillip McGuire ; with a foreword by Benjamin Quarles. — Santa Barbara, Calif. : ABC-Clio, c1983. — li, 278 p. . — *Includes index. — Bibliography: p. 263*

WORLD WAR, 1939-1945 — Personal narratives, Japanese

Women against war / compiled by Women's Division of Soka Gakkai ; translated by Richard L. Gage ; introduction by Richard H. Minnear. — Tokyo ; New York ; San Francisco : Kodansha International Ltd., 1986. — 247p

WORLD WAR, 1939-1945 — Posters

The Soviet political poster, 1917-1980 : from the USSR Lenin Library collection / [text and selection by Nina Baburina ; designed by Mikhail Anikst ; English translation by Boris Rubalsky]. — Harmmondsworth, Middx. : Penguin Books ; New York : Viking Penquin, 1985. — 9,183p. — *Originally published in 3 vols. in English and Russian under the title: Sovetskii politicheskii plakat*

WORLD WAR, 1939-1945 — Prisoners and prisons, British

VLAEMYNCK, Carlos H.
Naar Engeland gedeporteerd : Vlaamse geïnterneerden of het eiland Man 1940-1945 / Carlos H. Vlaemynck. — Antwerpen : De Nederlandsche Boekhandel, 1984. — 80p. — *Bibliography: p75-76*

WORLD WAR, 1939-1945 — Public Opinion

DOWER, John W
War without mercy / John Dower. — New York : Pantheon Books, 1986. — p. cm. — *Includes index. — Bibliography: p*

WORLD WAR, 1939-1945 — Refugees

JACOBMEYER, Wolfgang
Vom Zwangsarbeiter zum heimatlosen Ausländer : die Displaced Persons in Westdeutschland 1945-1951 / Wolfgang Jacobmeyer. — Göttingen : Vandenhoeck & Ruprecht, 1985. — 323p. — (Kritische Studien zur Geschichtswissenschaft ; 65). — *Bibliography: p311-319*

WORLD WAR, 1939-1945 — Regimental histories — Soviet Union

ANDREYEV, Catherine
Vlasov and the Russian Liberation Movement : Soviet reality and émigré theories / Catherine Andreyev. — Cambridge : Cambridge University Press, 1987. — xiv,251p. — (Soviet and East European studies). — *Bibliography: p224-239. — Includes index*

WORLD WAR, 1939-1945 — Reparations — Congresses

Japanese Americans, from relocation to redress / edited by Roger Daniels, Sandra C. Taylor, and Harry H.L. Kitano ; contributions by Leonard J. Arrington ... [et al.]. — Salt Lake City, Utah : University of Utah Press, c1986. — xxi, 216 p.. — *Based on the International Conference on Relocation and Redress held in Salt Lake City in March 1983. — Includes bibliographies*

WORLD WAR, 1939-1945 — Secret Service — Canada

STAFFORD, David
Camp X / David Stafford. — New York : Dodd, Mead, 1987. — p. cm. — *Includes index. — Bibliography: p*

WORLD WAR, 1939-1945 — Social aspects — Great Britain

LEWIS, Peter, 1928-
A people's war / Peter Lewis. — London : Thames Methuen, 1986. — vi,250p. — *Bibliography: p245. — Includes index*

War and social change : British society in the Second World War / edited by Harold L. Smith. — Manchester : Manchester University Press, c1986. — [288]p. — *Includes index*

WORLD WAR, 1939-1945 — Technology

BOWER, Tom, 1946-
The paperclip conspiracy : the battle for the spoils and secrets of Nazi Germany / Tom Bower. — London : Joseph, 1987. — xiv,336p,[12]p of plates. — *Bibliography: p326-327. — Includes index*

WORLD WAR, 1939-1945 — Underground literature

LUND, Erik
A girdle of truth : the underground news service "Information" 1943-1945 / Erik Lund. — [Copenhagen : Ministry of Foreign Affairs, 1970]. — 25p. — *A condensed version of the book "Fire millioner frie ord" by Erik Lund*

WORLD WAR, 1939-1945 — Underground movements — Czechoslovakia — Slovak Socialist Republic

CHŇOUPEK, Bohuš
Les résistants de la dernière chance : combattants français dans les maquis slovaques, 1944-45 / Bohuš Chňoupek. — Paris : Jacques Grancher, 1986. — 189p

WORLD WAR, 1939-1945 — Underground movements — France

BÉDARIDA, François
Résistants et collaborateurs : les français dans les années noires / présenté par François Bédarida. — Paris : Seuil, [1985]. — 129p

GANIER-RAYMOND, Philippe
L'affiche rouge / Philippe Ganier Raymond. — Verviers, Belgium : Marabout, [1985]. — 251p

ROBRIEUX, Phillippe
L'affaire Manouchian : vie et mort d'un héros communiste / Philippe Robrieux. — Paris : Fazard, [1986]. — 434p

ROSSITER, Margaret L
Women in the resistance / Margaret L. Rossiter. — New York, U.S.A. : Praeger, 1985. — p. cm. — *Includes index. — Bibliography: p*

WORLD WAR, 1939-1945 — Underground movements — France — Congresses

Jean Moulin et le Conseil national de la Résistance : études et témoignages / sous la direction de François Bédarida et Jean-Pierre Azéma ; textes de Daniel Cordier ; interventions de C. Andrieu ... [et al.]. — Paris : Institut d'histoire du temps présent, Editions du Centre national de la recherche scientifique, 1983. — 192 p.. — *"Journée d'études sur le Conseil national de la Résistance, Sorbonne, 9 juin 1983"--P. [5]. — Bibliography: p. 133-180*

WORLD WAR, 1939-1945 — Underground movements — Germany

JAHNKE, Karl Heinz
In einer Front : Junge Deutsche an der Seite der Sowjetunion im Grossen Vaterländischen Krieg / Karl Heinz Jahnke. — Berlin : Militärverlag der Deutschen Demokratischen Republik, 1986. — [252]p. — *Bibliography: p238-[239]*

WORLD WAR, 1939-1945 — Underground movements — Germany (West) — Munich

DUMBACH, Annette E
Shattering the German night : the story of the White Rose / by Annette E. Dumbach and Jud Newborn. — 1st ed. — Boston : Little, Brown, c1986. — xi, 259 p.. — *Includes index. — Bibliography: p. 243-247*

WORLD WAR, 1939-1945 — Underground movements — Greece

HONDROS, John Louis
Occupation and resistance : the Greek agony, 1941-44 / John Louis Hondros. — New York, NY : Pella Pub. Co., 1983. — 340 p.. — *Based on the author's thesis, Vanderbilt University. — Bibliography: p. 305-324*

WORLD WAR, 1939-1945 — Underground movements — Hungary

PINTÉR, István
Hungarian anti-fascism and resistance, 1941-1945 / by István Pintér. — Budapest : Akadémiai Kiadó, 1986. — 234p

WORLD WAR, 1939-1945 — Women — Canada

PIERSON, Ruth Roach
They're still women after all : the Second World War and Canadian womanhood / Ruth Roach Pierson. — Toronto, Ont. : McClelland and Stewart, c1986. — 301 p. — (The Canadian social history series). — *Includes index. — Bibliography: p. 221-236*

WORLD WAR, 1939-1945 — Women — France

ROSSITER, Margaret L
Women in the resistance / Margaret L. Rossiter. — New York, U.S.A. : Praeger, 1985. — p. cm. — *Includes index. — Bibliography: p*

WORLD WAR, 1939-1945 — Argentina and Chile — Patagonia

MORENO, Carlos Alberto
Patagonia punto crítico : la Patagonia Central en los proyectos geopolíticos y en dos guerras mundiales / Carlos Alberto Moreno. — Chubut : Fondo Editorial de Canal 9 de Comodoro Rivadavia, 1985. — 177p. — *Bibliography: p175-176*

WORLD WAR, 1939-1945 — Asia

IRIYE, Akira
The origins of the Second World War in Asia and the Pacific / Akira Iriye. — London : Longman, 1987. — 1v.. — (Origins of modern wars). — *Includes bibliography and index*

WORLD WAR, 1939-1945 — Europe, Eastern — Personal narratives

BUTSKO, O. V.
Memuary uchastnikov Velikoi Otechestvennoi voiny : voprosy internatsionalizma / O. V. Butsko. — Kiev : Naukova dumka, 1986. — 118p

WORLD WAR, 1939-1945 — France — Atrocities

Procès da'près-guerre : "Je suis partout", René Hardy, Orodour-sur-Glane, Oberg et Knochen / présenté et étobli par Jean-Marc Théolleyre. — Paris : Éditions la Découverte, 1985. — 221p

WORLD WAR, 1939-1945 — France — Brittany

FRELAUT, Bertrand
Les nationalistes bretons de 1939 à 1945 / Bertrand Frelaut. — [n.p] : Editions Beltan, 1985. — 236p

WORLD WAR, 1939-1945 — France — Franche-Comté — Resistance movements

MARCOT, François
La Franche-Comté sous l'occupation 1940-1944 / Françoise Marcot en collaboration avec Angèle Baud. — Besançon : Cêtre. — *Bibliography: p311-315*
Tome 1: La résistance dans le Jura. — 1985. — 332p

WORLD WAR, 1939-1945 — Germany

Deutschland im zweiten Weltkrieg / von einem Autorenkollektiv unter Leitung von Wolfgang Schumann ; Herausgeberkollegium, Walter Bartel...[et al.] ; Akademie der Wissenschaften der DDR, Zentralinstitut für Geschichte in Zusammenarbeit mit dem Militärgeschichtschen Institut der DDR ; Institut für Marxismus-Leninismus beim ZK der SED. — Köln : Pahl-Rugenstein
5: Der Zusammenbruch der Defensivstrategie des Hitlerfaschismus an allen Fronten (Januar bis August 1944) / Leitung Wolfgang Schumann unter Mitarbeit von Wolfgang Bleyer. — 1984. — 702p

SORGE, Martin K
The other price of Hitler's war : German military and civilian losses resulting from World War II / Martin K. Sorge. — New York : Greenwood Press, 1986. — xx, 175 p., [15] p. of plates. — (Contributions in military studies ; no. 55). — *Includes index. — Bibliography: p. [153]-164*

WORLD WAR, 1939-1945 — Germany — Bibliography

The Third Reich at war : a historical bibliography. — Santa Barbara, Calif. : ABC-Clio Information Services, [1984]. — xii, 270 p.. — (ABC-Clio research guides ; 11). — *Includes indexes*

WORLD WAR, 1939-1945 — Germany — Sources

Die geheimen Tagesberichte der deutschen Wehrmachtführung im zweiten Weltkrieg 1939-1945 / herausgegeben...von Kurt Mehner. — Osnabrück : Biblio. — (Veröffentlichungen deutschen Quellenmaterials zum zweiten Weltkrieg ; no.2)
Band 10: 1. März 1944-31. August 1944. — 1985. — 722p,48p of plates

Die geheimen Tagesberichte der deutschen Wehrmachtführung im zweiten Weltkrieg 1939-1945 / herausgegeben von Kurt Mehner. — Osnabrück : Biblio. — (Veröffentlichungen deutschen Quellenmaterials zum zweiten Weltkrieg)
Band 11: 1. September 1944-31. Dezember 1944. — 1984. — 492p,35p of plates

WORLD WAR, 1939-1945 — Germany — Sources *continuation*

Die geheimen Tagesberichte der deutschen Wehrmachtführung im zweiten Weltkrieg 1939-1945 / herausgegeben...von Kurt Mehner. — Osnabrück : Biblio. — (Veröffentlichungen deutschen Quellenmaterials zum zweiten Weltkrieg)
Band 12: 1. Januar 1945-9. Mai 1945. — 1984. — 611p,35p of plates

WORLD WAR, 1939-1945 — Great Britain

ROBERTSON, John
Turkey and Allied strategy, 1941-1945 / John Robertson. — New York : Garland Pub., 1986. — xvi, 309 p.. — (Outstanding theses from the London School of Economics and Political Science). — : *Originally presented as the author's thesis (Ph.D.--University of London, 1982) under title: Anglo-Turkish relations 1941-1945. — Includes index. — Bibliography: p. 272-295*

THORNE, Christopher
Allies of a kind : the United States, Britain, and the war against Japan, 1941-1945 / Christopher Thorne. — Oxford : Oxford University Press, 1979. — xxii, 772 p. — *Includes index. — Bibliography: p. [732]-746*

WORLD WAR, 1939-1945 — Hungary

The liberation of Hungary 1944-1945 : selected documents / [Introduction by Gyula Kállai, documents selected and explanatory texts written by Béla Estisf translated by Károly Ravasz]. — Budapest : Corvina, 1975. — 185p

VARGYAI, Gyula
Sisak és cilinder : a katonai vezetés és a politika magyarországon a második világháború elöestéjén / Vargyai Gyula. — Budapest : Kozmosz Könyvek, 1984. — 191p. — (Az én világom)

WORLD WAR, 1939-1945 — Indonesia

JONG, L. de
Het Koninkrijk der Nederlanden in de tweede wereldoorlog / L. de Jong
Deel 11c: Nederlands-Indië 3. — Leiden : Nijhoff, 1986. — viii,751p

WORLD WAR, 1939-1945 — Japan

IRIYE, Akira
The origins of the Second World War in Asia and the Pacific / Akira Iriye. — London : Longman, 1987. — 1v.. — (Origins of modern wars). — *Includes bibliography and index*

THORNE, Christopher
Allies of a kind : the United States, Britain, and the war against Japan, 1941-1945 / Christopher Thorne. — Oxford : Oxford University Press, 1979. — xxii, 772 p. — *Includes index. — Bibliography: p. [732]-746*

Women against war / compiled by Women's Division of Soka Gakkai ; translated by Richard L. Gage ; introduction by Richard H. Minnear. — Tokyo ; New York ; San Francisco : Kodansha International Ltd., 1986. — 247p

WORLD WAR, 1939-1945 — London

MACK, Joanna
London at war / Joanna Mack and Steve Humphries. — London : Sidgwick & Jackson, 1985. — 176p. — (The making of modern London ; 1939-1945)

WORLD WAR, 1939-1945 — Pacific Area

DOWER, John W
War without mercy / John Dower. — New York : Pantheon Books, 1986. — p. cm. — *Includes index. — Bibliography: p*

IRIYE, Akira
The origins of the Second World War in Asia and the Pacific / Akira Iriye. — London : Longman, 1987. — 1v.. — (Origins of modern wars). — *Includes bibliography and index*

WORLD WAR, 1939-1945 — Poland

COUTOUVIDIS, John
Poland 1939-1947 / John Coutouvidis & Jaime Reynolds. — [Leicester] : Leicester University Press, 1986. — xxi,393p,[8]p of plates. — (The Politics of liberation series). — *Bibliography: p372-382. — Includes index*

WORLD WAR, 1939-1945 — Poland — Gdańsk — Personal narratives

SCHOLZ, Joachim
Von Danzig nach Danzig - ein weiter Weg / Joachim Scholz. — Limburg an der Lahn : C. A. Starke, 1985. — 236p

WORLD WAR, 1939-1945 — Soviet Union

MOREKHINA, G. G.
Partiinoe stroitel'stvo v period Velikoi Otechestvennoi voiny Sovetskogo Soiuza 1941-1945 / G. G. Morekhina. — Moskva : Politizdat, 1986. — 391p

TOPITSCH, Ernst
Stalin's war : the Soviet long-term strategy against the West considered as rational power politics / Ernst Topitsch ; translated by Arthur Taylor. — London : Fourth Estate, 1987. — [192]p. — *Translation from the German. — Includes index*

WORLD WAR, 1939-1945 — Soviet Union — Atrocities

TOLSTOY, Nikolai
Trial and error : Canada's Commission of Inquiry on War Criminals and the Soviets / Nikolai Tolstoy. — Toronto : Justinian Press, 1986. — 28p

WORLD WAR, 1939-1945 — Soviet Union — Personal narratives

BUTSKO, O. V.
Memuary uchastnikov Velikoi Otechestvennoi voiny : voprosy internatsionalizma / O. V. Butsko. — Kiev : Naukova dumka, 1986. — 118p

WORLD WAR, 1939-1945 — Spain

TUSELL GÓMEZ, Javier
Franco y Mussolini : la política española durante la segunda guerra mundial / Xavier Tusell, Genoveva García Queipo de Llano. — Barcelona : Planeta, 1985. — 299p. — (Espejo de España ; 109). — *Bibliography: p293-296*

WORLD WAR, 1939-1945 — Turkey

ROBERTSON, John
Turkey and Allied strategy, 1941-1945 / John Robertson. — New York : Garland Pub., 1986. — xvi, 309 p.. — (Outstanding theses from the London School of Economics and Political Science). — : *Originally presented as the author's thesis (Ph.D.--University of London, 1982) under title: Anglo-Turkish relations 1941-1945. — Includes index. — Bibliography: p. 272-295*

WORLD WAR, 1939-1945 — Ukraine

PETLIAK, F. A.
Partiinoe rukovodstvo Sovetami na Ukraine v gody Velikoi Otechestvennoi voiny (1941-1945) / F. A. Petliak. — Kiev : Vyshcha shkola, 1986. — 181p

Sovetskaia Ukraina v gody Velikoi Otechestvennoi voiny 1941-1945 : dokumenty i materialy / [glav. red. kollegiia: V. I. Iurchuk...et al.]. — Izd. 2-e, dop.. — Kiev : Naukova dumka. — *In 3 vols.*
1: Ukrainskaia SSR v pervyi period Velikoi Otechestvennoi voiny (22 iiunia 1941 g.-18 noiabria 1942) / [red. kollegiia: D. F. Grigorovich...et al.]. — 1985. — 516p

Sovetskaia Ukraina v gody Velikoi Otechestvennoi voiny 1941-1945 / [glav. red. kollegiia: V. I. Iurchuk...et al.]. — Izd. 2-e, dop.. — Kiev : Naukova dumka. — *In 3 vols.*
2: Ukrainskaia SSR v period korennogo pereloma v khode Velikoi Otechestvennoi voiny (19 noiabria 1942g.-konets 1943g.) / red. kollegiia: V. N. Nemiatyi...et al.]. — 1985. — 509p

Sovetskaia Ukraina v gody Velikoi Otechestvennoi voiny 1941-1945 : dokumenty i materialy / [glav. red. kollegiia: V. I. Iurchuk...et al.]. — Izd. 2-e, dop.. — Kiev : Naukova dumka
3: Ukrainskaia SSR v zavershaiushchii period Velikoi Otechestvennoi voiny (1944-1945 gg.) / [red. kollegiia: P. I. Denisenko...et al.]. — 1985. — 508p

Ukraine during World War II : history and its aftermath : a symposium / edited by Yury Boshyk with the assistance of Roman Waschuk and Andriy Wynnyckyj. — Edmonton : Canadian Institute of Ukrainian Studies, University of Alberta ; Downsview, Ont., Canada : Distributed by University of Toronto Press, 1986. — xviii, 291 p., [8] p. of plates. — (The Canadian library in Ukrainian studies). — *Includes index. — Bibliography: p. [267]-285*

WORLD WAR, 1939-1945 — United States

THORNE, Christopher
Allies of a kind : the United States, Britain, and the war against Japan, 1941-1945 / Christopher Thorne. — Oxford : Oxford University Press, 1979. — xxii, 772 p. — *Includes index. — Bibliography: p. [732]-746*

WORLD WAR, 1939-1945 — Yugoslavia

War and revolution in Yugoslavia, 1941-1945 / prepared by Ivan Jelić ... [et al.] ; editor, Novak Strugar ; translation Margot and Boško Milosavljević. — [Belgrade] : Socialist Thought and Practice, c1985. — 284 p.. — *Translated from the Serbo-Croatian. — Includes bibliographical references*

WORLD WAR, 1939-1945 — Yugoslavia — Bibliography

IMPERIAL WAR MUSEUM. Library
Second World War Yugoslavia : selected list of references. — [London : the Library, 1975]. — 15p. — (Booklist / Imperial War Museum [Library] ; no.1236)

WORLD WAR III

HAYES, Peter
American lake : nuclear peril in the Pacific / Peter Hayes, Lyuba Zarsky, Walden Bello. — Harmondsworth : Penguin, 1987. — xiv, 529p. — *First published by Penguin in Australia in 1986*

SABIN, Philip A. G.
The Third World War scare in Britain : a critical analysis / Philip A.G. Sabin ; foreword by Lawrence Freedman. — Basingstoke : Macmillan, 1986. — xiv,191p. — *Bibliography: p172-185. — Includes index*

W.R. GRACE & CO — History

CLAYTON, Lawrence A
Grace : W.R. Grace & Co., the formative years, 1850-1930 / Lawrence A. Clayton. — Ottawa, Ill. : Jameson Books, c1985. — xiii, 403 p., [35] p. of plates. — *Includes index. — Bibliography: p. 387-394*

WRAN, NEVILLE

The Wran model : electoral politics in New South Wales 1981 and 1984 / edited by Ernie Chaples, Helen Nelson [and] Ken Turner. — Melbourne : Oxford University Press, 1985. — vi,289p

WRIGHT, PETER

HALL, Richard V.
A spy's revenge / Richard V. Hall. — Harmondsworth : Penguin, 1987. — 193p

WRIGLEY, JOSEPH

PHILANDER
A manufacturer's business a hundred years ago : notes on the account books of Joseph Wrigley of Stonebreaks (1711-1781) / compiled by 'Philander' (Samuel Andrew). — Oldham : Saddleworth Historical Society, 1879. — 46p. — *Reprinted from the Oldham Chronicle*

WRITERS' PROGRAM (Minn.)
The Bohemian Flats / compiled by the workers of the Writers' Program of the Work Projects Administration in the State of Minnesota ; with an introduction by Thaddeus Radzilowsky. — St. Paul : Minnesota Historical Society Press, 1986. — p. cm. — (Borealis books). — : Reprint. Originally published: Minneapolis : University of Minnesota Press, 1941. With new introd. and index. — Bibliography: p[189]-203

WRITING — History
GAUR, Albertine
A history of writing / Albertine Gaur. — London : British Library, c1984. — 224p. — Bibliography: p210-213. — Includes index

SAMPSON, Geoffrey
Writing systems : a linguistic introduction / Geoffrey Sampson. — Stanford, Calif. : Stanford University Press, 1985. — 234p. — Bibliography: p218-225

WRITING — Social aspects
GOODY, Jack
The logic of writing and the organization of society / Jack Goody. — Cambridge : Cambridge University Press, 1986. — xvii,213p. — (Studies in literacy, family, culture and the state). — Bibliography: p194-205. — Includes index

WYSZYŃSKI, STEFAN, Cardinal
KĄKOL, Kazimierz
Kardynał Stefan Wyszyński jakim go znałem / Kazimierz Kąkol. — Warszawa : Instytut Wydawniczy Związków Zawodowych, 1985. — 145,[30]p

X, MALCOLM, 1925-1965
The black book : the true political philosophy of Malcolm X (El Hajj Malik el Shabazz / edited and compiled by Y. N. Kly. — Ottawa ; Atlanta : Clarity Press, 1986. — viii,91p. — Bibliography: p89-91

XENOPHOBIA
The Sociobiology of ethnocentrism : evolutionary dimensions of xenophobia, discrimination, racism and nationalism / edited by Vernon Reynolds, Vincent Falger and Ian Vine. — London : Croom Helm, c1987. — xx,327p. — Bibliography: p274-314. — Includes index

XHOSA (AFRICAN PEOPLE)
BLONDEL, Alain
The parrot's egg / Alain Blondel and Shena Lamb ; photographs by Ali Hashemian. — Johannesburg : Ravan Press, 1985. — 159p. — Bibliography: p158-159

SHOOTER, Joseph
The Kafirs of Natal and the Zulu country. — New York : Negro Universities Press, [1969]. — x, 403 p. — Reprint of the 1857 ed

YAGÜE, JUAN
GARRIGA, Ramón
El general Juan Yagüe : figura clave para conocer nuestra historia / Ramón Garriga. — Barcelona : Planeta, 1985. — 282p

YAKUZA
KAPLAN, David E.
Yakuza : the explosive account of Japan's criminal underworld / David E. Kaplan and Alec Dubro. — London : Macdonald, 1987. — ix,336p,[20]p of plates. — (A Queen Anne Press book). — Originally published: Reading, Mass. : Addison-Wesley, 1986. — Bibliography: p315-321. — Includes index

YALE UNIVERSITY — Students — History
OREN, Dan A.
Joining the club : a history of Jews and Yale / Dan A. Oren. — New Haven : Yale University Press, c1985. — xiv, 440 p.. — (The Yale scene. University series ; 4). — Published in cooperation with the American Jewish Archives. — Includes index. — Bibliography: p. 397-423

YALTA CONFERENCE (1945)
KARSKI, Jan
The Great Powers & Poland, 1919-1945 : from Versailles to Yalta / Jan Karski. — Lanham, MD : University Press of America, c1985. — xvi, 697 p. — Includes index. — Bibliography: p. 627-671

YAQUI INDIANS — Ethnic identity
MCGUIRE, Thomas R
Politics and ethnicity on the Río Yaqui : Potam revisited / Thomas R. McGuire. — Tucson : University of Arizona Press, c1986. — xiv, 186p. — (Profmex monograph series ; 1). — Includes index. — Bibliography: p.165-178

YAQUI INDIANS — Government relations
MCGUIRE, Thomas R
Politics and ethnicity on the Río Yaqui : Potam revisited / Thomas R. McGuire. — Tucson : University of Arizona Press, c1986. — xiv, 186p. — (Profmex monograph series ; 1). — Includes index. — Bibliography: p.165-178

YAQUI INDIANS — Water rights
MCGUIRE, Thomas R
Politics and ethnicity on the Río Yaqui : Potam revisited / Thomas R. McGuire. — Tucson : University of Arizona Press, c1986. — xiv, 186p. — (Profmex monograph series ; 1). — Includes index. — Bibliography: p.165-178

YARUR MANUFACTURAS CHILENAS DE ALGODÓN
WINN, Peter
Weavers of revolution : the Yarur workers and Chile's road to socialism / Peter Winn. — New York : Oxford University Press, 1986. — xiv, 328 p.. — Includes index. — Bibliography: p. 300-315

YELLOW FEVER — Control — Africa
Prevention and control of yellow fever in Africa. — Geneva : World Health Organization, 1986. — v,94p. — Bibliographical references: p74-78

YELLOW FEVER — Africa — Prevention
Prevention and control of yellow fever in Africa. — Geneva : World Health Organization, 1986. — v,94p. — Bibliographical references: p74-78

YEMEN — Economic conditions
EL MALLAKH, Ragaei
The economic development of the Yemen Arab Republic / Ragaei El Mallakh. — London : Croom Helm, c1986. — [224]p

YEMEN — Ethnic relations
AHRONI, Reuben
Yemenite Jewry : origins, culture and literature / Reuben Ahroni. — Bloomington : Indiana University Press, 1986. — x,227. — (Jewish literature and culture). — Bibliography: p [204]-220

YEMEN — Foreign relations — Soviet Union
PAGE, Stephen
The Soviet Union and the Yemens : influence on asymmetrical relationships / Stephen Page. — New York : Praeger, 1985. — p. cm. — (Studies of influence in international relations). — Includes index. — Bibliography: p

YEMEN — History — 1962-
BADEEB, Saeed M
The Saudi-Egyptian conflict over North Yemen, 1962-1970 / Saeed M. Badeeb ; foreword by J.E. Peterson. — Boulder, Colo. : Westview Press ; Washington, D.C. : American-Arab Affairs Council, 1986. — xv, 148 p., [1] p. of plates. — Includes index. — Bibliography: p. 137-142

YEMEN — Population — Statistics — Evaluation
AL—TOHAMY, Abdel—Malik
Evaluation of the Yemen Arab Republic Fertility Survey 1979 / Abdel—Malik Al—Tohamy, Ishmael Kalule—Sabiti. — Voorburg : International Statistical Institute, 1985. — 47p. — (Scientific reports / World Fertility Survey ; no.76)

YEMEN (PEOPLE'S DEMOCRATIC REPUBLIC) — Foreign relations — Soviet Union
PAGE, Stephen
The Soviet Union and the Yemens : influence on asymmetrical relationships / Stephen Page. — New York : Praeger, 1985. — p. cm. — (Studies of influence in international relations). — Includes index. — Bibliography: p

YESTE (SPAIN) — Population
MARTÍNEZ CARRIÓN, José-Miguel
La población de Yeste en los inicios de la transición demográfica, 1850-1935 / José-Miguel Martínez Carrión. — Albacete : Instituto de Estudios Albacetenses : Confederación Española de Centros Locales, 1983. — 441p. — (Serie 1 : Ensayos históricos y científicos / Instituto de Estudios Albacetenses ; núm.18). — Bibliography: p [421]-441

YEZIDIS — History
GUEST, John S.
The Yezidis : a study in survival / John S. Guest. — London : KP1, 1987. — xviii,299p. — Bibliography: p251-282

YORK RETREAT
DIGBY, Anne
Madness, morality and medicine : a study of the York Retreat, 1796-1914 / Anne Digby. — Cambridge : Cambridge University Press, 1985. — xvi,323p. — (Cambridge history of medicine)

YOUNG ADULTS — Great Britain
SAUNDERS, Barbara
Homeless young people in Britain : the contribution of the voluntary sector / written for ERICA and DSU by Barbara Saunders ; with cartoons by Peter Kneebone. — London : published in association with ERICA and DSU by Bedford Square Press NCVO, 1986. — iv,108p. — Bibliography: p108

YOUNG ADULTS — Great Britain — Political activity
BLUMLER, Jay G.
Political communication and the young voter : a panel study, 1970-1971, examining the role of election communication in the political socialisation of first time voters / Jay G. Blumler, Denis McQuail and T. J. Nossiter ; report to the Social Science Research Council, October 1975. — [London : Social Science Research Council, 1975]. — 1v. (various pagings). — Bibliographical references: end of vol.

BLUMLER, Jay G.
Political communication and the young voter in the general election of February 1974 : a panal study, 1970-1974, examining influences on the political socialisation of young voters between their first and second election campaigns / Jay G. Blumler, Denis McQuail and T. J. Nossiter ; report to the Social Science Research Council, July 1976. — [London : Social Science Research Council, 1976]. — 99 leaves. — Bibliographical references: p98-99

YOUNG ADULTS — United States — Psychology
LITTWIN, Susan
The postponed generation : why America's kids are growing up later / Susan Littwin. — New York : Morrow, c1986. — p. cm

YOUNG ENGLAND (Political movement)
FABER, Richard
Young England / Richard Faber. — London : Faber, 1987. — [260]p. — Includes index

YOUNG WOMEN — Employment — Germany (West) — Case studies

GÄRTNER, Hans J.
Efforts to equalize opportunities for young women : case studies on the impact of new technologies on the vocational training for technicians / Hans J. Gärtner, Rainald von Gizycki ; Korreferent: Camilla Krebsbach—Gnath. — Luxembourg : Office for Official Publications of the European Communities, 1984. — xiii, 105p. — At head of title page: Commission of the European Communities

YOUNG WOMEN — Employment — Great Britain — Case studies

GÄRTNER, Hans J.
Efforts to equalize opportunities for young women : case studies on the impact of new technologies on the vocational training for technicians / Hans J. Gärtner, Rainald von Gizycki ; Korreferent: Camilla Krebsbach—Gnath. — Luxembourg : Office for Official Publications of the European Communities, 1984. — xiii, 105p. — At head of title page: Commission of the European Communities

YOUNG WOMEN — Training of — England

BREAKWELL, Glynis M.
Young women in 'gender-atypical' jobs : the case of trainee technicians in the engineering industry / Glynis M. Breakwell, Barbara Weinberger. — [London] : Department of Employment, [1987]. — 39p. — (Research paper / Department of Employment ; no.49). — Bibliographical references: p22

YOUNG WOMEN'S CHRISTIAN ASSOCIATIONS — New Zealand

CONEY, Sandra
Every girl : a social history of women and the YWCA in Auckland, 1885-1985 / Sandra Coney. — Auckland, N.Z. : Auckland YWCA, 1986. — 292p

YOUTH

GROSS, Fanny A.
Youth in crisis / Fanny A. Gross. — Cape Town : Juta, 1985. — xv,134p

YOUTH — Bibliography

Tuttogiovani notizie / Observatorio della Gioventù. — Rome : Observatorio della Gioventù, 1986-. — Quarterly

YOUTH — c Training of — Great Britain

FINN, Dan
Training without jobs : new deals and broken promises : from raising the school leaving age to the Youth Training Scheme / Dan Finn. — London : Macmillan, 1987. — xxi,242p. — (Youth questions). — Bibliography: p217-231. — Includes index

YOUTH — Care and hygiene — Denmark

The Children and Young Persons Act, 1964. — [Copenhagen : Ministry of Social Affairs?], 1964. — 33 leaves

YOUTH — Conduct of life

The revolution of everyday life : a new translation...of Traité de savoir-vivre à l'usage des jeunes générations / Raoul Vaneigem ; [translated by] Donald Nicholson-Smith. — [London?] : Left Bank Books : Rebel Press, 1983. — 216p

YOUTH — Crimes against — Psychological aspects

Psychological maltreatment of children and youth / [compiled by] Marla R. Brassard, Robert Germain, Stuart N. Hart. — New York ; Oxford : Pergamon, 1987. — xii, 296p. — (Pergamon general psychology series ; 143). — Includes index

YOUTH — Economic aspects — Québec (Province)

PERREAULT, Géraldine
La situation des jeunes à l'aide sociale. — Québec : [Ministère de la main-d'oeuvre et de la sécurité du revenu], 1984. — iv,103p. — (Études monographiques en sécurité du revenu ; no.1)

YOUTH — Education — England

CLOUGH, Elizabeth
Futures in black and white / by Elizabeth Clough and David Drew with Tony Wojciechowski. — Sheffield : PAVIC Publications, 1985. — 53p. — Bibliography: p52-53

YOUTH — Education — United States

HOSEK, James R
Educational expectations and enlistment decisions / James R. Hosek, Christine E. Peterson, Rick A. Eden. — Santa Monica, CA. : Rand, [1986]. — xiii, 41 p. — "Prepared for the Office of the Assistant Secretary of Defense/Force Management and Personnel.". — "March 1986.". — R-3350-FMP.". — Bibliography: p. 41

YOUTH — Employment

Child labour : a briefing manual. — Geneva : International Labour Office, 1986. — [83]. — Includes bibliographical references

Youth, unemployment and training : a collection of national perspectives / edited by Rob Fiddy. — London : Falmer, 1985. — 247 p. — (Politics and education series)

YOUTH — Employment — Australia — Longitudinal studies

The first wave of the Australian longitudinal survey : facts and figures about young CES registrants / Jan Muir...[et al.]. — Canberra : Australian Government Publishing Service, 1986. — xxi,220p. — (Monograph series / Bureau of Labour Market Research ; no.12). — Bibliographical references: p219-220

YOUTH — Employment — Denmark — Copenhagen — Statistics

Unges uddannelses- og beskaeftigelsesforhold i København, 1981. — [København : Københavns Statistiske Kontor, 1984. — 26p. — (Undersøgelser fra Københavns Statistiske Kontor ; nr.22). — Includes English summary

YOUTH — Employment — Developing countries — Bibliography

CORVALÁN-VÁSQUEZ, Oscar E.
Youth employment and training in developing countries : an annotated bibliography / Oscar Corvalán-Vásquez. — Geneva : International Labour Office, 1984. — vii,172p. — Includes indexes

YOUTH — Employment — England

ASHTON, David N.
Young adults in the labour market / by D. N. Ashton and M. J. Maguire ; with the assistance of D. Bowden... [et al.]. — [London] : Department of Employment, [1986]. — xiii, 163p. — (Research paper / Department of Employment ; no.55)

BANKS, Michael H.
Youth unemployment : social and psychological perspectives / Michael H. Banks, Philip Ullah. — [London] : Department of Employment, [1987]. — 91p. — (Research paper / Department of Employment ; no.61). — Bibliographical references: p86-88

CLOUGH, Elizabeth
Futures in black and white / by Elizabeth Clough and David Drew with Tony Wojciechowski. — Sheffield : PAVIC Publications, 1985. — 53p. — Bibliography: p52-53

YOUTH — Employment — England — Bolton (Greater Manchester)

THURNHAM, Peter
Operation long-stop : a time limit to unemployment : a redirection of the Community Programme based on the Bolton Pilot Scheme / Peter Thurnham. — London : Conservative Political Centre, 1987. — 55p. — Bibliography: p52-53

YOUTH — Employment — European Economic Community countries

MARSDEN, David, 19——
Wage differential between young and adults and its relation with youth unemployment / by David Marsden. — Luxembourg : Office for Official Publications of the European Communities, 1985. — 96p. — (Programme of research and actions on the development of the labour market). — At head of title: Commission of the European Communities

YOUTH — Employment — Germany — History

BRÜLLS, Klaus
Neubeginn oder Wiederaufbau? : Gewerkschaftsjugend in der britischen Zone 1945-1950 / Klaus Brülls. — Marburg : Verlag Arbeiterbewegung und Gesellschaftswissenschaft, 1985. — 384p. — (Schriftenreihe der Studiengesellschaft für Sozialgeschichte und Arbeiterbewegung ; Bd.52). — Bibliography: p349-384

YOUTH — Employment — Germany (West)

CASEY, Bernard
Worksharing and young persons : recent experiences in Great Britain, the Federal Republic of Germany and The Netherlands : main report / by Bernard Casey. — Luxembourg : Office for Official Publications of the European Communities, 1984. — 62p. — At head of title page: Commission of the European Communities

YOUTH — Employment — Germany (West) — Statistics

Massnahmen der Jugendarbeit im Rahmen der Jugendhilfe. — Wiesbaden : Statistisches Bundesamt, 1982-. — Annual

YOUTH — Employment — Great Britain

CASEY, Bernard
Worksharing and young persons : recent experiences in Great Britain, the Federal Republic of Germany and The Netherlands : main report / by Bernard Casey. — Luxembourg : Office for Official Publications of the European Communities, 1984. — 62p. — At head of title page: Commission of the European Communities

CHAPMAN, Paul G.
The Youth Training Scheme in the United Kingdom / Paul G. Chapman and Michael J. Tooze. — Aldershot : Avebury, c1987. — x,124p. — Includes index

EICHENGREEN, Barry
Juvenile unemployment in interwar Britain : the emergence of a problem / Barry Eichengreen. — London : Centre for Economic Policy Research, 1987. — 27p. — (Discussion paper series / Centre for Economic Policy Research ; no.194)

Getting into life / edited by Halla Beloff ; afterword by David Hargreaves ; contributions from Michael Billig ... [et al.]. — London : Methuen, 1986. — xii,157p. — Includes bibliographies and index

GREAT BRITAIN. Parliament. House of Commons. Library. Research Division
Education, training and income support for young people / Kay Andrews, Richard Cracknell, Christine Gillie. — [London] : the Division, 1985. — 52p. — (Background paper ; no.167). — Bibliographical references: p50-52

HORTON, Claire
Nothing like a job / Claire Horton. — London : Lasso Co-operative, 1985. — 70p. — Bibliography: p70

YOUTH — Employment — Great Britain
continuation

KEEP, Ewart
Designing the stable door : a study of how the Youth Training Scheme was planned / Ewart Keep. — Coventry : University of Warwick. School of Industrial and Business Studies, 1986. — 31p. — (Warwick papers in industrial relations ; no.8). — *Bibliography: p[1-4]*

MARSDEN, David, 19—
Wage differential between young and adults and its relation with youth unemployment / by David Marsden. — Luxembourg : Office for Official Publications of the European Communities, 1985. — 96p. — (Programme of research and actions on the development of the labour market). — *At head of title: Commission of the European Communities*

METCALF, David
Alternatives to unemployment : special employment measures in Britain / David Metcalf. — London : Policy Studies Institute, 1982. — 66p. — (Policy Studies Institute ; no. 610)

NG, Stephanie
The Youth Opportunities Programme in three local economies / Stephanie Ng. — London : London School of Economics. Graduate School of Geography, 1985. — 17p. — (Geography discussion papers / London School of Economics and Political Science. Graduate School of Geography. New series ; no.20). — *Bibliography: p18-20*

ROBERTS, Kenneth, 1940-
The changing structure of youth labour markets / K. Roberts, Sally Dench, Deborah Richardson. — [London] : Department of Employment, [1987]. — 181p. — (Research paper ; no.59). — *Bibliography: p172-175*

WILLMORE, Ian
The Youth Training Scheme : a basic guide / Ian Willmore [and] Paul Lewis. — [S.l] : [s.n.], 1985. — 33p

YOUTH — Employment — Netherlands

CASEY, Bernard
Worksharing and young persons : recent experiences in Great Britain, the Federal Republic of Germany and The Netherlands : main report / by Bernard Casey. — Luxembourg : Office for Official Publications of the European Communities, 1984. — 62p. — *At head of title page: Commission of the European Communities*

YOUTH — Employment — O.E.C.D. countries

ORGANISATION FOR ECONOMIC CO-OPERATION AND DEVELOPMENT
Entry of young people into working life : general report / [Organisation for Economic Co-operation and Development]. — Paris : O.E.C.D. ; [London] : [H.M.S.O.], 1977. — 106p. — *Bibliography: p.103-106*

YOUTH — Employment — Sweden — Addresses, essays, lectures

HARTMANN, Jürgen
Youth in the welfare society : a reader on theoretical concepts and empirical studies in youth research / Jürgen Hartmann. — Uppsala, Sweden : Distribution, Dept. of Sociology, Uppsala University, [1984]. — 103 p.. — *Includes bibliographies*

YOUTH — Employment — United States

LATIMORE, James
Weeding out the target population : the law of accountability in a manpower program / James Latimore. — Westport, Conn. : Greenwood Press, 1985. — x, 176 p.. — (Contributions in sociology ; no. 54). — *Includes index. — Bibliography: p. [173]-174*

YOUTH — Employment — United States — Addresses, essays, lectures

Becoming a worker / edited by Kathryn M. Borman. — Norwood, N.J. : Ablex Pub. Co., 1986. — p. cm. — *Based on a symposium held in October 1983 at the Ohio State University. — Includes index. — Bibliography: p*

YOUTH — Government policy — Great Britain

DAVIES, Bernard
Threatening youth : towards a national youth policy / Bernard Davies. — Milton Keynes : Open University Press, 1986. — viii,167p. — *Bibliography: p148-162. — Includes index*

YOUTH — Great Britain

Getting into life / edited by Halla Beloff ; afterword by David Hargreaves ; contributions from Michael Billig ... [et al.]. — London : Methuen, 1986. — xii,157p. — *Includes bibliographies and index*

YOUTH — Housing — England — Gloucester (Gloucestershire)

COWEN, Harry
The hidden homeless : a report of a survey on homelessness and housing amongst single young Blacks in Gloucester / Harry Cowen with Richard Lording. — Gloucester (15 Brunswick Rd, Gloucester GL1 1HG) : Gloucester Community Relations Council, 1982. — 54p

YOUTH — Legal status, laws, etc. — Great Britain

CRONIN, Kathryn
Children, nationality and immigration : a handbook on nationality, immigration and international family law affecting children and young people / written by Kathryn Cronin for the Children's Legal Centre. — London : Children's Legal Centre, 1985. — 146p. — *Bibliography: p127-132*

YOUTH — Political activity

MANN, John
Labour and youth : the missing generation / John Mann [and] Phil Woolas. — London : Fabian Society, 1986. — 19 p. — (Fabian tract ; 515)

YOUTH — Political activity — Cross-cultural studies

GALLATIN, Judith E.
Democracy's children : the development of political thinking in adolescents / Judith Gallatin. — Ann Arbor, Mich. : Quod Pub. Co., c1985. — xx, 391 p.. — *Includes indexes. — Bibliography: p. 355-370*

YOUTH — Services for — Great Britain

DAVIES, Bernard
Threatening youth : towards a national youth policy / Bernard Davies. — Milton Keynes : Open University Press, 1986. — viii,167p. — *Bibliography: p148-162. — Includes index*

YOUTH — Substance use

WATSON, Joyce
Solvent abuse : the adolescent epidemic? / Joyce M. Watson. — London : Croom Helm, c1986. — 234p. — *Includes index*

YOUTH — Suicidal behavior

HAWTON, Keith
Suicide and attempted suicide among children and adolescents / by Keith Hawton. — Beverly Hills ; London : Sage, c1986. — 159 p.. — (Developmental clinical psychology and psychiatry series ; v. 5). — *Includes index. — Bibliography: p. 145-153*

YOUTH — Suicidal behavior — Addresses, essays, lectures

Suicide in adolescence : suicidal behaviour among adolescents / edited by René F.W. Diekstra and Keith Hawton. — Dordrecht ; Boston : Nijhoff, 1986. — p. cm. — *Includes indexes*

YOUTH — Training of — Great Britain

GREAT BRITAIN. Parliament. House of Commons. Library. Research Division
Education, training and income support for young people / Kay Andrews, Richard Cracknell, Christine Gillie. — [London] : the Division, 1985. — 52p. — (Background paper ; no.167). — *Bibliographical references: p50-52*

YOUTH — Australia

EWEN, John
Youth in Australia : a new deal and a new role / by John Ewen. — Bundoora, Vic. : PIT Press, 1983. — 138p. — *Cover title: Youth in Australia: a new role and a new deal for the 80s. — Bibliography: p133-138*

YOUTH — England — London — Social conditions

DIG. — London : [S.n.], 1987-. — *Monthly*

YOUTH — England, Northern — Drug use

PEARSON, Geoffrey
Young people and heroin : an examination of heroin use in the North of England : a report to the Health Education Council / by Geoffrey Pearson, Mark Gilman, Shirley McIver. — Aldershot : Gower, c1987. — [72]p. — *Includes bibliography*

YOUTH — Finland — Statistics

FINLAND. Tilastokeskus
Kulttuuritilasto : Tilastotietoja taiteesta, tiedonvälityksestä, vapaa-ajasta, urheilusta ja nuorisotoiminnasta vuosilta 1930-1977 = Cultural statistics : Statistical information on arts, communication, leisure, sports and youth activities in 1930-1977. — Helsinki : Tilastokeskus, 1978. — 256p. — (Tilastollisia tiedonantoja = Statistical surveys ; no.60). — *In Finnish, Swedish and English*

FINLAND. Tilastokeskus
Kulttuuritilasto 1981 : Tilastotietoja taiteesta, tiedonvälityksestä, vapaa-ajasta, urheilusta ja nuorisotojminnasta = Cultural statistics 1981 : Statistical information on arts, communication, leisure, sports and youth activities. — Helsinki : Tilastokeskus, 1984. — 683p. — (Tilastollisia tiedonantoja = Statistical surveys ; no.73). — *In Finnish, Swedish and English*

Nuorten elinolot. — Helsinki : Tilastokeskus, 1984. — 128p. — (Tutkimuksia / Finland. Tilastokeskus ; no.108).

YOUTH — France

MAJASTRE, Jean-Olivier
La culture en Archipel : pratiques culturelles et mode de vie chez des jeunes en situation d'apprentissage précaire / par Jean-Olivier Majastre. — [Paris] : Documentation Française, [1986]. — 212p

YOUTH — France — Attitudes

LAGRÉE, Jean-Charles
La galère : marginalisations juvéniles et collectivités locales / par Jean-Charles Lagrée et Paula Lew-Foi. — Paris : Centre National de la Recherche Scientifique, 1985. — 280p

YOUTH — France — Emigration and immigration

JAZOULI, Adil
Dynamiques collectives et initiatives d'intégration sociale chez les jeunes d'origine immigrée / Adil Jazouli. — [Paris] : Agence de développement des relations interculturelles, 1984. — 76 leaves. — *Includes bibliographical references*

YOUTH — France — Sociological aspects

LAGRÉE, Jean-Charles
La galère : marginalisations juvéniles et collectivités locales / par Jean-Charles Lagrée et Paula Lew-Foi. — Paris : Centre National de la Recherche Scientifique, 1985. — 280p

YOUTH — Germany — History

BOESCH, Hermann
Jugend in der Weimarer Republik : erlebte Zeitgeschichte / Hermann Boesch. — Isenbüttel : Aurora Verlag, 1986. — 495p

YOUTH — Germany — Political activity

FRÖHER, Lothar
Der weite Weg : die deutsche Jugendbewegung seit Ende des 19. Jahrhunderts / Lothar Fröher. — Heidenheim : Südmarkverlag Fritsch, 1984. — vii,158p. — *Bibliography: p156-158*

YOUTH — Germany — Political activity
continuation

JAHNKE, Karl Heinz
In einer Front : Junge Deutsche an der Seite der Sowjetunion im Grossen Vaterländischen Krieg / Karl Heinz Jahnke. — Berlin : Militärverlag der Deutschen Demokratischen Republik, 1986. — [252]p. — *Bibliography: p238-[239]*

YOUTH — Germany — Political activity — History

BOESCH, Hermann
Jugend in der Weimarer Republik : erlebte Zeitgeschichte / Hermann Boesch. — Isenbüttel : Aurora Verlag, 1986. — 495p

YOUTH — Germany (West) — Political activity

DUDEK, Peter
Jugendliche Rechtsextremisten : zwischen Hakenkreuz und Odalsrune 1945 bis heute / Peter Dudek. — Köln : Bund-Verlag, 1985. — 243p. — *Bibliography: p237-240*

FRÖHER, Lothar
Der weite Weg : die deutsche Jugendbewegung seit Ende des 19. Jahrhunderts / Lothar Fröher. — Heidenheim : Südmarkverlag Fritsch, 1984. — vii,158p. — *Bibliography: p156-158*

HARTMANN, Ulrich
Rechtsextremismus bei Jugendlichen : Anregungen, der wachsenden Gefahr entgegenzuwirken / Ulrich Hartmann, Hans-Peter und Sigrid Steffen. — München : Kösel-Verlag, c1985. — 160p. — *Bibliography: p154-[160]*

YOUTH — Great Britain

Options for youth / John Fethney (ed.) ; with a foreword by Philip Morgan. — [Chichester] : Angel, [c1985]. — 144p. — *Cover title*

YOUTH — Great Britain — Alcohol use

MARSH, Alan
Adolescent drinking : a survey carried out on behalf of the Department of Health and Social Security and the Scottish Home and Health Department / Alan Marsh, Joy Dobbs, Amanda White ; [for the] Office of Population Censuses and Surveys, Social Survey Division. — London : H.M.S.O., 1986. — xii,65p. — *Bibliographical references: p65. — Social Survey no.: SS1209*

YOUTH — Great Britain — Attitudes

HEWITT, Roger
White talk black talk : inter-racial friendship and communication amongst adolescents / Roger Hewitt. — Cambridge : Cambridge University Press, 1986. — [264]p. — (Comparative ethnic and race relations). — *Includes bibliography and index*

JONES, Ray, 1949-
Like distant relatives : adolescents' perceptions of social work and social workers / Ray Jones. — Aldershot : Gower, c1987. — [200]p. — *Includes bibliography and index*

YOUTH — Great Britain — Drug use

MANNING, Mary, 1925-
The drugs menace / Mary Manning ; foreword by Michael Meacher. — London : Columbus, c1985. — x,190p. — *Bibliography: p166. — Includes index*

YOUTH — Great Britain — History

SPRINGHALL, John
Coming of age : adolescence in Britain, 1860-1960 / John Springhall. — Dublin : Gill and Macmillan, c1986. — 270p. — *Bibliography: p250-264. — Includes index*

YOUTH — Great Britain — Psychology

Getting into life / edited by Halla Beloff ; afterword by David Hargreaves ; contributions from Michael Billig ... [et al.]. — London : Methuen, 1986. — xii,157p. — *Includes bibliographies and index*

YOUTH — Great Britain — social conditions

Education and youth / edited and introduced by David Marsland. — London ; Philadelphia : Falmer Press, 1987. — (Contemporary analysis in education series ; 14)

YOUTH — Great Britain — Societies and clubs

RITCHIE, Neil
An inspector calls : a critical review of Her Majesty's Inspectorate reports on youth provision / Neil Ritchie. — Leicester : National Youth Bureau, 1986. — [10p]. — (Occasional paper / National Youth Bureau ; 1)

YOUTH — Hungary — Attitudes

A magyar ifjúság a nyolcvanas években / Ancsel Éva...[et al.]. — Budapest : MSZMP KB Társadalomtudományi Intézete : Kossuth Könyvkiadó, 1984. — 263p

YOUTH — Hungary — Social aspects

A magyar ifjúság a nyolcvanas években / Ancsel Éva...[et al.]. — Budapest : MSZMP KB Társadalomtudományi Intézete : Kossuth Könyvkiadó, 1984. — 263p

YOUTH — Nigeria — Political activity — History

SCHÄRER, Therese
Das Nigerian Youth Movement : eine Untersuchung zur Politisierung der afrikanischen Bildungsschicht vor dem Zweiten Weltkrieg / Therese Schärer. — Bern : Lang, 1986. — xiii,376,76p. — (Europäische Hochschulschriften. Reihe 31, Politikwissenschaft ; Bd.89). — *Bibliography: pA/67-A/76*

YOUTH — South Africa

GROSS, Fanny A.
Youth in crisis / Fanny A. Gross. — Cape Town : Juta, 1985. — xv,134p

YOUTH — South Africa — Political activity

HARRIES, Ann
The child is not dead : youth resistance in South Africa 1976-86 / compiled by Ann Harries, Roger Diski [and] Alasdair Brown. — London : British Defence and Aid Fund for Southern Africa : Inner London Education Authority, 1986. — 64p. — *Bibliography: p62*

YOUTH — Soviet Union — Political activity

PETROVA, N. K.
Obshchestvenno-politicheskii oblik sovetskoi rabochei molodezhi [70-e gody] / N. K. Petrova ; otv. redaktor V. E. Poletaev. — Moskva : Nauka, 1986. — 157p

YOUTH — Sweden — Addresses, essays, lectures

HARTMANN, Jürgen
Youth in the welfare society : a reader on theoretical concepts and empirical studies in youth research / Jürgen Hartmann. — Uppsala, Sweden : Distribution, Dept. of Sociology, Uppsala University, [1984]. — 103 p.. — *Includes bibliographies*

YOUTH — United States

BOCK, R. Darrell
Advantage and disadvantage : a profile of American youth / R. Darrell Bock, Elsie G.J. Moore. — Hillsdale, N.J. : L. Erlbaum Associates, 1986. — x, 230 p.. — *Includes indexes. — Bibliography: p. 210-221*

YOUTH — United States — Alcohol use — Addresses, essays, lectures

Youth and alcohol abuse : readings and resources / edited by Carla Martindell Felsted. — Phoenix, AZ : Oryx Press, 1986. — xvi, 219 p.. — *Includes bibliographies and index*

YOUTH — United States — Attitudes

MCAULEY, E. Nancy
Faith without form : beliefs of Catholic youth / E. Nancy McAuley and Moira Mathiesen ; introduction, George Gallup. — Kansas City : Sheed and Ward, 1986. — vi,166p. — *Bibliography: p165-6*

YOUTH — United States — Drug use

GLASSNER, Barry
Drugs in adolescent worlds : burnouts to straights / Barry Glassner and Julia Loughlin. — Basingstoke : Macmillan, 1987. — x,301p. — *Bibliography: p285-295. — Includes index*

YOUTH — United States — Drug use — Addresses, essays, lectures

Teen drug use / edited by George Beschner, Alfred S. Friedman. — Lexington, Mass. : Lexington Books, c1986. — x, 243 p.. — *Includes bibliographies and index*

YOUTH — United States — Public opinion

GILBERT, James Burkhart
A cycle of outrage : juvenile delinquency and mass media in the 1950s / James Gilbert. — New York ; Oxford : Oxford University Press, 1986. — vi, 258p, [6]p of plates. — *Includes bibliographical references and index. — Bibliography: p*

YOUTH — United States — Religious life

MCAULEY, E. Nancy
Faith without form : beliefs of Catholic youth / E. Nancy McAuley and Moira Mathiesen ; introduction, George Gallup. — Kansas City : Sheed and Ward, 1986. — vi,166p. — *Bibliography: p165-6*

YOUTH — United States — Social conditions

BOCK, R. Darrell
Advantage and disadvantage : a profile of American youth / R. Darrell Bock, Elsie G.J. Moore. — Hillsdale, N.J. : L. Erlbaum Associates, 1986. — x, 230 p.. — *Includes indexes. — Bibliography: p. 210-221*

YOUTH AS CONSUMERS

MCNEAL, James U
Children as consumers : insights and implications / James U. McNeal. — Lexington, Mass. : Lexington Books, c1987. — xvi, 211 p.. — *Includes index. — Bibliography: p. [191]-205*

YOUTH AS CONSUMERS — Great Britain

GREAT BRITAIN. Office of Population Censuses and Surveys
Contract law and minors : expenditure of 16 and 17 year olds in the FES; report to the Law Commission / W.F.F. Kemsley. — [London : the Office, 1978]. — 9leaves

YOUTH, BLACK — Training of — Great Britain

Black youth futures : ethnic minorities and the Youth Training Scheme / edited by Malcolm Cross and Douglas I. Smith. — [S.l.] : National Youth Bureau, 1987. — 113 p

YOUTH EMPLOYMENT AGENCY (U.S.)

LATIMORE, James
Weeding out the target population : the law of accountability in a manpower program / James Latimore. — Westport, Conn. : Greenwood Press, 1985. — x, 176 p.. — (Contributions in sociology ; no. 54). — *Includes index. — Bibliography: p. [173]-174*

YOUTH HOSTELS ASSOCIATION OF GREAT BRITAIN

YOUTH HOSTELS ASSOCIATION OF GREAT BRITAIN
Youth Hostels Association of Great Britain. — Welwyn Garden City : Youth Hostels Association, 1930. — 6p

YOUTH IN MASS MEDIA — United States
GILBERT, James Burkhart
A cycle of outrage : juvenile delinquency and mass media in the 1950s / James Gilbert. — New York ; Oxford : Oxford University Press, 1986. — vi, 258p, [6]p of plates. — *Includes bibliographical references and index. — Bibliography: p*

YOUTH MOVEMENT — Germany
FRÖHER, Lothar
Der weite Weg : die deutsche Jugendbewegung seit Ende des 19. Jahrhunderts / Lothar Fröher. — Heidenheim : Südmarkverlag Fritsch, 1984. — vii,158p. — *Bibliography: p156-158*

YOUTH MOVEMENT — Germany (West)
HARTMANN, Ulrich
Rechtsextremismus bei Jugendlichen : Anregungen, der wachsenden Gefahr entgegenzuwirken / Ulrich Hartmann, Hans-Peter und Sigrid Steffen. — München : Kösel-Verlag, c1985. — 160p. — *Bibliography: p154-[160]*

YOUTH MOVEMENT — Germany (West) — History
FRÖHER, Lothar
Der weite Weg : die deutsche Jugendbewegung seit Ende des 19. Jahrhunderts / Lothar Fröher. — Heidenheim : Südmarkverlag Fritsch, 1984. — vii,158p. — *Bibliography: p156-158*

YOUTH MOVEMENTS — Germany (West)
DUDEK, Peter
Jugendliche Rechtsextremisten : zwischen Hakenkreuz und Odalsrune 1945 bis heute / Peter Dudek. — Köln : Bund-Verlag, 1985. — 243p. — *Bibliography: p237-240*

YOUTH OPPORTUNITIES PROGRAMME
GLENDON, A. I.
A study of 1700 accidents on the Youth Opportunities Programme / A.I. Glendon, A. R. Hale. — [Sheffield] : Manpower Services Commission, 1985. — 1v. (various pagings)

NG, Stephanie
The Youth Opportunities Programme in three local economies / Stephanie Ng. — London : London School of Economics. Graduate School of Geography, 1985. — 17p. — (Geography discussion papers / London School of Economics and Political Science. Graduate School of Geography. New series ; no.20). — *Bibliography: p18-20*

YOUTH SERVICES — Commonwealth of Nations
COMMONWEALTH SECRETARIAT. Youth Division
Commonwealth youth programme. — [London] : the Secretariat, [1978]. — [12]p

YOUTH TRAINING SCHEME
Black youth futures : ethnic minorities and the Youth Training Scheme / edited by Malcolm Cross and Douglas I. Smith. — [S.l.] : National Youth Bureau, 1987. — 113 p

CHALLIS, Bob
YTS and the local authority / Bob Challis, Charlie Mason, David Parkes, Further Education Staff College. — [Sheffield] : Manpower Services Commission, [1986]. — vii,31p. — (Research & development ; no.37)

CHALLIS, Bob10
YTS and the local authority : interim project report / Bob Challis, Charlie Mason, David Parkes, Further Education Staff College. — Sheffield : Manpower Services Commission, 1984. — 71p

CHAPMAN, Paul G.
The Youth Training Scheme in the United Kingdom / Paul G. Chapman and Michael J. Tooze. — Aldershot : Avebury, c1987. — x,124p. — *Includes index*

COCKBURN, Cynthia
Two track training : sex inequalities and the YTS / Cynthia Cockburn. — Basingstoke : Macmillan Education, 1987. — [256]p. — (Youth questions)

Core skills in YTS. — [Sheffield : Manpower Services Commission]
Part 1: Number, communication, problem solving, practical. — [1984]. — 37p. — (Youth Training Scheme manual)

Core skills in YTS. — [Sheffield : Manpower Services Commission] 260.01/1, [1985]
Part 2: Computer and information technology. — 11p. — (Youth Training Scheme manual)

CRAIG, Rachel
The Youth Training Scheme : a study of non participants and early leavers / Rachel Craig, British Market Research Bureau Ltd. — [Sheffield] : Manpower Services Commission, [1986]. — 60p. — (YTS evaluation series ; no.2) (Research & development ; no.34)

CROW, Iain
Youth training and young offenders / Iain Crow, Paul Richardson, National Association for the Care and Resettlement of Offenders. — [Sheffield] : Manpower Services Commission, [1985]. — 28p. — (Research & development ; no.24)

Development of the Youth Training Scheme : a report. — Sheffield : Manpower Services Commission, c1985. — 52p. — *Cover title*

DOWNS, Sylvia
Developing skilled learners : learning to learn in YTS / Sylvia Downs, Patricia Perry. — [Sheffield] : Manpower Services Commission, [1984]. — 49p. — (Research & development ; no.22). — *Bibliographical references: p43-44*

GRAY, Duncan
The Youth Training Scheme : the first three years / Duncan Gray, Suzanne King. — [Sheffield] : Manpower Services Commission, [1986]. — 62p. — (YTS evaluation series ; no.1) (Research & development ; no.35)

GREAT BRITAIN. Manpower Services Commission
Development of the Youth Training Scheme : approved training organisations : an information paper on which comment is invited. — [Sheffield : the Commission, 1985]. — [8p]

GREAT BRITAIN. Working Group on Training Objectives and Content
A report (Youth Training Scheme). — [Sheffield : Manpower Services Commission, 1985]. — 17p

Residential training in YTS. — [Sheffield : Manpower Services Commission, 1985]. — 56p. — (Youth Training Scheme manual)

WOLF, Alison
Work based learning : trainee assessment by supervisors / Alison Wolf, Ruth Silver. — [Sheffield] : Manpower Services Commission, [1986]. — 35p. — (Research & development ; no.33). — *Bibliographical references: p34-35*

HORTON, Claire
Nothing like a job / Claire Horton. — London : Lasso Co-operative, 1985. — 70p. — *Bibliography: p70*

KEEP, Ewart
Designing the stable door : a study of how the Youth Training Scheme was planned / Ewart Keep. — Coventry : University of Warwick. School of Industrial and Business Studies, 1986. — 31p. — (Warwick papers in industrial relations ; no.8). — *Bibliography: p[1-4]*

WILLMORE, Ian
The Youth Training Scheme : a basic guide / Ian Willmore [and] Paul Lewis. — [S.l.] : [s.n.], 1985. — 33p

YOUTH TRAINING SCHEME (GREAT BRITAIN)
COCKBURN, Cynthia
Two track training : sex inequalities and the YTS / Cynthia Cockburn. — Basingstoke : Macmillan Education, 1987. — [256]p. — (Youth questions)

YRIGOYEN, HIPÓLITO
ALEN LASCANO, Luis C
Yrigoyen, Sandino y el panamericanismo / Luis C. Alen Lascano. — Buenos Aires : Centro Editor de América Latina, 1986. — 138p. — (Biblioteca Política Argentina ; 131). — *Bibliography: p138*

YUCATÁN (MEXICO) — Rural conditions
BRANNON, Jeffery
Agrarian reform & public enterprise in Mexico : the political economy of Yucatán's henequen industry / Jeffery Brannon, Eric N. Baklanoff ; a foreword by Edward H. Moseley. — Tuscaloosa, Ala. : University of Alabama Press, c1987. — xv, 237 p.. — *Includes index. — Bibliography: p. 220-230*

YUCATÁN (MEXICO : STATE) — Historiography
JOSEPH, G. M
Rediscovering the past at Mexico's periphery : essays on the history of modern Yucatán / Gilbert M. Joseph. — University, Ala. : University of Alabama Press, c1986. — xvii, 203 p.. — *Includes index. — Bibliography: p. 179-198*

YUGOSLAVIA — Census, 1981
YUGLOSLAVIA. Savezni zavod za statistiku
[Census (1981)]. Popis stanovništva, domačinstava i stanova u 1981. godini. — Beograd : Savezni zavod za statistiku, 1983-

YUGOSLAVIA — Constitution
YUGOSLAVIA
[Constitution]. The Constitution of the Socialist Federal Republic of Yugoslavia. — [S.l. : s.n., 198-?]. — 167p

YUGOSLAVIA — Economic conditions — 1945-
ANDREEVSKI, Urosh
Geneza na sotsio-ekonomskite razliki vo Jugoslavija / Urosh Andreevski. — Skopje : Misla, 1985. — 410p

BILANDŽIĆ, Dušan
Jugoslavija posle Tita (1980-1985) / Dušan Bilandžić. — Zagreb : Globus, [1986]. — 253p. — (Plava biblioteka)

HORVAT, Branko
Jugoslavensko društo u Krizi : kritički ogledi i prijedlozi reformi / Branko Horvat. — Zagreb : Globus, 1985. — 382p

MARSENI'C, Dragutin V.
Sumnje u privredni sistem Jugoslavije / Dragutin V. Marseni'c. — Beograd : Ekonomika, 1986. — 373p. — *Summary in English*

YUGOSLAVIA — Economic policy — 1945-
KRAIGHER, Sergej
Kako iz krize : o Dugoročnom programu ekonomske stabilizacije i njegovom ostvarivanju / Sergej Kraigher. — Zagreb : Globus, [1985]. — 398p. — (Biblioteka Globus)

MARSENI'C, Dragutin V.
Sumnje u privredni sistem Jugoslavije / Dragutin V. Marseni'c. — Beograd : Ekonomika, 1986. — 373p. — *Summary in English*

SAVEZ KOMUNISTA JUGOSLAVIJE. Centralni komitet. Sednica (3 : 1982)
Aktuelna idejno-politička pitanja društveno-ekonomske situacije i zadaci Saveza komunista u ostvarivanju stavova 12. kongresa SKJ : uvodno izlaganje Mitje Ribičiča, diskusija, zaključci. — Beograd : Izdavački Centae Komunist, 1982. — 212p

YUGOSLAVIA — Economic policy — 1945-
continuation

SAVEZ KOMUNISTA JUGOSLAVIJE.
Centralni komitet. Sednica (4 : 1983)
Ostvarivanje zaključaka 3. sednice CKSKJ i zadataka SKJ u ostvarivanju ekonomske politike u 1983. godini. — Beograd : Izdavački Centar Komunist, 1983. — 167p

SAVEZ KOMUNISTA JUGOSLAVIJE.
Centralni komitet. Sednica (15 : 1980)
15. Sednica CKSKJ : idejno-politička pitanja dništveno- ekonomskog razvoja Jugoslavije za period od 1981. do 1985. god. — Beograd : Izdavački Centar Komunist, 1982. — 141p. — (Dokumenti SKJ)

SAVEZ KOMUNISTA JUGOSLAVIJE.
Centralni komitet. Sednica (18 : 1985)
O ulozi i radu CKSKJ ; Ostavarivanje ustavnog položaja radnika u odlučivanju i raspolaganju dohotkom i sredstvima društvene reprodukcije. — Beograd : Izdavački Centar Komunist, 1985. — 220p

YUGOSLAVIA — Emigration and immigration — Government policy

ZIMMERMAN, William
Open borders, nonalignment, and the political evolution of Yugoslavia / William Zimmerman. — Princeton, N.J. : Princeton University Press, c1987. — p. cm. — *Includes index. — Bibliography: p*

YUGOSLAVIA — Foreign economic relations — Poland

RYŚ, Bronisław
Rozwój polsko-jugosłowiańskich stosunków gospodarczych / Bronisław Ryś. — Łódź : Wydawnictwo Łódskie, 1986. — 485p. — *Summary in Serbo Croat and German. — Bibliography: p467-[478]*

YUGOSLAVIA — Foreign relations — 1945-

Dokumenti o spoljnoj politici Socijalističke Federativne Republike Jugoslavije 1945- / redakcija: Dragomir Vučinić...[et al.]. — Beograd : Jugoslovenski pregled, 1984-. — *At head of title: Savezni sekretarijat za Inostrane poslove. Centar za informaciono-dokumentacione poslove [and] Institut za međunarodnu politiku i privredu*

YUGOSLAVIA — Foreign relations — Italy

PAVLOWITCH, Stevan K.
"Il caso Mirošević" : l`expulsion du ministre de Yougoslavie au Vatican par le gouvernement fasciste en 1941 / Stevan K. Pavlowitch. — Thessaloniki : [s.n.], 1978. — p107-137. — *Offprint from Balkan Studies*

YUGOSLAVIA — Foreign relations — Soviet Union

GIBIANSKII, L. Ia.
Sovetskii Soiuz i novaia Iugoslaviia 1941-1947 gg. / L. Ia. Gibianskii ; otv. redaktor V. K. Volkov. — Moskva : Nauka, 1987. — 201p

YUGOSLAVIA — History — 1918-1945 — Bibliography

IMPERIAL WAR MUSEUM. Library
Second World War Yugoslavia : selected list of references. — [London : the Library, 1975]. — 15p. — (Booklist / Imperial War Museum [Library] ; no.1236)

YUGOSLAVIA — History — Axis occupation, 1941-1945

War and revolution in Yugoslavia, 1941-1945 / prepared by Ivan Jelić ... [et al.] ; editor, Novak Strugar ; translation Margot and Boško Milosavljević. — [Belgrade] : Socialist Thought and Practice, c1985. — 284 p.. — *Translated from the Serbo-Croatian. — Includes bibliographical references*

YUGOSLAVIA — Industries

ARTISIEN, Patrick F. R.
Joint ventures in Yugoslav industry / Patrick F.R. Artisien. — Aldershot : Gower, c1985. — [xv,240]p. — *Bibliography: p210-218. — Includes index*

RESEARCH PROJECT ON NATIONAL INCOME IN EAST CENTRAL EUROPE
Occasional papers Nos.90-94 of the Research Project on National Income in East Central Europe / [by] Thad P. Alton...[et al.]. — New York : L. W. International Financial Research, Inc., 1986. — 1v(various pagings). — *Bibliography: [11p]. — Contents: Economic growth in Eastern Europe, 1970, and 1975-1985: Agricultural output, expenses and depreciation, gross product, and net product in Eastern Europe, 1965, 1970 and 1975-1985: Eastern Europe: Domestic Final Uses of Gross Product, 1970 and 1975-1985: Money Income of the Population and Standard of Living in Eastern Europe, 1970-1985: Measuring Industrial Growth of Yugoslavia, 1970-1985*

YUGOSLAVIA — Nonalignment

ZIMMERMAN, William
Open borders, nonalignment, and the political evolution of Yugoslavia / William Zimmerman. — Princeton, N.J. : Princeton University Press, c1987. — p. cm. — *Includes index. — Bibliography: p*

YUGOSLAVIA — Politics and government — 1945-

BILANDŽIĆ, Dušan
Jugoslavija posle Tita (1980-1985) / Dušan Bilandžić. — Zagreb : Globus, [1986]. — 253p. — (Plava biblioteka)

SEROKA, Jim
Political organizations in Yugoslavia / Jim Seroka and Rados Smiljkovic. -- Durham, NC : Duke University Press, 1986. — p. cm. — (Duke Press policy studies). — *Includes index*

Socijalistički savez radnog naroda u razvoju socijalističkog samoupravnog društva / redakcioni odbor: Ilija Globačnik...[et al.]. — Beograd : Izdavački centar Komunist ; Ljubljana : Jugoslovenski centar za teoriju i praksu samoupravljanja "Edvard Kardelj", [1986]. — 902p. — *U zborniku objavljuju se saopštenja i diskusije sa naučnog skupa, 26. i 27. januara 1984 godine u okviru Teorijskih rasprava "Misao i revolucionarno delo Edvarda Kardelja". — Summaries in Serbian, Croat, Macedonian, Hungarian, Albanian and English*

ZIMMERMAN, William
Open borders, nonalignment, and the political evolution of Yugoslavia / William Zimmerman. — Princeton, N.J. : Princeton University Press, c1987. — p. cm. — *Includes index. — Bibliography: p*

YUGOSLAVIA — Population

YUGLOSLAVIA. Savezni zavod za statistiku
[Census (1981)]. Popis stanovništva, domačinstava i stanova u 1981. godini. — Beograd : Savezni zavod za statistiku, 1983-

YUGOSLAVIA — Relations — Albania

VUKOVI´C, Ilija
Autonomaštvo i separatizam na Kosovu / Ilija Vukovi´c. — Beograd : Nova Knjiga, 1985. — 238p

YUGOSLAVIA — Social conditions

JOVANOVIĆ, Batrić
Kosovo, inflacija, socijalne razlike : istupanja u Skupštini SFRJ, 1982-85 / Batrić Jovanović. — Beograd : [Partizanska knjiga], 1985. — 331p. — (Sučeljavanja)

YUGOSLAVIA — Social conditions — 1945-

ANDREEVSKI, Urosh
Geneza na sotsio-ekonomiskite razliki vo Jugoslavija / Urosh Andreevski. — Skopje : Misla, 1985. — 410p

HORVAT, Branko
Jugoslavensko društо u Krizi : kritički ogledi i prijedlozi reformi / Branko Horvat. — Zagreb : Globus, 1985. — 382p

YUGOSLAVIA — Social policy

SAVEZ KOMUNISTA JUGOSLAVIJE.
Centralni komitet. Sednica (3 : 1982)
Aktuelna idejno-politička pitanja društveno-ekonomske situacije i zadaci Saveza komunista u ostvarivanju stavova 12. kongresa SKJ : uvodno izlaganje Mitje Ribičiča, diskusija, zaključci. — Beograd : Izdavački Centae Komunist, 1982. — 212p

YUKON — Economic conditions

CANADA. Parliament. House of Commons. Standing Committee on Aboriginal Affairs and Northern Development
Minutes of proceedings and evidence... = Procès verbaux et témoignages. — Ottawa : Government Printer, 1986-. — *Continues: Canada. Parliament. House of Commons. Standing Committee on Indian Affairs and Northern Development. Minutes of proceedings and evidence...*

CANADA. Parliament. House of Commons. Standing Committee on Indian Affairs and Northern Development
Minutes of proceedings and evidence... = Procès-verbaux et témoignages.... — Ottawa : Government Printer, 1968-1986. — *Irregular. — Continued by: Canada. Parliament. House of Commons. Standing Committee on Aboriginal Affairs and Northern Development*

YUKON TERRITORY — Politics and government

ROBERTSON, Gordon
Northern Provinces : a mistaken goal / Gordon Robertson. — Montréal : Institute for Research on Public Policy, 1985. — 77p

ZAIRE — Economic conditions

La réunion du Groupe consultatif de la Banque Mondiale pour le Zaire, Novembre 1973. — Kinshasa : Université Nationale du Zaire, Institut de Recherches Economiques, 1974. — 16p. — (Document du mois / Université Nationale du Zaire. Institute de Recherches Economiques ; vol.1, no.1)

ZAIRE — Economic conditions — 1960- — Congresses

The Crisis in Zaire : myths and realities / edited by Nzongola-Ntalaja. — Trenton, N.J. : Africa World Press, 1986. — vii, 327 p.. — *Selected papers from an international conference on "Myths and Realities of the Zairian Crisis," held at Howard Univ., Oct. 1984. — Includes index. — Bibliography: p. 297-312*

ZAIRE — Foreign relations — Congresses

The Crisis in Zaire : myths and realities / edited by Nzongola-Ntalaja. — Trenton, N.J. : Africa World Press, 1986. — vii, 327 p.. — *Selected papers from an international conference on "Myths and Realities of the Zairian Crisis," held at Howard Univ., Oct. 1984. — Includes index. — Bibliography: p. 297-312*

ZAIRE — History — 1960-

MARTENS, Ludo
Pierre Mulele : ou la seconde vie de Patrice Lumumba / Ludo Martens. — [Antwerp] : Editions EPO, 1985. — 384p. — *Bibliography: p363-365*

ZAIRE — Politics and government

Les enseignements du discours présidentiel devant le Conseil Legislatif National 30 Novembre 1973. — Kinshasa : Université Nationale du Zaire, 1974. — 21p. — (Document du mois / Université Nationale du Zaire. Institut de Recherches Economiques ; vol.1, no.2)

MOUVEMENT POPULAIRE DE LA REVOLUTION
Manifeste de la N´sele. — [S.l.] : Mouvement Populaire de la Revolution, [1960]. — 32p

MOUVEMENT POPULAIRE DE LA RÉVOLUTION
Statut et reglement d´ordre interieur. — [s.l.] : Mouvement Populaire de la Révolution, 1975. — 34p

ZAIRE — Politics and government
continuation
République du Zaire : manifeste du mouvement populaire de la révolution. — [S.l.] : [s.n.], [1970]. — 32p

ZAIRE — Politics and government — 1960- — Congresses
The Crisis in Zaire : myths and realities / edited by Nzongola-Ntalaja. — Trenton, N.J. : Africa World Press, 1986. — vii, 327 p.. — *Selected papers from an international conference on "Myths and Realities of the Zairian Crisis," held at Howard Univ., Oct. 1984. — Includes index. — Bibliography: p. 297-312*

ZAIRE — Religion
MACGAFFEY, Wyatt
Religion and society in central Africa : the BaKongo of lower Zaire / Wyatt MacGaffey. — Chicago : University of Chicago Press, 1986. — xi, 295 p.. — *Includes index. — Bibliography: p. 273-287*

ZAMBIA — Census, 1963
Preliminary report of the May/June, 1963 census of Africans in Northern Rhodesia. — Lusaka : Ministry of Finance, 1964. — 14p,xxi

ZAMBIA — Economic policy
CHILESHE, Jonathan H
Third World countries and development options, Zambia / Jonathan H. Chileshe. — New Delhi : Vikas Pub. House, c1986. — xii, 220 p., [2] leaves of plates. — *Includes index. — Bibliography: p. [213]-215*

Third national development plan: annual plan / Republic of Zambia. — Lusaka : Government Printer, 1983-. — *Annual*

ZAMBIA — History — 1964-
WINA, Sikota
The night without a president / Sikota Wina. — Lusaka : Multimedia Publications, 1985. — iv,91p

ZAMBIA — Industries
MUSAMPA, Christopher
Industrialization in Zambia : some industrial geographical perspectives / by Christopher Musampa. — 282 leaves. — *PhD (Econ) 1987 LSE. — Leaves 203-222 are appendices*

ZAMBIA — Politics and government — 1964-
WINA, Sikota
The night without a president / Sikota Wina. — Lusaka : Multimedia Publications, 1985. — iv,91p

ZAMBIA — Population — Statistics
Preliminary report of the May/June, 1963 census of Africans in Northern Rhodesia. — Lusaka : Ministry of Finance, 1964. — 14p,xxi

ZAMBIA — Social life and customs — History
STIRKE, D. E. C. R.
Barotseland : eight years among the Barotse / by D. W. Stirke ; with an introductory chapter by Sir Harry Johnston. — New York : Negro Universities Press, 1969. — xii,135p. — *Reprint of 1922 edition*

ZAMBIA — Social policy
Third national development plan: annual plan / Republic of Zambia. — Lusaka : Government Printer, 1983-. — *Annual*

ZANDE (AFRICAN PEOPLE)
EVANS-PRITCHARD, Sir Edward Evan
Witchcraft, oracles and magic among the Azande / Sir Edward Evans-Pritchard ; with a foreword by C. G. Seligman. — Oxford : Clarendon Press, 1937. — 558p

ZANZIBAR — Commerce — History
SHERIFF, Abdul
Slaves, spices & ivory in Zanzibar : integration of an East African commercial empire into the world economy, 1770-1873 / Abdul Sheriff. — London : Currey, 1987. — xx,297p. — *(Eastern African studies). — Bibliography: p259-281. — Includes index*

ZANZIBAR — History — To 1890
BENNETT, Norman Robert
Arab versus European : diplomacy and war in nineteenth-century east central Africa / Norman Robert Bennett. — New York ; London : Africana Publishing, 1986. — 325p. — *Includes index. — Bibliography: p*

ZAPOTEC INDIANS — Rites and ceremonies
EL GUINDI, Fadwa
The myth of ritual : a native's ethnography of Zapotec life-crisis rituals / Fadwa El Guindi, with the collaboration of Abel Hernández Jiménez. — Tucson : University of Arizona Press, c1986. — xvii, 147p. — *Includes index. — Bibliography: p.125-139*

ZAPOTEC INDIANS — Social life and customs
CHIÑAS, Beverly
The Isthmus Zapotecs : women's roles in cultural context / Beverly Chiñas. — Prospect Heights, Ill. : Waveland Press, 1983. — ix,129p. — *First published in 1973. — Bibliography: p128-129*

ZARAGOZA (SPAIN) — History
PINILLA NAVARRO, Vicente
Conflictividad social y revuelta politica en Zaragoza (1854-1856) / Vicente Pinilla Navarro. — Zaragoza : Diputación General de Aragon, 1985. — 244p. — *Bibliography: p234-244*

ZARAGOZA (SPAIN) — History — 19th century
INIGO GÍAS, María Pilar
Zaragoza esparterista (1840-1843) / Maria Pilar Inigo Gias. — Zaragoza : Ayuntamiento de Zaragoza, 1983. — 111p. — *Bibliography: p77-81*

ZIA-UL-HAQ, MOHAMMAD — Interviews
ZIA-UL-HAQ, Mohammad
President of Pakistan, General Mohammad Zia-ul-Haq : interviews to foreign media. — Islamabad : Directorate of Films & Publications, Ministry of Information & Broadcasting, Government of Pakistan, <[1980?-1984? >. — 5v.. — *Includes indexes. — Contents: v. 1. March-December 1978 -- v. 2. January-December 1979 -- v. 3. January-December 1980 -- v. 4. January-December 1981 -- v. 5. January-December 1982*

ZIA-UL-HAQ, MOHAMMED
SAWHNEY, R. G.
Zia's Pakistan : implications for India's security / R. G. Sawhney. — New Delhi : ABC Publishing House, 1985. — xv,200p. — *Bibliography: p[181]-193*

ZIMBABWE — Antiquities
KEANE, A. H.
The gold of Ophir : whence brought and by whom? / by A.H.Keane. — New York : Negro Universities Press, 1969. — xviii,244p. — *Originally published in 1901*

ZIMBABWE — Economic conditions — 1980-
Zimbabwe : the political economy of transition 1980-1986 / edited by Ibbo Mandaza. — Dakar : Codesria, 1986. — xii,430p. — *Bibliography: p405-424*

ZIMBABWE — Foreign economic relations — Bibliography
GREAT BRITAIN. Parliament. House of Commons. Library. International Affairs Section
The Bingham Report : a background bibliography / [Carole B. Mann]. — [London] : the Library, 1978. — 6leaves. — *(Reference sheet / House of Commons. Library. Research Division ; no.78/9)*

GREAT BRITAIN. Parliament. House of Commons. Library. International Affairs Section
The Bingham Report : a background bibliography; addenda: November 1978-January 1979 / [Carole B. Mann]. — [London] : the Library, 1979. — 2leaves. — *([Reference sheet] / House of Commons. Library. [Research Division] ; no.78/9: Addenda)*

ZIMBABWE — Foreign relations
DAVIDOW, Jeffrey
Dealing with international crises : lessons from Zimbabwe / Jeffrey Davidow. — Muscatine (Iowa) : Stanley Foundation, 1983. — 23p. — *(Occasional paper / Stanley Foundation ; 34)*

ZIMBABWE — Politics and government — 1980-
SPRING, William
The long fields : Zimbabwe since independence / William Spring. — Basingstoke : Pickering, 1986. — 191p

Zimbabwe : the political economy of transition 1980-1986 / edited by Ibbo Mandaza. — Dakar : Codesria, 1986. — xii,430p. — *Bibliography: p405-424*

ZIMBABWE — Social conditions — 1980-
Zimbabwe : the political economy of transition 1980-1986 / edited by Ibbo Mandaza. — Dakar : Codesria, 1986. — xii,430p. — *Bibliography: p405-424*

ZIMBABWE CONFERENCE ON RECONSTRUCTION AND DEVELOPMENT (1981 : Salisbury)
ZIMBABWE CONFERENCE ON RECONSTRUCTION AND DEVELOPMENT (1981 : Salisbury)
Let's build Zimbabwe together : Conference documentation. — Causeway : Ministry of Economic Planning and Development, [1981]. — 111p. — *Cover title*

ZIONISM
COHEN, Mitchell
Zion and state : nation, class and the shaping of modern Israel / Mitchell Cohen. — Oxford : Basil Blackwell, 1987. — [288]p. — *Includes bibliography and index*

DAVIS, Uri
On zionism and Jewish identity / Uri Davis. — London : Ithaca Press, 1983. — 19p. — *Bibliography: p19*

ELON, Amos
The Israelis : founders and sons / Amos Elon. — New York : Penguin, 1983. — xiv, 359 p.. — : *Previously published: New York : Holt, Rinehart, and Winston, 1971. — Includes index. — Bibliography: p. 336-348*

FYVEL, T. R.
And there my trouble began : uncollected writings, 1945-1985 / T. R. Fyvel. — London : Weidenfeld and Nicolson, 1986. — xii,240p

SEMENIUK, V. A.
Sovremennyi sionizm : kursom politicheskikh i voennykh avantiur / V. A. Semeniuk. — Minsk : Belarus', 1986. — 236p

ZIONISM — History
GORNY, Joseph
The British Labour movement and Zionism 1917-1948 / Joseph Gorny. — London : Cass, 1983. — xvi,251p. — *Bibliography: p239-242. — Includes index*

VITAL, David
Zionism : the crucial phase / David Vital. — Oxford : Clarendon, 1987. — [450]p,[8]p plates. — *Includes bibliography and index*

ZIONISM — Palestine — History
BLACK, Ian
Zionism and the Arabs, 1936-1939 / Ian Black. — New York : Garland, 1986. — 435 p.. — (Outstanding theses from the London School of Economics and Political Science). — *Thesis (Ph. D.)--University of London, 1978. — Bibliography: p. 426-435*

ZIONISTS — Attitudes — History
GORNI, Yosef
Zionism and the Arabs 1882-1948 : a study of ideology / Yosef Gorny. — Oxford : Clarendon, 1987. — x,342p. — *Translation of: Ha-She' elah ha-'Arvit veha-be 'ayah ha-Yehundit. — Bibliography: p326-330. — Includes index*

ZIONISTS — Correspondence, reminiscences, etc
RUPPIN, Arthur
Arthur Ruppin : memoirs, diaries, letters / edited with an introduction by Alex Bein ; translated from the German [MSS.] by Karen Gershon ; afterword by Moshe Dayan. — London : Weidenfeld and Nicolson, 1971. — xix,332,[16]p. — *Includes index*

ZIONISTS — United States — Biography
GOLDSTEIN, Israel
My world as a Jew : the memoirs of Israel Goldstein. — New York : Herzl Press ; London : Cornwall Books, c1984. — p. cm. — *Includes index*

ZULULAND (SOUTH AFRICA) — Description and travel
LESLIE, David
Among the Zulus and Amatongas : with sketches of the natives, their language and customs; and the country, products, climate, wild animals, &c. being principally contributions to magazines and newspapers / David Leslie ; edited by W. H. Drummond. — New York : Negro Universities Press, 1969. — xvi,436p. — *Originally published in 1875 by Edmonston & Douglas, Edinburgh*

ZULULAND (SOUTH AFRICA) — Social life and customs
LESLIE, David
Among the Zulus and Amatongas : with sketches of the natives, their language and customs; and the country, products, climate, wild animals, &c. being principally contributions to magazines and newspapers / David Leslie ; edited by W. H. Drummond. — New York : Negro Universities Press, 1969. — xvi,436p. — *Originally published in 1875 by Edmonston & Douglas, Edinburgh*

ZULUS
SHOOTER, Joseph
The Kafirs of Natal and the Zulu country. — New York : Negro Universities Press, [1969]. — x, 403 p. — *Reprint of the 1857 ed*

ZUNDEL, ERNST — Trials, litigation, etc. — Public opinion
WEIMANN, Gabriel
Hate on trial : the Zundel Affair : thr media public opinion in Canada / Gabriel Weimann and Conrad Winn. — Oakville, Ontario : Mosaic Press, 1986. — 201p. — *Includes references*

ZÜRICH (SWITZERLAND) — Economic conditions
ALLEN, Frederick S
Zürich, the 1820's to the 1870's : a study in modernization / Frederick S. Allen. — Lanham, MD : University Press of America, c1986. — xiii, 132 p.. — *Includes index. — Bibliography: p. 113-122*

ZÜRICH (SWITZERLAND) — Politics and government
ALLEN, Frederick S
Zürich, the 1820's to the 1870's : a study in modernization / Frederick S. Allen. — Lanham, MD : University Press of America, c1986. — xiii, 132 p.. — *Includes index. — Bibliography: p. 113-122*

ZÜRICH (SWITZERLAND : CANTON) — Economic conditions
ALLEN, Frederick S
Zürich, the 1820's to the 1870's : a study in modernization / Frederick S. Allen. — Lanham, MD : University Press of America, c1986. — xiii, 132 p.. — *Includes index. — Bibliography: p. 113-122*

ZÜRICH (SWITZERLAND : CANTON) — Politics and government
ALLEN, Frederick S
Zürich, the 1820's to the 1870's : a study in modernization / Frederick S. Allen. — Lanham, MD : University Press of America, c1986. — xiii, 132 p.. — *Includes index. — Bibliography: p. 113-122*

ŽUŽEK (Family)
DAVIS, James C
Rise from want : a peasant family in the machine age / James C. Davis. — Philadelphia : University of Pennsylvania Press, 1986. — xv, 165 p.. — *Includes index. — Bibliography: p. [153]-161*

List of subject headings used

A NICARAGUA — Social conditions — 1979-
AALBORG (DENMARK) — Civic improvement
ABDUCTION
ABDUL RAHMAN, Tunku, Putra Al-Haj
ABERDEEN (GRAMPIAN) — History
ABERDEEN (GRAMPIAN) — Social conditions
ABIDJAN (IVORY COAST) — Population — Statistics
ABIDJAN (IVORY COAST) — Statistics, vital
ABNORMALITIES, HUMAN — Denmark — Statistics
ABOLITION OF DOMESTIC RATES ETC. [SCOTLAND] BILL 1986-87
ABOLITIONISTS
ABOLITIONISTS — History — 19th century — Sources
ABOLITIONISTS — Great Britain — History
ABOLITIONISTS — United States — History
ABOLITIONISTS — United States — History — 19th century — Sources
ABORTION
ABORTION — Law and legislation — Great Britain
ABORTION — Moral and ethical aspects
ABORTION — Political aspects
ABORTION — Political aspects — United States
ABORTION — Social aspects — United States
ABORTION — Great Britain
ABORTION — United States
ABORTION — United States — History — 19th century
ABORTION (AMENDMENT) BILL 1979-80
ABORTION, INDUCED — United States
ABSENTEEISM (LABOR) — Great Britain
ABSENTEEISM (LABOR) — Québec (Province)
ABSTRACT DATA TYPES (COMPUTER SCIENCE)
ABSTRACTING AND INDEXING SERVICES — Great Britain — Directories
ABUSED AGED — Services for — United States — Directories
ABUSED WIVES — Services for — Québec (Province)
ACADEMIC FREEDOM
ACADEMIC FREEDOM — South Africa
ACADEMIC FREEDOM — United States
ACADEMIC FREEDOM — United States — History — 20th century
ACADÉMIE ROYALE DES SCIENCES (Paris)
ACADIA — History
ACADIA — Lieutenant-governors — Biography
ACCIDENT LAW — England
ACCIDENT LAW — England — Greater Manchester
ACCION ESPANOLA
ACCIÓN NACIONALISTA VASCA
ACCIÓN SINDICAL URUGUAYA — History
ACCOUNTANTS — Denmark
ACCOUNTANTS — Great Britain
ACCOUNTING
ACCOUNTING — Bibliography
ACCOUNTING — Books of Account
ACCOUNTING — Data processing
ACCOUNTING — Information storage and retrieval systems
ACCOUNTING — Research
ACCOUNTING — Standards
ACCOUNTING — Standards — Great Britain
ACCOUNTING — Standards — United States
ACCOUNTING — Denmark
ACCOUNTING — Europe
ACCOUNTING — Japan
ACCOUNTING — Spain — Effect of inflation upon
ACCOUNTING AND PRICE FLUCTUATIONS
ACCOUNTING FIRMS — South Africa — Statistics
ACCOUNTING LITERATURE
ACCULTURATION — Congresses
ACCULTURATION — Ethiopia — Case studies
ACCULTURATION — United States
ACEH (INDONESIA) — History — Autonomy and independence movements
ACHIEVEMENT MOTIVATION
ACID PRECIPITATION
ACID RAIN
ACID RAIN — Bibliography
ACID RAIN — Environmental aspects
ACID RAIN — Environmental aspects — Government policy — Canada
ACID RAIN — Environmental aspects — Government policy — United States
ACID RAIN — Environmental aspects — Canada
ACID RAIN — Environmental aspects — United States
ACID RAIN — Law and legislation
ACORN (Organization)
ACQUIRED IMMUNE DEFICIENCY SYNDROME
ACQUIRED IMMUNODEFICIENCY SYNDROME
ACQUIRED IMMUNODEFICIENCY SYNDROME — psychology
ACQUIRED IMMUNODEFICIENCY SYNDROME — psychology — congresses
ACQUISITION OF AUDIO-VISUAL MATERIALS
ACQUISITIONS (LIBRARIES)
ACTING — Social aspects
ACTION DIRECTE
ACTION RESEARCH
ACTIONS AND DEFENSES — Great Lakes Region
ACTRESSES — Soviet Union — Biography
ACUPUNCTURE — Great Britain — Professional ethics
ADAMS, JOHN BODKIN — Trials, litigation, etc.
ADAMS, JOHN QUINCY
ADELAIDE (SOUTH AUSTRALIA) — Planning
ADENAUER, KONRAD
ADJUSTMENT (PSYCHOLOGY)
ADMINISTRATIVE AGENCIES — Data processing
ADMINISTRATIVE AGENCIES — Data processing — Congresses
ADMINISTRATIVE AGENCIES — Handbooks, manuals, etc — Bibliography
ADMINISTRATIVE AGENCIES — Legal status, laws, etc. — Ecuador
ADMINISTRATIVE AGENCIES — Legal status, laws, etc. — Peru
ADMINISTRATIVE AGENCIES — Australia — Economic aspects
ADMINISTRATIVE AGENCIES — Great Britain — Bibliography
ADMINISTRATIVE AGENCIES — Peru
ADMINISTRATIVE AGENCIES — Puerto Rico — Handbooks, manuals, etc.
ADMINISTRATIVE AGENCIES — Sweden
ADMINISTRATIVE AGENCIES — United States
ADMINISTRATIVE AGENCIES — United States — History
ADMINISTRATIVE AGENCIES — United States — Management — Decision making
ADMINISTRATIVE AND POLITICAL DIVISIONS — Dictionaries
ADMINISTRATIVE COURTS
ADMINISTRATIVE COURTS — Australia
ADMINISTRATIVE DISCRETION — Great Britain
ADMINISTRATIVE LAW — Argentina
ADMINISTRATIVE LAW — Australia
ADMINISTRATIVE LAW — Canada
ADMINISTRATIVE LAW — England
ADMINISTRATIVE LAW — France
ADMINISTRATIVE LAW — Great Britain
ADMINISTRATIVE LAW — India
ADMINISTRATIVE LAW — Ireland
ADMINISTRATIVE LAW — Netherlands
ADMINISTRATIVE LAW — Peru
ADMINISTRATIVE LAW — Quebec (Province)
ADMINISTRATIVE LAW — Spain
ADMINISTRATIVE LAW — United States — Dictionaries
ADMINISTRATIVE PROCEDURE — Economic aspects — United States
ADMINISTRATIVE PROCEDURE — Australia
ADMINISTRATIVE REMEDIES — Australia
ADMINISTRATIVE REMEDIES — India
ADMINISTRATIVE RESPONSIBILITY — Great Britain
ADMINSTRATIVE LAW — Spain
ADMIRALS — Great Britain — Biography
ADMIRALTY — South Africa
ADOLESCENCE
ADOLESCENCE — Congresses
ADOLESCENCE — Physiological aspects — Addresses, essays, lectures
ADOLESCENCE — Social aspects — Addresses, essays, lectures
ADOLESCENT BEHAVIOR
ADOLESCENT PSYCHOLOGY
ADOLESCENT PSYCHOLOGY — Addresses, essays, lectures
ADOLESCENT PSYCHOLOGY — Congresses
ADOLESCENT PSYCHOPATHOLOGY — Addresses, essays, lectures
ADOPTION — Law and legislation — Scotland
ADOPTION — Psychological aspects
ADOPTION — Great Britain
ADOPTION — Great Britain — Bibliography
ADORNO, THEODOR W.
ADULT CHILDREN — United States

ADULT EDUCATION
ADULT EDUCATION — Government policy — Great Britain
ADULT EDUCATION — Government policy — Great Britain — History — 20th century
ADULT EDUCATION — Africa, West
ADULT EDUCATION — Alberta
ADULT EDUCATION — Developing countries
ADULT EDUCATION — England
ADULT EDUCATION — England — Liverpool (Merseyside)
ADULT EDUCATION — Finland — Statistics
ADULT EDUCATION — France
ADULT EDUCATION — Great Britain
ADULT EDUCATION — Ireland
ADULT EDUCATION — New York (N.Y.) — History
ADULT EDUCATION — Québec (Province)
ADULT EDUCATION — United States
ADULT EDUCATION OF WOMEN — Great Britain
ADULTERY — United States
ADULTHOOD — Michigan — Psychological aspects — Longitudinal studies
ADVANCED SCHOOL FOR GIRLS (South Australia)
ADVENTURE AND ADVENTURES — Africa, Central
ADVERTISING
ADVERTISING — Charities — Great Britain
ADVERTISING — Economic aspects
ADVERTISING — Psychological aspects
ADVERTISING — Research
ADVERTISING — Social aspects
ADVERTISING — Tobacco trade
ADVERTISING — Great Britain — Case studies
ADVERTISING — Québec (Province)
ADVERTISING — United States — History
ADVERTISING LAWS — Peru
ADVERTISING LAWS — United States
ADVERTISING MEDIA PLANNING
ADVERTISING, POLITICAL
ADVERTISING, POLITICAL — United States
ADVISORY, CONCILIATION AND ARBITRATION SERVICE
AER LINGUS
AERONAUTICS — Law and legislation
AERONAUTICS — European Economic Community Countries
AERONAUTICS AND STATE — Canada
AERONAUTICS AND STATE — Canada — History
AERONAUTICS, COMMERCIAL
AERONAUTICS, COMMERCIAL — Government policy — Canada — History
AERONAUTICS, COMMERCIAL — Law and legislation
AERONAUTICS, COMMERCIAL — Political aspects — History
AERONAUTICS, COMMERCIAL — Europe, Western
AERONAUTICS, COMMERCIAL — Great Britain — Freight — Statistics
AERONAUTICS, COMMERCIAL — Great Britain — Passenger traffic — Statistics
AEROSPACE INDUSTRIES
AEROSPACE INDUSTRIES — Australia
AEROSPACE INDUSTRIES — Great Britain — Statistics
AESTHETICS
AFFIRMATIVE ACTION PROGRAMS — England — London
AFFIRMATIVE ACTION PROGRAMS — United States — Congresses
AFGHANISTAN — Constitutional law
AFGHANISTAN — Description and travel
AFGHANISTAN — Ethnic relations — Congresses
AFGHANISTAN — Foreign relations

AFGHANISTAN — Foreign relations — Pakistan
AFGHANISTAN — Foreign relations — Soviet Union
AFGHANISTAN — History — Soviet occupation, 1979-
AFGHANISTAN — History — Soviet Occupation, 1979-
AFGHANISTAN — History — Soviet occupation, 1979-
AFGHANISTAN — History — Soviet occupation — 1979-
AFGHANISTAN — Politics and government
AFGHANISTAN — Politics and government — 1973- — Congresses
AFRICA
AFRICA — Bibliography
AFRICA — Civilization
AFRICA — Civilization — Islamic influences
AFRICA — Civilization — Occidental influences
AFRICA — Colonization
AFRICA — Constitutional history
AFRICA — Description and travel — To 1900
AFRICA — Economic conditions
AFRICA — Economic conditions — Bibliography
AFRICA — Economic conditions — 1945-1960
AFRICA — Economic conditions — 1960-
AFRICA — Economic policy
AFRICA — Economic policy — Congresses
AFRICA — Economic policy — Public opinion
AFRICA — Emigration and immigration
AFRICA — Famines
AFRICA — Famines — Bibliography
AFRICA — Famines — Information services
AFRICA — Foreign economic relations
AFRICA — Foreign economic relations — Japan
AFRICA — Foreign economic relations — United States
AFRICA — Foreign relations
AFRICA — Foreign relations — 1960-
AFRICA — Foreign relations — Germany
AFRICA — Foreign relations — Soviet Union
AFRICA — Foreign relations — United States
AFRICA — Historiography — Addresses, essays, lectures
AFRICA — History
AFRICA — History — To 1498
AFRICA — History — 19th century — Sources
AFRICA — History — 1884-1960
AFRICA — History — 1960-
AFRICA — Industries
AFRICA — Industries — Bibliography
AFRICA — Politics and government
AFRICA — Politics and government — 1960-
AFRICA — Politics and government — 1960- — Congresses
AFRICA — Population — Statistics
AFRICA — Presidents
AFRICA — Relations — United States
AFRICA — Religion
AFRICA — Social conditions
AFRICA — Social policy — Congresses
AFRICA — Yearbooks
AFRICA — History — Bibliography
AFRICA, CENTRAL — Courts and courtiers
AFRICA, CENTRAL — History — To 1884
AFRICA, EAST — Bibliography
AFRICA, EAST — Description and travel
AFRICA, EAST — Foreign relations
AFRICA, EAST — History — To 1886
AFRICA, EAST — Officials and employees — Biography
AFRICA, EAST — Politics and government

AFRICA, EAST — Politics and government — 1884-1960
AFRICA, EASTERN — Economic integration
AFRICA, EASTERN — Industries
AFRICA, NORTH — Emigration and immigration
AFRICA, NORTH — Politics and government
AFRICA, NORTHEAST — Politics and government
AFRICA, PORTUGUESE-SPEAKING — Economic conditions — Bibliography
AFRICA, PORTUGUESE-SPEAKING — Foreign relations — Bibliography
AFRICA, PORTUGUESE-SPEAKING — History — Bibliography
AFRICA, PORTUGUESE-SPEAKING — Politics and government — Bibliography
AFRICA, SOUTHERN — Dependency on South Africa
AFRICA, SOUTHERN — Economic integration
AFRICA, SOUTHERN — Economic policy
AFRICA, SOUTHERN — Foreign economic relations — South Africa
AFRICA, SOUTHERN — Foreign relations — 1975-
AFRICA, SOUTHERN — Foreign relations — South Africa
AFRICA, SOUTHERN — Foreign relations — United States
AFRICA, SOUTHERN — History
AFRICA, SOUTHERN — Military relations — South Africa
AFRICA, SOUTHERN — Politics and government
AFRICA, SOUTHERN — Politics and government — Bibliography
AFRICA, SOUTHERN — Politics and government — 1975-
AFRICA, SOUTHERN — Social conditions
AFRICA, SOUTHERN — Social policy
AFRICA, SUB-SAHARAN — Armed Forces — Political activity
AFRICA, SUB-SAHARAN — Economic conditions — 1960-
AFRICA, SUB-SAHARAN — Economic conditions — 1960- — Bibliography
AFRICA, SUB-SAHARAN — Economic policy
AFRICA, SUB-SAHARAN — Economic policy — Bibliography
AFRICA, SUB-SAHARAN — Famines — Bibliography
AFRICA, SUB-SAHARAN — Politics and government
AFRICA, SUB-SAHARAN — Politics and government — Addresses, essays, lectures
AFRICA, SUB-SAHARAN — Politics and government — 1960-
AFRICA, SUB-SAHARAN — Population
AFRICA, SUB-SAHARAN — Population policy
AFRICA, SUB-SAHARAN — Economic policy
AFRICA, SUB-SARHARAN — Economic conditions — 1960-
AFRICA, WEST — Discovery and exploration
AFRICA, WEST — Economic integration
AFRICA, WEST — Economic integration — History
AFRICA, WEST — Economic policy
AFRICA, WEST — Foreign economic relations
AFRICA, WEST — History — To 1884
AFRICA, WEST — Kings and rulers — Folklore
AFRICA, WEST — Politics and government — 1960-
AFRICAN STUDENTS — Relations — United States
AFRICAN STUDENTS — Attitudes
AFRICANS — Sudan — Bibliography
AFRIKANERS — South Africa — Gamkaskloof Valley

AFRO-AMERICAN COLLEGE STUDENTS — Political activity — History — 20th century
AFRO-AMERICAN COMMUNISTS — History — Sources
AFRO-AMERICAN ENTERTAINERS — Biography
AFRO-AMERICAN FAMILIES
AFRO-AMERICAN FAMILIES — Bibliography
AFRO-AMERICAN FAMILIES — Case studies
AFRO-AMERICAN FAMILIES — History
AFRO-AMERICAN HISTORIANS — History — 20th century — Addresses, essays, lectures
AFRO-AMERICAN IRON AND STEEL WORKERS — Pennsylvania — History
AFRO-AMERICAN SCIENTISTS — United States
AFRO-AMERICAN SOCIOLOGISTS — United States — Biography
AFRO-AMERICAN SOLDIERS — Congresses
AFRO-AMERICAN SOLDIERS — Correspondence
AFRO-AMERICAN STUDENT MOVEMENTS
AFRO-AMERICAN STUDENT MOVEMENTS — New York (N.Y.) — Case studies
AFRO-AMERICAN WOMEN
AFRO-AMERICAN WOMEN — Employment — History
AFRO-AMERICAN WOMEN — History
AFRO-AMERICAN YOUTH — Employment — Congresses
AFRO-AMERICANS
AFRO-AMERICANS — Addresses, essays, lectures
AFRO-AMERICANS — Biography
AFRO-AMERICANS — Civil rights
AFRO-AMERICANS — Civil rights — Addresses, essays, lectures
AFRO-AMERICANS — Civil rights — Case studies
AFRO-AMERICANS — Civil rights — History
AFRO-AMERICANS — Civil rights — Alabama — Tuskegee
AFRO-AMERICANS — Civil rights — Illinois — Chicago
AFRO-AMERICANS — Economic conditions
AFRO-AMERICANS — Economic conditions — Bibliography
AFRO-AMERICANS — Education
AFRO-AMERICANS — Employment — Pennsylvania — History
AFRO-AMERICANS — Historiography — Addresses, essays, lectures
AFRO-AMERICANS — History
AFRO-AMERICANS — History — To 1863 — Sources
AFRO-AMERICANS — History — 1877-1964 — Sources
AFRO-AMERICANS — Legal status, laws, etc.
AFRO-AMERICANS — Politics and government
AFRO-AMERICANS — Politics and government — Addresses, essays, lectures
AFRO-AMERICANS — Politics and suffrage
AFRO-AMERICANS — Race identity
AFRO-AMERICANS — Social conditions — Bibliography
AFRO-AMERICANS — Social conditions — To 1964
AFRO-AMERICANS — Social conditions — 1964-
AFRO-AMERICANS — Social conditions — 1975-
AFRO-AMERICANS — Social life and customs
AFRO-AMERICANS — Statistics, Vital
AFRO-AMERICANS — Study and teaching (Higher) — United States — History — 20th century — Addresses, essays, lectures
AFRO-AMERICANS — Suffrage
AFRO-AMERICANS — Alabama — Tuskegee — Politics and government
AFRO-AMERICANS — Chicago
AFRO-AMERICANS — Georgia — History — 19th century
AFRO-AMERICANS — Georgia — Politics and suffrage
AFRO-AMERICANS — Sea Islands — History — 19th century
AFRO-AMERICANS — St. Louis
AFRO-AMERICANS — Tennessee — History — 19th century
AFRO-AMERICANS IN THE PERFORMING ARTS
AFRO-AMERICANS IN THE PERFORMING ARTS — Bibliography
AFRO-AMERICANS IN THE TELEVISION INDUSTRY — Bibliography
AFRO-AMERICANS, RELIGION
AGE
AGE AND EMPLOYMENT — Great Britain
AGE AND EMPLOYMENT — United States
AGE DISCRIMINATION IN EMPLOYMENT — Australia
AGE DISTRIBUTION (DEMOGRAPHY)
AGE DISTRIBUTION (DEMOGRAPHY) — Statistics
AGE DISTRIBUTION (DEMOGRAPHY) — Canada
AGE DISTRIBUTION (DEMOGRAPHY) — United States — Addresses, essays, lectures
AGE DISTRIBUTION (DEMOGRAPHY) — United States — Statistics
AGE FACTORS
AGE GROUPS — Classification
AGE GROUPS — Developing countries — Statistics
AGED — England — Liverpool (Merseyside) — Crimes against
AGED
AGED — Care — Great Britain
AGED — Care and hygiene
AGED — Care and hygiene — Great Britain
AGED — Care and hygiene — Wales
AGED — Employment
AGED — Employment — Australia
AGED — Employment — United States
AGED — Family relationships
AGED — Government policy — Great Britain
AGED — Health and hygiene — United States
AGED — Home care — France
AGED — Home care — Great Britain
AGED — Home care — United States
AGED — Hospital care — England — London
AGED — Institutional care — Great Britain
AGED — Medical care — Great Britain
AGED — Medical care — United States — Addresses, essays, lectures
AGED — Mental health services — Great Britain
AGED — Psychology
AGED — Services for — Great Britain
AGED — Services for — United States
AGED — Suicidal behavior — Bibliography
AGED — Australia — Economic conditions
AGED — Australia — Social conditions
AGED — Australia — Brisbane — Case studies
AGED — Australia — Sydney (N.S.W.) — Family relationships
AGED — Australia — Sydney (N.S.W.) — Social conditions
AGED — California — Los Angeles — Case studies
AGED — Canada
AGED — Canada — Social conditions
AGED — Denmark — Dwellings
AGED — Denmark — Odense — Services for
AGED — England — Hampshire — Mental health services
AGED — England — Sheffield (South Yorkshire) — Care and hygiene
AGED — England — Shropshire — Care and hygiene
AGED — England — West Sussex — Care and hygiene
AGED — Europe — Dwellings
AGED — France — Economic conditions
AGED — France — Social conditions
AGED — France — Normandy — Care and hygiene
AGED — Germany (West) — Political activity
AGED — Great Britain — Care and Hygiene
AGED — Great Britain — Dwellings
AGED — Great Britain — Dwellings — Quality control
AGED — Great Britain — Economic aspects
AGED — Great Britain — Family relationships
AGED — Great Britain — Services for
AGED — Great Britain — Social conditions
AGED — Great Britain — Statistics
AGED — Great Britain — Transportation
AGED — India — Social conditions
AGED — Ireland — Dublin (Dublin)
AGED — London — Chelsea — Dwellings
AGED — London — Kensington — Dwellings
AGED — Netherlands — Statistics
AGED — Oceania
AGED — Poland — Statistics
AGED — Scotland
AGED — South Asia — Social conditions
AGED — Spain — Political activity
AGED — Spain — Social conditions
AGED — United States
AGED — United States — Abuse of
AGED — United States — Abuse of — Bibliography
AGED — United States — Congresses
AGED — United States — Crimes against
AGED — United States — Drug use
AGED — United States — Dwellings
AGED — United States — Dwellings — Addresses, essays, lectures
AGED — United States — Dwellings — Addressses, essays, lectures
AGED — United States — Economic conditions
AGED — United States — Economic conditions — Addresses, essays, lectures
AGED — United States — Family relationships
AGED — United States — Family relationships — Addresses, essays, lectures
AGED — United States — Family relationships — History
AGED — United States — Interviews
AGED — United States — Social conditions
AGED — United States — Social conditions — Addresses, essays, lectures
AGED — United States — Statistics
AGED — United States — Statistics — Handbooks, manuals, etc
AGED — Wales — South Glamorgan
AGED — Wales — Torfaen (Gwent) — Dwellings
AGED — West Sussex — Dwellings — England
AGED MEN — United States
AGED OFFENDERS — United States
AGED OFFENDERS — United States — Case studies
AGED WOMEN
AGENCIA DE PUBLICIDAD DEL ESTADO (Peru) — Legal status, laws, etc.
AGGRESSION (INTERNATIONAL LAW)
AGGRESSIVENESS IN CHILDREN
AGGRESSIVENESS IN CHILDREN — Cross-cultural studies

AGGRESSIVENESS (PSYCHOLOGY)
AGGRESSIVENESS (PSYCHOLOGY) — Congresses
AGGRESSIVENESS (PSYCHOLOGY) — Testing
AGING
AGING — Psychological aspects
AGING — Social aspects
AGING — Social aspects — Addresses, essays, lectures
AGING — Social aspects — Canada
AGRESSIVENESS IN CHILDREN
AGRICULTURAL ASSISTANCE
AGRICULTURAL ASSISTANCE, AMERICAN
AGRICULTURAL ASSISTANCE, BRITISH — Africa
AGRICULTURAL ASSISTANCE, CANADIAN — Bibliography
AGRICULTURAL COLONIES — Legal status, laws, etc — Ecuador
AGRICULTURAL COLONIES — Legal status, laws, etc. — Ecuador
AGRICULTURAL COLONIES — Big Sioux River Valley (S.D. and Iowa) — History — 19th century
AGRICULTURAL CONSERVATION
AGRICULTURAL COOPERATIVE CREDIT ASSOCIATIONS — India
AGRICULTURAL CREDIT — Addresses, essays, lectures
AGRICULTURAL CREDIT — Colombia
AGRICULTURAL CREDIT — India
AGRICULTURAL CREDIT — Peru
AGRICULTURAL CREDIT — Romania
AGRICULTURAL CREDIT — Sierra Leone
(AGRICULTURAL) DEVELOPMENT PROJECTS
AGRICULTURAL DEVELOPMENT PROJECTS — Developing countries
AGRICULTURAL DEVELOPMENT PROJECTS — Evaluation — Statistical methods
AGRICULTURAL DEVELOPMENT PROJECTS — Management — Statistical methods
AGRICULTURAL DEVELOPMENT PROJECTS — Political aspects — Africa
AGRICULTURAL DEVELOPMENT PROJECTS — Africa
AGRICULTURAL DEVELOPMENT PROJECTS — Developing countries
AGRICULTURAL DEVELOPMENT PROJECTS — Developing countries — Cost effectiveness
AGRICULTURAL DEVELOPMENT PROJECTS — Sierra Leone
AGRICULTURAL DEVELOPMENT PROJECTS — Taiwan
AGRICULTURAL ECOLOGY
AGRICULTURAL ECOLOGY — Africa
AGRICULTURAL ECOLOGY — Developing countries
AGRICULTURAL ECOLOGY — Great Britain
AGRICULTURAL ECOLOGY — Kenya
AGRICULTURAL ECOLOGY — Tanzania
AGRICULTURAL EDUCATION — Developing countries
AGRICULTURAL ESTIMATING AND REPORTING
AGRICULTURAL ESTIMATING AND REPORTING — Taiwan
AGRICULTURAL EXTENSION WORK
AGRICULTURAL EXTENSION WORK — Economic aspects
AGRICULTURAL EXTENSION WORK — Asia — Congresses
AGRICULTURAL EXTENSION WORK — Developing countries
AGRICULTURAL EXTENSION WORK — Developing countries — Evaluation
AGRICULTURAL EXTENSION WORK — Puerto Rico
AGRICULTURAL GEOGRAPHY — England — History

AGRICULTURAL HOLDINGS BILL 1983-84
AGRICULTURAL IMPLEMENTS — Hungary — Economic aspects
AGRICULTURAL INDUSTRIES — Government policy — Colombia
AGRICULTURAL INDUSTRIES — Developing countries — Case studies
AGRICULTURAL INDUSTRIES — Soviet Union
AGRICULTURAL INDUSTRIES — Soviet Union — Dictionaries
AGRICULTURAL INDUSTRIES — Soviet Union — Management
AGRICULTURAL INNOVATIONS
AGRICULTURAL INNOVATIONS — Africa, Sub-Saharan
AGRICULTURAL INNOVATIONS — Asia — Congresses
AGRICULTURAL INNOVATIONS — India — Punjab
AGRICULTURAL LABORERS — Government policy — Developing countries — Case studies
AGRICULTURAL LABORERS — Argentina — History — 20th century
AGRICULTURAL LABORERS — Byelorussian S.S.R.
AGRICULTURAL LABORERS — Developing countries
AGRICULTURAL LABORERS — Developing countries — Case studies
AGRICULTURAL LABORERS — France — Statistics
AGRICULTURAL LABORERS — India
AGRICULTURAL LABORERS — India — Hyderabad (State) — History
AGRICULTURAL LABORERS — Indonesia — Jawa Tengah
AGRICULTURAL LABORERS — Mexico
AGRICULTURAL LABORERS — Mexico — History — Congresses
AGRICULTURAL LABORERS — Soviet Union — History
AGRICULTURAL LABORERS — Spain — Andalusia
AGRICULTURAL LABORERS — United States — Congresses
AGRICULTURAL LAWS AND LEGISLATION — Ecuador
AGRICULTURAL LAWS AND LEGISLATION — European Economic Community countries
AGRICULTURAL LAWS AND LEGISLATION — Peru
AGRICULTURAL MACHINERY — Hungary — Economic aspects
AGRICULTURAL MARKETING BILL 1982-83
AGRICULTURAL POLICY
AGRICULTURAL POLICY — Mexico
AGRICULTURAL PRICES — Government policy — Bolivia
AGRICULTURAL PRICES — Government policy — Developing countries — Congresses
AGRICULTURAL PRICES — Government policy — Philippines
AGRICULTURAL PRICES — Government policy — United States
AGRICULTURAL PRICES — France — Statistics
AGRICULTURAL PRICES — Great Britain
AGRICULTURAL PRICES — Poland
AGRICULTURAL PROCESSING INDUSTRIES — France — Energy consumption — Statistics
AGRICULTURAL PROCESSING INDUSTRIES — France — Statistics
AGRICULTURAL PROCESSING INDUSTRIES — Soviet Union
AGRICULTURAL PRODUCTIVITY
AGRICULTURAL PRODUCTIVITY — Africa
AGRICULTURAL PRODUCTIVITY — Africa, Sub-Saharan

AGRICULTURAL PRODUCTIVITY — Africa, Sub-Saharan — Congresses
AGRICULTURAL PRODUCTIVITY — China — Hunan Province — History
AGRICULTURAL PRODUCTIVITY — Communist countries
AGRICULTURAL PRODUCTIVITY — Communist countries — Case studies
AGRICULTURAL PRODUCTIVITY — Denmark
AGRICULTURAL PRODUCTIVITY — India — Bihar
AGRICULTURAL PRODUCTIVITY — India — Orissa
AGRICULTURAL PRODUCTIVITY — India — Uttar Pradesh
AGRICULTURAL PRODUCTIVITY — India — West Bengal
AGRICULTURAL PRODUCTIVITY — Nepal
AGRICULTURAL PRODUCTIVITY — Philippines
AGRICULTURAL RESOURCES
AGRICULTURAL SOCIETIES — Poland
AGRICULTURAL SYSTEMS
AGRICULTURAL SYSTEMS — Research
AGRICULTURAL SYSTEMS — Tropics
AGRICULTURAL SYSTEMS — Africa, Sub-Saharan
AGRICULTURE — Thailand — Statistics
AGRICULTURE — Bibliography
AGRICULTURE — Economic aspects
AGRICULTURE — Economic aspects — Northwest, Pacific — History
AGRICULTURE — Economic aspects — Africa, Southern
AGRICULTURE — Economic aspects — Africa, Sub-Saharan
AGRICULTURE — Economic aspects — Argentina
AGRICULTURE — Economic aspects — Argentina — History
AGRICULTURE — Economic aspects — Australia
AGRICULTURE — Economic aspects — Bangladesh
AGRICULTURE — Economic aspects — Bangladesh — History — 20th century
AGRICULTURE — Economic aspects — Bolivia
AGRICULTURE — Economic aspects — Burkina Faso
AGRICULTURE — Economic aspects — Canada
AGRICULTURE — Economic aspects — Congo (Brazzaville)
AGRICULTURE — Economic aspects — Denmark
AGRICULTURE — Economic aspects — Denmark — Mathematical models
AGRICULTURE — Economic aspects — Developing countries — Congresses
AGRICULTURE — Economic aspects — England — History
AGRICULTURE — Economic aspects — Europe — Societies, etc.
AGRICULTURE — Economic aspects — European Economic Community Countries
AGRICULTURE — Economic aspects — European Economic Commynity countries — Mathematical models
AGRICULTURE — Economic aspects — Fiji
AGRICULTURE — Economic aspects — France
AGRICULTURE — Economic aspects — Great Britain
AGRICULTURE — Economic aspects — India
AGRICULTURE — Economic aspects — India — Case studies
AGRICULTURE — Economic aspects — India — Punjab
AGRICULTURE — Economic aspects — India — Rānchī — Case studies

AGRICULTURE — Economic aspects — India — West Bengal — History — 20th century
AGRICULTURE — Economic aspects — Japan
AGRICULTURE — Economic aspects — Japan — History
AGRICULTURE — Economic aspects — Jordan
AGRICULTURE — Economic aspects — Mali
AGRICULTURE — Economic aspects — Nepal
AGRICULTURE — Economic aspects — Nicaragua
AGRICULTURE — Economic aspects — Nigeria
AGRICULTURE — Economic aspects — Pakistan
AGRICULTURE — Economic aspects — Peru
AGRICULTURE — Economic aspects — Portugal
AGRICULTURE — Economic aspects — Romania
AGRICULTURE — Economic aspects — South Africa — History
AGRICULTURE — Economic aspects — South Australia
AGRICULTURE — Economic aspects — South Australia — Research
AGRICULTURE — Economic aspects — Southern States
AGRICULTURE — Economic aspects — Soviet Union
AGRICULTURE — Economic aspects — Soviet Union — Dictionaries
AGRICULTURE — Economic aspects — Spain
AGRICULTURE — Economic aspects — Spain — Andalucia
AGRICULTURE — Economic aspects — Sudan
AGRICULTURE — Economic aspects — Swaziland
AGRICULTURE — Economic aspects — Taiwan
AGRICULTURE — Economic aspects — United States
AGRICULTURE — Economic aspects — United States — History — 19th century
AGRICULTURE — Research — Economic aspects
AGRICULTURE — Research — Government policy
AGRICULTURE — Research — International cooperation
AGRICULTURE — Research — On-farm
AGRICULTURE — Research — Philippines
AGRICULTURE — Research — Syria
AGRICULTURE — Research — Africa, Sub-Saharan
AGRICULTURE — Research — Asia — Congresses
AGRICULTURE — Research — Burkina Faso
AGRICULTURE — Research — Burma
AGRICULTURE — Research — Chile
AGRICULTURE — Research — Cuba
AGRICULTURE — Research — Developing countries — Evaluation
AGRICULTURE — Research — Ecuador
AGRICULTURE — Research — Peru
AGRICULTURE — Research — Thailand
AGRICULTURE — Social aspects — United States — Congresses
AGRICULTURE — Statistical methods
AGRICULTURE — Taxation — Belgium
AGRICULTURE — Africa, sub-Saharan — Addresses, essays, lectures
AGRICULTURE — Albania
AGRICULTURE — Argentina
AGRICULTURE — Argentina — History — 1943-
AGRICULTURE — Asia
AGRICULTURE — Australia
AGRICULTURE — Australia — Finance
AGRICULTURE — Australia — Tasmania
AGRICULTURE — Bangladesh — Economic aspects
AGRICULTURE — Botswana — Statistics
AGRICULTURE — Brazil — Statistics
AGRICULTURE — Burkina Faso
AGRICULTURE — Canada
AGRICULTURE — Colombia — Statistics
AGRICULTURE — Czechoslovakia — History
AGRICULTURE — Denmark — History
AGRICULTURE — Developing countries — Addresses, essays, lectures
AGRICULTURE — Developing countries — Technology transfer — Evaluation
AGRICULTURE — England — Bedfordshire
AGRICULTURE — European Economic Community Countries
AGRICULTURE — European Economic Community countries
AGRICULTURE — European Economic Community countries — Accounting
AGRICULTURE — Finland
AGRICULTURE — Finland — Accounting
AGRICULTURE — Finland — Statistics
AGRICULTURE — France
AGRICULTURE — France — Statistics
AGRICULTURE — Great Britain
AGRICULTURE — Great Britain — Technological innovations
AGRICULTURE — Guadeloupe — Statistics
AGRICULTURE — Hungary
AGRICULTURE — India — Statistics
AGRICULTURE — Ireland — History
AGRICULTURE — Italy — Statistics
AGRICULTURE — Japan
AGRICULTURE — Jordan — Statistics
AGRICULTURE — Malawi — Statistics
AGRICULTURE — Mexico
AGRICULTURE — New Caledonia — Statistics
AGRICULTURE — New Zealand — Statistics
AGRICULTURE — Nigeria — Statistics
AGRICULTURE — Oregon — History
AGRICULTURE — Pakistan
AGRICULTURE — Portugal
AGRICULTURE — Puerto Rico
AGRICULTURE — Russian S.F.S.R. — Moscow — Statistics
AGRICULTURE — Sahel — Congresses
AGRICULTURE — San Marino — Statistics
AGRICULTURE — Scotland
AGRICULTURE — Sierra Leone
AGRICULTURE — Soviet Union — Statistics
AGRICULTURE — Spain
AGRICULTURE — Spain — History
AGRICULTURE — Spain — History — 19th century
AGRICULTURE — Spain — Statistics
AGRICULTURE — Spain — El Ejido
AGRICULTURE — Sri Lanka — Statistics
AGRICULTURE — Syria — Statistics
AGRICULTURE — Taiwan
AGRICULTURE — Taiwan — Planning
AGRICULTURE — Tanzania
AGRICULTURE — Trinidad and Tobago — Statistics
AGRICULTURE — Wales — Clwyd
AGRICULTURE — Zaire
AGRICULTURE — Zaire — Economic aspects
AGRICULTURE AND POLITICS — Germany (West)
AGRICULTURE AND POLITICS — South Africa — History
AGRICULTURE AND STATE
AGRICULTURE AND STATE — Congresses
AGRICULTURE AND STATE — Africa
AGRICULTURE AND STATE — Africa, Sub-Saharan
AGRICULTURE AND STATE — Africa, Sub-Saharan — Congresses
AGRICULTURE AND STATE — Argentina
AGRICULTURE AND STATE — Argentina — History
AGRICULTURE AND STATE — Asia — Congresses
AGRICULTURE AND STATE — Canada
AGRICULTURE AND STATE — China — Hunan Province — History
AGRICULTURE AND STATE — Colombia — Addresses, essays, lectures
AGRICULTURE AND STATE — Developing countries
AGRICULTURE AND STATE — Egypt
AGRICULTURE AND STATE — Ethiopia
AGRICULTURE AND STATE — Europe, Eastern
AGRICULTURE AND STATE — European Economic Community countries
AGRICULTURE AND STATE — European Economic Community countries — Sources — Bibliography
AGRICULTURE AND STATE — France
AGRICULTURE AND STATE — Germany — History — 20th century
AGRICULTURE AND STATE — Ghana
AGRICULTURE AND STATE — Great Britain
AGRICULTURE AND STATE — Honduras
AGRICULTURE AND STATE — Hungary
AGRICULTURE AND STATE — India
AGRICULTURE AND STATE — India — Haryana
AGRICULTURE AND STATE — India — Punjab
AGRICULTURE AND STATE — Jordan
AGRICULTURE AND STATE — Kazakh S.S.R.
AGRICULTURE AND STATE — Lithuania
AGRICULTURE AND STATE — Mexico
AGRICULTURE AND STATE — Mongolia (Mongolian People's Republic)
AGRICULTURE AND STATE — Near East
AGRICULTURE AND STATE — Nigeria
AGRICULTURE AND STATE — Organisation for Economic Co-operation and Development countries
AGRICULTURE AND STATE — Pakistan
AGRICULTURE AND STATE — Panama
AGRICULTURE AND STATE — Portugal
AGRICULTURE AND STATE — Puerto Rico
AGRICULTURE AND STATE — Russsian S.F.S.R. — Ural Mountains region
AGRICULTURE AND STATE — Soviet Union
AGRICULTURE AND STATE — Soviet Union — History
AGRICULTURE AND STATE — Spain
AGRICULTURE AND STATE — Spain — Andalucia
AGRICULTURE AND STATE — Tanzania
AGRICULTURE AND STATE — United States
AGRICULTURE AND STATE — United States — History
AGRICULTURE AND STATE — Uzbek S.S.R.
AGRICULTURE AND STATE — Zaire
AGRICULTURE, COOPERATIVE
AGRICULTURE, COOPERATIVE — Byelorussian S.S.R.
AGRICULTURE, COOPERATIVE — Developing countries — Finance
AGRICULTURE, COOPERATIVE — European Economic Community countries
AGRICULTURE, COOPERATIVE — Mongolia (Mongolian People's Republic)
AGRICULTURE, COOPERATIVE — Soviet Union — History
AGRICULTURE, PREHISTORIC — Congresses

AGRICULTUREAL DEVELOPMENT PROJECTS — Developing countries — Evaluation
AGRICULTUREOFF. PUBNS. — Employment — European Economic Community countries 986
AGUARUNA INDIANS — Ethnobotany
AGUARUNA INDIANS — Magic
AGUARUNA INDIANS — Religion and mythology
AIDS (DISEASE) — Congresses
AIDS (DISEASE) — Political aspects — Great Britain
AIDS (DISEASE) — Political aspects — United States
AIDS (DISEASE) — Psychological aspects
AIDS (DISEASE) — Psychological aspects — Congresses
AIDS (DISEASE) — See Acquired immune deficiency syndrome
AIDS (DISEASE) — Social aspects
AIDS (DISEASE) — Social aspects — United States
AIDS (DISEASE) — Transmission
AIDS (DISEASE — Developing countries
AIDS (DISEASE) — Europe
AIDS (DISEASE) — Great Britain — Prevention
AIR — Pollution
AIR — Pollution — Government policy — Europe
AIR — Pollution — Law and legislation
AIR — Pollution — Law and legislation — Great Britain
AIR — Pollution — Physiological effect
AIR — Pollution — England — London — History
AIR — Pollution — England — London — Statistics
AIR — Pollution — France
AIR — Pollution — Germany (West)
AIR — Pollution — Great Britain
AIR — Pollution — Italy
AIR — Pollution — Japan
AIR — Pollution — Organisation for Economic Co-operation and Development countries
AIR — Pollution — Scandinavia
AIR — Pollution — Soviet Union
AIR — Pollution — United States
AIR — Pollution
AIR LINES — Government policy — Canada
AIR LINES — Government policy — Canada — History
AIR LINES — Management
AIR LINES — Canada — History
AIR LINES — Great Britain — Finance — Statistics
AIR LINES — Great Britain — Statistics
AIR LINES — Ireland — History
AIR MAIL SERVICE — Great Britain — Statistics
AIR POWER
AIR QUALITY — Statistics
AIR QUALITY AND MANAGEMENT — Great Britain
AIR QUALITY MANAGEMENT — International cooperation
AIR TRAVEL — Great Britain — Statistics
AIR-TURBINES — European Economic Community countries
AIRCRAFT INDUSTRY — Corrupt practices
AIRCRAFT INDUSTRY — Technological innovations
AIRCRAFT INDUSTRY — United States
AIRPORTS — Employees — Scotland
AIRPORTS — Law and legislation — Great Britain
AIRPORTS — England — Location
AIRPORTS — England — Price policy
AIRPORTS — Great Britain — Statistics
AIRPORTS BILL 1985-86
AIT ATTA (BERBER TRIBE)
AKADEMIIA NAUK UKRAINSKOI SSR. Institut ekonomiki

AKAN POETRY
AL-ḤIZB AL-SHUYŪʻĪ AL-ʻIRĀQĪ
AL - QADHDHʻAFʻI, MUʻAMMAR
AL-QADHDHAFI, MUʻAMMAR
ALABAMA — Politics and government
ALASKA — Economic conditions — Addresses, essays, lectures
ALASKA — History — To 1867
ALASKA HIGHWAY — History — Congresses
ALBA, FERNANDO ALVAREZ DE TOLEDO, duque de
ALBANIA — Economic policy — Congresses
ALBANIA — Foreign relations
ALBANIA — Foreign relations — 1944-
ALBANIA — Foreign relations — China
ALBANIA — Politics and government
ALBANIA — Population
ALBANIA — Relations — Yugoslavia
ALBANIANS — Yugoslavia
ALBANY (N.Y.) — Industries — History — 19th century
ALBERTA — Apropriations and expenditures
ALBERTA — Economic conditions — Addresses, essays, lectures
ALBERTA — Economic conditions — Statistics
ALBERTA — Politics and government
ALBERTA. Bureau of Statistics
ALBERTA. Treasury
ALBERTA AGENCY FOR INTERNATIONAL DEVELOPMENT
ALCHEMY
ALCOHOL — Physiological effect
ALCOHOL DRINKING — dictionaries
ALCOHOL FUEL INDUSTRY — Brazil
ALCOHOLICS — Legal status, laws, etc — Australia
ALCOHOLICS — Rehabilitation — Australia
ALCOHOLICS — Middle Atlantic States — Case studies
ALCOHOLICS ANONYMOUS — Case studies
ALCOHOLISM
ALCOHOLISM — Addresses, essays, lectures
ALCOHOLISM — Law and legislation
ALCOHOLISM — Study and teaching — England — West Country
ALCOHOLISM — Treatment
ALCOHOLISM — Denmark
ALCOHOLISM — France — Statistical methods
ALCOHOLISM — France — Statistics
ALCOHOLISM — Great Britain
ALCOHOLISM — United States — Prevention
ALCOHOLISM AND EMPLOYMENT
ALEMÁN, MIGUEL
ALGEBRA, ABSTRACT
ALGEBRAS, LINEAR
ALGERIA — Emigration and immigration
ALGERIA — Foreign relations — France
ALGERIA — Foreign relations — Soviet Union
ALGERIA — History — Dictionaries
ALGERIA — History — Revolution, 1954-1962
ALGERIA — History — 1962-
ALGERIA — Population — Statistics
ALGERIA — Social conditions
ALGERIA — Statistics
ALGERIANS — France
ALGERIANS — France — Congress
ALGERIANS — France — Paris
ALGORITHMS
ALICANTE (SPAIN) — Politics and government
ALICANTE (SPAIN: PROVINCE) — Economic conditions
ALIEN LABOR — Government policy — France
ALIEN LABOR — Government policy — Germany (West)

ALIEN LABOR — Social aspects — Denmark
ALIEN LABOR — Denmark
ALIEN LABOR — Europe
ALIEN LABOR — Europe — Congresses
ALIEN LABOR — Germany — Government policy
ALIEN LABOR — Germany — History
ALIEN LABOR — Germany — History — 19th century
ALIEN LABOR — Germany — History — 20th century
ALIEN LABOR — Germany (West)
ALIEN LABOR — Great Britain — History
ALIEN LABOR CRIMINALS — Netherlands
ALIEN LABOR, HAITIAN — Dominican Republic
ALIEN LABOR, ITALIAN — Bibliography
ALIEN LABOR, MEXICAN — California, Northern
ALIEN LABOR, PHILIPPINE
ALIEN LABOR, TURKISH — Germany (West)
ALIEN PROPERTY
ALIENATION (PHILOSOPHY)
ALIENATION (SOCIAL PSYCHOLOGY)
ALIENATION (SOCIAL PSYCHOLOGY) — France
ALIENS — Legal status, laws, etc.
ALIENS — France — Public opinion
ALIENS — Germany (West)
ALIENS — Great Britain — History
ALIENS, ILLEGAL — Nigeria
ALIENS, ILLEGAL — United States
ALIENS, ILLEGAL — United States — Bibliography
ALKALI INDUSTRY AND TRADE — Energy conservation
ALKALI INDUSTRY AND TRADE — Taiwan
ALLIANCES
ALLIANCES — Psychological aspects
ALLIED HEALTH PERSONNEL — Legal status, laws, etc. — Commonwealth of Nations
ALMIRALL, VALENTÍ
ALSACE (FRANCE) — Population — Statistics
ALTERNATIVE MEDICINE See Therapeutic systems
ALTRUISM
ALUMINIUM INDUSTRY AND TRADE — European Economic Community countries
ALUMINIUM INDUSTRY AND TRADE — Ghana
AMALGAMATED CLOTHING AND TEXTILE WORKERS UNION — Case studies
AMALGAMATED ENGINEERING UNION
AMALGAMATED SOCIETY OF ENGINEERS
AMALGAMATED UNION OF ENGINEERING WORKERS
AMALGAMATED UNION OF ENGINEERING WORKERS. Technical, Administrative and Supervisory Section
AMALGAMATED UNION OF OPERATIVE BAKERS, CONFECTIONERS AND ALLIED WORKERS
AMBASSADORS — Finland — Biography
AMBASSADORS — United States — Biography
AMBIGUITY
AMERICA — Emigration and immigration — Congresses
AMERICA — Foreign economic relations — Spain — Valencia — History — 18th century
AMERICAN DILEMMA
AMERICAN FEDERATION OF LABOR
AMERICAN FEDERATION OF LABOR — History
AMERICAN JEWISH COMMITTEE

AMERICAN LITERATURE — 20th century
AMERICAN LITERATURE — 20th century — History and criticism
AMERICAN MISSIONARY ASSOCIATION
AMERICAN NATIONAL RED CROSS — History
AMERICAN PROSE LITERATURE — Colonial period, ca. 1600-1775 — History and criticism
AMERICAN PROSE LITERATURE — Puritan authors — History and criticism
AMERICAN TELEPHONE AND TELEGRAPH COMPANY
AMERICAN TELEPHONE AND TELEGRAPH COMPANY — Reorganization
AMERICANISMS — Dictionaries
AMERICANIZATION
AMERICANS — Employment — Nicaragua
AMERICANS — Foreign countries — Australia
AMERICANS — Nicaragua
AMISTAD (Schooner)
AMMONIA INDUSTRY — Great Britain — Employees
AMUESHA INDIANS — Religion and mythology
AMUSEMENTS — Europe — History
ANAA (TUAMOTU ISLANDS) — Population — Statistics
ANALYSIS OF VARIANCE — Mathematical models
ANALYSIS (PHILOSOPHY)
ANARCHISM
ANARCHISM — History
ANARCHISM — Spain — History
ANARCHISM AND ANARCHISTS
ANARCHISM AND ANARCHISTS — Bibliography
ANARCHISM AND ANARCHISTS — History — 19th century
ANARCHISM AND ANARCHISTS — Argentina
ANARCHISM AND ANARCHISTS — China
ANARCHISM AND ANARCHISTS — England — London
ANARCHISM AND ANARCHISTS — France — History
ANARCHISM AND ANARCHISTS — Great Britain
ANARCHISM AND ANARCHISTS — Italy
ANARCHISM AND ANARCHISTS — Soviet Union
ANARCHISM AND ANARCHISTS — Soviet Union — History
ANARCHISM AND ANARCHISTS — Spain
ANARCHISM AND ANARCHISTS — Spain — Aragon — History
ANARCHISTS — Germany (West) — Biography
ANARCHISTS — Great Britain — Addresses, essays, lectures
ANAS, MOHAMMAD
ANC See African National Congress
ANDALUCIA (SPAIN) — Economic ploicy
ANDALUSIA (SPAIN) — Biography
ANDALUSIA (SPAIN) — Civilization
ANDALUSIA (SPAIN) — Economic conditions
ANDALUSIA (SPAIN) — History
ANDALUSIA (SPAIN) — Politics and government
ANDALUSIA (SPAIN) — Social conditions
ANDAMAN AND NICOBAR ISLANDS (INDIA) — Population — Statistics
ANDES REGION — Rural conditions
ANDES REGION — Social conditions — Addresses, essays, lectures
ANDHRA PRADESH (INDIA) — Economic conditions — Maps
ANDHRA PRADESH (INDIA) — Social conditions — Maps
ANDORRA — Economic conditions — Statistics
ANDORRA — Social conditions — Statistics
ANDREEV, A. A.
ANDREEVA, M. F.
ANGLICAN CHURCH OF CANADA — History
ANGLICAN COMMUNION — England — History — 16th century
ANGLICAN COMMUNION — England — History — 17th century
ANGLO AMERICAN CORPORATION OF SOUTH AFRICA — History
ANGLO-FRENCH WAR, 1755-1763 — Economic aspects — France
ANGLO-SAXONS
ANGOLA — History — Dictionaries
ANGOLA — History — Revolution, 1961-1975
ANGOLA — History — Civil War, 1975-
ANGOLA — Politics and government
ANGOLA — Politics and government — 1961-1975
ANGRY BRIGADE
ANIMAL BEHAVIOR
ANIMAL BEHAVIOR — Measurement
ANIMAL COMMUNICATION
ANIMAL INDUSTRY — Bibliography
ANIMAL INDUSTRY — China
ANIMAL INDUSTRY — Developing countries — Forecasting
ANIMAL INDUSTRY — Latin America
ANIMAL INDUSTRY — New Caledonia — Statistics
ANIMAL INTELLIGENCE — Addresses, essays, lectures
ANIMAL PRODUCTS — Canada
ANIMAL PRODUCTS — United States
ANIMAL TRACTION — Africa, Sub-Saharan
ANIMALS, PROSECUTION AND PUNISHMENT OF — Europe — History
ANIMALS, TREATMENT OF
ANIMALS, TREATMENT OF — England — History
ANISEMITISM — United States — History — Addresses, essays, lectures
ANNUITIES
ANSCHLUSS MOVEMENT, 1918-1938
ANSELLS BREWERY STRIKE, GREAT BRITAIN, 1981
ANTARCTIC REGIONS
ANTARCTIC REGIONS — Discovery and exploration — Congresses
ANTARCTIC REGIONS — International status
ANTARCTIC REGIONS — International status — Congresses
ANTENUPTIAL CONTRACTS — United States
ANTHROPO-GEOGRAPHY
ANTHROPO-GEOGRAPHY — Addresses, essays, lectures
ANTHROPO-GEOGRAPHY — Dictionaries
ANTHROPO-GEOGRAPHY — Alberta — Addresses, essays, lectures
ANTHROPO-GEOGRAPHY — Amazon Valley
ANTHROPO-GEOGRAPHY — Europe
ANTHROPO-GEOGRAPHY — France
ANTHROPO-GEOGRAPHY — Great Britain
ANTHROPO-GEOGRAPHY — Nigeria
ANTHROPO-GEOGRAPHY — United States
ANTHROPOLOGICAL ETHICS
ANTHROPOLOGICAL LINGUISTICS
ANTHROPOLOGY
ANTHROPOLOGY — Dictionaries
ANTHROPOLOGY — History — Congresses
ANTHROPOLOGY — Philosophy
ANTHROPOLOGY — Philosophy — Congresses
ANTHROPOLOGY — Research — Finance — Directories
ANTHROPOLOGY — Research grants — United States — Directories
ANTHROPOLOGY, CULTURAL — Nepal
ANTHROPOLOGY-GEOGRAPHY — Great Britain
ANTI-APARTHEID MOVEMENTS — Biography
ANTI-CATHOLICISM — Scotland — History
ANTI-COMMUNIST MOVEMENTS — France — History
ANTI-COMMUNIST MOVEMENTS — Soviet Union
ANTI-COMMUNIST MOVEMENTS — United States — History
ANTI-COMMUNIST MOVEMENTS — United States — History — 20th century
ANTI-COMMUNIST MOVEMENTS — Yugoslavia
ANTI-FASCIST MOVEMENTS — Europe
ANTI-FASCIST MOVEMENTS — Hungary
ANTI-FASCIST MOVEMENTS — Spain — Catalonia
ANTI-NAZI MOVEMENT
ANTI-NAZI MOVEMENT — Germany
ANTI-NAZI MOVEMENT — Germany (West) — Munich
ANTI-SATELLITE WEAPONS — Soviet Union
ANTI-SATELLITE WEAPONS — United States
ANTIGUA AND BARBUDA — Economic conditions
ANTIGUA AND BARBUDA — Economic policy
ANTIMISSILE MISSILES
ANTINUCLEAR MOVEMENT
ANTINUCLEAR MOVEMENT — Australia
ANTINUCLEAR MOVEMENT — Germany (West)
ANTINUCLEAR MOVEMENT — Great Britain
ANTINUCLEAR MOVEMENT — United States
ANTINUCLEAR MOVEMENT — Washington (State)
ANTINUCLEAR MOVEMENT — Washington (State) — Addresses, essays, lectures
ANTINUCLEAR MOVEMENTS — Great Britain
ANTISEMITISM
ANTISEMITISM — History — 20th century
ANTISEMITISM — Argentina — History — 20th century
ANTISEMITISM — Canada
ANTISEMITISM — France
ANTISEMITISM — France — Biography
ANTISEMITISM — Germany — Congresses
ANTISEMITISM — Germany — History — 19th century
ANTISEMITISM — Soviet Union
ANTITRUST LAW — Economic aspects — United States
ANTITRUST LAW — Canada
ANTITRUST LAW — European Economic Community countries
ANTITRUST LAW — Great Britain
ANTITRUST LAW — United States
ANXIETY IN CHILDREN
APARTHEID
APARTHEID — Congresses
APARTHEID — Economic aspects — Namibia
APARTHEID — Economic aspects — South Africa
APARTHEID — Legal status, laws, etc. — South Africa
APARTHEID — Religious aspects
APARTHEID — Religious aspects — Christianity
APARTHEID — South Africa

APARTHEID — South Africa — Bibliography
APARTHEID — South Africa — History
APARTHEID — South Africa — Religious aspects — Catholic Church
APARTMENT HOUSES — Law and legislation — Great Britain
APARTMENT HOUSES — England — London
APPALACHIAN REGION — Economic conditions
APPALACHIAN REGION — Social conditions
APPELLATE PROCEDURE — European Economic Community Countries
APPETITE DISORDERS
APPLE — Canada — Marketing
APPLIED ANTHROPOLOGY
APPLIED ANTHROPOLOGY — Addresses, essays, lectures
APPLIED ANTHROPOLOGY — Case studies
APPRENTICES — France — Champagne-Ardenne
APPRENTICES — United States — History
AQUACULTURE — Waste disposal
AQUITAINE BASIN (FRANCE) — Economic policy
AQUITAINE BASIN (FRANCE) — Politics and government
AQUITAINE (FRANCE) — Politics and government
ARAB AMERICANS — History
ARAB COUNTRIES — Foreign economic relations — United States — Addresses, essays, lectures
ARAB COUNTRIES — Foreign relations — Soviet Union — History — 20th century
ARAB COUNTRIES — Intellectual life
ARAB COUNTRIES — Politics and government
ARAB COUNTRIES — Politics and government — 1945-
ARAB COUNTRIES — Population
ARAB COUNTRIES — Relations — Egypt
ARAB COUNTRIES — Social conditions
ARABIAN PENINSULA — Commerce — History
ARABIAN PENINSULAR — Economic conditions
ARABIAN PENINSULAR — Economic policy
ARABIAN PENINSULAR — Politics and government
ARABIC LANGUAGE — Addresses, Forms of
ARABIC LANGUAGE — Dialects — Egypt
ARABIC LANGUAGE — Social aspects — Egypt
ARABISM
ARABS
ARABS — History
ARABS — Social life and customs
ARABS — Africa, East — History — 19th century
ARABS — Australia — Public opinion
ARABS — Sahara — History
ARABS — Tanzania — Zanzibar — History — 19th century
ARAFAT, YASIR
ARAGON (SPAIN) — Economic conditions
ARAGON (SPAIN) — Economic policy
ARAGON (SPAIN) — History — Autonomy and Independence movements
ARAGON (SPAIN) — Politics and government
ARAPESH TRIBE — Religion
ARBEJDERNES OPLYSNINGSFORBUND
ARBITRAGE
ARBITRATION AND AWARD — England
ARBITRATION AND AWARD, INTERNATIONAL
ARBITRATION, INDUSTRIAL — Australia
ARBITRATION, INDUSTRIAL — United States
ARBITRATION, INDUSTRIAL — United States — Congresses
ARBITRATION, INTERNATIONAL
ARCHAEOLOGISTS — Biography
ARCHITECTS — Germany (West) — Taxation
ARCHITECTURE — Environmental aspects — United States
ARCHITECTURE — Human factors
ARCHITECTURE — Indian — Lucknow — History
ARCHITECTURE — United States — Human factors
ARCHITECTURE AND SOCIETY — United States
ARCHITECTURE AND THE AGED — Europe
ARCHITECTURE, INDUSTRIAL — Great Britain
ARCHITECTURE, MODERN — 19th century — Austria — Vienna
ARCHITECTURE, MODERN — 19th century — England — London
ARCHITECTURE, MODERN — 19th century — France — Paris
ARCHITECTURE, MODERN — 20th century — Austria — Vienna
ARCHITECTURE, MODERN — 20th century — England — London
ARCHITECTURE, MODERN — 20th century — France — Paris
ARCHITECTURE, MODERN — 20th century — Great Britain
ARCHITECTURE, SCOTTISH — History — 20th century
ARCHITECTURE, VICTORIAN — England
ARCHIVES — Administration — Addresses, essays, lectures
ARCHIVES — Data processing
ARCHIVES — Dictionaries — Polyglot
ARCHIVES — Law and legislation — Great Britain
ARCHIVES — Reference services
ARCHIVES — United States — Administration — Addresses, essays, lectures
ARCHTECTURE, MODERN — 19th century — Great Britain
ARCTIC REGIONS
ARENDT, HANNAH
ARGENTINA — Armed Forces — Appropriations and expenditures
ARGENTINA — Boundaries
ARGENTINA — Boundaries — Chile
ARGENTINA — Census, 1980
ARGENTINA — Commerce
ARGENTINA — Commerce — Statistics
ARGENTINA — Defenses
ARGENTINA — Economic conditions
ARGENTINA — Economic conditions — Statistics
ARGENTINA — Economic conditions — 1918-
ARGENTINA — Economic conditions — 1918- — Bibliography
ARGENTINA — Economic conditions — 1945-1983
ARGENTINA — Economic conditions — 1945-
ARGENTINA — Economic policy
ARGENTINA — Emigration and immigration
ARGENTINA — Emigration and Immigration
ARGENTINA — Emigration and immigration — History
ARGENTINA — Foreign economic relations — Brazil
ARGENTINA — Foreign population
ARGENTINA — Foreign population — History — 19th century
ARGENTINA — Foreign relations — Great Britain
ARGENTINA — History — 1810-
ARGENTINA — History — 1817-1860
ARGENTINA — History — 1910-1943
ARGENTINA — History — 1910-1943 — Bibliography
ARGENTINA — History — 1943-
ARGENTINA — History — 1955-1983
ARGENTINA — History — 1955-
ARGENTINA — History — 1943-
ARGENTINA — History, Naval
ARGENTINA — Politics and government
ARGENTINA — Politics and government — 1860-1910
ARGENTINA — Politics and government — 20th century
ARGENTINA — Politics and government — 1910-1943
ARGENTINA — Politics and government — 1910-
ARGENTINA — Politics and government — 1910- — Bibliography
ARGENTINA — Politics and government — 1943-1955
ARGENTINA — Politics and government — 1943-
ARGENTINA — Politics and government — 1955-1983
ARGENTINA — Politics and government — 1955-
ARGENTINA — Politics and government — 1983-
ARGENTINA — Presidents — Wives — Biography
ARGENTINA — Relations — Soviet Union
ARGENTINA — Relations — Spain
ARGENTINA — Social conditions — 1945-1983
ARGENTINA — Social conditions — 1945-
ARGENTINA. Armada — History
ARICAN NATIONAL CONGRESS
ARID REGIONS AGRICULTURE — Congresses
ARID REGIONS AGRICULTURE — Developing countries — Congresses
ARISTOTELES
ARISTOTLE
ARMADA, 1588 — History — Sources
ARMAGH PRISON — Security measures
ARMAMENTS
ARMAMENTS — Economic aspects — Congresses
ARMAMENTS — Economic aspects — Italy — History — 20th century
ARMED FORCES
ARMED FORCES — Appropriations and expenditures
ARMED FORCES — Political activity
ARMED FORCES — Spain — Political activity
ARMENIA — History
ARMENIA — History — 1801-1900
ARMENIA — History — 1901-
ARMENIA — History — 1901- — Addresses, essays, lectures
ARMENIA — Relations — Turkey
ARMENIAN MASSACRES, 1915-1923 — Turkey — Addresses, essays, lectures
ARMENIAN QUESTION
ARMENIAN S.S.R — Population
ARMINIANISM — England — History — 16th century
ARMINIANISM — England — History — 17th century
ARMOUR, J. B. — Archives
ARMS CONTROL
ARMS CONTROL — Congresses
ARMS CONTROL — Verification
ARMS CONTROL — Verification — Congresses
ARMS RACE
ARMS RACE — History — 20th century
ARMS RACE — Caribbean Area — History — 20th century
ARMS RACE — Europe — History — 19th century
ARMS RACE — Europe — History — 20th century
ARMS RACE — Soviet Union

ARNIM, HEINRICH ALEXANDER VON — Biography
AROMANIANS — History
ARON, RAYMOND
ARREST OF SHIPS
ARROW, KENNETH J.
ART — Addresses, essays, lectures
ART — Psychological aspects
ART — Psychology
ART — Sociological aspects
ART — Africa, West
ART — Oceania
ART AND SCIENCE
ART AND SOCIETY
ART AND SOCIETY — Congresses
ART AND STATE — Great Britain
ART AUCTIONS
ART, AUSTRALIAN (ABORIGINAL) — Congresses
ART CENTERS — Great Britain
ART CRITICISM — History
ART CRITICISM — History — 20th century
ART, EUROPEAN — Congresses
ART HISTORIANS — Great Britain — Biography
ART, MODERN — 17th-18th centuries — Europe
ART PATRONAGE — United States — Addresses, essays, lectures
ART, PRIMITIVE
ART, PRIMITIVE — Africa, West
ART, PRIMITIVE — New Guinea
ART, PRIMITIVE — Oceania
ART, PRIMITIVE — Papua New Guinea
ART, RENAISSANCE
ART, SENUFO (AFRICAN PEOPLE)
ARTIC OCEAN — Congresses
ARTIFICIAL INTELLIGENCE
ARTIFICIAL INSEMINATION, HUMAN — Social aspects
ARTIFICIAL INTELLIGENCE
ARTIFICIAL INTELLIGENCE — Addresses, essays, lectures
ARTIFICIAL INTELLIGENCE — Data processing
ARTIFICIAL INTELLIGENCE — Scientific applications
ARTIFICIAL SATELLITES IN TELECOMMUNICATION
ARTIFICIAL SATELLITES IN TELECOMMUNICATION — Congresses
ARTIFICIAL SATELLITES IN TELECOMMUNICATION — Law and legislation
ARTIFICIAL SATELLITES IN TELECOMMUNICATION — Australia
ARTISANS — Italy — Statistics
ARTIST COLONIES — Switzerland — Ascona
ARTISTS — Homes and haunts — United States
ARTISTS — Psychology
ARTISTS' STUDIOS — United States
ARTS — Political aspects — England — History — 17th century
ARTS — Political aspects — Great Britain
ARTS — England — London
ARTS — Finland — Statistics
ARTS — Great Britain — Finance
ARTS — Switzerland — Ascona
ARTS — United States — Finance — Addresses, essays, lectures
ARTS AND CRAFTS MOVEMENT — Exhibitions
ARTS AND CRAFTS MOVEMENT — United States
ARTS AND SOCIETY
ARTS AND SOCIETY — Great Britain — History — 20th century
ARTS AND SOCIETY — United States
ARTS, AUSTRALIAN — History — 18th century
ARTS, AUSTRALIAN — History — 19th century
ARTS, ENGLISH
ARTS FACILITIES — Great Britain

ARTS, GERMAN — Congresses
ARTS, MODERN — 20th century — Addresses, essays, lectures
ARTS, MODERN — 20th century — Germany — Congresses
ARUE (TAHITI : REGION) — Population — Statistics
ARUNACHAL PRADESH (INDIA) — Population — Statistics
ARUTUA (TUAMOTU ISLANDS) — Population — Statistics
ASBESTOS
ASBESTOS — Environmental aspects
ASBESTOS — Toxicology
ASBESTOS INDUSTRY — Australia — Employees — Diseases and hygiene
ASCONA (SWITZERLAND) — Intellectual life
ASEAN
ASEAN — Addresses, essays, lectures
ASEAN — Congresses
ASEAN — Emigration and immigration
ASEAN — Foreign relations — New Zealand
ASEAN — History
ASHANTIS (AFRICAN PEOPLE)
ASIA — Cities and towns
ASIA — Commerce
ASIA, — Commerce — Statistics
ASIA — Commercial policy
ASIA — Economic conditions — Social aspects
ASIA — Economic conditions — 1945-
ASIA — Economic policy
ASIA — Economic policy — Social aspects
ASIA — Foreign relations — Great Britain — History
ASIA — Industries
ASIA — Politics and government
ASIA — Population
ASIA — Population — Statistics
ASIA — Religion
ASIA — Rural conditions
ASIA — Social conditions
ASIA — Strategic aspects
ASIA — Study and teaching — Germany
ASIA — Yearbooks
ASIA, EASTERN — Foreign relations
ASIA, SOUTH — Social life and customs
ASIA, SOUTHEASTERN — Civilization
ASIA, SOUTHEASTERN — Commerce
ASIA, SOUTHEASTERN — Defenses
ASIA, SOUTHEASTERN — Economic conditions
ASIA, SOUTHEASTERN — Economic conditions — Congresses
ASIA, SOUTHEASTERN — Economic integration — Congresses
ASIA, SOUTHEASTERN — Economic policy
ASIA, SOUTHEASTERN — Foreign economic relations — Addresses, essays, lectures
ASIA, SOUTHEASTERN — Foreign economic relations — South Asia
ASIA, SOUTHEASTERN — Foreign relations
ASIA, SOUTHEASTERN — Foreign relations — Treaties
ASIA, SOUTHEASTERN — Foreign relations — Kampuchea
ASIA, SOUTHEASTERN — Foreign relations — Soviet Union
ASIA, SOUTHEASTERN — Foreign relations — United States
ASIA, SOUTHEASTERN — Industries
ASIA, SOUTHEASTERN — Library resources — Great Britain
ASIA, SOUTHEASTERN — Manufactures
ASIA, SOUTHEASTERN — Politics and government
ASIA, SOUTHEASTERN — Politics and government — Congresses
ASIA, SOUTHEASTERN — Relations — China
ASIA, SOUTHEASTERN — Religion

ASIA, SOUTHEASTERN — Rural conditions
ASIA, SOUTHEASTERN — Social conditions — Congresses
ASIA, SOUTHEASTERN — Study and teaching — Great Britain
ASIA, SOUTHEASTERN — Study and teaching — United States — Congresses
ASIAN AMERICANS — History — Addresses, essays, lectures
ASIAN AMERICANS — History — Dictionaries
ASIAN PRODUCTIVITY ORGANIZATION — Bibliography
ASIANS — Housing — Great Britain
ASIANS — Medical care — Great Britain
ASIANS — Australia — Public opinion
ASIANS — Canada
ASIANS — England
ASIANS — Great Britain
ASIANS — Great Britain — Social conditions
ASIATIC MODE OF PRODUCTION
ASMAT (Tribe) — New Guinea — Art
ASQUITH, H. H.
ASSAM (INDIA) — Politics and government
ASSAM (INDIA) — Rural conditions — Case studies
ASSASSINATION
ASSASSINATION — France — Paris
ASSEMBLER LANGUAGE (COMPUTER PROGRAM LANGUAGE)
ASSIMILATION (SOCIOLOGY) — Addresses, essays, lectures
ASSIMILATION (SOCIOLOGY) — History
ASSISTANCE IN EMERGENCIES — Planning — Congresses
ASSOCIATION OF COUNTY COUNCILS
ASSOCIATION OF PROFESSIONAL, EXECUTIVE, CLERICAL AND COMPUTER STAFF
ASSOCIATION OF UNIVERSITY TEACHERS
ASSOCIATIONS, INSTITUTIONS, — Great Britain
ASSOCIATIONS, INSTITUTIONS, ETC. — Europe — Finance — Handbooks, manuals, etc.
ASSOCIATIONS, INSTITUTIONS, ETC. — European Economic Community countries — Directories
ASSOCIATIONS, INSTITUTIONS, ETC. — France
ASSOCIATIONS, INSTITUTIONS, ETC. — Germany — History
ASSOCIATIONS, INSTITUTIONS, ETC. — Great Britain — Bibliography
ASSOCIATIONS, INSTITUTIONS, ETC. — Ireland — Directories
ASSOCIATIONS, INSTITUTIONS, ETC — United States
ASSOCIATIVE STORAGE
ASTRONAUTICS — Soviet Union — History
ASTRONAUTICS — United States — History
ASTRONAUTICS AND CIVILIZATION
ASTRONAUTICS AND STATE — France
ASTRONAUTICS AND STATE — Soviet Union
ASTRONAUTICS AND STATE — United States
ASTRONAUTICS IN METEOROLOGY — Congresses
ASTRONAUTICS, MILITARY — Soviet Union
ASTRONAUTICS, MILITARY — United States
ASTRONOMY
ASTURIAS (SPAIN) — Economic conditions
ASTURIAS (SPAIN) — Emigration and Immigration — Economic aspects — History
ASTURIAS (SPAIN) — History

ASTURIAS (SPAIN) — History — Autonomy and independence movements
ASTURIAS (SPAIN) — History — Revolution, 1934
ASTURIAS (SPAIN) — Industries — History
ASTURIAS (SPAIN) — Social conditions
ASYLUM, RIGHT OF — Biblical teaching — Congresses
ASYLUM, RIGHT OF — Congresses
ASYLUM, RIGHT OF — Germany (West)
ASYLUMS — France
ATATÜRK, KAMÂL
ATHEISM — Soviet Union
ATHENS (GREECE) — Politics and government
ATLANTIC FISHERIES RESTRUCTURING ACT 1983
ATLANTIC OCEAN — Commerce
ATLANTIC SALMON — Congresses
ATLASES
ATOMIC BOMB
ATOMIC BOMB — Moral and ethical aspects
ATOMIC ENERGY
ATOMIC POWER
ATOMIC POWER — Law and legislation — Mexico
ATOMIC POWER-PLANTS
ATOMIC POWER PLANTS — England — Sizewell (Suffolk)
ATOMIC POWER-PLANTS — Great Britain — Accidents — Economic aspects
ATOMIC POWER-PLANTS — Great Britain — Accidents — Social aspects
ATOMIC WARFARE
ATOMIC WARFARE — Moral and ethical aspects
ATOMIC WARFARE — Moral and religious aspects
ATOMIC WARFARE — Religious aspects — Catholic Church
ATOMIC WARFARE — Religious aspects — Catholic Church — Addresses, essays, lectures
ATOMIC WEAPONS
ATOMIC WEAPONS — Testing
ATOMIC WEAPONS AND DISARMAMENT
ATTACHMENT BEHAVIOR IN CHILDREN
ATTENTION — Congresses
ATTIKÍ (GREECE) — Politics and government
ATTIKÍ (GREECE) — Social conditions
ATTITUDE CHANGE
ATTITUDE (PSYCHOLOGY) — Testing
ATTORNEYS-GENERAL — Ontario — History
ATTRIBUTION (SOCIAL PSYCHOLOGY)
AUCTIONS
AUDIT COMMISSION FOR LOCAL AUTHORITIES IN ENGLAND AND WALES
AUDITING
AUDITING — Data processing
AUDITING — Research
AUDITING — Standards — United States
AUDITORS' REPORTS — Great Britain
AUGUSTA REGION (GA.) — Economic conditions
AUGUSTA REGION (GA.) — Social conditions
AUSTEN, JANE — Criticism and interpretation
AUSTIN MOTOR COMPANY — History
AUSTIN OF LONGBRIDGE, HERBERT AUSTIN, Baron
AUSTRAL ISLANDS — Population — Statistics
AUSTRALIA. Broadcasting and Television Act 1942
AUSTRALIA. Migration Act 1958
AUSTRALIA — Appropriations and expenditures
AUSTRALIA — Bibliography
AUSTRALIA — Civilization
AUSTRALIA — Commerce
AUSTRALIA — Commerce — Statistics
AUSTRALIA — Commerce — New Zealand
AUSTRALIA — Constitution
AUSTRALIA — Constitutional law
AUSTRALIA — Defenses
AUSTRALIA — Economic condition
AUSTRALIA — Economic conditions
AUSTRALIA — Economic conditions — 1945-
AUSTRALIA — Economic conditions — Maps
AUSTRALIA — Economic conditions — Mathematical models
AUSTRALIA — Economic conditions — 1945-
AUSTRALIA — Economic policy
AUSTRALIA — Economic policy — 1976-
AUSTRALIA — Emigration and immigration
AUSTRALIA — Emigration and immigration — Education
AUSTRALIA — Emigration and immigration — Government policy
AUSTRALIA — Emigration and immigration — History
AUSTRALIA — Emigration and immigration — Legal status, laws, etc
AUSTRALIA — Emigration and immigration — Public opinion
AUSTRALIA — Emigration and immigration — Social aspects
AUSTRALIA — Emigration and Immigration — United States
AUSTRALIA — Ethnic relations
AUSTRALIA — Exiles
AUSTRALIA — Foreign economic relations
AUSTRALIA — Foreign Economic Relations — European Economic Community countries
AUSTRALIA — Foreign economic relations — Great Britain
AUSTRALIA — Foreign opinion, American
AUSTRALIA — Foreign population
AUSTRALIA — Foreign relations
AUSTRALIA — Foreign relations — 1945-
AUSTRALIA — Foreign relations — Great Britain
AUSTRALIA — Foreign relations — Indochina
AUSTRALIA — Foreign relations — New Zealand — Sources
AUSTRALIA — History
AUSTRALIA — History — Sources
AUSTRALIA — History — 1788-1851
AUSTRALIA — History — 1788-1900
AUSTRALIA — History — 20th century
AUSTRALIA — Industries
AUSTRALIA — Industries — Location
AUSTRALIA — Manufactures
AUSTRALIA — Maps
AUSTRALIA — Military policy
AUSTRALIA — Moral conditions
AUSTRALIA — National security
AUSTRALIA — Native races
AUSTRALIA — Neutrality
AUSTRALIA — Politics and government
AUSTRALIA — Politics and government — Addresses, essays, lectures
AUSTRALIA — Politics and government — Bibliography
AUSTRALIA — Politics and government — Congresses
AUSTRALIA — Politics and government — 20th century
AUSTRALIA — Politics and government — 1945-
AUSTRALIA — Population
AUSTRALIA — Population policy
AUSTRALIA — Rural conditions — Government policy
AUSTRALIA — Social conditions
AUSTRALIA — Social policy
AUSTRALIA — Statistics
AUSTRALIA — Statistics, Vital
AUSTRALIA — Study and teaching — Great Britain — Directories
AUSTRALIA. Administrative Appeals Tribunal
AUSTRALIA. Bureau of Agricultural Economics
AUSTRALIA. Bureau of Industry Economics. Conference on Evaluation of Public Support for Industrial Research and Development (1986 : Canberra)
AUSTRALIA. Bureau of Industry Economics. Conference on Revitalising Australian Industry (1986 : Sydney)
AUSTRALIA. Committee of Review of Aboriginal Employment and Training Programs
AUSTRALIA. Commonwealth Bureau of Census and Statistics
AUSTRALIA. Federal Court
AUSTRALIA. Industries Assistance Commission
AUSTRALIA. Joint Select Committee on an Australia Card
AUSTRALIA. Parliament. House of Representatives — Rules and practice
AUSTRALIA. Parliament. House of Representavies — Elections, 1984
AUSTRALIA. Parliament. Senate — Elections, 1984
AUSTRALIA. Royal Commission into British Nuclear Tests in Australia
AUSTRALIA AND NEW ZEALAND BANKING GROUP
AUSTRALIA CONSTITUTIONAL LAW
AUSTRALIAN ABORIGINES
AUSTRALIAN ABORIGINES — Congresses
AUSTRALIAN ABORIGINES — Economic conditions
AUSTRALIAN ABORIGINES — Education — Case studies
AUSTRALIAN ABORIGINES — Employment
AUSTRALIAN ABORIGINES — Employment — South Australia
AUSTRALIAN ABORIGINES — Law and legislation
AUSTRALIAN ABORIGINES — Legal status, laws, etc
AUSTRALIAN ABORIGINES — Legal status, laws, etc. — Australia
AUSTRALIAN ABORIGINES — Religion
AUSTRALIAN ABORIGINES — Social conditions
AUSTRALIAN ABORIGINES — Social conditions — Congresses
AUSTRALIAN ABORIGINES — Training of
AUSTRALIAN ABORIGINES — Australia — Western Australia
AUSTRALIAN ABORIGINES — South Australia — Education
AUSTRALIAN HOSPITAL ASSOCIATION
AUSTRALIAN LABOR PARTY
AUSTRALIAN OVERSEAS AID PROGRAM
AUSTRALIAN UNIVERSITIES COMMISSION — History
AUSTRALIAN VICE-CHANCELLORS' COMMITTEE
AUSTRALIANS — Fiji — History — 19th century
AUSTRIA — Bibliography
AUSTRIA — Economic conditions
AUSTRIA — Economic conditions — 1945-
AUSTRIA — Foreign relations — 18th century
AUSTRIA — Foreign relations — 19th century
AUSTRIA — Foreign relations — 1955-
AUSTRIA — Foreign relations — Great Britain
AUSTRIA — History — 1867-1918
AUSTRIA — History — Allied occupation, 1945-1955
AUSTRIA — History — 1918-1938

AUSTRIA — History, Military
AUSTRIA — Military policy
AUSTRIA — Politics and government
AUSTRIA — Politics and government — 1918-1938
AUSTRIA — Politics and government — 1918-
AUSTRIA — Politics and government — 1945-
AUSTRIA — Social conditions
AUSTRIA — Statistics — Bibliography
AUSTRIA — 1918-1938
AUSTRIAN SCHOOL OF ECONOMISTS
AUSTRIANS — Spain — History
AUSTRO-HUNGARIAN MONARCHY
AUTHORITARIANISM
AUTHORITARIANISM — Case studies
AUTHORITARIANISM — Brazil — Addresses, essays, lectures
AUTHORITARIANISM — Europe, Southern — Case studies
AUTHORITARIANISM — Latin America — Addresses, essays, lectures
AUTHORITARIANISM — Latin America — Case studies
AUTHORITY
AUTHORS — Biography — Directories
AUTHORS — Directories
AUTHORS — Legal status, laws, etc. — Australia
AUTHORS AND PUBLISHERS
AUTHORS AND PUBLISHERS — Addresses, essays, lectures
AUTHORS AND PUBLISHERS — Australia
AUTHORS AND READERS
AUTHORS, ENGLISH — Homes and haunts
AUTHORS, ENGLISH — 19th century — Biography
AUTHORS, FRENCH — 18th century — Biography
AUTHORS, POLISH
AUTHORS, RUSSIAN — Biography
AUTHORS, SPANISH — Biography
AUTHORSHIP — Addresses, essays, lectures
AUTHORSHIP — Data processing — Handbooks, manuals, etc
AUTHORSHIP — Economic aspects
AUTHORSHIP — Social aspects
AUTHORSHIP — Style manuals
AUTOMATION — Economic aspects
AUTOMATION — Economic aspects — France — Normandy
AUTOMATION — Social aspects
AUTOMATION — Social aspects — France — Normandy
AUTOMOBILE INDUSTRY AND TRADE — Forecasting — Congresses
AUTOMOBILE INDUSTRY AND TRADE — Government policy — United States
AUTOMOBILE INDUSTRY AND TRADE — History
AUTOMOBILE INDUSTRY AND TRADE — Law and legislation — Peru
AUTOMOBILE INDUSTRY AND TRADE — Management
AUTOMOBILE INDUSTRY AND TRADE — Australia
AUTOMOBILE INDUSTRY AND TRADE — Germany — History
AUTOMOBILE INDUSTRY AND TRADE — Great Britain
AUTOMOBILE INDUSTRY AND TRADE — Latin America
AUTOMOBILE INDUSTRY AND TRADE — Michigan — Case studies
AUTOMOBILE INDUSTRY AND TRADE — Sweden
AUTOMOBILE INDUSTRY AND TRADE — United States — Automation — History
AUTOMOBILE INDUSTRY AND TRADE — United States — History
AUTOMOBILE INDUSTRY AND TRADE — United States — Management — History — 20th century
AUTOMOBILE INDUSTRY WORKERS — England — Stoke-on-Trent (Staffordshire)
AUTOMOBILE INDUSTRY WORKERS — Great Britain — Political activity
AUTOMOBILE INDUSTRY WORKERS — Sweden
AUTOMOBILE INDUSTRY WORKERS — United States — History
AUTOMOBILE OWNERSHIP — Forecasting — Congresses
AUTOMOBILE OWNERSHIP — Ireland — Statistics
AUTOMOBILE PARKING — Law and legislation — Great Britain
AUTOMOBILES — Marketing — Congresses
AUTOMOBILES — Registration and transfer — Great Britain — Statistics
AUTOMOBILES — Great Britain — Statistics
AUTOMOBILES — South Australia — Statistics
AUTOMOBILES, COMPANY — Taxation — Great Britain
AUTOMOBILES, COMPANY — England — London
AUTONOMY
AUTONOMY (PSYCHOLOGY)
AVILA CAMACHO, MANUEL
AVILA (SPAIN) — Economic conditions
AVILA (SPAIN) — Social conditions
AYER, A. J.. Language, truth and logic
AZERBAIJAN (IRAN) — Relations — Soviet Union
AZTECS — Economic conditions
BAARD, FRANCIS
BABY FOODS — Composition
BADAJOZ (SPAIN) — Economic conditions — 19th century
BADAJOZ (SPAIN) — Social conditions — 19th century
BADEN-POWELL OF GILWELL, ROBERT STEPHENSON SMYTH BADEN-POWELL, Baron
BAGEMDER (ETHIOPIA) — Economic conditions — Case studies
BAGEMDER (ETHIOPIA) — Economic conditions — Regional disparities — Case studies
BAGEMDER (ETHIOPIA) — Social conditions — Case studies
BAGUIO, PHILIPPINES — Markets
BAGUIO, PHILIPPINES — Social conditions
BAHAMAS — Census, 1980
BAHAMAS — Census, 1980
BAHAMAS — Economic conditions
BAHAMAS — Economic conditions — Statistics
BAHAMAS — Emigration and immigration — Statistics
BAHAMAS — Population — Statistics
BAHAMAS — Social conditions — Statistics
BAHIA (BRAZIL: STATE) — Economic conditions — Statistics
BAHRAIN — Census, 1971
BAHRAIN — Population — Statistics
BAIL — England
BAIL — South Africa
BAKERS AND BAKERIES — Great Britain
BAKERS', FOOD AND ALLIED WORKERS' UNION
BAKERS' UNION
BAKONGO (AFRICAN PEOPLE) — Religion
BAKUNIN, MIKHAIL
BALANCE OF PAYMENTS
BALANCE OF PAYMENTS — Africa, West
BALANCE OF PAYMENTS — Canada
BALANCE OF PAYMENTS — Developing countries
BALANCE OF PAYMENTS — Great Britain
BALANCE OF PAYMENTS — Hong Kong
BALANCE OF PAYMENTS — Hungary
BALANCE OF PAYMENTS — Japan
BALANCE OF PAYMENTS — Korea (South)
BALANCE OF PAYMENTS — Peru
BALANCE OF PAYMENTS — Singapore
BALANCE OF PAYMENTS — Taiwan
BALANCE OF PAYMENTS — United States
BALANCE OF PAYMENTS — United States — Mathematical models
BALANCE OF POWER
BALANCE OF TRADE
BALANCE OF TRADE — Hungary
BALANCE OF TRADE — United States
BALANCE OF TRADE — United States — Mathematical models
BALDWIN OF BEWDLEY, STANLEY BALDWIN, Earl
BALI (INDONESIA : PROVINCE) — Population
BALKAN PENINSULA — History — Autonomy and independence movements
BALKAN PENINSULA — History — 19th century
BALKAN PENINSULA — History, Military
BALLISTIC MISSILE DEFENSES
BALLISTIC MISSILE DEFENSES — North America — History
BALLISTIC MISSILE DEFENSES — Soviet Union
BALLISTIC MISSILE DEFENSES — United States
BALTIC SEA — Defenses
BALTIC STATES — Annexation to the Soviet Union
BALTIC STATES — Foreign relations — Germany
BALTIC STATES — History
BALTIC STATES — History — German occupation, 1941-1944
BALTIC STATES — Politics and government
BALTIMORE (MD.) — Economic conditions — Econometric models
BANCA CATALANA
BANDARANAIKE, Family — History
BANGKOK (THAILAND) — Social conditions
BANGLADESH — Commerce — Statistics
BANGLADESH — Economic policy
BANGLADESH — History — Revolution, 1971 — Sources
BANGLADESH — Politics and government
BANGLADESH — Rural conditions
BANGLADESH — Social life and customs
BANK DEPOSITS — Developing countries
BANK DEPOSITS — United States
BANK EMPLOYEES — United States — Supply and demand — Forecasting
BANK FAILURES — United States
BANK INVESTMENTS — Great Britain
BANK LOANS
BANK LOANS — Mathematical models
BANK LOANS — European Economic Community countries
BANK LOANS — United States
BANK MARKAZI JOMHOURI IRAN
BANK OF BARODA
BANK OF CANADA — Officials and employees — Biography
BANK OF ENGLAND
BANK OF ENGLAND — History
BANK OF UGANDA
BANKERS — Biography
BANKERS — Canada — Biography
BANKERS — Great Britain — Biography
BANKERS — Switzerland — Biography
BANKING — England
BANKING LAW — Ecuador
BANKING LAW — Germany (West)
BANKING LAW — Great Britain
BANKING LAW — United States
BANKING LAW (ISLAMIC LAW)
BANKRUPTCY — Great Britain
BANKRUPTCY — Netherlands

BANKS AND BANKING
BANKS AND BANKING — Accounting — Mathematical models
BANKS AND BANKING — Archival resources — Great Britain
BANKS AND BANKING — Directories
BANKS AND BANKING — Government guaranty of deposits
BANKS AND BANKING — Service charges
BANKS AND BANKING — Statistics
BANKS AND BANKING — Australia — History
BANKS AND BANKING — Brazil
BANKS AND BANKING — British Virgin Islands — Statistics
BANKS AND BANKING — Chile — Statistics
BANKS AND BANKING — Developing countries
BANKS AND BANKING — England — History — 20th century
BANKS AND BANKING — England — Hertfordshire
BANKS AND BANKING — England — Sussex — History
BANKS AND BANKING — France
BANKS AND BANKING — France — Statistics
BANKS AND BANKING — Germany — Hamburg
BANKS AND BANKING — Great Britain
BANKS AND BANKING — Great Britain — Directories
BANKS AND BANKING — Great Britain — History
BANKS AND BANKING — Great Britain — Statistics
BANKS AND BANKING — Great Britain — Technological innovations
BANKS AND BANKING — Hong Kong
BANKS AND BANKING — Hungary
BANKS AND BANKING — India — History
BANKS AND BANKING — Iran
BANKS AND BANKING — Islamic countries
BANKS AND BANKING — Italy
BANKS AND BANKING — Malaysia
BANKS AND BANKING — Netherlands — Statistics
BANKS AND BANKING — New Zealand — History
BANKS AND BANKING — Nigeria — Congresses
BANKS AND BANKING — Organisation for Economic Co-operation and Development countries — State supervision
BANKS AND BANKING — Pakistan
BANKS AND BANKING — Singapore
BANKS AND BANKING — South Africa
BANKS AND BANKING — Spain
BANKS AND BANKING — Spain — Catalonia
BANKS AND BANKING — Sweden
BANKS AND BANKING — Switzerland
BANKS AND BANKING — Turkey — Statistics
BANKS AND BANKING — United States
BANKS AND BANKING — United States — Accounting — Mathematical models
BANKS AND BANKING — United States — Service charges
BANKS AND BANKING — United States — State supervision
BANKS AND BANKING — United States — Statistics
BANKS AND BANKING — Uruguay
BANKS AND BANKING 4Z ASIA SOUTHEASTERN
BANKS AND BANKING, AUSTRALIA
BANKS AND BANKING, BRITISH
BANKS AND BANKING, BRITISH — Iran
BANKS AND BANKING, BRITISH — Near East
BANKS AND BANKING, CENTRAL
BANKS AND BANKING, CENTRAL — Decision making
BANKS AND BANKING, CENTRAL — France
BANKS AND BANKING, COOPERATIVE — France
BANKS AND BANKING, COOPERATIVE — Germany (West)
BANKS AND BANKING, COOPERATIVE — India
BANKS AND BANKING, INTERNATIONAL
BANKS AND BANKING, INTERNATIONAL — Accounting
BANKS AND BANKING, INTERNATIONAL — History
BANKS AND BANKING, INTERNATIONAL — Law and legislation
BANKS AND BANKING, INTERNATIONAL — Statistics — Sources
BANQUE DE FRANCE
BANQUE DE FRANCE — Statistics
BANYORO
BAPTISTS — Georgia
BARBADOS — Census, 1970
BARBADOS — Census, 1980
BARBADOS — Economic conditions
BARBADOS — Economic policy
BARBADOS — population — Statistics
BARBADOS. Legislature. House of Assembly — Elections, 1981
BARBIE, KLAUS
BARBOSA, RUY, 1849-1923
BARCELONA (SPAIN) — Economic conditions
BARCELONA (SPAIN) — Social conditions
BARCLAYS BANK
BARCLAYS BANK INTERNATIONAL
BARNSLEY WOMEN AGAINST PIT CLOSURES
BAROTSE (AFRICAN PEOPLE) — See Lozi (Afican people)
BARRE, RAYMOND
BARRY (SOUTH GLAMORGAN) — History
BARTER — Addresses, essays, lectures
BARUYA (PAPUAN PEOPLE) — Social life and customs
BASEL (SWITZERLAND) — Industries
BASIC (COMPUTER PROGRAM LANGUAGE)
BASIC NEEDS
BASIC NEEDS — Africa
BASIC NEEDS — Brazil
BASIC NEEDS — Kenya
BASILDON (ESSEX) — History
BASQUE PROVINCES — History
BASQUE PROVINCES (SPAIN) — Boundaries — France
BASQUE PROVINCES (SPAIN) — Economic conditions — Congresses
BASQUE PROVINCES (SPAIN) — History — Autonomy and independence movements
BASQUE PROVINCES (SPAIN) — History — 20th century
BASQUE PROVINCES (SPAIN) — History — Autonomy and independence movements
BASQUE PROVINCES (SPAIN) — Politics and government
BASQUES
BASQUES — Argentina — History
BASQUES — Latin America — History
BASTÜRK, ABDULLAH
BATH (AVON) — City planning
BATH PARTY See Hizb al-Báth al-Árabí al-Ishtirāki (Syria)
BAUER, OTTO — History and criticism
BAVARIA (GERMANY) — Politics and government — 1918-1945
BAYESIAN STATISTICAL DECISION THEORY
BAYESIAN STATISTICAL DECISION THEORY — Congresses
BAZAINE, ACHILLE FRANÇOIS, 1811-1888
BEAGLE CHANNEL — International status
BEBEL, AUGUST
BED AND BREAKFAST ACCOMODATIONS — England — London
BEDFORDSHIRE — Population
BEDFORDSHIRE (ENGLAND) — Population
BEDLINGTON (NORTHUMBERLAND) — Social life and customs
BEDOUINS
BEEF INDUSTRY — Botswana
BEEF INDUSTRY — Central America
BEHAVIOR
BEHAVIOR MODIFICATION
BEHAVIOR THERAPY
BEHAVIORAL ASSESSMENT
BEHAVIORAL ASSESSMENT OF CHILDREN
BEHAVIORISM (PSYCHOLOGY) — Congresses
BEHAVIORISM (PSYCHOLOGY) — History
BEHRSTOCK, JULIAN
BEIRUT — Politics and government
BELFAST (NORTHERN IRELAND) — City planning
BELFAST (NORTHERN IRELAND) — City planning — History
BELFAST (NORTHERN IRELAND) — Social life and customs
BELGIANS — South Africa — History
BELGIUM — Census, 1981
BELGIUM — Commerce — Statistics
BELGIUM — Economic conditions — 1945- — Congresses
BELGIUM — Economic conditions — 1945- — Mathematical models
BELGIUM — Economic policy — Congresses
BELGIUM — Foreign economic relations
BELGIUM — History — To 1555
BELGIUM — History — Revolution, 1789-1790
BELGIUM — History — Invasion of 1792
BELGIUM — History — 19th century
BELGIUM — Industries
BELGIUM — Industries — Statistics
BELGIUM — Languages — Political aspects
BELGIUM — Politics and government
BELGIUM — Population — Statistics
BELGIUM — Social conditions — 1945-
BELGIUM — Social policy
BELIZE — Description and travel
BELIZE — Economic conditions
BELIZE — Economic policy
BELIZE — Foreign economic relations
BELIZE — Population — Statistics
BELIZE — Social conditions
BELIZE — Statistics, Vital
BELLO, Sir AHMADU
BEN-GURION, DAVID
BENDE (NIGERIA) — Politics and government
BENEŠ, EDVARD
BENEVOLENCE
BENEVOLENCE — Mora! and ethical aspects
BENGAL (INDIA) — Rural conditions
BENGAL (INDIA) — Social conditions
BENIN CITY, NIGERIA — Kings and rulers
BENNETT, RICHARD BEDFORD BENNETT, 1st viscount
BENNETT, WILLIAM R
BENTHAM, JEREMY
BENZENE — Environmental aspects — Organisation for Economic Co-operation and Development countries
BERBERS
BEREAVEMENT
BEREAVEMENT — Psychological aspects
BERGEN-BELSEN (GERMANY: CONCENTRATION CAMP)
BERKELEY, GEORGE
BERKSHIRE COUNTY (MASS.) — History

BERLIN. Conference (1884-1885)
BERLIN (GERMANY) — Archives
BERLIN (GERMANY) — History
BERLIN (GERMANY) — History — Allied occupation, 1945-
BERLIN (GERMANY) — Politics and government
BERLIN (GERMANY) — Politics and government — 1945-
BERLIN QUESTION (1945-)
BERLIN QUESTION (1945-)
BERLIN QUESTION (1945-)
BESANT, ANNIE
BESEDOVSKIĬ, GRIGORIĬ ZINOV'EVICH
BEVAN, ANEURIN
BEVERAGE INDUSTRY — European Economic Community countries
BEVERAGE INDUSTRY
BEVERAGE INDUSTRY — Political aspects — Great Britain
BHARAT HEAVY ELECTRICALS LIMITED
BHARIAS
BHILAI STEEL PLANT
BHOPAL UNION CARBIDE PLANT DISASTER, BHOPAL, INDIA, 1984
BHUTTO, ZULFIKAR ALI
BIBLE — Versions
BIBLIOGRAPHICAL SERVICES — Directories
BIBLIOGRAPHY — Bibliography — Afro-Americans
BIBLIOGRAPHY — Bibliography — Catalogs
BIBLIOGRAPHY — Bibliography — History
BIBLIOGRAPHY — Bibliography — Sociology, Rural
BIBLIOGRAPHY — Rare books
BIBLIOGRAPHY — Soviet Union
BIBLIOGRAPHY, NATIONAL — Catalogs
BIBLIOGRAPHY, NATIONAL — Directories
BICULTURALISM — Québec (Province)
BIG BUSINESS — History — 20th century
BIG BUSINESS — United States
BIG SIOUX RIVER VALLEY (S.D. AND IOWA) — History
BIHAR (INDIA) — Economic conditions
BIHAR (INDIA) — Population density
BILBO, THEODORE GILMORE
BILINGUALISM
BILINGUALISM — Political aspects — Manitoba — History
BILINGUALISM — Belgium — Brussels
BILINGUALISM — Mexico — Statistics
BILL DRAFTING
BILLS, LEGISLATIVE — Canada
BILLS OF LADING
BILLS, PRIVATE — Great Britain
BINANDELI (PAPUAN PEOPLE)
BINGHAM, THOMAS HENRY. Report on the supply of petroleum and petroleum products to Rhodesia — Bibliography
BIOETHICS
BIOGAS — Developing countries
BIOLOGICAL WARFARE
BIOLOGY — Philosophy — History
BIOLOGY — Social aspects
BIOLOGY, ECONOMIC — Canada
BIOLOGY, ECONOMIC — United States
BIOMASS ENERGY — Congresses
BIOMASS ENERGY — European Economic Community countries
BIOPOLITICS
BIOTECHNOLOGY
BIOTECHNOLOGY — Developing countries
BIOTECHNOLOGY — Europe — Government policy
BIOTECHNOLOGY INDUSTRIES
BIOTECHNOLOGY INDUSTRIES — Europe
BIRLA, G. D.
BIRTH CONTROL
BIRTH CONTROL — Cross-cultural studies

BIRTH CONTROL — Evaluation — Methodology
BIRTH CONTROL — Government policy — Louisiana
BIRTH CONTROL — Africa, Sub-Saharan
BIRTH CONTROL — Africa, Subsaharan
BIRTH CONTROL — India
BIRTH CONTROL — India — Bibliography
BIRTH CONTROL — India — Congresses
BIRTH CONTROL — Indonesia — Bali (Province)
BIRTH CONTROL — Louisiana
BIRTH CONTROL — Pakistan
BIRTH CONTROL — United States — History — Bibliography
BIRTH INTERVALS — Great Britain
BIRTH INTERVALS — Jordan
BISERICA ORTODOXA ROMANA — History
BISMARCK, OTTO, Fürst von
BISMARK, OTTO, Fürst von
BITBURG (GERMANY) — Addresses, essays, lectures
BLACK ENGLISH — United States
BLACK FAMILIES — United States
BLACK MARKET
BLACK MARKET — Great Britain
BLACK MILITANT ORGANIZATIONS — France
BLACK MUSLIMS
BLACK MUSLIMS — Biography
BLACK MUSLIMS — United States
BLACK NATIONALISM
BLACK NATIONALISM — United States
BLACK NATIONALISM — United States — History
BLACK POWER
BLACK THEOLOGY
BLACKBURN (LANCASHIRE) — Social life and customs
BLACKS
BLACKS — Civil rights — South Africa
BLACKS — Education — Great Britain
BLACKS — Education — South Africa
BLACKS — Employment — Law and legislation — South Africa
BLACKS — Employment — South Africa
BLACKS — Services for — Great Britain — Case studies
BLACKS — Africa — Religion
BLACKS — Africa, Sub-Saharan — Psychology
BLACKS — England
BLACKS — England — London
BLACKS — England — London — Political activity
BLACKS — England — London — Social conditions
BLACKS — France — History — 20th century
BLACKS — Great Britain
BLACKS — Great Britain — Education
BLACKS — Great Britain — Language
BLACKS — Great Britain — Political activity
BLACKS — Great Britain — Politics and government
BLACKS — Haiti
BLACKS — Panama — History — 20th century
BLACKS — South Africa
BLACKS — South Africa — Biography
BLACKS — South Africa — Civil rights
BLACKS — South Africa — Economic conditions
BLACKS — South Africa — History
BLACKS — South Africa — Politics and government
BLACKS — South Africa — Race identity
BLACKS — South Africa — Religion
BLACKS — South Africa — Relocation
BLACKS — South Africa — Relocation — History — 20th century
BLACKS — South Africa — Segregation
BLACKS — South Africa — Social conditions

BLACKS — South Africa — Natal
BLACKS IN ART — Congresses
BLACKS IN LITERATURE — Congresses
BLEICHRODER, GERSON VON
BLOCK GRANTS — England
BLUMENFELD, HANS — Congresses
BLUNT, ANTHONY
BMDP (COMPUTER SYSTEM)
BOARD OF GOVERNORS OF THE FEDERAL RESERVE SYSTEM (U.S.)
BOARD OF GOVERNORS OF THE FEDERAL RESERVE SYSTEM (U.S.)
BODICHON, BARBARA LEIGH SMITH
BODIN, JEAN
BODY, HUMAN — Social aspects — United States
BODY IMAGE
BOER WAR, 1899-1902 See South African War, 1899-1902
BOGOTÁ (COLOMBIA) — Economic conditions
BOGOTÁ (COLOMBIA) — History
BOHEMIAN FLATS (MINNEAPOLIS, MINN.) — Social life and customs
BOHEMIANISM — France — Paris — History — 19th century
BOHR, NIELS
BOLIVIA — Politics and government — 1879-1938
BOLIVIA — Politics and government — 1938-1952
BOLIVIA — Politics and government — 1952-1982
BOLIVIA — Rural conditions
BOLIVIAN NEWSPAPERS — History — 20th century
BOLLISHE MISSILE DEFENSES — United States
BOLOGNA (ITALY) — Politics and government
BOMBAY (INDIA) — Social conditions
BOMBING INVESTIGATION — England — Guildford (Surrey)
BOMBINGS — England — Birmingham (West Midlands) — History — 20th century
BOND, JAMES (FICTITIOUS CHARACTER)
BONUZZI, PIERRE
BOOK DESIGN
BOOK INDUSTRIES AND TRADE
BOOK INDUSTRIES AND TRADE — Management
BOOK INDUSTRIES AND TRADE — Commonwealth of Nations
BOOK INDUSTRIES AND TRADE — Soviet Union
BOOK REVIEWING
BOOK SELECTION
BOOKS — History — Dictionaries
BOOKS — Purchasing — Statistics
BOOKS — France — Prices
BOOKS — Great Britain — Conservation and restoration
BOOKS — Great Britain — Mutilation, defacement, etc.
BOOKS — Great Britain — Prices
BOOKS — New Zealand — Statistics
BOOKS — Soviet Union
BOOKS — Sweden — History
BOOKS AND READING — Addresses, essays, lectures
BOOKS AND READING — Soviet Union — History
BOOKSELLERS AND BOOKSELLING — France
BOOKSELLERS AND BOOKSELLING — Great Britain — Directories
BOOKSELLERS AND BOOKSELLING — Latin America
BOOKSELLERS AND BOOKSELLING — London (England) — Directories
BOOKSELLERS AND BOOKSELLING — Sweden — History
BOPHUTHATSWANA (AFRICAN PEOPLE) — Social life and customs

BORA-BORA (SOCIETY ISLANDS) — Population — Statistics
BORIS III, King of Bulgaria
BOROUGH (LONDON, ENGLAND) — Social conditions
BOSTON (MASS.) — Commerce — History — 18th century
BOSTON (MASS.) — History — Revolution, 1775-1783 — Economic aspects
BOSTON (MASS.) — Race relations
BOTHA, PIETER WILLEM
BOTSWANA — Census, 1981
BOTSWANA — Commerce
BOTSWANA — Economic conditions
BOTSWANA — Economic conditions — 1966-
BOTSWANA — Foreign relations — South Africa
BOTSWANA — Social conditions
BOUNDARIES
BOUNDARIES — Legal status, laws, etc.
BOUNDARIES — Political aspects
BOY SCOUTS — Biography
BOY SCOUTS — History
BOYES, GEORGE THOMAS WILLIAM BLAMEY
BOYS — Psychology — Longitudinal studies
BRADFORD (WEST YORKSHIRE) — Economic conditions
BRADFORD (WEST YORKSHIRE) — Politics and government
BRAIN
BRAIN — popular works
BRAIN DRAIN — Argentina
BRAND NAME PRODUCTS
BRAZIL — Church history
BRAZIL — Civilization
BRAZIL — Civilization — 19th century
BRAZIL — Civilization — 20th century
BRAZIL — Economc policy
BRAZIL — Economic conditions
BRAZIL — Economic conditions — 19th century
BRAZIL — Economic conditions — 1918-
BRAZIL — Economic conditions — 1964-1985
BRAZIL — Economic conditions — 1964-
BRAZIL — Economic policy
BRAZIL — Economic policy — Addresses, essays, lectures
BRAZIL — Foreign economic relations
BRAZIL — Foreign economic relations — Argentina
BRAZIL — Foreign relations — Netherlands
BRAZIL — History — 1763-1821
BRAZIL — History — 1822-1889
BRAZIL — History — 1889-1930
BRAZIL — Industries — Statistics
BRAZIL — Kings and rulers — Biography
BRAZIL — Politics and government
BRAZIL — Politics and government — 1822-1889
BRAZIL — Politics and government — 1889-1930
BRAZIL — Politics and government — 20th century
BRAZIL — Politics and government — 1930-1954
BRAZIL — Politics and government — 1954-1964
BRAZIL — Politics and government — 1964-1985 — Addresses, essays, lectures
BRAZIL — Race relations
BRAZIL — Social conditions
BRAZIL — Social conditions — 19th century
BRAZIL — Social conditions — 1964-
BRAZIL — Social policy
BRAZIL — Statistics
BRAZIL, NORTH — Population — Statistics
BREACH OF CONTRACT — Canada
BREACH OF CONTRACT — England
BREACH OF THE PEACE — Great Britain
BREAD
BREAST — Cancer
BREAST — Radiography
BREAST FEEDING
BREAST FEEDING — Pakistan
BREATH TESTS — Great Britain
BRENT (LONDON, ENGLAND) — Social policy
BREWERY WORKERS — Effect of technological innovations on
BREWING INDUSTRY — Great Britain — Corrupt practices
BREWING INDUSTRY — Great Britain — History
BRICKMAKING — European Economic Community countries — Energy consumption
BRIDGES — England — London — Drawings
BRIGGS, RAYMOND. When the wind blows
BRIGGS, RAYMOND — Adaptations
BRIGHOUSE (YORKSHIRE) — Civic improvement
BRIGHT, JOHN
BRISBANE (QLD.) — History
BRISBANE STOCK EXCHANGE — History
BRISTOL (AVON) — Economic conditions
BRISTOL (AVON) — Economic policy
BRITISH — Argentina
BRITISH — Australia — Social conditions
BRITISH — Big Sioux River Valley (S.D. and Iowa) — History — 19th century
BRITISH — Canada
BRITISH — China
BRITISH — Spain — History — 20th century
BRITISH — United States
BRITISH AIRPORTS AUTHORITY — Price policy
BRITISH BANK OF THE MIDDLE EAST — history
BRITISH BROADCASTING CORPORATION
BRITISH BROADCASTING CORPORATION — History
BRITISH COLUMBIA — Appropriations and expenditures — Statistics
BRITISH COLUMBIA — Commerce
BRITISH COLUMBIA — Economic conditions
BRITISH COLUMBIA — Economic conditions — Statistics
BRITISH COLUMBIA — Economic policy
BRITISH COLUMBIA — Politics and government
BRITISH COLUMBIA — Politics and government — 1975-
BRITISH GAS CORPORATION
BRITISH GAS CORPORATION — Legal status, laws, etc.
BRITISH GENERAL TARIFF (1932)
BRITISH HOSPITALS CONTRIBUTORY SCHEMES ASSOCIATION
BRITISH LEYLAND MOTOR CORPORATION — History
BRITISH NATIONAL OIL CORPORATION
BRITISH NEWSPAPERS — History — Bibliography
BRITISH NORTH AMERICA ACT, 1867
BRITISH NUCLEAR FUELS LIMITED
BRITISH RAIL
BRITISH RAIL — History
BRITISH RAIL. Scottish Region — Management
BRITISH SHIPBUILDERS
BRITISH SOCIOLOGICAL ASSOCIATION
BRITISH STEEL CORPORATION
BRITISH STEEL CORPORATION — Legal status, laws, etc.
BRITISH TELECOM
BRITISH TELECOM — Legal status, laws, etc.
BRITISH TRANSPORT COMMISSION — History
BRITISH VIRGIN ISLANDS — Economic policy
BRITISH WATERWAYS BOARD
BRITOIL PLC
BRITTANY (FRANCE)
BRITTANY (FRANCE) — Economic conditions — Statistics
BRIXTON (LONDON, ENGLAND) — Riot, 1981
BROADCASTING
BROADCASTING — History
BROADCASTING — Law and legislation — Canada
BROADCASTING — Law and legislation — Ecuador
BROADCASTING — Law and legislation — United States — Digests
BROADCASTING — Management
BROADCASTING — Political aspects — Germany — History
BROADCASTING — Social aspects
BROADCASTING — Africa, Sub-Saharan
BROADCASTING — Australia
BROADCASTING — Developing countries
BROADCASTING — Great Britain — Public opinion
BROADCASTING AND TELEVISION ACT 1942
BROADCASTING BILL 1979-80
BROADCASTING POLICY — Germany — History
BROCK, WILLIAM REES
BROCKDORFF-RANTZAU, ULRICH, Graf von — Biography
BROCKWAY, FENNER
BROILERS (POULTRY) — Trinidad and Tobago — Statistics
BROKEN HILL (N.S.W.) — History
BROKEN HILL (N.S.W.) — Race relations — History
BROKEN HOMES — Denmark
BROKERS — United States
BROWN, ED — Trials, litigation, etc
BRUCE, S. M.
BRUGMANS, HENDRIK
BRUNEI — Constitution
BRUNEI — Economic conditions
BRUNEI — Economic policy
BRUSSELS (BELGIUM) — History
BRYANT, JOHN EMORY
BRYANT & MAY — History
BUBBITT, IRVING, 1865-1933
BUCHANAN, JAMES M.
BUDGET
BUDGET — Law and legislation — United States
BUDGET — Political aspects
BUDGET — Australia
BUDGET — Canada
BUDGET — China — Congresses
BUDGET — Ecuador
BUDGET — France
BUDGET — Great Britain
BUDGET — Hungary
BUDGET — Mauritius
BUDGET — Mexico
BUDGET — Mexico — Mexico (State)
BUDGET — Nigeria
BUDGET — Puerto Rico
BUDGET — Sudan
BUDGET — United States
BUDGET DEFICITS — Canada
BUDGET DEFICITS — Europe
BUDGET DEFICITS — United States
BUDGETS, PERSONAL — Netherlands — Methodology
BUDGETS, PERSONAL — Netherlands — Statistics
BUFFER STATES
BUILDING — Estimates — Finland
BUILDING — Great Britain — Safety measures
BUILDING — Nigeria — Statistics
BUILDING AND LOAN ASSOCIATIONS — Law and legislation — Great Britain
BUILDING AND LOAN ASSOCIATIONS — France — History

BUILDING AND LOAN ASSOCIATIONS — Great Britain
BUILDING AND LOAN ASSOCIATIONS — Great Britain — Statistics
BUILDING LAWS — Great Britain
BUILDING LAWS — Illinois — Chicago
BUILDING MATERIALS — Prices — Peru
BUILDING RESEARCH ESTABLISHMENT
BUILDING TRADES — Social aspects — United States
BUILDINGS — England — Maintenance
BUILDINGS — Great Britain — Repair and reconstruction
BULGARIA — Civilization
BULGARIA — Foreign relations — 1878-1944
BULGARIA — History — 1878-1944
BULGARIA — History — 1944-
BULGARIA — Politics and government — 1878-1944
BULGARIA — Politics and government — 1944-
BULGARIA — Population
BULGARIA — Relations — Soviet Union
BŬLGARSKA KOMUNISTICHESKA PARTIIA
BŬLGARSKA KOMUNISTICHESKA PARTIIA — History
BULK CARRIER CARGO SHIPS
BULK SOLIDS — Transportation
BUNGE & BORN
BURDEN OF PROOF — Great Britain
BUREAUCRACY
BUREAUCRACY — Congresses
BUREAUCRACY — Arabian Peninsula
BUREAUCRACY — China — History
BUREAUCRACY — Hongkong
BUREAUCRACY — India
BUREAUCRACY — Indonesia
BUREAUCRACY — Italy — Florence — History
BUREAUCRACY — Mexico — History
BUREAUCRACY — United States
BURGLARY — Great Britain
BURIAT A.S.S.R. (R.S.F.S.R.) — Social conditions
BURKINA FASO — Census, 1975
BURKINA FASO — Census, 1985
BURKINA FASO — Economic conditions
BURKINA FASO — Economic conditions — Statistics
BURKINA FASO — Economic policy
BURKINA FASO — Population — Statistics
BURKINA FASO — Social conditions — Statistics
BURKINA FASO — Social policy
BURKINA FASO — Statistics
BURMA — History — 1948-
BURMA — Rural conditions
BURTON, JOHN W — Addresses, essays, lectures
BURTON, ORMOND
BURUNDI — Economic Policy
BURUNDI — Social Policy
BUS DRIVERS — Great Britain
BUS LINES — Law and legislation — Great Britain
BUS LINES — Licenses — Great Britain
BUS LINES — Australia
BUS LINES — Great Britain
BUS LINES — Great Britain — Fares — Special rates
BUS LINES — Scotland — History
BUS LINES — Wales, South — History
BUSAN CITY (KOREA (SOUTH)) — Statistics
BUSES — England — London
BUSES — Great Britain
BUSINESS
BUSINESS — Archives
BUSINESS — Data processing
BUSINESS — Dictionaries
BUSINESS — Dictionaries — German
BUSINESS — Information services
BUSINESS — Information services — Directories
BUSINESS — Information services — Great Britain — Directories
BUSINESS — Law and legislation
BUSINESS — Periodicals — Indexes
BUSINESS AND POLITICS — Europe
BUSINESS AND POLITICS — France — Reims — History — 19th century
BUSINESS AND POLITICS — France — Saint Étienne (Loire) — History — 19th century
BUSINESS AND POLITICS — Great Britain
BUSINESS AND POLITICS — Michigan — Case studies
BUSINESS AND POLITICS — United States
BUSINESS ARCHIVES COUNCIL
BUSINESS CYCLES
BUSINESS CYCLES — Congresses
BUSINESS CYCLES — History
BUSINESS CYCLES — Mathematical models
BUSINESS CYCLES — Mathematical models — Congresses
BUSINESS CYCLES — Europe
BUSINESS CYCLES — Europe — Congresses
BUSINESS CYCLES — United States
BUSINESS CYCLES — United States — Addresses, essays, lectures
BUSINESS EDUCATION — United States
BUSINESS EDUCATION GRADUATES — United States
BUSINESS ENTERPRISES
BUSINESS ENTERPRISES — Accounting
BUSINESS ENTERPRISES — Employment — Organization for Economic Co-operation and Development countries
BUSINESS ENTERPRISES — Finance
BUSINESS ENTERPRISES — Finance — Data processing
BUSINESS ENTERPRISES — Finance — Research
BUSINESS ENTERPRISES — Foreign — Government ownership — Bibliography
BUSINESS ENTERPRISES — Political aspects — France
BUSINESS ENTERPRISES — Research
BUSINESS ENTERPRISES — Belgium
BUSINESS ENTERPRISES — Belgium — History — 19th century
BUSINESS ENTERPRISES — Belize — Rules and practice
BUSINESS ENTERPRISES — Burkina Faso
BUSINESS ENTERPRISES — England — London
BUSINESS ENTERPRISES — France
BUSINESS ENTERPRISES — France — Statistics
BUSINESS ENTERPRISES — Germany
BUSINESS ENTERPRISES — Great Britain
BUSINESS ENTERPRISES — Great Britain — History — Bibliography
BUSINESS ENTERPRISES — Great Britain — History — 19th century
BUSINESS ENTERPRISES — Hungary
BUSINESS ENTERPRISES — India — Statistics
BUSINESS ENTERPRISES — Manitoba
BUSINESS ENTERPRISES — Netherlands
BUSINESS ENTERPRISES — Netherlands — Corrupt practices
BUSINESS ENTERPRISES — Norway
BUSINESS ENTERPRISES — Spain
BUSINESS ENTERPRISES — Spain — Finance
BUSINESS ENTERPRISES — Switzerland
BUSINESS ENTERPRISES, FOREIGN — Yugoslavia
BUSINESS ENTREPRISES — Ile-de-France (France)
BUSINESS ETHICS
BUSINESS ETHICS — Addresses, essays, lectures
BUSINESS ETHICS — Congresses
BUSINESS FORECASTING
BUSINESS INTELLIGENCE
BUSINESS MATHEMATICS
BUSINESS MATHEMATICS — Data processing
BUSINESS RECORDS
BUSINESS TAX — Germany (West)
BUSINESS TAX — Great Britain
BUSINESSMEN — Canada — Biography
BUSINESSMEN — Great Britain — Biography
BUSINESSMEN — great Britain — Biography
BUSINESSMEN — Great Britain — Biography
BUSINESSMEN — Great Britain — Political activity
BUSINESSMEN — India — Case studies
BUSINESSMEN — Japan — Biography
BUSINESSMEN — Mexico — History
BUSINESSMEN — Nigeria — Case studies
BUSINESSMEN — Pennsylvania — Philadelphia — History — 18th century
BUSINESSMEN — United States
BUSINESSMEN — United States — Biography
BUSING FOR SCHOOL INTEGRATION — Law and legislation — United States
BUSING FOR SCHOOL INTEGRATION — Massachusetts — Boston
BUSING FOR SCHOOL INTEGRATION — Tennessee — Nashville — History
BUSOGA (UGANDA) — Social life and customs
BUTLER, RICHARD AUSTEN BUTLER, Baron
BYELORUSSIAN S.S.R. — History — February Revolution, 1917
BYELORUSSIAN S.S.R. — Politics and government
BYELORUSSIAN S.S.R. — Religion
BYRDCLIFFE (Art colony) — Exhibitions
BYZANTINE EMPIRE — History
C O B O L (COMPUTER PROGRAM LANGUAGE)
C.1673-1717
CABINET MINISTERS — Canada — Biography
CABINET OFFICERS — Handbooks, manuals, etc
CABINET OFFICERS — Canada — Biography
CABINET OFFICERS — Great Britain
CABINET OFFICERS — Great Britain — History — 19th century
CABINET OFFICERS — Great Britain — History — 20th century
CABINET OFFICERS — Ontario — Biography
CABINET OFFICERS — Poland
CABINET OFFICERS — United States — Biography
CABINET SYSTEM — Great Britain
CABLE TELEVISION — Management
CABLE TELEVISION — Canada — Statistics
CABLE TELEVISION — Great Britain
CACAO
CACAO — Research
CADASTERS — Soviet Union — History — 17th century
CÁDIZ (SPAIN) — Politics and government — History — 19th century
CAJUNS — Louisiana — Henderson — Social conditions
CALCULUS
CALCULUS, DIFFERENTIAL
CALCULUS, INTEGRAL
CALCULUS OF VARIATIONS
CALI (COLOMBIA) — Economic conditions
CALIFORNIA, SOUTHERN — History
CALIFORNIA, SOUTHERN — Social life and customs
CALIFORNIA STATE UNIVERSITIES AND COLLEGES — Faculty — Statistics
CALLAGHAN, JAMES

CALVINISTS — England — South East — History — 16th century
CALVINISTS — England — South East — Social conditions
CALVINSIM — France — History
CAMBODIA — Biography
CAMBODIA — History — 20th century
CAMBODIA — History — Civil War, 1970-1975
CAMBODIA — History — 1975-
CAMBODIA — Politics and government
CAMBODIA — Social life and customs
CAMBODIAN-VIETNAMESE CONFLICT, 1977-
CAMBRIDGE (CAMBRIDGESHIRE) — Intellectual life
CAMBRIDGE SCIENTIFIC INSTRUMENT COMPANY — History
CAMBRIDGE UNIVERSITY — History — 20th century
CAMDEN. Borough Council
CAMDEN. Housing Department
CAMDEN (LONDON, ENGLAND) — Economic conditions — Statistics
CAMDEN (LONDON, ENGLAND) — Population
CAMDEN (LONDON, ENGLAND) — Population — Statistics
CAMEROON — Bibliography
CAMEROON — Constitution
CAMEROON — Economic conditions — Statistics
CAMEROON — Economic Conditions — 1960- — Statistics
CAMEROON — History — Chronology
CAMEROON — History — Dictionaries
CAMEROON — Politics and government
CAMEROON — Population — Bibliography
CAMEROON — Population — Statistics
CAMEROON — Population — Statistics — Evaluation
CAMEROON — Statistics
CAMPAIGN FOR A SCOTTISH ASSEMBLY
CAMPAIGN FOR NUCLEAR DISARMAMENT
CAMPAIGN FOR NUCLEAR DISARMAMENT — History
CAMPAIGN FUNDS — United States
CAMPALANS, ALBERT
CAMPBELL, JOHN LOGAN
CAMPBELL, TUNIS
CAMRAN (YEMEN) — Social conditions
CAMRAN (YEMEN) — Social life and customs
CANADA. Atlantic Fisheries Restructuring Act 1983
CANADA. Canada Health Act 1984
CANADA. Canadian Charter of Rights and Freedoms
CANADA. Constitution Act, 1982
CANADA. Constitutional Act 1982
CANADA. Public Service Superannuation Act (Canada)
CANADA — Air defenses, Military
CANADA — Bibliography
CANADA — Canadian Charter of Rights and Freedoms
CANADA — Civilization — 1945- — Congresses
CANADA — Combines Investigation Act
CANADA — Commerce
CANADA — Commerce — History
CANADA — Commerce — Communist countries
CANADA — Commerce — European Economic Community
CANADA — Commerce — France — History — 18th century
CANADA — Commerce — Great Britain
CANADA — Commerce — Japan
CANADA — Commerce — United States
CANADA — Commercial policy
CANADA — Commercial policy — History — 19th century
CANADA — Constitution
CANADA — Constitutional law
CANADA — Constitutional law — Amendments
CANADA — Cultural policy — Congresses
CANADA — Defenses
CANADA — Department of Industry, Trade and Commerce
CANADA — Department of Regional Economic Expansion
CANADA — Department of Regional Industrial Expansion
CANADA — Diplomatic and consular service — History
CANADA — Economic conditions
CANADA — Economic conditions — Addresses, essays, lectures
CANADA — Economic conditions — Bibliography
CANADA — Economic conditions — Statistics
CANADA — Economic conditions — 1918-1945
CANADA — Economic conditions — 1918-
CANADA — Economic conditions — 1945-
CANADA — Economic conditions — 1945- — Regional disparities
CANADA — Economic conditions — 1971-
CANADA — Economic policy
CANADA — Economic policy — Congresses
CANADA — Economic policy — 1971-
CANADA — Economics condition — 1945-
CANADA — Emigration and immigration
CANADA — emigration and immigration
CANADA — Emigration and immigration
CANADA — Emigration and immigration — History
CANADA — Foreign economic relations
CANADA — Foreign economic relations — United States
CANADA — Foreign economic relations — United States — Congresses
CANADA — Foreign population
CANADA — Foreign relations
CANADA — Foreign relations — Congresses
CANADA — Foreign relations — History
CANADA — Foreign relations — 1945-
CANADA — Foreign relations — 1945- — Citizen participation
CANADA — Foreign relations — Great Britain
CANADA — Foreign relations — South Africa
CANADA — Foreign relations — United States
CANADA — Foreign relations — Vietnam
CANADA — Foreign relations administration
CANADA — Government publications
CANADA — Historiography
CANADA — History
CANADA — History — To 1763
CANADA — History — To 1763 (New France)
CANADA — History — 1867-1914
CANADA — History — 1914-1945
CANADA — Indexes
CANADA — Indian Act — 1984
CANADA — Industries — Statistics
CANADA — Intellectual life — History
CANADA — Library resources — Europe
CANADA — Manufactures
CANADA — Manufactures — Statistics
CANADA — Maps
CANADA — Military policy
CANADA — Military policy — Economic aspects
CANADA — Military relations — United States
CANADA — National security — Congresses
CANADA — Native races — Bibliography
CANADA — Occupations
CANADA — Officials and employees
CANADA — Politics and government
CANADA — Politics and government — 1867-1896
CANADA — Politics and government — 20th century
CANADA — Politics and government — 1914-1945
CANADA — Politics and government — 1945-1980
CANADA — Politics and government — 1945-
CANADA — Politics and government — 1957-1963
CANADA — Politics and government — 1963-1968
CANADA — Politics and government — 1963-
CANADA — Politics and government — 1968-1969
CANADA — Politics and government — 1980-1984
CANADA — Politics and government — 1980-
CANADA — Politics and government — 1981-
CANADA — Politics and government — 1984-
CANADA — Population
CANADA — Population — Bibliography
CANADA — Race relations
CANADA — Relations — East Asia
CANADA — Relations — Foreign countries
CANADA — Relations — Newfoundland
CANADA — Relations — Pacific Ocean Region — Congresses
CANADA — Relations — United States
CANADA — Religion
CANADA — Social conditions
CANADA — Social conditions — 20th century
CANADA — Social conditions — 1945-
CANADA — Social policy
CANADA — Social policy — Congresses
CANADA — Study and teaching — Europe
CANADA. Agriculture Canada. Research Branch
CANADA. Canadian armed forces — History
CANADA. Chief Electoral Officer
CANADA. Commission of Inquiry on War Criminals
CANADA. Department of External Affairs
CANADA. Department of Finance — History
CANADA. Department of Industry, Trade and Commerce
CANADA. Department of Regional Economic Expansion
CANADA. Department of Regional Industrial Expansion
CANADA. Emergency Planning Canada
CANADA. Indian Affairs Branch — History
CANADA. Investment Canada
CANADA. Northern Pipeline Agency
CANADA. Parlament. House of Commons. Standing Committee on External Affairs and National Defence
CANADA. Parliament — Elections, 1984
CANADA. Parliament. House of Commons
CANADA. Parliament. House of Commons — Biography
CANADA. Parliament. House of Commons — Speaker — Biography
CANADA. Parliament. House of Commons. Standing Committee on Finance and Economic Affairs
CANADA. Parliament. House of Commons. Standing Committee on Justice and Legal Affairs
CANADA. Parliament. House of Commons. Standing Committee on Justice and Solicitor General
CANADA. Parliament. House of Commons. Standing Committee on Labour, Employment and Immigration
CANADA. Parliament. House of Commons. Standing Committee on Labour, Manpower and Immigration

CANADA. Parliament. House of Commons. Standing Committee on Priviledges and Elections
CANADA. Parliament. House of Commons. Standing Committee on Secretary of State
CANADA. Parliament. Senate — Biography
CANADA. Parliament. Senate. Standing Committee on Foreign Affairs
CANADA. Petroleum Incentives Administration
CANADA. Royal Commission on Equality in Employment
CANADA. Security Intelligence Review Committee
CANADA. Supreme Court — History
CANADA, EASTERN — Commerce — New England
CANADA EMPLOYMENT AND IMMIGRATION ADVISORY COUNCIL
CANADA HEALTH ACT 1984
CANADA LABOUR RELATIONS BOARD
CANADA, NORTHERN — History
CANADA OIL AND GAS LANDS ADMINISTRATION
CANADA-ONTARIO-INDUSTRY ROCKBURST PROJECT
CANADA, WESTERN — Bibliography
CANADA, WESTERN — History — Bibliography
CANADIAN AIR LINE FLIGHT ATTENDANTS' ASSOCIATION — History
CANADIAN AVIATION SAFETY BOARD
CANADIAN BAR ASSOCIATION
CANADIAN HUMAN RIGHTS COMMISSION
CANADIAN SEAMEN'S UNION
CANADIAN SEAMEN'S UNION — History
CANADIAN SECURITY INTELLIGENCE SERVICE
CANADIAN WHO'S WHO — Indexes
CANALS — Law and legislation — Egypt
CANALS — Great Britain — Recreational use
CANARY ISLANDS — Appropriations and expenditures
CANARY ISLANDS — Commerce
CANARY ISLANDS — Politics and government
CANBERRA (A.C.T.) — History
CANCER — Government policy — United States — History
CANCER — Mortality — Netherlands — Statistics
CANCER — Reporting — Great Britain
CANCER — England — Cumbria
CANCER — England — West Cumbria
CANCER — Great Britain — Statistics
CANCER — United States — Statistics
CANNABIS
CANNABIS — Physiological effect
CANNIBALISM
CANNIBALISM — Congresses
CANNING AND PRESERVING — Industry and trade — Hawaii — History
CANTABRIA (SPAIN) — History
CANTABRIA (SPAIN) — History — 20th century
CANTABRIA (SPAIN) — Social conditions
CANTERBURY CATHEDRAL — History
CANTILLON, RICHARD
CANVASSING
CAPE OF GOOD HOPE (SOUTH AFRICA) — Frontier troubles
CAPE OF GOOD HOPE (SOUTH AFRICA) — History — 1795-1872
CAPE VERDE — Bibliography
CAPE VERDE — Census, 1970
CAPE VERDE — Census, 1980
CAPE VERDE — Commerce — Statistics
CAPE VERDE — History — Dictionaries
CAPE VERDE — Politics and government
CAPE VERDE — Population — Statistics
CAPITAL
CAPITAL — Mathematical models

CAPITAL — Canada
CAPITAL — Great Britain
CAPITAL — India
CAPITAL — Soviet Union
CAPITAL — United States
CAPITAL — United States — Congresses
CAPITAL ASSETS PRICING MODEL
CAPITAL BUDGET
CAPITAL GAINS TAX — Law and legislation — United States
CAPITAL GAINS TAX — Great Britain
CAPITAL INVESTMENTS
CAPITAL INVESTMENTS — Evaluation
CAPITAL INVESTMENTS — Colombia
CAPITAL INVESTMENTS — Finland
CAPITAL INVESTMENTS — Great Britain
CAPITAL LEVY
CAPITAL LEVY — Mathematical models
CAPITAL LEVY — Turkey
CAPITAL LEVY — United States
CAPITAL MARKET
CAPITAL MARKET — Australia
CAPITAL MOVEMENTS
CAPITAL MOVEMENTS — Law and legislation — Organisation for Economic Co-operation and Development countries
CAPITAL MOVEMENTS — Japan
CAPITAL MOVEMENTS — Organisation for Economic Co-operation and Development countries — Statistics
CAPITAL MOVEMENTS — Pacific Area
CAPITAL PRODUCTIVITY — Norway
CAPITAL PUNISHMENT — Great Britain
CAPITAL PUNISHMENT — Great Britain — History — 20th century
CAPITAL STOCK — Great Britain
CAPITAL STOCK — Organisation for Economic Co-operation and Development countries — Statistics
CAPITALISM
CAPITALISM — Addresses, essays, lectures
CAPITALISM — Congresses
CAPITALISM — History
CAPITALISM — Moral and ethical aspects
CAPITALISM — Religious aspects
CAPITALISM — Australia
CAPITALISM — China — History — 19th century
CAPITALISM — Developing countries
CAPITALISM — Hungary
CAPITALISM — Ivory coast — History
CAPITALISM — Kenya — History
CAPITALISM — Latin America
CAPITALISM — Latin America — History
CAPITALISM — Nigeria — History
CAPITALISM — North Carolina — History
CAPITALISM — Puerto Rico — History
CAPITALISM — South Africa
CAPITALISM — Soviet Union — History
CAPITALISTS AND FINANCIERS — Ivory Coast — History
CAPITALISTS AND FINANCIERS — Kenya — History
CAPITALISTS AND FINANCIERS — Nigeria — History
CAPITALISTS AND FINANCIERS — Southern States — History — 19th century
CAPITALISTS AND FINANCIERS — United States — Biography
CAPITALS (CITIES) — Dictionaries
CARACAS (VENEZUELA) — History
CARDANHA (PORTUGAL) — Population, Rural — History
CARDANHA (PORTUGAL) — Statistics, Vital — History
CARDIAC PACEMAKER INDUSTRY — France
CARDIGANSHIRE — Industries — Statistics
CARDINALS — Poland — Biography
CARDIOVASCULAR SYSTEM — Diseases — Nutritional aspects
CAREER DEVELOPMENT — United States
CAREER EDUCATION — European Economic Community countries

CAREER EDUCATION — Great Britain
CAREER EDUCATION — Great Britain — Management
CARIB INDIANS — Saint Vincent — Folklore
CARIBBEAN AREA — Archival resources
CARIBBEAN AREA — Armed Forces
CARIBBEAN AREA — Census — Handbooks, manuals, etc
CARIBBEAN AREA — Congresses
CARIBBEAN AREA — Economic conditions — 1945- — Congresses
CARIBBEAN AREA — Foreign relations
CARIBBEAN AREA — Foreign relations — Soviet Union
CARIBBEAN AREA — Foreign relations — United States
CARIBBEAN AREA — Politics and government — 1945-
CARIBBEAN AREA — Politics and government — 1945- — Congresses
CARIBBEAN AREA — Relations — Europe
CARIBBEAN AREA — Research
CARIBBEAN AREA — Social conditions — 1945-
CARINTHIA (AUSTRIA) — Ethnic relations
CARINTHIA (AUSTRIA) — Politics and government
CARINTHIA (AUSTRIA) — Social conditions
CARLISTS
CARLISTS — Biography
CARLOS, Prince of Bourbon
CARRERO BLANCO, LUIS
CARROLL, LEWIS — Biography
CARTER, JIMMY — Views on civil rights
CARTOGRAPHY
CARTOGRAPHY — Data processing
CARTULARIES
CASELY HAYFORD, ADELAIDE SMITH
CASEY, RICHARD GARDINER CASEY, Baron
CASH FLOW
CASH FLOW — Accounting
CASH FLOW — Great Britain — Management
CASSAVA INDUSTRY — India — Kerala
CAST
CAST-IRON — Economic aspects
CASTE — India
CASTE — India — Bengal
CASTE — India — Nagpur
CASTELLÓN DE LA PLANA (SPAIN) — Politics and government
CASTILE (SPAIN) — Economic conditions
CASTILLA-LA MANCHA (SPAIN) — Politics and government
CASTILLO RIVAS, ANA MARÍA — Biography
CASTRO, FIDEL
CASTRO, FIDEL — Psychology
CASTRO, FIDEL — Public opinion — Congresses
CATALAN LANGUAGE — Political aspects — Spain
CATALANS — Ethnic identity
CATALOGS, ON-LINE
CATALOGS, UNION — United States
CATALONIA (SPAIN) — Economic conditions
CATALONIA (SPAIN) — Economic conditions — Congresses
CATALONIA (SPAIN) — Emigration and immigration
CATALONIA (SPAIN) — Foreign economic relations
CATALONIA (SPAIN) — History
CATALONIA (SPAIN) — History — Autonomy and independence movements
CATALONIA (SPAIN) — History — 20th century
CATALONIA (SPAIN) — History — Autonomy and independence movements
CATALONIA (SPAIN) — Politics and government

CATALONIA (SPAIN) — Politics and government — 20th century
CATALONIA (SPAIN) — Public works — History
CATALONIA (SPAIN) — Relations — Europe
CATALONIA (SPAIN) — Social conditions
CATERERS AND CATERING — Great Britain
CATERERS AND CATERING — Great Britain — Statistics
CATHOLIC CHURCH — Doctrines
CATHOLIC CHURCH — Doctrines — Addresses, essays, lectures
CATHOLIC CHURCH — History — 20th century
CATHOLIC CHURCH — Argentina — History
CATHOLIC CHURCH — Brazil — History
CATHOLIC CHURCH — Brazil — History — 20th century
CATHOLIC CHURCH — Byelorussian S.S.R.
CATHOLIC CHURCH — Guatemala — History
CATHOLIC CHURCH — Ireland — History
CATHOLIC CHURCH — Latin America — History — 20th century — Addresses, essays, lectures
CATHOLIC CHURCH — Nicaragua
CATHOLIC CHURCH — Nicaragua — History — 20th century
CATHOLIC CHURCH — Poland
CATHOLIC CHURCH — Poland — Clergy
CATHOLIC CHURCH — Poland — Clergy — Biography
CATHOLIC CHURCH — Spain
CATHOLIC CHURCH — Spain — Congresses
CATHOLIC CHURCH — Spain — History
CATHOLIC CHURCH — Spain — History — Congresses
CATHOLIC CHURCH — Spain — History — 20th century
CATHOLIC CHURCH — United States
CATHOLIC CHURCH. National Conference of Catholic Bishops. Challenge of peace — Addresses, essays, lectures
CATHOLIC CHURCH. National Conference of Catholic Bishops
CATHOLIC CHURCH (Poland)
CATHOLIC CHURCH — Social aspects
CATHOLIC CHURCH — Argentina — Social aspects
CATHOLIC CHURCH AND WORLD POLITICS — History — 20th century
CATHOLICS — England — History — 20th century
CATHOLICS — Ireland — History
CATHOLICS — Northern Ireland — History
CATHOLICS — United States — Attitudes
CATT, CARRIE CHAPMAN
CATTLE — Prices — Peru
CATTLE — Denmark
CATTLE TRADE — Central America
CAUCASIAN RACE
CAUSATION
CAYMAN ISLANDS — Census, 1960
CAYMAN ISLANDS — Census, 1979
CAYMAN ISLANDS — Population — Statistics
CAYMAN ISLANDS. Legislative Assembly — Elections, 1976
CELTIC LANGUAGES
CELTS — Political activity
CELTS — Great Britain
CEMENT INDUSTRIES
CEMENT INDUSTRIES — Japan
CENSORSHIP
CENSORSHIP — Addresses, essays, lectures
CENSORSHIP — Great Britain — History
CENSORSHIP — United States
CENSUS — Handbooks, manuals, etc
CENSUS — Methodology
CENTRAL AFRICAN REPUBLIC — History — Dictionaries
CENTRAL AMERICA — Archival resources
CENTRAL AMERICA — Economic conditions
CENTRAL AMERICA — Economic conditions — 1979- — Congresses
CENTRAL AMERICA — Economic integration
CENTRAL AMERICA — Foreign relations — 1979-
CENTRAL AMERICA — Foreign relations — United States
CENTRAL AMERICA — History — 1951-
CENTRAL AMERICA — Politics and government
CENTRAL AMERICA — Politics and government — 1979-
CENTRAL AMERICA — Politics and government — 1979- — Congresses
CENTRAL AMERICA — Relations (Military) — United States
CENTRAL AMERICA — Research
CENTRAL COMPUTER AND TELECOMMUNICATIONS AGENCY
CENTRAL COUNCIL FOR EDUCATION AND TRAINING IN SOCIAL WORK
CENTRAL EUROPEAN CANADIANS — Congresses
CENTRAL INTELLIGENCE AGENCY
CENTRAL PLANNING — Communist countries
CENTRAL PLANNING — Great Britain
CENTRAL PLANNING — Poland
CENTRAL PLANNING — Soviet Union
CENTRAL PLANNING — Soviet Union — Data processing
CENTRAL PLANNING — Ukraine
CENTRAL PROVINCE (PAPUA NEW GUINEA) — Population — Statistics
CENTRE FOR POLICY RESEARCH (New Delhi, India)
CENTRE ON INTEGRATED RURAL DEVELOPMENT FOR ASIA AND THE PACIFIC
CEREAL PRODUCTS — European Economic Community countries
CEREMONIAL EXCHANGE — Papua New Guinea
CHAADAEV, P. IA.
CHACO WAR, 1932-1935 — Campaigns
CHAD — Bibliography
CHAD — History — Dictionaries
CHAD — Social conditions
CHAFEE, ZECHARIAH
CHAGA (AFRICAN PEOPLE) — Social life and customs
CHAIANOV, A. V.
CHALLENGE OF PEACE
CHAMBRI (PAPUA NEW GUINEA PEOPLE)
CHANGE (PSYCHOLOGY)
CHANNEL ISLANDS — Economic conditions
CHANNEL ISLANDS — History
CHANNEL TUNNEL
CHARITABLE USES, TRUSTS, AND FOUNDATIONS — United States — History
CHARITABLE USES, TRUSTS, AND FOUNDATIONS (ISLAMIC LAW) — India
CHARITIES — History
CHARITIES — Denmark
CHARITIES — England
CHARITIES — England — Cambridge (Cambridgeshire) — History
CHARITIES — France — Grenoble — History — 17th century
CHARITIES — France — Grenoble — History — 18th century
CHARITIES — Great Britain
CHARITIES — Great Britain — Finance
CHARITIES — Spain — Valladolid — History
CHARITIES — United States
CHARITIES, MEDICAL — Great Britain
CHARITY LAWS AND LEGISLATION — Great Britain
CHARTER-PARTIES — Great Britain
CHARTERED ASSOCIATION OF CERTIFIED ACCOUNTANTS
CHARTISM
CHARWOMEN AND CLEANERS — India — Delhi — Economic conditions
CHASE MANHATTAN BANK, N.A — History — 20th century
CHEBYSHEV APPROXIMATION
CHECKS — Legal status, laws, etc. — Ecuador
CHEMICAL INDUSTRY — Government policy — Germany — History
CHEMICAL INDUSTRY — Government policy — Ukraine
CHEMICAL INDUSTRY — Germany — History
CHEMICAL INDUSTRY — Germany (West) — History
CHEMICAL INDUSTRY — Switzerland — History
CHEMICAL INDUSTRY — Ukraine
CHEMICAL WARFARE
CHEMICAL WARFARE — History
CHEMICAL WARFARE — Germany (West)
CHEMICAL-WEAPON-FREE ZONES
CHEMICALS — Hygienic aspects
CHEMISTRY, FORENSIC
CHEMISTRY, FORENSIC — England
CHENG, NIEN
CHESHIRE — History
CHESHIRE (ENGLAND) — Population
CHIANG, KAI-SHEK
CHICAGO (Ill.). Department of Buildings
CHICAGO (ILL.) — Ethnic relations
CHICAGO (ILL.) — Race relations
CHICAGO SCHOOL OF ECONOMICS
CHICAGO SCHOOL OF ECONOMISTS
CHICAGO SCHOOL OF SOCIOLOGY — History
CHILD ABUSE
CHILD ABUSE — Bibliography
CHILD ABUSE — Congresses
CHILD ABUSE — Psychological aspects
CHILD ABUSE — Services
CHILD ABUSE — Services — Scotland
CHILD ABUSE — Canada
CHILD ABUSE — Great Britain
CHILD ABUSE — Great Britain — Bibliography
CHILD ABUSE — South Africa
CHILD ABUSE — United States
CHILD ABUSE — United States — Addresses, essays, lectures
CHILD CARE
CHILD CARE — Law and legislation — Great Britain
CHILD CARE — Great Britain
CHILD CARE — Great Britain — Case studies
CHILD CARE SERVICES — Government policy
CHILD CARE SERVICES — Government policy — Great Britain
CHILD CARE SERVICES — England — London
CHILD CARE SERVICES — Great Britain
CHILD DEVELOPMENT
CHILD DEVELOPMENT — Congresses
CHILD DEVELOPMENT — popular works
CHILD DEVELOPMENT — Testing
CHILD DEVELOPMENT — Great Britain — Case studies
CHILD DEVELOPMENT — Japan
CHILD DEVELOPMENT DEVIATIONS — Diagnosis
CHILD HEALTH SERVICES — Africa, Sub-Saharan
CHILD HEALTH SERVICES — United States
CHILD HEALTH SERVICES — United States — Cost control
CHILD HEALTH SERVICES — Wales

CHILD LABOR
CHILD LABOR — Case studies
CHILD LABOR — Statistics
CHILD MOLESTERS
CHILD MOLESTING
CHILD MOLESTING — Investigation
CHILD MOLESTING — South Australia
CHILD MOLESTING — United States
CHILD MOLESTING — United States — Addresses, essays, lectures
CHILD POVERTY ACTION GROUP
CHILD PSYCHOLOGY
CHILD PSYCHOLOGY — Addresses, essays, lectures
CHILD PSYCHOLOGY — popular works
CHILD PSYCHOTHERAPY
CHILD PSYCHOTHERAPY — Residential treatment
CHILD PSYCHOTHERAPY — Residential treatment — England — London Metropolitan Area
CHILD REARING — Economic aspects — Great Britain
CHILD REARING — Great Britain — Case studies
CHILD REARING — United States
CHILD SUPPORT — Great Britain
CHILD WELFARE — Bibliography
CHILD WELFARE — Government policy — Australia — History — 20th century
CHILD WELFARE — Law and legislation — England
CHILD WELFARE — Canada
CHILD WELFARE — Developing countries — History
CHILD WELFARE — England
CHILD WELFARE — England — History — 20th century
CHILD WELFARE — France — Nomenclature
CHILD WELFARE — Great Britain
CHILD WELFARE — United States
CHILD WELFARE — United States — Addresses, essays, lectures
CHILDBIRTH — Psychology
CHILDBIRTH — Great Britain — History
CHILDBIRTH — Great Britain — Statistics
CHILDE, V. GORDON
CHILDHOOD FRIENDSHIP
CHILDREN
CHILDREN — Attitudes — Addresses, essays, lectures
CHILDREN — Care and hygiene
CHILDREN — Care and hygiene — Denmark
CHILDREN — Care and hygiene — Developing countries
CHILDREN — Care and hygiene — France — Costs
CHILDREN — Death — Psychological aspects
CHILDREN — Economic aspects — Sri Lanka
CHILDREN — Employment
CHILDREN — Employment — Bibliography
CHILDREN — Employment — Bangladesh
CHILDREN — Government policy — Great Britain
CHILDREN — Institutional care — Law and legislation — England
CHILDREN — Institutional care — Australia
CHILDREN — Institutional care — Denmark
CHILDREN — Institutional care — England
CHILDREN — Institutional care — England — Congresses
CHILDREN — Institutional care — England — Formby (Lancashire)
CHILDREN — Institutional care — Great Britain
CHILDREN — Institutional care — Scotland
CHILDREN — Interviews
CHILDREN — Language
CHILDREN — Language — Congresses
CHILDREN — Legal status, laws, etc
CHILDREN — Legal status, laws, etc — Canada
CHILDREN — Legal status, laws, etc. — Great Britain
CHILDREN — Mortality — Social aspects — Bangladesh
CHILDREN — Mortality — Statistical methods
CHILDREN — Nutrition
CHILDREN — Suicidal behavior
CHILDREN — Africa — Mortality — Bibliography
CHILDREN — Africa, Southern
CHILDREN — Africa, Sub-saharan — Care and hygiene
CHILDREN — Africa, Subsaharan — Mortality
CHILDREN — Belgium — Ghent — History
CHILDREN — Ecuador — Mortality
CHILDREN — England — Buckinghamshire — Longitudinal studies
CHILDREN — Great Britain — History
CHILDREN — Great Britain — Nutrition
CHILDREN — Great Britain — Social conditions
CHILDREN — Guyana — Mortality
CHILDREN — Haiti — Mortality — Statistics
CHILDREN — India
CHILDREN — Jamaica — Mortality
CHILDREN — Northern Ireland
CHILDREN — Peru — Mortality — Statistics
CHILDREN — Scotland
CHILDREN — Scotland — Care and hygiene
CHILDREN — Spain
CHILDREN — Syria — Mortality — Statistics
CHILDREN — Trinidad and Tobago — Mortality
CHILDREN — Uganda — Social conditions
CHILDREN — United States — History
CHILDREN, ADOPTED — Canada — Interviews
CHILDREN AND DEATH
CHILDREN AND WAR — Bibliography
CHILDREN AND YOUNG PERSONS ACT, 1964
CHILDREN, BLACK — South Africa
CHILDREN, DEAF — Language
CHILDREN, FIRST-BORN
CHILDREN OF DIVORCED PARENTS — Finance
CHILDREN OF DIVORCED PARENTS — Mental health
CHILDREN OF DIVORCED PARENTS — Denmark
CHILDREN OF DIVORCED PARENTS — United States
CHILDREN OF HOLOCAUST SURVIVORS — Austria — Biography
CHILDREN OF HOLOCAUST SURVIVORS — Germany (West) — Biography
CHILDREN OF IMMIGRANTS — Education — Organisation for Economic Co-operation and Development countries
CHILDREN OF IMMIGRANTS — France
CHILDREN OF INTERRACIAL MARRIAGE — Great Britain
CHILDREN OF MIGRANT LABORERS — Education — Germany (West) — Munich
CHILDREN OF MIGRANT LABORERS — European Economic Community countries
CHILDREN OF MINORITIES — Government policy — Great Britain
CHILDREN OF MINORITIES — Great Britain
CHILDREN OF MINORITIES — Great Britain — Books and reading
CHILDREN OF PRISONERS — Great Britain
CHILDREN OF WORKING MOTHERS — United States
CHILDREN OF WORKING PARENTS — United States
CHILDREN'S ACCIDENTS — Prevention
CHILDREN'S CLUBS
CHILDREN'S LITERATURE
CHILDREN'S LITERATURE — Great Britain
CHILE — Bibliography — Union lists
CHILE — Biography — 20th century
CHILE — Boundaries — Argentina
CHILE — Commerce
CHILE — Commerce — Great Britain — History — 19th century
CHILE — Constitutional history
CHILE — Econmic policy
CHILE — Economic conditions — 1970-
CHILE — Economic conditions — 1970- — Addresses, essays, lectures
CHILE — History — 1824-1920
CHILE — History — 1920-
CHILE — History — Coup d'état, 1973
CHILE — Imprints — Union lists
CHILE — Politics and government
CHILE — Politics and government — 1970-1973
CHILE — Politics and government — 1970-
CHILE — Politics and government — 1973- — Addresses, essays, lectures
CHILE — Social conditions
CHILE — Statistics
CHILEANS — Scotland
CHIMBU PROVINCE (PAPUA NEW GUINEA) — Population — Statistics
CHINA
CHINA — Armed Forces
CHINA — Biography
CHINA — Boundaries — India
CHINA — Civilization — Congresses
CHINA — Commerce — History — 19th century
CHINA — Commerce — Great Britain — History — 19th century
CHINA — Commerce — United States — History — 19th century
CHINA — Commercial policy
CHINA — Description and travel — To 1900
CHINA — Descriptions and travel — 1949-
CHINA — Econmic conditions — 1976-
CHINA — Economic conditions
CHINA — Economic conditions — 1912-1949
CHINA — Economic conditions — 1949-1976
CHINA — Economic conditions — 1949-
CHINA — Economic conditions — 1976-
CHINA — Economic policy
CHINA — Economic policy — 1976-
CHINA — Economic policy — 1976- — Congresses
CHINA — Emigration and immigration — History
CHINA — Foreign economic relations
CHINA — Foreign economic relations — United States
CHINA — Foreign relations — 1644-1912
CHINA — Foreign relations — 1949-1976
CHINA — Foreign relations — 1949-
CHINA — Foreign relations — 1976-
CHINA — Foreign relations — 1976- — Addresses, essays, lectures
CHINA — Foreign relations — Albania
CHINA — Foreign relations — Great Britain
CHINA — Foreign relations — Indochina
CHINA — Foreign relations — Nepal
CHINA — Foreign relations — Soviet Union
CHINA — Foreign relations — Sri Lanka
CHINA — Foreign relations — Tibet (China)
CHINA — Foreign relations — United States

CHINA — Foreign relations — United States — Case studies
CHINA — History — 1861-1912
CHINA — History — Hsüan-t'ung, 1908-1912
CHINA — History — Revolution, 1911-1912
CHINA — History — Revolution, 1911-1912 — Addresses, essays, lectures
CHINA — History — Republic, 1912-1949 — Addresses, essays, lectures
CHINA — History — May Fourth Movement, 1919
CHINA — History — 1937-1945
CHINA — History — Civil war, 1945-1949
CHINA — History — 1949- — Addresses, essays, lectures
CHINA — History — 1949- — Chronology
CHINA — Industries — Research
CHINA — Intellectual life — 20th century
CHINA — Kings and rulers — Biography
CHINA — Library resources — Europe
CHINA — Politics and government
CHINA — Politics and government — 1368-1644
CHINA — Politics and government — 1644-1912
CHINA — Politics and government — 1912-1949
CHINA — Politics and government — 1949-1976
CHINA — Politics and government — 1949-
CHINA — Politics and government — 1976-
CHINA — Politics and government — 1976- — Congresses
CHINA — Politics and government — 1949-
CHINA — Population density — History
CHINA — Presidents — Biography
CHINA — Relations — Asia, Southeastern
CHINA — Relations — India
CHINA — Relations — United States
CHINA — Relations — United States — Bibliography
CHINA — Religion
CHINA — Religious life and customs
CHINA — Social conditions
CHINA — Social conditions — 1644-1912
CHINA — Social conditions — 1912-1949
CHINA — Social conditions — 1976-
CHINA — Social life and customs — Addresses, essays, lectures
CHINA — Study and teaching — Taiwan
CHINA — Study and teaching — United States
CHINA. Chung-kuo jen min chieh fang chün — Biography
CHINA. National People's Congress
CHINA — History — 1912-1937
CHINA, SOUTHWEST — Politics and government
CHINESE — Asia, Southeastern
CHINESE — East Asia
CHINESE — Foreign countries — History
CHINESE — Great Britain
CHINESE — Singapore — Economic conditions
CHINESE — Singapore — History
CHINESE — Singapore — Social conditions
CHINESE — Singapore — Societies, etc
CHINESE — South Africa
CHINESE — United States — History — 19th century
CHINESE AMERICANS — Ethnic identity
CHINESE AMERICANS — History
CHINESE AMERICANS — Social conditions
CHINESE IN AUSTRALIA — History
CHINESE REUNIFICATION QUESTION, 1949-
CHIROL, VALENTINE
CHLORIDES
CHLORINE INDUSTRY — Taiwan
CHOICE OF TRANSPORTATION
CHOICE (PSYCHOLOGY) — Congresses
CHOLERA, ASIATIC — France — Paris — History — 19th century
CHOU, EN-LAI
CHRÉTIEN, JEAN
CHRISTIAN COMMUNITIES — Catholic Church
CHRISTIAN COMMUNITIES — Brazil
CHRISTIAN COMMUNITIES — Philippines
CHRISTIAN LIFE
CHRISTIAN SAINTS — Biography
CHRISTIAN SAINTS — Dictionaries
CHRISTIAN SOCIALIST MOVEMENT — History
CHRISTIAN ZIONISM — History of doctrines — 20th century
CHRISTIANITY
CHRISTIANITY — Psychology
CHRISTIANITY — Canada — 19th century
CHRISTIANITY — Great Britain — Attitudes
CHRISTIANITY — Philippines
CHRISTIANITY — Sweden
CHRISTIANITY AND ECONOMICS
CHRISTIANITY AND JUSTICE — Georgia
CHRISTIANITY AND POLITICS
CHRISTIANS — Soviet Union
CHRISTLICH DEMOKRATISCHE VOLKSPARTEI DER SCHWEIZ
CHRONIC DISEASES — Epidemiology
CHRONICALLY SICK AND DISABLED PERSONS (AMENDMENT) BILL 1983-84
CHRONOLOGY, HISTORICAL
CHRONOLOGY, HISTORICAL — Charts, diagrams, etc
CHRYSLER CORPORATION — History
CH'UNG, HSUAN-T'UNG, Emperor of China, 1906-1967
CHUNGCHEONG BUG DO (KOREA (SOUTH)) — Statistics
CHUNGCHEONG NAM DO (KOREA (SOUTH)) — Statistics
CHURCH AND LABOR
CHURCH AND LABOR — Spain
CHURCH AND MINORITIES — Great Britain
CHURCH AND RACE PROBLEMS — Great Britain
CHURCH AND SOCIAL PROBLEMS
CHURCH AND SOCIAL PROBLEMS — Anglican Church of Canada — History
CHURCH AND SOCIAL PROBLEMS — Catholic Church
CHURCH AND SOCIAL PROBLEMS — Great Britain
CHURCH AND SOCIAL PROBLEMS — Scotland
CHURCH AND SOCIAL PROBLEMS — South Africa
CHURCH AND SOCIAL PROBLEMS — United States
CHURCH AND STATE
CHURCH AND STATE — Bibliography
CHURCH AND STATE — Brazil — History — 20th century
CHURCH AND STATE — Germany — History — 1933-1945
CHURCH AND STATE — Great Britain — History
CHURCH AND STATE — Great Britain — History — 16th century — Sources
CHURCH AND STATE — Great Britain — History — 19th century
CHURCH AND STATE — Great Britain — History — 20th century
CHURCH AND STATE — Nicaragua
CHURCH AND STATE — Nicaragua — History — 20th century
CHURCH AND STATE — Poland — History
CHURCH AND STATE — Scotland
CHURCH AND STATE — Soviet Union — History — 20th century
CHURCH AND STATE — Spain
CHURCH AND STATE — Spain — Congresses
CHURCH AND STATE IN GREAT BRITAIN
CHURCH AND THE POOR
CHURCH AND THE POOR — Scotland
CHURCH AND THE WORLD
CHURCH CHARITIES — United States
CHURCH HISTORY
CHURCH HISTORY — Middle Ages, 600-1500
CHURCH LANDS — England — Reading (Berkshire)
CHURCH OF ENGLAND
CHURCH OF ENGLAND — History — 16th century
CHURCH OF ENGLAND — History — 17th century
CHURCH OF SCOTLAND — Doctrines — Addresses, essays, lectures
CHURCH RECORDS AND REGISTERS — Portugal
CHURCH RENEWAL — Catholic church
CHURCH SCHOOLS — United States
CHURCH SOCIETIES — Directories
CHURCH WORK WITH ALCOHOLICS — United States
CHURCH WORK WITH YOUTH — United States — Catholic Church
CHURCHES, ANGLICAN — London — History — 18th century — Sources
CHURCHILL, Sir WINSTON
CHURCHILL, WINSTON S.
CHURCHILL, WINSTON S. (Winston Spencer), 1874-1965
CICERO, MARCUS TULLIUS
CIGAR INDUSTRY — Germany — History
CIGAR MAKERS — Germany — Social conditions
CIGARETTE HABIT
CILICIA (TURKEY) — History
CINCINNATI (OHIO) — Politics and government
CIRCULAR VELOCITY OF MONEY — Great Britain
CIRCUMCISION
CITIES AND TOWNS
CITIES AND TOWNS — Addresses, essays, lectures
CITIES AND TOWNS — Congresses
CITIES AND TOWNS — Growth
CITIES AND TOWNS — Growth — Congresses
CITIES AND TOWNS — Growth — History
CITIES AND TOWNS — Handbooks, manuals, etc
CITIES AND TOWNS — History
CITIES AND TOWNS — Mathematical models
CITIES AND TOWNS — Quotations, maxims, etc — Dictionaries
CITIES AND TOWNS — Research
CITIES AND TOWNS — Research — Great Britain
CITIES AND TOWNS — Social conditions
CITIES AND TOWNS — Statistics
CITIES AND TOWNS — Africa
CITIES AND TOWNS — Africa — Bibliography
CITIES AND TOWNS — Ahmedabad
CITIES AND TOWNS — Arab countries
CITIES AND TOWNS — Australia
CITIES AND TOWNS — Australia — Growth
CITIES AND TOWNS — Australia — Brisbane (Qld.) — Growth
CITIES AND TOWNS — Botswana — Statistics
CITIES AND TOWNS — Brazil — History
CITIES AND TOWNS — Canada
CITIES AND TOWNS — Canada — Growth
CITIES AND TOWNS — Canada — Growth — Addresses, essays, lectures
CITIES AND TOWNS — Canada — History
CITIES AND TOWNS — Canada — History — Addresses, essays, lectures
CITIES AND TOWNS — Caribbean Area — Growth
CITIES AND TOWNS — China — Growth

CITIES AND TOWNS — Developing countries
CITIES AND TOWNS — Ethiopia — Bagēmder — Case studies
CITIES AND TOWNS — Europe — Growth — History
CITIES AND TOWNS — Finland
CITIES AND TOWNS — France
CITIES AND TOWNS — Great Britain
CITIES AND TOWNS — Great Britain — Conservation and restoration
CITIES AND TOWNS — Great Britain — History
CITIES AND TOWNS — India
CITIES AND TOWNS — India — Growth
CITIES AND TOWNS — India — History
CITIES AND TOWNS — India — Bihar — Growth
CITIES AND TOWNS — India — Growth
CITIES AND TOWNS — Mexico
CITIES AND TOWNS — Middle West — Case studies
CITIES AND TOWNS — Middle West — Economic conditions
CITIES AND TOWNS — Middle West — Social conditions
CITIES AND TOWNS — Poland
CITIES AND TOWNS — Poland — Growth
CITIES AND TOWNS — Russian S.F.S.R. — Moscow
CITIES AND TOWNS — Russian S.F.S.R. — Siberia
CITIES AND TOWNS — Scotland — History — 16th century
CITIES AND TOWNS — Scotland — History — 17th century
CITIES AND TOWNS — Soviet Union
CITIES AND TOWNS — Soviet Union — History — Addresses, essays, lectures
CITIES AND TOWNS — Sunbelt States — Growth
CITIES AND TOWNS — United States
CITIES AND TOWNS — United States — Addresses, essays, lectures
CITIES AND TOWNS — United States — Growth
CITIES AND TOWNS — United States — Growth — Case studies
CITIES AND TOWNS — United States — History — 19th century
CITIES AND TOWNS — United States — History — 20th century
CITIES AND TOWNS — Uzbek S.S.R. — History
CITIES AND TOWNS — Wales — Clwyd
CITIES AND TOWNS, ISLAMIC — Middle East — History — Congresses
CITIES AND TOWNS, MEDIEVAL — England — Winchester (Hampshire)
CITIESA AND TOWNS — Vanuatu — Statistics
CITIZENS' ASSOCIATIONS — England — London
CITIZENS' ASSOCIATIONS — Missouri — Kansas City
CITIZENS' ASSOCIATIONS — Ohio — Cincinnati
CITIZENS' ASSOCIATIONS — United States
CITIZENSHIP — France
CITIZENSHIP — France — Philosophy
CITIZENSHIP — Great Britain
CITIZENSHIP — Puerto Rico
CITIZENSHIP — United States
CITY AND TOWN LIFE
CITY AND TOWN LIFE — Canada
CITY AND TOWN LIFE — European Economic Community countries
CITY AND TOWN LIFE — Spain — Catalonia
CITY OF LONDON — Periodicals
CITY PLANNING
CITY PLANNING — Addresses, essays, lectures
CITY PLANNING — Congresses
CITY PLANNING — Dictionaries — Polyglot
CITY PLANNING — Dictionaries, Polyglot
CITY PLANNING — Economic aspects — Zambia — Lusaka
CITY PLANNING — Environmental aspects — United States — History — 19th century
CITY PLANNING — Evaluation — Handbooks, manuals, etc
CITY PLANNING — Evaluation — Handbooks, manuals, etc.
CITY PLANNING — History
CITY PLANNING — Mathematical models
CITY PLANNING — Mathematical models — Congresses
CITY PLANNING — Moral and ethical aspects
CITY PLANNING — Asia — Congresses
CITY PLANNING — Australia
CITY PLANNING — Canada
CITY PLANNING — Canada — Addresses, essays, lectures
CITY PLANNING — Canada — History — 19th century
CITY PLANNING — Canada — History — 20th century
CITY PLANNING — China
CITY PLANNING — Denmark — Abstracts
CITY PLANNING — Developing countries — Evaluation — Handbooks, manuals, etc,
CITY PLANNING — Developing countries — Evaluation — Handbooks, manuals, etc.
CITY PLANNING — England
CITY PLANNING — England — Central Lancashire New Town (Lancashire) — Citizen participation
CITY PLANNING — England — Hertfordshire
CITY PLANNING — England — Leicestershire
CITY PLANNING — England — London
CITY PLANNING — England — Redditch
CITY PLANNING — France — History — Congresses
CITY PLANNING — Great Britain
CITY PLANNING — Great Britain — Citizen participation
CITY PLANNING — Great Britain — History
CITY PLANNING — India
CITY PLANNING — Ireland — History — Congresses
CITY PLANNING — London metropolitan area — Westminster
CITY PLANNING — Middle West
CITY PLANNING — Northern Ireland — History — 20th century
CITY PLANNING — Northern Ireland — Belfast
CITY PLANNING — Quebec (Province)
CITY PLANNING — South Australia — Adelaide
CITY PLANNING — Sweden
CITY PLANNING — Turkey — Ankara
CITY PLANNING — Turkey — Istanbul
CITY PLANNING — United States
CITY PLANNING — United States — History
CITY PLANNING — Wales — Glamorgan
CITY PLANNING AND REDEVELOPMENT LAW — Canada
CITY PLANNING AND REDEVELOPMENT LAW — England
CITY PLANNING AND REDEVELOPMENT LAW — Europe
CITY PLANNING AND REDEVELOPMENT LAW — France
CITY PLANNING AND REDEVELOPMENT LAW — Great Britain
CITY PLANNING AND REDEVELOPMENT LAW — Nigeria
CITY-STATES — Greece
CITY TRAFFIC — Mathematical models
CIUDAD JUAREZ (MEXICO) — Economic conditions
CIUDAD JUAREZ (MEXICO) — Social conditions
CIVICS — Study and teaching (Secondary) — United States
CIVIL DEFENSE — History — 20th century
CIVIL ENGINEERING — Cold weather conditions
CIVIL LAW
CIVIL LAW — Congresses
CIVIL LAW — Economic aspects
CIVIL LAW — California — History
CIVIL LAW — England — History — Sources
CIVIL LAW — France
CIVIL LAW — Hungary
CIVIL LAW — Spain
CIVIL-MILITARY RELATIONS — Latin America
CIVIL-MILITARY RELATIONS — Latin America — History — 20th century
CIVIL-MILITARY RELATIONS — Spain
CIVIL-MILITARY RELATIONS — Spain
CIVIL-MILITARY RELATIONS — United States — History — 20th century — Addresses, essays, lectures
CIVIL PROCEDURE — England
CIVIL RIGHTS — New Zealand
CIVIL RIGHTS
CIVIL RIGHTS — Addresses, essays, lectures
CIVIL RIGHTS — Bibliography
CIVIL RIGHTS — Evaluation
CIVIL RIGHTS — Legal status, laws, etc. — Indonesia
CIVIL RIGHTS — Moral and ethical aspects
CIVIL RIGHTS — Africa
CIVIL RIGHTS — America
CIVIL RIGHTS — Argentina
CIVIL RIGHTS — Asia
CIVIL RIGHTS — Australia
CIVIL RIGHTS — Australia — Bibliography
CIVIL RIGHTS — Canada
CIVIL RIGHTS — Canada — History
CIVIL RIGHTS — Chile
CIVIL RIGHTS — Communist countries
CIVIL RIGHTS — Cuba
CIVIL RIGHTS — Developing countries
CIVIL RIGHTS — Developing countries — Addresses, essays, lectures
CIVIL RIGHTS — England — London
CIVIL RIGHTS — Europe
CIVIL RIGHTS — Europe, Eastern
CIVIL RIGHTS — Finland
CIVIL RIGHTS — Great Britain
CIVIL RIGHTS — Great Britain — History
CIVIL RIGHTS — Guatemala
CIVIL RIGHTS — Haiti
CIVIL RIGHTS — Honduras
CIVIL RIGHTS — India
CIVIL RIGHTS — Japan — History
CIVIL RIGHTS — Korea (South) — History
CIVIL RIGHTS — Mexico
CIVIL RIGHTS — Namibia
CIVIL RIGHTS — New Zealand
CIVIL RIGHTS — Nicaragua
CIVIL RIGHTS — Philippines
CIVIL RIGHTS — Puerto Rico
CIVIL RIGHTS — Scandinavia
CIVIL RIGHTS — South Africa
CIVIL RIGHTS — Soviet Union
CIVIL RIGHTS — Spain — Congresses
CIVIL RIGHTS — Surinam
CIVIL RIGHTS — Switzerland
CIVIL RIGHTS — United States
CIVIL RIGHTS — United States — History
CIVIL RIGHTS — Zambia
CIVIL RIGHTS AND SOCIALISM
CIVIL RIGHTS DEMONSTRATIONS — United States
CIVIL RIGHTS (INTERNATIONAL LAW)
CIVIL RIGHTS (INTERNATIONAL LAW) — Bibliography

CIVIL RIGHTS (INTERNATIONAL LAW) — Cases
CIVIL RIGHTS (INTERNATIONAL LAW) — Developing Countries
CIVIL RIGHTS MOVEMENTS — Southern States
CIVIL RIGHTS MOVEMENTS — United States — History — 20th century
CIVIL RIGHTS WORKERS — United States — Biography
CIVIL SERVICE
CIVIL SERVICE — Congresses
CIVIL SERVICE — Training of — Denmark
CIVIL SERVICE — Denmark — Study and teaching
CIVIL SERVICE — Europe — Effect of technological innovations on
CIVIL SERVICE — Great Britain
CIVIL SERVICE — Great Britain — Bibliography
CIVIL SERVICE — Great Britain — Communication systems
CIVIL SERVICE — Great Britain — Effect of technological innovations on
CIVIL SERVICE — Great Britain — Management
CIVIL SERVICE — Great Britain — Management — Evaluation
CIVIL SERVICE — India — History
CIVIL SERVICE — India — History — 20th century
CIVIL SERVICE — New Zealand
CIVIL SERVICE — Peru
CIVIL SERVICE — South Australia — Minority employment
CIVIL SERVICE — Spain — History — 20th century
CIVIL SERVICE — Trinidad and Tobago — Statistics
CIVIL SERVICE — United States — History — 19th century
CIVIL SERVICE PENSIONS — Canada
CIVIL SERVICE POSITIONS — Great Britain — Bibliography
CIVIL SERVICE RECRUITING — Great Britain
CIVIL SERVICE REFORM — United States
CIVIL SUPREMACY OVER THE MILITARY — Great Britain — History — 19th century
CIVIL SUPREMACY OVER THE MILITARY — Great Britain — History — 20th century
CIVIL SUPREMACY OVER THE MILITARY — Nigeria
CIVIL WAR
CIVILIZATION
CIVILIZATION — Congresses
CIVILIZATION — History — Congresses
CIVILIZATION — Philosophy
CIVILIZATION — Philosophy — Congresses
CIVILIZATION, ANCIENT
CIVILIZATION, ANGLO-SAXON
CIVILIZATION, CELTIC
CIVILIZATION, CLASSICAL
CIVILIZATION, ISLAMIC
CIVILIZATION, ISLAMIC — History
CIVILIZATION, ISLAMIC — Occidental influences
CIVILIZATION, MEDIEVAL
CIVILIZATION, MODERN — 19th century
CIVILIZATION, MODERN — 20th century
CIVILIZATION, MODERN — 1950-
CIVILIZATION, OCCIDENTAL
CIVILIZATION, OCCIDENTAL — Addresses, essays, lectures
CIVILIZATION, ORIENTAL
CK COACHES
CLAIMS
CLANS — Indonesia — Mamboru
CLANS AND CLAN SYSTEMS — Scotland — History

CLARK, WILLIAM, 1916-1985
CLASS ACTIONS (CIVIL PROCEDURE) — United States
CLASS CONSCIOUSNESS — Norway
CLASSICAL SCHOOL OF ECONOMICS
CLASSICAL SCHOOL OF ECONOMICS — History
CLASSIFICATION
CLASSIFICATION, PRIMITIVE — Addresses, essays, lectures
CLAUSEWITZ, CARL VON
CLAY — Biography
CLAY INDUSTRIES — European Economic Community countries — Energy consumption
CLERGY — England
CLERGY — Great Britain — Directories
CLERGY — Great Britain — Minor orders — History
CLERGY — Northern Ireland — Biography
CLERKS — Salaries, pensions, etc — Great Britain
CLERKS — France
CLERKS — Germany — History
CLERKS — Great Britain
CLEVELAND — Economic conditions
CLEVELAND — Population
CLEVELAND — Social conditions
CLIMATIC CHANGES — Economic aspects
CLIMATIC CHANGES — Social aspects
CLIMATIC CHANGES — Great Britain
CLIMATOLOGY — Economic aspects
CLOSE COLONY (IOWA) — History
CLOTHING, PROTECTIVE
CLOTHING TRADE — Great Britain — Statistics
CLOTHING TRADE — New York (N.Y.)
CLOTHING WORKERS
CLOTHING WORKERS — New York (N.Y.)
CLUSTER ANALYSIS
CLWYD (WALES) — Economic conditions
CLWYD (WALES) — Population
CLWYD (WALES) — Rural conditions
CLYDESIDE (STRATHCLYDE) — Economic conditions
CLYDESIDE (STRATHCLYDE) — Economic policy
CO-OPERATIVE COMMONWEALTH FEDERATION — History — Congresses
CO-OPERATIVE PARTY
CO-OPERATIVE PRODUCTION — Great Britain
CO-OPERATIVE SOCIETIES — Canada
CO-OPERATIVE SOCIETIES — Great Britain — Finance
COACHING — Great Britain — History
COAL — Economic aspects — Great Britain
COAL — Environmental aspects — Great Britain
COAL — Environmental aspects — International Energy Agency countries
COAL — Environmental aspects — Organisation for Economic Co-operation and Development countries
COAL MINERS — England — Thurcroft (South Yorkshire) — Interviews
COAL MINERS — France — Decazeville — History
COAL-MINERS — Great Britain
COAL MINERS — Spain — Asturias — History — 20th century
COAL MINERS' STRIKE, GREAT BRITAIN, 1984-1985
COAL MINERS' WIVES — England — Nottinghamshire
COAL MINERS' WIVES — Great Britain
COAL MINES AND MINING — Economic aspects — Great Britain
COAL MINES AND MINING — Environmental aspects — Bibliography
COAL MINES AND MINING — Environmental aspects — England — Woolley
COAL MINES AND MINING — Environmental aspects — Great Britain

COAL MINES AND MINING — Environmental aspects — Organisation for Economic Co-operation and Development countries
COAL MINES AND MINING — Government ownership — Great Britain
COAL MINES AND MINING — England — Newcastle-upon-Tyne (Tyne and Wear) — History
COAL MINES AND MINING — England — Vale of Belvoir (Leicestershire: District) — Designs and plans
COAL MINES AND MINING — England — Vale of Belvoir (Leicestershire: District) — Planning
COAL MINES AND MINING — France — Decazeville — history
COAL MINES AND MINING — Great Britain
COAL MINES AND MINING — Great Britain — History
COAL MINES AND MINING — Spain — Asturias
COAL STRIKE, GREAT BRITAIN, 1984-5
COAL STRIKE, GREAT BRITAIN, 1984-1985
COAL STRIKE, GREAT BRITAIN, 1984-1985 — Social aspects
COAL STRIKE, GREAT BRITAIN, 1984-1985 — England — Nottinghamshire
COAL TRADE
COAL TRADE — Great Britain — Economic aspects
COAL TRADE — Scotland — Hamilton (Strathclyde) — History
COALITION GOVERNMENTS — Europe
COALITION GOVERNMENTS — Great Britain
COALITION GOVERNMENTS — Israel
COALITION (POLITICAL SCIENCE)
COASTAL ZONE MANAGEMENT — Greece
COASTAL ZONE MANAGEMENT — United States — Congresses
COBBETT, WILLIAM
COBDEN, RICHARD
COBOL (COMPUTER PROGRAM LANGUAGE)
COCA-COLA
COCA-COLA — Marketing
COCA-COLA COMPANY — History
COCAINE
COCAINE HABIT
COCAINE HABIT — Canada
COCAINE HABIT — United States
COCKBURN, CLAUDE
COCOA
COCOA — Research
COCOA TRADE — Ghana
COCONUT — Fiji
COD-FISHERIES — Economic aspects — Newfoundland
COFFEE — Guatemala — History — 19th century
COFFEE TRADE — Brazil — History
COFFEE TRADE — Colombia — Addresses, essays, lectures
COFFEE TRADE — Guatemala — History — 19th century
COGENERATION OF ELECTRIC POWER AND HEAT — Great Britain
COGNITION
COGNITION — Age factors
COGNITION — Congresses
COGNITION — Handbooks
COGNITION — in adulthood
COGNITION — physiology
COGNITION — Research
COGNITION — Social aspects
COGNITION IN CHILDREN
COLLECTION DEVELOPMENT (LIBRARIES)
COLLECTIVE BARGAINING
COLLECTIVE BARGAINING — Government employees — Great Britain

COLLECTIVE BARGAINING — International business enterprises — Asia — Congresses
COLLECTIVE BARGAINING — Mathematical models
COLLECTIVE BARGAINING — Transportation — New Zealand
COLLECTIVE BARGAINING — Canada
COLLECTIVE BARGAINING — Great Britain
COLLECTIVE BARGAINING — United States
COLLECTIVE BARGAINING UNIT — United States
COLLECTIVE FARMS — Soviet Union — Officials and employees
COLLECTIVE LABOR AGREEMENTS — European Economic Community countries
COLLECTIVE LABOR AGREEMENTS — Great Britain
COLLECTIVE SETTLEMENTS
COLLECTIVE SETTLEMENTS — United States — History
COLLECTIVIZATION OF AGRICULTURE — Soviet Union — History
COLLEGE CREDITS — Europe
COLLEGE GRADUATES — Employment — Great Britain
COLLEGE GRADUATES — United States
COLLEGE INTEGRATION — New York (N.Y.) — Case studies
COLLEGE LIBRARIANS — Great Britain
COLLEGE STUDENTS — Finland — Statistics
COLLEGE STUDENTS — Germany — Political activity — History — 20th century
COLLEGE STUDENTS — South Africa
COLLEGE STUDENTS, BLACK — South Africa — Intellectual life — History
COLLEGE STUDENTS, JEWISH — Connecticut — New Haven — History
COLLEGE STUDENTS' SOCIO-ECONOMIC STATUS — Australia — Statistics
COLLEGE TEACHERS — Political activity
COLLEGE TEACHERS — Salaries, pensions, etc — California — Statistics
COLLEGE TEACHERS — Tenure — Great Britain
COLLEGE TEACHERS — Australia
COLLEGE TEACHERS — Germany — History
COLLEGE TEACHERS — Germany — Political activity — History — 20th century
COLLEGE TEACHERS — India
COLLEGE TEACHERS — Spain — Biography
COLLEGE TEACHERS — Spain — Catalonia — Biography
COLLEGE TEACHERS — United States — Political activity — History — 20th century
COLLEGE TEACHING — Vocational guidance — Australia
COLLEGE TEACHING — Vocational guidance — India
COLLISIONS AT SEA — Cases
COLLISIONS AT SEA — Prevention
COLLOQUE NATIONAL SUR LA FÉCONDITÉ EN TUNISIE
COLOMBIA — Administrative and political divisions
COLOMBIA — Comnmercial policy — Addresses, essays, lectures
COLOMBIA — Constitution
COLOMBIA — Constitutional history
COLOMBIA — Constitutional law
COLOMBIA — Economic conditions
COLOMBIA — Economic conditions — Regional disparities
COLOMBIA — Economic conditions — Statistics
COLOMBIA — Economic conditions — 1970-

COLOMBIA — Economic policy
COLOMBIA — Economic policy — Addresses, essays, lectures
COLOMBIA — Manufactures
COLOMBIA — Politics and government — 1930-1946
COLOMBIA — Politics and government — 1946-1974
COLOMBIA — Politics and government — 1946-
COLOMBIA — Politics and government — 1974-
COLOMBIA — Rural conditions
COLOMBIA — Social conditions
COLOMBIA — Social conditions — Statistics
COLOMBIA — Statistics
COLOMBIA — Statistics, vital
COLONIAL ADMINISTRATORS — Africa — Biography
COLONIAL ADMINISTRATORS — Great Britain — Biography
COLONIES
COLONIES — History
COLONIES — Africa
COLONIES (INTERNATIONAL LAW)
COLONIES (INTERNATIONAL LAW) — Bibliography
COLORED PEOPLE (SOUTH AFRICA) — Addresses, essays, lectures
COLORED PEOPLE (SOUTH AFRICA) — Relocation
COLUMBIA — Politics and government — 1863-1885
COMBINATORIAL ANALYSIS
COMBINATORIAL OPTIMIZATION
COMMERCE
COMMERCE — Classification
COMMERCE — Congresses
COMMERCE — Dictionaries
COMMERCE — Dictionaries — Russian
COMMERCE — Directories
COMMERCE — Directories — Bibliography
COMMERCE — Econometric models
COMMERCE 650/2INVESTMENTS,
COMMERCE, PRIMITIVE — Nepal — Dolpā
COMMERCE, PRIMITIVE — New Guinea
COMMERCIAL ASSOCIATIONS — Switzerland
COMMERCIAL CRIMES — Soviet Union
COMMERCIAL CRIMES — United States
COMMERCIAL FINANCE COMPANIES — Great Britain — Statistics
COMMERCIAL LAW
COMMERCIAL LAW — Bibliography
COMMERCIAL LAW — Congresses
COMMERCIAL LAW — Australia
COMMERCIAL LAW — Belgium
COMMERCIAL LAW — England
COMMERCIAL LAW — European Economic Community countries
COMMERCIAL LAW — France
COMMERCIAL LAW — Great Britain
COMMERCIAL LAW — Iran
COMMERCIAL LAW — Korea (South)
COMMERCIAL LAW — Nigeria
COMMERCIAL LAW — Singapore
COMMERCIAL LAW — Spain
COMMERCIAL LAW — Yugoslavia
COMMERCIAL LAW — Zimbabwe
COMMERCIAL POLICY
COMMERCIAL POLICY — Addresses, essays, lectures
COMMERCIAL PRODUCTS
COMMERCIAL PRODUCTS — Classification
COMMERCIAL PRODUCTS — Prices — Mathematical models
COMMERCIAL PRODUCTS — Netherlands — Nomenclature
COMMERCIAL PRODUCTS — Soviet Union
COMMERCIAL STATISTICS
COMMERCIAL STATISTICS — Bibliography

COMMERCIAL STATISTICS — Methodology
COMMERCIAL TREATIES
COMMERCIAL TREATIES — Congresses
COMMISSION FOR BUILDING FIFTY NEW CHURCHES
COMMISSION OF THE EUROPEAN COMMUNITIES
COMMISSION OF THE EUROPEAN COMMUNITIES — Documentation — Bibliography
COMMISSION OF THE EUROPEAN COMMUNITIES. Library — Catalogs
COMMISSION OF THE EUROPEAN COMMUNITIES. London Information Office
COMMITTEE FOR COORDINATION OF INVESTIGATIONS OF THE LOWER MEKONG BASIN
COMMODITY CONTROL
COMMODITY CONTROL — Bibliography
COMMODITY EXCHANGES
COMMODITY EXCHANGES — Law and legislation — United States — History
COMMODITY EXCHANGES — Mathematical models
COMMODITY EXCHANGES — United States — History
COMMON AGRICULTURAL POLICY See Agriculture and state - European Economic Community countries
COMMON LAW — Congresses
COMMON LAW — England — History and criticism
COMMON LAW — Great Britain
COMMON LAW — United States
COMMON MARKET See European Economic Community
COMMONWEALTH DEVELOPMENT CORPORATION
COMMONWEALTH FOUNDATION
COMMONWEALTH OF NATIONS
COMMONWEALTH OF NATIONS — Constitutional History
COMMONWEALTH OF NATIONS — Foreign relations
COMMONWEALTH OF NATIONS — History
COMMONWEALTH OF NATIONS — Research — Bibliography
COMMONWEALTH OF NATIONS
COMMONWEALTH PARLIAMENTARY ASSOCIATION — History
COMMONWEALTH SCIENTIFIC AND INDUSTRIAL RESEARCH ORGANIZATION (Australia)
COMMONWEALTH YOUTH PROGRAMME
COMMUNICABLE DISEASES — Mortality — History
COMMUNICATION
COMMUNICATION — Dictionaries
COMMUNICATION — International cooperation
COMMUNICATION — International cooperation — Addresses, essays, lectures
COMMUNICATION — International cooperation — Bibliography
COMMUNICATION — International cooperation — Congresses
COMMUNICATION — Philosophy
COMMUNICATION — Political aspects — Addresses, essays, lectures
COMMUNICATION — Political aspects — United States
COMMUNICATION — Psychological aspects
COMMUNICATION — Research — Latin America
COMMUNICATION — Sex differences
COMMUNICATION — Social aspects
COMMUNICATION — Social aspects — Congresses
COMMUNICATION — Social aspects — United States
COMMUNICATION — Technological innovations

COMMUNICATION — Technological innovations — Addresses, essays, lectures
COMMUNICATION — Finland — Accounting
COMMUNICATION — Finland — Statistics
COMMUNICATION — Iran
COMMUNICATION — United States — Statistics
COMMUNICATION — West Bank
COMMUNICATION AND TRAFFIC
COMMUNICATION AND TRAFFIC — India
COMMUNICATION AND TRAFFIC — Taiwan
COMMUNICATION DISORDERS — Age factors
COMMUNICATION IN ECONOMIC DEVELOPMENT — Malaysia
COMMUNICATION IN MANAGEMENT
COMMUNICATION IN MANAGEMENT — Congresses
COMMUNICATION IN MANAGEMENT — Great Britain
COMMUNICATION IN MARRIAGE
COMMUNICATION IN MEDICINE
COMMUNICATION IN ORGANIZATIONS
COMMUNICATION IN ORGANIZATIONS — Addresses, essays, lectures
COMMUNICATION IN POLITICS
COMMUNICATION IN POLITICS — Addresses, essays, lectures
COMMUNICATION IN POLITICS — France
COMMUNICATION IN POLITICS — Great Britain
COMMUNICATION IN POLITICS — United States
COMMUNICATION IN RURAL DEVELOPMENT — Developing countries
COMMUNICATION IN SCIENCE
COMMUNICATION IN THE HUMANITIES — Great Britain
COMMUNICATION IN THE HUMANITIES — United States
COMMUNICATION IN THE SOCIAL SCIENCES
COMMUNICATION IN THE SOCIAL SCIENCES — Case studies
COMMUNICATION, INTERNATIONAL
COMMUNICATION, INTERNATIONAL — Congresses
COMMUNICATION MANAGERS' ASSOCIATION
COMMUNICATION OF TECHNICAL INFORMATION
COMMUNICATION POLICY — Congresses
COMMUNICATION, PRIMITIVE — Congresses
COMMUNICATIONS WORKERS OF AMERICA — History
COMMUNISM
COMMUNISM — Dictionaries
COMMUNISM — History
COMMUNISM — History — 20th century
COMMUNISM — History — 20th century — Sources
COMMUNISM — 1945-
COMMUNISM — 1945- — Bibliography
COMMUNISM — Argentina — History — 20th century
COMMUNISM — Austria
COMMUNISM — Bulgaria
COMMUNISM — Bulgaria — History
COMMUNISM — China
COMMUNISM — Cuba
COMMUNISM — Cuba — History
COMMUNISM — Developing countries
COMMUNISM — Egypt
COMMUNISM — Europe
COMMUNISM — Europe — History — 20th century
COMMUNISM — Europe — History — 20th century — Bibliography
COMMUNISM — Europe, Eastern
COMMUNISM — France
COMMUNISM — France — History
COMMUNISM — France — History — 20th century
COMMUNISM — Germany — History
COMMUNISM — Germany (East)
COMMUNISM — Germany (West) — History and criticism
COMMUNISM — Great Britain — History
COMMUNISM — Great Britain — History — 20th century
COMMUNISM — India
COMMUNISM — Ireland — History
COMMUNISM — Italy — History — 20th century
COMMUNISM — Japan — History
COMMUNISM — Japan — History — 20th century
COMMUNISM — Mexico
COMMUNISM — Netherlands
COMMUNISM — New York (N.Y.) — History — 20th century
COMMUNISM — Norway — History
COMMUNISM — Paraguay
COMMUNISM — Poland
COMMUNISM — Poland — History
COMMUNISM — Portugal
COMMUNISM — Russia
COMMUNISM — South Africa
COMMUNISM — Soviet Union
COMMUNISM — Soviet Union — History
COMMUNISM — Spain — Congresses
COMMUNISM — Spain — History
COMMUNISM — Sweden — History
COMMUNISM — Switzerland
COMMUNISM — Turkey — History
COMMUNISM — United States — History
COMMUNISM — United States — History — Sources
COMMUNISM — United States — History — 20th century
COMMUNISM — United States — 1917-
COMMUNISM — Yugoslavia
COMMUNISM — Yugoslavia — History
COMMUNISM AND CHRISTIANITY
COMMUNISM AND CHRISTIANITY — Catholic Church — Poland
COMMUNISM AND CHRISTIANITY — History
COMMUNISM AND CULTURE — Hungary
COMMUNISM AND INTELLECTUALS — China — Addresses, essays, lectures
COMMUNISM AND INTELLECTUALS — Soviet Union
COMMUNISM AND NUCLEAR WARFARE
COMMUNISM AND PHILOSOPHY
COMMUNISM AND RELIGION
COMMUNISM AND SCIENCE — Soviet Union
COMMUNIST COUNTRIES
COMMUNIST COUNTRIES — Commerce
COMMUNIST COUNTRIES — Commerce — Canada
COMMUNIST COUNTRIES — Economic conditions
COMMUNIST COUNTRIES — Economic policy
COMMUNIST COUNTRIES — Foreign economic relations
COMMUNIST COUNTRIES — Foreign economic relations — Cuba
COMMUNIST COUNTRIES — Foreign economic relations — Nicaragua
COMMUNIST COUNTRIES — Foreign relations
COMMUNIST COUNTRIES — Politics and government
COMMUNIST COUNTRIES — Social conditions
COMMUNIST COUNTRIES — Social policy
COMMUNIST EDUCATION — Soviet Union
COMMUNIST INTERNATIONAL *See also* Third International
COMMUNIST INTERNATIONAL
COMMUNIST INTERNATIONAL — Biography — Dictionaries
COMMUNIST INTERNATIONAL — History — Sources
COMMUNIST INTERNATIONAL. Congress (7th : 1935)
COMMUNIST LEADERSHIP — Russian S.F.S.R. — Biography — Directories
COMMUNIST ORGANISATION IN THE BRITISH ISLES
COMMUNIST PARTIES
COMMUNIST PARTIES — Directories
COMMUNIST PARTIES — Communist countries
COMMUNIST PARTIES — Soviet Union
COMMUNIST PARTY OF GREAT BRITAIN
COMMUNIST PARTY OF GREAT BRITAIN — History
COMMUNIST PARTY OF GREAT BRITAIN — History — Addresses, essays, lectures
COMMUNIST STATE
COMMUNIST STATE — History — 19th century
COMMUNIST STATES — Politics and government
COMMUNIST STRATEGY
COMMUNIST STRATEGY — Congresses
COMMUNISTS — Biography
COMMUNISTS — Biography — Dictionaries
COMMUNISTS — Argentina
COMMUNISTS — Bulgaria — Addresses, essays, lectures
COMMUNISTS — Bulgaria — Biography
COMMUNISTS — Czechoslovakia — Biography
COMMUNISTS — France
COMMUNISTS — Great Britain — Directories
COMMUNISTS — Ireland — History
COMMUNISTS — Italy — Biography
COMMUNISTS — Poland — Interviews
COMMUNISTS — Russian S.F.S.R. — Moscow — Biography
COMMUNISTS — Russian S.F.S.R. — Tatar A.S.S.R.
COMMUNISTS — Soviet Union — Biography
COMMUNISTS — Soviet Union — History
COMMUNISTS — Spain — Biography
COMMUNISTS — United States — Biography
COMMUNISTS — United States — Biography — Dictionaries
COMMUNITY
COMMUNITY AND SCHOOL — Great Britain
COMMUNITY AND SCHOOL — Virginia — History — 19th century
COMMUNITY AND SCHOOL — Virginia — History — 20th century
COMMUNITY ART PROJECTS — England — Lancashire
COMMUNITY-BASED CORRECTIONS — Europe
COMMUNITY-BASED CORRECTIONS — Massachusetts
COMMUNITY-BASED CORRECTIONS — Netherlands
COMMUNITY DEVELOPMENT
COMMUNITY DEVELOPMENT — Research — Case studies
COMMUNITY DEVELOPMENT — Brazil — São Paulo (State) — History
COMMUNITY DEVELOPMENT — Developing countries
COMMUNITY DEVELOPMENT — Developing countries — Evaluation
COMMUNITY DEVELOPMENT — England — London
COMMUNITY DEVELOPMENT — Great Britain

COMMUNITY DEVELOPMENT — Ireland
COMMUNITY DEVELOPMENT — Nicaragua
COMMUNITY DEVELOPMENT — Norway
COMMUNITY DEVELOPMENT — South Australia
COMMUNITY DEVELOPMENT — Wales — Cardiff
COMMUNITY DEVELOPMENT — Wales — West Glamorgan
COMMUNITY DEVELOPMENT, URBAN — Case studies
COMMUNITY DEVELOPMENT, URBAN — Study and teaching — Great Britain
COMMUNITY DEVELOPMENT, URBAN — Asia
COMMUNITY DEVELOPMENT, URBAN — India
COMMUNITY DEVELOPMENT, URBAN — Pakistan — Lahore
COMMUNITY DEVELOPMENT, URBAN — United States
COMMUNITY HEALTH AIDES — Tanzania
COMMUNITY HEALTH SERVICES
COMMUNITY HEALTH SERVICES — Case studies
COMMUNITY HEALTH SERVICES — Developing countries — Case studies
COMMUNITY HEALTH SERVICES — Developing countries — Finance — Evaluation
COMMUNITY HEALTH SERVICES — England
COMMUNITY HEALTH SERVICES — Europe
COMMUNITY HEALTH SERVICES — Great Britain
COMMUNITY HEALTH SERVICES — Great Britain — Bibliography
COMMUNITY HEALTH SERVICES — Great Britain — Citizen participation — Bibliography
COMMUNITY HEALTH SERVICES — United States
COMMUNITY HEALTH SERVICES FOR CHILDREN — Africa, Sub-Saharan
COMMUNITY HEALTH SERVICES FOR THE AGED — Great Britain
COMMUNITY MENTAL HEALTH SERVICES — organization & administration — United States
COMMUNITY MENTAL HEALTH SERVICES — China — Congresses
COMMUNITY MENTAL HEALTH SERVICES — Great Britain
COMMUNITY MENTAL HEALTH SERVICES — United States — Management — Addresses, essays, lectures
COMMUNITY ORGANIZATION — Great Britain
COMMUNITY ORGANIZATION — North Carolina
COMMUNITY ORGANIZATION — United States
COMMUNITY ORGANIZATION — United States — Case studies
COMMUNITY POWER
COMMUNITY SCHOOLS
COMMUNITY SCHOOLS — England — Coventry (West Midlands)
COMMUNITY SCHOOLS — Great Britain
COMMUTING — England
COMMUTING — England — Bedfordshire
COMMUTING — England — Surrey
COMMUTING — Spain — Statistics
COMORERA, JOAN, 1895-1958
COMOROS
COMOROS — Census, 1980
COMOROS — Economic conditions
COMOROS — Economic policy
COMOROS — Population — Statistics
COMOROS — Population — Statistiques
COMOROS — Social conditions
COMOROS — Social policy

COMPANIES ACT 1985
COMPARATIVE ACCOUNTING
COMPARATIVE ADVANTAGE (COMMERCE) — Case studies
COMPARATIVE ECONOMICS
COMPARATIVE EDUCATION — Congresses
COMPARATIVE GOVERNMENT
COMPARATIVE GOVERNMENT — Addresses, essays, lectures
COMPARATIVE LAW
COMPARATIVE MANAGEMENT — Addresses, essays, lectures
COMPASS
COMPENSATION (LAW)
COMPENSATION (LAW) — England
COMPENSATION (LAW) — England — Greater Manchester
COMPENSATION (LAW) — Great Britain
COMPETITION
COMPETITION — Congresses
COMPETITION — Law and legislation — European Economic Community Countries
COMPETITION — Mathematical models
COMPETITION — Mathematical models — Congresses
COMPETITION — Europe
COMPETITION — European Economic Community countries
COMPETITION — Organisation for Economic Co-operation and Development countries
COMPETITION — United States
COMPETITION — United States — Case studies
COMPETITION, IMPERFECT
COMPETITION, IMPERFECT — Mathematical models
COMPETITION, INTERNATIONAL
COMPETITION, UNFAIR — Canada
COMPETITION, UNFAIR — European Economic Community countries
COMPOST
COMPREHENSION
COMPREHENSIVE HIGH SCHOOLS — England
COMPROMISE (LAW) — England
COMPUTABLE FUNCTIONS — Data processing
COMPUTER-AIDED DESIGN
COMPUTER ARCHITECTURE
COMPUTER-ASSISTED INSTRUCTION
COMPUTER ASSISTED INSTRUCTION
COMPUTER-ASSISTED INSTRUCTION
COMPUTER-ASSISTED INSTRUCTION — Addresses, essays, lectures
COMPUTER-ASSISTED INSTRUCTION — European Economic Community countries
COMPUTER-ASSISTED INSTRUCTION — Great Britain
COMPUTER CRIMES
COMPUTER CRIMES — Legal status, laws, etc. — Organisation for Economic Co-operation and Development countries
COMPUTER CRIMES — United States
COMPUTER ENGINEERING
COMPUTER GRAPHICS
COMPUTER INDUSTRY — Government policy — United States
COMPUTER INDUSTRY — Canada
COMPUTER INDUSTRY — Great Britain
COMPUTER INDUSTRY — United States — History
COMPUTER INDUSTRY — United States — Technological innovations
COMPUTER INTEGRATED MANUFACTURING SYSTEMS
COMPUTER NETWORK PROTOCOLS — Bibliography
COMPUTER NETWORKS
COMPUTER NETWORKS — Congresses
COMPUTER NETWORKS — Great Britain
COMPUTER PROGRAMMING MANAGEMENT
COMPUTER PROGRAMS

COMPUTER PROGRAMS — Simulation methods
COMPUTER PROGRAMS — Specifications
COMPUTER PROGRAMS — Testing
COMPUTER SCIENCE LITERATURE — Indexes
COMPUTER SERVICE INDUSTRY — Great Britain — Statistics
COMPUTER SIMULATION
COMPUTER SOFTWARE
COMPUTER SOFTWARE — Design
COMPUTER SOFTWARE — Development
COMPUTER SOFTWARE — Development — Mathematical models
COMPUTER SOFTWARE INDUSTRY — Great Britain
COMPUTERS See also Electronic digital computers
COMPUTERS
COMPUTERS — Access control
COMPUTERS — Bibliography
COMPUTERS — Congresses
COMPUTERS — Economic aspects — Organisation for Economic Co-operation and Development countries
COMPUTERS — History
COMPUTERS — Law and legislation
COMPUTERS — Management
COMPUTERS — Research — Government policy — United States
COMPUTERS — Social aspects
COMPUTERS — Social aspects — Congresses
COMPUTERS — Study and teaching
COMPUTERS — Study and teaching — Great Britain
COMPUTERS — Vocational guidance
COMPUTERS — Great Britain
COMPUTERS — Scotland
COMPUTERS — United States — Access control
COMPUTERS AND CHILDREN
COMPUTERS AND CIVILIZATION
CONACHER, J. B
CONCEICAO, MANUEL DA
CONCENTRATION CAMPS — France
CONCENTRATION CAMPS — Germany — History — 20th century
CONCENTRATION CAMPS — Great Britain — History
CONCEPTS
CONCERT OF EUROPE
CONDEGA (NICARAGUA) — Social conditions
CONDUCT OF COURT PROCEEDINGS — Australia
CONDUCT OF LIFE
CONFEDERACION NACIONAL DE TRABAJO (SPAIN)
CONFEDERATE STATES OF AMERICA — Historiography — Addresses, essays, lectures
CONFÉDÉRATION FRANÇAISE DEMOCRATIQUE DU TRAVAIL
CONFÉDÉRATION GÉNÉRALE DU TRAVAIL
CONFEDERATION OF BRITISH INDUSTRY
CONFEDERATION OF THE SOCIALIST PARTIES OF THE EUROPEAN COMMUNITY
CONFERENCE ON INTERNATIONAL COMPARISONS OF THE DISTRIBUTION OF HOUSEHOLD WEALTH (1983 : New York, N.Y.)
CONFERENCE ON SECURITY AND CO-OPERATION IN EUROPE
CONFERENCE ON SECURITY AND COOPERATION IN EUROPE
CONFERENCE ON SECURITY AND COOPERATION IN EUROPE — Addresses, essays, lectures
CONFERENCE ON SECURITY AND COOPERATION IN EUROPE (1975 : Helsinki, Finland)
CONFESSION (LAW) — England
CONFESSION (LAW) — United States

CONFLICT MANAGEMENT
CONFLICT MANAGEMENT — Mathematical models
CONFLICT MANAGEMENT — Europe — History
CONFLICT MANAGEMENT — Georgia
CONFLICT OF LAWS
CONFLICT OF LAWS — Competition, Unfair
CONFLICT OF LAWS — Persons — Africa, Southern
CONFLICT OF LAWS — Products liability
CONFLICT OF LAWS — Canada — Cases
CONFLICT OF LAWS — England
CONFLICT OF LAWS — European Economic Community countries
CONFLICT OF LAWS — Great Britain — Cases
CONFUCIANISM — Korea — Rituals
CONGLOMERATE CORPORATIONS
CONGO (BRAZZAVILLE) — Economic policy
CONGRÉS CATALANISTA (1st : 1880 : Barcelona)
CONGRÈS INTERNATIONAL DE LA RÉSISTANCE (1951 : Vienne)
CONGRESS OF INDUSTRIAL ORGANIZATIONS
CONGRESS OF VIENNA (1814-1815)
CONJUGAL VIOLENCE — Bibliography
CONJUGAL VIOLENCE — United States
CONNOLLY, JAMES
CONQUISTA DEL ESTADO, LA (PERIODICAL)
CONRAD HINRICH DONNER (MERCHANT BANK)
CONSCIENTIOUS OBJECTORS — Legal status, laws, etc — United States — History
CONSCIENTIOUS OBJECTORS — United States — History
CONSCIOUSNESS
CONSCIOUSNESS — Addresses, essays, lectures
CONSEIL NATIONAL DE LA RÉSISTANCE (France) — Congresses
CONSEIL NATIONAL DES CHARGEURS DU CAMEROUN
CONSEJO NACIONAL PARA LA SEGURIDAD SOCIAL (Peru)
CONSENT (LAW)
CONSERVATION OF HUMAN RESOURCES PROJECT (Columbia University)
CONSERVATION OF NATURAL RESOURCES
CONSERVATION OF NATURAL RESOURCES — Citizen participation
CONSERVATION OF NATURAL RESOURCES — Law and legislation — France
CONSERVATION OF NATURAL RESOURCES — Europe
CONSERVATION OF NATURAL RESOURCES — France
CONSERVATION OF NATURAL RESOURCES — Great Britain
CONSERVATION OF NATURAL RESOURCES — Southern States
CONSERVATION OF NATURAL RESOURCES — Switzerland
CONSERVATION OF NATURAL RESOURCES — United States
CONSERVATISM
CONSERVATISM — Analysis
CONSERVATISM — Germany
CONSERVATISM — Germany (West)
CONSERVATISM — Great Britain
CONSERVATISM — Great Britain — History — Sources
CONSERVATISM — Great Britain — History — 19th century
CONSERVATISM — Great Britain — History — 20th century
CONSERVATISM — Israel
CONSERVATISM — Poland
CONSERVATISM — Poland — History
CONSERVATISM — United States
CONSERVATISM — United States — History — 20th century
CONSERVATISM — United States — Periodicals — Bibliography
CONSERVATIVE PARTY
CONSERVATIVE PARTY (Great Britain)
CONSOLIDATED GOLD FIELDS
CONSOLIDATED GOLD FIELDS LIMITED — History
CONSOLIDATION AND MERGER OF CORPORATIONS — Denmark
CONSOLIDATION AND MERGER OF CORPORATIONS — Great Britain
CONSOLIDATION AND MERGER OF CORPORATIONS — Great Britain — Statistics
CONSOLIDATION AND MERGER OF CORPORATIONS — United States — Bibliography
CONSPIRACIES — United States — History — Miscellanea
CONSTABLES — England — History — 16th century
CONSTABLES — England — History — 17th century
CONSTITUTION
CONSTITUTIONAL LAW
CONSTITUTIONAL LAW — Interpretation and construction
CONSTITUTIONS
CONSTITUTIONS, STATE — Colombia
CONSTRUCTION INDUSTRY
CONSTRUCTION INDUSTRY — Economic aspects — Northeastern States — Mathematical models
CONSTRUCTION INDUSTRY — Social aspects — United States
CONSTRUCTION INDUSTRY — Argentina — Costs
CONSTRUCTION INDUSTRY — Australia — New South Wales
CONSTRUCTION INDUSTRY — Australia — Tasmania
CONSTRUCTION INDUSTRY — Australia — Western Australia
CONSTRUCTION INDUSTRY — Employment — European Economic Community countries
CONSTRUCTION INDUSTRY — Finland — Accounting
CONSTRUCTION INDUSTRY — Great Britain
CONSTRUCTION INDUSTRY — Hungary — Budapest
CONSTRUCTION INDUSTRY — Netherlands — Statistics
CONSTRUCTION INDUSTRY — Nigeria — Statistics
CONSTRUCTION WORKERS — Diseases and hygiene — West Virginia — Gauley Bridge
CONSTRUCTION WORKERS — United States
CONSULTATIVE GROUP ON INTERNATIONAL AGRICULTURAL RESEARCH
CONSUMER CREDIT — Law and legislation — Canada
CONSUMER CREDIT — Law and legislation — Great Britain
CONSUMER CREDIT — Licenses — Great Britain
CONSUMER CREDIT — Great Britain — Statistics
CONSUMER CREDIT ACT 1974
CONSUMER EDUCATION
CONSUMER PANELS
CONSUMER PRICE INDEXES — Peru — Arequipa (City)
CONSUMER PRICE INDEXES — Peru — Chiclayo
CONSUMER PRICE INDEXES — Peru — Cuzco (City)
CONSUMER PRICE INDEXES — Peru — Huancayo
CONSUMER PRICE INDEXES — Peru — Iquitos
CONSUMER PRICE INDEXES — Peru — Piura (City)
CONSUMER PRICE INDEXES — Peru — Trujillo
CONSUMER PROTECTION — Law and legislation — European Economic Community Countries
CONSUMER PROTECTION — Law and legislation — Great Britain
CONSUMER PROTECTION — Law and legislation — United States
CONSUMER PROTECTION — European Economic Community countries
CONSUMER PROTECTION — United States
CONSUMERS
CONSUMERS — Addresses, essays, lectures
CONSUMERS — Attitudes
CONSUMERS — Research — Addresses, essays, lectures
CONSUMERS — Argentina — Statistics
CONSUMERS — England — Attitudes
CONSUMERS — Great Britain
CONSUMERS — India
CONSUMERS — India — Statistical methods
CONSUMERS — Pakistan
CONSUMERS' PREFERENCES
CONSUMPTION (ECONOMICS)
CONSUMPTION (ECONOMICS) — Mathematical models
CONSUMPTION (ECONOMICS) — Surveys
CONSUMPTION (ECONOMICS) — France
CONSUMPTION (ECONOMICS) — France — Statistics
CONSUMPTION (ECONOMICS) — Great Britain
CONSUMPTION (ECONOMICS) — Hungary — Statistics
CONSUMPTION (ECONOMICS) — India
CONSUMPTION (ECONOMICS) — Japan — Statistics
CONSUMPTION (ECONOMICS) — Jordan — Statistics
CONSUMPTION (ECONOMICS) — Latin America
CONSUMPTION (ECONOMICS) — Nepal
CONSUMPTION (ECONOMICS) — Netherlands — Statistics
CONSUMPTION (ECONOMICS) — Soviet Union
CONTADINI, FRA
CONTAINERIZATION
CONTEMPT OF COURT — Legal status, laws, etc. — Great Britain
CONTEMPT OF COURT — Australia
CONTEMPT OF COURT BILL 1980-1981
CONTENTMENT
CONTINENTAL SHELF — United States
CONTINGENCY TABLES
CONTINUING EDUCATION — Philosophy
CONTRACEPTION — Guyana
CONTRACEPTION — Jamaica
CONTRACEPTION — Trinidad and Tobago
CONTRACT LABOR — History
CONTRACT LABOR — Canada
CONTRACT SYSTEM (LABOR) — Great Britain
CONTRACTING OUT — Great Britain
CONTRACTING OUT — Great Britain — Auditing
CONTRACTING PARTIES TO THE GENERAL AGREEMENT ON TARIFFS AND TRADE
CONTRACTS
CONTRACTS — Congresses
CONTRACTS — Economic aspects
CONTRACTS — Australia
CONTRACTS — Canada
CONTRACTS — Canada — Cases
CONTRACTS — England
CONTRACTS — England — Cases

CONTRACTS — Great Britain
CONTRACTS — Ireland
CONTRACTS — Switzerland
CONTRACTS, LETTING OF
CONTRACTS, MARITIME — Great Britain
CONTRIBUTIONS IN POLITICAL SCIENCE
CONTROL THEORY
CONTROL THEORY — Econometric models — Congresses
CONVENTION ON A CODE OF CONDUCT FOR LINER CONFERENCES
CONVERSATION
CONVERSION
CONVEYANCING — England
CONVICT LABOR — New York (State) — Albany — History — 19th century
CONWAY, MONCURE
COOK ISLANDS — Census, 1981
COOK ISLANDS — Population — Statistics
COOKE, JOHN WILLIAM
COOKERY — England — Yorkshire
COOPERATION — Great Britain — History
COOPERATION
COOPERATION — European Economic Community countries
COOPERATION — Finland
COOPERATION — Germany — Biography
COOPERATION — Germany (West)
COOPERATION — Nigeria — Addresses, essays, lectures
COOPERATION — Poland
COOPERATIVE SOCIETIES
COOPERATIVE SOCIETIES — Government policies — Hungary
COOPERATIVE SOCIETIES — Law and legislation — Hungary
COOPERATIVE SOCIETIES — Canada — Auditing — Social aspects
COOPERATIVE SOCIETIES — Canada — History
COOPERATIVE SOCIETIES — European Economic Community countries
COOPERATIVE SOCIETIES — France
COOPERATIVE SOCIETIES — Germany (West)
COOPERATIVE SOCIETIES — Great Britain
COOPERATIVE SOCIETIES — Italy
COOPERATIVE UNION OF CANADA — History
COOPERATIVES — Africa — Addresses, essays, lectures
COPENHAGEN (DENMARK) — Economic conditions — Statistics
COPERNICUS (Nicolaus)
COPPER INDUSTRY AND TRADE — Mathematical models
COPPER INDUSTRY AND TRADE — Poland
COPPS, SHEILA, 1952-
COPYRIGHT — Computer programs
COPYRIGHT — Music — Canada
COPYRIGHT — Australia
COPYRIGHT — Great Britain
CORBY (NORTHAMPTONSHIRE) — Industries
CORDAGE INDUSTRY — Mexico — Yucatán — History
CORN — Indonesia
CORN — Indonesia — Utilization
CORN INDUSTRY — Indonesia
CORONERS
CORPORAL PUNISHMENT — Legal status, laws, etc. — Great Britain
CORPORATE CULTURE
CORPORATE CULTURE — United States
CORPORATE DIVESTITURE
CORPORATE IMAGE — United States — History
CORPORATE PLANNING
CORPORATE PLANNING — Addresses, essays, lectures
CORPORATE PLANNING — Case studies
CORPORATE PROFITS

CORPORATE RE-ORGANIZATIONS
CORPORATE STATE
CORPORATE STATE — Congresses
CORPORATE STATE — Europe
CORPORATE STATE — Latin America — Addresses, essays, lectures
CORPORATION — Great Britain — Accounting — Study and teaching
CORPORATION LAW — Austria
CORPORATION LAW — Belgium
CORPORATION LAW — Canada — Cases
CORPORATION LAW — France
CORPORATION LAW — Great Britain
CORPORATION LAW — Great Britain — Accounting
CORPORATION LAW — Great Britain — Cases
CORPORATION LAW — Great Britain — Handbooks, manuals, ect.
CORPORATION LAW — Great Britain — Handbooks, manuals, etc
CORPORATION LAW — Hong Kong
CORPORATION LAW — United States
CORPORATION REPORTS — France
CORPORATIONS
CORPORATIONS — Accounting
CORPORATIONS — Accounting — Law and legislation — Ireland
CORPORATIONS — Addresses, essays, lectures
CORPORATIONS — Charitable contributions — Great Britain
CORPORATIONS — Corrupt practices — Bibliography
CORPORATIONS — Finance
CORPORATIONS — Finance — Data processing
CORPORATIONS — History — 20th century
CORPORATIONS — Social aspects
CORPORATIONS — Social aspects — Spain
CORPORATIONS — Statistics
CORPORATIONS — Taxation
CORPORATIONS — Taxation — Germany (West)
CORPORATIONS — Taxation — Great Britain
CORPORATIONS — Valuation
CORPORATIONS — Australia — Finance
CORPORATIONS — Canada
CORPORATIONS — Canada — Charitable contributions
CORPORATIONS — European Economic Community countries — Finance
CORPORATIONS — France
CORPORATIONS — Great Britain
CORPORATIONS — Great Britain — Accounting
CORPORATIONS — Great Britain — Charitable contributions
CORPORATIONS — Great Britain — Finance
CORPORATIONS — Great Britain — Finance — Mathematical models
CORPORATIONS — India
CORPORATIONS — Japan — Finance
CORPORATIONS — Netherlands — Corrupt practices
CORPORATIONS — United States
CORPORATIONS — United States — Case studies
CORPORATIONS — United States — Finance
CORPORATIONS — United States — Finance — Congresses
CORPORATIONS — United States — Investor relations
CORPORATIONS — United States — Political activity
CORPORATIONS, BRITISH
CORPORATIONS, DEVELOPING COUNTRIES'
CORPORATIONS, EUROPEAN — Management
CORPORATIONS, FOREIGN — Taxation

CORPORATIONS, FOREIGN — Taxation — Canada
CORPORATIONS, FOREIGN — Asia — Personnel management — Congresses
CORPORATIONS, FOREIGN — South Africa
CORPORATIONS, GOVERNMENT — Great Britain
CORPORATIONS, GOVERNMENT — Great Britain — Accounting — Effect of inflation on
CORPORATIONS, GOVERNMENT — Great Britain — Finance
CORPORATIONS, GOVERNMENT — Great Britain — Management — Employee participation
CORPORATIONS, JAPANESE — European Economic Community countries
CORPORATIONS, JAPANESE — United States
CORPORATIONS, NONPROFIT — Finland — Accounting
CORPORATIONS, NONPROFIT
CORPORATIONS, NONPROFIT — Legal status, laws, etc. — France
CORPORATIONS, NONPROFIT — Management
CORPORATIONS, NONPROFIT — Management — Case studies
CORPORATIONS, NONPROFIT — United States — Finance — Addresses, essays, lectures
CORPORATIONS — Taxation — United States
CORRECTIONAL PERSONNEL — Addresses, essays, lectures
CORRECTIONS — Addresses, essays, lectures
CORRECTIONS — Canada
CORRECTIONS — Great Britain — History — 19th century
CORRECTIONS — New York (State)
CORRECTIONS — United States
CORRESPONDENCE SCHOOLS AND CLASSES — Addresses, essays, lectures
CORRUPTION (IN POLITICS) — Bibliography
CORRUPTION (IN POLITICS) — Africa, Sub. Saharan
CORRUPTION (IN POLITICS) — Canada
CORRUPTION (IN POLITICS) — Great Britain
CORRUPTION (IN POLITICS) — Hong Kong — History
CORRUPTION (IN POLITICS) — Hongkong
CORRUPTION (IN POLITICS) — Illinois — Chicago
CORRUPTION (IN POLITICS) — India
CORRUPTION (IN POLITICS) — Indonesia
CORRUPTION (IN POLITICS) — United States
CORRUPTION (IN POLITICS) — United States — 20th century
CORRUPTION INVESTIGATION — Hong Kong — History
CORSICA — History — French Revolution, 1789-1793
CORSICA — History — British occupation, 1794-1796
CORYNDON, ROBERT THORNE
COSSACKS — History
COST ACCOUNTING
COST ACCOUNTING — Technological innovations
COST AND STANDARD OF LIVING
COST AND STANDARD OF LIVING — Statistical methods
COST AND STANDARD OF LIVING — Africa
COST AND STANDARD OF LIVING — Armenian S.S.R.
COST AND STANDARD OF LIVING — Asia
COST AND STANDARD OF LIVING — Bulgaria — Statistics

COST AND STANDARD OF LIVING — Developing countries
COST AND STANDARD OF LIVING — Developing countries — Case studies
COST AND STANDARD OF LIVING — Developing countries — Congresses
COST AND STANDARD OF LIVING — Developing countries — Methodology
COST AND STANDARD OF LIVING — France
COST AND STANDARD OF LIVING — Germany (West) — Statistics
COST AND STANDARD OF LIVING — Hong Kong — Statistics
COST AND STANDARD OF LIVING — Hungary — Statistical methods — Congresses
COST AND STANDARD OF LIVING — India — Assam — Case studies
COST AND STANDARD OF LIVING — India — Sibsāgar District — Case studies
COST AND STANDARD OF LIVING — Italy
COST AND STANDARD OF LIVING — Ivory Coast
COST AND STANDARD OF LIVING — Ivory Coast — Statistical methods
COST AND STANDARD OF LIVING — Japan — Statistics
COST AND STANDARD OF LIVING — Jordan — Statistics
COST AND STANDARD OF LIVING — Latin America
COST AND STANDARD OF LIVING — Malaysia
COST AND STANDARD OF LIVING — Netherlands — Methodology
COST AND STANDARD OF LIVING — Netherlands — Statistics
COST AND STANDARD OF LIVING — Norway — Statistics
COST AND STANDARD OF LIVING — Sri Lanka
COST AND STANDARD OF LIVING — Thailand
COST CONTROL
COST CONTROL — trends — United States
COST EFFECTIVENESS
COSTA RICA — Census, 1984
COSTA RICA — Population
COSTA RICA — Population — Psychological aspects
COSTA RICA — Population — Statistics
COSTS, INDUSTRIAL — Great Britain — Mathematical models
COSTS, INDUSTRIAL — United States
COSTUME — Social aspects
COTTAGE INDUSTRIES — Cyprus — Statistics
COTTAGE INDUSTRIES — Italy, Northern — History — 19th century
COTTON TRADE — Alabama — Mobile — History — 19th century
COTTON TRADE — Central America
COTTON TRADE — European Economic Community countries
COTTON TRADE — France
COUNCIL FOR MUTUAL ECONOMIC ASSISTANCE
COUNCIL FOR NATIONAL ACADEMIC AWARDS
COUNCIL FOR NATIONAL PARKS
COUNCIL OF EUROPE. Parliamentary Assembly — Comparative studies
COUNCIL OF EUROPE. Symposium on Legal Data Processing in Europe (8th : 1985 : Luxembourg)
COUNCIL OF MINISTERS OF THE EUROPEAN COMMUNITIES — Sources — Bibliography
COUNCIL OF THE EUROPEAN COMMUNITIES — History
COUNSELING
COUNTERFACTUALS (LOGIC) — History — 18th century
COUNTERINSURGENCY
COUNTERINSURGENCY — United States — History — 20th century — Bibliography
COUNTERREVOLUTIONS — Nicaragua
COUNTERTRADE
COUNTERTRADE — Congresses
COUNTRY HOMES — England — History — 19th century
COUNTRY LIFE — England — History
COUNTY COURTS — Great Britain
COUPS DE´ÉTAT — Spain
COUPS D´ÉTAT
COUPS D´ÉTAT — History — 20th century
COUPS D´ÉTAT — Developing countries
COUPS D´ÉTAT — Latin America — History — 20th century
COURT ADMINISTRATION — England
COURT OF JUSTICE OF THE EUROPEAN COMMUNITIES
COURT OF JUSTICE OF THE EUROPEAN COMMUNITIES — Sources — Bibliography
COURT RECORDS — England — History
COURT RULES — Australia
COURTS
COURTS — England
COURTS — European Economic Community countries
COURTS — European Economic Community Countries
COURTS — France
COURTS — Great Britain
COURTS — Great Britain — Directories
COURTS — Northern Ireland — History
COURTS — United States
COURTS — United States — History
COURTS — Zambia
COURTS AND COURIERS
COURTS AND COURTIERS — History
COURTS, ISLAMIC — Afghanistan
COURTS, JEWISH
COURTS-MARTIAL AND COURTS OF INQUIRY — Great Britain — History — 20th century
COURTSHIP
COURTSHIP — Great Britain — History
COVENTRY (WEST MIDLANDS, ENGLAND) — History
COVENTRY (WEST MIDLANDS, ENGLAND) — Population — Statistics
COWAN, JAMES
COWAN, WALTER
COWLES COMMISSION FOR RESEARCH IN ECONOMICS
COX, JAMES M
COX, OLIVER C
COX, REAVIS
CREATIVE ABILITY
CREATIVE ABILITY IN SCIENCE
CREDIT
CREDIT — Dictionaries — Russian
CREDIT — Management
CREDIT — Brazil
CREDIT — Communist countries
CREDIT — Great Britain — Statistics
CREDIT — Peru
CREDIT — Soviet Union — Bibliography
CREDIT — Uruguay
CREDIT CONTROL — Mathematical models
CREDIT CONTROL — Developing countries
CREDIT CONTROL — United States
CREOLE DIALECTS
CRICHEL DOWN (WIMBORNE, DORSET) — History
CRIME
CRIME AND AGE — Case studies
CRIME AND CRIMINALS
CRIME AND CRIMINALS — Addresses, essays, lectures
CRIME AND CRIMINALS — Congresses
CRIME AND CRIMINALS — Developing countries
CRIME AND CRIMINALS — Public opinion
CRIME AND CRIMINALS — Research
CRIME AND CRIMINALS — Social aspects
CRIME AND CRIMINALS — Social aspects — Great Britain
CRIME AND CRIMINALS — Sociological aspects
CRIME AND CRIMINALS — Africa, Southern
CRIME AND CRIMINALS — Australia
CRIME AND CRIMINALS — Brazil — Pernambuco — History — 19th century
CRIME AND CRIMINALS — Canada
CRIME AND CRIMINALS — Canada — History
CRIME AND CRIMINALS — Council of Europe countries — Congresses
CRIME AND CRIMINALS — Council of Europe countries — History — Congresses
CRIME AND CRIMINALS — Council of Europe countries — Public opinion
CRIME AND CRIMINALS — Cyrprus — Statistics
CRIME AND CRIMINALS — England — London
CRIME AND CRIMINALS — England — London — History
CRIME AND CRIMINALS — France
CRIME AND CRIMINALS — France — Statistics
CRIME AND CRIMINALS — Great Britain
CRIME AND CRIMINALS — India — Assam
CRIME AND CRIMINALS — India — Meghalaya
CRIME AND CRIMINALS — Nepal
CRIME AND CRIMINALS — Netherlands
CRIME AND CRIMINALS — Netherlands — Citizen participation
CRIME AND CRIMINALS — Netherlands — Public opinion
CRIME AND CRIMINALS — Norway
CRIME AND CRIMINALS — Prussia — History
CRIME AND CRIMINALS — Soviet Union — Case studies
CRIME AND CRIMINALS — Soviet Union — Public opinion
CRIME AND CRIMINALS — United States
CRIME AND CRIMINALS — United States — Bibliography
CRIME AND CRIMINALS — United States — Case studies
CRIME AND CRIMINALS — United States — Congresses
CRIME AND CRIMINALS — United States — History — 19th century
CRIME AND CRIMINALS — United States — History — 20th century
CRIME AND CRIMINALS — United States — Public opinion
CRIME AND CRIMINALS — United States — Public opinion — History
CRIME AND CRIMINALS — United States — Research
CRIME AND THE PRESS — United States
CRIME IN TELEVISION
CRIME LABORATORIES — England
CRIME PREVENTION — Congresses
CRIME PREVENTION — Netherlands — Evaluation
CRIME PREVENTION — United States
CRIME PREVENTION — United States — Citizen participation
CRIMEAN WAR, 1853-1856 — Diplomatic history
CRIMES ABOARD BUSES — Great Britain
CRIMINAL ANTHROPOLOGY
CRIMINAL BEHAVIOR
CRIMINAL BEHAVIOR — Congresses
CRIMINAL BEHAVIOR, PREDICTION OF
CRIMINAL BEHAVIOR, PREDICTION OF — Statistical methods
CRIMINAL COURTS — England

CRIMINAL IINVESTIGATION — Canada
CRIMINAL INVESTIGATION
CRIMINAL INVESTIGATION — England
CRIMINAL INVESTIGATION — England — Birmingham (West Midlands) — History — 20th century
CRIMINAL INVESTIGATION — Great Britain
CRIMINAL JURISDICTION — Canada
CRIMINAL JUSTICE, ADMINISTRATION OF
CRIMINAL JUSTICE, ADMINISTRATION OF — Bibliography
CRIMINAL JUSTICE, ADMINISTRATION OF — Religious aspects — Christianity
CRIMINAL JUSTICE, ADMINISTRATION OF — Social aspects — United States
CRIMINAL JUSTICE, ADMINISTRATION OF — Canada
CRIMINAL JUSTICE, ADMINISTRATION OF — England
CRIMINAL JUSTICE, ADMINISTRATION OF — England — London
CRIMINAL JUSTICE, ADMINISTRATION OF — Great Britain
CRIMINAL JUSTICE, ADMINISTRATION OF — India
CRIMINAL JUSTICE, ADMINISTRATION OF — Poland
CRIMINAL JUSTICE, ADMINISTRATION OF — Prussia — History
CRIMINAL JUSTICE, ADMINISTRATION OF — United States
CRIMINAL JUSTICE, ADMINISTRATION OF — United States — Addresses, essays, lectures
CRIMINAL JUSTICE, ADMINISTRATION OF — United States — Bibliography
CRIMINAL JUSTICE, ADMINISTRATION OF — United States — Data processing
CRIMINAL JUSTICE, ADMINISTRATION OF — United States — Mathematical models
CRIMINAL JUSTICE BILL 1981-82
CRIMINAL JUSTICE BILL 1986-87
CRIMINAL LAW
CRIMINAL LAW — Congresses, conferences, etc.
CRIMINAL LAW — Moral and religious aspects
CRIMINAL LAW — Philosophy
CRIMINAL LAW — Public opinion
CRIMINAL LAW — Canada
CRIMINAL LAW — China
CRIMINAL LAW — England
CRIMINAL LAW — England — Cases
CRIMINAL LAW — England — Digests
CRIMINAL LAW — Europe
CRIMINAL LAW — France
CRIMINAL LAW — Great Britain — Congresses
CRIMINAL LAW — Indonesia
CRIMINAL LAW — Soviet Union — Cases
CRIMINAL LAW — Soviet Union — Congresses
CRIMINAL LAW — United States
CRIMINAL LAW — United States — History
CRIMINAL LIABILITY — Council of Europe countries
CRIMINAL PROCEDURE — Canada
CRIMINAL PROCEDURE — Canada — History
CRIMINAL PROCEDURE — China
CRIMINAL PROCEDURE — England
CRIMINAL PROCEDURE — Europe — Congresses
CRIMINAL PROCEDURE — Great Britain
CRIMINAL PROCEDURE — Great Britain — Congresses
CRIMINAL PROCEDURE — Soviet Union — Cases
CRIMINAL PROCEDURE — Soviet Union — Congresses
CRIMINAL PROCEDURE — Spain
CRIMINAL PROCEDURE (INTERNATIONAL LAW)
CRIMINAL PSYCHOLOGY
CRIMINAL PSYCHOLOGY — Addresses, essays, lectures
CRIMINAL PSYCHOLOGY — Congresses
CRIMINAL PSYCHOLOGY — Testing
CRIMINAL REGISTERS — Australia
CRIMINAL STATISTICS — Netherlands
CRIMINAL STATISTICS — Northern Ireland
CRIMINAL STATISTICS — United States
CRIMINOLOGISTS — England — Biography
CRISES
CRITICAL CARE MEDICINE — Moral and ethical aspects — Congresses
CRITICAL CARE MEDICINE — Social aspects — Congresses
CRITICISM
CRITICISM — Social aspects
CRITICISM (PHILOSOPHY)
CRITIQUE DE LA RAISON DIALECTIQUE. 1, THÉORIE DES ENSEMBLES PRATIQUES
CROP YIELDS
CROP YIELDS — Malawi — Statistics
CROP YIELDS — Soviet Union
CROP YIELDS — Zimbabwe — Statistics
CROPS — Nutrition
CROPS — Nutrition — Congresses
CROPS — Research — India
CROPS — Fiji
CROPS AND SOILS
CROWN AGENTS FOR OVERSEA GOVERNMENTS AND ADMINISTRATIONS
CROWN LANDS — Hong Kong
CROYDON (LONDON, ENGLAND) — Social policy
CRUELTY TO CHILDREN — England — London
CRUSADES
CRUSADES — First, 1096-1099
CRUTCHFIELD, JAMES ARTHUR
CRYPTOGRAPHY — History
CUBA — Armed forces
CUBA — Economic conditions — 1959-
CUBA — Economic conditions — 1959- — Statistics
CUBA — Foreign economic relations — Communist Countries
CUBA — Foreign relations
CUBA — Foreign relations — 1959-
CUBA — Foreign relations — Puerto Rica
CUBA — Foreign relations — United States
CUBA — History — Revolution, 1959
CUBA — History — 1878-1895
CUBA — History — Revolution, 1895-1898
CUBA — History — 1899-1906
CUBA — History — Revolution, 1959 — Journalists — Congresses
CUBA — Politics and government — 1933-1959
CUBA — Politics and government — Revolution, 1959
CUBA — Politics and government — 1959-
CUBA — Relations — Soviet Union
CUBA — Relations — United States
CUBA — Social conditions — 1959-
CUBA — History
CUBA — Politics and government — 1909-1933
CUBA. Treaties, etc. United States (1903 May 22)
CUBAN MISSILE CRISIS, OCT. 1962
CUBAN MISSILE CRISIS, OCT. 1962 — Bibliography
CUBAN MISSILE CRISIS, OCT. 1962 — Sources
CUBEO INDIANS
CULTS
CULTS — Congresses
CULTS — Controversial literature — History and criticism
CULTS — United States
CULTURAL PROPERTY EXPORT AND IMPORT ACT (CANADA)
CULTURAL RELATIONS
CULTURAL RELATIONS — Addresses, essays, lectures
CULTURE
CURIEL, HENRI
CURRAGH (KILDARE : COUNTY) MUTINY, 1914
CURRENCY QUESTION
CURRENCY QUESTION — History
CURRENCY QUESTION — Germany
CURRENCY QUESTION — Great Britain — History
CURRENCY QUESTION — Hungary
CURRENCY QUESTION — Hungary — Congress
CURRENCY QUESTION — Poland
CURRENCY QUESTION — Soviet Union — History
CURRENT COST ACCOUNTING
CURRENT VALUE ACCOUNTING — Great Britain
CURRICULUM PLANNING
CURRICULUM PLANNING — England — Suffolk
CURRICULUM PLANNING — United States
CURRYS GROUP PLC — History
CURTIN, PHILIP D
CURZON, GEORGE NATHANIEL CURZON, Marquess
CUSTODY OF CHILDREN
CUSTODY OF CHILDREN — Psychological aspects
CUSTODY OF CHILDREN — England
CUSTODY OF CHILDREN — Great Britain
CUSTODY OF CHILDREN — United States
CUSTOMARY LAW — Africa, Southern
CUSTOMARY LAW — Australia
CUSTOMARY LAW — Tanzania — Kilimanjaro
CUSTOMER SERVICE — Great Britain — Management
CUSTOMS ADMINISTRATION — China — History
CUSTOMS UNIONS
CYBERNETICS
CYPRIOTES — England — London — Ethnic identity
CYPRIOTES — England — London — Social life and customs
CYPRUS — Economic conditions
CYPRUS — Economic policy
CYPRUS — Ethnic relations
CYPRUS — Foreign relations
CYPRUS — History
CYPRUS — History — Cyprus crisis, 1974-
CYPRUS — Politics and government
CYPRUS — Population — Statistics
CYPRUS — Statistics, Vital
CZECH AMERICANS — Minnesota — Minneapolis — Social life and customs
CZECH SOCIALIST REPUBLIC (CZECHOSLOVAKIA) — Census — 1980
CZECH SOCIALIST REPUBLIC (CZECHOSLOVAKIA) — Statistics
CZECHOSLAVAKIA — Presidents — Correspondence
CZECHOSLOVAKIA
CZECHOSLOVAKIA — Bibliography
CZECHOSLOVAKIA — Census — 1980
CZECHOSLOVAKIA — Census — 1980-
CZECHOSLOVAKIA — Commerce
CZECHOSLOVAKIA — Foreign relations — Germany
CZECHOSLOVAKIA — Foreign relations — Soviet Union
CZECHOSLOVAKIA — History
CZECHOSLOVAKIA — History — 1918-1938

CZECHOSLOVAKIA — History — 1938-1945
CZECHOSLOVAKIA — History — 1938-1945 — Sources
CZECHOSLOVAKIA — History — Intervention, 1968
CZECHOSLOVAKIA — Intellectual life
CZECHOSLOVAKIA — Intellectual life — 1945-
CZECHOSLOVAKIA — Politics and government
CZECHOSLOVAKIA — Politics and government — 1938-1945
CZECHOSLOVAKIA — Politics and government — 1945-
CZECHOSLOVAKIA — Presidents — Biography
CZECHOSLOVAKIA — Presidents — Correspondence
CZECHOSLOVAKIA — Social conditions
CZECHOSLOVAKIA — Social policy
CZECHOSLOVAKIA — Statistics
DACCA (BANGLADESH) — Social conditions
DADRA AND NAGAR HAVELI (INDIA) — Population — Statistics
DAIMLER-BENZ AKTIENGESELLSCHAFT — History
DAIRY CATTLE — Denmark
DAIRY FARMING — England — West Country — Finance
DAIRY PRODUCTS — Statistics
DAIRYING — Economic aspects — European Economic Community Countries
DAIRYING — Denmark
DALHOUSIE OCEAN STUDIES PROGRAMME
DALTON, HUGH
DANSKE BOGHANDLERMEDHJÆLPERFORENING
DANVILLE (VA.) — Economic conditions
DANVILLE (VA.) — Social conditions
DARIBI
DARLING, Sir RALPH
DARRÉ, WALTHUR
DARWIN, CHARLES
DARWIN, CHARLES — Influence
DAS KAPITAL
DATA BASE MANAGEMENT
DATA BASES — Models
DATA LIBRARIES — Congresses
DATA PROTECTION — Great Britain
DATA PROTECTION ACT
DATA PROTECTION ACT 1984
DATA PROTECTION BILL 1982-83
DATA PROTECTION BILL 1983-84
DATA REDUCTION
DATA STRUCTURES (COMPUTER SCIENCE)
DATA TRANSMISSION EQUIPMENT INDUSTRY — Canada
DATABASE MANAGEMENT
DATING (SOCIAL CUSTOMS)
DAUPHINÉ (FRANCE) — Economic conditions
DAUPHINÉ (FRANCE) — History
DAVEY, KEITH
DAVIS, WILLIAM G
DAY CARE CENTERS — Denmark
DAY CARE CENTERS — England
DAY CARE CENTERS — European Economic Community countries
DAY CARE CENTERS — United States
DBASE III (COMPUTER PROGRAM)
DBASE III (COMPUTER PROGRAM)
DBASE III PLUS (COMPUTER PROGRAM)
DE FINETTI, BRUNO
DE GASPERI, ALEIDE
DE SECONDAT, CHARLES, baron de Montesquieu See Montesquieu, Charles de Secondat, baron de
DE TOCQUEVILLE, ALEXIS See Tocqueville, Alexis de
DEAF — Means of communication
DEAF — Great Britain — Public opinion
DEAF — United States — Biography
DEAF — United States — History
DEATH — Political aspects — France — History — 18th century
DEATH — Proof and certification — United States
DEATH — Psychological aspects
DEATH — Social aspects
DEATH — Social aspects — Oceania
DEBREU, GERARD
DEBT — Brazil
DEBT — Germany (West) — Statistics
DEBT — Great Britain
DEBT RELIEF
DEBT RELIEF — Brazil
DEBT RELIEF — Developing countries
DEBTOR AND CREDITOR — England
DEBTOR AND CREDITOR — Scotland
DEBTS, EXTERNA
DEBTS, EXTERNAL
DEBTS, EXTERNAL — Dictionaries — Polyglot
DEBTS, EXTERNAL — Reporting — Handbooks, manuals, etc.
DEBTS, EXTERNAL — Brazil
DEBTS, EXTERNAL. — Brazil
DEBTS, EXTERNAL -- Brazil
DEBTS, EXTERNAL — Caribbean Area
DEBTS, EXTERNAL — Developing countries
DEBTS, EXTERNAL — Developing countries
DEBTS, EXTERNAL — Developing countries — Congresses
DEBTS, EXTERNAL — Developing countries — Management
DEBTS, EXTERNAL — Developing countries — Statistics
DEBTS, EXTERNAL — Germany
DEBTS, EXTERNAL — Latin America
DEBTS, EXTERNAL — United States
DEBTS, PUBLIC
DEBTS, PUBLIC — Congresses
DEBTS, PUBLIC — Australia
DEBTS, PUBLIC — Germany
DEBTS, PUBLIC — India
DEBTS, PUBLIC — United States
DEBTS,PUBLIC — Organisation for Economic Co-operation and Development countries
DEBUGGING IN COMPUTER SCIENCE
DECAZEVILLE (FRANCE) — Industries — History
DECEDENTS' FAMILY MAINTENANCE — England
DECEMBRISTS
DECENTRALISATION IN GOVERNMENT — Europe
DECENTRALISATION IN GOVERNMENT — France — Bordeaux
DECENTRALIZATION IN GOVERNMENT — England — Bristol
DECENTRALIZATION IN GOVERNMENT — England — London
DECENTRALIZATION IN GOVERNMENT — Europe
DECENTRALIZATION IN GOVERNMENT — France
DECENTRALIZATION IN GOVERNMENT — Great Britain
DECENTRALIZATION IN GOVERNMENT — Iran — Case studies
DECENTRALIZATION IN GOVERNMENT — Spain
DECISION MAKING
DECISION-MAKING
DECISION-MAKING
DECISION-MAKING
DECISION MAKING
DECISION-MAKING
DECISION MAKING — Case studies
DECISION-MAKING — Congresses
DECISION-MAKING — Mathematical models
DECISION MAKING — mathematical models
DECISION-MAKING — Mathematical models — Congresses
DECISION-MAKING (ETHICS)
DECISION-MAKING, GROUP — Congresses
DECISION SUPPORT SYSTEMS
DECLARATION ON THE RIGHT TO DEVELOPMENT [DRAFT]
DECOLONIZATION — History
DECORATION AND ORNAMENT — Psychological aspects
DECORATIONS OF HONOR — Great Britain
DECORATIVE ARTS — England
DECORATIVE ARTS — New York (State) — Woodstock — History — 20th century — Exhibitions
DECORATIVE ARTS, HUGUENOT — England
DEFAULT (FINANCE) — New York (N.Y.)
DEFECTORS — Poland
DEFECTORS — Poland — Biography
DEFECTORS — United States — Biography
DEFENSES — Technological innovations
DEFICIT FINANCING — Canada
DEFICIT FINANCING — India
DEFICIT FINANCING — United States
DEFORESTATION
DEFORESTATION — Social aspects
DEGREES, ACADEMIC — Europe
DELAUNAY, VADIM
DELEGATED LEGISLATION — Great Britain
DELHI (INDIA) — History
DELIERY OF HEALTH CARE — trends — United States
DELINQUENT GIRLS — Scotland
DELIVERY OF HEALTH CARE
DELIVERY OF HEALTH CARE — economics — United States
DELIVERY OF HEALTH CARE — history — Great Britain
DELIVERY OF HEALTH CARE — history — United States
DELIVERY OF HEALTH CARE — trends — United States — congresses
DEMENTIA
DEMING, BARBARA
DEMOCRACY
DEMOCRACY — Addresses, essays, lectures
DEMOCRACY — Case studies
DEMOCRACY — Congresses
DEMOCRACY — Economic aspects
DEMOCRACY — History
DEMOCRACY — Public opinion
DEMOCRATIC CENTRALISM
DEMOCRATIC PARTY (Ill.)
DEMOCRATIC PARTY (N.Y.) — History — 20th century
DEMOCRATIC PARTY (U.S.) — History
DEMOGRAPHERS — Biography
DEMOGRAPHERS — Soviet Union — Directories
DEMOGRAPHIC ANTHROPOLOGY
DEMOGRAPHIC SURVEYS
DEMOGRAPHIC SURVEYS — Data processing
DEMOGRAPHIC SURVEYS — Cyprus
DEMOGRAPHIC SURVEYS — Yugoslavia — Vojvodina
DEMOGRAPHIC TRANSITION
DEMOGRAPHIC TRANSITION — Congresses
DEMOGRAPHIC TRANSITION — England
DEMOGRAPHIC TRANSITION — India
DEMOGRAPHY
DEMOGRAPHY — Cross-cultural studies
DEMOGRAPHY — Data processing
DEMOGRAPHY — Dictionaries — Polyglot
DEMOGRAPHY — History
DEMOGRAPHY — Mathematical models
DEMOGRAPHY — Statistical methods
DEMOGRAPHY — Canada — Bibliography

DEMOGRAPHY — Europe — Bibliography
DEMOGRAPHY — Finland — Bibliography
DEMOGRAPHY — Great Britain — History
DEMOGRAPHY — North America
DEMOGRAPHY — Poland
DEMOGRAPHY — Russian S.F.S.R. — Ural Mountains region
DEMOGRAPHY — Soviet Union
DEMOGRAPHY — Soviet Union — History
DEMOGRAPHY — Soviet Union — Study and teaching
DEMONSTRATIONS — Germany (West)
DENAZIFICATION
DENG, XIAOPING
DENMARK — Administrative and political divisions — Population — Statistics
DENMARK — Census, 1981
DENMARK — Commerce — Statistics
DENMARK — Defenses
DENMARK — Defenses — Bibliography
DENMARK — Diplomatic and consular service
DENMARK — Economic conditions
DENMARK — Economic conditions — Statistics
DENMARK — Economic conditions — 1945-
DENMARK — Economic conditions — 1945- — Mathematical models
DENMARK — Economic policy
DENMARK — Emigration and immigration
DENMARK — Foreign relations
DENMARK — History — German occupation, 1940-1945
DENMARK — Military policy
DENMARK — Military policy — Bibliography
DENMARK — National security
DENMARK — Officials and employees
DENMARK — Politics and government
DENMARK — Politics and government — 1900-
DENMARK — Politics and government — 1940-1945
DENMARK — Politics and government — 1947-
DENMARK — Politics and government — 1972-
DENMARK — Population
DENMARK — Population — Statistics
DENMARK — Social conditions
DENMARK — Social conditions — 1945-
DENMARK — Social policy
DENMARK — Statistics, Vital
DENMARK. Folketinget. Children and Young Persons Act, 1964
DENMARK. Folketinget. Employment Service and Unemployment Insurance Act, 1970
DENMARK. Folketinget. Holidays with Pay Act, 1971
DENMARK. Folketinget. National Health Security Act, 1975
DENMARK. Folketinget. Occupational Safety, Health and Welfare (General) Act, 1968
DENMARK. Folketinget. Old Age Pension Act, 1969
DENMARK. Folketinget. Old Age Pension (Amendment) Act, 1972
DENMARK. Folketinget. Public Health Security Act, 1971
DENMARK. Folketinget. Rehabilitation Act, 1970
DENMARK. Folketinget
DENMARK. Miljøministeriet
DENTAL LAWS AND LEGISLATION — Great Britain
DENTISTRY AS A PROFESSION
DENTISTS — England — History — 19th century
DENTISTS — South Africa — Statistics
DENTISTS BILL 1982-83
DEPARTMENT STORES — Canada — Statistics
DEPENDENCY — Addresses, essays, lectures
DEPORTATION — Sri Lanka
DEPRESSION — psychology
DEPRESSION, MENTAL — Social aspects
DEPRESSION, MENTAL — Social aspects — Research
DEPRESSION, MENTAL — Somatization — China
DEPRESSIONS
DEPRESSIONS — Social aspects — United States
DEPRESSIONS — 1929 — Canada
DEPRESSIONS — 1929 — Spain
DEPRESSIONS — 1929 — United States
DEPRESSIONS — 1929 — United States — Bibliography
DEPRESSIONS — 1929-
DEPTS, EXTERNAL — Developing countries
DERBYSHIRE — Population
DERBYSHIRE — Social policy
DEREGULATION — Germany (West)
DERRIDA, JACQUES
DESCARTES, RENÉ
DESERTIFICATION — Control
DESERTIFICATION — China — Control
DESERTIFICATION — Sudan
DESHMUKH, DURGABAI
DESIGN, INDUSTRIAL — Management
DESIGN, INDUSTRIAL — Great Britain — History
DESIGN, INDUSTRIAL — United States — History
DESPOTISM — Cross-cultural studies
DESRAMAULT, LUC
DET NORSKE TOTALARHOLDSSELSKAPS BARNEFORBUND
DETECTIVES
DETENTE
DETENTION OF PERSONS — Great Britain
DETENTION OF PERSONS — Scotland
DETERMINISM (PHILOSOPHY)
DETERRENCE (STATEGY)
DETERRENCE (STRATEGY)
DETERRENCE (STRATEGY) — Congresses
DETERRENCE (STRATEGY) — Moral and ethical aspects
DEUTSCHE DEMOKRATISCHE PARTEI — History
DEUTSCHE STAATSPARTEI — History
DEVALUATION OF CURRENCY
DEVALUATION OF CURRENCY — Australia
DEVALUATION OF CURRENCY — Germany
DEVELOPING COUNTRIES
DEVELOPING COUNTRIES — Abstracts
DEVELOPING COUNTRIES — Armed Forces — Appropriations and expenditures
DEVELOPING COUNTRIES — Armed forces — Appropriations and expenditures — Economic aspects
DEVELOPING COUNTRIES — Colonial influence
DEVELOPING COUNTRIES — Commerce
DEVELOPING COUNTRIES — Commerce — Statistics
DEVELOPING COUNTRIES — Commerce — European Economic Community countries
DEVELOPING COUNTRIES — Commercial policy
DEVELOPING COUNTRIES — Defenses
DEVELOPING COUNTRIES — Defenses — Economic aspects
DEVELOPING COUNTRIES — Economic conditions
DEVELOPING COUNTRIES — Economic conditions — Congresses
DEVELOPING COUNTRIES — Economic conditions — Mathematical models — Congresses
DEVELOPING COUNTRIES — Economic conditions — Regional disparities
DEVELOPING COUNTRIES — Economic integration
DEVELOPING COUNTRIES — Economic policy
DEVELOPING COUNTRIES — Economic policy — Congresses
DEVELOPING COUNTRIES — Emigration and immigration
DEVELOPING COUNTRIES — Emigration and immigration — History — 20th century
DEVELOPING COUNTRIES — Ethnic relations
DEVELOPING COUNTRIES — Foreign economic relations
DEVELOPING COUNTRIES — Foreign economic relations — Bibliography
DEVELOPING COUNTRIES — Foreign economic relations — Congresses
DEVELOPING COUNTRIES — Foreign relations
DEVELOPING COUNTRIES — Foreign relations — Congresses
DEVELOPING COUNTRIES — Foreign relations — Soviet Union
DEVELOPING COUNTRIES — Foreign relations — Soviet Union — Congresses
DEVELOPING COUNTRIES — Foreign relations — United States
DEVELOPING COUNTRIES — Foreign relations — United States — Congresses
DEVELOPING COUNTRIES — Full employment policies — Congresses
DEVELOPING COUNTRIES — History, Military
DEVELOPING COUNTRIES — Industries
DEVELOPING COUNTRIES — Industries — Energy conservation
DEVELOPING COUNTRIES — Literatures — History and criticism
DEVELOPING COUNTRIES — Military relations — Soviet Union
DEVELOPING COUNTRIES — Military relations — United States
DEVELOPING COUNTRIES — Politics and government
DEVELOPING COUNTRIES — Population
DEVELOPING COUNTRIES — Population — Congresses
DEVELOPING COUNTRIES — Population — Statistics — Estimates — Handbooks, Manuals, etc
DEVELOPING COUNTRIES — Population policy
DEVELOPING COUNTRIES — Rural conditions
DEVELOPING COUNTRIES — Rural conditions — Case studies
DEVELOPING COUNTRIES — Social conditions
DEVELOPING COUNTRIES — Social policy
DEVELOPING COUNTRIES — Statistics, Vital
DEVELOPING COUNTRIES — Economic policy
DEVELOPING COUNTRIES — Foreign economic relations
DEVELOPING COUNTRIES — Industries — Addresses, essays, lectures
DEVELOPING COUNTRIES — Politics and government
DEVELOPMENT BANKS
DEVELOPMENT BANKS — Law and legislation
DEVELOPMENT BANKS — India
DEVELOPMENT BANKS — Mexico
DEVELOPMENT BANKS — Puerto Rico
DEVELOPMENT CREDIT CORPORATIONS

DEVELOPMENT CREDIT
CORPORATIONS — Organisation for
Economic Co-operation and Development
countries
DEVELOPMENTAL PSYCHOLOGY
DEVELOPMENTAL PSYCHOLOGY —
Congresses
DEVELOPMENTAL PSYCHOLOGY —
Dictionaries
DEVIANT BEHAVIOR
DEVIANT BEHAVIOR — Congresses
DEVIANT BEHAVIOR — History
DEVIANT BEHAVIOR IN MASS MEDIA
— United States
DEVIL — History of doctrines
DEVON — Statistics
DEVON. County Council
DHIMAL (NEPALESE PEOPLE) — Social
life and customs
DHOFAR (OMAN) — Social conditions
DIALECTIC
DIALECTICAL MATERIALISM
DICKEY, CHRISTOPHER
DICTATORS
DICTATORS — Europe — History — 20th
century
DICTATORSHIP OF THE
PROLETARIAT
DICTIONARIES — Polyglot
DICTIONARIES, POLYGLOT
DIESEL, RUDOLF
DIESEL MOTOR — History
DIET
DIET — History
DIET — China
DIET — Developing countries
DIET — United States
DIFFUSION OF INNOVATIONS
DIGITAL MAPPING
DILL, Sir JOHN
DILTHEY, WILHELM
DIMITROV, GEORGI
DINKA (AFRICAN PEOPLE) —
Biography
DIPLOMACY
DIPLOMACY — Dictionaries — Russian
DIPLOMACY — Directories
DIPLOMACY — Moral and ethical aspects
DIPLOMATIC AND CONSULAR
SERVICE IN GREAT BRITAIN
DIPLOMATIC NEGOTIATIONS IN
INTERNATIONAL DISPUTES
DIPLOMATS — United States — Biography
DIPLOMATS — Canada — Biography
DIPLOMATS — Germany — Biography
DIPLOMATS — Great Britain — Biography
DIPLOMATS — Philippines — Biography
DIPLOMATS — Russia — Biography
DIPLOMATS — United States — Biography
DIPLOMATS — United States — History
— 18th century
DIPLOMATS — United States — History
— 19th century
DIRECT BROADCAST SATELLITE
TELEVISION — Australia
DIRECTORS OF CORPORATIONS —
Legal status, laws etc. — Great Britain
DIRECTORS OF CORPORATIONS —
Great Britain
DIRGES
DISABLED PERSONS (SERVICES,
CONSULTATION AND
REPRESENTATION) BILL 1985-86
DISARMAMENT
DISARMAMENT — Congresses
DISARMAMENT — Economic aspects —
Sweden
DISARMAMENT — History
DISARMAMENT — Public opinion
DISASTER HOSPITALS
DISASTER RELIEF
DISASTER RELIEF — Congresses
DISASTER RELIEF — Economic aspects
DISASTER RELIEF — Equipment and
supplies
DISASTER RELIEF — Legal status, laws,
etc.

DISASTER RELIEF — Management —
Congresses
DISASTER RELIEF — Planning —
Congresses
DISASTER RELIEF — Public relations
DISASTER RELIEF — Social aspects
DISASTER RELIEF — Angola
DISASTER RELIEF — California —
Planning
DISASTER RELIEF — Ethiopia
DISASTER VICTIMS
DISASTERS
DISASTERS — Economic aspects
DISASTERS — Law and legislation
DISASTERS — Legal status, laws, etc.
DISASTERS — Planning
DISASTERS — Prevention
DISASTERS — Psychological aspects
DISASTERS — Research
DISASTERS — United States —
Psychological aspects — Case studies
DISCOUNT
DISCOURSE ANALYSIS
DISCRIMINATION IN EMPLOYMENT —
Great Britain
DISCRIMINATION
DISCRIMINATION — Great Britain
DISCRIMINATION IN EDUCATION —
Law and legislation — United States
DISCRIMINATION IN EDUCATION —
Connecticut — New Haven
DISCRIMINATION IN EDUCATION —
Great Britain
DISCRIMINATION IN EMPLOYMENT
DISCRIMINATION IN EMPLOYMENT
— Canada
DISCRIMINATION IN EMPLOYMENT
— Cyprus — Statistics
DISCRIMINATION IN EMPLOYMENT
— England — London
DISCRIMINATION IN EMPLOYMENT
— Great Britain
DISCRIMINATION IN EMPLOYMENT
— Pennsylvania — History
DISCRIMINATION IN HOUSING — Law
and legislation — United States
DISCRIMINATION IN HOUSING —
England
DISCRIMINATION IN HOUSING —
Great Britain
DISCRIMINATION IN HOUSING —
London metropolitan area — Tower
Hamlets
DISCRIMINATION IN HOUSING —
United States
DISEASE — History
DISEASE — Tanzania — Causes and
theories of causation — History
DISEASES — Great Britain
DISEASES — Great Britain — Statistics
DISINFORMATION
DISINVESTMENTS — South Africa
DISINVESTMENTS — South Africa —
Public opinion
DISPOSITION (PHILOSOPHY)
DISPUTE RESOLUTION (LAW) — United
States
DISRAELI, BENJAMIN
DISSENTERS — Argentina
DISSENTERS — Czechoslovakia
DISSENTERS — Soviet Union
DISSENTERS — Soviet Union — Biography
DISSENTERS — Spain — La Rioja —
History
DISSENTERS — United States —
Biography
DISSENTERS — United States — History
— 19th century
DISSENTERS, RELIGIOUS
DISSERTATIONS, ACADEMIC
DISSERTATIONS, ACADEMIC —
England — London — Bibliography
DISSERTATIONS, ACADEMIC — Great
Britain
DISTANCE EDUCATION — Addresses,
essays, lectures
DISTRESS (LAW) — England

DISTRIBUTION (PROBABILITY
THEORY)
DISTRIBUTIVE JUSTICE
DISTRIBUTIVE JUSTICE — Congresses
DIVER (Family)
DIVERSIFICATION IN INDUSTRY —
Great Britain
DIVERSIFICATION IN INDUSTRY —
United States — Case studies
DIVIDENDS — Australia — Reinvestment
DIVIDENDS — Great Britain
DIVIDENDS — United States —
Reinvestment
DIVISION OF LABOR — Canada
DIVORCE — Law and legislation — Great
Britain
DIVORCE — Law and legislation —
Netherlands
DIVORCE — Law and legislation — United
States
DIVORCE — Australia
DIVORCE — Denmark
DIVORCE — England
DIVORCE — Great Britain
DIVORCE — Netherlands
DIVORCE — Trinidad and Tobago —
Statistics
DIVORCE — United States
DIVORCE MEDIATION — Canada
DIVORCE MEDIATION — Great Britain
DIVORCE MEDIATION — United States
DIVORCE SUITS — Great Britain
DIVORCE THERAPY
DIVORCED MOTHERS — Legal status,
laws, etc. — United States
DIVORCED MOTHERS — United States
DIVORCED MOTHERS — United States
— Economic conditions
DIVORCED MOTHERS — United States
— Social conditions
DIVORCED PARENTS — Denmark
DIVORCED WOMEN — United States —
Economic conditions
DIVORCED WOMEN — United States —
Social conditions
DLUGOS, GÜNTER
DOCTOR OF PHILOSOPHY DEGREE —
Great Britain
DOCUMENTARY CREDIT
DOGON LANGUAGE — Social aspects
DOGONS (AFRICAN PEOPLE) — Social
life and customs
DOLLAR, AMERICAN
DOLPĀ (NEPAL) — Economic conditions
DOLPĀ (NEPAL) — Ethnic relations
DOMESDAY BOOK — Bibliography
DOMESTIC ANIMALS, EFFECT OF
RADIATION ON
DOMESTIC EDUCATION — United States
DOMESTIC RELATIONS
DOMESTIC RELATIONS — Australia
DOMESTIC RELATIONS — Belgium —
Ghent — History
DOMESTIC RELATIONS — England
DOMESTIC RELATIONS — Hong Kong
DOMESTIC RELATIONS — Ontario —
History
DOMESTIC RELATIONS — Scotland
DOMESTIC RELATIONS — United States
DOMESTIC RELATIONS (ISLAMIC
LAW)
DOMESTIC RELATIONS (KURIA LAW)
— Tanzania
DOMICILE IN PUBLIC WELFARE —
New York (State) — History — 20th
century
DOMICILE IN PUBLIC WELFARE —
United States
DOMINICA — Economic conditions
DOMINICA — Economic policy
DOMINICAN REPUBLIC — Census, 1970
— Methodology
DOMINICAN REPUBLIC — Commercial
policy
DOMINICAN REPUBLIC — Economic
policy
DOMINICAN REPUBLIC — History

DOMINICAN REPUBLIC — Population — Statistics — Evaluation
DOMINICAN REPUBLIC — Population — Statistics — Methodology
DONALD, DAVID HERBERT — Addresses, essays, lectures
DONALD — Bibliography
DONATION OF ORGANS, TISSUES, ETC. — Great Britain — Attitudes
DORSEY, JASPER N
DOVER, STRAIT OF — International status
DOW CHEMICAL COMPANY — Trials, litigation, etc
DOWNES, JOHN
DRAINAGE — Government policy — Great Britain
DRAMATISTS, IRISH — 19th century — Diaries
DRENTHE (NETHERLANDS) — Economic policy
DREYFUS, ALFRED
DRINKING AND TRAFFIC ACCIDENTS
DRINKING OF ALCOHOLIC BEVERAGES — England — West Country
DRINKING OF ALCOHOLIC BEVERAGES — Switzerland — Statistics
DROPOUTS — Tanzania — Bukumbi
DROUGHT RELIEF — Southern States — History
DROUGHT RELIEF — Sudan
DROUGHTS
DROUGHTS — Economic aspects
DROUGHTS — Social aspects
DROUGHTS — Sahel — Congresses
DROUGHTS — Southern States — History
DROUGHTS — Sudan
DRUG ABUSE
DRUG ABUSE — Treatment — Denmark
DRUG ABUSE — Treatment — Great Britain
DRUG ABUSE — Canada
DRUG ABUSE — Denmark
DRUG ABUSE — Germany (West)
DRUG ABUSE — Scandinavia
DRUG ABUSE — United States
DRUG ABUSE — United States — Prevention
DRUG ABUSE AND CRIME
DRUG ABUSE AND CRIME — United States
DRUG ABUSE AND EMPLOYMENT
DRUG ABUSE SURVEYS — Canada
DRUG ABUSE SURVEYS — United States
DRUG TRADE
DRUG TRADE — Bangladesh
DRUG TRADE — Germany (West)
DRUG TRADE — Great Britain
DRUG TRADE — Great Britain — History
DRUGS — dictionaries
DRUGS — Law and legislation — Great Britain
DRUGS — Law and legislation — Northern Ireland
DRUGS — Physiological effect
DRUGS — Physiological effect — Addresses, essays, lectures
DRUGS — Denmark
DRUGS — Germany (West)
DRUGS AND EMPLOYMENT
DRUGS AND PRISONERS — Great Britain
DRUGS AND YOUTH — South Africa
DRUMONT, EDOUARD-ADOLPHE
DRUNK DRIVING — Great Britain
DRUZHININ, N. M.
DRY FARMING — Research — India
DU BOIS, W. E. B — Views on world politics
DUAL-CAREER FAMILIES — United States
DUALITY THEORY (MATHEMATICS)
DUARTE, JOSÉ NAPOLEÓN
DUHEM, PIERRE MAURICE MARIE, b.1861
DULLES, JOHN FOSTER

DUMFRIES AND GALLOWAY — Economic conditions
DUMFRIES AND GALLOWAY — Population
DUMONT
DUNANTUL (HUNGARY) — Industries
DURABLE GOODS, CONSUMER — France — Statistics
DURABLE GOODS, CONSUMER — Great Britain — Statistics
DURABLE GOODS, CONSUMER — Netherlands — Statistics
DURBAN METROPOLITAN CHAMBER OF COMMERCE
DURESS (LAW)
DURHAM (ENGLAND: COUNTY) — Bibliography — Union lists
DURKHEIM, ÉMILE. Suicide
DURKHEIM, ÉMILE
DURKHEIM, EMILE
DURKHEIM, EMILE
DURKHEIMIAN SCHOOL OF SOCIOLOGY
DURRUTI, BUENAVENTURA
DURY, E. C. (Ernest Charles)
DUTCH — New York (State) — History — 17th century
DUTCH LANGUAGE
DUTCH LANGUAGE — Dictionaries
DUTSCHKE, RUDI
DUTTON, HARRY
DUTY
DUTY-FREE IMPORTATION — European Economic Community countries
DWELLINGS — Energy conservation — Econometric models
DWELLINGS — Great Britain — Handbooks, manuals, etc.
DWELLINGS — Great Britain — Maintenance and repair — Finance
DWELLINGS — Japan — Statistics
DWELLINGS — South Africa — Johannesburg
DWELLINGS — United States — History — 19th century
DWELLINGS — United States — History — 20th century
DYNAMIC PROGRAMMING
DYNO INDUSTRIER A.S.
DZERZHINSKII, F. E.
EARTHQUAKE PREDICTION
EARTHQUAKE PREDICTION — Social aspects — California
EARTHQUAKES — Social aspects — California
EAST ASIA
EAST ASIA — Commercial policy — Congresses
EAST ASIA — Economic conditions
EAST ASIA — Economic policy
EAST ASIA — Economic policy — Congresses
EAST ASIA — Foreign economic relations
EAST ASIA — Foreign relations
EAST ASIA — Foreign relations — United States
EAST ASIA — History
EAST ASIA — Industries
EAST ASIA — Manufactures
EAST ASIA — Politics and government
EAST ASIA — Politics and government — Congresses
EAST ASIA — Relations — Canada
EAST BURRA (SCOTLAND) — Social conditions
EAST-CENTRAL STATE (NIGERIA) — Politics and government — Congresses
EAST EUROPEAN CANADIANS — Congresses
EAST INDIA COMPANY — Employees — History
EAST INDIAN AMERICANS
EAST INDIANS — Great Britain — Social conditions
EAST INDIANS — South Africa — Relocation

EAST SEPIK (PAPUA NEW GUINEA) — Population — Statistics
EAST-WEST TRADE (1945-)
EAST-WEST TRADE (1945-)
EAST-WEST TRADE (1945-)
EAST-WEST TRADE (1945-)
EAST-WEST TRADE (1945-)
EASTER ISLAND — History
EASTERN CAPE (SOUTH AFRICA) — Politics and government
EASTERN HIGHLANDS PROVINCE (PAPUA NEW GUINEA) — Population — Statistics
EASTERN QUESTION (BALKAN)
EASTERN SCOTTISH — History
EASTLEIGH. Council — History
EAVESDROPPING — Government policy — Great Britain
EAVESDROPPING — Ireland
ECCLESIASTICAL LAW — Spain
ECOLE NATIONALE D'ADMINISTRATION (France)
ECOLOGY
ECOLOGY — Bibliography
ECOLOGY — Philosophy
ECOLOGY — Statistics
ECOLOGY — Statistics — Bibliography
ECOLOGY — Germany (West) — Political aspects
ECOLOGY — Malaysia
ECONOMETRIC MODELS
ECONOMETRIC MODELS — Addresses, essays, lectures
ECONOMETRIC MODELS — Congresses
ECONOMETRICS
ECONOMETRICS — Addresses, essays, lectures
ECONOMETRICS — Computer programs
ECONOMIC — Computer programs
ECONOMIC AND SOCIAL COMMITTEE OF THE EUROPEAN COMMUNITIES 986OFF. PUBNS.. (270/2)
ECONOMIC ANTHROPOLOGY
ECONOMIC ANTHROPOLOGY — Australia
ECONOMIC ANTHROPOLOGY — Indonesia — Saroako
ECONOMIC ANTHROPOLOGY — Papua New Guinea
ECONOMIC ANTHROPOLOGY — Papua New Guinea — Goroka District
ECONOMIC ASSISTANCE
ECONOMIC ASSISTANCE — Dictionaries
ECONOMIC ASSISTANCE — Statistics
ECONOMIC ASSISTANCE — Developing countries
ECONOMIC ASSISTANCE — Africa, Sub-Saharan
ECONOMIC ASSISTANCE — Bangladesh
ECONOMIC ASSISTANCE — Developing countries
ECONOMIC ASSISTANCE — European Economic Community countries
ECONOMIC ASSISTANCE — Nepal
ECONOMIC ASSISTANCE — Rwanda
ECONOMIC ASSISTANCE, AMERICAN
ECONOMIC ASSISTANCE, AMERICAN — Addresses, essays, lectures
ECONOMIC ASSISTANCE, AMERICAN — Developing countries
ECONOMIC ASSISTANCE, AMERICAN — Egypt
ECONOMIC ASSISTANCE, AMERICAN — Europe
ECONOMIC ASSISTANCE, AMERICAN — Europe — History
ECONOMIC ASSISTANCE, AMERICAN — India
ECONOMIC ASSISTANCE, AMERICAN — Nepal
ECONOMIC ASSISTANCE, AMERICAN — Vietnam
ECONOMIC ASSISTANCE, AUSTRALIAN — Developing countries
ECONOMIC ASSISTANCE, BRITISH
ECONOMIC ASSISTANCE, BRITISH — Administration

ECONOMIC ASSISTANCE, BRITISH — Bibliography
ECONOMIC ASSISTANCE, BRITISH — Evaluation
ECONOMIC ASSISTANCE, BRITISH — Africa
ECONOMIC ASSISTANCE, CANADIAN
ECONOMIC ASSISTANCE, CANADIAN — Bibliography
ECONOMIC ASSISTANCE, CHINESE
ECONOMIC ASSISTANCE, COMMUNIST — Grenada — History
ECONOMIC ASSISTANCE, DOMESTIC
ECONOMIC ASSISTANCE, DOMESTIC — India
ECONOMIC ASSISTANCE, DOMESTIC — India — Congresses
ECONOMIC ASSISTANCE, DOMESTIC — India — Chakrabhavi
ECONOMIC ASSISTANCE, DOMESTIC — India — Gujarat
ECONOMIC ASSISTANCE, DOMESTIC — United States
ECONOMIC ASSISTANCE, NORWEGIAN
ECONOMIC ASSISTANCE, RUSSIAN — India
ECONOMIC COMMUNITY OF WEST AFRICAN STATES — History
ECONOMIC CONDITIONS — Burkina Faso — Statistics
ECONOMIC COOPERATION
ECONOMIC DEVELOPMENT
ECONOMIC DEVELOPMENT — Addresses, essays, lectures
ECONOMIC DEVELOPMENT — Case studies
ECONOMIC DEVELOPMENT — Congresses
ECONOMIC DEVELOPMENT — Dictionaries
ECONOMIC DEVELOPMENT — Effect of education on
ECONOMIC DEVELOPMENT — Effect of education on — Congresses
ECONOMIC DEVELOPMENT — Environmental aspects
ECONOMIC DEVELOPMENT — Mathematical models
ECONOMIC DEVELOPMENT — Religious aspects
ECONOMIC DEVELOPMENT — Research
ECONOMIC DEVELOPMENT — Social aspects
ECONOMIC DEVELOPMENT — Social aspects — Addresses, essays, lectures
ECONOMIC DEVELOPMENT — Social aspects — Developing countries — Case studies — Congresses
ECONOMIC DEVELOPMENT — Statistics
ECONOMIC DEVELOPMENT — Caribbean Area
ECONOMIC DEVELOPMENT — India
ECONOMIC DEVELOPMENT PROJECTS
ECONOMIC DEVELOPMENT PROJECTS — Environmental aspects
ECONOMIC DEVELOPMENT PROJECTS — Evaluation
ECONOMIC DEVELOPMENT PROJECTS — Evaluation — Bibliography
ECONOMIC DEVELOPMENT PROJECTS — Finance
ECONOMIC DEVELOPMENT PROJECTS — Finance — Kenya
ECONOMIC DEVELOPMENT PROJECTS — Social aspects — Bibliography
ECONOMIC DEVELOPMENT PROJECTS — Asia
ECONOMIC DEVELOPMENT PROJECTS — Bolivia — La Paz — Evaluation
ECONOMIC DEVELOPMENT PROJECTS — Caribbean area
ECONOMIC DEVELOPMENT PROJECTS — Developing countries
ECONOMIC DEVELOPMENT PROJECTS — Developing countries — Citizen participation
ECONOMIC DEVELOPMENT PROJECTS — Developing countries — Evaluation
ECONOMIC DEVELOPMENT PROJECTS — Ecuador — Guayaquil — Evaluation
ECONOMIC DEVELOPMENT PROJECTS — Egypt
ECONOMIC DEVELOPMENT PROJECTS — European Economic Community countries
ECONOMIC DEVELOPMENT PROJECTS — Latin America
ECONOMIC DEVELOPMENT PROJECTS — Saint Kitts-Nevis
ECONOMIC DEVELOPMENTECONOMIC DEVELOPMENT — Social aspects
ECONOMIC FORECASTING
ECONOMIC FORECASTING — Computer programs
ECONOMIC FORECASTING — Mathematical models
ECONOMIC FORECASTING — Bahamas
ECONOMIC FORECASTING — Great Britain
ECONOMIC FORECASTING — Great Britain — Simulation methods
ECONOMIC FORECASTING — Hong Kong
ECONOMIC FORECASTING — Netherlands
ECONOMIC FORECASTING — New Zealand
ECONOMIC FORECASTING — Soviet Union
ECONOMIC FORECASTING — Spain — Catalonia
ECONOMIC FORECASTING — Thailand
ECONOMIC HISTORY
ECONOMIC HISTORY — Congresses
ECONOMIC HISTORY — 1600-1750
ECONOMIC HISTORY — 1750-1918
ECONOMIC HISTORY — 19th century
ECONOMIC HISTORY — 20th century
ECONOMIC HISTORY — 20th century — Environmental aspects
ECONOMIC HISTORY — 1918-1945
ECONOMIC HISTORY — 1945-1971
ECONOMIC HISTORY — 1945-
ECONOMIC HISTORY — 1945- — Congresses
ECONOMIC HISTORY — 1971-
ECONOMIC HISTORY — 1971- — Congresses
ECONOMIC HISTORY — 1971- — Mathematical models
ECONOMIC HISTORY — Great Britain — History
ECONOMIC INDICATORS — Paraguay
ECONOMIC PLANNING
ECONOMIC POLICY
ECONOMIC POLICY — Addresses, essays, lectures
ECONOMIC POLICY — Case studies
ECONOMIC POLICY — Congresses
ECONOMIC POLICY — Decision making — Congresses
ECONOMIC POLICY — Econometric models
ECONOMIC POLICY — Econometric models — Congresses
ECONOMIC POLICY — Mathematical models
ECONOMIC RECOVERY TAX ACT
ECONOMIC RESEARCH
ECONOMIC SANCTIONS — South Africa
ECONOMIC SANCTIONS — South Africa — Bibliography
ECONOMIC SANCTIONS — Zimbabwe — Bibliography
ECONOMIC STABILIZATION
ECONOMIC STABILIZATION — Mathematical models
ECONOMIC STABILIZATION — Africa, West
ECONOMIC STABILIZATION — Central America
ECONOMIC STABILIZATION — Chile
ECONOMIC STABILIZATION — Developing countries
ECONOMIC STABILIZATION — Developing countries — Congresses
ECONOMIC STABILIZATION — Latin America
ECONOMIC STABILIZATION — Peru
ECONOMIC STABILIZATION — Southern Cone of South America
ECONOMIC STABILIZATION — Switzerland
ECONOMIC SURVEYS
ECONOMIC ZONES (MARITIME LAW)
ECONOMIC ZONES (MARITIME LAW) — Japan
ECONOMIC ZONING — Congresses
ECONOMIC ZONING — China
ECONOMIC ZONING — Spain — Congresses
ECONOMICS
ECONOMICS — Addresses, essays, lectures
ECONOMICS — Collected works
ECONOMICS — Congresses
ECONOMICS — Decision making
ECONOMICS — Dictionaries — Swedish
ECONOMICS — Dictionaries, indexes, etc.
ECONOMICS — History
ECONOMICS — History — To 1800
ECONOMICS — History — 19th century
ECONOMICS — History — 20th century
ECONOMICS — Law and legislation
ECONOMICS — Mathematical models
ECONOMICS — Mathematical models — Congresses
ECONOMICS — Methodology
ECONOMICS — Methodology — Addresses, essays, lectures
ECONOMICS — Moral and ethical aspects
ECONOMICS — Periodicals — Bibliography
ECONOMICS — Periodicals — Indexes
ECONOMICS — Philosophy
ECONOMICS — Philosophy — Addresses, essays, lectures
ECONOMICS — Political aspects
ECONOMICS — Psychological aspects
ECONOMICS — Religious aspects — Islam
ECONOMICS — Research
ECONOMICS — Statistical methods — Addresses, essays, lectures
ECONOMICS — Study and teaching
ECONOMICS — Study and teaching — Ukraine
ECONOMICS — Study and teaching (Higher) — Thailand
ECONOMICS — Denmark — Bibliography
ECONOMICS — France — History — 20th century
ECONOMICS — Great Britain — History
ECONOMICS — Great Britain — History — 19th century
ECONOMICS — Great Britain — History — 19th century — Sources
ECONOMICS — Great Britain — History — 20th century
ECONOMICS — Soviet Union
ECONOMICS, MATHEMATICAL
ECONOMICS, MATHEMATICAL — Addresses, essays, lectures
ECONOMICS, MATHEMATICAL — Congresses
ECONOMICS, MATHEMATICAL — Research
ECONOMICS, MEDICAL — history — Great Britain
ECONOMICS, MEDICAL — history — United States
ECONOMICS, MEDICAL — trends — United Staes
ECONOMICS, MEDICAL — trends — United States
ECONOMICS, MEDICAL — United States — congresses
ECONOMIS ASSISTANCE
ECONOMISTS — Biography
ECONOMISTS — Austria — Biography
ECONOMISTS — Germany — Biography

ECONOMISTS — Great Britain — Biography
ECONOMISTS — Great Britain — History
ECONOMISTS — Poland
ECONOMISTS — Poland — Biography
ECONOMISTS — Scotland — Correspondence
ECONOMISTS — Soviet Union — Directories
ECONOMISTS — Spain — Biography
ECONOMISTS — United States — Biography
ECONOMISTS — United States — Collected works
ECUADOR — Economic conditions — 1918-1972
ECUADOR — Economic policy
ECUADOR — Politics and government — 1944-
ECUADOR — Social policy
ECUADOR — Statistics, Vital
ECUADOR. Comisión de Valores - Corporación Financiera Nacional — Legal status, laws, etc.
EDEL, ABRAHAM
EDEN, ANTHONY
EDEN, ANTHONY — Career in international relations
EDITING
EDITORS — Addresses, essays, lectures
EDMONDS, LLOYD — Correspondence
EDUCATION
EDUCATION — Aims and objectives
EDUCATION — Aims and objectives — Congresses
EDUCATION — Data processing
EDUCATION — Data processing — Addresses, essays, lectures
EDUCATION — Economic aspects
EDUCATION — Economic aspects — Bibliography
EDUCATION — Economic aspects — Congresses
EDUCATION — Economic aspects — Developing countries
EDUCATION — Economic aspects — Europe — History
EDUCATION — Economic aspects — India
EDUCATION — Economic aspects — Sudan
EDUCATION — Experimental methods
EDUCATION — Finance — Law and legislation — Great Britain
EDUCATION — Philosophy — History
EDUCATION — Philosophy — 1965-
EDUCATION — Research
EDUCATION — Research — France
EDUCATION — Social aspects
EDUCATION — Social aspects — Canada
EDUCATION — Social aspects — Europe — History — 19th century
EDUCATION — Social aspects — Peru — Bibliography
EDUCATION — Social aspects — United States
EDUCATION — Social aspects — United States — History
EDUCATION — Africa, Southern
EDUCATION — Australia
EDUCATION — Australia — New South Wales
EDUCATION — Bahamas — Statistics
EDUCATION — Barbados — Statistics
EDUCATION — Canada
EDUCATION — Cuba — History — 20th century
EDUCATION — Developing countries — Aims and objectives
EDUCATION — Developing countries — Congresses
EDUCATION — Developing countries — Finance
EDUCATION — Developing countries — Political aspects
EDUCATION — England
EDUCATION — England — London
EDUCATION — Europe — History — 19th century
EDUCATION — Europe — History — 20th century
EDUCATION — Gambia — Statistics
EDUCATION — Germany (West) — Curricula
EDUCATION — Great Britain
EDUCATION — Great Britain — Aims and objectives
EDUCATION — Great Britain — Curricula
EDUCATION — Great Britain — History — 19th century
EDUCATION — Great Britain — Models
EDUCATION — India — History — Sources
EDUCATION — Japan
EDUCATION — Japan — History
EDUCATION — Mauritius — Statistics
EDUCATION — Morocco — Statistics
EDUCATION — New Brunswick — History
EDUCATION — Nicaragua
EDUCATION — Organisation for Economic Co-operation and Development countries
EDUCATION — Peru — Bibliography
EDUCATION — Quebec (Province)
EDUCATION — Scotland
EDUCATION — South Africa — History
EDUCATION — Southern States — History — Congresses
EDUCATION — Soviet Union — Aims and objectives — Addresses, essays, lectures
EDUCATION — Soviet Union — Curricula — Addresses, essays, lectures
EDUCATION — Spain — History — 20th century
EDUCATION — Spain — Castile
EDUCATION — Spain — Catalonia — History
EDUCATION — Spain — León
EDUCATION — Sweden — Addresses, essays, lectures
EDUCATION — Taiwan
EDUCATION — Tanzania — Bukumbi
EDUCATION — Thailand — Statistics
EDUCATION — Togo — Statistics
EDUCATION — Trinidad and Tobago — Statistics
EDUCATION — United States — Aims and objectives
EDUCATION — United States — Curricula
EDUCATION — United States — Evaluation — Methodology
EDUCATION — United States — Finance
EDUCATION — United States — History
EDUCATION — United States — Statistics
EDUCATION (AMENDMENT) BILL 1985-86
EDUCATION AND STATE
EDUCATION AND STATE — California — San Francisco
EDUCATION AND STATE — Chile — History — 20th century
EDUCATION AND STATE — Cuba — History — 20th century
EDUCATION AND STATE — Europe — History
EDUCATION AND STATE — Great Britain
EDUCATION AND STATE — Nicaragua
EDUCATION AND STATE — Pakistan
EDUCATION AND STATE — Papua New Guinea
EDUCATION AND STATE — South Africa — History
EDUCATION AND STATE — Soviet Union — Addresses, essays, lectures
EDUCATION AND STATE — Spain
EDUCATION AND STATE — Spain — History
EDUCATION AND STATE — United States
EDUCATION AND STATE — United States — History
EDUCATION, BILINGUAL — Political aspects — United States
EDUCATION, BILINGUAL — United States
EDUCATION, BILINGUAL — Wales
EDUCATION BILL 1980-81
EDUCATION BILL 1985-86
EDUCATION (CORPORAL PUNISHMENT) BILL 1984-85
EDUCATION (FEES AND AWARDS) BILL 1982-83
EDUCATION (GRANTS AND AWARDS) BILL 1983-84
EDUCATION, HIGHER — Congresses
EDUCATION, HIGHER — Data processing
EDUCATION, HIGHER — Political aspects — Argentina — History — 20th century
EDUCATION, HIGHER — Social aspects — United States — History
EDUCATION, HIGHER — Africa
EDUCATION, HIGHER — Africa, Sub-Saharan
EDUCATION, HIGHER — Australia
EDUCATION, HIGHER — China
EDUCATION, HIGHER — Denmark
EDUCATION, HIGHER — Denmark — Planning
EDUCATION, HIGHER — England
EDUCATION, HIGHER — Europe — 1965-
EDUCATION, HIGHER — European Economic Community countries
EDUCATION, HIGHER — France — History
EDUCATION, HIGHER — Great Britain
EDUCATION, HIGHER — Great Britain — Supply and demand — Forecasting
EDUCATION, HIGHER — Kenya
EDUCATION, HIGHER — Soviet Union
EDUCATION, HIGHER — United States — History
EDUCATION, HIGHER — United States — Philosophy
EDUCATION, HIGHER — Wales — Management
EDUCATION, HIGHER — West Bank
EDUCATION OF CHILDREN
EDUCATION, PRIMARY — Brazil — Finance
EDUCATION, PRIMARY — England — London
EDUCATION, PRIMARY — England — Suffolk
EDUCATION, PRIMARY — Great Britain
EDUCATION, RURAL — Africa, West
EDUCATION, RURAL — Developing countries
EDUCATION, RURAL — Developing countries — Communication systems
EDUCATION, RURAL — India
EDUCATION, RURAL — Virginia — History — 19th century
EDUCATION, RURAL — Virginia — History — 20th century
EDUCATION, RURAL — Wales
EDUCATION (SCOTLAND) BILL 1980-81
EDUCATION, SECONDARY — Australia — South Australia — History — Case studies
EDUCATION, SECONDARY — Colombia — Curricula — Case studies
EDUCATION, SECONDARY — Denmark — Copenhagen — Statistics
EDUCATION, SECONDARY — England
EDUCATION, SECONDARY — England — History — 19th century
EDUCATION, SECONDARY — England — London — History
EDUCATION, SECONDARY — England — Suffolk
EDUCATION, SECONDARY — Great Britain
EDUCATION, SECONDARY — Great Britain — Curricula
EDUCATION, SECONDARY — Great Britain — 1945- — Social aspects
EDUCATION, SECONDARY — Papua New Guinea

EDUCATION, SECONDARY — Tanzania — Curricula — Case studies
EDUCATION, SECONDARY — Wales — Cardiff (South Glamorgan) — Administration — History — 20th century
EDUCATION SOCIOLOGY — Canada
EDUCATION, URBAN — United States — History
EDUCATIONAL ACCOUNTABILITY
EDUCATIONAL ACCOUNTABILITY — United States
EDUCATIONAL ANTHROPOLOGY
EDUCATIONAL EQUALIZATION
EDUCATIONAL EQUALIZATION — Social aspects — England
EDUCATIONAL EQUALIZATION — England — History — 20th century
EDUCATIONAL EQUALIZATION — European Economic Community countries
EDUCATIONAL EQUALIZATION — Great Britain
EDUCATIONAL EQUALIZATION — Texas — History — 20th century
EDUCATIONAL EQUALIZATION — United States
EDUCATIONAL EQUALIZATION — United States — Case studies
EDUCATIONAL EXCHANGES — Bibliography
EDUCATIONAL EXCHANGES — European Economic Community countries — Congresses
EDUCATIONAL INNOVATIONS
EDUCATIONAL INNOVATIONS — Great Britain
EDUCATIONAL LAW AND LEGISLATION — Great Britain
EDUCATIONAL LAW AND LEGISLATION — Scotland
EDUCATIONAL LAW AND LEGISLATION — United States
EDUCATIONAL PLANNING
EDUCATIONAL PLANNING — Statistical methods
EDUCATIONAL PLANNING — Papua New Guinea
EDUCATIONAL PLANNING — Peru — Congresses
EDUCATIONAL PSYCHOLOGY
EDUCATIONAL SOCIOLOGY
EDUCATIONAL SOCIOLOGY — Australia
EDUCATIONAL SOCIOLOGY — Great Britain
EDUCATIONAL SOCIOLOGY — Japan — History
EDUCATIONAL SOCIOLOGY — United States
EDUCATIONAL STATISTICS
EDUCATIONAL SURVEYS
EDUCATIONAL SURVEYS — United States
EDUCATIONAL TECHNOLOGY
EDUCATIONAL VOUCHERS
EDUCATORS — Biography
EDUCATORS — History
EDUCATORS — Denmark — Biography
EDUCATORS — Sierra Leone — Biography
EEC See European Economic Community
EFFICIENCY, INDUSTRIAL
EFFICIENCY, INDUSTRIAL — Soviet Union
EFFICIENCY, INDUSTRIAL — United States
EFFICIENCY, INDUSTRIAL — United States — Case studies
EGG TRADE — Australia
EGG TRADE — European Economic Community Countries
EGGLESTON, JOHN
EGGLESTON REPORT
EGGPLANT INDUSTRY — Mexico
EGNA PROVINCE (PAPUA NEW GUINEA) — Population — Statistics
EGYPT — Boundaries
EGYPT — Census, 1976
EGYPT — Economic policy

EGYPT — Foreign relations — Italy
EGYPT — Foreign relations — Saudi Arabia
EGYPT — Foreign relations — United States
EGYPT — History — British Occupation 1882-1936
EGYPT — History — British occupation, 1882-1936
EGYPT — History — Insurrection, 1919
EGYPT — History — 19th century
EGYPT — History — Intervention, 1956
EGYPT — Industries
EGYPT — Politics and government — 640-1882
EGYPT — Politics and government — 1882-1936
EGYPT — Politics and government — 1952-
EGYPT — Population
EGYPT — Population — Statistics
EGYPT — Relations — Arab countries
EGYPT — Rural conditions
EGYPT — Statistics, Vital
EGYPT. Legislative Council. Egyptian Canal Act
EGYPTIAN CANAL ACT
EHRLICH, EUGEN
EIGHT-HOUR MOVEMENT
EINSTEIN, ALBERT — Views on realism
EISENHOWER, DWIGHT D
EISENHOWER, DWIGHT D.
EL EJIDO (SPAIN) — Social conditions
EL SALVADOR — Description and travel
EL SALVADOR — Dictionaries and encyclopedias
EL SALVADOR — Foreign relations — United States
EL SALVADOR — History — 1944-1979
EL SALVADOR — History — 1979-
EL SALVADOR — Politics and government — 1979-
EL SALVADOR — Presidents — Biography
ELECTIC UTILITIES — Great Britain — Bibliography
ELECTION DISTRICTS — Great Britain
ELECTION DISTRICTS — Wales
ELECTION LAW
ELECTION LAW — France
ELECTION LAW — Germany (West)
ELECTION LAW — Great Britain
ELECTIONEERING — History — 20th century
ELECTIONEERING — United States
ELECTIONS
ELECTIONS — History
ELECTIONS — Maps
ELECTIONS — Social aspects — Spain — Basque Provinces
ELECTIONS — Social aspects — Wales — Brecknock (Powys)
ELECTIONS — Social aspects — Wales — Radnor (Powys)
ELECTIONS — Africa — History — 20th century
ELECTIONS — Arab countries
ELECTIONS — Australia — Statistics
ELECTIONS — Australia — New South Wales
ELECTIONS — Canada
ELECTIONS — England — History — Bibliography
ELECTIONS — England — History — 17th century
ELECTIONS — France
ELECTIONS — France — Statistics
ELECTIONS — France — Meaux
ELECTIONS — Germany (West)
ELECTIONS — Great Britain
ELECTIONS — Great Britain — History — 19th century
ELECTIONS — Great Britain — History — 20th century
ELECTIONS — Great Britain — Law and legislation
ELECTIONS — India
ELECTIONS — Israel — Addresses, essays, lectures

ELECTIONS — Italy
ELECTIONS — Italy — Emilia Romagna
ELECTIONS — Kenya
ELECTIONS — Near East
ELECTIONS — New Zealand — Administration
ELECTIONS — Nigeria
ELECTIONS — North Carolina — History — 20th century
ELECTIONS — Norway — Statistics
ELECTIONS — Puerto Rico — Statistics
ELECTIONS — Spain
ELECTIONS — Spain — History — 20th century
ELECTIONS — Spain — Basque Provinces
ELECTIONS — Spain — Castilla-La Mancha
ELECTIONS — Spain — Catalonia
ELECTIONS — Spain — Galicia — Statistics
ELECTIONS — Spain — Lerida
ELECTIONS — Spain — Madrid (Province) — Statistics
ELECTIONS — Switzerland
ELECTIONS — Uganda
ELECTIONS — United States
ELECTIONS — United States — Addresses, essays, lectures
ELECTIONS — United States — History — Bibliography
ELECTRIC INDUSTRIES — European Economic Community countries
ELECTRIC INDUSTRIES — France
ELECTRIC INDUSTRIES — Portugal
ELECTRIC LIGHTING — England — Godalming (Surrey) — History
ELECTRIC NETWORKS
ELECTRIC POWER — Congresses
ELECTRIC POWER — Conservation
ELECTRIC POWER — Environmental aspects — Great Britain
ELECTRIC POWER — Egypt
ELECTRIC POWER CONSUMPTION — Bibliography
ELECTRIC POWER CONSUMPTION — Econometric models
ELECTRIC POWER CONSUMPTION — Forecasting — Economic aspects — United States
ELECTRIC POWER-PLANTS — Load — Mathematical models
ELECTRIC POWER PRODUCTION — Economic aspects — United States
ELECTRIC POWER PRODUCTION — Great Britain
ELECTRIC UTILITIES — Environmental aspects — Great Britain
ELECTRIC UTILITIES — Government ownership — United States — History
ELECTRIC UTILITIES — Rates
ELECTRIC UTILITIES — Rates — Bibliography
ELECTRIC UTILITIES — Asia — Costs
ELECTRIC UTILITIES — Asia — Rates
ELECTRIC UTILITIES — Australia
ELECTRIC UTILITIES — Developing countries — Costs
ELECTRIC UTILITIES — Developing countries — Rates
ELECTRIC UTILITIES — Europe — Bibliography
ELECTRIC UTILITIES — Great Britain
ELECTRIC UTILITIES — Great Britain — Bibliography
ELECTRIC UTILITIES — Great Britain — History
ELECTRIC UTILITIES — Great Britain — History — Bibliography
ELECTRIC UTILITIES — Great Britain — Technological innovations — Bibliography
ELECTRIC UTILITIES — Mexico — Energy consumption
ELECTRIC UTILITIES — Organisation for Economic Co-operation and Development countries — Costs
ELECTRIC UTILITIES — Sweden

ELECTRIC UTILITIES — Washington (State) — Rates — Public opinion
ELECTRICITY — Prices — European Economic Community Countries
ELECTRIFICATION — Finland
ELECTRONIC DATA PROCESSING
ELECTRONIC DATA PROCESSING — Addresses, essays, lectures
ELECTRONIC DATA PROCESSING — Congresses
ELECTRONIC DATA PROCESSING — Directories
ELECTRONIC DATA PROCESSING — Distributed processing
ELECTRONIC DATA PROCESSING — Economic research
ELECTRONIC DATA PROCESSING — Government policy — Congresses
ELECTRONIC DATA PROCESSING — Handbooks, manuals, etc
ELECTRONIC DATA PROCESSING — Research
ELECTRONIC DATA PROCESSING — Social aspects
ELECTRONIC DATA PROCESSING — Social sciences
ELECTRONIC DATA PROCESSING — Structured techniques
ELECTRONIC DATA PROCESSING — Vocational guidance
ELECTRONIC DATA PROCESSING DEPARTMENTS — Auditing
ELECTRONIC DATA PROCESSING DEPARTMENTS — Management
ELECTRONIC DATA PROCESSING IN RESEARCH
ELECTRONIC DATA PROCESSING PERSONNEL
ELECTRONIC DIGITAL COMPUTERS See also Computers
ELECTRONIC DIGITAL COMPUTERS
ELECTRONIC DIGITAL COMPUTERS — Programming
ELECTRONIC DIGITAL COMPUTERS — Developing countries
ELECTRONIC FUNDS TRANSFERS — Australia
ELECTRONIC FUNDS TRANSFERS — Great Britain
ELECTRONIC INDUSTRIES — Great Britain
ELECTRONIC INDUSTRIES — Japan — Technological innovations
ELECTRONIC INTELLIGENCE
ELECTRONIC OFFICE MACHINES — Great Britain
ELECTRONIC PUBLISHING
ELECTRONIC PUBLISHING — Costs
ELECTRONIC PUBLISHING — Directories
ELECTRONIC PUBLISHING — Handbooks, manuals, etc
ELECTRONIC PUBLISHING — Great Britain
ELECTRONIC TRAFFIC CONTROLS
ELECTRONICS — Study and teaching — Addresses, essays, lectures
ELEMENTARY SCHOOLS — Wales
ELGIN (NAME)
ELITE (SOCIAL SCIENCES)
ELITE (SOCIAL SCIENCES) — Research
ELITE (SOCIAL SCIENCES) — Bolivia
ELITE (SOCIAL SCIENCES) — Brazil — History — 19th century
ELITE (SOCIAL SCIENCES) — Canada
ELITE (SOCIAL SCIENCES) — China — Case studies
ELITE (SOCIAL SCIENCES) — China — History
ELITE (SOCIAL SCIENCES) — Developing countries
ELITE (SOCIAL SCIENCES) — Germany — History
ELITE (SOCIAL SCIENCES) — India — Punjab
ELITE (SOCIAL SCIENCES) — Italy — Florence — History
ELITE (SOCIAL SCIENCES) — Mexico
ELITE (SOCIAL SCIENCES) — Mexico — History
ELITE (SOCIAL SCIENCES) — Ouaddai (Chad)
ELITE (SOCIAL SCIENCES) — Soviet Union
ELITE (SOCIAL SCIENCES) — Spain
ELITE (SOCIAL SCIENCES) — Spain — Barcelona — History
ELITE (SOCIAL SCIENCES) — Syria
ELITE (SOCIAL SCIENCES) — Turkey — History
ELITE (SOCIAL SCIENCES) — United States
ELITE (SOCIAL SCIENCES) — United States — Addresses, essays, lectures
EMBARGO
EMIGRANT REMITTANCES — Portugal — History
EMIGRATION AND IMMIGRATION
EMIGRATION AND IMMIGRATION — Government policy
EMIGRATION AND IMMIGRATION — History — Congresses
EMIGRATION AND IMMIGRATION — Religious aspects — Christianity
EMIGRATION AND IMMIGRATION — Denmark — Public opinion
EMIGRATION AND IMMIGRATION LAW — Australia
EMIGRATION AND IMMIGRATION LAW — Great Britain
EMIGRATION AND IMMIGRATION LAW — Great Britain — Handbooks, manuals, etc
EMIGRATION AND IMMIGRATION LAW — New Zealand
EMIGRATION AND IMMIGRATION LAW — Organisation for Economic Co-operation and Development countries
EMIGRATION AND IMMIGRATION LAW — United States
EMILIA ROMAGNA (ITALY) — Politics and government
EMINANT DOMAIN — Sudan
EMINENT DOMAIN — Great Britain
EMINENT DOMAIN — Malaysia
EMINENT DOMAIN — Singapore
EMINENT DOMAIN — United States
EMINENT DOMAIN (INTERNATIONAL LAW)
EMOTIONS
EMPIRICISM
EMPLOYEE ASSISTANCE PROGRAMS
EMPLOYEE FRINGE BENEFITS
EMPLOYEE FRINGE BENEFITS — Taxation — Great Britain
EMPLOYEE FRINGE BENEFITS — Great Britain
EMPLOYEE FRINGE BENEFITS — Japan
EMPLOYEE MOTIVATION
EMPLOYEE MOTIVATION — Germany (West)
EMPLOYEE OWNERSHIP
EMPLOYEE OWNERSHIP — Chile — Santiago
EMPLOYEE OWNERSHIP — Great Britain
EMPLOYEE OWNERSHIP — United States
EMPLOYEE SELECTION
EMPLOYEE SELECTION — Great Britain
EMPLOYEE STOCK OPTIONS — Legal status, Laws, etc. — Great Britain
EMPLOYEES, DISMISSAL OF
EMPLOYEES, DISMISSAL OF — Law and legislation — Great Britain
EMPLOYEES, DISMISSAL OF — Great Britain — Law and legislation
EMPLOYEES, DISMISSAL OF — Japan — Law and legisatlion
EMPLOYEES, DISMISSAL OF — United States — Law and legislation
EMPLOYEES, DISMISSAL OF — Wales, South
EMPLOYEES' REPRESENTATION IN MANAGEMENT
EMPLOYEES' REPRESENTATION IN MANAGEMENT — England — Liverpool (Merseyside)
EMPLOYEES' REPRESENTATION IN MANAGEMENT — Great Britain
EMPLOYEES' REPRESENTATION IN MANAGEMENT — Poland
EMPLOYEE'S REPRESENTATION IN MANAGEMENT — Quebec (Province)
EMPLOYEES' REPRESENTATION IN MANAGEMENT — Sweden — Case studies
EMPLOYEES, TRAINING OF
EMPLOYEES, TRAINING OF — Commonwealth of Nations
EMPLOYEES, TRAINING OF — England — Bolton (Greater Manchester)
EMPLOYEES, TRAINING OF — England — Humberside
EMPLOYEES, TRAINING OF — England — London
EMPLOYEES, TRAINING OF — England — Yorkshire
EMPLOYEES, TRAINING OF — France
EMPLOYEES, TRAINING OF — Great Britain
EMPLOYEES, TRAINING OF — Great Britain — Evaluation
EMPLOYEES, TRAINING OF — Great Britain — History — 20th century
EMPLOYEES, TRAINING OF — London
EMPLOYEES, TRANSFER OF
EMPLOYERS' ASSOCIATIONS — Germany (West)
EMPLOYERS' ASSOCIATIONS — Great Britain
EMPLOYERS' ASSOCIATIONS — Great Britain — Directories
EMPLOYMENT — Research — France
EMPLOYMENT — Manitoba
EMPLOYMENT — Norway — Statistics
EMPLOYMENT AGENCIES
EMPLOYMENT AGENCIES — Denmark
EMPLOYMENT AGENCIES — France — History — 19th century
EMPLOYMENT AGENCIES — Great Britain
EMPLOYMENT BILL 1979-80
EMPLOYMENT BILL 1981-82
EMPLOYMENT (ECONOMIC THEORY)
EMPLOYMENT (ECONOMIC THEORY) — Graphic methods
EMPLOYMENT FORECASTING
EMPLOYMENT FORECASTING — France
EMPLOYMENT FORECASTING — Ireland
EMPLOYMENT FORECASTING — United States — Econometric models
EMPLOYMENT SERVICE AND UNEMPLOYMENT INSURANCE ACT, 1970
EMPLOYMENT STABILIZATION — Australia
EMPRESA DE RADIODIFUSIÓN (Peru) — Legal status, laws, etc.
EMPRESA EDITORA PERÚ — Legal status, laws, etc.
ENCOMIENDAS (LATIN AMERICA)
END OF THE WORLD
ENDOWMENTS — Directories
ENDOWMENTS — Canada
ENDOWMENTS — United States — History
ENERGY CONSERVATION
ENERGY CONSERVATION — Great Britain
ENERGY CONSERVATION — Great Britain — Bibliography
ENERGY CONSERVATION — International Energy Agency countries
ENERGY CONSERVATION — Mexico
ENERGY CONSUMPTION
ENERGY CONSUMPTION — Environmental aspects — Switzerland
ENERGY CONSUMPTION — Brazil

ENERGY CONSUMPTION — France — Statistics
ENERGY CONSUMPTION — Mexico
ENERGY CONSUMPTION — Netherlands — Statistics
ENERGY CONSUMPTION — Scotland
ENERGY CONSUMPTION — Switzerland
ENERGY CONSUMPTION — Zambia — Statistics
ENERGY DEVELOPMENT — Asia — Statistics
ENERGY DEVELOPMENT — Soviet Union
ENERGY DEVELOPMENT — United States — Addresses, essays, lectures
ENERGY INDUSTRIES
ENERGY INDUSTRIES — Congresses
ENERGY INDUSTRIES — Economic aspects — Spain — Congresses
ENERGY INDUSTRIES — Forecasting — Case studies
ENERGY INDUSTRIES — Government policy
ENERGY INDUSTRIES — Government policy — United States
ENERGY INDUSTRIES — Political aspects — Europe
ENERGY INDUSTRIES — Political aspects — Soviet Union
ENERGY INDUSTRIES — Brazil
ENERGY INDUSTRIES — Developing countries
ENERGY INDUSTRIES — Germany (West)
ENERGY INDUSTRIES — Great Britain
ENERGY INDUSTRIES — Scotland
ENERGY INDUSTRIES — Siberia, Western (R.S.F.S.R.) — Government policy
ENERGY INDUSTRIES — Spain — Congresses
ENERGY INDUSTRIES — United States
ENERGY POLICY
ENERGY POLICY — Case studies
ENERGY POLICY — Congresses
ENERGY POLICY — Economic aspects
ENERGY POLICY — Environmental aspects — Australia
ENERGY POLICY — Statistics
ENERGY POLICY — Asia — Congresses
ENERGY POLICY — Brazil
ENERGY POLICY — Canada
ENERGY POLICY — Denmark
ENERGY POLICY — Denmark — Statistics
ENERGY POLICY — Europe — Bibliography
ENERGY POLICY — European Economic Community
ENERGY POLICY — European Economic Community Countries
ENERGY POLICY — European Economic Community countries
ENERGY POLICY — European Economic Community countries — Congresses
ENERGY POLICY — France
ENERGY POLICY — Great Britain
ENERGY POLICY — Pacific Area — Congresses
ENERGY POLICY — Scotland — Strathclyde
ENERGY POLICY — Soviet Union
ENERGY POLICY — Spain — Congresses
ENERGY POLICY — Sweden
ENERGY POLICY — Switzerland
ENERGY POLICY — United States — Addresses, essays, lectures
ENFIELD (MASS.) — Social life and customs
ENGA (NEW GUINEA PEOPLE) — Commerce
ENGA (NEW GUINEA PEOPLE) — Rites and ceremonies
ENGELS, FRIEDERICH — Bibliography
ENGELS, FRIEDRICH
ENGELS, FRIEDRICH — Chronology
ENGELS, FRIEDRICH — Language — Glossaries, etc
ENGINEERING — Great Britain — Employees
ENGINEERING DESIGN — Data processing
ENGINEERING FIRMS — Great Britain — Employees
ENGINEERS — England — Supply and demand
ENGINEERS — Germany (West) — Taxation
ENGINEERS — Russian S.F.S.R. — Siberia
ENGLAND — Census, 1676
ENGLAND — Church history — Modern period, 1485-
ENGLAND — Church history — 16th century
ENGLAND — Church history — 17th century
ENGLAND — Church history — 20th century
ENGLAND — Civilization
ENGLAND — Civilization — 19th century
ENGLAND — Civilization — 20th century
ENGLAND — Constitutional law — Historiography
ENGLAND — Economic conditions — Medieval period, 1066-1485
ENGLAND — Emigration and immigration — History
ENGLAND — Emigration and immigration — History — 19th century
ENGLAND — History — Medieval period, 1066-1485
ENGLAND — Nobility — History
ENGLAND — Population
ENGLAND — Population — History
ENGLAND — Population — History — Addresses, Essays, Lectures
ENGLAND — Population, rural
ENGLAND — Race relations
ENGLAND — Royal household — History
ENGLAND — Rural conditions
ENGLAND — Social conditions
ENGLAND — Social conditions — Medieval period, 1066-1485
ENGLAND — Social conditions — 19th century
ENGLAND — Social life and customs
ENGLAND — Social life and customs — 16th century
ENGLAND — Social life and customs — 17th century
ENGLAND — Social life and customs — 18th century
ENGLAND. Court of Star Chamber — History
ENGLAND. Parliament. House of Commons — History — Bibliography
ENGLAND — Church history — 16th century
ENGLAND AND WALES. Army. New Model Army — History
ENGLAND AND WALES. Court of Star Chamber — History
ENGLAND AND WALES. Parliamant. House of Commons — History — Bibliography
ENGLAND AND WALES. Parliament — History
ENGLISH — Spain — Valverde — History
ENGLISH CHANNEL (ENGLAND AND FRANCE) — History
ENGLISH DRAMA — 20th century
ENGLISH IMPRINTS
ENGLISH LANGUAGE — Data processing
ENGLISH LANGUAGE — Dialects
ENGLISH LANGUAGE — Dictionaries
ENGLISH LANGUAGE — Dictionaries — French
ENGLISH LANGUAGE — Dictionaries — German
ENGLISH LANGUAGE — Dictionaries — Greek language, Modern
ENGLISH LANGUAGE — Dictionaries — Spanish
ENGLISH LANGUAGE — Gender
ENGLISH LANGUAGE — Jargon
ENGLISH LANGUAGE — Jargon — Dictionaries
ENGLISH LANGUAGE — Modality
ENGLISH LANGUAGE — Reform
ENGLISH LANGUAGE — Rhetoric
ENGLISH LANGUAGE — Sex differences
ENGLISH LANGUAGE — Slang — Dictionaries
ENGLISH LANGUAGE — Social aspects
ENGLISH LANGUAGE — Social aspects — Great Britain
ENGLISH LANGUAGE — Spoken English
ENGLISH LANGUAGE — Spoken English — Australia — Social aspects
ENGLISH LANGUAGE — Study and teaching — German speakers
ENGLISH LANGUAGE — Style
ENGLISH LANGUAGE — Synonyms and antonyms
ENGLISH LANGUAGE — Tense
ENGLISH LANGUAGE — Word formation
ENGLISH LANGUAGE — United States — Dictionaries
ENGLISH LANGUAGE — United States — Slang — Dictionaries
ENGLISH LITERATURE — Dictionaries
ENGLISH LITERATURE — 19th century — History and criticism
ENGLISH LITERATURE — 20th century
ENGLISH NEWSPAPERS — History — 17th century
ENGLISH NEWSPAPERS — History — 18th century
ENGLISH NEWSPAPERS — England — Derbyshire — Bibliography
ENGLISH NEWSPAPERS — England — Kent — Bibliography
ENGLISH NEWSPAPERS — England — Nottinghamshire — Bibliography
ENGLISH NEWSPAPERS — England — Wiltshire — Bibliography — Union lists
ENGLISH NEWSPAPERS — England, Northern — Bibliography
ENGLISH NEWSPAPERS — Japan
ENGLISH PERIODICALS — History — 17th century
ENGLISH PROSE LITERATURE — Puritan authors — History and criticism
ENGLISH PROSE LITERATURE — 17th century — History and criticism
ENGLISH WIT AND HUMOR
ENTEBBE AIRPORT RAID, 1976
ENTERPRISE ZONES — Great Britain
ENTERPRISE ZONES — Greece
ENTRAPMENT (CRIMINAL LAW)
ENTRAPMENT (CRIMINAL LAW) — Canada
ENTREPRENEUR
ENTREPRENEUR — Addresses, essays, lectures
ENTREPRENEUR — Biography
ENTREPRENEUR — Social aspects
ENTREPRENEURSHIP — Europe
ENVIRONMENT
ENVIRONMENTAL ARCHAEOLOGY
ENVIRONMENTAL EDUCATION
ENVIRONMENTAL HEALTH
ENVIRONMENTAL HEALTH — Moral and ethical aspects
ENVIRONMENTAL HEALTH — Statistics — Bibliography
ENVIRONMENTAL IMPACT ANALYSIS
ENVIRONMENTAL IMPACT ANALYSIS — Australia
ENVIRONMENTAL IMPACT ANALYSIS — Canada
ENVIRONMENTAL IMPACT ANALYSIS — Great Britain
ENVIRONMENTAL IMPACT ANALYSIS — United States
ENVIRONMENTAL IMPACT STATEMENTS — United States
ENVIRONMENTAL LAW

ENVIRONMENTAL LAW — Great Lakes Region
ENVIRONMENTAL LAW — New Zealand
ENVIRONMENTAL LAW — Nigeria
ENVIRONMENTAL LAW — United States — Cases
ENVIRONMENTAL LAW, INTERNATIONAL
ENVIRONMENTAL POLICY
ENVIRONMENTAL POLICY — Economic aspects — Australia
ENVIRONMENTAL POLICY — Information services — Developing countries
ENVIRONMENTAL POLICY — Statistics — Standards
ENVIRONMENTAL POLICY — Antarctic regions — Congresses
ENVIRONMENTAL POLICY — Denmark
ENVIRONMENTAL POLICY — Developing countries
ENVIRONMENTAL POLICY — Europe
ENVIRONMENTAL POLICY — European Economic Community countries
ENVIRONMENTAL POLICY — Germany (West)
ENVIRONMENTAL POLICY — Great Britain
ENVIRONMENTAL POLICY — Great Britain — Finance
ENVIRONMENTAL POLICY — Great Britain — History
ENVIRONMENTAL POLICY — Japan — Tokyo
ENVIRONMENTAL POLICY — North America
ENVIRONMENTAL POLICY — Organisation for Economic Co-operation and Development countries
ENVIRONMENTAL POLICY — Organisation for Economic Co-operation and Development countries — Statistics
ENVIRONMENTAL POLICY — Pakistan — Statistics
ENVIRONMENTAL POLICY — Soviet Union
ENVIRONMENTAL POLICY — Sudan
ENVIRONMENTAL POLICY — United States
ENVIRONMENTAL POLICY — United States — Addresses, essays, lectures
ENVIRONMENTAL POLICY — United States — History
ENVIRONMENTAL POLICY — United States — History — 20th century
ENVIRONMENTAL POLICY — Wales — Statistics
ENVIRONMENTAL POLICY — Yugoslavia
ENVIRONMENTAL PROTECTION
ENVIRONMENTAL PROTECTION — Bibliography
ENVIRONMENTAL PROTECTION — Information services — Developing countries
ENVIRONMENTAL PROTECTION — Moral and ethical aspects
ENVIRONMENTAL PROTECTION — Africa
ENVIRONMENTAL PROTECTION — Africa, Sub-Saharan — Bibliography
ENVIRONMENTAL PROTECTION — Europe
ENVIRONMENTAL PROTECTION — France — Statistics
ENVIRONMENTAL PROTECTION — Great Britain
ENVIRONMENTAL PROTECTION — Switzerland
ENVIRONMENTAL PROTECTION — Ukraine
ENVIRONMENTAL PSYCHOLOGY
ENVIRONMENTAL PSYCHOLOGY — Congresses
EPIDEMICS — History — 18th century
EPIDEMICS — Mathematical models
EPIDEMICS — Japan — History

EPIDEMIOLOGY
EPIDEMIOLOGY — Government policy
EPIDEMIOLOGY — England — West Cumbria
EPILEPSY — Great Britain
EPILEPTICS — Services for — Great Britain
EPISTEMICS
EQUAL PAY FOR EQUAL WORK
EQUAL PAY FOR EQUAL WORK — Law and legislation
EQUAL PAY FOR EQUAL WORK — Canada
EQUAL PAY FOR EQUAL WORK — Great Britain
EQUAL PAY FOR EQUAL WORK — Pennsylvania
EQUAL PAY FOR EQUAL WORK — United States
EQUAL RIGHTS AMENDMENTS — United States
EQUAL RIGHTS AMENDMENTS — United States — Bibliography
EQUALITY
EQUALITY — Addresses, essays, lectures
EQUALITY — Cross-cultural studies — Congresses
EQUALITY — Public opinion
EQUALITY — Developing countries
EQUALITY — India
EQUALITY — Scandinavia
EQUALITY — United States — Public opinion
EQUALITY BEFORE THE LAW — Australia
EQUALITY BEFORE THE LAW — Canada
EQUALITY BEFORE THE LAW — South Australia
EQUALITY OF STATES
EQUATORIAL GUINEA — Bibliography
EQUATORIAL GUINEA — Census, 1983
EQUATORIAL GUINEA — Constitution
EQUATORIAL GUINEA — History — Dictionaries
EQUATORIAL GUINEA — Population — Statistics
EQUILIBRIUM (ECONOMICS)
EQUILIBRIUM (ECONOMICS) — Mathematical models
EQUITABLE REMEDIES — Canada
EQUITABLE REMEDIES — Great Britain
EQUITY — Australia
EQUITY — Australia — Addresses, Essays, Lectures
EQUITY — England
ERITREA (ETHIOPIA) — Social conditions
EROS AND CIVILIZATION
EROTICA — Addresses, essays, lectures
ERROR ANALYSIS (MATHEMATICS)
ERSHAD, HOSSAIN MOHAMMAD
ESCALATION (MILITARY SCIENCE)
ESCHER, M. C. — Criticism and interpretation
ESCRIVA DE BALAGUER, JOSEMARÍA — Interviews
ESKIMOS — Alaska — Claims
ESKIMOS — Alaska — Economic conditions — Addresses, essays, lectures
ESKIMOS — Alaska — Government relations
ESKIMOS — Alaska — Land tenure
ESPARTERO, BALDOMERO
ESPIONAGE — Bibliography
ESPIONAGE — Canada
ESPIONAGE — France
ESPIONAGE — Germany (West)
ESPIONAGE — Great Britain — History — 20th century
ESPIONAGE — Ireland
ESPIONAGE, AMERICAN — Soviet Union — History
ESPIONAGE, BRITISH
ESPIONAGE, RUSSIAN
ESPIONAGE, RUSSIAN — History — 20th century
ESPIONAGE, RUSSIAN — Australia

ESPIONAGE, RUSSIAN — Great Britain — History — 20th century
ESPIONAGECANADA
ESTIMATION THEORY
ETA
ETHICAL RELATIVISM
ETHICS
ETHICS — Addresses, essays, lectures
ETHICS, MEDICAL
ETHICS, MEDICAL — congresses
ETHICS, MEDICAL — United States
ETHICS, MODERN — 20th century — Addresses, essays, lectures
ETHIOPIA — Description and travel — To 1900
ETHIOPIA — Description and travel — to 1900
ETHIOPIA — Famines
ETHIOPIA — Foreign relations — Somalia
ETHIOPIA — Foreign relations — United States
ETHIOPIA — History — Autonomy and independence movements
ETHIOPIA — History — Dictionaries
ETHIOPIA — History — 1889-1974
ETHIOPIA — Kings and rulers — Biography
ETHIOPIA — Politics and government
ETHIOPIA — Politics and government — 1974-
ETHNIC GROUPS — Civil rights
ETHNIC GROUPS — Dictionaries and encyclopedias
ETHNIC GROUPS — Government policy — Developing countries
ETHNIC GROUPS — Political activity
ETHNIC PRESS — Great Britain
ETHNIC PRESS — Great Britain — Directories
ETHNIC RELATIONS
ETHNIC RELATIONS — Political aspects — Case studies
ETHNICITY
ETHNICITY — Case studies
ETHNICITY — Economic aspects — Cross-cultural studies
ETHNICITY — Political aspects — Cross-cultural studies
ETHNICITY — Canada
ETHNICITY — Canada — Congresses
ETHNICITY — New Zealand — Statistics
ETHNICITY — Singapore
ETHNICITY — Thailand
ETHNICITY — United States
ETHNOBOTANY — Addresses, essays, lectures
ETHNOCENTRISM
ETHNOGRAPHY
ETHNOLOGICAL JURISPRUDENCE — Addresses, essays, lectures
ETHNOLOGISTS — Biography
ETHNOLOGY
ETHNOLOGY — Biographical methods
ETHNOLOGY — Field work
ETHNOLOGY — Field work — Case studies
ETHNOLOGY — Fieldwork
ETHNOLOGY — Methodology
ETHNOLOGY — Philosophy
ETHNOLOGY — Research
ETHNOLOGY — Africa
ETHNOLOGY — Africa, Central
ETHNOLOGY — Asia, South
ETHNOLOGY — Asia, Southeastern
ETHNOLOGY — Australia
ETHNOLOGY — Canada
ETHNOLOGY — Ethiopia — Gamo
ETHNOLOGY — Europe
ETHNOLOGY — India
ETHNOLOGY — India — Research — India
ETHNOLOGY — India — Madhya Pradesh
ETHNOLOGY — India — West Bengal
ETHNOLOGY — Indonesia
ETHNOLOGY — Indonesia — Mamboru
ETHNOLOGY — Israel
ETHNOLOGY — Japan

ETHNOLOGY — Japan — Ryukyu Islands
ETHNOLOGY — Latvia
ETHNOLOGY — Mediterranean region
ETHNOLOGY — Melanesia
ETHNOLOGY — Morocco
ETHNOLOGY — Nepal
ETHNOLOGY — Netherlands
ETHNOLOGY — New Guinea
ETHNOLOGY — New Guinea — Art
ETHNOLOGY — New Zealand — Statistics
ETHNOLOGY — Oceania
ETHNOLOGY — Papua New Guinea
ETHNOLOGY — Papua New Guinea — Field work
ETHNOLOGY — Papua New Guinea — Gawa
ETHNOLOGY — Scotland
ETHNOLOGY — Somalia
ETHNOLOGY — South Africa
ETHNOLOGY — Soviet Union
ETHNOLOGY — Soviet Union, Northern
ETHNOLOGY — Spain
ETHNOLOGY — Spain — Ronda
ETHNOLOGY — United States — Addresses, essays, lectures
ETHNOLOGY — United States — Congresses
ETHNOMETHODOLOGICAL
ETHNOMETHODOLOGY
ETHNOPHILOSOPHY — Africa, Sub-Saharan
ETHNOPSYCHOLOGY
ETHNOPSYCHOLOGY — Case studies
ETHNOZOOLOGY — Addresses, essays, lectures
EUGENICS
EUORPEAN ECONOMIC COMMUNITY — Spain
EURATOM SUPPLY AGENCY
EURO-DOLLAR MARKET
EUROPE — Armed Forces
EUROPE — Biography
EUROPE — Church history
EUROPE — Civilization
EUROPE — Civilization — 18th century — Sources
EUROPE — Commerce — Japan
EUROPE — Defences
EUROPE — Defenses
EUROPE — Defenses — Addresses, essays, lectures
EUROPE — Defenses — Congresses
EUROPE — Dependency on foreign countries
EUROPE — Economic and conditions — 1945-
EUROPE — Economic co-operation
EUROPE — Economic conditions
EUROPE — Economic conditions — Statistics
EUROPE — Economic conditions — To 1492
EUROPE — Economic conditions — 1945-
EUROPE — Economic integration
EUROPE — Economic integration — Congresses
EUROPE — Economic policy
EUROPE — Economic policy — Congresses
EUROPE — Emigration and immigration
EUROPE — Foreign economic relations
EUROPE — Foreign economic relations — Eastern Europe
EUROPE — Foreign economic relations — Latin America — Bibliography
EUROPE — Foreign economic relations — Persian Gulf States
EUROPE — Foreign economic relations — United States — Addresses, essays, lectures
EUROPE — Foreign relations
EUROPE — Foreign relations — 1871-1918
EUROPE — Foreign relations — 20th century
EUROPE — Foreign relations — 1945-
EUROPE — Foreign relations — 1945- — Addresses, essays, lectures
EUROPE — Foreign relations — Germany — Addresses, essays, lectures
EUROPE — Foreign relations — Germany (East)
EUROPE — Foreign relations — Germany (West)
EUROPE — Foreign relations — Great Britain
EUROPE — Foreign relations — Japan
EUROPE — Foreign relations — Near East
EUROPE — Foreign relations — Soviet Union
EUROPE — Foreign relations — United States
EUROPE — Foreign relations — United States — Congresses
EUROPE — Frontier troubles
EUROPE — Gentry — History
EUROPE — History — 392-814
EUROPE — History — 15th century
EUROPE — History — To 1492
EUROPE — History — 1492-1648
EUROPE — History — 1648-1789
EUROPE — History — 18th century
EUROPE — History — 1789-1815
EUROPE — History — 1789-1815 — Dictionaries
EUROPE — History — 1789-1900
EUROPE — History — 19th century
EUROPE — History — 1815-1848
EUROPE — History — 1815-1871
EUROPE — History — 1848-1871
EUROPE — History — 1871-1918
EUROPE — History — 20th century
EUROPE — History — 1945-
EUROPE — History, Military
EUROPE — History, Military — 17th century
EUROPE — History, Military — 18th century
EUROPE — Industries — History
EUROPE — Kings and rulers
EUROPE — Literature — History — 19th century
EUROPE — Literature — Political aspects
EUROPE — Military policy
EUROPE — National security
EUROPE — National security — Addresses, essays, lectures
EUROPE — Neutrality
EUROPE — Occupations — History — Addresses, essays, lectures
EUROPE — Politics — 1945-
EUROPE — Politics and government
EUROPE — Politics and government — 1789-1815
EUROPE — Politics and government — 20th century
EUROPE — Politics and government — 1918-1945
EUROPE — Politics and government — 1945-
EUROPE — Politics and government — 1945- — Addresses, essays, lectures
EUROPE — Politics and government — 1945- — Dictionaries
EUROPE — Popular culture — History
EUROPE — Population — Congresses
EUROPE — Public opinion
EUROPE — Race relations
EUROPE — Relations — Caribbean Area
EUROPE — Relations — Soviet Union
EUROPE — Relations — Spain
EUROPE — Relations — United States
EUROPE — Social conditions
EUROPE — Social conditions — Statistics
EUROPE — Social conditions — To 1492
EUROPE — Social conditions — 20th century
EUROPE — Social conditions — 1945-
EUROPE — Statistics, Vital
EUROPE — Strategic aspects
EUROPE — Politics and government — 1815-1848
EUROPE, EASTERN
EUROPE, EASTERN — Bibliography
EUROPE, EASTERN — Commercial policy
EUROPE, EASTERN — Description and travel
EUROPE, EASTERN — Economic conditions
EUROPE, EASTERN — Economic conditions — 1945-
EUROPE, EASTERN — Economic integration
EUROPE, EASTERN — Economic policy
EUROPE, EASTERN — Foreign economic relations
EUROPE, EASTERN — Foreign economic relations — Europe
EUROPE, EASTERN — Foreign economic relations — Soviet Union
EUROPE, EASTERN — Foreign relations — 1945-
EUROPE, EASTERN — Foreign relations — Soviet Union
EUROPE, EASTERN — Foreign relations — United States
EUROPE, EASTERN — History
EUROPE, EASTERN — History — 1945-
EUROPE, EASTERN — Library resources
EUROPE, EASTERN — Military policy
EUROPE, EASTERN — Nobility
EUROPE, EASTERN — Politics and government
EUROPE, EASTERN — Politics and government — 1945-
EUROPE, EASTERN — Population policy
EUROPE, EASTERN — Relations — Soviet Union
EUROPE, EASTERN — Social conditions
EUROPE, GERMAN-SPEAKING — Bibliography
EUROPE, NORTHERN — National security
EUROPE, NORTHERN — National security — Congresses
EUROPE, NORTHERN — Strategic aspects
EUROPE, SOUTHERN — Economic conditions — Congresses
EUROPE, SOUTHERN — Economic conditions — Regional disparities
EUROPE, SOUTHERN — Politics and government — Congresses
EUROPE, WESTERN — Economic conditions
EUROPE, WESTERN — Politics and government
EUROPE, WESTERN — Social conditions
EUROPEAN COMMUNITIES
EUROPEAN COMMUNITIES — Bibliography
EUROPEAN COMMUNITIES — Economic and Social Committee
EUROPEAN COMMUNITIES — Statistics
EUROPEAN COMMUNITIES. Economic and Social Committee
EUROPEAN COMMUNITIES
EUROPEAN COMMUNITIES — Appropriations and expenditures
EUROPEAN COMMUNITIES — Constitution
EUROPEAN COMMUNITIES — Dictionaries
EUROPEAN COMMUNITIES — Directories
EUROPEAN COMMUNITIES — Economic aspects — Bibliography — Catalogs
EUROPEAN COMMUNITIES — Finance — Bibliography — Catalogs
EUROPEAN COMMUNITIES — Foreign relations — Bibliography — Catalogs
EUROPEAN COMMUNITIES — Legal status, laws, etc.
EUROPEAN COMMUNITIES — Periodicals — Handbooks, manuals, etc.
EUROPEAN COMMUNITIES — Sources
EUROPEAN COMMUNITIES — Sources — Bibliography
EUROPEAN COMMUNITIES — Statistics — Bibliography
EUROPEAN COMMUNITIES — Statistics — Catalogs
EUROPEAN COMMUNITIES — Statistics — Indexes

EUROPEAN COMMUNITIES (AMENDMENT) BILL 1985-86
EUROPEAN COMMUNITIESOFF. PUBNS. — Foreign relations 986
EUROPEAN CONVENTION ON HUMAN RIGHTS
EUROPEAN COOPERATION
EUROPEAN COOPERATION — Addresses, essays, lectures
EUROPEAN COUNCIL *See* Council of the European Communities
EUROPEAN CURRENCY UNIT
EUROPEAN ECONOMIC COMMUNITY. Laws, statutes, etc
EUROPEAN ECONOMIC COMMUNITY
EUROPEAN ECONOMIC COMMUNITY — Bibliography
EUROPEAN ECONOMIC COMMUNITY — Commerce — Canada
EUROPEAN ECONOMIC COMMUNITY — Congresses
EUROPEAN ECONOMIC COMMUNITY — Economic assistance
EUROPEAN ECONOMIC COMMUNITY — Economic conditions
EUROPEAN ECONOMIC COMMUNITY — Economic conditions — Regional disparities
EUROPEAN ECONOMIC COMMUNITY — Economic conditions — Regional disparities — Statistics
EUROPEAN ECONOMIC COMMUNITY — Foreign relations
EUROPEAN ECONOMIC COMMUNITY — History
EUROPEAN ECONOMIC COMMUNITY — Industries
EUROPEAN ECONOMIC COMMUNITY — Industries — Statistics
EUROPEAN ECONOMIC COMMUNITY — Information services — Directories
EUROPEAN ECONOMIC COMMUNITY — Transportation
EUROPEAN ECONOMIC COMMUNITY — Transportion — Statistics
EUROPEAN ECONOMIC COMMUNITY — Australia
EUROPEAN ECONOMIC COMMUNITY — Europe, Southern — Congresses
EUROPEAN ECONOMIC COMMUNITY — Germany (West)
EUROPEAN ECONOMIC COMMUNITY — Great Britain
EUROPEAN ECONOMIC COMMUNITY — Greece
EUROPEAN ECONOMIC COMMUNITY — Mexico
EUROPEAN ECONOMIC COMMUNITY — Spain
EUROPEAN ECONOMIC COMMUNITY — Spain — Andalucia
EUROPEAN ECONOMIC COMMUNITY — Spain — Catalonia
EUROPEAN ECONOMIC COMMUNITY — Switzerland
EUROPEAN ECONOMIC COMMUNITY — Economic policy
EUROPEAN ECONOMIC COMMUNITY — Politics and government
EUROPEAN ECONOMIC COMMUNITY — Denmark
EUROPEAN ECONOMIC COMMUNITY — Portugal
EUROPEAN ECONOMIC COMMUNITY — Spain
EUROPEAN ECONOMIC COMMUNITY COUNTRIES
EUROPEAN ECONOMIC COMMUNITY COUNTRIES — Commerce — Statistics
EUROPEAN ECONOMIC COMMUNITY COUNTRIES — Commerce — Developing countries
EUROPEAN ECONOMIC COMMUNITY COUNTRIES — Commerce — Great Britain
EUROPEAN ECONOMIC COMMUNITY COUNTRIES — Commerce — Spain
EUROPEAN ECONOMIC COMMUNITY COUNTRIES — Commercial policy
EUROPEAN ECONOMIC COMMUNITY COUNTRIES — Economic conditions — Regional disparities
EUROPEAN ECONOMIC COMMUNITY COUNTRIES — Economic integration
EUROPEAN ECONOMIC COMMUNITY COUNTRIES — Economic policy
EUROPEAN ECONOMIC COMMUNITY COUNTRIES — Foreign economic relations — Australia
EUROPEAN ECONOMIC COMMUNITY COUNTRIES — Foreign economic relations — Hungary
EUROPEAN ECONOMIC COMMUNITY COUNTRIES — Foreign economic relations — Mexico
EUROPEAN ECONOMIC COMMUNITY COUNTRIES — Foreign economic relations — Scandinavia
EUROPEAN ECONOMIC COMMUNITY COUNTRIES — Foreign economic relations — United States
EUROPEAN ECONOMIC COMMUNITY COUNTRIES — Foreign relations — Bibliography — Catalogs
EUROPEAN ECONOMIC COMMUNITY COUNTRIES — Foreign relations — Treaties
EUROPEAN ECONOMIC COMMUNITY COUNTRIES — Industries
EUROPEAN ECONOMIC COMMUNITY COUNTRIES — Languages
EUROPEAN ECONOMIC COMMUNITY COUNTRIES — Politics and government
EUROPEAN ECONOMIC COMMUNITY COUNTRIES — Social conditions
EUROPEAN ECONOMIC COMMUNITY COUNTRIES — Social policy
EUROPEAN ECONOMIC COMMUNITY COUNTRIES — Statistics
EUROPEAN ECONOMIC COMMUNITY COUNTRIES — Statistics — Indexes
EUROPEAN ECONOMIC COMMUNITY COUNTRIES — Terminology
EUROPEAN ECONOMIC COMMUNITY COUNTRIES — Economic conditions
EUROPEAN ECONOMIC COMMUNITY COUNTRIES — Social conditions
EUROPEAN ECONOMIC COMMUNITY COUNTRIESOFF. PUBNS. — Economic conditions — Regional disparities 986
EUROPEAN ECONOMIC COMMUNITY COUNTRIESOFF. PUBNS. — Economic policy 986
EUROPEAN ECONOMIC COMMUNITY COUNTRIESOFF. PUBNS. — Social policy 986
EUROPEAN ECONOMIC COMMUNITYOFF. PUBNS. — Portugal 986. (271/6)
EUROPEAN FEDERATION
EUROPEAN FEDERATION — Bibliography
EUROPEAN FEDERATION — Congresses
EUROPEAN FEDERATION — History — Documentation
EUROPEAN FOUNDATION FOR THE IMPROVEMENT OF LIVING AND WORKING CONDITIONS
EUROPEAN FREE TRADE ASSOCIATION
EUROPEAN GROUP OF PUBLIC ADMINISTRATION
EUROPEAN INTEGRATION
EUROPEAN PARLIAMENT
EUROPEAN PARLIAMENT — Comparative studies
EUROPEAN PARLIAMENT — Sources
EUROPEAN PARLIAMENT — Sources — Bibliography
EUROPEAN PARLIAMENT. Information Office
EUROPEAN POPULATION CONFERENCE (1982 : Strasbourg)
EUROPEANS — Relations — United States
EUROPEANS — Migrations
EUROPEN COMMUNITIES
EUTHANASIA
EUTHANASIA — Moral and ethical aspects — Congresses
EUTROPHICATION — Control
EVALUATION RESEARCH (SOCIAL ACTION PROGRAMS)
EVALUATION RESEARCH (SOCIAL ACTION PROGRAMS) — Bibliography
EVALUATION RESEARCH (SOCIAL ACTION PROGRAMS) — United States
EVANGELISCHE KIRCHE IN DEUTSCHLAND — History
EVICTION — London — Westminster
EVICTION — Northern Ireland
EVIDENCE, CRIMINAL — United States
EVIDENCE, EXPERT — Congresses
EVIDENCE, EXPERT — United States
EVIDENCE (LAW) — England
EVIDENCE (LAW) — Scotland
EVIDENCE (LAW) — United States
EVIDENCE (LAW) — United States — Statistical methods
EVOLUTION
EVOLUTION — History
EVOLUTION — Philosophy
EVOLUTION — Philosophy — Addresses, essays, lectures
EWE (AFRICAN PEOPLE) — Social conditions
EX-NUNS — United States
EXAMINATIONS — Great Britain
EXAMINERS (ADMINISTRATIVE PROCEDURE) — United States
EXCHANGE
EXCHANGE — Social aspects — Papua New Guinea
EXCHANGES, LITERARY AND SCIENTIFIC — Addresses, essays, lectures
EXECUTIVE ABILITY
EXECUTIVE ADVISORY BODIES — Netherlands — Directories
EXECUTIVE ADVISORY BODIES — United States
EXECUTIVE POWER — New Zealand
EXECUTIVE POWER — France — History
EXECUTIVE POWER — India
EXECUTIVE POWER — United States
EXECUTIVE PRIVILEGE (GOVERNMENT INFORMATION) — United States
EXECUTIVES
EXECUTIVES — Addresses, essays, lectures
EXECUTIVES — Training of — Developing countries
EXECUTIVES — Europe, Eastern — Training of
EXECUTIVES — France
EXECUTIVES — Great Britain
EXECUTIVES — Soviet Union — Training of
EXECUTIVES — United States
EXISTENTIALISM
EXISTENTIALISM — Study and teaching (Higher) — Israel
EXORCISM
EXPATRIATION — Israel — History
EXPENDITURES, PUBLIC
EXPENDITURES, PUBLIC — Classification
EXPENDITURES, PUBLIC — Congresses
EXPENDITURES, PUBLIC — Forecasting
EXPERIMENTAL DESIGN
EXPERIMENTAL THEATER — Great Britain — History
EXPERT SYSTEMS
EXPERT SYSTEMS (COMPUTER SCIENCE)
EXPERT SYSTEMS (COMPUTER SCIENCE) — Congresses
EXPLORERS — Africa
EXPORT CONTROLS
EXPORT CONTROLS — United States
EXPORT CREDIT
EXPORT CREDIT — Great Britain
EXPORT CREDIT — United States

EXPORT-IMPORT BANK OF THE UNITED STATES
EXPORT MARKETING
EXPORT MARKETING — Management
EXPORT MARKETING — Canada
EXPORT MARKETING — European Economic Community countries
EXPORT MARKETING — Great Britain
EXPORT MARKETING — Sri Lanka
EXPORT MARKETING — United States — Decision making
EXPORT-PROCESSING ZONES — Asia, Southeastern
EXPORT PROCESSING ZONES — Caribbean Area
EXPORT-PROCESSING ZONES — Pacific area
EXPORT SALES
EXPORT SALES — Legal aspects, laws, etc.
EXPORT SALES — Europe
EXPORT SALES — Great Britain — Finance
EXPORT SALES — Middle East
EXPORT SALES — United States
EXPORT TRADING COMPANIES
EXPRESS HIGHWAYS — Developing countries
EXPRESS HIGHWAYS — France
EXTERNAL PROBLEMS (MATHEMATICS)
EXTERNALITIES (ECONOMICS) — Addresses, essays, lectures
FAAA (TAHITI : REGION) — Population — Statistics
FABIAN SOCIETY
FACTORIES — Location — Bibliography
FACTORY AND TRADE WASTE
FACTORY AND TRADE WASTE — Bibliography
FACTORY AND TRADE WASTE — Economic aspects
FACTORY AND TRADE WASTE — England
FACTORY MANAGEMENT — Germany (West)
FACTORY MANAGEMENT — Great Britain
FACTORY MANAGEMENT — Hungary — History
F.A.I. (Organization : Spain)
FAILURE (PSYCHOLOGY)
FAIRBAIRN, JOHN
FAKARAVA (TUAMOTU ISLANDS) — Population — Statistics
FALKLAND ISLAND — International status
FALKLAND ISLANDS
FALKLAND ISLANDS — Bibliography
FALKLAND ISLANDS — Census, 1986
FALKLAND ISLANDS — Economic policy
FALKLAND ISLANDS — History
FALKLAND ISLANDS — International status
FALKLAND ISLANDS — Population — Statistics
FALKLAND ISLANDS DEVELOPMENT CORPORATION
FALKLAND ISLANDS WAR, 1982
FALKLAND ISLANDS WAR, 1982 — Bibliography
FALKLAND ISLANDS WAR, 1982 — Influence
FALKLAND ISLANDS WAR, 1982 — Journalists
FALKLAND ISLANDS WAR, 1982 — Political aspects
FALKLANDS ISLANDS WAR, 1982 — Bibliography
FALKLANDS ISLANDS WAR, 1982 — Economic aspects
FALLS ROAD (BELFAST, NORTHERN IRELAND)
FALWELL, JERRY
FAME
FAMILY
FAMILY — Addresses, essays, lectures
FAMILY — Economic aspects

FAMILY — Economic aspects — Canada
FAMILY — Economic aspects — Great Britain — Congresses
FAMILY — Handbooks, manuals, etc
FAMILY — History
FAMILY — Research
FAMILY — Research — Methodology
FAMILY — Australia — Finance
FAMILY — Australia — Statistics
FAMILY — Belgium — Ghent — History
FAMILY — Brazil — Paraíba (State) — Case studies
FAMILY — Caribbean Area
FAMILY — Egypt
FAMILY — England — History
FAMILY — Europe — History
FAMILY — Great Britain
FAMILY — Great Britain — Case studies
FAMILY — Great Britain — Congresses
FAMILY — Great Britain — Finance — Statistics
FAMILY — Great Britain — History
FAMILY — Iran
FAMILY — Latin America — Statistics — Methodology
FAMILY — London
FAMILY — Scotland — History
FAMILY — Southern States — History — Congresses
FAMILY — Sudan
FAMILY — Switzerland — Law and legislation
FAMILY — Turkey — History
FAMILY — United States
FAMILY — United States — Addresses, essays, lectures
FAMILY — United States — Congresses
FAMILY — United States — History
FAMILY — United States — Psychological aspects — Congresses
FAMILY — United States — Religious life — History — 19th century
FAMILY — West Bank
FAMILY ALLOWANCES — Australia
FAMILY ALLOWANCES — Denmark
FAMILY ALLOWANCES — Great Britain
FAMILY CORPORATIONS — Management
FAMILY CORPORATIONS — East Asia — History — Congresses
FAMILY CORPORATIONS — Europe — History — Congresses
FAMILY CORPORATIONS — United States — History — Congresses
FAMILY CORPORATIONS — United States — Management
FAMILY CORPORATIONS — United States — Psychological aspects
FAMILY DEMOGRAPHY — Methodology
FAMILY FARMS
FAMILY FARMS — Africa, Sub-Saharan
FAMILY HEALTH FOUNDATION (La.)
FAMILY LIFE EDUCATION — Great Britain
FAMILY LIFE EDUCATION — United States — Addresses, essays, lectures
FAMILY LIFE SURVEYS — India — Maps
FAMILY LIFE SURVEYS — Pakistan — Lahore
FAMILY LIFE SURVEYS — United States
FAMILY MEDICINE
FAMILY MEDICINE — Data processing
FAMILY MEDICINE — Great Britain — Data processing
FAMILY MEDICINE — Great Britain — Evaluation
FAMILY MEDICINE — Wales
FAMILY PLANNING — history — United States — abstracts
FAMILY PLANNING — United States
FAMILY POLICY
FAMILY POLICY — Australia
FAMILY POLICY — China — Congresses
FAMILY POLICY — Germany (East)
FAMILY POLICY — Great Britain
FAMILY POLICY — United States

FAMILY POLICY — United States — Addresses, essays, lectures
FAMILY PSYCHOTHERAPY
FAMILY SIZE — Cross-cultural studies
FAMILY SIZE — Australia — Addresses, essays, lectures
FAMILY SIZE — Egypt
FAMILY SIZE — Poland
FAMILY SOCIAL WORK
FAMILY SOCIAL WORK — England
FAMILY SOCIAL WORK — Great Britain
FAMILY SOCIAL WORK — New York (State) — Syracuse — Case studies
FAMILY SOCIAL WORK — United States
FAMILY VIOLENCE — Law and legislation — South Australia
FAMILY VIOLENCE — Law and legislation — Council of Europe countries
FAMILY VIOLENCE — United States
FAMILY VIOLENCE — United States — Addresses, essays, lectures
FAMILY VIOLENCE — United States — Prevention
FAMINES
FAMINES — Economic aspects
FAMINES — Handbooks, manuals, etc.
FAMINES — Research
FAMINES — Africa
FAMINES — Ethiopia
FAMINES — Malawi — History
FAMINES — Sahel — Congresses
FAMINES — Ukraine — Congresses
FANGATAU (TUAMOTU ISLANDS) — Population — Statistics
FANON, FRANTZ
FARM INCOME — Australia — Forecasting
FARM INCOME — France
FARM INCOME — France — Statistics
FARM INCOME — Southern States
FARM INCOME — Taiwan
FARM MANAGEMENT
FARM MANAGEMENT — Great Britain — Bibliography
FARM MANAGEMENT — Hungary — Economic aspects
FARM MANAGEMENT — Soviet Union
FARM MECHANIZATION — Economic aspects — Developing countries
FARM MECHANIZATION — Government policy — Africa
FARM MECHANIZATION — Social aspects — Developing countries
FARM MECHANIZATION — Africa, Sub-Saharan
FARM MECHANIZATION — Denmark
FARM PRODUCE — Marketing — Government policy — Developing countries — Congresses
FARM PRODUCE — Prices — Peru
FARM PRODUCE — Central America — Supply and demand — Forecasting
FARM PRODUCE — Chile
FARM PRODUCE — England — London — Marketing
FARM PRODUCE — Mexico — Marketing
FARM RENTS — Legal status, laws, etc — Great Britain
FARM SUPPLIES — France — Marketing
FARM SUPPLIES — Great Britain — Marketing
FARM TENANCY — Georgia — History — 19th century
FARM TENANCY — Great Britain
FARMERS — Asia — Congresses
FARMERS — Denmark — Socioeconomic status
FARMERS — Ghana — Social conditions
FARMERS — India — Political activity
FARMERS — Ireland
FARMERS — United States — Congresses
FARMERS INSTITUTES — Africa
FARMS — India — Statistics
FARMS — United States — Congresses
FARMS, SMALL
FARMS, SMALL — Soviet Union
FAROE ISLANDS — Economic conditions

FAROE ISLANDS — Foreign relations
FAROE ISLANDS — History — 20th Century
FAROE ISLANDS — Politics and government
FAROE ISLANDS — Social conditions
FAROE ISLANDS — Yearbooks
FARRIS (FIRM) — History
FASCISM
FASCISM — Argentina
FASCISM — Europe
FASCISM — France
FASCISM — France — History
FASCISM — Germany — History
FASCISM — Great Britain
FASCISM — Great Britain — History
FASCISM — Italy
FASCISM — Italy — Turin — History — 20th century
FASCISM — New Zealand
FASCISM — Spain
FASCISM — United States
FASCISM AND WOMEN — Germany
FASCIST ETHICS
FASCISTS — Germany — Attitudes
FASCISTS — Great Britain
FATHER AND CHILD
FATHER AND CHILD — Addresses, essays, lectures
FATHER AND CHILD — United States
FATHERS
FATHERS — Psychology
FATHERS — United States — Psychology
FATHERS AND DAUGHTERS
FATU HIVA (MARQUESAS ISLANDS) — Population — Statistics
FEAR
FEDERACIÓN OBRERA REGIONAL ARGENTINA — History
FEDERAL AID TO CHILD WELFARE — United States
FEDERAL AID TO HIGHER EDUCATION — Australia — History
FEDERAL AID TO HIGHER EDUCATION — United States
FEDERAL AID TO PUBLIC WELFARE — Political aspects — Puerto Rico
FEDERAL AID TO RESEARCH — United States — Directories
FEDERAL AID TO TRANSPORTATION — Europe
FEDERAL-CITY RELATIONS — United States
FEDERAL-CITY RELATIONS — United States — Addresses, essays, lectures
FEDERAL DEPOSIT INSURANCE CORPORATION
FEDERAL GOVERNMENT
FEDERAL GOVERNMENT — Legal aspects
FEDERAL GOVERNMENT — Canada
FEDERAL GOVERNMENT — Canada — Congresses
FEDERAL GOVERNMENT — European Economic Community countries
FEDERAL GOVERNMENT — Germany (West) — Bibliography
FEDERAL GOVERNMENT — India
FEDERAL GOVERNMENT — India — Case studies
FEDERAL GOVERNMENT — India — Legal aspects
FEDERAL GOVERNMENT — Malaysia
FEDERAL GOVERNMENT — Netherlands
FEDERAL GOVERNMENT — Nigeria
FEDERAL GOVERNMENT — Switzerland
FEDERAL GOVERNMENT — United States
FEDERAL REFORMATORY FOR WOMEN (Alderson (West Virginia))
FEDERAL RESERVE BANKS
FEDERALISM — Argentina — History
FEDERALISM — European Economic Community countries — History
FEDERALIST

FEDERALLY ADMINISTERED TRIBAL AREAS (PAKISTAN) — Population — Statistics
FÉDÉRATION DES ENTREPRISES DE BELGIQUE
FÉDÉRATION DES ÉTUDIANTS D'AFRIQUE NOIRE EN FRANCE
FÉDÉRATION DES TRAVAILLEURS DU QUÉBEC
FEED ADDITIVE RESIDUES
FEIERABEND, LADISLAV
FEMALE OFFENDERS
FEMALE OFFENDERS — Poland
FEMALE OFFENDERS — United States
FEMININITY
FEMININITY (PSYCHOLOGY)
FEMINISM
FEMINISM — Congresses
FEMINISM — Cross-cultural studies
FEMINISM — History
FEMINISM — History — Addresses, essays, lectures
FEMINISM — History — 20th century
FEMINISM — Periodicals — Bibliography
FEMINISM — Philosophy
FEMINISM — Philosphy
FEMINISM — Australia
FEMINISM — Europe — History
FEMINISM — France
FEMINISM — France — History
FEMINISM — Germany — History — 19th century
FEMINISM — Great Britain
FEMINISM — Great Britain — History
FEMINISM — Great Britain — History — 19th century
FEMINISM — Great Britain — History — 19th century — Sources
FEMINISM — Israel — Congresses
FEMINISM — Nevada — History — 20th century
FEMINISM — Pakistan — History — 20th century
FEMINISM — Puerto Rico
FEMINISM — Spain — History
FEMINISM — United States
FEMINISM — United States — History — Addresses, essays, lectures
FEMINIST LITERARY CRITICISM
FEMINISTS — Biography
FEMINISTS — England — Biography
FEMINISTS — Great Britain — Biography
FEMINISTS — Ireland — Biography
FEMINISTS — Nevada — Biography
FEMINISTS — New Jersey — History — 20th century
FEMINISTS — Sierra Leone — Biography
FENCES — Law and legislation — Australia — New South Wales
FERBER, ROBERT
FERRARO, GERALDINE
FERROL DEL CAUDILLO (SPAIN) — Social conditions
FERTILITY, HUMAN
FERTILITY, HUMAN — Addresses, essays, lectures
FERTILITY, HUMAN — Cross-cultural studies
FERTILITY, HUMAN — Econometric models
FERTILITY, HUMAN — Economic aspects
FERTILITY, HUMAN — Economic aspects — Mexico — Baviacora
FERTILITY, HUMAN — Mathematical models
FERTILITY, HUMAN — Political aspects
FERTILITY, HUMAN — Research
FERTILITY, HUMAN — Statistical methods
FERTILITY, HUMAN — England — History
FERTILITY, HUMAN — Africa, Subsaharan
FERTILITY, HUMAN — Asia
FERTILITY, HUMAN — Asia, Southeastern

FERTILITY, HUMAN — Australia — Addresses, essays, lectures
FERTILITY, HUMAN — Bahamas — Statistics
FERTILITY, HUMAN — Bangladesh
FERTILITY, HUMAN — Cameroon
FERTILITY, HUMAN — Cameroon — Statistics
FERTILITY, HUMAN — China
FERTILITY, HUMAN — Costa Rica
FERTILITY, HUMAN — Costa Rica — Attitudes
FERTILITY, HUMAN — Developing countries
FERTILITY, HUMAN — Developing countries — Case studies
FERTILITY, HUMAN — Developing countries — Statistical methods
FERTILITY, HUMAN — Dominican Republic
FERTILITY, HUMAN — Ecuador
FERTILITY, HUMAN — Egypt — Statistics
FERTILITY, HUMAN — England — History
FERTILITY, HUMAN — England — Cleveland
FERTILITY, HUMAN — England — London — Statistics
FERTILITY, HUMAN — Europe — History
FERTILITY, HUMAN — France — Statistics
FERTILITY, HUMAN — Ghana
FERTILITY, HUMAN — Ghana — Statistics
FERTILITY, HUMAN — Great Britain
FERTILITY, HUMAN — Great Britain — Statistics
FERTILITY, HUMAN — Guyana
FERTILITY, HUMAN — Haiti
FERTILITY, HUMAN — Haiti — Forecasting
FERTILITY, HUMAN — Hungary — Statistics
FERTILITY, HUMAN — India — Case studies — Addresses, essays, lectures
FERTILITY, HUMAN — India — Arunachal Pradesh — Statistics
FERTILITY, HUMAN — India — Gujarat — Statistics
FERTILITY, HUMAN — Indonesia
FERTILITY, HUMAN — Indonesia — Bali (Province)
FERTILITY, HUMAN — Italy — Statistics
FERTILITY, HUMAN — Ivory Coast
FERTILITY, HUMAN — Jamaica
FERTILITY, HUMAN — Jordan
FERTILITY, HUMAN — Kenya
FERTILITY, HUMAN — Korea (South — Satatistics
FERTILITY, HUMAN — Lesotho
FERTILITY, HUMAN — Netherlands — Statistics
FERTILITY, HUMAN — Nigeria
FERTILITY, HUMAN — Pakistan
FERTILITY, HUMAN — Paraguay
FERTILITY, HUMAN — Paraguay — Statistics
FERTILITY, HUMAN — Peru — Statistical methods
FERTILITY, HUMAN — Portugal — Statistics
FERTILITY, HUMAN — Portugal — Lanhezes — History
FERTILITY, HUMAN — Senegal
FERTILITY, HUMAN — Seychelles
FERTILITY, HUMAN — Singapore
FERTILITY, HUMAN — South Asia
FERTILITY, HUMAN — Southern Africa
FERTILITY, HUMAN — Soviet Union — History — 19th century
FERTILITY, HUMAN — Soviet Union — History — 20th century
FERTILITY, HUMAN — Statistical methods

FERTILITY, HUMAN — Sweden — Statistics
FERTILITY, HUMAN — Syria — Statistics
FERTILITY, HUMAN — Thailand
FERTILITY, HUMAN — Thailand — Statistics
FERTILITY, HUMAN — Trinidad and Tobago
FERTILITY, HUMAN — Trinidad and Tobago — Statistics
FERTILITY, HUMAN — Tunisia — Statistics
FERTILITY, HUMAN — Turkey
FERTILITY, HUMAN — Yemen
FERTILIZATION IN VITRO, HUMAN — Law and legislation
FERTILIZER INDUSTRY — European Economic Community countries
FERTILIZER INDUSTRY
FERTILIZER INDUSTRY — Energy conservation
FERTILIZER INDUSTRY — Environmental aspects
FERTILIZER INDUSTRY — Great Britain
FERTILIZER INDUSTRY — Latin America — Evaluation — Mathematical models
FERTILIZER INDUSTRY — Taiwan
FERTILIZERS
FERTILIZERS — Congresses
FERTILIZERS — Developing countries
FERTILIZERS — Economic aspects
FERTILIZERS — Environmental aspects — Organisation for Economic Co-operation and Development countries
FERTILIZERS — Developing countries — Price policy — Case studies — Congresses
FERTILIZERS — Developing countries — Price policy — Congresses
FERTILIZERS — United States
FERTILIZERS AND MANURES — Great Britain
FESTIVALS — Sri Lanka
FEUDALISM — Soviet Union — History
FICTION — History and criticism
FICTION IN ENGLISH
FIFE (SCOTLAND) — Antiquities
FIJI — Economic conditions
FIJI — History
FIJI — Industries — Statistics
FIJI — Politics and government
FIJI — Social conditions
FIJIAN LANGUAGE — History
FILE ORGANIZATION (COMPUTER SCIENCE)
FILMS See Moving-pictures
FILTERS (MATHEMATICS)
FINANCE
FINANCE — Dictionaries — Russian
FINANCE — Periodicals
FINANCE — Africa
FINANCE — Asia
FINANCE — Asia, South-Eastern
FINANCE — Australia
FINANCE — Bangladesh
FINANCE — Brazil
FINANCE — Canada
FINANCE — Canada — Statistics
FINANCE — Chile — Statistics
FINANCE — Colombia
FINANCE — Communist countries
FINANCE — Developing countries
FINANCE — England — London
FINANCE — European Economic Community countries
FINANCE — France
FINANCE — Great Britain
FINANCE — Great Britain — History — 20th century
FINANCE — Great Britain — Statistical services
FINANCE — Indonesia — Statistics
FINANCE — Japan
FINANCE — Latin America
FINANCE — Nepal
FINANCE — Persian Gulf region
FINANCE — Soviet Union
FINANCE — Soviet Union — Bibliography
FINANCE — Spain
FINANCE — United States
FINANCE — United States — Statistics
FINANCE COMPANIES — European Economic Community countries
FINANCE DEPARTMENTS — Poland
FINANCE, PERSONAL
FINANCE, PERSONAL — Great Britain
FINANCE, PUBLIC
FINANCE, PUBLIC — Accounting
FINANCE, PUBLIC — Accounting — France
FINANCE, PUBLIC — Addresses, essays, lectures
FINANCE, PUBLIC — Congresses
FINANCE, PUBLIC — Decision making
FINANCE, PUBLIC — European Economic Community countries
FINANCE, PUBLIC — Law and legislation — Ecuador
FINANCE, PUBLIC — Law and legislation — Poland
FINANCE, PUBLIC — Management
FINANCE, PUBLIC — Political aspects — Central Europe — History
FINANCE, PUBLIC — Social aspects — Central Europe — History
FINANCE, PUBLIC — California — San Francisco — History
FINANCE, PUBLIC — Canada
FINANCE, PUBLIC — Canada — History
FINANCE, PUBLIC — England — London
FINANCE, PUBLIC — England — London — Statistics
FINANCE, PUBLIC — European Economic Community countries — Bibliography — Catalogs
FINANCE, PUBLIC — France — History — 18th century
FINANCE, PUBLIC — France — Statistics
FINANCE, PUBLIC — Georgia — History — 19th century
FINANCE, PUBLIC — Germany
FINANCE, PUBLIC — Great Britain
FINANCE, PUBLIC — Great Britain — To 1688
FINANCE, PUBLIC — Great Britain — To 1688 — Sources
FINANCE, PUBLIC — Ireland
FINANCE, PUBLIC — Japan
FINANCE, PUBLIC — Mexico
FINANCE, PUBLIC — Nepal
FINANCE, PUBLIC — New York (N.Y.)
FINANCE, PUBLIC — Newfoundland
FINANCE, PUBLIC — Nigeria
FINANCE, PUBLIC — Pakistan — Accounting
FINANCE, PUBLIC — Panama
FINANCE, PUBLIC — Peru
FINANCE, PUBLIC — Peru — History — 17th century
FINANCE, PUBLIC — Peru — Mathematical models
FINANCE, PUBLIC — Poland
FINANCE, PUBLIC — Saint Kitts-Nevis
FINANCE, PUBLIC — Saint Lucia
FINANCE, PUBLIC — Soviet Union
FINANCE, PUBLIC — Soviet Union — History
FINANCE, PUBLIC — Spain
FINANCE, PUBLIC — Spain — Colonies — History — 17th century
FINANCE, PUBLIC — United States — Accounting
FINANCE, PUBLIC — United States — States
FINANCE, PUBLIC — United States — States — Congresses
FINANCIAL ACCOUNTING STANDARDS BOARD
FINANCIAL FUTURES — United States
FINANCIAL INSTITUTIONS
FINANCIAL INSTITUTIONS — Government policy — Japan
FINANCIAL INSTITUTIONS — Law and legislation — Great Britain
FINANCIAL INSTITUTIONS — Law and legislation — Organisation for Economic Co-operation and Development countries
FINANCIAL INSTITUTIONS — Asia, South-Eastern
FINANCIAL INSTITUTIONS — Asia, Southeastern
FINANCIAL INSTITUTIONS — Canada
FINANCIAL INSTITUTIONS — Developing countries
FINANCIAL INSTITUTIONS — England — London
FINANCIAL INSTITUTIONS — France
FINANCIAL INSTITUTIONS — Great Britain
FINANCIAL INSTITUTIONS — Great Britain — Technological innovations
FINANCIAL INSTITUTIONS — Hong Kong
FINANCIAL INSTITUTIONS — Italy — Statistics
FINANCIAL INSTITUTIONS — Organisation for Economic Co-operation and Development countries — Investments
FINANCIAL INSTITUTIONS — Switzerland
FINANCIAL STATEMENTS
FINANCIAL STATEMENTS — France
FINANCIAL STATEMENTS — Great Britain
FINANCIAL STATEMENTS — Great Britain — Case studies
FINANCIAL STATEMENTS — United States
FINANCIAL STATEMENTS, CONSOLIDATED
FINANCIAL STATEMENTS, CONSOLIDATED — France
'FINANCIAL TIMES'
FINE GAEL — History
FINLAND — Appropriations and expenditures
FINLAND — Census, 1980
FINLAND — Commerce
FINLAND — Economic conditions
FINLAND — Economic policy
FINLAND — Foreign relations — Soviet Union
FINLAND — History — 1809-1917
FINLAND — History — 20th century
FINLAND — Industries — History
FINLAND — Industries — History — Statistics
FINLAND — Industries — Statistics
FINLAND — Military relations — Soviet Union
FINLAND — Politics and government
FINLAND — Politics and government — 1945-
FINLAND — Population — Bibliography
FINLAND — Population — Statistics
FINLAND — Presidents — Election
FINLAND — Social policy
FINLAND. Tilastokeskus
FIRE-DEPARTMENTS — Great Britain
FIRE-DEPARTMENTS — Great Britain — Auditing
FIRE PREVENTION — Great Britain
FIREARM OWNERSHIP — United States
FIREARMS — Law and legislation — United States
FIRES — Great Britain — Casualties
FIRMS — Great Britain — Archival resources
FIRMS — Great Britain — History — Sources
FISCAL POLICY
FISCAL POLICY — Congresses
FISCAL POLICY — Religious aspects — Islam
FISCAL POLICY — Australia
FISCAL POLICY — California — San Francisco — History
FISCAL POLICY — Canada
FISCAL POLICY — Communist countries
FISCAL POLICY — Developing countries
FISCAL POLICY — Dominican Republic

FISCAL POLICY — Georgia — History — 19th century
FISCAL POLICY — Islamic countries
FISCAL POLICY — Nepal
FISCAL POLICY — Organisation for Economic Co-operation and Development countries
FISCAL POLICY — Thailand
FISCAL POLICY — Turkey
FISCAL POLICY — Unied States
FISCAL POLICY — United States
FISCAL POLICY — United States — States — Congresses
FISH, MARY
FISH-CULTURE — Government policy — Great Britain
FISH, SALTED — Economic aspects — Newfoundland
FISH TRADE — Newfoundland — History — 19th century
FISHERIES — Bibliography
FISHERIES — Economic aspects — Newfoundland
FISHERIES — Argentina
FISHERIES — California — History
FISHERIES — Canada — History
FISHERIES — Finland — Accounting
FISHERIES — Georges Bank
FISHERIES — Newfoundland — History
FISHERIES — North Atlantic Ocean
FISHERIES — Taiwan
FISHERIES, CO-OPERATIVE — Zimbabwe — Kariba
FISHERIES, COOPERATIVE — Canada — History
FISHERMEN — Spain — Galicia
FISHERS — Canada — History
FISHERS — Ghana — Social conditions
FISHERS — Hong Kong
FISHERY CONSERVATION — Atlantic Ocean — Congresses
FISHERY CONSERVATION — North Atlantic Ocean
FISHERY LAW AND LEGISLATION — North Atlantic Ocean
FISHERY LAW AND LEGISLATION
FISHERY LAW AND LEGISLATION — Congresses
FISHERY LAW AND LEGISLATION — California — History
FISHERY LAW AND LEGISLATION — Caribbean Area
FISHERY MANAGEMENT
FISHERY MANAGEMENT — California — History
FISHERY POLICY — Social aspects — Canada
FISHERY POLICY — Social aspects — Newfoundland
FISHERY POLICY — Canada
FISHERY POLICY — France
FISHERY POLICY — Great Britain
FISHERY POLICY — Spain — Galicia
FISHING VILLAGES — Scotland — Burra (Shetland Islands)
FITZGERALD, GARRET
FITZGERALD, GARRET MICHAEL DESMOND
FLAGS OF CONVENIENCE
FLAT-RATE INCOME TAX — United States
FLEMING, DONALD M
FLEMING, IAN, 1908-1964 — Characters — James Bond
FLEMINGS — Biography
FLEMISH MOVEMENT
FLETCHER, ERIC GEORGE MOLYNEUX, Baron
FLEXIBLE MANUFACTURING SYSTEMS
FLOOD CONTROL
FLOOD CONTROL — Government policy — Great Britain
FLORENCE (ITALY) — Politics and government — 1421-1737
FLORENCE (ITALY) — Politics and government — 1737-1860
FLORENCE (ITALY) — Social conditions
FLOUR
FLOUR AND FEED TRADE — Developing countries — Forecasting
FLOW OF FUNDS — Australia
FLOW OF FUNDS — Great Britain
FLOW OF FUNDS — Great Britain — Econometric models
FLOW OF FUNDS — Japan
FLOW OF FUNDS — Taiwan
FM BROADCASTING — Government policy — Australia
FODIO, USMAN DAN
FOLK ART
FOLK MEDICINE — Cross-cultural studies
FOLK MEDICINE — Thailand
FOOD
FOOD — Drying
FOOD — Religious aspects
FOOD ADDITIVES
FOOD ADULTERATION AND INSPECTION — Law and legislation — New York (State) — History — 19th century
FOOD ADULTERATION AND INSPECTION — Law and legislation — United States — History — 19th century
FOOD ADULTERATION AND INSPECTION — New York (State) — History — 19th century
FOOD ADULTERATION AND INSPECTION — United States — History — 19th century
FOOD AND AGRICULTURE ORGANIZATION
FOOD AND AGRICULTURE ORGANIZATION — Bibliography
FOOD AND AGRICULTURE ORGANIZATION — Catalogs
FOOD AND AGRICULTURE ORGANIZATION. Fisheries Department — Catalogs
FOOD AND AGRICULTURE ORGANIZATION. Forestry Department — Catalogs
FOOD AND AGRICULTURE ORGANIZATION. Human Resources, Institutions and Agrarian Reform Division — Catalogs
FOOD AND AGRICULTURE ORGANIZATION OF THE UNITED NATIONS. Forestry Department
FOOD CONSUMPTION
FOOD CONSUMPTION — History
FOOD CONSUMPTION — Statistical methods
FOOD CONSUMPTION — Statistics
FOOD CONSUMPTION — Chile
FOOD CONSUMPTION — China
FOOD CONSUMPTION — France — Statistics
FOOD CONSUMPTION — Kenya
FOOD CONSUMPTION — Netherlands — Statistics
FOOD CONSUMPTION — Sri Lanka
FOOD CONSUMPTION — Taiwan
FOOD CONTAMINATION
FOOD CROPS
FOOD FROM BRITAIN
FOOD HABITS
FOOD HABITS — England — Yorkshire
FOOD HABITS — France — Statistics
FOOD HABITS — Great Britain
FOOD HABITS — Papua New Guinea
FOOD HABITS — Scotland — History
FOOD HANDLING
FOOD HISTORY — 19th century — England — Yorkshire
FOOD INDUSTRY AND TRADE — European Economic Community countries
FOOD INDUSTRY AND TRADE
FOOD INDUSTRY AND TRADE — Political aspects — Developing countries
FOOD INDUSTRY AND TRADE — Political aspects — Great Britain
FOOD INDUSTRY AND TRADE — Asia
FOOD INDUSTRY AND TRADE — England — London
FOOD INDUSTRY AND TRADE — France — Energy consumption — Statistics
FOOD INDUSTRY AND TRADE — France — Statistics
FOOD INDUSTRY AND TRADE — Great Britain — Statistics
FOOD INDUSTRY AND TRADE — Soviet Union
FOOD INDUSTRY AND TRADE — United States
FOOD LAW AND LEGISLATION
FOOD PRICES — Government policy — Dominican Republic
FOOD PRICES — Government policy — United States
FOOD PRICES — France — Statistics
FOOD PRICES — Kenya
FOOD RELIEF
FOOD RELIEF — Government policy — Sri Lanka
FOOD RELIEF — Sri Lanka
FOOD RELIEF — United States — History
FOOD RELIEF, AMERICAN
FOOD STAMP PROGRAM — Sri Lanka
FOOD SUPPLY — European Economic Community countries
FOOD SUPPLY
FOOD SUPPLY — Congresses
FOOD SUPPLY — Government policy — Mexico
FOOD SUPPLY — Political aspects
FOOD SUPPLY — Statistics
FOOD SUPPLY — Africa
FOOD SUPPLY — Africa, Southern
FOOD SUPPLY — Africa, Sub-Saharan
FOOD SUPPLY — Africa, sub-Saharan — addresses, essays, lectures
FOOD SUPPLY — Africa, Sub-Saharan — Congresses
FOOD SUPPLY — Africa,sub-Saharan
FOOD SUPPLY — Developing countries
FOOD SUPPLY — Developing countries — Congresses
FOOD SUPPLY — England — London
FOOD SUPPLY — Europe, Eastern
FOOD SUPPLY — Germany
FOOD SUPPLY — Germany — Schleswig-Holstein
FOOD SUPPLY — Great Britain
FOOD SUPPLY — Soviet Union
FOOD SUPPLY — Tanzania
FOOD, WILD — Canada
FOOD, WILD — United States
FOOLS AND JESTERS — United States
FOOTWARE INDUSTRY — Employees
FOOTWEAR INDUSTRY — Great Britain — Statistics
FORCED LABOR — Bolivia — Potosí (Dept.) — History
FORCED LABOR — Brazil — Pernambuco — History — 19th century
FORCED LABOR — Soviet Union
FORCES LABOR — Dominican Republic
FORD (Family) — History
FORD MOTOR COMPANY — History
FORD MOTOR COMPANY — Management
FORD MOTOR COMPANY — Management — History — 20th century
FORECASTING
FOREGIN TRADE REGULATION
FOREIGN EXCHANGE
FOREIGN EXCHANGE — Accounting
FOREIGN EXCHANGE — Law and legislation — Taiwan
FOREIGN EXCHANGE — Mathematical models
FOREIGN EXCHANGE — Great Britain
FOREIGN EXCHANGE — Great Britain — Government policy
FOREIGN EXCHANGE
FOREIGN EXCHANGE ADMINISTRATION — Addresses, essays, lectures

FOREIGN EXCHANGE ADMINISTRATION — Developing countries — Congresses
FOREIGN EXCHANGE ADMINISTRATION — Latin America
FOREIGN EXCHANGE ADMINISTRATION — Nigeria
FOREIGN EXCHANGE PROBLEM
FOREIGN EXCHANGE PROBLEM — Addresses, essays, lectures
FOREIGN EXCHANGE PROBLEM — Australia
FOREIGN EXCHANGE PROBLEM — Developing countries
FOREIGN EXCHANGE PROBLEM — Japan — Congresses
FOREIGN EXCHANGE PROBLEM — Norway
FOREIGN EXCHANGE PROBLEM — Sweden
FOREIGN EXCHANGE PROBLEM — United States
FOREIGN EXCHANGE PROBLEM — United States — Congresses
FOREIGN EXCHANGE PROBLEMS — Switzerland
FOREIGN LICENSING AGREEMENTS
FOREIGN NEWS — Congresses
FOREIGN NEWS — United States
FOREIGN STUDY — Bibliography
FOREIGN TRADE AND EMPLOYMENT
FOREIGN TRADE AND EMPLOYMENT — Japan
FOREIGN TRADE AND EMPLOYMENT — United States
FOREIGN TRADE PROMOTION — Morocco
FOREIGN TRADE REGULATION
FOREIGN TRADE REGULATION — Bibliography
FOREIGN TRADE REGULATION — Congresses
FOREIGN TRADE REGULATION — Political aspects
FOREIGN TRADE REGULATION — Taxation
FOREIGN TRADE REGULATION — European Economic Community countries
FOREIGN TRADE REGULATION — Great Britain
FOREIGN TRADE REGULATION — Great Britain — History
FOREIGN TRADE REGULATION — Japan — Congresses
FOREIGN TRADE REGULATION — United States — Congresses
FOREIGN TRADE REGULATIONS — European Economic Community countries
FORENSIC PSYCHIATRY — North America
FOREST AND FORESTRY — Scotland
FOREST CONSERVATION — Canada
FOREST MANAGEMENT — United States
FOREST POLICY — Canada
FOREST POLICY — United States
FOREST POLICY — United States — History
FOREST PRODUCTS — Prices
FOREST PRODUCTS INDUSTRY — Canada
FOREST PRODUCTS INDUSTRY — New Brunswick — Statistics
FORESTS AND FORESTRY — Bibliography
FORESTS AND FORESTRY — Dictionaries
FORESTS AND FORESTRY — Dictionaries — French
FORESTS AND FORESTRY — Economic aspects — Southern States
FORESTS AND FORESTRY — Economic aspects — United States
FORESTS AND FORESTRY — Asia, Southeastern
FORESTS AND FORESTRY — Finland — c Accounting
FORESTS AND FORESTRY — Finland — Statistics
FORESTS AND FORESTRY — Great Britain — Statistics
FORESTS AND FORESTRY — Taiwan
FORESTS AND FORESTRY — United States — History
FORESTS AND FORESTRY — Wales — Clwyd
FORMAN, JAMES
FORONDA, VALENTÍN DE
FORTE, CHARLES
FORTRAN (COMPUTER PROGRAM LANGUAGE) — Handbooks, manuals, etc.
FOSTER HOME CARE — Law and legislation
FOSTER HOME CARE — Great Britain
FOSTER HOME CARE — Wales
FOUCAULT, MICHEL
FOUNDRYMEN — South Africa — History
FOURIER, CHARLES
FRAGA IRIBARNE, MANUEL
FRANCE
FRANCE — Appropriations and expenditures
FRANCE — Appropriations and expenditures — Statistics
FRANCE — Armed Forces — History — World War, 1939-1945
FRANCE — Boundaries — Spain
FRANCE — Cencus, 1982 — Classification
FRANCE — Census, 1982
FRANCE — Census, 1982 — Classification
FRANCE — Church history — 16th century
FRANCE — Civilization — Addresses, essays, lectures
FRANCE — Civilization — 1830-1900
FRANCE — Colonies
FRANCE — Commerce
FRANCE — Commerce — History — Congresses
FRANCE — Commerce — Statistics
FRANCE — Commerce — Canada — History — 18th century
FRANCE — Commercial policy
FRANCE — Constitution
FRANCE — Constitution — Dictionaries
FRANCE — Description and travel — 1600-1799
FRANCE — Economic conditions
FRANCE — Economic conditions — Regional disparities
FRANCE — Economic conditions — 1918-
FRANCE — Economic conditions — 1945-
FRANCE — Economic conditions — 1945- — Statistics
FRANCE — Economic conditions — 1945- — Statistics Economiques
FRANCE — Economic policy
FRANCE — Economic policy — 20th century
FRANCE — Economic policy — 1945-
FRANCE — Economic policy — 1965-
FRANCE — Emigration and immigration
FRANCE — Emigration and immigration — History
FRANCE — Emigration and immigration — Statistics
FRANCE — Ethnic relations
FRANCE — Foreign economic relations
FRANCE — Foreign economic relations — Switzerland
FRANCE — Foreign population — Public opinion
FRANCE — Foreign population — Statistics
FRANCE — Foreign relations
FRANCE — Foreign relations — Treaties
FRANCE — Foreign relations — 1715-1793
FRANCE — Foreign relations — 1945-1958
FRANCE — Foreign relations — Algeria
FRANCE — Foreign relations — Germany
FRANCE — Foreign relations — Germany (West)
FRANCE — Foreign relations — Spain
FRANCE — Foreign relations — Turkey
FRANCE — Foreign relations — United States
FRANCE — Foreign relations by 1914-1940
FRANCE — Handbooks, manuals, etc.
FRANCE — History — Consulate and Empire, 1799-1815
FRANCE — History — Revolution — 1789-1793
FRANCE — History — Revolution, 1789-1799 — Causes
FRANCE — History — 16th century
FRANCE — History — Wars of the Huguenots, 1562-1598
FRANCE — History — Bourbons, 1589-1789 — Historiography
FRANCE — History — 18th century
FRANCE — History — Revolution, 1789-1792
FRANCE — History — Revolution, 1789-1793
FRANCE — History — Revolution, 1789-1794
FRANCE — History — Revolution, 1789-1797
FRANCE — History — Revolution, 1789-1799
FRANCE — History — Revolution, 1789-1799 — Biography
FRANCE — History — Revolution, 1789-1799 — Causes
FRANCE — History — Revolution, 1789-1799 — Dictionaries
FRANCE — History — 1789-1815
FRANCE — History — Revolution, 1789-1815
FRANCE — History — Revolution, 1795-1799
FRANCE — History — Consulate and Empire, 1799-1815
FRANCE — History — Consulate and Empire, 1799-1815 — Dictionaries
FRANCE — History — Restoration, 1814-1830 — Dictionaries
FRANCE — History — Louis Philip, 1830-1848
FRANCE — History — Louis Philip, 1830-1848 — Dictionaries
FRANCE — History — Second Republic, 1848-1852 — Dictionaries
FRANCE — History — 1848-1870
FRANCE — History — Second Empire, 1852-1870 — Dictionaries
FRANCE — History — Third Republic, 1870-1940
FRANCE — History — Third Republic, 1870-1940 — Dictionaries
FRANCE — History — 20th century
FRANCE — History — 1914-1940
FRANCE — History — German occupation, 1940-1945
FRANCE — History — German Occupation: 1940-45
FRANCE — History — German occupation, 1940-1945
FRANCE — History — 1945-
FRANCE — History — 1958-
FRANCE — History, Military — 1789-1815
FRANCE — Industries
FRANCE — Industries — Statistics
FRANCE — Kings and rulers
FRANCE — Kings and rulers — Biography
FRANCE — Law and legislation
FRANCE — Manufactures — Statistics
FRANCE — Maps, mental
FRANCE — Military policy
FRANCE — National security
FRANCE — Nobility — Biography
FRANCE — Nobility — History — 16th century
FRANCE — Nobility — History — 17th century
FRANCE — Nobility — History — 19th century
FRANCE — Officials and employees
FRANCE — Officials and employees — Classification

FRANCE — Officials and employees — Salaries, allowances, etc. — Statistics
FRANCE — Politics and goverment — 1958-
FRANCE — Politics and government
FRANCE — Politics and government — To 987
FRANCE — Politics and government — 18th century
FRANCE — Politics and government — 1870-1940
FRANCE — Politics and government — 20th century
FRANCE — Politics and government — 1945-1958
FRANCE — Politics and government — 1945-
FRANCE — Politics and government — 1958-
FRANCE — Politics and government — 1969-
FRANCE — Politics and government — 1974-1981
FRANCE — Politics and government — 1981
FRANCE — Politics and government — 1981-
FRANCE — Politics and government — 1981- — Biography
FRANCE — Popular culture — History
FRANCE — Population
FRANCE — Population — Classification
FRANCE — Population — History
FRANCE — Population — Statistical methods
FRANCE — Population — Statistics
FRANCE — Population, Rural
FRANCE — Presidents
FRANCE — Race relations
FRANCE — Relations — Germany (West)
FRANCE — Relations — Indian Ocean Region
FRANCE — Relations — Japan
FRANCE — Relations — Red Sea
FRANCE — Relations — Spain
FRANCE — Relations (general) with Germany
FRANCE — Rural conditions
FRANCE — Social conditions
FRANCE — Social conditions — 19th century
FRANCE — Social conditions — 1945-
FRANCE — Social life and customs
FRANCE — Social life and customs — 1328-1600
FRANCE — Social life and customs — 17th-18th centuries
FRANCE — Social policy
FRANCE — Statistics — Bibliography
FRANCE — Statistics, Vital
FRANCE — Politics and government
FRANCE — Census, 1982
FRANCE — Foreign relations
FRANCE — Foreign relations — Great Britain
FRANCE. Armée — Biography
FRANCE. Armée — History — 20th century
FRANCE. Assemblée Consultative Provisoire, [1943-45]
FRANCE. Assemblée de L'Union Francaise, [Dec.1947-58]
FRANCE. Assemblée de L'Union Francaise, Dec.1947-58
FRANCE. Assemblée Nationale — Biography
FRANCE. Assemblée Nationale — Elections,1876
FRANCE. Assemblée Nationale Constituante, [1945-46]
FRANCE. Caisse Nationale des Allocations Familiales
FRANCE. Conseil Economique
FRANCE. Conseil économique et social
FRANCE. Haut Conseil du Secteur Public
FRANCE. Institut National de la Statistique et des Etudes Economiques — Bibliography

FRANCE. Ministère de la Justice — Statistics
FRANCE.. Ministère de l'Économie, des Finances et de la Privatisation
FRANCE. Parlement — Biography
FRANCE. Parlement. Assemblée Constituante
FRANCE. Parlement. Assemblée Consultative Provisoire
FRANCE. Parlement. Assemblée Nationale
FRANCE. Parlement. Senat
FRANCE. Parlement (Paris) — History
FRANCE. Présidence — Biography
FRANCE. President
FRANCE, PUBLIC — Hungary
FRANCE, SOUTHERN — History
FRANCHISES (RETAIL TRADE)
FRANCHISES (RETAIL TRADE) — Great Britain
FRANCO BAHAMONDE, FRANCISCO
FRANCO-GERMAN WAR, 1870-1871
FRANCOISM
FRANCOISM — History — Philosophy
FRANKENTHAL, KÄTE
FRANKFURT SCHOOL OF SOCIOLOGY
FRANKLIN, BENJAMIN
FRANKS — France — Kings and rulers
FRAUD
FRAUD — Canada
FRAUD INVESTIGATION
FREDERICK II, King of Prussia
FREE PORTS AND ZONES — China
FREE PRESBYTERIAN CHURCH OF ULSTER — History
FREE THOUGHT — Spain — History
FREE TRADE
FREE TRADE AND PROTECTION
FREE TRADE AND PROTECTION — Congresses
FREE TRADE AND PROTECTION — Free trade
FREE TRADE AND PROTECTION — History — 19th century
FREE TRADE AND PROTECTION — Protection
FREE TRADE AND PROTECTION — Protection — Case studies
FREE WILL AND DETERMINISM
FREE WILL AND DETERMINISM — History — 20th century
FREEDMEN — Education
FREEDMEN — Religion
FREEDMEN — Georgia
FREEDOM OF ASSOCIATION
FREEDOM OF ASSOCIATION — Digests
FREEDOM OF INFORMATION
FREEDOM OF INFORMATION — Bibliography
FREEDOM OF INFORMATION — Legal status, laws, etc. — Great Britain
FREEDOM OF INFORMATION — Canada
FREEDOM OF INFORMATION — Colombia
FREEDOM OF INFORMATION — Great Britain
FREEDOM OF INFORMATION — Great Britain — Bibliography
FREEDOM OF INFORMATION — United States
FREEDOM OF INFORMATION BILL 1980-81
FREEDOM OF MOVEMENT — European Economic Community countries
FREEDOM OF MOVEMENT (INTERNATIONAL LAW)
FREEDOM OF SPEECH — Addresses, essays, lectures
FREEDOM OF SPEECH — Australia
FREEDOM OF SPEECH — United States
FREEDOM OF THE PRESS
FREEDOM OF THE PRESS — Canada
FREEDOM OF THE PRESS — Great Britain
FREEDOM OF THE PRESS — India — History

FREEDOM OF THE PRESS — Spain — Cádiz (Province) — History — 19th century
FREEDOM OF THE PRESS — Tanzania
FREEDOM OF THE PRESS — United States
FREEMASONRY — United States — History
FREEMASONS — Soviet Union — History — 20th century
FREEMASONS — Spain — History
FREEMASONS — Spain — Catalonia — History
FREGE, GOTTLOB
FREIBURG IM BREISGAU REGION (GERMANY) — Social conditions
FREIE DEMOKRATISCHE PARTEI
FREIGHT AND FREIGHTAGE — Statistics
FREIGHT AND FREIGHTAGE — Canada
FREIGHT AND FREIGHTAGE — Great Britain
FREIGHT AND FREIGHTAGE — Ireland
FREIGHT AND FREIGHTAGE — Nigeria — Kaduna
FRENCH — Czechoslovakia — Slovak Socialist Republic
FRENCH — England — History
FRENCH — Germany — Saarland
FRENCH — History
FRENCH-CANADIAN DRAMA — History and criticism
FRENCH-CANADIANS — New England — History
FRENCH GUIANA — Census, 1974
FRENCH GUIANA — Population — Statistics
FRENCH GUIANA — Statistics, Vital
FRENCH LANGUAGE — Dictionaires — English
FRENCH LANGUAGE — Dictionaries
FRENCH LANGUAGE — Dictionaries — English
FRENCH LANGUAGE — Political aspects — Manitoba — History
FRENCH LITERATURE — 17th century — History and criticism
FRENCH POLYNESIA — Census, 1983
FRENCH POLYNESIA — Politics and government
FRENCH POLYNESIA — Population — Statistics
FRENTE POPULAR
FRENTE SANDINISTA DE LIBERACIÓN NACIONAL
FREUD, SIGMUND. Totem und Tabu
FREUD, SIGMUND
FREY, ROBERT SEITZ
FRIEDMAN, MILTON
FRIENDLY SOCIETIES — Singapore
FRIENDSHIP
FRIENDSHIP — Research
FRIENDSHIP — London
FRIESLAND (NETHERLANDS) — Economic policy
FRIMODTS FORLAG — History
FRONT LIBÉRATION DE QUÉBEC
FRONT NATIONAL
FRONTIER AND PIONEER LIFE — Oklahoma
FROZEN GROUND
FRUIT — England — London — Marketing
FUEL — Prices — Congresses
FUEL — Great Britain
FUKUSHIMA-KEN (JAPAN) — Social conditions
FULBRIGHT, J. WILLIAM
FULHAM (LONDON) — Economic policy
FULL EMPLOYMENT POLICIES
FULL EMPLOYMENT POLICIES — Great Britain
FUNCTIONALISATION (SOCIAL SCIENCES)
FUNCTIONALISM
FUNCTIONALISM (LINGUISTICS)
FUNCTIONALISM (SOCIAL SCIENCES) — Addresses, essays, lectures

FUNCTIONS, CONTINUOUS
FUND RAISING — Canada
FUND RAISING — Great Britain
FUNDAMENTALISM — History of doctrines — 20th century
FUNERAL RITES AND CEREMONIES — Ghana
FUNERAL RITES AND CEREMONIES, SENUFO (AFRICAN PEOPLE)
FUR TRADE — Canada — History
FUR TRADE — Soviet Union — History
FURNITURE WORKERS — Great Britain — Recruiting
FUTUNA See Wallis and Futuna
FYVEL, T. R.
GABON — History — Dictionaries
GAELIC ATHLETIC ASSOCIATION — History
GAHUKU (PAPUA NEW GUINEA PEOPLE)
GAITÁN, JORGÉ ELIÉCER — Assassination
GALBRAITH, JOHN KENNETH
GALICIA (POLAND AND UKRAINE) — History — Uprising, 1848
GALICIA (POLAND AND UKRAINE) — Politics and government
GALICIA (SPAIN) — Economic conditions
GALICIA (SPAIN) — Politics and government — 20th century
GALIEV, MIRSAID SULTAN See Sultan Galiev, Mirsaid
GALLIFFET, GASTON ALEXANDRE AUGUSTE DE, 1930-1909
GÁLVEZ, MANUEL
GAMBIA — Commerce — Statistics
GAMBIA — Economic ploicy
GAMBIA — Economic policy
GAMBIA — History
GAMBIA — History — Dictionaries
GAMBIA — Social policy
GAMBIER ISLANDS — Population — Statistics
GAMBLING — Economic aspects — Australia
GAMBLING — Economic aspects — United States
GAMBLING — Legal status, laws, etc. — Australia
GAMBLING — Social aspects — France
GAMBLING — Social aspects — United States
GAMBLING — Australia
GAMBLING — France — History — 17th century
GAMBLING — France — History — 18th century
GAMBLING — United States
GAME THEORY
GAME THEORY — Congresses
GAMES — History
GAMKASKLOOF VALLEY, SOUTH AFRICA
GAMO (AFRICAN PEOPLE)
GAMO (ETHIOPIA) — History
GAMO (ETHIOPIA) — Politics and government
GANDHI, Mahatma — Bibliography
GANDHI, INDIRA
GANDHI, INDIRA, 1917-1984 — Assassination
GANDHI, M. K.
GANDHI, MAHATMA
GANDHI, MAHATMA — Views on peace
GANDHI, MAHATMA — Views on war
GANG-WEON DO (KOREA (SOUTH)) — Statistics
GARANG, JOHN
GARDEN CITIES — United States
GARDEN CITIES — United States — Case studies
GARIBALDI, GIUSEPPE
GARVEY, MARCUS
GARY (IND.) — Ethnic relations
GARY (IND.) — History
GARY (IND.) — Social conditions
GAS — Law and legislation — Great Britain
GAS — Prices — European Economic Community Countries
GAS — Prices — European Economic Community Countries — Statistics
GAS BILL 1985-86
GAS COMPANIES — England — Lincoln (Lincolnshire) — History
GAS COMPANIES — England — Nottingham (Nottinghamshire) — History
GAS INDUSTRY
GAS INDUSTRY — Accounting
GAS INDUSTRY — Political aspects
GAS INDUSTRY — Political aspects — Soviet Union
GAS INDUSTRY — England — Grimsby (Humberside)
GAS INDUSTRY — Great Britain
GAS, NATURAL
GAS, NATURAL — Developing countries — Reserves
GAS, NATURAL — Political aspects
GAS, NATURAL — Ecuador — Statistics
GAS, NATURAL — Great Britain
GAS, NATURAL — North Sea
GAUDOIS, JEAN
GAULLE, CHARLES DE
GAWA (PAPUA NEW GUINEA) — Social life and customs
GAZETTEERS
GDAŃSK (POLAND) — History
GEBUSI (PAPUA NEW GUINEA PEOPLE) — Rites and ceremonies
GEBUSI (PAPUA NEW GUINEA PEOPLE) — Social life and customs
GEMS
GENE BANKS, PLANT
GENERAL AGREEMENT ON TARIFFS AND TRADE
GENERAL AGREEMENT ON TARIFFS AND TRADE (1947)
GENERAL ELECTRIC COMPANY
GENERAL MOTORS CORPORATION
GENERAL MOTORS CORPORATION — Management
GENERAL MOTORS CORPORATION — Management — History — 20th century
GENERAL THEORY OF EMPLOYMENT, INTEREST AND MONEY
GENERAL WILL — History
GENERALS — China — Biography
GENERALS — Great Britain — Biography
GENERALS — Spain — Bibliography
GENERALS — Spain — Biography
GENERALS — United States — Biography
GENERATIVE GRAMMAR
GENETIC ENGINEERING — Law and legislation — United States
GENETIC ENGINEERING — Organisation for Economic Co-operation and Development countries — Safety measures
GENIUS
GENTILE, GIOVANNI
GENTRIFICATION — England — Norfolk
GENTRIFICATION — England — Nottinghamshire
GEO A. HORMEL AND CO.
GEOGRAPHICAL DISTRIBUTION OF PLANTS AND ANIMALS
GEOGRAPHICAL PERCEPTION
GEOGRAPHY
GEOGRAPHY — Bibliography
GEOGRAPHY — Dictionaries
GEOGRAPHY — Mathematical models
GEOGRAPHY — Mathematics
GEOGRAPHY — Methodology
GEOGRAPHY — Philosophy
GEOGRAPHY — Psychological aspects
GEOGRAPHY — Social aspects — Great Britain
GEOGRAPHY — Statistical methods
GEOGRAPHY — Statistical methods — Congresses
GEOGRAPHY — Great Britain — Data processing
GEOGRAPHY, ECONOMIC
GEOGRAPHY, ECONOMIC — Maps
GEOGRAPHY, HISTORICAL
GEOGRAPHY, POLITICAL
GEOLOGY — England
GEOLOGY — Scotland — Midland Valley
GEOMORPHOLOGY — History
GEOPOLITICS — Asia, Southeastern
GEOPOLITICS — Great Britain
GEORGE I, King of Great Britain
GEORGIA — Census, 1860
GEORGIA — History — 1775-1865
GEORGIA — History — Civil War, 1861-1865
GEORGIA — Politics and government — 1865-1950
GEORGIA — Race relations
GEORGIA — Social life and customs
GEORGIAN S.S.R. — Economic policy
GERIATRIC PSYCHIATRY — England — Hampshire
GERMAN AMERICANS — History — Congresses
GERMAN LANGUAGE — Dictionaries — English
GERMAN LANGUAGE — Grammar — 1950-
GERMAN LANGUAGE — Slang — Dictionaries
GERMAN LITERATURE — 20th century — History and criticism
GERMAN LITERATURE — Germany (East) — History and criticism — Congresses
GERMAN REUNIFICATION QUESTION (1949-)
GERMAN REUNIFICATION QUESTION (1949-) — Sources
GERMANS — Argentina
GERMANS — Brazil — São Pedro (Rio Grande do Sul)
GERMANS — Canada — History
GERMANS — Hungary
GERMANS — Ontario — Renfrew (County) — History
GERMANY. Enabling Act 1933
GERMANY — Armed forces — History — Sources
GERMANY — Bibliography
GERMANY — Biography
GERMANY — Boundaries — Poland
GERMANY — Colonies
GERMANY — Colonies — History
GERMANY — Constitutional history
GERMANY — Diplomatic and consular service — History
GERMANY — Economic conditions
GERMANY — Economic conditions — 19th century
GERMANY — Economic conditions — 20th century
GERMANY — Economic conditions — 1918-1945
GERMANY — Economic history
GERMANY — Economic policy
GERMANY — Economic policy — 1933-1945
GERMANY — Emigration and immigration — History
GERMANY — Ethnic relations
GERMANY — Ethnic relations — Congresses
GERMANY — Foreign economic relations — Italy
GERMANY — Foreign relations
GERMANY — Foreign relations — Sources — Great Britain
GERMANY — Foreign relations — Sources — United States
GERMANY — Foreign relations — 1871-1918
GERMANY — Foreign relations — 20th century — Addresses, essays, lectures
GERMANY — Foreign relations — 1918-1933
GERMANY — Foreign relations — 1933-1945
GERMANY — Foreign relations — 1945-
GERMANY — Foreign relations — Africa

GERMANY — Foreign relations — Baltic States
GERMANY — Foreign relations — Czechoslovakia
GERMANY — Foreign relations — Europe — Addresses, essays, lectures
GERMANY — Foreign relations — France
GERMANY — Foreign relations — Great Britain
GERMANY — Foreign relations — Japan
GERMANY — Foreign relations — Poland
GERMANY — Foreign relations — Silesia, Upper (Poland and Czechoslovakia)
GERMANY — Foreign relations — Soviet Union
GERMANY — Foreign relations — Spain
GERMANY — Foreign relations — United States
GERMANY — Foreign relations — United States — Addresses, essays, lectures
GERMANY — Foreign relations — United States — Congresses
GERMANY — Foreign relations — Venezuela
GERMANY — History
GERMANY — History — 20th century
GERMANY — History — 843-1273
GERMANY — History — To 1517
GERMANY — History — 1618-1648
GERMANY — History — 19th century
GERMANY — History — 1871-1918
GERMANY — History — William II, 1888-1918
GERMANY — History — 20th century
GERMANY — History — Revolution, 1918 — Sources
GERMANY — History — Allied occupation, 1918-1930 — Bibliography
GERMANY — History — 1918-1933
GERMANY — History — 1918-1933 — Bibliography
GERMANY — History — Revolution, 1918- — Sources
GERMANY — History — 1933-1945
GERMANY — History — 1933-45
GERMANY — History — 1933-1945 — Bibliography
GERMANY — History — 1933-1945 — Maps
GERMANY — History — Allied occupation, 1945-
GERMANY — Intellectual life — Congresses
GERMANY — Kings and rulers — Biography
GERMANY — Officials and employees — Political activity — History — 20th century
GERMANY — Politics and government — 1871-1888
GERMANY — Politics and government — 1871-1918
GERMANY — Politics and government — 1871-1933
GERMANY — Politics and government — 1871-1933 — Addresses, essays, lectures
GERMANY — Politics and government — 1888-1918
GERMANY — Politics and government — 20th century
GERMANY — Politics and government — 1918-1933
GERMANY — Politics and government — 1933-1945
GERMANY — Politics and government — 1933-1945 — Addresses, essays, lectures
GERMANY — Politics and government — 1933-1945 — Bibliography
GERMANY — Politics and government — 1945-
GERMANY — Politics and government — 1945- — Bibliography
GERMANY — Popular culture — History
GERMANY — Relations — Soviet Union
GERMANY — Relations — Spain
GERMANY — Relations (general) with France
GERMANY — Social conditions
GERMANY — Social conditions — 1871-1918
GERMANY — Social conditions — 1918-1933
GERMANY — Social conditions — 1933-1945
GERMANY — Social conditions — 1945-
GERMANY — Social life and customs — 20th century
GERMANY — Social policy
GERMANY — Territorial expansion — History
GERMANY. Heer — Political activity
GERMANY. Reichstag — Elections, 1930-1933
GERMANY (Federal Republic). Bundestag
GERMANY — Civilization — Congresses
GERMANY — Foreign relations — Soviet Union
GERMANY (EAST)
GERMANY (EAST) — Armed Forces
GERMANY (EAST) — Bibliography
GERMANY (EAST) — Congresses
GERMANY (EAST) — Economic conditions
GERMANY (EAST) — Economic policy
GERMANY (EAST) — Foreign relations
GERMANY (EAST) — Foreign relations — Europe
GERMANY (EAST) — Foreign relations — Germany (West)
GERMANY (EAST) — Foreign relations — Germany (West) — History
GERMANY (EAST) — Foreign relations — Poland
GERMANY (EAST) — Foreign relations — Soviet Union
GERMANY (EAST) — Government policy — Germany (West) — History
GERMANY (EAST) — Intellectual life — Congresses
GERMANY (EAST) — Militia
GERMANY (EAST) — Politics and government
GERMANY (EAST) — Social conditions
GERMANY (EAST) — Social conditions — Congresses
GERMANY (EAST) — Statistics
GERMANY (FEDERAL REPUBLIC). Bundesregierung
GERMANY (FEDERAL REPUBLIC). Deutscher Bundestag
GERMANY (FEDERAL REPUBLIC). Parlamentarischer Rat
GERMANY (FEDERAL REPUBLIC). Parlamentarischer Rat. Ausschuss für Zuständigkeitsabgrenzung
GERMANY (WEST) — Armed Forces — Procurement
GERMANY (WEST) — Commerce — Classification
GERMANY (WEST) — Commerce — Statistics
GERMANY (WEST) — Constitutional history — Sources
GERMANY (WEST) — Economic conditions
GERMANY (WEST) — Economic history
GERMANY (WEST) — Economic policy
GERMANY (WEST) — Economic policy — 1974-
GERMANY (WEST) — Finance
GERMANY (WEST) — Foreign economic relations — France
GERMANY (WEST) — Foreign economic relations — Netherlands
GERMANY (WEST) — Foreign economic relations — Switzerland
GERMANY (WEST) — Foreign population
GERMANY (WEST) — Foreign relations
GERMANY (WEST) — Foreign relations — Europe
GERMANY (WEST) — Foreign relations — Germany (East)
GERMANY (WEST) — Foreign relations — Germany (East) — History
GERMANY (WEST) — Foreign relations — Israel
GERMANY (WEST) — Foreign relations — Middle East
GERMANY (WEST) — Foreign relations — United States — Addresses, essays, lectures
GERMANY (WEST) — Government policy — Germany (East) — History
GERMANY (WEST) — History
GERMANY (WEST) — Industries
GERMANY (WEST) — Industries — Classification
GERMANY (WEST) — Manufactures — Classification
GERMANY (WEST) — Politics and government
GERMANY (WEST) — Politics and government — Sources
GERMANY (WEST) — Politics and government — 1982-
GERMANY (WEST) — Politics and governmernt
GERMANY (WEST) — Relations — France
GERMANY (WEST) — Relations — Netherlands
GERMANY (WEST) — Social conditions
GERMANY (WEST) — Social policy
GERMANY (WEST) — Social policy — Statisitcs
GERMAY (WEST) — Constitution
GERMENY (FEDERAL REPUBLIC). Bundestag — History
GERMPLASM RESOURCES, PLANT
GERONTOLOGY
GERONTOLOGY — Addresses, essays, lectures
GERONTOLOGY — Bibliography
GERONTOLOGY — Congresses
GERONTOLOGY — Canada
GERONTOLOGY — United States
GERONTOLOGY — United States — History
GEWERKSCHAFT NAHRUNG-GENUSS-GASTSTÄTTEN
GHANA — Foreign relations
GHANA — History — 1957-
GHANA — Politics and government
GHANA — Population
GHANA — Population — Statistics
GHANA — Population — Statistics Evaluation
GHANA — Presidents — Biography
GHANA — Rural conditions
GHANA — Social conditions
GHANDI, M. K.
GHOST DANCE
GIBRALTAR — Strategic aspects
GIFTED CHILDREN — Counseling of — Congresses
GIFTED CHILDREN — Identification — Congresses
GIFTED CHILDREN — Psychology
GILBERT AND ELLICE ISLANDS COLONY
GILBERT ISLANDS
GIPSIES — Scotland — Grampian
GIRONDISTS — History
GLADSTONE, W. E
GLADSTONE, W. E. (William Ewart)
GLAMORGAN — City planning
GLASGOW (STRATHCLYDE) — History
GLASGOW (STRATHCLYDE) — Social conditions
GLASS MANUFACTURE — European Economic Community countries
GLEISPRACH, WENZESLAUS K.
GLENCOE MASSACRE, 1692
GOA (INDIA) — Politics and government
GODDESSES, GREEK
GODWIN, WILLIAM
GOFF (Family)
GOKALP, ZIYA
GOLD INDUSTRY — Russian S.F.S.R. — Siberia, Eastern
GOLD INDUSTRY — South Africa — History

GOLD MINERS — Russian S.F.S.R. — Siberia, Eastern
GOLD MINES AND MINING — History
GOLD MINES AND MINING — South Africa
GOLD STANDARD
GOLD STANDARD — Addresses, essays, lectures
GOLD STANDARD — History
GOLDSTEIN, ISRAEL
GOLLANCZ, VICTOR
GOMPERS, SAMUEL
GOMUŁKA, WŁADYSŁAW
GOODNESS-OF-FIT TESTS
GORBACHEV, M. S.
GORBACHEV, MIKHAIL SERGEEVICH
GORBALS (LANARKSHIRE) — Social life and customs
GÖRING, HERMANN
GOR'KII, MAKSIM
GOROKA DISTRICT (PAPUA NEW GUINEA) — Economic conditions
GOROKA DISTRICT (PAPUA NEW GUINEA) — Social conditions
GOSSAGE, PATRICK
GOTTWALD, KLEMENT
GOVERNESSES — Soviet Union
GOVERNMENT AND THE PRESS — Australia
GOVERNMENT AND THE PRESS — Canada
GOVERNMENT AND THE PRESS — Great Britain
GOVERNMENT AND THE PRESS — India — History
GOVERNMENT AND THE PRESS — South Africa
GOVERNMENT AND THE PRESS — Tanzania
GOVERNMENT AND THE PRESS — United States
GOVERNMENT AND THE PRESS — United States — Bibliography
GOVERNMENT AND THE PRESS — United States — History — 20th century
GOVERNMENT BUSINESS ENTERPRISES — Developing countries — Bibliography
GOVERNMENT BUSINESS ENTERPRISES
GOVERNMENT BUSINESS ENTERPRISES — Accounting — France
GOVERNMENT BUSINESS ENTERPRISES — Bibliography
GOVERNMENT BUSINESS ENTERPRISES — Congresses
GOVERNMENT BUSINESS ENTERPRISES — Employment — Egypt
GOVERNMENT BUSINESS ENTERPRISES — Finance — Congresses
GOVERNMENT BUSINESS ENTERPRISES — Management
GOVERNMENT BUSINESS ENTERPRISES — Price policy — Congresses
GOVERNMENT BUSINESS ENTERPRISES — Africa
GOVERNMENT BUSINESS ENTERPRISES — Africa, Sub-Saharan
GOVERNMENT BUSINESS ENTERPRISES — Developing countries — Case studies
GOVERNMENT BUSINESS ENTERPRISES — Developing countries — Congresses
GOVERNMENT BUSINESS ENTERPRISES — Developing countries — Employees — Training of
GOVERNMENT BUSINESS ENTERPRISES — Developing countries — Finance
GOVERNMENT BUSINESS ENTERPRISES — Developing countries — Management
GOVERNMENT BUSINESS ENTERPRISES — Egypt — Labor productivity
GOVERNMENT BUSINESS ENTERPRISES — Egypt — Management
GOVERNMENT BUSINESS ENTERPRISES — Europe
GOVERNMENT BUSINESS ENTERPRISES — France
GOVERNMENT BUSINESS ENTERPRISES — Great Britain
GOVERNMENT BUSINESS ENTERPRISES — Great Britain — Finance
GOVERNMENT BUSINESS ENTERPRISES — India
GOVERNMENT BUSINESS ENTERPRISES — India — Location
GOVERNMENT BUSINESS ENTERPRISES — India — Orissa — Personnel management
GOVERNMENT BUSINESS ENTERPRISES — Pakistan — Statistics
GOVERNMENT BUSINESS ENTERPRISES — Poland — Finance
GOVERNMENT EXECUTIVES — Handbooks, manuals, etc — Bibliography
GOVERNMENT EXECUTIVES — Training of — Great Britain
GOVERNMENT EXECUTIVES — United States
GOVERNMENT FINANCIAL INSTITUTIONS — Congresses
GOVERNMENT FINANCIAL INSTITUTIONS — Developing countries — Congresses
GOVERNMENT FINANCIAL INSTITUTIONS — India
GOVERNMENT INFORMATION
GOVERNMENT INFORMATION — Legal status, laws, etc. — Great Britain
GOVERNMENT INFORMATION — Canada
GOVERNMENT INFORMATION — Colombia
GOVERNMENT INFORMATION — Great Britain
GOVERNMENT INFORMATION — United States
GOVERNMENT LENDING — United States
GOVERNMENT LIABILITY
GOVERNMENT LIABILITY — United States
GOVERNMENT OWNERSHIP
GOVERNMENT OWNERSHIP — Economic aspects
GOVERNMENT OWNERSHIP — Great Britain
GOVERNMENT OWNERSHIP — Great Britain — Statistics
GOVERNMENT OWNERSHIP — Poland
GOVERNMENT OWNERSHIP — United States — Addresses, essays, lectures
GOVERNMENT PAPERWORK — Great Britain
GOVERNMENT, PRIMITIVE — Ethiopia
GOVERNMENT PRODUCTIVITY — United States — Measurement
GOVERNMENT PUBLICITY — France
GOVERNMENT PUBLICITY — Great Britain
GOVERNMENT PUBLICITY — United States
GOVERNMENT PUBLICITY — United States — Addresses, essays, lectures
GOVERNMENT PURCHASING — Great Britain — Management
GOVERNMENT, RESISTANCE TO
GOVERNMENT, RESISTANCE TO — England — London
GOVERNMENT SPENDING POLICY — Australia
GOVERNMENT SPENDING POLICY — Canada
GOVERNMENT SPENDING POLICY — Great Britain
GOVERNMENT SPENDING POLICY — Pakistan — Statistics
GOVERNMENT SPENDING POLICY — United States
GOVERNMENT TRADING — Developing countries
GOVERNMENTAL INVESTIGATIONS — Australia
GOVERNMENTAL INVESTIGATIONS — Canada
GOVERNMENTAL INVESTIGATIONS — Great Britain
GOVERNORS — United States — Election — Case studies
GOVERNORS — United States — History
GOVERNORS GENERAL — Canada — Biography
GRADUATE MANAGEMENT ADMISSION COUNCIL
GRADUATE STUDENTS — Great Britain
GRAF BROCKDORFF-RANTZAN, ULRICH See Brockdorff-Rantzan, Ulrich, Graf von
GRAHAM, JOHN
GRAIN
GRAIN — Economic aspects — Hungary — Congresses
GRAIN — Fertilizers and manures
GRAIN — European Economic Community Countries
GRAIN — Soviet Union — Climatic factors
GRAIN TRADE
GRAIN TRADE — Australia
GRAIN TRADE — Baltic States — History
GRAIN TRADE — Developing countries — Forecasting
GRAIN TRADE — Soviet Union
GRAIN TRADE — United States
GRAMMAR, COMPARATIVE AND GENERAL — Morphology
GRAMMAR, COMPARATIVE AND GENERAL — Syntax
GRAMSCI, ANTONIO
GRANADA — History — American invasion, 1983
GRAND ALLIANCE, WAR OF THE, 1689-1697 — Diplomatic history
GRAND-SÉMINAIRE DE SAINT-SULPICE — History
GRANTS-IN-AID — Council of Europe countries
GRANTS-IN-AID — Great Britain
GRANTS-IN-AID — United States
GRANTS-IN-AID — Wales
GRAPHIC METHODS
GRAUE PANTHER
GREAT BITAIN. MI5 — History — 20th century
GREAT BRITAIN, Judicial Committee — History
GREAT BRITAIN. British North America Act, 1867
GREAT BRITAIN. Building Societies Bill
GREAT BRITAIN. Companies Act 1980
GREAT BRITAIN. Companies Act 1981
GREAT BRITAIN. Companies Act 1985
GREAT BRITAIN. Consumer Credit Act 1974
GREAT BRITAIN. Data Protection Act
GREAT BRITAIN. Data Protection Act 1984
GREAT BRITAIN. Financial Services Act 1986
GREAT BRITAIN. Financial Services Act, 1986
GREAT BRITAIN. Housing Act 1985
GREAT BRITAIN. Housing (Homeless Persons) Act 1977
GREAT BRITAIN. Industry Act 1972
GREAT BRITAIN. National Insurance (Industrial Injuries) Act 1946
GREAT BRITAIN. Police and Criminal Evidence Act, 1984
GREAT BRITAIN. Police and Criminal Evidence Act 1984
GREAT BRITAIN. Prevention of Terrorism (Temporary Provisions) Act 1974
GREAT BRITAIN. Prevention of Terrorism (Temporary Provisions) Act 1976
GREAT BRITAIN. Public Health Act 1936
GREAT BRITAIN. Public Order Act 1936

GREAT BRITAIN. Public Order Act, 1986
GREAT BRITAIN. Public Order Act 1986
GREAT BRITAIN. Public Utilities Street Works Act 1950
GREAT BRITAIN. Registered Homes Act 1984
GREAT BRITAIN. Rehabilitation of Offenders Act, 1974
GREAT BRITAIN. Transport Act 1978
GREAT BRITAIN. Transport Act 1985
GREAT BRITAIN. Wages Act 1986
GREAT BRITAIN
GREAT BRITAIN — Appropriations and expenditures
GREAT BRITAIN — Appropriations and expentitures
GREAT BRITAIN — Armed forces — Appropriations and expenditures
GREAT BRITAIN — Armed Forces — Colonial forces — History
GREAT BRITAIN — Armed Forces — History — World War, 1939-1945
GREAT BRITAIN — Bibliography
GREAT BRITAIN — Biography
GREAT BRITAIN — Census, 1981
GREAT BRITAIN — Census, 1981 — Bibliography
GREAT BRITAIN — Church history — Sources
GREAT BRITAIN — Church history — 19th century
GREAT BRITAIN — Church history — 20th century
GREAT BRITAIN — Church history — 19th century
GREAT BRITAIN — Civil defence — Bibliography
GREAT BRITAIN — Civil defense — Bibliography
GREAT BRITAIN — Civil defense — History — 20th century — Bibliography
GREAT BRITAIN — Civilization — 18th century
GREAT BRITAIN — Climate
GREAT BRITAIN — Colonies
GREAT BRITAIN — Colonies — Administration — History
GREAT BRITAIN — Colonies — Constitutional History
GREAT BRITAIN — Colonies — Economic conditions
GREAT BRITAIN — Colonies — History
GREAT BRITAIN — Colonies — History — 20th century
GREAT BRITAIN — Colonies — Social policy
GREAT BRITAIN — Colonies — Africa
GREAT BRITAIN — Colonies — Africa — Administration
GREAT BRITAIN — Colonies — Asia
GREAT BRITAIN — Colonies — India — Administration — Collected works
GREAT BRITAIN — Commerce
GREAT BRITAIN — Commerce — Near East
GREAT BRITAIN — Commerce — Statistics
GREAT BRITAIN — Commerce — Canada
GREAT BRITAIN — Commerce — Chile — History — 19th century
GREAT BRITAIN — Commerce — China — History — 19th century
GREAT BRITAIN — Commerce — European Economic Community countries
GREAT BRITAIN — Commerce — Poland
GREAT BRITAIN — Commerce — Romania
GREAT BRITAIN — Constitution
GREAT BRITAIN — Constitutional history
GREAT BRITAIN — Constitutional law
GREAT BRITAIN — Defenses
GREAT BRITAIN — Defenses — Appropriations and expenditures
GREAT BRITAIN — Defenses — Public opinion
GREAT BRITAIN — Description and travel — 1971-

GREAT BRITAIN — Diplomatic and consular service — History
GREAT BRITAIN — Economic condition — 1945
GREAT BRITAIN — Economic conditions — Addresses, Essays, Lectures
GREAT BRITAIN — Economic conditions — Regional disparities
GREAT BRITAIN — Economic conditions — Sources
GREAT BRITAIN — Economic conditions — Statistics
GREAT BRITAIN — Economic conditions — 1760-1860
GREAT BRITAIN — Economic conditions — 19th century
GREAT BRITAIN — Economic conditions — 20th century
GREAT BRITAIN — Economic conditions — 1918-1945
GREAT BRITAIN — Economic conditions — 1945-
GREAT BRITAIN — Economic conditions — 1945- — Addresses, essays, lectures
GREAT BRITAIN — Economic conditions — 1945- — Econometric models
GREAT BRITAIN — Economic conditions — 1945- — Regional disparities
GREAT BRITAIN — Economic conditions — 1979-
GREAT BRITAIN — Economic history
GREAT BRITAIN — Economic policy
GREAT BRITAIN — Economic policy — 1918-1945
GREAT BRITAIN — Economic policy — 1945-
GREAT BRITAIN — Economic policy — 1945- — Forcasting
GREAT BRITAIN — Economic policy — 1945- — Forecasting
GREAT BRITAIN — Economic policy — 1945- — Simulation methods
GREAT BRITAIN — Economic policy — 1970-
GREAT BRITAIN — Economic policy — 1979-
GREAT BRITAIN — Emigration and Immigration
GREAT BRITAIN — Emigration and immigration
GREAT BRITAIN — Emigration and Immigration
GREAT BRITAIN — Emigration and immigration
GREAT BRITAIN — Emigration and immigration — Bibliography
GREAT BRITAIN — Emigration and immigration — Government policy
GREAT BRITAIN — Emigration and immigration — History — 18th century
GREAT BRITAIN — Emigration and immigration — History — 19th century
GREAT BRITAIN — Emigration and immigration — Law and legislation
GREAT BRITAIN — Executive departments — Management
GREAT BRITAIN — Foreign economic relations
GREAT BRITAIN — Foreign economic relations — Australia
GREAT BRITAIN — Foreign economic relations — Nigeria — History
GREAT BRITAIN — Foreign economic relations — Poland
GREAT BRITAIN — Foreign economic relations — South Africa
GREAT BRITAIN — Foreign economic relations — Sudan
GREAT BRITAIN — Foreign population — Photograph collections
GREAT BRITAIN — Foreign relations — Sources
GREAT BRITAIN — Foreign relations — Sources — Germany
GREAT BRITAIN — Foreign relations — 1689-1702

GREAT BRITAIN — Foreign relations — 18th century
GREAT BRITAIN — Foreign relations — 1702-1714
GREAT BRITAIN — Foreign relations — 1714-1727
GREAT BRITAIN — Foreign relations — 1714-1927
GREAT BRITAIN — Foreign relations — 19th century
GREAT BRITAIN — Foreign relations — 19th century — Dictionaries
GREAT BRITAIN — Foreign relations — 1837-1901
GREAT BRITAIN — Foreign relations — 20th century
GREAT BRITAIN — Foreign relations — 20th century — Dictionaries
GREAT BRITAIN — Foreign relations — 1901-1910
GREAT BRITAIN — Foreign relations — 1901-1936
GREAT BRITAIN — Foreign relations — 1910-1936
GREAT BRITAIN — Foreign relations — 1936-1945
GREAT BRITAIN — Foreign relations — 1945-
GREAT BRITAIN — Foreign relations — Africa, Southern
GREAT BRITAIN — Foreign relations — Argentina
GREAT BRITAIN — Foreign relations — Asia — History
GREAT BRITAIN — Foreign relations — Australia
GREAT BRITAIN — Foreign relations — Austria
GREAT BRITAIN — Foreign relations — Canada
GREAT BRITAIN — Foreign relations — China
GREAT BRITAIN — Foreign relations — Europe
GREAT BRITAIN — Foreign relations — France
GREAT BRITAIN — Foreign relations — Germany
GREAT BRITAIN — Foreign relations — Hong Kong
GREAT BRITAIN — Foreign relations — Iceland
GREAT BRITAIN — Foreign relations — India
GREAT BRITAIN — Foreign relations — Iraq
GREAT BRITAIN — Foreign relations — Ireland
GREAT BRITAIN — Foreign relations — Israel
GREAT BRITAIN — Foreign relations — Japan
GREAT BRITAIN — Foreign relations — Near East
GREAT BRITAIN — Foreign relations — Palestine
GREAT BRITAIN — Foreign relations — Poland
GREAT BRITAIN — Foreign relations — Prussia (Germany)
GREAT BRITAIN — Foreign relations — Scandinavia
GREAT BRITAIN — Foreign relations — South Asia
GREAT BRITAIN — Foreign relations — Soviet Union
GREAT BRITAIN — Foreign relations — Spain
GREAT BRITAIN — Foreign relations — Turkey
GREAT BRITAIN — Foreign relations — United States
GREAT BRITAIN — Foreign relations — United States — History
GREAT BRITAIN — Foreign relations — Vatican City
GREAT BRITAIN — Forest policy

GREAT BRITAIN — Full employment policies
GREAT BRITAIN — Full employment policies — History — 20th century
GREAT BRITAIN — Full employment policy
GREAT BRITAIN — Gazetteers
GREAT BRITAIN — Government publications
GREAT BRITAIN — Historical geography
GREAT BRITAIN — Historiography
GREAT BRITAIN — History — Chronology — Tables
GREAT BRITAIN — History — Civil War, 1642-1649
GREAT BRITAIN — History — Handbooks, manuals, etc
GREAT BRITAIN — History — Anglo-Saxon period, 449-1066
GREAT BRITAIN — History — Anglo-Saxon period, 449-1066 — Addresses, essays, lectures
GREAT BRITAIN — History — To 1066
GREAT BRITAIN — History — Norman period, 1066-1154
GREAT BRITAIN — History — Medieval period, 1066-1485
GREAT BRITAIN — History — Medieval period, 1066-1485 — Addresses, essays, lectures
GREAT BRITAIN — History — Medieval period, 1066-1485 — Sources — Bibliography
GREAT BRITAIN — History — 1154-1399
GREAT BRITAIN — History — Henry III, 1216-1272 — Sources
GREAT BRITAIN — History — 14th century
GREAT BRITAIN — History — Henry IV, 1399-1413
GREAT BRITAIN — History — 15th century
GREAT BRITAIN — History — Edward IV, 1461-1483
GREAT BRITAIN — History — Henry VII, 1485-1509
GREAT BRITAIN — History — Tudors, 1485-1603
GREAT BRITAIN — History — Elizabeth, 1558-1603
GREAT BRITAIN — History — James I, 1603-1625
GREAT BRITAIN — History — Stuarts, 1603-1714
GREAT BRITAIN — History — Stuarts, 1603-1714 — Sources
GREAT BRITAIN — History — Civil War, 1642-1649
GREAT BRITAIN — History — Charles II, 1660-1685
GREAT BRITAIN — History — 1689-1714 — Sources
GREAT BRITAIN — History — 18th century
GREAT BRITAIN — History — George I-II, 1714-1760
GREAT BRITAIN — History — 1714-1837
GREAT BRITAIN — History — 1789-1820
GREAT BRITAIN — History — 1800-1857
GREAT BRITAIN — History — 19th century
GREAT BRITAIN — History — 1837-1901 — Historiography
GREAT BRITAIN — History — 20th century
GREAT BRITAIN — History — 1901-1910
GREAT BRITAIN — History — George V, 1910-1936
GREAT BRITAIN — History — George VI, 1936-1952
GREAT BRITAIN — History — Elizabeth II, 1952-
GREAT BRITAIN — History, Military — Stuarts, 1603-1714
GREAT BRITAIN — History, Military — 20th century
GREAT BRITAIN — Industries
GREAT BRITAIN — Industries — Addresses, essays, lectures
GREAT BRITAIN — Industries — Classification
GREAT BRITAIN — Industries — Energy consumption
GREAT BRITAIN — Industries — Environmental aspects
GREAT BRITAIN — Industries — History
GREAT BRITAIN — Industries — History — Maps
GREAT BRITAIN — Industries — Location
GREAT BRITAIN — Industries — Power supply
GREAT BRITAIN — Industries — Statistics
GREAT BRITAIN — Industries — Technological innovations
GREAT BRITAIN — Intellectual life — 18th century
GREAT BRITAIN — Intellectual life — 19th century
GREAT BRITAIN — Kings and rulers
GREAT BRITAIN — Kings and rulers — Biography
GREAT BRITAIN — Kings and rulers — Succession
GREAT BRITAIN — Manufacturers — Accounting
GREAT BRITAIN — Manufacturers — Employees
GREAT BRITAIN — Manufactures — Statistics
GREAT BRITAIN — Military policy
GREAT BRITAIN — Military policy — Bibliography
GREAT BRITAIN — Military relations — Japan
GREAT BRITAIN — Military relations — United States
GREAT BRITAIN — National Health Service
GREAT BRITAIN — National Health Service — Bibliography
GREAT BRITAIN — National health service — Employees
GREAT BRITAIN — National Health Service — Employees
GREAT BRITAIN — National Health Service — Employees — Supply and demand
GREAT BRITAIN — National Health Service — Equipment and supplies
GREAT BRITAIN — National Health Service — Officials and employees
GREAT BRITAIN — National Health Service — Procurement
GREAT BRITAIN — National security
GREAT BRITAIN — Nobility — Biography
GREAT BRITAIN — Nobility — History
GREAT BRITAIN — Occupations
GREAT BRITAIN — Officials and employees
GREAT BRITAIN — Officials and employees — Health and hygiene
GREAT BRITAIN — Officials and employees — Statistics
GREAT BRITAIN — Officials and employees — Training of — Evaluation
GREAT BRITAIN — Parliament — Elections, 1983
GREAT BRITAIN — Political events — 1910-1936
GREAT BRITAIN — Politics and goverment — 1945-
GREAT BRITAIN — Politics and government
GREAT BRITAIN — Politics and government — Addresses, essays, lectures
GREAT BRITAIN — Politics and government — Bibliography
GREAT BRITAIN — Politics and government — 449-1066
GREAT BRITAIN — Politics and government — 1066-1154
GREAT BRITAIN — Politics and government — 1066-1485
GREAT BRITAIN — Politics and government — 1399-1485
GREAT BRITAIN — Politics and government — 1485-1509
GREAT BRITAIN — Politics and government — 1558-1603
GREAT BRITAIN — Politics and government — 1603-1649
GREAT BRITAIN — Politics and government — 1603-1714
GREAT BRITAIN — Politics and government — 1625-1649
GREAT BRITAIN — Politics and government — 1642-1649
GREAT BRITAIN — Politics and government — 1642-1660
GREAT BRITAIN — Politics and government — 1660-1668
GREAT BRITAIN — Politics and government — 1660-1688
GREAT BRITAIN — Politics and government — Revolution of 1688
GREAT BRITAIN — Politics and government — 1689-1702
GREAT BRITAIN — Politics and government — 1702-1714
GREAT BRITAIN — Politics and government — 1714-1727
GREAT BRITAIN — Politics and government — 1714-1760
GREAT BRITAIN — Politics and government — 1714-1820
GREAT BRITAIN — Politics and government — 1760-1820
GREAT BRITAIN — Politics and government — 1800-1837
GREAT BRITAIN — Politics and government — 19th century
GREAT BRITAIN — Politics and government — 1837-1901
GREAT BRITAIN — Politics and government — 1894-1895
GREAT BRITAIN — Politics and government — 20th century
GREAT BRITAIN — Politics and government — 1910-1936
GREAT BRITAIN — Politics and government — 1936-1945
GREAT BRITAIN — Politics and government — 1945-
GREAT BRITAIN — Politics and Government — 1945-
GREAT BRITAIN — Politics and government — 1945-
GREAT BRITAIN — Politics and government — 1964-1979
GREAT BRITAIN — Politics and government — 1964-
GREAT BRITAIN — Politics and government — 1979-
GREAT BRITAIN — Politics and Government — 1979-
GREAT BRITAIN — Politics and government — 1979-
GREAT BRITAIN — Politics and government — 1979- — Addresses, essays, lectures
GREAT BRITAIN — Politics and government — 1837-1901
GREAT BRITAIN — Popular culture — History — 20th century
GREAT BRITAIN — Population
GREAT BRITAIN — Population — Forecasting
GREAT BRITAIN — Public lands — Management
GREAT BRITAIN — Race relations
GREAT BRITAIN — Race relations — Bibliography
GREAT BRITAIN — Race relations — History — 20th century
GREAT BRITAIN — Relations — Soviet Union
GREAT BRITAIN — Religion — Statistical services

GREAT BRITAIN — Religious life and customs — History — 19th century
GREAT BRITAIN — Road maps
GREAT BRITAIN — Roads — Bibliography
GREAT BRITAIN — Royal household — Finance
GREAT BRITAIN — Royal Household — Finance
GREAT BRITAIN — Rural conditions
GREAT BRITAIN — Rural conditions — Sources
GREAT BRITAIN — Social conditions
GREAT BRITAIN — Social conditions — Sources
GREAT BRITAIN — Social conditions — 16th century
GREAT BRITAIN — Social conditions — 18th century
GREAT BRITAIN — Social conditions — 19th century
GREAT BRITAIN — Social conditions — 20th century
GREAT BRITAIN — Social conditions — 1945-
GREAT BRITAIN — Social life and customs
GREAT BRITAIN — Social life and customs — 19th century — Bibliography
GREAT BRITAIN — Social life and customs — 20th century
GREAT BRITAIN — Social life and customs — 20th century — Bibliography
GREAT BRITAIN — Social life and customs — 1945-
GREAT BRITAIN — Social policy
GREAT BRITAIN — Social policy — Sources
GREAT BRITAIN — Statistical services
GREAT BRITAIN — Statistics
GREAT BRITAIN — Statistics, Medical
GREAT BRITAIN — Statistics, Vital
GREAT BRITAIN. Admiralty. Compass Department
GREAT BRITAIN. Army
GREAT BRITAIN. Army — Biography
GREAT BRITAIN. Army — History — Military life
GREAT BRITAIN. Army. Cavalry Brigade, 3rd — History
GREAT BRITAIN. Army. Home Guard — History — Sources
GREAT BRITAIN. Army. Special Operations Executive — History
GREAT BRITAIN. Board of Trade
GREAT BRITAIN. Commission for Racial Equality
GREAT BRITAIN. Committee of Enforcement Powers of Revenue Departments
GREAT BRITAIN. Department of Education and Science. Inspectorate of Schools — History
GREAT BRITAIN. Department of Health and Social Security
GREAT BRITAIN. Department of Health and Social Security — Bibliography
GREAT BRITAIN. Department of Health and Social Security — Management
GREAT BRITAIN. Department of Health and Social Security. Library
GREAT BRITAIN. Department of Health and Social Security. Social Work Service. Development Group
GREAT BRITAIN. Department of the Director of Public Prosecutions
GREAT BRITAIN. Department of the Environment. Streamlining the cities
GREAT BRITAIN. Department of Trade and Industry
GREAT BRITAIN. Department of Trade and Industry. Radio Regulatory Division
GREAT BRITAIN. Foreign and Commonwealth Office
GREAT BRITAIN. Foreign Office — History
GREAT BRITAIN. Forensic Science Service

GREAT BRITAIN. General Register Office — History
GREAT BRITAIN. Government Communications Headquarters
GREAT BRITAIN. Her Majesty's Stationery Office — Officials and employees
GREAT BRITAIN. Home Office. Review of the Public Order Act 1936 and related legislation
GREAT BRITAIN. Medicines Commission
GREAT BRITAIN. National Health Service
GREAT BRITAIN. National Rivers Authority
GREAT BRITAIN. Office of Population Censuses and Surveys. Social Survey Division
GREAT BRITAIN. Parliament
GREAT BRITAIN. Parliament — Committees
GREAT BRITAIN. Parliament — Elections
GREAT BRITAIN. Parliament — Elections — History — Chronology
GREAT BRITAIN. Parliament — Elections — Statistics
GREAT BRITAIN. Parliament — Elections, 1970
GREAT BRITAIN. Parliament — Elections, 1974 (February)
GREAT BRITAIN. Parliament — Elections, 1983
GREAT BRITAIN. Parliament — Elections, 1987
GREAT BRITAIN. Parliament — Reform
GREAT BRITAIN. Parliament. House of Commons. Abolition of Domestic Rates etc. [Scotland] Bill 1986-87
GREAT BRITAIN. Parliament. House of Commons. Abortion (Amendment) Bill 1979-80
GREAT BRITAIN. Parliament. House of Commons. Agricultural Marketing Bill 1982-83
GREAT BRITAIN. Parliament. House of Commons. Airports Bill 1985-86
GREAT BRITAIN. Parliament. House of Commons. Broadcasting Bill 1979-80
GREAT BRITAIN. Parliament. House of Commons. Chronically Sick and Disabled Persons (Amendment) Bill 1983-84
GREAT BRITAIN. Parliament. House of Commons. Criminal Justice Bill 1981-82
GREAT BRITAIN. Parliament. House of Commons. Criminal Justice Bill 1986-87
GREAT BRITAIN. Parliament. House of Commons. Data Protection Bill 1983-84
GREAT BRITAIN. Parliament. House of Commons. Disabled Persons (Services, Consultation and Representation) Bill 1985-86
GREAT BRITAIN. Parliament. House of Commons. Education (Amendment) Bill 1985-86
GREAT BRITAIN. Parliament. House of Commons. Education Bill 1980-81
GREAT BRITAIN. Parliament. House of Commons. Education (Corporal Punishment) Bill 1984-85
GREAT BRITAIN. Parliament. House of Commons. Education (Fees and Awards) Bill 1982-83
GREAT BRITAIN. Parliament. House of Commons. Education (Grants and Awards) Bill 1983-84
GREAT BRITAIN. Parliament. House of Commons. Education (Scotland) Bill 1980-81
GREAT BRITAIN. Parliament. House of Commons. Employment Bill 1979-80
GREAT BRITAIN. Parliament. House of Commons. Employment Bill 1981-82
GREAT BRITAIN. Parliament. House of Commons. European Communities (Amendment) Bill 1985-86
GREAT BRITAIN. Parliament. House of Commons. Freedom of Information Bill 1980-81

GREAT BRITAIN. Parliament. House of Commons. Gas Bill 1985-86
GREAT BRITAIN. Parliament. House of Commons. Health and Social Security Bill 1983-84
GREAT BRITAIN. Parliament. House of Commons. Health Services Bill 1979-80
GREAT BRITAIN. Parliament. House of Commons. Housing and Building Control Bill 1983-84
GREAT BRITAIN. Parliament. House of Commons. Housing and Planning Bill 1985-86
GREAT BRITAIN. Parliament. House of Commons. Housing Defects Bill 1983-84
GREAT BRITAIN. Parliament. House of Commons. Iron and Steel Bill 1980-81
GREAT BRITAIN. Parliament. House of Commons. Landlord and Tenant (No.2) Bill 1986-87
GREAT BRITAIN. Parliament. House of Commons. Local Government Bill 1984-85
GREAT BRITAIN. Parliament. House of Commons. Local Government Finance Bill 1981-82
GREAT BRITAIN. Parliament. House of Commons. Local Government Finance (No.2) Bill 1981-82
GREAT BRITAIN. Parliament. House of Commons. Local Government (Interim Provisions) Bill 1983-84
GREAT BRITAIN. Parliament. House of Commons. London Regional Transport Bill 1983-84
GREAT BRITAIN. Parliament. House of Commons. National Health Service (Amendment) Bill 1985-86
GREAT BRITAIN. Parliament. House of Commons. Oil and Gas (Enterprise) Bill 1981-82
GREAT BRITAIN. Parliament. House of Commons. Oil Taxation Bill 1983-84
GREAT BRITAIN. Parliament. House of Commons. Police and Criminal Evidence Bill 1982-83
GREAT BRITAIN. Parliament. House of Commons. Police and Criminal Evidence Bill 1983-84
GREAT BRITAIN. Parliament. House of Commons. Ports (Financial Assistance) Bill 1980-81
GREAT BRITAIN. Parliament. House of Commons. Prevention of Terrorism Bill 1983-84
GREAT BRITAIN. Parliament. House of Commons. Public Order Bill 1985-86
GREAT BRITAIN. Parliament. House of Commons. Rates Bill 1983-84
GREAT BRITAIN. Parliament. House of Commons. Rating and Valuation (Amendment) (Scotland) Bill 1983-84
GREAT BRITAIN. Parliament. House of Commons. Representation of the People Bill 1980-81
GREAT BRITAIN. Parliament. House of Commons. Shops Bill 1980-81
GREAT BRITAIN. Parliament. House of Commons. Shops Bill 1985-86
GREAT BRITAIN. Parliament. House of Commons. Social Security (Age of Retirement) Bill 1983-84
GREAT BRITAIN. Parliament. House of Commons. Social Security and Housing Benefits Bill 1982-83
GREAT BRITAIN. Parliament. House of Commons. Social Security Bill 1979-80 — Bibliography
GREAT BRITAIN. Parliament. House of Commons. Social Security Bill 1980-81
GREAT BRITAIN. Parliament. House of Commons. Social Security Bill 1984-85
GREAT BRITAIN. Parliament. House of Commons. Social Security Bill 1985-86
GREAT BRITAIN. Parliament. House of Commons. Social Security (Contributions) Bill 1980-81

GREAT BRITAIN. Parliament. House of Commons. Social Security (No.2) Bill 1979-80
GREAT BRITAIN. Parliament. House of Commons. Teachers' Pay and Conditions Bill 1986-87
GREAT BRITAIN. Parliament. House of Commons. Telecommunications Bill 1982-83
GREAT BRITAIN. Parliament. House of Commons. Telecommunications Bill 1983-84
GREAT BRITAIN. Parliament. House of Commons. Trade Union Bill 1983-84
GREAT BRITAIN. Parliament. House of Commons. Transport Bill 1980-81
GREAT BRITAIN. Parliament. House of Commons. Transport Bill 1981-82
GREAT BRITAIN. Parliament. House of Commons. Transport Bill 1982-83
GREAT BRITAIN. Parliament. House of Commons. Transport Bill 1984-85
GREAT BRITAIN. Parliament. House of Commons. Wages Bill 1985-86
GREAT BRITAIN. Parliament. House of Commons
GREAT BRITAIN. Parliament. House of Commons — Biography
GREAT BRITAIN. Parliament. House of Commons — Election districts
GREAT BRITAIN. Parliament. House of Commons — Elections — History — 17th ceentury
GREAT BRITAIN. Parliament. House of Commons — History
GREAT BRITAIN. Parliament. House of Commons — History — Bibliography
GREAT BRITAIN. Parliament. House of Commons — Qualifications
GREAT BRITAIN. Parliament. House of Commons — Salaries, pensions, etc.
GREAT BRITAIN. Parliament. House of Commons. Committee on Welsh Affairs — History
GREAT BRITAIN. Parliament. House of Lords. Agricultural Holdings Bill 1983-84
GREAT BRITAIN. Parliament. House of Lords. Contempt of Court Bill 1980-1981
GREAT BRITAIN. Parliament. House of Lords. Data Protection Bill 1982-83
GREAT BRITAIN. Parliament. House of Lords. Education Bill 1985-86
GREAT BRITAIN. Parliament. House of Lords. Matrimonial and Family Proceedings Bill 1983-84
GREAT BRITAIN. Parliament. House of Lords. Mental Health (Amendment) (Scotland) Bill 1982-83
GREAT BRITAIN. Parliament. House of Lords. Mobile Homes Bill 1982-83
GREAT BRITAIN. Parliament. House of Lords. National Heritage Bill 1982-83
GREAT BRITAIN. Parliament. House of Lords. Sex Discrimination Bill 1985-86
GREAT BRITAIN. Parliament. House of Lords. Select Committee on the European Communities
GREAT BRITAIN. Planning Inspectorate
GREAT BRITAIN. Resource Allocation Working Party
GREAT BRITAIN. Royal Air Force
GREAT BRITAIN. Royal Navy — Biography
GREAT BRITAIN. Royal Navy — History
GREAT BRITAIN. Royal Navy — History — 19th century
GREAT BRITAIN. Royal Navy — History — 20th century
GREAT BRITAIN. Royal Navy — Societies, etc
GREAT BRITAIN. Special Operations Executive. Special Training School 103 (Whitby, Ont.)
GREAT BRITAIN. Standing Advisory Committee on Trunk Road Assessment. Urban road appraisal
GREAT BRITAIN. Treasury — History — 20th century
GREAT BRITAIN — Economic conditions
GREAT BRITAIN — 1970-
GREAT BRITIAN — Law and legislation
GREAT BRITIAN — Race relations
GREAT BRITIAN. Parliament. House of Lords. Dentists Bill 1982-83
GREAT POWERS
GREAT WESTERN RAILWAY — History
GREAT WESTERN RAILWAY (GREAT BRITAIN) — History
GREATER LONDON ARTS
GREATER LONDON COUNCIL
GREATER LONDON COUNCIL — History
GREECE — Census 1981
GREECE — Census, 1981
GREECE — Economic conditions — 1974-
GREECE — Foreign relations — Turkey
GREECE — History — Occupation, 1941-1944
GREECE — Politics and government — To 146 B.C
GREECE — Politics and government — 19th century
GREECE — Population — Statistics
GREECE — Rural conditions
GREECE — Social life and customs
GREEK AMERICANS — Politics and government
GREEK DRAMA (TRAGEDY) — History and criticism
GREEK LANGUAGE, MODERN — Dictionaries — English
GREEN PARTY
GREEN REVOLUTION — India
GREENBELTS
GREENBELTS — England — London
GREENLAND — — Population — Statistics
GREENLAND — Defenses
GREENLAND — Foreign relations
GREENLAND — Statistics, Vital
GREENLAND EMIGRATION AND IMMIGRATION — Statistics
GREENWICH (LONDON, ENGLAND) — City planning
GREG (Family)
GREGORY, Sir WILLIAM
GRENADA — Economic conditions
GRENADA — Economic policy
GRENADA — Foreign relations — United States
GRENADA — Politics and government — 1974-
GRENOBLE (FRANCE) — Social conditions
GREW, JOSEPH C
GRIFFITHS, W. J.
GRIMES, SARA
GRIMM, ROBERT
GROCERY TRADE — Latin America — History — 18th century
GROCERY TRADE — Latin America — History — 19th century
GRONINGEN (NETHERLANDS: PROVINCE) — Economic policy
GRØNLAND — Statistics, Vital
GROSS NATIONAL PRODUCT
GROSS NATIONAL PRODUCT — Canada
GROSS NATIONAL PRODUCT — European Economic Community countries — Statistics
GROSS NATIONAL PRODUCT — Gambia — Statistics
GROSS NATIONAL PRODUCT — Kiribati — Statistics
GROSS NATIONAL PRODUCT — Tuvalu — Statistics
GROSSMAN, ALLAN
GROTIUS, HUGO — Congresses
GROUP IDENTITY
GROUP PSYCHOANALYSIS
GROUP RELATIONS TRAINING
GRUNDTVIG, N. F. S.
GRÜNEN, DIE
GRÜNEN, DIE — Economic policy
GRÜNEN, DIE
GUADELOUPE — Economic conditions
GUADELOUPE — Economic conditions — Statistics
GUADELOUPE — Economic policy
GUADELOUPE — Politics and government
GUADELOUPE — Social conditions
GUADELOUPE — Social policy
GUARANTEED ANNUAL INCOME — Great Britain
GUARANTEED ANNUAL INCOME — United States
GUARDIAN AND WARD — Australia
GUARDIAN AND WARD — England
GUATEMALA — Foreign relations — United States
GUATEMALA — History — To 1821
GUATEMALA — History — Revolution, 1954
GUATEMALA — Politics and government — 1945-
GUATEMALA — Social conditions
GUAYAQUIL (ECUADOR) — Social conditions
GUERILLAS — Argentina — History — 20th century
GUERRILLA WARFARE — United States — History — 20th century — Bibliography
GUERRILLAS — Central America
GUERRILLAS — Nicaragua — History — 20th century
GUERRILLAS — Uruguay
GUILD SOCIALISM
GUILDFORD (SURREY) — History
GUILDS — Europe — History
GUINEA — Bibliography
GUINEA — History — Dictionaries
GUINEA-BISSAU — Bibliography
GUINEA BISSAU — Economic conditions — To 1974
GUINEA BISSAU — Economic conditions — 1974-
GUINEA-BISSAU — Economic policy
GUINEA-BISSAU — Foreign relations — Portugal
GUINEA-BISSAU — History — Dictionaries
GUINEA-BISSAU — Nationalism
GUINEA-BISSAU — Politics and government
GUINEA BISSAU — Politics and government — To 1974
GUINEA BISSAU — Politics and government — 1974-
GUINEA BISSAU — Social conditions
GUINEA-BISSAU — Social policy
GUINNESS GROUP — History
GUISE, HOUSE OF
GUJARAT (INDIA) — Population — Statistics
GUJARAT (INDIA) — Rural conditions
GULF COOPERATION COUNCIL
GULF STATES — Relations — Iraq
GUN CONTROL — United States
GURWITSCH, ARON — Correspondence
GUYANA — Economic conditions — 1966-
GUYANA — Economic policy
GUYANA — Politics and government — 1966-
GUYANA — Population
GUYANA — Population — Statistics
GUYANA — Social policy
GUYANA — Statistics, Vital
GWYNEDD — Economic policy
GYNECOLOGIST AND PATIENT
GYNECOLOGISTS — United States — Interviews
GYNECOLOGY — Decision making
GYNECOLOGY, OPERATIVE — Decision making
GYPSIES — Bibliography
GYPSIES — History
GYPSIES — Information services
HABERMAS, JÜRGEN. Theorie des kommunikativen Handelns
HABERMAS, JÜRGEN

HABERMAS, JÜRGEN — Contributions in science
HACIENDAS — Mexico — History — Congresses
HACIENDAS — Peru — Cajamarca — History
HACKNEY (LONDON, ENGLAND) — City planning
HACKNEY (LONDON, ENGLAND) — Population
HACKNEY (LONDON, ENGLAND) — Social policy
HAGUE. Permanent Court of International Justice
HAILE SELASSIE I, Emperor of Ethiopia
HAIN, PETER
HAIRDRESSING — Great Britain
HAITI — Economic conditions — 1971 — Statistics
HAITI — Economic conditions — 1971-
HAITI — Economic policy
HAITI — History — Revolution, 1791-1804
HAITI — Politics and government
HAITI — Population — Statistics
HAITI — Population — Statistics — Evaluation
HAITI — Statistics, Vital
HAITIANS — Employment — Dominican Republic
HALFWAY HOUSES
HALL, EMMETT M.
HAMLET
HAMMER, ARMAND
HAMMERSMITH AND FULHAM (LONDON, ENGLAND) — Economic conditions
HAMMERSMITH (LONDON) — Economic policy
HAMMERSMITH (LONDON : ENGLAND)
HANDICAPPED
HANDICAPPED — Care and treatment
HANDICAPPED — Education — European Economic Community countries
HANDICAPPED — Employment
HANDICAPPED — Employment — European Economic Community countries
HANDICAPPED — Employment — European Economic Community countries — Statistics
HANDICAPPED — Employment — Great Britain
HANDICAPPED — Government policy — Great Britain
HANDICAPPED — Government policy — New Brunswick
HANDICAPPED — Housing — Denmark
HANDICAPPED — Legal status, laws, etc. — European Economic Community countries
HANDICAPPED — Legal status, laws, etc. — Great Britain
HANDICAPPED — Pensions — Denmark
HANDICAPPED — Services for — France — Nomenclature
HANDICAPPED — Taxation — Australia
HANDICAPPED — Training of — European Economic Community countries
HANDICAPPED — Australia — Legal status, laws, etc.
HANDICAPPED — Cyprus — Statistics
HANDICAPPED — England — Milton Keynes (Buckinghamshire)
HANDICAPPED — European Economic Community countries
HANDICAPPED — Great Britain — Transportation
HANDICAPPED — India — Dadra and Nagar Haveli — Statistics
HANDICAPPED CHILDREN — Education — European Economic Community countries
HANDICAPPED CHILDREN — Services for — Great Britain
HANDICRAFT — Taiwan
HANOVER, HOUSE OF
HANSA TOWNS

HANSA TOWNS — History
HAO (TUAMOTU ISLANDS) — Population — Statistics
HAOUZ (MOROCCO) — Economic conditions
HAPPINESS
HARBORS
HARBORS — Design and contruction
HARBORS — Management
HARBORS — Maps
HARBORS — Planning
HARBORS — Canada — Finance
HARBORS — Developing countries
HARBORS — France — Normandy
HARBORS — Great Britain — Finance — Law and legislation
HARD-CORE UNEMPLOYED — France
HARD-CORE UNEMPLOYED — United States
HARDINGE, HENRY HARDINGE, Viscount
HARE KRISHNAS — Psychology
HAREM
HARINGEY (LONDON, ENGLAND) — Industries
HARINGEY (LONDON, ENGLAND) — Population — Statistics
HARINGEY (LONDON, ENGLAND) — Social conditions
HARLAND AND WOLFF — Northern Ireland — Belfast — History
HARRIMAN, EDWARD HENRY
HARRIS, CHAUNCY DENNISON
HARROW (LONDON, ENGLAND) — Social conditions
HART, H. L. A.
HARVARD INSTITUTE FOR INTERNATIONAL DEVELOPMENT
HARVARD UNIVERSITY — Presidents — Biography
HASINA, SHEIKH
HASKALAH — Congresses
HAULTIN, PIERRE
HAUTES-PYRÉNÉES (FRANCE)
HAVEL, VÁCLAV
HAVERING (LONDON, ENGLAND) — History
HAWAII — Economic conditions
HAWAII — Economic conditions — 1959-
HAWAII — Kings and rulers — Religious aspects
HAWAII — Politics and government — 1959-
HAWAII — Religion
HAWAII — Social conditions
HAWAII — Social life and customs
HAWKS, ESTHER HILL
HAWKS NEST TUNNEL (W. VA.)
HAWLEY GROUP PLC
HAYEK, F. A.
HAZARDOUS SUBSTANCES — Accidents
HAZARDOUS SUBSTANCES — Packaging — Law and legislation — Great Britain
HAZARDOUS SUBSTANCES — Great Britain
HAZARDOUS WASTE SITES — Hygienic aspects — United States — Statistics
HAZARDOUS WASTE SITES — Location
HAZARDOUS WASTE SITES — Management
HAZARDOUS WASTES
HAZARDOUS WASTES — Organisation for Economic Co-operation and Development countries
HAZLETON (PA.) — Population
HAZLETON (PA.) — Social conditions
HEADS OF HOUSEHOLDS — England — Statistics
HEADS OF HOUSEHOLDS — England — London — Statistics
HEADS OF HOUSEHOLDS — France — Statistics
HEADS OF HOUSEHOLDS — Poland
HEADS OF STATE — Handbooks, manuals etc.
HEADS OF STATE — Health and hygiene
HEADS OF STATE — China — Biography

HEADS OF STATE — Cuba — Biography
HEADS OF STATE — Germany — Biography
HEADS OF STATE — Soviet Union — Biography
HEADS OF STATE — Soviet Union — Succession
HEALING — Thailand
HEALTH
HEALTH — Addresses, essays, lectures
HEALTH — Moral and ethical aspects
HEALTH — United States
HEALTH AND RACE — England
HEALTH AND SOCIAL SECURITY BILL 1983-84
HEALTH ATTITUDES
HEALTH ATTITUDES — Great Britain
HEALTH BEHAVIOR
HEALTH BEHAVIOR — Congresses
HEALTH EDUCATION — Political aspects — Great Britain
HEALTH EDUCATION — Europe
HEALTH EDUCATION — Wales
HEALTH FACILITIES — Albania
HEALTH FACILITIES — England
HEALTH FACILITIES — France — Nomenclature
HEALTH FACILITIES — Greenland
HEALTH FACILITIES — Namibia
HEALTH FACILITIES — South Africa
HEALTH FACILITIES — Sweden
HEALTH FACILITIES, PROPRIETARY — Great Britain — Surveys
HEALTH INSURANCE FOR AGED AND DISABLED, TITLE 18 — history
HEALTH MAINTENANCE ORGANIZATIONS — Great Britain
HEALTH MAINTENANCE ORGANIZATIONS — United States
HEALTH PLANNING — Africa
HEALTH PLANNING
HEALTH PLANNING — Africa
HEALTH PLANNING — Denmark
HEALTH PLANNING — Developing countries
HEALTH PLANNING — England
HEALTH PLANNING — Europe — Methodology
HEALTH PLANNING — Great Britain
HEALTH PLANNING — Nepal
HEALTH PLANNING — Wales
HEALTH POLICY
HEALTH POLICY — Congresses
HEALTH POLICY — economics — United States
HEALTH POLICY — history — Great Britain
HEALTH POLICY — trends — United States
HEALTH POLICY — trends — United States — congresses
HEALTH POLICY — United States
HEALTH RESORTS, WATERING PLACES, ETC. — Norway
HEALTH RESORTS, WATERING PLACES, ETC. — Soviet Union
HEALTH RISK ASSESSMENT — Congresses
HEALTH RISK ASSESSMENT — Government policy — United States — History
HEALTH SERVICES — economics — United States
HEALTH SERVICES — organization & administration
HEALTH SERVICES — Nepal
HEALTH SERVICES ADMINISTRATION
HEALTH SERVICES ADMINISTRATION — England — London
HEALTH SERVICES ADMINISTRATION — France
HEALTH SERVICES ADMINISTRATION — Great Britain
HEALTH SERVICES ADMINISTRATION — Great Britain — Case studies
HEALTH SERVICES ADMINISTRATION — Wales — Statistics

HEALTH SERVICES BILL 1979-80
HEALTH STATUS INDICATORS
HEALTH STATUS INDICATORS — Developing countries
HEALTH SURVEYS
HEALTH SURVEYS — Great Britain
HEARING AIDS
HEAT
HEBREW LANGUAGE
HEDGING (FINANCE)
HEGEL, GEORG WILHELM FRIEDRICH
HEGEL, GEORG WILHELM FRIEDRICH — Contributions in theory of knowledge
HEGEL, GEORG WILHELM FRIEDRICH — Influence
HEGEL, GEORG WILHELM FRIEDRICH — Metaphysics
HEIDEGGER, MARTIN
HEJAZ — History
HELCEL, ANTONI ZYGMUNT
HELMS, JESSE
HELSINKI CONSULTATIONS
HENDERSON, Sir NICHOLAS
HENDERSON (LA.) — Social conditions
HENDERSON (LA.) — Social life and customs
HENEQUEN INDUSTRY — Mexico — Yucatán — History
HENRY VIII, King of England
HENRY, Duke of Saxony and Bavaria
HERBERG, WILL
HEREDITY, HUMAN
HEREROS — Psychology
HEREROS — Social conditions
HERMENEUTICS
HEROES — Mexico
HEROIN HABIT
HEROIN HABIT — England, Northern
HEROIN HABIT — Great Britain
HEROINES — India
HERRIOT, EDOUARD
HERSHEY, LEWIS BLAINE
HESSE-KASSEL (GERMANY) — History
HEYDRICH, REINHARD — Biography
HEYWORTH OF OXTON, GEOFFREY HEYWORTH, Baron
HIERARCHIES — Fiji
HIGH SCHOOL GRADUATES — Employment — O.E.C.D. countries
HIGH SCHOOL STUDENTS — South Arica
HIGH SPEED GROUND TRANSPORTATION
HIGH TECHNOLOGY — Government policy — United States
HIGH TECHNOLOGY — Social aspects
HIGH TECHNOLOGY INDUSTRIES
HIGH TECHNOLOGY INDUSTRIES — Government ownership — Brazil
HIGH TECHNOLOGY INDUSTRIES — Government ownership — India
HIGH TECHNOLOGY INDUSTRIES — Government policy — Case studies
HIGH TECHNOLOGY INDUSTRIES — Government policy — Japan
HIGH TECHNOLOGY INDUSTRIES — Government policy — Pennsylvania
HIGH TECHNOLOGY INDUSTRIES — Government policy — United States
HIGH TECHNOLOGY INDUSTRIES — Germany (West)
HIGH TECHNOLOGY INDUSTRIES — United States
HIGH TECHNOLOGY INDUSTRIES — Wales — Wrexham Region (Denbighshire)
HIGHER EDUCATION AND STATE — England
HIGHER EDUCATION AND STATE — Europe
HIGHER EDUCATION AND STATE — Great Britain
HIGHER EDUCATION AND STATE — India
HIGHER EDUCATION AND STATE — United States

HIGHER EDUCATION OF WOMEN — Great Britain
HIGHLANDS (SCOTLAND) — Description and travel
HIGHLANDS (SCOTLAND) — Rural conditions
HIGHWAY DEPARTMENTS — Great Britain
HIGHWAY PLANNING — Great Britain
HIKUERU (TUAMOTU ISLANDS) — Population — Statistics
HILL FARMING — Philippines — Mindoro
HILLINGDON (LONDON, ENGLAND) — Social policy
HIMACHAL PRADESH (INDIA) — Statistics
HINDI LANGUAGE — Political aspects
HINDUISM — Congresses
HINDUISM — Great Britain — History
HINDUISM — Sri Lanka — Rituals
HIRSCHMAN, ALBERT O
HISPANIC AMERICANS — Economic conditions — Addresses, essays, lectures
HISPANIC AMERICANS — Employment — Addresses, essays, lectures
HISPANIC AMERICANS — History
HISPANIC AMERICANS — History — Bibliography
HISPANIC AMERICANS — Social conditions — Addresses, essays, lectures
HISTORIAL MATERIALISM
HISTORIANS — Canada
HISTORIANS — Canada — Biography
HISTORIANS — France
HISTORIANS — Poland — Biography
HISTORIANS — Soviet Union — Biography
HISTORIANS — United States — Biography
HISTORIC BUILDINGS — Law and legislation — Great Britain
HISTORIC BUILDINGS — Great Britain — Conservation and restoration
HISTORIC BUILDINGS — Scotland — Fife
HISTORIC BUILDINGS — Scotland — Tayside
HISTORIC BUILDINGS — United States — Conservation and restoration
HISTORIC BUILDINGS — United States — Maintenance and repair
HISTORIC SITES — Great Britain — Conservation and restoration
HISTORICAL LINGUISTICS — Congresses
HISTORICAL MATERIALISM
HISTORICAL RESEARCH
HISTORIOGRAPHY
HISTORIOGRAPHY — Data processing
HISTORIOGRAPHY — Dictionaries
HISTORIOGRAPHY — Dictionaries and encyclopedias
HISTORIOGRAPHY — Czechoslavakia
HISTORIOGRAPHY — France
HISTORIOGRAPHY — Great Britain — History
HISTORIOGRAPHY — Spain
HISTORY
HISTORY — Abstracts — Periodicals — Bibliography
HISTORY — Bibliography — Periodicals — Bibliography
HISTORY — Methodology
HISTORY — Philosophy
HISTORY — Philosophy — Addresses, essays, lectures
HISTORY — Statistical methods
HISTORY — Study and teaching
HISTORY — Study and teaching (Higher) — England — History — 19th century
HISTORY — Study and teaching (Secondary) — England — London
HISTORY, MODERN
HISTORY, MODERN — 20th century
HISTORY, MODERN — 1945-
HISTORY OF MEDICINE

HITIAA O TE RA (TAHITI : REGION) — Population — Statistics
HITLER, Adolf
HITLER, ADOLF
HITLER, ADOLF — Diaries — Forgeries
HITLER, ADOLF — Political and social views
HITLER, ADOLF — Views on foreign relations
HIVA OA (MARQUESAS ISLANDS) — Population — statistics
HIZB AL-BA'TH AL-'ARABĪ AL-ISHTIRĀKI (SYRIA)
HJØRRING (DENMARK) — Economic conditions
HMONG (ASIAN PEOPLE) — Thailand, Northern
HOBBES, THOMAS. Contributions in political science
HOBBES, THOMAS. Leviathan
HOBBES, THOMAS
HOBBES, THOMAS — Contributions in political science
HOBBES, THOMAS — Ethics
HOBBES, THOMAS — Political science
HOBHOUSE, EMILY — Correspondence
HOECHST (Firm) — History
HOELZ, MAX — Biography
HOFER, ANDREAS
HOFSTADTER, RICHARD
HOLCH, KNUD Ø.
HOLDEN, ISAAC
HOLIDAYS WITH PAY ACT, 1971
HOLISM
HOLLOWAY, EDWARD — Biography
HOLOCAUST (CHRISTIAN THEOLOGY)
HOLOCAUST, JEWISH (1939-1945)
HOLOCAUST, JEWISH (1939-1945) — Addresses, essays, lectures
HOLOCAUST, JEWISH (1939-1945) — Anniversaries, etc — Addresses, essays, lectures
HOLOCAUST, JEWISH (1939-1945) — Bibliography
HOLOCAUST, JEWISH (1939-1945) — Causes
HOLOCAUST, JEWISH (1939-1945) — Congresses
HOLOCAUST, JEWISH (1939-1945) — Maps
HOLOCAUST, JEWISH (1939-1945) — Moral and ethical aspects
HOLOCAUST, JEWISH (1939-1945) — Psychological aspects
HOLOCAUST, JEWISH (1939-1945) — Public opinion — Addresses, essays, lectures
HOLOCAUST, JEWISH (1939-1945) — France
HOLOCAUST, JEWISH (1939-1945) — Italy
HOLOCAUST (JEWISH THEOLOGY)
HOLY ROMAN EMPIRE — Kings and rulers — Biography
HOME AND SCHOOL — European Economic Community countries
HOME CARE SERVICES — Great Britain
HOME CARE SERVICES — Netherlands — Statistics
HOME ECONOMICS
HOME ECONOMICS — Bangladesh
HOME ECONOMICS — Bulgaria — Accounting — Statistics
HOME ECONOMICS — Finland — Accounting
HOME ECONOMICS — Hong Kong — Accounting — Statistics
HOME ECONOMICS — Nepal — Accounting — Statistics
HOME ECONOMICS — Netherlands — Accounting
HOME GUARD *See* Great Britain. Army. Home Guard
HOME LABOR — Germany — History
HOME LABOR — Great Britian
HOME OWNERSHIP — Government policy — Great Britain

HOME OWNERSHIP — Great Britain
HOME RULE (IRELAND)
HOME RULE (IRELAND) — History — Sources
HOMELANDS (SOUTH AFRICA)
HOMELANDS (SOUTH AFRICA) — Constitutional law
HOMELESS MEN — England — Gloucester (Gloucestershire)
HOMELESS PERSONS — Legal status, laws, etc. — Great Britain
HOMELESS PERSONS — Great Britain
HOMELESS WOMEN — England — Gloucester (Gloucestershire)
HOMELESS YOUTH — Great Britain
HOMELESSNESS — Government policy — Great Britain
HOMELESSNESS — Government policy — London metropolitan area
HOMELESSNESS — Law and legislation — Great Britain
HOMELESSNESS — England — London
HOMELESSNESS — Great Britain
HOMELESSNESS — Great Britain — Government policy
HOMELESSNESS — London
HOMELESSNESS — New York (State) — History — 20th century
HOMELESSNESS — Scotland
HOMELESSNESS — United States
HOMESITES — Government policy — Great Britain
HOMICIDE — Great Britain — Statistics
HOMICIDE — Kentucky — History
HOMICIDE — Tennesee — History
HOMOSEXUALITY
HOMOSEXUALITY — Bibliography
HOMOSEXUALITY — Law and legislation — Germany
HOMOSEXUALITY — Law and legislation — Great Britain
HOMOSEXUALITY — Canada
HOMOSEXUALITY — Canada — Bibliography
HOMOSEXUALITY, MALE — Cross-cultural studies
HOMOSEXUALITY, MALE — Germany — History — 20th century
HOMOSEXUALITY, MALE — Papua New Guinea
HOMOSEXUALS — Great Britain
HOMOSEXUALS — United States — Political activity
HOMOSEXUALS, MALE — Employment — England — London
HONDURANS — Scotland
HONDURAS — Economic conditions — 1918-
HONDURAS — Foreign relations
HONDURAS — Politics and government — 1982-
HONG KONG — Census, 1976
HONG KONG — Census, 1986
HONG KONG — Description and travel
HONG KONG — Economic conditions
HONG KONG — Economic conditions — Statistics
HONG KONG — Economic policy
HONG KONG — Foreign relations — Great Britain
HONG KONG — Languages
HONG KONG — Politics and government
HONG KONG — Population — Statistics
HONG KONG — Social conditions
HONG KONG — Social conditions — Statistics
HONG KONG — Social conditions — Addresses, essays, lectures
HONG KONG — Social policy
HONG KONG ISLAND (HONG KONG) — Statistics
HONGKONG TRAMWAYS LIMITED
HONK KONG — Social conditions — Statistics
HOOKER, RICHARD, 1553 or 4-1600
HOOVER, HERBERT — Views on race relations

HOOVER INSTITUTION ON WAR, REVOLUTION, AND PEACE
HOOVER INSTITUTION ON WAR, REVOLUTION, AND PEACE — Catalogs
HORKHEIMER, MAX
HORNE, MICHAEL R.. Review of the Public Utilities Street Works Act 1950
HORNEY, KAREN
HORROR FILMS
HORTICULTURAL PRODUCTS INDUSTRY — Europe, Southern — Congresses
HORTICULTURAL PRODUCTS INDUSTRY — European Economic Community countries — Congresses
HORTICULTURAL PRODUCTS INDUSTRY — Mediterranean Region — Congresses
HORTICULTURE — Bibliography
HOSIERY INDUSTRY — Great Britain — History — 19th century
HOSIERY INDUSTRY — Great Britain — History — 20th century
HOSPITAL CARE
HOSPITAL UTILIZATION — Length of stay — United States
HOSPITALS — Administration — Australia — Political aspects
HOSPITALS — Finance — Australia
HOSPITALS — Management and regulation — United States
HOSPITALS — Australia — Finance
HOSPITALS — Canada
HOSPITALS — Canada — Statistics
HOSPITALS — Denmark — Statistics
HOSPITALS — England
HOSPITALS — England — London — After care
HOSPITALS — England — London — History
HOSPITALS — Finland
HOSPITALS — France — Statistics
HOSPITALS — Great Britain — Admission and discharge
HOSPITALS — Great Britain — Waiting lists
HOSPITALS — London — Hackney
HOSPITALS — Scotland — Edinburgh (Lothian) — History — 18th century
HOSPITALS — South Australia — Administration
HOSPITALS — Sweden
HOSPITALS — Wales — Personnel management
HOSPITALS — Wales — Staff
HOSPITALS, MOBILE
HOSPITALS, PROPRIETARY — England — South East — Planning
HOSPITALS, PUBLIC — Australia
HOSTAGES — Iran
HOSTAGES — United States
HOTELS, TAVERNS, ETC — Employees — Bermuda
HOTELS, TAVERNS, ETC. — Employees — Great Britain
HOTELS, TAVERNS, ETC. — England — West Country
HOTELS, TAVERNS, ETC. — Great Britain — Employees — Statistics
HOTELS, TAVERNS, ETC. — Netherlands — Statistics
HOTELS, TAVERNS, ETC. — Singapore — Statistics
HOTHAM, Sir CHARLES
HOTU MATÚ´A, Easter Island Chief
HOURS OF LABOR
HOURS OF LABOR — Bibliography
HOURS OF LABOR — Flexible
HOURS OF LABOR — Societies, etc. — Directories
HOURS OF LABOR — Statistics — Sources
HOURS OF LABOR — Cyprus — Statistics
HOURS OF LABOR — European Economic Community countries — Statistics
HOURS OF LABOR — Germany
HOURS OF LABOR — Great Britain
HOURS OF LABOR — Japan

HOURS OF LABOR — Québec (Province)
HOURS OF LABOR — Sri Lanka — Statistics
HOURS OF LABOR — United States
HOURS OF LABOR, FLEXIBLE
HOUSE BUYING — Decision-making — Great Britain
HOUSE BUYING — Law and legislation — Great Britain
HOUSE BUYING — Great Britain
HOUSE CONSTRUCTION — Congresses
HOUSEHOLD ELECTRONICS
HOUSEHOLD SURVEYS — Africa
HOUSEHOLD SURVEYS — Asia
HOUSEHOLD SURVEYS — Developing countries
HOUSEHOLD SURVEYS — Developing countries — Case studies
HOUSEHOLD SURVEYS — Developing countries — Congresses
HOUSEHOLD SURVEYS — Hong Kong
HOUSEHOLD SURVEYS — Ivory Coast
HOUSEHOLD SURVEYS — Netherlands — Methodology
HOUSEHOLD SURVEYS — Sri Lanka
HOUSEHOLD SURVEYS — Thailand
HOUSEHOLDS — Economics aspects
HOUSEHOLDS — Africa, Sub-Saharan
HOUSEHOLDS — Brazil — São Paulo (State) — History
HOUSEHOLDS — Canada
HOUSEHOLDS — England — Statistics
HOUSEHOLDS — Europe — History
HOUSEHOLDS — European Economic Community countries — Statistics
HOUSEHOLDS — Finland — Statistics — Methodolgy
HOUSEHOLDS — France
HOUSEHOLDS — Great Britain — Forecasting
HOUSEHOLDS — Hong Kong — Statistics
HOUSEHOLDS — Israel — Statistics
HOUSEHOLDS — Italy — Economic aspects
HOUSEHOLDS — Ivory Coast
HOUSEHOLDS — Nigeria — Statistics
HOUSEHOLDS — Pakistan
HOUSEWIVES
HOUSEWIVES — United States — History
HOUSING
HOUSING — Finance
HOUSING — Korea (South) — Statistics
HOUSING — Law and legislation — England
HOUSING — Law and legislation — Great Britain
HOUSING — Law and legislation — Northern Ireland
HOUSING — Montserrat — Statistics
HOUSING — Taxation — Organisation for Economic Co-operation and Development countries
HOUSING — Argentina — Statistics
HOUSING — Australia — Western Australia
HOUSING — Austria — Statistics
HOUSING — Barbados — Statistics
HOUSING — Belgium — Statistics
HOUSING — Botswana — Statistics
HOUSING — Brazil — Salvador
HOUSING — Canada
HOUSING — Cape Verde — Statistics
HOUSING — Colombia — Finance
HOUSING — Comoros — Statistics
HOUSING — Costa Rica — Statistics
HOUSING — Cyprus — Statistics
HOUSING — Denmark
HOUSING — Developing countries
HOUSING — Developing countries — Congresses
HOUSING — Egypt — Statistics
HOUSING — England — Societies, etc.
HOUSING — England — Brighton
HOUSING — England — Hertfordshire
HOUSING — England — Liverpool (Merseyside)
HOUSING — England — London

HOUSING — England — London — History
HOUSING — England — London — Statistics
HOUSING — England — Sheffield (South Yorkshire)
HOUSING — England — Southampton (Hampshire) — History
HOUSING — England — West Midlands
HOUSING — Equatorial Guinea — Statistics
HOUSING — Europe
HOUSING — Finland — Statistics
HOUSING — FRance
HOUSING — France — Finance
HOUSING — France — Statistics
HOUSING — Great Britain
HOUSING — Great Britain — Finance
HOUSING — Great Britain — History
HOUSING — Great Britain — Law and legislation
HOUSING — Great Britain — Social aspects
HOUSING — Great Britain — Statistics
HOUSING — Great Britain — Statistics — Bibliography
HOUSING — Hungary — Statistics
HOUSING — Hungary — Budapest
HOUSING — India — Dadra and Nagar Haveli — Statistics
HOUSING — Ireland — Statistics
HOUSING — Israel — Statistics
HOUSING — Ivory Coast
HOUSING — Japan — Statistics
HOUSING — Korea (South) — Finance
HOUSING — Korea (South) — Statisitics
HOUSING — Korea (South) — Statistics
HOUSING — Korea (South — Statistics
HOUSING — London metropolitan area — Societies, etc.
HOUSING — Malaysia — Statistics
HOUSING — Malaysia — Sabah — Statistics
HOUSING — Malaysia — Selangor — Statistics
HOUSING — Malaysia — Wilayah Persekutuan — Statistics
HOUSING — Mauritius — Statistics
HOUSING — Mexico — Statistics
HOUSING — Netherlands — Mathematical models
HOUSING — New Zealand
HOUSING — Norway — Statistics
HOUSING — Panama — Statistics
HOUSING — Philippines — Finance
HOUSING — San Marino — Statistics
HOUSING — Scotland
HOUSING — Scotland — Dumfries and Galloway
HOUSING — Scotland — Strathclyde — Glasgow
HOUSING — Sri Lanka — Statistics
HOUSING — Sweden — Finance — Statistics
HOUSING — Sweden — Statistics
HOUSING — United States
HOUSING — United States — Addresses, essays, lectures
HOUSING — United States — Finance
HOUSING — United States — Forecasting
HOUSING — United States — History
HOUSING — Wales — Clwyd
HOUSING — Washington, D.C — Addresses, essays, lectures
HOUSING AND BUILDING CONTROL BILL 1983-84
HOUSING AND PLANNING BILL 1985-86
HOUSING ASSOCIATION MOVEMENT See National Federation of Housing Associations
HOUSING AUTHORITIES — Great Britain — Employees
HOUSING AUTHORITIES — Scotland
HOUSING, COOPERATIVE — Law and legislation — England
HOUSING, COOPERATIVE — Britain
HOUSING, COOPERATIVE — Great Britain
HOUSING, COOPERATIVE — Great Britain — Finance
HOUSING, COOPERATIVE — Great Britain — History
HOUSING DEFECTS BILL 1983-84
HOUSING DEVELOPMENT
HOUSING DEVELOPMENT — England — Leicester (Leicestershire)
HOUSING DEVELOPMENT — England — Leicester (Leicestershire) — Case studies
HOUSING DEVELOPMENT — England — Leicestershire
HOUSING DEVELOPMENT — Hungary — Budapest
HOUSING DEVELOPMENT — United States
HOUSING FORECASTING — United States
HOUSING MANAGEMENT — Great Britain
HOUSING POLICY
HOUSING POLICY — Australia
HOUSING POLICY — Botswana
HOUSING POLICY — Canada
HOUSING POLICY — England — Bedfordshire
HOUSING POLICY — England — Birmingham (West Midlands)
HOUSING POLICY — England — Kent
HOUSING POLICY — England — Liverpool (Merseyside)
HOUSING POLICY — England — London
HOUSING POLICY — England — London — History
HOUSING POLICY — England — Manchester (Greater Manchester)
HOUSING POLICY — England — Sheffield (South Yorkshire)
HOUSING POLICY — England — Southampton (Hampshire) — History
HOUSING POLICY — Europe
HOUSING POLICY — Great Britain
HOUSING POLICY — Great Britain — History
HOUSING POLICY — Great Britain — History — 20th century
HOUSING POLICY — Guinea-Bissau
HOUSING POLICY — Malaysia
HOUSING POLICY — Northern Ireland
HOUSING POLICY — Scotland
HOUSING POLICY — Scotland — Edinburgh
HOUSING POLICY — United States
HOUSING POLICY — United States — History
HOUSING POLICY — Wales — West Glamorgan
HOUSING REHABILITATION
HOUSING REHABILITATION — Finance — Law and legislation — Great Britain
HOUSING REHABILITATION — Government policy — Great Britain
HOUSING REHABILITATION — England
HOUSING REHABILITATION — England — London
HOUSING REHABILITATION — England — Newcastle-upon-Tyne (Tyne and Wear)
HOUSING REHABILITATION — England — Newcastle-upon-Tyne (Tyne and Wear)
HOUSING REHABILITATION — European Economic Community countries
HOUSING SUBSIDIES — Great Britain
HOUSING SUBSIDIES — United States
HOUSING SURVEYS
HOUSING SURVEYS — England — London
HOUSING SURVEYS — Great Britain
HOVAS — History
HOVAS — Rites and ceremonies
HOWMAN, H. R. G.
HSÜAN-T'UNG See Pu Yi, Emperor of China
HUA (PAPUA NEW GUINEA PEOPLE) — Religion
HUA (PAPUA NEW GUINEA PEOPLE) — Sexual behavior
HUAHINE (SOCIETY ISLANDS) — Population — Statistics
HUDSON'S BAY COMPANY — History
HUGUENOTS — Canada — History — 18th century
HUGUENOTS — England — History
HUGUENOTS — France — History
HUMAN BEHAVIOR
HUMAN BEHAVIOR — Mathematical models
HUMAN BIOLOGY — Social aspects
HUMAN CAPITAL — Congresses
HUMAN CAPITOL
HUMAN DEVELOPMENT — Congresses
HUMAN ECOLOGY
HUMAN ECOLOGY — Addresses, essays, lectures
HUMAN ECOLOGY — Congresses
HUMAN ECOLOGY — Economic aspects
HUMAN ECOLOGY — Moral and ethical aspects
HUMAN ECOLOGY — Moral and ethical aspects — Congresses
HUMAN ECOLOGY — Public opinion
HUMAN ECOLOGY — Religious aspects — Congresses
HUMAN ECOLOGY — Social aspects
HUMAN ECOLOGY — Statistics — Bibliography
HUMAN ECOLOGY — Indonesia
HUMAN ECOLOGY — Southwest, New
HUMAN ECOLOGY — United States
HUMAN ENGINEERING
HUMAN EVOLUTION
HUMAN EXPERIMENTATION IN MEDICINE — Law and legislation
HUMAN GENETICS — Law and legislation — United States
HUMAN INFORMATION PROCESSING
HUMAN POPULATION GENETICS — Philosophy
HUMAN POPULATION GENETICS — Social aspects
HUMAN POPULATION GENETICS — Wales
HUMAN REPRODUCTION — Moral and ethical aspects
HUMAN REPRODUCTION — Political aspects
HUMAN REPRODUCTION — Social aspects
HUMAN REPRODUCTION — Social aspects — Cross-cultural studies
HUMAN REPRODUCTION — Great Britain — Statistics
HUMAN SETTLEMENTS
HUMAN SETTLEMENTS — Societies, etc. — Directories
HUMAN SETTLEMENTS — Guinea-Bissau
HUMAN TERRITORIALITY
HUMANISM — Knowledge, Theory of
HUMANISM — Great Britain
HUMANITIES
HUMANITIES — Information services — Great Britain
HUMANITIES — Information services — United States
HUMANITIES — Scholarships, fellowships, etc. — Great Britain
HUMANITIES — China
HUMANITIES — Great Britain — Research grants
HUMBER RIVER VALLEY (ONT.) — Economic conditions
HUMBER RIVER VALLEY (ONT.) — History
HUME, DAVID
HUME, DAVID, 1711-1776
HUNAN PROVINCE (CHINA) — Population — History
HUNGARIAN LITERATURE — 20th century

HUNGARIAN WORKER' PARTY See
  Magyar Dolgozók Pártja
HUNGARY — Bibliography
HUNGARY — Census — 1984
HUNGARY — Census,1984
HUNGARY — Commerce — Bibliography
HUNGARY — Commercial policy
HUNGARY — Economic conditions
HUNGARY — Economic conditions —
  1918-1945
HUNGARY — Economic conditions —
  1945-
HUNGARY — Economic conditions —
  1968-
HUNGARY — Economic policy — 1945-
HUNGARY — Economic policy — 1968
HUNGARY — Economic policy — 1968-
HUNGARY — Ethnic relations
HUNGARY — Foreign economic relations
  — European Economic Community
  countries
HUNGARY — Foreign economic relations
  — Romania
HUNGARY — Foreign population
HUNGARY — Foreign relations
HUNGARY — Foreign relations — 1945-
HUNGARY — Foreign relations — Soviet
  Union
HUNGARY — History — German
  occupation, 1944-1945
HUNGARY — History — Revolution,
  1918-1919
HUNGARY — History — 1867-1918
HUNGARY — History — 1918-1945
HUNGARY — History — 1945-
HUNGARY — History — Revolution, 1956
HUNGARY — History — Revolution, 1956
  — Personal narratives
HUNGARY — Industries
HUNGARY — Industries — Statistics
HUNGARY — Intellectual life
HUNGARY — Politics and government —
  1918-1945
HUNGARY — Politics and government —
  1945-
HUNGARY — Popular culture
HUNGARY — Population
HUNGARY — Population — Statistics
HUNGARY — Relations — Romania —
  History
HUNGARY — Social conditions — 1968-
HUNGARY — Statistics
HUNGARY — Ethnic relations —
  Congresses
HUNGER
HUNGER STRIKES — Northern Ireland
HUNT, JAMES B.
HUNTING — Congresses
HUNTING — Finland — Accounting
HUNTING AND GATHERING
  SOCIETIES
ḤUSAYNĪ, AMĪN, Grand Mufti of
  Jerusalem
HUSBAND AND WIFE
HUSBAND AND WIFE — Taxation —
  Great Britain
HUSBAND AND WIFE — United States
HUSBANDS — Addresses, essays, lectures
HUTTERITE BRETHREN
HUTTERITE BRETHREN — Social
  conditions
HYDERABAD (INDIA : STATE) —
  History
HYDROELECTRIC POWER PLANTS —
  Economic aspects — Latin America
HYDROELECTRIC POWER PLANTS —
  Québec (Province)
HYDROELETRIC POWER PLANTS —
  Peru — Mantaro River Valley
HYDROGRAPHIC SURVEYING —
  Congresses
HYDROLOGY
HYSTERECTOMY
HYSTERECTOMY — Patients —
  Interviews
HYSTERECTOMY — Psychological aspects
IACOCCA, LEE

IBÁRRURI, DOLORES
IBM DISK OPERATING SYSTEM
  VERSION 3.20
IBM PERSONAL COMPUTER
IBM PERSONAL COMPUTER —
  Programming
IBN SA'UD, 'ABD AL-'AZ̄IZ IBN 'ABD
  AR-RAHM̄AN, King of Saudia Arabia
ICELAND — Economic conditions
ICELAND — Foreign relations — Great
  Britain
ICELAND — Social conditions
IDAHO — Economic conditions
IDAHO — Social conditions
IDENTIFICATION CARDS — Australia
IDENTIFICATION CARDS — United
  States
IDENTITY
IDENTITY (PSYCHOLOGY)
IDENTITY (PSYCHOLOGY) — Social
  aspects
IDENTITY (PSYCHOLOGY) IN
  CHILDREN — Great Britain
IDEOLOGY
IDEOLOGY — Addresses, essays, lectures
IDEOLOGY — History
IG DRUCK UND PAPIER
IG METALL
IGBO (AFRICAN PEOPLE) — Rites and
  ceremonies
IGBO (AFRICAN PEOPLE) — Nigeria
IGLESIAS, PABLO
ILE-DE-FRANCE (FRANCE) — Industries
  — Statistics
ILLAWARRA (N.S.W. : REGION) —
  Economic conditions
ILLUSTRATION OF BOOKS
IMAGERY (PSYCHOLOGY)
IMAGINARY CONVERSATIONS
IMAGINATION
IMMUNITIES OF FOREIGN STATES
IMPERIAL CHEMICAL INDUSTRIES —
  History
IMPERIALISM
IMPERIALISM — Addresses, essays,
  lectures
IMPERIALISM — Economic aspects —
  Soviet Union
IMPERIALISM — History
IMPERIALISM IN LITERATURE
IMPERIALIZM: KAK VYSSHAIA
  STADIIA KAPITALIZMA
IMPORT QUOTAS — Great Britain
IMPORT QUOTAS — Taiwan
IMPRISONMENT — Congress
INCAS
INCAS — Politics and government
INCAS — Social conditions — Addresses,
  essays, lectures
INCENTIVES IN INDUSTRY
INCENTIVES IN INDUSTRY — European
  Economic Community countries
INCENTIVES IN INDUSTRY — Great
  Britain
INCENTIVES IN INDUSTRY — Hungary
INCENTIVES IN INDUSTRY — Soviet
  Union
INCENTIVES IN INDUSTRY — United
  States
INCEST
INCEST — Cross-cultural studies
INCEST — United States
INCEST IN ART
INCEST IN LITERATURE
INCEST IN POPULAR CULTURE —
  United States
INCEST VICTIMS — Case studies
INCEST VICTIMS — United States —
  Psychology
INCOME
INCOME — Government policy — India
INCOME — Mathematical models
INCOME — Statistics
INCOME — Asia
INCOME — Australia — Statistics
INCOME — Bahamas — Statistics
INCOME — Denmark

INCOME — Egypt
INCOME — France
INCOME — Great Britain
INCOME — Great Britain — Statistical
  methods
INCOME — Great Britain — Statistics
INCOME — Hungary
INCOME — Japan — Statistics
INCOME — Northeastern States —
  Forecasting
INCOME — Norway — Statistics
INCOME DISTRIBUTION
INCOME DISTRIBUTION — Addresses,
  essays, lectures
INCOME DISTRIBUTION — Congresses
INCOME DISTRIBUTION — Data
  processing
INCOME DISTRIBUTION — Government
  policy
INCOME DISTRIBUTION —
  Mathematical models
INCOME DISTRIBUTION — Statistical
  methods
INCOME DISTRIBUTION — Statistics
INCOME DISTRIBUTION — Statistics —
  Bibliography
INCOME DISTRIBUTION — Denmark
INCOME DISTRIBUTION — Developing
  countries
INCOME DISTRIBUTION — Developing
  countries — Addresses, essays, lectures
INCOME DISTRIBUTION — Developing
  countries — Case studies
INCOME DISTRIBUTION — Egypt
INCOME DISTRIBUTION — Great Britain
INCOME DISTRIBUTION — Hungary
INCOME DISTRIBUTION — India —
  Case studies
INCOME DISTRIBUTION — India —
  Punjab
INCOME DISTRIBUTION — Indonesia —
  Jawa Tengah
INCOME DISTRIBUTION — Kenya
INCOME DISTRIBUTION — Latin
  America
INCOME DISTRIBUTION — Nepal
INCOME DISTRIBUTION — Netherlands
  — Statistics
INCOME DISTRIBUTION — Poland
INCOME DISTRIBUTION — Sweden
INCOME DISTRIBUTION — United States
INCOME DISTRIBUTION — Uruguay
INCOME MAINTENANCE PROGRAMS
INCOME MAINTENANCE PROGRAMS
  — Mathematical models
INCOME MAINTENANCE PROGRAMS
  — Australia
INCOME MAINTENANCE PROGRAMS
  — Canada — Statistics
INCOME MAINTENANCE PROGRAMS
  — Great Britain
INCOME MAINTENANCE PROGRAMS
  — Ireland
INCOME TAX
INCOME TAX — Foreign income
INCOME TAX — Law and legislation —
  Australia
INCOME TAX — Law and legislation —
  Canada
INCOME TAX — Law and legislation —
  United States
INCOME TAX — Mathematical models
INCOME TAX — Political aspects —
  United States — History
INCOME TAX — Australia
INCOME TAX — Great Britain
INCOME TAX — Nigeria — Law
INCOME TAX — Peru
INCOME TAX — Québec (Province)
INCOME TAX — United States
INCOME TAX — United States —
  Addresses, essays, lectures
INCOME TAX — United States — History
INDECENT ASSAULT — England —
  History
INDECENT ASSAULT — South Australia
INDENTURED SERVANTS — Mauritius

INDEPENDENT BROADCASTING AUTHORITY
INDEPENDENT COMMISSION AGAINST CORRUPTION
INDEPENDENT LABOUR PARTY — Biography
INDEXING
INDIA — Biography — Directories
INDIA — Boundaries — China
INDIA — Census — Statistics
INDIA — Census, 1981
INDIA — Census 1981
INDIA — Census, 1981
INDIA — Commerce
INDIA — Commerce — History
INDIA — Commercial policy
INDIA — Constitutional history
INDIA — Constitutional law
INDIA — Economic conditions
INDIA — Economic conditions — Addresses, essays, lectures
INDIA — Economic conditions — Bibliography
INDIA — Economic conditions — Maps
INDIA — Economic conditions — Statistics
INDIA — Economic conditions — 1947-
INDIA — Economic conditions — 1947- — Addresses, essays, lectures
INDIA — Economic conditions — 1947- — Mathematical models
INDIA — Economic policy
INDIA — Economic policy — 1947-
INDIA — Economic policy — 1947- — Addresses, essays, lectures
INDIA — Economic policy — 1974-
INDIA — Economic policy — 1980-
INDIA — Economic policy — 1980- — Congresses
INDIA — Economic policy — 1980- — Econometric models
INDIA — Exiles
INDIA — Foreign economic relations
INDIA — Foreign relations
INDIA — Foreign relations — Great Britain
INDIA — Foreign relations — Nepal
INDIA — Foreign relations — Pakistan
INDIA — Foreign relations — Soviet Union
INDIA — Foreign relations — Tibet
INDIA — Foreign relations — United States — History
INDIA — Government publications (State Governments) — Bibliograpahy
INDIA — Government publications (State governments) — Bibliography
INDIA — Governors
INDIA — Governors — Biography
INDIA — History
INDIA — History — Sepoy Rebellion, 1857-1858
INDIA — History — 19th century — Addresses, essays, lectures
INDIA — History — Sepoy Rebellion, 1857-1858
INDIA — History — 20th century
INDIA — History — 20th Century
INDIA — History — 20th century
INDIA — History — 20th century — Addresses, essays, lectures
INDIA — History — 1947-
INDIA — Imprints
INDIA — Industries
INDIA — Industries — History
INDIA — Industries — Statistics
INDIA — Military policy
INDIA — National security
INDIA — Nonalignment
INDIA — Politics and government
INDIA — Politics and government — 1765-1947
INDIA — Politics and government — 1765-1947 — Addresses, essays, lectures
INDIA — Politics and government — 19th century
INDIA — Politics and government — 1857-1919
INDIA — Politics and government — 1857-1919 — Sources
INDIA — Politics and government — 20th century
INDIA — Politics and government — 20th century — Bibliography
INDIA — Politics and government — 1919-1947
INDIA — Politics and government — 1919-1947 — Sources
INDIA — Politics and government — 1945-
INDIA — Politics and government — 1947-
INDIA — Politics and government — 1977-
INDIA — Population
INDIA — Population — Bibliography
INDIA — Population — Statistics
INDIA — Population policy
INDIA — Population, Rural
INDIA — President
INDIA — Presidents — Correspondence
INDIA — Relations — China
INDIA — Relations — Japan
INDIA — Relations — South Asia
INDIA — Relations — Soviet Union
INDIA — Relations — Sri Lanka
INDIA — Religion — History
INDIA — Rural conditions
INDIA — Rural conditions — Collected works
INDIA — Rural conditions — Maps
INDIA — Scheduled tribes
INDIA — Scheduled tribes — Economic conditions — Bibliography
INDIA — Scheduled tribes — Government policy — Bibliography
INDIA — Social conditions
INDIA — Social conditions — Addresses, essays, lectures
INDIA — Social conditions — Statistics
INDIA — Social conditions — 20th century
INDIA — Social conditions — 1945-
INDIA — Social conditions — 1947-
INDIA — Social life and customs
INDIA — Social policy
INDIA — Social policy — Congresses
INDIA — Statistics
INDIA — Karnataka — Population
INDIA — West Bengal — Scheduled tribes
INDIA. Imperial Legislative Council
INDIA. Parliament
INDIA. Parliament. Lok Sabha
INDIA. Parliament. Lok Sabha — Speaker
INDIA — Statistics
INDIA FOREIGN RELATIONS
INDIA, NORTHEASTERN — Economic policy — Congresses
INDIA, NORTHEASTERN — Ethnic relations — Congresses
INDIA, NORTHEASTERN — Politics and government — Congresses
INDIAN NATIONAL CONGRESS
INDIAN NATIONAL CONGRESS — History
INDIAN NATIONAL CONGRESS — History — Sources
INDIAN OCEAN — Strategic aspects
INDIAN OCEAN REGION — Politics and government
INDIAN OCEAN REGION — Relations — France
INDIAN OCEAN REGION — Strategic aspects
INDIANA — Politics and government
INDIANS OF CENTRAL AMERICA — Guatemala — History
INDIANS OF CENTRAL AMERICA — Nicaragua — Cultural assimilation
INDIANS OF CENTRAL AMERICAN — Nicaragua — History
INDIANS OF MEXICO — Government relations
INDIANS OF MEXICO — Rites and ceremonies
INDIANS OF MEXICO — Women
INDIANS OF MEXICO — Mexico, Valley of — Economic conditions
INDIANS OF MEXICO — Sonora (State) — Ethnic identity
INDIANS OF MEXICO — Sonora (State) — Water rights
INDIANS OF NORTH AMERICA — Biography
INDIANS OF NORTH AMERICA — Courts
INDIANS OF NORTH AMERICA — Crime
INDIANS OF NORTH AMERICA — Cultural assimilation — History
INDIANS OF NORTH AMERICA — Government relations
INDIANS OF NORTH AMERICA — Government relations — Addresses, essays, lectures
INDIANS OF NORTH AMERICA — Government relations — History
INDIANS OF NORTH AMERICA — Government relations — 1934-
INDIANS OF NORTH AMERICA — History — 20th century
INDIANS OF NORTH AMERICA — Hunting — Congresses
INDIANS OF NORTH AMERICA — Juvenile delinquency
INDIANS OF NORTH AMERICA — Legal status, laws, etc
INDIANS OF NORTH AMERICA — Legal status, laws, etc — History
INDIANS OF NORTH AMERICA — Population
INDIANS OF NORTH AMERICA — Social conditions
INDIANS OF NORTH AMERICA — Statistics
INDIANS OF NORTH AMERICA — Alaska — Claims
INDIANS OF NORTH AMERICA — Alaska — Economic conditions — Addresses, essays, lectures
INDIANS OF NORTH AMERICA — Alaska — Government relations
INDIANS OF NORTH AMERICA — Alaska — Land tenure
INDIANS OF NORTH AMERICA — Canada
INDIANS OF NORTH AMERICA — Canada — Civil rights
INDIANS OF NORTH AMERICA — Canada — Constitutional law
INDIANS OF NORTH AMERICA — Canada — Councils — Bibliography
INDIANS OF NORTH AMERICA — Canada — First contact with Occidental civilization
INDIANS OF NORTH AMERICA — Canada — Government relations
INDIANS OF NORTH AMERICA — Canada — Government relations — Bibliography
INDIANS OF NORTH AMERICA — Canada — History
INDIANS OF NORTH AMERICA — Canada — Legal status, laws, etc
INDIANS OF NORTH AMERICA — Canada — Legal status, laws, etc.
INDIANS OF NORTH AMERICA — Canada — Mixed bloods — Addresses, essays, lectures
INDIANS OF NORTH AMERICA — Canada — Mixed bloods — History — Addresses, essays, lectures
INDIANS OF NORTH AMERICA — Canada — Treaties
INDIANS OF NORTH AMERICA — Great Plains — History — 20th century — Addresses, essays, lectures
INDIANS OF NORTH AMERICA — Kansas — History
INDIANS OF NORTH AMERICA — Kansas — Land tenure
INDIANS OF NORTH AMERICA — Northwestern States — Government relations
INDIANS OF NORTH AMERICA — Northwestern States — Legal status, laws, etc

INDIANS OF NORTH AMERICA — Northwestern States — Treaties
INDIANS OF NORTH AMERICA — South Dakota — Social life and customs
INDIANS OF NORTH AMERICA — South Dakota — Women
INDIANS OF NORTH AMERICA — Southwest, New — Art
INDIANS OF NORTH AMERICA — Southwest, New — Economic conditions
INDIANS OF NORTH AMERICA — Southwest, New — Philosophy
INDIANS OF SOUTH AMERICA — Congresses
INDIANS OF SOUTH AMERICA — Ethics
INDIANS OF SOUTH AMERICA — Amazon Valley
INDIANS OF SOUTH AMERICA — Andes region — Addresses, essays, lectures
INDIANS OF SOUTH AMERICA — Bolivia — Government relations
INDIANS OF SOUTH AMERICA — Bolivia — Potosí (Dept.) — Employment — History
INDIANS OF SOUTH AMERICA — Brazil — Sexual behavior
INDIANS OF SOUTH AMERICA — Brazil — Social life and customs
INDIANS OF SOUTH AMERICA — Brazil — Women
INDIANS OF SOUTH AMERICA — Ecuador — Quito region — Economic conditions
INDIANS OF SOUTH AMERICA — Ecuador — Quito region — Politics and government
INDIANS OF SOUTH AMERICA — Paraguay — Economic conditions
INDIANS OF SOUTH AMERICA — Paraguay — Social conditions
INDIANS OF SOUTH AMERICA — Peru — Ethnobotany
INDIANS OF SOUTH AMERICA — Peru — Magic
INDIANS OF SOUTH AMERICA — Peru — Religion and mythology
INDIANS OF THE WEST INDIES — Government relations
INDIANS OF THE WEST INDIES — Saint Vincent — Folklore
INDIANS, TREATMENT OF — Latin America
INDIANS, TREATMENT OF — Nicaragua — History
INDIVIDUALISM
INDIVIDUALISM — Addresses, essays, lectures
INDIVIDUALISM — History
INDIVIDUALITY — Addresses, essays, lectures
INDOCHINA — Emigration and immigration
INDOCHINA — Foreign relations — Australia
INDOCHINA — Foreign relations — China
INDOCHINA — Foreign relations — United States
INDOCHINESE — France
INDOCHINESE WAR, 1946-1954 — United States
INDONESIA — Constitutional law
INDONESIA — Economic conditions — 1945- — Statistics
INDONESIA — Foreign relations — Netherlands — Sources
INDONESIA — Foreign relations — Papua New Guinea
INDONESIA — History — Java War, 1825-1830
INDONESIA — History — Revolution, 1945-1949
INDONESIA — History, Local
INDONESIA — Military policy
INDONESIA — Politics and government
INDONESIA — Population — Statistics — Forecasting
INDONESIA — Social conditions
INDONESIA — Social conditions — Statistics
INDUCTION (LOGIC)
INDUSTRIAL ACCIDENTS
INDUSTRIAL ACCIDENTS — Costs
INDUSTRIAL ACCIDENTS — Legal status, laws, etc. — Great Britain
INDUSTRIAL ACCIDENTS — Australia — Tasmania — Statistics
INDUSTRIAL ACCIDENTS — Great Britain
INDUSTRIAL ACCIDENTS — United States — Case studies
INDUSTRIAL ARTS — Study and teaching — Evaluation
INDUSTRIAL BUILDINGS — Economic aspects — Great Britain
INDUSTRIAL BUILDINGS — Great Britain
INDUSTRIAL CAPACITY — Finance — Mathematical models
INDUSTRIAL CONCENTRATION — France — Statistics
INDUSTRIAL CONCENTRATION — Great Britain — Statistics
INDUSTRIAL CONCENTRATION — United States
INDUSTRIAL DESIGN COORDINATION
INDUSTRIAL DEVELOPMENT BANK OF INDIA
INDUSTRIAL DEVELOPMENT PROJECTS — Australia
INDUSTRIAL DEVELOPMENT PROJECTS — Greece
INDUSTRIAL DISTRICTS — Law and legislation — Colombia
INDUSTRIAL EQUIPMENT — Netherlands — Statistics
INDUSTRIAL EQUIPMENT INDUSTRY — Developing countries
INDUSTRIAL HYGIENE
INDUSTRIAL HYGIENE — Bibliography
INDUSTRIAL HYGIENE — Government — India
INDUSTRIAL HYGIENE — Law and legislation — Denmark
INDUSTRIAL HYGIENE — Moral and ethical aspects
INDUSTRIAL HYGIENE — Societies, etc. — Directories
INDUSTRIAL HYGIENE — Denmark
INDUSTRIAL HYGIENE — Great Britain
INDUSTRIAL HYGIENE — Norway — Management — Employee participation
INDUSTRIAL HYGIENE — Spain — History — 19th century
INDUSTRIAL HYGIENE — United States
INDUSTRIAL HYGIENE — United States — History — 20th century
INDUSTRIAL LAWS AND LEGISLATION — Congresses
INDUSTRIAL LAWS AND LEGISLATION — Africa
INDUSTRIAL LAWS AND LEGISLATION — Ecuador
INDUSTRIAL LAWS AND LEGISLATION — India — History
INDUSTRIAL LAWS AND LEGISLATION — United States — History
INDUSTRIAL MANAGEMENT
INDUSTRIAL MANAGEMENT — Dictionaries
INDUSTRIAL MANAGEMENT — Belgium — Case studies
INDUSTRIAL MANAGEMENT — Developing countries
INDUSTRIAL MANAGEMENT — Europe
INDUSTRIAL MANAGEMENT — Europe, Eastern
INDUSTRIAL MANAGEMENT — France
INDUSTRIAL MANAGEMENT — Germany (West)
INDUSTRIAL MANAGEMENT — Great Britain
INDUSTRIAL MANAGEMENT — Great Britain — Case studies
INDUSTRIAL MANAGEMENT — Great Britain — Employee participation
INDUSTRIAL MANAGEMENT — India — Employee participation
INDUSTRIAL MANAGEMENT — Japan
INDUSTRIAL MANAGEMENT — Northwest, Pacific — Employee participation — Case studies
INDUSTRIAL MANAGEMENT — Romania — Employee representation
INDUSTRIAL MANAGEMENT — South Africa
INDUSTRIAL MANAGEMENT — Soviet Union
INDUSTRIAL MANAGEMENT — Soviet Union — Dictionaries
INDUSTRIAL MANAGEMENT — Soviet Union — Mathematical models
INDUSTRIAL MANAGEMENT — United States
INDUSTRIAL MANAGEMENT — United States — Case Studies
INDUSTRIAL MANAGEMENT — United States — Case studies
INDUSTRIAL MANAGEMENT — United States — Employee participation
INDUSTRIAL MARKETING
INDUSTRIAL MARKETING — Research — Germany (West)
INDUSTRIAL MARKETING — Research — United States
INDUSTRIAL ORGANIZATION
INDUSTRIAL ORGANIZATION — Case studies
INDUSTRIAL ORGANIZATION — Congresses
INDUSTRIAL ORGANIZATION — History
INDUSTRIAL ORGANIZATION — Germany (West)
INDUSTRIAL ORGANIZATION — Great Britain
INDUSTRIAL ORGANIZATION — Japan
INDUSTRIAL ORGANIZATION — Japan — Case studies
INDUSTRIAL ORGANIZATION — Soviet Union
INDUSTRIAL ORGANIZATION — Ukraine
INDUSTRIAL ORGANIZATION — United States
INDUSTRIAL ORGANIZATION (ECONOMIC THEORY)
INDUSTRIAL ORGANIZATION (ECONOMIC THEORY) — Mathematical models
INDUSTRIAL PROCUREMENT — Contracts and specifications
INDUSTRIAL PRODUCTIVITY — Congresses
INDUSTRIAL PRODUCTIVITY — Mathematical models
INDUSTRIAL PRODUCTIVITY — Measurement — Computer programs
INDUSTRIAL PRODUCTIVITY — Measurement — Data processing
INDUSTRIAL PRODUCTIVITY — Australia
INDUSTRIAL PRODUCTIVITY — Communist countries
INDUSTRIAL PRODUCTIVITY — Great Britain — History — 20th century
INDUSTRIAL PRODUCTIVITY — Norway
INDUSTRIAL PRODUCTIVITY — Soviet Union
INDUSTRIAL PRODUCTIVITY — United States — Case studies
INDUSTRIAL PRODUCTIVITY — United States — History — 20th century
INDUSTRIAL PRODUCTIVITY — United States — Measurement
INDUSTRIAL PROMOTION — Australia
INDUSTRIAL PROMOTION — Australia — Tasmania
INDUSTRIAL PROMOTION — Developing countries

INDUSTRIAL PROMOTION — England
INDUSTRIAL PROMOTION — European Economic Community countries
INDUSTRIAL PROMOTION — Morocco
INDUSTRIAL PROMOTION — Northern Ireland
INDUSTRIAL PROMOTION — Pennsylvania
INDUSTRIAL PROMOTION — Scotland
INDUSTRIAL PROMOTION — Wales
INDUSTRIAL PROPERTY
INDUSTRIAL PROPERTY — European Economic Community countries
INDUSTRIAL PROPERTY — Korea (South)
INDUSTRIAL PROPERTY — Spain
INDUSTRIAL PROPERTY (INTERNATIONAL LAW)
INDUSTRIAL RELATIONS
INDUSTRIAL RELATIONS — Bibliography
INDUSTRIAL RELATIONS — Congresses
INDUSTRIAL RELATIONS — Dictionaries
INDUSTRIAL RELATIONS — Economic aspects — Great Britain
INDUSTRIAL RELATIONS — History — Addresses, essays, lectures
INDUSTRIAL RELATIONS — Legal status laws, etc.
INDUSTRIAL RELATIONS — Africa
INDUSTRIAL RELATIONS — Asia — Congresses
INDUSTRIAL RELATIONS — Australia
INDUSTRIAL RELATIONS — Austria
INDUSTRIAL RELATIONS — British Columbia — Vancouver — History
INDUSTRIAL RELATIONS — Canada
INDUSTRIAL RELATIONS — Canada — History
INDUSTRIAL RELATIONS — Colombia — Case studies
INDUSTRIAL RELATIONS — Denmark
INDUSTRIAL RELATIONS — Denmark — Bibliography
INDUSTRIAL RELATIONS — England — History — 20th century
INDUSTRIAL RELATIONS — Europe
INDUSTRIAL RELATIONS — European Economic Community countries
INDUSTRIAL RELATIONS — France
INDUSTRIAL RELATIONS — Great Britain
INDUSTRIAL RELATIONS — Great Britain — Dictionaries
INDUSTRIAL RELATIONS — Great Britain — Effect of technological innovations on
INDUSTRIAL RELATIONS — Great Britain — History
INDUSTRIAL RELATIONS — Great Britain — Law and legislation
INDUSTRIAL RELATIONS — Hungary
INDUSTRIAL RELATIONS — India
INDUSTRIAL RELATIONS — India — History
INDUSTRIAL RELATIONS — Indonesia — Java — History
INDUSTRIAL RELATIONS — Japan
INDUSTRIAL RELATIONS — New York (State) — Albany — History — 19th century
INDUSTRIAL RELATIONS — New Zealand
INDUSTRIAL RELATIONS — Norway
INDUSTRIAL RELATIONS — Philippines
INDUSTRIAL RELATIONS — Singapore
INDUSTRIAL RELATIONS — South Africa
INDUSTRIAL RELATIONS — Spain
INDUSTRIAL RELATIONS — Sri Lanka
INDUSTRIAL RELATIONS — Turkey
INDUSTRIAL RELATIONS — United States — Addresses, essays, lectures
INDUSTRIAL RELATIONS — United States — History — 20th century
INDUSTRIAL RELATIONS — Yugoslavia
INDUSTRIAL SAFETY
INDUSTRIAL SAFETY — Bibliography
INDUSTRIAL SAFETY — Law and legislation — Denmark
INDUSTRIAL SAFETY — Europe — Congresses
INDUSTRIAL SAFETY — Great Britain
INDUSTRIAL SAFETY — United States
INDUSTRIAL SITES — Great Britain
INDUSTRIAL SOCIOLOGY
INDUSTRIAL SOCIOLOGY — Canada
INDUSTRIAL SOCIOLOGY — Canada — History
INDUSTRIAL SOCIOLOGY — Colombia — Case studies
INDUSTRIAL SOCIOLOGY — Europe, Eastern
INDUSTRIAL SOCIOLOGY — France
INDUSTRIAL SOCIOLOGY — Great Britain
INDUSTRIAL SOCIOLOGY — United States
INDUSTRIAL SOCIOLOGY — United States — Addresses, essays, lectures
INDUSTRIAL SOCIOLOGY — United States — History
INDUSTRIAL STATISTICS
INDUSTRIAL STATISTICS — Bibliography
INDUSTRIAL STATISTICS — Standards
INDUSTRIAL TOXICOLOGY — India — Bhopal
INDUSTRIAL WORKERS OF THE WORLD — Bibliography
INDUSTRIALISTS — Great Britain — History — 19th century
INDUSTRIALISTS — Great Britain — History — 20th century
INDUSTRIALISTS — Mexico
INDUSTRIALISTS — United States — Biography
INDUSTRIALIZATION
INDUSTRIALIZATION — Addresses, essays, lectures
INDUSTRIALIZATION — Bibliography
INDUSTRIALIZATION — History — Addresses, essays, lectures
INDUSTRIES — Germany (West) — Statistics
INDUSTRIES, LOCATION OF — Great Britain
INDUSTRIES, SIZE OF
INDUSTRIES, SIZE OF — United States
INDUSTRY
INDUSTRY — Directories — Bibliography
INDUSTRY — Location
INDUSTRY — Power supply
INDUSTRY — Social apects
INDUSTRY — Social aspects
INDUSTRY — Social aspects — England
INDUSTRY — Social aspects — Great Britain
INDUSTRY — Social aspects — India
INDUSTRY — Social aspects — United States
INDUSTRY — Social aspects — United States — Case studies
INDUSTRY ACT 1972
INDUSTRY AND EDUCATION — Australia
INDUSTRY AND EDUCATION — Great Britain
INDUSTRY AND EDUCATION — United States
INDUSTRY AND STATE
INDUSTRY AND STATE — Case studies
INDUSTRY AND STATE — Congresses
INDUSTRY AND STATE — Australia
INDUSTRY AND STATE — Brazil
INDUSTRY AND STATE — Canada
INDUSTRY AND STATE — Canada — Congresses
INDUSTRY AND STATE — Canada — History — 19th century
INDUSTRY AND STATE — Colombia
INDUSTRY AND STATE — Communist countries
INDUSTRY AND STATE — East Asia — Congresses
INDUSTRY AND STATE — Europe
INDUSTRY AND STATE — Europe — History — 20th century
INDUSTRY AND STATE — European Economic Community countries
INDUSTRY AND STATE — European Economic Community countries — Directories
INDUSTRY AND STATE — France
INDUSTRY AND STATE — France — History — 20th century
INDUSTRY AND STATE — Great Britain
INDUSTRY AND STATE — India
INDUSTRY AND STATE — India — History
INDUSTRY AND STATE — India — Hyderabad (State) — History
INDUSTRY AND STATE — Japan
INDUSTRY AND STATE — Korea (South)
INDUSTRY AND STATE — Mexico
INDUSTRY AND STATE — Mexico — History — 19th century
INDUSTRY AND STATE — Organisation for Economic Co-operation and Development countries
INDUSTRY AND STATE — Pakistan
INDUSTRY AND STATE — Panama
INDUSTRY AND STATE — Pennsylvania
INDUSTRY AND STATE — Poland — History
INDUSTRY AND STATE — Soviet Union
INDUSTRY AND STATE — Spain
INDUSTRY AND STATE — Sudan
INDUSTRY AND STATE — Tanzania
INDUSTRY AND STATE — Ukraine
INDUSTRY AND STATE — United States
INDUSTRY AND STATE — United States — Addresses, essays, lectures
INDUSTRY AND STATE — United States — History
INDUSTRY AND STATES — Europe
INFANT
INFANT — popular works
INFANT PSYCHOLOGY
INFANTS — Development
INFANTS — Mortality — Social aspects — Bangladesh
INFANTS — Mortality — Statistical methods
INFANTS — Nutrition — History
INFANTS — Ecuador — Mortality
INFANTS — Great Britain — Mortality
INFANTS — Great Britain — Nutrition
INFANTS — Guyana — Mortality
INFANTS — Haiti — Mortality — Statistics
INFANTS — Italy — Mortality — Statistics
INFANTS — Jamaica — Mortality
INFANTS — Syria — Mortality — Statistics
INFANTS — Thailand — Mortality — Statistics
INFANTS — Trinidad and Tobago — Mortality
INFANTS — Mortality — Bibliography
INFANTS (NEWBORN) — Diseases — Treatment — Government policy — Congresses
INFANTS (NEWBORN) — Diseases — Treatment — Moral and ethical aspects — Congresses
INFANTS (NEWBORN) — Great Britain — Statistics
INFERENCE
INFERENCE (LOGIC)
INFLATION — Developing countries
INFLATION (FINANCE)
INFLATION (FINANCE) — Effect of energy costs on — Mathematical models
INFLATION (FINANCE) — Social aspects
INFLATION (FINANCE) — Social aspects — Germany — History — 20th century
INFLATION (FINANCE) — Yugoslavia
INFLATION (FINANCE) — Belgium
INFLATION (FINANCE) — Canada
INFLATION (FINANCE) — Developing countries

INFLATION (FINANCE) — Great Britain
INFLATION (FINANCE) — Great Britain — Measurement
INFLATION (FINANCE) — Peru
INFLATION (FINANCE) — Spain
INFLATION (FINANCE) — Switzerland
INFLATION (FINANCE) — United States
INFLUENCE (PSYCHOLOGY)
INFLUENZA
INFORMAL SECTOR (ECONOMICS)
INFORMAL SECTOR (ECONOMICS) — Egypt
INFORMAL SECTOR (ECONOMICS) — France
INFORMATION NETWORKS
INFORMATION NETWORKS — Directories
INFORMATION RESOURCES MANAGEMENT
INFORMATION RESOURCES MANAGEMENT — Security measures
INFORMATION RETRIEVAL
INFORMATION SCIENCE
INFORMATION SCIENCE — Economic aspects — Organisation for Economic Co-operation and Development countries
INFORMATION SCIENCE — Social aspects
INFORMATION SCIENCE — Great Britain
INFORMATION SERVICES
INFORMATION SERVICES — Cost control
INFORMATION SERVICES — Directories
INFORMATION SERVICES — Economic aspects — Organisation for Economic Co-operation and Development countries
INFORMATION SERVICES — Finance
INFORMATION SERVICES — Legal status, laws, etc. — Peru
INFORMATION SERVICES — Management
INFORMATION SERVICES — Australia
INFORMATION SERVICES — Canada
INFORMATION SERVICES — Great Britain
INFORMATION SERVICES — New Zealand
INFORMATION SERVICES — South Asia
INFORMATION SERVICES — United States — Statistics
INFORMATION SERVICES AND STATE
INFORMATION SERVICES AND STATE — Legal status, laws, etc. — Peru
INFORMATION SERVICES AND STATE — Peru
INFORMATION SERVICES EMPLOYEES — Great Britain
INFORMATION STORAGE AND RETRIEVAL SYSTEMS
INFORMATION STORAGE AND RETRIEVAL SYSTEMS — Addresses, essays, lectures
INFORMATION STORAGE AND RETRIEVAL SYSTEMS — Archival material
INFORMATION STORAGE AND RETRIEVAL SYSTEMS — Business
INFORMATION STORAGE AND RETRIEVAL SYSTEMS — Directories
INFORMATION STORAGE AND RETRIEVAL SYSTEMS — Evaluation
INFORMATION STORAGE AND RETRIEVAL SYSTEMS — Geography
INFORMATION STORAGE AND RETRIEVAL SYSTEMS — Humanities — Congresses
INFORMATION STORAGE AND RETRIEVAL SYSTEMS — Labor supply
INFORMATION STORAGE AND RETRIEVAL SYSTEMS — Law
INFORMATION STORAGE AND RETRIEVAL SYSTEMS — Law — Bibliography
INFORMATION STORAGE AND RETRIEVAL SYSTEMS — Law — Europe
INFORMATION STORAGE AND RETRIEVAL SYSTEMS — Law — Europe — Public opinion
INFORMATION STORAGE AND RETRIEVAL SYSTEMS — Law — Great Britain
INFORMATION STORAGE AND RETRIEVAL SYSTEMS — Management
INFORMATION STORAGE AND RETRIEVAL SYSTEMS — Names, Geographical — Code numbers
INFORMATION STORAGE AND RETRIEVAL SYSTEMS — Social aspects
INFORMATION STORAGE AND RETRIEVAL SYSTEMS — Social aspects — Great Britain — Forecasting
INFORMATION STORAGE AND RETRIEVAL SYSTEMS — Social sciences — Congresses
INFORMATION STORAGE AND RETRIEVAL SYSTEMS — Technological innovations
INFORMATION STORAGE AND RETRIEVAL SYSTEMS — Technology — Great Britain
INFORMATION STORAGE AND RETRIEVAL SYSTEMS — Experiments
INFORMATION STORAGE AND RETRIEVAL SYSTEMS — Great Britain — Labor supply
INFORMATION STORAGE AND RETRIEVAL SYSTEMS — Portugal — Congresses
INFORMATION STORAGE AND RETRIEVAL SYSTEMS — Spain — Congresses
INFORMATION THEORY — Statistical methods
INFORMATION THEORY IN BIOLOGY — Data processing
INFRASTRUCTURE (ECONOMICS)
INFRASTRUCTURE (ECONOMICS) — Saint Lucia
INFRASTRUCTURE (ECONOMICS) — Saint Vincent and the Grenadines
INFRASTRUCTURE (ECONOMICS) — Soviet Union
INFRASTRUCTURE (ECONOMICS) — Spain — Vizcaya
INGESTION DISORDERS
INHERITANCE AND SUCCESSION — France
INIESTA CANO, CARLOS
INITIATION RITES — Papua New Guinea
INJUNCTIONS — England
INLAND NAVIGATION — Government policy — Great Britain
INLAND NAVIGATION — History
INLAND NAVIGATION — Great Britain — Management
INLAND NAVIGATION — Great Britain — Recreational use
INLAND REVENUE STAFF FEDERATION
INLAND WATER TRANSPORTATION — Statistics — European Economic Community countries
INLAND WATER TRANSPORTATION — Statistics
INLAND WATER TRANSPORTATION — Europe — Congresses
INMATES OF INSTITUTIONS — Great Britain
INNER LONDON EDUCATION AUTHORITY
INPUT-OUTPUT ANALYSIS
INPUT-OUTPUT TABLES — Denmark — Mathematical models
INPUT-OUTPUT TABLES — Developing countries
INPUT-OUTPUT TABLES — European Economic Community countries
INPUT-OUTPUT TABLES — Ghana
INPUT-OUTPUT TABLES — Ghana — Methodolgy
INPUT-OUTPUT TABLES — Indonesia
INPUT-OUTPUT TABLES — Italy
INPUT-OUTPUT TABLES — Switzerland
INPUT-OUTPUT TABLES — United States
INQUISITION — Europe
INQUISITION — Spain — Congresses
INSANE — Commitment and detention — Great Britain
INSANE — Commitment and detention — Great Britain — History
INSANE — Commitment and detention — Netherlands
INSANE, CRIMINAL AND DANGEROUS — England
INSANE, CRIMINAL AND DANGEROUS — Netherlands
INSANITY — Jurisprudence — Council of Europe countries
INSIDER TRADING IN SECURITIES — Law and legislation — Australia
INSTALMENT PLAN — Great Britain — Statistics
INSTITUTE OF CHARTERED ACCOUNTANTS IN ENGLAND AND WALES. Current cost accounting
INSTITUTE OF CHARTERED ACCOUNTANTS IN ENGLAND AND WALES
INSTITUTE OF COST AND MANAGEMENT ACCOUNTANTS — History
INSTITUTE OF PUBLIC ADMINISTRATION (Dublin, Dublin, Ireland)
INSTITUTE OF SOUTHEAST ASIAN STUDIES. Southeast Asian Studies Program
INSTITUTIONAL CARE
INSTITUTIONAL CARE — Great Britain
INSTITUTIONAL CARE — Great Britain — Finance
INSTITUTIONAL ECONOMICS — Addresses, essays, lectures
INSTITUTIONAL MARKET
INSTITUTO MEXICANO DEL SEGURO SOCIAL. Unidad de Promoción Voluntaria
INSTITUTO NACIONAL DE ADMINISTRACIÓN PÚBLICA (Peru) — Legal status, laws, etc
INSTITUTO NACIONAL DE PREVISIÓN (Spain) — History
INSURANCE — Economic aspects
INSURANCE — Finance
INSURANCE — Mathematics
INSURANCE — State supervision
INSURANCE — Austria — Statistics
INSURANCE — Developing countries
INSURANCE — England — London
INSURANCE — European Economic Community countries
INSURANCE — Great Britain — Statistics
INSURANCE — Netherlands — Statistics
INSURANCE — Organisation for Economic Co-operation and Development countries — Statistics
INSURANCE — Turkey — Statistics
INSURANCE, ACCIDENT — Denmark
INSURANCE, ACCIDENT — Switzerland
INSURANCE COMPANIES — Employees — Great Britain
INSURANCE COMPANIES — European Economic Community countries
INSURANCE COMPANIES — Great Britain — Finance
INSURANCE COMPANIES — Great Britain — Investments — Statistics
INSURANCE COMPANIES — Netherlands
INSURANCE COMPANIES — United States — Employees — Supply and demand — Forecasting
INSURANCE COMPANIES — United States — Investments — History
INSURANCE, CREDIT
INSURANCE, DISABILITY — Denmark
INSURANCE, DISABILITY — Denmark — Statistics
INSURANCE, FIRE — Great Britain
INSURANCE, FIRE — Great Britain — Policies
INSURANCE, HEALTH

INSURANCE, HEALTH — history — United States
INSURANCE, HEALTH — Law and legislation — Great Britain
INSURANCE, HEALTH — Law and legislation — India
INSURANCE, HEALTH — Social aspects — United States
INSURANCE, HEALTH — Canada
INSURANCE, HEALTH — Canada — History
INSURANCE, HEALTH — Denmark
INSURANCE, HEALTH — Great Britain
INSURANCE, HEALTH — India
INSURANCE, HEALTH — United States
INSURANCE LAW — Great Britain
INSURANCE LAW — United States
INSURANCE LIFE
INSURANCE, LIFE — Rates and tables — Mathematical models
INSURANCE, LIFE — Netherlands — Statistics
INSURANCE, LIFE — Organisation for Economic Co-operation and Development countries
INSURANCE, LIFE — United States — History
INSURANCE, MALPRACTICE — United States
INSURANCE, MARINE — Law and legislation — Great Britain
INSURANCE, SOCIAL
INSURANCE, UNEMPLOYMENT
INSURANCE, UNEMPLOYMENT — Denmark
INSURANCE, UNEMPLOYMENT — Great Britain
INSURANCE, UNEMPLOYMENT — United States
INTEGRATED WATER DEVELOPMENT — Political aspects — Africa
INTEL 8086 (COMPUTER)
INTEL 8088 (COMPUTER)
INTELLECT
INTELLECT — Addresses, essays, lectures
INTELLECT — Genetic aspects
INTELLECTUAL COOPERATION
INTELLECTUAL PROPERTY — Great Britain — Statistical services
INTELLECTUALS — Political activity — Addresses, essays, lectures
INTELLECTUALS — Algeria — Biography
INTELLECTUALS — Canada
INTELLECTUALS — China
INTELLECTUALS — Germany — History
INTELLECTUALS — Mexico
INTELLECTUALS — New York (N.Y.) — History — 20th century
INTELLECTUALS — Soviet Union — Political activity
INTELLECTUALS — Soviet Union — Sociological aspects
INTELLIGENCE LEVELS — Social aspects
INTELLIGENCE OFFICERS — Great Britain — Biography
INTELLIGENCE SERVICE
INTELLIGENCE SERVICE — International cooperation
INTELLIGENCE SERVICE — Canada — History — 20th century
INTELLIGENCE SERVICE — France
INTELLIGENCE SERVICE — Great Britain
INTELLIGENCE SERVICE — Great Britain — History — 20th century
INTELLIGENCE SERVICE — Soviet Union
INTELLIGENCE SERVICE — United States
INTER-AMERICAN COMMISSION ON HUMAN RIGHTS
INTER-AMERICAN COURT OF HUMAN RIGHTS
INTER-LIBRARY LOANS — Great Britain
INTERACTIVE COMPUTER SYSTEMS
INTERACTIVE VIDEO
INTERCULTURAL COMMUNICATION
INTERCULTURAL COMMUNICATION — Congresses
INTERCULTURAL EDUCATION — Great Britain
INTERDISCIPLINARY APPROACH IN EDUCATION
INTERDISCIPLINARY APPROACH TO KNOWLEDGE
INTEREST
INTEREST AND USURY — Europe
INTEREST RATE FUTURES
INTEREST RATES
INTEREST RATES — Government policy — Developing countries
INTEREST RATES — Developing countries
INTEREST RATES — Italy
INTEREST RATES — United States
INTERGENERATIONAL RELATIONS
INTERGENERATIONAL RELATIONS — Congresses
INTERGOVERNMENTAL FISCAL RELATIONS — Great Britain
INTERGOVERNMENTAL FISCAL RELATIONS — India
INTERGOVERNMENTAL FISCAL RELATIONS — Nigeria
INTERGOVERNMENTAL FISCAL RELATIONS — Switzerland
INTERGOVERNMENTAL FISCAL RELATIONS — United States
INTERLOCKING DIRECTORATES — Scotland — History — 20th century
INTERMEDIATION (FINANCE)
INTERNAL REVENUE — Australia — Statistics
INTERNAL SECURITY — Great Britain
INTERNAL SECURITY — United States — History
INTERNATIONAL ACCOUNTING STANDARDS COMMITTEE
INTERNATIONAL AGENCIES
INTERNATIONAL AGENCIES — Addresses, essays, lectures
INTERNATIONAL AGENCIES — Administration
INTERNATIONAL AGENCIES — Bibliography
INTERNATIONAL AGENCIES — Bibliography — Catalogs
INTERNATIONAL AGENCIES — Foreign relations — Treaties — Bibliography
INTERNATIONAL AGENCIES — officials and employees
INTERNATIONAL AND MUNICIPAL LAW — European Economic Community countries
INTERNATIONAL BANK FOR RECONSTRUCTION AND DEVELOPMENT
INTERNATIONAL BUSINES ENTERPRISES — Eployees — Effect of technological innovations on
INTERNATIONAL BUSINESS ENTERPRISES
INTERNATIONAL BUSINESS ENTERPRISES — Accounting
INTERNATIONAL BUSINESS ENTERPRISES — Employees
INTERNATIONAL BUSINESS ENTERPRISES — Employment
INTERNATIONAL BUSINESS ENTERPRISES — Employment — Developing countries
INTERNATIONAL BUSINESS ENTERPRISES — Employment — Germany (West)
INTERNATIONAL BUSINESS ENTERPRISES — Employment — India
INTERNATIONAL BUSINESS ENTERPRISES — Employment — Liberia
INTERNATIONAL BUSINESS ENTERPRISES — Employment — Sierra Leone
INTERNATIONAL BUSINESS ENTERPRISES — Finance
INTERNATIONAL BUSINESS ENTERPRISES — Finance — Addresses, essays, lectures
INTERNATIONAL BUSINESS ENTERPRISES — Government ownership — Bibliography
INTERNATIONAL BUSINESS ENTERPRISES — Government policy — Colombia
INTERNATIONAL BUSINESS ENTERPRISES — History — 19th century
INTERNATIONAL BUSINESS ENTERPRISES — Law and legislation — Developing countries
INTERNATIONAL BUSINESS ENTERPRISES — Law and legislation — Ghana
INTERNATIONAL BUSINESS ENTERPRISES — Management
INTERNATIONAL BUSINESS ENTERPRISES — Management — Environmental aspects — Developing countries
INTERNATIONAL BUSINESS ENTERPRISES — Moral and ethical aspects — Congresses
INTERNATIONAL BUSINESS ENTERPRISES — Personnel management
INTERNATIONAL BUSINESS ENTERPRISES — Reorganization
INTERNATIONAL BUSINESS ENTERPRISES — Safety measures
INTERNATIONAL BUSINESS ENTERPRISES — Social aspects
INTERNATIONAL BUSINESS ENTERPRISES — Taxation — Law and legislation
INTERNATIONAL BUSINESS ENTERPRISES — Argentina
INTERNATIONAL BUSINESS ENTERPRISES — Australia
INTERNATIONAL BUSINESS ENTERPRISES — Canada
INTERNATIONAL BUSINESS ENTERPRISES — Caribbean Area
INTERNATIONAL BUSINESS ENTERPRISES — Developing countries
INTERNATIONAL BUSINESS ENTERPRISES — Germany (West)
INTERNATIONAL BUSINESS ENTERPRISES — Ghana
INTERNATIONAL BUSINESS ENTERPRISES — Great Britain — Management
INTERNATIONAL BUSINESS ENTERPRISES — Kenya
INTERNATIONAL BUSINESS ENTERPRISES — Latin America
INTERNATIONAL BUSINESS ENTERPRISES — Latin America — History
INTERNATIONAL BUSINESS ENTERPRISES — Namibia
INTERNATIONAL BUSINESS ENTERPRISES — Nigeria
INTERNATIONAL BUSINESS ENTERPRISES — Peru — History
INTERNATIONAL BUSINESS ENTERPRISES — Poland
INTERNATIONAL BUSINESS ENTERPRISES — South Africa
INTERNATIONAL BUSINESS ENTERPRISES — United States
INTERNATIONAL BUSINESS ENTERPRISES — Yugoslavia
INTERNATIONAL BUSINESS MACHINES CORPORATION — History
INTERNATIONAL CLEARING — Finland
INTERNATIONAL CLEARING — Soviet Union
INTERNATIONAL COMMITTEE OF THE RED CROSS — Greece — Political activity
INTERNATIONAL CONVENTION FOR THE SAFETY OF LIFE AT SEA (1974). Protocols, amendments, etc.

INTERNATIONAL CONVENTION RELATING TO THE LIMITATION OF THE LIABILITY OF OWNERS OF SEA-GOING SHIPS
INTERNATIONAL COOPERATION
INTERNATIONAL COOPERATION — Communist countries
INTERNATIONAL COOPERATION — Persian Gulf Region
INTERNATIONAL COURT OF JUSTICE
INTERNATIONAL COURTS
INTERNATIONAL COVENANT ON ECONOMIC, SOCIAL, AND CULTURAL RIGHTS
INTERNATIONAL CROPS RESEARCH INSTITUTE FOR THE SEMI-ARID TROPICS
INTERNATIONAL DEVELOPMENT ASSOCIATION
INTERNATIONAL DEVELOPMENT ASSOCIATION — Legal status, laws, etc.
INTERNATIONAL DIVISION OF LABOR
INTERNATIONAL DIVISION OF LABOR — Congresses
INTERNATIONAL DRINKING WATER SUPPLY AND SANITATION DECADE, 1981-1990 — Statistics
INTERNATIONAL ECONOMIC INTEGRATION
INTERNATIONAL ECONOMIC RELATIONS
INTERNATIONAL ECONOMIC RELATIONS — Addresses, essays, lectures
INTERNATIONAL ECONOMIC RELATIONS — Bibliography
INTERNATIONAL ECONOMIC RELATIONS — Congresses
INTERNATIONAL ECONOMIC RELATIONS — History — 20th century
INTERNATIONAL ECONOMIC RELATIONS — Law and legislation
INTERNATIONAL ECONOMIC RELATIONS — Mathematical models
INTERNATIONAL ECONOMIC RELATIONS — Mathematical models — Congresses
INTERNATIONAL ECONOMIC RELATIONS — Research
INTERNATIONAL EDUCATION
INTERNATIONAL FEDERATION FOR INFORMATION PROCESSING. Technical Committee for Information Systems
INTERNATIONAL FEDERATION OF LIBRARY ASSOCIATIONS — Bibliography
INTERNATIONAL FINANCE
INTERNATIONAL FINANCE — Bibliography
INTERNATIONAL FINANCE — Congresses
INTERNATIONAL FINANCE — History — 20th century
INTERNATIONAL FINANCE — Law and legislation
INTERNATIONAL FINANCE — Moral and ethical aspects
INTERNATIONAL FINANCE — Research
INTERNATIONAL FINANCE CORPORATION — Legal status, laws, etc.
INTERNATIONAL LABOR ACTIVITIES
INTERNATIONAL LABOUR CONFERENCE — Rules and practice
INTERNATIONAL LABOUR OFFICE
INTERNATIONAL LABOUR ORGANISATION
INTERNATIONAL LABOUR ORGANISATION — Constitution
INTERNATIONAL LABOUR ORGANISATION. Jobs and Skills Programme for Africa
INTERNATIONAL LABOUR ORGANIZATION — History
INTERNATIONAL LAW
INTERNATIONAL LAW — Addresses, essays, lectures
INTERNATIONAL LAW — Bibliography
INTERNATIONAL LAW — Codification
INTERNATIONAL LAW — Congresses
INTERNATIONAL LAW — Dictionaries
INTERNATIONAL LAW — Sources
INTERNATIONAL LAW — Study and teaching
INTERNATIONAL LAW — China
INTERNATIONAL LAW — Developing countries
INTERNATIONAL LAW — Developing countries — Bibliography
INTERNATIONAL LAW (ISLAMIC LAW) — Congresses
INTERNATIONAL LIBRARIANSHIP — Addresses, essays, lectures
INTERNATIONAL MONETARY FUND
INTERNATIONAL MONETARY FUND — Bibliography
INTERNATIONAL MONETARY FUND — Legal status, laws, etc.
INTERNATIONAL MONETARY FUND — Developing countries
INTERNATIONAL MONETARY FUND — Jamaica
INTERNATIONAL MONETARY FUND — Nigeria — Bibliography
INTERNATIONAL MONETARY FUND — Peru
INTERNATIONAL MONETARY FUND — Finance
INTERNATIONAL MONETARY FUND — History
INTERNATIONAL NORTH PACIFIC FISHERIES COMMISSION — History
INTERNATIONAL OFFENSES
INTERNATIONAL OFFICIALS AND EMPLOYEES — Biography
INTERNATIONAL ORGANIZATION
INTERNATIONAL ORGANIZATION — Addresses, essays, lectures
INTERNATIONAL ORGANIZATION — History
INTERNATIONAL RELATIONS
INTERNATIONAL RELATIONS — Addresses, essays, lectures
INTERNATIONAL RELATIONS — Congresses
INTERNATIONAL RELATIONS — Methodology
INTERNATIONAL RELATIONS — Moral and ethical aspects
INTERNATIONAL RELATIONS — Philosophy
INTERNATIONAL RELATIONS — Psychological aspects
INTERNATIONAL RELATIONS — Research
INTERNATIONAL RELATIONS — Research — Congresses
INTERNATIONAL RELATIONS — Study and teaching
INTERNATIONAL RELATIONS — Yearbooks
INTERNATIONAL SOCIETY FOR KRISHNA CONSCIOUSNESS — United States
INTERNATIONAL SOCIETY OF KRISHNA CONSCIOUSNESS
INTERNATIONAL TRANSPORT WORKERS' FEDERATION — Archives
INTERNATIONAL WOMEN'S DECADE, 1976-1985
INTERNATIONAL WORKERS ASSOCIATION
INTERNATIONALISTS — Biography
INTERNAYIONAL BUSINESS ENTERPRISES — Management
INTERPERSONAL ATTRACTION
INTERPERSONAL COMMUNICATION
INTERPERSONAL COMMUNICATION — Addresses, essays, lectures
INTERPERSONAL COMMUNICATION IN CHILDREN
INTERPERSONAL CONFLICT — Congresses
INTERPERSONAL CONFLICT — Papua New Guinea
INTERPERSONAL RELATIONS
INTERPERSONAL RELATIONS — Addresses, essays, lectures
INTERPERSONAL RELATIONS IN CHILDREN
INTERRACIAL ADOPTION — Government policy — Great Britain
INTERSTATE BANKING — United States — Congresses
INTERVENTION (INTERNATIONAL LAW)
INTERVIEWING
INTERVIEWING IN DEMOGRAPHY
INTERVIEWING IN ETHNOLOGY
INTERVIEWS — Nicaragua
INTIMACY (PSYCHOLOGY)
INTRINSIC MOTIVATION
INVENTIONS — England
INVENTORIES
INVENTORS — Great Britain — Biography
INVESTIGATION OF THE POSSIBLE INCREASED INCIDENCE OF CANCER IN WEST CUMBRIA
INVESTMENT ANALYSIS
INVESTMENT ANALYSIS — Great Britain
INVESTMENT BANKING
INVESTMENT BANKING — Colombia
INVESTMENT BANKING — Developing countries
INVESTMENT OF PUBLIC FUNDS — Soviet Union
INVESTMENT TRUSTS — Great Britain
INVESTMENTS
INVESTMENTS — Accounting
INVESTMENTS — Decision making
INVESTMENTS — Law and legislation — Taiwan
INVESTMENTS — Mathematical models
INVESTMENTS — Social aspects — United States
INVESTMENTS — Taxation — Finland
INVESTMENTS — Australia
INVESTMENTS — Bolivia
INVESTMENTS — Canada
INVESTMENTS — Denmark — Statistics
INVESTMENTS — Developing countries
INVESTMENTS — Dominica
INVESTMENTS — European Economic Community countries
INVESTMENTS — Finland
INVESTMENTS — Great Britain
INVESTMENTS — Great Britain — Mathematical models
INVESTMENTS — Great Britain — Statistics
INVESTMENTS — India
INVESTMENTS — Japan
INVESTMENTS — Organisation for Economic Co-operation and Development countries
INVESTMENTS — Puerto Rico — History
INVESTMENTS — United States
INVESTMENTS, AMERICAN
INVESTMENTS, AMERICAN — Social aspects
INVESTMENTS, AMERICAN — Europe
INVESTMENTS, AMERICAN — South Africa
INVESTMENTS, BRAZILIAN
INVESTMENTS, BRITISH — Argentina
INVESTMENTS, BRITISH — South Africa
INVESTMENTS, DUTCH
INVESTMENTS, FOREIGN
INVESTMENTS, FOREIGN — Accounting
INVESTMENTS, FOREIGN — Addresses, essays, lectures
INVESTMENTS, FOREIGN — Government policy — Colombia
INVESTMENTS, FOREIGN — Government policy — Mexico
INVESTMENTS, FOREIGN — Law and legislation
INVESTMENTS, FOREIGN — Law and legislation — Developing countries

INVESTMENTS, FOREIGN — Law and legislation — Korea (South)
INVESTMENTS, FOREIGN — Mathematical models
INVESTMENTS, FOREIGN — Statistics
INVESTMENTS, FOREIGN — Asia
INVESTMENTS, FOREIGN — Asia, Southeastern
INVESTMENTS, FOREIGN — Canada
INVESTMENTS, FOREIGN — Canada, Western — History — Bibliography
INVESTMENTS, FOREIGN — Canada, Western — History — Sources
INVESTMENTS, FOREIGN — Communist countries
INVESTMENTS, FOREIGN — Developing countries
INVESTMENTS, FOREIGN — Ecuador
INVESTMENTS, FOREIGN — France — Statistics
INVESTMENTS, FOREIGN — Great Britain
INVESTMENTS, FOREIGN — Great Britain — Statistics
INVESTMENTS, FOREIGN — Mexico
INVESTMENTS, FOREIGN — Nigeria
INVESTMENTS, FOREIGN — Organisation for Economic Co-operation and Development countries
INVESTMENTS, FOREIGN — Taiwan
INVESTMENTS, FOREIGN — United States
INVESTMENTS, FOREIGN — West (U.S.) — History — Bibliography
INVESTMENTS, FOREIGN — West (U.S.) — History — Sources
INVESTMENTS, FOREIGN — Yugoslavia
INVESTMENTS, FOREIGN AND EMPLOYMENT — Australia
INVESTMENTS, FOREIGN (INTERNATIONAL LAW)
INVESTMENTS, INDIAN
INVESTMENTS, IRANIAN — United States
INVESTMENTS, JAPANESE — European Economic Community countries
INVESTMENTS, JAPANESE — United States
INVESTMENTS, KOREAN
INVISIBLE ITEMS OF TRADE
IRAN
IRAN — Bibliography
IRAN — Boundaries — Iraq
IRAN — Economic conditions
IRAN — Economic conditions — Addresses, essays, lectures
IRAN — Economic conditions — 1945
IRAN — Economic conditions — 1945- — Case studies
IRAN — Ethnic relations — Congresses
IRAN — Foreign relations — 1979-
IRAN — Foreign relations — Iraq
IRAN — Foreign relations — Middle East
IRAN — Foreign relations — Soviet Union
IRAN — Foreign relations — United States
IRAN — History — Qajar dynasty, 1779-1925
IRAN — History — 20th century
IRAN — History — Revolution, 1979
IRAN — Politics and government — 1941-1979
IRAN — Politics and government — 1941-1979 — Case studies
IRAN — Politics and government — 1979
IRAN — Politics and government — 1979-
IRAN — Politics and government — 1979- — Congresses
IRAN — Relations — Soviet Union
IRAN — Social conditions
IRAN — Social life and customs
IRAN-CONTRA AFFAIR, 1985-
IRAN HOSTAGE CRISIS, 1979-1981
IRAN-IRAQ WAR, 1980- See Iraqi-Iranian Conflict, 1980-
IRAQ — Armed Forces — Political activity
IRAQ — Boundaries — Iran
IRAQ — Foreign relations — Great Britain
IRAQ — Foreign relations — Iran
IRAQ — History — Hashemite Kingdom, 1921-1958
IRAQ — History — 1921-
IRAQ — Politics and government
IRAQ — Relations — Gulf States
IRAQI-IRANIAN CONFLICT, 1980-
IRAQI-IRANIAN CONFLICT, 1980
IRELAND — Appropriations and expenditures
IRELAND — Appropriations and expenditures — Congresses
IRELAND — Bibliography
IRELAND — Census, 1981
IRELAND — Census, 1986
IRELAND — Commerce — History — Congresses
IRELAND — Description and travel — 1801-1900
IRELAND — Directories
IRELAND — Economic conditions
IRELAND — Economic conditions — 1949- — Econometric models
IRELAND — Economic conditions — 1949-
IRELAND — Economic policy
IRELAND — Emigration and immigration — History
IRELAND — Foreign economic relations
IRELAND — Foreign relations — Great Britain
IRELAND — Handbooks, manuals, etc.
IRELAND — History
IRELAND — History — 16th century
IRELAND — History — 17th century
IRELAND — History — 1837-1901
IRELAND — History — 1837-1901 — Quotations
IRELAND — History — 20th century — Quotations
IRELAND — History — 1901-1910
IRELAND — History — 1910-1921
IRELAND — History — 1910-1921 — Bibliography
IRELAND — History — Civil War, 1922-1923
IRELAND — History — 1922-
IRELAND — Nobility — History
IRELAND — Occupations — Forecasting
IRELAND — Politics and government
IRELAND — Politics and government — 1172-1603
IRELAND — Politics and government — 19th century
IRELAND — Politics and government — 1837-1901
IRELAND — Politics and government — 20th century
IRELAND — Politics and government — 20th century — Quotations
IRELAND — Politics and government — 1901-1910
IRELAND — Politics and government — 1910-1921
IRELAND — Politics and government — 1922-1949
IRELAND — Politics and government — 1949-
IRELAND — Population — Statistics
IRELAND — Religious life and customs
IRELAND — Rural conditions
IRELAND — Rural conditions — Congresses
IRELAND — Social conditions
IRELAND — Social conditions — Statistics
IRELAND — Social life and customs — 19th century
IRELAND — Statistics, Vital
IRELAND — Voting registers — Analysis
IRELAND. Department of Labour
IRELAND. Garda Síochána
IRELAND. Oireachtas. Dail. Committee on Public Expenditure
IRELAND. Select Committee on Statutory Instruments
IRIAN JAYA (INDONESIA) — Politics and government
IRISH — Attitudes
IRISH — Australia — History
IRISH — Great Britain — History — Bibliography
IRISH — Scotland — Strathclyde — History
IRISH — United States
IRISH AMERICANS — History — Addresses, essays, lectures
IRISH AMERICANS — Public opinion — History — 19th century
IRISH AMERICANS — Social conditions — Addresses, essays, lectures
IRISH REPUBLICAN ARMY — Biography
IRISH UNIFICATION QUESTION
IRISH UNIFICATION QUESTION — Public opinion
IRON AND STEEL BILL 1980-81
IRON AND STEEL WORKERS — Employment
IRON AND STEEL WORKERS — Labor productivity
IRON AND STEEL WORKERS — Great Britain
IRON AND STEELWORKERS — Germany
IRON-FOUNDING — Economic aspects
IRON INDUSTRY AND TRADE
IRON INDUSTRY AND TRADE — Forecasting
IRON INDUSTRY AND TRADE — Government policy — Europe
IRON INDUSTRY AND TRADE — Canada
IRON INDUSTRY AND TRADE — Finland
IRON INDUSTRY AND TRADE — France — Lorraine
IRON INDUSTRY AND TRADE — India
IRON INDUSTRY AND TRADE — Spain — Basque provinces — History
IRON INDUSTRY AND TRADE — Sweden
IRON INDUSTRY AND TRADE — Wales, South — History — 18th century
IRON INDUSTRY AND TRADE — Wales, South — History — 19th century
IROQUOIS INDIANS — Government relations
IROQUOIS INDIANS — History
IRRELIGION — History
IRRELIGION — United States — History
IRRIGATION — Economic aspects
IRRIGATION — History — Congresses
IRRIGATION — Management
IRRIGATION — Social aspects — Congresses
IRRIGATION — Philippines — Pampanga River Project — Management
IRRIGATION — Sudan
IRRIGATION — Thailand
IRRIGATION ENGINEERING — Thailand
ISHIBASHI, TANZAN
ISKON See International Society for Krishna Consciousness
ISKRA
ISLAM
ISLAM — Biography
ISLAM — Congresses
ISLAM — History
ISLAM — Political aspects
ISLAM — 20th century
ISLAM — Arab countries — History
ISLAM — Indonesia
ISLAM — Senegal
ISLAM AND POLITICS
ISLAM AND POLITICS — Afghanistan
ISLAM AND POLITICS — Libya
ISLAM AND POLITICS — Near East
ISLAM AND POLITICS — Pakistan
ISLAM AND POLITICS — Turkey
ISLAM AND SOCIAL PROBLEMS
ISLAM AND STATE
ISLAM AND STATE — Afghanistan — Congresses
ISLAM AND STATE — Iran — Congresses
ISLAM AND STATE — Pakistan

ISLAM AND STATE — Pakistan — Congresses
ISLAM AND WORLD POLITICS
ISLAMIC COUNTRIES — Economic integration
ISLAMIC COUNTRIES — Foreign relations — Congresses
ISLAMIC COUNTRIES — Relations
ISLAMIC COUNTRIES
ISLAMIC COUNTRIES — History
ISLAMIC LAW
ISLAMIC LAW — History
ISLAMIC LAW — Social aspects
ISLANDS — Scotland — Rural conditions
ISLINGTON (LONDON, ENGLAND) — Economic conditions
ISLINGTON (LONDON, ENGLAND) — Economic policy
ISRAEL
ISRAEL — Armed forces — History
ISRAEL — Census, 1983
ISRAEL — Defenses
ISRAEL — Economic conditions
ISRAEL — Economic policy
ISRAEL — Foreign opinion, American
ISRAEL — Foreign relations
ISRAEL — Foreign relations — Addresses, essays, lectures
ISRAEL — Foreign relations — Germany (West)
ISRAEL — Foreign relations — Great Britain
ISRAEL — Foreign relations — United States
ISRAEL — History, Military
ISRAEL — Military policy
ISRAEL — Military relations — United States
ISRAEL — Politics and government
ISRAEL — Politics and government — Addresses, essays, lectures
ISRAEL — Politics and government — 1948-
ISRAEL — Population — Statistics
ISRAEL — Presidents — Biography
ISRAEL — Social conditions — Statistics
ISRAEL — Statistics, Vital
ISRAEL — Yearbooks
ISRAEL. Keneset
ISRAEL. Keneset — Elections, 1981 — Addresses, essays, lectures
ISRAEL. National Insurance Institute
ISRAEL AND THE DIASPORA — Addresses, essays, lectures
ISRAEL-ARAB BORDER CONFLICTS — 1949-
ISRAEL-ARAB BORDER CONFLICTS, 1949-
ISRAEL-ARAB BORDER CONFLICTS, 1949- — Lebanon
ISRAEL-ARAB WAR, 1948-1949
ISRAEL-ARAB WAR, 1967 — Diplomatic history
ISRAEL-ARAB WAR, 1967 — Occupied territories
ISRAELIS — Psychology
ITALIAN AMERICAN WOMEN — Folklore
ITALIAN AMERICAN WOMEN — New York (N.Y.) — History
ITALIAN AMERICANS — Folklore
ITALIAN AMERICANS — New Jersey — History
ITALIAN AMERICANS — New Jersey — History — Bibliography
ITALIANS — Foreign countries — Bibliography
ITALIANS — Argentina — History — 19th century
ITALIANS — Switzerland
ITALIANS IN FOREIGN COUNTRIES
ITALY — Census, 1981
ITALY — Civilization — 1559-1789
ITALY — Economic conditions
ITALY — Economic conditions — 1870-1918
ITALY — Economic conditions — 1945-
ITALY — Economic policy
ITALY — Elections
ITALY — Emigration and immigration — Bibliography
ITALY — Foreign economic relations — Germany
ITALY — Foreign relations — 1870-1915
ITALY — Foreign relations — 1922-1945
ITALY — Foreign relations — 1945-
ITALY — Foreign relations — Egypt
ITALY — Foreign relations — Poland
ITALY — Foreign relations — Spain
ITALY — Foreign relations — United States
ITALY — Foreign relations — Yugoslavia
ITALY — History — 1559-1789
ITALY — History — 18th century
ITALY — History — 19th century
ITALY — History — 1849-1870
ITALY — History — 1914-1945
ITALY — History — 1945-
ITALY — Industries
ITALY — Industries — Statistics
ITALY — Politics and government — 1922-1945
ITALY — Politics and government — 1922-1945 — Sources
ITALY — Politics and government — 1945-
ITALY — Politics and government — 1976-
ITALY — Population — Statistics
ITALY — Social conditions
ITALY. Parlamento — Elections
IVORY COAST — Cencus, 1975
IVORY COAST — Census, 1975
IVORY COAST — Commerce — Statistics
IVORY COAST — Constitution
IVORY COAST — Economic conditions — Statistics
IVORY COAST — Economic policy
IVORY COAST — Population — Statistics
IVORY COAST — Population — Statistics — Evaluation
IVORY COAST — Social policy
IVORY COAST — Statistics, vital
JACA (SPAIN) — History
JACKSON, ANDREW
JACKSON, HENRY M — Views on national security
JACKSON, JESSE
JACKSON STRUCTURED PROGRAMMING
JACOBINS — France
JACOBITE REBELLION, 1715
JACOBITE REBELLION, 1719
JACOBITE REBELLION, 1745-1746
JACOBITES
JAHANZEB, MIANGUL, Wali of Swat — Bibliography
JAILS — Social aspects — California — Case studies
JAKOBSON, MAX
JALISCO (MEXICO) — Governors
JAMAICA — Census, 1970
JAMAICA — Economic conditions
JAMAICA — Economic conditions — Statistics
JAMAICA — Economic policy
JAMAICA — Population
JAMAICA — Population — Statistics
JAMAICA — Statistics, Vital
JAMES, HENRY — Authorship
JAMES, HENRY — Criticism and interpretation
JAMES, WILLIAM
JAMMU AND KASHMIR (INDIA) — Kings and rulers — Biography
JAMMU AND KASHMIR (INDIA) — Politics and government
JAPAN — Bibliography
JAPAN — Census, 1980
JAPAN — Civilization
JAPAN — Civilization — 1945-
JAPAN — Colonies — History
JAPAN — Commerce
JAPAN — Commerce — Near East
JAPAN — Commerce — Canada
JAPAN — Commerce — Europe
JAPAN — Commerce — United States
JAPAN — Commercial policy
JAPAN — Constitutional history
JAPAN — Economic conditions
JAPAN — Economic conditions — Statistics
JAPAN — Economic conditions — To 1868
JAPAN — Economic conditions — 1868-1918
JAPAN — Economic conditions — 1868-1945
JAPAN — Economic conditions — 1868-
JAPAN — Economic conditions — 1918-1945
JAPAN — Economic conditions — 1945-
JAPAN — Economic history
JAPAN — Economic policy
JAPAN — Economic policy — 1945- — Congresses
JAPAN — Foreign economic relations
JAPAN — Foreign economic relations — Africa
JAPAN — Foreign economic relations — Malaysia
JAPAN — Foreign economic relations — United States — Congresses
JAPAN — Foreign opinion, British
JAPAN — Foreign relations — 1868-1912
JAPAN — Foreign relations — 1912-1945
JAPAN — Foreign relations — 1945-
JAPAN — Foreign relations — Europe
JAPAN — Foreign relations — Germany
JAPAN — Foreign relations — Great Britain
JAPAN — Foreign relations — New Zealand
JAPAN — Foreign relations — United States
JAPAN — History — Tokigawa period, 1600-1868
JAPAN — History — Tokugawa period, 1600-1868 — Addresses, essays, lectures
JAPAN — History — 1787-1868
JAPAN — History — 19th century
JAPAN — History — Meiji period, 1868-1912
JAPAN — History — 1868-1945
JAPAN — History — 1868-
JAPAN — History — 1868- — Historiography
JAPAN — History — 20th century
JAPAN — History — Taishō period, 1912-1926
JAPAN — History — 1912-1945
JAPAN — History — Allied occupation, 1945-1952
JAPAN — History, Military
JAPAN — History, Military — 1945-
JAPAN — Industries
JAPAN — Industries — Reorganization
JAPAN — Industries — 1945-
JAPAN — Intellectual life — 20th century
JAPAN — Military policy
JAPAN — Military relations — Great Britain
JAPAN — National security
JAPAN — Occupations — Statistics
JAPAN — Politics and government — 1868-1912
JAPAN — Politics and government — 1926-1945
JAPAN — Politics and government — 1945-
JAPAN — Population
JAPAN — Population — History
JAPAN — Population — Statistics
JAPAN — Relations — France
JAPAN — Relations — India
JAPAN — Relations — Middle East — Congresses
JAPAN — Rural conditions
JAPAN — Social conditions — 1600-1868
JAPAN — Social conditions — 1868-1912
JAPAN — Social conditions — 1945-
JAPAN — Social conditions — 1945- — Statistics
JAPAN — Social life and customs
JAPAN. Kaigun — History
JAPANESE AMERICANS — Civil rights

JAPANESE AMERICANS — Cultural assimilation
JAPANESE AMERICANS — Evacuation and relocation, 1942-1945
JAPANESE AMERICANS — Evacuation and relocation, 1942-1945 — Congresses
JAPANESE AMERICANS — Legal status, laws, etc
JAPANESE AMERICANS — Evacuation and relocation, 1942-1945
JAPANESE COMMUNIST PARTY See Nihon Kyosanto
JAPANESE IN CANADA
JAPANESE LANGUAGE — Dictionaries
JAPANESE LITERATURE — Meiji period, 1868-1912 — translations into English
JAPANESE LITERATURE — 20th century — translations into English
JAPANESE STUDIES — Europe
JAVA (INDONESIA) — History
JAVANESE LANGUAGE — Social aspects
JAWA TENGAH (INDONESIA) — Rural conditions
JEJU DO (KOREA (SOUTH)) — Statistics
JENKINS, DAFYDD — Bibliography
JEONRA BUG DO (KOREA(SOUTH)) — Statistics
JEONRA NAM DO (KOREA (SOUTH)) — Statistics
JEROME, JAMES
JERUSALEM — History
JERUSALEM — International status
JERUSALEM — Politics and government
JESUS CHRIST — Political and social views
JEVONS, WILLIAM STANLEY — Addresses, essays, lectures
JEWISH-ARAB RELATIONS
JEWISH-ARAB RELATIONS — Public opinion
JEWISH-ARAB RELATIONS — To 1917
JEWISH-ARAB RELATIONS — 1917-1949
JEWISH-ARAB RELATIONS — 1917-
JEWISH-ARAB RELATIONS — 1949-
JEWISH-ARAB RELATIONS — 1949- — Public opinion
JEWISH-ARAB RELATIONS — 1967-1973
JEWISH-ARAB RELATIONS — 1973-
JEWISH-ARAB RELATIONS — 1973- — Study and teaching (Higher) — Israel
JEWISH BANKERS — Biography
JEWISH CHILDREN — Israel
JEWISH COLLEGE TEACHERS — Connecticut — New Haven — History
JEWISH CRIMINALS — New York (State) — Brooklyn — Case studies
JEWISH CRIMINALS — Soviet Union
JEWISH FAMILIES — Bibliography
JEWISH LAW
JEWISH TRADE-UNIONS — France — Paris
JEWS
JEWS — Cultural assimilation — Congresses
JEWS — Education — Connecticut — New Haven — History
JEWS — Education — Europe, Eastern — History
JEWS — History
JEWS — History — Atlases
JEWS — History — 1789-1945 — Congresses
JEWS — History — 1945-
JEWS — Languages
JEWS — Politics and government
JEWS — Public opinion — History — 19th century
JEWS — Social conditions — Bibliography
JEWS — Argentina — Persecutions
JEWS — Austria — Biography
JEWS — California — Los Angeles — Cultural assimilation
JEWS — California — Los Angeles — Identify
JEWS — Canada
JEWS — Ethiopia
JEWS — France
JEWS — France — Persecutions
JEWS — France — Politics and government
JEWS — France — Paris
JEWS — Germany — History
JEWS — Germany — Intellectual life — Congresses
JEWS — Germany (West) — Biography
JEWS — Great Britain
JEWS — Great Britain — History — 1789-1945
JEWS — Great Britain — Social conditions
JEWS — Hungary — History
JEWS — Hungary — Persecutions — Congresses
JEWS — Italy — Persecutions
JEWS — Lithuania — Vilnius — Addresses, essays, lectures
JEWS — Palestine — Economic conditions
JEWS — Palestine — History
JEWS — Palestine — History — 19th century
JEWS — Poland
JEWS — Poland — Bibliography
JEWS — Poland — History
JEWS — Soviet Union
JEWS — Soviet Union — Economic conditions — Addresses, essays, lectures
JEWS — Soviet Union — History — 18th century
JEWS — Soviet Union — History — 19th century
JEWS — Soviet Union — Identity — Addresses, essays, lectures
JEWS — Soviet Union — Social conditions
JEWS — United States
JEWS — United States — Abstracts
JEWS — United States — Attitudes toward Israel
JEWS — United States — Biography
JEWS — United States — Economic conditions — Addresses, essays, lectures
JEWS — United States — History
JEWS — United States — Intellectual life
JEWS — United States — Politics and government — History
JEWS — United States — Social conditions
JEWS — Yemen — History
JEWS, EAST EUROPEAN — Education — New York (N.Y.) — History
JEWS, EAST EUROPEAN — France — Paris
JEWS, EAST EUROPEAN — United States — Economic conditions — Addresses, essays, lectures
JEWS, GERMAN — Netherlands
JEWS IN ART
JEWS, RUSSIAN — Education — New York (N.Y.) — History
JEWS, RUSSIAN — Israel — Cultural assimilation
JEWS, RUSSIAN — United States
JIHAD
JIYŪ MINSHUTŌ
JOB ANALYSIS
JOB EVALUATION
JOB EVALUATION — Great Britain
JOB EVALUATION — Ontario
JOB HUNTING — Great Britain
JOB SATISFACTION
JOB SATISFACTION — Great Britain
JOB SHARING — Québec (Province)
JOB STRESS — United States
JOB VACANCIES
JOB VACANCIES — Information services
JOB VACANCIES — England — Cleveland
JOB VACANCIES — England — Sheffield (South Yorkshire)
JOB VACANCIES — Great Britain
JOB VACANCIES — Kenya
JOB VACANCIES — United States
JOB VACANCIES — Wales — Clwyd
JOHANNESBURG (SOUTH AFRICA) — Buildings, structures, etc
JOHANNESBURG (SOUTH AFRICA) — History
JOHANNESBURG (SOUTH AFRICA) — Race relations — History
JOHN LEWIS PARTNERSHIP
JOHN SUMMERS & SONS
JOHNSEN AND JORGENSEN LTD
JOHNSON, HUGH S
JOHNSON, LYNDON B
JOHNSON, LYNDON B.
JOHNSTON, DONALD J.
JOINT ADVENTURES — Yugoslavia
JOINT VENTURES
JOINT VENTURES — Personnel management
JOINT VENTURES — Europe
JOINT VENTURES — Japan
JOINT VENTURES — Poland
JOINT VENTURES — United States
JONS (PERIODICAL)
JONSSON, Family
JORDAN — Economic conditions
JORDAN — Population — Statistics — Evaluation
JORDAN — Social conditions
JORDAN — Statistics, Vital
JOSEPH II, Holy Roman Emperor
JOSEPH, MICHAEL, 1897-1958
JOURNALISM
JOURNALISM — Authorship
JOURNALISM — Moral and ethical aspects
JOURNALISM — Political aspects
JOURNALISM — Political aspects — Mexico
JOURNALISM — Political aspects — United States
JOURNALISM — Social aspects — Great Britain — History
JOURNALISM — Germany (East)
JOURNALISM — Soviet Union — History
JOURNALISM — United States — Objectivity
JOURNALISM, MILITARY
JOURNALISM, SCIENTIFIC
JOURNALISTIC ETHICS
JOURNALISTS — Legal status, laws, etc — Ecuador
JOURNALISTS — Brazil — Biography
JOURNALISTS — Czechoslovakia — Biography
JOURNALISTS — France — Biography
JOURNALISTS — Germany — Biography
JOURNALISTS — Great Britain
JOURNALISTS — Great Britain — Biography
JOURNALISTS — Ohio — Biography
JOURNALISTS — United States
JOURNALISTS — United States — Biography
J.P. MORGAN & CO — History
J.P. STEVENS & CO — Case studies
JUAN CARLOS I, King of Spain
JUDAISM — History
JUDAISM — Germany — History — Congresses
JUDAISM — Yemen — History
JUDAISM AND POLITICS — History
JUDAISM AND SOCIAL PROBLEMS
JUDGE-MADE LAW — United States — History
JUDGEMENT — Congresses
JUDGEMENTS, CRIMINAL — France — Statistics
JUDGEMENTS, FOREIGN — Asia
JUDGEMENTS, FOREIGN — European Economic Community countries
JUDGES
JUDGES — Canada — Biography
JUDGES — Developing countries
JUDGES — England
JUDGES — England — History
JUDGES — France — History
JUDGES — Great Britain — Directories
JUDGES — Scotland — Biography
JUDGES — Spain
JUDGES — United States — Appointment, qualifications, tenure, etc
JUDGES — United States — Biography
JUDGES — United States — History — Addresses, essays, lectures
JUDGMENT
JUDICIAL ASSISTANCE — Asia

JUDICIAL ASSISTANCE — European Economic Community countries
JUDICIAL OPINIONS — United States
JUDICIAL POWER — United States — History
JUDICIAL PROCESS
JUDICIAL PROCESS — Data processing
JUDICIAL PROCESS — Social aspects — United States
JUDICIAL PROCESS — European Economic Community countries
JUDICIAL PROCESS — Spain
JUDICIAL PROCESS — United States
JUDICIAL REVIEW
JUDICIAL REVIEW — European Economic Community countries — Addresses, essays, lectures
JUDICIAL REVIEW — United Satates
JUDICIAL REVIEW — United States — History
JUDICIAL REVIEW OF ADMINISTRATIVE ACTS — Australia
JUDICIAL REVIEW OF ADMINISTRATIVE ACTS — Canada
JUDICIAL REVIEW OF ADMINISTRATIVE ACTS — Great Britain
JUDICIAL REVIEW OF ADMINISTRATIVE ACTS — Scotland
JUDICIAL REVIEW OF ADMINISTRATIVE ACTS — United States
JUNG, C. G.
JUNG, C. G — Interviews
JUNGLE ECOLOGY
JUNIOR MINISTERS (POLITICAL SCIENCE) — Great Britain — History
JUNTAS DE OFENSIVA NACIONAL-SINDICALISTA
JURA (SWITZERLAND) — History — Autonomy and independence movements
JURISDICTION — America
JURISDICTION — United States — History
JURISPRUDENCE
JURISPRUDENCE — Addresses, essays, lectures
JURISPRUDENCE — History
JURISPRUDENCE — Russia — History
JURISPRUDENCE — Russia — Philosophy
JURY — Spain
JURY — United States
JUST WAR DOCTRINE
JUSTICE
JUSTICE — Addresses, essays, lectures
JUSTICE, ADMINISTRATION OF
JUSTICE, ADMINISTRATION OF — Canada
JUSTICE, ADMINISTRATION OF — Canada — Public opinion — Congresses
JUSTICE, ADMINISTRATION OF — England
JUSTICE, ADMINISTRATION OF — Japan — History
JUSTICE, ADMINISTRATION OF — New Zealand
JUSTICE, ADMINISTRATION OF — Ontario — History
JUSTICE, ADMINISTRATION OF — Spain
JUSTICE, ADMINISTRATION OF — Sri Lanka
JUSTICE, ADMINISTRATION OF — United States
JUSTICE, ADMINSTRATION OF — Germany — History — 20th century
JUSTICE AND POLITICS — Spain
JUSTICE (PHILOSOPHY)
JUSTICES ACT
JUSTICES OF THE PEACE — England
JUSTICES OF THE PEACE — Great Britain
JUSTICES OF THE PEACE — Scotland
JUSTIFICATION
JUSTIFICATION (THEORY OF KNOWLEDGE)
JUTE INDUSTRY — Forecasting
JUTE INDUSTRY — Bangladesh
JUVENILE CORRECTIONS
JUVENILE CORRECTIONS — Legal status, laws, etc — Great Britain
JUVENILE CORRECTIONS — England — History — 20th century
JUVENILE CORRECTIONS — France — Statistics
JUVENILE CORRECTIONS — Massachusetts
JUVENILE CORRECTIONS — Netherlands
JUVENILE COURTS — England — London
JUVENILE COURTS — France — Statistics
JUVENILE COURTS — United States
JUVENILE DELINQUENCY
JUVENILE DELINQUENCY — Prevention
JUVENILE DELINQUENCY — Research
JUVENILE DELINQUENCY — Canada
JUVENILE DELINQUENCY — Denmark
JUVENILE DELINQUENCY — England — Durham (Durham)
JUVENILE DELINQUENCY — Great Britain — Bibliography
JUVENILE DELINQUENCY — Massachusetts
JUVENILE DELINQUENCY — Netherlands
JUVENILE DELINQUENCY — South Australia
JUVENILE DELINQUENCY — United States
JUVENILE DELINQUENCY — United States — Public opinion
JUVENILE DELINQUENTS
JUVENILE DELINQUENTS — Training of — Great Britain
JUVENILE DELINQUENTS — Great Britain
JUVENILE DELINQUENTS — Great Britain — Alcohol use
JUVENILE DELINQUENTS — South Australia — Services for
JUVENILE DETENTION HOMES — Australia
JUVENILE DETENTION HOMES — England — Management
JUVENILE DETENTION HOMES — England — Derbyshire
JUVENILE DETENTION HOMES — England — Isle of Wight
JUVENILE DETENTION HOMES — England — Lincolnshire
JUVENILE DETENTION HOMES — England — London
JUVENILE DETENTION HOMES — Great Britain
JUVENILE JUSTICE, ADMINISTRATION OF
JUVENILE JUSTICE, ADMINISTRATION OF — England
JUVENILE JUSTICE, ADMINISTRATION OF — Great Britain
JUVENILE JUSTICE, ADMINISTRATION OF — Poland
JUVENILE JUSTICE, ADMINISTRATION OF — United States
JUVENILE PAROLE
KAFIRS (KAFIRISTAN)
KAGURU (AFRICAN PEOPLE)
KALECKI, MICHAŁ
KAMPUCHEA — Foreign relations — Asia, Southeastern
KAMUNISTYCHNAIA PARTYIA BELARUSI — History — Sources
KAMUNISTYCHNAIA PARTYIA BELARUSI — History — Sources
KANATCHIKOV, S
KANSAS — History
KANSAS CITY (MO.) — Politics and government
KANT, IMMANUEL
KANT, IMMANUEL. Metaphysische Anfangsgründe der Naturwissenschaft
KANT, IMMANUEL
KANT, IMMANUEL — Ethics
KANT, IMMANUEL — Metaphysics
KANT, IMMANUEL — Political science
KAPITAL
KARAN SINGH, Sadar-i-Riyasat of Jammu and Kashmir
KARDELJ, EDVARD
KARST (YUGOSLAVIA AND ITALY) — Economic conditions
KARST (YUGOSLAVIA AND ITALY) — Social conditions
KASHKAI TRIBE
KASPRZAK, MARCIN
KAUTSKY, KARL
KAWAI, EIJIRO
KAZAKH S.S.R. — History — Revolution of 1905
KAZAKH S.S.R. — History — Revolution, 1917-1921
KAZAKH S.S.R. — Population
KELANTAN — Population — Statistics
KENNEDY, JOHN F. (John Fitzgerald)
KENT — Social policy
KENTUCKY — Rural conditions
KENYA — Bibliography
KENYA — Constitution
KENYA — Economic policy
KENYA — Government Publications — Bibliography
KENYA — History — Dictionaries
KENYA — History — 1895-1963
KENYA — Officials and employees — Salaries, allowances, etc
KENYA — Politics and government
KENYA — Population
KENYA — Race relations
KENYA — Rural conditions
KENYA — Rural conditions — Statistics
KENYA — Social policy
KERENSKY, ALEKSANDR FYODOROVICH
KERN, ALFRED
KEWA (PAPUA NEW GUINEA PEOPLE) — Folklore
KEYNES
KEYNES, JOHN MAYNARD. General theory of employment, interest and money
KEYNES, JOHN MAYNARD
KEYNES, JOHN MAYNARD — Congresses
KEYNESIAN ECONOMICS
KHARLAMOV, N. M.
KHRUSHCHEV, N.
KIBBUTZIM
KILLINGHOLME (HUMBERSIDE) — Economic policy
KINGS AND RULERS
KINGS AND RULERS (IN RELIGION, FOLK-LORE, ETC.)
KINMEN (TAIWAN) — Economic conditions
KINSHIP
KINSHIP — China — History — Addresses, essays, lectures
KINSHIP — England — History
KINSHIP — Europe — History
KINSHIP — India — Bengal
KINSHIP — India — Tirunelveli District
KINSHIP — Indonesia — Mamboru
KINSHIP — North Carolina
KINSHIP — Soviet Union
KINSHIP — Spain — Barcelona — History
KINSHIP — West Bank
KIRGHIZ S.S.R. — Population
KIRIBATI — Economic policy
KIRIBATI — Social ploicy
KIRIBATI — Social policy
KIRIWINIAN LANGUAGE
KIROV, S. M.
KISSINGER, HENRY A.
KITCHENS — Manufactures
KITH AND KIDS
KITSON, NORMA
KLEIN, MELANIE
KLEIVAN, HELGE
KLIMENT, GUSTAV
KNOWLEDGE, SOCIOLOGY OF — Addresses, essays, lectures
KNOWLEDGE, THEORY OF

KNOWLEDGE, THEORY OF — Congresses
KNOWLEDGE, THEORY OF — History — 20th century
KOESTLER, ARTHUR — Archives — Catalogs
KOMITET OSVOBOZHDENIIA NARODOV ROSSI — History
KOMMUNISTICHESKAIA PARTIIA SOVETSKAIA SOIUZA — Biography — Directories
KOMMUNISTICHESKAIA PARTIIA SOVETSKOGO SOIUZA
KOMMUNISTICHESKAĨÃ PARTIĨÃ SOVETSKOGO SOĨŨZA
KOMMUNISTICHESKAIA PARTIIA SOVETSKOGO SOIUZA — Congresses
KOMMUNISTICHESKAĨÃ PARTIĨÃ SOVETSKOGO SOĨŨZA — History
KOMMUNISTICHESKAIA PARTIIA SOVETSKOGO SOIUZA — History
KOMMUNISTICHESKAIA PARTIIA SOVETSKOGO SOIUZA — History — Sources
KOMMUNISTICHESKAIA PARTIIA SOVETSKOGO SOIUZA — Membership
KOMMUNISTICHESKAIA PARTIIA SOVETSKOGO SOIUZA — Party work
KOMMUNISTICHESKAIA PARTIIA SOVETSKOGO SOIUZA — Party work — Dictionaries
KOMMUNISTICHESKAIA PARTIIA SOVETSKOGO SOIUZA. Tsentral'nyi komitet. Politbiuro
KOMMUNISTISCHE PARTEI DEUTSCHLANDS
KOMMUNISTISCHE PARTEI DEUTSCHLANDS — History
KOMMUNISTISCHE PARTEI DEUTSCHLANDS (MARXISTEN-LENINISTEN)
KOMMUNISTISCHER BUND WESTDEUTSCHLAND
KOMUNISTIČKA PARTIJA CRNE GORE — History
KOMUNISTYCHNA PARTIIA UKRAINY — Party work
KOMUNISTYCZNA PARTIA POLSKI — History
KONDRAT'EV, N. D
KONJUNKTÚRA-ÉS PIACKUTATÓ INTÉZET. Kulkereskedelmi Információs Köspont — Bibliography
KONSERVATIVE FOLKEPARTI (Denmark)
KOPÁCSI, SÁNDOR
KORAN — Commentaries
KOREA — Civilization — Addresses, essays, lectures
KOREA — Economic conditions — 1945-
KOREA — Foreign relations — 1864-1910
KOREA — Foreign relations — United States
KOREA — Foreign relations — United States — Congresses
KOREA — History — 1864-
KOREA — History — Japanese occupation, 1910-1945 — Congresses
KOREA — History — Allied occupation, 1945-1948
KOREA — History — War and intervention, 1950-1953 — Bibliography
KOREA — Politics and government
KOREA — Popular culture — Addresses, essays, lectures
KOREA — Rural conditions — Addresses, essays, lectures
KOREA — Social conditions — Addresses, essays, lectures
KOREA — Social conditions — 1945-
KOREA (NORTH) — Defenses
KOREA (NORTH) — Foreign relations
KOREA (NORTH) — Foreign relations — Korea (South)
KOREA (NORTH) — Military policy
KOREA (NORTH) — Politics and government
KOREA (SOUTH) — Census. 1970
KOREA (SOUTH) — Census, 1970
KOREA (SOUTH — Census, 1970
KOREA (SOUTH) — Census, 1970
KOREA (SOUTH) — Commercial policy
KOREA (SOUTH) — Defenses
KOREA (SOUTH) — Economic conditions — 1960-
KOREA (SOUTH) — Economic policy
KOREA (SOUTH) — Economic policy — 1960-
KOREA (SOUTH) — Foreign relations
KOREA (SOUTH) — Foreign relations — Korea (North)
KOREA (SOUTH) — Foreign relations — United States
KOREA (SOUTH) — Military policy
KOREA (SOUTH) — National security
KOREA (SOUTH) — Politics and government
KOREA (SOUTH) — Politics and government — 1945-1948
KOREA (SOUTH) — Politics and government — 1948-1960
KOREA (SOUTH) — Politics and government — 1960-
KOREA (SOUTH) — Population — Statistics
KOREAN AIR LINES INCIDENT, 1983
KOREAN REUNIFICATION QUESTION (1945-)
KOREAN REUNIFICATION QUESTION (1945)-
KOREAN WAR, 1950-1953
KOSEDA, HEIDI
KOSOVA (YUGOSLAVIA) — Politics and government
KOSOVO (SERBIA) — Constitutional law
KOSOVO (SERBIA) — History
KOSOVO (SERBIA) — Politics and government
KOWLOON (HONG KONG) — Statistics
KRISTELIGT FOLKEPARTI (Denmark)
KUBEL, ALFRED
KUCZYNSKI, JÜRGEN
KUN, BÉLA
KUOMINTANG
KURDS — Civil rights
KUWAIT — Economic conditions — Econometric models
KWAIO (MELANESIAN PEOPLE) — Religion
KWOMA (PAPUAN PEOPLE) — Social life and customs
LA RIOJA (SPAIN) — History
LA TOUR, CHARLES DE ST. ETIENNE
LABOR AND LABORING CLASSES
LABOR AND LABORING CLASSES — Attitudes
LABOR AND LABORING CLASSES — Dwellings — Brazil — Salvador
LABOR AND LABORING CLASSES — Dwellings — Great Britain — History
LABOR AND LABORING CLASSES — Education
LABOR AND LABORING CLASSES — Education — Australia
LABOR AND LABORING CLASSES — Education — England — Liverpool (Merseyside)
LABOR AND LABORING CLASSES — Education — Finland
LABOR AND LABORING CLASSES — Education — Germany — History
LABOR AND LABORING CLASSES — History — Addresses, essays, lectures
LABOR AND LABORING CLASSES — History — 20th century
LABOR AND LABORING CLASSES — Moral and ethical aspects
LABOR AND LABORING CLASSES — Political activity
LABOR AND LABORING CLASSES — Social aspects — Soviet Union
LABOR AND LABORING CLASSES — Argentina — History
LABOR AND LABORING CLASSES — America — Congresses
LABOR AND LABORING CLASSES — Argentina
LABOR AND LABORING CLASSES — Argentina — History
LABOR AND LABORING CLASSES — Argentina — History — 19th century
LABOR AND LABORING CLASSES — Argentina — History — 20th century
LABOR AND LABORING CLASSES — Argentina — Political activity — History
LABOR AND LABORING CLASSES — Australia — History
LABOR AND LABORING CLASSES — Australia — Tasmania
LABOR AND LABORING CLASSES — Austria
LABOR AND LABORING CLASSES — British Columbia — History
LABOR AND LABORING CLASSES — British Columbia — Vancouver — History
LABOR AND LABORING CLASSES — Bulgaria
LABOR AND LABORING CLASSES — Canada
LABOR AND LABORING CLASSES — Canada — Bibliography
LABOR AND LABORING CLASSES — Canada — History
LABOR AND LABORING CLASSES — Canada — Atlantic Provinces
LABOR AND LABORING CLASSES — Chicago (Illinois) — History
LABOR AND LABORING CLASSES — Colombia — Bogota
LABOR AND LABORING CLASSES — Colombia — Cali
LABOR AND LABORING CLASSES — Denmark
LABOR AND LABORING CLASSES — Denmark — Political activity
LABOR AND LABORING CLASSES — Egypt — Political activity
LABOR AND LABORING CLASSES — England
LABOR AND LABORING CLASSES — England — History
LABOR AND LABORING CLASSES — England — Coventry — History
LABOR AND LABORING CLASSES — England — London
LABOR AND LABORING CLASSES — England — Oldham, Lancs. — History
LABOR AND LABORING CLASSES — England — West Country — Alcohol use
LABOR AND LABORING CLASSES — Europe — History
LABOR AND LABORING CLASSES — Europe — History — 20th century
LABOR AND LABORING CLASSES — Europe, Eastern
LABOR AND LABORING CLASSES — France
LABOR AND LABORING CLASSES — France — History — 19th century
LABOR AND LABORING CLASSES — France — Ladrecht — Language (New words, slang, etc)
LABOR AND LABORING CLASSES — Germany — History
LABOR AND LABORING CLASSES — Germany — History — 19th century
LABOR AND LABORING CLASSES — Germany — Political activity
LABOR AND LABORING CLASSES — Germany — Political activity — History
LABOR AND LABORING CLASSES — Germany — Social conditions
LABOR AND LABORING CLASSES — Germany (West)
LABOR AND LABORING CLASSES — Great Britain
LABOR AND LABORING CLASSES — Great Britain — History
LABOR AND LABORING CLASSES — Great Britain — History — Bibliography

LABOR AND LABORING CLASSES — Great Britain — History — 19th century
LABOR AND LABORING CLASSES — Great Britain — Law and legislation
LABOR AND LABORING CLASSES — Iceland
LABOR AND LABORING CLASSES — India
LABOR AND LABORING CLASSES — India — History
LABOR AND LABORING CLASSES — India — Political activity
LABOR AND LABORING CLASSES — India — Statistics
LABOR AND LABORING CLASSES — India — Hyderabad (State) — History
LABOR AND LABORING CLASSES — India — Manipur — Statistics
LABOR AND LABORING CLASSES — Iran
LABOR AND LABORING CLASSES — Iran — Political activity
LABOR AND LABORING CLASSES — Italy — Turin — History — 20th century
LABOR AND LABORING CLASSES — Japan — Statistics
LABOR AND LABORING CLASSES — Louisiana — History
LABOR AND LABORING CLASSES — Mexico — History
LABOR AND LABORING CLASSES — Moldavian S.S.R.
LABOR AND LABORING CLASSES — Namibia
LABOR AND LABORING CLASSES — Netherlands
LABOR AND LABORING CLASSES — New York (State) — Albany — History — 19th century
LABOR AND LABORING CLASSES — Nigeria, Northern — History
LABOR AND LABORING CLASSES — Peru
LABOR AND LABORING CLASSES — Poland
LABOR AND LABORING CLASSES — Poland — History
LABOR AND LABORING CLASSES — Poland — Łódź
LABOR AND LABORING CLASSES — Russian S.F.S.R. — Gor'kii
LABOR AND LABORING CLASSES — Russian S.F.S.R. — Moscow — Political activity
LABOR AND LABORING CLASSES — Russian S.F.S.R. — Siberia
LABOR AND LABORING CLASSES — Russian S.F.S.R. — Siberia — Historiography
LABOR AND LABORING CLASSES — Scotland — History
LABOR AND LABORING CLASSES — Scotland — Glasgow (Strathclyde) — History
LABOR AND LABORING CLASSES — South Africa — History
LABOR AND LABORING CLASSES — South America — History
LABOR AND LABORING CLASSES — Soviet Union
LABOR AND LABORING CLASSES — Soviet Union — Biography
LABOR AND LABORING CLASSES — Soviet Union — Historiography
LABOR AND LABORING CLASSES — Soviet Union — History
LABOR AND LABORING CLASSES — Soviet Union — Political activity
LABOR AND LABORING CLASSES — Soviet Union, Northern
LABOR AND LABORING CLASSES — Spain
LABOR AND LABORING CLASSES — Spain — Bibliography
LABOR AND LABORING CLASSES — Spain — History — 19th century
LABOR AND LABORING CLASSES — Spain — Statistics
LABOR AND LABORING CLASSES — Spain — Andalusia — History
LABOR AND LABORING CLASSES — Spain — Asturias — History — 20th century
LABOR AND LABORING CLASSES — Spain — Cantabria — History — 20th century
LABOR AND LABORING CLASSES — Spain — Madrid — History — 20th century
LABOR AND LABORING CLASSES — Spain — Seville — History
LABOR AND LABORING CLASSES — Spain — Valladolid
LABOR AND LABORING CLASSES — Spain — Vitoria — History
LABOR AND LABORING CLASSES — Sweden
LABOR AND LABORING CLASSES — Ukraine — History
LABOR AND LABORING CLASSES — United States
LABOR AND LABORING CLASSES — United States — Attitudes
LABOR AND LABORING CLASSES — United States — History
LABOR AND LABORING CLASSES — United States — History — Sources
LABOR AND LABORING CLASSES — United States — History — 19th century
LABOR AND LABORING CLASSES — United States — 1914-
LABOR AND LABORING CLASSES IN ART
LABOR AND LABORING CLASSES IN LITERATURE
LABOR CAMPS — Canada
LABOR CONTRACT
LABOR CONTRACT — Economic aspects
LABOR CONTRACT — Graphic methods
LABOR CONTRACT — Great Britain
LABOR COSTS
LABOR COSTS — France
LABOR COSTS — Great Britain
LABOR COSTS — Peru — Statistics
LABOR COURTS — Great Britain
LABOR DISPUTES
LABOR DISPUTES — Law and legislation
LABOR DISPUTES — European Economic Community countries
LABOR DISPUTES — Germany (West)
LABOR DISPUTES — Great Britain
LABOR DISPUTES — India
LABOR ECONOMICS
LABOR LAW AND LEGISLATION — Canada
LABOR LAWS AND LEAGISLATION — Canada
LABOR LAWS AND LEGISLATION
LABOR LAWS AND LEGISLATION — Addresses, essays, lectures
LABOR LAWS AND LEGISLATION — Australia
LABOR LAWS AND LEGISLATION — Canada
LABOR LAWS AND LEGISLATION — Europe — History
LABOR LAWS AND LEGISLATION — France
LABOR LAWS AND LEGISLATION — Great Britain
LABOR LAWS AND LEGISLATION — Iran — History — 20th century
LABOR LAWS AND LEGISLATION — Nigeria
LABOR LAWS AND LEGISLATION — Singapore
LABOR LAWS AND LEGISLATION — South Africa
LABOR LAWS AND LEGISLATION — Soviet Union
LABOR LAWS AND LEGISLATION — Turkey
LABOR LAWS AND LEGISLATION — United States
LABOR LAWS AND LEGISLATION, INTERNATIONAL
LABOR LAWS AND LEGISLATIONOFF. PUBNS. — European Economic Community countries 986
LABOR MARKET
LABOR MARKET — Great Britain
LABOR MOBILITY
LABOR MOBILITY — Australia
LABOR MOBILITY — Denmark
LABOR MOBILITY — France
LABOR MOBILITY — Germany (West)
LABOR MOBILITY — Great Britain
LABOR MOBILITY — India — Bombay
LABOR MOBILITY — Organisation for Economic Co-operation and Development countries
LABOR MOBILITY — Scotland
LABOR MOBILITY — Soviet Union
LABOR MOBILITY — Sudan — Statistics
LABOR POLICY
LABOR POLICY — Canal Zone — History — 20th century
LABOR POLICY — Egypt
LABOR POLICY — Europe, Eastern
LABOR POLICY — Great Britain — History — 20th century
LABOR POLICY — India
LABOR POLICY — Japan — History
LABOR POLICY — Netherlands
LABOR POLICY — Soviet Union
LABOR POLICY — United States
LABOR POLICY — United States — History
LABOR POLICY — United States — History — 20th century
LABOR PRODUCTIVITY
LABOR PRODUCTIVITY — Australia
LABOR PRODUCTIVITY — Australia — Measurement
LABOR PRODUCTIVITY — Canada
LABOR PRODUCTIVITY — Papua New Guinea
LABOR PRODUCTIVITY — Soviet Union
LABOR SUPPLY
LABOR SUPPLY — Addresses, essays, lectures
LABOR SUPPLY — Effect of technological innovations on
LABOR SUPPLY — Effect of technological innovations on — Congresses
LABOR SUPPLY — Government policy — Peru
LABOR SUPPLY — Great Britain — Statistics
LABOR SUPPLY — Mathematical models
LABOR SUPPLY — Regional disparities
LABOR SUPPLY — Research — Bibliography
LABOR SUPPLY — Statistical methods
LABOR SUPPLY — Statistics
LABOR SUPPLY — Statistics — Sources
LABOR SUPPLY — Africa
LABOR SUPPLY — Africa — Statistics
LABOR SUPPLY — Alsace (France) — Statistics
LABOR SUPPLY — Asia — Statistics
LABOR SUPPLY — Australia
LABOR SUPPLY — Australia — Longitudinal studies
LABOR SUPPLY — Australia — Methodology
LABOR SUPPLY — Belgium — Statistics
LABOR SUPPLY — Botswana — Statistics
LABOR SUPPLY — Brazil
LABOR SUPPLY — Brazil — Salvador
LABOR SUPPLY — Bulgaria
LABOR SUPPLY — Cape Verde
LABOR SUPPLY — Caribbean Area
LABOR SUPPLY — Costa Rica — Statistics
LABOR SUPPLY — Cyprus
LABOR SUPPLY — Cyprus — Statistics
LABOR SUPPLY — Denmark
LABOR SUPPLY — Developing countries

LABOR SUPPLY — Egypt
LABOR SUPPLY — England — Avon
LABOR SUPPLY — England — Bristol (Avon)
LABOR SUPPLY — England — Cheshire
LABOR SUPPLY — England — London
LABOR SUPPLY — Europe
LABOR SUPPLY — European Economic Community countries
LABOR SUPPLY — European Economic Community countries — Statistics
LABOR SUPPLY — Finland — Statistics
LABOR SUPPLY — France
LABOR SUPPLY — France — Statistics
LABOR SUPPLY — France — Ile-de-France — Statistics
LABOR SUPPLY — Germany (West)
LABOR SUPPLY — Great Britain
LABOR SUPPLY — Great Britain — Effect of automation on
LABOR SUPPLY — Great Britain — Effect of technological innovations on
LABOR SUPPLY — Great Britain — History — 20th century
LABOR SUPPLY — Great Britain — Statistical services
LABOR SUPPLY — Great Britain — Statistics
LABOR SUPPLY — India
LABOR SUPPLY — India — Statistics
LABOR SUPPLY — India — Karnataka
LABOR SUPPLY — Ireland — Statistics
LABOR SUPPLY — Italy — Statistics
LABOR SUPPLY — Jamaica — Statistics
LABOR SUPPLY — Japan — Statistics
LABOR SUPPLY — Jordan — Statistics
LABOR SUPPLY — Kenya
LABOR SUPPLY — Korea (South) — Statistics
LABOR SUPPLY — Latin America — Statistics
LABOR SUPPLY — London
LABOR SUPPLY — Mexico
LABOR SUPPLY — Nepal
LABOR SUPPLY — Netherlands
LABOR SUPPLY — Netherlands — Statistics
LABOR SUPPLY — Nigeria — Statistics
LABOR SUPPLY — Northeastern States
LABOR SUPPLY — Northeastern States — Forecasting
LABOR SUPPLY — Organisation for Economic Co-operation and Development countries
LABOR SUPPLY — Panama
LABOR SUPPLY — Portugal
LABOR SUPPLY — Québec (Province) — Effect of technological innovations on
LABOR SUPPLY — Québec (Province) — Statistics
LABOR SUPPLY — Réunion — Statistics
LABOR SUPPLY — San Marino — Statistics
LABOR SUPPLY — Scotland — Clydeside (Strathclyde)
LABOR SUPPLY — Singapore
LABOR SUPPLY — Southern Africa
LABOR SUPPLY — Soviet Union
LABOR SUPPLY — Spain
LABOR SUPPLY — Sri Lanka — Statistics
LABOR SUPPLY — Sweden
LABOR SUPPLY — Sweden — History — 20th century
LABOR SUPPLY — Thailand — Statistics
LABOR SUPPLY — Togo — Statistics
LABOR SUPPLY — Tonga — Statistics
LABOR SUPPLY — Trinidad and Tobago — Statistics
LABOR SUPPLY — Ukraine
LABOR SUPPLY — United States
LABOR SUPPLY — United States — Effect of technological innovations on
LABOR SUPPLY — United States — Statistics
LABOR SUPPLY — Wales
LABOR SUPPLY — Wales — Clwyd
LABOR SUPPLY OFF. PUBNS. — European Economic Community countries 986
LABOR THEORY OF VALUE
LABOR TURNOVER — Great Britain
LABOR TURNOVER — Russian S.F.S.R. — Siberia
LABOR TURNOVER — Soviet Union
LABOR UND LABORING CLASSES — Germany — History
LABORATORY ANIMALS
LABOUR CAMPAIGN FOR ELECTORAL REFORM
LABOUR CONTRACT — India
LABOUR-MANAGEMENT COMMITTEES — Hungary — History
LABOUR PARTY, Great Britain — History
LABOUR PARTY (Great Britain)
LABOUR PARTY (Great Britain) — Biography
LABOUR PARTY (Great Britain) — Decision making
LABOUR PARTY (Great Britain) — History
LABOUR PARTY (Great Britain). Deptford Constituency Labour Party
LABOUR PARTY (Ireland)
LABOUR PARTY (GREAT BRITAIN)
LABOUR SUPPLY — Egypt
LABOUR SUPPLY — England — London
LABOUR SUPPLY — Great Britain
LABOUR SUPPLY — Malaysia
LABOUR SUPPLY — New Zealand — Statistics
LABOUR SUPPLY — Réunion — Statistics
LADRECHT (FRANCE) — Social conditions
LADRECHT (FRANCE) — Coal Miners' Strike, 1981-1982
LAGOS (NIGERIA) — Social conditions
LAISSEZ-FAIRE
LAISSEZ-FAIRE — Congresses
LAISSEZ-FAIRE — History
LAISZEZ-FAIRE
LAKSHMI BAI, Rani of Jhansi
LAMBETH (LONDON, ENGLAND) — City planning
LAMBETH (LONDON, ENGLAND) — Economic conditions
LAMBETH (LONDON, ENGLAND) — Economic policy
LAMBETH (LONDON, ENGLAND) — Social policy
LANCASHIRE — Bibliography
LANCASHIRE — Social conditions
LANCASHIRE ASSOCIATION OF TRADES COUNCILS
LAND
LAND — Australia
LAND — Czechoslovakia
LAND — Great Britain
LAND — Kazakh S.S.R.
LAND COMPANIES — Argentina
LAND REFORM — Law and legislation — Ecuador
LAND REFORM — Law and legislation — Peru
LAND REFORM — Botswana
LAND REFORM — Great Britain
LAND REFORM — India
LAND REFORM — India — Government policy
LAND REFORM — India — History
LAND REFORM — Kenya — Case studies
LAND REFORM — Mexico — Yucatán — History
LAND REFORM — Peru
LAND SETTLEMENT — Nigeria — Kainji Reservoir Region
LAND SETTLEMENT — Oregon — History
LAND SETTLEMENT — Prairie Provinces — History
LAND SETTLEMENT — Zimbabwe — Statistics
LAND TENURE — Law and legislation — Ecuador
LAND TENURE — Law and legislation — Hong Kong
LAND TENURE — Law and legislation — Peru
LAND TENURE — Political aspects — England — Wimborne (Dorset)
LAND TENURE — Political aspects — India
LAND TENURE — Political aspects — Ireland
LAND TENURE — Appalachian Region
LAND TENURE — Colombia — History
LAND TENURE — Great Britain
LAND TENURE — Greece — History — 19th century
LAND TENURE — India
LAND TENURE — India — History — 18th century
LAND TENURE — Ireland — History — 19th century
LAND TENURE — Ivory Coast
LAND TENURE — Japan — History
LAND TENURE — Peru
LAND TENURE — Peru — Cajamarca — History
LAND TENURE — Poland — History
LAND TENURE — Singapore — Law
LAND TENURE — Soviet Union — History
LAND TENURE — Soviet Union — History — 17th century
LAND TENURE — Spain — History — 20th century
LAND TENURE — Taiwan
LAND TENURE — Taiwan — Kinmen
LAND TENURE — Transcaucasia — History
LAND TITLES — Registration and transfer — England
LAND USE
LAND USE — Dictionaries — Polyglot
LAND USE — Environmental aspects — Kenya
LAND USE — Environmental aspects — Tanzania
LAND USE — Government policy — Great Britain
LAND USE — Planning
LAND USE — Planning — Case studies
LAND USE — Planning — Dictionaries, Polyglot
LAND USE — Social aspects — Great Britain
LAND USE — Barbados — Planning
LAND USE — Bermuda
LAND USE — China — History
LAND USE — England — Bedfordshire
LAND USE — England — Kent
LAND USE — England — Killingholme (Humberside)
LAND USE — Great Britain
LAND USE — Great Britain — Planning
LAND USE — Greece — History — 19th century
LAND USE — Indonesia — History
LAND USE — Nepal
LAND USE — Netherlands
LAND USE — Scotland
LAND USE — South Africa
LAND USE — Wales — Flintshire
LAND USE — Wales — West Glamorgan
LAND USE, RURAL
LAND USE, RURAL — Environmental aspects — Developing countries
LAND USE, RURAL — Appalachian Region
LAND USE, RURAL — China — Hunan Province — History
LAND USE, RURAL — Colombia
LAND USE, RURAL — England — Bedfordshire
LAND USE, RURAL — England — Leicester (Leicestershire) — Case studies
LAND USE, RURAL — Fiji
LAND USE, RURAL — France
LAND USE, RURAL — Great Britain

LAND USE, RURAL — Ireland — Congresses
LAND USE, RURAL — Southern States
LAND USE, RURAL — Wales — West Glamorgan
LAND USE, URBAN
LAND USE, URBAN — England — London
LAND USE, URBAN — Great Britain
LAND VALUE TAXATION — England — History
LAND VALUE TAXATION — France
LANDER, J. R. — Bibliography
LANDFORMS
LANDLORD AND TENANT — Great Britain
LANDLORD AND TENANT — England
LANDLORD AND TENANT — England — London
LANDLORD AND TENANT — Great Britain
LANDLORD AND TENANT — Northern Ireland
LANDLORD AND TENANT (NO.2) BILL 1986-87
LANDOWNERS — Mexico — History — Congresses
LANDSCAPE
LANDSCAPE — Ireland — Congresses
LANDSCAPE ARCHITECTURE — History — 19th century
LANDSCAPE ARCHITECTURE — History — 20th century
LANDSCAPE PROTECTION — Great Britain
LANGE, OSKAR
LANGUAGE
LANGUAGE ACQUISITION
LANGUAGE ACQUISITION — Congresses
LANGUAGE AND CULTURE
LANGUAGE AND CULTURE — Mali
LANGUAGE AND EDUCATION
LANGUAGE AND LANGUAGES
LANGUAGE AND LANGUAGES — Study and teaching
LANGUAGE AND LANGUAGES — Study and teaching — Congresses
LANGUAGE AND LANGUAGES — Study and teaching — United States
LANGUAGE AND LANGUAGES — Vocational guidance — Congresses
LANGUAGE AWARENESS
LANGUAGE PLANNING
LANGUAGE PLANNING — Wales
LANGUAGE POLICY
LANGUAGE POLICY — India
LANGUAGE POLICY — Manitoba — History
LANGUAGE, TRUTH AND LOGIC
LANGUAGES — Philosophy
LANGUAGES — Political aspects
LANHEZES (PORTUGAL) — Population — History
LANZ VON LIEBENFELS, JÖRG
LAOS — History — 1975-
LAOS — Politics and government
LAPLACE TRANSFORMATION
LAPPS — Norway
LARKIN, J.
LARVIK (NORWAY) — Industries
LASSALLE, FERDINAND — Biography
LATCHKEY CHILDREN — United States
LATENT VARIABLES
LATIN AMERICA
LATIN AMERICA — Appropriations and expenditures
LATIN AMERICA — Armed Forces — Addresses, essays, lectures
LATIN AMERICA — Armed Forces — Appropriations and expenditures
LATIN AMERICA — Armed Forces — Political activity
LATIN AMERICA — Armed Forces — Political activity — History — 20th century
LATIN AMERICA — Census — Handbooks, manuals, etc
LATIN AMERICA — Church history — Addresses, essays, lectures
LATIN AMERICA — Civilization
LATIN AMERICA — Civilization — 1948- — Congresses
LATIN AMERICA — Commerce
LATIN AMERICA — Commerce — Bibliography
LATIN AMERICA — Commerce — Information services
LATIN AMERICA — Commerce — Spain
LATIN AMERICA — Commercial policy
LATIN AMERICA — Congresses
LATIN AMERICA — Defenses
LATIN AMERICA — Dependency on foreign countries — Addresses, essays, lectures
LATIN AMERICA — Description and travel — Bibliography
LATIN AMERICA — Economic conditions
LATIN AMERICA — Economic conditions — 1945-
LATIN AMERICA — Economic conditions — 1945- — Addresses, essays, lectures
LATIN AMERICA — Economic conditions — 1945- — Bibliography
LATIN AMERICA — Economic conditions — 1945- — Congresses
LATIN AMERICA — Economic conditions — 1945- — Information services
LATIN AMERICA — Economic integration
LATIN AMERICA — Economic policy
LATIN AMERICA — Emigration and immigration
LATIN AMERICA — Emigration and immigration — History
LATIN AMERICA — Foreign economic relations — Europe — Bibliography
LATIN AMERICA — Foreign economic relations — United States
LATIN AMERICA — Foreign relations — 1948-
LATIN AMERICA — Foreign relations — Soviet Union — Congresses
LATIN AMERICA — Foreign relations — United States
LATIN AMERICA — History
LATIN AMERICA — History — Archival resources
LATIN AMERICA — History — Wars of Independence, 1806-1830
LATIN AMERICA — Library resources — England — London
LATIN AMERICA — Manufactures
LATIN AMERICA — Military relations — United States
LATIN AMERICA — Politics and government
LATIN AMERICA — Politics and government — To 1830 — Congresses
LATIN AMERICA — Politics and government — 1945- — Addresses, essays, lectures
LATIN AMERICA — Politics and government — 1948 — Addresses, essays, lectures
LATIN AMERICA — Politics and government — 1948-
LATIN AMERICA — Politics and government — 1948- — Bibliography
LATIN AMERICA — Politics and government — 1948- — Congresses
LATIN AMERICA — Politics and government — 1948- — Philosophy
LATIN AMERICA — Population
LATIN AMERICA — Population — Statistics
LATIN AMERICA — Population — Statistics — Methodology
LATIN AMERICA — Relations — Soviet Union
LATIN AMERICA — Relations — Spain
LATIN AMERICA — Relations — United States
LATIN AMERICA — Social conditions — 1945-
LATIN AMERICA — Social conditions — 1945- — Congresses
LATIN AMERICA — Strategic aspects
LATIN AMERICA — Yearbooks
LATIN AMERICAN — Relations — Spain
LATVIA — Economic conditions — Statistics
LAUNDRESSES — England — History
LAUNDRESSES — England — Social conditions
LAUNDRY WORKERS — England — History
LAVAL, PIERRE
LAW
LAW — Addresses, essays, lectures
LAW — Bibliography
LAW — Congresses
LAW — Dictionaries
LAW — Economic aspects
LAW — Interpretation and construction
LAW — Language
LAW — Methodology
LAW — Methodology — Addresses, essays, lectures
LAW — Methodology — Data processing
LAW — Philosophy
LAW — Philosophy — Addresses, essays, lectures
LAW — Philosphy
LAW — Quotations
LAW — Sociological aspects
LAW — Study and teaching — Egypt
LAW — Study and teaching — England
LAW — Study and teaching — Great Britain
LAW — Study and teaching — Latin America — Bibliography
LAW — Afghanistan
LAW — Africa
LAW — Asia
LAW — Canada
LAW — Canada — Public opinion — Congresses
LAW — Canada, Northern — History and criticism
LAW — Canada, Western — History and criticism
LAW — Developing countries
LAW — England
LAW — England — History
LAW — England — History and criticism
LAW — Europe — Bibliography
LAW — European Communities countries
LAW — European Economic Community
LAW — European Economic Community countries
LAW — European Economic Community Countries
LAW — European Economic Community countries
LAW — European Economic Community Countries — Bibliography — Catalogs
LAW — Finland — Addresses, essays, lectures
LAW — Finland — Bibliography
LAW — France
LAW — France — Dictionaries
LAW — Germany — History
LAW — Germany — History — 20th century
LAW — Germany (West) — Bibliography
LAW — Great Britain
LAW — Greece — Athens
LAW — India — Public opinion
LAW — Korea (South)
LAW — Latin America — Bibliography
LAW — Netherlands
LAW — Netherlands — Addresses, essays, lectures
LAW — Russian S.F.S.R. — Moscow
LAW — Scotland — Dictionaries
LAW — South Africa
LAW — South Africa — Addresses, essays, lectures
LAW — Soviet Union
LAW — Spain
LAW — Spain — Autonomous communities

LAW — Spain — History and criticism
LAW — Sparta (Ancient city)
LAW — Sri Lanka — Language
LAW — United States
LAW — United States — Methodology
LAW — Wales — History and criticism
LAW — Yemen
LAW — Yugoslavia
LAW — Zambia
LAW AND ETHICS
LAW AND ETHICS — Addresses, essays, lectures
LAW AND POLITICS
LAW AND SOCIALISM
LAW, ASHANTI
LAW, CHAGA (AFRICAN PEOPLE)
LAW ENFORCEMENT
LAW, GREEK
LAW LIBRARIES
LAW LIBRARIES — Great Britain — Directories
LAW OF THE SEA See Maritime law
LAW PUBLISHING — Ireland
LAW PUBLISHING — Isle of Man
LAW PUBLISHING — Scotland
LAW REFORM — Australia
LAW REFORM — Canada
LAW REFORM — Great Britain
LAW REFORM — New Zealand
LAW REFORM — Northern Ireland — History
LAW REPORTS, DIGESTS, ETC. — England — History
LAW REPORTS, DIGESTS, ETC. — Soviet Union
LAW TEACHERS — United States — Biography
LAWYERS — Brazil — Biography
LAWYERS — Denmark
LAWYERS — Denmark — Fees
LAWYERS — England
LAWYERS — England — History — 16th century
LAWYERS — England — History — 17th century
LAWYERS — Great Britain — Directories
LAWYERS — Ireland — Biography
LAWYERS — Mississippi — Biography
LAWYERS — United States
LAWYERS — United States — History — Addresses, essays, lectures
LAY JUDGES — United States
LAYOFF SYSTEMS — Case studies
LAYOFF SYSTEMS — England — Stoke-on-Trent (Staffordshire)
LAYTON, WALTER
LAZARE, BERNARD
LE PEN, JEAN-MARIE
LE PEN, JEAN MARIE
LEA, HOMER
LEAD — Environmental aspects — Great Britain
LEAD MINES AND MINING — Wales — Cardiganshire — Statistics
LEAD POISONING — Law and legislation — Great Britain
LEADERSHIP
LEADERSHIP — Addresses, essays, lectures
LEADERSHIP — Congresses
LEADERSHIP — History — Congresses
LEADERSHIP — India — Case studies
LEAGUE OF WOMEN VOTERS (U.S.)
LEARNING
LEARNING AND SCHOLARSHIP — Data processing
LEARNING AND SCHOLARSHIP — California — Stanford — Case studies
LEARNING AND SCHOLARSHIP — United States — Statistics
LEARNING DISABILITIES
LEARNING DISABILITIES — United States — History
LEARNING, PSYCHOLOGY OF
LEARNING, PSYCHOLOGY OF — Congresses
LEASES — Accounting

LEAST DEVELOPED COUNTRIES See Developing countries
LEATHER INDUSTRY AND TRADE — Mexico
LEBANON — Foreign relations — Near East
LEBANON — Foreign relations — Syria
LEBANON — History
LEBANON — History — Israeli intervention, 1982-
LEBANON — History — French occupation, 1918-1946
LEBANON — History — 1946-
LEBANON — History — Civil War, 1975-1976
LEBANON — History — Israeli intervention, 1982-
LEBANON — Politics and government — 1946-
LEBANON — Politics and government — 1975-
LEBANON — History — Israeli intervention, 1982-
LEBERGOTT, STANLEY
LECLERC, EDOUARD
LECLERC, MICHEL-EDOUARD
LECTURES AND LECTURING — United States — History — 19th century — Addresses, essays, lectures
LEDESMA RAMOS, RAMIRO
LEEWARD ISLANDS (SOCIETY ISLANDS) — Population — Statistics
LEGA NAZIONALE DELLE COOPERATIVE E MUTUE — History
LEGAL AID — Directories
LEGAL AID — Handbooks, manuals, etc.
LEGAL AID — Australia
LEGAL AID — England — Greater Manchester
LEGAL AID — Great Britain
LEGAL AID — Great Britain — Handbooks, manuals, etc.
LEGAL ASSISTANCE TO CHILDREN — Canada
LEGAL COMPOSITION
LEGAL DEPOSIT (OF BOOKS, ETC.) — Great Britain
LEGAL POSITIVISM
LEGAL RESEARCH — Europe — Data processing — Public opinion
LEGAL RESEARCH — France
LEGAL RESEARCH — Great Britain
LEGAL SERVICES — Canada — Economic aspects
LEGAL SERVICES — Great Britain
LEGAL TENDER — Hungary
LEGENDS — Australia — Victoria
LEGENDS — India — History and criticism
LEGISLATION — Great Britain — History — 16th century
LEGISLATION — Great Britain — History — 20th century
LEGISLATION — Soviet Union
LEGISLATIVE BODIES
LEGISLATIVE BODIES — Addresses, essays, lectures
LEGISLATIVE BODIES — Bibliography
LEGISLATIVE BODIES — Great Britain — Reform
LEGISLATIVE BODIES — India
LEGISLATIVE BODIES — India — Privileges and immunities
LEGISLATIVE BODIES — United States — States — Ethics — Addresses, essays, lectures
LEGISLATIVE OVERSIGHT — India
LEGISLATIVE POWER — France — History
LEGISLATIVE POWER — India
LEGISLATIVE POWER — United States
LEGISLATORS — Addresses, essays, lectures
LEGISLATORS — Canada — Biography
LEGISLATORS — France — Lower Normandy
LEGISLATORS — Great Britain

LEGISLATORS — Great Britain — Biography
LEGISLATORS — Great Britain — History
LEGISLATORS — United States
LEGISLATORS — United States — Biography
LEGISLATORS — United States — History — 19th century
LEGITIMACY OF GOVERNMENTS
LEGITIMACY OF GOVERNMENTS — Asia
LEGITIMACY OF GOVERNMENTS — United States — History
LEHMAN BROTHERS
LEHMANN, E. L
LEIBNIZ, GOTTFRIED WILHELM
LEICESTER (LEICESTERSHIRE) — City planning
LEISURE
LEISURE — Economic aspects — Great Britain
LEISURE — Social aspects — Great Britain
LEISURE — Finland — Statistics
LEISURE — Great Britain
LEISURE — Norway — Statistics
LENIN, V. I.. Imperializm: kak vysshaia stadiia kapitalizma
LENIN, V. I.
LENIN, V. I. — Bibliography
LENINGRAD (R.S.F.S.R.) — History — Revolution, 1917-1921
LENINGRAD (R.S.F.S.R.) — Politics and government
LENINGRAD (R.S.F.S.R.) — Siege, 1941-1944
LENINGRAD (R.S.F.S.R.) — Politics and government
LERDO DE TEJADA, SEBASTIÁN
LERIDA (SPAIN) — Politics and government
LEROUX, PIERRE
LERROUX, ALEJANDRO
LESAGE, JEAN
LESBIAN MOTHERS — Legal status, laws, etc. — England
LESBIANISM — France — Paris — History
LESOTHO — Foreign relations — South Africa
LESOTHO — History — Dictionaries
LESOTHO — Population — Statistics
LESOTHO — Population — Statistics — Evaluation
LETTERS OF CREDIT — United States
LETTERS ROGATORY — Canada
LETTERS ROGATORY — Soviet Union
LETTERS ROGATORY — United States
LÉVÊQUE, JEAN-MAXIME
LEVIATHAN
LEVY, LEONARD WILIAMS
LEWISHAM (LONDON, ENGLAND) — Economic conditions
LIABILITY FOR MARINE ACCIDENTS
LIABILITY (LAW) — England
LIBEL AND SLANDER — England — Cases
LIBEL AND SLANDER — Ireland
LIBEL AND SLANDER — United States — Cases
LIBERAL PARTY
LIBERAL PARTY — Finance
LIBERAL PARTY — History
LIBERAL PARTY — History — 19th century
LIBERAL PARTY. SDP Liberal Alliance See SDP Liberal Alliance
LIBERAL PARTY — History — 19th century
LIBERAL PARTY (CANADA)
LIBERAL PARTY OF CANADA
LIBERAL PARTY OF CANADA — Biography
LIBERAL SDP ALLIANCE See SDP Liberal Alliance
LIBERALISM
LIBERALISM — Brazil — History — 19th century

LIBERALISM — Canada
LIBERALISM — England — History — 19th century
LIBERALISM — Germany — History
LIBERALISM — Japan
LIBERALISM — Japan — History
LIBERALISM — Poland — History
LIBERALISM — South Africa — Congresses
LIBERALISM — Soviet Union — History
LIBERALISM — Spain — History
LIBERALISM — Switzerland
LIBERALISM — United States
LIBERALISM — United States — History
LIBERALISM — United States — History — 20th century
LIBERATION THEOLOGY
LIBERIA — Foreign relations
LIBERIA — History — Dictionaries
LIBERIA — Politics and government
LIBERTARIANISM — United States
LIBERTARIONISM
LIBERTY
LIBERTY — History
LIBERTY — Philosophy
LIBERTY OF THE PRESS — Hungary
LIBRARIANS
LIBRARIES
LIBRARIES — Automation
LIBRARIES — Cost control
LIBRARIES — Handbooks
LIBRARIES — Special collections — Government publications
LIBRARIES — Asia, Southeastern
LIBRARIES — Europe — Automation
LIBRARIES — Europe — Special collections — China
LIBRARIES — Great Britain
LIBRARIES — Great Britain — Directories
LIBRARIES — Great Britain — Security measures
LIBRARIES — Great Britian
LIBRARIES — London (England)
LIBRARIES AND THE PHYSICALLY HANDICAPPED
LIBRARIES, DEPOSITORY — Great Britain
LIBRARIES, DEPOSITORY — United States
LIBRARIES, UNIVERSITY AND COLLEGE — Administration
LIBRARIES, UNIVERSITY AND COLLEGE — Evaluation — Statistical methods
LIBRARIES, UNIVERSITY AND COLLEGE — Australia
LIBRARIES, UNIVERSITY AND COLLEGE — Great Britain
LIBRARIES, UNIVERSITY AND COLLEGE — Great Britain — Acquisitions
LIBRARY ADMINISTRATION
LIBRARY COOPERATION — Great Britain
LIBRARY EMPLOYEES — Training of
LIBRARY FINANCE
LIBRARY FINES AND FEES
LIBRARY ORIENTATION
LIBRARY PERSONNEL MANAGEMENT
LIBRARY PERSONNEL MANAGEMENT — Great Britain
LIBRARY PUBLICATIONS
LIBRARY RESOURCES — Great Britain — Statistics
LIBRARY SCIENCE — Bibliography
LIBRARY SCIENCE — Terminology
LIBRARY SCIENCE — Vocational guidance — Great Britain
LIBRARY SCIENCE — Great Britain
LIBRARY STATISTICS
LIBRARY SURVEYS
LIBYA — Dictionaries and encyclopedias
LIBYA — Economic conditions
LIBYA — Economic policy
LIBYA — Foreign relations — Soviet Union
LIBYA — Foreign relations — United States
LIBYA — History
LIBYA — Politics and government

LIBYA — Rural conditions
LIBYA — Social policy
LICENSES — Hungary
LIDDELL, HENRY. c.1673-1717 — Correspondence
LIECHTENSTEIN — Biography
LIETUVOS KOMMUNISTA PARTYA
LIFE — Economic aspects — Congresses
LIFE CHANGE EVENTS
LIFE CYCLE, HUMAN
LIFE CYCLE, HUMAN — Handbooks, manuals, etc
LIFE EXPECTANCY — Great Britain
LIFE SKILLS — Study and teaching — Great Britain — History
LIFE SPAN, PRODUCTIVE — Japan — Statistics
LIFE SPAN, PRODUCTIVE — New Zealand — Statistics
LIFE STYLE
LIFESPAN, PRODUCTIVE
LIGA DER FREMDVÖLKER RUSSLANDS
LIMA (PERU) — Population
LIMITED LIABILITY
LIMITED LIABILITY — Austria
LINCOLN, ABRAHAM
LINCOLN, ABRAHAM — Addresses, essays, lectures
LINCOLN (LINCOLNSHIRE) — Industries — History
LINE AND STAFF ORGANIZATION
LINEAR MODELS (STATISTICS)
LINEAR PROGRAMMING
LINGUISTIC MINORITIES — Education
LINGUISTIC MINORITIES — England — London
LINGUISTIC MINORITIES — India
LINGUISTICS
LINGUISTICS — Data processing
LINGUISTICS — History
LINGUISTICS — History — 19th century
LINGUISTICS — History — 20th century
LINGUISTICS — Periodicals — Bibliography
LIQUIDATION
LIQUIDATION — England
LIQUIDATION — Netherlands
LIQUIDITY (ECONOMICS)
LIQUOR LAWS — Great Britain
LISP (COMPUTER PROGRAM LANGUAGE)
LIST, FRIEDRICH
LISTENING
LISTENING COMPREHENSION TESTS
LITERACY
LITERACY — Social aspects
LITERACY — Social aspects — England — History — 19th century
LITERACY — Social aspects — Europe — History — 19th century
LITERACY — Cuba — History — 20th century
LITERACY — Developing countries
LITERACY — European Economic Community countries
LITERACY — Nicaragua
LITERACY — Pakistan — Statistics
LITERACY — Soviet Union — History
LITERARY FORGERIES AND MYSTIFICATIONS
LITERARY LANDMARKS
LITERATURE — Directories
LITERATURE — Philosophy
LITERATURE — Women authors
LITERATURE AND SOCIETY — France
LITERATURE AND SOCIETY — Great Britain — History — 20th century
LITERATURE AND STATE
LITERATURE, MODERN — 20th century — translations from Japanese
LITHUANIANS — Canada
LIVERPOOL COMMUNITY ORGANISATIONS COMMITTEE
LIVERPOOL (MERSEYSIDE) — Politics and government

LIVERPOOL (MERSEYSIDE) — Population
LIVERPOOL (MERSEYSIDE) — Race relations
LIVERPOOL (MERSEYSIDE) — Social conditions
LIVESTOCK — Genetics — History
LIVESTOCK — Australia — Statistics
LIVESTOCK — China
LIVESTOCK — England — Breeding — History
LIVESTOCK — European Economic Community Countries
LIVESTOCK — India — Statistics
LIVESTOCK — Latin America
LIVESTOCK PRODUCTIVITY — Africa — Statistics
LIVING ALONE — United States
LIVINGSTONE, KEN
LLOYD GEORGE, DAVID
LLOYD'S OF LONDON
LOANS — Europe
LOANS — European Economic Community countries — Directories
LOANS — United States — Government guaranty
LOANS, AMERICAN — Developing countries
LOANS, FOREIGN
LOANS, FOREIGN — Asia
LOANS, FOREIGN — Contracts and specifications
LOANS, FOREIGN — Dictionaries — Polyglot
LOANS, FOREIGN — Africa, West
LOANS, FOREIGN — Brazil
LOANS, FOREIGN — Developing countries
LOANS, FOREIGN — India
LOANS, FOREIGN — Jamaica
LOANS, FOREIGN — Nigeria
LOANS, FOREIGN — Peru
LOBBYING — Canada
LOBBYING — Great Britain
LOBBYING — Great Britain — Handbooks, manuals, etc.
LOBBYING — United States
LOBBYING — United States — Case studies
LOBBYISTS — United States
LOCAL AREA NETWORKS (COMPUTER NETWORKS)
LOCAL AREA NETWORKS (COMPUTER NETWORKS) — Congresses
LOCAL BUDGETS — Great Britain
LOCAL ELECTIONS — England — Statistics
LOCAL ELECTIONS — Scotland — Statistics
LOCAL FINANCE — Accounting
LOCAL FINANCE — Law and legislation — Great Britain
LOCAL FINANCE — Law and legislation — Scotland
LOCAL FINANCE — Mathematical models — Congresses
LOCAL FINANCE — Statistical methods — Congresses
LOCAL FINANCE — Appalachian Region
LOCAL FINANCE — Australia
LOCAL FINANCE — Canary Islands
LOCAL FINANCE — Council of Europe countries
LOCAL FINANCE — Denmark — Copenhagen — Statistics
LOCAL FINANCE — England — London
LOCAL FINANCE — Europe
LOCAL FINANCE — France — Statistics
LOCAL FINANCE — Great Britain
LOCAL FINANCE — Great Britain — Auditing
LOCAL FINANCE — Iceland — Statistics
LOCAL FINANCE — Illinois
LOCAL FINANCE — Japan — Tokyo
LOCAL FINANCE — Northern Ireland
LOCAL FINANCE — Scotland — Dumfries and Galloway
LOCAL FINANCE — Switzerland — Berne

LOCAL FINANCE — Switzerland — Jura Sud
LOCAL FINANCE — United States
LOCAL FINANCE — Zambia — Statistics
LOCAL GOVERNMENT — Information services — Europe
LOCAL GOVERNMENT — Information services — Great Britain
LOCAL GOVERNMENT — Information services — Great Britain — Bibliography
LOCAL GOVERNMENT — Law and legislation — Spain
LOCAL GOVERNMENT — Law and legislation — United States
LOCAL GOVERNMENT — Planning
LOCAL GOVERNMENT — Research — Great Britain — Registers
LOCAL GOVERNMENT — Social aspects — France
LOCAL GOVERNMENT — Alabama
LOCAL GOVERNMENT — Alberta
LOCAL GOVERNMENT — Argentina
LOCAL GOVERNMENT — Australia — Brisbane (Qld.) — History
LOCAL GOVERNMENT — Bangladesh
LOCAL GOVERNMENT — British Columbia — Statistics
LOCAL GOVERNMENT — Colombia
LOCAL GOVERNMENT — Council of Europe countries — Management
LOCAL GOVERNMENT — Denmark — State supervision
LOCAL GOVERNMENT — Egypt
LOCAL GOVERNMENT — England
LOCAL GOVERNMENT — Europe
LOCAL GOVERNMENT — Europe — Citizen participation
LOCAL GOVERNMENT — Europe — Congresses
LOCAL GOVERNMENT — Europe — Data processing
LOCAL GOVERNMENT — France
LOCAL GOVERNMENT — France — Data processing
LOCAL GOVERNMENT — Germany (West)
LOCAL GOVERNMENT — Great Britain
LOCAL GOVERNMENT — Great Britain — Data processing
LOCAL GOVERNMENT — Great Britain — Data processing — Auditing
LOCAL GOVERNMENT — Great Britain — History — 17th century
LOCAL GOVERNMENT — Great Britain — History — 20th century
LOCAL GOVERNMENT — Great Britain — Management
LOCAL GOVERNMENT — Great Britain — Research — Bibliography
LOCAL GOVERNMENT — Great Britain — State supervision
LOCAL GOVERNMENT — Greece — Attikí
LOCAL GOVERNMENT — Illinois
LOCAL GOVERNMENT — Mexico
LOCAL GOVERNMENT — Nigeria — East-Central State — Congresses
LOCAL GOVERNMENT — Norway
LOCAL GOVERNMENT — Pakistan
LOCAL GOVERNMENT — Russian S.F.S.R. — Moscow
LOCAL GOVERNMENT — Scotland
LOCAL GOVERNMENT — Soviet Union
LOCAL GOVERNMENT — Spain
LOCAL GOVERNMENT — Spain — Madrid
LOCAL GOVERNMENT — Sudan
LOCAL GOVERNMENT — United States
LOCAL GOVERNMENT — Wales
LOCAL GOVERNMENT BILL 1984-85
LOCAL GOVERNMENT FINANCE BILL 1981-82
LOCAL GOVERNMENT FINANCE (NO.2) BILL 1981-82
LOCAL GOVERNMENT (INTERIM PROVISIONS) BILL 1983-84
LOCAL OFFICIALS AND EMPLOYEES
LOCAL OFFICIALS AND EMPLOYEES — England
LOCAL OFFICIALS AND EMPLOYEES — France
LOCAL OFFICIALS AND EMPLOYEES — Great Britain — History
LOCAL OFFICIALS AND EMPLOYEES — United States — Salaries, allowances, etc — Congresses
LOCAL TAXATION — Great Britain
LOCAL TRANSIT
LOCAL TRANSIT — Finance — Law and legislation — England
LOCAL TRANSIT — Statistics
LOCAL TRANSIT — Asia, Southeastern
LOCAL TRANSIT — England — Fares
LOCKE, ALAIN LEROY
LOCKE, JOHN, 1632-1704
LOCKE, JOHN, 1632-1704 — Bibliography
LOCKHEED AIRCRAFT CORPORATION
LOCKNEVI (SWEDEN) — History
LODGING-HOUSES — Great Britain
ŁÓDŹ (POLAND) — History
ŁÓDŹ (POLAND) — Industries — Location
ŁÓDŹ (POLAND) — Politics and government
LOFTHOUSE, GEOFF — Biography
LOGIC
LOGIC — Addresses, essays, lectures
LOGIC, SYMBOLIC AND MATHEMATICAL
LOKEREN (BELGIUM) — Economic conditions
LOKEREN (BELGIUM) — History
LOME CONVENTION
LOMÉ CONVENTION
LONDON — History
LONDON — Social conditions
LONDON — Social policy — History
LONDON CHAMBER OF COMMERCE AND INDUSTRY
LONDON (ENGLAND) — Airports
LONDON (ENGLAND) — Buildings, structures, etc
LONDON (ENGLAND) — Census, 1981
LONDON (ENGLAND) — City planning
LONDON (ENGLAND) — Civil defense
LONDON (ENGLAND) — Docks, wharves, etc
LONDON (ENGLAND) — Dwellings
LONDON (ENGLAND) — Economic conditions
LONDON (ENGLAND) — Economic conditions — Statistics
LONDON (ENGLAND) — Economic policy
LONDON (ENGLAND) — Full employment policies
LONDON (ENGLAND) — Harbor
LONDON (ENGLAND) — History — 18th century
LONDON (ENGLAND) — History — 1800-1950
LONDON (ENGLAND) — History — 20th century
LONDON (ENGLAND) — Languages
LONDON (ENGLAND) — Markets
LONDON (ENGLAND) — Office buildings
LONDON (ENGLAND) — Politics and government
LONDON (ENGLAND) — Politics and government — Legal status, laws, etc
LONDON (ENGLAND) — Politics and government — Legal status, laws, etc.
LONDON (ENGLAND) — Population
LONDON (ENGLAND) — Race relations
LONDON (ENGLAND) — Recreational facilities
LONDON (ENGLAND) — Schools
LONDON (ENGLAND) — Social conditions
LONDON (ENGLAND) — Social conditions — Statistics
LONDON (ENGLAND) — Social conditions — 20th century
LONDON (ENGLAND) — Social life and customs — 19th century
LONDON (ENGLAND) — Statistics, Vital
LONDON (ENGLAND) — Transit systems
LONDON (ENGLAND) — Transit systems — Law and legislation
LONDON METROPOLITAN AREA — Manufactures
LONDON METROPOLITAN AREA — Politics and government
LONDON REGIONAL TRANSPORT
LONDON REGIONAL TRANSPORT — Legal status, laws, etc.
LONDON REGIONAL TRANSPORT BILL 1983-84
LONDON RESIDUARY BODY
LONDON REVIEW OF BOOKS — Indexes
LONDON SCHOOL ECONOMICS AND POLITICAL SCIENCE
LONDON SCHOOL OF ECONOMICS AND POLITICAL SCIENCE — Fiction
LONDON SCHOOL OF ECONOMICS AND POLITICAL SCIENCE — Students
LONDON SCHOOL OF ECONOMICS AND POLITICAL SCIENCE. Centre for Labour Economics
LONDON TRANSPORT — Legal status, laws, etc.
LONDON TRANSPORT EXECUTIVE
LONDONDERRY, ROBERT STEWARD, 2nd Marquis of
LONDONDERRY (NORTHERN IRELAND) — History
LONELINESS
LONERGAN, BERNARD J. F — Congresses
LONG, HUEY PIERCE
LONG-TERM CARE OF THE SICK — Moral and ethical aspects — Congresses
LONG WAVES (ECONOMICS)
LONG WAVES (ECONOMICS) — Great Britain
LONGEVITY — Georgian S.S.R. — Abkhazian A.S.S.R.
LORRAINE (FRANCE) — Industries
LOS ANGELES (CALIF.) — Ethnic relations
LOTUS 1-2-3 (COMPUTER PROGRAM)
LOUGHEED, PETER
LOVE
LOVE — Psychological aspects
LOWER SAVONY (GERMANY) — Statistics
LOWER SAXONY (GERMANY) — Politics and government
:LOYALTY — security programs, 1947-
LOZI (AFRICAN PEOPLE) — Social life and customs
LUCKNOW (INDIA) — Buildings, structures, etc.
LUDDITES
LUKÁCS, GYÖRGY
LUMBER TRADE — Soviet Union
LUNDA, NORTHERN (AFRICAN PEOPLE)
LUNGS — Dust diseases
LURISTAN (IRAN) — Social conditions
LUTHERAN CHURCH — Soviet Union
LUTTE OUVRIÈRE
LUXEMBOURG — Description and travel
LUXEMBOURG — Economic conditions
LUXEMBOURG — Social conditions
LUXEMBOURG — Statistics
LUXEMBOURG — Statistics — Bibliography
LUXEMBOURG (BELGIUM) — Emigration and immigration — Statistics
LUXEMBOURG CONFERENCE ON THE COMMUNITY PATENT — 1975
LUXEMBURG, ROSA
LYNCH, LIAM
LYNDON BAINES JOHNSON LIBRARY
LYSERGIC ACID DIETHYLAMIDE
M. D. P. See Magyar Dolgozók Pártja
MCCARTHY, JOSEPH
MACDONALD, JAMES RAMSAY

MCDONALD'S CORPORATION — History
MACDOUGALL, DONALD
MCDOUGALL, F. L.
MACEO, ANTONIO
MCGILL UNIVERSITY — History
MACHINE LEARNING
MACHINE-TOOL INDUSTRY — Technological innovations — Government policy
MACHINE-TOOL INDUSTRY — Developing countries
MACHINE TRANSLATING
MACHINERY — Trade and manufacture
MACHINERY IN INDUSTRY
MACHINERY INDUSTRY — Developing countries
MACIEL, MERVYN — Biography
MACLAREN, ROY, 1934-
MACROECONOMICS
MACROECONOMICS — Addresses, essays, lectures
MACROECONOMICS — Computer programs
MACROECONOMICS — Econometric models — Congresses
MACROECONOMICS — Mathematical models
MACROECONOMICS — Mathematical models — Congresses
MACSWINEY, MARY
MACWRITE (COMPUTER PROGRAM) — Handbooks, manuals, etc.
MADAGASCAR — Description and travel
MADAGASCAR — History
MADAGASCAR — History — Revolution, 1947
MADAGASCAR — Politics and government — 1960
MADHYA PRADESH (INDIA) — Population — Statistics
MADRID OFFICE EUROPEAN COMMUNITIES
MADRID (SPAIN) — Census, 1981
MADRID (SPAIN) — History
MADRID (SPAIN) — Politics and government
MADRID (SPAIN) — Population — Statistics
MAFETENG (LESOTHO) — Economic conditions — Statistics
MAFETENG (LESOTHO) — Social conditions — Statistics
MAFIA — Italy — History
MAGARS — Commerce
MAGARS — Economic conditions
MAGIC — Africa, Central
MAGISTRATES' ASSOCIATION
MAGOMERO (MALAWI) — History
MAGOMERO (MALAWI) — Social life and customs
MAGYAR DOLGOZÓK PÁRTJA — History
MAGYAR SZOCIALISTA MUNKÁSPÁRT
MAGYAR SZOCIALISTA MUNKÁSPÁRT — Congresses
MAHARASHTRA (INDIA) — Economic conditions — Statistics
MAHINA (TAHITI) — Population — Statistics
MAIAO (SOCIETY ISLANDS) — Population — Statistics
MAJOK, DENG
MAKEMO (TUAMOTU ISLANDS) — Population — Statistics
MALAGA (SPAIN) — History — Civil War, 1936-1939
MALAGA (SPAIN) — Politics and government
MALAWI — History — Dictionaries
MALAWI — Politics and government — 1964-
MALAYA — Economic conditions
MALAYA — Social conditions
MALAYSIA — Census, 1980
MALAYSIA — Constitutional law
MALAYSIA — Economic conditions
MALAYSIA — Economic policy
MALAYSIA — Foreign economic relations — Japan
MALAYSIA — Foreign relations
MALAYSIA — Industries
MALAYSIA — Politics and government
MALAYSIA — Bibliography
MALI — Census, 1976
MALI — Economic policy
MALI — History — Dictionaries
MALI — Population — Statistics
MALMÖ (SWEDEN) — City planning
MALNUTRITION — Latin America
MALOHS (BORNEAN PEOPLE)
MALPRACTICE — Trends — United States — Legislation
MALPRACTICE — England
MALTHUS, T. R.
MALTHUSIANISM
MAMBAI (INDONESIAN PEOPLE) — Rites and ceremonies
MAMBORU (INDONESIA) — Social life and customs
MAN, HENDRIK DE
MAN
MAN — History
MAN — Influence of environment
MAN — Influence on nature
MAN — Influence on nature — China
MAN — Influence on nature — Developing countries
MAN — Machine systems
MAN — Migrations
MAN (CHRISTIAN THEOLOGY) — History of doctrines
MAN-MACHINE SYSTEMS
MANAGEMENT
MANAGEMENT — Case studies
MANAGEMENT — Data processing
MANAGEMENT — Data processing — Addresses, essays, lectures
MANAGEMENT — Employee participation
MANAGEMENT — Employee participation — Bibliography
MANAGEMENT — Social aspects
MANAGEMENT — Study and teaching — Developing countries
MANAGEMENT — Study and teaching — European Economic Community countries
MANAGEMENT — Study and teaching — France
MANAGEMENT — Study and teaching — Great Britain
MANAGEMENT — Australia — Employee participation
MANAGEMENT — China
MANAGEMENT — Costa Rica — Employee participation
MANAGEMENT — Developing countries — Employee participation
MANAGEMENT — England
MANAGEMENT — Europe
MANAGEMENT — Germany (West)
MANAGEMENT — Great Britain — Employee participation
MANAGEMENT — Hungary — Employee participation — History
MANAGEMENT — Ireland — Employee participation
MANAGEMENT — Japan
MANAGEMENT — Japan — Employee participation — History
MANAGEMENT — Norway — Employee participation
MANAGEMENT — Romania — Employee representation
MANAGEMENT — Sri Lanka — Employee participation
MANAGEMENT — Zambia — Employee participation
MANAGEMENT BUYOUTS — Great Britain
MANAGEMENT BY OBJECTIVES
MANAGEMENT BY OBJECTIVES — Evaluation
MANAGEMENT INFORMATION SYSTEMS
MANAGEMENT INFORMATION SYSTEMS — Data processing
MANAGEMENT INFORMATION SYSTEMS — Design and construction
MANAGEMENT INFORMATION SYSTEMS — Evaluation
MANAGEMENT INFORMATION SYSTEMS — Great Britain
MANAGEMENT SCIENCE
MANAGERIAL ACCOUNTING
MANAGERIAL ACCOUNTING — History
MANAGERIAL ACCOUNTING — United States — History
MANAGERIAL ECONOMICS
MANAGERIAL ECONOMICS — Congresses
MANAGERIAL ECONOMICS — Canada
MANAYUNK (PHILADELPHIA, PA.)
MANCHESTER (GREATER MANCHESTER) — Economic conditions
MANCHESTER SHIP CANAL COMPANY
MANCHURIA (CHINA) — History
MANDELA, WINNIE
MANDEVILLE, BERNARD
MANGANESE — Metallurgy
MANGANESE MINES AND MINING, SUBMARINE
MANGANESE NODULES
MANGOLIA — Economic conditions — Statistics
MANGYANS
MANIHI (TUAMOTU ISLANDS) — Population — Statistics
MANIPUR (INDIA) — Population — Statistics
MANITOBA — Politics and government
MANITOBA. Department of Industry, Trade and Technology
MANITOBA LABOUR
MANNERHEIM, CARL
MANNERHEIM, CARL GUSTAF EMIL, Frihene
MANNERHEIM, CARL GUSTAF EMIL, friherre
MANNERHEIM, CARL GUSTAF EMIL, Friherre
MANORS — England — Essex — History
MANOUCHIAN, MISSAK
MANPOWER — Cyprus — Statistics
MANPOWER — Jordan — Statistics
MANPOWER — United States
MANPOWER PLANNING — Mathematical models
MANPOWER PLANNING — Statistical methods
MANPOWER PLANNING — Denmark
MANPOWER PLANNING — Great Britain
MANPOWER PLANNING — Great Britain — Bibliography
MANPOWER PLANNING — United States — Addresses, essays, lectures
MANPOWER POLICY
MANPOWER POLICY — Congresses
MANPOWER POLICY — Models
MANPOWER POLICY — Australia
MANPOWER POLICY — Australia — Methodology
MANPOWER POLICY — Brazil
MANPOWER POLICY — Developing countries
MANPOWER POLICY — Egypt
MANPOWER POLICY — England — Cleveland
MANPOWER POLICY — England — London
MANPOWER POLICY — England — Sheffield (South Yorkshire)
MANPOWER POLICY — England — Stoke-on-Trent (Staffordshire)
MANPOWER POLICY — England — Surrey

MANPOWER POLICY — Europe — Congresses
MANPOWER POLICY — European Economic Community countries
MANPOWER POLICY — France
MANPOWER POLICY — France — Statistics
MANPOWER POLICY — Great Britain
MANPOWER POLICY — India
MANPOWER POLICY — Nigeria
MANPOWER POLICY — Northern Ireland — Statistics
MANPOWER POLICY — Québec (Province)
MANPOWER POLICY — Soviet Union
MANPOWER POLICY — Sweden — History — 20th century
MANPOWER POLICY — United States
MANPOWER POLICY — United States — Addresses, essays, lectures
MANPOWER POLICY — Wales — West Glamorgan
MANPOWER POLICY, RURAL — France — Statistics
MANPOWER SERVICES COMMISSION
MANUFACTURES — Finland — Accounting
MANUS PROVINCE (PAPUA NEW GUINEA) — Population — Statistics
MANUSCRIPT PREPARATION (AUTHORSHIP) — Handbooks, manuals, etc
MANUSCRIPTS — Soviet Union — Bibliography
MANUSCRIPTS, AMERICAN — United States — Catalogs
MAO, ZEDONG
MAORIS — Social conditions
MAORIS
MAORIS — Education — Case studies
MAORIS — Government relations
MAORIS — History
MAORIS — Land tenure
MAORIS — Social conditions
MAPS
MARBURG (GERMANY) — Politics and government
MARBURG (GERMANY) — Social life and customs
MARCEL, GABRIEL
MARCHLEWSKI, JULIAN BALTAZAR
MARCOS, FERDINAND E
MARCUSE, HERBERT. Eros and civilization
MARCUSE, HERBERT. One-dimensional man
MARCUSE, HERBERT
MARCUSE, HERBERT — Contributions in science
MARCUSE, HERBERT — Criticism and interpretation
MARCUSE, HERBERT, 1898-
MARGINALITY, SOCIAL
MARGINALITY, SOCIAL — France
MARGINALITY, SOCIAL — Germany (West)
MARGINALITY, SOCIAL — Great Britain
MARGINALITY, SOCIAL — Peru — Lima
MARIHUANA — Addresses, essays, lectures
MARINE ACCIDENTS — Legal aspects, laws, etc.
MARINE MINERAL RESOURCES
MARINE MINERAL RESOURCES — Law and legislation — Congresses
MARINE MINERAL RESOURCES — South Pacific Ocean
MARINE POLLUTION
MARINE POLLUTION — Government policy — European Economic Community countries
MARINE POLLUTION — Law and legislation
MARINE POLLUTION — Legal status, laws, etc.

MARINE POLLUTIONOFF. PUBNS. — Prevention 986
MARINE RESOURCES
MARINE RESOURCES — Economic aspects
MARINE RESOURCES — British Virgin Islands
MARINE RESOURCES — Caribbean Area — Management
MARINE RESOURCES CONSERVATION
MARINE RESOURCES CONSERVATION — Law and legislation
MARINE RESOURCES CONSERVATION — Law and legislation — Great Britain
MARINE RESURCES AND STATE — Caribbean Area
MARINE SCIENCES
MARING (NEW GUINEA PEOPLE) — Addresses, essays, lectures
MARITAL PROPERTY — History
MARITAL PROPERTY — Australia
MARITAL PROPERTY — England
MARITAL PSYCHOTHERAPY
MARITAL STATUS — Bahamas — Statistics
MARITIME LAW
MARITIME LAW — Bibliography
MARITIME LAW — Congresses
MARITIME LAW — Sources
MARITIME LAW — Artic Ocean — Congresses
MARITIME LAW — Asia, Southeastern
MARITIME LAW — Caribbean Area
MARITIME LAW — Caribbean Area — Congresses
MARITIME LAW — East Asia
MARITIME LAW — England
MARITIME LAW — Great Britain
MARITIME LAW — Malaysia
MARITIME LAW — South Africa
MARITIME LAW — Soviet Union
MARITIME LAW — United States
MARITIME PROVINCES — History
MARITIME PROVINCES — Industries — History
MARKET SEGMENTATION
MARKET SURVEYS
MARKET SURVEYS — Canada
MARKETING
MARKETING — Congresses
MARKETING — Decision making
MARKETING — Management
MARKETING — Management — Social aspects
MARKETING — Social aspects
MARKETING — Developing countries
MARKETING — Great Britain
MARKETING — Great Britain — History
MARKETING — United States — Decision making
MARKETING CHANNELS — Congresses
MARKETING RESEARCH
MARKETING RESEARCH — Addresses, essays, lectures
MARKETING RESEARCH — Case studies
MARKETING RESEARCH — Great Britain — Case studies
MARKETS
MARKETS — India — Tirunelveli District
MARKS & SPENCER (Firm)
MARQUESAS ISLANDS — Population — Statistics
MARR, WILHELM
MARRIAGE
MARRIAGE — Handbooks, manuals, etc
MARRIAGE — Religious aspects — Judaism
MARRIAGE — Religious aspects — Unification Church
MARRIAGE — Developing countries — Statistics
MARRIAGE — England — History
MARRIAGE — France — Statistics
MARRIAGE — Great Britain — History
MARRIAGE — Ireland — History
MARRIAGE — Pakistan

MARRIAGE — Portugal — Lanhezes — History
MARRIAGE — Southern Africa
MARRIAGE — Thailand — Statistics
MARRIAGE — Trinidad and Tobago
MARRIAGE — United States
MARRIAGE — United States — Addresses, essays, lectures
MARRIAGE COUNSELING
MARRIAGE COUNSELLING
MARRIAGE CUSTOMS AND RITES — Social aspects
MARRIAGE CUSTOMS AND RITES — England — History
MARRIAGE (ISLAMIC LAW) — Afghanistan
MARRIAGE LAW — Australia
MARRIAGE, MIXED — United States
MARRIED PEOPLE — Employment — Canada
MARRIED PEOPLE — Employment — United States
MARRIED PEOPLE — Psychology
MARRIED WOMEN — United States — Case studies
MARRIED WOMEN — United States — History
MARSHAL, WILLIAM
MARSHALL, ALFRED, 1842-1924 — Contributions in economics
MARSHALL PLAN, 1948-1952
MARSHALS — France — Biography
MARSHALS — Great Britain — Biography
MARSILIUS, of Padua
MARTENS, JOACHIM FRIEDRICH
MARTIAL LAW — Gaza Strip
MARTIAL LAW — West Bank
MARTIN, ANNE
MARTÍNEZ DEL RÍO (Family)
MARX, KARL. Das kapital — Addresses, essays, lectures
MARX, KARL. Kapital
MARX, KARL
MARX, KARL — Bibliography
MARX, KARL — Chronology
MARX, KARL — Congresses
MARX, KARL — Language — Glossaries, etc
MARX, KARL, 1818-1833
MARX, KARL, 1818-1883
MARX, KARL, 1818-1883 — Contributions in economics
MARX, KARL, 1818-1883 — Dictionaries
MARX, KARL, 1818-1883 — Dictionaries, indexes, etc.
MARXIAN ECONOMICS
MARXIAN ECONOMICS — History and criticism
MARXIAN HISTORIOGRAPHY — Soviet Union
MARXIAN SCHOOL OF SOCIOLOGY
MARXIST ECONOMICS
MARXIST THEORY AND SOCIAL SCIENCES
MARY, Blessed Virgin, Saint — Apparitions and miracles
MARY, Blessed Virgin, Saint — Cult
MASARYK, TOMAS GARRIGUE
MASCULINITY (PSYCHOLOGY)
MASCULINITY (PSYCHOLOGY) — Papua New Guinea
MASDEU, JUAN FRANCISCO — Contributions in historiography
MASDEU, JUAN FRANCISCO — Contributions in political science
MASHONALAND (ZIMBABWE) — Economic conditions — Statistics
MASHONALAND (ZIMBABWE) — Population — Statistics
MASHONALAND (ZIMBABWE) — Social conditions — Statistics
MASKS (SCULPTURE) — Nigeria
MASON, GEORGE
MASS MEDIA — United States — History
MASS MEDIA
MASS MEDIA — Addresses, essays, lectures

MASS MEDIA — Audiences — Research — Addresses, essays, lectures
MASS MEDIA — Censorship
MASS MEDIA — Economic aspects — Australia
MASS MEDIA — Influence
MASS MEDIA — Law and legislation — Australia
MASS MEDIA — Law and legislation — United States — Digests
MASS MEDIA — Methodology
MASS MEDIA — Moral and ethical aspects
MASS MEDIA — Political aspects
MASS MEDIA — Political aspects — Italy
MASS MEDIA — Political aspects — Canada
MASS MEDIA — Political aspects — Great Britain
MASS MEDIA — Psychological aspects
MASS MEDIA — Psychological aspects — Addresses, essays, lectures
MASS MEDIA — Social aspects
MASS MEDIA — Social aspects — Great Britain
MASS MEDIA — Social aspects — Great Britain — History — 20th century
MASS MEDIA — Social aspects — Italy
MASS MEDIA — Social aspects — United States
MASS MEDIA — Social aspects — United States — Addresses, essays, lectures
MASS MEDIA — Study and teaching
MASS MEDIA — Australia — Technological innovations
MASS MEDIA — Canada
MASS MEDIA — Canada — Influence
MASS MEDIA — Europe — Bibliography
MASS MEDIA — Great Britain
MASS MEDIA — Great Britain — History — 20th century
MASS MEDIA — Québec (Province) — Statistics
MASS MEDIA — Syria — Damascus
MASS MEDIA — United States — History — 20th century
MASS MEDIA — United States — Technological innovations
MASS MEDIA — West Bank
MASS MEDIA AND THE ARTS — United States
MASS MEDIA IN EDUCATION
MASS MEDIA POLICY
MASS MEDIA POLICY — Australia
MASS MEDIA SURVEYS
MASS MURDER — United States — Psychological aspects — Case studies
MASSEY, VINCENT
MATCH INDUSTRY — Sweden — History
MATE SELECTION
MATERIALISM
MATERNAL AGE
MATERNAL AND INFANT WELFARE — Great Britain
MATERNAL HEALTH SERVICES — Developing countries
MATERNAL HEALTH SERVICES — England
MATERNITY LEAVE
MATERNITY LEAVE — Great Britain
MATFORS PAPPERSBRUK
MATHABANE, MARK
MATHEMATICAL ABILITY — Great Britain
MATHEMATICAL ANALYSIS
MATHEMATICAL MODELS
MATHEMATICAL OPTIMIZATION
MATHEMATICAL OPTIMIZATION — Congresses
MATHEMATICAL PHYSICS — History
MATHEMATICAL STATISTICS
MATHEMATICAL STATISTICS — Addresses, essays, lectures
MATHEMATICAL STATISTICS — Collected works
MATHEMATICAL STATISTICS — Dictionaries
MATHEMATICS

MATHEMATICS — Collected works
MATHEMATICS — Computer-assisted instruction
MATHEMATICS — Dictionaries
MATHEMATICS — History
MATHEMATICS — Indexes
MATHEMATICS — Popular works
MATHEMATICS — 1961-
MATLAB (BANGLADESH) — Population — Statistics
MATRIARCHY — Caribbean Area
MATRIARCHY — Nigeria
MATRICES
MATRIMONIAL ACTIONS — England
MATRIMONIAL AND FAMILY PROCEEDINGS BILL 1983-84
MATRIX INVERSION
MATTEI, ENRICO
MAU MAU — History
MAUPITI (SOCIETY ISLANDS) — Population — Statistics
MAURA Y MONTANER, ANTONIO
MAURÍN, JOAQUÍN
MAURITANIA — History — Dictionaries
MAURITIUS — Census, 1983
MAURITIUS — History — Dictionaries
MAURITIUS — Population — Statistics
MAURRAS, CHARLES
MAUS, HEINZ — Bibliography
MAUSS, MARCEL
MAXIMA AND MINIMNA
MAXIMOFF, GREGORI PETROVICH
MAXTON, JAMES
MAXWELL, ROBERT, 1923-
MAY, SOMETH
MAY DAY (LABOR HOLIDAY) — United States — History
MAYDAY
MAYER, HENRY — Bibliography
MAYORS — United States
MBERE (AFRICAN PEOPLE) — Land tenure
MBERE (AFRICAN PEOPLE) — Social conditions
MEAD, GEORGE HERBERT
MEAD, GEORGE HERBERT, 1863-1931
MEANING (PHILOSOPHY)
MEANING (PSYCHOLOGY)
MEAT INDUSTRY AND TRADE — Statistics
MEAT INDUSTRY AND TRADE — Australia
MECCA (SAUDI ARABIA) — Commerce — History
MECHANICAL ENGINEERS — Germany — Biography
MEDIATION
MEDIATION — Delaware
MEDIATION AND CONCILIATION, INDUSTRIAL
MEDIATION AND CONCILIATION, INDUSTRIAL — European Economic Community countries
MEDIATION AND CONCILIATION, INDUSTRIAL — Great Britain
MEDIATION AND CONCILIATION, INDUSTRIAL — United States
MEDIATION, INTERNATIONAL
MEDICAID
MEDICAID — United States
MEDICAL ANTHROPOLOGY — Thailand
MEDICAL ASSISTANCE, SWISS — Nepal
MEDICAL ASSISTANCE, TITLE 19 — history
MEDICAL CARE
MEDICAL CARE — Congresses
MEDICAL CARE — Cost effectiveness
MEDICAL CARE — Cost effectiveness — Congresses
MEDICAL CARE — Cross-cultural studies
MEDICAL CARE — Economic aspects — Great Britain
MEDICAL CARE — Economic aspects — United States
MEDICAL CARE — Social aspects
MEDICAL CARE — Africa — Addresses, essays, lectures

MEDICAL CARE — Albania
MEDICAL CARE — Canada
MEDICAL CARE — Canada — Finance
MEDICAL CARE — China
MEDICAL CARE — Denmark
MEDICAL CARE — Developing countries — Finance
MEDICAL CARE — Developing countries — Finance — Evaluation
MEDICAL CARE — England
MEDICAL CARE — Europe — Needs assessment
MEDICAL CARE — European Economic Community countries — Cost control
MEDICAL CARE — European Economic Community countries — Finance
MEDICAL CARE — France — Nomenclature
MEDICAL CARE — France — Utilization — Statistics
MEDICAL CARE — Great Britain
MEDICAL CARE — Great Britain — Bibliography
MEDICAL CARE — Great Britain — Citizen participation
MEDICAL CARE — Great Britain — Finance
MEDICAL CARE — Great Britain — History
MEDICAL CARE — Great Britain — Statistics
MEDICAL CARE — Ireland
MEDICAL CARE — New York (N.Y.) — History
MEDICAL CARE — Scotland — History — 20th century
MEDICAL CARE — Switzerland
MEDICAL CARE — Tanzania — History
MEDICAL CARE — United States
MEDICAL CARE — United States — Congresses
MEDICAL CARE — United States — Cost effectiveness
MEDICAL CARE — United States — Finance
MEDICAL CARE — United States — History
MEDICAL CARE — Wales
MEDICAL CARE, COST OF — Organisation for Economic Co-operation and Development countries — Statistics
MEDICAL CARE, COST OF — United States
MEDICAL CENTERS — Government policy — England — Lancashire
MEDICAL CENTERS — London (England) — Peckham
MEDICAL ECONOMICS
MEDICAL ECONOMICS — Addresses, essays, lectures
MEDICAL ECONOMICS — Moral and ethical aspects — Congresses
MEDICAL ECONOMICS — Canada
MEDICAL ECONOMICS — Great Britain
MEDICAL ECONOMICS — New York (N.Y.) — History
MEDICAL ECONOMICS — Scotland
MEDICAL ECONOMICS — Tanzania — History
MEDICAL ECONOMICS — United States
MEDICAL ECONOMICS — Wales
MEDICAL EDUCATION — Social aspects — United States
MEDICAL EDUCATION — Africa
MEDICAL EDUCATION — Africa — Addresses, essays, lectures
MEDICAL EDUCATION — England
MEDICAL ETHICS
MEDICAL ETHICS — Congresses
MEDICAL GEOGRAPHY
MEDICAL GEOGRAPHY — Great Britain
MEDICAL INNOVATIONS — Social aspects
MEDICAL LAWS AND LEGISLATION — Canada — History
MEDICAL LAWS AND LEGISLATION — Commonwealth of Nations

MEDICAL LAWS AND LEGISLATION — England
MEDICAL LAWS AND LEGISLATION — Great Britain — Dictionaries
MEDICAL ONCOLOGY — United States — legislation
MEDICAL PERSONNEL
MEDICAL PERSONNEL — Malpractice — Economic aspects — United States
MEDICAL PERSONNEL — Malpractice — United States
MEDICAL PERSONNEL — Great Britain — Bibliography
MEDICAL PERSONNEL — Great Britain — Supply and demand
MEDICAL PERSONNEL — South Africa — Statistics
MEDICAL PERSONNEL — United States
MEDICAL POLICY
MEDICAL POLICY — Addresses, essays, lectures
MEDICAL POLICY — Social aspects
MEDICAL POLICY — Social aspects — Congresses
MEDICAL POLICY — Social aspects — United States
MEDICAL POLICY — Australia
MEDICAL POLICY — Canada — History — 20th century
MEDICAL POLICY — Developing countries
MEDICAL POLICY — Europe
MEDICAL POLICY — Great Britain
MEDICAL POLICY — Great Britain — History
MEDICAL POLICY — Ireland
MEDICAL POLICY — Nepal
MEDICAL POLICY — North America
MEDICAL POLICY — Tanzania — History
MEDICAL POLICY — United States — Congresses
MEDICAL POLICY — United States — History
MEDICAL RECORDS
MEDICAL RESEARCH
MEDICAL SOCIAL WORK
MEDICAL SOCIAL WORK — France — Nomenclature
MEDICAL STUDENTS — United States
MEDICAL SUPPLIES — Great Britain
MEDICAL TECHNOLOGY
MEDICARE
MEDICARE — United States
MEDICINE
MEDICINE — Addresses, essays, lectures
MEDICINE — Decision making — Moral and ethical aspects
MEDICINE — History
MEDICINE — History — 18th century
MEDICINE — History — 19th century
MEDICINE — Political aspects — Great Britain
MEDICINE — Research
MEDICINE — Research — Social aspects — Addresses, essays, lectures
MEDICINE — Research — Great Britain — Endowments
MEDICINE — Specialties and specialists — Congresses
MEDICINE — Specialties and specialists — Europe — Congresses
MEDICINE — Study and teaching
MEDICINE — Canada — History — 20th century
MEDICINE — England
MEDICINE — Great Britain
MEDICINE, CHINESE — Philosophy
MEDICINE, MAGIC, MYSTIC, AND SPAGIRIC — Thailand
MEDICINE, PREVENTIVE
MEDICINE, PREVENTIVE — Cost effectiveness — Congresses
MEDICINE, STATE — England
MEDICINE, STATE — European Economic Community countries
MEDICINE, STATE — Great Britain — Bibliography
MEDICINE, STATE — Northern Ireland
MEDIEVALISM — Great Britain — History
MEDITERRANEAN REGION — Defenses
MEDITERRANEAN REGION — History — 16th century
MEDITERRANEAN REGION — Politics and government
MEGHALAYA (INDIA) — Population — Statistics
MEHINACU INDIANS — Sexual behavior
MEKEO (PAPUA NEW GUINEA PEOPLE)
MELANESIA
MELANESIA — Social life and customs
MELBOURNE (VIC.) — Dwellings — History
MEMORIAL UNIVERSITY OF NEWFOUNDLAND. Institute of Social and Economic Research
MEMORY
MEN
MENDÈS FRANCE, PIERRE
MENDOZA, BERNARDINO DE
MENNONITES — Case studies
MENTAL HEALTH — Cross-cultural studies
MENTAL HEALTH — Social aspects
MENTAL HEALTH — Social aspects — Bibliography
MENTAL HEALTH — China — Congresses
MENTAL HEALTH — England — History
MENTAL HEALTH (AMENDMENT) (SCOTLAND) BILL 1982-83
MENTAL HEALTH FACILITIES — Denmark — Utilization — Statistics
MENTAL HEALTH LAWS — Australia
MENTAL HEALTH LAWS — Great Britain
MENTAL HEALTH LAWS — Great Britain — History
MENTAL HEALTH LAWS — Scotland
MENTAL HEALTH PLANNING — Great Britain
MENTAL HEALTH PLANNING — United States — Addresses, essays, lectures
MENTAL HEALTH SERVICES — Great Britain
MENTAL HEALTH SERVICES — Great Britain — Bibliography
MENTAL ILLNESS
MENTAL ILLNESS — Diagnosis
MENTAL ILLNESS — Social aspects
MENTAL ILLNESS — England — History
MENTAL ILLNESS — France
MENTAL ILLNESS — Great Britain — Diagnosis
MENTAL ILLNESS IN LITERATURE
MENTAL RETARDATION — Diagnosis
MENTAL RETARDATION — Social aspects
MENTALLY HANDICAPPED — Abuse of
MENTALLY HANDICAPPED — Care and treatment
MENTALLY HANDICAPPED — Case studies
MENTALLY HANDICAPPED — Civil rights — Australia
MENTALLY HANDICAPPED — Institutional care — England — London — Statistics
MENTALLY HANDICAPPED — Medical care — Moral and ethical aspects
MENTALLY HANDICAPPED — Services for — Great Britain
MENTALLY HANDICAPPED — Training of — Wales
MENTALLY HANDICAPPED — England — Gateshead (Tyne and Wear)
MENTALLY HANDICAPPED — England — London
MENTALLY HANDICAPPED — Great Britain
MENTALLY HANDICAPPED — Wales — Statistics
MENTALLY HANDICAPPED CHILDREN — United States — Family relationships
MENTALLY ILL — Care and treatment — England — History
MENTALLY ILL — Care and treatment — England — Shropshire
MENTALLY ILL — Care and treatment — Great Britain
MENTALLY ILL — Care and treatment — Ireland — History
MENTALLY ILL — Civil rights
MENTALLY ILL — Housing — Great Britain
MENTALLY ILL — Institutional care — Great Britain
MENTALLY ILL — Rehabilitation
MENTALLY ILL — Rehabilitation — Great Britain
MENTALLY ILL — Services for — United States
MENTALLY ILL — Great Britain — Home care
MENTALLY ILL — Wales — Statistics
MENZIES, Sir ROBERT, 1894-1978
MERCANTILE SYSTEM — History
MERCENARY TROOPS
MERCHANT BANKS
MERCHANT BANKS — Germany — Hamburg
MERCHANT MARINE
MERCHANT MARINE — Management
MERCHANT MARINE — Safety measures — Congresses
MERCHANT MARINE — Australia
MERCHANT MARINE — Europe — History
MERCHANT MARINE — South Africa — History
MERCHANT MARINE — Soviet Union
MERCHANT SEAMEN — Canada
MERCHANT SEAMEN — Canada — History
MERCHANT SEAMEN — Pacific States — History
MERCHANT SHIPS — Great Britain — Statistics
MERCHANTS — Canada — History — 18th century
MERCHANTS — China — History
MERCHANTS — New Zealand — Auckland — Biography
MERCHANTS, FOREIGN — Chile — History — 19th century
MERINO SHEEP — History
MERRHEIM, ALPHONSE
MERRIAM, CHARLES E.
MESSIANISM
MESSIANISM — Comparative studies
METAL TRADE
METAL TRADE — Employees — Effect of technological innovations on
METAL-WORKERS — Germany (West)
METAL-WORKERS' STRIKE, U.S., 1935 — History
METALS — Miscellanea
METALS — Religious aspects
METAPHOR
METAPHYSICS
METAPHYSISCHE ANFANGSGRÜNDE DER NATURWISSENSCHAFT
MÉTAYER SYSTEM
MÉTAYER SYSTEM — Africa
METEOROLOGY
METHADONE MAINTENANCE — Denmark
METHODISM
METHYL ISOCYANATE — Environemental aspects — India — Bhopal
METROPOLITAN AREAS — Congresses
METROPOLITAN AREAS — Asia
METROPOLITAN AREAS — Canada — Congresses
METROPOLITAN AREAS — Middle West
METROPOLITAN AREAS — Middle West — Case studies

METROPOLITAN AREAS — Sunbelt States
METROPOLITAN AREAS — United States — Congresses
METROPOLITAN GOVERNMENT — Legal status, laws, etc — England
METROPOLITAN GOVERNMENT — Legal status, laws, etc. — England
METROPOLITAN GOVERNMENT — Asia
METROPOLITAN GOVERNMENT — Australia — Addresses, essays, lectures
METROPOLITAN GOVERNMENT — England
METROPOLITAN GOVERNMENT — England — Bibliography
METROPOLITAN GOVERNMENT — Great Britain
METROPOLITAN GOVERNMENT — Middle West — Case studies
METROPOLITAN POLICE
METTERNICH, CLEMENS, Fürst von
MEXICAN AMERICAN AGRICULTURAL LABORERS — Employment — California, Northern
MEXICAN AMERICAN AGRICULTURAL LABORERS — California, Northern — Economic conditions
MEXICAN-AMERICAN BORDER REGION — Industries
MEXICAN AMERICAN LEADERSHIP — Politics and government
MEXICAN AMERICANS — Congresses
MEXICAN AMERICANS — Economic conditions
MEXICAN AMERICANS — Education — Texas — History — 20th century
MEXICAN AMERICANS — Politics and government
MEXICAN AMERICANS — Politics and suffrage
MEXICAN AMERICANS — Social conditions
MEXICAN AMERICANS — Arizona — Tucson — History
MEXICAN AMERICANS — Illinois — Chicago — Ethnic identity
MEXICAN AMERICANS — Texas — History — 19th century
MEXICANS — Employment — California, Northern
MEXICANS — California, Northern — Economic conditions
MEXICO — Commerce — History — 19th century
MEXICO — Description and travel
MEXICO — Description and travel — 1951-1980
MEXICO — Dictionaries and encyclopedias
MEXICO — Economic conditions — 1918-
MEXICO — Economic conditions — 1970-
MEXICO — Economic policy
MEXICO — Economic policy — 1970-
MEXICO — Emigration and immigration
MEXICO — Foreign economic relations — European Economic Community countries
MEXICO — Foreign relations — United States
MEXICO — History — Spanish Colony, 1540-1810
MEXICO — History — 1810-
MEXICO — History — 1821-1861
MEXICO — History — 1910-1946
MEXICO — Industries — Case studies
MEXICO — Officials and employees
MEXICO — Politics and government — 1810-
MEXICO — Politics and government — 20th century
MEXICO — Politics and government — 1946-
MEXICO — Politics and government — 1970-
MEXICO — Presidents
MEXICO — Presidents — Biography
MEXICO — Relations — United States — Congresses
MEXICO — Rural conditions
MEXICO — Social conditions
MEXICO — Social conditions — 1970-
MEXICO — Social policy
MEXICO. Comisión Federal de Electricidad
MEXICO. Secretaría de Relaciones Exteriores — Officials and employees
MEXICO, VALLEY OF (MEXICO) — Economic conditions
MICHAEL HENLEY AND SON — History
MICHIGAN — Industries — Location — Case studies
MICHNIK, ADAM — Addresses, essays, lectures
MICROCOMPUTERS
MICROCOMPUTERS — Congresses
MICROCOMPUTERS — Design and construction
MICROCOMPUTERS — Library applications
MICROCOMPUTERS — Programming
MICROECONOMICS
MICROECONOMICS — Addresses, essays, lectures
MICROECONOMICS — Mathematical models
MICROELECTRONICS
MICROELECTRONICS — Economic aspects
MICROELECTRONICS — Economic aspects — Great Britain
MICROELECTRONICS — Popular works
MICROELECTRONICS — Social aspects
MICROELECTRONICS — Social aspects — Great Britain — Forecasting
MICROELECTRONICS — Social aspects — United States
MICROELECTRONICS — Great Britain
MICROELECTRONICS CONSULTANCY SUPPORT
MICROELECTRONICS INDUSTRY — Government policy — North Carolina — Addresses, essays, lectures
MICROELECTRONICS INDUSTRY — California — Santa Clara County
MICROELECTRONICS INDUSTRY — Great Britain
MICROPHOTOGRAPHY
MIDDLE AGED WOMEN — United States — Employment
MIDDLE AGED WOMEN — United States — Social conditions
MIDDLE AGES — History
MIDDLE CLASSES — History
MIDDLE CLASSES — Australia
MIDDLE CLASSES — California — Santa Monica — Case studies
MIDDLE CLASSES — England — History
MIDDLE CLASSES — England — London — History — 19th century
MIDDLE CLASSES — Europe — Conduct of life
MIDDLE CLASSES — Germany (West) — Marburg — Political activity
MIDDLE CLASSES — Great Britain
MIDDLE CLASSES — Poland — History
MIDDLE CLASSES — Rhode Island — Providence — History
MIDDLE CLASSES — Spain — Political activity
MIDDLE CLASSES — Spain — Castellón de la Plana — History — 19th century
MIDDLE CLASSES — Spain — Catalonia
MIDDLE CLASSES — United States
MIDDLE EAST — Economic conditions
MIDDLE EAST — Foreign relations — Germany (West)
MIDDLE EAST — Foreign relations — Iran
MIDDLE EAST — Foreign relations — United States
MIDDLE EAST — Politics and government
MIDDLE EAST — Politics and government — 1945-
MIDDLE EAST — Relations
MIDDLE EAST — Relations — Japan — Congresses
MIDDLE EAST — Social conditions
MIDDLE WEST — Race relations
MIDDLESEX — History
MIDLAND BANK GROUP — History
MIDLANDS (ENGLAND) — Industries — History — Bibliography
MIGRANT AGRICULTURAL LABORERS — Kenya — History — 20th century
MIGRANT LABOR
MIGRANT LABOR — Health and hygiene — United States
MIGRANT LABOR — Legal status, laws, etc. — Europe — Congresses
MIGRANT LABOR — Medical care — Europe
MIGRANT LABOR — Medical care — United States
MIGRANT LABOR — America — Congresses
MIGRANT LABOR — Europe — History
MIGRANT LABOR — European Economic Community countries
MIGRANT LABOR — France
MIGRANT LABOR — Panama Canal (Panama)
MIGRANT LABOR — Switzerland — Geneva
MIGRANT LABORERS — Soviet Union — History
MIGRANT LABOUR — Scotland
MIGRANT LABOUR — South Africa
MIGRATION ACT 1958
MIGRATION, INTERNAL — Case studies
MIGRATION, INTERNAL — Cross-cultural studies
MIGRATION, INTERNAL — Developing countries — Research
MIGRATION, INTERNAL — Economic aspects — Portugal — History
MIGRATION, INTERNAL — History — Congresses
MIGRATION, INTERNAL — Measurement — Methodology
MIGRATION, INTERNAL — Africa
MIGRATION, INTERNAL — Asia, Southeastern — Congresses
MIGRATION, INTERNAL — Australia
MIGRATION, INTERNAL — Bahamas — Statistics
MIGRATION, INTERNAL — Bolivia — Santa Cruz (Dept.)
MIGRATION, INTERNAL — Botswana — Statistics
MIGRATION, INTERNAL — Comoros — Statistics
MIGRATION, INTERNAL — Egypt — Statistics
MIGRATION, INTERNAL — England — Surrey
MIGRATION, INTERNAL — Europe
MIGRATION, INTERNAL — Greenland — Statistics
MIGRATION, INTERNAL — India — Andaman and Nicobar Islands — Statistics
MIGRATION, INTERNAL — India — Arunachal Pradesh — Statistics
MIGRATION, INTERNAL — India — Chandigarh
MIGRATION, INTERNAL — India — Dadra and Nagar Haveli — Statistics
MIGRATION, INTERNAL — India — Pondicherry — Statistics
MIGRATION, INTERNAL — Japan — Statistics
MIGRATION, INTERNAL — Korea (South)
MIGRATION INTERNAL — Korea (South
MIGRATION, INTERNAL — Latin America — History
MIGRATION, INTERNAL — Mexico
MIGRATION, INTERNAL — Morocco
MIGRATION, INTERNAL — Nigeria — Kainji Reservoir Region
MIGRATION, INTERNAL — Pakistan

MIGRATION, INTERNAL — Pennsylvania — Hazleton
MIGRATION, INTERNAL — Peru
MIGRATION, INTERNAL — Poland
MIGRATION, INTERNAL — Spain
MIGRATION, INTERNAL — Thailand
MIGRATION, INTERNAL — Togo — Statistics
MIGRATION, INTERNAL — United States
MIGRATION, INTERNATIONAL — India — Statistics
MILITARISM — Germany
MILITARISM — Japan — History — 20th century
MILITARISM — Spain — History
MILITARY ART AND SCIENCE
MILITARY ART AND SCIENCE — History
MILITARY ART AND SCIENCE — History — 19th century
MILITARY ART AND SCIENCE — Europe — History
MILITARY ART AND SCIENCE — France
MILITARY ART AND SCIENCE — France — History — 20th century
MILITARY ART AND SCIENCE — Soviet Union
MILITARY ART AND SCIENCE — United States — History
MILITARY ASSISTANCE
MILITARY ASSISTANCE, AMERICAN — Middle East
MILITARY ASSISTANCE, AMERICAN — Turkey
MILITARY ASSISTANCE, AMERICAN — Turkey — History — 20th century
MILITARY ASSISTANCE, BRITISH — Middle East
MILITARY ASSISTANCE, FRENCH — Middle East
MILITARY ASSISTANCE, RUSSIAN — Middle East
MILITARY BASES, AMERICAN — Great Britain — History
MILITARY GEOGRAPHY — Great Britain
MILITARY GOVERNMENT — Germany (West) — Nuremberg
MILITARY GOVERNMENT — Latin America — History — 20th century
MILITARY HISTORY, MEDIEVAL
MILITARY HISTORY, MODERN
MILITARY HISTORY, MODERN — 18th century — Congresses
MILITARY HISTORY, MODERN — 20th century
MILITARY INTELLIGENCE — Canada
MILITARY PLANNING — Europe
MILITARY PLANNING — Germany — History — 20th century
MILITARY POLICY
MILITARY SERVICE, COMPULSORY — Great Britain — History — 20th century
MILITARY SERVICE, COMPULSORY — United States
MILITARY SERVICE, COMPULSORY — United States — Draft resisters
MILITARY SERVICE, COMPULSORY — United States — History — 20th century
MILK, HUMAN
MILK TRADE — European Economic Community Countries
MILL, JOHN STUART
MILL, JOHN STUART — Economics
MILL, JOHN STUART, 1806-1873
MILLENIALISM — United States — History — 18th century
MILLENNIALISM — Indians — New Harmony
MILLENNIALISM IN LITERATURE
MILLIONAIRES — Great Britain — Biography
MILTON KEYNES (BUCKINGHAMSHIRE : DISTRICT)
MIND AND BODY

MIND-BRAIN IDENTITY THEORY
MINE DUSTS
MINE SANITATION
MINERAL INDUSTRIES
MINERAL INDUSTRIES — Economic aspects — South Africa
MINERAL INDUSTRIES — Finance
MINERAL INDUSTRIES — Government policy — Canada
MINERAL INDUSTRIES — government policy — Canada — History
MINERAL INDUSTRIES — Taxation — Appalachian Region
MINERAL INDUSTRIES — Asia, Southeastern
MINERAL INDUSTRIES — Australia
MINERAL INDUSTRIES — Canada
MINERAL INDUSTRIES — Developing countries
MINERAL INDUSTRIES — East Asia
MINERAL INDUSTRIES — Great Britain — Statistics
MINERAL INDUSTRIES — South Africa — Statistics
MINERAL INDUSTRIES — Spain — History — 19th century
MINERAL INDUSTRIES — Spain — Almería — History
MINERAL INDUSTRIES — Spain — Murcia (Province) — History
MINERAL INDUSTRIES — Wales — Cardiganshire — Statistics
MINERAL INDUSTRIES — Wales — Flintshire
MINERAL INDUSTRY — South Africa
MINERAL WATERS — Norway
MINERS — Australia — Broken Hill (N.S.W.)
MINERS — Great Britain — Social life and customs
MINERS — South Africa — Johannesburg
MINES AND MINERAL RESOURCES — Bibliography
MINES AND MINERAL RESOURCES — Commerce — South Africa
MINES AND MINERAL RESOURCES — Information services — England — London
MINES AND MINERAL RESOURCES — Taxation
MINES AND MINERAL RESOURCES — Union lists
MINES AND MINERAL RESOURCES — British Columbia
MINES AND MINERAL RESOURCES — Great Britain
MINES AND MINERAL RESOURCES — Netherlands — Statistics
MINES AND MINERAL RESOURCES — Ontario — History
MINES AND MINERAL RESOURCES — Tanzania
MINES AND MINERAL RESOURCES — United States
MINES AND MINERAL RESOURCES — Wales — Clwyd
MINES AND MINERAL RESOURCES — Wales — West Glamorgan
MINET HOLDINGS
MINIMUM WAGE — Great Britain
MINING DISTRICTS — Canada
MINING DISTRICTS — Great Britain — Social conditions
MINING ENGINEERING — Ontario — History
MINING ENGINEERS — Great Britain — Biography
MINING LAW — Antarctic regions
MINING LAW — United States
MINISTERIAL RESPONSIBILITY — Great Britain — Bibliography
MINITAB (COMPUTER SYSTEM)
MINNEAPOLIS (MINN.) — Social life and customs
MINORITIES
MINORITIES — Civil rights
MINORITIES — Civil rights — Canada

MINORITIES — Dictionaries and encyclopedias
MINORITIES — Education
MINORITIES — Education — Government policy — Great Britain
MINORITIES — Education — Denmark — Case studies
MINORITIES — Education — England
MINORITIES — Education — Great Britain
MINORITIES — Education — Great Britain — Language arts
MINORITIES — Education — Organisation for Economic Co-operation and Development countries
MINORITIES — Education — United States
MINORITIES — Education (Higher) — Israel
MINORITIES — Education (Secondary) — England — Coventry (West Midlands)
MINORITIES — Education (Secondary) — Great Britain
MINORITIES — Employment — Great Britain
MINORITIES — Government policy — Canada
MINORITIES — Health and hygiene — England
MINORITIES — Health and hygiene — England — London
MINORITIES — Housing — Government policy — United States
MINORITIES — Housing — England
MINORITIES — Housing — England — Bedford (Bedfordshire)
MINORITIES — Housing — England — Gloucester (Gloucestershire)
MINORITIES — Housing — England — Leeds (West Yorkshire)
MINORITIES — Housing — Great Britain
MINORITIES — Housing — Great Britian
MINORITIES — Housing — London metropolitan area — Tower Hamlets
MINORITIES — Housing — United States
MINORITIES — Legal status, laws, etc
MINORITIES — Medical care — England
MINORITIES — Medical care — Great Britain
MINORITIES — Mental health services — Great Britain
MINORITIES — Political activity — Case studies
MINORITIES — Belgium
MINORITIES — Canada
MINORITIES — Canada — Employment
MINORITIES — China
MINORITIES — England
MINORITIES — England — Bristol (Avon) — Socioeconomic status
MINORITIES — England — Coventry (West Midlands) — Statistics
MINORITIES — England — London
MINORITIES — England — London — Statistics
MINORITIES — Europe — History
MINORITIES — Great Britain
MINORITIES — Great Britain — History
MINORITIES — Great Britain — Languages
MINORITIES — Great Britain — Photograph collections
MINORITIES — Great Britain — Political activity
MINORITIES — Great Britain — Services for
MINORITIES — Great Britain — Social conditions
MINORITIES — Great Britain — Statistics
MINORITIES — India — History — Sources
MINORITIES — Indiana — Gary — History — 20th century
MINORITIES — Iran
MINORITIES — Iraq
MINORITIES — Israel
MINORITIES — Kenya

MINORITIES — Middle West — History
MINORITIES — Middle West (U.S.) — History
MINORITIES — Poland
MINORITIES — South Africa — Civil rights
MINORITIES — Soviet Union
MINORITIES — Soviet Union — Historiography
MINORITIES — United States
MINORITIES — United States — Addresses, essays, lectures
MINORITIES — United States — Political activity — Case studies
MINORITIES — United States — Psychology — Case studies
MINORITIES — Venezuela — Political activity
MINORITIES IN MEDICINE — Great Britain
MINORITY AGED — England — London — Societies and clubs
MINORITY BUSINESS ENTERPRISES — United States — Addresses, essays, lectures
MIRABEAU, GABRIEL-HONORE DE RIQUETTI, Comte de
MISES, LUDWIG VON
MISSING PERSONS
MISSIONARIES — Asia — Biography
MISSIONARIES — Germany — Biography
MISSIONARIES — Middle East — Biography
MISSIONARIES — South Africa — Biography
MISSIONS — Asia
MISSIONS — Middle East
MISSIONS — South Africa — Educational work — History
MISSIONS, MEDICAL — Nepal
MISSIONS, NORWEGIAN — Africa — History
MISSIONS TO AFRO-AMERICANS
MISSIONS TO BURIATS — History — 19th century
MISSIONS TO JEWS — History — 19th century
MISSIONS TO MUSLIMS — History — 19th century
MISSISSIPPI — Governors — Biography
MISSISSIPPI — Politics and government — To 1865
MISSISSIPPI — Politics and government — 1865-1950
MISSOURI — Politics and government
MISTRESSES — United States
MITCHELL, ANDREW
MITO-HAN (JAPAN) — History
MITOGAKU
MITTERRAND, FRANÇOIS
MIYAMOTO, KENJI
MŁYNARSKI, FELIKS
MOBILE (ALA.) — Economic conditions
MOBILE (ALA.) — History — 19th century
MOBILE HOMES — Law and legislation — Great Britain
MOBILE HOMES — Great Britain — Handbooks, manuals, etc.
MOBILE HOMES BILL 1982-83
MOBILE POST OFFICES — Great Britain
MODELS, PSYCHOLOGICAL
MODERNISM — Catholic Church
MODIGLIANI, FRANCO. The contribution of intergenerational transfer to total wealth
MOERAN, BRIAN
MOHAMMED REZA PAHLAVI, Shah of Iran
MOLDAVIA — Politics and government
MOLDAVIA — Relations — Soviet Union
MOLDAVIAN S.S.R. — Economic conditions
MOLDAVIAN S.S.R. — Economic conditions — Statistics
MOLDAVIAN S.S.R. — Industries
MONACO — Population
MONACO — Statistics, Vital
MONARCHY
MONARCHY, BRITISH — Finance

MONASTERIES — Great Britain
MONDOÑEDO (SPAIN) — Economic conditions
MONETARY POLICY
MONETARY POLICY — Addresses, essays, lectures
MONETARY POLICY — Bibliography
MONETARY POLICY — Congresses
MONETARY POLICY — History
MONETARY POLICY — Mathematical models
MONETARY POLICY — Argentina — History — 20th century
MONETARY POLICY — Australia — History
MONETARY POLICY — Canada
MONETARY POLICY — Chile
MONETARY POLICY — Developing countries
MONETARY POLICY — France
MONETARY POLICY — Great Britain
MONETARY POLICY — Great Britain — History
MONETARY POLICY — Great Britain — History — 20th century
MONETARY POLICY — Hungary
MONETARY POLICY — India
MONETARY POLICY — Japan
MONETARY POLICY — Korea (South)
MONETARY POLICY — Latin America
MONETARY POLICY — Papua New Guinea
MONETARY POLICY — Southern Cone of South America
MONETARY POLICY — Switzerland
MONETARY POLICY — United States
MONETARY POLICYOFF. PUBNS. — European Economic Community countries 986
MONETARY REFORMERS — Great Britain — Biography
MONEY
MONEY — Economic aspects — Europe
MONEY — History
MONEY — Mathematical models
MONEY — Social aspects — Europe
MONEY — Australia
MONEY — Canada
MONEY — Chile — Statistics
MONEY — Europe — History
MONEY — Europe — History — 18th century
MONEY — Europe — History — 19th century
MONEY — European Economic Community countries
MONEY — European Economic Community countries — Bibliography — Catalogs
MONEY — France
MONEY — France — Statistics
MONEY — Great Britain — History
MONEY — Great Britain — History — 20th century
MONEY — Hungary
MONEY — Malaysia
MONEY — Peru
MONEY — Singapore
MONEY — Soviet Union — Bibliography
MONEY — Swaziland
MONEY — United States — Statistics
MONEY MARKET
MONEY MARKET — History — 20th century
MONEY MARKET — Australia
MONEY MARKET — Canada
MONEY MARKET — Japan
MONEY MARKET — United States
MONEY SUPPLY — Bibliography
MONEY SUPPLY — Government policy — Great Britain
MONEY SUPPLY — Spain
MONEY SUPPLY — United States
MONGOLIA (MONGOLIAN PEOPLE'S REPUBLIC)
MONOPOLIES
MONOPOLIES — United States
MONTAGNARDS — History

MONTAGNE, ROBERT
MONTENEGRO
MONTESQUIEU, CHARLES DE SECONDAT, Baron de
MONTRÉAL METROPOLITAN AREA (QUÉBEC) — Languages — Political aspects
MONTRÉAL METROPOLITAN AREA (QUÉBEC) — Politics and government
MONTREAL (QUEBEC) — City planning
MONTSERRAT — Census, 1980
MONTSERRAT — Economic conditions — Statistics
MONTSERRAT — Population — Statistics
MONUMENTS — Law and legislation — Great Britain
MOOREA (SOCIETY ISLANDS) — Population — Statistics
MOOT COURTS
MORAL CONDITIONS
MORAL DEVELOPMENT — Addresses, essays, lectures
MORAL EDUCATION — United States
MORBIDITY
MORELOS (MEXICO) — Moral conditions — Case studies
MORELOS (MEXICO) — Social conditions — Case studies
MORGAN, J. PIERPONT
MORGAN, JUNIUS SPENCER
MORITA, AKIO
MORO, ALDO — Kidnapping, 1978
MOROBE PROVINCE (PAPUA NEW GUINEA) — Population — Statistics
MOROCCANS — France
MOROCCANS — Germany (West) — Social conditions
MOROCCO — Dictionaries and encyclopedias
MOROCCO — Economic conditions
MOROCCO — Economic conditions — Statistics
MOROCCO — Emigration and immigration
MOROCCO — Foreign Relations — United States
MOROCCO — History — Dictionaries
MOROCCO — History — 20th century
MOROCCO — Manufactures
MOROCCO — Politics and government
MOROCCO — Population — Statistics
MOROCCO — Relations — Spain
MOROCCO — Social conditions — Statistics
MOROCCO — Social life and customs
MOROCCO. Ministere du Plan, de la Formation des Cadres et de la Formation Professionnelle
MORRIS, WILLIAM — Influence
MORTALITY
MORTALITY — Addresses, essays, lectures
MORTALITY — History — Congresses
MORTALITY — Social aspects — Great Britain
MORTALITY — Statistical methods
MORTALITY — Statistical methods — Congresses
MORTALITY — Tables
MORTALITY — Australia
MORTALITY — Cyprus — Statistics
MORTALITY — Denmark — Statistics
MORTALITY — Developing countries
MORTALITY — England — Cleveland
MORTALITY — England — London — Tables
MORTALITY — Europe
MORTALITY — Finland — Tables
MORTALITY — Israel — Statistics
MORTALITY — Japan — History
MORTALITY — Jordan — Statistics
MORTALITY — Lesotho
MORTALITY — Netherlands — Tables
MORTALITY — Peru — Statistics
MORTALITY — South Asia
MORTALITY — United States — Statistics
MORTALITY AND RACE — Australia
MORTALITY AND RACE — Israel — Statistics
MORTGAGE LOANS — Great Britain
MORTGAGE LOANS — United States

1067

MORTGAGES — England
MOSCA, GAETANO, 1858-1941 — Contributions in political science
MOSCOW (R.S.F.S.R.) — Economic conditions
MOSCOW (R.S.F.S.R.) — History — Revolution of 1905
MOSCOW (R.S.F.S.R.) — History — 1925-1953
MOSCOW (R.S.F.S.R.) — Politics and government
MOSCOW (R.S.F.S.R.) — Statistics
MOSCOW (R.S.F.S.R.: GUBERNIIA) — Economic conditions
MOSCOW (R.S.F.S.R.: GUBERNIIA) — Politics and government
MOSQUITO INDIANS — Civil rights
MOTHER AND CHILD
MOTHER-CHILD RELATIONS
MOTHERHOOD — Psychological aspects
MOTHERHOOD — Developing countries
MOTHERHOOD — Great Britain — History
MOTHERS
MOTHERS — Attitudes
MOTHERS — Employment
MOTHERS — Employment — France
MOTHERS — Employment — United States
MOTHERS — Employment — United States — History
MOTHERS — Legal status, laws, etc — United States
MOTHERS — Mortality — England
MOTHERS — psychology
MOTHERS — Developing countries — Mortality — Prevention
MOTHERS — Great Britain — Attitudes — History
MOTHERS — Great Britain — Interviews
MOTHERS AND DAUGHTERS — Cross-cultural studies
MOTHERS AND DAUGHTERS — United States
MOTIVATION (PSYCHOLOGY)
MOTIVATION RESEARCH (MARKETING) — Addresses, essays, lectures
MOTOR BUS TERMINALS — England — London
MOULIN, JEAN — Congresses
MOUNTBATTEN, LOUIS MOUNTBATTEN, Earl
MOUVEMENT RÉPUBLICAIN POPULAIRE
MOVEMENT, PSYCHOLOGY OF
MOVIMENTO POPULAR DE LIBERTACAO DE ANGOLA
MOVING-PICTURE INDUSTRY — Legal status, laws, etc — Peru
MOVING-PICTURE INDUSTRY — Legal status, laws, etc. — Peru
MOVING-PICTURE THEATRERS — Great Britain — Statistics
MOVING-PICTURES — Censorship — Great Britain
MOVING PICTURES — Political aspects — Great Britain
MOVING-PICTURES — Social aspects
MOVING-PICTURES, AMERICAN — Social aspects — Great Britain
MOVING PICTURES AND CHILDREN
MOVING PICTURES, CHILEAN — Political aspects
MOVING PICTURES, DOCUMENTARY — Great Britain — History and criticism
MOVING-PICTURES IN PROPAGANDA — Great Britain — History
MOZAMBIQUE. Treaties, etc. South Africa (1984 Mar. 16)
MS-DOS (COMPUTER OPERATING SYSTEM) — Handbooks, manuals, etc.
MUGGING — England — London
MUHAMMAD, FAQIR
MUHAMMED, MURTALA
MULDOON, ROBERT
MULELE, PIERRE
MULRONEY, BRIAN

MULTICULTURALISM — Canada
MULTILINGUALISM
MULTILINGUALISM — Belgium
MULTIPLE COMPARISONS (STATISTICS)
MULTIPLE IMPUTATION (STATISTICS)
MULTIVARIATE ANALYSIS
MUNAZZAMAT AL-TAḤRĪR AL-FILASṬĪNIYAH
MUNAZZAMAT AL-TAḤRĪR AL FILASṬĪNIYAH
MUNDURUCU INDIANS — Social life and customs
MUNDURUCU INDIANS — Women
MUNICH FOUR-POWER AGREEMENT, 1938
MUNICH (GERMANY) — History
MUNICIPAL CORPORATIONS — Canada
MUNICIPAL CORPORATIONS — Finland
MUNICIPAL FINANCE
MUNICIPAL FINANCE — Addresses, essays, lectures
MUNICIPAL FINANCE — Iceland — Statistics
MUNICIPAL FINANCE — Mexico — Mexico (State)
MUNICIPAL FINANCE — United States — Addresses, essays, lectures
MUNICIPAL GOVERNMENT — Addresses, essays, lectures
MUNICIPAL GOVERNMENT — Congresses
MUNICIPAL GOVERNMENT — Alberta
MUNICIPAL GOVERNMENT — Australia — Addresses, essays, lectures
MUNICIPAL GOVERNMENT — Australia — Tasmania — Statistics
MUNICIPAL GOVERNMENT — Belgium
MUNICIPAL GOVERNMENT — British Columbia — Statistics
MUNICIPAL GOVERNMENT — Denmark
MUNICIPAL GOVERNMENT — Great Britain
MUNICIPAL GOVERNMENT — Middle West — Case studies
MUNICIPAL GOVERNMENT — Organisation for Economic Co-operation and Development countries
MUNICIPAL GOVERNMENT — Russian S.F.S.R. — Leningrad
MUNICIPAL GOVERNMENT — South Africa
MUNICIPAL GOVERNMENT — Spain — Barcelona
MUNICIPAL GOVERNMENT — United States
MUNICIPAL GOVERNMENT — United States — Case studies
MUNICIPAL GOVERNMENT — Zambia — Lusaka
MUNICIPAL HEALTH SERVICES PROGRAM (U.S.)
MUNICIPAL OWNERSHIP — United States — History
MUNICIPAL SERVICES
MUNICIPAL SERVICES — Addresses, essays, lectures
MUNICIPAL SERVICES — France — Paris region
MUNICIPAL SERVICES — Great Britain
MUNICIPAL SERVICES — Illinois — Finance
MUNICIPAL SERVICES — Mexico
MUNICIPAL WATER SUPPLY — Developing Countries — Planning
MUNITIONS
MUNITIONS — International cooperation
MUNITIONS — Political aspects — Canada
MUNITIONS — Canada
MUNITIONS — Developing countries
MUNITIONS — Europe
MUNITIONS — Great Britain
MUNITIONS — Japan
MUNITIONS — Netherlands
MUNITIONS — Sweden

MUNITIONS — United States — History — 19th century — Addresses, essays, lectures
MUNITIONS — United States — History — 20th century — Addresses, essays, lectures
MURCIA (SPAIN : PROVINCE) — Politics and government — 1975-
MURDER — England, Northern
MURDER — Great Britain — Statistics
MŪSÁ, SALĀMAH
MUSEUMS — Law and legislation — Great Britain
MUSEUMS — Pakistan
MUSEUMS — Scotland
MUSIC — Publishing — Canada
MUSIC, POPULAR (SONGS, ETC.) — United States
MUSIC TRADE — Canada
MUSICIANS — Legal status, laws, etc. — Canada
MUSLIMS — India — Political activity
MUSLIMS — India — Assam
MUSLIMS — India — Tirunelveli District
MUSLIMS — Lebanon — Beirut — Political activity — History
MUSLIMS — Lebanon — Beirut — Social conditions
MUSLIMS — Nigeria, Northern — History
MUSLIMS — Soviet Union
MUSLIMS — Soviet Union — Political activity
MUSSOLINI, BENITO
MYER, DILLON S
MYRDAL, GUNNAR. American dilemma
MYSORE REGION — Population, Rural
MYSORE REGION (INDIA) — Rural conditions
MYTHOLOGY, AFRICAN
MYTHOLOGY, GREEK
NACIONAL FINANCIERA, S.A. (Mexico)
NAGALAND (INDIA) — Population — Statistics
NALGO ACTION GROUP
NAMBIA — Foreign economic relations
NAMES, GEOGRAPHICAL — Australia
NAMES, GEOGRAPHICAL — England — Scandinavian
NAMES, GEOGRAPHYCAL — England — Anglo-Saxon
NAMIBIA — Economic conditions
NAMIBIA — Foreign economic relations
NAMIBIA — International status
NAMIBIA — Politics and government
NAMIBIA — Politics and government — 1946-
NAMIBIA — Social conditions
NAMIBIA — Economic conditions
NANTUCKET (MASS.) — Politics and government
NANTUCKET (MASS.) — Social conditions
NAPOLÉON I, Emperor of the French
NAPOLEON I, Emperor of the French — Biography
NAPUKA (TUAMOTU ISLANDS) — Population — Statistics
NARAYAN, JAYAPRAKASH
NARCOTIC ADDICTS — Legal status, laws, etc — Australia
NARCOTIC ADDICTS — Rehabilitation — Australia
NARCOTIC ADDICTS — Rehabilitation — England — Portsmouth
NARCOTIC ADDICTS — Rehabilitation — Great Britain
NARCOTIC ADDICTS — Great Britain — Social aspects
NARCOTIC HABIT
NARCOTIC HABIT — Treatment
NARCOTIC HABIT — Netherlands
NARCOTIC LAWS
NARCOTIC LAWS — United States — Addresses, essays, lectures
NARCOTICS AND CRIME — Denmark
NARCOTICS, CONTROL OF — Canada
NARCOTICS, CONTROL OF — Scandinavia

NARCOTICS, CONTROL OF — United States
NASSER, GAMAL ABDEL
NATAL (SOUTH AFRICA)
NATAL (SOUTH AFRICA) — Economic conditions
NATAL (SOUTH AFRICA) — History — 1843-1893
NATAL (SOUTH AFRICA) — History — 1893-1910
NATAL (SOUTH AFRICA) — Social conditions
NATIONAL ACADEMY OF PEACE AND CONFLICT RESOLUTION
NATIONAL AND LOCAL GOVERNMENT OFFICERS' ASSOCIATION
NATIONAL AND LOCAL GOVERNMENT OFFICERS ASSOCIATION
NATIONAL ASSOCIATION FOR THE ADVANCEMENT OF COLORED PEOPLE — History
NATIONAL ASSOCIATIONS OF ACCOUNTANTS
NATIONAL BUILDING SOCIETY
NATIONAL BUREAU OF ECONOMIC RESEARCH
NATIONAL CAPITAL DISTRICT (PAPUA NEW GUINEA) — Population — Statistics
NATIONAL CHARACTERISTICS, AFRICAN
NATIONAL CHARACTERISTICS, AMERICAN
NATIONAL CHARACTERISTICS, CANADIAN
NATIONAL CHARACTERISTICS, CHINESE
NATIONAL CHARACTERISTICS, CHINESE — Congresses
NATIONAL CHARACTERISTICS, ENGLISH
NATIONAL CHARACTERISTICS, ISRAELI
NATIONAL CHARACTERISTICS, JAPANESE
NATIONAL CHARACTERISTICS, JAPANESE — Addresses, essays, lectures
NATIONAL CHARACTERISTICS, LATIN AMERICAN
NATIONAL CHARACTERISTICS, MEXICAN
NATIONAL CHARACTERISTICS, SPANISH
NATIONAL COAL BOARD
NATIONAL COMMUNICATIONS UNION
NATIONAL COUNCIL FOR CIVIL LIBERTIES — History
NATIONAL DISTRICT DEVELOPMENT CONFERENCE
NATIONAL FEDERATION OF HOUSING ASSOCIATIONS
NATIONAL FREIGHT CORPORATION — Government policy
NATIONAL FRONT
NATIONAL GIRO
NATIONAL HEALTH SECURITY ACT, 1975
NATIONAL HEALTH SERVICE (Great Britain)
NATIONAL HEALTH SERVICE (Great Britain) — Administration
NATIONAL HEALTH SERVICE (Great Britain) — Finance
NATIONAL HEALTH SERVICE (Great Britain) — Legal status, laws, etc.
NATIONAL HEALTH SERVICE (Great Britain) — Statistics
NATIONAL HEALTH SERVICE (AMENDMENT) BILL 1985-86
NATIONAL HEALTH SERVICE (GREAT BRITAIN) — Management
NATIONAL HEALTH SERVICE (GREAT BRITAIN)
NATIONAL HEALTH SERVICE (GREAT BRITAIN) — Appropriations and expenditures
NATIONAL HEALTH SERVICE (GREAT BRITAIN) — Finance
NATIONAL HERITAGE BILL 1982-83
NATIONAL INCOME
NATIONAL INCOME — Accounting
NATIONAL INCOME — Accounting — Congresses
NATIONAL INCOME — Accounting — Canada
NATIONAL INCOME — Australia
NATIONAL INCOME — Austria
NATIONAL INCOME — Burkina Faso — Accounting
NATIONAL INCOME — Chile — Accounting
NATIONAL INCOME — Denmark — Accounting
NATIONAL INCOME — Developing countries — Case studies
NATIONAL INCOME — Finland — Accounting
NATIONAL INCOME — France — Accounting
NATIONAL INCOME — Gambia — Accounting
NATIONAL INCOME — Germany (West) — Accounting
NATIONAL INCOME — Germany (West) — Statistics
NATIONAL INCOME — Great Britain — Accounting
NATIONAL INCOME — Hungary
NATIONAL INCOME — India — Accounting — Statistics
NATIONAL INCOME — India — Case studies
NATIONAL INCOME — Indonesia
NATIONAL INCOME — Japan — Accounting — Nomenclature — Translations into English
NATIONAL INCOME — Kiribati — Accounting
NATIONAL INCOME — Switzerland — Accounting
NATIONAL INCOME — Tanzania — Accounting — Methodolgy
NATIONAL INCOME — Tuvalu — Accounting
NATIONAL INQUIRY INTO LOCAL GOVERNMENT FINANCE (Australia)
NATIONAL INSTITUTE OF PUBLIC AFFAIRS (U.S.)
NATIONAL LIBERATION MOVEMENTS — Africa, Southern
NATIONAL LIBERATION MOVEMENTS — Ethiopia
NATIONAL PARKS AND RESERVES — Government policy — Great Britain
NATIONAL PARKS AND RESERVES — England — Broads
NATIONAL PARKS AND RESERVES — Great Britain
NATIONAL SECURITY
NATIONAL SERVICE — United States
NATIONAL SOCIALISM
NATIONAL SOCIALISM — History
NATIONAL SOCIALISM — Law and legislation
NATIONAL SOCIALISM — Germany
NATIONAL SOCIALISM AND EDUCATION — History
NATIONAL SOCIALISM AND EDUCATION — History — 20th century
NATIONAL SOCIALISTS — Germany (West)
NATIONAL STATE
NATIONAL UNION OF MINEWORKERS
NATIONAL UNION OF PUBLIC EMPLOYEES
NATIONAL UNION OF PUBLIC EMPLOYEES — History
NATIONAL UNION OF RAILWAYMEN. Darlington Branch — History
NATIONAL UNION OF TEACHERS
NATIONAL UNION PUBLIC EMPLOYEES
NATIONAL WAGES COUNCIL (Singapore)
NATIONAL WOMAN'S PARTY — History
NATIONALISM
NATIONALISM — History
NATIONALISM — Arab countries
NATIONALISM — Argentina — History
NATIONALISM — Canada
NATIONALISM — China
NATIONALISM — Czechoslovakia
NATIONALISM — Developing countries
NATIONALISM — Egypt
NATIONALISM — England — History
NATIONALISM — France
NATIONALISM — France — Brittany — History — 20th century
NATIONALISM — Germany
NATIONALISM — Germany — Addresses, essays, lectures
NATIONALISM — India — History
NATIONALISM — India — History — Sources
NATIONALISM — India — Punjab — History
NATIONALISM — Iraq — History
NATIONALISM — Ireland — History
NATIONALISM — Islamic countries
NATIONALISM — Kenya
NATIONALISM — Northern Ireland
NATIONALISM — Québec (Province)
NATIONALISM — Singapore
NATIONALISM — South Africa — History — 20th century
NATIONALISM — Soviet Union
NATIONALISM — Spain
NATIONALISM — Spain — History — 19th century
NATIONALISM — Spain — Basque Provinces
NATIONALISM — Spain — Basque Provinces — Congresses
NATIONALISM — Spain — Catalonia
NATIONALISM — Spain — Catalonia — Congresses
NATIONALISM — Spain — Catalonia — History
NATIONALISM — Spain — Galacia — History
NATIONALISM — Spain — Galicia — History
NATIONALISM — Spain — Valencia
NATIONALISM — Sudan — History
NATIONALISM — Thailand
NATIONALISM — Yugoslavia
NATIONALISM AND EDUCATION — Germany — History — 20th century
NATIONALISM AND EDUCATION — India
NATIONALISM AND SOCIALISM — Soviet Union
NATIONALISM AND SOCIALISM — Soviet Union — History
NATIONALISTS — France — Biography
NATIONALISTS — India — Biography
NATIONALISTS — Indonesia — Biography
NATIONALISTS — Ireland — Biography
NATIONALSOZIALISTISCHE DEUTSCHE ARBEITER-PARTEI. Sturmabteilung — History
NATIONWIDE BUILDING SOCIETY
NATIVE RACES
NATIVE RACES — Addresses, essays, lectures
NATIVISM — History — 19th century
NATURAL DISASTERS — Prevention
NATURAL DISASTERS — Prevention — Public relations
NATURAL ENVIRONMENT RESEARCH COUNCIL
NATURAL HISTORY — Gambia
NATURAL LAW
NATURAL RESOURCES
NATURAL RESOURCES — Addresses, essays, lectures

1069

NATURAL RESOURCES — Economic aspects — Canada
NATURAL RESOURCES — Government policy
NATURAL RESOURCES — Government policy — Canada
NATURAL RESOURCES — Government policy — India
NATURAL RESOURCES — Government policy — United States
NATURAL RESOURCES — Law and legislation
NATURAL RESOURCES — Law and legislation — Antarctic regions — Congresses
NATURAL RESOURCES — Law and legislation — Canada
NATURAL RESOURCES — Management
NATURAL RESOURCES — Political aspects
NATURAL RESOURCES — Remote sensing
NATURAL RESOURCES — Antarctic regions — Congresses
NATURAL RESOURCES — Asia, Southeastern — Congresses
NATURAL RESOURCES — Australia — Maps
NATURAL RESOURCES — Developing countries
NATURAL RESOURCES — Developing countries — Management
NATURAL RESOURCES — France — Statistics
NATURAL RESOURCES — Great Britain
NATURAL RESOURCES — India
NATURAL RESOURCES — India — Andhra Pradesh — Maps
NATURAL RESOURCES — Malaysia
NATURAL RESOURCES — United States
NATURAL RESOURCES — United States — Management
NATURAL SELECTION
NATURALISM
NATURALISTS — England — Biography
NATURE
NATURE (AESTHETICS)
NATURE AND NURTURE
NATURE CONSERVATION — England — Somerset
NATURE CONSERVATION — France
NATURE CONSERVATION — Great Britain
NATURE CONSERVATION — Law and legislation — Great Britain
NATURE CONSERVATION — Wales — West Glamorgan
NAVAHO INDIANS — Art
NAVAHO INDIANS — Philosophy
NAVAHO LANGUAGE
NAVAJO INDIANS — Economic conditions
NAVAL ART AND SCIENCE — History
NAVAL HISTORIANS — Great Britain — Biography
NAVIGATION — Channel Islands — History
NAVIGATION — United States — Bibliography
NAXALITE MOVEMENT
NEAR EAST — Boundaries
NEAR EAST — Commerce
NEAR EAST — Commerce — Great Britain
NEAR EAST — Commerce — Japan
NEAR EAST — Economic policy
NEAR EAST — Emigration and immigration
NEAR EAST — Foreign relations
NEAR EAST — Foreign relations — Europe
NEAR EAST — Foreign relations — Great Britain
NEAR EAST — Foreign relations — Lebanon
NEAR EAST — Foreign relations — Soviet Union
NEAR EAST — Foreign relations — United States
NEAR EAST — Historical geography
NEAR EAST — History — 20th century
NEAR EAST — Military relations — Soviet Union
NEAR EAST — Nationalism
NEAR EAST — Politics and government
NEAR EAST — Politics and government — 1945-
NEAR EAST — Social conditions
NEAR EAST — Statistics — Bibliography
NEAR EAST — Strategic aspects
NEGATIVE INCOME TAX — Great Britain
NEGATIVE INCOME TAX — United States
NEGLIGENCE — England
NEGOTIATION — Mathematical models
NEGOTIATION — Psychological aspects
NEGOTIATION IN BUSINESS — Japan
NEGOTIATION IN BUSINESS — United States
NEGOTIORUM GESTIO — South Africa — History
NEGROES — Addresses, essays, lectures
NEHRU, JAWAHARLAL
NEHRU, JAWAHARLAL — Correspondence
NEIGHBORHOOD — Michigan — Detroit — Case studies
NEIGHBORHOOD — New York (State) — Buffalo — Case studies
NEIGHBORHOOD — United States
NEIGHBORHOOD — United States — Case studies
NEIGHBORHOOD GOVERNMENT — Ohio — Cincinnati
NEIGHBORHOOD GOVERNMENT — United States
NEIGHBORHOOD JUSTICE CENTERS — Delaware
NEIGHBORHOOD JUSTICE CENTERS — United States
NEIGHBORLINESS — London
NEKRASOV, N. A.
NEOCLASSICAL SCHOOL OF ECONOMICS
NEOPLASMS — history
NEPAL — Census, 1981
NEPAL — Economic conditions
NEPAL — Economic conditions — Statistics
NEPAL — Economic policy
NEPAL — Economic policy — Bibliography
NEPAL — Foreign relations — China
NEPAL — Foreign relations — India
NEPAL — Industries
NEPAL — Industries — Statistics
NEPAL — Politics and government
NEPAL — Population
NEPAL — Population — Bibliography
NEPAL — Population — Statistics
NEPAL — Social policy
NEPAL — Statistics
NEPAL — Economic policy
NERVOUS SYSTEM — Illnesses
NETHERLANDS — Bibliography
NETHERLANDS — Constitution
NETHERLANDS — Constitutional law
NETHERLANDS — Economic conditions — 1945-
NETHERLANDS — Economic conditions — 1945- — Statistics
NETHERLANDS — Economic conditions — 1945- — Statistics — Methodology
NETHERLANDS — Economic policy
NETHERLANDS — Emigration and immigration
NETHERLANDS — Ethnic relations
NETHERLANDS — Foreign economic relations — Germany (West)
NETHERLANDS — Foreign relations — History
NETHERLANDS — Foreign relations — Brazil
NETHERLANDS — Foreign relations — Indonesia — Sources
NETHERLANDS — History — 1648-1795
NETHERLANDS — Industries — Statistics
NETHERLANDS — Manufactures — Statistics
NETHERLANDS — Maps
NETHERLANDS — Politics and government — 1945-
NETHERLANDS — Population — Forecasting
NETHERLANDS — Population — Statistics
NETHERLANDS — Population policy
NETHERLANDS — Relations — Germany (West)
NETHERLANDS — Social conditions
NETHERLANDS — Social conditions — 1945-
NETHERLANDS — Social policy
NETHERLANDS — Statistical services
NETHERLANDS — Statistics
NETHERLANDS. Centraal Bureau voor de Statistiek
NETHERLANDS. Werkgroep Beleidsdoelstellingen Analyse Noorden
NETHERLANDS. Werkgroep Bevolkingsaspecten Noorden des Lands
NETHERLANDS ANTILLES — Dictionaries and encyclopedias
NETO, AGOSTINHO — Biography
NETTLER, GWYNN — Congresses
NETWORK ANALYSIS — Transportation
NEURASTHENIA — psychology
NEURASTHENIA — Somatization — China
NEUROLINGUISTICS
NEUROLOGY — Philosophy
NEUROPSYCHOLOGY
NEUROPSYCHOLOGY — Philosophy
NEUROSES
NEVADA — Politics and government
NEW BRUNSWICK — Commerce — Statistics
NEW BRUNSWICK. Department of Education — History
NEW BRUNSWICK. Legislative Assembly — Rules and practice
NEW BUSINESS ENTERPRISES
NEW CALEDONIA — Economic conditions
NEW CALEDONIA — Economic conditions — Statistics
NEW CALEDONIA — Population — Statistics
NEW DEAL, 1933-1939
NEW DEAL, 1933-1939 — Dictionaries
NEW DEMOCRATIC PARTY
NEW DEMOCRATIC PARTY — History — Congresses
NEW DIRECTIONS FOR NEW BRUNSWICK: A CONFERENCE FOR WOMEN (Memramcook : 1974)
NEW ENGLAND — Church history
NEW ENGLAND — Commerce — Canada
NEW ENGLAND — History
NEW ENGLAND — History — Colonial period, ca. 1600-1775 — Congresses
NEW GUINEA — History
NEW HALFA AGRICULTURAL PRODUCTION SCHEME
NEW HALFA (SUDAN) — Economic conditions
NEW HARMONY (IND.) — History — 19th century
NEW IRELAND PROVINCE (PAPUA NEW GUINEA) — Population — Statistics
NEW JERSEY — History
NEW JERSEY — History — Bibliography
NEW KOWLOON (HONG KONG) — Statistics
NEW PRODUCTS
NEW REPUBLIC (NEW YORK, N.Y.)
NEW SCHOOL FOR SOCIAL RESEARCH (NEW YORK, N.Y.) — History
NEW SOUTH WALES — Civilization — 1788-1900
NEW SOUTH WALES — Governors — Biography
NEW SOUTH WALES — History — 1788-1851

NEW SOUTH WALES — Politics and government — 1976-
NEW SOUTH WALES. Australian Bureau of Statistics. New South Wales Office
NEW SOUTH WALES. Commonwealth Bureau of Census and Statistics. New South Wales Office
NEW TERRITORIES (HONG KONG) — Statistics
NEW TOWNS
NEW TOWNS — Government policy — Great Britain
NEW TOWNS — England — Essex
NEW TOWNS — France
NEW TOWNS — Great Britain
NEW TOWNS — United States
NEW WAVE MUSIC — California — History and criticism
NEW YORK (N.Y.) — Biography
NEW YORK (N.Y.) — Commerce
NEW YORK (N.Y.) — Economic conditions
NEW YORK (N.Y.) — Economic conditions — Econometric models
NEW YORK (N.Y.) — Emigration and immigration
NEW YORK (N.Y.) — Social life and customs
NEW YORK (STATE) — Emigration and immigration — Case studies
NEW YORK (STATE) — History — Colonial period, ca. 1600-1775
NEW YORK (STATE) — Politics and government — 1865-1950
NEW YORK UNIVERSITY — Students — Case studies
NEW ZEALAND — Bibliography
NEW ZEALAND — Commerce — Australia
NEW ZEALAND — Economic conditions
NEW ZEALAND — Economic conditions — 1945-
NEW ZEALAND — Economic policy — Mathematical models
NEW ZEALAND — Emigration and immigration — Government policy
NEW ZEALAND — Foreign relations
NEW ZEALAND — Foreign relations — ASEAN
NEW ZEALAND — Foreign relations — 1945-
NEW ZEALAND — Foreign relations — Australia — Sources
NEW ZEALAND — Foreign relations — Japan
NEW ZEALAND — Foreign relations — Oceania
NEW ZEALAND — History — 1843-1870
NEW ZEALAND — History — 1870-
NEW ZEALAND — Military policy
NEW ZEALAND — Military relations
NEW ZEALAND — Parliament — Membership — Biography
NEW ZEALAND — Politics and government
NEW ZEALAND — Politics and Government — 1972-
NEW ZEALAND — Politics and government — 1972-
NEW ZEALAND — Population
NEW ZEALAND — Population — Statistics
NEW ZEALAND — Race relations
NEW ZEALAND — Race relations — Political aspects
NEW ZEALAND — Social conditions
NEW ZEALAND — Statistics
NEW ZEALAND — Study and teaching — Great Britain — Directories
NEW ZEALAND — Yearbooks
NEW ZEALAND. Department of Justice
NEWFOUNDLAND — Annexation to Canada
NEWFOUNDLAND — Appropriations and expenditures
NEWFOUNDLAND — Commerce — History — 19th century
NEWFOUNDLAND — History

NEWFOUNDLAND — Relations — Canada
NEWFOUNDLAND — Social conditions
NEWFOUNDLAND — Statistics
NEWFOUNDLAND. House of Assembly. Public accounts committee
NEWFOUNDLAND. Treasury Board. Budgeting Division — Statistics
NEWFOUNDLAND. Workmen's Compensation Board
NEWFOUNDLAND AND LABRADOR. Worker's Compensation Commission
NEWFOUNDLAND AND LABRADOR FEDERATION OF LABOUR
NEWFOUNDLAND FISHERMEN, FOOD AND ALLIED WORKERS — History
NEWHAM (LONDON, ENGLAND) — Population
NEWS AGENCIES — Great Britain
NEWS INTERNATIONAL
NEWS INTERNATIONAL STRIKE, GREAT BRITAIN, 1986
NEWSPAPER PUBLISHING — Great Britain
NEWSPAPERS
NEWSPAPERS — History
NEWSPAPERS — Sections, columns, etc
NEWSPAPERS — Argentina
NEWSPAPERS — Great Britain
NEWSPAPERS ON MICROFILM
NEWTON, Sir ISAAC
NICARAGUA — Church history
NICARAGUA — Description and travel
NICARAGUA — Economic conditions
NICARAGUA — Economic conditions — 1979-
NICARAGUA — Foreign economic relations — Communist countries
NICARAGUA — Foreign relations — 1979-
NICARAGUA — Foreign relations — United States
NICARAGUA — History
NICARAGUA — History — 1909-1937
NICARAGUA — History — 1937-1979
NICARAGUA — History — Revolution, 1979
NICARAGUA — History — Revolution, 1979 — Influence
NICARAGUA — History — 1979-
NICARAGUA — Military relations — United States
NICARAGUA — Politics and government
NICARAGUA — Politics and government — 1937-1979
NICARAGUA — Politics and government — 1970-
NICARAGUA — Politics and government — 1979-
NICARAGUA — Rural conditions
NICARAGUA — Social conditions
NICARAGUA — Social conditions — 1979-
NICKEL INDUSTRY — Indonesia — Saroako
NIETZSCHE, FRIEDRICH
NIETZSCHE, FRIEDRICH — History and criticism
NIETZSCHE, FRIEDRICH — Influence
NIETZSCHE, FRIEDRICH — Metaphysics
NIETZSCHE, FRIEDRICH WILHELM
NIÈVRE (FRANCE) — Economic conditions
NIÈVRE (FRANCE) — Social conditions
NIGAM, SHYAM B. L.
NIGER — History — Dictionaries
NIGER — Statistics
NIGERIA — Appropriations and expenditures
NIGERIA — Commercial policy
NIGERIA — Economic conditions — History — To 1960
NIGERIA — Economic conditions — Statistics
NIGERIA — Economic conditions — 1960-
NIGERIA — Economic conditions — 1970-
NIGERIA — Economic policy
NIGERIA — Economic policy — 1970-

NIGERIA — Foreign economic relations — Bibliography
NIGERIA — Foreign economic relations — Great Britain — History
NIGERIA — Foreign relations — United States
NIGERIA — History — Dictionaries
NIGERIA — History — Civil War, 1967-1970
NIGERIA — History — Coup d'état, 1983
NIGERIA — Industries — Statistics
NIGERIA — Manufactures — Statistics
NIGERIA — Politics and government
NIGERIA — Politics and government — To 1960
NIGERIA — Politics and government — 1979-1983
NIGERIA — Politics and government — 1979-
NIGERIA — Population
NIGERIA — Population — Statistics
NIGERIA — Population — Statistics — Evaluation
NIGERIA — Presidents — Election — 1979
NIGERIA — Relations — United States
NIGERIA — Rural conditions — Statistics
NIGERIA — Social conditions — Statistics
NIGERIA — Social conditions — 1960-
NIGERIA. Industrial Research Council of Nigeria
NIGERIA, NORTHERN. Public Service Commission
NIGERIAN YOUTH MOVEMENT
NIGERIANS — Attitudes
NIGERIANS — Relations — United States
NIGHT WORK — Bibliography
NIHON KYOSANTO — History — 20th century
NIKOLAEV, E. B.
NIKOLAEV, LEV NIKOLAEVICH — Journeys — Afghanistan
NIN, ANDRES
NINETEEN FORTY-SEVEN, A.D.
NITRATES
NITROGEN
NITROGEN INDUSTRIES
NIXON, RICHARD
NIXON, RICHARD M
NIXON, RICHARD M — Views on public television
NKRUMAH, KWAME
NO-STRIKE CLAUSE — Great Britain
NOBEL PRIZES — Biography
NOBILITY — Europe — History
NOISE — Physiological aspects
NOISE — Psychological aspects
NOISE CONTROL — Organisation for Economic Co-operation and Development countries
NOMADS — Jordan — History
NOMADS — Oman — Dhofar
NOMADS — Sahel — Congresses
NOMADS — Sudan
NOMADS — Syria — History
NON-ALIGNED MOVEMENT — History
NON-FORMAL EDUCATION — Addresses, essays, lectures
NON-VIOLENCE
NON-WAGE PAYMENTS
NONALIGNMENT
NONALIGNMENT — Bibliography
NONLINEAR MECHANICS — Collected works
NONPARAMETRIC STATISTICS
NONRENEWABLE NATURAL RESOURCES — Econometric models
NONVERBAL COMMUNICATION
NONVERBAL COMMUNICATION (PSYCHOLOGY)
NONVIOLENCE
NORFOLK — Population
NORGES KOMMUNISTISKE PARTIE
NORMAN, E. HERBERT
NORMANDY (FRANCE) — Population — Statistics
NORMANTON (WEST YORKSHIRE) — Civic improvement

NORTH AFRICANS — France
NORTH AMERICA — Air defenses, Military — History
NORTH AMERICA — Census — Handbooks, manuals, etc
NORTH AMERICA — Economic conditions
NORTH AMERICA — Economic integration — Congresses
NORTH ATLANTIC ASSEMBLY
NORTH ATLANTIC ASSEMBLY. Civilian Affairs Committee
NORTH ATLANTIC ASSEMBLY. Economic Committee
NORTH ATLANTIC ASSEMBLY. Military Committee
NORTH ATLANTIC ASSEMBLY. Political Committee
NORTH ATLANTIC ASSEMBLY. Scientific and Technical Committee
NORTH ATLANTIC ASSEMBLY. Special Committee on Nuclear Strategy and Arms Control
NORTH ATLANTIC TREATY, 1949
NORTH ATLANTIC TREATY ORGANIZATION
NORTH ATLANTIC TREATY ORGANIZATION — Addresses, essays, lectures
NORTH ATLANTIC TREATY ORGANIZATION — Armed Forces
NORTH ATLANTIC TREATY ORGANIZATION — Armed Forces — Procurement
NORTH ATLANTIC TREATY ORGANIZATION — Armed Forces — Weapons systems
NORTH ATLANTIC TREATY ORGANIZATION — Congresses
NORTH ATLANTIC TREATY ORGANIZATION — History
NORTH ATLANTIC TREATY ORGANIZATION — Great Britain
NORTH ATLANTIC TREATY ORGANIZATION — Spain
NORTH CAROLINA — Economic conditions
NORTH CAROLINA — Economic policy
NORTH CAROLINA — Industries — History
NORTH CAROLINA — Politics and government — 1951-
NORTH CAROLINA — Rural conditions
NORTH-EAST ATLANTIC FISHERIES COMMISSION
NORTH-EAST METROPOLITAN REGIONAL HOSPITAL BOARD
NORTH-WEST TERRITORIES — Economic conditions
NORTH WEST TERRITORIES — Economic Conditions
NORTH WEST THAMES REGIONAL HEALTH AUTHORITY
NORTH YORKSHIRE — Civil defense
NORTHAMPTON GAS-LIGHT COMPANY — History
NORTHEASTERN STATES — Economic conditions
NORTHEASTERN STATES — Population — Forecasting
NORTHEASTERN STATES — Population — Statistics
NORTHEN IRELAND — Politics and government
NORTHERN IRELAND — Bibliography
NORTHERN IRELAND — Church history
NORTHERN IRELAND — Ethnic relations
NORTHERN IRELAND — Foreign opinion
NORTHERN IRELAND — History
NORTHERN IRELAND — History — Autonomy and independence movements
NORTHERN IRELAND — History — Sources
NORTHERN IRELAND — History — 1969-
NORTHERN IRELAND — Politics and government
NORTHERN IRELAND — Politics and government — Addresses, essays, lectures
NORTHERN IRELAND — Politics and government — Pictorial works
NORTHERN IRELAND — Politics and government — 1969-
NORTHERN IRELAND — Religion
NORTHERN IRELAND — Social conditions
NORTHERN IRELAND — politics and government
NORTHERN TERRITORY — Economic conditions
NORTHERN TERRITORY (AUSTRALIA) — History
NORTHERN TERRITORY (AUSTRALIA) — Politics and government
NORTHMEN
NORTHUMBERLAND — Bibliography — Union lists
NORTHWEST, CANADIAN — History
NORTHWEST, CANADIAN — Politics and government
NORWAY — Census, 1980
NORWAY — Economic conditions
NORWAY — Economic conditions — Statistics
NORWAY — Economic conditions — 1945-
NORWAY — Economic policy
NORWAY — Foreign relations — 1945-
NORWAY — Officials and employees — Salaries, allowances, etc. — Statistics
NORWAY — Politics and government — 1905-
NORWAY — Politics and government — 1945-
NORWAY — Population — Forecasting
NORWAY — Population — Statistics
NORWAY — Social conditions
NORWAY — Social conditions — 1945-
NORWAY — Social policy
NORWEGIAN ESSAYS
NORWEGIAN LANGUAGE — Dictionaries — English
NORWEGIAN LANGUAGE — Social aspects
NOTTINGHAM (NOTTINGHAMSHIRE) — Industries — History
NOVOSELENGINSK (R.S.F.S.R.) — Church history
NOWLAN, GEORGE CLYDE, 1898-1965
NUCLEAR ARMS CONTROL
NUCLEAR ARMS CONTROL — Congresses
NUCLEAR ARMS CONTROL — Verification
NUCLEAR ARMS CONTROL — Verification — Congresses
NUCLEAR ARMS CONTROL — Europe
NUCLEAR ARMS CONTROL — Soviet Union
NUCLEAR ARMS CONTROL — United States
NUCLEAR DISARMAMENT
NUCLEAR DISARMAMENT — Addresses, essays, lectures
NUCLEAR DISARMAMENT — History
NUCLEAR DISARMAMENT — Great Britain — Political activity
NUCLEAR DISARMAMENT — United States
NUCLEAR DISARMAMENT — United States — History
NUCLEAR ENERGY
NUCLEAR ENERGY — Bibliography
NUCLEAR ENERGY — Government policy — United States
NUCLEAR ENERGY — Government policy — United States — History
NUCLEAR ENERGY — Political aspects
NUCLEAR ENERGY — Religious aspects — Christianity
NUCLEAR ENERGY — Great Britain
NUCLEAR ENERGY — Korea (South)
NUCLEAR ENERGY — Pakistan
NUCLEAR ENERGY — Yugoslavia
NUCLEAR FACILITIES — Environmental aspects — Great Britain — Statistics
NUCLEAR FACILITIES — Mexico — Location
NUCLEAR INDUSTRY
NUCLEAR INDUSTRY — Government policy
NUCLEAR INDUSTRY — Government policy — Case studies
NUCLEAR INDUSTRY — Government policy — Great Britain
NUCLEAR INDUSTRY — Political aspects — History
NUCLEAR INDUSTRY — Australia
NUCLEAR INDUSTRY — Canada
NUCLEAR INDUSTRY — Germany, West
NUCLEAR INDUSTRY — Germany (West)
NUCLEAR INDUSTRY — Great Britain
NUCLEAR INDUSTRY — Great Britain — Accidents — Economic aspects
NUCLEAR INDUSTRY — Great Britain — Accidents — Social aspects
NUCLEAR INDUSTRY — Soviet Union — Safety measures
NUCLEAR INDUSTRY — United States
NUCLEAR NONPROLIFERATION
NUCLEAR PHYSICS — Research — Australia
NUCLEAR POWER PLANTS — Accidents — Mathematical models
NUCLEAR POWER PLANTS — Decommissioning
NUCLEAR POWER PLANTS — Environment aspects — England — Cumbria
NUCLEAR POWER PLANTS — Environmental aspects — England — Cumbria
NUCLEAR POWER PLANTS — Environmental aspects — England — Suffolk
NUCLEAR POWER PLANTS — Environmental aspects — Great Britain
NUCLEAR POWER PLANTS — Environmental aspects — Spain
NUCLEAR POWER PLANTS — England — Sizewell (Suffolk)
NUCLEAR POWER PLANTS — England — Suffolk
NUCLEAR POWER PLANTS — Spain
NUCLEAR POWER PLANTS — Ukraine — Chernobyl
NUCLEAR POWER PLANTS — Ukraine — Chernobyl — Accidents
NUCLEAR POWER PLANTS — United States — Safety measures
NUCLEAR POWER PLANTS — Washington (State) — Design and construction — Costs
NUCLEAR POWER PLANTS — Yugoslavia
NUCLEAR REACTORS — England — West Cumbria
NUCLEAR TERRORISM — United States
NUCLEAR WARFARE
NUCLEAR WARFARE — Congresses
NUCLEAR WARFARE — Dictionaries
NUCLEAR WARFARE — Moral and ethical aspects
NUCLEAR WARFARE — Psychological aspects
NUCLEAR WARFARE — Religious aspects — Christianity
NUCLEAR WARFARE — Social aspects — Australia
NUCLEAR-WEAPON-FREE ZONES
NUCLEAR-WEAPON-FREE ZONES — Great Britain — Planning
NUCLEAR-WEAPON-FREE ZONES — Indian Ocean Region — Congresses
NUCLEAR WEAPONS
NUCLEAR WEAPONS — Government policy
NUCLEAR WEAPONS — Government policy — Great Britain

NUCLEAR WEAPONS — Government policy — Soviet Union
NUCLEAR WEAPONS — History
NUCLEAR WEAPONS — Political aspects
NUCLEAR WEAPONS — Religious aspects — Christianity
NUCLEAR WEAPONS — Research — Great Britain — History
NUCLEAR WEAPONS — Testing
NUCLEAR WEAPONS — Europe
NUCLEAR WEAPONS — Great Britain
NUCLEAR WEAPONS — Great Britain — Testing
NUCLEAR WEAPONS — Korea (South)
NUCLEAR WEAPONS — Pakistan
NUCLEAR WEAPONS — Soviet Union
NUCLEAR WEAPONS — United States
NUCLEAR WEAPONS — United States — Safety measures
NUCLEAR WEAPONS TESTING VICTIMS — Australia
NUDE IN ART — Addresses, essays, lectures
NUISANCES — Legal status, laws, etc — Great Britain
NUKU HIVA (MARQUESAS ISLANDS) — Population — Statistics
NUKUTAVAKE (TUAMOTU ISLANDS) — Population — Statistics
NULLIFICATION
NÚÑEZ, RAFAEL, 1825-1894
NUREMBERG (GERMANY) — Politics and government
NUREMBERG (GERMANY (WEST)) — Politics and government
NURSERY SCHOOLS — Great Britain
NURSERY SCHOOLS — Wales — Languages
NURSES — In-service training — Great Britain
NURSES AND NURSING — Great Britain
NURSING — Political aspects — Great Britain
NURSING — Study and teaching — Great Britain
NURSING — Great Britain
NURSING HOMES — England — Sheffield (South Yorkshire)
NURSING SERVICE ADMINISTRATION — Political aspects — Great Britain
NUTRITION
NUTRITION — Great Britain
NUTRITION POLICY — Africa, sub-Saharan — Addresses, essays, lectures
NUTRITION POLICY — Canada
NUTRITION POLICY — Developing countries
NUTRITION SURVEYS
NUTRITION SURVEYS — China
NUTRITION SURVEYS — Developing countries
NUTRITIONALLY INDUCED DISEASES — Epidemiology
NUTRITIONALLY INDUCED DISEASES — United States
NYERERE, JULIUS K
OAKLAND (CALIF.) — Politics and government
OBESITY — Social aspects — United States — History
OBÓZ ZJEDNOCZENIA NARODOWEGO OBRERO, EL (NEWSPAPER)
OBSTETRICIANS — United States — Interviews
OBSTETRICS
OBSTETRICS — Decision making
OCCULT SCIENCES — France — History — 19th century
OCCUPATIONAL DISEASES — Costs
OCCUPATIONAL DISEASES — Epidemiology
OCCUPATIONAL DISEASES — Great Britain — Statistics
OCCUPATIONAL MOBILITY — Great Britain
OCCUPATIONAL MOBILITY — South Africa
OCCUPATIONAL MORTALITY — Finland — Statistics
OCCUPATIONAL PRESTIGE — United States
OCCUPATIONAL SAFETY, HEALTH AND WELFARE (GENERAL) ACT, 1968
OCCUPATIONAL TRAINING
OCCUPATIONAL TRAINING — Government policy
OCCUPATIONAL TRAINING — Bangladesh
OCCUPATIONAL TRAINING — Developing countries — Bibliography
OCCUPATIONAL TRAINING — Developing countries — Evaluation
OCCUPATIONAL TRAINING — France
OCCUPATIONAL TRAINING — Great Britain
OCCUPATIONAL TRAINING — Great Britain — Evaluation
OCCUPATIONAL TRAINING — Sri Lanka
OCCUPATIONAL TRAINING — Thailand
OCCUPATIONAL TRAINING FOR WOMEN — Germany (West) — Case studies
OCCUPATIONAL TRAINING FOR WOMEN — Great Britain — Case studies
OCCUPATIONS
OCCUPATIONS — Classification
OCCUPATIONS — Moral and ethical aspects
OCCUPATIONS — Netherlands — Classification
OCEAN
OCEAN BOTTOM (MARITIME LAW)
OCEAN ENERGY RESOURCES
OCEAN ENGINEERING
OCEAN LINERS
OCEAN MINING
OCEAN MINING — Law and legislation
OCEANIA — Bibliography
OCEANIA — Census — Handbooks, manuals, etc
OCEANIA — Economic conditions
OCEANIA — Foreign relations — New Zealand
OCEANIA — Social life and customs
OCEANIA — Yearbooks
OCEANOGRAPHY
OCHOLLO (ETHIOPIA) — Economic conditions
OCHOLLO (ETHIOPIA) — Politics and government
OCHOLLO (ETHIOPIA) — Social conditions
O'CONNELL, DANIEL
ODENSE (DENMARK) — Civic improvement
ODENSE (DENMARK) — Social conditions
ODESSA (UKRAINE) — History
ODORS — Social aspects — France
OFFENSES AGAINST PROPERTY — Prussia — History
OFFICE EQUIPMENT AND SUPPLIES
OFFICE MANAGEMENT
OFFICE PRACTICE — Automation
OFFICE PRACTICE — Automation — Congresses
OFFICE PRACTICE — Automation — Psychological aspects
OFFICE PRACTICES — Automation — Periodicals
OFFICES — Location — Government policy — Great Britain — History
OFFICES — Location — England — London
OFFICIAL JOURNAL OF THE EUROPEAN COMMUNITIES — Handbooks, manuals, etc.
OFFICIAL SECRETS
OFFICIAL SECRETS — Great Britain
OFFICIAL SECRETS — Soviet Union
OFFICIAL SECRETS — United States
OFFSHORE GAS INDUSTRY — Government policy — United States
OFFSHORE GAS INDUSTRY — Great Britain — Security measures
OFFSHORE GAS INDUSTRY — North Sea
OFFSHORE OIL FIELD EQUIPMENT INDUSTRY — Great Britain
OFFSHORE OIL INDUSTRY — Government policy — Canada
OFFSHORE OIL INDUSTRY — Government policy — Soviet Union
OFFSHORE OIL INDUSTRY — Government policy — United States
OFFSHORE OIL INDUSTRY — Taxation — Great Britain
OFFSHORE OIL INDUSTRY — Asia, Southeastern
OFFSHORE OIL INDUSTRY — Barents Sea
OFFSHORE OIL INDUSTRY — Great Britain — Security measures
OFFSHORE OIL INDUSTRY — Newfoundland
OFFSHORE OIL INDUSTRY — North Sea
OFFSHORE OIL INDUSTRY — Venezuela — Equipment and supplies
OFFSHORE PETROLEUM INDUSTRY — Environmental aspects — Georges Bank
OGAREV, N. P.
OGLALA INDIANS — Social life and customs
OGLALA INDIANS — Women
OHIO — Economic conditions — Congresses
OHIO — Economic policy — Congresses
OHIO — Governors — Biography
OHIO — Politics and government — 1787-1865
OHIO — Politics and government — 1865-1950
OIL AND GAS (ENTERPRISE) BILL 1981-82
OIL AND GAS LEASES — Canada
OIL AND GAS LEASES — United States
OIL FIELDS — Oklahoma — Osage County
OIL INDUSTRIES — Prices
OIL POLLUTION OF THE SEA — Prevention — History
OIL SPILLS — Great Britain
OIL TAXATION BILL 1983-84
OIL WELL DRILLING, SUBMARINE
OKLAHOMA — History
OLD AGE
OLD AGE — Bibliography
OLD AGE — Social aspects
OLD AGE — Georgian S.S.R. — Abkhazian A.S.S.R.
OLD AGE ASSISTANCE — Australia
OLD AGE ASSISTANCE — France — Nomenclature
OLD AGE HOMES — Australia — History — 20th century
OLD AGE HOMES — England — London
OLD AGE HOMES — Great Britain
OLD AGE HOMES — Great Britain — Quality control
OLD AGE HOMES — Ireland
OLD AGE PENSION ACT, 1969
OLD AGE PENSION (AMENDMENT) ACT, 1972
OLD AGE PENSIONS — Law and legislation — Denmark
OLD AGE PENSIONS — Law and legislation — Great Britain
OLD AGE PENSIONS — Canada
OLD AGE PENSIONS — Denmark
OLD AGE PENSIONS — Denmark — Statistics
OLD-AGE PENSIONS — Finland
OLD AGE PENSIONS — France
OLD AGE PENSIONS — Germany (West)
OLD AGE PENSIONS — Great Britain
OLD AGE PENSIONS — United States
OLD AGE PENSIONS — United States — History
OLIGARCHY — Brazil — Paraíba (State) — History
OLIGOPOLIES
OLIGOPOLIES — Econometric models

OLIVARES, GASPAR DE GUZMÁN, conde-duque de
O'MALLEY, DES
OMAN — Economic conditions
OMAN — History
OMAN — National security
OMAN — Social conditions
OMBUDSMAN — Great Britain — Bibliography
OMBUDSMAN — Ireland
ON-LINE BIBLIOGRAPHIC SEARCHING
ONE-DIMENSIONAL MAN
ONE PARTY SYSTEMS — Africa, West
ONION INDUSTRY — Mexico
ONTARIO — Constitutional history
ONTARIO — Economic conditions
ONTARIO — Economic policy
ONTARIO — History
ONTARIO — Politics and government
ONTARIO — Politics and government — 19th century
ONTARIO LIBERAL PARTY
ONTOLOGY
OPEC See Organization of the Petroleum Exporting Countries
OPEN AND CLOSED SHOP — Religious aspects — Catholic Church
OPEN AND CLOSED SHOP — Great Britain
OPEN AND CLOSED SHOP — United States
OPERATIONS RESEARCH
OPERATIONS RESEARCH — Data processing — Congresses
OPHIR
OPPOSITION (POLITICAL SCIENCE)
OPPOSITION (POLITICAL SCIENCE) — Mexico — History — 20th century
OPPOSITION (POLITICAL SCIENCE) — United States
OPPRESSION (PSYCHOLOGY)
OPTICAL DISKS — United States — Library applications
OPTICAL STORAGE DEVICES
OPUS DEI
ORAL COMMUNICATION
ORAL HISTORY
ORDEAL — History
ORDZHONIKIDZE, G. K.
ORGANIC WASTES AS FERTILIZER — United States
ORGANISATION COMMUNISTE INTERNATIONALISTE
ORGANISATION DE L'ARMÉE SECRÈTE — History
ORGANISATION FOR ECONOMIC CO-OPERATION AND DEVELOPMENT — Economic assistance — Statistics
ORGANISATION FOR ECONOMIC CO-OPERATION AND DEVELOPMENT. Development Centre
ORGANISATION FOR ECONOMIC CO—OPERATION AND DEVELOPMENT. Development Centre — Research
ORGANISATION FOR ECONOMIC CO-OPERATION AND DEVELOPMENT. Water Management Research Group
ORGANISATION FOR ECONOMIC CO-OPERATION AND DEVELOPMENT COUNTRIES — Economic conditions — Mathematical models
ORGANISATION FOR ECONOMIC CO-OPERATION AND DEVELOPMENT COUNTRIES — Economic policy
ORGANISATION OF THE PETROLEUM EXPORTING COUNTRIES — History
ORGANIZATION
ORGANIZATION — Addresses, essays, lectures
ORGANIZATION — Case studies
ORGANIZATION — Congresses
ORGANIZATION — Dictionaries and encyclopedias
ORGANIZATION — Mathematical models
ORGANIZATION — Research

ORGANIZATION — Research — Congresses
ORGANIZATION OF AFRICAN UNITY
ORGANIZATION OF AFRICAN UNITY — History
ORGANIZATION OF AMERICAN STATES
ORGANIZATION OF AMERICAN STATES — Bibliography
ORGANIZATION OF ARAB PETROLEUM EXPORTING COUNTRIES — Bibliography
ORGANIZATION OF EASTERN CARIBBEAN STATES
ORGANIZATION OF PETROLEUM EXPORTING COUNTRIES
ORGANIZATION OF REVOLUTIONARY WORKERS OF IRAN
ORGANIZATION OF THE PETROLEUM EXPORTING COUNTRIES
ORGANIZATION OF THE PETROLEUM EXPORTING COUNTRIES — History
ORGANIZATIONAL BEHAVIOR
ORGANIZATIONAL BEHAVIOR — Addresses, essays, lectures
ORGANIZATIONAL BEHAVIOR — Research
ORGANIZATIONAL CHANGE
ORGANIZATIONAL CHANGE — Addresses, essays, lectures
ORGANIZATIONAL CHANGE — Dictionaries
ORGANIZATIONAL CHANGE — Colombia — Case studies
ORGANIZATIONAL CHANGE — Great Britain — Management — Case studies
ORGANIZATIONAL CHANGE — Scotland
ORGANIZATIONAL EFFECTIVENESS
ORGANIZATIONAL EFFECTIVENESS — Case studies
ORGANIZATIONAL EFFECTIVENESS — Measurement
ORGANIZATIONS
ORGANIZATSIIA VARSHAVSKOGO DOGOVORA
ORGANIZED CRIME — Australia
ORIENTATION (PSYCHOLOGY) — Congresses
ORIGIN OF SPECIES
ORIGINS OF MUHAMMADAN JURISPRUDENCE
ORISSA (INDIA) — Politics and government — Addresses, essays, lectures
ORISSA (INDIA) — Statistics
ORREFORS GLASSWORKS
ORTHODOX EASTERN CHURCH — Romania — History
ORTHOPEDIC SHOES — England
ORWELL, GEORGE. 1984
ORWELL, GEORGE — Criticism and interpretation
OSAGE COUNTY (OKLA.) — Economic conditions
OSAGE INDIANS — Economic conditions
OSAGE INDIANS — History
OSTARA
OSTEOMALACIA — Prevention
OTECHESTVENNYE ZAPISKI
OUADDAI (CHAD) — Social conditions
OUTER SPACE — Bibliography
OUTER SPACE — Exploration
OVERIJSSEL (NETHERLANDS) — Economic policy
OVERPRODUCTION — History
OVERSEAS DEVELOPMENT INSTITUTE — History
OWEN, ROBERT, 1771-1858
PACEMAKER, ARTIFICIAL (HEART)
PACIFIC AREA
PACIFIC AREA — Commerce
PACIFIC AREA — Economic conditions
PACIFIC AREA — Foreign economic relations
PACIFIC AREA — Foreign relations
PACIFIC AREA — Strategic aspects
PACIFIC AREA — Yearbooks

PACIFIC AREA CO-OPERATION
PACIFIC OCEAN — Bibliography
PACIFIC OCEAN REGION — Relations — Canada — Congresses
PACIFIC OCEAN REGION — Strategic aspects
PACIFIC STATES — Commercial policy
PACIFICISM
PACIFISM
PACIFISM — History
PACIFISM — Germany (West)
PACIFISTS — Germany
PACIFISTS — New Zealand
PAEA (TAHITI : REGION) — Population — Statistics
PAGANISM IN ART
PAIN
PAIN — Psychological aspects
PAIN — psychology
PAINE, THOMAS
PAINTING
PAISLEY, IAN
PAKISTAN — Military policy
PAKISTAN
PAKISTAN — Appropriations and expenditures
PAKISTAN — Bibliography
PAKISTAN — Census, 1981
PAKISTAN — Commercial policy
PAKISTAN — Constitution, 1985
PAKISTAN — Constitutional history
PAKISTAN — Defenses
PAKISTAN — Economic conditions
PAKISTAN — Economic conditions — Statistics
PAKISTAN — Economic policy
PAKISTAN — Economic policy — Statistics
PAKISTAN — Emigration and immigration
PAKISTAN — Ethnic relations — Congresses
PAKISTAN — Foreign relations — Addresses, essays, lectures
PAKISTAN — Foreign relations — Afghanistan
PAKISTAN — Foreign relations — India
PAKISTAN — Foreign relations — United States
PAKISTAN — Foreign relations — United States — Addresses, essays, lectures
PAKISTAN — Government publications — Bibliography
PAKISTAN — History
PAKISTAN — Military policy
PAKISTAN — Military relations — Soviet Union
PAKISTAN — Politics and government
PAKISTAN — Politics and government — 1971-
PAKISTAN — Politics and government — 1971- — Congresses
PAKISTAN — Population
PAKISTAN — Population — Statistics
PAKISTAN — Population, Rural
PAKISTAN — Social conditions
PAKISTAN — Social policy
PAKISTAN. Agricultural Enquiry Committee
PAKISTAN. National Assembly. Public Accounts Committee
PAKISTAN INSTITUTE OF DEVELOPMENT ECONOMICS — History
PAKISTAN MOVEMENT
PALACIO, ALFREDO L.
PALACIOS, ALFREDO L.
PALENCIA (SPAIN) — Economic conditions
PALESTINE — Emigration and immigration
PALESTINE — Foreign opinion
PALESTINE — Foreign relations — Great Britain
PALESTINE — History — Addresses, essays, lectures
PALESTINE — History — 1799-1917
PALESTINE — History — Arab riots, 1929
PALESTINE — History — 1929-1948
PALESTINE — History — Arab rebellion, 1936-1939

PALESTINE — History — Partition, 1947
PALESTINE — International status
PALESTINE — Politics and government
PALESTINE — Politics and government — 1929-1948
PALESTINE — Politics and government — 1948-
PALESTINE ARABS — Legal status, laws, etc.
PALESTINE LIBERATION ORGANISATION
PALESTINIAN ARABS
PALESTINIAN ARABS — Biography
PALESTINIAN ARABS — Education (Higher)
PALESTINIAN ARABS — History
PALESTINIAN ARABS — Legal status, laws, etc. — Israel
PALESTINIAN ARABS — Politics and government
PALESTINIAN ARABS — Gaza Strip — Social conditions
PALESTINIAN ARABS — Israel
PALESTINIAN ARABS — Lebanon — Politics and government
PALESTINIAN ARABS — West Bank
PALMERSTON, HENRY JOHN TEMPLE, Viscount
PAN-AFRICANISM
PAN-AMERICANISM
PAN-AMERICANISM — History
PANAMA — Census, 1980
PANAMA — Economic conditions — 1979-
PANAMA — Economic conditions — 1979- — Statistics
PANAMA — Economic policy
PANAMA — Population — Statistics
PANAMA — Race relations
PANAMA — Statistics, Vital
PANARABISM
PANKHURST, CHRISTABEL
PANKHURST, E. SYLVIA
PANSLAVISM
PAPACY — History
PAPARA (TAHITI) — Population — Statistics
PAPAU NEW GUINEA — Population — Statistics
PAPEETE (TAHITI) — Population — Statistics
PAPER INDUSTRY — Environmental aspects
PAPERMAKING — History
PAPERMAKING — Massachusetts — Berkshire County — History
PAPUA NEW GUINEA — Census, 1980
PAPUA NEW GUINEA — Economic conditions
PAPUA NEW GUINEA — Economic conditions — 1975-
PAPUA NEW GUINEA — Economic policy
PAPUA NEW GUINEA — Foreign relations — Indonesia
PAPUA NEW GUINEA — Industries — Statistics
PAPUA NEW GUINEA — Population — Statistics
PAPUA NEW GUINEA — Social conditions
PAPUA NEW GUINEA — Social life and customs
PAPUA NEW GUINEA — Social life and customs — Addresses, essays, lectures
PARADIGMS (SOCIAL SCIENCES) — Congresses
PARAGUAY — Economic conditions — Statistics
PARAGUAY — History — To 1811
PARAGUAY — History — 1870-1938
PARAGUAY — Politics and government — 1938-1954
PARAGUAY — Population — Statistics
PARAGUAY — Population — Statistics — Evaluation
PARAÍBA (BRAZIL : STATE) — Politics and government

PARAPROFESSIONALS IN SOCIAL SERVICE
PARAPROFESSIONALS IN SOCIAL SERVICE — England
PARATRANSIT SERVICES — Europe — Congresses
PARENT AND CHILD
PARENT AND CHILD — Longitudinal studies
PARENT AND CHILD — Denmark
PARENT AND CHILD — England
PARENT AND CHILD (LAW)
PARENT AND CHILD (LAW) — Great Britain
PARENTAL ACCEPTANCE — Cross-cultural studies
PARENTAL BEHAVIOR IN ANIMALS
PARENTAL REJECTION — Cross-cultural studies
PARENTHOOD
PARENTING
PARENTING — United States
PARENTS — Interviews
PARENTS-IN-LAW
PARETO, VILFREDO
PARIS — History — Commune, 1871
PARIS. Parlement — History — 18th century
PARIS (FRANCE) — Ethnic relations
PARIS (FRANCE) — History — Revolution, 1789-1799
PARIS (FRANCE) — Politics and government
PARIS (FRANCE) — Popular culture — History — 19th century
PARIS (FRANCE) — Population — Statistics
PARIS (FRANCE) — Social classes
PARIS (FRANCE) — Social life and customs — 18th century
PARIS PEACE CONFERENCE (1919-1920)
PARKS — United States — History — 19th century
PARLIAMENTARY PRACTICE — England
PARLIAMENTARY PRACTICE — European Economic Community countries — Comparative studies
PARLIAMENTARY PRACTICE — New Brunswick
PARSONS, TALCOTT — Criticism and interpretation
PART-TIME EMPLOYMENT — Great Britain
PART-TIME EMPLOYMENT — United States
PART-TIME FARMING — Ireland
PARTI COMMUNISTE FRANÇAIS
PARTI COMMUNISTE FRANÇAIS — History
PARTI LIBÉRAL SUISSE
PARTI QUÉBÉCOIS
PARTI RADICAL-DÉMOCRATIQUE SUISSE
PARTI REPUBLICAIN
PARTI ROYALISTE (France)
PARTI SOCIALISTE BELGE
PARTIDO AFRICANO DA INDEPENDENCIA DE LA GUINEE "PORTUGAISE" ET DES ILES DU CAP VERT
PARTIDO COMUNISTA DE ESPAÑA
PARTIDO COMUNISTA DE ESPAÑA — History
PARTIDO COMUNISTA PORTUGUÊS
PARTIDO OBRERO DE UNIFICACIÓN MARXISTA
PARTIDO REVOLUCIONARIO FEBRERISTA
PARTIDO REVOLUCIONARIO INSTITUCIONAL
PARTIDO SOCIALISTA DE CHILE — History
PARTIDO SOCIALISTA OBERO ESPAÑOL — Congresses
PARTIDO SOCIALISTA OBRERO ESPAÑOL

PARTIDO SOCIALISTA OBRERO ESPAÑOLA
PARTIDUL COMUNIST ROMÂN — Congresses
PARTIDUL COMUNIST ROMÂN — History — Sources
PARTIIA SOTSIALISTOV-REVOLIUTSIONEROV
PARTIJ VAN DE ARBEID
PARTISAN REVIEW (NEW YORK, N.Y. : 1934) — History
PARTIT SOCIALISTA UNIFICAT DE CATALUNYA
PARTNERSHIP — Taxation — Great Britain
PARTNERSHIP — Canada — Cases
PARTY AFFILIATION — India
PARTY AFFILIATION — West (U.S.)
PARTY OF LABOUR OF ALBANIA
PASCAL (COMPUTER PROGRAM LANGUAGE)
PASSIVE RESISTANCE — Great Britain
PASSIVE RESISTANCE — United States
PASSIVE RESISTENCE — India
PASTURE, RIGHT OF — Australia — New South Wales
PATAGONIA (ARGENTINA AND CHILE) — Description and travel
PATAGONIA (ARGENTINA AND CHILE) — History, military — 20th century
PATAGONIA (ARGENTINA AND CHILE) — Rural conditions
PATAGONIA (ARGENTINA AND CHILE) — Social life and customs
PATAGONIA (ARGENTINA AND CHILE) — Strategic aspects
PATEL, I. G
PATENT LAWS AND LEGISLATION — European Economic Community Countries
PATENT LAWS AND LEGISLATION — Spain
PATENT LICENSES — European Economic Community countries
PATENT MEDICINES — Denmark
PATENTS — European Economic Community countries
PATENTS (INTERNATIONAL LAW)
PATERNAL DEPRIVATION
PATERNALISM — Moral and ethical aspects
PATERNALISM — Asia
PATRIARCHY
PATRIARCHY — Europe, Northern — History
PATRIOTISM — France
PATRIOTYCZNY RUCH ODRODZENIA NARODOWY
PATRONAGE, POLITICAL — Scotland
PATTERN PERCEPTION
PAUL, ALICE
PAVEMENTS — Organisation for Economic Co-operation and Development countries — Maintenance and repair
PAY EQUITY
PAY EQUITY — New York (State)
PAY EQUITY — United States
PAY EQUITY — United States — Case studies
PAYMENT — Australia
PAYMENT — Developing countries
PAYMENT — Finland
PAYMENT — Soviet Union
PC-DOS (COMPUTER OPERATING SYSTEM)
PC DOS (COMPUTER OPERATING SYSTEM) — Handbooks, manuals, etc.
PEACE
PEACE — Archival resources — United States — Directories
PEACE — Dictionaries
PEACE — Library resources — United States — Directories
PEACE — Religious aspects — Catholic Church — Addresses, essays, lectures
PEACE — Research
PEACE — Research — Directories
PEACE — Research — Africa

PEACE — Societies, etc. — Directories
PEACE — Study and teaching
PEACE — Study and teaching — Africa
PEACE — Study and teaching — Germany (West)
PEACE — Study and teaching — United States
PEACE CORPS (U.S.) — History
PEACE MOVEMENTS
PEACE NEWS
PEACE (PHILOSOPHY) — Study and teaching (Higher) — Israel
PEARL HARBOR (HAWAII), ATTACK ON, 1941
PEARL HARBOR (HAWAII), ATTACK ON, 1941 — Historiography
PEASANT UPRISINGS — India
PEASANT UPRISINGS — Japan
PEASANT UPRISINGS — Japan — History
PEASANT UPRISINGS — Mexico — History
PEASANTRY
PEASANTRY — Asia
PEASANTRY — Legal status, laws, etc. — Peru
PEASANTRY — Africa
PEASANTRY — Argentina — Political activity — History
PEASANTRY — Bangladesh
PEASANTRY — Byelorussian S.S.R.
PEASANTRY — China — History — 20th century
PEASANTRY — China — Hunan Province — History
PEASANTRY — Colombia — History
PEASANTRY — Colombia — Political activity — History — 20th century
PEASANTRY — Developing countries
PEASANTRY — Egypt
PEASANTRY — France
PEASANTRY — France — History — 16th century
PEASANTRY — France — History — 17th century
PEASANTRY — Germany — Political activity — History — 20th century
PEASANTRY — Guatemala — History — 19th century
PEASANTRY — India
PEASANTRY — India — Hyderabad (State) — History
PEASANTRY — Japan — Political activity — History
PEASANTRY — Karst (Yugoslavia and Italy)
PEASANTRY — Latin American
PEASANTRY — Mexico
PEASANTRY — Peru
PEASANTRY — Peru — Cajamarca — History
PEASANTRY — Philippines — Mindoro
PEASANTRY — Poland — Political activity
PEASANTRY — Romania — Political activity
PEASANTRY — Russian S.F.S.R. — Siberia — History
PEASANTRY — Soviet Union
PEASANTRY — Soviet Union — History
PEASANTRY — Soviet Union — Social life and customs
PEASANTRY — Transcaucasia — History
PEASANTRY — Yugoslavia — Slovenia — Case studies
PEASANTS' WAR, 1524-1525
PEAT INDUSTRY — Developing countries
PEDDLERS AND PEDDLING — Peru — Lima
PEDDLERS AND PEDDLING — United States — History
PEDESTRIANS — Great Britain
PEDIATRICS — Great Britain
PEDRO I, Emperor of Brazil
PEINADO PEINADO, RUFINO
PEKING (CHINA) — History
PEMBROKE, WILLIAM MARSHAL, Earl of

PENAL COLONIES — Australia
PENAL COLONIES, BRITISH
PENDLE (LANCASHIRE) — Industries — History
P'ENG TE-HUAI
PENN, WILLIAM
PENNSYLVANIA — Economic policy
PENNSYLVANIA — History — Insurrection of 1794
PENNSYLVANIA — History — Colonial period, ca.1600-1775 — Sources
PENSION TRUSTS — Investments — Law and legislation — Great Britain
PENSION TRUSTS — Social aspects — United States — Congresses
PENSION TRUSTS — Great Britain — Accounting
PENSION TRUSTS — Great Britain — Investments
PENSION TRUSTS — Great Britain — Investments — Statistics
PENSION TRUSTS — United States — Addresses, essays, lectures
PENSION TRUSTS — United States — Congresses
PENSION TRUSTS — United States — Investments
PENSION TRUSTS — United States — Investments — Congresses
PENSIONS — Law and legislation — Great Britain
PENSIONS — Australia
PENSIONS — Canada
PENSIONS — Denmark
PENSIONS — Finland
PENSIONS — France
PENSIONS — Great Britain
PENSIONS — Great Britain — Taxation
PENSIONS — United States
PENSIONS — United States — Addresses, essays, lectures
PENSIONS — United States — Finance — Congresses
PEOPLE'S ACTION PARTY (Singapore)
PEOPLES TEMPLE
PERAK (MALAYSIA) — Population — Statistics
PERCEPTION
PERELMAN, CHAIM
PEREZ, ANTONIO — Correspondence
PERFECTION (PHILOSOPHY) — History
PERFORMANCE — Congresses
PERFORMANCE — Evaluation
PERFORMING ARTS
PERFORMING ARTS — Psychological aspects
PERINATAL MORTALITY — Great Britain
PERINATAL MORTALITY — Italy — Statistics
PERINATAL MORTALITY — Syria — Statistics
PERIODICALS
PERIODICALS — Directories
PERIODICALS, PUBLISHING OF — Costs
PERLIS (MALAYSIA) — Population — Statistics
PERNAMBUCO (BRAZIL) — Economic conditions
PERÓN, EVA DUARTE
PERÓN, JUAN DOMINGO
PERONISM
PERSECUTION — Europe — History
PERSECUTION — Europe — History — 16th century
PERSECUTION — Europe — History — 17th century
PERSECUTION — Soviet Union
PERSIAN GULF REGION — Armed Forces
PERSIAN GULF REGION — Defenses
PERSIAN GULF REGION — Foreign relations — Russia
PERSIAN GULF REGION — Foreign relations — United States

PERSIAN GULF REGION — Foreign relations — United States — Bibliography
PERSIAN GULF REGION — History
PERSIAN GULF REGION — Military relations — Soviet Union
PERSIAN GULF REGION — Military relations — United States
PERSIAN GULF REGION — Politics and government
PERSIAN GULF REGION — Politics and government — Bibliography
PERSIAN GULF REGION — Strategic aspects
PERSIAN GULF STATES — Foreign economic relations — Europe
PERSIAN LANGUAGE — Discourse analysis
PERSIAN LANGUAGE — Social aspects — Iran
PERSONAL INJURIES — England — Greater Manchester
PERSONALITY
PERSONALITY — Research
PERSONALITY AND CULTURE
PERSONALITY AND OCCUPATION — Michigan — Longitudinal studies
PERSONALITY ASSESSMENT
PERSONALITY (LAW) — Australia
PERSONALITY TESTS
PERSONALS — Great Britain — History
PERSONNEL MANAGEMENT
PERSONNEL MANAGEMENT — Case studies
PERSONNEL MANAGEMENT — Libraries
PERSONNEL MANAGEMENT — methods
PERSONNEL MANAGEMENT — Research
PERSONNEL MANAGEMENT — Canada
PERSONNEL MANAGEMENT — Great Britain
PERSONNEL MANAGEMENT — Great Britain — Automation
PERSONNEL MANAGEMENT — Great Britain — Case studies
PERSONNEL MANAGEMENT — United States
PERSONNEL SERVICE IN SECONDARY EDUCATION — European Economic Community countries
PERSONS (ISLAMIC LAW)
PERSUASION (PSYCHOLOGY)
PERU — Economic conditions
PERU — Economic conditions — 1968-
PERU — Economic policy
PERU — Executive departments — Legal status, laws, etc.
PERU — History — Dictionaries
PERU — Officials and employees
PERU — Politics and government — 1968-
PERU — Population — Statistics
PERU — Rural conditions
PERU — Rural population
PERU — Social conditions — Addresses, essays, lectures
PERU — Statistics, Vital
PERU. Junta de Supervigilancia de Películas — Legal status, laws, etc.
PERU. Junta Nacional de Mano de Obra
PERU. Ministerio de Economía y Finanzas — Legal status, laws, etc.
PERU. Ministerio de Hacienda — Legal status, laws, etc.
PERU. Sistema Nacional de Información — Legal status, laws, etc.
PESSOA (Family)
PESTICIDE RESIDUES IN FOOD
PESTICIDES — Environmental aspects — Organisation for Economic Co-operation and Development countries
PESTICIDES INDUSTRY — Developing countries
PESTICIDES INDUSTRY — India — Accidents
PETRÓLEOS MEXICANOS
PETROLEUM — Developing countries — Reserves

PETROLEUM — Taxation — Law and legislation — Great Britain
PETROLEUM — South Africa — Transportation
PETROLEUM CHEMICALS INDUSTRY
PETROLEUM CHEMICALS INDUSTRY — Management
PETROLEUM CHEMICALS INDUSTRY — China — Congresses
PETROLEUM IN SUBMERGED LANDS — Asia, Southeastern
PETROLEUM IN SUBMERGED LANDS — Georges Bank
PETROLEUM IN SUBMERGED LANDS — North Sea
PETROLEUM INDUSTRY AND TRADE
PETROLEUM INDUSTRY AND TRADE — Accounting
PETROLEUM INDUSTRY AND TRADE — Congresses
PETROLEUM INDUSTRY AND TRADE — Government ownership
PETROLEUM INDUSTRY AND TRADE — Government ownership — Case studies
PETROLEUM INDUSTRY AND TRADE — Government policy — Case studies
PETROLEUM INDUSTRY AND TRADE — Government policy — Congresses
PETROLEUM INDUSTRY AND TRADE — Government policy — Great Britain
PETROLEUM INDUSTRY AND TRADE — Government policy — United States
PETROLEUM INDUSTRY AND TRADE — History
PETROLEUM INDUSTRY AND TRADE — History — 20th century
PETROLEUM INDUSTRY AND TRADE — International cooperation — Congresses
PETROLEUM INDUSTRY AND TRADE — Licenses — Great Britain
PETROLEUM INDUSTRY AND TRADE — Licenses — Norway
PETROLEUM INDUSTRY AND TRADE — Management — Case studies
PETROLEUM INDUSTRY AND TRADE — Political aspects — Near East
PETROLEUM INDUSTRY AND TRADE — Political aspects — Soviet Union
PETROLEUM INDUSTRY AND TRADE — Taxation
PETROLEUM INDUSTRY AND TRADE — Argentina — History
PETROLEUM INDUSTRY AND TRADE — Canada
PETROLEUM INDUSTRY AND TRADE — China — Congresses
PETROLEUM INDUSTRY AND TRADE — Ecuador
PETROLEUM INDUSTRY AND TRADE — Ecuador — Statistics
PETROLEUM INDUSTRY AND TRADE — France
PETROLEUM INDUSTRY AND TRADE — Great Britain
PETROLEUM INDUSTRY AND TRADE — Italy
PETROLEUM INDUSTRY AND TRADE — Mexico — Energy consumption
PETROLEUM INDUSTRY AND TRADE — Nigeria
PETROLEUM INDUSTRY AND TRADE — Norway
PETROLEUM INDUSTRY AND TRADE — South Africa
PETROLEUM INDUSTRY AND TRADE — United States
PETROLEUM INDUSTRY AND TRADE — United States — Consolidation
PETROLEUM INDUSTRY AND TRADE — United States — History
PETROLEUM INDUSTRY AND TRADE — Zimbabwe — Bibliography
PETROLEUM LAW AND LEGISLATION
PETROLEUM LAW AND LEGISLATION — Great Britain
PETROLEUM LAW AND LEGISLATION — Nigeria
PETROLEUM PRODUCTS — Prices
PETROLEUM PRODUCTS — Prices — Congresses
PETROLEUM PRODUCTS — Prices — Mathematical models
PETROLEUM PRODUCTS — Prices — Great Britain
PETROV, EVDOKIA
PETROV, VLADIMIR MIKHAĬLOVICH
PHARMACEUTICAL POLICY — Bangladesh
PHILADELPHIA (PA.) — Commerce — History — 18th century
PHILADELPHIA (PA.) — Economic conditions
PHILANTHROPISTS — Moral and ethical aspects
PHILANTHROPISTS — Great Britain — Biography
PHILANTHROPISTS — United States — Biography
PHILIP, JOHN
PHILIPPART, SIMON
PHILIPPINES — Commercial policy
PHILIPPINES — Economic conditions — 1946-
PHILIPPINES — Economic policy
PHILIPPINES — Foreign relations — United States
PHILIPPINES — History — 1946-
PHILIPPINES — Politics and government
PHILIPPINES — Politics and government — 1946-
PHILIPPINES — Politics and government — 1973-
PHILIPPINES — Relations — United States
PHILIPPINES — Social conditions
PHILIPPINES — Social policy
PHILLIPS CURVE
PHILOSOPHERS — Directories
PHILOSOPHERS — Austria — History and criticism — Congresses
PHILOSOPHERS — Canada — Directories
PHILOSOPHERS — England — Biography
PHILOSOPHERS — England — History and criticism — Congresses
PHILOSOPHERS — France — Biography
PHILOSOPHERS — Germany — Biography
PHILOSOPHERS — Germany — Correspondence
PHILOSOPHERS — Germany — History and criticism
PHILOSOPHERS — Great Britain — Biography
PHILOSOPHERS — Hungary
PHILOSOPHERS — Italy — Biography
PHILOSOPHERS — Scotland
PHILOSOPHERS — United States — Biography
PHILOSOPHERS — United States — Directories
PHILOSOPHERS — Wales — Biography
PHILOSOPHERS, MODERN
PHILOSOPHICAL ANTHROPOLOGY
PHILOSOPHY
PHILOSOPHY — Addresses, essays, lectures
PHILOSOPHY — Bibliography
PHILOSOPHY — Collected works
PHILOSOPHY — Correspondence
PHILOSOPHY — Dictionaries
PHILOSOPHY — Library resources
PHILOSOPHY — Political aspects — History
PHILOSOPHY — United States — History
PHILOSOPHY, AMERICAN
PHILOSOPHY, ANCIENT
PHILOSOPHY, BRITISH
PHILOSOPHY, CHINESE — 20th century
PHILOSOPHY, ENGLISH — 19th century
PHILOSOPHY, ENGLISH — 18th century
PHILOSOPHY, EUROPEAN
PHILOSOPHY, EUROPEAN — History
PHILOSOPHY, FRENCH
PHILOSOPHY, FRENCH — Addresses, essays, lectures
PHILOSOPHY, FRENCH — 18th century
PHILOSOPHY, FRENCH — 20th century
PHILOSOPHY, GERMAN
PHILOSOPHY, KAGURU (AFRICAN PEOPLE)
PHILOSOPHY, MARXIST
PHILOSOPHY, MARXIST — Congresses
PHILOSOPHY, MARXIST — Hungary
PHILOSOPHY, MODERN — 19th century
PHILOSOPHY, MODERN — 20th century
PHILOSOPHY OF NATURE
PHILOSOPHY, PRIMITIVE
PHILOSOPHY, SPANISH — 20th century
PHOSPHORUS INDUSTRY — Netherlands — Statistics
PHOTOGRAPHY, INDUSTRIAL — United States
PHOTOGRAPHY OF WOMEN
PHYSICAL GEOGRAPHY — Hong Kong
PHYSICALLY HANDICAPPED — Employment — Great Britain
PHYSICALLY HANDICAPPED — Home care — Great Britain
PHYSICALLY HANDICAPPED — Institutional care — Great Britain
PHYSICALLY HANDICAPPED — Transportation — Government policy — United States
PHYSICALLY HANDICAPPED — Transportation — Law and legislation — United States
PHYSICALLY HANDICAPPED — Great Britain — Bibliography
PHYSICIAN AND PATIENT
PHYSICIAN AND PATIENT — Wales
PHYSICIAN-PATIENT RELATIONS
PHYSICIANS
PHYSICIANS — economics — United States
PHYSICIANS — Malpractice — Economic aspects — United States
PHYSICIANS — Malpractice — Germany — History — 20th century
PHYSICIANS — Malpractice — United States
PHYSICIANS — Supply and demand
PHYSICIANS — Australia — Social aspects
PHYSICIANS — Canada — History
PHYSICIANS — Germany (West)
PHYSICIANS — Great Britain — Supply and demand
PHYSICIANS — United States — Biography
PHYSICIANS — United States — Supply and demand
PHYSICIANS (GENERAL PRACTICE) — Denmark
PHYSICIANS (GENERAL PRACTICE) — Great Britain — History
PHYSICISTS — Great Britain — Biography
PHYSICS
PHYSICS — Forecasting
PHYSICS — History
PHYSICS — History — 20th century
PHYSICS — Philosophy
PHYSIOCRATS
PI SUNYER, CARLES
PIAGET, JEAN
PIAGET, JEAN — Congresses
PIAGET, JEAN — Contributions in theory of knowledge
PICKENS, F. W
PICKERSGILL, J. W.
PICKETING — England — Orgreave (South Yorkshire)
PICTURE-WRITING — Australia — Northern Territory
PIDGIN LANGUAGES
PINEAPPLE INDUSTRY — Hawaii — History
PINTUBI (AUSTRALIAN PEOPLE)
PIONEER HEALTH CENTRE
PIONEERS — Pennsylvania — Correspondence
PIRAE (TAHITI) — Population — Statistics
PIRATE RADIO BROADCASTING — Great Britain
PIRATES — Persian Gulf — History — 18th century

PIRATES — Persian Gulf — History — 19th century
PITTERMANN, BRUNO
PLAGUE — Italy — Florence — History
PLAID CYMRU
PLANNING
PLANNING — Methodology
PLANNING — Social aspects
PLANNING — Barbados
PLANNING — Bermuda
PLANNING — Great Britain
PLANNING — India
PLANNING — Soviet Union — Mathematical models
PLANNING — Spain — Madrid
PLANNING TECHNICS
PLANT LAYOUT — Bibliography
PLANT PRODUCTS — Canada
PLANT PRODUCTS — United States
PLANT SHUTDOWNS
PLANT SHUTDOWNS — Law and legislation — United States
PLANT SHUTDOWNS — England — Corby (Northamptonshire)
PLANT SHUTDOWNS — France
PLANT SHUTDOWNS — United States
PLANTATION LIFE — Brazil — History
PLANTATION LIFE — Caribbean Area — History
PLANTATION LIFE — Georgia — History
PLANTATION LIFE — Georgia — History — 19th century
PLANTATION LIFE — Latin America — History
PLANTATION LIFE — Southern States — History
PLANTATION LIFE — Virgin Islands of the United States — Saint John
PLANTATION LIFE — Virginia — History — 18th century
PLANTATION OWNERS — Virginia — History — 18th century
PLANTATIONS — Guatemala — History — 19th century
PLANTATIONS — Sri Lanka
PLANTS, PROTECTION OF — Bibliography
PLASTICS INDUSTRY AND TRADE — Great Britain
PLASTICS INDUSTRY AND TRADE — Wales
PLATO. Republic
PLATO. Republic. Book 1
PLATO
PLEA BARGAINING — England
PLEA BARGAINING — England — Birmingham
PLEBISCITE
PLEBISCITE — Puerto Rico
PLUNKETT, HORACE
PLURALISM (SOCIAL SCIENCES)
PLURALISM (SOCIAL SCIENCES) — History
PLURALISM (SOCIAL SCIENCES) — Canada
PLURALISM (SOCIAL SCIENCES) — Poland
PLURALISM (SOCIAL SCIENCES) — Venezuela
PLYWOOD INDUSTRY — Northwest, Pacific — Management — Employee participation — Case studies
POETS, CUBAN — 20th century — Biography
POHER, ALAIN
POLAND
POLAND — Boundaries — Germany
POLAND — Commerce
POLAND — Commerce — Great Britain
POLAND — Economic conditions — 1918-1945
POLAND — Economic conditions — 1945-
POLAND — Economic Policy
POLAND — Economic policy — 1945-
POLAND — Economic policy — 1966-1980
POLAND — Economic policy — 1981-
POLAND — Emigration and immigration
POLAND — Ethnic relations
POLAND — Ethnic relations — Bibliography
POLAND — Foreign economic relations
POLAND — Foreign economic relations — Great Britain
POLAND — Foreign economic relations — Yugoslavia
POLAND — Foreign relations — 1918-1945
POLAND — Foreign relations — 1945-
POLAND — Foreign relations — Germany
POLAND — Foreign relations — Germany (East)
POLAND — Foreign relations — Great Britain
POLAND — Foreign relations — Italy
POLAND — Foreign relations — Soviet Union
POLAND — Foreign relations — United States
POLAND — History
POLAND — History — Study and teaching — Poland
POLAND — History — Revolution, 1863-1864
POLAND — History — 20th century
POLAND — History — 1918-1945
POLAND — History — 1945-1980
POLAND — History — 1945-
POLAND — History — 1980-
POLAND — Industries
POLAND — Poilitics and government — 1945-
POLAND — Politics and government
POLAND — Politics and government — 1796-1918
POLAND — Politics and government — 1918-1945
POLAND — Politics and government — 1945-1980
POLAND — Politics and government — 1945-
POLAND — Politics and government — 1980
POLAND — Politics and government — 1980-
POLAND — Politics and government — 1980- — Addresses, essays, lectures
POLAND — Population
POLAND — Relations — Silesia
POLAND — Relations — Slavic countries
POLAND — Social conditions — 1945-
POLAND — Social life and customs — 1945-
POLAND — Social policy
POLANYI, KARL
POLANYI, MICHAEL
POLAR REGIONS
POLAR REGIONS — Juvenile literature
POLES — Brazil
POLES — Germany — Berlin
POLES — United States
POLICE
POLICE — Complaints against — England — Manchester (Greater Manchester)
POLICE — Cross-cultural studies
POLICE — Handbooks, manuals, etc
POLICE — Political aspects — India
POLICE — Recruiting — Congresses
POLICE — Australia — Complaints against
POLICE — Canada — History
POLICE — England — Complaints against
POLICE — England — London
POLICE — England — London — Public opinion
POLICE — Europe
POLICE — France — Finance
POLICE — Great Britain
POLICE — Great Britain — Attitudes
POLICE — Great Britain — Complaints against
POLICE — Great Britain — Complaints aganist
POLICE — Great Britain — Equipment and supplies
POLICE — Great Britain — History
POLICE — Great Britain — Public opinion
POLICE — India
POLICE — India — Complaints against
POLICE — New Zealand
POLICE — South Africa
POLICE — South Africa — Complaints against
POLICE — South Australia — Corrupt practices
POLICE — Spain — History
POLICE — United States
POLICE — United States — Complaints against
POLICE ADMINISTRATION — India
POLICE AND CRIMINAL EVIDENCE ACT 1984
POLICE AND CRIMINAL EVIDENCE BILL 1982-83
POLICE AND CRIMINAL EVIDENCE BILL 1983-84
POLICE CHIEFS — Hungary — Biography
POLICE CORRUPTION — Bibliography
POLICE CORRUPTION — Great Britain
POLICE CORRUPTION — Hong Kong — History
POLICE MAGISTRATES — England
POLICE PATROL
POLICE PATROL — England
POLICE PATROL — Great Britain
POLICE POWER — England
POLICE POWER — Great Britain
POLICE POWER — India — Tamil Nadu — History
POLICE, PRIVATE
POLICE QUESTIONING — Scotland
POLICE SERVICES FOR JUVENILES — Great Britain
POLICE SHOOTINGS — Northern Ireland — Investigation
POLICE SOCIAL WORK — Great Britain
POLICE TRAINING — Congresses
POLICE TRAINING — Great Britain
POLICEWOMEN — Great Britain
POLICY SCIENCES
POLICY SCIENCES — Addresses, essays, lectures
POLICY SCIENCES — Dictionaries
POLICY SCIENCES — Methodology
POLICY SCIENCES — Moral and ethical aspects
POLICY SCIENCES — Research
POLICY SCIENCES — United States
POLISARIO
POLISH LITERATURE — Foreign countries
POLITBURO See Kommunisticheskaia partiia Sovetskogo Soiuza. Tsentral'nyi komitet. Politbiuro
POLITICAL ANTHROPOLOGY — Africa, East
POLITICAL ANTHROPOLOGY — Australia
POLITICAL ANTHROPOLOGY — Mexico
POLITICAL BALLADS AND SONGS — Netherlands
POLITICAL CLUBS — Yugoslavia
POLITICAL CONSULTANTS — Australia
POLITICAL CONVENTIONS — United States — Addresses, essays, lectures
POLITICAL CRIMES AND OFFENSES
POLITICAL CRIMES AND OFFENSES — United States
POLITICAL CRIMES AND OFFENSES — United States — Bibliography
POLITICAL ETHICS
POLITICAL LEADERSHIP
POLITICAL LEADERSHIP — India
POLITICAL LEADERSHIP — Soviet Union
POLITICAL PARTICIPATION
POLITICAL PARTICIPATION — Social aspects — Argentina
POLITICAL PARTICIPATION — Belgium
POLITICAL PARTICIPATION — India
POLITICAL PARTICIPATION — Malawi
POLITICAL PARTICIPATION — Michigan — Detroit — Case studies

POLITICAL PARTICIPATION — Missouri — Kansas City
POLITICAL PARTICIPATION — New York (State) — Buffalo — Case studies
POLITICAL PARTICIPATION — Ohio — Cincinnati
POLITICAL PARTICIPATION — Papua New Guinea
POLITICAL PARTICIPATION — Peru
POLITICAL PARTICIPATION — Spain
POLITICAL PARTICIPATION — Spain — Castellón de la Plana — History — 19th century
POLITICAL PARTICIPATION — Texas — San Antonio — Addresses, essays, lectures
POLITICAL PARTICIPATION — United States
POLITICAL PARTICIPATION — United States — Case studies
POLITICAL PARTICIPATION — United States — History
POLITICAL PARTIES
POLITICAL PARTIES — Germany
POLITICAL PARTIES — Manifestos — History — 20th century
POLITICAL PARTIES — Membership — Great Britain
POLITICAL PARTIES — Religious aspects — Christianity
POLITICAL PARTIES — Asia
POLITICAL PARTIES — Brazil
POLITICAL PARTIES — British Columbia
POLITICAL PARTIES — Canada
POLITICAL PARTIES — Chile
POLITICAL PARTIES — China
POLITICAL PARTIES — Denmark
POLITICAL PARTIES — Europe — Addresses, essays, lectures
POLITICAL PARTIES — Europe — History — 20th century
POLITICAL PARTIES — France
POLITICAL PARTIES — Germany — History
POLITICAL PARTIES — Germany (West)
POLITICAL PARTIES — Germany (West) — History
POLITICAL PARTIES — Great Britain
POLITICAL PARTIES — Great Britain — Finance
POLITICAL PARTIES — Great Britain — History — 19th century
POLITICAL PARTIES — India
POLITICAL PARTIES — India — States
POLITICAL PARTIES — Ireland
POLITICAL PARTIES — Israel
POLITICAL PARTIES — Israel — Addresses, essays, lectures
POLITICAL PARTIES — Japan
POLITICAL PARTIES — Kenya — Bibliography
POLITICAL PARTIES — Mexico — History — 20th century
POLITICAL PARTIES — Nigeria
POLITICAL PARTIES — Northern Ireland
POLITICAL PARTIES — Norway — History
POLITICAL PARTIES — Pacific Area
POLITICAL PARTIES — Paraguay
POLITICAL PARTIES — Quebec (Province)
POLITICAL PARTIES — Southern States — History — 20th century — Addresses, essays, lectures
POLITICAL PARTIES — Spain
POLITICAL PARTIES — Spain — History
POLITICAL PARTIES — United States
POLITICAL PARTIES — United States — Addresses, essays, lectures
POLITICAL PARTIES — United States — History
POLITICAL PARTIES — United States — History — Addresses, essays, lectures
POLITICAL PARTIES — Uruguay
POLITICAL PARTIES — West (U.S.)
POLITICAL PARTIES — Yugoslavia

POLITICAL PERSECUTION — Addresses, essays, lectures
POLITICAL PERSECUTION — Germany — History — 20th century
POLITICAL PERSECUTION — Philippines
POLITICAL PLANNING
POLITICAL PLANNING — Econometric models
POLITICAL PLANNING — Economic aspects
POLITICAL PLANNING — Evaluation
POLITICAL PLANNING — Canada
POLITICAL PLANNING — France — Evaluation
POLITICAL PLANNING — Great Britain
POLITICAL PLANNING — Japan — History
POLITICAL PLANNING — Latin America
POLITICAL PLANNING — United States
POLITICAL POSTERS, RUSSIAN
POLITICAL PRISONERS
POLITICAL PRISONERS — Biography
POLITICAL PRISONERS — Brazil
POLITICAL PRISONERS — China — Biography
POLITICAL PRISONERS — Cuba
POLITICAL PRISONERS — Greece
POLITICAL PRISONERS — Iran
POLITICAL PRISONERS — Northern Ireland
POLITICAL PRISONERS — Poland
POLITICAL PRISONERS — Poland — Correspondence
POLITICAL PRISONERS — Soviet Union
POLITICAL PRISONERS — Soviet Union — Personal narratives
POLITICAL PRISONERS — Vietnam
POLITICAL PSCYHOLOGY
POLITICAL PSYCHOLOGY
POLITICAL QUESTIONS AND JUDICIAL POWER — European Economic Community countries
POLITICAL QUESTIONS AND JUDICIAL POWER — Great Britain
POLITICAL QUESTIONS AND JUDICIAL POWER — Netherlands
POLITICAL QUESTIONS AND JUDICIAL POWER — United States
POLITICAL QUESTIONS AND JUDICIAL POWER — United States — History
POLITICAL RIGHTS — New Zealand
POLITICAL RIGHTS — Legal status, laws, etc. — Indonesia
POLITICAL RIGHTS — Great Britain
POLITICAL RIGHTS — India
POLITICAL SATIRE
POLITICAL SCIENCE
POLITICAL SCIENCE — Anecdotes, facetiae, satire, etc.
POLITICAL SCIENCE — Bibliography
POLITICAL SCIENCE — Decision-making
POLITICAL SCIENCE — Decision making — Mathematical models
POLITICAL SCIENCE — Dictionaries
POLITICAL SCIENCE — Dictionaries and encyclopedias
POLITICAL SCIENCE — Early works to 1700
POLITICAL SCIENCE — History
POLITICAL SCIENCE — Language — History
POLITICAL SCIENCE — Mathematical models
POLITICAL SCIENCE — Philosophy
POLITICAL SCIENCE — Research
POLITICAL SCIENCE — Study and teaching — Soviet Union
POLITICAL SCIENCE — Early works to 1700
POLITICAL SCIENCE — England — History
POLITICAL SCIENCE — England — History — 17th century
POLITICAL SCIENCE — Europe
POLITICAL SCIENCE — Europe — History

POLITICAL SCIENCE — France — History
POLITICAL SCIENCE — Germany
POLITICAL SCIENCE — Great Britain — History — 17th century
POLITICAL SCIENCE — Great Britain — History — 19th century
POLITICAL SCIENCE — Hungary
POLITICAL SCIENCE — India — Addresses, essays, lectures
POLITICAL SCIENCE — Italy — History
POLITICAL SCIENCE — Poland
POLITICAL SCIENCE — Russia
POLITICAL SCIENCE — Soviet Union — History
POLITICAL SCIENCE — United States
POLITICAL SCIENCE — United States — Addresses, essays, lectures
POLITICAL SCIENCE — United States — History
POLITICAL SCIENCE — United States — History — 18th century
POLITICAL SOCIALIZATION
POLITICAL SOCIALIZATION — Great Britain
POLITICAL SOCIALIZATION — India — Case studies
POLITICAL SOCIALIZATION — India — Delhi
POLITICAL SOCIOLOGY
POLITICAL SOCIOLOGY — History
POLITICAL STABILITY
POLITICAL STABILITY — Developing countries
POLITICAL STABILITY — Hong Kong
POLITICIANS — Addresses, essays, lectures
POLITICIANS — Ireland — Biography
POLITICIANS — Argentina
POLITICIANS — Argentina — Biography
POLITICIANS — Australia
POLITICIANS — Australia — Biography
POLITICIANS — Bangladesh
POLITICIANS — Canada — Biography
POLITICIANS — China — Biography
POLITICIANS — Denmark — Biography
POLITICIANS — England — London — Biography
POLITICIANS — Georgia — Biography
POLITICIANS — Germany — Biography
POLITICIANS — Germany — History
POLITICIANS — Germany — Lower Saxony — Biography
POLITICIANS — Germany — Prussia — Biography
POLITICIANS — Germany (West) — Interviews
POLITICIANS — Great Britain
POLITICIANS — Great Britain — Biography
POLITICIANS — Great Britain — History — 19th century
POLITICIANS — Great Britain — History — 20th century
POLITICIANS — Hungary — Biography
POLITICIANS — India
POLITICIANS — India — Biography
POLITICIANS — Indiana — History
POLITICIANS — Ireland — Biography
POLITICIANS — Mexico
POLITICIANS — Nevada — Biography
POLITICIANS — Northern Ireland — Biography
POLITICIANS — Ontario — Biography
POLITICIANS — Palestine — Biography
POLITICIANS — Poland — Biography
POLITICIANS — Poland — Interviews
POLITICIANS — Soviet Union
POLITICIANS — Spain — Biography
POLITICIANS — Spain — Catalonia
POLITICIANS — Sweden — Biography
POLITICIANS — United States — Biography
POLITICS — history — United States
POLITICS AND CULTURE — Hungary
POLITICS AND EDUCATION
POLITICS AND EDUCATION — Chile — History — 20th century

POLITICS AND EDUCATION — Soviet Union — Addresses, essays, lectures
POLITICS AND EDUCATION — United States
POLITICS AND EDUCATION — United States — History
POLITICS AND GOVERNMENT — Classification
POLITICS AND LITERATURE
POLITICS AND LITERATURE — Soviet Union — History
POLITICS IN LITERATURE
POLITICS, PRACTICAL — Canada
POLITICS, PRACTICAL — United States
POLL-TAX — Great Britain
POLLUTANTS — Toxicology
POLLUTION — Economic aspects — England
POLLUTION — Environmental aspects — Bibliography
POLLUTION — Law and legislation — Great Britain
POLLUTION — Law and legislation — United States
POLLUTION — Statistics — Bibliography
POLLUTION — Europe
POLLUTION — Great Britain
POLLUTION — Japan — Tokyo
POLLUTION — Organisation for Economic Co-operation and Development countries
POLLUTION — Switzerland
POLLUTION CONTROL INDUSTRY — Cost effectiveness
POLSKA PARTIA ROBOTNICZA
POLSKA PARTIA ROBOTNICZA — History
POLSKA PARTIA SOCJALISTYCZNA
POLSKA PARTIA SOCJALNO-DEMOKRATYCZNA
POLYGAMY — Cross-cultural studies
POLYNESIANS IN EASTER ISLAND — History
POLYTECHNICS AND COLLEGES FUNDING COUNCIL
PONDICHERRY (INDIA) — Population — Statistics
PONDOS
POOR
POOR — Great Britain
POOR — Health and hygiene — Great Britain
POOR — History
POOR — Hospital care — Scotland — Edinburgh (Lothian) — History — 18th century
POOR — Housing — United States
POOR — Services for — England — History — 19th century
POOR — Asia
POOR — Canada
POOR — Developing countries
POOR — England — Liverpool (Merseyside)
POOR — England — London — History — 19th century
POOR — England — Manchester (Greater Manchester)
POOR — France — Grenoble — History — 17th century
POOR — France — Grenoble — History — 18th century
POOR — Great Britain
POOR — Great Britain — Medical care
POOR — Great Britain — Nutrition
POOR — Great Britain — Political aspects
POOR — Great Britain — Statistics
POOR — India
POOR — India — Addresses, essays, lectures
POOR — India — Karnataka
POOR — Kenya
POOR — Latin America
POOR — Namibia
POOR — Pakistan
POOR — Pennsylvania — Philadelphia — History — 19th century
POOR — Peru — Lima
POOR — Scotland
POOR — Soviet Union — History — 20th century
POOR — Spain
POOR — Spain — Castile
POOR — Spain — Valladolid — History
POOR — Swaziland
POOR — Switzerland
POOR — United States
POOR — United States — Case Studies
POOR AS CONSUMERS — Great Britain
POPIEŁUSZKO, JERZY
POPPER, KARL R.
POPPER, KARL R. — Congresses
POPULAR CULTURE
POPULAR FRONTS — History
POPULAR FRONTS — Poland
POPULAR LITERATURE — Soviet Union — History and criticism
POPULAR MOVEMENT FOR THE LIBERATION OF ANGOLA
POPULATION
POPULATION — Dictionaries — English
POPULATION — Dictionaries — Polyglot
POPULATION — Forecasting — Statistics
POPULATION — Genetic aspects
POPULATION — Government policy
POPULATION — History
POPULATION — History — Congresses
POPULATION — History — 18th century
POPULATION — Mathematical models
POPULATION — Political aspects
POPULATION — Statistical methods
POPULATION — Statistics
POPULATION — Statistics — Data processing
POPULATION — Statistics — Methodology
POPULATION — Italy — Statistics
POPULATION — Netherlands — Statistics
POPULATION ASSISTANCE, AMERICAN
POPULATION BIOLOGY — Mathematical models
POPULATION FORECASTING — Statistical methods
POPULATION FORECASTING — Statistics
POPULATION FORECASTING — England — London
POPULATION FORECASTING — Great Britain
POPULATION FORECASTING — Ireland
POPULATION POLICY
POPULATION POLICY — Addresses, essays, lectures
POPULATION POLICY — Economic aspects
POPULATION POLICY — Mathematical models
POPULATION POLICY — Social aspects
POPULATION PROJECTIONS — Algeria
POPULATION PROJECTIONS — Nigeria
POPULATION PROJECTIONS — Seychelles
POPULATION TRANSFERS — Serbs
POPULISM — Soviet Union
POPULISM — United States
POPULISM — United States — Addresses, essays, lectures
POPULISM — United States — History — 20th century
PORNOGRAPHY — Social aspects
PORT, Sir JOHN
PORT DISTRICTS — Alabama — Mobile — History — 19th century
PORTFOLIO MANAGEMENT
PORTFOLIO MANAGEMENT — Great Britain
PORTLAND, WILLIAM CAVENDISH-BENTINCK, Duke of
PORTLAND (OR.) — Description and travel
PORTS (FINANCIAL ASSISTANCE) BILL 1980-81
PORTUGAL — Bibliography
PORTUGAL — Colonies — History
PORTUGAL — Commerce
PORTUGAL — Description and travel — 1981-
PORTUGAL — Economic conditions — 20th century
PORTUGAL — Economic conditions — 1974-
PORTUGAL — Economic conditions — 1974- — Addresses, essays, lectures
PORTUGAL — Economic conditions — 1974- — Econometric models
PORTUGAL — Emigration and immigration
PORTUGAL — Emigration and immigration — History — Case studies
PORTUGAL — Foreign relations — 1974- — Addresses, essays, lectures
PORTUGAL — Foreign relations — Guinea-Bissau
PORTUGAL — Foreign relations — Spain
PORTUGAL — History — 1789-1900
PORTUGAL — History — 1974-
PORTUGAL — Politics and government — 1974- — Addresses, essays, lectures
PORTUGAL — Population — Statistics
PORTUGAL — Rural conditions
PORTUGAL — Social conditions — 20th century
PORTUGAL — Social conditions — 20th century — Addresses, essays, lectures
PORTUGUESE — France
PORTUGUESE IN CANADA
PORTUGUESE LANGUAGE — Acquisition
PORTUGUESE LANGUAGE — Relative clauses
POSADA, ADOLFO
POSITIVISM
POST OFFICE ENGINEERING UNION
POSTAL CARDS — Algeria
POSTAL CARDS — Germany — History — 20th century
POSTAL CARDS — Northern Ireland
POSTAL SERVICE — Denmark — Employees
POSTAL SERVICE — France — Statistics
POSTAL SERVICE — Great Britain
POSTAL SERVICE — Great Britain — History
POSTAL SERVICES — Spain — History
POTOSÍ (BOLIVIA : DEPT.) — Economic conditions
POTTERS — England — Longton (Staffordshire)
POTTERY, ENGLISH — History
POTTERY INDUSTRY — England — History
POULTRY INDUSTRY — Trinidad and Tobago — Statitics
POUND, BRITISH
POVERTY
POVERTY — Comparative studies
POVERTY — History
POVERTY — Measurement — Mathematical models
POVERTY — Prevention — Great Britain
POVERTY — Psychological aspects
POVERTY — India
POVERTY — Latin America
POWER RESOURCES
POWER RESOURCES — Bibliography
POWER RESOURCES — Economic aspects — East Asia
POWER RESOURCES — Forecasting — Social aspects — Case studies
POWER RESOURCES — Information services — England — London
POWER RESOURCES — Law and legislation — European Economic Community countries
POWER RESOURCES — Political aspects — East Asia
POWER RESOURCES — Prices — Government policy — Developing countries
POWER RESOURCES — Research — Great Britain
POWER RESOURCES — Research — International Energy Agency countries

POWER RESOURCES — Research — Soviet Union
POWER RESOURCES — Research — Sweden
POWER RESOURCES — Research — United States — Addresses, essays, lectures
POWER RESOURCES — Union lists
POWER RESOURCES — Asia — Congresses
POWER RESOURCES — Asia — Statistics
POWER RESOURCES — European Economic Community countries
POWER RESOURCES — European Economic Community Countries — Statistics
POWER RESOURCES — France
POWER RESOURCES — France — Statistics
POWER RESOURCES — Great Britain — Forecasting
POWER RESOURCES — Siberia, Western (R.S.F.S.R.) — Government policy
POWER RESOURCES — Spain — Congresses
POWER RESOURCES — Switzerland — Costs
POWER RESOURCES — United States
POWER RESOURCES — Zambia — Statistics
POWER RESOURES — Pacific Area — Congresses
POWER (SOCIAL SCIENCES)
POWER (SOCIAL SCIENCES) — Addresses, essays, lectures
POWER (SOCIAL SCIENCES) — Case studies
POWER (SOCIAL SCIENCES) — Congresses
POWER (SOCIAL SCIENCES) — History
PRAGMATICS — Addresses, essays, lectures
PRAIRIE PROVINCES — History — 19th century
PRAIRIE PROVINCES — History — 20th century
PRASAD, RAJENDRA
PRAVDA — History
PRE-SENTENCE INVESTIGATION REPORTS
PRECIOUS METALS
PREFABRICATED BUILDINGS — Hungary — Budapest
PREFECTS (FRENCH GOVERNMENT)
PREGNANCY
PREGNANCY — Psychological aspects
PREGNANCY — Bangladesh — Matlab
PREGNANCY, ADOLESCENT — Canada
PREGNANCY, ADOLESCENT — Europe
PREGNANCY, ADOLESCENT — United States
PREJUDICE
PREMIER-ALBANIAN COACHES — History
PRENATAL CARE — Great Britain
PRENATAL DIAGNOSIS — Denmark — Statistics
PRESBYTERIAN CHURCH — United States — Clergy — History — 18th century — Addresses, essays, lectures
PRESBYTERIANS — Northern Ireland — Biography
PRESIDENTIAL CANDIDATES — United States — Biography
PRESIDENTS — Transition periods
PRESIDENTS — Pakistan — Interviews
PRESIDENTS — Turkey — Biography
PRESIDENTS — United States
PRESIDENTS — United States — Addresses, essays, lectures
PRESIDENTS — United States — Archives — Catalogs
PRESIDENTS — United States — Biography
PRESIDENTS — United States — Correspondence
PRESIDENTS — United States — Election
PRESIDENTS — United States — Election — History — Statistics
PRESIDENTS — United States — Election — 1920
PRESIDENTS — United States — Election — 1952
PRESIDENTS — United States — Election — 1984
PRESIDENTS — United States — Election — 1984 — Addresses, essays, lectures
PRESIDENTS — United States — Evaluation
PRESIDENTS — United States — History
PRESIDENTS — United States — History — 20th century
PRESIDENTS — United States — History — 20th century — Manuscripts — Catalogs
PRESIDENTS — United States — History — 20th century — Sources — Bibliography — Catalogs
PRESIDENTS — United States — Journeys
PRESIDENTS — United States — Nomination — Addresses, essays, lectures
PRESIDENTS — United States — Press conferences
PRESIDENTS — United States — Staff
PRESIDENTS — United States — Transition periods
PRESIDENTS — Zaire
PRESIDENT'S PRIVATE SECTOR SURVEY ON COST CONTROL (U.S.)
PRESS
PRESS — Africa
PRESS — England — History — 18th century
PRESS — France — Bibliography
PRESS — France — History — 18th century
PRESS — Germany — History — 19th century
PRESS — India — History
PRESS — Scotland — History — 19th century
PRESS — Soviet Union
PRESS AGENTS — Canada — Biography
PRESS AND POLITICS
PRESS AND POLITICS — Bolivia — History — 20th century
PRESS AND POLITICS — Germany — History — 19th century
PRESS AND POLITICS — Great Britain
PRESS AND POLITICS — Spain — History
PRESS, LABOR — Great Britain
PRESS LAW — United States — Cases
PRESS, SOCIALIST — Germany — History — 19th century
PRESS, SOCIALIST — Sweden — Karlstad — History
PRESSURE GROUPS — Canada
PRESSURE GROUPS — Great Britain
PRESSURE GROUPS — Great Britain — History
PRESSURE GROUPS — Kenya — Bibliography
PRESSURE GROUPS — Manitoba — Winnipeg
PRESSURE GROUPS — Siberia, Western (R.S.F.S.R.)
PRESSURE GROUPS — United States
PRESSURE GROUPS — United States — Finance
PRESSURE GROUPS — United States — History
PRESSURIZED WATER REACTORS
PRESTEL (VIDEOTEX SYSTEM)
PREVENTION OF TERRORISM BILL 1983-84
PREVENTION OF TERRORISM (TEMPORARY PROVISIONS) ACT 1974
PREVENTION OF TERRORISM (TEMPORARY PROVISIONS) ACT 1976
PREVENTIVE DETENTION — North /America
PRICE INDEXES
PRICE INDEXES — Finland
PRICE INDEXES — Trinidad and Tobago
PRICE POLICY
PRICE POLICY — Colombia — Addresses, essays, lectures
PRICE POLICY — Communist countries
PRICE POLICY — Developing countries
PRICE POLICY — United States
PRICE REGULATION
PRICE REGULATION — Great Britain
PRICE REGULATION — Poland
PRICES — Peru — Iquitos
PRICES
PRICES — Government policy — India — Congresses
PRICES — Mathematical models
PRICES — Mathematical models — Congresses
PRICES — Statistical methods
PRICES — Argentina — Statistics
PRICES — Australia — Tasmania
PRICES — Egypt
PRICES — Great Britain
PRICES — Great Britain — History
PRICES — Hungary — Statistics
PRICES — Japan
PRICES — Netherlands — Econometric models
PRICES — Nigeria — Statistics
PRICES — Organisation for Economic Co-operation and Development countries — Mathematical models
PRICES — Pakistan
PRICES — Peru — Arequipa (City)
PRICES — Peru — Chiclayo
PRICES — Peru — Cuzco (City)
PRICES — Peru — Huancayo
PRICES — Peru — Piura (City)
PRICES — Peru — Trujillo
PRICES — Poland
PRICES — Soviet Union
PRICES — United States
PRICING POLICY
PRIMARY HEALTH CARE — Nepal
PRIME MINISTERS — Alberta — Biography
PRIME MINISTERS — British Columbia — Biography
PRIME MINISTERS — Canada — Biography
PRIME MINISTERS — Canada — History
PRIME MINISTERS — China — Biography
PRIME MINISTERS — Great Britain — Biography
PRIME MINISTERS — India — Biography
PRIME MINISTERS — India — Correspondence
PRIME MINISTERS — Ontario — Biography
PRIME MINISTERS — Québec (Province) — Biography
PRIME MINISTERS — Quebec (Province) — Biography
PRIME MINISTERS — Soviet Union — Biography
PRIME MINISTERS — Trinidad and Tobago — Biography — Addresses, essays, lectures
PRIME RATE — United States
PRIMO DE RIVERA, MIGUEL
PRIMROSE, ARCHIBALD PHILIP, Earl of Rosebery See Rosebery, Archibald Philip Primose, Earl of
PRINCESSES — Social conditions
PRINCIPAL COMPONENTS ANALYSIS
PRINTERS — Germany (West)
PRINTING — France — History
PRINTING — Sweden — History
PRINTING, PUBLIC — Legal status, laws, etc. — Peru
PRISON ADMINISTRATION — India
PRISON ADMINISTRATION — United States
PRISON ADMINISTRATION — United States — History
PRISON DISCIPLINE — Addresses, essays, lectures
PRISON DISCIPLINE — England

PRISON PSYCHOLOGY
PRISON REFORM TRUST
PRISON REFORMERS — United States — History
PRISON RIOTS — Mathematical models
PRISON SENTENCES — California
PRISON WARDENS — Training of — Great Britain — Evaluation
PRISONERS — Addresses, essays, lectures
PRISONERS — Legal status, laws, etc.
PRISONERS — Legal status, laws, etc. — United States — History
PRISONERS — Psychiatric care — Netherlands
PRISONERS — California — Case studies
PRISONERS — England — London
PRISONERS — Germany (West) — Suicidal behavior
PRISONERS — Great Britain
PRISONERS — Great Britain — Mortality
PRISONERS — India
PRISONERS — India — Assam
PRISONERS — India — Meghalaya
PRISONERS — Scotland
PRISONERS — United States — Psychology
PRISONERS, FOREIGN — Netherlands
PRISONERS OF WAR — Belgium
PRISONERS OF WAR — Isle of Man
PRISONERS OF WAR — United States
PRISONERS OF WAR, GERMAN
PRISONERS' WRITINGS
PRISONS — Political aspects — Great Britain
PRISONS — California — Alcatraz — Rules and practice
PRISONS — Canada
PRISONS — Great Britain
PRISONS — Great Britain — History — Bibliography
PRISONS — India
PRISONS — Netherlands
PRISONS — Scotland
PRISONS — United States
PRISONS — United States — Officials and employees
PRIVACY, RIGHT OF — Legal status, laws, etc. — Quebec (Province)
PRIVACY, RIGHT OF — Canada
PRIVACY, RIGHT OF — Great Britain
PRIVACY, RIGHT OF — United States
PRIVACY, RIGHT OF — United States — History
PRIVATE COMPANIES — Registration and transfer — England
PRIVATE COMPANIES — Germany (West)
PRIVATE EYE
PRIVATE HEALTH CARE See Health facilities, Proprietary
PRIVATE PLOT AGRICULTURE — Soviet Union
PRIVATE PRACTICE — United States
PRIVATE SCHOOLS — Great Britain
PRIVATIZATION
PRIVATIZATION — Congresses
PRIVATIZATION — Canada
PRIVATIZATION — Great Britain
PRIVATIZATION — Norway
PRO-LIFE MOVEMENT — New York (State)
PROBABILITIES
PROBATION — California
PROBATION — England
PROBATION — England — Sheffield (South Yorkshire)
PROBATION — Great Britain
PROBATION — United States — Addresses, essays, lectures
PROBATION OFFICERS — Great Britain
PROBLEM CHILDREN
PROBLEM FAMILIES — Counseling of — United States
PROBLEM FAMILIES — United States
PROBLEM FAMILIES — United States — Addresses, essays, lectures
PROBLEM SOLVING
PROCEDURE (JEWISH LAW)

PROCEDURE (LAW) — Great Britain
PRODUCE TRADE
PRODUCE TRADE — Government policy — Philippines
PRODUCE TRADE — Government policy — United States
PRODUCE TRADE — Law and legislation — Great Britain
PRODUCE TRADE — Canada
PRODUCE TRADE — Europe, Eastern
PRODUCE TRADE — Hong Kong
PRODUCE TRADE — Soviet Union
PRODUCE TRADE — Tanzania — Dar Es Salaam
PRODUCER COOPERATIVES
PRODUCER COOPERATIVES — European Economic Community countries
PRODUCER COOPERATIVES — France
PRODUCER COOPERATIVES — Great Britain
PRODUCER COOPERATIVES — Great Britain — Employees
PRODUCER COOPERATIVES — Italy
PRODUCER COOPERATIVES — Northwest, Pacific — Management — Employee participation — Case studies
PRODUCER COOPERATIVES — Wales
PRODUCT COUNTERFEITING
PRODUCT MANAGEMENT
PRODUCT SAFETY
PRODUCT SAFETY — Organisation for Economic Co-operation and Development countries
PRODUCTION (ECONOMIC THEORY)
PRODUCTION ENGINEERING
PRODUCTION ENGINEERING — Data processing
PRODUCTION FUNCTIONS (ECONOMIC THEORY)
PRODUCTION FUNCTIONS (ECONOMIC THEORY) — Case studies
PRODUCTION MANAGEMENT — Data processing
PRODUCTION MANAGEMENT — Japan
PRODUCTS LIABILITY
PRODUCTS LIABILITY — Agent Orange — United States
PRODUCTS LIABILITY — Congresses
PRODUCTS LIABILITY — Great Britain
PROFESSIONAL EDUCATION — France — Champagne-Ardenne
PROFESSIONAL EDUCATION — Great Britain — Directories
PROFESSIONAL ETHICS
PROFESSIONS
PROFESSIONS — Law and legislation — European Economic Community countries
PROFESSIONS — Social aspects — England
PROFESSIONS — Social aspects — United States — Addresses, essays, lectures
PROFESSIONS — Sociological aspects
PROFESSIONS — Egypt — History
PROFESSIONS — England — History
PROFESSIONS — France — Statistical methods
PROFESSIONS — Soviet Union
PROFESSIONS — Soviet Union — Sociological aspects
PROFIT — Government policy — Great Britain
PROFIT — Great Britain
PROFIT — Great Britain — Accounting
PROFIT — Norway
PROFIT — Organisation for Economic Co-operation and Development countries — Mathematical models
PROFIT-SHARING
PROFIT SHARING
PROFIT SHARING — Taxation — Great Britain
PROFIT-SHARING — Great Britain
PROFUMO, JOHN D.
PROGESSIVE CONSERVATIVE PARTY OF CANADA
PROGRAM BUDGETING
PROGRAMMING LANGUAGES (ELECTRONIC COMPUTERS)

PROGRAMMING LANGUAGES (ELECTRONIC COMPUTERS) — Semantics
PROGRAMMING (MATHEMATICS)
PROGRESS
PROGRESSIVE CONSERVATIVE PARTY OF CANADA
PROGRESSIVE CONSERVATIVE PARTY OF ONTARIO
PROGRESSIVISM (UNITED STATES POLITICS)
PROGRESSIVISM (UNITED STATES POLITICS) — Addresses, essays, lectures
PROHIBITED BOOKS — Bibliography
PROLETARIAT
PROLOG (COMPUTER PROGRAM LANGUAGE)
PROPAGANDA
PROPAGANDA — Addresses, essays, lectures
PROPAGANDA, BRITISH
PROPAGANDA, COMMUNIST — Latin America — Congresses
PROPAGANDA, COMMUNIST — Soviet Union
PROPAGANDA, GERMAN — Soviet Union
PROPAGANDA, RUSSIAN
PROPERTY
PROPERTY — Law and legislation — Great Britain
PROPERTY — Moral and ethical aspects
PROPERTY — Germany (West) — Statistics
PROPERTY TAX — United States — States — Congresses
PROPORTIONAL REPRESENTATION — Great Britain
PROSECUTION — Europe — Decision-making — Congresses
PROSECUTION — Scotland — Decision making
PROSELYTES AND PROSELYTING, JEWISH — Biography
PROSPECTING — Environmental aspects — Georges Bank
PROSPECTING — British Columbia
PROSTITUTES — India — Calcutta
PROSTITUTES — New South Wales — Sydney — Interviews
PROSTITUTION — Australia — History
PROSTITUTION — Canada
PROSTITUTION — Great Britain — Law and legislation
PROSTITUTION — India — Calcutta
PROSTITUTION — Ontario — Toronto
PROSTITUTION, MALE — New South Wales — Sydney
PROTEST SONGS — Netherlands
PROTESTANT CHURCHES — Brazil — History
PROTESTANT CHURCHES — Germany — Political aspects
PROTESTANTISM
PROTESTANTISM — Doctrines — History
PROTESTANTS — Germany — Biography
PROTESTANTS — Northern Ireland — Political activity
PROTESTANTS — Scotland — History
PROTESTANTS — Ulster (Northern Ireland and Ireland) — History
PROVIDENCE (R.I.) — History
PROVIDENCE (R.I.) — Social conditions
PROVIDER MOVEMENT
PROVINCIAL GOVERNMENTS — Canada
PROVISIONAL IRA
PROVISIONAL IRA — History
PRUSSIA — Politics and government — 1871-1888
PRUSSIA — Social conditions
PRUSSIA (GERMANY) — Foreign relations — 1740-1786
PRUSSIA (GERMANY) — Foreign relations — Great Britain
PRUSSIA (GERMANY) — History

PRUSSIA (GERMANY) — History — 19th century
PRUSSIA (GERMANY) — History — 1918-1933
PRUSSIA (GERMANY) — Industries
PRUSSIA (GERMANY) — Politics and government — 1815-1870
PSYCHIATRIC HOSPITAL CARE — Denmark — Statistics
PSYCHIATRIC HOSPITAL CARE — Wales
PSYCHIATRIC HOSPITALS — England — History
PSYCHIATRIC HOSPITALS — England — Hampshire
PSYCHIATRIC HOSPITALS — Great Britain
PSYCHIATRISTS — Algeria — Biography
PSYCHIATRY
PSYCHIATRY — England — History
PSYCHIATRY — Soviet Union
PSYCHICAL RESEARCH — Collected works
PSYCHOANALYSIS
PSYCHOANALYSIS — Case studies
PSYCHOANALYSIS — History
PSYCHOANALYSIS — in infancy & childhood
PSYCHOANALYSIS — Political aspects
PSYCHOHISTORY
PSYCHOLINGUISTIC
PSYCHOLINGUISTICS
PSYCHOLINGUISTICS — Periodicals
PSYCHOLINGUISTICS — Social aspects
PSYCHOLOGICAL LITERATURE
PSYCHOLOGICAL RESEARCH
PSYCHOLOGICAL THEORY
PSYCHOLOGISTS
PSYCHOLOGY
PSYCHOLOGY — Addresses, essays, lectures
PSYCHOLOGY — Cross-cultural studies
PSYCHOLOGY — Field work
PSYCHOLOGY — Handbooks
PSYCHOLOGY — History
PSYCHOLOGY — Library resources
PSYCHOLOGY — Philosophy
PSYCHOLOGY — Research
PSYCHOLOGY — India
PSYCHOLOGY — India — History
PSYCHOLOGY — United States — History
PSYCHOLOGY — United States — History — 19th century
PSYCHOLOGY — United States — History — 20th century
PSYCHOLOGY AND RELIGION — United States — History
PSYCHOLOGY, CLINICAL
PSYCHOLOGY, COMPARATIVE
PSYCHOLOGY, FORENSIC — Congresses
PSYCHOLOGY, INDUSTRIAL
PSYCHOLOGY, INDUSTRIAL — Addresses, essays, lectures
PSYCHOLOGY, INDUSTRIAL — methods
PSYCHOLOGY, INDUSTRIAL — Research
PSYCHOLOGY, INDUSTRIAL — Europe
PSYCHOLOGY, INDUSTRIAL — Soviet Union
PSYCHOLOGY, PATHOLOGICAL
PSYCHOLOGY, PHYSIOLOGICAL
PSYCHOLOGY, SOCIAL
PSYCHOMETRICS
PSYCHOSEXUAL DEVELOPMENT
PSYCHOTHERAPY
PSYCHOTHERAPY PATIENTS
PSYCHOTROPIC DRUGS — United States
PU YI, Emperor of China
PUBERTY RITES — Papua New Guinea — Addresses, essays, lectures
PUBIC HEALTH PERSONNEL — Education — Africa
PUBLIC ADMINISTRATION
PUBLIC ADMINISTRATION — Classification
PUBLIC ADMINISTRATION — Data processing
PUBLIC ADMINISTRATION — Data processing — Congresses
PUBLIC ADMINISTRATION — Decision making
PUBLIC ADMINISTRATION — Dictionaries
PUBLIC ADMINISTRATION — Study and teaching
PUBLIC ADMINISTRATION — Study and teaching — Great Britain
PUBLIC ADMINISTRATION — Argentina
PUBLIC ADMINISTRATION — Europe
PUBLIC ADMINISTRATION — Europe — Technological innovations
PUBLIC ADMINISTRATION — Great Britain
PUBLIC ADMINISTRATION — Great Britain — Data processing
PUBLIC ADMINISTRATION — Great Britain — Decision making
PUBLIC ADMINISTRATION — Great Britain — Effect of technological innovations on
PUBLIC ADMINISTRATION — Hungary
PUBLIC ADMINISTRATION — India
PUBLIC ADMINISTRATION — Ireland
PUBLIC ADMINISTRATION — New Zealand
PUBLIC ADMINISTRATION — New Zealand — Congresses
PUBLIC ADMINISTRATION — Organisation for Economic Co-operation and Development countries — Public relations
PUBLIC ADMINISTRATION — Spain
PUBLIC ADMINISTRATION — United States
PUBLIC ADMINISTRATION — United States — History
PUBLIC CONTRACTS — Price policy — Great Britain
PUBLIC CONTRACTS — European Economic Community countries
PUBLIC CONTRACTS — Great Britain
PUBLIC FINANCE — Finland — Statistics
PUBLIC GOODS — Cost effectiveness
PUBLIC GOODS — Mathematical models
PUBLIC GOODS — Valuation
PUBLIC HEALTH
PUBLIC HEALTH — Congresses
PUBLIC HEALTH — Economic aspects — Africa
PUBLIC HEALTH — Economic aspects — Denmark
PUBLIC HEALTH — Government policy
PUBLIC HEALTH — History
PUBLIC HEALTH — History — 18th century
PUBLIC HEALTH — Information services — Great Britain
PUBLIC HEALTH — Moral and ethical aspects
PUBLIC HEALTH — Social aspects
PUBLIC HEALTH — Social aspects — Great Britain — Bibliography
PUBLIC HEALTH — Africa
PUBLIC HEALTH — Africa — Addresses, essays, lectures
PUBLIC HEALTH — Africa — Evaluation
PUBLIC HEALTH — Bangladesh
PUBLIC HEALTH — Canada
PUBLIC HEALTH — China
PUBLIC HEALTH — Colombia
PUBLIC HEALTH — Denmark
PUBLIC HEALTH — Denmark — Statistics
PUBLIC HEALTH — Developing countries — Finance
PUBLIC HEALTH — Economic aspects — Developing countries
PUBLIC HEALTH — Europe — Forecasting
PUBLIC HEALTH — Finland
PUBLIC HEALTH — Great Britain
PUBLIC HEALTH — Great Britain — Bibliography
PUBLIC HEALTH — Great Britain — Finance
PUBLIC HEALTH — Great Britain — Statistics
PUBLIC HEALTH — Italy — Statistics
PUBLIC HEALTH — Namibia
PUBLIC HEALTH — Organisation for Economic Co-operation and Development countries
PUBLIC HEALTH — South Africa
PUBLIC HEALTH — Tanzania — History
PUBLIC HEALTH — Wales — Citizen administration
PUBLIC HEALTH ACT 1936
PUBLIC HEALTH ADMINISTRATION — Denmark
PUBLIC HEALTH ADMINISTRATION — Great Britain — Finance
PUBLIC HEALTH ADMINISTRATION — Nepal
PUBLIC HEALTH ADMINISTRATION — Wales
PUBLIC HEALTH LAWS
PUBLIC HEALTH LAWS — Peru
PUBLIC HEALTH PERSONNEL
PUBLIC HEALTH PERSONNEL — Education — Europe
PUBLIC HEALTH PERSONNEL — Africa
PUBLIC HEALTH SECURITY ACT, 1971
PUBLIC HOUSING — Law and legislation — England
PUBLIC HOUSING — Law and legislation — Great Britain
PUBLIC HOUSING — Standards — England — London
PUBLIC HOUSING — England
PUBLIC HOUSING — England — London
PUBLIC HOUSING — England — London — Management
PUBLIC HOUSING — England — Manchester (Greater Manchester)
PUBLIC HOUSING — Great Britain
PUBLIC HOUSING — Great Britain — Finance
PUBLIC HOUSING — Great Britain — Maintenance and repair
PUBLIC HOUSING — Great Britain — Management
PUBLIC HOUSING — Great Britain — Management — History
PUBLIC HOUSING — London metropolitan area — Tower Hamlets
PUBLIC HOUSING — Northern Ireland
PUBLIC HOUSING — United States
PUBLIC HOUSING — United States — Case studies
PUBLIC INTEREST — United States
PUBLIC INTEREST LAW
PUBLIC INTEREST LAW — Great Britain
PUBLIC INVESTMENTS — Evaluation — Mathematical models — Case studies
PUBLIC INVESTMENTS — Dominica
PUBLIC INVESTMENTS — Grenada
PUBLIC INVESTMENTS — Haiti
PUBLIC INVESTMENTS — Kenya
PUBLIC INVESTMENTS — Latin America
PUBLIC INVESTMENTS — Saint Kitts-Nevis
PUBLIC INVESTMENTS — Saint Lucia
PUBLIC LAW — Great Britain
PUBLIC LAW — Spain
PUBLIC LIBRARIES — England
PUBLIC LIBRARIES — England — Services to the aged
PUBLIC LIBRARIES — England — Somerset
PUBLIC LIBRARIES — Great Britain
PUBLIC LIBRARIES — Great Britain — Acquisitions
PUBLIC LIBRARIES — Great Britain — Services to the blind
PUBLIC OFFICERS — Political activity — Bibliography
PUBLIC OPINION
PUBLIC OPINION — Addresses, essays, lectures
PUBLIC OPINION — Africa
PUBLIC OPINION — Canada

PUBLIC OPINION — Canada — Congresses
PUBLIC OPINION — Europe
PUBLIC OPINION — European Economic Community countries
PUBLIC OPINION — France
PUBLIC OPINION — Georgia — Augusta Region — History — 19th century
PUBLIC OPINION — Great Britain
PUBLIC OPINION — Great Britain — History — 19th century
PUBLIC OPINION — Greece — Athens
PUBLIC OPINION — India
PUBLIC OPINION — South Africa
PUBLIC OPINION — Southern States
PUBLIC OPINION — Soviet Union
PUBLIC OPINION — United States
PUBLIC OPINION — United States — History
PUBLIC OPINION — United States — History — 19th century
PUBLIC OPINION — Washington (State)
PUBLIC OPINION POLLS
PUBLIC ORDER ACT 1936
PUBLIC ORDER ACT 1986
PUBLIC ORDER BILL 1985-86
PUBLIC POLICY — United States
PUBLIC POLICY (INTERNATIONAL LAW)
PUBLIC POLICY (LAW)
PUBLIC POLICY (LAW) — Great Britain
PUBLIC POLICY (LAW) — Great Britain — Bibliography
PUBLIC POLICY (LAW) — Great Britain — Information Services
PUBLIC POLICY (LAW) — United States
PUBLIC PROSECUTORS — Canada — History
PUBLIC RECORDS — Great Britain
PUBLIC RECORDS — Great Britain — Access control
PUBLIC RECORDS — Sri Lanka
PUBLIC RECORDS — United States — Access control
PUBLIC RECORDS — United States — Data processing
PUBLIC RELATIONS — England — Police
PUBLIC RELATIONS — Great Britain — Police
PUBLIC RELATIONS — United States
PUBLIC RELATIONS — United States — Police
PUBLIC SCHOOLS — Brazil — Finance
PUBLIC SCHOOLS — New York (N.Y.) — History
PUBLIC SCHOOLS — United States
PUBLIC SCHOOLS — United States — Curricula — Censorship
PUBLIC SERVICE EMPLOYMENT — Great Britain
PUBLIC SERVICE SUPERANNUATION ACT (CANADA)
PUBLIC SERVICES INTERNATIONAL
PUBLIC TELEVISION — Government policy — United States
PUBLIC UNIVERSITIES AND COLLEGES — United States — Directories
PUBLIC UTILITIES — Employees — Great Britain
PUBLIC UTILITIES — Law and legislation — United States
PUBLIC UTILITIES — Belize
PUBLIC UTILITIES — Canada — History
PUBLIC UTILITIES — France
PUBLIC UTILITIES — Great Britain
PUBLIC UTILITIES — Netherlands — Statistics
PUBLIC UTILITIES — Scotland — Dumfries and Galloway
PUBLIC UTILITIES — United States
PUBLIC UTILITIES STREET WORKS ACT 1950
PUBLIC WELFARE
PUBLIC WELFARE — Bibliography
PUBLIC WELFARE — Cost effectiveness — Bibliography
PUBLIC WELFARE — Data processing
PUBLIC WELFARE — Government policy — Great Britain
PUBLIC WELFARE — Law and legislation — Great Britain
PUBLIC WELFARE — Political aspects — Australia
PUBLIC WELFARE — Political aspects — New Zealand
PUBLIC WELFARE — Religious aspects — Christianity
PUBLIC WELFARE — Australia — History
PUBLIC WELFARE — Canada
PUBLIC WELFARE — Canada — Congresses
PUBLIC WELFARE — England — History
PUBLIC WELFARE — England — History — 19th century
PUBLIC WELFARE — Germany (West)
PUBLIC WELFARE — Great Britain
PUBLIC WELFARE — Great Britain — Bibliography
PUBLIC WELFARE — Great Britain — History
PUBLIC WELFARE — Great Britain — History — 19th century
PUBLIC WELFARE — Great Britain — History — 20th century
PUBLIC WELFARE — India
PUBLIC WELFARE — Ireland — Statistics
PUBLIC WELFARE — Mexico
PUBLIC WELFARE — Middle East
PUBLIC WELFARE — New Zealand — History
PUBLIC WELFARE — Northern Ireland
PUBLIC WELFARE — Pennsylvania — Philadelphia — History — 19th century
PUBLIC WELFARE — Scandinavia
PUBLIC WELFARE — Spain — Valladolid — History
PUBLIC WELFARE — Switzerland
PUBLIC WELFARE — United States
PUBLIC WELFARE — Wales
PUBLIC WELFARE ADMINSTRATION — Australia
PUBLISHERS AND PUBLISHING — Data processing — Handbooks, manuals, etc
PUBLISHERS AND PUBLISHING — Directories
PUBLISHERS AND PUBLISHING — Management
PUBLISHERS AND PUBLISHING — Technological innovation
PUBLISHERS AND PUBLISHING — Technological innovations
PUBLISHERS AND PUBLISHING — Canada — Statistics
PUBLISHERS AND PUBLISHING — Commonwealth of Nations — Directories
PUBLISHERS AND PUBLISHING — Denmark — History
PUBLISHERS AND PUBLISHING — European Economic Community Countries — Congresses
PUBLISHERS AND PUBLISHING — Germany — History
PUBLISHERS AND PUBLISHING — Great Britain — Biography
PUBLISHERS AND PUBLISHING — Wales
PUEBLA (MEXICO) — Industries
PUERTO RICA — Foreign relations — Cuba
PUERTO RICANS — Illinois — Chicago — Ethnic identity
PUERTO RICO — Commerce — History
PUERTO RICO — Economic conditions
PUERTO RICO — Economic conditions — 1952-
PUERTO RICO — Emigration and immigration
PUERTO RICO — Executive departments
PUERTO RICO — Executive departments — Handbooks, manuals, etc.
PUERTO RICO — Foreign relations — United States
PUERTO RICO — History
PUERTO RICO — Politics and government
PUERTO RICO — Politics and government — 1952-
PUERTO RICO. Department of the Treasury
PUGLIA (ITALY) — Social conditions
PUKA PUKA (TUAMOTU ISLANDS) — Population — Statistics
PULAU PINANG (MALAYSIA) — Population — Statistics
PULITZER PRIZES
PUNAAUIA (TAHITI : REGION) — Population — Statistics
PUNISHMENT — Congresseses
PUNISHMENT — Canada
PUNISHMENT — Great Britain — History — 19th century
PUNISHMENT — Nepal
PUNISHMENT — United States
PUNISHMENT — United States — Bibliography
PUNJAB (INDIA) — Politics and government
PUNK ROCK MUSIC — California — History and criticism
PURCHASING POWER — Netherlands — Statistics
PURITANS
PURITANS — New England — Religious life
PUSHKARNA BRAHMANS
PUSHKIN, A. S.
PUT AND CALL TRANSACTIONS — United States
PYGMIES — Addresses, essays, lectures
QANTAS AIRWAYS — History
QUADRATIC PROGRAMMING
QUADRIPARTITE AGREEMENT ON BERLIN (1971)
QUADRUPLE ALLIANCE, 1718
QUALITY CIRCLES — Great Britain
QUALITY CONTROL — Law and legislation — Addresses, essays, lectures
QUALITY CONTROL — Great Britain
QUALITY OF LIFE
QUALITY OF LIFE — Handbooks, manuals, etc
QUALITY OF LIFE — Moral and ethical aspects
QUALITY OF LIFE — Asia
QUALITY OF LIFE — Communist countries
QUALITY OF LIFE — Hungary — Statistical methods — Congresses
QUALITY OF LIFE — Norway — Statistics
QUALITY OF LIFE — Scandinavia
QUALITY OF LIFE — Soviet Union
QUALITY OF LIFE — Soviet Union — Congresses
QUALITY OF LIFE — Sri Lanka
QUALITY OF LIFE — United States
QUALITY OF LIFE — United States — Statistics
QUALITY OF PRODUCTS — United States — Case studies
QUALITY OF WORK LIFE
QUALITY OF WORK LIFE — Societies, etc. — Directories
QUALITY OF WORK LIFE — Canada
QUALITY OF WORK LIFE — Europe
QUALITY OF WORK LIFE — Japan
QUALITY OF WORK LIFE — United States
QUALITY OF WORK LIFE — United States — Case studies
QUALITY OF WORKLIFE
QUANTUM THEORY
QUARTZ FIBERS — Toxicology — West Virginia — Gauley Bridge
QUEBEC (PROVINCE) — Autonomy and independence movements
QUÉBEC (PROVINCE) — Economic conditions
QUÉBEC (PROVINCE) — Economic conditions — Statistics

QUÉBEC (PROVINCE) — Ethnic relations
QUÉBEC (PROVINCE) — History
QUÉBEC (PROVINCE) — History — Autonomy and independence movements
QUÉBEC (PROVINCE) — History — 1936-1960
QUÉBEC (PROVINCE) — History — 1960-
QUÉBEC (PROVINCE) — Politics and government
QUÉBEC (PROVINCE) — Politics and government — 1960-
QUÉBEC (PROVINCE) — Politics and government — 1960-
QUÉBEC (PROVINCE) — Population — Statistics
QUÉBEC (PROVINCE) — Population — Statistics — Forecasting
QUÉBEC (PROVINCE) — Social conditions
QUÉBEC (PROVINCE) — Social conditions
QUÉBEC (PROVINCE) — Social policy
QUEENS — Social conditions
QUEENSLAND — Emigration and immigration — History — 19th century
QUESTIONNAIRES
QUETELET, ADOLPHE
QUINE, W. V
QUINE, W. V.
QUINE, WILLARD VAN ORMAN
QUINET, EDGAR
QUITMAN, JOHN ANTHONY
QUITO REGION (ECUADOR) — History
RABBIS — United States — Biography
RABKRIN See Soviet Union. Narodnyi kommissariat raboche-krest'iansko inspektsii
RACE AWARENESS
RACE AWARENESS — Austria
RACE AWARENESS IN CHILDREN — Great Britain
RACE DISCRIMINATION — Great Britain
RACE DISCRIMINATION
RACE DISCRIMINATION — Government policy — Great Britain
RACE DISCRIMINATION — Law and legislation — Great Britain
RACE DISCRIMINATION — Psychological aspects
RACE DISCRIMINATION — England — Liverpool (Merseyside)
RACE DISCRIMINATION — England — London
RACE DISCRIMINATION — Great Britain
RACE DISCRIMINATION — Great Britain — Bibliography
RACE DISCRIMINATION — Israel
RACE DISCRIMINATION — South Africa
RACE DISCRIMINATION — United States — History
RACE DISCRIMINATION IN EMPLOYMENT — Great Britain
RACE RELATIONS
RACE RELATIONS — Religious aspects — Christianity
RACE RELATIONS — Religious aspects — Christianity — Public opinion
RACE RELATIONS — Great Britain
RACE RELATIONS IN SCHOOL MANAGEMENT — Great Britain
RACISM
RACISM — History
RACISM — Political aspects — New Zealand
RACISM — Study and teaching
RACISM — Australia — Broken Hill (N.S.W.)
RACISM — Canada
RACISM — England — West Midlands
RACISM — Europe
RACISM — France
RACISM — Great Britain
RACISM — Great Britain — History — 20th century
RACISM — South Africa
RACISM — South Africa — Johannesburg
RACISM — United States
RACISM — United States — Addresses, essays, lectures
RACISM — United States — History
RACISM — United States — History — 20th century
RACISM IN TEXTBOOKS
RACISM IN TEXTBOOKS — Canada
RADIALISM — United States — Periodicals — Biography
RADIATION
RADICALISM
RADICALISM — Addresses, essays, lectures
RADICALISM — History
RADICALISM — Islam
RADICALISM — Songs and music
RADICALISM — British Columbia — History
RADICALISM — California — Santa Monica — History
RADICALISM — Europe
RADICALISM — Germany (West)
RADICALISM — Great Britain — History — 17th century
RADICALISM — Ireland — History
RADICALISM — Moldavia
RADICALISM — Oklahoma — History
RADICALISM — Soviet Union — History
RADICALISM — Soviet Union — History — 19th century
RADICALISM — United States
RADICALISM — United States — History — 20th century
RADICALISM — United States — History — 20th century — Addresses, essays, lectures
RADICALISM — United States — Literary collections
RADICALS — Great Britain — Biography
RADICALS — Great Britain — Directories
RADICALS — South Africa — Biography
RADICALS — Soviet Union — Biography
RADIO — Social aspects — Denmark
RADIO BROADCASTING
RADIO BROADCASTING — Legal status, laws, etc. — Peru
RADIO BROADCASTING — Australia
RADIO BROADCASTING — Great Britain
RADIO BROADCASTING POLICY — Australia
RADIO BROADCASTING POLICY — Cuba
RADIO BROADCASTING POLICY — Peru
RADIO BROADCASTING POLICY — United States
RADIO CORPORATION OF AMERICA
RADIO FREE EUROPE
RADIO FREQUENCY ALLOCATION — Great Britain
RADIO IN PROPAGANDA
RADIO IN PROPAGANDA — Europe
RADIO LIBERTY (Munich)
RADIOACTIVE CONTAMINATION OF FOOD
RADIOACTIVE POLLUTION — Mathematical models
RADIOACTIVE POLLUTION — England — West Cumbria
RADIOACTIVE POLLUTION — Great Britain
RADIOACTIVE POLLUTION OF THE SEA
RADIOACTIVE WASTE DISPOSAL
RADIOACTIVE WASTE DISPOSAL — England — Killingholme (Humberside)
RADIOACTIVE WASTE DISPOSAL — Great Britain
RADIOACTIVE WASTES
RADIOACTIVITY — Safety measures
RADIOISOTOPES IN AGRICULTURE
RAHMAN, SHEIKH MUJIBUR
RAIATEA (SOCIETY ISLANDS) — Population — Statistics
RAIFFEISEN, FRIEDRICH WILHELM — Biography
RAILRAODS — Statistics — European Economic Community countries
RAILROAD TERMINALS — England — London
RAILROADS — Economic aspects
RAILROADS — Freight — Statistics
RAILROADS — History — 19th century
RAILROADS — Noise
RAILROADS — Passenger traffic
RAILROADS — Africa, Southern
RAILROADS — Australia
RAILROADS — Belgium — History — 19th century
RAILROADS — Brazil — History
RAILROADS — England — Commuting traffic
RAILROADS — England — Management — History
RAILROADS — England — Passenger traffic
RAILROADS — England — Kent — Passenger traffic
RAILROADS — England — London
RAILROADS — England — London Metropolitan Area — Commuting traffic — Evaluation
RAILROADS — England, Northern — History
RAILROADS — France — History — 19th century
RAILROADS — Great Britain
RAILROADS — Great Britain — Employees
RAILROADS — Great Britain — History
RAILROADS — Kazakh S.S.R. — History
RAILROADS — Luxembourg — History — 19th century
RAILROADS — Soviet Central Asia — History
RAILROADS — United States — History
RAILROADS — United States — History — 20th century
RAILROADS — Wales — Management — History
RAILROADS, LOCAL AND LIGHT — England — London
RAILWAY MAIL SERVICE — Great Britain
RAILWAYS See Railroads
RAIN AND RAINFALL — Europe
RAIN FOREST — Asia, Southeastern
RAIN FOREST ECOLOGY
RAIN FOREST ECOLOGY — Asia, Southeastern
RAIVAVAE (AUSTRAL ISLANDS) — Population — Statistics
RAMMOHUN ROY, Raja
RAMMOHUN ROY, Raja — Ethics
RANGIROA (TUAMOTU ISLANDS) — Population — Statistics
RAPA (AUSTRAL ISLANDS) — Population — Statistics
RAPE
RAPE — Bibliography
RAPE — Law and legislation — England
RAPE — Legal status, laws, etc. — Bibliography
RAPE — Prevention
RAPE — England
RAPE — England — History — 18th century
RAPE — England — History — 19th century
RAPE IN MARRIAGE — United States
RAS TAFARI MOVEMENT
RASKOLNIKS
RASSEMBLEMENT DU PEUPLE TOGOLAIS. Secretariat Administratif
RATE OF RETURN
RATE OF RETURN — Great Britain
RATES BILL 1983-84
RATING AND VALUATION (AMENDMENT) (SCOTLAND) BILL 1983-84
RATIO ANALYSIS
RATIONAL EXPECTATIONS (ECONOMIC THEORY)

RATIONAL EXPECTATIONS (ECONOMIC THEORY) — Mathematical models
RATIONALISM
RATIONALISM — Addresses, essays, lectures
RATIONALISM IN LITERATURE
RATIONALIZATION (PSYCHOLOGY)
RAW MATERIALS
RAW MATERIALS — Economic aspects
RAW MATERIALS — Government policy — Canada
RAW MATERIALS — Prices — Mathematical models
RAW MATERIALS — Pacific area
RAWLS, JOHN. Theory of justice
REACTOR FUEL REPROCESSING — England — Cumbria
READ, KENNETH E
READING
READING ABBEY
READING (ELEMENTARY)
REAGAN, RONALD
REAGAN, RONALD — Addresses, essays, lectures
REAGAN, RONALD — Congresses
REAGAN, RONALD — Journeys — Germany (West) — Addresses, essays, lectures
REAL ANALYSIS
REAL ESTATE DEVELOPMENT — Environmental aspects — Great Britain
REAL ESTATE DEVELOPMENT — Government policy — Great Britain
REAL ESTATE DEVELOPMENT — Argentina — History
REAL ESTATE DEVELOPMENT — Australia — Melbourne (Vic.) — History — 20th century
REAL ESTATE DEVELOPMENT — England — Hertfordshire
REAL ESTATE DEVELOPMENT — England — Reading (Berkshire) — History — 20th century
REAL ESTATE DEVELOPMENT — Great Britain
REAL ESTATE DEVELOPMENT — Southern States
REAL ESTATE INVESTMENT — Taxation — Law and legislation — United States — Congresses
REAL ESTATE INVESTMENT — Taxation — United States — Congresses
REAL ESTATE INVESTMENT — Argentina
REAL ESTATE INVESTMENT — Pacific Area
REAL PROPERTY — Economic aspects — Great Britain
REAL PROPERTY — Law and legislation — Great Britain
REAL PROPERTY — Valuation — Hong Kong
REAL PROPERTY — England — Bibliography
REAL PROPERTY — England — Cases
REAL PROPERTY — England — London
REAL PROPERTY — Spain — Barcelona
REAL PROPERTY AND TAXATION — United States — Congresses
REAL PROPERTY, EXCHANGE OF — United States
REAL PROPERTY TAX — Law and legislation — Great Britain
REAL PROPERTY TAX — Law and legislation — Peru
REAL PROPERTY TAX — Law and legislation — Scotland
REAL PROPERTY TAX — Appalachian Region
REAL-TIME DATA PROCESSING
REALISM
REALITY — Philosophy
REAO (TUAMOTU ISLANDS) — Population — Statistics
REASON OF STATE
REASONING

REASONING (PSYCHOLOGY)
RECALL — United States
RECEIVERS — Canada
RECEIVERS — England
RECEIVERS — Ontario
RECEIVERS — Scotland
RECIDIVISM — California
RECIDIVISM — Netherlands
RECIDIVISTS — United States — Case studies
RECIFE HOUSE OF DETENTION — History — 19th century
RECIPROCITY
RECLAMATION OF LAND — England
RECLAMATION OF LAND — Great Britain
RECLAMATION OF LAND — Ukraine
RECLAMATION OF LAND — United States
RECOGNITION(PSYCHOLOGY)
RECOLLECTION(PSYCHOLOGY)
RECOMBINANT DNA — Safety measures
RECONCILIATION
RECONSTRUCTION
RECONSTRUCTION — Georgia
RECONSTRUCTION (1939-1951) — Poland
RECREATION — Economic aspects — United States
RECREATION — Canada — Statistics
RECREATION — England — Devon
RECRUITING OF EMPLOYEES
RECRUITING OF EMPLOYEES — Great Britain
RECRUITING OF EMPLOYEES — London
RECURSIVE FUNCTIONS — Data processing
RECYCLING (WASTE, ETC.)
RECYCLING (WASTE, ETC.) — Bibliography
RECYCLING (WASTE, ETC.) — Developing countries
RED SEA — Relations — France
REDDITCH (WORCESTERSHIRE) — City planning
REDUCING — Social aspects — United States — History
REFERENCE BOOKS — Bibliography
REFERENCE BOOKS — Criminal justice, Administration of
REFERENCE BOOKS — Philosophy
REFERENCE LIBRARIANS
REFERENCE LIBRARIES — Australia
REFERENCE SERVICES (LIBRARIES)
REFERENCE SERVICES (LIBRARIES) — England
REFERENCE SERVICES (LIBRARIES) — Great Britain
REFERENDUM — Bibliography
REFERENDUM — Europe
REFERENDUM — United States
REFORM JUDAISM — Great Britain — History
REFORMATION — Great Britain — Sources
REFORMATION — Wales
REFORMATORIES FOR WOMEN — England — London
REFORMATORIES FOR WOMEN — United States
REFORMED CHURCH — Doctrines — Addresses, essays, lectures
REFORMERS — India — Biography
REFORMERS — Mexico — Jalisco
REFORMERS — United States — Biography
REFUGEES
REFUGEES — Addresses, essays, lectures
REFUGEES — Education — Africa — Directories
REFUGEES — Government policy — Great Britain — Handbooks, manuals, etc
REFUGEES — Government policy — United States — History — 20th century
REFUGEES — Services for
REFUGEES — Afghanistan
REFUGEES — Africa

REFUGEES — Africa — Education (Higher)
REFUGEES — Central America
REFUGEES — Central America — Congresses
REFUGEES — Denmark — Public opinion
REFUGEES — Germany (West)
REFUGEES — Pakistan
REFUGEES — United States
REFUGEES, AFRICA
REFUGEES, ARAB
REFUGEES, ARAB — Social conditions
REFUGEES, JEWISH — Netherlands
REFUGEES, JEWISH — United States — History
REFUGEES, POLITICAL — Biography
REFUGEES, POLITICAL — Education — New York (N.Y.) — History
REFUGEES, POLITICAL — Germany (West)
REFUGEES, POLITICAL — Great Britain
REFUGEES, POLITICAL — Netherlands
REFUSE AND REFUSE DISPOSAL
REFUSE AND REFUSE DISPOSAL — Economic aspects
REFUSE AND REFUSE DISPOSAL — Belgium — East Flanders
REFUSE AND REFUSE DISPOSAL — England — Bedfordshire
REFUSE AND REFUSE DISPOSAL — England — South East
REFUSE AS FUEL — Europe
REGENTS — Great Britain — Biography
REGIONAL DEVELOPMENT — Economic aspects — Case studies
REGIONAL DEVELOPMENT — Switzerland
REGIONAL ECONOMIC DISPARITIES
REGIONAL ECONOMIC DISPARITIES — Spain
REGIONAL ECONOMICS
REGIONAL ECONOMICS — Congresses
REGIONAL ECONOMICS — Mathematical models
REGIONAL MEDICAL PROGRAMS — Great Britain
REGIONAL PLANNING
REGIONAL PLANNING — Case studies
REGIONAL PLANNING — Congresses
REGIONAL PLANNING — Dictionaries — Polyglot
REGIONAL PLANNING — Economic aspects
REGIONAL PLANNING — European Economic Community countries
REGIONAL PLANNING — Government policy
REGIONAL PLANNING — Law and legislation — England
REGIONAL PLANNING — Law and legislation — Europe
REGIONAL PLANNING — Law and legislation — Great Britain
REGIONAL PLANNING — Law and legislation — Nigeria
REGIONAL PLANNING — Political aspects
REGIONAL PLANNING — Bedfordshire — Citizen participation
REGIONAL PLANNING — Botswana
REGIONAL PLANNING — Canada
REGIONAL PLANNING — Colombia
REGIONAL PLANNING — Colombia — Bucaramanga
REGIONAL PLANNING — Developinmg countries — Mathematical models — Case studies — Congresses
REGIONAL PLANNING — Ecuador
REGIONAL PLANNING — England
REGIONAL PLANNING — England — History — 20th century
REGIONAL PLANNING — England — Avon
REGIONAL PLANNING — England — Berkshire
REGIONAL PLANNING — England — Buckinghamshire — Citizen participation

REGIONAL PLANNING — England — Cornwall
REGIONAL PLANNING — England — Devon
REGIONAL PLANNING — England — Essex — History — 20th century
REGIONAL PLANNING — England — Hereford and Worcester
REGIONAL PLANNING — England — Hertfordshire
REGIONAL PLANNING — England — Hertfordshire — Citizen participation
REGIONAL PLANNING — England — Lancashire
REGIONAL PLANNING — England — London
REGIONAL PLANNING — England — Somerset
REGIONAL PLANNING — England — Surrey
REGIONAL PLANNING — England — Sussex
REGIONAL PLANNING — England — Warwickshire
REGIONAL PLANNING — England — West Midlands
REGIONAL PLANNING — Europe, Southern
REGIONAL PLANNING — European Economic Community countries
REGIONAL PLANNING — European Economic Community Countries — Statistics
REGIONAL PLANNING — France
REGIONAL PLANNING — Great Britain
REGIONAL PLANNING — Great Britain — Citizen participation
REGIONAL PLANNING — Great Britain — Evaluation
REGIONAL PLANNING — Great Britain — History
REGIONAL PLANNING — Great Britain — Law and legislation
REGIONAL PLANNING — Guadeloupe
REGIONAL PLANNING — India
REGIONAL PLANNING — India — Andhra Pradesh
REGIONAL PLANNING — Libya
REGIONAL PLANNING — Netherlands
REGIONAL PLANNING — Nièvre, France (Dept.)
REGIONAL PLANNING — Peru
REGIONAL PLANNING — Québec (Province)
REGIONAL PLANNING — Scotland — Dumfries and Galloway
REGIONAL PLANNING — Scotland — Lothian
REGIONAL PLANNING — Scotland — Lothian — Citizen participation
REGIONAL PLANNING — Scotland — Strathclyde
REGIONAL PLANNING — Scotland — Strathclyde — Citizen participation
REGIONAL PLANNING — Sunbelt States
REGIONAL PLANNING — Wales — Anglesey
REGIONAL PLANNING — Wales — Caernarvonshire
REGIONAL PLANNING — Wales — Clwyd
REGIONAL PLANNING — Wales — Clwyd — Citizen participation
REGIONAL PLANNING — Wales — Clwyd — citizen participation
REGIONAL PLANNING — Wales — Clwyd — Citizen participation
REGIONAL PLANNING — Wales — Dyfed
REGIONAL PLANNING — Wales — Dyfed — Citizen participation
REGIONAL PLANNING — Wales — Ghent
REGIONAL PLANNING — Wales — Glamorgan
REGIONAL PLANNING — Wales — Gwent
REGIONAL PLANNING — Wales — Gwynedd
REGIONAL PLANNING — Wales — Powys
REGIONAL PLANNING — Wales — South Glamorgan
REGIONAL PLANNING — Wales — West Glamorgan
REGIONAL POWER UTILITY TARIFF SYMPOSIUM (1982 : Manila)
REGIONALISM
REGIONALISM — Australia
REGIONALISM — Canada
REGIONALISM — Canary Islands
REGIONALISM — Colombia — History — 19th century
REGIONALISM — Developing countries
REGIONALISM — Europe
REGIONALISM — France
REGIONALISM — South Asia — Congresses
REGIONALISM — Spain
REGIONALISM (INTERNATIONAL ORGANIZATION)
REGISTERED HOMES ACT 1984
REGISTERS OF BIRTHS, ETC — Congresses
REGISTERS OF BIRTHS, ETC. — Great Britain — History
REGISTERS OF BIRTHS, ETC. — Portugal
REHABILITATION
REHABILITATION — Law and legislation — Denmark
REHABILITATION — Great Britain
REHABILITATION ACT, 1970
REHABILITATION CENTERS — Great Britain
REHABILITATION OF CRIMINALS — Addresses, essays, lectures
REHABILITATION OF CRIMINALS — Canada
REHABILITATION OF CRIMINALS — Great Britain
REHABILITATION OF CRIMINALS — United States
REHABILITATION OF JUVENILE DELINQUENTS
REHABILITATION OF JUVENILE DELINQUENTS — England
REHABILITATION OF JUVENILE DELINQUENTS — England — Derbyshire
REHABILITATION OF JUVENILE DELINQUENTS — England — Durham (Durham)
REHABILITATION OF JUVENILE DELINQUENTS — England — Isle of Wight
REHABILITATION OF JUVENILE DELINQUENTS — England — Lincolnshire
REHABILITATION OF JUVENILE DELINQUENTS — England — London
REHABILITATION OF JUVENILE DELINQUENTS — France
REHABILITATION OF JUVENILE DELINQUENTS — Great Britain
REHABILITATION OF JUVENILE DELINQUENTS — Great Britain — Case studies
REHABILITATION OF JUVENILE DELINQUENTS — United States
REHABILITATION OF JUVENILE DELINQUENTS — Wales
REHABILITATION OF JUVENILE DELINQUENTS — Wales — Congresses
REIMS (FRANCE) — Politics and government
RELATIVITY
RELIABILITY (ENGINEERING) — Mathematical models
RELIGION
RELIGION — Dictionaries
RELIGION — History — 20th century — Congresses
RELIGION — Philosophy
RELIGION AND CIVILIZATION
RELIGION AND CULTURE — Congresses
RELIGION AND POLITICS — Congresses
RELIGION AND POLITICS — India — History
RELIGION AND RACE
RELIGION AND SOCIETY
RELIGION AND SOCIOLOGY
RELIGION AND SOCIOLOGY — Addresses, essays, lectures
RELIGION AND SOCIOLOGY — Bibliography
RELIGION AND STATE — Bibliography
RELIGION AND STATE — India — History
RELIGION AND STATE — Near East
RELIGION AND STATE — Soviet Union
RELIGION HISTORIANS — United States — Biography
RELIGIONS
RELIGIOUS BROADCASTING — Great Britain — History
RELIGIOUS EDUCATION — England — London
RELIGIOUS LIBERTY — Great Britain
RELIGIOUS LIBERTY — Soviet Union
RELIGIOUS LIBERTY — Spain
RELIGIOUS LIBERTY — United States
REMEDIAL TEACHING
REMEDIES (LAW)
REMINISCING
RENAISSANCE
RENAISSANCE — Wales
RENEWABLE ENERGY SOURCES
RENEWABLE ENERGY SOURCES — Economic aspects
RENEWABLE ENERGY SOURCES — Environmental aspects — Great Britain
RENEWABLE ENERGY SOURCES — International Energy Agency countries
RENFREW (ONT. : COUNTY) — History
RENT — Great Britain
RENT CONTROL — Great Britain
RENT CONTROL — United States
RENT (ECONOMIC THEORY)
RENT STRIKES — England — London
RENTAL HOUSING — Law and legislation — England
RENTAL HOUSING — Law and legislation — Great Britain
RENTAL HOUSING — Law and legislation — Northern Ireland
RENTAL HOUSING — Maintenance and repair — Great Britain
RENTAL HOUSING — England
RENTAL HOUSING — England — London
RENTAL HOUSING — Great Britain
RENTAL HOUSING — London — Chelsea — Resident satisfaction
RENTAL HOUSING — London — Kensington — Resident satisfaction
REPARATION — Great Britain
REPARATION — Netherlands
REPORT ON THE SUPPLY OF PETROLEUM AND PETROLEUM PRODUCTS TO RHODESIA
REPORT WRITING
REPORTERS AND REPORTING — Africa
REPORTERS AND REPORTING — Canada
REPRESENTATION OF THE PEOPLE BILL 1980-81
REPRESENTATIVE GOVERNMENT AND REPRESENTATION
REPRESENTATIVE GOVERNMENT AND REPRESENTATION — Case studies
REPRESENTATIVE GCVERNMENT AND REPRESENTATION — Congresses
REPRESENTATIVE GOVERNMENT AND REPRESENTATION — Europe, Southern — Case studies
REPRESENTATIVE GOVERNMENT AND REPRESENTATION — Finland
REPRESENTATIVE GOVERNMENT AND REPRESENTATION — Germany
REPRESENTATIVE GOVERNMENT AND REPRESENTATION — Great Britain

REPRESENTATIVE GOVERNMENT AND REPRESENTATION — Latin America — Case studies
REPRESENTATIVE GOVERNMENT AND REPRESENTATION — Spain — Congresses
REPRESENTATIVE GOVERNMENT AND REPRESENTATION — United States
REPRESENTATIVE GOVERNMENT AND REPRESENTATION — Venezuela
REPRESENTATIVE GOVERNMENT AND REPRESENTATION — Wales
REPRODUCTION
REPUBLIC
REPUBLIC. BOOK 1
REPUBLICAN PARTY (U.S. : 1854-)
REPUBLICANISM — Ireland
REPUBLICANISM — Spain — History
REPUBLICANISM — Spain — Catalonia
REPUBLICANISM — Spain — Malaga
RESEARCH
RESEARCH — Government policy — Great Britain
RESEARCH — Methodology
RESEARCH — Methodology — Handbooks
RESEARCH — Methods — Handbooks
RESEARCH — Social aspects
RESEARCH — Australia
RESEARCH — European Economic Community countries
RESEARCH — Germany (West)
RESEARCH — Great Britain
RESEARCH — Great Britain — Finance
RESEARCH — Organisation for Economic Co-operation and Development countries — Evaluation
RESEARCH — Taiwan — Bibliography
RESEARCH — United States — Finance
RESEARCH AND DEVELOPMENT CONTRACTS — Developing countries
RESEARCH AND DEVELOPMENT CONTRACTS — United States
RESEARCH GRANTS — Europe
RESEARCH GRANTS — Europe — Handbooks, manuals, etc.
RESEARCH, INDUSTRIAL — Government policy — Australia
RESEARCH, INDUSTRIAL — Australia
RESEARCH, INDUSTRIAL — Australia — Public opinion
RESEARCH, INDUSTRIAL — European Economic Community countries — Finance — Directories
RESEARCH, INDUSTRIAL — Great Britain — Finance
RESEARCH, INDUSTRIAL — Soviet Union
RESEARCH, INDUSTRIES — United States
RESEARCH INSTITUTES — United States — History
RESEARCH LIBRARIES — Evaluation — Statistical methods
RESEARCH LIBRARIES — Finance
RESEARCH PARKS
RESEARCHOFF. PUBNS. — European Economic Community countries 986
RESERVOIRS — Environmental aspects — England
RESIDENTIAL MOBILITY — England — Bristol (Avon)
RESIDENTIAL MOBILITY — United States
RESOURCE ALLOCATION
RESOURCE RECOVERY FACILITIES — Europe
RESPECT FOR PERSONS
RESPIRATORY ORGANS — Diseases — Great Britain — Mortality
RESPONSIBILITY
RESTAURANTS, LUNCH ROOMS, ETC. — Netherlands — Statistics
RESTAURANTS, LUNCH ROOMS, ETC. — Singapore — Statistics
RESTITUTION — Great Britain
RESTRAINT OF TRADE
RESTRAINT OF TRADE — Canada
RESTRAINT OF TRADE — England
RESTRAINT OF TRADE — European Economic Community countries
RETAIL TRADE — Congresses
RETAIL TRADE — Canada — Statistics
RETAIL TRADE — European Economic Community countries — Employees
RETAIL TRADE — European Economic Community Countries — Statistics
RETAIL TRADE — Fiji — Statistics
RETAIL TRADE — France
RETAIL TRADE — Great Britain
RETAIL TRADE — Great Britain — Statistics
RETAIL TRADE — Italy — Statistics
RETAIL TRADE — Nigeria — Statistics
RETAIL TRADE — Singapore — Statistics
RETAIL TRADE — Thailand — Statistics
RETAIL TRADE — United States — Foreign ownership
RETIREMENT
RETIREMENT — Bibliography
RETIREMENT — Denmark
RETIREMENT — Great Britain
RETIREMENT — Netherlands
RETIREMENT AGE — Legal status, laws, etc. — Great Britain
RETIREMENT COMMUNITIES — California — Los Angeles — Case studies
RETIREMENT INCOME — Germany (West)
RETIREMENT INCOME — Great Britain
RETIREMENT INCOME — United States
RÉUNION
REUTERS — History
REUTERSHAN, PAUL — Trials, litigation, etc
REUTHER, WALTER
REVENUE — Belgium
REVENUE — Canada
REVERSE DISCRIMINATION — Great Britain
REVIEW OF THE PUBLIC ORDER ACT 1936 AND RELATED LEGISLATION
REVIEW OF THE PUBLIC UTILITIES STREET WORKS ACT 1950
REVOLUČNÍ ODBOROVÉ HNUTI
REVOLUTIONISTS — Mexico
REVOLUTIONISTS — Algeria — Biography
REVOLUTIONISTS — Angola — Biography
REVOLUTIONISTS — Colombia — History — 20th century
REVOLUTIONISTS — Cuba — 19th Century — Biography
REVOLUTIONISTS — England — History — 17th century
REVOLUTIONISTS — Germany — Biography
REVOLUTIONISTS — India — Biography
REVOLUTIONISTS — Ireland — Biography
REVOLUTIONISTS — Latin America — History
REVOLUTIONISTS — Nigeria, Northern — Biography
REVOLUTIONISTS — Russian S.F.S.R. — Leningrad
REVOLUTIONISTS — Russian S.F.S.R. — Siberia
REVOLUTIONISTS — Soviet Union
REVOLUTIONISTS — Soviet Union — Bibliography
REVOLUTIONISTS — Soviet Union — Biography
REVOLUTIONISTS — Soviet Union — History
REVOLUTIONISTS — Soviet Union — History — 19th century
REVOLUTIONS
REVOLUTIONS — Cross-cultural studies — Congresses
REVOLUTIONS — History
REVOLUTIONS — History — 20th century
REVOLUTIONS — Religious aspects — Christianity
REVOLUTIONS — Europe — History
REVOLUTIONS — Latin America
REVOLUTIONS — Mexico — History
REVOLUTIONS — Spain — History
REVOLUTIONS — Spain — Jaca
REYKJAVIK SUMMIT (1986)
REYKJAVIK SUMMIT MEETING (1986 : Reykjavik)
RHETORIC
RHETORIC — Political aspects — United States
RHINELAND (GERMANY) — History
RHINELAND (GERMANY) — History — 20th century — Bibliography
RHINELAND (GERMANY) — Politics and government — History
RHODESIA — Description and travel
RHODESIA — Politics and government
RHODESIA, SOUTHERN — History — 1965-
RHODESIA, SOUTHERN — Politics and government — 1966-
RHÔNE-ALPES (FRANCE) — Industries — Statistics
RIBBON INDUSTRY — Switzerland — Basel — History
RICARDO, DAVID
RICE — Taiwan — Linear programming
RICE — Taiwan — Marketing
RICE TRADE — Asia, Southeastern
RICE TRADE — East Asia
RICE TRADE — Georgia — History
RICE TRADE — Ghana
RICHMOND, Sir HERBERT
RICKETS — Prevention
RIEBEN, HENRI
RIEL, LOUIS
RIEL REBELLION — Collected works
RIEL REBELLION, 1885
RIEL REBELLION 1885 — Collected works
RIGHT AND LEFT (PHILOSOPHY)
RIGHT AND LEFT (POLITICAL SCIENCE)
RIGHT AND LEFT (POLITICAL SCIENCE) — Documentation — Germany (West)
RIGHT AND LEFT (POLITICAL SCIENCE) — Periodicals — Bibliography
RIGHT OF PROPERTY
RIGHT OF PROPERTY — United States
RIGHT TO COUNSEL — United States
RIGHT TO DIE
RIGHT TO DIE — Law and legislation — United States
RIGHT TO LABOR — France
RIGHT TO LIFE PARTY
RIGHTS (PHILOSOPHY)
RIMATARA (AUSTRAL ISLANDS) — Population — Statistics
RIO DE LA PLATA REGION (ARGENTINA AND URUGUAY — History
RIO TINTO COMPANY — History — 19th century
RIOTS
RIOTS — Colombia — Bogotá
RIOTS — England
RIOTS — Great Britain
RIOTS — Great Britain — Bibliography
RIOTS — Great Britain — Information Services
RIOTS — Peru — History — 20th century
RISK
RISK — Congresses
RISK — Mathematical models
RISK (INSURANCE) — Congresses
RISK (INSURANCE) — United States
RISK MANAGEMENT
RISK PERCEPTION — Social aspects
RITCHIE
RITES AND CEREMONIES
RITES AND CEREMONIES — Addresses, essays, lectures
RITES AND CEREMONIES — Congresses
RITES AND CEREMONIES — Hawaii

RITES AND CEREMONIES — New Guinea
RIVAS, ANA MARÍA CASTILLO See Castillo Rivas, Ana María
RIVERS — Great Britain
R.J. REYNOLDS INDUSTRIES — History
ROAD CONSTRUCTION — Government policy — Great Britain
ROAD CONSTRUCTION — Great Britain — Bibliography
ROAD METERS — Calibration
ROADS — Riding qualities — Measurement
ROADS — Riding qualities — Testing
ROADS — England — Surrey
ROADS — Great Britain
ROADS — Great Britain — Maintenance and Repair — Bibliography
ROADS — Great Britain — Management
ROADS — Great Britain — Safety measures — Congresses
ROADS — Scotland — Fife — History
ROADS — Spain — History
ROBARTS, JOHN P.
ROBBERY — England
ROBBERY — Great Britain
ROBESPIERRE, MAXIMILIEN
ROBOTICS — Great Britain — Industrial applications
ROBOTS, INDUSTRIAL
ROBSON, W. A., 1895-1980 — Bibliography
ROBUST STATISTICS
ROCKETS (ORDNANCE) — Government policy — Germany (West)
ROCKINGHAM WHIG FACTION
ROCKWELL, NORMAN
ROLE CONFLICT
ROLFE (Family)
ROLPH, C. H.
ROMANIA — Church History
ROMANIA — Commerce — Great Britain
ROMANIA — Economic conditions
ROMANIA — Foreign economic relations — Hungary
ROMANIA — History
ROMANIA — History — To 1711
ROMANIA — Politics and government
ROMANIA — Politics and government — 1914-1944
ROMANIA — Politics and government — 1944-
ROMANIA — Relations — Hungary — History
ROMANIA. Consiliul Dirigent
ROME — History
ROME — History — Republic, 265-30 B.C.
ROME — History — Empire, 284-476
ROME — History, Military
ROME — Social conditions
ROME — Social life and customs
ROME (ITALY) — Statistics
ROME&XHISTORY — Germanic Invasions, 3rd-6th centuries
ROMULO, CARLOS PEÑA
RONDA (SPAIN) — Social life and customs
ROOSEVELT, FRANKLIN D.
ROOSEVELT, FRANKLIN D
RÖSCH, AUGUSTIN
ROSEBERY, ARCHIBALD PHILIP PRIMROSE, Earl of
ROSENBERG, HILARY
RÖSRATH (GERMANY) — Politics and government
RÖSRATH (GERMANY) — Social conditions
ROSSENDALE (LANCASHIRE : DISTRICT) — Economic history
ROSSIISKAIA SOTSIAL-DEMOKRATICHESKAIA RABOCHAIA PARTIIA
ROSSIISKAIA SOTSIAL-DEMOKRATICHESKAIA RABOCHAIA PARTIIA — History
ROTE ARMEE FRAKTION
ROTHFELS, HANS
ROUSSEAU, JEAN-JACQUES — Contributions in philosophy of war
ROUSSEAU, JEAN-JACQUES — Contributions in political science
ROUSSEAU, JEAN-JACQUES — Contributions in sociology
ROUSSEAU, JEAN-JACQUES — Political and social views
ROUSSEAU, JEAN-JACQUES, 1712-1778 — Criticism and interpretation
ROVERE, RICHARD HALWORTH
ROY, GABRIELLE
ROYAL CANADIAN MOUNTED POLICE — History
ROYAL COLLEGE OF NURSING
ROYAL COMMISSION ON THE ECONOMIC UNION AND DEVELOPMENT PROSPECTS FOR CANADA
ROYAL EXCHANGE ASSURANCE
ROYAL INFIRMARY OF EDINBURGH — History
ROYAL ULSTER CONSTABULARY
ROYALISTS — France
RUBBER, ARTIFICIAL — History
RUBBER INDUSTRY AND TRADE — United States — History
RUDOLF II, Holy Roman Emperor
RUEFF, JACQUES
RUG AND CARPET INDUSTRY — Management — Case studies
RUHR (GERMANY: REGION) — History — French occupation, 1923-1925
RUHR (GERMANY: REGION) — Politics and government
RULE OF LAW
RULE OF LAW — Gaza Strip
RULE OF LAW — South Africa
RULE OF LAW — West Bank
RUPPIN, ARTHUR
RURAL CONDITIONS
RURAL DEVELOPMENT — Government policy — Australia
RURAL DEVELOPMENT — Congo (Brazzaville)
RURAL DEVELOPMENT
RURAL DEVELOPMENT — Addresses, essays, lectures
RURAL DEVELOPMENT — Bibliography
RURAL DEVELOPMENT — Congresses
RURAL DEVELOPMENT — Government policy — Great Britain
RURAL DEVELOPMENT — Social aspects — Great Britain
RURAL DEVELOPMENT — Statistical methods
RURAL DEVELOPMENT — Africa
RURAL DEVELOPMENT — Africa, Sub-Saharan
RURAL DEVELOPMENT — Alaska — Addresses, essays, lectures
RURAL DEVELOPMENT — Asia
RURAL DEVELOPMENT — Asia — Case studies
RURAL DEVELOPMENT — Asia — Citizen participation
RURAL DEVELOPMENT — Bangladesh
RURAL DEVELOPMENT — Botswana
RURAL DEVELOPMENT — Colombia
RURAL DEVELOPMENT — Developing countries
RURAL DEVELOPMENT — Egypt
RURAL DEVELOPMENT — England
RURAL DEVELOPMENT — Ethiopia
RURAL DEVELOPMENT — Ethiopia — Case studies
RURAL DEVELOPMENT — Europe
RURAL DEVELOPMENT — India
RURAL DEVELOPMENT — India — Punjab
RURAL DEVELOPMENT — Ireland
RURAL DEVELOPMENT — Kenya
RURAL DEVELOPMENT — Korea (South)
RURAL DEVELOPMENT — Nigeria — Congresses
RURAL DEVELOPMENT — Organisation for Economic Co-operation and Development
RURAL DEVELOPMENT — Pakistan
RURAL DEVELOPMENT — Scotland
RURAL DEVELOPMENT — Singapore
RURAL DEVELOPMENT — Sudan
RURAL DEVELOPMENT — Tanzania
RURAL DEVELOPMENT — Wales
RURAL DEVELOPMENT — Zimbabwe
RURAL DEVELOPMENT PROJECTS — Congresses
RURAL DEVELOPMENT PROJECTS — Evaluation — Statistical methods
RURAL DEVELOPMENT PROJECTS — Management — Statistical methods
RURAL DEVELOPMENT PROJECTS — Social aspects
RURAL DEVELOPMENT PROJECTS — Bangladesh
RURAL DEVELOPMENT PROJECTS — Developing countries
RURAL DEVELOPMENT PROJECTS — Developing countries — Management
RURAL DEVELOPMENT PROJECTS — Developing countries — Management — Case studies
RURAL DEVELOPMENT PROJECTS — Egypt
RURAL DEVELOPMENT PROJECTS — India
RURAL ELECTRIFICATION — Economic aspects
RURAL ELECTRIFICATION — Government policy
RURAL FAMILIES — Africa, Sub-Saharan
RURAL FAMILIES — Developing countries — Case studies
RURAL FAMILIES — Great Britain — Bibliography
RURAL FAMILIES — India — Maps
RURAL GEOGRAPHY
RURAL HEALTH — Nepal
RURAL HEALTH SERVICES — Planning — International cooperation
RURAL HEALTH SERVICES — Nepal
RURAL HEALTH SERVICES — Tanzania
RURAL HEALTH SERVICES — United States
RURAL POOR
RURAL POOR — Asia
RURAL POOR — Great Britain
RURAL POOR — India
RURAL POOR — India — Chakrabhavi
RURAL POOR — India — Gujarat
RURAL POOR — Kenya
RURAL POPULATION
RURAL POPULATION — Lesotho — Statistics
RURAL PORT — India — Government policy
RURAL SCHOOLS — Developing countries
RURAL SCHOOLS — Virginia — History — 19th century
RURAL SCHOOLS — Virginia — History — 20th century
RURAL TRANSIT — Europe
RURAL-URBAN MIGRATION — Asia, Southeastern — Congresses
RURAL-URBAN MIGRATION — Bolivia — Santa Cruz (Dept.) — Case studies
RURAL-URBAN MIGRATION — Caribbean Area
RURAL-URBAN MIGRATION — Ethiopia — Bagëmder — Case studies
RURAL-URBAN MIGRATION — Europe
RURAL-URBAN MIGRATION — Middle East — History — Congresses
RURAL-URBAN MIGRATION — Russian S.F.S.R — Moscow — History
RURAL-URBAN MIGRATION — Thailand
RURAL WOMEN — Africa
RURAL WOMEN — Asia — Congresses
RURAL WOMEN — Developing countries — Economic conditions
RURAL WOMEN — Developing countries — Social conditions
RURAL WOMEN — Iowa — Case studies

RURAL WOMEN — Middle Atlantic States — History
RURAL WOMEN — United States — Case studies
RURUTU (AUSTRAL ISLANDS) — Population — Statistics
RUSKIN, JOHN — Influence
RUSSELL, BERTRAND
RUSSIA — Diplomatic and consular service
RUSSIA — Foreign relations — 1917-1945
RUSSIA — Foreign relations — Persian Gulf region
RUSSIA — Politics and government
RUSSIA — Politics and government — 19th century
RUSSIA — Politics and government — 20th century
RUSSIA — Politics and government — 1917-
RUSSIA. Gosudarstvennaia duma. 1st, 1906-1907
RUSSIA. Gosudarstvennaia duma. 4th, 1912-1917
RUSSIA (1923- U.S.S.R.). Ob'edirennoe gosudarstvennoe politicheskoe upravlenie
RUSSIAN DIARIES — Bibliography
RUSSIAN LITERATURE — History and criticism — 19th century
RUSSIAN LITERATURE — 20th century — History and criticism
RUSSIAN PERIODICALS — Indexes
RUSSIAN S.F.S.R. — Officials and employees — Biography — Directories
RUSSIANS — Foreign countries — Political activity
RUSSIANS — Alaska — History
RUSSIANS — Europe
RUSSIANS — Latvia
RUSSIANS — United States
RUSSKAIA OSVOBODITEL'NAIA ARMIIA — History
RUSSO-JAPANESE WAR, 1904-1905 — Diplomatic history
RUSSO-POLISH WAR, 1919-1920 — Diplomatic history
RUTKOWSKI, JAN
RYUKYU ISLANDS — Social life and customs
S. G. WARBURG & CO.
SAARLAND (GERMANY) — History — 20th century
SAARLAND (GERMANY) — Politics and government
SAARLAND (GERMANY) — Statistics
SABBATHAIANS
SACRIFICE
SACRIFICE — Hinduism
SAFETY EDUCATION, INDUSTRIAL
SAFETY REGULATIONS — Economic aspects — Congresses
SAILORS' UNION OF THE PACIFIC — History
SAINT ÉTIENNE (LOIRE, FRANCE) — Politics and government
SAINT JOHN (NEW BRUNSWICK) — History
SAINT JOHN (V.I.) — Race relations
SAINT KITTS-NEVIS — Economic conditions
SAINT LUCIA — Constitution
SAINT LUCIA — Economic conditions
SAINT VINCENT AND THE GRENADINES — Economic conditions
SAINT VINCENT AND THE GRENADINES — Economic policy
SAIONJI, KINMOCHI, Prince
SAKATA, TOSHIBOMI
SALES — England
SALES — Great Britain
SALES — Great Britain — Cases
SALES, CONDITIONAL — Canada
SALES TAX — Denmark
SALINE WATER CONVERSION — Developing countries
SALISBURY, ROBERT ARTHUR TALBOT GASCOYNE-CECIL, Marquess of
SALMON-FISHERIES — Atlantic Ocean — Congresses
SALMON INDUSTRY — United States — Pacific States
SALT INDUSTRY AND TRADE — Mexico — History
SALT INDUSTRY AND TRADE — Taiwan
SALTYKOV, M. E.
SALVAGE (WASTE, ETC.)
SALVAGE (WASTE, ETC.) — Developing countries
SALVATION ARMY. Men's Social Service Department — History
SAMBIA (PAPUA NEW GUINEA PEOPLE)
SAMBO (FICTITIOUS CHARACTER)
SAMOANS — Anthropometry
SAMOANS — Health and hygiene
SAMPLING (STATISTICS)
SAN ANTONIO (TEX.) — Politics and government — Addresses, essays, lectures
SAN FERNANDO (TRINIDAD AND TOBAGO) — Social conditions
SAN FRANCISCO (CALIF.) — Economic conditions
SAN FRANCISCO (CALIF.) — Politics and government
SAN FRANCISCO (CALIF.) — Social conditions
SAN MARINO — Census, 1976
SAN MARINO — Industries — Statistics
SAN MARINO — Population — Statistics
SAN MARINO — Social conditions — Statistics
SAN MARINO — Statistics
SANATORIUMS — Soviet Union
SANCTIONS (INTERNATIONAL LAW)
SANCTIONS (INTERNATIONAL LAW) — Bibliography
SANCTIONS (LAW)
SANCTUARY MOVEMENT
SANDINO, AUGUSTO CÉSAR — Political and social views
SANDINO, AUGUSTO CÉSAR — 1895-1934
SANDOZ, EDOUARD
SANDOZ AG (Basel)
SANE, INC — History
SANGER, MARGARET
SANGER, MARGARET — Bibliography
SANITARY ENGINEERING — Study and teaching (Higher) — Europe
SANITARY ENGINEERS — Training of — Europe
SANITATION — Statistics
SANITATION ENGINEERING
SANTA CATARINA (BRAZIL)
SÃO PAULO (BRAZIL : STATE) — Economic conditions
SÃO PEDRO (RIO GRANDE DO SUL, BRAZIL) — History
SAPINY (AFRICAN PEOPLE)
SARAWAK (MALAYSIA) — Population — Statistics
SAROAKO (INDONESIA) — Economic conditions
SAROAKO (INDONESIA) — Social conditions
SARTRE, JEAN PAUL. Critique de la raison dialectique. 1, Théorie des ensembles pratiques
SARTRE, JEAN-PAUL
SARTRE, JEAN PAUL — Contributions in political science
SARTRE, JEAN PAUL, 1905-1980
SAS (COMPUTER SYSTEM) — Handbooks, manuals, etc
SATURDAY EVENING POST — Illustrations
SAUDI ARABIA — Economic conditions
SAUDI ARABIA — Economic policy
SAUDI ARABIA — Foreign relations
SAUDI ARABIA — Foreign relations — Egypt
SAUDI ARABIA — Politics and government
SAUDI ARABIA — Social policy
SAUVÉ, JEANNE, 1922-
SAVEZ KOMUNISTA JUGOSLAVIJE
SAVEZ KOMUNISTA JUGOSLAVIJE — Congresses
SAVEZ KOMUNISTA JUGOSLAVIJE — History
SAVIGNY, FRIEDRICH KARL VON, 1779-1861
SAVIMBI, JONAS
SAVIMBI, JONAS MALHEIRO
SAVING AND INVESTMENT — Addresses, essays, lectures
SAVING AND INVESTMENT — Taxation — United States
SAVING AND INVESTMENT — Bangladesh
SAVING AND INVESTMENT — China — History
SAVING AND INVESTMENT — Denmark
SAVING AND INVESTMENT — Europe
SAVING AND INVESTMENT — Great Britain
SAVING AND INVESTMENT — Japan
SAVING AND INVESTMENT — Nigeria
SAVING AND INVESTMENT — Taiwan
SAVING AND INVESTMENT — United States
SAVING AND INVESTMENT — United States — Addresses, essays, lectures
SAVING AND INVESTMENT — United States — Congresses
SAVING AND INVESTMENT — Uruguay — History
SAVING AND THRIFT
SAVING AND THRIFT — Italy
SAVING SNF THRIFT — Developing countries
SAVINGS-BANKS — Europe
SCALES, JUNIUS IRVING
SCANDINAVIA — Emigration and immigration — History — 19th century
SCANDINAVIA — Foreign economic relations — European Economic Community countries
SCANDINAVIA — Foreign relations — Great Britain
SCANDINAVIA — Military relations — Soviet Union
SCANDINAVIA — National security
SCANDINAVIA — Politics and government
SCANDINAVIA — Social conditions
SCANDINAVIA — Social policy
SCANDINAVIA — Strategic aspects
SCHACHT, JOSEPH. Origins of Muhammadan jurisprudence
SCHEDULING (MANAGEMENT)
SCHELLING, CEES
SCHELSKY, HELMUT
SCHILLER, HERBERT I.
SCHIZOPHRENIA — Treatment
SCHIZOPHRENIA — Treatment — Economic aspects
SCHIZOPHRENIA — Treatment — Political aspects
SCHLESWIG-HOLSTEIN (GERMANY) — History
SCHLESWIG-HOLSTEIN (GERMANY) — Social conditions
SCHMITT, CARL
SCHOLARLY PUBLISHING — Technological innovations
SCHOLARLY PUBLISHING — Asia, Southeastern — Congresses
SCHOLARS, JEWISH — United States — Biography
SCHOLARSHIPS — Directories
SCHOOL CHILDREN — Food — Great Britain
SCHOOL CHILDREN — Denmark — Recreation
SCHOOL EMPLOYEES — Salaries, pensions, etc. — Norway — Statistics
SCHOOL FACILITIES — Extended use
SCHOOL INTEGRATION — California — San Francisco

SCHOOL INTEGRATION — Massachusetts — Boston
SCHOOL INTEGRATION — Tennessee — Nashville — History
SCHOOL INTEGRATION — United States — Case studies
SCHOOL LANDS — United States — History
SCHOOL MANAGEMENT AND ORGANISATION — England
SCHOOL MANAGEMENT AND ORGANIZATION — Decision making
SCHOOL MANAGEMENT AND ORGANIZATION — California — San Francisco
SCHOOL MANAGEMENT AND ORGANIZATION — Great Britain
SCHOOL MANAGEMENT AND ORGANIZATION — Great Britain — History — 20th century
SCHOOL MANAGEMENT AND ORGANIZATION — Japan
SCHOOL MANAGEMENT AND ORGANIZATION — Quebec (Province)
SCHOOL MANAGEMENT AND ORGANIZATION — United States
SCHOOL MANAGEMENT AND ORGANIZATION — Wales — Cardiff (South Glamorgan) — History — 20th century
SCHOOLS — Great Britain — Social aspects
SCHOOLS — United States
SCHOOLS OF SOCIOLOGY
SCHUMAN, ROBERT
SCHUMPETER, JOSEPH ALOIS — Congresses
SCHURZ, CARL
SCHÜTZ, ALFRED — Correspondence
SCHWARZHAUPT, ELISABETH
SCHWENKE, OLAF
SCIENCE
SCIENCE — Bibliography
SCIENCE — History
SCIENCE — History — 19th century
SCIENCE — International cooperation
SCIENCE — Methodology
SCIENCE — Methodology — History
SCIENCE — Periodicals
SCIENCE — Philosophy
SCIENCE — Philosophy — History
SCIENCE — Philosophy — History — 20th century
SCIENCE — Social aspects
SCIENCE — Social aspects — Great Britain
SCIENCE — Social aspects — United States
SCIENCE — Social aspects — United States — Addresses, essays, lectures
SCIENCE — Study and teaching (Higher)
SCIENCE — Great Britain
SCIENCE — Great Britain — History — 19th century
SCIENCE — Great Britain — History — 20th century
SCIENCE — Soviet Union — History — 20th century
SCIENCE — United States — History
SCIENCE AND CIVILIZATION
SCIENCE AND INDUSTRY — Soviet Union
SCIENCE AND STATE
SCIENCE AND STATE — Australia
SCIENCE AND STATE — European Economic Community countries
SCIENCE AND STATE — Finland
SCIENCE AND STATE — Great Britain
SCIENCE AND STATE — Netherlands
SCIENCE AND STATE — Portugal
SCIENCE AND STATE — Sweden
SCIENCE NEWS
SCIENTISTS, GERMAN
SCIENTISTS IN GOVERNMENT
SCIENTOLOGY
SCOTLAND — Antiquities
SCOTLAND — Economic conditions
SCOTLAND — Economic conditions — 1973-
SCOTLAND — Emigration and immigration
SCOTLAND — History — 16th century
SCOTLAND — History — James VI, 1567-1625
SCOTLAND — History — 17th century
SCOTLAND — History — Charles I, 1625-1649
SCOTLAND — History — 18th century
SCOTLAND — Industries
SCOTLAND — Learned institutions and societies
SCOTLAND — Nobility
SCOTLAND — Politics and government
SCOTLAND — Politics and government — 18th century
SCOTLAND — Politics and government — 19th century
SCOTLAND — Politics and government — 20th century
SCOTLAND — Rural conditions
SCOTLAND — Social conditions
SCOTLAND — Social conditions — 20th century
SCOTLAND — Social life and customs
SCOTS — Australia — History — 19th century
SCOTS IN CANADA
SCOTT, DUNCAN CAMPBELL, 1862-1947
SCOTT, JEANNINE B
SCOTTISH EQUITABLE LIFE ASSURANCE SOCIETY
SCOTTISH NATIONAL PARTY
SCOTTISH TRADES UNION CONGRESS — History
SDP/LIBERAL ALLIANCE
SDP LIBERAL ALLIANCE
SDP-LIBERAL ALLIANCE
SDP/LIBERAL ALLIANCE
SEA ISLANDS — History
SEA LEVEL
SEA-POWER — North Atlantic Ocean
SEAFARERS' INTERNATIONAL UNION OF NORTH AMERICA
SEASONAL VARIATIONS — Mathematical models
SECESSION
SECONDAT, CHARLES DE, baron de Montesquieu See Montesquieu, Charles de Secondat, baron de
SECRET SERVICE — Great Britain
SECRET SERVICE — Great Britain — History — 20th century
SECRET SERVICE — Soviet Union — History — 20th century
SECRET SOCIETIES — Italy
SECTS
SECTS — Congresses
SECTS — Law and legislation — United States
SECTS — Great Britain
SECTS — United States
SECULARISM
SECURITIES
SECURITIES — Canada
SECURITIES — United States
SECURITY CLASSIFICATION (GOVERNMENT DOCUMENTS) — United States
SECURITY, INTERNATIONAL
SECURITY, INTERNATIONAL — Congresses
SECURITY, INTERNATIONAL — History — 20th century
SECURITY, INTERNATIONAL — Moral and ethical aspects
SECURITY (PSYCHOLOGY)
SEED INDUSTRY AND TRADE — Argentina
SEGREGATION — South Africa
SEGREGATION — South Africa — History
SEGREGATION IN EDUCATION — Law and legislation — Louisiana — History
SEGREGATION IN EDUCATION — Law and legislation — United States — History
SEGREGATION IN TRANSPORTATION — Law and legislation — Louisiana — History
SEGREGATION IN TRANSPORTATION — Law and legislation — United States — History
SEIGNIORIAL TENURE — Québec (Province) — Montréal (Region) — History
SEISMOLOGY — France
SELANGOR (MALAYSIA) — Population — Statistics
SELECTIVITY (PSYCHOLOGY) — Congresses
SELF
SELF — Addresses, essays, lectures
SELF-ACTUALIZATION (PSYCHOLOGY)
SELF-CONSCIOUSNESS — History — Addresses, essays, lectures
SELF-DEFENSE (INTERNATIONAL LAW)
SELF-DETERMINATION, NATIONAL
SELF-DETERMINATION, NATIONAL — Addresses, essays, lectures
SELF-DETERMINATION, NATIONAL — Bibliography
SELF-DETERMINATION, NATIONAL — Western Sahara
SELF-EMPLOYED — European Economic Community countries
SELF-EMPLOYED — Great Britain
SELF-GOVERNMENT IN EDUCATION — United States — History
SELF HELP GROUPS — Ecuador — Guayaquil
SELF-HELP GROUPS — Europe
SELF-HELP GROUPS — United States
SELF-HELP HOUSING — Botswana
SELF-PERCEPTION
SELF (PHILOSOPHY)
SELF (PHILOSOPHY) — History — Addresses, essays, lectures
SELF (PHILOSOPHY) — History — 20th century
SELF-PRESENTATION
SELF-REALIZATION
SELLING — Automobiles — Congresses
SEMANTICS
SEMANTICS (LAW)
SEMANTICS (PHILOSOPHY)
SEMICONDUCTOR INDUSTRY — Europe
SEMICONDUCTOR INDUSTRY — Japan
SEMICONDUCTOR INDUSTRY — United States
SEMINAR ON ECONOMIC MODELLING IN NEW ZEALAND (1984 : Wellington)
SEMINAR ON INDUSTRIAL DEMOCRACY AND EMPLOYEE PARTICIPATION (1984 : Melbourne)
SEMIOTICS
SEMIOTICS — Social aspects
SENEGAL — History — Dictionaries
SENEGAL — Population — Statistics — Evaluation
SENEGAL — Relations — United States
SENEGALESE — Attitudes
SENILE DEMENTIA — Australia
SENILE DEMENTIA — Great Britain
SENTENCES (CRIMINAL PROCEDURE) — Legal status, laws, etc — Great Britain
SENTENCES (CRIMINAL PROCEDURE) — England
SENTENCES (CRIMINAL PROCEDURE) — Great Britain
SENTENCES (CRIMINAL PROCEDURE) — United States
SENUFO (AFRICAN PEOPLE)
SEPARATE PROPERTY — United States — History
SEPARATION OF POWERS — India
SEPARATION OF POWERS — United States
SEPARATION (PSYCHOLOGY)
SERBIA — History — 1945-
SERFDOM — Soviet Union
SERFDOM — Soviet Union — History
SERIAL PUBLICATIONS — Scotland — Bibliography

SERRA I MORET, MANUEL
SERRA Y MORET, MANUEL
SERRANO SUÑER, RAMÓN
SERVANTS — England — Liverpool (Merseyside)
SERVICE B
SERVICE INDUSTRIES
SERVICE INDUSTRIES — Government policy — Congresses
SERVICE INDUSTRIES — International cooperation — Congresses
SERVICE INDUSTRIES — Law and legislation — European Economic Community countries
SERVICE INDUSTRIES — Asia, Southeastern
SERVICE INDUSTRIES — Denmark
SERVICE INDUSTRIES — East Asia
SERVICE INDUSTRIES — Europe — Technological innovations — Bibliography
SERVICE INDUSTRIES — France — Statistics
SERVICE INDUSTRIES — Great Britain — Forecasting
SERVICE INDUSTRIES — Italy — Statistics
SERVICE INDUSTRIES — London
SERVICE INDUSTRIES — Organisation for Economic Co-operation and Development countries — Statistics — Measurement
SERVICE INDUSTRIES — Singapore — Statistics
SERVICE INDUSTRIES — Thailand — Statistics
SERVICE INDUSTRIES — Togo — Statistics
SERVICE INDUSTRIES — United States
SERVICE INDUSTRIES — United States — Communication systems — Congresses
SERVICE INDUSTRIES WORKERS — Europe — Effect of technological innovations on — Bibliography
SERVICE INDUSTRIES WORKERS — Great Britain — Supply and demand — Forecasting
SETTLEMENTS (LAW) — England
SEVEN YEARS' WAR, 1756-1763
SEVEN YEARS' WAR, 1756-1763 — Diplomatic history
SEVEN YEARS' WAR, 1756-1763 — Economic aspects — France
SEVERN, RIVER, ESTUARY (ENGLAND AND WALES) — Bridges
SEVERN TUNNEL (ENGLAND) AND WALES
SEVILLE (SPAIN) — History — 20th century
SEWAGE DISPOSAL — England — South East
SEWAGE IRRIGATION — Hygienic aspects — Developing countries
SEX
SEX — Addresses, essays, lectures
SEX — Religious aspects — Unification Church
SEX — Statistics
SEX AND LAW — Europe — Congresses
SEX (BIOLOGY)
SEX CRIMES — United States
SEX CUSTOMS
SEX CUSTOMS — Cross-cultural studies
SEX CUSTOMS — Barbados
SEX CUSTOMS — Canada
SEX CUSTOMS — Europe — History
SEX CUSTOMS — Germany — Case studies
SEX CUSTOMS — Great Britain — Case studies
SEX CUSTOMS — Great Britain — History — Sources
SEX CUSTOMS — Papua New Guinea
SEX CUSTOMS — Rome
SEX CUSTOMS — United States
SEX DIFFERENCES
SEX DIFFERENCES — Addresses, essays, lectures
SEX DIFFERENCES IN EDUCATION
SEX DIFFERENCES IN EDUCATION — Great Britain
SEX DIFFERENCES (PSYCHOLOGY)
SEX DISCRIMINATION — Law and legislation — South Australia
SEX DISCRIMINATION — Law and legislation — United States
SEX DISCRIMINATION AGAINST WOMEN
SEX DISCRIMINATION AGAINST WOMEN — Cross-cultural studies
SEX DISCRIMINATION AGAINST WOMEN — Law and legislation — Great Britain
SEX DISCRIMINATION AGAINST WOMEN — Law and legislation — United States
SEX DISCRIMINATION AGAINST WOMEN — European Economic Community countries
SEX DISCRIMINATION AGAINST WOMEN — Great Britain
SEX DISCRIMINATION AGAINST WOMEN — Great Britain — Statistics
SEX DISCRIMINATION BILL 1985-86
SEX DISCRIMINATION IN CRIMINAL JUSTICE ADMINISTRATION — United States
SEX DISCRIMINATION IN EDUCATION — Great Britain
SEX DISCRIMINATION IN EMPLOYMENT
SEX DISCRIMINATION IN EMPLOYMENT — Law and legislation — Great Britain
SEX DISCRIMINATION IN EMPLOYMENT — Canada
SEX DISCRIMINATION IN EMPLOYMENT — Cyprus
SEX DISCRIMINATION IN EMPLOYMENT — Developing countries
SEX DISCRIMINATION IN EMPLOYMENT — Great Britain
SEX DISCRIMINATION IN EMPLOYMENT — Great Britain — History
SEX DISCRIMINATION IN EMPLOYMENT — Palestine
SEX DISCRIMINATION IN EMPLOYMENT — United States
SEX DISCRIMINATION IN EMPOLYMENT — United States — History
SEX IN TELEVISION
SEX INSTRUCTION FOR CHILDREN — Great Britain
SEX OF CHILDREN, PARENTAL PREFERENCES FOR
SEX OFFENSES
SEX ORIENTED BUSINESSES — Law and legislation — England
SEX PRESELECTION
SEX (PSYCHOLOGY)
SEX ROLE
SEX ROLE — Addresses, essays, lectures
SEX ROLE — Case studies
SEX ROLE — Brazil
SEX ROLE — Denmark
SEX ROLE — Developing countries — Case studies
SEX ROLE — Great Britain — Case studies
SEX ROLE — Greece
SEX ROLE — Papua New Guinea
SEX ROLE — United States
SEX ROLE IN CHILDREN — Longitudinal studies
SEX ROLE IN THE WORK ENVIRONMENT
SEX ROLE IN THE WORK ENVIRONMENT — United States
SEX ROLES
SEX ROLES — Public opinion
SEX ROLEWOMEN — Developing countries 976/3 — Developing countries — Social conditions
SEXISM
SEXISM — Australia
SEXISM — Mexico
SEXISM — U.S
SEXISM IN LANGUAGE
SEXISM IN TEXTBOOKS
SEXUAL BEHAVIOR IN ANIMALS
SEXUAL BEHAVIOR SURVEYS — Caribbean Area
SEXUAL CUSTOMS — Caribbean Area
SEXUAL DEVIATION
SEXUAL DISORDERS — Addresses, essays, lectures
SEXUAL DIVISION OF LABOR
SEXUAL DIVISION OF LABOR — Developing countries
SEXUAL DIVISION OF LABOR — England
SEXUAL DIVISION OF LABOR — France — Auffay — History
SEXUAL DIVISION OF LABOR — Great Britain — History
SEXUAL DIVISION OF LABOR — United States
SEXUAL ETHICS — Addresses, essays, lectures
SEXUAL ETHICS — Canada
SEXUAL ETHICS — Europe — History
SEXUAL INTERCOURSE
SEXUALLY ABUSED CHILDREN
SEXUALLY ABUSED CHILDREN — Case studies
SEXUALLY TRANSMITTED DISEASES — Study and teaching — Great Britain
SEYCHELLES — Appropriations and expenditures — Statistics
SEYCHELLES — Economic policy
SEYCHELLES — Population
SEYCHELLES — Population — Statistics
SEYCHELLES — Social conditions (— 1976)
SEYCHELLES — Social policy
SEYN, F. A.
SH'I'AH — History — 20th century
SH'I'AH — Near East — History
SHAKERS — United States
SHAKESPEARE, WILLIAM. Hamlet
SHAMANISM — Korea (South)
SHAMANS — Korea (South)
SHAME — Social aspects — Melanesia
SHANGHAI (CHINA) — Economic conditions
SHARED HOUSING — Great Britain
SHATT AL'-ARAB RIVER (IRAQ AND IRAN)
SHAW, BERNARD
SHAYKH AL-ISLÁM — Turkey
SHEEP BREEDING — Australia — History
SHEFFIELD (SOUTH YORKSHIRE) — Economic conditions
SHEFFIELD (SOUTH YORKSHIRE) — Economic policy
SHEFFIELD (SOUTH YORKSHIRE) — Social conditions
SHEFFIELD (SOUTH YORKSHIRE) — Social policy
SHELTER
SHENZHEN (CHINA) — Economic policy
SHERPAS — Social life and customs
SHETLAND ISLANDS — Historical geography
SHIFT SYSTEMS
SHIFT SYSTEMS — Bibliography
SHIFT SYSTEMS — Effect of technological innovations on
SHIFTING CULTIVATION — Philippines — Mindoro
SHIMAMURA, HŌGETSU
SHIPBUILDING — Employees
SHIPBUILDING INDUSTRY — Safety regulations — Great Britain
SHIPBUILDING INDUSTRY — Europe
SHIPBUILDING INDUSTRY — Great Britain
SHIPBUILDING INDUSTRY — Sweden
SHIPBUILDING INDUSTRY — United States

SHIPHAM (SOMERSET) — Social conditions
SHIPMENT OF GOODS — Australia — Costs
SHIPMENT OF GOODS — Canada — Costs
SHIPPING
SHIPPING — Argentina — Statistics
SHIPPING — Asia, Southeastern
SHIPPING — Cameroon — Statistics
SHIPPING — Canada — Statistics
SHIPPING — France
SHIPPING — Pacific States
SHIPPING — Soviet Union
SHIPPING — Wales — Cardiff
SHIPPING CONFERENCE — History
SHIPPING CONFERENCES — Law and legislation
SHIPPING CONFERENCES — Law and legislation — United States
SHIPS — Cargo
SHIPS — Maintenance and repair — Safety regulations — Great Britain
SHIPS — Safety regulations
SHIPS — Safety regulations — Congresses
SHIPS — Great Britain — Nationality — Statistics
SHIPS — Greece — Scrapping
SHIPYARDS — British Columbia — History
SHIPYARDS — Northern Ireland — Belfast — History
SHOPLIFTING — England
SHOPPING — England — Devon
SHOPPING — England — East Sussex
SHOPPING — England — Exeter (Devon)
SHOPPING — Great Britain
SHOPPING CENTERS — England — Chelmsford (Essex)
SHOPPING CENTERS — Singapore
SHOPS BILL 1980-81
SHOPS BILL 1985-86
SHORE PROTECTION — United States — Congresses
SHORT-TERM COUNSELING
SHORT-TERM MEMORY
SHORTIS, VALENTINE FRANCIS CUTHBERT
SHOTTON (CLWYD) — Industries — History
SHROPSHIRE — Rural conditions
SIBERIA (R.S.F.S.R.) — Economic conditions
SIBERIA (R.S.F.S.R.) — Historiography
SIBERIA (R.S.F.S.R.) — History — 1904-1914
SIBERIA (R.S.F.S.R.) — Rural conditions
SIBSAGAR DISTRICT (INDIA) — Rural conditions — Case studies
SICILY — History
SICK — Psychology
SICK LEAVE — Great Britain
SICKLE CELL ANEMIA — Great Britain
SIDAMO (AFRICAN PEOPLE)
SIEFF, MARCUS JOSEPH SIEFF, Baron
SIEMENS, CARL FRIEDRICH VON
SIEMENS, WILHELM VON
SIEMENS AG — History
SIENKIEWICZ, HENRYK
SIERRA LEONE — Description and travel
SIERRA LEONE — History — Dictionaries
SIERRA LEONE — Rural conditions
SIERRA LEONE — Statistics, Vital — Estimates
SIGN LANGUAGE — Case studies
SIKHS — Education — Great Britain
SIKHS — British Columbia — Vancouver — Economic conditions
SIKHS — British Columbia — Vancouver — Social conditions
SIKHS — India — Punjab
SIKKIM (INDIA) — Economic policy
SIKKIM (INDIA) — Politics and government
SIKKIM (INDIA) — Social policy
SILESIA — Relations — Poland
SILESIA — Social conditions

SILESIA, UPPER (POLAND AND CZECHOSLOVAKIA) — Foreign relations — Germany
SILESIA, UPPER (POLAND AND CZECHOSLOVAKIA) — History — Partition, 1919-1922
SILICOSIS — West Virginia — Gauley Bridge
SILK INDUSTRY — Connecticut — South Manchester — Employees — History — 19th century
SILK INDUSTRY — England — Employees — History — 19th century
SILK INDUSTRY — New Jersey — Paterson — Employees — History — 19th century
SILK MANUFACTURE AND TRADE — China
SILVER MINES AND MINING — Bolivia — Potosí (Dept.) — History
SILVER MINES AND MINING — Wales — Cardiganshire — Statistics
SIMON, SHENA
SIMPLEXES (MATHEMATICS)
SIN, ORIGINAL
SINCLAIR, Sir CLIVE, 1940-
SINGAPORE
SINGAPORE — Civilization
SINGAPORE — Commerce
SINGAPORE — Economic conditions
SINGAPORE — Economic conditions — Statistics
SINGAPORE — Economic policy
SINGAPORE — Ethnic relations
SINGAPORE — History
SINGAPORE — Industries
SINGAPORE — Politics and government
SINGAPORE — Social conditions
SINGAPORE — Social conditions — Statitics
SINGLE MEN — United States
SINGLE-PARENT FAMILY
SINGLE-PARENT FAMILY — Canada
SINGLE-PARENT FAMILY — Canada — Bibliography
SINGLE PARENT FAMILY — Great Britain
SINGLE PARENT FAMILY — Great Britain — Medical care
SINGLE-PARENT FAMILY — United States
SINGLE-PARENT FAMILY — United States — Bibliography
SINGLE PARENTS — Employment — Australia
SINGLE PARENTS — Government policy — Australia
SINGLE PARENTS — Legal status, laws, etc. — England
SINGLE PARENTS — Australia
SINGLE PARENTS — Australia — Finance
SINGLE PARENTS — Great Britain — Medical care
SINGLE PEOPLE — Housing — England — Gloucester (Gloucestershire)
SINGLE PEOPLE — Housing — England — London
SINGLE PEOPLE — California — Los Angeles — Case studies
SINGLE TAX
SINGLE WOMEN — United States — Psychology
SINKIANG PROVINCE (CHINA) — Foreign relations — Soviet Union
SINKIANG PROVINCE (CHINA) — History
SINKIANG PROVINCE (CHINA) — Politics and government
SINKIANG UIGHUR AUTONOMOUS REGION (CHINA) — Politics and government
SINN FEIN
SINO-INDIAN BORDER DISPUTE — 1957-
SINO-JAPANESE CONFLICT, 1937-1945
SIRACKY, ANDREJ
SIT-DOWN STRIKES — Netherlands

SKEPTICISM
SKILLED LABOR — Europe — History
SKILLED LABOR — Great Britain — History
SKILLS DEVELOPMENT FUND (Singapore)
SLAVE TRADE — Bibliography
SLAVE-TRADE — Africa
SLAVE-TRADE — America
SLAVE-TRADE — American
SLAVE TRADE — Brazil — History
SLAVE TRADE — Caribbean Area — History
SLAVE-TRADE — England — Bristol (Avon) — History — 18th century
SLAVE-TRADE — Great Britain
SLAVE TRADE — Latin America — History
SLAVE-TRADE — United States — History — 18th century
SLAVE TRADE — Virginia — Danville — History
SLAVEHOLDERS — Georgia — Augusta Region — Attitudes
SLAVERY
SLAVERY — Bibliography
SLAVERY — Law and legislation — United States — History
SLAVERY — Political aspects — Africa — History
SLAVERY — Political aspects — Caribbean Area — History
SLAVERY — Political aspects — United States — History
SLAVERY — Africa
SLAVERY — America
SLAVERY — Brazil — History
SLAVERY — Caribbean Area — History
SLAVERY — Georgia — Condition of slaves
SLAVERY — Georgia — History
SLAVERY — Georgia — Augusta Region — Public opinion
SLAVERY — Great Britain — Anti-slavery movements
SLAVERY — Latin America — History
SLAVERY — Southern States
SLAVERY — Southern States — Addresses, essays, lectures
SLAVERY — Southern States — Condition of slaves
SLAVERY — Tennessee — Emancipation
SLAVERY — United States
SLAVERY — United States — Anti-slavery movements
SLAVERY — United States — Anti-slavery movements — Sources
SLAVERY — United States — Emancipation
SLAVERY — United States — Historiography
SLAVERY — United States — Insurrections, etc
SLAVERY — Virgin Islands of the United States — Saint John — History
SLAVERY — West Indies, British
SLAVERY AND ISLAM — Africa
SLAVERY IN THE UNITED STATES — History
SLAVIC COUNTRIES — Library resources
SLAVIC COUNTRIES — Relations — Poland
SLAVIC LANGUAGES — Library resources
SLAVS, SOUTHERN — Hungary
SLOVAK AMERICANS — Minnesota — Minneapolis — Social life and customs
SLOVAK SOCIALIST REPUBLIC (CZECHOSLOVAKIA) — History
SLOVAK SOCIALIST REPUBLIC (CZECHOSLOVAKIA) — History — Uprising, 1944
SLOVENES — Austria — Carinthia
SLUMS
SLUMS — Denmark
SLUMS — England — London — History
SLUMS — India — Bombay

SLUMS — Pakistan — Layāri
SMALL BUSINESS
SMALL BUSINESS — Information services — Great Britain
SMALL BUSINESS — Management
SMALL BUSINESS — Asia
SMALL BUSINESS — Australia
SMALL BUSINESS — Developing countries
SMALL BUSINESS — Developing countries — Finance
SMALL BUSINESS — Europe
SMALL BUSINESS — European Economic Community countries
SMALL BUSINESS — France — Finance
SMALL BUSINESS — Great Britain
SMALL BUSINESS — Great Britain — Societies, etc
SMALL BUSINESS — Great Britain — Technological innovations
SMALL BUSINESS — Netherlands
SMALL BUSINESS — United States
SMART (COMPUTER PROGRAM)
ŠMERAL, BOHUMÍR
SMITH, ADAM
SMOKING
SMOKING — Government policy — Addresses, essays, lectures
SMOKING — Social aspects — Addresses, essays, lectures
SMOKING — Australia — History
SMOKING — Great Britain
SNOWDEN, PHILIP
SOAP OPERAS — United States
SOAP OPERAS — United States — Addresses, essays, lectures
SOCCER — Great Britain
SOCCER — Great Britain — Fans — Bibliography
SOCIAL ACCOUNTING — Statistical methods
SOCIAL ACCOUNTING — Developinmg countries — Case studies — Congresses
SOCIAL ACCOUNTING — Developinmg countries — Methodology — Congresses
SOCIAL ACCOUNTING — Indonesia — Statistics
SOCIAL ACTION
SOCIAL ADJUSTMENT — Congresses
SOCIAL CASE WORK
SOCIAL CASE WORK — Great Britain
SOCIAL CASEWORK
SOCIAL CHANGE
SOCIAL CHANGE — Case studies
SOCIAL CHANGE — Congresses
SOCIAL CHANGE — Cross-cultural studies
SOCIAL CHANGE — History
SOCIAL CHANGE — Mathematical models
SOCIAL CHOICE
SOCIAL CHOICE — Congresses
SOCIAL CHOICE — Mathematical models
SOCIAL CLASSES — India
SOCIAL CLASSES
SOCIAL CLASSES — Case studies
SOCIAL CLASSES — Health and hygiene — Great Britain — Bibliography
SOCIAL CLASSES — History — Addresses, essays, lectures
SOCIAL CLASSES — Australia — History
SOCIAL CLASSES — Bangladesh
SOCIAL CLASSES — Canada
SOCIAL CLASSES — China — History
SOCIAL CLASSES — Egypt
SOCIAL CLASSES — England — Oldham, Lancs. — History
SOCIAL CLASSES — England — West Midlands
SOCIAL CLASSES — Europe
SOCIAL CLASSES — Europe, Eastern
SOCIAL CLASSES — Fiji
SOCIAL CLASSES — France — Nomenclature
SOCIAL CLASSES — France — Statistics
SOCIAL CLASSES — France — Paris region
SOCIAL CLASSES — Germany — History
SOCIAL CLASSES — Ghana
SOCIAL CLASSES — Great Britain

SOCIAL CLASSES — Great Britain — Case studies
SOCIAL CLASSES — Guyana
SOCIAL CLASSES — India
SOCIAL CLASSES — India — Congresses
SOCIAL CLASSES — India — West Bengal
SOCIAL CLASSES — Iraq
SOCIAL CLASSES — Malaya
SOCIAL CLASSES — Nicaragua
SOCIAL CLASSES — Nigeria, Northern
SOCIAL CLASSES — Poland
SOCIAL CLASSES — Russian S.F.S.R — Moscow — History
SOCIAL CLASSES — Scotland
SOCIAL CLASSES — Southern States
SOCIAL CLASSES — Soviet Union
SOCIAL CLASSES — Spain — Barcelona — History
SOCIAL CLASSES — Spain — Catalonia
SOCIAL CLASSES — United States
SOCIAL CLASSES — United States — History
SOCIAL CLASSES — Uzbek S.S.R. — History
SOCIAL CONDITIONS — Burkina Faso — Statistics
SOCIAL CONFLICT
SOCIAL CONFLICT — Economic aspects
SOCIAL CONFLICT — Religious aspects — Christianity
SOCIAL CONFLICT — Arab countries
SOCIAL CONFLICT — Denmark
SOCIAL CONFLICT — Mexico — Morelos — Case studies
SOCIAL CONFLICT — Near East
SOCIAL CONFLICT — Norway
SOCIAL CONFLICT — Spain — Basque Provinces
SOCIAL CONFLICT — Spain — Cantabria
SOCIAL CONFLICT — Spain — Catalonia
SOCIAL CONFLICT — Spain — Madrid — History — 20th century
SOCIAL CONFLICT — Spain — Zaragoza
SOCIAL CONTRACT
SOCIAL CONTROL
SOCIAL CREDIT
SOCIAL DARWINISM
SOCIAL DEMOCRATIC PARTY
SOCIAL DEMOCRATIC PARTY. SDP Liberal Alliance See SDP Liberal Alliance
SOCIAL ENVIRONMENT — United States
SOCIAL ETHICS
SOCIAL ETHICS — Addresses, essays, lectures
SOCIAL EVOLUTION
SOCIAL EVOLUTION — Congresses
SOCIAL EXCHANGE
SOCIAL GROUP WORK
SOCIAL GROUP WORK — Great Britain
SOCIAL GROUP WORK — Great Britain — Abstracts
SOCIAL GROUPS
SOCIAL HISTORY
SOCIAL HISTORY — Medieval, 500-1500
SOCIAL HISTORY — Modern, 1500-
SOCIAL HISTORY — 16th century
SOCIAL HISTORY — 1945-
SOCIAL HISTORY — 1960-1970
SOCIAL INDICATORS — Colombia
SOCIAL INDICATORS — Indonesia
SOCIAL INDICATORS — Japan
SOCIAL INDICATORS — Scandinavia
SOCIAL INSTITUTIONS — Addresses, essays, lectures
SOCIAL INSTITUTIONS — Congresses
SOCIAL INSTITUTIONS — Pennsylvania — Hazleton
SOCIAL INTEGRATION — Russian S.F.S.R — Moscow — History
SOCIAL INTERACTION
SOCIAL INTERACTION — Congresses
SOCIAL INTERACTION — Great Britain
SOCIAL INTERACTION — Michigan — Detroit — Case studies
SOCIAL INTERACTION — New York (State) — Buffalo — Case studies

SOCIAL INTERACTION — Papua New Guinea
SOCIAL INTERACTION — West Bank
SOCIAL JUSTICE
SOCIAL JUSTICE — Congresses
SOCIAL LEARNING
SOCIAL LEARNING — Congresses
SOCIAL LEGISLATION
SOCIAL LEGISLATION — Canada — Addresses, essays, lectures
SOCIAL LEGISLATION — European Economic Community countries
SOCIAL LEGISLATION — France — History
SOCIAL LEGISLATION — Near East
SOCIAL MEDICINE
SOCIAL MEDICINE — Addresses, essays, lectures
SOCIAL MEDICINE — Bibliography
SOCIAL MEDICINE — China
SOCIAL MEDICINE — France
SOCIAL MEDICINE — Great Britain
SOCIAL MEDICINE — Tanzania — History
SOCIAL MEDICINE — United States
SOCIAL MOBILITY
SOCIAL MOBILITY — Cross-cultural studies
SOCIAL MOBILITY — Canada
SOCIAL MOBILITY — China — Case studies
SOCIAL MOBILITY — Great Britain
SOCIAL MOBILITY — Hungary
SOCIAL MOBILITY — India
SOCIAL MOBILITY — Poland
SOCIAL MOBILITY — United States — Case studies
SOCIAL MOVEMENTS
SOCIAL MOVEMENTS — England — History — 19th century
SOCIAL MOVEMENTS — England — History — 20th century
SOCIAL MOVEMENTS — India — History
SOCIAL MOVEMENTS — Latin America
SOCIAL MOVEMENTS — Netherlands
SOCIAL MOVEMENTS — Peru
SOCIAL MOVEMENTS — Quebec (Province)
SOCIAL MOVEMENTS — United States — History
SOCIAL NORMS
SOCIAL PARTICIPATION
SOCIAL PERCEPTION
SOCIAL PERCEPTION — Addresses, essays, lectures
SOCIAL PERCEPTION — Congresses
SOCIAL PERCEPTION — Handbooks
SOCIAL PERCEPTION IN CHILDREN
SOCIAL POLICY
SOCIAL POLICY — Congresses
SOCIAL POLICY — Decision making
SOCIAL POLICY — United States — Addresses, essays, lectures
SOCIAL PREDICTION — Mathematical models
SOCIAL PROBLEMS
SOCIAL PROBLEMS — Congresses
SOCIAL PROBLEMS — Literary collections
SOCIAL PSYCHIATRY
SOCIAL PSYCHOLOGY
SOCIAL PSYCHOLOGY — Addresses, essays, lectures
SOCIAL PSYCHOLOGY — Congresses
SOCIAL PSYCHOLOGY — Dictionaries
SOCIAL PSYCHOLOGY — History — 20th century
SOCIAL PSYCHOLOGY — Russian S.F.S.R — Leningrad — Addresses, essays, lectures
SOCIAL PSYCHOLOGY — Soviet Union — Addresses, essays, lectures
SOCIAL REFORMERS — Alabama — Fairhope — History — Addresses, essays, lectures
SOCIAL REFORMERS — Great Britain — Biography

SOCIAL REFORMERS — Great Britian — Biography
SOCIAL REFORMERS — United States — Biography
SOCIAL ROLE — Cross-cultural studies
SOCIAL ROLE — Denmark
SOCIAL SCIENCE — Data processing
SOCIAL SCIENCE LITERATURE — Publishing
SOCIAL SCIENCE RESEARCH
SOCIAL SCIENCE RESEARCH — Great Britain
SOCIAL SCIENCES
SOCIAL SCIENCES — Abstracting and indexing
SOCIAL SCIENCES — Addresses, essays, lectures
SOCIAL SCIENCES — Bibliography
SOCIAL SCIENCES — Computer programs
SOCIAL SCIENCES — Data processing
SOCIAL SCIENCES — Dictionaries and encyclopedias
SOCIAL SCIENCES — Forecasting
SOCIAL SCIENCES — History
SOCIAL SCIENCES — History — 20th century
SOCIAL SCIENCES — Information services
SOCIAL SCIENCES — International cooperation — Case studies
SOCIAL SCIENCES — Mathematical models
SOCIAL SCIENCES — Mathematics
SOCIAL SCIENCES — Methodology
SOCIAL SCIENCES — Methodology — Congresses
SOCIAL SCIENCES — Methodology — History
SOCIAL SCIENCES — Methodology — Moral and ethical aspects
SOCIAL SCIENCES — Philosophy
SOCIAL SCIENCES — Philosophy — Congresses
SOCIAL SCIENCES — Philosophy — History
SOCIAL SCIENCES — Philosophy — History — 19th century
SOCIAL SCIENCES — Research
SOCIAL SCIENCES — Research — Case studies
SOCIAL SCIENCES — Research — Congresses
SOCIAL SCIENCES — Research — Data processing
SOCIAL SCIENCES — Research — Methodology
SOCIAL SCIENCES — Research — Moral and ethical aspects
SOCIAL SCIENCES — Research — Great Britain
SOCIAL SCIENCES — Research — Great Britain — Directories
SOCIAL SCIENCES — Research — Great Britain — Government policy — History — 20th century
SOCIAL SCIENCES — Research — United States — Case studies
SOCIAL SCIENCES — Research — United States — Congresses
SOCIAL SCIENCES — Research — United States — Finance
SOCIAL SCIENCES — Research — United States — Government policy — History — 20th century
SOCIAL SCIENCES — Scholarships, fellowships, etc. — Great Britain
SOCIAL SCIENCES — Statistical methods
SOCIAL SCIENCES — statistical methods
SOCIAL SCIENCES — Statistical methods
SOCIAL SCIENCES — Statistical methods — Congresses
SOCIAL SCIENCES — Statistical methods — Mathematical models
SOCIAL SCIENCES — Study and teaching
SOCIAL SCIENCES — Study and teaching — Philippines
SOCIAL SCIENCES — Study and teaching (Secondary) — England — London
SOCIAL SCIENCES — Terminology
SOCIAL SCIENCES — Africa, Sub-Saharan
SOCIAL SCIENCES — China
SOCIAL SCIENCES — Europe — History
SOCIAL SCIENCES — Great Britain — Research
SOCIAL SCIENCES — Great Britain — Research grants
SOCIAL SCIENCES — Spain
SOCIAL SCIENCES AND ETHICS
SOCIAL SCIENTISTS — Japan — Biography
SOCIAL SECURITY
SOCIAL SECURITY — Congresses
SOCIAL SECURITY — Finance
SOCIAL SECURITY — Government policy — Australia
SOCIAL SECURITY — Law and legislation — Addresses, essays, lectures
SOCIAL SECURITY — Law and legislation — Australia
SOCIAL SECURITY — Law and legislation — European Economic Community countries
SOCIAL SECURITY — Law and legislation — Great Britain
SOCIAL SECURITY — Law and legislation — Great Britain — Bibliography
SOCIAL SECURITY — Law and legislation — Spain
SOCIAL SECURITY — Law and legislation — United States
SOCIAL SECURITY — Argentina — History
SOCIAL SECURITY — Australia
SOCIAL SECURITY — Austria
SOCIAL SECURITY — Brazil
SOCIAL SECURITY — Canada
SOCIAL SECURITY — Denmark
SOCIAL SECURITY — Denmark — Copenhagen — Statistics
SOCIAL SECURITY — Egypt
SOCIAL SECURITY — European Economic Community countries
SOCIAL SECURITY — Finland
SOCIAL SECURITY — Germany — History
SOCIAL SECURITY — Germany. West — Statistics
SOCIAL SECURITY — Great Britain
SOCIAL SECURITY — Great Britain — History
SOCIAL SECURITY — Great Britain — Law and legislation
SOCIAL SECURITY — Great Britain — Statistics
SOCIAL SECURITY — India
SOCIAL SECURITY — Law and legislation
SOCIAL SECURITY — Netherlands — Statistics
SOCIAL SECURITY — New Zealand — Finance
SOCIAL SECURITY — Peru
SOCIAL SECURITY — Québec (Province)
SOCIAL SECURITY — Scandinavia — Statistics
SOCIAL SECURITY — Spain
SOCIAL SECURITY — United States
SOCIAL SECURITY — United States — Congresses
SOCIAL SECURITY — United States — Finance
SOCIAL SECURITY — United States — History
SOCIAL SECURITY — United States — Law and Legislation
SOCIAL SECURITY (AGE OF RETIREMENT) BILL 1983-84
SOCIAL SECURITY AND HOUSING BENEFITS BILL 1982-83
SOCIAL SECURITY BENEFICIARIES — Legal status, laws, etc. — Quebec (Province)
SOCIAL SECURITY BILL 1979-80
SOCIAL SECURITY BILL 1980-81
SOCIAL SECURITY BILL 1984-85
SOCIAL SECURITY BILL 1985-86
SOCIAL SECURITY (CONTRIBUTIONS) BILL 1980-81
SOCIAL SECURITY COURTS — Great Britain — Bibliography
SOCIAL SECURITY COURTS — United States
SOCIAL SECURITY (NO.2) BILL 1979-80
SOCIAL SERVICE
SOCIAL SERVICE — Addresses, essays, lectures
SOCIAL SERVICE — Data processing
SOCIAL SERVICE — Psychological aspects
SOCIAL SERVICE — Team-work
SOCIAL SERVICE — Vocational guidance — Great Britain
SOCIAL SERVICE — Africa
SOCIAL SERVICE — Denmark
SOCIAL SERVICE — Denmark — Bibliography
SOCIAL SERVICE — Developing countries — Finance
SOCIAL SERVICE — France
SOCIAL SERVICE — France — Nomenclature
SOCIAL SERVICE — Great Britain
SOCIAL SERVICE — Great Britain — Bibliography
SOCIAL SERVICE — Great Britain — Finance
SOCIAL SERVICE — Hong Kong
SOCIAL SERVICE — India
SOCIAL SERVICE — Ireland — Tallaght (Dublin) — Case studies
SOCIAL SERVICE — South Africa
SOCIAL SERVICE — South Australia
SOCIAL SERVICE — Taiwan
SOCIAL SERVICE — United States
SOCIAL SERVICE — United States — Addresses, essays, lectures
SOCIAL SERVICE AND RACE RELATIONS — Great Britain
SOCIAL SERVICE, RURAL — Great Britain
SOCIAL SERVICE, RURAL — Northern Ireland
SOCIAL SETTLEMENTS — Scotland — Dumfries and Galloway
SOCIAL SKILLS
SOCIAL SKILLS IN CHILDREN
SOCIAL SKILLS IN CHILDREN — Therapeutic use
SOCIAL STATUS — Cross-cultural studies
SOCIAL STATUS — Canada
SOCIAL STATUS — United States
SOCIAL STRUCTURE
SOCIAL STRUCTURE — Comparative studies
SOCIAL STRUCTURE — Psychological aspects — Bibliography
SOCIAL STRUCTURE — Africa, Sub-Saharan — History
SOCIAL STRUCTURE — Denmark
SOCIAL STRUCTURE — Europe — History
SOCIAL STRUCTURE — Europe, Eastern
SOCIAL STRUCTURE — France
SOCIAL STRUCTURE — Germany (West)
SOCIAL STRUCTURE — Iran — Case studies
SOCIAL STRUCTURE — Japan
SOCIAL STRUCTURE — Libya
SOCIAL STRUCTURE — Pennsylvania — Hazleton
SOCIAL STRUCTURE — Portugal — History
SOCIAL STRUCTURE — Russian S.F.S.R. — Buriat A.S.S.R.
SOCIAL STRUCTURE — Soviet Union
SOCIAL STRUCTURE — Spain
SOCIAL STRUCTURE — Tunisia
SOCIAL STRUCTURE — United States
SOCIAL SURVEYS
SOCIAL SURVEYS — Response rate
SOCIAL SURVEYS — Australia — Sydney (N.S.W.)
SOCIAL SURVEYS — Great Britain
SOCIAL SURVEYS — India

SOCIAL SURVEYS — India — Nagpur
SOCIAL SURVEYS — Southern States
SOCIAL SYSTEMS
SOCIAL SYSTEMS — Congresses
SOCIAL VALUES
SOCIAL VALUES — Congresses
SOCIAL WORK ADMINISTRATION
SOCIAL WORK EDUCATION — Great Britain
SOCIAL WORK WITH BLACKS — Great Britain
SOCIAL WORK WITH CHILDREN — Great Britain
SOCIAL WORK WITH DELINQUENTS AND CRIMINALS — Great Britain
SOCIAL WORK WITH DELINQUENTS AND CRIMINALS — Great Britain — Congresses
SOCIAL WORK WITH DELINQUENTS AND CRIMINALS — Massachusets
SOCIAL WORK WITH DELINQUENTS AND CRIMINALS — Scotland — Strathclyde
SOCIAL WORK WITH IMMIGRANTS — Denmark
SOCIAL WORK WITH IMMIGRANTS — Great Britain
SOCIAL WORK WITH MINORITIES — Great Britain
SOCIAL WORK WITH MINORITY YOUTH — Great Britain — Case studies
SOCIAL WORK WITH THE AGED
SOCIAL WORK WITH THE AGED — Great Britain
SOCIAL WORK WITH THE MENTALLY HANDICAPPED — Great Britain
SOCIAL WORK WITH YOUTH
SOCIAL WORK WITH YOUTH — Great Britain
SOCIAL WORK WITH YOUTH — Scotland
SOCIAL WORK WITH YOUTH — South Africa
SOCIAL WORK WITH YOUTH — Wales — Cardiff
SOCIAL WORKERS
SOCIAL WORKERS — In-service training — Great Britain
SOCIAL WORKERS — Great Britain
SOCIAL WORKERS — Great Britain — Attitudes
SOCIAL WORKERS — Great Britain — Job stress
SOCIAL WORKERS — United States
SOCIAL WORKERS — United States — Biography — Dictionaries
SOCIALDEMOKRATISCHE PARTEI DEUTSCHLANDS
SOCIALE SERURITY — Italy — Statistics
SOCIALE SERVICE — Italy — Statistics
SOCIALISM — Spain
SOCIALISM
SOCIALISM — Addresses, essays, lectures
SOCIALISM — Bibliography
SOCIALISM — Collected works
SOCIALISM — Economic aspects — Great Britain
SOCIALISM — History
SOCIALISM — History — Sources
SOCIALISM — History — 20th century
SOCIALISM — Spain — Catalonia
SOCIALISM — Uruguay
SOCIALISM — Africa
SOCIALISM — Albania
SOCIALISM — Argentina — History
SOCIALISM — Australia
SOCIALISM — Australia — History
SOCIALISM — Austria
SOCIALISM — Belgium
SOCIALISM — Canada
SOCIALISM — Canada — History — Congresses
SOCIALISM — Chile
SOCIALISM — Czechoslovakia — History
SOCIALISM — Denmark
SOCIALISM — Developing countries
SOCIALISM — Europe

SOCIALISM — Europe — History
SOCIALISM — Europe — History — 20th century
SOCIALISM — Europe, Eastern
SOCIALISM — France
SOCIALISM — France — History
SOCIALISM — France — History — 20th century
SOCIALISM — Germany
SOCIALISM — Germany — History
SOCIALISM — Germany (West)
SOCIALISM — Great Britain
SOCIALISM — Great Britain — History
SOCIALISM — Great Britain — History — 19th century
SOCIALISM — Great Britain — History — 20th century
SOCIALISM — Grenada — History
SOCIALISM — Hungary
SOCIALISM — India
SOCIALISM — Latin America
SOCIALISM — Latin America — History
SOCIALISM — Netherlands
SOCIALISM — Poland — History
SOCIALISM — Poland — Łódz
SOCIALISM — South Africa
SOCIALISM — Soviet Union
SOCIALISM — Soviet Union — History
SOCIALISM — Spain
SOCIALISM — Spain — Bibliography
SOCIALISM — Spain — Chronology
SOCIALISM — Spain — History
SOCIALISM — Spain — History — 20th Century
SOCIALISM — Spain — History — 20th century
SOCIALISM — Spain — Andalusia — History
SOCIALISM — Spain — Asturias — History
SOCIALISM — Spain — Catalonia
SOCIALISM — Spain — Catalonia — History — 20th century
SOCIALISM — Spain — Seville — History
SOCIALISM — Spain — Vitoria
SOCIALISM — Sweden — History
SOCIALISM — Switzerland
SOCIALISM — Ukraine — History
SOCIALISM — United States — History
SOCIALISM AND CHRISTIANITY
SOCIALISM AND RELIGION
SOCIALISM AND YOUTH — Great Britain
SOCIALISM, CHRISTIAN — Great Britain
SOCIALISM IN ZAMBIA
SOCIALIST PARTIES — Directories
SOCIALIST PARTIES — History
SOCIALIST PARTIES — Poland — History
SOCIALISTS — Argentina
SOCIALISTS — Austria — Biography
SOCIALISTS — Canada — Biography
SOCIALISTS — France — Biography
SOCIALISTS — Germany — Biography
SOCIALISTS — Great Britain — Biography
SOCIALISTS — Great Britain — Directories
SOCIALISTS — Ireland — Biography
SOCIALISTS — New York (N.Y.) — History — 20th century
SOCIALISTS — Poland — Biography
SOCIALISTS — Spain — Catalonia — Biography
SOCIALISTS — United States — Biography — Dictionaries
SOCIALIZATION
SOCIALIZATION — Addresses, essays, lectures
SOCIALIZATION — Cross-cultural studies
SOCIALLY HANDICAPPED — Health and hygiene — Great Britain
SOCIALLY HANDICAPPED — India — Government policy — Congresses
SOCIALLY HANDICAPPED YOUTH — United States — Case studies
SOCIALOGISTS — Germany — Bibliography
SOCIETY ISLANDS — Population — Statistics

SOCIETY OF FRIENDS — Biography
SOCIETY OF FRIENDS — History — 17th century — Sources
SOCIETY OF FRIENDS — History — 18th century — Sources
SOCIETY, PRIMITIVE
SOCIOBIOLOGY
SOCIOBIOLOGY — Addresses, essays, lectures
SOCIOECONOMIC FACTORS
SOCIOLINGUISTICS
SOCIOLINGUISTICS — Cross-cultural studies
SOCIOLINGUISTICS — Methodology
SOCIOLINGUISTICS — Belgium
SOCIOLINGUISTICS — Fiji
SOCIOLINGUISTICS — Hong Kong
SOCIOLOGICAL JURISPRUDENCE
SOCIOLOGICAL JURISPRUDENCE — Addresses, essays, lectures
SOCIOLOGISTS — Germany — Biography
SOCIOLOGISTS — Germany (West)
SOCIOLOGISTS — Soviet Union — Directories
SOCIOLOGY
SOCIOLOGY — Addresses, essays, lectures
SOCIOLOGY — Bibliography
SOCIOLOGY — Biographical method
SOCIOLOGY — Congresses
SOCIOLOGY — Correspondence
SOCIOLOGY — Dictionaries
SOCIOLOGY — History
SOCIOLOGY — History — 20th century
SOCIOLOGY — Methodology
SOCIOLOGY — Philosophy
SOCIOLOGY — Political aspects — Soviet Union
SOCIOLOGY — Quotations, maxims, etc — History — Sources
SOCIOLOGY — Research
SOCIOLOGY — Study and teaching
SOCIOLOGY — Canada — History
SOCIOLOGY — German — History
SOCIOLOGY — Germany
SOCIOLOGY — Germany — Bibliography
SOCIOLOGY — Germany — History
SOCIOLOGY — Great Britain
SOCIOLOGY — Great Britain — History
SOCIOLOGY — Hungary — History
SOCIOLOGY — India — Research — India
SOCIOLOGY — Italy
SOCIOLOGY — Korea — Addresses, essays, lectures
SOCIOLOGY — Quebec (Province)
SOCIOLOGY — Southern States — Addresses, essays, lectures
SOCIOLOGY — Soviet Union
SOCIOLOGY — United Satates
SOCIOLOGY — United States
SOCIOLOGY AND RELIGION — Congresses
SOCIOLOGY, CHRISTIAN
SOCIOLOGY, CHRISTIAN — Addresses, essays, lectures
SOCIOLOGY, CHRISTIAN — Canada — 19th century
SOCIOLOGY, CHRISTIAN — Latin America
SOCIOLOGY, CHRISTIAN (BAPTIST)
SOCIOLOGY, MEDICAL — China
SOCIOLOGY, MILITARY — History — 18th century — Congresses
SOCIOLOGY, MILITARY — Latin America — Addresses, essays, lectures
SOCIOLOGY, RURAL
SOCIOLOGY, RURAL — Sweden — Locknevi (Småland)
SOCIOLOGY, URBAN
SOCIOLOGY, URBAN — Australia — Jabiru (Northern Territory)
SOCIOLOGY, URBAN — France — Paris region
SOCIOLOGY, URBAN — India
SOCIOLOGY, URBAN — United States
SOCIOMETRY
SOCJALDEMOCRACJA KROLESTWA POLSKIEGO I LITWY — History

SODOMY
SOETOMO, RADEN
SOFTWARE, COMPUTER — Accounting
SOIL CONSERVATION — Southern States
SOIL DEGRADATION
SOIL EROSION — Tanzania
SOIL MANAGEMENT — Congresses
SOIL POLLUTION — England — Shipham (Somerset)
SOIL RESEARCH
SOILS
SOLAR ACCESS RIGHTS — Australia
SOLAR ENERGY
SOLAR ENERGY — Law and legislation — Australia
SOLAR NEUTRINOS — Measurement
SOLAR RADIATION — Great Britain
SOLDIERS — Education, Non-military — Soviet Union
SOLDIERS — United States — Biography
SOLIDARNOŚĆ
SOLIDARNOŚĆ — Biography
SOLO (INDONESIA) — Social conditions
SOLOMON ISLANDS — Religion
SOLVENT ABUSE
SOMALIA — Foreign relations — Ethiopia
SOMALIA — History
SOMALIA — History — Dictionaries
SOMALIA — Politics and government
SOMALIA — Social life and customs
SOMARY, FELIX
SOMATOFORM DISORDERS — China
SOMERSET. Library Service
SOREL, GEORGES
SOTHEBY'S (Firm)
SOTHO (AFRICAN PEOPLE)
SOUQ AL-MANAKH
SOUTH AFRICA — Bibliography
SOUTH AFRICA — Census, 1985
SOUTH AFRICA — Commerce
SOUTH AFRICA — Commercial policy — History — 20th century
SOUTH AFRICA — Constitutional history
SOUTH AFRICA — Economic conditions
SOUTH AFRICA — Economic conditions — Statistics
SOUTH AFRICA — Economic conditions — 1918-
SOUTH AFRICA — Economic conditions — 1961-
SOUTH AFRICA — Economic policy
SOUTH AFRICA — Ethnic relations
SOUTH AFRICA — Ethnic relations — Addresses, essays, lectures
SOUTH AFRICA — Foreign economic relations
SOUTH AFRICA — Foreign economic relations — Africa, Southern
SOUTH AFRICA — Foreign enonomic relations — Great Britain
SOUTH AFRICA — Foreign relations
SOUTH AFRICA — Foreign relations — Bibliography
SOUTH AFRICA — Foreign relations — 1948-1961
SOUTH AFRICA — Foreign relations — 1948-1961 — Bibliography
SOUTH AFRICA — Foreign relations — Africa, Southern
SOUTH AFRICA — Foreign relations — Botswana
SOUTH AFRICA — Foreign relations — Canada
SOUTH AFRICA — Foreign relations — Lesotho
SOUTH AFRICA — Foreign relations — Soviet Union
SOUTH AFRICA — Foreign relations — United States
SOUTH AFRICA — Foreign relations — United States — Bibliography
SOUTH AFRICA — History
SOUTH AFRICA — History — Great Trek, 1836-1840
SOUTH AFRICA — History — 1836-1909
SOUTH AFRICA — History — 1836-1909 — Sources
SOUTH AFRICA — History — 1909-1961
SOUTH AFRICA — History — 1961-
SOUTH AFRICA — Industries — Statistics
SOUTH AFRICA — Military relations — Africa, Southern
SOUTH AFRICA — National security
SOUTH AFRICA — Occupations
SOUTH AFRICA — Occupations — Statistics
SOUTH AFRICA — Politics and government
SOUTH AFRICA — Politics and government — 1948-1961 — Bibliography
SOUTH AFRICA — Politics and government — 20th century
SOUTH AFRICA — Politics and government — 1909-1948
SOUTH AFRICA — Politics and government — 1909-1948 — Bibliography
SOUTH AFRICA — Politics and government — 1948-1961
SOUTH AFRICA — Politics and government — 1948-1961 — Bibliography
SOUTH AFRICA — Politics and government — 1961-1978
SOUTH AFRICA — Politics and government — 1969-
SOUTH AFRICA — Politics and government — 1978-
SOUTH AFRICA — Politics and government — 1978- — Government
SOUTH AFRICA — Politics and government — 1978- — Public opinion
SOUTH AFRICA — Population — Statistics
SOUTH AFRICA — Population density — Statistics
SOUTH AFRICA — Race relations
SOUTH AFRICA — Race relations — Addresses, essays, lectures
SOUTH AFRICA — Race relations — Bibliography
SOUTH AFRICA — Race relations — Public opinion
SOUTH AFRICA — Relations — Foreign countries
SOUTH AFRICA — Relations — United States
SOUTH AFRICA — Religion
SOUTH AFRICA — Social conditions
SOUTH AFRICA — Social conditions — 1961-
SOUTH AFRICA — Social life and customs
SOUTH AFRICA — Social policy
SOUTH AFRICA — Statistics
SOUTH AFRICA — Statistics, Vital
SOUTH AFRICA — Relations — United States
SOUTH AFRICA. Department of Home Affairs
SOUTH AFRICA. Department of Mineral and Energy Affairs
SOUTH AFRICA. Department of Trade and Industry
SOUTH AFRICA. Directorate Agricultural Economic Trends
SOUTH AFRICA WAR, 1899-1902 — Correspondence
SOUTH AFRICAN ESSAYS (ENGLISH)
SOUTH AFRICAN WAR, 1899-1902 — History
SOUTH AMERICA — Politics and government — 20th century — Case studies
SOUTH ASIA — Atlases
SOUTH ASIA — Bibliography
SOUTH ASIA — Economic policy — Congresses
SOUTH ASIA — Foreign economic relations — Asia, Southeastern
SOUTH ASIA — Foreign relations — Great Britain
SOUTH ASIA — Foreign relations — Soviet Union
SOUTH ASIA — Foreign relations — United States
SOUTH ASIA — History — Addresses, essays, lectures
SOUTH ASIA — Library resources — Great Britain — Directories
SOUTH ASIA — Politics and government
SOUTH ASIA — Politics and government — Congresses
SOUTH ASIA — Relations — India
SOUTH ASIA — Rural conditions
SOUTH ASIA — Social conditions — Addresses, essays, lectures
SOUTH ASIA — Social policy — Congresses
SOUTH ATLANTIC REGION — Defenses
SOUTH ATLANTIC REGION — Economic aspects
SOUTH AUSTRALIA. Justices Act
SOUTH AUSTRALIA — Officials and employees
SOUTH AUSTRALIA. Committee on Aboriginal Employment
SOUTH AUSTRALIA. Department for Community Welfare
SOUTH AUSTRALIA. Department of Agriculture. Economics Division — Research
SOUTH AUSTRALIA. Enquiry into Hospital Services in South Australia
SOUTH AUSTRALIA. Police Department — Corrupt practices
SOUTH AUSTRALIA. Task Force on Child Sexual Abuse
SOUTH CAROLINA — Governors — Biography
SOUTH CAROLINA — Politics and government — 1775-1865
SOUTH-EAST ASIA LIBRARY GROUP
SOUTH EAST (ENGLAND) — Economic conditions — Statistics
SOUTH EAST (ENGLAND) — Social conditions — Statistics
SOUTH GLAMORGAN — Economic conditions
SOUTH GLAMORGAN — Economic conditions — Statistics
SOUTH GLAMORGAN — Population
SOUTH GLAMORGAN — Population — Statistics
SOUTH GLAMORGAN — Social conditions
SOUTH PACIFIC FORUM
SOUTHALL (MIDDLESEX) — Race relations
SOUTHAMPTON INSURRECTION, 1831 — Fiction
SOUTHERN CONE OF SOUTH AMERICA — Economic policy
SOUTHERN STATES — Civilization
SOUTHERN STATES — Civilization — 1775-1865
SOUTHERN STATES — Economic conditions
SOUTHERN STATES — Economic conditions — Addresses, essays, lectures
SOUTHERN STATES — Economic conditions — 1945-
SOUTHERN STATES — Historiography
SOUTHERN STATES — History — 1775-1865
SOUTHERN STATES — History — 1865-1877
SOUTHERN STATES — History — 20th century
SOUTHERN STATES — Industries — History
SOUTHERN STATES — Politics and government — 1865-1950
SOUTHERN STATES — Politics and government — 1951- — Addresses, essays, lectures
SOUTHERN STATES — Popular culture
SOUTHERN STATES — Race relations
SOUTHERN STATES — Race relations — Addresses, essays, lectures
SOUTHERN STATES — Rural conditions
SOUTHERN STATES — Social conditions
SOUTHERN STATES — Social conditions — Congresses

SOUTHERN STATES — Social life and customs
SOUTHPORT LIBERAL ASSOCIATION — History
SOUTHWARK (LONDON, ENGLAND) — Economic conditions
SOUTHWARK (LONDON, ENGLAND) — Social conditions
SOUTHWARK (LONDON, ENGLAND) — Social policy
SOVEREIGNTY
SOVET EKONOMICHESKOI VZAIMOPOMOSHCHI
SOVET EKONOMICHESKOI VZAIMOPOMOSHCHI — Commerce — Statistics
SOVET EKONOMICHESKOI VZAIMOPOMOSHCHI — Foreign economic relations — Statistics
SOVET EKONOMICHESKOI VZAIMOPOMOSHCHI — History
SOVIET CENTRAL ASIA — History — Revolution of 1905
SOVIET FAR EAST (R.S.F.S.R.) — History — Revolution, 1917-1921
SOVIET UNION
SOVIET UNION — Administrative and political divisions
SOVIET UNION — Appropriations and expenditures
SOVIET UNION — Armed forces
SOVIET UNION — Armed Forces — Appropriations and expenditures
SOVIET UNION — Armed forces — History
SOVIET UNION — Armed forces — Political activity
SOVIET UNION — Armed Forces — Political activity
SOVIET UNION — Bibliography
SOVIET UNION — Biography — Bibliography
SOVIET UNION — Boundaries
SOVIET UNION — Census — History — Study and teaching
SOVIET UNION — Church history — 17th century
SOVIET UNION — Civilization
SOVIET UNION — Civilization — 18th century — Ukrainian influences
SOVIET UNION — Civilization — 18th century — Ukranian influences
SOVIET UNION — Civilization — 19th century — Ukrainian influences
SOVIET UNION — Civilization — 1917-
SOVIET UNION — Commerce
SOVIET UNION — Commerce — United States
SOVIET UNION — Commercial policy
SOVIET UNION — Constitution
SOVIET UNION — Constitution — Dictionaries
SOVIET UNION — Constitutional law
SOVIET UNION — Defences — History
SOVIET UNION — Defenses
SOVIET UNION — Economic conditions
SOVIET UNION — Economic conditions — To 1861
SOVIET UNION — Economic conditions — 1861-1917 — Addresses, essays, lectures
SOVIET UNION — Economic conditions — 1917-
SOVIET UNION — Economic conditions — 1918-1945
SOVIET UNION — Economic conditions — 1918-
SOVIET UNION — Economic conditions — 1965-1975
SOVIET UNION — Economic conditions — 1976-
SOVIET UNION — Economic conditions — 1981-
SOVIET UNION — Economic integration
SOVIET UNION — Economic policy
SOVIET UNION — Economic policy — Data processing
SOVIET UNION — Economic policy — Dictionaries
SOVIET UNION — Economic policy — Mathematical models
SOVIET UNION — Economic policy — 1917-1928
SOVIET UNION — Economic policy — 1917-
SOVIET UNION — Economic policy — 1928-1932
SOVIET UNION — Economic policy — 1946-1950
SOVIET UNION — Economic policy — 1981-
SOVIET UNION — Economic policy — 1985-
SOVIET UNION — Economic policy 1981-
SOVIET UNION — Emigration and immigration — Case studies
SOVIET UNION — Emigration and immigration — History
SOVIET UNION — Ethnic relations
SOVIET UNION — Ethnic relations — Addresses, essays, lectures
SOVIET UNION — Ethnic relations — Historiography
SOVIET UNION — Foreign economic relations
SOVIET UNION — Foreign economic relations — Europe, Eastern
SOVIET UNION — Foreign economic relations — Sweden
SOVIET UNION — Foreign opinion — 1917-
SOVIET UNION — Foreign opinion, American
SOVIET UNION — Foreign relatins — 1975-
SOVIET UNION — Foreign relations
SOVIET UNION — Foreign relations — 19th century
SOVIET UNION — Foreign relations — Historiography
SOVIET UNION — Foreign relations — 1689-1725
SOVIET UNION — Foreign relations — 19th century
SOVIET UNION — Foreign relations — 1894-1917
SOVIET UNION — Foreign relations — 1917-1945
SOVIET UNION — Foreign relations — 1945-
SOVIET UNION — Foreign relations — 1945- — Bibliography
SOVIET UNION — Foreign relations — 1953-1975
SOVIET UNION — Foreign relations — 1953-1975 — Congresses
SOVIET UNION — Foreign relations — 1975-
SOVIET UNION — Foreign relations — 1975- — Congresses
SOVIET UNION — Foreign relations — 1975- — Sources
SOVIET UNION — Foreign relations — Afghanistan
SOVIET UNION — Foreign relations — Africa
SOVIET UNION — Foreign relations — Algeria
SOVIET UNION — Foreign relations — Arab countries — History — 20th century
SOVIET UNION — Foreign relations — Asia, Southeastern
SOVIET UNION — foreign relations — Caribbean Area
SOVIET UNION — Foreign relations — China
SOVIET UNION — Foreign relations — China — Sinkiang Province
SOVIET UNION — Foreign relations — Czechoslovakia
SOVIET UNION — Foreign relations — Developing countries
SOVIET UNION — Foreign relations — Developing countries — Congresses
SOVIET UNION — Foreign relations — Europe
SOVIET UNION — Foreign relations — Europe, Eastern
SOVIET UNION — Foreign relations — Finland
SOVIET UNION — Foreign relations — Germany
SOVIET UNION — Foreign relations — Germany (East)
SOVIET UNION — Foreign relations — Great Britain
SOVIET UNION — Foreign relations — Hungary
SOVIET UNION — Foreign relations — India
SOVIET UNION — Foreign relations — Iran
SOVIET UNION — Foreign relations — Latin America — Congresses
SOVIET UNION — Foreign relations — Libya
SOVIET UNION — Foreign relations — Near East
SOVIET UNION — Foreign relations — Poland
SOVIET UNION — Foreign relations — South Africa
SOVIET UNION — Foreign relations — South Asia
SOVIET UNION — Foreign relations — United States
SOVIET UNION — Foreign relations — United States — Addresses, essays, lectures
SOVIET UNION — Foreign relations — United States — Case studies
SOVIET UNION — Foreign relations — United States — Congresses
SOVIET UNION — Foreign relations — Yemen
SOVIET UNION — Foreign relations — Yemen (People's Democratic Republic)
SOVIET UNION — Foreign relations — Yugoslavia
SOVIET UNION — Historiography
SOVIET UNION — History
SOVIET UNION — History — Bibliography
SOVIET UNION — History — Philosophy
SOVIET UNION — History — Sources
SOVIET UNION — History — Peter I, 1689-1725
SOVIET UNION — History — 19th century
SOVIET UNION — History — Conspiracy of December, 1825 — Historiography
SOVIET UNION — History — Nicholas II, 1894-1917
SOVIET UNION — History — 1894-1917
SOVIET UNION — History — Nicholas II, 1894-1917
SOVIET UNION — History — 20th century
SOVIET UNION — History — Revolution of 1905
SOVIET UNION — History — Revolution of 1905 — Congresses
SOVIET UNION — History — February Revolution, 1917
SOVIET UNION — History — Revolution, 1917-1921
SOVIET UNION — History — Revolution 1917-1921
SOVIET UNION — History — Revolution, 1917-1921
SOVIET UNION — History — Revolution, 1917-1921 — Causes
SOVIET UNION — History — Revolution, 1917-1921 — Chronology
SOVIET UNION — History — Revolution, 1917-1921 — Foreign public opinion, German — Sources
SOVIET UNION — History — Revolution, 1917-1921 — Historiography
SOVIET UNION — History — Revolution, 1917-1921 — Influence
SOVIET UNION — History — 1917-1936
SOVIET UNION — History — 1917-
SOVIET UNION — History — 1917- — Historiography

SOVIET UNION — History — 1917- —
    Sources
SOVIET UNION — History — 1925-1953
SOVIET UNION — History — 1925-1953
    — Bibliography
SOVIET UNION — History — 1939-1945
SOVIET UNION — History — 1953-1980
SOVIET UNION — History — 1953-
SOVIET UNION — History — 1953- —
    Bibliography
SOVIET UNION — History, Military —
    1917-
SOVIET UNION — Industries — Location
SOVIET UNION — Military policy
SOVIET UNION — Military relations —
    Finland
SOVIET UNION — Military relations —
    Near East
SOVIET UNION — Military relations —
    Pakistan
SOVIET UNION — Military relations —
    Persian Gulf Region
SOVIET UNION — Military relations —
    Scandinavia
SOVIET UNION — Military relations —
    United States
SOVIET UNION — National security
SOVIET UNION — Politics and government
SOVIET UNION — Politics and
    Government
SOVIET UNION — Politics and government
SOVIET UNION — Politics and government
    — To 1533
SOVIET UNION — Politics and government
    — 1533-1613
SOVIET UNION — Politics and government
    — 19th century
SOVIET UNION — Politics and government
    — 1881-1894
SOVIET UNION — Politics and government
    — 1894-1917
SOVIET UNION — Politics and government
    — 20th century — Addresses, essays,
    lectures
SOVIET UNION — Politics and government
    — 1904-1914
SOVIET UNION — Politics and government
    — 1917 — Posters
SOVIET UNION — Politics and government
    — 1917-1936
SOVIET UNION — Politics and government
    — 1917-
SOVIET UNION — Politics and government
    — 1936-1953
SOVIET UNION — Politics and government
    — 1953-1982
SOVIET UNION — Politics and government
    — 1953-
SOVIET UNION — Politics and government
    — 1982-
SOVIET UNION — Popular culture
SOVIET UNION — Population
SOVIET UNION — Population — Study
    and teaching
SOVIET UNION — Population policy
SOVIET UNION — Public opinion
SOVIET UNION — Relations — Argentina
SOVIET UNION — Relations — Bulgaria
SOVIET UNION — Relations — Cuba
SOVIET UNION — Relations — Europe,
    Eastern
SOVIET UNION — Relations — Germany
SOVIET UNION — Relations — Great
    Britain
SOVIET UNION — Relations — India
SOVIET UNION — Relations — Iran —
    Azerbaijan
SOVIET UNION — Relations — Latin
    America
SOVIET UNION — Relations — Moldavia
SOVIET UNION — Relations — United
    States
SOVIET UNION — Relations (Military)
    with the United States
SOVIET UNION — Religion
SOVIET UNION — Revolution, 1917-1921
    — Personal narratives
SOVIET UNION — Rural conditions
SOVIET UNION — Social conditions
SOVIET UNION — Social conditions —
    1801-1917
SOVIET UNION — Social conditions —
    1917-
SOVIET UNION — Social conditions —
    1970-
SOVIET UNION — Social conditions —
    1970- — Congresses
SOVIET UNION — Social life and customs
    — 19th century
SOVIET UNION — Social life and customs
    — 1970-
SOVIET UNION — Social policy
SOVIET UNION — Statistics
SOVIET UNION — Statistics —
    Handbooks, manuals, etc — Bibliography
SOVIET UNION — Relations — Europe
SOVIET UNION. Armiia — History
SOVIET UNION. Armiia — History
SOVIET UNION. Armiia — Political
    activity
SOVIET UNION. Ministerstvo inostrannykh
    del
SOVIET UNION. Voenno-morskoĭ flot
SOVIET UNION — Foreign relations —
    1975-
SOVIET UNION — Foreign relations —
    Germany
SOVIET UNION, NORTHERN — Ethnic
    relations
SOVIET UNION, NORTHERN — Native
    races
SOVIET UNION, NORTHERN — Social
    conditions
SOVIET UNION X HISTORY — February
    Revolution, 1917
SOVIETS — Russian S.F.S.R. — Leningrad
SOVIETS — Russian S.F.S.R. — Moscow
SOVIETS — Ukraine
SOZIALDEMOKRATISCHE PARTEI
    DEUTSCHLANDS
SOZIALDEMOKRATISCHE PARTEI
    DEUTSCHLANDS — History
SOZIALDEMOKRATISCHE PARTIE
    DEUTSCHLANDS — History
SOZIALISTISCHE EINHEITSPARTEI
    DEUTSCHLANDS — History
SOZIALISTISCHE EINHEITSPARTEI
    DEUTSCHLANDS — History — Sources
SOZIALISTISCHE FRONT
SPACE COLONIES
SPACE FLIGHT
SPACE IN ECONOMICS
SPACE IN ECONOMICS — Mathematical
    models
SPACE LAW
SPACE PERCEPTION
SPACE SCIENCES — France
SPACE STATIONS — Legal status, laws,
    etc
SPACE WARFARE
SPACE WEAPONS
SPAIN — Armed Forces
SPAIN — Armed forces — Civil rights —
    Congresses
SPAIN — Armed forces — Political activity
SPAIN — Boundaries — France
SPAIN — Census, 1981
SPAIN — Civilization
SPAIN — Colonies — America
SPAIN — Colonies — America —
    Administration
SPAIN — Colonies — America — Economic
    policy
SPAIN — Commerce
SPAIN — Commerce — European
    Economic Community countries
SPAIN — Commerce — Latin America
SPAIN — Commercial policy
SPAIN — Constitution
SPAIN — Constitutional history
SPAIN — Constitutional law
SPAIN — Defenses
SPAIN — Description and travel — 1981
SPAIN — Economic conditions
SPAIN — Economic conditions — 19th
    century
SPAIN — Economic conditions — 20th
    century
SPAIN — Economic conditions —
    1918-1975
SPAIN — Economic conditions — 1975-
SPAIN — Economic policy
SPAIN — Economic policy — 1975-
SPAIN — Foreign economic relations
SPAIN — Foreign opinion, British
SPAIN — Foreign relations — Treaties
SPAIN — Foreign relations — 18th century
SPAIN — Foreign relations — 20th century
SPAIN — Foreign relations — 1939-1975
SPAIN — Foreign relations — France
SPAIN — Foreign relations — Germany
SPAIN — Foreign relations — Great Britain
SPAIN — Foreign relations — Italy
SPAIN — Foreign relations — Portugal
SPAIN — History — Civil War, 1936-1939
SPAIN — History — Civil War, 1936-1939
    — Personal narratives
SPAIN — History — Republic, 1931-1939
SPAIN — History — Ferdinand and
    Isabella, 1479-1516
SPAIN — History — Charles I, 1516-1556
SPAIN — History — House of Austria,
    1516-1700
SPAIN — History — Philip II, 1556-1598
SPAIN — History — Philip V, 1700-1746
SPAIN — History — 19th century
SPAIN — History — Napoleonic Conquest,
    1808-1813
SPAIN — History — Revolution, 1854
SPAIN — History — 1868-1931
SPAIN — History — Carlist War, 1873-1876
SPAIN — History — 20th century
SPAIN — History — Dictatorship,
    1923-1930
SPAIN — History — 1923-1930 —
    Congresses
SPAIN — History — Revolution, 1931
SPAIN — History — Republic, 1931-1939
SPAIN — History — Civil War, 1936-39
SPAIN — History — Civil War, 1936-1939
SPAIN — History — Civil war, 1936-1939
SPAIN — History — Civil War, 1936-1939
SPAIN — History — Civil war, 1936-1939
SPAIN — History — Civil War, 1936-1939
SPAIN — History — Civil War, 1936-1939
    — Bibliography
SPAIN — History — Civil War, 1936-1939
    — Foreign participation
SPAIN — History — Civil War, 1936-1939
    — Foreign participation — French
SPAIN — History — Civil War, 1936-1939
    — Foreign public opinion
SPAIN — History — Civil War, 1936-1939
    — Participation, American
SPAIN — History — Civil War, 1936-1939
    — Participation, British
SPAIN — History — Civil War, 1936-1939
    — Participation, Canadian
SPAIN — History — Civil War, 1936-1939
    — Participation, Foreign
SPAIN — History — Civil War, 1936-1939
    — Personal narratives
SPAIN — History — Civil war, 1936-1939
    — Personal narratives
SPAIN — History — Civil War, 1936-1939
    — Personal narratives, American
SPAIN — History — Civil War, 1936-1939
    — Personal narratives, British
SPAIN — History — Civil War, 1936-1939
    — Personal narratives, Canadian
SPAIN — History — Civil War. 1936-1939
    — Photography
SPAIN — History — Civil War, 1936-1939
    — Refugees
SPAIN — History — Civil War, 1936-1939
    — Sources
SPAIN — History — 1939-1975
SPAIN — History — 1975-
SPAIN — Industries
SPAIN — Industries — Finance
SPAIN — Industries — History

SPAIN — Intellectual life — 20th century
SPAIN — Kings and rulers — Biography
SPAIN — Military policy
SPAIN — Nobility — Biography
SPAIN — Politics and government
SPAIN — Politics and government — 1621-1665
SPAIN — Politics and government — 19th century
SPAIN — Politics and government — 1808-1814
SPAIN — Politics and government — 1868-1875
SPAIN — Politics and government — 1886-1931
SPAIN — Politics and government — 20th century
SPAIN — Politics and government — 1923-1930
SPAIN — Politics and government — 1923-1930 — Congresses
SPAIN — Politics and government — 1931-1939
SPAIN — Politics and government — 1939-1945
SPAIN — Politics and government — 1939-1975
SPAIN — Politics and government — 1975-
SPAIN — Politics and government — 1976-
SPAIN — Population
SPAIN — Population — Statistics
SPAIN — Relations — Argentina
SPAIN — Relations — Europe
SPAIN — Relations — France
SPAIN — Relations — Germany
SPAIN — Relations — Latin America
SPAIN — Relations — Morocco
SPAIN — Rural conditions
SPAIN — Rural conditions — History
SPAIN — Social conditions
SPAIN — Social conditions — 19th century
SPAIN — Social conditions — 1886-1939
SPAIN — Social conditions — 20th century
SPAIN — Social conditions — 1939-1975
SPAIN — Social conditions — 1975-
SPAIN — Social life and customs
SPAIN — Social policy
SPAIN. Comisión de Reformas Sociales — History
SPAIN. Guardia Civil — History
SPAIN. Ministerio de Industria y Energía
SPAIN. Ministerio de Trabajo y Seguridad Social
SPAIN. Tribunal Supremo
SPANISH LANGUAGE — Dictionaries — English
SPANISH LANGUAGE — Social aspects — United States — Addresses, essays, lectures
SPANISH LANGUAGE — United States — Addresses, essays, lectures
SPARE SURVEILLANCE
SPASOWSKI, ROMUALD
SPATIAL ANALYSIS (STATISTICS)
SPATIAL SYSTEMS
SPECIAL DISTRICTS — Illinois
SPECIAL DRAWING RIGHTS
SPECULATION
SPECULATION — Mathematical models
SPEECH ACTS (LINGUISHES)
SPEECH ACTS (LINGUISTICS)
SPEECH AND SOCIAL STATUS — Indonesia — Solo
SPEECH PERCEPTION
SPEECH SYNTHESIS
SPENCER, JOHN POYNTZ SPENCER, Earl — Correspondence
SPENDINGS TAX — United States
SPIES — Canada
SPIES — Great Britain
SPIES — Great Britain — Biography
SPINOZA, BENEDICTUS DE
SPIRITUALITY — History of doctrines — 16th century
SPIRITUALITY — History of doctrines — 17th century

SPOKANE (WASH.) — Economic conditions
SPOKANE (WASH.) — Social conditions
SPONSORS — Europe — History
SPORTS — History
SPORTS — Political aspects — Argentina
SPORTS — Political aspects — Ireland
SPORTS — Social aspects
SPORTS — Social aspects — History
SPORTS — Social aspects — Great Britain
SPORTS — Finland — Statistics
SPORTS — Great Britain — History
SPORTS AND STATE
SPORTS AND STATE — South Africa
SPORTS SPECTATORS — History
SPRY, IRENE M — Addresses, essays, lectures
SPSS/PC⁺ (COMPUTER SYSTEM)
SPY STORIES
SQUATTER SETTLEMENTS — Great Britain — Handbooks, manuals, etc.
SQUATTER SETTLEMENTS — Pakistan — Lahore
SQUATTERS — England
SQUATTERS — Kenya — History — 20th century
SRI LANKA — Census, 1981
SRI LANKA — Commerce
SRI LANKA — Economic conditions
SRI LANKA — Ethnic relations
SRI LANKA — Foreign relations
SRI LANKA — Foreign relations — China
SRI LANKA — Foreign relations — India
SRI LANKA — Governors — Biography
SRI LANKA — History
SRI LANKA — Languages
SRI LANKA — Neutrality
SRI LANKA — politics and govenment
SRI LANKA — Politics and government
SRI LANKA — Population — Statistics
SRI LANKA — Relations — India
SRI LANKA — Bibliography
SRI LANKA. Department of National Archives
SRI LANKA. Ministry of Industries and Scientific Affairs
ST. HUGH'S COLLEGE — History
ST. VINCENT'S COMMUNITY HOME
STABLE POPULATION MODEL
STADIA — Great Britain — Safety measures
STALIN, JOSEPH
STALIN, JOSEPH, 1879-1953
STALKER, JOHN
STAMP-DUTIES — Legal aspects, laws, etc. — Great Britain
STANDARD CHARTERED PLC
STANFORD UNIVERSITY — Students — Attitudes — Case studies
STARVATION
STATE AID TO HIGHER EDUCATION — Great Britain
STATE BONDS — Law and legislation — United States — History
STATE FARMS — Russsian S.F.S.R. — Ural Mountains region
STATE GOVERNMENTS
STATE GOVERNMENTS — India
STATE-LOCAL RELATIONS — England — Bristol
STATE-LOCAL RELATIONS — France — Bordeaux
STATE-LOCAL RELATIONS — United States
STATE SUCCESSION
STATE, THE
STATE, THE — Addresses, essays, lectures
STATE, THE — History
STATE UNIVERSITIES AND COLLEGES — United States — Directories
STATES, SIZE OF
STATES, SMALL
STATESMAN — Canada — Biography
STATESMAN — Soviet Union — Biography
STATESMAN — United States — Biography
STATESMEN

STATESMEN — Addresses, essays, lectures
STATESMEN — Italy — Biography
STATESMEN — Australia — Biography
STATESMEN — Brazil — Biography
STATESMEN — Bulgaria — Addresses, essays, lectures
STATESMEN — Bulgaria — Biography
STATESMEN — Canada — Biography
STATESMEN — Finland — Biography
STATESMEN — Germany — Biography
STATESMEN — Great Britain — Biography
STATESMEN — Great Britain — Correspondence
STATESMEN — India — Biography
STATESMEN — Japan — Biography
STATESMEN — Nigeria — Biography
STATESMEN — Soviet Union — Biography
STATESMEN — Spain — Biography
STATESMEN — United States — Biography
STATESMEN — United States — Interviews
STATICS AND DYNAMICS (SOCIAL SCIENCES)
STATISICAL SERVICES
STATISTICAL DICISION
STATISTICAL HYPOTHESIS TESTING
STATISTICAL OFFICE OF THE EUROPEAN COMMUNITIES
STATISTICAL OFFICE OF THE EUROPEAN COMMUNITIES — Catalogs
STATISTICAL SERVICES
STATISTICAL SERVICES — Finland
STATISTICS
STATISTICS — Charts, diagrams, etc.
STATISTICS — Data processing — Handbooks, manuals, etc
STATISTICS — Dictionaries
STATISTICS — Graphic methods
STATISTICS — History
STATISTICS — History — 19th century — Bibliography
STATISTICS — History — 20th century — Bibliography
STATISTICS — Programmed instruction
STATISTICS — Finland
STATISTICS CANADA. Travel, Tourism and Recreation Section
STATUS OFFENDERS — Government policy — United States
STATUS OFFENDERS — United States — Case studies
STATUTES — England
STATUTES — United States
STEAMBOATS — History — 19th century
STEDELIJK HOGER INSTITUUT VOOR SOCIALE STUDIE
STEEL INDUSTRY AND TRADE
STEEL INDUSTRY AND TRADE — Government policy — Europe
STEEL INDUSTRY AND TRADE — Government policy — European Economic Community countries
STEEL INDUSTRY AND TRADE — Government policy — United States
STEEL INDUSTRY AND TRADE — Planning — Mathematical models
STEEL INDUSTRY AND TRADE — Belgium — Management — Case studies
STEEL INDUSTRY AND TRADE — Canada
STEEL INDUSTRY AND TRADE — England — Sheffield Region (South Yorkshire) — History
STEEL INDUSTRY AND TRADE — Europe
STEEL INDUSTRY AND TRADE — European Economic Community countries
STEEL INDUSTRY AND TRADE — France — Lorraine
STEEL INDUSTRY AND TRADE — Germany — Rhineland
STEEL INDUSTRY AND TRADE — Germany — Ruhr River Valley
STEEL INDUSTRY AND TRADE — Germany — Saarland
STEEL INDUSTRY AND TRADE — Germany (West)

STEEL INDUSTRY AND TRADE — Great Britain
STEEL INDUSTRY AND TRADE — Great Britain — History — 19th century
STEEL INDUSTRY AND TRADE — Great Britain — History — 20th century
STEEL INDUSTRY AND TRADE — India
STEEL INDUSTRY AND TRADE — Mexico — Planning — Mathematical models
STEEL INDUSTRY AND TRADE — Spain — Basque provinces — History
STEEL INDUSTRY AND TRADE — Sweden — History
STEEL INDUSTRY AND TRADE — United States
STEEL INDUSTRY AND TRADE — United States — History
STEEL INDUSTRY AND TRADE — Wales — Shotton (Clwyd) — History
STEEL INDUSTRY MANAGEMENT ASSOCIATION
STEEL MINIMILLS — United States
STEREOTYPE (PSYCHOLOGY)
STEREOTYPE (PSYCHOLOGY) — Case studies
STERILIZATION, EUGENIC — Germany
STERILIZATION OF WOMEN — Germany
STERN
STEVENS, ISAAC INGALLS
STIGMA (SOCIAL PSYCHOLOGY)
STOCHASTIC ANALYSIS
STOCHASTIC PROCESSES
STOCHASTIC PROGRAMMING
STOCK EXCHANGE (London)
STOCK EXCHANGE
STOCK-EXCHANGE
STOCK-EXCHANGE — Periodicals
STOCK-EXCHANGE — Great Britain
STOCK-EXCHANGE — Ireland — History
STOCK-EXCHANGE — Queensland — Brisbane — History
STOCK EXCHANGE — United States
STOCK OWNERSHIP
STOCK OWNERSHIP — Great Britain
STOCK OWNERSHIP — United States
STOCKHOLDERS
STOCKHOLDERS — Great Britain
STOCKHOLDERS — United States
STOCKMAN, DAVID ALAN
STOCKMANN, DAVID ALAN
STOCKS — Law and legislation — Great Britain
STOCKS — Prices
STOCKS — Great Britain
STOCKS — India
STOCZNIA GDAŃSKA IM. LENINA
STRIKE, GDAŃSK, POLAND, 1980
STOKES, CHARLES
STOLIAROV, IVAN
STOLYPIN, P. A.
STONEHENGE (WILTSHIRE, ENGLAND)
STORAGE AND MOVING TRADE — Netherlands — Statistics
STORE HOURS — Law and legislation — Great Britain
STORE HOURS — Great Britain
STORE LOCATION — Great Britain
STORES, RETAIL
STORES, RETAIL — England — London
STORY, JOSEPH
STORYTELLERS — Italy
STORYTELLERS — United States
STRATEGIC DEFENCE INITIATIVE
STRATEGIC DEFENSE INITIATIVE
STRATEGIC DEFENSE INITIATIVE — Bibliography
STRATEGIC DEFENSE INITIATIVE — Congresses
STRATEGIC DEFENSE INITIATIVE — Study and teaching
STRATEGIC FORCES — Soviet Union
STRATEGIC MATERIALS — Commerce — South Africa
STRATEGIC PLANNING
STRATEGIC PLANNING — Case studies
STRATEGIC PLANNING — Great Britain
STRATEGIC PLANNING — Japan
STRATEGIC PLANNING — United States
STRATEGY
STRATEGY — History
STRATEGY — History — 20th century
STRATEGY — Political aspects — Soviet Union — History — 20th century
STRATHCLYDE — Emigration and immigration — History
STRATHCLYDE — Religious life and customs
STRATHCLYDE (SCOTLAND) — Economic conditions
STRATHCLYDE (SCOTLAND) — Economic policy
STREET-RAILROADS — Hongkong — Employees
STRESS IN CHILDREN — Bibliography
STRESS (PHYSIOLOGY)
STRESS (PSYCHOLOGY)
STRESS (PSYCHOLOGY) — Social aspects
STRESS (PSYCHOLOGY) — Social aspects — Research
STRIKERS AND LOCK-OUTS — Coal mining — England — Barnsley (South Yorkshire)
STRIKES AND LOCK-OUTS
STRIKES AND LOCK-OUTS — Coal-miners — Great Britain
STRIKES AND LOCK-OUTS — Coal mining — Great Britain
STRIKES AND LOCK-OUTS — Newspapers — England — London
STRIKES AND LOCK-OUTS — Social aspects
STRIKES AND LOCK-OUTS — Transport workers — Ireland — Dublin
STRIKES AND LOCK-OUTS — England — London — Printers
STRIKES AND LOCKOUTS — Agricultural laborers — Patagonia (Argentina and Chile)
STRIKES AND LOCKOUTS — Coal mining — England — Doncaster (South Yorkshire)
STRIKES AND LOCKOUTS — Coal mining — Scotland — Mauchline (Ayrshire)
STRIKES AND LOCKOUTS — Law and legislation
STRIKES AND LOCKOUTS — Law and legislation — United States
STRIKES AND LOCKOUTS — Meat industry — Minnesota — Austin
STRIKES AND LOCKOUTS — Metal workers — Germany (West)
STRIKES AND LOCKOUTS — Printers — Germany (West)
STRIKES AND LOCKOUTS — Public utilities — Law and legislation — Great Britain
STRIKES AND LOCKOUTS — Railroads — Argentina — History
STRIKES AND LOCKOUTS — Argentina — History
STRIKES AND LOCKOUTS — Europe
STRIKES AND LOCKOUTS — France — History — 19th century
STRIKES AND LOCKOUTS — France — Paris
STRIKES AND LOCKOUTS — Germany (West)
STRIKES AND LOCKOUTS — Netherlands
STRIKES AND LOCKOUTS — Poland
STRIKES AND LOCKOUTS — Spain
STRIKES AND LOCKOUTS — Spain — Cantabria — History — 20th century
STRIKES AND LOCKOUTS — Spain — Madrid — History — 20th century
STRIKES AND LOCKOUTS — United States
STRIP MINING — Environmental aspects — Ukraine
STRIP MINING — Law and legislation — United States
STRUCTURAL ANTHROPOLOGY
STRUCTURALISM
STRUCTURALISM — Addresses, essays, lectures
STRUCTURALISM — History
STRUCTURALISM (LITERARY ANALYSIS)
STRUCTURED PROGRAMMING
STUART, HOUSE OF
STUDENT ADJUSTMENT
STUDENT ASPIRATION — United States
STUDENT ASPIRATIONS — California — Stanford — Case studies
STUDENT MOBILITY — Egypt — Statistics
STUDENT MOVEMENTS — Great Britain
STUDENT NONVIOLENT COORDINATING COMMITTEE (U.S.) — Biography
STUDENTS — Belgium
STUDENTS — Crimes against — England — Manchester (Greater Manchester)
STUDENTS — Political activity
STUDENTS — Belgium — Statistics
STUDENTS — Finland — Socioeconomic status
STUDENTS — France
STUDENTS — Great Britain — Political activity
STUDENTS — United States — Psychology
STUDENTS, BLACK — France
STUDENTS, FOREIGN
STUDENTS, FOREIGN — Bibliography
STUDENTS, FOREIGN — Legal status, laws, etc. — Great Britain
STUDENTS, INTERCHANGE OF — European Economic Community countries
STUDENTS, RATING OF — Germany (West)
STUDY, METHOD OF
STURGE, JOSEPH
SUBCONSCIOUSNESS
SUBCONSIOUSNESS
SUBJECT HEADINGS — Bibliography
SUBSIDIARY CORPORATIONS — Management
SUBSIDIARY CORPORATIONS — Taxation
SUBSIDIES — England
SUBSIDIES — Europe — Handbooks, manuals, etc.
SUBSIDIES — European Economic Community countries — Directories
SUBSIDIES — Great Britain
SUBSIDIES — Scotland
SUBSIDIES — Wales
SUBSISTENCE ECONOMY — Alaska — Addresses, essays, lectures
SUBSTANCE ABUSE
SUBSTANCE ABUSE — Dictionaries
SUBSTANCE ABUSE — dictionaries
SUBSTANCE ABUSE — Slang — Dictionaries
SUBSTANCE ABUSE — Terminology
SUBSTANCE ABUSE — United States
SUBURBAN LIFE — California — Orange County — Case studies
SUBURBAN LIFE — United States
SUBURBS — Congresses
SUBURBS — California — Orange County — Case studies
SUBURBS — United States
SUBVERSIVE ACTIVITIES — France
SUBVERSIVE ACTIVITIES — Great Britain — History — 17th century
SUBVERSIVE ACTIVITIES — United States
SUBVERSIVE ACTIVITIES — United States — History — 20th century
SUBWAYS — England — London
SUCCESS
SUCCESS IN BUSINESS — Great Britain
SUCCESS IN BUSINESS — Japan
SUCCESS IN BUSINESS — United States — Addresses, essays, lectures

SUCCESS IN BUSINESS — United States — Case studies
SUDAN — Biography
SUDAN — Economic conditions
SUDAN — Economic policy
SUDAN — Foreign economic relations — Great Britain
SUDAN — History
SUDAN — History — 1899-1956
SUDAN — History — Civil War, 1955-1972
SUDAN — History — 1956-
SUDAN — Industries
SUDAN — Politics and government
SUDAN — Social conditions
SUDDEN DEATH IN INFANTS — Government policy — United States
SUDDEN DEATH IN INFANTS — United States — Political aspects
SUDDEN INFANT DEATH — prevention & control — United States
SUDETENLAND (CZECHOSLOVAKIA) — History — 20th century — Sources
SUEZ CANAL — History
SUEZ CANAL (EGYPT)
SUEZ CANAL (EGYPT) — History
SUFFOLK — History
SUFFRAGE — Germany (West)
SUFFRAGE — South Africa
SUFFRAGETTES — Spain — History
SUFFRAGETTES — United States
SUFFRAGETTES — United States — Biography
SUFISM — Soviet Union — History
SUGAO (INDIA) — Economic conditions
SUGAO (INDIA) — Social conditions
SUGAR — Manufacture and refining — Taiwan
SUGAR CANE INDUSTRY — Dominican Republic
SUGAR GROWING — Taiwan
SUGAR GROWING — Taiwan — Linear programming
SUGAR TRADE
SUGAR TRADE — Government policy
SUGAR WORKERS — Dominican Republic
SUGARCANE — Fiji
SUGARCANE — Taiwan
SUICIDE
SUICIDE — Bibliography
SUICIDE — in adolescence
SUICIDE — in infancy & childhood
SUICIDE — Prevention
SUICIDE — Prevention — Addresses, essays, lectures
SUICIDE — prevention & control
SUICIDE — Japan
SUICIDE — United States — Bibliography
SUICIDE
SUKARNO, President of Indonesia
SUKYO MAHIKARI
SULPHUR — Environmental aspects
SULTAN GALIEV, MIRSAID
SUN, YAT-SEN
SUN, YAT-SEN — Exile, 1896-1897 — England — London
SUN FIRE OFFICE
SUNDAY LEGISLATION — Great Britain
SUNDAY-SCHOOLS — England — History
SUNDERLAND (TYNE AND WEAR) — Religion
SUNTORY-TOYOTA INTERNATIONAL CENTRE FOR ECONOMICS AND RELATED DISCIPLINES
SUOMEN KOMUNISTINEN PUOLUE
SUPERCALC (COMPUTER PROGRAM)
SUPERCOMPUTERS
SUPERMARKETS — Denmark
SUPERVISION OF SOCIAL WORKERS
SUPERVISORS, INDUSTRIAL
SUPERVISORS, INDUSTRIAL — Great Britain
SUPPLEMENTAL SECURITY INCOME PROGRAM — Australia
SUPPLEMENTAL SECURITY INCOME PROGRAM — Great Britain
SUPPLEMENTAL SECURITY INCOME PROGRAM — Great Britain — Statistics
SUPPLEMENTARY EMPLOYMENT — European Economic Community countries — Statistics
SUPPLEMENTARY EMPLOYMENT — Germany (West)
SUPPLEMENTARY EMPLOYMENT — Great Britain
SUPPLY AND DEMAND
SUPPLY AND DEMAND — Transportation — Mathematical models
SUPPLY-SIDE ECONOMICS
SUPPLY-SIDE ECONOMICS — Organisation for Economic Co-operation and Development countries — Mathematical models
SUPPLY-SIDE ECONOMICS — United States
SUPPLY-SIDE ECONOMICS — United States — Congresses
SUPPORT (DOMESTIC RELATIONS) — Great Britain
SURETY OF THE PEACE — England
SURETYSHIP AND GUARANTY — South Africa
SURFACE ROUGHNESS — Measurement
SURINAM — Social conditions
SURREY — Economic conditions
SURREY — Population — Statistics
SURREY — Statistics, Vital
SURVEYS
SURVIVORS' BENEFITS — France
SUTCLIFFE, PETER, 1946-
SUTTNER, BERTHA VON
SVARĀJYA PARṬĪ (India)
SVENSKA KYRKAN
SVENSKA TÄNDSTICKS AKTIEBOLAGET — History
SVERIGES KOMMUNISTISKA PARTI
SWAT KOHISTAN (PAKISTAN) — History
SWAHILI LANGUAGE — Zaire — History
SWALCAP
SWAZILAND — Population
SWAZILAND — Rural conditions
SWEDEN — Commerce
SWEDEN — Economic conditions — 1945-
SWEDEN — Economic policy
SWEDEN — Foreign economic relations — Soviet Union
SWEDEN — Foreign relations
SWEDEN — Foreign relations — 1950-
SWEDEN — History — Christina, 1632-1654
SWEDEN — History — House of Pfalz-Zweibrücken, 1654-1718
SWEDEN — Industries
SWEDEN — Industries — History — 18th century
SWEDEN — Industries — History — 19th century
SWEDEN — Manufactures
SWEDEN — Politics and government — 1905-
SWEDEN — Politics and government — 1950-1973
SWEDEN — Politics and government — 1973-
SWEDEN — Population — Statistics
SWEDEN — Religious life and customs
SWEDEN — Social conditions — 1945-
SWEDES — Germany — History
SWEDES — Germany — Schleswig-Holstein — History
SWEDES — Soviet Union
SWEDISH LANGUAGE — Dictionaries — English
SWEDISH MATCH COMPANY See Svenska Tändsticks Aktiebologet
ŚWIATŁO, JÓZEF
SWINE — Ecomomic aspects — Denmark
SWISS — Argentina — History — 19th century
SWITZERLAND — Biography
SWITZERLAND — Boundaries
SWITZERLAND — Constitution
SWITZERLAND — Economic conditions — 1918-
SWITZERLAND — Economic conditions — 1945-
SWITZERLAND — Emigration and immigration
SWITZERLAND — Emigration and immigration — History — 19th century
SWITZERLAND — Foreign economic relations
SWITZERLAND — Foreign economic relations — France
SWITZERLAND — Foreign economic relations — Germany (West)
SWITZERLAND — Foreign relations — Sources
SWITZERLAND — History
SWITZERLAND — Industries
SWITZERLAND — Intellectual life — 20th century
SWITZERLAND — Politics and government
SWITZERLAND — Politics and government — 1945- — Addresses, essays, lectures
SWITZERLAND — Population
SWITZERLAND — Social conditions
SWITZERLAND — Social policy
SWITZERLAND. Commission d'experts chargée d'examiner la revision de l'assurance-accidents
SWITZERLAND. Office fédéral de la protection de l'environnement
SYMBOLIC INTERACTIONISM
SYMBOLISM
SYMBOLISM IN ART
SYMPOSIUM ON ARTIFICIAL AUDITORY STIMULATION (1982 : Erlangen)
SYNDICALISM — France — History
SYNDICALISM — France — History — 19th century
SYNDICALISM — Great Britain — History
SYNDICATES (FINANCE) — Great Britain
SYRIA — Boundaries
SYRIA — Census, 1970
SYRIA — Foreign relations — Lebanon
SYRIA — History — 20th century
SYRIA — Politics and government
SYRIA — Population — Statistics
SYRIA — Social conditions
SYRIA — Statistics, vital
SYRIAN AMERICANS — History
SYSTEM ANALYSIS
SYSTEM ANALYSIS — Collected works
SYSTEM ANALYSIS — Congresses
SYSTEM DESIGN
SYSTEM THEORY
TABLE RONDE DES AIDES EXTÉRIEURES AU RWANDA (3ièm : 1982 : Kigali)
TABOO
TACITUS, COMELIUS
TAHAA (SOCIETY ISLANDS) — Population — Statistics
TAHITI (SOCIETY ISLANDS) — Economic conditions — Statistics
TAHITI (SOCIETY ISLANDS) — Population — Statistics
TAHUATA (MARQUESAS ISLANDS) — Population — Statistics
TAIARAPU-EST (TAHITI : REGION) — Population — Statistics
TAIARAPU-OUEST (TAHITI : REGION) — Population — Statistics
TAIWAN
TAIWAN — Economic conditions
TAIWAN — Economic conditions — 1945
TAIWAN — Economic conditions — 1945-
TAIWAN — Economic policy
TAIWAN — Economic policy — 1945-
TAIWAN — Foreign relations — 1945-
TAIWAN — Foreign relations — United States
TAIWAN — History — 1945- — Addresses, essays, lectures

TAIWAN — Industries
TAIWAN — Politics and government — 1945-1975
TAIWAN — Politics and government — 1945-
TAIWAN — Rural conditions
TAIWAN — Social conditions
TAIWAN — Social policy
TAIWAN FERTILIZER CO., LTD.
TAIWAN RELATIONS ACT
TAKAROA (TUAMOTU ISLANDS) — Population — Statistics
TALES — Italy
TALES — Papua New Guinea — History and criticism
TALES — United States
TALK SHOWS — United States
TALLENSI (AFRICAN PEOPLE)
TAMIL NADU (INDIA) — Economic conditions — Statistics
TAMILS — India
TAMILS — Sri Lanka
TANAKA, ŌDŌ
TANKERS — Law and legislation — Great Britain
TANKS (MILITARY SCIENCE) — History
TANZANIA — Economic policy
TANZANIA — Industries
TANZANIA — Politics and government — 1964-
TANZANIA — Rural conditions
TAPESTRY, FLEMISH
TAPUTAPUATEA (RAIATEA : REGION) — Population — Statistics
TARIFF — Law and legislation
TARIFF — Law and legislation — Canada — Congresses
TARIFF — Law and legislation — European Economic Community countries
TARIFF — Law and legislation — Mexico
TARIFF — Law and legislation — United States — Congresses
TARIFF — Canada
TARIFF — Canada — History — 19th century
TARIFF — Great Britain
TARIFF — Great Britain — History
TARIFF — United States
TARIFF PREFERENCES — Congresses
TARIFF PREFERENCES — European Economic Community countries
TARPENBEK (Ship)
TASCA, ANGELO
TASMANIA — History — 1803-1851
TASMANIA — Population
TASMANIAN DEVELOPMENT AUTHORITY
TATAKOTO (TUAMOTU ISLANDS) — Population — Statistics
TATAR A.S.S.R. — Politics and government
TATARS — Russian S.F.S.R — Tatarskaīa A.S.S.R — History
TATARSKAĪA A.S.S.R. (R.S.F.S.R.) — History
TAX ADMINISTRATION AND PROCEDURE
TAX ADMINISTRATION AND PROCEDURE — Great Britain
TAX COLLECTION — China — History
TAX EVASION — Mathematical models
TAX EVASION — Germany (West)
TAX EVASION — Great Britain
TAX HAVENS
TAX INCIDENCE — Québec (Province)
TAX PLANNING — Great Britain
TAXATION
TAXATION — Environmental aspects — Australia
TAXATION — Law and legislation — France
TAXATION — Law and legislation — Great Britain
TAXATION — Law and legislation — Hong Kong
TAXATION — Law and legislation — Korea (South)
TAXATION — Law and legislation — Peru
TAXATION — Law and legislation — Scotland
TAXATION — Law and legislation — Soviet Union
TAXATION — Law and legislation — United States
TAXATION — Asia, Southeastern
TAXATION — Australia
TAXATION — Developing countries
TAXATION — France — Dauphiné — History
TAXATION — Great Britain
TAXATION — Great Britain — Forms
TAXATION — Great Britain — Statistics
TAXATION — India
TAXATION — Pakistan
TAXATION — Puerto Rico
TAXATION — South Africa
TAXATION — Soviet Union — History
TAXATION — Taiwan
TAXATION — United States
TAXATION — United States — Mathematical models
TAXATION — United States — States — Congresses
TAXATION, DOUBLE
TAXATION, DOUBLE — Treaties
TAXATION, DOUBLE — Soviet Union
TAXATION OF ALIENS
TAXATION OF ALIENS — Soviet Union
TAXATION OF ARTICLES OF CONSUMPTION — Mathematical models
TAXATION OF ARTICLES OF CONSUMPTION — United States
TAXATION OF BONDS, SECURITIES, ETC. — Peru
TAXATION OF PERSONAL PROPERTY — Great Britain
TAYLOR, ZACHARY
TAYSIDE (SCOTLAND) — Antiquities
TEA — Sri Lanka
TEA PLANTATION WORKERS — Sri Lanka
TEA TRADE
TEA TRADE — Mathematical models
TEACHERS — In-service training — European Economic Community countries
TEACHERS — Salaries, pensions, etc. — Law and legislation — Great Britain
TEACHERS — Salaries, pensions, etc — United States — Congresses
TEACHERS — England — London — Political activity
TEACHERS' PAY AND CONDITIONS BILL 1986-87
TEACHERS, TRAINING OF — Great Britain
TEACHING
TEACHING TEAMS — England — Suffolk
TECHNICAL ASSISTANCE
TECHNICAL ASSISTANCE — Anthropological aspects
TECHNICAL ASSISTANCE — Anthropological aspects — Case studies
TECHNICAL ASSISTANCE — Dictionaries
TECHNICAL ASSISTANCE — Evaluation
TECHNICAL ASSISTANCE, AMERICAN — Nepal
TECHNICAL ASSISTANCE, BRITISH
TECHNICAL ASSISTANCE, BRITISH — Administration
TECHNICAL ASSISTANCE, BRITISH — Directories
TECHNICAL ASSISTANCE, BRITISH — Evaluation
TECHNICAL ASSISTANCE, BRITISH — Bangladesh
TECHNICAL ASSISTANCE, BRITISH — Bangladesh — Evaluation
TECHNICAL ASSISTANCE, BRITISH — Sri Lanka
TECHNICAL ASSISTANCE, BRITISH — Thailand
TECHNICAL ASSISTANCE, CANADIAN — Bibliography
TECHNICAL EDUCATION — Evaluation
TECHNICAL EDUCATION — Europe — Directories
TECHNICAL EDUCATION — United States
TECHNICAL INNOVATIONS — Developing countries
TECHNOCRACY
TECHNOLOGICAL FORECASTING
TECHNOLOGICAL INNOVATION — Economic aspects
TECHNOLOGICAL INNOVATION — Social aspects
TECHNOLOGICAL INNOVATIONS
TECHNOLOGICAL INNOVATIONS — Congresses
TECHNOLOGICAL INNOVATIONS — Economic aspects
TECHNOLOGICAL INNOVATIONS — Economic aspects — Developing countries
TECHNOLOGICAL INNOVATIONS — Economic aspects — Europe
TECHNOLOGICAL INNOVATIONS — Economic aspects — Great Britain
TECHNOLOGICAL INNOVATIONS — Economic aspects — Japan
TECHNOLOGICAL INNOVATIONS — Economic aspects — Latin America
TECHNOLOGICAL INNOVATIONS — Economic aspects — United States
TECHNOLOGICAL INNOVATIONS — Government policy
TECHNOLOGICAL INNOVATIONS — Government policy — France
TECHNOLOGICAL INNOVATIONS — Government policy — Ireland
TECHNOLOGICAL INNOVATIONS — History — Addresses, essays, lectures
TECHNOLOGICAL INNOVATIONS — Law and legislation
TECHNOLOGICAL INNOVATIONS — Law and legislation — Québec (Province)
TECHNOLOGICAL INNOVATIONS — Management — Congresses
TECHNOLOGICAL INNOVATIONS — Social aspects
TECHNOLOGICAL INNOVATIONS — Social aspects — Argentina
TECHNOLOGICAL INNOVATIONS — Social aspects — Switzerland
TECHNOLOGICAL INNOVATIONS — Argentina
TECHNOLOGICAL INNOVATIONS — Australia
TECHNOLOGICAL INNOVATIONS — Canada
TECHNOLOGICAL INNOVATIONS — Developing countries
TECHNOLOGICAL INNOVATIONS — Developing countries — Case studies
TECHNOLOGICAL INNOVATIONS — Europe
TECHNOLOGICAL INNOVATIONS — European Economic Community countries
TECHNOLOGICAL INNOVATIONS — European Economic community countries — Bibliography — Catalogs
TECHNOLOGICAL INNOVATIONS — France
TECHNOLOGICAL INNOVATIONS — Great Britain
TECHNOLOGICAL INNOVATIONS — India
TECHNOLOGICAL INNOVATIONS — Ireland
TECHNOLOGICAL INNOVATIONS — Nigeria
TECHNOLOGICAL INNOVATIONS — Québec (Province)
TECHNOLOGICAL INNOVATIONS — Soviet Union
TECHNOLOGICAL INNOVATIONS — Soviet Union — Finance
TECHNOLOGICAL INNOVATIONS — Spain
TECHNOLOGICAL INNOVATIONS — United States

TECHNOLOGICAL INNOVATIONS — United States — Congresses
TECHNOLOGY
TECHNOLOGY — Bibliography
TECHNOLOGY — Congresses
TECHNOLOGY — Economic aspects — Soviet Union
TECHNOLOGY — History
TECHNOLOGY — International cooperation
TECHNOLOGY — Moral and ethical aspects
TECHNOLOGY — Philosophy
TECHNOLOGY — Religious aspects
TECHNOLOGY — Social aspects
TECHNOLOGY — Social aspects — Bibliography
TECHNOLOGY — Social aspects — Germany (West)
TECHNOLOGY — Social aspects — Soviet Union
TECHNOLOGY — Social aspects — Yugoslavia
TECHNOLOGY — China — Government policy
TECHNOLOGY — Developing countries — Case studies
TECHNOLOGY — Europe
TECHNOLOGY — Great Britain
TECHNOLOGY — Netherlands
TECHNOLOGY — United States
TECHNOLOGY — United States — History — 19th century — Addresses, essays, lectures
TECHNOLOGY — United States — History — 20th century — Addresses, essays, lectures
TECHNOLOGY AND CIVILIZATION
TECHNOLOGY AND CIVILIZATION — Congresses
TECHNOLOGY AND CIVILIZATION — Forecasting
TECHNOLOGY AND STATE
TECHNOLOGY AND STATE — Case studies
TECHNOLOGY AND STATE — Australia
TECHNOLOGY AND STATE — Finland
TECHNOLOGY AND STATE — Great Britain
TECHNOLOGY AND STATE — Nigeria
TECHNOLOGY AND STATE — Portugal
TECHNOLOGY AND STATE — Soviet Union
TECHNOLOGY AND STATE — Sweden
TECHNOLOGY ASSESSMENT
TECHNOLOGY ASSESSMENT — Congresses
TECHNOLOGY TRANSFER
TECHNOLOGY TRANSFER — Addresses, essays, lectures
TECHNOLOGY TRANSFER — Bibliography
TECHNOLOGY TRANSFER — Congresses
TECHNOLOGY TRANSFER — Economic aspects — Europe
TECHNOLOGY TRANSFER — Economic aspects — Japan
TECHNOLOGY TRANSFER — Economic aspects — United States
TECHNOLOGY TRANSFER — Government policy — United States
TECHNOLOGY TRANSFER — China
TECHNOLOGY TRANSFER — Communist countries
TECHNOLOGY TRANSFER — Developing countries
TECHNOLOGY TRANSFER — Europe, Eastern
TECHNOLOGY TRANSFER — Japan
TECHNOLOGY TRANSFER — Soviet Union
TECHNOLOGY TRANSFER — United States
TEESSIDE (YORKSHIRE) — Social conditions
TEHERAN CONFERENCE (1943)
TELECOMMUNICATION

TELECOMMUNICATION — Bibliography
TELECOMMUNICATION — Economic aspects — Australia
TELECOMMUNICATION — Law and legislation — Economic aspects — United States
TELECOMMUNICATION — Law and legislation — Australia
TELECOMMUNICATION — Law and legislation — Great Britain
TELECOMMUNICATION — Law and legislation — United States
TELECOMMUNICATION — Management
TELECOMMUNICATION — Political aspects — Europe
TELECOMMUNICATION — Research — Australia
TELECOMMUNICATION — Denmark — Employees
TELECOMMUNICATION — Developing countries
TELECOMMUNICATION — European Economic Community countries
TELECOMMUNICATION — France — Statistics
TELECOMMUNICATION — Great Britain
TELECOMMUNICATION — United States
TELECOMMUNICATION CABLES — Great Britain
TELECOMMUNICATION EQUIPMENT INDUSTRY
TELECOMMUNICATION EQUIPMENT INDUSTRY — Technological innovations
TELECOMMUNICATION POLICY
TELECOMMUNICATION POLICY — Bibliography
TELECOMMUNICATION POLICY — Australia
TELECOMMUNICATION POLICY — Canada
TELECOMMUNICATION POLICY — Great Britain
TELECOMMUNICATION POLICY — Organisation for Economic Co-operation and Development countries
TELECOMMUNICATIONS
TELECOMMUNICATIONS — Law and legislation — Great Britain
TELECOMMUNICATIONS — Denmark
TELECOMMUNICATIONS — France — Statistics
TELECOMMUNICATIONS BILL 1982-83
TELECOMMUNICATIONS BILL 1983-84
TELECOMMUTING — United States
TELECONFERENCING
TELEPHONE — United States — Rates — Peak-load pricing — Mathematical models
TELEVISION — Censorship — United States
TELEVISION — Law and legislation
TELEVISION — Social aspects
TELEVISION — Social aspects — Denmark
TELEVISION ADVERTISING AND CHILDREN
TELEVISION AND CHILDREN
TELEVISION AND CHILDREN — Cross-cultural studies
TELEVISION AND CHILDREN — United States
TELEVISION AND POLITICS — Great Britain
TELEVISION AUDIENCES — Great Britain
TELEVISION BROADCASTING
TELEVISION BROADCASTING — Research — Addresses, essays, lectures
TELEVISION BROADCASTING — Social aspects
TELEVISION BROADCASTING — Social aspects — Canada
TELEVISION BROADCASTING — Australia
TELEVISION BROADCASTING — Canada — History
TELEVISION BROADCASTING — European Economic Community countries — Congresses

TELEVISION BROADCASTING — European Economic Community Countries — Congresses
TELEVISION BROADCASTING — Great Britain
TELEVISION BROADCASTING — Ireland — History — Congresses
TELEVISION BROADCASTING OF NEWS
TELEVISION BROADCASTING OF NEWS — Great Britain
TELEVISION BROADCASTING POLICY — Australia
TELEVISION BROADCASTING POLICY — Great Britain
TELEVISION IN POLITICS — Great Britain
TELEVISION PLAYS — Ireland — History and criticism — Congresses
TELEVISION PROGRAMS
TELEVISION SERIALS — United States
TELEVISION SERIALS — United States — Addresses, essays, lectures
TELLICO DAM (TENN.)
TEMPERANCE SOCIETIES — Norway — History
TEMPORARY EMPLOYMENT — France — Statistics
TEMPORARY EMPLOYMENT — Great Britain
TENNESEE — Rural conditions
TENNESSEE — History — Civil War, 1861-1865
TENNESSEE — History — Civil War, 1861-1865 — Social aspects
TENNESSEE — Race relations
TENNESSEE VALLEY AUTHORITY
TENSE (LOGIC)
TERMINAL CARE — Law and legislation — United States
TERMINAL CARE — Great Britain
TERMINALS (TRANSPORTATION)
TERRITORIAL WATERS — Political aspects
TERRITORIAL WATERS — Asia, Southeastern
TERRORISM
TERRORISM — Addresses, essays, lectures
TERRORISM — Bibliography
TERRORISM — Finance
TERRORISM — History — Dictionaries
TERRORISM — Legal status, laws, etc — Great Britain
TERRORISM — Prevention
TERRORISM — Statistics
TERRORISM — Armenia
TERRORISM — Europe
TERRORISM — France
TERRORISM — Germany (West)
TERRORISM — Great Britain
TERRORISM — Great Britain — Prevention
TERRORISM — Ireland
TERRORISM — Italy
TERRORISM — Near East
TERRORISM — Northern Ireland — History — Addresses, essays, lectures
TERRORISM — Pakistan
TERRORISM — Spain — History — 20th century
TERRORISM — Turkey
TERRORISM — United States
TERRORISM — United States — Congresses
TERRORISM — Yugoslavia
TERRORISM IN MASS MEDIA — Italy
TERRORISM IN MASS MEDIA — United States
TERRORISTS — Germany (West)
TEVA I UTA (TAHITI : REGION) — Population — Statistics
TEXAS — History — Republic, 1836-1846
TEXAS — History — 1846-1950
TEXAS — Race relations
TEXT PROCESSING (COMPUTER SCIENCE)
TEXTILE INDUSTRY — Automation

TEXTILE INDUSTRY — Economic aspects
TEXTILE INDUSTRY — Colombia — Location
TEXTILE INDUSTRY — France — Auffay — Employees
TEXTILE INDUSTRY — Mexico — Puebla — History
TEXTILE INDUSTRY — Pennsylvania — Philadelphia — History
TEXTILE INDUSTRY — Peru
TEXTILE INDUSTRY — Sweden
TEXTILE INDUSTRY — Taiwan
TEXTILE INDUSTRY AND TRADE — England — Oldham (Lancashire)
TEXTILE MACHINERY INDUSTRY — European Economic Community countries
TEXTILE WORKERS
TEXTILE WORKERS — Chile
TEXTILE WORKERS — Egypt — Political activity
THAILAND — Civilization
THAILAND — Economic conditions
THAILAND — Economic policy
THAILAND — Foreign relations
THAILAND — Industries — Statistics
THAILAND — Native races
THAILAND — Occupations — Statistics
THAILAND — Politics and government
THAILAND — Population
THAILAND — Population — Statistics
THAILAND — Social conditions
THAILAND — Social policy
THAMES RIVER (ENGLAND) — Bridges — Drawings
THATCHER, MARGARET
THEATER — History — 20th century
THEATER — Political aspects
THEATER — Political aspects — Québec (Province)
THEATER — Québec (Province) — History — 20th century
THEATER AND SOCIETY — Québec (Province)
THEOLOGY — Addresses, essays, lectures
THEOLOGY, DOCTRINAL — History
THEORIE DES KOMMUNIKATIVEN HANDELNS
THEORY OF JUSTICE
THEOSOPHISTS — Great Britain — Biography
THERAPEUTIC SYSTEMS
THERAPEUTIC SYSTEMS — Religious aspects
THERAPEUTIC SYSTEMS — Social aspects
THESAURI — Bibliography
THIEVES — United States — Case studies
THIRD INTERNATIONAL
THIRD INTERNATIONAL — History
THIRD INTERNATIONAL — History — Sources
THIRD PARTIES (UNITED STATES POLITICS)
THIRTY YEARS WAR, 1618-1648
THIRTY YEAR'S WAR, 1618-1648
THISTED (DENMARK) — Economic conditions
THOMAS, Aquinas, Saint
THOMPSON-FREY, NANCY
THOUGHT AND THINKING
TIBET — Foreign relations — India
TIBET — Politics and government
TIBET — Religion
TIBET (CHINA) — Foreign relations — China
TIBET (CHINA) — History
TIBET (CHINA) — International status
TIBET (CHINA) — Politics and government — 1951-
TIBUAI (AUSTRAL ISLANDS) — Population — Statistics
TIENTSIN (CHINA) — Industries — History
TIKHOMIROV, M. N.
TILLAGE — Economic aspects — Denmark
TILLAGE — Denmark — Energy conservation

TILLICH, PAUL
TIME
TIME — Psychological aspects
TIME — Social aspects
TIME AND ECONOMIC REACTIONS
TIME MANAGEMENT
TIME MANAGEMENT — United States
TIME MANAGEMENT — United States — Social aspects
TIME MANAGEMENT SURVEYS — Developing countries
TIME MANAGEMENT SURVEYS — United States
TIME-SERIES ANALYSIS
TIME-SERIES ANALYSIS — Congresses
TIMES
TIMOR ISLAND (INDONESIA) — History
TIMOR ISLAND (INDONESIA) — Politics and government
TIN INDUSTRY — Bolivia
TIN MINES AND MINING — Bolivia
TIN MINES AND MINING — England — Dartmoor — History — Pictorial works
TINIDAD AND TOBAGO — Statistics, Vital
TIRUNELVELI DISTRICT (INDIA) — Social conditions
TITHES — Wales — Clwyd
TOBACCO — Economic aspects — Addresses, essays, lectures
TOBACCO — Physiological effect — Addresses, essays, lectures
TOBACCO HABIT
TOBACCO HABIT — Treatment — Great Britain
TOBACCO HABIT — Australia — History
TOBACCO INDUSTRY
TOBACCO INDUSTRY — Social aspects — Developing countries
TOBACCO INDUSTRY — Developing countries
TOBACCO INDUSTRY — Germany — History
TOBACCO INDUSTRY — United States — History
TOBACCO INDUSTRY — Virginia — History — 18th century
TOBACCO INDUSTRY — Virginia — Danville — History
TOCQUEVILLE, ALEXIS DE
TOCQUEVILLE, ALEXIS DE — Correspondence
TODESCO, CLEMENTINA
TOGO — Census, 1981
TOGO — Commerce — Statistics
TOGO — Economic conditions — Statistics
TOGO — Industries — Statistics
TOGO — Politics and government
TOGO — Population — Statistics
TOGO — Statistics, Vital
TOKYO (JAPAN) — Economic conditions
TOKYO (JAPAN) — Politics and government
TOKYO (JAPAN) — Social conditions
TOKYO ROUND (1973-1979)
TOKYO ROUND (1973-1979)
TOKYO ROUND AGREEMENTS
TŌKYŌ SHIBAURA DENKI KABUSHIKI KAISHA
TOKYO TRIAL, 1946-1948 — Congresses
TOLL ROADS — Developing countries
TOLL ROADS — Great Britain
TOM, PETRUS
TOMATO INDUSTRY — Mexico
TONGA — Industries — Statistics
TORADJAS — Rites and ceremonies
TORADJAS — Social conditions
TORFAEN (GWENT) — Social policy
TORONTO GENERAL HOSPITAL
TORRES STRAIT ISLANDERS — Employment
TORRES STRAIT ISLANDERS — Training of
TORT LIABILITY OF HOSPITALS — United States
TORTS
TORTS — Australia

TORTS — England
TORTS — Germany (West)
TORTS — Great Britain
TORTURE
TORTURE — Congresses
TOTALITARIANISM
TOTALITARIANISM — Addresses, essays, lectures
TOTEM UND TABU
TOTEMISM
TOURISM — Pakistan
TOURIST CAMPS, HOSTELS, ETC. — Great Britain — History
TOURIST TRADE
TOURIST TRADE — Environmental aspects
TOURIST TRADE — Political aspects
TOURIST TRADE — Social aspects
TOURIST TRADE — Statistics — Standards
TOURIST TRADE — Canada — Statistics
TOURIST TRADE — Caribbean area
TOURIST TRADE — Developing countries
TOURIST TRADE — England
TOURIST TRADE — England — Planning
TOURIST TRADE — England — Yorkshire
TOURIST TRADE — European Economic Community countries
TOURIST TRADE — Fiji
TOURIST TRADE — France
TOURIST TRADE — Gambia — Statistics
TOURIST TRADE — Great Britain
TOURIST TRADE — Great Britain — Statistics
TOURIST TRADE — Jamaica — Statistics
TOURIST TRADE — Louisiana — Henderson
TOURIST TRADE — Malaysia
TOURIST TRADE — Manitoba
TOURIST TRADE — Pakistan
TOURIST TRADE — Pakistan — Galliat
TOURIST TRADE — Pakistan — Murree
TOURIST TRADE — Scotland
TOURIST TRADEOFF. PUBNS. — European Economic Community countries 986
TOWER HAMLETS (LONDON) — Race relations
TOWER HAMLETS (LONDON, ENGLAND) — City planning
TOWER HAMLETS (LONDON, ENGLAND) — Economic conditions
TOWER HAMLETS (LONDON, ENGLAND) — Population
TOWERS, GRAHAM F.
TRADE ADJUSTMENT ASSISTANCE
TRADE ADJUSTMENT ASSISTANCE — United States
TRADE AND PROFESSIONAL ASSOCIATIONS — Europe — Directories
TRADE AND PROFESSIONAL ASSOCIATIONS — Great Britain — Directories
TRADE-MARKS (INTERNATIONAL LAW)
TRADE REGULATION
TRADE REGULATION — Congresses
TRADE REGULATION — History
TRADE REGULATION — Canada — Addresses, essays, lectures
TRADE REGULATION — Great Britain
TRADE REGULATION — India — History
TRADE REGULATION — Soviet Union
TRADE REGULATION — United States
TRADE UNION BILL 1983-84
TRADE-UNIONS
TRADE UNIONS
TRADE-UNIONS
TRADE-UNIONS — Agricultural laborers — Patagonia (Argentina and Chile)
TRADE-UNIONS — Automobile industry workers — Great Britain
TRADE-UNIONS — Automobile industry workers — United States
TRADE-UNIONS — Bank employees — Australia

1105

TRADE-UNIONS — Building trades — United States
TRADE-UNIONS — Carpenters — Nova Scotia — Halifax — History
TRADE-UNIONS — Communication and traffic — United States — History
TRADE-UNIONS — Directories
TRADE-UNIONS — Electric industry workers — France
TRADE-UNIONS — Fishers — Canada — History
TRADE-UNIONS — Fishers — Newfoundland — History
TRADE-UNIONS — Foundrymen — South Africa — History
TRADE-UNIONS — Health facilities — Soviet Union
TRADE-UNIONS — Industrial technicians — Great Britain
TRADE-UNIONS — Information services — Great Britain
TRADE-UNIONS — Insurance companies — Australia
TRADE UNIONS — International cooperation
TRADE-UNIONS — Law and legislation — Digests
TRADE-UNIONS — Law and legislation — Australia
TRADE-UNIONS — Law and legislation — Great Britain
TRADE-UNIONS — Law and legislation — Great Britain
TRADE-UNIONS — Law and legislation — Great Britain
TRADE-UNIONS — Law and legislation — Nigeria
TRADE-UNIONS — Law and legislation — United States
TRADE-UNIONS — Law and legislation — United States — Congresses
TRADE-UNIONS — Merchant seamen — Canada — History
TRADE-UNIONS — Merchant seamen — Pacific States — History
TRADE-UNIONS — Metal workers — Germany (West)
TRADE-UNIONS — Periodicals — Bibliography
TRADE-UNIONS — Postal Service — Great Britain
TRADE UNIONS — Railway workers — Germany — History
TRADE UNIONS — Railway workers — Great Britain — History
TRADE-UNIONS — Recognition — Elections — Law and legislation — United States
TRADE-UNIONS — Shipbuilding industry employees — Sweden
TRADE-UNIONS — Sugar workers — Indonesia — Java — History
TRADE-UNIONS — Telephone workers — United States — History
TRADE UNIONS — Tobacco workers — Germany — History
TRADE-UNIONS — Transport workers — United States
TRADE UNIONS — Uruguay
TRADE-UNIONS — Africa
TRADE-UNIONS — Africa — Political activity
TRADE-UNIONS — Argentina — History
TRADE UNIONS — Argentina — History
TRADE-UNIONS — Argentina — History
TRADE-UNIONS — Australia — History
TRADE-UNIONS — Austria
TRADE-UNIONS — Belgium
TRADE-UNIONS — British Columbia — History
TRADE UNIONS — Canada — History
TRADE-UNIONS — Canada — Atlantic Provinces
TRADE UNIONS — Chile
TRADE-UNIONS — China
TRADE-UNIONS — China — Shanghai — Political activity — History — 20th century
TRADE-UNIONS — Communist countries
TRADE-UNIONS — Czechoslovakia
TRADE-UNIONS — Europe — History
TRADE-UNIONS — France
TRADE-UNIONS — France — Officials and employees — Biography
TRADE UNIONS — Germany — History
TRADE-UNIONS — Germany — History
TRADE-UNIONS — Germany (East)
TRADE-UNIONS — Germany (West)
TRADE UNIONS — Great Britain
TRADE UNIONS — Great Britain
TRADE UNIONS — Great Britain — Dictionaries
TRADE UNIONS — Great Britain — Directories
TRADE UNIONS — Great Britain — Elections
TRADE UNIONS — Great Britain — History
TRADE UNIONS — Great Britain — History — 20th century
TRADE-UNIONS — Great Britain — Political activity
TRADE-UNIONS — Hungary
TRADE-UNIONS — Iceland
TRADE-UNIONS — India
TRADE-UNIONS — India — History
TRADE-UNIONS — India — Officials and employees
TRADE-UNIONS — India — Punjab — Officials and employees — Case studies
TRADE-UNIONS — Indonesia — Java — History
TRADE-UNIONS — Iran — History — 20th century
TRADE-UNIONS — Ireland — History
TRADE-UNIONS — Louisiana — History
TRADE UNIONS — Netherlands
TRADE-UNIONS — New Zealand — Directories
TRADE-UNIONS — New Zealand — History
TRADE-UNIONS — Newfoundland — History
TRADE-UNIONS — Norway
TRADE-UNIONS — Poland — Biography
TRADE-UNIONS — Poland — History
TRADE-UNIONS — Russian S.F.S.R. — Moscow
TRADE-UNIONS — Scotland
TRADE-UNIONS — Scotland — History
TRADE-UNIONS — Senegal — Political activity
TRADE-UNIONS — South Africa — Biography
TRADE-UNIONS — South Africa — History
TRADE-UNIONS — South America — History
TRADE-UNIONS — Soviet Union
TRADE UNIONS — Spain
TRADE UNIONS — Spain
TRADE UNIONS — Spain
TRADE-UNIONS — Spain — History
TRADE-UNIONS — Spain — History — Sources
TRADE-UNIONS — Spain — Political activity
TRADE-UNIONS — Spain — Asturias — History
TRADE-UNIONS — Spain — Asturias — Political activity — History
TRADE-UNIONS — Spain — Cantabria — History
TRADE-UNIONS — Spain — Cantabria — History — 20th century
TRADE-UNIONS — Spain — Madrid — History — 20th century
TRADE-UNIONS — Sweden
TRADE-UNIONS — Sweden — History
TRADE-UNIONS — Turkey
TRADE-UNIONS — United States — Bibliography
TRADE-UNIONS — United States — Biography
TRADE-UNIONS — United States — History
TRADE-UNIONS — United States — History — Sources
TRADE-UNIONS — United States — History — 20th century
TRADE-UNIONS — United States — Organizing — History
TRADE-UNIONS — United States — Political activity
TRADE-UNIONS — West Bank
TRADE-UNIONS — Yugoslavia
TRADE-UNIONS AND COMMUNISM
TRADE-UNIONS AND MASS MEDIA — United States — History
TRADE-UNIONS AND YOUTH — Germany — History
TRADE-UNIONS, BLACK — South Africa
TRADE-UNIONS, BLACK — South Africa — Biography
TRADE-UNIONS, BLACK — South Africa — History
TRADE-UNIONS, CATHOLIC — Spain
TRADEMARKS — Great Britain
TRADES UNION CONGRESS
TRADES UNION CONGRESS — Decision making
TRADES-UNIONS — Economic aspects
TRADES-UNIONS — Public utilities
TRADING COMPANIES
TRADING COMPANIES — Developing countries
TRAFFIC ACCIDENTS — Great Britain — Congresses
TRAFFIC CONGESTION — Great Britain
TRAFFIC ENGINEERING — England — Reading (Berkshire)
TRAFFIC ENGINEERING — Great Britain — Congresses
TRAFFIC ESTIMATION — Great Britain — Mathematical models
TRAFFIC FLOW — Sweden — Stockholm
TRAFFIC REGULATIONS
TRAFFIC REGULATIONS — Great Britain
TRAFFIC SAFETY
TRAFFIC SAFETY — Canada
TRAFFIC SAFETY — Europe — Congresses
TRAFFIC SAFETY — Great Britain
TRAFFIC SIGNS AND SIGNALS — Great Britain
TRAFFIC SURVEYS — England
TRAFFIC SURVEYS — England — London
TRAFFIC SURVEYS — Great Britain — Methodology
TRAFFIC SURVEYS — Sweden — Stockholm
TRANQUILIZING DRUGS
TRANSACTION COSTS — Mathematical models
TRANSFER OF TRAINING
TRANSFER PAYMENTS — Organisation for Economic Co-operation and Development countries — Data processing
TRANSFER PAYMENTS — Organisation for Economic Co-operation and Development countries — Statistics
TRANSFER PAYMENTS — Québec (Province)
TRANSFER PRICING
TRANSFERENCE (PSYCHOLOGY)
TRANSIENTS, RELIEF OF — Government policy — United States
TRANSIENTS, RELIEF OF — New York (State) — History — 20th century
TRANSIT, INTERNATIONAL — Europe — Congresses
TRANSIT, INTERNATIONAL — Great Britain
TRANSKEI — History
TRANSKEI — Politics and government
TRANSKEI — Social conditions
TRANSLATING AND INTERPRETING

TRANSLATION OF: DEL BUEN SALVAJE AL BUEN REVOLUCIONARIO
TRANSPLANTATION OF ORGANS, TISSUES, ETC — Law and legislation
TRANSPORT ACT 1978
TRANSPORT, AUTOMOTIVE — Law and legislation — Great Britain
TRANSPORT BILL 1980-81
TRANSPORT BILL 1981-82
TRANSPORT BILL 1982-83
TRANSPORT BILL 1984-85
TRANSPORTATION — Statistics — European Economic Community countries
TRANSPORTATION
TRANSPORTATION — Bibliography
TRANSPORTATION — Congresses
TRANSPORTATION — Cost effectiveness
TRANSPORTATION — Cost effectiveness — Case studies
TRANSPORTATION — Dictionaries — Polyglot
TRANSPORTATION — History
TRANSPORTATION — Law and legislation — Great Britain
TRANSPORTATION — Management
TRANSPORTATION — Mathematical models
TRANSPORTATION — Passenger traffic
TRANSPORTATION — Passenger traffic — Finance
TRANSPORTATION — Planning
TRANSPORTATION — Planning — Congresses
TRANSPORTATION — Planning — Social aspects
TRANSPORTATION — Australia — Passenger traffic
TRANSPORTATION — Belize
TRANSPORTATION — Brazil — Statistics
TRANSPORTATION — Denmark — Copenhagen
TRANSPORTATION — England — London — Passenger traffic
TRANSPORTATION — England — London — Passenger Traffic
TRANSPORTATION — England — London — Passenger traffic
TRANSPORTATION — England — South Yorkshire
TRANSPORTATION — England — West Yorkshire — Passenger traffic
TRANSPORTATION — Europe — Congresses
TRANSPORTATION — Europe — Passenger traffic
TRANSPORTATION — Europe — Planning
TRANSPORTATION — Finland — Accounting
TRANSPORTATION — France — Statistics
TRANSPORTATION — Great Britain — History
TRANSPORTATION — Great Britain — Passenger traffic
TRANSPORTATION — Great Britain — Planning
TRANSPORTATION — Great Britain — Statistics
TRANSPORTATION — Malaysia — History
TRANSPORTATION — Netherlands — Statistics
TRANSPORTATION — New Zealand
TRANSPORTATION — Northeastern States — Finance — Mathematical models
TRANSPORTATION — Northeastern States — Mathematical models
TRANSPORTATION — Northeastern States — Passenger traffic — Statistical methods
TRANSPORTATION — Northeastern States — Planning
TRANSPORTATION — Northeastern States — Planning — Mathematical models
TRANSPORTATION — Portugal — Statistics
TRANSPORTATION — Spain — History
TRANSPORTATION — Spain — Passenger traffic — Statistics
TRANSPORTATION — Sri Lanka — Statistics
TRANSPORTATION — Taiwan
TRANSPORTATION — Wales — Planning
TRANSPORTATION — Wales — Statistics
TRANSPORTATION — Wales — Clwyd — Citizens participation
TRANSPORTATION — Wales — West Glamorgan
TRANSPORTATION AND STATE
TRANSPORTATION AND STATE — Europe
TRANSPORTATION AND STATE — France
TRANSPORTATION, AUTOMOTIVE
TRANSPORTATION, AUTOMOTIVE — Environmental aspects — Organisation for Economic Co-operation and Development countries
TRANSPORTATION, AUTOMOTIVE — Forecasting — Congresses
TRANSPORTATION, AUTOMOTIVE — Law and legislation — Great Britain
TRANSPORTATION, AUTOMOTIVE — Social aspects
TRANSPORTATION, AUTOMOTIVE — Statistics
TRANSPORTATION, AUTOMOTIVE — Great Britain — Congresses
TRANSPORTATION, AUTOMOTIVE — Ireland — Freight
TRANSPORTATION, AUTOMOTIVE — South Australia — Statistics
TRANSPORTATION PLANNING — Methodology
TRANSPORTATION PLANNING — England — West Midlands
TRANSPORTATION POLICY
TRANSVAAL (SOUTH AFRICA) — Finance
TRANSVESTISM — Cross-cultural studies
TRANSYLVANIA (ROMANIA) — History
TRANSYLVANIA (ROMANIA) — History — 1919-
TRAVELERS — German
TRAVELERS — Africa
TRAVELLING-SALESMAN PROBLEM
TREASON — Bibliography
TREASON — England — History — 16th century
TREATIES
TREATIES — Bibliography
TREATIES — Collections
TREATIES — History — 19th century
TREATIES — History — 20th century
TREATIES, ETC. SOUTH AFRICA
TREATIES, ETC. UNITED STATES
TREATY-MAKING POWER — United States
TREATY OF PARIS (1783) — Addresses, essays, lectures
TREATY OF VERSAILLES (1919)
TREE CROPS — Great Britain
TREES — Great Britain — Statistics
TRENTINO-ALTO ADIGE (ITALY) — History
TRENTINO-ALTO ADIGE (ITALY) — Politics and government
TRESPASS — England
TRESPASS — Great Britain
TRIAGE (MEDICINE) — Moral and ethical aspects — Congresses
TRIALS — France — Statistics
TRIALS (COMMERCIAL CRIMES) — Soviet Union
TRIALS (FORGERY) — Germany (West)
TRIALS (FRAUD) — England
TRIALS (HATE PROPAGANDA) — Canada — Public opinion
TRIALS (LIBEL) — England
TRIALS (MURDER) — Canada — History
TRIALS (MURDER) — England — London
TRIALS (MURDER) — Mississippi — DeKalb
TRIALS (POLITICAL CRIMES AND OFFENSES)
TRIALS (POLITICAL CRIMES AND OFFENSES) — United States
TRIALS (RIOTS) — England — Sheffield (South Yorkshire)
TRIALS (SEX CRIMES) — Scotland
TRIBES — Congresses
TRIBES — Iran — Luristan
TRIBES AND TRIBAL SYSTEM — India
TRIDENT (WEAPONS SYSTEMS) — Bibliography
TRIDENT (WEAPONS SYSTEMS) — Government policy — Great Britain
TRINIDAD AND TOBAGO — Description and travel
TRINIDAD AND TOBAGO — Economic conditions
TRINIDAD AND TOBAGO — Economic conditions — Statistics
TRINIDAD AND TOBAGO — Officials and employees — Statistics
TRINIDAD AND TOBAGO — Politics and government
TRINIDAD AND TOBAGO — Politics and government — Addresses, essays, lectures
TRINIDAD AND TOBAGO — Population
TRINIDAD AND TOBAGO — Population — Statistics
TRINIDAD AND TOBAGO — Social conditions
TRINIDAD AND TOBAGO — Statistics, Vital
TRINIDAD AND TOBAGO — Bibliography
TRIP GENERATION — Spain — Statistics
TRIPARTITE DECLARATION OF PRINCIPLES CONCERNING MULTINATIONAL ENTERPRISES AND SOCIAL POLICY
TRIPLE ALLIANCE, 1717
TRIPURA (INDIA) — Population — Statistics
TROTSKIĬ, L.
TROTSKII, L.
TROTSKII, LEV
TRUCK DRIVERS — Europe — Congresses
TRUCKING — Government policy — United States — History
TRUCKING — Law and legislation — Great Britain
TRUCKING — Law and legislation — United States — History
TRUCKING — Canada — Statistics
TRUCKING — Europe — Labor productivity — Congresses
TRUCKING — United States — History
TRUCKS — Environmental aspects — Great Britain
TRUCKS — Legal status, laws, etc. — Great Britain
TRUCKS — Routes — Great Britain
TRUCKS — Great Britain
TRUDEAU, PIERRE ELLIOTT — Friends and associates
TRUMAN, HARRY S.
TRUMAN, HARRY S. — Congresses
TRUST (PSYCHOLOGY)
TRUSTS AND TRUSTEES — England
TRUSTS, INDUSTRIAL — History — Congresses
TRUTH
TSK KPSS. Politbi͡uro
TSWANA (AFRICAN PEOPLE)
TUAMOTU ISLANDS — Population — Statistics
TUBERCULOSIS — Kenya — Prevention
TUCHOLSKY, KURT — Biography
TUCHOLSKY, KURT — History and criticism
TUCSON (ARIZ.) — History
TUMARAA (RAIATEA : REGION) — Population — Statistics
TUMORS IN CHILDREN — Statistics

TUNISIA — Emigration and immigration
TUNISIA — Politics and government
TUNISIA — Rural conditions
TUNISIANS — France
TUNNELS — English Channel
TUPAMAROS
TURBO PASCAL (COMPUTER PROGRAM)
TUREIA (TUAMOTU ISLANDS) — Population — Statistics
TURIN (ITALY) — Politics and government — 1860-1954
TURIN (ITALY) — Social conditions
TURKEY — Armed Forces — Political activity
TURKEY — Economic conditions — 1918-1960
TURKEY — Economic conditions — 1960-
TURKEY — Economic policy
TURKEY — Emigration and immigration
TURKEY — Foreign relations
TURKEY — Foreign relations — France
TURKEY — Foreign relations — Great Britain
TURKEY — Foreign relations — Greece
TURKEY — History
TURKEY — History — Ottoman Empire, 1288-1918
TURKEY — History — Ottoman Empire, 1288-1918 — Addresses, essays, lectures
TURKEY — History — 1918-1960
TURKEY — History — 1960-
TURKEY — Military policy
TURKEY — Military relations — United States
TURKEY — Neutrality
TURKEY — Politics and government
TURKEY — Politics and government — 1909—
TURKEY — Politics and government — 1918-1960
TURKEY — Politics and government — 1960-
TURKEY — Politics and government — 1918-1960
TURKEY — Population — Statistics — Evaluation
TURKEY — Relations — Armenia
TURKEY — Strategic aspects
TURKEY. Ba̅g-Kur — Statistics
TURKS — France
TURKS — Germany (West)
TURNER, JOHN N
TURNER, NAT — Fiction
TUSKEGEE (ALA.) — Race relations
TUSKEGEE INSTITUTE
TUVALU — Economic policy
TUVALU — Social policy
TVARDOVSKII, ALEKSANDR — Correspondence
TWENTIETH CENTURY
TWENTIETH CENTURY — Forecasts
TWENTIETH CENTURY — Forecasts — Congresses
TWENTY-FIRST CENTURY — Forecasts
TWYMAN (Family)
TYPEWRITING — Psychological aspects
TYROL (AUSTRIA) — History — Uprising of 1809
UA HUKA (MARQUESAS ISLANDS) — Population — Statistics
UA POU (MARQUESAS ISLANDS) — Population — Statistics
UBALDI, BALDO DEGLI — Contributions in political science
UGANDA — Armed Forces — Political activity
UGANDA — History — 1979-
UGANDA — Politics and government
UKRAINE — Dictionaries and encyclopedias
UKRAINE — Economic policy
UKRAINE — History — 1921-1944
UKRAINE — History — 1921-1944 — Congresses
UKRAINE — History — German occupation, 1941-1944
UKRAINE — History — German occupation, 1941-1945
UKRAINE — Politics and government
UKRAINE — Population policy
UKRAINE, WESTERN — History
UKRAINIANS — Government policy — History
UKRAINIANS — Canada — History
UKRAINIANS — Canada — History — Sources
UKRAINIANS — Galicia (Poland and Ukraine) — History
UKRAINIANS — Poland
UKRAINIANS — Prairie Provinces — History
ULSTER (NORTHERN IRELAND AND IRELAND) — History
ULSTER (NORTHERN IRELAND AND IRELAND) — Politics and government
ULSTER UNIONIST PARTY — History
ULTRA VIRES — Great Britain
UNCERTAINTY
UNDERDEVELOPED AREAS — Economic policy
UNDERDEVELOPED AREAS — Peasantry
UNDERDEVELOPED AREAS — Social conditions
UNDERDEVELOPED AREAS — Unemployed
UNDERDEVELOPED ARES — Taxation
UNDEREMPLOYMENT — Brazil
UNDERGROUND LITERATURE — China — Bibliography — Catalogs
UNDERGROUND PRESS — United States
UNDERGROUND RAILROAD
UNDERHILL, FRANK H.
UNEMPLOYED
UNEMPLOYED — Diseases and hygiene
UNEMPLOYED — Education — England
UNEMPLOYED — Education — Great Britain
UNEMPLOYED — Government policy — Great Britain
UNEMPLOYED — Health and hygiene
UNEMPLOYED — Training of — Denmark
UNEMPLOYED — Training of — Great Britain
UNEMPLOYED — Australia
UNEMPLOYED — Australia — Interviews
UNEMPLOYED — Australia — Illawarra (N.S.W. : Region)
UNEMPLOYED — Austria
UNEMPLOYED — Brazil
UNEMPLOYED — Canada
UNEMPLOYED — Canada — History
UNEMPLOYED — England — Attitudes
UNEMPLOYED — England — Bolton (Greater Manchester)
UNEMPLOYED — England — London
UNEMPLOYED — England — Skelmersdale (Lancashire)
UNEMPLOYED — France
UNEMPLOYED — Great Britain
UNEMPLOYED — Great Britain — Rehabilitation
UNEMPLOYED — Great Britain — Services for
UNEMPLOYED — India
UNEMPLOYED — Netherlands
UNEMPLOYED — O.E.C.D. countries
UNEMPLOYED — Puerto Rico
UNEMPLOYED — United States
UNEMPLOYMENT
UNEMPLOYMENT — Bibliography
UNEMPLOYMENT — Effect of inflation on
UNEMPLOYMENT — Effect of inflation on — History — 20th century
UNEMPLOYMENT — Government policy — Great Britain
UNEMPLOYMENT — History
UNEMPLOYMENT — Mathematical models
UNEMPLOYMENT — Psychological aspects
UNEMPLOYMENT — Religious aspects — Christianity
UNEMPLOYMENT — Research — Bibliography
UNEMPLOYMENT — Social aspects
UNEMPLOYMENT — Social aspects — Denmark
UNEMPLOYMENT — Social aspects — England — Teesside (Yorkshire) — History — 20th century
UNEMPLOYMENT — Social aspects — Great Britain
UNEMPLOYMENT — Australia
UNEMPLOYMENT — Australia — Congresses
UNEMPLOYMENT — Australia — Longitudinal studies
UNEMPLOYMENT — Canada
UNEMPLOYMENT — Denmark
UNEMPLOYMENT — Egypt
UNEMPLOYMENT — England — Bristol (Avon)
UNEMPLOYMENT — England — London
UNEMPLOYMENT — European Economic Community countries
UNEMPLOYMENT — Finland — Mathematical models
UNEMPLOYMENT — France — Costs
UNEMPLOYMENT — France — Statistics
UNEMPLOYMENT — Germany — History — 20th century
UNEMPLOYMENT — Germany (West) — Costs
UNEMPLOYMENT — Great Britain
UNEMPLOYMENT — Great Britain — History — 20th century
UNEMPLOYMENT — Great Britain — Statistics
UNEMPLOYMENT — India — Karnataka
UNEMPLOYMENT — Ireland
UNEMPLOYMENT — Italy — Costs
UNEMPLOYMENT — London
UNEMPLOYMENT — London Metropolitan Area
UNEMPLOYMENT — Netherlands
UNEMPLOYMENT — Organisation for Economic Co-operation and Development countries
UNEMPLOYMENT — Scotland — Clydeside (Strathclyde)
UNEMPLOYMENT — Scotland — Strathclyde
UNEMPLOYMENT — United States
UNEMPLOYMENT — United States — Congresses
UNEMPLOYMENT — United States — History
UNEMPLOYMENT — Wales — South Glamorgan
UNEMPLOYMENT, STRUCTURAL — Great Britain
UNEMPLOYMENTOFF. PUBNS. — Great Britain — Costs 986
UNESCO
UNESCO — History
UNESCO — United States
UNIÃO NACIONAL PARA A INDEPENDÊNCIA TOTAL DE ANGOLA
UNICEF
UNICEF — Bibliography
UNICEF — History
UNIFICATION CHURCH
UNIFICATION CHURCH — Doctrines
UNIFORMS — Social aspects
UNILEVER LIMITED — Management
UNIMAR GROUP
UNION CARBIDE CORPORATION
UNION CARBIDE LTD. (India)
UNION CASTLE MAIL STEAMSHIP COMPANY — History
UNION DE CENTRO DEMOCRATICO
UNIÓN GENERAL DE TRABAJADORES DE ESPAÑA — History
UNIÓN GENERAL DE TRABAJADORES DE ESPAÑA — History — Sources
UNION GÉNÉRALE DES ISRAÉLITES DE FRANCE
UNION LIBÉRALE-DEMOCRATIQUE SUISSE

UNIÓN MILITAR DEMOCRÁTICA
UNION OF COMMUNICATION WORKERS
UNION OF CONSTRUCTION, ALLIED TRADES AND TECHNICIANS
UNION OF LIBERAL AND PROGRESSIVE SYNAGOGUES — History
UNION PACIFIC CORPORATION
UNION PROGRESSISTE SÉNÉGALAISE
UNITED ARAB EMIRATES
UNITED ARAB EMIRATES — History
UNITED ARAB REPUBLIC — Statistics
UNITED AUTOMOBILE WORKERS UNION
UNITED BISCUITS
UNITED BROTHERHOOD OF CARPENTERS AND JOINERS OF AMERICA. Local 83 (Halifax, N.S.) — History
UNITED COUNTIES OMNIBUS COMPANY
UNITED FRUIT COMPANY
UNITED KINGDOM IMMIGRANTS ADVISORY SERVICE
UNITED NATIONS
UNITED NATIONS — Armed Forces — History
UNITED NATIONS — Documentation
UNITED NATIONS — Government publications
UNITED NATIONS — History
UNITED NATIONS — Management
UNITED NATIONS — Officials and employees, American
UNITED NATIONS — Developing countries
UNITED NATIONS — Nepal — Economic assistance
UNITED NATIONS — Palestine
UNITED NATIONS — Philippines — History
UNITED NATIONS — South Africa
UNITED NATIONS — Spain
UNITED NATIONS — United States
UNITED NATIONS. Conference on the Law of the Sea (3rd : 1973-1982 : New York, etc.) — Documentation
UNITED NATIONS. Conference on Trade and Development
UNITED NATIONS. Conference on Trade and Development — Bibliography
UNITED NATIONS. Development Programme
UNITED NATIONS. Economic and Social Commission for Asia and the Pacific
UNITED NATIONS. Economic and Social Commission for Asia and the Pacific — Relations — Nepal
UNITED NATIONS. Economic and Social Commission for Western Asia — Statistics
UNITED NATIONS. Economic Commission for Africa
UNITED NATIONS. Environment Programme
UNITED NATIONS. General Assembly
UNITED NATIONS. General Assembly. Charter of Economic Rights and Duties of States
UNITED NATIONS. Industrial Development Organization — Documentation — Bibliography
UNITED NATIONS
UNITED NATIONS — Membership
UNITED NATIONS — Resolutions
UNITED NATIONS — Taiwan
UNITED NATIONS CHILDREN'S FUND
UNITED NATIONS COMMISSION ON INTERNATIONAL TRADE LAW
UNITED NATIONS CONFERENCE ON THE LAW OF THE SEA
UNITED NATIONS CONVENTION ON THE LAW OF THE SEA (1982 : Montego Bay)
UNITED NATIONS. ECONOMIC COMMISSION FOR AFRICA
UNITED NATIONS ENVIRONMENT PROGRAMME — Catalogs

UNITED NATIONS HIGH COMMISSIONER FOR REFUGEES IN AFRICA
UNITED STATED — History — 1815-1861 — Collected works
UNITED STATES. Constitution
UNITED STATES. Economic Recovery Tax Act
UNITED STATES. Migrant Health Act 1962
UNITED STATES. Taiwan Relations Act
UNITED STATES
UNITED STATES — Air defenses, Military
UNITED STATES — Appropriations and expenditures
UNITED STATES — Armed Forces
UNITED STATES — Armed Forces — Addresses, essays, lectures
UNITED STATES — Armed Forces — Afro-American troops
UNITED STATES — Armed Forces — Appropriations and expenditures
UNITED STATES — Armed Forces — History — 19th century — Addresses, essays, lectures
UNITED STATES — Armed Forces — History — 20th century — Addresses, essays, lectures
UNITED STATES — Armed Forces — Military life
UNITED STATES — Armed Forces — Pay, allowances, etc — Congresses
UNITED STATES — Armed Forces — Recruiting, enlistment, etc
UNITED STATES — Armed forces — Recruiting, enlistment, etc. — Forecasting
UNITED STATES — Armed Forces — Search and rescue operations — History — 20th century
UNITED STATES — Biography
UNITED STATES — Census — Indexes
UNITED STATES — Civilization
UNITED STATES — Civilization — Addresses, essays, lectures
UNITED STATES — Civilization — 20th century
UNITED STATES — Civilization — 1945-
UNITED STATES — Commerce
UNITED STATES — Commerce — Case studies
UNITED STATES — Commerce — History — 19th century
UNITED STATES — Commerce — Canada
UNITED STATES — Commerce — China — History — 19th century
UNITED STATES — Commerce — Japan
UNITED STATES — Commerce — Soviet Union
UNITED STATES — Commercial policy
UNITED STATES — Commercial policy — Case studies
UNITED STATES — Congress
UNITED STATES — Constitution
UNITED STATES — Constitutional history
UNITED STATES — Constitutional history — Bibliography
UNITED STATES — Constitutional history — Sources
UNITED STATES — Constitutional law
UNITED STATES — Constitutional law — Amendments — 11th
UNITED STATES — Constitutional law — Amendments — 14th — History
UNITED STATES — Constitutional law — Interpretation and construction
UNITED STATES — Constitutional law — Interpretation and construction — History
UNITED STATES — Defenses
UNITED STATES — Defenses — Addresses, essays, lectures
UNITED STATES — Diplomatic and consular service
UNITED STATES — Diplomatic and consular service — Australia — History
UNITED STATES — Directories — Bibliography
UNITED STATES — Economic conditions

UNITED STATES — Economic conditions — Maps
UNITED STATES — Economic conditions — Regional disparities
UNITED STATES — Economic conditions — To 1865 — Congresses
UNITED STATES — Economic conditions — 1865-1918 — Congresses
UNITED STATES — Economic conditions — 1918-1945
UNITED STATES — Economic conditions — 1918-1945 — Bibliography
UNITED STATES — Economic conditions — 1945-
UNITED STATES — Economic conditions — 1971-1981
UNITED STATES — Economic conditions — 1971-1981 — Congresses
UNITED STATES — Economic conditions — 1981-
UNITED STATES — Economic conditions — 1981- — Congresses
UNITED STATES — Economic policy
UNITED STATES — Economic policy — Congresses
UNITED STATES — Economic policy — Mathematical models
UNITED STATES — Economic policy — To 1933
UNITED STATES — Economic policy — 1933-1945 — Addresses, essays, lectures
UNITED STATES — Economic policy — 1933-1945 — Bibliography
UNITED STATES — Economic policy 1971-1981
UNITED STATES — Economic policy — 1971-1981 — Congresses
UNITED STATES — Economic policy — 1971-
UNITED STATES — Economic policy — 1981-
UNITED STATES — Economic policy — 1981- — Congresses
UNITED STATES — Economic polity — 1981-
UNITED STATES — Emigration and immigration
UNITED STATES — Emigration and Immigration
UNITED STATES — Emigration and immigration
UNITED STATES — Emigration and immigration — Bibliography
UNITED STATES — Emigration and immigration — History
UNITED STATES — Emigration and immigration — History — Addresses, essays, lectures
UNITED STATES — Emigration and immigration — History — 18th century
UNITED STATES — Emigration and immigration — History — 19th century
UNITED STATES — Emigration and immigration — History — 20th century
UNITED STATES — Emigration and Immigration — Australia
UNITED STATES — Ethnic relations
UNITED STATES — Ethnic relations — Abstracts
UNITED STATES — Ethnic relations — Addresses, essays, lectures
UNITED STATES — Executive departments
UNITED STATES — Executive departments — Reorganization — History — 20th century
UNITED STATES — Foreign economic relations
UNITED STATES — Foreign economic relations — Mathematical models
UNITED STATES — Foreign economic relations — Africa
UNITED STATES — Foreign economic relations — Arab countries — Addresses, essays, lectures
UNITED STATES — Foreign economic relations — Canada

UNITED STATES — Foreign economic relations — Canada — Congresses
UNITED STATES — Foreign economic relations — China
UNITED STATES — Foreign economic relations — Europe — Addresses, essays, lectures
UNITED STATES — Foreign economic relations — European Economic Community countries
UNITED STATES — Foreign economic relations — Japan — Congresses
UNITED STATES — Foreign economic relations — Latin America
UNITED STATES — Foreign opinion
UNITED STATES — Foreign opinion, African
UNITED STATES — Foreign opinion, European
UNITED STATES — Foreign opinion, Nigerian
UNITED STATES — Foreign opinion, Russian
UNITED STATES — Foreign population
UNITED STATES — Foreign public opinion
UNITED STATES — Foreign relations
UNITED STATES — Foreign relations — Bibliography
UNITED STATES — Foreign relations — Chronology
UNITED STATES — Foreign relations — Dictionaries
UNITED STATES — Foreign relations — Law and legislation
UNITED STATES — Foreign relations — Philosophy
UNITED STATES — Foreign relations — Public opinion — History
UNITED STATES — Foreign relations — Sources — Germany
UNITED STATES — Foreign relations — 1783-1815
UNITED STATES — Foreign relations — 1829-1837
UNITED STATES — Foreign relations — 20th century
UNITED STATES — Foreign relations — 20th century — Philosophy
UNITED STATES — Foreign relations — 1913-1921
UNITED STATES — Foreign relations — 1921-1923
UNITED STATES — Foreign relations — 1923-1929
UNITED STATES — foreign relations — 1929-1933
UNITED STATES — Foreign relations — 1933-1945
UNITED STATES — Foreign relations — 1945-1953
UNITED STATES — Foreign relations — 1945-1953 — Congresses
UNITED STATES — Foreign relations — 1945-
UNITED STATES — Foreign relations — 1945- — Decision making
UNITED STATES — Foreign relations — 1945- — Decision making — Case studies
UNITED STATES — Foreign relations — 1963-1969 — Sources — Bibliography
UNITED STATES — Foreign relations — 1969-1974
UNITED STATES — Foreign relations — 1974-1977
UNITED STATES — Foreign relations — 1977-1981
UNITED STATES — Foreign relations — 1981-
UNITED STATES — Foreign relations — 1981- — Addresses, essays, lectures
UNITED STATES — Foreign relations — 1981- — Congresses
UNITED STATES — Foreign relations — Africa
UNITED STATES — Foreign relations — Africa, Southern
UNITED STATES — Foreign relations — Asia, Southeastern
UNITED STATES — Foreign relations — Canada
UNITED STATES — Foreign relations — Caribbean area
UNITED STATES — Foreign relations — Central America
UNITED STATES — Foreign relations — China
UNITED STATES — Foreign relations — China — Case studies
UNITED STATES — Foreign relations — Cuba
UNITED STATES — Foreign relations — Developing countries
UNITED STATES — Foreign relations — Developing countries — Congresses
UNITED STATES — Foreign relations — East Asia
UNITED STATES — Foreign relations — Egypt
UNITED STATES — Foreign relations — El Salvador
UNITED STATES — Foreign relations — Ethiopia
UNITED STATES — Foreign relations — Europe
UNITED STATES — Foreign relations — Europe — Congresses
UNITED STATES — Foreign relations — Europe, Eastern
UNITED STATES — Foreign relations — France
UNITED STATES — Foreign relations — Germany
UNITED STATES — Foreign relations — Germany — Addresses, essays, lectures
UNITED STATES — Foreign relations — Germany — Congresses
UNITED STATES — Foreign relations — Germany (West) — Addresses, essays, lectures
UNITED STATES — Foreign relations — Great Britain
UNITED STATES — Foreign relations — Great Britain — History
UNITED STATES — Foreign relations — Grenada
UNITED STATES — Foreign relations — Guatemala
UNITED STATES — Foreign relations — India — History
UNITED STATES — Foreign relations — Indochina
UNITED STATES — Foreign relations — Iran
UNITED STATES — Foreign relations — Israel
UNITED STATES — Foreign relations — Italy
UNITED STATES — Foreign relations — Japan
UNITED STATES — Foreign relations — Korea
UNITED STATES — Foreign relations — Korea — Congresses
UNITED STATES — Foreign relations — Korea (South)
UNITED STATES — Foreign relations — Latin America
UNITED STATES — Foreign relations — Libya
UNITED STATES — Foreign relations — Mexico
UNITED STATES — Foreign relations — Middle East
UNITED STATES — Foreign Relations — Morocco
UNITED STATES — Foreign relations — Near East
UNITED STATES — Foreign relations — Nicaragua
UNITED STATES — Foreign relations — Nigeria
UNITED STATES — Foreign relations — Pakistan
UNITED STATES — Foreign relations — Pakistan — Addresses, essays, lectures
UNITED STATES — Foreign relations — Persian Gulf Region
UNITED STATES — Foreign relations — Persian Gulf region
UNITED STATES — Foreign relations — Persian Gulf Region — Bibliography
UNITED STATES — Foreign relations — Philippines
UNITED STATES — Foreign relations — Poland
UNITED STATES — Foreign relations — Puerto Rico
UNITED STATES — Foreign relations — South Africa
UNITED STATES — Foreign relations — South Africa — Bibliography
UNITED STATES — Foreign relations — South Asia
UNITED STATES — Foreign relations — Soviet Union
UNITED STATES — Foreign relations — Soviet Union — Addresses, essays, lectures
UNITED STATES — Foreign relations — Soviet Union — Case studies
UNITED STATES — Foreign relations — Soviet Union — Congresses
UNITED STATES — Foreign relations — Taiwan
UNITED STATES — Foreign relations — Vietnam
UNITED STATES — Foreign Relations — Western Sahara
UNITED STATES — Foreign relations administration
UNITED STATES — Government policy — Developing countries
UNITED STATES — Government publications
UNITED STATES — Government publications — Bibliography
UNITED STATES — Government publications — Handbooks, manuals, etc.
UNITED STATES — Government publications — Indexes
UNITED STATES — Historical geography
UNITED STATES — Historiography
UNITED STATES — Historiography — Addresses, essays, lectures
UNITED STATES — History
UNITED STATES — History — Philosophy
UNITED STATES — History — Colonial period, ca. 1600-1775 — Addresses, essays, lectures
UNITED STATES — History — Revolution, 1775-1783
UNITED STATES — History — Revolution, 1775-1783 — Causes
UNITED STATES — History — Revolution, 1775-1783 — Causes — Case studies
UNITED STATES — History — Revolution, 1775-1783 — Economic aspects
UNITED STATES — History — Revolution, 1775-1783 — Foreign public opinion
UNITED STATES — History — Revolution, 1775-1783 — Peace — Addresses, essays, lectures
UNITED STATES — History — Revolution, 1775-1783 — Religious aspects
UNITED STATES — History — Revolution, 1775-1783 — Social aspects — Addresses, essays, lectures
UNITED STATES — History — 1801-1809 — Collected works
UNITED STATES — History — 1809-1817 — Collected works
UNITED STATES — History — 1815-1861 — Collected works
UNITED STATES — History — War with Mexico, 1845-1848 — Campaigns
UNITED STATES — History — Civil War, 1861-1865 — Causes
UNITED STATES — History — Civil War, 1861-1865 — Civilian relief

UNITED STATES — History — Civil War, 1861-1865 — Historiography — Addresses, essays, lectures
UNITED STATES — History — Civil War, 1861-1865 — Medical care
UNITED STATES — History — Civil War, 1861-1865 — Personal narratives
UNITED STATES — History — Civil War, 1861-1865 — Religious aspects
UNITED STATES — History — Civil War, 1861-1865 — Social aspects
UNITED STATES — History — Civil War, 1861-1865 — Women
UNITED STATES — History — 1933-1945
UNITED STATES — History — 1933-1945 — Dictionaries
UNITED STATES — History, Military — 20th century
UNITED STATES — History, Military — 20th century — Bibliography
UNITED STATES — History, Naval — Bibliography
UNITED STATES — History, Naval — To 1900
UNITED STATES — Industries
UNITED STATES — Industries — Case studies
UNITED STATES — Industries — History
UNITED STATES — Industries — History — Congresses
UNITED STATES — Industries — Location
UNITED STATES — Industries — Reorganization
UNITED STATES — Industries — Statistics
UNITED STATES — Intellectual life
UNITED STATES — Intellectual life — Addresses, essays, lectures
UNITED STATES — Intellectual life — 1865-1918
UNITED STATES — Intellectual life — 20th century
UNITED STATES — Manufactures
UNITED STATES — Military policy
UNITED STATES — Military policy — Addresses, essays, lectures
UNITED STATES — Military relations — Canada
UNITED STATES — Military relations — Developing countries
UNITED STATES — Military relations — Great Britain
UNITED STATES — Military relations — Israel
UNITED STATES — Military relations — Latin America
UNITED STATES — Military relations — Nicaragua
UNITED STATES — Military relations — Persian Gulf Region
UNITED STATES — Military relations — Turkey
UNITED STATES — Moral conditions
UNITED STATES — National security
UNITED STATES — National security — Addresses, essays, lectures
UNITED STATES — National security — Law and legislation — History
UNITED STATES — Officials and employees
UNITED STATES — Officials and employees — Biography
UNITED STATES — Officials and employees — Salaries, allowances, etc — Congresses
UNITED STATES — Politics and government
UNITED STATES — Politics and government — Addresses, essays, lectures
UNITED STATES — Politics and government — Miscellanea
UNITED STATES — Politics and government — Periodicals — Bibliography
UNITED STATES — Politics and government — Statistics
UNITED STATES — Politics and government — Colonial period, ca. 1600-1775
UNITED STATES — Politics and government — Colonial period, ca. 1600-1775 — Addresses, essays, lectures
UNITED STATES — Politics and government — Revolution, 1775-1783
UNITED STATES — Politics and government — 1783-1789
UNITED STATES — Politics and government — 1783-1865
UNITED STATES — Politics and government — 1789-1815
UNITED STATES — Politics and government — 19th century
UNITED STATES — Politics and government — 1815-1861
UNITED STATES — Politics and government — 1815-1861 — Literary collections
UNITED STATES — Politics and government — 1825-1829
UNITED STATES — Politics and government — 1829-1837
UNITED STATES — Politics and government — 1849-1877
UNITED STATES — Politics and government — 1849-1877 — Addresses, essays, lectures
UNITED STATES — Politics and government — 1865-1900
UNITED STATES — Politics and government — 1865-1933
UNITED STATES — Politics and government — 1865-1933 — Addresses, essays, lectures
UNITED STATES — Politics and government — 20th century
UNITED STATES — Politics and government — 20th century — Manuscripts — Catalogs
UNITED STATES — Politics and government — 20th century — Sources — Bibliography — Catalogs
UNITED STATES — Politics and government — 1901-1953
UNITED STATES — Politics and government — 1913-1921
UNITED STATES — Politics and government — 1933-1945
UNITED STATES — Politics and government — 1933-1945 — Addresses, essays, lectures
UNITED STATES — Politics and government — 1945-1953
UNITED STATES — Politics and government — 1945-1953 — Congresses
UNITED STATES — Politics and government — 1945-
UNITED STATES — Politics and government — 1945- — Congresses
UNITED STATES — Politics and government — 1945- — Decision making — Case studies
UNITED STATES — Politics and government — 1945- — Public opinion
UNITED STATES — Politics and government — 1961-1963
UNITED STATES — Politics and government — 1961-1963 — Addresses, essays, lectures
UNITED STATES — Politics and government — 1963-1969
UNITED STATES — Politics and government — 1963-1969 — Addresses, essays, lectures
UNITED STATES — Politics and government — 1963-1969 — Sources — Bibliography
UNITED STATES — Politics and government — 1965-1969
UNITED STATES — Politics and government — 1974-
UNITED STATES — Politics and government — 1977-
UNITED STATES — Politics and government — 1981
UNITED STATES — Politics and government — 1981-
UNITED STATES — Politics and government — 1981- — Addresses. essays, lectures
UNITED STATES — Politics and government — 1981- — Congresses
UNITED STATES — Popular culture
UNITED STATES — Population
UNITED STATES — Population — History — 19th century — Sources — Indexes
UNITED STATES — Population policy
UNITED STATES — Population policy — Addresses, essays, lectures
UNITED STATES — Public lands — History
UNITED STATES — Race question — Addresses, essays, lectures
UNITED STATES — Race relations
UNITED STATES — Race relations — Addresses, essays, lectures
UNITED STATES — Relations — Europeans
UNITED STATES — Relations — Nigerians
UNITED STATES — Relations — Africa
UNITED STATES — Relations — African
UNITED STATES — Relations — Canada
UNITED STATES — Relations — China
UNITED STATES — Relations — China — Bibliography
UNITED STATES — Relations — Cuba
UNITED STATES — Relations — Europe
UNITED STATES — Relations — Latin America
UNITED STATES — Relations — Mexico — Congresses
UNITED STATES — Relations — Nigeria
UNITED STATES — Relations — Philippines
UNITED STATES — Relations — Senegal
UNITED STATES — Relations — South Africa
UNITED STATES — Relations — Soviet Union
UNITED STATES — Relations (Military) — Central America — Moral and ethical aspects
UNITED STATES — Relations (Military) with the Soviet Union
UNITED STATES — Religion
UNITED STATES — Religion — Biography — Dictionaries
UNITED STATES — Religion — To 1800
UNITED STATES — Religion — 19th century
UNITED STATES — Religion — 1960-
UNITED STATES — Rural conditions
UNITED STATES — Social conditions
UNITED STATES — Social conditions — Congresses
UNITED STATES — Social conditions — To 1865
UNITED STATES — Social conditions — To 1865 — Addresses, essays, lectures
UNITED STATES — Social conditions — To 1865 — Literary collections
UNITED STATES — Social conditions — 1865-1918 — Addresses, essays, lectures
UNITED STATES — Social conditions — 1918-1932
UNITED STATES — Social conditions — 1933-1945
UNITED STATES — Social conditions — 1933-1945 — Bibliography
UNITED STATES — Social conditions — 1945-
UNITED STATES — Social conditions — 1960-1980
UNITED STATES — Social conditions — 1960-1980 — Public opinion
UNITED STATES — Social conditions — 1960-
UNITED STATES — Social conditions — 1980-
UNITED STATES — Social life and customs — 1783-1865
UNITED STATES — Social life and customs — 1971-
UNITED STATES — Social policy

UNITED STATES — Social policy — Addresses, essays, lectures
UNITED STATES — Social policy — Case studies
UNITED STATES — Social policy — Congresses
UNITED STATES — Social policy — 1980-
UNITED STATES — Statistical services
UNITED STATES — Statistical services — Bibliography
UNITED STATES — Statistics
UNITED STATES — Statistics, Vital
UNITED STATES — Foreign relations — 1945-1953
UNITED STATES — Relations — South Africa
UNITED STATES. Army — Biography
UNITED STATES. Central Intelligence Agency — History. Congress
UNITED STATES. Congress — Biography
UNITED STATES. Congress — Committees — History — Handbooks, manuals, etc
UNITED STATES. Congress — Committees — Seniority system
UNITED STATES. Congress — Elections, 1984
UNITED STATES. Congress — Elections, 1984 — Addresses, essays, lectures
UNITED STATES. Congress — Ethics — Addresses, essays, lectures
UNITED STATES. Congress — History — 19th century
UNITED STATES. Congress — Powers and duties
UNITED STATES. Congress. House — Biography
UNITED STATES. Congress. House — Committees
UNITED STATES. Congress. House — Election districts
UNITED STATES. Congress. House — Election districts — History
UNITED STATES. Congress. House — Election districts — Maps
UNITED STATES. Congress. House — Election districts — Statistics
UNITED STATES. Congress. House — Voting
UNITED STATES. Congress. Senate — Biography
UNITED STATES. Congress. Senate — Elections, 1984
UNITED STATES. Constitutional Convention (1787)
UNITED STATES. Department of Defense
UNITED STATES. Department of Defense — Appropriations and expenditures
UNITED STATES. Department of State — Bibliography
UNITED STATES. Environmental Protection Agency
UNITED STATES. Environmental Protection Agency — Management — Decision making
UNITED STATES. Federal Trade Commission
UNITED STATES. Forest Service — History
UNITED STATES. Government Printing Office
UNITED STATES. Immigration and Naturalization Service
UNITED STATES. Joint Chiefs of Staff — Reorganization
UNITED STATES. National Labor Relations Board
UNITED STATES. National Recovery Administration — Officials and employees — Biography
UNITED STATES. National Technical Information Service — Catalogs
UNITED STATES. Navy
UNITED STATES. Navy — History
UNITED STATES. Navy — History — 19th century
UNITED STATES. Office of Surface Mining Reclamation and Enforcement
UNITED STATES. Office of the Comptroller of the Currency
UNITED STATES. Social Security Administration
UNITED STATES. Supreme Court
UNITED STATES. Supreme Court — History
UNITED STATES PENITENTIARY, ALCATRAZ, CALIFORNIA — Rules and practice
UNITES STATES — Armed forces — Germany
UNIVERSAL NEGRO IMPROVEMENT ASSOCIATION — History
UNIVERSITÄT MÜNCHEN — Riot, 1943
UNIVERSITIES AND COLLEGES
UNIVERSITIES AND COLLEGES — Directories
UNIVERSITIES AND COLLEGES — Government policy — Great Britain
UNIVERSITIES AND COLLEGES — Graduate work
UNIVERSITIES AND COLLEGES — Political aspects — Argentina — History
UNIVERSITIES AND COLLEGES — Africa — Directories
UNIVERSITIES AND COLLEGES — Australia — Finance — History
UNIVERSITIES AND COLLEGES — Australia — Statistics
UNIVERSITIES AND COLLEGES — Canada — Finance
UNIVERSITIES AND COLLEGES — Canada — Finance — Statistics
UNIVERSITIES AND COLLEGES — China — Administration
UNIVERSITIES AND COLLEGES — China — Finance
UNIVERSITIES AND COLLEGES — Denmark
UNIVERSITIES AND COLLEGES — Developing countries — Admission
UNIVERSITIES AND COLLEGES — Europe — Entrance requirements
UNIVERSITIES AND COLLEGES — Germany — Faculty — Attitudes — History — 20th century
UNIVERSITIES AND COLLEGES — Great Britain — Administration
UNIVERSITIES AND COLLEGES — Great Britain — Data processing
UNIVERSITIES AND COLLEGES — Great Britain — Directories
UNIVERSITIES AND COLLEGES — Great Britain — Finance
UNIVERSITIES AND COLLEGES — Great Britain — Graduate work
UNIVERSITIES AND COLLEGES — Nigeria
UNIVERSITIES AND COLLEGES — Organisation for Economic Co-operation and Development countries
UNIVERSITIES AND COLLEGES — Organisation for Economic Co-operation and Development countries — Graduate work
UNIVERSITIES AND COLLEGES — South Africa
UNIVERSITIES AND COLLEGES — United States
UNIVERSITIES AND COLLEGES — Finance — Statistics
UNIVERSITIES AND COLLEGES, BLACK — South Africa — History
UNIVERSITIES FUNDING COUNCIL
UNIVERSITY COLLEGE OF NORTH WALES
UNIVERSITY COLLEGE OF NORTH WALES — History
UNIVERSITY COOPERATION — Commonwealth of Nations
UNIVERSITY COOPERATION — European Economic Community countries
UNIVERSITY OF ASTON IN BIRMINGHAM
UNIVERSITY OF ESSEX — Students
UNIVERSITY OF KANSAS. School of Medicine
UNIVERSITY OF KUWAIT
UNIVERSITY OF LONDON — Dissertations — Bibliography
UNIVERSITY OF LONDON — History
UNIVERSITY OF LONDON — Libraries — Directories
UNIVERSITY OF LONDON. Institute of Education — History
UNIVERSITY OF WARWICK. Library. Modern Records Centre
UNIVERSITY PRESSES — Asia, Southeastern — Congresses
UNMARRIED COUPLES — Legal status, laws, etc — United States
UNMARRIED MOTHERS — Legal status, laws, etc. — England
UNTOUCHABLES
UNTOUCHABLES — Case studies
UNTOUCHABLES — Politics and suffrage — History
UPPER CLASSES — Great Britain — Attitudes
UPPER CLASSES — Great Britain — History
UPPER CLASSES — United States — Case studies
UPPER VOLTA — Bibliography
UPPER VOLTA — History — Chronology
UPPER VOLTA — History — Dictionaries
URAL MOUNTAINS REGION (R.S.F.S.R.) — Population
URANIUM INDUSTRY
URANIUM INDUSTRY — Political aspects — History
URANIUM INDUSTRY — United States
URANIUM MINES AND MINING — Social aspects — Australia — Jabiru (Northern Territory)
URANIUM MINES AND MINING — Mexico — Hygienic aspects
URBAN ANTHROPOLOGY — Case studies
URBAN BEAUTIFICATION — England
URBAN ECONOMICS
URBAN ECONOMICS — Congresses
URBAN ECONOMICS — History
URBAN HEALTH — United States
URBAN HOMESTEADING — United States
URBAN POLICY
URBAN POLICY — Congresses
URBAN POLICY — Moral and ethical aspects
URBAN POLICY — Research — Great Britain
URBAN POLICY — Asia
URBAN POLICY — Asia — Congresses
URBAN POLICY — Australia
URBAN POLICY — Australia — Addresses, essays, lectures
URBAN POLICY — Caribbean Area
URBAN POLICY — China
URBAN POLICY — Developing countries — Congresses
URBAN POLICY — England
URBAN POLICY — England — Birmingham (West Midlands)
URBAN POLICY — England — Hertfordshire
URBAN POLICY — Great Britain
URBAN POLICY — India — Punjab — Congresses
URBAN POLICY — Japan
URBAN POLICY — Manitoba — Winnipeg — Citizen participation
URBAN POLICY — Middle West
URBAN POLICY — Nigeria
URBAN POLICY — Organisation for Economic Co-operation and Development countries
URBAN POLICY — Pakistan — Layāri
URBAN POLICY — Sweden — Malmö
URBAN POLICY — Turkey
URBAN POLICY — United States

URBAN POLICY — United States — Addresses, essays, lectures
URBAN POLICY — United States — History
URBAN POOR — Services for
URBAN POOR — United States — Case studies
URBAN PROGRAMME
URBAN PROGRAMMME
URBAN RENEWAL
URBAN RENEWAL — Case studies
URBAN RENEWAL — Citizen participation — Case studies
URBAN RENEWAL — England
URBAN RENEWAL — England — Finance
URBAN RENEWAL — Great Britain
URBAN RENEWAL — India — Addresses, essays, lectures
URBAN RENEWAL — London — Fulham
URBAN RENEWAL — London — Hammersmith
URBAN RENEWAL — Middle West
URBAN RENEWAL — Northern Ireland — Belfast
URBAN RENEWAL — Organisation for Economic Co-operation and Development countries
URBAN RENEWAL — Scotland — Glasgow (Strathclyde)
URBAN RENEWAL — United States
URBAN RENEWAL — United States — Case studies
URBAN RENEWAL — United States — Citizen participation
URBAN-RURAL MIGRATION
URBAN-RURAL MIGRATION — History — Addresses, essays, lectures
URBAN-RURAL MIGRATION — Korea (South)
URBAN TRANSPORTATION
URBAN TRANSPORTATION — Mathematical models
URBAN TRANSPORTATION — Statistics
URBAN TRANSPORTATION — Asia, Southeastern
URBAN TRANSPORTATION — Great Britain
URBAN TRANSPORTATION — Great Britain — Planning
URBAN TRANSPORTATION — India
URBAN TRANSPORTATION — Japan
URBAN TRANSPORTATION POLICY — France
URBAN WOMEN — Employment — United States
URBANIZATION
URBANIZATION — Addresses, essays, lectures
URBANIZATION — History
URBANIZATION — Research
URBANIZATION — Social aspects — India
URBANIZATION — Africa — Bibliography
URBANIZATION — Africa, Sub-Saharan
URBANIZATION — Ahmedabad
URBANIZATION — Asia, Southeastern — Congresses
URBANIZATION — Canada
URBANIZATION — Colombia
URBANIZATION — Developing countries
URBANIZATION — Developing countries — Congresses
URBANIZATION — Ethiopia — Bagēmder — Case studies
URBANIZATION — India
URBANIZATION — India — Addresses, essays, lectures
URBANIZATION — India — History
URBANIZATION — India — Maharashtra
URBANIZATION — India — Punjab — Congresses
URBANIZATION — Kenya
URBANIZATION — Latin America
URBANIZATION — Mexico
URBANIZATION — Middle East — History — Congresses
URBANIZATION — Nigeria

URBANIZATION — Nigeria — Congresses
URBANIZATION — Nigeria — Lagos — History
URBANIZATION — Norway
URBANIZATION — Russian S.F.S.R — Moscow — History
URBANIZATION — Russian S.F.S.R. — Siberia
URBANIZATION — Southern States — History — 19th century
URBANIZATION — Soviet Union — History — Addresses, essays, lectures
URBANIZATION — Sudan
URBANIZATION — Tanzania — Dar Es Salaam
URBANIZATION — Turkey
URBANIZATION — United States — History — 20th century
URIBURU, JOSÉ FÉLIX
URQUHART, LESLIE
URUGUAY — Dictionaries and encyclopedias
URUGUAY — Economic conditions — 1973-
URUGUAY — Economic policy
URUGUAY — History — 1904-1973
URUGUAY — Politics and government
U.S. NUCLEAR REGULATORY COMMISSION
USURY
UTILITARIANISM
UTILITARIANISM — England
UTOPIAN SOCIALISM
UTOPIAN SOCIALISM — History
UTOPIAN SOCIALISM — France
UTOPIAS
UTOPIAS — History
UTOPIAS IN LITERATURE
UTTAR PRADESH (INDIA) — Politics and government
UTUROA (RAIATEA) — Population — Statistics
UZBEK S.S.R. — Economic conditions
UZBEK S.S.R. — Economic policy
UZBEK S.S.R. — Industries
UZBEK S.S.R. — Social conditions
VACATIONS — Great Britain — Statistics
VACATIONS, EMPLOYEE — Law and legislation — Denmark
VAGRANCY — Brazil — Pernambuco — History — 19th century
VAIZEY, JOHN
VALCO See Volta Aluminium Company
VALE OF BELVOIR (LEICESTERSHIRE DISTRICT) — Industries
VALE OF BELVOIR (LEICESTERSHIRE: DISTRICT) — Industries
VALENCIA (SPAIN) — Foreign economic relations — America — History — 18th century
VALENCIA (SPAIN) — History — Auntonomy and independence movements
VALENCIA (SPAIN: REGION) — History
VALLADARES, ARMANDO — Biography — Imprisonment
VALLADOLID (SPAIN) — Economic conditions — History
VALLADOLID (SPAIN) — Social conditions
VALLADOLID (SPAIN) — Social conditions — History
VALLARTA, IGNACIO LUIS
VALOIS TAPESTRIES
VALUE
VALUE — Addresses, essays, lectures
VALUE ADDED
VALUE ADDED — Great Britain
VALUE ADDED — Great Britain — Industries — Statistics
VALUE ADDED — Organisation for Economic Co-operation and Development countries — Statistical methods
VALUE-ADDED TAX — Great Britain
VALUE-ADDED TAX — Spain
VALUES
VALVERDE (SPAIN) — Emigration and immigration

VANCOUVER (B.C.) — Economic conditions
VANCOUVER (B.C.) — History
VANCOUVER (B.C.) — Social conditions
VANCOUVER (B.C.) — Social conditions — History
VANDALISM — Great Britain
VÄNSTERPARTIET KOMMUNISTERNA
VANUATU — Census, 1946
VANUATU — Population — Statistics
VANUATU — Statistics
VÄRMLANDS FOLKBLAD
VATICAN CITY — Foreign relations — Great Britain
VATICAN COUNCIL (2nd : 1962-1965)
VATICAN COUNCIL (2ND: 1962-1965)
VATTENFALL
VEGETABLES — England — London — Marketing
VENDETTA — Scotland — History
VENEZUELA — Armed Forces — Appropriations and expenditures
VENEZUELA — Defenses
VENEZUELA — Description and travel
VENEZUELA — Foreign relations — Germany
VENEZUELA — History — Anglo-German Blockade, 1902
VENEZUELA — Politics and government — 1958-
VENSTRE (Norway)
VENTURE CAPITAL
VENTURE CAPITAL — European Economic Community countries
VENTURE CAPITAL — Great Britain
VENTURE CAPITAL — Japan
VENTURE CAPITAL — United States
VENTURE CAPITAL — United States — Addresses, essays, lectures
VENTURE CAPITAL — United States — Congresses
VERBAL ABILITY
VERBAL BEHAVIOR
VERENIGDE OOST-INDISCHE COMPAGNIE
VERLAG ERNST WASMUTH — History
VESTNIK MOSKOVSKOGO UNIVERSITETA — Indexes
VETERANS — Education — Law and legislation — United States — History
VETERANS — Tennessee
VICE-PRESIDENTIAL CANDIDATES — United States — Biography
VICEROYS — India — Biography
VICO, GIAMBATTISTA — Contributions in political science
VICTIMS OF CRIME — Great Britain
VICTIMS OF CRIMES
VICTIMS OF CRIMES — Congresses
VICTIMS OF CRIMES — Government policy — Canada
VICTIMS OF CRIMES — Services for — Great Britain
VICTIMS OF CRIMES — Council of Europe countries
VICTIMS OF CRIMES — England — Liverpool (Merseyside)
VICTIMS OF CRIMES — Netherlands
VICTIMS OF CRIMES — United States
VICTORIA, Queen of Great Britain
VICTORIA — Governors — Biography
VIDEO DISC PLAYERS — Design and construction
VIDEO DISCS
VIDEO DISPLAY TERMINALS — Hygienic aspects
VIDEO RECORDINGS
VIDEOTEX SYSTEMS
VIENNA (AUSTRIA) — History — Siege, 1683 — Bibliography
VIET CONG
VIETNAM — Economic conditions
VIETNAM — Economic policy
VIETNAM — Foreign relations — Canada
VIETNAM — Foreign relations — United States

VIETNAM — Government publications — Bibliography
VIETNAM — History — 1945-1975
VIETNAM — History — 1975-
VIETNAM — Politics and government
VIETNAM — Politics and government — 20th century
VIETNAM — Politics and government — 1945-1975
VIETNAM — Rural conditions
VIETNAMESE CONFLICT, 1961-1975
VIETNAMESE CONFLICT, 1961-1975 — Influence
VIETNAMESE CONFLICT, 1961-1975 — Literature and the war
VIETNAMESE CONFLICT, 1961-1975 — Motion pictures and the war
VIETNAMESE CONFLICT, 1961-1975 — personal narratives
VIETNAMESE CONFLICT, 1961-1975 — Personal narratives, American
VIETNAMESE CONFLICT, 1961-1975 — Protest movements
VIETNAMESE CONFLICT, 1961-1975 — Protest movements — United States
VIETNAMESE CONFLICT, 1961-1975 — Psychological aspects
VIETNAMESE CONFLICT, 1961-1975 — Social aspects — United States
VIETNAMESE CONFLICT, 1961-1975 — United States
VILLAGES — Botswana — Statistics
VILLAGES — England — Planning
VILLAGES — Great Britain
VILLAGES — Japan
VILLAGES — Mexico
VILLAGES — Portugal — History
VILLAGES — Soviet Union
VILLAGES — Tanzania
VILNIUS (LITHUANIA) — Ethnic relations — Addresses, essays, lectures
VIOLENCE
VIOLENCE — Prediction — North America
VIOLENCE — Research
VIOLENCE — Canada — History
VIOLENCE — Great Britain
VIOLENCE — India
VIOLENCE — Kentucky — History
VIOLENCE — Mexico — Morelos — Case studies
VIOLENCE — Netherlands
VIOLENCE — Northern Ireland — History
VIOLENCE — Southern States — History — 19th century
VIOLENCE — Spain — Basque provinces
VIOLENCE — Tennessee — History
VIOLENCE — United States
VIOLENCE — United States — Congresses
VIOLENCE IN HOSPITALS — Great Britain
VIOLENCE IN MOTION PICTURES
VIOLENCE IN SPORTS — History
VIOLENCE IN SPORTS — Argentina
VIOLENCE IN TELEVISION
VIOLENCE IN TELEVISION — Cross-cultural studies
VIOLENCE IN TELEVISION — United States
VIOLENT CRIMES — Denmark
VIOLENT CRIMES — England — Liverpool (Merseyside)
VIOLENT CRIMES — Great Britain
VIOLENT CRIMES — United States — Prevention
VIRGINIA — History — Colonial period, ca. 1600-1775
VIRGINIA — History — Revolution, 1775-1783 — Causes — Case studies
VIRGINIA — Rural conditions
VISICALC (COMPUTER PROGRAM)
VISITS OF STATE — Germany (West) — Addresses, essays, lectures
VISITS OF STATE — United States
VISUAL PERCEPTION
VISUALIZATION
VITAMIN D
VITORIA (SPAIN) — History

VIVISECTION — England — History
VIZCAYA (SPAIN) — Economic conditions
VLACHS See Aromanians
VLASOV, A. A.
VOCATIONAL EDUCATION
VOCATIONAL EDUCATION — Evaluation
VOCATIONAL EDUCATION — Colombia — Case studies
VOCATIONAL EDUCATION — Great Britain
VOCATIONAL EDUCATION — Ireland
VOCATIONAL EDUCATION — Japan
VOCATIONAL EDUCATION — Tanzania — Case studies
VOCATIONAL GUIDANCE — European Economic Community countries
VOCATIONAL GUIDANCE — Great Britain — Management
VOCATIONAL INTERESTS
VOCATIONAL INTERESTS — California — Stanford — Case studies
VOCATIONAL QUALIFICATIONS — Great Britain
VOCATIONAL REHABILITATION
VOCATIONAL REHABILITATION — European Economic Community countries
VOGEL, JULIUS
VOLCANISM
VOLGGER, FRIEDL
VOLTA ALUMINIUM COMPANY
VOLTAIRE — Biography
VOLUNTARISM
VOLUNTARISM — England — Liverpool (Merseyside)
VOLUNTARISM — England — London
VOLUNTARISM — Great Britain
VOLUNTARISM — Great Britain — Bibliography
VOLUNTARISM — Ireland — Directories
VOLUNTARISM — Mexico
VOLUNTARISM — United States
VOLUNTARISM — United States — Congresses
VOLUNTARY EUTHANASIA SOCIETY
VOLUNTEER WORKERS IN EDUCATION
VOLUNTEER WORKERS IN SOCIAL SERVICE — Northern Ireland
VOLUNTEER WORKERS IN SOCIAL SERVICE — Pakistan — Layāri
VOLUNTEERS — Nicaragua
VOLUNTEERS — United States
VOLVO KALMAR
VOTERS, REGISTRATION OF — United States
VOTING
VOTING — History
VOTING — British Columbia
VOTING — Canada
VOTING — Great Britain
VOTING — Great Britain — History — 20th century
VOTING — United States
VOTING — United States — History — Bibliography
VOYAGES AND TRAVELS
VUYLSTEKE, JULIUS
VYGOTSKII, L. S.
VYGOTSKII, LEV SEMENOVICH
WAGE — Cost-of-living adjustments — United States
WAGE PAYMENT SYSTEMS — Legal status, laws, etc. — Great Britain
WAGE PAYMENT SYSTEMS — Belgium
WAGE PAYMENT SYSTEMS — European Economic Community countries
WAGE PAYMENT SYSTEMS — France
WAGE PAYMENT SYSTEMS — Germany (West)
WAGE PAYMENT SYSTEMS — Great Britain
WAGE PAYMENT SYSTEMS — Italy
WAGE PAYMENT SYSTEMS — Luxembourg
WAGE-PRICE POLICY
WAGE-PRICE POLICY — Congresses

WAGE-PRICE POLICY — History
WAGE-PRICE POLICY — Pennsylvania
WAGES — Netherlands — Statistics
WAGES
WAGES — Clothing workers — Great Britain — History — 20th century
WAGES — Cost-of-living adjustments
WAGES — Econometric models
WAGES — Effect of business cycles on
WAGES — Government policy — Mexico
WAGES — Hairdressing — Great Britain
WAGES — Hispanic Americans — Addresses, essays, lectures
WAGES — Law and legislation — Belgium
WAGES — Law and legislation — Great Britain
WAGES — Mathematical models
WAGES — Medical personnel — England
WAGES — Metal workers — Germany (West)
WAGES — Minimum wage
WAGES — Minimum wage — Great Britain
WAGES — Printers — Germany (West)
WAGES — Public utilities
WAGES — Public utilities — Great Britain
WAGES — Statistical methods
WAGES — Statistics
WAGES — Statistics — Sources
WAGES — Women — England — London
WAGES — Women — France
WAGES — Women — Great Britain
WAGES — Women — Great Britain — History
WAGES — Youth — European Economic Community countries
WAGES — Youth — Great Britain
WAGES — Asia — Congresses
WAGES — Australia
WAGES — Australia — Tasmania
WAGES — Caribbean Area — Congresses
WAGES — Cyprus — Statistics
WAGES — Denmark — Statistics
WAGES — Developing countries
WAGES — Egypt
WAGES — European Economic Community countries
WAGES — European Economic Community countries — Statistics — Sources
WAGES — France
WAGES — France — Statistics
WAGES — Germany (West)
WAGES — Germany (West) — Statistics
WAGES — Great Britain
WAGES — Great Britain — History
WAGES — Great Britain — Statistics
WAGES — Hungary
WAGES — India — Manufactures — Statistics
WAGES — India — Statistics
WAGES — Japan
WAGES — Luxembourg — Statistics
WAGES — Mexico
WAGES — Netherlands — Statistics
WAGES — Norway — Statistics
WAGES — Pacific Area — Congresses
WAGES — Scotland
WAGES — Sri Lanka — Statistics
WAGES — United States
WAGES — Statistics
WAGES AND LABOR PRODUCTIVITY
WAGES BILL 1985-86
WALBIRI (AUSTRALIAN PEOPLE)
WALDEGRAVE, WILLIAM
WALES — Administrative and political divisions
WALES — History
WALES — History — To 1536
WALES — Industries
WALES — Industries — Statistics
WALES — Politics and government
WALES — Politics and government — 20th century
WALES — Population
WALES — Rural conditions
WALES, SOUTH — Gentry — History
WAŁĘSA, LECH
WALKER, PETER, 1932-

WALL STREET
WALLINGFORD COMMUNITY HOSPITAL
WALLIS AND FUTUNA — Census, 1983
WALLIS AND FUTUNA — Population — Statistics
WALLO (ETHIOPIA) — Politics and government
WALLO (ETHIOPIA) — Rural conditions
WALPOLE, ROBERT
WAMIRA (PAPUA NEW GUINEA PEOPLE)
WANDSWORTH (LONDON, ENGLAND)
WANG, AN
WANG LABORATORIES, INC — History
WAPPING POST
WAR
WAR — History
WAR — Moral and ethical aspects
WAR — Religious aspects — Islam
WAR AND EMERGENCY LEGISLATION
WAR AND EMERGENCY LEGISLATION — Ireland — History
WAR AND EMERGENCY LEGISLATION — Northern Ireland — History
WAR AND EMERGENCY POWERS
WAR AND EMERGENCY POWERS — Great Britain
WAR AND EMERGENCY POWERS — United States
WAR AND EMERGENCY POWERS — United States — History
WAR AND SOCIALISM
WAR AND SOCIETY
WAR CRIME TRIALS — Bibliography
WAR CRIME TRIALS — Canada
WAR CRIME TRIALS — France
WAR CRIME TRIALS — United States
WAR CRIMES — Bibliography
WAR CRIMES — Germany
WAR CRIMINALS — Bibliography
WAR CRIMINALS — Canada
WAR CRIMINALS — Germany — Biography
WAR CRIMINALS — Germany (West)
WAR CRIMINALS — Ukraine
WAR (INTERNATIONAL LAW)
WAR OF THE PACIFIC, 1879-1884 — Chile
WAR (PHILOSOPHY) — History — 18th century
WAR VICTIMS — Legal status, laws, etc
WAR WIDOWS — Services for — Israel
WAR WIDOWS — Israel — Psychology
WAR WIDOWS — Israel — Social conditions
WARBURG, Sir SIEGMUND
WARD, STEPHEN
WARSAW TREATY ORGANIZATION
WARSAW TREATY ORGANIZATION — Congresses
WARSAW TREATY ORGANIZATION — History — Sources
WARSHIPS — Europe
WASHINGTON, GEORGE — Influence
WASHINGTON, GEORGE — Military leadership
WASHINGTON, D.C — Social conditions — Addresses, essays, lectures
WASHINGTON PUBLIC POWER SUPPLY SYSTEM — Finance
WASHINGTON (STATE) — Economic conditions
WASHINGTON (STATE) — Social conditions
WASTE DISPOSAL IN THE OCEAN — Government policy — European Economic Community countries
WASTE IN GOVERNMENT SPENDING — United States
WASTE LANDS — Great Britain
WASTE LANDS — Ukraine
WASTE PRODUCTS AS FUEL — Europe
WATER — Economic aspects — Bibliography
WATER — Law and legislation — Ghana
WATER — Nitrogen content
WATER — Pollution
WATER — Pollution — Law and legislation — Great Lakes Region
WATER — Pollution — Law and legislation — United States
WATER — Pollution — England
WATER — Pollution — Organisation for Economic Co-operation and Development countries
WATER — Purification
WATER-MELON INDUSTRY — Mexico
WATER-POWER — Economic aspects — United States — History
WATER-POWER — Finland
WATER QUALITY MANAGEMENT — United States — Cost effectiveness
WATER RESOURCES BOARD
WATER RESOURCES DEVELOPMENT
WATER RESOURCES DEVELOPMENT — Bibliography
WATER RESOURCES DEVELOPMENT — Eanvironmental aspects — Netherlands
WATER RESOURCES DEVELOPMENT — Economic aspects
WATER RESOURCES DEVELOPMENT — Environmental aspects — Great Britain
WATER RESOURCES DEVELOPMENT — Environmental aspects — Canada
WATER RESOURCES DEVELOPMENT — Environmental aspects — England
WATER RESOURCES DEVELOPMENT — Environmental aspects — Finland
WATER RESOURCES DEVELOPMENT — Environmental aspects — France
WATER RESOURCES DEVELOPMENT — Environmental aspects — Germany (West)
WATER RESOURCES DEVELOPMENT — Environmental aspects — Japan
WATER RESOURCES DEVELOPMENT — Government policy — Brazil
WATER RESOURCES DEVELOPMENT — Planning — Bibliography
WATER RESOURCES DEVELOPMENT — Research
WATER RESOURCES DEVELOPMENT — Social aspects
WATER RESOURCES DEVELOPMENT — Developing countries
WATER RESOURCES DEVELOPMENT — Great Britain
WATER RESOURCES DEVELOPMENT — Mexico — Mexico (State)
WATER RESOURCES DEVELOPMENT — Québec (Province)
WATER RESOURCES DEVELOPMENT — Scotland
WATER RESOURCES DEVELOPMENT — Sudan
WATER RESOURCES DEVELOPMENT — United States
WATER REUSE — Hygienic aspects — Developing countries
WATER RIGHTS — United States — History
WATER-SUPPLY — Canada — Management
WATER-SUPPLY — Colorado River Watershed (Colo.-Mexico) — Collected works
WATER-SUPPLY — Finland — Management
WATER-SUPPLY — France
WATER-SUPPLY — Germany (West) — Management
WATER-SUPPLY — Great Britain
WATER-SUPPLY — Great Britain — Bibliography
WATER-SUPPLY — Great Britain — Congresses
WATER-SUPPLY — Great Britain — Management
WATER-SUPPLY — Japan
WATER-SUPPLY — Netherlands
WATER-SUPPLY — Organisation for Economic Co-operation and Development Countries — Price policy
WATER-SUPPLY — Statistics
WATER-SUPPLY — United States
WATER-SUPPLY ENGINEERING — Developing countries
WATER USE — Great Britain — Congresses
WATERWORKS — Developing countries — Planning
WATKINSON, HAROLD
WAYFARING LIFE — Law and legislation — England
WEALTH
WEALTH — Addresses, essays, lectures
WEALTH — Congresses
WEALTH — Denmark
WEALTH — Germany (West) — Statistics
WEALTH — Great Britain
WEALTH — Hungary
WEALTH, ETHICS OF
WEAPONS SYSTEMS
WEATHER CONTROL — Steamboat Springs region — Collected works
WEATHER FORECASTING — Economic aspects
WEBB, BEATRICE
WEBER, ALFRED — History and criticism
WEBER, MAX
WEBER, MAX — criticism and interpretation
WEBER, MAX — Criticism and interpretation
WEBER, MAX — History and criticism
WEBSTER, DANIEL, 1782-1852
WEBSTER, DANIEL, 1782-1852 — Correspondence
WEEKLY REST-DAY
WEHNER, HERBERT — Interviews
WEIHAIWEI (CHINA) — Politics and government
WEISSE ROSE (Resistance group)
WEIZMANN, CHAIM
WELFARE ECONOMICS
WELFARE ECONOMICS — Addresses, essays, lectures
WELFARE ECONOMICS — Econometric models
WELFARE ECONOMICS — Mathematical models
WELFARE FRAUD — Great Britain
WELFARE RECIPIENTS — Employment — Australia
WELFARE RECIPIENTS — Employment — United States
WELFARE RECIPIENTS — United States
WELFARE STATE
WELFARE STATE — Addresses, essays, lectures
WELFARE STATE — Congresses
WELFARE STATE — History
WELFARE STATE — Political aspects
WELFARE WORK IN INDUSTRY — Germany — History
WELLCOME, Sir HENRY SOLOMON
WELLCOME FOUNDATION — History
WELLCOME TRUST
WELLINGTON, ARTHUR WELLESLEY, Duke of
WELLINGTON
WELSH — Canada
WELSH — United States
WELSH AGRICULTURAL ORGANISATION SOCIETY
WELSH LANGUAGE
WELSH LANGUAGE — Study and teaching (Preschool) — Wales
WELWYN GARDEN CITY (HERTFORDSHIRE) — City planning
WEST BANK — Defenses
WEST BANK — Family relationships
WEST BANK — History
WEST BANK — International status
WEST BANK — Politics and government
WEST BENGAL (INDIA) — Economic conditions

WEST BENGAL (INDIA) — Ethnic relations
WEST BENGAL (INDIA) — Politics and government
WEST BENGAL (INDIA) — Population — Statistics
WEST BENGAL (INDIA) — Scheduled tribes
WEST BURRA (SCOTLAND) — Social conditions
WEST GLAMORGAN (WALES) — Economic conditions
WEST INDIANS — Canada
WEST INDIANS — Europe — History — 20th century
WEST INDIANS — Great Britain — History — 20th century
WEST INDIANS — Great Britain — Languages
WEST INDIANS — Panama Canal (Panama)
WEST INDIES — Emigration and immigration
WEST INDIES, BRITISH — Dictionaries and encyclopedias
WEST INDIES, FRENCH — Dictionaries and encyclopedias
WEST INDIES, FRENCH — History
WEST INDIES, FRENCH — History — Archival resources
WEST MIDLANDS — Economic conditions
WEST MIDLANDS — Social conditions
WEST MIDLANDS (ENGLAND) — Economic conditions
WEST MIDLANDS (ENGLAND) — Economic policy
WEST MIDLANDS (ENGLAND) — Race relations
WEST MIDLANDS (ENGLAND) — Social conditions
WEST (U.S.) — Politics and government
WESTERN AND NORTHERN TERRITORIES (POLAND) — History
WESTERN AUSTRALIA. Commonwealth Bureau of Census and Statistics. Western Australian Office
WESTERN HIGHLANDS PROVINCE (PAPUA NEW GUINEA) — Population — Statistics
WESTERN SAHARA — Dictionaries and encyclopedias
WESTERN SAHARA — Foreign Relations — United States
WESTERN SAHARA — History — 1975-
WESTMAN, KARL GUSTAF
WESTMINSTER, HUGH RICHARD ARTHUR GROSVENOR, Duke of, F45, 11843468
WESTMINSTER (LONDON) — City planning
WESTMINSTER (LONDON, ENGLAND) — Economic conditions
WESTMINSTER (LONDON, ENGLAND) — Industries
WETLAND CONSERVATION — Government policy — Great Britain
WETLAND CONSERVATION — United States
WETLAND ECOLOGY — England — Somerset
WETLANDS — United States
WEY AND ARUN CANAL (ENGLAND) — History
WHALES
WHALING — Arctic Ocean — History
WHEAT — Economic aspects — Hungary — Congresses
WHEAT — Prices — Pakistan
WHEAT — Taiwan
WHEAT TRADE — Australia
WHEATLEY, JOHN WHEATLEY, Lord
WHELAN, EUGENE F.
WHEN THE WIND BLOWS
WHIG PARTY (GREAT BRITAIN)
WHISKEY INSURRECTION, 1794
WHITE COLLAR CRIMES

WHITE COLLAR CRIMES — United States
WHITE COLLAR WORKERS — Germany — History
WHITE COLLAR WORKERS — Germany — Political activity — History
WHITE COLLAR WORKERS — Great Britain
WHITE COLLAR WORKERS — Switzerland — History
WHITE COLLAR WORKERS — United States — Effect of technological innovations on — Congresses
WHITEHEAD, ALFRED NORTH
WHITNEY, Sir JAMES PLINY
WHOLESALE TRADE — Denmark
WHOLESALE TRADE — Fiji — Statistics
WHOLESALE TRADE — Great Britain — Statistics
WHOLESALE TRADE — Singapore — Statistics
WHOLESALE TRADE — Thailand — Statistics
WIDOWERS — United States — Life skills guides
WIDOWS — Economic aspects — France
WIEHN, ERHARD R. — Collected works
WIFE ABUSE — Bibliography
WIGGINS, BEN T
WIKMANSHYTTAN (Firm) — History
WILAYAH PERSEKUTUAN (MALAYSIA) — Population — Statistics
WILDLIFE CONSERVATION
WILDLIFE CONSERVATION — Great Britain
WILDLIFE CONSERVATION — Kenya
WILDLIFE CONSERVATION — Tanzania
WILDLIFE CONSERVATION — Yukon Territory — History
WILDLIFE MANAGEMENT — Law and legislation — Yukon Territory — History
WILDLIFE MANAGEMENT — Yukon Territory — History
WILKES, JOHN, 1727-1797
WILLARD, FRANCES ELIZABETH
WILLIAM III, King of England
WILLIAMS, DAVID, 1738-1816
WILLIAMS, ERIC EUSTACE — Addresses, essays, lectures
WILSON, HAROLD, 1916-
WILSON, WALTER
WILSON, WOODROW
WILTSHIRE — Bibliography — Union lists
WINCHESTER (HAMPSHIRE) — Social conditions — History
WIND POWER — European Economic Community countries
WINDWARD ISLANDS (SOCIETY ISLANDS) — Population — Statistics
WINNIPEG (MAN.) — Politics and government
WIRE-TAPPING — Government policy — Great Britain
WIT AND HUMOR — Therapeutic use
WITCHCRAFT — History
WITCHCRAFT — Africa, Central
WITCHCRAFT — Europe
WITCHCRAFT — Europe — History — 16th century
WITCHCRAFT — Europe — History — 17th century
WITCHCRAFT — France, Southern — History
WITCHCRAFT — Papua New Guinea
WITNESSES — Great Britain
WITTGENSTEIN, LUDWIG
WITTGENSTEIN, LUDWIG — History and Criticism
WIVES — Employment — Canada
WIVES — Employment — Germany (East)
WIVES — Employment — Great Britain — Mathematical models
WOLA (PAPUA NEW GUINEA PEOPLE)
WOLFF
WOLFF, JOSEPH
WOMAN (CHRISTIAN THEOLOGY) — Addresses, essays, lectures

WOMAN (PHILOSOPHY)
WOMAN'S CHRISTIAN TEMPERANCE UNION
WOMEN — Finland — Social conditions — Statistics
WOMEN
WOMEN — Bibliography
WOMEN — Congresses
WOMEN — Drug use
WOMEN — Education — Australia — South Australia — History — Case studies
WOMEN — Education — European Economic Community countries
WOMEN — Education — Great Britain — History
WOMEN — Education — India
WOMEN — Education — Spain — Statistics
WOMEN — Employment
WOMEN — Employment — Government policy — United States
WOMEN — Employment — Law and legislation — Canada — Congresses
WOMEN — Employment — Social aspects — United States
WOMEN — Employment — Australia — South Australia — History — Case studies
WOMEN — Employment — Canada
WOMEN — Employment — Canada — Congresses
WOMEN — Employment — Canada — History — 20th century
WOMEN — Employment — China
WOMEN — Employment — China — Tientsin — History
WOMEN — Employment — Cyprus — Statistics
WOMEN — Employment — Developing countries
WOMEN — Employment — Developing countries — Case studies
WOMEN — Employment — England — London
WOMEN — Employment — England — London — Bermondsey
WOMEN — Employment — Europe — Congresses
WOMEN — Employment — Europe — History — Addresses, essays, lectures
WOMEN — Employment — Europe, Northern — History
WOMEN — Employment — European Economic Community countries
WOMEN — Employment — Germany — History
WOMEN — Employment — Great Britain
WOMEN — Employment — Great Britain — History
WOMEN — Employment — Great Britain — History — 20th century
WOMEN — Employment — Great Britain — Religious aspects — Christianity
WOMEN — Employment — India
WOMEN — Employment — India — Bibliography
WOMEN — Employment — India — Delhi
WOMEN — Employment — Ireland — Statistics
WOMEN — Employment — Netherlands
WOMEN — Employment — Norway
WOMEN — Employment — Pakistan
WOMEN — Employment — Peru — Lima
WOMEN — Employment — Portugal
WOMEN — Employment — Puerto Rico
WOMEN — Employment — Puerto Rico — Statistics
WOMEN — Employment — Spain — Statistics
WOMEN — Employment — Swaziland
WOMEN — Employment — United States
WOMEN — Employment — United States — History
WOMEN — Employment — United States — History — 19th century — Congresses
WOMEN — Employment — United States — History — 20th century — Congresses
WOMEN — Employment — United States — Longitudinal studies

WOMEN — Employment — United States — Psychological aspects
WOMEN — Employment — Wales — South Glamorgan
WOMEN — Food — Psychological aspects
WOMEN — Food — Social aspects
WOMEN — Government policy — United States — Addresses, essays, lectures
WOMEN — Health and hygiene
WOMEN — Health and hygiene — Addresses, essays, lectures
WOMEN — Health and hygiene — Cross-cultural studies
WOMEN — Health and hygiene — England — London
WOMEN — Health and hygiene — Québec (Province)
WOMEN — History
WOMEN — History — Middle Ages, 500-1500
WOMEN — Housing — England — London
WOMEN — Language
WOMEN — Legal status, law, etc — Cross-cultural studies
WOMEN — Legal status, laws, etc — Canada — Congresses
WOMEN — Legal status, laws, etc. — Great Britain
WOMEN — Legal status, laws, etc — Spain
WOMEN — Legal status, laws, etc. — Spain — History
WOMEN — Legal status, laws. etc — Swaziland
WOMEN — Legal status, laws, etc — United States
WOMEN — Legal status, laws, etc — United States — Bibliography
WOMEN — Legal status, laws, etc — United States — History
WOMEN — Medical care
WOMEN — Medical care — Québec (Province)
WOMEN — Mental health — England — London — Bermondsey
WOMEN — Miscellanea — Addresses, essays, lectures
WOMEN — psychology
WOMEN — Psychology
WOMEN — Psychology — Cross-cultural studies
WOMEN — Services for — South Australia
WOMEN — Services for — United States
WOMEN — Sexual behavior — Addresses, essays, lectures
WOMEN — Social conditions
WOMEN — Social conditions — Atlases
WOMEN — Social conditions — Cross-cultural studies
WOMEN — Social conditions — New Zealand
WOMEN — Societies and clubs — New Zealand
WOMEN — Socioeconomic status
WOMEN — Suffrage — Great Britain
WOMEN — Suffrage — Great Britain — History
WOMEN — Suffrage — Great Britain — History — Bibliography
WOMEN — Suffrage — New Jersey — History — 20th century
WOMEN — Suffrage — Spain — History
WOMEN — Tobacco use
WOMEN — Africa, Southern — Economic conditions — Bibliography
WOMEN — Africa, Southern — Social conditions — Bibliography
WOMEN — Alabama — Fairhope — Biography — Addresses, essays, lectures
WOMEN — Albania — Social conditions
WOMEN — Algeria — Social conditions
WOMEN — Australia — History — Modern period, 1600-
WOMEN — Australia — Social conditions
WOMEN — Australia — South Australia — Social conditions — Case studies
WOMEN — Canada — Bibliography
WOMEN — Canada — Crimes against
WOMEN — Canada — Economic conditions
WOMEN — Canada — Economic conditions — Congresses
WOMEN — Canada — History — 20th century
WOMEN — Canada — Social conditions
WOMEN — Caribbean Area
WOMEN — Caribbean Area — Social conditions
WOMEN — Chile
WOMEN — China — Bibliography
WOMEN — China — Case studies
WOMEN — China — Social conditions
WOMEN — Developing countries
WOMEN — Developing countries — Economic conditions
WOMEN — Developing countries — Economic conditions — Case studies
WOMEN — Developing countries — Social conditions
WOMEN — Developing countries — Social conditions — Congresses
WOMEN — Ecuador — Guayaquil
WOMEN — Egypt — Social conditions
WOMEN — England — History — 16th century
WOMEN — England — History — 16th century — Sources
WOMEN — England — History — 17th century
WOMEN — England — History — 17th century — Sources
WOMEN — England — London — Social conditions
WOMEN — England — Nottinghamshire
WOMEN — England, Northern — Crimes against
WOMEN — Europe — Economic conditions — Addresses, essays, lectures
WOMEN — Finland — Statistics
WOMEN — France — Institutional care
WOMEN — France — Statistics
WOMEN — Germany — Economic conditions
WOMEN — Germany — History
WOMEN — Germany — History — 20th century
WOMEN — Germany — Social conditions
WOMEN — Germany — Social conditions — History
WOMEN — Germany (West)
WOMEN — Great Britain — Crimes against
WOMEN — Great Britain — Economic conditions
WOMEN — Great Britain — Health and hygiene
WOMEN — Great Britain — History
WOMEN — Great Britain — History — 17th century
WOMEN — Great Britain — Social conditions
WOMEN — Great Britain — Social conditions — History
WOMEN — Great Britain — Social conditions — Sources
WOMEN — Great Britain — Social conditions — Statistics
WOMEN — Greece — Social conditions
WOMEN — India — Bibliography
WOMEN — India — Economic conditions
WOMEN — India — Social conditions
WOMEN — India — Social conditions — Bibliography
WOMEN — Iowa — Case studies
WOMEN — Iran
WOMEN — Ireland — Social conditions
WOMEN — Japan
WOMEN — Korea (South) — Religious life
WOMEN — Latin America
WOMEN — Mediterranean Region — Social conditions
WOMEN — Mexican-American Border Region — Social conditions
WOMEN — New Brunswick — Bibliography
WOMEN — New Brunswick — Congresses
WOMEN — New Zealand — Social conditions
WOMEN — New Zealand — North Island — History
WOMEN — New Zealand — North Island — Social conditions
WOMEN — Nicaragua — Social conditions
WOMEN — Norway — Social conditions
WOMEN — Papua New Guinea
WOMEN — Papua New Guinea — Goroka District
WOMEN — Poland — Statistics
WOMEN — Puerto Rico
WOMEN — Puerto Rico — Social conditions
WOMEN — Québec (Province) — Social conditions
WOMEN — Russia — History — Congresses
WOMEN — Russia — Social conditions — Congresses
WOMEN — South Africa — Biography
WOMEN — South Australia
WOMEN — Southern States — Social conditions — Congresses
WOMEN — Soviet Union — Social conditions
WOMEN — Spain — Statistics
WOMEN — Sudan — Social conditions
WOMEN — Tanzania — History
WOMEN — Thailand — Bangkok — Social conditions
WOMEN — Turkey — History
WOMEN — United States
WOMEN — United States — Crimes against
WOMEN — United States — Economic conditions
WOMEN — United States — Economic conditions — Congresses
WOMEN — United States — Economic conditions — Maps
WOMEN — United States — History
WOMEN — United States — History — Sources
WOMEN — United States — History — 18th century
WOMEN — United States — History — 18th century — Bibliography
WOMEN — United States — History — 19th century — Bibliography
WOMEN — United States — Maps
WOMEN — United States — Psychology
WOMEN — United States — Social conditions
WOMEN — United States — Social conditions — Maps
WOMEN — United States — Social conditions — Sources
WOMEN AND LAND USE PLANNING
WOMEN AND MILITARISM
WOMEN AND PEACE
WOMEN AND PEACE — Addresses, essays, lectures
WOMEN AND POLITICS
WOMEN AND RELIGION
WOMEN AND RELIGION — Congresses
WOMEN AND RELIGION — Social aspects
WOMEN AND RELIGION — England — History
WOMEN AND SOCIALISM
WOMEN AND SOCIALISM — Great Britain — History
WOMEN AND WAR
WOMEN AS COLLEGE TEACHERS
WOMEN, AUSTRALIAN (ABORIGINAL)
WOMEN, AUSTRALIAN (ABORIGINAL) — Congresses
WOMEN, BLACK — Education
WOMEN, BLACK — Employment
WOMEN, BLACK — Africa, Southern — Social conditions
WOMEN, BLACK — South Africa
WOMEN, BLACK — South Africa — Social conditions
WOMEN CLERKS — Great Britain — History

WOMEN CLOTHING WORKERS — Canada
WOMEN CLOTHING WORKERS — Canada — Interviews
WOMEN CLOTHING WORKERS — Great Britain — Attitudes
WOMEN COLONIAL ADMINISTRATORS — Nigeria — History
WOMEN CORRECTIONAL PERSONNEL — United States
WOMEN DOMESTICS — Peru — Lima
WOMEN DOMESTICS — South Africa
WOMEN DOMESTICS — United States — History
WOMEN DOMESTICS — United States — Interviews
WOMEN ENGINEERS
WOMEN ENGINEERS — Australia
WOMEN EXECUTIVES
WOMEN EXECUTIVES — Training of — Great Britain
WOMEN HEADS OF HOUSEHOLDS — Developing countries
WOMEN HEADS OF HOUSEHOLDS — United States
WOMEN HEADS OF STATE — Addresses, essays, lectures
WOMEN IMMIGRANTS — Canada — History — Congresses
WOMEN IMMIGRANTS — Great Britain — History
WOMEN IMMIGRANTS — Ontario — History — Congresses
WOMEN IN AGRICULTURE — Great Britain
WOMEN IN AGRICULTURE — Middle Atlantic States — History
WOMEN IN ART
WOMEN IN ART — Addresses, essays, lectures
WOMEN IN BUSINESS — Developing countries — Case studies
WOMEN IN BUSINESS — Egypt
WOMEN IN CHRISTIANITY — History
WOMEN IN CIVIL SERVICE — United States — History — 19th century
WOMEN IN COOPERATIVE SOCIETIES — Great Britain — Case studies
WOMEN IN COOPERATIVE SOCIETIES — Italy — Case studies
WOMEN IN DEVELOPMENT
WOMEN IN DEVELOPMENT — Asia
WOMEN IN DEVELOPMENT — Developing countries — Congresses
WOMEN IN DEVELOPMENT — Pacific Area
WOMEN IN DEVELOPMENT — Turkey
WOMEN IN EDUCATION
WOMEN IN ENGINEERING
WOMEN IN ENGINEERING — Australia
WOMEN IN ENGINEERING — England
WOMEN IN FINANCE — California — San Francisco
WOMEN IN FINANCE — New York (N.Y.)
WOMEN IN LITERATURE
WOMEN IN MASS MEDIA
WOMEN IN MASS MEDIA — Great Britain
WOMEN IN POLITICS
WOMEN IN POLITICS — Australia
WOMEN IN POLITICS — Canada
WOMEN IN POLITICS — Canada — History — 20th century
WOMEN IN POLITICS — Egypt
WOMEN IN POLITICS — Germany (West)
WOMEN IN POLITICS — Great Britain
WOMEN IN POLITICS — Great Britain — History — 19th century
WOMEN IN POLITICS — India — Case studies
WOMEN IN POLITICS — India — History
WOMEN IN POLITICS — India — Delhi
WOMEN IN POLITICS — New Jersey — History — 20th century
WOMEN IN POLITICS — New Zealand
WOMEN IN POLITICS — Papua New Guinea
WOMEN IN POLITICS — Spain — History
WOMEN IN POLITICS — United States
WOMEN IN POLITICS — United States — Biography
WOMEN IN POLITICS — United States — History — Addresses, essays, lectures
WOMEN IN PUBLIC LIFE — Egypt
WOMEN IN PUBLIC LIFE — Middle Atlantic States — History
WOMEN IN RURAL DEVELOPMENT — Asia — Congresses
WOMEN IN RURAL DEVELOPMENT — Developing countries
WOMEN IN SCIENCE
WOMEN IN TECHNOLOGY — Great Britain
WOMEN IN THE CIVIL SERVICE
WOMEN IN THE CIVIL SERVICE — Great Britain
WOMEN IN THE COMPUTER SERVICE INDUSTRY
WOMEN IN THE PROFESSIONS — United States
WOMEN IN TRADE UNIONS
WOMEN IN TRADE UNIONS — Canada
WOMEN IN TRADE-UNIONS — Germany (West)
WOMEN IN TRADE-UNIONS — Great Britain
WOMEN, JEWISH — New York (N.Y.) — History
WOMEN, JEWISH — Palestine — Employment
WOMEN LEGISLATORS — Canada — Biography
WOMEN, MUSLIM — Turkey
WOMEN PETROLEUM INDUSTRY WORKERS — Norway
WOMEN PHYSICIANS — Great Britain — Congresses
WOMEN, POOR — Pakistan — Lahore
WOMEN, POOR — United States
WOMEN PRISONERS — Biography
WOMEN PRISONERS — Northern Ireland — Armagh — Searching
WOMEN PRISONERS — Poland
WOMEN PRISONERS — United States
WOMEN PSYCHOLOGISTS — United States — Biography
WOMEN REFUGEES — Bibliography
WOMEN SCHOLARS
WOMEN SCIENTISTS — Great Britain
WOMEN SLAVES — Southern States
WOMEN SOCIAL REFORMERS — Great Britain — Biography
WOMEN SOCIAL REFORMERS — New Jersey — History — 20th century
WOMEN SOLDIERS
WOMEN TEACHERS — Germany (West)
WOMEN TECHNICIANS
WOMEN TEXTILE WORKERS — China — Shanghai — History — 20th century
WOMEN VOLUNTEERS IN SOCIAL SERVICE — United States
WOMEN WHITE COLLAR WORKERS — Effect of automation on
WOMEN WHITE COLLAR WORKERS — Effect of technological innovations on
WOMEN WHITE COLLAR WORKERS — United States — Effect of technological innovations on
WOMEN'S CLOTHING INDUSTRY — Canada
WOMEN'S RIGHTS
WOMEN'S RIGHTS — History — Addresses, essays, lectures
WOMEN'S RIGHTS — Austria
WOMEN'S RIGHTS — Canada
WOMEN'S RIGHTS — Germany — History — 19th century
WOMEN'S RIGHTS — India
WOMEN'S RIGHTS — New Brunswick
WOMEN'S RIGHTS — New Brunswick — History
WOMEN'S RIGHTS — Spain
WOMEN'S RIGHTS — Swaziland
WOMEN'S RIGHTS — Turkey
WOMEN'S RIGHTS — United States
WOMEN'S RIGHTS — United States — History
WOMEN'S STUDIES
WOMEN'S STUDIES — Congresses
WOMEN'S STUDIES — United States
WOOD-CARVING, PRIMITIVE — New Guinea
WOOD-PULP INDUSTRY — Environmental aspects
WOODCRAFT FOLK
WOODWARD, C. VANN
WOODWORKERS — Great Britain — Recruiting
WOOL — Australia — Marketing — Mathematical models
WOOL-COMBING — History — 19th century
WOOL TRADE AND INDUSTRY — Australia
WOOL TRADE AND INDUSTRY — Australia — History
WOOL TRADE AND INDUSTRY — Australia — Statistics
WOOL TRADE AND INDUSTRY — Great Britain
WOOL TRADE AND INDUSTRY — Great Britain — History — 20th century
WOOLEN AND WORSTED MANUFACTURE — France — History — 19th century
WORD PROCESSING
WORDSTAR (COMPUTER PROGRAM) — Handbooks, manuals, etc.
WORK
WORK — Psychological aspects
WORK — Social aspects
WORK — Social aspects — South Africa
WORK AND FAMILY — Michigan — Longitudinal studies
WORK AND FAMILY — United States
WORK DESIGN — Social aspects
WORK DESIGN — Great Britain
WORK ENVIRONMENT
WORK ENVIRONMENT — Societies, etc. — Directories
WORK ENVIRONMENT — Europe — Congresses
WORK GROUPS
WORK GROUPS — Sweden
WORK IN LITERATURE
WORK MEASUREMENT
WORK SHARING
WORK SHARING — Germany (West)
WORK SHARING — Great Britain
WORK SHARING — Ireland
WORK SHARING — Netherlands
WORKERS' COMPENSATION — Law and legislation — Great Britain
WORKERS' COMPENSATION — Brazil
WORKER'S COMPENSATION — Denmark
WORKERS' COMPENSATION — Denmark
WORKERS' COMPENSATION — United States — Addresses, essays, lectures
WORKERS POWER
WORKING CAPITAL
WORKING CLASS WOMEN
WORKING CLASS WOMEN — Biography — History and criticism
WORKING CLASS WOMEN — England — Barnsley (South Yorkshire)
WORKING CLASS WOMEN — India — Bibliography
WORKING MOTHERS
WORKING MOTHERS — United States — Biography
WORKING MOTHERS — United States — Psychology
WORKS COUNCILS — Great Britain — Directories
WORKS COUNCILS — Hungary — History
WORKS COUNCILS — Iran

WORKSHOPS — Great Britain
WORLD BANK
WORLD BANK — Bibliography
WORLD BANK — Case studies
WORLD BANK — Finance
WORLD BANK — History
WORLD BANK — Language — Glossaries, etc.
WORLD BANK — Legal status, laws, etc.
WORLD BANK — Membership
WORLD BANK — Asia
WORLD BANK — Developing countries
WORLD BANK — Switzerland
WORLD BANK. Operations Evaluation Department
WORLD BANK
WORLD BANK — Congresses
WORLD DISARMAMENT CAMPAIGN (UK) — History
WORLD EMPLOYMENT PROGRAMME — Research — Bibliography
WORLD FEDERATION OF TRADE UNIONS
WORLD FERTILITY SURVEY — Data processing
WORLD FERTILITY SURVEY — Statistical methods
WORLD HEALTH
WORLD HEALTH — Addresses, essays, lectures
WORLD HEALTH ORGANIZATION
WORLD HEALTH ORGANIZATION. Regional Experts Meeting on Health Manpower Development (1977 : Brazzaville)
WORLD HISTORY
WORLD MAPS
WORLD POLITICS
WORLD POLITICS — Addresses, essays, lectures
WORLD POLITICS — Chronology
WORLD POLITICS — 1900-1945
WORLD POLITICS — 20th century
WORLD POLITICS — 20th century — Library resources — California — Stanford
WORLD POLITICS — 20th century — Philosophy
WORLD POLITICS — 1919-1932
WORLD POLITICS — 1933-1945
WORLD POLITICS — 1945-1955
WORLD POLITICS — 1945-
WORLD POLITICS — 1945- — Addresses, essays, lectures
WORLD POLITICS — 1965-1975
WORLD POLITICS — 1965-
WORLD POLITICS — 1975-1985
WORLD POLITICS — 1985-1995
WORLD POLITICS — 1986-
WORLD WAR — Economic aspects — Moldavian S.S.R.
WORLD WAR, 1914-1918 — Causes
WORLD WAR, 1914-1918 — Civilian relief — Poland
WORLD WAR, 1914-1918 — Diplomatic history
WORLD WAR, 1914-1918 — Economic aspects — Brazil
WORLD WAR, 1914-1918 — Economic aspects — Europe
WORLD WAR, 1914-1918 — Economic aspects — France
WORLD WAR, 1914-1918 — Finance
WORLD WAR, 1914-1918 — Moral and ethical aspects
WORLD WAR, 1914-1918 — Peace
WORLD WAR, 1914-1918 — Pictorial works
WORLD WAR, 1914-1918 — Reparations
WORLD WAR, 1914-1918 — Social aspects — Great Britain
WORLD WAR, 1914-1918 — Territorial questions — Near East
WORLD WAR, 1914-1918 — Africa
WORLD WAR, 1914-1918 — Argentina and Chile — Patagonia
WORLD WAR, 1914-1918 — China
WORLD WAR, 1914-1918 — Europe, Eastern
WORLD WAR, 1914-1918 — Germany
WORLD WAR, 1914-1918 — Great Britain
WORLD WAR, 1914-1918 — Great Britain — Propaganda
WORLD WAR, 1914-1918 — Ireland
WORLD WAR, 1914-1918 — Italy
WORLD WAR, 1914-1918 — Poland
WORLD WAR, 1914-1918 — Soviet Union
WORLD WAR, 1914-1918 — United States
WORLD WAR, 1939-1945
WORLD WAR, 1939-1945 — Atrocities
WORLD WAR, 1939-1945 — Atrocities — Bibliography
WORLD WAR, 1939-1945 — Campaigns — Western
WORLD WAR, 1939-1945 — Campaigns — Europe
WORLD WAR, 1939-1945 — Campaigns — Near East
WORLD WAR, 1939-1945 — Casualties (Statistics, etc.)
WORLD WAR, 1939-1945 — Catholic Church — Germany
WORLD WAR, 1939-1945 — Causes
WORLD WAR, 1939—1945 — Causes
WORLD WAR, 1939-1945 — Causes
WORLD WAR, 1939-1945 — Collaborationists — Czechoslovakia — Slovak Socialist Republic
WORLD WAR, 1939-1945 — Collaborationists — France
WORLD WAR, 1939-1945 — Collaborationists — Ukraine
WORLD WAR, 1939-1945 — Concentration camps — Germany (West)
WORLD WAR, 1939-1945 — Deportations from France
WORLD WAR, 1939-1945 — Destruction and pillage — Germany
WORLD WAR, 1939-1945 — Diplomatic history
WORLD WAR, 1939-1945 — Economic aspects — Germany
WORLD WAR, 1939-1945 — Economic aspects — Italy
WORLD WAR, 1939-1945 — Economic aspects — Soviet Union
WORLD WAR, 1939-1945 — Finance — Germany
WORLD WAR, 1939-1945 — Forced repatriation
WORLD WAR, 1939-1945 — Jews
WORLD WAR, 1939-1945 — Military intelligence — Great Britain
WORLD WAR, 1939-1945 — Participation, Afro-American
WORLD WAR, 1939-1945 — Participation, Female — Bibliography
WORLD WAR, 1939-1945 — Peace
WORLD WAR, 1939-1945 — Personal narratives, American
WORLD WAR, 1939-1945 — Personal narratives, Japanese
WORLD WAR, 1939-1945 — Posters
WORLD WAR, 1939-1945 — Prisoners and prisons, British
WORLD WAR, 1939-1945 — Public Opinion
WORLD WAR, 1939-1945 — Refugees
WORLD WAR, 1939-1945 — Regimental histories — Soviet Union
WORLD WAR, 1939-1945 — Reparations — Congresses
WORLD WAR, 1939-1945 — Secret Service — Canada
WORLD WAR, 1939-1945 — Social aspects — Great Britain
WORLD WAR, 1939-1945 — Technology
WORLD WAR, 1939-1945 — Underground literature
WORLD WAR, 1939-1945 — Underground movements — Czechoslovakia — Slovak Socialist Republic
WORLD WAR, 1939-1945 — Underground movements — France
WORLD WAR, 1939-1945 — Underground movements — France — Congresses
WORLD WAR, 1939-1945 — Underground movements — Germany
WORLD WAR, 1939-1945 — Underground movements — Germany (West) — Munich
WORLD WAR, 1939-1945 — Underground movements — Greece
WORLD WAR, 1939-1945 — Underground movements — Hungary
WORLD WAR, 1939-1945 — Women — Canada
WORLD WAR, 1939-1945 — Women — France
WORLD WAR, 1939-1945 — Argentina and Chile — Patagonia
WORLD WAR, 1939-1945 — Asia
WORLD WAR, 1939-1945 — Europe, Eastern — Personal narratives
WORLD WAR, 1939-1945 — France — Atrocities
WORLD WAR, 1939-1945 — France — Brittany
WORLD WAR, 1939-1945 — France — Franche-Comté — Resistance movements
WORLD WAR, 1939-1945 — Germany
WORLD WAR, 1939-1945 — Germany — Bibliography
WORLD WAR, 1939-1945 — Germany — Sources
WORLD WAR, 1939-1945 — Great Britain
WORLD WAR, 1939-1945 — Hungary
WORLD WAR, 1939-1945 — Indonesia
WORLD WAR, 1939-1945 — Japan
WORLD WAR, 1939-1945 — London
WORLD WAR, 1939-1945 — Pacific Area
WORLD WAR, 1939-1945 — Poland
WORLD WAR, 1939-1945 — Poland — Gdańsk — Personal narratives
WORLD WAR, 1939-1945 — Soviet Union
WORLD WAR, 1939-1945 — Soviet Union — Atrocities
WORLD WAR, 1939-1945 — Soviet Union — Personal narratives
WORLD WAR, 1939-1945 — Spain
WORLD WAR, 1939-1945 — Turkey
WORLD WAR, 1939-1945 — Ukraine
WORLD WAR, 1939-1945 — United States
WORLD WAR, 1939-1945 — Yugoslavia
WORLD WAR, 1939-1945 — Yugoslavia — Bibliography
WORLD WAR III
W.R. GRACE & CO — History
WRAN, NEVILLE
WRIGHT, PETER
WRIGLEY, JOSEPH
WRITERS' PROGRAM (Minn.)
WRITING — History
WRITING — Social aspects
WYSZYŃSKI, STEFAN, Cardinal
X, MALCOLM, 1925-1965
XENOPHOBIA
XHOSA (AFRICAN PEOPLE)
YAGÜE, JUAN
YAKUZA
YALE UNIVERSITY — Students — History
YALTA CONFERENCE (1945)
YAQUI INDIANS — Ethnic identity
YAQUI INDIANS — Government relations
YAQUI INDIANS — Water rights
YARUR MANUFACTURAS CHILENAS DE ALGODÓN
YELLOW FEVER — Control — Africa
YELLOW FEVER — Africa — Prevention
YEMEN — Economic conditions
YEMEN — Ethnic relations
YEMEN — Foreign relations — Soviet Union
YEMEN — History — 1962-
YEMEN — Population — Statistics — Evaluation
YEMEN (PEOPLE'S DEMOCRATIC REPUBLIC) — Foreign relations — Soviet Union
YESTE (SPAIN) — Population
YEZIDIS — History

YORK RETREAT
YOUNG ADULTS — Great Britain
YOUNG ADULTS — Great Britain — Political activity
YOUNG ADULTS — United States — Psychology
YOUNG ENGLAND (Political movement)
YOUNG WOMEN — Employment — Germany (West) — Case studies
YOUNG WOMEN — Employment — Great Britain — Case studies
YOUNG WOMEN — Training of — England
YOUNG WOMEN'S CHRISTIAN ASSOCIATIONS — New Zealand
YOUTH
YOUTH — Bibliography
YOUTH — c Training of — Great Britain
YOUTH — Care and hygiene — Denmark
YOUTH — Conduct of life
YOUTH — Crimes against — Psychological aspects
YOUTH — Economic aspects — Québec (Province)
YOUTH — Education — England
YOUTH — Education — United States
YOUTH — Employment
YOUTH — Employment — Australia — Longitudinal studies
YOUTH — Employment — Denmark — Copenhagen — Statistics
YOUTH — Employment — Developing countries — Bibliography
YOUTH — Employment — England
YOUTH — Employment — England — Bolton (Greater Manchester)
YOUTH — Employment — European Economic Community countries
YOUTH — Employment — Germany — History
YOUTH — Employment — Germany (West)
YOUTH — Employment — Germany (West) — Statistics
YOUTH — Employment — Great Britain
YOUTH — Employment — Netherlands
YOUTH — Employment — O.E.C.D. countries
YOUTH — Employment — Sweden — Addresses, essays, lectures
YOUTH — Employment — United States
YOUTH — Employment — United States — Addresses, essays, lectures
YOUTH — Government policy — Great Britain
YOUTH — Great Britain
YOUTH — Housing — England — Gloucester (Gloucestershire)
YOUTH — Legal status, laws, etc. — Great Britain
YOUTH — Political activity
YOUTH — Political activity — Cross-cultural studies
YOUTH — Services for — Great Britain
YOUTH — Substance use
YOUTH — Suicidal behavior
YOUTH — Suicidal behavior — Addresses, essays, lectures
YOUTH — Training of — Great Britain
YOUTH — Australia
YOUTH — England — London — Social conditions
YOUTH — England, Northern — Drug use
YOUTH — Finland — Statistics
YOUTH — France
YOUTH — France — Attitudes
YOUTH — France — Emigration and immigration
YOUTH — France — Sociological aspects
YOUTH — Germany — History
YOUTH — Germany — Political activity
YOUTH — Germany — Political activity — History
YOUTH — Germany (West) — Political activity
YOUTH — Great Britain
YOUTH — Great Britain — Alcohol use
YOUTH — Great Britain — Attitudes
YOUTH — Great Britain — Drug use
YOUTH — Great Britain — History
YOUTH — Great Britain — Psychology
YOUTH — Great Britain — social conditions
YOUTH — Great Britain — Societies and clubs
YOUTH — Hungary — Attitudes
YOUTH — Hungary — Social aspects
YOUTH — Nigeria — Political activity — History
YOUTH — South Africa
YOUTH — South Africa — Political activity
YOUTH — Soviet Union — Political activity
YOUTH — Sweden — Addresses, essays, lectures
YOUTH — United States
YOUTH — United States — Alcohol use — Addresses, essays, lectures
YOUTH — United States — Attitudes
YOUTH — United States — Drug use
YOUTH — United States — Drug use — Addresses, essays, lectures
YOUTH — United States — Public opinion
YOUTH — United States — Religious life
YOUTH — United States — Social conditions
YOUTH AS CONSUMERS
YOUTH AS CONSUMERS — Great Britain
YOUTH, BLACK — Training of — Great Britain
YOUTH EMPLOYMENT AGENCY (U.S.)
YOUTH HOSTELS ASSOCIATION OF GREAT BRITAIN
YOUTH IN MASS MEDIA — United States
YOUTH MOVEMENT — Germany
YOUTH MOVEMENT — Germany (West)
YOUTH MOVEMENT — Germany (West) — History
YOUTH MOVEMENTS — Germany (West)
YOUTH OPPORTUNITIES PROGRAMME
YOUTH SERVICES — Commonwealth of Nations
YOUTH TRAINING SCHEME
YOUTH TRAINING SCHEME (GREAT BRITAIN)
YRIGOYEN, HIPÓLITO
YUCATÁN (MEXICO) — Rural conditions
YUCATÁN (MEXICO : STATE) — Historiography
YUGOSLAVIA — Census, 1981
YUGOSLAVIA — Constitution
YUGOSLAVIA — Economic conditions — 1945-
YUGOSLAVIA — Economic policy — 1945-
YUGOSLAVIA — Emigration and immigration — Government policy
YUGOSLAVIA — Foreign economic relations — Poland
YUGOSLAVIA — Foreign relations — 1945-
YUGOSLAVIA — Foreign relations — Italy
YUGOSLAVIA — Foreign relations — Soviet Union
YUGOSLAVIA — History — 1918-1945 — Bibliography
YUGOSLAVIA — History — Axis occupation, 1941-1945
YUGOSLAVIA — Industries
YUGOSLAVIA — Nonalignment
YUGOSLAVIA — Politics and government — 1945-
YUGOSLAVIA — Population
YUGOSLAVIA — Relations — Albania
YUGOSLAVIA — Social conditions
YUGOSLAVIA — Social conditions — 1945-
YUGOSLAVIA — Social policy
YUKON — Economic conditions
YUKON TERRITORY — Politics and government
ZAIRE — Economic conditions
ZAIRE — Economic conditions — 1960- — Congresses
ZAIRE — Foreign relations — Congresses
ZAIRE — History — 1960-
ZAIRE — Politics and government
ZAIRE — Politics and government — 1960- — Congresses
ZAIRE — Religion
ZAMBIA — Census, 1963
ZAMBIA — Economic policy
ZAMBIA — History — 1964-
ZAMBIA — Industries
ZAMBIA — Politics and government — 1964-
ZAMBIA — Population — Statistics
ZAMBIA — Social life and customs — History
ZAMBIA — Social policy
ZANDE (AFRICAN PEOPLE)
ZANZIBAR — Commerce — History
ZANZIBAR — History — To 1890
ZAPOTEC INDIANS — Rites and ceremonies
ZAPOTEC INDIANS — Social life and customs
ZARAGOZA (SPAIN) — History
ZARAGOZA (SPAIN) — History — 19th century
ZIA-UL-HAQ, MOHAMMAD — Interviews
ZIA-UL-HAQ, MOHAMMED
ZIMBABWE — Antiquities
ZIMBABWE — Economic conditions — 1980-
ZIMBABWE — Foreign economic relations — Bibliography
ZIMBABWE — Foreign relations
ZIMBABWE — Politics and government — 1980-
ZIMBABWE — Social conditions — 1980-
ZIMBABWE CONFERENCE ON RECONSTRUCTION AND DEVELOPMENT (1981 : Salisbury)
ZIONISM
ZIONISM — History
ZIONISM — Palestine — History
ZIONISTS — Attitudes — History
ZIONISTS — Correspondence, reminiscences, etc
ZIONISTS — United States — Biography
ZULULAND (SOUTH AFRICA) — Description and travel
ZULULAND (SOUTH AFRICA) — Social life and customs
ZULUS
ZUNDEL, ERNST — Trials, litigation, etc. — Public opinion
ZÜRICH (SWITZERLAND) — Economic conditions
ZÜRICH (SWITZERLAND) — Politics and government
ZÜRICH (SWITZERLAND : CANTON) — Economic conditions
ZÜRICH (SWITZERLAND : CANTON) — Politics and government
ŽUŽEK (Family)

JUL 1 5 1988